Infants, Children, and Adolescents

EIGHTH EDITION

Laura E. Berk

Illinois State University

Adena B. Meyers

Illinois State University

PEARSON

Boston • Columbus • Indianapolis • New York • San Francisco • Hoboken
Amsterdam • Cape Town • Dubai • London • Madrid • Milan • Munich • Paris • Montréal • Toronto
Delhi • Mexico City • São Paulo • Sydney • Hong Kong • Seoul • Singapore • Taipei • Tokyo

In loving memory of my parents, Sofie and Philip Eisenberg   L. E. B.

For my grandmothers, Rose Honig and Edith Polin, with love and gratitude   A. B. M.

Senior Publisher: Roth Wilkofsky
Managing Editor: Tom Pauken
Development Editor: Judy Ashkenaz
Editorial Assistants: Rachel Trapp, Devon Bacso
Supplements Editors: Rachel Trapp, Judy Ashkenaz, Kim Michaud, Jeanie McHale
Team Lead—Project Management, Communication/Psychology: Linda Behrens
Senior Project Manager, Psychology: Donna Simons
Senior Digital Product Manager: Thomas Scalzo
Associate Digital Product Manager: Christopher Fegan
Senior Product Marketing Manager: Lindsey Prudhomme Gill
Senior Operations Specialist: Diane Peirano

Photo Researcher: Sarah Evertson—ImageQuest
Interior Designer: Carol Somberg
Cover Designer: Joel Gendron, Lumina Datamatics
Project Coordination and Editorial Services: MPS North America LLC
Art Rendering and Electronic Page Makeup: Jouve
Composition Specialist: Jeff Miller
Copyeditor and References Editor: Margaret Pinette
Proofreader: Julie Hotchkiss
Indexer: Linda Herr Hallinger
Printer/Binder and Cover Printer: Courier Corp., Kendallville, IN
Cover Art: "The Mango Tree Is Our Friend," Nilakna Disiwari Warushavithana, 7 years, Sri Lanka. Reprinted with permission from the International Museum of Children's Art, Oslo, Norway.

Page 510: Photo © 2015 by Child Lures, Ltd. All Rights Reserved. Excerpted from Child Lures® Prevention's *Think First & Stay Safe™* School Program/Student Workbook/Parent Guide by Kenneth Wooden, Rosemary Webb, and Jennifer Mitchell. Excerpted with permission of Child Lures, Ltd., Child Lures Prevention, 5166 Shelburne Road, Shelburne, Vermont 05482 (802) 985-8458, *www.childluresprevention.com.*

Library of Congress Cataloging-in-Publication Data
Berk, Laura E.
  Infants, children, and adolescents / Laura E. Berk and
Adena B. Meyers. — Eighth edition.
      pages cm
  Includes bibliographical references and index.
  ISBN 978-0-13-393673-5 — ISBN 0-13-393673-2
  1. Child development.   2. Infants—Development.
  3. Adolescence.   I. Meyers, Adena Beth   II. Title.
  RJ131.B387 2016
  618.92—dc23
                                        2015002431

10 9 8 7 6 5 4 3 2 1

Student Edition
ISBN 10: 0-13-393673-2
ISBN 13: 978-0-13-393673-5

Instructor's Review Edition
ISBN 10: 0-13-403567-4
ISBN 13: 978-0-13-403567-3

À la Carte Edition
ISBN 10: 0-13-403565-8
ISBN 13: 978-0-13-403565-9

www.pearsonhighered.com

About the Authors

Laura E. Berk is a distinguished professor of psychology at Illinois State University, where she has taught child, adolescent, and lifespan development for more than three decades. She received her bachelor's degree in psychology from the University of California, Berkeley, and her master's and doctoral degrees in child development and educational psychology from the University of Chicago.

Berk has been a visiting scholar at Cornell University, UCLA, Stanford University, and the University of South Australia. She has published widely on effects of school environments on children's development, the development of children's private speech, and the role of make-believe play in development. She has been featured on National Public Radio's *Morning Edition* and in *Parents Magazine, Wondertime,* and *Readers' Digest,* and has contributed to *Psychology Today* and *Scientific American.*

In addition to *Infants, Children, and Adolescents,* Berk's best-selling texts include *Child Development, Development Through the Lifespan,* and *Exploring Lifespan Development,* published by Pearson. Her other books include *Private Speech: From Social Interaction to Self-Regulation; Scaffolding Children's Learning: Vygotsky and Early Childhood Education; Awakening Children's Minds: How Parents and Teachers Can Make a Difference;* and *A Mandate for Playful Learning in Preschool: Presenting the Evidence.*

Berk is active in work for children's causes. She recently completed nine years of service on the national board of Jumpstart for Young Children and currently serves on the governing board of the Illinois Network of Child Care Resource and Referral Agencies. She is a fellow of the American Psychological Association, Division 7: Developmental Psychology.

Adena B. Meyers is a professor of psychology and member of the school psychology faculty at Illinois State University. She received her bachelor's degree in women's studies from Brown University and her doctoral degree in clinical-community psychology from the University of Illinois at Urbana-Champaign, and is a licensed clinical psychologist.

Meyers's areas of specialization include contextual influences on child and adolescent development, with an emphasis on family-, school-, and community-based interventions that promote children's social and emotional functioning. She has served as a consultant to the Collaborative for Academic, Social, and Emotional Learning (CASEL), and as a supervisor of mental health consultants working in Head Start preschool settings. She also supervises clinicians providing mental health services to elementary and secondary school students.

Meyers's publications have focused on school-based consultation; adolescent pregnancy, parenthood, and sexual development; school-based preventive interventions; and the role of pretend play in child development. Her clinical interests include therapeutic interventions related to stress and trauma, and mindfulness-based stress reduction. She has taught a wide variety of courses, including introductory psychology, child and adolescent development, human sexuality, introduction to women's studies, and statistics for the social sciences.

Berk and Meyers are faculty colleagues in the Department of Psychology at Illinois State University. They have collaborated on numerous projects, most recently coauthoring the chapter on make-believe play and self-regulation for the *Sage Handbook of Play and Learning in Early Childhood.*

Features at a Glance

Contents

chapter 4
Birth and the Newborn Baby 122

PART THREE
INFANCY AND TODDLERHOOD: THE FIRST TWO YEARS

chapter 5
Physical Development in Infancy and Toddlerhood 158

chapter 6

Cognitive Development in Infancy and Toddlerhood 200

chapter 7

Emotional and Social Development in Infancy and Toddlerhood 244

MILESTONES
Development in Infancy and Toddlerhood 282

PART FOUR
EARLY CHILDHOOD: TWO TO SIX YEARS

chapter 8

Physical Development in Early Childhood 284

chapter 9

Cognitive Development in Early Childhood   310

chapter 10

Emotional and Social Development in Early Childhood   356

MiLESTONES
Development in Early Childhood   402

PART FIVE

MIDDLE CHILDHOOD: SIX TO ELEVEN YEARS

PART SIX

ADOLESCENCE: THE TRANSITION TO ADULTHOOD

chapter 14
Physical Development in Adolescence   518

chapter 15
Cognitive Development in Adolescence   554

A Personal Note to Students

Our many years of teaching child development have brought us in contact with thousands of students like you—students with diverse college majors, future goals, interests, and needs. Some are affiliated with our own field of psychology, but many come from other related fields—education, sociology, anthropology, biology, family studies, social service, and health sciences, to name just a few. Each semester, our students' aspirations have proved to be as varied as their fields of study. Many look toward careers in applied work—teaching, caregiving, nursing, counseling, social work, school psychology, and program administration. Some want to teach, and a few want to do research. Most hope someday to become parents, whereas others are already parents who come with a desire to better understand and rear their children. And almost all arrive with a deep curiosity about how they themselves developed from tiny infants into the complex human beings they are today.

Our goal in preparing this eighth edition of *Infants, Children, and Adolescents* is to provide a textbook that meets the instructional goals of your course as well as your personal interests and needs. To achieve these objectives, we have grounded this book in a carefully selected body of classic and current theory and research brought to life with stories and vignettes about children and families, most of whom we have known personally. In addition, the text highlights the joint contributions of biology and environment to the developing child, explains how the research process helps solve real-world problems, illustrates commonalities and differences among ethnic groups and cultures, and pays special attention to policy issues that are crucial for safeguarding children's well-being in today's world. Woven throughout the text is a unique pedagogical program that will assist you in mastering information, integrating the various aspects of development, critically examining controversial issues, applying what you have learned, and relating the information to real life.

We hope that learning about child development will be as rewarding for you as we have found it over the years. We would like to know what you think about both the field of child development and this book. We welcome your comments; please contact us through our textbook website: *www.infantschildrenandadolescents.com*.

Laura E. Berk and Adena B. Meyers

Preface for Instructors

A Message from Laura Berk

It is my pleasure to introduce **Adena B. Meyers,** new coauthor of *Infants, Children, and Adolescents,* Eighth Edition. How excited I was when she readily responded "yes!" to my invitation to join in preparing this edition. Adena and I live and work in the same community: We have been departmental colleagues for many years and have written together on numerous occasions. Our coauthorship of the eighth edition is a natural extension of our previous joint endeavors.

Adena brings to the text outstanding scholarship, areas of specialization that complement my own, a similar writing style, a shared commitment to research-based applications, and wide-ranging direct experiences with children and families. In addition to her talents as a teacher, researcher, and clinician, she is an exemplary parent of two remarkable teenagers.

Adena's gracious partnership throughout the journey of preparing this revision realizes my fondest hopes when I first set my pen to page to craft *Infants, Children, and Adolescents:* that future editions will be numerous, and that instructor and student enthusiasm for the text will continue to be a deep source of author pride and satisfaction for many years to come.

Laura E. Berk

The Eighth Edition

In preparing this eighth edition of *Infants, Children, and Adolescents,* we drew inspiration from the hundreds of students of child development with whom we have worked in our combined half-century of college teaching. As in previous editions, we aimed for a text that is intellectually stimulating, provides depth as well as breadth of coverage, portrays the complexities of child development with clarity and excitement, and is relevant and useful in building a bridge from theory and research to children's everyday lives.

The more than two decades since *Infants, Children, and Adolescents* first appeared have been a period of unprecedented expansion and change in theory and research. This eighth edition represents these rapidly transforming aspects of the field, with a wealth of new content and enhanced teaching tools:

■ **Diverse pathways of change are highlighted.** Investigators have reached broad consensus that variations in biological makeup, everyday tasks, and the people who support children in mastery of those tasks lead to wide individual differences in children's paths of change and resulting competencies. This edition pays more attention to variability in development and to recent theories—including ecological, sociocultural, dynamic systems, and epigenesis—that attempt to explain it. Multicultural and cross-cultural findings,

including international comparisons, are enhanced throughout the text and in revised and expanded Cultural Influences boxes.

■ **The complex, bidirectional relationship between biology and environment is given greater attention.** Accumulating evidence on development of the brain, motor skills, cognitive and language competencies, temperament and personality, emotional and social understanding, and developmental problems underscores the way biological factors emerge in, are modified by, and share power with experience. The interconnection between biology and environment is revisited throughout the text narrative and in Biology and Environment boxes with new and updated topics.

■ **Inclusion of interdisciplinary research is expanded.** The move toward viewing thoughts, feelings, and behavior as an integrated whole, affected by a wide array of influences in biology, social context, and culture, has motivated developmental researchers to strengthen their ties with other areas of psychology and with other disciplines. Topics and findings included in this edition increasingly reflect the contributions of educational psychology, social psychology, health psychology, clinical psychology, neurobiology, pediatrics, sociology, anthropology, social service, and other fields.

■ **The links among theory, research, and applications—a theme of this book since its inception—are strengthened.** As researchers intensify their efforts to generate findings that can be applied to real-life situations, we have placed even greater weight on social policy issues and sound theory- and evidence-based interventions and practices. Further applications are provided in the Applying What We Know tables, which give students concrete ways of building bridges between their learning and the real world.

■ **The educational context of development becomes a stronger focus.** The home, school, and community are featured as vital educational contexts in which the child develops. Research on effective teaching practices appears in all chapters and in new and revised Social Issues: Education boxes.

■ **The role of active student learning is made more explicit.** The *Take a Moment…* feature, built into the chapter narrative, asks students to think deeply and critically as they read. Ask Yourself questions at the end of each major section have been revised to promote four approaches to engaging actively with the subject matter: *Review, Connect, Apply,* and *Reflect.* This feature assists students in thinking about what they have read from multiple vantage points. The *Look and Listen* feature presents students with opportunities to observe what real children say and do and attend to influences on children in their everyday environments.

Text Philosophy

The basic approach of this book has been shaped by our professional and personal histories as teachers, researchers, and parents. It consists of seven philosophical ingredients that we regard as essential for students to emerge from a course with a thorough understanding of child development:

1. *An understanding of major theories and the strengths and shortcomings of each.* The first chapter begins by emphasizing that only knowledge of multiple theories can do justice to the richness of child development. As we take up each age period and domain of development, we present a variety of theoretical perspectives, indicate how each highlights previously overlooked facets of development, and discuss research that evaluates it. Consideration of contrasting theories also serves as the context for an evenhanded analysis of many controversial issues.

2. *An appreciation of research strategies for investigating child development.* To evaluate theories, students must have a firm grounding in research methods and designs. In addition to a special section in Chapter 1 covering research strategies, numerous studies are discussed in sufficient detail throughout the book for students to use what they have learned to critically assess the findings, conclusions, and implications of research.

3. *Knowledge of both the sequence of child development and the processes that underlie it.* Students are provided with a description of the organized sequence of development along with processes of change. An understanding of *process*—how complex interactions of biological and environmental events produce development—has been the focus of most recent research. Accordingly, the text reflects this emphasis. But new information about the timetable of change is constantly emerging. In many ways, children are considerably more competent than they were believed to be in the past. Current evidence on the sequence and timing of development, along with its implications for process, is presented throughout the book.

4. *An appreciation of the impact of context and culture on child development.* A wealth of research indicates that children live in rich physical and social contexts that affect all domains of development. In each chapter, students travel to distant parts of the world as we review a growing body of cross-cultural evidence. The text narrative also discusses many findings on socioeconomically and ethnically diverse children within the United States and on children with varying abilities and challenges. Besides highlighting the role of immediate settings, such as family, neighborhood, and school, we make a concerted effort to underscore the impact of larger social structures—societal values, laws, and government programs—on children's well-being.

5. *An understanding of the joint contributions of biology and environment to development.* The field recognizes more powerfully than ever before the joint roles of hereditary/constitutional and environmental factors—that these contributions to development combine in complex ways and cannot be separated in a simple manner. Numerous examples of how biological dispositions can be maintained as well as transformed by social contexts are presented throughout the book.

6. *A sense of the interdependency of all domains of development—physical, cognitive, emotional, and social.* Every chapter takes an integrated approach to understanding children. We show how physical, cognitive, emotional, and social development are interwoven.

Within the text narrative and in a special series of Ask Yourself *Connect* questions at the end of major sections, students are referred to other sections of the book to deepen their grasp of relationships among various aspects of change.

7. *An appreciation of the interrelatedness of theory, research, and applications.* Throughout this book, we emphasize that theories of child development and the research stimulated by them provide the foundation for sound, effective practices with children. The links among theory, research, and applications are reinforced by an organizational format in which theory and research are presented first, followed by practical implications. In addition, a current focus in the field—harnessing child development knowledge to shape social policies that support children's needs—is reflected in every chapter. The text addresses the current condition of children in the United States and around the world and shows how theory and research have combined with public interest to spark successful interventions.

Text Organization

The chronological organization of this text assists students in thoroughly understanding each age period. It also eases the task of integrating the various domains of development because each is discussed in close proximity. At the same time, a chronologically organized book requires that theories covering several age periods be presented piecemeal. This creates a challenge for students, who must link the various parts together. To assist with this task, we frequently remind students of important earlier achievements before discussing new developments, referring back to related sections with page references. Also, chapters devoted to the same topic (for example, cognitive development) are similarly organized, making it easier for students to draw connections across age periods and construct an overall view of developmental change.

New Coverage in the Eighth Edition

Child development is a fascinating and ever-changing field, with constantly emerging new discoveries and refinements in existing knowledge. The eighth edition represents this burgeoning contemporary literature with more than 2,000 new citations. Cutting-edge topics throughout the text underscore the book's major themes. Here is a sampling:

CHAPTER 1 New chapter introduction, inviting readers to become acquainted with the coauthors • Revised and updated section on developmental neuroscience, with special attention to developmental social neuroscience • New Social Issues: Health box on how family chaos undermines children's well-being • Revised and updated Cultural Influences box on immigrant youths • Updated examples of research designs, including the benefits of massive longitudinal projects yielding multipurpose data banks • Inclusion of children's assent as part of informed consent guidelines for protection of human subjects

CHAPTER 2 Updated discussion of gene–gene interactions, including the distinction between protein-coding genes and regulator genes • Consideration of social and cultural influences on the male-to-female birth sex ratio • New evidence on older paternal age and increased risk of DNA mutations contributing to serious disorders, including autism and schizophrenia • Enhanced attention to the impact of poverty on development, with special attention to interventions that help children surmount developmental risks • Revised and updated Social Issues: Education box on the impact of worldwide education of girls • Updated research on neighborhood influences on children's physical and mental health • Expanded attention to the role of ethnic minority extended families in promoting resilience in the face of prejudice and economic deprivation • Current statistics on the condition of children and families in the United States compared with other Western nations • Enhanced discussion of gene–environment interaction • Expanded section on epigenesis, including the role of methylation

CHAPTER 3 Revised and updated section on motivations for parenthood • Enhanced attention to fetal brain development, sensory capacities, and behavior • Updated Biology and Environment box on the prenatal environment and health in later life • Expanded and updated consideration of a wide range of teratogens • New evidence on the long-term consequences of emotional stress during pregnancy • Updated Social Issues: Health box on the Nurse–Family Partnership—reducing maternal stress and enhancing child development through social support

CHAPTER 4 New statistics and research on benefits and risks of medical interventions during childbirth • Consideration of the role of chronic maternal stress in preterm and low birth weight • New findings on the risks of late preterm birth—as little as 1 or 2 weeks early • New research on parenting and development of preterm and low-birth-weight infants • Expanded and updated Social Issues: Health box on health care and other policies for parents and newborn babies • Updated findings on hormonal changes in both mothers and fathers around the time of birth, and in foster and adoptive mothers, that facilitate caregiving • New evidence on factors contributing to sudden infant death syndrome (SIDS), along with the importance of public education efforts • New research on the role of sleep in infant learning • Updated discussion of "proximal care"—extensive holding of young babies—in reducing infant crying • Enhanced discussion of techniques for reducing infant stress to painful medical procedures • New findings on prenatal influences on newborn taste perception

CHAPTER 5 Updated introduction to major measures of brain functioning, including the EEG geodesic sensor net (GSN) and near-infrared spectroscopy (NIRS) • Enhanced discussion of brain development, with special attention to the prefrontal cortex • Updated Biology and Environment box on early brain plasticity • New research on children adopted from Romanian orphanages, bearing on whether infancy is a sensitive period of development • Enhanced attention to cultural influences on infant sleep • New findings on long-term consequences of malnutrition in infancy and toddlerhood • New Social Issues: Health box on U.S. public policy changes that improve infant feeding practices in low-income families •

Updated discussion of the controversy surrounding newborns' capacity to imitate • New dynamic systems research on development of walking, reaching, and grasping • Updated findings on implications of infants' capacity to analyze the speech stream for later language progress • Enhanced discussion of the impact of crawling and walking experience on perception of depth-at-an-edge • New evidence on the perceptual narrowing effect in speech, music, and species-related face perception, and in gender- and race-related face perception

CHAPTER 6 Updated evidence on toddlers' grasp of pictures and videos as symbols, including experiences that enhance symbolic understanding • New research on infants' ability to discriminate and perform simple arithmetic operations on large sets of items • Revised section introducing information-processing concepts, including working memory, automatic processes, processing speed, and executive function • Updated Biology and Environment box on infantile amnesia, addressing contributions of neurological change, language, and adult–child conversations about past events to stable long-term memories • New research on cultural variations in scaffolding infant and toddler learning • New evidence on the importance of sustained, high-quality child care from infancy through the preschool years for cognitive, language, literacy, and math performance at kindergarten entry • Updated evaluation findings on Early Head Start • New Biology and Environment box on the capacity of deaf children to invent language when exposed to limited or grammatically inconsistent input • Updated findings on babies' participation in imitative exchanges and joint attention, revealing their developing capacity for effective communication • New research on toddlers' preverbal gestures, with implications for spoken language development • Enhanced attention to SES differences in early vocabulary development as a predictor of vocabulary size at kindergarten entry • New evidence highlighting the vital role of a responsive adult in early language development

CHAPTER 7 Enhanced discussion of cultural variations in infant emotional expressiveness, with special emphasis on the social smile • New research on consequences of effortful control for cognitive, emotional, and social development • Revised section on genetic and environmental influences on temperament, with updated section on ethnic and gender differences • New section on temperamental differences in toddlers' susceptibility to rearing experiences, highlighting research on the short 5-HTTLPR gene • Revised and updated section on consequences of early availability of a consistent caregiver for attachment security, with special attention to children adopted from Eastern European orphanages • New findings on the joint contributions of infant genotype, temperament, and parenting to disorganized/disoriented attachment, with evidence on the short 5-HTTLPR and DRD4-7 repeat genes • Revised and updated Social Issues: Health box on child care, attachment, and later development • Updated research on cultural variations in early self-development

CHAPTER 8 Updated consideration of early childhood brain development, with emphasis on the prefrontal cortex and executive function • New statistics and research on the health status of young children, including tooth decay and childhood immunizations •

Updated Biology and Environment box on low-level lead exposure and children's development • Enhanced discussion of the contribution of sleep to early childhood physical growth and cognitive development • Expanded attention to the impact of adult mealtime practices on children's eating behavior and weight status • New evidence on parenting practices and young children's unintentional injuries • Expanded attention to cultural variations in development of drawing, including a new Cultural Influences box on why children from Asian cultures are advanced in drawing progress and creativity

CHAPTER 9 New research on young children's natural and supernatural beliefs, including cultural variations • Updated evidence on early childhood categorization, highlighting cultural differences • New findings on cultural variations in effective scaffolding • New Social Issues: Education box on children's questions as a catalyst for cognitive development • Expanded discussion of gains in executive function in early childhood, including attention, inhibition, and planning • New evidence on neurobiological changes in the cerebral cortex accompanying young children's more effective problem solving • New findings on cognitive attainments and social experiences that contribute to mastery of false belief, with attention to cultural differences • Updated Biology and Environment box on autism and theory of mind • Enhanced discussion of SES differences in emergent literacy and math knowledge • New evidence on benefits of universal prekindergarten programs • Revised section on strengthening preschool intervention, including findings on Head Start REDI • Updated discussion of effects of educational television and computer activities on academic learning • New research on preschoolers' strategies for word learning, including cultural variations

CHAPTER 10 New research on the influence of parents' elaborative reminiscing on preschoolers' self-concept and emotional understanding • Updated Cultural Influences box on cultural variations in personal storytelling and its implications for early self-concept • New evidence addressing contributions of sociodramatic and rough-and-tumble play to young children's emotional and social development • Enhanced discussion of cultural variations in sociodramatic play • Expanded and updated section on contributions of early childhood peer relations to school readiness and academic performance • New research on corporal punishment and children's adjustment, with special attention to children at high genetic risk for behavior problems • Updated Cultural Influences box on ethnic differences in the consequences of physical punishment • Expanded discussion of parent training programs in intervening with aggressive children, with special attention to Incredible Years • Updated evidence on hormonal influences on gender typing • New Social Issues: Education box on mother–child conversations as a source of children's gender stereotypes • Updated section on styles of child rearing, including Baumrind's distinction between confrontive and coercive control

CHAPTER 11 Updated findings on brain development in middle childhood • New evidence on factors contributing to obesity, including parents' demanding work schedules, frequent eating out, and children's capacity for self-regulation • New Social Issues: Health box on family stressors and childhood obesity • Enhanced consideration of the effectiveness of school-based obesity prevention programs • New findings on unintentional injury in middle childhood, with special attention to parental supervision and to school and community safety education programs as preventive strategies • Expanded attention to informal, child-organized games in middle childhood, including SES and cultural variations • Updated statistics on U.S. schoolchildren's physical activity levels and access to physical education and recess

CHAPTER 12 Updated research on school-age children's spatial reasoning, focusing on cognitive maps of large-scale spaces • New sections on executive function and working memory in middle childhood, with implications for academic learning • Updated Biology and Environment box on children with attention-deficit hyperactivity disorder • New findings on the contribution of societal modernization to children's performance on diverse cognitive tasks • Updated evidence on the school-age child's theory of mind, with special attention to recursive thought • New Cultural Influences box on the Flynn effect, dramatic gains in IQ from one generation to the next • New research on contributions of language skills to test bias, with special attention to African-American English • Updated findings on reducing cultural bias in testing through countering the negative impact of stereotype threat • Implications of recursive thought for language development, including understanding irony and sarcasm • Expanded discussion of the diverse cognitive benefits of bilingualism • Enhanced consideration of the benefits of cooperative learning in classrooms • Revised and updated section on educational media, with special attention to the influence of video game play on diverse aspects of cognitive development • Updated section on U.S. academic achievement in international perspective

CHAPTER 13 New evidence addressing effects of person praise and process praise on children's mastery orientation • Expanded coverage of cognitive and cultural influences on achievement-related attributions • Updated section on peer acceptance and rejection • Revised and updated Biology and Environment box on bullies and their victims, with special attention to cyberbullying • Recent changes in children's stereotyped beliefs about achievement • Updated evidence on children's development in gay and lesbian families • Expanded coverage of effects of fathers' employment on child development • Updated discussion of children's fears, including school refusal • Revised and updated Cultural Influences box on the impact of ethnic and political violence on children • Updated evidence on child sexual abuse, including global prevalence estimates and long-term developmental consequences • Enhanced discussion of resilience, introducing the concept of developmental cascade • New research on social and emotional learning interventions, with special emphasis on the 4Rs program

CHAPTER 14 Consideration of adrenarche—hormonal changes preceding the physical events of puberty • New statistics on physical activity levels among U. S. adolescents • New research on effects of adverse family environments on pubertal timing • Updated evidence on the secular trend in age at menarche in industrialized nations • New research on adolescent brain development, with implications for adolescent risk taking and susceptibility to peer influence • New findings on pubertal timing and adjustment • Revised and updated evidence on eating disorders, with new section on binge-eating disorder • Updated Social Issues: Education box on parent–adolescent communication about sex • Expanded discussion of healthy and unhealthy sexual behavior during adolescence, with new evidence on consequences of early sexual activity • Updated Biology and Environment box on lesbian, gay, and bisexual identity development and coming-out experiences • Updated statistics on adolescent contraceptive use, pregnancy and parenthood, and sexually transmitted infections • New research on substance use prevention, including the Strong African American Families (SAAF) program

CHAPTER 15 Updated discussion of sex differences in mental abilities, including current U.S. and international evidence on reading, writing, and math achievement • Revised and updated Biology and Environment box on sex differences in spatial abilities, with new research on experiences influencing spatial skills • Expanded discussion of school transitions, including new findings on achievement of students in K–8 versus middle schools • Updated Social Issues: Education box on media multitasking, with new evidence on consequences for executive function • Updated Social Issues: Education box on high-stakes testing • Revised and updated discussion of high school dropout, with new statistics on U.S. dropout rates • New findings on the impact of gender-stereotyped messages on girls' career aspirations and confidence in entering STEM fields

CHAPTER 16 New research on personal and social factors contributing to identity development in adolescence • Updated Cultural Influences box on development of ethnic identity, including enhanced attention to peer influences • Enhanced consideration of

factors that promote moral identity, along with its relationship to moral behavior • New evidence on adolescent religious involvement and moral development • Updated Social Issues: Education box on development of civic engagement in adolescence, including school and community contributions through extracurricular activities and service learning • New findings on gender intensification in adolescence • Enhanced discussion of parent–child relationships and development of adolescent autonomy, including cultural variations • Expanded section on teenagers' communication with friends through social media, including implications for friendship quality and social adjustment • Updated evidence on adolescent depression, with special attention to gender differences • New research on family, school, and neighborhood contributions to delinquency • Updated findings on long-term outcomes of multisystemic therapy for violent juvenile offenders

CHAPTER 17 Expanded discussion of emerging adults' romantic relationships, including the Internet as an increasingly popular way to initiate relationships • New research on uncommitted sexual encounters during the college years, with implications for adjustment • Updated evidence on cohabitation among U.S. emerging-adult couples and its implications for a lasting intimate relationship • New research on the importance of a high-quality college education to securing favorable employment • Updated findings on challenges experienced by women who choose to purse male-dominated careers • New evidence on racial and ethnic biases in career opportunities • Enhanced consideration of the debate over whether emerging adults forge self-centered worldviews, as the descriptor "generation me" suggests • Expanded section on religion and spirituality among emerging adults, with implications for psychological adjustment • Enhanced discussion of emerging adults who flourish, developing favorably, versus those who flounder, appearing lost during these transitional years

Pedagogical Features

Maintaining a highly accessible writing style—one that is lucid and engaging without being simplistic—continues to be one of our major goals. We frequently converse with students, encouraging them to relate what they read to their own lives. In doing so, we aim to make the study of child development involving and pleasurable.

Chapter Introductions and Vignettes About Children

To provide a helpful preview of chapter content, we include an outline and overview in each chapter introduction. To help students construct a clear image of development and to enliven the text narrative, each chronological age division is unified by case examples woven throughout that set of chapters. For example, within the infancy and toddlerhood section, we look in on three children, observe dramatic changes and striking individual differences, and address the impact of family background, child-rearing practices, parents' and children's life experiences, and child-care quality on development. Besides a set of main characters, many additional vignettes offer vivid examples of development among children and adolescents.

End-of-Chapter Summaries

Comprehensive end-of-chapter summaries, organized according to the major divisions of each chapter and highlighting important terms, remind students of key points in the text discussion. Learning objectives are included in the summary to encourage focused review.

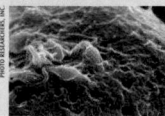

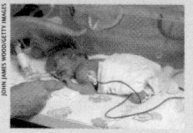

Ask Yourself Questions

Active engagement with the subject matter is supported by revised and expanded study questions at the end of each major section. Four types of questions prompt students to think about child development in diverse ways: **Review** questions help students recall and comprehend information they have just read. **Connect** questions help students build an image of the whole child by integrating what they have learned across age periods and domains of development. **Apply** questions encourage application of knowledge to controversial issues and problems faced by children, parents, and professionals who work with them. **Reflect** questions make the study of child development personally meaningful by asking students to reflect on their own development and life experiences. Each question is answered on the text's MyDevelopmentLab website.

Learning Objectives

New to this edition, learning objectives appear in the text margins next to each main head, guiding students' reading and study.

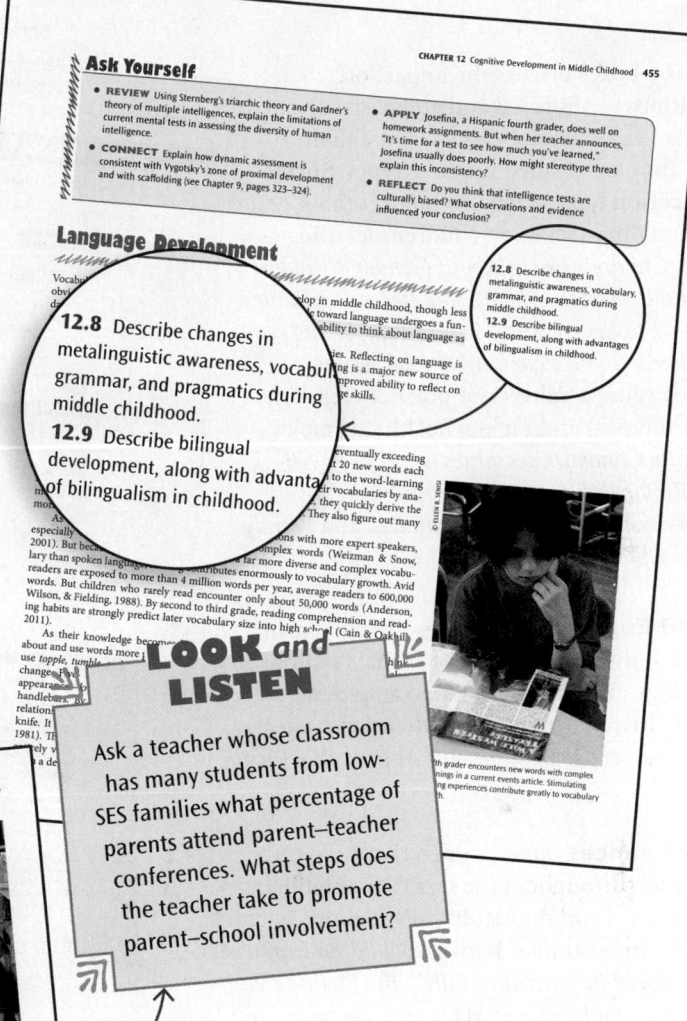

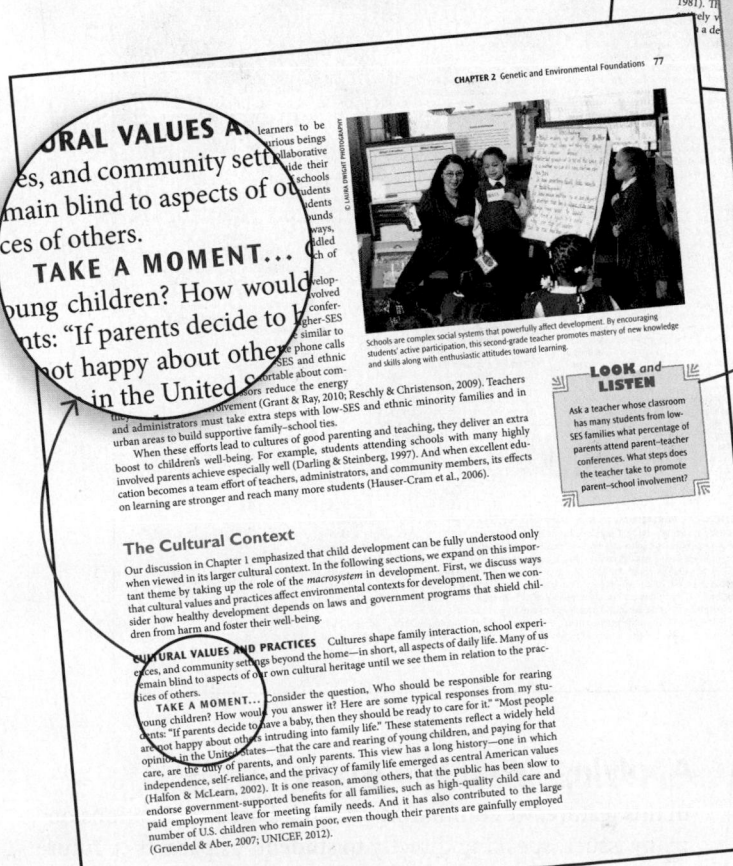

Take a Moment...

Built into the text narrative, this feature asks students to "take a moment" to think about an important point, integrate information on children's development, or engage in an exercise or an application to clarify a challenging concept. **TAKE A MOMENT...** highlights and reinforces the text's strength in conversing with and actively engaging students in learning and in inspiring critical thinking.

Look and Listen

This active-learning feature presents students with opportunities to observe what real children say and do and attend to influences on children in their everyday environments. "Look and Listen" experiences are tied to relevant text sections, with the goal of making the study of development more authentic and meaningful.

Three Types of Thematic Boxes

Thematic boxes accentuate the philosophical themes of this book:

Social Issues boxes discuss the impact of social conditions on children and emphasize the need for sensitive social policies to ensure their well-being. They are divided into two types: **Social Issues: Education** boxes focus on home, school, and community influences on children's learning—for example, *Children Learn About Gender Through Mother–Child Conversations; School Recess—A Time to Play, a Time to Learn;* and *Media Multitasking Disrupts Attention and Learning*. **Social Issues: Health** boxes address values and practices relevant to children's physical and mental health. Examples include *Family Chaos Undermines Children's Well-Being, U.S. Public Policy Changes Improve Infant Feeding Practices in Low-Income Families,* and *Family Stressors and Childhood Obesity*.

Biology and Environment boxes highlight growing attention to the complex, bidirectional relationship between biology and environment. Examples include *The Prenatal Environment and Health in Later Life, Deaf Children Invent Language,* and *Autism and Theory of Mind*.

Cultural Influences boxes deepen the attention to culture threaded throughout the text. They highlight both cross-cultural and multicultural variations in child development—for example, *Why Are Children from Asian Cultures Advanced in Drawing Skills?, The Flynn Effect: Massive Generational Gains in IQ,* and *Is Emerging Adulthood Really a Distinct Stage of Development?*

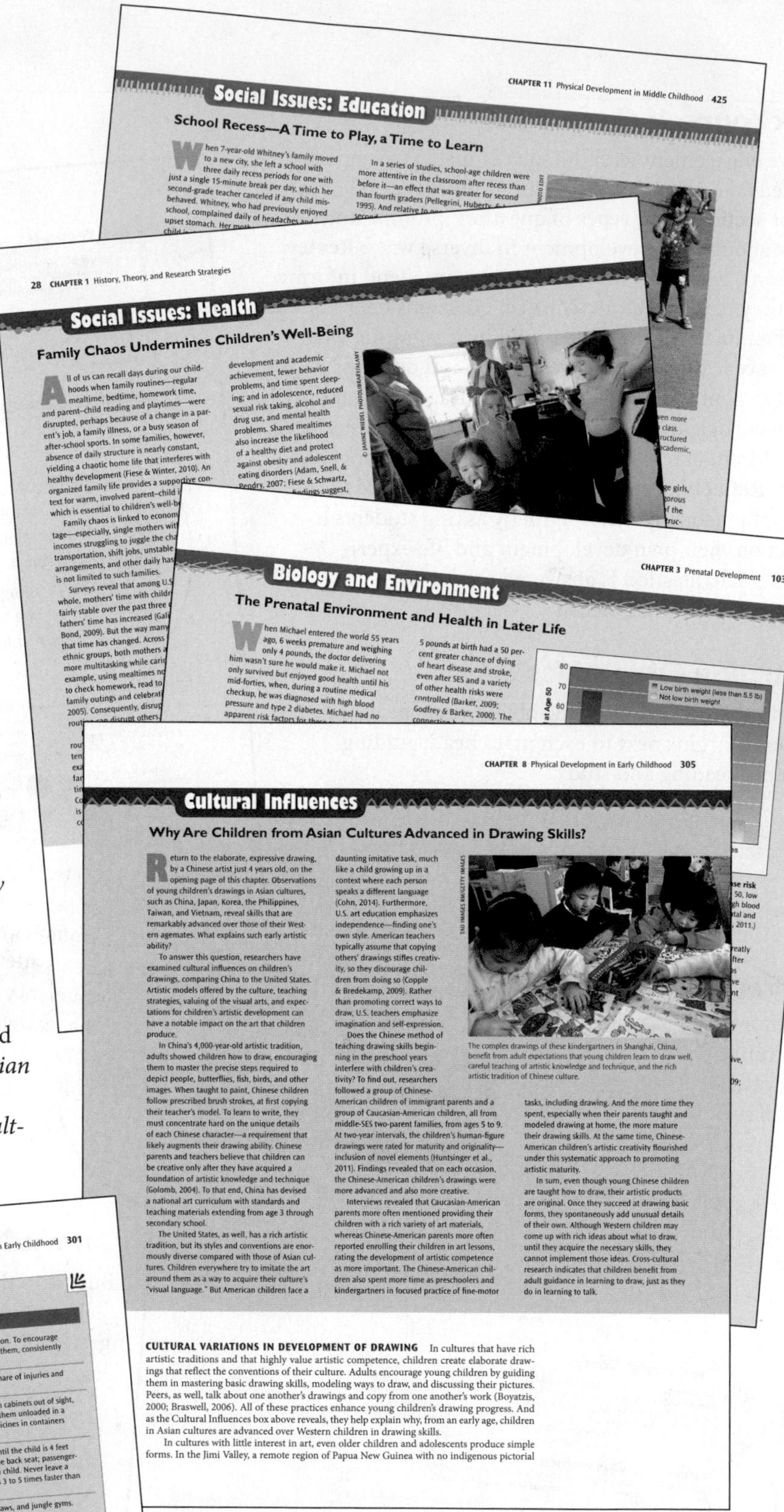

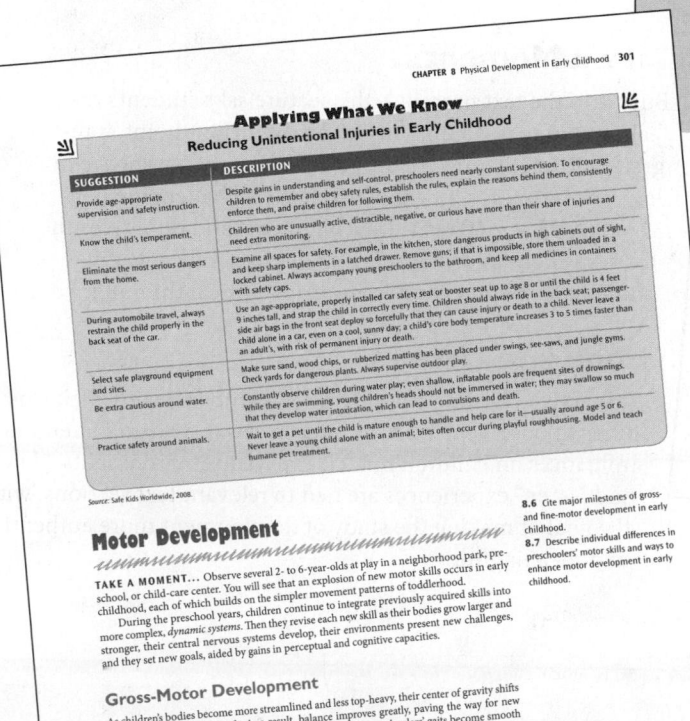

Applying What We Know Tables

In this feature, we summarize research-based applications on many issues, speaking directly to students as parents or future parents and to those pursuing different careers or areas of study, such as teaching, health care, counseling, or social work. The tables include *Supporting Early Language Learning, Helping Children Manage Common Fears of Early Childhood, Regulating Screen Media Use,* and *Supporting Healthy Identity Development*.

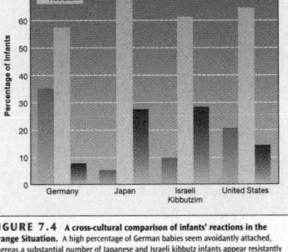

Milestones Tables

A Milestones table appears at the end of each age division of the text. The tables summarize major physical, cognitive, language, emotional, and social attainments, providing a convenient aid for reviewing the chronology of child development.

Enhanced Art and Photo Program

The art and page-layout style present concepts and research findings with clarity and attractiveness, thereby aiding student understanding and retention. Each photo has been carefully selected to complement the text discussion and to represent the diversity of children around the world.

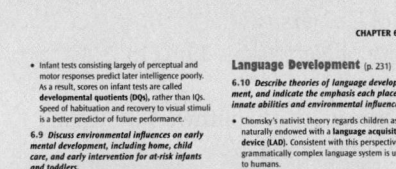

In-Text Key Terms with Definitions, End-of-Chapter Term List, and End-of-Book Glossary

Mastery of terms that make up the central vocabulary of the field is promoted through in-text highlighting of key terms and definitions, which encourages students to review the terminology of the field in greater depth by rereading related information. Key terms also appear in an end-of-chapter page-referenced term list and an end-of-book glossary.

Acknowledgments

The dedicated contributions of a great many individuals helped make this book a reality and contributed to refinements and improvements in this eighth edition.

Reviewers

An impressive cast of reviewers provided many helpful suggestions and constructive criticisms, as well as encouragement and enthusiasm, for the organization and content of the text. We are grateful to each one of them.

For the First Through Seventh Editions

Scott Adler, York University
Mark B. Alcorn, University of Northern Colorado
Joseph Allen, University of Virginia
William Aquilino, University of Wisconsin
Armin W. Arndt, Eastern Washington University
Martha Arterberry, Colby College
Lamia Barakat, Drexel University
Cecelia Benelli, Western Illinois University
Kathleen Bey, Palm Beach Community College
Heather Bouchey, University of Vermont
Donald Bowers, Community College of Philadelphia
Michele Y. Breault, Truman State University
Jerry Bruce, Sam Houston State College
Kristy Burkholder, University of Wisconsin, Madison
Melissa Burnham, University of Nevada, Reno
Lanthan D. Camblin, University of Cincinnati
Joseph J. Campos, University of California, Berkeley
Linda A. Camras, DePaul University
Gustavo Carlo, University of Nebraska—Lincoln
Lynn Caruso, Seneca College
Nancy Taylor Coghill, University of Southwest Louisiana
Raymond Collings, SUNY Cortland
Diane Brothers Cook, Gainesville College
Nicole Campione-Barr, University of Missouri, Columbia
Jennifer Cook, Kent State University
Roswell Cox, Berea College
Ronald Craig, Edinboro University of Pennsylvania
Zoe Ann Davidson, Alabama A&M University
Sheridan DeWolf, Grossmont College
Matthew DiCintio, Delaware County Community College
Constance DiMaria-Kross, Union County College
Jacquelynne Eccles, University of Michigan
Jeff Farrar, University of Florida
Bronwyn Fees, Kansas State University
F. Richard Ferraro, University of North Dakota
Kathleen Fite, Southwest Texas State University
Peter Flynn, Northern Essex Community College
Trisha Folds-Bennett, College of Charleston
Nancy Freeman, University of South Carolina
William Friedman, Oberlin College
Jayne Gackenbach, MacEwan University

Eugene Geist, Ohio University
Sabine Gerhardt, University of Akron
Abi Gewirtz, University of Minnesota
Kristine Hansen, University of Winnipeg
Vivian Harper, San Joaquin Delta College
Algea Harrison, Oakland University
Janice Hartgrove-Freile, North Harris Community College
Vernon Haynes, Youngstown State University
Bert Hayslip, Jr., University of North Texas
Sandra Hellyer, Butler University
Joan Herwig, Iowa State University
Paula Hillmann, University of Wisconsin, Waukesha
Robert Hiltonsmith, Radford University
Shayla Holub, University of Texas, Dallas
Christie Honeycutt, Stanly Community College
Malia Huchendorf, Normandale Community College
Lisa Huffman, Ball State University
Clementine Hansley Hurt, Radford University
Jennifer Jipson, California Polytechnic State University
Scott Johnson, New York University
Joline Jones, Worcester State University
Kate Kenney, Howard Community College
Shirin Khosropour, Austin Community College
Elisa Klein, University of Maryland
John S. Klein, Castleton State College
Claire Kopp, Claremont Graduate School
Eugene Krebs, California State University, Fresno
Carole Kremer, Hudson Valley Community College
Gary W. Ladd, University of Illinois, Urbana–Champaign
Deborah Laible, Lehigh University
Linda Lavine, State University of New York at Cortland
Sara Lawrence, California State University, Northridge
Gail Lee, Jersey City State College
Judith R. Levine, State University of New York at Farmingdale
Miriam Linver, Montclair State University
David Lockwood, Humber College
Frank Manis, University of Southern California
Martin Marino, Atlantic Cape Community College
Mary Ann McLaughlin, Clarion University of Pennsylvania
Megan McLelland, Oregon State University
Annie McManus, Parkland College
Trent Maurer, Georgia Southern University
Cloe Merrill, Weber State University
Daniel Messinger, University of Miami
Rich Metzger, University of Tennessee at Chattanooga
Karla Miley, Black Hawk College
Joyce Munsch, California State University, Northridge
Jennifer Trapp Myers, University of Michigan
Virginia Navarro, University of Missouri, St. Louis
Larry Nelson, Brigham Young University
Peggy Norwood, Red Rocks Community College
Peter V. Oliver, University of Hartford
Behnaz Pakizegi, William Patterson University
Virginia Parsons, Carroll College
Karen Peterson, University of Washington, Vancouver
Julie Poehlmann, University of Wisconsin—Madison

Tom Power, Washington State University
Kavita Prakash, Heritage College
Joe M. Price, San Diego State University
Cathy Proctor-Castillo, Long Beach Community College
Verna Raab, Mount Royal College
Raghu Rao, University of Minnesota
Mary Kay Reed, York College of Pennsylvania
Michael Rodman, Middlesex Community College
Alan Russell, Flinders University
Pamela Schulze, University of Akron
Tizrah Schutzengel, Bergen Community College
Johnna Shapiro, Illinois Wesleyan University
Elizabeth Short, Case Western Reserve University
Delores Smith, University of Tennessee
Gregory Smith, Dickinson College
Laura Sosinsky, Fordham University
Thomas Spencer, San Francisco State University
Carolyn Spies, Bloomfield College
Kathy Stansbury, University of New Mexico
Connie Steele, University of Tennessee, Knoxville
Janet Strayer, Simon Fraser University
Marcia Summers, Ball State University
Daniel Swingley, University of Pennsylvania
Christy Teranishi, Texas A&M International University
Dennis Thompson, Georgia State University
Tracy Thorndike-Christ, Western Washington University
Connie K. Varnhagen, University of Alberta
Athena Vouloumanos, McGill University
Judith Ward, Central Connecticut State University
Shawn Ward, Le Moyne College
Alida Westman, Eastern Michigan University
Jayne White, Drury University
Colin William, Columbus State Community College
Belinda Wholeben, Rockford College
Sue Williams, Southwest Texas State University
Deborah Winters, New Mexico State University
Ilona Yim, University of California, Irvine
Nicole Zarrett, University of South Carolina, Columbia

For the Eighth Edition

Shannon Audley-Piotrowski, Smith College
Janet J. Boseovski, University of North Carolina Greensboro
Kate Fogarty, University of Florida
Dominic Gullo, Drexel University
Shanta Hattikudur, Temple University
Hiu-Chin Hsu, University of Georgia
Zsuzsa Kaldy, University of Massachusetts Boston
Sarah Kollat, Pennsylvania State University
Murray Krantz, Florida State University
Stuart Marcovitch, University of North Carolina Greensboro
Amy H. Mezulis, Seattle Pacific University
Amanda Morris, Oklahoma State University—Tulsa
Winnie Mucherah, Ball State University
Dara Musher-Eisenman, Bowling Green State University
Angela Nievar, University of North Texas

Maggie Renken, Georgia State University
Dorothy Sluss, James Madison University
Joan E. Test, Missouri State University
Virginia Tompkins, Ohio State University

Editorial and Production Team

We have been fortunate to collaborate with a highly capable editorial team at Pearson Education. It has been a great pleasure to work once again with Tom Pauken, Managing Editor, who oversaw the preparation of the fourth and seventh editions of *Infants, Children, and Adolescents* and who returned to edit this eighth edition as well as its supplements package. We cannot capture in words Tom's amazing contributions: His careful review of manuscript, keen organizational skills, responsive day-to-day communication, insightful suggestions, astute problem solving, interest in the subject matter, patience, thoughtfulness, and sense of humor (at just the right moments) greatly enhanced the quality of the text and made it possible for us to keep pace with Pearson's tight revision time frame. Tom is truly our editor extraordinaire: We greatly look forward to working with him on future projects.

Donna Simons, Senior Production Project Manager, coordinated the complex production tasks for the seventh edition as well as for this eighth edition, transforming our manuscript into an exquisitely beautiful text. We are grateful for Donna's keen aesthetic sense, attention to detail, flexibility, efficiency, thoughtfulness, and incredible commitment. We cannot count the number of times Donna has been there for us, not just during typical working hours but virtually at all hours—finding a way to create a more convenient page layout, suggesting a more effective turn of phrase in our prose, improving on an artwork sketch to make the resulting figure more effective, and much, much more.

Rachel Trapp, Editorial Assistant, has been nothing short of amazing. In addition to spending countless hours expertly gathering and organizing scholarly literature, she assisted with so many editorial and production tasks that they are, literally, too numerous to list. Judy Ashkenaz, Development Editor, commented on each chapter prior to our revision, helping to ensure that we listened attentively to each of the reviewers' recommendations and suggestions. She also prepared the new Lecture Enhancements for the Instructor's Resource Manual and revised its chapter summaries and outlines. Our appreciation to Judy for her work on more editions of *Infants, Children, and Adolescents* than any other member of the publishing team.

We thank Sarah Evertson for helping to identify the exceptional photographs that so aptly illustrate the text narrative. Margaret Pinette provided outstanding copyediting and Julie Hotchkiss, impeccable proofreading.

The instructor resources package benefited from the talents and diligence of several other individuals. Kimberly Michaud, Jeanie McHale, and Rachel Trapp prepared a superb Test Bank along with excellent MyDevelopmentLab and REVEL assessments. Rachel Trapp is also responsible for the beautifully illustrated PowerPoint presentation. Maria Henneberry and Phil Vandiver of Contemporary Visuals in Bloomington, IL, collaborated with us in producing an artistic and inspiring set of new video segments covering diverse topics in child development.

Rachael Payne prepared the ad copy and informative e-mails to the sales representatives and the field about *Infants, Children, and Adolescents,* Eighth Edition. She also designed our text website, *www.infantschildrenandadolescents.com.* Rachael's insightful and creative work also appears within Pearson's product website, *www.pearsonhighered.com/berk-ica-8e-info.* We thank, as well, Lindsey Gill, Marketing Manager, for day-to-day marketing efforts aimed at ensuring that up-to-date information about the text and its instructor resources reaches Pearson Education's sales force.

Last but not least, our sincere thanks to Roth Wilkofsky, Senior Publisher of Arts and Sciences, for crafting a caring climate at Pearson in which to prepare this revision. We are indebted to Roth for valuing our work, bringing us to New York for the eighth edition planning meeting, visiting our community to get to know us in the everyday settings in which we work, and periodic problem solving and encouragement. We have benefited greatly from his wide-ranging knowledge and experience, and his cordiality.

Family, Colleagues, and Friends

Immeasurable gratitude goes to our families, colleagues, and friends for their patience, understanding, and support.

From Laura: I thank my family for being *there* for me during over a quarter-century of work on my suite of Pearson titles. My sons, David and Peter, grew up with my texts, passing from childhood to adolescence and then to adulthood as successive editions were written. David has a special connection with the books' subject matter as an inner-city elementary school teacher. Peter is now an experienced attorney, and his vivacious and talented wife Melissa joins a new generation of university faculty engaged in innovative teaching and research. All three continue to enrich my understanding through reflections on events and progress in their own lives. My husband, Ken, willingly put on hold much in our life together to accommodate the challenges and pace of this revision. His astute reflections and support made all the difference during the project's final months.

My appreciation, as well, to Richard Payne, colleague, friend, and fellow Pearson author, for many profitable discussions about the writing process, the condition of children and families, and other topics that have significantly influenced my work. Greg Simpson, Dean of the College of Arts and Sciences, has taught from my texts, repeatedly underscoring their importance to Illinois State University. In addition to warm friendship and advice on the cover image and design, Harold and Marlene Gregor have provided me with an unmatched model of lifelong creativity. Throughout the preparation of this project, my long-time friend Jana Edge ensured that a five- to six-mile early morning walk preceded my sitting down to write. For extraordinary counsel, I am immensely grateful to Paul LiCalsi and Devereux Chatillon.

From Adena: I am especially grateful to Cooper Cutting for encouraging me to pursue this project despite his own significant work commitments. I appreciate the many family dinners he prepared, rides to and from school he provided, and hours of homework he supervised while I was busy writing. My teenage children, Charlie and Isabel Cutting, are my best cheerleaders. As usual, they were good-natured about their mother's hectic schedule and periodic high stress levels. I also thank my parents, Barbara and Joel Meyers, for nurturing my writing skills, believing in me more than I believed in myself, and demonstrating all of the features of high-quality parenting that we describe throughout this text.

I am grateful to my friends and colleagues, Rocío Rivadeneyra, Maura Toro-Morn, Sue Sprecher, Rachel Bowden, Amy Wood, Corinne Zimmerman, and Renée Tobin, for camaraderie that kept me sane and balanced and for understanding when I was too busy. In addition to being an especially supportive department chair and a good friend, Scott Jordan imparted some of the most important professional advice I have ever received. Karina Diaz and Amanda Rohan proved to be exceptionally reliable and conscientious graduate assistants, whose help was indispensable throughout my work on this project.

Finally, I thank Laura Berk for the opportunity to collaborate with her on this remarkable textbook. Her mentorship and example inspire my best work.

Laura E. Berk and Adena B. Meyers

mydevelopmentlab

MyDevelopmentLab is a collection of online homework, tutorial, and assessment products, integrated with the eText, that is designed to improve students' learning. Authored by Laura Berk and Adena Meyers, MyDevelopmentLab for *Infants, Children, and Adolescents,* Eighth Edition, engages students through active learning and promotes in-depth mastery of the subject matter, thereby fostering more thorough preparation for class, quizzes, and exams.

- **A Personalized Study Plan** analyzes students' study needs into three levels: Remember, Understand, and Apply.

- **A Variety of Assessments** enable continuous evaluation of students' learning.

- **The Gradebook** helps students track progress and get immediate feedback. Automatically graded assessments flow into the Gradebook, which can be viewed in MyDevelopmentLab or exported.

- **The eText** allows students to highlight relevant passages and add notes. It can be accessed through a laptop, iPad®, or tablet. An app is available to facilitate download.

- **Extensive video footage** includes NEW segments produced by author Laura Berk.

- **Multimedia simulations** include NEW topics, with simulations designed by author Laura Berk to seamlessly complement the text.

- **Careers in Human Development** explains how studying human development is essential for a wide range of career paths. This tool features more than 25 career overviews, which contain interviews with actual practitioners, educational requirements, typical day-to-day activities, and links to websites for additional information.

- **Biographies** of major figures in the field. Examples include Erik Erikson, Jean Piaget, Lev Vygotsky, Eleanor Gibson, Lawrence Kohlberg, and Carol Gilligan.

- **MyVirtualChild** is an interactive web-based simulation that allows students to rear a child from birth to age 18 and monitor the effects of their parenting decisions over time.

For a sampling of MyDevelopmentLab's rich content, visit *www.mydevelopmentlab.com*.

REVEL™

Revel™ is an immersive learning experience designed for the way today's students read, think, and learn. Built in collaboration with educators and students nationwide, REVEL is Pearson's newest, fully digital method of delivering course content.

REVEL further enlivens the text by integrating into the authors' narrative interactive media and assessments, thereby offering students additional opportunities to engage deeply with course content while reading. Greater student engagement leads to more thorough understanding and improved performance throughout the course.

To learn more about REVEL, visit *www.pearsonhighered.com/ REVEL*.

Instructor Resources

In addition to MyDevelopmentLab and REVEL, several other author-produced student and instructor materials accompany *Infants, Children, and Adolescents,* Eighth Edition.

Instructor's Resource Manual (IRM) This thoroughly revised IRM can be used by first-time or experienced instructors to enrich classroom experiences. Two new lecture enhancements accompany each chapter, presenting cutting-edge topics, with article citations and suggestions for expanding on chapter content in class.

Test Bank The Test Bank contains over 2,000 multiple-choice and essay questions, all of which are page-referenced to chapter content and also classified by type.

Pearson MyTest This secure online environment allows instructors to easily create exams, study guide questions, and quizzes from any computer with an Internet connection.

PowerPoint Presentation The PowerPoint presentation provides outlines and illustrations of key topics for each chapter of the text.

"Explorations in Child Development" DVD and Guide This REVISED DVD WITH 10 NEW SEGMENTS is over five hours in length and contains more than 50 four- to ten-minute narrated segments, designed for classroom use, that illustrate the many theories, concepts, and milestones of child development. The DVD and Guide are available only to instructors who are confirmed adopters of the text.

About the Chapter Opening Art

We would like to extend grateful acknowledgments to the International Museum of Children's Art, Oslo, Norway; to the International Child Art Foundation, Washington, DC; and to the World Awareness Children's Museum, Glens Falls, New York, for the exceptional cover image and chapter opening art, which depict the talents, concerns, and viewpoints of young artists from around the world. The awe-inspiring collection of children's art gracing this text expresses family, school, and community themes; good times and personal triumphs; profound appreciation for beauty; and great depth of emotion. We are pleased to share with readers this window into children's creativity, insightfulness, sensitivity, and compassion.

"A Child's Dream of Parents with More Time"
Mia Koch
16 years, Norway

REPRINTED WITH PERMISSION FROM THE INTERNATIONAL MUSEUM OF CHILDREN'S ART, OSLO, NORWAY

Infants, Children, and Adolescents

History, Theory, and Research Strategies

"Me and My World"
Lizaveta Lenkevich
9 years, Belarus

With bold brush strokes and vibrant color, this artist conveys the energy and beauty of her town and the various pathways through it. Chapter 1 will introduce you to a multiplicity of ways to think about and study child development.

In a café not far from our university offices, we held our first meeting to discuss the exciting collaborative journey before us—preparing this eighth edition of *Infants, Children, and Adolescents*. As we delved into the task, our conversation turned to child development as we had personally experienced it. We exchanged stories about our own children—the amusing things they had said as preschoolers, their varied personalities and interests, and the differences in their childhood experiences, given that our two families are a generation apart in age.

Three decades ago, Laura noted, a free day usually meant that her sons David and Peter hurried out the door after breakfast to join neighborhood playmates in climbing trees, organizing a game of pickup baseball, or building a backyard fort. The out-of-school hours of today's children, in contrast, are more often devoted to a flurry of prearranged learning opportunities—dance, music, and karate lessons; academic tutoring; and parent-organized play dates—leaving little time for unstructured play. Similarly, school life for present-day children seems speeded up: Charlie and Isabel, Adena's son and daughter, mastered in kindergarten much of what David and Peter had been expected to learn in first and second grade. And Charlie and Isabel's world is replete with high-tech media—fast-action video games, cell phones, iPads, iPods, and countless other modern gadgets that didn't exist when David and Peter were young.

As we talked, we touched on our own childhood experiences and how they contributed to who we are today. Laura remembered weekends helping her father in his downtown clothing shop, the year her mother studied to become a high school teacher, and Sunday outings to museums and the seashore. Adena described frequent moves to new cities as her father, a professor, changed jobs every few years, along with the excitement and challenges of adapting to new neighborhoods, schools, and peer groups.

We also spoke about our childhood friends and what we know about their present lives. Laura's high school classmate Phil—shy, anxious, and cruelly teased because of his cleft lip—now owner of a thriving chain of hardware stores and member of his city council. Adena's inventive, extroverted friend Ally, who grew up in a low-income family, served as Adena's campaign manager when she ran for student council, and saved for college by crushing and selling pop cans—today a successful CEO of a nonprofit organization. Julio, immigrant from Mexico who joined Laura's class in third grade—currently director of an elementary school bilingual education program and single parent of an adopted Mexican boy. And finally, Laura's next-door neighbor Rick, who picked fights at recess, struggled with reading, dropped out of high school, and moved from one job to another over the following 10 years.

As you begin this course in child development, perhaps you, too, are wondering about some of the same questions that crossed our minds during our café conversation:

- In what ways are children's home, school, and neighborhood experiences the same today as they were in generations past, and in what ways are they different?
- How are young children's perceptions of the world similar to adults', and how are they different?

- What determines the features that humans have in common and those that make each of us unique—physically, mentally, and behaviorally?
- How did Julio, transplanted at age 8 to a new culture, master its language and customs and succeed in its society, yet remain strongly identified with his ethnic community?
- Why do some of us, like Kathryn and Rick, retain the same styles of responding that characterized us as children, whereas others, like Phil, change in essential ways?
- How do cultural changes—employed mothers, child care, divorce, smaller families, and new technologies—affect children's characteristics?

These are central questions addressed by **child development,** an area of study devoted to understanding constancy and change from conception through adolescence. Child development is part of a larger, interdisciplinary field known as **developmental science,** which includes all changes we experience throughout the lifespan (Lerner et al., 2011). Great diversity characterizes the interests and concerns of the thousands of investigators who study child development. But all have a common goal: to describe and identify those factors that influence the consistencies and changes in young people during the first two decades of life. ■

1.1 What is the field of child development, and what factors stimulated its expansion?

1.2 How is child development typically divided into domains and periods?

The Field of Child Development

The questions just listed are not just of scientific interest. Each has *applied,* or practical, importance as well. In fact, scientific curiosity is just one factor that led child development to become the exciting field of study it is today. Research about development has also been stimulated by social pressures to improve the lives of children. For example, the beginning of public education in the early twentieth century led to a demand for knowledge about what and how to teach children of different ages. Pediatricians' interest in improving children's health required an understanding of physical growth and nutrition. The social service profession's desire to treat children's emotional and behavior problems and to help them cope with challenging life circumstances, such as the birth of a sibling, parental divorce, poverty, bullying in school, or the death of a loved one, required information about personality and social development. And parents have continually sought advice about child-rearing practices and experiences that would promote their children's development and well-being.

Our large storehouse of information about child development is *interdisciplinary.* It has grown through the combined efforts of people from many fields. Because of the need to solve everyday problems concerning children, researchers from psychology, sociology, anthropology, biology, and neuroscience have joined forces with professionals from education, family studies, medicine, public health, and social service, to name just a few. Together, they have created the field

Child development research has great practical value. Findings on how children learn best in school have contributed to new approaches to education that emphasize exploration, discovery, and collaboration.

© ELLEN B. SENISI

of child development as it exists today—a body of knowledge that is not just scientifically important but also relevant and useful.

Domains of Development

To make the vast, interdisciplinary study of human constancy and change more orderly and convenient, development is often divided into three broad domains: *physical, cognitive,* and *emotional and social.* Refer to Figure 1.1 for a description and illustration of each. Within each period from infancy through adolescence, we will consider the three domains in the order just mentioned. Yet the domains are not really distinct. Rather, they combine in an integrated, holistic fashion to yield the living, growing child. Furthermore, each domain influences and is influenced by the others. For example, in Chapter 5 you will see that new motor capacities, such as reaching, sitting, crawling, and walking (physical), contribute greatly to infants' understanding of their surroundings (cognitive). When babies think and act more competently, adults stimulate them more with games, language, and expressions of delight at their new achievements (emotional and social). These enriched experiences, in turn, promote all aspects of development.

You will encounter instances of the interwoven nature of all domains on nearly every page of this book. In the margins of the text, you will find occasional *Look and Listen* activities—opportunities for you to see everyday illustrations of development by observing what real children say and do or by attending to everyday influences on children. Through these experiences, we hope to make your study of development more authentic and meaningful.

Also, look for the *Ask Yourself* feature at the end of major sections, designed to deepen your understanding. Within it, we have included *Review* questions, which help you recall and think about information you have just read; *Connect* questions, which help you form a coherent, unified picture of child development; *Apply* questions, which encourage you to apply your knowledge to controversial issues and problems faced by parents, teachers, and children; and *Reflect* questions, which invite you to reflect on your own development and that of people you know well.

Physical Development

Changes in body size, proportions, appearance, functioning of body systems, perceptual and motor capacities, and physical health

Cognitive Development

Changes in intellectual abilities, including attention, memory, academic and everyday knowledge, problem solving, imagination, creativity, and language

Emotional and Social Development

Changes in emotional communication, self-understanding, knowledge about other people, interpersonal skills, friendships, intimate relationships, and moral reasoning and behavior

FIGURE 1.1 **Major domains of development.** The three domains are not really distinct. Rather, they overlap and interact.

Periods of Development

Besides distinguishing and integrating the three domains, another dilemma arises in discussing development: how to divide the flow of time into sensible, manageable parts. Researchers usually use the following age periods, according to which we have organized this book. Each brings new capacities and social expectations that serve as important transitions in major theories:

- *The prenatal period: from conception to birth.* In this nine-month period, the most rapid time of change, a one-celled organism is transformed into a human baby with remarkable capacities for adjusting to life in the surrounding world.
- *Infancy and toddlerhood: from birth to 2 years.* This period brings dramatic changes in the body and brain that support the emergence of a wide array of motor, perceptual, and intellectual capacities; the beginnings of language; and first intimate ties to others. Infancy spans the first year; toddlerhood spans the second, during which children take their first independent steps, marking a shift to greater autonomy.
- *Early childhood: from 2 to 6 years.* The body becomes longer and leaner, motor skills are refined, and children become more self-controlled and self-sufficient. Make-believe play blossoms, reflecting and supporting many aspects of psychological development. Thought and language expand at an astounding pace, a sense of morality becomes evident, and children establish ties with peers.
- *Middle childhood: from 6 to 11 years.* Children learn about the wider world and master new responsibilities that increasingly resemble those they will perform as adults. Hallmarks of this period are improved athletic abilities; participation in organized games with rules; more logical thought processes; mastery of fundamental reading, writing, math, and other academic knowledge and skills; and advances in understanding the self, morality, and friendship.
- *Adolescence: from 11 to 18 years.* This period initiates the transition to adulthood. Puberty leads to an adult-sized body and sexual maturity. Thought becomes increasingly complex, abstract, and idealistic, and schooling is directed toward preparation for higher education and the world of work. Young people begin to establish autonomy from the family and to define personal values and goals.

For many contemporary youths in industrialized nations, the transition to adult roles has become increasingly prolonged—so much so that some researchers have posited a new period of development called *emerging adulthood,* extending from age 18 to the mid- to late-twenties. Although emerging adults have moved beyond adolescence, they have not yet fully assumed adult roles. Rather, during higher education and sometimes beyond, these young people intensify their exploration of options in love, career, and personal values before making enduring commitments. Because emerging adulthood first became apparent during the past few decades, researchers have just begun to study it (Arnett, 2007, 2011). Perhaps it is *your* period of development. In Chapter 17, we will consider milestones of emerging adulthood, which build on adolescent attainments.

With this introduction in mind, let's turn to some basic issues that have captivated, puzzled, and sparked debate among child development theorists. Then our discussion will trace the emergence of the field and survey major theories. We will return to each contemporary theory in greater detail in later chapters.

© UWE OMMER, 1,000 FAMILIES, TASCHEN

Child development is so dramatic that researchers divide it into periods. This large South African family includes children in infancy (child in arms), early childhood (seated boys), middle childhood (girl standing in front row), and adolescence (boy standing at far left).

Basic Issues

Research on child development did not begin until the late nineteenth and early twentieth centuries. But ideas about how children grow and change have a much longer history. As these speculations combined with research, they inspired the construction of *theories* of development. A **theory** is an orderly, integrated set of statements that describes, explains, and predicts behavior. For example, a good theory of infant–caregiver attachment would (1) *describe* the behaviors of babies around 6 to 8 months of age as they seek the affection and comfort of a familiar adult, (2) *explain* how and why infants develop this strong desire to bond with a caregiver, and (3) *predict* the consequences of this emotional bond for future relationships.

Theories are vital tools for two reasons. First, they provide organizing frameworks for our observations of children. In other words, they *guide and give meaning* to what we see. Second, theories that are verified by research often serve as a sound basis for practical action. Once a theory helps us *understand* development, we are in a much better position *to know how to improve* the welfare and treatment of children.

As we will see later, theories are influenced by the cultural values and belief systems of their times. But theories differ in one important way from mere opinion or belief: A theory's continued existence depends on *scientific verification*. Every theory must be tested using a fair set of research procedures agreed on by the scientific community, and its findings must endure, or be replicated over time.

Within the field of child development, many theories offer very different ideas about what children are like and how they change. The study of child development provides no ultimate truth because investigators do not always agree on the meaning of what they see. Also, children are complex beings; they change physically, cognitively, emotionally, and socially. No single theory has explained all these aspects. But the existence of many theories helps advance knowledge because researchers are continually trying to support, contradict, and integrate these different points of view.

Although there are many theories, we can easily organize them by looking at the stand they take on three basic issues: (1) Is the course of development continuous or discontinuous? (2) Does one course of development characterize all children, or are there many possible courses? (3) What are the roles of genetic and environmental factors—nature and nurture—in development? Let's look closely at each of these issues.

Continuous or Discontinuous Development?

A mother reported with amazement that her 20-month-old son Angelo had pushed a toy car across the living room floor while making a motorlike sound, "Brmmmm, brmmmm," for the first time. When he hit a nearby wall with a bang, Angelo let go of the car, exclaimed, "C'ash!" and laughed heartily.

"How come Angelo can pretend, but he couldn't a few months ago?" his mother asked. "And I wonder what 'Brmmmm, brmmmm' and 'Crash!' mean to Angelo. Does he understand motorlike sounds and collision the same way I do?"

Angelo's mother has raised a puzzling issue about development: How can we best describe the differences in capacities and behavior among small infants, young children, adolescents, and adults? As Figure 1.2 on page 8 illustrates, most major theories recognize two possibilities.

One view holds that infants and preschoolers respond to the world in much the same way as adults do. The difference between the immature and the mature being is simply one of *amount or complexity*. For example, little Angelo's thinking may be just as logical and well-organized as our own. Perhaps (as his mother reports) he can sort objects into simple categories, recognize whether he has more of one kind than of another, and remember where he left his favorite toy at child care the week before. Angelo's only limitation may be that he cannot perform these skills with as much information and precision as we can. If this is so, then

FIGURE 1.2 **Is development continuous or discontinuous?** (a) Some theorists believe that development is a smooth, continuous process. Children gradually add more of the same types of skills. (b) Other theorists think that development takes place in discontinuous stages. Children change rapidly as they step up to a new level and then change very little for a while. With each step, the child interprets and responds to the world in a qualitatively different way.

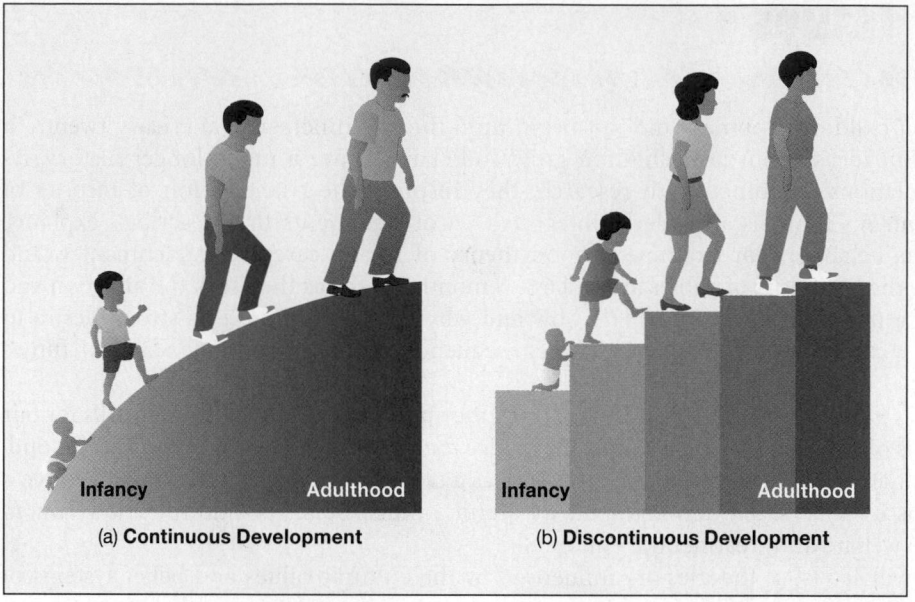

(a) **Continuous Development**   (b) **Discontinuous Development**

Angelo's development is **continuous**—a process of gradually adding more of the same types of skills that were there to begin with.

According to a second view, Angelo's thoughts, emotions, and behavior differ considerably from those of adults. His development is **discontinuous**—a process in which new ways of understanding and responding to the world emerge at specific times. From this perspective, Angelo is not yet able to organize objects or remember and interpret experiences as we do. Instead, he will move through a series of developmental steps, each with unique features, until he reaches the highest level of functioning.

Theories that accept the discontinuous perspective regard development as taking place in **stages**—*qualitative* changes in thinking, feeling, and behaving that characterize specific periods of development. In stage theories, development is much like climbing a staircase, with each step corresponding to a more mature, reorganized way of functioning. The stage concept also assumes that children undergo periods of rapid transformation as they step up from one stage to the next, alternating with plateaus during which they stand solidly within a stage. In other words, change is fairly sudden rather than gradual and ongoing.

Does development actually occur in a neat, orderly sequence of stages? This ambitious assumption has faced significant challenges (Collins & Hartup, 2013). Later in this chapter, we will review some influential stage theories.

One Course of Development or Many?

Stage theorists assume that people everywhere follow the same sequence of development. For example, in the domain of cognition, a stage theorist might try to identify the common influences that lead children to represent their world through language and make-believe play in early childhood, to think more logically and systematically in middle childhood, and to reason more systematically and abstractly in adolescence.

At the same time, the field of child development is becoming increasingly aware that children grow up in distinct **contexts**—unique combinations of personal and environmental circumstances that can result in different paths of change. For example, a shy child who fears social encounters develops in very different contexts from those of an outgoing agemate who readily seeks out other people. Children in non-Western village societies have experiences in their families and communities that differ sharply from those of children in large Western cities (Kagan, 2013a; Shweder et al., 2006). These different circumstances foster different cognitive capacities, social skills, and feelings about the self and others.

As you will see, contemporary theorists regard the contexts that shape development as many-layered and complex. On the personal side, these include heredity and biological makeup. On the environmental side, they include both immediate settings—home, child-care center, school, and neighborhood—and circumstances that are more remote from children's everyday lives: community resources, societal values and priorities, and historical time period. Finally, researchers today are more conscious than ever before of cultural diversity in development.

Relative Influence of Nature and Nurture?

In addition to describing the course of child development, each theory takes a stand on a major question about its underlying causes: Are genetic or environmental factors more important in influencing development? This is the age-old **nature–nurture controversy.** By *nature,* we mean the hereditary information we receive from our parents at the moment of conception. By *nurture,* we mean the complex forces of the physical and social world that influence our biological makeup and psychological experiences before and after birth.

Although all theories grant roles to both nature and nurture, they vary in emphasis. Consider the following questions: Is the older child's ability to think in more complex ways largely the result of a built-in timetable of growth, or is it primarily influenced by stimulation from parents and teachers? Do children acquire language because they are genetically predisposed to do so or because parents intensively teach them from an early age? And what accounts for the vast individual differences among children—in height, weight, physical coordination, intelligence, personality, and social skills? Is nature or nurture more responsible?

A theory's position on the roles of nature and nurture affects how it explains individual differences. Theorists who emphasize *stability*—that children who are high or low in a characteristic (such as verbal ability, anxiety, or sociability) will remain so at later ages—typically stress the importance of *heredity.* If they regard environment as important, they usually point to *early experiences* as establishing a lifelong pattern of behavior. Powerful negative events in the first few years, they argue, cannot be fully overcome by later, more positive ones (Bowlby, 1980; Sroufe, Coffino, & Carlson, 2010). Other theorists, taking a more optimistic view, see development as having substantial **plasticity** throughout life—as open to change in response to influential experiences (Baltes, Lindenberger, & Staudinger, 2006; Overton, 2010).

Throughout this book, you will see that investigators disagree, often sharply, on the question of *stability versus plasticity.* Their answers have great applied significance. If you believe that development is largely due to nature, then providing experiences aimed at promoting change would seem to be of little value. If, on the other hand, you are convinced of the supreme importance of early experience, then you would intervene as soon as possible, offering high-quality stimulation and support to ensure that children develop at their best. Finally, if you think that environment is profoundly influential throughout development, you would provide assistance any time children or adolescents face difficulties, in the belief that, with the help of favorable life circumstances, they can recover from early negative events.

A Balanced Point of View

So far, we have discussed basic issues of child development in terms of extremes—solutions favoring one side or the other. But as we trace the unfolding of the field in the rest of this chapter, you will see that the positions of many theorists have softened. Today, some theorists believe that both continuous and discontinuous changes occur. Many acknowledge that development has both universal features and features unique to the individual and his or her contexts. And a growing number regard heredity and environment as inseparably interwoven, each affecting the potential of the other to modify the child's traits and capacities (Goldhaber, 2012; Kagan, 2013b; Overton, 2010). We will discuss these new ideas about nature and nurture in Chapter 2.

Biology and Environment

Resilient Children

John and his best friend, Gary, grew up in a rundown, crime-ridden inner-city neighborhood. By age 10, each had experienced years of family conflict followed by parental divorce. Reared from then on in mother-headed households, John and Gary rarely saw their fathers. Both dropped out of high school and were in and out of trouble with the police.

Then their paths diverged. By age 30, John had fathered two children with women he never married, had spent time in prison, was unemployed, and drank alcohol heavily. In contrast, Gary had returned to finish high school, had studied auto mechanics at a community college, and became manager of a gas station and repair shop. Married with two children, he had saved his earnings and bought a home. He was happy, healthy, and well-adapted to life.

A wealth of evidence shows that environmental risks—poverty, negative family interactions and parental divorce, job loss, mental illness, and drug abuse—predispose children to future problems (Masten, 2007, 2011; Sameroff, 2006). Why did Gary "beat the odds" and come through unscathed?

Research on **resilience**—the ability to adapt effectively in the face of threats to development—

is receiving increased attention as investigators look for ways to protect young people from the damaging effects of stressful life conditions. This interest has been inspired by several long-term studies on the relationship of life stressors in childhood to competence and adjustment in adolescence and adulthood (Werner, 2013). In each study, some individuals were shielded from negative outcomes, whereas others had lasting problems. Four broad factors seemed to offer protection from the damaging effects of stressful life events.

Personal Characteristics

A child's genetically influenced characteristics can reduce exposure to risk or lead to experi-

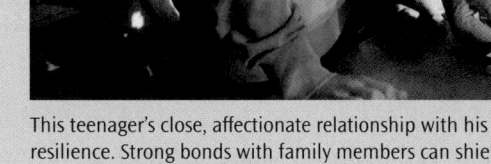

This teenager's close, affectionate relationship with his grandfather helps foster resilience. Strong bonds with family members can shield children from the damaging effects of stressful life conditions.

ences that compensate for early stressful events. High intelligence and socially valued talents (in music or athletics, for example) increase the chances that a child will have rewarding

---

Finally, as you will see later in this book, the relative impact of early and later experiences varies greatly from one domain of development to another and even—as the Biology and Environment box above indicates—across individuals! Because of the complex network of factors contributing to human change and the challenges of isolating the effects of each, many theoretical points of view have gathered research support. Although debate continues, this circumstance has also sparked more balanced visions of child development.

Ask Yourself

- **REVIEW** What is meant by a *stage* of development? Provide your own example of stagewise change. What stand do stage theorists take on the issue of continuous versus discontinuous development?

- **CONNECT** Provide an example of how one domain of development (physical, cognitive, or emotional/social) can affect development in another domain.

- **APPLY** Anna, a high school counselor, has devised a program that integrates classroom learning with vocational training to help adolescents at risk for school dropout stay in school and transition smoothly to work life. What is Anna's position on *stability versus plasticity* in development? Explain.

- **REFLECT** Describe an aspect of your development that differs from a parent's or a grandparent's when he or she was your age. How might *contexts* explain this difference?

experiences at school and in the community that offset the impact of a stressful home life. Temperament is particularly powerful. Children who have easygoing, sociable dispositions and who can readily inhibit negative emotions and impulses tend to have an optimistic outlook on life and a special capacity to adapt to change—qualities that elicit positive responses from others. In contrast, emotionally reactive and irritable children often tax the patience of people around them (Vanderbilt-Adriance & Shaw, 2008; Wang & Deater-Deckard, 2013). For example, both John and Gary moved several times during their childhoods. Each time, John became anxious and angry. Gary looked forward to making new friends and exploring a new neighborhood.

A Warm Parental Relationship

A close relationship with at least one parent who provides warmth, appropriately high expectations, monitoring of the child's activities, and an organized home environment fosters resilience (Masten & Shaffer, 2006; Taylor, 2010). But this factor (as well as the next one) is not independent of children's personal characteristics. Children who are relaxed, socially responsive, and able to deal with change are easier to rear and more likely to enjoy positive relationships with parents and other people. At the same time, children may develop more attractive dispositions as a result of parental warmth and attention (Gulotta, 2008).

Social Support Outside the Immediate Family

The most consistent asset of resilient children is a strong bond with a competent, caring adult. For children who do not have a close bond with either parent, a grandparent, aunt, uncle, or teacher who forms a special relationship with the child can promote resilience (Masten & Reed, 2002). Gary received support in adolescence from his grandfather, who listened to Gary's concerns and helped him solve problems. In addition, Gary's grandfather had a stable marriage and work life and handled stressors skillfully. Consequently, he served as a model of effective coping.

Associations with rule-abiding peers who value school achievement are also linked to resilience (Tiet, Huizinga, & Byrnes, 2010). But children who have positive relationships with adults are far more likely to establish these supportive peer ties.

Community Resources and Opportunities

Community supports—good schools, convenient and affordable health care and social services, libraries, and recreation centers—foster both parents' and children's well-being. In addition, opportunities to participate in community life help older children and adolescents overcome adversity. Extracurricular activities at school, religious youth groups, scouting, and other organizations teach important social skills, such as cooperation, leadership, and contributing to others' welfare. As participants acquire these competencies, they gain in self-reliance, self-esteem, and community commitment (Benson et al., 2006). As a college student, Gary volunteered for Habitat for Humanity, joining a team building affordable housing in low-income neighborhoods. Community involvement offered Gary opportunities to form meaningful relationships, which further strengthened his resilience.

Research on resilience highlights the complex connections between heredity and environment. Armed with positive characteristics, which stem from native endowment, favorable rearing experiences, or both, children and adolescents can act to reduce stressful situations.

But when many risks pile up, they are increasingly difficult to overcome (Obradović et al., 2009). To inoculate children against the negative effects of risk, interventions must not only reduce risks but also enhance children's protective relationships at home, in school, and in the community. This means attending to both the person and the environment—strengthening children's capacities while also reducing hazardous experiences.

Historical Foundations

1.4 Describe major historical influences on theories of child development.

Contemporary theories of child development are the result of centuries of change in Western cultural values, philosophical thinking about children, and scientific progress. To understand the field as it exists today, we must return to its early beginnings—to ideas about children that long preceded scientific child study but that linger as important forces in current theory and research.

Medieval Times

Childhood was regarded as a separate period of life as early as medieval Europe—the sixth through the fifteenth centuries. Medieval painters often depicted children wearing loose, comfortable gowns, playing games, and looking up to adults. Written texts contained terms that distinguished children under age 7 or 8 from other people and that recognized even young teenagers as not fully mature. By the fourteenth century, manuals offering advice on many aspects of child care, including health, feeding, clothing, and games, were common (Heywood, 2013; Lett, 1997). Laws recognized that children needed protection from people

As early as medieval times, adults viewed childhood as a distinct developmental period. In this sixteenth-century painting, *Children's Games*, by Pieter Bruegel the Elder, boys and girls wearing loose, comfortable clothing play lively outdoor games. [*Children's Games (Kinderspiele)*: Detail of top right-hand corner, 1560 (oil on panel) (detail of 68945), Bruegel, Pieter the Elder (c.1525–69).]

who might mistreat them, and courts exercised leniency with lawbreaking youths because of their tender years (Hanawalt, 1993).

In sum, in medieval times, if not before, clear awareness existed of children as vulnerable beings. Religious writings, however, contained contradictory depictions of children's basic nature, sometimes portraying them as possessed by the devil and in need of purification, at other times as innocent and close to angels (Hanawalt, 2003). Both ideas foreshadowed later views of childhood.

The Reformation

In the sixteenth century, the Puritan belief in original sin gave rise to the view that children were born evil and stubborn and had to be civilized (Heywood, 2013). Harsh, restrictive child-rearing practices were recommended to tame the depraved child. Children were dressed in stiff, uncomfortable clothing that held them in adultlike postures, and disobedient students were routinely beaten by their schoolmasters. Nevertheless, love and affection for their children prevented most Puritan parents from using extremely repressive measures (Moran & Vinovskis, 1986).

As the Puritans emigrated from England to the New World, they brought the belief that child rearing was one of their most important obligations. Although they continued to regard the child's soul as tainted by original sin, they tried to teach their sons and daughters to use reason to tell right from wrong (Clarke-Stewart, 1998). As they trained their children in self-reliance and self-control, Puritan parents gradually adopted a moderate balance between severity and permissiveness.

Philosophies of the Enlightenment

The seventeenth-century Enlightenment brought new philosophies that emphasized ideals of human dignity and respect. Conceptions of childhood were more humane than those of the past.

JOHN LOCKE The writings of British philosopher John Locke (1632–1704) served as the forerunner of a twentieth-century perspective that we will discuss shortly: behaviorism. Locke viewed the child as a *tabula rasa*—Latin for "blank slate." According to this idea, children begin as nothing at all; their characters are shaped entirely by experience. Locke (1690/1892) saw parents as rational tutors who can mold the child in any way they wish through careful instruction, effective example, and rewards for good behavior. He was ahead of his time in recommending child-rearing practices that present-day research supports—for example, the use of praise and approval as rewards, rather than money or sweets. He also opposed physical punishment: "The child repeatedly beaten in school cannot look upon books and teachers without experiencing fear and anger." Locke's philosophy led to a change from harshness toward children to kindness and compassion.

Look carefully at Locke's ideas, and you will see that he regarded development as *continuous*: Adultlike behaviors are gradually built up through the warm, consistent teachings of parents. His view of the child as a tabula rasa led him to champion *nurture*—the power of the environment to shape the child. And his faith in nurture suggests the possibility of *many courses of development* and of *high plasticity at later ages* due to new experiences. Finally,

Locke's philosophy characterizes children as doing little to influence their own destiny, which is written on "blank slates" by others. This vision of a passive child has been discarded. All contemporary theories view children as active, purposeful beings who contribute substantially to their own development.

JEAN-JACQUES ROUSSEAU   In the eighteenth century, French philosopher Jean-Jacques Rousseau (1712–1778) introduced a new view of childhood. Children, Rousseau claimed, are not blank slates to be filled by adult instruction. Instead, they are *noble savages,* naturally endowed with a sense of right and wrong and an innate plan for orderly, healthy growth. Unlike Locke, Rousseau believed that children's built-in moral sense and unique ways of thinking and feeling would only be harmed by adult training. His was a child-centered philosophy in which the adult should be receptive to the child's needs at each of four stages: infancy, childhood, late childhood, and adolescence.

Rousseau's philosophy includes two influential concepts. The first is the concept of *stage,* which we discussed earlier. The second is the concept of **maturation,** which refers to a genetically determined, naturally unfolding course of growth. In contrast to Locke, Rousseau saw children as determining their own destinies. And he viewed development as a *discontinuous, stagewise* process that follows a *single, unified course* mapped out by *nature.*

Scientific Beginnings

The study of child development evolved quickly in the late nineteenth and early twentieth centuries. Early observations of children were soon followed by improved methods and theories. Each advance contributed to the firm foundation on which the field rests today.

DARWIN: FOREFATHER OF SCIENTIFIC CHILD STUDY   British naturalist Charles Darwin (1809–1882) joined an expedition to distant parts of the world, where he observed infinite variation among plant and animal species. He also saw that within a species, no two individuals are exactly alike. From these observations, he constructed his famous *theory of evolution.*

The theory emphasized two related principles: *natural selection* and *survival of the fittest.* Darwin (1859/2003) explained that certain species survive in particular parts of the world because they have characteristics that fit with, or are adapted to, their surroundings. Other species die off because they are less well-suited to their environments. Individuals within a species who best meet the environment's survival requirements live long enough to reproduce and pass their more beneficial characteristics to future generations. Darwin's emphasis on the adaptive value of physical characteristics and behavior eventually found its way into important developmental theories.

During his explorations, Darwin discovered that early prenatal growth is strikingly similar in many species. Other scientists concluded from Darwin's observation that the development of the human child followed the same general plan as the evolution of the human species. Although this belief eventually proved inaccurate, efforts to chart parallels between child growth and human evolution prompted researchers to make careful observations of all aspects of children's behavior. Out of these first attempts to document an idea about development, scientific child study was born.

THE NORMATIVE PERIOD   G. Stanley Hall (1844–1924), one of the most influential American psychologists of the early twentieth century, is generally regarded as the founder of the child-study movement (Cairns & Cairns, 2006). Inspired by Darwin's work, Hall and his well-known student Arnold Gesell (1880–1961) devised theories based on evolutionary ideas. They regarded development as a *maturational process*—a genetically determined series of events that unfold automatically, much like a flower (Gesell, 1933; Hall, 1904).

Hall and Gesell are remembered less for their one-sided theories than for their intensive efforts to describe all aspects of child development. They launched the **normative approach,** in which measures of behavior are taken on large numbers of individuals and age-related

Theories of child development have sparked an extensive parenting-advice literature. These parents turn to an infant-care manual for guidance on how best to care for their new baby.

averages are computed to represent typical development. Using this procedure, Hall constructed elaborate questionnaires asking children of different ages almost everything they could tell about themselves—interests, fears, imaginary playmates, dreams, friendships, everyday knowledge, and more. Similarly, through observations and parent interviews, Gesell collected detailed normative information on the motor achievements, social behaviors, and personality characteristics of infants and children.

Gesell was also among the first to make knowledge about child development meaningful to parents by telling them what to expect at each age. If, as he believed, the timetable of development is the product of millions of years of evolution, then children are naturally knowledgeable about their needs. His child-rearing advice, in the tradition of Rousseau, recommended sensitivity to children's cues (Thelen & Adolph, 1992). Along with Benjamin Spock's *Baby and Child Care,* Gesell's books became a central part of a rapidly expanding popular literature for parents.

THE MENTAL TESTING MOVEMENT   While Hall and Gesell were developing their theories and methods in the United States, French psychologist Alfred Binet (1857–1911) was also taking a normative approach to child development, but for a different reason. In the early 1900s, Binet and his colleague Theodore Simon were asked by Paris school officials to find a way to identify children with learning problems who needed to be placed in special classes. To address these practical educational concerns, Binet and Simon constructed the first successful intelligence test.

Binet began with a well-developed theory of intelligence. Capturing the complexity of children's thinking, he defined intelligence as good judgment, planning, and critical reflection (Sternberg & Jarvin, 2003). Then he created age-graded test items that directly measured these abilities.

In 1916, at Stanford University, Binet's test was adapted for use with English-speaking children. Since then, the English version has been known as the *Stanford-Binet Intelligence Scale.* Besides providing a score that could successfully predict school achievement, the Binet test sparked tremendous interest in individual differences in development. Comparisons of the scores of children who vary in gender, ethnicity, birth order, family background, and other characteristics became a major focus of research. And intelligence tests rose quickly to the forefront of the nature–nurture controversy.

LOOK and LISTEN

Examine several recent parenting-advice books in your local bookstore or library, and identify the stance each book takes on the three basic issues about child development.

Ask Yourself

- **REVIEW** Imagine a debate between John Locke and Jean-Jacques Rousseau on the nature–nurture controversy. Summarize the argument that each historical figure is likely to present.

- **CONNECT** What do the ideas of Rousseau, Darwin, and Hall have in common?

- **REFLECT** Find out whether your parents read any child-rearing advice books when you were growing up. What questions most concerned them? Do you think the concerns of today's parents differ from those of your parents' generation? Explain.

1.5 What theories influenced child development research in the mid-twentieth century?

Mid-Twentieth-Century Theories

In the mid-twentieth century, the field of child development expanded. A variety of theories emerged, each of which continues to have followers today. In these theories, the European concern with the child's inner thoughts and feelings contrasts sharply with the North American academic focus on scientific precision and concrete, observable behavior.

The Psychoanalytic Perspective

By the 1930s and 1940s, parents increasingly sought professional help in dealing with children's emotional difficulties. The earlier normative movement had answered the question, What are children like? Now another question had to be addressed: How and why do children become the way they are? To treat psychological problems, psychiatrists and social workers turned to an emerging approach to personality development that emphasized each child's unique history.

According to the **psychoanalytic perspective,** children move through a series of stages in which they confront conflicts between biological drives and social expectations. How these conflicts are resolved determines the person's ability to learn, to get along with others, and to cope with anxiety. Among the many individuals who contributed to the psychoanalytic perspective, two were especially influential: Sigmund Freud, founder of the psychoanalytic movement, and Erik Erikson.

FREUD'S THEORY   Freud (1856–1939), a Viennese physician, sought a cure for emotionally troubled adults by having them talk freely about painful events of their childhoods. Working with these recollections, he examined his patients' unconscious motivations and constructed his **psychosexual theory,** which emphasizes that how parents manage their child's sexual and aggressive drives in the first few years is crucial for healthy personality development.

In Freud's theory, three parts of the personality—id, ego, and superego—become integrated during five stages, summarized in Table 1.1 on page 16. The *id,* the largest portion of the mind, is the source of basic biological needs and desires. The *ego,* the conscious, rational part of personality, emerges in early infancy to redirect the id's impulses so they are discharged in acceptable ways. Between 3 and 6 years of age, the *superego,* or conscience, develops as parents insist that children conform to the values of society. Now the ego faces the increasingly complex task of reconciling the demands of the id, the external world, and conscience—for example, the id impulse to grab an attractive toy from a playmate versus the superego's awareness that such behavior is wrong. According to Freud, the relations established between id, ego, and superego during the preschool years determine the individual's basic personality.

Freud (1938/1973) believed that during childhood, sexual impulses shift their focus from the oral to the anal to the genital regions of the body. In each stage, parents walk a fine line between permitting too much or too little gratification of their child's basic needs. If parents strike an appropriate balance, children grow into well-adjusted adults with the capacity for mature sexual behavior and investment in family life.

Freud's theory was the first to stress the influence of the early parent–child relationship on development—an emphasis that continues in many contemporary theories. But his perspective was eventually criticized. First, it overemphasized the influence of sexual feelings in development. Second, because it was based on the problems of sexually repressed, well-to-do adults in nineteenth-century Victorian society, it did not apply in other cultures. Finally, Freud had not studied children directly.

ERIKSON'S THEORY   Several of Freud's followers took what was useful from his theory and improved on his vision. The most important is Erik Erikson (1902–1994), who expanded the picture of development at each stage. In his **psychosocial theory,** Erikson emphasized that in addition to mediating between id impulses and superego demands, the ego makes a positive contribution to development, acquiring attitudes and skills that make the individual an active, contributing member of society. A basic psychological conflict, which is resolved along a continuum from positive to negative, determines healthy or maladaptive outcomes at each stage. As Table 1.1 on page 16 shows, Erikson's first five stages parallel Freud's stages, but Erikson added three adult stages. He was one of the first to recognize the lifespan nature of development.

Unlike Freud, Erikson pointed out that normal development must be understood in relation to each culture's life situation. For example, in the 1940s, he observed that the Yurok Indians of the U.S. northwest coast deprived newborns of breastfeeding for the first 10 days,

TABLE 1.1	Freud's Psychosexual Stages and Erikson's Psychosocial Stages Compared	
APPROXIMATE AGE	**FREUD'S PSYCHOSEXUAL STAGE**	**ERIKSON'S PSYCHOSOCIAL STAGE**
Birth–1 year	*Oral:* If oral needs are not met through sucking from breast or bottle, the individual may develop such habits as thumb sucking, fingernail biting, overeating, or smoking.	*Basic trust versus mistrust:* From warm, responsive care, infants gain a sense of trust that the world is good. Mistrust occurs if infants are neglected or handled harshly.
1–3 years	*Anal:* Toddlers and preschoolers enjoy holding and releasing urine and feces. If parents toilet train before children are ready or make too few demands, conflicts about anal control may appear in the form of extreme orderliness or disorder.	*Autonomy versus shame and doubt:* Using new mental and motor skills, children want to decide for themselves. Parents can foster autonomy by permitting reasonable free choice and not forcing or shaming the child.
3–6 years	*Phallic:* As preschoolers take pleasure in genital stimulation, Freud's Oedipus conflict for boys and Electra conflict for girls arise: Children feel a sexual desire for the other-sex parent. To avoid punishment, they give up this desire and adopt the same-sex parent's characteristics and values. As a result, the superego is formed, and children feel guilty when they violate its standards.	*Initiative versus guilt:* Through make-believe play, children gain insight into the person they can become. Initiative—a sense of ambition and responsibility—develops when parents support their child's sense of purpose. If parents demand too much self-control, children experience excessive guilt.
6–11 years	*Latency:* Sexual instincts die down, and the superego strengthens as the child acquires new social values from adults and same-sex peers.	*Industry versus inferiority:* At school, children learn to work and cooperate with others. Inferiority develops when negative experiences at home, at school, or with peers lead to feelings of incompetence.
Adolescence	*Genital:* With puberty, sexual impulses reappear. Successful development during earlier stages leads to marriage, mature sexuality, and child rearing.	*Identity versus role confusion:* By exploring values and vocational goals, the young person forms a personal identity. The negative outcome is confusion about future adult roles.
Early adulthood		*Intimacy versus isolation:* Young adults establish intimate relationships. Because of earlier disappointments, some individuals cannot form close bonds and remain isolated.
Middle adulthood		*Generativity versus stagnation:* Generativity means giving to the next generation through child rearing, caring for others, or productive work. The person who fails in these ways feels an absence of meaningful accomplishment.
Old age		*Integrity versus despair:* Integrity results from feeling that life was worth living as it happened. Older people who are dissatisfied with their lives fear death.

© OLIVE PIERCE/BLACK STAR

Erik Erikson

ANTONIA TOZER/GETTY IMAGES

A child of the Kasakh people of Mongolia learns from her grandfather how to train an eagle to hunt small animals, essential for the meat-based Kasakh diet. As Erikson recognized, this parenting practice is best understood in relation to the competencies valued and needed in Kasakh culture.

instead feeding them a thin soup. At age 6 months, infants were abruptly weaned—if necessary, by having the mother leave for a few days. From our cultural vantage point, these practices may seem cruel. But Erikson explained that because the Yurok depended on salmon, which fill the river just once a year, the development of self-restraint was essential for survival. In this way, he showed that child rearing is responsive to the competencies valued and needed by the child's society.

CONTRIBUTIONS AND LIMITATIONS OF PSYCHOANALYTIC THEORY A special strength of the psychoanalytic perspective is its emphasis on the individual's unique life history as worthy of study and understanding. Consistent with this view, psychoanalytic theorists accept the *clinical,* or *case study, method,* which synthesizes information from a variety of sources into a detailed picture of the personality of a single child. (We will discuss this method further at the end of this chapter.) Psychoanalytic theory has also inspired a wealth of research on many aspects of emotional and social development, including infant–caregiver attachment, aggression, sibling relationships, child-rearing practices, morality, gender roles, and adolescent identity.

Despite its extensive contributions, the psychoanalytic perspective is no longer in the mainstream of child development research. Psychoanalytic theorists may have become isolated from the rest of the field because they were so strongly committed to the clinical approach that they failed to consider other methods. In addition, many psychoanalytic ideas, such as psychosexual stages and ego functioning, are too vague to be tested empirically (Crain, 2010). Nevertheless, Erikson's broad outline of psychosocial change captures the essence of personality development during childhood and adolescence. Consequently, we will return to it in later chapters.

Behaviorism and Social Learning Theory

As the psychoanalytic perspective gained prominence, child study was also influenced by a very different perspective. According to **behaviorism,** directly observable events—stimuli and responses—are the appropriate focus of study. North American behaviorism began in the early twentieth century with the work of psychologist John Watson (1878–1958), who wanted to create an objective science of psychology.

TRADITIONAL BEHAVIORISM   Watson was inspired by Russian physiologist Ivan Pavlov's studies of animal learning. Pavlov knew that dogs release saliva as an innate reflex when they are given food. But he noticed that his dogs started salivating before they tasted any food—when they saw the trainer who usually fed them. The dogs, Pavlov reasoned, must have learned to associate a neutral stimulus (the trainer) with another stimulus (food) that produces a reflexive response (salivation). Because of this association, the neutral stimulus alone could bring about a response resembling the reflex. Eager to test this idea, Pavlov successfully taught dogs to salivate at the sound of a bell by pairing it with the presentation of food. He had discovered *classical conditioning*.

Watson wanted to find out if classical conditioning could be applied to children's behavior. In a historic experiment, he taught Albert, an 11-month-old infant, to fear a neutral stimulus—a soft white rat—by presenting it several times with a sharp, loud sound, which naturally scared the baby. Little Albert, who at first had reached out eagerly to touch the furry rat, began to cry and turn his head away at the sight of it (Watson & Raynor, 1920). In fact, Albert's fear was so intense that researchers eventually challenged the ethics of studies like this one. Consistent with Locke's tabula rasa, Watson concluded that environment is the supreme force in development and that adults can mold children's behavior by carefully controlling stimulus–response associations. He viewed development as continuous—a gradual increase with age in the number and strength of these associations.

Another form of behaviorism was B. F. Skinner's (1904–1990) *operant conditioning theory*. According to Skinner, the frequency of a behavior can be increased by following it with a wide variety of *reinforcers*—food, praise, a friendly smile, or a new toy—or decreased through *punishment,* such as disapproval or withdrawal of privileges. As a result of Skinner's work, operant conditioning became a broadly applied learning principle. We will consider these basic learning capacities further in Chapter 5.

SOCIAL LEARNING THEORY   Psychologists wondered whether behaviorism might offer a more direct and effective explanation of the development of children's social behavior than the less precise concepts of psychoanalytic theory. This sparked approaches that built on the principles of conditioning, offering expanded views of how children and adults acquire new responses.

Several kinds of **social learning theory** emerged. The most influential, devised by Albert Bandura (1977, 2011), emphasizes *modeling,* also known as *imitation* or *observational learning,* as a powerful source of development. The baby who claps her hands after her mother does so, the child who angrily hits a playmate in the same way that he has been punished at home, and the teenager who wears the same clothes and hairstyle as her friends are all displaying observational learning. In his early research, Bandura found that diverse factors influence children's

Social learning theory recognizes that children acquire many skills through modeling. By observing and imitating his father's behavior, this child learns an important skill.

LOOK and LISTEN

Describe an event you observed in which feedback from a parent or teacher likely strengthened a child's self-efficacy. How might the adult's message have influenced the child's self-perceptions and choice of models?

motivation to imitate—their own history of reinforcement or punishment for the behavior, the promise of future reinforcement or punishment, and even observations of the model being reinforced or punished.

Bandura's work continues to influence much research on children's social development. But today, like the field of child development as a whole, his theory stresses the importance of *cognition,* or thinking. Bandura has shown that children's ability to listen, remember, and abstract general rules from complex sets of observed behaviors affects their imitation and learning. In fact, the most recent revision of Bandura's (1992, 2001) theory places such strong emphasis on how children think about themselves and other people that he calls it a *social-cognitive* rather than a social learning approach.

In Bandura's revised view, children gradually become more selective in what they imitate. From watching others engage in self-praise and self-blame and through feedback about the worth of their own actions, children develop *personal standards* for behavior and a *sense of self-efficacy*—the belief that their own abilities and characteristics will help them succeed. These cognitions guide responses in particular situations (Bandura, 2001, 2011). For example, imagine a parent who often remarks, "I'm glad I kept working on that task, even though it was hard," and who encourages persistence by saying, "I know you can do a good job on that homework!" Soon the child starts to view herself as hardworking and high-achieving and selects people with these characteristics as models. In this way, as children acquire attitudes, values, and convictions about themselves, they control their own learning and behavior.

CONTRIBUTIONS AND LIMITATIONS OF BEHAVIORISM AND SOCIAL LEARNING THEORY   Behaviorism and social learning theory have had a major impact on practices with children. **Applied behavior analysis** consists of observations of relationships between behavior and environmental events, followed by systematic changes in those events based on procedures of conditioning and modeling. The goal is to eliminate undesirable behaviors and increase desirable responses. It has been used to relieve a wide range of difficulties in children and adults, ranging from poor time management and unwanted habits to serious problems such as language delays, persistent aggression, and extreme fears (Heron, Hewar, & Cooper, 2013).

In one study, researchers reduced toddlers' aggressive behavior in a child-care classroom by reinforcing them with adult attention and joint play when they behaved appropriately and punishing them for attacking other children or throwing objects by withdrawing adult attention and playing with nearby peers (Greer et al., 2013). In another investigation, children with acute burn injuries played a virtual reality game while nurses engaged in the painful process of changing their bandages. Visual images and sound effects delivered though a headset made the children feel as if they were in a fantasy world. As the game reinforced children's concentration and pleasure, it distracted them from the medical procedure, causing their pain and anxiety to drop sharply compared with dressing changes in which the game was unavailable (Das et al., 2005).

Nevertheless, many theorists believe that behaviorism and social learning theory offer too narrow a view of important environmental influences, which extend beyond immediate reinforcement, punishment, and modeled behaviors to children's rich physical and social worlds. Behaviorism and social learning theory have also been criticized for underestimating children's contributions to their own development. Bandura, with his emphasis on cognition, is unique among theorists whose work grew out of the behaviorist tradition in granting children an active role in their own learning.

TABLE 1.2	Piaget's Stages of Cognitive Development	

STAGE	PERIOD OF DEVELOPMENT	DESCRIPTION
Sensorimotor	Birth–2 years	Infants "think" by acting on the world with their eyes, ears, hands, and mouth. As a result, they invent ways of solving sensorimotor problems, such as pulling a lever to hear the sound of a music box, finding hidden toys, and putting objects into and taking them out of containers.
Preoperational	2–7 years	Preschool children use symbols to represent their earlier sensorimotor discoveries. Development of language and make-believe play takes place. However, thinking lacks the logic of the two remaining stages.
Concrete operational	7–11 years	Children's reasoning becomes logical and better organized. School-age children understand that a certain amount of lemonade or play dough remains the same even after its appearance changes. They also organize objects into hierarchies of classes and subclasses. However, children think in a logical, organized fashion only when dealing with concrete information they can perceive directly.
Formal operational	11 years on	The capacity for abstract, systematic thinking enables adolescents, when faced with a problem, to start with a hypothesis, deduce testable inferences, and isolate and combine variables to see which inferences are confirmed. Adolescents can also evaluate the logic of verbal statements without referring to real-world circumstances.

© BETTMANN/CORBIS

Jean Piaget

Piaget's Cognitive-Developmental Theory

If one individual has influenced the contemporary field of child development more than any other, it is Swiss cognitive theorist Jean Piaget (1896–1980). North American investigators had been aware of Piaget's work since 1930. But they did not grant it much attention until the 1960s, mainly because Piaget's ideas were at odds with behaviorism, which dominated North American psychology in the mid-twentieth century (Watrin & Darwich, 2012). Piaget did not believe that children's learning depends on reinforcers, such as rewards from adults. According to his **cognitive-developmental theory,** children actively construct knowledge as they manipulate and explore their world.

PIAGET'S STAGES   Piaget's view of development was greatly influenced by his early training in biology. Central to his theory is the biological concept of *adaptation* (Piaget, 1971). Just as structures of the body are adapted to fit with the environment, so structures of the mind develop to better fit with, or represent, the external world. In infancy and early childhood, Piaget claimed, children's understanding is different from adults'. For example, he believed that young babies do not realize that an object hidden from view— a favorite toy or even the mother—continues to exist. He also concluded that preschoolers' thinking is full of faulty logic. For example, children younger than age 7 commonly say that the amount of a liquid changes when it is poured into a different-shaped container. According to Piaget, children eventually revise these incorrect ideas in their ongoing efforts to achieve an *equilibrium,* or balance, between internal structures and information they encounter in their everyday worlds.

In Piaget's theory, as the brain develops and children's experiences expand, they move through four broad stages, each characterized by qualitatively distinct ways of thinking. Table 1.2 provides a brief description of Piaget's stages. Cognitive development begins in the *sensorimotor stage* with the baby's use of the senses and movements to explore the world. These action patterns evolve into the symbolic but illogical thinking of the preschooler

© LAURA DWIGHT PHOTOGRAPHY

In Piaget's sensorimotor stage, babies learn by acting on the world. As this 1-year-old bangs a wooden spoon on a coffee can, he discovers that his movements have predictable effects on objects, and that objects influence one another in regular ways.

In Piaget's preoperational stage, preschoolers represent their earlier sensorimotor discoveries with symbols, and language and make-believe play develop rapidly. These 4-year-olds use a variety of props to create an imaginary birthday party.

in the *preoperational stage*. Then cognition is transformed into the more organized reasoning of the school-age child in the *concrete operational stage*. Finally, in the *formal operational stage,* thought becomes the abstract, systematic reasoning system of the adolescent and adult.

Piaget devised special methods for investigating how children think. Early in his career, he carefully observed his three infant children and also presented them with everyday problems, such as an attractive object that could be grasped, mouthed, kicked, or searched for. From their responses, Piaget derived his ideas about cognitive changes during the first two years. To study childhood and adolescent thought, Piaget adapted the clinical method of psychoanalysis, conducting open-ended *clinical interviews* in which a child's initial response to a task served as the basis for Piaget's next question. We will look more closely at this technique when we discuss research methods later in this chapter.

CONTRIBUTIONS AND LIMITATIONS OF PIAGET'S THEORY Piaget convinced the field that children are active learners whose minds consist of rich structures of knowledge. Besides investigating children's understanding of the physical world, Piaget explored their reasoning about the social world. His stages have sparked a wealth of research on children's conceptions of themselves, other people, and human relationships. In practical terms, Piaget's theory encouraged the development of educational philosophies and programs that emphasize children's discovery learning and direct contact with the environment.

Despite Piaget's overwhelming contributions, his theory has been challenged. Research indicates that Piaget underestimated the competencies of infants and preschoolers. When

In Piaget's concrete operational stage, school-age children think in an organized, logical fashion about concrete objects. This 7-year-old understands that the amount of pie dough remains the same after he changes its shape from a ball to a flattened circle.

In Piaget's formal operational stage, adolescents think systematically and abstractly. These high school students participating in a robotics competition solve problems by generating hypotheses about procedures that might work and conducting systematic tests to observe their real-world consequences.

young children are given tasks scaled down in difficulty and relevant to their everyday experiences, their understanding appears closer to that of the older child and adult than Piaget assumed. Also, adolescents generally reach their full intellectual potential only in areas of endeavor in which they have had extensive education and experience. These findings have led many researchers to conclude that cognitive maturity depends heavily on the complexity of knowledge sampled and the individual's familiarity with the task (Miller, 2011). Furthermore, many studies show that children's performance on Piagetian problems can be improved with training—findings that call into question Piaget's assumption that discovery learning rather than adult teaching is the best way to foster development (Klahr, Matlin, & Jirout, 2013; Siegler & Svetina, 2006). Critics also point out that Piaget's stagewise account pays insufficient attention to social and cultural influences—and the resulting wide variation in thinking among children and adolescents of the same age.

Today, the field of child development is divided over its loyalty to Piaget's ideas. Those who continue to find merit in Piaget's stages often accept a modified view—one in which changes in children's thinking take place more gradually than Piaget believed (Case, 1998; Fischer & Bidell, 2006; Halford & Andrews, 2011; Morra et al., 2008). Among those who disagree with Piaget's stage sequence, some have embraced an approach that emphasizes continuous gains in children's cognition: information processing. And still others have been drawn to theories that highlight the role of children's social and cultural contexts. We take up these approaches in the next section.

Ask Yourself

- **REVIEW** What aspect of behaviorism made it attractive to critics of psychoanalytic theory? How did Piaget's theory respond to a major limitation of behaviorism?

- **CONNECT** Although social learning theory focuses on social development and Piaget's theory on cognitive development, each has enhanced our understanding of other domains. Mention an additional domain addressed by each theory.

- **APPLY** A 4-year-old becomes frightened of the dark and refuses to go to sleep at night. How would a psychoanalyst and a behaviorist differ in their views of how this problem developed?

- **REFLECT** Illustrate Bandura's ideas by describing a personal experience in which you observed and received feedback from another person that strengthened your self-efficacy—belief that your abilities and characteristics will help you succeed.

Recent Theoretical Perspectives

1.6 Describe recent theoretical perspectives on child development.

New ways of understanding the child are constantly emerging—questioning, building on, and enhancing the discoveries of earlier theories. Today, a burst of fresh approaches and research emphases is broadening our understanding of children's development.

Information Processing

In the 1970s and 1980s, researchers turned to the field of cognitive psychology for ways to understand the development of children's thinking. The design of digital computers that use mathematically specified steps to solve problems suggested to psychologists that the human mind might also be viewed as a symbol-manipulating system through which information flows—a perspective called **information processing** (Munakata, 2006). From the time information is presented to the senses at *input* until it emerges as a behavioral response at *output*, information is actively coded, transformed, and organized.

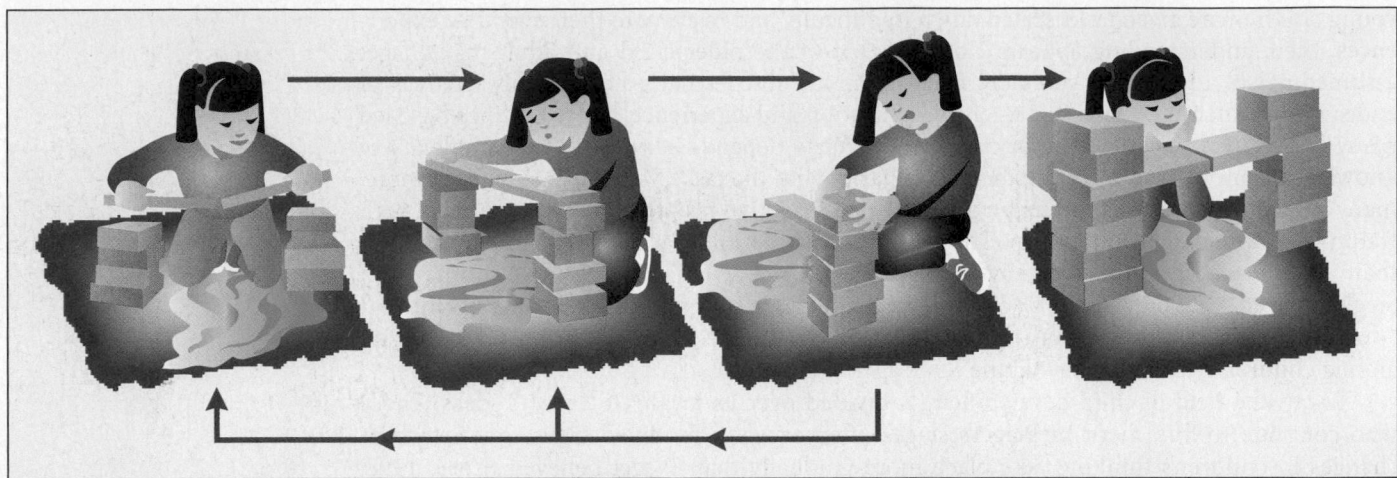

FIGURE 1.3 **Information-processing flowchart showing the steps that a 5-year-old used to solve a bridge-building problem.** Her task was to use blocks varying in size, shape, and weight, some of which were planklike, to construct a bridge across a "river" (painted on a floor mat) too wide for any single block to span. The child discovered how to counterweight and balance the bridge. The arrows reveal that even after building a successful counterweight, she returned to earlier, unsuccessful strategies, which seemed to help her understand why the counterweight approach worked. (Based on Thornton, 1999.)

Information-processing researchers often design flowcharts to map the precise steps individuals use to solve problems and complete tasks, much like the plans devised by programmers to get computers to perform a series of "mental operations." They seek to clarify how both task characteristics and cognitive limitations—for example, memory capacity or available knowledge—influence performance (Birney & Sternberg, 2011). To see the usefulness of this approach, let's look at an example.

In a study of problem solving, a researcher provided a pile of blocks varying in size, shape, and weight and asked school-age children to build a bridge across a "river" (painted on a floor mat) that was too wide for any single block to span (Thornton, 1999). Figure 1.3 shows one solution: Two planklike blocks span the water, each held in place by the counterweight of heavy blocks on the bridge's towers. Whereas older children easily built successful bridges, only one 5-year-old did. Careful tracking of her efforts revealed that she repeatedly tried unsuccessful strategies, such as pushing two planks together and pressing down on their ends to hold them in place. But eventually, her experimentation triggered the idea of using the blocks as counterweights. Her mistaken procedures helped her understand why the counterweight approach worked.

Many information-processing models exist. Some, like the one just considered, track children's mastery of one or a few tasks. Others describe the human cognitive system as a whole (Gopnik & Tenenbaum, 2007; Johnson & Mareschal, 2001; Westermann et al., 2006). These general models are used as guides for asking questions about broad age changes in children's thinking: Does a child's ability to solve problems become more organized and "planful" with age? What strategies do younger and older children use to remember new information, and how do those strategies affect children's recall?

The information-processing approach has also been used to clarify the processing of social information. For example, flowcharts exist that track the steps children use to solve social problems (such as how to enter an ongoing play group) and acquire gender-linked preferences and behaviors (Liben & Bigler, 2002; Rubin, Begle, & McDonald, 2012). If we can identify how social problem solving and gender stereotyping arise in childhood, then we can design interventions that promote more favorable social development.

Like Piaget's theory, the information-processing approach regards children as active, sense-making beings who modify their own thinking in response to environmental demands (Halford & Andrews, 2011; Munakata, 2006). But unlike Piaget's theory, it does not divide development into stages. Rather, most information-processing researchers regard the thought processes studied—perception, attention, memory, categorization of information, planning, problem solving, and comprehension of written and spoken prose—as similar at all ages but present to a lesser or greater extent. Their view of development is one of continuous change.

A great strength of the information-processing approach is its commitment to rigorous research methods. Because it has provided precise accounts of how children of different ages engage in many aspects of thinking, its findings have important implications for education (Blumenfeld, Marx, & Harris, 2006; Siegler, 2009). But information processing has fallen short in some respects. It has been better at analyzing thinking into its components than at putting them back together into a comprehensive theory. And it has had little to say about aspects of children's cognition that are not linear and logical, such as imagination and creativity (Birney & Sternberg, 2011).

Developmental Neuroscience

Over the past three decades, as information-processing research expanded, an area of investigation arose called **developmental cognitive neuroscience.** It brings together researchers from psychology, biology, neuroscience, and medicine to study the relationship between changes in the brain and the developing child's cognitive processing and behavior patterns.

Improved methods for analyzing brain activity while children perform various tasks have greatly enhanced knowledge of relationships between brain functioning and behavior (Blakemore et al., 2011). Armed with these brain electrical-recording and imaging techniques (which we will consider in Chapter 5), neuroscientists are tackling questions like these: How does genetic makeup combine with specific experiences at various ages to influence the growth and organization of the child's brain? How do changes in brain structures support rapid memory development in infancy and toddlerhood? What transformations in brain systems make it harder for adolescents and adults than for children to acquire a second language?

Recently, researchers spawned a complementary new area—**developmental social neuroscience**—devoted to studying the relationship between changes in the brain and emotional and social development. Developmental social neuroscience emerged later than its cognitive counterpart because techniques for measuring brain activity, which restrict movements in children, are hard to implement in most social situations, where children must move freely to interact with others (Zelazo & Paus, 2010). When researchers started to tap more convenient neurobiological measures that are sensitive to psychological state, such as heart rate, blood pressure, and hormone levels detected in saliva, an explosion of social-neuroscience investigations followed.

Active areas of investigation in developmental social neuroscience range widely. These include identification of the neural systems underlying infant gains in perception of facial expressions, risk-taking behaviors in adolescence, and individual differences in sociability, anxiety, aggression, and depression. A particularly energetic focus is the negative impact of extreme circumstances—such as early rearing in deprived orphanages or child abuse and neglect—on brain development and cognitive, emotional, and social skills (Anderson & Beauchamp, 2013; de Haan & Gunnar, 2009). Another burgeoning interest is uncovering the neurological bases of *autism*—the disrupted brain structures and networks that lead to the impaired social skills, language delays, and repetitive motor behavior of this disorder (Stoner et al., 2014). As these efforts illustrate, researchers are forging links between cognitive and social neuroscience, identifying brain systems that affect both domains of development.

Rapid progress in clarifying the types of experiences that support or undermine brain development at diverse ages is contributing to effective interventions for children with learning and behavior problems. Today, researchers are examining the impact of various treatment techniques on both brain functioning and behavior (Johnson, 2011; Schlaggar & Barnes, 2011). Although much remains to be discovered, developmental

A therapist encourages a 6-year-old with autism to master the alphabet and interact socially, giving her a high five for progress. Developmental social neuroscientists are intensely interested in identifying the neurological bases of autism and using those findings to devise effective interventions.

neuroscience is broadening our understanding of development and yielding major practical applications.

Nevertheless, neuroscience research has so captivated the field that it poses the risk that brain properties underlying children's behavior will be granted undue importance over powerful environmental influences, such as parenting, educational, and economic inequalities in families and communities. Although most neuroscientists are mindful of the complex interplay between heredity, children's experiences, and brain development, their findings have too often resulted in excessive emphasis being placed on biological processes (Kagan, 2013b). Consequently, instances exist in which psychological outcomes in children have been wrongly attributed mostly or entirely to genetic and brain-based causes.

Fortunately, an advantage of having many theories is that they encourage researchers to attend to previously neglected dimensions of children's lives. The final four perspectives we will discuss focus on *contexts* for development. The first of these views emphasizes that the development of many capacities is influenced by the environments to which humans were exposed over a long evolutionary history.

Ethology and Evolutionary Developmental Psychology

Ethology is concerned with the adaptive, or survival, value of behavior and its evolutionary history. Its roots can be traced to the work of Darwin. Two European zoologists, Konrad Lorenz and Niko Tinbergen, laid its modern foundations. Watching diverse animal species in their natural habitats, Lorenz and Tinbergen observed behavior patterns that promote survival. The best known of these is *imprinting*, the early following behavior of certain baby birds, such as geese, which ensures that the young will stay close to the mother and be fed and protected from danger (Lorenz, 1952). Imprinting takes place during an early, restricted period of development. If the mother goose is absent during this time but an object resembling her in important features is present, young goslings may imprint on it instead.

Observations of imprinting led to a major concept in child development: the *critical period*. It is a limited time span during which the child is biologically prepared to acquire certain adaptive behaviors but needs the support of an appropriately stimulating environment. Many researchers have investigated whether complex cognitive and social behaviors must be learned during certain periods. For example, if children are deprived of adequate food or physical and social stimulation during their early years, will their intelligence be impaired? If language is not mastered in early childhood, is the child's capacity to acquire it reduced?

In later chapters, we will discover that the term *sensitive period* applies better to human development than the strict notion of a critical period (Bornstein, 1989; Knudsen, 2004). A **sensitive period** is a time that is biologically optimal for certain capacities to emerge because the individual is especially responsive to environmental influences. However, its boundaries are less well-defined than are those of a critical period. Development can occur later, but it is harder to induce.

Inspired by observations of imprinting, British psychoanalyst John Bowlby (1969) applied ethological theory to understanding the human infant–caregiver relationship. He argued that infant smiling, babbling, grasping, and crying are built-in social signals that encourage the caregiver to approach, care for, and interact with the baby. By keeping the parent near, these behaviors help ensure that the baby will be fed, protected from danger, and provided with the stimulation and affection necessary for healthy growth. The development of attachment in human infants is a lengthy process involving changes in psychological structures that lead the baby to form a deep affectionate tie with the caregiver (Thompson, 2006). In Chapter 7, we will consider how infant, caregiver, and family context contribute to attachment and how attachment influences later development.

© MARTIN HARVEY/GALLO IMAGES/CORBIS

Ethology focuses on the adaptive, or survival, value of behavior and on similarities between human behavior and that of other species, especially our primate relatives. Observing this mother cuddling her 8-day-old infant helps us understand the human infant–caregiver relationship.

Observations by ethologists have shown that many aspects of children's social behavior, including emotional expressions, aggression, cooperation, and social play, resemble those of our primate relatives. Recently, researchers have extended this effort in a new area of research called **evolutionary developmental psychology.** It seeks to understand the adaptive value of species-wide cognitive, emotional, and social competencies as those competencies change with age (King & Bjorklund, 2010; Lickliter & Honeycutt, 2013). Evolutionary developmental psychologists ask questions like these: What role does the newborn's visual preference for face-like stimuli play in survival? Does it support older infants' capacity to distinguish familiar caregivers from unfamiliar people? Why do children play in gender-segregated groups? What do they learn from such play that might lead to adult gender-typed behaviors, such as male dominance and female investment in caregiving?

As these examples suggest, evolutionary psychologists are not just concerned with the genetic and biological roots of development. They recognize that humans' large brain and extended childhood resulted from the need to master an increasingly complex environment, so they are also interested in learning (Bjorklund, Causey, & Periss, 2009). And they realize that today's lifestyles differ so radically from those of our evolutionary ancestors that certain evolved behaviors—such as life-threatening risk taking by adolescents and male-to-male violence—are no longer adaptive (Blasi & Bjorklund, 2003). By clarifying the origins and development of such behaviors, evolutionary developmental psychology may help spark more effective interventions.

In sum, evolutionary developmental psychology aims to understand the entire *person–environment system.* The next contextual perspective we will discuss, Vygotsky's sociocultural theory, serves as an excellent complement to the evolutionary viewpoint because it highlights the social and cultural dimensions of children's experiences.

Vygotsky's Sociocultural Theory

The field of child development has recently seen a dramatic increase in studies addressing the cultural context of children's lives. Investigations that make comparisons across cultures, and between ethnic groups within cultures, provide insight into whether developmental pathways apply to all children or are limited to particular environmental conditions.

Today, much research is examining the relationship of *culturally specific beliefs and practices* to development (Goodnow, 2010). The contributions of Russian psychologist Lev Vygotsky (1896–1934) have played a major role in this trend. Vygotsky's perspective, known as **sociocultural theory,** focuses on how culture—the values, beliefs, customs, and skills of a social group—is transmitted to the next generation. According to Vygotsky, social interaction—in particular, cooperative dialogues with more knowledgeable members of society—is necessary for children to acquire the ways of thinking and behaving that make up a community's culture. Vygotsky (1934/ 1987) believed that as adults and more expert peers help children master culturally meaningful activities, the communication between them becomes part of children's thinking. As children internalize features of these dialogues, they can use the language within them to guide their own thought and actions and to acquire new skills (Lourenço, 2012; Winsler, Fernyhough, & Montero, 2009). The young child instructing herself while working a puzzle or preparing a table for dinner has begun to produce the same kinds of guiding comments that an adult previously used to help her master important tasks.

Vygotsky's theory has been especially influential in the study of children's cognition. Vygotsky agreed with Piaget that children are active, constructive beings. But whereas Piaget emphasized children's independent efforts to make sense of their world, Vygotsky viewed cognitive development as a *socially mediated process,* in which children depend on assistance from adults and more-expert peers as they tackle new challenges.

In Vygotsky's theory, children undergo certain stagewise changes. For example, when they acquire language, they gain in ability to participate in dialogues with

COURTESY OF JAMES V. WERTSCH/WASHINGTON UNIVERSITY IN ST. LOUIS

According to Lev Vygotsky, shown here with his daughter, many cognitive processes and skills are socially transferred from more knowledgeable members of society to children. Vygotsky's sociocultural theory helps explain the wide cultural variation in cognitive competencies.

With her teacher's guidance, this Chinese child practices calligraphy. She acquires a culturally valued skill through interaction with an older, more experienced calligrapher.

others, and mastery of culturally valued competencies surges forward. When children enter school, they spend much time discussing language, literacy, and other academic concepts—experiences that encourage them to reflect on their own thinking (Bodrova & Leong, 2007; Kozulin, 2003). As a result, they gain dramatically in reasoning and problem solving.

At the same time, Vygotsky stressed that dialogues with experts lead to continuous changes in thinking that vary greatly from culture to culture. Consistent with this view, a major finding of cross-cultural research is that cultures select different tasks for children's learning, and social interaction surrounding those tasks leads to competencies essential for success in a particular culture. For example, in industrialized nations, teachers help people learn to read, drive a car, or use a computer. Among the Zinacanteco Indians of southern Mexico, adult experts guide young girls as they master complicated weaving techniques (Greenfield, 2004). In Brazil and other developing nations, child candy sellers with little or no schooling develop sophisticated mathematical abilities as the result of buying candy from wholesalers, pricing it in collaboration with adults and experienced peers, and bargaining with customers on city streets (Saxe, 1988).

Research stimulated by Vygotsky's theory reveals that children in every culture develop unique strengths. But Vygotsky's emphasis on culture and social experience led him to neglect the biological side of development. Although he recognized the importance of heredity and brain growth, he said little about their role in cognitive change. Furthermore, Vygotsky's focus on social transmission of knowledge meant that, compared with other theorists, he placed less emphasis on children's capacity to shape their own development. Followers of Vygotsky stress that children strive for social connection, actively participating in the conversations and social activities from which their development springs. From these joint experiences, they not only acquire culturally valued practices but also modify and transform those practices (Daniels, 2011; Rogoff, 2003). Contemporary sociocultural theorists grant the individual and society balanced, mutually influential roles.

Ecological Systems Theory

Urie Bronfenbrenner (1917–2005) is responsible for an approach to child development that has moved to the forefront of the field over the past two decades because it offers the most differentiated and complete account of contextual influences on children's development. **Ecological systems theory** views the child as developing within a complex *system* of relationships affected by multiple levels of the surrounding environment. Since the child's biologically influenced dispositions join with environmental forces to mold development, Bronfenbrenner characterized his perspective as a *bioecological model* (Bronfenbrenner, 2005; Bronfenbrenner & Morris, 2006).

Bronfenbrenner envisioned the environment as a series of interrelated, nested structures that form a complex functioning whole, or *system*. These include but also extend beyond the home, school, and neighborhood settings in which children spend their everyday lives (see Figure 1.4). Each layer joins with the others to powerfully affect development.

THE MICROSYSTEM The innermost level of the environment, the **microsystem,** consists of activities and interaction patterns in the child's immediate surroundings. Bronfenbrenner emphasizes that to understand child development at this level, we must keep in mind that all relationships are *bidirectional:* Adults affect children's behavior, but children's biologically and socially influenced characteristics—their physical attributes, personalities, and capacities—also affect adults' behavior. A friendly, attentive child is likely to evoke positive, patient reactions from parents, whereas an irritable or distractible child is more likely to receive impatience, restriction, and punishment. When these reciprocal interactions occur often over time, they have an enduring impact on development (Crockenberg & Leerkes, 2003).

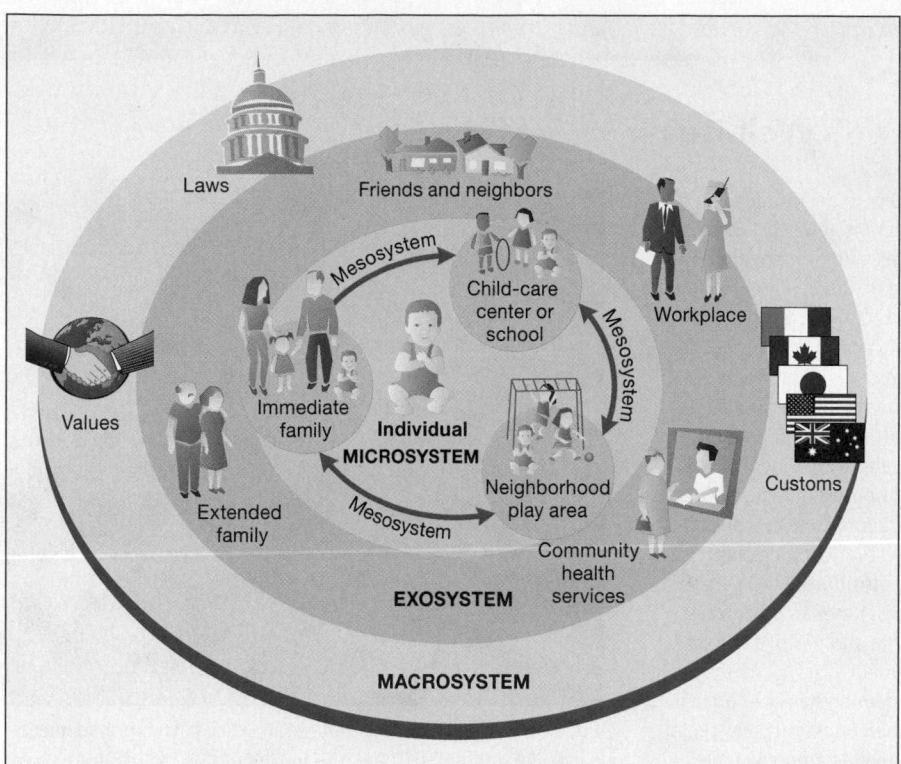

Third parties—other individuals in the microsystem—also affect the quality of any two-person relationship. If they are supportive, interaction is enhanced. For example, when parents encourage each other in their child-rearing roles, each engages in more effective parenting. In contrast, marital conflict is associated with inconsistent discipline and hostile reactions toward children. In response, children often react with fear and anxiety or with anger and aggression, and the well-being of both parent and child suffers (Caldera & Lindsey, 2006; Low & Stocker, 2012).

THE MESOSYSTEM The second level of Bronfenbrenner's model, the **mesosystem,** encompasses connections between microsystems, such as home, school, neighborhood, and child-care center. For example, a child's academic progress depends not just on activities that take place in classrooms but also on parent involvement in school life and on the extent to which academic learning is carried over into the home (Jeynes, 2012). Similarly, parent–child interaction at home is likely to affect caregiver–child interaction in the child-care setting, and vice versa. Each relationship is more likely to support development when there are links between home and child care, in the form of visits and cooperative exchanges of information.

THE EXOSYSTEM The **exosystem** consists of social settings that do not contain children but that nevertheless affect children's experiences in immediate settings. These can be formal organizations, such as parents' workplaces, their religious institutions, and community health and welfare services. Flexible work schedules, paid maternity and paternity leave, and sick leave for parents whose children are ill are examples of ways that work settings can support child rearing and, indirectly, enhance children's development. Exosystem supports also can be informal, such as parents' social networks—friends and

This father says good-bye to his daughter at the start of the school day. Her experiences at school (microsystem) and the father's experiences at work (exosystem) affect the father–daughter relationship.

Social Issues: Health

Family Chaos Undermines Children's Well-Being

All of us can recall days during our childhoods when family routines—regular mealtime, bedtime, homework time, and parent–child reading and playtimes—were disrupted, perhaps because of a change in a parent's job, a family illness, or a busy season of after-school sports. In some families, however, absence of daily structure is nearly constant, yielding a chaotic home life that interferes with healthy development (Fiese & Winter, 2010). An organized family life provides a supportive context for warm, involved parent–child interaction, which is essential to children's well-being.

Family chaos is linked to economic disadvantage—especially, single mothers with limited incomes struggling to juggle the challenges of transportation, shift jobs, unstable child-care arrangements, and other daily hassles. But chaos is not limited to such families.

Surveys reveal that among U.S. families as a whole, mothers' time with children has remained fairly stable over the past three decades, and fathers' time has increased (Galinsky, Aumann, & Bond, 2009). But the way many parents spend that time has changed. Across income levels and ethnic groups, both mothers and fathers report more multitasking while caring for children—for example, using mealtimes not just to eat but also to check homework, read to children, and plan family outings and celebrations (Bianchi & Raley, 2005). Consequently, disruption in one family routine can disrupt others.

Possibly because of this compression of family routines, today's parents and children consistently say they have too little time together. For example, only slightly more than half of U.S. families report eating together three to five times per week (CASA, 2006; Opinion Research Corporation, 2009). Frequency of family meals is associated with wide-ranging positive outcomes—in childhood, enhanced language development and academic achievement, fewer behavior problems, and time spent sleeping; and in adolescence, reduced sexual risk taking, alcohol and drug use, and mental health problems. Shared mealtimes also increase the likelihood of a healthy diet and protect against obesity and adolescent eating disorders (Adam, Snell, & Pendry, 2007; Fiese & Schwartz, 2008). As these findings suggest, regular mealtimes are a general indicator of an organized family life and positive parent involvement.

But family chaos can prevail even when families do engage in joint activities. Unpredictable, disorganized family meals involving harsh or lax parental discipline and hostile, disrespectful communication are associated with children's adjustment difficulties (Fiese, Foley, & Spagnola, 2006). As family time becomes pressured and overwhelming, its orderly structure diminishes, and warm parent–child engagement disintegrates.

Diverse circumstances can trigger a pileup of limited parental emotional resources, breeding family chaos. In addition to *microsystem* and *mesosytem* influences (parents with mental health problems, parental separation and divorce, single parents with few or no supportive relationships), the *exosystem* is powerful: When family time is at the mercy of external forces—parents commuting several hours a day to and from work, child-care arrangements often failing, parents experiencing excessive workplace pressures or job loss—family routines are threatened.

A chaotic home life interferes with warm, relaxed parent–child interaction and contributes to behavior problems. Exosystem influences, such as excessive workplace pressures, can trigger disorganized family routines.

Family chaos contributes to children's behavior problems, above and beyond its negative impact on parenting effectiveness (Coldwell, Pike, & Dunn, 2008; Fiese & Winter, 2010). Chaotic surroundings induce in children a sense of being hassled and feelings of powerlessness, which engender anxiety and low self-esteem.

Exosystem and macrosystem supports—including work settings with favorable family policies and high-quality child care that is affordable and reliable—can help prevent escalating demands on families that give way to chaos (Repetti & Wang, 2010). In one community, a child-care center initiated a take-home dinner program. Busy parents could special-order a healthy, reasonably priced family meal, ready to go at day's end to aid in making the family dinner a routine that enhances children's development.

extended-family members who provide advice, companionship, and even financial assistance. Research confirms the negative impact of a breakdown in exosystem activities. Families who are affected by unemployment or who are socially isolated, with few personal or community-based ties, show increased rates of conflict and child abuse (Coulton et al., 2007). Refer to the Social Issues: Health box above for an additional illustration of the power of the exosystem to affect family functioning and children's development.

THE MACROSYSTEM   The outermost level of Bronfenbrenner's model, the **macrosystem,** consists of cultural values, laws, customs, and resources. The priority that the macrosystem gives to children's needs affects the support they receive at inner levels of the environment. For example, in countries that require generous workplace benefits for employed parents and high-quality standards for child care, children are more likely to have favorable experiences in their immediate settings. As you will see in later chapters, such programs are far less available in the United States than in other industrialized nations (Pew Research Center, 2013a).

AN EVER-CHANGING SYSTEM According to Bronfenbrenner, the environment is not a static force that affects children in a uniform way. Instead, it is ever-changing. Important life events, such as the birth of a sibling, the beginning of school, a move to a new neighborhood, or parents' divorce, modify existing relationships between children and their environments, producing new conditions that affect development. In addition, the timing of environmental change affects its impact. The arrival of a new sibling has very different consequences for a homebound toddler than for a school-age child with many relationships and activities beyond the family.

Bronfenbrenner called the temporal dimension of his model the **chronosystem** (the prefix *chrono-* means "time"). Life changes can be imposed on the child, as in the examples just given. Alternatively, they can arise from within the child, since as children get older they select, modify, and create many of their own settings and experiences. How they do so depends on their physical, intellectual, and personality characteristics and their environmental opportunities. Therefore, in ecological systems theory, development is neither entirely controlled by environmental circumstances nor driven solely by inner dispositions. Rather, children and their environments form a network of interdependent effects. Notice how our discussion of resilient children on pages 10–11 illustrates this idea. You will see many more examples in this book.

Development as a Dynamic System

Today, researchers recognize both consistency and variability in children's development and want to do a better job of explaining variation. Consequently, a new wave of systems theorists focuses on how children, in interacting with their complex contexts, alter their behavior to attain more advanced functioning. According to this **dynamic systems perspective,** the child's mind, body, and physical and social worlds form an *integrated system* that guides mastery of new skills. The system is *dynamic,* or constantly in motion. A change in any part of it—from brain growth to physical or social surroundings—disrupts the current organism–environment relationship. When this happens, the child actively reorganizes his or her behavior so the various components of the system work together again but in a more complex, effective way (Fischer & Bidell, 2006; Spencer, Perone, & Buss, 2011; Thelen & Smith, 2006).

Researchers adopting a dynamic systems perspective try to find out just how children attain new levels of organization by studying their behavior while they are in transition (Thelen & Corbetta, 2002). For example, when presented with an attractive toy, how does a 3-month-old baby who engages in many, varied movements discover how to reach for it? On hearing a new word, how does a 2-year-old figure out the category of objects or events to which it refers?

Dynamic systems theorists acknowledge that a common human genetic heritage and basic regularities in children's physical and social worlds yield certain universal, broad outlines of development. But children's biological makeup, interests and goals, everyday tasks, and the people who support children in mastery of those tasks vary greatly, leading to wide individual differences in specific skills. Even when children master the same skills, such as walking, talking, or adding and subtracting, they often do so in unique ways. And because children build competencies by engaging in real activities in real contexts, different skills vary in maturity within the same child. From this perspective, development cannot be characterized as a single line of change. As Figure 1.5 on page 30 shows, it is more like a web of fibers branching out in many directions, each representing a different skill area that may undergo both continuous and stagewise transformations (Fischer & Bidell, 2006).

LOOK and LISTEN

Ask a parent to explain his or her most worrisome child-rearing challenge. Describe one source of support at each level of Bronfenbrenner's model that could ease parental stress and promote child development.

The dynamic systems perspective views the child's mind, body, and physical and social worlds as a continuously reorganizing, integrated system. In response to the physical and psychological changes of adolescence, this father and daughter must develop a new, more mature relationship.

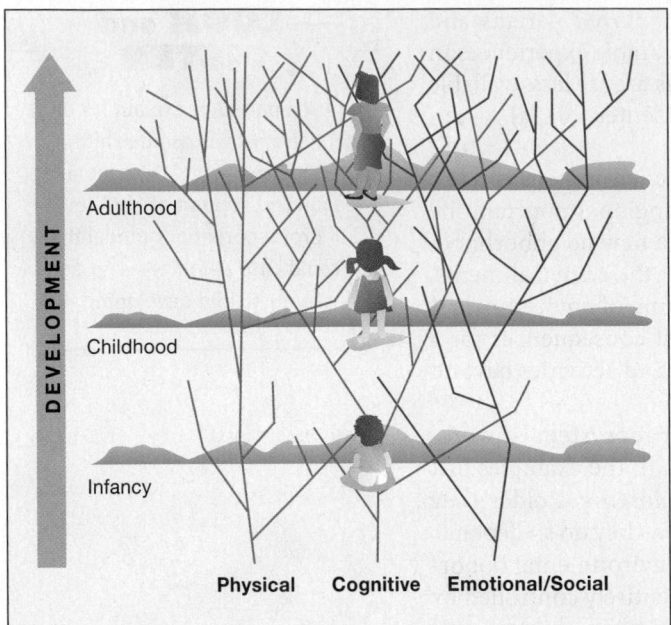

FIGURE 1.5 **The dynamic systems view of development.** Rather than envisioning a single line of stagewise or continuous change (refer to Figure 1.2 on page 8), dynamic systems theorists conceive of development as a web of fibers branching out in many directions. Each strand in the web represents a skill within the major domains of development—physical, cognitive, and emotional/social. The differing directions of the strands signify possible variations in paths and outcomes as the child masters skills necessary to participate in diverse contexts. The interconnections of the strands at each row of "hills" portray stagelike changes—periods of major transformation in which various skills work together as a functioning whole. As the web expands, skills become more numerous, complex, and effective. (Based on Fischer & Bidell, 2006.)

The dynamic systems view has been inspired by other scientific disciplines, especially biology and physics. It also draws on information-processing and contextual theories—evolutionary developmental psychology, sociocultural theory, and ecological systems theory. Dynamic systems research is still in its early stages. The perspective has been applied largely to children's motor and cognitive skills, but some investigators have drawn on it to explain emotional and social development as well (Fogel & Garvey, 2007; Kunnen, 2012). Consider the young teenager, whose body and reasoning powers are changing massively and who also is confronting a multiplicity of new academic and social challenges. Researchers following parent–child interaction over time found that the transition to adolescence disrupted family communication. It became unstable and variable for several years—a mix of positive, neutral, and negative exchanges (Granic et al., 2003). Gradually, as parent and adolescent devised new, more mature ways of relating to one another, the system reorganized and stabilized. Once again, interaction became predictable and mostly positive.

As dynamic systems research illustrates, today investigators are tracking and analyzing development in all its complexity. In doing so, they hope to move closer to an all-encompassing approach to understanding change.

Ask Yourself

- **REVIEW** Explain how each recent theoretical perspective regards children as active contributors to their own development.

- **CONNECT** Return to the Biology and Environment box on pages 10–11. How does the story of John and Gary illustrate bidirectional influences within the microsystem, as described in ecological systems theory?

- **APPLY** Mario wants to find out precisely how children of different ages recall stories. Anna is interested in how adult–child communication in different cultures influences children's storytelling. Which theoretical perspective has Mario probably chosen? How about Anna? Explain.

- **REFLECT** To illustrate the chronosystem in ecological systems theory, select an important event from your childhood, such as a move to a new neighborhood or a class with an inspiring teacher. How did the event affect you? How might its impact have differed had you been five years younger? How about five years older?

1.7 Identify the stand taken by each major theory on the basic issues of child development.

Comparing Child Development Theories

In the preceding sections, we reviewed theoretical perspectives in child development research. They differ in many respects. First, they focus on different domains of development. Some, such as the psychoanalytic perspective and ethology, emphasize emotional and social development. Others, such as Piaget's cognitive-developmental theory, information processing, and Vygotsky's sociocultural theory, stress changes in thinking. The remaining approaches—behaviorism,

TABLE 1.3	Stances of Major Theories on Basic Issues in Child Development		
THEORY	**CONTINUOUS OR DISCONTINUOUS DEVELOPMENT?**	**ONE COURSE OF DEVELOPMENT OR MANY?**	**RELATIVE INFLUENCE OF NATURE AND NURTURE?**
Psychoanalytic perspective	*Discontinuous:* Psychosexual and psychosocial development takes place in stages.	*One course:* Stages are assumed to be universal.	*Both nature and nurture:* Innate impulses are channeled and controlled through child-rearing experiences. *Early experiences* set the course of later development.
Behaviorism and social learning theory	*Continuous:* Development involves an increase in learned behaviors.	*Many possible courses:* Behaviors reinforced and modeled may vary from child to child.	*Emphasis on nurture:* Development results from conditioning and modeling. *Both early and later experiences* are important.
Piaget's cognitive-developmental theory	*Discontinuous:* Cognitive development takes place in stages.	*One course:* Stages are assumed to be universal.	*Both nature and nurture:* Development occurs as the brain grows and children exercise their innate drive to discover reality in a generally stimulating environment. *Both early and later experiences* are important.
Information processing	*Continuous:* Children gradually improve in perception, attention, memory, and problem-solving skills.	*One course:* Changes studied characterize most or all children.	*Both nature and nurture:* Children are active, sense-making beings who modify their thinking as the brain grows and they confront new environmental demands. *Both early and later experiences* are important.
Ethology and evolutionary developmental psychology	*Both continuous and discontinuous:* Children gradually develop a wider range of adaptive behaviors. Sensitive periods occur, in which qualitatively distinct capacities emerge fairly suddenly.	*One course:* Adaptive behaviors and sensitive periods apply to all members of a species.	*Both nature and nurture:* Evolution and heredity influence behavior, and learning lends greater flexibility and adaptiveness to it. In sensitive periods, *early experiences* set the course of later development.
Vygotsky's sociocultural theory	*Both continuous and discontinuous:* Language acquisition and schooling lead to stagewise changes. Dialogues with more expert members of society also lead to continuous changes that vary from culture to culture.	*Many possible courses:* Socially mediated changes in thought and behavior vary from culture to culture.	*Both nature and nurture:* Heredity, brain growth, and dialogues with more expert members of society jointly contribute to development. *Both early and later experiences* are important.
Ecological systems theory	*Not specified.*	*Many possible courses:* Children's characteristics join with environmental forces at multiple levels to mold development in unique ways.	*Both nature and nurture:* Children's characteristics and the reactions of others affect each other in a bidirectional fashion. Layers of the environment influence child-rearing experiences. *Both early and later experiences* are important.
Dynamic systems perspective	*Both continuous and discontinuous:* Change in the system is always ongoing. Stagelike transformations occur as children reorganize their behavior so components of the system work as a functioning whole.	*Many possible courses:* Biological makeup, everyday tasks, and social experiences vary, yielding wide individual differences in specific skills.	*Both nature and nurture:* The child's mind, body, and physical and social surroundings form an integrated system that guides mastery of new skills. *Both early and later experiences* are important.

social learning theory, evolutionary developmental psychology, ecological systems theory, and the dynamic systems perspective—encompass many aspects of children's functioning. Second, every theory contains a point of view about child development. **TAKE A MOMENT...** As we conclude our review of theoretical perspectives, identify the stand that each theory takes on the controversial issues presented at the beginning of this chapter. Then check your analysis of the theories against Table 1.3.

Finally, we have seen that every theory has strengths and limitations. Perhaps you found that you are attracted to some theories, but you have doubts about others. As you read more about child development in later chapters, you may find it useful to keep a notebook in which you test your own theoretical likes and dislikes against the evidence. Don't be surprised if you revise your ideas many times, just as theorists have done throughout the past century. By the end of the course, you will have built your own personal perspective on child development. Very likely, it will be an *eclectic position,* or blend of several theories, since every viewpoint we have considered has contributed to what we know about children.

1.8 Describe research methods commonly used to study children.

1.9 Distinguish between correlational and experimental research designs, noting strengths and limitations of each.

1.10 Describe designs for studying development, noting strengths and limitations of each.

1.11 What special ethical concerns arise in doing research on children?

Studying the Child

In every science, research usually begins with a *hypothesis*—a prediction drawn directly from a theory. Theories and hypotheses, however, merely initiate the many activities that result in sound evidence on child development. Conducting research according to scientifically accepted procedures involves many steps and choices. Investigators must decide which participants, and how many, to include. Then they must figure out what the participants will be asked to do and when, where, and how many times each will be seen. Finally, they must examine and draw conclusions from their data.

In the following sections, we look at research strategies commonly used to study children. We begin with common *research methods*—the specific activities of participants, such as taking tests, answering questionnaires, responding to interviews, or being observed. Then we turn to *research designs*—overall plans for research studies that permit the best possible test of the investigator's hypothesis. Finally, we discuss special ethical issues involved in doing research on children.

Why learn about research strategies? Why not leave these matters to research specialists and concentrate on what is already known about the child and how this knowledge can be applied? There are two reasons. First, each of us must be a wise and critical consumer of knowledge. Knowing the strengths and limitations of various research strategies is important in separating dependable information from misleading results. Second, individuals who work directly with children may be in a unique position to build bridges between research and practice by conducting studies, either on their own or in partnership with experienced investigators. Community agencies such as schools, mental health facilities, and parks and recreation programs sometimes collaborate with researchers in designing, implementing, and evaluating interventions aimed at enhancing children's development (Guerra, Graham, & Tolan, 2011). To broaden these efforts, a basic understanding of the research process is essential.

LOOK and LISTEN

Ask a teacher, counselor, social worker, or nurse to describe a question about development he or she would like researchers to address, as a means of facilitating applied work with children. After reading the rest of this chapter, recommend research strategies best suited to answering that question, citing their strengths and limitations.

Common Research Methods

How does a researcher choose a basic approach to gathering information about children? Common methods include systematic observation, self-reports (such as questionnaires and interviews), clinical or case studies of a single child, and ethnographies of the life circumstances of a specific group of children. Table 1.4 summarizes the strengths and limitations of each of these methods.

SYSTEMATIC OBSERVATION Observations of the behavior of children, and of adults who are important in their lives, can be made in different ways. One approach is to go into the field, or natural environment, and observe the behavior of interest—a method called **naturalistic observation.**

A study of preschoolers' responses to their peers' distress provides a good example of this technique (Farver & Branstetter, 1994). Observing 3- and 4-year-olds in child-care centers, the researchers recorded each instance of a child crying and the reactions of nearby children— whether they ignored, watched curiously, commented on the child's unhappiness, scolded or teased, or shared, helped, or expressed sympathy. Caregiver behaviors—explaining why a child was crying, mediating conflict, or offering comfort—were noted to see if adult sensitivity was related to children's caring responses. A strong relationship emerged. The great strength of naturalistic observation is that investigators can see directly the everyday behaviors they hope to explain.

TABLE 1.4	Strengths and Limitations of Common Information-Gathering Methods		
METHOD	**DESCRIPTION**	**STRENGTHS**	**LIMITATIONS**
Systematic Observation			
Naturalistic observation	Observation of behavior in natural contexts.	Reflects participants' everyday behaviors.	Cannot control conditions under which participants are observed.
Structured observation	Observation of behavior in a laboratory, where conditions are the same for all participants.	Grants each participant an equal opportunity to display the behavior of interest. Permits study of behaviors rarely seen in everyday life.	May not yield observations typical of participants' behavior in everyday life.
Self-Reports			
Clinical interview	Flexible interviewing procedure in which the investigator obtains a complete account of the participant's thoughts.	Comes as close as possible to the way participants think in everyday life. Great breadth and depth of information can be obtained in a short time.	May not result in accurate reporting of information. Flexible procedure makes comparing individuals' responses difficult.
Structured interview, questionnaires, and tests	Self-report instruments in which each participant is asked the same questions in the same way.	Permits comparisons of participants' responses and efficient data collection. Researchers can specify answer alternatives that participants might not think of in an open-ended interview.	Does not yield the same depth of information as a clinical interview. Responses are still subject to inaccurate reporting.
Clinical, or Case Study, Method			
	A full picture of one individual's psychological functioning, obtained by combining interviews, observations, and sometimes test scores.	Provides rich, descriptive insights into processes of development.	May be biased by researchers' theoretical preferences. Findings cannot be applied to individuals other than the participant.
Ethnography			
	Participant observation of a culture or distinct social group. By making extensive field notes, the researcher tries to capture the culture's unique values and social processes.	Provides a more complete and accurate description than can be derived from a single observational visit, interview, or questionnaire.	May be biased by researchers' values and theoretical preferences. Findings cannot be applied to individuals and settings other than the ones studied.

Naturalistic observation also has a major limitation: Not all individuals have the same opportunity to display a particular behavior in everyday life. In the study just described, some children might have witnessed a child crying more often than others or been exposed to more cues for positive social responses from caregivers. For this reason, they might have displayed more compassion.

Researchers commonly deal with this difficulty by making **structured observations,** in which the investigator sets up a laboratory situation that evokes the behavior of interest so that every participant has an equal opportunity to display the response. In one study, 2-year-olds' emotional reactions to harm that they thought they had caused were observed by asking them to take care of a rag doll that had been modified so its leg would fall off when the child picked it up. To make the child feel at fault, once the leg detached, an adult "talked for" the doll by saying, "Ow!" Researchers recorded children's facial expressions of sadness and concern for the injured doll, efforts to help the doll, and body tension—responses that indicated remorse and a desire to make amends. In addition, mothers were asked to engage in brief conversations about emotions with their children (Garner, 2003). Toddlers whose mothers more often explained the causes and consequences of emotion were more likely to express concern for the injured doll

© ELLEN B. SENISI

In naturalistic observation, the researcher goes into the field and records the behavior of interest. This researcher observes children at a preschool. She may be focusing on their playmate choices, cooperation, helpfulness, or conflicts.

Structured observation permits greater control over the research situation than does naturalistic observation. In addition, the method is especially useful for studying behaviors—such as parent–child or friendship interactions—that investigators rarely have an opportunity to see in everyday life. When aggressive and nonaggressive 10-year-old boys were observed playing games with their best friend in a laboratory, the aggressive boys and their friends more often violated game rules, cheated, and encouraged each other to engage in these dishonest acts. In addition, observers rated these boys' interactions as angrier and less cooperative than the interactions of nonaggressive boys and their friends (Bagwell & Coie, 2004). The researchers concluded that aggressive boys' close peer ties provide a context in which they practice hostility and other negative behaviors, which may contribute to their antisocial behavior.

The procedures used to collect systematic observations vary, depending on the purpose of the research. Some investigators choose to describe the entire stream of behavior—everything said and done over a certain time period. In one study, researchers wanted to find out whether maternal sensitivity in infancy and early childhood contributes to readiness for formal schooling at age 6 (Hirsh-Pasek & Burchinal, 2006). Between age 6 months and 4½ years, the investigators periodically videotaped 15-minute mother–child play sessions. Then they rated each session for maternal positive emotion, support, stimulating play, and respect for the child's autonomy—ingredients of sensitivity that did predict better language and academic progress when the children reached kindergarten.

Researchers have devised ingenious ways of observing difficult-to-capture behaviors. For example, to record instances of bullying, a group of investigators set up video cameras overlooking a classroom and a playground and had fourth to sixth graders wear small, remote microphones and pocket-sized transmitters (Craig, Pepler, & Atlas, 2000). Results revealed that bullying occurred often—at rates of 2.4 episodes per hour in the classroom and 4.5 episodes per hour on the playground. Yet only 15 to 18 percent of the time did teachers take steps to stop the harassment.

Systematic observation provides invaluable information on how children and adults behave, but it tells us little about the reasoning behind their responses. For this kind of information, researchers must turn to self-report techniques.

SELF-REPORTS   Self-reports ask research participants to provide information on their perceptions, thoughts, abilities, feelings, attitudes, beliefs, and past experiences. They range from relatively unstructured interviews to highly structured interviews, questionnaires, and tests.

In a **clinical interview,** a flexible, conversational style is used to probe for the participant's point of view. In the following example, Piaget questioned a 5-year-old child about his understanding of dreams:

> *Where does the dream come from?*—I think you sleep so well that you dream.—*Does it come from us or from outside?*—From outside.—*When you are in bed and you dream, where is the dream?*—In my bed, under the blanket. I don't really know. If it was in my stomach, the bones would be in the way and I shouldn't see it.—*Is the dream there when you sleep?*—Yes, it is in the bed beside me. (Piaget, 1926/1930, pp. 97–98)

Although a researcher conducting clinical interviews with more than one child would typically ask the same first question to establish a common task, individualized prompts are used to provide a fuller picture of each child's reasoning.

The clinical interview has two major strengths. First, it permits people to display their thoughts in terms that are as close as possible to the way they think in everyday life. Second, the clinical interview can provide a large amount of information in a fairly brief period. For example, in an hour-long session, we can obtain a wide range of child-rearing information from a parent—much more than we could capture by observing for the same amount of time.

A major limitation of the clinical interview has to do with the accuracy with which people report their thoughts, feelings, and experiences. Some participants, wishing to please the interviewer, may make up answers. When asked about past events, some may have trouble recalling exactly what happened. And because the clinical interview depends on verbal ability and expressiveness, it may underestimate the capacities of individuals who have difficulty putting their thoughts into words.

The clinical interview has also been criticized because of its flexibility. When questions are phrased differently for each participant, variations in responses may reflect the manner of interviewing rather than real differences in the way people think about a topic. **Structured interviews** (including tests and questionnaires), in which each participant is asked the same questions in the same way, eliminate this problem. These instruments are also much more efficient. Answers are briefer, and researchers can obtain written responses from an entire group at the same time. Furthermore, by listing answer alternatives, researchers can indicate the specific activities and behaviors of interest—ones that participants might not think of in an open-ended clinical interview. For example, when parents were asked what they considered "the most important thing for children to prepare them for life," 62 percent checked "to think for themselves" when this alternative appeared on a list. Yet only 5 percent thought of it during a clinical interview (Schwarz, 1999).

Nevertheless, structured interviews do not yield the same depth of information as a clinical interview. And they can still be affected by inaccurate reporting.

THE CLINICAL, OR CASE STUDY, METHOD An outgrowth of psychoanalytic theory, the **clinical,** or **case study, method** brings together a wide range of information on one child, including interviews, observations, and sometimes test scores. The aim is to obtain as complete a picture as possible of that child's psychological functioning and the experiences that led up to it.

The clinical method is well-suited to studying the development of certain types of individuals who are few in number but vary widely in characteristics. For example, the method has been used to find out what contributes to the accomplishments of *prodigies*—extremely gifted children who attain adult competence in a field before age 10 (Moran & Gardner, 2006).

In one investigation, researchers conducted case studies of eight child prodigies nationally recognized for talents in such areas as art, music, and mathematics (Ruthsatz & Urbach, 2012). One child began playing the violin at 28 months, had won regional competitions as a 5-year-old, and by age 7 had performed as a soloist at New York's Carnegie Hall and Lincoln Center. Another child started reading as an infant, took college-level classes beginning at age 8, and published a paper in a mathematics journal at 13. Across the eight cases, the researchers noticed interesting patterns, including above-average intelligence and exceptionally high scores on tests of memory and attention to detail. Notably, several prodigies in the study had relatives with autism, a condition that also involves intense attention to detail. The researchers concluded that although child prodigies generally do not display the social and cognitive deficits of individuals with autism, the two groups may share an underlying genetic trait that affects the functioning of certain brain regions, heightening perception and attention.

Using the clinical, or case study, method, this researcher interacts with a 3-year-old during a home visit. Interviews and observations will contribute to an in-depth picture of this child's psychological functioning.

The clinical method yields richly detailed case narratives that offer valuable insights into the multiplicity of factors affecting development. Nevertheless, like all other methods, it has drawbacks. Because information often is collected unsystematically and subjectively, researchers' theoretical preferences may bias their observations and interpretations. In addition, investigators cannot assume that their conclusions apply, or generalize, to anyone other than the child or children studied (Stanovich, 2013). Even when patterns emerge across several cases, as occurred in the study of child prodigies, it is wise to confirm these with other research strategies.

METHODS FOR STUDYING CULTURE To study the impact of culture on child development, researchers adjust the methods just considered or tap procedures specially devised for cross-cultural and multicultural research (Triandis, 2007). Which approach investigators choose depends on their research goals.

Sometimes researchers are interested in characteristics that are believed to be universal but that vary in degree from one culture to the next: Are parents warmer or more directive in

This Western ethnographer spent months living among the Efe people of the Republic of Congo. Here he observes young children sharing food. The Efe value and encourage cooperation and generosity at an early age.

some cultures than in others? How strong are gender stereotypes in different nations? In each instance, several cultural groups will be compared, and all participants must be questioned or observed in the same way. Therefore, researchers draw on the observational and self-report procedures we have already considered, adapting them through translation so they can be understood in each cultural context. For example, to study cultural variation in parent–adolescent relationships, the same questionnaire, asking for ratings on such items as "I often start a conversation with my parents about what happens in school" or "My parents can tell when I'm upset about something" is given to all participants (Qin & Pomerantz, 2013). Still, investigators must be mindful of cultural differences in familiarity with responding to self-report instruments that may bias their findings (van de Vijver, 2011).

At other times, researchers want to uncover the *cultural meanings* of children's and adults' behaviors by becoming as familiar as possible with their way of life. To achieve this goal, researchers rely on a method borrowed from the field of anthropology—**ethnography.** Like the clinical method, ethnographic research is a descriptive, qualitative technique. But instead of aiming to understand a single individual, it is directed toward understanding a culture or a distinct social group through *participant observation.* Typically, the researcher spends months and sometimes years in the cultural community, participating in its daily life. Extensive field notes are gathered, consisting of a mix of observations, self-reports from members of the culture, and careful interpretations by the investigator (Miller, Hengst, & Wang, 2003; Shweder et al., 2006). Later, these notes are put together into a description of the community that tries to capture its unique values and social processes.

The ethnographic method assumes that by entering into close contact with a social group, researchers can understand the beliefs and behaviors of its members in a way not possible with an observational visit, interview, or questionnaire. Some ethnographies take in many aspects of children's experience, as one researcher did in describing what it is like to grow up in a small American town. Others focus on one or a few settings, such as home, school, or neighborhood life (Calaff, 2008; MacLeod, 2009; Valdés, 1998). And still others are limited to a particular practice, such as uncovering cultural and religious influences on children's make-believe play. For example, ethnographic findings reveal that East Indian Hindu parents encourage preschoolers to communicate with "invisible" characters. They regard this activity as linked to *karma* (the cycle of birth and death) and believe that the child may be remembering a past life. In contrast, Christian fundamentalist parents often discourage children from pretending to be unreal characters, believing that such play promotes dangerous spiritual ideas and deceitful behavior (Taylor & Carlson, 2000). Researchers may supplement traditional self-report and observational methods with ethnography if they suspect that unique meanings underlie cultural differences, as the Cultural Influences box on the following page reveals.

Ethnographers strive to minimize their influence on the culture they are studying by becoming part of it. Nevertheless, as with clinical research, investigators' cultural values and theoretical commitments sometimes lead them to observe selectively or misinterpret what they see. Finally, the findings of ethnographic studies cannot be assumed to generalize beyond the people and settings in which the research was conducted.

Ask Yourself

- **REVIEW** Why might a researcher choose structured observation over naturalistic observation? How about the reverse? What might lead the researcher to opt for clinical interviewing over systematic observation?

- **CONNECT** What strengths and limitations do the clinical, or case study, method and ethnography have in common?

- **APPLY** A researcher wants to study the thoughts and feelings of children who have a parent on active duty in the military. Which method should she use? Why?

Cultural Influences

Immigrant Youths: Adapting to a New Land

Over the past several decades, increasing numbers of immigrants have come to North America, fleeing war and persecution in their homelands or seeking better life chances. Today, nearly one-fourth of U.S. children and adolescents have foreign-born parents, mostly originating from Latin America, the Caribbean, Asia, and Africa. Although some move with their parents, more than 80 percent of young people from immigrant families are U.S.-born citizens (Hernandez, Denton, & Blanchard, 2011; Hernandez et al., 2012).

How well are these youths—now the fastest growing sector of the U.S. youth population—adapting to their new country? To find out, researchers use multiple research methods: academic testing, questionnaires assessing psychological adjustment, and in-depth ethnographies.

Academic Achievement and Adjustment

Although educators and laypeople often assume that the transition to a new country has a negative impact on psychological well-being, evidence reveals that many children of immigrant parents adapt amazingly well. Students who are first generation (foreign-born) or second generation (American-born, with immigrant parents) often achieve in school as well as or better than students of native-born parents (Fuligni, 2004; Hao & Woo, 2012; Hernandez, Denton, & Blanchard, 2011). Findings on psychological adjustment are similar. Compared with their agemates, adolescents from immigrant families are less likely to commit delinquent and violent acts, to use drugs and alcohol, or to have early sex. They are also less likely to be obese or to have missed school because of illness. And they tend to report just as favorable, and at times higher, self-esteem as do young people with native-born parents (Fuligni, 1998; Saucier et al., 2002; Supple & Small, 2006).

These outcomes are strongest for Chinese, Filipino, Japanese, Korean, and East Indian youths, less dramatic for other ethnicities (Fuligni, 2004; Louie, 2001; Portes & Rumbaut, 2005). Variation in adjustment is greater among Mexican, Central American, and Southeast Asian (Hmong, Cambodian, Laotian, Thai, and Vietnamese) young people, who show elevated rates of school failure and dropout, delinquency, teenage parenthood, and drug use. Disparities in parental economic resources, education, English-language proficiency, and support of children contribute to these trends (García Coll & Marks, 2009; Pong & Landale, 2012).

Still, many first- and second-generation youths whose parents face considerable financial hardship and who speak little English are successful

(Hao & Woo, 2012; Hernandez et al., 2011). Factors other than income are responsible—notably, family values and strong ethnic-community ties.

Family and Ethnic-Community Influences

Ethnographies reveal that immigrant parents view education as the surest way to improve life chances (Garcia Coll & Marks, 2009; Goldenberg et al., 2001). Aware of the challenges their children face, they typically emphasize trying hard. They remind their children that, because educational opportunities were not available in their native countries, they themselves are often limited to menial jobs. And while preserving their culture's values, these parents also make certain adaptations—for example, supporting education for daughters even though their culture of origin endorses it only for sons.

Adolescents from immigrant families internalize their parents' valuing of academic achievement, endorsing it more strongly than agemates with native-born parents (Fuligni, 2004; Su & Costigan, 2008). Because minority ethnicities usually stress allegiance to family and community over individual goals, first- and second-generation young people often feel a strong sense of obligation to their parents. They view school success as an important way of repaying their parents for the hardships they have endured (Bacallao & Smokowski, 2007; van Geel & Vedder, 2011). Both family relationships and school achievement protect these youths from risky behaviors (see the Biology and Environment box on pages 10–11).

Immigrant parents of successful youths typically develop close ties to an ethnic community, which exerts additional control through a high consensus on values and constant monitoring of young people's activities. The following comments capture the power of these family and community forces:

- *A 16-year-old girl from Central America describes the supportive adults in her neighborhood*: They ask me if I need anything for school. If we go to a store and I see a notebook, they ask me if I want it. They give me advice, tell me that I should be careful of the friends I choose. They also tell me to stay in school to get prepared. They tell me I am smart. They give me encourage-

These Tibetan-American children march in an international immigrants parade in New York City. Cultural values that engender allegiance to family and community promote high achievement and protect many immigrant youths from involvement in risky behaviors.

ment. (Suárez-Orozco, Pimental, & Martin, 2009, p. 733)
- *A ninth-grade boy from Haiti explains how his mother encourages and monitors his homework efforts*: When she's at work she's always calling me, asking if I am doing my homework or if I don't understanding something, . . . I just go to the library to look up some books and finish it because I know she's gonna ask about it. (Bang, 2011, p. 14)
- *A teenage boy from Mexico discusses the importance of family in his culture:* A really big part of the Hispanic population [is] being close to family, and the family being a priority all the time. I hate people who say, "Why do you want to go to a party where your family's at? Don't you want to get away from them?" You know, I don't really get tired of them. I've always been really close to them. That connection to my parents, that trust that you can talk to them, that makes me Mexican. (Bacallao & Smokowski, 2007, p. 62)

The experiences of well-adjusted immigrant youths are not problem-free. Chinese adolescents who had arrived in the United States within the previous year described their adjustment as very difficult because they were not proficient in English and, as a result, found many everyday tasks challenging and felt socially isolated (Yeh et al., 2008). Young immigrants also encounter racial and ethnic prejudices and experience tensions between family values and the new culture—challenges we will take up in Chapter 16. In the long term, however, family and community cohesion, supervision, and high expectations promote favorable outcomes.

General Research Designs

In deciding on a research design, investigators choose a way of setting up a study that permits them to test their hypotheses with the greatest degree of certainty possible. Two main designs are used in all research on human behavior: *correlational* and *experimental*.

CORRELATIONAL DESIGN   In a **correlational design,** researchers gather information on individuals, generally in natural life circumstances, and make no effort to alter their experiences. Then they look at relationships between participants' characteristics and their behavior or development. Suppose we want to answer such questions as, Do parents' styles of interacting with their children have any bearing on children's intelligence? Does attending a child-care center promote children's friendliness with peers? How do child abuse and neglect affect children's feelings about themselves and their relationships with peers? In these and many other instances, the conditions of interest are difficult or impossible to arrange and control and must be studied as they currently exist.

Correlational studies have one major limitation: We cannot infer cause and effect. For example, if we find that parental interaction is related to children's intelligence, we would not know whether parents' behavior actually *causes* intellectual differences among children. In fact, the opposite is possible. The behaviors of highly intelligent children may be so attractive that they cause parents to interact more favorably. Or a third variable that we did not even consider, such as the amount of noise and distraction in the home, may cause changes in both parental interaction and children's intelligence.

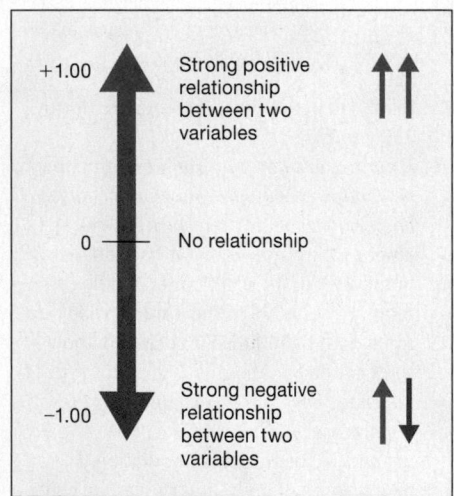

FIGURE 1.6   **The meaning of correlation coefficients.** The magnitude of the number indicates the *strength* of the relationship. The sign of the number (+ or –) indicates the *direction* of the relationship.

In correlational studies, and in other types of research designs, investigators often examine relationships by using a **correlation coefficient**—a number that describes how two measures, or variables, are associated with one another. We will encounter the correlation coefficient in discussing research findings throughout this book, so let's look at what it is and how it is interpreted. A correlation coefficient can range in value from +1.00 to −1.00. The *magnitude, or size, of the number* shows the *strength of the relationship.* A zero correlation indicates no relationship, but the closer the value is to either +1.00 or −1.00, the stronger the relationship (see Figure 1.6). For instance, a correlation of −.78 is high, −.52 is moderate, and −.18 is low. Note, however that correlations of +.52 and −.52 are equally strong. The *sign of the number* refers to the *direction of the relationship.* A positive sign (+) means that as one variable *increases,* the other also *increases.* A negative sign (−) indicates that as one variable *increases,* the other *decreases.*

Let's look at some examples of how a correlation coefficient works. One researcher reported a +.55 correlation between a measure of maternal language stimulation and the size of children's vocabularies at age 2 years (Hoff, 2003). This is a moderate correlation, which indicates that mothers who spoke more to their infants had children who were more advanced in language development. In two other studies, child-rearing practices were related to toddlers' compliance in consistent ways. First, maternal warmth and sensitivity during play correlated positively with 2-year-olds' willingness to comply with their mother's directive to clean up toys, at +.34 (Feldman & Klein, 2003). Second, the extent to which mothers spoke harshly, interrupted, and controlled their 4-year-olds' play correlated negatively with children's compliance, at −.31 for boys and −.42 for girls (Smith et al., 2004).

All these investigations found a relationship between parenting and young children's behavior. **TAKE A MOMENT...** Are you tempted to conclude that parenting influenced children's responses? Although the researchers in these studies suspected this was so, they could not be sure of cause and effect. Can you think of other possible explanations? Finding a relationship in a correlational study suggests that tracking down its cause—using a more powerful experimental strategy, if possible—would be worthwhile.

EXPERIMENTAL DESIGN   An **experimental design** permits inferences about cause and effect because researchers use an evenhanded procedure to assign people to two or more treatment conditions. In an experiment, the events and behaviors of interest are divided into two types: independent and dependent variables. The **independent variable** is the one the investigator expects to cause changes in another variable. The **dependent variable** is the one the investigator expects to be influenced by the independent variable. Cause-and-effect relationships can be detected because the researcher directly *controls* or *manipulates* changes in the independent variable by exposing participants to the treatment conditions. Then the researcher compares their performance on measures of the dependent variable.

In one *laboratory experiment,* researchers explored the impact of adults' angry interactions on children's adjustment (El-Sheikh, Cummings, & Reiter, 1996). They hypothesized that the way angry encounters end (independent variable) affects children's emotional reactions (dependent variable). Four- and 5-year-olds were brought one at a time to a laboratory, accompanied by their mothers. One group was exposed to an *unresolved-anger treatment,* in which two adult actors entered the room and argued but did not work out their disagreements. The other group witnessed a *resolved-anger treatment,* in which the adults ended their disputes by apologizing and compromising. As Figure 1.7 shows, when they witnessed a follow-up adult conflict, more children in the resolved-anger treatment showed a decline in distress, as measured by fewer anxious facial expressions, less freezing in place, and less seeking of closeness to their mothers. The experiment revealed that anger resolution can reduce the stressful impact of adult conflict on children.

In experimental studies, investigators must take special precautions to control for participants' characteristics that could reduce the accuracy of their findings. For example, in the study just described, if more children from homes high in parental conflict ended up in the unresolved-anger treatment, we could not tell what produced the results—the independent variable or the children's backgrounds. To protect against this problem, researchers engage in **random assignment** of participants to treatment conditions. By using an unbiased procedure, such as drawing numbers out of a hat or flipping a coin, investigators increase the chances that participants' characteristics will be equally distributed across treatment groups.

Sometimes researchers combine random assignment with another technique called *matching.* In this procedure, participants are measured before the experiment on the factor in question—in our example, exposure to parental conflict. Then children high and low on that factor are assigned in equal numbers to each treatment condition. In this way, the experimental groups are deliberately matched, or made equivalent, on characteristics that are likely to distort the results.

MODIFIED EXPERIMENTAL DESIGNS: FIELD AND NATURAL EXPERIMENTS Most experiments are conducted in laboratories, where researchers can achieve the maximum possible control over treatment conditions. But as we have already indicated, findings obtained in laboratories may not apply to everyday situations. In *field experiments,* investigators capitalize on rare opportunities to assign participants randomly to treatment conditions in natural settings. In the experiment just described, we can conclude that the emotional climate established by adults affects children's behavior in the laboratory. But does it also do so in daily life?

Another study helps answer this question. Ethnically diverse, poverty-stricken families with a 2-year-old child were scheduled for a home visit, during which researchers assessed family functioning and child problem behaviors by asking parents to respond to questionnaires and videotaping parent–child interaction. Then the families were randomly assigned to either an intervention condition, called the Family Check-Up, or a no-intervention control group. The intervention consisted of three home-based sessions in which a consultant gave parents feedback about their child-rearing practices and their child's adjustment, explored parents' willingness to improve, identified community services appropriate to each family's needs, and offered follow-up sessions on parenting practices and other concerns (Brennan et al., 2013; Dishion et al., 2008). Findings showed that families assigned to the Family Check-Up (but not controls) gained in positive parenting, which predicted a reduction in child problem behaviors and improved academic achievement.

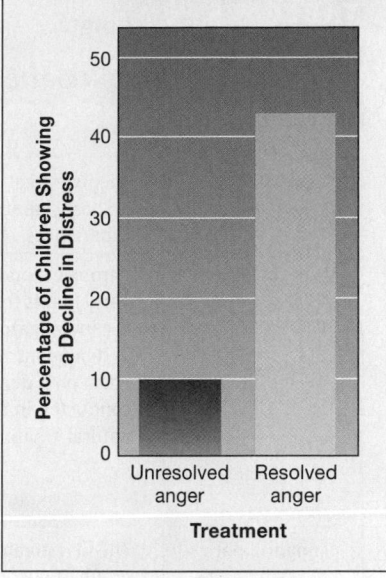

FIGURE 1.7 Does the way adults end their angry encounters affect children's emotional reactions? A laboratory experiment showed that children who had previously witnessed adults resolving their disputes by apologizing and compromising were more likely to decline in distress when witnessing subsequent adult conflicts than were children who witnessed adults leaving their arguments unresolved. Notice in this graph that only 10 percent of children in the unresolved-anger treatment declined in distress (see bar on left), whereas 42 percent of children in the resolved-anger treatment did so (see bar on right). (Based on El-Sheikh, Cummings, & Reiter, 1996.)

When researchers cannot randomly assign children to conditions in the real world, they sometimes conduct natural experiments using treatments that already exist. For example, the learning environments of different child-care centers might be compared to explore the impact of storybook reading on preschoolers' language and literacy development.

TABLE 1.5	Strengths and Limitations of Research Designs		
DESIGN	**DESCRIPTION**	**STRENGTHS**	**LIMITATIONS**
General			
Correlational	The investigator obtains information on participants without altering their experiences.	Permits study of relationships between variables.	Does not permit inferences about cause-and-effect relationships.
Experimental	Through random assignment of participants to treatment conditions, the investigator manipulates an independent variable and examines its effect on a dependent variable. Can be conducted in the laboratory or in the natural environment.	Permits inferences about cause-and-effect relationships.	When conducted in the laboratory, findings may not generalize to the real world. In *field experiments,* control over the treatment is usually weaker than in the laboratory. In *natural,* or *quasi-, experiments,* lack of random assignment substantially reduces the precision of research.
Developmental			
Longitudinal	The investigator studies the same group of participants repeatedly at different ages.	Permits study of common patterns and individual differences in development and relationships between early and later events and behaviors.	Age-related changes may be distorted because of biased sampling, selective attrition, practice effects, and cohort effects.
Cross-sectional	The investigator studies groups of participants differing in age at the same point in time.	More efficient than the longitudinal design.	Does not permit study of individual developmental trends. Age differences may be distorted because of cohort effects.
Sequential	The investigator conducts several similar cross-sectional or longitudinal studies (called sequences). These might study participants over the same ages but in different years, or they might study participants over different ages but during the same years.	Permits both longitudinal and cross-sectional comparisons. Reveals cohort effects. Permits tracking of age-related changes more efficiently than the longitudinal design.	May have the same problems as longitudinal and cross-sectional strategies, but the design itself helps identify difficulties.
Microgenetic	The investigator presents children with a novel task and follows their mastery over a series of closely spaced sessions.	Offers insights into how change occurs.	Requires intensive study of participants' moment-by-moment behaviors. The time required for participants to change is difficult to anticipate. Practice effects may distort developmental trends.

Often researchers cannot randomly assign participants and manipulate conditions in the real world, as these investigators were able to do. Sometimes they can compromise by conducting *natural,* or *quasi-, experiments.* Treatments that already exist, such as different family environments, child-care centers, or schools, are compared. These studies differ from correlational research only in that groups of participants are carefully chosen to ensure that their characteristics are as much alike as possible. In this way, investigators do their best to rule out alternative explanations for their treatment effects. But despite these efforts, natural experiments cannot achieve the precision and rigor of true experimental research.

To help you compare correlational and experimental designs, Table 1.5 summarizes their strengths and limitations. It also includes an overview of designs for studying development, to which we turn next.

Designs for Studying Development

Scientists interested in child development require information about the way research participants change over time. To answer questions about development, they must extend correlational and experimental approaches to include measurements at different ages. Longitudinal and cross-sectional designs are special *developmental research strategies.* In each, age comparisons form the basis of the research plan.

THE LONGITUDINAL DESIGN   In a **longitudinal design,** participants are studied repeatedly, and changes are noted as they get older. The time spanned may be relatively short (a few months to several years) or very long (a decade or even a lifetime).

The longitudinal approach has two major strengths. First, because it tracks the performance of each person over time, researchers can identify common patterns as well as individual differences in development. Second, longitudinal studies permit investigators to examine relationships between early and later events and behaviors. Let's illustrate these ideas.

A group of researchers wondered whether children who display extreme personality styles—either angry and explosive or shy and withdrawn—retain the same dispositions when they become adults. In addition, the researchers wanted to know what kinds of experiences promote stability or plasticity in personality and what consequences explosiveness and shyness have for long-term adjustment. To answer these questions, the researchers delved into the archives of the Guidance Study, a well-known longitudinal investigation initiated in 1928 at the University of California, Berkeley, that continued for several decades (Caspi, Elder, & Bem, 1987, 1988).

Results revealed that the two personality styles were moderately stable. Between ages 8 and 30, a good number of individuals remained the same, whereas others changed substantially. When stability did occur, it appeared to be due to a "snowballing effect," in which children evoked responses from adults and peers that acted to maintain their dispositions. Explosive youngsters were likely to be treated with anger, whereas shy children were apt to be ignored. As a result, the two types of children came to view their social worlds differently. Explosive children tended to view others as hostile; shy children regarded them as unfriendly (Caspi & Roberts, 2001). Together, these factors led explosive children to sustain or increase their unruliness and shy children to continue to withdraw.

Persistence of extreme personality styles affected many areas of adult adjustment. For men, the results of early explosiveness were most apparent in their work lives, in the form of conflicts with supervisors, frequent job changes, and unemployment. Since few women in this sample of an earlier generation worked after marriage, their family lives were most affected. Explosive girls grew up to be hotheaded wives and mothers who were especially prone to divorce. Sex differences in the long-term consequences of shyness were even greater. Men who had been withdrawn in childhood were delayed in marrying, becoming fathers, and developing stable careers. However, because a withdrawn, unassertive style was socially acceptable for females in the mid-twentieth century, women with shy personalities showed no special adjustment problems.

PROBLEMS IN CONDUCTING LONGITUDINAL RESEARCH   Despite their strengths, longitudinal investigations pose a number of problems. For example, *biased sampling*—the failure to enlist participants who adequately represent the population of interest—is a common problem. People who willingly participate in research that requires them to be observed and tested over many years are likely to have distinctive characteristics—perhaps a special appreciation for the scientific value of research, or a unique need or desire for medical, mental health, or educational services provided by the investigators. Furthermore, longitudinal samples generally become more biased as the investigation proceeds because of *selective attrition.* Participants may move away or drop out of the study for other reasons, and the ones who remain are likely to differ in important ways from the ones who do not continue. Also, from repeated study, people may become "test-wise." Their performance may improve as a result of *practice effects*—better test-taking skills and increased familiarity with the test—not because of factors commonly associated with development.

The most widely discussed threat to the accuracy of longitudinal findings is cultural–historical change, commonly called **cohort effects.** Longitudinal studies examine the development of *cohorts*—children born at the same time, who are influenced by particular cultural and historical conditions. Results based on one cohort may not apply to children developing at other times. For example, look back at the findings on female shyness described in the preceding section, which were gathered in the 1950s. Today's shy adolescent girls and young women tend to be poorly adjusted—a difference that may be due to changes in gender roles in Western societies. Shy adults, whether male or female, feel more anxious, depressed, have fewer

An 11-year-old helps his mother fix the grave of his father, who died in the typhoon that battered the Philippines in 2013. This powerfully destructive event is a cohort effect, with profound consequences for this child's development.

social supports, and may do less well in educational and career attainment than their agemates (Caspi et al., 2003; Karevold et al., 2012; Mounts et al., 2006). Similarly, a longitudinal study of social development would probably result in quite different findings if it were carried out in the second decade of the twenty-first century, around the time of World War II, or during the Great Depression of the 1930s.

Cohort effects don't just operate broadly on an entire generation. They also occur when specific experiences influence some children but not others in the same generation. For example, children who witnessed the terrorist attacks of September 11, 2001 (either because they were near Ground Zero or because they saw injury and death on TV), or who lost a parent in the disaster, were far more likely than other children to display persistent emotional problems, including intense fear, anxiety, and depression (Mullett-Hume et al., 2008; Pfeffer et al., 2007; Rosen & Cohen, 2010). A study of one New York City sample suggested that as many as one-fourth of the city's children were affected (Hoven et al., 2005).

Finally, longitudinal research, especially when conducted over multiple years, requires large investments of time, effort and resources. To maximize the benefits of these costly endeavors, investigators are increasingly carrying out massive longitudinal projects that gather information from large, representative samples on many aspects of development. Then they create multipurpose longitudinal data banks, which any researcher can access.

For example, the Early Childhood Longitudinal Study (ECLS), sponsored by the U.S. Department of Education in collaboration with other federal agencies, includes several nationally representative samples with thousands of participants, some followed from birth to kindergarten and others from kindergarten through eighth grade. The ECLS data bank has been used to study a wide variety of topics, including predictors of childhood obesity, effects of maternal stress during pregnancy on early development, the impact of family and preschool experiences on kindergarten readiness, and the influence of elementary school teaching practices on later academic performance. Investigations like the ECLS are enabling much more research to capitalize the unique strengths of the longitudinal design.

THE CROSS-SECTIONAL DESIGN   The length of time it takes for many behaviors to change, even in limited longitudinal studies, has led researchers to turn to a more efficient strategy for studying development. In the **cross-sectional design,** groups of people differing in age are studied at the same point in time. Because participants are measured only once, researchers need not be concerned about such difficulties as participant dropout or practice effects.

An investigation in which students in grades 3, 6, 9, and 12 filled out a questionnaire about their sibling relationships provides a good illustration (Buhrmester & Furman, 1990). Findings revealed that sibling interaction was characterized by greater equality and less power assertion with age. Also, feelings of sibling companionship declined during adolescence. The researchers thought that several factors contributed to these age differences. As later-born children become more competent and independent, they no longer need, and are probably less willing to accept, direction from older siblings. And as adolescents move from psychological dependence on the family to greater involvement with peers, they may have less time and emotional need to invest in siblings. As you will see in Chapter 16, subsequent research has confirmed these intriguing ideas about the development of sibling relationships.

PROBLEMS IN CONDUCTING CROSS-SECTIONAL RESEARCH   Despite its convenience, cross-sectional research does not provide evidence about change at the level at which it actually occurs: the individual. For example, in the cross-sectional study of sibling relationships just discussed, comparisons are limited to age-group averages. We cannot tell if important individual differences exist. Indeed, longitudinal findings reveal that adolescents vary considerably in the changing quality of their sibling relationships. Although many become more distant, others become more supportive and intimate, still others more rivalrous and antagonistic (Branje et al., 2004; Kim et al., 2006; Whiteman & Loken, 2006).

Cross-sectional studies—especially those that cover a wide age span—have another problem. Like longitudinal research, they can be threatened by cohort effects. For example, comparisons of 5-year-old cohorts and 15-year-old cohorts—groups born and reared in different years—may not really represent age-related changes. Instead, they may reflect unique experiences associated with the time period in which the age groups were growing up.

Improving Developmental Designs

Researchers have devised ways of building on the strengths and minimizing the weaknesses of longitudinal and cross-sectional approaches. Several modified developmental designs have resulted.

SEQUENTIAL DESIGNS To overcome some of the limitations of traditional developmental designs, investigators sometimes use **sequential designs,** in which they conduct several similar cross-sectional or longitudinal studies (called *sequences*) at varying times. As the illustration in Figure 1.8 reveals, some sequential designs combine longitudinal and cross-sectional strategies, an approach that has three advantages:

- We can find out whether cohort effects are operating by comparing participants of the same age who were born in different years. In Figure 1.8, for example, we can compare the longitudinal samples at seventh, eighth, and ninth grades. If they do not differ, we can rule out cohort effects.
- We can make both longitudinal and cross-sectional comparisons. If outcomes are similar, we can be especially confident about the findings.
- The design is efficient. In our example, we can find out about change over a five-year period by following each cohort for three years.

In a study that used the design in Figure 1.8, researchers wanted to find out if family harmony changed as young people experienced the dramatic physical and psychological changes of adolescence (Baer, 2002). A questionnaire assessing emotional bonding among family members was given to three adolescent cohorts, each born a year apart. In longitudinal follow-ups, each cohort again responded to the questionnaire during the following two years.

Findings for the three cohorts converged: All reported (1) a slight decline in family harmony with grade and (2) similar levels of family harmony as they reached the same grade, confirming that there were no cohort effects. Therefore, the researchers concluded that family closeness diminishes steadily from sixth to tenth grade, noting, however, that the change is mild—not enough to threaten supportive family ties. **TAKE A MOMENT...** Turn back to our discussion of parent–adolescent communication as a dynamic system on page 30 and our

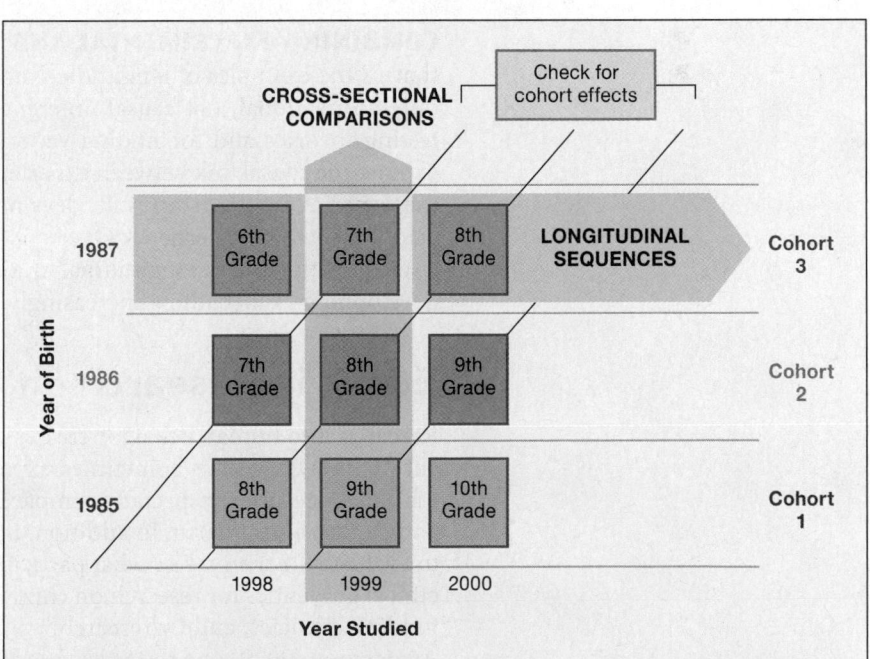

FIGURE 1.8 **Example of a sequential design.** Three cohorts, born in 1985 (blue), 1986 (orange), and 1987 (pink), respectively, are followed longitudinally for three years. Testing the cohorts in overlapping grades enables researchers to check for cohort effects by comparing participants born in different years when they reach the same grade (see diagonals). In a study using this design, same-grade adolescents who were members of different cohorts scored similarly on a questionnaire assessing family harmony, indicating no cohort effects. By following each cohort for just three years, the investigator could infer a developmental trend across five years, from sixth to tenth grade.

How do these first graders make use of manipulatives to master place value in arithmetic? A microgenetic design, which permits researchers to follow children's mastery of a challenging task, is uniquely suited to answering this question.

consideration of adolescent sibling relationships on page 42. How are those results helpful in interpreting the outcomes of the sequential study just described?

EXAMINING MICROCOSMS OF DEVELOPMENT In the examples of developmental research we have discussed, observations of children are fairly widely spaced. When we observe once a year or every few years, we can describe development, but we cannot easily capture the processes that produce it. The **microgenetic design,** an adaptation of the longitudinal approach, presents children with a novel task and follows their mastery over a series of closely spaced sessions. Within this "microcosm" of development, researchers observe how change occurs (Flynn & Siegler, 2007; Kuhn, 1995; Siegler & Crowley, 1991). The microgenetic design is especially useful for studying cognitive development—for example, the strategies children use to acquire new knowledge in reading, mathematics, and science (Siegler, 2002, 2006). As we will see in Chapter 5, the microgenetic design has also been used to trace infants' mastery of motor skills.

Nevertheless, microgenetic studies are difficult to carry out. Researchers must pore over hours of recorded information, analyzing each participant's behavior many times. In addition, the time required for children to change is hard to anticipate. It depends on a careful match between the child's capabilities and the demands of the task. Finally, as in other longitudinal research, practice effects can distort microgenetic findings. But when researchers overcome these challenges, they reap the benefits of seeing development as it takes place.

COMBINING EXPERIMENTAL AND DEVELOPMENTAL DESIGNS Perhaps you noticed that all the examples of longitudinal and cross-sectional research we have considered permit only correlational, not causal, inferences. Yet causal information is also desirable, both for testing theories and for finding ways to enhance development. Sometimes researchers can explore the causal link between experiences and development by experimentally manipulating the experiences. If, as a result, development improves, then we have strong evidence for a causal association (Lerner & Overton, 2008). Today, research that combines an experimental strategy with either a longitudinal or a cross-sectional approach, with the aim of augmenting development, is becoming increasingly common.

Ethics in Research on Children

Research into human behavior creates ethical issues because, unfortunately, the quest for scientific knowledge can sometimes exploit people. When children take part in research, the ethical concerns are especially complex. Children are more vulnerable than adults to physical and psychological harm. In addition, immaturity makes it difficult or impossible for children to evaluate for themselves what participation in research will mean. For these reasons, special ethical guidelines for research on children have been developed by the federal government, by funding agencies, and by research-oriented associations such as the American Psychological Association (2010) and the Society for Research in Child Development (2007).

Table 1.6 presents a summary of children's basic research rights. **TAKE A MOMENT...** After examining them, read about the following research situations, each of which poses a serious ethical dilemma. What precautions do you think should be taken in each instance? Is either so threatening to children's well-being that it should not be carried out?

- In a study of moral development, a researcher wants to assess children's ability to resist temptation by videotaping their behavior without their knowledge. She promises 7-year-

TABLE 1.6	Children's Research Rights
RESEARCH RIGHT	**DESCRIPTION**
Protection from harm	Children have the right to be protected from physical or psychological harm in research. If in doubt about the harmful effects of research, investigators should seek the opinion of others. When harm seems possible, investigators should find other means for obtaining the desired information or abandon the research.
Informed consent/assent	All research participants, including children, have the right to have explained to them, in language appropriate to their level of understanding, all aspects of the research that may affect their willingness to participate. When children are participants, informed consent of parents as well as others who act on the child's behalf (such as school officials) should be obtained, preferably in writing. Although minors cannot legally give consent, investigators are usually required to obtain children's written or verbal assent (agreement) for participation. Children, and the adults responsible for them, have the right to discontinue participation in the research at any time.
Privacy	Children have the right to concealment of their identity on all information collected in the course of research. They also have this right with respect to written reports and any informal discussions about the research.
Knowledge of results	Children have the right to be informed of the results of research in language that is appropriate to their level of understanding.
Beneficial treatments	If experimental treatments believed to be beneficial are under investigation, children in control groups have the right to alternative beneficial treatments (if available) or to the same treatment (if found to be effective) once the research is complete.

Sources: American Psychological Association, 2010; Society for Research in Child Development, 2007.

olds an attractive prize for solving difficult puzzles but tells them not to look at a classmate's correct solutions, which are deliberately placed at the back of the room. Telling children ahead of time that cheating is being studied or that their behavior is being monitored will defeat the purpose of the study.

- A researcher is interviewing fifth graders about their experiences with bullying. A girl describes frequent name-calling and derogatory comments by her older sister. Although the girl is unhappy, she wants to handle the problem on her own. If the researcher alerts the girl's parents to provide protection and help, he will violate his promise to keep participants' responses private.

Did you find it difficult to evaluate these examples? Virtually every organization that has devised ethical principles for research has concluded that conflicts arising in research situations do not have simple right or wrong answers. The ultimate responsibility for the ethical integrity of research lies with the investigator. But researchers are advised—and often required—to seek advice from others. Committees for this purpose exist in colleges, universities, and other institutions. These *institutional review boards (IRBs)* follow federal guidelines for the protection of human subjects, which balance the costs of the research to participants in terms of time, stress, and inconvenience against the study's value for advancing knowledge and improving conditions of life. If any risks to the safety and welfare of participants outweigh the worth of the research, then preference is always given to the interests of the participants.

The ethical principle of *informed consent* requires special interpretation when participants cannot fully appreciate the research goals and activities. Parental consent is meant to protect the safety of children whose ability to decide is not yet mature. In addition, researchers should obtain the agreement of other individuals who act on children's behalf, such as institutional officials when research is conducted in schools, child-care centers, or hospitals. This is especially important when research includes special groups, such as abused children, whose parents may not always represent their best interests (Fisher, 1993; Thompson, 1990).

© JOHN BIRDSALL/THE IMAGE WORKS

Extra steps must be taken to protect children's research rights. Although this 8-year-old responds to the interviewer's questions, she may not know why she is being interviewed, or realize that she has the right to withdraw from the study without negative consequences.

As soon as children are old enough to appreciate the purpose of the research, and certainly by 7 years of age, their own informed *assent*, or agreement, should be obtained in addition to parental consent. Around age 7, changes in children's thinking permit them to better understand basic scientific principles and the needs of others. Researchers should respect and enhance these capacities by giving school-age children a full explanation of research activities in language they can understand (Fisher, 1993). Extra care must be taken when telling children that the information they provide will be kept confidential and that they can end their participation at any time. Even adolescents may not understand, and sometimes do not believe, these promises (Bruzzese & Fisher, 2003; Ondrusek et al., 1998). And in certain ethnic minority communities, where deference to authority, maintaining pleasant relationships, and meeting the needs of a guest (the researcher) are highly valued, children and parents may be particularly likely to consent or assent when they would rather not do so (Fisher et al., 2002).

Careful attention to informed consent and assent helps resolve dilemmas about revealing children's responses to parents, teachers, or other authorities when those responses suggest that the child's welfare is in danger. Children can be told in advance that if they report that someone is harming them, the researcher will tell an appropriate adult to take action to ensure the child's safety (Jennifer & Cowie, 2009).

Finally, because young children rely on a basic faith in adults to feel secure in unfamiliar situations, they may find some types of research particularly disturbing. All ethical guidelines advise that special precautions be taken in the use of deception and concealment, as occurs when researchers observe children from behind one-way mirrors, give them false feedback about their performance, or misrepresent the real purpose of the research. When these procedures are used with adults, *debriefing,* in which the researcher provides a full account and justification of the activities, occurs after the research session is over. Debriefing should also be done with children, and it sometimes works well. But young children often lack the cognitive skills to understand the reasons for deceptive procedures, and, despite explanations, they may leave the research situation questioning the honesty of adults. Ethical standards permit deception in research with children if investigators satisfy IRBs that such practices are necessary. Nevertheless, because deception may have serious emotional consequences for some youngsters, many child development specialists believe that researchers should use it only if the risk of harm is minimal.

Ask Yourself

● **REVIEW** Explain how cohort effects can distort the findings of both longitudinal and cross-sectional studies. How does the sequential design reveal cohort effects?

● **CONNECT** Review the field experiment on the impact of the Family Check-Up on page 39. Why is it ethically important for researchers to offer the intervention to the no-intervention control group after completion of the study? (Hint: Refer to Table 1.6. on page 45)

● **APPLY** A researcher compares children who went to summer leadership camps with children who attended athletic camps. She finds that those who attended leadership camps are friendlier. Should the investigator tell parents that sending children to leadership camps will cause them to be more sociable? Why or why not?

● **REFLECT** Suppose a researcher asks you to enroll your baby in a 10-year longitudinal study. What factors would lead you to agree and to stay involved? Do your answers shed light on why longitudinal studies often have biased samples? Explain.

Summary

The Field of Child Development (p. 4)

1.1 What is the field of child development, and what factors stimulated its expansion?

- **Child development** is an area of study devoted to understanding constancy and change from conception through adolescence. It is part of a larger interdisciplinary field known as **developmental science,** which includes all changes we experience throughout the lifespan. Research on child development has been stimulated both by scientific curiosity and by social pressures to better children's lives.

1.2 How is child development typically divided into domains and periods?

- Development is often divided into physical, cognitive, and emotional and social domains. These domains are not really distinct; rather, they combine in an integrated, holistic fashion.

© UWE OMMER, 1,000 FAMILIES, TASCHEN

- Researchers generally divide the flow of time into the following age periods: (1) prenatal (conception to birth), (2) infancy and toddlerhood (birth to 2 years), (3) early childhood (2 to 6 years), (4) middle childhood (6 to 11 years), and (5) adolescence (11 to 18 years). To describe the prolonged transition to adulthood typical of contemporary young people in industrialized nations, researchers have posited a new period of development, emerging adulthood, spanning ages 18 to 25.

Basic Issues (p. 7)

1.3 Identify three basic issues on which theories of child development take a stand.

- Each **theory** of child development takes a stand on three fundamental issues: (1) Is development a **continuous** process, or is it **discontinuous,** following a series of distinct **stages?** (2) Does one general course of development characterize all children, or are there many possible courses, influenced by the distinct **contexts** in which children grow up? (3) Are genetic or environmental factors more important in influencing development (the **nature–nurture controversy**), and are individual differences stable or characterized by substantial **plasticity?**

- Recent theories take a balanced stand on these issues. And contemporary researchers realize that answers may vary across domains of development and even, as research on **resilience** illustrates, across individuals.

Historical Foundations (p. 11)

1.4 Describe major historical influences on theories of child development.

- As early as medieval times, the sixth through the fifteenth centuries, childhood was regarded as a separate phase of life.

- In the sixteenth and seventeenth centuries, the Puritan conception of original sin led to a harsh philosophy of child rearing. The seventeenth-century Enlightenment brought a new emphasis on human dignity and respect that led to more humane views of childhood. Locke's notion of the child as a tabula rasa ("blank slate") provided the basis for twentieth-century behaviorism, while Rousseau's idea that children were noble savages foreshadowed the concepts of stage and **maturation.**

- Inspired by Darwin's theory of evolution, efforts to observe the child directly began in the late nineteenth and early twentieth centuries. Hall and Gesell introduced the **normative approach,** in which many measures were gathered on large numbers of individuals, yielding descriptions of typical development. Binet and Simon constructed the first successful intelligence test, which sparked interest in individual differences and made intelligence central to the nature–nurture controversy.

Mid-Twentieth-Century Theories (p. 14)

1.5 What theories influenced child development research in the mid-twentieth century?

- In the 1930s and 1940s, psychiatrists and social workers turned to the **psychoanalytic perspective** for help in treating children's emotional problems. In Freud's **psychosexual theory,** children move through five stages, during which three portions of the personality—id, ego, and superego—become integrated.

- Erikson's **psychosocial theory** builds on Freud's theory, emphasizing the development of culturally relevant attitudes and skills and—with the addition of three adult stages—the lifespan nature of development. Despite its extensive contributions, the psychoanalytic perspective is no longer in the mainstream of child development research.

ANTONIA TOZER/GETTY IMAGES

- **Behaviorism** focused on directly observable events (stimuli and responses) in an effort to create an objective science of psychology. B. F. Skinner's operant conditioning theory emphasizes the role of reinforcement and punishment in increasing or decreasing the frequency of behaviors.

- A related approach, Albert Bandura's **social learning theory,** focuses on modeling as the major means through which children and adults acquire new responses. Its most recent revision stresses the role of cognition, or thinking, in children's imitation and learning and is known as a social-cognitive approach.

- Behaviorism and social learning theory gave rise to techniques of **applied behavior analysis,** in which procedures of conditioning and modeling are designed to eliminate undesirable behaviors and increase desirable responses.

- Piaget's **cognitive-developmental theory** emphasizes that children actively construct knowledge as they move through four stages, beginning with the baby's sensorimotor action patterns and ending with the abstract, systematic reasoning system of the adolescent and adult. Piaget's work has stimulated a wealth of research on children's thinking and has encouraged educational programs that emphasize children's discovery learning.

Recent Theoretical Perspectives
(p. 21)

1.6 Describe recent theoretical perspectives on child development.

- **Information processing** views the mind as a complex symbol-manipulating system, much like a computer. This approach helps investigators achieve a detailed understanding of how children of different ages respond to tasks and problems and has important implications for education.

- Over the past three decades, researchers in **developmental cognitive neuroscience** have studied the relationship between changes in the brain and the developing child's cognitive processing and behavior patterns. More recently, investigators in **developmental social neuroscience** have examined relationships between changes in the brain and social development. Findings on the types of experiences that support or undermine brain development is leading to effective interventions for children with learning and behavior problems.

- Four contemporary perspectives emphasize contexts for development. **Ethology** stresses the adaptive value and evolutionary history of behavior and inspired the **sensitive period** concept. Researchers in **evolutionary developmental psychology** have extended this emphasis, seeking to understand the adaptiveness of species-wide competencies as they change over time.

- Vygotsky's **sociocultural theory,** which focuses on how culture is transmitted from one generation to the next through social interaction, views cognitive development as a socially mediated process. Through cooperative dialogues with more expert members of society, children come to use language to guide their own thought and actions and acquire culturally relevant knowledge and skills.

- **Ecological systems theory** views the child as developing within a complex system of relationships affected by multiple, nested layers of the surrounding environment—**microsystem, mesosystem, exosystem,** and **macrosystem.** Each of these levels is seen as a major influence on children's well-being. The **chronosystem** represents the dynamic, ever-changing nature of children and their experiences.

- Theorists who adopt a **dynamic systems perspective** seek to understand how children alter their behavior to attain more advanced functioning. According to this view, the mind, body, and physical and social worlds form an integrated system that guides mastery of new skills. A change in any part of the system prompts the child to reorganize her behavior so the various components work together in a more complex, effective way.

Comparing Child Development Theories (p. 30)

1.7 Identify the stand taken by each major theory on the basic issues of child development.

- Major theories vary in their focus on different domains of development, in their view of how development occurs, and in their strengths and weaknesses. (For a full summary, see Table 1.3 on page 31.)

Studying the Child (p. 32)

1.8 Describe research methods commonly used to study children.

- **Naturalistic observations** are gathered in everyday environments and permit researchers to see directly the everyday behaviors they hope to explain. **Structured observations** take place in laboratories, where every participant has an equal opportunity to display the behaviors of interest.

- Self-report methods can be flexible and open-ended like the **clinical interview,** which permits participants to express their thoughts in ways similar to their thinking in everyday life. **Structured interviews,** tests, and questionnaires are more efficient and permit researchers to specify activities and behaviors that participants might not think of in an open-ended interview.

- Investigators use the **clinical,** or **case study, method** to obtain an in-depth understanding of a single child. It involves synthesizing a wide range of information, including interviews, observations, and sometimes test scores.

- Researchers have adapted observational and self-report methods to permit direct comparisons of cultures. To uncover the cultural meanings of behavior, they rely on **ethnography,** engaging in participant observation.

1.9 Distinguish between correlational and experimental research designs, noting strengths and limitations of each.

- The **correlational design** examines relationships between variables, generally as they occur in natural life circumstances, without altering participants' experiences. The **correlation coefficient** describes how two measures, or variables, are associated with one another. Correlational studies do not permit inferences about cause and effect, but they can be helpful in identifying relationships that are worth exploring with a more powerful experimental strategy.

- An **experimental design** permits inferences about cause and effect. Researchers manipulate an **independent variable** by exposing participants to two or more treatment conditions. Then they determine what effect this variable has on a **dependent variable. Random assignment** reduces the chances that characteristics of participants will affect the accuracy of experimental findings.

- Field and natural, or quasi-, experiments compare treatments in natural environments. However, these approaches are less rigorous than laboratory experiments.

1.10 Describe designs for studying development, noting strengths and limitations of each.

- In a **longitudinal design,** participants are studied repeatedly at different ages, revealing common patterns as well as individual differences in development and the relationship between early and later events and behaviors. Longitudinal research poses several problems, including biased sampling, selective attrition, **cohort effects** (difficulty generalizing to children developing under other cultural and historical conditions), and the need for large investments of time and resources.

- The **cross-sectional design,** in which groups of children differing in age are studied at the same point in time, offers an efficient approach to investigating development. However, it is limited to comparisons of age-group averages and can be vulnerable to cohort effects.
- **Sequential designs** compare groups of children born in different years to find out if cohort effects are operating. When sequential designs combine longitudinal and cross-sectional strategies, researchers can see if outcomes are similar, for added confidence in their findings.

- In the **microgenetic design,** researchers present children with a novel task and track their mastery over a series of closely spaced sessions, seeking to capture processes of development. However, the time required for children to change is hard to anticipate, and practice effects can bias findings.
- When researchers combine experimental and developmental designs, they can examine causal influences on development. This combined strategy is increasingly common today.

1.11 *What special ethical concerns arise in doing research on children?*

- Because of their immaturity, children are especially vulnerable to harm and often cannot evaluate the risks and benefits of research. Ethical guidelines and institutional review boards that weigh the risks and benefits of research help ensure that children's research rights are protected.
- Besides obtaining consent from parents and others who act on children's behalf, researchers should seek the informed assent of children 7 years and older. The use of deception in research with children is especially risky because it may undermine their basic faith in the honesty of adults.

Important Terms and Concepts

applied behavior analysis (p. 18)
behaviorism (p. 17)
child development (p. 4)
chronosystem (p. 29)
clinical interview (p. 34)
clinical, or case study, method (p. 35)
cognitive-developmental theory (p. 19)
cohort effects (p. 41)
contexts (p. 8)
continuous development (p. 8)
correlational design (p. 38)
correlation coefficient (p. 38)
cross-sectional design (p. 42)
dependent variable (p. 38)
developmental cognitive neuroscience (p. 23)
developmental social neuroscience (p. 23)
developmental science (p. 4)

discontinuous development (p. 8)
dynamic systems perspective (p. 29)
ecological systems theory (p. 26)
ethnography (p. 36)
ethology (p. 24)
evolutionary developmental
  psychology (p. 25)
exosystem (p. 27)
experimental design (p. 38)
independent variable (p. 38)
information processing (p. 21)
longitudinal design (p. 41)
macrosystem (p. 28)
maturation (p. 13)
mesosystem (p. 27)
microgenetic design (p. 44)
microsystem (p. 26)

naturalistic observation (p. 32)
nature–nurture controversy (p. 9)
normative approach (p. 13)
plasticity (p. 9)
psychoanalytic perspective (p. 15)
psychosexual theory (p. 15)
psychosocial theory (p. 15)
random assignment (p. 39)
resilience (p. 10)
sensitive period (p. 24)
sequential design (p. 43)
social learning theory (p. 17)
sociocultural theory (p. 25)
stage (p. 8)
structured interview (p. 35)
structured observation (p. 33)
theory (p. 7)

Genetic and Environmental Foundations

"Childhood"
Leticia Aparecida Da Silva
11 years, Brazil

As these children enjoy a summer day, their kite flying is influenced not only by their physical abilities but also by the direction and strength of the wind. Likewise, Chapter 2 addresses both genetic and environmental influences on child development.

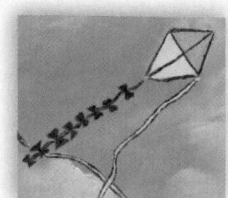

"It's a girl!" announces the doctor, holding up the squalling newborn baby as her parents gaze with amazement at their miraculous creation.

"A girl! We've named her Sarah!" exclaims the proud father to eager relatives waiting for news of their new family member.

As we join these parents in thinking about how this wondrous being came into existence and imagining her future, we are struck by many questions. How could this baby, equipped with everything necessary for life outside the womb, have developed from the union of two tiny cells? What ensures that Sarah will, in due time, roll over, reach for objects, walk, talk, make friends, learn, imagine, and create—just like other typical children born before her? Why is she a girl and not a boy, dark-haired rather than blond, calm and cuddly instead of wiry and energetic? What difference will it make that Sarah is given a name and place in one family, community, nation, and culture rather than another?

To answer these questions, this chapter takes a close look at the foundations of development: heredity and environment. Because nature has prepared us for survival, all humans have features in common. Yet each of us is also unique. **TAKE A MOMENT...** Think about several children you know well, and jot down the most obvious physical and behavioral similarities between them and their parents. Did you find that one child shows combined features of both parents, another resembles just one parent, whereas a third is not like either parent? These directly observable characteristics are called **phenotypes.** They depend in part on the individual's **genotype**—the complex blend of genetic information that determines our species and influences all our unique characteristics. Yet phenotypes are also affected by each person's lifelong history of experiences.

We begin our discussion at the moment of conception, an event that establishes the hereditary makeup of the new individual. First we review basic genetic principles that help explain similarities and differences among children in appearance and behavior. Then we turn to aspects of the environment that play powerful roles in children's lives. As our discussion proceeds, some findings about the influence of nature and nurture may surprise you. For example, many people believe that when children inherit unfavorable characteristics, not much can be done to help them. Others are convinced that the damage done to a child by a harmful environment can easily be corrected. As we will see, neither of these assumptions is true. Rather, heredity and environment continuously collaborate, each modifying—for better or for worse—the power of the other to shape the course of development. In the final section of this chapter, we consider how nature and nurture work together. ■

Genetic Foundations

Within each of the trillions of cells in the human body (except red blood cells) is a control center, or *nucleus,* that contains rodlike structures called **chromosomes,** which store and transmit genetic information. Human chromosomes come in 23 matching pairs (an exception is the XY pair in males, which we will discuss shortly). Each member of a pair corresponds to the other in size, shape, and genetic functions. One is inherited from the mother and one from the father (see Figure 2.1 on page 52).

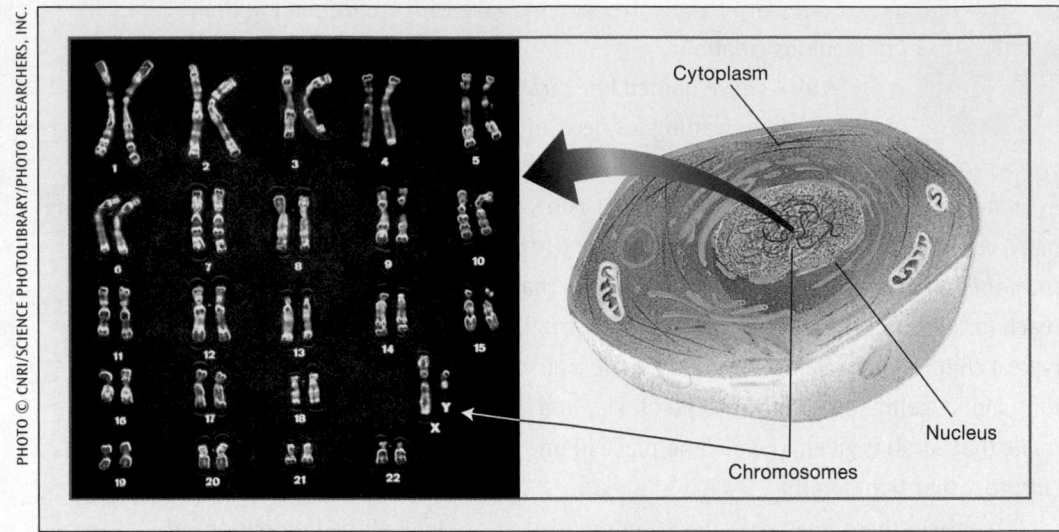

PHOTO © CNRI/SCIENCE PHOTOLIBRARY/PHOTO RESEARCHERS, INC.

FIGURE 2.1 **A karyotype, or photograph, of human chromosomes.** The 46 chromosomes shown on the left were isolated from a human cell, stained, greatly magnified, and arranged in pairs according to decreasing size of the upper "arm" of each chromosome. The twenty-third pair, XY, reveals that the cell donor is a male. In a female, this pair would be XX.

2.1 What are genes, and how are they transmitted from one generation to the next?

2.2 Describe various patterns of genetic inheritance.

2.3 Describe major chromosomal abnormalities, and explain how they occur.

The Genetic Code

Chromosomes are made up of a chemical substance called **deoxyribonucleic acid** or **DNA.** As Figure 2.2 shows, DNA is a long, double-stranded molecule that looks like a twisted ladder. Each rung of the ladder consists of a pair of chemical substances called *bases*. Although the bases always pair up in the same way across the ladder rungs—A with T and C with G—they can occur in any order along its sides. It is this sequence of base pairs that provides genetic instructions. A **gene i**s a segment of DNA along the length of the chromosome. Genes can be of different lengths—perhaps 100 to several thousand ladder rungs long. An estimated 21,000 **protein-coding genes,** which directly affect our body's characteristics, lie along the human chromosomes. They send instructions for making a rich assortment of proteins to the *cytoplasm,* the area surrounding the cell nucleus. Proteins, which trigger chemical reactions throughout the body, are the biological foundation on which our characteristics are built. An additional 18,000 **regulator genes** modify the instructions given by protein-coding genes, greatly complicating their genetic impact (Pennisi, 2012).

We share some of our genetic makeup with even the simplest organisms, such as bacteria and molds, and most of it with other mammals, especially primates. About 95 percent of chimpanzee and human DNA is identical. And the genetic variation from one human to the next is even less: Individuals around the world are about 99.6 percent genetically identical (Tishkoff & Kidd, 2004). But these straightforward comparisons are misleading. Many human DNA segments that appear like those of chimpanzees have undergone duplications and rearrangements with other segments. So in actuality, the species-specific genetic material responsible for the attributes that make us human, from our upright gait to our extraordinary language and cognitive capacities, is extensive (Preuss, 2012). Furthermore, it takes a change in only a single DNA base pair to influence human traits. And such tiny changes generally combine in unique ways across multiple genes, thereby amplifying variability within the human species.

How do humans, with far fewer genes than scientists once thought (only twice as many as the worm or fly), manage to develop into such complex beings? The answer lies in the proteins our genes make, which break up and reassemble in staggering variety—about 10 to 20 million altogether. Simpler species have far fewer proteins. Furthermore, the communication system between the cell nucleus and cytoplasm, which fine-tunes gene activity, is more intricate in humans than in simpler organisms. Finally, within the cell, a wide range of environmental factors modify gene expression. Recent evidence reveals that many such effects are unique to humans and influence brain development (Hernando-Herraez et al., 2013). So even at this microscopic level, biological events of profound developmental significance are the result of *both* genetic and nongenetic forces.

The Sex Cells

New individuals are created when two special cells called **gametes,** or sex cells—the sperm and ovum—combine. A gamete contains only 23 chromosomes, half as many as a regular body cell. Gametes are formed through a cell division process called **meiosis,** which halves the number of chromosomes normally present in body cells. When sperm and ovum unite at conception, the resulting cell, called a **zygote,** will again have 46 chromosomes. Meiosis ensures that a constant quantity of genetic material is transmitted from one generation to the next.

In meiosis, the chromosomes pair up and exchange segments, so that genes from one are replaced by genes from another. This shuffling of genes creates new hereditary combinations. Then chance determines which member of each pair will gather with other chromosomes and end up in the same gamete. These events make the likelihood extremely low—about 1 in 700 trillion—that nontwin siblings will be genetically identical (Gould & Keeton, 1996). The genetic variability produced by meiosis is adaptive: It increases the chances that at least some members of a species will cope with ever-changing environments and will survive.

In the male, four sperm are produced when meiosis is complete. Also, the cells from which sperm arise are produced continuously throughout life. For this reason, a healthy man can father a child at any age after sexual maturity. In the female, meiosis results in just one ovum; the remaining genetic material degenerates. In addition, the female is born with a bank of ova already present in her ovaries, though recent findings suggest that new ova may arise from ovarian stem cells later on (White et al., 2012). Still, there are plenty of female sex cells. About 1 to 2 million are present at birth, 40,000 remain at adolescence, and approximately 350 to 450 will mature during a woman's childbearing years (Moore, Persaud, & Torchia, 2013).

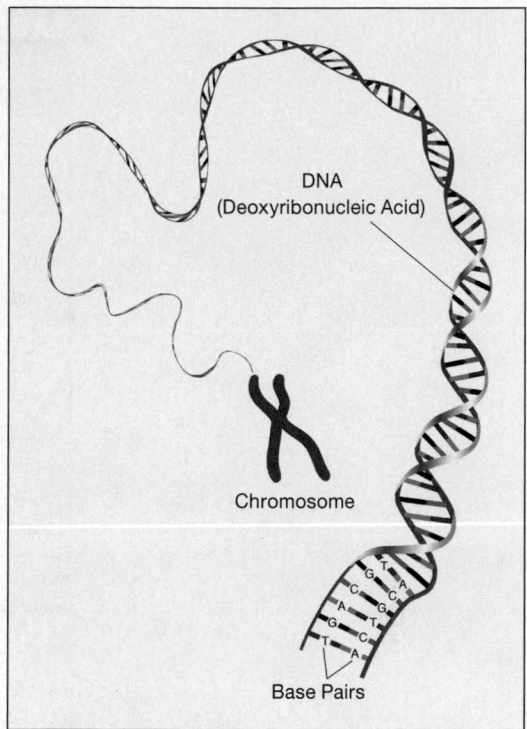

FIGURE 2.2 **DNA's ladderlike structure.** A gene is a segment of DNA along the length of the chromosome, varying from perhaps 100 to several thousand ladder rungs long. The pairings of bases across the rungs of the ladder are very specific: Adenine (A) always appears with thymine (T), and cytosine (C) always appears with guanine (G).

Boy or Girl?

Return to Figure 2.1 and note that 22 of the 23 pairs of chromosomes are matching pairs, called **autosomes** (meaning *not* sex chromosomes). The twenty-third pair consists of **sex chromosomes.** In females, this pair is called XX; in males, it is called XY. The X is a relatively large chromosome, whereas the Y is short and carries little genetic material. When gametes form in males, the X and Y chromosomes separate into different sperm cells. The gametes that form in females all carry an X chromosome. Therefore, the sex of the new organism is determined by whether an X-bearing or a Y-bearing sperm fertilizes the ovum. In fact, scientists have isolated a gene on the Y chromosome that initiates the formation of male sex organs during the prenatal period (Sekido & Lovell-Badge, 2009). But they also know that other genes, some yet to be identified, are involved in the development of sexual characteristics.

Multiple Offspring

Ruth and Peter, a couple your first author knows well, tried for several years to have a child, without success. When Ruth reached age 33, her doctor prescribed a fertility drug, and twins—Jeannie and Jason—were born. Jeannie and Jason are **fraternal,** or **dizygotic, twins,** the most common type of multiple offspring, resulting from the release and fertilization of two ova.

TABLE 2.1	Maternal Factors Linked to Fraternal Twinning
FACTOR	**DESCRIPTION**
Ethnicity	Occurs in 6 to 9 per 1,000 births among Asians and Hispanics, 9 to 12 per 1,000 births among white Europeans, and 11 to 18 or more per 1,000 births among black Africans[a]
Family history of twinning	Occurs more often among women whose mothers and sisters gave birth to fraternal twins, suggesting a hereditary influence through the female line
Age	Rises with maternal age, peaking between 35 and 39 years, and then rapidly falls
Nutrition	Occurs less often among women with poor diets; occurs more often among women who are tall and overweight or of normal weight as opposed to slight body build
Number of births	Is more likely with each additional birth
Fertility drugs and in vitro fertilization	Is more likely with fertility hormones and in vitro fertilization (see page 62), which also increase the chances of bearing triplets, quadruplets, or quintuplets

[a]Worldwide rates, not including multiple births resulting from use of fertility drugs.

Sources: Kulkarni et al., 2013; Lashley, 2007; Smits & Monden, 2011.

Genetically, they are no more alike than ordinary siblings. Table 2.1 summarizes genetic and environmental factors that increase the chances of giving birth to fraternal twins. Older maternal age, fertility drugs, and in vitro fertilization (to be discussed shortly) are major causes of the dramatic rise in fraternal twinning and other multiple births in industrialized nations over the past several decades—a trend that has recently leveled off with improved in vitro procedures (Kulkarni et al., 2013). Currently, fraternal twins account for 1 in about every 33 births in the United States (Martin et al., 2013).

Twins can be created in another way. Sometimes a zygote that has started to duplicate separates into two clusters of cells that develop into two individuals. These are called **identical,** or **monozygotic, twins** because they have the same genetic makeup. The frequency of identical twins is the same around the world—about 1 in every 350 to 400 births (Kulkarni et al., 2013). Animal research has uncovered a variety of environmental influences that prompt this type of twinning, including temperature changes, variation in oxygen levels, and late fertilization of the ovum (Lashley, 2007). In a minority of cases, identical twinning runs in families, but this occurs so rarely that it is likely due to chance rather than heredity.

During their early years, children of single births often are healthier and develop more rapidly than twins. Jeannie and Jason, like most twins, were born early—three weeks before Ruth's due date. And, like other premature infants—as you will see in Chapter 4—they required special care after birth. When the twins came home from the hospital, Ruth and Peter had to divide time between them. Perhaps because neither baby got quite as much attention as the average single infant, Jeannie and Jason walked and talked several months later than most other children their age. Most twins, however, catch up in development by early or middle childhood, as Jeannie and Jason eventually did (Lytton & Gallagher, 2002: Thorpe, 2006). Parental energies are further strained after the birth of triplets, whose early development is slower than that of twins (Feldman, Eidelman, & Rotenberg, 2004).

© F4FOTO/ALAMY

These identical, or monozygotic, twins were created when a duplicating zygote separated into two clusters of cells and developed into two individuals with the same genetic makeup. Identical twins look alike and tend to resemble each other in a variety of psychological characteristics.

Patterns of Gene–Gene Interactions

Jeannie has her parents' dark, straight hair; Jason is curly-haired and blond. The way genes from each parent interact helps explain these outcomes. Recall that except for the XY pair in males, all chromosomes come in matching pairs. Two forms of each gene occur at the same place on the chromosomes, one inherited from the mother and one from the father. Each form of a gene is called an **allele.** If the alleles from both parents are alike, the child is **homozygous** and will display the inherited trait. If the alleles are different, the child is **heterozygous,** and relationships between the alleles determine the phenotype.

DOMINANT–RECESSIVE PATTERN In many heterozygous pairings, **dominant–recessive inheritance** occurs: Only one allele affects the child's characteristics. It is called *dominant;* the second allele, which has no effect, is called *recessive.* Hair color is an example. The allele for dark hair is dominant (we can represent it with a capital *D*), whereas the one for blond hair is recessive (symbolized by a lowercase *b*). A child who inherits a homozygous pair of dominant alleles *(DD)* and a child who inherits a heterozygous pair *(Db)* will both be dark-haired, even though their genotypes differ. Blond hair (like Jason's) can result only from having two recessive alleles *(bb).* Still, heterozygous individuals with just one recessive allele *(Db)* can pass that trait to their children. Therefore, they are called **carriers** of the trait.

Most recessive alleles—like those for blond hair, pattern baldness, or nearsightedness—are of little developmental importance. But as Table 2.2 on page 56 illustrates, some cause serious disabilities and diseases. One of the most frequently occurring recessive disorders is *phenylketonuria,* or *PKU,* which affects the way the body breaks down proteins contained in many foods. Infants born with two recessive alleles lack an enzyme that converts one of the basic amino acids that make up proteins (phenylalanine) into a byproduct essential for body functioning (tyrosine). Without this enzyme, phenylalanine quickly builds to toxic levels that damage the central nervous system. By 1 year, infants with PKU suffer from permanent intellectual disability.

Despite its potentially damaging effects, PKU illustrates that inheriting unfavorable genes does not always lead to an untreatable condition. All U.S. states require that each newborn be given a blood test for PKU. If the disease is found, doctors place the baby on a diet low in phenylalanine. Children who receive this treatment nevertheless show mild deficits in certain cognitive skills, such as memory, planning, decision making, and problem solving, because even small amounts of phenylalanine interfere with brain functioning (DeRoche & Welsh, 2008; Fonnesbeck et al., 2013). But as long as dietary treatment begins early and continues, children with PKU usually attain an average level of intelligence and have a normal lifespan.

In dominant–recessive inheritance, if we know the genetic makeup of the parents, we can predict the percentage of children in a family who are likely to display or carry a trait. Figure 2.3 illustrates this for PKU. For a child to inherit the condition, each parent must have a recessive allele. But because of the action of regulator genes, children vary in the degree to which phenylalanine accumulates in their tissues and in the extent to which they respond to treatment.

Only rarely are serious diseases due to dominant alleles. Think about why this is so. Children who inherit the dominant allele always develop the disorder. They seldom live long enough to reproduce, so the harmful dominant allele is eliminated from the family's heredity in a single generation. Some dominant disorders, however, do persist. One is *Huntington disease,* a condition in which the central nervous system degenerates. Why has this disorder endured? Its symptoms usually do not appear until age 35 or later, after the person has passed the dominant allele to his or her children.

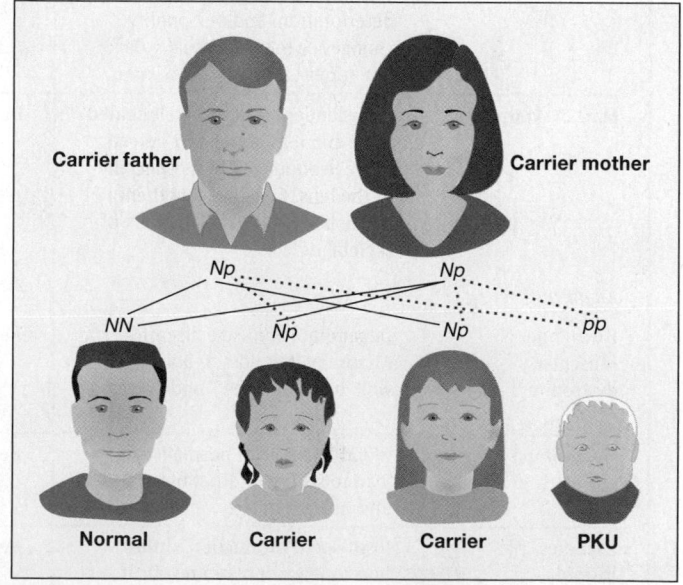

FIGURE 2.3 **Dominant–recessive mode of inheritance, as illustrated by PKU.** When both parents are heterozygous carriers of the recessive gene *(p),* we can predict that 25 percent of their offspring are likely to be normal *(NN),* 50 percent are likely to be carriers *(Np),* and 25 percent are likely to inherit the disorder *(pp).* Notice that the PKU-affected child, in contrast to his siblings, has light hair. The recessive gene for PKU affects more than one trait. It also leads to fair coloring.

TABLE 2.2	Examples of Dominant and Recessive Diseases			
DISEASE	**DESCRIPTION**	**MODE OF INHERITANCE**	**INCIDENCE**	**TREATMENT**
Autosomal Diseases				
Cooley's anemia	Pale appearance, delayed physical growth, and lethargic behavior begin in infancy.	Recessive	1 in 500 births to parents of Mediterranean descent	Frequent blood transfusions; death from complications usually occurs by adolescence.
Cystic fibrosis	Lungs, liver, and pancreas secrete large amounts of thick mucus, leading to breathing and digestive difficulties.	Recessive	1 in 2,000 to 2,500 Caucasian births; 1 in 16,000 births to North Americans of African descent	Bronchial drainage, prompt treatment of respiratory infection, dietary management. Advances in medical care allow survival with good life quality into adulthood.
Phenylketonuria (PKU)	Inability to metabolize the amino acid phenylalanine, contained in many proteins, causes severe central nervous system damage in the first year of life.	Recessive	1 in 8,000 births	Placing the child on a special diet results in average intelligence and normal lifespan. Subtle difficulties in memory, planning, decision making, and problem solving are often present.
Sickle cell anemia	Abnormal sickling of red blood cells causes oxygen deprivation, pain, swelling, and tissue damage. Anemia and susceptibility to infections, especially pneumonia, occur.	Recessive	1 in 500 births to North Americans of African descent	Blood transfusions, painkillers, prompt treatment of infection. No known cure; 50 percent die by age 55.
Tay-Sachs disease	Central nervous system degeneration, with onset at about 6 months, leads to poor muscle tone, blindness, deafness, and convulsions.	Recessive	1 in 3,600 births to Jews of European descent and to French Canadians	None. Death occurs by 3 to 4 years of age.
Huntington disease	Central nervous system degeneration leads to muscular coordination difficulties, mental deterioration, and personality changes. Symptoms usually do not appear until age 35 or later.	Dominant	1 in 18,000 to 25,000 births to North Americans	None. Death occurs 10 to 20 years after symptom onset.
Marfan syndrome	Tall, slender build; thin, elongated arms and legs; and heart defects and eye abnormalities, especially of the lens. Excessive lengthening of the body results in a variety of skeletal defects.	Dominant	1 in 5,000 to 10,000 births	Correction of heart and eye defects sometimes possible. Death from heart failure in early adulthood is common.
X-Linked Diseases				
Duchenne muscular dystrophy	Degenerative muscle disease. Abnormal gait, loss of ability to walk between ages 7 and 13 years.	Recessive	1 in 3,000 to 5,000 male births	None. Death from respiratory infection or weakening of the heart muscle usually occurs in adolescence.
Hemophilia	Blood fails to clot normally; can lead to severe internal bleeding and tissue damage.	Recessive	1 in 4,000 to 7,000 male births	Blood transfusions. Safety precautions to prevent injury.
Diabetes insipidus	Insufficient production of the hormone vasopressin results in excessive thirst and urination. Dehydration can cause central nervous system damage.	Recessive	1 in 2,500 male births	Hormone replacement.

Note: For recessive disorders, carrier status can be detected in prospective parents through a blood test or genetic analyses. For all disorders listed, prenatal diagnosis is available (see page 64).

Sources: Kliegman et al., 2008; Lashley, 2007; National Center for Biotechnology Information, 2014.

INCOMPLETE DOMINANCE PATTERN In some heterozygous circumstances, the dominant–recessive relationship does not hold completely. Instead, we see **incomplete dominance,** a pattern of inheritance in which both alleles are expressed in the phenotype, resulting in a combined trait, or one that is intermediate between the two.

The *sickle cell trait,* a heterozygous condition present in many black Africans, provides an example. *Sickle cell anemia* (see Table 2.2) occurs in full form when a child inherits two recessive alleles. They cause the usually round red blood cells to become sickle (crescent-moon) shaped, especially under low-oxygen conditions. The sickled cells clog the blood vessels and block the flow of blood, causing intense pain, swelling, and tissue damage. Despite medical advances that today allow 85 percent of affected children to survive to adulthood, North Americans with sickle cell anemia have a life expectancy of only 55 years (Driscoll, 2007). Heterozygous individuals are protected from the disease under most circumstances. However, when they experience oxygen deprivation—for example, at high altitudes or after intense physical exercise—the single recessive allele asserts itself, and a temporary, mild form of the illness occurs.

The sickle cell allele is common among black Africans for a special reason. Carriers of it are more resistant to malaria than are individuals with two alleles for normal red blood cells. In Africa, where malaria is common, these carriers have survived and reproduced more frequently than others, leading the gene to be maintained in the black population. But in regions of the world where the risk of malaria is low, the frequency of the gene is declining. For example, only 8 percent of African Americans are carriers, compared with 20 percent of black Africans (U.S. Department of Health and Human Services, 2012).

X-LINKED PATTERN Males and females have an equal chance of inheriting recessive disorders carried on the autosomes, such as PKU and sickle cell anemia. But when a harmful allele is carried on the X chromosome, **X-linked inheritance** applies. Males are more likely to be affected because their sex chromosomes do not match. In females, any recessive allele on one X chromosome has a good chance of being suppressed by a dominant allele on the other X. But the Y chromosome is only about one-third as long and therefore lacks many corresponding alleles to override those on the X. A well-known example is *hemophilia,* a disorder in which the blood fails to clot normally. Figure 2.4 shows its greater likelihood of inheritance by male children whose mothers carry the abnormal allele.

Besides X-linked disorders, many sex differences reveal the male to be at a disadvantage. Rates of miscarriage, infant and childhood deaths, birth defects, learning disabilities, behavior disorders, and intellectual disability all are higher for boys (Butler & Meaney, 2005). It is possible that these sex differences can be traced to the genetic code. The female, with two X chromosomes, benefits from a greater variety of genes. Nature, however, has adjusted for the male's disadvantage. Worldwide, about 106 boys are born for every 100 girls, and judging from miscarriage and abortion statistics, an even greater number of males are conceived (United Nations, 2012).

In cultures with strong gender-biased attitudes that induce expectant parents to prefer a male child, the male-to-female birth sex ratio is often much larger. In China, for example, the spread of ultrasound technology (which enables prenatal sex determination) and enforcement of a one-child family policy to control population growth—both of which began in the 1980s—led to a dramatic increase in sex-selective abortion (Chen, Li, & Meng, 2013). Today, China's birth sex ratio is 118 boys for every 100 girls—a gender imbalance with adverse social consequences, such as rising crime rates and male competition for marriage partners.

In contrast, in many Western countries, including the United States, Canada, and European nations, the proportion of male births has declined in recent decades. Some researchers attribute the trend

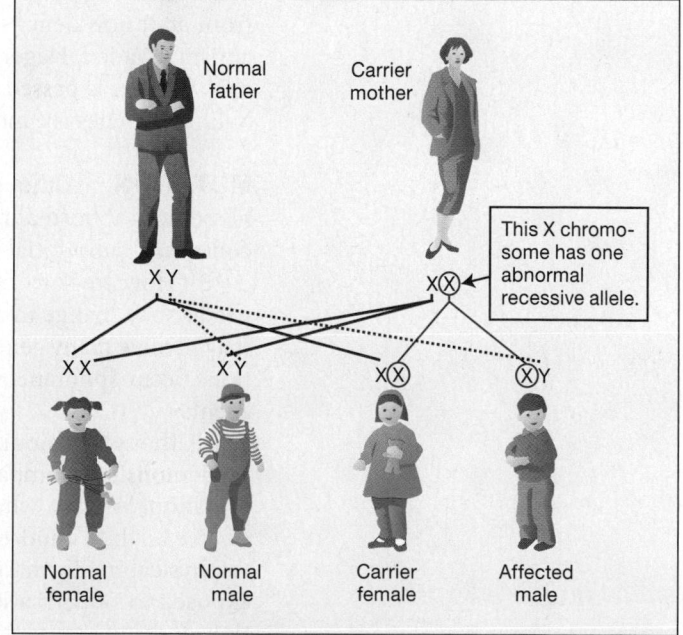

FIGURE 2.4 **X-linked inheritance.** In the example shown here, the allele on the father's X chromosome is normal. The mother has one normal and one abnormal recessive allele on her X chromosomes. By looking at the possible combinations of the parents' alleles, we can predict that 50 percent of these parents' male children are likely to have the disorder, and 50 percent of their female children are likely to be carriers of it.

to a rise in stressful living conditions, which heighten spontaneous abortions, especially of male fetuses (Catalano et al., 2010). In support of this hypothesis, a California study spanning the decade of the 1990s revealed that the percentage of male fetal deaths increased in months in which unemployment (a major stressor) also rose above its typical level (Catalano et al., 2009).

In sum, social and cultural factors can substantially modify the male-to-female birth sex ratio, in either direction. And they can readily undermine the ratio's assumed evolutionary role: compensating for males' greater genetic vulnerability.

GENOMIC IMPRINTING More than 1,000 human characteristics follow the rules of dominant–recessive and incomplete-dominance inheritance (National Center for Biotechnology Information, 2014). In these cases, whichever parent contributes a gene to the new individual, the gene responds in the same way. Geneticists, however, have identified some exceptions. In **genomic imprinting,** alleles are imprinted, or chemically marked through regulatory processes within the genome, in such a way that one pair member (either the mother's or the father's) is activated, regardless of its makeup (Hirasawa & Feil, 2010). The imprint is often temporary; it may be erased in the next generation, and it may not occur in all individuals. The number of genes subjected to genomic imprinting is believed to be small—less than 1 percent (Isles & Wilkinson, 2011). Nevertheless, these genes have a significant impact on brain development and physical health.

Imprinting helps us understand certain puzzling genetic patterns. For example, children are more likely to develop diabetes if their father, rather than their mother, suffers from it. And people with asthma or hay fever tend to have mothers, not fathers, with the illness. Imprinting is involved in several childhood cancers and in *Prader-Willi syndrome,* a disorder with symptoms of mental disability and severe obesity (Butler, 2009). It may also explain why Huntington disease, when inherited from the father, tends to emerge at an earlier age and to progress more rapidly (Gropman & Adams, 2007).

Genomic imprinting can also operate on the sex chromosomes, as *fragile X syndrome*— the most common inherited cause of intellectual disability—reveals. In this disorder, which affects about 1 in 4,000 males and 1 in 6,000 females, an abnormal repetition of a sequence of DNA bases occurs in a special spot on the X chromosome, damaging a particular gene. In addition to cognitive impairments, the majority of individuals with fragile X syndrome suffer from attention deficits and high anxiety, and about 30 to 35 percent also have symptoms of autism (Wadell, Hagerman, & Hessl, 2013). The defective gene at the fragile site is expressed only when it is passed from mother to child (Hagerman et al., 2009). Because the disorder is X-linked, males are more severely affected.

MUTATION Although less than 3 percent of pregnancies result in the birth of a baby with a hereditary abnormality, these children account for about 20 percent of infant deaths and contribute substantially to lifelong impaired physical and mental functioning (Martin et al., 2013). How are harmful genes created in the first place? The answer is **mutation,** a sudden but permanent change in a segment of DNA. A mutation may affect only one or two genes, or it may involve many genes, as in the chromosomal disorders we will discuss shortly. Some mutations occur spontaneously, simply by chance. Others are caused by hazardous environmental agents.

Although nonionizing forms of radiation—electromagnetic waves and microwaves—have no demonstrated impact on DNA, ionizing (high-energy) radiation is an established cause of mutation. Women who receive repeated doses before conception are more likely to miscarry or give birth to children with hereditary defects. The incidence of genetic abnormalities, such as physical malformations and childhood cancer, is also higher in children whose fathers are exposed to radiation in their occupations. However, infrequent and mild exposure to radiation does not cause genetic damage (Jacquet, 2004). Rather, high doses over a long period impair DNA.

The examples just given illustrate *germline mutation,* which takes place in the cells that give rise to gametes. When the affected individual mates, the defective DNA is passed on to the next generation. In a second type, called *somatic mutation,* normal body cells mutate, an event that can occur at any time of life. The DNA defect appears in every cell derived from the affected body cell, eventually becoming widespread enough to cause disease (such as cancer) or disability.

It is easy to see how disorders that run in families can result from germline mutation. But somatic mutation may be involved in these disorders as well. Some people harbor a genetic susceptibility that causes certain body cells to mutate easily in the presence of triggering events (Weiss, 2005). This helps explain why some individuals develop serious illnesses (such as cancer) as a result of smoking, exposure to pollutants, or psychological stress, while others do not.

Although virtually all mutations that have been studied are harmful, some spontaneous ones (such as the sickle cell allele in malaria-ridden regions of the world) are necessary and desirable. By increasing genetic variation, they help individuals adapt to unexpected environmental challenges. Scientists, however, seldom go looking for mutations that underlie favorable traits, such as an exceptional talent or an especially sturdy immune system. They are far more concerned with identifying and eliminating unfavorable genes that threaten health and survival.

POLYGENIC INHERITANCE So far, we have discussed patterns of gene–gene interaction in which people either display a particular trait or do not. These cut-and-dried individual differences are much easier to trace to their genetic origins than are characteristics that vary on a continuum among people, such as height, weight, intelligence, and personality. These traits are due to **polygenic inheritance,** in which many genes affect the characteristic in question. Polygenic inheritance is complex, and much about it is still unknown. In the final section of this chapter, we discuss how researchers infer the influence of heredity on human attributes when they do not know the precise patterns of inheritance.

Chromosomal Abnormalities

Besides harmful recessive alleles, abnormalities of the chromosomes are a major cause of serious developmental problems. Most chromosomal defects result from mistakes during meiosis, when the ovum and sperm are formed. A chromosome pair does not separate properly, or part of a chromosome breaks off. Because these errors involve far more DNA than problems due to single genes, they usually produce many physical and mental symptoms.

DOWN SYNDROME The most common chromosomal disorder, occurring in 1 out of every 700 live births, is *Down syndrome*. In 95 percent of cases, it results from a failure of the twenty-first pair of chromosomes to separate during meiosis, so the new individual receives three of these chromosomes rather than the normal two. For this reason, Down syndrome is sometimes called *trisomy 21*. In other, less frequent forms, an extra broken piece of a twenty-first chromosome is attached to another chromosome (called *translocation* pattern). Or an error occurs during the early stages of cell duplication, causing some but not all body cells to have the defective chromosomal makeup (called *mosaic* pattern) (U.S. Department of Health and Human Services, 2014). Because the mosaic type involves less genetic material, symptoms may be less extreme.

The consequences of Down syndrome include intellectual disability, memory and speech problems, limited vocabulary, and slow motor development. Measures of electrical brain activity reveal substantial disruption in connectivity among brain regions. This indicates that the brains of children with Down syndrome function in a far less coordinated fashion than do the brains of typical children (Ahmadlou et al., 2013). Affected individuals also have distinct physical features—a short, stocky build; a flattened face; a protruding tongue; almond-shaped eyes; and (in 50 percent of cases) an unusual crease running across the palm of the hand. In addition, infants with Down syndrome

An 8-year-old with Down syndrome, at right, plays with a typically developing classmate. Despite impaired intellectual development, this child benefits from exposure to stimulating environments and from opportunities to interact with peers.

© LAURA DWIGHT PHOTOGRAPHY

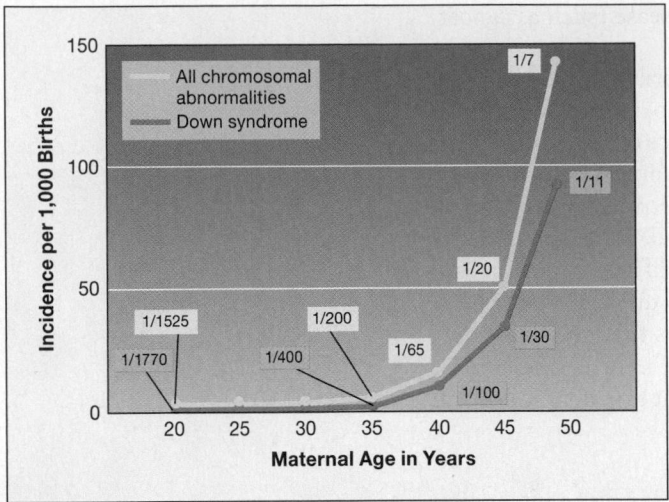

FIGURE 2.5 **Risk of Down syndrome and all chromosomal abnormalities by maternal age.** Risk rises sharply after age 35. (From R. L. Schonberg & C. J. Tifft, 2012, "Birth Defects and Prenatal Diagnosis," from *Children with Disabilities,* 7/e, M. L. Matshaw, N. J. Roizen, & G. R. Lotrecchiano, editors, p. 50. Baltimore: Paul H. Brookes Publishing Co, Inc. Adapted by permission.)

are often born with eye cataracts, hearing loss, and heart and intestinal defects (U.S. Department of Health and Human Services, 2014). Because of medical advances, life expectancy of individuals with Down syndrome has increased greatly: Today, it is about 60 years of age. However, more than half of affected individuals who live past age 40 show symptoms of *Alzheimer's disease,* the most common form of dementia (Davis & Escobar, 2013). Genes on chromosome 21 are linked to this disorder.

Infants with Down syndrome smile less readily, show poor eye-to-eye contact, have weak muscle tone, and explore objects less persistently (Slonims & McConachie, 2006). But when parents encourage them to engage with their surroundings, children with Down syndrome develop more favorably. They also benefit from infant and preschool intervention programs, although emotional, social, and motor skills improve more than intellectual performance (Carr, 2002). Clearly, environmental factors affect how well children with Down syndrome fare.

As Figure 2.5 shows, the risk of bearing a baby with Down syndrome, as well as other chromosomal abnormalities, rises dramatically with maternal age. But exactly why older mothers are more likely to release ova with meiotic errors is not yet known (Chiang, Schultz, & Lampson, 2012). In about 5 to 10 percent of cases, the extra genetic material originates with the father. Some studies suggest a role for advanced paternal age, while others show no age effects (De Souza, Alberman, & Morris, 2009; Dzurova & Pikhart, 2005; Sherman et al., 2005).

ABNORMALITIES OF THE SEX CHROMOSOMES Disorders of the autosomes other than Down syndrome usually disrupt development so severely that miscarriage occurs. When such babies are born, they rarely survive beyond early childhood. In contrast, abnormalities of the sex chromosomes usually lead to fewer problems. In fact, sex chromosome disorders often are not recognized until adolescence when, in some deviations, puberty is delayed. The most common problems involve the presence of an extra chromosome (either X or Y) or the absence of one X in females.

Research has discredited a variety of myths about individuals with sex chromosome disorders. For example, as Table 2.3 reveals, males with *XYY syndrome* are not necessarily more aggressive and antisocial than XY males (Stochholm et al., 2012). And most children with sex

TABLE 2.3	Sex Chromosomal Disorders		
DISORDER	**DESCRIPTION**	**INCIDENCE**	**TREATMENT**
XYY syndrome	Extra Y chromosome. Above-average height, large teeth, and sometimes severe acne. Intelligence, male sexual development, and fertility are normal.	1 in 1,000 male births	No special treatment necessary.
Triple X syndrome (XXX)	Extra X chromosome. Tallness and impaired verbal intelligence. Female sexual development and fertility are normal.	1 in 500 to 1,250 female births	Special education to treat verbal ability problems.
Klinefelter syndrome (XXY)	Extra X chromosome. Tallness, body fat distribution resembling females, incomplete development of sex characteristics at puberty, sterility, and impaired verbal intelligence.	1 in 900 male births	Hormone therapy at puberty to stimulate development of sex characteristics; special education to treat verbal ability problems.
Turner syndrome (XO)	Missing X chromosome. Short stature, webbed neck, incomplete development of sex characteristics at puberty, sterility, and impaired spatial intelligence.	1 in 2,500 to 8,000 female births	Hormone therapy in childhood to stimulate physical growth and at puberty to promote development of sex characteristics; special education to treat spatial ability problems.

Sources: Powell & Schulte, 2011; Ross et al., 2012; Saitta & Zackai, 2005.

chromosome disorders do not suffer from intellectual disabilities. Rather, their cognitive challenges are usually very specific. Verbal difficulties—for example, with reading and vocabulary—are common among girls with *triple X syndrome* and boys with *Klinefelter syndrome,* both of whom inherit an extra X chromosome. In contrast, girls with *Turner syndrome,* who are missing an X, have trouble with spatial relationships—for example, drawing pictures, telling right from left, following travel directions, and noticing changes in facial expressions (Otter et al., 2013; Ross et al., 2012; Temple & Shephard, 2012). Brain-imaging evidence confirms that adding to or subtracting from the usual number of X chromosomes alters the development of certain brain structures, yielding particular intellectual deficits (Bray et al., 2011; Bryant et al., 2012).

Ask Yourself

- **REVIEW** Cite evidence indicating that both heredity and environment contribute to the development of children with PKU and Down syndrome.

- **REVIEW** Using your knowledge of X-linked inheritance, explain why males are more vulnerable than females to miscarriage, infant death, genetic disorders, and other problems.

- **CONNECT** Referring to ecological systems theory (Chapter 1, pages 26–29), explain why parents of children with genetic disorders often experience increased stress. What factors, within and beyond the family, can help these parents support their children's development?

- **APPLY** Gilbert's genetic makeup is homozygous for dark hair. Jan's is homozygous for blond hair. What color is Gilbert's hair? How about Jan's? What proportion of their children are likely to be dark-haired? Explain.

Reproductive Choices

2.4 What procedures can assist prospective parents in having healthy children?

Two years after they married, Ted and Marianne gave birth to their first child. Kendra appeared to be a healthy infant, but by 4 months her growth had slowed, and she was diagnosed as having Tay-Sachs disease (see Table 2.2). When Kendra died at 2 years of age, Ted and Marianne were devastated. Although they did not want to bring another infant into the world who would endure such suffering, they badly wanted to have a child.

In the past, many couples with genetic disorders in their families chose not to bear a child at all rather than risk the birth of a baby with abnormalities. Today, genetic counseling and prenatal diagnosis help people make informed decisions about conceiving, carrying a pregnancy to term, or adopting a child.

Genetic Counseling

Genetic counseling is a communication process designed to help couples assess their chances of giving birth to a baby with a hereditary disorder and choose the best course of action in view of risks and family goals (Resta et al., 2006). Individuals likely to seek counseling are those who have had difficulties bearing children—for example, repeated miscarriages—or who know that genetic problems exist in their families. In addition, adults who delay childbearing are often candidates for genetic counseling. As maternal age rises beyond age 35, the rates of Down syndrome and other chromosomal abnormalities increase sharply (refer again to Figure 2.5). Older paternal age presents heightened risk of DNA mutations as well. After age 40, it is associated with increased risk of several serious psychological disorders (Zitzmann, 2013). These include *autism* (see page 23 in Chapter 1); *schizophrenia,* characterized by hallucinations, delusions, and irrational behavior; and *bipolar disorder,* marked by alternating periods of elation and depression. But because younger parents have children in far higher numbers than older parents, they still bear the majority of babies with genetic defects. Therefore, some experts argue that parental needs, not age, should determine referral for genetic counseling (Berkowitz, Roberts, & Minkoff, 2006).

Social Issues: Health

The Pros and Cons of Reproductive Technologies

Some couples decide not to risk pregnancy because of a history of genetic disease. Many others—in fact, one-sixth of all couples who try to conceive—discover that they are infertile. And some never-married adults and gay and lesbian partners want to bear children. Today, increasing numbers of individuals are turning to alternative methods of conception—technologies that, although they fulfill the wish for parenthood, have become the subject of heated debate.

Donor Insemination and In Vitro Fertilization

For several decades, *donor insemination*—injection of sperm from an anonymous man into a woman—has been used to overcome male reproductive difficulties. In recent years, it has also permitted women without a male partner to become pregnant. Donor insemination is 70 percent successful, resulting in about 40,000 deliveries and 52,000 newborn babies in the United States each year (Rossi, 2014).

In vitro fertilization is another reproductive technology that has become increasingly common. Since the first "test tube" baby was born in England in 1978, 1 percent of all children in developed countries—about 60,000 babies in the United States—have been conceived through this technique annually (Centers for Disease Control and Prevention, 2014a). With in vitro fertilization, a woman is given hormones that stimulate the ripening of several ova. These are removed surgically and placed in a dish of nutrients, to which sperm are added. Once an ovum is fertilized and begins to duplicate into several cells, it is injected into the mother's uterus.

By mixing and matching gametes, pregnancies can be brought about when either or both partners have a reproductive problem. Usually, in vitro fertilization is used to treat women whose fallopian tubes are permanently damaged. But a single sperm can now be injected directly into an ovum, thereby overcoming most male fertility problems. And a "sex sorter" method helps ensure that couples who carry X-linked diseases (which usually affect males) have a daughter. Fertilized ova and sperm can even be frozen and stored in embryo banks for use at some future time, thereby guaranteeing healthy zygotes should age or illness lead to fertility problems.

The overall success rate of assisted reproductive techniques, as measured by live births, is about 50 percent. However, success declines steadily with age, from 55 percent in women age 31 to 35 to 8 percent in women age 43 (Cetinkaya et al., 2013; Gnoth et al., 2011). Furthermore, assisted reproduction is associated with an elevated risk of pregnancy complications, miscarriage, and birth defects, due to the biological effects of in vitro techniques

AP IMAGES/HERALD & REVIEW, JIM BOWLING

Fertility drugs and in vitro fertilization often lead to multiple fetuses. These quadruplets are healthy, but babies born with the aid of reproductive technologies are at high risk for low birth weight and major birth defects.

and the older age of many people seeking treatment.

Children conceived through these methods may be genetically unrelated to one or both of their parents. In addition, most parents who have used the procedures do not tell their children how they were conceived. Does lack of genetic ties or secrecy surrounding these techniques interfere with parent–child relationships? Perhaps because of a strong desire for parenthood, caregiving is actually somewhat warmer for young children conceived through donor insemination or in vitro

If a family history of intellectual disability, psychological disorders, physical defects, or inherited diseases exists, the genetic counselor interviews the couple and prepares a *pedigree,* a picture of the family tree in which affected relatives are identified. The pedigree is used to estimate the likelihood that parents will have an abnormal child. For many disorders traceable to a single gene, blood tests or genetic analyses can reveal whether the parent is a carrier of the harmful allele. Carrier detection is possible for all the recessive diseases listed in Table 2.2, as well as others, and for fragile X syndrome.

Autism, schizophrenia, and bipolar disorder have each been linked to an array of DNA-sequence deviations (called *genetic markers*) distributed across multiple chromosomes. New *genomewide testing methods,* which look for these genetic markers, have enabled genetic counselors to estimate risk for these conditions. But the estimates are generally low because the

fertilization. Also, in vitro infants are as securely attached to their parents, and in vitro children and adolescents as well-adjusted, as their counterparts who were naturally conceived (Punamaki, 2006; Wagenaar et al., 2011). However, in one study, school-age children who had not been informed of their gamete-donor origins experienced less positive maternal interaction (Golombok et al., 2011). This suggests that families can benefit from open discussion with their children.

Although reproductive technologies have many benefits, serious questions have arisen about their use. In many countries, including the United States, doctors are not required to keep records of donor characteristics, though information about the child's genetic background might be critical in the case of serious disease (Murphy, 2013). Another concern is that the in vitro "sex sorter" method enables parental sex selection, eroding the moral value that boys and girls are equally precious.

Furthermore, about 45 percent of in vitro procedures result in multiple births. Most are twins, but 6 percent are triplets and higher-order multiples. Consequently, among in vitro babies, the rate of low birth weight is nearly four times as high as in the general population. In response, doctors have begun to reduce the number of fertilized ova injected into a woman's uterus, typically to no more than two (Kulkarni et al., 2013; Sunderam et al., 2013). Risk of pregnancy complications, miscarriage, and major birth defects also rises, due to the biological effects of in vitro techniques and the older age of many people seeking treatment. In sum, in vitro fertilization poses greater risks than natural conception to infant survival and healthy development.

Surrogate Motherhood

An even more controversial form of medically assisted conception is *surrogate motherhood*.

In this procedure, in vitro fertilization may be used to impregnate a woman (called a surrogate) with a couple's fertilized ovum. Alternatively, sperm from a man whose partner is infertile may be used to inseminate the surrogate, who agrees to turn the baby over to the natural father. The child is then adopted by his partner. In both cases, the surrogate is paid a fee for her childbearing services.

Most surrogate arrangements proceed smoothly, and the limited evidence available suggests that families usually function well, tell their children about the surrogacy, and stay in touch with and have positive relationships with the surrogate, especially if she is genetically related to the child (Golomobok et al., 2011; Jadva, Casey, & Golombok, 2012). The small number of children who have been studied appear to be as well-adjusted as agemates who were naturally conceived.

Nevertheless, because surrogacy usually involves the wealthy as contractors for infants and the less economically advantaged as surrogates, it may promote exploitation of financially needy women. In addition, most surrogates already have children of their own. Knowledge that their mother would give away a baby may cause these children to worry about the security of their own family circumstances.

New Reproductive Frontiers

Reproductive technologies are evolving faster than societies can weigh the ethics of these procedures. Doctors have used donor ova from younger women in combination with in vitro fertilization to help postmenopausal women become pregnant. Most recipients are in their forties, but several women in their fifties and sixties, and a few at age 70, have given birth. These cases raise questions about bringing children into the world whose parents may not live to see them reach adulthood.

Currently, experts are debating other reproductive options. At donor banks, customers can select ova or sperm on the basis of physical characteristics and even IQ. And scientists are devising ways to alter the DNA of human ova, sperm, and embryos to protect against hereditary disorders—techniques that could be used to engineer other desired characteristics. Many worry that these practices are dangerous steps toward selective breeding through "designer babies"—controlling offspring traits by manipulating genetic makeup.

Although new reproductive technologies permit many barren couples to rear healthy newborn babies, laws are needed to regulate such practices. In Australia, New Zealand, and Europe, in vitro gamete donors and applicants for the procedure must undergo highly regulated screening (Murphy, 2013). Denmark, France, and Italy have prohibited in vitro fertilization for women past menopause. Pressure from those working in the field of assisted reproduction may eventually lead to similar policies in the United States.

The ethical problems of surrogate motherhood are so complex that 13 U.S. states and the District of Columbia have sharply restricted the practice (Swain, 2014). Australia, Canada, and many European nations have banned commercial surrogacy, arguing that the status of a baby should not involve profit making. At present, not enough is known about the consequences of being a product of these procedures. More research on how such children grow up, including later-appearing medical conditions and feelings about their origins, is important for weighing the pros and cons of these techniques.

genetic markers are found in only a minority of affected people. Also, the genetic markers are not associated with mental illness every time they appear. Their expression—as we will illustrate at the end of this chapter—seems to depend on environmental conditions. Recently, geneticists have begun to identify rare repeats and deletions of DNA bases that are more consistently related to mental illness (Gershon & Alliey-Rodriguez, 2013). In a small number of cases, these discoveries may lead to more accurate prediction of the likelihood of passing a psychological disorder from parent to child.

When all the relevant hereditary information is in, genetic counselors help people consider appropriate options. These include taking a chance and conceiving, choosing from among a variety of reproductive technologies (see the Social Issues: Health box above), or adopting a child.

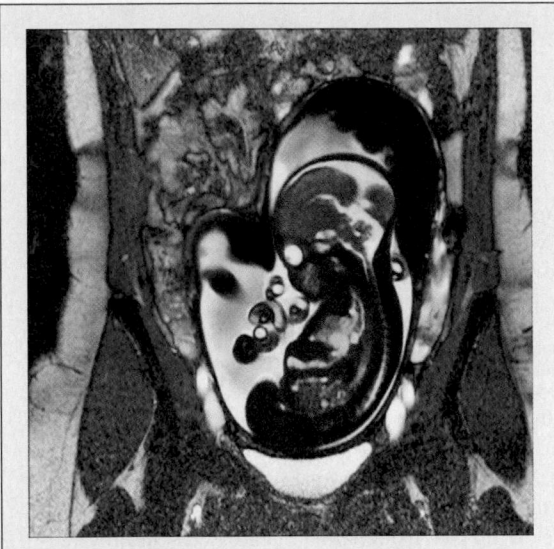

© SIMON FRASER/SCIENCE SOURCE

FIGURE 2.6 **Ultrafast MRI of a fetus, showing body structures.** Ultrafast MRI is increasingly being used as a supplement to ultrasound because it records detailed pictures of body structures, permitting greater diagnostic accuracy. In this colorized MRI of a 26-week-old fetus, the yellow area highlights a brain abnormality.

Prenatal Diagnosis and Fetal Medicine

If couples at risk for bearing a child with abnormalities decide to conceive, several **prenatal diagnostic methods**—medical procedures that permit detection of developmental problems before birth—are available (see Table 2.4). Women of advanced maternal age are prime candidates for *amniocentesis* or *chorionic villus sampling. Ultrasound,* commonly used during pregnancy to track fetal growth, permits detection of gross structural abnormalities. When ultrasound suggests problems but diagnosis is uncertain, *ultrafast fetal magnetic resonance imaging,* in which a scanner magnetically records detailed pictures of fetal structures, can be used for greater accuracy (see Figure 2.6). As Table 2.4 reveals, certain prenatal diagnostic techniques should not be used routinely because of risk of injury to the developing organism.

Prenatal diagnosis has led to advances in fetal medicine. For example, by inserting a needle into the uterus, doctors can administer drugs to the fetus. Surgery has been performed to repair such problems as heart, lung, and diaphragm malformations, urinary tract obstructions, and neural defects (Adzick, 2013; Bianchi, 2012). Fetuses with blood disorders have been given blood transfusions. And those with immune deficiencies have received bone marrow transplants that succeeded in creating a normally functioning immune system (Deprest et al., 2010).

These techniques frequently result in complications, the most common being premature labor and miscarriage (Danzer & Johnson, 2014). Yet parents

TABLE 2.4	Prenatal Diagnostic Methods
METHOD	**DESCRIPTION**
Amniocentesis	The most widely used technique. A hollow needle is inserted through the abdominal wall to obtain a sample of fluid in the uterus. Cells are examined for genetic defects. Can be performed by the 14th week after conception; 1 to 2 more weeks are required for test results. Small risk of miscarriage.
Chorionic villus sampling	A procedure that can be used if results are desired or needed very early in pregnancy. A thin tube is inserted into the uterus through the vagina, or a hollow needle is inserted through the abdominal wall. A small plug of tissue is removed from the end of one or more chorionic villi, the hairlike projections on the membrane surrounding the developing organism. Cells are examined for genetic defects. Can be performed at 9 weeks after conception; results are available within 24 hours. Entails a slightly greater risk of miscarriage than does amniocentesis. Also associated with a small risk of limb deformities, which increases the earlier the procedure is performed.
Fetoscopy	A small tube with a light source at one end is inserted into the uterus to inspect the fetus for defects of the limbs and face. Also allows a sample of fetal blood to be obtained, permitting diagnosis of such disorders as hemophilia and sickle cell anemia as well as neural defects (see below). Usually performed between 15 and 18 weeks after conception but can be done as early as 5 weeks. Entails some risk of miscarriage.
Ultrasound	High-frequency sound waves are beamed at the uterus; their reflection is translated into a picture on a video screen that reveals the size, shape, and placement of the fetus. By itself, permits assessment of fetal age, detection of multiple pregnancies, and identification of gross physical defects. Also used to guide amniocentesis, chorionic villus sampling, and fetoscopy. Sometimes combined with magnetic resonance imaging (see below) to detect physical abnormalities with greater accuracy. When used five or more times, may increase the chances of low birth weight.
Maternal blood analysis	By the second month of pregnancy, some of the developing organism's cells enter the maternal bloodstream. An elevated level of alpha-fetoprotein may indicate kidney disease, abnormal closure of the esophagus, or neural tube defects, such as anencephaly (absence of most of the brain) and spina bifida (bulging of the spinal cord from the spinal column). Isolated cells can be examined for genetic defects.
Ultrafast fetal magnetic resonance imaging (MRI)	Sometimes used as a supplement to ultrasound, where brain or other abnormalities are detected and MRI can provide greater diagnostic accuracy. Uses a scanner to magnetically record detailed pictures of fetal structures. The ultrafast technique overcomes image blurring due to fetal movements. No evidence of adverse effects.
Preimplantation genetic diagnosis	After in vitro fertilization and duplication of the zygote into a cluster of about 8 to 10 cells, 1 or 2 cells are removed and examined for hereditary defects. Only if that sample is free of detectable genetic disorders is the fertilized ovum implanted in the woman's uterus.

Sources: Hahn & Chitty, 2008; Jokhi & Whitby, 2011; Kollmann et al., 2013; Moore, Persaud, & Torchia, 2013; Sermon, Van Steirteghem, & Liebaers, 2004.

Applying What We Know

Steps Prospective Parents Can Take Before Conception to Increase the Chances of a Healthy Baby

RECOMMENDATION	EXPLANATION
Arrange for a physical exam.	A physical exam before conception permits detection of diseases and other medical problems that might reduce fertility, be difficult to treat during pregnancy, or affect the developing organism.
Consider your genetic makeup.	Find out if anyone in your family has had a child with a genetic disorder. If so, seek genetic counseling before conception.
Reduce or eliminate toxins under your control.	Because the developing organism is highly sensitive to damaging environmental agents during the early weeks of pregnancy (see Chapter 3), couples trying to conceive should avoid drugs, alcohol, cigarette smoke, radiation, pollution, chemical substances in the home and workplace, and infectious diseases. Furthermore, they should stay away from ionizing radiation and some industrial chemicals that are known to cause mutations.
Ensure proper nutrition.	A doctor-recommended vitamin–mineral supplement, begun before conception, helps prevent many prenatal problems. It should include folic acid, which reduces the chances of neural tube defects, prematurity, and low birth weight (see Chapter 3, page 112).
Consult your doctor after 12 months of unsuccessful efforts at conception.	Long periods of infertility may be due to undiagnosed spontaneous abortions, which can be caused by genetic defects in either partner. If a physical exam reveals a healthy reproductive system, seek genetic counseling.

may be willing to try almost any option, even one with only a slim chance of success. Currently, the medical profession is struggling with how to help parents make informed decisions about fetal surgery.

Advances in *genetic engineering* also offer new hope for correcting hereditary defects. As part of the Human Genome Project—an ambitious international research program extending from 1990 to 2003, aimed at deciphering the chemical makeup of human genetic material (genome)—researchers succeeded in mapping the sequence of all human DNA base pairs. Using this information, they are "annotating" the genome—identifying all its genes and their functions, including their protein products and what these products do. A major goal is to understand the estimated 4,000 human disorders, those due to single genes and those resulting from an interplay of multiple genes and environmental factors.

Already, thousands of genes have been identified, including those involved in hundreds of disorders of the heart, digestive, blood, eye, and nervous system; and many forms of cancer (National Institutes of Health, 2014). As a result, new treatments are being explored, such as *gene therapy*—correcting genetic abnormalities by delivering DNA carrying a functional gene to the cells. Recent testing of gene therapies for relieving symptoms of hemophilia and treating severe immune system dysfunction, leukemia, and several forms of cancer has been encouraging (Kaufmann et al., 2013). In another approach, called *proteomics,* scientists modify gene-specified proteins involved in disease (Ray et al., 2011).

Genetic treatments, however, seem some distance in the future for most single-gene defects and even farther off for diseases involving multiple genes that combine in complex ways with each other and the environment. Applying What We Know above summarizes steps that prospective parents can take before conception to protect the genetic health of their child.

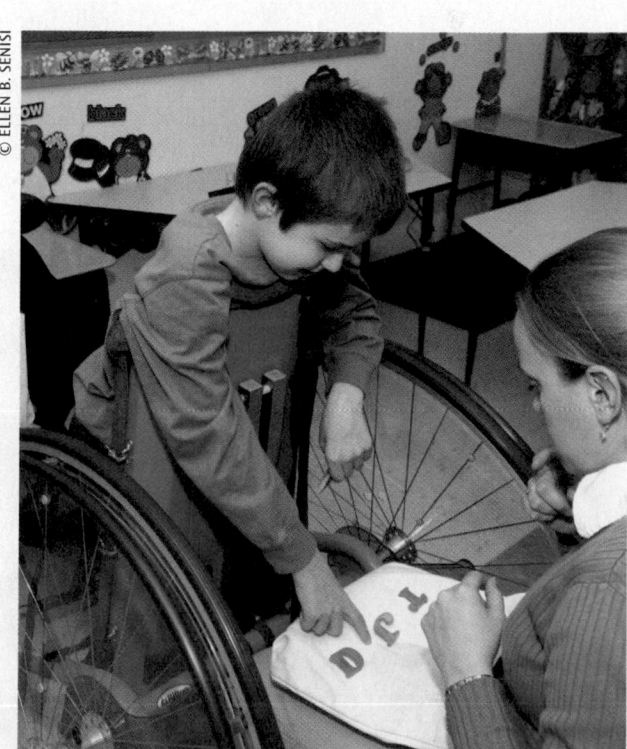

© ELLEN B. SENISI

This 10-year-old has Duchenne muscular dystrophy, a hereditary degenerative muscle disease that is likely to lead to early death. In the future, such children may benefit from gene-based treatments for hereditary disorders.

Adoption

Adults who are infertile, who are likely to pass along a genetic disorder, or who are older and single but want a family are turning to adoption in increasing numbers. Those who have children by birth, too, sometimes choose to expand their families through adoption. Adoption agencies try to ensure a good fit by seeking parents of the same ethnic and religious background as the child and, where possible, trying to choose parents who are the same age as typical biological parents. Because the availability of healthy babies has declined (fewer young unwed mothers give up their babies than in the past), more people in North America and Western Europe are adopting from other countries or accepting children who are past infancy or who have known developmental problems (Palacios & Brodzinsky, 2010).

Adopted children and adolescents—whether or not they are born in their adoptive parents' country—tend to have more learning and emotional difficulties than other children, a difference that increases with the child's age at time of adoption (van den Dries et al., 2009; van IJzendoorn, Juffer, & Poelhuis, 2005; Verhulst, 2008). Various explanations exist for adoptees' more problematic childhoods. The biological mother may have been unable to care for the child because of problems believed to be partly genetic, such as alcoholism or severe depression, and may have passed this tendency to her offspring. Or perhaps she experienced stress, poor diet, or inadequate medical care during pregnancy—factors that can affect the child (as we will see in Chapter 3). Furthermore, children adopted after infancy often have a preadoptive history of conflict-ridden family relationships, lack of parental affection, neglect and abuse, or deprived institutional rearing. Finally, adoptive parents and children, who are genetically unrelated, are less alike in intelligence and personality than are biological relatives—differences that may threaten family harmony.

Despite these risks, most adopted children fare well, and those with preexisting problems usually make rapid progress (Arcus & Chambers, 2008; Juffer & van IJzendoorn, 2012). In a study of internationally adopted children in the Netherlands, sensitive maternal care and secure attachment in infancy predicted cognitive and social competence at age 7 (Stams, Juffer, & van IJzendoorn, 2002).

Overall, international adoptees fare much better in development than birth siblings or institutionalized agemates who stay behind (Christoffersen, 2012). By middle childhood, those who were adopted in infancy have mental test scores resembling those of their nonbiological siblings and school classmates, although they tend to achieve less well in school, to have more learning problems that require special treatment, and to be slightly delayed in language skills (van IJzendoorn, Juffer, & Poelhuis, 2005). Children adopted at older ages generally improve in feelings of trust and affection for their adoptive parents as they come to feel loved and supported in their new families (Verissimo & Salvaterra, 2006). As we will see in Chapter 5, however, later-adopted children—especially those with multiple early-life adversities—are more likely than their agemates to have persistent cognitive, emotional, and social problems.

By adolescence, adoptees' lives are often complicated by unresolved curiosity about their roots. Some have difficulty accepting the possibility that they may never know their birth parents. Others worry about what they would do if their birth parents suddenly reappeared. Adopted teenagers also face a more challenging process of defining themselves as they try to integrate aspects of their birth family and their adoptive family into their emerging identity. Nevertheless, the decision to search for birth parents is usually postponed until early adulthood, when marriage and childbirth may trigger it.

© XINHUA/LANDOV

Adoption is one option for adults who are infertile or have a family history of genetic disorders. This couple, who adopted their daughters from China, can promote their children's adjustment by helping them learn about their birth heritage.

Despite concerns about their origins, most adoptees appear well-adjusted as adults. When parents have been warm, open, and supportive in their communication about adoption, their children typically forge a positive sense of self (Brodzinsky, 2011). And as long as their parents took steps to help them learn about their heritage in childhood, young people adopted into a different ethnic group or culture generally develop identities that are healthy blends of their birth and rearing backgrounds (Nickman et al., 2005; Thomas & Tessler, 2007).

As we conclude our discussion of reproductive choices, perhaps you are wondering how things turned out for Ted and Marianne. Through genetic counseling, Marianne discovered a history of Tay-Sachs disease on her mother's side of the family. Ted had a distant cousin who died of the disorder. The genetic counselor explained that the chances of giving birth to another affected baby were 1 in 4. Ted and Marianne took the risk. Their son Douglas is now 12 years old. Although Douglas is a carrier of the recessive allele, he is a normal, healthy boy. In a few years, Ted and Marianne will tell Douglas about his genetic history and explain the importance of genetic counseling and testing before he has children of his own.

Ask Yourself

● **REVIEW** Why is genetic counseling called a *communication process?* Who should seek it?

● **CONNECT** How does research on adoption reveal resilience? Which factor related to resilience (see Chapter 1, pages 10–11) is central in positive outcomes for adoptees?

● **APPLY** Imagine that you must counsel a couple considering in vitro fertilization using donor ova to overcome infertility. What medical and ethical risks would you raise?

● **REFLECT** Suppose you are a carrier of fragile X syndrome and want to have children. Would you choose pregnancy, adoption, or surrogacy? If you became pregnant, would you opt for prenatal diagnosis? Explain your decisions.

Environmental Contexts for Development

2.5 Describe family functioning from the perspective of ecological systems theory, along with aspects of the environment that support family well-being and children's development.

Just as complex as the genetic inheritance is the surrounding environment—a many-layered set of influences that combine to help or hinder physical and psychological well-being. **TAKE A MOMENT...** Think back to your own childhood, and jot down a brief description of events and people that significantly influenced your development. Do the items on your list resemble those of our students, who mostly mention experiences that involve their families? This emphasis is not surprising, since the family is the first and longest-lasting context for development. Other influences that make most students' top ten are friends, neighbors, school, and community and religious organizations.

Return to Bronfenbrenner's ecological systems theory, discussed in Chapter 1. It emphasizes that environments extending beyond the *microsystem*—the immediate settings just mentioned—powerfully affect development. Indeed, our students rarely mention one important context. Its impact is so pervasive that we seldom stop to think about it in our daily lives. This is the *macrosystem,* or broad social climate of society—its values and programs that support and protect children's development. All families need help in rearing children—through affordable housing and health care, safe neighborhoods, good schools, well-equipped recreational facilities, and high-quality child care and other services that permit parents to meet both work and family responsibilities. And some families, because of poverty or special tragedies, need considerably more help than others.

In the following sections, we take up these contexts for development. Because they affect every age and aspect of change, we will return to them in later chapters. For now, our discussion emphasizes that environments, as well as heredity, can enhance or create risks for development.

The family is a network of interdependent relationships, in which each person's behavior influences that of others. As this family plays a game, warm, considerate parental communication encourages children's cooperation, which promotes further parental warmth and caring.

The Family

In power and breadth of influence, no other micro-system context equals the family. The family introduces children to the physical world by providing opportunities for play and exploration of objects. It also creates unique bonds among people. Attachments to parents and siblings are usually lifelong and serve as models for relationships in the wider world. Within the family, children learn the language, skills, and social and moral values of their culture. And people of all ages turn to family members for information, assistance, and pleasurable interaction. In cultures around the world, warm, gratifying family ties predict physical and psychological health throughout development (Khaleque & Rohner, 2012; Parke & Buriel, 2006). In contrast, a sense of isolation or alienation from the family, especially from parents, is generally associated with developmental problems.

Contemporary researchers view the family as a network of interdependent relationships (Bornstein & Sawyer, 2006; Bronfenbrenner & Morris, 2006). Recall from ecological systems theory that *bidirectional influences* exist in which the behaviors of each family member affect those of others. Indeed, the very term *system* implies that the responses of all family members are related. These system influences operate both directly and indirectly.

DIRECT INFLUENCES   Recently, while passing through the checkout counter at the supermarket, one of us witnessed two episodes, each an example of how parents and children directly influence each other:

- Four-year-old Danny looked longingly at the tempting rows of candy as his mother lifted groceries from her cart onto the counter. "Pleeeeease, can I have it, Mom?" Danny begged, holding up a large package of bubble gum. "Do you have a dollar? Just one?"

  "No, not today," his mother answered. "Remember, we picked out your special cereal. That's what I need the dollar for." Gently taking the bubble gum from his hand, Danny's mother handed him the box of cereal. "Here, let's pay," she said, lifting Danny so he could see the cash register.
- Three-year-old Meg was sitting in the shopping cart while her mother transferred groceries to the counter. Suddenly Meg turned around, grabbed a bunch of bananas, and started pulling them apart.

  "Stop it, Meg!" shouted her mother, snatching the bananas from Meg's hand. But as she turned her attention to swiping her debit card, Meg reached for a chocolate bar from a nearby shelf. "Meg, how many times have I told you, don't touch!" Loosening the candy from Meg's tight little fist, Meg's mother slapped her hand. Meg's face turned red with anger as she began to wail.

These observations fit with a wealth of research on the family system. Studies of families of diverse ethnicities show that when parents are firm but warm, children tend to comply with their requests. And when children cooperate, their parents are likely to be warm and gentle in the future. In contrast, children whose parents discipline harshly and impatiently are likely to refuse and rebel. And because children's misbehavior is stressful, parents may increase their use of punishment, leading to more unruliness by the child (Stormshak et al., 2000; Whiteside-Mansell et al., 2003). In each case, the behavior of one family member helps sustain a form of interaction in the other that either promotes or undermines children's well-being.

LOOK and LISTEN

Observe several parent–young child pairs in a supermarket or department store, where parents are likely to place limits on children's behavior. How does quality of parent communication seem to influence the child's response? How does the child's response affect the parent's subsequent interaction?

INDIRECT INFLUENCES   The impact of family relationships on child development becomes even more complicated when we consider that interaction between any two members is affected by others present in the setting. Bronfenbrenner calls these indirect influences the effect of *third parties* (see Chapter 1, page 27).

Third parties can serve as supports for or barriers to development. For example, when a marital relationship is warm and considerate, mothers and fathers are more likely to engage in effective **coparenting,** mutually supporting each other's parenting behaviors. Such parents are warmer, praise and stimulate their children more, and nag and scold them less. Effective coparenting, in turn, fosters a positive marital relationship (Morrill et al., 2010). In contrast, parents whose relationship is tense and hostile often interfere with one another's child-rearing efforts, are less responsive to children's needs, and are more likely to criticize, express anger, and punish (Caldera & Lindsey, 2006; Pruett & Donsky, 2011).

Children who are chronically exposed to angry, unresolved parental conflict have serious emotional problems resulting from disrupted emotional security (Cummings & Davies, 2010). These include both *internalizing difficulties* (especially among girls), such as feeling worried and fearful and trying to repair their parents' relationship, and *externalizing difficulties* (especially among boys), including anger and aggression (Cummings, Goeke-Morey, & Papp, 2004; Goeke-Morey, Papp, & Cummings, 2013). These child problems can further disrupt parents' relationship.

Yet even when parental conflict strains children's adjustment, other family members may help restore effective interaction. Grandparents, for example, can promote children's development both directly, by responding warmly to the child, and indirectly, by providing parents with child-rearing advice, models of child-rearing skill, and even financial assistance. Of course, as with any indirect influence, grandparents can sometimes be harmful. When relations between parents and grandparents are quarrelsome, parent–child communication may suffer.

ADAPTING TO CHANGE   Think back to the *chronosystem* in Bronfenbrenner's theory (see page 29 in Chapter 1). The interplay of forces within the family is dynamic and ever-changing, as each member adapts to the development of other members.

For example, as children acquire new skills, parents adjust the way they treat their more competent youngsters. **TAKE A MOMENT...** The next time you have a chance, notice the way a parent relates to a tiny baby as compared with a walking, talking toddler. During the first few months, parents spend much time feeding, changing, bathing, and cuddling the infant. Within a year, things change dramatically. The 1-year-old points, shows, names objects, and makes his way through the household cupboards. In response, parents devote less time to physical care and more to talking, playing games, and disciplining. These new ways of interacting, in turn, encourage the child's expanding motor, cognitive, and social skills.

Parents' development affects children as well. The rise in parent–child conflict that often occurs in early adolescence is not solely due to teenagers' striving for independence. This is a time when most parents of adolescents have reached middle age and—conscious that their children will soon leave home and establish their own lives—are reconsidering their own commitments (Steinberg & Silk, 2002). Consequently, while the adolescent presses for greater autonomy, the parent presses for more togetherness. This imbalance promotes friction, which parent and teenager gradually resolve by accommodating to changes in each other. Indeed, no social unit other than the family is required to adjust to such vast changes in its members.

Historical time period also contributes to a dynamic family system. In recent decades, a declining birth rate, a high divorce rate, expansion of women's roles, increased acceptance of homosexuality, and postponement of parenthood have led to a smaller family size and a greater number of single parents, remarried parents, gay and lesbian parents, employed mothers, and dual-earner families. Clearly, families in industrialized nations have become more diverse than ever before. In later chapters we will take up these family forms, examining how each affects family relationships and, ultimately, children's development.

Social Issues: Education

Worldwide Education of Girls: Transforming Current and Future Generations

Malalah Yousafzai, a Pakistani schoolgirl, rose to international prominence for her persuasive activism favoring the rights of girls to education. Encouraged by her father, a schoolteacher and an educational activist himself, in 2009 at age 11 she wrote a blog for the BBC, using a pseudonym to protect her safety. In the blog, she described her experiences under rule of the Taliban, who had at times banned girls in her province from attending school. Later that year, the *New York Times* made a documentary about Malalah's life, and she started giving interviews that were broadcast around the world.

One afternoon in October 2012, a Taliban gunman boarded Malalah's school bus, asked for her by name, and fired three shots, critically wounding her. In the days following the assassination attempt, she hung between life and death, but gradually she recovered enough to travel to England for intensive treatment. The incident sparked worldwide support for Malalah and her cause. Among the outcomes of her persistent outspokenness was a United Nations petition called "I am Malalah," which demanded that all children be enrolled in school by the end of 2015. The petition led to Pakistan's first Compulsory Education Bill, passed by the National Assembly in 2012, which guarantees free education to all children between ages 5 and 16.

Over the past century, the percentage of children in the developing world who go to school has increased from a small minority of boys to a majority of all children in most regions. Still, some 57 million children of elementary school age, most of them poverty-stricken girls, are not in school, and 71 million of middle school age, again mostly girls, are out of school. Almost two-thirds of the world's 775 million illiterate adults are women (UNICEF, 2013b).

In research carried out in four countries—Mexico, Nepal, Venezuela, and Zambia—investigators examined the impact of variations in maternal language and literacy skills on family

Pakistani girls attend class on the first anniversary of the near-fatal shooting of Malalah Yousafzai, a teenage activist who advocates forcefully for education for girls. Malalah survived to see Pakistan's first compulsory education legislation and in 2014 was awarded the Nobel Peace Prize.

health, mother–child interaction, and young children's literacy skills (LeVine et al., 2012). Participating mothers' average levels of schooling ranged from 5 years in Nepal to 8 years in Zambia, with some attending for as little as 1 year and most leaving school by age 13.

Nevertheless, some general patterns in family functioning do exist. In the United States and other industrialized nations, one important source of these consistencies is socioeconomic status.

Socioeconomic Status and Family Functioning

People in industrialized nations are stratified on the basis of what they do at work and how much they earn for doing it—factors that determine their social position and economic well-being. Researchers assess a family's standing on this continuum through an index called **socioeconomic status (SES),** which combines three related, but not completely overlapping, variables: (1) years of education and (2) the prestige of one's job and the skill it requires, both of which measure social status, and (3) income, which measures economic status. As SES rises and falls, parents and children face changing circumstances that profoundly affect family functioning.

SES is linked to timing of parenthood and to family size. People who work in skilled and semiskilled manual occupations (for example, construction workers, truck drivers, and custodians) tend to marry and have children earlier as well as give birth to more children than people in professional and technical occupations. The two groups also differ in child-rearing values and expectations. For example, when asked about personal qualities they desire for

Findings in each country, and across rural and urban areas, were the same: Educating girls had an especially powerful impact on the welfare of children and families. The diverse benefits of girls' schooling largely accrued in two ways: (1) through enhanced verbal skills—reading, writing, and oral communication; and (2) through the cognitive abilities that literacy promotes. Together, these capacities enable girls, as they become adults and mothers, to navigate health and educational settings more effectively and to teach their children in ways that foster school success in the next generation.

Family Health

Maternal education in developing countries has played a powerful role in the dramatic worldwide gains in child survival and health over past half century (Gakidou et al., 2010). In the four-countries study, the greater mothers' school attainment, the better their comprehension of radio and TV health messages and the more clearly they could to explain an instance of their own or their child's illness to a clinic health professional. And mothers' literacy competence explained this link between maternal schooling and health-related cognitive processing.

Clearly, education gives women the communicative skills and knowledge to benefit from public health information. As a result, it strongly predicts preventive health behaviors: prenatal visits, child immunizations, healthy diet, and sanitary practices (LeVine et al., 2004). In addition, because women with more schooling have more life opportunities, they are more likely to take advantage of family planning services, delay marriage and childbearing, and have more widely spaced and fewer children (Stromquist, 2007). All these practices are linked to increased maternal and child survival and health.

Mother–Child Interaction and Children's Literacy Skills

Making home visits to observe mothers interacting with their babies, researchers in the four-countries study found that schooling was positively associated with mothers' verbal responsiveness to their infants' and toddlers' vocalizations. And once again, maternal literacy skills accounted for this relationship. Follow-ups as the children grew older revealed that mothers who talked more had children with larger vocabularies. The more literate mothers had adopted a style of interaction that promoted language development.

In Nepal, the investigators looked closely at literacy-related parenting behaviors in the preschool and early school years. Regardless of family income or husband's schooling, mothers with more education—especially those with better literacy skills—reported that they more often taught their children academic skills, enriched the home with literacy materials, modeled literacy behaviors, and had higher expectations for their children's education. These home supports for education, in turn, predicted children's language and literacy progress.

Implications

The opportunity to advance in language and literacy skills—even in the limited doses available to women in the four-country study, many of whom attended low-quality schools for just a few years—alters maternal behavior, with substantial health and educational gains in the next generation. A recent United Nations report concluded that educating girls is the most effective means of combating the most profound, global threats to human development: poverty, maternal and child mortality, disease, gender inequality, and economic and social instability in the world's poorest countries (UNICEF, 2013b). But because of cultural beliefs about gender roles or reluctance to give up a daughter's work at home, parents sometimes resist sending their daughters to school.

An even larger barrier is that many countries continue to charge parents a fee for each child enrolled in school, often amounting to nearly one-third of the income of poverty-stricken families. Under these conditions, parents—if they send any children—tend to send only sons. But when governments abolish enrollment fees, provide information about the benefits of education for girls, and create employment possibilities for women, the overwhelming majority of parents—including the very poor—choose to send their daughters to school and are willing to make sacrifices to do so.

---

their children, lower-SES parents tend to emphasize external characteristics, such as obedience, politeness, neatness, and cleanliness. In contrast, higher-SES parents emphasize psychological traits, such as curiosity, happiness, self-direction, and cognitive and social maturity (Duncan & Magnuson, 2003; Hoff, Laursen, & Tardif, 2002; Tudge et al., 2000).

These differences are reflected in family interaction. Parents higher in SES talk to, read to, and otherwise stimulate their infants and preschoolers more and grant them greater freedom to explore. With older children and adolescents, higher-SES parents use more warmth, explanations, and verbal praise; set higher academic and other developmental goals; and allow their children to make more decisions. Commands ("You do that because I told you to"), criticism, and physical punishment all occur more often in low-SES households (Bush & Peterson, 2008; Mandara et al., 2009).

Education contributes substantially to these variations in child rearing. Higher-SES parents' interest in providing verbal stimulation, nurturing inner traits, and promoting academic achievement is supported by years of schooling, during which they learned to think about abstract, subjective ideas and, thus, to invest in their children's cognitive and social development (Mistry et al., 2008; Vernon-Feagans et al., 2008). In diverse cultures around the world, as the Social Issues: Education box above makes clear, education of women in particular fosters patterns of thinking and behaving that greatly improve quality of life, for both parents and children.

Because of limited education and low social status, many lower-SES parents feel a sense of powerlessness and lack of influence in their relationships beyond the home. At work, for example, they must obey rules made by others in positions of authority. When they get home, their parent–child interaction seems to duplicate these experiences—but now they are in authority. High levels of stress contribute to low-SES parents' greater use of coercive discipline (Belsky, Schlomer, & Ellis, 2012; Conger & Donnellan, 2007). Higher-SES parents, in contrast, typically have more control over their own lives. At work, they are used to making independent decisions and convincing others of their point of view. At home, they are more likely to teach these skills to their children (Greenberger, O'Neil, & Nagel, 1994).

As early as the second year of life, higher SES is associated with enhanced cognitive and language development and with reduced incidence of behavior problems. And throughout childhood and adolescence, children from higher-SES families do better in school (Bradley & Corwyn, 2003; Hoff, 2013; Melby et al., 2008). As a result, they attain higher levels of education, which greatly enhances their opportunities for a prosperous adult life. Researchers believe that differences in family functioning have much to do with these outcomes.

Affluence

Despite their advanced education and great material wealth, affluent parents—those in prestigious and high-paying occupations—too often fail to engage in family interaction and parenting that promote favorable development. In several studies, researchers tracked the adjustment of youths growing up in wealthy suburbs (Luthar & Latendresse, 2005a). By seventh grade, a substantial number (as many as 10 percent) showed multiple, serious problems that worsened in high school. Their school grades were poor, and they were more likely than low-SES youths to engage in alcohol and drug use, to have been involved with the legal system, and to report high levels of anxiety and depression (Luthar & Goldstein, 2008; Racz, McMahon, & Luthar, 2011). Furthermore, among affluent (but not low-SES) teenagers, substance use was correlated with anxiety and depression, suggesting that wealthy youths took drugs to self-medicate—a practice that predicts persistent abuse (Luthar & Sexton, 2004).

Why are so many affluent youths troubled? Compared to their better-adjusted counterparts, poorly adjusted affluent young people report less emotional closeness, less supervision, and fewer serious consequences for misbehaviors from their parents, who lead professionally and socially demanding lives. As a group, wealthy parents are nearly as physically and emotionally unavailable to their youngsters as parents coping with serious financial strain. At the same time, affluent parents of troubled youths often make excessive demands for achievement and are critical when their youngsters perform less than perfectly (Luthar & Barkin, 2012). Adolescents whose parents value their accomplishments more than their character are more likely to have academic and emotional problems.

For both affluent and low-SES youths, a simple routine—eating dinner with parents—is associated with a reduction in adjustment difficulties, even after many other aspects of parenting are controlled (see Figure 2.7) (Luthar & Latendresse, 2005b). Interventions that make wealthy parents aware of the high costs of a competitive lifestyle and minimal family time are badly needed.

© INTI ST. CLAIR/GETTY IMAGES/PHOTODISC

Advanced education and material wealth do not guarantee a healthy family life. When children in affluent families lack parental supervision and emotional closeness, they are at risk for academic and emotional difficulties.

Parental affection, acceptance, and monitoring of the adolescent's whereabouts and activities predict favorable adjustment in affluent young people, just as they do for youths in general.

Poverty

When families slip into poverty, development is seriously threatened. In a TV documentary on childhood poverty, a PBS filmmaker explored the daily lives of several American children, along with the struggles of their families (Frontline, 2012). Asked what being poor is like, 10-year-old Kaylie replied, "We don't get three meals a day. . . . Sometimes we have cereal but no milk and have to eat it dry." Kaylie said she felt hungry much of the time, adding, "I'm afraid if we can't pay our bills, me and my brother will starve."

Kaylie lives with her 12-year-old brother Tyler and their mother, who suffers from depression and panic attacks and cannot work. The children sometimes gather discarded tin cans from around their rural neighborhood and sell them for a small amount of cash. When money to pay rent ran out, the family moved from its small house to an extended-stay motel room. Before the move, Kaylie and Tyler had to give up their dog Noah. During the ride to the animal shelter, Kaylie whispered, "I love you, Noah," bursting into tears.

In the cramped motel room with family belongings piled haphazardly around her, Kaylie complained, "I have no friends, no places to play. I pass the time by." Her mother had postponed the children's school enrollment, expecting soon to move to a trailer court in a new school district. Kaylie and Tyler had few books and indoor games; no outdoor play equipment such as bicycles, bats and balls, and roller skates; and no scheduled leisure pursuits like swimming or music lessons or youth organization activities. Asked to imagine her future, Kaylie wasn't hopeful. "I see my future poor, on the streets, in a box, asking for money from everyone, stealing stuff. . . . I'd like to explore the world, but I'm never going to be able to do that."

Although poverty rates in the United States declined slightly in the 1990s, in recent years they have risen. Today, about 15 percent—46 million Americans—are affected. Those hit hardest are parents under age 25 with young children and older adults who live alone. Poverty is also magnified among ethnic minorities and women. For example, 22 percent of U.S. children—about 14.5 million—live in families with incomes below the federal poverty level, the income judged necessary for a minimum living standard (about $23,500 for a family of four). Poverty rates climb to 32 percent for Hispanic children, 34 percent for Native-American children, and 38 percent for African-American children. For single mothers with preschool children, the poverty rate is close to 50 percent (DeNavas-Walt, Proctor, & Smith, 2011; U.S. Census Bureau, 2014b).

Joblessness, a high divorce rate, a high rate of adolescent parenthood, and (as we will see later) inadequate government programs to meet family needs are responsible for these disheartening statistics. The poverty rate is higher among children than any other age group. And of all Western nations, the United States has the highest percentage of extremely poor children. Nearly 10 percent of U.S. children

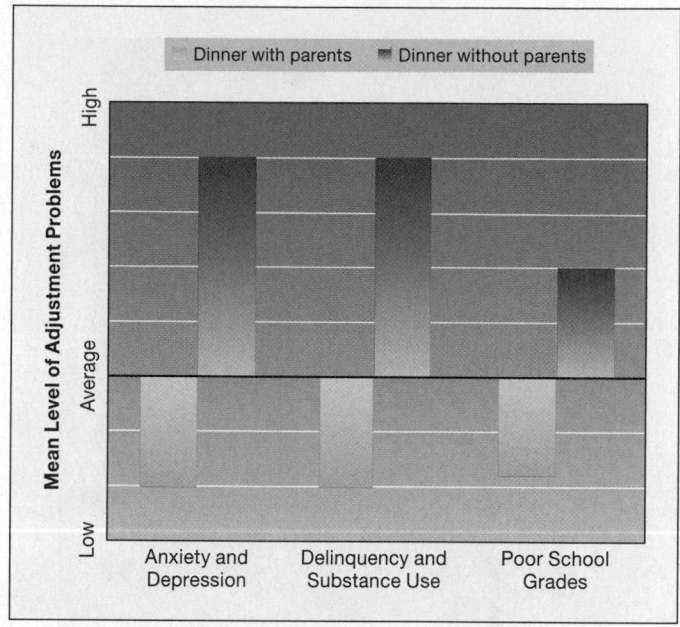

FIGURE 2.7   Relationship of regularly eating dinner with parents to affluent youths' adjustment problems. Compared with sixth graders who often ate dinner with their parents, those who rarely did so were far more likely to display anxiety and depression, delinquency and substance use, and poor school grades, even after many other aspects of parenting were controlled. In this study, frequent family mealtimes also protected low-SES youths from delinquency and substance use and from classroom learning problems. (Based on Luthar & Latendresse, 2005b.)

Homelessness poses enormous challenges for maintaining positive family relationships and physical and mental health. This mother and her three children prepare to move out of the motel room they share with her boyfriend and father.

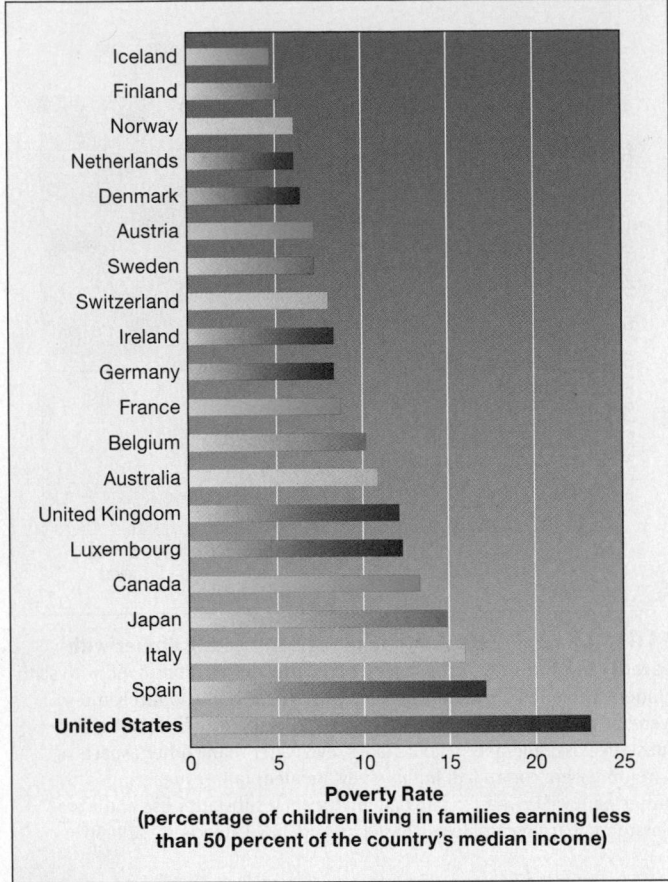

FIGURE 2.8 **Child poverty in 20 of the world's economically advanced nations.** Among the countries listed, the United States ranks last in having the highest percentage of children and youths under age 18 living in families with incomes below 50 percent of the national median income. (From UNICEF (2012). "Measuring Child Poverty: New League Tables of Child Poverty in the World's Rich Countries," *Innocenti Report Card No. 10*, UNICEF Innocenti Research Centre, Florence. Adapted by permission of UNICEF Innocenti Research Centre.)

live in deep poverty (at less than half the federal poverty threshold). In contrast, in most northern and central European countries, child poverty rates have remained below 10 percent for several decades (see Figure 2.8), and extreme child poverty is rare (UNICEF, 2013b). The earlier poverty begins, the deeper it is, and the longer it lasts, the more devastating are its effects. Children of poverty are more likely than other children to suffer from lifelong poor physical health, persistent deficits in cognitive development and academic achievement, high school dropout, mental illness, and impulsivity, aggression, and antisocial behavior (Morgan et al., 2009; Ryan, Fauth, & Brooks-Gunn, 2006; Yoshikawa, Aber, & Beardslee, 2012).

The constant stressors that accompany poverty gradually weaken the family system. Poor families have many daily hassles—the car breaking down, loss of welfare and unemployment payments, basic services—phone, TV, electricity, hot water—being shut off because of inability to pay bills, and limited or uncertain access to food—to name just a few. When daily crises arise, family members become depressed, irritable, and distracted; hostile interactions increase; and children's development suffers (Conger & Donnellan, 2007; Kohen et al., 2008). Negative outcomes are especially severe in single-parent families and families who must live in poor housing and dangerous neighborhoods—conditions that make everyday existence even more difficult while reducing social supports that help people cope with economic hardship (Hart, Atkins, & Matsuba, 2008; Leventhal & Brooks-Gunn, 2003).

A related problem—one that has become more common in the past 30 years—has reduced the life chances of many children. From 2.5 to 3.5 million people in the United States experience homelessness in a given year. The majority are adults on their own, many of whom suffer from serious mental illness. But about 40 percent of the homeless are children and youths (National Coalition for the Homeless, 2009). The rise in homelessness is mostly due to two factors: a decline in the availability of government-supported low-cost housing and an increase in poverty.

Most homeless families consist of women with children under age 5. Besides health problems (which affect the majority of homeless people), many homeless children suffer from developmental delays and chronic emotional stress due to their harsh, insecure daily lives (Kilmer et al., 2012). An estimated 25 to 30 percent of those who are old enough do not go to school. Those who do enroll achieve less well than other poverty-stricken children because of poor attendance, frequent moves from school to school due to time-limited shelters, and health and emotional difficulties (Cutuli et al., 2010; Obradović et al., 2009).

Although gaps in overall health, achievement, and emotional adjustment between poverty-stricken children and their economically better-off peers are substantial, a considerable number of children from financially stressed families fare well. In Chapter 1, we discussed a variety of factors that promote resilience in the face of environmental risks to development (see pages 10–11).

A host of interventions aimed at helping children surmount the developmental risks of poverty exist. In one, poverty-stricken families with preschool through adolescent children were randomly assigned to a family strengthening intervention or a no-intervention control group. The intervention involved 14 hours of intensive parent training devoted to learning about and practicing effective strategies for coping with stress, solving everyday problems, and engaging in positive family communication and parenting. Compared with controls, participating parents reported an improved capacity to manage stressful situations, lessening of economic strain, warmer parent–child interaction, and fewer depressive symptoms—benefits that translated into a reduction in child internalizing and externalizing difficulties (Wadsworth et al., 2013). Gains in family functioning, parent mental health, and children's adjustment were still evident 18 months after the intervention ended.

Some interventions, like the example just described, address family functioning and parenting skills, while others directly target children's academic, emotional, and social skills in preschools, elementary schools, and secondary schools. And an increasing number of programs recognize that because poverty-stricken children often experience multiple adversities, they benefit most from efforts that are multifaceted—that focus on family, parenting, and children's needs at once (Kagan, 2013a). We will discuss many such interventions, along with their impact on children's cognitive, emotional, and social development, later in this book.

Beyond the Family: Neighborhoods and Schools

As the concepts of *mesosystem* and *exosystem* in ecological systems theory make clear, connections between family and community are vital for children's well-being. From our discussion of poverty, perhaps you can see why: In poverty-stricken areas, community life is usually disrupted. Families move often, parks and playgrounds are in disarray, and community centers providing leisure-time activities do not exist. In poor urban neighborhoods, family violence, child abuse and neglect, children's problem behavior, youth antisocial activity, and adult criminal behavior are widespread (Chen, Howard, & Brooks-Gunn, 2011; Ingoldsby et al., 2012). And in poor rural communities—like the small town where Kaylie, Tyler, and their mother live—family isolation and scarcity of supportive services are especially high (Vernon-Feagans & Cox, 2013). In contrast, strong family ties to the community—as indicated by frequent contact with friends and relatives, organized youth activities, and regular church, synagogue, or mosque attendance—reduce family stress and enhance adjustment.

NEIGHBORHOODS Let's look closely at the functions of communities in the lives of children by beginning with the neighborhood. **TAKE A MOMENT...** What were your childhood experiences like in the yards, streets, parks, and community centers surrounding your home? How did you spend your time, whom did you get to know, and how important were these moments to you?

Neighborhoods offer resources and social ties that play an important part in children's development. In several studies, low-SES families were randomly assigned vouchers to move out of public housing into neighborhoods varying widely in affluence. Compared with their peers who remained in poverty-stricken areas, children and youths who moved into low-poverty neighborhoods showed substantially better physical and mental health and school achievement (Goering, 2003; Leventhal & Brooks-Gunn, 2003; Leventhal & Dupéré, 2011).

Neighborhood resources have a greater impact on economically disadvantaged than on well-to-do young people. Higher-SES families depend less on their immediate surroundings for social support, education, and leisure pursuits. They can afford to transport their children to lessons and entertainment and, if necessary, to better-quality schools in distant parts of the community. In low-income neighborhoods, in-school and after-school programs that substitute for lack of other resources by providing art, music, sports, scouting, and other enrichment activities staffed by caring adults are associated with improved school performance and a reduction in emotional and behavior problems in middle childhood (Kataoka & Vandell, 2013; Peters, Petrunka, & Arnold, 2003; Vandell, Reisner, & Pierce, 2007). Neighborhood organizations, such as religious youth groups and special-interest clubs, contribute to favorable development in adolescence, including increased

Elementary school students learn chess in an after-school program. Neighborhood and school resources are especially important for economically disadvantaged children and families.

LOOK and **LISTEN**

Ask several parents to list their school-age children's regular lessons and other enrichment activities. Then inquire about home and neighborhood factors that either encourage or impede their children's participation.

self-confidence, school achievement, and educational aspirations (Barnes et al., 2007; Gonzales et al., 1996).

Yet in dangerous, disorganized neighborhoods, high-quality activities for children and adolescents are usually scarce. Even when they are available, crime and social disorder limit young people's access, and attendance is low (Dynarski et al., 2004). Furthermore, home and neighborhood obstacles often combine to reduce involvement. Parents overwhelmed by financial and other stressors are less likely to provide the stimulation and encouragement that motivate their children to participate (Kohen et al., 2008). In an investigation of a large sample of elementary school students diverse in SES and neighborhood residence, those living in the least stimulating homes and the most chaotic neighborhoods were least likely to participate in after-school and community-center enrichment activities (Dearing et al., 2009). Thus, the neediest children were especially likely to miss out on these development-enhancing experiences.

Just how do family–neighborhood ties reduce parenting stress and promote child development? One answer lies in their provision of *social support*, which leads to the following benefits:

- *Parental self-worth.* A neighbor or relative who listens and tries to relieve a parent's concern enhances her self-esteem. The parent, in turn, is likely to interact in a more sensitive and involved manner with her children.
- *Parental access to valuable information and services.* A friend who suggests where a parent might find a job, housing, and affordable child care and youth activities helps make the multiple roles of spouse, parent, and provider easier to fulfill.
- *Child-rearing controls and role models.* Friends, relatives, and other community members may encourage and demonstrate effective parenting practices and discourage ineffective practices.
- *Direct assistance with child rearing.* As children and adolescents participate in their parents' social networks and in neighborhood settings, other adults can influence children through warmth, stimulation, and exposure to a wider array of competent models. In this way, family–neighborhood ties can reduce the impact of ineffective parenting (Silk et al., 2004). Nearby adults can also intervene when they see young people skipping school or behaving antisocially.

The Better Beginnings, Better Futures Project of Ontario, Canada, is a government-sponsored set of community enrichment programs aimed at preventing the dire consequences of home and neighborhood poverty, including child and adolescent school failure and antisocial activity. The most successful of these efforts, using a local elementary school as its base, provided children with in-class and summer enrichment activities (Gershoff & Aber, 2006; Peters, 2005; Peters, Petrunka, & Arnold, 2003). Workers also visited each child's parents regularly, informed them about community resources, and encouraged their involvement in the child's school and neighborhood life.

Evaluations as children reached grades 3, 6, and 9 revealed wide-ranging benefits compared with children and families living in other impoverished neighborhoods without this set of programs (Peters et al., 2010). Among these were parents' sense of improved family functioning and child rearing, and gains in children's academic achievement and social adjustment, including positive relationships with peers and adults and a reduction in emotional and behavior problems.

SCHOOLS   Unlike the informal worlds of family and neighborhood, the school is a formal institution designed to transmit knowledge and skills that children need to become productive members of their society. Children in the developed world spend many hours in school—6 hours a day, 5 days a week, 36 weeks a year—a total of about 14,000 hours, on average, by high school graduation. And today, because many children younger than age 5 attend "school-like" child-care centers or preschools, the impact of schooling begins even earlier and is more powerful than these figures suggest.

Schools are complex social systems that affect many aspects of development. Schools differ in their physical environments—student body size, number of children per class, and space available for work and play. They also vary in their educational philosophies—whether teachers regard children as passive learners to be molded by adult instruction; as active, curious beings who determine their own learning; or as collaborative partners assisted by adult experts, who guide their mastery of new skills. Finally, the social life of schools varies—for example, in the degree to which students cooperate or compete; in the extent to which students of different abilities, SES, and ethnic backgrounds learn together; and in whether classrooms, hallways, and play yards are safe, humane settings or are riddled with violence (Evans, 2006). We will discuss each of these aspects of schooling in later chapters.

Regular parent–school contact supports development at all ages. Students whose parents are involved in school activities and attend parent–teacher conferences show better academic achievement. Higher-SES parents, whose backgrounds and values are similar to those of teachers, are more likely to make phone calls and visits to school. In contrast, low-SES and ethnic minority parents often feel uncomfortable about coming to school, and daily stressors reduce the energy they have for school involvement (Grant & Ray, 2010; Reschly & Christenson, 2009). Teachers and administrators must take extra steps with low-SES and ethnic minority families and in urban areas to build supportive family–school ties.

When these efforts lead to cultures of good parenting and teaching, they deliver an extra boost to children's well-being. For example, students attending schools with many highly involved parents achieve especially well (Darling & Steinberg, 1997). And when excellent education becomes a team effort of teachers, administrators, and community members, its effects on learning are stronger and reach many more students (Hauser-Cram et al., 2006).

Schools are complex social systems that powerfully affect development. By encouraging students' active participation, this second-grade teacher promotes mastery of new knowledge and skills along with enthusiastic attitudes toward learning.

LOOK and **LISTEN**

Ask a teacher whose classroom has many students from low-SES families what percentage of parents attend parent–teacher conferences. What steps does the teacher take to promote parent–school involvement?

The Cultural Context

Our discussion in Chapter 1 emphasized that child development can be fully understood only when viewed in its larger cultural context. In the following sections, we expand on this important theme by taking up the role of the *macrosystem* in development. First, we discuss ways that cultural values and practices affect environmental contexts for development. Then we consider how healthy development depends on laws and government programs that shield children from harm and foster their well-being.

CULTURAL VALUES AND PRACTICES   Cultures shape family interaction, school experiences, and community settings beyond the home—in short, all aspects of daily life. Many of us remain blind to aspects of our own cultural heritage until we see them in relation to the practices of others.

TAKE A MOMENT... Consider the question, Who should be responsible for rearing young children? How would you answer it? Here are some typical responses from our students: "If parents decide to have a baby, then they should be ready to care for it." "Most people are not happy about others intruding into family life." These statements reflect a widely held opinion in the United States—that the care and rearing of young children, and paying for that care, are the duty of parents, and only parents. This view has a long history—one in which independence, self-reliance, and the privacy of family life emerged as central American values (Halfon & McLearn, 2002). It is one reason, among others, that the public has been slow to endorse government-supported benefits for all families, such as high-quality child care and paid employment leave for meeting family needs. And it has also contributed to the large number of U.S. children who remain poor, even though their parents are gainfully employed (Gruendel & Aber, 2007; UNICEF, 2012).

Cultural Influences

The African-American Extended Family

The African-American extended family can be traced to the African heritage of most black Americans. In many African societies, newly married couples do not start their own households. Instead, they live with a large extended family, which assists its members with all aspects of daily life. This tradition of maintaining a broad network of kinship ties traveled to North America during the period of slavery. Since then, it has served as a protective shield against the destructive impact of poverty and racial prejudice on African-American family life. Today, more black than white adults have relatives other than their own children living in the same household. African-American parents also live closer to kin, often establish family-like relationships with friends and neighbors, see more relatives during the week, and perceive them as more important in their lives (Boyd-Franklin, 2006; McAdoo & Younge, 2009).

By providing emotional support and sharing essential resources, the African-American extended family helps reduce the stress of poverty and single parenthood. Extended-family members often help with child rearing. As long as relationships with extended kin are warm, adolescent mothers of infants are more likely to complete high school and get a job than mothers living on their own—factors that benefit

children's well-being (Gordon, Chase-Lansdale, & Brooks-Gunn, 2004).

For single mothers rearing children and adolescents, extended-family living continues to be associated with more positive mother–child interaction. Even after establishing their own home, single mothers often invite family members or close friends to live with them. This kinship support increases the likelihood of effective parenting, which is related to gains in children's academic performance, social skills, and emotional well-being and to reduced antisocial behavior (Simons et al., 2006; Taylor, 2010; Washington, Gleeson, & Rulison, 2013).

Finally, the extended family plays an important role in transmitting African-American culture. Compared with nuclear-family households (which include only parents and their children), extended-family arrangements place more emphasis on cooperation and on moral and religious values. And older black adults, such as grandparents and great-grandparents, regard educating children about their African heritage as especially important (Mosely-Howard & Evans, 2000; Taylor, 2000). Family reunions—sometimes

Three generations celebrate together at a neighborhood festival. Strong bonds with extended family members have helped protect many African-American children against the destructive impact of poverty and racial prejudice.

held in grandparents' and great-grandparents' hometowns—are especially common among African Americans, giving young people a strong sense of their roots (Boyd-Franklin, 2006). These influences strengthen family bonds, enhance children's development, and increase the chances that the extended-family lifestyle will carry over to the next generation.

Although the culture as a whole may value independence and privacy, not all citizens share the same values. Some belong to **subcultures**—groups of people with beliefs and customs that differ from those of the larger culture. Many ethnic minority groups in the United States have cooperative family structures, which help protect their members from the harmful effects of poverty. As the Cultural Influences box above indicates, the African-American tradition of **extended-family households,** in which parent and child live with one or more adult relatives, is a vital feature of black family life that has promoted resilience in its members, despite a long history of prejudice and economic deprivation.

Active, involved extended families also characterize other minorities, such as Asian, Native-American, and Hispanic subcultures. Within these families, grandparents play meaningful roles in guiding younger generations; adults who face employment, marital, or child-rearing difficulties receive assistance and emotional support; and caregiving is enhanced for children and the elderly (Jones & Lindahl, 2011; Mutchler, Baker, & Lee, 2007). In Hispanic extended families, for example, grandparents are even more likely to share in rearing young children than are African-American grandparents—a collaborative parenting arrangement that has physical and emotional health benefits for grandparents, parents, and children alike (Goodman & Silverstein, 2006). A likely reason for such far-reaching effects is that intergenerational shared parenting is consistent with the Hispanic cultural ideal of *familism,* which places an especially high priority on close, harmonious family bonds, frequent contact, and meeting family needs.

Our discussion so far reflects two broad sets of values on which cultures and subcultures are commonly compared: *collectivism* versus *individualism* (Triandis, 2005; Triandis & Gelfand, 2012). In cultures that emphasize collectivism, people stress group goals over individual goals and value *interdependent* qualities, such as social harmony, obligations and responsibility to others, and collaborative endeavors. In cultures that emphasize individualism, people are largely concerned with their own personal needs and value *independence*— personal exploration, discovery, achievement, and choice in relationships. Though the most common basis for comparing cultures, the collectivism–individualism distinction is controversial because both sets of values exist, in varying mixtures, in most cultures. In addition, cultural values are complex, differing in myriad additional ways (Chen & Eisenberg, 2012; Taras et al., 2014). Nevertheless, consistent cross-national differences in collectivism–individualism remain, with important consequences: The United States is more individualistic than most Western European countries, which place greater weight on collectivism. These values powerfully affect a nation's approach to protecting the well-being of its children and families.

PUBLIC POLICIES AND CHILD DEVELOPMENT When widespread social problems arise, such as poverty, homelessness, hunger, and disease, nations attempt to solve them by developing **public policies**—laws and government programs designed to improve current conditions. For example, when poverty increases and families become homeless, a country might decide to build more low-cost housing, provide economic aid to homeowners having difficulty making mortgage payments, raise the minimum wage, and increase welfare benefits. When reports indicate that many children are not achieving well in school, federal and state governments might grant more tax money to school districts, strengthen teacher preparation, and make sure that help reaches children who need it most.

Nevertheless, U.S. public policies safeguarding children and youths have lagged behind policies in other developed nations. As Table 2.5 reveals, the United States does not rank well on any key measure of children's health and well-being.

The problems of children and youths extend beyond the indicators in Table 2.5. The Affordable Care Act, signed into law in 2010, extended government-supported health insurance to all children in low-income families. But expanded coverage for low-income adults,

TABLE 2.5	How Does the United States Compare to Other Nations on Indicators of Children's Health and Well-Being?		
INDICATOR		**U.S. RANK**[a]	**SOME COUNTRIES THE UNITED STATES TRAILS**
Childhood poverty (among 20 economically advanced nations with similar standards of living)		20th	Canada, Iceland, Germany, United Kingdom, Norway, Sweden, Spain[b]
Infant deaths in the first year of life (worldwide)		37th	Canada, Greece, Hungary, Ireland, Singapore, Spain
Teenage birth rate (among 28 industrialized nations)		28th	Australia, Canada, Czech Republic, Denmark, Hungary, Iceland, Poland, Slovakia
Public expenditure on education as a percentage of gross domestic product[c] (among 30 industrialized nations considered)		13th	Belgium, France, Iceland, New Zealand, Portugal, Spain, Sweden
Public expenditure on early childhood education and child care as a percentage of gross domestic product (among 36 industrialized nations considered)		32th	Austria, Germany, Italy, Netherlands, France, Sweden
Public expenditure on health as a percentage of total health expenditure, public plus private (among 34 industrialized nations considered)		34th	Austria, Australia, Canada, France, Hungary, Iceland, Switzerland, New Zealand

[a]1 = highest, or best, rank.

[b]U.S. childhood poverty rates greatly exceed poverty in these nations, which have standards of living similar to the United States (see Figure 2.8 on page 74).

[c]Gross domestic product is the value of all goods and services produced by a nation during a specified time period. It provides an overall measure of a nation's wealth.

Sources: OECD, 2013c, 2014; UNICEF, 2012; U.S. Census Bureau, 2014b; U.S. Department of Education, 2014a.

Upward Bound, a U.S. federally-funded enrichment program for high school students, serves as a pathway to college for many low-income students. Favorable public policies are vital for solving social problems and safeguarding development.

including parents, is optional for the states. Currently, 19 states have chosen not to participate, leaving millions of low-income parents without an affordable coverage option. Largely because uninsured parents lack knowledge of how to enroll their children, 11 percent of children eligible for the federally supported Children's Health Insurance Program (CHIP)—more than 5 million—do not receive coverage (Kaiser Family Foundation, 2014). Furthermore, the United States has been slow to move toward national standards and funding for child care. Affordable care is in short supply, and much of it is substandard in quality (Phillips & Lowenstein, 2011). In families affected by divorce, weak enforcement of child support payments heightens poverty in mother-headed households. When non-college-bound young people finish high school, many lack the vocational preparation they need to contribute fully to society. And 8 percent of 16- to 24-year olds who dropped out of high school have not returned to earn a diploma (U.S. Department of Education, 2014a).

Why have attempts to help children and youths been difficult to realize in the United States? A complex set of political and economic forces is involved. Cultural values of self-reliance and privacy have made government hesitant to become involved in family matters. Furthermore, good social programs are expensive, and they must compete for a fair share of a country's economic resources. Children can easily remain unrecognized in this process because they cannot vote or speak out to protect their own interests (Ripple & Zigler, 2003). Instead, they must rely on the goodwill of others to make them an important government priority.

Without vigilance from child advocates, policies directed at solving a particular social problem can work at cross-purposes with children's well-being, leaving them in dire straits or even worsening their condition. For example, U.S. welfare policy aimed at returning welfare recipients to the workforce—by reducing or terminating their welfare benefits after 24 continuous months—can either help or harm children, depending on whether it lifts a family out of poverty. When welfare-to-work reduces financial strain, it relieves maternal stress, improves quality of parenting, and is associated with cognitive gains and a reduction in child behavior problems (Dunifon, Kalil, & Danziger, 2003; Gennetian & Morris, 2003; Jackson, Bentler, & Franke, 2006). In contrast, former welfare recipients who must take very low-paying jobs that perpetuate poverty often engage in harsh, coercive parenting and have poorly adjusted children (Smith et al., 2001).

LOOKING TOWARD THE FUTURE Public policies aimed at fostering children's development can be justified on two grounds. The first is that children are the future—the parents, workers, and citizens of tomorrow. Investing in children yields valuable returns to a nation's quality of life. Second, child-oriented policies can be defended on humanitarian grounds—children's basic rights as human beings.

In 1989, the U.N. General Assembly, with the assistance of experts from many child-related fields, drew up the *Convention on the Rights of the Child,* a legal agreement among nations that commits each cooperating country to work toward guaranteeing environments that foster children's development, protect them from harm, and enhance their community participation and self-determination. Examples of rights include the highest attainable standard of health; an adequate standard of living; free and compulsory education; a happy, understanding, and loving family life; protection from all forms of abuse and neglect; and freedom of thought, conscience, and religion, subject to appropriate parental guidance and national law.

Although the United States played a key role in drawing up the Convention, it is one of only two countries in the world whose legislature has not yet ratified it (the other is Somalia).

American individualism has stood in the way (Scherrer, 2012). Opponents maintain that the Convention's provisions would shift the burden of child rearing from the family to the state.

Although the worrisome state of many children and families persists, efforts are being made to improve their condition. Throughout this book, we will discuss many successful programs that could be expanded. Also, growing awareness of the gap between what we know and what we do to better children's lives has led experts in child development to join with concerned citizens as advocates for more effective policies. As a result, several influential interest groups devoted to the well-being of children have emerged.

In the United States, one of the most vigorous is the Children's Defense Fund—a private, nonprofit organization founded by Marian Wright Edelman in 1973—that engages in research, public education, legal action, drafting of legislation, congressional testimony, and community organizing. It also publishes many reports on U.S. children's condition, government-sponsored programs that serve children and families, and proposals for improving those programs. To learn more about the Children's Defense Fund, visit its website at *www.childrensdefense.org.* Another energetic advocacy organization is the National Center for Children in Poverty, dedicated to advancing the economic security, health, and welfare of U.S. children in low-income families by informing policy makers of relevant research. To explore its activities, visit *www.nccp.org.*

Besides strong advocacy, public policies that enhance child development depend on policy-relevant research that documents needs and evaluates programs to spark improvements. Today, more researchers are collaborating with community and government agencies to enhance the social relevance of their investigations. They are also doing a better job of disseminating their findings to the public in easily understandable, compelling ways, through reports to government officials, websites aimed at increasing public understanding, and collaborations with the media to ensure accurate and effective reporting in news stories and radio and television documentaries (Shonkoff & Bales, 2011). In these ways, researchers are helping to create the sense of immediacy about the condition of children and families that is necessary to spur a society into action.

Ask Yourself

- **REVIEW** Links between family and community are essential for children's well-being. Provide examples and research findings from our discussion that support this idea.

- **CONNECT** How does poverty affect the functioning of the family system, placing all aspects of development at risk?

- **APPLY** Check your local newspaper or one or two national news websites to see how often articles appear on the condition of children and families. Why is it important for researchers to communicate with the general public about children's needs?

- **REFLECT** Do you agree with the widespread American sentiment that government should not become involved in family life? Explain.

Understanding the Relationship Between Heredity and Environment

2.6 Explain the various ways heredity and environment may combine to influence complex traits.

Throughout this chapter, we have discussed a wide variety of genetic and environmental influences, each of which has the power to alter the course of development. Yet children who are born into the same family (and who therefore share both genes and environments) are often quite different in characteristics. We also know that some children are affected more than others by their homes, neighborhoods, and communities. In some cases, a child who is given many advantages nevertheless does poorly, while another, though exposed to unfavorable rearing conditions, does well. How do scientists explain the impact of heredity and environment when they seem to work in so many different ways?

Children vary widely in intellectual abilities and personality traits. Contemporary researchers seek to clarify how heredity and environment jointly contribute to individual differences in these complex characteristics.

Behavioral genetics is a field devoted to uncovering the contributions of nature and nurture to this diversity in human traits and abilities. All contemporary researchers agree that both heredity and environment are involved in every aspect of development. But for polygenic traits (those due to many genes) such as intelligence and personality, scientists are a long way from knowing the precise hereditary influences involved. Although—as indicated earlier in this chapter—they are making progress in identifying variations in DNA sequences associated with complex traits, so far these genetic markers explain only a small amount of variation in human behavior, and a minority of cases of most psychological disorders (Plomin, 2013; Psychiatric Genomics Consortium, 2013). For the most part, scientists are still limited to investigating the impact of genes on complex characteristics indirectly.

Some believe that it is useful and possible to answer the question of *how much each factor contributes* to differences among children. A growing consensus, however, regards that question as unanswerable. These investigators believe that heredity and environment are inseparable (Gottlieb, Wahlsten, & Lickliter, 2006; Lerner & Overton, 2008). The important question, they maintain, is *how nature and nurture work together*. Let's consider each position in turn.

The Question, "How Much?"

To infer the role of heredity in complex human characteristics, researchers use special methods, the most common being the *heritability estimate*. Let's look closely at the information this procedure yields, along with its limitations.

HERITABILITY **Heritability estimates** measure the extent to which individual differences in complex traits in a specific population are due to genetic factors. We will take a brief look at heritability findings on intelligence and personality here and will return to them in later chapters, when we consider these topics in greater detail. Heritability estimates are obtained from **kinship studies,** which compare the characteristics of family members. The most common type of kinship study compares identical twins, who share all their genes, with fraternal twins, who share only some. If people who are genetically more alike are also more similar in intelligence and personality, then the researcher assumes that heredity plays an important role.

Kinship studies of intelligence provide some of the most controversial findings in the field of child development. Some experts claim a strong genetic influence, whereas others believe that heredity is barely involved. Currently, most kinship findings support a moderate role for heredity. When many twin studies are examined, correlations between the scores of identical twins are consistently higher than those of fraternal twins. In a summary of more than 10,000 twin pairs, the average correlation was .86 for identical twins and .60 for fraternal twins (Plomin & Spinath, 2004).

Researchers use a complex statistical procedure to compare these correlations, arriving at a heritability estimate ranging from 0 to 1.00. The value for intelligence is about .50 for child and adolescent twin samples in Western industrialized nations. This suggests that differences in genetic makeup explain half the variation in intelligence. Adopted children's mental test scores are more strongly related to their biological parents' scores than to those of their adoptive parents, offering further support for the role of heredity (Petrill & Deater-Deckard, 2004).

Heritability research also reveals that genetic factors are important in personality. For frequently studied traits, such as sociability, anxiety, agreeableness, and activity level, heritability estimates obtained on child, adolescent, and young adult twins are moderate, in the .40s and .50s (Caspi & Shiner, 2006; Rothbart & Bates, 2006; Wright et al., 2008).

Twin studies of schizophrenia, bipolar disorder, and autism generally yield high heritabilities, above .70. The role of heredity in antisocial behavior and major depression, though apparent, is less strong, with heritabilities in the .30s and .40s (Ronald & Hoekstra, 2014; Sullivan, Daley, & Donovan, 2012). Again, adoption studies support these results. Biological relatives of adoptees with schizophrenia, bipolar disorder, or autism are more likely than adoptive relatives to share the same disorder (Plomin, DeFries, & Knopik, 2013).

LIMITATIONS OF HERITABILITY The accuracy of heritability estimates depends on the extent to which the twin pairs studied reflect genetic and environmental variation in the population. Within a population in which all people have very similar home, school, and community experiences, individual differences in intelligence and personality would be largely genetic, and heritability estimates would be close to 1.00. Conversely, the more environments vary, the more likely they are to account for individual differences, yielding lower heritability estimates. In twin studies, most twin pairs are reared together under highly similar conditions. Even when separated twins are available for study, social service agencies have often placed them in advantaged homes that are alike in many ways (Rutter et al., 2001). Because the environments of most twin pairs are less diverse than those of the general population, heritability estimates are likely to exaggerate the role of heredity.

Heritability estimates are controversial measures because they can easily be misapplied. For example, high heritabilities have been used to suggest that ethnic differences in intelligence, such as the poorer performance of black children compared to white children, have a genetic basis (Jensen, 1969, 2001; Rushton, 2012; Rushton & Jensen, 2006). Yet this line of reasoning is widely regarded as incorrect. Heritabilities computed on mostly white twin samples do not tell us what causes test score differences between ethnic groups. We have already seen that large economic and cultural differences are involved. In Chapter 12, we will discuss research indicating that when black children are adopted into economically advantaged homes at an early age, their scores are well above average and substantially higher than those of children growing up in impoverished families.

Perhaps the most serious criticism of heritability estimates has to do with their limited usefulness. Though confirming heredity, these estimates offer no precise information on how intelligence and personality develop or how children might respond to environments designed to help them develop as far as possible (Baltes, Lindenberger, & Staudinger, 2006). Indeed, the heritability of children's intelligence increases as parental education and income increase—that is, as children grow up in conditions that allow them to make the most of their genetic endowment. In impoverished environments, children are prevented from realizing their potential. Consequently, enhancing these children's experiences through interventions—such as parent education and high-quality preschool or child care—has a greater impact on development (Bronfenbrenner & Morris, 2006; Phillips & Lowenstein, 2011).

Kasia Ofmanski, of Warsaw, Poland, holds photos of Nina (right), the identical twin from whom she was mistakenly separated at birth, and Edyta (left), who was assumed to be her twin and who grew up with her. When the twins first met at age 17, Kasia exclaimed, "She's just like me." They found many similarities: Both were physically active, extroverted, and earned similar grades in school. Clearly heredity contributes to personality traits, but generalizing from twin evidence to the population is controversial.

The Question, "How?"

Today, most researchers view development as the result of a dynamic interplay between heredity and environment. How do nature and nurture work together? Several concepts shed light on this question.

GENE–ENVIRONMENT INTERACTION The first of these ideas is **gene–environment interaction,** which means that because of their genetic makeup, individuals differ in their responsiveness to qualities of the environment (Rutter, 2011). Let's explore this idea in Figure 2.9 on page 84. Gene–environment interaction can apply to any characteristic; here it is illustrated for intelligence. Notice that when environments vary from extremely unstimulating to highly enriched, Ben's intelligence increases steadily, Linda's rises sharply and then falls

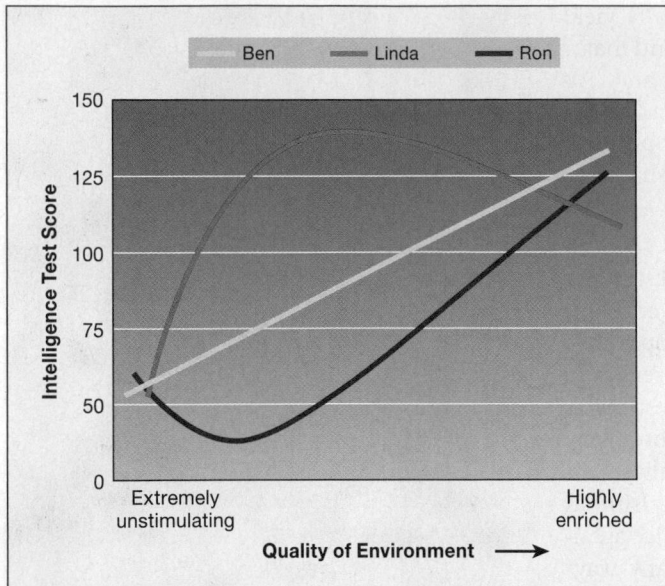

FIGURE 2.9   Gene–environment interaction, illustrated for intelligence by three children who differ in responsiveness to quality of the environment. As environments vary from extremely unstimulating to highly enriched, Ben's intelligence test score increases steadily, Linda's rises sharply and then falls off, and Ron's begins to increase only after the environment becomes modestly stimulating.

This mother shares her love of the piano with her daughter, who also may have inherited her mother's musical talent. When heredity and environment are correlated, the influence of one cannot be separated from the influence of the other.

off, and Ron's begins to increase only after the environment becomes modestly stimulating.

Gene–environment interaction highlights two important points. First, it shows that because each of us has a unique genetic makeup, we respond differently to the same environment. Notice in Figure 2.9 how a poor environment results in similarly low scores for all three individuals. But when the environment provides an intermediate level of stimulation, Linda is by far the best-performing child. And in a highly enriched environment, Ben does best, followed by Ron, both of whom now outperform Linda. Second, sometimes different gene–environment combinations can make two people look the same! For example, if Linda is reared in a minimally stimulating environment, her score will be about 100—average for children in general. Ben and Ron can also obtain this score, but to do so, they must grow up in a fairly enriched home (Gottlieb, Wahlsten, & Lickliter, 2006).

Recently, researchers have made strides in identifying gene–environment interactions in personality development. In Chapter 7 we will see that young children with a gene that increases their risk of an emotionally reactive temperament respond especially strongly to variations in parenting quality (Pluess & Belsky, 2011). When parenting is favorable, they gain control over their emotions and adjust as well as or better than other children. But when parenting is unfavorable, they become increasingly irritable, angry, and poorly adjusted, more so than children not at genetic risk.

GENE–ENVIRONMENT CORRELATION   A major problem in trying to separate heredity and environment is that they are often correlated (Rutter, 2011; Scarr & McCartney, 1983). According to the concept of **gene–environment correlation,** our genes influence the environments to which we are exposed. The way this happens changes with age.

Passive and Evocative Correlation   At younger ages, two types of gene–environment correlation are common. The first is called *passive* correlation because the child has no control over it. Early on, parents provide environments influenced by their own heredity. For example, parents who are good athletes emphasize outdoor activities and enroll their children in swimming and gymnastics. Besides being exposed to an "athletic environment," the children may have inherited their parents' athletic ability. As a result, they are likely to become good athletes for both genetic and environmental reasons.

The second type of gene–environment correlation is *evocative.* Children evoke responses that are influenced by the child's heredity, and these responses strengthen the child's original style. For example, an active, friendly baby is likely to receive more social stimulation than a passive, quiet infant. And a cooperative, attentive child probably receives more patient and sensitive interactions from parents than an inattentive, distractible child. In support of this idea, the less genetically alike siblings are, the more their parents treat them differently, in both warmth and negativity. Thus, parents' treatment of identical twins is highly similar, whereas their treatment of fraternal twins and nontwin biological siblings is only moderately so. And little resemblance exists in parents' warm and negative interactions with unrelated stepsiblings (see Figure 2.10) (Reiss, 2003).

Active Correlation   At older ages, *active* gene–environment correlation becomes common. As children extend their experiences beyond the immediate family and are given the freedom to make more choices, they actively seek environments that fit with their genetic tendencies. The well-coordinated, muscular child spends more time at after-school sports, the musically talented youngster joins the school orchestra and practices his violin, and the intellectually curious child is a familiar patron at her local library.

This tendency to actively choose environments that complement our heredity is called **niche-picking** (Scarr & McCartney, 1983). Infants and young children cannot do much niche-picking because adults select environments for them. In contrast, older children and adolescents are much more in charge of their environments.

Niche-picking explains why pairs of identical twins reared apart during childhood and later reunited may find, to their surprise, that they have similar hobbies, food preferences, and vocations—a trend that is especially marked when twins' environmental opportunities are similar (Plomin, 1994). Niche-picking also helps us understand why identical twins become somewhat more alike, and fraternal twins and adopted siblings less alike, in intelligence with age (Bouchard, 2004; Loehlin, Horn, & Willerman, 1997). And niche-picking sheds light on why adolescent identical twin pairs—far more often than same-sex fraternal pairs, ordinary siblings, and adopted siblings—report similar stressful life events influenced by personal decisions and actions, such as failing a course, quitting a job, or getting in trouble for drugtaking (Bemmels et al., 2008).

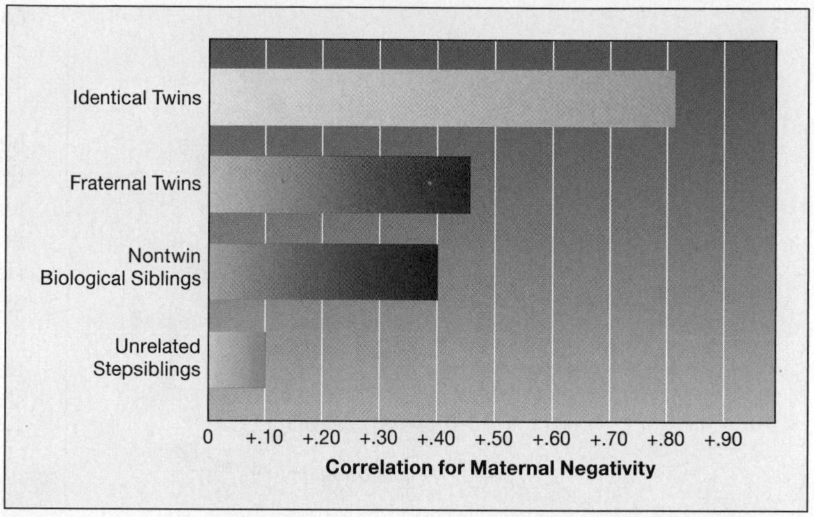

The influence of heredity and environment is not constant but changes over time. With age, genetic factors may become more important in influencing the environments we experience and choose for ourselves.

ENVIRONMENTAL INFLUENCES ON GENE EXPRESSION Notice how, in the concepts just considered, heredity is granted priority. In gene–environment interaction, it affects responsiveness to particular environments. Similarly, gene–environment correlation is viewed as driven by genetics, in that children's genetic makeup causes them to receive, evoke, or seek experiences that actualize their inborn tendencies (Plomin, 2009; Rutter, 2011).

A growing number of researchers take issue with the supremacy of heredity, arguing that it does not dictate children's experiences or development in a rigid way. In one study, boys with a genetic tendency toward antisocial behavior (based on the presence of a gene on the X chromosome known to predispose both animals and humans to aggression) were no more aggressive than boys without this gene, *unless* they also had a history of severe child abuse (Caspi et al., 2002). Boys with and without the gene did not differ in their experience of abuse, indicating that the "aggressive genotype" did not increase exposure to abuse. And in a large Finnish adoption study, children whose biological mothers had schizophrenia but who were being reared by healthy adoptive parents showed little mental illness—no more than a control group with healthy biological and adoptive parents. In contrast, schizophrenia and other psychological impairments piled up in adoptees whose biological and adoptive parents were both disturbed (Tienari et al., 2003; Tienari, Wahlberg, & Wynne, 2006).

Furthermore, parents and other caring adults can *uncouple* unfavorable gene–environment correlations by providing children with positive experiences that modify the expression of heredity, yielding favorable outcomes. For example, in a study that tracked the development of 5-year-old identical twins, pair members tended to resemble each other in level of aggression. And the more aggression they displayed, the more maternal anger and criticism they received (a gene–environment correlation). Nevertheless, some mothers treated their twins differently. When followed up at age 7, twins who had been targets of more maternal negativity engaged in even more antisocial behavior. In contrast, their better-treated, genetically identical

FIGURE 2.10 **Similarity in mothers' interactions for pairs of siblings differing in genetic relatedness.** The correlations shown are for maternal negativity. The pattern illustrates evocative genetic–environmental correlation. Identical twins evoke similar maternal treatment because of their identical heredity. As genetic resemblance between siblings declines, the strength of the correlation drops. Mothers vary their interactions as they respond to each child's unique genetic makeup. (Based on Reiss, 2003.)

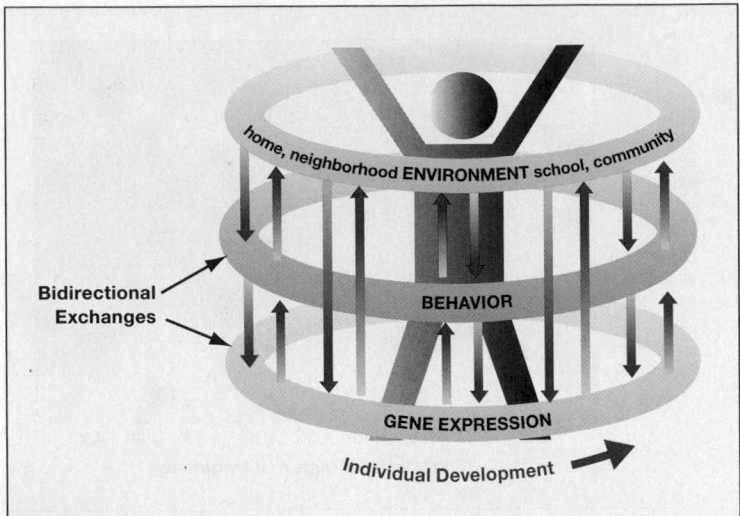

FIGURE 2.11 **Epigenesis.** Development takes place through ongoing, bidirectional exchanges between heredity and all levels of the environment. Genes affect behavior and experiences. Experiences and behavior also affect gene expression. (Based on Gottlieb, 2007.)

counterparts showed a reduction in disruptive acts (Caspi et al., 2004). Good parenting protected them from a spiraling, antisocial course of development.

Accumulating evidence reveals that the relationship between heredity and environment is not a one-way street, from genes to environment to behavior. Rather, like other system influences considered in this and the previous chapter, it is *bidirectional:* Genes affect children's behavior and experiences, but their experiences and behavior also affect gene expression (Diamond, 2009; Gottlieb, 2003; Rutter, 2007). Stimulation—whether *internal* to the child (activity within the cytoplasm of the cell, hormones released into the bloodstream) or *external* to the child (home, neighborhood, school, and society)—modifies gene activity.

This view of the relationship between heredity and environment, depicted in Figure 2.11, is called **epigenesis**, which means development resulting from ongoing, bidirectional exchanges between heredity and all levels of the environment (Gottlieb, 1998, 2007). Researchers are just beginning to clarify the precise mechanisms through which environment alters gene expression. One such mechanism is **methylation**—a biochemical process triggered by certain experiences, in which a set of chemical compounds (called a methyl group) lands on top of a gene and changes its impact, reducing or silencing its expression. Methylation levels can be measured, and they help explain why identical twins, though precisely the same in DNA sequencing, sometimes display strikingly different phenotypes with age.

A case study of a pair of identical-twin adults offers an illustration. Researchers reported that they had been highly similar in intelligence and personality throughout childhood. But after high school, one twin remained close to home, studied law, married, and had children, whereas the other left home, became a journalist, and traveled to war zones around the world, where she repeatedly encountered life-threatening situations and saw many people killed or wounded. Assessed again in their forties, the twins remained similar in intelligence. But compared with the "law twin," the "war twin" engaged in more risky behaviors, including drinking and gambling (Kaminsky et al., 2007). DNA analyses revealed greater methylation of a gene known to play a role in impulse control in the "war twin" than the "law twin"—a difference much larger than is typical for identical twin pairs.

Environmental modification of gene expression can occur at any age, even prenatally, with lasting consequences, as the Biology and Environment box on the following page reveals. And strong evidence exists, from both animal and human studies, that poor-quality parental care reshapes methylation levels of numerous genes, altering the expression of genes involved in children's neurological capacity to manage stress and, thus, elevating their risk for maladjustment (Devlin et al., 2010). The harsh conditions associated with chronic poverty, as well, are believed to exert their impact epigenetically, leaving behind a "biological residue" that compromises the child's potential for a physically and mentally healthy life (Miller et al., 2009). And at times, the impact can be so profound that later experiences can do little to modify the affected the characteristics. Furthermore, animal evidence indicates that some methylated genes are passed to offspring, affecting development in the next generation (Zhang & Meaney, 2010).

We must keep in mind, however, that epigenesis also operates positively: Favorable rearing experiences alter gene expression in ways that enhance development! And some negative epigenetic modifications in gene expression may be reversible through carefully designed interventions (van IJzendoorn, Bakermans-Kranenburg, & Ebstein, 2011). The concept of epigenesis reminds us that the genome is not static but is constantly in flux, both reflecting and affecting its ever-changing environment.

Epigenetics is still an emerging field, and clarifying its mechanisms may prove to be even more complex than efforts to understand DNA sequence variations (Duncan, Pollastri, &

Biology and Environment

Smoking During Pregnancy Alters Gene Expression

aternal smoking during pregnancy is among the risk factors for *attention-deficit hyperactivity disorder (ADHD)*—one of the most common disorders of childhood, which we will take up in greater detail in Chapter 12. ADHD symptoms—inattention, impulsivity, and overactivity—typically result in serious academic and social problems. Some studies report that individuals who are homozygous for a chromosome-5 gene (DD) containing a special repeat of base pairs are at increased risk for ADHD, though other research has not confirmed any role for this gene (Fisher et al., 2002; Gill et al., 1997; Waldman et al., 1998).

One reason for this inconsistency may be that environmental influences associated with ADHD—such as prenatal exposure to toxins—modify the gene's activity. To test this possibility, researchers recruited several hundred mothers and their 6-month-old babies, obtaining infant blood samples for genetic analysis and asking mothers whether they smoked regularly during pregnancy (Kahn et al., 2003). At a 5-year follow-up, parents responded to a widely used behavior rating scale that assesses children for ADHD symptoms.

Findings revealed that by itself, the DD genotype was unrelated to impulsivity, overactivity, or oppositional behavior. But children whose mothers had smoked during pregnancy scored higher in these behaviors than children of non-smoking mothers. Furthermore, as Figure 2.12 illustrates, 5-year-olds with both prenatal nicotine exposure and DD genetic makeup obtained substantially higher impulsivity, overactivity, and oppositional scores than all other groups—outcomes that persisted even after a variety of other factors (quality of the home environment and maternal ethnicity, marital status, and postbirth smoking) had been controlled.

Another investigation following participants into adolescence obtained similar findings, suggesting that the genotype–prenatal environment effect persists (Becker et al., 2008). What processes might account for it? In animal research, tobacco smoke stimulates the DD genotype to release chemicals in the brain that promote impulsivity and overactivity (Ernst, Moolchan, & Robinson,

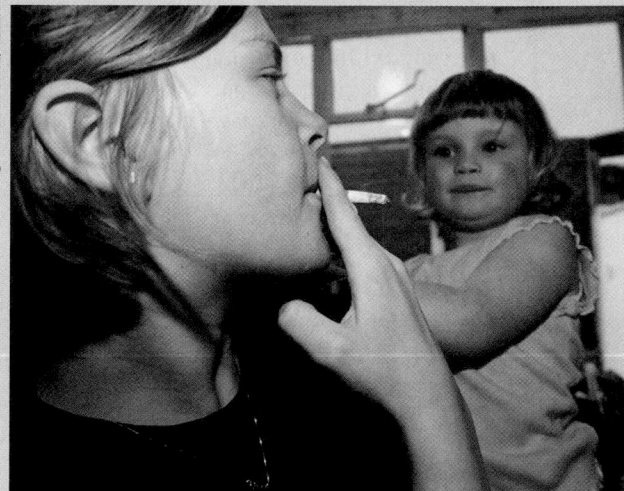

Because her mother smoked during pregnancy, this child may be at increased risk for attention-deficit hyperactivity disorder (ADHD). Prenatal exposure to nicotine seems to alter expression of a chromosome-12 gene in ways that greatly heighten impulsivity, overactivity, and oppositional behavior.

2001). These behaviors, in turn, often evoke harsh, punitive parenting, which triggers defiance in children.

The DD genotype is widespread, present in more than 50 percent of people. Thus, the majority of children prenatally exposed to nicotine are at high risk for learning and behavior problems (refer to page 106 in Chapter 3). Mounting evidence indicates that other genes, in epigenetic interplay with as yet unknown environmental factors, contribute to ADHD symptoms (Hudziak & Rettew, 2009).

FIGURE 2.12 Combined influence of maternal prenatal smoking and genotype on impulsivity and overactivity at age 5. In the absence of prenatal smoking, 5-year-olds who were homozygous for a chromosome-5 gene (DD) showed no elevation in impulsivity and overactivity (orange bar) compared with children of other genotypes (Dd or dd) (red bar). Among children of all genotypes, prenatal smoking was associated with an increase in these behaviors (green and purple bars). And the combination of prenatal smoking and the DD genotype greatly magnified impulsivity and overactivity (purple bar). Children's oppositional behavior followed a similar epigenetic pattern. (Based on Kahn et al., 2003.)

Smoller, 2014). But from what we already know, one lesson is clear: Development is best understood as a series of complex exchanges between nature and nurture. Although children cannot be changed in any way we might desire, environments are continuously transforming their genetic potential. The success of any attempt to improve development depends on the characteristics we want to change, the genetic makeup of the child, and the type and timing of our intervention.

Ask Yourself

- **REVIEW** What is epigenesis, and how does it differ from gene–environment interaction and gene–environment correlation?

- **CONNECT** Explain how each of the following concepts supports the conclusion that genetic influences on children's traits are not constant but change over time: somatic mutation (page 58), niche-picking (page 85), and epigenesis (page 86).

- **APPLY** Bianca's parents are accomplished musicians. At age 4, Bianca began taking piano lessons. By age 10, she was accompanying the school choir. At age 14, she asked if she could attend a special music high school. Explain how gene–environment correlation promoted Bianca's talent.

- **REFLECT** What aspects of your own development—for example, interests, hobbies, college major, or vocational choice—are probably due to niche-picking? Explain.

Summary

Genetic Foundations (p. 51)

2.1 What are genes, and how are they transmitted from one generation to the next?

- Each individual's **phenotype,** or directly observable characteristics, is a product of both **genotype** and environment. **Chromosomes,** rodlike structures within the cell nucleus, contain our hereditary endowment. Along their length are **genes,** segments of **deoxyribonucleic acid (DNA).** Protein-coding genes send instructions for making a rich assortment of proteins to the cytoplasm of the cell; **regulator genes** modify those instructions. A wide range of environmental factors also alter gene expression.

- **Gametes,** or sex cells, are produced through a cell division process called **meiosis,** which halves the number of chromosomes. In meiosis, genes shuffle to create new combinations, ensuring the uniqueness of individuals. Once sperm and ovum unite, the resulting **zygote** will again have the full complement of chromosomes.

- If the fertilizing sperm carries an X chromosome, the child will be a girl; if it contains a Y chromosome, a boy. **Fraternal,** or **dizygotic, twins** result when two ova are released from the mother's ovaries and each is fertilized. **Identical,** or **monozygotic, twins** develop when a zygote divides in two during the early stages of cell duplication.

© F4FOTO/ALAMY

2.2 Describe various patterns of genetic inheritance.

- Traits controlled by single genes follow **dominant–recessive** and **incomplete dominance** patterns of inheritance. **Homozygous** individuals have two identical **alleles,** or forms of a gene. **Heterozygous** individuals, with one dominant and one recessive allele, are **carriers** of the recessive trait. Most recessive genes have little developmental impact, but some bring serious consequences, such as PKU. In incomplete dominance, both alleles are expressed in the phenotype, resulting in a trait that combines aspects of both.

- **X-linked inheritance** applies when recessive disorders are carried on the X chromosome and, therefore, are more likely to affect males. In **genomic imprinting,** one parent's allele is activated, regardless of its makeup, at times profoundly affecting brain development and physical health.

- Harmful genes arise from **mutation,** which can occur spontaneously or be caused by hazardous environmental agents. Germline mutation occurs in the cells that give rise to gametes; somatic mutation can occur in body cells at any time of life.

- Human traits that vary continuously among people, such as intelligence and personality, result from **polygenic inheritance**—the effects of many genes. For such characteristics, scientists must study the influence of heredity indirectly.

2.3 Describe major chromosomal abnormalities, and explain how they occur.

- Most chromosomal abnormalities are due to errors in meiosis. The most common, Down syndrome, results in physical defects and intellectual disability. Disorders of the **sex chromosomes** are milder than defects of the **autosomes.**

Reproductive Choices (p. 61)

2.4 What procedures can assist prospective parents in having healthy children?

- **Genetic counseling** helps couples at risk for giving birth to children with genetic abnormalities consider appropriate reproductive options. **Prenatal diagnostic methods** allow early detection of genetic problems. Advances in genetic engineering and gene therapy offer hope for treating hereditary disorders.

- Reproductive technologies such as donor insemination, in vitro fertilization, surrogate motherhood, and postmenopausal-assisted childbirth permit many individuals to become parents who otherwise would not, but they raise serious legal and ethical concerns.

AP IMAGES/HERALD & REVIEW, JIM BOWLING

- Many parents who cannot conceive or who have a high likelihood of transmitting a genetic disorder decide to adopt. Although adopted children tend to have more learning and emotional problems than children in general, most fare well in the long run. Warm, sensitive parenting predicts favorable development.

Environmental Contexts for Development (p. 67)

2.5 Describe family functioning from the perspective of ecological systems theory, along with aspects of the environment that support family well-being and children's development.

- The first and foremost context for child development is the family, a dynamic system characterized by bidirectional influences, in which each family member's behaviors affect those of others. Both direct and indirect influences operate within the family system, which must continually adjust to new events and changes in its members. Warm, gratifying family ties, which foster effective **coparenting,** predict psychological health.

- **Socioeconomic status (SES)** profoundly affects family functioning. Higher-SES families tend to be smaller, to emphasize psychological traits, and to engage in warm, verbally stimulating interaction with children. Lower-SES families more often use commands, criticism, and physical punishment.

- Children's development in affluent families may be impaired by parents' physical and emotional unavailability. Poverty and homelessness undermine effective parenting and pose serious threats to children's development.

- Children benefit from supportive ties between the family and the surrounding environment, including stable, socially cohesive neighborhoods that provide constructive leisure and enrichment activities and that offer parents access to social support. High-quality schools with frequent parent–teacher contact are also vital.

- The values and practices of cultures and **subcultures** affect all aspects of children's daily lives. **Extended-family households,** which are common among many ethnic minority groups, help protect children from negative effects of poverty and other stressful conditions.

© JEFF GREENBERG/THE IMAGE WORKS

- Consistent cross-national differences in collectivism–individualism powerfully affect approaches to devising **public policies** to address social problems, including those affecting children. Largely because of its strongly individualistic values, the United States lags behind other developed nations in policies safeguarding children and youths.

Understanding the Relationship Between Heredity and Environment (p. 81)

2.6 Explain the various ways heredity and environment may combine to influence complex traits.

- **Behavioral genetics** examines the contributions of nature and nurture to complex traits. Some researchers use **kinship studies** to compute **heritability estimates,** which attempt to quantify the influence of genetic factors on such traits as intelligence and personality. However, the accuracy and usefulness of this approach have been challenged.

- In **gene–environment interaction,** individuals respond differently to varying environments because of their genetic makeup. **Gene–environment correlation** and **niche-picking** describe how children's genes affect the environments to which they are exposed. **Epigenesis** reminds us that development is best understood as a series of complex exchanges between nature and nurture.

Important Terms and Concepts

allele (p. 55)
autosomes (p. 53)
behavioral genetics (p. 82)
carrier (p. 55)
chromosomes (p. 51)
coparenting (p. 69)
deoxyribonucleic acid (DNA) (p. 52)
dominant–recessive inheritance (p. 55)
epigenesis (p. 86)
extended-family household (p. 78)
fraternal, or dizygotic, twins (p. 53)
gametes (p. 53)
gene (p. 52)

genetic counseling (p. 61)
gene–environment interaction (p. 83)
gene–environment correlation (p. 84)
genomic imprinting (p. 58)
genotype (p. 51)
heritability estimate (p. 82)
heterozygous (p. 55)
homozygous (p. 55)
identical, or monozygotic, twins (p. 54)
incomplete dominance (p. 57)
kinship studies (p. 82)
meiosis (p. 53)
methylation (p. 86)

mutation (p. 58)
niche-picking (p. 85)
phenotype (p. 51)
polygenic inheritance (p. 59)
prenatal diagnostic methods (p. 64)
protein-coding genes (p. 52)
public policies (p. 79)
regulator genes (p. 52)
sex chromosomes (p. 53)
socioeconomic status (SES) (p. 70)
subculture (p. 78)
X-linked inheritance (p. 57)
zygote (p. 53)

Prenatal Development

"Pregnant Mommy"
Eliska Kocová
5 years, Czech Republic

In this painting, the rapidly growing fetus claims a central place in the parent's world. How is the one-celled organism transformed into a baby with the capacity to participate in family life? What factors support or undermine this earliest period of development? Chapter 3 provides answers to these questions.

REPRINTED WITH PERMISSION FROM THE INTERNATIONAL MUSEUM OF CHILDREN'S ART, OSLO, NORWAY

One fall, Yolanda and Jay enrolled in an evening section of our department's child development course, when Yolanda was two months pregnant. In their early thirties, married for several years, and with their careers well under way, they had decided to have a baby. Each week, they arrived for class full of questions: "How does the baby grow before birth?" "When is each organ formed?" "Has its heart begun to beat?" "Can it hear, feel, or sense our presence?"

Most of all, Yolanda and Jay wanted to do everything possible to make sure their baby would be born healthy. Yolanda started to wonder about her diet and whether she should keep up her daily aerobic workout. And she asked whether an aspirin for a headache, a glass of wine at dinner, or a few cups of coffee during the workday might be harmful.

In this chapter, we answer Yolanda and Jay's questions, along with a great many more that scientists have asked about the events before birth. We begin our discussion with these puzzling questions: Why is it that generation after generation, most couples who fall in love want to become parents? And what factors influence their decision to have just one child or more than one?

Then we trace prenatal development, paying special attention to supports for healthy growth as well as damaging influences that threaten the child's health and survival. Because the changes taking place during these nine months are so astonishing, the prenatal environment can exert a powerful, lasting impact—for better or for worse—on physical and mental health. Finally, we look at how expectant parents prepare psychologically for the arrival of the baby and start to forge a new sense of self as mother or father. ∎

Motivations for Parenthood

TAKE A MOMENT... What, in your view, are the benefits and drawbacks of having children? How large would your ideal family be, and why? As part of her semester project, Yolanda interviewed her grandmother, asking why she had wanted children and how she had settled on a particular family size. Yolanda's grandmother, whose children were born in the 1960s, replied:

> We didn't think much about whether or not to have children in those days. We just had them—everybody did. It would have seemed odd not to! I was 22 years old when I had the first of my four children, and I had four because—well, I wouldn't have had just one because we all thought children needed brothers and sisters, and only children could end up spoiled and selfish. Life is more interesting and enjoyable with children, you know.

Why Have Children?

In the past, the issue of whether to have children was, for many adults, a biological given or a compelling social expectation. Today, in Western industrialized nations, it is a matter of true individual choice. Effective birth control techniques enable adults to avoid having children in most instances. And changing cultural values allow

3.1 How has decision making about childbearing changed over the past half century, and what are the consequences for child rearing and child development?

people to remain childless with far less fear of social criticism than a generation or two ago (Scott, 2009). Nevertheless, the 6 percent of American 18- to 40-year-olds who currently say they do not want children is just slightly higher than the 5 percent who said so a quarter century ago. Despite media messages suggesting that Americans are increasingly preferring a childless lifestyle, the desire for children remains the norm: A survey of over 5,000 U.S. adults of childbearing age revealed that more than 90 percent already have children or are planning to have them (Gallup, 2013). Whether people actually become parents is affected by a complex array of contextual factors, including economic conditions, partnership changes, career goals, religious values, health conditions, and availability of supportive government and workplace family policies (Mills et al., 2011; Theil, 2006).

Besides these influences, a vital personal factor called *childbearing motivations*—each person's disposition to respond positively or negatively to the idea of parenthood—affects people's decision to have children as well as their psychological adjustment to pregnancy and the new baby's arrival. In Western nations, these motivations have changed over time, increasingly emphasizing individual fulfillment and deemphasizing obligation to society (Frejka et al., 2008).

When Americans and Europeans are asked about their motivations for parenthood, they mention a variety of advantages and disadvantages, which are listed in Table 3.1. Although some ethnic and regional differences exist, in all groups highly rated reasons for having children include personal rewards—for example, the warm, affectionate relationship and opportunities for care and teaching that children provide. Also frequently mentioned are social and economic returns, such as affirmation of one's adult status and children as a source of caregiving and financial support in later life (Guedes et al., 2013). Less important, but still mentioned, is a sense of future continuity—having someone to carry on after one's own death. And occasionally, couples look to parenthood as a gratifying opportunity to share in a challenging but important life task and to deepen their relationship.

Most adults also realize that having children means years of extra burdens and responsibilities. Among disadvantages of parenthood, they most often cite concerns about role overload (not enough time for both family and work responsibilities), doubts about their own readiness for parenthood, and worries about bringing up children in a troubled world. The financial strains of child rearing follow close behind. According to a conservative estimate, new parents in the United States today will spend about $300,000 to rear a child from birth to age 18, and many will incur substantial additional expense for higher education and financial dependency during emerging adulthood—a reality that has contributed to the declining birthrate in industrialized nations (U.S. Department of Agriculture, 2013a).

Greater freedom to choose whether, when, and how to have children (see the discussion of reproductive choices in Chapter 2) makes contemporary family planning more challenging as well as intentional than it was in Yolanda's grandmother's day. Still, about 30 percent of U.S. newborn babies are the result of unintended pregnancies, with most born to low-income, less educated mothers—circumstances associated with delayed prenatal care, premature birth, and child health problems (Guttmacher Institute, 2013). Yet opportunities to explore childbearing motivations in high school, college, and community-based health education classes and through family-planning counseling might encourage more adults to make informed and personally meaningful decisions—a trend that would increase the chances that they would have children when ready, find parenting an enriching experience, and rear physically and mentally healthy children.

© ALAN CAREY/THE IMAGE WORKS

One reason often given for having children is the opportunity for care and teaching that a young child provides.

TABLE 3.1	Advantages and Disadvantages of Parenthood Mentioned by American and European Adults of Childbearing Age (in general order of importance)	
ADVANTAGES	**DISADVANTAGES**	
Giving and receiving warmth and affection, providing care and teaching	Constant worries over and responsibility for children's health, safety, and well-being	
Personal fulfillment, enhancing life's meaning		
Creating one's own family	Role overload—not enough time to meet both child-rearing and job responsibilities	
Nurturing a new person and personality		
Being accepted as a responsible and mature member of the community	Risks of bringing up children in a world plagued by crime, war, and pollution	
Having a source of caregiving and economic support in times of need	Fear that children will turn out badly, through no fault of one's own	
Carrying on one's family name, lineage, heritage, or values	Financial strain	
Strengthening the couple relationship through a shared project	Reduced time to spend with partner	
Fulfilling a partner's desire for parenthood	Loss of privacy	

Sources: Guedes et al., 2013; Miller, 2009.

How Large a Family?

In contrast to her grandmother, Yolanda—like most U.S. adults—plans to have no more than two children. And she and Jay are talking about whether to limit their family to a single child. In 1960, the average number of children per American woman of childbearing age was 3.1. Currently, it is 2.1 in the United States, 1.9 in the United Kingdom, 1.8 in Australia, 1.7 in Sweden, 1.6 in Canada, 1.4 in Germany, and 1.3 in Italy and Japan (U.S. Census Bureau, 2014a, 2014b). In addition to more effective birth control, a major reason for this decline is that a family size of one or two children is more compatible with a woman's decision to divide her energies between family and career. The tendency of many couples, like Yolanda and Jay, to delay having children until they are well-established professionally and secure economically also contributes to smaller family size. Furthermore, marital instability plays a role: More couples today get divorced before their childbearing plans are complete.

Popular advice to prospective parents often recommends limiting family size in the interests of "child-rearing quality"—more parental affection, involvement, and material resources per child, which enhance children's intellectual development. Do large families really make less intelligent children, as prevailing attitudes suggest?

For years, researchers thought that earlier birth order and wider spacing might grant children more parental attention and stimulation and, therefore, result in more favorable cognitive development. But recent evidence indicates that birth order and spacing are unrelated to children's intelligence (Kanazawa, 2012; Rodgers et al., 2000; Wichman, Rodgers, & MacCallum, 2007). Why is this so? Parents' differential treatment of siblings is far more responsive to children's personalities, interests, and behaviors than to these aspects of family structure.

Other evidence confirms that rather than parenting quality declining as new children are born, parents reallocate their energies. In a longitudinal study of Canadian two-parent families, new births led to a decrease in maternal affection toward older siblings, though most mothers probably remained generally warm. At the same time, the consistency of parenting—the extent to which mothers insisted older children meet their expectations for mature behavior, such as completing chores, doing homework, and treating others respectfully—rose over time (Strohschein et al., 2008). After a new baby joined the family, mothers seemed to reorganize their parenting practices to best meet all their children's needs.

Furthermore, the well-documented association between large family size and lower intelligence test scores of all siblings can be entirely explained by a

Average family size has declined in recent decades in most industrialized nations. But, contrary to popular belief, having more children does not reduce the intelligence or life chances of later-born children.

strong trend for low-SES mothers to give birth to more children. Among children of well-educated, economically advantaged mothers, the family size–intelligence relationship disappears (Guo & VanWey, 1999; Wichman, Rodgers, & MacCallum, 2007). In sum, although many good reasons exist for limiting family size, the concern that additional births will reduce parenting quality and, thus, impair children's skills and life chances is not warranted.

Is Yolanda's grandmother right when she says that parents who have just one child are likely to end up with a spoiled, selfish youngster? As we will see in Chapter 13, research also challenges this widely held belief. Overall, only children are just as well-adjusted as children with siblings.

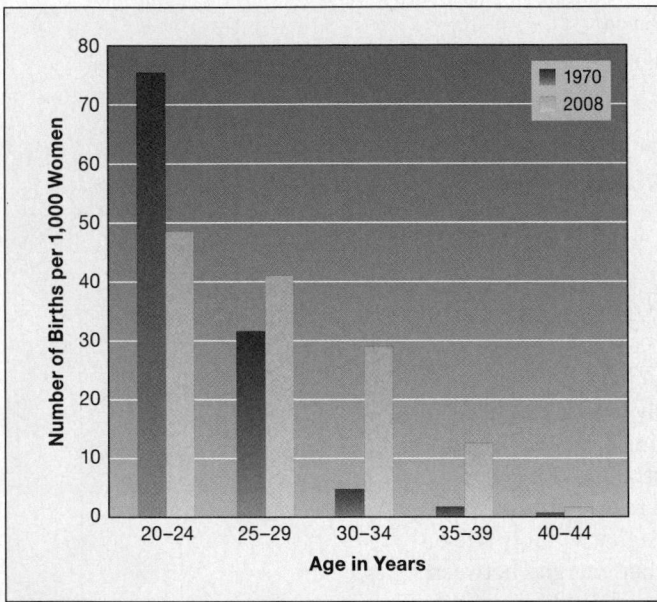

FIGURE 3.1 **First births to American women of different ages in 1970 and 2012.** The birthrate decreased during this period for women 20 to 24 years of age, whereas it increased for women 25 years of age and older. For women in their thirties, the birthrate rose nearly fivefold. Similar trends have occurred in other industrialized nations. (Based on U.S. Census Bureau, 2014b.)

Is There a Best Time During Adulthood to Have a Child?

Yolanda's grandmother gave birth to her first child in her early twenties. Yolanda, at age 32, is pregnant for the first time. Many people believe that couples should, ideally, have children in their twenties because the risk of having a baby with a chromosomal disorder increases with maternal age. Advanced paternal age is also associated with elevated risk of certain genetically influenced disorders, including autism and schizophrenia (see Chapter 2). Furthermore, younger parents have more energy to keep up with active children.

Nevertheless, as Figure 3.1 reveals, first births to women in their thirties have increased greatly over the past several decades. Many people are delaying childbearing until their education is complete, their careers are established, and they know they can support a child. Older parents may be somewhat less energetic than they once were, but they are financially better off and emotionally more mature. For these reasons, they may be better able to invest in parenting.

Nevertheless, reproductive capacity does decline with age. Fertility problems among women increase from age 15 to 50, with a sharp rise in the mid-thirties. Between ages 25 and 34, 12 percent of women are affected, a figure that climbs to 39 percent for 35- to 39-year-olds and to 47 percent for 40- to 44-year-olds. Age also affects male reproductive capacity. Amount of semen, concentration of sperm in each ejaculation, and quality of sperm decline gradually after age 35. Consequently, compared to a 25-year-old man, a 40-year-old is 12 times as likely to take more than two years to achieve a conception (Chandra, Copen, & Stephen, 2013; Lambert, Masson, & Fisch, 2006).

Women with demanding careers are especially likely to delay parenthood (Tough, Vekved, & Newburn-Cook, 2012). Many believe, incorrectly, that if they have difficulty conceiving, they can rely on reproductive technologies. But recall from Chapter 2 that the success of these procedures drops steadily with age. Although no one time during adulthood is best to begin parenthood, individuals who decide to put off pregnancy until well into their thirties or early forties risk having fewer children than they desire or none at all.

Ask Yourself

- **REVIEW** Explain why the common assumption that larger families reduce child-rearing quality, resulting in less intelligent children, is mistaken.

- **CONNECT** Why is it incorrect for couples who postpone childbearing until age 35 or later to conclude that medical advances can overcome fertility problems? (See Chapter 2, page 62.)

- **APPLY** Rhonda and Mark, a career-oriented couple in their early thirties, are thinking about having a baby. What factors should they keep in mind as they decide whether to add to their family at this time in their lives?

- **REFLECT** Ask one of your parents or grandparents to list his or her childbearing motivations. How do those motivations compare with your own? What factors—for example, education or cultural changes—might account for any differences?

Prenatal Development

3.2 List the three phases of prenatal development, and describe the major milestones of each.

The sperm and ovum that unite to form the new individual are uniquely suited for the task of reproduction. The ovum is a tiny sphere, measuring ¹⁄₁₇₅ inch in diameter, that is barely visible to the naked eye as a dot the size of the period at the end of this sentence. But in its microscopic world, it is a giant—the largest cell in the human body. The ovum's size makes it a perfect target for the much smaller sperm, which measure only ¹⁄₅₀₀ inch.

Conception

About once every 28 days, in the middle of a woman's menstrual cycle, an ovum bursts from one of her *ovaries,* two walnut-sized organs located deep inside her abdomen, and is drawn into one of two *fallopian tubes*—long, thin structures that lead to the hollow, soft-lined uterus (see Figure 3.2). While the ovum is traveling, the spot on the ovary from which it was released, now called the *corpus luteum,* secretes hormones that prepare the lining of the uterus to receive a fertilized ovum. If pregnancy does not occur, the corpus luteum shrinks, and the lining of the uterus is discarded two weeks later with menstruation.

The male produces sperm in vast numbers—an average of 300 million a day—in the *testes,* two glands located in the *scrotum,* sacs that lie just behind the penis. In the final process of maturation, each sperm develops a tail that permits it to swim

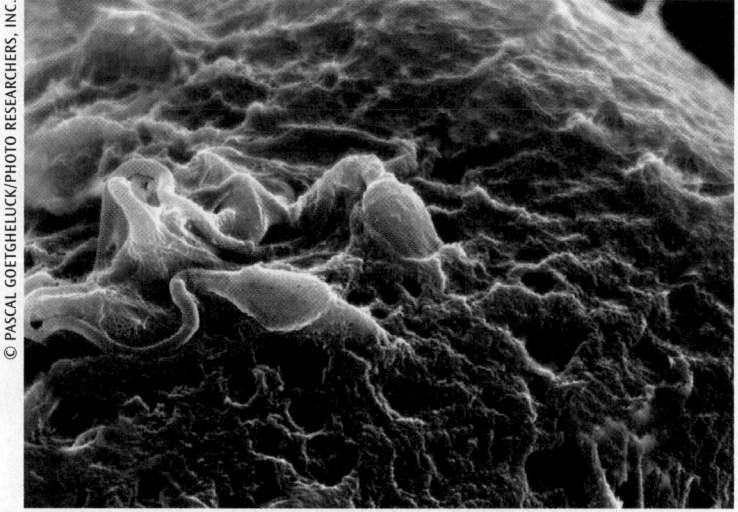

© PASCAL GOETGHELUCK/PHOTO RESEARCHERS, INC.

In this photo taken with the aid of a powerful microscope, sperm penetrate the surface of the enormous-looking ovum, the largest cell in the human body. When one sperm successfully fertilizes the ovum, the resulting zygote begins to duplicate.

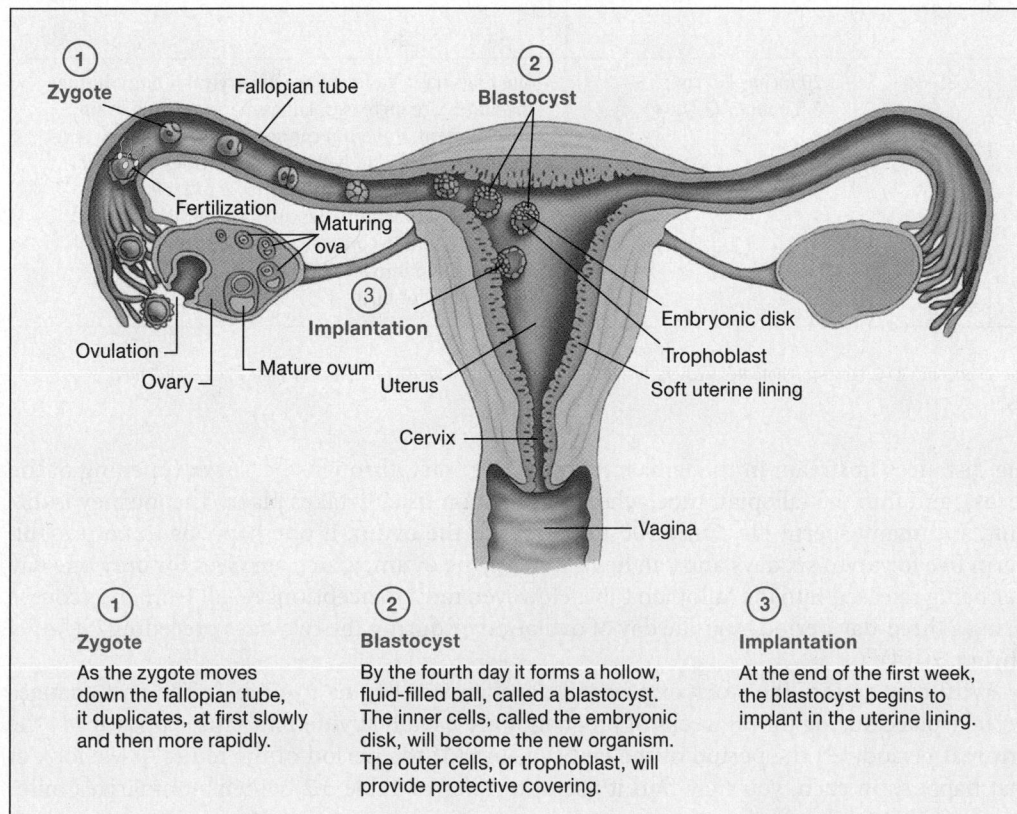

FIGURE 3.2 **Female reproductive organs, showing fertilization, early cell duplication, and implantation.** (From *Before We Are Born,* 6th ed., by K. L. Moore and T. V. N. Persaud, p. 87. Copyright © 2003, reprinted with permission from Elsevier, Inc.)

① Zygote
As the zygote moves down the fallopian tube, it duplicates, at first slowly and then more rapidly.

② Blastocyst
By the fourth day it forms a hollow, fluid-filled ball, called a blastocyst. The inner cells, called the embryonic disk, will become the new organism. The outer cells, or trophoblast, will provide protective covering.

③ Implantation
At the end of the first week, the blastocyst begins to implant in the uterine lining.

TABLE 3.2	Milestones of Prenatal Development			
TRIMESTER	**PRENATAL PHASE**	**WEEKS**	**LENGTH AND WEIGHT**	**MAJOR EVENTS**
First	Germinal	1		The one-celled zygote multiplies and forms a blastocyst.
		2		The blastocyst burrows into the uterine lining. Structures that feed and protect the developing organism begin to form—*amnion, chorion, yolk sac, placenta,* and *umbilical cord*.
	Embryo	3–4	¼ inch (6 mm)	A primitive brain and spinal cord appear. Heart, muscles, ribs, backbone, and digestive tract begin to develop.
		5–8	1 inch (2.5 cm); ½ ounce (4 g)	Many external body structures (face, arms, legs, toes, fingers) and internal organs form. The sense of touch begins to develop, and the embryo can move.
	Fetus	9–12	3 inches (7.6 cm); less than 1 ounce (28 g)	Rapid increase in size begins. Nervous system, organs, and muscles become organized and connected, and new behavioral capacities (kicking, thumb sucking, mouth opening, and rehearsal of breathing) appear. External genitals are well-formed, and the fetus's sex is evident.
Second		13–24	12 inches (30 cm); 1.8 pounds (820 g)	The fetus continues to enlarge rapidly. In the middle of this period, the mother can feel fetal movements. Vernix and lanugo keep the fetus's skin from chapping in the amniotic fluid. Most of the brain's neurons are in place by 24 weeks. Eyes are sensitive to light, and the fetus reacts to sound.
Third		25–38	20 inches (50 cm); 7.5 pounds (3,400 g)	The fetus has a good chance of survival if born during this time. Size increases. Lungs mature. Rapid brain development, in neural connectivity and organization, enables sensory and behavioral capacities to expand. In the middle of this period, a layer of fat is added under the skin. Antibodies are transmitted from mother to fetus to protect against disease. Most fetuses rotate into an upside-down position in preparation for birth.

Source: Moore, Persaud, & Torchia, 2013.
Photos (from top to bottom): © Claude Cortier/Photo Researchers, Inc.; © G. Moscoso/Photo Researchers, Inc.; © John Watney/Photo Researchers, Inc.; © James Stevenson/Photo Researchers, Inc.; © Lennart Nilsson, *A Child Is Born*/Scanpix.

long distances upstream in the female reproductive tract, through the *cervix* (opening of the uterus), and into the fallopian tube, where fertilization usually takes place. The journey is difficult, and many sperm die. Only 300 to 500 reach the ovum, if one happens to be present. Sperm live for up to six days and can lie in wait for the ovum, which survives for only one day after being released into the fallopian tube. However, most conceptions result from intercourse during a three-day period—on the day of ovulation or during the two days preceding it (Mu & Fehring, 2014).

With conception, the story of prenatal development begins to unfold. The vast changes that take place during the 38 weeks of pregnancy are usually divided into three phases: (1) the germinal period, (2) the period of the embryo, and (3) the period of the fetus. As we look at what happens in each, you may find it useful to refer to Table 3.2, which summarizes milestones of prenatal development.

Germinal Period

The germinal period lasts about two weeks, from fertilization and formation of the zygote until the tiny mass of cells drifts down and out of the fallopian tube and attaches itself to the wall of the uterus. The zygote's first cell duplication is long and drawn out; it is not complete until about 30 hours after conception. Gradually, new cells are added at a faster rate. By the fourth day, 60 to 70 cells exist that form a hollow, fluid-filled ball called a **blastocyst** (refer again to Figure 3.2). The cells on the inside of the blastocyst, called the **embryonic disk,** will become the new organism; the thin outer ring of cells, termed the **trophoblast,** will become the structures that provide protective covering and nourishment.

IMPLANTATION Between the seventh and ninth days, **implantation** occurs: The blastocyst burrows deep into the uterine lining. Surrounded by the woman's nourishing blood, it starts to grow in earnest. At first, the trophoblast (protective outer layer) multiplies fastest. It forms a membrane, called the **amnion,** that encloses the developing organism in **amniotic fluid,** which helps keep the temperature of the prenatal world constant and provides a cushion against any jolts caused by the woman's movement. A *yolk sac* emerges that produces blood cells until the developing liver, spleen, and bone marrow are mature enough to take over this function (Moore, Persaud, & Torchia, 2013).

The events of these first two weeks are delicate and uncertain. As many as 30 percent of zygotes do not survive this period. In some, the sperm and ovum did not join properly. In others, for some unknown reason, cell duplication never begins. By preventing implantation in these cases, nature eliminates most prenatal abnormalities (Sadler, 2010).

THE PLACENTA AND UMBILICAL CORD By the end of the second week, cells of the trophoblast form another protective membrane—the **chorion,** which surrounds the amnion. From the chorion, tiny fingerlike *villi,* or blood vessels, emerge.[1] As these villi burrow into the uterine wall, the placenta starts to develop. By bringing the mother's and the embryo's blood close together, the **placenta** permits food and oxygen to reach the developing organism and waste products to be carried away. A membrane forms that allows these substances to be exchanged but prevents the mother's and the embryo's blood from mixing directly (see Figure 3.3).

FIGURE 3.3 **Cross-section of the uterus, showing detail of the placenta.** The embryo's blood flows from the umbilical cord arteries into the chorionic villi and returns via the umbilical cord vein. The mother's blood circulates in spaces surrounding the chorionic villi. A membrane between the two blood supplies permits food and oxygen to be delivered and waste products to be carried away. The two blood supplies do not mix directly. The umbilical arteries carry oxygen-poor blood (shown in blue) to the placenta, and the umbilical vein carries oxygen-rich blood (shown in red) to the fetus. (From *Before We Are Born,* 6th ed., by K. L. Moore and T. V. N. Persaud, p. 95. Copyright © 2003, reprinted with permission from Elsevier, Inc.)

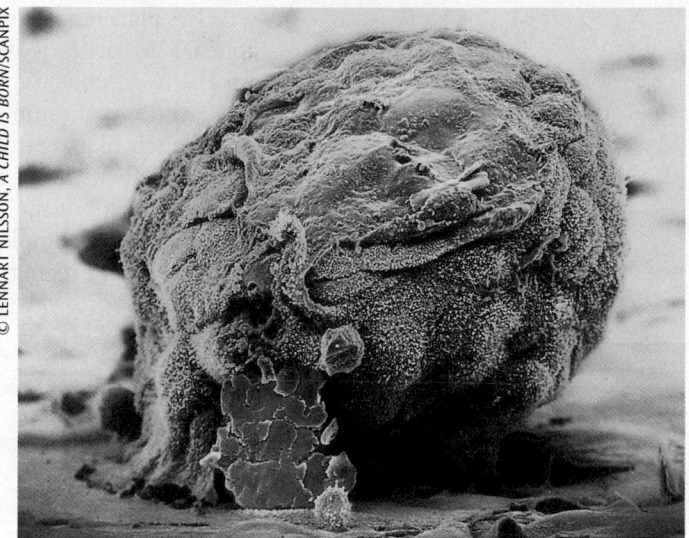

© LENNART NILSSON, *A CHILD IS BORN*/SCANPIX

Period of the zygote: seventh to ninth day. The fertilized ovum duplicates at an increasingly rapid rate, forming a hollow ball of cells, or blastocyst, by the fourth day after fertilization. Here the blastocyst, magnified thousands of times, burrows into the uterine lining between the seventh and ninth day.

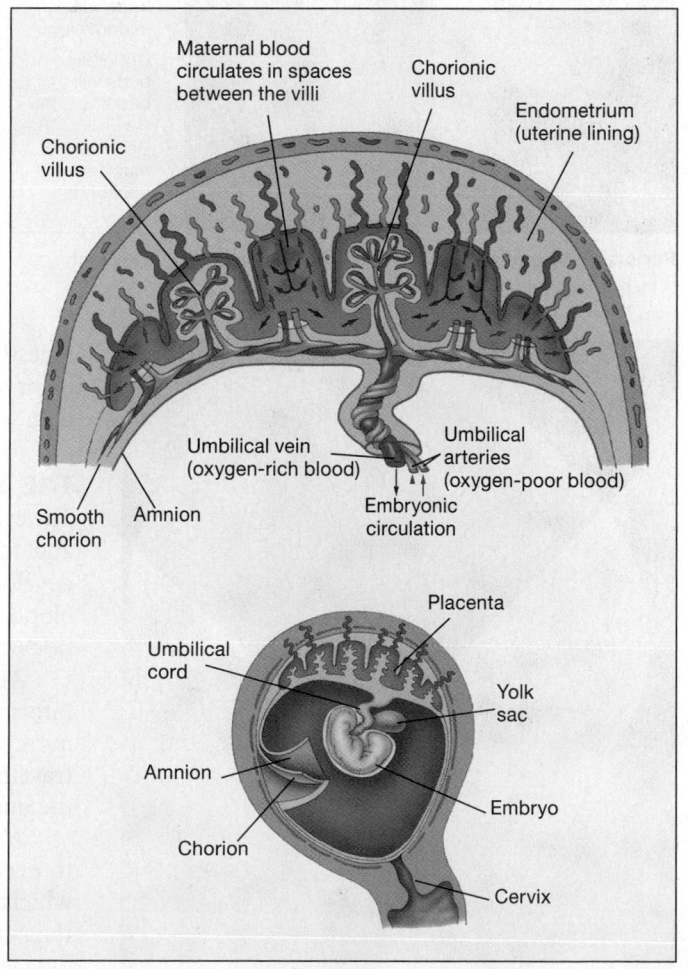

[1]Recall from Chapter 2 that *chorionic villus sampling* is the prenatal diagnostic method that can be performed earliest, at nine weeks after conception. In this procedure, tissues from the ends of the villi are removed and examined for genetic abnormalities.

The placenta is connected to the developing organism by the **umbilical cord,** which first appears as a primitive body stalk and, during the course of pregnancy, grows to a length of 1 to 3 feet. The umbilical cord contains one large vein that delivers blood loaded with nutrients and two arteries that remove waste products. The force of blood flowing through the cord keeps it firm, much like a garden hose, so it seldom tangles while the embryo, like a space-walking astronaut, floats freely in its fluid-filled chamber (Moore, Persaud, & Torchia, 2013).

By the end of the germinal period, the developing organism has found food and shelter. Already, it is a complex being. These dramatic beginnings take place before most mothers know they are pregnant.

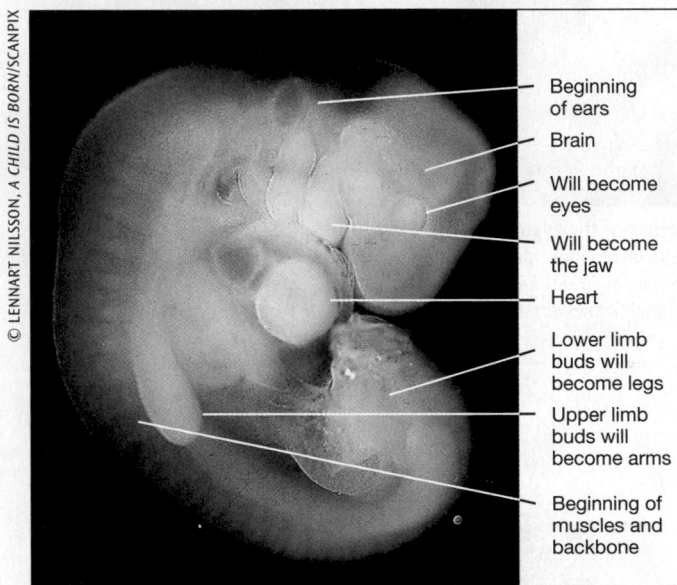

Beginning of ears

Brain

Will become eyes

Will become the jaw

Heart

Lower limb buds will become legs

Upper limb buds will become arms

Beginning of muscles and backbone

Period of the embryo: fourth week. This 4-week-old embryo is only ¼ inch long, but many body structures have begun to form.

Period of the Embryo

The period of the **embryo** lasts from implantation through the eighth week of pregnancy. During these brief six weeks, the most rapid prenatal changes take place, as the groundwork is laid for all body structures and internal organs. Because all parts of the body are forming, the embryo is especially vulnerable to interference with healthy development. But the short time span of embryonic growth helps limit opportunities for serious harm.

LAST HALF OF THE FIRST MONTH In the first week of this period, the embryonic disk forms three layers of cells: (1) the *ectoderm,* which will become the nervous system and skin; (2) the *mesoderm,* from which will develop the muscles, skeleton, circulatory system, and other internal organs; and (3) the *endoderm,* which will become the digestive system, lungs, urinary tract, and glands. These three layers give rise to all parts of the body.

At first, the nervous system develops fastest. The ectoderm folds over to form the **neural tube,** or spinal cord. At 3½ weeks, the top swells to form the brain. While the nervous system is developing, the heart begins to pump blood, and muscles, backbone, ribs, and digestive tract start to appear. At the end of the first month, the curled embryo—only ¼ inch long—consists of millions of organized groups of cells with specific functions.

THE SECOND MONTH In the second month, growth continues rapidly. The eyes, ears, nose, jaw, and neck form. Tiny buds become arms, legs, fingers, and toes. Internal organs are more distinct: The intestines grow, the heart develops separate chambers, and the liver and spleen take over production of blood cells so that the yolk sac is no longer needed. Changing body proportions cause the embryo's posture to become more upright.

At 7 weeks, production of neurons (nerve cells that store and transmit information) begins deep inside the neural tube at the astounding pace of more than 250,000 per minute (Nelson, 2011). Once formed, neurons begin traveling along tiny threads to their permanent locations, where they will form the major parts of the brain.

Around this time, ovaries in the female and testes in the male have begun to develop. By 8 weeks, the testes start to secrete the hormone testosterone, which will stimulate differentiation of male internal reproductive organs and the penis and scrotum during the coming month. In the absence of testosterone, female reproductive organs form.

At the end of this period, the embryo—about 1 inch long and ⅐ ounce in weight—can already sense its world. It responds to touch, particularly in the mouth area and on the soles of the feet. And it can move, although its tiny flutters are still too light to be felt by the mother (Moore, Persaud, & Torchia, 2013).

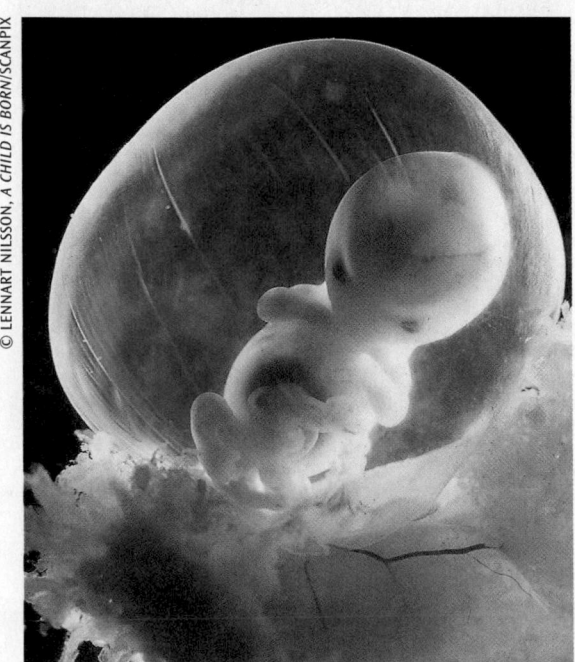

Period of the embryo: seventh week. The embryo's posture is more upright. Body structures—eyes, nose, arms, legs, and internal organs—are more distinct. The embryo now responds to touch. It also can move, although at less than one inch long and an ounce in weight, it is still too tiny to be felt by the mother.

Period of the Fetus

The period of the **fetus,** from the ninth week to the end of pregnancy, is the longest prenatal period. During this "growth and finishing" phase, the developing organism increases rapidly in size, especially from the ninth to the twentieth week.

THE THIRD MONTH   In the third month, the organs, muscles, and nervous system start to become organized and connected. When the brain signals, the fetus kicks, bends its arms, forms a fist, curls its toes, turns its head, opens its mouth, and even sucks its thumb, stretches, and yawns. Body position changes are frequent, occurring as often as 25 times per hour (Einspieler, Marschik, & Prechtl, 2008). The tiny lungs begin to expand and contract in an early rehearsal of breathing movements.

By the twelfth week, the external genitals are well-formed, and the sex of the fetus can be detected with ultrasound (Sadler, 2010). Other finishing touches appear, such as fingernails, toenails, tooth buds, eyebrows, eyelids, and eyelashes. The heartbeat can now be heard through a stethoscope.

Prenatal development is sometimes divided into **trimesters,** or three equal time periods. At the end of the third month, the *first trimester* is complete.

THE SECOND TRIMESTER   By the middle of the second trimester, between 17 and 20 weeks, the new being has grown large enough that the mother can feel its movements. A white, cheeselike substance called **vernix** protects its skin from chapping during the long months spent bathing in the amniotic fluid. White, downy hair called **lanugo** also appears over the entire body, helping the vernix stick to the skin.

At the end of the second trimester, many organs are well-developed. And most of the brain's billions of neurons are in place; few will be produced after this time. However, *glial cells,* which support and feed the neurons, continue to increase at a rapid rate throughout the remaining months of pregnancy, as well as after birth. Consequently, brain weight increases tenfold from the twentieth week until birth (Roelfsema et al., 2004). At the same time, neurons begin forming *synapses,* or connections, at a rapid pace.

Brain growth means new sensory and behavioral capacities. The 20-week-old fetus can be stimulated as well as irritated by sounds. Slow eye movements appear, with rapid eye movements following at 22 weeks. And if a doctor looks inside the uterus using fetoscopy (see Chapter 2, page 64), fetuses try to shield their eyes from the light with their hands, indicating that sight has begun to emerge (Moore, Persaud, & Torchia, 2013). Still, a fetus born at this time cannot survive. Its lungs are immature, and the brain cannot yet control breathing movements or body temperature.

THE THIRD TRIMESTER   During the final trimester, a fetus born early has a chance for survival. The point at which the baby can first survive, called the **age of viability,** occurs sometime between 22 and 26 weeks (Moore, Persaud, & Torchia, 2013). A baby born between the seventh and eighth month, however, usually needs oxygen assistance to breathe. Although the brain's respiratory center is now mature, tiny air sacs in the lungs are not yet ready to inflate and exchange carbon dioxide for oxygen.

The brain continues to make great strides. The *cerebral cortex,* the seat of human intelligence, enlarges. Convolutions and grooves in its surface appear, permitting a dramatic increase in surface area that allows

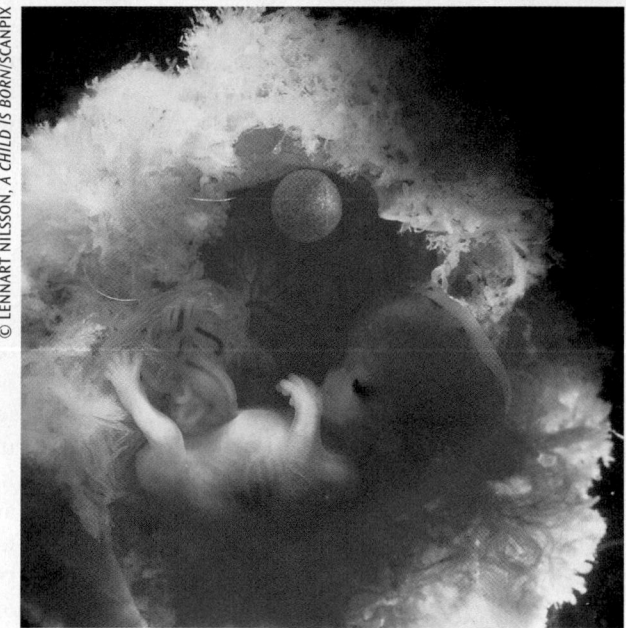

Period of the fetus: eleventh week. The organism grows rapidly, and body structures are completed. At 11 weeks, the brain and muscles are better connected. The fetus can kick, bend its arms, open and close its hands and mouth, and suck its thumb. Notice the yolk sac, which shrinks as pregnancy advances. The internal organs have taken over its function of producing blood cells.

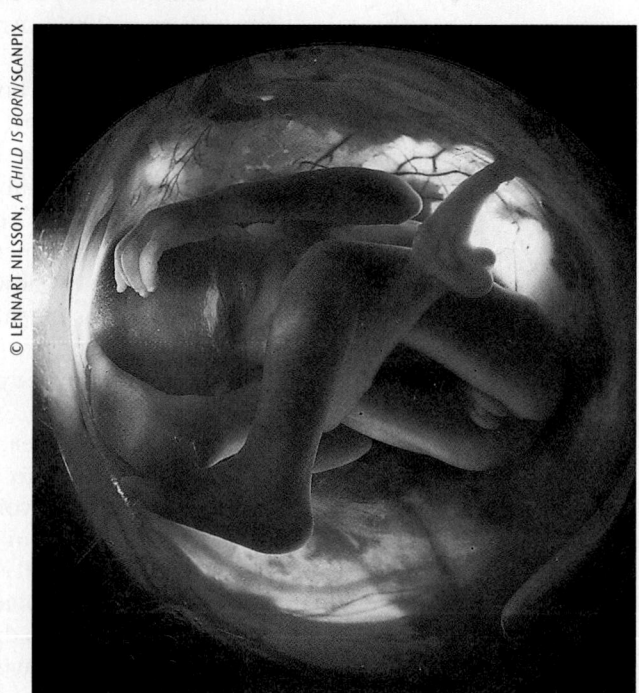

Period of the fetus: twenty-second week. This fetus is almost a foot long and weighs slightly more than one pound. Its movements can be felt easily by the mother and by other family members who place a hand on her abdomen. The fetus has reached the age of viability; if born, it has a slim chance of surviving.

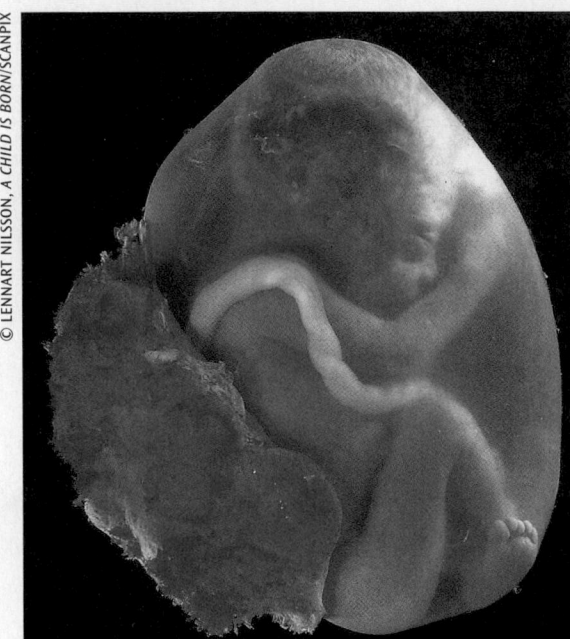

Period of the fetus: thirty-sixth week. This fetus fills the uterus. To support its need for nourishment, the umbilical cord and placenta have grown large. The vernix (cheeselike substance) on the skin protects it from chapping. The fetus has accumulated a layer of fat to assist with temperature regulation after birth. In two more weeks, it will be full-term.

for maximum prenatal brain growth without the full-term baby's head becoming too large to pass through the birth canal. As rapid gains in neural connectivity and organization continue, the fetus spends more time awake. At 20 weeks, fetal heart rate reveals no periods of alertness. But by 28 weeks, fetuses are awake about 11 percent of the time, a figure that rises to 16 percent just before birth (DiPietro et al., 1996). Between 30 and 34 weeks, fetuses show rhythmic alternations between sleep and wakefulness that gradually increase in organization (Rivkees, 2003). Around this time, synchrony between fetal heart rate and motor activity peaks: A rise in heart rate is usually followed within five seconds by a burst of motor activity (DiPietro et al., 2006). These are clear signs that coordinated neural networks are beginning to form in the brain.

By the end of pregnancy, the fetus also takes on the beginnings of a personality. Higher fetal activity in the final weeks predicts a more active infant in the first month of life—a relationship that, for boys, persists into early childhood (Groome et al., 1999). Fetal activity is linked in other ways to infant temperament. In one study, more active fetuses during the third trimester became 1-year-olds who could better handle frustration and 2-year-olds who were less fearful, in that they more readily interacted with toys and with an unfamiliar adult in a laboratory (DiPietro et al., 2002). Perhaps fetal activity level is an indicator of healthy neurological development, which fosters adaptability in childhood. The relationships just described, however, are only modest. As we will see in Chapter 7, sensitive caregiving can modify the temperaments of children who have difficulty adapting to new experiences.

The third trimester also brings greater responsiveness to external stimulation. As we will see later when we discuss newborn capacities, fetuses acquire taste and odor preferences from bathing in and swallowing amniotic fluid (its makeup is influenced by the mother's diet). Between 23 and 30 weeks, connections form between the cerebral cortex and brain regions involved in pain sensitivity. By this time, painkillers should be used in any surgical procedures performed on a fetus (Lee et al., 2005). Around 28 weeks, fetuses blink their eyes in reaction to nearby sounds (Kisilevsky & Low, 1998; Saffran, Werker, & Werner, 2006). And around 30 weeks, fetuses presented with a repeated auditory stimulus against the mother's abdomen initially react with a rise in heart rate, electrical brain-wave recordings, and body movements. Then responsiveness gradually declines, indicating *habituation* (adaptation) to the sound. If a new auditory stimulus is introduced, heart rate and brain waves recover to a high level, revealing that the fetus recognizes the new sound as distinct from the originally presented stimulus (Hepper, Dornan, & Lynch, 2012; Muenssinger et al., 2013). This indicates that fetuses can remember for at least a brief period.

Within the next six weeks, fetuses distinguish the tone and rhythm of different voices and sounds. They show systematic heart-rate and brain-wave changes in response to the mother's voice versus the father's or a stranger's, to their native language (English) versus a foreign language (Mandarin Chinese), and to a simple familiar melody (descending tones) versus an unfamiliar melody (ascending tones) (Granier-Deferre et al., 2003; Kisilevsky & Hains, 2011; Kisilevsky et al., 2009; Lecanuet et al., 1993; Lee & Kisilevsky, 2013; Voegtline et al., 2013). And in one clever study, mothers read aloud Dr. Seuss's lively book *The Cat in the Hat* each day during the last six weeks of pregnancy. After birth, their infants learned to turn on recordings of the mother's voice by sucking on nipples (DeCasper & Spence, 1986). They sucked hardest to hear *The Cat in the Hat*—the sound they had come to know while still in the womb.

TAKE A MOMENT... On the basis of these findings, would you recommend that expectant mothers provide fetuses with stimulation designed to enhance later development? Notice how risky it is to draw such conclusions. First, specific forms of fetal stimulation, such as reading aloud or playing classical music, are unlikely to have a long-lasting impact on cognitive development because of the developing child's constantly changing capacities and experiences, which can override the impact of fetal stimulation (Lecanuet, Granier-Deferre, & DeCasper, 2005). Second, although ordinary stimulation contributes to the functioning of sensory systems, excessive input can be dangerous. For example, animal studies indicate that a sensitive period (see page 24 in Chapter 1) exists in which the fetal ear is highly susceptible to injury. During that time, prolonged exposure to sounds that are harmless to the mature ear can permanently damage fetal inner-ear structures (Pierson, 1996).

In the final three months, the fetus gains more than 5 pounds and grows 7 inches. As it fills the uterus, it gradually moves less often. In addition, brain development, which enables the organism to inhibit behavior, contributes to a decline in physical activity (DiPietro et al., 1996). In the eighth month, a layer of fat is added to assist with temperature regulation. The fetus also receives antibodies from the mother's blood to protect against illnesses, since the newborn's immune system will not work well until several months after birth. In the last weeks, most fetuses assume an upside-down position, partly because of the shape of the uterus and partly because the head is heavier than the feet. Growth slows, and birth is about to take place.

Ask Yourself

- **REVIEW** Why is the period of the embryo regarded as the most dramatic prenatal period? Why is the period of the fetus called the "growth and finishing" phase?

- **CONNECT** How is brain development related to fetal capacities and behavior? What implications do individual differences in fetal behavior have for infant temperament after birth?

- **APPLY** Amy, two months pregnant, wonders how the embryo is being fed and what parts of the body have formed. "I don't look pregnant yet, so does that mean not much development has taken place?" she asks. How would you respond to Amy?

Prenatal Environmental Influences

Although the prenatal environment is far more constant than the world outside the womb, a great many factors can affect the embryo and fetus. Yolanda and Jay learned that parents—and society as a whole—can do a great deal to create a safe environment for development before birth.

Teratogens

The term **teratogen** refers to any environmental agent that causes damage during the prenatal period. Scientists chose this label (from the Greek word *teras,* meaning "malformation" or "monstrosity") because they first learned about harmful prenatal influences from cases in which babies had been profoundly damaged. But the harm done by teratogens is not always simple and straightforward. It depends on the following factors:

- *Dose.* As we discuss particular teratogens, you will see that larger doses over longer time periods usually have more negative effects.
- *Heredity.* The genetic makeup of the mother and the developing organism plays an important role. Some individuals are better able than others to withstand harmful environments.
- *Other negative influences.* The presence of several negative factors at once, such as additional teratogens, poor nutrition, and lack of medical care, can worsen the impact of a harmful agent.
- *Age.* The effects of teratogens vary with the age of the organism at time of exposure. To understand this last idea, think of the *sensitive period* concept. Recall that a sensitive period is a limited time span in which a part of the body or a behavior is biologically prepared to develop rapidly. During that time, it is especially sensitive to its surroundings. If the environment is harmful, then damage occurs, and recovery is difficult and sometimes impossible.

3.3 What are teratogens, and what factors influence their impact?

3.4 List agents known to be or suspected of being teratogens, and discuss evidence supporting their harmful impact.

3.5 Describe the impact of other maternal factors on prenatal development.

3.6 Why is early and regular health care vital during the prenatal period?

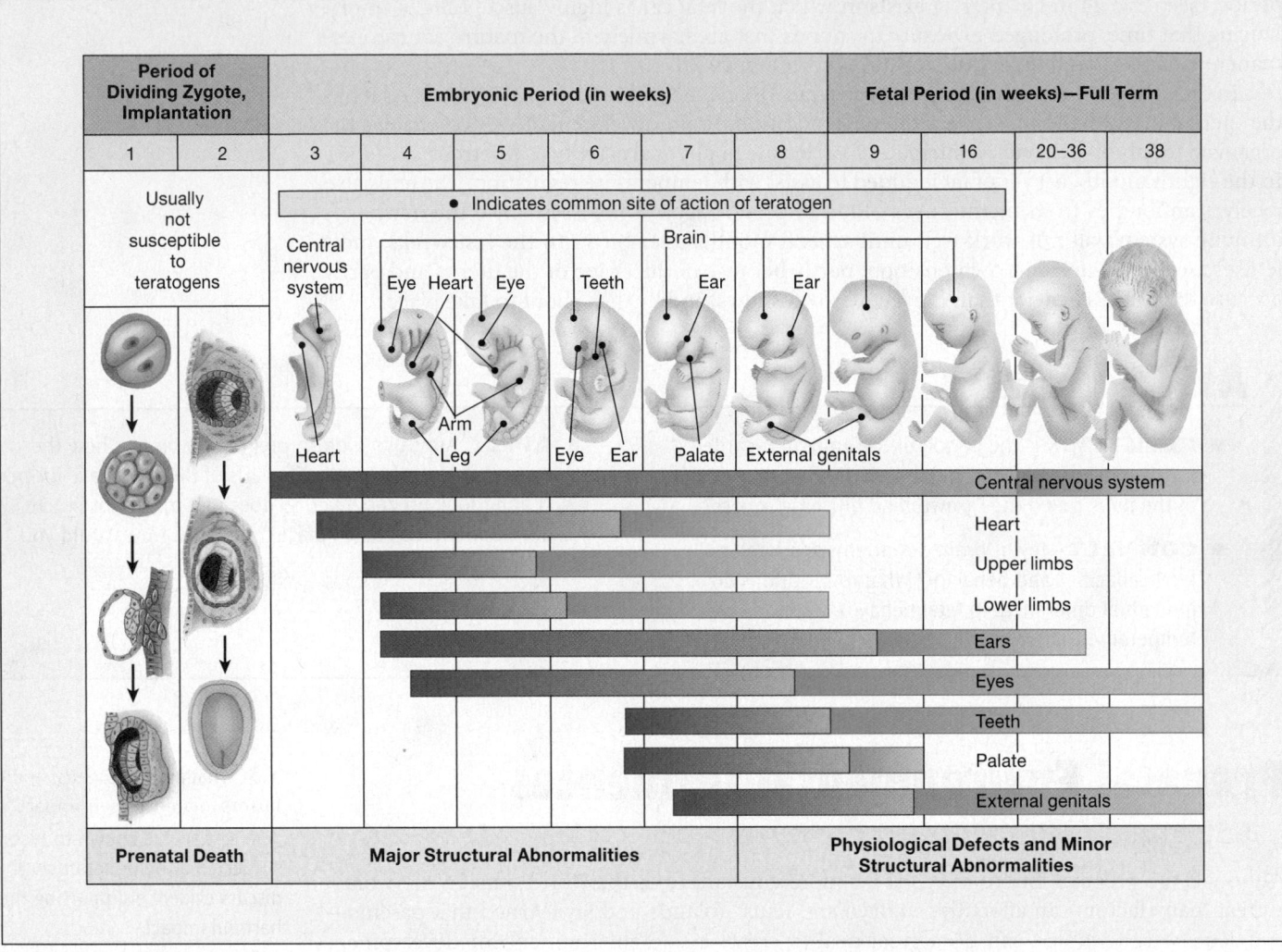

FIGURE 3.4 **Sensitive periods in prenatal development.** Each organ or structure has a sensitive period, during which its development may be disturbed. Blue horizontal bars indicate highly sensitive periods. Green horizontal bars indicate periods that are somewhat less sensitive to teratogens, although damage can occur. (Adapted from *Before We Are Born, 7th ed.,* by K. L. Moore and T. V. N. Persaud, p. 313. Copyright © 2008, reprinted with permission from Elsevier, Inc.)

Figure 3.4 summarizes prenatal sensitive periods. Look at it carefully, and you will see that some parts of the body, such as the brain and eye, have long sensitive periods that extend throughout prenatal development. Other sensitive periods, such as those for the limbs and palate, are much shorter. Figure 3.4 also indicates that we can make some general statements about the timing of harmful influences. In the *germinal period,* before implantation, teratogens rarely have any impact. If they do, the tiny mass of cells is usually so damaged that it dies. The *embryonic period* is the time when serious defects are most likely to occur because the foundations for all body parts are being laid down. During the *fetal period,* teratogenic damage is usually minor. However, organs such as the brain, ears, eyes, teeth, and genitals can still be strongly affected.

The effects of teratogens go beyond immediate physical damage. Some health effects are subtle and delayed. As the Biology and Environment box on the following page illustrates, they may not show up for decades. Furthermore, psychological consequences may occur indirectly, as a result of physical damage. For example, a defect resulting from drugs the mother took during pregnancy can affect others' reactions to the child as well as the child's ability to explore the environment. Over time, parent–child interaction, peer relations, and opportunities to learn may suffer. Furthermore, prenatally exposed children may be less resilient in the face of environmental risks, such as single parenthood, parental emotional disturbance, or maladaptive parenting (Yumoto, Jacobson, & Jacobson, 2008). As a result, their long-term adjustment may be compromised.

Biology and Environment

The Prenatal Environment and Health in Later Life

When Michael entered the world 55 years ago, 6 weeks premature and weighing only 4 pounds, the doctor delivering him wasn't sure he would make it. Michael not only survived but enjoyed good health until his mid-forties, when, during a routine medical checkup, he was diagnosed with high blood pressure and type 2 diabetes. Michael had no apparent risk factors for these conditions.

Could the roots of Michael's health problems date back to his prenatal development? Increasing evidence suggests that prenatal environmental factors—ones that are not toxic (as are tobacco or alcohol) but rather fairly subtle, such as the flow of nutrients and hormones across the placenta—can affect an individual's health decades later.

Low Birth Weight and Heart Disease, Stroke, and Diabetes

Carefully controlled animal experiments reveal that a poorly nourished, underweight fetus experiences changes in body structure and function that greatly increase the risk of cardiovascular disease in adulthood (Franco et al., 2002). To explore this relationship in humans, researchers tapped public records, gathering information on the birth weights of thousands of British men and women and the occurrence of disease in middle adulthood. Those weighing less than

5 pounds at birth had a 50 percent greater chance of dying of heart disease and stroke, even after SES and a variety of other health risks were controlled (Barker, 2009; Godfrey & Barker, 2000). The connection between birth weight and cardiovascular disease was strongest for people whose weight-to-length ratio at birth was very low—a sign of prenatal growth stunting.

In other large-scale studies, a consistent link between low birth weight and high blood pressure, heart disease, stroke, and diabetes in middle adulthood emerged—for both sexes and in diverse countries (see Figure 3.5) (Barker, 2009; Johnson & Schoeni, 2011). Researchers believe that complex factors associated with underweight are involved.

Some speculate that a poorly nourished fetus diverts large amounts of blood to the brain, causing organs in the abdomen, such as the liver and kidneys (involved in controlling cholesterol and blood pressure), to be undersized (Hales & Ozanne, 2003). The result is heightened later risk of heart disease and stroke. In the case of diabetes, inadequate prenatal nutrition may permanently impair the pancreas, leading glucose intolerance to rise as the person ages (Wu et al., 2004). Yet another hypothesis is that the malfunctioning placentas of some expectant mothers permit high levels of stress hormones to reach the fetus, which slows fetal growth, increases fetal blood pressure, and promotes excess blood glucose, predisposing the developing person to later disease (Barker & Thornberg, 2013).

Finally, prenatally growth-stunted babies often gain excessive weight in childhood, once they have access to plentiful food (Ojha et al., 2013). This excess weight usually persists, greatly increasing the risk of diabetes and heart disease.

High Birth Weight and Cancer

The other prenatal growth extreme—high birth weight—is linked to breast cancer, the most common malignancy in adult women (Barker et al., 2008). In a study of more than 2,000 British women, high birth weight—especially weight

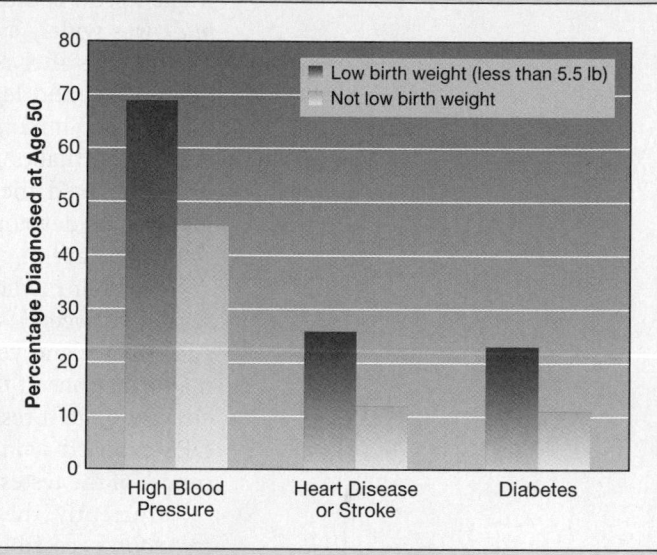

FIGURE 3.5 Relationship of low birth weight to disease risk in adulthood. In a follow-up of more than 2000 U.S. births at age 50, low birth weight was associated with a greatly increased incidence of high blood pressure, heart disease, stroke, and diabetes after many other prenatal and postnatal health risks were controlled. (Based on Johnson & Schoeni, 2011.)

above 8.8 pounds—was associated with a greatly increased incidence of breast cancer, even after other cancer risks were controlled (dos Santos Silva et al., 2004). The likely culprit is excessive maternal estrogen in the overweight expectant mother, which promotes large fetal size and alters the makeup of beginning breast tissue so that it responds to estrogen in adulthood by becoming malignant.

High birth weight is also associated with increases in prostate cancer in men and digestive, blood, and lymphatic cancers in both genders (Caughey & Michels, 2009; Cnattingius et al., 2009; McCormack et al., 2005). As yet, the reasons are unclear.

Prevention

The relationships between prenatal development and later-life illnesses do not mean that the illnesses are inevitable. Rather, the steps we take to protect our health can prevent prenatal risks from becoming reality. Researchers advise individuals who were low-weight or high-weight at birth to get regular medical checkups and screening tests that increase the odds of early disease detection. They also recommend consistent attention to diet, weight, fitness, and stress—controllable factors that contribute to cardiovascular disease, adult-onset diabetes, and cancer.

Prenatal environmental factors can affect health in later life. This baby's high birth weight places her at increased risk for breast cancer in adulthood.

© BLEND IMAGES/ALAMY

Notice how an important idea about development that we discussed in earlier chapters is at work here: *bidirectional influences* between child and environment. Now let's look at what scientists have discovered about a variety of teratogens.

PRESCRIPTION AND NONPRESCRIPTION DRUGS   In the early 1960s, the world learned a tragic lesson about drugs and prenatal development. At that time, a sedative called *thalidomide* was widely available in Canada, Europe, and South America. When taken by mothers 4 to 6 weeks after conception, thalidomide produced gross deformities of the embryo's developing arms and legs and, less frequently, damage to the ears, heart, kidneys, and genitals. About 7,000 infants worldwide were affected (Moore, Persaud, & Torchia, 2013). As children exposed to thalidomide grew older, many scored below average in intelligence. Perhaps the drug damaged the central nervous system directly, by modifying the expression of genes involved its development. Or the child-rearing conditions of these severely deformed youngsters may have impaired their intellectual development.

Another medication, a synthetic hormone called *diethylstilbestrol (DES),* was widely prescribed between 1945 and 1970 to prevent miscarriages. As daughters of these mothers reached adolescence and young adulthood, they showed unusually high rates of cancer of the vagina, malformations of the uterus, and infertility. When they tried to have children, their pregnancies more often resulted in prematurity, low birth weight, and miscarriage than those of non-DES-exposed women. Young men showed an increased risk of genital abnormalities and cancer of the testes (Goodman, Schorge, & Greene, 2011; Reed & Fenton, 2013).

Currently, the most widely used potent teratogen is a vitamin A derivative called *isotretinoin,* prescribed to treat severe acne and taken by hundreds of thousands of women of childbearing age in industrialized nations. Exposure during the first trimester results in eye, ear, skull, brain, heart, and immune system abnormalities (Yook et al., 2012). Isotretinoin's packaging warns users to avoid pregnancy by using two methods of birth control, but many women do not heed this advice (Garcia-Bournissen et al., 2008).

Indeed, any drug with a molecule small enough to penetrate the placental barrier can enter the embryonic or fetal bloodstream. Yet many pregnant women continue to take over-the-counter medications without consulting their doctors. Aspirin is one of the most common. Several studies suggest that regular aspirin use is linked to low birth weight, infant death around the time of birth, poorer motor development, and lower intelligence test scores in early childhood, although other research fails to confirm these findings (Barr et al., 1990; Kozer et al., 2003; Streissguth et al., 1987). Coffee, tea, cola, and cocoa contain another frequently consumed drug, caffeine. High doses increase the risk of low birth weight (Sengpiel et al., 2013). And persistent intake of antidepressant medication is linked to an elevated incidence of premature delivery and birth complications, including respiratory distress, and to high blood pressure in infancy (Lund, Pedersen, & Henriksen, 2009; Roca et al., 2011; Udechuku et al., 2010).

Because children's lives are involved, we must take findings like these seriously. At the same time, we cannot be sure that these frequently used drugs actually cause the problems just mentioned. Often mothers take more than one drug. If the embryo or fetus is injured, it is hard to tell which drug might be responsible or whether other factors correlated with drug taking are at fault. Until we have more information, the safest course of action is the one Yolanda took: Avoid these drugs entirely. Unfortunately, many women do not know that they are pregnant during the early weeks of the embryonic period, when exposure to medications (and other teratogens) can be of greatest threat.

ILLEGAL DRUGS   The use of highly addictive mood-altering drugs, such as cocaine and heroin, has become more widespread, especially in poverty-stricken inner-city areas, where these drugs provide a temporary escape from a daily life of hopelessness. Nearly 6 percent of U.S. pregnant women take these substances (Substance Abuse and Mental Health Services Administration, 2013).

Babies born to users of cocaine, heroin, or methadone (a less addictive drug used to wean people away from heroin) are at risk for a wide variety of problems, including prematurity, low birth weight, physical defects, breathing difficulties, and death around the time of birth

LOOK and LISTEN

On a trip to your grocery or drugstore, examine the fine print on nonprescription medication labels, such as pain relievers, and on energy drinks containing high levels of caffeine. Are the prenatal risks of these products clearly conveyed?

(Bandstra et al., 2010; Howell, Coles, & Kable, 2008; Schuetze & Eiden, 2006). In addition, these infants are born drug-addicted. They are often feverish and irritable and have trouble sleeping, and their cries are abnormally shrill and piercing—a common symptom among stressed newborns (Barthell & Mrozek, 2013). When mothers with many problems of their own must care for these babies, who are difficult to calm down, cuddle, and feed, behavior problems are likely to persist.

Throughout the first year, heroin- and methadone-exposed infants are less attentive to the environment than nonexposed babies, and their motor development is slow. After infancy, some children get better, while others remain jittery and inattentive. The kind of parenting they receive may explain why problems persist for some but not for others (Hans & Jeremy, 2001).

Evidence on cocaine suggests that some prenatally exposed babies develop lasting difficulties. Cocaine constricts the blood vessels, causing oxygen delivered to the developing organism to fall for 15 minutes following a high dose. It also can alter the production of neurons, formation of synaptic connections, and chemical balance in the fetus's brain. These effects may

This 3-day-old infant, born many weeks before his due date, breathes with the aid of a respirator. Prematurity and low birth weight can result from a variety of environmental influences during pregnancy, including maternal drug and tobacco use.

contribute to an array of cocaine-associated physical malformations, especially of the central nervous system and heart; brain hemorrhages and seizures; and growth retardation (Cain, Bornick, & Whiteman, 2013; Li et al., 2013; Salisbury et al., 2009). Several studies report perceptual, motor, attention, memory, language, and impulse-control problems that persist into adolescence (Bandstra et al., 2010; Buckingham-Howes et al., 2013; Lester & Lagasse, 2010).

Other investigations, however, reveal no major negative effects of prenatal cocaine exposure (Ackerman, Riggins, & Black, 2010; Behnke & Smith, 2013; Hurt et al., 2009). These contradictory findings indicate how difficult it is to isolate the precise damage caused by illegal drugs. Cocaine users vary greatly in the amount, potency, and purity of the cocaine they ingest. Also, they often take several drugs, display other high-risk behaviors, suffer from poverty and other stresses, and engage in insensitive caregiving—factors that worsen outcomes for children (Jones, 2006; Molnar et al., 2014). But researchers have yet to determine exactly what accounts for findings of cocaine-related damage in some studies but not in others.

Another illegal drug, marijuana, is used more widely than heroin and cocaine. Researchers have linked prenatal marijuana exposure to attention, memory, and academic achievement difficulties; impulsivity and overactivity; and depression as well as anger and aggression in childhood and adolescence (Behnke & Smith, 2013; Goldschmidt et al., 2004; Gray et al., 2005; Jutras-Aswad et al., 2009). As with cocaine, however, lasting consequences are not well-established. Overall, the effects of illegal drugs are far less consistent than the impact of two legal substances to which we now turn: tobacco and alcohol.

TOBACCO   Although smoking has declined in Western nations, about 11 percent of U.S. women smoke during their pregnancies (Centers for Disease Control and Prevention, 2014h). The best-known effect of smoking during the prenatal period is low birth weight. But the likelihood of other serious consequences, such as miscarriage, prematurity, cleft lip and palate, blood vessel abnormalities, impaired heart rate and breathing during sleep, infant death, and asthma and cancer later in childhood, also increases (Geerts et al., 2012; Havstad et al., 2012; Howell, Coles, & Kable, 2008; Mossey et al., 2009). The more cigarettes a mother smokes, the greater the chances that her baby will be affected. If a pregnant woman stops smoking at any time, even during the third trimester, she reduces the likelihood that her infant will be born underweight and suffer from future problems (Polakowski, Akinbami, & Mendola, 2009). And the earlier she stops, the more beneficial the effects.

Even when a baby of a smoking mother appears to be born in good physical condition, slight behavioral abnormalities may threaten the child's development. Newborns of smoking mothers are less attentive to sounds, display more muscle tension, are more excitable when touched and visually stimulated, and more often have colic (persistent crying). These findings suggest subtle negative effects on brain development (Espy et al., 2011; Law et al., 2003). Consistent with this view, prenatally exposed children and adolescents tend to have shorter attention spans, difficulties with impulsivity and overactivity, poorer memories, lower intelligence test scores, and higher levels of disruptive, aggressive behavior (Lindblad & Hjern, 2010; Thakur et al., 2013).

Exactly how can smoking harm the fetus? Nicotine, the addictive substance in tobacco, constricts blood vessels, lessens blood flow to the uterus, and causes the placenta to grow abnormally. This reduces the transfer of nutrients, so the fetus gains weight poorly. Also, nicotine raises the concentration of carbon monoxide in the bloodstreams of both mother and fetus. Carbon monoxide displaces oxygen from red blood cells, damaging the central nervous system and slowing body growth in the fetuses of laboratory animals. Similar effects may occur in humans. Also, recall from Chapter 2 that nicotine-exposed fetuses with a certain genotype are at high risk for becoming impulsive, overactive, and oppositional children and adolescents (see page 87).

From one-third to one-half of nonsmoking pregnant women are "passive smokers" because their husbands, relatives, or co-workers use cigarettes. Passive smoking is also related to low birth weight, infant death, childhood respiratory illnesses, and possible long-term attention, learning, and behavior problems (Best, 2009; Pattenden et al., 2006). Clearly, expectant mothers should avoid smoke-filled environments.

ALCOHOL   In his moving book *The Broken Cord*, Michael Dorris (1989) described what it was like to rear his adopted son Adam, whose biological mother drank heavily throughout pregnancy and died of alcohol poisoning shortly after his birth. A Sioux Indian, Adam was born with **fetal alcohol spectrum disorder (FASD),** a term that encompasses a range of physical, mental, and behavioral outcomes caused by prenatal alcohol exposure. As Table 3.3 shows, children with FASD are given one of three diagnoses, which vary in severity:

1. **Fetal alcohol syndrome (FAS),** distinguished by (a) slow physical growth, (b) a pattern of three facial abnormalities (short eyelid openings; a thin upper lip; a smooth or flattened philtrum, or indentation running from the bottom of the nose to the center of the upper lip), and (c) brain injury, evident in a small head and impairment in at least three areas of functioning—for example, memory, language and communication, attention span and activity level (overactivity), planning and reasoning, motor coordination, or social skills. Other defects—of the eyes, ears, nose, throat, heart, genitals, urinary tract, or immune system—may also be present. Adam was diagnosed as having FAS. As is typical for this disorder, his mother drank heavily throughout pregnancy.

2. **Partial fetal alcohol syndrome (p-FAS),** characterized by (a) two of the three facial abnormalities just mentioned and (b) brain injury, again evident in at least three areas of

TABLE 3.3	Fetal Alcohol Spectrum Disorder: Criteria for Diagnosis		
	DIAGNOSTIC CATEGORY		
Criteria	*FAS*	*p-FAS*	*ARND*
Slow physical growth	Yes	No	No
Facial abnormalities: ● Short eyelid openings ● Thin upper lip ● Smooth or flattened philtrum	All three are present	Two of the three are present	None are present
Brain injury	Impairment in a minimum of three areas of functioning	Impairment in a minimum of three areas of functioning	Impairment in a minimum of three areas of functioning

Source: Mattson, Crocker, & Nguyen, 2012.

impaired functioning. Mothers of children with p-FAS generally drank alcohol in smaller quantities, and children's defects vary with the timing and length of alcohol exposure. Furthermore, recent evidence suggests that paternal alcohol use around the time of conception can alter gene expression, thereby contributing to symptoms (Alati et al., 2013; Ouko et al., 2009).

3. **Alcohol-related neurodevelopmental disorder (ARND),** in which at least three areas of mental functioning are impaired, despite typical physical growth and absence of facial abnormalities. Again, prenatal alcohol exposure, though confirmed, is less pervasive than in FAS (Mattson, Crocker, & Nguyen, 2012).

Even when provided with enriched diets, FAS babies fail to catch up in physical size during infancy or childhood. Mental impairment associated with all three FASD diagnoses is also permanent: In his teens and twenties, Adam had trouble concentrating and keeping a routine job, and he suffered from poor judgment. For example, he would buy something and not wait for change or would wander off in the middle of a task. He died at age 23, after being hit by a car.

The more alcohol a woman consumes during pregnancy, the poorer the child's motor coordination, speed of information processing, reasoning, and intelligence and achievement test scores during the preschool and school years (Burden, Jacobson, & Jacobson, 2005; Mattson, Calarco, & Lang, 2006). In adolescence and early adulthood, FASD is associated with persisting attention and motor-coordination deficits, poor school performance, trouble with the law, inappropriate social and sexual behaviors, alcohol and drug abuse, and lasting mental health problems, including depression and high emotional reactivity to stress (Bertrand & Dang, 2012; Fryer, Crocker, & Mattson, 2008; Hellemans et al., 2010).

How does alcohol produce its devastating effects? First, it interferes with production and migration of neurons in the primitive neural tube. Brain-imaging research reveals reduced brain size, damage to many brain structures, and abnormalities in brain functioning, including the electrical and chemical activity involved in transferring messages from one part of the brain to another (Coles et al., 2011; Memo et al., 2013). Second, the body uses large quantities of oxygen to metabolize alcohol. A pregnant woman's heavy drinking draws away oxygen that the developing organism needs for cell growth.

This 5-year-old's mother drank heavily during pregnancy. Her widely spaced eyes, thin upper lip, and flattened philtrum are typical of fetal alcohol syndrome (FAS).

This 12-year-old has the small head and facial abnormalities of FAS. She also shows the cognitive impairments and slow growth that accompany the disorder.

About 25 percent of U.S. mothers reported drinking at some time during their pregnancies. As with heroin and cocaine, alcohol abuse is higher in poverty-stricken groups. It is especially high among Native Americans, for whom the risk of a baby born with FAS is 20 to 25 times greater than for the rest of the U.S. population (Rentner, Dixon, & Lengel, 2012). Unfortunately, when affected girls later become pregnant, the poor judgment caused by the syndrome often prevents them from understanding why they themselves should avoid alcohol. Thus, the tragic cycle is likely to be repeated in the next generation.

How much alcohol is safe during pregnancy? Even mild drinking, less than one drink per day, is associated with reduced head size (a measure of brain development), slow body growth, and behavior problems (Flak et al., 2014; Martinez-Frias et al., 2004). Recall that other factors—both genetic and environmental—can make some fetuses more vulnerable to teratogens.

This child's deformities are linked to radiation exposure during the Chernobyl nuclear power plant disaster of 1986, when her mother was just a few weeks pregnant. Prenatal radiation exposure also increases the risk of low intelligence and language and emotional disorders.

Therefore, no amount of alcohol is safe. Couples planning a pregnancy and expectant mothers should avoid alcohol entirely.

RADIATION In Chapter 2, we saw that ionizing radiation can cause mutation, damaging DNA in ova and sperm. When mothers are exposed to radiation during pregnancy, the embryo or fetus can suffer additional harm. Defects due to ionizing radiation were tragically apparent in children born to pregnant women who survived the bombing of Hiroshima and Nagasaki during World War II. Similar abnormalities surfaced in the nine months following the 1986 Chernobyl, Ukraine, nuclear power plant accident. After each disaster, the incidence of miscarriage and babies born with brain damage, physical deformities, and slow physical growth rose dramatically (Double et al., 2011; Schull, 2003). Evacuation of residents in areas near the Japanese nuclear facility damaged by the March 2011 earthquake and tsunami was intended to prevent these devastating outcomes.

Even when a radiation-exposed baby seems normal, problems may appear later. For example, even low-level radiation, resulting from industrial leakage or medical X-rays, can increase the risk of childhood cancer (Fushiki, 2013). In middle childhood, prenatally exposed Chernobyl children had abnormal brain-wave activity, lower intelligence test scores, and rates of language and emotional disorders two to three times greater than those of nonexposed children in the surrounding area. Furthermore, the more tension parents reported, due to forced evacuation from their homes and worries about living in irradiated areas, the poorer their children's emotional functioning (Loganovskaja & Loganovsky, 1999; Loganovsky et al., 2008). Stressful rearing conditions seemed to combine with the damaging effects of prenatal radiation to impair children's development.

Women should do their best to avoid medical X-rays during pregnancy. If dental, thyroid, chest, or other X-rays are necessary, insisting on the use of an abdominal X-ray shield is a key protective measure.

ENVIRONMENTAL POLLUTION In industrialized nations, an astounding number of potentially dangerous chemicals are released into the environment. More than 75,000 are in common use in the United States, and many new pollutants are introduced each year. When 10 newborns were randomly selected from U.S. hospitals for analysis of umbilical cord blood, researchers uncovered a startling array of industrial contaminants—287 in all (Houlihan et al., 2005). They concluded that many babies are "born polluted" by chemicals that not only impair prenatal development but also increase the chances of life-threatening diseases and health problems later on.

Certain pollutants cause severe prenatal damage. In the 1950s, an industrial plant released waste containing high levels of *mercury* into a bay providing seafood and water for the town of Minamata, Japan. Many children born at the time displayed physical deformities, intellectual disability, abnormal speech, difficulty in chewing and swallowing, and uncoordinated movements. High levels of prenatal mercury exposure disrupt production and migration of neurons, causing widespread brain damage (Caserta et al., 2013; Hubbs-Tait et al., 2005). Prenatal mercury exposure from maternal seafood diets predicts deficits in speed of cognitive processing and motor, attention, and verbal test performance during the school years (Boucher et al., 2010; Debes et al., 2006). Pregnant women are wise to avoid eating long-lived predatory fish, such as swordfish, albacore tuna, and shark, which are heavily contaminated with mercury.

For many years, *polychlorinated biphenyls (PCBs)* were used to insulate electrical equipment, until research showed that, like mercury, they entered waterways and the food supply. In Taiwan, prenatal exposure to high levels of PCBs in rice oil resulted in low birth weight, discolored skin, deformities of the gums and nails, brain-wave abnormalities, and delayed cognitive development (Chen & Hsu, 1994; Chen et al., 1994). Steady, low-level PCB exposure is also harmful. Women who frequently ate PCB-contaminated fish, compared with those who ate little or no fish, had infants with lower birth weights, smaller heads, persisting attention and memory difficulties, and lower intelligence test scores in childhood (Boucher, Muckle, & Bastien, 2009; Jacobson & Jacobson, 2003; Stewart et al., 2008).

Another teratogen, *lead,* is present in paint flaking off the walls of old buildings and in certain materials used in industrial occupations. High levels of prenatal lead exposure are consistently related to prematurity, low birth weight, brain damage, and a wide variety of physical defects. Even at low levels, affected infants and children show slightly poorer mental and motor development (Caserta et al., 2013; Jedrychowski et al., 2009).

Prenatal exposure to *dioxins*—toxic compounds resulting from commercial waste incineration and burning of fuels, such as coal or oil—has particularly injurious effects. In addition to the problems just mentioned, it is linked to thyroid abnormalities in infancy and to an increased incidence of breast and uterine cancers in women, perhaps through altering hormone levels (ten Tusscher & Koppe, 2004). Even tiny amounts of dioxin in the paternal bloodstream cause a dramatic change in sex ratio of offspring: Affected men father nearly twice as many girls as boys (Ishihara et al., 2007). Dioxin seems to impair the fertility of Y-bearing sperm prior to conception.

Finally, persistent air pollution inflicts substantial prenatal harm. Exposure to traffic-related fumes and smog is associated with reduced infant head size, low birth weight, elevated infant death rates, impaired lung and immune-system development, and later respiratory illnesses (Proietti et al., 2013; Ritz et al., 2014).

INFECTIOUS DISEASE During her first prenatal visit, Yolanda's doctor asked her if she and Jay had already had measles, mumps, chickenpox, and several other illnesses. In addition, Yolanda was checked for the presence of several infections—and for good reason. As Table 3.4 indicates, certain diseases are major causes of miscarriage and birth defects.

This pregnant woman wears a face mask as protection against Singapore's smog, which occasionally hits life-threatening levels. Prolonged exposure to polluted air poses serious risks to prenatal development.

TABLE 3.4	Effects of Some Infectious Diseases During Pregnancy			
DISEASE	**MISCARRIAGE**	**PHYSICAL MALFORMATIONS**	**INTELLECTUAL DISABILITY**	**LOW BIRTH WEIGHT AND PREMATURITY**
Viral				
Acquired immune deficiency syndrome (AIDS)	✔	?	✔	✔
Chickenpox	✔	✔	✔	✔
Cytomegalovirus	✔	✔	✔	✔
Herpes simplex 2 (genital herpes)	✔	✔	✔	✔
Mumps	✔	✗	✗	✗
Rubella (German measles)	✔	✔	✔	✔
Bacterial				
Chlamydia	✔	?	✗	✔
Syphilis	✔	✔	✔	?
Tuberculosis	✔	?	✔	✔
Parasitic				
Malaria	✔	✗	✗	✔
Toxoplasmosis	✔	✔	✔	✔

✔ = established finding; ✗ = no present evidence; ? = possible effect that is not clearly established.

Sources: Kliegman et al., 2008; Waldorf & McAdams, 2013.

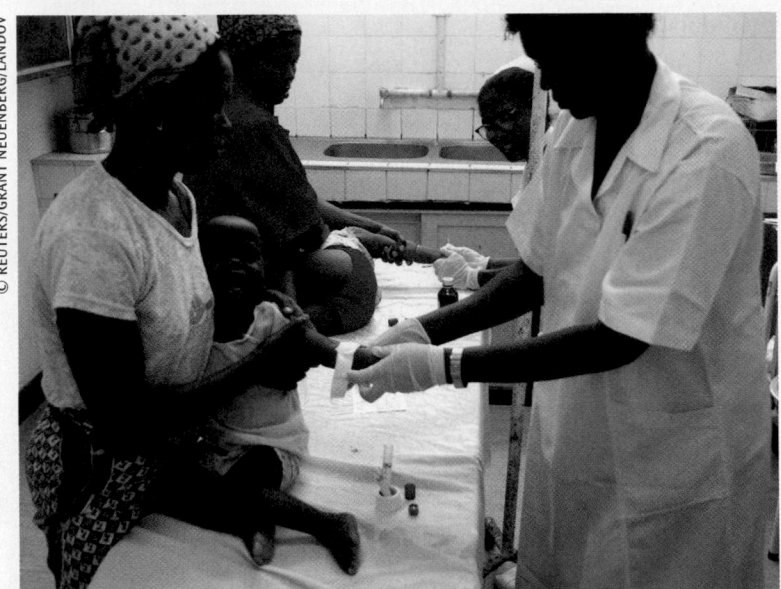

Babies are tested for the HIV virus in a clinic in Mozambique, Africa. Prenatal treatment with antiretroviral drugs reduces transmission of AIDS from mother to child by as much as 95 percent.

Viruses. In the mid-1960s, a worldwide epidemic of *rubella* (three-day, or German, measles) led to the birth of more than 20,000 American babies with serious defects and to 13,000 fetal and newborn deaths. Consistent with the sensitive-period concept, the greatest damage occurs when rubella strikes during the embryonic period. More than 50 percent of infants whose mothers become ill during that time show deafness; eye deformities, including cataracts; heart, genital, urinary, intestinal, bone, and dental defects; and intellectual disability. Infection during the fetal period is less harmful, but low birth weight, hearing loss, and bone defects may still occur. The organ damage inflicted by prenatal rubella often leads to lifelong health problems, including severe mental illness, diabetes, cardiovascular disease, and thyroid and immune-system dysfunction in adulthood (Duszak, 2009; Waldorf & McAdams, 2013). Routine vaccination in infancy and childhood has made new rubella outbreaks unlikely in industrialized nations. But an estimated 110,000 cases of prenatal infection continue to occur each year, primarily in developing countries in Africa and Asia with weak or absent immunization programs (World Health Organization, 2014b).

The *human immunodeficiency virus (HIV),* which can lead to *acquired immune deficiency syndrome (AIDS),* a disease that destroys the immune system, has infected increasing numbers of women over the past three decades. Currently, women account for one-fourth of cases in North America, Western Europe, and East Asia. Although the incidence of AIDS has declined in industrialized nations, the disease is rampant in developing countries, where 95 percent of new infections occur, more than half of which affect women. In South Africa, for example, nearly 30 percent of all pregnant women are HIV-positive (South African Department of Health, 2009). Untreated HIV-infected expectant mothers pass the deadly virus to the developing organism 10 to 20 percent of the time.

AIDS progresses rapidly in infants. By 6 months, weight loss, diarrhea, and repeated respiratory illnesses are common. The virus also causes brain damage, as indicated by seizures, gradual loss in brain weight, and delayed cognitive and motor development. Nearly half of prenatal AIDS babies die by 1 year of age and 90 percent by age 3 (Devi et al., 2009). Antiretroviral drug therapy reduces prenatal transmission by as much as 95 percent, with no harmful consequences of drug treatment for children. These medications have led to a dramatic decline in prenatally acquired AIDS in Western nations. And recently, several babies born with HIV who were given aggressive retroviral treatment within 2 days after birth appeared free of the disease (McNeil, 2014). Although distribution is increasing, antiretroviral drugs remain unavailable to about half of people needing treatment in impoverished regions of the world (UNAIDS, 2012).

As Table 3.4 reveals, the developing organism is especially sensitive to the family of herpes viruses, for which no vaccine or treatment exists. Among these, *cytomegalovirus* (the most frequent prenatal infection, transmitted through respiratory or sexual contact) and *herpes simplex 2* (which is sexually transmitted) are especially dangerous. In both, the virus invades the mother's genital tract, infecting babies either during pregnancy or at birth. Both diseases often have no symptoms, very mild symptoms, or symptoms with which people are unfamiliar, thereby increasing the likelihood of contagion. Pregnant women who are not in a mutually monogamous relationship are at greatest risk.

Bacterial and Parasitic Diseases. Table 3.4 also includes several bacterial and parasitic diseases. Among the most common is *toxoplasmosis,* an infection caused by a parasite found in many animals. Pregnant women may become infected from handling contaminated soil while gardening, contact with the feces of infected cats, or eating raw or undercooked meat or unwashed fruits and vegetables. About 40 percent of women who have the disease transmit it to the developing organism. If it strikes during the first trimester, it is likely to cause eye and brain damage. Later infection is linked to mild visual and cognitive impairments. And about 80 percent of affected newborns with no obvious signs of damage develop learning or visual disabilities in later life (Diav-Citrin, 2011; Jones, Lopez, & Wilson, 2003). Expectant mothers can avoid toxoplasmosis by making sure that the meat they eat is well-cooked, having pet cats checked for the disease, and turning over the care of litter boxes and the garden to other family members.

Other Maternal Factors

Besides avoiding teratogens, expectant parents can support the development of the embryo and fetus in other ways. Regular exercise, good nutrition, and emotional well-being of the mother are essential. Problems that may result from maternal and fetal blood type differences can be prevented. Finally, many prospective parents wonder how a mother's age affects the course of pregnancy. We examine each of these factors in the following sections.

EXERCISE   Yolanda continued her half-hour aerobic workout three times a week into the third trimester, although her doctor cautioned against bouncing, jolting, and jogging movements that might subject the fetus to too many shocks and startles. In healthy, physically fit women, regular moderate exercise, such as walking, swimming, biking, or an aerobic workout, is related to improved fetal cardiovascular functioning, higher birth weight, and a reduction in risk for certain complications, such as pregnancy-induced maternal diabetes and high blood pressure (May et al., 2010; Olson et al., 2009). However, frequent, vigorous exercise, especially late in pregnancy, results in lower birth weight than in healthy, nonexercising controls (Clapp et al., 2002; Leet & Flick, 2003). Hospital-sponsored childbirth education programs frequently offer exercise classes and suggest appropriate routines that help prepare for labor and delivery.

During the last trimester, when the abdomen grows very large, mothers have difficulty moving freely and often must cut back on exercise. Most women, however, do not engage in sufficient moderate exercise during pregnancy to promote their own and their baby's health (Poudevigne & O'Connor, 2006). An expectant mother who remains fit experiences fewer physical discomforts, such as back pain, upward pressure on the chest, or difficulty breathing in the final weeks.

Pregnant women with health problems, such as circulatory difficulties or a history of miscarriages, should consult their doctor about a physical fitness routine. For these mothers, exercise (especially the wrong kind) can endanger the pregnancy.

NUTRITION   During the prenatal period, when children are growing more rapidly than at any other time, they depend totally on the mother for nutrients. A healthy diet, consisting of a gradual increase in calories—an extra 100 calories a day in the first trimester, 265 in the second, and 430 in the third—resulting in a weight gain of 25 to 30 pounds (10 to 13.5 kilograms), helps ensure the health of mother and baby.

Consequences of Prenatal Malnutrition.   During World War II, a severe famine occurred in the Netherlands, giving scientists a rare opportunity to study the impact of nutrition on prenatal development. Findings revealed that the sensitive-period concept operates with nutrition, just as it does with teratogens. Women affected by the famine during the first trimester were more likely to have miscarriages or give birth to babies with physical defects. When women were past the first trimester, fetuses usually survived, but many were born underweight and had small heads (Stein et al., 1975).

Prenatal malnutrition can cause serious damage to the central nervous system. The poorer the mother's diet, the greater the loss in brain weight, especially if malnutrition occurred during the third trimester. During that time, the brain is increasing rapidly in size, and for it to reach its full potential, a maternal diet high in all the basic nutrients is necessary (Hovdenak & Haram, 2012). An inadequate diet during pregnancy can also distort the structure of other

Prenatal malnutrition can damage the central nervous system and other organs. A government-supported farmers' market nutrition program enables this low-income expectant mother to purchase fruits and vegetables.

organs, including the liver, kidney, and pancreas, resulting in lifelong health problems (refer again to the Biology and Environment box on page 103).

Because poor nutrition suppresses development of the immune system, prenatally malnourished babies frequently catch respiratory illnesses (Chandra, 1991). In addition, they often are irritable and unresponsive to stimulation. Like drug-addicted newborns, they have a high-pitched cry that is particularly distressing to their caregivers. In poverty-stricken families, these effects quickly combine with a stressful home life. With age, delays in motor, attention, and memory development, low intelligence test scores, and serious learning problems become more apparent (Monk, Georgieff, & Osterholm, 2013).

Prevention and Treatment. Many studies show that providing pregnant women with adequate food has a substantial impact on the health of their newborn babies. Yet the growth demands of the prenatal period require more than just increased quantity of food. Vitamin–mineral enrichment is also crucial. For example, taking a folic acid supplement around the time of conception reduces by more than 70 percent abnormalities of the neural tube, such as *anencephaly* and *spina bifida* (see Table 2.4 on page 64). Folic acid supplementation early in pregnancy also reduces the risk of other physical defects, including cleft lip and palate, circulatory system and urinary tract abnormalities, and limb deformities. Furthermore, adequate folic acid intake during the last 10 weeks of pregnancy cuts in half the risk of premature delivery and low birth weight (Goh & Koren, 2008; Hovdenak & Haram, 2012).

Because of these findings, U.S. government guidelines recommend that all women of childbearing age consume 0.4 milligrams of folic acid per day. For women who have previously had a pregnancy affected by neural tube defect, the recommended amount is 5 milligrams (dosage must be carefully monitored, as excessive intake can be harmful) (Talaulikar & Arulkumaran, 2011). Since many U.S. pregnancies are unplanned (see page 92), government regulations mandate that bread, flour, rice, pasta, and other grain products be fortified with folic acid.

Other vitamins and minerals also have established benefits. Enriching women's diets with calcium helps prevent maternal high blood pressure and low birth weight. Adequate magnesium and zinc reduce the risk of many prenatal and birth complications (Hovdenak & Haram, 2012). Fortifying table salt with iodine virtually eradicates *infantile hypothyroidism*—a condition of stunted growth and cognitive impairment caused by prenatal iodine deficiency, that is a common cause of intellectual disability in many parts of the world (Williams, 2008). And sufficient vitamins C and E and iron beginning early in pregnancy promote growth of the placenta and healthy birth weight (Gambling, Kennedy, & McArdle, 2011; Klemmensen et al., 2009). Nevertheless, a supplement program should complement, not replace, efforts to improve maternal diets during pregnancy. For women who do not get enough food or an adequate variety of foods, multivitamin tablets are a necessary, but not sufficient, intervention.

When poor nutrition continues throughout pregnancy, infants usually require more than dietary improvement. In response to their tired, restless behavior, parents tend to be less sensitive and stimulating. Babies, in turn, become even more passive and withdrawn. Successful interventions must break this cycle of apathetic caregiver–baby interaction. Some do so by teaching parents how to interact effectively with their infants; others focus on stimulating infants to promote active engagement with their physical and social surroundings (Grantham-McGregor, Schofield, & Powell, 1987; Grantham-McGregor et al., 1994).

Although prenatal malnutrition is highest in poverty-stricken regions of the world, it is not limited to developing countries. The U.S. Special Supplemental Nutrition Program for Women, Infants, and Children (WIC), which provides food packages and nutrition education to low-income pregnant women, reaches about 90 percent of those who qualify because of their extremely low incomes (U.S. Department of Agriculture, 2012). But many U.S. women who need nutrition intervention are not eligible for WIC.

TRACY A. WOODWARD/THE WASHINGTON POST VIA GETTY IMAGES

EMOTIONAL STRESS When women experience severe emotional stress during pregnancy, their babies are at risk for a wide variety of difficulties. Intense anxiety—especially during the first two trimesters—is associated with higher rates of miscarriage, prematurity, low birth weight, infant respiratory and digestive illnesses, colic (persistent infant crying), sleep disturbances, and irritability during the child's first three years (Dunkel-Shetter & Lobel, 2012; Field, 2011; Lazinski, Shea, & Steiner, 2008). Prenatal stressors consistently found to impair infant physical and psychological well-being include chronic strain due to poverty, neighborhood crime, or homelessness; major negative life events such as divorce or death of a family member; community-wide disasters such as earthquakes or terrorist attacks; and fears specific to pregnancy and childbirth, including anxiety about the health and survival of the baby and oneself.

How can maternal stress affect the developing organism? **TAKE A MOMENT...** To understand this process, list the changes you sensed in your own body the last time you were under stress. When we experience fear and anxiety, stimulant hormones released into our bloodstream—such as *epinephrine* (adrenaline) and *cortisol,* known as the "flight or fight" hormones—cause us to be "poised for action." Large amounts of blood are sent to parts of the body involved in the defensive response—the brain, the heart, and the muscles in the arms, legs, and trunk. Blood flow to other organs, including the uterus, is reduced. As a result, the fetus is deprived of a full supply of oxygen and nutrients.

Maternal stress hormones also cross the placenta, causing a dramatic rise in fetal stress hormones (evident in the amniotic fluid) and, therefore, in fetal heart rate, blood pressure, blood glucose, and activity level (Kinsella & Monk, 2009; Weinstock, 2008). Excessive fetal stress may permanently alter fetal neurological functioning, thereby heightening stress reactivity in later life. In several studies, infants and children of mothers who experienced severe prenatal anxiety displayed cortisol levels that were either abnormally high or abnormally low, both of which signal impaired physiological capacity to manage stress. Consistent with these findings, such children are more upset than their agemates when faced with novel or challenging experiences—effects that persist into adolescence and early adulthood (Entringer et al., 2009; Van den Bergh et al., 2008).

Furthermore, maternal emotional stress during pregnancy predicts weakened immune system functioning and increased susceptibility to infectious disease in childhood (Nielsen et al., 2011). It is also associated with diverse negative behavioral outcomes, including anxiety, short attention span, anger, aggression, overactivity, and lower intelligence test scores, above and beyond the impact of other risks, such as maternal smoking during pregnancy, low birth weight, postnatal maternal anxiety, and low SES (Loomans et al., 2011; Monk, Georgieff, & Osterholm, 2013).

But stress-related prenatal complications are greatly reduced when mothers have partners, other family members, and friends who offer social support (Bloom et al., 2013; Luecken et al., 2013). The relationship of social support to positive pregnancy outcomes and subsequent child development is particularly strong for economically disadvantaged women, who often lead highly stressful lives (see the Social Issues: Health box on page 114).

RH FACTOR INCOMPATIBILITY When inherited blood types of mother and fetus differ, serious problems sometimes result. The most common cause of these difficulties is **Rh factor incompatibility.** When the mother is Rh-negative (lacks the Rh blood protein) and the father is Rh-positive (has the protein), the baby may inherit the father's Rh-positive blood type. (Because Rh-positive blood is dominant and Rh-negative blood is recessive, the chances are good that the baby will be Rh-positive.) If even a little of a fetus's Rh-positive blood crosses the placenta into the Rh-negative mother's bloodstream, she begins to form antibodies to the foreign Rh protein. If these enter the fetus's system, they destroy red blood cells, reducing the oxygen supply to organs and tissues. Intellectual disability, miscarriage, heart damage, and infant death can occur.

It takes time for the mother to produce Rh antibodies, so firstborn children are rarely affected. The danger increases with each additional pregnancy. Fortunately, Rh incompatibility can be prevented in most cases. After the birth of each Rh-positive baby, Rh-negative mothers are routinely given a vaccine to prevent the buildup of antibodies. In emergency cases, blood transfusions can be performed immediately after delivery or, if necessary, even before birth.

LOOK and LISTEN

List prenatal environmental factors that can compromise later academic performance and social adjustment. Ask several adults who hope someday to be parents to explain what they know about each factor. How great is their need for prenatal education?

Social Issues: Health

The Nurse–Family Partnership: Reducing Maternal Stress and Enhancing Child Development Through Social Support

At age 17, Denise—an unemployed high-school dropout living with her disapproving parents—gave birth to Tara. Having no one to turn to for help during pregnancy and beyond, Denise felt overwhelmed and anxious much of the time. Tara was premature and cried uncontrollably, slept erratically, and suffered from frequent minor illnesses throughout her first year. When she reached school age, she had trouble keeping up academically, and her teachers described her as distractible, unable to sit still, angry, and uncooperative.

The Nurse–Family Partnership—currently implemented in hundreds of counties across 43 U.S. states, in six tribal communities, in the U.S. Virgin Islands, and internationally in Australia, Canada, the Netherlands, and the United Kingdom—is a voluntary home visiting program for first-time, low-income expectant mothers like Denise. Its goals are to reduce pregnancy and birth complications, promote competent early caregiving, and improve family conditions, thereby protecting children from lasting adjustment difficulties.

A registered nurse visits the home weekly during the first month after enrollment, twice a month during the remainder of pregnancy and through the middle of the child's second year, and then monthly until age 2. In these sessions, the nurse provides the mother with intensive social support—a sympathetic ear; assistance in accessing health and other community services and the help of family members (especially fathers and grandmothers); and encouragement to finish high school, find work, and engage in future family planning.

To evaluate the program's effectiveness, researchers randomly assigned large samples of mothers at risk for high prenatal stress (due to teenage pregnancy, poverty, and other negative life conditions) to nurse-visiting or comparison conditions (just prenatal care, or prenatal care plus infant referral for developmental problems). Families were followed through their child's school-age years and, in one experiment, into adolescence (Kitzman et al., 2010; Olds et al., 2004, 2007; Rubin et al., 2011).

As kindergartners, Nurse–Family Partnership children obtained higher language and intelligence test scores. And at both ages 6 and 9, children of home-visited mothers in the poorest mental health during pregnancy exceeded comparison children in academic achievement and displayed fewer behavior problems. Furthermore, from their baby's birth on, home-visited mothers were on a more favorable life course: They had fewer subsequent births, longer intervals between their first and second births, more frequent contact with the child's father, more stable intimate partnerships, less welfare dependence, and a greater sense of control over their lives—key factors in reducing subsequent prenatal stress and in protecting children's development. Perhaps for these reasons, adolescent children of home-visited mothers continued to be advantaged in academic achievement and reported less alcohol and drug use than comparison-group agemates.

Other findings revealed that professional nurses, compared with trained paraprofessionals,

COURTESY OF NURSE–FAMILY PARTNERSHIP

The Nurse–Family Partnership provides a first-time, low-income mother with regular home visits from a registered nurse, who offers social support and help in accessing community services. As a result, this child has a considerably better chance of developing favorably.

were far more effective in preventing outcomes associated with prenatal stress, including high infant fearfulness to novel stimuli and delayed mental development (Olds et al., 2002). Nurses were probably more proficient in individualizing program guidelines to fit the strengths and challenges faced by each family. They also might have had unique legitimacy as experts in the eyes of stressed mothers, more easily convincing them to take steps to reduce pregnancy complications that can trigger persisting developmental problems—such as those Tara displayed.

The Nurse–Family Partnership is highly cost-effective (Dawley, Loch, & Bindrich, 2007). For each $1 spent, it saves more than $5 in public spending on pregnancy complications, preterm births, and child and youth learning and behavior problems.

MATERNAL AGE AND PREVIOUS BIRTHS In Chapter 2, we noted that women who delay childbearing until their thirties or forties face increased risk of infertility, miscarriage, and babies with chromosomal defects. Are other pregnancy complications also more common for older mothers? Research consistently indicates that healthy women in their thirties have about the same rates as those in their twenties (Bianco et al., 1996; Dildy et al., 1996). Thereafter, as Figure 3.6 reveals, complication rates increase, with a sharp rise among women age 50 to 55—an age at which, because of menopause (end of menstruation) and aging reproductive organs, few women can conceive naturally (Salihu et al., 2003; Usta & Nassar, 2008).

In the case of teenage mothers, does physical immaturity cause prenatal problems? As we will see in Chapter 14, nature tries to ensure that once a girl can conceive, she is physically ready to carry and give birth to a baby. Infants born to teenagers have a higher rate of problems, but not directly because of maternal age. Most pregnant teenagers come from low-income backgrounds, where stress, poor nutrition, and health problems are common. Also, many are afraid to seek medical care. And in the United States, although the Affordable Care Act has greatly increased health insurance for pregnant adolescents, not all have full coverage.

The Importance of Prenatal Health Care

Yolanda had her first prenatal appointment three weeks after missing her menstrual period. After that, she visited the doctor's office once a month until she was seven months pregnant, then twice during the eighth month. As birth grew near, Yolanda's appointments increased to once a week. The doctor kept track of her general health, her weight gain, the capacity of her uterus and cervix to support the fetus, and the fetus's growth.

Yolanda's pregnancy, like most others, was free of complications. But unexpected difficulties can arise, especially if mothers have health problems. For example, the 5 percent of pregnant women who have diabetes need careful monitoring. Extra glucose in the diabetic mother's bloodstream increases the risk of pregnancy and birth problems, as well as brain damage and later learning difficulties (see the Biology and Environment box on page 116). Another complication, experienced by 5 to 10 percent of pregnant women, is *preeclampsia* (sometimes called *toxemia*), in which blood pressure increases sharply and the face, hands, and feet swell in the second half of pregnancy. If untreated, preeclampsia can cause convulsions in the mother and fetal death. Usually, hospitalization, bed rest, and drugs can lower blood pressure to a safe level (Vest & Cho, 2012). If not, the baby must be delivered at once.

Unfortunately, 6 percent of pregnant women in the United States wait until after the first trimester to seek prenatal care or receive none at all. As Figure 3.7 on page 117 shows, inadequate care is far more common among adolescent and low-income, ethnic minority mothers. Their infants are three times as likely to be born underweight and five times as likely to die as are babies of mothers who receive early medical attention (Child Trends, 2014b). Although government-sponsored health services for low-income pregnant women have been expanded, some do not qualify and must pay for at least part of their care. As we will see when we take up birth complications in Chapter 4, in nations where affordable medical care is universally available, such as Australia, Canada, Japan, and European countries, late-care pregnancies and maternal and infant health problems are greatly reduced.

Besides financial hardship, some mothers have other reasons for not seeking early prenatal care. These include *situational barriers* (difficulty finding a doctor, getting an appointment, and arranging transportation, and insensitive or unsatisfying experiences with clinic staff) and *personal barriers* (psychological stress, the demands of taking care of other young children, family crises, lack of knowledge about signs of pregnancy and benefits of prenatal care, and ambivalence about the pregnancy). Many also engage in high-risk behaviors, such as smoking and drug abuse, which they do not want to reveal to health professionals (Kitsantas, Gaffney, & Cheema, 2012). These women, who receive little or no prenatal care, are among those who need it most!

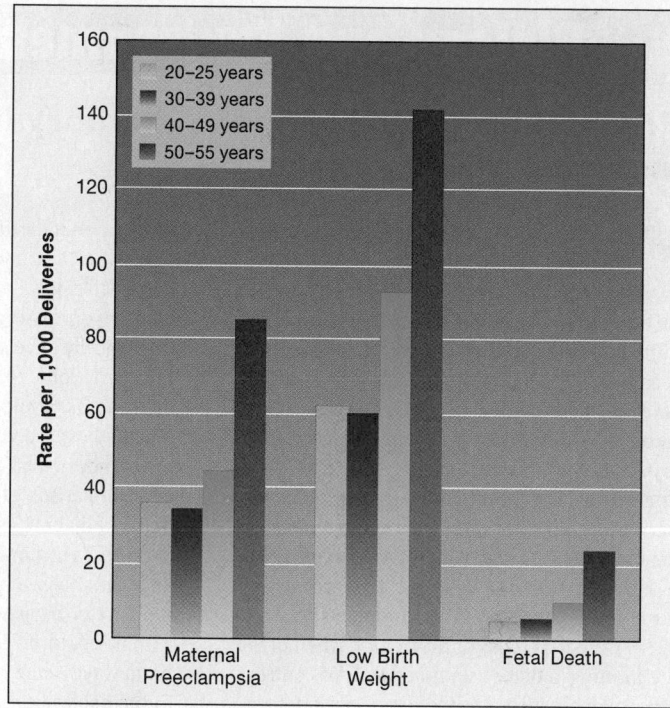

FIGURE 3.6   Relationship of maternal age to prenatal and birth complications. Complications increase after age 40, with a sharp rise between 50 and 55 years. (Based on Salihu et al., 2003.)

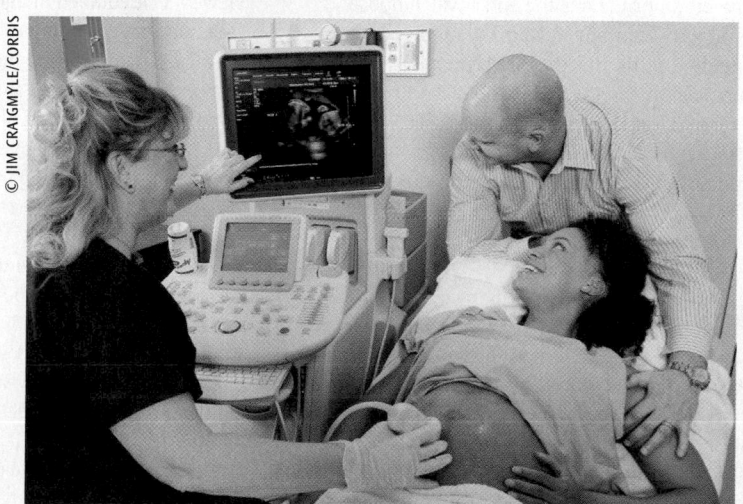

During a routine prenatal visit, a couple views an ultrasound image of twins. All pregnant women need regular prenatal care to protect their health and that of their babies.

Biology and Environment

Prenatal Iron Deficiency and Memory Impairments in Infants of Diabetic Mothers

Diabetes affects nearly 11 percent of Americans age 20 and older—a rate that has risen sharply over the past quarter century due to widespread overweight and obesity. Although its incidence is increasing among all sectors of the population, diabetes is at least twice as likely to affect low-income ethnic minority as white adults. Today, about 5 percent of expectant mothers are diabetic—twice as many as a decade ago. Most had the disease before becoming pregnant; others developed it during pregnancy (American Diabetes Association, 2014). In either case, their newborn babies are at risk for long-term developmental problems.

In the early weeks of pregnancy, when organs are forming, a diabetic mother's out-of-control blood glucose increases the risk of birth defects. Later in pregnancy, excess blood glucose causes the fetus to be "overfed" and to grow unusually large, often causing birth complications. Furthermore, to metabolize this flood of maternal glucose, the fetus secretes abnormally high levels of insulin—a circumstance that greatly increases demand for oxygen. To extract extra oxygen from the mother's system, the fetus increases production of oxygen-carrying red blood cells. This expanding red blood-cell mass requires extra iron, which the fetus can obtain only by taxing its own iron stores in the liver, muscles, heart, and brain.

In animal research on maternal diabetes, by late pregnancy iron stores decline sharply in the brain's temporal lobes (located on each side of the brain, just above the ears), which house structures centrally involved in memory development—specifically, the *hippocampus,* which plays a crucial role in the formation of new memories. Prenatal iron depletion interferes with growth of brain cells and their connections, permanently reducing the size and altering the structure of the hippocampus and impairing memory in laboratory rats (Jorgenson et al., 2005; Schmidt et al., 2007).

In human research, diabetic mothers bear children who, at later follow-ups, score lower than their agemates on intelligence tests (Nielson, Andersen, & Lundbye-Christensen, 2010). Is prenatal iron deficiency and resulting early damage to the brain's memory areas responsible? In a series of studies, Charles Nelson (2007a) and his collaborators recorded electrical brain waves to assess young infants' memory performance,

focusing on a particular slow brain wave in the temporal lobes believed to reflect memory processing.

Typically developing newborns come to recognize their mother's voice through repeated exposure during pregnancy (see page 100). In a comparison of newborns of diabetic mothers likely to have a brain iron deficiency (based on a measure of body iron stores) with normal-iron controls, brain waves were recorded as the babies listened to sound clips of their mother's or a stranger's voice (Sidappa et al., 2004). The controls showed a distinctive slow wave to each stimulus, indicating recognition of the mother's voice. The brain iron–deficient babies showed no difference in brain waves to the two stimuli, suggesting memory impairment of prenatal origin.

Do these memory deficits persist beyond the newborn period—evidence that diabetes-linked prenatal brain damage has lasting consequences? At 6 months, the researchers recorded brain waves while 6-month-old infants alternately viewed a videotaped image of their mother's face and that of an unfamiliar woman. Consistent with the newborn findings, control infants responded with distinct slow waves in the temporal lobes to the two faces, while infants of diabetic mothers displayed no difference (Nelson et al., 2000). Even after months of experience, they could not recognize their mother's facial image.

At an 8-month follow-up, babies were given a more challenging memory task. After feeling a novel object (an unusually shaped wooden block) held beneath an apron so they could not see it, the infants were tested visually: They viewed photos of the novel object interspersed with photos of familiar objects (Nelson et al., 2003). Again, infants of diabetic mothers showed no evidence of distinguishing the novel object from other stimuli. The control babies, in contrast,

© ARIEL SKELLEY/BLEND IMAGES/CORBIS

Maternal diabetes increases the fetus's risk of iron depletion and resulting damage to the brain's memory areas. This newborn of a diabetic mother is likely to have difficulty distinguishing his mother's voice from that of a stranger.

responded to the novel object with a stronger temporal-lobe slow wave, suggesting an ability to recognize the novel stimulus, even when presented in a different sensory modality.

Nelson and his colleagues have followed their research participants through the preschool years, amassing additional evidence for poorer memory (especially more rapid forgetting) in children born to diabetic mothers than in controls (Riggins et al., 2009). The findings highlight a previously hidden pregnancy complication: As a result of iron depletion in critical brain areas, a diabetic pregnancy places the fetus at risk for lasting memory deficits and thus for long-term learning and academic problems. The researchers believe that damage to the hippocampus, located deep inside the temporal lobes, is responsible.

Nelson's research underscores the need for more effective ways of intervening with iron supplementation in diabetic pregnancies, as well as the importance of sufficient dietary iron for every expectant mother and her fetus. Diabetes prevention is also vital, through weight control, increased exercise, and improved diet beginning in childhood.

Applying What We Know

Do's and Don'ts for a Healthy Pregnancy

DO	DON'T
Do make sure that you have been vaccinated against infectious diseases that are dangerous to the embryo and fetus, such as rubella, before you get pregnant. Most vaccinations are not safe during pregnancy.	Don't take any drugs without consulting your doctor.
Do see a doctor as soon as you suspect that you are pregnant, and continue to get regular medical checkups throughout pregnancy.	Don't smoke. If you have already smoked during part of your pregnancy, cut down or, better yet, quit. If other members of your family smoke, ask them to quit or to smoke outside.
Do eat a well-balanced diet and take vitamin–mineral supplements, as prescribed by your doctor, both prior to and during pregnancy. Gain 25 to 30 pounds gradually.	Don't drink alcohol from the time you decide to get pregnant.
Do obtain information about prenatal development from your doctor, local library, bookstore, and health organization websites. Ask your doctor about anything that concerns you.	Don't engage in activities that might expose your embryo or fetus to environmental hazards, such as radiation or chemical pollutants. If you work in an occupation that involves these agents, ask for a safer assignment or a leave of absence.
Do keep physically fit through moderate exercise. If possible, join a special exercise class for expectant mothers.	Don't engage in activities that might expose your embryo or fetus to harmful infectious diseases, such as toxoplasmosis.
Do avoid emotional stress. If you are a single expectant mother, find a relative or friend on whom you can rely for emotional support.	Don't choose pregnancy as a time to go on a diet.
Do get plenty of rest. An overtired mother is at risk for pregnancy complications.	Don't gain too much weight during pregnancy. A very large weight gain is associated with complications.
Do enroll in a prenatal and childbirth education class with your partner or other companion. When you know what to expect, the nine months before birth can be one of the most joyful times of life.	

Clearly, public education about the importance of early and sustained prenatal care for all pregnant women is badly needed. For women who are young, less-educated, low-income, or under stress and therefore at risk for inadequate prenatal care, assistance in making appointments, drop-in child-care centers, and convenient, free, or low-cost transportation are vital.

Culturally sensitive health-care practices are also helpful. Low-SES minority women often report depersonalizing experiences during prenatal appointments, including condescending interactions with medical staff and hurried checkups with no opportunity to ask questions. These behaviors are especially disturbing to women whose cultures emphasize warm, personalized interaction styles and a relaxed sense of time—causing many to avoid returning (Downe et al., 2009). In a strategy called *group prenatal care,* after each medical checkup, trained leaders provide minority expectant mothers with a group discussion session, which is conducted in their native language and encourages them to talk about important health issues (Massey, Rising, & Ickovics, 2006; Tandon et al., 2012). Compared to mothers receiving traditional brief appointments, participants engaged in more health-promoting behaviors and also gave birth to babies with a reduced incidence of prematurity and low birth weight—major predictors of newborn survival and healthy development. Applying What We Know above lists "do's and don'ts" for a healthy pregnancy, based on our discussion of the prenatal environment.

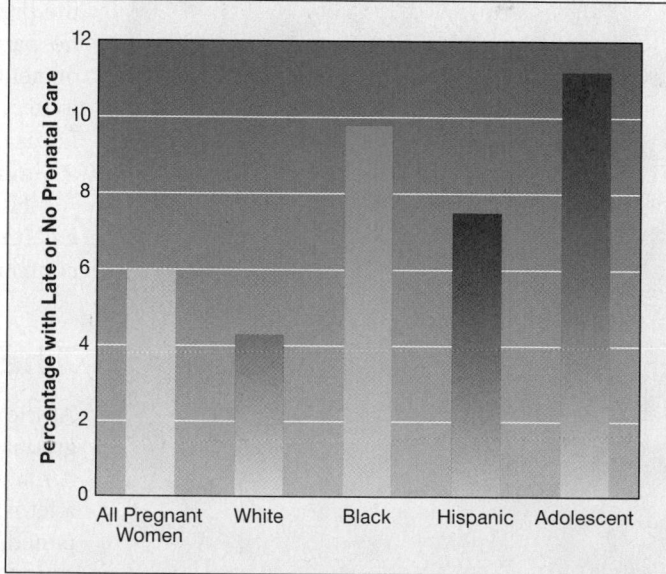

FIGURE 3.7 **Expectant mothers in the United States with late (after the first trimester) or no prenatal care.** More than 9 percent of low-income minority mothers, and about 10 percent of adolescent mothers, receive inadequate prenatal care. (Based on Child Trends, 2014b.)

Ask Yourself

- **REVIEW**   Why is it difficult to determine the prenatal effects of many environmental agents, such as drugs and pollution?

- **CONNECT**   How do teratogens illustrate the notion of epigenesis, presented in Chapter 2, that environments can affect gene expression? (See page 86 to review.)

- **APPLY**   Nora, pregnant for the first time, believes that a few cigarettes and a glass of wine a day won't be harmful. Provide Nora with research-based reasons for not smoking or drinking.

- **REFLECT**   If you had to choose five environmental influences to publicize in a campaign aimed at promoting healthy prenatal development, which ones would you choose, and why?

3.7 What factors contribute to preparation for parenthood during the prenatal period?

Preparing for Parenthood

Although we have discussed many ways that development can be thrown off course during the prenatal period, more than 90 percent of pregnancies in industrialized nations result in healthy newborn babies. For expectant parents fortunate enough to have stable relationships, sufficient income, and networks of social support, the prenatal period is not a time of medical hazard. Rather, it is a period of major life change accompanied by excitement, anticipation, and looking inward. The nine months before birth not only permit the fetus to grow but also give men and women time to develop a new sense of themselves as mothers and fathers.

This period of psychological preparation is vital. In one study, more than 100 U.S. first-time expectant married couples, varying in age and SES, were interviewed about their pregnancy experiences. Participants reported a wide range of reactions to learning they were expecting. Nearly two-thirds were positive, about one-third mixed or neutral, and only a handful negative (Feeney et al., 2001). An unplanned pregnancy was especially likely to spark negative or ambivalent feelings. But as the pregnancy moved along, these reactions subsided. By the third trimester, no participants felt negatively, and only about 10 percent remained mixed or neutral. Similarly, when a large sample of German expectant parents was followed over time, life satisfaction increased as birth approached (Dyrdal & Lucas, 2013). Couples' upbeat attitudes reflected acceptance of parenthood—a coming to terms with this imminent, radical change in their lives.

How effectively individuals construct a parental identity during pregnancy has important consequences for the parent–child relationship. Many factors contribute to the personal adjustments that take place.

The Baby Becomes a Reality

At the beginning of pregnancy, the baby's arrival seems far in the future. But gradually, as the woman's abdomen enlarges, the baby starts to become a reality. A major turning point occurs when expectant parents have concrete proof that a fetus is, indeed, developing inside the uterus. For Yolanda and Jay, this happened 13 weeks into the pregnancy, when their doctor showed them an ultrasound image. As Jay described the experience, "We saw it, these little hands and feet waving and kicking. It's really a baby in there!" Sensing the fetus's movements for the first time can be just as thrilling. Of course, the mother feels these "kicks" first, but soon after, the partner (and siblings) can participate by touching her abdomen.

Parents get to know the fetus as an individual through these signs of life. And both are likely to form an emotional attachment to the new being,

For many expectant parents, feeling the fetus's movements initiates an emotional attachment to the new being.

especially when their relationship is positive, extended family members are supportive, and the mother reports favorable psychological well-being (Alhusen, 2008; Bouchard, 2011). In a Swedish study, the stronger mothers' and fathers' attachment to their fetus, the more positively they related to each other and to their baby after birth, and the more upbeat the baby's mood at age 8 months (White et al., 1999).

Models of Effective Parenthood

As pregnancy proceeds, expectant parents think about important models of parenthood in their own lives. When men and women have had good relationships with their own parents, they are more likely to develop positive images of themselves as parents during pregnancy (Deutsch et al., 1988). These images, in turn, predict harmonious marital communication and effective parenting during infancy and early childhood (Curran et al., 2005; McHale et al., 2004).

If their own parental relationships are mixed or negative, expectant mothers and fathers may have trouble building a healthy picture of themselves as parents. Some adults handle this challenge by seeking other examples of effective parenthood. One expectant father named Roger shared these thoughts with his wife and several couples, who met regularly with a counselor to talk about their concerns during pregnancy:

> I rethink past experiences with my father and my family and am aware of how I was raised. I just think I don't want to do that again. . . . I wish there had been more connection and closeness and a lot more respect for who I was. For me, my father-in-law . . . is a mix of empathy and warmth plus stepping back and being objective that I want to be as a father. (Colman & Colman, 1991, p. 148)

Like Roger, many people come to terms with negative experiences in their own childhood, recognize that other options are available to them, and build healthier and happier relationships with their children (Thompson, 2006). Roger achieved this understanding after participating in a special intervention program for expectant parents. Couples who take part in such programs feel better about themselves and their relationships, communicate more effectively, feel more competent as parents after the baby arrives, and adapt more easily when family problems arise (Glade, Bean, & Vira, 2005; Petch & Halford, 2008).

© BLEND IMAGES/ALAMY

Couples who have a warm, respectful relationship and who look forward to parenthood often find that pregnancy brings them closer. As a result, they are well-equipped to handle the changes that will come after the baby arrives.

The Parental Relationship

The most important preparation for parenthood takes place in the context of the parents' relationship. Expectant couples who are unhappy in their marriages and who have difficulty working out their differences continue to be distant, dissatisfied, and poor problem solvers after childbirth (Houts et al., 2008; Kluwer & Johnson, 2007). Deciding to have a baby in hopes of improving a troubled relationship is a serious mistake. In a distressed marriage, pregnancy adds to rather than lessens family conflict (Perren et al., 2005). Furthermore, expectant couples experiencing prolonged anxiety and depressive symptoms influence prenatal development negatively (see page 113). They are in crucial need of intervention, starting as early as possible during pregnancy, directed at alleviating difficulties that contribute to poor family functioning.

When a couple's relationship is faring well and both partners want and plan for the baby, the excitement of a first pregnancy may bring husband and wife closer (Dyrdal & Lucas, 2013; Feeney et al., 2001). Parents who have forged a solid foundation of love and respect are well-equipped for the challenges of pregnancy. They are also prepared to handle the much more demanding changes that will take place once their baby is born. We will discuss the transition to parenthood in greater depth in the next chapter.

Ask Yourself

- **REVIEW** List psychological factors during pregnancy that predict parenting effectiveness after childbirth.

- **APPLY** Megan, who is expecting her first child, recalls her own mother as cold and distant. Suggest steps she can take to form a confident, positive picture of herself as a new parent.

- **REFLECT** Ask your parents and/or your grandparents to describe attitudes and experiences that fostered or interfered with their capacity to build a positive parental identity when they were expecting their first child. Do you think building a healthy picture of oneself as a parent is more challenging today than it was in your parents' or grandparents' generation?

Summary

Motivations for Parenthood (p. 91)

3.1 How has decision making about childbearing changed over the past half century, and what are the consequences for child rearing and child development?

- Adults in Western industrialized nations are freer today to choose whether, when, and how to have children. Motivations for parenthood have increasingly emphasized personal fulfillment and deemphasized societal obligations.

- In industrialized nations, family size has declined over the past half century, reflecting in part the need to balance career and family. Birth order and spacing are unrelated to children's intelligence. The greater number of births to low-SES mothers accounts for the link between large family size and children's lower intelligence test scores.

- Although older parents may be better equipped financially and emotionally to rear children, reproductive capacity declines with age, particularly as women reach their late thirties. Advanced maternal and paternal age is associated with increased risk of chromosomal and genetically influenced disorders.

Prenatal Development (p. 95)

3.2 List the three phases of prenatal development, and describe the major milestones of each.

- The first prenatal phase, the germinal period, lasts about two weeks, from fertilization and formation of the zygote through **implantation** of the **blastocyst** in the uterine lining. During this time, structures that will support prenatal growth begin to form, including the **placenta** and the **umbilical cord.**

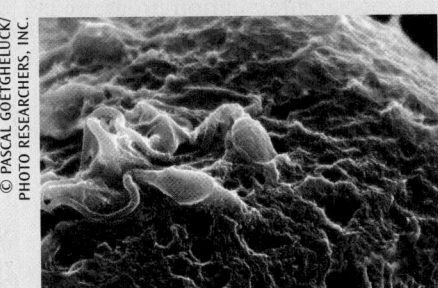

© PASCAL GOETGHELUCK/ PHOTO RESEARCHERS, INC.

- During the period of the **embryo,** from weeks 2 to 8, the foundations for all body structures are laid down. Initially, the nervous system develops fastest, forming the **neural tube,** the top of which swells to form the brain. Other organs, including the reproductive system, follow. At the end of this period, the embryo responds to touch and can move.

- The period of the **fetus,** lasting until the end of pregnancy, involves a dramatic increase in body size and completion of physical structures. At the end of the second **trimester,** most of the brain's neurons are in place. In the third trimester, between 22 and 26 weeks, the fetus reaches the **age of viability.** The brain continues to develop rapidly, and new sensory and behavioral capacities emerge: The fetus distinguishes different voices and language and musical sounds. Gradually, the lungs mature, and the fetus fills the uterus.

Prenatal Environmental Influences (p. 101)

3.3 What are teratogens, and what factors influence their impact?

- **Teratogens** are environmental agents that cause damage during the prenatal period. Their impact varies with the amount and length of exposure, the genetic makeup of mother and fetus, the presence or absence of other harmful agents, and the age of the organism at time of exposure. The developing organism is especially vulnerable during the embryonic period. In addition to immediate physical damage, some health outcomes may appear later in development, and physical defects may have indirect psychological consequences.

3.4 List agents known to be or suspected of being teratogens, and discuss evidence supporting their harmful impact.

- Drugs, cigarettes, alcohol, radiation, environmental pollution, and infectious diseases are teratogens that can endanger the developing organism. Currently, the most widely used potent teratogen is isotretinoin, a drug used to treat severe acne. The prenatal impact of many other commonly used medications, such as aspirin and caffeine, is hard to separate from other factors correlated with drug taking.

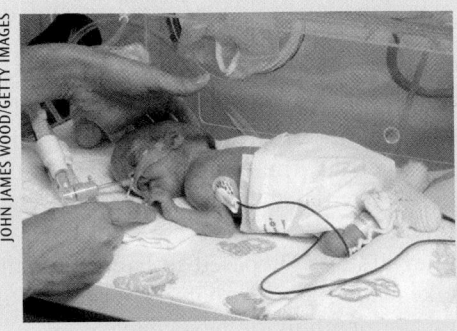

JOHN JAMES WOOD/GETTY IMAGES

- Babies born to users of heroin, methadone, or cocaine are at risk for a wide variety of problems, including prematurity, low birth weight, physical defects, and breathing difficulties around the time of birth. However, long-term consequences of maternal cocaine use are not well-established.

- Infants whose parents use tobacco are often born underweight and have attention, learning, and behavior problems in early childhood. Maternal alcohol consumption can lead to **fetal alcohol spectrum disorder (FASD)**. **Fetal alcohol syndrome (FAS)** involves slow physical growth, facial abnormalities, permanent intellectual impairment, and lasting mental health problems. Milder forms—**partial fetal alcohol syndrome (p-FAS)** or **alcohol-related neurodevelopmental disorder (ARND)**—affect children whose mothers consumed smaller quantities of alcohol.

- Prenatal exposure to high levels of radiation, mercury, PCBs, lead, and dioxins leads to physical malformations and severe brain damage; low-level exposure to these teratogens has also been linked to diverse impairments. Persistent exposure to air pollution also inflicts substantial prenatal harm.

- Among infectious diseases, rubella causes a wide variety of abnormalities. Babies with prenatally transmitted HIV rapidly develop AIDS, which leads to brain damage and early death; antiretroviral drug therapy dramatically reduces prenatal transmission. Cytomegalovirus, herpes simplex 2, and toxoplasmosis can also be devastating to the embryo and fetus.

3.5 Describe the impact of other maternal factors on prenatal development.

- Regular moderate exercise during pregnancy contributes to maternal health, fetal cardiovascular functioning, and higher birth weight. However, very vigorous exercise results in lower birth weight.

- When the mother's diet is inadequate, low birth weight and damage to the brain and other organs are major concerns. Vitamin–mineral supplementation, including folic acid, before conception and continuing during pregnancy can prevent prenatal and birth complications.

- Severe emotional stress is linked to pregnancy complications and permanent alteration of fetal neurological functioning, resulting in impaired capacity to manage stress. Long-term outcomes include a weakened immune system, anxiety, short attention span, behavior problems, and lower intelligence test scores. The negative impact of prenatal stress can be reduced by providing the mother with emotional support.

- **Rh factor incompatibility**—an Rh-positive fetus developing within an Rh-negative mother—can lead to oxygen deprivation, brain and heart damage, and infant death.

- Older mothers face increased risk of miscarriage and babies with chromosomal defects, and, after age 40, a rise in other pregnancy complications. Poor health and environmental risks associated with poverty are the strongest predictors of pregnancy complications in teenage mothers.

3.6 Why is early and regular health care vital during the prenatal period?

- Unexpected difficulties, such as preeclampsia, can arise, especially when pregnant women have health problems to begin with. Prenatal care is especially crucial for those women least likely to seek it—in particular, those who are young or poverty-stricken. Among low-SES ethnic minority mothers, culturally sensitive health-care practices—such as group prenatal care—can lead to more health-promoting behaviors.

Preparing for Parenthood (p. 118)

3.7 What factors contribute to preparation for parenthood during the prenatal period?

- The nine months of pregnancy provide an adjustment period for expectant parents, who typically become increasingly positive about their new roles as childbirth approaches. Ultrasound images and fetal movements make the baby a reality, and parents may form an emotional attachment to the new being. They also rely on effective models of parenthood to build positive images of themselves as mothers and fathers.

- The most important preparation for parenthood takes place in the context of the couple's relationship. A troubled relationship usually worsens with expectant parenthood, while preparing to welcome a baby may strengthen a good relationship.

Important Terms and Concepts

age of viability (p. 99)
alcohol-related neurodevelopmental disorder (ARND) (p. 107)
amnion (p. 97)
amniotic fluid (p. 97)
blastocyst (p. 97)
chorion (p. 97)
embryo (p. 98)

embryonic disk (p. 97)
fetal alcohol spectrum disorder (FASD) (p. 106)
fetal alcohol syndrome (FAS) (p. 106)
fetus (p. 99)
implantation (p. 97)
lanugo (p. 99)
neural tube (p. 98)
partial fetal alcohol syndrome (p-FAS) (p. 106)

placenta (p. 97)
Rh factor incompatibility (p. 113)
teratogen (p. 101)
trimesters (p. 99)
trophoblast (p. 97)
umbilical cord (p. 98)
vernix (p. 99)

Birth and the Newborn Baby

"A Happy Day"
Natthanan Inhusub
9 years, Thailand

Safely held and nurtured by her parents, this baby thrives both physically and emotionally. In Chapter 4, we explore the birth process, the marvelous competencies of the newborn, and the challenges of new parenthood.

REPRINTED WITH PERMISSION FROM THE INTERNATIONAL MUSEUM OF CHILDREN'S ART, OSLO, NORWAY

Although Yolanda and Jay completed their child development course three months before their baby was born, both agreed to return to share with next term's class their reactions to birth and new parenthood. Two-week-old Joshua came along as well. Yolanda and Jay's story revealed that the birth of a baby is one of the most dramatic and emotional events in human experience. Jay was present throughout Yolanda's labor and delivery. Yolanda explained:

> By morning, we knew I was in labor. It was Thursday, so we went in for my usual weekly appointment. The doctor said, yes, the baby was on the way, but it would be a while. He told us to go home and relax and come to the hospital in three or four hours. We checked in at 3 in the afternoon; Joshua arrived at 2 o'clock the next morning. When, finally, I was ready to deliver, it went quickly; a half hour or so and some good hard pushes, and there he was! His face was red and puffy, his head was misshapen, but I thought, "Our son! I can't believe he's really here."

Jay was also elated by Joshua's birth. "I wanted to support Yolanda and to experience as much as I could. It was awesome, indescribable," he said, holding little Joshua over his shoulder and patting and kissing him gently.

In this chapter, we explore the experience of childbirth, from both the parents' and the baby's point of view. Today, women in industrialized nations have many choices about where and how they give birth, and hospitals go to great lengths to make the arrival of a new baby a rewarding, family-centered event.

Joshua reaped the benefits of Yolanda and Jay's careful attention to his needs during pregnancy. He was strong, alert, and healthy at birth. Nevertheless, the birth process does not always go smoothly. We will consider the pros and cons of medical interventions, such as pain-relieving drugs and surgical deliveries, designed to ease a difficult birth and protect the health of mother and baby. Our discussion also addresses the problems of infants born underweight or too early.

Finally, Yolanda and Jay spoke candidly about how their lives had changed since Joshua's arrival. "It's exciting and wonderful," reflected Yolanda, "but the adjustments are enormous. I wasn't quite prepared for the intensity of Joshua's 24-hour-a-day demands." In the concluding sections of this chapter, we look closely at the remarkable capacities of newborns to adapt to the external world and to communicate their needs. We also consider how parents adjust to the realities of everyday life with a new baby. ■

The Stages of Childbirth

It is not surprising that childbirth is often referred to as labor. It is the hardest physical work a woman may ever do. A complex series of hormonal changes initiates the process. As pregnancy advances, the placenta releases increasing amounts of *corticotropin-releasing hormone (CRH)*, a hormone involved in the stress response. High levels of CRH trigger additional placental hormone adjustments that induce uterine contractions. And as CRH rises in the fetal bloodstream in the final prenatal weeks, it

4.1 Describe the three stages of childbirth, the baby's adaptation to labor and delivery, and the newborn baby's appearance.

stimulates fetal production of the stress hormone cortisol, which promotes development of the lungs in preparation for breathing (Li et al., 2014; Norwitz, 2009). An abnormal increase in maternal CRH in the third trimester of pregnancy is currently being evaluated as an early predictor of premature birth (Latendresse & Ruiz, 2011; Smith et al., 2009).

Several signs indicate that labor is near:

- Yolanda occasionally felt the upper part of her uterus contract. These contractions are often called *false labor* or *prelabor* because they remain brief and unpredictable for several weeks.
- About two weeks before birth, an event called *lightening* occurred; Joshua's head dropped low into the uterus. Placental hormone changes had caused Yolanda's cervix to soften, and it no longer supported Joshua's weight so easily.
- A sure sign that labor is only hours or days away is the *bloody show*. As the cervix begins to open, the plug of mucus that sealed it during pregnancy is released, producing a reddish discharge. Soon after, uterine contractions become more frequent, and mother and baby have entered the first of three stages of labor (see Figure 4.1).

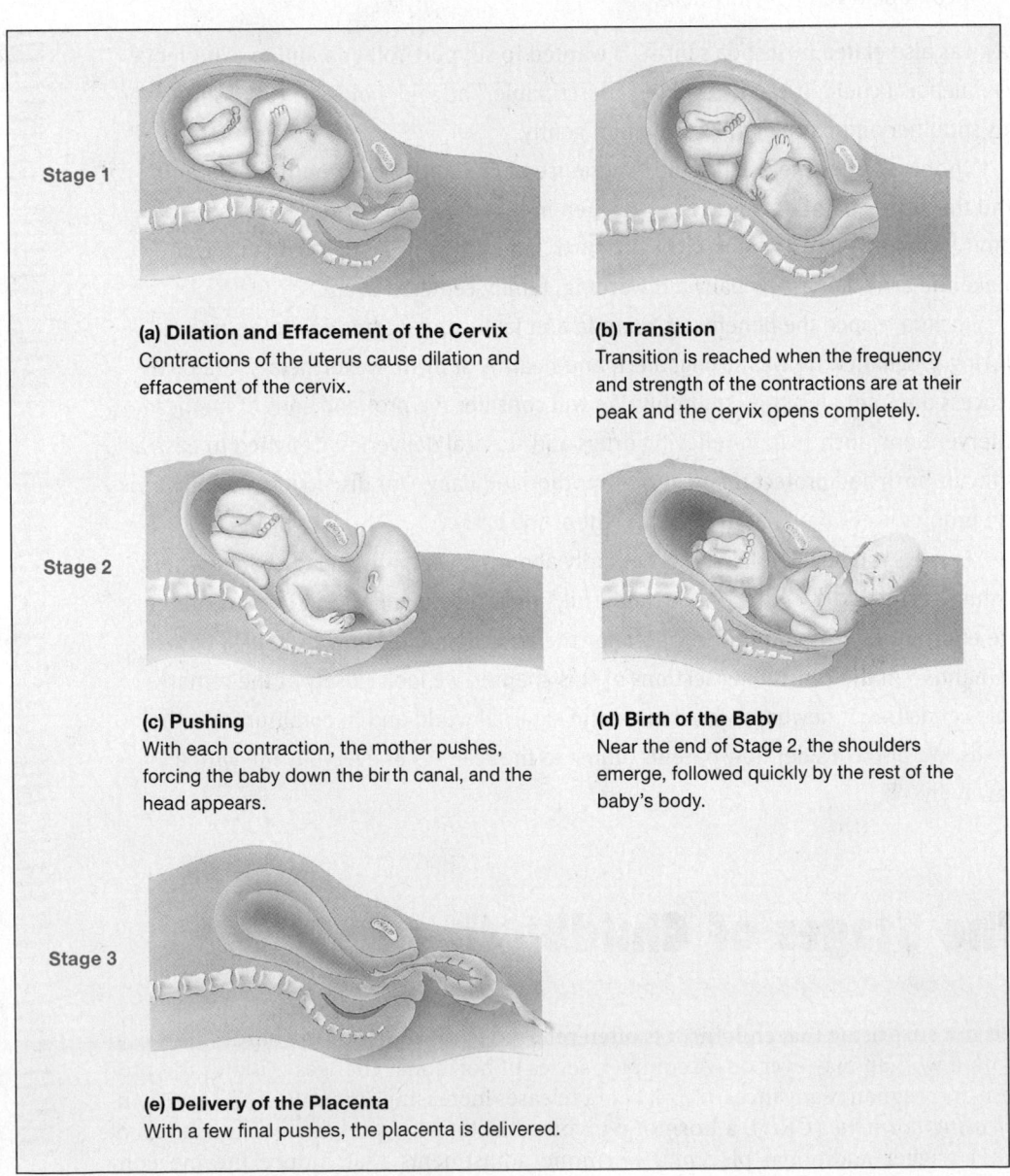

(a) Dilation and Effacement of the Cervix
Contractions of the uterus cause dilation and effacement of the cervix.

(b) Transition
Transition is reached when the frequency and strength of the contractions are at their peak and the cervix opens completely.

(c) Pushing
With each contraction, the mother pushes, forcing the baby down the birth canal, and the head appears.

(d) Birth of the Baby
Near the end of Stage 2, the shoulders emerge, followed quickly by the rest of the baby's body.

(e) Delivery of the Placenta
With a few final pushes, the placenta is delivered.

FIGURE 4.1 **The three stages of childbirth.**

Stage 1: Dilation and Effacement of the Cervix

Stage 1 is the longest, lasting an average of 12 to 14 hours with a first birth and 4 to 6 hours with later births. **Dilation and effacement of the cervix** take place—that is, as uterine contractions gradually become more frequent and powerful, they cause the cervix to open (dilate) and thin (efface), forming a clear channel from the uterus into the birth canal, or vagina. The uterine contractions that open the cervix are forceful and regular, starting out 10 to 20 minutes apart and lasting about 15 to 20 seconds. Gradually, they get closer together, occurring every 2 to 3 minutes, and become stronger, persisting for as long as 60 seconds.

During this stage, Yolanda could do nothing to speed up the process. Jay held her hand, provided sips of juice and water, and helped her get comfortable. Throughout the first few hours, Yolanda walked, stood, or sat upright. As the contractions became more intense, she leaned against pillows or lay on her side.

The climax of Stage 1 is a brief phase called **transition,** in which the frequency and strength of contractions are at their peak and the cervix opens completely. Although transition is the most uncomfortable part of childbirth, it is especially important that the mother relax. If she tenses or bears down with her muscles before the cervix is completely dilated and effaced, she may bruise the cervix and slow the progress of labor.

Stage 2: Delivery of the Baby

In Stage 2, which lasts about 50 minutes for a first baby and 20 minutes in later births, the infant is born. Strong contractions of the uterus continue, but the mother also feels a natural urge to squeeze and push with her abdominal muscles. As she does so with each contraction, she forces the baby down and out.

Between contractions, Yolanda dozed lightly. When the doctor announced that the baby's head was *crowning*—the vaginal opening had stretched around the entire head—Yolanda felt renewed energy; she knew that soon the baby would arrive. Quickly, with several more pushes, Joshua's forehead, nose, and chin emerged, then his upper body and trunk. The doctor held him up, wet with amniotic fluid and still attached to the umbilical cord. As air rushed into his lungs, Joshua cried. When the umbilical cord stopped pulsing, it was clamped and cut. A nurse placed Joshua on Yolanda's chest, where she and Jay could see, touch, and gently talk to him. Then the nurse wrapped Joshua snugly, to help with temperature regulation.

Stage 3: Birth of the Placenta

Stage 3 brings labor to an end. A few final contractions and pushes cause the placenta to separate from the wall of the uterus and be delivered in about 5 to 10 minutes. Yolanda and Jay were surprised at the large size of the thick 1½-pound red-gray organ, which had taken care of Joshua's basic needs for the previous nine months.

The Baby's Adaptation to Labor and Delivery

At first glance, labor and delivery seem like a dangerous ordeal for the baby. The strong contractions of Yolanda's uterus exposed Joshua's head to a great deal of pressure, and they squeezed the placenta and the umbilical cord repeatedly. Each time, Joshua's supply of oxygen was temporarily reduced.

Fortunately, healthy babies are equipped to withstand these traumas. The force of the contractions intensifies the baby's production of stress hormones. Unlike during pregnancy, when excessive stress endangers the fetus (see Chapter 3), during childbirth high levels of infant cortisol and other stress hormones are adaptive. They help the baby withstand oxygen deprivation by sending a rich supply of blood to the brain and heart (Gluckman, Sizonenko, & Bassett, 1999). And as noted earlier, they prepare the newborn's lungs to breathe. Finally, stress hormones arouse the infant into alertness. Joshua was born wide-awake, ready to interact with the surrounding world.

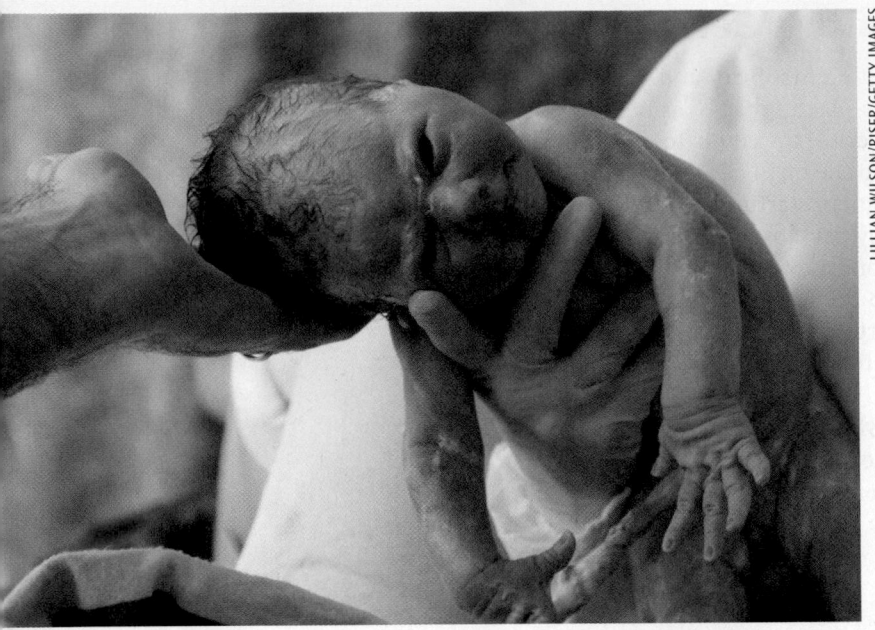

To accommodate the well-developed brain, a newborn's head is large in relation to the trunk and legs. This newborn's body readily turns pink as she takes her first few breaths.

The Newborn Baby's Appearance

Parents are often surprised at the odd-looking newborn—a far cry from the storybook image they may have had in their minds. The average newborn is 20 inches long and 7½ pounds in weight; boys tend to be slightly longer and heavier than girls. The head is large in comparison to the trunk and legs, which are short and bowed. Proportionally, if your head were as large as that of a newborn infant, you would be balancing something about the size of a watermelon between your shoulders! This combination of a large head (with its well-developed brain) and a small body means that human infants learn quickly in the first few months of life. But unlike most other mammals, they cannot get around on their own until much later.

Even though newborn babies may not match parents' idealized image, some features do make them attractive (Luo, Li, & Lee, 2011). Their round faces, chubby cheeks, large foreheads, and big eyes make adults feel like picking them up and cuddling them.

Assessing the Newborn's Physical Condition: The Apgar Scale

Infants who have difficulty making the transition to life outside the uterus must be given special help at once. To assess the newborn's physical condition quickly, doctors and nurses use the **Apgar Scale.** As Table 4.1 shows, a rating of 0, 1, or 2 on each of five characteristics is made at 1 minute and again at 5 minutes after birth. A combined Apgar score of 7 or better indicates that the infant is in good physical condition. If the score is between 4 and 6, the baby requires assistance in establishing breathing and other vital signs. If the score is 3 or below, the infant is in serious danger and requires emergency medical attention. Two Apgar ratings are given because some babies have trouble adjusting at first but do quite well after a few minutes (Apgar, 1953).

TABLE 4.1 **The Apgar Scale**

	SCORE		
Sign[a]	*0*	*1*	*2*
Heart rate	No heartbeat	Under 100 beats per minute	100 to 140 beats per minute
Respiratory effort	No breathing for 60 seconds	Irregular, shallow breathing	Strong breathing and crying
Reflex irritability (sneezing, coughing, and grimacing)	No response	Weak reflexive response	Strong reflexive response
Muscle tone	Completely limp	Weak movements of arms and legs	Strong movements of arms and legs
Color[b]	Blue body, arms, and legs	Body pink with blue arms and legs	Body, arms, and legs completely pink

[a]To remember these signs, you may find it helpful to use a technique in which the original labels are reordered and renamed as follows: color = **A**ppearance; heart rate = **P**ulse; reflex irritability = **G**rimace; muscle tone = **A**ctivity; and respiratory effort = **R**espiration. Together, the first letters of the new labels spell **Apgar.**

[b]The skin tone of nonwhite babies makes it difficult to apply the "pink" color criterion. However, newborns of all races can be rated for pinkish glow resulting from the flow of oxygen through body tissues.

Source: Apgar, 1953.

Ask Yourself

- **REVIEW** Name and briefly describe the three stages of labor.

- **CONNECT** Contrast the positive impact of the baby's production of high levels of stress hormones during childbirth with the negative impact of severe maternal stress on the fetus, discussed on page 113 in Chapter 3.

- **APPLY** On seeing her newborn baby for the first time, Caroline exclaimed, "Why is she so out of proportion?" What observations prompted Caroline to ask this question? Explain why her baby's appearance is adaptive.

Approaches to Childbirth

4.2 Describe natural childbirth and home delivery, noting benefits and concerns associated with each.

Childbirth practices, like other aspects of family life, are molded by the society of which mother and baby are a part. In many village and tribal cultures, expectant mothers are well-acquainted with the childbirth process. For example, the Jarara of South America and the Pukapukans of the Pacific Islands treat birth as a vital part of daily life. The Jarara mother gives birth in full view of the entire community, including small children. The Pukapukan girl is so familiar with the events of labor and delivery that she can frequently be seen playing at it. Using a coconut to represent the baby, she stuffs it inside her dress, imitates the mother's pushing, and lets the nut fall at the proper moment.

In most nonindustrialized cultures, women are assisted—though often not by medical personnel—during labor and delivery. Among the Mende of Sierra Leone, birth attendants are appointed by the village chief and are highly respected members of their communities. They visit expectant mothers before and after a birth to provide advice, can be called to help deliver a baby at any time, and practice traditional strategies to promote delivery, including massaging the abdomen and supporting the woman in a squatting position (Dorwie & Pacquiao, 2014). In Bolivia, a Siriono mother delivers her own baby in a hammock with a crowd of women close by, who keep her company. The father cuts the umbilical cord and joins the mother in tending to the newborn for the first few days (Jordan, 1993; Reed, 2005).

In Western nations, childbirth has changed dramatically over the centuries. Before the late 1800s, birth usually took place at home and was a family-centered event. The industrial revolution brought greater crowding to cities, along with new health problems. As a result, childbirth moved from home to hospital, where the health of mothers and babies could be protected. Once doctors assumed responsibility for childbirth, women's knowledge of it declined, and relatives and friends no longer participated (Borst, 1995).

By the 1950s and 1960s, women had begun to question the medical procedures that had come to be used during labor and delivery. Many felt that routine use of strong drugs and delivery instruments had robbed them of a precious experience and was often neither necessary nor safe for the baby. Gradually, a natural childbirth movement arose in Europe and spread to North America. Its purpose was to make hospital birth as comfortable and rewarding for mothers as possible. Today, most hospitals offer birth centers that are family-centered and homelike. *Freestanding birth centers,* which permit greater maternal control over labor and delivery, including choice of delivery

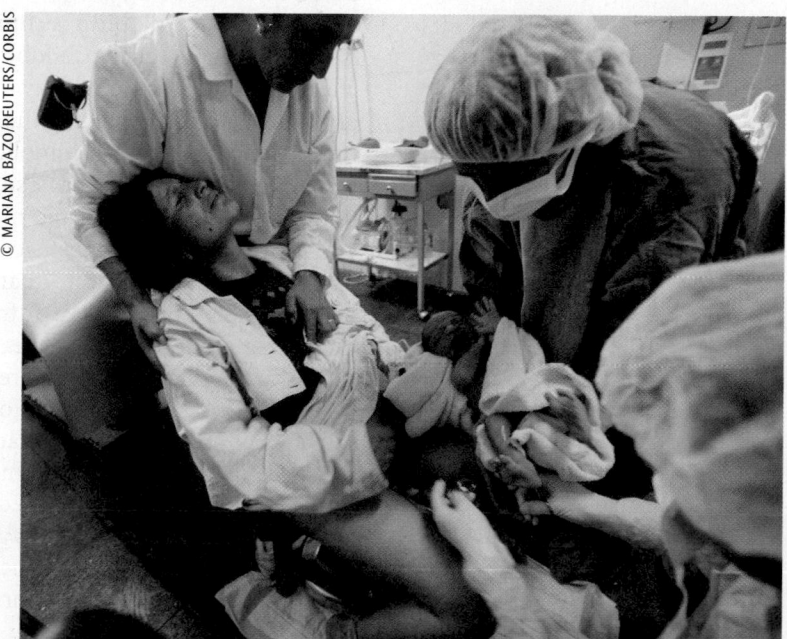

© MARIANA BAZO/REUTERS/CORBIS

In this Peruvian health clinic, families are encouraged to incorporate practices of their village culture into the birth experience. Here, a familiar attendant supports and soothes a new mother as her baby is delivered.

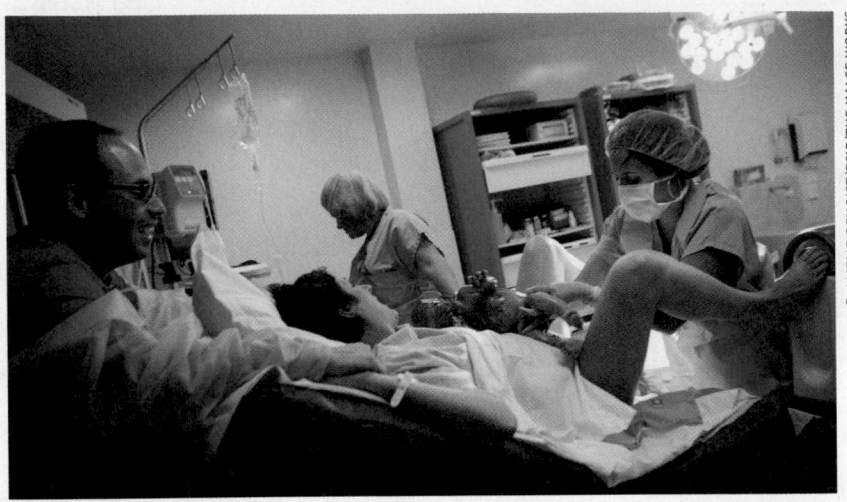

In a hospital birth center, a mother gives birth, assisted by the father. A companion's support is a vital part of natural childbirth, which is associated with shorter labors, fewer complications, and a more rewarding birth experience.

positions, presence of family members and friends, and early contact between parents and baby, also exist. And a small number of North American women reject institutional birth entirely and choose to have their babies at home.

Natural, or Prepared, Childbirth

Yolanda and Jay chose **natural,** or **prepared, childbirth**—a group of techniques aimed at reducing pain and medical intervention and making childbirth a rewarding experience. Most natural childbirth programs draw on methods developed by Grantly Dick-Read (1959) in England and Fernand Lamaze (1958) in France. These physicians recognized that cultural attitudes had taught women to fear the birth experience. An anxious, frightened woman in labor tenses her muscles, heightening the pain that usually accompanies strong contractions.

In a typical natural childbirth program, the expectant mother and a companion (a partner, relative, or friend) participate in three activities:

- *Classes.* Yolanda and Jay attended a series of classes in which they learned about the anatomy and physiology of labor and delivery. Knowledge about the birth process reduces a mother's fear.
- *Relaxation and breathing techniques.* During each class, Yolanda was taught relaxation and breathing exercises aimed at counteracting the pain of uterine contractions.
- *Labor coach.* Jay learned how to help Yolanda during childbirth by reminding her to relax and breathe, massaging her back, supporting her body, and offering encouragement and affection.

SOCIAL SUPPORT AND NATURAL CHILDBIRTH Social support is important to the success of natural childbirth techniques. In Guatemalan and American hospitals that routinely isolated patients during childbirth, some mothers were randomly assigned a *doula*—a Greek word referring to a trained lay attendant—who stayed with them throughout labor and delivery, talking to them, holding their hands, and rubbing their backs to promote relaxation. These mothers had fewer birth complications, and their labors were several hours shorter than those of women who did not have supportive companionship. Guatemalan mothers who received doula support also interacted more positively with their babies after delivery, talking, smiling, and gently stroking (Kennell et al., 1991; Sosa et al., 1980).

Other studies indicate that mothers who are supported during labor—either by a lay birth attendant or a relative or friend with doula training—less often have instrument-assisted or cesarean (surgical) deliveries or need medication to control pain. Also, their babies' Apgar scores are higher, and they are more likely to be breastfeeding at a two-month follow-up (Campbell et al., 2006, 2007; Hodnett et al., 2012; McGrath & Kennell, 2008).

The continuous rather than intermittent support of a doula during labor and delivery strengthens these benefits for mothers and babies—outcomes evident in studies conducted in both developing and developed nations and among women of diverse ethnicities (Hodnett et al., 2012). Furthermore, this aspect of natural childbirth makes Western hospital-birth customs more acceptable to women from parts of the world where assistance from family and community members is the norm (Dundek, 2006).

POSITIONS FOR DELIVERY When natural childbirth is combined with delivery in a birth center or at home, mothers often give birth in an upright, sitting position rather than lying flat on their backs with their feet in stirrups (the traditional hospital delivery room practice). Use of special seats to enable an upright birth has become more common.

LOOK *and* **LISTEN**

Talk to several mothers about social supports available to them during labor and delivery. From the mothers' perspectives, how did those supports (or lack of support) affect the birth experience?

When mothers are upright, labor is slightly shorter because contractions are stronger and pushing is more effective. The baby benefits from a richer supply of oxygen because blood flow to the placenta is increased, and fewer instances of infant heartbeat irregularities occur. Because the mother can see the delivery, she can work with the doctor or midwife, adjusting her pushing to ensure that the baby's head and shoulders emerge slowly, which reduces the chances of tearing the mother's tissues and, thus, the need for an *episiotomy* (incision that increases the size of the vaginal opening). Compared with those who give birth lying on their backs, women who choose an upright position are less likely to use pain-relieving medication or to have instrument-assisted deliveries (Gupta, Hofmeyr, & Shehmar, 2012; Romano & Lothian, 2008).

In another increasingly popular method, water birth, the mother sits in a warm tub of water, which supports her weight, relaxes her, and provides her with the freedom to move into any position she finds most comfortable. Among mothers at low risk for birth complications, water birth is associated with reduced maternal stress, shorter labor, lower episiotomy rate, and greater likelihood of medication-free delivery than both back-lying and seated positions (American Association of Birth Centers, 2014; Cluett & Burns, 2013). As long as water birth is carefully managed by skilled health professionals, it poses no additional risk of infection or safety to mothers or babies.

After a home birth, the midwife and a lay attendant provide support to the new mother. For healthy women attended by a well-trained doctor or midwife, home birth is as safe as hospital birth.

Home Delivery

Home birth has always been popular in certain industrialized nations, such as England, the Netherlands, and Sweden. The number of American women choosing to have their babies at home rose during the 1970s and 1980s but remains small, at less than 1 percent (Martin et al., 2013). Although some home births are attended by doctors, many more are handled by *certified nurse-midwives*, who have degrees in nursing and additional training in childbirth management.

The joys and perils of home delivery are well illustrated by the story that Don, a father of four, told us. "Our first child was delivered in the hospital," he said. "Even though I was present, Kathy and I found the atmosphere to be rigid and insensitive. We wanted a warmer, more personal birth environment." With a nurse-midwife's coaching, Don delivered their second child, Cindy, at their farmhouse, 3 miles out of town. Three years later, when Kathy went into labor with Marnie, a heavy snowstorm prevented the midwife from reaching the house on time, so Don delivered the baby alone. The birth was difficult, and Marnie failed to breathe for several minutes. With great effort, Don managed to revive her. The frightening memory of Marnie's limp, blue body convinced Don and Kathy to return to the hospital to have their last child. By then, the hospital's birth practices had changed, and the event was a rewarding one for both parents.

Don and Kathy's experience raises the question: Is it just as safe to give birth at home as in a hospital? For healthy women who are assisted by a well-trained doctor or midwife, it seems so because complications rarely occur (Fullerton, Navarro, & Young, 2007; Wax, Pinette, & Cartin, 2010). However, if attendants are not carefully trained and prepared to handle emergencies, the likelihood of infant disability and death is high. When mothers are at risk for any kind of complication, the appropriate place for labor and delivery is the hospital, where lifesaving treatment is available.

Medical Interventions

4.3 List common medical interventions during childbirth, circumstances that justify their use, and any dangers associated with each.

Medical interventions during childbirth occur in both industrialized and nonindustrialized cultures. For example, some tribal and village societies have discovered labor-inducing drugs and devised surgical techniques to deliver babies (Jordan, 1993). Yet childbirth in North America, more so than elsewhere in the world, is a medically monitored and controlled event.

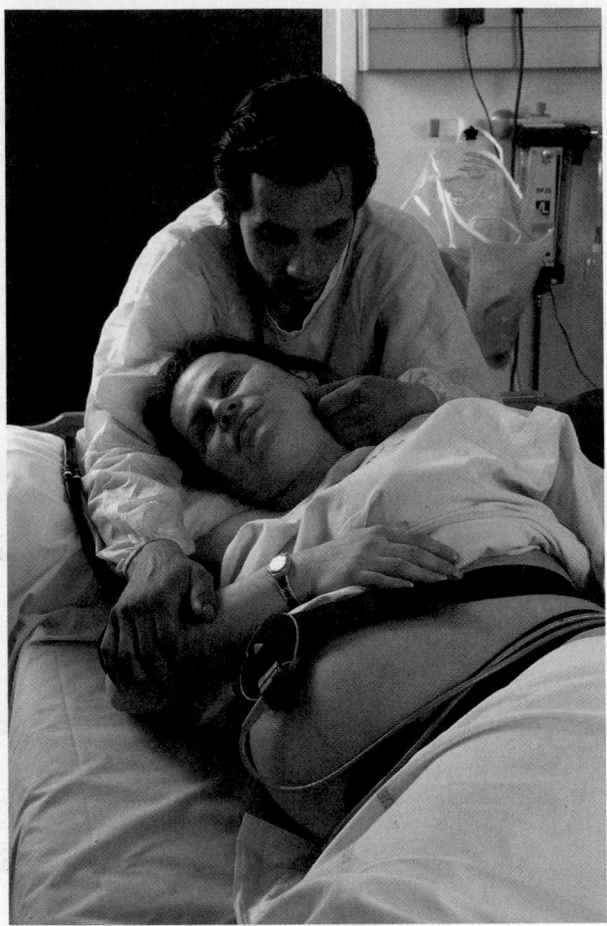

© BSIP SA/ALAMY

The fetal monitor strapped across this mother's abdomen uses ultrasound to record fetal heart rate throughout labor. In high-risk situations, fetal monitoring saves many lives. But it also may encourage unnecessary instrument and cesarean deliveries.

Use of some medical procedures has reached epic proportions—in part because of rising rates of multiple births and other high-risk deliveries, which are associated with increased maternal age and use of fertility treatments. But births unaffected by these factors are also medicalized.

What medical techniques are doctors likely to use during labor and delivery? When are they justified, and what dangers do they pose to mothers and babies?

Fetal Monitoring

Fetal monitors are electronic instruments that track the baby's heart rate during labor. An abnormal heartbeat pattern may indicate that the baby is in distress due to lack of oxygen and needs to be delivered immediately. Continuous fetal monitoring, which is required in most U.S. hospitals, is used in over 85 percent of U.S. births (Ananth et al., 2013). The most popular type of monitor is strapped across the mother's abdomen throughout labor. A second, more accurate method involves threading a recording device through the cervix and placing it directly under the baby's scalp.

Fetal monitoring is a safe medical procedure that has saved the lives of many babies in high-risk situations. But in healthy pregnancies, it does not reduce the already low rates of infant brain damage and death (Haws et al., 2009). Furthermore, most infants have some heartbeat irregularities during labor, so critics worry that fetal monitors identify many babies as in danger who, in fact, are not. Monitoring is linked to an increase in the number of instrument and cesarean (surgical) deliveries, practices we will discuss shortly (Wolfberg, 2012). In addition, some women complain that the devices are uncomfortable and interfere with the normal course of labor.

Still, fetal monitors will probably continue to be used routinely in the United States, even though they are not necessary in most cases. Doctors fear that they will be sued for malpractice if an infant dies or is born with problems and they cannot show that they did everything possible to protect the baby.

Labor and Delivery Medication

Some form of medication is used in over 60 percent of U.S. births (Osterman & Martin, 2011). *Analgesics,* drugs used to relieve pain, may be given in mild doses during labor to help a mother relax. *Anesthetics* are a stronger type of painkiller that blocks sensation. Currently, the most common approach to controlling pain during labor is *epidural analgesia,* in which a regional pain-relieving drug is delivered continuously through a catheter into a small space in the lower spine. Unlike older spinal block procedures, which numb the entire lower half of the body, epidural analgesia limits pain reduction to the pelvic region. Because the mother retains the capacity to feel the pressure of the contractions and to move her trunk and legs, she is able to push during the second stage of labor.

Although pain-relieving drugs help women cope with childbirth and enable doctors to perform essential medical interventions, they also can cause problems. Epidural analgesia, for example, weakens uterine contractions. As a result, labor is prolonged, and the chances of instrument delivery or cesarean (surgical) birth increase. And because drugs rapidly cross the placenta, exposed newborns are at risk for respiratory distress (Kumar et al., 2014). They also tend to have lower Apgar scores, to be sleepy and withdrawn, to suck poorly during feedings, and to be irritable when awake (Caton et al., 2002; Eltzschig, Lieberman, & Camann, 2003; Platt, 2014). Although no confirmed long-term consequences for development exist, the negative impact of these drugs on the newborn's adjustment supports the current trend to limit their use.

Instrument Delivery

Forceps, metal clamps placed around the baby's head to pull the infant from the birth canal, have been used since the sixteenth century to speed up delivery (see Figure 4.2). A more recent instrument, the *vacuum extractor,* consists of a plastic cup (placed on the baby's head) attached to a suction tube. Instrument delivery is appropriate if the mother's pushing during the second stage of labor does not move the baby through the birth canal in a reasonable period of time.

Instrument use has declined considerably over the past three decades, partly because doctors more often deliver babies surgically when labor problems arise. Today, forceps and (more often) vacuum extractors continue to be used in about 3 percent of U.S. births (Martin et al., 2013).

Using forceps to pull the baby through most or all of the birth canal greatly increases the risk of brain damage. As a result, forceps are seldom used this way today. Low-forceps delivery (carried out when the baby is most of the way through the vagina) is associated with injury to the baby's head and the mother's tissues. Vacuum extractors, which have rapidly replaced forceps as the dominant instrument, are less likely to tear the mother's tissues. Nevertheless, cup suction doubles the risk of bleeding beneath the baby's skin and on the outside of the skull compared with nonassisted deliveries. And the risk of more serious complications, including bleeding beneath the skull and seizures (which can damage the brain), increases tenfold (Ekéus, Högberg, & Norman, 2014). Consequently, neither instrument should be used when mothers can be encouraged to deliver normally and there is no special reason to hurry the birth.

Induced Labor

An **induced labor** is one that is started artificially, usually by breaking the amnion, or bag of waters (an event that typically occurs naturally in the first stage of labor), and giving the mother synthetic oxytocin, a hormone that stimulates contractions. About 23 percent of American labors are induced—a figure that has more than doubled over the past two decades (U.S. Census Bureau, 2014b).

Induced labors are justified when continuing the pregnancy threatens the well-being of mother or baby. Often, though, they are performed for the doctor's or the patient's convenience—a major reason they have increased. An induced labor often proceeds differently from a naturally occurring one. Contractions are longer, harder, and closer together, increasing the possibility of inadequate oxygen supply to the baby. In addition, mothers often find it more difficult to stay in control of an induced labor, even when they have been coached in natural childbirth techniques. As a result, labor and delivery medication is likely to be used in larger amounts, and the chances of instrument delivery are slightly greater (Hoffman et al., 2006; Ramirez, 2011).

Occasionally, induction is performed before the mother is physically ready to give birth, and the procedure fails. When this happens, a cesarean delivery is necessary. The rate of cesareans is substantially higher in induced than spontaneous labors. Ripening of the cervix—initial dilation and effacement—is the best predictor of the success of labor induction (Simpson, 2011).

Cesarean Delivery

A **cesarean delivery** is a surgical birth; the doctor makes an incision in the mother's abdomen and lifts the baby out of the uterus. Forty years ago, cesarean delivery was rare. Since then, cesarean rates have climbed internationally, reaching 16 percent in Finland, 24 percent in New Zealand, 26 percent in Canada, 32 percent in Australia and Switzerland, and 37 percent in the United States (Martin et al., 2013; OECD, 2013b).

Cesareans have always been warranted by medical emergencies, such as Rh incompatibility, premature separation of the placenta from the uterus, or serious maternal illness or

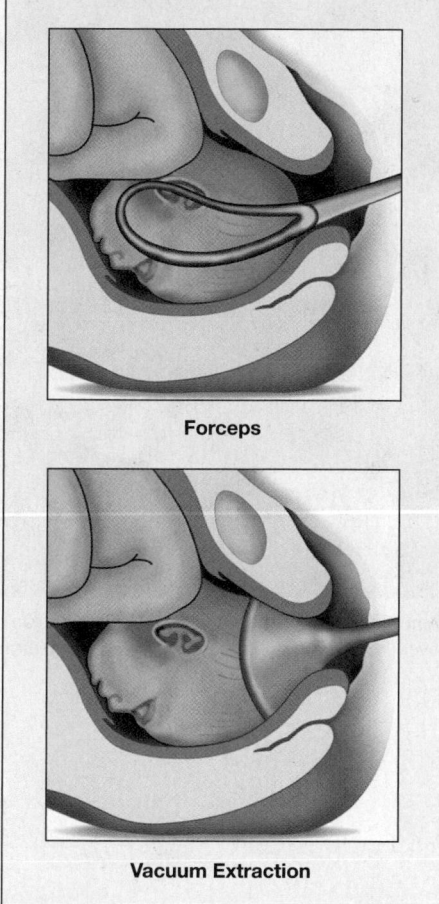

Forceps

Vacuum Extraction

FIGURE 4.2 **Instrument delivery.** The pressure that must be applied to pull the infant from the birth canal with forceps can injure the baby's head. An alternative method, the vacuum extractor, is less likely than forceps to injure the mother's tissues. Nevertheless, risk of infant scalp injuries and internal bleeding in the eyes and skull remains.

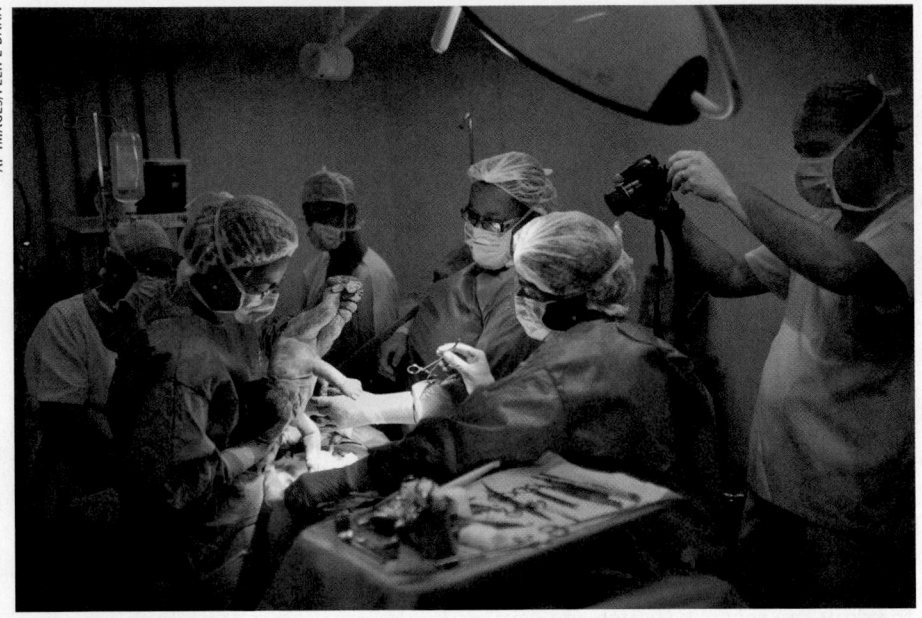

A new father records his baby's arrival by cesarean delivery. Cesareans have become increasingly common over the past forty years, largely because of medical control over childbirth.

infection (for example, the herpes simplex 2 virus, which can infect the baby during a vaginal delivery). Cesareans are also justified when babies are in **breech position,** turned so that the buttocks or feet would be delivered first (about 1 in every 25 births). The breech position increases the chances of squeezing of the umbilical cord as the large head moves through the birth canal, thereby depriving the infant of oxygen. Head injuries are also more likely. But the infant's exact position makes a difference. Certain breech babies fare just as well with a normal delivery as with a cesarean (Vistad et al., 2013). Sometimes the doctor can gently turn the baby into a head-down position during the early part of labor.

Until recently, many women who have had a cesarean have been offered the option of a vaginal birth in subsequent pregnancies. But growing evidence indicates that compared with repeated cesareans, a natural labor after a cesarean is associated with slightly increased rates of rupture of the uterus and infant death (Hunter, 2014). As a result, the rule "Once a cesarean, always a cesarean" has made a comeback.

Repeated cesareans, however, do not explain the worldwide rise in cesarean deliveries. Instead, medical control over childbirth is largely responsible. Because many needless cesareans are performed, pregnant women should ask questions about the procedure when choosing a doctor. Although the operation itself is safe, mother and baby require more time for recovery. Anesthetic may have crossed the placenta, making cesarean newborns sleepy and unresponsive and putting them at increased risk for breathing difficulties (Ramachandrappa & Jain, 2008).

Ask Yourself

- **REVIEW** Describe the features and benefits of natural childbirth. What aspect contributes greatly to favorable outcomes, and why?

- **CONNECT** How might use of epidural analgesia negatively affect the parent–newborn relationship? Explain how your answer illustrates bidirectional influences between parent and child, emphasized in ecological systems theory.

- **APPLY** Sharon, a heavy smoker, has just arrived at the hospital in labor. Which one of the medical interventions discussed in the preceding sections is her doctor justified in using? (For help in answering this question, review the prenatal effects of tobacco on pages 105–106 in Chapter 3.)

- **REFLECT** If you were an expectant parent, would you choose home birth? Why or why not?

4.4 What are the risks of oxygen deprivation, preterm birth, and low birth weight, and what factors can help infants who survive a traumatic birth?

Birth Complications

We have seen that some babies—in particular, those whose mothers are in poor health, do not receive good medical care, or have a history of pregnancy problems—are especially likely to experience birth complications. Inadequate oxygen, a pregnancy that ends too early, and a baby who is born underweight are serious risks to development that we have touched on many times. A baby remaining in the uterus too long is yet another risk. Let's look at the impact of each complication on later development.

Oxygen Deprivation

Some years ago, we got to know 4-year-old Melinda and her mother, Judy, both of whom participated in a special program for children with disabilities at our laboratory school. Melinda has *cerebral palsy,* a general term for a variety of impairments in muscle coordination caused by brain damage before, during, or just after birth. The disorder can range from mild tremors to severe physical and mental disability. One out of every 500 American children has cerebral palsy. About 10 percent experienced **anoxia,** or inadequate oxygen supply, along with a buildup of harmful acids and deficiency of vital blood substrates, as a result of decreased maternal blood supply during labor and delivery (Clark, Ghulmiyyah, & Hankins, 2008; McIntyre et al., 2013).

Melinda walks with a halting, lumbering gait and has difficulty keeping her balance. "Some mothers don't know how the palsy happened," confided Judy, "but I do. I got pregnant accidentally, and my boyfriend didn't want to have anything to do with it. I was frightened and alone most of the time. I arrived at the hospital at the last minute. Melinda was breech, and the cord was wrapped around her neck."

Squeezing of the umbilical cord, as in Melinda's case, is one cause of anoxia. Another cause is *placenta abruptio,* or premature separation of the placenta, a life-threatening event with a high rate of infant death. Factors related to it include multiple fetuses and teratogens that cause constriction of blood vessels and abnormal development of the placenta, such as tobacco and cocaine (Yamada et al., 2012). Just as serious is *placenta previa,* a condition caused by implantation of the blastocyst so low in the uterus that the placenta covers the cervical opening. As the cervix dilates and effaces in the third trimester, part of the placenta may detach. Women who have had previous cesareans or who are carrying multiple fetuses are at increased risk (Trønnes et al., 2014). Although placenta abruptio and placenta previa occur in only 1 to 2 percent of births, they can cause severe hemorrhaging, which requires that an emergency cesarean be performed.

In still other instances, the birth seems to go along all right, but the baby fails to start breathing within a few minutes. Healthy newborns can survive periods of little or no oxygen longer than adults can; they reduce their metabolic rate, thereby conserving the limited oxygen available. Nevertheless, brain damage is likely if regular breathing is delayed more than 10 minutes. **TAKE A MOMENT...** Can you think of other possible causes of oxygen deprivation that you learned about as you studied prenatal development and birth?

After initial brain injury from anoxia, another phase of cell death can occur several hours later. Placing anoxic newborns in a head-cooling device shortly after birth for 72 hours substantially reduces this secondary brain damage (detected through brain scans) and increases scores on a newborn behavioral assessment (Hoehn et al., 2008). Another alternative—whole-body cooling by having anoxic newborns lie on a precooled water blanket—leads to an impressive reduction in death and disability rates during the first two years (Allen, 2014).

How do children who experience anoxia during labor and delivery fare as they get older? Research suggests that the greater the oxygen deprivation, the poorer children's cognitive and language skills in early and middle childhood (Hopkins-Golightly, Raz, & Sander, 2003; Vohr et al., 2013). Although effects of even mild to moderate anoxia often persist, many children improve over time (Bass et al., 2004). In Melinda's case, her physical disability was permanent, but with warm, stimulating intervention services, she was just slightly behind in mental development as a preschooler.

When development is severely impaired, the anoxia was probably extreme. Perhaps it was caused by prenatal insult to the baby's respiratory system, or it may have happened because the infant's lungs were not yet mature enough to

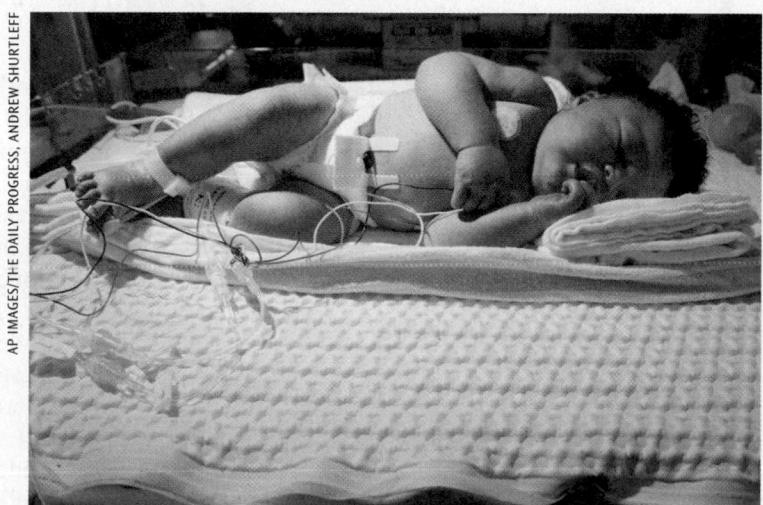

AP IMAGES/THE DAILY PROGRESS, ANDREW SHURTLEFF

Treatment for this newborn, who experienced oxygen deprivation, includes a cooling water blanket to lower the baby's body temperature, which helps prevent brain damage.

breathe. For example, infants born more than six weeks early commonly have *respiratory distress syndrome* (otherwise known as *hyaline membrane disease*). Their tiny lungs are so poorly developed that the air sacs collapse, causing serious breathing difficulties. Today, mechanical respirators keep many such infants alive. In spite of these measures, some babies suffer permanent brain damage from lack of oxygen, and in other cases their delicate lungs are harmed by the treatment itself. Respiratory distress syndrome is only one of many risks for babies born too soon, as we will see in the following section.

Preterm and Low-Birth-Weight Infants

Janet, almost six months pregnant, and her husband, Rick, boarded a flight in Hartford, Connecticut, on their way to a vacation in Hawaii. During a stopover in San Francisco, Janet told Rick she was bleeding. Rushed to a hospital, she gave birth to Keith, who weighed less than 1½ pounds. Delivered 23 weeks after conception, he had barely reached the age of viability (see Chapter 3, page 99).

During Keith's first month, he experienced one crisis after another. Three days after birth, an ultrasound scan suggested that fragile blood vessels feeding Keith's brain had hemorrhaged, a complication that can cause brain damage. Within three weeks, Keith had surgery to close a heart valve that seals automatically in full-term babies. Keith's immature immune system made infections difficult to contain. Repeated illnesses and the drugs used to treat them caused permanent hearing loss. Keith also had respiratory distress syndrome and breathed with the help of a respirator. Soon there was evidence of lung damage. More than three months of hospitalization passed before Keith's rough course of complications and treatment eased.

Babies born three weeks or more before the end of a full 38-week pregnancy or who weigh less than 5½ pounds (2,500 grams) have for many years been referred to as "premature." A wealth of research indicates that premature babies are at risk for many problems. Birth weight is the best available predictor of infant survival and healthy development. Many newborns who weigh less than 3½ pounds (1,500 grams) experience persisting difficulties, an effect that becomes stronger as length of pregnancy and birth weight decrease (see Figure 4.3) (Baron & Rey-Casserly, 2010; Bolisetty et al., 2006; Wilson-Ching et al., 2013). Brain abnormalities, frequent illness, inattention, overactivity, sensory impairments, poor motor coordination, language delays, low intelligence test scores, deficits in school learning, and emotional and behavior problems are some of the problems that persist through childhood and adolescence and into adulthood (Aarnoudse-Moens, Weisglas-Kuperus, & van Goudoever, 2009; Hutchinson et al., 2013; Nosarti et al., 2011; Tanskanen et al., 2011).

About 12 percent of American infants are born early, and 8 percent are born underweight. The two risk factors often co-occur, and they can strike unexpectedly, as Keith's case illustrates. But the problem is highest among poverty-stricken women (Martin et al., 2013). These mothers, as indicated in Chapter 3, are more likely to be under stress, undernourished, and exposed to other harmful environmental influences—factors strongly linked to low birth weight. In addition, they often do not receive adequate prenatal care.

African-American babies are especially vulnerable to early and underweight birth: They have about twice the rates of white and Hispanic infants, even after accounting for SES and other potentially contributing factors, such as single parenthood and young maternal age (Martin et al., 2013). Although the disparity is not yet fully understood, researchers suspect that African-American pregnant mothers' greater exposure to multiple chronic stressors, such as job strain (long hours at tiring work), crime-ridden inner-city neighborhoods, crowded living conditions, and prejudice and discrimination, is involved (Dunkel-Shetter, 2011; Dunkel-Shetter & Lobel, 2012). Many studies confirm, for example, that race-related stressors—

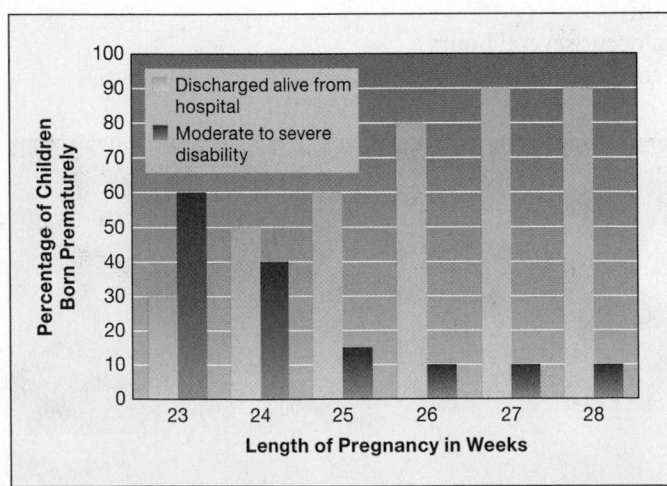

FIGURE 4.3 **Rates of infant survival and child disabilities by length of pregnancy.** In a follow-up of more than 2,300 babies born between 23 and 28 weeks gestation, the percentage of infants who survived decreased and the percentage who displayed moderate to severe disabilities (assessed during the preschool years) increased with reduced length of pregnancy. Severe disabilities included cerebral palsy (unlikely to ever walk), severely delayed mental development, deafness, and blindness. Moderate disabilities included cerebral palsy (able to walk with assistance), moderately delayed mental development, and hearing impairments partially correctable with a hearing aid. (Adapted from Bolisetty et al., 2006.)

biased treatment at school, at work, or in access to housing—predict lower birth weight, especially in African-American women (Giscombé & Lobel, 2005).

Furthermore, low birth weight is often transmitted across generations: Women who were underweight at birth themselves are twice as likely as other women to bear an underweight baby (Collins, Rankin, & David, 2011). The possible causes are diverse: They may be genetic, environmental, or epigenetic—for example, excessive prenatal stress may impair offspring's lifelong capacity to manage stress (see page 113 in Chapter 3). When a daughter becomes pregnant, she exposes her fetus to severe emotional stress and its negative consequences.

Finally, recall from Chapter 2 that prematurity is common in multiple births. About 60 percent of twins and more than 90 percent of triplets are born early and low birth weight (Martin et al., 2013). Because space inside the uterus is restricted, multiples gain less weight than singletons in the second half of pregnancy.

PRETERM VERSUS SMALL-FOR-DATE INFANTS   Although preterm and low-birth-weight infants face many obstacles to healthy development, most go on to lead normal lives; about half of those born at 23 to 24 weeks gestation and weighing only a couple of pounds at birth have no disability (refer again to Figure 4.3). To better understand why some babies do better than others, researchers divide them into two groups. **Preterm infants** are born several weeks or more before their due date. Although they are small, their weight may still be appropriate, based on time spent in the uterus. **Small-for-date infants** are below their expected weight considering length of the pregnancy. Some small-for-date infants are actually full-term. Others are preterm babies who are especially underweight.

Small-for-date infants—especially those who are also preterm—usually have more serious problems. During the first year, they are more likely to die, catch infections, and show evidence of brain damage. By middle childhood, they are smaller in stature, have lower intelligence test scores, are less attentive, achieve more poorly in school, and are socially immature (Katz et al., 2013; Sullivan et al., 2008; Wilson-Ching et al., 2013).

Small-for-date infants probably experienced inadequate nutrition before birth. Perhaps their mothers did not eat properly, the placenta did not function normally, or the babies themselves had defects that prevented them from growing as they should. In some of these babies, an abnormally functioning placenta permitted ready transfer of stress hormones from mother to fetus. Consequently, small-for-date infants are especially likely to suffer from neurological impairments that permanently weaken their capacity to manage stress (Osterholm, Hostinar, & Gunnar, 2012). Severe stress, in turn, heightens their susceptibility to later physical and psychological health problems.

Even among preterm newborns whose weight is appropriate for length of pregnancy, just 7 to 14 more days—from 34 to 35 or 36 weeks—greatly reduces rates of illness, costly medical procedures, and lengthy hospital stays (although they need greater medical intervention than full-term babies) (Ananth, Friedman, & Gyamfi-Bannerman, 2013). And despite being relatively low-risk for disabilities, a substantial number of 34-week preterms are below average in physical growth and mildly to moderately delayed in cognitive development in early and middle childhood (Morse et al., 2009; Stephens & Vohr, 2009). In an investigation of over 120,000 New York City births, babies born even 1 or 2 weeks early showed slightly lower reading and math scores at a third-grade follow-up than children who experienced a full-length prenatal period (Noble et al., 2012). These outcomes persisted even after controlling for other factors linked to achievement, such as birth weight and SES. Yet doctors often induce births several weeks preterm, under the misconception that these babies are developmentally "mature."

CONSEQUENCES FOR CAREGIVING   Imagine a scrawny, thin-skinned infant whose body is only a little larger than the size of your hand. You try to play with the baby by stroking and talking softly, but he is sleepy and unresponsive. When you feed him, he sucks poorly. During the short, unpredictable periods in which he is awake, he is usually irritable.

The appearance and behavior of preterm babies can lead parents to be less sensitive and responsive in caring for them. Compared to full-term infants, preterm babies—especially those who are very ill at birth—are less often held close, touched, and talked to gently. At times, mothers of these infants behave in an overly controlling fashion, resorting to interfering pokes and verbal commands in an effort to obtain a higher level of response from the baby (Feldman, 2007b; Forcada-Guex et al., 2006). This may explain why preterm babies as a group are at risk for child abuse.

Research reveals that distressed, emotionally reactive preterm infants are particularly susceptible to the effects of parenting quality: Among a sample of preterm 9-month-olds, the combination of infant negativity and angry or intrusive parenting yielded the highest rates of behavior problems at 2 years of age. But with warm, sensitive parenting, distressed preterm babies' rates of behavior problems were the lowest (Poehlmann et al., 2011). When they are born to isolated, poverty-stricken mothers who cannot provide good nutrition, health care, and parenting, the likelihood of unfavorable outcomes increases. In contrast, parents with stable life circumstances and social supports usually can overcome the stresses of caring for a preterm infant (Ment et al., 2003). In these cases, even sick preterm babies have a good chance of catching up in development by middle childhood.

These findings suggest that how well preterm babies develop has a great deal to do with the parent–child relationship. Consequently, interventions directed at supporting both sides of this tie are more likely to help these infants recover.

INTERVENTIONS FOR PRETERM INFANTS   A preterm baby is cared for in a special Plexiglas-enclosed bed called an *isolette*. Temperature is carefully controlled because these infants cannot yet regulate their own body temperature effectively. To help protect the baby from infection, air is filtered before it enters the isolette. When a preterm infant is fed through a stomach tube, breathes with the aid of a respirator, and receives medication through an intravenous needle, the isolette can be very isolating indeed! Physical needs that otherwise would lead to close contact and other human stimulation are met mechanically.

Special Infant Stimulation.   In proper doses, certain kinds of stimulation can help preterm infants develop. In some intensive care nurseries, preterm babies can be seen rocking in suspended hammocks or lying on waterbeds designed to replace the gentle motion they would have received while still in the mother's uterus. Other forms of stimulation have also been used—an attractive mobile or a tape recording of a heartbeat, soft music, or the mother's voice. These experiences promote faster weight gain, more predictable sleep patterns, and greater alertness (Arnon et al., 2006; Marshall-Baker, Lickliter, & Cooper, 1998).

Touch is an especially important form of stimulation. In baby animals, touching the skin releases certain brain chemicals that support physical growth—effects believed to occur in humans as well. When preterm infants were gently massaged several times each day in the hospital, they gained weight faster and, at the end of the first year, were more advanced in mental and motor development than preterm babies not given this stimulation (Field, 2001; Field, Hernandez-Reif, & Freedman, 2004).

In developing countries where hospitalization is not always possible, skin-to-skin "kangaroo care" is the most readily available intervention for promoting the survival and recovery of preterm babies. It involves placing the infant in a vertical position between the mother's breasts or next to the father's chest (under the parent's clothing) so the parent's body functions as a human incubator. Kangaroo care offers fathers a unique opportunity to increase their involvement in caring for the preterm newborn. Because of its many physical and psychological benefits, the technique is used often in Western nations as a supplement to hospital intensive care.

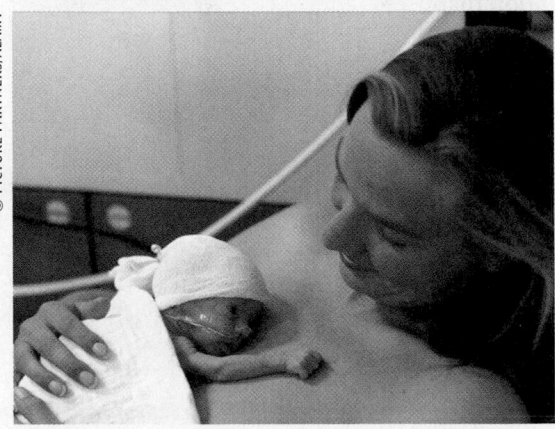

Top photo: A father in El Salvador uses skin-to-skin "kangaroo care" with his infant as part of a hospital program that teaches parents techniques for promoting survival and development in preterm and underweight babies. *Bottom photo:* In Western nations, kangaroo care may be used to supplement hospital intensive care. Here, a U.S. mother engages in the technique with her fragile newborn.

Kangaroo skin-to-skin contact fosters improved oxygenation of the baby's body, temperature regulation, sleep, breastfeeding, alertness, and infant survival (Conde-Agudelo, Belizan, & Diaz-Rossello, 2011; Kaffashi et al., 2013; Lawn et al., 2010). In addition, the kangaroo position provides the baby with gentle stimulation of all sensory modalities: hearing (through the parent's voice), smell (through proximity to the parent's body), touch (through skin-to-skin contact), and visual (through the upright position). Mothers and fathers practicing kangaroo care feel more confident about caring for their fragile babies, interact more sensitively and affectionately, and feel more attached to them (Dodd, 2005; Feldman, 2007a).

Together, these factors may explain why preterm babies given many hours of kangaroo care in their early weeks, compared to those given little or no such care, are more likely to explore novel toys and score higher on measures of mental and motor development during the first year (Bera et al., 2014; Feldman, 2007a). Because of its diverse benefits, most U.S. hospital nurseries now offer kangaroo care to parents and preterm newborns.

Training Parents in Infant Caregiving Skills. Interventions that support parents of preterm infants generally teach them about the infant's characteristics and promote caregiving skills. For parents with the economic and personal resources to care for a preterm infant, just a few sessions of coaching in recognizing and responding to the baby's needs are linked to enhanced parent–infant interaction, reduced infant crying and improved sleep, more rapid language development in the second year, and steady gains in mental test performance that equal those of full-term children by middle childhood (Achenbach, Howell, & Aoki, 1993; Newnham, Milgrom, & Skouteris, 2009).

When preterm infants live in stressed, economically disadvantaged households, long-term intensive intervention is necessary (Guralnick, 2012). In the Infant Health and Development Program, preterm babies born into poverty received a comprehensive intervention. It combined medical follow-up, weekly home visits beginning soon after hospital discharge in which mothers received training in infant care and everyday problem solving, and cognitively stimulating child care from 1 to 3 years of age. More than four times as many intervention children as no-intervention controls (39 versus 9 percent) were within normal range at age 3 in intelligence, psychological adjustment, and physical growth (Bradley et al., 1994). In addition, mothers in the intervention group were more affectionate and more often encouraged play and cognitive mastery in their children—one reason their 3-year-olds may have been developing so favorably (McCarton, 1998).

At ages 5 and 8, children who had attended the child-care program regularly—for more than 350 days over the three-year period—continued to show better intellectual functioning. The more they attended, the higher they scored, with greater gains among those whose birth weights were higher—between 4½ and 5½ pounds (2,001 to 2,500 grams) (see Figure 4.4). In contrast, children who attended only sporadically gained little or even lost ground (Hill, Brooks-Gunn, & Waldfogel, 2003). A follow-up at age 18 revealed persisting benefits for the higher-birth-weight participants: They remained advantaged over controls in academic achievement, and they also engaged in fewer risky behaviors such as unprotected sexual activity and alcohol and drug use (McCormick et al., 2006).

These findings confirm that babies who are both preterm and economically disadvantaged require *intensive* intervention. And special strategies, such as extra adult–child interaction both at home and in infant–toddler and early childhood programs, may be necessary to achieve lasting changes in children with the lowest birth weights.

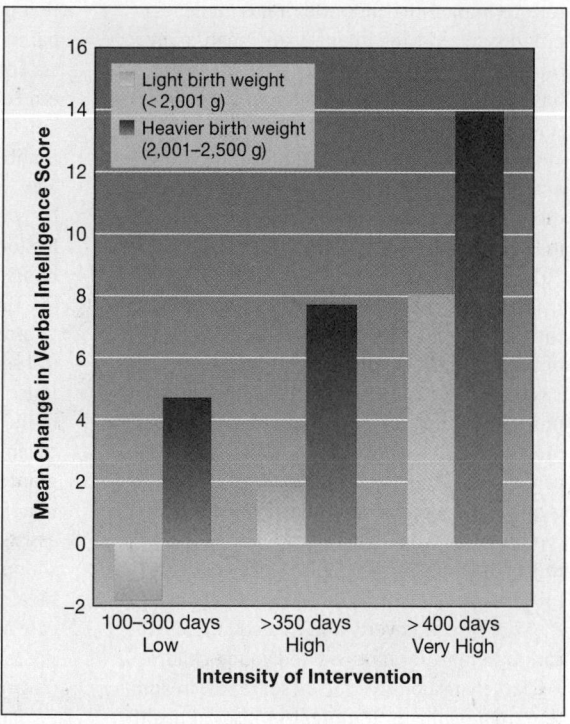

FIGURE 4.4 **Influence of intensity of early intervention for low-income, preterm babies on intellectual functioning at age 8.** Infants born preterm received cognitively stimulating child care from 1 through 3 years of age. Those who attended the program sporadically gained little in intellectual functioning (heavier-weight babies) or lost ground (lighter-weight babies). The more often children attended, the greater their intellectual gains. Heavier babies consistently gained more than light babies. But boosting the intensity of intervention above 400 days led to a dramatic increase in the performance of the light-weight group. (Adapted from Hill, Brooks-Gunn, & Waldfogel, 2003.)

VERY LOW BIRTH WEIGHT, ENVIRONMENTAL ADVANTAGES, AND LONG-TERM OUTCOMES

Although very low-birth-weight individuals often have lasting problems, in a Canadian study, young adults who weighed between 1 and 2.2 pounds (500 to 1,000 grams) at birth were doing well in overall quality of life (Saigal et al., 2006). At 22 to 25 years of age, they resembled normal-birth-weight individuals in educational attainment, rates of marriage and parenthood, and (for those who had no neurological or sensory impairments) employment status. What explains these excellent outcomes? Researchers believe that home, school, and societal advantages are largely responsible (Hack & Klein, 2006). Most participants in this study were reared in two-parent middle-SES homes, attended good schools where they received special services, and benefited from Canada's universal health care system.

Social Issues: Health

A Cross-National Perspective on Health Care and Other Policies for Parents and Newborn Babies

Infant mortality—the number of deaths in the first year of life per 1,000 live births— is an index used around the world to assess the overall health of a nation's children. Although the United States has the most up-to-date health-care technology in the world, it has made less progress in reducing infant deaths than many other countries. Over the past three decades, it has slipped in the international rankings, from seventh in the 1950s to thirty-seventh in 2014. Members of America's poor ethnic minorities are at greatest risk, with African-American infants more than twice as likely as white infants to die in the first year of life (U.S. Census Bureau, 2014a, 2014b).

Neonatal mortality, the rate of death within the first month of life, accounts for 67 percent of the infant death rate in the United States. Two factors are largely responsible for neonatal mortality. The first is serious physical defects, most of which cannot be prevented. The percentage of babies born with physical defects is about the same in all ethnic and income groups. The second leading cause of neonatal mortality is low birth weight, which is largely preventable.

Widespread poverty and inadequate health-care programs for mothers and young children are largely responsible for these trends. In addition to providing government-sponsored health-care benefits to all citizens, each country in Figure 4.5 takes extra steps to make sure that pregnant mothers and babies have access to good nutrition, high-quality medical care, and social and economic supports that promote effective parenting.

For example, all Western European nations guarantee women a certain number of prenatal visits at very low or no cost. After a baby is born, a health professional routinely visits the home to provide counseling about infant care and to arrange continuing medical services. Home assistance is especially extensive in the Netherlands. For a token fee, each mother is granted a specially trained maternity helper, who assists with infant care, shopping, housekeeping, meal preparation, and the care of other children during the days after delivery (Zwart, 2007).

Paid, job-protected employment leave is another vital societal

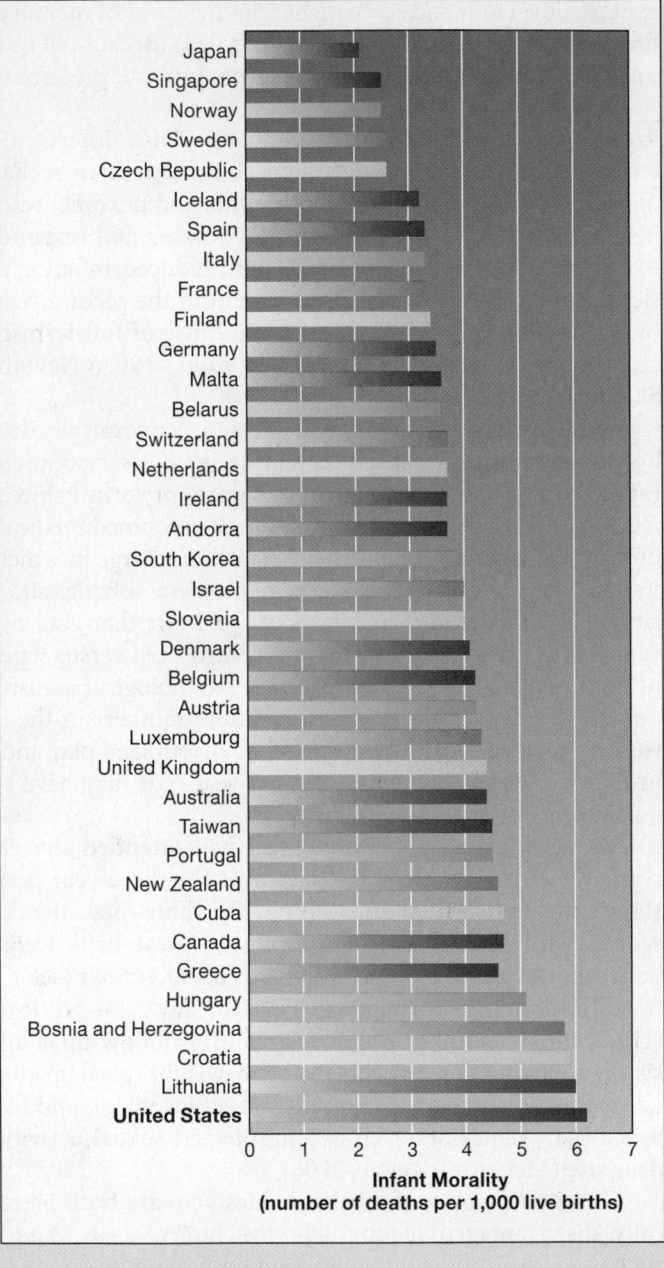

FIGURE 4.5 **Infant mortality in 37 nations.** Despite its advanced healthcare technology, the United States ranks poorly. It is thirty-seventh in the world, with a death rate of 6.2 infants per 1,000 births. (Adapted from U.S. Census Bureau, 2014a.)

Nevertheless, even the best environments cannot always overcome the enormous biological risks associated with very low birth weight. Think back to Keith, the very sick baby you met at the beginning of this section. Despite advanced medical technology and new ways of helping parents, most infants born as early and with as low a birth weight as Keith either die or end up with serious disabilities (Larroque et al., 2008). Six months after he was born, Keith died without ever having left the hospital.

Keith's premature birth was unavoidable, but the high rate of underweight babies in the United States—one of the worst in the industrialized world—could be greatly reduced by improving the health and social conditions described in the Social Issues: Health box above.

intervention for new parents. Canadian mothers are eligible for 15 weeks' maternity leave at 55 percent of prior earnings (up to a maximum of $413 per week), and Canadian mothers or fathers can take an additional 35 weeks of parental leave at the same rate. Paid maternal and paternal leave is widely available in other industrialized nations as well. Sweden has the most generous parental leave program in the world. Mothers can begin maternity leave 60 days prior to expected delivery, extending it to six weeks after birth; fathers are granted two weeks of birth leave. In addition, either parent can take full leave for 15 months at 80 percent of prior earnings, followed by an additional three months at a modest flat rate. Each parent is also entitled to another 18 months of unpaid leave. Even economically less well-off nations provide parental leave benefits. In Bulgaria, new mothers are granted 20 months paid leave, and fathers receive three weeks (Robila, 2012). Furthermore, many countries supplement basic paid leave. In Germany, for example, after a fully paid three-month leave, a parent may take one more year at a flat rate and additional leave at no pay until the child reaches age 3 years (Ray, Gornick, & Schmitt, 2008).

Yet in the United States, the federal government mandates *only 12 weeks of unpaid leave* for employees in companies with at least 50 workers. Most women, however, work in smaller businesses, and many of those who work in large enough companies cannot afford to take unpaid leave. And because of financial pressures, many new mothers who are eligible for unpaid work leave take far less than 12 weeks. Similarly, though paternal leave predicts fathers' increased involvement in infant care at the end of first year, many fathers take little or none at all (Nepomnyaschy & Waldfogel, 2007). In 2002, California became the first state to guarantee a mother or father paid leave—up to six weeks at half salary, regardless of the size of the company. Since then, the District of Columbia, Hawaii, New

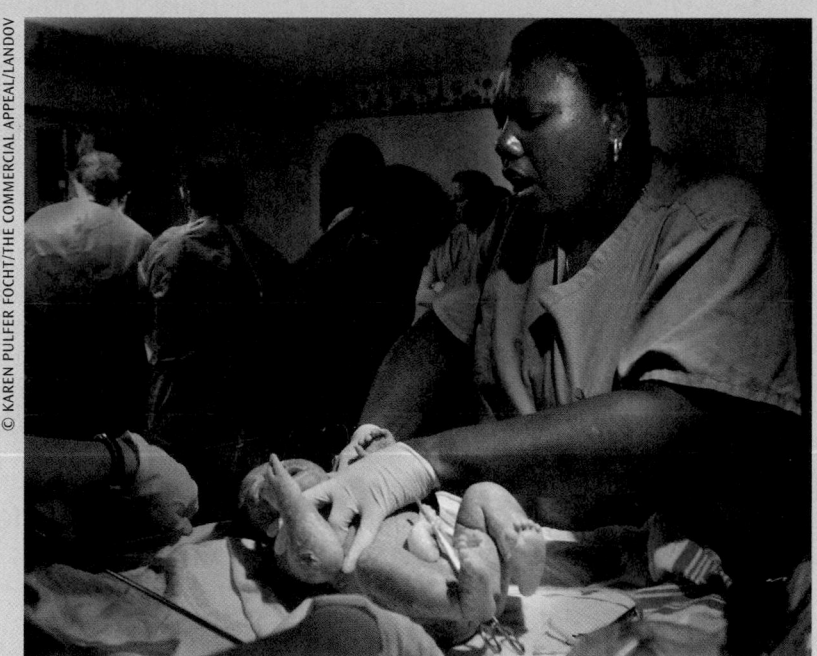

This doctor works with high-risk pregnancies, delivering infants whose poverty-stricken mothers have had little or no prenatal care. Nations with low poverty rates and government-supported, high-quality health care for pregnant mothers and babies outrank the United States in infant survival.

Jersey, New York, Rhode Island, Washington, and the territory of Puerto Rico have passed similar legislation.

Nevertheless, six weeks of childbirth leave (the norm in the United States) is not enough. When a family is stressed by a baby's arrival, leaves of six weeks or less are linked to increased maternal anxiety, depression, marital dissatisfaction, sense of role overload, and negative interactions with the baby. A longer leave (12 weeks or more) predicts favorable maternal mental health, supportive marital interaction, and sensitive, responsive caregiving (Feldman, Sussman, & Zigler, 2004; Hyde et al., 2001). Single women and their babies are most hurt by the absence of a generous national paid-leave policy. These

mothers, who are usually the sole source of support for their families, can least afford to take time from their jobs.

In countries with low infant mortality rates, expectant parents need not wonder how they will access essential resources for supporting their baby's development. The powerful impact of universal, high-quality health care; generous parental leave; and other social services on maternal and infant well-being provides strong justification for these policies. Responding to these findings, the Affordable Care Act provides generous grants to U.S. states to cover the cost of evidence-based home-visiting programs that provide comprehensive services to mothers, infants, and young children in high-risk families.

Fortunately, today we can save many preterm babies, but an even better course of action would be to prevent this serious threat to infant survival and development before it happens.

Birth Complications, Parenting, and Resilience

In the preceding sections, we considered a variety of birth complications. Now let's try to put the evidence together. Can any general principles help us understand how infants who survive a traumatic birth are likely to develop? A landmark study carried out in Hawaii provides answers to this question.

In 1955, Emmy Werner and Ruth Smith began to follow the development of nearly 700 infants on the island of Kauai who experienced either mild, moderate, or severe birth complications. Each was matched, on the basis of SES and ethnicity, with a healthy newborn (Werner & Smith, 1982). Findings showed that the likelihood of long-term difficulties increased if birth trauma was severe. But among mildly to moderately stressed children, those growing up in stable families with sensitive, involved parenting did almost as well on measures of intelligence and psychological adjustment as those with no birth problems. Children exposed to poverty, family disorganization, and mentally ill parents often developed serious learning difficulties, behavior problems, and emotional disturbance.

The Kauai study tells us that as long as birth injuries are not overwhelming, a supportive home can restore children's growth. But the most intriguing cases in this study were the handful of exceptions. A few children with both fairly serious birth complications and troubled family environments grew into competent adults who fared as well as controls in career attainment and psychological adjustment. Werner and Smith found that these children relied on factors outside the family and within themselves to overcome stress. Some had attractive personalities that drew positive responses from relatives, neighbors, and peers. In other instances, a grandparent, aunt, uncle, or babysitter provided the needed emotional support (Werner, 1989, 2001; Werner & Smith, 1992).

Do these outcomes remind you of the characteristics of resilient children, discussed in Chapter 1? The Kauai study and other similar investigations reveal that the impact of early biological risks often wanes as children's personal characteristics and social experiences contribute increasingly to their functioning (Werner, 2013). In sum, when the overall balance of life events tips toward the favorable side, children with serious birth problems can develop successfully. And when negative factors outweigh positive ones, even a sturdy newborn can become a lifelong casualty.

Ask Yourself

- **REVIEW** Sensitive care can help preterm infants recover, but they are less likely than full-term newborns to receive such care. Explain why.

- **CONNECT** List factors discussed in this chapter and in Chapter 3 that increase the chances that an infant will be born underweight. How many of these factors could be prevented by better health care for expectant mothers?

- **APPLY** Cecilia and Anna each gave birth to a 3-pound baby seven weeks preterm. Cecilia is single and on welfare. Anna and her husband are happily married and earn a good income. Plan an intervention appropriate for helping each baby develop.

- **REFLECT** Many people object to the use of extraordinary medical measures to save extremely low-birth-weight babies because of their high risk for serious developmental problems. Do you agree or disagree? Explain.

4.5 Is close parent–infant contact shortly after birth necessary for bonding?

Precious Moments After Birth

Yolanda and Jay's account of Joshua's birth revealed that the time spent holding and touching him right after delivery was filled with intense emotion. A mother given her infant at this time will usually stroke the baby gently, look into the infant's eyes, and talk softly (Klaus & Kennell, 1982). Fathers respond similarly. Most are overjoyed at their baby's birth; characterize the experience as "awesome," "indescribable," or "unforgettable"; and display intense interest in their newborn child (Rose, 2000). Regardless of SES or participation in childbirth classes, fathers touch, look at, talk to, and kiss their newborn infants just as much as mothers do.

Because effective caregiving is crucial for infant survival and optimal development, nature helps prepare mothers and fathers for their new role. Toward the end of pregnancy, mothers begin producing higher levels of the hormone *oxytocin,* which causes the breasts to "let down" milk; induces a calm, relaxed mood; and heightens responsiveness to the baby (Gordon et al., 2010).

Fathers show hormonal changes around the time of birth that are compatible with those of mothers—specifically, slight increases in *prolactin* (a hormone that stimulates milk production in females) and *estrogens* (sex hormones produced in larger quantities in females) and a drop in *androgens* (sex hormones produced in larger quantities in males) (Delahunty et al., 2007; Wynne-Edwards, 2001). These changes, which are induced by fathers' contact with the mother and baby, predict paternal positive emotional reactions and sensitivity to infants (Feldman et al., 2010; Leuner, Glasper, & Gould, 2010).

But do human parents require close physical contact in the hours after birth for **bonding,** or feelings of affection and concern for the infant, to develop—as many animal species do? Current evidence shows that the human parent–infant relationship does not depend on a precise, early period of togetherness. Some parents report sudden, deep feelings of affection on first holding their babies. For others, these emotions emerge gradually. And as successful adoption reveals (see pages 66–67 in Chapter 2), humans can parent effectively without experiencing birth-related hormonal changes. In fact, when foster and adoptive mothers hold and interact with their nonbiological infants, they typically release oxytocin (Bick et al., 2013; Galbally et al., 2011). And the greater their oxytocin production, the more they express affection and pleasure toward the infant.

Human bonding is a complex process that depends on many factors, not just on what happens during a short period after birth. Nevertheless, early contact with the baby may be one of several factors that help build a good parent–infant relationship. Realizing this, today hospitals offer **rooming in,** in which the infant stays in the mother's hospital room all or most of the time. If parents do not choose this option or cannot do so for medical reasons, there is no evidence that their competence as caregivers will be compromised or that the baby will suffer emotionally.

© ABK/BSIP/THE IMAGE WORKS

This father displays great affection for and involvement with his newborn baby. Like mothers, fathers typically express their elation by touching, looking at, talking to, and kissing the infant.

The Newborn Baby's Capacities

Newborn infants have a remarkable set of capacities that are crucial for survival and for evoking adult attention and care. In relating to the physical and social world, babies are active from the very start.

Reflexes

A **reflex** is an inborn, automatic response to a particular form of stimulation. Reflexes are the newborn baby's most obvious organized patterns of behavior. As Jay placed Joshua on a table in the classroom, we saw several. When Jay bumped the side of the table, Joshua reacted by flinging his arms wide and bringing them back toward his body. As Yolanda stroked Joshua's cheek, he turned his head in her direction. When she put her finger in Joshua's palm, he grabbed on tightly. **TAKE A MOMENT...** Look at Table 4.2 on page 142 and see if you can name the newborn reflexes that Joshua displayed. Then let's consider the meaning and purpose of these curious behaviors.

ADAPTIVE VALUE OF REFLEXES   Some reflexes have survival value. The rooting reflex helps a breastfed baby find the mother's nipple. Babies display it only when hungry and touched by another person, not when they touch themselves (Rochat & Hespos, 1997). And if sucking were not automatic, our species would be unlikely to survive for a single generation! At birth, babies adjust their sucking pressure to how easily milk flows from the nipple (Craig & Lee, 1999). The swimming reflex helps a baby who is accidentally dropped into water stay afloat, increasing the chances of retrieval by the caregiver.

4.6 Describe the newborn baby's reflexes and states of arousal, including sleep characteristics and ways to soothe a crying baby.

4.7 Describe the newborn baby's sensory capacities.

4.8 Why is neonatal behavioral assessment useful?

TABLE 4.2	Some Newborn Reflexes			
REFLEX	**STIMULATION**	**RESPONSE**	**AGE OF DISAPPEARANCE**	**FUNCTION**
Eye blink	Shine bright light at eyes or clap hand near head.	Infant quickly closes eyelids.	Permanent	Protects infant from strong stimulation
Rooting	Stroke cheek near corner of mouth	Head turns toward source of stimulation.	3 weeks (becomes voluntary head turning at this time)	Helps infant find the nipple
Sucking	Place finger in infant's mouth.	Infant sucks finger rhythmically.	Replaced by voluntary sucking after 4 months	Permits feeding
Swimming[a]	Occurs when infant is face down in pool of water.	Baby paddles and kicks in swimming motion.	4–6 months	Helps infant survive if dropped into water
Moro	Hold infant horizontally on back and let head drop slightly, or produce a sudden loud sound against surface supporting infant.	Infant makes an "embracing" motion by arching back, extending legs, throwing arms outward, and then bringing arms in toward the body	6 months	In human evolutionary past, may have helped infant cling to mother
Palmar grasp	Place finger in infant's hand and press against palm	Spontaneous grasp of finger	3–4 months	Prepares infant for voluntary grasping
Tonic neck	Turn baby's head to one side while infant is lying awake on back	Infant lies in a "fencing position." One arm is extended in front of eyes on side to which head is turned, other arm is flexed	4 months	May prepare infant for voluntary reaching
Stepping	Hold infant under arms and permit bare feet to touch a flat surface	Infant lifts one foot after another in stepping response	2 months in infants who gain weight quickly; sustained in lighter infants	Prepares infant for voluntary walking
Babinski	Stroke sole of foot from toe toward heel	Toes fan out and curl as foot twists in	8–12 months	Unknown

[a]Placing infants in a pool of water is dangerous. See discussion on the following page.

Sources: Knobloch & Pasamanick, 1974; Prechtl & Beintema, 1965; Thelen, Fisher, & Ridley-Johnson, 1984.

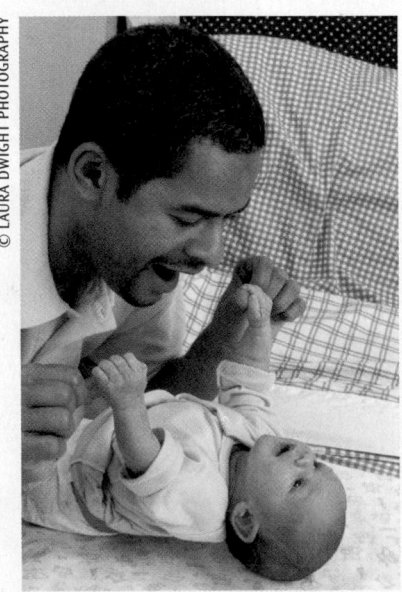

© LAURA DWIGHT PHOTOGRAPHY

The palmar grasp reflex is so strong during the first week after birth that many infants can use it to support their entire weight.

Other reflexes probably helped babies survive during our evolutionary past. For example, the Moro, or "embracing," reflex is believed to have helped infants cling to their mothers when they were carried about all day (Kessen, 1967). If the baby happened to lose support, the reflex caused the infant to embrace and, along with the palmar grasp reflex (so strong during the first week that it can support the baby's entire weight), regain its hold on the mother's body.

Several reflexes help parents and infants establish gratifying interaction. A baby who searches for and successfully finds the nipple, sucks easily during feedings, and grasps when her hand is touched encourages parents to respond lovingly and feel competent as caregivers. Reflexes can also help parents comfort the baby because they permit infants to control distress and amount of stimulation. For example, on short trips with Joshua to the grocery store, Yolanda brought along a pacifier. If he became fussy, sucking helped quiet him until she could feed, change, or hold him.

REFLEXES AND THE DEVELOPMENT OF MOTOR SKILLS   A few reflexes form the basis for complex motor skills that will develop later. For example, the tonic neck reflex may prepare the baby for voluntary reaching. When infants lie on their backs in this "fencing position," they naturally gaze at the hand in front of their eyes. The reflex may encourage them to combine vision with arm movements and, eventually, reach for objects (Knobloch & Pasamanick, 1974).

Certain reflexes—such as the palmar grasp, swimming, and stepping—drop out early, but the motor functions involved are renewed later. The stepping reflex, for example, looks like a primitive walking response. Unlike other reflexes, it appears in a wide range of situations—

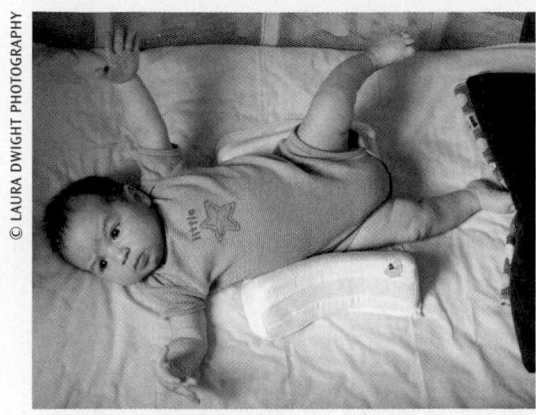

In the Moro reflex, loss of support or a sudden loud sound causes the baby to arch her back, extend her arms outward, and then bring them in toward her body.

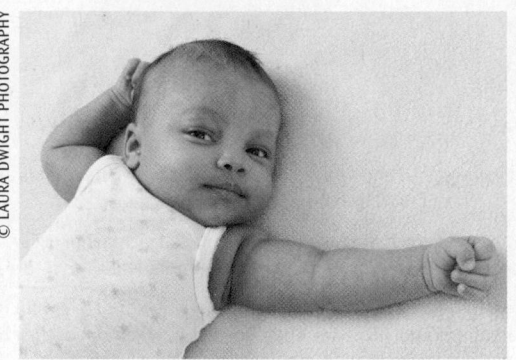

In the tonic neck reflex, infants lie on their backs in a "fencing position," which may help prepare them for voluntary reaching.

When held upright under the arms, newborn babies show reflexive stepping movements.

with the newborn's body in a sideways or upside-down position, with feet touching walls or ceilings, and even with legs dangling in the air (Adolph & Berger, 2006). One reason that babies frequently engage in the alternating leg movements of stepping is their ease compared with other movement patterns; repetitive movement of one leg or of both legs at once requires more effort.

In infants who gain weight quickly in the weeks after birth, the stepping reflex drops out because thigh and calf muscles are not strong enough to lift the baby's chubby legs. But if the lower part of the infant's body is dipped in water, the reflex reappears because the buoyancy of the water lightens the load on the baby's muscles (Thelen, Fisher, & Ridley-Johnson, 1984). When stepping is exercised regularly, babies make more spontaneous stepping movements and are likely to walk several weeks earlier than if stepping is not practiced (Zelazo et al., 1993). However, there is no special need for infants to practice the stepping reflex because all normal babies walk in due time.

In the case of the swimming reflex, trying to build on it is risky. Although young babies placed in a swimming pool will paddle and kick, they swallow large amounts of water. This lowers the concentration of salt in the baby's blood, which can cause brain swelling and seizures. Despite this remarkable reflex, swimming lessons are best postponed until at least 3 years of age.

THE IMPORTANCE OF ASSESSING NEWBORN REFLEXES   Look at Table 4.2 again, and you will see that most newborn reflexes disappear during the first six months. Researchers believe that this is due to a gradual increase in voluntary control over behavior as the cerebral cortex develops.

Pediatricians test reflexes carefully, especially if a newborn has experienced birth trauma, because reflexes can reveal the health of the baby's nervous system. Weak or absent reflexes, overly rigid or exaggerated reflexes, and reflexes that persist beyond the point in development when they should normally disappear can signal brain damage (Schott & Rossor, 2003; Zafeiriou, 2000). However, individual differences in reflexive responses exist that are not cause for concern. An observer must assess newborn reflexes along with other characteristics to accurately distinguish normal from abnormal central nervous system functioning.

States

Throughout the day and night, newborn infants move in and out of the five **states of arousal, or degrees of sleep and wakefulness,** described in Table 4.3 on page 144. During the first month, these states alternate frequently. The most fleeting is quiet alertness, which usually moves quickly toward fussing and crying. Much to the relief of their fatigued parents, newborns spend the greatest amount of time asleep—about 16 to 18 hours a day. Because the fetus tends to synchronize periods of rest and activity with those of the mother, newborns—even those who are 4 to 6 weeks preterm—sleep more at night than during the day (Heraghty et al.,

TABLE 4.3	Infant States of Arousal		
STATE	**DESCRIPTION**	**DAILY DURATION IN NEWBORN**
Regular, or NREM, sleep	The infant is at full rest and shows little or no body activity. The eyelids are closed, no eye movements occur, the face is relaxed, and breathing is slow and regular.	8–9 hours
Irregular, or REM, sleep	Gentle limb movements, occasional stirring, and facial grimacing occur. Although the eyelids are closed, occasional rapid eye movements can be seen beneath them. Breathing is irregular.	8–9 hours
Drowsiness	The infant is either falling asleep or waking up. Body is less active than in irregular sleep but more active than in regular sleep. The eyes open and close; when open, they have a glazed look. Breathing is even but somewhat faster than in regular sleep.	Varies
Quiet alertness	The infant's body is relatively inactive, with eyes open and attentive. Breathing is even.	2–3 hours
Waking activity and crying	The infant shows frequent bursts of uncoordinated body activity. Breathing is very irregular. Face may be relaxed or tense and wrinkled. Crying may occur.	1–4 hours

Source: Wolff, 1966.

2008). Nevertheless, young babies' sleep–wake cycles are affected more by fullness–hunger than by darkness–light (Davis, Parker, & Montgomery, 2004).

However, striking individual differences in daily rhythms exist that affect parents' attitudes toward and interactions with the baby. A few newborns sleep for long periods, increasing the energy their well-rested parents have for sensitive, responsive care. Other babies wake frequently and cry often, and their parents must exert great effort to soothe them. If these parents do not succeed, they may feel less competent and less positive toward their infant (Sadeh et al., 2007; Smart & Hiscock, 2007).

Furthermore, from birth on, arousal patterns have implications for cognitive development. Babies who spend more time alert probably receive more social stimulation and opportunities to explore and, therefore, may have a slight advantage in mental development. And as with adults, sleep enhances babies' learning and memory. In one study, eye-blink responses and brain-wave recordings revealed that sleeping newborns readily learned that a tone would be followed by a puff of air to the eye (Fifer et al., 2010). Because young infants spend so much time sleeping, the capacity to learn about external stimuli during sleep may be essential for babies' adaptation to their surroundings.

Of the states listed in Table 4.3 the two extremes—sleep and crying—have been of greatest interest to researchers. Each tells us something about normal and abnormal early development.

SLEEP   Observing Joshua as he slept, Yolanda and Jay wondered why his eyelids and body twitched and his rate of breathing varied. Sleep is made up of at least two states. During irregular, or **rapid-eye-movement (REM), sleep,** brain-wave activity is remarkably similar to that of the waking state. The eyes dart beneath the lids; heart rate, blood pressure, and breathing are uneven; and slight body movements occur. The expression "sleeping like a baby" was probably not meant to describe this state! In contrast, during regular, or **non-rapid-eye-movement (NREM), sleep,** the body is almost motionless, and heart rate, breathing, and brain-wave activity are slow and even.

Like children and adults, newborns alternate between REM and NREM sleep. However, they spend far more time in the REM state than they ever will again. REM sleep accounts for 50 percent of the newborn baby's sleep time. By 3 to 5 years, it has declined to an adultlike level of 20 percent (Louis et al., 1997).

Why do young infants spend so much time in REM sleep? In older children and adults, the REM state is associated with dreaming. Babies probably do not dream, at least not in the same way we do. But researchers believe that the stimulation of REM sleep is vital for growth of the central nervous system (Tarullo, Balsam, & Fifer, 2011). Young infants seem to have a special need for this stimulation because they spend so little time in an alert state, when they can get input from the environment. In support of this idea, the percentage of REM sleep is especially great in the fetus and in preterm babies, who are even less able than full-term newborns to take advantage of external stimulation (de Weerd & van den Bossche, 2003; Peirano, Algarin, & Uauy, 2003).

Social Issues: Health

The Mysterious Tragedy of Sudden Infant Death Syndrome

Millie awoke with a start one morning and looked at the clock. It was 7:30, and Sasha had missed both her night waking and her early morning feeding. Wondering if she was all right, Millie and her husband, Stuart, tiptoed into the room. Sasha lay still, curled up under her blanket. She had died silently during her sleep.

Sasha was a victim of **sudden infant death syndrome (SIDS),** the unexpected death, usually during the night, of an infant younger than 1 year of age that remains unexplained after thorough investigation. In industrialized nations, SIDS is the leading cause of infant mortality between 1 week and 12 months, accounting for about 11 percent of these deaths in the United States (Child Health USA, 2013).

SIDS victims usually show physical problems from the beginning. Early medical records of SIDS babies reveal higher rates of prematurity and low birth weight, poor Apgar scores, and limp muscle tone. Abnormal heart rate and respiration and disturbances in sleep–wake activity and in REM–NREM cycles while asleep are also involved (Cornwell & Feigenbaum, 2006; Garcia, Koschnitzky, & Ramirez, 2013). At the time of death, many SIDS babies have a mild respiratory infection (Blood-Siegfried, 2009). This seems to increase the chances of respiratory failure in an already vulnerable baby.

Mounting evidence suggests that impaired brain functioning is a major contributor to SIDS. Between 2 and 4 months, when SIDS is most likely to occur, reflexes decline and are replaced by voluntary, learned responses. Neurological weaknesses may prevent SIDS babies from acquiring behaviors that replace defensive reflexes (Lipsitt, 2003). As a result, when breathing difficulties occur during sleep, these infants do not wake up, shift their position, or cry out for help. Instead, they simply give in to oxygen deprivation and death. In support of this interpretation, autopsies reveal that the brains of SIDS babies

contain unusually low levels of serotonin (a brain chemical that assists with arousal when survival is threatened) as well as other abnormalities in centers that control breathing and arousal (Duncan et al., 2010).

Several environmental factors are linked to SIDS. Maternal cigarette smoking, both during and after pregnancy, as well as smoking by other caregivers, doubles risk of the disorder. Babies exposed to cigarette smoke arouse less easily from sleep and have more respiratory infections (Richardson, Walker, & Horne, 2008; Shah, Sullivan, & Carter, 2006). Prenatal abuse of drugs that depress central nervous system functioning (alcohol, opiates, and barbiturates) increases the risk of SIDS as much as fifteen-fold (Hunt & Hauck, 2006). Babies of drug-abusing mothers are especially likely to display SIDS-related brain abnormalities (Kinney, 2009).

SIDS babies are also more likely to sleep on their stomachs than on their backs and often are wrapped very warmly in clothing and blankets. Infants who sleep on their stomachs less often wake when their breathing is disturbed (Richardson, Walker, & Horne, 2008). In other cases, healthy babies sleeping face down in soft bedding may die from continually breathing their own exhaled breath.

SIDS rates are especially high among poverty-stricken minorities (Colson et al., 2009). In these families, parental stress, substance abuse, reduced access to health care, and lack of knowledge about safe sleep practices are widespread.

Public education efforts are vital for reducing the prevalence of SIDS. The U.S. government's Safe to Sleep campaign encourages parents to create safe sleep environments and engage in other protective practices. Among its recommendations are quitting smoking and drug taking, changing an infant's sleeping position, providing a firm sleep surface, and eliminating soft

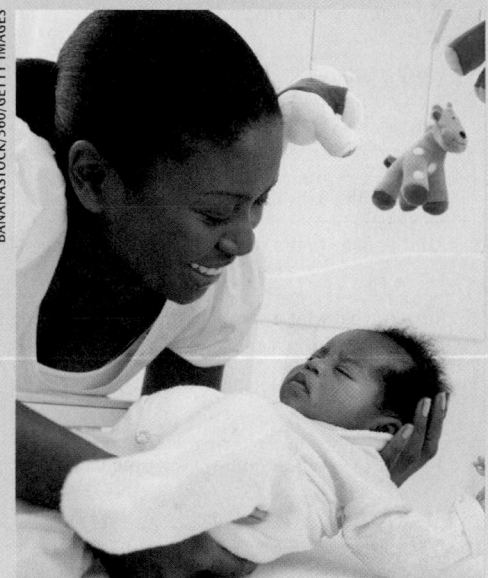

Public education campaigns encouraging parents to put their infants down on their backs to sleep have helped to reduce the incidence of SIDS, which has dropped by more than half in many Western nations.

bedding. An estimated 20 percent of SIDS cases would be prevented if all infants had smoke-free homes. Dissemination of information to parents about putting infants down on their backs has cut the incidence of SIDS by more than half in many Western nations (Behm et al., 2012; Moon, Horne, & Hauck, 2007). Another protective measure is pacifier use: Sleeping babies who suck arouse more easily in response to breathing and heart-rate irregularities (Li et al., 2006).

When SIDS does occur, surviving family members require a great deal of help to overcome a sudden and unexpected death. As Millie commented six months after Sasha's death, "It's the worst crisis we've ever been through. What's helped us most are the comforting words of others who've experienced the same tragedy."

Because newborn babies' normal sleep behavior is organized and patterned, observations of sleep states can help identify central nervous system abnormalities. In infants who are brain-damaged or who have experienced birth trauma, disturbed REM–NREM sleep cycles are often present. Both full-term and preterm babies with poor sleep organization are likely to be behaviorally disorganized and, therefore, to have difficulty learning and eliciting caregiver interactions that enhance their development. In follow-ups during the preschool years, they show delayed motor, cognitive, and language development (Feldman, 2006; Holditch-Davis, Belyea, & Edwards, 2005; Weisman et al., 2011). And the brain-functioning problems that underlie newborn sleep irregularities may culminate in sudden infant death syndrome, a major cause of infant mortality (see the Social Issues: Health box above).

Applying What We Know

Soothing a Crying Baby

TECHNIQUE	EXPLANATION
Talk softly or play rhythmic sounds.	Continuous, monotonous, rhythmic sounds (such as a clock ticking, a fan whirring, or peaceful music) are more effective than intermittent sounds.
Offer a pacifier.	Sucking helps babies control their own level of arousal.
Massage the baby's body.	Stroking the baby's torso and limbs with continuous, gentle motions relaxes the baby's muscles.
Swaddle the baby.	Restricting movement and increasing warmth often soothe a young infant.
Lift the baby to the shoulder and rock or walk.	This combination of physical contact, upright posture, and motion is an effective soothing technique, causing young infants to become quietly alert.
Take the baby for a short car ride or a walk in a baby carriage; swing the baby in a cradle.	Gentle, rhythmic motion of any kind helps lull the baby to sleep.
Combine several of the methods just listed.	Stimulating several of the baby's senses at once is often more effective than stimulating only one.
If these methods do not work, let the baby cry for a short period.	Occasionally, a baby responds well to just being put down and will, after a few minutes, fall asleep.

Sources: Campos, 1989; Evanoo, 2007; St James-Roberts, 2012.

To soothe his crying infant, this father holds the baby against his gently moving body and speaks softly. The combination of physical contact, motion, and gentle sounds causes infants to stop crying and become quietly alert.

CRYING   Crying is the first way that babies communicate, letting parents know that they need food, comfort, and stimulation. During the weeks after birth, all babies seem to have some fussy periods when they are difficult to console. But most of the time, the nature of the cry, combined with the experiences that led up to it, helps guide parents toward its cause. The baby's cry is a complex stimulus that varies in intensity, from a whimper to a message of all-out distress (Gustafson, Wood, & Green, 2000; Wood, 2009). As early as the first few weeks, infants can be identified by the unique vocal "signature" of their cries, which helps parents locate their baby from a distance (Gustafson, Green, & Cleland, 1994).

Young infants usually cry because of physical needs. Hunger is the most common cause, but babies may also cry in response to temperature change when undressed, a sudden noise, or a painful stimulus. Newborns (as well as older babies) often cry at the sound of another crying baby (Dondi, Simion, & Caltran, 1999; Geangu et al., 2010). Some researchers believe that this response reflects an inborn capacity to react to the suffering of others. Furthermore, crying typically increases during the early weeks, peaks at about 6 weeks, and then declines (Barr, 2001). Because this trend appears in many cultures with vastly different infant care practices, researchers believe that normal readjustments of the central nervous system underlie it.

TAKE A MOMENT... The next time you hear a baby cry, notice your own reaction. The sound stimulates strong feelings of arousal and discomfort in men and women, parents and nonparents alike (Murray, 1985). This powerful response is probably innately programmed to help ensure that babies receive the care and protection they need to survive.

Soothing a Crying Infant. Although parents do not always interpret their baby's cry correctly, their accuracy improves with experience. At the same time, they vary widely in responsiveness. Parents who are high in empathy (ability to take the perspective of others in distress) and who hold "child-centered" attitudes toward infant care—for example, believe that babies cannot be spoiled by being picked up—are more likely to respond quickly and sensitively to a crying baby (Leerkes, 2010; Zeifman, 2003).

Fortunately, there are many ways to soothe a crying baby when feeding and diaper changing do not work (see Applying What We Know above). The technique that Western parents usually try first, lifting the baby to the shoulder and rocking or walking, is highly effective. Another common soothing method is swaddling—wrapping the baby snugly in a blanket. The Quechua, who live in the cold, high-altitude desert regions of Peru, dress young infants in several layers of clothing and blankets that cover the head and body, a technique that reduces crying and promotes sleep (Tronick, Thomas, & Daltabuit, 1994). It also enables the baby to conserve energy for early growth in the harsh Peruvian highlands.

In many tribal and village societies and in non-Western developed nations, infants spend most of the day and night in close physical contact with their caregivers. Among the !Kung of Botswana, Africa, mothers carry their young babies in grass-lined, animal-skin slings hung on their hips, so the infants can see their surroundings and can nurse at will. Japanese mothers also spend much time holding their babies (Small, 1998). Infants in these cultures show shorter bouts of crying than their American counterparts (Barr, 2001). When Western parents choose to practice "proximal care" by holding their babies extensively, amount of crying in the early months is reduced by about one-third (St James-Roberts, 2012).

The Mongol people of Central Asia heavily swaddle their babies, a practice that reduces crying and promotes sleep while also protecting infants from the region's harsh winters.

Abnormal Crying. Like reflexes and sleep patterns, the infant's cry offers a clue to central nervous system distress. The cries of brain-damaged babies and those who have experienced prenatal and birth complications are often shrill, piercing, and shorter in duration than the cries of healthy infants (Green, Irwin, & Gustafson, 2000). Even newborns with a fairly common problem—*colic,* or persistent crying—tend to have high-pitched, harsh-sounding cries (Zeskind & Barr, 1997). Although the cause of colic is unknown, certain newborns, who react especially strongly to unpleasant stimuli, are susceptible. Because their crying is intense, they find it harder to calm down than other babies (Barr et al., 2005; St James-Roberts, 2007). Colic generally subsides between 3 and 6 months.

In an intervention aimed at reducing colic, nurses made periodic home visits, providing parents with help in identifying their baby's early warning signs of becoming overly aroused, in using effective soothing techniques, and in modifying light, noise, and activity in the home to promote predictable sleep–wake cycles (Keefe et al., 2005). Colicky infants who received the intervention spent far less time crying than no-intervention controls—1.3 versus 3 hours per day.

Most parents try to respond to a crying baby's call for help with extra care and attention, but sometimes the cry is so unpleasant and the infant so difficult to soothe that parents become frustrated, resentful, and angry. Preterm and ill babies are more likely to be abused by highly stressed parents, who sometimes mention a high-pitched, grating cry as one factor that caused them to lose control and harm the baby (Rautava et al., 2007; St James-Roberts, 2012). We will discuss a host of additional influences on child abuse in Chapter 10.

LOOK and LISTEN

In a public setting, watch several parents soothe their crying babies. What techniques did the parents use, and how successful were they?

Sensory Capacities

On his visit to class, Joshua looked wide-eyed at Yolanda's bright pink blouse and readily turned to the sound of her voice. During feedings, he lets Yolanda know by the way he sucks that he prefers the taste of breast milk to a bottle of plain water. Clearly, Joshua has some well-developed sensory capacities. In the following sections, we explore the newborn baby's responsiveness to touch, taste, smell, sound, and visual stimulation.

TOUCH   In our discussion of preterm infants, we saw that touch helps stimulate early physical growth. And as we will see in Chapter 7, it is vital for emotional development as well. Therefore, it is not surprising that sensitivity to touch is well-developed at birth.

The reflexes listed in Table 4.2 on page 142 reveal that the newborn baby responds to touch, especially around the mouth, on the palms, and on the soles of the feet. During the prenatal period, these areas, along with the genitals, are the first to become sensitive to touch

(Humphrey, 1978; Streri, 2005). Newborns, even those born several weeks preterm, use touch to investigate their world. When small objects are placed in their palms, they can distinguish shape (prism versus cylinder) and texture (smooth versus rough), as indicated by their tendency to hold on longer to an object with an unfamiliar shape or texture than to a familiar object (Lejeune et al., 2012; Sann & Streri, 2007, 2008).

At birth, infants are highly sensitive to pain. If male newborns are circumcised, anesthetic is sometimes not used because of the risk of giving drugs to a very young infant. Babies often respond with a high-pitched, stressful cry and a dramatic rise in heart rate, blood pressure, palm sweating, pupil dilation, and muscle tension (Lehr et al., 2007; Warnock & Sandrin, 2004). Brain-imaging research suggests that because of central nervous system immaturity, preterm and male babies feel the pain of a medical injection especially intensely (Bartocci et al., 2006).

Certain local analgesics for newborns ease the pain of these procedures. As a supplement to pain-relieving medication, offering a nipple that delivers a sugar solution is helpful; it quickly reduces crying and discomfort in young babies, preterm and full-term alike (Roman-Rodriguez et al., 2014). Breast milk may be especially effective: Even the smell of the milk of the baby's mother reduces infant stress to a routine blood-test heelstick more effectively than the odor of another mother's milk or of formula (Badiee, Asghari, & Mohammadizadeh, 2013; Nishitani et al., 2009). And combining sweet liquid with gentle holding by the parent lessens pain even more. Research on infant mammals indicates that physical touch releases *endorphins*—painkilling chemicals in the brain (Axelin, Salantera, & Lehtonen, 2006; Gormally et al., 2001).

Allowing a baby to endure severe pain overwhelms the nervous system with stress hormones, which can disrupt the child's developing capacity to handle common, everyday stressors (Walker, 2013). The result is heightened pain sensitivity, sleep disturbances, feeding problems, and difficulty calming down when upset.

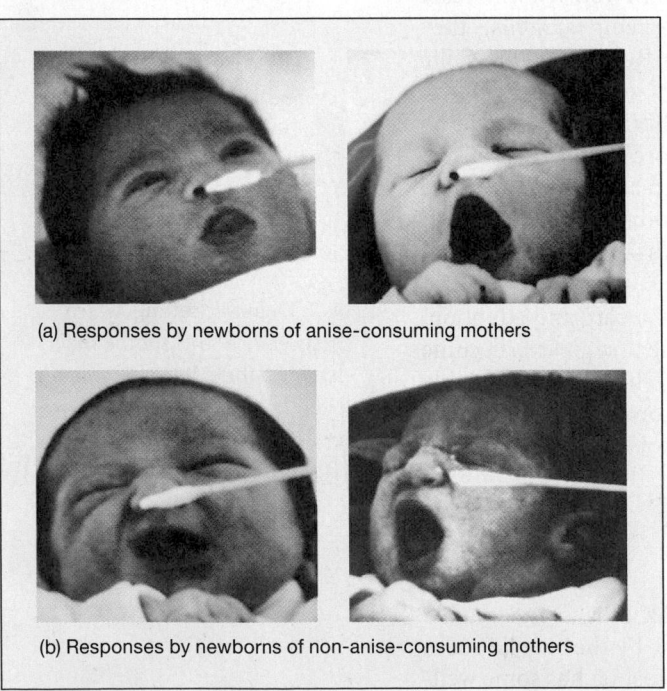

(a) Responses by newborns of anise-consuming mothers

(b) Responses by newborns of non-anise-consuming mothers

FIGURE 4.6   Examples of facial expressions of newborns exposed to the odor of anise whose mothers' diets differed in anise-flavored foods during late pregnancy. (a) Babies of anise-consuming mothers spent more time turning toward the odor and sucking, licking, and chewing. (b) Babies of non-anise-consuming mothers more often turned away with a negative facial expression. (From B. Schaal, L. Marlier, & R. Soussignan, 2000, "Human Foetuses Learn Odours from Their Pregnant Mother's Diet," *Chemical Senses, 25,* p. 731. Reprinted by permission of Oxford University Press, Inc., and Benoist Schaal.)

TASTE AND SMELL   Facial expressions reveal that newborns can distinguish several basic tastes. Like adults, they relax their facial muscles in response to sweetness, purse their lips when the taste is sour, and show a distinct archlike mouth opening when it is bitter. Similarly, certain odor preferences are present at birth. For example, the smell of bananas or chocolate causes a pleasant facial expression, whereas the odor of rotten eggs makes the infant frown (Steiner, 1979; Steiner et al., 2001). These reactions are important for survival: The food that best supports the infant's early growth is the sweet-tasting milk of the mother's breast. Not until 4 months do babies prefer a salty taste to plain water, a change that may prepare them to accept solid foods (Mennella & Beauchamp, 1998).

During pregnancy, the amniotic fluid is rich in tastes and smells that vary with the mother's diet—early experiences that influence newborns' preferences. In a study carried out in the Alsatian region of France, where anise is frequently used to flavor foods, researchers tested newborns for their reaction to the anise odor (Schaal, Marlier, & Soussignan, 2000). The mothers of some babies had regularly consumed anise during the last two weeks of pregnancy; the other mothers had never consumed it. When presented with the anise odor on the day of birth, the babies of non-anise-consuming mothers were far more likely to turn away with a negative facial expression (see Figure 4.6). These different reactions were still apparent four days later, even though all mothers had refrained from consuming anise during this time.

Other evidence indicates that exposure to a flavor, either prenatally in the amniotic fluid or during the weeks after birth in breast milk, continues to influence taste preferences well into the first year and possibly beyond. Fetuses and newborns exposed to the flavor of carrots (because their mothers drank carrot juice) reacted more positively than did unexposed counterparts to carrot-flavored cereal at age 6 months (Mennella, Jagnow, & Beauchamp, 2001).

Furthermore, young infants will readily learn to prefer a taste that at first evoked either a negative or neutral response. Bottle-fed newborns allergic to cow's milk formula who are given a soy or other vegetable-based substitute (typically very sour and bitter-tasting) soon prefer it to regular formula. When first given solid foods several months later, these infants display an unusual liking for bitter-tasting cereals (Beauchamp & Mennella, 2011). This taste preference is still evident at ages 4 to 5 years, in more positive responses to foods with sour and bitter tastes compared to agemates without early vegetable-based formula exposure.

In mammals, including humans, the sense of smell—in addition to playing an important role in feeding—helps mothers and babies identify each other. At 4 days of age, breastfed babies prefer the smell of their own mother's breast to that of an unfamiliar lactating woman (Cernoch & Porter, 1985). And both breast- and bottle-fed 3- to 4-day-olds orient more and display more mouthing to the smell of unfamiliar human milk than to formula milk, indicating that (even without postnatal exposure) the odor of human milk is more attractive to newborns (Marlier & Schaal, 2005). Newborns' dual attraction to the odors of their mother and of breast milk helps them locate an appropriate food source and, in the process, begin to distinguish their caregiver from other people.

HEARING   Although conduction of sound through the structures of the ear and transmission of auditory information to the brain are inefficient at birth, newborn infants can hear a wide variety of sounds—sensitivity that improves greatly over the first few months (Saffran, Werker, & Werner, 2006). At birth, infants prefer complex sounds, such as noises and voices, to pure tones. And babies only a few days old can tell the difference between a variety of sound patterns: a series of tones arranged in ascending versus descending order; tone sequences with a rhythmic downbeat (as in music) versus those without; utterances with two versus three syllables; the stress patterns of words, such as "*ma*-ma" versus "ma-*ma*"; happy-sounding speech as opposed to speech with negative or neutral emotional qualities; and even two languages spoken by the same bilingual speaker, as long as those languages differ in their rhythmic features—for example, French versus Russian (Mastropieri & Turkewitz, 1999; Ramus, 2002; Sansavini, Bertoncini, & Giovanelli, 1997; Trehub, 2001; Winkler et al., 2009).

Young infants listen longer to human speech than to structurally similar nonspeech sounds (Vouloumanos, 2010). And they can detect the sounds of any human language. Newborns make fine-grained distinctions among many speech sounds. For example, when given a nipple that turns on a recording of the "*ba*" sound, babies suck vigorously for a while and then slow down as the novelty wears off. When the sound switches to "*ga*," sucking picks up, indicating that infants detect this subtle difference. Using this method, researchers have found only a few speech sounds that newborns cannot discriminate. Their ability to perceive sounds not found in their own language is more precise than an adult's (Aldridge, Stillman, & Bower, 2001; Jusczyk & Luce, 2002). These capacities reveal that the baby is marvelously prepared for the awesome task of acquiring language.

Responsiveness to sound also supports the newborn baby's exploration of the environment. Infants as young as 3 days turn their eyes and head in the general direction of a sound. The ability to identify the precise location of a sound improves greatly over the first six months and shows further gains through the preschool years (Litovsky & Ashmead, 1997).

TAKE A MOMENT... Listen carefully to yourself the next time you talk to a young baby. You will probably speak in ways that highlight important parts of the speech stream—use a slow, high-pitched, expressive voice with a rising tone at the ends of phrases and sentences and a pause before continuing. Adults probably communicate this way with infants because they notice that babies are more attentive when they do so. Indeed, newborns prefer speech with these characteristics (Saffran, Werker, & Werner, 2006). They will also suck more on a nipple to hear a recording of their own mother's voice than that of an unfamiliar woman and to hear their native language as opposed to a foreign language (Moon, Cooper, & Fifer, 1993; Spence & DeCasper, 1987). These preferences may have developed from hearing the muffled sounds of the mother's voice before birth.

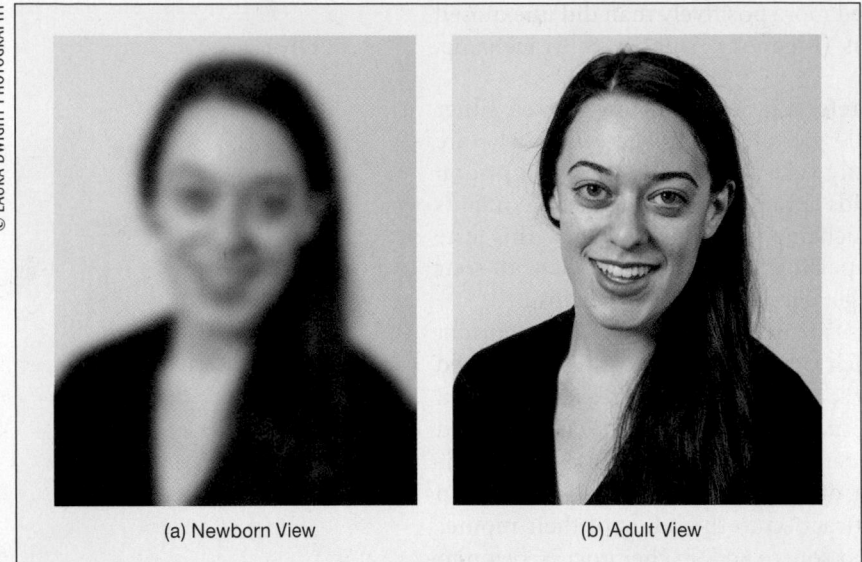

© LAURA DWIGHT PHOTOGRAPHY

(a) Newborn View   (b) Adult View

FIGURE 4.7 **View of the human face by the newborn and the adult.** The newborn baby's limited focusing ability and poor visual acuity lead the mother's face, even when viewed from close up, to look much like the fuzzy image in (a) rather than the clear image in (b). Also, newborn infants have some color vision, although they have difficulty discriminating colors. Researchers speculate that colors probably appear similar, but less intense, to newborns than to older infants and adults (From Kellman & Arterberry 2006; Slater et al., 2010.).

VISION   Vision is the least-developed of the newborn baby's senses. Visual structures in both the eye and the brain are not yet fully formed at birth. For example, cells in the *retina,* the membrane lining the inside of the eye that captures light and transforms it into messages that are sent to the brain, are not as mature or densely packed as they will be in several months. The optic nerve that relays these messages, and visual centers in the brain that receive them, will not be adultlike for several years. And muscles of the *lens,* which permit us to adjust our visual focus to varying distances, are weak (Kellman & Arterberry, 2006).

As a result, newborns cannot focus their eyes well, and their **visual acuity,** or fineness of discrimination, is limited. At birth, infants perceive objects at a distance of 20 feet about as clearly as adults do at 600 feet (Slater et al., 2010). In addition, unlike adults (who see nearby objects most clearly), newborn babies see unclearly across a wide range of distances (Banks, 1980; Hainline, 1998). As a result, images such as the parent's face, even from close up, look like the blurry image in Figure 4.7. Nevertheless, as we will see in Chapter 5, newborns can detect human faces. And as with their preference for their mother's smell and voice, from repeated exposures they quickly learn to prefer her face to that of an unfamiliar woman, although they are more sensitive to its broad outlines than its fine-grained, internal features (Bartrip, Morton, & de Schonen, 2001; Walton, Armstrong, & Bower, 1998).

Although they cannot yet see well, newborns actively explore their environment by scanning it for interesting sights and tracking moving objects. However, their eye movements are slow and inaccurate (von Hofsten & Rosander, 1998). Joshua's captivation with Yolanda's pink blouse reveals that he is attracted to bright objects. Nevertheless, once newborns focus on an object, they tend to look only at a single feature—for example, the corner of a triangle instead of the entire shape. And despite their preference for colored over gray stimuli, newborn babies are not yet good at discriminating colors. It will take about four months for color vision to become adultlike (Kellman & Arterberry, 2006).

Neonatal Behavioral Assessment

A variety of instruments permit doctors, nurses, and researchers to assess the behavior of newborn babies. The most widely used of these tests, T. Berry Brazelton's **Neonatal Behavioral Assessment Scale (NBAS),** evaluates the baby's reflexes, muscle tone, state changes, responsiveness to physical and social stimuli, and other reactions (Brazelton & Nugent, 1911). An instrument consisting of similar items, called the *Neonatal Intensive Care Unit Network Neurobehavioral Scale (NNNS),* is specially designed for use with newborns at risk for developmental problems because of low birth weight, preterm delivery, prenatal substance exposure, or other conditions (Tronick & Lester, 2013). Scores are used to recommend appropriate interventions and to guide parents in meeting their baby's unique needs.

The NBAS has been given to many infants around the world. As a result, researchers have learned about individual and cultural differences in newborn behavior and how child-rearing practices can maintain or change a baby's reactions. For example, NBAS scores of Asian and Native-American babies reveal that they are less irritable than Caucasian infants. Mothers in these cultures often encourage their babies' calm dispositions through holding and nursing at the first signs of discomfort (Muret-Wagstaff & Moore, 1989; Small, 1998). The Kipsigis of Kenya, who highly value infant motor maturity, massage babies regularly and begin exercising the stepping reflex shortly after birth. These customs contribute to Kipsigis babies' strong

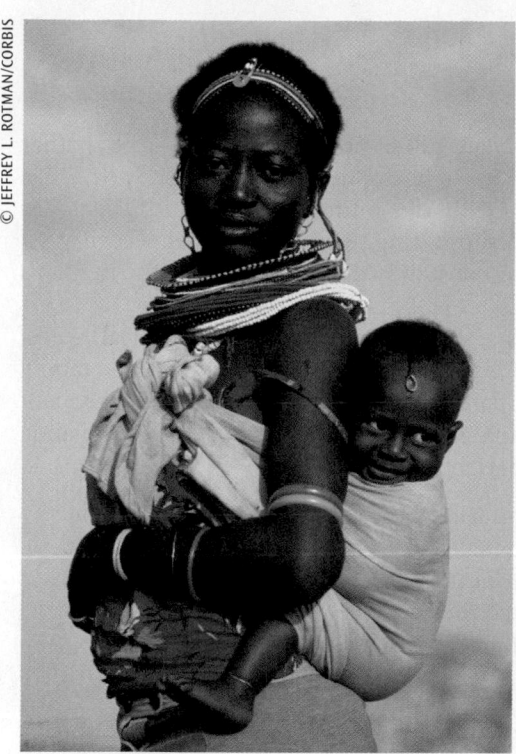

A mother of the El Molo people of northern Kenya carries her baby in a sling all day, providing close physical contact and a rich variety of stimulation. This practice, also adopted by many Western parents, promotes a calm, alert state in infants.

but flexible muscle tone at 5 days of age (Super & Harkness, 2009). In Zambia, Africa, close mother–infant contact throughout the day quickly changes the poor NBAS scores of undernourished newborns. When reassessed at 1 week of age, a once unresponsive baby appears alert and contented (Brazelton, Koslowski, & Tronick, 1976).

TAKE A MOMENT... Using these examples, can you explain why a single neonatal assessment score is not a good predictor of later development? Because newborn behavior and parenting styles combine to shape development, *changes in scores* over the first week or two of life (rather than a single score) provide the best estimate of the baby's ability to recover from the stress of birth. NBAS "recovery curves" predict intelligence and absence of emotional and behavior problems with moderate success well into the preschool years (Brazelton, Nugent, & Lester, 1987; Ohgi et al., 2003a, 2003b).

In some hospitals, health professionals use the NBAS or the NNNS to help parents get to know their newborns through discussion or demonstration of the capacities these instruments assess. Parents of both preterm and full-term newborns who participate in these programs, compared with no-intervention controls, interact more confidently and effectively with their babies (Browne & Talmi, 2005; Bruschweiler-Stern, 2004). Although lasting effects on development have not been demonstrated, NBAS-based interventions are useful in helping the parent–infant relationship get off to a good start.

Ask Yourself

- **REVIEW** What can newborn sleep patterns and crying tell us about the health of the central nervous system?

- **CONNECT** How do the diverse capacities of newborn babies contribute to their first social relationships? Provide as many examples as you can.

- **APPLY** After a difficult delivery, Jackie observes her 2-day-old daughter, Kelly, being given the NBAS. Kelly scores poorly on many items. Seeing this, Jackie wonders if Kelly will develop normally. How would you respond to Jackie's concern?

- **REFLECT** Are newborns more competent than you thought they were before you read this chapter? Which of their capacities most surprised you?

4.9 Describe typical changes in the family after the birth of a new baby, along with interventions that foster the transition to parenthood.

The Transition to Parenthood

The early weeks after a new baby enters the family are full of profound changes. The mother needs to recover from childbirth and adjust to massive hormone shifts in her body. If she is breastfeeding, energies must be devoted to working out this intimate relationship. The father must become a part of this new threesome while supporting the mother in her recovery. At times, he may feel ambivalent about the baby, who constantly demands and gets the mother's attention.

While all this is going on, the tiny infant is assertive about his urgent physical needs, demanding to be fed, changed, and comforted at odd times of the day and night. The family schedule becomes irregular and uncertain, and parental sleep deprivation and consequent daytime fatigue is often a major challenge (Insana & Montgomery-Downs, 2012). Yolanda spoke candidly about the changes she and Jay experienced:

> When we brought Joshua home, he seemed so small and helpless, and we worried about whether we would be able to take proper care of him. It took us 20 minutes to change the first diaper. I rarely feel rested because I'm up two to four times every night, and I spend a good part of my waking hours trying to anticipate Joshua's rhythms and needs. If Jay weren't so willing to help by holding and walking Joshua, I think I'd find it much harder.

Changes in the Family System

The demands of new parenthood—constant caregiving, added financial responsibilities, and less time for couples to devote to one another—usually cause the gender roles of husband and wife to become more traditional (Katz-Wise, Priess, & Hyde, 2010; Lawrence et al., 2010). This is true even for couples like Yolanda and Jay, who are strongly committed to gender equality and are used to sharing household tasks. Yolanda took a leave of absence from work, whereas Jay's career continued as it had before. As a result, Yolanda spent more time at home with the baby, while Jay focused more on his provider role.

For most new parents, however, the arrival of a baby—though often associated with mild declines in relationship satisfaction and communication quality—does not cause significant marital strain. Marriages that are gratifying and supportive tend to remain so (Doss et al., 2009; Feeney et al., 2001). But troubled marriages usually become more distressed after a baby is born (Houts et al., 2008; Kluwer & Johnson, 2007). And when expectant mothers anticipate lack of partner support in parenting, their prediction generally becomes reality, yielding an especially difficult post-birth adjustment (Driver et al., 2012; McHale & Rotman, 2007). For some new parents, problems are severe (see the Biology and Environment box on the following page).

Violated expectations about division of labor in the home powerfully affect family well-being. In dual-earner marriages, the larger the difference between men's and women's caregiving responsibilities, the greater the decline in marital satisfaction after childbirth, especially for women—with negative consequences for parent–infant interaction. In contrast, sharing caregiving predicts greater parental happiness and sensitivity to the baby (McHale et al., 2004; Moller, Hwang, & Wickberg, 2008). An exception exists, however, for employed lower-SES women who endorse traditional gender roles. When their husbands help extensively with child care, these mothers tend to report more distress, perhaps because they feel disappointed at being unable to fulfill their desire to do most of the caregiving (Goldberg & Perry-Jenkins, 2003).

Postponing parenthood until the late twenties or thirties, as more couples do today, eases the transition to parenthood. Waiting permits couples to pursue occupational goals and gain life experience. Under these circumstances, men are more enthusiastic about becoming fathers and therefore more willing to participate. And women whose careers are well under way and whose marriages are happy are more likely to encourage their husbands to share housework and child care, which fosters fathers' involvement (Lee & Doherty, 2007; Schoppe-Sullivan et al., 2008).

Biology and Environment

Parental Depression and Child Development

About 8 to 10 percent of women experience chronic depression—mild to severe feelings of sadness and withdrawal that continue for months or years. Often, the beginnings of this emotional state cannot be pinpointed. In other instances, depression emerges or strengthens after childbirth but fails to subside as the new mother adjusts to hormonal changes in her body and gains confidence in caring for her baby. This is called *postpartum depression.*

Although it is less recognized and studied, fathers, too, experience chronic depression. About 3 to 5 percent of fathers report symptoms after the birth of a child (Madsen & Juhl, 2007; Thombs, Roseman, & Arthurs, 2010). Parental depression can interfere with effective parenting and seriously impair children's development. As noted in Chapter 2, genetic makeup increases the risk of depressive illness, but social and cultural factors are also involved.

Maternal Depression

During Julia's pregnancy, her husband, Kyle, showed so little interest in the baby that Julia worried that having a child might be a mistake. Then, shortly after Lucy was born, Julia's mood plunged. She felt anxious and weepy, overwhelmed by Lucy's needs, and angry at loss of control over her own schedule. When Julia approached Kyle about her own fatigue and his unwillingness to help with the baby, he snapped that she was overreacting. Julia's childless friends stopped by just once to see Lucy but did not call again.

Julia's depressed mood quickly affected her baby. In the weeks after birth, infants of depressed mothers sleep poorly, are less attentive to their surroundings, and have elevated levels of the stress hormone cortisol (Field, 1998). The more extreme the depression and the greater the number of stressors in a mother's life (such as marital discord, little or no social support, and poverty), the more the parent–child relationship suffers (Simpson et al., 2003). Julia rarely smiled at, comforted, or talked to Lucy, who responded to her mother's sad, vacant gaze by turning away, crying, and often looking sad or angry herself (Feldman et al., 2009; Field, 2011). Julia, in turn, felt guilty and inadequate, and her depression deepened. By age 6 months, Lucy showed symptoms common in babies of depressed mothers—delays in motor and mental development, an irritable mood, and attachment difficulties (Hanington et al., 2012; McMahon et al., 2006).

When maternal depression persists, the parent–child relationship worsens. Depressed parents view their infants more negatively than independent observers do (Forman et al., 2007). And they use inconsistent discipline—sometimes lax, at other times too forceful. As we will see in later chapters, children who experience these maladaptive parenting practices often have serious adjustment problems. Some withdraw into a depressive mood themselves; others become impulsive and aggressive. In one study, children born to mothers who were depressed during pregnancy were four times as likely as children of nondepressed mothers to have engaged in violent antisocial behavior by age 16, after other stressors in the mother's life that could contribute to youth antisocial conduct had been controlled (Hay et al., 2010).

Paternal Depression

Paternal depression is also linked to dissatisfaction with marriage and family life after childbirth and to other life stressors, including job loss and divorce (Bielawska-Batorowicz & Kossakowska-Petrycka, 2006). In a study of a large representative sample of British parents and babies, researchers assessed depressive symptoms of fathers shortly after birth and again the following year. Then they tracked the children's development into the preschool years. Persistent paternal depression was, like maternal depression, a strong predictor of child behavior problems—especially overactivity, defiance, and aggression in boys (Ramchandani et al., 2008).

Paternal depression is linked to frequent father–child conflict as children grow older (Kane & Garber, 2004). Over time, children subjected to parental negativity develop a pessimistic worldview—one in which they lack self-confidence and perceive their parents and other people as threatening. Children who constantly feel in danger are especially likely to become overly aroused in stressful situations, easily losing control in the face of cognitive and social challenges (Sturge-Apple et al., 2008). Although children of depressed parents may inherit a tendency toward emotional and behavior problems, quality of parenting is a major factor in their adjustment.

© CATCHLIGHT VISUAL SERVICES/ALAMY

This father appears completely disengaged from his wife and toddler. If this continues, disruptions in the parent–child relationship will likely lead to serious child behavior problems.

Interventions

Early treatment is vital to prevent parental depression from interfering with the parent–child relationship. Julia's doctor referred her to a therapist, who helped Julia and Kyle with their marital problems. At times, antidepressant medication is prescribed.

In addition to alleviating parental depression, therapy that encourages depressed mothers to revise their negative views of their babies and to engage in emotionally positive, responsive caregiving is essential for reducing young children's attachment and other developmental problems (Forman et al., 2007). When a depressed parent does not respond easily to treatment, a warm relationship with the other parent or another caregiver can safeguard children's development (Mezulis, Hyde, & Clark, 2004).

Applying What We Know

How Couples Can Ease the Transition to Parenthood

STRATEGY	DESCRIPTION
Devise a plan for sharing household tasks.	As soon as possible, discuss division of household responsibilities. Decide who does a particular chore based on who has the needed skill and time, not gender. Schedule regular times to reevaluate your plan to fit changing family circumstances.
Begin sharing child care right after the baby's arrival.	For fathers, strive to spend equal time with the baby early. For mothers, refrain from imposing your standards on your partner. Instead, share the role of "child-rearing expert" by discussing parenting values and concerns often. Attend a new-parenthood course together.
Talk over conflicts about decision making and responsibilities.	Face conflict through communication. Clarify your feelings and needs, and express them to your partner. Listen and try to understand your partner's point of view. Then be willing to negotiate and compromise.
Establish a balance between work and parenting.	Critically evaluate the time you devote to work in view of new parenthood. If it is too much, try to cut back.
Press for workplace and public policies that assist parents in rearing children.	Difficulties faced by new parents may be partly due to lack of workplace and societal supports. Encourage your employer to provide benefits that help combine work and family roles, such as paid employment leave, flexible work hours, and on-site high-quality, affordable child care. Communicate with lawmakers and other citizens about improving policies for children and families, including paid, job-protected leave to support the transition to parenthood.

A second birth typically requires that fathers take an even more active role in parenting—by caring for the firstborn while the mother is recuperating and by sharing in the high demands of tending to both a baby and a young child. Consequently, well-functioning families with a newborn second child typically pull back from the traditional division of responsibilities that occurred after the first birth. In a study that tracked parents from the end of pregnancy through the first year after their second child's birth, fathers' willingness to place greater emphasis on the parenting role was strongly linked to mothers' adjustment after the arrival of a second baby (Stewart, 1990). And both parents must help their firstborn child adjust. Preschool-age siblings understandably may feel displaced and react with jealousy and anger—a topic we will take up in Chapter 7. For strategies couples can use to ease the transition to parenthood, refer to Applying What We Know above.

Single-Mother Families

About 40 percent of U.S. births are to single mothers, one-third of whom are teenagers (Martin et al., 2013). In Chapter 14, we will see that adolescent mothers and their newborns are at high risk for developmental problems.

At the other extreme, planned births and adoptions by single 30- to 45-year-old women are increasing. These mothers are generally financially secure, have readily available social support from family members and friends, and adapt to parenthood with relative ease. In fact, older single mothers in well-paid occupations who plan carefully for a new baby may encounter fewer parenting difficulties than married couples, largely because their family structure is simpler: They do not have to coordinate parenting roles with a partner, and they have no unfulfilled expectations for shared caregiving (Tyano et al., 2010). And because of their psychological maturity, these mothers are likely to cope effectively with parenting challenges.

The majority of nonmarital births are unplanned and to women in their twenties. Most of these mothers have incomes below the poverty level and experience a stressful transition to parenthood. Although many live with the baby's father or another partner, cohabiting relationships in the United States are less socially acceptable than those in Western Europe,

LOOK and LISTEN

Ask a couple or a single mother to describe the challenges of new parenthood, along with factors that aided or impeded this transition.

involve less commitment and cooperation, and are far more likely to break up—especially after an unplanned baby arrives (Jose, O'Leary, & Moyer, 2010). Single mothers often lack emotional and parenting support—strong predictors of psychological distress and infant caregiving difficulties (Keating-Lefler et al., 2004).

Parent Interventions

Special interventions are available to help parents adjust to life with a new baby. For those who are not at high risk for problems, counselor-led parenting groups are highly effective (Gottman, Gottman, & Shapiro, 2010). In one program, first-time expectant couples gathered once a week for six months to discuss their dreams for the family and the changes in relationships sparked by the baby's arrival. Eighteen months after the program ended, participating fathers described themselves as more involved with their child than did fathers in a no-intervention condition. Perhaps because of fathers' caregiving assistance, participating mothers maintained their prebirth satisfaction with family

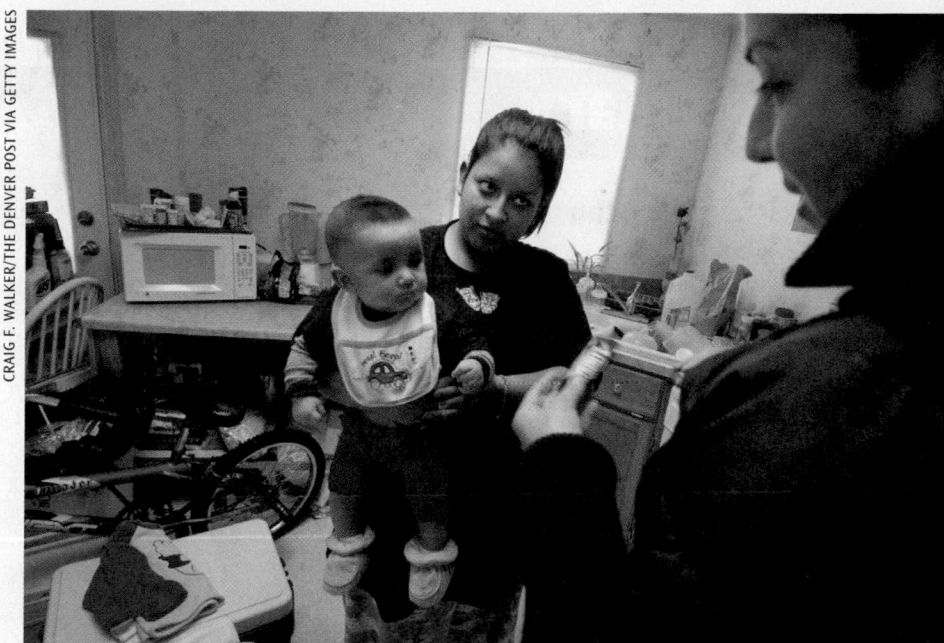

A counselor discusses options with this single mother for continuing her education. Parents struggling with poverty benefit from intensive intervention focusing on social support and effective parenting.

and work roles. Three years after the birth, the marriages of all participating couples were still intact and just as happy as they had been before parenthood (Cowan & Cowan, 1997; Schulz, Cowan, & Cowan, 2006). In contrast, 15 percent of couples receiving no intervention had divorced.

High-risk parents struggling with poverty or the birth of a child with disabilities need more intensive interventions. Programs in which a professional intervener visits the home and focuses on enhancing social support and parenting have resulted in improved parent–infant interaction and benefits for children's cognitive and social development into middle childhood (to review one example, return to page 114 in Chapter 3). Many low-income single mothers benefit from interventions that focus on sustaining the father's involvement and that provide training in effective coparenting (Jones, Charles, & Benson, 2013). These parents also require tangible support—money, food, transportation, and affordable child care—to ease stress so they have the psychological resources to engage in sensitive, responsive infant care.

When parents' relationships are positive and cooperative, social support is available, and families have sufficient income, the stress caused by the birth of a baby remains manageable. These family conditions, as we have already seen, consistently contribute to favorable development—in infancy and beyond.

Ask Yourself

- **REVIEW** Explain how persisting postpartum depression seriously impairs children's development.

- **CONNECT** Explain how generous employment leave for childbirth—at least 12 weeks of paid time off available to either the mother or father—can ease the transition to parenthood and promote positive parent–infant interaction. (*Hint:* Consult the Social Issues: Health box on pages 138–139.)

- **APPLY** Derek, father of a 3-year-old and a newborn, reported that he had a harder time adjusting to the birth of his second child than to that of his first. Explain why this might be so.

- **REFLECT** If you are a parent, what was the transition to parenthood like for you? What factors helped you adjust? What factors made it more difficult? If you are not a parent, pose these questions to someone you know who recently became a parent.

Summary

The Stages of Childbirth (p. 123)

4.1 Describe the three stages of childbirth, the baby's adaptation to labor and delivery, and the newborn baby's appearance.

- In the first stage of childbirth, **dilation and effacement of the cervix** occur as uterine contractions increase in strength and frequency. This stage culminates in **transition**, a brief period in which contractions are at their peak and the cervix opens completely. In the second stage, the mother feels an urge to bear down with her abdominal muscles, and the baby is born. In the final stage, the placenta is delivered.

- During labor, the force of the contractions causes infants to produce high levels of stress hormones, which help them withstand oxygen deprivation, clear the lungs for breathing, and arouse them into alertness at birth.

- Newborn infants have large heads and small bodies. The **Apgar Scale** is used to assess the baby's physical condition at birth.

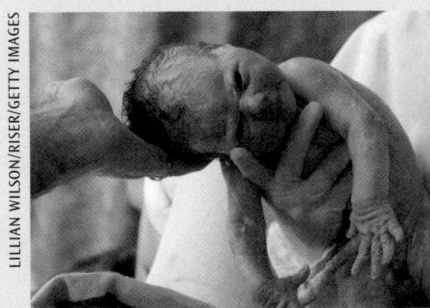

LILLIAN WILSON/RISER/GETTY IMAGES

Approaches to Childbirth (p. 127)

4.2 Describe natural childbirth and home delivery, noting benefits and concerns associated with each.

- In **natural**, or **prepared**, **childbirth**, the expectant mother and a companion typically attend classes where they learn about labor and delivery, master relaxation and breathing techniques to counteract pain, and prepare for coaching during childbirth. Social support from a doula reduces the length of labor, the need for instrument-assisted births and pain medication, and the incidence of birth complications.

- Home birth is relatively rare in the United States but is common in some other industrialized nations. It is safe for healthy mothers who are assisted by a well-trained doctor or midwife, but mothers at risk for any kind of complication are better off giving birth in a hospital.

ANDERSEN ROSS/BRAND X PICTURES/GETTY IMAGES

Medical Interventions (p. 129)

4.3 List common medical interventions during childbirth, circumstances that justify their use, and any dangers associated with each.

- **Fetal monitors** help save the lives of many babies whose mothers have a history of pregnancy and birth complications. But they also may identify infants as in danger who, in fact, are not, and are linked to an increase in cesarean deliveries.

- Use of analgesics and anesthetics to control pain during childbirth can prolong labor and cause newborns to be withdrawn and irritable. Instrument delivery using *forceps* or, more often, a *vacuum extractor* may be appropriate if the mother's pushing does not move the infant through the birth canal in a reasonable period of time. However, because they can cause serious complications, they should be avoided if possible.

- **Induced labor** is more difficult than naturally occurring labor and is more likely to be associated with the use of labor and delivery medication and instrument delivery. Inductions should be scheduled only when continuing the pregnancy threatens the well-being of mother or baby.

- **Cesarean deliveries** are justified in cases of medical emergency or serious maternal illness and when the baby is in **breech position**. A dramatic worldwide rise has occurred in cesarean deliveries, many of which are unnecessary.

Birth Complications (p. 132)

4.4 What are the risks of oxygen deprivation, preterm birth, and low birth weight, and what factors can help infants who survive a traumatic birth?

- Squeezing of the umbilical cord during childbirth, placenta abruptio, and placenta previa can cause **anoxia** (oxygen deprivation), with risk of brain damage and infant death. Effects of even mild to moderate anoxia on cognitive and language development are still evident in middle childhood, though many children improve over time. Infants born more than six weeks early commonly have respiratory distress syndrome, which can cause brain damage due to immaturity of the lungs and associated anoxia.

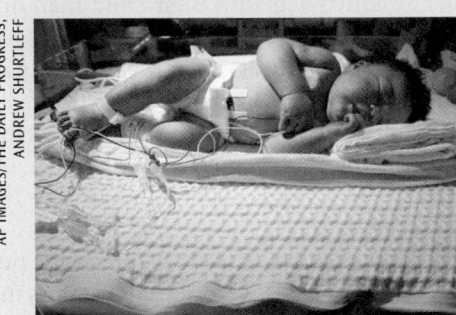

AP IMAGES/THE DAILY PROGRESS, ANDREW SHURTLEFF

- Low birth weight is a major cause of **neonatal** and **infant mortality** and wide-ranging developmental problems. It is most common in infants born to poverty-stricken women. Chronic maternal stress likely contributes to the high rate of low birth weight among African-American babies. Compared with **preterm** babies, whose weight is appropriate for time spent in the uterus, **small-for-date** infants usually have longer-lasting difficulties. However, even minimally preterm babies experience mild to moderate developmental delays.

- Some interventions provide special infant stimulation in the intensive care nursery. Others teach parents how to care for and interact with their babies. Preterm infants in stressed, low-income households need long-term, intensive intervention.

- When babies experience birth trauma, a supportive family environment or relationships with other caring adults can help restore their growth. Even infants with fairly serious birth complications can recover with the help of positive life events.

Precious Moments After Birth
(p. 140)

4.5 Is close parent–infant contact shortly after birth necessary for bonding?

- Human parents do not require close physical contact with the baby immediately after birth for **bonding** and effective parenting to occur. Nevertheless, early contact supports parents' feelings of caring and affection. Hospital practices that promote parent–infant closeness, such as **rooming in,** may help parents build a good relationship with their newborn.

The Newborn Baby's Capacities
(p. 141)

4.6 Describe the newborn baby's reflexes and states of arousal, including sleep characteristics and ways to soothe a crying baby.

- **Reflexes** are the newborn baby's most obvious organized patterns of behavior. Some have survival value, others help parents and infants establish gratifying interaction, and still others provide the foundation for voluntary motor skills.

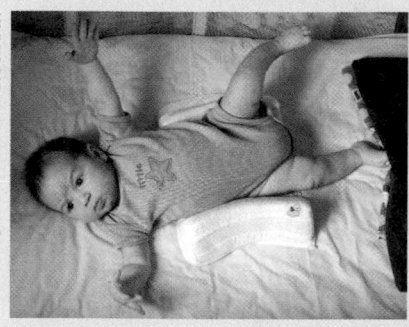

© LAURA DWIGHT PHOTOGRAPHY

- Although newborns move in and out of five **states of arousal,** they spend most of their time asleep. Sleep includes at least two states: **rapid-eye-movement (REM) sleep** and **non-rapid-eye-movement (NREM) sleep.** Newborns spend about 50 percent of their sleep time in REM sleep, far more than they ever will again. REM sleep provides young infants with stimulation essential for central nervous system development. Disturbed REM–NREM cycles are a sign of central nervous system abnormalities, which may lead to **sudden infant death syndrome (SIDS).**

- A crying baby stimulates strong feelings of discomfort in nearby adults. Once feeding and diaper changing have been tried, lifting the baby to the shoulder and rocking or walking is a highly effective soothing technique. Extensive parent–infant physical contact substantially reduces crying in the early months.

4.7 Describe the newborn baby's sensory capacities.

- The senses of touch, taste, smell, and sound are well-developed at birth. Newborns are sensitive to pain, prefer sweet tastes and smells, and orient toward the odor of their own mother's lactating breast and toward human milk rather than formula milk. Taste preferences developed through prenatal exposure to a mother's diet or through breast milk continue through the first year and possibly beyond.

- Newborns can distinguish a variety of sound patterns, as well as nearly all speech sounds. They are especially responsive to human speech, high-pitched expressive voices, their own mother's voice, and speech in their native language.

- Vision is the least developed of the newborn's senses. At birth, focusing ability and **visual acuity** are limited. Nevertheless, newborns can detect human faces and prefer their mother's familiar face to the face of a stranger. In exploring the visual field, they are attracted to bright objects but limit their looking to single features. Newborn babies have difficulty discriminating colors.

4.8 Why is neonatal behavioral assessment useful?

- The most widely used instrument for assessing the behavior of the newborn infant, Brazelton's **Neonatal Behavioral Assessment Scale (NBAS),** has helped researchers understand individual and cultural differences in newborn behavior. Sometimes it is used to teach parents about their baby's capacities.

The Transition to Parenthood
(p. 152)

4.9 Describe typical changes in the family after the birth of a new baby, along with interventions that foster the transition to parenthood.

- In response to the demands of new parenthood, the gender roles of husband and wife usually become more traditional. Parents in gratifying marriages who continue to support each other's needs generally adapt well. But a large difference between a husband's and wife's caregiving responsibilities can strain the marriage and negatively affect parent–infant interaction. Favorable adjustment to a second birth typically requires that fathers take an even more active role in parenting.

- Most nonmarital births are unplanned and to young mothers who have incomes below the poverty level and experience a stressful transition to parenthood. Planned births and adoptions by financially secure single women in their thirties and forties are increasing. These mothers typically adapt easily to new parenthood.

CRAIG F. WALKER/THE DENVER POST VIA GETTY IMAGES

- When parents are at low risk for problems, counselor-led parenting groups involving discussion of changing family relationships can ease the transition to parenthood. High-risk parents struggling with poverty or the birth of a baby with disabilities are more likely to benefit from intensive home interventions focusing on enhancing social support and parenting.

Important Terms and Concepts

anoxia (p. 133)
Apgar Scale (p. 126)
bonding (p. 141)
breech position (p. 132)
cesarean delivery (p. 131)
dilation and effacement of the cervix (p. 125)
fetal monitors (p. 130)
induced labor (p. 131)

infant mortality (p. 138)
natural, or prepared, childbirth (p. 128)
Neonatal Behavioral Assessment Scale (NBAS) (p. 150)
neonatal mortality (p. 138)
non-rapid-eye-movement (NREM) sleep (p. 144)
preterm infants (p. 135)
rapid-eye-movement (REM) sleep (p. 144)

reflex (p. 141)
rooming in (p. 141)
small-for-date infants (p. 135)
states of arousal (p. 143)
sudden infant death syndrome (SIDS) (p. 145)
transition (p. 125)
visual acuity (p. 150)

chapter 5

Physical Development in Infancy and Toddlerhood

"First Steps"
Irailde Alves Da Silva
14 years, Brazil

Encouraged and supported by his mother, a baby takes his first steps and experiences the physical potential of his growing body. During the first year, infants grow rapidly, move on their own, increasingly investigate their surroundings, and make sense of complex sights and sounds.

On a brilliant June morning, 16-month-old Caitlin emerged from her front door, ready for the short drive to the child-care home where she spent her weekdays while her mother, Carolyn, and her father, David, worked. Clutching a teddy bear in one hand and her mother's arm with the other, Caitlin descended the steps. "One! Two! Threeeee!" Carolyn counted as she helped Caitlin down. "How much she's changed!" Carolyn thought to herself, looking at the child who, not long ago, had been a newborn. With her first steps, Caitlin had passed from *infancy* to *toddlerhood*—a period spanning the second year of life. At first, Caitlin did, indeed, "toddle" with an awkward gait, tipping over frequently. But her face reflected the thrill of conquering a new skill.

As they walked toward the car, Carolyn and Caitlin spotted 3-year-old Eli and his father, Kevin, in the neighboring yard. Eli dashed toward them, waving a bright yellow envelope. Carolyn bent down to open the envelope and took out a card. It read, "Announcing the arrival of Grace Ann. Born: Cambodia. Age: 16 months." Carolyn turned toward Kevin and Eli. "That's wonderful news! When can we see her?"

"Let's wait a few days," Kevin suggested. "Monica's taken Grace to the doctor this morning. She's underweight and malnourished." Kevin described Monica's first night with Grace in a hotel room in Phnom Penh. Grace lay on the bed, withdrawn and fearful. Eventually she fell asleep, gripping crackers in both hands.

Carolyn felt Caitlin's impatient tug at her sleeve. Off they drove to child care, where Vanessa had just dropped off her 18-month-old son, Timmy. Within moments, Caitlin and Timmy were in the sandbox, shoveling sand into plastic cups and buckets with the help of their caregiver, Ginette.

A few weeks later, Grace joined Caitlin and Timmy at Ginette's child-care home. Although still unable to crawl or walk, she had grown taller and heavier, and her sad, vacant gaze had given way to an alert expression, a ready smile, and an enthusiastic desire to imitate and explore. When Caitlin headed for the sandbox, Grace stretched out her arms, asking Ginette to carry her there, too. Soon Grace was pulling herself up at every opportunity. Finally, at age 18 months, she walked!

This chapter traces physical growth during the first two years—one of the most remarkable and busiest times of development. We will see how rapid changes in the infant's body and brain support learning, motor skills, and perceptual capacities. Caitlin, Grace, and Timmy will join us along the way to illustrate individual differences and environmental influences on physical development. ∎

Body Growth

TAKE A MOMENT... The next time you're walking in your neighborhood park or at the mall, note the contrast between infants' and toddlers' physical capabilities. One reason for the vast changes in what children can do over the first two years is that their bodies change enormously—faster than at any other time after birth.

Changes in Body Size and Muscle–Fat Makeup

By the end of the first year a typical infant's height is about 32 inches—more than 50 percent greater than at birth. By 2 years, it is 75 percent greater (36 inches).

5.1 Discuss major changes in body size, muscle–fat makeup, body proportions, and variations in rate of physical growth over the first two years.

Similarly, by 5 months of age, birth weight has doubled, to about 15 pounds. At 1 year it has tripled, to 22 pounds, and at 2 years it has quadrupled, to about 30 pounds.

Figure 5.1 illustrates this dramatic increase in body size. But rather than making steady gains, infants and toddlers grow in little spurts. In one study, children who were followed over the first 21 months of life went for periods of 7 to 63 days with no growth, then added as much as half an inch in a 24-hour period! Almost always, parents described their babies as irritable, very hungry, and sleeping more on the days before a spurt (Lampl, 1993; Lampl & Johnson, 2011).

One of the most obvious changes in infants' appearance is their transformation into round, plump babies by the middle of the first year. This early rise in "baby fat," which peaks at about 9 months, helps the infant maintain a constant body temperature. In the second year, most toddlers slim down, a trend that continues into middle childhood (Fomon & Nelson, 2002). In contrast, muscle tissue increases very slowly during infancy and will not reach a peak until adolescence. Babies are not very muscular; their strength and physical coordination are limited.

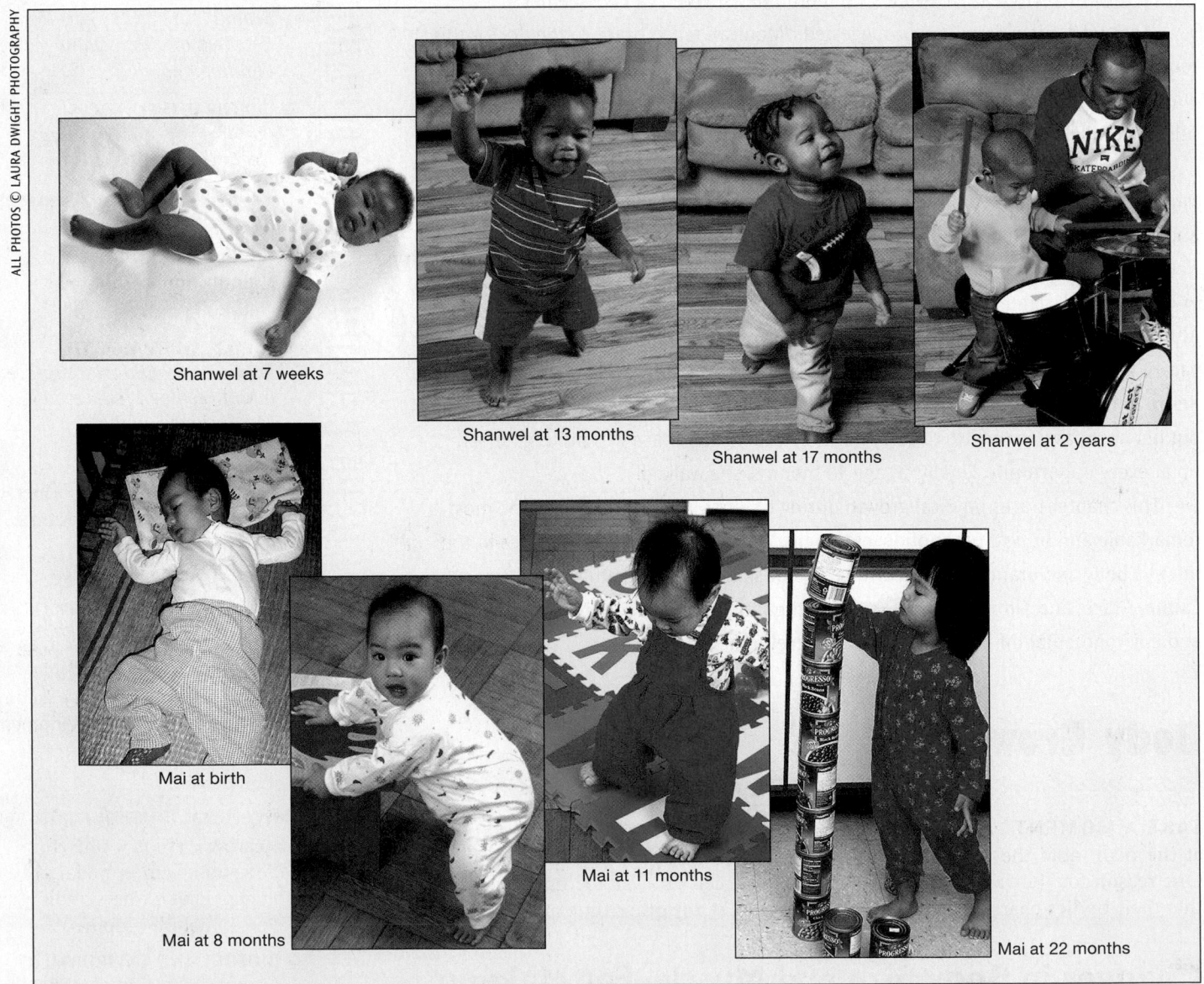

ALL PHOTOS © LAURA DWIGHT PHOTOGRAPHY

Shanwel at 7 weeks

Shanwel at 13 months

Shanwel at 17 months

Shanwel at 2 years

Mai at birth

Mai at 8 months

Mai at 11 months

Mai at 22 months

FIGURE 5.1 **Body growth during the first two years.** These photos depict the dramatic changes in body size and proportions during infancy and toddlerhood in two children—a boy, Shanwel, and a girl, Mai. In the first year, the head is quite large in proportion to the rest of the body, and height and weight gain are especially rapid. During the second year, the lower portion of the body catches up. Notice, also, how both children added "baby fat" in the early months of life and then slimmed down, a trend that continues into middle childhood.

Changes in Body Proportions

As the child's overall size increases, parts of the body grow at different rates. Two growth patterns describe these changes. The first is the **cephalocaudal trend**—from the Latin for "head to tail." During the prenatal period, the head develops more rapidly than the lower part of the body. At birth, the head takes up one-fourth of total body length, the legs only one-third. Notice how, in Figure 5.1, the lower portion of the body catches up. By age 2, the head accounts for only one-fifth and the legs for nearly one-half of total body length.

In the second pattern, the **proximodistal trend,** growth proceeds, literally, from "near to far"—from the center of the body outward. In the prenatal period, the head, chest, and trunk grow first; then the arms and legs; and finally the hands and feet. During infancy and childhood, the arms and legs continue to grow somewhat ahead of the hands and feet.

Individual and Group Differences

In infancy, girls are slightly shorter and lighter than boys, with a higher ratio of fat to muscle. These small sex differences persist throughout early and middle childhood and are greatly magnified at adolescence. Ethnic differences in body size are apparent as well. Grace was below the *growth norms* (height and weight averages for children her age). Early malnutrition played a part, but even after substantial catch-up, Grace—as is typical for Asian children—remained below North American norms. In contrast, Timmy is slightly above average in size, as African-American children tend to be (Bogin, 2001).

Children of the same age differ in *rate* of physical growth; some make faster progress toward mature body size than others. But current body size is not enough to tell us how quickly a child's physical growth is moving along. Although Timmy is larger and heavier than Caitlin and Grace, he is not physically more mature. In a moment, you will see why.

The best estimate of a child's physical maturity is *skeletal age,* a measure of bone development. It is determined by X-raying the long bones of the body to see the extent to which soft, pliable cartilage has hardened into bone, a gradual process that is completed in adolescence. When skeletal ages are examined, African-American children tend to be slightly ahead of Caucasian-American children in skeletal age. And girls are considerably ahead of boys—the reason Timmy's skeletal age lags behind that of Caitlin and Grace. At birth, the sexes differ by about 4 to 6 weeks, a gap that widens over infancy and childhood (Tanner, Healy, & Cameron, 2001). Girls are advanced in development of other organs as well. This greater physical maturity may contribute to girls' greater resistance to harmful environmental influences. As noted in Chapter 2, girls experience fewer developmental problems than boys and have lower infant and childhood mortality rates.

Brain Development

At birth, the brain is nearer to its adult size than any other physical structure, and it continues to develop at an astounding pace throughout infancy and toddlerhood. We can best understand brain growth by looking at it from two vantage points: (1) the microscopic level of individual brain cells and (2) the larger level of the cerebral cortex, the most complex brain structure and the one responsible for the highly developed intelligence of our species.

Development of Neurons

The human brain has 100 to 200 billion **neurons,** or nerve cells, that store and transmit information, many of which have thousands of direct connections with other neurons. Unlike other body cells, neurons are not tightly packed together. Between them are tiny gaps, or **synapses,** where fibers from different neurons come close together but do not touch (see Figure 5.2 on page 162). Neurons send messages to one another by releasing chemicals called **neurotransmitters,** which cross the synapse.

5.2 Describe brain development during infancy and toddlerhood, current methods of measuring brain functioning, and appropriate stimulation to support the brain's potential.

5.3 How does organization of sleep and wakefulness change over the first two years?

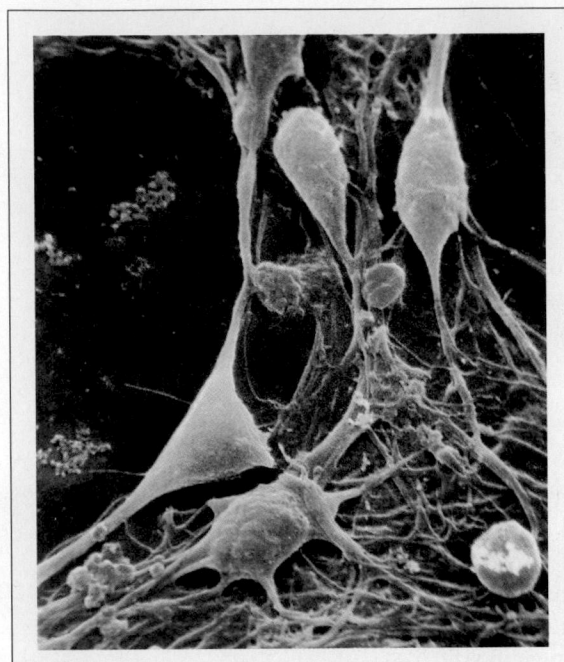

© CNRI/SCIENCE SOURCE

FIGURE 5.2 **Neurons and their connective fibers.** This photograph of several neurons, taken with the aid of a powerful microscope, shows the elaborate synaptic connections that form with neighboring cells.

The basic story of brain growth concerns how neurons develop and form this elaborate communication system. Figure 5.3 summarizes major milestones of brain development. In the prenatal period, neurons are produced in the embryo's primitive neural tube. From there, they migrate to form the major parts of the brain (see Chapter 3, page 98). Once neurons are in place, they differentiate, establishing their unique functions by extending their fibers to form synaptic connections with neighboring cells. During infancy and toddlerhood, neural fibers and synapses increase at an astounding pace (Gilmore et al., 2012; Moore, Persaud, & Torchia, 2013). Because developing neurons require space for these connective structures, a surprising aspect of brain growth is that as synapses form, many surrounding neurons die—20 to 80 percent, depending on the brain region (Stiles, 2008). Fortunately, during the prenatal period, the neural tube produces far more neurons than the brain will ever need.

As neurons form connections, *stimulation* becomes vital to their survival. Neurons that are stimulated by input from the surrounding environment continue to establish new synapses, forming increasingly elaborate systems of communication that support more complex abilities. At first, stimulation results in a massive overabundance of synapses, many of which serve identical functions, thereby ensuring that the child will acquire the motor, cognitive, and social skills that our species needs to survive. Neurons that are seldom stimulated soon lose their synapses, in a process called **synaptic pruning** that returns neurons not needed at the moment to an uncommitted state so they can support future development. In all, about 40 percent of synapses are pruned during childhood and adolescence (Webb, Monk, & Nelson, 2001). For this process to advance, appropriate stimulation of the child's brain is vital during periods in which the formation of synapses is at its peak (Bryk & Fisher, 2012).

If few neurons are produced after the prenatal period, what causes the extraordinary increase in brain size during the first two years? About half the brain's volume is made up of **glial cells,** which are responsible for **myelination,** the coating of neural fibers with an insulating fatty sheath (called *myelin*) that improves the efficiency of message transfer. Certain types of glial cells also participate directly in neural communication, by picking up and passing on neuronal signals and releasing neurotransmitters. Glial cells multiply rapidly from the end of

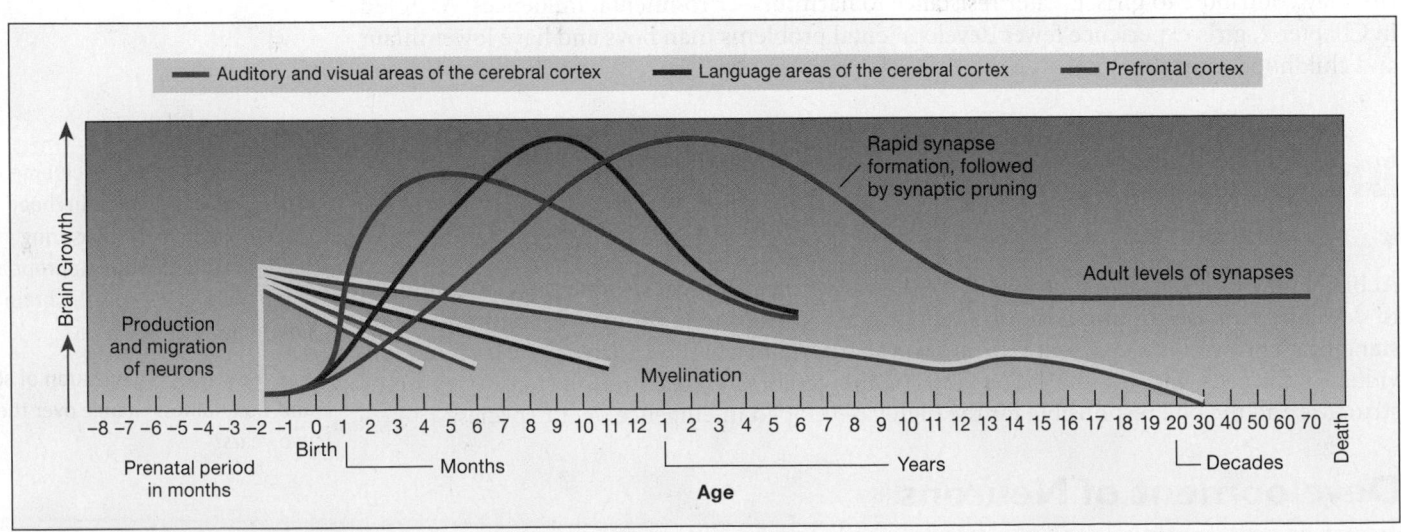

FIGURE 5.3 **Major milestones of brain development.** Formation of synapses is rapid during the first two years, especially in the auditory, visual, and language areas of the cerebral cortex. The prefrontal cortex undergoes more extended synaptic growth. In each area, overproduction of synapses is followed by synaptic pruning. The prefrontal cortex, responsible for thought (see page 165), is among the last regions to attain an adult level of synaptic connections—in mid- to late adolescence. Myelination occurs at a dramatic pace during the first two years and then at a slower pace through childhood, followed by an acceleration at adolescence. The multiple yellow lines indicate that the timing of myelination varies among different brain areas. For example, neural fibers myelinate over a longer period in the language areas, and especially in the prefrontal cortex, than in the visual and auditory areas. (Based on Thompson & Nelson, 2001.)

pregnancy through the second year of life—a process that continues at a slower pace through middle childhood and accelerates again in adolescence. Gains in neural fibers and myelination account for the overall increase in size of the brain, from nearly 30 percent of its adult weight at birth to 70 percent by age 2 (Johnson, 2011; Knickmeyer et al., 2008). Growth is especially rapid during the first year, when the brain more than doubles in size.

Brain development can be compared to molding a "living sculpture." First, neurons and synapses are overproduced. Then, cell death and synaptic pruning sculpt away excess building material to form the mature brain—a process jointly influenced by genetically programmed events and the child's experiences. The resulting "sculpture" is a set of interconnected regions, each with specific functions—much like countries on a globe that communicate with one another (Johnston et al., 2001). This "geography" of the brain permits researchers to study its organization and the activity of its regions using neurobiological techniques.

Measures of Brain Functioning

Table 5.1 describes major measures of brain functioning. Among these methods, the two most frequently used detect changes in *electrical activity* in the cerebral cortex. In an *electroencephalogram (EEG)*, researchers examine *brain-wave patterns* for stability and organization—signs of mature functioning of the cortex (see Figure 5.4). And as a child processes a particular stimulus, *event-related potentials (ERPs)* detect the general location of brain-wave activity—a technique often used to study preverbal infants' responsiveness to various stimuli, the impact of experience on specialization of specific regions of the cortex, and atypical brain functioning in children at risk for learning and emotional problems (DeBoer, Scott, & Nelson, 2007; Gunnar & de Haan, 2009).

Neuroimaging techniques, which yield detailed, three-dimensional computerized pictures of the entire brain and its active areas, provide the most precise information about which brain regions are specialized for certain capacities. The most promising of these methods is *functional magnetic resonance imaging (fMRI)*. Unlike *positron emission tomography (PET)*, fMRI does not depend on X-ray photography, which requires injection of a radioactive substance. Rather, when a child is exposed to a stimulus, fMRI detects changes in blood flow and oxygen metabolism throughout the

OLI SCHARFF/GETTY IMAGES

FIGURE 5.4 **Electroencephalogram (EEG) using the geodesic sensor net (GSN).** Interconnected electrodes embedded in the head cap record electrical brain-wave activity in the cerebral cortex.

TABLE 5.1	Measuring Brain Functioning
METHOD	**DESCRIPTION**
Electroencephalogram (EEG)	Electrodes embedded in a head cap record electrical brain-wave activity in the brain's outer layers—the cerebral cortex. Researchers use an advanced tool called a geodesic sensor net (GSN) to hold interconnected electrodes (up to 128 for infants and 256 for children and adults) in place through a cap that adjusts to each person's head shape, yielding improved brain-wave detection.
Event-related potentials (ERPs)	Using the EEG, the frequency and amplitude of brain waves in response to particular stimuli (such as a picture, music, or speech) are recorded in the cerebral cortex. Enables identification of general regions of stimulus-induced activity.
Functional magnetic resonance imaging (fMRI)	While the person lies inside a tunnel-shaped apparatus that creates a magnetic field, a scanner magnetically detects increased blood flow and oxygen metabolism in areas of the brain as the individual processes particular stimuli. The scanner typically records images every 1 to 4 seconds; these are combined into a computerized moving picture of activity anywhere in the brain (not just its outer layers). Not appropriate for children younger than age 5 to 6, who cannot remain still during testing.
Positron emission tomography (PET)	After injection or inhalation of a radioactive substance, the person lies on an apparatus with a scanner that emits fine streams of X-rays, which detect increased blood flow and oxygen metabolism in areas of the brain as the person processes particular stimuli. As with fMRI, the result is a computerized image of activity anywhere in the brain. Not appropriate for children younger than age 5 to 6.
Near-infrared spectroscopy (NIRS)	Using thin, flexible optical fibers attached to the scalp through a head cap, infrared (invisible) light is beamed at the brain; its absorption by areas of the cerebral cortex varies with changes in blood flow and oxygen metabolism as the individual processes particular stimuli. The result is a computerized moving picture of active areas in the cerebral cortex. Unlike fMRI and PET, NIRS is appropriate for infants and young children, who can move within limited range during testing.

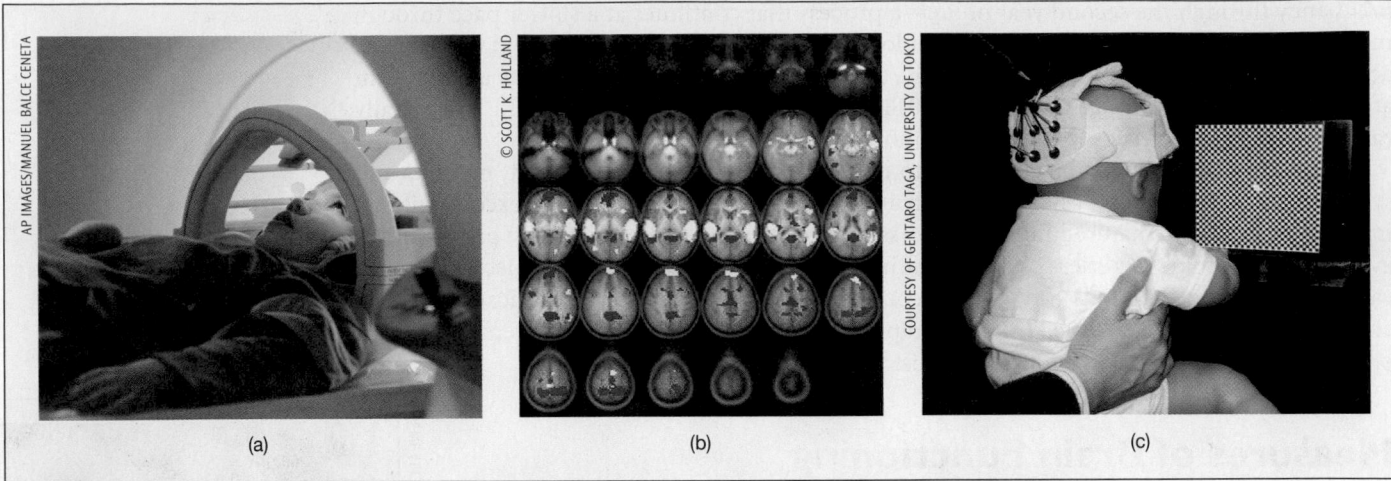

FIGURE 5.5 **Functional magnetic resonance imaging (fMRI) and near infrared spectroscopy (NIRS).** (a) This 6-year-old is part of a study that uses fMRI to find out how his brain processes light and motion. (b) The fMRI image shows which areas of the boy's brain are active while he views changing visual stimuli. (c) Here, NIRS is used to investigate a 2-month-old's response to a visual stimulus. During testing, the baby can move freely within a limited range. (Photo (c) From G. Taga, K. Asakawa, A. Maki, Y. Konishi, & H. Koisumi, 2003, "Brain Imaging in Awake Infants by Near-Infrared Optical Topography," *Proceedings of the National Academy of Sciences, 100,* p. 10723. Reprinted by permission.)

brain magnetically, yielding a colorful, moving picture of parts of the brain used to perform a given activity (see Figure 5.5a and b).

Because PET and fMRI require that the participant lie as motionless as possible for an extended time, they are not suitable for infants and young children. A neuroimaging technique that works well in infancy and early childhood is *near infrared spectroscopy (NIRS)*, in which infrared (invisible) light is beamed at regions of the cerebral cortex to measure blood flow and oxygen metabolism while the child attends to a stimulus (refer again to Table 5.1). Because the apparatus consists only of thin, flexible optical fibers attached to the scalp using a head cap, a baby can sit on the parent's lap and move during testing—as Figure 5.5c illustrates (Hespos et al., 2010). But unlike PET and fMRI, which map activity changes throughout the brain, NIRS examines only the functioning of the cerebral cortex.

The measures just reviewed are powerful tools for uncovering relationships between the brain and psychological development. But like all research methods, they have limitations. Even though a stimulus produces a consistent pattern of brain activity, investigators cannot be certain that an individual has processed it in a certain way (Kagan, 2013). And a researcher who takes a change in brain activity as an indicator of information processing must make sure that the change was not due instead to hunger, boredom, fatigue, or body movements. Consequently, other methods must be combined with brain-wave and -imaging findings to clarify their meaning (de Haan & Gunnar, 2009). Now let's turn to the developing organization of the cerebral cortex.

Development of the Cerebral Cortex

The **cerebral cortex** surrounds the rest of the brain, resembling half of a shelled walnut. It is the largest brain structure—accounting for 85 percent of the brain's weight and containing the greatest number of neurons and synapses. Because the cerebral cortex is the last part of the brain to stop growing, it is sensitive to environmental influences for a much longer period than any other part of the brain.

REGIONS OF THE CORTEX Figure 5.6 shows specific functions of regions of the cerebral cortex, such as receiving information from the senses, instructing the body to move, and thinking. The order in which cortical regions develop corresponds to the order in which various capacities emerge in the infant and growing child. For example, a burst of synaptic growth occurs in the auditory and visual cortexes and in areas responsible for body movement over the first year—a period of dramatic gains in auditory and visual perception and mastery of motor skills (Gilmore et al., 2012). Language areas are especially active from late infancy through the preschool years, when language development flourishes (Pujol et al., 2006).

The cortical regions with the most extended period of development are the *frontal lobes.* The **prefrontal cortex,** lying in front of areas controlling body movement, is responsible for thought—in particular, consciousness, inhibition of impulses, integration of information, and use of memory, reasoning, planning, and problem-solving strategies. From age 2 months on, the prefrontal cortex functions more effectively. But it undergoes especially rapid myelination and formation and pruning of synapses during the preschool and school years, followed by another period of accelerated growth in adolescence, when it reaches an adult level of synaptic connections (Nelson, 2002; Nelson, Thomas, & de Haan, 2006; Sowell et al., 2002).

LATERALIZATION AND PLASTICITY OF THE CEREBRAL CORTEX   The cerebral cortex has two *hemispheres,* or sides, that differ in their functions. Some tasks are done mostly by the left hemisphere, others by the right. For example, each hemisphere receives sensory information from the side of the body opposite to it and controls only that side.[1] For most of us, the left hemisphere is largely responsible for verbal abilities (such as spoken and written language) and positive emotion (for example, joy). The right hemisphere handles spatial abilities (judging distances, reading maps, and recognizing geometric shapes) and negative emotion (such as distress) (Nelson & Bosquet, 2000). In left-handed people, this pattern may be reversed or, more commonly, the cerebral cortex may be less clearly specialized than in right-handers.

Why does this specialization of the two hemispheres, called **lateralization,** occur? Studies using fMRI reveal that the left hemisphere is better at processing information in a sequential, analytic (piece-by-piece) way, a good approach for dealing with communicative information—both verbal (language) and emotional (a joyful smile). In contrast, the right hemisphere is specialized for processing information in a holistic, integrative manner, ideal for making sense of spatial information and regulating negative emotion. A lateralized brain may have evolved because it enabled humans to cope more successfully with changing environmental demands (Falk, 2005). It permits a wider array of functions to be carried out effectively than if both sides processed information in exactly the same way. However, the popular notion of a "right-brained" or "left-brained" person is an oversimplification. The two hemispheres communicate and work together, doing so more rapidly and effectively with age.

Researchers study the timing of brain lateralization to learn more about **brain plasticity.** A highly *plastic* cerebral cortex, in which many areas are not yet committed to specific functions, has a high capacity for learning. And if a part of the cortex is damaged, other parts can take over the tasks it would have handled. But once the hemispheres lateralize, damage to a specific region means that the abilities it controls cannot be recovered to the same extent or as easily as earlier.

At birth, the hemispheres have already begun to specialize. Most newborns favor the right side of the body in their head position and reflexive reactions (Grattan et al., 1992; Rönnqvist & Hopkins, 1998). Most also show greater activation (detected with either ERP or NIRS) in the left hemisphere while listening to speech sounds or displaying a positive state of arousal. In contrast, the right hemisphere reacts more strongly to nonspeech sounds and to stimuli (such as a sour-tasting fluid) that evoke a negative reaction (Fox & Davidson, 1986; Hespos et al., 2010).

Nevertheless, research on brain-damaged children and adults offers evidence for substantial plasticity in the young brain, summarized in the Biology and Environment box on page 166.

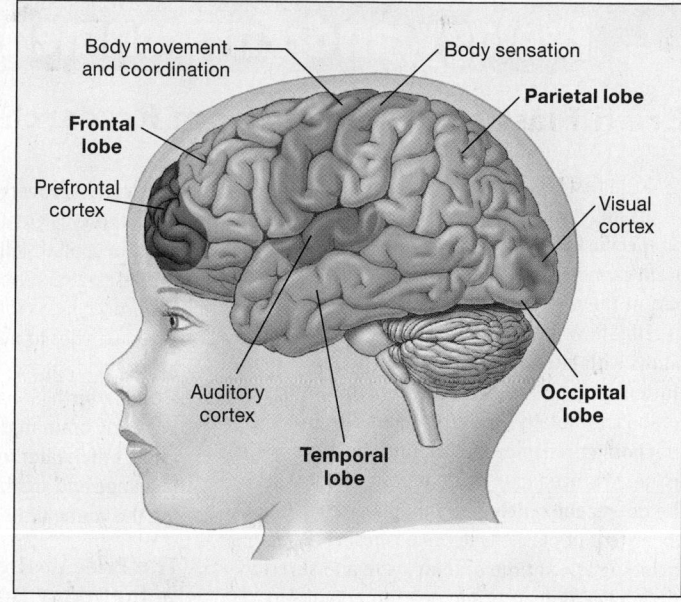

FIGURE 5.6 **The left side of the human brain, showing the cerebral cortex.** The cortex is divided into different lobes, each of which contains a variety of regions with specific functions. Some major regions are labeled here.

---

[1]The eyes are an exception. Messages from the right half of each retina go to the right hemisphere; messages from the left half of each retina go to the left hemisphere. Thus, visual information from *both* eyes is received by *both* hemispheres.

Biology and Environment

Brain Plasticity: Insights from Research on Brain-Damaged Children and Adults

In the first few years of life, the brain is highly plastic. It can reorganize areas committed to specific functions in a way that the mature brain cannot. Adults who suffered injury to a part of the brain in infancy and early childhood usually show fewer cognitive impairments than adults with later-occurring injury (Holland, 2004; Huttenlocher, 2002). Nevertheless, the young brain is not totally plastic. When it is injured, its functioning is compromised. And the more brain tissue destroyed in infancy or early childhood, the poorer the outcomes (Anderson et al., 2006). The extent of plasticity depends on several factors, including age at time of injury, site and severity of damage, skill area, and environmental supports for recovery.

Brain Plasticity in Infancy and Early Childhood

In a large study of children with injuries to the cerebral cortex that occurred around the time of birth or in the first six months of life, language and spatial skills were assessed repeatedly into adolescence (Stiles, Reilly, & Levine, 2012; Stiles et al., 2005, 2008, 2009). All the children had experienced early brain seizures or hemorrhages. Brain-imaging techniques (fMRI and PET) revealed the precise site of damage.

Regardless of whether injury occurred in the left or right cerebral hemisphere, the children showed delays in language development that persisted until about 3½ years of age. That damage to either hemisphere affected early language competence indicates that at first, language functioning is broadly distributed in the brain. But by age 5, the children caught up in vocabulary and grammatical skills. Undamaged areas—in either the left or the right hemisphere—had taken over these language functions.

Compared with language, spatial skills were more impaired after early brain injury. When preschool through adolescent-age youngsters were asked to copy designs, those with early right-hemispheric damage had trouble with holistic processing—accurately representing the overall shape. In contrast, children with left-hemispheric damage captured the basic shape but omitted fine-grained details. Nevertheless, the children showed improvements in their drawings with age—gains that did not occur in brain-injured adults (Stiles, Reilly, & Levine, 2012; Stiles et al., 2003, 2008, 2009).

Clearly, recovery after early brain injury is greater for language than for spatial skills. Why is this so? Researchers speculate that spatial processing is the older of the two capacities in our evolutionary history and, therefore, more lateralized at birth (Stiles et al., 2008). But early brain injury has less impact than later injury on both language and spatial skills, revealing the young brain's plasticity.

The Price of High Plasticity in the Young Brain

Despite impressive recovery of language and (to a lesser extent) spatial skills, children with early brain injuries show deficits in a wide variety of complex mental abilities during the school years. For example, their reading and math progress is slow. In telling stories, they produce simpler narratives than agemates without early brain injuries. And as the demands of daily life increase, they have difficulty managing homework and other responsibilities (Anderson, Spencer-Smith, & Wood, 2011; Stiles, Reilly, & Levine, 2012).

High brain plasticity, researchers explain, comes at a price. When healthy brain regions take over the functions of damaged areas, a "crowding effect" occurs: Multiple tasks must be done by a smaller-than-usual volume of brain tissue (Stiles, 2012). Consequently, the brain processes information less quickly and accurately than it would if it were intact. Complex mental abilities of all kinds suffer into middle childhood, and often longer, because performing them well requires the collaboration of many regions in the cerebral cortex. In sum, the full impact of an early brain injury may not be apparent for many years, until higher-order skills are expected to develop.

Age of Injury and Plasticity

In infancy and childhood, the goal of brain growth is to form neural connections that ensure mastery of essential skills. Animal research reveals that plasticity is greatest while the brain is forming many new synapses; it declines during synaptic pruning (Murphy & Corbett, 2009). At

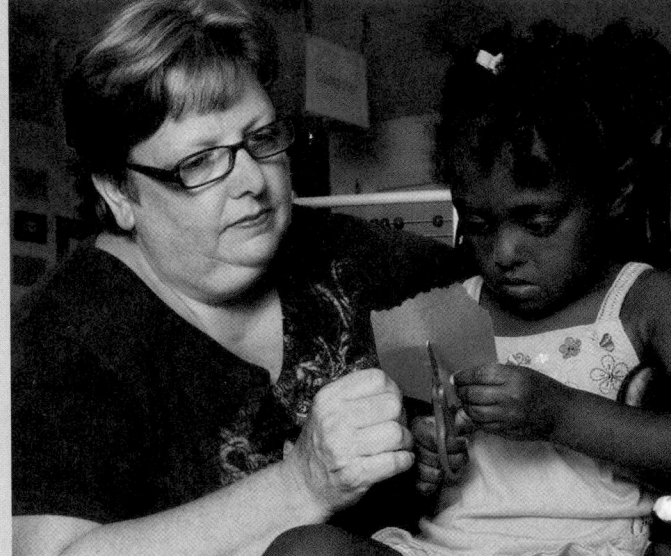

This preschooler, who experienced brain damage in infancy, has been spared massive impairments because of high plasticity of the brain. Here, a teacher encourages her to cut basic shapes to strengthen spatial skills, which remain more impaired than language after early brain injury.

the same time, for as yet unexplained reasons, some young children suffer permanent damage following a localized brain injury (Anderson, Spencer-Smith, & Wood, 2011). Age likely combines with other influences—insult site and severity and environmental factors, such as warm, stimulating parenting and access to intervention services—to affect outcomes.

Furthermore, brain plasticity is not restricted to early childhood. Though far more limited, reorganization in the brain can occur later, even in adulthood. For example, adult stroke victims often display considerable recovery, especially in response to stimulation of language and motor skills. Brain-imaging findings reveal that structures adjacent to the permanently damaged area or in the opposite cerebral hemisphere reorganize to support the impaired ability (Kalra & Ratan, 2007; Murphy & Corbett, 2009). When an individual practices relevant tasks, the brain strengthens existing synapses and generates new ones.

Plasticity seems to be a basic property of the nervous system. Researchers hope to discover how brain plasticity and experience work together throughout life, so they can help people of all ages—with and without brain injuries—develop at their best.

Furthermore, early experience greatly influences the organization of the cerebral cortex. For example, deaf adults who, as infants and children, learned sign language (a spatial skill) depend more than hearing individuals on the right hemisphere for language processing (Neville & Bavelier, 2002). And toddlers who are advanced in language development show greater left-hemispheric specialization for language than their more slowly developing agemates (Luna et al., 2001; Mills et al., 2005). Apparently, the very process of acquiring language and other skills promotes lateralization.

In sum, the brain is more plastic during the first few years than it will ever be again. An overabundance of synaptic connections supports brain plasticity and, therefore, young children's ability to learn, which is fundamental to their survival. And although the cortex is programmed from the start for hemispheric specialization, experience greatly influences the rate and success of its advancing organization.

Sensitive Periods in Brain Development

Animal studies confirm that early, extreme sensory deprivation results in permanent brain damage and loss of functions—findings that verify the existence of sensitive periods in brain development. For example, early, varied visual experiences must occur for the brain's visual centers to develop normally. If a 1-month-old kitten is deprived of light for just three or four days, these areas of the brain degenerate. If the kitten is kept in the dark during the fourth week of life and beyond, the damage is severe and permanent (Crair, Gillespie, & Stryker, 1998). And the general quality of the early environment affects overall brain growth. When animals reared from birth in physically and socially stimulating surroundings are compared with those reared in isolation, the brains of the stimulated animals are larger and show much denser synaptic connections (Sale, Berardi, & Maffei, 2009).

HUMAN EVIDENCE: VICTIMS OF DEPRIVED EARLY ENVIRONMENTS For ethical reasons, we cannot deliberately deprive some infants of normal rearing experiences and observe the impact on their brains and competencies. Instead, we must turn to natural experiments, in which children were victims of deprived early environments that were later rectified. Such studies have revealed some parallels with the animal evidence just described.

For example, when babies are born with cataracts in both eyes (clouded lenses, preventing clear visual images), those who have corrective surgery within four to six months show rapid improvement in vision, except for subtle aspects of face perception, which require early visual input to the right hemisphere to develop (Maurer & Lewis, 2013; Maurer, Mondloch, & Lewis, 2007). The longer cataract surgery is postponed beyond infancy, the less complete the recovery in visual skills. And if surgery is delayed until adulthood, vision is severely and permanently impaired (Lewis & Maurer, 2005).

Studies of infants placed in orphanages who were later exposed to family rearing confirm the importance of a generally stimulating environment for psychological development. In one investigation, researchers followed the progress of a large sample of children transferred between birth and 3½ years from extremely deprived Romanian orphanages to adoptive families in Great Britain (Beckett et al., 2006; O'Connor et al., 2000; Rutter et al., 1998, 2004, 2010). On arrival, most were impaired in all domains of development. Cognitive catch-up was impressive for children adopted before 6 months, who consistently attained average mental test scores in childhood and adolescence, performing as well as a comparison group of early-adopted British-born children.

But Romanian children who had been institutionalized for more than the first six months showed serious intellectual deficits (see Figure 5.7 on page 168). Although they improved in mental test scores during middle childhood and adolescence, they remained substantially below average. And most displayed at least three serious mental health problems, such as inattention, overactivity, unruly behavior, and autistic-like symptoms (social disinterest, stereotyped behavior) (Kreppner et al., 2007, 2010). A major correlate of both time spent in the institution and poor

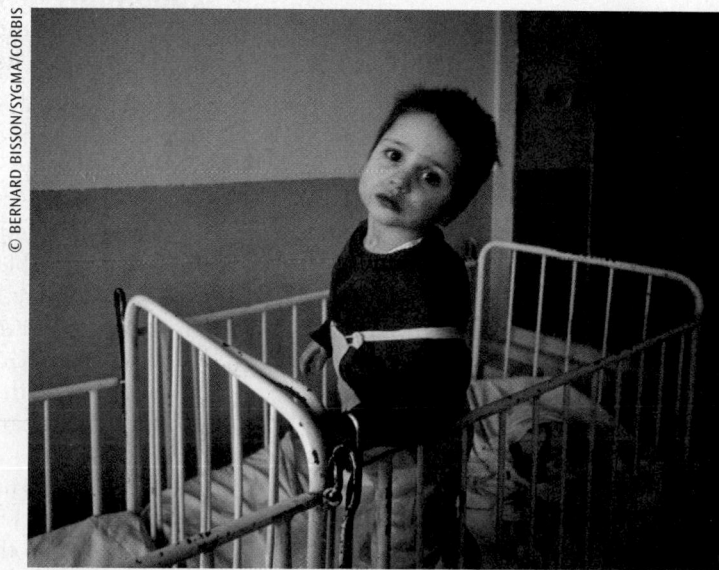

This Romanian orphan receives little adult contact or stimulation. The longer he remains in this barren environment, the greater his risk of brain damage and lasting impairments in all domains of development.

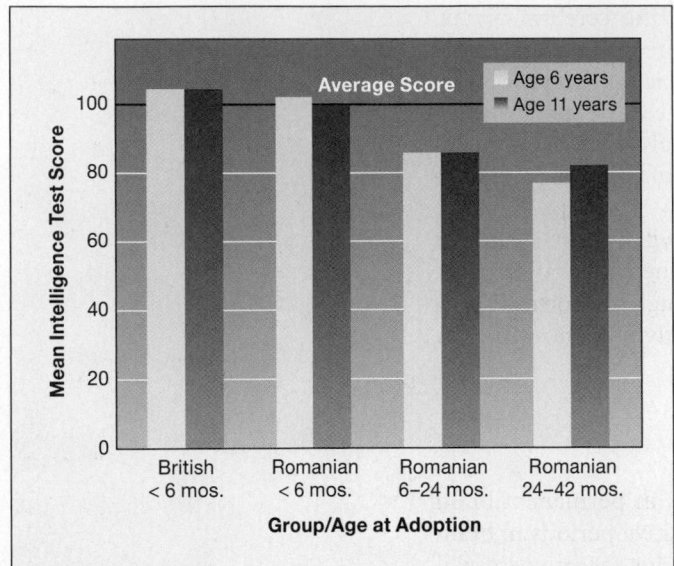

FIGURE 5.7 **Relationship of age at adoption to mental test scores at ages 6 and 11 among British and Romanian adoptees.** Children transferred from Romanian orphanages to British adoptive homes in the first six months of life attained average scores and fared as well as British early-adopted children, suggesting that they had fully recovered from extreme early deprivation. Romanian children adopted after 6 months of age performed well below average. And although those adopted after age 2 improved between ages 6 and 11, they continued to show serious intellectual deficits. (Adapted from Beckett et al., 2006.)

cognitive and emotional functioning was below-average head size, suggesting that early lack of stimulation permanently damaged the brain (Sonuga-Barke, Schlotz, & Kreppner, 2010).

Neurobiological findings indicate that early, prolonged institutionalization leads to a generalized decrease in activity of the cerebral cortex—especially the prefrontal cortex, which governs complex cognition and impulse control. Neural fibers connecting the prefrontal cortex with other brain structures involved in control of emotion are also reduced (Eluvathingal et al., 2006; Nelson, 2007b). And activation of the left cerebral hemisphere, governing positive emotion, is diminished relative to right cerebral activation, governing negative emotion (McLaughlin et al., 2011).

Additional evidence confirms that the chronic stress of early, deprived orphanage rearing disrupts the brain's capacity to manage stress. In another investigation, researchers followed the development of children who had spent their first eight months or more in Romanian institutions and were then adopted into Canadian homes (Gunnar & Cheatham, 2003; Gunnar et al., 2001). Compared with agemates adopted shortly after birth, these children showed extreme stress reactivity, as indicated by high concentrations of the stress hormone *cortisol* in their saliva—a physiological response linked to persistent illness, delayed physical growth, and learning and behavior problems, including deficits in attention and control of anger and other impulses. The longer the children spent in orphanage care, the higher their cortisol levels—even 6½ years after adoption. In other research, orphanage children displayed abnormally low cortisol—a blunted physiological stress response that may be the central nervous system's adaptation to earlier, frequent cortisol elevations (Loman & Gunnar, 2010).

Finally, early deprived rearing may also disrupt the brain's typical response to pleasurable social experiences. After sitting on their mother's lap and playing an enjoyable game, preschoolers adopted, on average, at age 1½ years from Romanian orphanages had abnormally low urine levels of *oxytocin*—a hormone released by the brain that evokes calmness and contentment in the presence of familiar, trusted people (Fries et al., 2005). As we will see in Chapter 7, children who spend their infancy in neglectful institutions often display attachment difficulties.

APPROPRIATE STIMULATION Unlike the orphanage children just described, Grace, whom Monica and Kevin had adopted in Cambodia at 16 months of age, showed favorable progress. Two years earlier, they had adopted Grace's older brother, Eli. When Eli was 2 years old, Monica and Kevin sent a letter and a photo of Eli to his biological mother, describing a bright, happy child. The next day, the Cambodian mother tearfully asked an adoption agency to send her baby daughter to join Eli and his American family.

Although Grace's early environment was very depleted, her biological mother's loving care—holding gently, speaking softly, playfully stimulating, and breastfeeding—may have prevented irreversible damage to her brain. Besides offering gentle, appropriate stimulation, sensitive adult care helps normalize cortisol production in both typically developing and emotionally traumatized infants and young children (Gunnar & Quevedo, 2007; Tarullo & Gunnar, 2006). Good parenting seems to protect the young brain from the potentially damaging effects of both excessive and inadequate stress-hormone exposure.

In the Bucharest Early Intervention Project, 136 institutionalized Romanian babies were randomized into conditions of either care as usual or transfer to high-quality foster families between 6 and 31 months of age. Specially trained social workers provided foster parents with counseling and support. Follow-ups between 2½ and 8 years revealed that the foster-care group exceeded the institutional-care group in intelligence test scores, language skills, emotional responsiveness, social skills, and EEG and ERP assessments of brain development (Fox, Nelson & Zeanah, 2013; Nelson, Fox, & Zeanah, 2014). On all measures, the earlier the foster placement, the better the outcome. But consistent with an early sensitive period, the foster-care group remained behind never-institutionalized agemates living with Bucharest families.

In addition to impoverished environments, ones that overwhelm children with expectations beyond their current capacities interfere with the brain's potential. In recent years, expensive early learning centers have sprung up, in which infants are trained with letter and number flash cards and slightly older toddlers are given a full curriculum of reading, math, science, art, gym, and more. There is no evidence that these programs yield smarter, better "super-babies" (Hirsh-Pasek & Golinkoff, 2003). To the contrary, trying to prime infants with stimulation for which they are not ready can cause them to withdraw, thereby threatening their interest in learning and creating conditions much like stimulus deprivation!

How, then, can we characterize appropriate stimulation during the early years? To answer this question, researchers distinguish between two types of brain development. The first, **experience-expectant brain growth,** refers to the young brain's rapidly developing organization, which depends on ordinary experiences—opportunities to explore the environment, interact with people, and hear language and other sounds. As a result of millions of years of evolution, the brains of all infants, toddlers, and young children *expect* to encounter these experiences and, if they do, grow normally. The second type of brain development, **experience-dependent brain growth,** occurs throughout our lives. It consists of additional growth and the refinement of established brain structures as a result of specific learning experiences that vary widely across individuals and cultures (Greenough & Black, 1992). Reading and writing, playing computer games, weaving an intricate rug, and practicing the violin are examples. The brain of a violinist differs in certain ways from the brain of a poet because each has exercised different brain regions for a long time.

Experience-expectant brain growth occurs naturally, through ordinary, stimulating experiences. This toddler exploring a mossy log engages in the type of activity that best promotes brain development in the early years.

Experience-expectant brain development occurs early and naturally, as caregivers offer babies and preschoolers age-appropriate play materials and engage them in enjoyable daily routines—a shared meal, a game of peekaboo, a bath before bed, a picture book to talk about, or a song to sing. The resulting growth provides the foundation for later-occurring, experience-dependent development (Belsky & de Haan, 2011; Huttenlocher, 2002). No evidence exists for a sensitive period in the first few years of life for mastering skills that depend on extensive training, such as reading, musical performance, or gymnastics (Bruer, 1999). To the contrary, rushing early learning also harms the brain by overwhelming its neural circuits, thereby reducing the brain's sensitivity to the everyday experiences it needs for a healthy start in life.

Changing States of Arousal

Rapid brain growth means that the organization of sleep and wakefulness changes substantially between birth and 2 years, and fussiness and crying also decline. The newborn baby takes round-the-clock naps that total about 16 to 18 hours. Total sleep time declines slowly; the average 2-year-old still needs 12 to 13 hours. But periods of sleep and wakefulness become fewer and longer, and the sleep–wake pattern increasingly conforms to a night–day schedule. Most 6- to 9-month-olds take two daytime naps; by about 18 months, children generally need only one nap (Galland et al., 2012). Finally, between ages 3 and 5, napping subsides.

These changing arousal patterns are due to brain development, but they are also affected by cultural beliefs and practices and parents' needs (Super & Harkness, 2002). Dutch parents, for example, view sleep regularity as far more important than U.S. parents do. And whereas U.S. parents regard a predictable sleep schedule as emerging naturally from within the child, Dutch parents believe that a schedule must be imposed, or the baby's development might suffer (Super & Harkness, 2010; Super et al., 1996). At age 6 months, Dutch babies are put to bed earlier and sleep, on average, 2 hours more per day than their U.S. agemates.

Motivated by demanding work schedules and other needs, many Western parents try to get their babies to sleep through the night as early as 3 to 4 months by offering an evening feeding—a practice that may be at odds with young infants' neurological capacities. Not until

Cultural Influences

Cultural Variation in Infant Sleeping Arrangements

Western child-rearing advice from experts strongly encourages the nighttime separation of baby from parent. For example, the most recent edition of Benjamin Spock's *Baby and Child Care* recommends that babies sleep in their own room by 3 months of age, explaining, "By 6 months, a child who regularly sleeps in her parents' room may feel uneasy sleeping anywhere else" (Spock & Needlman, 2012, p. 62). And the American Academy of Pediatrics (2012b) has issued a controversial warning that parent–infant bedsharing may increase the risk of sudden infant death syndrome (SIDS).

Yet parent–infant "cosleeping" is the norm for approximately 90 percent of the world's population, in cultures as diverse as the Japanese, the rural Guatemalan Maya, the Inuit of northwestern Canada, and the !Kung of Botswana. Japanese and Korean children usually lie next to their mothers throughout infancy and early childhood, and many continue to sleep with a parent or other family member until adolescence (Takahashi, 1990; Yang & Hahn, 2002). Among the Maya, mother–infant bedsharing is interrupted only by the birth of a new baby, when the older child is moved next to the father or to another bed in the same room (Morelli et al., 1992). Bedsharing is also common in U.S. ethnic minority families (McKenna & Volpe, 2007). African-American children, for example, frequently fall asleep with their parents and remain with them for part or all of the night (Buswell & Spatz, 2007).

Cultural values strongly influence infant sleeping arrangements. In one study, researchers interviewed Guatemalan Mayan mothers and American middle-SES mothers about their sleeping practices. Mayan mothers stressed the importance of promoting an *interdependent self,* explaining that cosleeping builds a close parent–child bond, which is necessary for children to learn the ways of people around them. In contrast, American mothers emphasized an *independent self,* mentioning their desire to instill early autonomy, prevent bad habits, and protect their own privacy (Morelli et al., 1992).

Over the past two decades, cosleeping has increased in Western nations. An estimated 11 percent of U.S. infants routinely bedshare, and an additional 30 to 35 percent sometimes do (Buswell & Spatz, 2007; Colson et al., 2013). Proponents of the practice say that it helps infants sleep, makes breastfeeding more convenient, and provides valuable bonding time (McKenna & Volpe, 2007).

During the night, cosleeping babies breastfeed three times longer than infants who sleep alone. Because infants arouse to nurse more often when sleeping next to their mothers, some researchers believe that cosleeping may actually help safeguard babies at risk for SIDS. Consistent with this view, SIDS is rare in Asian cultures where cosleeping is widespread, including Cambodia, China, Japan, Korea, Thailand, and Vietnam (McKenna, 2002; McKenna & McDade, 2005). And contrary to popular belief, cosleeping does not reduce mothers' total sleep time, although they experience more brief awakenings, which permit them to check on their baby (Mao et al., 2004).

Infant sleeping practices affect other aspects of family life. For example, Mayan babies doze off in the midst of ongoing family activities and are carried to bed by their mothers. In contrast, for many North American parents, bedtime often requires a lengthy, elaborate ritual. Perhaps bedtime struggles, so common in Western homes but rare elsewhere in the world, are related to the stress young children feel when they must fall asleep without assistance (Latz, Wolf, & Lozoff, 1999).

Critics warn that bedsharing will promote emotional problems, especially excessive dependency. Yet a longitudinal study following children from the end of pregnancy through age 18 years showed that young people who had bedshared in the early years were no different from others in any aspect of adjustment (Okami, Weisner, & Olmstead, 2002). Another concern is that infants might become trapped under the parent's body or in soft bedding and suffocate. Parents who are obese or who use alcohol, tobacco, or illegal drugs do pose a serious risk

A Vietnamese mother and child sleep together—a practice common in their culture and around the globe. Hard wooden sleeping surfaces protect cosleeping children from entrapment in soft bedding.

to their sleeping babies, as does the use of quilts and comforters or an overly soft mattress (American Academy of Pediatrics, 2012b).

But with appropriate precautions, parents and infants can cosleep safely (Ball & Volpe, 2013). In cultures where cosleeping is widespread, parents and infants usually sleep with light covering on hard surfaces, such as firm mattresses, floor mats, and wooden planks, or infants sleep in a cradle or hammock next to the parents' bed (McKenna, 2001, 2002). And when sharing the same bed, infants typically lie on their back or side facing the mother—positions that promote frequent, easy communication between parent and baby and arousal if breathing is threatened.

Finally, breastfeeding mothers usually assume a distinctive sleeping posture. They face the infant, with knees drawn up under the baby's feet and arm above the baby's head. Besides facilitating feeding, the position prevents the infant from sliding down under covers or up under pillows (Ball, 2006). Because this posture is also seen in female great apes while sharing sleeping nests with their infants, researchers believe it may have evolved to enhance infant safety.

the middle of the first year is the secretion of *melatonin,* a hormone within the brain that promotes drowsiness, much greater at night than during the day (Sadeh, 1997).

Furthermore, as the Cultural Influences box above reveals, isolating infants to promote sleep is rare elsewhere in the world. When babies sleep with their parents, their average sleep period remains constant at three hours from 1 to 8 months of age. Only at the end of the first year, as REM sleep (the state that usually prompts waking) declines, do infants move in the direction of an adultlike sleep–wake schedule (Ficca et al., 1999).

Even after infants sleep through the night, they continue to wake occasionally. When babies begin to crawl and walk, they often show temporary periods of disrupted sleep (Scher, Epstein, & Tirosh, 2004). In studies carried out in Australia, Israel, and the United States, night wakings increased around 6 months and again between 1½ and 2 years and then declined (Armstrong, Quinn, & Dadds, 1994; Scher, Epstein, & Tirosh, 2004; Scher et al., 1995). As Chapter 7 will reveal, around the middle of the first year, infants are forming a clear-cut attachment to their familiar caregiver and begin protesting when he or she leaves. And the challenges of toddlerhood—the ability to range farther from the caregiver and increased awareness of the self as separate from others—often prompt anxiety, evident in disturbed sleep and clinginess. When parents offer comfort, these behaviors subside.

LOOK *and* **LISTEN**

Interview a parent of a baby about sleep challenges. What strategies has the parent tried to ease these difficulties? Are the techniques likely to be effective, in view of evidence on infant sleep development?

Ask Yourself

- **REVIEW** How do overproduction of synapses and synaptic pruning support infants' and children's ability to learn?

- **CONNECT** Explain how inappropriate stimulation— either too little or too much—can impair cognitive and emotional development in the early years.

- **APPLY** Which infant enrichment program would you choose: one that emphasizes gentle talking and touching and social games, or one that includes reading and number drills and classical music lessons? Explain.

- **REFLECT** What is your attitude toward parent–infant cosleeping? Is it influenced by your cultural background? Explain.

Influences on Early Physical Growth

5.4 Cite evidence indicating that heredity, nutrition, and parental affection contribute to early physical growth.

Physical growth, like other aspects of development, results from the continuous and complex interplay between genetic and environmental factors. Heredity, nutrition, relative freedom from disease, and emotional well-being all affect early physical growth.

Heredity

Because identical twins are much more alike in body size than fraternal twins, we know that heredity is important in physical growth (Estourgie-van Burk et al., 2006). When diet and health are adequate, height and rate of physical growth are largely determined by heredity. In fact, as long as negative environmental influences such as poor nutrition or illness are not severe, children and adolescents typically show *catch-up growth*—a return to a genetically determined growth path—once conditions improve. After her adoption, Grace grew rapidly until, at age 2, she was nearly average in size by Cambodian standards. Still, the health of the brain, the heart, the digestive system, and many other internal organs may be permanently compromised. (Recall the consequences of inadequate prenatal nutrition for long-term health, discussed on pages 111–112 in Chapter 3.)

Genetic makeup also affects body weight: The weights of adopted children correlate more strongly with those of their biological than of their adoptive parents (Kinnunen, Pietilainen, & Rissanen, 2006). At the same time, environment—in particular, nutrition—plays an especially important role.

Nutrition

Nutrition is especially crucial for development in the first two years because the baby's brain and body are growing so rapidly. Pound for pound, an infant's energy needs are at least twice those of an adult. Twenty-five percent of infants' total caloric intake is devoted to growth, and babies need extra calories to keep rapidly developing organs functioning properly (Meyer, 2009).

Applying What We Know

Reasons to Breastfeed

NUTRITIONAL AND HEALTH ADVANTAGES	EXPLANATION
Provides the correct balance of fat and protein	Compared with the milk of other mammals, human milk is higher in fat and lower in protein. This balance, as well as the unique proteins and fats contained in human milk, is ideal for a rapidly myelinating nervous system.
Ensures nutritional completeness	A mother who breastfeeds need not add other foods to her infant's diet until the baby is 6 months old. The milks of all mammals are low in iron, but the iron contained in breast milk is much more easily absorbed by the baby's system. Consequently, bottle-fed infants need iron-fortified formula.
Helps ensure healthy physical growth	One-year-old breastfed babies are leaner (have a higher percentage of muscle to fat), a growth pattern that persists through the preschool years and that is associated with a reduction in later overweight and obesity.
Protects against many diseases	Breastfeeding transfers antibodies and other infection-fighting agents from mother to baby and enhances functioning of the immune system. Compared with bottle-fed infants, breastfed babies have far fewer allergic reactions and respiratory and intestinal illnesses. Breast milk also has anti-inflammatory effects, which reduce the severity of illness symptoms. Breastfeeding in the first four months (especially when exclusive) is linked to lower blood cholesterol levels in adulthood and, thereby, may help prevent cardiovascular disease.
Protects against faulty jaw development and tooth decay	Sucking the mother's nipple instead of an artificial nipple helps avoid malocclusion, a condition in which the upper and lower jaws do not meet properly. It also protects against tooth decay due to sweet liquid remaining in the mouths of infants who fall asleep while sucking on a bottle.
Ensures digestibility	Because breastfed babies have a different kind of bacteria growing in their intestines than do bottle-fed infants, they rarely suffer from constipation or other gastrointestinal problems.
Smooths the transition to solid foods	Breastfed infants accept new solid foods more easily than do bottle-fed infants, perhaps because of their greater experience with a variety of flavors, which pass from the maternal diet into the mother's milk.

Sources: American Academy of Pediatrics, 2012a; Druet et al., 2012; Ip et al., 2009; Owen et al., 2008.

BREASTFEEDING VERSUS BOTTLE-FEEDING Babies not only need enough food but also the right kind of food. In early infancy, breast milk is ideally suited to their needs, and bottled formulas try to imitate it. Applying What We Know above summarizes major nutritional and health advantages of breastfeeding.

Because of these benefits, breastfed babies in poverty-stricken regions of the world are much less likely to be malnourished and 6 to 14 times more likely to survive the first year of life. The World Health Organization recommends breastfeeding until age 2 years, with solid foods added at 6 months. These practices, if widely followed, would save the lives of more than 800,000 infants annually (World Health Organization, 2012b). Even breastfeeding for just a few weeks offers some protection against respiratory and intestinal infections, which are devastating to young children in developing countries. Also, because a nursing mother is less likely to get pregnant, breastfeeding helps increase spacing among siblings, a major factor in reducing infant and childhood deaths in nations with widespread poverty. (Note, however, that breastfeeding is not a reliable method of birth control.)

Yet many mothers in the developing world do not know about these benefits. In Africa, the Middle East, and Latin America, most babies get some breastfeeding, but fewer than 40 percent are exclusively breastfed for the first six months, and one-third are fully weaned from the breast before 1 year (UNICEF, 2013a). In place of breast milk, mothers give their babies commercial formula or low-grade nutrients, such as rice water or highly diluted cow or goat milk. Contamination of these foods as a result of poor sanitation is common and often leads to illness and infant death. The United Nations has encouraged all hospitals and maternity units in developing countries to promote breastfeeding as long as mothers do not have viral or bacterial infections (such as HIV or tuberculosis) that can be transmitted to the baby. Today, most developing countries have banned the practice of giving free or subsidized formula to new mothers.

Partly as a result of the natural childbirth movement, breastfeeding has become more common in industrialized nations, especially among well-educated women. Today, 77 percent of American mothers begin breastfeeding after birth, but more than one-third stop by 6 months (Centers for Disease Control and Prevention, 2013a). And despite the health benefits of breast milk, only 50 percent of preterm infants are breastfed at hospital discharge. Breastfeeding a preterm baby presents special challenges, including maintaining a sufficient milk supply with artificial pumping until the baby is mature enough to suck at the breast and providing the infant with enough sucking experience to learn to feed successfully. Kangaroo care (see page 136 in Chapter 4) and the support of health professionals are helpful.

Breast milk is so easily digestible that a breastfed infant becomes hungry quite often—every 1½ to 2 hours, compared to every 3 or 4 hours for a bottle-fed baby. This makes breastfeeding inconvenient for many employed women. Not surprisingly, mothers who return to work sooner wean their babies from the breast earlier (McCarter-Spaulding, Lucas, & Gore, 2011; Smith & Forrester, 2013). But mothers who cannot be with their babies all the time can still combine breast- and bottle-feeding. The U.S. Department of Health and Human Services (2010a) advises exclusive breastfeeding for the first 6 months and inclusion of breast milk in the baby's diet until at least 1 year.

Women who do not breastfeed sometimes worry that they are depriving their baby of an experience essential for healthy psychological development. Yet breastfed and bottle-fed infants in industrialized nations do not differ in quality of the mother–infant relationship or in later emotional adjustment (Jansen, de Weerth, & Riksen-Walraven, 2008; Lind et al., 2014). Some studies report a slight advantage in intelligence test performance for children and adolescents who were breastfed, after controlling for many factors. Most, however, find no cognitive benefits (Der, Batty, & Deary, 2006).

ARE CHUBBY BABIES AT RISK FOR LATER OVERWEIGHT AND OBESITY?

From early infancy, Timmy was an enthusiastic eater who nursed vigorously and gained weight quickly. By 5 months, he began reaching for food on his parents' plates. Vanessa wondered: Was she overfeeding Timmy and increasing his chances of long-term overweight?

Most chubby babies thin out during toddlerhood and the preschool years, as weight gain slows and they become more active. Infants and toddlers can eat nutritious foods freely without risk of becoming overweight. But recent evidence does indicate a strengthening relationship between rapid weight gain in infancy and later obesity (Druet et al., 2012). The trend may be due to the rise in overweight and obesity among adults, who promote unhealthy eating habits in their young children. Interviews with 1,500 U.S. parents of 4- to 24-month-olds revealed that many routinely served older infants and toddlers french fries, pizza, candy, sugary fruit drinks, and soda. On average, infants consumed 20 percent and toddlers 30 percent more calories than they needed (Siega-Riz et al., 2010). At the same time, as many as one-fourth ate no fruits and one-third no vegetables.

How can parents prevent their infants from becoming overweight children and adults? One way is to breastfeed for the first six months, which is associated with slower weight gain over the first year, leaner body build through early childhood, and 10 to 20 percent reduced obesity risk in later life (Gunnarsdottir et al., 2010; Koletzko et al., 2013). Another strategy is for parents to

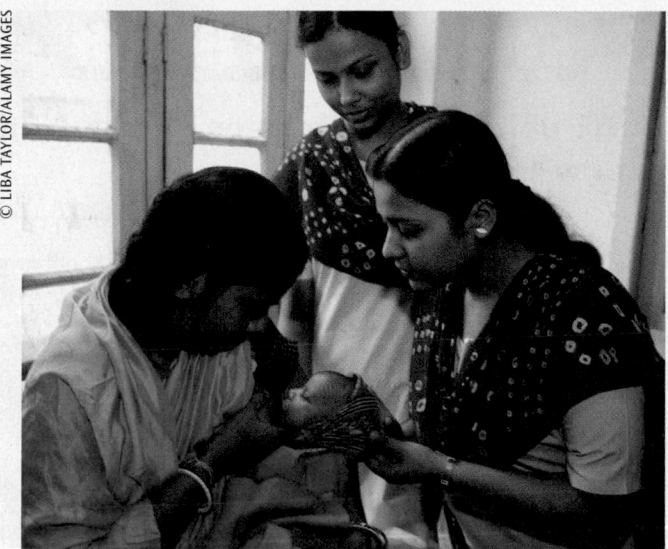

Midwives in India support a mother as she learns to breastfeed her infant. Breastfeeding is especially important in developing countries, where it helps protect babies against life-threatening infections and early death.

LOOK and LISTEN

Ask several parents of 1- to 2-year-olds to keep a diary of all the foods and drinks they offer their toddler over a weekend. How healthy are the toddlers' diets? Did any of the parents report heightened awareness of family nutrition as a result of the diary exercise?

A father supports his toddler's desire to feed himself while also modeling and encouraging healthy eating habits that protect against overweight and obesity.

Social Issues: Health

U.S. Public Policy Changes Improve Infant Feeding Practices in Low-Income Families

In a study in which researchers made periodic home visits to several hundred low-income first-time mothers and their babies, inappropriate feeding practices were pervasive. Rather than a mostly breast-milk diet for the first half-year, the majority of infants were fed formula. And more than 75 percent received solid foods and juices too soon—by age 3 months (Thompson & Bentley, 2013). Inappropriate feeding of solids and liquids in infancy is consistently associated with greater daily caloric intake and excessive weight gain during the first two years (Smith & Forrester, 2013).

The U.S. Special Supplemental Nutrition Program for Women, Infants, and Children (WIC) is a federally funded initiative that provides nutrition education and food to low-income mothers and to their children from birth to age 5. Though not reaching all families in need, WIC serves about half of U.S. infants—2 million annually, two-thirds of whom live in poverty (U.S. Department of Agriculture, 2014).

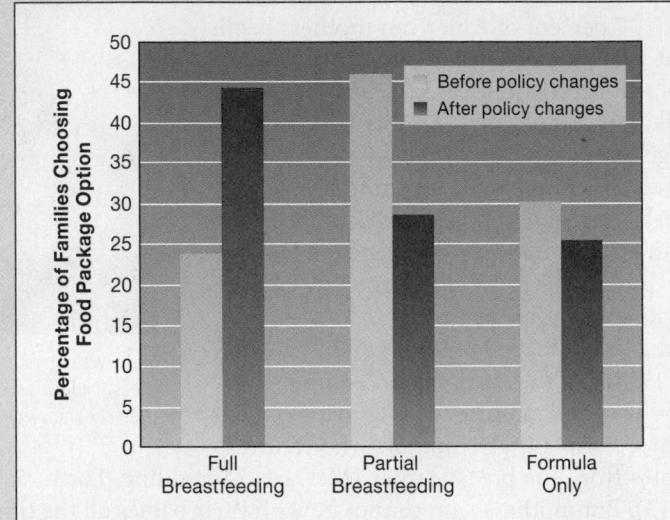

FIGURE 5.8 **Rates of breastfeeding by new mothers at WIC enrollment, as indicated by food package choice, before and after WIC policy changes.** Full breastfeeding nearly doubled after the policy changes, whereas partial breastfeeding and formula-only feeding declined. (Based on Whaley et al., 2012.)

A WIC counselor meets with breastfeeding mothers to provide nutrition education and enhanced food packages—incentives that increase the number of breastfed babies and the duration of breastfeeding.

To induce improvements in infant feeding practices, in 2009 WIC strengthened its breastfeeding counseling and educational materials for new mothers. It also offered mothers who breastfeed enhanced food packages for the first 12 months. A "fully breastfeeding package" includes no formula while providing the largest quantity and variety of healthy foods for the mother. A "partially breastfeeding package" includes some formula plus extra healthy foods for the mother, but less than in the fully breastfeeding package. A "formula only package" contains more formula for the baby but only a basic food package for the mother, limited to the first 6 months.

Are WIC's policy changes effective? To find out, researchers first confirmed that maternal food package choice is an accurate indicator of feeding practices at home (Whaley, Koleilat, & Jiang, 2012). Then they examined the distribution of the three types of food packages to 5,000 California families before and after the policy changes. As Figure 5.8 shows, following the new policies, enrollment in the fully breastfeeding option increased sharply—to double its former rate. In contrast, the partially breastfeeding and formula-only package options declined (Whaley et al., 2012). Furthermore, more mothers continued to select the fully breastfeeding packages when their babies reached ages 2 and 6 months, indicating that WIC incentives lengthened the duration of breastfeeding.

Full breastfeeding for the first half-year followed by a healthy infant diet is a WIC priority—part of a national early obesity prevention strategy. The findings just described are particularly impressive, given that the WIC policy changes coincided with the late-2000s recession and a rise in poverty, which is typically linked to reduced breastfeeding and increased unhealthy eating practices.

avoid giving babies foods loaded with sugar, salt, and saturated fats. As the Social Issues: Health box above illustrates, policy changes directed at low-income families, where breastfeeding rates are lowest and unhealthy feeding practices are highest, are a vital child health measure. And once toddlers learn to walk, climb, and run, parents can also provide plenty of opportunities for energetic play. Finally, as Chapter 11 will reveal, because excessive television viewing is linked to overweight in older children, parents should limit the time very young children spend in front of the TV.

Malnutrition

Osita is an Ethiopian 2-year-old whose mother has never had to worry about his gaining too much weight. When she weaned him at 1 year, he had little to eat besides starchy rice flour cakes. Soon his belly enlarged, his feet swelled, his hair fell out, and a rash appeared on his skin. His bright-eyed curiosity vanished, and he became irritable and listless.

In developing countries and war-torn areas where food resources are limited, malnutrition is widespread. Recent evidence indicates that about one-third of the world's children suffer from malnutrition before age 5 (World Health Organization, 2013b). The 8 percent who are severely affected suffer from two dietary diseases.

Marasmus is a wasted condition of the body caused by a diet low in all essential nutrients. It usually appears in the first year of life when a baby's mother is too malnourished to produce enough breast milk and bottle-feeding is also inadequate. Her starving baby becomes painfully thin and is in danger of dying.

Osita has **kwashiorkor,** caused by an unbalanced diet very low in protein. The disease usually strikes after weaning, between 1 and 3 years of age. It is common in regions where children get just enough calories from starchy foods but little protein. The child's body responds by breaking down its own protein reserves, which causes the swelling and other symptoms that Osita experienced.

Children who survive these extreme forms of malnutrition often grow to be smaller in all body dimensions and suffer from lasting damage to the brain, heart, liver, pancreas, and other organs (Müller & Krawinkel, 2005; Spoelstra et al., 2012). When their diets do improve, they tend to gain excessive weight (Black et al., 2013). A malnourished body protects itself by establishing a low basal metabolism rate, which may endure after nutrition improves. Also, malnutrition may disrupt appetite control centers in the brain, causing the child to overeat when food becomes plentiful.

Learning and behavior are also seriously affected. Animal evidence reveals that a deficient diet permanently reduces brain weight and alters the production of neurotransmitters in the brain—an effect that can disrupt all aspects of development (Bedi, 2003; Haller, 2005). Children who experienced marasmus or kwashiorkor show poor fine-motor coordination, have difficulty paying attention, often display conduct problems, and score low on intelligence tests into adulthood (Galler et al., 1990, 2012; Waber et al., 2014). They also display a more intense stress response to fear-arousing situations, perhaps caused by the constant, gnawing pain of hunger (Fernald & Grantham-McGregor, 1998).

Recall from our discussion of prenatal malnutrition in Chapter 3 that the passivity and irritability of malnourished children worsen the impact of poor diet. These behaviors may appear even when protein-calorie deprivation is only mild to moderate. They also accompany *iron-deficiency anemia,* a condition common among poverty-stricken infants and children that interferes with many central nervous system processes. Withdrawal and listlessness reduce the nutritionally deprived child's ability to pay attention, explore, and evoke sensitive caregiving from parents, whose lives are already disrupted by poverty and stressful living conditions (Corapci, Radan, & Lozoff, 2006; Grantham-McGregor & Ani, 2001). For this reason, interventions for malnourished children must improve the family situation as well as the child's nutrition.

Inadequate nutrition is not confined to developing countries. Because government-supported supplementary food programs do not reach all families in need, an estimated 22 percent of U.S. children suffer from *food insecurity*—uncertain access to enough food for a healthy, active life. Food insecurity is especially high among single-parent families (35 percent) and low-income ethnic minority families—for example, Hispanics and African Americans (23 and 25 percent, respectively) (U.S. Department of Agriculture, 2013b). Although few of these children have marasmus or kwashiorkor, their physical growth and ability to learn are still affected.

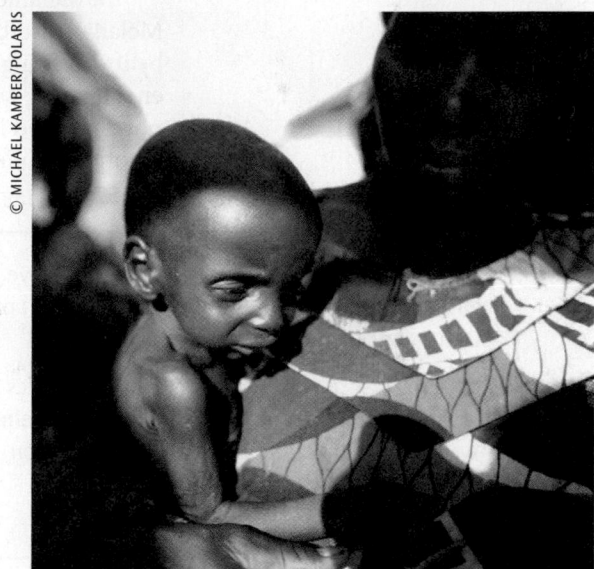

The baby on the top, of Niger, Africa, has marasmus, a wasted condition caused by a diet low in all essential nutrients. The swollen abdomen of the toddler on the bottom, also from Niger, is a symptom of kwashiorkor, which results from a diet very low in protein. If these children survive, they are likely to be growth stunted and to suffer from lasting organ damage as well as serious cognitive and emotional impairments.

Emotional Well-Being

We may not think of affection as necessary for healthy physical growth, but it is as vital as food. **Growth faltering** is a term applied to infants whose weight, height, and head circumference are substantially below age-related growth norms and who are withdrawn and apathetic (Black, 2005). In as many as half such cases, a disturbed parent–infant relationship contributes to this failure to grow normally.

Lana, an observant nurse at a public health clinic, became concerned about 8-month-old Melanie, who was 3 pounds lighter than she had been at her last checkup. Lana noted that Melanie kept her eyes on nearby adults, anxiously watching their every move, and rarely smiled at her mother. During feeding and diaper changing, Melanie's mother sometimes appeared depressed and distant, at other times impatient and hostile. Melanie tried to protect herself by tracking her mother's whereabouts and, when she approached, avoiding her gaze.

Often an unhappy marriage and parental psychological disturbance contribute to these serious caregiving problems. And most of the time, the baby is irritable and displays abnormal feeding behaviors, such as poor sucking or vomiting, that both disrupt growth and lead parents to feel anxious and helpless, which stress the parent–infant relationship further (Batchelor, 2008; Linscheid, Budd, & Rasnake, 2005).

In Melanie's case, her alcoholic father was out of work, and her parents argued constantly. Melanie's mother had little energy to meet Melanie's psychological needs. When treated early, by intervening in infant feeding problems, helping parents with their own life challenges, and encouraging sensitive caregiving, babies show quick catch-up growth. But if the disorder is not corrected in infancy, most of these children remain small and show lasting cognitive and emotional difficulties (Black et al., 2007; Crookston et al., 2013).

Ask Yourself

- **REVIEW** Explain why breastfeeding can have lifelong consequences for the development of babies born in poverty-stricken regions of the world.

- **CONNECT** How are bidirectional influences between parent and child involved in the impact of malnutrition on psychological development? After her adoption, how did those influences change for Grace?

- **APPLY** Eight-month-old Shaun is well below average in height and painfully thin. He cries during feedings and is listless and irritable. Shaun's single mother feels overwhelmed and discouraged. Why do Shaun and his mother need intervention quickly? What should health professionals do?

- **REFLECT** Imagine that you are the parent of a newborn baby. Describe feeding practices you would use, and ones you would avoid, to prevent overweight and obesity.

5.5 Describe infant learning capacities, the conditions under which they occur, and the unique value of each.

Learning Capacities

Learning refers to changes in behavior as the result of experience. Babies come into the world with built-in learning capacities that permit them to profit from experience immediately. Infants are capable of two basic forms of learning, which we introduced in Chapter 1: classical and operant conditioning. They also learn through their natural preference for novel stimulation. Finally, shortly after birth, babies learn by observing others; they can imitate the facial expressions and gestures of adults.

Classical Conditioning

Newborn reflexes, discussed in Chapter 4, make **classical conditioning** possible in the young infant. In this form of learning, a neutral stimulus is paired with a stimulus that leads to a reflexive response. Once the baby's nervous system makes the connection between the two stimuli, the neutral stimulus produces the behavior by itself. Classical conditioning helps infants recognize which events usually occur together in the everyday world, so they can anticipate what is about to happen next. As a result, the environment becomes more orderly and predictable. Let's take a closer look at the steps of classical conditioning.

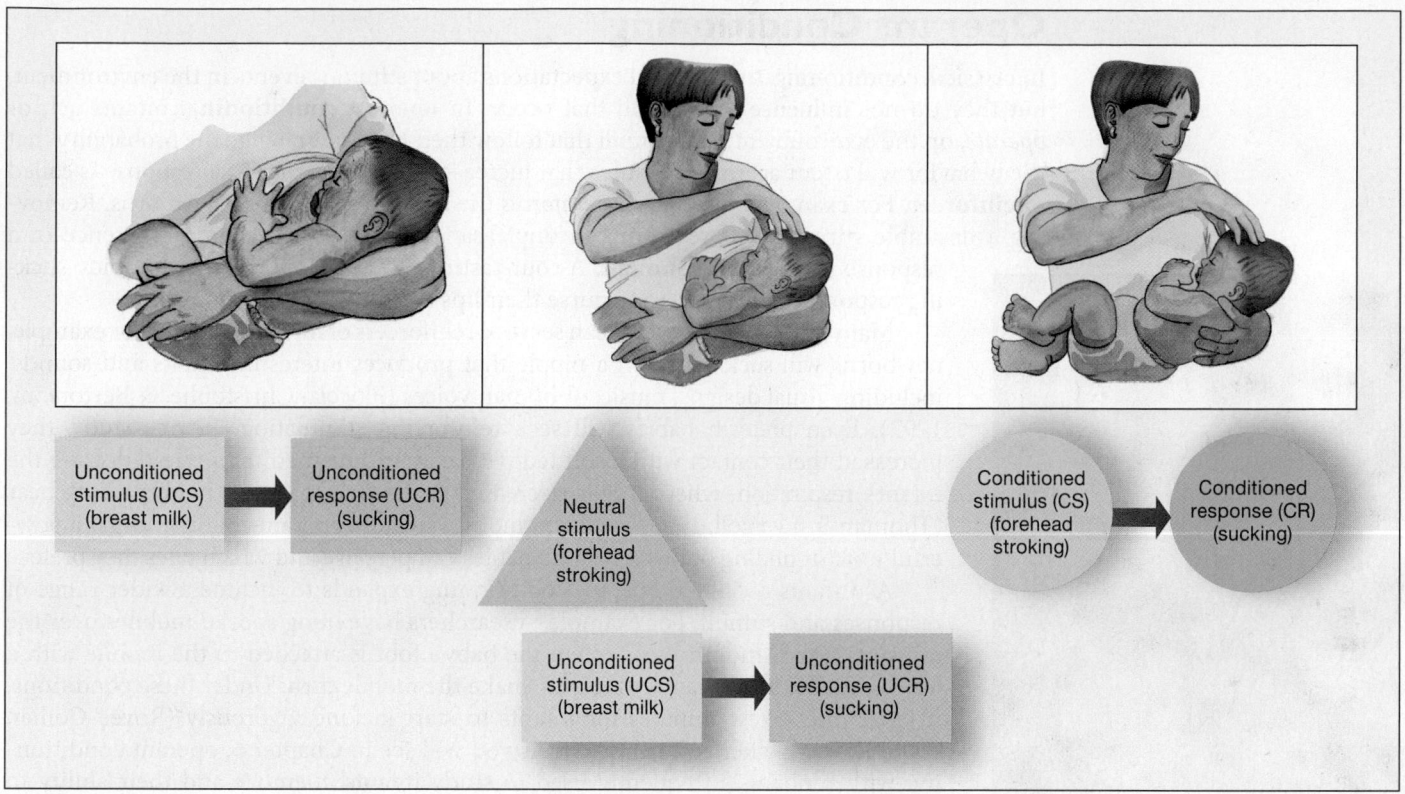

FIGURE 5.9   The steps of classical conditioning. This example shows how a mother classically conditioned her baby to make sucking movements by stroking the baby's forehead at the beginning of feedings.

As Carolyn settled down in the rocking chair to nurse Caitlin, she often stroked Caitlin's forehead. Soon Carolyn noticed that each time she did this, Caitlin made active sucking movements. Caitlin had been classically conditioned. Figure 5.9 shows how it happened:

1. Before learning takes place, an **unconditioned stimulus (UCS)** must consistently produce a *reflexive,* or **unconditioned, response (UCR).** In Caitlin's case, sweet breast milk (UCS) resulted in sucking (UCR).
2. To produce learning, a *neutral stimulus* that does not lead to the reflex is presented just before, or at about the same time as, the UCS. Carolyn stroked Caitlin's forehead as each nursing period began. The stroking (neutral stimulus) was paired with the taste of milk (UCS).
3. If learning has occurred, the neutral stimulus alone produces a response similar to the reflexive response. The neutral stimulus is then called a **conditioned stimulus (CS),** and the response it elicits is called a **conditioned response (CR).** We know that Caitlin has been classically conditioned because stroking her forehead outside the feeding situation (CS) results in sucking (CR).

If the CS is presented alone enough times, without being paired with the UCS, the CR will no longer occur, an outcome called *extinction.* In other words, if Carolyn repeatedly strokes Caitlin's forehead without feeding her, Caitlin will gradually stop sucking in response to stroking.

Young infants can be classically conditioned most easily when the association between two stimuli has survival value. In the example just described, learning which stimuli regularly accompany feeding improves the infant's ability to get food and survive (Blass, Ganchrow, & Steiner, 1984).

In contrast, some responses, such as fear, are very difficult to classically condition in young babies. Until infants have the motor skills to escape unpleasant events, they have no biological need to form these associations. After age 6 months, however, fear is easy to condition. **TAKE A MOMENT...** Return to Chapter 1, page 17, to review John Watson's well-known experiment in which he conditioned Little Albert to withdraw and cry at the sight of a furry white rat. Then test your knowledge of classical conditioning by identifying the UCS, UCR, CS, and CR in Watson's study.

Operant Conditioning

In classical conditioning, babies build expectations about stimulus events in the environment, but they do not influence the stimuli that occur. In **operant conditioning,** infants act, or *operate,* on the environment, and stimuli that follow their behavior change the probability that the behavior will occur again. A stimulus that increases the occurrence of a response is called a **reinforcer.** For example, sweet liquid *reinforces* the sucking response in newborns. Removing a desirable stimulus or presenting an unpleasant one to decrease the occurrence of a response is called **punishment.** A sour-tasting fluid *punishes* newborn babies' sucking response, causing them to purse their lips and stop sucking entirely.

As this baby and father imitate each other's facial expressions, the behavior of each reinforces the other, sustaining their pleasurable interaction.

Many stimuli besides food can serve as reinforcers of infant behavior. For example, newborns will suck faster on a nipple that produces interesting sights and sounds, including visual designs, music, or human voices (Floccia, Christophe, & Bertoncini, 1997). Even preterm babies will seek reinforcing stimulation. In one study, they increased their contact with a soft teddy bear that "breathed" at a rate reflecting the infant's respiration, whereas they decreased their contact with a nonbreathing bear (Thoman & Ingersoll, 1993). As these findings suggest, operant conditioning is a powerful tool for finding out what stimuli babies can perceive and which ones they prefer.

As infants get older, operant conditioning expands to include a wider range of responses and stimuli. For example, researchers have hung special mobiles over the cribs of 2- to 6-month-olds. When the baby's foot is attached to the mobile with a long cord, the infant can, by kicking, make the mobile turn. Under these conditions, it takes only a few minutes for infants to start kicking vigorously (Rovee-Collier, 1999; Rovee-Collier & Barr, 2001). As you will see in Chapter 6, operant conditioning with mobiles is frequently used to study infants' memory and their ability to group similar stimuli into categories. Once babies learn the kicking response, researchers see how long and under what conditions they retain it when exposed again to the original mobile or to mobiles with varying features.

Operant conditioning also plays a vital role in the formation of social relationships. As the baby gazes into the adult's eyes, the adult looks and smiles back, and then the infant looks and smiles again. As the behavior of each partner reinforces the other, both continue their pleasurable interaction. In Chapter 7, we will see that this contingent responsiveness contributes to the development of infant–caregiver attachment.

Habituation

At birth, the human brain is set up to be attracted to novelty. Infants tend to respond more strongly to a new element that has entered their environment, an inclination that ensures that they will continually add to their knowledge base. **Habituation** refers to a gradual reduction in the strength of a response due to repetitive stimulation. Time spent looking at the stimulus, heart rate, respiration rate, and brain activity may all decline, indicating a loss of interest. Once this has occurred, a new stimulus—a change in the environment—causes responsiveness to return to a high level, an increase called **recovery.** For example, when you walk through a familiar space, you notice things that are new and different—a recently hung picture on the wall or a piece of furniture that has been moved. Habituation and recovery promote learning by focusing our attention on those aspects of the environment we know least about.

Researchers studying infants' understanding of the world rely on habituation and recovery more than any other learning capacity. For example, a baby who first *habituates* to a visual pattern (a photo of a baby) and then *recovers* to a new one (a photo of a bald man) appears to remember the first stimulus and perceive the second one as new and different from it. This method of studying infant perception and cognition, illustrated in Figure 5.10, can be used with newborns, including preterm infants (Kavšek & Bornstein, 2010). It has even been used to study the fetus's sensitivity to external stimuli in the third trimester of pregnancy—for example, by measuring changes in fetal heart rate or brain waves when various repeated sounds are presented, followed by a different sound (see page 100 in Chapter 3).

Recovery to a new stimulus, or *novelty preference*, assesses infants' *recent memory*. **TAKE A MOMENT...** Think about what happens when you return to a place you have not seen for a long time. Instead of attending to novelty, you are likely to focus on aspects that are familiar: "I recognize that—I've been here before!" Like adults, infants shift from a novelty preference to a *familiarity preference* as more time intervenes between habituation and test phases in research. That is, babies recover to the familiar stimulus rather than to a novel stimulus (see Figure 5.10) (Colombo, Brez, & Curtindale, 2013; Courage & Howe, 1998; Flom & Bahrick, 2010; Richmond, Colombo, & Hayne, 2007). By focusing on that shift, researchers can also use habituation to assess *remote memory*, or memory for stimuli to which infants were exposed weeks or months earlier.

With age, babies habituate and recover to stimuli more quickly, indicating that they process information more efficiently. Habituation and recovery have been used to assess a wide range of infant perceptual and cognitive capacities—speech perception, musical and visual pattern perception, object perception, categorization, and knowledge of the social world. But despite the strengths of habituation research, its findings are not clear-cut. When looking, sucking, heart rate, or brain activity declines and recovers, what babies actually know about the stimuli to which they responded is uncertain. We will return to this difficulty in Chapter 6.

Imitation

Babies come into the world with a primitive ability to learn through **imitation**—by copying the behavior of another person. For example, Figure 5.11 on page 180 shows a human newborn imitating two adult facial expressions (Meltzoff & Moore, 1977). The newborn's capacity to imitate extends to certain gestures, such as head and index-finger movements, and has been demonstrated in many eth-nic groups and cultures (Meltzoff & Kuhl, 1994; Nagy et al., 2005). As the figure reveals, even newborn primates, including chimpanzees (our closest evolutionary relatives), imitate some behaviors (Ferrari et al., 2006; Myowa-Yamakoshi et al., 2004).

Nevertheless, some studies have failed to reproduce the human findings (see, for example, Anisfeld, 2005). And because newborn mouth and tongue movements occur with increased frequency to almost any arousing change in stimulation (such as lively music or flashing lights), some researchers argue that certain newborn "imitative" responses are actually mouthing—a common early exploratory response to interesting stimuli (Jones, 2009). Furthermore, imita-tion is harder to induce in babies 2 to 3 months old than just after birth. Therefore, skeptics believe that the newborn imitative response is little more than an automatic response that declines with age, much like a reflex (Heyes, 2005).

Others claim that newborns imitate a variety of facial expressions and head movements with effort and determination, even after short delays—when the adult is no longer demon-strating the behavior (Hayne, 2002; Meltzoff & Moore, 1999; Paukner, Ferrari, & Suomi, 2011). Furthermore, these investigators argue that imitation—unlike reflexes—does not decline. Rather, they claim, human babies several months old often do not imitate an adult's behavior right away because they first try to play familiar social games—mutual gazing, cooing, smil-ing, and waving their arms. But when an adult models a gesture repeatedly, older human infants soon get down to business and imitate (Meltzoff & Moore, 1994). Similarly, imitation declines in baby chimps around 9 weeks of age, when mother–baby mutual gazing and other face-to-face exchanges increase.

According to Andrew Meltzoff, newborns imitate much as older children and adults do—by actively trying to match body movements they *see* with ones they *feel* themselves make

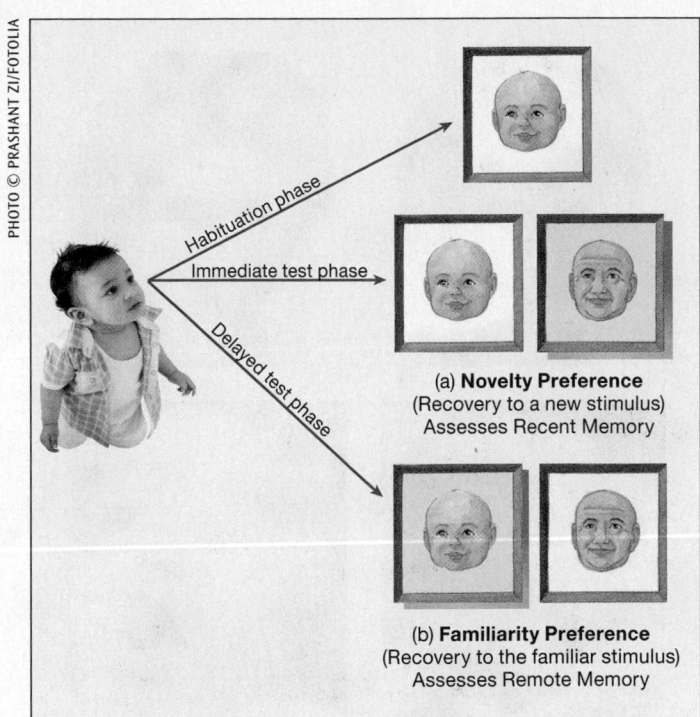

PHOTO © PRASHANT ZI/FOTOLIA

(a) Novelty Preference
(Recovery to a new stimulus)
Assesses Recent Memory

(b) Familiarity Preference
(Recovery to the familiar stimulus)
Assesses Remote Memory

FIGURE 5.10 **Using habituation to study infant perception and cognition.** In the habituation phase, infants view a photo of a baby until their looking declines. In the test phase, infants are again shown the baby photo, but this time it appears alongside a photo of a bald-headed man. (a) When the test phase occurs soon after the habituation phase (within minutes, hours, or days, depending on the age of the infants), participants who remember the baby face and distinguish it from the man's face show a *novelty preference;* they recover to (spend more time looking at) the new stimulus. (b) When the test phase is delayed for weeks or months, infants who continue to remember the baby face shift to a *familiarity preference;* they recover to the familiar baby face rather than to the novel man's face.

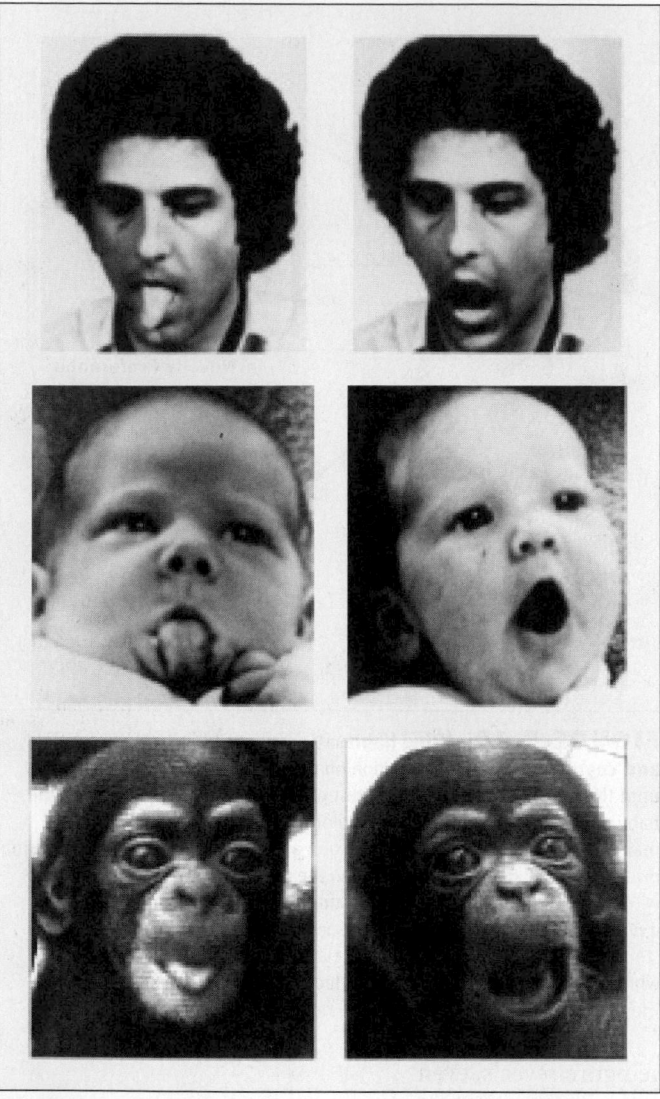

FIGURE 5.11 Imitation by human and chimpanzee newborns. The human infants in the middle row imitating (left) tongue protrusion and (right) mouth opening are 2 to 3 weeks old. The chimpanzee imitating both facial expressions is 2 weeks old. (From A. N. Meltzoff & M. K. Moore, 1977, "Imitation of Facial and Manual Gestures by Human Neonates," *Science, 198,* p. 75. Copyright © 1977 by AAAS. Reprinted by permission of the American Association for the Advancement of Science conveyed through Copyright Clearance Center, Inc., and Dr. Andrew Meltzoff. And from M. Myowa-Yamakoshi et al., 2004, "Imitation in Neonatal Chimpanzees [Pan Troglodytes]." *Developmental Science, 7,* p. 440. Copyright © 2004 by John Wiley and Sons. Reprinted with permission of John Wiley and Sons conveyed through Copyright Clearance Center, Inc.)

(Meltzoff, 2007). Later we will encounter evidence that young babies are remarkably adept at coordinating information across sensory systems.

Scientists have identified specialized cells in motor areas of the cerebral cortex in primates—called **mirror neurons**—that may underlie early imitative capacities (Ferrari & Coudé, 2011). Mirror neurons fire identically when a primate hears or sees an action and when it carries out that action on its own (Rizzolatti & Craighero, 2004). Humans have especially elaborate neural mirroring systems, which enable us to observe another person's behavior (such as smiling or throwing a ball) while simulating the behavior in our own brain. These systems are believed to be the biological basis of a variety of interrelated, complex social abilities, including imitation, empathic sharing of emotions, and understanding others' intentions (Iacoboni, 2009; Schulte-Ruther et al., 2007).

Brain-imaging findings support functioning neural mirroring systems in human infants as early as 6 months of age. Using NIRS, researchers found that the same motor areas of the cerebral cortex were activated in 6-month-olds and in adults when they observed a model engage in a behavior that could be imitated (tapping a box to make a toy pop out) as when they themselves engaged in the motor action (Shimada & Hiraki, 2006). In contrast, when infants and adults observed an object that appeared to move on its own, without human intervention (a ball hanging from the ceiling on a string, swinging like a pendulum), motor areas were not activated.

Still, Meltzoff's view of newborn imitation as a flexible, voluntary capacity remains controversial. Some critics contend that babies learn to imitate gradually through rich social experiences (Ray & Heyes, 2011). And even researchers who believe that newborns can imitate agree that many opportunities to see oneself act, to watch others' responses, and to engage in imitative games with caregivers are required for infants to become proficient imitators (Marshall & Meltzoff, 2011). Consistent with this view, human neural mirroring systems, though possibly functional at birth, undergo an extended period of development (Ferrari et al., 2013; Heyes, 2010). And as we will see in Chapter 6, the capacity to imitate expands greatly over the first two years.

However limited it is at birth, imitation is a powerful means of learning. Using imitation, infants explore their social world, learning from other people. As they notice similarities between their own actions and those of others, they experience other people as "like me" and learn about themselves (Meltzoff, 2007). By tapping into infants' ability to imitate, adults can get infants to exhibit desirable behaviors. Finally, caregivers take great pleasure in a baby who participates in imitative exchanges—a capacity that strengthens the parent–infant bond.

Ask Yourself

● **REVIEW** Provide an example of classical conditioning, of operant conditioning, and of habituation/recovery in young infants. Why is each type of learning useful?

● **CONNECT** Which learning capacities contribute to an infant's first social relationships? Explain, providing examples.

● **APPLY** Nine-month-old Byron has a toy with large, colored push buttons on it. Each time he pushes a button, he hears a nursery tune. Which learning capacity is the manufacturer of this toy taking advantage of? What can Byron's play with the toy reveal about his perception of sound patterns?

Motor Development

5.6 Discuss the general course of motor development during the first two years, along with factors that influence it.

Carolyn, Monica, and Vanessa each kept a baby book, filled with proud notations about when their children held up their heads, reached for objects, sat by themselves, and walked alone. Parents are understandably excited about these new motor skills, which allow babies to master their bodies and the environment in new ways. For example, sitting upright gives infants a new perspective on the world. Reaching permits babies to find out about objects by acting on them. And when infants can move on their own, their opportunities for exploration multiply.

Babies' motor achievements have a powerful effect on their social relationships. When Caitlin crawled at 7½ months, Carolyn and David began to restrict her movements by saying no and expressing mild impatience. When she walked three days after her first birthday, the first "testing of wills" occurred (Biringen et al., 1995). Despite her mother's warnings, she sometimes pulled items from shelves that were off limits. "I said, 'Don't do that!'" Carolyn would repeat firmly, taking Caitlin's hand and redirecting her attention.

At the same time, newly walking babies more actively attend to and initiate social interaction (Clearfield, 2011; Karasik et al., 2011). Caitlin frequently toddled over to her parents to express a greeting, give a hug, or show them an object of interest. Carolyn and David, in turn, increased their verbal responsiveness, expressions of affection, and playful activities. Caitlin's delight as she worked on new motor skills triggered pleasurable reactions in others, which encouraged her efforts further (Mayes & Zigler, 1992). Motor, social, cognitive, and language competencies developed together and supported one another.

The Sequence of Motor Development

Gross-motor development refers to control over actions that help infants get around in the environment, such as crawling, standing, and walking. *Fine-motor development* has to do with smaller movements, such as reaching and grasping. Table 5.2 on page 182 shows the average ages at which U.S. infants and toddlers achieve a variety of gross- and fine-motor skills. It also presents the age range during which most babies accomplish each skill, indicating large individual differences in *rate* of motor progress. Also, a baby who is a late reacher will not necessarily be a late crawler or walker. We would be concerned about a child's development only if many motor skills were seriously delayed.

Historically, researchers assumed that the motor milestones listed in Table 5.2 are separate, innate abilities that emerge in a fixed sequence governed by a built-in maturational timetable. This view has long been discredited. Rather, motor skills are interrelated: Each is a product of earlier motor attainments and a contributor to new ones. And children acquire motor skills in highly individual ways. For example, before her adoption, Grace spent most of her days lying in a hammock. Because she was rarely placed on her tummy and on firm surfaces that enabled her to move on her own, she did not try to crawl. As a result, she pulled to a stand and walked before she crawled! Babies display such skills as rolling, sitting, crawling, and walking in diverse orders rather than in the sequence implied by motor norms (Adolph, Karasik, & Tamis-LeMonda, 2010).

Many influences—both internal and external to the child—join together to support the vast transformations in motor competencies of the first two years. The *dynamic systems perspective,* introduced in Chapter 1 (see pages 29–30), helps us understand how motor development takes place.

Motor Skills as Dynamic Systems

According to the **dynamic systems theory of motor development,** mastery of motor skills involves acquiring increasingly *complex systems of action.* When motor skills work as a system, separate abilities blend together, each cooperating with others to produce more effective ways of exploring and controlling the environment. For example, control of the head and upper chest combine into sitting with support. Kicking, rocking on all fours, and reaching combine

TABLE 5.2	Gross- and Fine-Motor Development in the First Two Years	
MOTOR SKILL	**AVERAGE AGE ACHIEVED**	**AGE RANGE IN WHICH 90 PERCENT OF INFANTS ACHIEVE THE SKILL**
When held upright, holds head erect and steady	6 weeks	3 weeks–4 months
When prone, lifts self by arms	2 months	3 weeks–4 months
Rolls from side to back	2 months	3 weeks–5 months
Grasps cube	3 months, 3 weeks	2–7 months
Rolls from back to side	4½ months	2–7 months
Sits alone	7 months	5–9 months
Crawls	7 months	5–11 months
Pulls to stand	8 months	5–12 months
Plays pat-a-cake	9 months, 3 weeks	7–15 months
Stands alone	11 months	9–16 months
Walks alone	11 months, 3 weeks	9–17 months
Builds tower of two cubes	11 months, 3 weeks	10–19 months
Scribbles vigorously	14 months	10–21 months
Walks up stairs with help	16 months	12–23 months
Jumps in place	23 months, 2 weeks	17–30 months
Walks on tiptoe	25 months	16–30 months

Note: These milestones represent overall age trends. Individual differences exist in the precise age at which each milestone is attained.
Sources: Bayley, 1969, 1993, 2005.

© LAURA DWIGHT PHOTOGRAPHY

© LAURA DWIGHT PHOTOGRAPHY

© BSIP SA/ALAMY

to become crawling. Then crawling, standing, and stepping are united into walking (Adolph & Berger, 2006; Thelen & Smith, 1998).

Each new skill is a joint product of the following factors: (1) central nervous system development, (2) the body's movement capacities, (3) the goals the child has in mind, and (4) environmental supports for the skill. Change in any element makes the system less stable, and the child starts to explore and select new, more effective motor patterns. The factors that induce change vary with age. In the early weeks of life, brain and body growth are especially important as infants achieve control over the head, shoulders, and upper torso. Later, the baby's goals (getting a toy or crossing the room) and environmental supports (parental encouragement, objects in the infants' everyday setting) play a greater role.

The broader physical environment also profoundly influences motor skills. Infants with stairs in their home learn to crawl up stairs at an earlier age and also more readily master a back-descent strategy—the safest but also the most challenging position because the baby must turn around at the top, give up visual guidance of her goal, and crawl backward (Berger, Theuring, & Adolph, 2007). And if children were reared on the moon with its reduced gravity, they would prefer jumping to walking or running!

When a skill is first acquired, infants must refine it. For example, in trying to crawl, Caitlin often collapsed on her tummy and moved backward. Soon she figured out how to propel herself forward by alternately pulling with her arms and pushing with her feet, "belly-crawling" in various ways for several weeks. As they attempt a new skill, most babies move back and forth between its presence and absence: An infant might roll over, sit, crawl, or take a few steps but not do so again until the following week. And related, previously mastered skills often become less secure. As the novice walker experiments with balancing the body vertically over two small moving feet, balance during sitting may become temporarily less stable (Chen et al.,

LOOK and LISTEN

Spend an hour observing a newly crawling or walking baby. Note the goals that motivate the baby to move, along with the baby's effort and motor experimentation. Describe parenting behaviors and features of the environment that promote mastery of the skill.

2007). This variability is evidence of loss of stability in the system—in dynamic systems theory, a necessary transition between a less mature and a more mature stable state.

Motor mastery involves intense practice. In learning to walk, for example, toddlers practice six or more hours a day, traveling the length of 29 football fields! They fall, on average, 32 times per hour but rarely cry, returning to motion within a few seconds (Adolph et al., 2012). Gradually their small, unsteady steps change to a longer stride, their feet move closer together, their toes point to the front, and their legs become symmetrically coordinated (Adolph, Vereijken, & Shrout, 2003). As movements are repeated thousands of times, they promote new synaptic connections in the brain that govern motor patterns.

In tackling challenging motor tasks, babies are steadfast problem solvers, taking into account multiple sources of information. They explore ways of adapting to varied surfaces and openings, such as sliding down a steep slope and turning sideways to fit through a narrow doorway (Franchak & Adolph, 2012; Gill, Adolph, & Vereijken, 2009). And when conditions are uncertain—for instance, a ledge that may not be passable—toddlers are more likely to back off when the penalty for error is high (a fall). In these situations, they also place greater weight on caregivers' advice (Adolph et al., 2010). If their mother says "go," they usually proceed; if she says "no," they avoid.

Dynamic systems theory shows us why motor development cannot be genetically determined. Because it is motivated by exploration and the desire to master new tasks and varies with context, heredity can map it out only at a general level. Rather than being *hardwired* into the nervous system, motor behaviors are *softly assembled* from multiple components, allowing for different paths to the same motor skill (Spencer, Perone, & Buss, 2011; Thelen & Smith, 2006).

Dynamic Motor Systems in Action

To find out how infants acquire motor capacities, researchers conduct microgenetic studies (see Chapter 1, page 44), following babies from their first attempts at a skill until it becomes smooth and effortless. Using this strategy, James Galloway and Esther Thelen (2004) held sounding toys alternately in front of infants' hands and feet, from the time they first showed interest until they engaged in well-coordinated reaching and grasping. As Figure 5.12 illustrates, the infants violated the normative sequence of arm and hand control preceding leg and foot control, shown in Table 5.2. They first explored the toys with their feet—as early as 8 weeks of age, at least a month before reaching with their hands!

Why did babies reach "feet first"? Because the hip joint constrains the legs to move less freely than the shoulder joint constrains the arms, infants could more easily control their leg movements. Consequently, foot reaching required far less practice than hand reaching. As these findings confirm, rather than following a strict, predetermined pattern, the order in which motor skills develop depends on the anatomy of the body part being used, the surrounding environment, and the baby's efforts.

Furthermore, in building a more effective dynamic system, babies often use advances in one motor skill to support advances in others. For example, beginning to walk frees the hands for carrying, and new walkers like to fetch distant objects and transport them—often just for the fun of carrying but also to share with their caregivers (Karasik, Tamis-LeMonda, & Adolph, 2011). Observations of new walkers reveal that, surprisingly, they fall less often when carrying objects than when their hands are empty (Karasik et al., 2012). Even though combining walking with carrying is a more attention-demanding task, toddlers integrate object carrying into their emerging "walking system," using it to improve their balance (see Figure 5.13 on page 184).

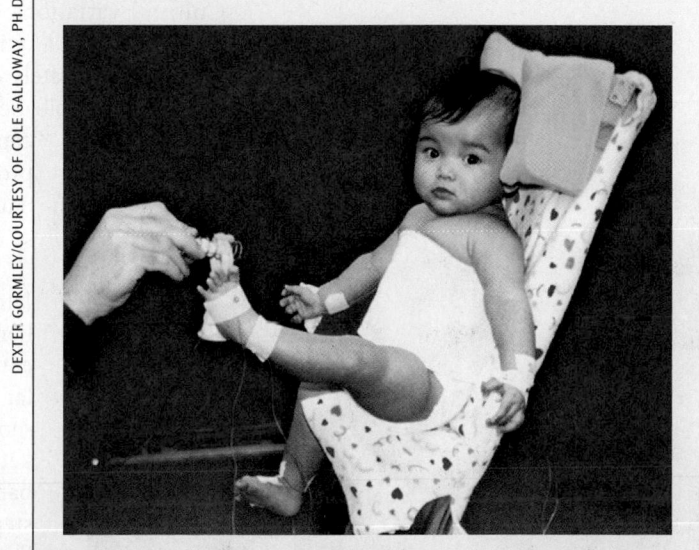

DEXTER GORMLEY/COURTESY OF COLE GALLOWAY, PH.D.

FIGURE 5.12 Reaching "feet first." When sounding toys were held in front of babies' hands and feet, they reached with their feet as early as 8 weeks of age, a month or more before they reached with their hands. This 2½-month-old skillfully explores an object with her foot.

FIGURE 5.13 **New walkers fall less often when carrying objects.** *Left:* When toddlers are first beginning to walk, carrying objects helps them focus attention and steady their balance. *Right:* An empty-handed new walker easily tips over.

Cultural Variations in Motor Development

Cross-cultural research further illustrates how early movement opportunities and a stimulating environment contribute to motor development. Half a century ago, Wayne Dennis (1960) observed infants in Iranian orphanages who were deprived of the tantalizing surroundings that induce infants to acquire motor skills. These babies spent their days lying on their backs in cribs, without toys to play with—conditions far worse than Grace experienced lying in a hammock in her Cambodian home. As a result, most did not move on their own until after 2 years of age. When they finally did move, the constant experience of lying on their backs led them to scoot in a sitting position rather than crawl on their hands and knees. Because babies who scoot come up against furniture with their feet (not their hands), they are far less likely to pull themselves to a standing position in preparation for walking. Indeed, by 3 to 4 years of age, only 15 percent of the Iranian orphans were walking alone.

Cultural variations in infant-rearing practices also affect motor development. **TAKE A MOMENT...** Take a quick survey of several parents you know: Should sitting, crawling, and walking be deliberately encouraged? Answers vary widely from culture to culture. Japanese mothers, for example, believe such efforts are unnecessary (Seymour, 1999). Among the Zinacanteco Indians of southern Mexico and the Gusii of Kenya, rapid motor progress is actively discouraged. Babies who walk before they know enough to keep away from cooking fires and weaving looms are viewed as dangerous to themselves and disruptive to others (Greenfield, 1992).

In contrast, among the Kipsigis of Kenya and the West Indians of Jamaica, babies hold their heads up, sit alone, and walk considerably earlier than North American infants. In both societies, parents emphasize early motor maturity, practicing formal exercises to stimulate particular skills (Adolph, Karasik, & Tamis-LeMonda, 2010). In the first few months, babies are seated in holes dug in the ground, with rolled blankets to keep them upright. Walking is promoted by frequently standing babies in adults' laps, bouncing them on their feet, and exercising the stepping reflex (see page 142 in Chapter 4) (Hopkins & Westra, 1988; Super, 1981). As parents in these cultures support babies in upright postures and rarely put them down on the floor, their infants usually skip crawling—a motor skill regarded as crucial in Western nations!

Finally, because it decreases exposure to "tummy time," the current Western practice of having babies sleep on their backs to protect them from SIDS (see page 145) delays gross-motor milestones of rolling,

The West Indians of Jamaica believe that exercise helps infants grow up strong and physically attractive. This mother "walks" her baby up her body—an activity that contributes to earlier mastery of walking.

sitting, and crawling (Scrutton, 2005). Regularly exposing infants to the tummy-lying position during waking hours prevents these delays.

Fine-Motor Development: Reaching and Grasping

Of all motor skills, reaching may play the greatest role in infant cognitive development. By grasping things, turning them over, and seeing what happens when they are released, infants learn a great deal about the sights, sounds, and feel of objects.

Reaching and grasping, like many other motor skills, start out as gross, diffuse activity and move toward mastery of fine movements. Figure 5.14 illustrates some milestones of reaching over the first nine months. Newborns will actively work to bring their hands into their field of vision: In a dimly lit room, they keep their hand within a narrow beam of light, moving the hand when the light beam moves (van der Meer, 1997). Newborns also make poorly coordinated swipes, called **prereaching**, toward an object in front of them, but because of poor arm and hand control they rarely contact the object. Like newborn reflexes, prereaching drops out around 7 weeks of age, when babies improve in eye movements involved in tracking and fixating on objects, which are essential for accurate reaching (von Hofsten, 2004). Yet these early behaviors suggest that babies are biologically prepared to coordinate hand with eye in the act of exploring.

DEVELOPMENT OF REACHING AND GRASPING At about 3 to 4 months, as infants develop the necessary eye, head, and shoulder control, reaching reappears as purposeful, forward arm movements in the presence of a nearby toy and gradually improves in accuracy (Bhat, Heathcock, & Galloway, 2005). By 5 to 6 months, infants reach for an object in a room that has been darkened during the reach by switching off the lights—a skill that improves over the next few months (Clifton et al., 1994; McCarty & Ashmead, 1999). This indicates that the baby does not need to use vision to guide the arms and hands in reaching. Rather, reaching is largely controlled by *proprioception*—our sense of movement and location in space, arising from stimuli within the body. When vision is freed from the basic act of reaching, it can focus on more complex adjustments, such as fine-tuning actions to fit the distance and shape of objects.

Reaching improves as depth perception advances and as infants gain greater control of body posture and arm and hand movements. Four-month-olds aim their reaches ahead of a moving object so they can catch it (von Hofsten, 1993). Around 5 months, babies reduce their efforts when an object is moved beyond their reach (Robin, Berthier, & Clifton, 1996). By 7 months, the arms become more independent: Infants reach for an object by extending one arm rather than both (Fagard & Pezé, 1997). During the next few months, infants become more efficient at reaching for moving objects—ones that spin, change direction, and move

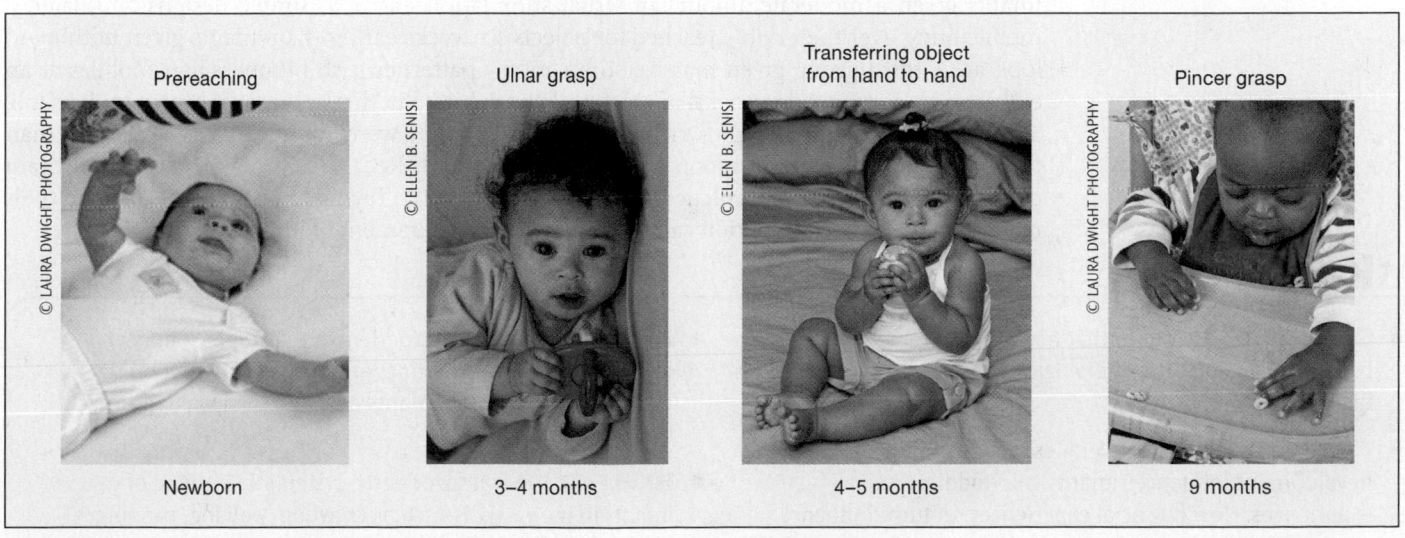

Prereaching	Ulnar grasp	Transferring object from hand to hand	Pincer grasp
Newborn	3–4 months	4–5 months	9 months

FIGURE 5.14 **Some milestones of reaching and grasping.** The average age at which each skill is attained is given. (Ages from Bayley, 1969; Rochat, 1989.)

To explore the surface of this uniquely textured ball, a 6-month-old coordinates both hands—and uses her mouth as well!

sideways, closer, or farther away (Fagard, Spelke, & von Hofsten, 2009; Wentworth, Benson, & Haith, 2000).

Once infants can reach, they increase the quantity and variety of their exploratory behaviors with objects—mouthing, fingering, looking, and combining these actions (Lobo & Galloway, 2013). They also modify their grasp. The newborn's grasp reflex is replaced by the **ulnar grasp,** a clumsy motion in which the young infant's fingers close against the palm. Still, even 4- to 5-month-olds modify their grasp to suit an object's size, shape, and texture (rigid versus soft)—a capacity that improves over the second half-year as infants adjust the hand more precisely and do so in advance of contacting the object (Cicuto et al., 2012; Witherington, 2005). Around 4 to 5 months, when infants begin to sit up, both hands become coordinated in exploring objects. Babies of this age can hold an object in one hand while the other scans it with the tips of the fingers, and they frequently transfer objects from hand to hand (Rochat & Goubet, 1995). By the end of the first year, infants use the thumb and index finger in a well-coordinated **pincer grasp.** Then the ability to manipulate objects greatly expands. The 1-year-old can pick up raisins and blades of grass, turn knobs, and open and close small boxes.

Between 8 and 11 months, reaching and grasping are well-practiced. As a result, attention is released from the motor skill to events that occur before and after obtaining the object. For example, 10-month-olds easily modify their reach to anticipate their next action. They reach for a ball faster when they intend to throw it than when they intend to drop it carefully through a narrow tube (Claxton, Keen, & McCarty, 2003). Around this time, too, infants begin to solve simple problems that involve reaching, such as searching for and finding a hidden toy.

Finally, the capacity to reach for and manipulate an object increases infants' attention to the way an adult reaches for and plays with that same object (Hauf, Aschersleben, & Prinz, 2007). As babies watch what others do, they broaden their understanding of others' behaviors and of the range of actions that can be performed on various objects, gradually incorporating those possibilities into their own object-related behaviors.

EARLY EXPERIENCE AND REACHING Like other motor milestones, reaching is affected by early experience. In cultures where mothers carry their infants on their hips or in slings for most of the day, babies have rich opportunities to explore with their hands. Among the !Kung of Botswana, infants grasp their mothers' colorful, beaded necklaces to steady themselves while breastfeeding as the mother moves. While riding along, they also frequently swipe at and manipulate their mother's jewelry and other dangling objects (Konner, 1977). As a result, !Kung infants are advanced in development of reaching and grasping. And because babies of Mali and Uganda spend half or more of their day held in sitting or standing positions, which facilitate reaching, they, too, develop manual skills earlier than Western infants, who spend much of their day lying down (Adolph, Karasik, & Tamis-LeMonda, 2010).

Babies' visual surroundings are also influential. In a well-known study, institutionalized infants given a moderate amount of visual stimulation—at first, simple designs and, later, a mobile hung over their crib—reached for objects six weeks earlier than infants given nothing to look at. A third group given massive stimulation—patterned crib bumpers and mobiles at an early age—also reached sooner than unstimulated babies. But this heavy enrichment took its toll. These infants looked away and cried a great deal, and they were less advanced in reaching than the moderately stimulated group (White & Held, 1966). Recall from our discussion of brain development that more stimulation is not necessarily better. Trying to push infants beyond their readiness to handle stimulation can undermine the development of important motor skills.

Ask Yourself

- **REVIEW** Cite evidence that motor development is a joint product of biological, psychological, and environmental factors.

- **CONNECT** Provide several examples of how motor development influences infants' and toddlers' social experiences. How do social experiences, in turn, influence motor development?

- **APPLY** List everyday experiences that support mastery of reaching, grasping, sitting, and crawling. Why should caregivers place young infants in a variety of waking-time body positions?

- **REFLECT** Do you favor early, systematic training of infants in motor skills such as crawling, walking, running, hopping, and stair climbing? Why or why not?

Perceptual Development

In Chapter 4, you learned that the senses of touch, taste, smell, and hearing—but not vision—are remarkably well-developed at birth. Now let's turn to a related question: How does perception change over the first year? Our discussion will address hearing and vision, the focus of almost all research. Unfortunately, little evidence exists on how touch, taste, and smell develop after birth. Also, in Chapter 4 we used the word *sensation* to talk about these capacities. It suggests a fairly passive process—what the baby's receptors detect when exposed to stimulation. Now we use the word *perception,* which is active: When we perceive, we organize and interpret what we see.

As we review the perceptual achievements of infancy, you may find it hard to tell where perception leaves off and thinking begins. The research we are about to discuss provides an excellent bridge to the topic of Chapter 6—cognitive development during the first two years.

5.7 What changes in hearing and in depth, pattern, object, and intermodal perception take place during infancy?

5.8 Explain differentiation theory of perceptual development.

Hearing

On Timmy's first birthday, Vanessa bought several CDs of nursery songs, and she turned one on each afternoon at naptime. Soon Timmy let her know his favorite tune. If she put on "Twinkle, Twinkle," he stood up in his crib and whimpered until she replaced it with "Jack and Jill." Timmy's behavior illustrates the greatest change in hearing over the first year of life: Babies start to organize sounds into complex patterns.

Between 4 and 7 months, infants display a sense of musical phrasing. They prefer Mozart minuets with pauses between phrases to those with awkward breaks (Krumhansl & Jusczyk, 1990). Around 6 to 7 months, they can distinguish musical tunes on the basis of variations in rhythmic patterns, including beat structure (duple or triple) and accent structure (emphasis on the first note of every beat unit or at other positions) (Hannon & Johnson, 2004). They are also sensitive to features conveying the purpose of familiar types of songs, preferring to listen to high-pitched playsongs (aimed at entertaining) and low-pitched lullabies (used to soothe) (Tsang & Conrad, 2010). By the end of the first year, infants recognize the same melody when it is played in different keys (Trehub, 2001). As we will see next, 6- to 12-month-olds make comparable discriminations in human speech: They readily detect sound regularities, which will facilitate later language learning.

SPEECH PERCEPTION Recall from Chapter 4 that newborns can distinguish nearly all sounds in human languages and that they prefer listening to speech over nonspeech sounds and to their native tongue rather than a rhythmically distinct foreign language. Brain-imaging evidence reveals that in young infants, discrimination of speech sounds activates *both* auditory and motor areas in the cerebral cortex (Kuhl et al., 2014). Researchers speculate that while perceiving speech sounds, babies also generate internal motor plans that prepare them for producing those sounds.

As infants listen to people talk, they learn to focus on meaningful sound variations. ERP brain-wave recordings reveal that around 5 months, infants become sensitive to syllable stress patterns in their own language (Weber et al., 2004). Between 6 and 8 months, they start to "screen out" sounds not used in their native tongue and, in the case of bilingual infants, in both native languages (Albareda-Castellot, Pons, & Sebastián-Gallés, 2010; Curtin & Werker, 2007). As the Biology and Environment box on page 188 explains, this increased responsiveness to native-language sounds is part of a general "tuning" process in the second half of the first year—a possible sensitive period in which babies acquire a range of perceptual skills for picking up socially important information.

Soon after, infants focus on larger speech units that are critical to figuring out meaning. They recognize familiar words in spoken passages and listen longer to speech with clear clause and phrase boundaries (Johnson & Seidl, 2008; Soderstrom et al., 2003). Around 7 to 9 months, infants extend this sensitivity to speech structure to individual words: They begin to divide the speech stream into wordlike units (Jusczyk, 2002; Saffran, Werker, & Werner, 2006).

A 6-month-old is a remarkable analyzer of the speech stream. While listening to her mother talk, she detects sound patterns, discriminating words and word sequences for which she will later learn meanings.

Biology and Environment

"Tuning in" to Familiar Speech, Faces, and Music: A Sensitive Period for Culture-Specific Learning

To share experiences with members of their family and community, babies must become skilled at making perceptual discriminations that are meaningful in their culture. As we have seen, at first babies are sensitive to virtually all speech sounds but, around 6 months, they narrow their focus, limiting the distinctions they make to the language they hear and will soon learn.

The ability to perceive faces shows a similar **perceptual narrowing effect**—perceptual sensitivity that becomes increasingly attuned with age to information most often encountered. After habituating to one member of each pair of faces in Figure 5.15, 6-month-olds were shown the familiar face and the novel face side by side. For both pairs, they recovered to (looked longer at) the novel face, indicating that they could discriminate the individual faces of both humans and monkeys equally well (Pascalis, de Haan, & Nelson, 2002). But at 9 months, infants no longer showed a novelty preference when viewing the monkey pair. Like adults, they could distinguish only the human faces. Similar findings emerge with sheep faces: Four- to 6-month-olds easily distinguish them, but 9- to 11-month-olds no longer do (Simpson et al., 2011).

This perceptual narrowing effect appears again in musical rhythm perception. Western adults are accustomed to the even-beat pattern of Western music—repetition of the same rhythmic structure in every measure of a tune—and easily notice rhythmic changes that disrupt this familiar beat. But present them with music that does not follow this typical Western rhythmic form—Baltic folk tunes, for example—and they fail to pick up on rhythmic-pattern deviations. In contrast, 6-month-olds can detect such disruptions in both Western and non-Western melodies. By 12 months, however, after added exposure to Western music, babies are no longer aware of deviations in foreign musical rhythms, although their sensitivity to Western rhythmic structure remains unchanged (Hannon & Trehub, 2005b).

Several weeks of regular interaction with a foreign-language speaker and of daily opportunities to listen to non-Western music fully restore 12-month-olds' sensitivity to wide-ranging speech sounds and music rhythms (Hannon & Trehub, 2005a; Kuhl, Tsao, & Liu, 2003). Similarly, 6-month-olds given three months of training in discriminating individual monkey faces, in which each image is verbally labeled with a distinct name ("Carlos," "Iona") instead of the generic label "monkey," retain their ability to discriminate monkey faces at 9 months (Scott & Monesson, 2009). Adults given similar extensive experiences, by contrast, show little improvement in perceptual sensitivity.

Taken together, these findings suggest a heightened capacity—or sensitive period—in the second half of the first year, when babies are biologically prepared to "zero in" on socially meaningful perceptual distinctions. Notice how,

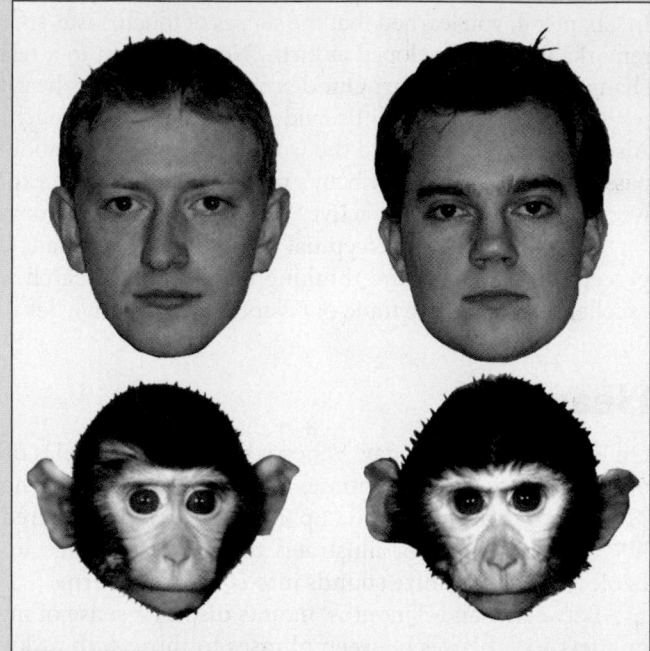

FIGURE 5.15 Discrimination of human and monkey faces. Which of these pairs is easiest for you to tell apart? After habituating to one of the photos in each pair, infants were shown the familiar and the novel face side-by-side. For both pairs, 6-month-olds recovered to (looked longer at) the novel face, indicating that they could discriminate human and monkey faces equally well. By 12 months, babies lost their ability to distinguish the monkey faces. Like adults, they showed a novelty preference only to human stimuli. (From O. Pascalis et al., 2002, "Is Face Processing Species-Specific During the First Year of Life?" *Science, 296,* p. 1322. Copyright © 2002 by AAAS. Republished with permission of American Association for the Advancement of Science conveyed through Copyright Clearance Center, Inc.)

between 6 and 12 months, learning is especially rapid across several domains (speech, faces, and music) and is easily modified by experience. This suggests a broad neurological change—perhaps a special time of experience-expectant brain growth (see page 169) in which babies analyze everyday stimulation of all kinds similarly, in ways that prepare them to participate in their cultural community.

ANALYZING THE SPEECH STREAM   How do infants make such rapid progress in perceiving the structure of speech? Research reveals that they have an impressive **statistical learning capacity.** By analyzing the speech stream for patterns—repeatedly occurring sequences of sounds—they acquire a stock of speech structures for which they will later learn meanings, long before they start to talk around age 12 months.

For example, when presented with controlled sequences of nonsense syllables, babies as young as 5 months listened for statistical regularities: They locate words by discriminating syllables that often occur together (indicating that they belong to the same word) from syllables that seldom occur together (indicating a word boundary) (Johnson & Tyler, 2010). Consider the English word sequence *pretty#baby.* After listening to the speech stream for just one minute (about 60 words), babies can distinguish a word-internal syllable pair *(pretty)* from a word-external syllable pair *(ty#ba).* They prefer to listen to new speech that preserves the word-internal pattern (Saffran, Aslin, & Newport, 1996; Saffran & Thiessen, 2003).

Once infants begin locating words, they focus on the words and discover additional statistical cues that signal word boundaries (Thiessen, Kronstein, & Hufnagle, 2012). For example, 7- to 8-month-olds detect regular syllable-stress patterns—for example, in English and Dutch, that the onset of a strong syllable (*hap*-py, *rab*-bit) often signals a new word (Swingley, 2005; Thiessen & Saffran, 2007). By 10 months, babies can detect words that start with weak syllables, such as "sur*prise*," by listening for sound regularities before and after the words (Kooijman, Hagoort, & Cutler, 2009).

Clearly, babies have a powerful ability to extract patterns from complex, continuous speech. Their remarkable statistical learning capacity also extends to visual stimuli and is present in the first weeks of life (Aslin & Newport, 2012). Statistical learning seems to be a general capacity that infants use to analyze complex stimulation.

By the middle of the first year, infants also attend to regularities in word sequences. In a study using nonsense words, 7-month-olds distinguished the ABA structure of "ga ti ga" and "li na li" from the ABB structure of "wo fe fe" and "ta la la" (Marcus et al., 1999). They seemed to detect simple word-order rules, a capacity that may eventually help them figure out basic grammar. And as with statistical learning, the capacity to extract ABA and ABB rules also applies to sequences of visual stimuli—and to musical stimuli as well (Dawson & Gerken, 2009; Johnson et al., 2009).

Finally, the more rapidly 10-month-olds detect words within the speech stream (as indicated by ERP recordings), the larger their vocabulary at age 2 years (Junge et al., 2012). Certain features of adults' utterances facilitate such rapid detection. Natural speech, for example, is full of both uninterrupted strings of words and pauses enabling listeners to hear isolated words. Infants exposed to a brief quantity of speech containing both isolated words and the same words embedded in the speech stream ("Doggie!" "See the doggie there?") are better able to discriminate those words when later exposed to fluent speech (Lew-Williams, Pelucchi, & Saffran, 2011). As we will see in Chapter 6, adults' style of communicating with infants greatly facilitates analysis of the structure of speech.

Vision

For exploring the environment, humans depend on vision more than any other sense. Although at first a baby's visual world is fragmented, it undergoes extraordinary changes during the first 7 to 8 months of life.

Visual development is supported by rapid maturation of the eye and visual centers in the cerebral cortex. Recall from Chapter 4 that the newborn baby focuses and perceives color poorly. Around 2 months, infants can focus on objects about as well as adults, and their color vision is adultlike by 4 months (Kellman & Arterberry, 2006). *Visual acuity* (fineness of discrimination) increases steadily throughout the first year, reaching 20/80 by 6 months and an adult level of about 20/20 by 4 years (Slater et al., 2010). Scanning the environment and tracking moving objects also improve over the first half-year as infants see more clearly and better control their eye movements. In addition, as young infants build an organized perceptual world, they scan more thoroughly and systematically, strategically picking up important information (Johnson, Slemmer, & Amso, 2004; von Hofsten & Rosander, 1998). Consequently, scanning enhances perception, and—in bidirectional fashion—perception also enhances scanning.

As babies explore their visual field, they figure out the characteristics of objects and how they are arranged in space. To understand how they do so, let's examine the development of three aspects of vision: depth, pattern, and object perception.

DEPTH PERCEPTION *Depth perception* is the ability to judge the distance of objects from one another and from ourselves. It is important for understanding the layout of the environment and for guiding motor activity.

FIGURE 5.16 The visual cliff. Plexiglas covers the deep and shallow sides. By refusing to cross the deep side and showing a preference for the shallow side, this infant demonstrates the ability to perceive depth.

Figure 5.16 shows the *visual cliff,* designed by Eleanor Gibson and Richard Walk (1960) and used in the earliest studies of depth perception. It consists of a Plexiglas-covered table with a platform at the center, a "shallow" side with a checkerboard pattern just under the glass, and a "deep" side with a checkerboard several feet below the glass. The researchers found that crawling babies readily crossed the shallow side, but most avoided the deep side. They concluded that around the time infants crawl, most distinguish deep from shallow surfaces and steer clear of drop-offs.

The visual cliff shows that crawling and avoidance of drop-offs are linked, but not how they are related or when depth perception first appears. Recent research has looked at babies' ability to detect specific depth cues, using methods that do not require that they crawl.

Emergence of Depth Perception How do we know when an object is near rather than far away? **TAKE A MOMENT...** Try these exercises to find out. Pick up a small object (such as your cup) and move it toward and away from your face. Did its image grow larger as it approached and smaller as it receded? Next time you take a bike or car ride, notice that nearby objects move past your field of vision more quickly than those far away.

Motion is the first depth cue to which infants are sensitive. Babies 3 to 4 weeks old blink their eyes defensively when an object moves toward their face as though it is going to hit (Nánez & Yonas, 1994). *Binocular depth cues* arise because our two eyes have slightly different views of the visual field. The brain blends these two images, resulting in perception of depth. Research in which two overlapping images are projected before the baby, who wears special goggles to ensure that each eye receives only one image, reveals that sensitivity to binocular cues emerges between 2 and 3 months and improves rapidly over the first year (Birch, 1993; Brown & Miracle, 2003). Finally, beginning at 3 to 4 months and strengthening between 5 and 7 months, babies display sensitivity to *pictorial depth cues*—the ones artists often use to make a painting look three-dimensional. Examples include receding lines that create the illusion of perspective, changes in texture (nearby textures are more detailed than faraway ones), overlapping objects (an object partially hidden by another object is perceived to be more distant), and shadows cast on surfaces (indicating a separation in space between the object and the surface) (Kavšek, Yonas, & Granrud, 2012; Shuwairi, Albert, & Johnson, 2007).

Why does perception of depth cues emerge in the order just described? Researchers speculate that motor development is involved. For example, control of the head during the early weeks of life may help babies notice motion and binocular cues. Around 5 to 6 months, the ability to turn, poke, and feel the surface of objects may promote perception of pictorial cues (Bushnell & Boudreau, 1993; Soska, Adolph, & Johnson, 2010). And as we will see next, one aspect of motor progress—independent movement—plays a vital role in refinement of depth perception.

Independent Movement and Depth Perception At 6 months, Timmy started crawling. "He's fearless!" exclaimed Vanessa. "If I put him down in the middle of the bed, he crawls right over the edge. The same thing happens by the stairs." Will Timmy become wary of the side of the bed and the staircase as he becomes a more experienced crawler? Research suggests that he will. Infants with more crawling experience (regardless of when they started to crawl) are far more likely to refuse to cross the deep side of the visual cliff (Campos et al., 2000).

From extensive everyday experience, babies gradually figure out how to use depth cues to detect the danger of falling. But because the loss of body control that leads to falling differs greatly for each body position, babies must undergo this learning separately for each posture (Adolph & Kretch, 2012). In one study, 9-month-olds, who were experienced sitters but novice crawlers, were placed on the edge of a shallow drop-off that could be widened (Adolph, 2002, 2008). While in the familiar sitting position, infants avoided leaning out for an attractive toy at distances likely to result in falling. But in the unfamiliar crawling position, they headed over the edge, even when the distance was extremely wide! And newly walking babies will step repeatedly over a risky drop-off (Kretch & Adolph, 2013a). They will also career down slopes and over uneven surfaces without making necessary postural adjustments (Adolph et al., 2008; Joh & Adolph, 2006). Thus, they fall frequently.

Even experienced crawlers and walkers encounter new depth-at-an-edge situations that require additional learning. In one study, researchers encouraged crawling and walking babies to cross bridges varying in width over drop-offs (with an adult following alongside to catch infants if they began to fall). Most avoided crossing impossibly narrow bridges. And the greater their experience, the narrower the bridge both crawlers and walkers attempted to cross. Nevertheless, walkers perceived the likelihood of falling from a narrow bridge more accurately than crawlers. While crossing, crawlers could not easily see and adjust the placement of their hind limbs to prevent falls. In contrast, experienced walkers had figured out how to turn their body to accommodate the narrow passageway (see Figure 5.17) (Kretch & Adolph, 2013b). As infants and toddlers discover how to avoid falling in different postures and situations, their understanding of depth expands.

Independent movement promotes other aspects of three-dimensional understanding. For example, seasoned crawlers are better than their inexperienced agemates at remembering object locations and finding hidden objects (Campos et al., 2000). Why does crawling make such a difference? **TAKE A MOMENT...** Compare your own experience of the environment when you are driven from one place to another with what you experience when you walk or drive yourself. When you move on your own, you are much more aware of landmarks and routes of travel, and you take more careful note of what things look like from different points of view. The same is true for infants. In fact, crawling promotes a new level of brain organization, as indicated by more organized EEG brain-wave activity in the cerebral cortex (Bell & Fox, 1996). Perhaps crawling strengthens certain neural connections, especially those involved in vision and understanding of space.

PATTERN PERCEPTION   Even newborns prefer to look at patterned rather than plain stimuli (Fantz, 1961). As they get older, infants prefer more complex patterns. For example, 3-week-olds look longest at black-and-white checkerboards with a few large squares, whereas 8- and 14-week-olds prefer those with many squares (Brennan, Ames, & Moore, 1966).

A general principle, called **contrast sensitivity,** explains early pattern preferences (Banks & Ginsburg, 1985). *Contrast* refers to the difference in the amount of light between adjacent regions in a pattern. If babies are *sensitive to* (can detect) the contrast in two or more

© ELLEN B. SENISI

Infants must learn to use depth cues to detect the danger of falling separately for each posture. When this experienced crawler—who avoids most drop-offs—starts to walk, he will be at risk for stepping off ledges and staircases.

FIGURE 5.17 **An experienced walker crosses a narrow bridge over a drop-off.** This 14-month-old has figured out how to turn his body sideways to accommodate the narrow passageway. (From K. S. Kretch & K. E. Adolph, 2013b, "No Bridge Too High: Infants Decide Whether to Cross Based on the Probability of Falling Not the Severity of the Potential Fall," *Developmental Science, 16,* p. 338. © 2013 Blackwell Publishing Ltd. Reprinted by permission of John Wiley and Sons, Inc., conveyed through Copyright Clearance Center, Inc.)

Bold checkerboard   Complex checkerboard

Appearance of checkerboards to very young infants

FIGURE 5.18 **The way two checkerboards differing in complexity look to infants in the first few weeks of life.** Because of their poor vision, very young infants cannot resolve the fine detail in the *complex checkerboard*. It appears blurred, like a gray field. The large, *bold checkerboard* appears to have more contrast, so babies prefer to look at it. (Adapted from M. S. Banks & P. Salapatek, 1983, "Infant Visual Perception," in M. M. Haith & J. J. Campos (Eds.), *Handbook of Child Psychology: Vol. 2. Infancy and Developmental Psychobiology* [4th ed.], New York: John Wiley & Sons, p. 504. Copyright © 1983 by John Wiley & Sons, Inc. Reproduced with permission of John Wiley & Sons, Inc.)

patterns, they prefer the one with more contrast. To understand this idea, look at the checkerboards in the top row of Figure 5.18. To us, the one with many small squares has more contrasting elements. Now look at the bottom row, which shows how these checkerboards appear to infants in the first few weeks of life. Because of their poor vision, very young babies cannot resolve the small features in more complex patterns, so they prefer to look at the large, bold checkerboard. Around 2 months, when detection of fine-grained detail has improved, infants become sensitive to the contrast in complex patterns and spend more time looking at them (Gwiazda & Birch, 2001).

Combining Pattern Elements In the early weeks of life, infants respond to the separate parts of a pattern. They stare at single high-contrast features, generally on the edges, and have difficulty shifting their gaze away toward other interesting stimuli (Hunnius & Geuze, 2004a, 2004b). At 2 to 3 months, when scanning ability and contrast sensitivity improve, infants thoroughly explore a pattern's internal features, pausing briefly to look at each part (Bronson, 1994).

Once babies can take in all aspects of a pattern, they integrate the parts into a unified whole. Around 4 months, babies are so good at detecting pattern organization that they perceive subjective boundaries that are not really present. For example, they perceive a square in the center of Figure 5.19a, just as you do (Ghim, 1990). And like adults, 3- to 4-month-olds engage in *boundary extension*: When re-exposed to a photo of a natural scene, they remember it as extending beyond its original boundaries. The visual system seems to interpret the photographed scene like a view through a window, which is understood to extend beyond the edges of the window (Quinn & Intraub, 2007).

Older infants carry this sensitivity to subjective form further. For example, 9-month-olds look much longer at an organized series of moving lights that resembles a human being walking than at an upside-down or scrambled version (Proffitt & Bertenthal, 1990). At 12 months, infants can detect familiar objects represented by incomplete drawings, even when as much as two-thirds of the drawing is missing (see Figure 5.19b) (Rose, Jankowski, & Senior, 1997). As these findings reveal, infants' increasing knowledge of objects and actions supports pattern perception.

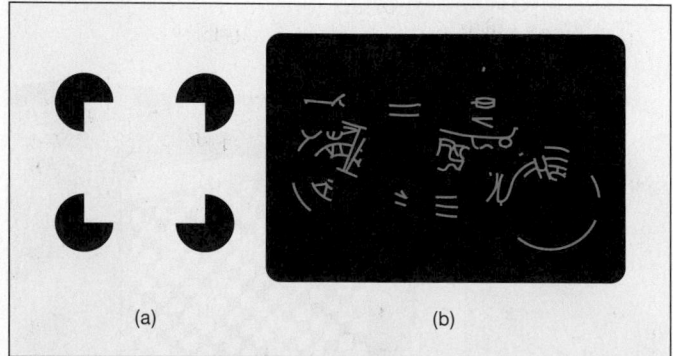

(a)   (b)

FIGURE 5.19 **Subjective boundaries in visual patterns.** (a) Do you perceive a square in the middle of the figure? By 4 months of age, infants do, too. (b) What does the image, missing two-thirds of its outline, look like to you? By 12 months, infants detect a motorcycle. After habituating to the incomplete motorcycle image, they were shown an intact motorcycle figure paired with a novel form. Twelve-month-olds recovered to (looked longer at) the novel figure, indicating that they recognized the motorcycle pattern on the basis of very little visual information. (Adapted from Ghim, 1990; Rose, Jankowski, & Senior, 1997.)

Face Perception Infants' tendency to search for structure in a patterned stimulus applies to face perception. Newborns prefer to look at photos and simplified drawings of faces with features arranged naturally (upright) rather than unnaturally (upside down or sideways) (see Figure 5.20a and b) (Cassia, Turati, & Simion, 2004; Mondloch et al., 1999). They also track a facelike pattern moving across their visual field farther than they track other stimuli (Johnson, 1999). And although they rely more on outer features (hairline and chin) than inner features to distinguish real faces, newborns prefer photos of faces with eyes open and a direct gaze (Farroni et al., 2002; Turati et al., 2006). Yet another amazing capacity is their tendency to look longer at both human and animal faces judged by adults as attractive—a preference that may be the origin of the widespread social bias favoring physically attractive people (Quinn et al., 2008; Slater et al., 2010).

Some researchers claim that these behaviors reflect a built-in capacity to orient toward members of one's own species, just as many newborn animals do (Johnson, 2001; Slater et al., 2011). Others assert that newborns simply prefer any stimulus in which the most

FIGURE 5.20 **Early face perception.** Newborns prefer to look at the photo of a face (a) and the simple pattern resembling a face (b) over the upside-down versions. (c) When the complex drawing of a face on the left and the equally complex, scrambled version on the right are moved across newborns' visual field, they follow the face longer. But if the two stimuli are stationary, infants show no preference for the face until around 2 months of age. (From Cassia, Turati, & Simion, 2004; Johnson, 1999; Mondloch et al., 1999.)

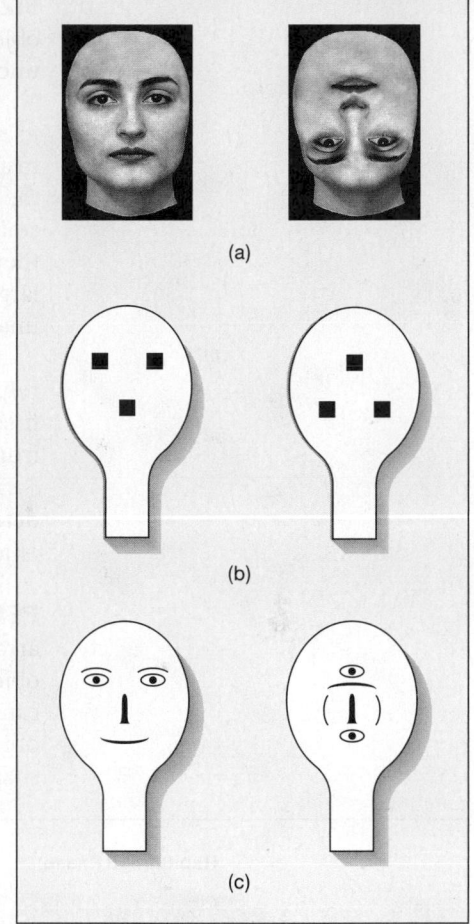

salient elements are arranged horizontally in the upper part of a pattern—like the "eyes" in Figure 5.20b. Indeed, newborns do prefer patterns with these characteristics over other arrangements (Cassia, Turati, & Simion, 2004; Simion et al., 2001). Possibly, however, a bias favoring the facial pattern promotes such preferences. Still other researchers argue that newborns are exposed to faces more often than to other stimuli—early experiences that could quickly "wire" the brain to detect faces and prefer attractive ones (Bukacha, Gauthier, & Tarr, 2006).

Although newborns respond to facelike structures, they cannot discriminate a complex facial pattern from other, equally complex patterns (see Figure 5.20c). But from repeated exposures to their mother's face, they quickly learn to prefer her face to that of an unfamiliar woman, although they mostly attend to its broad outlines. Around 2 months, when they can combine pattern elements into an organized whole, babies prefer a complex drawing of the human face to other equally complex stimulus arrangements (Dannemiller & Stephens, 1988). And they clearly prefer their mother's detailed facial features to those of another woman (Bartrip, Morton, & de Schonen, 2001).

Around 3 months, infants readily make fine distinctions among the features of different faces—for example, between photographs of two strangers, even when the faces are moderately similar (Farroni et al., 2007). At 5 months, infants perceive emotional expressions as meaningful wholes. They treat positive faces (happy and surprised) as different from negative ones (sad and fearful) (Bornstein & Arterberry, 2003). And by 7 months, they discriminate among a wider range of facial expressions, including happiness, surprise, sadness, fearfulness, and anger (Witherington et al., 2010).

Experience influences face processing, leading babies to form group biases at a tender age. As early as 3 months, infants prefer and more easily discriminate among female faces than among male faces (Quinn et al., 2002; Ramsey-Rennels & Langlois, 2006). The greater time infants spend with female adults explains this effect, since babies with a male primary caregiver prefer male faces. Furthermore, 3- to 6-month-olds exposed mostly to members of their own race prefer to look at the faces of members of that race, and between 6 and 9 months their ability to discriminate other-race faces weakens (Kelly et al., 2007, 2009). This own-race bias is absent in babies who have frequent contact with members of other races or who view picture books of other-race faces, and it can be reversed through exposure to racial diversity (Anzures et al., 2013; Heron-Delaney et al., 2011). **TAKE A MOMENT...** Notice how early experience promotes *perceptual narrowing* with respect to gender and racial information in faces, as occurs for species information, discussed in the Biology and Environment box on page 188.

Clearly, extensive face-to-face interaction with caregivers contributes to infants' refinement of face perception. And as babies recognize and respond to the expressive behavior of others, face perception supports their earliest social relationships.

Object Perception

Research on pattern perception involves only two-dimensional stimuli, but our environment is made up of stable, three-dimensional objects. Do young infants perceive a world of independently existing objects—knowledge essential for distinguishing among the self, other people, and things?

Exposure to racial diversity in her child-care center means that this baby is unlikely to have developed a preference for faces of her own race. When infants have limited social experiences, group biases emerge early.

SIZE AND SHAPE CONSTANCY As we move around the environment, the images that objects cast on our retina constantly change in size and shape. To perceive objects as stable and unchanging, we must translate these varying retinal images into a single representation.

Size constancy—perception of an object's size as the same, despite changes in the size of its retinal image—is evident in the first week of life. To test for it, researchers habituated infants to a small cube at varying distances from the eye, in an effort to desensitize them to changes in the cube's retinal image size and direct their attention to the object's actual size. When the small cube was presented together with a new, large cube—but at different distances so that they cast retinal images of the same size—all babies recovered to (looked longer at) the novel large cube, indicating that they distinguished objects on the basis of actual size, not retinal image size (Slater et al., 2010).

Perception of an object's shape as stable, despite changes in the shape projected on the retina, is called **shape constancy.** Habituation research reveals that it, too, is present within the first week of life, long before babies can actively rotate objects with their hands and view them from different angles (Slater & Johnson, 1999).

In sum, both size and shape constancy seem to be built-in capacities that assist babies in detecting a coherent world of objects. Yet they provide only a partial picture of young infants' object perception.

PERCEPTION OF OBJECT IDENTITY At first, babies rely heavily on motion and spatial arrangement to identify objects (Jusczyk et al., 1999; Spelke & Hermer, 1996). When two objects are touching and either move in unison or stand still, babies younger than 4 months cannot distinguish them. Infants, of course, are fascinated by moving objects. As they observe objects' motions, they pick up additional information about objects' boundaries, such as shape, color, and texture.

For example, as Figure 5.21 reveals, around 2 months, babies realize that a moving rod whose center is hidden behind a box is a complete rod rather than two rod pieces. Motion, a textured background, and a small box (so most of the rod is visible) are necessary for young infants to infer object unity. They need all these cues to heighten the distinction between objects in the display because their ability to scan for salient information is still immature (Amso & Johnson, 2006; Johnson, 2009).

As infants become familiar with many objects and improvements in scanning assist them in integrating each object's features into a unified whole, they rely more on shape, color, and pattern and less on motion (Johnson, 2011; Slater et al., 2010). Babies as young as 4½ months can discriminate two touching objects on the basis of their features in very simple, easy-to-process situations. And prior exposure to one of the test objects enhances 4½-month-olds' ability to discern the boundary between two touching objects—a finding that highlights the role of experience (Dueker, Modi, & Needham, 2003; Needham, 2001).

In everyday life, objects frequently move in and out of sight, so infants must keep track of their disappearance and reappearance to perceive their identity. Habituation research, in which a ball moves back and forth behind a screen, reveals that at age 4 months, infants first perceive the ball's path as continuous (Johnson et al., 2003). Between 4 and 5 months, infants can monitor more intricate paths of objects. As indicated by their future-oriented eye movements (looking ahead to where they expect an object to reappear from behind a barrier), 5-month-olds even keep track of an object that travels on a curvilinear course at varying speeds (Rosander & von Hofsten, 2004). Again, experience—the opportunity to track a moving object along a fully visible path of movement just before testing—enhances young infants' predictive eye tracking (Johnson & Shuwairi, 2009).

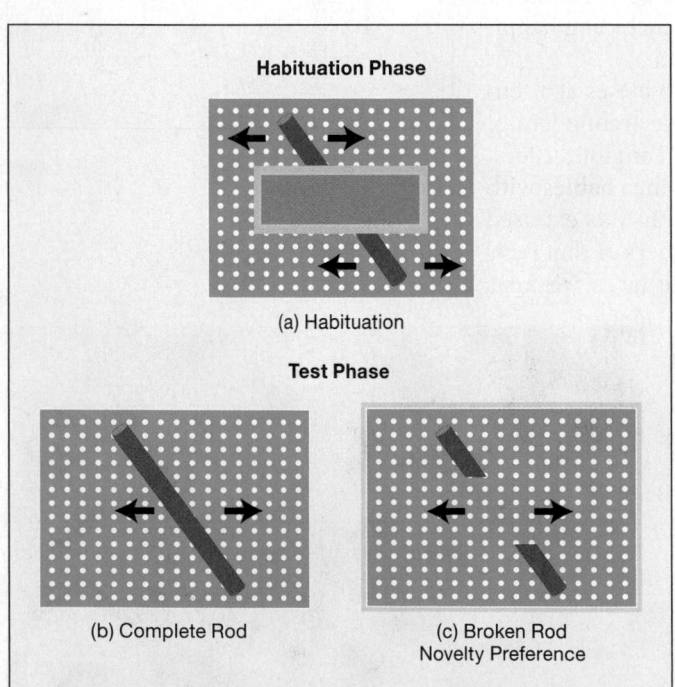

FIGURE 5.21 **Testing infants' ability to perceive object unity.** (a) Infants were habituated to a rod moving back and forth behind a box against a textured background. Next, they were shown two test displays in alternation: (b) a complete rod and (c) a broken rod with a gap corresponding to the location of the box. Each stimulus was moved back and forth against the textured background, in the same way as the habituation stimulus. Infants 2 months of age and older recovered to (looked longer at) the broken rod than the complete rod. Their novelty preference suggests that they perceive the rod behind the box in the first display as a single unit. (Based on Johnson, 1997.)

From 4 to 11 months, infants increasingly use featural information to detect the identity of an object traveling behind a screen. At first, they need strong featural cues—a change in two features (size and shape, or shape and color)—to signify that a disappearing object is distinct from an emerging object. Later in the first year, change in a single feature is sufficient (Bremner et al., 2013; Wilcox & Woods, 2009). And as before, experience—in particular, physically manipulating the object—boosts older infants' attention to its surface features.

In sum, perception of object identity is mastered gradually over the first year. We will consider a related attainment, infants' understanding of object permanence—awareness that an object still exists when hidden—in Chapter 6.

Intermodal Perception

Our world provides rich, continuous *intermodal stimulation*—simultaneous input from more than one *modality,* or sensory system. In **intermodal perception,** we make sense of these running streams of light, sound, tactile, odor, and taste information, perceiving them as integrated wholes. We know, for example, that an object's shape is the same whether we see it or touch it, that lip movements are closely coordinated with the sound of a voice, and that dropping a rigid object on a hard surface will cause a sharp, banging sound.

Recall that newborns turn in the general direction of a sound and reach for objects in a primitive way. These behaviors suggest that infants expect sight, sound, and touch to go together. Research reveals that babies perceive input from different sensory systems in a unified way by detecting **amodal sensory properties,** information that is not specific to a single modality but that overlaps two or more sensory systems, such as rate, rhythm, duration, intensity, temporal synchrony (for vision and hearing), and texture and shape (for vision and touch). Consider the sight and sound of a bouncing ball or the face and voice of a speaking person. In each event, visual and auditory information are conveyed simultaneously and with the same rate, rhythm, duration, and intensity.

Even newborns are impressive perceivers of amodal properties. After touching an object (such as a cylinder) placed in their palms, they recognize it visually, distinguishing it from a different-shaped object (Sann & Streri, 2007). And they require just one exposure to learn the association between the sight and sound of a toy, such as a rhythmically jangling rattle (Morrongiello, Fenwick, & Chance, 1998).

Within the first half-year, infants master a remarkable range of intermodal relationships. Three- to 5-month-olds can match faces with voices on the basis of lip–voice synchrony, emotional expression, and even age and gender of the speaker. Around 6 months, infants can perceive and remember the unique face–voice pairings of unfamiliar adults (Flom, 2013).

How does intermodal perception develop so quickly? Young infants seem biologically primed to focus on amodal information. Their detection of amodal relations—for example, the common tempo and rhythm in sights and sounds—precedes and provides the basis for detecting more specific intermodal matches, such as the relation between a particular person's face and the sound of her voice or between an object and its verbal label (Bahrick, 2010).

Intermodal sensitivity is crucial for perceptual development. In the first few months, when much stimulation is unfamiliar and confusing, it enables babies to notice meaningful correlations between sensory inputs and rapidly make sense of their surroundings. As a result, inexperienced perceivers notice a unitary event, such as a hammer's tapping, without being distracted by momentarily irrelevant aspects of the situation, such as the hammer's color or orientation (Bahrick, Lickliter, & Flom, 2004).

© LAURA DWIGHT PHOTOGRAPHY

This toddler exploring a tambourine readily detects amodal relations in the synchronous sounds and visual appearance of its metal jingles.

In addition to easing perception of the physical world, intermodal perception facilitates processing of the social world. For example, as 3- to 4-month-olds gaze at an adult's face, they initially require both vocal and visual input to distinguish positive from negative emotional expressions (Flom & Bahrick, 2007; Kahana-Kalman & Walker-Andrews, 2001). Only later do infants discriminate positive from negative emotion in each sensory modality—first in voices (around 5 months), later (from 7 months on) in faces (Bahrick, Hernandez-Reif, & Flom, 2005).

Research suggests that intermodal perception supports diverse aspects of learning. In one study, 3-month-olds were given an operant conditioning task in which kicking their foot made a mobile hung with cylinder-shaped blocks turn. Some babies held in their palms a cylinder, others held a cube, and still others were given no object. Infants given matching amodal information—who viewed the cylinders while holding a cylinder—learned the kicking response fastest (Kraebel, 2012). Those given mismatching information (who held a cube) showed inhibited learning.

Furthermore, because communication is often intermodal (simultaneously verbal, visual, and tactile), infants receive much support from other senses in acquiring language. When parents speak to infants, they often provide temporal synchrony between words, object motions, and touch—for example, saying "doll" while moving a doll and occasionally having the doll touch the infant (Gogate & Bahrick, 1998, 2001). In doing so, caregivers greatly increase the chances that babies will remember the association between the word and the object.

In sum, intermodal stimulation fosters all aspects of psychological development. When caregivers provide many concurrent sights, sounds, and touches, babies process more information and learn faster (Bahrick, 2010). Intermodal perception is yet another fundamental capacity that assists infants in their active efforts to build an orderly, understandable world.

LOOK and LISTEN

While watching a parent and infant playing, list instances of parental intermodal stimulation and communication. What is the baby likely learning about people, objects, or language from each intermodal experience?

Understanding Perceptual Development

Now that we have reviewed the development of infant perceptual capacities, how can we put together this diverse array of amazing achievements? Widely accepted answers come from the work of Eleanor and James Gibson. According to the Gibsons' **differentiation theory,** infants actively search for *invariant features* of the environment—those that remain stable—in a constantly changing perceptual world. In pattern perception, for example, young babies search for features that stand out and orient toward faces. Soon they explore internal features, noticing *stable relationships* among them. As a result, they detect patterns, such as complex designs and individual faces. Similarly, infants analyze the speech stream for regularities, detecting words, word-order sequences, and—within words—syllable-stress patterns. The development of intermodal perception also reflects this principle (Bahrick & Lickliter, 2012). Babies seek out invariant relationships—first, amodal properties, such as common rate and rhythm, in a voice and face, later more detailed associations, such as unique voice–face matches.

The Gibsons described their theory as *differentiation* (where *differentiate* means "analyze" or "break down") because over time the baby detects finer and finer invariant features among stimuli. In addition to pattern perception and intermodal perception, differentiation applies to depth and object perception: Recall how in each, sensitivity to motion precedes detection of fine-grained features. So one way of understanding perceptual development is to think of it as a built-in tendency to seek order and consistency—a capacity that becomes increasingly fine-tuned with age (Gibson, 1970; Gibson, 1979).

Acting on the environment is vital in perceptual differentiation. According to the Gibsons, perception is guided by the discovery of **affordances**—the action possibilities that a situation offers an organism with certain motor capabilities (Gibson, 2000, 2003). By moving about and exploring the environment, babies figure out which objects can be grasped, squeezed, bounced, or stroked and which surfaces are safe to cross or present the possibility of falling. Sensitivity to affordances means that we spend far less time correcting ineffective actions than we would otherwise: It makes our actions future-oriented and largely successful rather than reactive and blundering.

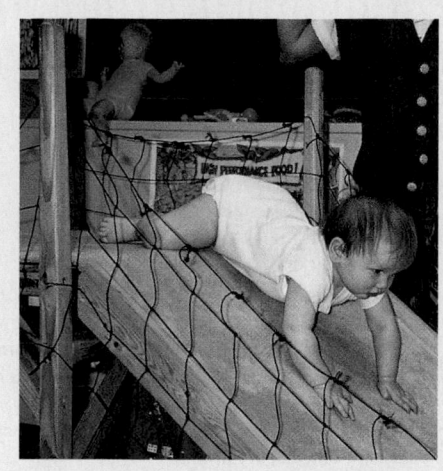 

FIGURE 5.22 **Acting on the environment plays a major role in perceptual differentiation.** Crawling and walking change the way babies perceive a sloping surface. The newly crawling infant on the left plunges headlong down the slope. He has not yet learned that it affords the possibility of falling. The toddler on the right, who has been walking for more than a month, approaches the slope cautiously. Experience in trying to remain upright but frequently tumbling over has made him more aware of the consequences of his movements. He perceives the incline differently than he did at a younger age.

To illustrate, recall how infants' changing capabilities for independent movement affect their perception. When babies crawl, and again when they walk, they gradually realize that a sloping surface *affords the possibility* of falling (see Figure 5.22). With added weeks of practicing each skill, they hesitate to crawl or walk down a risky incline. Experience in trying to keep their balance on various surfaces makes crawlers and walkers more aware of the consequences of their movements. Crawlers come to detect when surface slant places so much body weight on their arms that they will fall forward, and walkers come to sense when an incline shifts body weight so their legs and feet can no longer hold them upright.

Infants do not transfer their learning about slopes or drop-offs from crawling to walking because the affordances for each posture are different (Adolph, Kretch, & LoBue, 2014). Learning is gradual and effortful because newly crawling and walking babies cross many types of surfaces in their homes each day. As they experiment with balance and postural adjustments to accommodate each, they perceive surfaces in new ways that guide their movements. As a result, they act more competently.

As we conclude this chapter, it is only fair to note that some researchers believe that babies do more than make sense of experience by searching for invariant features and discovering affordances: They also *impose meaning on* what they perceive, constructing categories of objects and events in the surrounding environment. We have seen the glimmerings of this cognitive point of view in this chapter. For example, older babies *interpret* a familiar face as a source of pleasure and affection and a pattern of blinking lights as a moving human being. This cognitive perspective also has merit in understanding the achievements of infancy. In fact, many researchers combine these two positions, regarding infant development as proceeding from a perceptual to a cognitive emphasis over the first year of life.

Ask Yourself

● **REVIEW** Using examples, explain why intermodal stimulation is vital for infants' developing understanding of their physical and social worlds.

● **CONNECT** According to differentiation theory, perceptual development reflects infants' active search for invariant features. Provide examples from research on hearing, pattern perception, and intermodal perception.

● **APPLY** After several weeks of crawling, Ben learned to avoid going headfirst over a drop-off. Now he has started to walk. Can his mother trust him not to step over a risky drop-off? Explain, using the concept of affordances.

● **REFLECT** Are young infants more competent than you thought they were before you read this chapter? List the capacities that most surprised you.

Summary

Body Growth (p. 159)

5.1 Discuss major changes in body size, muscle–fat makeup, body proportions, and variations in rate of physical growth over the first two years.

- Height and weight gains are greater during the first two years than at any other time after birth. Body fat develops quickly during the first nine months, whereas muscle development is slow and gradual.

- Parts of the body grow at different rates, following **cephalocaudal** and **proximodistal trends,** resulting in changing body proportions.

- Girls are ahead of boys in physical maturity, and African-American children tend to be ahead of Caucasian-American children, based on skeletal age.

Brain Development (p. 161)

5.2 Describe brain development during infancy and toddlerhood, current methods of measuring brain functioning, and appropriate stimulation to support the brain's potential.

- Early in development, the brain grows faster than any other organ of the body. Once **neurons** are in place, they rapidly form **synapses** and release **neurotransmitters,** which cross synapses to send messages to other neurons. During the peak period of synaptic growth in any brain area, many surrounding neurons die. Neurons that are seldom stimulated lose their synapses in a process called **synaptic pruning. Glial cells,** responsible for **myelination,** multiply rapidly through the second year, contributing to large gains in brain weight.

- Measures of brain functioning include those that detect changes in electrical activity in the cerebral cortex (EEG, ERPs), neuroimaging techniques (PET, fMRI), and NIRS, which uses infrared light and is suitable for infants and young children.

- The **cerebral cortex** is the largest, most complex brain structure and the last to stop growing. Its regions develop in the general order in which various capacities emerge in the growing child, with the frontal lobes (which contain the **prefrontal cortex**) having the most extended period of development. The hemispheres of the cerebral cortex specialize, a process called **lateralization.** In the first few years of life, there is high **brain plasticity,** with many areas not yet committed to specific functions.

- Both heredity and early experience contribute to brain organization. Stimulation of the brain is essential during sensitive periods—periods in which the brain is developing most rapidly. Prolonged early deprivation, experienced by some babies in orphanages, can disrupt brain growth and interfere with the brain's capacity to manage stress, with long-term physical and psychological consequences.

- Appropriate early stimulation promotes **experience-expectant brain growth** through ordinary experiences. No evidence exists for a sensitive period in the first few years for **experience-dependent brain growth,** which relies on specific learning experiences. In fact, environments that overwhelm children with inappropriately advanced expectations can undermine the brain's potential.

© CULTURA CREATIVE (RF)/ALAMY

5.3 How does organization of sleep and wakefulness change over the first two years?

- Infants' changing arousal patterns are primarily affected by brain growth, but the social environment also plays a role. Periods of sleep and wakefulness become fewer but longer over the first two years, conforming to a night–day schedule. Most parents in Western nations try to get their babies to sleep through the night much earlier than parents throughout most of the world, who are more likely to sleep with their babies.

Influences on Early Physical Growth (p. 171)

5.4 Cite evidence indicating that heredity, nutrition, and parental affection contribute to early physical growth.

- Twin and adoption studies reveal that heredity contributes to body size and rate of physical growth.

- Breast milk is ideally suited to infants' growth needs. Breastfeeding protects against disease and prevents malnutrition and infant death in poverty-stricken areas of the world.

- Most infants and toddlers can eat nutritious foods freely without risk of becoming overweight. However, the relationship between rapid weight gain in infancy and obesity at older ages is strengthening, perhaps because of a rise in unhealthy early feeding practices, in which babies are given high-fat foods and sugary drinks.

© PHOTOALTO/ALAMY

- **Marasmus** and **kwashiorkor** are dietary diseases caused by malnutrition that affect many children in developing countries and, if prolonged, can permanently stunt body growth and brain development. **Growth faltering** illustrates the importance of parental affection and early emotional well-being for normal physical growth.

Learning Capacities (p. 176)

5.5 Describe infant learning capacities, the conditions under which they occur, and the unique value of each.

- **Classical conditioning** is based on the infant's ability to associate events that usually occur together in the everyday world. Infants can be classically conditioned most easily when the pairing of an **unconditioned stimulus (UCS)** and a **conditioned stimulus (CS)** has survival value—for example, learning which stimuli regularly accompany feeding.

- In **operant conditioning,** infants act on their environment and their behavior is followed by either **reinforcers,** which increase the occurrence of a preceding behavior, or **punishment,** which either removes a desirable stimulus or presents an unpleasant one to decrease the occurrence of a response. In young infants, interesting sights and sounds and pleasurable caregiver interaction serve as effective reinforcers.

- **Habituation** and **recovery** reveal that at birth, babies are attracted to novelty. Novelty preference (recovery to a novel stimulus) assesses recent memory, whereas familiarity preference (recovery to the familiar stimulus) assesses remote memory.

- Newborns also have a primitive ability to imitate adults' facial expressions and gestures. **Imitation** is a powerful means of learning, which contributes to the parent–infant bond. Scientists have identified specialized cells called **mirror neurons** that underlie these capacities. However, whether newborn imitation is a voluntary capacity remains controversial.

Motor Development (p. 181)

5.6 Discuss the general course of motor development during the first two years, along with factors that influence it.

- According to the **dynamic systems theory of motor development,** children acquire new motor skills by combining existing skills into increasingly complex systems of action. Each new skill is a joint product of central nervous system development, the body's movement possibilities, the child's goals, and environmental supports for the skill.

- Movement opportunities and a stimulating environment profoundly affect motor development, as shown by research on infants reared in deprived institutions. Cultural values and child-rearing customs contribute to the emergence and refinement of early motor skills.

© DON DESPAIR/ALAMY

- During the first year, infants perfect their reaching and grasping. The poorly coordinated **prereaching** of the newborn period drops out. Gradually, reaching becomes more flexible and accurate, and the clumsy **ulnar grasp** is transformed into a refined **pincer grasp** by the end of the first year.

Perceptual Development (p. 187)

5.7 What changes in hearing and in depth, pattern, object, and intermodal perception take place during infancy?

- Infants organize sounds into increasingly complex patterns and, in the middle of the first year, become more sensitive to the sounds of their own language. They have an impressive **statistical learning capacity,** which enables them to detect speech regularities for which they will later learn meanings.

- Rapid maturation of the eye and visual centers in the cerebral cortex supports the development of focusing, color discrimination, and visual acuity during the first few months. The ability to scan the environment and track moving objects also improves.

- Research on depth perception reveals that responsiveness to motion develops first, followed by sensitivity to binocular and then to pictorial depth cues. Experience in crawling enhances depth perception, but babies must learn to use depth cues for each body position in order to avoid drop-offs.

- **Contrast sensitivity** accounts for infants' early pattern preferences. At first, babies stare at single, high-contrast features. Over time, they discriminate increasingly complex and meaningful patterns.

- Newborns prefer to look at photos and simplified drawings of faces. Around 2 months, they recognize and prefer their mother's facial features, and at 3 months, they distinguish the features of different faces. From 5 months on, they perceive emotional expressions as meaningful wholes.

- At birth, **size** and **shape constancy** help babies begin to detect a coherent world of objects. At first, infants depend on motion and spatial arrangement to identify objects. After 4 months of age, they rely increasingly on object features, such as distinct shape and surface pattern. Soon they can monitor increasingly intricate paths of objects, and they look for featural information to detect the identity of a moving object.

- From the start, infants are capable of **intermodal perception**—combining information across sensory modalities. Detection of **amodal sensory properties,** such as common rate, rhythm, or intensity, provides the basis for detecting many intermodal matches.

5.8 Explain differentiation theory of perceptual development.

- According to **differentiation theory,** perceptual development is a matter of detecting increasingly fine-grained invariant features in a constantly changing perceptual world. Perceptual differentiation is guided by discovery of **affordances**—the action possibilities that a situation offers the individual.

Important Terms and Concepts

affordances (p. 196)
amodal sensory properties (p. 195)
brain plasticity (p. 165)
cephalocaudal trend (p. 161)
cerebral cortex (p. 164)
classical conditioning (p. 176)
conditioned response (CR) (p. 177)
conditioned stimulus (CS) (p. 177)
contrast sensitivity (p. 191)
differentiation theory (p. 196)
dynamic systems theory of motor development (p. 181)
experience-dependent brain growth (p. 169)
experience-expectant brain growth (p. 169)
glial cells (p. 162)

growth faltering (p. 176)
habituation (p. 178)
imitation (p. 179)
intermodal perception (p. 195)
kwashiorkor (p. 175)
lateralization (p. 165)
marasmus (p. 175)
mirror neurons (p. 180)
myelination (p. 162)
neurons (p. 161)
neurotransmitters (p. 161)
operant conditioning (p. 178)
perceptual narrowing effect (p. 188)
pincer grasp (p. 186)
prefrontal cortex (p. 165)

prereaching (p. 185)
proximodistal trend (p. 161)
punishment (p. 178)
recovery (p. 178)
reinforcer (p. 178)
shape constancy (p. 194)
size constancy (p. 194)
statistical learning capacity (p. 188)
synapses (p. 161)
synaptic pruning (p. 162)
ulnar grasp (p. 186)
unconditioned response (UCR) (p. 177)
unconditioned stimulus (UCS) (p. 177)

Cognitive Development in Infancy and Toddlerhood

"My Mother and My Brother"
Maisha Maliha Siddique
8 years, Bangladesh

This toddler delights in his mother's attention and speech as they play. In Chapter 6, you will see that a stimulating environment and the guidance of more mature members of their culture ensure that young children's cognition will develop at its best.

REPRINTED WITH PERMISSION FROM THE INTERNATIONAL MUSEUM OF CHILDREN'S ART, OSLO, NORWAY

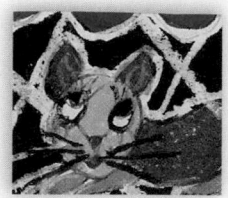

When Caitlin, Grace, and Timmy gathered at Ginette's child-care home, the playroom was alive with activity. The three spirited explorers, each nearly 18 months old, were bent on discovery. Grace dropped shapes through holes in a plastic box that Ginette held and adjusted so the harder ones would fall smoothly into place. Once a few shapes were inside, Grace grabbed the box and shook it, squealing with delight as the lid fell open and the shapes scattered around her. The clatter attracted Timmy, who picked up a shape, carried it to the railing at the top of the basement steps, and dropped it overboard, then followed with a teddy bear, a ball, his shoe, and a spoon. Meanwhile, Caitlin pulled open a drawer, unloaded a set of wooden bowls, stacked them in a pile, knocked it over, and then banged two bowls together. With each action, the children seemed to be asking, "How do things work? What makes interesting events happen? Which ones can I control?"

As the toddlers experimented, we could see the beginnings of spoken language—a whole new way of influencing the world. "All gone baw!" Caitlin exclaimed as Timmy tossed the bright red ball down the basement steps. "Bye-bye," Grace chimed in, waving as the ball disappeared from sight. Later that day, Grace revealed the beginnings of make-believe. "Night-night," she said, putting her head down and closing her eyes, ever so pleased that she could decide for herself when and where to go to bed.

Over the first two years, the small, reflexive newborn baby becomes a self-assertive, purposeful being who solves simple problems and starts to master the most amazing human ability: language. Parents wonder, how does all this happen so quickly? This question has also captivated researchers, yielding a wealth of findings along with vigorous debate over how to explain the astonishing pace of infant and toddler cognition.

In this chapter, we take up three perspectives on early cognitive development: Piaget's *cognitive-developmental theory, information processing,* and Vygotsky's *socio-cultural theory.* We also consider the usefulness of tests that measure infants' and toddlers' intellectual progress. Finally, we look at the beginnings of language. We will see how toddlers' first words build on early cognitive achievements and how, very soon, new words and expressions greatly increase the speed and flexibility of their thinking. Throughout development, cognition and language mutually support each other. ■

Piaget's Cognitive-Developmental Theory

Swiss theorist Jan Piaget inspired a vision of children as busy, motivated explorers whose thinking develops as they act directly on the environment. Influenced by his background in biology, Piaget believed that the child's mind forms and modifies psychological structures so they achieve a better fit with external reality. Recall from Chapter 1 that in Piaget's theory, children move through four stages between infancy and adolescence. During these stages, Piaget claimed, all aspects of cognition develop in an integrated fashion, changing in a similar way at about the same time.

Piaget's **sensorimotor stage** spans the first two years of life. Piaget believed that infants and toddlers "think" with their eyes, ears, hands, and other sensorimotor equipment. They cannot yet carry out many activities inside their heads. But by the

6.1 According to Piaget, how do schemes change over the course of development?

6.2 Describe major cognitive attainments of the sensorimotor stage.

6.3 What does follow-up research say about infant cognitive development and the accuracy of Piaget's sensorimotor stage?

end of toddlerhood, children can solve everyday practical problems and represent their experiences in speech, gesture, and play. To appreciate Piaget's view of how these vast changes take place, let's consider some important concepts.

Piaget's Ideas About Cognitive Change

According to Piaget, specific psychological structures—organized ways of making sense of experience called **schemes**—change with age. At first, schemes are sensorimotor action patterns. For example, at 6 months, Timmy dropped objects in a fairly rigid way, simply by letting go of a rattle or teething ring and watching with interest. By 18 months, his "dropping scheme" had become deliberate and creative. In tossing objects down the basement stairs, he threw some in the air, bounced others off walls, released some gently and others forcefully. Soon, instead of just acting on objects, he will show evidence of thinking before he acts. For Piaget, this change marks the transition from sensorimotor to preoperational thought.

In Piaget's theory, two processes, *adaptation* and *organization,* account for changes in schemes.

ADAPTATION **TAKE A MOMENT...** The next time you have a chance, notice how infants and toddlers tirelessly repeat actions that lead to interesting effects. **Adaptation** involves building schemes through direct interaction with the environment. It consists of two complementary activities: *assimilation* and *accommodation.* During **assimilation**, we use our current schemes to interpret the external world. For example, when Timmy dropped objects, he was assimilating them to his sensorimotor "dropping scheme." In **accommodation**, we create new schemes or adjust old ones after noticing that our current ways of thinking do not capture the environment completely. When Timmy dropped objects in different ways, he modified his dropping scheme to take account of the varied properties of objects.

According to Piaget, the balance between assimilation and accommodation varies over time. When children are not changing much, they assimilate more than they accommodate—a steady, comfortable state that Piaget called cognitive *equilibrium.* During times of rapid cognitive change, children are in a state of *disequilibrium,* or cognitive discomfort. Realizing that new information does not match their current schemes, they shift from assimilation to accommodation. After modifying their schemes, they move back toward assimilation, exercising their newly changed structures until they are ready to be modified again.

Each time this back-and-forth movement between equilibrium and disequilibrium occurs, more effective schemes are produced. Because the times of greatest accommodation are the earliest ones, the sensorimotor stage is Piaget's most complex period of development.

ORGANIZATION Schemes also change through **organization**, a process that occurs internally, apart from direct contact with the environment. Once children form new schemes, they rearrange them, linking them with other schemes to create a strongly interconnected cognitive system. For example, eventually Timmy will relate "dropping" to "throwing" and to his developing understanding of "nearness" and "farness." According to Piaget, schemes truly reach equilibrium when they become part of a broad network of structures that can be jointly applied to the surrounding world (Piaget, 1936/1952).

In the following sections, we will first describe infant development as Piaget saw it, noting research that supports his observations. Then we will consider evidence demonstrating that in some ways, babies' cognitive competence is more advanced than Piaget believed.

© LAURA DWIGHT PHOTOGRAPHY

In Piaget's theory, first schemes are sensorimotor action patterns. As this 12-month-old experiments with his dropping scheme, his behavior becomes more deliberate and varied.

The Sensorimotor Stage

The difference between the newborn baby and the 2-year-old child is so vast that Piaget divided the sensorimotor stage into six substages, summarized in Table 6.1. Piaget based this sequence on a very small sample: his own three children. He observed his son and two daughters carefully and also presented them with everyday problems (such as hidden objects) that helped reveal their understanding of the world.

According to Piaget, at birth infants know so little that they cannot explore purposefully. The **circular reaction** provides a special means of adapting their first schemes. It involves stumbling onto a new experience caused by the baby's own motor activity. The reaction is "circular" because, as the infant tries to repeat the event again and again, a sensorimotor response that originally occurred by chance strengthens into a new scheme. Consider Caitlin, who at age 2 months accidentally made a smacking sound after a feeding. Finding this new sound intriguing, she tried to repeat it until, after a few days, she became quite expert at smacking her lips.

The circular reaction initially centers on the infant's own body but later turns outward, toward manipulation of objects. In the second year, it becomes experimental and creative, aimed at producing novel outcomes. Infants' difficulty inhibiting new and interesting behaviors may underlie the circular reaction. This immaturity in inhibition seems to be adaptive, helping to ensure that new skills will not be interrupted before they strengthen (Carey & Markman, 1999). Piaget considered revisions in the circular reaction so important that, as Table 6.1 shows, he named the sensorimotor substages after them.

REPEATING CHANCE BEHAVIORS Piaget saw newborn reflexes as the building blocks of sensorimotor intelligence. In Substage 1, babies suck, grasp, and look in much the same way, no matter what experiences they encounter.

Around 1 month, as babies enter Substage 2, they start to gain voluntary control over their actions through the *primary circular reaction*, by repeating chance behaviors largely motivated by basic needs. This leads to some simple motor habits, such as sucking their fists or thumbs. Babies of this substage also begin to vary their behavior in response to environmental demands. For example, they open their mouths differently for a nipple than for a spoon. And they start to anticipate events. At age 3 months, when Timmy awoke from his nap, he cried out with hunger. But as soon as Vanessa entered the room, his crying stopped. He knew that feeding time was near.

During Substage 3, from 4 to 8 months, infants sit up and reach for and manipulate objects. These motor achievements strengthen the *secondary circular reaction*, through which babies try to repeat interesting events in the surrounding environment that are caused by their own actions. For example, 4-month-old Caitlin accidentally knocked a toy hung in front of her,

© ELLEN B. SENISI

This 3-month-old tries to repeat a newly discovered action—sucking her toes— in a primary circular reaction that helps her gain voluntary control over her behavior.

TABLE 6.1	Summary of Piaget's Sensorimotor Stage
SENSORIMOTOR SUBSTAGE	**TYPICAL ADAPTIVE BEHAVIORS**
1. Reflexive schemes (birth–1 month)	Newborn reflexes (see Chapter 4, page 142)
2. Primary circular reactions (1–4 months)	Simple motor habits centered around the infant's own body; limited anticipation of events
3. Secondary circular reactions (4–8 months)	Actions aimed at repeating interesting effects in the surrounding world; imitation of familiar behaviors
4. Coordination of secondary circular reactions (8–12 months)	Intentional, or goal-directed, behavior; ability to find a hidden object in the first location in which it is hidden (object permanence); improved anticipation of events; imitation of behaviors slightly different from those the infant usually performs
5. Tertiary circular reactions (12–18 months)	Exploration of the properties of objects by acting on them in novel ways; imitation of novel behaviors; ability to search in several locations for a hidden object (accurate A–B search)
6. Mental representation (18 months–2 years)	Internal depictions of objects and events, as indicated by sudden solutions to problems; ability to find an object that has been moved while out of sight (invisible displacement); deferred imitation; and make-believe play

When this 3-month-old accidentally hits a toy hung in front of her, her action causes it to swing. Using the secondary circular reaction, she tries to recapture this interesting effect. In the process, she forms a new "hitting scheme."

producing a fascinating swinging motion. Over the next three days, Caitlin tried to repeat this effect, gradually forming a new "hitting" scheme. Improved control over their own behavior permits infants to imitate others' behavior more effectively. However, Piaget noted, 4- to 8-month-olds cannot adapt flexibly and quickly enough to imitate novel behaviors. Although they enjoy watching an adult demonstrate a game of pat-a-cake, they are not yet able to participate.

INTENTIONAL BEHAVIOR   In Substage 4, 8- to 12-month-olds combine schemes into new, more complex action sequences. As a result, actions that lead to new schemes no longer have a random, hit-or-miss quality—*accidentally* bringing the thumb to the mouth or *happening* to hit the toy. Instead, 8- to 12-month-olds can engage in **intentional,** or **goal-directed, behavior**, coordinating schemes deliberately to solve simple problems. Consider Piaget's famous object-hiding task, in which he shows the baby an attractive toy and then hides it behind his hand or under a cover. Infants of this substage can find the object by coordinating two schemes—"pushing" aside the obstacle and "grasping" the toy. Piaget regarded these *means–end action sequences* as the foundation for all problem solving.

Retrieving hidden objects reveals that infants have begun to master **object permanence**, the understanding that objects continue to exist when they are out of sight. But this awareness is not yet complete. Babies make the **A-not-B search error:** If they reach several times for an object at a first hiding place (A), then see it moved to a second (B), they still search for it in the first hiding place (A). Consequently, Piaget concluded that they do not have a clear image of the object as persisting when hidden from view.

Infants in Substage 4, who can better anticipate events, sometimes use their capacity for intentional behavior to try to change those events. At 10 months, Timmy crawled after Vanessa when she put on her coat, whimpering to keep her from leaving. Also, babies can now imitate behaviors slightly different from those they usually perform. After watching someone else, they try to stir with a spoon, push a toy car, or drop raisins into a cup (Piaget, 1945/1951).

In Substage 5, from 12 to 18 months, the *tertiary circular reaction,* in which toddlers repeat behaviors with variation, emerges. Recall how Timmy dropped objects over the basement steps, trying this action, then that, then another. This deliberately exploratory approach makes 12- to 18-month-olds better problem solvers. For example, Grace figured out how to fit a shape through a hole in a container by turning and twisting it until it fell through and how to use a stick to get a toy that was out of reach. According to Piaget, this capacity to experiment leads to a more advanced understanding of object permanence. Toddlers look for a hidden toy in several locations, displaying an accurate A–B search. Their more flexible action patterns also permit them to imitate many more behaviors, such as stacking blocks, scribbling on paper, and making funny faces.

To find the toy hidden inside the pot, a 10-month-old engages in intentional, goal-directed behavior—the basis for all problem solving.

Using a tertiary circular reaction, this baby twists, turns, and pushes until a block fits through its matching hole in her shape sorter. Between 12 and 18 months, toddlers take a deliberately experimental approach to problem solving.

MENTAL REPRESENTATION Substage 6 brings the ability to create **mental representations**—internal depictions of information that the mind can manipulate. Our most powerful mental representations are of two kinds: (1) *images*—mental pictures of objects, people, and spaces; and (2) *concepts*—categories in which similar objects or events are grouped together. We use a mental image to retrace our steps when we've misplaced something or to imitate someone's behavior long after observing it. By thinking in concepts and labeling them (for example, "ball" for all rounded, movable objects used in play), we become more efficient thinkers, organizing our diverse experiences into meaningful, manageable, and memorable units.

Piaget noted that 18- to 24-month-olds arrive at solutions suddenly rather than through trial-and-error behavior. In doing so, they seem to experiment with actions inside their heads—evidence that they can mentally represent their experiences. For example, at 19 months, Grace—after bumping her new push toy against a wall—paused for a moment as if to "think," and then immediately turned the toy in a new direction.

Representation enables older toddlers to solve advanced object permanence problems involving *invisible displacement*—finding a toy moved while out of sight, such as into a small box while under a cover. It also permits **deferred imitation**—the ability to remember and copy the behavior of models who are not present. And it makes possible **make-believe play,** in which children act out everyday and imaginary activities. As the sensorimotor stage draws to a close, mental symbols have become major instruments of thinking.

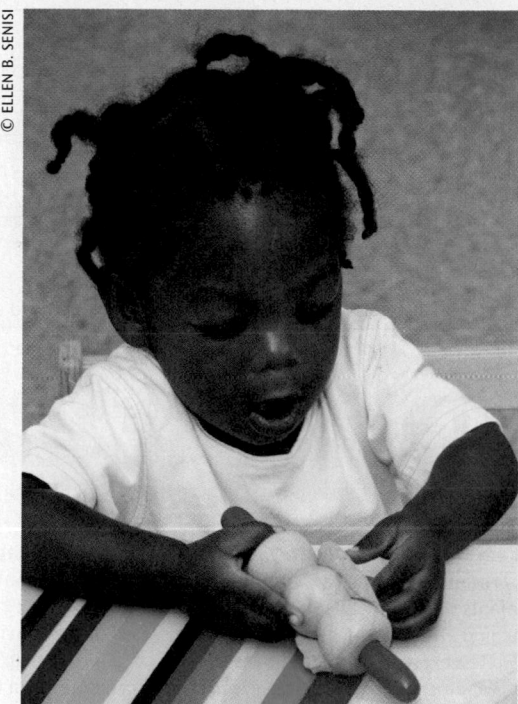

© ELLEN B. SENISI

Through deferred imitation, toddlers greatly expand their sensorimotor schemes. While imitating, this 2-year-old encounters a problem faced by all cookie bakers at one time or another.

Follow-Up Research on Infant Cognitive Development

Many studies suggest that infants display a wide array of understandings earlier than Piaget believed. Recall the operant conditioning research reviewed in Chapter 5, in which newborns sucked vigorously on a nipple to gain access to interesting sights and sounds. This behavior, which closely resembles Piaget's secondary circular reaction, shows that babies try to explore and control the external world long before 4 to 8 months. In fact, they do so as soon as they are born.

To discover what infants know about hidden objects and other aspects of physical reality, researchers often use the **violation-of-expectation method.** They may *habituate* babies to a physical event (expose them to the event until their looking declines) to familiarize them with a situation in which their knowledge will be tested. Or they may simply show babies an *expected event* (one that is consistent with reality) and an *unexpected event* (a variation of the first event that violates reality). Heightened attention to the unexpected event suggests that the infant is "surprised" by a deviation from physical reality and, therefore, is aware of that aspect of the physical world.

The violation-of-expectation method is controversial. Some critics believe that it indicates limited, implicit (nonconscious) awareness of physical events—not the full-blown, conscious understanding that was Piaget's focus in requiring infants to act on their surroundings, as in searching for hidden objects (Campos et al., 2008; Munakata, 2001). Others maintain that the method reveals only babies' perceptual preference for novelty, not their knowledge of the physical world (Bremner, 2010; Cohen, 2010; Kagan, 2008). Let's examine this debate in light of recent evidence.

OBJECT PERMANENCE In a series of studies using the violation-of-expectation method, Renée Baillargeon and her collaborators claimed to have found evidence for object permanence in the first few months of life. Figure 6.1 on page 206 describes and illustrates one of these studies, in which infants exposed to both an expected and an unexpected object-hiding event looked longer at the unexpected event (Aguiar & Baillargeon, 2002; Baillargeon & DeVos, 1991).

Additional violation-of-expectation studies yielded similar results, suggesting that infants look longer at a wide variety of unexpected events involving hidden objects (Newcombe,

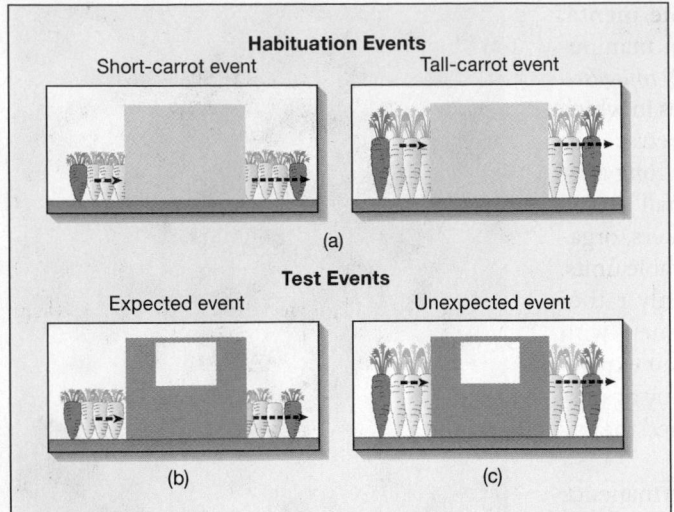

FIGURE 6.1 **Testing young infants for understanding of object permanence using the violation-of-expectation method.** (a) First, infants were habituated to two events: a short carrot and a tall carrot moving behind a yellow screen, on alternate trials. Next, the researchers presented two test events. The color of the screen was changed to help infants notice its window. (b) In the *expected event,* the carrot shorter than the window's lower edge moved behind the blue screen and reappeared on the other side. (c) In the *unexpected event,* the carrot taller than the window's lower edge moved behind the screen and did not appear in the window, but then emerged intact on the other side. Infants as young as 2½ to 3½ months looked longer at the *unexpected event,* suggesting that they had some understanding of object permanence. (Adapted from R. Baillargeon & J. DeVos, 1991, "Object Permanence in Young Infants: Further Evidence," *Child Development, 62,* p. 1230. © 1991, John Wiley and Sons. Reprinted with permission of John Wiley & Sons Ltd. conveyed through Copyright Clearance Center, Inc.)

Sluzenski, & Huttenlocher, 2005; Wang, Baillargeon, & Paterson, 2005). Still, several researchers using similar procedures failed to confirm some of Baillargeon's findings (Cohen & Marks, 2002; Schöner & Thelen, 2006; Sirois & Jackson, 2012). And, as previously noted, critics question what babies' looking preferences tell us about what they actually understand.

But another type of looking behavior suggests that young infants are aware that objects persist when out of view. Four- and 5-month-olds will track a ball's path of movement as it disappears and reappears from behind a barrier, even gazing ahead to where they expect it to emerge. As further support for such awareness, 5- to 9-month-olds more often engaged in such predictive tracking when a ball viewed on a computer screen gradually rolled behind a barrier than when it disappeared instantaneously or imploded (rapidly decreased in size) at the barrier's edge (Bertenthal, Gredebäck, & Boyer, 2013; Bertenthal, Longo, & Kenny, 2007). With age, babies are more likely to fixate on the predicted place of the ball's reappearance and wait for it—evidence of an increasingly secure grasp of object permanence.

If young infants do have some notion of object permanence, how do we explain Piaget's finding that even infants capable of reaching do not try to search for hidden objects before 8 months of age? Compared with looking reactions in violation-of-expectation tasks, searching for a hidden object is far more cognitively demanding: The baby must figure out where the hidden object is. Consistent with this idea, infants solve some object-hiding tasks before others: Eight- to 10-month-olds remove the cover from a partially hidden object before they are able to do so from a fully covered object (Moore & Meltzoff, 2008). And 10-month-olds search for an object placed on a table and covered by a cloth before they search for an object that a hand deposits under a cloth (Moore & Meltzoff, 1999). In the second, more difficult task, infants seem to expect the object to reappear in the hand from which it initially disappeared. When the hand emerges without the object, they conclude that there is no other place the object could be. Not until 14 months can most babies infer that the hand deposited the object under the cloth.

Around this age, toddlers also know that objects continue to exist in their hidden locations after the babies have left the location. After seeing an object hidden in a cupboard, when toddlers returned the next day, they correctly searched for the specific object in its original location (Moore & Meltzoff, 2004). When exposed to a similar cupboard in a new room, the toddlers behaved just as adults do: They saw no reason to search.

SEARCHING FOR OBJECTS HIDDEN IN MORE THAN ONE LOCATION Once 8- to 12-month-olds search for hidden objects, they make the A-not-B search error. Some research suggests that they search at A (where they found the object on previous reaches) instead of B (its most recent location) because they have trouble inhibiting a previously rewarded motor response (Diamond, Cruttenden, & Neiderman, 1994). Another possibility is that after finding the object several times at A, babies do not attend closely when it is hidden at B (Ruffman & Langman, 2002).

A more comprehensive explanation is that a complex, dynamic system of factors—having built a habit of reaching toward A, continuing to look at A, having the hiding place at B appear similar to the one at A, and maintaining a constant body posture—increases the chances that the baby will make the A-not-B search error. Disrupting any one of these factors increases 10-month-olds' accurate searching at B (Thelen et al., 2001). In addition, older infants are still perfecting reaching and grasping (see Chapter 5) (Berger, 2010). If these motor skills are challenging, babies have little attention left to focus on inhibiting their habitual reach toward A.

In sum, mastery of object permanence is a gradual achievement. Babies' understanding becomes increasingly complex with age: They must perceive an object's identity by integrating feature and movement information (see Chapter 5, pages 194–195), distinguish the object from the barrier concealing it and the surface on which it rests, keep track of the object's whereabouts, and use this knowledge to obtain the object (Moore & Meltzoff, 2008). Success at object search tasks coincides with rapid development of the frontal lobes of the cerebral cortex (Bell, 1998). Also crucial are a wide variety of experiences perceiving, acting on, and remembering objects.

MENTAL REPRESENTATION In Piaget's theory, before about 18 months, infants are unable to mentally represent experience. Yet 8- to 10-month-olds' ability to recall the location of hidden objects after delays of more than a minute, and 14-month-olds' recall after delays of a day or more, clearly indicate that babies construct mental representations of objects and their whereabouts (McDonough, 1999; Moore & Meltzoff, 2004). In studies of deferred imitation and problem solving, representational thought is evident even earlier. And toddlers make impressive strides in symbolic understanding, as their grasp of words and photos reveals.

Deferred and Inferred Imitation Piaget studied imitation by noting when his three children demonstrated it in their everyday behavior. Under these conditions, a great deal must be known about the infant's daily life to be sure that deferred imitation—which requires infants to represent a model's past behavior—has occurred.

Laboratory research reveals that deferred imitation is present at 6 weeks of age! Infants who watched an unfamiliar adult's facial expression imitated it when exposed to the same adult the next day (Meltzoff & Moore, 1994). As motor capacities improve, infants copy actions with objects. In one study, adults showed 6- and 9-month-olds a novel series of actions with a puppet: taking its glove off, shaking the glove to ring a bell inside, and replacing the glove. When tested a day later, infants who had seen the novel actions were far more likely to imitate them (see Figure 6.2). And when researchers paired a second, motionless puppet with the first puppet from 1 to 6 days before the demonstration, 6- to 9-month-olds generalized the actions to this new, very different-looking puppet (Barr, Marrott, & Rovee-Collier, 2003; Giles & Rovee-Collier, 2011). Even more impressive, after having seen Puppet A paired with B and

LOOK *and* **LISTEN**

Using an attractive toy and cloth, try several object-hiding tasks with 8- to 14-month-olds. Is their search behavior consistent with research findings?

COURTESY OF CAROLYN ROVEE-COLLIER

(a)   (b)

FIGURE 6.2 Testing infants for deferred imitation. After researchers performed a novel series of actions with a puppet, this 6-month-old imitated the actions a day later—(a) removing the glove; (b) shaking the glove to ring a bell inside. With age, gains in recall are evident in deferred imitation of others' behaviors over longer delays.

Puppet B paired with C on successive days, infants transferred modeled actions from A to C and from C to A, although they had not directly observed this pair together (Townsend & Rovee-Collier, 2007). Already, infants can form flexible mental representations that include chains of relevant associations.

Gains in recall, expressed through deferred imitation, are accompanied by changes in brain-wave activity during memory tasks, as measured by ERPs. This suggests that improvements in memory storage in the cerebral cortex contribute to these advances (Bauer et al., 2006). Between 12 and 18 months, toddlers use deferred imitation skillfully to enrich their range of schemes. They retain modeled behaviors for at least several months, copy the actions of peers as well as adults, and imitate across a change in context—for example, enact at home a behavior seen at child care (Meltzoff & Williamson, 2010; Patel, Gaylord, & Fagen, 2013). The ability to recall modeled behaviors in the order they occurred—evident as early as 6 months—also strengthens over the second year (Bauer, 2006; Rovee-Collier & Cuevas, 2009). And when babies imitate in correct sequence, they remember more behaviors (Knopf, Kraus, & Kressley-Mba, 2006).

Older infants and toddlers even imitate rationally, by *inferring* others' intentions! They are more likely to imitate purposeful than accidental or arbitrary behaviors on objects (Hamlin, Hallinan, & Woodward, 2008; Thoermer et al., 2013). And they adapt their imitative acts to a model's goals. If 12-month-olds see an adult perform an unusual action for fun (make a toy dog enter a miniature house by jumping through the chimney, even though its door is wide open), they copy the behavior. But if the adult engages in the odd behavior because she *must* (she makes the dog go through the chimney only after first trying to use the door and finding it locked), 12-month-olds typically imitate the more efficient action (putting the dog through the door) (Schwier et al., 2006).

Between 14 and 18 months, toddlers become increasingly adept at imitating actions an adult *tries* to produce, even if these are not fully realized (Bellagamba, Camaioni, & Colonnesi, 2006; Olineck & Poulin-Dubois, 2009). On one occasion, Ginette attempted to pour some raisins into a small bag but missed, spilling them onto the counter. A moment later, Grace began dropping the raisins into the bag, indicating that she had inferred Ginette's goal.

Though advanced in terms of Piaget's predictions, toddlers' ability to represent others' intentions—a cornerstone of social understanding and communication—has roots in earlier sensorimotor activity (Rosander & von Hofsten, 2011). Infants' skill at engaging in goal-directed actions—reaching for objects at 3 to 4 months, pointing to objects at 9 months—predicts their awareness of an adult's similar behavior as goal-directed (Gerson & Woodward, 2010; Woodward, 2009). And the better 10-month-olds are at detecting the goals of others' gazes and reaches, the more successful they are four months later at inferring an adult's intention from her incomplete actions in an imitation task (Olineck & Poulin-Dubois, 2009).

Problem Solving As Piaget indicated, around 8 months, infants develop intentional means–end action sequences, such as pulling on a cloth to obtain a toy resting on its far end (Willatts, 1999). Out of these explorations of object-to-object relations, the capacity for tool use in problem solving—flexibly manipulating an object as a means to a goal—emerges (Keen, 2011).

For example, 12-month-olds who were repeatedly presented with a spoon oriented so its handle pointed toward their preferred hand (usually the right) adapted their grip when the spoon's handle was presented in the opposite orientation (to the left). As a result, they succeeded in transporting food to their mouths most of the time (McCarty & Keen, 2005). With age, babies increasingly adjusted their grip to fit the spoon's orientation in advance, planning ahead for what they wanted to do with the tool.

By 10 to 12 months, infants can *solve problems by analogy*—apply a solution strategy from one problem to other relevant problems. In one study, babies of this age were given three similar problems, each requiring them to overcome a barrier, grasp a string, and pull it to get an attractive toy. The problems differed in many aspects of their superficial features—texture and color of the string, barrier, and floor mat and type of toy (horse, doll, or car). For the first problem, the parent demonstrated the solution and encouraged the infant to imitate (Chen, Sanchez, & Campbell, 1997). Babies obtained the toy more readily with each additional problem.

These findings suggest that around the end of the first year, infants form flexible mental representations of how to use tools to get objects. They have some ability to move beyond trial-and-error experimentation, represent a solution mentally, and use it in new contexts.

Symbolic Understanding One of the most momentous advances in early development is the realization that words can be used to cue mental images of things not physically present—a symbolic capacity called **displaced reference** that emerges around the first birthday. It greatly expands toddlers' capacity to learn about the world through communicating with others. Observations of 12-month-olds reveal that they respond to the label of an absent toy by looking at and gesturing toward the spot where it usually rests (Saylor, 2004). And on hearing the name of a parent or sibling who has just left the room, most 13-month-olds turn toward the door (DeLoache & Ganea, 2009). The more experience toddlers have with an object and its verbal label, the more likely they are to call up a mental representation when they hear the object's name. As memory and vocabulary improve, skill at displaced reference expands.

But at first, toddlers have difficulty using language to acquire new information about an absent object—an ability that is essential to learn from symbols. In one study, an adult taught 19- and 22-month-olds a name for a stuffed animal—"Lucy" for a frog. Then, with the frog out of sight, the toddler was told that some water had spilled, so "Lucy's all wet!" Finally, the adult showed the toddler three stuffed animals—a wet frog, a dry frog, and a pig—and said, "Get Lucy!" (Ganea et al., 2007). Although all the children remembered that Lucy was a frog, only the 22-month-olds identified the wet frog as Lucy. Nevertheless, older toddlers' reliance on verbal information is fragile. When a verbal message about a toy's new location conflicts with a previously observed location, most 23-month-olds simply go to the initial location. At 30 months, children succeed at finding the toy (Ganea & Harris, 2010). The capacity to use language as a flexible symbolic tool—to modify an existing mental representation—improves from the end of the second into the third year.

A beginning awareness of the symbolic function of pictures emerges in the first year, strengthening in the second. Even newborns perceive a relation between a picture and its referent, as indicated by their preference for looking at a photo of their mother's face (see page 193 in Chapter 5). And by 9 months and perhaps before, the majority of infants recognize that real objects can be grasped while pictures of objects cannot. Most touch, rub, or pat a color photo of an object but rarely try to grasp it (Ziemer, Plumert, & Pick, 2012). These behaviors suggest that 9-month-olds do not mistake a picture for the real thing, though they may not yet comprehend it as a symbol. Manual exploration of pictures declines after 9 months, becoming rare around 18 months (DeLoache & Ganea, 2009).

Around this time, toddlers clearly treat pictures symbolically, as long as pictures strongly resemble real objects. After hearing a novel label ("blicket") applied to a color photo of an unfamiliar object, most 15- to 24-month-olds—when presented with both the real object and its picture and asked to indicate the "blicket"—gave a symbolic response (Ganea et al., 2009). They selected either the real object or both the object and its picture, not the picture alone—a response that strengthened with age.

By the middle of the second year, toddlers often use pictures as vehicles for communicating with others and acquiring new knowledge. They point to, name, and talk about pictures, and they can apply something learned from a book with realistic-looking pictures to real objects, and vice versa (Ganea, Ma, & DeLoache, 2011; Simcock, Garrity, & Barr, 2011).

Picture-rich environments in which caregivers often direct babies' attention to the link between pictures and their referents facilitate pictorial understanding. In non-Western cultures where pictures are rare,

© ELLEN B. SENISI

A 17-month-old points to a picture in a book, revealing her beginning awareness of the symbolic function of pictures. But pictures must be highly realistic for toddlers to treat them symbolically.

Social Issues: Education

Baby Learning from TV and Video: The Video Deficit Effect

Children first become TV and video viewers in early infancy, as they are exposed to programs watched by parents and older siblings or to shows aimed at viewers not yet out of diapers, such as the Baby Einstein products. About 40 percent of U.S. 3-month-olds watch regularly, a figure that rises to 90 percent at age 2. During this period, average viewing time increases from just under an hour to 1½ hours a day (Zimmerman, Christakis, & Meltzoff, 2007). Although parents assume that babies learn from TV and videos, research indicates that they cannot take full advantage of them.

Initially, infants respond to videos of people as if viewing people directly—smiling, moving their arms and legs, and (by 6 months) imitating actions of a televised adult (Barr, Muentener, & Garcia, 2007; Marian, Neisser, & Rochat, 1996). But when shown videos of attractive toys, 9-month-olds touch and grab at the screen, suggesting that they confuse the images with the real thing. By the middle of the second year, manual exploration has declined in favor of pointing at the images (Pierroutsakos & Troseth, 2003). Nevertheless, toddlers have difficulty applying what they see on video to real situations.

In a series of studies, some 2-year-olds watched through a window while a live adult hid an object in an adjoining room, while others watched the same event on a video screen. Children in the direct viewing condition retrieved the toy easily; those in the video condition had difficulty (Troseth, 2003; Troseth & DeLoache, 1998). This **video deficit effect**—poorer performance after a video than a live demonstration—has also been found for 2-year-olds' deferred imitation, word learning, and means–end problem solving (Bellagamba et al., 2012; Hayne, Herbert, & Simcock, 2003; Krcmar, Grela, & Linn, 2007).

One explanation is that 2-year-olds typically do not view a video character as offering socially relevant information. After an adult on video announced where she had hidden a toy, few 2-year-olds searched (Schmidt, Crawley-Davis, & Anderson, 2007). In contrast, when the adult uttered the same words while standing in front of the child, 2-year-olds promptly retrieved the object.

Toddlers seem to discount information on video as relevant to their everyday experiences because the people onscreen do not look at and converse with them directly or establish a shared focus on objects, as their caregivers do. In one study, researchers gave some 2-year-olds an interactive video experience (using a two-way, closed-circuit video system). An adult on video interacted with the child for five minutes—calling the child by name, talking about the child's siblings and pets, waiting for the child to respond, and playing interactive games (Troseth, Saylor, & Archer, 2006). Compared with 2-year-olds who viewed the same adult in a noninteractive video, those in the interactive condition were far more successful in using a verbal cue from a person on video to retrieve a toy.

Around age 2½, the video deficit effect declines. Before this age, the American Academy of Pediatrics (2001) recommends against mass media exposure, emphasizing that babies require rich responsive exchanges with caregivers and exploration of their physical surroundings for optimal brain growth and psychological development (see Chapter 5, page 169). In support of

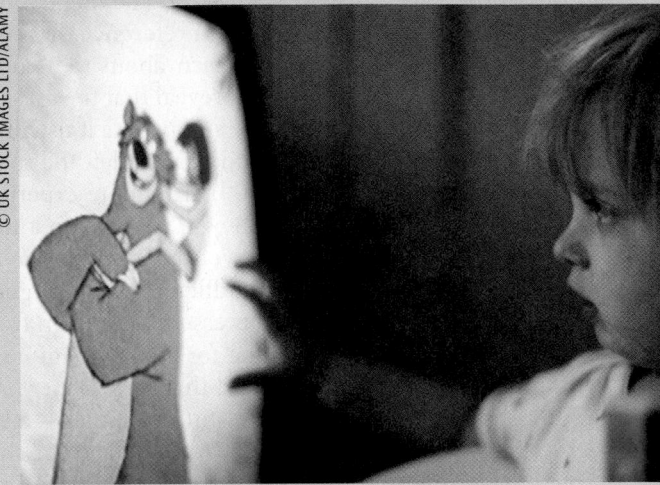

A 2-year-old looks puzzled by a video image. Perhaps she has difficulty grasping its meaning because onscreen characters do not converse with her directly, as adults in real life do.

this advice, amount of TV viewing is negatively related to 8- to 18-month-olds' language progress (Tanimura et al., 2004; Zimmerman, Christakis, & Meltzoff, 2007). And 1- to 3-year-old heavy viewers tend to have attention, memory, and reading difficulties in the early school years (Christakis et al., 2004; Zimmerman & Christakis, 2005).

Toddlers face a complex task in making sense of video: Although they no longer confuse it with reality, they do not know how to mentally represent the relationship between video images and real objects and people. When they do watch TV or video, it is likely to work best as teaching tools when it is rich in social cues (Lauricella et al., 2011). These include use of familiar characters and close-ups in which the character looks directly at the camera, addresses questions to viewers, and pauses to invite a response.

---

symbolic understanding of pictures is delayed (Callaghan et al., 2011). In a study carried out in a village community in Tanzania, Africa, where children receive no exposure to pictures before school entry, an adult taught 1½- to 3-year-olds a new name for an unfamiliar object during a picture-book interaction (Walker, Walker, & Ganea, 2012). When later asked to pick the named object from arrays of pictures and real objects, not until age 3 did the Tanzanian children's performance equal that of U.S. 15-month-olds.

But even after coming to appreciate the symbolic nature of pictures, young children continue to have difficulty grasping the distinction between some pictures (such as line drawings) and their referents, as we will see in Chapter 8. How do infants and toddlers interpret another ever-present, pictorial medium—video? See the Social Issues: Education box above to find out.

Evaluation of the Sensorimotor Stage

Table 6.2 summarizes the remarkable cognitive attainments we have just considered. **TAKE A MOMENT...** Compare this table with Piaget's description of the sensorimotor substages in Table 6.1 on page 203. You will see that infants anticipate events, actively search for hidden objects, master the A–B object search, flexibly vary their sensorimotor schemes, engage in make-believe play, and treat pictures and video images symbolically within Piaget's time frame. Yet other capacities—including secondary circular reactions, understanding of object properties, first signs of object permanence, deferred imitation, problem solving by analogy, and displaced reference of words—emerge earlier than Piaget expected. These findings show that the cognitive attainments of infancy and toddlerhood do not develop together in the neat, stepwise fashion that Piaget predicted.

Recent research raises questions about Piaget's view of how infant development takes place. Consistent with Piaget's ideas, sensorimotor action helps infants construct some forms of knowledge. For example, as we saw in Chapter 5, crawling enhances depth perception and ability to find hidden objects, and handling objects fosters awareness of object properties. Yet we have also seen that infants comprehend a great deal before they are capable of the motor behaviors that Piaget assumed led to those understandings. How can we account for babies' amazing cognitive accomplishments?

ALTERNATIVE EXPLANATIONS   Unlike Piaget, who thought babies constructed all mental representations out of sensorimotor activity, most researchers now believe that infants have some built-in cognitive equipment for making sense of experience. But intense disagreement exists over the extent of this initial understanding. As we have seen, much evidence on young infants' cognition rests on the violation-of-expectation method. Researchers who lack confidence in this method argue that babies' cognitive starting point is limited (Campos et al., 2008; Cohen, 2010; Kagan, 2008, 2013c). For example, some believe that newborns begin life with a set of biases for attending to certain information and with general-purpose learning procedures—such as powerful techniques for analyzing complex perceptual information (Bahrick, 2010; Huttenlocher, 2002; Quinn, 2008; Rakison, 2010). Together, these capacities enable infants to construct a wide variety of schemes.

Others, convinced by violation-of-expectation findings, believe that infants start out with impressive understandings. According to this **core knowledge perspective,** babies are born

TABLE 6.2	Some Cognitive Attainments of Infancy and Toddlerhood
AGE	**COGNITIVE ATTAINMENTS**
Birth–1 month	Secondary circular reactions using limited motor skills, such as sucking a nipple to gain access to interesting sights and sounds
1–4 months	Awareness of object permanence, object solidity, and gravity, as suggested by violation-of-expectation findings; deferred imitation of an adult's facial expression over a short delay (one day)
4–8 months	Improved knowledge of object properties and basic numerical knowledge, as suggested by violation-of-expectation findings; deferred imitation of an adult's novel actions on objects over a short delay (one to three days)
8–12 months	Ability to search for a hidden object when covered by a cloth; ability to solve simple problems by analogy to a previous problem
12–18 months	Ability to search in several locations for a hidden object (accurate A–B search); awareness that objects continue to exist in their hidden locations even after the toddler has left the location; deferred imitation of an adult's novel actions on objects after long delays (at least several months) and across a change in situation (from child care to home); rational imitation, inferring the model's intentions; displaced reference of words
18 months–2 years	Ability to find an object moved while out of sight (invisible displacement); deferred imitation of actions an adult tries to produce, even if these are not fully realized; deferred imitation of everyday behaviors in make-believe play; beginning awareness of pictures and video as symbols of reality

TAKE A MOMENT... Which of the capacities listed in this table indicate that mental representation emerges earlier than Piaget believed?

Did this toddler learn to build a block tower by repeatedly acting on objects, as Piaget assumed? Or did he begin life with innate knowledge that helps him understand objects and their relationships quickly, with little hands-on exploration?

with a set of innate knowledge systems, or *core domains of thought.* Each of these prewired understandings permits a ready grasp of new, related information and therefore supports early, rapid development (Carey & Markman, 1999; Leslie, 2004; Spelke & Kinzler, 2007). Core knowledge theorists argue that infants could not make sense of the complex stimulation around them without having been genetically "set up" in the course of evolution to comprehend its crucial aspects.

Researchers have conducted many studies of infants' *physical knowledge,* including object permanence, object solidity (that one object cannot move through another), and gravity (that an object will fall without support). Violation-of-expectation findings suggest that in the first few months, infants have some awareness of all these basic object properties and quickly build on this knowledge (Baillargeon et al., 2009, 2011). Core knowledge theorists also assume that an inherited foundation of *linguistic knowledge* enables swift language acquisition in early childhood—a possibility we will consider later in this chapter. Further, these theorists argue, infants' early orientation toward people initiates rapid development of *psychological knowledge*—in particular, understanding of mental states, such as intentions, emotions, desires, and beliefs, which we will address further in Chapter 7.

Research also suggests that infants have basic *numerical knowledge.* In the best-known study, 5-month-olds saw a screen raised to hide a single toy animal and then watched a hand place a second toy behind the screen. Finally, the screen was removed to reveal either one or two toys. If infants kept track of the two objects (requiring them to add one object to another), then they should look longer at the unexpected, one-toy display—which is what they did (see Figure 6.3)

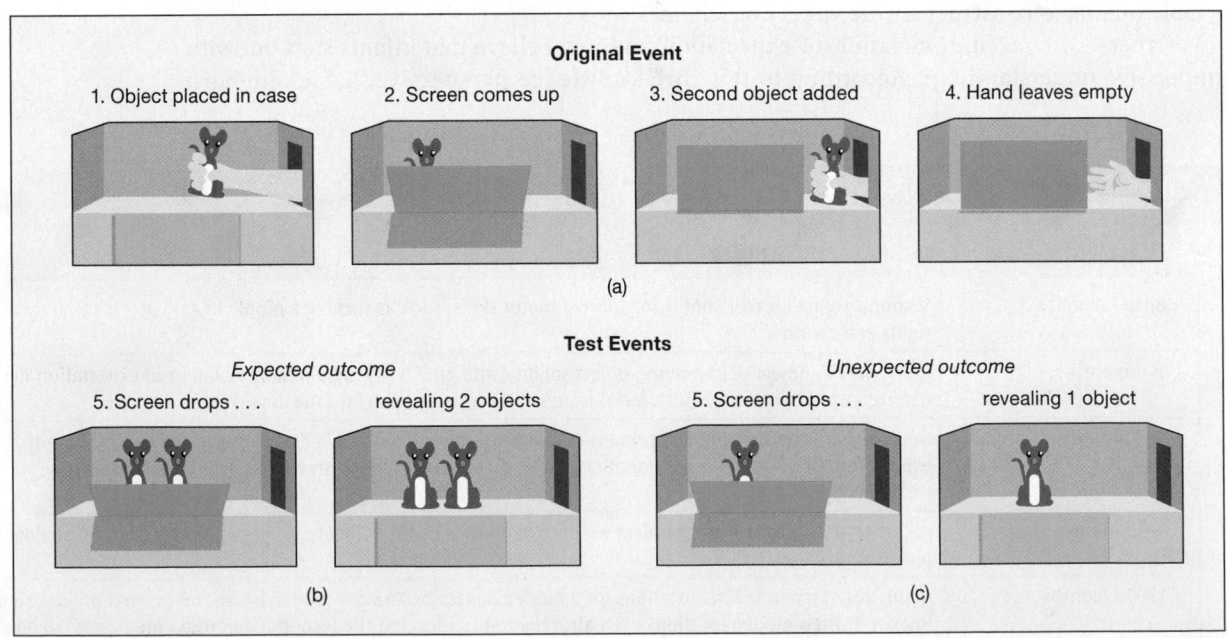

FIGURE 6.3 **Testing infants for basic number concepts.** (a) First, infants saw a screen raised in front of a toy animal. Then an identical toy was added behind the screen. Next, the researchers presented two outcomes. (b) In the *expected outcome,* the screen dropped to reveal two toy animals. (c) In the *unexpected outcome,* the screen dropped to reveal one toy animal. Five-month-olds shown the unexpected outcome looked longer than 5-month-olds shown the expected outcome. The researchers concluded that infants can discriminate the quantities "one" and "two" and use that knowledge to perform simple addition: 1 + 1 = 2. A variation of this procedure suggested that 5-month-olds could also do simple subtraction: 2 − 1 = 1. (From K. Wynn, 1992, "Addition and Subtraction by Human Infants," *Nature, 358,* p. 749. © 1992, Nature Publishing Group. Reprinted by permission from Macmillan Publishers Ltd.)

(Wynn, 1992). These findings and others suggest that babies can discriminate quantities up to three and use that knowledge to perform simple arithmetic—both addition and subtraction (in which two objects are covered and one is removed) (Kobayashi, Hiraki, & Hasegawa, 2005; Kobayashi et al., 2004; Wynn, Bloom, & Chiang, 2002). As further support, ERP brain-wave recordings taken while babies view correct and incorrect simple arithmetic solutions reveal a response pattern identical to the pattern adults show when detecting errors (Berger, Tzur, & Posner, 2006).

Additional evidence suggests that 6-month-olds can distinguish among large sets of items, as long as the difference between those sets is very great—at least a factor of two. For example, they can tell the difference between 8 and 16 dots but not between 8 and 12. At 9 months, babies can discriminate 8 and 12 but not 8 and 10 (Lipton & Spelke, 2003; Xu, Spelke, & Goddard, 2005). Furthermore, research resembling the experiment in Figure 6.3 reveals that 9-month-olds can perform operations on large sets of items, adding and subtracting (McCrink & Wynn, 2004). And by the middle of the first year, babies show distinct ERP brain-wave patterns like those of adults when processing large sets of items (Hyde & Spelke, 2011). As a result, some researchers believe that infants can represent approximate large-number values, and that processing of large-item and small-item sets is governed by different neural networks.

These impressive findings suggest that certain notions of quantity are present in the first year. But like other violation-of-expectation results, the evidence is controversial. Skeptics question whether other aspects of object displays, rather than numerical sensitivity, are responsible for the findings (Cohen & Marks, 2002; Langer, Gillette, & Arriaga, 2003). According to these investigators, claims for infants' knowledge of number concepts are surprising, in view of other research indicating that before 14 to 16 months, toddlers have difficulty making less-than and greater-than comparisons between small sets. And, as we will see in Chapter 9, not until the preschool years do children add and subtract small sets correctly.

Furthermore, critics take issue with the core knowledge assumption, based on violation-of-expectation findings, that infants are endowed with *knowledge* (Bremner, 2010; Cohen, 2009). They argue that young infants' looking behaviors may indicate only a perceptual preference, not the existence of concepts and reasoning. And indisputable evidence for built-in core knowledge requires that it be demonstrated at birth or close to it—in the absence of relevant opportunities to learn (Johnson, 2010). Although tentative support for distinct systems for processing small and large numerical values in newborns has been reported, contrary findings also exist (Coubart et al., 2014; Izard, Dehaene-Lambertz, & Dehaene, 2008; Izard et al., 2009). Thus, much more research is needed.

Finally, the core knowledge perspective, while emphasizing native endowment, acknowledges that experience is essential for children to extend this initial knowledge. But so far, it has said little about which experiences are most important in each core domain and how those experiences advance children's thinking. Despite challenges from critics, core knowledge research has sharpened the field's focus on clarifying the starting point for human cognition and on carefully tracking the changes that build on it.

PIAGET'S LEGACY   Follow-up research on Piaget's sensorimotor stage yields broad agreement on two issues. First, many cognitive changes of infancy are gradual and continuous rather than abrupt and stagelike, as Piaget thought (Bjorklund, 2012). Second, rather than developing together, various aspects of infant cognition change unevenly because of the challenges posed by different types of tasks and infants' varying experiences with them. These ideas serve as the basis for another major approach to cognitive development—*information processing*—which we take up next.

Before we turn to this alternative point of view, let's recognize Piaget's enormous contributions. Piaget's work inspired a wealth of research on infant cognition, including studies that challenged his theory. Today, researchers are far from consensus on how to modify or replace his account of infant cognitive development, and some believe that his general approach continues to make sense and fits most of the evidence (Cohen, 2010). Piaget's observations also have been of great practical value. Teachers and caregivers continue to look to the sensorimotor stage for guidelines on how to create developmentally appropriate environments for infants and toddlers.

Applying What We Know

Play Materials That Support Infant and Toddler Cognitive Development

FROM 2 MONTHS	FROM 6 MONTHS	FROM 1 YEAR
Crib mobile	Squeeze toys	Large dolls, toy dishes, toy telephone
Rattles and other handheld sound-making toys, such as a bell on a handle	Nesting cups	Cars and trucks
	Clutch and texture balls	Large blocks, cardboard boxes
Adult-operated music boxes and music recordings with gentle, regular rhythms, songs, and lullabies	Stuffed animals and soft-bodied dolls	Hammer-and-peg toy
	Filling and emptying toys	Pull and push toys, riding toys that can be pushed with feet
	Large and small blocks	Rhythm instruments for shaking and banging, such as bells, cymbals, and drums
	Pots, pans, and spoons from the kitchen	Simple puzzles
	Simple, floating objects for the bath	Sandbox, shovel, and pail
	Picture books with realistic color images	Shallow wading pool and water toys
		Balls of various sizes

TAKE A MOMENT... Now that you are familiar with some milestones of the first two years, what play materials do you think would support the development of sensorimotor and early representational schemes? Prepare a list, justifying it by referring to the cognitive attainments described in the previous sections. Then compare your suggestions to the ones given in Applying What We Know above.

Ask Yourself

- **REVIEW** Using the text discussion on pages 203–210, construct your own summary table of infant and toddler cognitive development. Which entries in your table are consistent with Piaget's sensorimotor stage? Which ones develop earlier than Piaget anticipated?

- **CONNECT** Recall from Chapter 5 (pages 195–196) that around the middle of the first year, infants identify objects by their features and by their paths of movement, even when they cannot observe the entire path. How might these attainments contribute to infants' understanding of object permanence?

- **APPLY** Several times, after her father hid a teething biscuit under a red cup, 12-month-old Mimi retrieved it easily. Then Mimi's father hid the biscuit under a nearby yellow cup. Why did Mimi persist in searching for it under the red cup?

- **REFLECT** What advice would you give the typical U.S. parent about permitting an infant or toddler to watch as much as 1 to 1½ hours of TV or video per day? Explain.

6.4 Describe the information-processing view of cognitive development and the general structure of the information-processing system.

6.5 What changes in attention, memory, and categorization take place over the first two years?

6.6 Describe the strengths and limitations of the information-processing approach to early cognitive development.

Information Processing

Information-processing researchers agree with Piaget that children are active, inquiring beings. But instead of providing a single, unified theory of cognitive development, they focus on many aspects of thinking, from attention, memory, and categorization skills to complex problem solving.

Recall from Chapter 1 that the information-processing approach frequently relies on computer-like flowcharts to describe the human cognitive system. Information-processing theorists are not satisfied with general concepts, such as assimilation and accommodation, to describe how children think. Instead, they want to know exactly what individuals of different ages do when faced with a task or problem (Birney & Sternberg, 2011). The computer model of human thinking is attractive because it is explicit and precise.

A General Model of Information Processing

Most information-processing researchers assume that we hold information in three parts of the mental system for processing: the *sensory register,* the *short-term memory store,* and the *long-term memory store* (see Figure 6.4). As information flows through each, we can use *mental strategies* to operate on and transform it, increasing the chances that we will retain the information, use it efficiently, and think flexibly, adapting it to changing circumstances. To understand this more clearly, let's look at each aspect of the mental system.

First, information enters the **sensory register**, where sights and sounds are represented directly and stored briefly. **TAKE A MOMENT...** Look around you, and then close your eyes. An image of what you saw persists for a few seconds, but then it decays, or disappears, unless you use mental strategies to preserve it. For example, by *attending to* some information more carefully than to other information, you increase the chances that it will transfer to the next step of the information-processing system.

In the second part of the mind, the **short-term memory store**, we retain attended-to information briefly so we can actively "work" on it to reach our goals. One way of looking at the short-term store is in terms of its *basic capacity,* often referred to as *short-term memory:* how many pieces of information can be held at once for a few seconds. But most researchers endorse a contemporary view of the short-term store, which offers a more meaningful indicator of its capacity, called **working memory**—the number of items that can be briefly held in mind while also engaging in some effort to monitor or manipulate those items. Working memory can be thought of as a "mental workspace" that we use to accomplish many activities in daily life. From childhood on, researchers assess changes in its capacity by presenting individuals with lists of items (such as numerical digits or short sentences), asking them to "work on" the items (for example, repeat the digits backward or remember the final word of each sentence in correct order), and seeing how well they do.

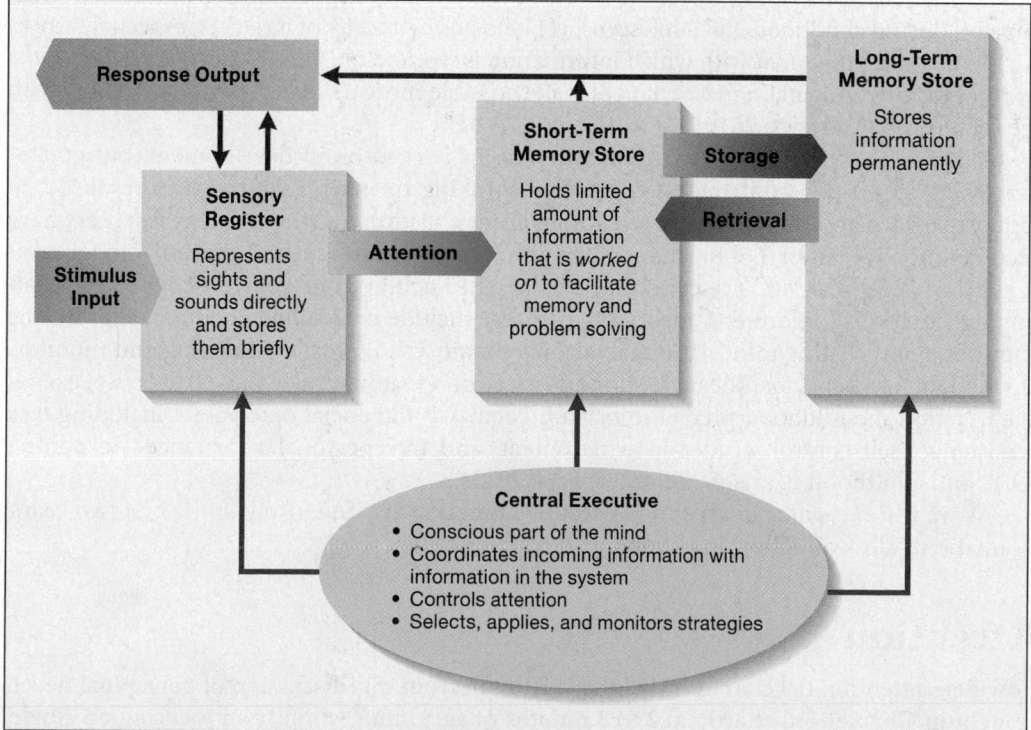

FIGURE 6.4 Model of the human information-processing system. Information flows through three parts of the mental system: the *sensory register,* the *short-term memory store,* and the *long-term memory store.* In each, mental strategies can be used to manipulate information, increasing the efficiency and flexibility of thinking and the chances that information will be retained. The *central executive* is the conscious, reflective part of working memory. It coordinates incoming information already in the system, decides what to attend to, and oversees the use of strategies.

The sensory register can take in a wide panorama of information. Short-term and working memory are far more restricted, though their capacity increases steadily from early childhood through adolescence—on a verbatim digit-span task tapping short-term memory, from about 2 to 7 items; and on working-memory tasks, from about 2 to 5 items (Cowan & Alloway, 2009). Still, individual differences are evident at all ages. By engaging in a variety of basic cognitive procedures, such as focusing attention on relevant items and repeating (rehearsing) them rapidly, we increase the chances that information will be retained and accessible to ongoing thinking.

To manage the cognitive system's complex activities, the **central executive** directs the flow of information, implementing the basic procedures just mentioned and also engaging in more sophisticated activities that enable complex, flexible thinking. For example, the central executive coordinates incoming information with information already in the system, and it selects, applies, and monitors strategies that facilitate memory storage, comprehension, reasoning, and problem solving (Pressley & Hilden, 2006). The central executive is the conscious, reflective part of our mental system. It ensures that we think purposefully, to attain our goals.

The more effectively the central executive joins with working memory to process information, the better learned cognitive activities will be and the more *automatically* we can apply them. Consider the richness of your thinking while you automatically drive a car. **Automatic processes** are so well-learned that they require no space in working memory and, therefore, permit us to focus on other information while performing them. Furthermore, the more effectively we process information in working memory, the more likely it will transfer to the third, and largest, storage area—**long-term memory**, our permanent knowledge base, which is unlimited. In fact, we store so much in long-term memory that *retrieval*—getting information back from the system—can be problematic. To aid retrieval, we apply strategies, just as we do in working memory. Information in long-term memory is *categorized* by its contents, much like a library shelving system that enables us to retrieve items by following the same network of associations used to store them in the first place.

Information-processing researchers believe that several aspects of the cognitive system improve during childhood and adolescence: (1) the *basic capacity* of its stores, especially working memory; (2) the *speed* with which information is worked on; and (3) the *functioning of the central executive.* Together, these changes make possible more complex forms of thinking with age (Halford & Andrews, 2010).

Gains in working-memory capacity are due in part to brain development, but greater processing speed also contributes. Fast, fluent thinking frees working-memory resources to support storage and manipulation of additional information. Furthermore, researchers have become intensely interested in studying the development of **executive function**—the diverse cognitive operations and strategies that enable us to achieve our goals in cognitively challenging situations (Zelazo & Carlson, 2012). These include controlling attention, suppressing impulses, coordinating information in working memory, and flexibly directing and monitoring thought and behavior. The reason for investigators' great interest is that measures of executive function in childhood predict important cognitive and social outcomes—including task persistence, self-control, academic achievement, and interpersonal acceptance—in adolescence and adulthood (Carlson, Zelazo, & Faja, 2013).

As we will see, gains in aspects of executive function are under way in the first two years. Dramatic strides will follow in childhood and adolescence.

Attention

How does attention develop in early infancy? Recall from our discussion of perceptual development in Chapter 5 that around 2 to 3 months of age, infants shift from focusing on single, high-contrast features to exploring objects and patterns more thoroughly. Besides attending to more aspects of the environment, infants gradually become more efficient at managing their attention, taking in information more quickly. Habituation research reveals that preterm and newborn babies require a long time—about 3 to 4 minutes—to habituate and recover to novel visual stimuli. But by 4 or 5 months, they need as little as 5 to 10 seconds to take in a complex visual stimulus and recognize it as different from a previous one (Colombo, Kapa, & Curtindale, 2011; Rose, Feldman, & Jankowski, 2001b).

One reason that very young babies' habituation times are so much longer is that they have difficulty disengaging attention from a stimulus (Colombo, 2002). When Carolyn held up a colorful rattle, 2-month-old Caitlin stared intently until, unable to break her gaze, she burst into tears. The ability to shift attention from one stimulus to another improves by 4 months—a change believed to be due to development of structures in the cerebral cortex controlling eye movements (Posner & Rothbart, 2007a).

Over the first year, infants attend to novel and eye-catching events. In the second year, as toddlers become increasingly capable of intentional behavior (refer back to Piaget's Substage 4), attraction to novelty declines (but does not disappear) and *sustained attention* improves, especially when children play with toys. A toddler who engages even in simple goal-directed behavior, such as stacking blocks or putting them in a container, must sustain attention to reach the goal (Ruff & Capozzoli, 2003). As plans and activities gradually become more complex, the duration of attention increases.

Adults can foster sustained attention by encouraging babies' current interest ("Oh, you like that bell!") and prompting the child to stay focused ("See, it makes a noise!"). Consistently helping infants focus attention at 10 months predicts higher intelligence test scores at 18 months (Bono & Stifter, 2003). Also, infants and toddlers gradually become more interested in what others are attending to. Later we will see that this joint attention between caregiver and child is important for language development.

By encouraging her toddler's goal-directed play, this mother promotes sustained attention.

Memory

Methods devised to assess infants' short-term memory, which require keeping in mind an increasingly longer sequence of very briefly presented visual stimuli, reveal that retention increases from 1 item at age 6 months to 2 to 4 items at 12 months (Rose, Feldman, & Janowski, 2001b; Ross-Sheehy, Oakes, & Luck, 2003). Operant conditioning and habituation techniques, which grant babies more extended time to process information, provide windows into early long-term memory. Both methods show that retention of visual events improves greatly with age.

OPERANT CONDITIONING RESEARCH Using operant conditioning, researchers study infant memory by teaching 2- to 6-month-olds to move a mobile by kicking a foot tied to it with a long cord. Two-month-olds remember how to activate the mobile for 1 to 2 days after training, and 3-month-olds for one week. By 6 months, memory increases to two weeks (Rovee-Collier, 1999; Rovee-Collier & Bhatt, 1993). Around the middle of the first year, babies can manipulate switches or buttons to control stimulation. When 6- to 18-month olds pressed a lever to make a toy train move around a track, duration of memory continued to increase with age; 13 weeks after training, 18-month-olds still remembered how to press the lever (Hartshorn et al., 1998b). Figure 6.5 on page 218 shows this dramatic rise in retention of operant responses over the first year and a half.

Even after 2- to 6-month-olds forget an operant response, they need only a brief prompt—an adult who shakes the mobile—to reinstate the memory (Hildreth & Rovee-Collier, 2002). And when 6-month-olds are given a chance to reactivate the response themselves for just a couple of minutes—

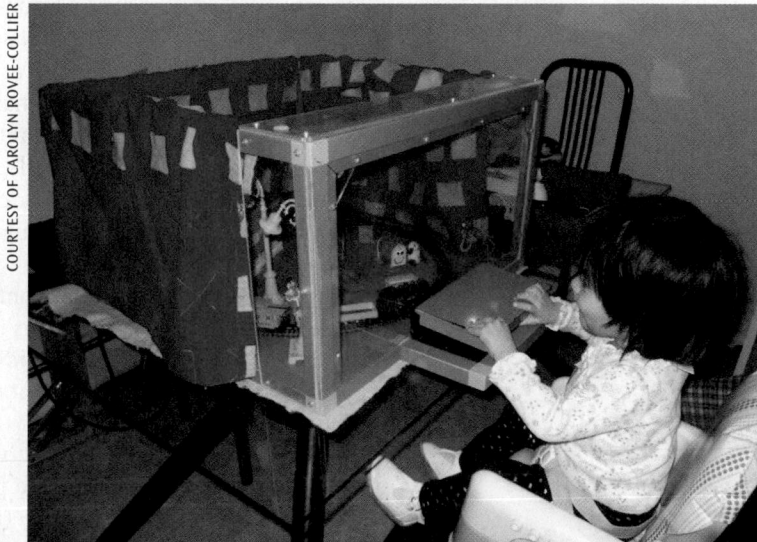

Memory for operant responses improves dramatically over the first 18 months. This 12-month-old has learned to press a lever to make a toy train move around a track—an operant response she is likely to remember when reexposed to the task many weeks later.

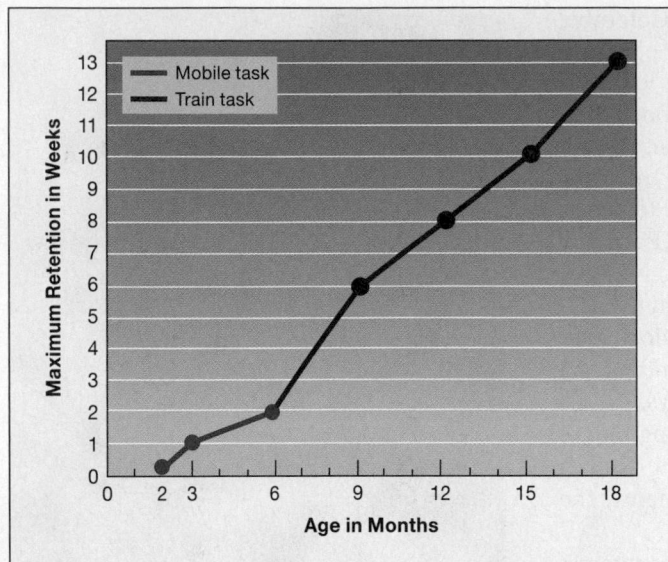

FIGURE 6.5 **Increase in retention in two operant conditioning tasks from 2 to 18 months.** Two- to 6-month-olds were trained to make a kicking response that turned a mobile. Six- to 18-month-olds were trained to press a lever that made a toy train move around a track. Six-month-olds learned both responses and retained them for an identical length of time, indicating that the tasks are comparable. Consequently, researchers could plot a single line of gains in retention from 2 to 18 months. The line shows that memory improves dramatically. (From C. Rovee-Collier & R. Barr, 2001, "Infant Learning and Memory," in G. Bremner & A. Fogel [Eds.], *Blackwell Handbook of Infant Development,* Oxford, U.K.: Blackwell, p. 150. © 2001, 2004 by Blackwell Publishing Ltd. Republished with permission of John Wiley & Sons Ltd. conveyed through Copyright Clearance Center, Inc.)

jiggling the mobile by kicking or moving the train by lever-pressing—their memory not only returns but also extends dramatically, to about 17 weeks (Hildreth, Sweeney, & Rovee-Collier, 2003). Perhaps permitting the baby to generate the previously learned behavior strengthens memory because it reexposes the child to more aspects of the original learning situation. Furthermore, with just five widely spaced adult-provided reminders of the train task extending over 1½ years, babies trained at age 6 months still remembered the response after reaching their second birthday (Hartshorn, 2003).

At first, infants' memory for operant responses is highly *context-dependent.* If 2- to 6-month-olds are not tested in the same situation in which they were trained—with the same mobile and crib bumper and in the same room—they remember poorly (Hayne, 2004). After 9 months, the importance of context declines. Older infants and toddlers remember how to make the toy train move even when its features are altered and testing takes place in a different room (Hartshorn et al., 1998a; Learmonth, Lamberth, & Rovee-Collier, 2004). Crawling is strongly associated with 9-month-olds' formation of an increasingly context-free memory (Herbert, Gross, & Hayne, 2007). As babies move on their own and experience frequent changes in context, they apply learned responses more flexibly, generalizing them to relevant new situations.

HABITUATION RESEARCH Habituation studies show that infants learn and retain a wide variety of information just by watching objects and events, without being physically active. Sometimes they do so for much longer time spans than in operant conditioning studies. Babies are especially attentive to the movements of objects and people. In one investigation, 5½-month-olds remembered a woman's captivating action (such as blowing bubbles or brushing hair) seven weeks later, as indicated by a *familiarity preference* (see page 179 in Chapter 5) (Bahrick, Gogate, & Ruiz, 2002). The babies were so attentive to the woman's action that they did not remember her face, even when tested 1 minute later for a *novelty preference.*

In Chapter 5, we saw that 3- to 5-month-olds are excellent at discriminating faces. But their memory for the faces of unfamiliar people and for other visual patterns is short-lived—at 3 months, only about 24 hours; at the end of the first year, several days to a few weeks (Fagan, 1973; Pascalis, de Haan, & Nelson, 1998). By contrast, 3-month-olds' memory for the unusual movements of objects (such as a metal nut swinging on the end of a string) persists for at least three months (Bahrick, Hernandez-Reif, & Pickens, 1997).

By 10 to 12 months, infants remember both novel actions and features of objects involved in those actions equally well (Baumgartner & Oakes, 2011). Thus, over the second half-year, sensitivity to object appearance increases. This change, as noted earlier, is fostered by infants' increasing ability to manipulate objects, which helps them learn about objects' observable properties.

Habituation research confirms that infants need not be physically active to acquire new information. Nevertheless, as illustrated by research presented in Chapter 5 on the facilitating role of crawling in finding hidden objects (see page 191), motor activity does promote certain aspects of learning and memory.

RECALL MEMORY So far, we have discussed only **recognition**—noticing when a stimulus is identical or similar to one previously experienced. It is the simplest form of memory: All babies have to do is indicate (by kicking, pressing a lever, or looking) whether a new experience is identical or similar to a previous one. **Recall** is more challenging because it involves remembering something not present. To recall, you must generate a mental image of the past experience. Can infants engage in recall? By the middle of the first year, they can, as indicated by their ability to find hidden objects and engage in deferred imitation.

Recall memory improves steadily with age. For example, 1-year-olds can retain short sequences of adult-modeled behaviors for up to 3 months, and 1½–year-olds can do so for as long as 12 months. The ability to recall modeled behaviors in the order in which the actions occurred—evident as early as 6 months—strengthens over the second year (Bauer, Larkina, & Deocampo, 2011; Rovee-Collier & Cuevas, 2009). And when toddlers imitate in correct sequence, processing not just separate actions but relations between actions, they remember more (Knopf, Kraus, & Kressley-Mba, 2006).

Long-term recall depends on connections among multiple regions of the cerebral cortex, especially with the prefrontal cortex. During infancy and toddlerhood, these neural circuits develop rapidly (Nelson, Thomas, & de Haan, 2006). The evidence as a whole indicates that infants' memory processing is remarkably similar to that of older children and adults: Babies have distinct short-term and long-term memories and display both recognition and recall. And they acquire information quickly, retain it over time, and apply it flexibly, doing so more effectively with age (Bauer, 2009; Rose et al., 2011). Furthermore, recall assessed through deferred imitation tasks at age 20 months predicts performance on memory tests at age 6, suggesting continuity of memory functions over time (Riggins et al., 2013). Yet a puzzling finding is that older children and adults no longer recall their earliest experiences! See the Biology and Environment box on page 220 for a discussion of *infantile amnesia*.

Categorization

Even young infants can *categorize,* grouping similar objects and events into a single representation. Categorization reduces the enormous amount of new information infants encounter every day, helping them learn and remember (Rakison, 2010).

Creative variations of operant conditioning research with mobiles have been used to find out about infant categorization. One such study, of 3-month-olds, is described and illustrated in Figure 6.6. Similar investigations reveal that in the first few months, babies categorize stimuli on the basis of shape, size, and other physical properties (Wasserman & Rovee-Collier, 2001). By 6 months of age, they can categorize on the basis of two correlated features—for example, the shape and color of an alphabet letter (Bhatt et al., 2004). This ability to categorize using clusters of features prepares babies for acquiring many complex everyday categories.

Habituation has also been used to study infant categorization. Researchers show babies a series of pictures belonging to one category and then see whether they recover to (look longer at) a picture that is not a member of the category (see Figure 6.8 on page 221). Findings reveal that in the second half of the first year, infants group familiar objects into an impressive array of categories—food items, furniture, birds, land animals, air animals, sea animals, plants, vehicles, kitchen utensils, and spatial location ("above" and "below," "on" and "in") (Bornstein, Arterberry, & Mash, 2010; Casasola & Park, 2013; Oakes, Coppage, & Dingel, 1997). Besides organizing the physical world, infants of this age categorize their emotional and social worlds. They sort people and their voices by gender and age, have begun to distinguish emotional expressions, can separate people's natural actions (walking) from other motions, and expect people (but not inanimate objects) to move spontaneously (Spelke, Phillips, & Woodward, 1995; see also Chapter 5, pages 192–193).

Babies' earliest categories are based on similar overall appearance or prominent object parts: legs for animals, wheels for vehicles. But as infants approach their first birthday, more categories appear to be based on subtle sets of features (Cohen, 2003; Mandler, 2004; Quinn, 2008). Older infants can even make categorical distinctions when the perceptual contrast between two categories is minimal (birds versus airplanes).

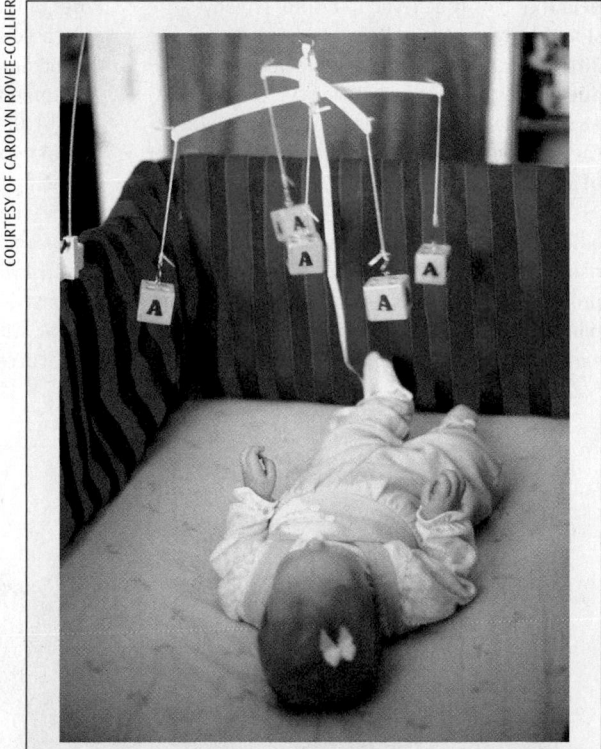

COURTESY OF CAROLYN ROVEE-COLLIER

FIGURE 6.6 Investigating infant categorization using operant conditioning. Three-month-olds were taught to kick to move a mobile that was made of small blocks, all with the letter *A* on them. After a delay, kicking returned to a high level only if the babies were shown a mobile whose blocks were labeled with the same form (the letter *A*). If the form was changed (from *A*s to *2*s), infants no longer kicked vigorously. While making the mobile move, the babies had grouped together its features. They associated the kicking response with the category *A* and, at later testing, distinguished it from the category *2*. (Bhatt, Rovee-Collier, & Weiner, 1994; Hayne, Rovee-Collier, & Perris, 1987)

Biology and Environment

Infantile Amnesia

I f infants and toddlers remember many aspects of their everyday lives, how do we explain **infantile amnesia**—that most of us cannot retrieve events that happened to us before age 3? The reason cannot be merely the passage of time because we can recall many personally meaningful one-time events from both the recent and the distant past: the day a sibling was born or a move to a new house—recollections known as **autobiographical memory.**

Several explanations of infantile amnesia exist. One theory credits brain development, pointing to the *hippocampus* (located just under the temporal lobes), which plays a vital role in the formation of new memories. Though its overall structure is formed prenatally, the hippocampus continues to add new neurons well after birth. Integrating those neurons into existing neural circuits is believed to disrupt already stored early memories (Josselyn & Frankland, 2012). In support of this view, the decline in production of hippocampal neurons—in monkeys and rats as well as in humans—coincides with the ability to form stable, long-term memories of unique experiences.

Another conjecture is that older children and adults often use verbal means for storing information, whereas infants' and toddlers' memory processing is largely nonverbal—an incompatibility that may prevent long-term retention of early experiences. To test this idea, researchers

sent two adults to the homes of 2- to 4-year-olds with an unusual toy that the children were likely to remember: The Magic Shrinking Machine, shown in Figure 6.7. One adult showed the child how, after inserting an object in an opening on top of the machine and turning a crank that activated flashing lights and musical sounds, the child could retrieve a smaller, identical object (discreetly dropped down a chute by the second adult) from behind a door on the front of the machine.

A day later, the researchers tested the children to see how well they recalled the event. Their nonverbal memory—based on acting out the "shrinking" event and recognizing the "shrunken" objects in photos—was excellent. But even when they had the vocabulary, children younger than age 3 had trouble describing features of the "shrinking" experience. Verbal recall increased sharply between ages 3 and 4—the period during which children "scramble over the amnesia barrier" (Simcock & Hayne, 2003, p. 813). In a follow-up study, which assessed verbal recall 6 years later, only 19 percent— including two children who were younger than age 3— remembered the "shrinking" event (Jack, Simcock, & Hayne, 2012). Those who recalled were more likely to have participated in conversations about the experience with a parent, which could have helped them gain verbal access to the memory.

These findings help us reconcile infants' and toddlers' remarkable memory skills with infantile amnesia. During the first few years, children rely heavily on nonverbal memory techniques, such as visual images and motor actions. As language develops, their ability to use it to refer to preverbal memories requires considerable support in translating the memory into words (Morris & Baker-Ward, 2007). Only after age 3 do children often represent events verbally. As children encode autobiographical events in verbal form, they use language-based cues to retrieve them, increasing the accessibility of memories at later ages (Peterson, Warren, & Short, 2011).

Other findings indicate that the advent of a clear self-image contributes to the end of infantile amnesia (Howe, Courage, & Rooksby, 2009). Toddlers who were advanced in development of a sense of self demonstrated better verbal memories a year later while conversing about past events with their mothers (Harley & Reese, 1999).

Very likely, both neurological change and social experience contribute to the decline of infantile amnesia. Brain development and adult–child interaction may jointly foster self-awareness, language, and improved memory, which enable children to talk with adults about significant past experiences (Bauer, 2007). As a result, preschoolers begin to construct a long-lasting autobiographical narrative of their lives and enter into the history of their family and community.

  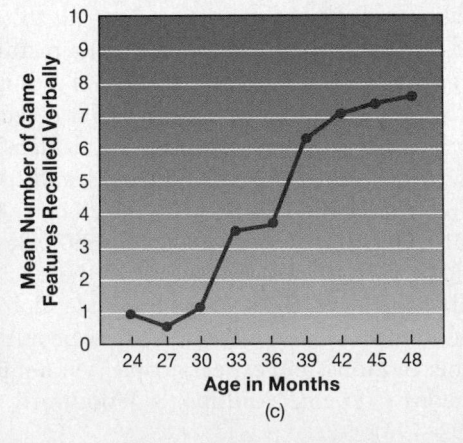

(a)   (b)   (c)

FIGURE 6.7   The Magic Shrinking Machine, used to test young children's verbal and nonverbal memory of an unusual event. After being shown how the machine worked, the child participated in selecting objects from a polka-dot bag, dropping them into the top of the machine (a), and turning a crank, which produced a "shrunken" object (b). When tested the next day, 2- to 4-year-olds' nonverbal memory for the event was excellent. But below 36 months, verbal recall was poor, based on the number of features recalled about the game during an open-ended interview (c). Recall improved between 36 and 48 months, the period during which infantile amnesia subsides. (From G. Simcock & H. Hayne, 2003, "Age-Related Changes in Verbal and Nonverbal Memory During Early Childhood," *Developmental Psychology, 39,* pp. 807, 809. Copyright © 2003 by the American Psychological Association. Reprinted by permission of the American Psychological Association.) *Photos:* Ross Coombes/Courtesy of Harlene Hayne.

As they gain experience in comparing to-be-categorized items in varied ways and their store of verbal labels expands, toddlers start to categorize flexibly: When 14-month-olds are given four balls and four blocks, some made of soft rubber and some of rigid plastic, their sequence of object touching reveals that after classifying by shape, they can switch to classifying by material (soft versus hard) if an adult calls their attention to the new basis for grouping (Ellis & Oakes, 2006).

In addition to touching and sorting, toddlers' categorization skills are evident in their play behaviors. After watching an adult give a toy dog a drink from a cup, most 14-month-olds shown a rabbit and a motorcycle offered the drink only to the rabbit (Mandler & McDonough, 1998). They clearly understood that certain actions are appropriate for some categories of items (animals) but not for others (vehicles).

By the end of the second year, toddlers' grasp of the animate–inanimate distinction expands. Nonlinear motions are typical of animates (a person or a dog jumping), linear motions of inanimates (a car or a table pushed along a surface). At 18 months, toddlers more often imitate a nonlinear motion with a toy that has animate-like parts (legs), even if it represents an inanimate (a bed). At 22 months, displaying a fuller understanding, they imitate a nonlinear motion only with toys in the animate category (a cat but not a bed) (Rakison, 2005). They seem to realize that whereas animates are self-propelled and therefore have varied paths of movement, inanimates move only when acted on, in highly restricted ways.

Researchers disagree on how babies arrive at these impressive attainments. One view holds that older infants and toddlers categorize more effectively because they become increasingly sensitive to fine-grained perceptual features and to stable relations among those features—for example, objects with flapping wings and feathers belong to one category; objects with rigid wings, windows, and a smooth surface belong to another category (Madole, Oakes, & Rakison, 2011; Schultz, 2011). An alternative view is that before the end of the first year, babies undergo a fundamental shift from a perceptual to a conceptual basis for constructing categories, increasingly grouping objects by their common function or behavior (birds versus airplanes, cars versus motorcycles, dogs versus cats) (Mandler, 2004; Träuble & Pauen, 2011).

But all acknowledge that exploration of objects and expanding knowledge of the world contribute (Mash & Bornstein, 2012). In addition, adult labeling of a set of objects with a consistently applied word ("Look at the car!" "Do you see the car?") calls babies' attention to commonalities among objects, fostering categorization as early as 3 to 4 months of age (Ferry, Hespos, & Waxman, 2010). Toddlers' vocabulary growth, in turn, promotes categorization by highlighting new categorical distinctions (Cohen & Brunt, 2009).

Variations among languages lead to cultural differences in development of categories. Korean toddlers, who learn a language in which object names are often omitted from sentences, develop object-sorting skills later than their English-speaking counterparts (Gopnik & Choi, 1990). At the same time, Korean contains a common word, *kkita,* with no English equivalent, referring to a tight fit between objects in contact (a ring on a finger, a cap on a pen). Hearing this label highlights the spatial category "tight-fit" for Korean toddlers, who are advanced in forming it (Choi et al., 1999). After English-speaking 18-month-olds heard the word *tight* while observing several instances of objects fitting together tightly, they readily acquired the tight-fit category (Casasola, Bhagwat, & Burke, 2009). Those who viewed the events without the label did not form the category.

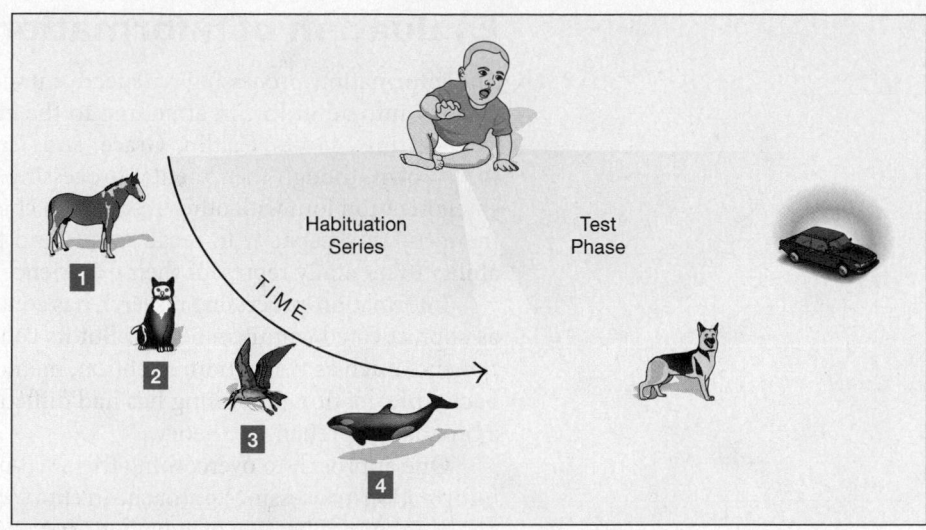

FIGURE 6.8 Using habituation to study infant categorization. After habituating to a series of items belonging to one category (in this example, animals), infants are shown two novel items, one that is a member of the category (dog) and one that is not (car). If infants recover to (look longer at or spend more time manipulating) the out-of-category item (car), this indicates that they distinguish it from the set of within-category items (animals). Habituating another group of infants to a series of vehicles and seeing if, when presented with the two test items above, they recover to the dog confirms that babies can distinguish animals from vehicles. This pattern of responding has been found in many infant categorization studies.

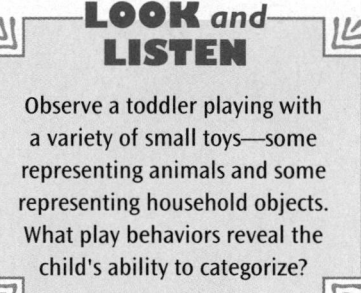

LOOK *and* **LISTEN**

Observe a toddler playing with a variety of small toys—some representing animals and some representing household objects. What play behaviors reveal the child's ability to categorize?

Evaluation of Information-Processing Findings

The information-processing perspective underscores the continuity of human thinking from infancy into adult life. In attending to the environment, remembering everyday events, and categorizing objects, Caitlin, Grace, and Timmy think in ways that are remarkably similar to our own, though their mental processing is far from proficient. Findings on memory and categorization join with other research in challenging Piaget's view of early cognitive development. Infants' capacity to recall events and to categorize stimuli attests, once again, to their ability to mentally represent their experiences.

Information-processing research has contributed greatly to our view of infants and toddlers as sophisticated cognitive beings. But its central strength—analyzing cognition into its components, such as perception, attention, memory, and categorization—is also its greatest drawback: Information processing has had difficulty putting these components back together into a broad, comprehensive theory.

One approach to overcoming this weakness has been to combine Piaget's theory with the information-processing approach, an effort we will explore in Chapter 12. A more recent trend has been the application of a *dynamic systems view* (see Chapter 1, page 29) to early cognition. In this approach, researchers analyze each cognitive attainment to see how it results from a complex system of prior accomplishments and the child's current goals (Spencer, Perone, & Buss, 2011; Thelen & Smith, 2006). Once these ideas are fully tested, they may move the field closer to a more powerful view of how the minds of infants and children develop.

6.7 How does Vygotsky's concept of the zone of proximal development expand our understanding of early cognitive development?

The Social Context of Early Cognitive Development

Recall the description at the beginning of this chapter of Grace dropping shapes into a container. Notice that she learns about the toy with Ginette's help. With adult support, Grace will gradually become better at matching shapes to openings and dropping them into the container. Then she will be able to perform this and similar activities on her own.

Vygotsky's sociocultural theory emphasizes that children live in rich social and cultural contexts that affect the way their cognitive world is structured (Bodrova & Leong, 2007; Rogoff, 2003). Vygotsky believed that complex mental activities, such as voluntary attention, deliberate memory, categorization, and problem solving, have their origins in social interaction. Through joint activities with more mature members of their society, children master activities and think in ways that have meaning in their culture.

A special Vygotskian concept explains how this happens. The **zone of proximal** (or potential) **development** refers to a range of tasks that the child cannot yet handle alone but can do with the help of more skilled partners. To understand this idea, think about how a sensitive adult (such as Ginette) introduces a child to a new activity. The adult picks a task that the child can master but that is challenging enough that the child cannot do it by herself. Or the adult capitalizes on an activity that the child has chosen. The adult guides and supports, adjusting the level of support offered to fit the child's current level of performance. As the child joins in the interaction and picks up mental strategies, her competence increases, and the adult steps back, permitting the child to take more responsibility for the task. This form of teaching—known as *scaffolding*—promotes learning at all ages, and we will consider it further in Chapter 9.

Vygotsky's ideas have been applied mostly to preschool and school-age children, who are more skilled in language and social communication. Recently, however, his theory has been extended to infancy and toddlerhood. Recall that babies are equipped with capabilities that ensure that caregivers will interact with them (Csibra & Gergely, 2011). Then adults adjust the environment and their communication in ways that promote learning adapted to their cultural circumstances.

A study by Barbara Rogoff and her collaborators (1984) illustrates this process. Placing a jack-in-the-box nearby, the researchers watched how several adults played with Rogoff's son and daughter over the first two years. In the early months, adults tried to focus the baby's attention by working the toy and, as the bunny popped out, saying something like "My, what happened?" By the end of the first year, when cognitive and motor skills had improved, interaction centered on how to use the toy: The adults guided the baby's hand in turning the crank and putting the bunny back in the box. During the second year, adults helped from a distance, using gestures and verbal prompts, such as making a turning motion with the hand near the crank. Research indicates that this fine-tuned support is related to advanced play, language, and problem solving during the second year (Bornstein et al., 1992; Charman et al., 2001; Tamis-LeMonda & Bornstein, 1989).

As early as the first year, cultural variations in social experiences affect mental strategies. In the jack-in-the-box example, adults and children focused their attention on a single activity. This strategy, common in Western middle-SES homes, is well-suited to lessons in which children master skills apart from the everyday situations in which they will later use those skills. In contrast, infants and young children in Guatemalan Mayan, Native American, and other indigenous communities often attend to several events at once. For example, one 12-month-old skillfully put objects in a jar while watching a passing truck and blowing into a toy whistle (Chavajay & Rogoff, 1999; Correa-Chavez, Roberts, & Perez, 2011).

© JAMES SHAFFER/PHOTOEDIT

By bringing the task within his son's zone of proximal development and adjusting his communication to suit the child's needs, the father transfers mental strategies to the child, promoting his cognitive development.

Processing several competing events simultaneously may be vital in cultures where children largely learn not through lessons but through keen observation of others' ongoing activities at home, at work, and in public life. In a comparison of 18-month-olds from German middle-SES homes and Nso farming villages in Cameroon, the Nso toddlers copied far fewer experimenter-demonstrated actions on toys than did the German toddlers (Borchert et al., 2013). Nso caregivers rarely create such child-focused teaching situations. Rather, they expect children to imitate observed behaviors without adult prompting. Nso children are motivated to do so because they want to be included in the major activities of their community.

Earlier we saw how infants and toddlers create new schemes by acting on the physical world (Piaget) and how certain skills become better-developed as children represent their experiences more efficiently and meaningfully (information processing). Vygotsky adds a third dimension to our understanding by emphasizing that many aspects of cognitive development are socially prompted and encouraged. The Cultural Influences box on page 224 presents additional evidence for this idea. And we will see even more evidence in the next section, where we look at individual differences in mental development during the first two years.

Ask Yourself

- **REVIEW** What impact does toddlers' more advanced play have on the development of attention?

- **CONNECT** List techniques that parents can use to scaffold the development of categorization in infancy and toddlerhood, and explain why each is effective.

- **APPLY** When Timmy was 18 months old, his mother stood behind him, helping him throw a large ball into a box. As his skill improved, she stepped back, letting him try on his own. Using Vygotsky's ideas, explain how Timmy's mother is supporting his cognitive development.

- **REFLECT** Describe your earliest autobiographical memory. How old were you when the event occurred? Do your responses fit with research on infantile amnesia?

Cultural Influences

Social Origins of Make-Believe Play

One of the activities that Ken, your first author's husband, used to do with their two young sons was to bake pineapple upside-down cake, a favorite treat. One Sunday afternoon when a cake was in the making, 21-month-old Peter stood on a chair at the kitchen sink, busily pouring water from one cup to another.

"He's in the way, Dad!" complained 4-year-old David, trying to pull Peter away from the sink.

"Maybe if we let him help, he'll give us room," Ken suggested. As David stirred the batter, Ken poured some into a small bowl for Peter, moved his chair to the side of the sink, and handed him a spoon.

"Here's how you do it, Petey," instructed David, with a superior air. Peter watched as David stirred, then tried to copy his motion. When it was time to pour the batter, Ken helped Peter hold and tip the small bowl.

"Time to bake it," said Ken.

"Bake it, bake it," repeated Peter, watching Ken slip the pan into the oven.

Several hours later, Ken observed one of Peter's earliest instances of make-believe play. He got his pail from the sandbox and, after filling it with a handful of sand, carried it into the kitchen and put it down on the floor in front of the oven. "Bake it, bake it," Peter called to Ken. Together, father and son placed the pretend cake in the oven.

Piaget and his followers concluded that toddlers discover make-believe independently, once they are capable of representational schemes. Vygotsky's theory has challenged this view. He believed that society provides children with opportunities to represent culturally meaningful activities in play. Make-believe, like other complex mental activities, is first learned under the guidance of experts (Meyers & Berk, 2014). In the example just described, Peter extended his capacity to represent daily events when Ken drew him into the baking task and helped him act it out in play.

Current evidence supports the idea that early make-believe is the combined result of children's readiness to engage in it and social experiences that promote it. In Western middle-SES families, play is culturally cultivated by adults, who value it as a developmentally beneficial activity and frequently play with their children (Gaskins, Haight, & Lancy, 2007). In one observational study of U.S. middle-SES toddlers, 75 to 80 percent of make-believe involved mother–child

interaction (Haight & Miller, 1993). At 12 months, make-believe was fairly one-sided: Almost all play episodes were initiated by mothers. But by the end of the second year, half of pretend episodes were initiated by each.

During make-believe, Western mothers offer toddlers a rich array of cues that they are pretending—looking and smiling at the child more, making more exaggerated movements, and using more "we" talk (acknowledging that pretending is a joint endeavor) than they do during the same real-life event (Lillard et al., 2007). These maternal cues encourage toddlers to join in and probably facilitate their ability to distinguish pretend from real acts, which strengthens over the second and third years (Lillard & Witherington, 2004; Ma & Lillard, 2006).

Also, when adults participate, toddlers' make-believe is more elaborate (Keren et al., 2005). They are more likely to combine pretend acts into complex sequences, as Peter did when he put the sand in the bucket (making the batter), carried it into the kitchen, and, with Ken's help, put it in the oven (baking the cake). The more parents pretend with their toddlers, the more time their children devote to make-believe.

In some cultures, such as those of Indonesia and Mexico, where extended-family households and sibling caregiving are common, make-believe is more frequent and more complex with older siblings than with mothers. As early as age 3 to 4, children provide rich, challenging stimulation to their younger brothers and sisters, take these teaching responsibilities seriously, and, with age, become better at them (Zukow-Goldring, 2002). In a study of Zinacanteco Indian children of southern Mexico, by age 8, sibling teachers were highly skilled at showing 2-year-olds how to play at everyday tasks, such as washing and cooking (Maynard, 2002). They often guided toddlers verbally and physically through the task and provided feedback.

In cultures where sibling caregiving is common, make-believe play is more frequent and complex with older siblings than with mothers. These Afghan children play "wedding," dressing the youngest as a bride.

In Western middle-SES families, older siblings less often teach deliberately but still serve as influential models of playful behavior. In New Zealand families of Western European descent, when both a parent and an older sibling were available, toddlers more often imitated the actions of the sibling, especially when siblings engaged in make-believe (Barr & Hayne, 2003).

As we will see in Chapters 9 and 10, make-believe play is a major means through which children extend their cognitive and social skills and learn about important activities in their culture (Nielsen, 2012). Vygotsky's theory, and the findings that support it, tell us that providing a stimulating physical environment is not enough to promote early cognitive development. In addition, toddlers must be invited and encouraged by more skilled members of their culture to participate in the social world around them. Parents and teachers can enhance early make-believe by playing often with toddlers, guiding and elaborating their make-believe themes.

Individual Differences in Early Mental Development

Because of Grace's deprived early environment, Kevin and Monica had a child psychologist give her one of many tests available for assessing mental development in infants and toddlers. Worried about Timmy's progress, Vanessa also arranged for him to be tested. At age 22 months, he had only a handful of words in his vocabulary, played in a less mature way than Caitlin and Grace, and seemed restless and overactive.

The cognitive theories we have just discussed try to explain the *process* of development—how children's thinking changes. Mental tests, in contrast, focus on cognitive *products*. Their goal is to measure behaviors that reflect development and to arrive at scores that *predict* future performance, such as later intelligence, school achievement, and adult vocational success. This concern with prediction arose nearly a century ago, when French psychologist Alfred Binet designed the first successful intelligence test, which predicted school achievement (see Chapter 1). It inspired the design of many new tests, including ones that measure intelligence at very early ages.

6.8 Describe the mental testing approach, the meaning of intelligence test scores, and the extent to which infant tests predict later performance.

6.9 Discuss environmental influences on early mental development, including home, child care, and early intervention for at-risk infants and toddlers.

Infant and Toddler Intelligence Tests

Accurately measuring infants' intelligence is a challenge because young babies cannot answer questions or follow directions. All we can do is present them with stimuli, coax them to respond, and observe their behavior. As a result, most infant tests emphasize perceptual and motor responses. But increasingly, tests are being developed that also tap early language, cognition, and social behavior, especially with older infants and toddlers.

One commonly used test, the *Bayley Scales of Infant and Toddler Development,* is suitable for children between 1 month and 3½ years. The most recent edition, the Bayley-III, has three main subtests: (1) the Cognitive Scale, which includes such items as attention to familiar and unfamiliar objects, looking for a fallen object, and pretend play; (2) the Language Scale, which taps understanding and expressions of language—for example, recognition of objects and people, following simple directions, and naming objects and pictures; and (3) the Motor Scale, which includes gross- and fine-motor skills, such as grasping, sitting, stacking blocks, and climbing stairs (Bayley, 2005).

Two additional Bayley-III scales depend on parental report: (4) the Social-Emotional Scale, which asks caregivers about such behaviors as ease of calming, social responsiveness, and imitation in play; and (5) the Adaptive Behavior Scale, which asks about adaptation to the demands of daily life, including communication, self-control, following rules, and getting along with others.

A trained examiner administers a test based on the Bayley Scales of Infant Development to a 1-year-old in her mother's lap. Current Bayley-III Cognitive and Language Scales predict preschool mental test performance better than earlier versions.

COMPUTING INTELLIGENCE TEST SCORES   Intelligence tests for infants, children, and adults are scored in much the same way—by computing an **intelligence quotient (IQ),** which indicates the extent to which the raw score (number of items passed) deviates from the typical performance of same-age individuals. To make this comparison possible, test designers engage in **standardization**—giving the test to a large, representative sample and using the results as the *standard* for interpreting scores. The standardization sample for the Bayley-III included 1,700 infants, toddlers, and young preschoolers, reflecting the U.S. population in SES and ethnic diversity.

Within the standardization sample, performances at each age level form a **normal distribution,** in which most scores cluster around the mean, or average, with progressively fewer falling toward the extremes (see Figure 6.9 on page 226). This *bell-shaped distribution* results

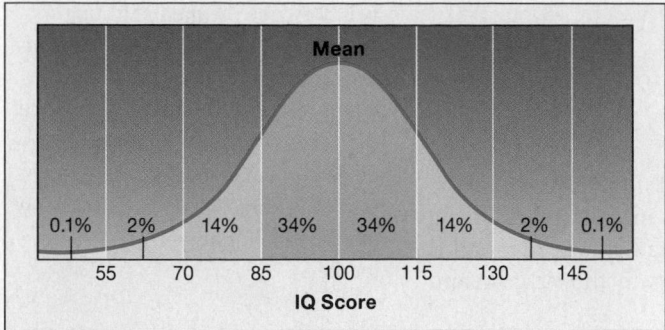

FIGURE 6.9   Normal distribution of intelligence test scores.
To determine what percentage of same-age individuals in the population a person with a certain IQ outperformed, add the figures to the left of that IQ score. For example, an 8-year-old child with an IQ of 115 scored better than 84 percent of the population of 8-year-olds.

whenever researchers measure individual differences in large samples. When intelligence tests are standardized, the mean IQ is set at 100. An individual's IQ is higher or lower than 100 by an amount that reflects how much his or her test performance deviates from the standardization-sample mean.

The IQ offers a way of finding out whether an individual is ahead, behind, or on time (average) in mental development compared with others of the same age. For example, if Timmy's score is 100, then he did better than 50 percent of his agemates. A child with an IQ of 85 did better than only 16 percent, whereas a child with an IQ of 130 outperformed 98 percent. The IQs of 96 percent of individuals fall between 70 and 130; only a few achieve higher or lower scores.

PREDICTING LATER PERFORMANCE FROM INFANT TESTS

Despite careful construction, most infant tests—including previous editions of the Bayley—predict later intelligence poorly. Infants and toddlers easily become distracted, fatigued, or bored during testing, so their scores often do not reflect their true abilities. And infant perceptual and motor items differ from the tasks given to older children, which increasingly emphasize verbal, conceptual, and problem-solving skills. In contrast, the Bayley-III Cognitive and Language Scales, which better dovetail with childhood tests, are good predictors of preschool mental test performance (Albers & Grieve, 2007). But because most infant test scores do not tap the same dimensions of intelligence measured at older ages, they are conservatively labeled **developmental quotients (DQs)** rather than IQs.

Infant tests are somewhat better at making long-term predictions for extremely low-scoring babies. Today, they are largely used for *screening*—helping to identify for further observation and intervention babies who are likely to have developmental problems.

As an alternative to infant tests, some researchers have turned to information-processing measures, such as habituation, to assess early mental progress. Their findings show that speed of habituation and recovery to novel visual stimuli is among the best available infant predictors of IQ from early childhood to early adulthood, with correlations ranging from the .30s to the .60s (Fagan, Holland, & Wheeler, 2007; Kavšek, 2004). Habituation and recovery seem to be an especially effective early index of intelligence because they assess memory as well as quickness and flexibility of thinking, which underlie intelligent behavior at all ages (Colombo et al., 2004). The consistency of these findings has prompted designers of the Bayley-III to include items that tap such cognitive skills as habituation, object permanence, and categorization.

Early Environment and Mental Development

In Chapter 2, we indicated that intelligence is a complex blend of hereditary and environmental influences. Many studies have examined the relationship of environmental factors to infant and toddler mental test scores. As we consider this evidence, you will encounter findings that highlight the role of heredity as well.

HOME ENVIRONMENT   The **Home Observation for Measurement of the Environment (HOME)** is a checklist for gathering information about the quality of children's home lives through observation and parental interview (Caldwell & Bradley, 1994). Applying What We Know on the following page lists the factors measured by the HOME Infant–Toddler Subscales—the most widely used home environment measure during the first three years. A briefer, exclusively observational HOME instrument is also available (Rijlaarsdam et al., 2012).

Each HOME subscale is positively related to toddlers' mental test performance. Regardless of SES and ethnicity, an organized, stimulating physical setting and parental affection, involvement, and encouragement of new skills repeatedly predict better language and IQ scores in toddlerhood and early childhood (Fuligni, Han, & Brooks-Gunn, 2004; Linver, Martin, & Brooks-Gunn, 2004; Tamis-LeMonda et al., 2004; Tong et al., 2007). The extent to which parents converse with infants and toddlers is particularly important. It contributes strongly to

Applying What We Know

Features of a High-Quality Home Life for Infants and Toddlers: The HOME Infant–Toddler Subscales

HOME SUBSCALE	SAMPLE ITEM
Organization of the physical environment	Child's play environment appears safe and free of hazards.
Provision of appropriate play materials	Parent provides toys or interesting activities for child during observer's visit.
Emotional and verbal responsiveness of the parent	Parent caresses or kisses child at least once during observer's visit.
	Parent spontaneously speaks to child twice or more (excluding scolding) during observer's visit.
Parental acceptance of the child	Parent does not interfere with child's actions or restrict child's movements more than three times during observer's visit.
Parental involvement with the child	Parent tends to keep child within view and to look at child often during observer's visit.
Opportunities for variety in daily stimulation	Child eats at least one meal per day with mother and/or father, according to parental report.
	Child frequently has a chance to get out of house (for example, accompanies parent on trips to grocery store).

Source: Bradley, 1994; Bradley et al., 2001. A brief, exclusively observational HOME instrument taps the first three subscales only. *See:* Rijlaarsdam et al., 2012.

early language progress, which, in turn, predicts intelligence and academic achievement in elementary school (Hart & Risley, 1995; Hoff, 2013).

Yet we must interpret these correlational findings cautiously. In all the studies, children were reared by their biological parents, with whom they share not just a common environment but also a common heredity. Parents who are genetically more intelligent may provide better experiences while also giving birth to genetically brighter children, who evoke more stimulation from their parents. Research supports this hypothesis, which refers to *genetic–environmental correlation* (see Chapter 2, pages 84–85) (Saudino & Plomin, 1997). But heredity does not account for the entire association between home environment and mental test scores. Family living conditions—both HOME scores and affluence of the surrounding neighborhood—continue to predict children's IQ beyond the contribution of parental IQ and education (Chase-Lansdale et al., 1997; Klebanov et al., 1998).

How can the research summarized so far help us understand Vanessa's concern about Timmy's development? Ben, the psychologist who tested Timmy, found that he scored only slightly below average. Ben talked with Vanessa about her child-rearing practices and watched her play with Timmy. A single parent who worked long hours, Vanessa had little energy for Timmy at the end of the day. Ben also noticed that Vanessa, anxious about Timmy's progress, tended to pressure him, dampening his active behavior and bombarding him with directions: "That's enough ball play. Stack these blocks."

Ben explained that when parents are intrusive in these ways, infants and toddlers are likely to be distractible, play immaturely, and do poorly on mental tests (Bono & Stifter, 2003). He coached Vanessa in how to interact sensitively with Timmy, while assuring her that Timmy's current performance need not forecast his future development. Warm, responsive parenting that builds on toddlers' current capacities is a much better indicator than an early mental test score of how children will do later.

INFANT AND TODDLER CHILD CARE Today, more than 60 percent of U.S. mothers with a child under age 2 are employed (U.S. Census Bureau, 2014b). Child care for infants and toddlers has become common, and its quality—though not as influential as parenting—affects mental development.

A mother plays affectionately with her baby. Warm, responsive parental interaction is a better indicator of how a child will do later than early mental test scores.

High-quality child care, with a generous caregiver–child ratio, well-trained caregivers, and developmentally appropriate activities, can be especially beneficial to children from low-SES homes.

Research consistently shows that young children exposed to long hours of mediocre to poor-quality child care—whether they come from middle-class or from low-SES homes—score lower on measures of cognitive, language, academic, and social skills during the pre-school, elementary, and secondary school years (Belsky et al., 2007b; Dearing, McCartney, & Taylor, 2009; NICHD Early Child Care Research Network, 2000b, 2001, 2003b, 2006; Vandell et al., 2010). In contrast, good child care can reduce the negative impact of a stressed, poverty-stricken home life, and it sustains the benefits of growing up in an economically advantaged family (Lamb & Ahnert, 2006; McCartney et al., 2007; NICHD Early Child Care Research Network, 2003b). As Figure 6.10 illustrates, the Early Childhood Longitudinal Study (see page 42 in Chapter 1), which included a large sample of children diverse in SES and ethnicity followed from birth through the preschool years, confirmed the importance of continuous high-quality child care from infancy through the preschool years (Li et al., 2013).

In contrast to most European countries and to Australia and New Zealand, where child care is nationally regulated and funded to ensure its quality, reports on U.S. child care raise serious concerns. Standards are set by the individual states and vary widely. In studies of quality, only 20 to 25 percent of child-care centers and family child-care homes provided infants and toddlers with sufficiently positive, stimulating experiences to promote healthy psychological development. Most settings offered substandard care (NICHD Early Child Care Research Network, 2000a, 2004). And the cost of child care in the United States is high: On average, full-time center-based care for one infant consumes from 7 to 19 percent of the median income for couples and over 40 percent for single mothers (Child Care Aware, 2013). The cost of a family child-care home is only slightly lower.

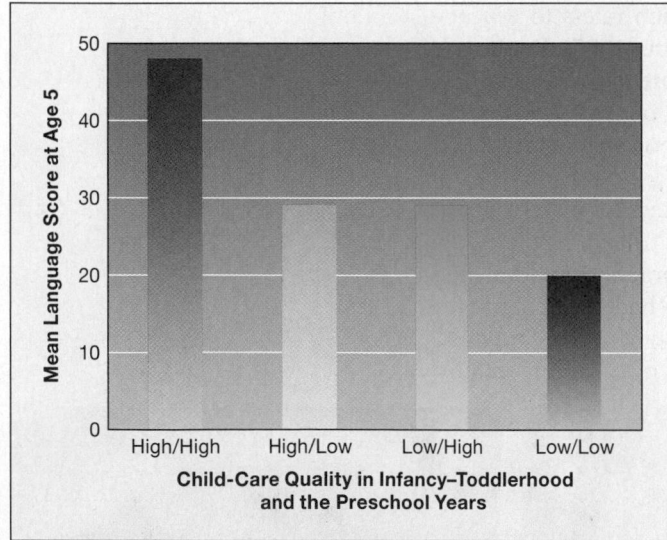

FIGURE 6.10 **Relationship of child-care quality in infancy–toddlerhood and the preschool years to language development at age 5.** When a nationally representative sample of more than 1,300 children was followed over the first five years, language scores were highest for those experiencing high-quality child care in both infancy–toddlerhood and the preschool years, intermediate for those experiencing high-quality care in just one of these periods, and lowest for those experiencing poor-quality care in both periods. Cognitive, literacy, and math scores also showed this pattern. (Adapted from Weilin Li; George Farkas; Greg J. Duncan; Margaret J. Burchinal & Deborah Lowe Vandell, 2013, "Timing of High-Quality Child Care and Cognitive, Language, and Preacademic Development," *Developmental Psychology*, 49, p. 1448. Copyright © 2013 by the American Psychological Association. Reprinted by permission of the American Psychological Association.)

Unfortunately, many U.S. children from low-income families experience inadequate child care (NICHD Early Child Care Research Network, 2005; Torquati et al., 2011). But U.S. settings providing the very worst care tend to serve middle-income families. These parents are especially likely to place their children in for-profit centers, where quality tends to be lowest. Economically disadvantaged children more often attend publicly subsidized, nonprofit centers, which are better equipped with learning materials and have smaller group sizes and more favorable teacher–child ratios (Johnson, Ryan, & Brooks-Gunn, 2012). Still, child-care quality for low-income children is often substandard.

See Applying What We Know on the following page for signs of high-quality child care for infants and toddlers, based on standards for **developmentally appropriate practice.** These standards, devised by the U.S. National Association for the Education of Young Children, specify program characteristics that serve young children's developmental and individual needs, based on both current research and consensus among experts. Caitlin, Grace, and Timmy are fortunate to be in family child care that meets these standards.

Child care in the United States is affected by a macrosystem of individualistic values and weak government regulation and funding. Furthermore, many parents think that their children's child-care experiences are better than they really are (Cryer, Tietz, & Wessels, 2002; Torquati et al., 2011). Unable to identify good care or without the financial means to purchase it, they do not demand it. In recent years, recognizing that child care is in a state of crisis, the U.S. federal government and some states have allocated additional funds to subsidize its cost, especially for low-income families (Matthews, 2014). Though far from meeting the need, this increase in resources has had a positive impact on child-care quality and accessibility.

Applying What We Know

Signs of Developmentally Appropriate Infant and Toddler Child Care

PROGRAM CHARACTERISTIC	SIGNS OF QUALITY
Physical setting	Indoor environment is clean, in good repair, well-lighted, and well-ventilated. Fenced outdoor play space is available. Setting does not appear overcrowded when children are present.
Toys and equipment	Play materials are appropriate for infants and toddlers and are stored on low shelves within easy reach. Cribs, highchairs, infant seats, and child-sized tables and chairs are available. Outdoor equipment includes small riding toys, swings, slide, and sandbox.
Caregiver–child ratio	In child-care centers, caregiver–child ratio is no greater than 1 to 3 for infants and 1 to 6 for toddlers. Group size (number of children in one room) is no greater than 6 infants with 2 caregivers and 12 toddlers with 2 caregivers. In family child-care homes, caregiver is responsible for no more than 6 children; within this group, no more than 2 are infants or toddlers. Staffing is consistent, so infants and toddlers can form relationships with particular caregivers.
Daily activities	Daily schedule includes times for active play, quiet play, naps, snacks, and meals. It is flexible rather than rigid, to meet the needs of individual children. Atmosphere is warm and supportive, and children are never left unsupervised.
Interactions among adults and children	Caregivers respond promptly to infants' and toddlers' distress; hold, talk to, sing, and read to them; and interact with them in a manner that respects the individual child's interests and tolerance for stimulation.
Caregiver qualifications	Caregiver has some training in child development, first aid, and safety.
Relationships with parents	Parents are welcome anytime. Caregivers talk frequently with parents about children's behavior and development.
Licensing and accreditation	Child-care setting, whether a center or a home, is licensed by the state. In the United States, voluntary accreditation by the National Association for the Education of Young Children *(www.naeyc.org/accreditation)* or the National Association for Family Child Care *(www.nafcc.org)* is evidence of an especially high-quality program.

Source: Copple & Bredekamp, 2009.

Early Intervention for At-Risk Infants and Toddlers

Children living in persistent poverty are likely to show gradual declines in intelligence test scores and to achieve poorly when they reach school age (Schoon et al., 2012). These problems are largely due to stressful home environments that undermine children's ability to learn and increase the likelihood that they will remain poor as adults (McLoyd, Aikens, & Burton, 2006). A variety of intervention programs have been developed to break this tragic cycle of poverty. Although most begin during the preschool years (we will discuss these in Chapter 9), some start during infancy and continue through early childhood.

In center-based interventions, children attend an organized child-care or preschool program where they receive educational, nutritional, and health services and their parents receive child-rearing and other social service supports. In home-based interventions, a skilled adult visits the home and works with parents, providing social support and teaching them how to stimulate a young child's development. In most programs of either type, participating children score higher than untreated controls on mental tests by age 2. The earlier intervention begins, the longer it lasts, and the greater its scope and intensity (for example, year-round high-quality child care plus generous support services for parents), the better participants' cognitive and academic performance throughout childhood and adolescence (Brooks-Gunn, 2004; Ramey, Ramey, & Lanzi, 2006; Sweet & Appelbaum, 2004).

The Carolina Abecedarian Project illustrates these positive outcomes. In the 1970s, more than 100 infants from poverty-stricken families, ranging in age from 3 weeks to 3 months, were randomly assigned to either a treatment group or a control group. Treatment infants were enrolled in full-time, year-round child care through the preschool years. There they received carefully planned educational experiences aimed at promoting motor, cognitive, language, and social skills and, after age 3, literacy and math concepts. Special emphasis was

LOOK and LISTEN

Ask several employed parents of infants or toddlers to describe what they sought in a child-care setting, along with challenges they faced in finding child care. Are the parents knowledgeable about the ingredients of high-quality care?

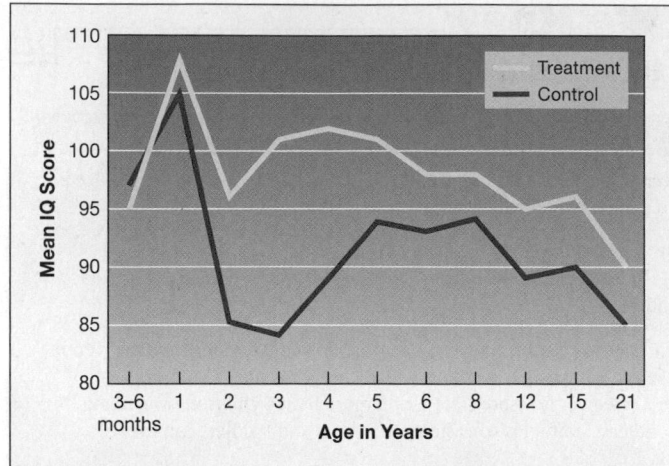

FIGURE 6.11 **IQ scores of treatment and control children from infancy to 21 years in the Carolina Abecedarian Project.** At 1 year, treatment children outperformed controls, an advantage consistently maintained through age 21. The IQ scores of both groups declined gradually during childhood and adolescence—a trend probably due to the damaging impact of poverty on mental development. (Based on Campbell et al., 2001.)

placed on rich, responsive adult–child verbal communication. All children received nutrition and health services; the primary difference between treatment and controls was the intensive child-care experience.

As Figure 6.11 shows, by 12 months of age, the IQs of the two groups diverged. Treatment children sustained an advantage until last tested—at age 21. In addition, throughout their years of schooling, treatment youths achieved considerably higher scores in reading and math. These gains translated into reduced enrollment in special education, more years of schooling completed, higher rates of college enrollment and employment in skilled jobs, and lower rates of drug use and adolescent parenthood (Campbell & Ramey, 2010; Campbell et al., 2001, 2002).

Recognition of the power of intervening as early as possible led the U.S. Congress to provide limited funding for intervention services directed at infants and toddlers who already have serious developmental problems or who are at risk for problems because of poverty. Early Head Start, begun in 1995, currently has 1,000 sites serving about 150,000 low-income children and their families (Schmidt, 2013). It offers an array of coordinated services—child care, educational experiences for infants and toddlers, parenting education, family social support, and health care—delivered through a center-based, home-based, or mixed approach, depending on community needs.

A recent evaluation, conducted when children reached age 3, showed that Early Head Start led to warmer, more stimulating parenting, a reduction in harsh discipline, gains in cognitive and language development, and lessening of child aggression (Love, Chazan-Cohen, & Raikes, 2007; Love et al., 2005; Raikes et al., 2010). The strongest effects occurred at sites mixing center- and home-visiting services.

By age 5, however, the benefits of Early Head Start had declined or disappeared, and a follow-up in fifth grade showed no persisting gains (U.S. Department of Health and Human Services, 2006; Vogel et al., 2010). One speculation is that more intentional educational experiences extending through the preschool years—as in the Abecedarian project—would increase the lasting impact of Early Head Start (Barnett, 2011). Also, some evidence suggests that the cognitive benefits of Early Head Start are greater for certain children—in particular, those who receive little stimulation at home (Bradley, McKelvey, & Whiteside-Mansell, 2011). Although Early Head Start is in need of refinement, it is a promising beginning at providing U.S. infants and toddlers living in poverty with publicly supported intervention.

© ELLEN B. SENISI

This Early Head Start program provides rich, educational experiences for toddlers plus parent education and family social supports. The most favorable outcomes of Early Head Start result from mixing center- and home-visiting services.

Ask Yourself

● **REVIEW** What probably accounts for the finding that speed of habituation and recovery to visual stimuli predicts later IQ better than an infant mental test score?

● **CONNECT** Using what you learned about brain development in Chapter 5, explain why it is best to initiate intervention for poverty-stricken children in the first two years rather than later.

● **APPLY** Fifteen-month-old Joey's developmental quotient (DQ) is 115. His mother wants to know exactly what this means and what she should do to support his intellectual development. How would you respond?

● **REFLECT** Suppose you were seeking a child-care setting for your baby. What would you want it to be like, and why?

Language Development

Improvements in perception and cognition during infancy pave the way for an extraordinary human achievement—language. In Chapter 5, we saw that by the second half of the first year, infants make dramatic progress in distinguishing the basic sounds of their language and in segmenting the flow of speech into word and phrase units. They also start to comprehend some word meanings and, around 12 months of age, say their first word. Sometime between 1½ and 2 years, toddlers combine two words (Gleason, 2013). By age 6, children understand the meaning of about 10,000 words, speak in elaborate sentences, and are skilled conversationalists.

To appreciate this awesome task, think about the many abilities involved in your own flexible use of language. When you speak, you must select words that match the underlying concepts you want to convey. To be understood, you must pronounce words correctly. Then you must combine them into phrases and sentences using a complex set of grammatical rules. Finally, you must follow the rules of everyday conversation—taking turns, making comments relevant to what your partner just said, and using an appropriate tone of voice. How do infants and toddlers make such remarkable progress in launching these skills?

6.10 Describe theories of language development, and indicate the emphasis each places on innate abilities and environmental influences.

6.11 Describe major milestones of language development in the first two years, individual differences, and ways adults can support infants' and toddlers' emerging capacities.

Theories of Language Development

In the 1950s, researchers did not take seriously the idea that very young children might be able to figure out important properties of language. Children's regular and rapid attainment of language milestones suggested a process largely governed by maturation, inspiring the nativist perspective on language development. In recent years, new evidence has spawned the interactionist perspective, which emphasizes the joint roles of children's inner capacities and communicative experiences.

THE NATIVIST PERSPECTIVE   According to linguist Noam Chomsky's (1957) *nativist* theory, language is a uniquely human accomplishment, etched into the structure of the brain. Focusing on grammar, Chomsky reasoned that the rules of sentence organization are too complex to be directly taught to or discovered by even a cognitively sophisticated young child. Rather, he proposed that all children have a **language acquisition device (LAD),** an innate system that contains a *universal grammar,* or set of rules common to all languages. It enables children, no matter which language they hear, to understand and speak in a rule-oriented fashion as soon as they pick up enough words.

Are children innately primed to acquire language? Recall from Chapter 4 that newborn babies are remarkably sensitive to speech sounds. And children everywhere reach major language milestones in a similar sequence (Parish-Morris, Golinkoff, & Hirsh-Pasek, 2013). Research reviewed in the Biology and Environment box on page 232, suggesting that children have an impressive ability to invent new language systems, provides some of the most powerful support for the nativist perspective.

Furthermore, the ability to master a grammatically complex language system seems to be unique to humans, as efforts to teach language to nonhuman primates—using either specially devised artificial symbol systems or sign language—have met with limited success. Even after extensive training, chimpanzees (who are closest to humans in terms of evolution) master only a basic vocabulary and short word combinations, and they produce these far less consistently than human preschoolers (Tomasello, Call, & Hare, 2003).

Evidence for specialized language areas in the brain and a sensitive period for language development have also been interpreted as supporting Chomsky's theory. Let's take a closer look at these findings.

© LAURA DWIGHT PHOTOGRAPHY

Infants communicate from the very beginning of life. How will this child become a fluent speaker of her native language within just a few years? Theorists disagree sharply.

Biology and Environment

Deaf Children Invent Language

Can children develop complex, rule-based language systems with minimal language input, or with input so inconsistent that grammatical rules are not readily apparent? If so, such evidence would support Chomsky's idea that the human brain is prewired for language development. Research reveals that deaf children can generate an intricate natural language, even when reared in language-deficient environments.

Minimal Language Input

In a series of studies, researchers tracked the language development of deaf toddlers and preschoolers whose parents discouraged signing and addressed them verbally (Goldin-Meadow, 2009). None of the children made progress in acquiring spoken language or used even the most common gestures of their nation's sign language. Nevertheless, in interacting with one another, they spontaneously produced a gestural communication system, called *homesign*, strikingly similar in basic structure to hearing children's verbal language.

The deaf children developed gestural vocabularies with distinct forms for nouns and verbs, similar to the meanings of spoken words. Furthermore, the children combined gestures into novel sentences conforming to basic grammatical rules that were not necessarily those of their parents' spoken language (Goldin-Meadow, Gelman, & Mylander, 2005). For example, to describe a large bubble he had blown, one child first pointed at a bubble jar and then used two open palms with fingers spread to denote the act of "blowing up big."

The children did not pick up their gesture systems from parents, whose gestures were limited—no different from the gestures that hearing speakers produce while talking (Goldin-Meadow, 2003). Rather the children created homesign as they interacted with one another, and they used it for the same diverse purposes as any language—to comment on present and nonpresent objects and events, to ask questions,

to influence others' actions, to tell stories, and to talk about their own and others' signs.

Hearing children acquire a larger vocabulary and a far more complex grammar than children inventing homesign. This indicates that a rich language environment with partners who "speak" the same language—for deaf children, exposure to adults fluent in an elaborate sign language—fosters typical language development. But without access to conventional language, children generate their own language system.

In Nicaragua, educators brought deaf children and adolescents, each with a unique homesign, together to form a community. Although they had no shared language, in less than two decades they developed Nicaraguan Sign Language, which matches other languages in complexity (Senghas et al., 2005).

Inconsistent Language Input

A study of Simon, a deaf child born to deaf parents who were late learners of American Sign Language (ASL), also illustrates children's remarkable capacity to invent language. As with the deaf children just described, Simon's parent were exposed only to oral language in childhood; only in adolescence did they start to learn ALS. As a result, they had not attained the grammatical competence of native signers, and they used many ASL structures inconsistently. (See the discussion of a sensitive period for language development on page 233.) Simon went to school with hearing teachers and children, so his only ASL input came from his parents.

When Simon was 7, researchers gave him a challenging ASL grammar task, which assessed his knowledge of the verb *to move* (Singleton and Newport, 2004). In ASL, expressing motion requires up to seven grammatical markers, which designate an object's path, orientation, style of movement,

In Nicaragua, educators brought deaf children and adolescents together to form a community. Within two decades, they devised a new language—Nicaraguan Sign Language.

and location, plus a secondary object's features and position relative to the first object and its path. Simon's performance was compared with the performance of several reference groups: his parents, deaf school-age children of deaf native-signing parents, and deaf native-signing adults.

Findings confirmed that Simon's parents' ASL grammar was much weaker than that of native-signing adults. Yet Simon introduced rule usage into his language that greatly exceeded his parents' scores. His performance even surpassed the average score of native-signing deaf children and approached that of native-signing deaf adults. Simon had managed to extract ASL regularities from his parents' imperfect language, arriving at a highly consistent grammar.

Deaf children's remarkable capacity to invent language, despite minimal or inconsistent input, is compatible with the existence of an innate LAD. As we will see, however, other theorists claim that nonlinguistic cognitive capacities, applied to the task of communicating, are responsible.

Language Areas in the Brain Recall from Chapter 5 that for most individuals, language is housed largely in the left hemisphere of the cerebral cortex. Within it are two important language-related structures (see Figure 6.12). To clarify their functions, researchers have, for several decades, studied adults who experienced damage to these structures and display *aphasias,* or communication disorders. *Broca's area,* located in the left frontal lobe, supports grammatical processing and language production. *Wernicke's area,* located in the left temporal lobe, plays a role in comprehending word meaning.

But recent brain-imaging research suggests that the relationship between these brain structures and language functions is complicated. Neither area is solely, or even mainly, responsible for specific language capacities. Rather, the impaired pronunciation and grammar of patients with Broca's aphasia and the meaningless speech streams of patients with Wernicke's aphasia involve the spread of injury to nearby cortical areas and widespread abnormal activity in the left cerebral hemisphere, triggered by the brain damage (Bates et al., 2003; Keller et al., 2009).

The broad association of language functions with left-hemispheric regions is consistent with Chomsky's notion of a brain prepared to process language. But critics point out that at birth, the brain is not fully lateralized; it is highly plastic. Language areas in the cerebral cortex *develop* as children acquire language (Mills & Conboy, 2005). Although the left hemisphere is biased for language processing, if it is injured in the first few years, other regions take over language functions, and most such children eventually attain normal language competence. Thus, left-hemispheric localization, though typical, is not necessary for effective language processing.

Nevertheless, when the young brain allocates language to the right hemisphere—as a result of left-hemispheric damage or learning of sign language (see pages 166–167 in Chapter 5)—it localizes it in roughly the same regions that typically support language in the left hemisphere (Stiles, Reilly, & Levine, 2012). This suggests that those brain structures are uniquely disposed for language processing.

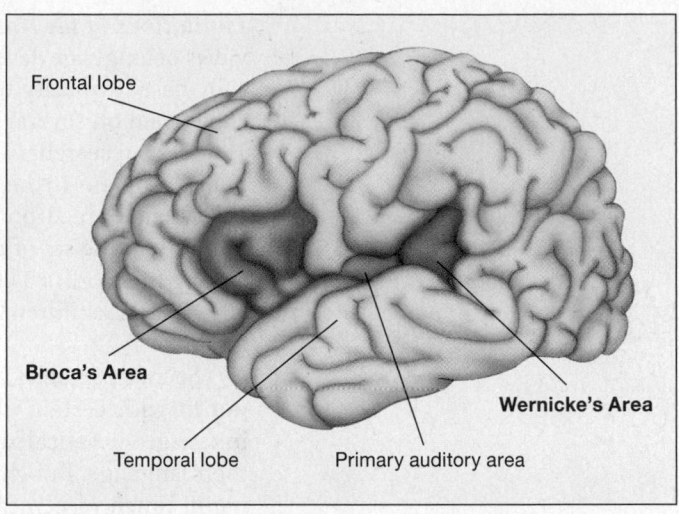

FIGURE 6.12 Broca's and Wernicke's areas, in the left hemisphere of the cerebral cortex. Broca's area, located in the frontal lobe, supports grammatical processing and language production. Wernicke's area, located in the temporal lobe, is involved in comprehending word meaning. Contrary to what was once believed, however, neither area is solely or even mainly responsible for these functions.

A Sensitive Period for Language Development Must language be acquired early in life, during an age span in which the brain is particularly responsive to language stimulation? Evidence for a sensitive period that coincides with brain lateralization would support the view that language development has unique biological properties.

To test this idea, researchers have examined the language competence of deaf adults who acquired their first language—American Sign Language (ASL), a gestural system just as complex as any spoken language—at different ages. The later learners, whose parents chose to educate them through the oral method, which relies on speech and lip-reading, did not acquire spoken language because of their profound deafness. Consistent with the sensitive-period notion, those who learned ASL in adolescence or adulthood never became as proficient as those who learned in childhood (Mayberry, 2010; Singleton & Newport, 2004). (Recall from the Biology and Environment box on page 232 that Simon's parents, who acquired ASL in adolescence, scored lower than he did on a test of complex grammar.) However, a precise age cutoff for a decline in first-language competence has not been established.

Is acquiring a second language also harder after a sensitive period has passed? In one study, researchers examined U.S. census data, selecting immigrants from non-English-speaking countries who had resided in the United States for at least ten years. The census form had asked the immigrants to rate how competently they spoke English, from "not at all" to "very well"—self-reports that correlate strongly with objective language measures. As age of immigration increased from infancy and early childhood into adulthood, English proficiency declined (Hakuta, Bialystok, & Wiley, 2003). Furthermore, ERP and fMRI measures of brain activity indicate that second-language processing is less lateralized in older than in younger learners (Neville & Bruer, 2001). But second-language competence does not drop sharply at a certain age. Rather, a continuous, age-related decrease occurs.

In sum, research on both first- and second-language learning reveals a biologically based timeframe for optimum language development. However, the boundaries of this sensitive period remain unclear.

© SYRACUSE NEWSPAPERS/MIKE GREENLAR/THE IMAGE WORKS

Childhood seems to be a sensitive period for optimum language development. This Ethiopian father, attending an English-as-a-second-language class, may never become as proficient an English speaker as his daughter.

Limitations of the Nativist Perspective Chomsky's theory has had a major impact on current views of language development. It is now widely accepted that humans have a unique, biologically based capacity to acquire language. Still, Chomsky's account of development has been challenged on several grounds.

First, researchers have had great difficulty specifying Chomsky's universal grammar. A major problem is the absence of a complete description of these abstract grammatical rules or even an agreed-on list of how many exist or the best examples of them. Chomsky's critics doubt that one set of rules can account for the extraordinary variation in grammatical forms among the world's 5,000 to 8,000 languages (Christiansen & Chater, 2008; Evans & Levinson, 2009). How children manage to link such rules with the strings of words they hear is also unclear.

Second, Chomsky's assumption that grammatical knowledge is innately determined does not fit with certain observations of language development. Once children begin to use an innate grammatical structure, we would expect them to apply it to all relevant instances in their language. But children refine and generalize many grammatical forms gradually, engaging in much piecemeal learning and making errors along the way. For example, one 3-year-old, in grappling with prepositions, initially added *with* to the verb *open* ("You open with scissors") but not to the word *hit* ("He hit me stick") (Tomasello, 2006). As we will see in Chapter 12, complete mastery of some grammatical forms, such as the passive voice, is not achieved until well into middle childhood. This suggests that more experimentation and learning are involved than Chomsky assumed.

THE INTERACTIONIST PERSPECTIVE   Recent ideas about language development emphasize *interactions* between inner capacities and environmental influences. One type of interactionist theory applies the information-processing perspective to language development. A second type emphasizes social interaction.

Some information-processing theorists assume that children make sense of their complex language environments by applying powerful cognitive capacities of a general kind (Bates, 2004; Munakata, 2006; Saffran, 2009). These theorists note that regions of the brain housing language also govern similar perceptual and cognitive abilities, such as the capacity to analyze musical and visual patterns (Saygin, Leech, & Dick, 2010; Saygin et al., 2004).

Other theorists blend this information-processing view with Chomsky's nativist perspective. They agree that infants are amazing statistical analyzers of speech and other information (see Chapter 5). But, they argue, these capacities probably are not sufficient to account for mastery of higher-level aspects of language, such as intricate grammatical structures (Aslin & Newport, 2012). They also point out that grammatical competence may depend more on specific brain structures than the other components of language. When 2- to 2½-year-olds and adults listened to short sentences—some grammatically correct, others with phrase-structure violations—both groups showed similarly distinct ERP brain-wave patterns for each sentence type in the left frontal and temporal lobes of the cerebral cortex (Oberecker & Friederici, 2006). This suggests that 2-year-olds process sentence structures using the same neural system as adults do. Furthermore, in studies of older children and adults with left-hemispheric brain damage, grammar is more impaired than other language functions (Curtiss & Schaeffer, 2005).

Still other interactionists emphasize that children's social skills and language experiences are centrally involved in language development. In this *social-interactionist* view, an active child strives to communicate, which cues her caregivers to provide appropriate language experiences, which in turn help her relate the content and structure of language to its social meanings (Bohannon & Bonvillian, 2013; Chapman, 2006).

Among social interactionists, disagreement continues over whether or not children are equipped with specialized language structures (Hsu, Chater, & Vitányi, 2013; Lidz, 2007; Tomasello, 2006). Nevertheless, as we chart the course of language development, we will encounter much support for their central premise—that children's social competencies and language experiences greatly affect their language progress. In reality, native endowment, cognitive-processing strategies, and social experience probably operate in different balances with respect to each aspect of language: pronunciation, vocabulary, grammar, and communication skills. Table 6.3 provides an overview of early language milestones that we will examine in the next few sections.

TABLE 6.3	Milestones of Language Development During the First Two Years
APPROXIMATE AGE	**MILESTONE**
2 months	Infants coo, making pleasant vowel sounds.
4 months on	Infants observe with interest as the caregiver plays turn-taking games, such as pat-a-cake and peekaboo.
6 months on	Infants babble, adding consonants to their cooing sounds and repeating syllables. By 7 months, babbling starts to include many sounds of spoken languages.
	Infants begin to comprehend a few commonly heard words.
8–12 months	Infants become more accurate at establishing joint attention with the caregiver, who often verbally labels what the baby is looking at.
	Infants actively participate in turn-taking games, trading roles with the caregiver.
	Infants use preverbal gestures, such as showing and pointing, to influence others' goals and behavior and to convey information.
12 months	Babbling includes sound and intonation patterns of the child's language community.
	Speed and accuracy of word comprehension increase rapidly.
	Toddlers say their first recognizable word.
18–24 months	Spoken vocabulary expands from about 50 to 200 to 250 words.
	Toddlers combine two words.

Getting Ready to Talk

Before babies say their first word, they make impressive progress toward understanding and speaking their native tongue. They listen attentively to human speech, and they make speech-like sounds. As adults, we can hardly help but respond.

COOING AND BABBLING Around 2 months, babies begin to make vowel-like noises, called **cooing** because of their pleasant "oo" quality. Gradually, consonants are added, and around 6 months **babbling** appears, in which infants repeat consonant–vowel combinations, often in long strings, such as "babababababa" or "nanananana."

Babies everywhere (even those who are deaf) start babbling at about the same age and produce a similar range of early sounds. But for babbling to develop further, infants must be able to hear human speech. In hearing-impaired babies, these speechlike sounds are greatly delayed and limited in diversity of sounds (Bass-Ringdahl, 2010). And a deaf infant not exposed to sign language will stop babbling entirely (Oller, 2000).

In one case, a deaf-born 5-month-old received a *cochlear implant*—an electronic device surgically inserted into the ear that converts external sounds into a signal to stimulate the auditory nerve. She showed typical babbling in infancy and resembled her hearing agemates in language development at 3 to 4 years (Schauwers et al., 2004). But if auditory input is not restored until after age 2 (the usual time for cochlear implant surgery), children remain behind in language development. And if implantation occurs after age 4, language delays are severe and persistent (Coene et al., 2011; Svirsky, Teoh, & Neuburger, 2004). These outcomes suggest an early sensitive period for the brain to develop the necessary organization for normal speech processing.

Babies initially produce a limited number of sounds and then expand to a much broader range. Around 7 months, babbling starts to include many sounds of spoken

Even babies who are deaf begin babbling at around 2 months. Those exposed to sign language from birth, as this child has been, babble with their hands, much as hearing babies do through speech.

languages. As caregivers respond to infant babbles, older infants modify their babbling to include sound patterns like those in the adult's speech (Goldstein & Schwade, 2008). By 8 to 10 months, babbling reflects the sound and intonation patterns of children's language community, some of which are transferred to their first words (Boysson-Bardies & Vihman, 1991).

TAKE A MOMENT... The next time you hear an older baby babbling, notice how certain sounds appear in particular contexts—for example, when exploring objects, looking at books, or walking upright (Blake & Boysson-Bardies, 1992). Infants seem to be experimenting with the sound system and meaning of language before they speak in conventional ways. Toddlers continue babbling for four or five months after they say their first words.

Deaf infants exposed to sign language from birth babble with their hands much as hearing infants do through speech (Petitto & Marentette, 1991). Furthermore, hearing babies of deaf, signing parents produce babblelike hand motions with the rhythmic patterns of natural sign languages (Petitto et al., 2001, 2004). This sensitivity to language rhythm—evident in both spoken and signed babbling—supports both discovery and production of meaningful language units.

BECOMING A COMMUNICATOR   At birth, infants are prepared for some aspects of conversational behavior. For example, newborns initiate interaction through eye contact and terminate it by looking away. By 3 to 4 months, infants start to gaze in the same general direction adults are looking—a skill that becomes more accurate at 10 to 11 months, as babies realize that others' focus offers information about their communicative intentions (to talk about an object) or other goals (to obtain an object) (Brooks & Meltzoff, 2005; Senju, Csibra, & Johnson, 2008). Around their first birthday, infants realize that a person's visual gaze signals a vital connection between the viewer and his or her surroundings, and they want to participate.

This **joint attention,** in which the child attends to the same object or event as the caregiver, who often labels it, contributes greatly to early language development. Infants and toddlers who frequently experience it sustain attention longer, comprehend more language, produce meaningful gestures and words earlier, and show faster vocabulary development through 2 years of age (Brooks & Meltzoff, 2008; Carpenter, Nagel, & Tomasello, 1998; Flom & Pick, 2003; Silvén, 2001). Gains in joint attention at the end of the first year enable babies to establish a "common ground" with the adult, through which they can figure out the meaning of the adult's verbal labels (Tomasello, 2003).

This baby uses a preverbal gesture to draw his caregiver's attention to a picture. The caregiver's verbal response promotes the baby's transition to spoken language.

Around 3 months, interactions between caregivers and babies begin to include *give-and-take*. Infants and mothers mutually imitate the pitch, loudness, and duration of each other's sounds. Mothers take the lead, imitating about twice as often as 3-month-olds, who limit their imitations to a small range of sounds—ones they find easier to produce (Gratier & Devouche, 2011). Between 4 and 6 months, imitation extends to social games, as in pat-a-cake and peekaboo. At first, the parent starts the game and the baby is an amused observer. Gradually, infants join in, and by the end of the first year, they participate actively, trading roles with the caregiver. Through these imitative exchanges, babies practice the turn-taking pattern of human conversation, a vital context for acquiring language and communication skills. Infants' vocalizations and play maturity during games predict advanced language progress during toddlerhood (Rome-Flanders & Cronk, 1995).

At the end of the first year, infants use *preverbal gestures* to direct adults' attention, influence their behavior, and convey helpful information (Tomasello, Carpenter, & Liszkowski, 2007). For example, Caitlin held up a toy to show it, pointed to the cupboard when she wanted a cookie, and pointed at her mother's car keys lying on the floor. Carolyn responded to these gestures and also labeled them ("That's your bear!" "You want a cookie!" "Oh, there are my keys!"). In this way, toddlers learn that using language leads to desired results.

Besides using preverbal gestures to serve their own goals, 12-month-olds adapt these gestures to the needs of others. In one study, they pointed more often to an object whose location a searching adult did not know than to an object whose location the adult did know (Liszkowski, Carpenter, & Tomasello, 2008). They also understand what an adult means when she points to the location of a hidden toy (Behne et al., 2012). Already, the cooperative processes essential for effective communication are under way—namely, modifying messages to suit others' intentions and knowledge and recognizing when others have done the same.

The more time caregivers and infants spend in joint activity with objects, the earlier and more often babies use preverbal gestures (Salomo & Liszkowski, 2013). Over time, some of these gestures become explicitly symbolic. For example, a toddler might flap her arms to indicate "butterfly" or raise her palms to signal "all gone." Soon toddlers integrate words with gestures, using the gesture to expand their verbal message, as in pointing to a toy while saying "give" (Capirci et al., 2005). Gradually, gestures recede, and words become dominant. But the greater the number of items toddlers gesture about and the earlier they form word–gesture combinations, the faster their vocabulary growth, the sooner they produce two-word utterances at the end of the second year, and the more complex their sentences are at age 3½ (Huttenlocher et al., 2010; Rowe & Goldin-Meadow, 2009a, 2009b).

LOOK and **LISTEN**

Observe a toddler for 30 to 60 minutes at home or child care. Jot down preverbal gestures, words, and word–gesture combinations that the baby produces. Do the toddler's language skills fit with research findings?

First Words

In the middle of the first year, infants begin to understand word meanings. By 5 months, they respond to their own name, preferring to listen to it than to another word matched in stress pattern (Mandel, Jusczyk, & Pisoni, 1995). And when 6-month-olds listened to the words "Mommy" or "Daddy" while viewing side-by-side videos of their parents, they looked longer at the video of the named parent (Tincoff & Jusczyk, 1999). At 9 months, after hearing a word paired with an object, babies looked longer at other objects in the same category than at those in a different category (Balaban & Waxman, 1997).

First spoken words, around 1 year, build on the sensorimotor foundations Piaget described and on categories infants have formed. In a study tracking the first 10 words used by several hundred U.S. and Chinese (both Mandarin- and Cantonese-speaking) babies, important people ("Mama," "Dada"), common objects ("ball," "bread"), and sound effects ("woof-woof," "vroom") were mentioned most often. Action words ("hit," "grab," "hug") and social routines ("hi," "bye"), though also appearing in all three groups, were more often produced by Chinese than U.S. babies—differences we will consider shortly (Tardif et al., 2008). Other investigations concur that earliest words usually include people, objects that move, foods, animals (in families with pets), familiar actions, outcomes of such actions ("hot," "wet"), and social terms (Hart, 2004; Nelson, 1973). In their first 50 words, toddlers rarely name things that just *sit there,* like "table" or "vase."

When young children first learn words, they sometimes apply them too narrowly, an error called **underextension.** At 16 months, Caitlin used "bear" only to refer to the worn and tattered teddy bear she carried nearly constantly. As vocabulary expands, a more common error is **overextension**—applying a word to a wider collection of objects and events than is appropriate. For example, Grace used "car" for buses, trains, trucks, and fire engines. Toddlers' overextensions reflect their sensitivity to categories (MacWhinney, 2005). They apply a new word to a group of similar experiences: "car" to wheeled objects, "open" to opening a door, peeling fruit, and untying shoelaces. This suggests that children often overextend deliberately because they have difficulty recalling or have not acquired a suitable word. And when a word is hard to pronounce, toddlers are likely to substitute a related one they can say (Bloom, 2000). As vocabulary expands and pronunciation improves, overextensions gradually decline.

The Two-Word Utterance Phase

Young toddlers add to their spoken vocabularies at a rate of one to three words a week. Because gains in word production between 18 and 24 months are so impressive (one or two words per day), many researchers concluded that toddlers undergo a *spurt in vocabulary*—a transition

Toddlers typically utter their first word around 1 year. As their experiences broaden, they label more objects and events, first with single words and then with two-word utterances known as telegraphic speech.

from a slower to a faster learning phase. In actuality, most children show a steady increase in rate of word learning that continues through the preschool years (Ganger & Brent, 2004).

How do toddlers build their vocabularies so quickly? In the second year, they improve in ability to categorize experience, recall words, and grasp others' social cues to meaning, such as eye gaze, pointing, and handling objects (Golinkoff & Hirsh-Pasek, 2006; Liszkowski, Carpenter, & Tomasello, 2007). Furthermore, as toddlers' experiences broaden, they have a wider range of interesting objects and events to label. For example, children approaching age 2 more often mention places to go ("park," "store"). And as they construct a clearer self-image, they add more words that refer to themselves ("me," "mine," "Katy") and to their own and others' bodies and clothing ("eyes," "mouth," "jacket" (Hart, 2004). In Chapter 9, we will consider the diverse strategies young children use to figure out word meanings.

Once toddlers produce 200 to 250 words, they start to combine two words: "Mommy shoe," "go car," "more cookie." These two-word utterances are called **telegraphic speech** because, like a telegram, they focus on high-content words, omitting smaller, less important ones ("can," "the," "to"). Children the world over use them to express an impressive variety of meanings.

Two-word speech consists largely of simple formulas ("more + X," "eat + X"), with different words inserted in the "X" position. Toddlers rarely make gross grammatical errors, such as saying "chair my" instead of "my chair." But their word-order regularities are usually copies of adult word pairings, as when Carolyn remarked to Caitlin, "How about *more sandwich?*" or "Let's see if you can *eat the berries?*" (Tomasello, 2003; Tomasello & Brandt, 2009). When 18- to 23-month-olds were taught noun and verb nonsense words (for example, "meek" for a doll and "gop" for a snapping action), they easily combined the new nouns with words they knew well ("more meek"). But they seldom formed word combinations with the new verbs (Tomasello, 2000; Tomasello et al., 1997). This suggests that they cannot yet flexibly form novel sentences that express subject–verb and verb–object relations, which are the foundation of grammar.

In sum, toddlers are absorbed in figuring out word meanings and using their limited vocabularies in whatever way possible to get their thoughts across. At first, they rely on "concrete pieces of language" they often hear, gradually generalizing from those pieces to word-order and other grammatical rules (Bannard, Lieven, & Tomasello, 2009; Tomasello, 2006). As we will see in Chapter 7, they make steady progress over the preschool years.

Comprehension versus Production

So far, we have focused on language **production**—the words and word combinations children use. What about **comprehension**—the language they understand? At all ages, comprehension develops ahead of production. A five-month lag exists between the time toddlers typically comprehend 50 words (around 13 months) and the time they produce that many (around 18 months) (Menyuk, Liebergott, & Schultz, 1995).

Think back to the distinction made earlier in this chapter between two types of memory—recognition and recall. Comprehension requires only that children *recognize* the meaning of a word. But for production, children must *recall,* or actively retrieve from their memories, not only the word but also the concept for which it stands. Still, the two capacities are related. The speed and accuracy of toddlers' comprehension of spoken language increase dramatically over the second year. And toddlers who are faster and more accurate in comprehension tend to show more rapid growth in words understood and produced over the following year (Fernald & Marchman, 2012). Quick comprehension frees space in working memory for picking up new words and for the more demanding task of using them to communicate.

Individual and Cultural Differences

Although children typically produce their first word around their first birthday, the range is large, from 8 to 18 months—variation due to a complex blend of genetic and environmental influences. Earlier we saw that Timmy's spoken language was delayed, in part because of Vanessa's tense, directive communication with him. But Timmy is also a boy, and research indicates that girls are slightly ahead of boys in early vocabulary growth (Fenson et al., 1994; Van Hulle, Goldsmith, & Lemery, 2004). The most common explanation is girls' faster rate of physical maturation, which is believed to promote earlier development of the left cerebral hemisphere.

Temperament matters, too. Shy toddlers often wait until they understand a great deal before trying to speak. Once they do speak, their vocabularies increase rapidly, although they remain slightly behind their agemates (Spere et al., 2004). Emotionally negative toddlers also acquire language more slowly because their high reactivity diverts them from processing linguistic information (Salley & Dixon, 2007).

Caregiver–child conversation—especially, the richness of adults' vocabularies—also play a strong role (Huttenlocher et al. 2010). Commonly used words for objects appear early in toddlers' speech, and the more often their caregivers use a particular noun, the sooner young children produce it (Goodman, Dale, & Li, 2008). Mothers talk more to toddler-age girls than to boys, and parents converse less often with shy than with sociable children (Leaper, Anderson, & Sanders, 1998; Patterson & Fisher, 2002).

Compared to their higher-SES agemates, children from low-SES homes usually have smaller vocabularies. By 18 to 24 months, they are slower at word comprehension and have acquired 30 percent fewer words (Fernald, Marchman & Weisleder, 2013). Limited parent–child conversation and book reading are major factors. Higher-SES parents typically interact more with their children, using a richer vocabulary, than do low-SES parents (Hoff, 2006). And on average, a middle-SES child is read to for 1,000 hours between 1 and 5 years, a low-SES child for only 25 hours (Neuman, 2003).

Not surprisingly, rate of early vocabulary growth is a strong predictor of low-SES children's vocabulary size at kindergarten entry, which forecasts their later literacy skills and school success (Rowe, Raudenbush, & Goldin-Meadow, 2012). Higher-SES toddlers who lag behind their agemates in word learning have more opportunities to catch up in early childhood.

Young children have distinct styles of early language learning. Caitlin and Grace, like most toddlers, used a **referential style;** their vocabularies consisted mainly of words that referred to objects. A smaller number of toddlers use an **expressive style;** compared to referential children, they produce many more social formulas and pronouns ("thank you," "done," "I want it"). These styles reflect early ideas about the functions of language. Grace, for example, thought words were for naming things. In the week after her adoption, she uttered only a single word in Khmer, her native language. But after two months of listening to English conversation, Grace added words quickly: "Eli," then "doggie," "kitty," "Mama," "Dada," "book," "ball," "car," "cup," "clock," and "chicken"—all within one week. In contrast, expressive-style children believe words are for talking about people's feelings and needs. The vocabularies of referential-style toddlers grow faster because all languages contain many more object labels than social terms (Bates et al., 1994).

What accounts for a toddler's language style? Rapidly developing referential-style children often have an especially active interest in exploring objects. They also eagerly imitate their parents' frequent naming of objects, and their parents imitate back, which helps children remember new labels (Masur & Rodemaker, 1999). Expressive-style children tend to be highly sociable, and their parents more often use verbal routines ("How are you?" "It's no trouble") that support social relationships (Goldfield, 1987).

The two language styles are also linked to culture. Object words (nouns) are particularly common in the vocabularies of English-speaking toddlers, but Chinese, Japanese, and Korean toddlers have more words for actions (verbs) and

This Chinese mother's communication with her toddler probably includes many words for actions and social routines. Her child—like other Chinese children—is likely to display an expressive style, focused on strengthening social relationships.

Applying What We Know

Supporting Early Language Learning

STRATEGY	CONSEQUENCE
Respond to coos and babbles with speech sounds and words.	Encourages experimentation with sounds that can later be blended into first words Provides experience with the turn-taking pattern of human conversation
Establish joint attention and comment on what child sees.	Predicts earlier onset of language and faster vocabulary development
Play social games, such as pat-a-cake and peekaboo.	Provides experience with the turn-taking pattern of human conversation
Engage toddlers in joint make-believe play.	Promotes all aspects of conversational dialogue
Engage toddlers in frequent conversations.	Predicts faster early language development and academic success during the school years
Read to toddlers often, engaging them in dialogues about picture books.	Provides exposure to many aspects of language, including vocabulary, grammar, communication skills, and information about written symbols and story structures

social routines. Mothers' speech in each culture reflects this difference (Chan, Brandone, & Tardif, 2009; Chan et al., 2011; Choi & Gopnik, 1995; Fernald & Morikawa, 1993). American mothers frequently label objects when interacting with their babies. Asian mothers, perhaps because of a cultural emphasis on the importance of group membership, emphasize actions and social routines. Also, in Mandarin, sentences often begin with verbs, making action words particularly salient to Mandarin-speaking toddlers.

At what point should parents become concerned if their child talks very little or not at all? If a toddler's development is greatly delayed when compared with the norms in Table 6.3 (page 235), then parents should consult the child's doctor or a speech and language therapist. Late babbling or gesturing may be signs of slow language development that can be prevented with early intervention (Rowe, Raudenbush, & Goldin-Meadow, 2012). Some toddlers who do not follow simple directions or who, after age 2, have difficulty putting their thoughts into words may suffer from a hearing impairment or a language disorder that requires immediate treatment.

Supporting Early Language Development

Consistent with the interactionist view, a rich social environment builds on young children's natural readiness to speak their native tongue. For a summary of how caregivers can consciously support early language learning, see Applying What We Know above. Caregivers also do so unconsciously—through a special style of speech.

Adults in many countries speak to young children in **infant-directed speech (IDS),** a form of communication made up of short sentences with high-pitched, exaggerated expression, clear pronunciation, distinct pauses between speech segments, clear gestures to support verbal meaning, and repetition of new words in a variety of contexts ("See the *ball.*" "The *ball* bounced!") (Fernald et al., 1989; O'Neill et al., 2005). Deaf parents use a similar style of communication when signing to their deaf babies (Masataka, 1996). From birth on, infants prefer IDS over other kinds of adult talk, and by 5 months they are more emotionally responsive to it (Aslin, Jusczyk, & Pisoni, 1998).

IDS builds on several communicative strategies we have already considered: joint attention, turn-taking, and caregivers' sensitivity to toddlers' preverbal gestures. In this example, Carolyn uses IDS with 18-month-old Caitlin:

> *Caitlin:* "Go car."
> *Carolyn:* "Yes, time to go in the car. Where's your jacket?"
> *Caitlin:* [Looks around; walks to the closet.] "Dacket!" [Points to her jacket.]

Carolyn:	"There's that jacket! *[She helps Caitlin into the jacket.]* On it goes! Let's zip up. *[Zips up the jacket.]* Now, say bye-bye to Grace and Timmy."
Caitlin:	"Bye-bye, G-ace. Bye-bye, Te-te."
Carolyn:	"Where's your bear?"
Caitlin:	*[Looks around.]*
Carolyn:	*[Pointing.]* "See? By the sofa." *[Caitlin gets the bear.]*

A mother speaks to her baby in short, clearly pronounced sentences with high-pitched, exaggerated intonation. This form of communication, called infant-directed speech, eases language learning for infants and toddlers.

Notice how Carolyn kept her utterance length just ahead of Caitlin's, creating a sensitive match between language stimulation and Caitlin's current capacities. Parents constantly fine-tune the length and content of their utterances in IDS to fit children's needs—adjustments that enable infants and toddlers to join in and that foster both language comprehension and production (Cameron-Faulkner, Lieven, & Tomasello, 2003; Ma et al., 2011; Rowe, 2008).

As we saw earlier, parent–toddler conversation strongly predicts language development and later academic success. It provides many examples of speech just ahead of the child's current level and a sympathetic environment in which children can try out new skills. Dialogues about picture books are particularly effective. They expose children to great breadth of language and literacy knowledge, from vocabulary, grammar, and communication skills to information about written symbols and story structures. From the end of the first year through early childhood, children who experience regular adult–child book reading are substantially ahead of their agemates in language skills (Karrass & Braungart-Rieker, 2005; Whitehurst & Lonigan, 1998).

Research also reveals that live interaction with a responsive adult is far better suited to spurring early language development than media sources. After a month's regular exposure to a commercial video for babies that labeled common household objects, 12- to 18-month-olds did not add any more words to their vocabulary than nonviewing controls. Rather, toddlers in a comparison group whose parents spent time teaching them the words in everyday activities learned best (DeLoache et al., 2010). Consistent with these findings, a video format that allows an adult to interact responsively with a 2-year-old—as in a Skype session—is an effective context for acquiring new verbs (Roseberry et al., 2014). But viewers younger than age 3 are unable to learn language from TV or video alone—even from programs specially designed for them (Krcmar, Grela, & Lin, 2007; Roseberry et al., 2009). **TAKE A MOMENT...** Return to page 210 to review the *video deficit effect,* noting how these findings illustrate it.

Do social experiences that promote early language development remind you of those that strengthen cognitive development in general? IDS and parent–child conversation create a *zone of proximal development* in which children's language expands. In contrast, adult behaviors that are unresponsive to children's needs or impatient with their efforts to talk result in immature language skills (Baumwell, Tamis-LeMonda, & Bornstein, 1997; Cabrera, Shannon, & Tamis-LeMonda, 2007). In the next chapter, we will see that adult sensitivity supports infants' and toddlers' emotional and social development as well.

Ask Yourself

- **REVIEW** Why is the social-interactionist perspective attractive to many investigators of language development? Cite evidence that supports it.

- **CONNECT** Cognition and language are interrelated. List examples of how cognition fosters language development. Next, list examples of how language fosters cognitive development.

- **APPLY** Fran frequently corrects her 17-month-old son Jeremy's attempts to talk and—fearing that he won't use words—refuses to respond to his gestures. How might Fran be contributing to Jeremy's slow language progress?

- **REFLECT** Find an opportunity to speak to an infant or toddler. Did you use IDS? What features of your speech are likely to promote early language development, and why?

Summary

Piaget's Cognitive-Developmental Theory (p. 201)

6.1 According to Piaget, how do schemes change over the course of development?

- By acting on the environment, children move through four stages in which psychological structures, or **schemes,** achieve a better fit with external reality.

- Schemes change in two ways: through **adaptation,** which is made up of two complementary activities—**assimilation** and **accommodation;** and through **organization,** the internal rearrangement of schemes into a strongly interconnected cognitive system.

6.2 Describe major cognitive attainments of the sensorimotor stage.

- In the **sensorimotor stage,** the **circular reaction** provides a means of adapting first schemes, and the newborn baby's reflexes gradually transform into the more flexible action patterns of the older infant. Around 8 months, infants develop **intentional, or goal-directed, behavior** and begin to understand **object permanence.**

- Twelve- to 18-month-olds engage in more deliberate, varied exploration and no longer make the **A-not-B search error.** Between 18 and 24 months, **mental representation** is evident in sudden solutions to sensorimotor problems, mastery of object-permanence problems involving invisible displacement, **deferred imitation,** and **make-believe play.**

6.3 What does follow-up research say about infant cognitive development and the accuracy of Piaget's sensorimotor stage?

- Many studies suggest that infants display a variety of understandings earlier than Piaget believed. Some awareness of object permanence, as revealed by the **violation-of-expectation method** and object-tracking research, may be evident in the first few months.

- Furthermore, young infants display deferred imitation, and by 10 to 12 months, they solve problems by analogy—attainments that require mental representation. Older infants and toddlers even imitate rationally, by inferring others' intentions.

- A major advance in symbolic understanding, occurring around the first birthday, is **displaced reference**—the realization that words can be used to cue mental images of things not physically present. The capacity to use language to modify mental representations improves from the end of the second into the third year. Awareness of the symbolic function of pictures emerges in the first year and strengthens in the second. Around 2½ years, the **video deficit effect** declines; children grasp the symbolic meaning of video.

- Today, researchers believe that newborns have more built-in equipment for making sense of their world than Piaget assumed, although they disagree on how much initial understanding infants have. According to the **core knowledge perspective,** infants are born with core domains of thought, including physical, psychological, linguistic, and numerical knowledge, that support rapid cognitive development.

© EDITH HELD/CORBIS

- Broad agreement exists that many cognitive changes of infancy are continuous rather than stagelike and that various aspects of cognition develop unevenly, rather than in an integrated fashion.

Information Processing (p. 214)

6.4 Describe the information-processing view of cognitive development and the general structure of the information-processing system.

- Information-processing researchers assume that we hold information in three parts of the mental system: the **sensory register;** the **short-term memory store;** and **long-term memory.** The **central executive** joins with **working memory**—our "mental workspace"—to process information effectively. Well-learned **automatic processes** require no space in working memory, permitting us to focus on other information while performing them.

- Gains in **executive function**—including attention, impulse control, coordinating information in working memory, and flexible thinking—predict important cognitive and social outcomes.

6.5 What changes in attention, memory, and categorization take place over the first two years?

- With age, infants attend to more aspects of the environment and take information in more quickly. In the second year, attention to novelty declines and sustained attention improves.

- Young infants are capable of **recognition** memory. By the middle of the first year, they also engage in **recall.** Both recognition and recall improve steadily with age.

- Infants group stimuli into an expanding array of categories. In the second year, toddlers begin to categorize flexibly, switching their basis of object sorting, and their grasp of the animate–inanimate distinction expands. Babies' exploration of objects, expanding knowledge of the world, and advancing language skills foster categorization.

6.6 Describe the strengths and limitations of the information-processing approach to early cognitive development.

- Information-processing findings challenge Piaget's view of infants as purely sensorimotor beings who cannot mentally represent experiences. But information processing has not yet provided a broad, comprehensive theory of children's thinking.

The Social Context of Early Cognitive Development (p. 222)

6.7 How does Vygotsky's concept of the zone of proximal development expand our understanding of early cognitive development?

- Vygotsky believed that children master tasks within the **zone of proximal development**—ones just ahead of their current capacities—through the support and guidance of more skilled partners. As early as the first year, cultural variations in social experiences affect mental strategies.

© JAMES SHAFFER/PHOTOEDIT

Individual Differences in Early Mental Development (p. 225)

6.8 Describe the mental testing approach, the meaning of intelligence test scores, and the extent to which infant tests predict later performance.

- The mental testing approach measures intellectual development in an effort to predict future performance. Scores are arrived at by computing an **intelligence quotient (IQ),** which compares an individual's performance with that of a **standardization** sample of same-age individuals, whose performances form a **normal distribution.**

- Infant tests consisting largely of perceptual and motor responses predict later intelligence poorly. As a result, scores on infant tests are called **developmental quotients (DQs),** rather than IQs. Speed of habituation and recovery to visual stimuli is a better predictor of future performance.

6.9 Discuss environmental influences on early mental development, including home, child care, and early intervention for at-risk infants and toddlers.

- Research with the **Home Observation for Measurement of the Environment (HOME)** shows that an organized, stimulating home environment and parental affection, involvement, and encouragement repeatedly predict higher mental test scores. Although the HOME–IQ relationship is partly due to heredity, family living conditions also affect mental development.

- Quality of infant and toddler child care influences cognitive, language, academic, and social skills. Standards for **developmentally appropriate practice** specify program characteristics that meet young children's developmental needs.

- Intensive intervention beginning in infancy and extending through early childhood can help prevent the gradual declines in intelligence and the poor academic performance evident in many poverty-stricken children.

Language Development (p. 231)

6.10 Describe theories of language development, and indicate the emphasis each places on innate abilities and environmental influences.

- Chomsky's nativist theory regards children as naturally endowed with a **language acquisition device (LAD).** Consistent with this perspective, a grammatically complex language system is unique to humans.

- Although language-related structures—Broca's and Wernicke's areas—exist in the left hemisphere of the cerebral cortex, their roles are more complex than previously assumed. But the broad association of language functions with left-hemispheric regions is consistent with Chomsky's notion of a brain prepared to process language. Evidence for a sensitive period for language development also supports this view.

- Recent theories suggest that language development results from *interactions* between inner capacities and environmental influences. Some interactionists apply the information-processing perspective to language development. Others emphasize the importance of children's social skills and language experiences.

6.11 Describe major milestones of language development in the first two years, individual differences, and ways adults can support infants' and toddlers' emerging capacities.

- Infants begin **cooing** at 2 months and **babbling** around 6 months. Around 10 to 11 months, their skill at establishing **joint attention** improves, and soon they use preverbal gestures. Adults can encourage language progress by responding to infants' coos and babbles, playing turn-taking games, establishing joint attention and labeling what babies see, and responding verbally to their preverbal gestures.

- Around 12 months, toddlers say their first word. Young children often make errors of **underextension** and **overextension.** Rate of word learning increases steadily, and once vocabulary reaches about 200 to 250 words, two-word utterances called **telegraphic speech** appear. At all ages, language **comprehension** develops ahead of **production.**

- Girls show faster progress than boys, and both shy and emotionally negative toddlers acquire language more slowly. Low-SES children, who receive less verbal stimulation than higher-SES children, have smaller vocabularies—a strong predictor of later language and literacy skills.

- Most toddlers use a **referential style** of language learning, in which early words consist largely of names for objects. A few use an **expressive style,** in which social formulas and pronouns are common and vocabulary grows more slowly.

- Adults in many cultures speak to young children in **infant-directed speech (IDS),** a simplified form of communication that is well-suited to their learning needs. Parent–toddler conversation is one of the best predictors of early language development and academic competence during the school years.

Important Terms and Concepts

Emotional and Social Development in Infancy and Toddlerhood

"The Mother and Child"
Ruvini Ariyaranthna
Kahingala
16 years, Sri Lanka

A mutual embrace reflects the strong, affectionate bond between this mother and child. Chapter 7 considers the importance of parental love and sensitivity for infants' and toddlers' feelings of security and competence.

REPRINTED WITH PERMISSION FROM THE INTERNATIONAL MUSEUM OF CHILDREN'S ART, OSLO, NORWAY

As Caitlin reached 8 months of age, her parents noticed that she had become more fearful. One evening, when Carolyn and David left her with a babysitter, she wailed as they headed for the door—an experience she had accepted easily a few weeks earlier. Caitlin and Timmy's caregiver Ginette also observed an increasing wariness of strangers. When she turned to go to another room, both babies dropped their play to crawl after her. At the mail carrier's knock at the door, they clung to Ginette's legs, reaching out to be picked up.

At the same time, each baby seemed more willful. Removing an object from the hand produced little response at 5 months. But at 8 months, when Timmy's mother, Vanessa, took away a table knife he had managed to reach, Timmy burst into angry screams and could not be consoled or distracted.

All Monica and Kevin knew about Grace's first year was that she had been deeply loved by her destitute, homeless mother. Separation from her, followed by a long journey to an unfamiliar home, had left Grace in shock. At first she was extremely sad, turning away when Monica or Kevin picked her up. But as Grace's new parents held her close, spoke gently, and satisfied her craving for food, Grace returned their affection. Two weeks after her arrival, her despondency gave way to a sunny, easygoing disposition. She burst into a wide grin, reached out at the sight of Monica and Kevin, and laughed at her brother Eli's funny faces. Among her first words were the names of family members—"Eli," "Mama," and "Dada." As her second birthday approached, she pointed to herself, exclaiming "Gwace!" and laid claim to treasured possessions. "Gwace's chicken!" she would announce at mealtimes, sucking the marrow from the drumstick, a practice she had brought with her from Cambodia.

Taken together, the children's reactions reflect two related aspects of personality that develop during the first two years: close ties to others and a sense of self. We begin with Erikson's psychosocial theory, which provides an overview of personality development during infancy and toddlerhood. Then, as we chart the course of emotional development, we will discover why fear and anger became more apparent in Caitlin's and Timmy's range of emotions by the end of the first year. Our attention then turns to individual differences in temperament. We will examine biological and environmental contributions to these differences and their consequences for future development.

Next, we take up attachment to the caregiver, the child's first affectionate tie. We will see how the feelings of security that grow out of this important bond support the child's exploration, sense of independence, and expanding social relationships.

Finally, we focus on early self-development. By the end of toddlerhood, Grace recognized herself in mirrors and photographs, labeled herself as a girl, and showed the beginnings of self-control. "Don't touch!" she instructed herself one day as she resisted the desire to pull a lamp cord out of its socket. Cognitive advances combine with social experiences to produce these changes during the second year. ■

7.1 What personality changes take place during Erikson's stages of basic trust versus mistrust and autonomy versus shame and doubt?

Erikson's Theory of Infant and Toddler Personality

Our discussion of major theories in Chapter 1 revealed that psychoanalytic theory is no longer in the mainstream of child development research. But one of its lasting contributions is its ability to capture the essence of personality during each period of development. Recall that although Freud's preoccupation with the channeling of biological drives and his neglect of important experiences beyond infancy and early childhood came to be heavily criticized, the basic outlines of his theory were accepted and elaborated in several subsequent theories. The most influential is Erik Erikson's *psychosocial theory,* also introduced in Chapter 1.

Basic Trust versus Mistrust

Erikson accepted Freud's emphasis on the importance of the parent–infant relationship during feeding, but he expanded and enriched Freud's view. A healthy outcome during infancy, Erikson believed, does not depend on the *amount* of food or oral stimulation offered but rather on the *quality* of caregiving: relieving discomfort promptly and sensitively, holding the infant gently, waiting patiently until the baby has had enough milk, and weaning when the infant shows less interest in breast or bottle.

Erikson recognized that no parent can be perfectly in tune with the baby's needs. Many factors affect parental responsiveness—feelings of personal happiness, current life conditions (for example, additional young children in the family), and culturally valued child-rearing practices. But when the *balance of care* is sympathetic and loving, the psychological conflict of the first year—**basic trust versus mistrust**—is resolved on the positive side. The trusting infant expects the world to be good and gratifying. As a result, he feels confident about venturing out and exploring it, and he emerges from this stage well-prepared for the challenges of toddlerhood. The mistrustful baby cannot count on the kindness and compassion of others, so she protects herself by withdrawing from people and things around her.

Autonomy versus Shame and Doubt

With the transition to toddlerhood, Freud viewed the parent's manner of toilet training as decisive for psychological health. In Erikson's view, toilet training is only one of many influential experiences. The familiar refrains of newly walking, talking toddlers—"No!" "Do it myself!"—reveal that they have entered a new period of budding selfhood. They want to decide for themselves, not just in toileting but also in other situations. The conflict of toddlerhood, **autonomy versus shame and doubt,** is resolved favorably when parents provide young children with suitable guidance and reasonable choices. A self-confident, secure 2-year-old has parents who do not criticize or attack him when he fails at new skills—using the toilet, eating with a spoon, or putting away toys. And they meet his assertions of independence with tolerance and understanding—for example, by giving him an extra five minutes to finish his play before leaving for the grocery store. In contrast, when parents are over- or undercontrolling, the outcome is a child who feels forced and shamed and who doubts his ability to control his impulses and act competently on his own.

In sum, basic trust and autonomy grow out of warm, sensitive parenting and reasonable expectations for impulse control starting in the second year. If children emerge from the first few years without sufficient trust in caregivers and without a healthy sense

On a visit to a science museum, a 2-year-old explores a flight simulator. As the mother supports her toddler's desire to "do it myself," she fosters a healthy sense of autonomy.

© SYRACUSE NEWSPAPERS/S. CANNERELLI/THE IMAGE WORKS

of individuality, the seeds are sown for adjustment problems. Adults who have difficulty establishing intimate ties, who are overly dependent on a loved one, or who continually doubt their own ability to meet new challenges may not have fully mastered the tasks of trust and autonomy during infancy and toddlerhood.

Emotional Development

TAKE A MOMENT... Observe several infants and toddlers, noting the emotions each displays, the cues you rely on to interpret the baby's emotional state, and how caregivers respond. Researchers have conducted many such observations to find out how babies convey their emotions and interpret those of others. They have discovered that emotions play powerful roles in organizing the attainments that Erikson regarded as so important: social relationships, exploration of the environment, and discovery of the self (Halle, 2003; Saarni et al., 2006).

Think back to the *dynamic systems perspective* introduced in Chapters 1 and 5. As you read about early emotional development in the sections that follow, notice how emotions are an integral part of young children's dynamic systems of action. Emotions energize development. At the same time, they are an aspect of the system that develops, becoming more varied and complex as children reorganize their behavior to attain new goals (Campos, Frankel, & Camras, 2004; Camras, 2011).

Because infants cannot describe their feelings, determining exactly which emotions they are experiencing is a challenge. Although vocalizations and body movements provide some information, facial expressions offer the most reliable cues. Cross-cultural evidence reveals that people around the world associate photographs of different facial expressions with emotions in the same way (Ekman & Friesen, 1972; Ekman & Matsumoto, 2011). These findings inspired researchers to analyze infants' facial patterns to determine the range of emotions they display at different ages.

Nevertheless, assuming a close correspondence between a pattern of behavior and an underlying emotional state can lead to error. Infants, children, and adults use diverse responses to express a particular emotion. For example, babies on the visual cliff (see page 190 in Chapter 5) generally do not display a fearful facial expression, though they do show signs of avoidance—drawing back and refusing to crawl over the deep side. And the emotional expressions of blind babies, who cannot make eye contact, are muted, prompting parents to withdraw. When therapists show parents how blind infants express emotions through finger movements, parents become more interactive (Fraiberg, 1971; Saarni et al., 2006). Furthermore, the same general response can express several emotions. Depending on the situation, a smile might convey joy, embarrassment, contempt, or a social greeting.

In line with the dynamic systems view, emotional expressions vary with the individual's developing capacities, goals, and context. To infer babies' emotions more accurately, researchers must attend to multiple interacting expressive cues—vocal, facial, and gestural—and see how they vary across situations believed to elicit different emotions (Lewis, 2008). With these ideas in mind, let's chart the course of early emotional development.

Basic Emotions

Basic emotions—happiness, interest, surprise, fear, anger, sadness, and disgust—are universal in humans and other primates and have a long evolutionary history of promoting survival. Do infants come into the world with the ability to express basic emotions? Although signs of some emotions are present, babies' earliest emotional life consists of little more than two global arousal states: attraction to pleasant stimulation and withdrawal from unpleasant stimulation (Camras et al., 2003). Only gradually do emotions become clear, well-organized signals.

The dynamic systems perspective helps us understand how this happens: Children coordinate separate skills into more effective, emotionally expressive systems as the central nervous system develops and the child's goals and experiences change (Camras & Shutter, 2010).

7.2 Describe the development of basic emotions over the first year, noting the adaptive function of each.

7.3 Summarize changes during the first two years in understanding others' emotions, self-conscious emotions, and emotional self-regulation.

Videotaping the facial expressions of her daughter from 6 to 14 weeks, Linda Camras (1992) found that in the early weeks, the baby displayed a fleeting angry face as she was about to cry and a sad face as her crying waned. At first, these expressions appeared on the way to or from full-blown distress and were not clearly linked to the baby's experiences and desires. With age, she was better able to sustain an angry signal when she encountered a blocked goal and a sad signal when she could not overcome an obstacle.

According to one view, sensitive, contingent caregiver communication, in which parents selectively mirror aspects of the baby's diffuse emotional behavior, helps infants construct emotional expressions that more closely resemble those of adults (Gergely & Watson, 1999). With age, face, gaze, voice, and posture form organized patterns that vary meaningfully with environmental events. For example, Caitlin typically responded to her parents' playful inter-action with a joyful face, pleasant babbling, and a relaxed posture, as if to say, "This is fun!" In contrast, an unresponsive parent often evokes a sad face, fussy sounds, and a drooping body (sending the message, "I'm despondent") or an angry face, crying, and "pick-me-up" gestures (as if to say, "Change this unpleasant event!") (Weinberg & Tronick, 1994). Gradually, emotional expressions become well-organized and specific—and therefore provide more pre-cise information about the infant's internal state.

Four basic emotions—happiness, anger, sadness, and fear—that have received the most research attention. Let's see how they develop.

HAPPINESS   Happiness—expressed first in blissful smiles, later through exuberant laugh-ter—contributes to many aspects of development. When infants achieve new skills, they smile and laugh, displaying delight in motor and cognitive mastery. As the smile encourages care-givers to be affectionate and stimulating, the baby smiles even more (Aksan & Kochanska, 2004). Happiness binds parent and baby into a warm, supportive relationship that fosters the infant's developing competencies.

During the early weeks, newborn babies smile when full, during REM sleep, and in response to gentle touches and sounds, such as stroking of the skin, rocking, and the mother's soft, high-pitched voice. By the end of the first month, infants smile at dynamic, eye-catching sights, such as a bright object jumping suddenly across their field of vision. As infants attend to the parent's face and the parent talks and smiles, babies knit their brows, open their mouths to coo, and move their arms and legs excitedly, gradually becoming more emotionally posi-tive until, between 6 and 10 weeks, the parent's communication evokes a broad grin called the **social smile** (Lavelli & Fogel, 2005; Sroufe & Waters, 1976). These changes parallel the development of infant perceptual capacities—in particular, sensitivity to visual patterns, including the human face (see Chapter 5). And social smiling becomes better-organized and stable as babies learn to use it to evoke and sustain pleasurable face-to-face interaction with the parent.

Development of the social smile, however, varies substantially with culture. The Nso people, a rural farming society of Cameroon, highly value infant calmness, so Nso caregivers discourage emotional express-iveness of all kinds and, instead, emphasize soothing (Keller & Otto, 2009). In contrast, Western middle-SES parents, who value self-expression, enthusiastically promote active social engagement in their babies. In line with these differences, observations of Nso and urban German mother–infant pairs between 6 and 12 weeks revealed that the Nso mothers participated in far fewer face-to-face imitative exchanges, including smil-ing. As a result, the social smile was considerably delayed in Nso babies (see Figure 7.1) (Wörmann et al., 2012). At 12 weeks, far fewer Nso than German infants smiled during mother–infant mutual gazing.

Laughter, which typically appears around 3 to 4 months, reflects faster processing of information than smiling. But as with smiling, the first laughs occur in response to very active stimuli, such as the parent saying playfully, "I'm gonna get you!" and kissing the baby's tummy. As infants understand more about their world, they laugh at events with subtler elements of surprise, such as a silent game of peekaboo (Sroufe & Wunsch, 1972).

© RADIUS IMAGES/ALAMY IMAGES

This baby's laughter encourages his mother to respond in kind, binding them together in a warm, affectionate relationship that promotes all aspects of development.

Around the middle of the first year, babies smile and laugh more often when interacting with familiar people, a preference that strengthens the parent–child bond. Between 8 and 10 months, infants more often interrupt their play with an interesting toy to relay their delight to an attentive adult (Venezia et al., 2004). And like adults, 10- to 12-month-olds have several smiles, which vary with context— a broad, "cheek-raised" smile in response to a parent's greeting; a reserved, muted smile for a friendly stranger; and a "mouth-open" smile during stimulating play (Bolzani et al., 2002; Messinger & Fogel, 2007). By the end of the first year, the smile has become a deliberate social signal.

ANGER AND SADNESS   Newborn babies respond with generalized distress to a variety of unpleasant experiences, including hunger, painful medical procedures, changes in body temperature, and too much or too little stimulation (see Chapter 4). From 4 to 6 months into the second year, angry expressions increase in frequency and intensity (Braungart-Rieker, Hill-Soderlund, & Karrass, 2010). Older infants also react with anger in a wider range of situations—when an interesting object or event is removed, an expected pleasant event does not occur, their arms are restrained, the caregiver leaves for a brief time, or they are put down for a nap (Camras et al., 1992; Stenberg & Campos, 1990; Sullivan & Lewis, 2003).

Why do angry reactions increase with age? As infants become capable of intentional behavior (see Chapter 6), they want to control their own actions and the effects they produce (Mascolo & Fischer, 2007). Furthermore, older infants are better at identifying who caused them pain or removed a toy. Their anger is particularly intense when a caregiver from whom they have come to expect warm behavior causes discomfort. And increased parental limit setting once babies crawl and walk contributes to babies' angry responses (Roben et al., 2012). The rise in anger is also adaptive. Independent movement enables an angry infant to defend herself or overcome an obstacle to obtain a desired object. Finally, anger motivates caregivers to relieve the infant's distress and, in the case of separation, may discourage them from leaving again soon.

Although expressions of sadness also occur in response to pain, removal of an object, and brief separations, they are less common than anger. In contrast, sadness occurs often when infants are deprived of a familiar, loving caregiver (as illustrated by Grace's despondency in the weeks after her adoption) and when parent–infant interaction is seriously disrupted. In several studies, researchers had parents interact with their babies and then, suddenly, assume either a still-faced, unreactive pose or a depressed emotional state. Their 2- to 7-month-olds tried facial expressions, vocalizations, and body movements to get the parent to respond again. When these efforts failed, they turned away, frowned, and cried (Moore, Cohn, & Campbell, 2001; Papousek, 2007). The still-face reaction is identical among American, Canadian, and Chinese babies, suggesting that it is a built-in withdrawal response to caregivers' lack of communication (Kisilevsky et al., 1998; Legerstee & Markova, 2007). Return to Chapter 4, page 153, and note that infants of depressed parents respond this way. When allowed to persist, a sad, vacant outlook disrupts all aspects of early development.

FEAR   Like anger, fear rises during the second half of the first year into the second year (Braungart-Rieker, Hill-Soderlund, & Karrass, 2010; Brooker et al., 2013). Older infants, for example, look wary, hesitating before playing with a new toy. But the most frequent expression of fear is to unfamiliar adults, a response called **stranger anxiety.** Many infants and toddlers are quite fearful of strangers, although the reaction does not always occur. It depends on several factors: temperament (some babies are generally more fearful), past experiences with strangers, and the current situation. When an unfamiliar adult picks up the infant in a new situation, stranger anxiety is likely. But if the adult sits still while the baby moves around and a parent is nearby, infants often show positive and curious behavior (Horner, 1980). The stranger's style of interaction—expressing warmth, holding out an attractive toy, playing a

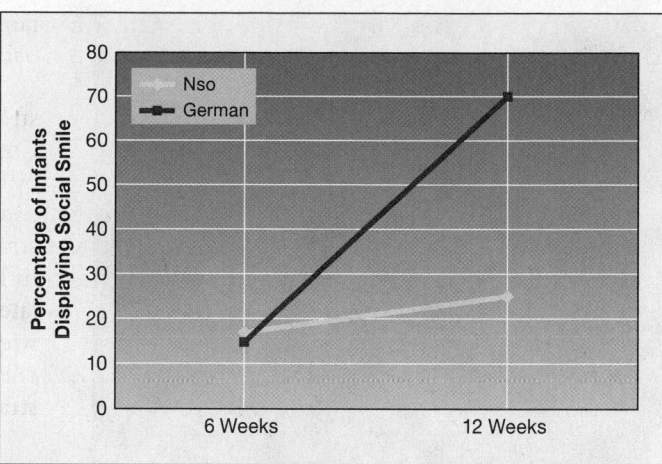

FIGURE 7.1 **Development of the social smile in German and Nso infants.** At 6 weeks, only a minority of Nso and German infants displayed the social smile during mother–infant mutual gazing. By 12 weeks, the majority of German infants smiled at their mothers. Among Nso infants, whose mothers less often engaged in face-to-face imitative exchanges, social smiling increased only slightly. (Based on Wörmann et al., 2012.)

LOOK and LISTEN

While observing an 8- to 18-month-old with his or her parent, gently approach the baby, offering a toy. Does the baby respond with stranger anxiety? To better understand the baby's behavior, ask the parent to describe his or her temperament and past experiences with strangers.

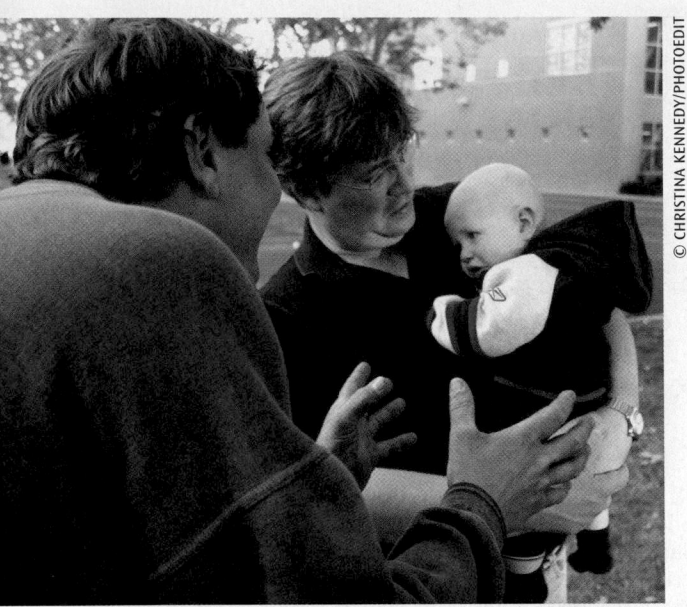

When an unfamiliar adult attempts to hold him, this baby makes it clear that he prefers his father. Fear rises during the second half of the first year. Its most frequent expression is stranger anxiety.

familiar game, and approaching slowly rather than abruptly—reduces the baby's fear.

Cross-cultural research reveals that infant-rearing practices can modify stranger anxiety. Among the Efe hunters and gatherers of the Republic of Congo, where the maternal death rate is high, infant survival is safeguarded by a collective caregiving system in which, starting at birth, Efe babies are passed from one adult to another. Consequently, Efe infants show little stranger anxiety (Tronick, Morelli, & Ivey, 1992). In contrast, among infants in Israeli kibbutzim (cooperative agricultural settlements), who live in isolated communities vulnerable to terrorist attacks, wariness of strangers is widespread. By the end of the first year, when infants look to others for cues about how to respond emotionally, kibbutz babies display far greater stranger anxiety than their city-reared counterparts (Saarni et al., 2006).

The rise in fear after 6 months of age keeps newly mobile babies' enthusiasm for exploration in check. Once wariness develops, infants use the familiar caregiver as a **secure base,** or point from which to explore, venturing into the environment and then returning for emotional support. As part of this adaptive system, encounters with strangers lead to two conflicting tendencies: approach (indicated by interest and friendliness) and avoidance (indicated by fear). The infant's behavior is a balance between the two.

As cognitive development permits toddlers to discriminate more effectively between threatening and nonthreatening people and situations, stranger anxiety and other fears of the first two years decline. Fear also wanes as children acquire a wider array of strategies for coping with it, as we will see when we discuss emotional self-regulation.

Understanding and Responding to the Emotions of Others

Infants' emotional expressions are closely tied to their ability to interpret the emotional cues of others. We have seen that in the first few months, babies match the feeling tone of the caregiver in face-to-face communication. Some researchers claim that young babies respond in kind to others' emotions through a built-in, automatic process of *emotional contagion* (Stern, 1985). Others believe that infants acquire these emotional contingencies through operant conditioning—for example, learning that a smile generally triggers caregiver responsiveness and that distress prompts a comforting response (Saarni et al., 2006).

Around 3 months, infants become sensitive to the structure and timing of face-to-face interactions (see Chapter 6, page 236). When they gaze, smile, or vocalize, they now expect their social partner to respond in kind, and they reply with positive vocal and emotional reactions (Markova & Legerstee, 2006). Within these exchanges, babies become increasingly aware of the range of emotional expressions (Montague & Walker-Andrews, 2001). According to some researchers, out of this early imitative communication, infants start to view others as "like me," which lays the foundation for understanding others' thoughts and feelings (Meltzoff, 2013).

By 4 to 5 months, infants distinguish positive from negative emotion in voices, and soon after, they do so in facial expressions, gradually discriminating a wider range of emotions (see Chapter 5). Around the middle of the first year, they match specific facial and vocal displays of emotion. Infants look longer at an appropriate face–voice pairing (such as a happy face with a happy voice) than at an inappropriate one (a happy face with an angry voice) (de Haan & Matheson, 2009; Vaillant-Molina, Bahrick, & Flom, 2013).

Responding to emotional expressions as organized wholes indicates that these signals are becoming meaningful to babies. From 7 months on, ERPs recorded while infants attend to facial expressions reveal reorganized brain-wave patterns resembling those of adults, suggesting enhanced processing of emotional cues (Grossmann, Striano, & Friederici, 2007). As skill at establishing joint attention improves (see Chapter 6), infants realize that an emotional expression not only has meaning but is also a meaningful reaction to a specific object or event (Moses et al., 2001).

Once these understandings are in place, beginning at 8 to 10 months, infants engage in **social referencing**—actively seeking emotional information from a trusted person in an uncertain situation (Mumme et al., 2007). Many studies show that a caregiver's emotional expression (happy, angry, or fearful) influences whether a 1-year-old will be wary of strangers, play with an unfamiliar toy, or cross the deep side of the visual cliff (de Rosnay et al., 2006; Stenberg, 2003; Striano & Rochat, 2000). The adult's voice—either alone or combined with a facial expression—is more effective than a facial expression alone (Kim, Walden, & Knieps, 2010; Vaish & Striano, 2004). The voice conveys both emotional and verbal information, and the baby need not turn toward the adult but, instead, can focus on evaluating the novel event.

As toddlers start to appreciate that others' emotional reactions may differ from their own, social referencing allows them to compare their own and others' assessments of events. In one study, an adult showed 14- and 18-month-olds broccoli and crackers. In one condition, she acted delighted with the taste of broccoli but disgusted with the taste of crackers. In the other condition, she showed the reverse preference. When asked to share the food, 14-month-olds offered only the type of food they themselves preferred—usually crackers. In contrast, 18-month-olds gave the adult whichever food she appeared to like, regardless of their own preferences (Repacholi & Gopnik, 1997).

In sum, in social referencing, toddlers use others' emotional messages to evaluate the safety and security of their surroundings, to guide their own actions, and to gather information about others' intentions and preferences. These experiences, along with cognitive and language development, probably help toddlers refine the meanings of emotions of the same valence—for example, happiness versus surprise, anger versus fear—during the second year (Gendler, Witherington, & Edwards, 2008; Saarni et al., 2006).

LOOK and LISTEN

Observe a toddler and parent at a playground, park, or shopping mall, noting circumstances that trigger social referencing. How does the parent convey emotional information? How does the toddler respond?

Emergence of Self-Conscious Emotions

Besides basic emotions, humans are capable of a second, higher-order set of feelings, including guilt, shame, embarrassment, envy, and pride. These are called **self-conscious emotions** because each involves injury to or enhancement of our sense of self. We feel guilt when we know that we have harmed someone and want to correct the wrongdoing. Envy arises when we desire something that another possesses, so we try to restore our sense of self-worth by securing that possession. When we are ashamed or embarrassed, we have negative feelings about our behavior, and we want to retreat so others will no longer notice our failings. In contrast, pride reflects delight in the self's achievements, and we are inclined to tell others what we have accomplished and to take on further challenges (Lewis, 2014).

Self-conscious emotions appear in the middle of the second year, as 18- to 24-month-olds become firmly aware of the self as a separate, unique individual. Toddlers show shame and embarrassment by lowering their eyes, hanging their heads, and hiding their faces with their hands. They show guiltlike reactions, too. After noticing Grace's unhappiness, 22-month-old Caitlin returned a toy she had grabbed and patted her upset playmate. Pride and envy also emerge around age 2 (Barrett, 2005; Garner, 2003; Lewis, 2014).

Besides self-awareness, self-conscious emotions require an additional ingredient: adult instruction in *when* to feel proud, ashamed, or guilty. Parents begin this tutoring early when they say, "Look how far you can throw that ball!" or "You should feel ashamed for grabbing that toy!" Self-conscious emotions play important roles in children's achievement-related and moral behaviors. The situations in which adults encourage these feelings vary from culture to culture. In Western nations, most children are taught to feel pride over personal achievement—throwing a ball the farthest, winning a game, and (later on) getting good grades. In cultures such as China and Japan, which promote an interdependent self, calling attention to individual success

A mother praises her 2-year-old's success at tower-building. To experience the self-conscious emotion of pride, young children need self-awareness as well as adult instruction in when to feel proud of an accomplishment.

evokes embarrassment and self-effacement. And violating cultural standards by failing to show concern for others—a parent, a teacher, or an employer—sparks intense shame (Akimoto & Sanbinmatsu, 1999; Lewis, 1992).

Beginnings of Emotional Self-Regulation

Besides expressing a wider range of emotions, infants and toddlers begin to manage their emotional experiences. **Emotional self-regulation** refers to the strategies we use to adjust our emotional state to a comfortable level of intensity so we can accomplish our goals (Eisenberg, 2006; Thompson & Goodvin, 2007). When you remind yourself that an anxiety-provoking event will be over soon, suppress your anger at a friend's behavior, or decide not to see a scary horror film, you are engaging in emotional self-regulation.

Emotional self-regulation requires voluntary, effortful management of emotions. This capacity for *effortful control* improves rapidly in early childhood, as the result of development of the prefrontal cortex and a history of support from caregivers, who help children manage intense emotion and teach them strategies for doing so (Rothbart, Posner, & Kieras, 2006). Individual differences in control of emotion are already evident in infancy and, by early childhood, play such a vital role in adjustment that—as we will see later—effortful control is regarded as a major dimension of temperament. A good start in regulating emotion during the first two years contributes greatly to autonomy and mastery of cognitive and social skills. Poorly regulated toddlers, by contrast, are at risk for long-lasting adjustment difficulties (Eisenberg et al., 2004; Lawson & Ruff, 2004).

In the early months, infants have only a limited capacity to regulate their emotional states. When their feelings get too intense, they are easily overwhelmed. They depend on the soothing interventions of caregivers for distraction and reorienting of attention—being lifted to the shoulder, rocked, gently stroked, and talked to softly.

More effective functioning of the prefrontal cortex increases the baby's tolerance for stimulation. Between 2 and 4 months, caregivers build on this capacity by initiating face-to-face play and attention to objects. In these interactions, parents arouse pleasure in the baby while adjusting the pace of their own behavior so the infant does not become overwhelmed and distressed (Kopp & Neufeld, 2003). As a result, the baby's tolerance for stimulation increases further.

By 4 to 6 months, the ability to shift attention away from unpleasant events and to engage in self-soothing helps infants control emotion. In the second half-year, they become better at communicating their need for help in regulating emotion by gesturing and vocalizing to the caregiver (Stifter & Braungart, 1995). And crawling and walking, which permit babies to approach or retreat from various situations, foster more effective self-regulation. Also, further gains in attention permit older infants and toddlers to sustain interest in their surroundings and in play activities for a longer time (Rothbart & Bates, 2006).

As caregivers help infants regulate their emotional states, they contribute to the child's style of emotional self-regulation. Infants whose parents "read" and respond contingently and sympathetically to their emotional cues tend to be less fussy, to express more pleasurable emotion, to be more interested in exploration, and to be easier to soothe (Braungart-Rieker, Hill-Soderlund, & Karrass, 2010; Crockenberg & Leerkes, 2004). In contrast, parents who respond impatiently or angrily or who wait to intervene until the infant has become extremely agitated reinforce the baby's rapid rise to intense distress. This makes it harder for parents to soothe the baby in the future—and for the baby to learn to calm herself. When caregivers fail to regulate stressful experiences for infants who cannot yet regulate them for themselves, brain structures that buffer stress may fail to develop properly, resulting in an anxious, reactive child who has a reduced capacity for managing emotional problems (Blair & Raver, 2012; Little & Carter, 2005).

Caregivers also provide lessons in socially approved ways of expressing feelings. Beginning in the first few months, parents encourage infants to suppress negative emotion by imitating their expressions of interest, happiness, and surprise more often than their expressions of anger and sadness. Boys get more of this training than girls, in part because boys have a harder time regulating negative emotion (Else-Quest et al., 2006; Malatesta et al., 1986). As a result, the well-known sex difference—females as emotionally expressive and males as emotionally controlled—is fostered at a tender age. Cultures that highly value social harmony place particular emphasis on socially appropriate emotional behavior. Compared with North Americans, Japanese and Chinese adults discourage the expression of strong emotion in babies (Camras, Kolmodin, & Chen, 2008; Friedlmeier, Corapci, & Cole, 2011). By the end of the first year, Chinese and Japanese infants smile, laugh, and cry less than American babies (Camras et al., 1998; Gartstein et al., 2010).

In the second year, growth in representation and language leads to new ways of regulating emotions. A vocabulary for talking about feelings—"happy," "love," "surprised," "scary," "yucky," "mad"—develops rapidly after 18 months, but toddlers are not yet good at using language to manage their emotions. Temper tantrums tend to occur because toddlers cannot control the intense anger that often arises when an adult rejects their demands, particularly when they are fatigued or hungry (Mascolo & Fischer, 2007). Toddlers whose parents are emotionally sympathetic but set limits (by not giving in to tantrums), who distract the child by offering acceptable alternatives, and who later suggest better ways to handle adult refusals display more effective anger-regulation strategies and social skills during the preschool years (Lecuyer & Houck, 2006).

Chinese and Japanese adults discourage the expression of strong emotion in infants. This baby's calm demeanor is typical of Chinese infants, who tend to smile and cry less than American babies.

Patient, sensitive parents also talk about emotions and encourage toddlers to describe their internal states. Then, when 2-year-olds feel distressed, they can guide caregivers in helping them (Cole, Armstrong, & Pemberton, 2010). For example, while listening to a story about monsters, Grace whimpered, "Mommy, scary." Monica put the book down and gave Grace a comforting hug.

Ask Yourself

- **REVIEW** Why do many infants show stranger anxiety in the second half of the first year? What factors can increase or decrease wariness of strangers?

- **CONNECT** Why do children of depressed parents have difficulty regulating emotion (see page 153 in Chapter 4)? What implications do their weak self-regulatory skills have for their response to cognitive and social challenges?

- **APPLY** At age 14 months, Reggie built a block tower and gleefully knocked it down. But at age 2, he called to his mother and pointed proudly to his tall block tower. What explains this change in Reggie's emotional behavior?

- **REFLECT** Describe several recent instances illustrating how you typically manage negative emotion. How might your early experiences, gender, and cultural background have influenced your style of emotional self-regulation?

Temperament and Development

7.4 What is temperament, and how is it measured?

7.5 Discuss the roles of heredity and environment in the stability of temperament, including the goodness-of-fit model.

From early infancy, Caitlin's sociability was unmistakable. She smiled and laughed while interacting with adults and, in her second year, readily approached other children. Meanwhile, Monica marveled at Grace's calm, relaxed disposition. At 19 months, she sat contentedly in a highchair through a two-hour family celebration at a restaurant. In contrast, Timmy was active and distractible. Vanessa found herself chasing him as he dropped one toy, moved on to the next, and climbed on chairs and tables.

When we describe one person as cheerful and upbeat, another as active and energetic, and still others as calm, cautious, or prone to angry outbursts, we are referring to **temperament**—early-appearing, stable individual differences in reactivity and self-regulation. *Reactivity* refers to quickness and intensity of emotional arousal, attention, and motor activity. *Self-regulation,* as we have seen, refers to strategies that modify that reactivity (Rothbart, 2011; Rothbart & Bates, 2006). The psychological traits that make up temperament are believed to form the cornerstone of the adult personality.

In 1956, Alexander Thomas and Stella Chess initiated the New York Longitudinal Study, a groundbreaking investigation of the development of temperament that followed 141 children from early infancy well into adulthood. Results showed that temperament can increase a child's chances of experiencing psychological problems or, alternatively, protect a child from the negative effects of a highly stressful home life. At the same time, Thomas and Chess (1977) discovered that parenting practices can modify children's emotional styles considerably.

These findings stimulated a growing body of research on temperament, including its stability, biological roots, and interaction with child-rearing experiences. Let's begin to explore these issues by looking at the structure, or makeup, of temperament and how it is measured.

The Structure of Temperament

Thomas and Chess's model of temperament inspired all others that followed. When detailed descriptions of infants' and children's behavior obtained from parental interviews were rated on nine dimensions of temperament, certain characteristics clustered together, yielding three types of children:

- The **easy child** (40 percent of the sample) quickly establishes regular routines in infancy, is generally cheerful, and adapts easily to new experiences.
- The **difficult child** (10 percent of the sample) is irregular in daily routines, is slow to accept new experiences, and tends to react negatively and intensely.
- The **slow-to-warm-up child** (15 percent of the sample) is inactive, shows mild, low-key reactions to environmental stimuli, is negative in mood, and adjusts slowly to new experiences.

Note that 35 percent of the children did not fit any of these categories. Instead, they showed unique blends of temperamental characteristics.

The difficult pattern has sparked the most interest because it places children at high risk for adjustment problems—both anxious withdrawal and aggressive behavior in early and middle childhood (Bates, Wachs, & Emde, 1994; Ramos et al., 2005). Compared with difficult children, slow-to-warm-up children present fewer problems initially. However, they tend to show excessive fearfulness and slow, constricted behavior in the late preschool and school years, when they are expected to respond actively and quickly in classrooms and peer groups (Chess & Thomas, 1984; Schmitz et al., 1999).

Today, the most influential model of temperament is Mary Rothbart's, described in Table 7.1. It combines related traits proposed by Thomas and Chess and other researchers, yielding a concise list of just six dimensions. For example, distractibility and persistence are considered opposite ends of the same dimension, which is labeled "attention span/persistence." A unique feature of Rothbart's model is inclusion of both "fearful distress" and "irritable distress," which distinguish between reactivity triggered by fear and reactivity due to frustration. And the model deletes overly broad dimensions such as regularity of body functions and intensity of reaction (Rothbart, 2011; Rothbart, Ahadi, & Evans, 2000). A child who is regular in sleeping is not necessarily regular in eating or bowel habits. And a child who smiles and laughs intensely is not necessarily intense in fear, irritability, or motor activity.

Rothbart's dimensions represent the three underlying components included in the definition of temperament: (1) *emotion* ("fearful distress," "irritable distress," "positive affect"), (2) *attention* ("attention span/persistence"), and (3) *action* ("activity level"). According to Rothbart, individuals differ not just in their reactivity on each dimension but also in the self-regulatory dimension of temperament, **effortful control**—the capacity to voluntarily suppress a dominant response in order

On a visit to a playground, this toddler reacts with irritable distress when he sees he must wait for a turn to use a swing. Patient, supportive parenting can help him modify his biologically based temperament and better manage his reactivity.

TABLE 7.1	Rothbart's Model of Temperament
DIMENSION	**DESCRIPTION**
Reactivity	
Activity level	Level of gross-motor activity
Attention span/persistence	Duration of orienting or interest
Fearful distress	Wariness and distress in response to intense or novel stimuli, including time to adjust to new situations
Irritable distress	Extent of fussing, crying, and distress when desires are frustrated
Positive affect	Frequency of expression of happiness and pleasure
Self-Regulation	
Effortful control	Capacity to voluntarily suppress a dominant, reactive response in order to plan and execute a more adaptive response
	In the first two years, called *orienting/regulation,* which refers to the capacity to engage in self-soothing, shift attention from unpleasant events, and sustain interest for an extended time

to plan and execute a more adaptive response (Rothbart, 2003; Rothbart & Bates, 2006). Variations in effortful control are evident in how effectively a child can focus and shift attention, inhibit impulses, and manage negative emotion.

Beginning in early childhood, capacity for effortful control predicts favorable development and adjustment in cultures as diverse as China and the United States (Zhou, Lengua, & Wang, 2009). Outcomes include persistence, task mastery, academic achievement, moral maturity (such as concern about wrongdoing and willingness to apologize), and social behaviors of cooperation, sharing, and helpfulness, which contribute to positive relationships with adults and peers (Eisenberg, 2010; Kochanska & Aksan, 2006; Posner & Rothbart, 2007b; Valiente, Lemery-Chalfant, & Swanson, 2010).

Measuring Temperament

Temperament is often assessed through interviews or questionnaires given to parents. Behavior ratings by pediatricians, teachers, and others familiar with the child and laboratory observations by researchers have also been used. Parental reports are convenient and take advantage of parents' depth of knowledge about their child across many situations (Gartstein & Rothbart, 2003). Although information from parents has been criticized as being biased, parental reports are moderately related to researchers' observations of children's behavior (Majdandžić & van den Boom, 2007; Mangelsdorf, Schoppe, & Buur, 2000). And parent perceptions are vital for understanding how parents view and respond to their child.

Observations by researchers in the home or laboratory avoid the subjectivity of parent reports but can lead to other inaccuracies. In homes, observers find it hard to capture rare but important events, such as infants' response to frustration. And in the unfamiliar lab setting, fearful children who calmly avoid certain experiences at home may become too upset to complete the session (Rothbart, 2011). Still, researchers can better control children's experiences in the lab. And they can conveniently combine observations of behavior with neurobiological measures to gain insight into the biological basis of temperament.

Most neurobiological research has focused on children who fall at opposite extremes of the positive-affect and fearful-distress dimensions of temperament: **inhibited,** or **shy, children,** who react negatively to and withdraw from novel stimuli, and **uninhibited,** or **sociable, children,** who display positive emotion and approach novel stimuli. As the Biology and Environment box on page 256 reveals, biologically based reactivity—evident in heart rate, hormone levels, and measures of brain activity—differentiates children with inhibited and uninhibited temperaments.

Biology and Environment

Development of Shyness and Sociability

Two 4-month-old babies, Larry and Mitch, visited the laboratory of Jerome Kagan, who observed their reactions to a variety of unfamiliar experiences. When exposed to new sights and sounds, such as a moving mobile decorated with colorful toys, Larry tensed his muscles, moved his arms and legs with agitation, and began to cry. In contrast, Mitch remained relaxed and quiet, smiling and cooing at the excitement around him.

As toddlers, Larry and Mitch returned to the laboratory, where they experienced a variety of procedures designed to induce uncertainty. Electrodes were placed on their bodies and blood pressure cuffs on their arms to measure heart rate; toy robots, animals, and puppets moved before their eyes; and unfamiliar people entered and behaved in unexpected ways or wore novel costumes. While Larry whimpered and quickly withdrew, Mitch watched with interest, laughed at the strange sights, and approached the toys and strangers.

On a third visit, at age 4½, Larry barely talked or smiled during an interview with an unfamiliar adult. In contrast, Mitch asked questions and communicated his pleasure at each new activity. In a playroom with two unfamiliar peers, Larry pulled back and watched, while Mitch made friends quickly.

In longitudinal research on several hundred Caucasian infants followed into adolescence, Kagan found that about 20 percent of 4-month-olds were, like Larry, easily upset by novelty; another 40 percent, like Mitch, were comfortable, even delighted, with new experiences. About 20 to 25 percent of these extreme groups retained their temperamental styles as they grew older (Kagan, 2003, 2013d; Kagan et al., 2007). But most children's dispositions became less extreme over time. Genetic makeup and child-rearing experiences jointly influenced stability and change in temperament.

Neurobiological Correlates of Shyness and Sociability

Individual differences in arousal of the *amygdala*, an inner brain structure devoted to processing of novelty and emotional information, contribute to these contrasting temperaments. In shy, inhibited children, novel stimuli easily excite the amygdala and its connections to the cerebral cortex and sympathetic nervous system, which prepares the body to act in the face of threat. In sociable, uninhibited children, the same level of stimulation

evokes minimal neural excitation (Kagan, 2013d). In support of this theory, while viewing photos of unfamiliar faces, adults who had been classified as inhibited in the second year of life showed greater fMRI activity in the amygdala than adults who had been uninhibited as toddlers (Schwartz et al., 2012). And additional neurobiological responses known to be mediated by the amygdala distinguish these two emotional styles:

● *Heart rate.* From the first few weeks of life, the heart rates of shy children are consistently higher than those of sociable children, and they speed up further in response to unfamiliar events (Schmidt et al., 2007; Snidman et al., 1995).

● *Cortisol.* Saliva concentrations of the stress hormone cortisol tend to be higher, and to rise more in response to a stressful event, in shy than in sociable children (Schmidt et al., 1997, 1999; Zimmermann & Stansbury, 2004).

● *Pupil dilation, blood pressure, and skin surface temperature.* Compared with sociable children, shy children show greater pupil dilation, rise in blood pressure, and cooling of the fingertips when faced with novelty (Kagan et al., 1999, 2007).

Another physiological correlate of approach–withdrawal to people and objects is the pattern of brain waves in the frontal lobes of the cerebral cortex. Shy infants and preschoolers show greater EEG activity in the right frontal lobe, which is associated with negative emotional reactivity; sociable children show the opposite pattern (Fox et al., 2008; Kagan et al., 2007). Inhibited children also show a stronger ERP brain-wave response to unfamiliar visual scenes (Kagan, 2013d). Neural activity in the amygdala, which is transmitted to the frontal lobes, probably contributes to these differences.

Child-Rearing Practices

According to Kagan, most extremely shy or sociable children inherit a physiology that biases them toward a particular temperamental style. Yet heritability research indicates that genes contribute only modestly to shyness and sociability (Kagan, 2013d). Experience has a profound impact.

Child-rearing practices affect the chances that an emotionally reactive baby will become a fearful child. Warm, supportive parenting reduces shy infants' and preschoolers' intense physiological

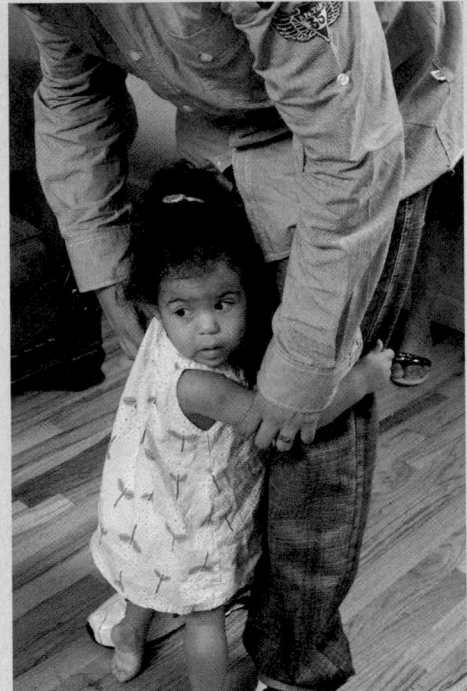

A strong physiological response to uncertain situations prompts this child to cling to her father. With patient, insistent encouragement, her parents can help her overcome the urge to retreat from unfamiliar events.

reaction to novelty, whereas cold, intrusive parenting that punishes or denies children's feelings heightens anxiety (Coplan & Arbeau, 2008; Davis & Buss, 2012). And if parents overprotect infants and young children who dislike novelty, they make it harder for the child to overcome an urge to retreat. Parents who make appropriate demands for their child to approach new experiences help shy youngsters overcome fear (Rubin & Burgess, 2002).

When inhibition persists, it leads to excessive cautiousness, low self-esteem, and loneliness (Fordham & Stevenson-Hinde, 1999; Rubin, Stewart, & Coplan, 1995). In adolescence, persistent shyness increases the risk of severe anxiety, depression, and other internalizing problems, including unrealistic worries about harm, illness, and criticism for mistakes as well as social phobia—intense fear of being humiliated in social situations (Kagan, 2013d; Karevold et al., 2012). For inhibited children to acquire effective social skills, parenting must be tailored to their temperaments—a theme we will encounter again in this and later chapters.

Stability of Temperament

Young children who score low or high on attention span, irritability, sociability, shyness, or effortful control tend to respond similarly when assessed again several months to a few years later and, occasionally, even into the adult years (Casalin et al., 2012; Caspi et al., 2003; Kochanska & Knaack, 2003; Majdandžić & van den Boom, 2007; van den Akker et al., 2010). However, the overall stability of temperament is low in infancy and toddlerhood and only moderate from the preschool years on (Putnam, Samson, & Rothbart, 2000). Some children remain the same, but many others change.

Why isn't temperament more stable? A major reason is that temperament itself develops with age. To illustrate, let's look at irritability and activity level. Recall from Chapter 4 that the early months are a period of fussing and crying for most babies. As infants better regulate their attention and emotions, many who initially seemed irritable become calm and content. In the case of activity level, the meaning of the behavior changes. At first, an active, wriggling infant tends to be highly aroused and uncomfortable, whereas an inactive baby is often alert and attentive. Once infants move on their own, the reverse is so! An active crawler is usually alert and interested in exploration, whereas an inactive baby may be fearful and withdrawn.

These discrepancies help us understand why long-term prediction from early temperament is best achieved after age 3, when children's styles of responding are better established (Roberts & DelVecchio, 2000). In line with this idea, between ages 2½ and 3, children improve substantially and also perform more consistently across a wide range of tasks requiring effortful control, such as waiting for a reward, lowering their voice to a whisper, succeeding at games like "Simon Says," and selectively attending to one stimulus while ignoring competing stimuli (Kochanska, Murray, & Harlan, 2000; Li-Grining, 2007). Researchers believe that around this time, areas in the prefrontal cortex involved in suppressing impulses develop rapidly (Rothbart, 2011).

Nevertheless, the ease with which children manage their reactivity in early childhood depends on the type and strength of the reactive emotion involved. Preschoolers who were highly fearful as toddlers score slightly better than their agemates in effortful control. In contrast, angry, irritable toddlers tend to be less effective at effortful control at later ages (Bridgett et al., 2009; Kochanska & Knaack, 2003). Other evidence confirms that child rearing plays an important role in modifying temperamental traits. Toddlers and young preschoolers who have fearful or negative, irritable temperaments but experience patient, supportive parenting gain most in capacity to manage their reactivity (Kim & Kochanska, 2012; Warren & Simmens, 2005). But if exposed to insensitive or unresponsive parenting, these emotionally negative children are especially likely to score low in effortful control, placing them at risk for adjustment problems.

In sum, many factors affect the extent to which a child's temperament remains stable, including development of the biological systems on which temperament is based, the child's capacity for effortful control, and the success of her efforts, which depend on the quality and intensity of her emotional reactivity. When we consider the evidence as a whole, the low to moderate stability of temperament makes sense. It also confirms that child rearing can modify biologically based temperamental traits considerably and that children with certain traits, such as negative emotionality, are especially susceptible to the influence of parenting—a finding we will return to shortly. With these ideas in mind, let's take a closer look at genetic and environmental contributions to temperament and personality.

Genetic and Environmental Influences

The word *temperament* implies a genetic foundation for individual differences in personality. Identical twins are more similar than fraternal twins across a wide range of temperamental traits (activity level, attention span, shyness/sociability, irritability, and effortful control) and personality measures (introversion/extroversion, anxiety, agreeableness, curiosity and imaginativeness, and impulsivity) (Bouchard, 2004; Caspi & Shiner, 2006; Krueger & Johnson, 2008; Roisman & Fraley, 2006). In Chapter 2, we noted that heritability estimates derived from twin studies suggest a moderate role for genetic factors in temperament and personality: About half of individual differences have been attributed to differences in genetic makeup.

Although genetic influences on temperament are clear, environment is also powerful. Recall from Chapter 5 that children exposed to severe malnutrition in infancy remain more distractible and fearful than their agemates, even after dietary improvement. And infants reared in deprived orphanages are easily overwhelmed by stressful events. Their poor regulation of emotion results in inattention and weak impulse control, including frequent expressions of anger (see pages 168 and 175).

Furthermore, heredity and environment often jointly contribute to temperament, since a child's initial approach to the world can be intensified or lessened by experience. To illustrate, let's begin by looking closely at ethnic and gender differences in temperament.

ETHNIC AND GENDER DIFFERENCES Compared with North American Caucasian infants, Chinese and Japanese babies tend to be less active, irritable, and vocal; more easily soothed when upset; and better at quieting themselves (Kagan, 2013d; Lewis, Ramsay, & Kawakami, 1993). Grace's capacity to remain contentedly seated in her highchair through a long family dinner certainly fits with this evidence. Chinese and Japanese babies are also more fearful and inhibited, remaining closer to their mothers in an unfamiliar playroom and displaying more anxiety when interacting with a stranger (Chen, Wang, & DeSouza, 2006).

These variations may have genetic roots, but they are supported by cultural beliefs and practices, yielding a possible *gene–environment correlation.* Japanese mothers usually say that babies come into the world as independent beings who must learn to rely on their parents through close physical contact. American mothers, in contrast, typically believe that they must wean the baby away from dependency toward autonomy. Consistent with these beliefs, Asian mothers interact gently, soothingly, and gesturally with their infants, whereas Caucasian mothers use a more active, stimulating, verbal approach (Kagan, 2010; Rothbaum et al., 2000). Also, recall from our discussion of emotional self-regulation that Chinese and Japanese adults discourage babies from expressing strong emotion, which contributes further to their infants' tranquility.

Similarly, gender differences in temperament are evident in infancy, suggesting a genetic foundation. Boys are more active and daring, more irritable when frustrated, more likely to express high-intensity pleasure in play, and slightly more impulsive than girls—factors that contribute to boys' higher injury rates throughout childhood and adolescence. Girls, in contrast, tend to be more anxious and timid. And girls' large advantage in effortful control undoubtedly contributes to their greater cooperativeness, better school performance, and lower incidence of behavior problems (Else-Quest, 2012; Else-Quest et al., 2006). At the same time, parents more often encourage their young sons to be physically active and their daughters to seek help and physical closeness—through activities they encourage and through more positive reactions when their child exhibits temperamental traits consistent with gender stereotypes (Bryan & Dix, 2009; Ruble, Martin, & Berenbaum, 2006).

DIFFERENTIAL SUSCEPTIBILITY TO REARING EXPERIENCES Earlier we discussed findings indicating that emotionally reactive toddlers function worse than other children when exposed to inept parenting, yet benefit most from good parenting. Researchers have become increasingly interested in temperamental differences in children's susceptibility (or responsiveness) to environmental influences (Pluess & Belsky, 2011). Using molecular genetic analyses, they are clarifying how these *gene–environment interactions* operate.

In one study, 2-year-olds with a chromosome 7 gene containing a certain repetition of DNA base pairs, called short 5-HTTLPR—which interferes with functioning of the inhibitory neurotransmitter serotonin and, thus, greatly increases the risk of negative mood, fear of the unfamiliar,

Gender differences in temperament are evident in children's play styles. Boys tend to engage in more active, high-intensity play. And girls' large advantage in effortful control helps explain their greater cooperativeness.

and self-regulation difficulties—became increasingly irritable as their mothers' anxiety about parenting increased (Ivorra et al., 2010). Maternal anxiety, however, had little impact on children without this gene. In another investigation, toddlers with the short 5-HTTLPR gene responded especially favorably to effective parenting (Kochanska, Philibert, & Barry, 2009; Kochanska et al. 2011). With maternal warmth and support in mastering new skills, their capacity for self-regulation improved during the preschool years, equaling that of agemates with a low-risk genotype. They were also advantaged in academic and social skills compared to their counterparts with less responsive mothers.

Consistently, the short 5-HTTLPR genotype combined with maladaptive parenting leads to externalizing problems, including defiance and aggression (van IJzendoorn, Belsky, & Bakermans-Kranenburg, 2012). Why is this so? A two-year follow-up of 1-year-olds from poverty-stricken families revealed that parenting quality had little impact on children with a low-risk genotype. In contrast, toddlers with a high-risk genotype became increasingly reactive emotionally to their mother's insensitive, hostile, and rejecting behavior, responding with distress, anger, and uncontrolled screaming (see Figure 7.2) (Davies & Cicchetti, 2014). Negative emotionality, in turn, predicted a sharp rise in aggression and defiance over the preschool years—externalizing difficulties that often persist.

As these outcomes reveal, children with the short 5-HTTLPR gene show unusually high early *plasticity* (see page 9 in Chapter 1 to review). They are particularly susceptible to the effects of both good and poor parenting. Because young children with this "susceptibility attribute" fare better than other children when parenting is supportive, they are likely to respond especially well to interventions aimed at reducing parental stress and promoting responsive child rearing.

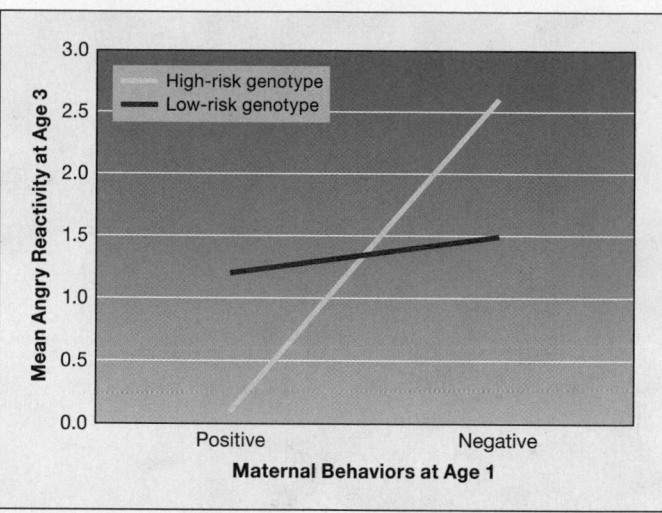

FIGURE 7.2 **Angry reactivity at age 3 in response to positive and negative maternal behaviors for children with and without the short 5-HTTLPR gene.** Children with a low-risk genotype (without the gene) responded little to quality of maternal behavior. Those with a high-risk genotype (with the gene), in contrast, were highly susceptible to parenting quality—both good and bad. They displayed little anger when exposed to maternal affection and encouragement but high anger to maternal insensitivity and hostility. (Adapted from P. T. Davies and D. Cicchetti, 2014, "How and Why Does the 5-HTTLPR Gene Moderate Associations Between Maternal Unresponsiveness and Children's Disruptive Problems?" *Child Development, 85,* p. 494. Copyright © 2013 Society for Research in Child Development, Inc., and The Authors. Reprinted with permission of John Wiley and Sons, Inc., conveyed through Copyright Clearance Center, Inc.)

SIBLINGS' UNIQUE EXPERIENCES   In families with several children, another influence on temperament is at work. Parents often look for differences between siblings: "She's a lot more active." "He's more sociable." "She's far more persistent." As a result, parents often view siblings as more distinct than other observers do.

In a large study of 1- to 3-year-old twin pairs, parents rated identical twins as less alike in temperament than researchers' ratings indicated. And whereas researchers rated fraternal twins as moderately similar, parents viewed them as somewhat opposite in temperament—one shy and the other sociable, one active and the other restrained, one persistent and the other distractible (Saudino, 2003). This tendency to emphasize each child's unique qualities affects parenting practices. Each child, in turn, evokes responses from caregivers that are consistent with parental beliefs and with the child's developing temperament.

Besides different experiences within the family, siblings have distinct experiences with teachers, peers, and others in their community that affect development. And as we will see in Chapter 13, in middle childhood and adolescence, siblings often seek ways to differ from one another. In sum, temperament and personality can be understood only in terms of complex interdependencies between genetic and environmental factors.

LOOK and LISTEN

Ask several parents of siblings to describe their children's temperaments, along with child-rearing practices they use with each. Do the parents tend to emphasize differences? Are their child-rearing practices responsive to their views of each child's unique qualities?

Temperament and Child Rearing: The Goodness-of-Fit Model

If a child's disposition interferes with learning or getting along with others, adults must gently but consistently counteract the child's maladaptive style. Thomas and Chess (1977) proposed a **goodness-of-fit model** to explain how temperament and environment can together produce favorable outcomes. Goodness of fit involves creating child-rearing environments

This parent's firm but affectionate approach to discipline is "a good fit" with his son's difficult temperament, helping the toddler gain in effortful control and manage negative emotion.

that recognize each child's temperament while simultaneously encouraging more adaptive functioning.

Goodness of fit helps explain why difficult children (who withdraw from new experiences and react negatively and intensely) frequently experience parenting that fits poorly with their dispositions. As infants, they are less likely to receive sensitive caregiving. By the second year, their parents tend to resort to angry, punitive discipline, which undermines the development of effortful control. As the child reacts with defiance and disobedience, parents become increasingly stressed (Bridgett et al., 2009; Paulussen-Hoogeboom et al., 2007). As a result, they continue their coercive tactics and also discipline inconsistently, sometimes rewarding the child's noncompliance by giving in to it (Pesonen et al., 2008; van Aken et al., 2007). These practices sustain and even increase the child's irritable, conflict-ridden style.

In contrast, when parents are positive and sensitive, which helps infants and toddlers—especially those who are emotionally reactive—regulate emotion, difficultness declines by age 2 or 3 (Raikes et al., 2007). In toddlerhood and childhood, parental sensitivity, support, clear expectations, and limits foster effortful control, reducing the likelihood that difficultness will persist and lead to emotional and social difficulties (Cipriano & Stifter, 2010; Jaffari-Bimmel et al., 2006).

Effective parenting of difficult children, however, also depends on life conditions—good parental mental health, marital happiness, and favorable economic conditions (Schoppe-Sullivan et al., 2007). In a comparison of the temperaments of Russian and U.S. babies, Russian infants were more emotionally negative, fearful, and upset when frustrated (Gartstein, Slobodskaya, & Kinsht, 2003). At the time of the study, Russian parents faced a severely depressed national economy. Because of financial worries and longer work hours, Russian parents may have lacked time and energy for patient parenting.

Cultural values also affect the fit between parenting and child temperament, as research in China illustrates. In the past, high valuing of social harmony, which discourages self-assertion, led Chinese adults to evaluate shy children positively. Chinese children of two decades ago appeared well-adjusted, both academically and socially (Chen, Rubin, & Li, 1995; Chen et al., 1998). But rapid expansion of a market economy in China, which requires assertiveness and sociability for success, may be responsible for a change in Chinese parents' and teachers' attitudes toward childhood shyness (Chen, Wang, & DeSouza, 2006; Yu, 2002). In an investigation of Shanghai fourth graders, the association between shyness and adjustment also changed over time. Whereas shyness was positively correlated with teacher-rated competence, peer acceptance, leadership, and academic achievement in 1990, these relationships weakened in 1998 and reversed in 2002, when they mirrored findings of Western research (Chen et al., 2005). But in rural areas of China, positive valuing of shyness persists, and shy children continue to enjoy high social status and are well-adjusted (Chen, Wang, & Cao, 2011). Cultural context makes a difference in whether shy children receive support or disapproval and whether they adjust well or poorly.

An effective match between rearing conditions and child temperament is best accomplished early, before unfavorable temperament–environment relationships produce maladjustment. Recall from Chapter 6 that Vanessa often behaved in an overly directive way with Timmy in an effort to contain his high activity level. A poor fit between her intrusive parenting and Timmy's active temperament may have contributed to his tendency to move from one activity to the next with little involvement.

The goodness-of-fit model reminds us that babies have unique dispositions that adults must accept. Parents can neither take full credit for their children's virtues nor be blamed for all their faults. But parents can turn an environment that exaggerates a child's problems into one that builds on the child's strengths. As we will see, goodness of fit is also at the heart of infant–caregiver attachment. This first intimate relationship grows out of interaction between parent and baby, to which the emotional styles of both partners contribute.

Ask Yourself

● **REVIEW** Describe emotionally reactive and easy-going children's differential susceptibility to rearing experiences. Why are emotionally reactive children who receive warm, supportive parenting at especially low risk for self-regulation difficulties?

● **CONNECT** Explain how findings on ethnic and gender differences in temperament illustrate gene–environment correlation, discussed on page 84 in Chapter 2.

● **APPLY** Mandy and Jeff are parents of 2-year-old inhibited Sam and 3-year-old emotionally reactive Maria. Explain the importance of effortful control to Mandy and Jeff, and suggest ways they can strengthen it in each of their children.

● **REFLECT** How would you describe your temperament as a young child? Do you think it has remained stable, or has it changed? What factors might be involved?

Development of Attachment

Attachment is the strong affectionate tie we have with special people in our lives that leads us to experience pleasure and joy when we interact with them and to be comforted by their nearness in times of stress. By the second half-year, infants have become attached to familiar people who have responded to their needs. **TAKE A MOMENT...** Watch how babies of this age single out their parents for special attention: When the parent enters the room, the baby breaks into a broad, friendly smile. When she picks him up, he pats her face, explores her hair, and snuggles against her. When he feels anxious or afraid, he crawls into her lap and clings closely.

Freud first suggested that the infant's emotional tie to the mother is the foundation for all later relationships. Contemporary research indicates that—although the infant–parent bond is vitally important—later development is influenced not just by early attachment experiences but also by the continuing quality of the parent–child relationship.

Attachment has also been the subject of intense theoretical debate. Recall that the *psychoanalytic perspective* regards feeding as the central context in which caregivers and babies build this close emotional bond. *Behaviorism,* too, emphasizes the importance of feeding but for different reasons. According to a well-known behaviorist account, infants learn to prefer the mother's soft caresses, warm smiles, and tender words because these events are paired with tension relief as she satisfies the baby's hunger.

Although feeding is an important context for building a close relationship, attachment does not depend on hunger satisfaction. In the 1950s, a famous experiment showed that rhesus monkeys reared with terry-cloth and wire-mesh "surrogate mothers" clung to the soft terry-cloth substitute, even though the wire-mesh "mother" held the bottle and infants had to climb onto it to be fed (Harlow & Zimmerman, 1959). Human infants, too, become attached to family members who seldom feed them, including fathers, siblings, and grandparents. And toddlers in Western cultures who sleep alone and experience frequent daytime separations from their parents sometimes develop strong emotional ties to cuddly objects, such as blankets and teddy bears, that play no role in infant feeding!

Both psychoanalytic and behaviorist accounts of attachment have another problem: They emphasize the caregiver's contribution to the attachment relationship but pay little attention to the importance of the infant's characteristics.

Bowlby's Ethological Theory

Today, **ethological theory of attachment,** which recognizes the infant's emotional tie to the caregiver as an evolved response that promotes survival, is the most widely accepted view. John Bowlby (1969), who first applied this perspective to the infant–caregiver bond, retained the psychoanalytic idea that quality of attachment to the caregiver has profound implications for the child's feelings of security and capacity to form trusting relationships.

7.6 What are the unique features of ethological theory of attachment?

7.7 Cite the four attachment patterns assessed by the Strange Situation and the Attachment Q-Sort, and discuss factors that affect attachment security.

7.8 Discuss infants' formation of multiple attachments, and indicate how attachment paves the way for early peer sociability.

7.9 Describe and interpret the relationship between secure attachment in infancy and psychological development in childhood.

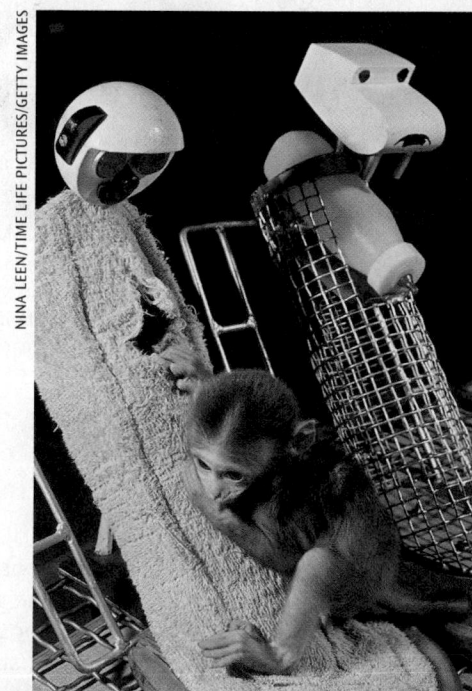

NINA LEEN/TIME LIFE PICTURES/GETTY IMAGES

Baby monkeys reared with "surrogate mothers" preferred to cling to a soft terry-cloth "mother" instead of a wire-mesh "mother" that held a bottle. These findings contradict the drive-reduction explanation of attachment, which assumes that the parent–infant relationship is based on feeding.

LOOK and LISTEN

Watch an 8- to 18-month-old at play for 20 to 30 minutes. Describe the baby's use of the parent or other familiar caregiver as a secure base from which to explore.

At the same time, Bowlby was inspired by Konrad Lorenz's studies of imprinting in baby geese (see Chapter 1). Bowlby believed that the human infant, like the young of other animal species, is endowed with a set of built-in behaviors that keep the parent nearby to protect the infant from danger and to provide support for exploring and mastering the environment. Contact with the parent also ensures that the baby will be fed, but Bowlby pointed out that feeding is not the basis for attachment. Rather, attachment can best be understood in an evolutionary context in which survival of the species—through ensuring both safety and competence—is of utmost importance.

According to Bowlby, the infant's relationship with the parent begins as a set of innate signals that call the adult to the baby's side. Over time, a true affectionate bond forms, supported by new cognitive and emotional capacities as well as by a history of warm, sensitive care. Attachment develops in four phases:

1. *Preattachment phase* (birth to 6 weeks). Built-in signals—grasping, smiling, crying, and gazing into the adult's eyes—help bring newborn babies into close contact with other humans, who comfort them. Babies of this age recognize their own mother's smell, voice, and face (see Chapter 4). But they are not yet attached to her, since they do not mind being left with an unfamiliar adult.

2. *"Attachment in the making" phase* (6 weeks to 6–8 months). During this phase, infants respond differently to a familiar caregiver than to a stranger. For example, at 4 months, Timmy smiled, laughed, and babbled more freely when interacting with his mother and quieted more quickly when she picked him up. As infants learn that their own actions affect the behavior of those around them, they begin to develop a *sense of trust*—the expectation that the caregiver will respond when signaled—but they still do not protest when separated from her.

3. *"Clear-cut" attachment phase* (6–8 months to 18 months–2 years). Now attachment to the familiar caregiver is evident. Babies display **separation anxiety,** becoming upset when their trusted caregiver leaves. Like stranger anxiety (see page 249), separation anxiety does not always occur; it depends on infant temperament and the current situation. But in many cultures, separation anxiety increases between 6 and 15 months, suggesting that infants have developed a clear understanding that the caregiver continues to exist when not in view. Besides protesting the parent's departure, older infants and toddlers try hard to maintain her presence. They approach, follow, and climb on her in preference to others. And they use the familiar caregiver as a secure base from which to explore.

4. *Formation of a reciprocal relationship* (18 months to 2 years and on). By the end of the second year, rapid growth in representation and language enables toddlers to understand some of the factors that influence the parent's coming and going and to predict her return. As a result, separation protest declines. Now children negotiate with the caregiver, using requests and persuasion to alter her goals. For example, at age 2, Caitlin asked Carolyn and David to read her a story before leaving her with a babysitter. The extra time with her parents, along with a better understanding of where they were going ("to have dinner with Uncle Sean") and when they would be back ("right after you go to sleep"), helped Caitlin withstand her parents' absence.

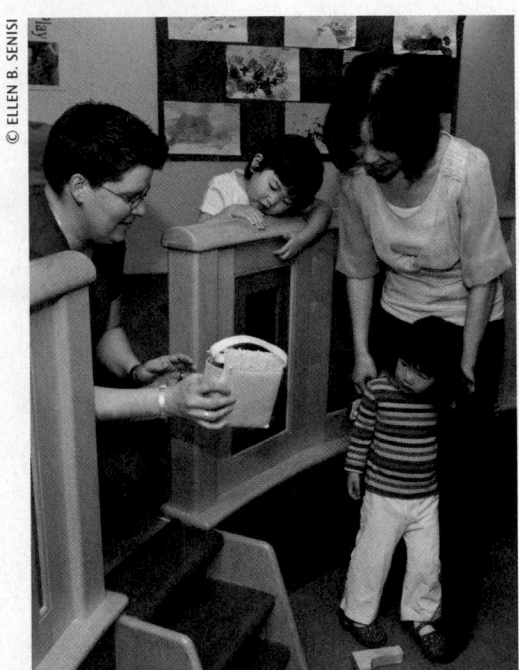

With her teacher's enticement to play and an explanation that her mother will be back soon, this 2-year-old is likely separate without tears. Her language and representational skills enable her to predict her mother's return, so separation anxiety declines.

According to Bowlby (1980), out of their experiences during these four phases, children construct an enduring affectionate tie to the caregiver that they can use as a secure base in the parent's absence. This image serves as an **internal working model,** or set of expectations about the availability of attachment figures, their likelihood of providing support during times of stress, and the self's interaction with those figures. The internal working model becomes a vital part of personality, serving as a guide for all future close relationships (Bretherton & Munholland, 2008).

Consistent with these ideas, as early as the second year, toddlers form attachment-related expectations about parental comfort and support. In one study, securely attached 12- to 16-month-olds looked longer at a video of an unresponsive caregiver (inconsistent with their expectations) than a video of a responsive caregiver. Insecurely attached toddlers, in contrast,

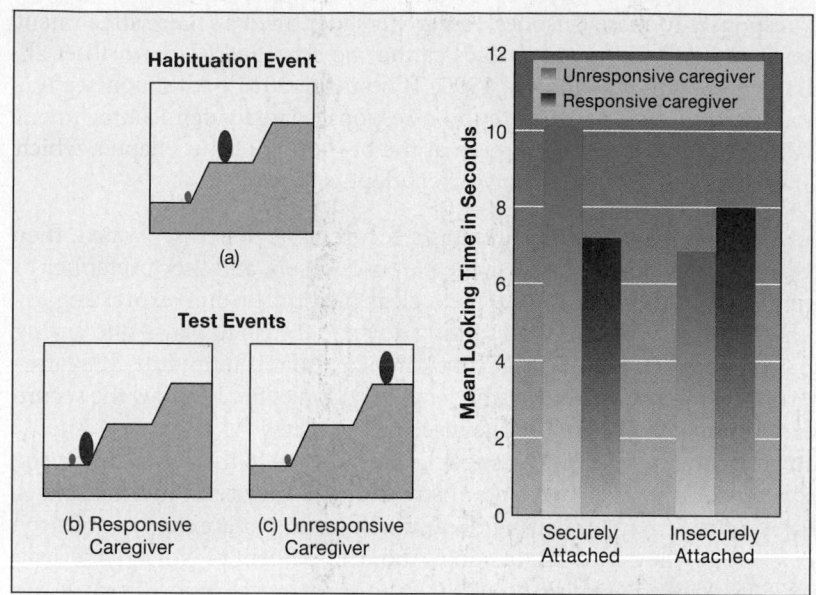

FIGURE 7.3 Testing toddlers for internal working models of attachment. (a) First, 12- to 16-month-olds were habituated to a video of two animated shapes, one large (the "caregiver") and one small (the "child"). The caregiver traveled halfway up an incline to a plateau, and the child began to "cry," depicted by pulsing and bouncing paired with an infant cry. Next the researchers presented two test events: (b) In the *responsive caregiver outcome,* the caregiver returned to the child. (c) In the *unresponsive caregiver outcome,* the caregiver continued up the slope away from the child. Securely attached toddlers looked longer at the unresponsive outcome, depicting caregiver behavior inconsistent with their expectations. Insecurely attached toddlers did not differentiate between the two test events. (Based on Johnson, Dweck, & Chen, 2007.)

did not distinguish between the two (see Figure 7.3) (Johnson, Dweck, & Chen, 2007; Johnson et al., 2010). With age, children continually revise and expand their internal working model as their cognitive, emotional, and social capacities increase and as they interact with parents and form other close bonds with adults, siblings, and friends.

Measuring the Security of Attachment

Although all family-reared babies become attached to a familiar caregiver by the second year, the quality of this relationship differs from child to child. Some infants appear relaxed and secure in the presence of the caregiver; they know they can count on her for protection and support. Others seem anxious and uncertain.

A widely used laboratory technique for assessing the quality of attachment between 1 and 2 years of age is the **Strange Situation.** In designing it, Mary Ainsworth and her colleagues reasoned that securely attached infants and toddlers should use the parent as a secure base from which to explore in an unfamiliar playroom. In addition, when the parent leaves, an unfamiliar adult should be less comforting than the parent. The Strange Situation takes the baby through eight short episodes in which brief separations from and reunions with the parent occur (see Table 7.2).

TABLE 7.2	Episodes in the Strange Situation	
EPISODE	**EVENTS**	**ATTACHMENT BEHAVIOR OBSERVED**
1	Researcher introduces parent and baby to playroom and then leaves.	
2	Parent is seated while baby plays with toys.	Parent as a secure base
3	Stranger enters, is seated, and talks to parent.	Reaction to unfamiliar adult
4	Parent leaves room. Stranger responds to baby and offers comfort if baby is upset.	Separation anxiety
5	Parent returns, greets baby, and offers comfort if necessary. Stranger leaves room.	Reaction to reunion
6	Parent leaves room.	Separation anxiety
7	Stranger enters room and offers comfort.	Ability to be soothed by stranger
8	Parent returns, greets baby, offers comfort if necessary, and tries to reinterest baby in toys.	Reaction to reunion

Note: Episode 1 lasts about 30 seconds; each of the remaining episodes lasts about 3 minutes. Separation episodes are cut short if the baby becomes very upset. Reunion episodes are extended if the baby needs more time to calm down and return to play.

Source: Ainsworth et al., 1978.

Observing infants' responses to these episodes, researchers identified a secure attachment pattern and three patterns of insecurity; a few babies cannot be classified (Ainsworth et al., 1978; Barnett & Vondra, 1999; Main & Solomon, 1990; Thompson, 2013). Although separation anxiety varies among the groups, the baby's reunion responses largely define attachment quality. **TAKE A MOMENT...** From the description at the beginning of this chapter, which pattern do you think Grace displayed after adjusting to her adoptive family?

- **Secure attachment.** These infants use the parent as a secure base. When separated, they may or may not cry, but if they do, it is because the parent is absent and they prefer her to the stranger. When the parent returns, they express clear pleasure—some expressing joy from a distance, others asking to be held until settling down to return to play—and crying is reduced immediately. About 60 percent of North American infants in middle-SES families show this pattern. (In low-SES families, a smaller proportion of babies show the secure pattern, with higher proportions falling into the insecure patterns.)
- **Insecure–avoidant attachment.** These infants seem unresponsive to the parent when she is present. When she leaves, they usually are not distressed, and they react to the stranger in much the same way as to the parent. During reunion, they avoid or are slow to greet the parent, and when picked up, they often fail to cling. About 15 percent of North American infants in middle-SES families show this pattern.
- **Insecure–resistant attachment.** Before separation, these infants seek closeness to the parent and often fail to explore. When the parent leaves, they are usually distressed, and on her return they combine clinginess with angry, resistive behavior (struggling when held, hitting and pushing) or with an anxious focus on the parent. Many continue to cry after being picked up and cannot be comforted easily. About 10 percent of North American infants in middle-SES families show this pattern.
- **Disorganized/disoriented attachment.** This pattern reflects the greatest insecurity. At reunion, these infants show confused, contradictory behaviors—for example, looking away while the parent is holding them or approaching the parent with flat, depressed emotion. Most display a dazed facial expression, and a few cry out unexpectedly after having calmed down or display odd, frozen postures. About 15 percent of North American infants in middle-SES families show this pattern.

An alternative method, the **Attachment Q-Sort,** suitable for children between 1 and 5 years, depends on home observations (Waters et al., 1995). Either the parent or a highly trained observer sorts 90 behaviors—such as "Child greets mother with a big smile when she enters the room," "If mother moves very far, child follows along," and "Child uses mother's facial expressions as a good source of information when something looks risky or threatening"—into nine categories ranging from "highly descriptive" to "not at all descriptive" of the child. Then a score, ranging from high to low in security, is computed.

Because the Q-Sort taps a wider array of attachment-related behaviors than the Strange Situation, it may better reflect the parent–infant relationship in everyday life. However, the Q-Sort method is time-consuming, requiring a nonparent informant to spend several hours observing the child before sorting the descriptors, and it does not differentiate between types of insecurity. The Q-Sort responses of expert observers correspond well with babies' secure-base behavior in the Strange Situation, but parents' Q-Sorts do not (van IJzendoorn et al., 2004). Parents of insecure children, especially, may have difficulty accurately reporting their child's attachment behaviors.

Stability of Attachment

Research on the stability of attachment patterns between 1 and 2 years of age yields a wide range of findings. In some studies, as many as 70 to 90 percent of children remain the same in their reactions to parents; in others, only 30 to 40 percent do (Thompson, 2006, 2008, 2013). A close look at which babies stay the same and which ones change yields a more consistent picture. Quality of attachment is usually secure and stable for middle-SES babies experiencing favorable life conditions. And infants who move from insecurity to security typically have well-adjusted mothers with positive family and friendship ties. Perhaps many became parents before they were psychologically ready but, with social support, grew into the role.

In contrast, in low-SES families with many daily stresses, attachment generally moves away from security or changes from one insecure pattern to another (Fish, 2004; Levendosky et al., 2011; Vondra et al., 2001). And in a long-term follow-up from infancy to early adulthood, child maltreatment, maternal depression, and poor family functioning were associated with shifts from security to insecurity (Weinfield, Sroufe, & Egeland, 2000; Weinfield, Whaley, & Egeland, 2004).

These findings indicate that securely attached babies more often maintain their attachment status than insecure babies, whose relationship with the caregiver is, by definition, fragile and uncertain. The exception is disorganized/disoriented attachment, an insecure pattern that is either highly stable or that consistently predicts insecurity of another type in adolescence and early adulthood (Aikens, Howes, & Hamilton, 2009; Hesse & Main, 2000; Weinfeld, Whaley, & Egeland, 2004). As you will soon see, many disorganized/disoriented infants experience extremely negative caregiving, which may disrupt emotional self-regulation so severely that confused, ambivalent feelings toward parents persist.

Cultural Variations

Cross-cultural evidence indicates that attachment patterns may have to be interpreted differently in certain cultures. For example, as Figure 7.4 reveals, German infants show considerably more avoidant attachment than American babies do. But German parents value independence and encourage their infants to be nonclingy, so the baby's behavior may be an intended outcome of cultural beliefs and practices (Grossmann et al., 1985). In contrast, a study of infants of the Dogon people of Mali, Africa, revealed that none showed avoidant attachment to their mothers (True, Pisani, & Oumar, 2001). Even when grandmothers are primary caregivers (as they are with firstborn sons), Dogon mothers remain available to their babies, holding them close and nursing them promptly in response to hunger and distress.

Japanese infants, as well, rarely show avoidant attachment (refer again to Figure 7.4). Rather, many are resistantly attached, but this reaction may not represent true insecurity. Japanese mothers rarely leave their babies in others' care, so the Strange Situation probably induces greater stress in them than in infants who frequently experience maternal separations (Takahashi, 1990). Also, Japanese parents view the attention seeking that is part of resistant attachment as a normal indicator of infants' efforts to satisfy dependency and security needs (Rothbaum et al., 2007). Likewise, infants in Israeli kibbutzim frequently show resistant attachment. For these babies, who can sense the fear of unfamiliar people that is pervasive in their communities (see page 250), the Strange Situation probably induces unusual distress (van IJzendoorn & Sagi, 1999). Despite these and other cultural variations, the secure pattern is still the most common attachment quality in all societies studied to date (van IJzendoorn & Sagi-Schwartz, 2008).

Factors That Affect Attachment Security

What factors might influence attachment security? Researchers have looked closely at four important influences: (1) early availability of a consistent caregiver, (2) quality of caregiving, (3) the baby's characteristics, and (4) family context, including parents' internal working models.

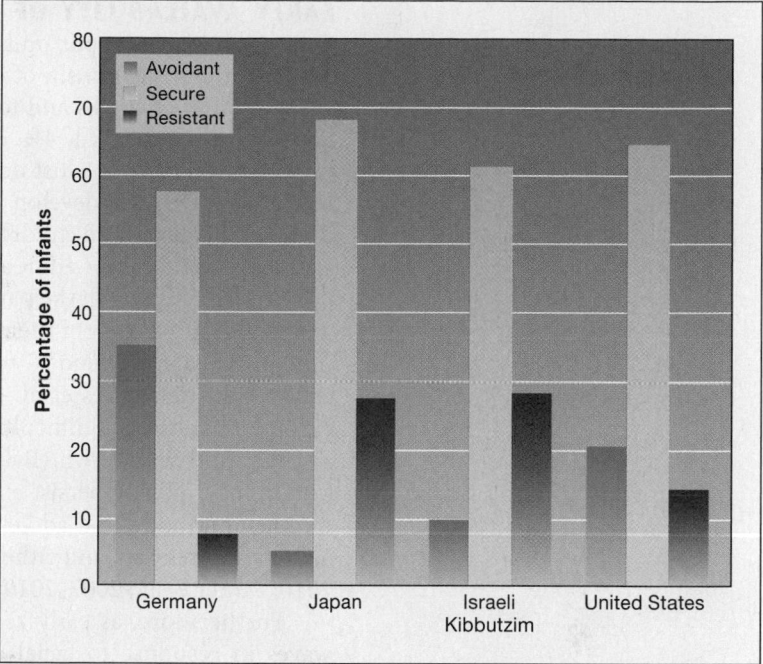

FIGURE 7.4 A cross-cultural comparison of infants' reactions in the Strange Situation. A high percentage of German babies seem avoidantly attached, whereas a substantial number of Japanese and Israeli kibbutz infants appear resistantly attached. Note that these responses may not reflect true insecurity. Instead, they are probably due to cultural differences in child-rearing practices. (Based on van IJzendoorn & Kroonenberg, 1988; van IJzendoorn & Sagi-Schwartz, 2008.)

© AFRIPICS.COM/ALAMY

Dogon mothers of Mali, West Africa, stay close to their babies and respond promptly and gently to infant hunger and distress. With their mothers consistently available, none of the Dogon babies show avoidant attachment.

EARLY AVAILABILITY OF A CONSISTENT CAREGIVER What happens when a baby does not have the opportunity to establish a close tie to a caregiver? To find out, researchers followed the development of infants in an institution with a good caregiver–child ratio and a rich selection of books and toys. However, staff turnover was so rapid that the average child had 50 caregivers by age 4½. Many of these children became "late adoptees" who were placed in homes after age 4. Most developed deep ties with their adoptive parents, indicating that a first attachment can develop as late as 4 to 6 years of age (Hodges & Tizard, 1989; Tizard & Rees, 1975). But these children were more likely to display attachment difficulties, including an excessive desire for adult attention, "overfriendliness" to unfamiliar adults and peers, failure to check back with the parent in anxiety-arousing situations, and few friendships.

Children who spent their first year or more in deprived Eastern European orphanages—though also able to bond with their adoptive parents—show elevated rates of attachment insecurity (van den Dries et al., 2009; Smyke et al., 2010). And they, too, are at high risk for emotional and social difficulties. Whereas many are indiscriminately friendly, others are sad, anxious, and withdrawn (Bakermans-Kranenberg et al., 2011; O'Connor et al., 2003). These symptoms typically persist and are associated with wide-ranging mental health problems in middle childhood and adolescence, including cognitive impairments, inattention and overactivity, depression, and either social avoidance or aggressive behavior (Kreppner et al., 2007, 2010; Rutter et al., 2007, 2010; Zeanah, 2000).

Furthermore, as early as 7 months, institutionalized children show reduced ERP brain waves in response to facial expressions of emotion and have trouble discriminating such expressions—outcomes that suggest disrupted formation of neural structures involved in "reading" emotions (Parker et al., 2005). These problems are still evident in preschoolers adopted during the second year, who find it hard to match appropriate facial expressions with situations in stories (Fries & Pollak, 2004). Consistent with these findings, in adopted children with longer institutional stays, the volume of the *amygdala* (see page 256) is atypically large (Tottenham et al., 2011). The larger the amygdala, the worse adopted children perform on tasks assessing understanding of emotion and the poorer their emotional self-regulation. Overall, the evidence indicates that fully normal emotional development depends on establishing a close tie with a caregiver early in life.

QUALITY OF CAREGIVING Dozens of studies report that **sensitive caregiving**—responding promptly, consistently, and appropriately to infants and holding them tenderly and carefully— is moderately related to attachment security in both biological and adoptive mother–infant pairs and in diverse cultures and SES groups (Belsky & Fearon, 2008; De Wolff & van IJzendoorn, 1997; van IJzendoorn et al., 2004). Mothers of securely attached babies also frequently refer to their infants' mental states and motives: "You really *like* that swing!" "Do you *remember* Grandma?" This tendency to treat the baby as a person with inner thoughts and feelings seems to promote sensitive caregiving (Meins et al., 2001, 2003). In contrast, insecurely attached infants tend to have mothers who engage in less physical contact, handle them awkwardly or in a "routine" manner, and are sometimes resentful and rejecting, particularly in response to infant distress (Ainsworth et al., 1978; Isabella, 1993; McElwain & Booth-LaForce, 2006; Pederson & Moran, 1996).

Also, in studies of Western babies, a special form of communication called **interactional synchrony** separates the experiences of secure from insecure babies. It is best described as a sensitively tuned "emotional dance," in which the caregiver responds to infant signals in a well-timed, rhythmic, appropriate fashion. In addition, both partners match emotional states, especially the positive ones (Bigelow et al., 2010; Isabella & Belsky, 1991; Nievar & Becker, 2008). For example, when Caitlin excitedly shook a rattle, Carolyn responded with a broad smile and an enthusiastic "That-a-girl!" In return, Caitlin smiled and cooed. And when Caitlin fussed and cried, Carolyn soothed with gentle touches and soft, sympathetic words.

Earlier we saw that sensitive face-to-face play, in which interactional synchrony occurs, increases babies' responsiveness to others' emotional

A father and baby engage in a sensitively tuned form of communication called interactional synchrony, in which they match emotional states, especially positive ones. Among Western infants, this style of communication predicts secure attachment.

© CHAD SPRINGER/CULTURA/CORBIS

messages and helps them regulate emotion. But moderate adult–infant coordination is a better predictor of attachment security than "tight" coordination, in which the adult responds to most infant cues (Jaffee et al., 2001). Perhaps warm, sensitive caregivers use a relaxed, flexible style of communication in which they comfortably accept and repair emotional mismatches, returning to a synchronous state.

Cultures vary in their view of sensitivity toward infants. Among the Gusii people of Kenya, mothers rarely cuddle, hug, or interact playfully with their babies, although they are very responsive to their babies' needs. Yet most Gusii infants appear securely attached (LeVine et al., 1994). This suggests that security depends on attentive caregiving, not necessarily on moment-by-moment contingent interaction. Puerto Rican mothers, who highly value obedience and socially appropriate behavior, often physically direct and limit their babies' actions—a caregiving style linked to attachment security in Puerto Rican culture (Carlson & Harwood, 2003). Yet in many Western cultures, such physical control and restriction of exploration are viewed as intrusive and predict insecurity (Belsky & Fearon, 2008; Whipple, Bernier, & Mageau, 2011).

Compared with securely attached infants, avoidant babies tend to receive overstimulating, intrusive care. Their mothers might, for example, talk energetically to them while they are looking away or falling asleep. By avoiding the mother, these infants appear to be escaping from overwhelming interaction. Resistant infants often experience inconsistent care. Their mothers are unresponsive to infant signals. Yet when the baby begins to explore, these mothers interfere, shifting the infant's attention back to themselves. As a result, the baby is overly dependent as well as angry at the mother's lack of involvement (Cassidy & Berlin, 1994; Isabella & Belsky, 1991).

Highly inadequate caregiving is a powerful predictor of disruptions in attachment. Child abuse and neglect (topics we will consider in Chapter 10) are associated with all three forms of attachment insecurity. Among maltreated infants, disorganized/disoriented attachment is especially high (Cyr et al., 2010). Persistently depressed mothers, mothers with very low marital satisfaction, and parents suffering from a traumatic event, such as serious illness or loss of a loved one, also tend to promote the uncertain behaviors of this pattern (Campbell et al., 2004; Madigan et al., 2006; Moss et al., 2005). And some mothers of disorganized/disoriented infants engage in frightening, contradictory, and unpleasant behaviors, such as looking scared, teasing the baby, holding the baby stiffly at a distance, roughly pulling the baby by the arm, or seeking reassurance from the upset child (Lyons-Ruth, Bronfman, & Parsons, 1999; Moran et al., 2008; Solomon & George, 2011). Perhaps the baby's disorganized behavior reflects a conflicted reaction to the parent, who sometimes comforts but at other times arouses fear.

INFANT CHARACTERISTICS   Because attachment is the result of a *relationship* between two partners, infant characteristics should affect how easily it is established. In Chapters 3 and 4 we saw that prematurity, birth complications, and newborn illness make caregiving more taxing. In families under stress, these difficulties are linked to attachment insecurity. In one study, the *combination* of preterm birth with either socioeconomic risk (poverty, single parenthood, high-school dropout) or maternal psychological risk (depression, high emotional stress)—but not preterm birth alone—reduced maternal sensitivity, which predicted insecure attachment at 12 months (Candelaria, Teti, & Black, 2011). Infants with special needs probably require greater parental sensitivity, which stressed parents often cannot provide. But at-risk newborns whose parents have adequate time and patience to care for them fare quite well in attachment security (Brisch et al., 2005; Cox, Hopkins, & Hans, 2000).

With respect to temperament, babies who are emotionally reactive are more likely to develop later insecure attachments (van IJzendoorn et al., 2004; Vaughn, Bost, & Van IJzendoorn, 2008). And disorganized newborn behavior, evident in scores on the Neonatal Behavioral Assessment Scale (NBAS, see Chapter 4), increases the risk of disorganized/disoriented attachment at the end of the first year (Spangler, Fremmer-Bomik, & Grossmann, 1996).

Again, however, evidence highlighting gene–environment interactions suggests that parental mental health and caregiving are involved. For example, babies with the short 5-HTTLPR gene, which is associated with emotional reactivity (see pages 258–259), are more likely than infants with a low-risk genotype to exhibit disorganized-disoriented attachment, but only when their mothers display low responsiveness or other negative parenting characteristics

(Spangler et al., 2009). In other research, mothers' experience of unresolved loss of a loved one or other trauma was associated with attachment disorganization, but only in infants with a chromosome-11 gene having a certain repetition of DNA base pairs (called DRD4 7-repeat), which is linked to impulsive, overactive behavior (Gervai, 2009; van IJzendoorn & Bakermans-Kranenburg, 2006). Babies with this genetic marker, who face special self-regulation challenges, were more susceptible to the negative impact of maternal adjustment problems.

If children's temperaments alone determined attachment quality, we would expect attachment, like temperament, to be at least moderately heritable. Yet twin comparisons reveal that the heritability of attachment is virtually nil (O'Connor & Croft, 2001; Roisman & Fraley, 2008). Rather, babies with certain genotypes are at increased risk for attachment insecurity when they also experience insensitive parenting. Consistent with this conclusion, about two-thirds of siblings establish similar attachment patterns with their parents, although the siblings often differ in temperament (Cole, 2006; Dozier et al., 2001). This suggests that most parents try to adjust their caregiving to each child's individual needs.

Interventions that teach parents to interact sensitively with difficult-to-care-for infants and toddlers enhance both sensitive care and attachment security (Velderman et al., 2006). One program that focused on both maternal sensitivity and effective discipline was particularly effective in reducing stress reactivity (as indicated by lower cortisol levels) and disruptive behavior among toddlers with the DRD4 7-repeat gene (Bakermans-Kranenburg & van IJzendoorn, 2011; Bakermans-Kranenburg et al., 2008a, 2008b). These findings suggest that the DRD4 7-repeat—like the short 5-HTTLPR gene—makes children more susceptible to the effects of both negative and positive parenting.

FAMILY CIRCUMSTANCES Shortly after Timmy's birth, his parents divorced, and his father moved to a distant city. Anxious and distracted, Vanessa placed 2-month-old Timmy in Ginette's child-care home and began working 50-hour weeks to make ends meet. On days Vanessa stayed late at the office, a babysitter picked Timmy up, gave him dinner, and put him to bed. Once or twice a week, Vanessa went to get Timmy from child care. As he neared his first birthday, Vanessa noticed that, unlike the other children, who reached out, crawled, or ran to their parents, Timmy ignored her.

Timmy's behavior reflects a repeated finding: Job loss, a failing marriage, financial difficulties, or parental psychological problems (such as anxiety or depression) can undermine attachment indirectly by interfering with parental sensitivity. These stressors can also affect babies' sense of security directly by altering the emotional climate of the family (for example, exposing them to angry adult interactions) or by disrupting familiar daily routines (Finger et al., 2009; Thompson, 2013). By reducing parental stress and improving the quality of parent–child communication, social support fosters attachment security (Moss et al., 2005). Ginette's sensitivity toward Timmy was helpful, as was the parenting advice Vanessa received from Ben, a psychologist. As Timmy turned 2, his relationship with his mother seemed warmer.

PARENTS' INTERNAL WORKING MODELS Parents bring to the family context their own history of attachment experiences, from which they construct internal working models that they apply to the bonds they establish with their babies. Monica, who recalled her mother as tense and preoccupied, expressed regret that they had not had a closer relationship. Is her image of parenthood likely to affect Grace's attachment security?

To assess parents' internal working models, researchers ask them to evaluate childhood memories of attachment experiences (Main & Goldwyn, 1998). Parents who discuss their childhoods with objectivity and balance, regardless of whether their experiences were positive or negative, tend to have securely attached infants and to behave sensitively toward them. In contrast, parents who dismiss the importance of early relationships or describe them in angry, confused ways usually have insecurely attached children and are less warm, sensitive, and encouraging of learning and mastery (Behrens, Hesse, & Main, 2007; Coyl, Newland, & Freeman, 2010; McFarland-Piazza et al., 2012; Steele, Steele, & Fonagy, 1996).

© IMAGEBROKER/ALAMY

Family circumstances are linked to attachment quality. Observing her parents' heated quarrels may undermine this child's sense of emotional security.

But we must not assume any direct transfer of parents' childhood experiences to quality of attachment with their own children. Internal working models are *reconstructed memories* affected by many factors, including relationship experiences over the life course, personality, and current life satisfaction. Longitudinal research reveals that negative life events can weaken the link between an individual's own attachment security in infancy and a secure internal working model in adulthood. And insecurely attached babies who become adults with insecure internal working models often have lives that, based on self-reports in adulthood, are filled with family crises (Waters et al., 2000; Weinfield, Sroufe, & Egeland, 2000).

In sum, our early rearing experiences do not destine us to become either sensitive or insensitive parents. Rather, the way we *view* our childhoods—our ability to come to terms with negative events, to integrate new information into our working models, and to look back on our own parents in an understanding, forgiving way—is far more influential in how we rear our children than the actual history of care we received (Bretherton & Munholland, 2008).

ATTACHMENT IN CONTEXT   Carolyn and Vanessa returned to work when their babies were 2 to 3 months old. Monica did the same a few weeks after Grace's adoption. When parents divide their time between work and parenting and place their infants and toddlers in child care, is quality of attachment and child adjustment affected? See the Social Issues: Health box on page 270 for research that addresses this issue.

After reading the box, consider each factor that influences the development of attachment—infant and parent characteristics, parents' relationship with each other, outside-the-family stressors, the availability of social supports, parents' views of their attachment history, and child-care arrangements. Although attachment builds within the warmth and intimacy of caregiver–infant interaction, it can be fully understood only from an ecological systems perspective. **TAKE A MOMENT...** Return to Chapter 1, pages 26–29, to review Bronfenbrenner's ecological systems theory. Notice how research confirms the importance of each level of the environment for attachment security.

Multiple Attachments

As we have indicated, babies develop attachments to a variety of familiar people—not just mothers, but also fathers, grandparents, siblings, and professional caregivers. Although Bowlby (1969) believed that infants are predisposed to direct their attachment behaviors to a single special person, especially when they are distressed, his theory allows for these multiple attachments.

FATHERS   An anxious, unhappy 1-year-old who is permitted to choose between the mother and the father as a source of comfort and security will usually choose the mother. But this preference typically declines over the second year. And when babies are not distressed, they approach, vocalize to, and smile equally often at both parents, who in turn are equally responsive to their infant's social bids (Bornstein, 2006; Parke, 2002).

Fathers' sensitive caregiving predicts infant attachment security, though somewhat less strongly than mothers' (Brown, Mangelsdorf, & Neff, 2012; Lucassen et al., 2011). At the same time, interventions aimed at increasing parental sensitivity and attachment security, though successful with both mothers and fathers, appear more effective with fathers (Bakermans-Kranenburg, Van IJzendoorn, & Juffer, 2003). As infancy progresses, mothers and fathers in many cultures, including Australia, Canada, Germany, India, Israel, Italy, Japan, and the United States, tend to interact differently with their babies: Mothers devote more time to physical care and expressing affection, fathers to playful interaction (Freeman & Newland, 2010; Roopnarine et al., 1990).

Also, mothers and fathers tend to play differently. Mothers more often provide toys, talk to infants, and gently play conventional games like pat-a-cake and peekaboo. In contrast, fathers—especially with their infant sons—tend to engage in highly stimulating physical play with bursts of excitement and surprise that increase as play progresses (Feldman, 2003). As long as fathers are also sensitive, this stimulating, startling play style helps babies regulate

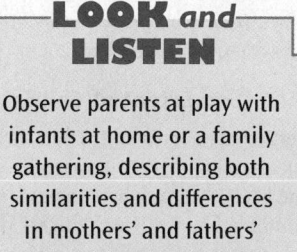

LOOK and LISTEN

Observe parents at play with infants at home or a family gathering, describing both similarities and differences in mothers' and fathers' behaviors. Are your observations consistent with research findings?

Social Issues: Health

Does Child Care Threaten Attachment Security and Later Adjustment?

Are infants who experience daily separations from their employed parents and early placement in child care at risk for attachment insecurity and developmental problems? Some researchers think so, but others disagree. Let's look closely at the evidence.

Attachment Quality

Some studies suggest that babies placed in full-time child care before 12 months of age are more likely to display insecure attachment in the Strange Situation (Belsky, 2001, 2005). But the best current evidence—from the U.S. National Institute of Child Health and Development (NICHD) Study of Early Child Care, the largest longitudinal investigation to date, including more than 1,300 infants and their families—confirms that use of nonparental care by itself does not affect attachment quality (NICHD Early Child Care Research Network, 1997, 2001). Rather, the relationship between child care and emotional well-being depends on both family and child-care experiences.

Family Circumstances

We have seen that family conditions affect children's attachment security and later adjustment. Findings of the NICHD Study confirmed that parenting quality, assessed using a combination of maternal sensitivity and HOME scores (see page 227 in Chapter 6), exerted a more powerful impact on children's adjustment than did exposure to child care (NICHD Early Childhood Research Network, 1998; Watamura et al., 2011).

For employed parents, balancing work and caregiving can be stressful. Mothers who are fatigued and anxious because they feel overloaded by work and family pressures may respond less sensitively to their babies, thereby risking the infant's security. And as paternal involvement in caregiving has risen (see page 271), many more U.S. fathers in dual-earner families also report work–family life conflict (Galinsky, Aumann, & Bond, 2009).

Quality and Extent of Child Care

Nevertheless, poor-quality child care may contribute to a higher rate of insecure attachment. In the NICHD Study, when babies were exposed to combined home and child-care risk factors—insensitive caregiving at home along with insensitive caregiving in child care, long hours in child care, or more than one child-care arrangement—the rate of insecurity increased. Overall, mother–child interaction was more favorable when

children attended higher-quality child care and also spent fewer hours in child care (NICHD Early Child Care Research Network, 1997, 1999).

Furthermore, when these children reached age 3, a history of higher-quality child care predicted better social skills (NICHD Early Child Care Research Network, 2002b). However, at age 4½ to 5, children averaging more than 30 child-care hours per week displayed more externalizing problems, especially defiance, disobedience, and aggression. For those who had been in child-care centers as opposed to family child-care homes, this outcome persisted through elementary school (Belsky et al., 2007b; NICHD Early Child Care Research Network, 2003a, 2006).

But these findings do not necessarily mean that child care causes behavior problems. Rather, heavy exposure to substandard care, which is widespread in the United States, may promote these difficulties, especially when combined with family risk factors. A closer look at the NICHD participants during the preschool years revealed that those in both poor-quality home and child-care environments fared worst in social skills and problem behaviors, whereas those in both high-quality home and child-care environments fared best. In between were preschoolers in high-quality child care but poor-quality homes (Watamura et al., 2011). These children benefited from the *protective influence* of high-quality child care.

Evidence from other industrialized nations confirms that full-time child care need not harm children's development. For example, amount of time spent in child care in Australia and Norway, which also offer high-quality, government-subsidized center-based care, is unrelated to children's behavior problems (Love et al., 2003; Zachrisson et al. 2013).

Still, some children may be particularly stressed by long child-care hours. Many infants, toddlers, and preschoolers attending child-care centers for full days show a mild increase in saliva concentrations of the stress hormone cortisol across the day—a pattern that does not occur on days they spend at home. In one study, children rated as highly fearful by their caregivers experienced an especially sharp increase in cortisol levels (Watamura et al., 2003). Inhibited children may find the constant company of large numbers of peers particularly stressful. Nevertheless, a secure attachment to a professional caregiver is protective (Badanes, Dmitrieva & Watamura, 2012). It is associated with falling cortisol levels across the child-care day.

High-quality child care, with generous caregiver–child ratios, small group sizes, and knowledgeable caregivers, can be part of a system that promotes all aspects of development, including attachment security.

Conclusions

Taken together, research suggests that some infants may be at risk for attachment insecurity and adjustment problems due to inadequate child care, long hours in such care, and the joint pressures their parents experience from full-time employment and parenthood. But it is inappropriate to use these findings to justify a reduction in child-care services. When family incomes are limited or mothers who want to work are forced to stay at home, children's emotional security is not promoted.

Instead, it makes sense to increase the availability of high-quality child care and to relieve work–family-life conflict by providing parents with paid employment leave (see page 139 in Chapter 4) and opportunities for part-time work. In the NICHD study, part-time (as opposed to full-time) employment during the baby's first year was associated with greater maternal sensitivity and a higher-quality home environment, which yielded more favorable development in early childhood (Brooks-Gunn, Han, & Waldfogel, 2010).

Finally, the professional caregiver's relationship with the baby is vital. When caregiver–child ratios are generous, group sizes are small, and caregivers are educated about child development, caregivers' interactions are more positive, their attachments to babies are more secure, and children develop more favorably—cognitively, emotionally, and socially (Biringen et al., 2012; NICHD Early Child Care Research Network, 2000b, 2002a, 2006). Child care with these characteristics can become part of an ecological system that relieves parental and child stress, thereby promoting healthy attachment and development.

emotion in intensely arousing situations and may prepare them to venture confidently into active, unpredictable contexts, including novel physical environments and play with peers (Cabrera et al., 2007; Hazen et al., 2010). In a German study, fathers' sensitive, challenging play with preschoolers predicted favorable emotional and social adjustment from kindergarten to early adulthood (Grossmann et al, 2008).

Play is a vital context in which fathers build secure attachments (Newland, Coyl, & Freeman, 2008). It may be especially influential in cultures where long work hours prevent most fathers from sharing in infant caregiving, such as Japan (Hewlett, 2004; Shwalb et al., 2004). In many Western nations, however, a strict division of parental roles—mother as caregiver, father as playmate—has changed over the past several decades in response to women's workforce participation and to cultural valuing of gender equality.

A U.S. national survey of several thousand employed workers indicated that U.S. fathers under age 29 devote about 85 percent as much time as mothers do to children—on average, just over 4 hours per workday, nearly double the hours young fathers reported three decades ago. Although fathers age 29 to 42 spend somewhat less time with children, their involvement has also increased substantially (see Figure 7.5). Today, nearly one-third of U.S. employed women say that their spouse or partner shares equally in or takes most responsibility for child-care tasks (Galinsky, Aumann, & Bond, 2009). Paternal availability to children is fairly similar across SES and ethnic groups, with one exception: Hispanic fathers spend more time engaged, probably because of the particularly high value that Hispanic cultures place on family involvement (Cabrera & García Coll, 2004; Parke et al., 2004a).

A warm marital bond and supportive coparenting (see page 69 in Chapter 2) promote both parents' sensitivity and involvement and children's attachment security, but they are especially important for fathers (Brown et al., 2010; Lamb & Lewis, 2004; Laurent, Kim, & Capaldi, 2008). See the Cultural Influences box on page 272 for cross-cultural evidence documenting this conclusion—and also highlighting the powerful role of paternal warmth in children's development.

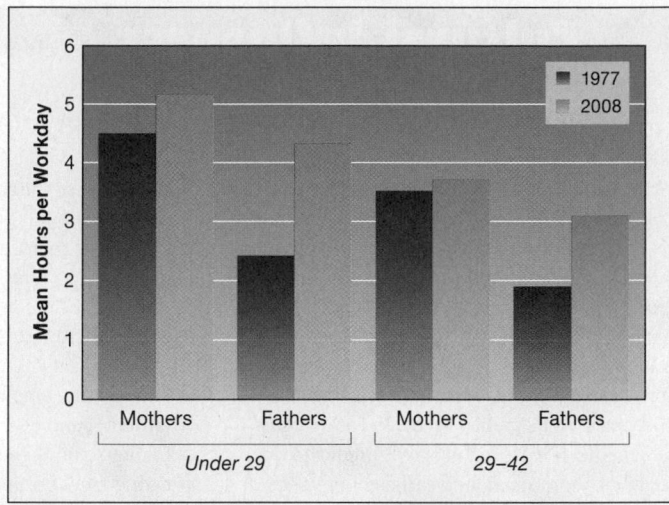

FIGURE 7.5 **Average amount of time per workday U.S. employed mothers and fathers reported spending with their children (age 12 and younger) in 1977 and 2008.** In national surveys of several thousand employed parents, mothers' time with children remained fairly stable from 1977 to 2008; fathers' time increased substantially. (Based on Galinsky, Aumann, & Bond, 2009.)

GRANDPARENT PRIMARY CAREGIVERS Nearly 2.4 million U.S. children—4 to 5 percent of the child population—live with their grandparents but apart from parents, in so-called *skipped-generation families* (U.S. Census Bureau, 2014b). The number of grandparents rearing grandchildren has increased over the past two decades. The arrangement occurs in all ethnic groups, though more often in African-American, Hispanic, and Native-American families than in Caucasian families. Although grandparent caregivers are more likely to be women than men, many grandfathers participate (Fuller-Thomson & Minkler, 2005, 2007; Minkler & Fuller-Thomson, 2005). Grandparents generally step in when parents' troubled lives—as a result of substance abuse, child abuse and neglect, mental illness, or adolescent parenthood—threaten children's well-being (Langosch, 2012). Often these families take in two or more children.

As a result, grandparents usually assume the parenting role under highly stressful life circumstances. Unfavorable child-rearing experiences have left their mark on children, who show high rates of learning difficulties, depression, and antisocial behavior. Absent parents' adjustment difficulties strain family relationships. Parents may interfere by violating the grandparents' behavioral limits, taking grandchildren away without permission, or making promises to children that they do not keep. These youngsters also introduce financial burdens into households

Despite stressful family conditions, grandparents who provide long-term physical and emotional care form deep attachments with their grandchildren.

Cultural Influences

The Powerful Role of Paternal Warmth in Development

R esearch in diverse cultures demonstrates that fathers' warmth contributes greatly to children's long-term favorable development. In studies of many societies and ethnic groups around the world, researchers coded paternal expressions of love and nurturance—evident in such behaviors as cuddling, hugging, comforting, playing, verbally expressing love, and praising the child's behavior. Fathers' sustained affectionate involvement predicted later cognitive, emotional, and social competence as strongly as did mothers' warmth—and occasionally more strongly (Rohner & Veneziano, 2001; Veneziano, 2003). And in Western cultures, paternal warmth and secure attachment are associated with children's mature social behavior and a reduction in a wide range of difficulties, including childhood emotional and behavior problems and adolescent substance abuse and delinquency (Lamb & Lewis, 2013; Michiels et al., 2010; Nelson & Coyne, 2009; Tacon & Caldera, 2001).

Fathers who devote little time to physical caregiving express warmth through play. In a German study, fathers' play sensitivity—accepting toddlers' play initiatives, adapting play behaviors to toddlers' capacities, and responding appropriately to toddlers' expressions of emotion—predicted children's secure internal working models of attachment during middle childhood and adolescence (Grossmann et al., 2002). Through play, fathers seemed to transfer to young children

a sense of confidence about parental support, which may strengthen their capacity to master many later challenges.

What factors promote paternal warmth? Cross-cultural research reveals a consistent association between the amount of time fathers spend near infants and toddlers and their expressions of caring and affection (Rohner & Veneziano, 2001). Consider the Aka hunters and gatherers of Central Africa, where fathers spend more time in physical proximity to their babies than in any other known society. Observations reveal that Aka fathers are within arm's reach of infants more than half the day. They pick up, cuddle, and play with their babies at least five times as often as fathers in other hunting-and-gathering societies. Why are Aka fathers so involved? The bond between Aka husband and wife is unusually cooperative and intimate. Throughout the day, couples share hunting, food preparation, and social and leisure activities (Hewlett, 1992). The more Aka parents are together, the greater the father's loving interaction with his baby.

In Western cultures as well, happily married fathers whose partners coparent effectively with

In both Western and non-Western nations, paternal warmth predicts long-term favorable cognitive, emotional, and social development.

them spend more time with and interact more effectively with their infants. In contrast, marital dissatisfaction is associated with insensitive paternal care (Brown et al., 2010; Lundy, 2002; Sevigny & Loutzenhiser, 2010). Clearly, fathers' warm relationships with their partners and with their babies are closely linked. Evidence for the power of fathers' affection, reported in virtually every culture and ethnic group studied, is reason to encourage more men to engage in nurturing care of young children.

that often are already low-income (Mills, Gomez-Smith, & De Leon, 2005; Williamson, Softas-Nall, & Miller, 2003). And grandparent caregivers, at a time when they anticipated having more time for spouses, friends, and leisure, instead have less. Many report feeling emotionally drained, depressed, and worried about what will happen to the children if their own health fails (Hayslip & Kaminski, 2005; Langosch, 2012).

Nevertheless, because they provide physical and emotional care for an extended time and are invested in the child's well-being, grandparent caregivers forge significant attachment relationships with their grandchildren (Poehlmann, 2003). Warm grandparent–grandchild bonds help protect children from worsening adjustment problems, even under conditions of great hardship (Hicks & Goedereis, 2009). Still, grandparent caregivers have a tremendous need for social and financial support and intervention services for their at-risk grandchildren.

SIBLINGS   Despite declines in family size, 80 percent of North American and European children grow up with at least one sibling (Dunn, 2004). The arrival of a new baby is a difficult experience for most preschoolers, who—realizing that they must now share their parents' attention and affection—often become demanding, clingy, deliberately naughty, and less affectionate with their parents for a time. Attachment security also typically declines, especially for children over age 2 (old enough to feel threatened and displaced) and for those with mothers under stress (Teti et al., 1996; Volling, 2012).

Applying What We Know

Encouraging Affectionate Ties Between Infants and Their Preschool Siblings

SUGGESTION	DESCRIPTION
Spend extra time with the older child.	Parents can minimize the older child's feelings of being deprived of affection and attention by setting aside time to spend with her. Fathers can be especially helpful, planning special outings with the preschooler and taking over care of the baby so the mother can be with the older child.
Handle sibling misbehavior with patience.	When parents respond patiently to the older sibling's misbehavior and demands for attention, these reactions are usually temporary. Parents can give the preschooler opportunities to feel proud of being more grown-up than the baby—for example, by encouraging the older child to assist with feeding, bathing, dressing, and offering toys, and showing appreciation for these efforts.
Discuss the baby's wants and needs.	By helping the older sibling understand the baby's point of view, parents can promote friendly, considerate behavior. They can say, for example, "He's so little that he just can't wait to be fed" or "He's trying to reach his rattle, and he can't."
Express positive emotion toward your partner and engage in joint problem solving.	When parents mutually support each other's parenting behavior, their good communication helps the older sibling cope adaptively with jealousy and conflict.

Yet resentment is only one feature of the rich emotional relationship that starts to build between siblings after a baby's birth. Older children also show affection and concern—kissing and patting the baby and calling out, "Mom, he needs you," when the infant cries. By the end of the first year, babies typically spend much time with older siblings and are comforted by the presence of a preschool-age brother or sister during short parental absences. Throughout childhood, children continue to treat older siblings as attachment figures, turning to them for comfort in stressful situations when parents are unavailable (Seibert & Kerns, 2009). And in the second year, as toddlers imitate and join in play with their brothers and sisters, siblings start to become gratifying sources of companionship (Barr & Hayne, 2003).

Nevertheless, individual differences in sibling relationships emerge soon after the new baby's arrival. Temperament plays an important role. For example, conflict is greater when one sibling is emotionally intense or highly active (Brody, Stoneman, & McCoy, 1994; Dunn, 1994). And maternal warmth toward both children is related to positive sibling interaction and to preschoolers' support of a distressed younger sibling (Volling, 2001; Volling & Belsky, 1992). Mothers who frequently play with their children and explain the toddler's wants and needs to the preschool sibling foster sibling cooperation. In contrast, maternal harshness and lack of involvement are linked to antagonistic sibling relationships (Howe, Aquan-Assee, & Bukowski, 2001).

Finally, a good marriage is correlated with older preschool siblings' capacity to cope adaptively with jealousy and conflict (Volling, McElwain, & Miller, 2002). Perhaps good communication between parents serves as a model of effective problem solving. It may also foster a generally happy family environment, giving children less reason to feel jealous.

Refer to Applying What We Know above for ways to promote positive relationships between babies and their preschool siblings. Siblings offer a rich social context in which children learn and practice a wide range of skills, including affectionate caring, conflict resolution, and control of hostile and envious feelings.

© ELLEN B. SENISI

The arrival of a baby brother or sister is a difficult experience for most preschoolers. Maternal warmth toward both children assures the older sibling of continuing parental love, models affectionate caring, and is related to positive sibling interaction.

Advances in peer sociability during the second year are evident in toddlers' coordinated interaction, mostly in the form of mutual imitation.

From Attachment to Peer Sociability

In cultures where agemates have regular contact during the first year of life, peer sociability begins early. By age 6 months, Caitlin and Timmy occasionally looked, reached, smiled, and babbled when they saw each other. These isolated social acts increased until, by the end of the first year, an occasional reciprocal exchange occurred in which the children grinned, gestured, or otherwise imitated a playmate's behavior (Vandell & Mueller, 1995).

Between 1 and 2 years, as toddlers appreciate that others have intentions, desires, and emotions distinct from their own, they increasingly view one another as playmates (Brownell & Kopp, 2007). As a result, coordinated interaction occurs more often, largely in the form of offering each other objects, sharing positive emotions, and mutual imitation involving jumping, chasing, or banging a toy (Vandell et al., 2006; Williams, Mastergeorge, & Ontai, 2010). These exchanges promote peer engagement and create joint understandings that aid verbal communication.

Around age 2, toddlers use words to talk about and influence a peer's behavior, as when Caitlin said to Grace, "Let's play chase," and after the game got going, "Hey, good running!" (Eckerman & Peterman, 2001). Reciprocal play and positive emotion are especially frequent in toddlers' interactions with familiar agemates, suggesting that they are building true peer relationships (Ross et al., 1992).

Though limited, peer sociability is present in the first two years and is promoted by the early caregiver–child bond. From interacting with sensitive adults, babies learn how to send and interpret emotional signals in their first peer associations (Trevarthen, 2003). Toddlers who have a warm parental relationship or who attend high-quality child care with a small group size and a generous caregiver–child ratio—features that promote warm, stimulating caregiving and gentle support for engaging with peers—display more positive and extended peer exchanges. These children, in turn, display more socially competent behavior as preschoolers (Deynoot-Schaub & Riksen-Walraven, 2006a, 2006b; Howes & Matheson, 1992; Williams, Mastergeorge, & Ontai, 2010).

Attachment and Later Development

According to psychoanalytic and ethological theories, the inner feelings of affection and security that result from a healthy attachment relationship support all aspects of psychological development. Consistent with this view, an extended longitudinal study found that preschoolers who had been securely attached as babies were rated by their teachers as higher in self-esteem, social skills, and empathy than were their insecurely attached counterparts, who displayed more behavior problems. When studied again at age 11 in summer camp, children who had been secure infants had more favorable relationships with peers, closer friendships, and better social skills, as judged by camp counselors. And as these well-functioning school-age children became adolescents and young adults, they continued to benefit from more supportive social networks, formed more stable and gratifying romantic relationships, and attained higher levels of education (Elicker, Englund, & Sroufe, 1992; Sroufe, 2002; Sroufe et al., 2005).

For some researchers, these findings indicate that secure attachment in infancy causes improved cognitive, emotional, and social competence in later years. Yet contrary evidence exists. In other longitudinal studies, secure infants generally fared better than insecure infants, but not always (Fearon et al., 2010; McCartney et al., 2004; Schneider, Atkinson, & Tardif, 2001; Stams, Juffer, & van IJzendoorn, 2002).

What accounts for the inconsistency in research findings on the consequences of early attachment quality? Mounting evidence indicates that *continuity of caregiving* determines whether attachment security is linked to later development (Lamb et al., 1985; Thompson, 2013). Children whose parents respond sensitively not just in infancy but also in later years are likely to develop favorably. In contrast, children whose parents react insensitively or who, over a long period, are exposed to a negative family climate tend to establish lasting patterns of avoidant, resistant, or disorganized behavior and are at greater risk for developmental difficulties.

A close look at the relationship between parenting and children's adjustment in the first few years supports this emphasis on continuity of caregiving. Disorganized/disoriented attachment, a pattern associated with serious parental psychological problems and highly maladaptive caregiving, is strongly linked to internalizing and externalizing difficulties in childhood (Lyons-Ruth, Bronfman, & Parsons, 1999; Moss, Cyr, & Dubois-Comtois, 2004; Moss et al., 2006). And when a large sample of children were tracked from age 1 to 3 years, those with histories of secure attachment followed by sensitive parenting scored highest in cognitive, emotional, and social outcomes. Those with histories of insecure attachment followed by insensitive parenting scored lowest, while those with mixed histories of attachment and maternal sensitivity scored in between (Belsky & Fearon, 2002). Specifically, insecurely attached infants whose mothers became more positive and supportive in early childhood showed signs of developmental recovery.

Does this trend remind you of our discussion of *resilience* in Chapter 1? A child whose parental caregiving improves or who has other compensating affectionate ties can bounce back from adversity. In contrast, a child who experiences tender care in infancy but lacks sympathetic ties later on is at risk for problems.

Although a secure attachment in infancy does not guarantee continued good parenting, it does launch the parent–child relationship on a positive path. An early warm, positive parent–child tie, sustained over time, promotes many aspects of children's development: a more confident and complex self-concept, more advanced emotional understanding, better emotional self-regulation, more effective social skills, a stronger sense of moral responsibility, and higher motivation to achieve in school (Drake, Belsky, & Fearon, 2014; Groh et al., 2014; Thompson, 2013). But the effects of early attachment security are *conditional*—dependent on the quality of the baby's future relationships. Finally, as we will see again in future chapters, attachment is just one of the complex influences on children's psychological development.

Ask Yourself

- **REVIEW** What factors explain stability in attachment pattern for some children and change for others? Are these factors also involved in the link between attachment in infancy and later development? Explain.

- **CONNECT** Review research on emotional self-regulation on pages 252–253. How do the caregiving experiences of securely attached infants promote the development of emotional self-regulation?

- **APPLY** What attachment pattern did Timmy display when Vanessa picked him up from child care, and what factors probably contributed to it?

- **REFLECT** How would you characterize your internal working model? What factors, in addition to your early relationship with your parents, might have influenced it?

Self-Development

Infancy is a rich formative period for the development of physical and social understanding. In Chapter 6, you learned that infants develop an appreciation of the permanence of objects. And in this chapter, we have seen that over the first year, infants recognize and respond appropriately to others' emotions and distinguish familiar from unfamiliar people. That both objects and people achieve an independent, stable existence for the infant implies that knowledge of the self as a separate, permanent entity is also emerging.

7.10 Describe the development of self-awareness in infancy and toddlerhood, along with the emotional and social capacities it supports.

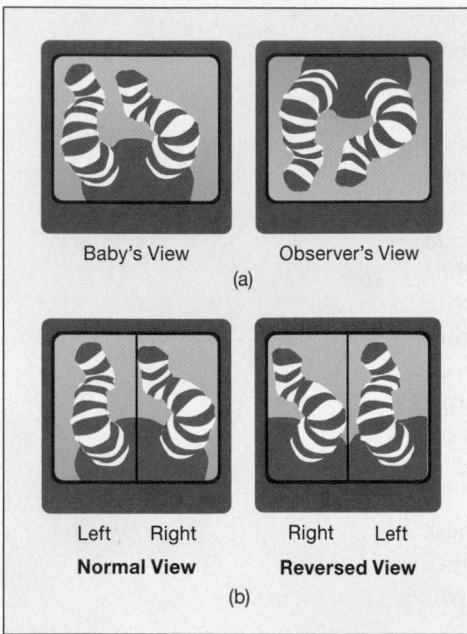

FIGURE 7.6   Three-month-olds' emerging self-awareness, as indicated by reactions to video images. (a) When shown two side-by-side views of their kicking legs, babies looked longer at the novel, observer's view than at their own view. (b) When shown a normal view of their leg positions alongside a reversed view, infants looked longer at the novel, reversed view. (Based on Rochat, 1998.)

This 18-month-old makes silly faces in a mirror, a playful response to her reflection that indicates she is aware of herself as a separate being and recognizes her unique physical features.

Self-Awareness

After Caitlin's bath, Carolyn often held her in front of the bathroom mirror. As early as the first few months, Caitlin smiled and returned friendly behaviors to her image. At what age did she realize that the charming baby gazing and grinning back was herself?

BEGINNINGS OF SELF-AWARENESS   At birth, infants sense that they are physically distinct from their surroundings. For example, newborns display a stronger rooting reflex in response to external stimulation (an adult's finger touching their cheek) than to self-stimulation (their own hand contacting their cheek) (Rochat & Hespos, 1997). Newborns' remarkable capacity for intermodal perception (see page 195 in Chapter 5) supports the beginnings of self-awareness (Rochat, 2013). As they feel their own touch, feel and watch their limbs move, and feel and hear themselves cry, babies experience intermodal matches that differentiate their own body from surrounding bodies and objects.

Over the first few months, infants distinguish their own visual image from other stimuli, but their self-awareness is limited—expressed only in perception and action. When shown two side-by-side video images of their kicking legs, one from their own perspective (camera behind the baby) and one from an observer's perspective (camera in front of the baby), 3-month-olds looked longer at the observer's view (see Figure 7.6a). In another video-image comparison, they looked longer at a reversal of their leg positions than at a normal view (see Figure 7.6b) (Rochat, 1998). This suggests that young babies have a sense of their own body as a distinct entity, since they have habituated to it, as indicated by their interest in novel views of the body. By 4 months, infants look and smile more at video images of others than video images of themselves (Rochat & Striano, 2002). This indicates that they distinguish between the two and treat another person (as opposed to the self) as a potential social partner.

This discrimination of one's own limb and facial movements from those of others in real-time video presentations reflects an *implicit sense of self–world differentiation*. Implicit self-awareness is also evident in young infants' social expectations—for example, in protest or withdrawal when face-to-face interaction with a responsive adult is disrupted (see page 249). As early as 2 months, infants display a sense of their own agency in relation to other people. These early signs of self-experience serve as the foundation for development of *explicit self-awareness*: an objective understanding that the self is a unique object in a world of objects, which includes representations of one's own physical features and body dimensions.

EXPLICIT SELF-AWARENESS   During the second year, toddlers become consciously aware of the self's physical features. In several studies, 9- to 28-month-olds were placed in front of a mirror. Then, under the pretext of wiping the baby's face, each mother rubbed red dye on her child's nose or forehead. Younger babies touched the mirror as if the red mark had nothing to do with them. But the majority of those older than 18 to 20 months touched or rubbed their strange-looking noses or foreheads, a response indicating clear awareness of their unique facial appearance (Bard et al., 2006; Lewis & Brooks-Gunn, 1979). And some toddlers act silly or coy in front of the mirror, playfully experimenting with the way the self looks (Bullock & Lutkenhaus, 1990).

Around age 2, *self-recognition*—identification of the self as a physically unique being—is well under way. Children point to themselves in photos and refer to themselves by name or with a personal pronoun ("I" or "me") (Lewis & Ramsay, 2004). And soon they will identify themselves in images with less detail and fidelity than mirrors. Around age 2½, most reach for a sticker surreptitiously placed on top of their heads when shown themselves in a live video, and around age 3 most recognize their own shadow (Cameron & Gallup, 1988; Suddendorf, Simcock, & Nielsen, 2007).

As self-recognition takes shape, older toddlers also construct an explicit *body self-awareness*. At the end of the second year, they realize that their own body can serve as an obstacle. When asked to push a shopping cart while standing on a mat attached to its rear axle, most 18- to 21-month-olds (but not younger children) figured out how to remove themselves from the mat so the cart would move—an ability that improved with age (Moore et al., 2007).

Nevertheless, toddlers make **scale errors,** attempting to do things that their body size makes impossible. For example, they will try to put on dolls' clothes, sit in a doll-sized chair or walk through a doorway too narrow for them to pass through (Brownell, Zerwas, & Ramani, 2007; DeLoache, Uttal, & Rosengren, 2004). They are amazingly persistent, even seeking an adult's help after they repeatedly do not succeed! Possibly, toddlers lack an accurate understanding of their own body dimensions. Alternatively, they may simply be exploring the consequences of squeezing into restricted spaces, as they are far less likely to try when the risk of harming themselves is high (for example, if the too-narrow doorway is next to a ledge where they could fall) (Franchak & Adolph, 2012). Scale errors decline between ages 2 and 3½. Young preschoolers are still learning to process physical information when acting with their own bodies.

INFLUENCES ON SELF-AWARENESS What experiences contribute to gains in self-awareness? During the first year, as infants act on the environment, they probably notice effects that help them sort out self, other people, and objects (Nadel, Prepin, & Okanda, 2005; Rochat, 2001). For example, batting a mobile and seeing it swing in a pattern different from the infant's own actions gives the baby information about the relation between self and physical world. Smiling and vocalizing at a caregiver who smiles and vocalizes back helps specify the relation between self and social world. And watching the movements of one's own hands and feet provides still another kind of feedback—one under much more direct control than the movements of other people or objects. The contrast between these experiences helps infants sense that they are separate from external reality.

Researchers do not yet know exactly how toddlers acquire the various aspects of explicit self-awareness. But sensitive caregiving seems to play a role. Compared to their insecurely attached agemates, securely attached toddlers display more complex self-related actions during play, such as making a doll labeled as the self take a drink or kiss a teddy bear. They also show greater knowledge of their own physical features—for example, in labeling body parts (Pipp, Easterbrooks, & Brown, 1993; Pipp, Easterbrooks, & Harmon, 1992). And 18-month-olds who often establish joint attention with their caregivers are advanced in mirror self-recognition (Nichols, Fox, & Mundy, 2005). Joint attention offers toddlers many opportunities to engage in social referencing—to compare their own and others' reactions to objects and events—which may enhance toddlers' awareness of their own physical uniqueness.

Cultural variations exist in early self-development. In one investigation, urban middle-SES German and East Indian toddlers attained mirror self-recognition earlier than toddlers of non-Western farming communities, such as the Nso people of rural Cameroon and rural families of East India (see Figure 7.7) (Kärtner et al., 2012). Urban German and, to a lesser extent, urban East Indian mothers placed considerable emphasis on *autonomous child-rearing goals,* including promoting personal talents and interests and expressing one's own preferences, which strongly predicted earlier mirror self-recognition. In contrast, Nso and East Indian rural mothers valued *relational child rearing goals*—doing what parents say and sharing with others. In related research, Nso toddlers, though delayed in mirror self-recognition, displayed an earlier capacity to comply with adult requests than did middle-SES urban Greek toddlers, whose mothers encouraged child autonomy (Keller et al., 2004).

LOOK and LISTEN

Ask several parents of 1½- to 3-year-olds if they have observed any instances of scale errors. Have the parent hand the toddler doll-sized clothing (hat, jacket, or shoe) or furniture (table, slide, or car) and watch for scale errors.

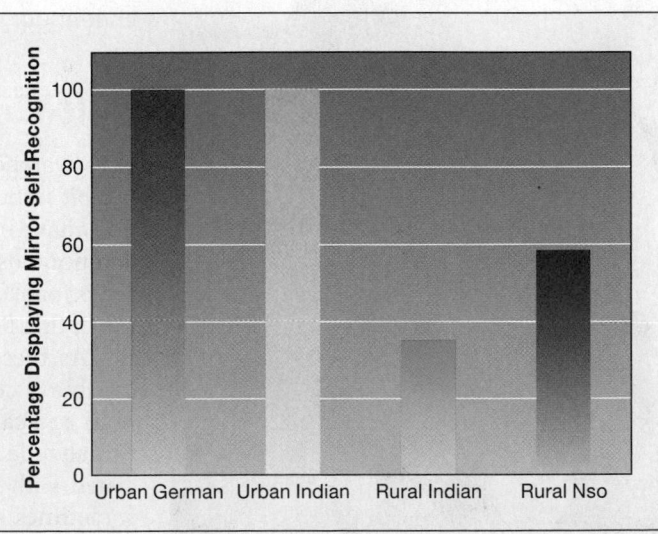

FIGURE 7.7 Mirror self-recognition at 19 months in four cultures. Urban middle-SES German and East Indian toddlers attained mirror self-recognition earlier than Nso toddlers of rural Cameroon and toddlers of rural East India—a finding that held even after toddlers were provided considerable experience in seeing themselves in mirrors. Urban German and East Indian mothers emphasized autonomous child-rearing goals, which strongly predicted earlier self-recognition. In contrast, rural Nso and East Indian mothers valued relational child-rearing goals. (Based on Kärtner et al., 2012.)

SELF-AWARENESS AND EARLY EMOTIONAL AND SOCIAL DEVELOPMENT   Self-awareness quickly becomes a central part of children's emotional and social lives. Recall that self-conscious emotions depend on a strengthening sense of self. Self-awareness also leads to first efforts to understand another's perspective. We have seen that toddlers increasingly appreciate others' intentions, feelings, and desires. Older toddlers who have experienced sensitive caregiving and emotionally available parents draw on their advancing capacity to distinguish what happens to oneself from what happens to others to express first signs of **empathy**—the ability to understand another's emotional state and feel with that person, or respond emotionally in a similar way. For example, they communicate concern when others are distressed and may offer what they themselves find comforting—a hug, a reassuring comment, or a favorite doll or blanket (Hoffman, 2000; Moreno, Klute, & Robinson, 2008).

At the same time, toddlers demonstrate clearer awareness of how to upset others. One 18-month-old heard her mother talking to another adult about an older sibling: "Anny is really frightened of spiders. In fact, there's a particular toy spider that we've got that she just hates" (Dunn, 1989, p. 107). The innocent-looking toddler ran to the bedroom, returned with the toy spider, and pushed it in front of Anny's face!

Categorizing the Self

By the end of the second year, language becomes a powerful tool in self-development. Between 18 and 30 months, children develop a **categorical self** as they classify themselves and others on the basis of age ("baby," "boy," or "man"), sex ("boy" or "girl"), physical characteristics ("big," "strong"), and even goodness and badness ("I good girl." "Tommy mean!"). They also start to refer to the self's competencies ("Did it!" "I can't") (Stipek, Gralinski, & Kopp, 1990).

Toddlers use their limited understanding of these social categories to organize their own behavior. As early as 17 months, children select and play in a more involved way with toys that are stereotyped for their own gender—dolls and tea sets for girls, trucks and cars for boys. Their ability to label their own gender predicts a sharp rise in these play preferences over the next few months (Zosuls et al., 2009). Then parents encourage gender-typed behavior by responding more positively when toddlers display it (Ruble, Martin, & Berenbaum, 2006). As we will see in Chapter 10, gender typing increases dramatically during early childhood.

Self-Control

Self-awareness also contributes to *effortful control*, the extent to which children can inhibit impulses, manage negative emotion, and behave in socially acceptable ways. To behave in a self-controlled fashion, children must think of themselves as separate, autonomous beings who can direct their own actions. And they must have the representational and memory capacities to recall a caregiver's directive ("Caitlin, don't touch that light socket!") and apply it to their own behavior.

As these capacities emerge between 12 and 18 months, toddlers first become capable of **compliance:** They show clear awareness of caregivers' wishes and expectations and can obey simple requests and commands. And, as every parent knows, they can also decide to do just the opposite! Although defiance in preschoolers is associated with negative parent–child relationships and poor adjustment, toddlers who sometimes strongly resist parental demands tend to have sensitive, supportive parents with whom they interact positively. These parents recognize the young child's need for self-assertion and autonomy (Dix et al., 2007).

Indeed, active resistance in toddlerhood does not predict later, persisting defiance. Rather, for most toddlers, assertiveness and opposition occur alongside compliance with an eager, willing spirit, which suggests that the child is beginning to adopt the adult's directives as his own (Kochanska, Murray, & Harlan, 2000). Compliance quickly leads to toddlers' first consciencelike verbalizations—for example, correcting the self by saying "No, can't" before reaching for a treat or jumping on the sofa.

SW PRODUCTIONS/PHOTODISC GREEN/GETTY IMAGES

This father encourages compliance and the beginnings of self-control. The toddler joins in the task with an eager, willing spirit, which suggests he is adopting the adult's directive as his own.

Applying What We Know

Helping Toddlers Develop Compliance and Self-Control

SUGGESTION	RATIONALE
Respond to the toddler with sensitivity and encouragement.	Toddlers whose parents are sensitive and supportive at times actively resist, but they are also are more compliant and self-controlled.
Provide advance notice when the toddler must stop an enjoyable activity.	Toddlers find it more difficult to stop a pleasant activity that is already under way than to wait before engaging in a desired action.
Offer many prompts and reminders.	Toddlers' ability to remember and comply with rules is limited; they need continuous adult oversight and patient assistance.
Respond to self-controlled behavior with verbal and physical approval.	Praise and hugs reinforce appropriate behavior, increasing the likelihood that it will occur again.
Encourage selective and sustained attention (see Chapter 6, page 217).	Development of attention is related to self-control. Children who can shift attention from a captivating stimulus and focus on a less attractive alternative are better at controlling their impulses.
Support language development (see Chapter 6, pages 240–241).	Early language development is related to self-control. In the second year, children begin to use language to remind themselves of adult expectations and to delay gratification.
Gradually increase rules in a manner consistent with the toddler's developing capacities.	As cognition and language improve, toddlers can follow more rules related to safety, respect for people and property, family routines, manners, and simple chores.

Researchers often study the early emergence of self-control by giving children tasks that, like the situations just mentioned, require **delay of gratification**—waiting for an appropriate time and place to engage in a tempting act. Between ages 1½ and 4, children show an increasing capacity to wait before eating a treat, opening a present, or playing with a toy (Cole, LeDonne, & Tan, 2013; Vaughn, Kopp, & Krakow, 1984). Children who are advanced in development of attention, language, and suppressing negative emotion tend to be better at delaying gratification—findings that help explain why girls are typically more self-controlled than boys (Else-Quest et al., 2012). Some toddlers already use verbal and other attention-diverting techniques—talking to themselves, singing, or looking away—to keep from engaging in prohibited acts.

Like effortful control in general, young children's capacity to delay gratification is influenced by both temperament and quality of caregiving (Kochanska & Aksan, 2006; Kochanska & Knaack, 2003). Inhibited children find it easier to wait than angry, irritable children do. But toddlers and preschoolers who experience parental warmth and gentle encouragement are more likely to be cooperative and to resist temptation. Such parenting—which encourages and models patient, nonimpulsive behavior—is particularly important for temperamentally reactive babies and preschoolers (Kochanska, Aksan, & Carlson, 2005; Kochanska & Kim, 2013). **TAKE A MOMENT...** Turn back to page 260, and note how these findings provide yet another example of the importance of goodness of fit between temperament and child rearing.

As self-control improves, parents gradually expand the rules they expect toddlers to follow, from safety and respect for property and people to family routines, manners, and simple chores (Gralinski & Kopp, 1993). Still, toddlers' control over their own actions depends on constant parental oversight and reminders. Several prompts ("Remember, we're going to go in just a minute") and gentle insistence were usually necessary to get Caitlin to stop playing so that she and her parents could go on an errand. Applying What We Know above summarizes ways to help toddlers develop compliance and self-control.

As the second year of life drew to a close, Carolyn, Monica, and Vanessa were delighted at their children's readiness to learn the rules of social life. As we will see in Chapter 10, advances in cognition and language, along with parental warmth and reasonable demands for maturity, lead preschoolers to make tremendous strides in this area.

Ask Yourself

- **REVIEW** Why is insisting that infants comply with parental directives inappropriate? What competencies are necessary for the emergence of compliance and self-control?

- **CONNECT** What type of early parenting fosters the development of emotional self-regulation, secure attachment, and self-control? Why, in each instance, is it effective?

- **APPLY** Len, a caregiver of 1- and 2-year-olds, wonders whether toddlers recognize themselves. List signs of self-recognition in the second year that Len can observe. What behaviors reveal that toddlers are still forming objective representations of their own physical features?

- **REFLECT** In view of research on toddlers' compliance, active resistance, and budding capacity to delay gratification, do you think that "the terrible twos," a commonly used expression to characterize typical toddler behavior, is an apt description? Explain.

Summary

Erikson's Theory of Infant and Toddler Personality (p. 246)

7.1 What personality changes take place during Erikson's stages of basic trust versus mistrust and autonomy versus shame and doubt?

- Warm, responsive caregiving leads infants to resolve Erikson's psychological conflict of **basic trust versus mistrust** on the positive side. During toddlerhood, **autonomy versus shame and doubt** is resolved favorably when parents provide appropriate guidance and reasonable choices. If children emerge from the first few years without sufficient trust and autonomy, the seeds are sown for adjustment problems.

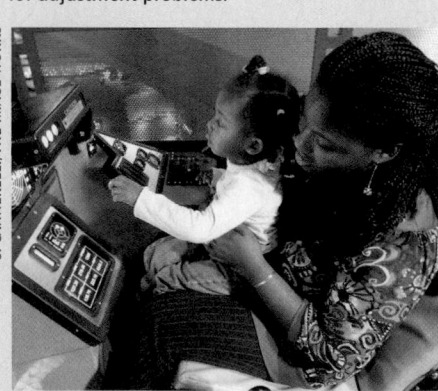

Emotional Development (p. 247)

7.2 Describe the development of basic emotions over the first year, noting the adaptive function of each.

- During the first half-year, **basic emotions** gradually become clear, well-organized signals. The **social smile** appears between 6 and 10 weeks, laughter around 3 to 4 months. Happiness strengthens the parent–child bond and reflects as well as supports physical and cognitive mastery.

- Anger and fear, especially in the form of **stranger anxiety,** increase in the second half of the first year as infants' cognitive and motor capacities improve. Newly mobile babies use the familiar caregiver as a **secure base** from which to explore.

7.3 Summarize changes during the first two years in understanding others' emotions, self-conscious emotions, and emotional self-regulation.

- The ability to understand others' emotional expressions expands over the first year. Beginning at 8 to 10 months, infants engage in **social referencing.** By the middle of the second year, infants become aware that others' emotional reactions may differ from their own.

- During toddlerhood, self-awareness and adult instruction provide the foundation for **self-conscious emotions:** guilt, shame, embarrassment, envy, and pride. **Emotional self-regulation** emerges as the prefrontal cortex functions more effectively and as caregivers sensitively assist infants in adjusting their emotional reactions. In the second year, growth in representation and language leads to more effective ways of regulating emotion.

Temperament and Development (p. 253)

7.4 What is temperament, and how is it measured?

- Children differ greatly in **temperament**—early appearing, stable individual differences in reactivity and self-regulation. The New York Longitudinal Study identified three patterns: the **easy child,** the **difficult child,** and the **slow-to-warm-up child.** The most influential model of temperament, devised by Mary Rothbart, includes dimensions representing emotion, attention, and action, along with **effortful control,** the ability to regulate one's reactivity.

- Temperament is assessed through parental reports, behavior ratings by others familiar with the child, and laboratory observations. Most neurobiological research has focused on distinguishing **inhibited, or shy, children** from **uninhibited, or sociable, children.**

7.5 Discuss the roles of heredity and environment in the stability of temperament, including the goodness-of-fit model.

- Temperament has low to moderate stability: It develops with age and can be modified by experience. Long-term prediction from early temperament is best achieved after age 3, when children improve substantially in effortful control.

- Temperament has a genetic foundation, but child rearing and cultural beliefs and practices have much to do with maintaining or changing it. Children with the short 5-HTTLPR gene, which heightens risk of negative mood, fearfulness, and self-regulation difficulties, are more susceptible to the effects of rearing experiences: They function worse than other children when exposed to inept parenting but benefit most from good parenting. Parents tend to emphasize temperamental differences between siblings.

- According to the **goodness-of-fit model,** parenting practices that fit well with the child's temperament help children achieve more adaptive functioning.

Development of Attachment

(p. 261)

7.6 *What are the unique features of ethological theory of attachment?*

- **Ethological theory,** the most widely accepted perspective on **attachment,** recognizes the infant's emotional tie to the caregiver as an evolved response that promotes survival. In early infancy, a set of built-in behaviors encourages the parent to remain close to the baby.

- Around 6 to 8 months, **separation anxiety** and use of the parent as a secure base indicate the existence of a true attachment bond. As representation and language develop, separation anxiety declines. From early caregiving experiences, children construct an **internal working model** that guides future close relationships.

7.7 *Cite the four attachment patterns assessed by the Strange Situation and the Attachment Q-Sort, and discuss factors that affect attachment security.*

- Using the **Strange Situation,** a laboratory technique for measuring the quality of attachment between 1 and 2 years of age, researchers have identified four attachment patterns: **secure, insecure-avoidant, insecure-resistant,** and **disorganized/disoriented attachment.** The **Attachment Q-Sort,** based on home observations of children between ages 1 and 5, yields a score ranging from low to high security.

- Securely attached babies in middle-SES families with favorable life conditions more often maintain their attachment pattern than insecure babies. However, the disorganized/disoriented pattern is highly stable. Cultural conditions must be considered in interpreting the meaning of attachment patterns.

- Attachment security is influenced by early availability of a consistent caregiver, quality of caregiving, the fit between the baby's temperament and parenting practices, and family circumstances. **Sensitive caregiving** is moderately related to secure attachment. In Western cultures, **interactional synchrony** characterizes the experiences of securely attached babies.

- Parents' internal working models are good predictors of infant attachment patterns. However, parents' childhood experiences do not transfer directly to quality of attachment with their own children.

7.8 *Discuss infants' formation of multiple attachments, and indicate how attachment paves the way for early peer sociability.*

- Infants develop strong affectionate ties to fathers, who tend to engage in more exciting, physical play than do mothers. Especially in cultures where fathers devote little time to infant care, play is a vital context in which fathers and babies build secure attachments, predicting favorable emotional and social adjustment.

© CHAD SPRINGER/CULTURA/CORBIS

- Grandparents who serve as primary caregivers for grandchildren forge significant attachment ties that help protect children with troubled family lives from adjustment problems.

- Early in the first year, infants start to form rich emotional relationships with siblings that combine rivalry and resentment with affection and sympathetic concern. Individual differences in quality of sibling relationships are influenced by temperament, parenting, and marital quality.

- Peer sociability begins in infancy with isolated social acts, followed by reciprocal exchanges (largely in the form of mutual imitation) in the second year of life. A warm caregiver–child bond promotes peer sociability.

7.9 *Describe and interpret the relationship between secure attachment in infancy and psychological development in childhood.*

- Continuity of caregiving determines whether attachment security is linked to later development. If caregiving improves, children can recover from an insecure attachment history.

Self-Development (p. 275)

7.10 *Describe the development of self-awareness in infancy and toddlerhood, along with the emotional and social capacities it supports.*

- At birth, infants sense that they are physically distinct from their surroundings, an implicit self-awareness that expands over the early months and serves as the foundation for explicit self-awareness. In the middle of the second year, self-recognition emerges as toddlers become consciously aware of the self's physical features. However, toddlers make **scale errors,** attempting to do things their body size makes impossible.

- Self-awareness leads to toddlers' first efforts to appreciate others' perspectives, including early signs of **empathy.** Between 18 and 30 months, as language develops, children develop a **categorical self,** classifying themselves and others on the basis of age, sex, physical characteristics, and competencies.

- Self-awareness also contributes to gains in self-control. **Compliance** emerges between 12 and 18 months, followed by **delay of gratification,** which strengthens between 1½ and 4 years. Toddlers who experience parental warmth and gentle encouragement are likely to be advanced in self-control.

Important Terms and Concepts

attachment (p. 261)
Attachment Q-Sort (p. 264)
autonomy versus shame and doubt (p. 246)
basic emotions (p. 247)
basic trust versus mistrust (p. 246)
categorical self (p. 278)
compliance (p. 278)
delay of gratification (p. 279)
difficult child (p. 254)
disorganized/disoriented attachment (p. 264)
easy child (p. 254)
effortful control (p. 254)

emotional self-regulation (p. 252)
empathy (p. 278)
ethological theory of attachment (p. 261)
goodness-of-fit model (p. 259)
inhibited, or shy, child (p. 255)
insecure–avoidant attachment (p. 264)
insecure–resistant attachment (p. 264)
interactional synchrony (p. 266)
internal working model (p. 262)
scale errors (p. 277)
secure attachment (p. 264)
secure base (p. 250)

self-conscious emotions (p. 251)
sensitive caregiving (p. 266)
separation anxiety (p. 262)
slow-to-warm-up child (p. 254)
social referencing (p. 251)
social smile (p. 248)
stranger anxiety (p. 249)
Strange Situation (p. 263)
temperament (p. 253)
uninhibited, or sociable, child (p. 255)

MILESTONES
Development in Infancy and Toddlerhood

BIRTH–6 MONTHS

ARIEL SKELLY/BLEND IMAGES/GETTY IMAGES

PHYSICAL

- Height and weight increase rapidly. (159–160)
- Newborn reflexes decline. (143)
- Distinguishes basic tastes and odors; shows preference for sweet-tasting foods. (148)
- Responses can be classically and operantly conditioned. (176–178)
- Habituates to unchanging stimuli; recovers to novel stimuli. (178–179)
- Sleep is increasingly organized into a night–day schedule. (169)
- Holds head up, rolls over, and grasps objects. (182)
- Shows sensitivity to motion, then binocular, and finally pictorial depth cues. (189–190)
- Recognizes and prefers human facial pattern; recognizes features of mother's face. (192–193)
- Perceives auditory and visual stimuli as organized patterns. (187, 195)
- Moves from relying on motion and spatial arrangement to using featural information—shape, color, and pattern—to visually detect the identity of an object. (194)
- Masters a wide range of intermodal (visual, auditory, and tactile) relationships. (195–196)

COGNITIVE

- Engages in immediate and deferred imitation of adults' facial expressions. (207)
- Repeats chance behaviors that lead to pleasurable and interesting results. (203–204)
- Has some awareness of many physical properties (including object permanence) and basic numerical knowledge. (205–206)
- Attention becomes more efficient and flexible. (216–217)
- Recognition memory for visual events improves. (217–218)
- Forms categories based on objects' similar physical properties. (219)

LANGUAGE

- Coos and, by the end of this period, babbles. (235)
- Begins to establish joint attention with caregiver, who labels objects and events. (236)

EMOTIONAL/SOCIAL

- Social smile and laughter emerge. (248)
- Matches feeling tone of caregiver in face-to-face communication; later, expects matched responses. (250)
- Distinguishes positive from negative emotion in voices and facial expressions. (250)
- Emotional expressions become well organized and meaningfully related to environmental events (250)

© TETRA IMAGES/ALAMY

- Regulates emotion by shifting attention and self-soothing. (252)
- Smiles, laughs, and babbles more to caregiver than to a stranger. (262)
- Awareness of self as physically distinct from surroundings increases. (276)

7–12 MONTHS

PHYSICAL

- Approaches adultlike sleep–wake schedule. (169)
- Sits alone, crawls, and walks. (182)

© LAURA DWIGHT PHOTOGRAPHY

- Reaching and grasping improve in flexibility and accuracy; shows refined pincer grasp. (185–186)

- "Screens out" sounds not used in own language; perceives meaningful speech. (187–189)
- Increasingly uses featural information to detect the identity of an object. (194–195)
- Intermodal perception continues to improve. (196)

COGNITIVE

- Engages in intentional, or goal-directed, behavior. (204)
- Finds an object hidden in an initial location. (204)

© LAURA DWIGHT PHOTOGRAPHY

- Recall memory improves, as indicated by gains in deferred imitation of adults' actions with objects. (207–208)
- Solves simple problems by analogy to a previous problem. (208)
- Categorizes objects on the basis of subtle sets of features, even when the perceptual contrast between categories is minimal. (219)

LANGUAGE

- Babbling expands to include many sounds of spoken languages and patterns of the child's language community. (235–236)
- Joint attention with caregiver becomes more accurate. (236)
- Takes turns in games, such as pat-a-cake and peekaboo. (236)

© ELLEN B. SENISI

- Uses preverbal gestures (showing, pointing) to influence others' goals and behavior and to convey information. (236)
- Comprehends some word meanings. (237)
- Around end of this period, understands displaced reference of words and says first words. (237)

Note: Numbers in parentheses indicate the page or pages on which each milestone is discussed.

EMOTIONAL/SOCIAL

- Smiling and laughter increase in frequency and expressiveness. (249)
- Anger and fear increase in frequency and intensity. (249–250)
- Stranger anxiety and separation anxiety appear. (250, 262)
- Uses caregiver as a secure base for exploration. (250)
- Shows "clear-cut" attachment to a familiar caregiver. (262)
- Increasingly detects the meaning of others' emotional expressions and engages in social referencing. (250–251)
- Regulates emotion by approaching and retreating from stimulation. (252)

13–18 MONTHS

PHYSICAL

- Height and weight gain are rapid, but not as great as in first year; toddlers slim down. (159–160)
- Walking is better coordinated (182)
- Manipulates small objects with improved coordination. (186, 204)

COGNITIVE

- Explores the properties of objects by acting on them in novel ways. (203)
- Searches in several locations for a hidden object. (206)
- Engages in deferred imitation of adults' actions with objects over longer delays and across a change in context—for example, from child care to home. (208)
- Sustained attention improves. (217)
- Recall memory improves further. (219)
- Sorts objects into categories. (221)
- Realizes that pictures can symbolize real objects. (209)

LANGUAGE

- Steadily adds to vocabulary. (237)
- By end of this period, produces 50 words. (235)

EMOTIONAL/SOCIAL

- Joins in play with familiar adults, siblings, and peers. (273–274)

- Realizes that others' emotional reactions may differ from one's own. (251)
- Complies with simple directives. (278)

19–24 MONTHS

PHYSICAL

- Jumps, walks on tiptoe, runs, and climbs. (182)

- Manipulates small objects with good coordination. (186, 204)

COGNITIVE

- Solves simple problems suddenly, through representation. (205)
- Finds a hidden object that has been moved while out of sight. (205)
- Engages in make-believe play, using simple actions experienced in everyday life. (205)

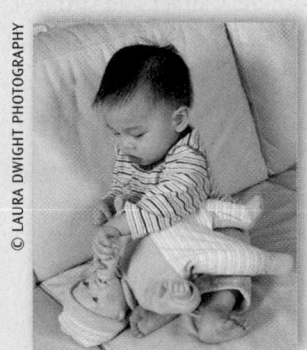

- Engages in deferred imitation of actions an adult tries to produce, even if not fully realized. (208)
- Categorizes objects conceptually, on the basis of common function or behavior. (221)
- Begins to use language as a flexible symbolic tool, to modify existing mental representations. (209)

LANGUAGE

- Produces 200 to 250 words. (235)
- Combines two words. (238)

EMOTIONAL/SOCIAL

- Self-conscious emotions (shame, embarrassment, guilt, envy, and pride) emerge. (251)
- Acquires a vocabulary for talking about feelings. (253)
- Begins to use language to assist with emotional self-regulation. (253)
- Begins to tolerate caregiver's absences more easily; separation anxiety declines. (262)
- Recognizes image of self and, by end of this period, uses own name or personal pronoun to refer to self. (276)

- Less often makes scale errors. (276–277)
- Shows signs of empathy. (278)
- Categorizes self and others on the basis of age, sex, physical characteristics, goodness and badness, and competencies. (278)
- Shows gender-stereotyped toy preferences. (278)
- Self-control, as indicated by delay of gratification, emerges. (279)
- Starts to use words to influence a playmate's behavior. (274)

Physical Development in Early Childhood

"My Strength Is Greater Than Yours"
Gao Ao
4 years, China

As this boy grows larger and stronger, he eagerly demonstrates his newly acquired arm-wrestling skills with his father. Chapter 8 highlights the close link between physical growth and other aspects of development in early childhood.

For more than a decade, our fourth-floor office windows have overlooked the preschool and kindergarten play yard of our university laboratory school. On mild fall and spring mornings, classroom doors swing open, and sand table, easels, and large blocks spill out into a small courtyard. Alongside the building is a grassy area with jungle gyms, swings, a playhouse, and a flower garden planted by the children; beyond it, a circular path lined with tricycles and wagons. Each day, the setting is alive with activity.

Even from our distant vantage points, the physical changes of early childhood are evident. Children's bodies are longer and leaner than they were a year or two earlier. The awkward gait of toddlerhood has disappeared in favor of more refined movements that include running, climbing, jumping, galloping, and skipping. Children scale the jungle gym, race across the lawn, turn somersaults, and vigorously pedal tricycles. Just as impressive as these gross-motor achievements are gains in fine-motor skills. At the sand table, children build hills, valleys, caves, and roads and prepare trays of pretend cookies and cupcakes. And as they grew older, their paintings at the outdoor easels took on greater structure and detail as family members, houses, trees, birds, sky, monsters, and letterlike forms appeared in the colorful creations.

The years from 2 to 6 are often called "the play years"—aptly so, since play blossoms during this time and supports every aspect of development. Our discussion of early childhood opens with the physical achievements of this period—growth in body size, improvements in motor coordination, and refinements in perception. We pay special attention to genetic and environmental factors that support these changes, as well as to their intimate connection with other domains of development. The children we came to know well, first by watching from our office windows and later by observing at close range in their classrooms, will provide many examples of developmental trends and individual differences. ■

Body Growth

In early childhood, the rapid increase in body size of the first two years tapers off into a slower growth pattern. On average, children add 2 to 3 inches in height and about 5 pounds in weight each year. Boys continue to be slightly larger than girls. As the "baby fat" that began to decline in toddlerhood drops off further, children gradually become thinner, although girls retain somewhat more body fat than boys, who are slightly more muscular. As the torso lengthens and widens, internal organs tuck neatly inside, and the spine straightens. As Figure 8.1 on page 286 shows, by age 5 the top-heavy, bowlegged, potbellied toddler has become a more streamlined, flat-tummied, longer-legged child with body proportions similar to those of adults. Consequently, posture and balance improve—changes that foster gains in motor coordination.

Individual differences in body size are even more apparent during early childhood than in infancy and toddlerhood. Speeding around the bike path in the play yard, 5-year-old Darryl—at 48 inches tall and 55 pounds—towered over his kindergarten classmates. (The average North American 5-year-old boy is 43 inches tall and weighs 42 pounds.) Priti, an Asian-Indian child, was unusually small because of genetic factors linked to her cultural ancestry. And Lynette and Hal, two Caucasian children with impoverished home lives, were well below average for reasons we will discuss shortly.

8.1 Describe changes in body size, proportions, and skeletal maturity during early childhood.

8.2 Describe brain development in early childhood.

The existence of these variations in body size reminds us that growth norms for one population are not good standards for children elsewhere in the world. Consider the Efe of the Republic of Congo, whose typical adult height is less than 5 feet. For genetic reasons, the impact of hormones controlling body size is reduced in Efe children (Meazza, Pagani, & Bozzola, 2011). By age 5, the average Efe child is shorter than more than 97 percent of North American and European 5-year-olds, and Efe children reach puberty and stop growing at an earlier age than U.S. comparison children. Researchers disagree on why the Efe's small size evolved. Some suggest that it reduces their caloric requirements in the face of food scarcity in the rain forests of Central Africa, others that it permits easy movement through the dense forest underbrush, and still others that it enables earlier childbearing to compensate for the Efe's extremely high mortality rate (Migliano, Vinicius, & Lahr, 2007; Perry & Dominy, 2009). Efe children's short stature is not a sign of growth or health problems. But for other children, such as Lynette and Hal, extremely slow growth is cause for concern.

PHOTOS OF WILSON: DIAHANNE LUCAS; PHOTOS OF MARIEL: © JIM WEST PHOTOGRAPHY

Wilson at 3 years

Wilson at 3½ years

Wilson at 4½ years

Wilson at 5 years

Mariel at 2½ years

Mariel at 4 years

Mariel at 4½ years

Mariel at 5 years

FIGURE 8.1 **Body growth during early childhood.** During the preschool years, children grow more slowly than in infancy and toddlerhood. Wilson and Mariel's bodies became more streamlined, flat-tummied, and longer-legged. Boys continue to be slightly taller, heavier, and more muscular than girls. But generally, the two sexes are similar in body proportions and physical capacities.

Skeletal Growth

The skeletal changes of infancy continue throughout early childhood. Between ages 2 and 6, approximately 45 new *epiphyses,* or growth centers in which cartilage hardens into bone, emerge in various parts of the skeleton. Other epiphyses will appear in middle childhood. X-rays of these growth centers enable doctors to estimate children's *skeletal age,* or progress toward physical maturity (see page 161 in Chapter 5)—information helpful in diagnosing growth disorders.

By the end of the preschool years, children start to lose their primary, or "baby," teeth. The age at which they do so is heavily influenced by genetic factors. For example, girls, who are ahead of boys in physical development, lose their primary teeth sooner. Cultural ancestry also makes a difference. North American children typically get their first secondary (permanent) tooth at 6½ years, children in Ghana at just over 5 years, and children in Hong Kong around the sixth birthday (Burns, 2000). But nutritional factors also influence dental development. Prolonged malnutrition delays the appearance of permanent teeth, whereas overweight and obesity accelerate it (Costacurta et al., 2012; Heinrich-Weltzien et al., 2013).

Diseased baby teeth can affect the health of permanent teeth, so preventing decay in primary teeth is essential—by brushing consistently, avoiding sugary foods, drinking fluoridated water, and getting topical fluoride treatments and sealants (plastic coatings that protect tooth surfaces). Another factor is exposure to tobacco smoke, which suppresses children's immune system, including the ability to fight bacteria responsible for tooth decay. The risk associated with this suppression is greatest in infancy and early childhood, when the immune system is not yet fully mature (Aligne et al., 2003). Young children in homes with regular smokers are at increased risk for decayed teeth (Hanioka et al., 2011).

Unfortunately, an estimated 28 percent of U.S. preschoolers have tooth decay, a figure that rises to 50 percent in middle childhood and 60 percent by age 18. Causes include poor diet and inadequate health care—factors that are more likely to affect low-SES children. About 30 percent of U.S. children living in poverty have untreated dental caries (National Institutes of Health, 2011).

During early childhood, body fat declines, the torso enlarges to better accommodate the internal organs, and the spine straightens. This 5-year-old appears more streamlined than his younger playmate.

Brain Development

Between ages 2 and 6, the brain increases from 70 percent of its adult weight to 90 percent. At the same time, preschoolers improve in a wide variety of skills—physical coordination, perception, attention, memory, language, logical thinking, and imagination.

In addition to increasing in weight, the brain undergoes much reshaping and refining. By age 4 to 5, many parts of the cerebral cortex have overproduced synapses. In some regions, such as the prefrontal cortex, the number of synapses is nearly double the adult value. Together, synaptic growth and myelination of neural fibers result in a high energy need. In fact, fMRI evidence reveals that energy metabolism in the cerebral cortex reaches a peak around this age (Huttenlocher, 2002; Nelson, Thomas, & de Haan, 2006).

Recall from Chapter 5 that overabundance of synaptic connections supports *plasticity* of the young brain, helping to ensure that the child will acquire certain abilities even if some areas are damaged. *Synaptic pruning* follows: Neurons that are seldom stimulated lose their connective fibers, and the number of synapses is reduced (see page 162). As the structures of stimulated neurons become more elaborate and require more space, surrounding neurons die, and brain plasticity declines. By age 8 to 10, energy consumption of most cortical regions diminishes to near-adult levels (Lebel & Beaulieu, 2011; Nelson, 2002). In addition, cognitive functions are no longer as widely distributed in the cerebral cortex. Rather, they increasingly localize in distinct neural systems that become better integrated, reflecting a developmental shift toward a more fine-tuned, efficient neural organization (Bathelt et al., 2013; Markant & Thomas, 2013).

EEG, NIRS, and fMRI measures of neural activity reveal especially rapid growth from early to middle childhood in prefrontal-cortical areas devoted to various aspects of executive

A 5-year-old illustrates gains in executive function, supported by rapid growth of the prefrontal cortex, as she engages in an activity that challenges her capacity to attend, remember, and plan.

function. These include inhibition of impulses, attention, working memory, and planning and organizing behavior—capacities that advance markedly during the preschool years (Bunge & Wright, 2007; Durston & Casey, 2006). Furthermore, for most children, the left cerebral hemisphere is especially active between 3 and 6 years and then levels off. In contrast, activity in the right hemisphere increases steadily throughout early and middle childhood, with a slight spurt between ages 8 and 10 (Thatcher, Walker, & Giudice, 1987; Thompson et al., 2000).

These findings fit nicely with what we know about several aspects of cognitive development. Early childhood is a time of marked gains on tasks that depend on the prefrontal cortex—ones that require suppression of impulses in favor of thoughtful responses (Rothbart, 2011). Further, language skills (typically housed in the left hemisphere) increase at an astonishing pace in early childhood, and they support children's increasing control over behavior, also mediated by the prefrontal cortex. In contrast, spatial skills (usually located in the right hemisphere), such as giving directions, drawing pictures, and recognizing geometric shapes, develop gradually over childhood and adolescence.

Differences in rate of development between the two hemispheres suggest that they are continuing to *lateralize* (specialize in functions). Let's take a closer look at brain lateralization during early childhood by focusing on handedness.

HANDEDNESS On a visit to the preschool, we watched 3-year-old Moira as she drew pictures, worked puzzles, ate a snack, and played outside. Unlike most of her classmates, Moira does most things—drawing, eating, and zipping her jacket—with her left hand. But she uses her right hand for a few activities, such as throwing a ball. Research on handedness, along with other evidence covered in Chapter 5, supports the joint contribution of nature and nurture to brain lateralization.

As early as the tenth prenatal week, most fetuses show a right-hand preference during thumb-sucking (Hepper, McCartney, & Shannon, 1998). And by age 6 months, infants typically display a smoother, more efficient movement when reaching with their right than their left arm. These early tendencies may contribute to the right-handed bias of most children by the end of the first year (Nelson, Campbell, & Michel, 2013; Rönnqvist & Domellöf, 2006). During toddlerhood and early childhood, handedness gradually extends to a wider range of skills.

Handedness reflects the greater capacity of one side of the brain—the individual's **dominant cerebral hemisphere**—to carry out skilled motor action. Other important abilities are generally located on the dominant side as well. For right-handed people—in Western nations, 90 percent of the population—language is housed in the left hemisphere with hand control. For the left-handed 10 percent, language is occasionally located in the right hemisphere or, more often, shared between the hemispheres (Szaflarski et al., 2012). This indicates that the brains of left-handers tend to be less strongly lateralized than those of right-handers. Consistent with this idea, many left-handed individuals (like Moira) are also *ambidextrous*. Although they prefer their left hand, they sometimes use their right hand skillfully as well.

Left-handed parents show only a weak tendency to have left-handed children (Vuoksimaa et al., 2009). One genetic theory proposes that most children inherit a gene that *biases* them for right-handedness and a left-dominant cerebral hemisphere. But that bias is not strong enough to overcome experiences that might sway children toward a left-hand preference (Annett, 2002). Even prenatal events may profoundly affect handedness. Both identical and fraternal twins are more likely than ordinary siblings to differ in hand preference, probably because twins usually lie in opposite orientations in the uterus (Derom et al., 1996). The orientation of most singleton fetuses—facing toward the left—is believed to promote greater control over movements on the body's right side (Previc, 1991).

Handedness also involves practice. Newborns' bias in head position causes them to spend more time looking at and using one hand, which contributes to greater skillfulness of that hand

Twins are more likely than ordinary siblings to differ in hand preference, perhaps because twins usually lie in opposite orientations in the uterus.

(Hinojosa, Sheu, & Michael, 2003). Handedness is strongest for complex skills requiring extensive training, such as eating with utensils, writing, and engaging in athletic activities. Also, wide cultural differences exist in rates of left-handedness. For example, in tribal and village cultures, the rate of left-handedness is relatively high. But in a study of one such society in New Guinea, individuals who had attended school in childhood were far more likely to be extremely right-handed—findings that highlight the role of experience (Geuze et al., 2012).

Although rates of left-handedness are elevated among people with intellectual disabilities and mental illness, atypical brain lateralization is probably not responsible for these individuals' problems. Rather, early damage to the left hemisphere may have caused their disabilities while also leading to a shift in handedness. In support of this idea, left-handedness is associated with prenatal and birth difficulties that can result in brain damage, including maternal stress, prolonged labor, prematurity, Rh incompatibility, and breech delivery (Domellöf, Johansson, & Rönnqvist, 2011; Kurganskaya, 2011).

Most left-handers, however, have no developmental problems—in fact, unusual lateralization may have certain advantages. Left- and mixed-handed young people are slightly advantaged in speed and flexibility of thinking, and they are more likely than their right-handed agemates to develop outstanding verbal and mathematical talents (Beratis et al., 2013; Noroozian et al., 2012). More even distribution of cognitive functions across both hemispheres may be responsible.

OTHER ADVANCES IN BRAIN DEVELOPMENT Besides the cerebral cortex, several other areas of the brain make strides during early childhood (see Figure 8.2). All of these changes involve establishing links between parts of the brain, increasing the coordinated functioning of the central nervous system.

At the rear and base of the brain is the **cerebellum,** a structure that aids in balance and control of body movement. Fibers linking the cerebellum to the cerebral cortex grow and myelinate from birth through the preschool years. This change contributes to dramatic gains in motor coordination: By the end of the preschool years, children can play hopscotch, throw a ball with well-coordinated movements, and print letters of the alphabet. Connections between the cerebellum and the cerebral cortex also support thinking. Children with damage to the cerebellum usually display both motor and cognitive deficits, including problems with memory, planning, and language (Noterdaeme et al., 2002; Riva & Giorgi, 2000).

The **reticular formation,** a structure in the brain stem that maintains alertness and consciousness, generates synapses and myelinates throughout early childhood and into adolescence. Neurons in the reticular formation send out fibers to other areas of the brain. Many go to the prefrontal cortex, contributing to improvements in sustained, controlled attention.

An inner-brain structure called the **hippocampus,** which plays a vital role in memory and in images of space that help us find our way, undergoes rapid synapse formation and myelination in the second half of the first year, when recall memory and independent movement emerge. Over the preschool and elementary school years, the hippocampus and surrounding areas of the cerebral cortex continue to develop swiftly, establishing connections with one another and with the prefrontal cortex and lateralizing toward greater right-sided activation (Hopf et al., 2013; Nelson, Thomas, & de Haan, 2006). These changes make possible the

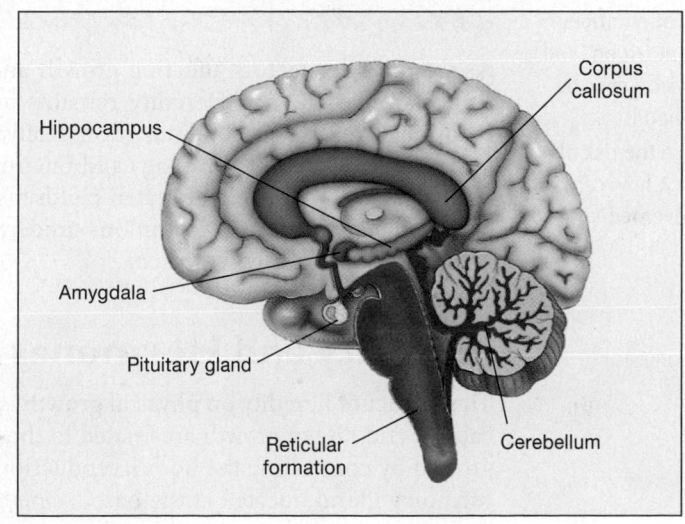

FIGURE 8.2 **Cross-section of the human brain, showing the location of the cerebellum, the reticular formation, the hippocampus, the amygdala, and the corpus callosum.** These structures undergo considerable development during early childhood. Also shown is the pituitary gland, which secretes hormones that control body growth (see page 290).

Continued growth of the corpus callosum in early childhood contributes to improved motor coordination, enabling this child to keep his balance while hopping across a path of circles.

dramatic gains in memory and spatial understanding of early and middle childhood—ability to use strategies to store and retrieve information, expansion of autobiographical memory (which brings an end to infantile amnesia), and drawing and reading of maps (which we will take up in Chapter 9).

Also located in the inner brain, adjacent to the hippocampus, is the **amygdala,** a structure that plays a central role in processing of novelty and emotional information. The amygdala is sensitive to facial emotional expressions, especially fear (Adolphs, 2010). It also enhances memory for emotionally salient events, thereby ensuring that information relevant for survival—stimuli that evoke fear or signify safety—will be retrieved on future occasions. This capacity for emotional learning seems to emerge in early childhood: Damage to the amygdala in the first few years leads to loss of ability to learn about fear and safety signals and wide-ranging socially inappropriate behaviors (Shaw, Brierley, & David, 2005). Throughout childhood and adolescence, connections between the amygdala and the prefrontal cortex, which governs regulation of emotion, form and myelinate (Tottenham, Hare, & Casey, 2009). Recall from Chapter 7 that in socially anxious children, the amygdala is overly reactive to threatening situations (see page 256).

The **corpus callosum** is a large bundle of fibers connecting the two cerebral hemispheres. Production of synapses and myelination of the corpus callosum increase at 1 year, peak between 3 and 6 years, then continue at a slower pace through middle childhood and adolescence (Thompson et al., 2000). The corpus callosum supports smooth coordination of movements on both sides of the body and integration of many aspects of thinking, including perception, attention, memory, language, and problem solving. The more complex the task, the more essential communication is between the hemispheres.

Ask Yourself

- **REVIEW** What aspects of brain development support the tremendous gains in language, thinking, and motor control of early childhood?

- **CONNECT** What stand on the nature–nurture issue do findings on development of handedness support? Explain, using research findings.

- **APPLY** Dental checkups revealed a high incidence of untreated tooth decay in a U.S. preschool program serving low-income children. Using findings presented in this and previous chapters, list possible contributing factors.

- **REFLECT** How early, and to what extent, did you experience tooth decay in childhood? What factors might have been responsible?

8.3 Explain how heredity influences physical growth.

8.4 Describe the effects of emotional well-being, restful sleep, nutrition, and infectious disease on physical growth and health in early childhood.

8.5 What factors increase the risk of unintentional injuries, and how can childhood injuries be prevented?

Influences on Physical Growth and Health

As we consider factors affecting growth and health in early childhood, you will encounter some familiar themes. Heredity remains important, but environmental factors—including emotional well-being, good nutrition, relative freedom from disease, and physical safety—are also essential. And as the Biology and Environment box on the following page illustrates, environmental pollutants can threaten children's healthy development. The extent to which low-level lead—one of the most common—undermines children's mental and emotional functioning is the focus of intensive research.

Heredity and Hormones

The impact of heredity on physical growth is evident throughout childhood. Children's physical size and rate of growth are related to those of their parents (Bogin, 2001). Genes influence growth by controlling the body's production of hormones. Figure 8.2 on page 289 shows the **pituitary gland,** located at the base of the brain, which plays a critical role by releasing two hormones that induce growth.

Biology and Environment

Low-Level Lead Exposure and Children's Development

Lead is a highly toxic element that, at blood levels exceeding 60 μg/dL (micrograms per deciliter), causes brain swelling, hemorrhaging, disrupted functioning of neurons, and widespread cell death. Before 1980, exposure to lead resulted from use of lead-based paints for the interiors of residences (infants and young children often ate paint flakes) and from use of leaded gasoline (car exhaust resulted in a highly breathable form of lead). Laws limiting the lead content of paint and mandating lead-free gasoline led to a sharp decline in children's lead levels, from an average of 15 μg/dL in 1980 to 1.3 μg/dL today (Kennedy et al., 2014).

But in areas near airports with significant burning of jet fuel, near industries using lead production processes, or where lead-based paint remains in older homes, children's blood levels are still markedly elevated. In some areas, water-pipe corrosion has caused lead to rise in drinking water. Contaminated soil and imported consumer products, such as toys made of leaded plastic, are additional sources of exposure (Cole & Winsler, 2010). Today, about 5 percent of U.S. children have blood-lead levels exceeding 5 μg/dL—the level deemed high enough by the U.S. government to warrant immediate efforts to reduce exposure (Centers for Disease Control and Prevention, 2014c). Most live in large central cities and come from low-SES ethnic minority families.

Does lead contamination, even in small quantities, impair children's cognitive functioning?

Until recently, answers were unclear. Studies reporting a negative relationship between children's current lead levels and intelligence test performance had serious limitations. Researchers knew nothing about children's history of lead exposure and often failed to control for factors associated with both blood-lead levels and mental test scores (such as SES, home environmental quality, and nutrition) that might account for the findings.

Over the past quarter century, eight longitudinal studies of the developmental consequences of lead have been conducted in multiple countries, including the United States, Australia, Mexico, and Yugoslavia. Some focused on inner-city, low-SES minority children, others on middle- and upper-middle-SES suburban children, and one on children living close to a lead smelter. Each tracked children's lead exposure over an extended time and included relevant controls.

All but one site reported negative relationships between lead exposure and children's IQs (Canfield et al., 2003; Hubbs-Tait et al., 2005; Lanphear et al., 2005). Higher blood levels were also associated with deficits in verbal and visual-motor skills and with distractibility, overactivity, poor organization, and behavior problems. And an array of additional findings suggested that persistent childhood lead exposure contributes to antisocial behavior in adolescence (Needleman et al., 2002; Nevin, 2006; Stretesky & Lynch, 2004).

The investigations did not agree on an age period of greatest vulnerability. In some, relationships were strongest in toddlerhood and early childhood; in others, in middle childhood, suggesting cumulative effects over time. Still other studies reported similar lead-related cognitive deficits from infancy through adolescence. Overall, poorer intelligence test scores associated with lead exposure seemed to be permanent. Children given drugs to induce excretion of lead (chelation) did not improve

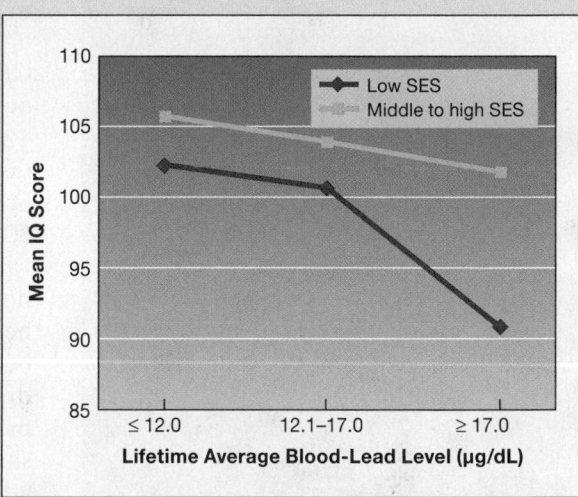

FIGURE 8.3 **Relationship of lifetime average lead exposure to 11-to-13-year-olds' IQ by SES.** In this study, conducted in the lead-smelting city of Port Pirie, Australia, blood-lead levels of 375 children were measured repeatedly from birth to age 11 to 13. The lead-exposure-related drop in IQ was much greater for low-SES than higher-SES children. (Based on Tong, McMichael, & Baghurst, 2000.)

(Dietrich et al., 2004; Rogan et al., 2001). Negative cognitive consequences were evident at all levels of lead exposure, with one study reporting persisting effects into early adulthood (Canfield et al., 2003; Lanphear et al., 2005; Mazumdar et al., 2011; Wright et al., 2008).

Furthermore, in several investigations, cognitive consequences were much greater for low-SES than middle- and higher-SES children (see, for example, Figure 8.3) (Bellinger, Leviton, & Sloman, 1990; Ris et al., 2004; Tong, McMichael, & Baghurst, 2000). A stressed, disorganized home life seems to heighten lead-induced damage. Dietary factors can also magnify lead's toxic effects. Iron and zinc deficiencies, especially common in low-SES children, increase lead concentration in the blood (Noonan et al., 2003; Wolf, Jimenez, & Lozoff, 2003; Wright et al., 2003).

In sum, lead impairs cognitive development and contributes to behavior problems. Low-SES children are more likely both to live in lead-contaminated areas and to experience additional risks that magnify lead-induced damage. Because lead is a stable element, its release into the air and soil is difficult to reverse. Therefore, in addition to laws that control lead pollution, interventions that reduce the negative impact of lead—through involved parenting, dietary enrichment, better schools, and public education about lead hazards—are vital.

These children play near a smelting factory in Copsa Mica, Romania, which ranks among the world's most polluted cities in levels of lead and other toxins. Longitudinal studies consistently show lasting negative effects of lead exposure, including learning impairments and behavior problems.

© ELLEN B. SENISI

These preschoolers are the same age but differ greatly in body size. Early treatment of growth hormone (GH) deficiency leads to substantial gains in height, but little justification exists for intervention with normal-GH children whose short stature simply reflects human diversity.

The first, **growth hormone (GH),** is necessary from birth on for development of almost all body tissues. GH acts directly but also accomplishes its task with the help of an intermediary. It stimulates the liver and epiphyses of the skeleton to release another hormone called *insulin-like growth factor 1 (IGF-1),* which triggers cell duplication throughout the body, especially the skeleton, muscles, nerves, bone marrow (origin of blood cells), liver, kidney, skin, and lungs.

About 2 percent of children suffer from inherited conditions that cause either GH deficiency or IGF-1 deficiency (in which GH fails to stimulate IGF-1). Without medical intervention, such children reach an average mature height of only 4 to 4½ feet. When treated early with injections of GH or IGF-1 (depending on the disorder), such children show catch-up growth and then grow at a normal rate, becoming much taller than they would have without treatment (Bright, Mendoza, & Rosenfeld, 2009; Saenger, 2003).

The availability of synthetic GH has also made it possible to treat short, normal-GH children with hormone injections, in hopes of increasing their final height. Thousands of parents, concerned that their children will suffer social stigma because of their shortness, have sought this GH therapy. But most normal-GH children given GH treatment grow only slightly taller than their previously predicted mature height (Rosenbloom, 2009). And contrary to popular belief, normal-GH short children are not deficient in self-esteem or other aspects of psychological adjustment (Gardner & Sandberg, 2011). So despite the existence of "heightism" in Western cultures, little justification exists for medically intervening in short stature that is merely the result of biologically normal human diversity.

A second pituitary hormone, **thyroid-stimulating hormone (TSH),** prompts the thyroid gland in the neck to release *thyroxine,* which is necessary for brain development and for GH to have its full impact on body size. Infants born with inadequate thyroxine must receive it at once, or they will be intellectually disabled. Once the most rapid period of brain development is complete, children with too little thyroxine grow at a below-average rate, but the central nervous system is no longer affected (Donaldson & Jones, 2013). With prompt treatment, such children catch up in body growth and eventually reach normal size.

Emotional Well-Being

In childhood as in infancy, emotional well-being can profoundly affect growth and health. Preschoolers with very stressful home lives (due to divorce, financial difficulties, or parental job loss) suffer more respiratory and intestinal illnesses and more unintentional injuries than others (Kemeny, 2003).

In addition, high stress suppresses the release of GH (Deltondo et al., 2008). Consequently, extreme emotional deprivation can lead to **psychosocial dwarfism,** a growth disorder that appears between ages 2 and 15. Typical characteristics include decreased secretion of GH and *melatonin,* a hormone within the brain that promotes sleep (during which GH is released), very short stature, and immature skeletal age. Also, these children display serious adjustment problems, which help distinguish psychosocial dwarfism from normal shortness (Muños-Hoyos et al., 2011; Tarren-Sweeney, 2006). Lynette, the 4-year-old mentioned earlier in this chapter, was diagnosed with this condition. She was placed in foster care after child welfare authorities discovered that she spent most of the day at home alone, unsupervised, and also might have been physically abused. When children like Lynette are removed from their emotionally inadequate environments, their GH levels quickly return to normal, and they grow rapidly. But if treatment is delayed, the dwarfism can be permanent.

Sleep Habits and Problems

Because GH is released during the child's sleeping hours, sleep contributes to body growth. And a well-rested child is better able to play, learn, and contribute positively to family functioning. Many studies confirm that sleep difficulties are associated with impaired cognitive performance, including decreased attention, speed of thinking, working memory, and intelligence and achievement test scores, as well as with internalizing and externalizing problems. The impact of disrupted sleep on cognitive functioning and emotional adjustment is more pronounced for low-SES children. Perhaps insufficient sleep heightens the impact of other environmental stressors prevalent in their daily lives (Buckhalt et al., 2009; El-Sheikh et al., 2010, 2013; Goodnight et al., 2007). Also, children who sleep poorly disturb their parents' sleep, which can generate significant family stress—a major reason that sleep difficulties are among the most frequent concerns parents raise with their preschooler's doctor.

Total sleep declines in early childhood; on average, 2- and 3-year-olds sleep 11 to 12 hours, 4- to 6-year-olds 10 to 11 hours. But substantial variability exists, with lesser- or greater-than-average sleep remaining fairly stable over time (Jenni & Carskadon, 2012). Younger preschoolers typically take a 1- to 2-hour nap in the early afternoon, although daytime sleep need also varies widely. Some continue to take two naps, as they did in toddlerhood; others give up napping entirely. Most Caucasian-American children stop napping between ages 3 and 4, although a quiet rest period after lunch helps them rejuvenate for the rest of the day. Perhaps because of greater cultural acceptance, napping remains common among African-American, Asian, and Hispanic children throughout early childhood, balanced by a tendency to go to bed later and to sleep less at night (Crosby, LeBourgeois, & Harsh, 2005; Mindell et al., 2013). And napping at preschool enhances memories acquired earlier in the day, especially for children who nap regularly at home (Kurdziel, Duclos, & Spencer, 2013). Consequently, replacing nap opportunities with additional learning activities in early childhood programs may be counterproductive.

The majority of Western parents engage in bedtime routines with their preschoolers, though in the United States this is slightly more common among white than African-American and Hispanic parents. As Figure 8.4 shows, Caucasian preschoolers are less likely to cosleep with their parents than their African-American and Hispanic agemates. White children more often go to bed with a security object, which may help them adjust to feelings of uneasiness at being left by themselves in a darkened room. African-American preschoolers are especially likely to share a bedroom with siblings (Milan, Snow, & Belay, 2007). In most cases, parent–child cosleeping is not associated with problems during the preschool years, other than more frequent night wakings by parents due to children's movements (Gaylor et al., 2005; Worthman, 2011). Western cosleeping children generally ask to sleep in their own bed by age 6 or 7.

Difficulty falling asleep—calling to the parent or asking for another drink of water—is common in early childhood, occurring in about one-third of preschoolers. But Caucasian parents more often express concern about their child falling asleep at a regular time than do African-American parents (Milan, Snow, & Belay, 2007). Perhaps Caucasian parents more highly value a scheduled bedtime and tend to view falling asleep without protest as a sign of maturity—expectations likely to be unmet at least occasionally.

Sleep problems frequently result from inadequate parental control over young children's TV, computer, and video game use, which is linked to later bedtimes, longer delay in falling asleep, and greater number of night wakings (Mindell et al., 2013). Sleep difficulties may also stem from a mismatch between parental demands and children's biology. The parent may step up pressure on the child, who vigorously resists because of a lower-than-average need for sleep. Consequently, sleep interventions should include parent education about individual differences in young children's sleep requirements (Johnson & Mindell, 2011). Intense bedtime struggles sometimes result from family turmoil, as children worry about how their parents

Compared with their Caucasian peers, African-American preschoolers are more likely to share a bedroom with siblings or cosleep with parents. As a result, they less often depend on a security object to reduce the discomfort of being left alone in a darkened room.

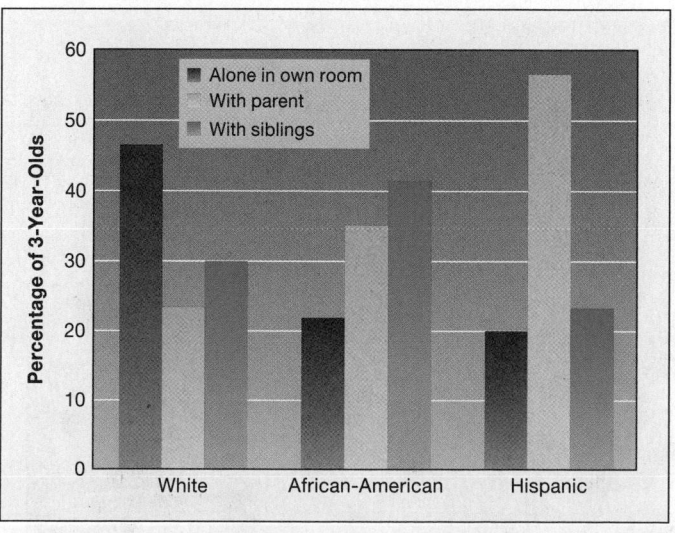

FIGURE 8.4 Sleeping arrangements of U.S. 3-year-olds by ethnicity. A survey of several thousand mothers who were asked about their 3-year-old's typical sleep location revealed that white preschoolers were far more likely to sleep alone in their own bedroom than African-American and Hispanic preschoolers. Among minority children, more Hispanic preschoolers slept with a parent, more African-American preschoolers with siblings. (Based on Milan, Snow, & Belay, 2007.)

may get along when they are asleep and not available to distract them. In these cases, addressing family stress and conflict is key to improving children's sleep.

Finally, most children waken during the night from time to time, and those who cannot return to sleep on their own may suffer from a sleep disorder. Because young children have vivid imaginations and difficulty separating fantasy from reality, *nightmares* are common; half of 3- to 6-year-olds experience them from time to time. And about 4 percent of children are frequent *sleepwalkers,* who are unaware of their wanderings during the night. Gently awakening and returning the child to bed helps avoid self-injury. *Sleep terrors,* which affect 3 percent of young children, are perhaps the most upsetting sleep problem to parents. In these panic-stricken arousals from deep sleep, the child may scream, thrash, speak incoherently, show a sharp rise in heart rate and breathing, and initially be unresponsive to parents' attempts to comfort. Sleepwalking and sleep terrors tend to run in families, suggesting a genetic influence (Guilleminault et al., 2003; Moore & Mindell, 2012). But they can also be triggered by stress or extreme fatigue.

Fortunately, sleep disorders of early childhood usually subside without treatment. In the few cases that persist, children require a medical and psychological evaluation. Their disturbed sleep may be a sign of neurological or emotional difficulties.

Nutrition

With the transition to early childhood, many children become unpredictable, picky eaters. One father we know wistfully recalled how his son, as a toddler, eagerly sampled Chinese food: "He ate rice, chicken chow mein, egg rolls—and now, at age 3, the only thing he'll try is the ice cream!"

Preschoolers' appetites decline because their growth has slowed. Their wariness of new foods is also adaptive: If they stick to familiar foods, they are less likely to swallow dangerous substances when adults are not around to protect them (Birch & Fisher, 1995). Parents need not worry about variations in amount eaten from meal to meal. Over the course of a day, preschoolers compensate for eating little at one meal by eating more at a later one (Hursti, 1999).

Though they eat less, preschoolers need a high-quality diet, including the same foods adults need, but in smaller amounts. These include milk and milk products, meat or meat alternatives (such as eggs, dried peas or beans, and peanut butter), vegetables and fruits, and breads and cereals. Fats, oils, and salt are best kept to a minimum because of their link to high blood pressure and heart disease in adulthood. And foods high in sugar should be eaten only in small amounts to prevent tooth decay and protect against overweight and obesity—a topic we will take up in Chapter 11.

Children tend to imitate the food choices and eating practices of people they admire, both adults and peers. For example, mothers who drink milk or soft drinks tend to have 5-year-old daughters with a similar beverage preference (Fisher et al., 2001). In Mexico, where children see family members delighting in the taste of peppery foods, preschoolers enthusiastically eat chili peppers, whereas most U.S. children reject them (Birch, Zimmerman, & Hind, 1980).

Repeated, unpressured exposure to a new food also increases acceptance (Fuller et al., 2005). In one study, preschoolers were given one of three versions of a food they had never eaten before (sweet, salty, or plain tofu). After 8 to 15 exposures, they readily ate the food. But they preferred the version they had already tasted. For example, children in the "sweet" condition liked sweet tofu best, and those in the "plain" condition liked plain tofu best (Sullivan & Birch, 1990). These findings reveal that adding sugar or salt in hopes of increasing a young child's willingness to eat healthy foods simply strengthens the child's desire for a sugary or salty taste. Similarly, offering children sweet fruit drinks or soft drinks promotes "milk avoidance." Compared to their milk-drinking agemates, milk-avoiders are shorter in

© ADAM HESTER/CORBIS

This Mexican 3-year-old helps his mother prepare refried beans for dinner. Children tend to imitate the food preferences of those they admire—both adults and peers.

Applying What We Know

Encouraging Good Nutrition in Early Childhood

SUGGESTION	DESCRIPTION
Offer a varied, healthy diet.	Provide a well-balanced variety of nutritious foods that are colorful and attractively served. Avoid including sweets and "junk" foods in the child's regular food environment.
Offer predictable meals as well as several snacks each day.	Preschoolers' stomachs are small, and they may not be able to eat enough in three meals to satisfy their energy requirements. They benefit from extra opportunities to eat.
Offer small portions, and permit the child to serve him- or herself and to ask for seconds.	When too much food is put on the plate, preschoolers (like adults) often overeat, increasing the risk of obesity. On average, preschoolers consume 25 percent less at a meal when permitted to serve themselves.
Offer healthy new foods early in a meal and repeatedly at subsequent meals, and respond with patience if the child rejects the food.	Introduce healthy new foods before the child's appetite is satisfied. Let children see you eat and enjoy the new food. If the child rejects it, accept the refusal and serve it again at another meal. As foods become more familiar, they are more readily accepted.
Keep mealtimes pleasant, include the child in mealtime conversations, and refrain from coercing the child to eat.	A pleasant, relaxed eating environment helps children develop positive attitudes about food. Refrain from constantly offering food, pressuring the child to eat, or engaging in confrontations over disliked foods and table manners—practices associated with children's refusal to eat.
Avoid using food as a reward and restricting access to certain foods.	Saying "No dessert until you clean your plate" tells children that they must eat even if they are not hungry and that dessert is the best part of the meal. Restricting access to a food increases children's valuing of that food and efforts to obtain it.

Sources: Fisher, Rolls, & Birch, 2003; Jansen et al., 2012.

stature and have a lower bone density—a condition that leads to a lifelong reduction in strength and to increased risk of bone fractures (Black et al., 2002).

The emotional climate at mealtimes has a powerful impact on children's eating habits. When parents are worried about how well their preschoolers are eating, meals can become unpleasant and stressful. Coercing children to eat—for example, by offering bribes, such as "Finish your vegetables, and you get an extra cookie"—causes children to like the healthy food less and the treat more (Birch, Fisher, & Davison, 2003). Similarly, restricting access to tasty foods focuses children's attention on those foods and increases their desire to eat them. In a study of nearly 5,000 Dutch 4-year-olds, maternal feeding practices were strongly associated with children's unhealthy weight, in both directions. The more mothers reported pressuring their child to eat, the greater the likelihood of an underweight child. And the more mothers reported restricting their child's eating, the greater the chances of an overweight or obese child (see Figure 8.5) (Jansen et al., 2012). Too much parental control over eating seems to interfere with children's responsiveness to hunger cues, resulting either in withdrawal from food or in excessive eating.

Children's healthy eating depends on a healthy food environment, but too much adult control limits their opportunities to develop self-control, thereby promoting overeating. For ways to encourage healthy, varied eating in young children, refer to Applying What We Know above.

Finally, as indicated in earlier chapters, many children in the United States and in developing countries lack access to sufficient high-quality food to support healthy growth. Five-year-old Hal rode a bus from a poor neighborhood to our laboratory preschool. His mother's paycheck barely covered her rent, let alone food. Hal's diet was deficient in protein and in essential vitamins and minerals—iron

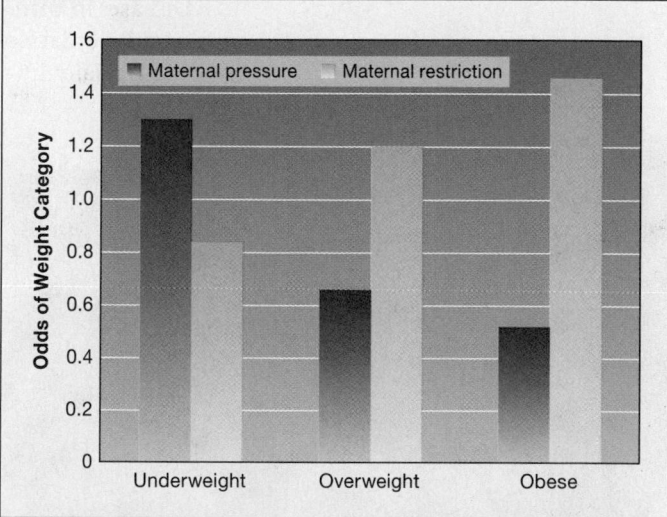

FIGURE 8.5 Relationship of maternal feeding practices to preschoolers' risk of underweight, overweight, and obesity. In a Dutch study of nearly 5,000 four-year-olds, mothers who pressured their child to eat were more likely to have an underweight child. Mothers who restricted their child's eating increased their chances of having an overweight or obese child. These relationships held even after controlling for many factors that could have influenced maternal feeding practices and preschoolers' weight gain, including parents' SES, ethnicity, height, and weight and children's enjoyment of eating. (Based on Jansen et al., 2012.)

LOOK and LISTEN

Arrange to join a family with at least one preschooler for a meal, and closely observe parental mealtime practices. Are they likely to promote healthy eating habits? Explain.

(to prevent anemia), calcium (to support development of bones and teeth), zinc (to support immune system functioning, neural communication, and cell duplication), vitamin A (to help maintain eyes, skin, and a variety of internal organs), and vitamin C (to facilitate iron absorption and wound healing). These are the most common dietary deficiencies of the preschool years (Yousafzai, Yakoob, & Bhutta, 2013).

Hal was small for his age, pale, inattentive, and unruly at preschool. By the school years, low-SES U.S. children are, on average, about ½ to 1 inch shorter than their economically advantaged counterparts (Cecil et al., 2005). And throughout childhood and adolescence, a nutritionally deficient diet is associated with attention and memory difficulties, poorer intelligence and achievement test scores, and behavior problems—especially hyperactivity and aggression—even after family factors that might account for these relationships (such as stressors, parental psychological health, education, warmth, and stimulation of the child) are controlled (Liu et al., 2004; Lukowski et al., 2010; Slack & Yoo, 2005).

Infectious Disease

One day, we noticed that Hal had been absent from the play yard for several weeks, so we asked Leslie, his preschool teacher, what was wrong. "Hal's been hospitalized with the measles," she explained. "He's had difficulty recovering—lost weight when there wasn't much to lose in the first place." In well-nourished children, ordinary childhood illnesses have no effect on physical growth. But when children are undernourished, disease interacts with malnutrition in a vicious spiral, with potentially severe consequences.

INFECTIOUS DISEASE AND MALNUTRITION Hal's reaction to the measles is commonplace in developing nations, where a large proportion of the population lives in poverty and children do not receive routine immunizations. Illnesses such as measles and chicken pox, which typically do not appear until after age 3 in industrialized nations, occur much earlier. Poor diet depresses the body's immune system, making children far more susceptible to disease. Of the 6.6 million annual deaths of children under age 5 worldwide, 98 percent are in developing countries, and 65 percent are due to infectious diseases (World Health Organization, 2012a, 2013a).

Disease, in turn, is a major contributor to malnutrition, hindering both physical growth and cognitive development. Illness reduces appetite and limits the body's ability to absorb foods, especially in children with intestinal infections. In developing countries, widespread diarrhea, resulting from unsafe water and contaminated foods, leads to growth stunting and an estimated one million childhood deaths each year (Unger et al., 2014). Studies carried out in the slums and shantytowns of Brazil and Peru reveal that the more persistent diarrhea is in early childhood, the shorter children are in height and the lower their intelligence test scores during the school years (Checkley et al., 2003; Niehaus et al., 2002).

Most developmental impairments and deaths due to diarrhea can be prevented with nearly cost-free *oral rehydration therapy (ORT)*, in which sick children are given a glucose, salt, and water solution that quickly replaces fluids the body loses. Since 1990, public health workers have taught nearly half the families in the developing world how to administer ORT. Also, supplements of zinc (essential for immune system functioning), which cost only 25 cents for a ten-day supply, substantially reduce the incidence of severe and prolonged diarrhea, especially when combined with ORT (Galvao et al., 2013). Through these interventions, the lives of millions of children are saved each year.

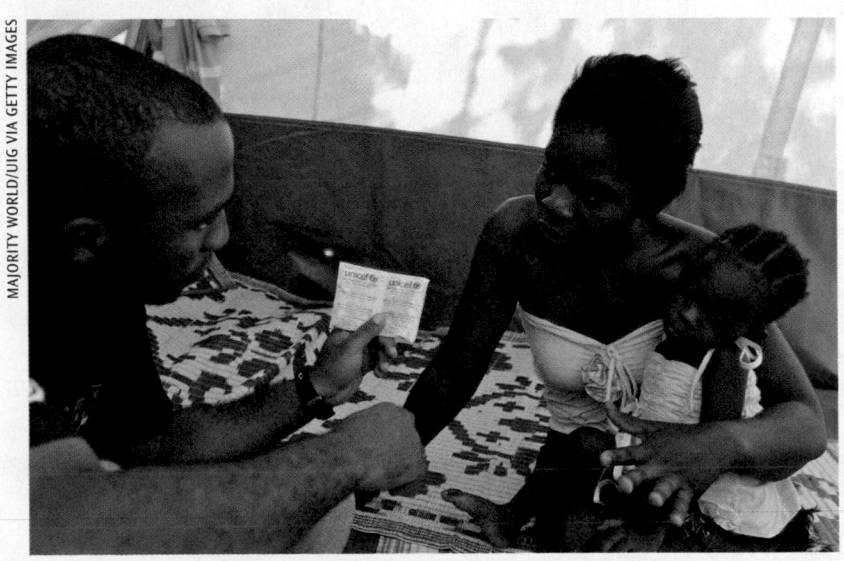

MAJORITY WORLD/UIG VIA GETTY IMAGES

A public health worker teaches a Haitian mother how to prepare an oral rehydration therapy (ORT) packet for her child, who is suffering from diarrhea. This nearly cost-free treatment saves the lives of millions of children in developing countries each year.

IMMUNIZATION In industrialized nations, childhood diseases have declined dramatically during the past half century, largely as a result of widespread immunization of infants and young children. Hal got the measles because, unlike his classmates from more advantaged homes, he did not receive a full program of immunizations.

In the United States, routine childhood immunizations have prevented an estimated 322 million illnesses and 700,000 deaths over the past two decades (Whitney et al., 2014). Yet about 20 percent of U.S. infants and toddlers are not fully immunized. Of the 80 percent who receive a complete schedule of vaccinations in the first two years, some do not receive the immunizations they need later, in early childhood. Overall, 17 percent of U.S. preschoolers lack essential immunizations. The rate rises to 22 percent for poverty-stricken children, many of whom do not receive full protection until age 5 or 6, when it is required for school entry (Centers for Disease Control and Prevention, 2013b). In contrast, fewer than 10 percent of preschoolers lack immunizations in Australia, Denmark, and Norway, and fewer than 5 percent in Canada, the Netherlands, Sweden, and the United Kingdom (World Health Organization, 2014a).

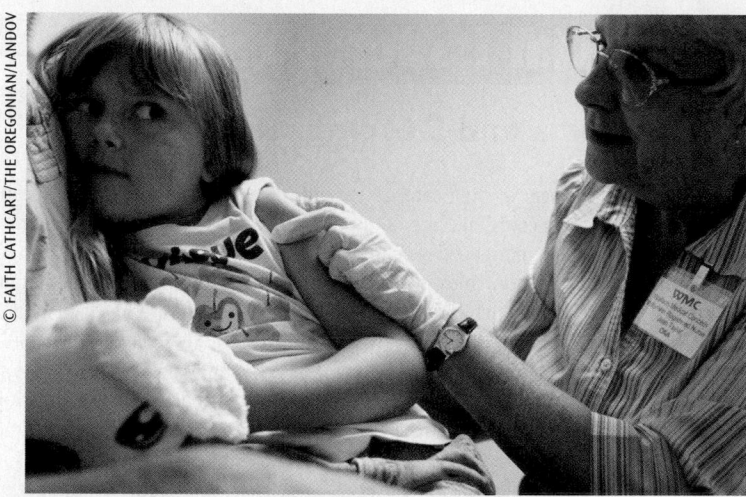

Although routine childhood immunizations prevent illness and death, fewer preschoolers in the United States receive timely essential vaccinations than do their counterparts in many Western nations.

Why does the United States lag behind these countries in immunization? Although the U.S. Affordable Care act greatly improved health insurance coverage for American children, many low-income children remain without coverage (return to pages 79–80 in Chapter 2 to review) and, therefore, may not receive timely vaccinations. In 1994, all U.S. children whose parents are unable to pay were guaranteed free immunizations, a program that has led to gains in vaccination rates.

But inability to pay for vaccines is not the only cause of U.S. inadequate immunization. Parents with little education and with stressful daily lives often fail to schedule vaccination appointments, and those without a primary-care physician do not want to endure long waits in crowded U.S. public health clinics (Falagas & Zarkadoulia, 2008). Some parents have been influenced by media reports—now widely discredited—suggesting a link between a mercury-based preservative used for decades in vaccines and a rise in the number of children diagnosed with autism. In fact, large-scale studies show no association with autism and no consistent effects on cognitive performance (Hensley & Briars, 2010; Richler et al., 2006; Stehr-Green et al., 2003; Thompson et al., 2007). Still, as a precautionary measure, mercury-free versions of childhood vaccines are now available. Other parents have religious or philosophical objections—for example, the belief that children should develop immunities naturally.

In areas where many parents refuse to immunize their children, disease outbreaks of whooping cough and rubella have occurred, with life-threatening consequences (Kennedy & Gust, 2008). Public education programs directed at increasing parental knowledge about the importance and safety of timely immunizations, and convenient opportunities to obtain them free or at low cost, are badly needed. The Netherlands achieves its high child immunization rate by giving parents of every newborn baby a written schedule that shows exactly when and where the child should be immunized (Lernout et al., 2013). If a parent does not bring the child at the specified time, a public health nurse calls the family. When appointments are missed repeatedly, the nurse goes to the home to ensure that the child receives the recommended vaccines.

A final point regarding communicable disease in early childhood deserves mention. Childhood illness rises with child-care attendance. On average, an infant or toddler in child care becomes sick 9 to 10 times a year, a preschooler 6 to 7 times. The diseases that spread most rapidly are those most frequently suffered by young children—diarrhea and respiratory infections. The risk that a respiratory infection will result in *otitis media,* or middle ear infection, is greatly elevated. To learn about the consequences of otitis media and how to prevent it, consult the Social Issues: Health box on page 298.

Social Issues: Health

Otitis Media and Development

During his first year in child care, 2-year-old Alex caught five colds, had the flu on two occasions, and experienced repeated *otitis media* (middle ear infection). Alex is not unusual. By age 3, 75 percent of U.S. children have had respiratory illnesses that resulted in at least one bout of otitis media; nearly half of these have had three or more bouts (Aronson & Henderson, 2006). Although antibiotics eliminate the bacteria responsible for otitis media, they do not reduce fluid buildup in the middle ear, which causes mild to moderate hearing loss that can last for weeks or months.

The incidence of otitis media is greatest between 6 months and 3 years, when children are first acquiring language. Frequent infections predict delayed language progress in early childhood and poorer academic performance, including reading deficits, after school entry (Racanello & McCabe, 2010).

How might otitis media disrupt language and academic progress? Difficulties in perceiving and processing speech sounds, particularly in noisy settings, may be responsible. Children with many bouts are less attentive to others' speech and less persistent at tasks (Asbjornsen et al., 2005; Polka & Rvachew, 2005). Their distractibility may result from an inability to make out what people around them are saying—which, in turn, may reduce the quality of others' interactions with them.

Because otitis media is so widespread, current evidence argues strongly in favor of early prevention. Crowded living conditions and exposure to cigarette smoke and other pollutants are linked to the disease, probably accounting for its high incidence among low-SES children. And compared with children remaining at home, rates of otitis media nearly double in children who attend child-care centers, where severe, antibacterial-resistant strains of respiratory infections can easily develop and spread. Risk increases further with the number of daily child-care settings a child experiences, which magnifies the number of peers with whom the child comes in contact (Morrissey, 2013).

Early otitis media can be prevented in the following ways:

Otitis media is widespread among children who attend child-care centers, where close contact leads to rapid spread of respiratory infection.

- *Frequent screening for the disease, followed by prompt medical intervention.* Plastic tubes that drain the narrow Eustachian tubes of the middle ear often are used to treat chronic otitis media in children, although their effectiveness has been disputed.
- *Child-care settings that control infection.* Because infants and young children often put toys in their mouths, these objects should be rinsed frequently with a disinfectant. Pacifier use has also been linked to a greater risk of otitis media (Rovers et al., 2008). Spacious, well-ventilated rooms and small group sizes help limit spread of the disease.
- *Verbally stimulating adult–child interaction.* Developmental problems associated with otitis media are reduced or eliminated in high-quality child-care centers. When caregivers are verbally stimulating and keep noise to a minimum, children have more opportunities to hear, and benefit from, spoken language (Vernon-Feagans et al., 2007).
- *Vaccines.* Many cases of otitis media are associated with influenza infection, making regular flu vaccination a helpful preventive measure (Principi, Baggi, & Esposito, 2012).

Childhood Injuries

More than any other child in the preschool classroom, 3-year-old Tommy had trouble sitting still and paying attention. Instead, he darted from one place and activity to another. One day, he narrowly escaped serious injury when he put his mother's car in gear while she was outside scraping ice from its windows. The vehicle rolled through a guardrail and over the side of a 10-foot concrete underpass, where it hung until rescue workers arrived. Police charged Tommy's mother with failing to use a restraint seat for a child younger than age 8.

Unintentional injuries are the leading cause of childhood mortality in industrialized nations. Although U.S. childhood injury fatalities have declined steadily over the past 35 years due to state laws and community policies aimed at improving child safety, the United States nevertheless ranks poorly in these largely preventable events, as Figure 8.6 reveals. About 35 percent of U.S. childhood deaths and 50 percent of adolescent deaths result from injuries, causing over 8,000 children to die annually (Child Trends, 2014d). And among the hundreds of thousands of injured children and youths who survive, many suffer pain, brain damage, and permanent physical disabilities.

FIGURE 8.6 International death rates due to unintentional injury among 1- to 14-year-olds. Compared with other industrialized nations, the United States has a high injury death rate, largely because of widespread childhood poverty and shortages of high-quality child care. Injury death rates are many times higher in developing nations, where poverty, rapid population growth, overcrowding in cities, and inadequate safety measures endanger children's lives. (Based on World Health Organization, 2008.)

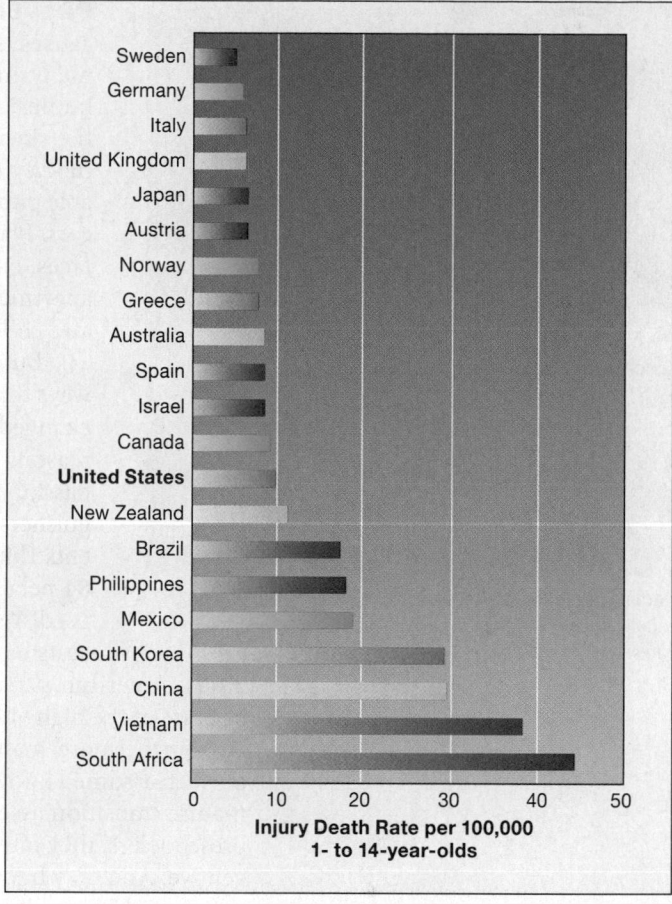

Injury Death Rate per 100,000
1- to 14-year-olds

Auto and traffic accidents, drownings, and burns are the most common childhood injuries (Safe Kids Worldwide, 2013). Motor vehicle collisions are by far the most frequent source of injury. They rank as the second leading U.S. cause of death from birth to age 5 (after suffocation among infants and drowning among toddlers and preschoolers) and as the leading cause of death among school-age children and adolescents.

FACTORS RELATED TO CHILDHOOD INJURIES The common view of childhood injuries as "accidental" suggests that they are due to chance and cannot be prevented. In fact, these injuries occur within a complex *ecological system* of individual, family, community, and societal influences—and we can do something about them.

As Tommy's case suggests, individual differences exist in the safety of children's behaviors. Because of their higher activity level and greater impulsivity and risk taking, boys are nearly twice as likely as girls to be injured, and their injuries are more severe (Child Trends, 2014d). Parents realize that they need to take more steps to protect their young sons than daughters from injury, and most do so. Still, mothers judge the chances of preventing injury in sons to be lower (Morrongiello & Kiriakou, 2004; Morrongiello, Ondejko, & Littlejohn, 2004). This belief may keep parents from sufficiently monitoring the most injury-prone boys.

Children with certain temperamental characteristics—inattentiveness, overactivity, irritability, defiance, and aggression—are also at greater risk for injury (Ordonana, Caspi, & Moffitt, 2008; Schwebel & Gaines, 2007). As we saw in Chapter 7, these children present child-rearing challenges. They are likely to protest when placed in auto seat restraints, to refuse to take a companion's hand when crossing the street, and to disobey after repeated instruction and discipline.

Poverty, single parenthood, and low parental education are also strongly associated with injury (Dudani, Macpherson, & Tamim, 2010; Schwebel & Brezausek, 2007). Parents who must cope with many daily stresses often have little time or energy to monitor the safety of their children. And their homes and neighborhoods are likely to be noisy, crowded, and rundown, posing further risks.

Broad societal conditions also affect childhood injury. In developing countries, the rate of death from injury before age 15 is five times as high as in developed nations and soon may exceed disease as the leading cause of childhood mortality (refer again to Figure 8.6). Rapid population growth, overcrowding in cities, and heavy road traffic combined with weak safety measures are major causes. Safety devices, such as car safety seats and bicycle helmets, are neither readily available nor affordable.

Childhood injury rates are high in the United States because of extensive poverty, shortages of high-quality child care (to supervise children in their parents' absence), and a high rate of births to teenagers, who are neither psychologically nor financially ready for parenthood (Child Trends, 2014a; Ekéus, Christensson, & Hjern, 2003). But U.S. children from advantaged families are also at considerably greater risk for injury than children in Western Europe. This indicates that besides reducing poverty and teenage pregnancy and upgrading the status of child care, additional steps are needed to ensure children's safety.

GARY S. CHAPMAN/GETTY IMAGES

Boys' higher activity level and greater impulsivity and risk taking explain why they are more likely to be injured and to suffer severe injuries than girls.

© GODONG/BSIP/THE IMAGE WORKS

Parental attention to simple precautions—such as wearing bicycle helmets—can substantially reduce childhood injury rates.

PREVENTING CHILDHOOD INJURIES Childhood injuries have many causes, so a variety of approaches are needed to control them. Laws prevent many injuries by requiring car safety seats, child-resistant caps on medicine bottles, flameproof clothing, and fencing around backyard swimming pools—the site of 50 percent of early childhood drownings. Communities can help by modifying their physical environments. Providing inexpensive and widely available public transportation can reduce the amount of time that children spend in cars. Playgrounds, a common site of injury, can be covered with protective surfaces. Free, easily installed window guards can be given to families in high-rise apartment buildings to prevent falls. And media campaigns can inform parents and children about safety issues.

But even though they know better, many parents and children behave in ways that compromise safety. During the past several decades, U.S. parents have changed very little in how much they do to protect their children, citing such reasons as "the chances of serious injury are slim," taking necessary steps "is a hassle," and (among low-income families) safety devices (such as home fire extinguishers and bicycle helmets) "cost too much." For example, 27 percent of U.S. parents (like Tommy's mother) fail to place their children in car safety seats, and 84 percent of infant seats and 40 percent of child booster seats are improperly used. Yet research confirms that young children properly restrained in car safety seats have an 80 percent reduced risk of fatal injury (Safe Kids Worldwide, 2008, 2011). American parents, especially, seem willing to ignore familiar safety practices, perhaps because of the high value they place on individual rights and personal freedom.

Furthermore, many parents overestimate young children's knowledge of safety rules, relying on such assumed knowledge rather than monitoring and controlling access to hazards—a premature transition associated with a rise in home injuries. When parents teach safety rules to preschoolers, they often do so as a reaction to unsafe behaviors, rather than as an advance preventive. And they frequently fail to explain the basis for the rules—despite evidence that explanations enhance children's retention, understanding, and compliance (Morrongiello, Ondejko, & Littlejohn, 2004; Morrongiello et al., 2014). Even with well-learned rules, preschoolers need supervision to ensure that they comply (Morrongiello, Midgett, & Shields, 2001).

Interventions aimed at parents that highlight risk factors and that model and reinforce safety practices are effective in reducing home hazards and childhood injuries (Kendrick et al., 2008). Attention must also be paid to family conditions that can prevent childhood injury: relieving crowding in the home, providing social supports to ease parental stress, and teaching parents to use effective discipline—a topic we will take up in Chapter 10. Positive parenting—an affectionate, supportive relationship with the child; consistent, reasonable expectations for maturity; and oversight to ensure safety-rule compliance—substantially reduces injury rates, especially in overactive, emotionally reactive, and impulsive children (Schwebel & Gaines, 2007). But to implement these strategies, parents must have ample time and emotional resources as well as relevant knowledge and skills. Refer to Applying What We Know on the following page for ways to minimize unintentional injuries in early childhood.

Ask Yourself

- **REVIEW** Describe factors that contribute to sleep problems during the preschool years.

- **CONNECT** Using research on malnutrition or on unintentional injuries, show how physical growth and health in early childhood result from a continuous, complex interplay between heredity and environment.

- **APPLY** One day, Leslie prepared a new snack to serve at preschool: celery stuffed with ricotta cheese and pineapple. The first time she served it, few children touched it. How can Leslie encourage her students to accept the snack? What tactics should she avoid?

- **REFLECT** Ask a parent or other family member whether, as a preschooler, you were a picky eater, suffered from many infectious diseases, or sustained any serious injuries. In each instance, what factors might have been responsible?

Applying What We Know

Reducing Unintentional Injuries in Early Childhood

SUGGESTION	DESCRIPTION
Provide age-appropriate supervision and safety instruction.	Despite gains in understanding and self-control, preschoolers need nearly constant supervision. To encourage children to remember and obey safety rules, establish the rules, explain the reasons behind them, consistently enforce them, and praise children for following them.
Know the child's temperament.	Children who are unusually active, distractible, negative, or curious have more than their share of injuries and need extra monitoring.
Eliminate the most serious dangers from the home.	Examine all spaces for safety. For example, in the kitchen, store dangerous products in high cabinets out of sight, and keep sharp implements in a latched drawer. Remove guns; if that is impossible, store them unloaded in a locked cabinet. Always accompany young preschoolers to the bathroom, and keep all medicines in containers with safety caps.
During automobile travel, always restrain the child properly in the back seat of the car.	Use an age-appropriate, properly installed car safety seat or booster seat up to age 8 or until the child is 4 feet 9 inches tall, and strap the child in correctly every time. Children should always ride in the back seat; passenger-side air bags in the front seat deploy so forcefully that they can cause injury or death to a child. Never leave a child alone in a car, even on a cool, sunny day; a child's core body temperature increases 3 to 5 times faster than an adult's, with risk of permanent injury or death.
Select safe playground equipment and sites.	Make sure sand, wood chips, or rubberized matting has been placed under swings, see-saws, and jungle gyms. Check yards for dangerous plants. Always supervise outdoor play.
Be extra cautious around water.	Constantly observe children during water play; even shallow, inflatable pools are frequent sites of drownings. While they are swimming, young children's heads should not be immersed in water; they may swallow so much that they develop water intoxication, which can lead to convulsions and death.
Practice safety around animals.	Wait to get a pet until the child is mature enough to handle and help care for it—usually around age 5 or 6. Never leave a young child alone with an animal; bites often occur during playful roughhousing. Model and teach humane pet treatment.

Source: Safe Kids Worldwide, 2008.

Motor Development

8.6 Cite major milestones of gross- and fine-motor development in early childhood.

8.7 Describe individual differences in preschoolers' motor skills and ways to enhance motor development in early childhood.

TAKE A MOMENT... Observe several 2- to 6-year-olds at play in a neighborhood park, preschool, or child-care center. You will see that an explosion of new motor skills occurs in early childhood, each of which builds on the simpler movement patterns of toddlerhood.

During the preschool years, children continue to integrate previously acquired skills into more complex, *dynamic systems*. Then they revise each new skill as their bodies grow larger and stronger, their central nervous systems develop, their environments present new challenges, and they set new goals, aided by gains in perceptual and cognitive capacities.

Gross-Motor Development

As children's bodies become more streamlined and less top-heavy, their center of gravity shifts downward, toward the trunk. As a result, balance improves greatly, paving the way for new motor skills involving large muscles of the body. By age 2, preschoolers' gaits become smooth and rhythmic—secure enough that soon they leave the ground, at first by running and later by jumping, hopping, galloping, and skipping.

As children become steadier on their feet, their arms and torsos are freed to experiment with new skills—throwing and catching balls, steering tricycles, and swinging on horizontal bars and rings. Then upper- and lower-body skills combine into more refined actions. Five- and 6-year-olds simultaneously steer and pedal a tricycle and flexibly move their whole body when throwing, catching, hopping, and jumping. By the end of the preschool years, all skills

TABLE 8.1	Changes in Gross- and Fine-Motor Skills During Early Childhood	
AGE	**GROSS-MOTOR SKILLS**	**FINE-MOTOR SKILLS**
2–3 years	Walks more rhythmically; hurried walk changes to run Jumps, hops, throws, and catches with rigid upper body Pushes riding toy with feet; little steering	Puts on and removes simple items of clothing Zips and unzips large zippers Uses spoon effectively
3–4 years	Walks up stairs, alternating feet, and down stairs, leading with one foot Jumps and hops, flexing upper body Throws and catches with slight involvement of upper body; still catches by trapping ball against chest Pedals and steers tricycle	Fastens and unfastens large buttons Serves self food without assistance Uses scissors Copies vertical line and circle Draws first picture of person, using tadpole image
4–5 years	Walks down stairs, alternating feet Runs more smoothly Gallops and skips with one foot Throws ball with increased body rotation and transfer of weight from one foot to the other; catches ball with hands Rides tricycle rapidly, steers smoothly	Uses fork effectively Cuts with scissors following line Copies triangle, cross, and some letters
5–6 years	Increases running speed to 12 feet per second Gallops more smoothly; engages in true skipping Displays mature throwing and catching pattern Rides bicycle with training wheels	Uses knife to cut soft food Ties shoes Draws person with six parts Copies some numbers and simple words

Sources: Cratty, 1986; Haywood & Getchell, 2014.

are performed with greater speed and endurance. Table 8.1 provides a closer look at gross-motor development in early childhood.

Changes in ball skills provide an excellent illustration of preschoolers' gross-motor progress. Young preschoolers stand still, facing the target, throwing with their arm thrust forward (see Figure 8.7a). Catching is equally awkward. Two-year-olds extend their arms and hands rigidly, using them as a single unit to trap the ball. By age 3, children flex their elbows enough to trap the ball against the chest. But if the ball arrives too quickly, they cannot adapt, and it may bounce off the body (Haywood & Getchell, 2014).

Gradually, children call on the shoulders, torso, trunk, and legs to support throwing and catching. By age 4, children rotate the body and take a step forward to add force to their throw.

Throwing style typical of young preschoolers
(a)

Throwing style typical of older children
(b)

FIGURE 8.7 **Changes in throwing during early childhood.** At age 2 to 3, children stand still, simply bringing the hand back and throwing rigidly without taking a step. Gradually, they involve the entire body. By age 5 to 6, they typically engage in arm, leg, and trunk rotation and preparatory action before executing the throw. Integrated throwing movements become increasingly refined and adapted to the throwing situation during middle childhood. (Adapted figures drawn from film tracings taken in the Motor Development and Child Study Laboratory, University of Wisconsin–Madison and now available from the Motor Development Film Collection, Kinesiology Division, Bowling Green State University. © Mary Ann Roberton. Reprinted by permission of Mary Ann Roberton.).

Around 5 to 6 years, they begin by shifting their weight to a rear foot in a preparatory back-swing and then shift forward, rotating the trunk and stepping into the throw as they release the ball (see Figure 8.7b). As a result, the ball travels faster and farther. When the ball is returned, older preschoolers predict its place of landing by moving forward, backward, or sideways. Soon, they can catch the ball with their hands and fingers, "giving" with arms and body to absorb the force of the ball.

LOOK and LISTEN

Play a game of catch with a 2- to 3-year-old, then with a 4- to 6-year-old. What differences in movement and coordination are evident?

Fine-Motor Development

Like gross-motor development, fine-motor skills take a giant leap forward in the preschool years. As control of the hands and fingers improves, young children put puzzles together, build with small blocks, cut and paste, and string beads. To parents, fine-motor progress is most apparent in two areas: (1) children's care of their own bodies, and (2) the drawings and paintings that fill the walls at home, child care, and preschool.

SELF-HELP SKILLS   As Table 8.1 shows, young children gradually become self-sufficient at dressing and feeding. Two-year-olds put on and take off simple items of clothing. By age 3, children can dress and undress well enough to take care of toileting needs by themselves. Between ages 4 and 5, children can dress and undress without supervision. At mealtimes, young preschoolers use a spoon well, and they can serve themselves. By age 4 they are adept with a fork, and around 5 to 6 years they can use a knife to cut soft foods. Roomy clothing with large buttons and zippers and child-sized eating utensils help children master these skills.

Preschoolers get great satisfaction from managing their own bodies. They are proud of their independence, and their new skills also make life easier for adults. But parents must be patient about these abilities: When tired and in a hurry, young children often revert to eating with their fingers. And the 3-year-old who dresses himself in the morning sometimes ends up with his shirt on inside out, his pants on backward, and his left snow boot on his right foot! Perhaps the most complex self-help skill of early childhood is shoe tying, mastered around age 6. Success requires a longer attention span, memory for an intricate series of hand movements, and the dexterity to perform them. Shoe tying illustrates the close connection between motor and cognitive development, as do two other skills: drawing and writing.

DRAWING   When given crayon and paper, even toddlers scribble in imitation of others. As the young child's ability to mentally represent the world expands, marks on the page take on meaning. A variety of factors combine with fine-motor control in the development of children's artful representations (Golomb, 2004). These include the realization that pictures can serve as symbols, improved planning and spatial understanding, and the emphasis that the child's culture places on artistic expression.

Typically, drawing progresses through the following sequence:

Preschoolers gradually become more proficient at self-help skills of dressing and feeding themselves. Most master shoe tying, the most complex self-help skill, around age 6.

1. *Scribbles*. Western children begin to draw during the second year. At first, the intended representation is contained in gestures rather than in the resulting marks on the page. For example, one 18-month-old made her crayon hop and, as it produced a series of dots, explained, "Rabbit goes hop-hop" (Winner, 1986).

   Recall from Chapter 6 that 2-year-olds treat realistic-looking pictures symbolically, but they have difficulty interpreting line drawings. When an adult held up a drawing indicating which of two objects preschoolers should drop down a chute, 3-year-olds used the drawing as a symbol to guide their behavior, but 2-year-olds did not (Callaghan, 1999).

2. *First representational forms*. Around age 3, children's scribbles start to become pictures. Often children make a gesture with the crayon, notice that they have drawn a recognizable shape, and then label it. In one case, a 2-year-old made some random marks on a page and then, realizing the resemblance between his scribbles and noodles, named the creation "chicken pie and noodles" (Winner, 1986).

╫ **LOOK** *and* ╫
LISTEN

Visit a preschool or child-care center where artwork by 3- to 5-year-olds is plentiful. Note developmental progress in drawings of human and animal figures and in the complexity of children's pictures.

Few 3-year-olds spontaneously draw so others can tell what their picture represents. However, after an adult demonstrated how drawings can be used to stand for objects in a game, more 3-year-olds drew recognizable forms (Callaghan & Rankin, 2002). Western parents and teachers spend much time promoting 2- and 3-year-olds' language and make-believe play but relatively little time showing them how they can use drawings to represent their world (Cohn, 2014). When adults draw with children and point out resemblances between drawings and objects, preschoolers' pictures become more comprehensible and detailed (Braswell & Callanan, 2003).

A major milestone in drawing occurs when children use lines to represent the boundaries of objects. This enables 3- and 4-year-olds to draw their first picture of a person. Fine-motor and cognitive limitations lead the preschooler to reduce the figure to the simplest form that still looks human—the universal "tadpole" image, a circular shape with lines attached, shown on the left in Figure 8.8. Four-year-olds add features, such as eyes, nose, mouth, hair, fingers, and feet, as the tadpole drawings illustrate.

3. *More realistic drawings.* Five- and 6-year-olds create more complex drawings, like the one on the right in Figure 8.8, containing more conventional human and animal figures, with the head and body differentiated. Older preschoolers' drawings still contain perceptual distortions because they have just begun to represent depth. Use of depth cues, such as overlapping objects, smaller size for distant than for near objects, diagonal placement, and converging lines, increases during middle childhood (Nicholls & Kennedy, 1992).

Realism in drawings appears gradually, as perception, language (ability to describe visual details), sustained attention, memory, and fine-motor capacities improve (Riggs, Jolley, & Simpson, 2013; Toomela, 2002). Drawing of geometric objects follows the steps illustrated in Figure 8.9. (1) Three- to 7-year olds draw a single unit to stand for an object. To represent a cube, they draw a square; to represent a cylinder, they draw a circle, an oval, or a rectangle. (2) During the late preschool and school years, children represent salient object parts. They draw several squares to stand for a cube's sides and draw two circles and some lines to represent a cylinder. However, the parts are not joined properly. (3) Older school-age children and adolescents integrate object parts into a realistic whole (Toomela, 1999).

Drawing Category and Approximate Age Range	Cube	Cylinder
Single Units (3 to 7 years)		
Object Parts (4 to 13 years)		
Integrated Whole (8 years and older)		

FIGURE 8.8 Examples of young children's drawings. The universal tadpolelike shape that children use to draw their first picture of a person is shown on the left. The tadpole soon becomes an anchor for greater detail as arms, fingers, toes, and facial features sprout from the basic shape. By the end of the preschool years, children produce more complex, differentiated pictures like the one on the right, drawn by a 6-year-old child. (*Left:* From H. Gardner, 1980, *Artful Scribbles: The Significance of Children's Drawing*, New York: Basic Books, p. 64. Copyright © 1980 by Howard Gardner. Reprinted by permission of Basic Books, a member of the Perseus Books, conveyed through Copyright Clearance Center. *Right:* From E. Winner, "Where Pelicans Kiss Seals," *Psychology Today, 20*[8], August 1986, p. 35. Reprinted by permission from the collection of Ellen Winner.)

FIGURE 8.9 Development of children's drawings of geometric objects—a cube and a cylinder. As these examples show, drawings change from single units to representation of object parts. Then the parts are integrated into a realistic whole. (Based on Toomela, 1999.)

Cultural Influences

Why Are Children from Asian Cultures Advanced in Drawing Skills?

Return to the elaborate, expressive drawing, by a Chinese artist just 4 years old, on the opening page of this chapter. Observations of young children's drawings in Asian cultures, such as China, Japan, Korea, the Philippines, Taiwan, and Vietnam, reveal skills that are remarkably advanced over those of their Western agemates. What explains such early artistic ability?

To answer this question, researchers have examined cultural influences on children's drawings, comparing China to the United States. Artistic models offered by the culture, teaching strategies, valuing of the visual arts, and expectations for children's artistic development can have a notable impact on the art that children produce.

In China's 4,000-year-old artistic tradition, adults showed children how to draw, encouraging them to master the precise steps required to depict people, butterflies, fish, birds, and other images. When taught to paint, Chinese children follow prescribed brush strokes, at first copying their teacher's model. To learn to write, they must concentrate hard on the unique details of each Chinese character—a requirement that likely augments their drawing ability. Chinese parents and teachers believe that children can be creative only after they have acquired a foundation of artistic knowledge and technique (Golomb, 2004). To that end, China has devised a national art curriculum with standards and teaching materials extending from age 3 through secondary school.

The United States, as well, has a rich artistic tradition, but its styles and conventions are enormously diverse compared with those of Asian cultures. Children everywhere try to imitate the art around them as a way to acquire their culture's "visual language." But American children face a

daunting imitative task, much like a child growing up in a context where each person speaks a different language (Cohn, 2014). Furthermore, U.S. art education emphasizes independence—finding one's own style. American teachers typically assume that copying others' drawings stifles creativity, so they discourage children from doing so (Copple & Bredekamp, 2009). Rather than promoting correct ways to draw, U.S. teachers emphasize imagination and self-expression.

Does the Chinese method of teaching drawing skills beginning in the preschool years interfere with children's creativity? To find out, researchers followed a group of Chinese-American children of immigrant parents and a group of Caucasian-American children, all from middle-SES two-parent families, from ages 5 to 9. At two-year intervals, the children's human-figure drawings were rated for maturity and originality—inclusion of novel elements (Huntsinger et al., 2011). Findings revealed that on each occasion, the Chinese-American children's drawings were more advanced and also more creative.

Interviews revealed that Caucasian-American parents more often mentioned providing their children with a rich variety of art materials, whereas Chinese-American parents more often reported enrolling their children in art lessons, rating the development of artistic competence as more important. The Chinese-American children also spent more time as preschoolers and kindergartners in focused practice of fine-motor

TAO IMAGES RM/GETTY IMAGES

The complex drawings of these kindergartners in Shanghai, China, benefit from adult expectations that young children learn to draw well, careful teaching of artistic knowledge and technique, and the rich artistic tradition of Chinese culture.

tasks, including drawing. And the more time they spent, especially when their parents taught and modeled drawing at home, the more mature their drawing skills. At the same time, Chinese-American children's artistic creativity flourished under this systematic approach to promoting artistic maturity.

In sum, even though young Chinese children are taught how to draw, their artistic products are original. Once they succeed at drawing basic forms, they spontaneously add unusual details of their own. Although Western children may come up with rich ideas about what to draw, until they acquire the necessary skills, they cannot implement those ideas. Cross-cultural research indicates that children benefit from adult guidance in learning to draw, just as they do in learning to talk.

CULTURAL VARIATIONS IN DEVELOPMENT OF DRAWING In cultures that have rich artistic traditions and that highly value artistic competence, children create elaborate drawings that reflect the conventions of their culture. Adults encourage young children by guiding them in mastering basic drawing skills, modeling ways to draw, and discussing their pictures. Peers, as well, talk about one another's drawings and copy from one another's work (Boyatzis, 2000; Braswell, 2006). All of these practices enhance young children's drawing progress. And as the Cultural Influences box above reveals, they help explain why, from an early age, children in Asian cultures are advanced over Western children in drawing skills.

In cultures with little interest in art, even older children and adolescents produce simple forms. In the Jimi Valley, a remote region of Papua New Guinea with no indigenous pictorial

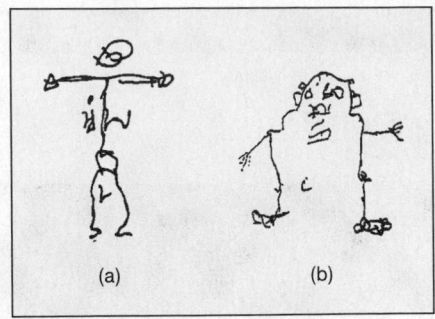

FIGURE 8.10 **Human figure drawings produced by nonschooled 10- to 15-year-olds of the Jimi Valley of Papua New Guinea.** Many produced (a) "stick" figures or (b) "contour" figures, which resemble the tadpole form of young preschoolers. (From M. Martlew & K. J. Connolly, 1996, "Human Figure Drawings by Schooled and Unschooled Children in Papua New Guinea," *Child Development, 67*, pp. 2750–2751. © The Society for Research in Child Development. Adapted with permission of John Wiley and Sons, Inc., conveyed through Copyright Clearance Center, Inc.)

Gains in fine-motor control and perception, along with experience with written materials, contribute to this 5-year-old's skill at printing.

art, many children do not go to school and therefore have little opportunity to develop drawing skills. When a Western researcher asked nonschooled Jimi 10- to 15-year-olds to draw a human figure for the first time, most produced nonrepresentational scribbles and shapes or simple "stick" or "contour" images (see Figure 8.10) (Martlew & Connolly, 1996). These forms, which resemble those of preschoolers, seem to be a universal beginning in drawing. Once children realize that lines must evoke human features, they find solutions to figure drawing that vary somewhat from culture to culture but, overall, follow the sequence described earlier.

EARLY PRINTING When preschoolers first try to write, they scribble, making no distinction between writing and drawing. As they experiment with lines and shapes, notice print in storybooks, and observe people writing, they attempt to print letters and, later, words. Around age 4, children's writing shows some distinctive features of print, such as separate forms arranged in a line on the page. But children often include picturelike devices. For example, they might use a circular shape to write "sun." Or they might call a large scribble the word *lion,* a small scribble the word *caterpillar,* and a red scribble the word *apple* (Ehri & Roberts, 2006; Levin & Bus, 2003). Applying their understanding of the symbolic function of drawings, 4-year-olds asked to write typically make a "drawing of print." Only gradually, as they learn to name the letters of the alphabet and to link them with language sounds, do preschoolers realize that writing stands for language.

Preschoolers' first attempts to print often involve their name, generally using a single letter. "How do you make a *D*?" your first author's older son David asked at age 3½. When his mother printed a large uppercase *D*, he tried to copy. "*D* for David," he proclaimed, quite satisfied with his backward, imperfect creation. A year later, David added several letters, and around age 5, he printed his name clearly enough that others could read it.

Between ages 3 and 5, children acquire skill in gripping a pencil. As Figure 8.11 shows, 3-year-olds display diverse grip patterns and pencil angles, varying their grip depending on the direction and location of the marks they want to make. By trying out different forms of pencil-holding, they discover the grip and angle that maximize stability and writing efficiency (Greer & Lockman, 1998). By age 5, most children use an adult grip pattern and a fairly constant pencil angle across a range of drawing and writing conditions.

In addition to gains in fine-motor control, advances in perception contribute to the ability to print. Like many children, David continued to reverse letters until well into second grade. Once preschoolers distinguish writing from nonwriting around age 4, they make progress in identifying individual letters. Many preschoolers confuse letter pairs that are alike in shape with subtle distinctive features, such as *C* and *G, E* and *F,* and *M* and *W* (Bornstein & Arterberry, 1999). Mirror-image letter pairs (*b* and *d, p* and *q*) are especially hard to discriminate. Until children start to read, they do not find it especially useful to notice the difference between these forms.

The ability to tune in to mirror images and to scan a printed line from left to right improves as children gain experience with written materials (Casey, 1986). The more parents and teachers assist preschoolers in their efforts to print, the more advanced children are in writing and other aspects of literacy development (Aram & Levin, 2011). We will consider early childhood literacy in greater detail in Chapter 9.

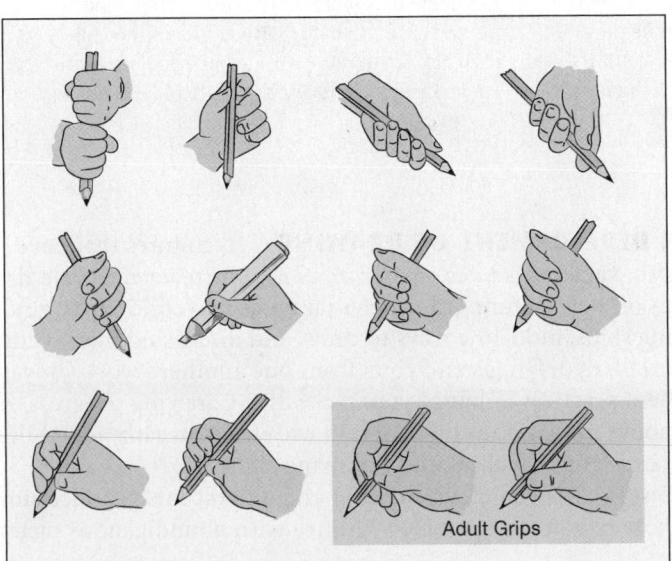

Adult Grips

FIGURE 8.11 **Variations in 3-year-olds' pencil grip.** Through experimenting with different grips, preschoolers gradually discover an adult grip with one or two fingers on top of the pencil, which maximizes writing stability and efficiency. (Based on Greer & Lockman, 1998.)

Individual Differences in Motor Skills

Wide individual differences exist in the ages at which children reach motor mile-stones. A child with a tall, muscular body tends to move more quickly and to acquire certain skills earlier than a short, stocky youngster. And as in other domains, parents and teachers probably provide more encouragement to children with biologically based motor-skill advantages.

Sex differences in motor skills are evident in early childhood. Boys are ahead of girls in skills that emphasize force and power. By age 5, they can broad-jump slightly farther, run slightly faster, and throw a ball about 5 feet farther. Girls have an edge in fine-motor skills and in certain gross-motor skills that require a combination of good balance and foot movement, such as hopping and skipping (Fischman, Moore, & Steele, 1992; Haywood & Getchell, 2014). Boys' greater muscle mass and, in the case of throwing, slightly longer forearms contribute to their skill advantages. And girls' greater overall physical maturity may be partly responsible for their better balance and precision of movement.

From an early age, boys and girls are usually channeled into different physical activities. For example, fathers are more likely to play catch with their sons than with their daughters. Baseballs and footballs are purchased for boys, jump ropes and sewing materials for girls. Sex differences in motor skills increase with age, but they remain small throughout childhood (Greendorfer, Lewko, & Rosengren, 1996). This suggests that social pressures for boys to be active and physically skilled and for girls to play quietly at fine-motor activities exaggerate small genetically based sex differences. In support of this view, boys can throw a ball much farther than girls only when using their dominant hand. When they use their nondominant hand, the sex difference is minimal (Williams, Haywood, & Painter, 1996). Boys' superior throwing largely results from practice.

Sex differences in motor development are already apparent in early childhood. Girls have an edge in skills that require balance and precision of movement, like jumping rope, but boys benefit from greater encouragement to improve their skill levels in throwing, catching, and running.

Enhancing Early Childhood Motor Development

Many Western parents provide preschoolers with early training in gymnastics, tumbling, dance, soccer, and other movement skills through organized classes. These experiences can offer excellent opportunities for exercise and social interaction. But aside from throwing (where direct instruction is helpful), formal lessons during the preschool years have little added impact on gross-motor progress. Rather, children master the gross-motor skills of early childhood through everyday play.

Nevertheless, the physical environment in which play takes place can affect mastery of complex motor skills. The National Association for Sport and Physical Education (2009) recommends that preschoolers engage in at least 60 minutes of adult-planned physical experiences in which parents and teachers provide enjoyable games and other playful activities, and up to several hours of child-directed physical activity, every day. When children have play spaces and equipment appropriate for running, climbing, jumping, and throwing and are encouraged to use them, they respond eagerly to these challenges. But if balls are too large and heavy to be properly grasped and thrown, or jungle gyms, ladders, and horizontal bars are suitable for only the largest and strongest children, then preschoolers cannot easily acquire new motor skills. Playgrounds must offer a range of equipment to meet the diverse needs of individual children.

Similarly, development of fine-motor skills can be supported through daily routines, such as dressing and pouring juice, and through richly equipped early childhood environments that include puzzles, construction sets, drawing, painting, sculpting, cutting, and pasting. And as the Cultural Influences box on page 305 revealed, adults who guide and support children in acquiring drawing skills foster artistic development.

When play spaces are properly designed and equipped, young children respond eagerly to motor challenges and develop new skills through informal play.

Finally, the social climate created by adults can enhance or dampen preschoolers' motor development. When parents and teachers criticize a child's performance, push specific motor skills, or promote a competitive attitude, they risk undermining children's self-confidence and, in turn, their motor progress (Berk, 2006). Adult involvement in young children's motor activities should focus on fun rather than on winning or perfecting the "correct" technique.

Ask Yourself

- **REVIEW** Describe typical changes in children's drawings in early childhood, along with factors that contribute to those changes. Why are children from Asian cultures advanced in drawing skills?

- **CONNECT** How are experiences that best support preschoolers' gross-motor development consistent with experience-expectant brain growth of the early years? (Return to page 169 in Chapter 5 to review.)

- **APPLY** Mabel and Chad want to do everything they can to support their 3-year-old daughter's athletic development. What advice would you give them?

- **REFLECT** Do you think American children should be provided with systematic instruction in drawing skills beginning in early childhood, similar to the direct teaching Chinese children receive? Explain.

Summary

Body Growth (p. 285)

8.1 Describe changes in body size, proportions, and skeletal maturity during early childhood.

- Gains in body size taper off in early childhood as children become longer and leaner, and individual differences in body size and rate of growth are more apparent. In various parts of the skeleton, new epiphyses emerge, where cartilage hardens into bone.

LAYLAND MASUDA/MOMENT OPEN/GETTY IMAGES

- By the end of the preschool years, children start to lose their primary teeth. Care of primary teeth is essential because diseased baby teeth can affect the health of permanent teeth. Childhood tooth decay remains common, especially among low-SES children.

8.2 Describe brain development in early childhood.

- Neural fibers in the brain continue to form synapses and myelinate. By this time, many parts of the cerebral cortex have overproduced synapses, and *synaptic pruning* occurs. To make room for the connective structures of stimulated neurons, many surrounding neurons die, leading to reduced brain plasticity.

- Prefrontal-cortical areas devoted to various aspects of executive function show rapid growth from early to middle childhood. In addition, for most children, the left cerebral hemisphere develops ahead of the right, supporting rapidly expanding language skills.

- Hand preference, which reflects an individual's **dominant cerebral hemisphere,** strengthens during early childhood. Research on handedness supports the joint contribution of nature and nurture to brain lateralization.

- During early childhood, connections are established between brain structures. Fibers linking the **cerebellum** to the cerebral cortex grow and myelinate, enhancing motor coordination and cognition. The **reticular formation,** responsible for alertness and consciousness; the **hippocampus,** which plays a vital role in memory and understanding of space; the **amygdala,** which plays a central role in processing novelty and emotional information; and the **corpus callosum,** which connects the two cortical hemispheres, also form synapses and myelinate.

Influences on Physical Growth and Health (p. 290)

8.3 Explain how heredity influences physical growth.

- Heredity influences physical growth by controlling production and release of two vital hormones from the **pituitary gland: growth hormone (GH),** which affects the development of almost all body tissues, and **thyroid-stimulating hormone (TSH),** which affects brain growth and body size.

8.4 Describe the effects of emotional well-being, restful sleep, nutrition, and infectious disease on physical growth and health in early childhood.

- Emotional well-being continues to influence growth and health. Extreme emotional deprivation can lead to **psychosocial dwarfism.**

- Restful sleep contributes to body growth, since GH is released during the child's sleeping hours. Sleep difficulties impair cognitive functioning and emotional adjustment, especially for low-SES children. Although total sleep need declines, substantial variability exists.

- Sleep problems sometimes stem from inadequate parental control over young children's use of electronic devices, as well as a mismatch between parental demands and children's sleep needs. Many preschoolers have difficulty falling asleep, and most awaken occasionally at night. A few children suffer from sleep disorders, such as sleepwalking or sleep terrors, which run in families, suggesting a genetic influence. These problems can also be triggered by stress or extreme fatigue. Most subside with age.

- As growth rate slows, preschoolers' appetites decline, and they often become wary of new foods. Modeling by others, repeated exposure to new foods, and a positive emotional climate at mealtimes can promote healthy, varied eating.

- Dietary deficiencies—most commonly in protein, vitamins, and minerals—are associated with attention and memory difficulties, academic and behavior problems, and greater susceptibility to infectious diseases. Disease also contributes to malnutrition, especially when intestinal infections cause persistent diarrhea. In developing countries, inexpensive oral rehydration therapy (ORT) and supplements of zinc can prevent most developmental impairments and deaths due to diarrhea.

- Immunization rates are lower in the United States than in other industrialized nations because many economically disadvantaged children lack access to necessary health care. Parental stress and misconceptions about vaccine safety also contribute.

8.5 What factors increase the risk of unintentional injuries, and how can childhood injuries be prevented?

- Unintentional injuries are the leading cause of childhood mortality in industrialized nations. Injury victims are more likely to be boys; to be temperamentally irritable, inattentive, overactive, and aggressive; and to live in stressed, poverty-stricken, crowded family environments.

- Effective injury prevention includes passing laws that promote child safety; creating safer home, travel, and play environments; relieving sources of family stress; improving public education; and changing parent and child behaviors.

Motor Development (p. 301)

8.6 Cite major milestones of gross- and fine-motor development in early childhood.

- As the child's center of gravity shifts toward the trunk, balance improves, paving the way for new gross-motor achievements. Preschoolers' gaits become smooth and rhythmic; they run, jump, hop, gallop; eventually skip, throw, and catch; and generally become better coordinated.

- Increasing control of the hands and fingers leads to dramatic improvements in fine-motor skills. Preschoolers gradually dress themselves and use a fork and knife.

- By age 3, children's scribbles become pictures. As perceptual, cognitive, and fine-motor capacities improve, children's drawings increase in complexity and realism. Children's drawings are also influenced by their culture's artistic traditions.

- Between 3 and 5 years, children experiment with pencil grip; by age 5, most use an adultlike grip that maximizes stability and writing efficiency.

- Advances in perception and exposure to written materials contribute to progress in discriminating and accurately printing individual letters. When parents and teachers support children's efforts to print, preschoolers are more advanced in writing and other aspects of literacy development.

8.7 Describe individual differences in preschoolers' motor skills and ways to enhance motor development in early childhood.

- Body build and opportunity for physical play affect early childhood motor development. Sex differences that favor boys in skills requiring force and power and girls in skills requiring good balance and fine movements are partly genetic, but social pressures exaggerate them.

- Children master the motor skills of early childhood through informal play experiences, with little benefit from exposure to formal training. Richly equipped play environments that accommodate a wide range of physical abilities are important. Emphasizing pleasure in motor activities is the best way to foster motor development during the preschool years.

Important Terms and Concepts

amygdala (p. 290)
cerebellum (p. 289)
corpus callosum (p. 290)
dominant cerebral hemisphere (p. 288)

growth hormone (GH) (p. 292)
hippocampus (p. 289)
pituitary gland (p. 290)
psychosocial dwarfism (p. 292)

reticular formation (p. 289)
thyroid-stimulating hormone (TSH) (p. 292)

Cognitive Development in Early Childhood

Untitled
Bermain Samil Belajar
6 years, Indonesia

Storybooks expose these children to a wealth of language and literacy experiences and encourage discovery of the wider world. Mental representation blossoms in early childhood, contributing greatly to cognitive and language development.

One rainy morning, as we observed in our laboratory preschool, Leslie, the children's teacher, joined us at the back of the room for a moment. "Preschoolers' minds are such a curious blend of logic, fantasy, and faulty reasoning," Leslie reflected. "Every day, I'm startled by the maturity and originality of what they say and do. Yet at other times, their thinking seems limited and inflexible."

Leslie's comments sum up the puzzling contradictions of early childhood cognition. That day, for example, 3-year-old Sammy looked up, startled, after a loud crash of thunder outside. "A magic man turned on the thunder!" he pronounced. Even when Leslie patiently explained that thunder is caused by lightning, not by a person turning it on or off, Sammy persisted: "Then a magic lady did it."

In other respects, Sammy's thinking was surprisingly advanced. At snack time, he accurately counted, "One, two, three, four!" and then got four cartons of milk, one for each child at his table. Sammy's keen memory and ability to categorize were also evident. He could recite by heart *The Very Hungry Caterpillar*, a story he had heard many times. And he could name and classify dozens of animals.

But when his snack group included more than four children, Sammy's counting broke down. And some of his notions about quantity seemed as fantastic as his understanding of thunder. After Priti dumped out her raisins, scattering them in front of her, Sammy asked, "How come you got lots, and I only got this little bit?" He didn't realize that he had just as many raisins; his were simply all bunched up in a tiny red box. While Priti was washing her hands after snack, Sammy put her remaining raisins in her cubby. When Priti returned and looked for her raisins, Sammy pronounced, "You know where they are!" He failed to grasp that Priti, who hadn't seen him move the raisins, would expect them to be where she had left them.

In this chapter, we explore early childhood cognition, drawing on three theories with which you are already familiar. To understand Sammy's reasoning, we turn first to Piaget's and Vygotsky's theories along with evidence highlighting the strengths and limitations of each. Then we examine additional research on young children's cognition inspired by the information-processing perspective. Next, we address factors that contribute to individual differences in mental development—the home environment, the quality of preschool and child care, and the many hours young children spend with electronic media. Our chapter concludes with the dramatic expansion of language in early childhood. ■

Piaget's Theory: The Preoperational Stage

As children move from the sensorimotor to the **preoperational stage,** which spans the years 2 to 7, the most obvious change is an extraordinary increase in representational, or symbolic, activity. Recall that infants and toddlers have considerable ability to mentally represent their world. In early childhood, this capacity blossoms.

9.1 Describe advances in mental representation, and limitations of thinking, during the preoperational stage.

9.2 What does follow-up research imply about the accuracy of Piaget's preoperational stage?

9.3 What educational principles can be derived from Piaget's theory?

Advances in Mental Representation

Piaget acknowledged that language is our most flexible means of mental representation. By detaching thought from action, it permits far more efficient thinking than was possible earlier. When we think in words, we overcome the limits of our momentary experiences. We can deal with past, present, and future at once and combine concepts in unique ways, as when we imagine a hungry caterpillar eating bananas or monsters flying through the forest at night.

But Piaget did not regard language as a primary ingredient in childhood cognitive change. Instead, he believed that sensorimotor activity leads to internal images of experience, which children then label with words (Piaget, 1936/1952). In support of Piaget's view, recall from Chapter 6 that children's first words have a strong sensorimotor basis. And toddlers acquire an impressive range of categories long before they use words to label them (see page 219). But as we will see, Piaget underestimated the power of language to spur children's cognition.

Make-Believe Play

Make-believe play is another excellent example of the development of representation in early childhood. Piaget believed that through pretending, young children practice and strengthen newly acquired representational schemes. Drawing on his ideas, several investigators have traced changes in make-believe play during the preschool years.

DEVELOPMENT OF MAKE-BELIEVE   One day, Sammy's 20-month-old brother, Dwayne, visited the classroom. Dwayne wandered around, picked up a toy telephone receiver, eyed his mother, said, "Hi, Mommy," and then dropped it. Next, he found a cup, pretended to drink, and then toddled off again. Meanwhile, Sammy joined Vance and Lynette in the block area for a space shuttle launch.

"That can be our control tower," Sammy suggested, pointing to a corner by a bookshelf. "Countdown!" he announced, speaking into his "walkie-talkie"—a small wooden block. "Five, six, two, four, one, blastoff!" Lynette made a doll push a pretend button, and the rocket was off!

Comparing Dwayne's pretend play with Sammy's, we see three important changes that reflect the preschool child's growing symbolic mastery:

- *Play detaches from the real-life conditions associated with it.* In early pretending, toddlers use only realistic objects—a toy telephone to talk into or a cup to drink from. Their earliest pretend acts usually imitate adults' actions and are not yet flexible. Children younger than age 2, for example, will pretend to drink from a cup but refuse to pretend a cup is a hat (Rakoczy, Tomasello, & Striano, 2005). They have trouble using an object (cup) that already has an obvious use as a symbol of another object (hat).

  After age 2, children pretend with less realistic toys—for example, a block for a telephone receiver. Gradually, they can imagine objects and events without any support from the real world, as Sammy's imaginary control tower illustrates (O'Reilly, 1995; Striano, Tomasello, & Rochat, 2001). And by age 3, they flexibly understand that an object (a yellow stick) may take on one fictional identity (a toothbrush) in one pretend game and another fictional identity (a carrot) in a different pretend game (Wyman, Rakoczy, & Tomasello, 2009).
- *Play becomes less self-centered.* At first, make-believe is directed toward the self. For example, Dwayne pretends to feed only himself. Soon, children begin to direct pretend actions toward objects, as when a child feeds a doll. Early in the third year, they become detached participants, making a doll feed itself or pushing a button to launch a rocket (McCune, 1993). Make-believe becomes less self-centered as children realize that agents and recipients of pretend actions can be independent of themselves.
- *Play includes more complex combinations of schemes.* Dwayne can pretend to drink from a cup, but he does not yet combine drinking with pouring. Later, children combine schemes with those of peers in **sociodramatic play,** the make-believe with others that is under way by the end of the second year and that increases rapidly in complexity during early childhood (Kavanaugh, 2006a). Already, Sammy and his classmates can create and coordinate several roles in an elaborate plot. By the end of the preschool years, children have a sophisticated understanding of role relationships and story lines.

LOOK and LISTEN

Observe the make-believe play of several 2- to 4-year-olds at home or in a preschool or child-care center. Describe pretend acts that exemplify important developmental changes.

Children as young as age 2 display awareness that make-believe is a representational activity. They distinguish make-believe from real experiences and grasp that pretending is a deliberate effort to act out imaginary ideas—an understanding that strengthens over early childhood (Rakoczy, Tomasello, & Striano, 2004; Sobel, 2006). **TAKE A MOMENT...** Listen closely to preschoolers as they assign roles and negotiate plans in sociodramatic play: "*You pretend to be* the astronaut, *I'll act like* I'm operating the control tower!*" "Wait, *I gotta set up* the spaceship." In communicating about pretend, children think about their own and others' fanciful representations—evidence that they have begun to reason about people's mental activities, a topic we will return to later in this chapter.

BENEFITS OF MAKE-BELIEVE   Today, Piaget's view of make-believe as mere practice of representational schemes is regarded as too limited. Play not only reflects but also contributes to children's cognitive and social skills. Sociodramatic play has been studied most thoroughly. Compared with social nonpretend activities (such as drawing or putting puzzles together), during sociodramatic play preschoolers' interactions last longer, show more involvement, draw more children into the activity, and are more cooperative (Creasey, Jarvis, & Berk, 1998).

It is not surprising, then, that preschoolers who spend more time in sociodramatic play are rated by observers as more socially competent a year later (Lindsey & Colwell, 2013). And many studies reveal that make-believe strengthens a wide variety of cognitive capacities: sustained attention, inhibiting impulses, memory, logical reasoning, language and literacy (including story comprehension and storytelling skills), imagination, creativity, and the ability to reflect on one's own thinking, regulate one's own behavior, and take another's perspective (Berk & Meyers, 2013; Buchsbaum et al., 2012; Carlson & White, 2013; Mottweiler & Taylor, 2014; Nicolopoulou & Ilgaz, 2013; Roskos & Christie, 2013).

Between 25 and 45 percent of preschoolers and young school-age children spend much time in solitary make-believe, creating *imaginary companions*—special fantasized friends endowed with humanlike qualities. For example, one preschooler created Nutsy and Nutsy, a pair of boisterous birds who lived outside her bedroom window and often went along on family outings (Gleason, Sebanc, & Hartup, 2000; Taylor et al., 2004). Imaginary companions were once viewed as a sign of maladjustment, but research challenges this assumption. Children with an invisible playmate typically treat it with care and affection and say it offers caring, comfort, and good company, just as their real friendships do (Gleason & Hohmann, 2006; Hoff, 2005). Such children also display more complex and imaginative pretend play, are advanced in understanding others' viewpoints and emotions, and are more sociable with peers (Bouldin, 2006; Gleason, 2013; Taylor & Carlson, 1997; Trionfi & Reese, 2009).

Applying What We Know on page 314 lists ways to enhance preschoolers' make-believe. Later we will return to the origins and consequences of make-believe from an alternative perspective—that of Vygotsky.

Make-believe play increases in sophistication during the preschool years. Children increasingly coordinate make-believe roles and pretend with less realistic toys. These children "drive," using plastic flower plates as steering wheels.

Symbol–Real-World Relations

In a corner of the classroom, Leslie set up a dollhouse, replete with tiny furnishings. Sammy liked to arrange the furniture to match his real-world living room, kitchen, and bedroom. Representations of reality, like Sammy's, are powerful cognitive tools. When we understand that a picture, model, or map corresponds to something specific in everyday life, we can use these tools to find out about objects and places we have not experienced.

In Chapter 6, we saw that by the middle of the second year, children grasp the symbolic function of realistic-looking pictures (such as photos). When do children comprehend scale

Applying What We Know

Enhancing Make-Believe Play in Early Childhood

STRATEGY	DESCRIPTION
Provide sufficient space and play materials.	Generous space and materials allow for many play options and reduce conflict.
Encourage children's play without controlling it.	Model, guide, and build on young preschoolers' play themes. Provide open-ended suggestions (for example, "Would the animals like a train ride?"), and talk with the child about the thoughts, motivations, and emotions of play characters. These forms of adult support lead to more elaborate pretending. Refrain from directing the child's play; excessive adult control destroys the creativity and pleasure of make-believe.
Offer a variety of both realistic materials and materials without clear functions.	Children use realistic materials, such as trucks, dolls, tea sets, dress-up clothes, and toy scenes (house, farm, garage, airport) to act out everyday roles in their culture. Materials without clear functions (such as blocks, cardboard cylinders, paper bags, and sand) inspire fantastic role play, such as "pirate" and "creature from outer space."
Ensure that children have many rich, real-world experiences to inspire positive fantasy play.	Opportunities to participate in real-world activities with adults and to observe adult roles in the community provide children with rich social knowledge to integrate into make-believe. Restricting television viewing, especially programs with violent content, limits the degree to which violent themes and aggressive behavior become part of children's play. (See Chapter 10, pages 381–383.)
Help children solve social conflicts constructively.	Cooperation is essential for sociodramatic play. Guide children toward positive relationships with agemates by helping them resolve disagreements constructively. For example, ask, "What could you do if you want a turn?" If the child cannot think of possibilities, suggest options, and assist the child in implementing them.

Sources: Nielsen & Christie, 2008; Weisberg et al., 2013.

Children who experience a variety of symbols come to understand dual representation—for example, that this dollhouse is both an object in its own right and can stand for another, a full-sized house that people live in.

models as symbols for real-world spaces? In one study, 2½- and 3-year-olds watched an adult hide a small toy (Little Snoopy) in a scale model of a room and then were asked to retrieve it. Next, they had to find a larger toy (Big Snoopy) hidden in the room that the model represented. Not until age 3 could most children use the model as a guide to finding Big Snoopy in the real room (DeLoache, 1987). The 2½-year-olds did not realize that the model could be both *a toy room* and *a symbol of another room.* They had trouble with **dual representation**—viewing a symbolic object as both an object in its own right and a symbol.

In support of this interpretation, when researchers made the model room less prominent as an object, by placing it behind a window and preventing children from touching it, more 2½-year-olds succeeded at the search task (DeLoache, 2002). Recall, also, that in make-believe play, 1½- to 2-year-olds cannot use an object that has an obvious use (cup) to stand for another object (hat). Likewise, most 2-year-olds do not yet grasp that a line drawing—an object in its own right—also represents real-world objects (see page 304 in Chapter 8).

Similarly, when presented with objects disguised in various ways and asked what each "looks like" and what each "is really and truly," preschoolers have difficulty. For example, when asked whether a stone painted to look like an egg is "really and truly" an egg, children younger than age 6 often responded "yes" (Flavell, Green, & Flavell, 1987). But simplify these *appearance–reality tasks* by permitting children to solve them nonverbally, by selecting from an array of objects the one that "really" has a particular identity, and most 3-year-olds perform well (Deák, Ray, & Brenneman, 2003). They realize that an object can be one thing (a stone) while symbolizing another (an egg).

How do children grasp the dual representation of symbolic objects? When adults point out similarities between models and real-world spaces, 2½-year-olds perform better on the find-Snoopy task (Peralta de Mendoza & Salsa, 2003). Also, insight into one type of symbol–real-world relation helps preschoolers master others. For example, children regard realistic-looking pictures as symbols early, around 1½ to 2 years, because a picture's primary purpose is to stand for something; it is not an interesting object in its own right (Simcock & DeLoache, 2006). And 3-year-olds who can use a model of a room to locate Big Snoopy readily transfer their understanding to a simple map (Marzolf & DeLoache, 1994).

In sum, exposing young children to diverse symbols—picture books, photographs, drawings, make-believe, and maps—helps them appreciate that one object can stand for another. With age, children come to understand a wide range of symbols that have little physical similarity to what they represent (Liben, 2009). As a result, doors open to vast realms of knowledge.

Limitations of Preoperational Thought

Aside from gains in representation, Piaget described preschoolers in terms of what they *cannot* understand. As the term *pre*operational suggests, he compared them to older, more competent children who have reached the concrete operational stage. According to Piaget, young children are not capable of *operations*—mental representations of actions that obey logical rules. Rather, their thinking is rigid, limited to one aspect of a situation at a time, and strongly influenced by the way things appear at the moment.

EGOCENTRIC AND ANIMISTIC THINKING For Piaget, the most fundamental deficiency of preoperational thinking is **egocentrism**—failure to distinguish the symbolic viewpoints of others from one's own. He believed that when children first mentally represent the world, they tend to focus on their own viewpoint and assume that others perceive, think, and feel the same way they do.

Piaget's most convincing demonstration of egocentrism involves his *three-mountains problem,* described in Figure 9.1. He also regarded egocentrism as responsible for preoperational children's **animistic thinking**—the belief that inanimate objects have lifelike qualities, such as thoughts, wishes, feelings, and intentions (Piaget, 1926/1930). Recall Sammy's insistence that someone must have turned on the thunder. According to Piaget, because young children egocentrically assign human purposes to physical events, magical thinking is common during the preschool years.

Piaget argued that preschoolers' egocentric bias prevents them from *accommodating,* or reflecting on and revising their faulty reasoning in response to their physical and social worlds. To understand this shortcoming, let's consider some additional tasks that Piaget gave to children.

INABILITY TO CONSERVE Piaget's famous conservation tasks reveal several deficiencies of preoperational thinking. **Conservation** refers to the idea that certain physical characteristics of objects remain the same, even when their outward appearance changes. At snack time, Sammy and Priti had identical boxes of raisins, but when Priti spread her raisins out on the table, Sammy was convinced that she had more.

In another conservation task involving liquid, the child is shown two identical tall glasses of water and asked if they contain equal

FIGURE 9.1 Piaget's three-mountains problem. Each mountain is distinguished by its color and by its summit. One has a red cross, another a small house, and the third a snow-capped peak. Children at the preoperational stage respond egocentrically. They cannot select a picture that shows the mountains from the doll's perspective. Instead, they simply choose the photo that reflects their own vantage point.

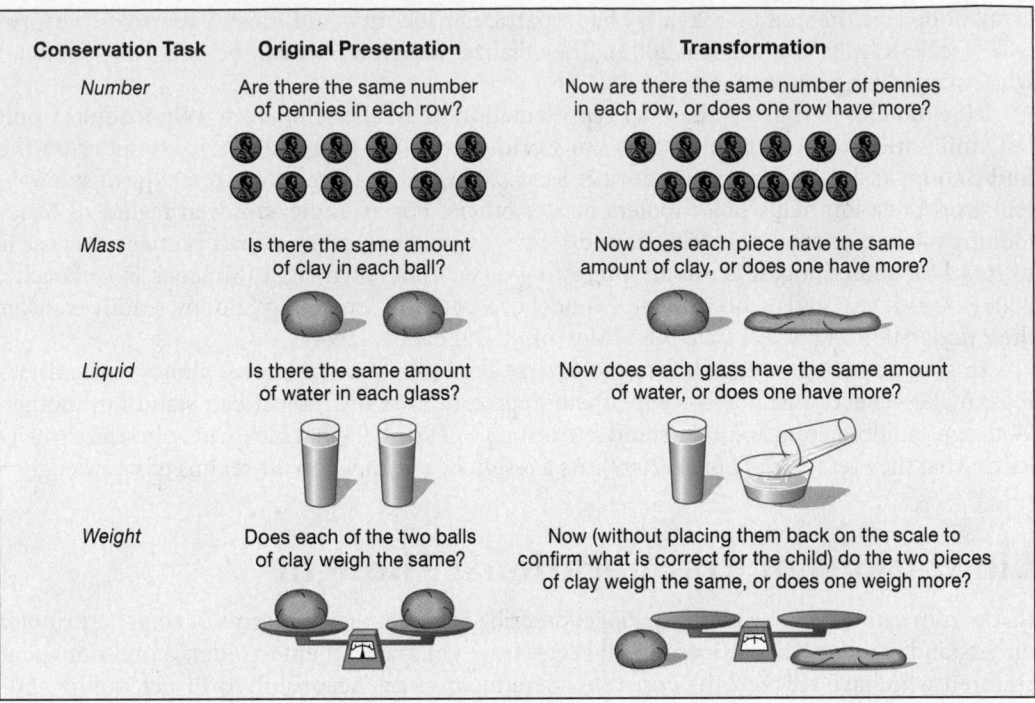

FIGURE 9.2 **Some Piagetian conservation tasks.** Children at the preoperational stage cannot yet conserve. These tasks are mastered gradually over the concrete operational stage. Children in Western nations typically acquire conservation of number, mass, and liquid sometime between 5 and 7 years and conservation of weight between 8 and 10 years.

amounts. Once the child agrees, the water in one glass is poured into a short, wide container, changing its appearance but not its amount. Then the child is asked whether the amount of water is the same or has changed. Preoperational children think the quantity has changed. They explain, "There is less now because the water is way down here" (that is, its level is so low) or, "There is more now because it is all spread out." Figure 9.2 illustrates other conservation tasks that you can try with children.

The inability to conserve highlights several related aspects of preoperational children's thinking. First, their understanding is *centered,* or characterized by **centration.** They focus on one aspect of a situation, neglecting other important features. In conservation of liquid, the child *centers* on the height of the water, failing to realize that changes in width compensate for the changes in height. Second, children are easily distracted by the *perceptual appearance* of objects. Third, children treat the initial and final *states* of the water as unrelated events, ignoring the *dynamic transformation* (pouring of water) between them.

The most important illogical feature of preoperational thought is its **irreversibility**—an inability to mentally go through a series of steps in a problem and then reverse direction, returning to the starting point. *Reversibility* is part of every logical operation. After Priti spills her raisins, Sammy cannot reverse by thinking, "I know Priti doesn't have more raisins than I do. If we put them back in that little box, her raisins and mine would look just the same."

LACK OF HIERARCHICAL CLASSIFICATION Preoperational children have difficulty with **hierarchical classification**—the organization of objects into classes and subclasses on the basis of similarities and differences. Piaget's famous *class inclusion problem,* illustrated in Figure 9.3, demonstrates this limitation. Preoperational children *center* on the overriding feature, red. They do not think reversibly, moving from the whole class (flowers) to the parts (red and blue) and back again.

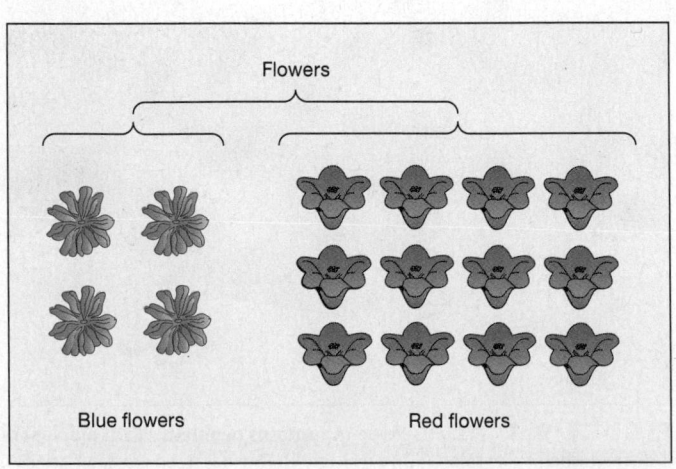

FIGURE 9.3 **A Piagetian class inclusion problem.** Children are shown 16 flowers, 4 of which are blue and 12 of which are red. Asked, "Are there more red flowers or flowers?" the preoperational child responds, "More red flowers," failing to realize that both red and blue flowers are included in the category "flowers."

Follow-Up Research on Preoperational Thought

Over the past three decades, researchers have challenged Piaget's view of preschoolers as cognitively deficient. Because many Piagetian problems contain unfamiliar elements or too many pieces of information for young children to handle at once, preschoolers' responses often do not reflect their true abilities. Piaget also missed many naturally occurring instances of effective reasoning by preschoolers. Let's look at some examples.

EGOCENTRIC, ANIMISTIC, AND MAGICAL THINKING Do young children really believe that a person standing elsewhere in a room sees exactly what they see? When researchers use simplified tasks with familiar objects, 3-year-olds show clear awareness of others' vantage points, such as recognizing how something looks to another person who is looking at it through a color filter (Moll & Meltzoff, 2011). Even 2-year-olds realize that what they see sometimes differs from what another person sees. When asked to help an adult look for a lost object, 24-month-olds (but not 18-month-olds) handed her a toy resting behind a bucket that was within their line of sight but not the adult's (Moll & Tomasello, 2006).

Nonegocentric responses also appear in young children's conversations. For example, preschoolers adapt their speech to fit the needs of their listeners. Four-year-olds use shorter, simpler expressions when talking to 2-year-olds than to agemates or adults (Gelman & Shatz, 1978). And in describing objects, children do not use such words as "big" and "little" in a rigid, egocentric fashion. Instead, they *adjust* their descriptions to allow for context. By age 3, children judge a 2-inch shoe as little when seen by itself (because it is much smaller than most shoes) but as big for a tiny 5-inch-tall doll (Ebeling & Gelman, 1994).

In previous chapters, we saw that toddlers have already begun to infer others' intentions and perspectives. And in his later writings, Piaget (1945/1951) did describe preschoolers' egocentrism as a *tendency* rather than an inability. As we revisit the topic of perspective taking, we will see that it develops gradually throughout childhood and adolescence.

Piaget also overestimated preschoolers' animistic beliefs. Even infants have begun to distinguish animate from inanimate, as indicated by their remarkable categorical distinctions among living and nonliving things (see Chapter 6, page 219). By age 2½, children give psychological explanations ("he likes to" or "she wants to") for people and other animals but rarely for objects (Hickling & Wellman, 2001). And 3- to 5-year-olds asked whether a variety of animals and objects can eat, grow, talk, think, remember, see, or feel mostly attribute these capacities to animals, not objects. In addition, they rarely attribute biological properties (like eating and growing) to robots, indicating that they are well aware that even a self-moving object with lifelike features is not alive. But unlike adults, preschoolers often say that robots have perceptual and psychological capacities—for example, seeing, thinking, and remembering (Jipson & Gelman, 2007; Subrahmanyam, Gelman, & Lafosse, 2002). These responses result from incomplete knowledge about certain objects, and they decline with age.

Similarly, preschoolers think that magic accounts for events they otherwise cannot explain, as in Sammy's magical explanation of thunder in the opening to this chapter. But their notions of magic are flexible and appropriate. For example, older 3-year-olds and 4-year-olds think that violations of physical laws (walking through a wall) and mental laws (turning on the TV just by thinking about it) require magic more than violations of social conventions (taking a bath with shoes on) (Browne & Woolley, 2004). And they are more likely to say that a magical process—wishing—caused an event (an object to appear in a box) when a person made the wish before the event occurred, the event was consistent with the wish (the wished-for object rather than another object appeared in the box), and no alternative causes

© TATSUYUKI TAYAMA/FUJIFOTOS/THE IMAGE WORKS

Three- to 5-year-olds distinguish between animate and inanimate and realize, for example, that a robot with lifelike features cannot eat or grow. But because of incomplete knowledge, they often claim that robots have perceptual and psychological capacities, such as seeing, thinking, and remembering.

were apparent (Woolley, Browne, & Boerger, 2006). These features of causality are the same ones preschoolers rely on in ordinary situations.

Between ages 4 and 8, as children gain familiarity with physical events and principles, their magical beliefs decline. They figure out who is really behind Santa Claus and the Tooth Fairy, and they realize that magicians' feats are due to trickery (Woolley & Cornelius, 2013). And increasingly, children say that events in fantastical stories couldn't really happen and that characters in such stories aren't real (Woolley & Cox, 2007). Still, because children entertain the possibility that something they imagine might materialize, they may react with anxiety to scary stories, TV shows, and nightmares.

Religion and culture play a role in children's fantastic and supernatural ideas. For example, Jewish children are more likely than their Christian agemates to express disbelief in Santa Claus and the Tooth Fairy. Having heard at home that Santa is imaginary, they seem to generalize this attitude to other unseen agents (Woolley, 1997). And cultural myths about wishing—for example, the custom of making a wish before blowing out birthday candles—probably underlie the conviction of most 3- to 6-year-olds that by wishing, you can sometimes make your desires come true (Woolley, 2000).

In actuality, both children and adults endorse natural and supernatural accounts of hard-to-explain events, with these types of explanations coexisting. Children, however, prefer natural over supernatural explanations, even in cultures that strongly endorse supernatural beliefs (Woolley, Cornelius, & Lacey, 2011). In one study, researchers asked 5- to 15-year-olds living in South African communities where witchcraft beliefs were widespread to explain why certain people got AIDS (Legare & Gelman, 2008). Children of all ages—even 5-year-olds—more often gave biological explanations (contact with a sick person, exposure to germs) than bewitchment explanations (a neighbor cast a spell). Bewitchment accounts increased in middle childhood, as children acquired their culture's belief system, but they did not replace biological explanations. And children mentioned witchcraft as a cause of serious illness far less often than did adults!

LOGICAL THOUGHT   Many studies show that when preschoolers are given tasks that are simplified and made relevant to their everyday lives, they do not display the illogical characteristics that Piaget saw in the preoperational stage. For example, when a conservation-of-number task is scaled down to include only three items instead of six or seven, 3-year-olds perform well (Gelman, 1972). And when preschoolers are asked carefully worded questions about what happens to substances (such as sugar) after they are dissolved in water, they give accurate explanations. Most 3- to 5-year-olds know that the substance is conserved—that it continues to exist, can be tasted, and makes the liquid heavier, even though it is invisible in the water (Au, Sidle, & Rollins, 1993; Rosen & Rozin, 1993).

Preschoolers' ability to reason about transformations is evident on other problems. They can engage in impressive *reasoning by analogy* about physical changes. When presented with the picture-matching problem "Play dough is to cut-up play dough as apple is to . . .?," even 3-year-olds choose the correct answer (a cut-up apple) from a set of alternatives, several of which (a bitten apple, a cut-up loaf of bread) share physical features with the right choice (Goswami, 1996). These findings indicate that in familiar contexts, preschoolers can overcome appearances and think logically about cause and effect.

Finally, even without detailed biological or mechanical knowledge, preschoolers realize that the insides of animals are responsible for certain cause–effect sequences (such as willing oneself to move) that are impossible for nonliving things, such as machines (Gelman, 2003; Keil & Lockhart, 1999). Preschoolers seem to use illogical reasoning only when they must grapple with unfamiliar topics, too much information, or contradictory facts that they cannot reconcile.

CATEGORIZATION   Despite their difficulty with Piagetian class inclusion tasks, preschoolers organize their everyday knowledge into nested categories at an early age. By the beginning of early childhood, children's categories include objects that go together because of their common function, behavior, or natural kind (animate versus inanimate), challenging Piaget's assumption that preschoolers' thinking is wholly governed by perceptual appearances.

LOOK and LISTEN

Try the conservation of number and mass tasks in Figure 9.2 with a 3- or 4-year-old. Next, simplify conservation of number by reducing the number of pennies, and relate conservation of mass to the child's experience by pretending the clay is baking dough and transforming it into cupcakes. Did the child perform more competently?

Indeed, 2- to 5-year-olds readily draw appropriate inferences about non-observable characteristics shared by category members. For example, after being told that a bird has warm blood and that a stegosaurus (dinosaur) has cold blood, preschoolers infer that a pterodactyl (labeled a dinosaur) has cold blood, even though it closely resembles a bird (Gopnik & Nazzi, 2003). And when shown a set of three characters—two of whom look different but share an inner trait ("outgoing") and two of whom look similar but have different inner traits (one "shy," one "outgoing")—preschoolers rely on the trait category, not physical appearance, to predict similar preferred activities (Heyman & Gelman, 2000).

Nevertheless, when most instances of a category have a certain perceptual property (such as long ears), preschoolers readily categorize on the basis of perceptual features. This indicates that they flexibly use different types of information to classify, depending on the situation (Rakison & Lawson, 2013). And past experiences influence which information they decide to use. When Native-American 5-year-olds growing up on the Menominee Reservation in northern Wisconsin were compared with 5-year-olds growing up in Boston, the Menominee children often used relations in the natural world to categorize animals. For example, they grouped together wolves and eagles because of their shared forest habitat (Ross et al., 2003). The Boston children, in contrast, mostly relied on common features of the animals.

During the second and third years, and perhaps earlier, children's categories differentiate. They form many *basic-level categories*—ones at an intermediate level of generality, such as "chairs," "tables," and "beds." By the third year, children easily move back and forth between basic-level categories and *general categories,* such as "furniture." And they break down basic-level categories into *subcategories,* such as "rocking chairs" and "desk chairs."

These 4-year-olds understand that a category ("dinosaurs") can be based on underlying characteristics ("cold-blooded"), not just on perceptual features such as upright posture and scaly skin.

Preschoolers' rapidly expanding vocabularies and general knowledge support their impressive skill at categorizing, and they benefit greatly from conversations with adults, who frequently label and explain categories to young children. When adults use the word *bird* for hummingbirds, turkeys, and swans, they signal to children that something other than physical similarity binds these instances together (Gelman, 2003, 2006; Gelman & Kalish, 2006). Picture-book reading is an especially rich context for understanding categories. In conversing about books with their preschoolers, parents provide information that guides children's inferences about the structure of categories: "Penguins live at the South Pole, swim, catch fish, and have thick layers of fat and feathers that help them stay warm." Furthermore, as the Social Issues: Education box on page 320 indicates, young children ask many questions about their world and generally get informative answers, which are particularly well-suited to advancing their conceptual understanding.

In sum, although preschoolers' category systems are less complex than those of older children and adults, they already have the capacity to classify hierarchically and on the basis of nonobvious properties. And they use logical, causal reasoning to identify the features that form the basis of a category and to classify new members.

Evaluation of the Preoperational Stage

Table 9.1 on page 321 provides an overview of the cognitive attainments of early childhood just considered. **TAKE A MOMENT...** Compare them with Piaget's description of the preoperational child on pages 315–316. The evidence as a whole indicates that Piaget was partly wrong and partly right about young children's cognitive capacities. When given simplified tasks based on familiar experiences, preschoolers show the beginnings of logical thinking. How can we make sense of the contradictions between Piaget's conclusions and the findings of recent research?

That preschoolers have some logical understandings that strengthen with age indicates that they attain logical operations gradually. Over time, children rely on increasingly effective mental (as opposed to perceptual) approaches to solving problems. For example, children who

Social Issues: Education

Children's Questions: Catalyst for Cognitive Development

"Dad, what's that?" asked 4-year-old Emily as her father chopped vegetables for dinner.

"It's an onion," her father said.

"Is an onion a fruit?" Emily asked.

"It's a vegetable," her father replied. "A root vegetable because it grows underground."

Emily wrinkled her nose. "Why does it smell yucky?"

"I don't know," her father admitted. "But after dinner we can look it up online and find out."

When young children converse with adults, they ask, on average, more than one question per minute! Do inquisitive children like Emily really want answers to their many questions? Or are they—as their parents sometimes conclude—merely clamoring for attention?

An analysis of diaries that parents diverse in SES and ethnicity kept of their children's questions and of audio recordings of parent–child interactions revealed that at every age between 1 and 5 years, 70 to 90 percent of children's questions were information-seeking ("What's that [pointing to a crawfish]?") as opposed to non-information-seeking ("Can I have a cookie?") (Chouinard, 2007). And from age 2 on, children increasingly built on their fact-oriented questions with follow-up questions that asked for causes and explanations ("What do crawfish eat?" "Why does it have claws?"). By age 3½, these sets of "building questions" made up about half of children's questions, confirming that preschoolers ask questions purposefully, to obtain clarifying information about things that puzzle them.

Answers to children's questions provide them with the precise knowledge they need at the precise moment they need it. Even before children can talk, they ask questions by gesturing at objects in their environment. A pointing gesture, for example, might lead a parent to say, "That's a ball. See, it bounces!" And the content

of children's questions is related to their cognitive development. At a time when vocabulary is advancing rapidly, about 60 percent of 1½- to 2-year-olds' questions ask for names of objects. With age, preschoolers increasingly ask about function ("What's it do?"), activity ("What's he doing?"), state ("Is she hungry?"), and theory of mind ("How does the pilot *know* where to fly?").

Context also makes a difference. Compared with everyday situations, a visit to a zoo elicits many more questions about biological information from 2- to 4-year-olds: "Why is the lion sleeping?" "Is he dead?" "What do bats eat?" "Will the baby lion grow bigger?" Biological questions calling for explanations increased with age as 3- and 4-year-olds tried to make sense of such processes as growth, life, illness, and death—concepts they are currently grappling with and that will soon advance (see page 418 in Chapter 11).

The usefulness of children's questions depends on adults' answers. Most of the time, parents respond informatively. If they do not, preschoolers often express dissatisfaction (Frazier, Gelman, & Wellman, 2009). And they can be amazingly persistent, asking again until they get the information they want. Especially for 1- and 2-year-olds, parents often respond with additional relevant knowledge aimed at enhancing children's understanding and guiding further thinking. Parents also adjust the complexity of their answers to fit their children's maturity (Callanan & Oakes, 1992). To a question like "Why does the light come on?" 3-year-olds typically get simpler, "prior cause" explanations ("I turned on the switch"). Slightly older children

Preschoolers' questions are often purposeful efforts to understand things that puzzle them. Because adults' answers provide the precise knowledge children need at the precise moment they need it, question-asking is a powerful source of cognitive development.

frequently get "mechanism" explanations ("The switch allows electricity to reach the light bulb").

In non-Western village cultures, young children engage in question asking just as often as their Western counterparts, but they rarely ask why-questions, aimed at getting explanations. As we will see later in this chapter, preschoolers in village societies are included in nearly all aspects of family and community life, reducing their need to ask adults to explain (Gauvain, Munroe, & Beebe, 2012). In contrast, Western children's explanatory questions are important for acquiring the wide-ranging knowledge needed to make sense of their complex world, much of which children cannot directly experience.

Clearly, asking questions is a major means through which Western children strive to attain adultlike understandings. Children's questions offer parents and teachers a fascinating window into their factual and conceptual knowledge, along with a wealth of opportunities to help them learn.

cannot use counting to compare two sets of items do not conserve number. Rather, they rely on perceptual cues to compare the amounts in two sets of items (Rouselle, Palmers, & Noël, 2004). Once preschoolers can count, they apply this skill to conservation-of-number tasks involving just a few items. As counting improves, they extend the strategy to problems with more items. By age 6, they understand that number remains the same after a transformation in the length and spacing of a set of items as long as nothing is added or taken away (Halford & Andrews, 2011). Consequently, they no longer need to count to verify their answer.

Evidence that preschool children can be trained to perform well on Piagetian problems also supports the idea that operational thought is not absent at one point in time and present at another (Ping & Goldin-Meadow, 2008; Siegler & Svetina, 2006). Children who possess some understanding would naturally benefit from training, unlike those with no understanding at

| TABLE 9.1 | Some Cognitive Attainments of Early Childhood |

APPROXIMATE AGE	COGNITIVE ATTAINMENTS
2–4 years	Shows a dramatic increase in representational activity, as reflected in the development of language, make-believe play, understanding of dual representation, and categorization
	Takes the perspective of others in simplified, familiar situations and in everyday, face-to-face communication
	Distinguishes animate beings from inanimate objects; prefers natural over supernatural explanations for events
	Grasps conservation, notices transformations, reverses thinking, and understands many cause-and-effect relationships in simplified, familiar situations
	Categorizes objects on the basis of common function, behavior, and natural kind as well as perceptual features, depending on context; uses inner causal features to categorize objects varying widely in external appearance
	Sorts familiar objects into hierarchically organized categories
4–7 years	Becomes increasingly aware that make-believe (and other thought processes) are representational activities
	Replaces beliefs in magical creatures and events with plausible explanations
	Passes Piaget's conservation of number, mass, and liquid problems

© ELLEN B. SENISI/THE IMAGE WORKS

RYAN McVAY/ PHOTODISC/GETTY IMAGES

all. The gradual development of logical operations poses a serious challenge to Piaget's assumption of abrupt change toward logical reasoning around age 6 or 7. Does a preoperational stage really exist? Some no longer think so. Recall from Chapter 6 that according to the information-processing perspective, children work out their understanding of each type of task separately, and their thought processes are basically the same at all ages—just present to a greater or lesser extent.

Other experts think that the stage concept is still valid, with modifications. For example, some *neo-Piagetian theorists* combine Piaget's stage approach with the information-processing emphasis on task-specific change (Case, 1998; Halford & Andrews, 2011). They believe that Piaget's strict stage definition must be transformed into a less tightly knit concept, one in which a related set of competencies develops over an extended period, depending on brain development and specific experiences. These investigators point to findings indicating that as long as the complexity of tasks and children's exposure to them are carefully controlled, children approach those tasks in similar, stage-consistent ways (Andrews & Halford, 2002; Case & Okamoto, 1996). For example, in drawing pictures, preschoolers depict objects separately, ignoring their spatial arrangement (return to the drawing in Figure 8.9 on page 304 for an example). In understanding stories, they grasp a single story line but have trouble with a main plot plus one or more subplots.

This flexible stage notion recognizes the unique qualities of early childhood thinking. At the same time, it provides a better account of why, as Leslie put it, "Preschoolers' minds are such a blend of logic, fantasy, and faulty reasoning."

Piaget and Education

Three educational principles derived from Piaget's theory continue to influence teacher training and classroom practices, especially during early childhood:

● *Discovery learning.* In a Piagetian classroom, children are encouraged to discover for themselves through spontaneous interaction with the environment. Instead of presenting ready-made knowledge verbally, teachers provide a rich variety of activities designed to promote exploration and discovery, including art, puzzles, table games, dress-up clothing, building blocks, books, measuring tools, natural science tasks, and musical instruments.

- *Sensitivity to children's readiness to learn.* In a Piagetian classroom, teachers introduce activities that build on children's current thinking, challenging their incorrect ways of viewing the world. But they do not try to speed up development by imposing new skills before children indicate they are interested and ready.
- *Acceptance of individual differences.* Piaget's theory assumes that all children go through the same sequence of development, but at different rates. Therefore, teachers must plan activities for individual children and small groups, not just for the whole class. In addition, teachers evaluate each child's educational progress in relation to the child's previous development, rather than on the basis of normative standards, or average performance of same-age peers.

Like his stages, educational applications of Piaget's theory have met with criticism, especially his insistence that young children learn primarily through acting on the environment (Brainerd, 2003). As we have already seen, children also use language-based routes to knowledge—a point emphasized by Vygotsky's sociocultural theory, to which we now turn. Nevertheless, Piaget's influence on education has been powerful. He gave teachers new ways to observe, understand, and enhance young children's development and offered strong theoretical justification for child-oriented approaches to classroom teaching and learning.

Ask Yourself

- **REVIEW** Select two of the following features of preoperational thought: egocentrism, a focus on perceptual appearances, difficulty reasoning about transformations, and lack of hierarchical classification. Present evidence indicating that preschoolers are more capable thinkers than Piaget assumed.

- **CONNECT** Make-believe play promotes both cognitive and social development (see page 313). Explain why this is so.

- **APPLY** Three-year-old Will understands that his tricycle isn't alive and can't feel or move on its own. But at the beach, while watching the sun dip below the horizon, Will exclaimed, "The sun is tired. It's going to sleep!" What explains this apparent contradiction in Will's reasoning?

- **REFLECT** Did you have an imaginary companion as a young child? If so, what was your companion like, and why did you create it? Were your parents aware of your companion? What was their attitude toward it?

9.4 Describe Vygotsky's perspective on the social origins and significance of children's private speech.

9.5 Describe applications of Vygotsky's theory to education, and evaluate his major ideas.

Vygotsky's Sociocultural Theory

Piaget's de-emphasis on language as a source of cognitive development brought on yet another challenge, this time from Vygotsky's sociocultural theory, which stresses the social context of cognitive development. In Vygotsky's view, the child and the social environment collaborate to mold cognition in culturally adaptive ways. During early childhood, rapid growth of language broadens preschoolers' participation in social dialogues with more knowledgeable individuals, who encourage them to master culturally important tasks. Soon children start to communicate with themselves in much the same way they converse with others. This greatly enhances the complexity of their thinking and their ability to control their own behavior. Let's see how this happens.

Private Speech

TAKE A MOMENT... Watch preschoolers as they play and explore the environment, and you will see that they frequently talk out loud to themselves. For example, as Sammy worked a puzzle, he said, "Where's the red piece? I need the red one. Now, a blue one. No, it doesn't fit. Try it here."

Piaget (1923/1926) called these utterances *egocentric speech,* reflecting his belief that young children have difficulty taking the perspectives of others. Their talk, he said, is often "talk for self" in which they express thoughts in whatever form they happen to occur, regardless of whether a listener can understand. Piaget believed that cognitive development and certain social experiences eventually bring an end to egocentric speech. Specifically, through disagreements with peers, children see that others hold viewpoints different from their own. As a result, egocentric speech declines in favor of social speech, in which children adapt what they say to their listeners.

Vygotsky (1934/1987) disagreed strongly with Piaget's conclusions. Because language helps children think about their mental activities and behavior and select courses of action, Vygotsky saw it as the foundation for all higher cognitive processes, including controlled attention, deliberate memorization and recall, categorization, planning, problem solving, and self-reflection. In Vygotsky's view, children speak to themselves for self-guidance. As they get older and find tasks easier, their self-directed speech is internalized as silent, *inner speech*—the internal verbal dialogues we carry on while thinking and acting in everyday situations.

Over the past three decades, almost all studies have supported Vygotsky's perspective (Berk & Harris, 2003; Winsler, 2009). As a result, children's self-directed speech is now called **private speech** instead of egocentric speech. Research shows that children use more of it when tasks are appropriately challenging—neither too easy nor too hard but within their *zone of proximal development,* or range of mastery (see page 222 in Chapter 6). For example, Figure 9.4 shows how 5- and 6-year-olds' private speech increased as researchers made a problem-solving task moderately difficult, then decreased as the task became very difficult (Fernyhough & Fradley, 2005).

With age, as Vygotsky predicted, private speech goes underground, changing into whispers and silent lip movements. Furthermore, children who freely use private speech during a challenging activity are more attentive and involved and show better task performance than their less talkative agemates (Al-Namlah, Fernyhough, & Meins, 2006; Benigno et al., 2011; Lidstone, Meins, & Fernyhough, 2010).

Finally, compared with their agemates, children with learning and behavior problems engage in more private speech over a longer period of development (Berk, 2001b; Bono & Bizri, 2014; Winsler et al., 2007). They seem to use private speech to help compensate for impairments in attention and cognitive processing that make many tasks more difficult for them.

Social Origins of Early Childhood Cognition

Where does private speech come from? Recall from Chapter 6 that Vygotsky believed children's learning takes place within the *zone of proximal development*—a range of tasks too difficult for the child to do alone but possible with the help of others. Consider the joint activity of Sammy and his mother, who helps him put together a difficult puzzle:

> Sammy: "I can't get this one in." *[Tries to insert a piece in the wrong place.]*
>
> Mother: "Which piece might go down here?" *[Points to the bottom of the puzzle.]*

A 4-year-old talks to herself as she draws. Research supports Vygotsky's theory that children use private speech to guide their thinking and behavior.

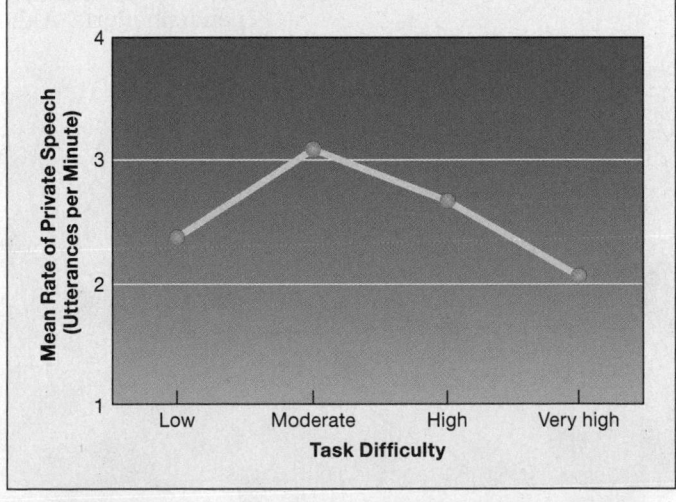

FIGURE 9.4 Relationship of private speech to task difficulty among 5- and 6-year-olds. Researchers increased the difficulty of a problem-solving task. Private speech rose as the task became moderately difficult, then declined as it became highly difficult. Children are more likely to use private speech for self-guidance when tasks are within their zone of proximal development, or range of mastery. (Adapted from Fernyhough & Fradley, 2005.)

Sammy: "His shoes." *[Looks for a piece resembling the clown's shoes but tries the wrong one.]*

Mother: "Well, what piece looks like this shape?" *[Pointing again to the bottom of the puzzle.]*

Sammy: "The brown one." *[Tries it, and it fits; then attempts another piece and looks at his mother.]*

Mother: "Try turning it just a little." *[Gestures to show him.]*

Sammy: "There!" *[Puts in several more pieces while his mother watches.]*

By questioning, prompting, and suggesting strategies, Sammy's mother keeps the puzzle within his zone of proximal development, at a manageable level of difficulty.

EFFECTIVE SOCIAL INTERACTION   To promote cognitive development, social interaction must have two vital features. The first is **intersubjectivity,** the process by which two participants who begin a task with different understandings arrive at a shared understanding (Newson & Newson, 1975). Intersubjectivity creates a common ground for communication, as each partner adjusts to the other's perspective. Adults try to promote it when they translate their own insights in ways that are within the child's grasp. As the child stretches to understand the adult, she is drawn into a more mature approach to the situation.

The capacity for intersubjectivity is present early, in parent–infant mutual gaze, exchange of vocal and emotional signals, imitation, and joint play with objects; and in toddlers' capacity to infer others' intentions (Csibra, 2010; Feldman, 2007c). Later, language facilitates intersubjectivity. As conversational skills improve, preschoolers increasingly seek others' help and direct that assistance to ensure that it is beneficial. Between ages 3 and 5, children strive for intersubjectivity in dialogues with peers, as when they affirm a playmate's message, add new ideas, and make contributions to ongoing play to sustain it. They can also be heard saying, "I think [this way]. What do you think?"—evidence of a willingness to share viewpoints (Berk, 2001b). In these ways, children create zones of proximal development for one another.

A second important feature of social experience is **scaffolding**—adjusting the support offered during a teaching session to fit the child's current level of performance. When the child has little notion of how to proceed, the adult uses direct instruction, breaking the task into manageable units, suggesting strategies, and offering rationales for using them. As the child's competence increases, effective scaffolders—like Sammy's mother—gradually and sensitively withdraw support, turning over responsibility to the child. Then children take the language of these dialogues, make it part of their private speech, and use this speech to organize their independent efforts. Although preschoolers freely use private speech when alone or when others are nearby, they use more in the presence of others (McGonigle-Chalmers, Slater, & Smith, 2014). This suggests that some private speech retains a social purpose, perhaps as an indirect appeal for renewed scaffolding should the child need additional help.

Scaffolding captures the form of teaching interaction that occurs as children work on school or school-like tasks, such as puzzles, model building, picture matching, and (later) academic assignments. It may not apply to other contexts that are equally vital for cognitive development—for example, play or everyday activities, during which adults usually support children's efforts without deliberately teaching. To encompass children's diverse opportunities to learn through involvement with others, Barbara Rogoff (1998, 2003) suggests the term **guided participation,** a broader concept than scaffolding. It refers to shared endeavors between more expert and less expert participants, without specifying the precise features of communication. Consequently, it allows for variations across situations and cultures.

A grandfather engages in scaffolding by breaking a challenging construction task into manageable units, suggesting strategies, and gradually turning over responsibility to his 3-year-old grandchild.

© LAURA DWIGHT PHOTOGRAPHY

> ## LOOK *and* LISTEN
>
> Ask a preschooler to join you in working a difficult puzzle or another challenging task. How did you scaffold the child's progress? Did the child display any self-guiding private speech?

RESEARCH ON SOCIAL INTERACTION AND COGNITIVE DEVELOPMENT What evidence supports Vygotsky's ideas on the social origins of cognitive development? In previous chapters, we reviewed evidence indicating that when adults establish intersubjectivity by being stimulating, responsive, and supportive, they foster many competencies—attention, language, complex play, and understanding of others' perspectives. In several studies, children whose parents were effective scaffolders used more private speech, were more successful when attempting difficult tasks on their own, and were advanced in overall cognitive development (Berk & Spuhl, 1995; Conner & Cross, 2003; Mulvaney et al., 2006).

Nevertheless, effective scaffolding can take different forms in different cultures. In an investigation of Hmong families who had emigrated from Southeast Asia to the United States, once again, parental cognitive support was associated with children's advanced reasoning skills. But unlike Caucasian-American parents, who emphasize independence by encouraging their children to think of ways to approach a task, Hmong parents—who highly value interdependence and child obedience—frequently tell their children what to do (for example, "put this block piece here, then this piece on top of it") (Stright, Herr, & Neitzel, 2009). Among Caucasian-American children, such directive scaffolding is associated with kindergartners' lack of self-control and behavior problems (Neitzel & Stright, 2003). Among the Hmong children, however, it predicted capacity to follow rules, be organized, and finish assignments.

Vygotsky and Early Childhood Education

Both Piagetian and Vygotskian classrooms emphasize active participation and acceptance of individual differences. But a Vygotskian classroom goes beyond independent discovery to promote *assisted discovery.* Teachers guide children's learning with explanations, demonstrations, and verbal prompts, tailoring their interventions to each child's zone of proximal development. Assisted discovery is aided by *peer collaboration,* as children with varying abilities work in groups, teaching and helping one another.

Vygotsky (1935/1978) saw make-believe play as the ideal social context for fostering cognitive development in early childhood. As children create imaginary situations, they learn to follow internal ideas and social rules rather than their immediate impulses. For example, a child pretending to go to sleep follows the rules of bedtime behavior. A child imagining himself as a father and a doll as a child conforms to the rules of parental behavior (Meyers & Berk, 2014). According to Vygotsky, make-believe play is a unique, broadly influential zone of proximal development in which children try out a wide variety of challenging activities and acquire many new competencies.

Turn back to page 313 to review findings that make-believe play enhances a diverse array of cognitive and social skills. Pretending is also rich in private speech—a finding that supports its role in helping children bring action under the control of thought (Krafft & Berk, 1998). Preschoolers who spend more time engaged in sociodramatic play are better at inhibiting impulses, regulating emotion, and taking personal responsibility for following classroom rules (Kelly & Hammond, 2011; Lemche et al., 2003; Ogan & Berk, 2009). These findings support the role of make-believe in children's increasing self-control.

In this Vygotksy-inspired classroom, preschoolers benefit from peer collaboration as they jointly create an elaborate block structure.

© LAURA DWIGHT PHOTOGRAPHY

Evaluation of Vygotsky's Theory

In granting social experience a fundamental role in cognitive development, Vygotsky's theory underscores the vital role of teaching and helps us understand the wide cultural variation in children's cognitive skills. Nevertheless, it has not gone unchallenged. In some cultures, verbal dialogues are not the only—or even the most important—means through which children learn. When Western parents scaffold their young children's mastery of challenging tasks, they

Cultural Influences

Children in Village and Tribal Cultures Observe and Participate in Adult Work

In Western societies, children are largely excluded from participating in adult work, which generally takes place outside the home. The role of equipping children with the skills they need to become competent workers is assigned to school. In early childhood, middle-SES parents' interactions with children emphasize child-focused activities designed to prepare children to succeed academically—especially adult–child conversations and play that enhance language, literacy, and other school-related knowledge. In village and tribal cultures, children receive little or no schooling, spend their days in contact with or participating in adult work, and start to assume mature responsibilities in early childhood (Gaskins, 2013a). Consequently, parents have little need to rely on conversation and play to teach children.

A study comparing 2- and 3-year-olds' daily lives in four cultures—two U.S. middle-SES suburbs, the Efe hunters and gatherers of the Republic of Congo, and a Mayan agricultural town in Guatemala—documented these differences (Morelli, Rogoff, & Angelillo, 2003). In the U.S. communities, young children had little access to adult work and spent much time conversing and playing with adults. In contrast, the Efe and Mayan children rarely engaged in these child-focused activities. Instead, they spent their days close to—and frequently observing—adult work, which often took place in or near the Efe campsite or the Mayan family home.

An ethnography of a remote Mayan village in Yucatán, Mexico, shows that when young children are legitimate onlookers and participants in a daily life structured around adult work, their competencies differ from those of Western preschoolers (Gaskins, 1999; Gaskins, Haight, & Lancy, 2007). Yucatec Mayan adults are subsistence farmers. Men tend cornfields, aided by sons age 8 and older. Women prepare meals, wash clothes, and care for the livestock and garden, assisted by daughters and by sons too young to work in the fields. Children join in these activities from the second year on. When not participating, they are expected to be self-sufficient. Young children make many nonwork decisions for themselves—how much to sleep and eat, what to wear, when to take their daily bath, and even when to start school. As a result, Yucatec Mayan preschoolers are highly competent at self-care. In contrast, their make-believe play is limited; when it occurs, they usually imitate adult work. Otherwise, they watch others—for hours each day.

Yucatec Mayan parents rarely converse or play with preschoolers or scaffold their learning. Rather, when children imitate adult tasks, parents conclude that they are ready for more responsibility. Then they assign chores, selecting tasks the child can do with little help so that adult work is not disturbed. If a child cannot do a task, the adult takes over and the child observes, reengaging when able to contribute.

A Mayan 3-year-old imitates her mother in balancing a basket of laundry on her head. Children in Guatemalan Mayan culture observe and participate in the work of their community from an early age.

Expected to be autonomous and helpful, Yucatec Mayan children seldom display attention-getting behaviors or ask others for something interesting to do. From an early age, they can sit quietly for long periods—through a lengthy religious service or a three-hour truck ride. And when an adult interrupts their activity and directs them to do a chore, they respond eagerly to the type of command that Western children frequently avoid or resent. By age 5, Yucatec Mayan children spontaneously take responsibility for tasks beyond those assigned.

assume much responsibility for children's motivation by frequently giving verbal instructions and conversing with the child. Their communication resembles the teaching that occurs in school, where their children will spend years preparing for adult life. But in cultures that place less emphasis on schooling and literacy, parents often expect children to take greater responsibility for acquiring new skills through keen observation and participation in community activities (Rogoff, 2003; Rogoff, Correa-Chavez, & Silva, 2011). See the Cultural Influences box above for research illustrating this difference.

Vygotsky's theory has also been criticized for saying little about how basic motor, perceptual, attention, memory, and problem-solving skills, discussed in Chapters 5 and 6, contribute to socially transmitted higher cognitive processes. For example, his theory does not address how these elementary capacities spark changes in children's social experiences, from which more advanced cognition springs (Daniels, 2011; Miller, 2009). Piaget paid far more attention than Vygotsky to the development of basic cognitive processes. It is intriguing to speculate about the broader theory that might exist today had Piaget and Vygotsky—the two twentieth-century giants of cognitive development—had a chance to meet and weave together their extraordinary accomplishments.

Ask Yourself

- **REVIEW** Describe features of social interaction that support children's cognitive development. How does such interaction create a zone of proximal development?

- **CONNECT** Explain how Piaget's and Vygotsky's theories complement each other. How would classroom practices inspired by these theories be similar? How would they differ?

- **APPLY** Tanisha sees her 5-year-old son Toby talking aloud to himself as he plays. She wonders whether she should discourage this behavior. Use Vygotsky's theory to explain why Toby talks to himself. How would you advise Tanisha?

- **REFLECT** When do you use private speech? Does it serve a self-guiding function for you, as it does for children? Explain.

Information Processing

Return to the model of information processing discussed on pages 215–216 in Chapter 6. Recall that information processing focuses on cognitive operations and mental strategies that children use to transform stimuli flowing into their mental systems. As we have already seen, early childhood is a period of dramatic strides in mental representation. And the various components of executive function that enable children to succeed in cognitively challenging situations—attention, impulse control, working memory, and planning—show impressive gains, leading to more efficient and flexible ways of manipulating information and solving problems (Carlson, Zelazo, & Faja, 2013). Preschoolers also become more aware of their own mental life and begin to acquire academically relevant knowledge important for school success.

9.6 How do attention, memory, and problem solving change during early childhood?

9.7 Describe the young child's theory of mind.

9.8 Summarize children's literacy and mathematical knowledge during early childhood.

Attention

As parents and teachers know, preschoolers—compared with school-age children—spend shorter times involved in tasks and are more easily distracted. But recall from Chapter 6 that sustained attention improves in toddlerhood, a trend that continues during early childhood.

INHIBITION A major reason is a steady gain in children's ability to inhibit impulses and keep their mind on a competing goal. Consider a task in which the child must tap once when the adult taps twice and tap twice when the adult taps once, or must say "night" to a picture of the sun and "day" to a picture of the moon with stars. As Figure 9.5 shows, 3- and 4-year-olds make many errors. But by age 6 to 7, children find such tasks easy (Kirkham, Cruess, & Diamond, 2003; Zelazo et al., 2003). They can resist the "pull" of their attention toward a dominant stimulus—a skill that, as early as age 3 to 5, predicts social maturity as well as subsequent reading and math achievement from kindergarten through high school (Blair & Razza, 2007; Duncan et al., 2007; Rhoades, Greenberg, & Domitrovich, 2009). Simultaneously, ERP and fMRI measures reveal a steady age-related increase in activation of the prefrontal cortex while children engage in activities requiring suppression of inappropriate responses (Bartgis, Lilly, & Thomas, 2003; Luna et al., 2001).

Gains in working memory, enabling preschoolers to hold in mind and manipulate more information at once (see page 215 in Chapter 6), contribute to the development of attention. A larger working memory permits preschoolers to generate increasingly complex play and problem-solving goals, which require concentration to attain (Senn, Espy, & Kaufmann, 2004). Greater working-memory capacity

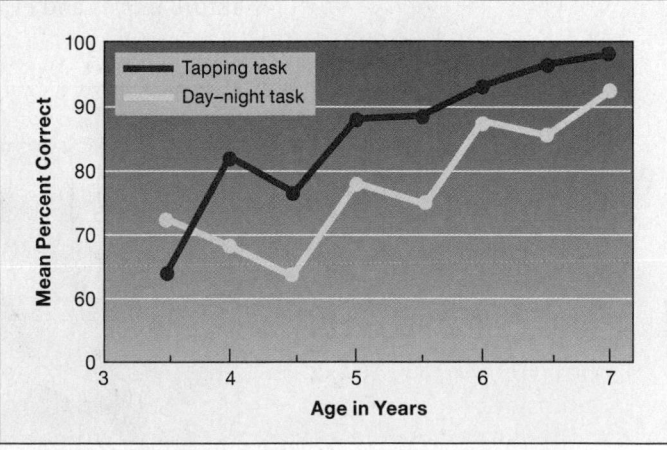

FIGURE 9.5 **Gains between ages 3 and 7 in performance on tasks requiring children to inhibit an impulse and focus on a competing goal.** In the tapping task, children had to tap once when the adult tapped twice and tap twice when the adult tapped once. In the day–night task, children had to say "night" to a picture of the sun and "day" to a picture of the moon with stars. (From A. Diamond, 2004, "Normal Development of Prefrontal Cortex from Birth to Young Adulthood: Cognitive Functions, Anatomy, and Biochemistry," as appeared in D. T. Stuss & R. T. Knight, [Eds.], *Principles of Frontal Lobe Function*, New York: Oxford University Press, p. 474. Reprinted by permission of Adele Diamond.)

Playing Simon Says requires inhibition—refraining from acting when the teacher's command omits "Simon says." These 3- and 4-year-olds find the game challenging. By the end of early childhood, it will be easy.

also eases effort in inhibiting incorrect responses, thereby improving performance.

Adult scaffolding of attention also makes a difference. Preschoolers whose parents offer suggestions, questions, and comments that help the child overcome frustration and sustain direction on a challenging task are more mature, cognitively and socially, when reassessed a year or two later (Bono & Stifter, 2003). In one study, parents' effective scaffolding of 2- and 3-year-olds while solving a complex puzzle predicted higher scores on diverse executive function tasks at age 4, including measures of inhibition and working memory (which, as noted earlier, contributes to attention) (Hammond et al., 2012). Among the 2-year-olds, effective scaffolding was associated with gains in language, which in turn fostered improved executive function, likely by augmenting children's ability to verbally regulate their own behavior through private speech.

PLANNING During early childhood, children also become better at **planning**—thinking out a sequence of acts ahead of time and allocating attention accordingly to reach a goal. As long as tasks are familiar and not too complex, older preschoolers can follow a plan.

Consider a task, devised to resemble real-world planning, in which 3- to 5-year-olds were shown a doll named Molly, a camera, and a miniature zoo with a path, along which were three animal cages. The first and third cages had storage lockers next to them; the middle cage, with no locker, housed a kangaroo (see Figure 9.6). The children were told that Molly could follow the path only once and that she wanted to take a picture of the kangaroo. Then they were asked, "What locker could you leave the camera in so Molly can get it and take a photo of the kangaroo?" (McColgan & McCormack, 2008). Not until age 5 children were children able to plan effectively, selecting the locker at the first cage. On this and other planning tasks, younger preschoolers seem to have difficulty postponing action in favor of mapping out a sequence of future moves and evaluating the consequences of each (McCormack & Atance, 2011; Russell,

FIGURE 9.6 **Miniature zoo used to assess children's planning.** After having been told that Molly wanted to take a picture of the kangaroo but could follow the path only once, preschoolers were asked which locker the camera should be left in so Molly could get it and take the photo. Not until age 5 did children plan, more often selecting the first locker. (Based on McColgan & McCormack, 2008.)

Alexis, & Clayton, 2010). These procedures require inhibition and increased working memory, in addition to planning skill.

Children learn much from cultural tools that support planning—directions for playing games, patterns for construction, recipes for cooking—especially when they collaborate with more expert planners. When 4- to 7-year-olds were observed jointly constructing a toy with their mothers, the mothers provided basic information about the usefulness of plans and how to implement specific steps: "Do you want to look at the picture and see what goes where? What piece do you need first?" After working with their mothers, younger children more often referred to the plan when building on their own (Gauvain, 2004; Gauvain, de la Ossa, & Hurtado-Ortiz, 2001). When parents encourage planning in everyday activities, from loading the dishwasher to packing for a vacation, they help children plan more effectively.

Memory

Unlike infants and toddlers, preschoolers have the language skills to describe what they remember, and they can follow directions on simple memory tasks. As a result, memory becomes easier to study in early childhood.

RECOGNITION AND RECALL   TAKE A MOMENT... Show a young child a set of 10 pictures or toys. Then mix them up with some unfamiliar items, and ask the child to point to the ones in the original set. You will find that preschoolers' *recognition* memory—ability to tell whether a stimulus is the same as or similar to one they have seen before—is remarkably good. In fact, 4- and 5-year-olds perform nearly perfectly.

Now keep the items out of view, and ask the child to name the ones she saw. This more demanding task requires *recall*—generating a mental image of an absent stimulus. Young children's recall is much poorer than their recognition. At age 2, they can recall no more than one or two items, and at age 4 only about three or four (Perlmutter, 1984).

Of course, recognition is much easier than recall for adults as well, but in comparison to adults, children's recall is quite deficient. Improvement in recall over the preschool years is strongly associated with language development, which greatly enhances long-lasting representations of both lists of items and past experiences (Melby-Lervag & Hulme, 2010; Ornstein, Haden, & Elischberger, 2006). But even preschoolers with good language skills recall poorly because they are not skilled at using **memory strategies,** deliberate mental activities that improve our chances of remembering. For example, to retain information, you may *rehearse,* repeating the items over and over, or *organize,* intentionally grouping items that are alike so that you can easily retrieve them by thinking of their similar characteristics.

Why do young children seldom use memory strategies? One reason is that strategies tax their limited working memories. Preschoolers have difficulty holding on to pieces of information and applying a strategy at the same time.

MEMORY FOR EVERYDAY EXPERIENCES   Think about the difference between your recall of listlike information and your memory for everyday experiences—what researchers call **episodic memory.** In remembering lists, you recall isolated bits, reproducing them exactly as you originally learned them. In remembering everyday experiences, you recall complex, meaningful information. Between 3 and 6 years, children improve sharply in memory for relations among stimuli. For example, in a set of photos, they remember not just the animals they saw but also their contexts, such as a bear emerging from a tunnel or a zebra tied to a tree on a city street (Lloyd, Doydum, & Newcombe, 2009). The capacity to *bind together stimuli* when encoding and retrieving them supports the development of an increasingly rich event memory during early childhood.

Memory for Familiar Events.   Like adults, preschoolers remember familiar, repeated events— what you do when you go to child care or have dinner—in terms of **scripts,** general descriptions of what occurs and when it occurs in a particular situation. Young children's scripts begin as a structure of main acts. For example, when asked to tell what happens at a restaurant, a 3-year-old might say, "You go in, get the food, eat, and then pay." Although children's first

Like adults, preschoolers remember familiar, repeated events, such as brushing teeth, in terms of scripts. Over time, children construct more elaborate scripts: "You squeeze out the toothpaste and brush your teeth. You rinse your mouth and then your toothbrush."

scripts contain only a few acts, as long as events in a situation take place in logical order, they are almost always recalled in correct sequence (Bauer, 2002, 2006). With age, scripts become more spontaneous and elaborate, as in this 5-year-old's account of going to a restaurant: "You go in. You can sit in a booth or at a table. Then you tell the waitress what you want. You eat. If you want dessert, you can have some. Then you pay and go home" (Hudson, Fivush, & Kuebli, 1992).

Scripts help children organize, interpret, and predict everyday experiences. Once formed, they can be used to predict what will happen on similar occasions in the future. Children rely on scripts to assist recall when listening to and telling stories. They also act out scripts in make-believe play as they pretend to put the baby to bed, go on a trip, or play school. And scripts support children's earliest efforts at planning by helping them represent sequences of actions that lead to desired goals (Hudson & Mayhew, 2009).

Memory for One-Time Events. In Chapter 6, we considered a second type of episodic memory—*autobiographical memory,* or representations of personally meaningful, one-time events. As 3- to 6-year-olds' cognitive and conversational skills improve, their descriptions of special events become better organized in time, more detailed, enriched with a personal perspective, and related to the larger context of their lives. A young preschooler simply reports, "I went camping." Older preschoolers include specifics: where and when the event happened and who was present. And with age, preschoolers increasingly include subjective information—why, for example, an event was exciting, funny, sad, or made them feel proud or embarrassed—that explains the event's personal significance (Bauer, 2013; Fivush, 2001; Pathman et al., 2013). For example, they might say, "I loved sleeping all night in the tent!"

Adults use two styles to elicit children's autobiographical narratives. In the *elaborative style,* they follow the child's lead, ask varied questions, add information to the child's statements, and volunteer their own recollections and evaluations of events. For example, after a field trip to the zoo, Leslie asked, "What was the first thing we did? Why weren't the parrots in their cages? I thought the roaring lion was scary. What did you think?" In this way, she helped the children reestablish and reorganize their memory of the field trip. In contrast, adults who use the *repetitive style* provide little information and keep repeating the same questions, regardless of the child's interest: "Do you remember the zoo? What did we do at the zoo? What did we do there?"

Preschoolers who experience the elaborative style recall more information about past events and also produce more organized and detailed personal stories when followed up one to two years later (Cleveland & Reese, 2005; Farrant & Reese, 2000). Parents can be trained to use an elaborative style, which also enhances the richness of preschoolers' event memories (Reese & Newcombe, 2007).

As children converse with adults about the past, they not only improve their autobiographical memory but also create a shared history that strengthens close relationships and self-understanding. Parents and preschoolers with secure attachment bonds engage in more elaborate reminiscing (Bost et al., 2006; Reese, Newcombe, & Bird, 2006). And 5- and 6-year-olds of elaborative-style parents describe themselves in clearer, more consistent ways (Bird & Reese, 2006).

Girls tend to have more organized and detailed narratives about past events than boys (Bauer et al., 2007). And compared with Asian children, Western children produce narratives with more talk about their own thoughts and emotions—knowledge that contributes to an appreciation of the personal meaning of events and, therefore, to better recall (Wang, 2008). These differences fit with variations in parent–child conversations. Parents

As this toddler talks about past experiences, his mother responds in an elaborative style, asking varied questions and contributing her own recollections and evaluations of events. Through such conversations, she enriches his autobiographical memory.

reminisce in more detail and talk more about the emotional significance of events with daughters (Fivush, 2009). And cultural valuing of interdependence leads many Asian parents to discourage children from talking about themselves. Chinese parents, for example, engage in less detailed and evaluative past-event dialogues with their preschoolers (Fivush & Wang, 2005; Wang, 2006a).

Consistent with these early experiences, women report an earlier age of first memory and more vivid early memories than men. And Western adults' autobiographical memories include earlier, more detailed events that focus more on their own roles than do the memories of Asians, who tend to highlight the roles of others (Wang, 2006b).

Problem Solving

How do preschoolers use their cognitive competencies to discover new problem-solving strategies? To find out, let's look in on 5-year-old Darryl as he adds marbles tucked into pairs of small bags that Leslie set out on a table.

As Darryl deals with adding each pair, his strategies vary. Sometimes he guesses, without applying any strategy. At other times, he counts from one on his fingers. For example, for bags containing 2 + 4 marbles, his fingers pop up one by one as he exclaims, "One, two, three, four, five, six!" On still other occasions, he starts with the lower digit, 2, and "counts on" ("two, three, four, five, six"). Or he begins with the higher digit, 4, and "counts on" ("four, five, six")— a strategy called *min* because it minimizes the work. Sometimes, he simply retrieves the answer from memory.

To study children's problem solving, Robert Siegler (1996, 2006) used the microgenetic research design (see Chapter 1, page 44), presenting children with many problems over an extended time. He found that children experiment with diverse strategies on many types of problems—basic math facts, numerical estimation, conservation, memory for lists of items, reading first words, spelling, even tic-tac-toe. And their strategy use follows the overlapping-waves pattern shown in Figure 9.7. According to **overlapping-waves theory,** when given challenging problems, children try out various strategies and observe which work best, which work less well, and which are ineffective. Gradually, they select strategies on the basis of two criteria: *accuracy* and *speed*—for basic addition, the *min* strategy. As children home in on effective strategies for solving the problems at hand, correct solutions become more strongly associated with problems, and children display the most efficient strategy—automatic retrieval of the answer.

How do children move from less to more effective strategies? Often they discover faster, more accurate strategies by using more time-consuming techniques. For example, by repeatedly counting on fingers, Darryl began to recognize the number of fingers he held up. Also, certain problems dramatize the need for a better strategy. When Darryl opened a pair of bags, one containing ten marbles and the other with only two, he realized that *min* would be best. Teaching children to reason logically with concepts relevant to the problems is also helpful (Alibali, Phillips, & Fischer, 2009; Siegler & Svetina, 2006). Once Darryl understood that he got the same result regardless of the order in which he combined two sets (3 + 6 = 9 and 6 + 3 = 9), he more often used *min* and arrived at correct answers. Finally, a large improvement in the accuracy of a newly discovered strategy over previous strategies generally leads to rapid adoption of the new approach (Siegler, 2006).

As children transition to automatic retrieval, fMRI evidence reveals reorganized and better integrated activity in networks of brain regions involved in memory-based problem solving (Cho et al.,

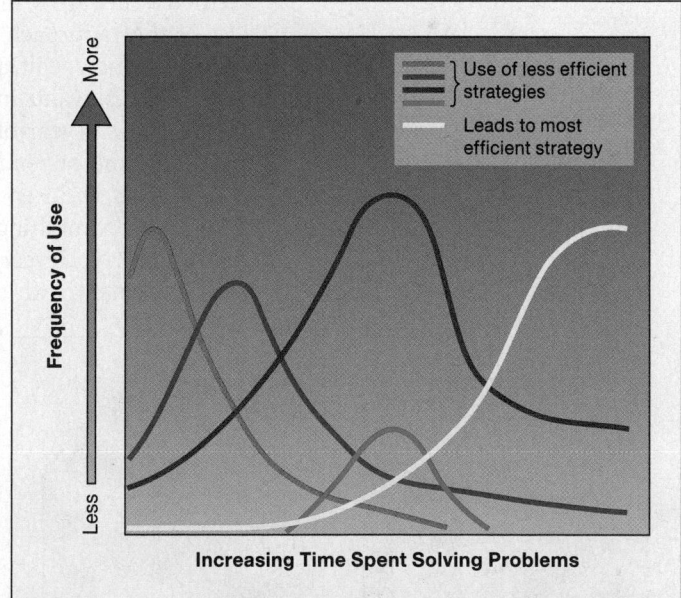

FIGURE 9.7 Overlapping-waves pattern of strategy use in problem solving. When given challenging problems, a child generates a variety of strategies, each represented by a wave. The waves overlap because the child tries several different strategies at the same time. Use of each strategy, depicted by the height of the wave, is constantly changing. As the child observes which strategies work best, which work less well, and which are ineffective, the strategy that results in the most rapid, accurate solutions wins out. (From R. S. Siegler, *Emerging Minds: The Process of Change in Children's Thinking.* Copyright © 1996 by Oxford University Press, Inc. Adapted by permission of Oxford University Press, Inc.)

2011). These include the prefrontal cortex, the hippocampus, and other areas in the cerebral cortex known to support long-term retention. Augmented brain functioning, in turn, likely enhances future problem solving.

Many factors, including practice, reasoning, tasks with new challenges, and adult assistance, contribute to gains in problem solving. And experimenting with less mature strategies lets children see the limitations of those techniques. In sum, overlapping-waves theory emphasizes that trying many strategies is vital for developing new, more effective solution techniques. The overlapping-waves pattern characterizes problem solving across a wide range of ages. And in the tradition of the information-processing approach, the theory views development as occurring gradually, rather than in discontinuous stages.

The Young Child's Theory of Mind

As representation of the world, memory, and problem solving improve, children start to reflect on their own thought processes. They begin to construct a *theory of mind,* or coherent set of ideas about mental activities. This understanding is also called **metacognition,** or "thinking about thought" (the prefix *meta-* means "beyond" or "higher"). As adults, we have a complex appreciation of our inner mental worlds, which we use to interpret our own and others' behavior and to improve our performance on various tasks. How early are children aware of their mental lives, and how complete and accurate is their knowledge?

AWARENESS OF MENTAL LIFE At the end of the first year, babies view people as intentional beings who can share and influence one another's mental states, a milestone that opens the door to new forms of communication—joint attention, social referencing, preverbal gestures, and spoken language. These early milestones serve as the foundation for later mental understandings. In longitudinal research, 10-month-olds' ability to discern others' intentions predicted theory-of-mind competence at age 4 (Wellman et al., 2008).

As they approach age 2, children display a clearer grasp of others' emotions and desires, evident in their realization that people often differ from one another and from themselves in likes, dislikes, wants, needs, and wishes ("Mommy like broccoli. Daddy like carrots. I no like carrots."). As 2-year-olds' vocabularies expand, their first verbs include such words as *think, remember,* and *pretend* (Wellman, 2002).

By age 3, children realize that thinking takes place inside their heads and that a person can think about something without seeing, touching, or talking about it (Flavell, Green, & Flavell, 1995). But 2- to 3-year-olds' verbal responses indicate that they think people always behave in ways consistent with their *desires;* they do not understand that less obvious, more interpretive mental states, such as *beliefs,* also affect behavior. Between ages 3 and 4, children use *think* and *know* to refer to their own and others' thoughts and beliefs (Wellman, 2011). And from age 4 on, they realize that both *beliefs* and *desires* determine behavior.

Dramatic evidence for this advance comes from games that test whether preschoolers realize that *false beliefs*—ones that do not represent reality accurately—can guide people's behavior. **TAKE A MOMENT...** For example, show a child two small closed boxes—a familiar Band-Aid box and a plain, unmarked box (see Figure 9.8). Then say, "Pick the box you think has the Band-Aids in it." Children usually pick the marked container. Next, open the boxes and show the child that, contrary to her own belief, the marked one is empty, and the unmarked one contains the Band-Aids. Finally, introduce the child to a hand puppet and explain, "Here's Pam. She has a cut, see? Where do you think she'll look for Band-Aids? Why would she look in there? Before you looked inside, did you think that the plain box contained the Band-Aids? Why?" (Bartsch & Wellman, 1995). Only a handful of 3-year-olds can explain Pam's—and their own—false beliefs, but many 4-year-olds can.

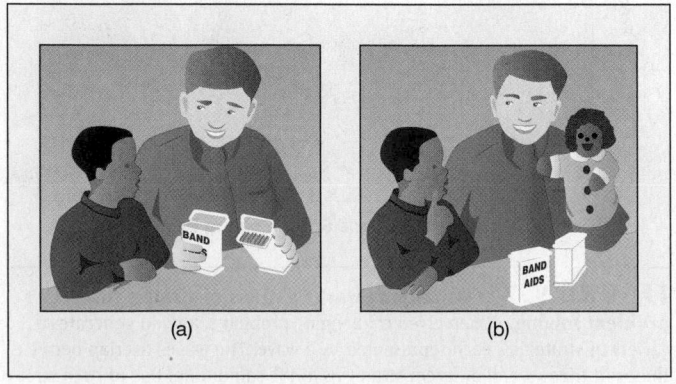

FIGURE 9.8 **Example of a false-belief task.** (a) An adult shows a child the contents of a Band-Aid box and of an unmarked box. The Band-Aids are in the unmarked container. (b) The adult introduces the child to a hand puppet named Pam and asks the child to predict where Pam would look for the Band-Aids and to explain Pam's behavior. The task reveals whether children understand that without having seen that the Band-Aids are in the unmarked container, Pam will hold a false belief.

Some researchers claim that the procedures just described, which require verbal responses, grossly underestimate younger children's ability to attribute false beliefs to others. Relying on the violation-of-expectation method (which depends on looking behavior), these investigators assert that children comprehend others' false beliefs by age 15 months (Baillargeon, Scott, & He, 2010). But like other violation-of-expectation evidence, this conclusion is controversial (see page 206 in Chapter 6) (Sirios & Jackson, 2007). Yet in a study relying on active behavior (helping), most 18-month-olds—after observing an adult reach for a box previously used for blocks that now contained a spoon—based their choice of how to help her on her false belief about the contents of the box: They gave her a block rather than a spoon (Buttelmann et al., 2014). This suggests that toddlers *implicitly* understand that people's actions can be guided by false beliefs, though more evidence is needed to confirm this conclusion (Astington & Hughes, 2013). Researchers cannot yet explain the striking contrast between toddlers' success on nonverbal tasks and 3-year-olds' consistent failure on verbal assessments.

Among children of diverse cultural and SES backgrounds, *explicit* false-belief understanding, assessed with verbal tasks, strengthens after age 3½, becoming more secure between ages 4 and 6 (Wellman, 2012). During that time, it becomes a powerful tool for reflecting on the thoughts and emotions of oneself and others and a good predictor of social skills (Hughes, Ensor, & Marks, 2010). Understanding the mind contributes to *selective trust*—the realization that some people are more credible sources of information than others. For example, preschooler's developing grasp of mental states, including false belief, predicts greater willingness to follow the advice of a helpful person as opposed to a trickster, which emerges around age 5 (Vanderbilt, Liu, & Heyman, 2011).

Finally, mastery of false belief is associated with early reading ability, probably because it helps children comprehend story narratives (Astington & Pelletier, 2005). To follow a story line, children generally must link plot actions with characters' motives and beliefs.

FACTORS CONTRIBUTING TO PRESCHOOLERS' THEORY OF MIND How do children develop a theory of mind beginning at such a young age? Research indicates that language, executive function, make-believe play, and social experiences all contribute.

Language and Verbal Reasoning. The prefrontal cortex seems to play a crucial role in theory-of-mind development. ERP brain-wave recordings obtained while 4- to 6-year-olds reasoned about others' beliefs revealed that children who pass false-belief tasks (as opposed to those who fail) display a distinct pattern of activity in the left prefrontal cortex (Liu et al., 2009). This left-prefrontal ERP pattern also appears when adults reason verbally about mental concepts.

Understanding the mind requires the ability to reflect on thoughts, which language makes possible. Many studies indicate that language ability strongly predicts preschoolers' grasp of false belief (Milligan, Astington, & Dack, 2007). Children who spontaneously use, or who are trained to use, complex sentences with mental-state words are especially likely to pass false-belief tasks (de Villiers & de Villiers, 2000; Hale & Tager-Flusberg, 2003). The Quechua village people of the Peruvian highlands refer to mental states such as "think" and "believe" indirectly, because their language lacks mental-state terms. Quechua children have difficulty with false-belief tasks for years after children in industrialized nations have mastered them (Vinden, 1996).

Executive Function. Several aspects of preschoolers' executive function—ability to inhibit inappropriate responses, think flexibly, and plan—predict mastery of false-belief (Benson et al., 2013; Hughes & Ensor, 2007). Like language, these cognitive skills enhance children's ability to reflect on experiences and mental states. Gains in inhibition are strongly related to mastery of false belief, perhaps because false-belief tasks require suppression of an irrelevant response—the tendency to assume that others' knowledge and beliefs are the same as one's own (Birch & Bloom, 2003; Carlson, Moses, & Claxton, 2004).

Make-Believe Play. Make-believe offers a rich context for thinking about the mind. As children act out roles, they often express the thoughts and emotions of the characters they portray and then reason about their implications (Kavanaugh, 2006b). These experiences may increase children's awareness that belief influences behavior. In support of this idea, preschoolers who engage in extensive fantasy play or who have imaginary companions—and, thus, are deeply absorbed in creating make-believe characters—are advanced in understanding false belief and other aspects of the mind (Astington & Jenkins, 1995; Lalonde & Chandler, 1995).

Social Interaction. Social experiences also promote understanding of the mind. In longitudinal research, mothers of securely attached babies were more likely to comment appropriately on their infants' mental states: "Do you *remember* Grandma?" "You really *like* that swing!" These mothers continued to describe their children, when they reached preschool age, in terms of mental characteristics: "She's got *a mind of her own!*" This maternal "mind-mindedness" was positively associated with later performance on false-belief and other theory-of-mind tasks (Laranjo et al., 2010; Meins et al., 2003; Ruffman et al., 2006). As we saw earlier, secure attachment is related to more elaborative parent–child narratives, which often include discussions of mental states (Ontai & Thompson, 2008; Taumoepeau & Ruffman, 2006). These conversations expose preschoolers to concepts and language that help them think about their own and others' mental lives.

Interaction with siblings, especially older siblings, contributes to preschoolers' awareness of others' perspectives and, therefore, promotes understanding of false belief.

Also, preschoolers with siblings who are children (but not infants)—especially those with older siblings or two or more siblings—tend to be more aware of false belief. Children with older siblings close in age, and those with more siblings, are exposed to and participate in more family talk about varying thoughts, beliefs, and emotions (Hughes et al., 2010; McAlister & Peterson, 2006, 2007). Similarly, preschool friends who often engage in mental-state talk are advanced in false-belief and other mental-state understandings (de Rosnay & Hughes, 2006; Hughes & Dunn, 1998). These social experiences offer extra opportunities to observe different viewpoints and talk about inner states.

Children from interdependent cultural backgrounds, where talk about one's own opinions and emotions is discouraged, are delayed in passing false-belief tasks in relation to Western children. Preschoolers growing up in China and Iran, for example, attain a grasp of explicit false-belief somewhat later than their Australian and American agemates (Shahaeian et al., 2011; Wellman et al., 2006). Both Chinese and Iranian parents teach children to respect their elders' authority and to avoid disagreeing with the viewpoints of parents and other family members.

Core knowledge theorists (see Chapter 6, pages 211–213) believe that to profit from the social experiences just described, children must be biologically prepared to develop a theory of mind. They claim that children with *autism*, for whom mastery of false belief is either greatly delayed or absent, are deficient in the brain mechanism that enables humans to detect mental states. See the Biology and Environment box on the following page to find out more about the biological basis of reasoning about the mind.

LIMITATIONS OF THE YOUNG CHILD'S THEORY OF MIND Though surprisingly advanced, preschoolers' awareness of mental activities is far from complete. For example, 3- and 4-year-olds are unaware that people continue to think while they wait, look at pictures, listen to stories, or read books—that is, when there are no obvious cues that they are thinking. Preschoolers also do not realize that when two people view the same object, their trains of thought will differ because of variations in their knowledge and other characteristics (Eisbach, 2004; Flavell, Green, & Flavell, 1995; Flavell et al., 1997).

A major reason for these findings is that children younger than age 6 pay little attention to the *process* of thinking. When asked about subtle distinctions between mental states, such as *know* and *forget*, they express confusion (Lyon & Flavell, 1994). And they often insist that they have always known information they just learned (Taylor, Esbenson, & Bennett, 1994). Finally, they believe that all events must be directly observed to be known. They do not understand that *mental inferences* can be a source of knowledge (Miller, Hardin, & Montgomery, 2003).

Biology and Environment

Autism and Theory of Mind

Michael stood at the water table in Leslie's classroom, repeatedly filling a plastic cup and dumping out its contents—dip-splash, dip-splash—until Leslie came over and redirected his actions. Without looking at Leslie's face, Michael moved to a new repetitive pursuit: pouring water from one cup into another and back again. As other children entered the play space and conversed, Michael hardly noticed. He rarely spoke, and when he did, he usually used words to get things he wanted, not to exchange ideas.

Michael has *autism*, a term meaning "absorbed in the self." Autism varies in severity along a continuum, called *autistic spectrum disorder*. Michael's difficulties are substantial. Like other similarly affected children, by age 3 he displayed deficits in three core areas of functioning. First, he had only limited ability to engage in nonverbal behaviors required for successful social interaction, such as eye gaze, facial expressions, gestures, imitation, and give-and-take. Second, his language was delayed and stereotyped. He used words to echo what others said and to get things he wanted, not to exchange ideas. Third, he engaged in much less make-believe play than other children (American Psychiatric Association, 2013; Walenski, Tager-Flusberg, & Ullman, 2006). And Michael showed another typical feature of autism: His interests were narrow and overly intense. For example, one day he sat for more than an hour spinning a toy Ferris wheel.

Researchers agree that autism stems from abnormal brain functioning, usually due to genetic or prenatal environmental causes. Beginning in the first year, children with the disorder have larger-than-average brains, with the greatest excess in brain-region volume occurring in the prefrontal cortex (Courchesne et al., 2011). This brain overgrowth is believed to result from lack of synaptic pruning, which accompanies typical development of cognitive, language, and communication skills.

The amygdala, especially, grows abnormally large in childhood, followed by a greater than average reduction in size in adolescence and adulthood. This deviant growth pattern is believed to contribute to deficits in emotion processing and social interaction involved in the disorder (Allely, Gillberg, & Wilson, 2014; Hobson et al., 2013). fMRI studies also reveal that autism is associated with reduced activity in areas of the cerebral cortex involved in emotional and social responsiveness and with weaker connections between the amygdala and the temporal lobes (important for processing facial expressions) (Monk et al., 2010).

Furthermore, brain-imaging evidence reveals that preschoolers with autism show a deficient left-hemispheric response to speech sounds (Eyler, Pierce, & Courchesne, 2012). Failure of the left hemisphere of the cerebral cortex to lateralize for language may underlie these children's language deficits.

Mounting evidence reveals that children with autism are impaired in theory of mind. Long after they reach the intellectual level of an average 4-year-old, they have great difficulty with false belief. Most find it hard to attribute mental states to themselves or others (Steele, Joseph, & Tager-Flusberg, 2003). They rarely use mental-state words such as *believe, think, know, feel,* and *pretend.*

As early as the second year, children with autism show deficits in emotional and social capacities believed to contribute to an understanding of mental life. Compared with other children, they less often establish eye contact, have difficulty distinguishing facial expressions, and seldom engage in social referencing or imitate an adult's novel behaviors (Chawarska, Macari, & Shic, 2013; Vivanti et al., 2008). Furthermore, they are relatively insensitive to eye gaze as a cue to what a speaker is talking about. Instead, they often assume that another person's language refers to what they themselves are looking at—a possible reason for their frequent nonsensical expressions.

Do these findings indicate that autism is due to impairment in an innate, core brain function that leaves the child unable to detect others' mental states and therefore deficient in human sociability? Some researchers think so (Baron-Cohen, 2011; Baron-Cohen & Belmonte, 2005). But others point out that individuals with general intellectual disability but not autism also do poorly on tasks assessing mental understanding

This child, who has autism, is barely aware of his teacher and classmates. Researchers disagree on whether the deficient emotional and social capacities accompanying autism result from a basic impairment in ability to detect others' mental states, a deficit in executive function, or a style of information processing that focuses on parts rather than patterns and coherent wholes.

(Yirmiya et al., 1998). This suggests that cognitive deficits are largely responsible.

One conjecture is that children with autism are impaired in executive function. This leaves them deficient in skills involved in flexible, goal-oriented thinking, including shifting attention to address relevant aspects of a situation, inhibiting irrelevant responses, applying strategies, and generating plans (Joseph & Tager-Flusberg, 2004; Robinson et al., 2009). Another possibility is that children with autism display a peculiar style of information processing, preferring to process the parts of stimuli over patterns and coherent wholes (Happé & Frith, 2006). Deficits in thinking flexibly and in holistic processing of stimuli would each interfere with understanding the social world because social interaction requires quick integration of information from various sources and evaluation of alternative possibilities.

It is not clear which of these hypotheses is correct. Some research suggests that impairments in social awareness, flexible thinking, processing coherent wholes, and verbal ability contribute independently to autism (Pellicano et al., 2006). Perhaps several biologically based deficits underlie the tragic social isolation of children like Michael.

These findings suggest that preschoolers view the mind as a passive container of information. Consequently, they greatly underestimate the amount of mental activity that people engage in and are poor at inferring what people know or are thinking about (Wellman, 2002). In contrast, older children view the mind as an active, constructive agent that selects and interprets information—a change we will consider in Chapter 12.

Early Literacy and Mathematical Development

Researchers are studying how children's information-processing capacities affect the development of basic reading, writing, and mathematical skills that prepare them for school. The way preschoolers begin to master these complex activities gives us additional information about their cognitive strengths and limitations—knowledge we can use to foster early literacy and mathematical development.

LITERACY One week, Leslie's students created a make-believe grocery store. They brought empty food boxes from home, placed them on shelves in the classroom, labeled items with prices, made shopping lists, and wrote checks at the cash register. A sign at the entrance announced the daily specials: "APLS BNS 5¢" ("apples bananas 5¢").

As such play reveals, preschoolers understand a great deal about written language long before they learn to read or write in conventional ways. This is not surprising: Children in industrialized nations live in a world filled with written symbols. Each day, they observe and participate in activities involving storybooks, calendars, lists, and signs. Children's active efforts to construct literacy knowledge through informal experiences are called **emergent literacy.**

Young preschoolers search for units of written language as they "read" memorized versions of stories and recognize familiar signs ("PIZZA"). But they do not yet understand the symbolic function of the elements of print (Bialystok & Martin, 2003). Many preschoolers think that a single letter stands for a whole word or that each letter in a person's signature represents a separate name. Initially, as we noted in Chapter 8, preschoolers do not distinguish between drawing and writing but often believe that letters (like pictures) resemble the meanings they represent. For example, one child explained that the word *sun* begins with the letter *O* because that letter is shaped like the sun; to demonstrate, he drew an *O* surrounded with rays to produce a picture of the sun.

Children revise these ideas as their perceptual and cognitive capacities improve, as they encounter writing in many contexts, and as adults help them with written communication. Gradually preschoolers notice more features of written language and depict writing that varies in function, as in the "story" and "grocery list" in Figure 9.9.

Eventually children figure out that letters are parts of words and are linked to sounds in systematic ways, as 5- to 7-year-olds' invented spellings illustrate. At first, children rely on sounds in the names of letters: "ADE LAFWTS KRMD NTU A LAVATR" ("eighty elephants crammed into a[n] elevator"). Over time, they grasp sound–letter correspondences and learn that some letters have more than one common sound and that context affects their use (*a* is pronounced differently in "cat" than in "table") (McGee & Richgels, 2012).

Literacy development builds on a broad foundation of spoken language and knowledge about the world (Dickinson, Golinkoff, & Hirsh-Pasek, 2010). **Phonological awareness**—the ability to reflect on and manipulate the sound structures of spoken language, as indicated by sensitivity to changes in sounds within words, to rhyming, and to incorrect pronunciation—is a strong predictor of emergent literacy and later reading and spelling achievement (Dickinson et al., 2003; Paris & Paris, 2006). When combined with sound–letter knowledge, it enables children to isolate speech segments and link them with their written symbols. Vocabulary

© LAURA DWIGHT PHOTOGRAPHY

Preschoolers acquire literacy knowledge informally by participating in everyday activities involving written symbols. These young chefs "write down" orders they need to fill.

and grammatical knowledge are also influential. And preschoolers' narrative competence, assessed through having them retell stories, fosters diverse language skills essential for literacy progress, including phonological awareness (Hipfner-Boucher et al., 2014). Coherent storytelling requires attention to large language structures, such as character, setting, problem, and resolution. It seems to support the smaller-scale analysis involved in awareness of sound structures.

The more informal literacy experiences young children have, the better their language and emergent literacy development and their later reading skills (Dickinson & McCabe, 2001; Speece et al., 2004). Pointing out letter–sound correspondences and playing language–sound games enhance children's awareness of the sound structures of language and how they are represented in print (Ehri & Roberts, 2006; Foy & Mann, 2003). *Interactive reading,* in which adults discuss storybook content with preschoolers, promotes many aspects of language and literacy development. And adult-supported writing activities that focus on narrative, such as preparing a letter or a story, also have wide-ranging benefits (Purcell-Gates, 1996; Wasik & Bond, 2001). In longitudinal research, each of these literacy experiences is linked to improved reading achievement in middle childhood (Hood, Conlon, & Andrews, 2008; Senechal & LeFevre, 2002; Storch & Whitehurst, 2001).

Preschoolers from low-SES families have fewer home and preschool language and literacy learning opportunities—a major reason that they are behind in emergent literacy skills and in reading achievement throughout the school years (Foster & Miller, 2007; Turnbull et al., 2009). Age-appropriate books, for example, are scarce in their environments. In one survey of four middle- and low-income communities, the middle-income neighborhoods averaged 13 books per child, the low-income neighborhoods just 1 book for every 300 children (Neuman & Celano, 2001).

On average, a low-SES child is read to for a total of 25 hours during the preschool years, a higher-SES child for 1,000 hours. The SES gap in early literacy experiences translates into large differences in knowledge and skills that are vital for reading readiness at kindergarten entry (see Figure 9.10). Kindergartners who are behind in emergent literacy development tend to remain behind, performing poorly in reading in the early grades (National Early Literacy Panel, 2008). Over time, skilled readers acquire wide-ranging knowledge more efficiently, progressing more rapidly than poor readers in all achievement areas (Neuman, 2006). In this way, literacy deficiencies at the start of school contribute to widening achievement disparities between economically advantaged and disadvantaged children that often persist into high school.

High-quality intervention can reduce the SES gap in early literacy development substantially. Providing low-SES parents with children's books, along with guidance in how to stimulate emergent literacy, greatly enhances literacy activities in the home (High et al., 2000; Huebner & Payne, 2010). And when teachers are shown how to engage in effective early childhood instruction of diverse literacy skills, low-SES preschoolers gain in emergent literacy components included in their classroom experiences (Hilbert & Eis, 2014; Lonigan et al., 2013). For ways to support early childhood literacy development, refer to Applying What We Know on page 338.

FIGURE 9.9 **A story (a) and a grocery list (b) written by a 4-year-old child.** This child's writing has many features of real print. It also reveals an awareness of different kinds of written expression. (From McGee, Lea M.; Richgels, Donald J., *Literacy's Beginnings: Supporting Young Readers and Writers,* 4th Ed., © 2004. Reprinted and Electronically reproduced by permission of Pearson Education, Inc., Upper Saddle River, New Jersey.)

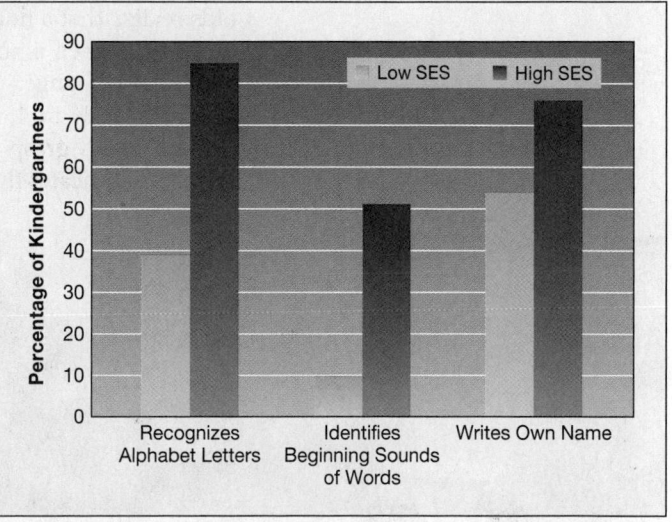

FIGURE 9.10 **Some reading readiness skills at kindergarten entry by SES.** The SES gap in emergent literacy development is large. (Adapted from Lee & Burkham, 2002.)

MATHEMATICAL REASONING Mathematical reasoning, like literacy, builds on informal knowledge. Between 14 and 16 months, toddlers display a beginning grasp of **ordinality,** or order relationships between quantities—for example, that 3 is more than 2, and 2 is more than 1. In the early preschool years, children attach verbal labels *(lots, little, big, small)* to

Applying What We Know

Supporting Emergent Literacy in Early Childhood

STRATEGY	EXPLANATION
Provide literacy-rich home and preschool environments.	Homes and preschools with abundant reading and writing materials—including a wide variety of children's storybooks, some relevant to children's ethnic backgrounds—open the door to a wealth of language and literacy experiences. Make-believe play in which children have many opportunities to use newly acquired literacy skills in meaningful ways spurs literacy development.
Engage in interactive book reading.	When adults discuss story content, ask open-ended questions about story events, explain the meaning of words, and point out features of print, they promote language development, comprehension of story content, knowledge of story structure, and awareness of units of written language.
Provide outings to libraries, museums, parks, zoos, and other community settings.	Visits to child-oriented community settings enhance children's general knowledge and offer many opportunities to see how written language is used in everyday life. They also provide personally meaningful topics for narrative conversation, which promote many language skills essential for literacy development.
Point out letter–sound correspondences, play rhyming and other language–sound games, and read rhyming poems and stories.	Experiences that help children isolate the sounds in words foster *phonological awareness*—a powerful predictor of early childhood literacy knowledge and later reading and spelling achievement.
Support children's efforts at writing, especially narrative products.	Assisting children in their efforts to write—especially letters, stories, and other narratives—fosters many language and literacy skills.
Model literacy activities.	When children see adults engaged in reading and writing activities, they better understand the diverse everyday functions of literacy skills and the knowledge and pleasure that literacy brings. As a result, children's motivation to become literate is strengthened.

Sources: McGee & Richgels, 2012; Neuman, 2006.

amounts and sizes. Sometime in the third year, they begin to count. By the time children turn 3, most can count rows of about five objects, although they do not yet know what the words mean. For example, when asked for *one,* they give one item, but when asked for *two, three, four,* or *five,* they usually give a larger, but incorrect, amount. Nevertheless, 2½- to 3½-year-olds realize that a number word refers to a unique quantity (Sarnecka & Gelman, 2004). They know that when a number label changes (for example, from *five* to *six*), the number of items should also change.

By age 3½ to 4, most children have mastered the meaning of numbers up to *ten,* count correctly, and grasp the vital principle of **cardinality**—that the last number in a counting sequence indicates the quantity of items in the set (Sarnecka & Wright, 2013). In the preschool scene described in the opening of this chapter, Sammy showed an understanding of cardinality when he counted four children at his snack table and then retrieved four milk cartons. Mastery of cardinality increases the efficiency of counting. By age 4, children use counting to solve simple arithmetic problems. At first, their strategies are tied to the order of numbers presented; when given 2 + 4, they count on from 2 (Bryant & Nunes, 2002). But soon they experiment with other strategies and master the *min* strategy, a more efficient approach (see page 331). Around this time, children realize that subtraction cancels out addition. Knowing, for example, that 4 + 3 = 7, they infer without counting that 7 − 3 = 4 (Rasmussen, Ho, & Bisanz, 2003). Grasping basic arithmetic rules greatly facilitates rapid, accurate computation.

© ELLEN B. SENISI

Preschoolers "hop" a toy frog along a number line, measuring the length of each jump. Through informal exploration of number concepts, they construct basic understandings essential for learning math skills later on.

Understanding basic arithmetic makes possible beginning *estimation*—the ability to generate approximate answers, which are useful for evaluating the accuracy of exact answers. After watching several doughnuts being added to or removed from a plate of four to ten doughnuts, 3- and 4-year-olds make sensible predictions about how many are on the plate (Zur & Gelman, 2004). Still, children can estimate only just beyond their calculation competence. For example, preschoolers who can solve addition problems with sums up to 10 can estimate answers with sums up to about 20 (Dowker, 2003). And as with arithmetic operations, children try out diverse estimation strategies, gradually moving to more efficient, accurate techniques.

The arithmetic knowledge just described emerges universally around the world. But when adults provide many occasions for counting, comparing quantities, and talking about number concepts, children acquire these understandings sooner (Ginsburg, Lee, & Boyd, 2008). Math proficiency at kindergarten entry strongly predicts math achievement years later, in elementary and secondary school (Duncan et al., 2007; Geary, 2006).

As with emergent literacy, children from low-SES families begin kindergarten with considerably less math knowledge than their higher-SES agemates—a gap due to differences in environmental supports. Just a few sessions devoted to playing a number board game with an adult (see Figure 9.11) led to a dramatic improvement in low-SES 4-year-olds' number concepts and proficiency at counting from 1 to 10 (Siegler, 2009). And in an early childhood math curriculum called *Building Blocks,* materials that promote math concepts and skills through three types of media—computers, manipulatives, and print—enable teachers to weave math into many preschool daily activities, from building blocks to art and stories (Clements et al., 2011). Compared with agemates randomly assigned to other preschool programs, low-SES preschoolers experiencing Building Blocks showed substantially greater year-end gains in math concepts and skills, including counting, sequencing, arithmetic computation, and geometric shapes.

FIGURE 9.11 A number board game. An adult and child took turns using a spinner with a "1" section and a "2" section, which indicated how far to move a token on each turn. Children were asked to say the number spun and the numbers on the spaces as they moved. For example, a child on 5 who spun 2 would say "6, 7." Compared with agemates who played a color version of the game (it had only colored spaces on the board and a spinner with matching color sections), low-SES 4-year-olds who played the number board game showed large gains in number concepts and counting proficiency from 1 to 10. (From R. S. Siegler, 2009, "Improving Preschoolers' Number Sense Using Information-Processing Theory," in O. A. Barbarin & B. H. Wasik, eds., *Handbook of Child Development and Early Education.* New York: Guilford, p. 438. Reprinted by permission of Guilford Publications, Inc.)

LOOK and LISTEN

Ask several parents of preschoolers what they routinely do to help their children learn about math. Then ask what they do to support literacy. Do the parents promote math as much as literacy learning?

Ask Yourself

- **REVIEW** Describe a typical 4-year-old's understanding of mental activities, noting both strengths and limitations.

- **CONNECT** Cite evidence on the development of preschoolers' memory, theory of mind, and literacy and mathematical understanding that is consistent with Vygotsky's sociocultural theory.

- **APPLY** Lena wonders why her 4-year-old son Gregor's teacher provides extensive playtime in learning centers during each preschool day. Explain to Lena how adult-supported play can promote literacy and math skills essential for academic success.

- **REFLECT** Describe informal experiences important for literacy and math development that you experienced while growing up.

Individual Differences in Mental Development

9.9 Describe the content of early childhood intelligence tests and the impact of home, preschool and kindergarten programs, child care, and educational media on mental development.

Psychologists and educators typically measure how well preschoolers are developing mentally by giving them intelligence tests. Scores are computed in the same way as they are for infants and toddlers (return to Chapter 6, pages 225–226, to review). But instead of emphasizing perceptual and motor responses, tests for preschoolers sample a wide range of mental abilities. Understanding the link between early childhood experiences and mental test performance highlights ways to intervene in support of children's cognitive development.

Early Childhood Intelligence Tests

Five-year-old Hal sat in a small, unfamiliar testing room while Sarah gave him an intelligence test. Some of Sarah's questions were *verbal*. For example, she showed Hal a picture of a shovel and said, "Tell me what this is"—an item measuring vocabulary. She tested Hal's memory by asking him to repeat sentences and lists of numbers back to her. She probed his quantitative knowledge and problem solving by seeing if he could count and solve simple addition and subtraction problems. Finally, to assess Hal's spatial reasoning, Sarah used *nonverbal* tasks: Hal copied designs with special blocks, figured out the pattern in a series of shapes, and indicated what a piece of paper folded and cut would look like when unfolded (Roid, 2003; Wechsler, 2002).

Sarah knew that Hal came from an economically disadvantaged family. When low-SES and certain ethnic minority preschoolers are bombarded with questions by an unfamiliar adult, they sometimes react with anxiety. Also, such children may not define the testing situation in achievement terms (Ford, Kozey, & Negreiros, 2012). Instead, they may look for attention and approval from the adult and may settle for lower performance than their abilities allow. Sarah spent time playing with Hal before she began testing and encouraged him while the test was in progress. Under these conditions, low-SES preschoolers improve in performance (Bracken, 2000).

The questions Sarah asked Hal tap knowledge and skills that not all children have had an equal opportunity to learn. In Chapter 12, we will take up the hotly debated issue of *cultural bias* in mental testing. For now, keep in mind that intelligence tests do not sample all human abilities, and performance is affected by cultural and situational factors. Nevertheless, test scores remain important: By age 6 to 7, they are good predictors of later IQ and academic achievement, which are related to vocational success in industrialized societies. Let's see how the environments in which children spend their days—home, preschool, and child care—affect mental test performance.

Home Environment and Mental Development

A special version of the *Home Observation for Measurement of the Environment (HOME)*, covered in Chapter 6, assesses aspects of 3- to 6-year-olds' home lives that foster intellectual growth (see Applying What We Know on the following page). Preschoolers who develop well intellectually have homes rich in educational toys and books. Their parents are warm and affectionate, stimulate language and academic knowledge, and arrange interesting outings. They also make reasonable demands for socially mature behavior—for example, that the child perform simple chores and behave courteously toward others. And these parents resolve conflicts with reason instead of physical force and punishment (Bradley & Caldwell, 1982; Espy, Molfese, & DiLalla, 2001; Roberts, Burchinal, & Durham, 1999).

As we saw in Chapter 2, these characteristics are less often seen in low-SES families. When parents manage, despite low education and income, to obtain high HOME scores, their preschoolers do substantially better on intelligence tests and measures of language and emergent literacy skills (Berger, Paxson, & Waldfogel, 2009; Mistry et al., 2008). In a study of African-American 3- and 4-year-olds from low-income families, HOME cognitive stimulation and emotional support subscales predicted reading achievement four years later (Zaslow et al., 2006). These findings (along with others we will discuss in Chapter 12) indicate that the home plays a major role in the generally poorer intellectual performance of low-SES children compared to their higher-SES peers.

Applying What We Know

Features of a High-Quality Home Life for Preschoolers: The HOME Early Childhood Subscales

HOME SUBSCALE	SAMPLE ITEMS
Cognitive stimulation through toys, games, and reading material	Home includes toys that teach colors, sizes, and shapes.
Language stimulation	Parent converses with child at least twice during observer's visit.
Organization of the physical environment	All visible rooms are reasonably clean and minimally cluttered.
Emotional support; parental pride, affection, and warmth	Parent spontaneously praises child's qualities or behavior twice during observer's visit. Parent caresses, kisses, or hugs child at least once during observer's visit.
Stimulation of academic behavior	Child is encouraged to learn colors.
Parental modeling and encouragement of social maturity	Parent introduces interviewer to child.
Opportunities for variety in daily stimulation	Family member takes child on one outing (picnic, shopping) at least every other week.
Avoidance of physical punishment	Parent neither slaps nor spanks child during observer's visit.

Sources: Bradley, 1994; Bradley et al., 2001.

Preschool, Kindergarten, and Child Care

Children between ages 2 and 6 spend even more time away from their homes and parents than infants and toddlers do. Largely because of the rise in maternal employment, over the past several decades the number of young children enrolled in preschool or child care has steadily increased, to more than 60 percent in the United States (U.S. Census Bureau, 2014b).

A *preschool* is a program with planned educational experiences aimed at enhancing the development of 2- to 5-year-olds. In contrast, *child care* refers to a variety of arrangements for supervising children of employed parents, ranging from care in the caregiver's or the child's home to some type of center-based program. The line between preschool and child care is fuzzy. Parents often select a preschool as a child-care option. And in response to the needs of employed parents, many U.S. preschools, as well as most public school kindergartens, have increased their hours from half to full days (Child Trends, 2013).

With age, preschoolers tend to shift from home-based to center-based early childhood programs. In the United States, children of higher-income parents and children of very low-income parents are especially likely to be in preschools or child-care centers (Federal Interagency Forum on Child and Family Statistics, 2013). Many low-income working parents rely on care by relatives because they are not eligible for public preschool or government-subsidized child-care centers. A few states offer government-funded prekindergarten programs located within public schools to all 4-year-olds (Barnett et al., 2013). The goal of these universal prekindergartens is to ensure that as many children as possible, from all SES levels, enter kindergarten prepared to succeed.

TYPES OF PRESCHOOL AND KINDERGARTEN Preschool and kindergarten programs range along a continuum from child-centered to teacher-directed. In **child-centered programs,** teachers provide activities from which children select, and much learning takes place through play. In contrast, in **academic programs,** teachers structure children's learning, teaching letters, numbers, colors, shapes, and other academic skills through formal lessons, often using repetition and drill.

Despite evidence that formal academic training undermines young children's motivation and emotional well-being, early childhood teachers have felt increased pressure to take this approach. Preschoolers and kindergartners who spend much time in large-group

Five-year-olds in a Montessori classroom benefit cognitively and socially from materials designed to promote exploration and discovery and ample time for both individual and small-group learning.

teacher-directed academic instruction and completing worksheets—as opposed to being actively engaged in learning centers by warm, responsive teachers—display more stress behaviors (such as wiggling and rocking), have less confidence in their abilities, prefer less challenging tasks, and are less advanced in motor, academic, language, and social skills at the end of the school year (Stipek, 2011; Stipek et al., 1995). Follow-ups reveal lasting effects through elementary school in poorer study habits and lower achievement test scores (Burts et al., 1992; Hart et al., 1998, 2003). These outcomes are strongest for low-SES children, with whom teachers more often use a directive, academic approach—a disturbing trend in view of its negative impact on motivation and learning (Stipek, 2004).

Although government spending for universal prekindergarten is controversial in the United States, in Western Europe such programs are widespread and child-centered in their daily activities. Enrolled preschoolers of all SES backgrounds show gains in cognitive and social development still evident in elementary and secondary school (Rindermann & Ceci, 2008; Waldfogel & Zhai, 2008). Findings on some U.S universal prekindergarten programs that meet rigorous state standards of quality—especially, provision of rich teacher–child interactions and stimulating learning activities—reveal up to a one-year advantage in kindergarten and first-grade language, literacy, and math scores relative to those of children not enrolled (Gormley & Phillips, 2009; Weiland & Yoshikawa, 2013). Children from low-SES families benefit most.

A special type of child-centered approach is *Montessori education,* devised more than a century ago by Italian physician and child development researcher Maria Montessori, who originally applied her method to poverty-stricken children. Features of Montessori schooling include multiage classrooms, teaching materials specially designed to promote exploration and discovery, long time periods for individual and small-group learning in child-chosen activities, and equal emphasis on academic and social development (Lillard, 2007). In an evaluation of public preschools serving mostly urban minority children in Milwaukee, researchers compared students randomly assigned to either Montessori or other classrooms (Lillard & Else-Quest, 2006). Five-year-olds who had completed two years of Montessori education outperformed controls in literacy and math skills, cognitive flexibility, false-belief understanding, concern with fairness in solving conflicts with peers, and cooperative play with agemates.

As for the dramatic rise in U.S. full-day kindergartens, the longer school day is associated with better academic achievement in the early elementary grades. But benefits for social development are mixed (Cooper et al., 2010). Some evidence suggests that kindergartners in full-day as opposed to half-day classrooms have more behavior problems.

EARLY INTERVENTION FOR AT-RISK PRESCHOOLERS   In the 1960s, as part of the "War on Poverty" in the United States, many intervention programs for low-SES preschoolers were initiated, in an effort to address learning problems prior to school entry. The most extensive of these federal programs, **Project Head Start,** began in 1965. A typical Head Start center provides children with a year or two of preschool, along with nutritional and health services. Parent involvement is central to the Head Start philosophy. Parents serve on policy councils, contribute to program planning, work directly with children in classrooms, attend special programs on parenting and child development, and receive services directed at their own emotional, social, and vocational needs. Currently, Head Start serves about 904,000 children and their families across the nation (Office of Head Start, 2014).

Benefits of Preschool Intervention. More than two decades of research have established the long-term benefits of preschool intervention. The most extensive of these studies combined data from seven interventions implemented by universities or research foundations. Results showed that poverty-stricken children who attended programs scored higher in IQ and achievement than controls during the first two to three years of elementary school. After that, differences declined (Lazar & Darlington, 1982). But on real-life measures of school adjustment, children and adolescents who had received intervention remained ahead. They were less likely to be placed in special education or retained in grade, and a greater number graduated from high school.

A separate report on one program—the High/Scope Perry Preschool Project—revealed benefits lasting well into adulthood. Two years' exposure to cognitively enriching preschool was associated with increased employment and reduced pregnancy and delinquency rates in adolescence. At age 27, those who had attended preschool were more likely than their no-preschool counterparts to have graduated from high school and college, have higher earnings, be married, and own their own home—and less likely to have been involved with the criminal justice system (see Figure 9.12) (Weikart, 1998). In the most recent follow-up, at age 40, the intervention group sustained its advantage on all measures of life success, including education, income, family life, and law-abiding behavior (Schweinhart, 2010; Schweinhart et al., 2005).

Do effects on school adjustment of these excellent interventions generalize to Head Start and other community-based preschool interventions? Gains are similar, though not as strong. Head Start preschoolers, who are more economically disadvantaged than children in university-based programs, have more severe learning and behavior problems. And quality of Head Start—though better than in most preschool programs serving low-SES children—often does not equal that of model university-based programs (Resnick, 2010; U.S. Department of Health and Human Services, 2010b). But community-based interventions of documented high quality are associated with diverse life-success outcomes, including higher rates of high school graduation and college enrollment and lower rates of adolescent drug use and delinquency (Yoshikawa et al., 2013).

A consistent finding is that gains in IQ and achievement test scores from attending Head Start and other interventions quickly dissolve. In the Head Start Impact Study, a nationally representative sample of 5,000 Head Start–eligible 3- and 4-year-olds was randomly assigned to one year of Head Start or to a control group that could attend other types of preschool programs (Puma et al., 2012; U.S. Department of Health and Human Services, 2010b). By year's end, Head Start 3-year-olds had gained relative to controls in vocabulary, emergent literacy, and math skills; 4-year-olds in vocabulary, emergent literacy, and color identification. Head Start 3-year-olds also benefited socially, displaying declines in overactivity and withdrawn behavior. But except for language skills, academic test-score advantages were no longer evident by the end of first grade. And Head Start graduates did not differ from controls on any achievement measures at the end of third grade.

What explains these disappointing outcomes? Head Start children typically enter inferior public schools in poverty-stricken neighborhoods, which undermine the

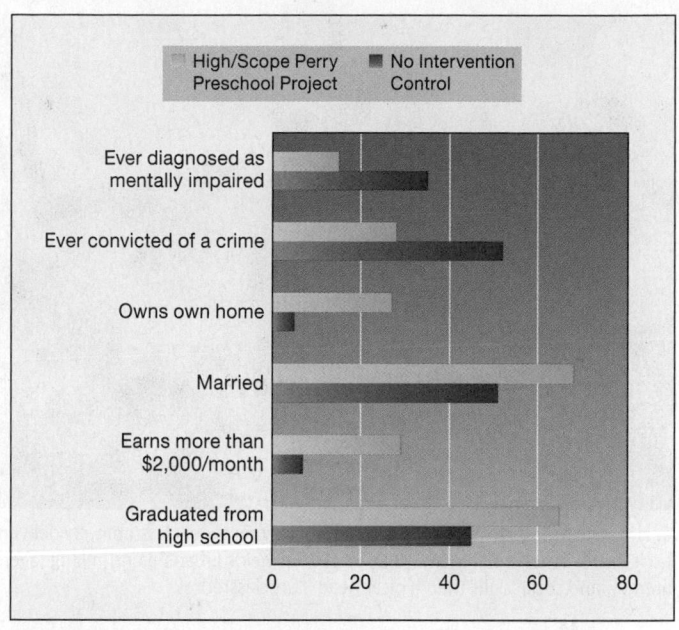

FIGURE 9.12 **Some outcomes of the High/Scope Perry Preschool Project on follow-up at age 27.** Although two years of a cognitively enriching preschool program did not eradicate the effects of growing up in poverty, children who received intervention were advantaged over no-intervention controls on all measures of life success when they reached adulthood. (Adapted from Schweinhart, 2010; Schweinhart et al., 2005.)

Project Head Start provides children from poverty-stricken families with preschool education and nutritional and health services. High-quality early educational intervention has benefits lasting into adulthood.

This teacher integrates Head Start REDI into her preschool classroom. By delivering extra educational enrichment, Head Start REDI yields greater gains in language, literacy, and social skills than typical Head Start classrooms.

benefits of preschool education (Brooks-Gunn, 2003; Ramey, Ramey, & Lanzi, 2006). An exception is the Chicago Child–Parent Centers—a program emphasizing literacy intervention and parent involvement that began at age 3 and continued through third grade—in which gains in academic achievement were still evident in middle school (Reynolds & Temple, 1998). And recall from Chapter 6 that when intensive intervention persists from infancy through early childhood, IQ gains are more likely to endure into adulthood (see pages 229–230).

Still, the improved school adjustment that results from attending a one- or two-year Head Start program is impressive. Program effects on parents may contribute: The more involved parents are in Head Start, the better their child-rearing practices and the more stimulating their home learning environments. These factors are positively related to preschoolers' independence, task persistence in the classroom, and year-end academic, language, and social skills (Bulotsky-Shearer et al., 2012; Marcon, 1999; McLoyd, Aikens, & Burton, 2006).

Strengthening Preschool Intervention. A few supplementary programs have responded to the need to intensify preschool intervention to augment its impact. One of the most widely implemented is *Head Start REDI* (Research-based Developmentally Informed), an enrichment curriculum designed for integration into existing Head Start classrooms. Before school begins, Head Start teachers—60 percent of whom do not have teaching certificates—take workshops in which they learn research-based strategies for enhancing language, literacy, and social skills. Throughout the school year, they receive one-to-one mentoring from master teachers, aimed at ensuring effective delivery of REDI.

Relative to typical Head Start classrooms, Head Start plus REDI yields higher year-end language, literacy, and social development scores. These advantages are still evident at the end of kindergarten, with stronger effects in elementary schools with many poorly achieving students (Bierman et al., 2008, 2014). REDI's powerful impact on teaching quality is believed to be responsible. Teachers trained in REDI converse with preschoolers in more cognitively complex ways and more often use management strategies that prevent disruptive behavior (Domitrovich et al., 2009).

Head Start is highly cost-effective when compared with the price of providing special education, treating criminal behavior, and supporting unemployed adults. Economists estimate a lifetime return to society of more than $300,000 to $500,000 on an investment of about $17,000 per preschool child—a potential savings of many billions of dollars if every poverty-stricken preschooler in the United States were enrolled (Heckman et al., 2010). Because of limited funding, however, only 60 percent of 3- and 4-year-olds living in poverty attend some type of preschool program, with Head Start serving just half of these children (Magnuson & Shager, 2010).

CHILD CARE We have seen that high-quality early intervention can enhance the development of economically disadvantaged children. As noted in Chapter 6, however, much U.S. child care lacks quality. Preschoolers exposed to substandard child care, particularly for long hours, score lower in cognitive and social skills and display more behavior problems (Lamb & Ahnert, 2006; NICHD Early Child Care Research Network, 2003b, 2006). Externalizing difficulties

Ingredients of high-quality child care include small group size, generous caregiver–child ratios, richly equipped activity areas, and well-educated caregivers. Child care that meets these criteria enhances development, especially for low-SES preschoolers.

Applying What We Know

Signs of Developmentally Appropriate Early Childhood Programs

PROGRAM CHARACTERISTIC	SIGNS OF QUALITY
Physical setting	Indoor environment is clean, in good repair, and well-ventilated. Classroom space is divided into richly equipped activity areas, including make-believe play, blocks, science, math, games and puzzles, books, art, and music. Fenced outdoor play space is equipped with swings, climbing equipment, tricycles, and sandbox.
Group size	In preschools and child-care centers, group size is no greater than 18 to 20 children with two teachers.
Teacher–child ratio	In preschools and child-care centers, teacher is responsible for no more than 8 to 10 children. In family child-care homes, caregiver is responsible for no more than 6 children.
Daily activities	Children select many of their own activities and learn through experiences relevant to their own lives, mainly in small groups or individually. Teachers facilitate children's involvement, accept individual differences, and adjust expectations to children's developing capacities.
Interactions between adults and children	Teachers move among groups and individuals, asking questions, offering suggestions, and adding more complex ideas. Teachers use positive guidance techniques, such as modeling and encouraging expected behavior and redirecting children to more acceptable activities.
Teacher qualifications	Teachers have college-level specialized preparation in early childhood development, early childhood education, or a related field.
Relationships with parents	Parents are encouraged to observe and participate. Teachers talk frequently with parents about children's behavior and development.
Licensing and accreditation	Preschool and child-care programs are licensed by the state. Voluntary accreditation by the National Association for the Education of Young Children (www.naeyc.org/academy) or the National Association for Family Child Care (www.nafcc.org) is evidence of an especially high-quality program.

Sources: Copple & Bredekamp, 2009.

are especially likely to endure into the school years after extensive exposure to mediocre care (Belsky et al., 2007b; Vandell et al., 2010). Psychological well-being also declines when children experience the instability of several child-care settings. The emotional problems of temperamentally difficult preschoolers worsen considerably (De Schipper, van IJzendoorn, & Tavecchio, 2004; De Schipper et al., 2004).

In contrast, good child care enhances language, cognitive, and social development, especially for low-SES children—effects that persist into elementary school and, for academic achievement in one investigation, adolescence (Burchinal, Vandergrift, & Pianta, 2010; Dearing, McCartney, & Taylor, 2009; Vandell et al., 2010). Center-based care is more strongly associated with cognitive gains than are other child-care arrangements (Abner et al., 2013). Good-quality child-care centers are more likely than family child-care homes to provide a systematic educational program.

What are the ingredients of high-quality early childhood education? Large-scale studies identify several important factors: group size (number of children in a single space), teacher–child ratio, teachers' educational preparation, and teachers' personal commitment to learning about and caring for children. When these characteristics are favorable, adults are more verbally stimulating and sensitive to children's developmental needs (Lamb & Ahnert, 2006).

Applying What We Know above summarizes characteristics of high-quality early childhood programs, based on standards for developmentally appropriate practice devised by the U.S. National Association for the Education of Young Children. These standards offer a set of worthy goals as the United States strives to upgrade child-care, preschool, and kindergarten services for young children.

LOOK and LISTEN

Arrange to observe at a child-care center and to talk to its director. Jot down signs of quality, referring to Applying What We Know above. How would you rate the center's overall quality?

Educational Media

Besides home and preschool, young children spend much time in another learning environment: screen media, including both television and computers. In the industrialized world, nearly all homes have at least one television set, and most have two or more. And more than 90 percent of U.S. children live in homes with one or more computers, 80 percent of which have an Internet connection, usually a high-speed link (Rideout, Foehr, & Roberts, 2010; U.S. Census Bureau, 2014b).

EDUCATIONAL TELEVISION   Sammy's favorite TV program, *Sesame Street,* uses lively visual and sound effects to stress basic literacy and number concepts and presents engaging puppet and human characters to teach general knowledge, emotional and social understanding, and social skills. Today, *Sesame Street* is broadcast in more than 140 countries, making it the most widely viewed children's program in the world (Sesame Workshop, 2014).

Time devoted to watching children's educational programs, including *Sesame Street,* is associated with gains in early literacy and math skills and with academic progress in elementary school (Ennemoser & Schneider, 2007; Mares & Pan, 2013). One study reported a link between preschool viewing of *Sesame Street* (and similar educational programs) and getting higher grades, reading more books, and placing more value on achievement in high school (Anderson et al., 2001).

Sesame Street has modified its previous rapid-paced format in favor of more leisurely episodes with a clear story line. Programs with slow-paced action and easy-to-follow narratives, such as *Arthur* and *The Magic School Bus,* are associated with improved executive function, greater recall of program content, gains in vocabulary and reading skills, and more elaborate make-believe play than programs presenting quick, disconnected bits of information (Lillard & Peterson, 2011; Linebarger & Piotrowski, 2010; Singer & Singer, 2005). Narratively structured educational TV eases processing demands, facilitating sustained attention and freeing up space in working memory for applying program content to real-life situations.

Despite the spread of computers, television remains the dominant form of youth media, with children first becoming viewers in early infancy. About 40 percent of U.S. 3-month-olds regularly watch either TV or videos, a figure that rises to 90 percent by age 2 (Zimmerman, Christakis, & Meltzoff, 2007). The average U.S. 2- to 6-year-old watches TV programs and videos from 1½ to 2⅔ hours a day. In middle childhood, viewing time increases to an average of 3½ hours a day, then declines slightly in adolescence (Common Sense Media, 2013; Rideout, Foehr, & Roberts, 2010).

Low-SES children are more frequent TV viewers, perhaps because few alternative forms of entertainment are available in their neighborhoods or affordable for their parents. On the positive side, preschoolers in low-SES families watch as much educational television as their economically advantaged agemates (Common Sense Media, 2013). But parents with limited education are more likely to engage in practices that heighten TV viewing of all kinds, including leaving the TV on all day and eating family meals in front of it (Rideout, Foehr, & Roberts, 2010).

The average U.S. child, from infancy to middle childhood, experiences nearly 4 hours of background television a day (Lapierre, Piotrowski, & Klinebarger, 2012). Background TV impairs young children's sustained attention to play activities and reduces the quantity and quality of parent–child interaction (Courage & Howe, 2010; Kirkorian et al., 2009). Kindergartners and first graders in families where the TV is on nearly constantly are far less likely than their agemates to have acquired beginning reading skills (Vandewater et al., 2005).

About 35 percent of U.S. preschoolers and 45 percent of school-age children have a TV set in their bedroom. These children are exposed to even more background TV than their agemates and spend from 40 to 90 minutes more per day watching programs, usually with no parental restrictions on what they view (Common Sense Media, 2013; Rideout & Hamel, 2006).

Does extensive TV viewing take children away from worthwhile activities? The more preschool and school-age children watch prime-time shows and cartoons, the less time they spend reading and interacting with others and the poorer their academic skills (Ennemoser &

Schneider, 2007; Huston et al., 1999; Wright et al., 2001). Whereas educational programs can be beneficial, watching entertainment TV—especially heavy viewing—detracts from children's school success and social experiences.

LEARNING WITH COMPUTERS The majority of 2- to 4-year-olds have used a computer at one time or another, with more than one-third doing so regularly—from once a week to every day. But although almost all young children from higher-income families have access to a computer at home, only about half of those from low-income families do (Common Sense Media, 2013; Fletcher et al., 2014).

Because computers can have rich educational benefits, most early childhood classrooms include computer-learning centers. Computer literacy and math programs, including online storybooks, expand children's general knowledge and encourage diverse language, literacy, and arithmetic skills (Karemaker, Pitchford, & O'Malley, 2010; Li, Atkins, & Stanton, 2006). Turning over control of the mouse to preschoolers, allowing them to interact directly with the activity, enhances attention and interest (Calvert, Strong, & Gallagher, 2005). Kindergartners who use computers to draw or write produce more elaborate pictures and text, make fewer writing errors, and edit their work much as older children do.

Simplified computer languages that children can use to make designs or build structures introduce them to programming skills. As long as adults support children's efforts, these activities promote problem solving and metacognition (awareness of thought processes) because children must plan and reflect on their thinking to get their programs to work. Furthermore, while programming, children are especially likely to help one another and to persist in the face of challenge (Resnick & Silverman, 2005; Tran & Subrahmanyam, 2013). Small groups often gather around classroom computers, and children more often collaborate than in other pursuits.

In a classroom computer-learning center, preschoolers play a game in which they construct an imaginary landscape of mountains, lakes, rivers, and roads in an on-screen sandbox. The game is designed to support their developing understanding of symbol–real-world relations.

As with television, children spend much time using computers and other screen media for entertainment, especially game playing. Parental reports suggest that about half of U.S. preschoolers play electronic games at least occasionally. In addition to computers, many use mobile devices, including smart phones and tablets, where parents have downloaded game apps for them. Still, preschoolers typically spend little time playing electronic games—on average, just 12 minutes per day (Common Sense Media, 2013). Time devoted to doing so rises sharply in middle childhood and adolescence, when—as we will see in Chapter 12—a large sex difference favoring boys emerges.

Games designed for young children generally have specific educational goals, including literacy, math, science, colors, and other concepts. But on the whole, TV and game media are rife with gender stereotypes and violence. We will consider the impact of screen media on emotional and social development in the next chapter.

Ask Yourself

- **REVIEW** What findings indicate that child-centered rather than academic preschools and kindergartens are better suited to fostering academic development?

- **CONNECT** Compare outcomes resulting from preschool intervention programs with those from interventions beginning in infancy (see pages 229–230 in Chapter 6). Which are more likely to lead to lasting cognitive gains? Explain.

- **APPLY** Your senator has heard that IQ gains resulting from Head Start do not last, so he plans to vote against additional funding. Write a letter explaining why he should support Head Start.

- **REFLECT** How much and what kinds of TV viewing and computer use did you engage in as a child? How do you think your home media environment influenced your development?

Language Development

Language is intimately related to virtually all the cognitive changes discussed in this chapter. Between ages 2 and 6, children make momentous advances in language. Their remarkable achievements, as well as their mistakes along the way, reveal their active, rule-oriented approach to mastering their native tongue.

Vocabulary

At age 2, Sammy had a spoken vocabulary of 250 words. By age 6, he will have acquired around 10,000 words (Byrnes & Wasik, 2009). To accomplish this feat, Sammy will learn about five new words each day. How do children build their vocabularies so quickly? Research shows that they can connect new words with their underlying concepts after only a brief encounter, a process called **fast-mapping.** Even toddlers comprehend new labels remarkably quickly, but they need more repetitions of the word's use across several situations than preschoolers, who process speech-based information faster and are better able to categorize and recall it (Akhtar & Montague, 1999; Fernald, Perfors, & Marchman, 2006). Still, fast-mapping does not imply that children immediately acquired adultlike word meanings.

TYPES OF WORDS   One day, Leslie announced to the children that they would soon take a field trip. That night, Sammy excitedly told his mother, "We're going on a field trip!" When she asked where the class would go, Sammy responded matter-of-factly, "To a field!" Sammy's error suggests that young children fast-map some words more easily than others.

Children in many Western and non-Western language communities fast-map labels for objects especially rapidly because these refer to concepts that are easy to perceive (McDonough et al., 2011; Parish-Morris et al., 2010). When adults point to, label, and talk about an object, they help the child figure out the word's meaning (Gershoff-Stowe & Hahn, 2007). Soon children add verbs *(go, run, broke),* which require understandings of relationships between objects and actions. Because learning verbs is more cognitively challenging, preschoolers speaking quite different languages take longer to extend a new verb ("*push* the bike") to other instances of the same action ("*push* the box") than they do to extend a novel noun to other objects in the same category (Imai et al., 2008; Scott & Fisher, 2012). In mastering verb meanings, they benefit from multiple examples of the same verb used in a consistent manner in different contexts.

Nevertheless, young children learning Chinese, Japanese, and Korean—languages in which nouns are often omitted from adults' sentences, while verbs are stressed—acquire verbs much sooner (early in the second year) and more readily than their English-speaking agemates (Chan et al., 2011; Tardif, 2006). Besides increased exposure to verbs, Chinese-speaking children hear a greater variety of verbs denoting physical actions, which are visually obvious and therefore easiest to master (Ma et al., 2009). For example, Mandarin Chinese has several verbs for *carry,* each referring to a different way of carrying, such as on one's back, in one's arms, or with one's hands.

As young children acquire verbs, they also add modifiers *(red, round, sad).* First they make general distinctions *(big–small),* then more specific ones *(tall–short, high–low, wide–narrow)* (Stevenson & Pollitt, 1987).

STRATEGIES FOR WORD LEARNING   Children figure out the meanings of words by contrasting them with words they already know and assigning the new label to a gap in their vocabulary. On hearing a new word, 2-year-olds repeat the word or acknowledge it with "yeah" or "uh-huh" in their next verbalization 60 percent of the time (Clark, 2007). This suggests that they assign the word a preliminary meaning and often start to use it right away. Over time, they refine its meaning, striving to match its conventional use in their language community.

When learning a new noun, toddlers and preschoolers acquiring diverse languages tend to assume it refers to an object category at the basic level—an intermediate level of generality (see page 319). This preference helps young children narrow the range of possible meanings.

Once they acquire a basic-level name *(dog),* they add names at other hierarchical levels—both more general *(animal)* and more specific *(beagle, greyhound)* (Imai & Haryu, 2004; Waxman & Lidz, 2006).

How do children discover which concept each word picks out? This process is not yet fully understood. One speculation is that early in vocabulary growth, children adopt a **mutual exclusivity bias**—the assumption that words refer to entirely separate (nonoverlapping) categories (Markman, 1992). Two-year-olds seem to rely on mutual exclusivity when the objects named are perceptually distinct—for example, differ clearly in shape. After hearing the labels for two distinct novel objects (for example, *clip* and *horn*), they assign each word correctly, to the whole object, not just a part of it (Waxman & Senghas, 1992).

Indeed, children's first several hundred nouns refer mostly to objects well-organized by shape. In a study in which toddlers repeatedly played with and heard names for novel objects of different shapes ("That's a *wif* ") over a nine-week period, they soon formed the generalization that only similar-shaped objects have the same name (Smith et al., 2002; Yoshida & Smith, 2003). Tod-

To engage in effective verbal communication, preschoolers must master and combine principles of word meaning, grammar, and everyday conversation. How they accomplish this feat so rapidly is the focus of intensive research and debate.

dlers with this training added more than three times as many object names to their vocabularies outside the laboratory as did untrained controls. Because shape is a perceptual property relevant to most object categories for which they have already learned names, this *shape bias* helps preschoolers master additional names of objects, and vocabulary accelerates.

Once the name of a whole object is familiar, on hearing a new name for the object, 2- and 3-year-olds set aside the mutual exclusivity assumption. For example, if the object *(bottle)* has a part that stands out *(spout),* children readily apply the new label to it (Hansen & Markman, 2009). In these instances, mutual exclusivity helps limit the possibilities the child must consider. Still, mutual exclusivity and object shape cannot account for preschoolers' remarkably flexible responses when objects have more than one name.

By age 3, preschoolers' memory, categorization, and language skills have expanded, and they assign multiple labels to many objects (Deák, Yen, & Pettit, 2001). For example, they refer to a sticker of a gray goose as "sticker," "goose," and "gray." In these instances, children often call on other aspects of language. According to one proposal, preschoolers discover many word meanings by observing how words are used in syntax, or the structure of sentences—a strategy called **syntactic bootstrapping** (Gleitman et al., 2005; Naigles & Swenson, 2007). Consider an adult who says, "This is a *citron* one," while showing the child a yellow car. Two- and 3-year-olds conclude that a new word used as an adjective for a familiar object (car) refers to a property of that object (Imai & Haryu, 2004). As children hear the word in various sentence structures ("That lemon is bright *citron*"), they use syntactic information to refine the word's meaning and generalize it to other categories. Preschoolers' capacity to use syntactic cues to discern word meanings predicts vocabulary growth in diverse languages (McBride-Chang et al., 2008).

Young children also take advantage of the rich social information that adults frequently provide when they introduce new words. In one study, an adult performed an action on an object and then used a new label while looking back and forth between the child and the object, as if inviting the child to play. Two-year-olds concluded that the label referred to the action, not the object (Tomasello & Akhtar, 1995). And when an adult first designates the whole object ("The bird has something . . .") and then points to a part of it ("in its beak"), 3-year-olds realize that *beak* is a certain part, not the whole bird (Saylor, Sabbagh, & Baldwin, 2002).

Adults also inform children directly about word meanings. Parents commonly highlight the meaning of adjectives by using the new label with several objects (a "red car," a "red truck")—information that helps children infer that the word refers to an object property (Hall, Burns, & Pawluski, 2003). And adults often explain which of two or more words to use, by saying, for example, "You can call it a sea creature, but it's better to say *dolphin*" (Callanan & Sabbagh, 2004). In these situations, preschoolers often call on their expanding theory of mind to facilitate word learning. For example, by age 3 they can use a speaker's recently expressed

Young children rely on any useful information available to add to their vocabularies. As he makes a bird feeder, this preschooler attends to a variety of perceptual, social, and linguistic cues to grasp the meanings of unfamiliar words, such as *pine cone, spread, dip, bird seed,* and *munching sparrow.*

desire ("I really want to play with the *riff*") to figure out the label belonging to one of two novel objects (Saylor & Troseth, 2006).

Furthermore, to fill in for words they have not yet learned, children as young as age 3 coin new words using ones they already know—for example, "plant-man" for a gardener or "crayoner" for a child using crayons. Preschoolers also extend language meanings through metaphor—like the 3-year-old who described a stomachache as a "fire engine in my tummy" (Winner, 1988). Young preschoolers' metaphors involve concrete sensory comparisons: "Clouds are pillows," "Leaves are dancers." As their vocabulary and general knowledge expand, they appreciate nonsensory comparisons: "Friends are like magnets," "Time flies by" (Keil, 1986; Özçalişkan, 2005). Metaphors permit young children to communicate in amazingly vivid and memorable ways.

EXPLAINING VOCABULARY DEVELOPMENT Children acquire vocabulary so efficiently and accurately that some theorists believe that they are innately biased to induce word meanings using certain principles, such as mutual exclusivity and syntactic bootstrapping (Lidz, Gleitman, & Gleitman, 2004). But critics observe that a small set of built-in, fixed principles cannot account for the varied, flexible manner in which children master vocabulary (Parish-Morris, Golinkoff, & Hirsh-Pasek, 2013). And many word-learning strategies cannot be innate because children acquiring different languages use different approaches to mastering the same meanings.

An alternative view is that vocabulary growth is governed by the same cognitive strategies that children apply to nonlinguistic information. According to one account, children draw on a *coalition* of cues—perceptual, social, and linguistic—which shift in importance with age (Golinkoff & Hirsh-Pasek, 2006, 2008). Infants rely solely on perceptual features. Toddlers and young preschoolers, while still sensitive to perceptual features (such as object shape and physical action), increasingly attend to social cues—the speaker's direction of gaze, gestures, expressions of intention and desire, and soon the speaker's knowledge (Hollich, Hirsh-Pasek, & Golinkoff, 2000; Pruden et al., 2006). And as language develops further, linguistic cues—sentence structure and intonation (stress, pitch, and loudness)—play larger roles.

Preschoolers are most successful at figuring out new word meanings when several kinds of information are available (Parish-Morris, Golinkoff, & Hirsh-Pasek, 2013). Researchers have just begun to study the multiple cues that children use for different kinds of words and how their combined strategies change with development.

Grammar

Grammar refers to the way we combine words into meaningful phrases and sentences. Between ages 2 and 3, English-speaking children use simple sentences that follow a subject–verb–object word order. Children learning other languages adopt the word orders of the adult speech to which they are exposed.

BASIC RULES Toddlers' greater looking times at scenes that match sentences they hear reveal that they comprehend the meaning of basic grammatical structures that they cannot yet produce, such as "Big Bird is tickling Cookie Monster" or "What did the ball hit?" (Seidl, Hollich, & Jusczyk, 2003). First use of grammatical rules, however, is piecemeal—limited to just a few verbs. As children listen for familiar verbs in adults' speech, they expand their own utterances containing those verbs, relying on adult speech as their model (Gathercole, Sebastián, & Soto, 1999). Sammy, for example, added the preposition *with* to the verb *open* ("You open with scissors") but not to the word *hit* ("He hit me stick").

To test preschoolers' ability to generate novel sentences that conform to basic English grammar, researchers had them use a new verb in the subject–verb–object form after hearing it in a different construction, such as passive: "Ernie is getting *gorped* by the dog." When children were asked what the dog was doing, the percentage who could respond, "He's *gorping* Ernie," rose steadily with age. But not until age 3½ to 4 could the majority of children apply the fundamental subject–verb–object structure broadly, to newly acquired verbs (Chan et al., 2010; Tomasello, 2003, 2006).

As these examples suggest, once children form three-word sentences, they also make small additions and changes in words that enable speakers to express meanings flexibly and efficiently. For example, they add *-ing* for ongoing actions *(playing)*, *-s* for plural *(cats)*, use prepositions *(in* and *on)*, and form various tenses of the verb *to be (is, are, were, has been, will)*. All English-speaking children master these grammatical markers in a regular sequence, from the simplest meanings and structures *(-ing, in* and *on, -s)* to the most complex (tenses of the verb *to be)* (Brown, 1973). As with basic word order, comprehension of these small units proceeds ahead of production (Soderstrom, 2008; Wood, Kouider, & Carey, 2009). Even 1½- to 2-year-olds can discriminate an adult's correct from incorrect application of the plural *-s* months in advance of using it themselves.

Once children acquire these markers, they sometimes overextend the rules to words that are exceptions, a type of error called **overregularization.** "We each got two *foots*" and "My toy car *breaked*" are expressions that appear between ages 2 and 3 and persist into middle childhood (Maratsos, 2000; Marcus, 1995). Children less often make this error on frequently used irregular verbs, such as the past tense of *go (went)* and *say (said)*, which they hear often enough to learn by rote. For rarely used verbs such as *grow* and *sing*, children alternate for months—or even several years—between overregularized forms *(growed, singed)* and correct forms, until the irregular form eventually wins out. Overregularization provides evidence that children apply grammatical rules creatively.

COMPLEX STRUCTURES Gradually, preschoolers master more complex grammatical structures, although they make errors along the way. In first creating questions, 2- and 3-year-olds use many formulas: "Where's *X*?" "Can I *X*?" (Dabrowska, 2000; Tomasello, 2003). Question asking remains variable for the next couple of years. An analysis of one child's questions revealed that he inverted the subject and verb when asking certain questions but not others ("What she will do?" "Why he can go?"). The correct expressions were the ones he heard most often in his mother's speech (Rowland & Pine, 2000). And sometimes children produce errors in subject–verb agreement ("Where does the dogs play?") and subject case ("Where can me sit?") (Rowland, 2007).

Similarly, children have trouble with some passive sentences. When told, "The car is pushed by the truck," young preschoolers often make a toy car push a truck. By age 4½, they understand such expressions, whether they contain familiar or novel verbs (Dittmar et al., 2014). Nevertheless, full mastery of the passive form is not complete until the end of middle childhood.

Though grammatical development takes place gradually, preschoolers' grasp of language structures is remarkable. By age 4 to 5, they form embedded sentences ("I think *he will come*"), tag questions ("Dad's going to be home soon, *isn't he?*"), and indirect objects ("He showed *his friend* the present") (Zukowski, 2013). As the preschool years draw to a close, children use most of the grammatical constructions of their language competently.

EXPLAINING GRAMMATICAL DEVELOPMENT Evidence that grammatical development is an extended process has raised questions about Chomsky's *language acquisition device (LAD)*, which assumes that children have innate knowledge of grammatical rules (see Chapter 6, page 231). Some experts believe that grammar is a product of general cognitive development—children's tendency to search the environment for consistencies and patterns of all sorts (Bloom, 1999; Chang, Dell, & Bock, 2006; Tomasello, 2003). Yet among these theorists, debate continues over just how children master grammar.

According to one view, young children rely on *semantics*, or word meanings, to figure out grammatical rules—an approach called **semantic bootstrapping.** For example, children might begin by grouping together words with "agent qualities" (things that cause actions) as *subjects* and words with "action qualities" as *verbs*. Then they merge these categories with observations of how words are used in sentences (Bates & MacWhinney, 1987; Braine, 1994).

Others believe that children master grammar through direct observation of the structure of language: They notice which words appear in the same positions in sentences and are combined in the same way with other words. Over time, they group words into grammatical categories and use them appropriately in sentences (Bannard, Lieven, & Tomasello, 2009; Chang, Dell, & Bock, 2006; Tomasello, 2011).

Still other theorists agree with the essence of Chomsky's theory. One idea accepts semantic bootstrapping but proposes that the grammatical categories into which children group word meanings are innate—present at the outset (Pinker, 1999; Tien, 2013). Critics, however, point out that toddlers' two-word utterances do not reflect a flexible grasp of grammar (return to Chapter 6, page 238, to review). In sum, controversy persists over whether a universal, built-in language-processing device exists or whether children draw on general cognitive-processing procedures, devising unique strategies adapted to the specific language that they hear (Howell & Becker, 2013; Lidz, 2007).

Conversation

Besides acquiring vocabulary and grammar, children must learn to engage in effective and appropriate communication—by taking turns, staying on the same topic, stating their messages clearly, and conforming to cultural rules for social interaction. This practical, social side of language is called **pragmatics,** and preschoolers make considerable headway in mastering it.

As early as age 2, children are skilled conversationalists. In face-to-face interaction, they take turns and respond appropriately to their partner's remarks (Pan & Snow, 1999). With age, the number of turns over which children can sustain interaction, ability to maintain a topic over time, and responsiveness to queries requesting clarifications increase (Comeau, Genesee, & Mendelson, 2010; Snow et al., 1996). By age 3, children can infer a speaker's intention when the speaker expresses it indirectly. For example, most know that an adult who, in response to an offer of cereal, says, "We have no milk," is declining the cereal (Schulze, Grassmann, & Tomasello, 2013). These surprisingly advanced abilities probably grow out of early interactive experiences (see Chapter 6).

Indeed, the presence of a sibling seems to be especially conducive to acquiring the pragmatics of language. Preschoolers closely monitor conversations between their twin or older siblings and parents, and they often try to join in. When they do, these verbal exchanges last longer, with each participant taking more turns (Barton & Strosberg, 1997; Barton & Tomasello, 1991). As they listen to these conversations, young language learners pick up important skills, such as use of personal pronouns (*I* versus *you*), which are more common in the early vocabularies of later-born than of firstborn siblings (Pine, 1995). Furthermore, older siblings' remarks to a younger brother or sister often focus on regulating interaction:

These preschoolers likely use more assertive language when speaking for a male puppet than they would if speaking for a female puppet. In doing so, they reveal their early grasp of stereotypic features of social roles in their culture.

"Do you like Kermit?" "OK, your turn" (Oshima-Takane & Robbins, 2003). This emphasis probably contributes to younger siblings' conversational skills.

By age 4, children adapt their language to social expectations. For example, in acting out roles with hand puppets, they show that they understand the stereotypic features of different social positions. They use more commands when playing socially dominant and male roles (teacher, doctor, father) but speak more politely and use more indirect requests when playing less dominant and female roles (student, patient, mother) (Andersen, 2000).

Preschoolers' conversational skills occasionally do break down—for example, when talking on the phone. Here is an excerpt from one 4-year-old's phone conversation with his grandfather:

Grandfather: "How old will you be?"
John: "Dis many." *[Holding up four fingers.]*
Grandfather: "Huh?"
John: "Dis many." *[Again holding up four fingers.]* (Warren & Tate, 1992, pp. 259–260)

Young children's conversations appear less mature in highly demanding situations in which they cannot see their listeners' reactions or rely on typical conversational aids, such as gestures and objects to talk about. But when asked to tell a listener how to solve a simple puzzle, 3- to 6-year-olds give more specific directions over the phone than in person, indicating that they realize that more verbal description is necessary on the phone (Cameron & Lee, 1997). Between ages 4 and 8, both conversing and giving directions over the phone improve greatly.

Supporting Language Learning in Early Childhood

How can adults foster preschoolers' language development? As in toddlerhood, interaction with more skilled speakers remains vital in early childhood. Conversational give-and-take with adults, either at home or in preschool, is consistently related to

Adults can support preschoolers' grammatical learning through indirect feedback, including recasts and expansions, which model grammatical alternatives to incorrect constructions.

language progress (Hart & Risley, 1995; Hoff, 2006; Huttenlocher et al, 2010). Furthermore, recall that language learning and literacy development are closely linked. Return to Applying What We Know on page 338, and notice how each strategy for supporting emergent literacy also fosters language progress.

Sensitive, caring adults use additional techniques that promote language skills. When children use words incorrectly or communicate unclearly, they give helpful, explicit feedback: "I can't tell which ball you want. Do you mean a large or small one or a red or green one?" But they do not overcorrect, especially when children make grammatical mistakes. Criticism discourages children from freely using language in ways that lead to new skills.

Instead, adults often provide indirect feedback about grammar by using two strategies, often in combination: **recasts**—restructuring inaccurate speech into correct form, and **expansions**—elaborating on children's speech, increasing its complexity (Bohannon & Stanowicz, 1988; Chouinard & Clark, 2003). For example, if a child says, "I gotted new red shoes," the parent might respond, "Yes, you got a pair of new red shoes." In one study, after such corrective input, 2- to 4-year-olds often shifted to correct forms—improvements still evident several months later (Saxton, Backley, & Gallaway, 2005). However, the impact of such feedback has been challenged. The techniques are not used in all cultures and, in a few investigations, had no impact on children's grammar (Strapp & Federico, 2000; Valian, 1999). Rather than eliminating errors, perhaps expansions and recasts model grammatical alternatives and encourage children to experiment with them.

In language, as in other aspects of cognitive development, parents and teachers gently prompt young children to take the next developmental step forward. Children strive to master language because they want to connect with other people. Adults, in turn, respond to children's desire to become competent speakers by listening attentively, elaborating on what children say, modeling correct usage, and stimulating children to talk further. In the next chapter, we will see that this combination of warmth and encouragement of mature behavior is at the heart of early childhood emotional and social development as well.

LOOK and LISTEN

Observe a parent conversing with a 2- or 3-year-old child during play or picture-book reading. List examples of how the parent promotes the child's vocabulary, grammar, and pragmatic skills. Do the findings just described remind you once again of Vygotsky's theory?

Ask Yourself

● **REVIEW** Provide a list of recommendations for promoting language development in early childhood, noting research that supports each.

● **CONNECT** Explain how children's strategies for word learning support the interactionist perspective on language development, described on page 234 in Chapter 6.

● **APPLY** Sammy's mother explained to him that the family would take a vacation in Miami. The next morning, Sammy announced, "I gotted my bags packed. When are we going to Your-ami?" What explains Sammy's errors?

Summary

Piaget's Theory: The Preoperational Stage (p. 311)

9.1 Describe advances in mental representation, and limitations of thinking, during the preoperational stage.

- Rapid advances in mental representation, notably language and make-believe play, mark the beginning of Piaget's **preoperational stage.** With age, make-believe becomes increasingly complex, evident in **sociodramatic play** with peers. Make-believe supports many aspects of cognitive and social development. **Dual representation** improves rapidly over the third year of life as children realize that models, drawings, and simple maps correspond to circumstances in the real world.

- Aside from representation, Piaget described preschoolers in terms of deficits rather than strengths. Because **egocentrism** prevents them from reflecting on their own thinking and accommodating, it contributes to **animistic thinking, centration,** and **irreversibility.** These difficulties cause preschoolers to fail **conservation** and **hierarchical classification** tasks.

9.2 What does follow-up research imply about the accuracy of Piaget's preoperational stage?

- When young children are given familiar and simplified problems, their performance appears more mature than Piaget assumed. Preschoolers recognize differing perspectives, distinguish animate from inanimate objects, have flexible and appropriate notions of magic, and notice and reason about transformations and cause-and-effect relations. They also show impressive skill at flexibly categorizing on the basis of both perceptually apparent and nonobservable characteristics, depending on the situation.

- Rather than being absent in the preschool years, operational thinking develops gradually. These findings challenge Piaget's concept of stage.

9.3 What educational principles can be derived from Piaget's theory?

- A Piagetian classroom promotes discovery learning, sensitivity to children's readiness to learn, and acceptance of individual differences.

Vygotsky's Sociocultural Theory (p. 322)

9.4 Describe Vygotsky's perspective on the social origins and significance of children's private speech.

- In contrast to Piaget, Vygotsky regarded language as the foundation for all higher cognitive processes. According to Vygotsky, **private speech,** or language used for self-guidance, emerges out of social communication as adults and more skilled peers help children master challenging tasks within the zone of proximal development. Eventually, private speech is internalized as inner, verbal thought.

- **Intersubjectivity** and **scaffolding** are two features of social interaction that promote transfer of cognitive processes to children. **Guided participation** recognizes situational and cultural variations in adult support of children's efforts.

9.5 Describe applications of Vygotsky's theory to education, and evaluate his major ideas.

- A Vygotskian classroom emphasizes assisted discovery, in which both teacher guidance and peer collaboration are vitally important. Make-believe play is a unique, broadly influential zone of proximal development in early childhood.

- Vygotsky's theory helps us understand the wide cultural variation in cognitive skills. In some cultures, verbal communication is not the only means—or even the most important means—through which children learn. Vygotsky said little about how basic cognitive and motor capacities, which develop in infancy, contribute to socially transmitted higher cognitive processes.

Information Processing (p. 327)

9.6 How do attention, memory, and problem solving change during early childhood?

- Preschoolers' executive function shows impressive gains. Sustained attention increases sharply, due to gains in inhibition and in working memory, which allows more complex play and problem-solving goals. Adult scaffolding supports gains in attention, and **planning** also improves.

- Young children's recognition memory is remarkably accurate. But their recall of listlike information is poor because they use **memory strategies** less effectively than older children.

- **Episodic memory,** or memory for everyday experiences, improves greatly in early childhood. Like adults, preschoolers remember recurring events as **scripts,** which become more elaborate with age.

- As cognitive and conversational skills improve, children's autobiographical memories become more organized, detailed, and related to the larger context of their lives, especially when adults use an elaborative style to talk about the past.

- According to **overlapping-waves theory,** children try out various strategies to solve challenging problems, gradually selecting those that result in rapid, accurate solutions. Practice with strategies, reasoning, tasks with new challenges, and adult assistance contribute to improved problem solving.

9.7 Describe the young child's theory of mind.

- Preschoolers begin to construct a theory of mind, indicating that they are capable of **metacognition,** or thinking about thought. From age 4 on, they realize that both beliefs and desires can influence behavior, in that they pass verbal false-belief tasks. False-belief understanding enhances children's capacity to reflect on the thoughts and emotions of oneself and others.

- Language, executive function, make-believe play, and mental-state talk with adults, older siblings, and friends contribute to young children's awareness of false belief and other mental-state understandings.

- Preschoolers regard the mind as a passive container of information. As a result, they have difficulty inferring what people know or are thinking about.

9.8 Summarize children's literacy and mathematical knowledge during early childhood.

- Young children's **emergent literacy** reveals that they understand a great deal about written language before they read and write in conventional ways. Preschoolers gradually revise incorrect ideas about the meaning of written symbols as their perceptual and cognitive capacities improve, as they encounter writing in many contexts, and as adults help them make sense of written information.

- Literacy development builds on a foundation of spoken language and knowledge about the world. **Phonological awareness** strongly predicts emergent literacy and later reading and spelling achievement. Preschoolers' vocabulary, grammatical knowledge, and narrative competence are also influential. Informal literacy experiences, including adult–child interactive storybook reading, foster literacy development.

- Mathematical reasoning also builds on informal knowledge. Toddlers' beginning grasp of **ordinality** serves as the basis for more complex understandings. By age 3½ to 4, they grasp the principle of **cardinality,** which increases the efficiency of counting. Soon children experiment with diverse strategies to solve simple arithmetic problems. When adults provide many occasions for counting and comparing quantities, children construct basic numerical concepts sooner.

Individual Differences in Mental Development (p. 339)

9.9 Describe the content of early childhood intelligence tests and the impact of home, preschool and kindergarten programs, child care, and educational media on mental development.

- Intelligence tests in early childhood sample a range of verbal and nonverbal skills, including vocabulary, memory, quantitative knowledge, problem solving, and spatial reasoning. By age 6 to 7, scores are good predictors of later IQ and academic achievement.

- A warm, stimulating home and parental reasonable demands for mature behavior promotes children's intellectual development. Home environment plays a major role in the poorer intellectual performance of low-SES children in comparison to their higher-SES peers.

- Preschools and kindergartens range along a continuum from **child-centered programs,** in which much learning occurs through play, to **academic programs,** in which teachers structure children's learning, often using repetition and drill. Emphasizing formal academic training undermines children's motivation and negatively influences later achievement.

© ELLEN B. SENISI

- **Project Head Start** is the most extensive federally funded preschool program for low-income children in the United States. High-quality preschool intervention results in immediate IQ and achievement gains and long-term improvements in school adjustment, educational attainment, and life success. Parental involvement in Head Start, and the implementation of Head Start REDI, yield higher year-end academic, language, and social skills.

- Poor-quality child care undermines preschoolers' cognitive and social skills. In contrast, good child care enhances cognitive, language, and social development, especially for low-SES children.

- Children pick up academic knowledge from educational television and computer software. TV programs with slow-paced action and easy-to-follow narratives help preschoolers comprehend program content. Introducing children to computer programming skills promotes problem solving and metacognition. But heavy exposure to prime-time TV, cartoons, and inappropriate electronic games reduces time spent reading and interacting with others and is associated with poorer academic skills.

Language Development (p. 348)

9.10 Trace the development of vocabulary, grammar, and conversational skills in early childhood.

- Supported by **fast-mapping,** preschoolers' vocabularies increase dramatically. According to one view, children are innately biased to induce word meanings using a **mutual exclusivity bias** and **syntactic bootstrapping.** Another proposal is that children use the same cognitive strategies they apply to nonlinguistic information. An alternative perspective is that preschoolers figure out word meanings from a coalition of cues—perceptual, social, and linguistic—which shift in importance with age.

- Between ages 2 and 3, children adopt the word order of their language. As they master grammatical constructions, they sometimes **overregularize,** applying the rules to words that are exceptions. By the end of the preschool years, children have acquired a wide variety of complex grammatical forms.

- Some experts believe that grammar is a product of general cognitive development. According to one view, children engage in **semantic bootstrapping,** relying on word meanings to figure out grammatical rules. Others agree with the essence of Chomsky's theory that children's brains are innately tuned for acquiring grammar.

- **Pragmatics** refers to the practical, social side of language. In face-to-face interaction with peers, young preschoolers are already skilled conversationalists. By age 4, they adapt their language to social expectations.

9.11 Cite factors that support language learning in early childhood.

- Conversational give-and-take with more skilled speakers fosters preschoolers' language skills. Adults provide both explicit feedback on the clarity of children's utterances and indirect feedback about grammar through **recasts** and **expansions.** However, the impact of these strategies, which are not used in all cultures, has been challenged.

Important Terms and Concepts

Emotional and Social Development in Early Childhood

REPRINTED WITH PERMISSION FROM THE INTERNATIONAL MUSEUM OF CHILDREN'S ART, OSLO, NORWAY

"My Wonderful Birthday"
Anonymous
7 years, India

First friendships serve as important contexts for acquiring emotional and social skills, including understanding of emotion, capacity to solve social problems, and morality. Chapter 10 considers these and other facets of emotional and social development in early childhood.

As the children in Leslie's classroom moved through the preschool years, their personalities took on clearer definition. By age 3, they voiced firm likes and dislikes as well as new ideas about themselves. "Stop bothering me," Sammy said to Mark, who had reached for Sammy's beanbag as Sammy aimed it toward the mouth of a large clown face. "See, I'm great at this game," Sammy announced with confidence, an attitude that kept him trying, even though he missed most of the throws.

The children's conversations also revealed their first notions about morality. Often they combined statements about right and wrong with forceful attempts to defend their own desires. "You're 'posed to share," stated Mark, grabbing the beanbag out of Sammy's hand.

"I was here first! Gimme it back," demanded Sammy, pushing Mark. The two boys struggled for the beanbag until Leslie intervened, provided an extra set of beanbags, and showed them how they could both play.

As the interaction between Sammy and Mark reveals, preschoolers quickly become complex social beings. Young children argue, grab, and push, but cooperative exchanges are far more frequent. Between ages 2 and 6, first friendships form, in which children converse, act out complementary roles, and learn that their own desires for companionship and toys are best met when they consider others' needs and interests.

The children's developing understanding of their social world was especially apparent in their growing attention to the dividing line between male and female. While Lynette and Karen cared for a sick baby doll in the housekeeping area, Sammy, Vance, and Mark transformed the block corner into a busy intersection. "Green light, go!" shouted police officer Sammy as Vance and Mark pushed large wooden cars and trucks across the floor. Already, the children preferred peers of their own gender, and their play themes mirrored their culture's gender stereotypes.

This chapter is devoted to the many facets of early childhood emotional and social development. We begin with Erik Erikson's theory, which provides an overview of personality change in the preschool years. Then we consider children's concepts of themselves, their insights into their social and moral worlds, their gender typing, and their increasing ability to manage their emotional and social behaviors. Finally, we ask, What is effective child rearing? And we consider the complex conditions that support good parenting or lead it to break down, including the serious and widespread problems of child abuse and neglect. ■

Erikson's Theory: Initiative versus Guilt

Erikson (1950) described early childhood as a period of "vigorous unfolding." Once children have a sense of autonomy, they become less contrary than they were as toddlers. Their energies are freed for tackling the psychological conflict of the preschool years: **initiative versus guilt.** As the word *initiative* suggests, young children have a

10.1 What personality changes take place during Erikson's stage of initiative versus guilt?

new sense of purposefulness. They are eager to tackle new tasks, join in activities with peers, and discover what they can do with the help of adults. They also make strides in conscience development.

Erikson regarded play as a means through which young children learn about themselves and their social world. Play permits preschoolers to try new skills with little risk of criticism and failure. It also creates a small social organization of children who must cooperate to achieve common goals. Around the world, children act out family scenes and highly visible occupations—police officer, doctor, and nurse in Western societies, rabbit hunter and potter among the Hopi Indians, hut builder and spear maker among the Baka of West Africa (Gaskins, 2013).

Recall that Erikson's theory builds on Freud's psychosexual stages (see Chapter 1, page 15). In Freud's Oedipus and Electra conflicts, to avoid punishment and maintain the affection of parents, children form a *superego*, or conscience, by *identifying* with the same-sex parent. As a result, they adopt the moral and gender-role standards of their society. For Erikson, the negative outcome of early childhood is an overly strict superego that causes children to feel too much guilt because they have been threatened, criticized, and punished excessively by adults. When this happens, preschoolers' exuberant play and bold efforts to master new tasks break down.

Although Freud's ideas are no longer accepted as satisfactory explanations of conscience development, Erikson's image of initiative captures the diverse changes in young children's emotional and social lives. Early childhood is, indeed, a time when children develop a confident self-image, more effective control over their emotions, new social skills, the foundations of morality, and a clear sense of themselves as boy or girl. Now let's look closely at each of these aspects of development.

A Guatemalan 3-year-old pretends to shell corn. By acting out family scenes and adult occupations, young children around the world develop a sense of initiative, gaining insight into what they can do and become in their culture.

10.2 Describe the development of self-concept and self-esteem in early childhood.

Self-Understanding

As we saw in Chapter 7, infants and toddlers make strides in acquiring *body self-awareness*. *Psychological self-awareness* emerges in early childhood, as language development enables children to talk about their own subjective experience of being. In Chapter 9, we noted that preschoolers acquire a vocabulary for talking about their inner mental lives and refine their understanding of mental states. As self-awareness strengthens, children focus more intently on qualities that make the self unique. They begin to develop a **self-concept,** the set of attributes, abilities, attitudes, and values that an individual believes defines who he or she is. This mental representation of the self has profound implications for children's emotional and social lives, influencing their preferences for activities and social partners and their vulnerability to stress.

Foundations of Self-Concept

Ask a 3- to 5-year-old to tell you about him- or herself, and you are likely to hear something like this: "I'm Tommy. I'm 4 years old. I can wash my hair all by myself. I have a new Tinkertoy set, and I made this big, big tower." Preschoolers' self-concepts largely consist of observable characteristics, such as their name, physical appearance, possessions, and everyday behaviors (Harter, 2012a; Watson, 1990).

By age 3½, children also describe themselves in terms of typical emotions and attitudes ("I'm happy when I play with my friends"; "I don't like scary TV programs"; "I usually do what Mommy says"), suggesting a beginning understanding of their unique psychological characteristics (Eder & Mangelsdorf, 1997). And by age 5, children's degree of agreement with a battery of such statements coincides with maternal reports of their personality traits, indicating that older preschoolers have a sense of their own timidity, agreeableness, and positive or negative affect (Brown et al., 2008). As further support for this emerging grasp of personality, when given a trait label ("shy," "mean"), 4-year-olds infer appropriate motives and feelings. For example, they know that a shy person doesn't like to be with unfamiliar people (Heyman & Gelman, 1999). But most preschoolers do not yet say "I'm helpful" or "I'm shy." Direct references to personality traits must wait for greater cognitive maturity.

A warm, sensitive parent–child relationship seems to foster a more positive, coherent early self-concept. In one study, 4-year-olds with a secure attachment to their mothers were more likely than their insecurely attached agemates to describe themselves in favorable terms at age 5—with statements reflecting agreeableness and positive affect (Goodvin et al., 2008). Also, recall from Chapter 9 that securely attached preschoolers participate in more elaborative parent–child conversations about personally experienced events, which help them understand themselves (see page 330). When, in past-event conversations, a child discovers that she finds swimming, getting together with friends, and going to the zoo fun, she can begin to connect these specific experiences into a general understanding of "what I enjoy." The result is a clearer image of herself (Fivush, 2011).

Elaborative reminiscing that focuses on young children's *internal states*— their thoughts, feelings, and subjective experiences—plays an especially important role in early self-concept development. Although preschoolers rarely describe themselves with reference to personality traits, they are more likely to mention traits ("I'm smart," "I'm really strong!") and typical emotions ("My brother makes me feel cranky") if their parents talk to them about causes and consequences of internal states ("Tell mommy why you were crying") (Wang, Doan, & Song, 2010). Also, 4- and 5-year-olds describe their emotional tendencies more favorably—"I'm not scared, not me!"—if their parents reminisce with them about times when they successfully resolved upsetting feelings (Goodvin & Romdall, 2013). By emphasizing the personal meaning of past events, conversations about internal states facilitate development of self-knowledge.

As early as age 2, parents use narratives of past events to impart rules, standards for behavior, and evaluative information about the child: "You added the milk when we made the mashed potatoes. That's a very important job!" (Nelson, 2003). As the Cultural Influences box on page 360 reveals, these self-evaluative narratives are a major means through which caregivers imbue the young child's self-concept with cultural values.

As they talk about personally significant events and as their cognitive skills advance, preschoolers gradually come to view themselves as persisting over time. Around age 4, children first become certain that a video image of themselves replayed shortly after it was filmed is still "me" (Povinelli, 2001). Similarly, when researchers asked 3- to 5-year-olds to imagine a future event (walking next to a waterfall) and to envision a future personal state by choosing from three items (a raincoat, money, a blanket) the one they need to bring with them, performance— along with future-state justifications ("I'm gonna get wet")—increased sharply from age 3 to 4 (Atance & Meltzoff, 2005).

When asked to tell about themselves, preschoolers typically mention observable characteristics—physical appearance, possessions, and everyday behaviors and skills, such as "I can tie my own shoes." They also have an emerging grasp of their unique psychological characteristics—for this 5-year-old, persistence and determination!

Emergence of Self-Esteem

Another aspect of self-concept emerges in early childhood: **self-esteem,** the judgments we make about our own worth and the feelings associated with those judgments. **TAKE A MOMENT...** Make a list of your own self-judgments. Notice that, besides a global appraisal of your worth as a person, you have a variety of separate self-evaluations concerning different activities. These evaluations are among the most important aspects of self-development because they affect our emotional experiences, future behavior, and long-term psychological adjustment.

Cultural Influences

Cultural Variations in Personal Storytelling: Implications for Early Self-Concept

Preschoolers of many cultural backgrounds participate in personal storytelling with their parents. Striking cultural differences exist in parents' selection and interpretation of events in these narratives, affecting the way children view themselves.

In one study, researchers spent hundreds of hours over a two-year period studying the storytelling practices of six middle-SES Irish-American families in Chicago and six middle-SES Chinese families in Taiwan. From extensive videotapes of adults' conversations with the children from age 2½ to 4, the investigators identified personal stories and coded them for content, quality of their endings, and evaluation of the child (Miller, Fung, & Mintz, 1996; Miller et al., 1997, 2012).

Parents in both cultures discussed pleasurable holidays and family excursions in similar ways and with similar frequency. But five times more often than the Irish-American parents, the Chinese parents told long stories about their preschoolers' previous misdeeds—using impolite language, writing on the wall, or playing in an overly rowdy way. These narratives, often sparked by a current misdeed, were conveyed with warmth and caring, stressed the impact of misbehavior on others ("You made Mama lose face"), and often ended with direct teaching of proper behavior

("Saying dirty words is not good"). By contrast, in the few instances in which Irish-American stories referred to transgressions, parents downplayed their seriousness, attributing them to the child's spunk and assertiveness.

Early narratives about the child launch preschoolers' self-concepts on culturally distinct paths (Miller, Fung, & Koven, 2007). Influenced by Confucian traditions of strict discipline and social obligations, Chinese parents integrated these values into their stories, affirming the importance of not disgracing the family and explicitly conveying expectations in the story's conclusion. Although Irish-American parents disciplined their children, they rarely dwelt on misdeeds in storytelling. Rather, they cast the child's shortcomings in a positive light, perhaps to promote self-esteem.

Whereas most Americans believe that favorable self-esteem is crucial for healthy development, Chinese adults generally see it as unimportant or even negative—as impeding the child's willingness to listen and be corrected (Miller et al., 2002). Consistent with this view, the Chinese parents did little to cultivate their child's individuality. Instead, they used storytelling to guide the child toward socially responsible behavior. Hence, by the end of the preschool years, the Chinese

A Chinese mother speaks gently to her child about proper behavior. Chinese parents often use storytelling to point out how their child's misdeeds affect others. The Chinese child's self-concept, in turn, emphasizes social obligations.

child's self-image emphasizes a sense of belonging and obligations to others ("I belong to the Lee family"; "I like to help my mom wash dishes"), whereas the American child's is more autonomous, consisting largely of personal descriptions ("I do lots of puzzles"; "I like hockey") (Wang, 2004; Wang, Doan, & Song, 2010).

After creating a "camera" and "flash," this preschooler pretends to take pictures. Her high self-esteem contributes greatly to her initiative in mastering many new skills.

By age 4, preschoolers have several self-judgments—for example, about learning things well in school, making friends, getting along with parents, and treating others kindly (Marsh, Ellis, & Craven, 2002). But young children lack the cognitive maturity necessary to develop a global sense of self-esteem. They are not yet able to assimilate the judgments of other people, and they cannot combine information about their competencies in different domains. Thus, their self-appraisals are fragmented. Also, because they have difficulty distinguishing between their desired and their actual competence, they usually rate their own ability as extremely high and often underestimate task difficulty, as Sammy did when he asserted, despite his many misses, that he was great at beanbag throwing (Harter, 2012a).

High self-esteem contributes greatly to preschoolers' initiative during a period in which they must master many new skills. By age 3, children whose parents patiently encourage while offering information about how to succeed are enthusiastic and highly motivated. In contrast, children with a history of parental criticism of their worth and performance give up easily when faced with challenges and express shame and despondency after failing (Kelley, Brownell, & Campbell, 2000). When preschool nonpersisters use dolls to act out an adult's reaction to failure, they anticipate disapproval—saying, for example, "He's punished because he can't do the puzzle" (Burhans & Dweck, 1995). They are also likely to report that their parents berate them for making small mistakes (Heyman, Dweck, & Cain, 1992). Adults can avoid promoting these self-defeating reactions by adjusting their expectations to children's capacities, scaffolding children's attempts at difficult tasks (see Chapter 9, page 324), and pointing out effort and improvement in children's work or behavior.

Ask Yourself

- **REVIEW** Why is self-esteem typically extremely high in early childhood?

- **APPLY** Joshua wants to know how he can help his 3-year-old daughter build a positive self-concept. Provide several recommendations.

- **REFLECT** When you were a child, did your parents actively promote your self-esteem? How did their efforts reflect your family's cultural background? Explain.

Emotional Development

10.3 Identify changes in understanding and expressing emotion during early childhood, citing factors that influence those changes.

Gains in representation, language, and self-concept support emotional development in early childhood. Between ages 2 and 6, children make strides in the emotional abilities that, collectively, researchers refer to as *emotional competence* (Denham et al., 2011; Saarni et al., 2006). First, preschoolers gain in emotional understanding, becoming better able to talk about feelings and to respond appropriately to others' emotional signals. Second, they become better at emotional self-regulation—in particular, at coping with intense negative emotion. Finally, preschoolers more often experience *self-conscious emotions* and *empathy*, which contribute to their developing sense of morality.

Parenting strongly influences preschoolers' emotional competence. Emotional competence, in turn, is vital for successful peer relationships and overall mental health.

Understanding Emotion

Preschoolers' vocabulary for talking about emotion expands rapidly, and they use it skillfully to reflect on their own and others' behavior. Here are some excerpts from conversations in which 2-year-olds and 6-year-olds commented on emotionally charged experiences:

> *Two-year-old: [After father shouted at child, she became angry, shouting back.]* "I'm mad at you, Daddy. I'm going away. Good-bye."
>
> *Two-year-old: [Commenting on another child who refused to nap and cried.]* "Mom, Annie cry. Annie sad."
>
> *Six-year-old: [In response to mother's comment, "It's hard to hear the baby crying."]* "Well, it's not as hard for me as it is for you." *[When mother asked why]* "Well, you like Johnny better than I do! I like him a little, and you like him a lot, so I think it's harder for you to hear him cry."
>
> *Six-year-old: [Trying to comfort a small boy in church whose mother had gone up to communion.]* "Aw, that's all right. She'll be right back. Don't be afraid. I'm here." (Bretherton et al., 1986, pp. 536, 540, 541)

COGNITIVE DEVELOPMENT AND EMOTIONAL UNDERSTANDING As these examples show, young preschoolers refer to causes, consequences, and behavioral signs of emotion, and over time their understanding becomes more accurate and complex (Thompson, Winer, & Goodvin, 2011). By age 4 to 5, they correctly judge the causes of many basic emotions ("He's happy because he's swinging very high"; "He's sad because he misses his mother"). Preschoolers' explanations tend to emphasize external factors over internal states, a balance that changes with age (Rieffe, Terwogt, & Cowan, 2005). In Chapter 9, we saw that after age 4, children appreciate that both desires and beliefs motivate behavior. Once these understandings are secure, children's grasp of how internal factors can trigger emotion expands.

Preschoolers are good at inferring how others are feeling based on their behavior. For example, they can tell that a child who jumps up and down and claps his hands is probably happy, and one who is tearful and withdrawn is sad (Widen & Russell, 2011). And they are beginning to realize that thinking and feeling are interconnected—that a person reminded of a

This child's carefree gestures and humorous words suggest to her playmates that she feels joyful, and they respond in kind with laughter.

previous sad experience is likely to feel sad and that unpleasant feelings can be eased by changing one's thoughts (Davis et al., 2010; Lagattuta, Wellman, & Flavell, 1997; Sayfan & Lagattuta, 2009). Furthermore, they come up with effective ways to relieve others' negative emotions, such as hugging to reduce sadness (Fabes et al., 1988). Overall, preschoolers have an impressive ability to interpret, predict, and change others' feelings.

At the same time, preschoolers have difficulty interpreting situations that offer conflicting cues about how a person is feeling. When shown a picture of a happy-faced child with a broken bicycle, 4- and 5-year-olds tended to rely only on the emotional expression: "He's happy because he likes to ride his bike." Older children more often reconciled the two cues: "He's happy because his father promised to help fix his broken bike" (Gnepp, 1983; Hoffner & Badzinski, 1989). As in their approach to Piagetian tasks, young children focus on the most obvious aspect of a complex emotional situation to the neglect of other relevant information.

SOCIAL EXPERIENCE AND EMOTIONAL UNDERSTANDING The more parents label emotions, explain them, and express warmth and enthusiasm when conversing with pre-schoolers, the more "emotion words" children use and the better developed their emotional understanding (Fivush & Haden, 2005; Laible & Song, 2006). Discussions focusing on negative experiences or involving disagreements are particularly helpful.

In one study, mothers engaged in more detailed dialogues about causes of emotion and more often validated their preschoolers' feelings when discussing negative (as opposed to positive) topics. And the more elaborative the discussions, the higher the children scored in emotional understanding (Laible, 2011). In another study, when mothers explained feelings, negotiated, and compromised during conflicts with their 2½-year-olds, their children, at age 3, were advanced in emotional understanding and used similar strategies to resolve disagreements (Laible & Thompson, 2002). Such dialogues seem to help children reflect on the causes and consequences of emotion while also modeling mature communication skills. Furthermore, preschoolers who are securely attached better understand emotion (Thompson, 2011). Attachment security, as we have seen, is related to more elaborative parent–child narratives, including discussions of feelings that highlight the emotional significance of past events.

Knowledge about emotion helps children in their efforts to get along with others. As early as 3 to 5 years of age, it is related to friendly, considerate behavior, constructive responses to disputes with agemates, and perspective-taking ability (Garner & Estep, 2001; Hughes & Ensor, 2010; O'Brien at al., 2011). As children learn about emotion from interacting with adults, they engage in more emotion talk with siblings and friends (Hughes & Dunn, 1998). And preschoolers who refer to feelings when interacting with playmates are better liked by their peers (Fabes et al., 2001). Children seem to recognize that acknowledging others' emotions and explaining their own enhance the quality of relationships.

Emotional Self-Regulation

Language also contributes to preschoolers' improved *emotional self-regulation,* or ability to manage the experience and expression of emotion (Cole, Armstrong, & Pemberton, 2010). By age 3 to 4, children verbalize a variety of strategies for adjusting their emotional arousal to a more comfortable level (Thompson & Goodvin, 2007). For example, they know they can blunt emotions by restricting sensory input (covering their eyes or ears to block out a scary sight or sound), talking to themselves ("Mommy said she'll be back soon"), or changing their goals (deciding that they don't want to play anyway after being excluded from a game).

As children use these strategies, emotional outbursts decline. *Effortful control*—in particular, inhibiting impulses and shifting attention—is vital in managing emotion in early childhood. Three-year-olds who can distract themselves when frustrated tend to become

Applying What We Know

Helping Children Manage Common Fears of Early Childhood

FEAR	SUGGESTION
Monsters, ghosts, and darkness	Reduce exposure to frightening stories and TV programs until the child is better able to distinguish appearance from reality. "Search" the child's room for monsters, showing him that none are there. Use a night-light, sit by the child's bed until he falls asleep, and tuck in a favorite toy for protection.
Preschool or child care	If the child resists going to preschool but seems content once there, the fear is probably separation. Provide warmth and caring while gently encouraging independence. If the child fears being at preschool, try to find out why—the teacher, the children, or a crowded, noisy environment. Provide support by accompanying the child and gradually lessening the amount of time you stay.
Animals	Do not force the child to approach a dog, cat, or other animal that arouses fear. Let the child move at her own pace. Demonstrate how to hold and pet the animal, showing that when treated gently, the animal is friendly. If the child is larger than the animal, emphasize this: "You're so big. That kitty is probably afraid of *you!*"
Intense fears	If a child's fear is intense, persists for a long time, interferes with daily activities, and cannot be reduced in any of the ways just suggested, it has reached the level of a *phobia*. Some phobias are linked to family problems and require counseling. Other phobias diminish without treatment as the child's emotional self-regulation improves.

cooperative school-age children with few problem behaviors (Gilliom et al., 2002). By age 3, effortful control predicts children's skill at portraying an emotion they do not feel—for example, reacting cheerfully after receiving an undesirable gift (Kieras et al., 2005). These emotional "masks" are largely limited to the positive feelings of happiness and surprise. Children of all ages (and adults as well) find it harder to act sad, angry, or disgusted than pleased (Denham, 1998). To promote good social relations, most cultures teach children to communicate positive feelings and inhibit unpleasant ones.

Temperament affects the development of emotional self-regulation. Children who experience negative emotion intensely find it harder to inhibit feelings and shift attention away from disturbing events. They are more likely to be anxious and fearful, respond with irritation to others' distress, react angrily or aggressively when frustrated, and get along poorly with teachers and peers (Eisenberg, Smith, & Spinrad, 2011; Raikes et al., 2007).

To avoid social difficulties, emotionally reactive children must develop effective emotion-regulation strategies. By watching parents manage their feelings, children learn strategies for regulating their own. Parents who are in tune with their own emotional experiences tend to be supportive and patient with their preschoolers, offering suggestions and explanations of emotion-regulation strategies that strengthen children's capacity to handle stress (Meyer et al., 2014; Morris et al., 2011). In contrast, when parents rarely express positive emotion, dismiss children's feelings as unimportant, and fail to control their own anger, children's emotion management and psychological adjustment suffer (Hill et al., 2006; Thompson & Meyer, 2007). And because emotionally reactive children become increasingly difficult to rear, they are often targets of ineffective parenting, which compounds their poor self-regulation.

Adult–child conversations that prepare children for difficult experiences also foster emotional self-regulation (Thompson & Goodman, 2010). Parents who discuss what to expect and ways to handle anxiety offer coping strategies that children can apply. Nevertheless, preschoolers' vivid imaginations and incomplete grasp of the distinction between appearance and reality make fears common in early childhood. Consult Applying What We Know above for ways adults can help young children manage fears.

Self-Conscious Emotions

One morning in Leslie's classroom, a group of children crowded around for a bread-baking activity. Leslie asked them to wait patiently while she got a baking pan. But Sammy reached over to feel the dough, and the bowl tumbled off the table. When Leslie returned, Sammy looked at her, then covered his eyes with his hands, and said, "I did something bad." He felt ashamed and guilty.

As their self-concepts develop, preschoolers become increasingly sensitive to praise and blame or (as Sammy did) to the possibility of such feedback. As a result, they more often experience *self-conscious emotions*—feelings that involve injury to or enhancement of their sense of self (see Chapter 7). By age 3, self-conscious emotions are clearly linked to self-evaluation (Lagattuta & Thompson, 2007; Lewis, 1995). But because preschoolers are still developing standards of excellence and conduct, they depend on messages from parents, teachers, and others who matter to them to know *when* to feel proud, ashamed, or guilty, often viewing adult expectations as obligatory rules ("Dad said you're 'posed to take turns") (Thompson, Meyer, & McGinley, 2006).

When parents repeatedly comment on the worth of the child and her performance ("That's a bad job! I thought you were a good girl"), children experience self-conscious emotions intensely—more shame after failure, more pride after success. In contrast, when parents focus on how to improve performance ("You did it this way; now try doing it that way"), they induce moderate, more adaptive levels of shame and pride and greater persistence on difficult tasks (Kelley, Brownell, & Campbell, 2000; Lewis, 1998).

Among Western children, intense shame is associated with feelings of personal inadequacy ("I'm stupid"; "I'm a terrible person") and with maladjustment—withdrawal and depression as well as intense anger and aggression toward those who participated in the shame-evoking situation (Lindsay-Hartz, de Rivera, & Mascolo, 1995; Mills, 2005). In contrast, guilt—when it occurs in appropriate circumstances and is neither excessive nor accompanied by shame—is related to good adjustment. Guilt helps children resist harmful impulses, and it motivates a misbehaving child to repair the damage and behave more considerately (Mascolo & Fischer, 2007; Tangney, Stuewig, & Mashek, 2007). But overwhelming guilt—involving such high emotional distress that the child cannot make amends—is linked to depressive symptoms as early as age 3 (Luby et al., 2009).

Finally, the consequences of shame for children's adjustment may vary across cultures. As illustrated in the Cultural Influences box on page 360, people in Asian societies, who tend to define themselves in relation to their social group, view shame as an adaptive reminder of an interdependent self and of the importance of others' judgments (Friedlmeier, Corapci, & Cole, 2011).

Empathy and Sympathy

Empathy is another emotional capacity that becomes more common in early childhood. It serves as a motivator of **prosocial, or altruistic, behavior**—actions that benefit another person without any expected reward for the self (Spinrad & Eisenberg, 2009). Compared with toddlers, preschoolers rely more on words to communicate empathic feelings, a change that indicates a more reflective level of empathy. When a 4-year-old received a Christmas gift that she hadn't included on her list for Santa, she assumed it belonged to another little girl and pleaded with her parents, "We've got to give it back—Santa's made a big mistake. I think the girl's crying 'cause she didn't get her present!" As the ability to take the perspective of others improves, empathic responding increases.

Yet empathy—*feeling with* another person and responding emotionally in a similar way—does not always yield acts of kindness and helpfulness. For some children, empathizing with an upset adult or peer escalates into *personal distress*. In trying to reduce these feelings, the child focuses on her own anxiety rather than on the person in need. As a result, empathy does not lead to **sympathy**—feelings of concern or sorrow for another's plight.

Temperament plays a role in whether empathy prompts sympathetic, prosocial behavior or a personally distressed, self-focused response. Children who are sociable, assertive, and good at regulating emotion are more likely to help, share, and comfort others in distress. But poor emotion regulators less often display sympathetic concern and prosocial behavior (Eisenberg, Fabes, & Spinrad, 2006; Eisenberg et al., 1998). When faced with someone in need, they react with behavioral and physiological distress—frowning, lip biting, thumb sucking, comfort seeking, a rise in heart rate, and a sharp increase in EEG brain-wave activity in the right cerebral hemisphere, which houses negative emotion—indications that they are overwhelmed by their feelings (Liew et al., 2010; Pickens, Field, & Nawrocki, 2001).

Preschoolers develop empathic concern in the context of secure parent–child attachment relationships (Murphy & Laible, 2013). When parents are warm, encourage emotional expressiveness, and show sensitive, empathic concern for their preschoolers' feelings, children react with concern to others' distress—a response that persists into adolescence and young adulthood (Michalik et al., 2007; Strayer & Roberts, 2004; Taylor et al., 2013). Besides modeling sympathy, parents can teach children the importance of kindness and can intervene when they display inappropriate emotion—strategies that predict high levels of sympathetic responding (Eisenberg, 2003).

In contrast, angry, punitive parenting disrupts the development of empathy at an early age—particularly among children who are poor emotion regulators and who therefore respond to parental hostility with especially high personal distress (Valiente et al., 2004). In one study, physically abused preschoolers at a child-care center rarely expressed concern at a peer's unhappiness but, rather, reacted with fear, anger, and physical attacks (Klimes-Dougan & Kistner, 1990). The children's behavior resembled their parents' insensitive responses to the suffering of others.

As children's language skills and ability to take the perspective of others improve, empathy also increases, motivating prosocial, or altruistic, behavior.

Ask Yourself

- **REVIEW** What do preschoolers understand about emotion, and how do cognition and social experience contribute to their understanding?

- **CONNECT** Cite ways that parenting contributes to preschoolers' self-concept, self-esteem, emotional understanding, emotional self-regulation, self-conscious emotions, and empathy and sympathy. Do you see any patterns? Explain.

- **APPLY** On a hike with his family, 5-year-old Ryan became frightened when he reached a very steep section of the trail. His father gently helped him climb up while saying, "Can you be brave? Being brave is when you feel scared but you do it anyway." What aspect of emotional development is Ryan's father trying to promote, and why is his intervention likely to help Ryan?

Peer Relations

10.4 Describe peer sociability, friendship, and social problem solving in early childhood, along with cultural and parental influences on early peer relations.

As children become increasingly self-aware and better at communicating and understanding the thoughts and feelings of others, their skill at interacting with peers improves rapidly. Peers provide young children with learning experiences they can get in no other way. Because peers interact on an equal footing, they must keep a conversation going, cooperate, and set goals in play. With peers, children form friendships—special relationships marked by attachment and common interests. Let's look at how peer interaction changes over the preschool years.

Advances in Peer Sociability

Mildred Parten (1932), one of the first to study peer sociability among 2- to 5-year-olds, noticed a dramatic rise with age in joint, interactive play. She concluded that social development proceeds in a three-step sequence. It begins with **nonsocial activity**—unoccupied, onlooker behavior and solitary play. Then it shifts to **parallel play,** a limited form of social participation in which a child plays near other children with similar materials but does not try to influence their behavior. At the highest level are two forms of true social interaction. In **associative play,** children engage in separate activities but exchange toys and comment on one another's behavior. Finally, in **cooperative play,** a more advanced type of interaction, children orient toward a common goal, such as acting out a make-believe theme.

FOLLOW-UP RESEARCH ON PEER SOCIABILITY Longitudinal evidence indicates that these play forms emerge in the order Parten suggested but that later-appearing ones do not replace earlier ones in a developmental sequence (Rubin, Bukowski, & Parker, 2006). Rather, all types coexist in early childhood.

TAKE A MOMENT... Watch preschool children move from one type of play to another in a play group or classroom. You will see that they often transition from onlooker to parallel to cooperative play and back again (Robinson et al., 2003). Preschoolers seem to use parallel play as a way station. To successfully join the ongoing play of peers, they often first engage in parallel play nearby, easing into the group's activities—a strategy that increases the likelihood of being accepted. Later, they may return to parallel play as a respite from the high demands of complex social interaction and as a crossroad to new activities.

Although nonsocial activity declines with age, it is still the most frequent form among 3- to 4-year-olds. Even among kindergartners it continues to occupy about one-third of children's free-play time. Both solitary and parallel play remain fairly stable from 3 to 6 years, accounting for as much of the young child's play as highly social, cooperative interaction (Rubin, Fein, & Vandenberg, 1983).

We now understand it is the *type,* not the amount, of solitary and parallel play that changes during early childhood. In studies of preschoolers' play in Taiwan and the United States, researchers rated the *cognitive maturity* of nonsocial, parallel, and cooperative play by applying the categories shown in Table 10.1. Within each of Parten's play types, older children displayed more cognitively mature behavior than younger children (Pan, 1994; Rubin, Watson, & Jambor, 1978).

Often parents wonder whether a preschooler who spends large amounts of time playing alone is developing normally. But only *certain types* of nonsocial activity—aimless wandering, hovering near peers, and functional play involving immature, repetitive motor action—are cause for concern. Children who behave reticently, by watching peers without playing, are usually temperamentally inhibited—high in social fearfulness (Coplan & Ooi, 2014). Their parents frequently overprotect them, criticize their social awkwardness, and unnecessarily control their play activities instead of patiently encouraging them to approach other children and helping them form at least one rewarding friendship, which protects against persisting

LOOK and **LISTEN**

Observe several 3- to 5-year-olds during a free-play period in a preschool or child-care program. How much time does each child devote to nonsocial activity, parallel play, and socially interactive play? Do children seem to use parallel play as a way station between activities?

Four-year-olds *(left)* engage in parallel play. Cooperative play *(right)* develops later than parallel play, but preschoolers continue to move back and forth between the two types of sociability. They often use parallel play as a respite from the complex demands of cooperation.

TABLE 10.1	Developmental Sequence of Cognitive Play Categories	
PLAY CATEGORY	**DESCRIPTION**	**EXAMPLES**
Functional play	Simple, repetitive motor movements with or without objects, especially common during the first two years	Running around a room, rolling a car back and forth, kneading clay with no intent to make something
Constructive play	Creating or constructing something, especially common between 3 and 6 years	Making a house out of toy blocks, drawing a picture, putting together a puzzle
Make-believe play	Acting out everyday and imaginary roles, especially common between 2 and 6 years	Playing house, school, or police officer; acting out storybook or television characters

Source: Rubin, Fein, & Vandenberg, 1983.

adjustment problems (Guimond et al., 2012; Rubin, Bukowski, & Parker, 2006; Rubin, Burgess, & Hastings, 2002). And preschoolers who engage in solitary, repetitive behavior (banging blocks, making a doll jump up and down) tend to be immature, impulsive children who find it difficult to regulate anger and aggression (Coplan et al., 2001). In the classroom, both reticent and impulsive children experience peer ostracism, with boys at greater risk for rejection than girls (Coplan & Arbeau, 2008).

But other preschoolers with low rates of peer interaction are not socially anxious or impulsive. They simply prefer to play alone, and their solitary activities are positive and constructive. Teachers encourage such play by setting out art materials, books, puzzles, and building toys. Children who spend much time at these activities are usually well-adjusted, and when they do play with peers, they show socially skilled behavior (Coplan & Armer, 2007). Still, a few preschoolers who engage in age-appropriate solitary play—again, more often boys—are rebuffed by peers (Coplan et al., 2001, 2004). Perhaps because quiet play is inconsistent with the "masculine" gender role, boys who engage in it are at risk for negative reactions from both parents and peers and, eventually, for adjustment problems.

As noted in Chapter 9, *sociodramatic play*—an advanced form of cooperative play—becomes especially common over the preschool years and supports cognitive, emotional, and social development. In joint make-believe, preschoolers act out and respond to one another's pretend feelings. They also explore and gain control of fear-arousing experiences when they play doctor or pretend to search for monsters in a magical forest. As a result, they can better understand others' feelings and regulate their own (Meyers & Berk, 2014). Finally, preschoolers spend much time negotiating roles and rules in sociodramatic play. To create and manage complex plots, they must resolve disputes through discussion and compromise.

When researchers observed free-play periods in preschools, they found that girls participated more in sociodramatic play, whereas boys participated more in friendly, vigorous interactions called *rough-and-tumble play*. Each type of play was associated with gains in emotional competence one year later (Lindsey & Colwell, 2013). Both sociodramatic play and rough-and-tumble play require children to understand emotions, exercise self-control, and respond to other children's verbal and nonverbal cues. We will return to the topic of rough-and-tumble play in Chapter 11.

CULTURAL VARIATIONS   Peer sociability takes different forms, depending on the relative importance cultures place on group harmony as opposed to individual autonomy (Chen, 2012). For example, children in India generally play in large groups. Much of their behavior is imitative, occurs in unison, and involves close physical contact—a play style requiring high levels of cooperation. In a game called Bhatto Bhatto, children act out a script about a trip to the market, touching one another's elbows and hands as they pretend to cut and share a tasty vegetable (Roopnarine et al., 1994).

As another example, young Chinese children—unlike their North American agemates, who tend to reject reticent peers—are typically accepting of passive, reticent behaviors among their playmates (Chen et al., 2006; French et al., 2011). In Chapter 7, we saw that until recently, cultural values that discourage self-assertion led to positive evaluations of shyness in China

© JACOB MAENTZ/CORBIS

Agta village children in the Philippines play a tug-of-war game. Large group, highly cooperative play occurs more often in societies that value group harmony rather than individual autonomy.

(see page 260). Apparently, this benevolent attitude is still evident in the play behaviors of young Chinese children.

Cultural beliefs about the importance of play also affect early peer associations. Caregivers who view play as mere entertainment are less likely to provide props or to encourage pretend than those who value its cognitive and social benefits (Gaskins, 2014). Recall the description of children's daily lives in village and tribal cultures, described on page 326 in Chapter 9. Mayan parents, for example, do not promote children's play—yet Mayan children are socially competent. When Mayan children do pretend, their play themes are *interpretive* of daily life—involving a limited number of scripts that reflect everyday roles and experiences. Children in industrialized, urban contexts more often engage in *inventive* play, generating make-believe scenarios unconstrained by actual experience (Gaskins, 2013). Perhaps Western-style sociodramatic play, with its elaborate materials and wide-ranging imaginative themes, is particularly important for social development in societies where the worlds of adults and children are distinct. It may be less crucial in village cultures where children participate in adult activities from an early age.

First Friendships

As preschoolers interact, first friendships form that serve as important contexts for emotional and social development. **TAKE A MOMENT...** Jot down a description of what *friendship* means to you. You probably pictured a mutual relationship involving companionship, sharing, understanding of thoughts and feelings, and caring for and comforting one another in times of need. In addition, mature friendships endure over time and survive occasional conflicts.

Preschoolers understand something about the uniqueness of friendship. They say that a friend is someone "who likes you" and with whom you spend a lot of time playing. Yet their ideas about friendship are far from mature. Four- to 7-year-olds regard friendship as pleasurable play and sharing of toys. But friendship does not yet have a long-term, enduring quality based on mutual trust (Damon, 1988; Hartup, 2006). "Mark's my best friend," Sammy would declare on days when the boys got along well. But when a dispute arose, he would reverse himself: "Mark, you're not my friend!" When researchers asked preschoolers to identify their best friends—the children they most liked to play with—less than one-third mentioned the same best friend one year later, and only about one-fourth identified playmates who reciprocally named them as best friends (Eivers et al., 2012).

Nevertheless, interactions between young friends are unique. Preschoolers give twice as much reinforcement—greetings, praise, and compliance—to children they identify as friends, and they also receive more from them. Friends play together in more complex ways and are more cooperative and emotionally expressive—talking, laughing, and looking at each other more often than nonfriends do (Hartup, 2006; Vaughn et al., 2001). And early childhood friendships offer social support: Children who begin kindergarten with friends in their class or readily make new friends adjust to school more favorably (Ladd, Birch, & Buhs, 1999; Proulx & Poulin, 2013). Perhaps the company of friends serves as a secure base from which to develop new relationships, enhancing children's feelings of comfort in the new classroom.

Peer Relations and School Readiness

The ease with which kindergartners make new friends and are accepted by classmates predicts cooperative participation in classroom activities and self-directed completion of learning tasks. These behaviors, in turn, promote gains in achievement (Ladd, Birch, & Buhs, 1999;

Ladd, Buhs, & Seid, 2000). Of course, kindergartners with friendly, prosocial behavioral styles make new friends easily, whereas those with weak emotional self-regulation skills and argumentative, aggressive, or peer-avoidant styles establish poor-quality relationships and make few friends.

In Chapter 7, we indicated that certain genetically influenced temperamental traits—negative mood, emotional reactivity, and weak effortful control—place children at risk for adjustment problems, including peer difficulties (Boivin et al., 2013). But recall, also, that environment—in particular, parenting quality—contributes profoundly to outcomes for these children. Early childhood classroom contexts also make a difference. In research in which identical-twin pair members' kindergarten experiences differed, those encountering peer rejection or conflict-ridden teacher relationships performed less well academically in first grade than their twin counterparts with more favorable classroom social experiences (Vitaro et al. 2012).

The capacity to form mutually rewarding friendships, cooperate with peers, and build positive ties with teachers enables young children to integrate themselves into classroom environments in ways that foster both academic and social competence. Socially competent preschoolers are more motivated and persistent, consistently exceeding their less socially skilled peers in language, literacy, and math scores in the early school grades (Walker & Henderson, 2012; Ziv, 2013). Because social maturity in early childhood contributes to later academic performance, readiness for kindergarten must be assessed in terms of not only academic skills but also social skills.

In evaluating readiness for school, children's capacity for friendly, cooperative interaction is just as important as their academic skills.

Positive peer interactions among young children occur most often in unstructured situations such as free play, making it important for preschools to provide space, time, materials, and adult scaffolding to support child-directed activities (Booren, Downer, & Vitiello, 2012). Warm, responsive teacher–child interaction is also vital, especially for shy, impulsive, emotionally negative, and aggressive children, who are at high risk for social difficulties (Brendgen et al., 2011; McClelland et al., 2007). In studies involving several thousand 4-year-olds in public preschools in six states, teacher sensitivity and emotional support were potent predictors of children's social competence during preschool and in a follow-up after kindergarten entry (Curby et al., 2009; Mashburn et al., 2008). Along with excellent teacher preparation, other indicators of program quality—small group sizes, generous teacher–child ratios, and developmentally appropriate daily activities (see page 345)—create classroom conditions that make positive teacher and peer relationships more likely.

Social Problem Solving

As noted earlier, children, even those who are best friends, come into conflict—events that provide invaluable learning experiences in resolving disputes constructively. Preschoolers' disagreements only rarely result in hostile encounters. Although friends argue more than other peers do, they are also more likely to work out their differences through negotiation and to continue interacting (Rubin et al., 2011).

TAKE A MOMENT... At your next opportunity, observe preschoolers' play, noting disputes over objects ("That's mine!" "I had it first!"), entry into and control over play activities ("I'm on your team, Jerry." "No, you're not!"), and disagreements over facts, ideas, and beliefs ("I'm taller than he is." "No, you aren't!"). Children take these matters quite seriously. Social conflicts provide repeated occasions for **social problem solving**—generating and applying strategies that prevent or resolve disagreements, resulting in outcomes that are both acceptable to others and beneficial to the self. To engage in social problem solving, children must bring together diverse social understandings.

FIGURE 10.1 **An information-processing model of social problem solving.** The model is circular because children often engage in several information-processing activities at once—for example, interpreting information as they notice it and continuing to consider the meaning of another's behavior while they generate and evaluate problem-solving strategies. The model also takes into account the impact of mental state on social information processing—in particular, children's knowledge of social rules, their representations of past social experiences, and their expectations for future experiences. Peer evaluations and responses to enacted strategies are also important factors in social problem solving. (Adapted from N. R. Crick & K. A. Dodge, 1994, "A Review and Reformulation of Social Information-Processing Mechanisms in Children's Social Adjustment," *Psychological Bulletin, 115,* 74–101, Figure 2 [adapted], p. 76. Copyright © 1994 by the American Psychological Association. Reprinted with permission of the American Psychological Association.)

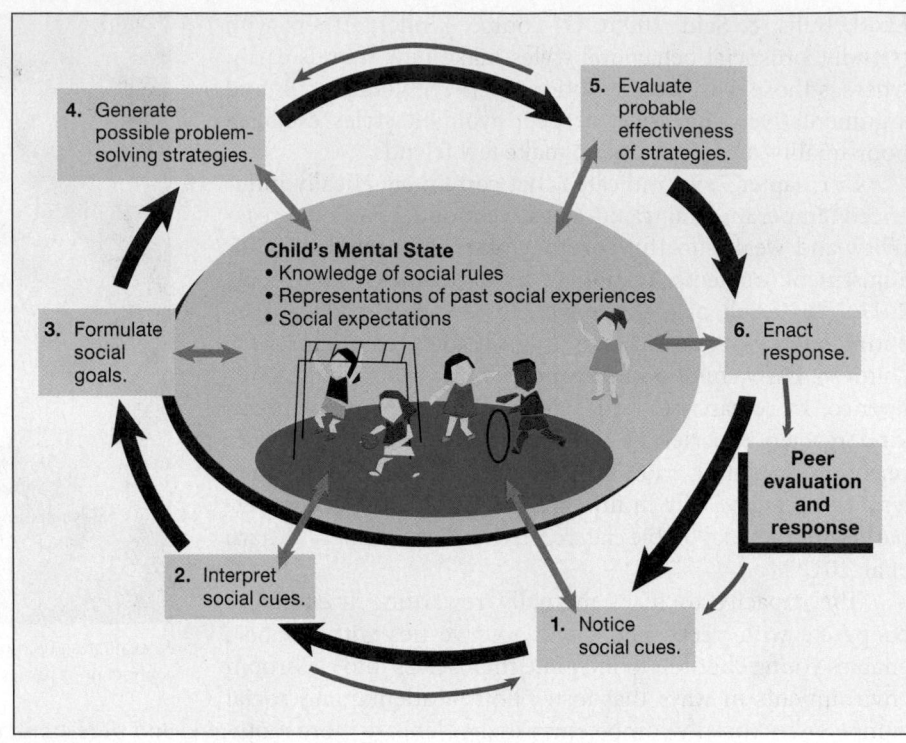

THE SOCIAL PROBLEM-SOLVING PROCESS Nicki Crick and Kenneth Dodge (1994) organize the steps of social problem solving into the circular model shown in Figure 10.1. Notice how this flowchart takes an *information-processing approach,* clarifying exactly what a child must do to grapple with and solve a social problem. It enables identification of processing deficits, so intervention can be tailored to meet individual needs.

Social problem solving profoundly affects peer relations. Children who get along well with agemates interpret social cues accurately, formulate goals (helping or cooperating with peers) that enhance relationships, and have a repertoire of effective problem-solving strategies—for example, politely asking to play, requesting an explanation when they do not understand a peer's behavior, and working out a compromise when faced with peer disagreement. In contrast, children with peer difficulties often hold biased social expectations. Consequently, they attend selectively to social cues (such as hostile acts) and misinterpret others' behavior (view an unintentional jostle as hostile). Their social goals (satisfying an impulse, getting even with or avoiding a peer) often lead to strategies that damage relationships (Dodge, Coie, & Lynam, 2006; Meece & Mize, 2011). They might barge into a play group without asking, use threats and physical force, or fearfully hover around peers' activities.

Children improve greatly in social problem solving over the preschool and early school years. Between ages 2 and 4, they increasingly display positive emotion and sociable behavior when negotiating with peers (Walker et al., 2013). Five- to 7-year-olds tend to rely on persuasion and compromise, to think of alternative strategies when an initial one does not work, and to resolve disagreements without adult intervention (Mayeux & Cillessen, 2003). Sometimes they suggest creating new, mutual goals, reflecting awareness that how they solve current problems will influence the future of the relationship (Yeates, Schultz, & Selman, 1991). By kindergarten, the accuracy and effectiveness of each component of social problem solving are related to socially competent behavior (Dodge et al., 1986).

ENHANCING SOCIAL PROBLEM SOLVING Intervening with children who have weak social problem-solving skills can foster development in several ways. Besides improving peer relations, effective social problem solving offers children a sense of mastery in the face of stressful life events. It reduces the risk of adjustment difficulties in children from low-SES and troubled families (Goodman, Gravitt, & Kaslow, 1995).

In one intervention—the *Promoting Alternative Thinking Strategies (PATHS)* curriculum for preschool children—teachers provide children with weekly lessons in the ingredients of social problem solving. Using stories, puppet characters, discussion, and role-play demonstrations, they teach such skills as detecting others' feelings, planning sequences of action, generating effective strategies, and anticipating probable outcomes. In evaluations of PATHS, preschoolers who completed 30 lessons in their Head Start classrooms scored higher than no-intervention controls in accurately "reading" others' emotions, inferring how others are likely to feel based on situational cues, selecting competent solutions to social conflicts, and cooperating and communicating with peers (Bierman et al., 2008; Domitrovich, Cortes, & Greenberg, 2007).

Parental Influences on Early Peer Relations

Children first acquire skills for interacting with peers within the family. Parents influence children's peer sociability both *directly,* through attempts to influence children's peer relations, and *indirectly,* through their child-rearing practices and play.

DIRECT PARENTAL INFLUENCES   Outside preschool, child care, and kindergarten, young children depend on parents to help them establish rewarding peer associations. Preschoolers whose parents frequently arrange informal peer play activities tend to have larger peer networks and to be more socially skilled (Ladd, LeSieur, & Profilet, 1993). In providing play opportunities, parents show children how to initiate peer contacts and encourage them to be good "hosts" who consider their playmates' needs.

Parents also influence children's peer interaction skills by offering guidance on how to act toward others. Their skillful suggestions for managing conflict, discouraging teasing, and entering a play group are associated with preschoolers' social competence and peer acceptance (Mize & Pettit, 2010; Parke et al., 2004b).

INDIRECT PARENTAL INFLUENCES   Many parenting behaviors not directly aimed at promoting peer sociability nevertheless influence it. For example, secure attachments to parents are linked to more responsive, harmonious peer interactions; larger peer networks; and warmer, more supportive friendships throughout childhood and adolescence (Laible, 2007; Lucas-Thompson & Clarke-Stewart, 2007; Wood, Emmerson, & Cowan, 2004). The sensitive, emotionally expressive communication that contributes to attachment security may be responsible. In several studies, highly involved, emotionally positive parent–child conversations and play predicted prosocial behavior and positive peer relations in preschool children (Clark & Ladd, 2000; Lindsey & Mize, 2000).

Parent–child play seems particularly effective for promoting peer interaction skills. During play, parents interact with their child on a "level playing field," much as peers do. And perhaps because parents play more with children of their own sex, mothers' play is more strongly linked to daughters' competence, fathers' play to sons' competence (Lindsey & Mize, 2000; Pettit et al., 1998).

As we have seen, some preschoolers already have great difficulty with peer relations. In Leslie's classroom, Robbie was one of them. Wherever he happened to be, comments like "Robbie ruined our block tower" and "Robbie hit me for no reason" could be heard. As we take up moral development in the next section, you will learn more about how parenting contributed to Robbie's peer problems.

Parents' play with young children, especially same-sex children, is linked to social competence. By playing with his father as he would with a peer, this child acquires social skills that facilitate peer interaction.

Ask Yourself

- **REVIEW** How is social competence related to children's school readiness, and what can early childhood teachers do to promote positive peer relations?

- **CONNECT** Illustrate the influence of temperament on social problem solving by explaining how an impulsive child and a shy child might respond at each social problem-solving step in Figure 10.1 on page 370.

- **APPLY** Three-year-old Ben lives in the country, with no other preschoolers nearby. His parents wonder whether it is worth driving Ben into town once a week to participate in a peer play group. What advice would you give Ben's parents, and why?

- **REFLECT** What forms of play do you recall engaging in as a young child? In what ways might those early experiences reflect your gender, culture, and family background?

10.5 What are the central features of psychoanalytic, social learning, and cognitive-developmental approaches to moral development?

10.6 Describe the development of aggression in early childhood, including family and media influences.

Foundations of Morality

Young children's behavior provides many examples of their budding moral sense. In Chapter 4, we noted that newborn (and older) infants often cry in response to the cries of other babies, a possible precursor of empathy. And after watching scenes in which one puppet helps another by returning a dropped ball while a second takes the ball away, babies as young as 3 months overwhelmingly preferred (looked longer at) the helpful character over the hinderer (Hamlin & Wynn, 2011). They seem implicitly drawn to the "nice" guy and repelled by the "mean" guy.

By the middle of the second year, toddlers expect others to act fairly, by dividing resources equally among recipients (Geraci & Surian, 2011). As children reach age 2, they often use language to evaluate their own and others' actions: "I naughty. I wrote on the wall" or (after being hit by another child) "Connie not nice." And we have seen that children of this age share toys, help others, and cooperate in games—early indicators of considerate, responsible, prosocial attitudes.

Adults everywhere take note of this developing capacity to distinguish right from wrong and to accommodate the needs of others. Some cultures have special terms for it. The Utku Indians of Hudson Bay say the child develops *ihuma* (reason). The Fijians believe that *vakayalo* (sense) appears. In response, parents hold children more responsible for their actions (Dunn, 2005). By the end of early childhood, children can state many moral rules: "Don't take someone's things without asking." "Tell the truth!" In addition, they argue over matters of justice: "You sat there last time, so it's my turn." "It's not fair. He got more!"

All theories of moral development recognize that conscience begins to take shape in early childhood. And most agree that at first, the child's morality is *externally controlled* by adults. Gradually, it becomes regulated by *inner standards*. Truly moral individuals do not do the right thing just to conform to others' expectations. Rather, they have developed compassionate concerns and principles of good conduct, which they follow in many situations.

Each major theory of development emphasizes a different aspect of morality. Psychoanalytic theory stresses the *emotional side* of conscience development—in particular, identification and guilt as motivators of good conduct. Social learning theory focuses on how *moral behavior* is learned through reinforcement and modeling. Finally, the cognitive-developmental perspective emphasizes *thinking*—children's ability to reason about justice and fairness.

The Psychoanalytic Perspective

Recall that according to Freud, young children form a *superego*, or conscience, by *identifying* with the same-sex parent, whose moral standards they adopt. Children obey the superego to avoid *guilt*, a painful emotion that arises each time they are tempted to misbehave. Moral development, Freud believed, is largely complete by 5 to 6 years of age.

Today, most researchers disagree with Freud's view of conscience development. In his theory (see page 16 in Chapter 1), fear of punishment and loss of parental love motivate conscience formation and moral behavior. Yet children whose parents frequently use threats, commands, or physical force tend to violate standards often and feel little guilt, whereas parental warmth and responsiveness predict greater guilt following transgressions (Kochanska et al., 2005, 2008). And if a parent withdraws love after misbehavior—for example, refuses to speak to or states a dislike for the child—children often respond with high levels of self-blame, thinking, "I'm no good," or "Nobody loves me." Eventually, to protect themselves from overwhelming guilt, these children may deny the emotion and, as a result, also develop a weak conscience (Kochanska, 1991; Zahn-Waxler et al., 1990).

INDUCTIVE DISCIPLINE   In contrast, conscience formation is promoted by a type of discipline called **induction,** in which an adult helps make the child aware of feelings by pointing out the effects of the child's misbehavior on others, especially noting their distress and making clear that the child caused it. For example, a parent might say, "If you keep pushing him, he'll fall down and cry" or "She's crying because you won't give back her doll" (Hoffman, 2000). When generally warm parents provide explanations that match the child's capacity to understand, while firmly insisting that the child listen and comply, induction is effective as early as age 2. Preschoolers whose parents use it are more likely to refrain from wrongdoing, confess and repair damages after misdeeds, and display prosocial behavior (Choe, Olson, & Sameroff, 2013; Volling, Mahoney, & Rauer, 2009).

This teacher uses inductive discipline to explain to a child how her misbehavior affects others. She indicates how the child should behave, encouraging empathy and sympathetic concern.

The success of induction may lie in its power to motivate children's active commitment to moral standards, in the following ways:

- Induction gives children information about how to behave that they can use in future situations.
- By emphasizing the impact of the child's actions on others, induction encourages empathy and sympathetic concern, which motivate prosocial behavior.
- Giving children reasons for changing their behavior encourages them to adopt moral standards because those standards make sense.
- Children who consistently experience induction may form a *script* for the negative emotional consequences of harming others: Child causes harm, inductive message points out harm, child feels empathy for victim, child makes amends (Hoffman, 2000). The script deters future transgressions.

In contrast, discipline that relies too heavily on threats of punishment or withdrawal of love makes children so anxious and frightened that they cannot think clearly enough to figure out what they should do. As a result, these practices do not get children to internalize moral rules and—as noted earlier—also interfere with empathy and prosocial responding (Eisenberg, Fabes, & Spinrad, 2006; Padilla-Walker, 2008). Nevertheless, warnings, disapproval, and commands are sometimes necessary to get an unruly child to listen to an inductive message (Grusec, 2006).

THE CHILD'S CONTRIBUTION   Although good discipline is crucial, children's characteristics also affect the success of parenting techniques. Twin studies suggest a modest genetic contribution to empathy (Knafo et al., 2009). More empathic children require less power assertion and are more responsive to induction.

Temperament is also influential. Mild, patient tactics—requests, suggestions, and explanations—are sufficient to prompt guilt reactions and conscience development in anxious, fearful preschoolers (Kochanska et al., 2002). But with fearless, impulsive children, gentle discipline has little impact. As a result, parents of preschoolers high in externalizing behavior

When children are impulsive and low in anxiety, a secure attachment relationship motivates conscience development. This preschooler wants to follow parental rules to preserve an affectionate, supportive relationship with her father.

are unlikely to use induction, relying instead on power assertive methods including physical punishment. But power assertion also works poorly. It undermines the child's capacity for effortful control, which strongly predicts good conduct, empathy, sympathy, and prosocial behavior (Kochanska & Aksan, 2006). Parents of impulsive children can foster conscience development by ensuring a warm, harmonious relationship and combining firm correction of misbehavior with induction (Kim et al., 2014; Kochanska & Kim, 2014). When children are so low in anxiety that parental disapproval causes them little discomfort, a close parent–child bond provides an alternative foundation for morality. It motivates children to listen to parents as a means of preserving an affectionate, supportive relationship.

In sum, to foster early moral development, parents must tailor their disciplinary strategies to their child's personality. Does this remind you of *goodness of fit,* discussed in Chapter 7? Return to page 259 to review this idea.

THE ROLE OF GUILT　Although little support exists for Freudian ideas about conscience development, Freud was correct that guilt motivates moral action. By the end of toddlerhood, guilt reactions are evident, and preschoolers' assertions reveal that they have internalized the parent's moral voice: "Didn't you hear my mommy? We'd better not play with these toys."

Inducing *empathy-based* guilt (expressions of personal responsibility and regret, such as "I'm sorry I hurt him") by explaining that the child is causing someone distress and has disappointed the parent is a means of influencing children without using coercion. Empathy-based guilt reactions are associated with stopping harmful actions, repairing damage caused by misdeeds, and engaging in future prosocial behavior (Eisenberg, Eggum, & Edwards, 2010). At the same time, parents must help children deal with guilt feelings constructively—by guiding them to make up for immoral behavior rather than minimizing or excusing it (Bybee, Merisca, & Velasco, 1998).

But contrary to what Freud believed, guilt is not the only force that compels us to act morally. Nor is moral development complete by the end of early childhood. Rather, it is a gradual process that extends into adulthood, building on foundations that emerge during early childhood.

Social Learning Theory

According to social learning theory, morality does not have a unique course of development. Rather, moral behavior is acquired just like any other set of responses: through reinforcement and modeling.

IMPORTANCE OF MODELING　*Operant conditioning*—reinforcement for good behavior, in the form of approval, affection, and other rewards—is not enough for children to acquire moral responses. For a behavior to be reinforced, it must first occur spontaneously. Yet many prosocial acts—sharing, helping, comforting an unhappy playmate—occur so rarely at first that reinforcement cannot explain their rapid development in early childhood. Rather, social learning theorists believe that children learn to behave morally largely through *modeling*—by observing and imitating people who demonstrate appropriate behavior (Grusec, 1988). Once children acquire a moral response, such as sharing or telling the truth, reinforcement in the form of praise for the act ("That was a very nice thing to do") and for the child's character ("You're a very kind and considerate boy") increases its frequency (Mills & Grusec, 1989).

Nevertheless, certain characteristics of models affect children's willingness to imitate:

- *Warmth and responsiveness.* Preschoolers are more likely to copy prosocial actions of warm, responsive (as opposed to cold, distant) adults (Yarrow, Scott, & Waxler, 1973). Warmth seems to make children more attentive and receptive to the model and is itself an example of a prosocial response.

- *Competence and power.* Children admire and therefore tend to imitate competent, powerful models—especially older peers and adults (Bandura, 1977).
- *Consistency between assertions and behavior.* When models say one thing and do another—for example, announce that "it's important to help others" but rarely engage in helpful acts—children generally choose the most lenient standard of behavior (Mischel & Liebert, 1966).

Models are most influential in the early years. In one study, toddlers' eager, willing imitation of their mothers' behavior predicted moral conduct (not cheating in a game) and guilt following transgressions at age 3 (Forman, Aksan, & Kochanska, 2004). At the end of the preschool years, children who have had consistent exposure to caring adults tend to behave prosocially whether or not a model is present (Mussen & Eisenberg-Berg, 1977). They have internalized prosocial rules from repeated observations and encouragement by others.

EFFECTS OF PUNISHMENT   Many parents realize that angrily yelling at, slapping, and spanking children are ineffective disciplinary tactics. A sharp reprimand or physical force to restrain or move a child is justified when immediate obedience is necessary—for example, when a 3-year-old is about to run into the street. In fact, parents are most likely to use forceful methods under these conditions. But to foster long-term goals, such as acting kindly toward others, they tend to rely on warmth and reasoning (Kuczynski, 1984; Lansford et al., 2012). And in response to serious transgressions, such as lying or stealing, they often combine power assertion with reasoning (Grusec, 2006).

Frequent punishment promotes immediate compliance but not lasting changes in behavior. For example, Robbie's parents often punished by hitting, shouting, and criticizing. But as soon as they were out of sight, Robbie usually engaged in the unacceptable behavior again. The more harsh threats, angry physical control, and physical punishment children experience, the more likely they are to develop serious, lasting problems. These include weak internalization of moral rules; depression, aggression, antisocial behavior, and poor academic performance in childhood and adolescence; and depression, alcohol abuse, criminality, physical health problems, and family violence in adulthood (Afifi et al., 2006, 2013; Bender et al., 2007; Kochanska, Aksan, & Nichols, 2003; Lynch et al., 2006).

Repeated harsh punishment has several undesirable side effects:

- Parents often spank in response to children's aggression. Yet the punishment itself models aggression!
- Harshly treated children react with anger, resentment, and a chronic sense of being personally threatened, which prompts a focus on the self's distress rather than a sympathetic orientation to others' needs.
- Children who are frequently punished develop a more conflict-ridden and less supportive parent–child relationship and also learn to avoid the punitive parent (McLoyd & Smith, 2002; Shaw, Lacourse, & Nagin, 2005). Consequently, the parent's effectiveness at teaching desirable behaviors is substantially reduced.
- By stopping children's misbehavior temporarily, harsh punishment gives adults immediate relief, reinforcing them for using coercive discipline. For this reason, a punitive adult is likely to punish with greater frequency over time, a course of action that can spiral into serious abuse.
- Children, adolescents, and adults whose parents used *corporal punishment*—physical force that inflicts pain but not injury—are more accepting of such discipline (Deater-Deckard et al., 2003; Vitrup & Holden, 2010). In this way, use of physical punishment may transfer to the next generation.

Although corporal punishment spans the SES spectrum, its frequency and harshness are elevated among less educated, economically disadvantaged parents (Giles-Sims, Straus, & Sugarman, 1995; Lansford et al., 2009). And consistently, parents with conflict-ridden marriages and with mental health problems (who are emotionally reactive, depressed, or aggressive) are more likely to be punitive and also to have hard-to-manage children, whose disobedience evokes more parental harshness (Erath et al., 2006; Knafo & Plomin, 2006). But even after

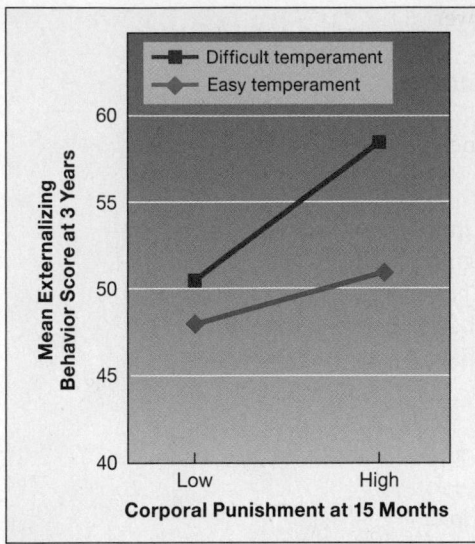

FIGURE 10.2 Relationship of parental corporal punishment at age 15 months to externalizing behavior, by child temperament. Corporal punishment was associated with increased externalizing behavior (anger and aggression) for both easy and difficult children, even after controlling for family and parenting characteristics. The rise in externalizing behavior was greater for difficult children—a difference also evident in a follow-up during first grade. (From M. K. Mulvaney & C. J. Mebert, 2007, "Parental Corporal Punishment Predicts Behavior Problems in Early Childhood," *Journal of Family Psychology, 21,* p. 394. Copyright © 2007 by the American Psychological Association. Reprinted with permission of the American Psychological Association.)

controlling for child, parenting, and family characteristics that might otherwise account for the relationship, longitudinal findings reveal a link between physical punishment and later child and adolescent aggression (Lansford et al., 2011; Lee et al., 2013; MacKenzie et al., 2013; Taylor et al., 2010).

On average, the negative effects of physical punishment are small after controlling for the factors just mentioned (Ferguson, 2013). But physical punishment affects children with vulnerable temperaments more negatively than others. For example, in a longitudinal study extending from 15 months to 3 years, early corporal punishment predicted externalizing behavior problems in preschoolers of diverse temperaments, but negative outcomes were more pronounced among temperamentally difficult children (see Figure 10.2) (Mulvaney & Mebert, 2007). Similar findings emerged from a twin study in which physical punishment was most detrimental for children at high genetic risk for behavior problems (Boutwell et al., 2011). **TAKE A MOMENT...** Return to page 85 in Chapter 2 to review findings indicating that good parenting can shield children genetically at risk for aggression and antisocial activity from developing those behaviors.

In view of these findings, the widespread use of corporal punishment by American parents is cause for concern. Surveys of nationally representative samples of U.S. households reveal that although corporal punishment increases from infancy to age 5 and then declines, it is high at all ages (see Figure 10.3) (Gershoff et al., 2012; Straus & Stewart, 1999). Furthermore, over the past 40 years, the prevalence of physical punishment has remained stable among preschoolers and declined only slightly (remaining high) among school-age children (Zolotor et al., 2011). And more than one-fourth of physically punishing U.S. parents report having used a hard object, such as a brush or a belt (Gershoff, 2002).

A prevailing American belief is that corporal punishment, if implemented by caring parents, is harmless, perhaps even beneficial. In one opinion poll, 72 percent of adults agreed that it is "OK to spank a child" (Survey USA, 2005). But as the Cultural Influences box on the following page reveals, this assumption is valid only under conditions of limited use in certain social contexts.

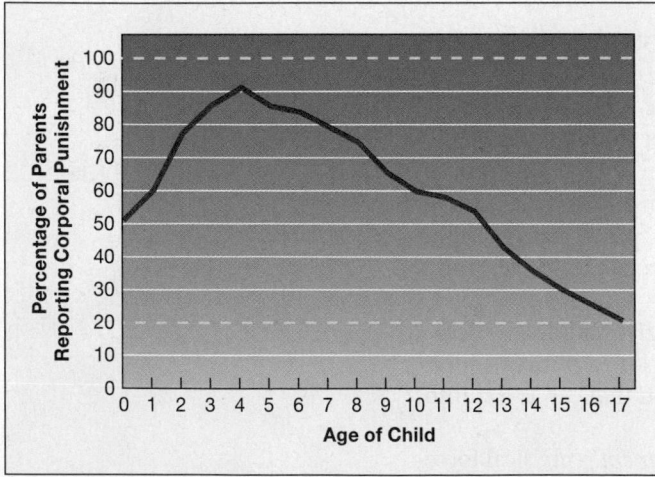

FIGURE 10.3 Prevalence of corporal punishment by child's age. Estimates are based on the percentage of parents in a nationally representative U.S. sample of nearly 1,000 reporting one or more instances of spanking, slapping, pinching, shaking, or hitting with a hard object in the past year. Physical punishment increases sharply during early childhood and then declines, but it is high at all ages. (Adapted from M. A. Straus & J. H. Stewart, 1999, "Corporal Punishment by American Parents: National Data on Prevalence, Chronicity, Severity, and Duration in Relation to Child and Family Characteristics," *Clinical Child and Family Psychology Review, 2,* p. 59. Reprinted with permission from Springer Science+Business Media conveyed through Copyright Clearance Center, Inc.)

ALTERNATIVES TO HARSH PUNISHMENT Alternatives to criticism, slaps, and spankings can reduce the side effects of punishment. A technique called **time out** involves removing children from the immediate setting—for example, by sending them to their rooms—until they are ready to act appropriately. When a child is out of control, a few minutes in time out can be enough to change behavior while also giving angry parents time to cool off (Morawska & Sanders, 2011). Another approach is *withdrawal of privileges,* such as playing outside or watching a favorite TV program. Like time out, removing privileges allows parents to avoid using harsh techniques that can easily intensify into violence.

When parents do decide to use punishment, they can increase its effectiveness in three ways:

- *Consistency.* Permitting children to act inappropriately on some occasions but scolding them on others confuses children, and the unacceptable act persists (Acker & O'Leary, 1996).
- *A warm parent–child relationship.* Children of involved, caring parents find the interruption in parental affection that accompanies punishment especially unpleasant. They want to regain parental warmth and approval as quickly as possible.
- *Explanations.* Providing reasons for mild punishment helps children relate the misdeed to expectations for future behavior. This approach leads to far greater reduction in misbehavior than using punishment alone (Larzelere et al., 1996).

Cultural Influences

Ethnic Differences in the Consequences of Physical Punishment

In an African-American community, six elders, all of whom had volunteered to serve as mentors for parents facing child-rearing challenges, met to discuss parenting issues at a social service agency. Their attitudes toward discipline were strikingly different from those of the white social workers who had brought them together. Each elder argued that successful child rearing required appropriate physical tactics. At the same time, they voiced strong disapproval of screaming or cursing at children, calling such out-of-control parental behavior "abusive." Ruth, the oldest and most respected member of the group, characterized good parenting as a complex combination of warmth, teaching, talking nicely, and disciplining physically. She related how an older neighbor advised her to handle her own children when she was a young parent:

> She said to me says, don't scream . . . you talk to them real nice and sweet and when they do something ugly . . . she say you get a nice little switch and you won't have any trouble with them and from that day that's the way I raised 'em. (Mosby et al., 1999, pp. 511–512)

In several studies, corporal punishment predicted externalizing problems similarly among white, black, Hispanic, and Asian children (Gershoff et al., 2012; MacKenzie et al., 2013). But other studies point to ethnic variations. In one longitudinal investigation, researchers followed several hundred families, collecting information from mothers on disciplinary strategies and from teachers on children's problem behaviors from kindergarten through fourth grade. Regardless of ethnicity, reasoning was the most common approach to discipline, spanking the least common. But predictors and outcomes

of spanking varied, depending on family ethnicity.

Among white families, externalizing behavior in kindergarten predicted parental physical punishment in first through third grades, which in turn led to more externalizing behavior by fourth grade. In contrast, among African-American families, kindergarten externalizing behavior was unrelated to later physical punishment, and physical punishment did not augment externalizing behavior (Lansford et al., 2012). The investigators concluded that white parents more often use physical discipline in reaction to challenging behaviors, causing those behaviors to escalate. African-American parents, in contrast, seem to use physical punishment to prevent child difficulties, thereby reducing its negative consequences.

Consistent with this interpretation, African-American and Caucasian-American parents report meting out physical punishment differently. In black families, such discipline is typically culturally approved, mild, delivered in a context of parental warmth, accompanied by verbal teaching, and aimed at helping children become responsible adults. White parents, in contrast, usually consider physical punishment to be wrong, so when they resort to it, they are often highly agitated and rejecting of the child (Dodge, McLoyd, & Lansford, 2006; LeCuyer et al., 2011). As a result, most black children may view spanking as a practice carried out with their best interests in mind, whereas white children may regard it as an act of aggression.

In support of this view, when several thousand ethnically diverse children were followed from the preschool through the early school

© ELLEN B. SENISI

In African-American families, physical discipline is often culturally approved, generally mild, and delivered in a context of parental warmth. As a result, children may view it as an effort to encourage maturity, not as an act of aggression.

years, spanking was associated with a rise in behavior problems if parents were cold and rejecting but not if they were warm and supportive (McLoyd & Smith, 2002). In another study, spanking predicted depressive symptoms only among a small number of African-American children whose mothers disapproved of the practice and, as a result, tended to use it when they were highly angry and frustrated (McLoyd et al., 2007).

These findings are not an endorsement of physical punishment. Other forms of discipline, such as time out, and the positive parenting strategies listed on page 378, are far more effective (Simons, Simons, & Su, 2013). But it is noteworthy that the meaning and impact of physical discipline vary sharply with its intensity, context of warmth and support, and cultural approval.

POSITIVE RELATIONSHIPS, POSITIVE PARENTING The most effective forms of discipline encourage good conduct—by building a mutually respectful bond with the child, letting the child know ahead of time how to act, and praising mature behavior. When sensitivity, cooperation, and shared positive emotion are evident in joint activities between parents and preschoolers, children show firmer conscience development—expressing empathy after transgressions, behaving responsibly, playing fairly in games, and considering others' welfare (Kochanska et al., 2005, 2008). Parent–child closeness leads children to heed parental demands because children feel a sense of commitment to the relationship.

Consult Applying What We Know on page 378 for ways to parent positively. Parents who use these strategies focus on long-term social and life skills—cooperation, problem solving, and consideration for others. As a result, they greatly reduce the need for punishment.

Applying What We Know

Positive Parenting

STRATEGY	EXPLANATION
Use transgressions as opportunities to teach.	When a child engages in harmful or unsafe behavior, intervene firmly, and then use induction, which motivates children to make amends and behave prosocially.
Reduce opportunities for misbehavior.	On long car trips, bring back-seat activities that relieve children's restlessness. At the supermarket, converse with children, and let them help with shopping. Children then learn to occupy themselves constructively when options are limited.
Provide reasons for rules.	When children appreciate that rules are fair to all concerned, not arbitrary, they strive to follow the rules because they are reasonable and rational.
Arrange for children to participate in family routines and duties.	By joining with adults in preparing a meal, washing dishes, or raking leaves, children develop a sense of responsible participation in family and community life and acquire many practical skills.
When children are obstinate, try compromising and problem solving.	When a child refuses to obey, express understanding of the child's feelings ("I know it's not fun to clean up"), suggest a compromise ("You put those away, I'll take care of these"), and help the child think of ways to avoid the problem in the future. Responding firmly but kindly and respectfully increases the likelihood of willing cooperation.
Encourage mature behavior.	Express confidence in children's capacity to learn and appreciation for effort and cooperation, as in "You gave that your best!" "Thanks for helping!" Adult encouragement fosters pride and satisfaction in succeeding, thereby inspiring children to improve further.
Be sensitive to children's physical and emotional resources.	When children are tired, ill, or bored, they are likely to engage in attention-getting, disorganized, or otherwise improper behavior as a reaction to discomfort. In these instances, meeting the child's needs makes more sense than disciplining.

Sources: Berk, 2001a; Grusec, 2006.

The Cognitive-Developmental Perspective

The psychoanalytic and behaviorist approaches to morality focus on how children acquire ready-made standards of good conduct from adults. In contrast, the cognitive-developmental perspective regards children as *active thinkers* about social rules. As early as the preschool years, children make moral judgments, deciding what is right or wrong on the basis of concepts they construct about justice and fairness (Gibbs, 2010; Helwig & Turiel, 2011).

PRESCHOOLERS' MORAL UNDERSTANDING   Young children have some well-developed ideas about morality. As long as researchers emphasize people's intentions, 3-year-olds say that a person with bad intentions—someone who deliberately frightens, embarrasses, or otherwise hurts another—is more deserving of punishment than a well-intentioned person. They also protest when they see one person harming another (Helwig, Zelazo, & Wilson, 2001; Vaish, Missana, & Tomasello, 2011). Around age 4, children know that a person who expresses an insincere intention—saying, "I'll come over and help you rake leaves"—while not intending to do so—is lying (Maas, 2008). And 4-year-olds approve of telling the truth and disapprove of lying, even when a lie remains undetected (Bussey, 1992).

Furthermore, preschoolers in diverse cultures distinguish **moral imperatives,** which protect people's rights and welfare, from two other types of rules and expectations: **social conventions,** customs determined solely by consensus, such as table manners and politeness rituals (saying "please" and "thank you"); and **matters of personal choice,** such as choice of friends, hairstyle, and leisure activities, which do not violate rights and are up to the individual (Killen, Margie, & Sinno, 2006; Nucci & Gingo, 2011; Smetana, 2006). Interviews with 3- and 4-year-olds reveal that they consider moral violations (unprovoked hitting, stealing an apple) as more wrong than violations of social conventions (eating ice cream with your fingers). They also say that moral violations would still be wrong even if an adult did not see them and no rules existed to prohibit them because they harm others (Smetana et al, 2012). And preschoolers' concern with personal choice, conveyed through statements like "I'm gonna wear *this* shirt," serves as the springboard for moral concepts of individual rights, which will expand greatly in middle childhood and adolescence.

Young children's moral reasoning tends to be *rigid,* emphasizing salient features and consequences while neglecting other important information. For example, they have difficulty distinguishing between accidental and intentional transgressions (Killen et al. 2011). And they are more likely than older children to claim that stealing and lying are always wrong, even when a person has a morally sound reason for engaging in these acts (Lourenço, 2003; Poplinger et al., 2011). Furthermore, their explanations for why hitting others is wrong are simplistic and centered on physical harm: "When you get hit, it hurts, and you start to cry" (Nucci, 2008).

Still, preschoolers' ability to distinguish moral imperatives from social conventions is impressive. How do they do so? According to cognitive-developmental theorists, they *actively make sense* of their experiences (Helwig & Turiel, 2011). They observe that after a moral offense, peers respond with strong negative emotion, describe their own injury or loss, tell another child to stop, or retaliate. And an adult who intervenes is likely to call attention to the rights and feelings of the victim. In contrast, violations of social convention elicit less intense peer reactions. And in these situations, adults usually demand obedience without explanation or point to the importance of keeping order.

This preschooler understands that his choice of a toy is a matter of personal choice, distinct from moral imperatives and social conventions.

SOCIAL EXPERIENCE AND MORAL UNDERSTANDING   Cognition and language support preschoolers' moral understanding, but social experiences are vital. Disputes with siblings and peers over rights, possessions, and property allow preschoolers to negotiate, compromise, and work out their first ideas about justice and fairness. Children also learn from warm, sensitive parental communication and from observing how adults handle rule violations (Turiel & Killen, 2010). And they benefit greatly from adult–child discussions of moral issues. Children who are advanced in moral thinking tend to have parents who adapt their communications about fighting, honesty, and ownership to what their children can understand, tell stories with moral implications, encourage prosocial behavior, and gently stimulate the child to think further, without being hostile or critical (Janssens & Deković, 1997; Walker & Taylor, 1991a).

Preschoolers who verbally and physically assault others, often with little or no provocation, are already delayed in moral reasoning (Helwig & Turiel, 2004). Without special help, such children show long-term disruptions in moral development, deficits in self-control, and ultimately an antisocial lifestyle.

The Other Side of Morality: Development of Aggression

Beginning in late infancy, all children display aggression from time to time, and as opportunities to interact with siblings and peers increase, aggressive outbursts occur more often (Dodge, Coie, & Lynam, 2006; Nærde et al. 2014). By the second year, aggressive acts with two distinct purposes emerge. Initially, the most common is **proactive** (or *instrumental*) **aggression,** in which children act to fulfill a need or desire—to obtain an object, privilege, space, or social reward, such as adult or peer attention—and unemotionally attack a person to achieve their goal. The other type, **reactive** (or *hostile*) **aggression,** is an angry, defensive response to provocation or a blocked goal and is meant to hurt another person (Dodge, Coie, & Lynam, 2006; Vitaro & Brendgen, 2012).

Proactive and reactive aggression come in three forms, which are the focus of most research:

- **Physical aggression** harms others through physical injury—pushing, hitting, kicking, or punching others, or destroying another's property.
- **Verbal aggression** harms others through threats of physical aggression, name-calling, or hostile teasing.

© BOB EBBESEN/ALAMY

These preschoolers display proactive aggression, pushing and grabbing as they argue over a game. Proactive aggression declines with age as children learn to compromise and share, and as their capacity to delay gratification improves.

- **Relational aggression** damages another's peer relationships through social exclusion, malicious gossip, or friendship manipulation.

Although verbal aggression is always direct, physical and relational aggression can be either *direct* or *indirect*. For example, hitting injures a person directly, whereas destroying property indirectly inflicts physical harm. Similarly, saying, "Do what I say, or I won't be your friend," conveys relational aggression directly, while spreading rumors, refusing to talk to a peer, or manipulating friendship by saying behind someone's back, "Don't play with her; she's a nerd," does so indirectly.

In early childhood, verbal aggression gradually replaces physical aggression as language develops and adults and peers react negatively and strongly to physical attacks (Alink et al., 2006; Vitaro & Brendgen, 2012). And proactive aggression declines as preschoolers' improved capacity to delay gratification enables them to resist grabbing others' possessions. But reactive aggression in verbal and relational forms tends to rise over early and middle childhood (Côté et al., 2007; Tremblay, 2000). Older children are better able to recognize malicious intentions and, as a result, more often retaliate in hostile ways.

By age 17 months, boys are more physically aggressive than girls—a difference found throughout childhood in many cultures (Baillargeon et al., 2007; Card et al., 2008; Lussier, Corrado, & Tzoumakis, 2012). The sex difference is due in part to biology—in particular, to male sex hormones (androgens) and temperamental traits (activity level, irritability, impulsivity) on which boys score higher. Gender-role conformity is also important. For example, parents respond far more negatively to physical fighting in girls (Arnold, McWilliams, & Harvey-Arnold, 1998).

Although girls have a reputation for being both verbally and relationally more aggressive than boys, the sex difference is small (Crick, Ostrov, & Werner, 2006; Crick et al., 2006). Beginning in the preschool years, girls concentrate most of their aggressive acts in the relational category. Boys inflict harm in more variable ways. Physically and verbally aggressive boys also tend to be relationally aggressive (Card et al., 2008). Therefore, boys display overall rates of aggression that are much higher than girls'.

At the same time, girls more often use indirect relational tactics that—in disrupting intimate bonds especially important to girls—can be particularly mean. Whereas physical attacks are usually brief, acts of indirect relational aggression may extend for hours, weeks, or even months (Nelson, Robinson, & Hart, 2005; Underwood, 2003). In one instance, a 6-year-old girl formed a "pretty-girls club" and—for nearly an entire school year—convinced its members to exclude several classmates by saying they were "dirty and smelly."

An occasional aggressive exchange between preschoolers is normal. Children sometimes assert their sense of self through these encounters, which become important learning experiences as adults intervene and teach social problem solving (Vaughn et al., 2003). But some children—especially those who are emotionally negative, impulsive, and disobedient—are at risk for early, high rates of physical or relational aggression (or both) that can persist. Persistent aggression, in turn, predicts later internalizing and externalizing difficulties and social skills deficits, including loneliness, anxiety, depression, peer relationship problems, and antisocial activity in middle childhood and adolescence (Côté et al., 2007; Crick, Ostrov, & Werner, 2006; Ostrov et al., 2013).

THE FAMILY AS TRAINING GROUND FOR AGGRESSIVE BEHAVIOR "I can't control him; he's impossible," Robbie's mother, Nadine, complained to Leslie one day. When Leslie asked if Robbie might be troubled by something happening at home, she discovered that his parents fought constantly and resorted to harsh, inconsistent discipline. The same child-rearing practices that undermine moral internalization—love withdrawal, power assertion, physical punishment, negative comments and emotions, and inconsistency—are linked to aggression from early childhood through adolescence, in children of both sexes and in many cultures, with most of these practices predicting both physical and relational forms (Côté et al., 2007; Gershoff et al., 2010; Kuppens et al., 2013; Nelson et al., 2013; Olson et al. 2011).

In families like Robbie's, anger and punitiveness quickly create a conflict-ridden family atmosphere and an "out-of-control" child. The pattern begins with forceful discipline, which occurs more often with stressful life experiences (such as economic hardship or an unhappy marriage), a parent with an unstable personality, or a temperamentally difficult child (Dodge, Coie, & Lynam, 2006). Typically, the parent threatens, criticizes, and punishes, and the child whines, yells, and refuses until the parent "gives in." At the end of each exchange, both parent and child get relief from stopping the unpleasant behavior of the other, so the behaviors repeat and escalate.

As these cycles become more frequent, they generate anxiety and irritability among other family members, who soon join in the hostile interactions. Compared with siblings in typical families, preschool siblings who have critical, punitive parents are more aggressive toward one another. Physically, verbally, and relationally destructive sibling conflict, in turn, quickly spreads to peer relationships, contributing to poor impulse control and antisocial behavior by the early school years (Garcia et al., 2000; Miller et al., 2012; Ostrov, Crick, & Stauffacher, 2006).

Boys are more likely than girls to be targets of harsh, inconsistent discipline because they are more active and impulsive and therefore harder to control. When children who are extreme in these characteristics are exposed to emotionally negative, inept parenting, their capacity for emotional self-regulation, empathic responding, and guilt after transgressions is severely disrupted (Eisenberg, Eggum, & Edwards, 2010). Consequently, they lash out when disappointed, frustrated, or faced with a sad or fearful victim.

SOCIAL INFORMATION-PROCESSING DEFICITS Children who are products of these family processes soon acquire a distorted view of the social world. Those who are high in reactive aggression often see hostile intent where it does not exist—in situations where peers' intentions are unclear, where harm is accidental, and even where peers are trying to be helpful (Lochman & Dodge, 1998; Orobio de Castro et al., 2002). When such children feel threatened (for example, a researcher tells them that a peer they will work with is in a bad mood and might pick a fight), they are especially likely to interpret accidental mishaps as hostile (Williams et al., 2003). As a result, they make many unprovoked attacks, which trigger aggressive retaliations.

Children high in proactive aggression have different deficits in social information processing. Compared with agemates, they believe there are more benefits and fewer costs for engaging in destructive acts (Arsenio, 2010; Dodge et al., 1997). And they are more likely to think that aggression "works," producing material rewards and reducing others' unpleasant behaviors (Arsenio & Lemerise, 2001; Goldstein & Tisak, 2004). Thus, they callously use aggression to advance their own goals and are relatively unconcerned about causing suffering in others—an aggressive style associated with later, more severe conduct problems, violent behavior, and delinquency (Marsee & Frick, 2010).

TAKE A MOMENT... Return to the information-processing model of social problem solving on page 370. Notice how reactive aggression is linked to deficiencies in recognizing and interpreting social cues. In contrast, proactive aggression is associated with deficiencies in formulating social goals (caring more about satisfying one's own needs than getting along with others) and generating and evaluating strategies (engaging in aggression and evaluating it favorably) (Arsenio, 2010). A substantial number of aggressive children engage in both reactive and proactive acts, while others largely display one type (Fite et al., 2008).

Highly aggressive children tend to be rejected by peers, to fail in school, and (by adolescence) to seek out deviant peers. Together, these factors contribute to the long-term stability of aggression. We will consider this life-course path of antisocial activity in Chapter 16.

MEDIA AND AGGRESSION In the United States, 57 percent of TV programs between 6 A.M. and 11 P.M. contain violent scenes, often portraying repeated aggressive acts that go unpunished. TV victims of violence are rarely shown experiencing serious harm, and few programs condemn violence or depict other ways of solving problems (Center for Communication and Social Policy, 1998). Verbally and relationally aggressive acts are particularly frequent in reality

TV violence increases the likelihood of hostile thoughts and emotions and tolerance of real-world aggression. Playing violent video and computer games has similar effects.

TV shows (Coyne, Robinson, & Nelson, 2010). And violent content is 9 percent above average in children's programming, with cartoons being the most violent.

Reviewers of thousands of studies—using a wide variety of research designs, methods, and participants from diverse cultures—have concluded that TV violence increases the likelihood of hostile thoughts and emotions and of verbally, physically, and relationally aggressive behavior (Bushman & Huesmann, 2012; Comstock & Scharrer, 2006). A growing number of studies show that playing violent video and computer games has similar effects (Anderson et al., 2010; Hofferth, 2010). Although young people of all ages are susceptible, preschool and young school-age children are especially likely to imitate TV violence because they believe that much TV fiction is real and accept what they see uncritically.

Violent programming not only creates short-term difficulties in parent and peer relations but also has lasting negative consequences. In several longitudinal studies, time spent watching TV in childhood and adolescence predicted aggressive behavior in early adulthood, after other factors linked to TV viewing (such as prior child and parent aggression, IQ, parent education, family income, and neighborhood crime) were controlled (see Figure 10.4) (Graber et al., 2006; Huesmann et al., 2003; Johnson et al., 2002). Aggressive children and adolescents have a greater appetite for violent media fare. And boys devote more time to violent media than girls, in part because of male-oriented themes of conquest and adventure and use of males as lead characters. But even in nonaggressive children, violent TV sparks hostile thoughts and behavior; its impact is simply less intense.

Furthermore, media violence "hardens" children to aggression, making them more willing to tolerate it in others (Anderson et al., 2003, 2010). Viewers quickly habituate, responding with reduced arousal and greater acceptance when exposed to real-world instances.

Preschoolers, as we saw in Chapter 9, spend much time watching educational programs for young children. Although beneficial for cognitive and academic progress, high exposure to educational programs is associated with a rise in relational aggression in young children (Ostrov, Gentile, & Mullins, 2013). The likely reason is that these programs often present social-conflict scenes, in a well-intentioned effort to model social problem solving. But preschoolers have difficulty connecting characters' relational conflicts to their eventual favorable resolutions, so they readily imitate the relationally aggressive acts they see. When brief explanations are inserted, alerting young viewers to an educational program's prosocial message, they more often respond as intended (Mares & Acosta, 2010).

The ease with which screen media can manipulate children's beliefs and behavior has led to strong public pressure to improve its content. In Canada, a nationwide broadcasting code bans from children's shows realistic scenes of violence that minimize consequences and cartoons with violence as the central theme. Further, violent programming intended for adults cannot be shown on Canadian channels before 9 P.M. In the United States, however, the First Amendment right to free speech has hampered efforts to regulate TV broadcasting (and many Canadian children have access to violent TV fare on U.S. channels).

As a result, parents bear most responsibility for regulating their children's exposure to media violence and other inappropriate content. In the United States, TV programs are rated for violent and sexual content, and since 2000 new TV sets have been required to contain the V-chip, which allows parents to block undesired material. And parents can control children's Internet access by using filters or programs that monitor website visits.

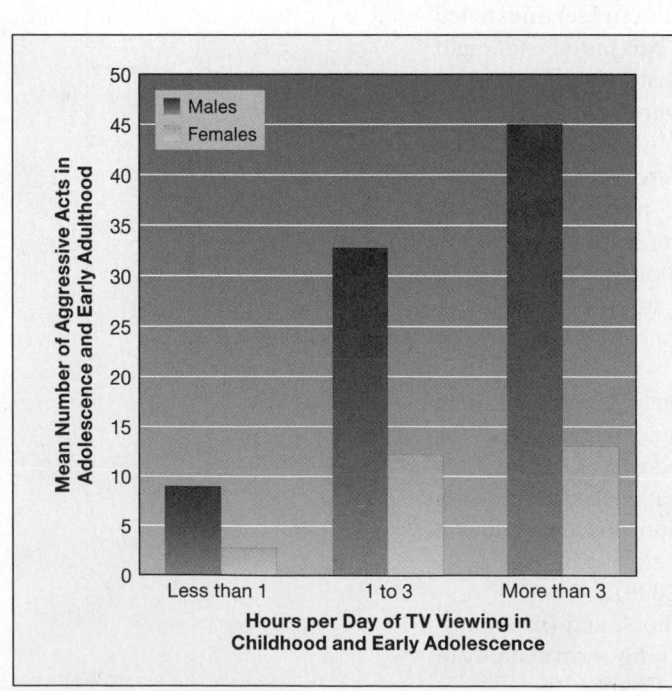

FIGURE 10.4 **Relationship of television viewing in childhood and early adolescence to aggressive acts in adolescence and early adulthood.** Interviews with more than 700 parents and youths revealed that the more TV watched in childhood and early adolescence, the greater the annual number of aggressive acts committed by the young person, as reported in follow-up interviews at ages 16 and 22. (Based on Johnson et al., 2002.)

Applying What We Know

Regulating Screen Media Use

STRATEGY	EXPLANATION
Limit TV viewing and computer and tablet use.	Parents should provide clear rules limiting children's TV viewing and computer and tablet use and should stick to the rules. The TV or computer should not be used as a babysitter. Placing a TV or a computer in a child's bedroom substantially increases use and makes the child's activity hard to monitor.
Avoid using screen media as a reward.	When media access is used as a reward or withheld as punishment, children become increasingly attracted to it.
When possible, watch TV and view online content with children, helping them understand what they see.	By raising questions about realism in media depictions, expressing disapproval of on-screen behavior, and encouraging discussion, adults help children understand and critically evaluate TV and online content.
Link TV and online content to everyday learning experiences.	Parents can extend TV and online learning in ways that encourage children to engage actively with their surroundings. For example, a program on animals might spark a trip to the zoo, a visit to the library for books about animals, or new ways of observing and caring for the family pet.
Model good media practices.	Parents' media behavior influences children's behavior. Parents should avoid excessive TV and computer use, limit their own exposure to harmful media content, and limit mobile device use during family interactions.
Use a warm, rational approach to child rearing.	Children of warm parents who make reasonable demands for mature behavior prefer media experiences with educational and prosocial content and are less attracted to violent programming.

Yet surveys of U.S. parents indicate that 20 to 30 percent of preschoolers and 40 percent of school-age children experience no limits on TV or computer use at home. Some children begin visiting websites without parental supervision as early as age 4 (Rideout & Hamel, 2006; Roberts, Foehr, & Rideout, 2005; Varnhagen, 2007). Also, parents often model excessive, inappropriate screen media use. In a naturalistic study of adults with children in fast food restaurants, almost one-third of the adults spent the entire meal absorbed with mobile devices instead of engaging with the children in their care (Radesky et al., 2014).

To help parents improve their children's "media diet," one group of researchers devised a 12-month intervention in which they guided parents in replacing violent programs with age-appropriate prosocial programs. Compared to a control group, children in intervention families displayed lower rates of externalizing behavior and improved social competence (Christakis et al., 2013). Applying What We Know above lists strategies parents can use to regulate children's screen media use.

HELPING CHILDREN AND PARENTS CONTROL AGGRESSION Treatment for aggressive children must begin early, before their antisocial behavior becomes well-practiced and difficult to change. Breaking the cycle of hostilities between family members and promoting effective ways of relating to others is crucial. The coercive cycles of punitive parents and aggressive children are so persistent that these children often are punished when they do behave appropriately!

Leslie suggested that Robbie's parents see a family therapist, who observed their ineffective practices and coached them in alternatives. They learned not to give in to Robbie, to pair commands with reasons, and to replace verbal insults and spankings with more effective punishments, such as time out and withdrawal of privileges. The therapist also encouraged Robbie's parents to be warmer and to give him attention and approval for prosocial acts. Finally, she helped them with their marital problems. This, in addition to their improved ability to manage Robbie's behavior, greatly reduced tension and conflict in the household.

Parent training programs based on social learning theory have been devised to improve parenting in families like Robbie's. In one highly effective approach called *Incredible Years*, parents complete 18 weekly group sessions facilitated by two professionals, who teach parenting techniques for promoting children's academic, emotional, and social skills and for managing disruptive behaviors. Sessions include coaching, modeling, and practicing effective

LOOK and LISTEN

Watch a half-hour of children's cartoons and a prime-time movie on TV, and tally the number of violent acts, including those that go unpunished. How often did violence occur in each type of program? What do young viewers learn about the consequences of violence?

parenting behaviors—experiences aimed at interrupting parent–child destructive interaction while promoting positive relationships and competencies (Webster-Stratton & Reid, 2010). A special focus is positive parenting, including attention, encouragement, and praise for pro-social behaviors.

Evaluations in which families with aggressive children were randomly assigned to either Incredible Years or control groups reveal that the program is highly effective at improving parenting and reducing child behavior problems. And the effects endure. In one 8- to 12- year follow-up, 75 percent of young children with serious conduct problems whose parents participated in Incredible Years were well-adjusted as teenagers (Webster-Stratton, Rinaldi, & Reid, 2011).

At preschool, Leslie began teaching Robbie more successful ways of relating to peers, had him practice these skills, and praised him for using them. As opportunities arose, she encouraged Robbie to talk about a playmate's feelings and to express his own. As he increasingly took the perspective of others, empathized, and felt sympathetic concern, his lashing out at peers declined (Izard et al., 2008). Robbie participated in a social problem-solving intervention as well (return to pages 370–371 to review).

Finally, relieving stressors that stem from poverty and neighborhood disorganization and providing families with social supports help prevent childhood aggression (Boyle & Lipman, 2002; Bugental, Corpuz, & Schwartz, 2012). When parents better cope with difficulties in their own lives, interventions aimed at reducing children's aggression are even more effective.

Ask Yourself

- **REVIEW** What experiences help preschoolers differentiate moral imperatives, social conventions, and matters of personal choice?

- **CONNECT** What must parents do to foster conscience development in fearless, impulsive children? How does this illustrate the concept of goodness of fit (see pages 259–260 in Chapter 7)?

- **APPLY** Alice and Wayne want their two young children to become morally mature, caring individuals. List some parenting practices they should use and some they should avoid.

- **REFLECT** Which types of punishment for a misbehaving preschooler do you endorse, and which types do you reject? Why?

10.7 Discuss biological and environmental influences on preschoolers' gender-stereotyped beliefs and behavior.

10.8 Describe and evaluate major theories that explain the emergence of gender identity.

Gender Typing

Gender typing refers to any association of objects, activities, roles, or traits with one sex or the other in ways that conform to cultural stereotypes (Blakemore, Berenbaum, & Liben, 2009). In Leslie's classroom, girls spent more time in the housekeeping, art, and reading corners, while boys gathered more often in spaces devoted to blocks, woodworking, and active play. Already, the children had acquired many gender-linked beliefs and preferences and tended to play with peers of their own sex.

The same theories that provide accounts of morality have been used to explain children's gender typing: *social learning theory,* with its emphasis on modeling and reinforcement, and *cognitive-developmental theory,* with its focus on children as active thinkers about their social world. As we will see, neither is adequate by itself. *Gender schema theory,* a third perspective that combines elements of both, has gained favor. In the following sections, we consider the early development of gender typing.

Gender-Stereotyped Beliefs and Behaviors

Even before children can label their own sex consistently, they have begun to acquire subtle associations with gender that most of us hold—men as rough and sharp, women as soft and round. In one study, 18-month-olds linked such items as fir trees and hammers with males, although they had not yet learned comparable feminine associations (Eichstedt et al., 2002). Recall from Chapter 7 that around age 2, children use such words as *boy, girl, lady,* and *man* appropriately. As soon as gender categories are established, children sort out what they mean in terms of activities and behaviors.

Preschoolers associate toys, clothing, tools, household items, games, occupations, colors (pink and blue), and behaviors (physical and relational aggression) with one sex or the other (Banse et al., 2010; Giles & Heyman, 2005; Poulin-Dubois et al., 2002). And their actions reflect their beliefs, not only in play preferences but in personality traits as well. As we have seen, boys tend to be more active, impulsive, assertive, and physically aggressive. Girls tend to be more fearful, dependent, emotionally sensitive, compliant, advanced in effortful control, and skilled at understanding self-conscious emotions and at inflicting indirect relational aggression (Bosacki & Moore, 2004; Else-Quest, 2012; Underwood, 2003).

Gender typing is well under way in the preschool years. Girls tend to play with girls and are drawn to toys and activities that emphasize nurturance, cooperation, and physical attractiveness.

Between ages 3 and 4, gender-stereotyped beliefs strengthen—so much so that many children apply them as blanket rules rather than flexible guidelines (Halim, Ruble, & Tamis-LeMonda, 2013). When children were asked whether gender stereotypes could be violated, half or more of 3- and 4-year-olds answered "no" to clothing, hairstyle, certain play styles (girls playing roughly), and play with certain toys (Barbie dolls and G.I. Joes) (Blakemore, 2003). Furthermore, most 3- to 6-year-olds are firm about not wanting to be friends with a child who violates a gender stereotype (a boy who wears nail polish, a girl who plays with trucks) or to attend a school where such violations are allowed (Ruble et al., 2007).

The rigidity of preschoolers' gender stereotypes helps us understand some commonly observed everyday behaviors. When Leslie showed her class a picture of a Scottish bagpiper wearing a kilt, the children insisted, "Men don't wear skirts!" During free play, they often exclaimed that girls can't be police officers and boys don't take care of babies. These one-sided judgments are a joint product of gender stereotyping in the environment and young children's cognitive limitations—in particular, their difficulty coordinating conflicting sources of information (Trautner et al., 2005). Most preschoolers do not yet realize that characteristics *associated with* one's sex—activities, toys, occupations, hairstyle, and clothing—do not *determine* whether a person is male or female. They have trouble understanding that males and females can be different in terms of their bodies but similar in many other ways.

Biological Influences on Gender Typing

The sex differences in play and personality traits just described appear in many cultures around the world (Munroe & Romney, 2006; Whiting & Edwards, 1988). Certain ones—male activity level and physical aggression, female emotional sensitivity, and a preference for same-sex playmates—are widespread among mammalian species (de Waal, 1993, 2001). According to an evolutionary perspective, the adult life of our male ancestors was oriented toward competing for mates, that of our female ancestors toward rearing children. Therefore, males became genetically primed for dominance and females for intimacy, responsiveness, and cooperativeness. Evolutionary theorists claim that family and cultural forces can influence the intensity of genetically based sex differences, leading some individuals to be more gender-typed than others. But experience cannot eradicate those aspects of gender typing that served adaptive functions in human history (Konner, 2010; Maccoby, 2002).

Experiments with animals reveal that prenatally administered androgens increase active play and suppress maternal caregiving in both male and female mammals (Sato et al., 2004). Research with humans reveals similar patterns. Girls exposed prenatally to high levels of androgens (due to normal variation in hormone levels or to a genetic defect) show more "masculine" behaviors—a preference for trucks and blocks over dolls, for active over quiet play, and for boys as playmates—even when their parents encourage them to engage in gender-typical play (Berenbaum & Beltz, 2011; Cohen-Bendahan, van de Beek, & Berenbaum, 2005). Maternal stress during pregnancy—such as unemployment, divorce, or death of a close relative—may influence prenatal hormones, and it has been linked to "masculine" behaviors among preschool girls (Barrett et al., 2014). Similarly, boys with reduced prenatal androgen exposure (due to hereditary defects or maternal contact with industrial chemicals that interfere with androgen production) tend to engage in "feminine" behaviors, including toy choices, play behaviors, and preference for girl playmates (Jürgensen et al., 2007; Swan et al., 2010).

Eleanor Maccoby (1998) argues that biologically based sex differences, which affect children's play styles, lead children to choose same-sex playmates whose interests and behaviors are compatible with their own. Preschool girls like to play in pairs with other girls because they share a preference for quieter activities involving cooperative roles. Boys prefer larger-group play with other boys, who desire to run, climb, play-fight, compete, and build up and knock down (Fabes, Martin, & Hanish, 2003). At age 4, children spend three times as much time with same-sex as with other-sex playmates. By age 6, this ratio has climbed to 11 to 1 (Martin & Fabes, 2001).

Environmental Influences on Gender Typing

In a study following almost 14,000 British children from ages 2½ to 13, gender-typed behavior rose steadily over early childhood and persisted into early adolescence, with the most gender-typed young preschoolers showing the sharpest increase (Golombok et al., 2008; 2012). A wealth of evidence reveals that environmental forces—at home, at school, and in the community—build on genetic influences to promote vigorous gender typing in early childhood.

THE FAMILY Beginning at birth, parents have different expectations of sons than of daughters (see Chapter 7). Many parents prefer that their children play with "gender-appropriate" toys (Blakemore & Hill, 2008). They tend to describe achievement, competition, and control of emotion as important for sons and warmth, polite behavior, and closely supervised activities as important for daughters (Brody, 1999; Turner & Gervai, 1995).

Actual parenting practices reflect these beliefs. Parents give their sons toys that stress action and competition (guns, cars, tools, and footballs) and their daughters toys that emphasize nurturance, cooperation, and physical attractiveness (dolls, tea sets, and jewelry) (Leaper, 1994; Leaper & Friedman, 2007). Fathers of preschoolers report more physical interactions—chasing, playing ball, playing outdoors—with sons, and more literacy activities—singing, reading, storytelling—with daughters (Leavell et al., 2011). Parents also tend to react more positively when a son plays with cars and trucks, demands attention, runs and climbs, or tries to take toys from others. When interacting with daughters, they more often direct play activities, provide help, encourage participation in household tasks, make supportive statements (approval, praise, and agreement), and refer to emotions (Clearfield & Nelson, 2006; Fagot & Hagan, 1991; Leaper, 2000). For example, when playing housekeeping, mothers engage in high rates of supportive emotion talk with girls.

As these findings suggest, language is a powerful indirect means for teaching children about gender stereotypes. Earlier we saw that most young children hold rigid beliefs about gender. Although their strict views are due in part to cognitive limitations, they also draw on relevant social experiences to construct these beliefs. Even parents who believe strongly in gender equality unconsciously use language that highlights gender

CAVAN IMAGES/GETTY IMAGES

Of the two sexes, boys are more gender-typed. Fathers, especially, promote "masculine" behavior in their preschool sons through activities that stress action and competition.

distinctions and informs children about traditional gender roles (see the Social Issues box on pages 388–389).

Of the two sexes, boys are more gender-typed. Fathers, especially, tend to insist that boys conform to gender roles. They place more pressure to achieve on sons than on daughters and are less tolerant of "cross-gender" behavior in sons—more concerned when a boy acts like a "sissy" than when a girl acts like a "tomboy" (Blakemore & Hill, 2008; Wood, Desmarais, & Gugula, 2002). Yet some parents have more flexible views. Recognizing the negative effects of restrictive norms for males, they want their sons to be comfortable expressing feelings. As one father explained: "I'm more reserved than my wife emotionally. I realize that it is better to have our son be more open emotionally. . . . So, that's a challenge. You want him to open up, and you have to do the same thing. I'm not used to doing that" (Parker et al., 2012, p. 61).

Parents who hold nonstereotyped values and behave accordingly have children who are less gender-typed (Brody, 1997; Tenenbaum & Leaper, 2002). Young children with gay or lesbian parents are less gender-typed than agemates with heterosexual parents, perhaps because of their parents' more egalitarian gender norms (Fulcher, Sutfin, & Patterson, 2008; Goldberg, Kashy, & Smith, 2012).

Other family members may also reduce gender typing. For example, children with older, other-sex siblings have many more opportunities to imitate and participate in "cross-gender" activities and, as a result, are less gender-typed in play preferences, attitudes, and personality traits (McHale et al., 2001; Rust et al., 2000).

TEACHERS   Teachers often act in ways that extend gender-role learning. Several times, Leslie caught herself emphasizing gender distinctions when she called out, "Will the girls line up on one side and the boys on the other?" or pleaded "Boys, I wish you'd quiet down like the girls!"

Like parents, preschool teachers encourage girls to participate in adult-structured activities. Girls frequently cluster around the teacher, following directions, while boys are attracted to play areas where adults are minimally involved (Campbell, Shirley, & Candy, 2004). As a result, boys and girls engage in different social behaviors. Compliance and bids for help occur more often in adult-structured contexts; assertiveness, leadership, and creative use of materials in unstructured pursuits.

As early as kindergarten, teachers give more overall attention (both positive and negative) to boys than to girls—a difference evident in diverse countries, including China, England, and the United States. They praise boys more for their academic knowledge but also use more disapproval and controlling discipline with them (Chen & Rao, 2011; Davies, 2008; Swinson & Harrop, 2009). Teachers seem to expect boys to misbehave more often—a belief based partly on boys' actual behavior and partly on gender stereotypes.

PEERS   Children's same-sex peer associations make the peer context an especially potent source of gender-role learning. The more preschoolers play with same-sex partners, the more their behavior becomes gender-typed—in toy choices, activity level, aggression, and adult involvement (Martin et al., 2011, 2013).

By age 3, same-sex peers positively reinforce one another for gender-typed play by praising, imitating, or joining in. In contrast, when preschoolers engage in "cross-gender" activities—for example, when boys play with dolls or girls with cars and trucks—peers criticize them. Boys are especially intolerant of cross-gender play in other boys (Thorne, 1993). A boy who frequently crosses gender lines is likely to be ignored by other boys, even when he does engage in "masculine" activities!

Children also develop different styles of social influence in gender-segregated peer groups. To get their way in large-group play, boys often rely on commands, threats, and physical force. Girls' preference for playing in pairs leads to greater concern with a partner's needs, evident in girls' use of polite requests, persuasion, and acceptance. When girls communicate assertively with commands, other girls tend to respond with aggression (Hanish et al., 2012).

LOOK and LISTEN

While observing 3- to 5-year-olds during a free-play period in a preschool or child-care program, note the extent of gender segregation and gender-typed play. Did styles of social influence differ in boys' and girls' gender-segregated groups? Jot down examples.

© ELLEN B. SENISI

© LAURA DWIGHT PHOTOGRAPHY

Children develop different styles of interaction in gender-segregated play. Boys more often use commands and physical force to get their way. Girls, out of greater concern for their playmate's feelings, rely on polite requests and persuasion.

Social Issues: Education

Children Learn About Gender Through Mother–Child Conversations

In an investigation of the power of language to shape children's beliefs and expectations about gender, mothers were asked to converse with their 2- to 6-year-olds about picture books containing images of male and female children and adults engaged in various activities, half consistent and half inconsistent with gender stereotypes. Each picture was accompanied by the question, "Who can X?" where X was the activity on the page.

One mother, who believed in gender equality, turned to a picture of a boy driving a boat and asked, "Who's driving the boat?"

Her 4-year-old son replied, "A sail-man."

The mother affirmed, "A sail-man. Yup, a sailor." Then she asked, "Who can be a sailor? Boys and girls?"

"Boys," the child replied.

"Boys . . . OK," the mother again affirmed. The child stated more decisively, "Only boys."

Again the mother agreed, "Only boys," and turned the page (Gelman, Taylor, & Nguyen, 2004, p. 104).

A detailed analysis of picture-book conversations revealed that mothers' directly expressed attitudes about gender stereotypes were neutral, largely because, like this mother, they typically posed questions to their children. But by age 4,

children often voiced stereotypes, and—nearly one-third of the time—mothers affirmed them! Some mothers either moved on with the conversation or repeated the question, as in the conversation above, but rarely—just 2 percent of the time—did they explicitly counter a child's stereotype, and usually only when the book itself included stereotype-inconsistent pictures.

Although the researchers did not ask mothers to discuss gender, the mothers called attention to it even when they did not need to do so. In the English language, many nouns referring to people convey age-related information (*kid, baby, 2-year-old, preschooler, teenager, grownup, senior*), whereas only a few encode gender (*male, female, sister, brother, aunt, uncle*). Yet when using a noun to refer to a person, mothers explicitly called attention to gender more than half the time, even though the people shown in the books varied as much in age (children versus adults) as in gender. Mothers labeled gender, either with nouns or with pronouns (which in English always refer to gender), especially often when conversing with 2-year-olds: "Is that a he or a she?" "That's a boy." "There's a girl." Such statements encourage toddlers to sort their social world into gender categories, even when the statements themselves do not explicitly convey stereotypes.

While reading, this mother may unconsciously teach her child to see the world in gender-linked terms—by referring to gender unnecessarily or by making generic gender statements ("Most girls prefer X"; "Boys usually don't like X").

Furthermore, both mothers and children frequently expressed *generic utterances*—ones that were broad in scope, referring to many, or nearly all, males and females: "Boys can be

---

LOOK and LISTEN

Observe a parent discussing a picture book with a 3- to 6-year-old. How many times did the parent make generic statements about gender? How about the child? Did the parent accept or correct the child's generic utterances?

Girls soon find that gentle tactics succeed with other girls but not with boys, who ignore their courteous overtures (Leaper, 1994). Boys' unresponsiveness gives girls another reason to stop interacting with them.

Over time, children come to believe in the "correctness" of gender-segregated play and to perceive themselves as more similar to same-sex than other-sex peers, which further strengthen gender segregation and gender-stereotyped activities (Martin et al., 1999, 2011). As boys and girls separate, *in-group favoritism*—more positive evaluations of members of one's own gender—becomes another factor that sustains the separate social worlds of boys and girls, resulting in "two distinct subcultures" of shared knowledge, beliefs, interests, and behaviors (Maccoby, 2002; Ruble, Martin, & Berenbaum, 2006).

THE BROADER SOCIAL ENVIRONMENT Although children's everyday environments have changed to some degree, they continue to present many examples of gender typing—in occupations, leisure activities, media portrayals, and achievements of men and women. For example, although today's TV programs include more career-oriented women than in the past, female characters continue to be young, attractive, caring, emotional, and victimized and to be seen in romantic and family contexts. In contrast, male characters are usually dominant and powerful. Stereotypes are especially prevalent in cartoons and computer games. These media depictions contribute to young children's biased beliefs about roles and behaviors suitable for males and females (Halim, Ruble, & Tamis-LeMonda, 2013; Leaper, 2013).

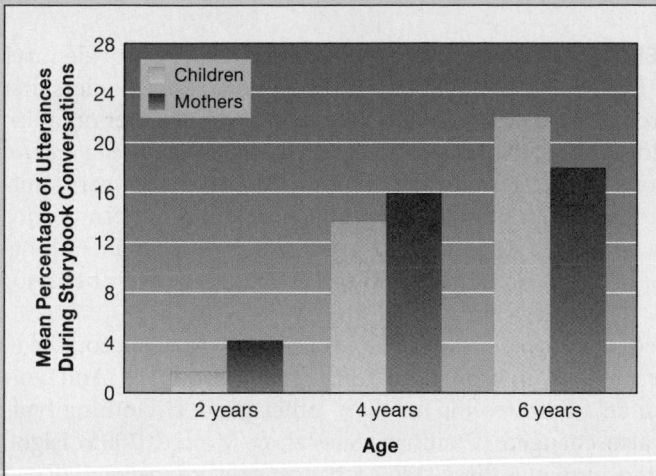

FIGURE 10.5 Mothers' and children's use of generic references to gender during storybook conversations. Generic utterances were broad in scope, in that they referred to many, or nearly all, males and females. Mothers' and children's use of generics increased dramatically between ages 2 and 6. At age 2, mothers produced more generics than children. By age 6, children produced more generics than mothers. (From S. A. Gelman, M. G. Taylor, & S. P. Nguyen, "Mother–Child Conversations About Gender," *Monographs of the Society for Research in Child Development, 69*[1, Serial No. 275], p. 46. © 2004 The Society for Research in Child Development, Inc. Republished with permission of John Wiley and Sons, Inc., conveyed through Copyright Clearance Center, Inc.)

sailors." "Most girls don't like trucks." Even generics that were gender-neutral ("Lots of girls in this book") or denied a stereotype ("Boys can be ballet dancers, too") prompted children to view individuals of the same gender as alike and to ignore exceptions. As we will see later in this chapter, generics promote gender-role conformity. Statements such as "This toy is for girls" induce children to prefer the toy labeled for their own sex and to avoid the toy labeled for the other sex.

Mothers' and children's use of generics increased sharply between ages 2 and 6, a period in which gender stereotyping and gender-role conformity rise dramatically (See Figure 10.5). Initially, mothers led the way in generic talk; at age 2 they introduced these category-wide generalizations nearly three times as often as children. By age 6, however, children were producing generics more often than mothers. In addition, mother–child pairs produced more generics about males than about females, and generics were especially common in speech to and from boys, who are the more gender typed of the two sexes.

Even though these mothers overwhelmingly believed in gender equality, they did little to instill those ideas in their children. To the contrary, their most common response to children's stereotypical comments was to affirm them! In this way, even without directly teaching stereotypes, parents—through language—provide a wealth of implicit cues that enable children to readily construct them.

Adults can combat stereotypical thinking in children through concerted efforts to avoid gendered language. Here are some suggestions:

- Refrain from labeling gender when it is unnecessary, substituting *child, friend, adult,* or *person,* for *boy, girl, man,* or *woman.*
- Substitute references to individuals ("That person wants to be a firefighter") for generic expressions, or use qualifiers ("Some boys and some girls want to be firefighters"). Experimental research confirms that generic statements strongly induce in preschoolers social biases of all kinds—gender, ethnic, and racial (Rhodes, Leslie, & Tworek, 2012).
- Monitor your own inclination to affirm children's stereotypical claims, countering these as often as possible.
- Discuss gender biases in language with children, pointing out how words can shape inappropriate beliefs and expectations and asking children to avoid using gender labels and generics.

As we will see next, children do more than imitate the many gender-linked responses they observe. They soon come to view not just their social surroundings but also themselves through a "gender-biased lens"—a perspective that can seriously restrict their interests and learning opportunities.

Gender Identity

As adults, each of us has a **gender identity**—an image of oneself as relatively masculine or feminine in characteristics. By middle childhood, researchers can measure gender identity by asking children to rate themselves on personality traits. A child or adult with a "masculine" identity scores high on traditionally masculine items (such as *ambitious, competitive,* and *self-sufficient*) and low on traditionally feminine items (such as *affectionate, cheerful,* and *soft-spoken*). Someone with a "feminine" identity does the reverse. And a substantial minority (especially females) have a gender identity called **androgyny,** scoring high on both masculine and feminine personality characteristics.

Gender identity is a good predictor of psychological adjustment. "Masculine" and androgynous children and adults have higher self-esteem than "feminine" individuals, perhaps because many typically feminine traits are not highly valued by society (DiDonato & Berenbaum, 2011; Harter, 2012a). Also, androgynous individuals are more adaptable—able to show masculine independence or feminine sensitivity, depending on the situation (Huyck, 1996; Taylor &

Hall, 1982). The existence of an androgynous identity demonstrates that children can acquire a mixture of positive qualities traditionally associated with each gender—an orientation that may best help them realize their potential.

EMERGENCE OF GENDER IDENTITY   How do children develop a gender identity? According to *social learning theory,* behavior comes before self-perceptions. Preschoolers first acquire gender-typed responses through modeling and reinforcement and only later organize these behaviors into gender-linked ideas about themselves. In contrast, *cognitive-developmental theory* maintains that self-perceptions come before behavior. Over the preschool years, children acquire **gender constancy**—a full understanding of the biologically based permanence of their gender, including the realization that sex remains the same over time, even if clothing, hairstyle, and play activities change. Then children use this knowledge to guide their behavior (Kohlberg, 1966).

When 3- to 5-year-olds are asked such questions as "When you (a girl) grow up, could you ever be a daddy?" or "Could you be a boy if you wanted to?" they freely answer yes. And children younger than age 6 who watch an adult dressing a doll in "other-gender" clothing typically insist that the doll's sex has also changed (Chauhan, Shastri, & Mohite, 2005; Fagot, 1985). Mastery of gender constancy occurs in a three-step sequence: *gender labeling* (correct naming of one's own and others' sex), *gender stability* (understanding that gender remains the same over time), and *gender consistency* (realization that gender is not altered by superficial changes in clothing or activities). Full attainment of gender constancy is strongly related to ability to pass Piagetian conservation and verbal appearance–reality tasks (see page 314 in Chapter 9) (De Lisi & Gallagher, 1991; Trautner, Gervai, & Nemeth, 2003). Indeed, gender constancy tasks can be considered a type of appearance–reality problem, in that children must distinguish what a person looks like from who he or she really is.

Is cognitive-developmental theory correct that gender constancy is responsible for children's gender-typed behavior? Evidence for this assumption is weak. Although outcomes are not entirely consistent, some evidence suggests that gender constancy actually contributes to the emergence of more flexible gender-role attitudes during the school years (Ruble et al., 2007). But overall, the impact of gender constancy on gender typing is not great. As research in the following section reveals, gender-role adoption is more powerfully affected by children's beliefs about how close the connection must be between their own gender and their behavior.

GENDER SCHEMA THEORY   **Gender schema theory** is an information-processing approach to gender typing that combines social learning and cognitive-developmental features. It explains how environmental pressures and children's cognitions work together to shape gender-role development (Martin & Halverson, 1987; Martin, Ruble, & Szkrybalo, 2002). Young children pick up gender-stereotyped preferences and behaviors from others. At the same time, they organize their experiences into *gender schemas,* or masculine and feminine categories, that they use to interpret their world. As soon as preschoolers can label their own gender, they select gender schemas consistent with it ("Only boys can be doctors" or "Cooking is a girl's job") and apply those categories to themselves.

We have seen that individual differences exist in the extent to which children endorse gender-typed views. Figure 10.6 shows different cognitive pathways for children who often apply gender schemas to their experiences and those who rarely do (Liben & Bigler, 2002). Consider Billy, who encounters a doll. If Billy is a *gender-schematic child,* his *gender-salience filter* immediately makes gender highly relevant. Drawing on his prior learning, he asks himself, "Should boys play with dolls?" If he answers "yes" and the toy interests him, he will approach it, explore it, and learn more about it. If he answers "no," he will respond by avoiding the "gender-inappropriate" toy. But if Billy is a *gender-aschematic child*—one who seldom views the world in gender-linked terms—he simply asks himself, "Do I like this toy?" and responds on the basis of his interests.

To examine the consequences of gender-schematic processing, researchers showed 4- and 5-year-olds gender-neutral toys that varied in attractiveness. An adult labeled some as boys' toys and others as girls' toys, leaving a third group unlabeled. Most children engaged

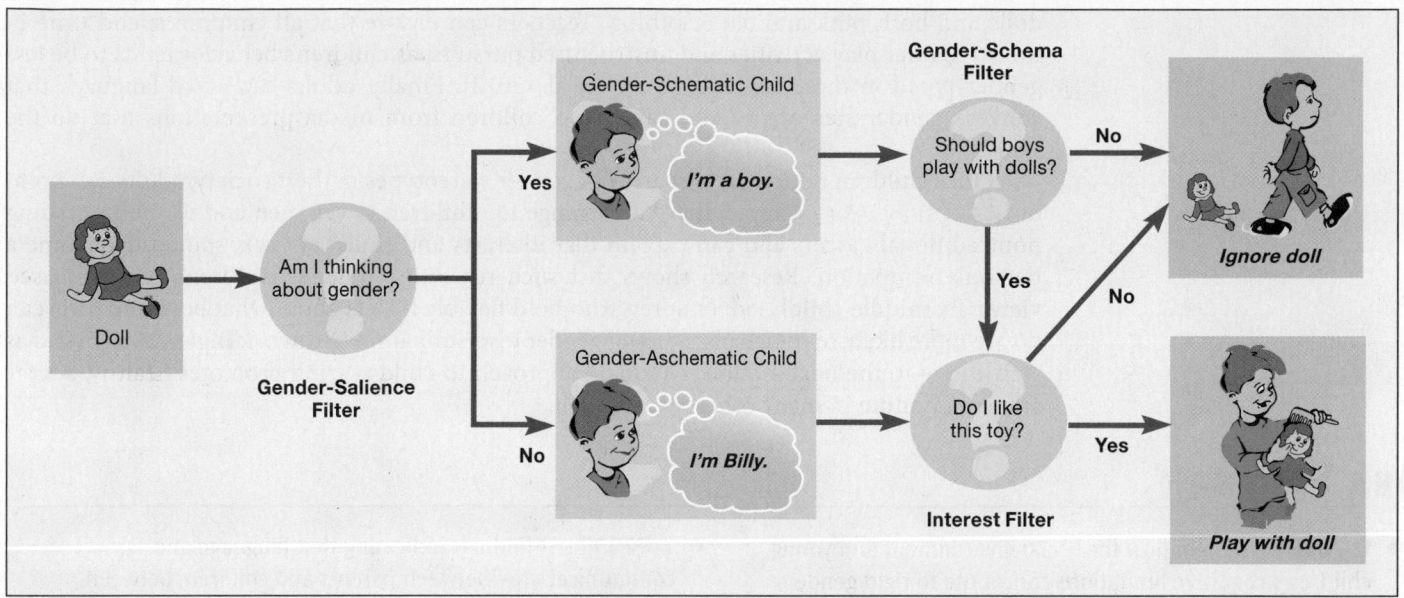

FIGURE 10.6 Cognitive pathways for gender-schematic and gender-aschematic children. In *gender-schematic children,* the gender-salience filter immediately makes gender highly relevant: Billy sees a doll and thinks, "I'm a boy. Should boys play with dolls?" Drawing on his experiences, he answers "yes" or "no." If he answers "yes" and the doll interests him, he plays with the doll. If he answers "no," he avoids the "gender-inappropriate" toy. *Gender-aschematic children* rarely view the world in gender-linked terms. Billy simply asks, "Do I like this toy?" and responds on the basis of his interests. (Reprinted by permission of Rebecca Bigler.)

in gender-schematic reasoning, preferring toys labeled for their gender and predicting that same-sex peers would also like those toys (Martin, Eisenbud, & Rose, 1995). Highly attractive toys, especially, lost their appeal when they were labeled as for the other gender.

Gender-schematic thinking is so powerful that when children see others behaving in "gender-inconsistent" ways, they often distort their memory to make it "gender-consistent." For example, when shown a picture of a male nurse, they may remember him as a doctor (Martin & Ruble, 2004). And, because gender-schematic preschoolers typically conclude, "What I like, children of my own sex will also like," they often use their own preferences to add to their gender biases (Liben & Bigler, 2002). For example, a girl who dislikes oysters may declare, "Only boys like oysters!" even though she has never actually been given information supporting such a stereotype. At least partly for this reason, young children's gender schemas contain both culturally standard and nonstandard ideas (Tenenbaum et al., 2010). Not until well into the school years do children's gender schemas fully resemble those of adults.

Reducing Gender Stereotyping in Young Children

How can we help young children avoid rigid gender schemas that restrict their behavior and learning opportunities? No easy recipe exists. Biology clearly affects children's gender typing, channeling boys, on average, toward active, competitive play and girls toward quieter, more intimate interaction. But most aspects of gender typing are not built into human nature (Ruble, Martin, & Berenbaum, 2006).

Because young children's cognitive limitations lead them to assume that cultural practices determine gender, parents and teachers are wise to delay preschoolers' exposure to gender-stereotyped messages. Adults can begin by limiting traditional gender roles in their own behavior and provide children with nontraditional alternatives. For example, parents can take turns making dinner, bathing children, and driving the family car, and they can give their sons and daughters both trucks and

Parents and teachers can reduce preschoolers' gender stereotyping by modeling nonstereotyped behaviors and providing nontraditional alternatives. For this boy, making cookies is not "for girls." It's an activity he and his mother enjoy together.

dolls and both pink and blue clothing. Teachers can ensure that all children spend time in mixed-gender play activities and unstructured pursuits, as children's behavior tends to be less gender-typed in these contexts (Goble et al., 2012). Finally, adults can avoid language that conveys gender stereotypes and can shield children from media presentations that do the same.

Once children notice the vast array of gender stereotypes in their society, adults can point out exceptions. For example, they can arrange for children to see men and women pursuing nontraditional careers and can explain that interests and skills, not sex, should determine a person's occupation. Research shows that such reasoning reduces children's gender-biased views. By middle childhood, children who hold flexible beliefs about what boys and girls can do are more likely to notice instances of gender discrimination (Brown & Bigler, 2004). And as we will see in the next section, a rational approach to child rearing promotes healthy, adaptable functioning in many other areas as well.

Ask Yourself

- **REVIEW** Explain how the social environment and young children's cognitive limitations contribute to rigid gender stereotyping in early childhood.

- **CONNECT** In addition to gender-stereotyped beliefs, what other aspects of young children's social understanding tend to be rigid and one-sided in early childhood?

- **APPLY** List findings indicating that language and communication—between parents and children, between teachers and children, and between peers—powerfully affect children's gender typing. What recommendations would you make to counteract these influences?

- **REFLECT** Would you describe your own gender identity as "masculine," "feminine," or "androgynous"? What biological and social factors might have influenced your gender identity?

10.9 Describe the impact of child-rearing styles on development, and explain why authoritative parenting is effective.

10.10 Discuss the multiple origins of child maltreatment, its consequences for development, and prevention strategies.

Child Rearing and Emotional and Social Development

In this and previous chapters, we have seen how parents can foster children's competence—by building a parent–child relationship based on affection and cooperation, by modeling and reinforcing mature behavior, by using reasoning and inductive discipline, and by guiding and encouraging mastery of new skills. Now let's put these practices together into an overall view of effective parenting.

Styles of Child Rearing

Child-rearing styles are combinations of parenting behaviors that occur over a wide range of situations, creating an enduring child-rearing climate. In a landmark series of studies, Diana Baumrind gathered information on child rearing by watching parents interact with their pre-schoolers (Baumrind, 1971). Her findings, and those of others who have extended her work, reveal three features that consistently differentiate an effective style from less effective ones: (1) acceptance and involvement, (2) control, and (3) autonomy granting (Gray & Steinberg, 1999; Hart, Newell, & Olsen, 2003). Table 10.2 shows how child-rearing styles differ in these features. Let's discuss each style in turn.

AUTHORITATIVE CHILD REARING The **authoritative child-rearing style**—the most successful approach—involves high acceptance and involvement, adaptive control techniques, and appropriate autonomy granting. Authoritative parents are warm, attentive, and sensitive

TABLE 10.2	Features of Child-Rearing Styles		
CHILD-REARING STYLE	**ACCEPTANCE AND INVOLVEMENT**	**CONTROL**	**AUTONOMY GRANTING**
Authoritative	Is warm, responsive, attentive, and sensitive to the child's needs	Engages in confrontive behavioral control: Makes reasonable demands for mature behavior and consistently enforces and explains them	Permits the child to make decisions in accord with readiness Encourages the child to express thoughts, feelings, and desires When parent and child disagree, engages in joint decision making when possible
Authoritarian	Is cold and rejecting and frequently degrades the child	Engages in coercive behavioral control: Makes excessive demands for mature behavior, uses force and punishment Often uses psychological control, withdrawing love and manipulating and intruding on the child's individuality and attachment to parents	Makes decisions for the child Rarely listens to the child's point of view
Permissive	Is warm but overindulgent or inattentive	Is lax in behavioral control: Makes few or no demands for mature behavior	Permits the child to make many decisions before the child is ready
Uninvolved	Is emotionally detached and withdrawn	Is lax in behavioral control: Makes few or no demands for mature behavior	Is indifferent to the child's decision making and point of view

to their child's needs. They establish an enjoyable, emotionally fulfilling parent–child relationship that draws the child into close connection. When necessary, authoritative parents exercise firm, reasonable control called *confrontive control:* They insist on mature behavior, give reasons for their expectations, and use disciplinary encounters as "teaching moments" to promote the child's self-regulation. They avoid using *coercive control,* which is arbitrary, rigid, intrusive, and punitive. Finally, authoritative parents engage in gradual, appropriate *autonomy granting,* allowing the child to make decisions in areas where he is ready to do so (Baumrind, 2013; Kuczynski & Lollis, 2002; Russell, Mize, & Bissaker, 2004).

Throughout childhood and adolescence, authoritative parenting is linked to many aspects of competence—an upbeat mood, self-control, task persistence, cooperativeness, high self-esteem, social and moral maturity, and favorable school performance (Amato & Fowler, 2002; Aunola, Stattin, & Nurmi, 2000; Gonzalez & Wolters, 2006; Mackey, Arnold, & Pratt, 2001; Milevsky et al., 2007; Steinberg, Darling, & Fletcher, 1995).

AUTHORITARIAN CHILD REARING The **authoritarian child-rearing style** is low in acceptance and involvement, high in coercive control, and low in autonomy granting. Authoritarian parents appear cold and rejecting. To exert control, they yell, command, criticize, and threaten. "Do it because I said so!" is their attitude. They make decisions for their child and expect their child to accept their word unquestioningly. If the child resists, authoritarian parents resort to force and punishment.

Children of authoritarian parents are more likely to be anxious, unhappy, and low in self-esteem and self-reliance. When frustrated, they tend to react with hostility and, like their parents, use force to get their way. Boys, especially, show high rates of anger and defiance. Although girls also engage in acting-out behavior, they are more likely to be dependent, lacking interest in exploration, and overwhelmed by challenging tasks (Hart, Newell, & Olsen, 2003; Kakihara et al., 2010; Thompson, Hollis, & Richards, 2003). Children and adolescents exposed to the authoritarian style typically do poorly in school. However, because of their parents' concern with control, they tend to achieve better and to commit fewer antisocial acts than peers with undemanding parents—that is, those whose parents use one of the two styles we will consider next (Steinberg, Blatt-Eisengart, & Cauffman, 2006).

In addition to unwarranted direct control, authoritarian parents engage in a more subtle type called **psychological control,** in which they attempt to take advantage of children's psychological needs by intruding on and manipulating their verbal expressions, individuality, and attachments to parents. These parents frequently interrupt or put down the child's ideas, decisions, and choice of friends. When they are dissatisfied, they withdraw love, making their affection contingent on the child's compliance. Children subjected to psychological control exhibit adjustment problems involving both anxious, withdrawn behavior and defiance and aggression—especially the relational form, which (like parental psychological control) damages relationships through manipulation and exclusion (Barber, Stolz, & Olsen, 2005; Barber & Xia, 2013; Kuppens et al., 2013).

PERMISSIVE CHILD REARING   The **permissive child-rearing style** is warm and accepting but uninvolved. Permissive parents are either overindulgent or inattentive and, thus, engage in little control. Instead of gradually granting autonomy, they allow children to make many of their own decisions at an age when they are not yet capable of doing so. Their children can eat meals and go to bed when they feel like it and watch as much television as they want. They do not have to learn good manners or do household chores. Although some permissive parents truly believe in this approach, many others simply lack confidence in their ability to influence their child's behavior (Oyserman et al., 2005).

Children of permissive parents are impulsive, disobedient, and rebellious. They are also overly demanding and dependent on adults, and they show less persistence on tasks, poorer school achievement, and more antisocial behavior. The link between permissive parenting and dependent, nonachieving, rebellious behavior is especially strong for boys (Barber & Olsen, 1997; Steinberg, Blatt-Eisengart, & Cauffman, 2006).

UNINVOLVED CHILD REARING   The **uninvolved child-rearing style** combines low acceptance and involvement with little control and general indifference to issues of autonomy. Often these parents are emotionally detached and depressed and so overwhelmed by life stress that they have little time and energy for children. At its extreme, uninvolved parenting is a form of child maltreatment called *neglect*. Especially when it begins early, it disrupts virtually all aspects of development (see Chapter 4, page 153). Even with less extreme parental disengagement, children and adolescents display many problems—poor emotional self-regulation, school achievement difficulties, and antisocial behavior (Aunola, Stattin, & Nurmi, 2000; Schroeder et al., 2010).

What Makes Authoritative Child Rearing Effective?

Like other correlational findings, the association between authoritative parenting and children's competence is open to interpretation. Perhaps parents of well-adjusted children are authoritative because their youngsters have especially cooperative dispositions. But although temperamentally fearless, impulsive children and emotionally negative children are more likely to evoke coercive, inconsistent discipline, extra warmth and firm control succeed in modifying these children's maladaptive styles (Cipriano & Stifter, 2010; Kochanska, Philibert, & Barry, 2009; Larzelere, Cox, & Mandara, 2013). With fearful, inhibited children, parents must suppress their tendency to overprotect and take over solving the child's social problems. Instead, inhibited children benefit from extra encouragement to be assertive and express their autonomy (Nelson et al., 2006; Rubin & Burgess, 2002).

Longitudinal research indicates that among children of diverse temperaments, authoritative child rearing in the preschool years predicts maturity and adjustment in adolescence, whereas authoritarian or permissive child rearing predicts adolescent immaturity and adjustment difficulties. And a variant of authoritativeness in which parents exert strong control over the child's behavior—becoming directive but not coercive—yields just as favorable long-term outcomes as a more democratic approach (Baumrind, Larzelere, & Owens, 2010). Indeed, some children, because of their dispositions, require "heavier doses" of certain authoritative features.

In sum, authoritative child rearing seems to create a positive emotional context for parental influence in the following ways:

● Warm, involved parents who are secure in the standards they hold for their children model caring concern as well as confident, self-controlled behavior.
● Children are far more likely to comply with and internalize control that appears fair and reasonable, not arbitrary.
● By adjusting demands and autonomy granting to children's capacities, authoritative parents convey to children that they are competent and can do things successfully for themselves. In this way, parents foster favorable self-esteem and cognitive and social maturity.
● Supportive aspects of the authoritative style, including parental acceptance, involvement, and rational control, are a powerful source of *resilience,* protecting children from the negative effects of family stress and poverty (Beyers et al., 2003).

LOOK and LISTEN

Ask several parents to explain their style of child rearing, inquiring about acceptance and involvement, control, and autonomy granting. Look, especially, for variations in amount and type of control over children's behavior along with parents' rationales.

Cultural Variations

Although authoritative parenting is broadly advantageous, ethnic minority parents often have distinct child-rearing beliefs and practices reflecting cultural values. Let's look at some examples.

Compared with Western parents, Chinese parents describe their parenting as more controlling. They are more directive in teaching and scheduling their children's time, as a way of fostering self-control and high achievement. Chinese parents may appear less warm than Western parents because they withhold praise, which they believe results in self-satisfied, poorly motivated children (Cheah & Li, 2010; Ng, Pomerantz, & Deng, 2014). High control reflects the Confucian belief in strict discipline, respect for elders, and socially desirable behavior, taught by deeply involved parents. Chinese parents report expressing affection and concern and using induction and other reasoning-oriented discipline as much as American parents do, but they more often shame a misbehaving child, withdraw love, and use physical punishment (Cheah et al., 2009; Shwalb et al., 2004). When these practices become excessive, resulting in an authoritarian style high in psychological or coercive control, Chinese children display the same negative outcomes as Western children: poor academic achievement, anxiety, depression, impaired self-regulation, and aggressive behavior (Chan, 2010; Lee et al., 2012; Pomerantz & Wang, 2009; Pong, Johnston, & Chen, 2010; Sorkhabi & Mandara, 2013).

In Hispanic families, Asian Pacific Island families, and Caribbean families of African and East Indian origin, firm insistence on respect for parental authority is paired with high parental warmth—a combination suited to promoting cognitive and social competence and family loyalty (Halgunseth, Ispa, & Rudy, 2006; Harrison et al., 1994; Roopnarine & Evans, 2007). Hispanic fathers typically spend much time with their children and are warm and sensitive (Cabrera & Bradley, 2012). In Caribbean families that immigrated to the United States, fathers' authoritativeness—but not mothers'—predicted preschoolers' literacy and math skills, probably because Caribbean fathers take a larger role in guiding their children's academic progress (Roopnarine et al., 2006).

Although wide variation exists, low-SES African-American parents tend to expect immediate obedience. They believe strict parenting fosters self-control and vigilance in risky surroundings. African-American parents who use controlling strategies tend to have cognitively and socially competent children who view parental control as a sign of love and concern (Mason et al., 2004). Recall, also, that a history of mild physical punishment is associated with a reduction in antisocial behavior among African-American youths but with an increase among Caucasian Americans (refer to the Cultural Influences box on page 377). Most African-American parents who use strict, "no-nonsense" discipline use physical punishment sparingly and combine it with warmth and reasoning.

These cultural variations remind us that child-rearing styles must be viewed in their larger context. As we have seen, many factors contribute to good parenting:

In Caribbean families of African origins, respect for parental authority is paired with high parental warmth—a combination that promotes competence and family loyalty.

personal characteristics of the child and parent, SES, extended family and community supports, cultural values and practices, and public policies.

As we turn to the topic of child maltreatment, our discussion will underscore, once again, that effective child rearing is sustained not just by the desire of mothers and fathers to be good parents. Almost all want to be. Unfortunately, when vital supports for parenting break down, children—as well as parents—can suffer terribly.

Child Maltreatment

Child maltreatment is as old as human history, but only in recent decades has the problem been widely acknowledged and studied. Perhaps public concern has increased because child maltreatment is especially common in large industrialized nations. In the most recently reported year, nearly 700,000 U.S. children (9 out of every 1,000) were identified as victims (U.S. Department of Health and Human Services, 2013a). Because most cases go unreported, the true figures are much higher.

Child maltreatment takes the following forms:

- *Physical abuse:* Assaults, such as kicking, biting, shaking, punching, or stabbing, that inflict physical injury
- *Sexual abuse:* Fondling, intercourse, exhibitionism, commercial exploitation through prostitution or production of pornography, and other forms of sexual exploitation
- *Neglect:* Failure to meet a child's basic needs for food, clothing, medical attention, education, or supervision
- *Emotional abuse:* Acts that could cause serious emotional harm, including social isolation, repeated unreasonable demands, ridicule, humiliation, intimidation, or terrorizing

Neglect accounts for about 78 percent of reported cases, physical abuse for 18 percent, emotional abuse for 9 percent, and sexual abuse for 9 percent (U.S. Department of Health and Human Services, 2013a). But these figures are only approximate, as many children experience more than one form.

Parents commit more than 80 percent of abusive incidents. Other relatives account for about 6 percent, and the remainder are perpetrated by parents' unmarried partners, school personnel, camp counselors, and other adults. Infants, toddlers, and preschoolers are at greatest risk for neglect, physical abuse, and emotional abuse. Sexual abuse is perpetrated more often against school-age and early adolescent children. But each type occurs at every age (Trocmé & Wolfe, 2002; U.S. Department of Health and Human Services, 2013a). Because many sexual abuse victims are identified in middle childhood, we will pay special attention to this form of maltreatment in Chapter 13.

ORIGINS OF CHILD MALTREATMENT Early findings suggested that child maltreatment was rooted in adult psychological disturbance (Kempe et al., 1962). But although child maltreatment is more common among disturbed parents, it soon became clear that a single "abusive personality type" does not exist. Parents who were abused as children do not necessarily become abusers (Jaffee et al., 2013). And sometimes even "normal" parents harm their children!

For help in understanding child maltreatment, researchers turned to *ecological systems theory* (see Chapters 1 and 2). They discovered that many interacting variables—at the family, community, and cultural levels—contribute. The more risks present, the greater the likelihood that abuse or neglect will occur. Table 10.3 summarizes factors associated with child maltreatment.

The Family. Within the family, children whose characteristics make them more challenging to rear are more likely to become targets of abuse. These include premature or very sick babies and children who are temperamentally difficult, are inattentive and overactive, or have other developmental problems. Child factors, however, only slightly increase the risk of abuse (Jaudes & Mackey-Bilaver, 2008; Sidebotham et al., 2003). Whether such children are maltreated largely depends on parents' characteristics.

TABLE 10.3	Factors Related to Child Maltreatment
FACTOR	**DESCRIPTION**
Parent characteristics	Psychological disturbance; alcohol and drug abuse; history of abuse as a child; belief in harsh physical discipline; desire to satisfy unmet emotional needs through the child; unreasonable expectations for child behavior; young age (most under 30); low educational level; lack of parenting skills
Child characteristics	Premature or very sick baby; difficult temperament; inattentiveness and overactivity; other developmental problems
Family characteristics	Low income or poverty; homelessness; marital instability; social isolation; partner abuse; frequent moves; large families with closely spaced children; overcrowded living conditions; nonbiological caregivers present; disorganized household; lack of steady employment; other signs of high life stress
Community	Characterized by violence and social isolation; few parks, child-care centers, preschool programs, recreation centers, or religious institutions to serve as family supports
Culture	Approval of physical force and violence as ways to solve problems

Sources: Centers for Disease Control and Prevention, 2014e; Wekerle & Wolfe, 2003; Whipple, 2006.

Maltreating parents are less skillful than other parents in handling discipline confrontations and getting children to cooperate in working toward common goals. They also suffer from biased thinking about their child. For example, they often attribute their baby's crying or their child's misdeeds to a stubborn or bad disposition, evaluate children's transgressions as worse than they are, and feel powerless in parenting—perspectives that lead them to move quickly toward physical force (Bugental & Happaney, 2004; Crouch et al., 2008).

Most parents have enough self-control not to respond to their children's misbehavior or developmental problems with abuse. Other factors combine with these conditions to prompt an extreme response. Unmanageable parental stress is strongly associated with maltreatment. Abusive parents respond to stressful situations with high emotional arousal. And low income, low education (less than a high school diploma), unemployment, alcohol and drug use, marital conflict, overcrowded living conditions, frequent moves, and extreme household disorganization are common in abusive homes (Dakil et al., 2012; Wulczyn, 2009). These conditions increase the chances that parents will be too overwhelmed to meet basic child-rearing responsibilities or will vent their frustrations by lashing out at their children.

The Community. The majority of abusive and neglectful parents are isolated from both formal and informal social supports. Because of their life histories, many have learned to mistrust and avoid others and are poorly skilled at establishing and maintaining positive relationships. Also, maltreating parents are more likely to live in unstable, rundown neighborhoods that provide few links between family and community, such as parks, recreation centers, and religious institutions (Guterman et al., 2009; Tomyr, Ouimet, & Ugnat, 2012). These parents lack "lifelines" to others and have no one to turn to for help during stressful times.

The Larger Culture. Cultural values, laws, and customs profoundly affect the chances that child maltreatment will occur when parents feel overburdened. Societies that view violence as an appropriate way to solve problems set the stage for child abuse.

Although the United States has laws to protect children from maltreatment, widespread support exists for use of physical force with children (refer back to page 376). Many countries—including Austria, Croatia, Cyprus, Denmark, Finland, Germany, Israel, Latvia, Norway, Spain, Sweden, and Uruguay—have outlawed corporal

© JEFF GREENBERG/PHOTOEDIT

High parental stress, low income and education, and extreme household disorganization are often associated with child maltreatment. Abusive parents are more likely to live in rundown neighborhoods that offer few sources of social support.

punishment, a measure that dampens both physical discipline and abuse (Zolotor & Puzia, 2010). Furthermore, all industrialized nations except the United States prohibit corporal punishment in schools. The U.S. Supreme Court has twice upheld the right of school officials to use corporal punishment. Fortunately, 31 U.S. states and the District of Columbia have passed laws that ban it.

CONSEQUENCES OF CHILD MALTREATMENT The family circumstances of maltreated children impair the development of attachment security, emotional self-regulation, empathy and sympathy, self-concept, social skills, and academic motivation. Over time, these youngsters show serious adjustment problems—cognitive deficits including impaired executive function, school failure, severe depression, aggressive behavior, peer difficulties, substance abuse, and violent crime (Gould et al., 2010; Kaplow & Widom, 2007; Nikulina & Widom, 2013; Stronach et al., 2011).

How do these damaging consequences occur? Recall our earlier discussion of hostile cycles of parent–child interaction. For abused children, these are especially severe. Also, a family characteristic strongly associated with child abuse is partner abuse (Graham-Bermann & Howell, 2011). Clearly, the home lives of abused children overflow with adult conduct that leads to profound distress, including emotional insecurity (see page 69 in Chapter 2), and to aggression as a way of solving problems.

Furthermore, demeaning parental messages, in which children are ridiculed, humiliated, rejected, or terrorized, result in low self-esteem, high anxiety, self-blame, and efforts to escape from extreme psychological pain—at times severe enough to lead to attempted suicide in adolescence. At school, maltreated children present serious discipline problems (Wolfe, 2005). Their noncompliance, poor motivation, and cognitive immaturity interfere with academic achievement, further undermining their chances for life success.

Finally, repeated abuse is associated with central nervous system damage, including abnormal EEG brain-wave activity; fMRI-detected reduced size and impaired functioning of the cerebral cortex, corpus callosum, cerebellum, and hippocampus; and atypical production of the stress hormone cortisol—initially too high but, after months of abuse, often too low. Over time, the massive trauma of persistent abuse seems to blunt children's normal physiological response to stress (Cicchetti, 2007; Hart & Rubia, 2012; Jaffee & Christian, 2014). These effects increase the chances that cognitive and emotional problems will endure.

PREVENTING CHILD MALTREATMENT Because child maltreatment is embedded in families, communities, and society as a whole, efforts to prevent it must be directed at each of these levels. Many approaches have been suggested, including teaching high-risk parents effective child-rearing strategies, providing direct experience with children in high school child development courses, and developing broad social programs aimed at improving economic conditions and community services.

We have seen that providing social supports to families is effective in easing parental stress. This approach sharply reduces child maltreatment as well. A trusting relationship with another person is the most important factor in preventing mothers with childhood histories of abuse from repeating the cycle with their own children (Egeland, Jacobvitz, & Sroufe, 1988). Parents Anonymous, a U.S. organization with affiliate programs around the world, helps child-abusing parents learn constructive parenting practices, largely through social supports. Its local chapters offer self-help group meetings, daily phone calls, and regular home visits to relieve social isolation and teach responsible child-rearing skills.

Early intervention aimed at strengthening both child and parent competencies can improve parenting practices, thereby preventing child maltreatment (Howard & Brooks-Gunn, 2009). Healthy Families America, a program that

Each year, fourth to sixth graders across Los Angeles County enter a poster contest to celebrate Child Abuse Prevention Month. This recent winner appeals to parents to treat children with warmth and caring. (Katrina Weng, 4th Grade, Ya Ya Fine Art, Arcadia, CA. Courtesy ICAN Associates, Los Angeles County InterAgency Council on Child Abuse & Neglect, *ican4kids.org*.)

began in Hawaii and has spread to 430 sites across the United States and Canada, identifies families at risk for maltreatment during pregnancy or at birth. Each receives three years of home visitation, in which a trained worker helps parents manage crises, encourages effective child rearing, and puts parents in touch with community services to meet their own and their children's needs (Healthy Families America, 2011). In an evaluation in which over 600 families were randomly assigned to intervention and control groups, Healthy Families home visitation alone reduced only neglect, not abuse (Duggan et al., 2004). But adding a *cognitive component* dramatically increased its impact. When home visitors helped parents change negative appraisals of their children—by countering inaccurate interpretations (for example, that the baby is behaving with malicious intent) and by working on solving child-rearing problems—physical punishment and abuse dropped sharply after one year of intervention (see Figure 10.7) (Bugental et al., 2002). Another home-visiting program shown to reduce child abuse and neglect is the Nurse–Family Partnership, discussed on page 114 in Chapter 3 (Olds et al., 2009).

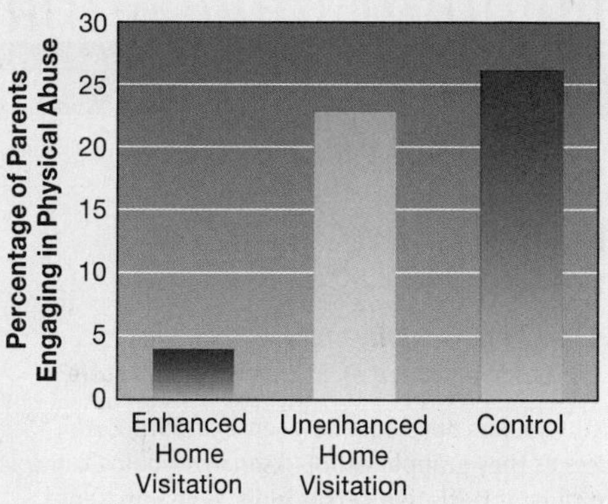

Still, many experts believe that child maltreatment cannot be eliminated as long as violence is widespread and harsh physical punishment is regarded as acceptable. In addition, combating poverty and its diverse correlates—family stress and disorganization, inadequate food and medical care, teenage parenthood, low-birth-weight babies, and parental hopelessness—would protect many children.

Although more cases reach the courts than in decades past, child maltreatment is difficult to prove. Usually, the only witnesses are the child victims or other loyal family members. And even when the evidence is strong, judges hesitate to impose the ultimate safeguard against further harm: permanently removing the child from the family. There are several reasons for their reluctance. First, in the United States, government intervention into family life is viewed as a last resort. Second, despite destructive family relationships, maltreated children and their parents usually are attached to one another, and neither desires separation. Finally, the U.S. legal system tends to regard children as parental property rather than as human beings in their own right, and this also has stood in the way of court-ordered protection.

Even with intensive treatment, some adults persist in their abusive acts. An estimated 1,600 U.S. children, most of them infants and preschoolers, die from maltreatment annually. Nearly half suffered from physical abuse, including beatings, drownings, suffocation, or *shaken baby syndrome,* in which shaking an infant or young child inflicts brain and neck injuries. About 70 percent were neglected, some so severely that it caused their deaths (U.S. Department of Health and Human Services, 2013a). When parents are unlikely to change their behavior, the drastic step of separating parent from child and legally terminating parental rights is the only justifiable course of action.

Child maltreatment is a sad note on which to end our discussion of a period of childhood that is so full of excitement, awakening, and discovery. But there is reason to be optimistic. Great strides have been made over the past several decades in understanding and preventing child maltreatment.

FIGURE 10.7 Impact of a home visitation program with a cognitive component on preventing physical abuse of young children. In an enhanced home visitation condition, home visitors not only provided social support, encouraged effective child rearing, and connected families with community resources but also helped at-risk parents change their negative appraisals of their babies and solve child-rearing problems. After one year of intervention, this cognitive component sharply reduced physical abuse of babies (hitting, shaking, beating, kicking, biting) compared with an unenhanced home visitation condition and a no-intervention control. (Adapted from Bugental et al., 2002.)

Ask Yourself

- **REVIEW** Summarize findings on ethnic variations in child-rearing styles. Is the concept of authoritative parenting useful for understanding effective parenting across cultures? Explain.

- **CONNECT** Which child-rearing style is most likely to be associated with inductive discipline, and why?

- **APPLY** Chandra heard a news report about 10 severely neglected children, living in squalor in an inner-city tenement. She wondered, "Why would parents so mistreat their children?" How would you answer Chandra?

- **REFLECT** How would you classify your parents' child-rearing styles? What factors might have influenced their approach to parenting?

Summary

Erikson's Theory: Initiative versus Guilt (p. 357)

10.1 What personality changes take place during Erikson's stage of initiative versus guilt?

● Preschoolers develop a new sense of purposefulness as they grapple with Erikson's psychological conflict of **initiative versus guilt.** A healthy sense of initiative depends on exploring the social world and trying new skills through play and experiencing supportive child rearing that fosters a secure (but not overly strict) conscience.

Self-Understanding (p. 358)

10.2 Describe the development of self-concept and self-esteem in early childhood.

● As preschoolers think more intently about themselves, they construct a **self-concept** that consists largely of observable characteristics and typical emotions and attitudes. Older preschoolers also have an emerging grasp of their own personalities.

● Securely attached preschoolers have a more positive, coherent self-concept. More elaborative parent–child conversations about past events contribute to a clearer self-image, and conversations about internal states facilitate self-knowledge.

● Preschoolers' **self-esteem** consists of several self-judgments. Their high self-esteem contributes to a mastery-oriented approach to the environment.

Emotional Development (p. 361)

10.3 Identify changes in understanding and expressing emotion during early childhood, citing factors that influence those changes.

● Preschoolers have an impressive understanding of the causes, consequences, and behavioral signs of basic emotions, which is supported by cognitive development, secure attachment, and conversations about feelings.

● By age 3 to 4, children are aware of various strategies for emotional self-regulation. Temperament, parental modeling, and parental communication about coping strategies influence preschoolers' capacity to handle negative emotion.

● As their self-concepts become better developed, preschoolers experience self-conscious emotions, such as pride, shame, and guilt, more often. However, they depend on parental feedback to know when to feel these emotions.

● Empathy also becomes more common in early childhood. The extent to which empathy leads to **sympathy** and results in **prosocial, or altruistic, behavior** depends on temperament and parenting.

Peer Relations (p. 365)

10.4 Describe peer sociability, friendship, and social problem solving in early childhood, along with cultural and parental influences on early peer relations.

● During early childhood, peer interaction increases as children move from **nonsocial activity** to **parallel play** and then to **associative** and **cooperative play.** Nevertheless, both solitary and parallel play remain common.

● With age, sociodramatic play occurs more often, supporting cognitive, emotional, and social development. Cultural valuing of group harmony versus individual autonomy influences play, as do beliefs about the importance of play.

● Preschoolers view friendship in concrete, activity-based terms. Compared to other peer interactions, those with friends are more cooperative and emotionally expressive. Early childhood friendship and peer acceptance contribute to academic and social adjustment in kindergarten.

© GAETANO IMAGES INC./ALAMY

● Social conflicts offer occasions for **social problem solving,** which improves over the preschool and early school years. By kindergarten, each of its information-processing components is related to socially competent behavior.

● Parents influence early peer relations both directly, through attempts to influence their child's interactions with peers, and indirectly, through their child-rearing practices.

Foundations of Morality (p. 372)

10.5 What are the central features of psychoanalytic, social learning, and cognitive-developmental approaches to moral development?

● The psychoanalytic perspective emphasizes the emotional side of moral development. Although guilt is an important motivator of moral action, contrary to Freud's theory, discipline promoting fear of punishment and loss of parental love does not foster conscience development. **Induction** is far more effective.

● Social learning theory focuses on how children learn moral behavior through reinforcement and modeling. Effective adult models of morality are warm, powerful, and consistent in what they say and do.

● Alternatives such as **time out** and withdrawal of privileges can help parents avoid the undesirable side effects of harsh punishment. When parents use punishment, they can increase its effectiveness by being consistent, maintaining a warm parent–child relationship, and offering explanations. The most effective discipline encourages good conduct by building a mutually respectful bond with the child.

● The cognitive-developmental perspective views children as active thinkers about social rules. By age 4, children consider intentions in making moral judgments and distinguish truthfulness from lying. Preschoolers also distinguish **moral imperatives** from **social conventions** and **matters of personal choice,** but they tend to reason rigidly about morality.

● Through sibling and peer interaction, children work out their first ideas about justice and fairness. Parents who discuss moral issues with their children help them reason about morality.

10.6 Describe the development of aggression in early childhood, including family and media influences.

● During early childhood, **proactive aggression** declines while **reactive aggression** increases. Proactive and reactive aggression come in three forms: **physical aggression** (more common in boys), **verbal aggression,** and **relational aggression** (where girls' aggression tends to concentrate).

● Ineffective discipline and a conflict-ridden family atmosphere promote children's aggression. Children high in reactive aggression see hostility where it does not exist, making many unprovoked attacks. Those high in proactive aggression callously use it to advance their own goals—a style that predicts severe conduct problems. Media violence also triggers aggression.

- Teaching parents effective child-rearing practices, intervening to enhance children's emotional and social skills, relieving family stress through social supports, and shielding children from violent media reduce aggressive behavior.

Gender Typing (p. 384)

10.7 *Discuss biological and environmental influences on preschoolers' gender-stereotyped beliefs and behavior.*

- **Gender typing** is well under way in early childhood. Preschoolers acquire a wide range of gender-stereotyped beliefs, which operate as blanket rules rather than flexible guidelines for behavior.

- Prenatal hormones contribute to boys' higher activity level and rowdier play and to children's preference for same-sex playmates. But parents, same-sex older siblings, teachers, peers, and the broader social environment encourage many gender-typed responses. Parents apply more pressure for gender-role conformity to sons, and boys are more gender-typed than girls.

10.8 *Describe and evaluate major theories that explain the emergence of gender identity.*

- Although most people have a traditional **gender identity**, some are **androgynous**, combining both masculine and feminine characteristics. Masculine and androgynous identities are linked to better psychological adjustment.

- According to social learning theory, preschoolers first acquire gender-typed responses through modeling and reinforcement, then organize these into gender-linked ideas about themselves. Cognitive-developmental theory suggests that **gender constancy** must be mastered before children develop gender-typed behavior, but evidence for this assumption is weak.

- **Gender schema theory** combines features of social learning and cognitive-developmental perspectives. As children acquire gender-stereotyped preferences and behaviors, they form masculine and feminine categories, or gender schemas, that they apply to themselves and their world.

Child Rearing and Emotional and Social Development (p. 392)

10.9 *Describe the impact of child-rearing styles on development, and explain why authoritative parenting is effective.*

- Three features distinguish the major **child-rearing styles:** (1) acceptance and involvement, (2) control, and (3) autonomy granting. Compared with the **authoritarian, permissive,** and **uninvolved styles,** the **authoritative style** promotes cognitive, emotional, and social competence. Warmth, confrontive rather than coercive control, and gradual autonomy granting account for the effectiveness of the authoritative style. **Psychological control** is associated with authoritarian parenting and contributes to adjustment problems.

- Certain ethnic groups, including Chinese, Hispanic, Asian Pacific Island, and African-American, combine parental warmth with high levels of control. But when control becomes harsh and excessive, it impairs academic and social competence.

10.10 *Discuss the multiple origins of child maltreatment, its consequences for development, and prevention strategies.*

- Child maltreatment is related to factors within the family, community, and larger culture. Maltreating parents use ineffective discipline and hold a negatively biased view of their child. Unmanageable parental stress and social isolation greatly increase the chances that abuse and neglect will occur. When a society approves of force and violence as a means for solving problems, child abuse is promoted.

- Maltreated children are impaired in attachment security, emotional self-regulation, empathy and sympathy, self-concept, social skills, and academic motivation. They are also likely to suffer central nervous system damage. Successful prevention of child maltreatment requires efforts at the family, community, and societal levels.

Important Terms and Concepts

MILESTONES
Development in Early Childhood

2 YEARS

PHYSICAL

- Throughout early childhood, height and weight increase more slowly than in toddlerhood. (285)
- Balance improves; walking becomes smooth and rhythmic; running emerges. (301–302)

- Jumps, hops, throws, and catches with rigid upper body. (302)
- Puts on and removes simple items of clothing. (302–303)
- Uses spoon effectively. (302)
- First drawings are gestural scribbles. (303)

COGNITIVE

- Increasingly uses language as a flexible symbolic tool, to modify existing mental representations. (312)
- Make-believe becomes less dependent on realistic objects, less self-centered, and more complex; sociodramatic play increases. (312)
- Takes the perspective of others in simplified, familiar situations and in face-to-face communication. (317, 332)
- Recognition memory is well developed. (329)
- Shows awareness of the difference between inner mental and outer physical events. (332)
- Begins to count. (338)

LANGUAGE

- Vocabulary increases rapidly. (348)
- Uses a coalition of cues—perceptual and, increasingly, social and linguistic—to figure out word meanings. (350)
- Speaks in simple sentences that follow basic word order of native language. (350)
- Adds grammatical markers. (351)
- Displays effective conversational skills. (352)

EMOTIONAL/SOCIAL

- Understands causes, consequences, and behavioral signs of basic emotions. (361)
- Begins to develop self-concept and self-esteem. (358–360)
- Shows early signs of developing moral sense—verbal evaluations of own and others' actions and distress at harmful behaviors. (372, 378)
- May display proactive (or instrumental) aggression. (379)
- Gender-stereotyped beliefs and behavior increase. (385)

3–4 YEARS

PHYSICAL

- May no longer need a daytime nap. (293)
- Running, jumping, hopping, throwing, and catching become more refined, with flexible upper body. (302)
- Galloping and one-foot skipping appear. (302)
- Pedals and steers tricycle. (302)

- Uses scissors. (302)
- Uses fork effectively. (302)
- Draws first picture of a person, using tadpole image. (304)
- Distinguishes writing from nonwriting. (306)

COGNITIVE

- Understands the symbolic function of drawings and of models of real-world spaces. (303–304, 314–315)
- Grasps conservation, reasons about transformations, reverses thinking, and understands cause-and-effect relationships in simplified, familiar situations. (318)
- Sorts familiar objects into hierarchically organized categories. (319)
- Distinguishes appearance from reality. (314–315)
- Uses private speech to guide behavior during challenging tasks. (323)
- Improves in sustained attention. (327–328)
- Uses scripts to recall familiar events. (329)
- Understands that both beliefs and desires determine behavior. (332)
- Knows meaning of numbers up to ten, counts correctly, and grasps cardinality. (338)

Note: Numbers in parentheses indicate the page or pages on which each milestone is discussed.

LANGUAGE

- Aware of some meaningful features of written language. (336)
- Coins new words based on known words; extends language meanings through metaphor. (350)

- Masters increasingly complex grammatical structures, occasionally overextending grammatical rules to exceptions. (351)
- Adjusts speech to fit the age, sex, and social status of listeners. (317, 352)

EMOTIONAL/SOCIAL

- Describes self in terms of observable characteristics and typical emotions and attitudes. (358)
- Has several self-esteems, such as learning things in school, making friends, and getting along with parents. (360)
- Emotional self-regulation improves. (362)
- Experiences self-conscious emotions more often. (364)
- Relies more on language to express empathy. (364)
- Engages in associative and cooperative play with peers, in addition to parallel play. (366)

- Proactive aggression declines, while reactive aggression (verbal and relational) increases. (380)
- Forms first friendships, based on pleasurable play and sharing of toys. (368)
- Distinguishes moral imperatives from social conventions and matters of personal choices. (378)
- Preference for same-sex playmates strengthens. (386)

5–6 YEARS

PHYSICAL

- Starts to lose primary teeth. (287)
- Increases running speed, gallops more smoothly, and engages in true skipping. (302)
- Displays mature, flexible throwing and catching patterns. (302)
- Uses knife to cut soft foods. (302, 303)
- Ties shoes. (302, 303)
- Draws more complex pictures. (304)

- Uses an adult pencil grip, writes name, copies some numbers and simple words, and discriminates letters of the alphabet. (302, 306)

COGNITIVE

- Replaces beliefs in magical creatures and events with natural, plausible explanations. (318)
- Improves in ability to distinguish appearance from reality. (314–315)
- Passes Piaget's conservation of number, mass, and liquid problems. (316)
- Continues to improve in sustained attention; begins to plan effectively. (327–329)

- Improves in recognition, recall, scripted memory, and autobiographical memory. (329–330)

- Understanding of false belief strengthens. (333)

LANGUAGE

- Understands that letters and sounds are linked in systematic ways. (336)
- Uses invented spellings. (336)
- By age 6, has acquired a vocabulary of about 10,000 words. (348)
- Uses most grammatical constructions competently. (351)

EMOTIONAL/SOCIAL

- Improves in emotional understanding (ability to interpret, predict, and influence others' emotional reactions). (361–362)

- Becomes better at social problem solving. (370)
- Has acquired many morally relevant rules and behaviors. (372)
- Gender-stereotyped beliefs and behavior, and preference for same-sex playmates, continue to strengthen. (387)
- Understands gender constancy. (390)

Physical Development in Middle Childhood

"My Favorite Sport"
Su Degirmenci & Miray Celik
9 years, Turkey

This confident swimmer's exploration of the undersea world is aided by gains in strength, agility, and flexibility. Chapter 11 takes up the diverse physical attainments of middle childhood and their close connection with other domains of development.

"I'm on my way, Mom!" hollered 10-year-old Joey as he stuffed the last bite of toast into his mouth, slung his book bag over his shoulder, dashed out the door, jumped on his bike, and headed down the street for school. Joey's 8-year-old sister Lizzie followed, kissing her mother goodbye and pedaling furiously until she caught up with Joey. Rena, the children's mother and one of our colleagues at the university, watched from the front porch as her son and daughter disappeared in the distance.

"They're branching out," Rena commented over lunch that day, as she described the children's expanding activities and relationships. Homework, household chores, soccer teams, music lessons, scouting, friends at school and in the neighborhood, and Joey's new paper route were all part of the children's routine. "It seems as if the basics are all there; I don't have to monitor Joey and Lizzie so constantly anymore. Being a parent is still very challenging, but it's more a matter of refinements—helping them become independent, competent, and productive individuals."

Joey and Lizzie have entered middle childhood—the years from 6 to 11. Around the world, children of this age are assigned new responsibilities. For children in industrialized nations, like Joey and Lizzie, middle childhood is often called the "school years" because its onset is marked by the start of formal schooling. In village and tribal cultures, the school may be a field or a jungle. But universally, mature members of society guide children of this age period toward real-world tasks that increasingly resemble those they will perform as adults.

This chapter focuses on physical growth in middle childhood—changes less spectacular than those of earlier years. By age 6, the brain has reached 90 percent of its adult weight, and the body continues to grow slowly. In this way, nature gives school-age children the mental powers to master challenging tasks as well as added time—before reaching physical maturity—to acquire the knowledge and skills essential for life in a complex social world.

We begin by reviewing typical growth trends and special health concerns. Then we turn to rapid gains in motor abilities, which support practical everyday activities, athletic skills, and participation in organized games. We will see that each of these achievements is affected by and also contributes to cognitive, emotional, and social development. Our discussion will echo a familiar theme—that all domains are interrelated. ■

Body Growth

Physical growth during the school years continues at the slow, regular pace of early childhood. At age 6, the average North American child weighs about 45 pounds and is 3½ feet tall. Over the next few years, children will add about 2 to 3 inches in height and 5 pounds in weight each year (see Figure 11.1 on page 407). Between ages 6 and 8, girls are slightly shorter and lighter than boys. By age 9, this trend reverses. Already, Rena noticed, Lizzie was starting to catch up with Joey in physical size as she approached the dramatic adolescent growth spurt, which occurs two years earlier in girls than in boys.

Because the lower portion of the body is growing fastest, Joey and Lizzie appeared longer-legged than they had in early childhood. They grew out of their jeans more quickly than their jackets and frequently needed larger shoes. As in early childhood,

11.1 Describe changes in body size, proportions, and skeletal maturity during middle childhood.

11.2 Describe brain development in middle childhood.

girls have slightly more body fat and boys more muscle. After age 8, girls begin accumulating fat at a faster rate, and they will add even more during adolescence (Hauspie & Roelants, 2012).

Worldwide Variations in Body Size

TAKE A MOMENT... Glance into any elementary school classroom, and you will see wide individual differences in body growth. Diversity in physical size is especially apparent when we travel to different nations. Worldwide, a 9-inch gap exists between the smallest and the largest 8-year-olds. The shortest children, found in South America, Asia, the Pacific Islands, and parts of Africa, include such ethnic groups as Colombian, Burmese, Thai, Vietnamese, Ethiopian, and Bantu. The tallest children—living in Australia, northern and central Europe, Canada, and the United States—come from Czech, Dutch, Latvian, Norwegian, Swiss, and African populations (Meredith, 1978; Ruff, 2002). These findings remind us that *growth norms* (age-related averages for height and weight) must be applied cautiously, especially in countries with high immigration rates and many ethnic minorities.

Body size sometimes results from evolutionary adaptations to a particular climate. These Tanzanian boys live on the hot African plains. Their long, lean physiques permit their bodies to cool easily.

What accounts for these vast differences in physical size? Both heredity and environment are involved. Body size sometimes reflects evolutionary adaptations to a particular climate. Long, lean physiques are typical in hot, tropical regions and short, stocky ones in cold, Arctic areas (Katzmarzyk & Leonard, 1998). Also, children who grow tallest usually live in developed countries, where food is plentiful and infectious diseases are largely controlled. Physically small children tend to live in less developed regions, where poverty, hunger, and disease are common (Steckel, 2012). When families move from poor to wealthy nations, their children not only grow taller but also change to a longer-legged body shape. (Recall that during childhood, the legs are growing fastest.) For example, U.S.-born school-age children of immigrant Guatemalan Mayan parents are, on average, 4½ inches taller, with legs nearly 3 inches longer, than their agemates in Guatemalan Mayan villages (Bogin et al., 2002; Varela-Silva et al., 2007).

Secular Trends in Physical Growth

Over the past 150 years, **secular trends in physical growth**—changes in body size from one generation to the next—have occurred in industrialized nations. Joey and Lizzie are taller and heavier than their parents and grandparents were as children. These trends have been found in Australia, Canada, Japan, New Zealand, the United States, and nearly all European countries (Ong, Ahmed, & Dunger, 2006). The secular gain appears early in life, increases over childhood and early adolescence, then declines as mature body size is reached. This pattern suggests that the larger size of today's children is mostly due to a faster rate of physical development.

Although varying considerably in physical size, these second graders are taller and heavier than previous generations were at the same age. Improved health and nutrition account for this secular trend throughout the industrialized world.

Once again, improved health and nutrition are largely responsible for these growth gains. As developing nations make socioeconomic progress, they also show secular gains (Ji & Chen, 2008). Secular increases are smaller for low-income children, who have poorer diets and are more likely to suffer from growth-stunting illnesses. And in regions with widespread poverty, famine, and disease, either no secular change or a secular decrease in body size has occurred (Bogin, 2013; Cole, 2000). In most industrialized nations, the secular gain in height has slowed in recent decades. Weight gain, however, is continuing. As we will see later, overweight and obesity have reached epic proportions.

Skeletal Growth

During middle childhood, the bones of the body lengthen and broaden. However, ligaments are not yet firmly attached to bones. This, combined with increasing muscle strength, gives children

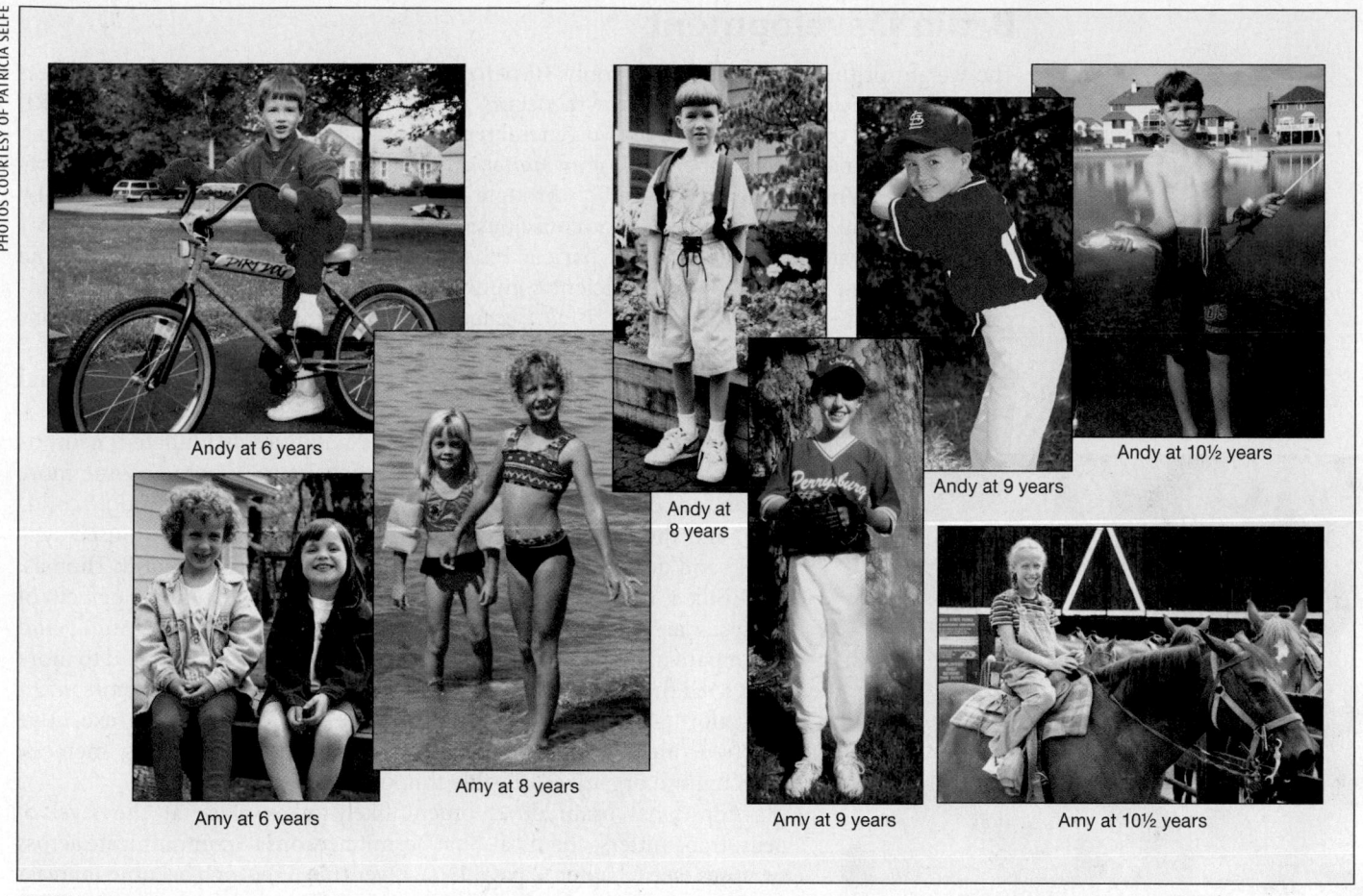

PHOTOS COURTESY OF PATRICIA SELFE

Andy at 6 years

Andy at 8 years

Andy at 9 years

Andy at 10½ years

Amy at 6 years

Amy at 8 years

Amy at 9 years

Amy at 10½ years

FIGURE 11.1 **Body growth during middle childhood.** Andy and Amy continued the slow, regular pattern of growth that they showed in early child-hood (see Chapter 8, page 286). But around age 9, Amy began to grow at a faster rate than Andy. At age 10½, she was taller, heavier, and more mature-looking.

unusual flexibility of movement. School-age children often seem like "physical contortionists," turning cartwheels and doing splits and handstands. As their bodies become stronger, many children experience a greater desire for physical exercise. Nighttime "growing pains"—stiffness and aches in the legs—are common (Uziel et al., 2012). These subside as bones strengthen to accommodate increased physical activity and as muscles adapt to an enlarging skeleton.

Between ages 6 and 12, all 20 primary teeth are lost and replaced by permanent ones, with girls losing their teeth slightly earlier than boys. The first teeth to go are the lower and then upper front teeth, giving many first and second graders a "toothless" smile. For a while, the permanent teeth seem much too large. Gradually, growth of the facial bones, especially those of the jaw and chin, causes the child's face to lengthen and the mouth to widen, accommodating the newly erupting teeth.

Care of the teeth is essential during the school years because dental health affects the child's appearance, speech, and ability to chew properly. Parents need to remind children to brush their teeth thoroughly, and most children need help with flossing until about 9 years of age. More than 50 percent of U.S. school-age children have at least some tooth decay. Low-SES children have especially high levels, with about 30 percent untreated (National Institutes of Health, 2011). As decay progresses, they experience pain, embarrassment at damaged teeth, distraction from play and learning, and school absences due to dental-related illnesses.

Malocclusion, a condition in which the upper and lower teeth do not meet properly, occurs in one-third of school-age children. In about 14 percent of cases, serious difficulties in biting and chewing result. Malocclusion can be caused by thumb sucking after permanent teeth erupt. School-age children who continue to engage in the habit may require gentle but persistent encouragement to give it up (Garde et al., 2014). A more frequent cause of malocclusion is crowding of permanent teeth. In some children, this problem clears up as the jaw grows. Others need braces, a common sight by the end of elementary school.

Brain Development

The weight of the brain increases by only 10 percent during middle childhood and adolescence. Nevertheless, considerable growth occurs in certain brain structures. Using fMRI, researchers can detect the volume of two general types of brain tissue: *white matter*, consisting largely of myelinated nerve fibers, and *gray matter*, consisting mostly of neurons and supportive material. White matter rises steadily throughout childhood and adolescence, especially in the prefrontal cortex (responsible for consciousness, impulse control, integration of information, and strategic thinking), in the parietal lobes (supporting spatial abilities), and in the corpus callosum (leading to more efficient communication between the two cortical hemispheres) (Giedd et al., 2009; Smit et al., 2012). Because interconnectivity among distant regions of the cerebral cortex increases, the prefrontal cortex becomes a more effective "executive"— coordinating integrated functioning of various areas, yielding more complex, flexible, and adaptive behavior.

SKIP BROWN/LIFESIZE/GETTY IMAGES

In middle childhood, the prefrontal cortex becomes a more effective "executive," coordinating integrated functioning of various brain regions. These changes support more complex, flexible abilities, such as this kayaker's deft maneuvering.

As children acquire more complex abilities, stimulated neurons increase in synaptic connections, and their neural fibers become more elaborate and myelinated. As a result, gray matter peaks in middle childhood and then declines as synaptic pruning (reduction of unused synapses) and death of surrounding neurons proceed (Markant & Thomas, 2013; Silk & Wood, 2011). Recall from Chapter 5 that about 40 percent of synapses are pruned over childhood and adolescence. Pruning and accompanying reorganization and selection of brain circuits lead to more optimized functioning of specific brain regions and, thus, to more effective information processing. In particular, children gain in executive function, including sustained attention, inhibition, working memory capacity, and organized, flexible thinking.

Additional brain development likely takes place at the level of neurotransmitters, chemicals that permit neurons to communicate across synapses (see Chapter 5, page 161). Over time, neurons become increasingly selective, responding only to certain chemical messages. This change may add to school-age children's more efficient thinking. Secretions of particular neurotransmitters are related to cognitive performance, social and emotional adjustment, and ability to withstand stress. When neurotransmitters are not present in appropriate balances, children may suffer serious developmental problems, such as inattention and overactivity, emotional disturbance, and epilepsy (an illness involving brain seizures and loss of motor control) (Brooks et al., 2006; Kurian et al., 2011; Weller, Kloos, & Weller, 2006).

Researchers also believe that brain functioning may change in middle childhood because of the influence of hormones. Around age 7 to 8, an increase in androgens (male sex hormones), secreted by the adrenal glands (located on top of the kidneys), occurs in children of both sexes. Androgens will rise further among boys at puberty, when the testes release them in large amounts. Androgens affect brain organization and behavior in many animal species, including humans. Recall from Chapter 10 that androgens contribute to boys' higher activity level and physical aggression. They may also promote social dominance and play-fighting, topics we will take up at the end of this chapter (Azurmendi et al., 2006).

Ask Yourself

- **REVIEW** What aspects of physical growth account for the long-legged appearance of many 8- to 12-year-olds?

- **CONNECT** Relate secular trends in physical growth to the concept of cohort effects, discussed on page 41 in Chapter 1.

- **APPLY** Joey complained to his mother that it wasn't fair that his younger sister Lizzie was almost as tall as he was. He worried that he wasn't growing fast enough. How should Rena respond to Joey's concern?

- **REFLECT** How does your height compare with that of your parents and grandparents when they were your age? Do your observations illustrate secular trends?

Common Health Problems

Children from economically advantaged homes, like Joey and Lizzie, are at their healthiest in middle childhood, full of energy and play. Growth in lung size permits more air to be exchanged with each breath, so children are better able to exercise vigorously without tiring. The cumulative effects of good nutrition, combined with rapid development of the body's immune system, offer greater protection against disease. In fact, children who spent much time in child-care centers during the preschool years, and therefore experienced frequent respiratory and ear infections, are sick less often than their agemates after reaching elementary school (Côté et al., 2010). Their increased immunity may grant them a learning advantage, as they miss fewer days of school.

Not surprisingly, poverty continues to be a powerful predictor of poor health during middle childhood. Because economically disadvantaged U.S. children often lack health insurance and, if they are publicly insured, generally receive a lower standard of care (see Chapter 8, page 297), many do not have regular access to a doctor. A substantial number also lack such basic necessities as a comfortable home and regular meals.

Nutrition

Children need a well-balanced, plentiful diet to provide energy for successful learning in school and increased physical activity. With their increasing focus on play, friendships, and new activities, many children spend little time at the table. Joey's hurried breakfast, described at the beginning of this chapter, is a common event in middle childhood. The percentage of children who eat meals with their families drops sharply between ages 9 and 14. Family dinnertimes have waned in general over the past two decades. Yet eating an evening meal with parents leads to a diet higher in fruits, vegetables, grains, and milk products and lower in soft drinks and fast foods (Burgess-Champoux et al., 2009; Hammons & Fiese, 2011).

School-age children report that they "feel better" and "focus better" after eating healthy foods and that they feel sluggish, "like a blob," after eating junk foods. In a longitudinal study of nearly 14,000 U.S. children, a parent-reported diet high in sugar, fat, and processed food in early childhood predicted slightly lower IQ at age 8, after many factors that might otherwise account for this association were controlled (Northstone et al., 2012). Even mild nutritional deficits can affect cognitive functioning. Among school-age children from middle- to high-SES families, insufficient dietary iron and folate are related to poorer concentration and mental test performance (Arija et al., 2006; Low et al., 2013). Children say that a major barrier to healthy eating is the ready availability of unhealthy options, even in their homes. As one sixth grader commented, "When I get home from school, I think, 'I should eat some fruit,' but then I see the chips" (O'Dea, 2003, p. 498).

Recall from Chapter 8 that food familiarity and food preferences are strongly linked: Children like best foods they have eaten repeatedly in the past. Readily available, healthy between-meal snacks—such as cheese, fruit, raw vegetables, and peanut butter—can help meet school-age children's nutritional needs and increase their liking for healthy foods.

As we have seen in earlier chapters, many poverty-stricken children in developing countries and in the United States suffer from serious and prolonged malnutrition. By middle childhood, the effects are apparent in delayed physical growth, impaired motor coordination, inattention, and low IQ. The negative impact of malnutrition on learning and behavior may intensify as children encounter new academic and social challenges at school. First, as in earlier years, growth-stunted school-age children show greater stress reactivity, as indicated by a sharper rise in heart rate and in saliva levels of the stress hormone cortisol (Fernald & Grantham-McGregor, 1998). Second, animal evidence reveals that a deficient diet alters the production of neurotransmitters in the brain—an effect that can disrupt all aspects of psychological functioning (Haller, 2005).

Unfortunately, malnutrition that persists from infancy or early childhood into the school years usually results in permanent physical and mental damage (Grantham-McGregor, Walker, & Chang, 2000; Liu et al., 2003). Government-sponsored supplementary food programs from the early years through adolescence can prevent these effects.

11.3 Describe the causes and consequences of serious nutritional problems in middle childhood, giving special attention to obesity.

11.4 What factors contribute to myopia, otitis media, nocturnal enuresis, and asthma, and how can these health problems be reduced?

11.5 Describe changes in the occurrence of unintentional injuries during middle childhood, and cite effective interventions.

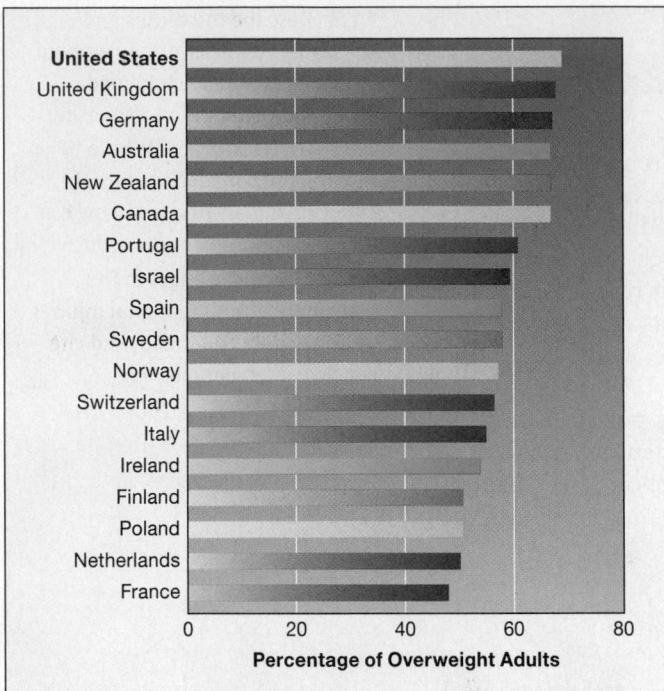

FIGURE 11.2 Overweight adults in eighteen industrialized nations. The United States outranks all other developed nations in pervasiveness of overweight in the adult population, defined here according to the widely accepted adult standard of a BMI greater than 25. (Based on World Health Organization, 2014c.)

Overweight and Obesity

Mona, a very heavy child in Lizzie's class, often watched from the sidelines during recess. When she did join in games, she was slow and clumsy, the target of unkind comments: "Move it, Tubs!" Although Mona was a good student, the other children rejected her in the classroom as well. When they chose partners for special activities, Mona was among the last to be selected. Most afternoons, she walked home alone while her schoolmates gathered in groups, talking, laughing, and chasing. At home, Mona sought comfort in high-calorie snacks.

Mona suffers from **obesity,** a greater-than-20-percent increase over healthy weight, based on *body mass index (BMI)*—a ratio of weight to height associated with body fat. A BMI above the 85th percentile for a child's age and sex is considered *overweight,* a BMI above the 95th percentile *obese.* During the past several decades, a rise in overweight and obesity has occurred in many Western nations (see Figure 11.2), with large increases in Canada, Germany, Israel, Greece, Ireland, New Zealand, United Kingdom, and the United States. Today, 32 percent of U.S. children and adolescents are overweight, more than half of them extremely so: 17 percent are obese (Ogden et al., 2014; World Health Organization, 2014d). Smaller increases have occurred in other industrialized nations, including Finland, the Netherlands, Norway, and Sweden.

Obesity rates have also risen in developing countries, as urbanization shifts the population toward sedentary lifestyles and diets high in meats and energy-dense refined foods (World Health Organization, 2014d). In China, for example, where obesity was nearly nonexistent a generation ago, today 20 percent of urban children are overweight and 8 percent obese—a fortyfold increase over the past 25 years, with obesity affecting twice as many boys as girls (Sun et al., 2014). In addition to lifestyle changes, a prevailing belief in Chinese culture that excess body fat represents prosperity and health—carried over from a half-century ago, when famine caused millions of deaths—has contributed to this alarming upsurge. High valuing of sons may induce Chinese parents to offer boys especially generous portions of meat, dairy products, and other energy-dense foods that were once scarce but are now widely available.

Overweight rises with age, from 23 percent among U.S. preschoolers to 35 percent among school-age children and adolescents to an astronomical 69 percent among adults (Ogden et al., 2014). In a longitudinal study of more than 1,000 U.S. children, overweight preschoolers were five times more likely than their normal-weight peers to be overweight at age 12 (Nader et al., 2006). And few young people who are persistently overweight in adolescence attain a normal weight in adulthood (Patton et al., 2011).

Besides serious emotional and social difficulties, obese children are at risk for lifelong health problems. Symptoms that begin to appear in the early school years—high blood pressure, high cholesterol levels, respiratory abnormalities, insulin resistance, and inflammatory reactions—are powerful predictors of heart disease, circulatory difficulties, type 2 diabetes, gallbladder disease, sleep and digestive disorders, many forms of cancer, and early death. Furthermore, obesity has caused a dramatic rise in cases of diabetes in children, sometimes leading to early, severe complications, including stroke, kidney failure, and circulatory problems that heighten the risk of eventual blindness and leg amputation (Biro & Wien, 2010; Lakshman, Elks, & Ong, 2012). As you can see from Table 11.1, childhood obesity is a complex physical disorder with multiple causes.

CAUSES OF OBESITY Not all children are equally at risk for excessive weight gain. Overweight children tend to have overweight parents, and identical twins are more likely to share the disorder than fraternal twins. But heredity accounts for only a *tendency* to gain weight (Kral & Faith, 2009). The importance of environment is evident in the consistent relationship of low SES to overweight and obesity in industrialized nations, especially among ethnic

TABLE 11.1	Factors Contributing to Childhood Obesity
FACTOR	**DESCRIPTION**
Heredity	Obese children are likely to have at least one obese parent, and identical twins are more likely than fraternal twins to share the disorder.
Socioeconomic status	Obesity is more common in low-SES families.
Early growth pattern	Infants who gain weight rapidly are at greater risk for obesity, probably because their parents promote unhealthy eating habits (see Chapter 5).
Family eating habits	When parents purchase high-calorie fast foods, treats, and junk food; use them as rewards; anxiously overfeed; or control their children's intake, their children are more likely to be obese.
Responsiveness to food cues	Obese children often decide when to eat on the basis of external cues, such as taste, smell, sight, time of day, and food-related words, rather than hunger.
Physical activity	Obese children are less physically active than their normal-weight peers.
Television viewing	Children who spend many hours watching television are more likely to become obese.
Early malnutrition	Early, severe malnutrition that results in growth stunting increases the risk of later obesity.

minorities—in the United States, African-American, Hispanic, and Native-American children and adults (Martinson, McLanahan, & Brooks-Gunn, 2012; Ogden et al., 2014). Factors responsible include lack of knowledge about healthy diet; a tendency to buy high-fat, low-cost foods; neighborhoods that lack convenient access to affordable, healthy foods in grocery stores and restaurants; and family stress, which can prompt overeating.

Furthermore, children who were undernourished in their early years are at risk for later excessive weight gain. Studies in many poverty-stricken regions of the world reveal that growth-stunted children are more likely to be overweight than their nonstunted agemates (Branca & Ferrari, 2002). In industrialized nations, many studies confirm that children whose mothers smoked during pregnancy and who therefore are often born underweight (see Chapter 3) are at elevated risk for later overweight and obesity (Rogers, 2009). A malnourished body protects itself by establishing a low basal metabolism rate, which may endure after nutrition improves. Also, malnutrition may disrupt appetite control centers in the brain, causing the child to overeat when food becomes plentiful. Nevertheless, in the developing world (unlike in industrialized countries), obesity risk is greatest for individuals living in economically well-off households, probably because of greater food availability and reduced activity levels (Subramanian et al., 2011).

Parental feeding practices also contribute to childhood obesity. Overweight children are more likely to eat larger quantities of high-calorie sugary and fatty foods, perhaps because these foods are plentiful in the diets offered by their parents, who also tend to be overweight (Kit, Ogden, & Flegal, 2014). Frequent eating out—which increases parents' and children's consumption of high-calorie fast foods—is linked to overweight. And it likely plays a major role in the consistent relationship between mothers' employment hours and elevated BMI among school-age children (Morrissey, Dunifon, & Kalil, 2011). Demanding work schedules reduce the time parents have for healthy meal preparation.

Furthermore, some parents anxiously overfeed, interpreting almost all their child's discomforts as a desire for food—a practice common among immigrant parents and grandparents who, as children themselves, survived deadly famines or periods of food deprivation due to poverty. Still other parents are overly controlling, restricting when, what, and how much their child eats and worrying about weight gain (Jansen et al., 2012). In each case, parents undermine children's ability to regulate their own food intake. Also, parents of overweight

ROLF BRUDERER/BLEND IMAGES/GETTY IMAGES

Frequent eating out, which increases both parents' and children's consumption of high-calorie fast foods, contributes to excessive weight gain.

Social Issues: Health

Family Stressors and Childhood Obesity

In response to chronic stress, many adults and children increase their food consumption—especially foods high in sugar and fat—and gain excessive weight. How can a stressful daily life prompt overeating?

One route is through elevated stress hormones, including cortisol, which signal the body to increase energy expenditure and the brain, in turn, to boost caloric intake (Zellner et al., 2006). In a second pathway, chronic stress triggers insulin resistance—a prediabetic condition that frequently induces a raging appetite (Dallman et al., 2003).

Furthermore, the effort required to manage persistent stress can easily strain self-regulatory capacity, leaving the individual unable to limit excessive eating (Blair, 2010). In several studies, the greater the number of home-life stressors in school-age children's lives, the poorer their regulation of negative emotion and behavior (Evans, 2003; Evans et al., 2005). Impaired self-regulation, then, might be a major intervening factor in the link between childhood chronic stress and obesity.

To find out, researchers followed several hundred children from economically disadvantaged families, assessing family stressors and self-regulatory ability at age 9 and change in BMI four years later, at age 13 (Evans et al., 2012). Number of stressors experienced—including poverty, single-parent household, residential crowding, noise, household clutter, lack of books and play materials, child separation from the family, and exposure to violence—strongly predicted impaired self-regulation, as indicated by children's delay of gratification (ability to wait for a reward). Poor self-regulation, in turn, largely accounted for the relationship between family stressors and gain in BMI over time.

In obesity prevention programs, children given self-regulation training—instructions to "stop and think" in eating situations—show beneficial outcomes in terms of improved eating behaviors and weight

ZACK WITTMAN FOR THE BOSTON GLOBE VIA GETTY IMAGES

This 9-year-old, living in shelter housing with her mother, is at high risk for obesity. Home-life stressors, including poverty, single-parenthood, noise, crowding, and clutter, contribute to overeating by impairing children's self-regulation.

loss (Johnson, 2000). But such training is likely to be fully effective only when stressors in children's family lives are manageable, not overwhelming.

LOOK and LISTEN

Observe in the check-out area of a supermarket for an hour on a weekend, recording the percentage of families with children whose carts contain large quantities of high-calorie processed foods and soft drinks. In how many of these families are parents and children overweight?

children often use high-fat, sugary foods to reinforce other behaviors, leading children to attach great value to treats (Sherry et al., 2004).

Because of these experiences, obese children soon develop maladaptive eating habits. They are more responsive than normal-weight individuals to external stimuli associated with food—taste, sight, smell, time of day, and food-related words—and less responsive to internal hunger cues (Jansen et al., 2003; Temple et al., 2007). Furthermore, a stressful family life contributes to children's diminished self-regulatory capacity, amplifying uncontrolled eating (see the Social Issues: Health box above).

Another factor implicated in weight gain is insufficient sleep (Nielsen, Danielsen, & Sørensen, 2011). A follow-up of more than 2,000 U.S. 3- to 12-year-olds revealed that children who got less nightly sleep were more likely to be overweight five years later (Snell, Adam, & Duncan, 2007). Reduced sleep may increase time available for eating, leave children too fatigued for physical activity, or disrupt the brain's regulation of hunger and metabolism.

Overweight children are less physically active than their normal-weight peers. Inactivity is both cause and consequence of excessive weight gain. Research reveals that the rise in childhood obesity is due in part to the many hours U.S. children spend watching television. In a study that tracked children's TV viewing from ages 4 to 11, the more TV children watched, the more body fat they added. Children who devoted more than 3 hours per day to TV accumulated 40 percent more fat than those devoting less than 1¾ hours (see Figure 11.3) (Proctor et al., 2003). Watching TV reduces time devoted to physical exercise, and TV ads encourage children to eat fattening, unhealthy snacks. Children permitted to have a TV in their bedroom—a practice linked to especially high TV viewing—are at even further risk for overweight (de Jong et al., 2013).

Finally, the broader food environment affects the incidence of obesity. The Pima Indians of Arizona, who two decades ago changed from a traditional diet of plant foods to a high-fat, typically American diet, have one of the world's highest obesity rates. Compared with descendants of their ancestors living in the remote Sierra Madre region of Mexico, the Arizona Pima have body weights 50 percent greater. Half the population has diabetes (8 times the national average), with many in their twenties and thirties already disabled by the disease—blind, in wheelchairs, and on kidney dialysis. The Pima have a genetic susceptibility to overweight, but it emerges only under Western dietary conditions. U.S. Pima children who are obese display double the rate of illness-related premature deaths after they reach adulthood as their normal-weight peers (Franks et al., 2010; Traurig et al., 2009). Other ethnic groups with a hereditary tendency to gain weight include Pacific Islanders, including native Hawaiians and Samoans (Furusawa et al., 2010). Many now eat an Americanized diet of high-calorie processed and fast foods, and over 80 percent are overweight.

CONSEQUENCES OF OBESITY Unfortunately, physical attractiveness is a powerful predictor of social acceptance. In Western societies, both children and adults rate obese youngsters as unlikable, stereotyping them as lazy, sloppy, dirty, ugly, stupid, and deceitful (Penny & Haddock, 2007; Tiggemann & Anesbury, 2000). In school, obese children and adolescents are often socially isolated. They report more emotional, social, and school difficulties, including peer teasing, rejection, and consequent low self-esteem (van Grieken et al., 2013; Zeller & Modi, 2006). They also tend to achieve less well than their healthy-weight agemates (Datar & Sturm, 2006).

Because unhappiness and overeating contribute to each other, the child remains overweight. Persistent obesity from childhood into adolescence predicts serious behavior problems, including defiance, aggression, severe depression, and suicidal thoughts and behavior (Puhl & Latner, 2007; Young-Hyman et al., 2006). As we will see in Chapter 14, overweight girls are more likely to reach puberty early, increasing their risk for early sexual activity and other adjustment problems.

The psychological consequences of obesity combine with continuing discrimination to result in reduced life chances. Overweight adults are less likely than their normal-weight agemates to receive financial aid for college, be rented apartments, find mates, and be offered jobs. And they report frequent mistreatment by family members, peers, co-workers, and health-care professionals, which intensifies physical and psychological health problems (Carr & Friedman, 2005; Puhl, Heuer, & Brownell, 2010).

TREATING OBESITY Childhood obesity is difficult to treat because it is a family disorder. In Mona's case, the school nurse suggested that Mona and her obese mother enter a weight-loss program together. But Mona's mother, unhappily married for many years, had her own reasons for overeating. She rejected this idea, claiming that Mona would eventually decide to lose weight on her own. In one study, only one-fourth of overweight parents judged their overweight children to have a weight problem (Jeffrey, 2004). Consistent with these findings, fewer than 20 percent of obese children get any treatment. Although many try to slim down in adolescence, they often go on crash diets that make matters worse. Temporary starvation leads to physical stress, discomfort, and fatigue. Soon the child returns to old eating patterns, and weight rebounds to a higher level. Then, to protect itself, the body burns calories more slowly and becomes more resistant to future weight loss.

The most effective interventions are family-based and focus on changing behaviors (Oude et al., 2009). In one program, both parent and child revised eating patterns, exercised daily, and reinforced each other with praise and points for progress, which they exchanged for special activities and times together. The more weight parents lost, the more their children lost (Wrotniak et al., 2004). Follow-ups after five and ten years showed that children maintained their weight loss more effectively than adults—a finding that underscores the importance of

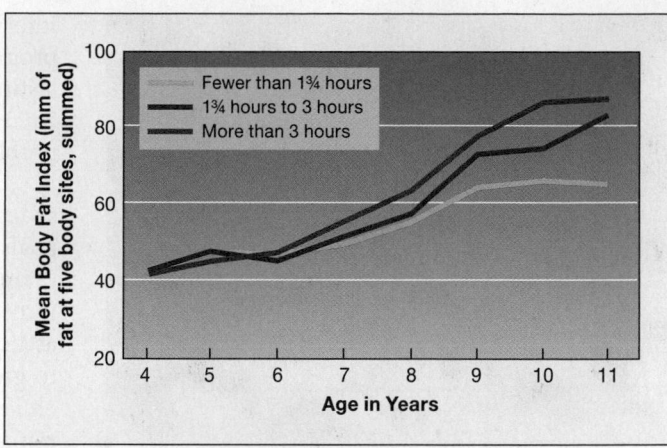

FIGURE 11.3 **Relationship of television viewing to gains in body fat from ages 4 to 11.** Researchers followed more than 100 children from ages 4 to 11, collecting information on hours per day of television viewing and on body fat, measured in millimeters of skinfold thickness at five body sites (upper arms, shoulders, abdomen, trunk, and thighs). The more TV children watched, the greater the gain in body fat. At ages 10 to 11, the difference between children watching fewer than 1¾ hours and those watching more than 3 hours had become large. (Adapted from M. H. Proctor et al., 2003, "Television Viewing and Change in Body Fat from Preschool to Early Adolescence: The Framingham Children's Study," *International Journal of Obesity, 27,* p. 831. Reprinted by permission from Macmillan Publishers Ltd.)

ARIEL SKELLEY/BLEND IMAGES/GETTY IMAGES

This mother and son reinforce each other's efforts to lose weight and get in shape. The most effective interventions for childhood obesity focus on changing the whole family's behaviors, emphasizing fitness and healthy eating.

intervening at an early age (Epstein, Roemmich, & Raynor, 2001). Treatment programs that focus on both diet and lifestyle can yield substantial, long-lasting weight reduction among children and adolescents (Nemet et al., 2005). But these interventions work best when parents' and children's weight problems are not severe.

Getting obese children to exercise is challenging because they find being sedentary pleasurable. Approaches that encourage setting personal exercise goals and keeping a record of success at meeting those goals are helpful (Staniford, Breckon, & Copeland, 2012). One successful technique is to reinforce obese children for spending less time inactive. Providing rewards (such as tickets to the zoo or a baseball game) for reducing sedentary time leads to greater liking for physical activity and more weight loss than reinforcing children directly for exercising or punishing them (by loss of privileges) for remaining inactive (Epstein et al., 1997). Rewarding children for giving up inactivity seems to increase their sense of personal control over exercising—a factor linked to sustained physical activity.

Children consume one-third of their daily energy intake at school. Therefore, schools can help reduce obesity by serving healthier meals and ensuring regular physical activity (Lakshman, Elks, & Ong, 2012). Because obesity is expected to rise further without broad prevention strategies, many U.S. states and cities have passed obesity-reduction legislation. Among measures taken are weight-related school screenings for all children, improved nutrition standards and limited vending machine access in schools, additional recess time in the elementary grades and physical education time in all grades, and obesity awareness and weight-reduction programs as part of school curricula. A review of school-based efforts reported impressive benefits (Waters et al., 2011). Obesity prevention in schools was more successful in reducing 6- to 12-year-olds' BMIs than programs delivered in other community settings, perhaps because schools are better able to provide long-term, comprehensive intervention.

Finally, obesity prevention and reduction are becoming U.S. national priorities. The *Let's Move* campaign, launched by First Lady Michelle Obama in 2010, aims to create partnerships among federal and state governments, communities, businesses, schools, and health organizations to solve the childhood obesity problem within a generation. Among its goals are:

- increased public education about healthy eating and physical activity, including limiting time devoted to TV viewing
- greater access to healthy, affordable foods in low-income neighborhoods, where overweight and obesity are highest
- laws mandating improved labels on foods and menus specifying nutritional content and calories
- improved quality of government-supported school breakfasts and lunches
- expanded opportunities for physical activity in schools as well as in communities, by building more parks, recreation centers, and walking and bike paths

For more information, visit *www.letsmove.gov*.

LOOK and **LISTEN**

Contact your state and city governments to find out about their childhood obesity prevention legislation. Can policies be improved?

Vision and Hearing

The most common vision problem in middle childhood is *myopia,* or nearsightedness. By the end of the school years, it affects nearly 25 percent of children—a rate that rises to 60 percent by early adulthood (Rahi, Cumberland, & Peckham, 2011).

Heredity plays a role: Identical twins are more likely than fraternal twins to share the condition (Pacella et al., 1999). And compared to children with no myopic parents, those with one myopic parent have twice the risk, and those with two myopic parents two to five times the risk, of becoming myopic themselves. Worldwide, myopia occurs far more frequently in Asian than in Caucasian populations (Morgan, Ohno-Matsui, & Saw, 2012). Early biological trauma can also induce myopia. School-age children with low birth weights show an especially high rate, believed to result from immaturity of visual structures, slower eye growth, and a greater incidence of eye disease (Molloy et al., 2013).

When parents warn their children not to read in dim light or sit too close to the TV or computer screen, their concern ("You'll ruin your eyes!") is well-founded. In diverse cultures, the more time children spend reading, writing, using the computer, and doing other close work, the more likely they are to be myopic. Conversely, the incidence of myopia is reduced in school-age children who spend more time playing outdoors (Pan, Ramamurthy, & Saw, 2012; Russo et al., 2014). Myopia is one of the few health conditions to increase with SES, and it has become more prevalent in recent generations. Fortunately, myopia can be overcome easily with corrective lenses.

During middle childhood, the Eustachian tube (canal that runs from the inner ear to the throat) becomes longer, narrower, and more slanted, preventing fluid and bacteria from traveling so easily from the mouth to the ear. As a result, *otitis media* (middle ear infection), common in infancy and early childhood (see Chapter 8), becomes less frequent. Still, about 3 to 4 percent of the school-age population, and as many as 20 percent of low-SES children, develop some hearing loss as a result of repeated infections (Ryding et al., 2002). With regular screening for both vision and hearing, defects can be corrected before they lead to serious learning difficulties.

Bedwetting

One Friday afternoon, Terry called Joey to see if he could sleep over, but Joey refused. "I can't," said Joey anxiously, without offering an explanation.

"Why not? We can take our sleeping bags out in the backyard. Come on, it'll be cool!"

"My mom won't let me," Joey responded, unconvincingly. "I mean, well, I think we're busy. We're doing something tonight."

"Gosh, Joey, this is the third time you've said no. See if I'll ask you again!" snapped Terry as he hung up the phone.

Joey is one of 10 percent of U.S. school-age children who suffer from **nocturnal enuresis,** or bedwetting during the night. At all ages, more boys than girls are affected. In the overwhelming majority of cases, the problem has biological roots. Heredity is a major contributing factor: Parents with a history of bedwetting are far more likely to have a child with the problem, and identical twins are more likely than fraternal twins to share it (von Gontard, Heron, & Joinson, 2011). Most often, enuresis is caused by a failure of muscular responses that inhibit urination or by a hormonal imbalance that permits too much urine to accumulate during the night. Some children also have difficulty awakening to the sensation of a full bladder (Becker, 2013). Punishing a school-age child for wetting is only likely to make matters worse.

To treat enuresis, doctors often prescribe a synthetic hormone called desmopressin, which reduces the amount of urine produced. Although medication is a short-term solution for children attending camp or visiting a friend's house, once children stop taking it, they typically begin wetting again (Kwak et al., 2010). The most effective treatment is a urine alarm that wakes the child at the first sign of dampness and works according to conditioning principles. Success rates of about 55 to 75 percent occur after four to six months of treatment (Glazener, Evans, & Petro, 2005). The few children who relapse achieve dryness after trying the alarm a second time.

Although a decade ago, only a minority of U.S. school-age children with nocturnal enuresis saw a health professional about the problem, today increasing numbers of parents seek treatment (Kushnir, Kushnir, & Sadeh, 2013). Doing so has immediate, positive psychological consequences. It leads to gains in restful sleep, parents' evaluation of their child's behavior, and children's self-esteem (Longstaffe, Moffatt, & Whalen, 2000). Although many children outgrow enuresis without intervention, this generally takes years.

Illnesses

Children experience a somewhat higher rate of illness during the first two years of elementary school than later, because of exposure to sick children and an immune system that is still developing. Typically, illness causes children to miss from 1 to 5 days of school per year (National Survey of Children's Health, 2012). Longer absences usually can be traced to a few students with chronic health problems.

About 20 to 25 percent of U.S. children living at home have chronic diseases and conditions (including physical disabilities) (Compas et al., 2012). By far the most common—accounting for about one-third of childhood chronic illness and the most frequent cause of school absence and childhood hospitalization—is *asthma,* in which the bronchial tubes (passages that connect the throat and lungs) are highly sensitive (Basinger, 2013). In response to a variety of stimuli, such as cold weather, infection, exercise, allergies, and emotional stress, they fill with mucus and contract, leading to coughing, wheezing, and serious breathing difficulties.

The prevalence of asthma in the United States has increased steadily over the past several decades. It is now at its highest level, with nearly 10 percent of children affected. Although heredity contributes to asthma, researchers believe that environmental factors are necessary to spark the illness. Boys, African-American children, and children who were born underweight, whose parents smoke, and who live in poverty are at greatest risk (Centers for Disease Control and Prevention, 2012; Pearlman et al., 2006). The higher rate and greater severity of asthma among African-American and poverty-stricken children may be the result of pollution in inner-city areas (which triggers allergic reactions), stressful home lives, and lack of access to good health care. Childhood obesity is also related to asthma (Hampton, 2014). High levels of blood-circulating inflammatory substances associated with body fat and the pressure of excess weight on the chest wall may be responsible.

These children, who live in an inner-city community where asthma is common, use a meter to measure the daily concentration of air pollutants. The device will warn them when pollution reaches a level likely to trigger asthma attacks.

About 2 percent of U.S. children have more severe chronic illnesses, such as sickle cell anemia, cystic fibrosis, diabetes, arthritis, cancer, and acquired immune deficiency syndrome (AIDS). Painful medical treatments, physical discomfort, and changes in appearance often disrupt the sick child's daily life, making it difficult to concentrate in school and separating the child from peers. As the illness worsens, family and child stress increases (Marin et al., 2009; Rodriguez, Dunn, & Compas, 2012). For these reasons, chronically ill children are at risk for academic, emotional, and social difficulties. In adolescence, they are more likely than their agemates to suffer from low self-esteem and depression and report more often smoking cigarettes, using illegal drugs, and thinking about and attempting suicide (Erickson et al., 2005).

A strong link exists between good family functioning and child well-being for chronically ill children, just as it does for physically healthy children (Compas et al., 2012). Interventions that foster positive family relationships help parent and child cope effectively with the disease and improve adjustment. These include:

- Health education, in which parents and children learn about the illness and get training in how to manage it
- Home visits by health professionals, who offer counseling and social support to enhance parents' and children's strategies for managing the stress of chronic illness
- Schools that accommodate children's special health and education needs
- Disease-specific summer camps, which teach children self-help skills and give parents time off from the demands of caring for an ill youngster
- Parent and peer support groups

Unintentional Injuries

As we conclude our discussion of threats to school-age children's health, let's return to the topic of unintentional injuries (discussed in detail in Chapter 8). As Figure 11.4 shows, injury fatalities increase from middle childhood into adolescence, with rates for boys rising considerably above those for girls. Poverty and either rural or inner-city residence—factors associated with dangerous environments and reduced parental monitoring of children—are also linked to high injury rates (Birken et al., 2006; Schwebel et al., 2004).

Motor vehicle accidents, involving children as passengers or pedestrians, continue to be the leading cause of injury, followed by bicycle accidents (Bailar-Heath & Valley-Gray, 2010). Pedestrian injuries most often result from midblock dart-outs, bicycle accidents from disobeying traffic signals and rules. When many stimuli impinge on them at once, young school-age children often fail to think before they act. They need frequent reminders, supervision, and prohibitions against venturing into busy traffic on their own. Yet a study that tracked routine supervision provided to middle-SES 7- to 10-year-olds at home revealed that the children were unsupervised 35 percent of the time (Morrongiello, Kane, Zdzieborski, 2011). Both nonsupervision and indirect supervision (parent checking on the child intermittently) were associated with increased injuries.

As children range farther from home, safety education related to their widening world becomes important. Effective school- and community-based prevention programs use extensive modeling and rehearsal of safety practices, give children feedback about their performance along with praise and tangible rewards for acquiring safety skills, and provide occasional booster sessions. Targeting specific injury risks (such as traffic safety) rather than many risks at once yields longer-lasting results (Nauta et al., 2014). As part of these programs, parents, who often overestimate their child's safety knowledge and physical abilities, must be educated about children's age-related safety capacities (Schwebel & Bounds, 2003).

One vital safety measure is legally requiring that children wear protective helmets while bicycling, in-line skating, skateboarding, or using scooters. This precaution leads to a 9 percent reduction in head injuries, a leading cause of permanent physical disability and death in school-age children (Karkhaneh et al., 2013). Combining helmet use with preventive education and other community-based prevention strategies is especially effective. In the Harlem Hospital Injury Prevention Program, inner-city children attended bicycle safety clinics, during which helmets were distributed. They also received traffic safety education in their classrooms and in a simulated traffic environment. In addition, existing playgrounds were improved and new ones constructed to provide expanded off-street play areas, and more community-sponsored, supervised recreational activities were offered (Durkin et al., 1999). As a result, motor vehicle and bicycle injuries declined by 36 percent.

Not all children respond to efforts to increase their safety. By middle childhood, the greatest risk-takers tend to be those whose parents do not act as safety-conscious models, rarely supervise their children's activities, or use punitive or inconsistent discipline to enforce rules (Rowe, Maughan, & Goodman, 2004; Tuchfarber, Zins, & Jason, 1997). These child-rearing tactics, as we saw in Chapter 10, spark children's defiance, reduce their willingness to comply, and actually promote high-risk behavior.

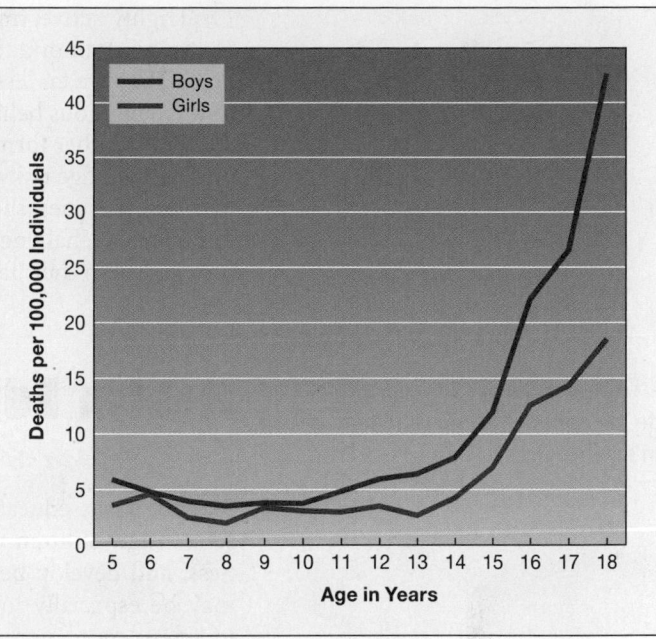

FIGURE 11.4 **U.S. rates of injury mortality from middle childhood to adolescence.** Injury fatalities increase with age, and the gap between boys and girls expands. Motor vehicle (passenger and pedestrian) accidents are the leading cause, with bicycle injuries next in line. (Based on National Center for Injury Prevention and Control, 2013.)

These Oglala children of South Dakota risk serious injury when they don't wear helmets while riding bikes and horses. Head injuries are a leading cause of permanent disability and death in school-age children.

Highly active, impulsive children, many of whom are boys, remain particularly susceptible to injury in middle childhood. Although they have just as much safety knowledge as their peers, they are far less likely to implement it. Parents tend to be particularly lax in intervening in the dangerous behaviors of such children, especially under conditions of persistent marital conflict or other forms of distress (Schwebel et al., 2011, 2012). Furthermore, compared with girls, boys judge risky play activities as less likely to result in injury, and they pay less attention to injury risk cues, such as a peer who looks hesitant or fearful (Morrongiello & Rennie, 1998). The greatest challenge for injury-control programs is reaching these children, altering high-risk factors in their families, and reducing the dangers to which they are exposed.

11.6 What can parents and teachers do to encourage good health practices in school-age children?

Health Education

Psychologists, educators, and pediatricians are intensely interested in finding ways to help school-age children understand their bodies, acquire mature conceptions of health and illness, and develop behaviors that foster good health throughout life. The school-age period may be especially important for fostering healthy lifestyles because of the child's growing independence, increasing cognitive capacities, and rapidly developing self-concept, which includes a sense of physical well-being.

During middle childhood, children can comprehend a wide range of health information—about the structure and functioning of their bodies, about good nutrition, and about the causes and consequences of physical injuries and diseases. When given scientific facts, they build on basic biological concepts acquired during the preschool years, and their understanding advances. For example, a 5-year-old is likely to say, "You get a cold when your friend sneezes and gives you her germs" (Legare, Zhu, & Wellman, 2013). A 10-year-old, in contrast, offers a deeper, more detailed explanation: "You get a cold when your sinuses fill with mucus. Sometimes your lungs do, too, and you get a cough. Colds come from viruses. They get into the bloodstream and make your platelet count go down" (Myant & Williams, 2005).

Without effective teaching, however, school-age children readily generalize their knowledge of familiar health conditions to less familiar ones. As a result, they may conclude that risk factors for colds (getting sneezed on, sharing a Coke) can cause AIDS or that cancer (like a cold) is contagious (González-Rivera & Bauermeister, 2007). Furthermore, supernatural accounts of illness widespread in certain cultures—such as "Maybe his sickness is punishment for bad behavior"—must be gently countered with scientific facts (Raman & Gelman, 2004). Otherwise, these incorrect ideas can lead to unnecessary anxiety about getting a serious disease.

A visiting doctor discusses biological information about the human body with fifth graders. When school-age children are provided with scientific facts, they gain in understanding of health and illness.

Nevertheless, most efforts to impart health information to school-age children have little impact on behavior (Tinsley, 2003). Several related reasons underlie this gap between knowledge and practice:

- Health is seldom an important goal for children, who feel good most of the time. They are far more concerned about schoolwork, friends, and play.
- Children do not yet have an adultlike time perspective that relates past, present, and future. They cannot see the connection between engaging in preventive behaviors now and experiencing later health consequences.
- Much health information given to children is contradicted by other sources, such as television advertising and the examples of adults and peers.

Consequently, teaching school-age children health-related facts, though important, must be supplemented by other efforts. As we have seen, a powerful means of fostering children's

Applying What We Know

Strategies for Fostering Healthy Lifestyles in School-Age Children

STRATEGY	DESCRIPTION
Increase health-related knowledge and encourage healthy behaviors.	Provide health education that imparts scientific information about health concepts and healthy lifestyles and that includes modeling, role playing, rehearsal, and reinforcement of good health practices.
Involve parents in supporting health education.	Communicate with parents about health education goals in school, encouraging them to extend these efforts at home. Teach parents about unhealthy dietary practices and how to create healthy food environments at home. Promote proper parental supervision by providing information on children's age-related safety capacities.
Provide healthy environments in schools.	Ask school administrators to ensure that school breakfasts and lunches follow widely accepted dietary guidelines. Limit access to vending machines with junk food. Work for daily recess periods in elementary school and mandatory daily physical education at all grade levels.
Make voluntary screening for risk factors available as part of health education.	Offer periodic measures of height, weight, body mass, blood pressure, and adequacy of diet. Educate children about the meaning of each index, and encourage improvement.
Promote pleasurable physical activity.	Provide opportunities for regular, vigorous physical exercise through activities that de-emphasize competition and stress skill building and personal and social enjoyment.
Teach children to be critical of media advertising.	Besides teaching children to be skeptical of ads for unhealthy foods on TV and other screen media, reduce such advertising in schools—for example, on sports scoreboards.
Work for safer, healthier community environments for children.	Form community action groups to improve child safety, school nutrition, and play environments, and initiate community programs that foster healthy physical activity.

health is to reduce hazards, such as pollution, an unhealthy diet, and inadequate medical and dental care. At the same time, because environments will never be totally free of health risks, parents and teachers must coach children in good health practices and must model and reinforce these behaviors. Refer to Applying What We Know above for ways to foster healthy lifestyles in school-age children.

Ask Yourself

● **REVIEW** Select one of the following health problems of middle childhood: obesity, myopia, bedwetting, asthma, or unintentional injuries. Explain how both genetic and environmental factors contribute to it.

● **CONNECT** Children who were undernourished in the early years are more likely to become overweight when their food environments improve. Explain how this finding illustrates epigenesis, described on page 86 in Chapter 2.

● **APPLY** Nine-year-old Talia is afraid to hug and kiss her grandmother, who has cancer. What explains Talia's mistaken belief that the same behaviors that cause colds to spread might lead her to catch cancer? What would you do to change her thinking?

● **REFLECT** List unintentional injuries that you experienced as a child. Were you injury-prone? Why or why not?

Motor Development and Play

TAKE A MOMENT... Visit a park on a pleasant weekend afternoon, and watch several preschool and school-age children at play. You will see that gains in body size and muscle strength support improved motor coordination during middle childhood. And greater cognitive and social maturity enables older children to use their new motor skills in more complex ways. A major change in children's play takes place at this time.

11.7 Cite major changes in gross- and fine-motor development during middle childhood.

11.8 Describe individual differences in motor performance during middle childhood.

11.9 What qualities of children's play are evident in middle childhood?

11.10 What steps can schools take to promote physical fitness in middle childhood?

Improved physical flexibility, balance, agility, and force, along with more efficient information processing, promote gains in school-age children's gross-motor skills.

Gross-Motor Development

During the school years, running, jumping, hopping, and ball skills become more refined. At Joey and Lizzie's school, we watched during the third to sixth graders' recess. Children burst into sprints as they raced across the playground, jumped quickly over rotating ropes, engaged in intricate hopscotch patterns, kicked and dribbled soccer balls, batted at balls pitched by their classmates, and balanced adeptly as they walked heel-to-toe across narrow ledges. Table 11.2 summarizes gross-motor achievements between 6 and 12 years of age. These diverse skills reflect gains in four basic motor capacities:

- *Flexibility.* Compared with preschoolers, school-age children are physically more pliable and elastic, a difference evident as they swing bats, kick balls, jump over hurdles, and execute tumbling routines.
- *Balance.* Improved balance supports many athletic skills, including running, hopping, skipping, throwing, kicking, and the rapid changes of direction required in many team sports.
- *Agility.* Quicker and more accurate movements are evident in the fancy footwork of dance and cheerleading and in the forward, backward, and sideways motions used to dodge opponents in tag and soccer.
- *Force.* Older children can throw and kick a ball harder and propel themselves farther off the ground when running and jumping than they could at earlier ages (Haywood & Getchell, 2014).

Along with body growth, more efficient information processing plays a vital role in improved motor performance. Younger children often have difficulty with skills that require rapid responding, such as dribbling and batting. During middle childhood, the capacity to react only to relevant information increases. And steady gains in reaction time occur, including anticipatory

TABLE 11.2	**Changes in Gross-Motor Skills During Middle Childhood**	
	SKILL	**DEVELOPMENTAL CHANGE**
	Running	Running speed increases from 12 feet per second at age 6 to over 18 feet per second at age 12.
	Other gait variations	Skipping improves. Sideways stepping appears around age 6 and becomes more continuous and fluid with age.
	Vertical jump	Height jumped increases from 4 inches at age 6 to 12 inches at age 12.
	Standing broad jump	Distance jumped increases from 3 feet at age 6 to over 5 feet at age 12.
	Precision jumping and hopping (on a mat divided into squares)	By age 7, children can accurately jump and hop from square to square, a performance that improves until age 9 and then levels off.
	Throwing	Throwing speed, distance, and accuracy increase for both sexes, but much more for boys than for girls. At age 6, a ball thrown by a boy travels 39 feet per second, one by a girl 29 feet per second. At age 12, a ball thrown by a boy travels 78 feet per second, one by a girl 56 feet per second.
	Catching	Ability to catch small balls thrown over greater distances improves with age.
	Kicking	Kicking speed and accuracy improve, with boys considerably ahead of girls. At age 6, a ball kicked by a boy travels 21 feet per second, one by a girl 13 feet per second. At age 12, a ball kicked by a boy travels 34 feet per second, one by a girl 26 feet per second.
	Batting	Batting motions become more effective with age, increasing in speed and accuracy and involving the entire body.
	Dribbling	Style of hand dribbling gradually changes, from awkward slapping of the ball to continuous, relaxed, even stroking.

Sources: Haywood & Getchell, 2014; Malina & Bouchard, 1991.

responding to repeated visual stimuli, such as a thrown ball in a game of catch or a turning rope in a game of jump rope: Ten-year-olds react twice as quickly as 5-year-olds (Debrabant et al., 2012; Kail, 2003). These differences in speed of reaction have practical implications for physical education. Because 5- to 7-year-olds are seldom successful at batting a thrown ball, T-ball is more appropriate for them than baseball. Similarly, handball, four-square, and kickball should precede instruction in tennis, basketball, and football.

Fine-Motor Development

Fine-motor development also improves over the school years. On rainy afternoons, Joey and Lizzie experimented with yo-yos, built model airplanes, and wove potholders on small looms. Like many children, they took up musical instruments, which demand considerable fine-motor control. And gains in fine-motor skill are especially evident in children's writing and drawing.

By age 6, most children can print the alphabet, their first and last names, and the numbers from 1 to 10 with reasonable clarity. Their writing is large, however, because they make strokes using the entire arm rather than just the wrist and fingers. Children usually master uppercase letters first because their horizontal and vertical motions are easier to control than the small curves of the lowercase alphabet. Legibility of writing gradually increases as children produce more accurate letters with uniform height and spacing.

Children's drawings show dramatic gains in organization, detail, and representation of depth during middle childhood. By the end of the preschool years, children can accurately copy many two-dimensional shapes, and they integrate these into their drawings. Some depth cues have also begun to appear, such as making distant objects smaller than near ones (Braine et al., 1993). Yet recall from Chapter 8 that before age 8, children have trouble accurately copying a three-dimensional form, such as a cube or cylinder (see page 304). Around 9 to 10 years, the third dimension is clearly evident through overlapping objects, diagonal placement, and converging lines. Furthermore, as Figure 11.5 shows, school-age children not only depict objects in considerable detail but also relate them to one another as part of an organized whole (Case, 1998; Case & Okamoto, 1996).

INTERNATIONAL COLLECTION OF CHILD ART, MILNER LIBRARY, ILLINOIS STATE UNIVERSITY, NORMAL, IL

FIGURE 11.5 Increase in organization, detail, and depth cues in school-age children's drawings. TAKE A MOMENT... Compare both drawings to the one by a 6-year-old in Figure 8.8 on page 304. In the drawing by an 8-year-old on the top, notice how all parts are depicted in relation to one another and with greater detail. Integration of depth cues increases dramatically over the school years, as shown in the drawing on the bottom by an 11-year-old. Here, depth is indicated by overlapping objects, diagonal placement, and converging lines, as well as by making distant objects smaller than near ones.

Individual Differences in Motor Skills

As at younger ages, school-age children show marked individual differences in motor capacities that are influenced by both heredity and environment. Body build is one factor: Taller, more muscular children excel at many motor tasks. And children whose parents encourage physical exercise tend to enjoy it more and also to be more skilled.

Family income affects children's access to lessons needed to develop abilities in areas such as ballet, tennis, gymnastics, and instrumental music. For low-SES children, school and community provisions for nurturing athletics and other motor skills by making lessons, equipment, and opportunities for regular practice available and affordable are crucial. When these experiences combine with parental encouragement, many low-SES children become highly skilled.

Sex differences in motor skills that appeared during the preschool years extend into middle childhood and, in some instances, become more pronounced. Girls have an edge in fine-motor skills of handwriting and drawing and in gross-motor capacities that depend on balance and agility, such as hopping and skipping (Haywood & Getchell, 2014). But boys out-perform girls on all other skills listed in Table 11.2, especially throwing and kicking.

School-age boys' genetic advantage in muscle mass is not large enough to account for their gross-motor superiority. Rather, the social environment plays a larger role. Research confirms that parents hold higher expectations for boys' athletic performance, and children readily absorb these messages. From first through twelfth grades, girls are less positive than boys about the value of sports and their own sports ability—differences explained in part by parental beliefs (Fredricks & Eccles, 2002; Gentile et al., 2009). The more strongly girls believe that females are incompetent at sports (such as hockey or soccer), the lower they judge their own ability and the poorer they actually perform (Belcher et al., 2003; Chalabaev, Sarrazin, & Fontayne, 2009). But girls and older school-age children regard boys' advantage in sports as unjust. They indicate, for example, that coaches should spend equal time with children of each sex and that female sports should command just as much media attention as male sports (Solomon & Bredemeier, 1999).

Educating parents about the minimal differences between school-age boys' and girls' physical capacities and sensitizing them to unfair biases against promotion of girls' athletic ability may help increase girls' self-confidence and participation in athletics. Greater emphasis on skill training for girls, along with increased attention to their athletic achievements, is also likely to help. As a positive sign, compared with a generation ago, many more girls now participate in individual and team sports such as gymnastics and soccer, though their involvement continues to lag behind boys' (Kanters et al., 2013; Sabo & Veliz, 2011). Middle childhood is a crucial time to encourage girls' sports participation because during this period, children start to discover what they are good at and make some definite skill commitments.

Games with Rules

The physical activities of school-age children reflect an important advance in quality of play: Games with rules become common. Children around the world engage in an enormous variety of informally organized games, including variants on popular sports such as soccer, baseball, and basketball. In addition to the best-known childhood games, such as tag, jacks, and hopscotch, children have also invented hundreds of other games, including red rover, statues, leapfrog, kick the can, and prisoner's base.

Gains in perspective taking—in particular, the ability to understand the roles of several players in a game—permit this transition to rule-oriented games. These play experiences, in turn, contribute greatly to emotional and social development. Child-invented games usually rely on simple physical skills and a sizable element of luck. As a result, they rarely become contests of individual ability. Instead, they permit children to try out different styles of cooperating, competing, winning, and losing with little personal risk. Also, in their efforts to organize a game, children discover why rules are necessary and which ones work well. In fact, they often spend as much time working out the details of how a game should proceed as they do playing the game! As we will see in Chapter 13, these experiences help children form more mature concepts of fairness and justice.

Compared with past generations, children today spend less time gathering informally on sidewalks and in playgrounds. In part, this change reflects parental concern about neighborhood safety, as well as competition for children's time from TV, video games, and the Internet. Another factor is the rise in adult-organized sports, such as Little League baseball and soccer and hockey leagues, which fill many hours that children from economically advantaged families used to devote to spontaneous play.

Still, in village societies in developing countries and in many low-SES communities in industrialized nations, children's informal sports and games remain common. In an ethnographic study

A group of boys gather in their school yard for a pick-up game of basketball. Unlike their economically advantaged agemates, children in low-SES communities often play child-organized games, which serve as rich contexts for social learning.

in two communities—one a refugee camp in Angola, Africa, the other a Chicago public housing complex—the overwhelming majority of 6- to 12-year-olds engaged in child-organized games at least once a week, and half or more did so nearly every day. Play in each context reflected distinct cultural values (Guest, 2013). In the Angolan community, games emphasized imitation of social roles—soccer moves of admired professional players, the intricate operation of a cooking spice shop. Games in Chicago, in contrast, were competitive and individualistic. In ballgames, for example, children often made sure peers noticed when they batted or fielded balls particularly well.

Adult-Organized Youth Sports

About half of U.S. children—60 percent of boys and 37 percent of girls—participate in organized sports outside of school hours at some time between ages 5 and 18 (National Council of Youth Sports, 2008; SFIA, 2013). Children in low-SES communities, however, are profoundly underserved, with girls and ethnic minorities having especially limited opportunities. In a comparison of two neighborhoods in Oakland, Calfornia, 67 percent of teenage girls in a well-to-do area were members of athletic teams (Team Up for Youth, 2014). But just a few miles away, in a poverty-stricken, largely minority part of the city, a mere 11 percent were involved in organized sports.

With their coach's encouragement, these young softball players are likely to view themselves as good at sports and to continue playing. In contrast, coaches who criticize and overemphasize competition promote early athletic dropout.

For most children, joining community athletic teams is associated with increased self-esteem and social skills (Daniels & Leaper, 2006; Fletcher, Nickerson, & Wright, 2003). Among shy children, sports participation seems to play a protective role, fostering self-confidence and a decline in social anxiety, perhaps because it provides a sense of group belonging and a basis for communicating with peers (Findlay & Coplan, 2008). And children who view themselves as good at sports are more likely to continue playing on teams in adolescence, which predicts greater participation in sports and other physical fitness activities in early adulthood (Kjønniksen, Anderssen, & Wold, 2009; Marsh et al., 2007).

In some cases, though, the arguments of critics—that youth sports overemphasize competition and substitute adult control for children's natural experimentation with rules and strategies—are valid. When coaches make winning paramount, weaker performers generally experience social ostracism, with boys—for whom competence at sports is linked to peer admiration—affected more than girls (Stryer, Tofler, & Lapchick, 1998). And children who join teams so early that the necessary skills are beyond their abilities soon lose interest.

Parents, even more than coaches, influence children's athletic attitudes and abilities. At the extreme are parents who value sports so highly that they punish their child for making mistakes, insist that the child keep playing after injury, hold the child back in school to ensure a physical advantage, or even seek medical interventions to improve the child's performance (Wall & Côté, 2007). High parental pressure sets the stage for emotional difficulties and early athletic dropout, not elite performance.

In most organized youth sports, health and safety rules help ensure that injuries are infrequent and mild. An exception is football, which has a high incidence of serious injury. Eight- to 12-year-old boys in tackle football leagues experience rates of *concussion*—brain injuries resulting from a blow to the head or body—that equal those of high school and college players (Kontos et al., 2013). And in any sport, frequent, intense practice can lead to painful "overuse" injuries that, in extreme cases, cause stress-related fractures resulting in impaired physical growth (Frank et al., 2007). On highly competitive teams with year-round training, overuse injuries are common.

When parents and coaches emphasize effort, improvement, participation, and teamwork, young athletes enjoy sports more, exert greater effort to improve their skills, and perceive themselves as more competent at their chosen sport (Ullrich-French & Smith, 2006). See Applying What We Know on page 424 for ways to ensure that athletic leagues provide children with positive learning experiences.

LOOK and LISTEN

Observe a youth athletic-league game, such as soccer, baseball, or hockey. Do coaches and parents encourage children's effort and skill gains, or are they overly focused on winning? Cite examples of adult and child behaviors.

Applying What We Know

Providing Developmentally Appropriate Organized Sports in Middle Childhood

STRATEGY	DESCRIPTION
Build on children's interests.	Permit children to select from among appropriate activities the ones that suit them best. Do not push children into sports they do not enjoy.
Teach age-appropriate skills.	For children younger than age 9, emphasize basic skills, such as kicking, throwing, and batting, and simplified games that grant all participants adequate playing time.
Emphasize enjoyment.	Permit children to progress at their own pace and to play for the fun of it, whether or not they become expert athletes.
Limit the frequency and length of practices.	Adjust practice time to children's attention spans and need for unstructured time with peers, with family, and for homework. Two practices a week, each no longer than 30 minutes for younger school-age children and 60 minutes for older school-age children, are sufficient.
Focus on personal and team improvement.	Emphasize effort, skill gains, and teamwork rather than winning. Avoid criticism for errors and defeat, which promotes anxiety and avoidance of athletics.
Discourage unhealthy competition.	Avoid all-star games and championship ceremonies that recognize individuals. Instead, acknowledge all participants.
Permit children to contribute to rules and strategies.	Involve children in decisions aimed at ensuring fair play and teamwork. To strengthen desirable responses, reinforce compliance rather than punishing noncompliance.

Shadows of Our Evolutionary Past

TAKE A MOMENT... While watching children in your neighborhood park, notice how they occasionally wrestle, roll, hit, and run after one another, alternating roles while smiling and laughing. This friendly chasing and play-fighting is called **rough-and-tumble play.** It emerges in the preschool years and peaks in middle childhood, and children in many cultures engage in it with peers whom they like especially well (Pellegrini, 2004). After a rough-and-tumble episode, children continue interacting rather than separating, as they do after an aggressive encounter.

Children's rough-and-tumble play resembles the social behavior of many other young mammals. It seems to originate in parents' physical play with babies, especially fathers' play with sons (see page 269 in Chapter 7). And it is more common among boys, probably because prenatal exposure to androgens predisposes boys toward active play (see Chapter 10, page 385). Boys' rough-and-tumble largely consists of playful wrestling and hitting, whereas girls tend to engage in running and chasing, with only brief physical contact.

In middle childhood, rough-and-tumble accounts for as much as 10 percent of free-play behavior, before declining in adolescence. In our evolutionary past, it may have been important for developing fighting skill. It also helps children form a **dominance hierarchy**—a stable ordering of group members that predicts who will win when conflict arises. Observations of arguments, threats, and physical attacks between children reveal a consistent lineup of winners and losers that becomes increasingly stable in middle childhood and adolescence, especially among boys. Once school-age children establish a dominance hierarchy, hostility is rare. Children seem to use play-fighting as a safe context to assess the strength of a peer before challenging that peer's dominance (Fry, 2014; Roseth et al., 2007). Rough-and-tumble play offers lessons in how to handle combative interactions with restraint.

As children reach puberty, individual differences in strength become apparent, and rough-and-tumble play declines. When it does occur, its meaning changes: Adolescent boys' rough-and-tumble is linked to aggression (Pellegrini, 2003). Unlike children, teenage rough-and-tumble players "cheat," hurting their opponent. In explanation, boys often say that they are retaliating, apparently to reestablish dominance. Thus, a play behavior that limits aggression in childhood becomes a context for hostility in adolescence.

© CLEVE BRYANT/PHOTOEDIT

In our evolutionary past, rough-and-tumble play—which can be distinguished from aggression by its friendly quality—may have been important for developing fighting skill and establishing dominance hierarchies.

Social Issues: Education

School Recess—A Time to Play, a Time to Learn

When 7-year-old Whitney's family moved to a new city, she left a school with three daily recess periods for one with just a single 15-minute break per day, which her second-grade teacher canceled if any child misbehaved. Whitney, who had previously enjoyed school, complained daily of headaches and an upset stomach. Her mother, Jill, thought, "My child is stressing out because she can't move all day!" After Jill and other parents successfully appealed to the school board to add a second recess period, Whitney's symptoms vanished (Rauber, 2006).

In recent years, recess—along with its rich opportunities for child-organized play and peer interaction—has diminished or disappeared in many U.S. schools (American Academy of Pediatrics, 2013). Under the assumption that extra time for academics will translate into achievement gains, 80 percent of school districts no longer require daily recess for elementary school students. Among districts that do, fewer than half mandate at least 20 minutes of recess per day (Centers for Disease Control and Prevention, 2014b).

Yet rather than subtracting from classroom learning, recess periods boost it! Research dating back more than 100 years confirms that distributing cognitively demanding tasks over a longer time by introducing regular breaks, rather than consolidating intensive effort within one period, enhances attention and performance at all ages. Such breaks are particularly important for young children.

In a series of studies, school-age children were more attentive in the classroom after recess than before it—an effect that was greater for second than fourth graders (Pellegrini, Huberty, & Jones, 1995). And relative to nonparticipating agemates, second and third graders randomly assigned to a program of 10-minute periods of physical activity distributed across the school day scored substantially higher in academic achievement at a three-year follow-up (Donnelly et al., 2009). Teacher ratings of classroom disruptive behavior also decline for children who have more than 15 minutes of recess a day (Barros, Silver, & Stein, 2009).

In another investigation, kindergartners' and first graders' engagement in peer conversation and games during recess positively predicted later academic achievement, even after other factors that might explain the relationship (such as previous achievement) were controlled (Pellegrini et al., 2002). Recall from Chapter 10 that children's social maturity contributes substantially to early academic competence. Recess is one of the few remaining contexts devoted to child-organized games that provide practice in vital social skills—cooperation, leadership, followership, and inhibition of aggression—under adult supervision rather than direction. As children transfer these skills to the classroom, they may join in discussions, collaborate, follow rules, and enjoy academic pursuits more—factors that enhance motivation and achievement.

Finally, children are even more physically active during recess than in gym class (U.S.

School-age children, especially girls, are even more physically active during recess than in gym class. By providing regular opportunities for unstructured play and games, recess promotes physical, academic, and social competence.

Department of Education, 2006). School-age girls, especially, engage in more moderate-to-vigorous exercise during recess than at other times of the day (Mota et al., 2005). In sum, regular, unstructured recess fosters children's health and competence—physically, academically, and socially.

Physical Education

Physical activity supports many aspects of children's development—their health, their sense of self-worth as physically active and capable beings, and the cognitive and social skills necessary for getting along with others. A large body of evidence links school-based physical activity to improved academic achievement (Centers for Disease Control and Prevention, 2010). Yet to devote more time to academic instruction, U.S. elementary schools have cut back on recess (see the Social Issues: Education box above).

Similarly, although most U.S. states require some physical education, only six require it in every grade, and only one mandates at least 30 minutes per school day in elementary school and 45 minutes in middle and high school. Nearly half of U.S elementary and secondary school students do not attend any physical education classes during a typical school week. Not surprisingly, physical inactivity among children and adolescents is

These children participate in a friendly running race where finishing—not winning—is the goal. Many experts believe that physical education classes should emphasize informal games, individual exercise, and personal progress rather than competitive sports.

pervasive. Fewer than one-third of 6- to 17-year-olds engage in at least moderate-intensity activity for 60 minutes per day, including some vigorous activity (involving breathing hard and sweating) on three of those days—the U.S. government recommendations for good health (National Association for Sport and Physical Education, 2012). With the transition to adolescence, physical activity declines, more for girls than for boys.

Many experts believe that schools should not only offer more frequent physical education classes but also change the content of these programs. Training in competitive sports, often a high priority, is unlikely to reach the least physically fit youngsters, who avoid activities demanding a high level of skill. Instead, programs should emphasize enjoyable, informal games and individual exercise (walking, running, jumping, tumbling, and climbing)—pursuits most likely to endure. Furthermore, children of varying skill levels are more likely to sustain physical activity when teachers focus on each child's personal progress and contribution to team accomplishment (Connor, 2003). Then physical education fosters a healthy sense of self while satisfying school-age children's need to participate with others.

Physically fit children take great pleasure in their rapidly developing motor skills. As a result, they develop rewarding interests in physical activity and sports and are more likely to become active adolescents and adults who reap many benefits (Kjønniksen, Torsheim, & Wold, 2008). These include greater physical strength, resistance to many illnesses (from colds and flu to cancer, diabetes, and heart disease), enhanced psychological well-being, and a longer life.

Ask Yourself

- **REVIEW** Explain the adaptive value of rough-and-tumble play and dominance hierarchies.

- **CONNECT** On Saturdays, 10-year-old Billy gathers with friends on the driveway of his house to play basketball. Besides improved ball skills, what else is he learning?

- **APPLY** Nine-year-old Allison thinks she isn't good at sports, and she doesn't like physical education class. Suggest some strategies her teacher can use to improve her pleasure and involvement in physical activity.

- **REFLECT** Did you participate in adult-organized sports as a child? If so, what kind of climate for learning did coaches and parents create? What impact do you think your experiences had on your development?

Summary

Body Growth (p. 405)

11.1 Describe changes in body size, proportions, and skeletal maturity during middle childhood.

- School-age children's growth is slow and regular, though large individual and ethnic variations exist in physical growth. On average, they add about 2 to 3 inches in height and 5 pounds in weight each year. By age 9, girls overtake boys in physical size.

- **Secular trends in physical growth** have occurred in industrialized nations. Because of improved health and nutrition, many children are growing larger and reaching physical maturity earlier than their ancestors.

- Bones continue to lengthen and broaden, and permanent teeth replace primary teeth. Tooth decay affects over half of U.S. school-age children, with especially high levels among low-SES children. One-third of school-age children suffer from **malocclusion**, making braces common by the end of elementary school.

11.2 Describe brain development in middle childhood.

- Only a small gain in brain size occurs during middle childhood. White matter (myelinated nerve fibers) rises steadily. As interconnectivity among distant areas of the cerebral cortex increases, the prefrontal cortex becomes a more effective "executive." Gray matter (neurons and supportive material) peaks and then declines as a result of synaptic pruning. Accompanying reorganization and selection of brain circuits lead to more effective information processing, especially executive function.

Common Health Problems (p. 409)

11.3 Describe the causes and consequences of serious nutritional problems in middle childhood, giving special attention to obesity.

- Poverty-stricken children in developing countries and in the United States continue to suffer from serious and prolonged malnutrition, which can permanently impair physical and mental development.

ZACK WITTMAN FOR THE BOSTON GLOBE VIA GETTY IMAGES

- Overweight and **obesity** have increased dramatically in both industrialized and developing nations. Although heredity contributes to obesity, parental feeding practices, maladaptive eating habits, reduced sleep, lack of exercise, and Western high-fat diets are more powerful influences. Obese children are often socially rejected, are more likely to report feeling depressed, and display more behavior problems than their normal-weight peers.

- Family-based interventions aimed at changing parents' and children's eating patterns and lifestyles are the most effective approaches to treating childhood obesity. Rewarding obese children for reducing sedentary time is effective in getting them to enjoy and engage in more physical activity. Schools can help by ensuring regular physical activity and serving healthier meals.

11.4 What factors contribute to myopia, otitis media, nocturnal enuresis, and asthma, and how can these health problems be reduced?

- The most common vision problem, myopia, is influenced by heredity, early biological trauma, and time spent reading and doing other close work. It is one of the few health conditions that increases with family education and income. Although ear infections decline during the school years, many low-SES children experience some hearing loss because of chronic, untreated otitis media.

- Heredity is responsible for most cases of **nocturnal enuresis,** through a failure of muscular responses that inhibit urination or a hormonal imbalance that permits too much urine to accumulate. The most effective treatment is a urine alarm that works according to conditioning principles.

- Asthma is the most frequent cause of school absence and hospitalization in U.S. children. It occurs more often among African-American and poverty-stricken children, perhaps because of inner-city pollution, stressful home lives, and lack of access to good health care. Childhood obesity is also a factor.

- Children with severe chronic illnesses are at risk for academic, emotional, and social difficulties, but positive family interactions improve adjustment.

11.5 Describe changes in the occurrence of unintentional injuries during middle childhood, and cite effective interventions.

- Unintentional injuries increase over middle childhood and adolescence, especially for boys, with motor vehicle and bicycle accidents accounting for most of the rise. Parental supervision is key to preventing such injuries.

- Effective school- and community-based safety education programs use modeling and rehearsal of safety practices and reward children for good performance. Parents also must be educated about children's age-related safety capacities. One vital safety measure is insisting that children wear protective bicycle helmets, which dramatically reduces the risk of serious head injury.

Health Education (p. 418)

11.6 What can parents and teachers do to encourage good health practices in school-age children?

- Besides providing health-related information, adults must reduce health hazards in children's environments, coach children in good health practices, and model and reinforce these behaviors.

Motor Development and Play (p. 419)

11.7 Cite major changes in gross- and fine-motor development during middle childhood.

- Gross-motor improvements in flexibility, balance, agility, and force occur, and gains in responding only to relevant information and in reaction time also contribute to athletic performance.

- Fine-motor development also improves. Handwriting becomes more legible, and children's drawings show dramatic increases in organization, detail, and representation of depth.

11.8 Describe individual differences in motor performance during middle childhood.

- Wide individual differences in children's motor capacities are influenced by both heredity and environment, including such factors as body build, parental encouragement, and opportunities to take lessons.

- Gender stereotypes, which affect parental expectations for children's athletic performance, largely account for school-age boys' superiority on a wide range of gross-motor skills. Greater emphasis on skill training for girls and attention to their athletic achievements can help increase their involvement and performance.

11.9 What qualities of children's play are evident in middle childhood?

- Games with rules become common during the school years, contributing to emotional and social development. Expansion of adult-organized youth sports programs is associated with increased self-esteem and social competence in most players, but such programs are less available to low SES children. For some children, adult overemphasis on competition promotes undue anxiety and avoidance of sports. Encouraging effort, improvement, participation, and teamwork makes organized sports enjoyable and beneficial for self-esteem.

- Some features of children's physical activity reflect our evolutionary past. **Rough-and-tumble play** may once have been important for the development of fighting skill and may help children establish a **dominance hierarchy.** In middle childhood, dominance hierarchies become increasingly stable, especially among boys, and serve the adaptive function of limiting aggression among group members.

11.10 What steps can schools take to promote physical fitness in middle childhood?

- In addition to providing an opportunity for physical activity, school recess is a rich context for child-organized games and social interaction.

- Despite cutbacks in U.S. elementary schools, regular physical education classes help ensure that all children have access to the physical, cognitive, and social benefits of exercise and play, which translate into lifelong psychological and physical health benefits.

Important Terms and Concepts

dominance hierarchy (p. 424)
malocclusion (p. 407)

nocturnal enuresis (p. 415)
obesity (p. 410)

rough-and-tumble play (p. 424)
secular trends in physical growth (p. 406)

Cognitive Development in Middle Childhood

"Game of Sanga"
Florence Faure
10 years, Gabon

Middle childhood brings dramatic gains in attention, memory, categorization, reasoning, and problem solving. These children use their advancing cognitive skills to play a popular game.

"Finally!" 6-year-old Lizzie exclaimed the day Rena enrolled her in elementary school. "Now I get to go to real school just like Joey!" Lizzie confidently walked into a combined kindergarten–first-grade class in her neighborhood school, pencils, crayons, and writing pad in hand, ready for a more disciplined approach to learning than she had experienced previously. As a preschooler, Lizzie had loved playing school, giving assignments as the "teacher" and pretending to read and write as the "student." Now she was eager to master the tasks that had sparked her imagination as a 4- and 5-year-old.

Lizzie had entered a whole new world of challenging activities. In a single morning, she and her classmates met in reading groups, wrote in journals, worked on addition and subtraction, and sorted leaves gathered for a science project. As Lizzie and Joey moved through the elementary school grades, they tackled increasingly complex projects and became more accomplished at reading, writing, math skills, and general knowledge of the world.

To understand the cognitive attainments of middle childhood, we turn to research inspired by Piaget's theory and the information-processing approach. And we look at expanding definitions of intelligence that help us appreciate individual differences in mental development. We also examine the genetic and environmental roots of IQ scores, which often influence important educational decisions. Our discussion continues with language, which blossoms further in these years. Finally, we consider the role of schools in children's development. ■

Piaget's Theory:
The Concrete Operational Stage

When Lizzie was 4, Piaget's conservation problems confused her (see Chapter 9, page 316). For example, when water was poured from a tall, narrow container into a short, wide one, she insisted that the amount of water had changed. Three years later, when one of our child development students interviewed her, she found this task easy. "Of course it's the same!" she exclaimed. "The water's shorter, but it's also wider. Pour it back," she instructed. "You'll see, it's the same amount!"

Attainments of the
Concrete Operational Stage

Lizzie has entered Piaget's **concrete operational stage,** which extends from about 7 to 11 years. Compared with early childhood, thought is more logical, flexible, and organized.

CONSERVATION The ability to pass *conservation tasks* provides clear evidence of *operations*—mental actions that obey logical rules. Notice how Lizzie is capable of **decentration,** focusing on several aspects of a problem and relating them, rather than centering on just one. She also demonstrates **reversibility,** the capacity to think through a series of steps and then mentally reverse direction, returning to the starting point. Recall from Chapter 9 that reversibility is part of every logical operation. It is solidly achieved in middle childhood.

12.1 What are the major characteristics of concrete operational thought?

12.2 Discuss follow-up research on concrete operational thought.

CLASSIFICATION   Between ages 7 and 10, children pass Piaget's *class inclusion problem* (see page 316). This indicates that they are more aware of classification hierarchies and can focus on relations between a general category and two specific categories at the same time—on three relations at once. Children of this age are better able to inhibit their habitual strategy of perceptually comparing the two specific categories (blue flowers and yellow flowers) in favor of relating each specific category to its less-obvious general category (flowers) (Borst et al., 2013; Ni, 1998). School-age children's enhanced classification skills are evident in their enthusiasm for collecting treasured objects. At age 10, Joey spent hours sorting and resorting his baseball cards, grouping them first by league and team, then by playing position and batting average. He could separate the players into a variety of classes and subclasses and easily rearrange them.

SERIATION   The ability to order items along a quantitative dimension, such as length or weight, is called **seriation.** To test for it, Piaget asked children to arrange sticks of different lengths from shortest to longest. Older preschoolers can put the sticks in a row to create the series, but they do so haphazardly, making many errors. In contrast, 6- to 7-year-olds create the series efficiently, moving in an orderly sequence from the smallest stick, to the next largest, and so on.

The concrete operational child can also seriate mentally, an ability called **transitive inference.** In a well-known transitive inference problem, Piaget showed children pairings of sticks of different colors. From observing that stick *A* is longer than stick *B* and that stick *B* is longer than stick *C*, children must infer that *A* is longer than *C*. Like Piaget's class inclusion task, transitive inference requires children to integrate three relations at once—in this instance, *A–B*, *B–C*, and *A–C*. As long as they receive help in remembering the premises (*A–B* and *B–C*), 7- to 8-year-olds can grasp transitive inference (Wright, 2006). And when the task is made relevant to children's everyday experiences—for example, based on winners of races between pairs of cartoon characters—6-year-olds perform well (Wright, Robertson, & Hadfield, 2011).

An improved ability to categorize underlies children's interest in collecting objects during middle childhood. Here, a 9-year-old sorts and organizes her extensive shell collection.

SPATIAL REASONING   Piaget found that school-age children's understanding of space is more accurate than that of preschoolers. To illustrate, let's consider children's **cognitive maps**—their mental representations of spaces, such as a classroom, school, or neighborhood. Drawing or reading a map of a large-scale space (school or neighborhood) requires considerable perspective-taking skill. Because the entire space cannot be seen at once, children must infer its overall layout by relating its separate parts.

Preschoolers and young school-age children include *landmarks* on maps they draw of a single room, but their arrangement is not always accurate. They do better when asked to place stickers showing the location of furniture and people on a map of the room. But if the map is rotated to a position other than the room's orientation, they have difficulty (Liben & Downs, 1993). In identifying landmarks on a rotated map, 7-year-olds are aided by the opportunity to walk through the room (Lehnung et al., 2003). Actively exploring it permits them to experience landmarks from different vantage points, which fosters a more flexible mental representation.

With respect to large-scale outdoor environments, not until age 9 can many children accurately place stickers on a map to indicate the location of landmarks. Children who spontaneously use strategies that help them align the map with their current location in the space—rotating the map or tracing their route on it—show better performance (Liben et al., 2013). Around this age, the maps children draw of large-scale spaces become better organized, showing landmarks along an *organized route of travel.* At the same time, children are able to give clear, well-organized instructions for getting from one place to another by using a "mental walk" strategy—imagining another person's movements along a route (Gauvain & Rogoff, 1989b).

At the end of middle childhood, most children can form an accurate *overall view of a large-scale space.* And they readily draw and read maps, even when the orientation of the map and the space it represents do not match (Liben, 2009). Ten- to 12-year-olds also grasp the notion of *scale*—the proportional relation between a space and its map representation (Liben, 2006). And they appreciate that in interpreting map symbols, a mapmaker's assigned meaning supersedes physical resemblance—for example, that green dots (not red dots) may indicate where red fire trucks are located (Myers & Liben, 2008).

Map-related experiences greatly improve children's map skills. When teachers asked fourth graders to write down the clues they used to decide where stickers (signifying landmark locations) should go on a map of an outdoor space, the accuracy of children's performance improved (Kastens & Liben, 2007). Such self-generated explanations seem to induce learners to reflect on and revise their own thinking, sparking gains in many types of problem solving among students from elementary school through college. And a computer-based curriculum called *Where Are We,* consisting of 12 map-reading and map-making lessons, led to substantial improvements in second to fourth graders' performance on diverse mapping tasks (Liben, Kastens, & Stevenson, 2001).

Cultural frameworks influence children's map making. In many non-Western communities, people rarely use maps for way finding but rely on information from neighbors, street vendors, and shopkeepers. Also, compared to their Western agemates, non-Western children less often ride in cars and more often walk, which results in intimate neighborhood knowledge. When a researcher had 12-year-olds in small cities in India and in the United States draw maps of their neighborhoods, the Indian children represented a rich array of landmarks and aspects of social life, such as people and vehicles, in a small area surrounding their home. The U.S children, in contrast, drew a more formal, extended space, highlighting main streets and key directions (north–south, east–west) but including few landmarks (see Figure 12.1) (Parameswaran, 2003). Although the U.S. children's maps scored higher in cognitive maturity, this difference reflected cultural interpretations of the task: When asked to create a map to "help people find their way," the Indian children drew spaces as far-reaching and organized as the U.S. children's.

Third graders locate landmarks on a trail map of a nearby park. Map-related classroom experiences support their advancing mental representations of large-scale spaces.

LOOK and LISTEN

Ask a 6- to 8-year-old and a 9- to 12-year-old to draw a neighborhood map showing important landmarks, such as the school, a friend's house, or a shopping area. In what ways do the children's maps differ?

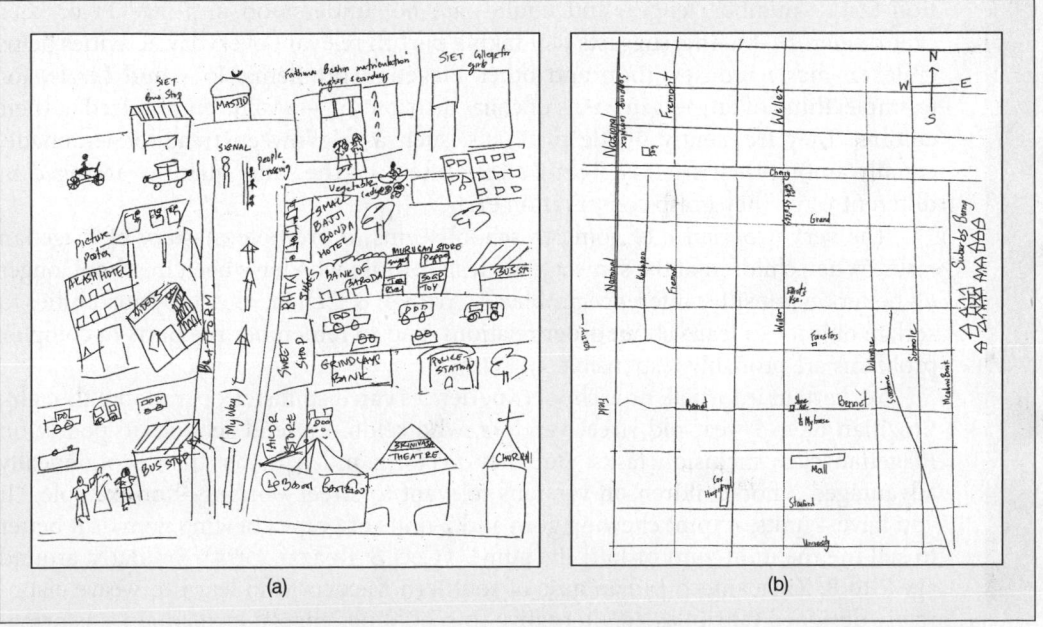

FIGURE 12.1   Maps drawn by older school-age children from India and the United States. (a) The Indian child depicted many landmarks and features of social life in a small area near her home. (b) The U.S. child drew a more extended space and highlighted main streets and key directions. (From G. Parameswaran, 2003, "Experimenter Instructions as a Mediator in the Effects of Culture on Mapping One's Neighborhood," *Journal of Environmental Psychology, 23*, pp. 415–416. Copyright © 2003, reprinted with permission from Elsevier, Ltd., conveyed through Copyright Clearance Center, Inc.)

Limitations of Concrete Operational Thought

As the name of this stage suggests, concrete operational thinking suffers from one important limitation: Children think in an organized, logical fashion only when dealing with concrete information they can perceive directly. Their mental operations work poorly with abstract ideas—ones not apparent in the real world. Consider children's solutions to transitive inference problems. When shown pairs of sticks of unequal length, Lizzie easily engaged in transitive inference. But she had great difficulty with a hypothetical version of this task: "Susan is taller than Sally, and Sally is taller than Mary. Who is the tallest?" Not until age 11 or 12 can children typically solve this problem.

That logical thought is at first tied to immediate situations helps account for a special feature of concrete operational reasoning. Children master concrete operational tasks step by step, not all at once. For example, they usually grasp conservation of number first, followed by length, liquid, and mass, and then weight. This *continuum of acquisition* (or gradual mastery) of logical concepts is another indication of the limitations of concrete operational thinking (Fischer & Bidell, 1991). Rather than coming up with general logical principles that they apply to all relevant situations, children seem to work out the logic of each problem separately.

Follow-Up Research on Concrete Operational Thought

According to Piaget, brain development combined with experience in a rich and varied external world should lead children everywhere to reach the concrete operational stage. Yet recent evidence indicates that cultural and school practices have much to do with mastery of Piagetian tasks (Rogoff, 2003). And information-processing research helps explain the gradual mastery of logical concepts in middle childhood.

This Brazilian street vendor might not perform well on Piagetian class inclusion tasks, but he is likely to understand versions relevant to street vending—for example, that "all the chewing gum" represents a larger quantity than the amount of any one flavor.

THE IMPACT OF CULTURE AND SCHOOLING   In village societies, conservation is often delayed. For example, among the Hausa of Nigeria, who live in small agricultural settlements and rarely send their children to school, even basic conservation tasks—number, length, and liquid—are not understood until age 11 or later (Fahrmeier, 1978). This suggests that taking part in relevant everyday activities helps children master conservation and other Piagetian problems. Joey and Lizzie, for example, think of fairness in terms of equal distribution—a value emphasized in their culture. They frequently divide materials, such as Halloween treats or lemonade, equally among their friends. Because they often see the same quantity arranged in different ways, they grasp conservation early.

The very experience of going to school seems to promote mastery of Piagetian tasks. When children of the same age are tested, those who have been in school longer do better on transitive inference problems (Artman & Cahan, 1993). Opportunities to seriate objects, to learn about order relations, and to remember the parts of complex problems are probably responsible.

Yet certain informal, nonschool experiences can also foster operational thought. Brazilian 6- to 9-year-old street vendors, who seldom attend school, do poorly on Piagetian class inclusion tasks. But they perform much better than economically advantaged schoolchildren on versions relevant to street vending—for example, "If you have 4 units of mint chewing gum and 2 units of grape chewing gum, is it better to sell me the mint gum or [all] the gum?" (Ceci & Roazzi, 1994). Similarly, around age 7 to 8, Zinacanteco Indian girls of southern Mexico, who learn to weave elaborately designed fabrics as an alternative to schooling, engage in mental transformations to figure out how a warp strung on a loom will turn out as woven cloth—reasoning expected at the concrete operational stage (Maynard & Greenfield, 2003). North American children of the same age, who do much better than Zinacanteco children on Piagetian tasks, have great difficulty with these weaving problems.

On the basis of such findings, some investigators have concluded that the forms of logic required by Piagetian tasks do not emerge spontaneously in children but, rather, are heavily influenced by training, context, and cultural conditions. Does this view remind you of Vygotsky's sociocultural theory, which we discussed in earlier chapters?

AN INFORMATION-PROCESSING VIEW OF CONCRETE OPERATIONAL THOUGHT

As we saw in Chapter 9, preschoolers show the beginnings of logical thinking on simplified and familiar tasks. The gradual mastery of logical concepts in middle childhood raises a familiar question about Piaget's theory: Is an abrupt stagewise transition to logical thought the best way to describe cognitive development in middle childhood?

Some *neo-Piagetian theorists* argue that the development of operational thinking can best be understood in terms of expansion of information-processing capacity rather than a sudden shift to a new stage. For example, Robbie Case (1996, 1998) proposed that change within each Piagetian stage, and movement from one stage to the next, are largely due to gains in the efficiency with which children use their limited working memories. According to Case, with practice, cognitive schemes demand less attention and are applied more rapidly, becoming automatic. This frees up space in working memory (see Chapter 6, page 216) so children can focus on combining old schemes and generating new ones. For instance, a child who sees water poured from one container to another recognizes that the height of the liquid changes. As this understanding becomes routine, the child notices that the width of the water changes as well. Soon children coordinate these observations, and they grasp conservation of liquid. Then, as this logical idea becomes well-practiced, the child transfer it to more demanding situations, such as weight.

Once the schemes of a Piagetian stage are sufficiently automatic, enough working memory is available to integrate them into an improved representation. As a result, children acquire *central conceptual structures*—networks of concepts and relations that permit them to think more effectively in a wide range of situations. The central conceptual structures that emerge from integrating concrete operational schemes are broadly applicable principles that result in increasingly complex, systematic reasoning, which we will discuss in Chapter 15 in the context of formal operational thought.

Case and his colleagues—along with other information processing researchers—have examined children's performance on a wide variety of Piagetian and other tasks. In each, preschoolers typically focus on only one or two dimensions. In understanding stories, for example, they grasp only a single story line. In drawing pictures, they depict objects separately. By the early school years, children coordinate two or three dimensions—two story lines in a single plot, and drawings that show both the features of objects and their relationships. Around 9 to 11 years, children integrate multiple dimensions (Case, 1998; Halford & Andrews, 2006). They tell coherent stories with a main plot and several subplots. And their drawings follow a set of rules for representing perspective and, therefore, include several points of reference, such as near, midway, and far.

As this child pours milk from one container to another, he recognizes the change first in height and then, as this observation becomes automatic, in width. Eventually he coordinates these observations and grasps conservation of liquid.

Case's theory, along with other similar neo-Piagetian perspectives, helps explain why many understandings appear in specific situations at different times rather than being mastered all at once (Barrouillet & Gaillard, 2011a). First, different forms of the same logical insight, such as the various conservation tasks, vary in their processing demands, with those acquired later requiring more space in working memory. Second, children's experiences vary widely. A child who often listens to and tells stories but rarely draws pictures displays more advanced central conceptual structures in storytelling than in drawing. Compared with Piaget's theory, neoPiagetian approaches better account for unevenness in cognitive development (Andrews & Halford, 2011). When tasks make similar processing demands, such as Piaget's class inclusion and transitive inference problems (each of which requires children to consider three relations at once), children with relevant experiences master those tasks at about the same time.

Evaluation of the Concrete Operational Stage

Piaget was correct that school-age children approach many problems in more organized, rational ways than preschoolers. But disagreement continues over whether this difference occurs because of *continuous* improvement in logical skills or *discontinuous* restructuring of children's thinking (as Piaget's stage idea assumes). Many researchers think that both types of change may be involved (Andrews & Halford, 2011; Barrouillet & Gaillard, 2011b; Case, 1998; Fischer & Bidell, 2006).

During the school years, children apply logical schemes to many more tasks. In the process, their thought seems to change qualitatively—toward a more comprehensive grasp of the underlying principles of logical thought. Piaget himself seems to have recognized this possibility in evidence for gradual mastery of conservation and other tasks. So perhaps some blend of Piagetian and information-processing ideas holds the greatest promise for explaining cognitive development in middle childhood.

Ask Yourself

- **REVIEW** Children's performance on conservation tasks illustrates a continuum of acquisition of logical concepts. Review the preceding sections, and list additional examples of gradual development of operational reasoning.

- **CONNECT** Explain how advances in perspective taking contribute to school-age children's improved ability to draw and use maps.

- **APPLY** Nine-year-old Adrienne spends many hours helping her father build furniture in his woodworking shop. How might this experience facilitate Adrienne's advanced performance on Piagetian seriation problems?

- **REFLECT** Which aspects of Piaget's description of the concrete operational child do you accept? Which do you doubt? Explain, citing research evidence.

12.3 Cite basic changes in information processing, and describe the development of attention and memory in middle childhood.

12.4 Describe the school-age child's theory of mind and capacity to engage in self-regulation.

12.5 Discuss current perspectives on teaching reading and mathematics to elementary school children.

Information Processing

In contrast to Piaget's focus on overall cognitive change, the information-processing perspective examines separate aspects of thinking. As noted in our discussion of Case's theory, capacity of working memory continues to increase in middle childhood, as does speed of thinking. And school-age children make strides in other facets of executive function, including attention, planning, strategic memory, and self-regulation. Each contributes vitally to academic learning.

Executive Function

During the school years, a time of continued development of the prefrontal cortex, executive function undergoes marked improvement, and its various aspects become more strongly interrelated (Xu et al., 2013). Children handle increasingly difficult tasks that require the integration of working memory, inhibition, and flexible thinking, which, in turn, support gains in planning, strategic thinking, and self-monitoring and self-correction of behavior.

Heritability evidence suggests substantial genetic influence on various aspects of executive function, including combining information in working memory, controlling attention, and inhibiting inappropriate responses (Hansell et al., 2001; Polderman et al., 2009; Young et al., 2009) And molecular genetic analyses are identifying specific genes related to severely deficient function of executive components, such as attention and inhibition, which (as we will soon see) contribute to learning and behavior disorders, such as attention-deficit hyperactivity disorder (ADHD).

But in both typically and atypically developing children, heredity combines with environmental factors to influence executive function. In Chapter 3, we reviewed evidence indicating that prenatal teratogens can impair impulse control, attention, planning, and other executive processes. And poverty and stressful living conditions can undermine executive function, with powerfully negative consequences for academic achievement and social competence (Blair & Raver, 2012). As we turn now to the development of an array of executive processes, our discussion will confirm once more that supportive home and school experiences are essential for their optimal development.

Middle childhood is a period of marked gains in executive function. In this science project on how flood plains are formed, fifth graders must plan, flexibly implement strategies, and monitor their progress, redirecting unsuccessful efforts.

Working-Memory Capacity

Gains in working-memory capacity, like other aspects of executive function, are supported by brain development (Cowan et al., 2011). And as Case's theory emphasizes, working memory benefits from increased efficiency of thinking. Time needed to process information on a wide variety of cognitive tasks declines rapidly between ages 6 and 12 in diverse cultures, likely due to myelination and synaptic pruning in the cerebral cortex (Kail & Ferrer, 2007; Kail et al., 2013). A faster thinker can hold on to and operate on more information at once. Still, individual differences in working-memory capacity exist, and they are of particular concern because they predict intelligence test scores and academic achievement in many subjects (DeMarie & Lopez, 2014).

Many studies confirm that children with persistent learning difficulties in reading and math are often deficient in working memory (Alloway, 2009; Alloway et al., 2009). Observations of elementary school children with limited working memories revealed that they often failed at school assignments that made heavy memory demands (Gathercole, Lamont, & Alloway, 2006). They could not follow complex instructions, lost their place in tasks with multiple steps, and frequently gave up before finishing their work. The children struggled because they could not hold in mind sufficient information to complete assignments.

Compared to their economically advantaged agemates, children from poverty-stricken families are more likely to score low on working-memory tasks. In one study, years of childhood spent in poverty predicted reduced working memory in early adulthood (Evans & Schamberg, 2009). Childhood neurobiological measures of stress (elevated blood pressure and stress hormone levels, including cortisol) largely explained this poverty–working-memory association. Chronic stress, as we saw in Chapter 5, can impair brain structure and function, especially in the prefrontal cortex and its connections with the hippocampus, which govern working-memory capacity.

About 15 percent of children have very low working-memory scores, the majority of whom struggle in school (Holmes, Gathercole, & Dunning, 2010). Interventions are needed to reduce memory loads so these children can learn. Effective approaches include communicating in short sentences with familiar vocabulary, repeating task instructions, breaking complex tasks into manageable parts, and encouraging children to use external memory aids (such as lists of useful spellings when writing or number lines when doing math).

In addition, direct training with working-memory tasks is effective. In one study, researchers embedded such training in interactive computer games. Ten-year-olds with learning difficulties were randomly assigned to low-frequency training (once a week), high-frequency training (four times a week), or a no-training control (Alloway, Bibile, & Lau, 2013). Compared with the other groups, students experiencing high-frequency training improved substantially in working-memory capacity, IQ, and spelling achievement—gains still evident 8 months after training had ended.

Attention

During middle childhood, gains in sustained attention continue. In addition, attention becomes more selective, flexible, and planful.

SELECTIVITY AND FLEXIBILITY As Joey and Lizzie moved through elementary school, they became better at deliberately attending to relevant aspects of a task and inhibiting irrelevant responses. One way researchers study this increasing selectivity of attention is by introducing irrelevant stimuli into a task and seeing how well children attend to its central elements. For example, they might present a stream of numbers on a computer screen and ask children to press a button whenever a particular two-digit sequence (such as "1" followed by "9") appears. Findings show that selective attention improves sharply between ages 6 and 10, with gains continuing through adolescence (Gomez-Perez & Ostrosky-Solis, 2006; Tabibi & Pfeffer, 2007; Vakil et al., 2009).

Older children also flexibly adapt their attention to situational requirements. For example, when asked to sort cards with pictures that vary in both color and shape, children age 5 and older readily switch their basis of sorting from color to shape when asked to do so; younger children have difficulty (Brooks et al., 2003; Zelazo, Carlson, & Kesek, 2008). Notice how this task requires working memory to retain relevant sorting rules (color and shape), inhibition of the irrelevant rule, and cognitive flexibility in responding to a rule switch by updating working memory and inhibition accordingly.

Over middle childhood, selectivity and flexibility of attention become better controlled and more efficient (Carlson, Zelazo, & Faja, 2013). Children can focus and adapt their attention in the face of increasingly complex distractors—skills that contribute to more organized, strategic, and planful approaches to challenging tasks with age.

PLANNING Planning on multistep tasks improves over the school years. When 5- to 9-year-olds were given lists of items to obtain from a play grocery store, older children more often took time to scan the store before shopping, figuring out the best sequence in which to gather the items. They also paused more often to look for each item before moving to get it (Gauvain & Rogoff, 1989a; Szepkouski, Gauvain, & Carberry, 1994). Consequently, they followed shorter routes through the aisles.

Effective planning often goes beyond implementing a sequence of moves: In many instances, children must evaluate the entire sequence *in advance* to see if it will get them to their goal. To assess both sequential and advance planning, 4- to 10-year-olds were presented with the paddle-box illustrated in Figure 12.2. On each trial, they had to get a small item from the paddle on which an adult placed it to the open goal at the bottom of the box. The paddles

FIGURE 12.2 Examples of sequential- and advance-planning solutions using the paddle box. An adult placed a small item on one of the horizontal paddles within the box, visible to the child through its transparent cover. Children had to get the item to the open goal at the bottom of the box. The paddles could be rotated to three positions—flat, diagonal, or left—using handles extending out the front of the box. (a) In sequential planning, rotating the start paddle first, without presetting other paddles, leads to success. (b) In advance planning, children must preset at least one other paddle before rotating the start paddle. (From E. C. Tecwyn, S. K. S. Thorpe, & J. Chappell, 2014, "Development of Planning in 4- to 10-Year-Old Children: Reducing Inhibitory Demands Does Not Improve Performance," *Journal of Experimental Child Psychology, 125,* p. 92. Copyright © 2014 with permission from Elsevier, Ltd., conveyed through Copyright Clearance Center, Inc.)

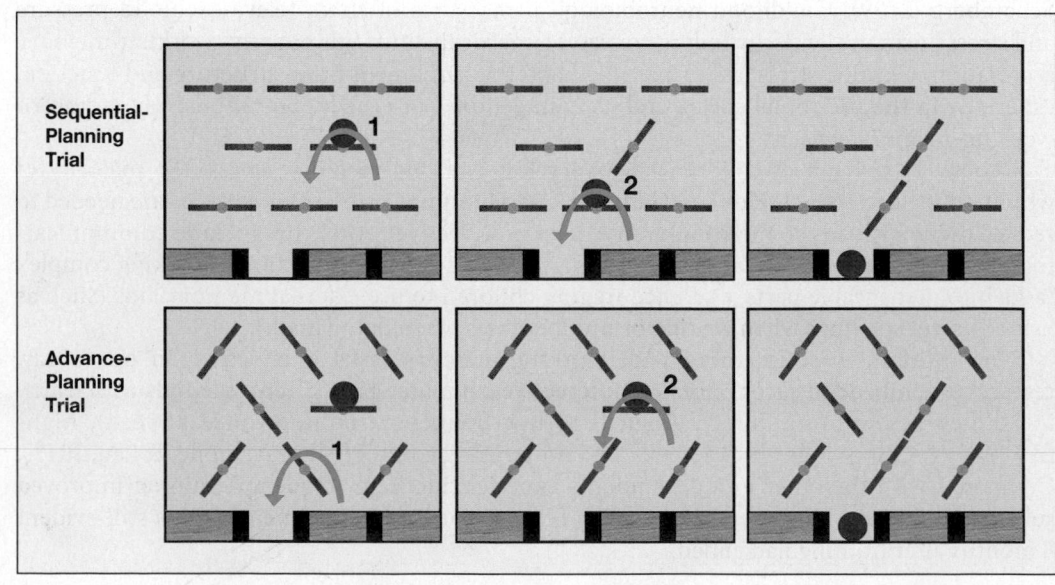

could be rotated to three positions: flat, diagonal left, or diagonal right. On sequential trials, children could rotate the start paddle first and still succeed. On advance-planning trials, to prevent the object from being trapped, children needed to preset one or two other paddles before rotating the start paddle (Tecwyn, Thorpe, & Chappell, 2014). Many of the youngest children succeeded at sequential planning, but advance planning was difficult: Not until age 9 to 10 did children consistently perform well.

The development of planning illustrates how attention becomes coordinated with other cognitive processes. Children must postpone action in favor of weighing alternatives, organizing an efficient sequence of steps, and remembering the steps so they can attend to each one. Along the way, they must monitor how well the plan works and revise it if necessary.

As Chapter 9 revealed, children learn much about planning by collaborating with more expert planners. With age, they take more responsibility in these joint endeavors, such as suggesting planning strategies and organizing task materials. The demands of school tasks—and teachers' explanations of how to plan—also contribute to gains in planning.

But adult-controlled activities may rob children of opportunities to plan. In one study, researchers videotaped small groups of first and second graders devising plays that they would perform for their class (Baker-Sennett, Matusov, & Rogoff, 2008). Some groups were child-led; others were led by adult volunteers. Child-led groups engaged in extensive planning—brainstorming themes and working out the details of their improvisations. But when adults planned the play in advance, the children spent most of their time in nonplanning pursuits, such as rehearsing lines and making play props. The adults missed a rich opportunity to scaffold learning (see page 324 in Chapter 9) by turning over responsibility for play planning to the children and guiding and supporting, as needed.

The attentional and planning strategies just considered are crucial for success in school. Unfortunately, some children have great difficulty paying attention. See the Biology and Environment box on pages 438–439 for a discussion of the serious learning and behavior problems of children with attention-deficit hyperactivity disorder.

Memory Strategies

As attention improves, so do *memory strategies,* the deliberate mental activities we use to store and retain information. When Lizzie had a list of things to learn, such as the capitals of the United States or the names of geometric shapes, she immediately used **rehearsal**—repeating the information to herself. Language proficiency predicts the emergence of rehearsal in the early grade school years, perhaps because a certain vocabulary size and ability to automatically name items is necessary for children to use the strategy (Bebko et al., 2014). Soon after, a second strategy becomes common: **organization**—grouping related items together (for example, all state capitals in the same part of the country), an approach that greatly improves recall (Schneider, 2002).

Perfecting memory strategies requires time and effort. For example, 8-year-old Lizzie rehearsed in a piecemeal fashion. After being given the word *cat* in a list of words, she said, "Cat, cat, cat." But 10-year-old Joey combined previous words with each new item, saying, "Desk, man, yard, cat, cat." This active, cumulative approach, in which neighboring words create contexts for each other that trigger recall, yields much better memory (Lehman & Hasselhorn, 2007, 2012). Furthermore, whereas Lizzy often organized by everyday association (hat–head, carrot–rabbit), Joey grouped items *taxonomically,* based on common properties (clothing, food, animals) and, thus, into fewer categories—an efficient procedure yielding dramatic memory gains (Bjorklund et al., 1994). And Joey used organization in a wide range of memory tasks, whereas Lizzie used it only when categorical relations among items were obvious.

As children gain in familiarity with strategies and in working-memory capacity, they combine several strategies—for example, organizing items, stating the category names, and finally rehearsing. The more strategies children apply simultaneously, the better they remember (DeMarie et al., 2004; Schwenck, Bjorklund, & Schneider, 2007). Younger children often try out various memory strategies but use them less systematically and successfully than older children. Still, their tendency to experiment allows them to discover which strategies work best and how to combine them effectively. Recall from *overlapping-waves theory,* discussed in Chapter 9,

Biology and Environment

Children with Attention-Deficit Hyperactivity Disorder

While the other fifth graders worked quietly at their desks, Calvin squirmed, dropped his pencil, looked out the window, fiddled with his shoelaces, and talked aloud. "Hey Joey," he yelled across the room, "wanna play ball after school?" But the other children weren't eager to play with Calvin, who was physically awkward and failed to follow the rules of the game. He had trouble taking turns at bat. In the outfield, he tossed his mitt up in the air and looked elsewhere when the ball came his way. Calvin's desk was a chaotic mess. He often lost pencils, books, and other school materials, and he had difficulty remembering assignments and due dates.

Symptoms of ADHD

Calvin is one of 3 to 7 percent of U.S. school-age children with **attention-deficit hyperactivity disorder (ADHD),** which involves inattention, impulsivity, and excessive motor activity resulting in academic and social problems (American Psychiatric Association, 2013; Goldstein, 2011). Boys are diagnosed three to nine times as often as girls. However, many girls with ADHD seem to be overlooked, either because their symptoms are less flagrant or because of a gender bias:

A difficult, disruptive boy is more likely to be referred for treatment (Faraone, Biederman, & Mick, 2006).

Children with ADHD cannot stay focused on a task that requires mental effort for more than a few minutes. They often act impulsively, ignoring social rules and lashing out with hostility when frustrated. Many, though not all, are *hyperactive,* exhausting parents and teachers and irritating other children with their excessive motor activity. For a child to be diagnosed with ADHD, these symptoms must have appeared before age 12 as a persistent problem.

Because of their difficulty concentrating, ADHD children score lower in IQ than other children, though the difference is mostly accounted for by a small subgroup with substantially below-average scores (Biederman et al., 2012). Researchers agree that deficient executive function underlies ADHD symptoms. According to one view, children with ADHD are impaired in capacity to inhibit action in favor of thought—a basic difficulty that results in wide-ranging inadequacies in executive processing and, therefore, in impulsive, disorganized behavior (Barkley, 2003a). Another hypothesis is that ADHD is the direct result of a cluster of executive-processing

problems that interfere with ability to guide one's own actions (Brown, 2006). Research confirms that children with ADHD do poorly on tasks requiring sustained attention; find it hard to ignore irrelevant information; have difficulty with memory, planning, reasoning, and problem solving in academic and social situations; and often fail to manage frustration and intense emotion (Barkley, 2003b, 2006).

Origins of ADHD

ADHD runs in families and is highly heritable. Identical twins share it more often than fraternal twins (Freitag et al., 2010; Rasmussen et al., 2004). Children with ADHD show abnormal brain functioning, including reduced electrical and blood-flow activity and structural abnormalities in the prefrontal cortex and in other areas involved in attention, inhibition of behavior, and other aspects of motor control (Mackie et al., 2007). Also, the brains of children with ADHD grow more slowly and are about 3 percent smaller in overall volume, with a thinner cerebral cortex, than the brains of unaffected agemates (Narr et al., 2009; Shaw et al., 2007). Several genes that disrupt functioning of the neurotransmitters serotonin (involved in

---

that children experiment with strategies when faced with many cognitive challenges—an approach that enables them to gradually "home in" on the most effective techniques.

By the end of middle childhood, children start to use **elaboration**—creating a relationship, or shared meaning, between two or more pieces of information that are not members of the same category. For example, to learn the words *fish* and *pipe,* you might generate the verbal statement or mental image, "The fish is smoking a pipe." This highly effective memory technique, which requires considerable effort and space in working memory, becomes increasingly common in adolescence and early adulthood (Schneider & Pressley, 1997).

Because organization and elaboration combine items into *meaningful chunks,* they permit children to hold onto much more information and, as a result, further expand working memory. In addition, when children link a new item to information they already know, they can *retrieve* it easily by thinking of other items associated with it. As we will see, this also contributes to improved memory during the school years.

Knowledge and Memory Performance

During middle childhood, the long-term knowledge base grows larger and becomes organized into increasingly elaborate, hierarchically structured networks. This rapid growth of knowledge helps children use strategies and remember (Schneider, 2002). In other words, knowing more about a topic makes new information more meaningful and familiar, so it is easier to store and retrieve.

inhibition and self-control) and dopamine (required for effective cognitive processing) have been implicated in the disorder (Akutagava-Martins et al., 2013).

At the same time, ADHD is associated with environmental factors. Prenatal teratogens—such as tobacco, alcohol, illegal drugs, and environmental pollutants—are linked to inattention and hyperactivity (see Chapter 3). And they can combine with certain genotypes to greatly increase risk of the disorder (see page 87 in Chapter 2). Furthermore, children with ADHD are more likely to have parents with psychological disorders and to come from homes where family stress is high (Law et al., 2014). These circumstances often intensify the child's preexisting difficulties.

Treating ADHD

Calvin's doctor eventually prescribed stimulant medication, the most common treatment for ADHD. As long as dosage is carefully regulated, these drugs reduce impulsivity and hyperactivity and improve attention for about 70 percent of children who take them (Greenhill, Halperin, & Abikoff, 1999). Stimulant medication seems to increase activity in the prefrontal cortex, thereby improving the child's capacity to sustain attention and to inhibit off-task and self-stimulating behavior. However, if stimulant treatment is initiated late, after age 9 or 10, it does not reduce the decline in academic performance associated with ADHD (Zoëga et al., 2012).

By itself, drug treatment is insufficient for helping children compensate for inattention and impulsivity in everyday situations. So far, the most effective treatments combine medication with interventions that model and reinforce appropriate academic and social behaviors (Smith, Barkley, & Shapiro, 2006). New approaches that provide children with adult-guided activities designed to augment executive-function skills yield improved performance on attention, working memory, cognitive flexibility, and planning tasks (Miranda et al., 2013; Tamm, Nakonezny, & Hughes, 2014). But more research is needed on the extent to which these gains generalize to the classroom.

Family intervention is also vital. Inattentive, hyperactive children strain the patience of parents, who are likely to react punitively and inconsistently—a child-rearing style that strengthens defiant, aggressive behavior. In fact, in 50 to 75 percent of cases, these two sets of

This child frequently engages in disruptive behavior at school. Children with ADHD have great difficulty staying on task and often act impulsively, ignoring social rules.

behavior problems occur together (Goldstein, 2011).

ADHD is usually a lifelong disorder. Affected individuals are at risk for persistent antisocial behavior, depression, alcohol and drug abuse, and other problems (Kessler et al., 2005, 2006). Adults with ADHD continue to need help in structuring their environments, regulating negative emotion, selecting appropriate careers, and understanding their condition as a biological deficit rather than a character flaw.

To investigate this idea, school-age children who were expert chess players were tested on how well they could remember complex chessboard arrangements. Then their performance was compared with that of adults who knew how to play chess but were not especially knowledgeable. The children's expert knowledge enabled them to reproduce the chessboard configurations considerably better than the adults could (Bédard & Chi, 1992).

In another study, researchers classified fourth graders as either experts or novices in knowledge of soccer and then gave both groups lists of soccer and nonsoccer items to learn. Experts remembered far more items on the soccer list (but not on the nonsoccer list) than novices. And during recall, the experts' listing of items was better organized, as indicated by clustering of items into categories (Schneider & Bjorklund, 1992). This superior organization at retrieval suggests that highly knowledgeable children organize information in their area of expertise with little or no effort—by rapidly associating new items with the large number they already know (Bjorklund & Douglas, 1997). Consequently, experts can devote more working-memory resources to using recalled information to reason and solve problems.

But knowledge is not the only important factor in children's strategic memory processing. Children who are expert in an area are usually highly motivated. As a result, they not only acquire knowledge more quickly but also *actively use what they know* to add more. In contrast, academically unsuccessful children often fail to ask how previously stored information can clarify new material. This, in turn, interferes with the development of a broad knowledge base (Schneider & Bjorklund, 1998). So extensive knowledge and use of memory strategies support one another.

Children in a shanty town on the outskirts of Lima use laptops provided by the Peruvian government. Societal modernization—access to contemporary resources for communication and literacy—is broadly associated with improved cognitive performance.

Culture, Schooling, and Memory Strategies

Rehearsal, organization, and elaboration are techniques that children and adults usually use when they need to remember information for its own sake. On many other occasions, memory occurs as a natural byproduct of participation in daily activities. For example, Joey can spout a wealth of facts about baseball teams and players—information he picked up from watching ball games, discussing the game, and trading baseball cards with his friends. And without prior rehearsal, he can recount the story line of an exciting movie or novel—narrative material that is already meaningfully organized.

A repeated finding is that people in village cultures who have little formal schooling do not use or benefit from instruction in memory strategies because they see no practical reason to use these techniques (Rogoff, 2003). Tasks requiring children to engage in isolated recall, which are common in classrooms, strongly motivate memory strategies. In fact, children in developed nations get so much practice with this type of learning that they do not refine techniques that rely on cues available in everyday life, such as spatial location and arrangement of objects. For example, Guatemalan Mayan 9-year-olds do slightly better than their U.S. agemates when told to remember the placement of 40 familiar objects in a play scene (Rogoff & Waddell, 1982). U.S. children often rehearse object names when it would be more effective to keep track of spatial relations.

Societal *modernization,* as indicated by the presence of communication, literacy, and other economically advantageous resources in homes—such as books, writing tablets, electricity, radio, TV, and car ownership—is broadly associated with performance on cognitive tasks commonly administered to children in industrialized nations. In an investigation in which researchers rated towns in Belize, Kenya, Nepal, and American Samoa for degree of modernization, Belize and American Samoa exceeded Kenya and Nepal (Gauvain & Munroe, 2009). Modernity predicted both extent of schooling and 5- to 9-year-olds' cognitive scores—on a memory test plus an array of other measures.

In sum, the development of memory strategies and other cognitive skills valued in complex societies is not just a product of a more competent information-processing system. It also depends on task demands, schooling, and cultural circumstances.

The School-Age Child's Theory of Mind

During middle childhood, children's *theory of mind,* or set of beliefs about mental activities, becomes much more elaborate and refined. Recall from Chapter 9 that this awareness of thought is often called *metacognition.* Children's improved ability to reflect on their own mental life is another reason that their thinking and problem solving advance.

KNOWLEDGE OF COGNITIVE CAPACITIES Unlike preschoolers, who view the mind as a passive container of information, older children regard it as an active, constructive agent that selects and transforms information (Astington & Hughes, 2013). Consequently, they have a much better understanding of cognitive processes and the impact of psychological factors on performance. For example, with age, elementary school children become increasingly aware of effective memory strategies and why they work (Alexander et al., 2003). And they gradually grasp relationships between mental activities—for example, that remembering is crucial for understanding and that understanding strengthens memory (Schwanenflugel, Henderson, & Fabricius, 1998).

Furthermore, school-age children's understanding of sources of knowledge expands. They are aware that people can extend their knowledge not only by directly observing events and talking to others but also by making *mental inferences* (Miller, Hardin, & Montgomery,

2003). This grasp of inference enables knowledge of false belief to expand. In several studies, researchers told children complex stories involving one character's belief about a second character's belief. Then the children answered questions about what the first character thought the second character would do (see Figure 12.3). By age 6 to 7, children were aware that people form beliefs about other people's beliefs and that these *second-order beliefs* can be wrong!

Appreciation of *second-order false belief* enables children to pinpoint the reasons that another person arrived at a certain belief (Astington, Pelletier, & Homer, 2002; Miller, 2009; Naito & Seki, 2009). Notice how it requires the ability to view a situation from at least two perspectives—that is, to reason simultaneously about what two or more people are thinking, a form of perspective taking called **recursive thought.** We think recursively when we make such statements as, "*Lisa believes* that *Jason believes* the letter is under his pillow, but that's *not what Jason really believes; he knows* the letter is in the desk."

The capacity for recursive thought greatly assists children in appreciating that people can harbor quite different interpretations of the same situation. For example, 6- to 7-year-olds realize that when two people view the same object, their trains of thought will differ because of variations in their knowledge, experiences, or other characteristics (Eisbach, 2004). Children of this age also understand that two people can make sense of the same event—such as an ambiguous fragment taken from a larger drawing they have never seen—quite differently, no matter what beliefs or biases they bring to the situation (Lalonde & Chandler, 2002). They recognize that the same reality can legitimately be construed in multiple ways. Indeed, school-age children's newfound awareness of varying viewpoints is so powerful that, at first, they overextend it (Lagattuta, Sayfan, & Blattman, 2010). Six- and 7-year-olds are especially likely to overlook the fact that people with differing past experiences sometimes agree!

ERP and fMRI evidence reveals that from age 6 to 11, children become increasingly selective in the brain regions they recruit when thinking about another's mental states (Bowman et al., 2012; Gweon et al., 2012). In addition to the prefrontal cortex, they activate an area connecting the right temporal and parietal lobes (known to play a crucial role in theory-of-mind processes), just as adults do.

As with other cognitive attainments, schooling contributes to a more reflective, process-oriented view of the mind. In a study of rural children of Cameroon, Africa, those who attended school performed much better on theory-of-mind tasks (Vinden, 2002). In school, teachers often call attention to the workings of the mind when they remind children to pay attention, remember mental steps, share points of view with peers, and evaluate their own and others' reasoning. As recursive perspective taking becomes more secure, children more often use persuasive strategies to try to change others' viewpoints (Bartsch, London, & Campbell,

LOOK and LISTEN

Watch a teacher explain a learning activity to 6- to 8-year-olds. How often did the teacher call attention to the workings of the mind?

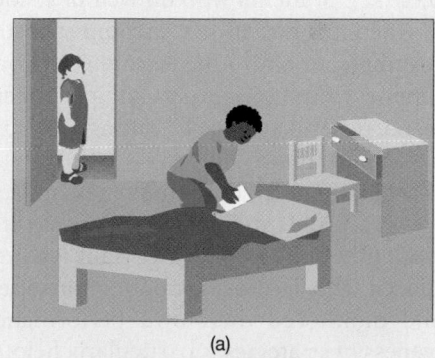 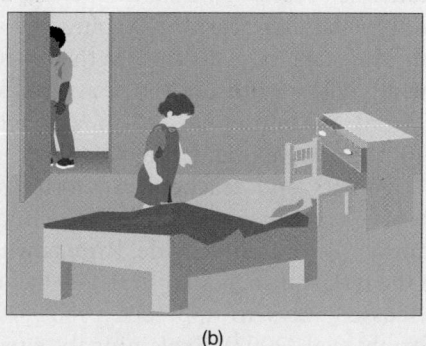 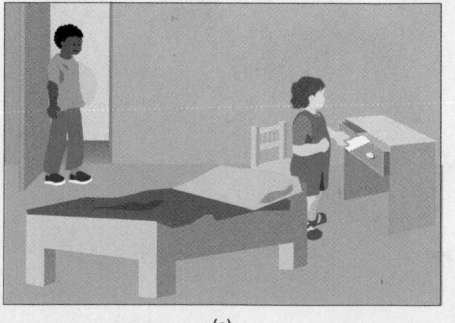

(a) Jason has a letter from a friend. Lisa wants to read the letter, but Jason doesn't want her to. Jason puts the letter under his pillow.

(b) Jason leaves the room to help his mother.

(c) While Jason is gone, Lisa takes the letter and reads it. Jason returns and watches Lisa, but Lisa doesn't see Jason. Then Lisa puts the letter in Jason's desk.

FIGURE 12.3 A second-order false belief task. After relating the story in the sequence of pictures, the researcher asks a second-order false-belief question: "Where does Lisa think Jason will look for the letter? Why?" Around age 7, children answer correctly—that Lisa thinks Jason will look under his pillow because Lisa doesn't know that Jason saw her put the letter in the desk. (Adapted from Astington, Pelletier, & Homer, 2002.)

2007). They also grasp complex, recursive verbal expressions, such as irony and sarcasm, as we will see later when we address language development.

KNOWLEDGE OF STRATEGIES　Consistent with their more active view of the mind, school-age children are far more conscious of mental strategies than preschoolers. When shown video clips depicting two children using different recall strategies and asked which one is likely to produce better memory, kindergarten and young elementary school children knew that rehearsing or organizing is better than looking or naming (Justice, 1986; Schneider, 1986). Older children were aware of more subtle differences—that organizing is better than rehearsing.

Between third and fifth grade, children develop a much better appreciation of how and why strategies work (Alexander et al., 2003). Consequently, fifth graders are considerably better than younger children at discriminating good from bad reasoning. When given examples varying in quality, fifth graders consistently rated "good" reasoning as based on weighing of possibilities (rather than jumping to conclusions) and gathering of evidence (rather than ignoring important facts), even if such reasoning led to an unfavorable result (Amsterlaw, 2006).

Cognitive Self-Regulation

Although metacognition expands, school-age children frequently have difficulty putting what they know about thinking into action. They are not yet good at **cognitive self-regulation,** the process of continuously monitoring progress toward a goal, checking outcomes, and redirecting unsuccessful efforts. For example, Lizzie is aware that she should attend closely to her teacher's directions, group items when memorizing, reread a complicated paragraph to make sure she understands it, and relate new information to what she already knows. But she does not always engage in these activities.

To study cognitive self-regulation, researchers sometimes look at the impact of children's awareness of memory strategies on how well they remember. By second grade, the more children know about memory strategies, the more they recall—a relationship that strengthens over middle childhood (DeMarie et al., 2004). And when children apply a strategy consistently, their knowledge of strategies strengthens, resulting in a bidirectional relationship between metacognition and strategic processing that enhances self-regulation (Schlagmüller & Schneider, 2002).

Why does cognitive self-regulation develop gradually? Monitoring learning outcomes is cognitively demanding, requiring constant evaluation of effort and progress. Throughout elementary and secondary school, self-regulation predicts academic success (Zimmerman & Labuhn, 2012). Students who do well in school know when their learning is going well and when it is not. If they encounter obstacles, they take steps to address them—for example, organize the learning environment, review confusing material, or seek support from more expert adults or peers (Schunk & Zimmerman, 2013). This active, purposeful approach contrasts sharply with the passive orientation of students who achieve poorly.

Parents and teachers can foster self-regulation. In one study, researchers observed parents instructing their children on a problem-solving task during the summer before third grade. Parents who patiently pointed out important features of the task and suggested strategies had children who, in the classroom, more often discussed ways to approach problems and monitored their own performance (Stright et al., 2002). Explaining the effectiveness of strategies is particularly helpful because it provides a rationale for future action.

Children who acquire effective self-regulatory skills develop a sense of *academic self-efficacy*—confidence in their own ability, which supports future self-regulation (Schunk & Pajares, 2005). Unfortunately, some children receive messages from parents and teachers that seriously undermine their academic self-esteem and self-regulatory skills. We will consider these *learned-helpless* students, along with ways to help them, in Chapter 13.

© ELLEN B. SENISI

This fifth grader's capacity for cognitive self-regulation is evident in the convenient way she organizes materials, making sure her textbook glossary and dictionary are handy. When she encounters an unfamiliar word, she can quickly look up its definition.

Applications of Information Processing to Academic Learning

When Joey completed kindergarten, he recognized some familiar written words, used what he knew about letter–sound relations to decode simple words, predicted what might happen next in a beginning-reader story, and could retell its main events in sequence. In second grade, he read grade-level books independently, used story context to help identify unfamiliar words, and read aloud with expression. By fourth grade, he was a proficient reader who understood different types of texts, including biographies, fiction, and poetry.

In math, as a new first grader Joey counted to 100 by ones and tens, perform one-digit addition and subtraction with ease, and could decompose the numbers from 11 to 19 to determine, "How many more than 10" as the foundation for understanding place value. In third grade, he used his grasp of place value to perform two-digit arithmetic, multiplied and divided within 100, and had begun to master fractions and percentages.

Fundamental discoveries about the development of information processing have been applied to children's learning of reading and mathematics. Researchers are identifying the cognitive ingredients of skilled performance, tracing their development, and distinguishing good from poor learners by pinpointing differences in cognitive skills. They hope, as a result, to design teaching methods that will improve children's learning.

READING   Reading makes use of many skills at once, taxing all aspects of our information-processing systems. We must perceive single letters and letter combinations, translate them into speech sounds, recognize the visual appearance of many common words, hold chunks of text in working memory while interpreting their meaning, and combine the meanings of various parts of a text passage into an understandable whole. And because reading is so demanding, most or all of these skills must be done automatically. If one or more are poorly developed, they will compete for resources in our limited working memories, and reading performance will decline.

As children make the transition from emergent literacy to conventional reading, *phonological awareness*—the ability to reflect on and manipulate the sound structure of spoken language—continues to facilitate their progress (see page 336 in Chapter 9). Other information-processing skills also contribute. Gains in processing speed foster children's rapid conversion of visual symbols into sounds (Moll et al., 2014). Visual scanning and discrimination play important roles and improve with reading experience (Rayner, Pollatsek, & Starr, 2003). Performing all these skills efficiently releases working memory for higher-level activities involved in comprehending the text's meaning.

In this second-grade classroom, teaching of phonics is embedded in captivating stories. Combining instruction in basic skills with whole-language teaching is more effective in promoting children's reading progress than either approach alone.

Until recently, researchers were involved in an intense debate over how to teach beginning reading. Those who took a **whole-language approach** argued that from the beginning, children should be exposed to text in its complete form—stories, poems, letters, posters, and lists—so that they can appreciate the communicative function of written language. According to this view, as long as reading is kept meaningful, children will be motivated to discover the specific skills they need (Goodman, 2005). Other experts advocated a **phonics approach,** believing that children should first be coached on *phonics*—the basic rules for translating written symbols into sounds. Only after mastering these skills should they get complex reading material (Adams, 2002).

Many studies show that children learn best with a mixture of both approaches. In kindergarten, first, and second grades, teaching that includes phonics boosts reading scores, especially for children who lag behind in reading progress (Block, 2012; Brady, 2011). And when teachers combine real reading and writing with teaching of phonics and engage in other excellent teaching practices—encouraging children to tackle reading challenges and integrating reading into all school subjects—first graders show far greater literacy progress (Pressley et al., 2002).

TABLE 12.1	**Sequence of Reading Development**
GRADE/AGE	**DEVELOPMENT**
Preschool 2–5 years	"Pretends" to read; recognizes some familiar signs ("ON," "OFF," "PIZZA"); "pretends" to write; prints own name and other words
Kindergarten 5–6 years	Knows the most frequent letter–sound correspondences; recognizes some familiar written words; decodes simple, one-syllable words; retells story main events in sequence
Grades 1 and 2 6–7 years	Knows letter–sound correspondences for common double consonants; decodes regularly spelled one-syllable words; recognizes some irregularly spelled words; reads grade-level texts with increasing accuracy on repeated readings
Grades 2 and 3 7–8 years	Reads grade-level stories more fluently; knows letter–sound correspondences for common vowel combinations; decodes multisyllable words and an increasing number of irregularly spelled words; reads grade-level stories more fluently and expressively, while also comprehending
Grades 4 to 9 9–15 years	Reads to acquire new knowledge, usually without questioning the reading material; understands different types of texts, including biographies, fiction, and poetry
Grades 10 to 12 15–18 years	Reads more widely, tapping materials with diverse viewpoints

Source: Chall, 1983; Common Core, 2010.

Why might combining phonics with whole language work best? Learning the relationships between letters and sounds enables children to *decode,* or decipher, words they have never seen before. Children who enter school low in phonological awareness make far better reading progress when given training in phonics (Casalis & Cole, 2009). Soon they detect new letter–sound relations while reading on their own, and as their fluency in decoding words increases, they are freer to attend to text meaning. Without early phonics training, such children (many of whom come from poverty-stricken families) are substantially behind their agemates in text comprehension skills by third grade (Foster & Miller, 2007).

Yet too much emphasis on basic skills may cause children to lose sight of the goal of reading: understanding. Children who read aloud fluently without registering meaning know little about effective reading strategies—for example, that they must read more carefully if they will be tested than if they are reading for pleasure, that relating ideas in the text to personal experiences and general knowledge will deepen understanding, and that explaining a passage in one's own words is a good way to assess comprehension. Teaching aimed at increasing awareness and use of reading strategies enhances reading performance from third grade on (Paris & Paris, 2006).

Table 12.1 charts the general sequence of reading development. Notice the major shift, around age 7 to 8, from "learning to read" to "reading to learn" (Melzi & Schick, 2013). As decoding and comprehension skills reach a high level of efficiency, older readers become actively engaged with the text. They adjust the way they read to fit their current purpose—sometimes seeking new facts and ideas, sometimes questioning, agreeing with, or disagreeing with the writer's viewpoint.

MATHEMATICS   Mathematics teaching in elementary school builds on and greatly enriches children's informal knowledge of number concepts and counting. Written notation systems and formal computational techniques enhance children's ability to represent numbers and compute. Over the early elementary school years, children acquire basic math facts through a combination of frequent practice, experimentation with diverse computational procedures (through which they discover faster, more accurate techniques), reasoning about number concepts, and teaching that conveys effective strategies. (Return to Chapter 9, page 339, for research supporting the importance of both extended practice and a grasp of concepts.) Eventually children retrieve answers automatically and apply this basic knowledge to more complex problems.

Arguments about how to teach mathematics resemble those about reading, pitting drill in computing against "number sense," or understanding. Again, a blend of both approaches is most beneficial (Fuson, 2009). In learning basic math, poorly performing students use cumbersome, error-prone techniques or try to retrieve answers from memory too soon. They have not sufficiently experimented with strategies to see which are most effective and to reorganize their observations in logical, efficient ways—for example, noticing that multiplication problems involving 2 (2 × 8) are equivalent to addition doubles (8 + 8). On tasks assessing their grasp of math concepts, their performance is weak (Clements & Sarama, 2012). This suggests that encouraging students to apply strategies and making sure they know why certain strategies work well are essential for solid mastery of basic math.

A similar picture emerges for more complex skills, such as carrying in addition, borrowing in subtraction, and operating with decimals and fractions. Children taught by rote cannot apply the procedure to new problems. Instead, they persistently make mistakes, following a "math rule" that they recall incorrectly because they do not understand it (Carpenter et al., 1999). Look at the following subtraction errors:

$$
\begin{array}{r} 427 \\ -138 \\ \hline 311 \end{array}
\qquad
\begin{array}{r} 7002 \\ -5445 \\ \hline 1447 \end{array}
$$

In the first problem, the child consistently subtracts a smaller from a larger digit, regardless of which is on top. In the second, the child skips columns with zeros in a borrowing operation and, whenever there is a zero on top, writes the bottom digit as the answer.

Children who are given rich opportunities to experiment with problem solving, to appreciate the reasons behind strategies, and to evaluate solution techniques seldom make such errors. In one study, second graders who were taught in these ways not only mastered correct procedures but even invented their own successful strategies, some of which were superior to standard, school-taught methods! Consider this solution:

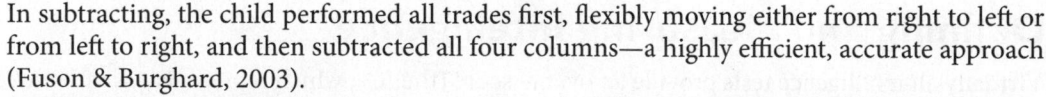

$$
\begin{array}{cccc} 3 & 15 & 14 & 12 \\ \cancel{4} & \cancel{6} & \cancel{5} & \cancel{2} \\ -1 & 9 & 6 & 8 \\ \hline 2 & 6 & 8 & 4 \end{array}
$$

In subtracting, the child performed all trades first, flexibly moving either from right to left or from left to right, and then subtracted all four columns—a highly efficient, accurate approach (Fuson & Burghard, 2003).

In a German study, the more teachers emphasized conceptual knowledge, by having children actively construct meanings in word problems before practicing computation and memorizing math facts, the more children gained in math achievement from second to third grade (Staub & Stern, 2002). Children taught in this way draw on their solid knowledge of relationships between operations (for example, that the inverse of division is multiplication) to generate efficient, flexible procedures: To solve the division problem 360/9, they might multiply 9 × 40 = 360. And because such children have been encouraged to estimate answers, if they go down the wrong track in computation, they are usually self-correcting. Furthermore, they appreciate connections between math operations and problem contexts. They can solve a word problem ("Jesse spent $3.45 for bananas, $2.62 for bread, and $3.55 for peanut butter. Can he pay for it all with a $10 bill?") quickly through estimation instead of exact calculation (De Corte & Verschaffel, 2006).

In Asian countries, students receive a variety of supports for acquiring mathematical knowledge and often excel at math computation and reasoning. Use of the metric system helps Asian children grasp place value. The consistent structure of number words in Asian languages (*ten-two* for 12, *ten-three* for 13) also makes this idea clear (Miura & Okamoto, 2003). And because Asian number words are shorter and more quickly pronounced, more digits can be held in working memory at once, increasing speed of thinking. Furthermore, Chinese parents provide their children with extensive everyday practice in counting and

This fourth grader uses paper cut in different sizes to clarify the concept of fractions. The most effective math teaching combines frequent practice with instruction emphasizing conceptual understanding.

computation—experiences that contribute to the superiority of Chinese over U.S. children's math knowledge, even before school entry (Siegler & Mu, 2008; Zhou et al., 2006). Finally, as we will see later in this chapter, compared with lessons in the United States, those in Asian classrooms devote more time to exploring math concepts and less to drill and repetition.

Ask Yourself

- **REVIEW** Cite evidence indicating that school-age children view the mind as an active, constructive agent.

- **APPLY** After viewing a slide show on endangered species, second and fifth graders in Lizzie and Joey's school were asked to remember as many animals as they could. Explain why fifth graders recalled much more than second graders.

- **APPLY** Lizzie knows that if you have difficulty learning part of a task, you should devote extra attention to that part. But she plays each of her piano pieces from beginning to end instead of practicing the hard parts. Explain why Lizzie does not engage in cognitive self-regulation.

- **REFLECT** In your elementary school math education, how much emphasis was placed on computational drill and how much on understanding concepts? How do you think that balance affected your interest and performance in math?

12.6 Describe major approaches to defining intelligence.

12.7 Describe evidence indicating that both heredity and environment contribute to intelligence.

Individual Differences in Mental Development

Around age 6, IQ becomes more stable than it was at earlier ages, and it correlates moderately well with academic achievement, typically around .50 to .60. And children with higher IQs are more likely when they grow up to attain higher levels of education and enter more prestigious occupations (Brody, 1997; Deary et al., 2007). Because IQ predicts school performance and educational attainment, it often enters into educational decisions. Do intelligence tests accurately assess the school-age child's ability to profit from academic instruction? Let's look closely at this controversial issue.

Defining and Measuring Intelligence

Virtually all intelligence tests provide an overall score (the IQ), which represents *general intelligence* or reasoning ability, along with an array of separate scores measuring specific mental abilities. But intelligence is a collection of many capacities, not all of which are included on currently available tests (Carroll, 2005; Sternberg, 2008). Test designers use a complicated statistical technique called *factor analysis* to identify the various abilities that intelligence tests measure. It identifies which sets of test items cluster together, meaning that test-takers who do well on one item in the cluster tend to do well on the others. Distinct clusters are called *factors*, each of which represents an ability. See Figure 12.4 for items typically included in intelligence tests for children.

The intelligence tests given from time to time in classrooms are *group-administered tests*. They permit large numbers of students to be tested at once and are useful for instructional planning and for identifying children who require more extensive evaluation with *individually administered tests*. Unlike group tests, which teachers can give with minimal training, individually administered tests demand considerable training and experience to give well. The examiner not only considers the child's answers but also observes the child's behavior, noting such reactions as attention to and interest in the tasks and wariness of the adult. These observations provide insight into whether the test score accurately reflects the child's abilities. Two individual tests—the Stanford-Binet and the Wechsler—are often used to identify highly intelligent children and to diagnose children with learning problems.

The contemporary descendent of Alfred Binet's first successful intelligence test is the *Stanford-Binet Intelligence Scales,* Fifth Edition, for individuals from age 2 to adulthood. In addition to general intelligence, it assesses five intellectual factors: general knowledge, quantitative reasoning, visual–spatial processing, working memory, and basic information processing (such as speed of analyzing information). Each factor includes both a verbal mode and a nonverbal mode of testing, yielding 10 subtests in all (Roid, 2003; Roid & Pomplun, 2012). The nonverbal subtests, which do not require spoken language, are especially useful when assessing individuals with limited English, hearing impairments, or communication disorders. The knowledge and quantitative reasoning factors emphasize culturally loaded, fact-oriented information, such as vocabulary and arithmetic problems. In contrast, the visual–spatial processing, working-memory, and basic information-processing factors are assumed to be less culturally biased because they require little specific information (see the spatial visualization item in Figure 12.4).

The *Wechsler Intelligence Scale for Children–IV (WISC–IV)* is the fourth edition of a widely used test for 6- through 16-year-olds. A downward extension of it, the *Wechsler Preschool and Primary Scale of Intelligence–Revised (WPPSI–III),* is appropriate for children 2 years 6 months through 7 years 3 months (Wechsler, 2002, 2003). The Wechsler tests offered both a measure of general intelligence and a variety of factor scores long before the Stanford-Binet. As a result, many psychologists and educators came to prefer them. The WISC–IV has four broad intellectual factors: verbal reasoning, perceptual (or visual–spatial) reasoning, working memory, and processing speed. Each factor is made up of two or three subtests, yielding 10 separate scores in all. The WISC-IV was designed to downplay culture-dependent information, which is emphasized on only one factor (verbal reasoning). According to the test designers, the result is the most "culture-fair" intelligence test available (Williams, Weiss, & Rolfhus, 2003). The WISC was also the first test to be standardized on children representing the total population of the United States, including ethnic minorities.

Recent Efforts to Define Intelligence

As we have seen, intelligence tests now tap important aspects of information processing. In line with this trend, some researchers have combined the mental-testing approach to defining intelligence with the information-processing approach. They believe that once we identify the processing skills that separate individuals who test well from those who test poorly, we will know more about how to intervene to improve performance. These investigators conduct *componential analyses* of children's test scores. This means that they look for relationships between aspects (or components) of information processing and children's intelligence test scores.

Processing speed, measured in terms of reaction time on diverse cognitive tasks, is moderately related to IQ (Coyle, 2013; Li et al., 2004). Individuals whose nervous systems function more efficiently, permitting them to take in more information and manipulate it quickly, appear to have an edge in intellectual skills. In support of this interpretation, fast, strong ERPs (EEG brain waves in response to stimulation) predict both speedy cognitive processing and higher mental test scores (Rijsdijk & Boomsma, 1997; Schmid, Tirsch, & Scherb, 2002). And measures of working-memory capacity, to which processing speed contributes, correlate well with IQ (Giofré, Mammarella, & Cornoldi, 2013; Swanson, 2011).

But other factors, including flexible attention, memory, and reasoning strategies, are as important as efficient thinking in predicting IQ, and they explain some of the association between response speed and good test performance (Lohman, 2000). Children who apply

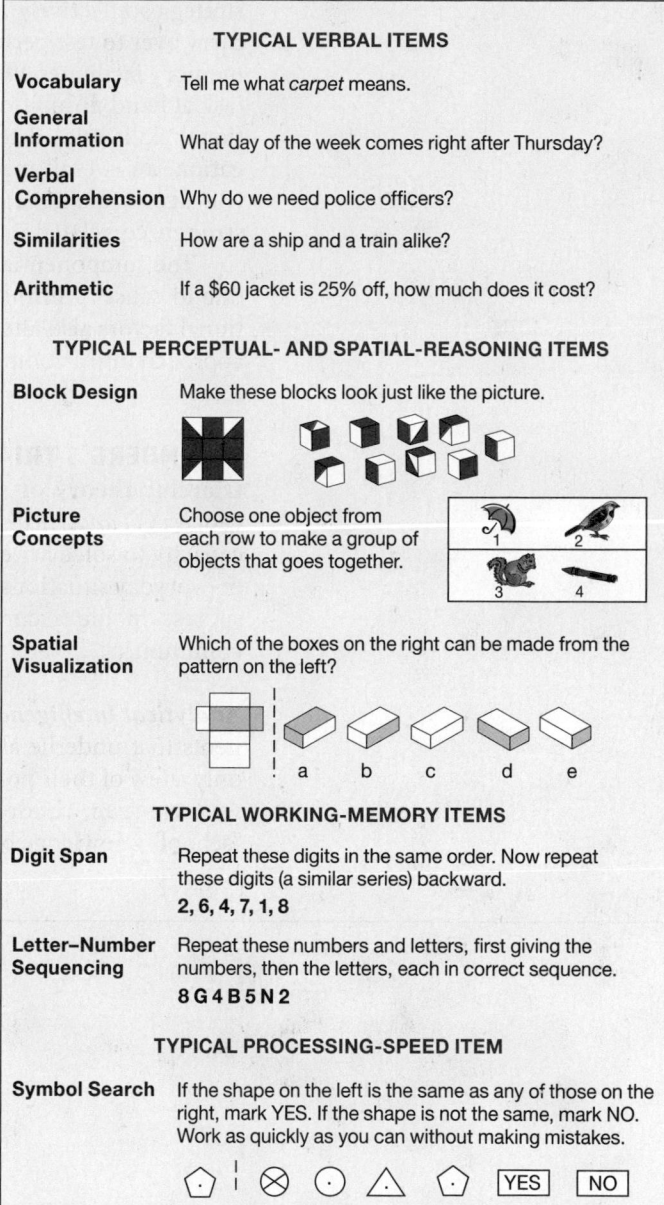

FIGURE 12.4 **Test items like those on commonly used intelligence tests for children.** The verbal items emphasize culturally loaded, fact-oriented information. The perceptual- and spatial-reasoning, working-memory, and processing-speed items emphasize aspects of information processing and are assumed to assess more biologically based skills.

strategies effectively acquire more knowledge and can retrieve it rapidly—advantages that carry over to test performance. Similarly, recall from page 436 that available space in working memory facilitates effective inhibition—keeping irrelevant information from intruding on the task at hand. Inhibition and sustained and selective attention are among a wide array of attentional skills related to IQ (Schweizer, Moosbrugger, & Goldhammer, 2006). In one investigation, an overall measure of executive function predicted intelligence in 7- to 9-year-olds (Brydges et al., 2012). Recall from page 434 that aspects of executive function become more strongly correlated in middle childhood: They unify into a single factor.

The componential approach has one major shortcoming: It regards intelligence as entirely due to causes within the child. Throughout this book, we have seen how cultural and situational factors also affect children's thinking. Robert Sternberg has expanded the componential approach into a comprehensive theory that regards intelligence as a product of inner and outer forces.

STERNBERG'S TRIARCHIC THEORY As Figure 12.5 shows, Sternberg's (2005, 2008, 2013) **triarchic theory of successful intelligence** is made up of three broad, interacting intelligences: (1) *analytical intelligence,* or information-processing skills; (2) *creative intelligence,* the capacity to solve novel problems; and (3) *practical intelligence,* application of intellectual skills in everyday situations. Intelligent behavior involves balancing all three intelligences to achieve success in life according to one's personal goals and the requirements of one's cultural community.

Analytical Intelligence. *Analytical intelligence* consists of the information-processing components that underlie all intelligent acts. But on intelligence tests, processing skills are used in only a few of their potential ways, resulting in far too narrow a view of intelligent behavior. As we have seen, children in village societies do not necessarily perform well on measures of "school" knowledge but thrive when processing information in out-of-school situations.

Creative Intelligence. In any context, success depends not only on processing familiar information but also on generating useful solutions to new problems. People who are *creative* think more skillfully than others when faced with novelty. Given a new task, they apply their information-processing skills in exceptionally effective ways, rapidly making these skills automatic so that working memory is freed for more complex aspects of the situation. Consequently, they quickly move to high-level performance. Although all of us are capable of some creativity, only a few individuals excel at generating novel solutions.

Practical Intelligence. Finally, intelligence is a *practical,* goal-oriented activity aimed at *adapting to, shaping,* or *selecting environments.* Intelligent people skillfully *adapt* their thinking to fit with both their desires and the demands of their everyday worlds. When they cannot adapt to a situation, they try to *shape,* or change, it to meet their needs. If they cannot shape it, they *select* new contexts that better match their skills, values, or goals. Practical intelligence reminds us that intelligent behavior is never culture-free. Children with certain life histories do well at the behaviors required for success on intelligence tests and adapt easily to the testing conditions and tasks. Others, with different backgrounds, may misinterpret or reject the testing context. Yet such children often display sophisticated abilities in daily life—for example, telling stories, engaging in complex artistic activities, or interacting skillfully with other people.

The triarchic theory emphasizes the complexity of intelligent behavior and the limitations of current intelligence tests in assessing

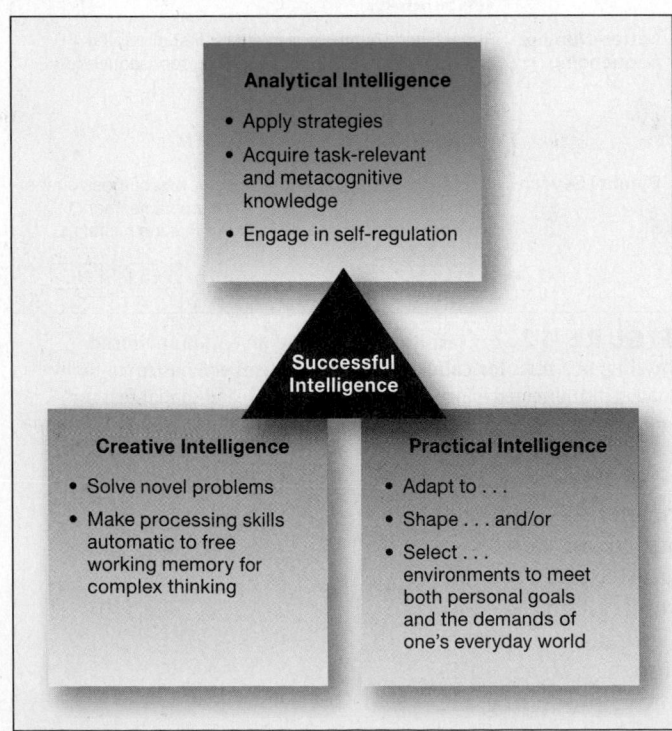

FIGURE 12.5 **Sternberg's triarchic theory of successful intelligence.** People who behave intelligently balance three interrelated intelligences—analytical, creative, and practical—to achieve success in life, defined by their personal goals and the requirements of their cultural communities.

that complexity. For example, out-of-school, practical forms of intelligence are vital for life success and help explain why cultures vary widely in the behaviors they regard as intelligent (Sternberg, 2011). When researchers asked ethnically diverse parents for their idea of an intelligent first grader, Caucasian Americans mentioned cognitive traits. In contrast, ethnic minorities (Cambodian, Filipino, Vietnamese, and Mexican immigrants) saw noncognitive capacities—motivation, self-management, and social skills—as particularly important (Okagaki & Sternberg, 1993). According to Sternberg, intelligence tests can easily underestimate, and even overlook, the cognitive strengths of some children, especially ethnic minorities.

According to Gardner, people are capable of at least eight distinct intelligences. Through a project aimed at improving sea turtle nesting habitats, these children expand and enrich their naturalist intelligence.

GARDNER'S THEORY OF MULTIPLE INTELLIGENCES

In yet another view of how information-processing skills underlie intelligence behavior, Howard Gardner's (1983, 1993, 2011) **theory of multiple intelligences** defines intelligence in terms of distinct sets of processing operations that permit individuals to engage in a wide range of culturally valued activities. Dismissing the idea of general intelligence, Gardner proposes at least eight independent intelligences (see Table 12.2).

Gardner believes that each intelligence has a unique neurological basis, a distinct course of development, and different expert, or "end-state," performances. At the same time, he emphasizes that a lengthy process of education is required to transform any raw potential into a mature social role (Gardner, 2011). Cultural values and learning opportunities affect the extent to which a child's intellectual strengths are realized and the way they are expressed.

Gardner's list of abilities has yet to be firmly grounded in research. Neurological evidence for the independence of his abilities is weak. Some exceptionally gifted individuals have abilities that are broad rather than limited to a particular domain (Piirto, 2007). And research with mental tests suggests that several of Gardner's intelligences (linguistic, logico-mathematical, and spatial) have at least some features in common. Nevertheless, Gardner calls attention to several intelligences not tapped by IQ scores.

TABLE 12.2	Gardner's Multiple Intelligences	
INTELLIGENCE	**PROCESSING OPERATIONS**	**END-STATE PERFORMANCE POSSIBILITIES**
Linguistic	Sensitivity to the sounds, rhythms, and meaning of words and the functions of language	Poet, journalist
Logico-mathematical	Sensitivity to, and capacity to detect, logical or numerical patterns; ability to handle long chains of logical reasoning	Mathematician
Musical	Ability to produce and appreciate pitch, rhythm (or melody), and aesthetic quality of the forms of musical expressiveness	Instrumentalist, composer
Spatial	Ability to perceive the visual–spatial world accurately, to perform transformations on those perceptions, and to re-create aspects of visual experience in the absence of relevant stimuli	Sculptor, navigator
Bodily-kinesthetic	Ability to use the body skillfully for expressive as well as goal-directed purposes; ability to handle objects skillfully	Dancer, athlete
Naturalist	Ability to recognize and classify all varieties of animals, minerals, and plants	Biologist
Interpersonal	Ability to detect and respond appropriately to the moods, temperaments, motivations, and intentions of others	Therapist, salesperson
Intrapersonal	Ability to discriminate complex inner feelings and to use them to guide one's own behavior; knowledge of one's own strengths, weaknesses, desires, and intelligences	Person with detailed, accurate self-knowledge

Sources: Gardner, 1983, 1993, 2011.

For example, Gardner's interpersonal and intrapersonal intelligences include a set of skills for accurately perceiving, reasoning about, and regulating emotion that has become known as *emotional intelligence.* Among school-age children and adolescents, measures of emotional intelligence are positively associated with self-esteem, empathy, prosocial behavior, cooperation, leadership skills, and academic performance and negatively associated with internalizing and externalizing problems (Brackett, Rivers, & Salovey, 2011; Ferrando et al., 2011). These findings have increased teachers' awareness that providing classroom lessons that coach students in emotional abilities can improve their adjustment.

TAKE A MOMENT... Review the *core knowledge perspective,* discussed on page 211 in Chapter 6, and compare it with Gardner's view. Gardner also accepts the existence of innately specified, core domains of thought, present at birth or emerging early in life. Then, as children respond to the demands of their culture, they transform those intelligences to fit the activities they are called on to perform. Gardner's multiple intelligences have been helpful in efforts to understand and nurture children's special talents, a topic we will take up at the end of this chapter.

In this fifth-grade class at an urban elementary school, IQ scores may vary with ethnicity and SES. Research aimed at explaining these differences has generated heated controversy.

Explaining Individual and Group Differences in IQ

When we compare individuals in terms of academic achievement, years of education, and occupational status, it is clear that certain sectors of the population are advantaged over others. In trying to explain these differences, researchers have compared the IQ scores of ethnic and SES groups. American black children and adolescents score, on average, 10 to 12 IQ points below American white children. Although the difference has been shrinking over the past several decades, a substantial gap remains (Flynn, 2007; Nisbett, 2009; Nisbett et al., 2012). Hispanic children fall midway between black and white children, and Asian Americans score slightly higher than their white counterparts—about 3 points (Ceci, Rosenblum, & Kumpf, 1998).

The IQ gap between middle-SES and low-SES children—about 9 points—accounts for some of the ethnic differences in IQ, but not all (Brooks-Gunn et al., 2003). Of course, IQ varies greatly *within* each ethnic and SES group, and minority top performers are typically indistinguishable from top performers in the white majority. Still, these group differences are large enough and of serious enough consequence that they cannot be ignored.

In the 1970s, the IQ nature–nurture controversy escalated after psychologist Arthur Jensen (1969) published a controversial monograph entitled, "How Much Can We Boost IQ and Scholastic Achievement?" Jensen's answer was "not much." He claimed—and still maintains—that heredity is largely responsible for individual, ethnic, and SES variations in intelligence (Jensen, 1998, 2001; Rushton & Jensen, 2006, 2010). Jensen's work prompted an outpouring of research studies and responses, including ethical challenges reflecting deep concern that his conclusions would fuel social prejudices. Richard Herrnstein and Charles Murray rekindled the controversy with *The Bell Curve* (1994). Like Jensen, they argued that heredity contributes substantially to individual and SES differences in IQ, and they implied that heredity plays a sizable role in the black–white IQ gap. Let's look closely at some important evidence.

NATURE VERSUS NURTURE In Chapter 2 we introduced the *heritability estimate.* Recall that heritabilities are obtained from *kinship studies,* which compare family members. The most powerful evidence on the heritability of IQ involves twin comparisons. The IQ scores of identical twins (who share all their genes) are more similar than those of fraternal twins (who are genetically no more alike than ordinary siblings). On the basis of this and other kinship evidence, researchers estimate that about half the differences in IQ among children can be traced to their genetic makeup.

Recall, however, that heritabilities risk overestimating genetic influences and underestimating environmental influences. Although these measures offer convincing evidence that genes contribute to IQ, disagreement persists over how large a role heredity plays. As we saw in Chapter 2, the heritability of children's intelligence rises with parental education and income—conditions that enable children to realize their genetic potential. And heritability estimates do not reveal the complex processes through which genes and experiences influence intelligence as children develop. So far, little progress has been made in identifying genetic markers associated with typical variation in IQ (Butcher et al., 2008; Nisbett et al., 2012). Among the few markers found, relationships with intellectual ability are weak and inconsistent.

Compared with heritability evidence, adoption studies offer a wider range of information. Findings consistently reveal that when young children are adopted into caring, stimulating homes, their IQs rise substantially compared with the IQs of nonadopted children who remain in economically deprived families (Hunt, 2011; van IJzendoorn, Juffer, & Poelhuis, 2005). But adopted children benefit to varying degrees. In one investigation, children of two extreme groups of biological mothers—those with IQs below 95 and those with IQs above 120—were adopted at birth by parents who were well above average in income and education. During the school years, the children of the low-IQ biological mothers scored above average in IQ, indicating that test performance can be greatly improved by an advantaged home life. But they did not do as well as children of high-IQ biological mothers placed in similar adoptive families (Loehlin, Horn, & Willerman, 1997). Adoption research confirms that heredity and environment jointly contribute to IQ.

Adoption studies also shed light on the black–white IQ gap. In two investigations, African-American children adopted into economically well-off white homes during the first year of life scored high on intelligence tests, attaining mean IQs of 110 and 117 by middle childhood—20 to 30 points higher than the typical scores of children growing up in low-income black communities (Moore, 1986; Scarr & Weinberg, 1983). IQ gains of black children "reared in the culture of the tests and schools" are consistent with a wealth of evidence that poverty severely depresses the intelligence of ethnic minority children (Nisbett et al., 2012).

Dramatic gains in IQ from one generation to the next offer additional support for the conclusion that, given new experiences and opportunities, members of oppressed groups can move far beyond their current test performance. See the Cultural Influences box on page 452 to learn about the *Flynn effect*.

CULTURAL INFLUENCES   A controversial question raised about ethnic differences in IQ has to do with whether they result from *test bias*. If a test samples knowledge and skills that not all groups of children have had equal opportunity to learn, or if the testing situation impairs the performance of some groups but not others, the resulting score is a biased, or unfair, measure.

Some experts reject the idea that intelligence tests are biased, claiming that they are intended to represent success in the common culture. According to this view, because IQ predicts academic achievement equally well for majority and minority children, IQ tests are fair to both groups (Edwards & Oakland, 2006; Jensen, 2002). Others believe that lack of exposure to certain communication styles and knowledge, along with negative stereotypes about the test-taker's ethnic group, can undermine children's performance (McKown, 2013; Sternberg, 2005). Let's look at the evidence.

Language and Communication Styles.   Ethnic minority families often foster unique language skills that do not match the expectations of most classrooms and testing situations. African-American English is a complex, rule-governed dialect used by most African Americans in the United States (Craig & Washington, 2006). Nevertheless, it is often inaccurately viewed as a deficient form of standard American English rather than as different from it, and as a low-status dialect associated with poverty.

The majority of African-American children entering school speak African-American English, though they vary greatly in the extent to which they use it. Greater users tend to come from low-SES families, who quickly learn that the language they bring from home is devalued in school, whereas standard American English is respected. Teachers

Many African-Amercan children enter school speaking African-American English. Their home discourse differs from standard English, on which school learning is based.

Cultural Influences

The Flynn Effect: Massive Generational Gains in IQ

After gathering IQ scores from diverse nations that had either military mental testing or frequent testing of other large, representative samples, James Flynn (1999, 2007) reported a finding so consistent and intriguing that it became known as the **Flynn effect:** IQs have increased steadily from one generation to the next. Evidence for the Flynn effect now exists for 30 nations (Nisbett et al., 2012). This dramatic *secular trend* in intelligence test performance holds for industrialized and developing nations, both genders, and individuals varying in ethnicity and SES (Ang, Rodgers, & Wänström, 2010; Rodgers & Wänström, 2007.) Gains are greatest on tests of spatial reasoning—tasks often assumed to be "culture-fair" and, therefore, mostly genetically based.

The amount of increase depends on extent of societal modernization (see page 440 to review). Among European and North American nations that modernized by the early twentieth century, IQ gains have been about 3 points per decade (Flynn, 2007). IQ has continued to increment at that pace in England and the United States, but gains have slowed in certain nations with especially favorable economic and social conditions, such as Norway and Sweden (Schneider, 2006; Sundet, Barlaug, & Torjussen, 2004).

Among nations that modernized later, around the mid-twentieth century (such as Argentina), IQ gains tend to be larger, as much as 5 to 6 points per decade (Flynn & Rossi-Casé, 2011). And nations that began to modernize in the late-twentieth century (Caribbean countries, Kenya, Sudan) show even greater increments, especially in spatial reasoning (Daley et al., 2003; Khaleefa, Sulman, & Lynn, 2009). The degree of societal modernity possible today is far greater than it was a century ago.

Diverse aspects of modernization probably underlie the better reasoning ability of each successive generation. These include improved education, health, and technology (TV, computers, the Internet); more cognitively demanding jobs and leisure activities (reading, chess, video games); a generally more stimulating world; and greater test-taking motivation.

As developing nations continue to advance in IQ, they are projected to catch up with the industrialized world by the end of the twenty-first century (Nisbett et al., 2012). Large, environmentally induced gains in IQ over time present a major challenge to the assumption that black–white and other ethnic variations in IQ are genetic.

Dramatic generational gains in IQ may result, in part, from greater participation by each successive generation in cognitively stimulating leisure activities.

---

frequently try to "correct" or eliminate their use of African-American English forms, replacing them with standard English (Washington & Thomas-Tate, 2009). Because their home discourse is distinctly different from the linguistic knowledge required to learn to read, children who speak mostly African-American English in school generally progress slowly in reading and achieve poorly (Charity, Scarborough, & Griffin, 2004).

Many African-American children learn to flexibly shift between African-American English and standard English by third grade. But those who continue to speak mostly their African-American dialect through the later grades—the majority of whom live in poverty and therefore have few opportunities outside of school for exposure to standard English—fall further behind in reading and in overall achievement (Washington & Thomas-Tate, 2009). These children have a special need for school programs that facilitate mastery of standard English while respecting and accommodating their home language in the classroom.

Research also reveals that many ethnic minority parents without extensive education prefer a *collaborative style of communication* when completing tasks with children. They work together in a coordinated, fluid way, each focused on the same aspect of the problem. This pattern of adult–child engagement has been observed in Native-American, Canadian Inuit, Hispanic, and Guatemalan Mayan cultures (Chavajay & Rogoff, 2002; Crago, Annahatak, & Ningiuruvik, 1993; Paradise & Rogoff, 2009). With increasing education, parents establish a *hierarchical style of communication*, like that of classrooms and tests. The parent directs each child to carry out an aspect of the task, and children work independently (Greenfield, Suzuki, & Rothstein-Fish, 2006). This sharp discontinuity between home and school communication practices likely contributes to low-SES minority children's lower IQ and school performance.

Knowledge. Many researchers argue that IQ scores are affected by specific information acquired as part of majority-culture upbringing. Consistent with this view, low-SES African-American children often miss vocabulary words on intelligence tests that have alternative meanings in their cultural community—for example, interpreting the word *frame* as "physique" or *wrapping* as "rapping," referring to the style of music (Champion, 2003).

Knowledge affects ability to reason effectively. When researchers assessed black and white community college students' familiarity with vocabulary taken from items on an intelligence test, the whites had considerably more knowledge (Fagan & Holland, 2007). But the African-American students were just as capable at learning new words, either from dictionary definitions or from their use in sentences. When verbal comprehension, similarities, and analogies test items depended on words and concepts that the white students knew better, the whites scored higher than the blacks. But when the same types of items involved words and concepts that the two groups knew equally well, the two groups did not differ. Prior knowledge, not reasoning ability, fully explained ethnic differences in performance.

Even nonverbal test items, such as spatial reasoning, depend on learning opportunities. For example, among children, adolescents, and adults alike, playing video games that require fast responding and mental rotation of visual images increases success on spatial test items (Uttal et al., 2013). Low-income minority children, who often grow up in more "people-oriented" than "object-oriented" homes, may lack opportunities to use games and objects that promote certain intellectual skills.

Furthermore, the sheer amount of time a child spends in school predicts IQ. In comparisons of children of the same age who are in different grades, those who have been in school longer score higher in verbal intelligence—a difference that increases as the children advance further in school (Bedard & Dhuey, 2006). Similarly, the earlier young people leave school, the greater their loss of IQ points (Ceci, 1999). And over the summer months, IQ and academic skills decline for low-SES children but rise for higher-SES children, who have greater access to educational activities (Burkam et al., 2004). Taken together, these findings indicate that children's exposure to the knowledge and ways of thinking valued in classrooms has a sizable impact on their intelligence test performance.

Stereotypes. **TAKE A MOMENT...** Imagine trying to succeed at an activity when the prevailing attitude is that members of your group are incompetent. What might you be feeling? **Stereotype threat**—the fear of being judged on the basis of a negative stereotype—can trigger anxiety that interferes with performance. Mounting evidence confirms that stereotype threat undermines test taking in children and adults (McKown & Strambler, 2009). For example, researchers gave African-American, Hispanic-American, and Caucasian-American 6- to 10-year-olds verbal tasks. Some children were told that the tasks were "not a test." Others were told that they were "a test of how good children are at school problems"—a statement designed to induce stereotype threat in the ethnic minority children. Among children who were aware of ethnic stereotypes (such as "black people aren't smart"), African Americans and Hispanics performed far worse in the "test" condition than in the "not a test" condition (McKown & Weinstein, 2003). Caucasian children, in contrast, performed similarly in both conditions.

From third grade on, children become increasingly conscious of ethnic stereotypes, and those from stigmatized groups are especially mindful of them. When confronted with stereotype threat, they well up with anxiety, which reduces mental resources available for doing well on challenging tasks. By early adolescence, many low-SES minority students start to devalue doing well in school, saying it is not important to them (Cooper & Huh, 2008; Killen, Rutland, & Ruck, 2011). Self-protective disengagement, sparked by stereotype threat, may be responsible. This weakening of motivation can have serious long-term consequences. Research shows that self-discipline—effort and delay of gratification—predicts changes in school performance, as measured by report card grades, better than IQ does (Duckworth, Quinn, & Tsukayama, 2012).

School-age children become increasingly conscious of ethnic stereotypes, and those from stigmatized groups are especially mindful of them. Fear of being judged on the basis of a negative stereotype may undermine this Hispanic fourth grader's performance on a spelling test.

Reducing Cultural Bias in Testing

Although not all experts agree, many acknowledge that IQ scores can underestimate the intelligence of children from ethnic minority groups. A special concern exists about incorrectly labeling minority children as slow learners and assigning them to remedial classes, which are far less stimulating than regular school experiences. Because of this danger, test scores need to be combined with assessments of children's adaptive behavior—their ability to cope with the demands of their everyday environments. The child who does poorly on an IQ test yet plays a complex game on the playground or figures out how to rewire a broken TV is unlikely to be intellectually deficient.

In addition, flexible testing procedures enhance minority children's performance. In an approach called **dynamic assessment,** an innovation consistent with Vygotsky's zone of proximal development, the adult introduces purposeful teaching into the testing situation to find out what the child can attain with social support (Lidz, 2001; Robinson-Zañartu & Carlson, 2013). While intervening, the adult seeks the teaching style best suited to the individual child and communicates strategies that the child can apply in new situations.

Research shows that "static" assessments, such as IQ scores, frequently underestimate how well children do on test items after adult assistance. Children's receptivity to teaching and their capacity to transfer what they have learned to novel problems add considerably to the prediction of future performance (Haywood & Lidz, 2007; Sternberg & Grigorenko, 2002). In one study, first graders diverse in SES and ethnicity participated in two dynamic assessment sessions in which they were asked to solve a series of unfamiliar math equations that increased in difficulty, such as __+1 = 4 (easier) and 3 + 6 = 5 + __ (difficult). When a child could not solve an equation, an adult provided increasingly explicit teaching until the child either succeeded or still had trouble, in which case the session ended. Over and above static IQ-like measures of children's verbal, math, and reasoning abilities, performance during dynamic assessment strongly predicted end-of-year scores on a test of math story problems, which children usually find highly challenging (Seethaler et al., 2012). Dynamic assessment seemed to evoke reasoning skills and conceptual understandings that children readily transferred to a very different and demanding type of math.

Cultural bias in testing can also be reduced by countering the negative impact of stereotype threat. A variety of brief, school-based interventions are effective. Persuading students that their intelligence depends heavily on effort, not on a stereotype of native endowment, is helpful (Blackwell, Trzesniewski, & Dweck, 2007). Another approach is to encourage minority students to affirm their self-worth by writing a short essay about their most important values (for example, a close friendship or a self-defining skill). This self-affirmation intervention was just as successful in boosting end-of-term grades of poorly performing middle school students as it was for students doing moderately well in school (see Figure 12.6) (Cohen, Garcia, & Master, 2006).

In view of its many problems, should intelligence testing in schools be suspended? Most experts regard this solution as unacceptable. Without testing, important educational decisions would be based only on subjective impressions, perhaps increasing discriminatory placement of minority children. Intelligence tests are useful when interpreted carefully by examiners who are sensitive to cultural influences on test performance. And despite their limitations, IQ scores continue to be valid measures of school learning potential for the majority of Western children.

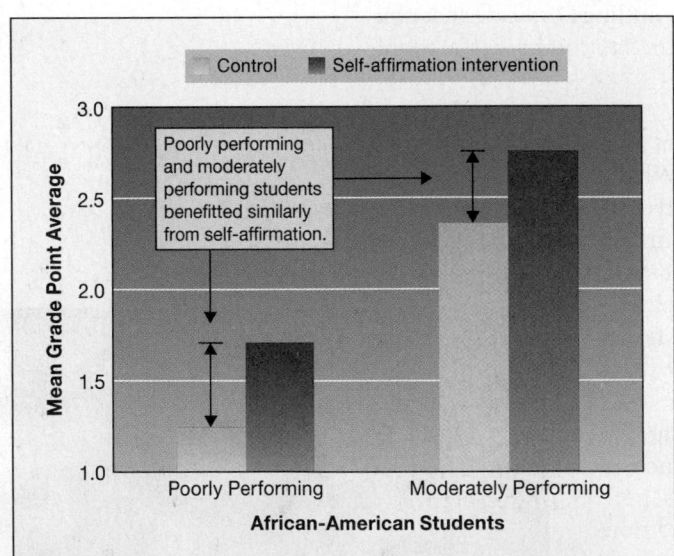

FIGURE 12.6 Impact of a self-affirmation intervention on African-American middle school students' end-of-term grade-point average. Early in the fall term, several hundred middle-school students were randomly assigned to either a self-affirmation intervention, in which they wrote brief essays about why their most important values were important to them, or a control condition, in which they wrote essays about why their least important values might be important to someone else. African-American students experiencing the self-affirmation condition attained substantially higher end-of-term course grades than did controls; poorly performing and moderately performing students benefited similarly. White students' grades (not shown) were unaffected, indicating that the treatment succeeded by lessening the negative impact of stereotype threat on African Americans. (Based on Cohen, Garcia, & Master, 2006.)

Ask Yourself

- **REVIEW** Using Sternberg's triarchic theory and Gardner's theory of multiple intelligences, explain the limitations of current mental tests in assessing the diversity of human intelligence.

- **CONNECT** Explain how dynamic assessment is consistent with Vygotsky's zone of proximal development and with scaffolding (see Chapter 9, pages 323–324).

- **APPLY** Josefina, a Hispanic fourth grader, does well on homework assignments. But when her teacher announces, "It's time for a test to see how much you've learned," Josefina usually does poorly. How might stereotype threat explain this inconsistency?

- **REFLECT** Do you think that intelligence tests are culturally biased? What observations and evidence influenced your conclusion?

Language Development

Vocabulary, grammar, and pragmatics continue to develop in middle childhood, though less obviously than at earlier ages. In addition, children's attitude toward language undergoes a fundamental shift. They develop **metalinguistic awareness,** the ability to think about language as a system.

Schooling contributes greatly to these language competencies. Reflecting on language is extremely common during reading instruction. And fluent reading is a major new source of language learning (Ravid & Tolchinsky, 2002). As we will see, an improved ability to reflect on language grows out of literacy and supports many complex language skills.

12.8 Describe changes in metalinguistic awareness, vocabulary, grammar, and pragmatics during middle childhood.

12.9 Describe bilingual development, along with advantages of bilingualism in childhood.

Vocabulary

During the elementary school years, vocabulary increases fourfold, eventually exceeding comprehension of 40,000 words. On average, children learn about 20 new words each day—a rate of growth greater than in early childhood. In addition to the word-learning strategies discussed in Chapter 9, school-age children enlarge their vocabularies by analyzing the structure of complex words. From *happy* and *decide,* they quickly derive the meanings of *happiness* and *decision* (Larsen & Nippold, 2007). They also figure out many more word meanings from context.

As at earlier ages, children benefit from conversations with more expert speakers, especially when their partners use and explain complex words (Weizman & Snow, 2001). But because written language contains a far more diverse and complex vocabulary than spoken language, reading contributes enormously to vocabulary growth. Avid readers are exposed to more than 4 million words per year, average readers to 600,000 words. But children who rarely read encounter only about 50,000 words (Anderson, Wilson, & Fielding, 1988). By second to third grade, reading comprehension and reading habits are strongly predict later vocabulary size into high school (Cain & Oakhill, 2011).

As their knowledge becomes better organized, older school-age children think about and use words more precisely: In addition to the verb *fall,* for example, they also use *topple, tumble,* and *plummet* (Berman, 2007). Word definitions also illustrate this change. Five- and 6-year-olds offer concrete descriptions referring to functions or appearance—*knife:* "when you're cutting carrots"; *bicycle:* "it's got wheels, a chain, and handlebars." By the end of elementary school, synonyms and explanations of categorical relationships appear—for example, *knife:* "something you could cut with. A saw is like a knife. It could also be a weapon" (Uccelli & Pan, 2013; Wehren, De Lisi, & Arnold, 1981). This advance reflects older children's ability to deal with word meanings on an entirely verbal plane. They can add new words to their vocabulary simply by being given a definition.

A fifth grader encounters new words with complex meanings in a current events article. Stimulating reading experiences contribute greatly to vocabulary growth.

School-age children's more reflective and analytical approach to language permits them to appreciate the multiple meanings of words—to recognize, for example, that many words, such as *cool* or *neat,* have psychological as well as physical meanings: "Cool shirt!" or "That movie was really neat!" This grasp of double meanings permits 8- to 10-year-olds to comprehend subtle metaphors, such as "sharp as a tack" and "spilling the beans" (Nippold, Taylor, & Baker, 1996; Wellman & Hickling, 1994). It also leads to a change in children's humor. Riddles and puns that alternate between different meanings of a key word are common: "Hey, did you take a bath?" "Why, is one missing?"

Grammar

During the school years, mastery of complex grammatical constructions improves. For example, English-speaking children use the passive voice more frequently, and they more often extend it from an abbreviated structure ("It broke") into full statements ("The glass was broken by Mary") (Israel, Johnson, & Brooks, 2000; Tomasello, 2006). Older children also apply their grasp of the passive voice to a wider range of nouns and verbs. Preschoolers comprehend the passive best when the subject of the sentence is an animate being and the verb is an action word: "The boy is *kissed* by the girl." School-age children extend the passive to inanimate subjects *(drum, hat)* and include experiential verbs *(like, know)* (Lempert, 1989; Pinker, Lebeaux, & Frost, 1987). Although the passive form is challenging, language input makes a difference. When adults speak a language that emphasizes full passives, such as Inuktitut (spoken by the Inuit people of Arctic Canada), children produce them earlier (Allen & Crago, 1996).

Another grammatical achievement of middle childhood is advanced understanding of infinitive phrases—the difference between "John is eager to please" and "John is easy to please" (Berman, 2007; Chomsky, 1969). Like gains in vocabulary, appreciation of these subtle grammatical distinctions is supported by improved ability to analyze and reflect on language.

Pragmatics

The school years also bring dramatic gains in *pragmatics,* the communicative side of language. Opportunities to communicate in many situations with a variety of people help children refine these skills.

COMMUNICATING CLEARLY In middle childhood, children can adapt to the needs of listeners in challenging communicative situations, such as describing one object among a group of very similar objects. Whereas preschoolers tend to give ambiguous descriptions ("the red one"), school-age children are precise: "the round red one with stripes on it" (Deutsch & Pechmann, 1982). Because peers challenge unclear messages that adults accept, peer interaction probably contributes greatly to this aspect of conversational competence.

The ability to evaluate the clarity of others' messages improves as well, and children become better at resolving inconsistencies. Consider the instruction, "Put the frog on the book in the box." Preschoolers cannot make sense of the ambiguity, even though they use similar embedded phrases in their own speech. They respond by attending only to the first prepositional phrase ("on the book") and place a toy frog on a book. School-age children, in contrast, can attend to and integrate two competing representations ("on the book" and "in the box") (Hurewitz et al., 2000). They quickly figure out the speaker's meaning and pick up a toy frog resting on a book and place it in a box.

Furthermore, a more advanced theory of mind—in particular, the capacity for recursive thought—enables children to detect increasingly subtle, indirect expressions of meaning with age (Lee, Torrance, & Olson, 2001). Seven-year-old Lizzie often avoided her daily garbage-disposal chore, so she knew that her mother's comment, "The garbage is beginning to smell," really meant, "Take that garbage out!" Around age 8, children begin to grasp irony and sarcasm (Glenright & Pexman, 2010). After Rena prepared a dish for dinner that Joey didn't like, he quipped sarcastically, "Oh boy, my favorite!" Notice how these remarks require the speaker to consider at least two perspectives simultaneously—in Joey's case, his mother's desire to serve a particular dish despite his objection, expressed through a critical comment with a double meaning.

NARRATIVES   As a result of improved memory, ability to take the perspective of listeners, and conversations with adults about past experiences, children's narratives increase in organization, detail, and expressiveness. A typical 4- or 5-year-old's narrative states what happened: "We went to the lake. We fished and waited. Paul caught a huge catfish!" Six- and 7-year-olds add orienting information (time, place, participants) and connectives ("next," "then," "so," "finally") that lend coherence to the story. Gradually, narratives lengthen into a *classic form* in which events not only build to a high point but resolve: "After Paul reeled in the catfish, Dad cleaned and cooked it. Then we ate it all up!" And evaluative comments rise dramatically, becoming common by age 8 to 9: "The catfish tasted great. Paul was so proud!" (Melzi & Schick, 2013; Ukrainetz et al., 2005).

Because children pick up the narrative styles of significant adults in their lives, their narratives vary widely across cultures. For example, instead of the *topic-focused style* of most American school-age children, who describe an experience from beginning to end, African-American children often use a *topic-associating style* in which they blend several similar experiences. One 9-year-old related having a tooth pulled, then described seeing her sister's tooth pulled, next told how she had removed one of her baby teeth, and concluded, "I'm a pullin-teeth expert . . . call me, and I'll be over" (McCabe, 1997, p. 164). Like adults in their families and communities, African-American children are more attuned to keeping their listeners interested than relating a linear sequence of story events.

Children's narratives vary widely across cultures, reflecting the styles of significant adults in their lives. African-American children like this second grader tend to tell longer, more complex stories than white children.

They often embellish their narratives by including fictional elements and many references to characters' motives and intentions (Gorman et al., 2011). As a result, African-American children's narratives are usually longer and more complex than those of white children.

The ability to generate clear oral narratives enhances reading comprehension and prepares children for producing longer, more explicit written narratives. In families who regularly eat meals together, children are advanced in language and literacy development, perhaps because mealtimes offer many opportunities to relate personal stories (Snow & Beals, 2006).

Learning Two Languages

Joey and Lizzie speak only one language—English, their native tongue. Yet throughout the world, many children grow up *bilingual*, learning two languages and sometimes more than two. An estimated 22 percent of U.S. children—11 million in all—speak a language other than English at home (U.S. Census Bureau, 2014b).

BILINGUAL DEVELOPMENT   Children can become bilingual in two ways: (1) by acquiring both languages at the same time in early childhood or (2) by learning a second language after mastering the first. Children of bilingual parents who teach them both languages in infancy and early childhood separate the language systems early on and attain early language milestones according to a typical timetable (Hoff et al., 2012; Weikum et al., 2007). Preschoolers acquire normal native ability in the language of their surrounding community and good-to-native ability in the second language, depending on their exposure to it (Serratrice, 2013). When school-age children acquire a second language, they generally take 5 to 7 years to attain speaking and writing skills on a par with those of native-speaking agemates (Paradis, 2007).

Like many bilingual adults, bilingual children sometimes engage in *code switching*—producing an utterance in one language that contains one or more "guest" words from the other—without violating the grammar of either language. Rather than a sign of confusion, code switching is adaptive, reflecting deliberate control of the two languages (Bhatt & Bolonyai, 2011). Children may engage in code switching because they lack the vocabulary to convey a particular thought in one language, so they use the other. And children who code-switch the most are those whose parents often do so. Bilingual adults frequently code-switch to express cultural identity, and children may follow suit—as when a Korean child speaking English switches to Korean on mentioning her piano teacher, as a sign of respect for authority (Chung, 2006). Opportunities to listen to code switching may facilitate bilingual development. For example, a child accustomed to hearing French sentences with English guest words may rely on sentence-level cues to figure out English word meanings.

Recall from Chapter 6 that, just as with first-language development, a *sensitive period* for second-language development exists. Although mastery must begin sometime in childhood for full development to occur, a precise age cutoff for a decline in second-language learning has not been established (see page 233).

Children who become fluent in two languages develop denser gray matter (neurons and connective fibers) in areas of the left hemisphere devoted to language. And compared to monolinguals, bilinguals show greater activity in these areas and in the prefrontal cortex during linguistic tasks, likely due to the high executive-processing demands of controlling two languages (Costa & Sebastián-Gallés, 2014). Because both languages are always active, bilingual speakers must continuously decide which one to use in particular social situations, resisting attention to the other.

This increase in executive processing has diverse cognitive benefits as bilinguals acquire more efficient executive-function skills and apply those to other tasks (Bialystok, 2011). Bilingual children and adults outperform others on tests of sustained and selective attention, inhibition of irrelevant information, flexible thinking, analytical reasoning, concept formation, and false-belief (Bialystok, Craik, & Luk, 2012; Carlson & Meltzoff, 2008). They are also advanced in certain aspects of metalinguistic awareness, such as detection of errors in grammar, meaning, and conventions of conversation (responding politely, relevantly, and informatively). And children transfer their phonological awareness skills in one language to the other, especially if their two languages share phonological features and letter–sound correspondences, as Spanish and English do (Bialystok, 2013; Siegal, Iozzi, & Surian, 2009). These capacities enhance reading achievement.

BILINGUAL EDUCATION   The advantages of bilingualism provide strong justification for bilingual education programs in schools. In Canada, about 7 percent of elementary school students are enrolled in *language immersion programs,* in which English-speaking children typically are taught entirely in French from kindergarten through second grade. Gradually, English is introduced as a subject in third grade, though French continues to be the main classroom language. This strategy succeeds in developing children who are proficient in both languages. Though initial delays in English literacy achievement are common, by grade 6 immersion students achieve as well in reading, writing, and math as their counterparts in the regular English program (Genesee & Jared, 2008; Lyster & Genesee, 2012).

In the United States, fierce disagreement exists over the question of how best to educate ethnic minority children with limited English proficiency. Some believe that time spent communicating in the child's native tongue detracts from English-language achievement, which is crucial for success in the worlds of school and work. Other educators, committed to developing minority children's native language while fostering mastery of English, note that providing instruction in the native tongue lets minority children know that their heritage is respected. It also prevents inadequate proficiency in both languages. Minority children who gradually lose their first language as a result of being taught the second end up limited in both languages for a time (McCabe et al., 2013). This circumstance leads to serious academic difficulties and is believed to contribute to the high rates of school failure and dropout among low-SES Hispanic youngsters, who make up over 60 percent of the U.S. language-minority population.

At present, public opinion and educational practice favor English-only instruction. Many U.S. states have passed laws declaring English to be their official language, creating conditions in which schools have no obligation to teach minority students in languages other than English. Where bilingual education exists, its goal is to transition students to English-only instruction as soon as possible (Wright, 2013). Yet in classrooms where both languages are integrated into the curriculum, minority children are more involved in learning, participate more actively in class discussions,

The child on the left, a native Spanish speaker, benefits from an English–Spanish bilingual classroom, which sustains her native language while she masters English. And her native-English-speaking classmate has the opportunity to begin learning Spanish!

and acquire the second language more easily—gains that predict better academic achievement (Guglielmi, 2008). In contrast, when teachers speak only in a language that children can barely understand, minority children display frustration, boredom, and withdrawal. Under these conditions, U.S. kindergartners with limited English proficiency quickly fall behind their English-proficient counterparts in oral language and reading skills and are likely to struggle academically throughout their school years (Paradis, Genesee, & Crago 2011). This downward spiral in achievement is greatest in high-poverty schools, where resources to support the needs of language-minority children are especially scarce.

Supporters of U.S. English-only education often point to the success of Canadian language immersion programs, in which classroom lessons are conducted in the second language. But Canadian parents enroll their children in immersion classrooms voluntarily, and students in those programs are native speakers of the dominant language of their region. Furthermore, teaching in the child's native language is merely delayed, not ruled out. For U.S. non-English-speaking minority children, whose native languages are not valued by the larger society, a different strategy is necessary: one that promotes children's native-language and literacy skills while they learn English.

Ask Yourself

- **REVIEW** Cite examples of how metalinguistic awareness fosters school-age children's language progress.

- **CONNECT** How can bilingual education promote ethnic minority children's cognitive and academic development?

- **APPLY** After soccer practice, 10-year-old Shana remarked, "I'm wiped out!" Megan, her 5-year-old sister, responded, "What did'ya wipe out?" Explain Shana's and Megan's different understandings.

- **REFLECT** Considering research on bilingualism, what changes would you make in your own second-language learning, and why?

Children's Learning in School

Evidence cited throughout this chapter indicates that schools are vital forces in children's cognitive development. How do schools exert such a powerful influence? Research looking at schools as complex social systems—class size, educational philosophies, teacher–student relationships, and larger cultural context—provides important insights. As you read about these topics, refer to Applying What We Know on page 460, which summarizes characteristics of high-quality education in elementary school.

Class Size

As each school year began, Rena telephoned the principal's office to ask, "How large will Joey's and Lizzie's classes be?" Her concern is well-founded. In a large field experiment, more than 6,000 Tennessee kindergartners were randomly assigned to three class types: "small" (13 to 17 students), "regular" (22 to 25 students) with only a teacher, and regular with a teacher plus a full-time teacher's aide. These arrangements continued into third grade. Small-class students scored higher in reading and math achievement each year (Mosteller, 1995). Placing teacher's aides in regular-size classes had no impact. Rather, experiencing small classes from kindergarten through third grade predicted substantially higher achievement from fourth through ninth grades, after children had returned to regular-size classes. It also predicted greater likelihood of graduating from high school, particularly for low-SES students (Finn, Gerber, & Boyd-Zaharias, 2005; Nye, Hedges, & Konstantopoulos, 2001).

Small class size, especially if introduced at school entry, is associated with better academic progress even after diverse measures of teacher quality have been controlled (Brühweiler &

12.10 Describe the impact of class size and educational philosophies on children's motivation and academic achievement.

12.11 Discuss the role of teacher–student interaction and grouping practices in academic achievement.

12.12 Describe benefits of, as well as concerns about, educational media.

12.13 Under what conditions is placement of children with mild intellectual disability or learning disabilities in regular classrooms successful?

12.14 Describe the characteristics of gifted children and efforts to meet their educational needs.

12.15 How well-educated are U.S. children compared with children in other industrialized nations?

Applying What We Know

Signs of High-Quality Education in Elementary School

CLASSROOM CHARACTERISTICS	SIGNS OF QUALITY
Class size	Optimum class size is no larger than 18 to 20 children.
Physical setting	Space is divided into richly equipped activity centers—for reading, writing, playing math or language games, exploring science, working on construction projects, using computers, and engaging in other academic pursuits. Spaces are used flexibly for individual and small-group activities and whole-class gatherings.
Curriculum	The curriculum helps children both achieve academic standards and make sense of their learning. Subjects are integrated so that children apply knowledge in one area to others. The curriculum is implemented through activities responsive to children's interests, ideas, and everyday lives, including their cultural backgrounds.
Daily activities	Teachers provide challenging activities that include opportunities for small-group and independent work. Groupings vary in size and makeup of children, depending on the activity and on children's learning needs. Teachers encourage cooperative learning and guide children in attaining it.
Interactions between teachers and children	Teachers foster each child's progress and use intellectually engaging strategies, including posing problems, asking thought-provoking questions, discussing ideas, and adding complexity to tasks. They also demonstrate, explain, coach, and assist in other ways, depending on each child's learning needs.
Evaluations of progress	Teachers regularly evaluate children's progress through written observations and work samples, which they use to enhance and individualize teaching. They help children reflect on their work and decide how to improve it. They also seek information and perspectives from parents on how well children are learning and include parents' views in evaluations.
Relationship with parents	Teachers forge partnerships with parents. They hold periodic conferences and encourage parents to visit the classroom anytime, to observe and volunteer.

Source: Copple & Bredekamp, 2009.

Blatchford, 2011). Why is it beneficial? With fewer children, teachers spend less time disciplining and more time teaching and giving individual attention. Also, children who learn in smaller groups show better concentration, higher-quality class participation, and more favorable attitudes toward school (Blatchford, 2012; Blatchford, Bassett, & Brown, 2005, 2011).

Educational Philosophies

Each teacher brings to the classroom an educational philosophy that plays a major role in children's learning. Two philosophical approaches have received the most research attention. They differ in what children are taught, in the way they are believed to learn, and in how their progress is evaluated.

TRADITIONAL VERSUS CONSTRUCTIVIST CLASSROOMS   In a **traditional classroom,** the teacher is the sole authority for knowledge, rules, and decision making and does most of the talking. Students are relatively passive—listening, responding when called on, and completing teacher-assigned tasks. Their progress is evaluated by how well they keep pace with a uniform set of standards for their grade.

A **constructivist classroom,** in contrast, encourages students to *construct* their own knowledge. Although constructivist approaches vary, many are grounded in Piaget's theory, which views children as active agents who reflect on and coordinate their own thoughts, rather than absorbing those of others. A glance inside a constructivist classroom reveals richly equipped learning centers, small groups and individuals solving self-chosen problems, and a teacher who guides and supports in response to children's needs. Students are evaluated by considering their progress in relation to their own prior development.

In the United States, the pendulum has swung back and forth between these two views. In the 1960s and early 1970s, constructivist classrooms gained in popularity. Then, as concern arose over the academic progress of children and youths, a "back-to-basics" movement arose, and classrooms returned to traditional instruction. This style, still prevalent today, has become increasingly pronounced as a result of the U.S. No Child Left Behind Act, signed into law in 2001 (Darling-Hammond, 2010; Kew et al., 2012). Because it places heavy pressure on teachers and school administrators to improve achievement test scores, it has narrowed the curricular focus in many schools to preparing students to take such tests.

Although older elementary school children in traditional classrooms have a slight edge in achievement test scores, constructivist settings are associated with many other benefits—gains in critical thinking, greater social and moral maturity, and more positive attitudes toward school (DeVries, 2001; Rathunde & Csikszentmihalyi, 2005; Walberg, 1986). And as noted in Chapter 9, when teacher-directed instruction is emphasized in preschool and kindergarten, it actually undermines academic motivation and achievement, especially in low-SES children.

The emphasis on knowledge absorption in many kindergarten and primary classrooms has contributed to a trend among parents to delay their child's school entry—especially among higher-SES families and if the child is a boy with a birth date close to the cutoff for kindergarten enrollment. But research reveals no long-term academic or social benefits (Bassok & Reardon, 2013; Lincove & Painter, 2006). To the contrary, younger first graders reap achievement gains from on-time enrollment, outperforming same-age children a year behind them (Stipek & Byler, 2001). An alternative perspective is that school readiness can be cultivated through classroom experiences that foster children's individual progress.

NEW PHILOSOPHICAL DIRECTIONS New approaches to education, grounded in Vygotsky's sociocultural theory, capitalize on the rich social context of the classroom to spur children's learning. In these **social-constructivist classrooms,** children participate in a wide range of challenging activities with teachers and peers, with whom they jointly construct understandings. As children *appropriate* (take for themselves) the knowledge and strategies generated through working together, they become competent, contributing members of their classroom community and advance in cognitive and social development (Bodrova & Leong, 2007; Lourenço, 2012). Vygotsky's emphasis on the social origins of complex mental activities has inspired the following educational themes:

- *Teachers and children as partners in learning.* A classroom rich in both teacher–child and child–child collaboration transfers culturally valued ways of thinking to children.
- *Experience with many types of symbolic communication in meaningful activities.* As children master reading, writing, and mathematics, they become aware of their culture's communication systems, reflect on their own thinking, and bring it under voluntary control. **TAKE A MOMENT...** Can you identify research presented earlier in this chapter that supports this theme?
- *Teaching adapted to each child's zone of proximal development.* Assistance that both responds to current understandings and encourages children to take the next step helps ensure that each child makes the best progress possible.

Let's look at two examples of a growing number of programs that have translated these ideas into action.

Reciprocal Teaching. Originally designed to improve reading comprehension in poorly achieving students, this Vygotsky-inspired teaching method has been extended to other subjects and all schoolchildren (Palincsar & Herrenkohl, 1999). In **reciprocal teaching,** a teacher and two to four students form a cooperative group and take turns leading dialogues on the content of a text passage. Within the dialogues, group members apply four cognitive strategies: questioning, summarizing, clarifying, and predicting.

The dialogue leader (at first a teacher, later a student) begins by *asking questions* about the content of the text passage. Students offer answers, raise additional questions, and, in case of disagreement, reread the original text. Next, the leader *summarizes* the passage, and children discuss the summary and *clarify* unfamiliar ideas. Finally, the leader encourages students to *predict* upcoming content based on clues in the passage.

Elementary and middle school students exposed to reciprocal teaching show impressive gains in reading comprehension compared to controls taught in other ways (Schunemann, Sporer, & Brunstein, 2013; Sporer, Brunstein, & Kieschke, 2009). Notice how reciprocal teaching creates a zone of proximal development in which children learn to scaffold one another's

LOOK *and* **LISTEN**

Ask an elementary school teacher to sum up his or her educational philosophy. Is it closest to a traditional, constructivist, or social-constructivist view? Has the teacher encountered any obstacles to implementing that philosophy? Explain.

progress and assume more responsibility for comprehending text passages. Also, by collaborating with others, children forge group expectations for high-level thinking, more often apply their metacognitive knowledge, and acquire skills vital for learning and success in everyday life.

Communities of Learners. Recognizing that collaboration requires a supportive context to be most effective, another Vygotsky-based innovation makes it a schoolwide value. Classrooms become **communities of learners** where teachers guide the overall process of learning but no other distinction is made between adult and child contributors: All participate in joint endeavors and have the authority to define and resolve problems. This approach is based on the assumption that different people have different expertises that can benefit the community and that students, too, may become experts (Sewell, St George, & Cullen, 2013). Classroom activities are often long-term projects addressing complex, real-world problems. In working toward project goals, children and teachers draw on the expertises of one another and of others within and outside the school.

A teacher and students form a community of learners to plan, plant, and track the growth of a vegetable garden. During this complex, long-term project, all participants—adults as well as children—may become experts who share knowledge, teaching one another.

In one classroom, students studied animal–habitat relationships in order to design an animal of the future, suited to environmental changes. The class formed small research groups, each of which selected a subtopic—for example, defense against predators, protection from the elements, reproduction, or food getting. Each group member assumed responsibility for part of the subtopic, consulting diverse experts and preparing teaching materials. Then group members taught one another, assembled their contributions, and brought them to the community as a whole so the knowledge gathered could be used to solve the problem (Brown, 1997; Stone, 2005). The result was a multifaceted understanding of the topic that would have been too difficult and time-consuming for any learner to accomplish alone.

In communities of learners, collaboration is created from within by teachers and children and supported from without by the culture of the school (Sullivan & Glanz, 2006). As a result, the approach broadens Vygotsky's concept of the zone of proximal development, from a child in collaboration with a more expert partner (adult or peer) to multiple, interrelated zones.

Teacher–Student Interaction

Elementary and secondary school students describe good teachers as caring, helpful, and stimulating—behaviors associated with gains in motivation, achievement, and positive peer relations (Hughes & Kwok, 2006, 2007; Hughes, Zhang, & Hill, 2006; O'Connor & McCartney, 2007). But too many U.S. teachers—especially those in schools with many students from low-income families—emphasize repetitive drill over higher-level thinking, such as grappling with ideas and applying knowledge to new situations (Valli, Croninger, & Buese, 2012). This focus on low-level skills becomes increasingly pronounced over the school year as state-mandated achievement testing draws nearer.

Of course, teachers do not interact in the same way with all children. Well-behaved, high-achieving students typically get more support and praise, whereas unruly students have more conflicts with teachers and receive more criticism (Henricsson & Rydell, 2004). Warm, low-conflict teacher–student relationships have an especially strong impact on academic self-esteem, achievement, and social behavior of low-SES minority students and other children at risk for learning difficulties (Hughes, 2011; Hughes et al., 2012; Spilt et al., 2012). But overall, higher-SES students—who tend to be higher-achieving and to have fewer learning and behavior problems—have more sensitive and supportive relationships with teachers (Jerome, Hamre, & Pianta, 2008).

Unfortunately, once teachers' attitudes toward students are established, they can become more extreme than is warranted by children's behavior. Of special concern are **educational self-fulfilling prophecies:** Children may adopt teachers' positive or negative views and start to live up to them. This effect is particularly strong when teachers emphasize competition and publicly compare children, regularly favoring the best students (Weinstein, 2002).

Teacher expectations have a greater impact on low-achieving than high-achieving students (McKown, Gregory, & Weinstein, 2010). When a teacher is critical, high achievers can fall back on their history of success. Low-achieving students' sensitivity to self-fulfilling prophecies can be beneficial when teachers believe in them. But biased teacher judgments are usually slanted in a negative direction.

Furthermore, much evidence confirms that academic stereotypes about ethnic minority students have self-fulfilling effects on their behavior (Madon et al., 2011). In one study, African-American and Hispanic elementary school students taught by high-bias teachers (who expected them to do poorly) showed substantially lower end-of-year achievement than their counterparts taught by low-bias teachers (McKown & Weinstein, 2008). Recall our discussion of *stereotype threat*. A child in the position of confirming a negative stereotype may respond with especially intense anxiety and reduced motivation, amplifying a negative self-fulfilling prophecy.

Grouping Practices

In many schools, students are assigned to *homogeneous* groups or classes, in which children of similar ability levels are taught together. Homogeneous grouping can be a potent source of self-fulfilling prophecies. Low-group students—who as early as first grade are more likely to be low-SES, minority, and male—get more drill on basic facts and skills, engage in less discussion, and progress at a slower pace. Gradually, they decline in self-esteem and motivation and fall further behind in achievement (Lleras & Rangel, 2009; Worthy, Hungerford-Kresser, & Hampton, 2009).

Unfortunately, widespread SES and ethnic segregation in U.S. schools consigns large numbers of low-SES, minority students to a form of school-wide, deleterious homogeneous grouping. Refer to the Social Issues: Education box on page 464 to find out how magnet schools foster heterogeneous learning contexts, thereby reducing achievement differences between SES and ethnic minority groups.

Fourth graders work together to complete an assignment. Successful cooperative learning enhances children's enjoyment of learning and academic achievement.

However, small, heterogeneous groups of students working together often engage in poorer-quality interaction (less accurate explanations and answers) than homogeneous groups of above-average students (Webb, Nemer, & Chizhik, 1998). For collaboration between heterogeneous peers to succeed, children need extensive training and guidance in **cooperative learning,** in which small groups of classmates work toward common goals—by considering one another's ideas, appropriately challenging one another, providing sufficient explanations to correct misunderstandings, and resolving differences of opinion on the basis of reasons and evidence. When teachers prompt, explain, model, and have children role-play how to work together effectively, cooperative learning among heterogeneous peers results in more complex reasoning, greater enjoyment of learning, and achievement gains across a wide range of subjects (Gillies, 2003b; Jadallah et al., 2011; Webb et al., 2008).

Consider an investigation in which teachers taught heterogeneous groups of fourth graders to collaborate in reasoning about controversial issues, such as whether zoos are good places for animals. Over 10 group sessions, the students increasingly engaged in more advanced reasoning by analogy—comparisons that moved beyond surface features ("In a zoo it would be just like being in jail") to higher-order relations ("Pretend this classroom is like a cage. And who would rather be here or recess?"). During discussions, use of analogies "snowballed." When one student introduced an analogy, other students often elaborated on it and contributed new analogies ("Cause it's like your mom locking you in your room for a week") (Lin et al., 2012). Together, students used analogy as a powerfully persuasive tool, capitalizing on it to introduce new information and perspectives.

Educational Media

Virtually all public schools in industrialized nations have integrated computers into their instructional programs and can access the Internet. And, as noted in Chapter 9, most U.S. children have access to a home computer, usually with an Internet connection. Although the

Social Issues: Education

Magnet Schools: Equal Access to High-Quality Education

Each school-day morning, Emma leaves her affluent suburban neighborhood, riding a school bus 20 miles to a magnet school in an impoverished, mostly Hispanic inner-city neighborhood. In her fifth-grade class, she settles into a science project with her friend Maricela, who lives in the local neighborhood. For the first hour of the day, the girls use a thermometer, ice water, and a stopwatch to determine which of several materials is the best insulator, recording and graphing their data. Throughout the school, which specializes in innovative math and science teaching, students diverse in SES and ethnicity learn side-by-side.

Despite the 1954 U.S. Supreme Court *Brown v. Board of Education* decision ordering schools to desegregate, school integration receded over the 1990s as federal courts canceled their integration orders and returned this authority to states and cities. Since 2000, the racial divide in American education has improved only modestly (Stroub & Richards, 2013). When minority students attend ethnically mixed schools, they typically do so with other minorities.

U.S. schools in inner-city, low-income neighborhoods are vastly disadvantaged in funding and therefore in educational opportunities, largely because public education is primarily supported by local property taxes. Federal and state grants-in-aid are not sufficient to close this funding gap between rich and poor districts. Consequently, in inner-city segregated neighborhoods, dilapidated school buildings; inexperienced teachers; outdated, poor-quality educational resources; and school cultures that fail to encourage strong teaching are widespread (Condron, 2013). The negative impact on student achievement is severe.

A promising solution is the establishment of magnet schools. In addition to the usual curriculum, they emphasize a specific area of interest—such as performing arts, math and science, or technology. Families outside the school neighborhood are attracted to magnet schools (hence the name) by their rich academic offerings. Often magnets are located in low-income, minority areas, where they serve the neighborhood student population. Other students, who apply and are admitted by lottery, are bussed in—many from well-to-do city and suburban neighborhoods. In another model, all students—including those in the surrounding neighborhood—must apply. In either case, magnet schools are voluntarily desegregated.

Do magnet schools enhance minority student achievement? A Connecticut study comparing students enrolled in magnet middle schools with those whose lottery numbers were not drawn and who therefore attended other city schools confirmed that the magnets served a far more diverse student population. Although magnet-

A magnet-school teacher receives hugs from her first-grade students at a party celebrating news that she is a finalist for Texas Elementary Teacher of the Year. Magnet schools typically attract students diverse in ethnicity and SES because of their rich academic offerings and innovative teaching.

school enrollees and nonadmitted applicants were similar in ethnicity, SES, and prior academic achievement, magnet students showed greater gains in reading and math achievement over a two-year period—outcomes especially pronounced for low-SES, ethnic minority students (Bifulco, Cobb, & Bell, 2009).

By high school, the higher-achieving peer environments of ethnically diverse schools encourage more students to pursue higher education (Franklin, 2012). In sum, magnet schools are a promising approach for overcoming the negative forces of SES and ethnic isolation in American schools.

---

overwhelming majority of higher-SES homes have computers and Internet, more than 70 percent of U.S. low-SES families with school-age children and adolescents now have them (Common Sense Media, 2013; U.S. Census Bureau, 2014b).

Computer use is associated with academic progress. Word processing, for example, enables children to write freely, without having to struggle with handwriting. Because they can revise their text's meaning and style and also check their spelling, they worry less about making mistakes. As a result, their written products tend to be longer and of higher quality (Clements & Sarama, 2003). And as in early childhood, computer programming projects promote problem solving and metacognition and are common classroom contexts for peer collaboration (see page 346 in Chapter 9).

As children get older, they increasingly use screen media for schoolwork, mostly to search the Web for information and to prepare written assignments—activities linked to improved problem-solving skills and academic achievement (Judge, Puckett, & Bell, 2006; Tran & Subrahmanyam, 2013). The more low-SES middle school students use the Internet for information gathering (either for school or for personal interests), the better their subsequent reading achievement and school grades (Jackson et al., 2011). Perhaps those who use the Web to find information also devote more time to reading, given that many Web pages are heavily text-based.

With age, video game play rises dramatically: two-thirds of U.S. 6- to 8-year-olds, and the overwhelming majority of 8- to 18-year-olds, have played at one time or another. Young school-age children, on average, devote 20 minutes per day to gaming, older school-age children and adolescents 73 minutes. Boys are two to three times more likely than girls to be daily players (Common Sense Media, 2013; Rideout, Foehr, & Roberts, 2010).

Although video games with violent content are harmful (see Chapter 10), game play is also rich in cognitive benefits. These include gains in eye-and-hand coordination, visual processing speed, attention, strategic thinking, and spatial reasoning (see page 453) (Tran & Subrahmanyam, 2013). Games emphasizing academic skills, such as reading or math, succeed in teaching their intended content (Murphy et al., 2002). And because adventure games typically involve substantial cognitive challenge—navigating a series of worlds and manipulating variables to overcome obstacles—successful play requires strategic thinking, planning, self-regulation, problem solving, and (in fantasy role-play games) imagination (Boyan & Sherry, 2011; Valkenburg & Calvert, 2012). These cognitive demands usually increase as games progress. Furthermore, playing video games collaboratively with peers can promote cooperative skills, which may transfer to other contexts.

The learning advantages of screen media raise concerns about a "digital divide" between SES and gender groups. Computers and Internet connections are less prevalent in low-SES than in middle-SES homes, and the SES gap in access to tablets and educational apps is even larger (Common Sense Media, 2013; Lenhart et al., 2010). Boys spend more time with screen media than girls and use them somewhat differently. Boys, as mentioned earlier, play games far more often, and they also devote more time to downloading music, creating Web pages, writing computer programs, and using graphics programs. Girls emphasize information gathering and social communication (Lenhart et al., 2010; Looker & Thiessen, 2003; Rideout, Foehr, & Roberts, 2010). Schools need to ensure that girls and economically disadvantaged students have many opportunities to benefit from the diverse, cognitively enriching aspects of screen-media technology.

Because children find mastering complex game elements highly motivating, designing video games to teach academic content is likely to boost achievement for all children. But devoting too much time to computer use—especially playing entertainment video games, even those with nonviolent content—is linked to poorer school performance (Gentile, 2011; Hofferth, 2010). Like entertainment TV (see Chapter 10), excessive game play detracts from time devoted to homework, reading, and other activities that have greater educational benefits.

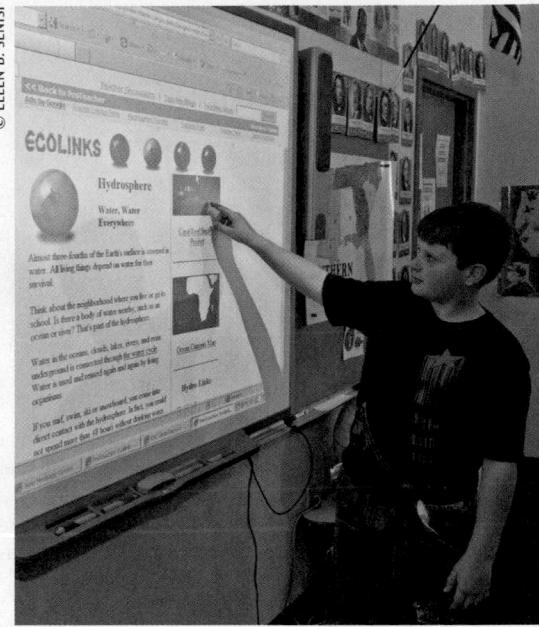

This fifth grader uses a digital whiteboard to interact with an environmental education website. Using the Internet to search for information is linked to better reading achievement and school grades.

Teaching Children with Special Needs

We have seen that effective teachers flexibly adjust their teaching strategies to accommodate students with a wide range of abilities and characteristics. But such adjustments are increasingly difficult at the very low and high ends of the ability distribution. How do schools serve children with special learning needs?

CHILDREN WITH LEARNING DIFFICULTIES U.S. legislation mandates that schools place children who require special supports for learning in the "least restrictive" (as close to normal as possible) environments that meet their educational needs. In **inclusive classrooms,** students with learning difficulties learn alongside typical students in the regular educational setting for part or all of the school day—a practice designed to prepare them for participation in society and to combat prejudices against individuals with disabilities. Largely as the result of parental pressures, an increasing number of students experience *full inclusion*—full-time placement in regular classrooms.

Students with mild intellectual disability are sometimes integrated into inclusive classrooms. Typically, their IQs fall between 55 and 70, and they also show problems in adaptive behavior, or skills of everyday living (American Psychiatric Association, 2013). But the largest number designated for inclusion—5 to 10 percent of school-age children—have **learning disabilities,** great difficulty with one or more aspects of learning, usually reading. As a result,

In this inclusive classroom, children with special needs learn alongside typical students. Such arrangements can be beneficial, but some students with disabilities are overwhelmed by the academic and social demands of a regular classroom.

their achievement is considerably behind what would be expected on the basis of their IQ. Sometimes, deficits express themselves in other ways—for example, as severe inattention (see page 438), which depresses both intelligence and achievement test scores. The problems of students with learning disabilities cannot be traced to any obvious physical or emotional difficulty or to environmental disadvantage. Instead, deficits in brain functioning are involved (Waber, 2010). Some learning disabilities run in families, and in certain cases, specific genes have been identified that contribute to the problem (Goldstein, 2011). In many instances, the cause is unknown.

Although some students benefit academically from inclusion, many do not. Achievement gains depend on both the severity of the disability and the support services available (Downing, 2010). Furthermore, children with disabilities often are rejected by regular-classroom peers. Students with intellectual disability are overwhelmed by the social skills of their classmates; they cannot interact adeptly in a conversation or game. And the processing deficits of some students with learning disabilities lead to problems in social awareness and responsiveness (Lohrmann & Bambara, 2006; Nowicki, Brown, & Stepien, 2014).

Does this mean that students with special needs cannot be served in regular classrooms? Not necessarily. Often these children do best when they receive instruction in a resource room for part of the day and in the regular classroom for the remainder (McLeskey & Waldron, 2011). In the resource room, a special education teacher works with students on an individual and small-group basis. Then, depending on their progress, children join typically developing classmates for different subjects and amounts of time.

Special steps must be taken to promote positive peer relations in inclusive classrooms. Peer tutoring experiences in which teachers guide typical students in supporting the academic progress of classmates with learning difficulties lead to friendly interaction, improved peer acceptance, and achievement gains (Mastropieri et al., 2013). Teachers can also prepare their class for the arrival of a student with special needs. Under these conditions, inclusion may foster emotional sensitivity and prosocial behavior among regular classmates.

GIFTED CHILDREN In Joey and Lizzie's school, some children were **gifted,** displaying exceptional intellectual strengths. One or two students in every grade have IQ scores above 130, the standard definition of giftedness based on intelligence test performance (Pfeiffer & Yermish, 2014). High-IQ children, as we have seen, have keen memories and an exceptional capacity to solve challenging academic problems. Yet recognition that intelligence tests do not sample the entire range of human cognitive skills, as noted earlier in this chapter, has led to an expanded conception of giftedness.

As sixth graders rehearse a play they have written, they gain experience in generating original ideas, evaluating those ideas, and choosing the most promising—vital ingredients of creativity.

Creativity and Talent. **Creativity** is the ability to produce work that is *original* yet *appropriate*—something that others have not thought of that is useful in some way (Lubart, 2003). A child with high potential for creativity can be designated as gifted. Tests of creative capacity tap **divergent thinking**—the generation of multiple and unusual possibilities when faced with a task or problem. Divergent thinking contrasts sharply with **convergent thinking,** which involves arriving at a single correct answer and is emphasized on intelligence tests (Guilford, 1985).

Because highly creative children (like high-IQ children) are often better at some types of tasks than others, a variety of tests of divergent thinking are available (Runco, 1992; Torrance, 1988). A verbal measure might ask children to name uses for common objects (such as a newspaper). A figural measure might ask them to come up with drawings based on a circular motif (see Figure 12.7). A "real-world problem" measure requires students to suggest solutions to everyday problems. Responses can be scored for the number of ideas generated and their originality.

Yet critics point out that these measures are poor predictors of creative accomplishment in everyday life because they tap only one of the complex cognitive contributions to creativity (Plucker & Makel, 2010). Also involved are defining new and important problems, evaluating divergent ideas, choosing the most promising, and calling on relevant knowledge to understand and solve problems (Lubart, Georgsdottir, & Besançon, 2009).

Consider these ingredients, and you will see why people usually demonstrate expertise and creativity in only one or a few related areas. Even individuals designated as gifted by virtue of their high IQ often show uneven ability across academic subjects. Partly for this reason, definitions of giftedness have been extended to include **talent—** outstanding performance in a specific field. Case studies reveal that excellence in such endeavors as creative writing, mathematics, science, music, visual arts, athletics, and leadership have roots in specialized skills that first appear in childhood (Moran & Gardner, 2006). Highly talented children are biologically prepared to master their domain of interest, and they display a passion for doing so.

But talent must be nurtured. Studies of the backgrounds of talented children and highly accomplished adults often reveal parents who are warm and sensitive, provide a stimulating home life, are devoted to developing their child's abilities, and provide models of hard work and high achievement. These parents are reasonably demanding but not driving or overambitious (Winner, 2000). They arrange for caring teachers while the child is young and for more rigorous master teachers as the child's talent develops.

Although most are well-adjusted, gifted children and adolescents are more likely than their typical classmates to experience social isolation, partly because their highly driven, independent styles leave them out of step with peers and partly because they enjoy solitude, which is necessary to develop their talents (Pfeiffer & Yermish, 2014). Still, gifted children desire gratifying peer relationships, and some—more often girls than boys—try to become better-liked by hiding their abilities (Reis, 2004).

Finally, whereas many talented youths become experts in their fields and solve problems in new ways, few become highly creative. Rapidly mastering an existing field and thinking flexibly within it require different skills than innovating in that field. Gifted individuals who are restless with the status quo and daring about changing it are rare. And before these individuals become creative masters, they typically spend a decade or more becoming proficient in their field of interest (Simonton, 2009). The world, however, needs both experts and creators.

Educating the Gifted. Gifted children thrive in learning environments that permit them to choose topics for extended projects, take intellectual risks, reflect on ideas, and interact with like-minded peers. When not sufficiently challenged, they sometimes lose their drive to excel. And when parents and teachers push them too hard, by adolescence they are likely to ask, "Who am I doing this for?" If the answer is not "myself," they may decide not to pursue their gift (Winner, 2000, p. 166).

Although many schools offer programs for the gifted, debate about their effectiveness usually focuses on factors irrelevant to giftedness—whether to provide enrichment in regular classrooms, to pull children out for special instruction (the most common practice), or to advance brighter students to a higher grade. Overall, gifted children fare well within each of these models, as long as special activities promote problem solving, critical thinking, and creativity (Guignard & Lubart, 2007).

Gardner's theory of multiple intelligences has inspired several model programs that provide enrichment to all students in diverse subjects, so any child capable of high-level performance

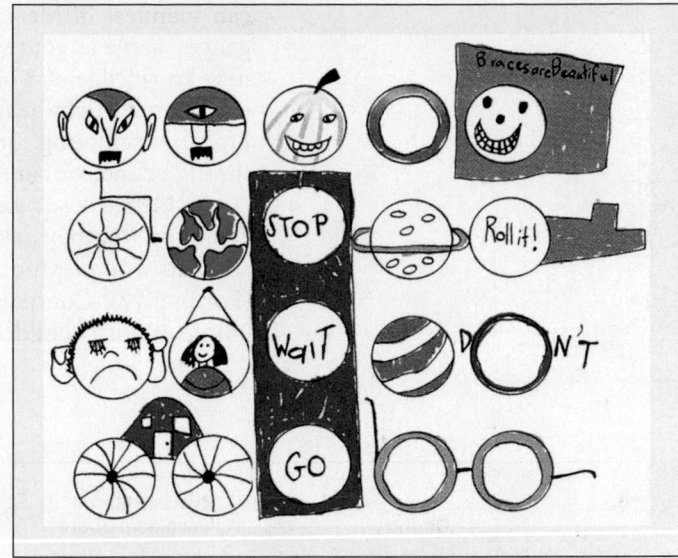

FIGURE 12.7 **Responses of an 8-year-old who scored high on a figural measure of divergent thinking.** This child was asked to make as many pictures as she could from the circles on the page. The titles she gave her drawings, from left to right, are as follows: "Dracula," "one-eyed monster," "pumpkin," "Hula-Hoop," "poster," "wheelchair," "earth," "stoplight," "planet," "movie camera," "sad face," "picture," "beach ball," "the letter *O*," "car," "glasses." Tests of divergent thinking tap only one of the complex cognitive contributions to creativity. (Reprinted by permission of Laura E. Berk.)

can manifest it. Meaningful activities, each tapping a specific intelligence or set of intelligences, serve as contexts for assessing strengths and weaknesses and, on that basis, teaching new knowledge and original thinking (Gardner, 2000; Hoerr, 2004). For example, linguistic intelligence might be fostered through storytelling or playwriting; spatial intelligence through drawing, sculpting, or taking apart and reassembling objects; and kinesthetic intelligence through dance or pantomime.

Evidence is still needed on how effectively these programs nurture children's talents and creativity. But they have already succeeded in one way—by highlighting the strengths of some students who previously had been considered unexceptional or even at risk for school failure (Ford, 2012). Consequently, they may be especially useful in identifying talented low-SES, ethnic minority children, who are often underrepresented in programs for the gifted.

	Country	Average Math Achievement Score
High-Performing Nations	China (Shanghai)	613
	Singapore	573
	China (Hong Kong)	561
	Taiwan	560
	Korea	554
	China (Macao)	538
	Japan	536
	Switzerland	531
	Netherlands	523
	Estonia	521
	Finland	519
	Canada	518
	Poland	518
	Belgium	515
	Germany	514
Intermediate-Performing Nations	Austria	506
	Australia	504
	Ireland	501
	Slovenia	501
	Denmark	500
	New Zealand	500
	Czech Republic	499
	France	495
International Average = 494	United Kingdom	494
	Iceland	493
	Luxembourg	490
	Norway	489
	Portugal	487
	Italy	485
	Spain	484
	Russian Federation	482
	United States	**481**
	Sweden	478
	Hungary	477
Low-Performing Nations	Israel	466
	Greece	453
	Turkey	448
	Romania	445

FIGURE 12.8 Average mathematics scores of 15-year-olds by country. The Programme for International Student Assessment measured achievement in many nations around the world. In recent comparisons of countries' performance, the United States performed below the international average in math; in reading and science, its performance was about average. (Adapted from Programme for International Student Assessment, 2012.)

How Well-Educated Are U.S. Children?

Our discussion of schooling has largely focused on how teachers can support the education of children. Yet we have also seen that many factors—both within and outside schools—affect children's learning. Societal values, school resources, quality of teaching, and parental encouragement all play important roles. These multiple influences are especially apparent when schooling is examined in cross-cultural perspective.

In international studies of reading, mathematics, and science achievement, young people in China, Korea, and Japan are consistently top performers. Among Western nations, Canada, Finland, the Netherlands, and Switzerland are also in the top tier. But U.S. students typically perform at or below the international averages (see Figure 12.8) (Programme for International Student Assessment, 2012).

Why do U.S. students fall behind in academic accomplishments? According to international comparisons, instruction in the United States is less challenging, more focused on absorbing facts, and less focused on high-level reasoning and critical thinking than in other countries. A growing number of experts believe that the U.S. No Child Left Behind Act has contributed to these trends because it mandates severe sanctions for schools whose students do not meet targeted goals on achievement tests—initially, student transfers to higher-performing schools; and ultimately, staff firing, closure, state takeover, or other restructuring (Darling-Hammond, 2010; Kew et al., 2012; Ravitch, 2010).

Furthermore, countries with large socioeconomic inequalities (such as the United States) rank lower in achievement, in part because low-SES children tend to live in less favorable families and neighborhoods (Condron, 2013). But the United States is also far less equitable than top achieving countries in the quality of education it provides its low-SES and ethnic minority students. U.S. teachers, for example, vary much more in training, salaries, and teaching conditions.

Finland is a case in point. In the 1980s, it abandoned a national testing system used to ability-group students and replaced it with curricula, teaching practices, and assessments aimed at cultivating initiative, problem solving, and creativity—vital abilities needed for success in the twenty-first century. Finnish teachers are highly trained: They must complete several years of graduate-level education at government expense (Ripley, 2013). And Finnish education is grounded in equal opportunity for all—a policy that has nearly eliminated SES variations in achievement, despite an influx of immigrant students from low-income families into Finnish schools over the past decade.

In-depth research on learning environments in Asian nations, such as Japan, Korea, and Taiwan, also highlights social forces that foster strong student learning. Among these is cultural valuing of effort. Whereas American parents and teachers tend to regard native ability as the key to academic success, Japanese, Korean, and Taiwanese parents and teachers believe that all children can succeed academically as long as they try hard. Asian parents devote many more hours to helping their children with homework (Stevenson, Lee, & Mu, 2000). And Asian children, influenced by interdependent values, typically view striving to do well in school as a moral obligation—part of their responsibility to family and community (Hau & Ho, 2010).

As in Finland, all students in Japan, Korea, and Taiwan receive the same nationally mandated, high-quality instruction, delivered by teachers who are well-prepared, highly respected in their society, and far better paid than U.S. teachers (Kang & Hong, 2008; U.S. Department of Education, 2014). Academic lessons are particularly well-organized and presented in ways that capture children's attention and encourage high-level thinking (Grow-Maienza, Hahn, & Joo, 2001). And Japanese teachers are three times as likely as U.S. teachers to work outside class with students who need extra help (Woodward & Ono, 2004).

Finnish students explain the results of a static electricity experiment. Their country's education system—designed to cultivate initiative, problem solving, and creativity in all students—has nearly eliminated SES variations in achievement.

The Finnish and Asian examples underscore the need for American families, schools, and the larger society to work together to upgrade education. Over the past fifteen years, U.S. international rankings in reading, math, and science achievement have declined. And although the U.S. National Assessment of Educational Progress—in which challenging achievement tests are given to nationally representative samples of 9-, 13-, and 17-year-olds—has shown slight gains in reading and moderate gains in math since 1990, the increments have not been sufficient to catch up internationally (U.S. Department of Education, 2014).

These disappointing achievement outcomes underscore the need for "a broader, bolder approach to U.S. education." Recommended strategies, verified by research, include:

- supporting parents in attaining economic security, creating stimulating home learning environments, monitoring their children's academic progress, and communicating often with teachers
- investing in high-quality preschool education, so every child arrives at school ready to learn
- strengthening teacher education
- providing intellectually challenging, relevant instruction with real-world applications
- vigorously pursuing school improvements that reduce the large inequities in quality of education between SES and ethnic groups.

Ask Yourself

- **REVIEW** List some teaching practices that foster children's academic achievement and some that undermine it. For each practice, explain why it is or is not effective.

- **CONNECT** Review research on child-rearing styles on pages 392–394 in Chapter 10. What style do gifted children who realize their potential typically experience? Explain.

- **APPLY** Sandy wonders why her daughter Mira's teacher often has students work on assignments in small, cooperative groups. Explain the benefits of this approach to Sandy. What must Mira's teacher do to ensure that cooperative learning succeeds?

- **REFLECT** What grouping practices were used in your elementary education—homogeneous, heterogeneous, or a combination? What impact do you think those practices had on your motivation and achievement?

Summary

Piaget's Theory: The Concrete Operational Stage (p. 429)

12.1 What are the major characteristics of concrete operational thought?

- In the **concrete operational stage,** children's thought becomes more logical, flexible, and organized. Mastery of conservation requires **decentration** and **reversibility** in thinking.

- School-age children are also better at hierarchical classification and **seriation,** including **transitive inference,** the ability to seriate mentally. Their spatial reasoning improves, as illustrated by their understanding of **cognitive maps.** By the end of middle childhood, they form accurate overall views of large-scale spaces and grasp the meaning of scale and map symbols.

© LAURA DWIGHT PHOTOGRAPHY

12.2 Discuss follow-up research on concrete operational thought.

- Concrete operational children think logically only when dealing with concrete, tangible information, and mastery of concrete operational tasks occurs gradually. Specific cultural practices, especially those associated with schooling, promote mastery of Piagetian tasks.

- Some researchers attribute the gradual development of operational thought to expansion of information-processing capacity. Case's neo-Piagetian theory proposes that gains in working-memory efficiency explain cognitive change, within and between stages. With practice, cognitive schemes become more automatic, freeing up space in working memory for combining old schemes and generating new ones. Eventually, children consolidate schemes into central conceptual structures and are increasingly able to coordinate multiple dimensions.

Information Processing (p. 434)

12.3 Cite basic changes in information processing, and describe the development of attention and memory in middle childhood.

- Marked improvement in executive function enables school-age children to handle increasingly complex tasks that require integration of working memory, inhibition, and flexible thinking. Heredity and environment combine to influence various executive processes.

- Increased speed of thinking supports gains in working-memory capacity. Children with working-memory deficits suffer from persistent learning difficulties in school.

- During middle childhood, attention becomes more sustained, selective, and flexible. Deficits in executive processing and inhibition may underlie symptoms of **attention-deficit hyperactivity disorder (ADHD),** which leads to serious academic and social problems.

- Children become better at planning, particularly when adults turn over responsibility to them and guide and support them as needed.

- Memory strategies also improve. **Rehearsal** appears first, followed by **organization** and then **elaboration.** With age, children use several memory strategies at once.

- Development of the long-term knowledge base facilitates strategic memory processing, as does children's motivation to use what they know. Memory strategies are not used by children in village cultures who have no formal schooling. Societal modernization is broadly associated with improved cognitive performance.

12.4 Describe the school-age child's theory of mind and capacity to engage in self-regulation.

- Metacognition expands as school-age children view the mind as an active, constructive agent. Consequently, they better understand cognitive processes and factors that influence them. Awareness of the role of mental inferences enables mastery of second-order false belief and promotes **recursive thought.** School-age children also become increasingly conscious of how and why mental strategies work and able to discriminate good from bad reasoning.

- **Cognitive self-regulation** develops gradually. It improves with adult instruction in effective strategy use and predicts academic success.

12.5 Discuss current perspectives on teaching reading and mathematics to elementary school children.

- Skilled reading draws on all aspects of the information-processing system. A combination of **whole-language** and **phonics** is most effective for teaching beginning reading.

- Teaching that combines practice in basic skills with conceptual understanding also is best in mathematics. Students benefit from extensive opportunities to experiment with strategies and reason about number concepts.

Individual Differences in Mental Development (p. 446)

12.6 Describe major approaches to defining intelligence.

- During the school years, IQ becomes more stable and correlates moderately with academic achievement. Most intelligence tests yield an overall score as well as scores for separate intellectual factors. The *Stanford-Binet Intelligence Scales,* Fifth Edition, and the *Wechsler Intelligence Scale for Children–IV (WISC–IV)* are widely used individually administered intelligence tests.

- The componential approach to defining intelligence seeks to identify the inner, information-processing skills that contribute to mental test performance. Speed of thinking, working-memory capacity, flexible attention, and memory and reasoning strategies are positively related to IQ.

- Sternberg's **triarchic theory of successful intelligence** views intelligence as an interaction of analytical intelligence (information-processing skills), creative intelligence (ability to solve novel problems), and practical intelligence (application of intellectual skills in everyday situations).

- Gardner's **theory of multiple intelligences** identifies at least eight mental abilities, each with a distinct biological basis and course of development. It has been helpful in stimulating efforts to define, measure, and foster emotional intelligence.

© AGE FOTOSTOCK/ROBERT HARDING

12.7 Describe evidence indicating that both heredity and environment contribute to intelligence.

- Heritability estimates and adoption research reveal that intelligence is a product of both heredity and environment. Adoption studies along with the **Flynn effect**—dramatic generational gains in IQ—suggest that environmental factors account for the black–white IQ gap.

- IQ scores are affected by culturally influenced language and communication styles, knowledge, and sheer amount of time spent in school. **Stereotype threat** can trigger anxiety that impairs test performance. **Dynamic assessment** helps many minority children perform more competently on mental tests.

Language Development (p. 455)

12.8 Describe changes in metalinguistic awareness, vocabulary, grammar, and pragmatics during middle childhood.

- Schooling, especially reading, contributes greatly to **metalinguistic awareness** and other complex language competencies. Vocabulary continues to grow rapidly, and children have a more precise and flexible understanding of word meanings. They also use more complex grammatical constructions and conversational strategies, and their narratives increase in organization, detail, and expressiveness.

12.9 Describe bilingual development, along with advantages of bilingualism in childhood.

- Children who learn two languages in early childhood acquire each according to a typical timetable. When school-age children acquire a second language, they typically take 5 to 7 years to attain the competence of native-speaking agemates.

- Bilingual children are better at diverse executive-function skills and certain aspects of metalinguistic awareness. They transfer their phonological awareness skills in one language to the other, which enhances reading achievement.

- In Canada, language immersion programs succeed in developing children who are proficient in both English and French. In the United States, bilingual education that combines instruction in the native language and in English supports academic learning in children with limited English proficiency.

Children's Learning in School (p. 459)

12.10 Describe the impact of class size and educational philosophies on children's motivation and academic achievement.

- As class size declines, academic achievement improves. Older students in **traditional classrooms** have a slight edge in academic achievement over those in **constructivist classrooms,** who gain in academic motivation, critical thinking, and social and moral maturity.

- Vygotsky-inspired **social-constructivist classrooms** use the rich social context of the classroom to promote learning, often employing such methods as **reciprocal teaching** and **communities of learners.** Students benefit from working collaboratively and from teaching adapted to each child's zone of proximal development.

ALISTAIR BERG/DIGITAL VISION/ GETTY IMAGES

12.11 Discuss the role of teacher–student interaction and grouping practices in academic achievement.

- Caring, helpful, and stimulating teaching fosters children's motivation and academic achievement. **Educational self-fulfilling prophecies** have a greater impact on low achievers and are most likely to occur in homogenous classrooms and ones that emphasize competition and public evaluation.

- To benefit from collaboration with heterogeneous peers, children need extensive training in **cooperative learning.** Ethnically diverse magnet schools are also associated with higher achievement.

12.12 Describe benefits of, as well as concerns about, educational media.

- Using screen media for schoolwork, including searching for information, preparing assignments, and playing academic and nonviolent adventure games, has cognitive benefits and is linked to improved achievement. Low-SES children are disadvantaged in computer and Internet use, and boys tend to be more skilled at complex computer activities than girls.

12.13 Under what conditions is placement of children with mild intellectual disability or learning disabilities in regular classrooms successful?

- Students with mild intellectual disability and **learning disabilities** are often placed in **inclusive classrooms** where they learn alongside typical students. Success depends on meeting individual academic needs and promoting positive peer relations.

12.14 Describe the characteristics of gifted children and efforts to meet their educational needs.

- **Giftedness** includes high IQ, **creativity,** and **talent.** Tests of creativity that tap **divergent thinking** rather than **convergent thinking** focus on only one of the complex cognitive ingredients of creativity. Gifted children are more likely than their peers to experience social isolation.

- Gifted children who thrive have parents and teachers who nurture their extraordinary abilities and make reasonable demands. They are best served by educational programs that build on their special strengths.

12.15 How well-educated are U.S. children compared with children in other industrialized nations?

- In international studies, U.S. students typically display average or below-average performance. Compared with education in top-achieving nations, U.S. instruction is less focused on high-level reasoning and critical thinking. Whereas high-achieving nations emphasize equal opportunity for all, U.S. low-income and ethnic minority students typically attend inferior-quality schools.

Important Terms and Concepts

attention-deficit hyperactivity disorder (ADHD) (p. 438)

cognitive maps (p. 430)

cognitive self-regulation (p. 442)

communities of learners (p. 462)

concrete operational stage (p. 429)

constructivist classroom (p. 460)

convergent thinking (p. 466)

cooperative learning (p. 463)

creativity (p. 466)

decentration (p. 429)

divergent thinking (p. 466)

dynamic assessment (p. 454)

educational self-fulfilling prophecies (p. 462)

elaboration (p. 438)

Flynn effect (p. 452)

gifted (p. 466)

inclusive classrooms (p. 465)

learning disabilities (p. 465)

metalinguistic awareness (p. 455)

organization (p. 437)

phonics approach (p. 443)

reciprocal teaching (p. 461)

recursive thought (p. 441)

rehearsal (p. 437)

reversibility (p. 429)

seriation (p. 430)

social-constructivist classroom (p. 461)

stereotype threat (p. 453)

talent (p. 467)

theory of multiple intelligences (p. 449)

traditional classroom (p. 460)

transitive inference (p. 430)

triarchic theory of successful intelligence (p. 448)

whole-language approach (p. 443)

chapter 13

Emotional and Social Development in Middle Childhood

"Our Multiracial and Multireligious Society"
Tay Xue Er
9 years, Singapore

As this artist's colorful portrayal of ethnic and religious diversity suggests, school-age children become capable of viewing themselves and others from multiple perspectives. This change contributes to improved self-understanding, a more flexible grasp of moral obligations, declining racial and ethnic prejudices, and deepening friendships.

One afternoon as school dismissed, Joey urgently tapped his best friend Terry on the shoulder. "Gotta talk to you," Joey pleaded. "Everything was going great until I got that word—*porcupine,*" Joey went on, referring to the fifth-grade spelling bee that day. "Just my luck! *P-o-r-k,* that's how I spelled it! I can't believe it. Maybe I'm not so good at social studies," Joey confided, "but I *know* I'm better at spelling than that stuck-up Belinda Brown. I knocked myself out studying those spelling lists. Then *she* got all the easy words. If I *had* to lose, why couldn't it be to a nice person?"

Joey's conversation reflects new emotional and social capacities. By entering the spelling bee, he shows *industriousness,* the energetic pursuit of meaningful achievement in his culture—a major change of middle childhood. Joey's social understanding has also expanded. He can size up strengths, weaknesses, and personality characteristics. Furthermore, friendship means something different to Joey than it did earlier: He counts on his best friend, Terry, for understanding and emotional support.

For an overview of the personality changes of middle childhood, we return to Erikson's theory. Then we look at children's views of themselves and of others, their moral understanding, and their peer relationships. Each increases in complexity as children reason more effectively and spend more time in school and with agemates.

Despite changing parent–child relationships, the family remains powerfully influential in middle childhood. Today, family lifestyles are more diverse than ever before. Through Joey's and his younger sister Lizzie's experiences with parental divorce, we will see that family functioning is far more important than family structure in ensuring children's well-being. Finally, we look at some common emotional problems of middle childhood. ■

Erikson's Theory: Industry versus Inferiority

According to Erikson (1950), children whose previous experiences have been positive enter middle childhood prepared to redirect their energies from the make-believe of early childhood into realistic accomplishment. Erikson believed that the combination of adult expectations and children's drive toward mastery sets the stage for the psychological conflict of middle childhood: **industry versus inferiority,** which is resolved positively when experiences lead children to develop a sense of competence at useful skills and tasks.

In cultures everywhere, adults respond to children's improved physical and cognitive capacities by making new demands, and children are ready to benefit from those challenges. Among the Baka hunters and gatherers of Cameroon, 5- to 7-year-olds fetch and carry water, bathe and mind younger siblings, and accompany adults on food-gathering missions. In a miniature village behind the main camp, children practice hut building, spear shaping, and fire making (Avis & Harris, 1991). The Ngoni of Malawi, Central Africa, believe that when children shed their first teeth,

13.1 What personality changes take place during Erikson's stage of industry versus inferiority?

they are mature enough for intensive skill training. Six and 7-year-old boys move out of family huts into dormitories, where they enter a system of male domination and instruction (Rogoff, 1996). All children of this age are expected to show independence and are held accountable for irresponsible and disrespectful behavior.

The industriousness of middle childhood involves responding to new expectations for realistic accomplishment. In the informal, encouraging atmosphere of this classroom in India, children come to view themselves as responsible, capable, and cooperative.

In industrialized nations, the beginning of formal schooling marks the transition to middle childhood. With it comes literacy training, which prepares children for a vast array of specialized careers. In school, children discover their own and others' unique capacities, learn the value of division of labor, and develop a sense of moral commitment and responsibility. The danger at this stage is *inferiority,* reflected in the pessimism of children who have little confidence in their ability to do things well. This sense of inadequacy can develop when family life has not prepared children for school life or when teachers and peers destroy children's feelings of competence and mastery with negative responses.

Erikson's sense of industry combines several developments of middle childhood: a positive but realistic self-concept, pride in accomplishment, moral responsibility, and cooperative participation with agemates. How do these aspects of self and social relationships change over the school years?

13.2 Describe school-age children's self-concept and self-esteem, and discuss factors that affect their achievement-related attributions.

Self-Understanding

In middle childhood, children become able to describe themselves in terms of psychological traits, to compare their own characteristics with those of their peers, and to speculate about the causes of their strengths and weaknesses. These transformations in self-understanding have a major impact on children's self-esteem.

Self-Concept

During the school years, children refine their self-concept, organizing their observations of behaviors and internal states into general dispositions. A major change takes place between ages 8 and 11, as the following self-description by an 11-year-old illustrates:

> My name is A. I'm a human being. I'm a girl. I'm a truthful person. I'm not pretty. I do so-so in my studies. I'm a very good cellist. I'm a very good pianist. I'm a little bit tall for my age. I like several boys. I like several girls. I'm old-fashioned. I play tennis. I am a very good swimmer. I try to be helpful. I'm always ready to be friends with anybody. Mostly I'm good, but I lose my temper. I'm not well liked by some girls and boys. I don't know if I'm liked by boys or not. (Montemayor & Eisen, 1977, pp. 317–318)

Instead of specific behaviors, this child emphasizes competencies: "a very good cellist," "so-so in my studies" (Damon & Hart, 1988). She also describes her personality, mentioning both positive and negative traits: "truthful" but short-tempered. Older school-age children are far less likely than younger children to describe themselves in extreme, all-or-none ways (Harter, 2012a).

These evaluative self-descriptions result from school-age children's frequent **social comparisons**—judgments of their appearance, abilities, and behavior in relation to those of others. For example, Joey observed that he was "better at spelling" than his peers but "not so good at social studies." Whereas 4- to 6-year-olds can compare their own performance to that of a single peer, older children can compare multiple individuals, including themselves (Butler, 1998; Harter, 2012a).

Cognitive, Social, and Cultural Influences on Self-Concept

What factors account for these revisions in self-concept? Cognitive development affects the changing *structure* of the self. School-age children, as we saw in Chapter 12, can better coordinate several aspects of a situation in reasoning about their physical world. Similarly, in the social realm, they combine typical experiences and behaviors into stable psychological dispositions, blend positive and negative characteristics, and compare their own characteristics with those of many peers (Harter, 2012a). In middle childhood, children also gain a clearer understanding that traits are linked to specific desires (a "generous" person *wants* to share) and, therefore, are causes of behavior (Yuill & Pearson, 1998).

The changing *content* of self-concept is a product of both cognitive capacities and feedback from others. Sociologist George Herbert Mead (1934) proposed that a well-organized psychological self emerges when children adopt a view of the self that resembles others' attitudes toward the child. Mead's ideas indicate that *perspective-taking skills*—in particular, an improved ability to infer what other people are thinking and to distinguish those viewpoints from one's own—are crucial for developing a self-concept based on personality traits. As we saw in Chapter 12, middle childhood brings the capacity for recursive thought, which enables school-age children to "read" others' messages more accurately and internalize their expectations. As they do so, they form an *ideal self* that they use to evaluate their real self. As we will see, a large discrepancy between the two can greatly undermine self-esteem, leading to sadness, hopelessness, and depression.

As school-age children enter a wider range of settings beyond the family, their self-concepts include frequent reference to social groups. When asked about themselves, these baseball players are likely to mention being a member of a Little League team.

Parental support for self-development continues to be vitally important. School-age children with a history of elaborative parent–child conversations about past experiences construct a rich, positive narrative about the self and thus have more complex, favorable, and coherent self-concepts (Harter, 2012a). Children also look to more people beyond the family for information about themselves as they enter a wider range of settings in school and community. And self-descriptions now include frequent reference to social groups: "I'm a Boy Scout, a paper boy, and a Prairie City soccer player," said Joey. As children move into adolescence, their sources of self-definition become more selective. Although parents and other adults remain influential, self-concept is increasingly vested in feedback from close friends (Oosterwegel & Oppenheimer, 1993).

But recall that the content of self-concept varies from culture to culture. In earlier chapters, we noted that Asian parents stress harmonious interdependence, whereas Western parents emphasize independence and self-assertion. When asked to recall personally significant past experiences (their last birthday, a time their parent scolded them), U.S. school-age children gave longer accounts including more personal preferences, interests, skills, and opinions. Chinese children, in contrast, more often referred to social interactions and to others rather than themselves. Similarly, in their self-descriptions, U.S. children listed more personal attributes ("I'm smart," "I like hockey"), Chinese children more attributes involving group membership and relationships with others ("I'm in second grade," "My friends are crazy about me") (Wang, 2006b; Wang, Shao, & Li, 2010).

LOOK *and* **LISTEN**

Ask several 8- to 11-year-old children to tell you about themselves. Do their self-descriptions include personality traits (both positive and negative), social comparisons, and references to social groups, as is typical in middle childhood?

Self-Esteem

Recall that most preschoolers have extremely high self-esteem. But as children enter school and receive much more feedback about how well they perform compared with their peers, self-esteem differentiates and also adjusts to a more realistic level.

To study school-age children's self-esteem, researchers ask them to indicate the extent to which statements such as "I'm good at reading" or "I'm usually the one chosen for games" are true of themselves. By age 6 to 7, children in diverse Western cultures have formed at least four

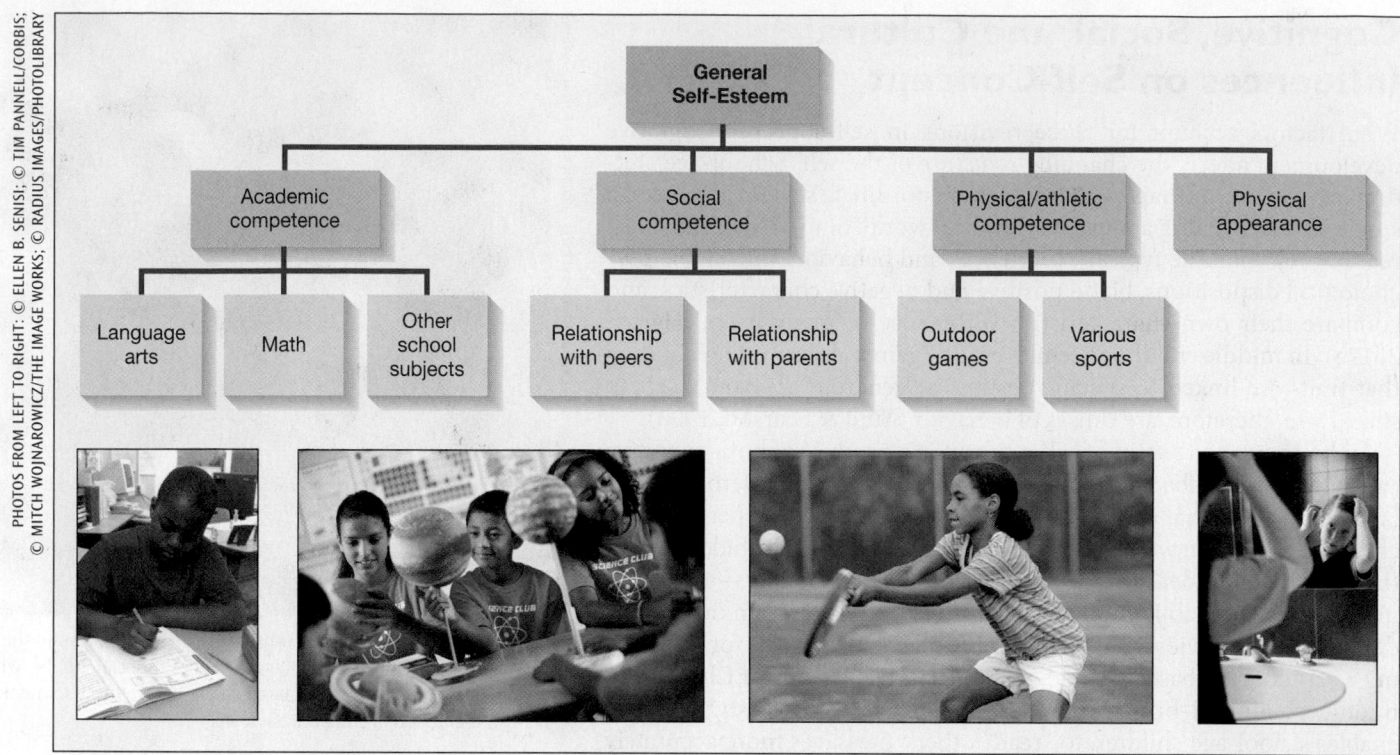

FIGURE 13.1 **Hierarchical structure of self-esteem in the mid-elementary school years.** From their experiences in different settings, children form at least four separate self-esteems: academic competence, social competence, physical/athletic competence, and physical appearance. These differentiate into additional self-evaluations and combine to form a general sense of self-esteem.

broad self-evaluations: academic competence, social competence, physical/athletic competence, and physical appearance. Within these are more refined categories that become increasingly distinct with age (Marsh, 1990; Marsh & Ayotte, 2003; Van den Bergh & De Rycke, 2003). Furthermore, the capacity to view the self in terms of stable dispositions permits school-age children to combine their separate self-evaluations into a general psychological image of themselves—an overall sense of self-esteem (Harter, 2012a). As a result, self-esteem takes on the hierarchical structure shown in Figure 13.1.

Children attach greater importance to certain self-evaluations than to others. Although individual differences exist, during childhood and adolescence perceived physical appearance correlates more strongly with overall self-worth than does any other self-esteem factor (O'Dea, 2012; Shapka & Keating, 2005). Emphasis on appearance—in the media, by parents and peers, and in society—has major implications for young people's overall satisfaction with themselves.

Self-esteem generally remains high during elementary school but becomes more realistic and nuanced as children evaluate themselves in various areas (Marsh, Craven, & Debus, 1998; Wigfield et al., 1997). These changes occur as children receive more competence-related feedback, as their performances are increasingly judged in relation to those of others, and as they become cognitively capable of social comparison (Harter, 2012a).

Influences on Self-Esteem

From middle childhood on, individual differences in self-esteem become increasingly stable (Trzesniewski, Donnellan, & Robins, 2003). And positive relationships among self-esteem, valuing of various activities, and success at those activities emerge and strengthen with age. Academic self-esteem predicts how important, useful, and enjoyable children judge school subjects to be, their willingness to try hard, and their achievement (Denissen, Zarrett, & Eccles, 2007; Valentine, DuBois, & Cooper, 2004; Whitesell et al., 2009). Children with high social self-esteem are consistently better-liked by classmates (Jacobs et al., 2002). And as we saw in Chapter 11, sense of athletic competence is positively associated with investment in and performance at sports.

Furthermore, across age, sex, SES, and ethnic groups, individuals with favorable self-esteem tend to be well-adjusted, sociable, and conscientious. In contrast, a profile of low self-esteem in all areas is linked to anxiety, depression, and antisocial behavior (DuBois et al., 1999; Robins et al., 2001; Sowislo & Orth, 2013).

CULTURE AND GENDER   Cultural forces profoundly affect self-esteem. An especially strong emphasis on social comparison in school may explain why Chinese and Japanese children, despite their higher academic achievement, score lower than U.S. children in self-esteem—a difference that widens with age (Harter, 2012a; Twenge & Crocker, 2002). At the same time, because their culture values modesty and social harmony, Asian children rely less on social comparisons to promote their own self-esteem. Rather, they tend to be reserved in positive self-judgments but generous in praise of others (Falbo et al., 1997).

Gender-stereotyped beliefs also affect self-esteem. In one study, the more 5- to 8-year-old girls talked with friends about the way people look, watched TV shows focusing on physical appearance, and perceived their friends as valuing thinness, the greater their dissatisfaction with their physical self and the lower their overall self-esteem a year later (Dohnt & Tiggemann, 2006). And in an investigation of third-graders, being overweight was more strongly linked to negative body image for girls than boys (Shriver et al., 2013). By the end of middle childhood, girls feel less confident than boys about their physical appearance and athletic abilities. With respect to academic self-esteem, boys, again, are somewhat advantaged: Whereas girls score higher in language-arts self-esteem, boys have higher math and science self-esteem—even when children of equal skill levels are compared (Jacobs et al., 2002; Kurtz-Costes et al., 2008). At the same time, girls exceed boys in self-esteem dimensions of close friendship and social acceptance.

Children learn African drumming skills at a community center during Kwanzaa, a holiday honoring their African heritage. A stronger sense of ethnic pride may contribute to slightly higher self-esteem among African-American children compared with their Caucasian agemates.

Compared with their Caucasian agemates, African-American children tend to have slightly higher self-esteem, perhaps because of warm extended families and a stronger sense of ethnic pride (Gray-Little & Hafdahl, 2000; Harter, 2012a). But media exposure has the opposite effect: The more TV African-American children watch, the lower their self-esteem—an association that also applies to Caucasian girls. In contrast, TV viewing predicts higher self-esteem among Caucasian boys (Martins & Harrison, 2012). Ethnic and gender stereotypes in TV programs may explain these findings. Finally, children and adolescents who attend schools or live in neighborhoods where their SES and ethnic groups are well-represented feel a stronger sense of belonging and have fewer self-esteem problems (Gray-Little & Carels, 1997).

CHILD-REARING PRACTICES   Children whose parents use an *authoritative* child-rearing style (see Chapter 10) feel especially good about themselves (Lindsey et al, 2008; McKinney, Donnelly, & Renk, 2008). Warm, positive parenting lets children know that they are accepted as competent and worthwhile. And firm but appropriate expectations, backed up with explanations, help them evaluate their own behavior against reasonable standards.

Controlling parents—those who too often help or make decisions for their child—communicate a sense of inadequacy to children. Having parents who are repeatedly disapproving and insulting is also linked to low self-esteem (Kernis, 2002; Pomerantz & Eaton, 2000). Children subjected to such parenting need constant reassurance, and many rely heavily on peers to affirm their self-worth—a risk factor for adjustment difficulties, including aggression and antisocial behavior (Donnellan et al., 2005). In contrast, indulgent parenting is associated with unrealistically high self-esteem, which also undermines development. These children—whom researchers label *narcissistic* because they combine an inflated sense of superiority with obsessive worry about what others think of them—are vulnerable to temporary, sharp drops in self-esteem when their overblown self-images are challenged (Thomaes et al., 2013). They tend to lash out at peers who express disapproval and display adjustment problems, including meanness and aggression (Hughes, Cavell, & Grossman, 1997; Thomaes et al., 2008).

American cultural values have increasingly emphasized a focus on the self that may lead parents to indulge children and boost their self-esteem too much. The self-esteem of U.S. youths has risen sharply in recent decades—a period in which parenting literature, educational policies, and social programs have advised promoting children's self-esteem (Gentile, Twenge, & Campbell, 2010). Research, however, confirms that children do not benefit from compliments ("You're terrific") that have no basis in real accomplishment (Wentzel & Brophy, 2014). Rather, the best way to foster a positive, secure self-image is to encourage children to strive for worthwhile goals. Over time, a bidirectional relationship emerges: Achievement fosters self-esteem, which contributes to further effort and gains in performance (Marsh et al., 2005).

What can adults do to promote, and to avoid undermining, this mutually supportive relationship between motivation and self-esteem? Some answers come from research on the precise content of adults' messages to children in achievement situations. Let's look first at the meanings children assign to their successes and failures.

ACHIEVEMENT-RELATED ATTRIBUTIONS   *Attributions* are our common, everyday explanations for the causes of behavior. Notice how Joey, in talking about the spelling bee at the beginning of this chapter, attributes his disappointing performance to *luck* (Belinda got all the easy words) and his usual success to *ability* (he *knows* he's a better speller than Belinda). Joey also appreciates that *effort* matters: "I knocked myself out studying those spelling lists."

The combination of improved reasoning skills and frequent evaluative feedback permits 10- to 12-year-olds to separate all these variables in explaining performance (Dweck, 2002). Those who are high in academic self-esteem and motivation make **mastery-oriented attributions,** crediting their successes to ability—a characteristic they can improve by trying hard and can count on when faced with new challenges. This *incremental view of ability*—that it can increase through effort—influences the way mastery-oriented children interpret negative events. They attribute failure to factors that can be changed and controlled, such as insufficient effort or a difficult task (Dweck & Molden, 2013). So whether these children succeed or fail, they take an industrious, persistent approach to learning.

In contrast, children who develop **learned helplessness** attribute their failures, not their successes, to ability. When they succeed, they are likely to conclude that external factors, such as luck, are responsible. Unlike their mastery-oriented counterparts, they hold a *fixed view of ability*—that it cannot be improved by trying hard (Dweck & Molden, 2013). When a task is difficult, these children experience an anxious loss of control—in Erikson's terms, a pervasive sense of inferiority. They give up without really trying.

Children's attributions affect their goals. Mastery-oriented children focus on *learning goals*—seeking information on how best to increase their ability through effort. Hence, their performance improves over time (Dweck & Molden, 2013). In contrast, learned-helpless children focus on *performance goals*—obtaining positive and avoiding negative evaluations of their fragile sense of ability. Gradually their ability ceases to predict how well they do. In one study, the more fourth to sixth graders held self-critical attributions, the lower they rated their competence, the less they knew about effective study strategies, the more they avoided challenge, and the poorer their academic performance. These outcomes strengthened their fixed view of ability (Pomerantz & Saxon, 2001). Because learned-helpless children fail to connect effort with success, they do not develop the metacognitive and self-regulatory skills necessary for high achievement (see Chapter 12). Lack of effective learning strategies, reduced persistence, and a sense of loss of control sustain one another in a vicious cycle.

INFLUENCES ON ACHIEVEMENT-RELATED ATTRIBUTIONS   What accounts for the different attributions of mastery-oriented and learned-helpless children? Adult communication plays a key role. When parents hold a fixed view of ability, their perceptions of children's academic competence tend to act as self-fulfilling prophecies (see page 462 in Chapter 12). Their children's self-evaluations and school grades conform more closely to parental ability judgments than do those of children whose parents deny that ability is fixed (Pomerantz & Dong, 2006). Parents who believe little can be done to improve ability may ignore information that is inconsistent with their perceptions, giving their child little opportunity to counteract a negative parental evaluation. Indeed, children with a learned-helpless style often have parents who believe their child is not very capable and must work much harder than others to succeed.

When the child fails, the parent might say, "You can't do that, can you? It's OK if you quit" (Hokoda & Fincham, 1995).

When a child succeeds, adults can offer **person praise,** which emphasizes the child's traits ("You're so smart"; "you're very artistic"), or **process praise,** which emphasizes behavior and effort ("you worked really hard"; "you figured it out"). Research indicates that adults use more person praise with children low in self-esteem and more process praise with children high in self-esteem. Perhaps they believe that any positive messages about children's characteristics can help raise self-esteem. But children—especially those with low self-esteem—respond unfavorably to person praise. They feel more shame following failure if they previously received person praise, less shame if they previously received process praise or no praise at all (Brummelman et al., 2014). Consistent with a learned-helpless orientation, person praise teaches children that abilities are fixed, which leads them to question their competence in the face of failure and retreat from challenges (Pomerantz & Kempner, 2013; Skipper & Douglas, 2012). In contrast, process praise implies that competence develops through persistence and hard work, consistent with a mastery orientation (Pomerantz, Grolnick, & Price, 2013).

When adults offer process praise emphasizing behavior and effort, children learn that persistence and hard work build competence. Teacher remarks such as, "You found a good way to solve that problem!" will foster a mastery-oriented approach in this student.

Teachers' messages also affect children's attributions. Teachers who are caring and helpful and who emphasize learning over getting good grades tend to have mastery-oriented students (Anderman et al., 2001). In a study of third to eighth graders, students who viewed their teachers as providing positive, supportive learning conditions worked harder and participated more in class—factors that predicted high achievement, which sustained children's belief in the role of effort. In contrast, students with unsupportive teachers regarded their performance as externally controlled (by their teachers or by luck). This attitude predicted withdrawal from learning activities and declining achievement—outcomes that led children to doubt their ability (Skinner, Zimmer-Gembeck, & Connell, 1998).

For some children, performance is especially likely to be undermined by adult feedback. Despite their higher achievement, girls more often than boys attribute poor performance to lack of ability. When girls do not do well, they tend to receive messages from teachers and parents that their ability is at fault, and negative stereotypes (for example, that girls are weak at math) undermine their interest and performance (Gunderson et al., 2012; Tomasetto, Alparone, & Cadinu, 2011). And as Chapter 12 revealed, low-SES ethnic minority students often receive less favorable feedback from teachers, especially when assigned to homogeneous groups of poorly achieving students—conditions that result in a drop in academic self-esteem and achievement (Harris & Graham, 2007).

Cognitive development also affects attributions. Five- and 6-year-olds tend to believe, optimistically, that undesirable traits such as messiness, clumsiness, attention problems, or learning difficulties will improve greatly with age. In contrast, 7- to 10-year-olds' views are more realistic. They recognize that negative traits can change but expect only moderate improvement, and they understand that such change requires effort. Still, they are more optimistic than adults about the possibility of altering undesirable characteristics (Lockhart, Chang, & Story, 2002; Lockhart et al., 2008). This positive but realistic outlook is adaptive for school-age children, who must exert effort to develop competence and behave responsibly.

Finally, cultural values influence children's views about success and failure. Asian parents and teachers are more likely than their American counterparts to hold an incremental view of ability (see page 469 in Chapter 12) and to view effort as key to success and also as a moral responsibility—messages they transmit to children (Mok, Kennedy, & Moore, 2011; Pomerantz, Ng, & Wang, 2008). Asians also attend more to failure than to success because failure indicates where corrective action is needed. Americans, in contrast, focus more on success because it enhances self-esteem. Observations of U.S. and Chinese mothers' responses to their fourth and fifth graders' puzzle solutions revealed that the U.S. mothers offered more praise after success, whereas the Chinese mothers more often pointed out the child's inadequate performance. And regardless of success or failure, Chinese mothers made more task-relevant

LOOK *and* **LISTEN**

Observe a school-age child working on a challenging homework assignment under the guidance of a parent or other adult. What features of the adult's communication likely foster mastery-oriented attributions? How about learned helplessness? Explain.

Applying What We Know

Fostering a Mastery-Oriented Approach to Learning

CONTEXT	DESCRIPTION
Provision of tasks	Select tasks that are meaningful, responsive to a diversity of student interests, and appropriately matched to current competence so that the child is challenged but not overwhelmed.
Parent and teacher encouragement	Communicate warmth, confidence in the child's abilities, the value of achievement, and the importance of effort in success.
	Resist the urge to praise children's personal qualities; focus instead on their competent behavior, sustained effort, and successful strategies.
	Model high effort in overcoming failure.
	(For teachers) Communicate often with parents, suggesting ways to foster children's effort and progress.
	(For parents) Monitor schoolwork; provide scaffolded assistance that promotes knowledge of effective strategies and self-regulation.
Performance evaluations	Make evaluations private; avoid publicizing success or failure through wall posters, stars, privileges to "smart" children, and prizes for "best" performance.
	Emphasize individual progress and self-improvement.
	Provide accurate, constructive feedback to children about their performance.
School environment	Offer small classes, which permit teachers to provide individualized support for mastery.
	Provide for cooperative learning (see page 463 in Chapter 12), in which children assist one another; avoid ability grouping, which makes evaluations of children's progress public.
	Accommodate individual and cultural differences in styles of learning.
	Create an atmosphere that sends a clear message that all students can learn.

Sources: Hilt, 2004; Wentzel & Brophy, 2014; Wigfield et al., 2006.

statements aimed at ensuring that children exerted sufficient effort to do well ("You concentrated on it"; "You only got 6 out of 12") (see Figure 13.2). When children continued with the task after mothers left the room, the Chinese children showed greater gains in performance (Ng, Pomerantz, & Lam, 2007).

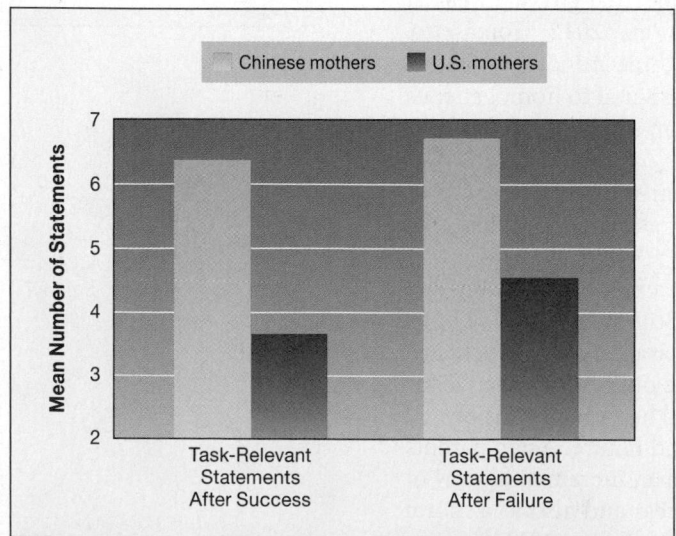

FIGURE 13.2 Chinese and U.S. mothers' task-relevant statements in response to their fourth-grade child's success or failure on puzzle tasks. Observations revealed that regardless of whether their child had just succeeded or failed, Chinese mothers were more likely than U.S. mothers to make task-relevant statements aimed at ensuring that the child exerted high effort. (Based on Ng, Pomerantz, & Lam, 2007.)

FOSTERING A MASTERY-ORIENTED APPROACH An intervention called **attribution retraining** encourages learned-helpless children to believe they can overcome failure by exerting more effort and using more effective strategies. Children are given tasks difficult enough that they will experience some failure, followed by repeated feedback that helps them revise their attributions: "You can do it if you try harder." After they succeed, children are given process praise—"Your strategies worked"; "You really tried hard on that one"—so that they attribute their success to both effort and effective strategies, not chance. Another approach is to encourage low-effort children to focus less on grades, more on mastering a task for its own sake, and more on individual performance improvement than on comparisons with classmates (Horner & Gaither, 2004; Wentzel & Brophy, 2014). Instruction in effective strategies and self-regulation is also vital, to compensate for development lost in this area and to ensure that renewed effort pays off (Berkeley, Mastropieri, & Scruggs, 2011; Wigfield et al., 2006).

Attribution retraining is best begun in middle childhood, before children's views of themselves become hard to change. An even better approach is to prevent learned helplessness, using the techniques summarized in Applying What We Know above.

Ask Yourself

- **REVIEW** How do cultural values, parent and teacher communication, and attribution styles affect self-esteem in middle childhood?

- **CONNECT** What cognitive changes, described in Chapter 12 (pages 440–441), support the transition to a self-concept emphasizing competencies, personality traits, and social comparisons?

- **APPLY** Should parents try to promote children's self-esteem by telling them they're "smart" or "wonderful"? Are children harmed if they do not feel good about everything they do? Explain.

- **REFLECT** Recall your own attributions for academic successes and failures when you were in elementary school. What are those attributions like now? What messages from others may have contributed to your attributions?

Emotional Development

13.3 Cite changes in the expression and understanding of emotion in middle childhood.

Greater self-awareness and social sensitivity support advances in emotional competence in middle childhood. Gains take place in experience of self-conscious emotions, emotional understanding, and emotional self-regulation.

Self-Conscious Emotions

As children integrate social expectations into their self-concepts, self-conscious emotions of pride and guilt become clearly governed by personal responsibility. Unlike preschoolers, school-age children experience pride in a new accomplishment and guilt over a transgression even when no adult is present (Harter, 2012a). Also, children no longer report guilt for any mishap, as they did earlier, but only for intentional wrongdoing, such as ignoring responsibilities, cheating, or lying (Ferguson, Stegge, & Damhuis, 1991). These changes reflect the older child's more mature sense of morality, a topic addressed later in this chapter.

When school-age children feel pride or guilt, they connect success or failure to specific aspects of the self: "I tried hard on that difficult task, and it paid off" (pride) or "I made a mistake, and now I have to deal with it" (guilt). They tend to feel shame when their violation of a standard is not under their control (Lewis & Ramsay, 2002; Saarni et al., 2006). For example, Lizzie felt ashamed when she dropped a spoonful of spaghetti and had a large spot on her shirt for the rest of the school day. But as children develop an overall sense of self-esteem, they may also experience shame after a controllable breach of standards if someone blames them for it (Harter, 2012a; Mascolo & Fischer, 1995). For example, the child whose teacher or parent reprimands him following poor performance ("Everyone else can do it! Why can't you?") may hang his head in shame, repeating to himself, "I'm stupid! I'm a terrible kid!"

Pride motivates children to take on further challenges, whereas guilt prompts them to make amends and to strive for self-improvement. But profound feelings of shame (as noted in Chapter 10) are particularly destructive. A sharp, shame-induced drop in self-esteem can trigger withdrawal and depression or intense anger at those who participated in the shame-evoking situation, followed by lashing out with aggression (Mills, 2005). A summary of findings from many studies confirmed that children and adolescents who experience guilt after transgressions tend to be well-adjusted—unlikely to react with depression, anger, or aggression. In contrast, those who experience shame are prone to these adjustment problems (Muris & Meesters, 2014).

If this child reacts with guilt to wrongdoing, he is likely to make amends. But adult blame and criticism may cause him to experience intense shame, leading to depression, anger, and a sharp drop in self-esteem.

Third graders help prepare meal packages to be sent to Africa to feed children in need. Gains in emotional understanding and perspective taking in middle childhood enable children to respond with empathy to people's general life condition.

AP IMAGES/THE EVANSVILLE COURIER & PRESS, JASON CLARK

Emotional Understanding

School-age children's understanding of mental activity means that, unlike preschoolers, they are likely to explain emotion by referring to internal states, such as happy or sad thoughts, rather than to external events (Flavell, Flavell, & Green, 2001). Also, between ages 6 and 12, children become more aware of circumstances likely to spark mixed emotions, each of which may be positive or negative and may differ in intensity, and they increasingly report experiencing more than one emotion at a time (Pons et al., 2003; Zadjel et al., 2013). For example, recalling the birthday present he received from his grandmother, Joey reflected, "I was very happy I got something but a little sad that I didn't get just what I wanted."

Appreciating mixed emotions helps children realize that people's expressions may not reflect their true feelings (Misailidi, 2006). It also fosters awareness of self-conscious emotions. For example, between ages 6 and 7, children improve sharply in ability to distinguish pride from happiness and surprise (Tracy, Robins, & Lagattuta, 2005). And 8- and 9-year-olds understand that pride combines two sources of happiness—joy in accomplishment and joy that a significant person recognized that accomplishment (Harter, 1999).

Furthermore, children of this age can reconcile contradictory facial and situational cues in figuring out another's feelings. And they can use information about "what might have happened" to predict how people will feel in a new situation—realizing, for example, that someone will feel a sense of relief when an actual outcome is more favorable than what might have occurred (Guttentag & Ferrell, 2004).

As with self-understanding, gains in emotional understanding are supported by cognitive development and social experiences, especially adults' sensitivity to children's feelings and willingness to discuss emotions. Together, these factors contribute to a rise in empathy as well. As children move closer to adolescence, advances in recursive perspective taking permit an empathic response not just to people's immediate distress but also to their general life condition (Hoffman, 2000). As at early ages, emotional understanding and empathy are linked to favorable social relationships and prosocial behavior (Eisenberg, Spinrad, & Morris, 2013). As Joey and Lizzie imagined how people who are chronically ill or hungry feel and evoked those emotions in themselves, they gave part of their allowance to charity and joined in fundraising projects through school, community center, and scouting.

Emotional Self-Regulation

In Chapter 10, we saw that emotional understanding and effortful control, along with parents' modeling and teaching of emotion-regulation strategies, contribute to young children's ability to manage emotions. These factors continue to play important roles during middle childhood, a period of rapid gains in emotional self-regulation (Morris et al., 2007; Zalewski et al., 2011).

By age 10, most children shift adaptively between two general strategies for managing emotion. In **problem-centered coping,** they appraise the situation as changeable, identify the difficulty, and decide what to do about it. If problem solving does not work, they engage in **emotion-centered coping,** which is internal, private, and aimed at controlling distress when little can be done about an outcome (Kliewer, Fearnow, & Miller, 1996; Lazarus & Lazarus, 1994). For example, when faced with an anxiety-provoking test or an angry friend, older school-age children view problem solving and seeking social support as the best strategies. But when outcomes are beyond their control—after receiving a bad grade—they opt for distraction or try to redefine the situation in ways that help them accept it: "Things could be worse. There'll be another test." School-age children's improved ability to appraise situations and reflect on thoughts and feelings means that, compared with preschoolers, they more often use these internal strategies to manage emotion (Brenner & Salovey, 1997).

Cognitive development and a wider range of social experiences permit children to flexibly vary their coping strategies (Zimmer-Gembeck & Skinner, 2011). Furthermore, through interacting with parents, teachers, and peers, school-age children become more knowledgeable about socially approved ways to display negative emotion. With age, they increasingly prefer verbal expression ("Please stop pushing and wait your turn") to crying, sulking, or aggression (Shipman et al., 2003; Waters & Thompson, 2014). Young school-age children justify these more mature displays of emotion by mentioning avoidance of punishment or disapproval, but by third grade, they begin to emphasize concern for others' feelings. Children with this awareness are rated as especially helpful, cooperative, and socially responsive by teachers and as better-liked by peers (Garner, 1996; McDowell & Parke, 2000).

When emotional self-regulation has developed well, school-age children acquire a sense of *emotional self-efficacy*—a feeling of being in control of their emotional experience (Saarni, 2000; Thompson & Goodman, 2010). This fosters a favorable self-image and an optimistic outlook, which further help children face emotional challenges. As at younger ages, children whose parents respond sensitively and helpfully when the child is distressed are emotionally well-regulated—generally upbeat in mood and also empathic and prosocial (Abraham & Kerns, 2013; Vinik, Almas, & Grusec, 2011). When mothers supported their 5-year-olds' emotional development in this way, children demonstrated more effective emotional self-regulation at age 7, which in turn predicted better quality friendships at age 10 (Blair et al., 2014). In contrast, poorly regulated children often experience hostile, dismissive parental reactions to distress (Morris et al., 2007). These children are overwhelmed by negative emotion, a response that interferes with empathy and prosocial behavior.

Finally, culture influences emotional self-regulation. In a striking illustration, researchers studied children in two subcultures in rural Nepal. In response to stories about emotionally charged situations (such as peer aggression or an unjust parental punishment), Hindu children more often said they would feel angry but would try to mask their feelings. Buddhist children, in contrast, interpreted the situation so that they felt "just OK" rather than angry. "Why be angry?" they explained. "The event already happened." Accordingly, Hindu mothers reported that they often teach their children how to control their emotional behavior, whereas Buddhist mothers pointed to the value their religion places on a calm, peaceful disposition (Cole & Tamang, 1998; Cole, Tamang, & Shrestha, 2006). Compared to both Nepalese groups, U.S. children preferred conveying anger verbally in these situations; for example, to an unjust punishment, they answered, "If I say I'm angry, he'll stop hurting me!" (Cole, Bruschi, & Tamang, 2002). Notice how this response fits with the Western emphasis on personal rights and self-expression.

© ELLEN B. SENISI

Through interacting with adults and peers, school-age children acquire socially approved ways to express negative emotion. These friends use words rather than crying, sulking, or aggression to confront a disagreement.

LOOK and LISTEN

Ask several school-age children how they would manage their emotions in the following situations: (1) a friend is angry with them, and (2) they receive a bad grade on an important test. Do their responses reflect flexible, adaptive coping?

Moral Development

13.4 Describe changes in moral understanding during middle childhood, including children's understanding of diversity and inequality.

Recall from Chapter 10 that preschoolers pick up many morally relevant behaviors through modeling and reinforcement. By middle childhood, they have had time to internalize rules for good conduct: "It's good to help others in trouble" or "It's wrong to take something that doesn't belong to you." This change leads children to become considerably more independent and trustworthy.

In Chapter 10, we also saw that children do not just copy their morality from others. As the cognitive-developmental approach emphasizes, they actively think about right and wrong. An expanding social world, the capacity to consider more information when reasoning, and gains in recursive perspective taking lead moral understanding to advance greatly in middle childhood.

School-age children recognize that certain social conventions have a clear purpose—such as separating recyclables from trash to reduce waste. They regard violations of these types of conventions as closer to moral transgressions.

Moral and Social-Conventional Understanding

During middle childhood, children construct a flexible appreciation of moral rules. They take into account an increasing number of variables, including both an actor's intentions and the context of his behavior in terms of harm done to others. For example, between ages 7 and 11, children increasingly say it is acceptable to hit another child in certain situations—in self-defense, to protect someone else from serious bodily injury, or to prevent the other child from hurting herself (Jambon & Smetana, 2014). Older children focus less on the actor's transgression (hitting) and more on the positive aim of his actions (trying to prevent harm).

Similarly, by age 7 to 8, children no longer say truth telling is always good and lying is always bad but also consider prosocial and antisocial intentions and the context of the behavior. They evaluate certain types of truthfulness very negatively—for example, blunt statements, particularly when made in public contexts where they are especially likely to have negative social consequences (telling a friend that you don't like her drawing) (Ma et al., 2011).

Although both Chinese and Canadian schoolchildren consider lying about antisocial acts "very naughty," Chinese children more often rate lying favorably when the intention is modesty, as when a student who has thoughtfully picked up litter from the playground says, "I didn't do it" (Cameron et al., 2012; Lee et al., 2001). Similarly, Chinese children are more likely to favor lying to support the group at the expense of the individual (claiming you're sick so, as a poor singer, you won't harm your class's chances of winning a singing competition). In contrast, Canadian children more often favor lying to support the individual at the expense of the group (asserting that a friend who is a poor speller is actually a good speller because the friend wants to participate in a spelling competition) (Fu et al., 2007; Lau et al., 2012). These judgments reflect school-age children's increasingly sophisticated understanding of different reasons for deception (Mills, 2013). They realize that people may convey inaccurate information because they are biased, trying to be persuasive, or concerned about how others will react.

As children construct more advanced ideas about justice, they clarify and link moral imperatives and social conventions. School-age children distinguish social conventions with a clear *purpose* (not running in school hallways to prevent injuries) from ones with no obvious justification (crossing a "forbidden" line on the playground). They regard violations of purposeful conventions as closer to moral transgressions (Buchanan-Barrow & Barrett, 1998).

Furthermore, as with moral rules, older children realize that people's intentions and the context of their actions affect the moral implications of violating a social convention. In one study, 8- to 10-year-olds judged that because of a flag's symbolic value, burning it to express disapproval of a country or to start a cooking fire is worse than burning it accidentally. They also stated that public flag burning is worse than private flag burning because it inflicts emotional harm on others. But they recognized that flag burning is a form of freedom of expression, and most agreed it would be acceptable in a country that treated its citizens unfairly (Helwig & Prencipe, 1999).

In middle childhood, children also realize that people whose *knowledge* differs may not be equally responsible for moral transgressions. Many 7-year-olds tolerate a teacher's decision to give more snack to girls than to boys because she thinks (incorrectly) that girls need more food. But when a teacher gives girls more snack because she holds an *immoral belief* ("it's all right to be nicer to girls than boys"), almost all children judge her actions negatively (Wainryb & Ford, 1998).

Understanding Individual Rights

When children challenge adult authority, they typically do so within the personal domain. As their grasp of moral imperatives and social conventions strengthens, so does their conviction that certain choices, such as hairstyle, friends, and leisure activities, are up to the individual (Nucci, 2005).

Notions of personal choice, in turn, enhance children's moral understanding. As early as age 6, children view freedom of speech and religion as individual rights, even if laws exist that deny those rights (Helwig, 2006). And they regard laws that discriminate against individuals—for example, denying certain people access to medical care or education—as wrong and worthy of violating (Helwig & Jasiobedzka, 2001). In justifying their responses, children appeal to personal privileges and, by the end of middle childhood, to the importance of individual rights for maintaining a fair society.

At the same time, older school-age children place limits on individual choice. Fourth graders faced with conflicting moral and personal concerns—such as whether or not to befriend a classmate of a different race or gender—typically decide in favor of kindness and fairness (Killen et al., 2002). Partly for this reason, prejudice generally declines in middle childhood.

Culture and Moral Understanding

Children and adolescents in diverse cultures use similar criteria to reason about moral, social-conventional, and personal concerns (Neff & Helwig, 2002; Nucci, 2005, 2008). For example, Chinese young people, whose culture places a high value on respect for and deference to adult authority, nevertheless say that adults have no right to interfere in children's personal matters, such as how they spend free time (Hasebe, Nucci, & Nucci, 2004). A Colombian child illustrated this passionate defense of personal control when asked if a teacher had the right to tell a student where to sit during circle time. In the absence of a moral reason from the teacher, the child declared, "She should be able to sit wherever she wants" (Ardila-Rey & Killen, 2001, p. 249).

Furthermore, American and Korean children alike claim that a child with no position of authority should be obeyed when she gives a directive that is fair and caring, such as telling others to share candy or to return lost money to its owner. And even in Korean culture, which places a high value on deference to authority, 7- to 11-year-olds evaluate negatively an adult's order to engage in immoral acts, such as stealing or refusing to share—a response that strengthens with age (Kim, 1998). In sum, children everywhere seem to realize that higher principles, independent of rule and authority, must prevail when people's personal rights and welfare are at stake.

Understanding Diversity and Inequality

By the early school years, children absorb prevailing societal attitudes, associating power and privilege with white people and poverty and inferior status with people of color. They do not necessarily acquire these views directly from parents or friends, whose attitudes often differ from their own (Aboud & Doyle, 1996). Perhaps white parents are reluctant to discuss their racial and ethnic views with children, and friends also say little. Given limited or ambiguous information, children may fill in the gaps with information they encounter in the media and elsewhere in their environments.

Consistent with this idea, research indicates that children pick up much information about group status from implicit messages in their surroundings. In one investigation, 7- to 12-year-olds attending a summer school were randomly assigned to social groups, identified by colored T-shirts (yellow or blue) that the children wore. The researchers hung posters in the classroom depicting yellow-group members as having higher status—for example, as having won more athletic and spelling competitions. When teachers used the groups as the basis for seating arrangements, assignments, and bulletin-board displays, the children in the high-status group evaluated their own group more favorably than the other group, and the children in the low-status group viewed their own group less favorably (Bigler, Brown, & Markell, 2001). But when teachers ignored the social groupings, no prejudice emerged.

These findings indicate that children do not necessarily form stereotypes even when some basis for them exists—in this instance, information on wall posters. But when an authority figure behaves in ways that endorse group status distinctions, children form biased attitudes.

© SYRACUSE NEWSPAPERS/MIKE GREENLAR/THE IMAGE WORKS

Fourth graders participate in a nature walk during a school lunch break. Around age 7 or 8, voicing of negative attitudes toward minorities declines, and most children judge exclusion based on skin color to be unfair.

IN-GROUP AND OUT-GROUP BIASES: DEVELOPMENT OF PREJUDICE   Studies in diverse Western nations confirm that by age 5 to 6, white children generally evaluate their own racial group favorably and other racial groups less favorably or negatively (Aboud, 2003; Bennett et al., 2004; Nesdale et al., 2004). Many minority children of this age, in a reverse pattern, assign positive characteristics to the privileged white majority and negative characteristics to their own group (Corenblum, 2003; Newheiser et al., 2014).

But recall that with age, children pay more attention to inner traits. The capacity to classify the social world in multiple ways enables school-age children to understand that people can be both "the same" and "different"—those who look different need not think, feel, or act differently. Consequently, voicing of negative attitudes toward minorities declines after age 7 or 8 (Aboud, 2008; Raabe & Beelman, 2011). Around this time, both majority and minority children express *in-group favoritism,* and white children's prejudice against *out-group* members often weakens (Nesdale et al., 2005; Ruble et al., 2004). Most school-age children and adolescents are also quick to verbalize that it is wrong to exclude others from peer-group and learning activities on the basis of skin color—discrimination they evaluate as unfair (Killen et al., 2002).

Yet even in children aware of the injustice of discrimination, prejudice often operates unintentionally and without awareness—as it does in many adults (Dunham, Baron, & Banaji, 2006). Consider a study in which U.S. children and adults were shown pictures of computer-generated racially ambiguous faces displaying happy and angry expressions and asked to classify them by race. White participants more often categorized happy faces as white and angry faces as African American or Asian. These implicit biases were evident across all ages tested—as early as 3 or 4. In contrast, African-American participants did not show any racial biases in their responses (Dunham, Chen, & Banaji, 2013). The absence of any in-group favoritism (classifying happy faces as black) suggests an early emerging, implicit sensitivity to prevailing racial attitudes among African Americans.

These findings raise the question of whether the decline in white children's explicit racial bias during middle childhood is a true decrease, or whether it reflects their growing awareness of widely held standards that deem prejudice to be inappropriate—or both. Around age 10, white children start to avoid talking about race in order to appear unbiased, just as many adults do (Apfelbaum et al., 2008). At least to some degree, then, older school-age children's desire to present themselves in a socially acceptable light may contribute to reduced explicit out-group prejudice, while implicit racial bias persists.

Nevertheless, the extent to which children hold racial and ethnic biases varies, depending on the following personal and situational factors:

- *A fixed view of personality traits.* Children who believe personality traits are fixed rather than changeable often judge others as either "good" or "bad." Ignoring motives and circumstances, they readily form prejudices based on limited information. For example, they might infer that "a new child at school who tells a lie to get other kids to like her" is simply a bad person (Levy & Dweck, 1999).
- *Overly high self-esteem.* Children (and adults) with very high self-esteem are more likely to hold racial and ethnic prejudices (Baumeister et al., 2003; Bigler, Brown, & Markell, 2001). These individuals seem to belittle disadvantaged individuals or groups to justify their own extremely favorable self-evaluation. Children who say their own ethnicity makes them feel especially "good"—and thus perhaps socially superior—are more likely to display in-group favoritism and out-group prejudice (Pfeifer et al., 2007).
- *A social world in which people are sorted into groups.* The more adults highlight group distinctions for children and the less interracial contact children experience, the more likely white children will express in-group favoritism and out-group prejudice (Killen et al., 2010).

REDUCING PREJUDICE Research confirms that an effective way to reduce prejudice is through intergroup contact, in which racially and ethnically different children have equal status, work toward common goals, and become personally acquainted, and in which authority figures (such as parents and teachers) expect them to engage in such interaction. Children assigned to cooperative learning groups with peers of diverse backgrounds show low levels of prejudice in their expressions of likability and in their behavior. For example, they form more cross-race friendships (Pettigrew & Tropp, 2006). Sharing thoughts and feelings with close, cross-race friends, in turn, reduces even subtle, unintentional prejudices (Turner, Hewstone, & Voci, 2007). But positive effects seem not to generalize to out-group members who are not part of these learning teams.

Third graders perform a traditional Chinese dance at their culturally diverse school. Opportunities to work together toward common goals can reduce even subtle, unintentional prejudices as racially and ethnically different children get to know one another.

Long-term contact and collaboration among neighborhood, school, and community groups may be the best way to reduce prejudice (Rutland, Killen, & Abrams, 2010). School environments that expose children to broad ethnic diversity, teach them to understand and value those differences, directly address the damage caused by prejudice, and encourage perspective taking and empathy both prevent children from forming negative biases and reduce already acquired biases (Dweck, 2009). Unfortunately, as noted in Chapter 12, segregation is widespread in U.S. schools, which seldom offer exposure to the diversity necessary for countering negative racial and ethnic biases. Return to page 464 to review efforts of magnet schools to reduce this racial divide.

Finally, inducing children to view others' traits as changeable, by discussing with them the many possible influences on those traits, is helpful. The more children believe that people can change their personalities, the more they report liking, wanting to spend time with, and perceiving themselves as similar to members of disadvantaged out-groups. Furthermore, children who believe that human attributes are changeable spend more time volunteering to help people in need—for example, by serving meals to homeless people or reading to poverty-stricken preschoolers (Karafantis & Levy, 2004). Volunteering may, in turn, promote a view of others as changeable by helping children take the perspective of the underprivileged and appreciate the social conditions that lead to disadvantage.

Ask Yourself

- **REVIEW** How does emotional self-regulation improve in middle childhood? What implications do these advances have for children's self-esteem?

- **CONNECT** Cite examples of how older children's capacity to take more information into account enhances their emotional understanding, perspective taking, and moral understanding.

- **APPLY** Ten-year-old Marla says her classmate Bernadette will never get good grades because she's lazy. Jane believes that Bernadette tries but can't concentrate because her parents are divorcing. Why is Marla more likely than Jane to develop prejudices?

- **REFLECT** Did you attend an integrated elementary school? Why is school integration vital for reducing racial and ethnic prejudice?

Peer Relations

In middle childhood, the society of peers becomes an increasingly important context for development. Advances in recursive perspective taking permit more sophisticated understanding of self and others. These developments, in turn, enhance peer interaction. Compared with preschoolers, school-age children resolve conflicts more effectively, using persuasion and

13.5 How do peer sociability and friendship change in middle childhood?

13.6 Describe major categories of peer acceptance and ways to help rejected children.

compromise (Mayeux & Cillessen, 2003). Sharing, helping, and other prosocial acts also increase. In line with these changes, aggression declines. But the drop is greatest for physical attacks (Côté et al., 2007; Tremblay, 2000). As we will see, verbal and relational aggression continue as children form peer groups.

Peer Groups

TAKE A MOMENT... Watch children in the schoolyard or neighborhood, and notice how they often gather in groups of three to a dozen or more. In what ways are members of the same group noticeably alike?

By the end of middle childhood, children display a strong desire for group belonging. They form **peer groups,** collectives that generate unique values and standards for behavior and a social structure of leaders and followers. Peer groups organize on the basis of proximity (being in the same classroom) and similarity in sex, ethnicity, academic achievement, popularity, and aggression (Rubin et al., 2013). When groups are tracked for 3 to 6 weeks, membership changes very little. When they are followed for a year or longer, substantial change can occur, depending on whether children are reshuffled into different classrooms. For children who remain together, 50 to 70 percent of groups consist mostly of the same children from year to year (Cairns, Xie, & Leung, 1998).

The practices of these informal groups lead to a "peer culture" that typically involves a specialized vocabulary, dress code, and place to "hang out." Joey and three other boys formed a club whose "uniform" was T-shirts, jeans, and sneakers. They met at recess and on Saturdays in the tree house in Joey's backyard. Calling themselves "the pack," the boys devised a secret handshake and chose Joey as their leader. Their activities included improving the clubhouse, trading baseball cards, playing basketball and video games, and—just as important—keeping unwanted peers and adults out!

As children develop these exclusive associations, the codes of dress and behavior that grow out of them become more broadly influential. Peers who deviate—by "kissing up" to teachers, wearing the wrong clothes, or tattling on classmates—are often rebuffed, becoming targets of critical glances and comments. These customs bind peers together, creating a sense of group identity. Within the group, children acquire many social skills—cooperation, leadership, followership, and loyalty to collective goals. Through these experiences, children experiment with and learn about social organizations.

As with other aspects of social reasoning, children evaluate a group's decision to exclude a peer in complex ways. Most view exclusion as wrong, even when they see themselves as different from the excluded child. And with age, children are less likely to endorse excluding someone because of unconventional appearance or behavior. Girls, especially, regard exclusion as unjust, perhaps because they experience it more often than boys (Killen, Crystal, & Watanabe, 2002). But when a peer threatens group functioning, by acting disruptively or by lacking skills to participate in a valued group activity (such as sports), both boys and girls say that exclusion is justified—a perspective that strengthens with age (Killen & Stangor, 2001).

Despite these sophisticated understandings, children do exclude unjustly, often using relationally aggressive tactics. Peer groups—at the instigation of their leaders, who can be skillfully aggressive—frequently oust no longer "respected" children. Some of these cast-outs, whose own previous hostility toward outsiders reduces their chances of being included elsewhere, turn to other low-status peers with poor social skills (Farmer et al., 2010). Socially anxious children, when ousted, often become increasingly peer-avoidant and thus more isolated (Buhs, Ladd, & Herald-Brown, 2010). In either case, opportunities to acquire socially competent behavior diminish.

School-age children's desire for group belonging can also be satisfied through formal group ties such as scouting, 4-H, and religious

© BJARKI REYR MR/ALAMY

Peer groups first form in middle childhood. These boys have probably established a social structure of leaders and followers as they gather for a soccer game. Their relaxed body language and similar dress suggest a strong sense of group belonging.

youth groups. Adult involvement holds in check the negative behaviors associated with children's informal peer groups. And through working on joint projects and helping in their communities, children gain in social and moral maturity (Vandell & Shumow, 1999).

Friendships

Whereas peer groups provide children with insight into larger social structures, friendships contribute to the development of trust and sensitivity. During the school years, friendship becomes more complex and psychologically based. Consider the following 8-year-old's ideas:

Why is Shelly your best friend? Because she helps me when I'm sad, and she shares. . . . *What makes Shelly so special?* I've known her longer, I sit next to her and got to know her better. . . . *How come you like Shelly better than anyone else?* She's done the most for me. She never disagrees, she never eats in front of me, she never walks away when I'm crying, and she helps me on my homework. . . . *How do you get someone to like you?* . . . If you're nice to [your friends], they'll be nice to you. (Damon, 1988, pp. 80–81)

As these responses show, friendship has become a mutually agreed-on relationship in which children like each other's personal qualities and respond to one another's needs and desires. And once a friendship forms, *trust* becomes its defining feature. School-age children state that a good friendship is based on acts of kindness, signifying that each person can be counted on to support the other (Hartup & Abecassis, 2004). Consequently, older children regard violations of trust, such as not helping when others need help, breaking promises, and gossiping behind the other's back, as serious breaches of friendship.

Because of these features, school-age children's friendships are more selective. Whereas preschoolers say they have lots of friends, by age 8 or 9 children name only a handful of good friends. Girls, who demand greater closeness than boys, are more exclusive in their friendships. In addition, children tend to select friends similar to themselves in age, sex, race, ethnicity, and SES. Friends also resemble one another in personality (sociability, inattention/hyperactivity, aggression, depression), peer popularity, academic achievement, and prosocial behavior (Hartup, 2006; Rubin et al., 2013). But friendship opportunities offered by children's environments also affect their choices. As noted earlier, in integrated classrooms with mixed-race collaborative learning groups, students form more cross-race friendships.

Over middle childhood, high-quality friendships remain fairly stable: About 50 to 70 percent endure over a school year, and some last for several years (Berndt, 2004). Friendships spanning several contexts—such as school, religious institution, and children of parents' friends—are more enduring (Troutman & Fletcher, 2010). Through friendships, children learn the importance of emotional commitment. They come to realize that close relationships can survive disagreements if friends are secure in their liking for each other (Hartup, 2006). Friendship provides an important context in which children learn to tolerate criticism and resolve disputes in ways that meet both partners' needs.

Yet the impact of friendships on children's development depends on the nature of their friends. Children who bring kindness and compassion to their friendships strengthen each other's prosocial tendencies. But when aggressive children make friends, the relationship is often riddled with hostile interaction and is at risk for breakup, especially when just one member of the pair is aggressive (Ellis & Zarbatany, 2007). Aggressive girls' friendships are high in exchange of private feelings but also full of relational hostility, including jealousy, conflict, and betrayal. Aggressive boys' friendships involve frequent expressions of anger, coercive statements, physical attacks, and enticements to rule breaking (Bagwell & Coie, 2004; Rubin et al., 2013; Werner & Crick, 2004). These findings indicate that the social problems of aggressive children operate within their closest peer ties. As we will see next, these children often acquire negative reputations in the wider world of peers.

LOOK and LISTEN

Ask an 8- to 11-year-old to tell you what he or she looks for in a best friend. Is *trust* centrally important? Does the child mention personality traits, just as school-age children do in describing themselves (see page 474)?

© ELLEN B. SENISI

During middle childhood, concepts of friendship become more psychologically based. School-age friendships are more selective than those of younger children, and girls demand greater friendship closeness than do boys.

Peer Acceptance

Peer acceptance refers to likability—the extent to which a child is viewed by a group of age-mates, such as classmates, as a worthy social partner. Unlike friendship, peer acceptance is not a mutual relationship but a one-sided perspective, involving the group's view of an individual. Nevertheless, better-accepted children tend to be socially competent and, thus, to have more friends and more positive relationships with them (Mayeux, Houser, & Dyches, 2011).

To assess peer acceptance, researchers usually use self-reports that measure *social preferences*—for example, asking children to identify classmates whom they "like most" or "like least" (Cillessen, 2009). These self-reports yield five general categories of peer acceptance:

- **Popular children,** who get many positive votes (are well-liked)
- **Rejected children,** who get many negative votes (are disliked)
- **Controversial children,** who receive many votes, both positive and negative (are both liked and disliked)
- **Neglected children,** who are seldom mentioned, either positively or negatively
- **Average children,** who receive average numbers of positive and negative votes

Another approach assesses *perceived popularity*—children's judgments of whom most of their classmates admire. Only moderate correspondence exists between the classmates children perceive as popular (believe are admired by many others) and those classified as popular based on peer preferences (receive many "like most" ratings) (Mayeux, Houser, & Dyches, 2011).

Peer acceptance is a powerful predictor of current as well as later psychological adjustment. Rejected children, especially, are anxious, unhappy, disruptive, and low in self-esteem. Both teachers and parents rate them as having a wide range of emotional and social problems. Peer rejection in middle childhood is also strongly associated with poor school performance, absenteeism, dropping out, substance use, depression, antisocial behavior, and delinquency in adolescence and with criminality in adulthood (Ladd, 2005; Rubin, et al., 2013).

However, earlier influences—children's characteristics combined with parenting practices—may largely explain the link between peer acceptance and adjustment. School-age children with peer-relationship problems are more likely to have preexisting, weak emotional self-regulation skills and to have experienced family stress due to low income, insensitive child rearing, and coercive discipline (Blair et al., 2014; Trentacosta & Shaw, 2009). Nevertheless, as we will see, rejected children evoke reactions from peers that contribute to their unfavorable development.

DETERMINANTS OF PEER ACCEPTANCE   Why is one child liked while another is rejected? A wealth of research reveals that social behavior plays a powerful role.

Peers gather around a popular classmate. Most popular children are prosocial—academically successful, socially sensitive, and cooperative. But some are antisocial, admired for their skill at controlling peer relationships through relational aggression.

Popular Children.   Socially successful children include those who are well-liked (socially accepted) and those who are admired (high in perceived popularity). **Popular-prosocial children,** who are both socially accepted and admired, combine academic and social competence. They perform well in school, communicate with peers in friendly and cooperative ways, and solve social problems constructively (Cillessen & Bellmore, 2004; Mayeux, Houser, & Dyches, 2011).

But other popular children are admired for their socially adept yet belligerent behavior. **Popular-antisocial children** include "tough" boys—athletically skilled but poor students who cause trouble and defy adult authority—and relationally aggressive boys and girls who enhance their own status by ignoring, excluding, and spreading rumors about other children (Rose, Swenson, & Waller, 2004; Vaillancourt & Hymel, 2006). Despite their aggressiveness, peers often view these youths as "cool," perhaps because of their athletic abilities and sophisticated but devious social skills.

Although peer admiration gives these children some protection against lasting adjustment difficulties, their antisocial acts require intervention (Rodkin et al., 2006). With age, peers like these high-status, aggressive youths less and less, a trend that is stronger for relationally aggressive girls. The more socially prominent and controlling these girls become, the more they engage in relational aggression (Mayeux, Houser, & Dyches, 2011). Eventually peers condemn their nasty tactics and reject them.

Rejected Children. Rejected children display a wide range of negative social behaviors. The largest subtype, **rejected-aggressive children,** show high rates of conflict, physical and relational aggression, and hyperactive, inattentive, and impulsive behavior. They are usually deficient in perspective taking, and they tend to misinterpret innocent behaviors of peers as hostile and to blame others for their social difficulties (Dodge, Coie, & Lynam, 2006; Rubin et al., 2013). Compared with popular-antisocial children, they are more extremely antagonistic.

In contrast, **rejected-withdrawn children** are passive and socially awkward. Overwhelmed by social anxiety, they hold negative expectations about interactions with peers and worry about being scorned and attacked. Like their aggressive counterparts, they typically feel like retaliating rather than compromising when conflicts arise, although they less often act on those feelings (Hart et al., 2000; Rubin et al., 2013; Troop-Gordon & Asher, 2005).

Rejected children are excluded by peers as early as kindergarten. Rejection, in turn, further impairs biased social information processing, heightening hostility (Lansford et al., 2010). Soon their classroom participation declines, their feelings of loneliness rise, their academic achievement falters, and they want to avoid school (Buhs, Ladd, & Herald-Brown, 2010; Gooren et al., 2011). Most have few friends, and some have none—a circumstance linked to low self-esteem, mistrust of peers, and severe adjustment difficulties (Ladd et al., 2011; Pedersen et al., 2007).

Both types of rejected children are at risk for peer harassment. But as the Biology and Environment box on page 492 reveals, rejected-aggressive children also act as bullies, and rejected-withdrawn children are especially likely to be victimized (Putallaz et al., 2007).

Controversial and Neglected Children. Consistent with the mixed peer opinion they engender, controversial children display a blend of positive and negative social behaviors. They are hostile and disruptive, but they also engage in positive, prosocial acts. Even though some peers dislike them, they have qualities that protect them from exclusion. They have many friends and are happy with their peer relationships (de Bruyn & Cillessen, 2006). But like their popular-antisocial counterparts, they often bully others and engage in calculated relational aggression to sustain their dominance (Putallaz et al., 2007).

Perhaps the most surprising finding on peer acceptance is that neglected children, once thought to be in need of treatment, are usually well-adjusted. Although they engage in low rates of interaction and are considered shy by their classmates, most are just as socially skilled as average children and do not report feeling unhappy about their social life. When they want to, they can break away from their usual, preferred pattern of playing alone, cooperating well with peers and forming positive, stable friendships (Ladd & Burgess, 1999; Ladd et al., 2011). Consequently, neglected status (like controversial status) is often temporary. Neglected, socially competent children remind us that an outgoing, gregarious personality style is not the only path to emotional well-being. Nevertheless, a few neglected children are socially anxious and poorly skilled and, thus, at risk for peer rejection.

HELPING REJECTED CHILDREN A variety of interventions exist to improve the peer relations and psychological adjustment of rejected children. Most involve coaching, modeling, and reinforcing positive social skills, such as how to initiate interaction with a peer, cooperate in play, and respond to another child with friendly emotion and approval. Several of these programs have produced gains in social competence and peer acceptance still present from several weeks to a year later (Asher & Rose, 1997; DeRosier, 2007).

Combining social-skills training with other treatments increases its effectiveness. Rejected children are often poor students, whose low academic self-esteem magnifies their negative interactions with teachers and classmates. Intensive academic tutoring improves both school achievement and social acceptance (O'Neil et al., 1997).

Still another approach focuses on training in perspective taking and social problem solving. But many rejected-aggressive children are unaware of their poor social skills and do not take responsibility for their social failures (Mrug, Hoza, & Gerdes, 2001). Rejected-withdrawn

Biology and Environment

Bullies and Their Victims

Follow the activities of aggressive children over a school day, and you will see that they reserve their hostilities for certain peers. A highly destructive form of interaction is **peer victimization,** in which particular children become targets of verbal and physical attacks or other forms of abuse. What sustains these repeated assault–retreat cycles between pairs of children?

Almost 20 percent of children are bullies, while 25 percent are repeatedly victimized. Most bullies who engage in face-to-face physical and verbal attacks are boys, but a considerable number of girls have bombarded vulnerable classmates with verbal and relational hostility (Cook et al., 2010).

As bullies move into adolescence, an increasing number attack through electronic means. About 20 to 40 percent of youths have experienced "cyberbullying" through text messages, e-mail, chat rooms, or other electronic tools (Kowalski & Limber, 2013). Compared with face-to-face bullying, gender differences in cyberbullying are less pronounced; the indirectness of online aggression may lead girls to prefer it (Menesini & Spiel, 2012). Girls more often use text messages, e-mail, or chat rooms to cyberbully, whereas boys more often distribute embarrassing photos or videos (Menesini, Nicocenti, & Calussi, 2011).

"Traditional" bullying and cyberbullying frequently co-occur: Bullies and victims in one context are frequently involved in the other. But electronic bullying is not always an extension of traditional bullying (Smith et al., 2008). And victims are far less likely to report cyberbullying to parents or adults at school. Most of the time, the cyberbully's identity is unknown to the victim and audience.

Many bullies are disliked, or become so, because of their cruelty. But a substantial number are socially prominent, powerful youngsters who are broadly admired for their physical attractiveness, leadership, or athletic abilities (Vaillancourt et al., 2010b). To preserve their high social status, bullies often target already peer-rejected children, whom classmates are unlikely to defend (Veenstra et al., 2010). This helps explain why peers rarely intervene to help victims, and why about 20 to 30 percent of onlookers encourage bullies, even joining in (Salmivalli & Voeten, 2004). Bullying occurs more often in schools where teachers are viewed as unfair and uncaring and where many students judge bullying behaviors to be "OK" (Guerra, Williams, & Sadek, 2011).

Indeed, bullies, and the peers who assist them, typically display social-cognitive deficits, including overly high self-esteem, pride in their acts, and indifference to harm done to their victims (Hymel et al., 2010).

Depression and other internalizing difficulties increase children's risk of both real-life and cyber victimization (Kochel, Ladd, & Rudolph, 2012; Vaillancourt et al., 2013). Biologically based traits—an inhibited temperament and a frail physical appearance—contribute. But victims also have histories of resistant attachment, overly controlling child rearing, and maternal overprotection—parenting that prompts anxiety, low self-esteem, and dependency, resulting in a fearful demeanor that marks these children and youths as vulnerable (Snyder et al., 2003).

Other adjustment problems associated with victimization include loneliness, low peer acceptance, poor school performance, disruptive behavior, and school avoidance (Kochel, Ladd, & Rudolph, 2012; Paul & Cillessen, 2003). And like persistent child abuse, victimization is linked to impaired production of cortisol, suggesting a chronically disrupted physiological response to stress (Vaillancourt, Hymel, & McDougall, 2013).

As instances of traditional bullying and cyberbullying accumulate, victims report substantial interference with daily functioning. Both forms of victimization are related to rising anxiety, depression, and suicidal thoughts (Menesini, Calussi, & Nocentini, 2012; van den Eijnden et al., 2014). Repeated cyberattacks directed at widespread damage to the victim's reputation—for example, circulating malicious videos on cell phones or social networking sites—magnify these effects.

Aggression and victimization are not polar opposites. One-third to one-half of victims are also aggressive, meeting out physical, relational, or cyberhostilities. Bullies usually respond by abusing them again—a cycle that sustains their victim status. Among rejected children, these bully/victims are the most despised. They often have histories of extremely maladaptive parenting, including child abuse. This combination of highly negative home and peer experiences places them at severe risk for maladjustment (Kowalski, Limber, & Agatston, 2008).

Interventions that change victimized children's negative opinions of themselves and that teach them to respond in nonreinforcing ways to their attackers are helpful. Another way to assist victimized children is to help them acquire the social skills needed to form and maintain a

Many bullies are socially prominent, admired youngsters who target peer-rejected children as a means of preserving their high social status. Classmates are unlikely to defend these victims, and some join in the verbal and physical attacks.

gratifying friendship. When children have a close friend to whom they can turn for help, bullying episodes typically end quickly. Anxious, withdrawn children with a close friend have fewer adjustment problems than those with no friends (Fox & Boulton, 2006; Laursen et al., 2007).

Although modifying victimized children's behavior can help, the best way to reduce bullying is to change youth environments (including school, sports programs, recreation centers, and neighborhoods), promoting prosocial attitudes and behaviors. Effective approaches include developing school and community codes against both traditional bullying and cyberbullying; teaching child bystanders to intervene; strengthening parental oversight of children and youths' use of cell phones, computers, and the Internet; and increasing adult supervision of high-bullying areas in schools, such as hallways, lunchroom, and schoolyard (Kiriakidis & Kavoura, 2010; Vaillancourt et al., 2010a).

The U.S. Department of Health and Human Services manages an antibullying website, *www.stopbullying.gov,* which raises awareness of the harmfulness of bullying and provides parents, teachers, and students with information on prevention.

children, in contrast, are likely to develop a *learned-helpless* approach to peer acceptance—concluding, after repeated rebuffs, that they will never be liked (Wichmann, Coplan, & Daniels, 2004). Both types of rejected children need help attributing their peer difficulties to internal, changeable causes.

As rejected children gain in social skills, teachers must encourage peers to alter their negative opinions. Accepted children often selectively recall their negative acts while overlooking their positive ones (Mikami, Lerner, & Lun, 2010). Consequently, even in the face of contrary evidence, rejected children's negative reputations tend to persist. Teachers' praise and expressions of liking, along with classroom expectations for social acceptance, can modify peer judgments (De Laet at al., 2014; Mikami et al., 2013).

Finally, because rejected children's socially incompetent behaviors often originate in a poor fit between the child's temperament and parenting practices, interventions focusing on the child may not be sufficient (Bierman & Powers, 2009). Without improving the quality of parent–child interaction, rejected children will continue to practice poor interpersonal skills at home and, as a result, may soon return to their old behavior patterns.

LOOK *and* LISTEN

Contact a nearby elementary school or a school district office to find out what practices are in place to prevent bullying. Inquire about a written antibullying policy, and request a copy.

Gender Typing

Children's understanding of gender roles broadens in middle childhood, and their gender identities (views of themselves as relatively masculine or feminine) change as well. We will see how gender stereotypes influence children's attitudes, behaviors, peer relations, and self-perceptions.

13.7 What changes in gender-stereotyped beliefs and gender identity occur during middle childhood?

Gender-Stereotyped Beliefs

By age 5, gender stereotyping of activities and occupations is well-established. During the school years, knowledge of stereotypes increases in the less obvious areas of personality traits and achievement.

PERSONALITY TRAITS　Research in many cultures reveals that stereotyping of personality traits increases steadily in middle childhood, becoming adultlike around age 11 (Best, 2001; Heyman & Legare, 2004). For example, children regard "tough," "aggressive," "rational," and "dominant" as masculine and "gentle," "affectionate," and "dependent" as feminine.

Children derive these distinctions from observing sex differences in behavior as well as from adult treatment. When helping a child with a task, for example, parents (especially fathers) behave in a more mastery-oriented fashion with sons, setting higher standards, explaining concepts, and pointing out important features of tasks—particularly during gender-typed pursuits, such as science activities (Tenenbaum & Leaper, 2003; Tenenbaum et al., 2005). Furthermore, parents less often encourage girls to make their own decisions. And both parents and teachers more often praise boys for knowledge and accomplishment, girls for obedience (Good & Brophy, 2003; Pomerantz & Ruble, 1998).

ACHIEVEMENT AREAS　Shortly after entering elementary school, school-age children figure out which academic subjects and skill areas are "masculine" and which are "feminine." They often regard reading, spelling, art, and music as more for girls and mathematics, athletics, and mechanical skills as more for boys (Cvencek, Meltzoff, & Greenwald, 2011; Eccles, Jacobs, & Harold, 1990). These stereotypes—and the attitudes and behaviors of parents and teachers that promote them—influence children's preferences for and sense of competence at certain subjects. As we saw in our discussion of self-esteem, boys tend to feel more competent than girls at math, science, and athletics, whereas girls feel more competent than boys at language arts (see page 477).

Adults' gender-typed judgments of children's competence can have lasting consequences. In one study, mothers' early perceptions of their children's competence at math continued to predict daughters' self-perceptions and also career choices in their mid-twenties. Young

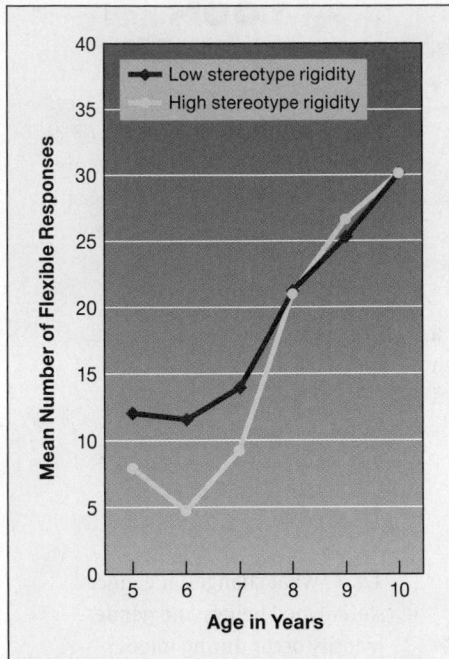

FIGURE 13.3 **Changes in gender-stereotype flexibility between ages 5 and 10.** German schoolchildren responded annually to a questionnaire assessing the flexibility of their gender-stereotyped beliefs (whether they thought both genders could display a personality trait or engage in an activity). Children differing in degree of gender-stereotype rigidity at age 5 eventually became equally flexible. Findings support the powerful role of cognitive changes in inducing flexibility, since early individual differences in rigidity were not sustained. (From H. M. Trautner et al., 2005, "Rigidity and Flexibility of Gender Stereotypes in Childhood: Developmental or Differential?," *Infant and Child Development, 14,* p. 371. Copyright © 2005 John Wiley & Sons Limited. Reprinted by permission of John Wiley and Sons, Ltd., conveyed through Copyright Clearance Center, Inc.)

women whose mothers had regarded them as highly capable at math were far more likely to choose a physical science career (Bleeker & Jacobs, 2004). Yet mothers rarely made such optimistic judgments about girls.

An encouraging sign is that some gender-stereotyped beliefs about achievement may be changing. In several recent investigations carried out in Canada, France, and the United States, a majority of elementary and secondary students disagreed with the idea that math is a "masculine" subject (Martinot, Bagès, & Désert, 2012; Martinot & Désert, 2007; Plante, Théoret, & Favreau, 2009; Rowley et al., 2007). And when Canadian students were given the option of rating math as a "feminine" subject (not offered in previous studies), an impressive number—though more girls than boys—expressed the view that it is predominantly feminine. The overwhelming majority of these young people, however, continued to view language arts traditionally—as largely "feminine." And they still perceived girls to do better in language arts than in math.

TOWARD GREATER FLEXIBILITY   Although school-age children are aware of many gender stereotypes, they also develop a more flexible, open-minded view of what males and females *can do,* a trend that continues into adolescence.

In studying gender stereotyping, researchers usually ask children whether or not both genders can display a personality trait or engage in an activity—responses that measure **gender-stereotype flexibility,** or overlap in the characteristics of males and females. In a German study that followed children from ages 5 to 10, regardless of the degree of early gender-stereotype rigidity, flexibility increased dramatically from age 7 on (see Figure 13.3) (Trautner et al., 2005). As they develop the capacity to integrate conflicting social cues, children realize that a person's sex is not a certain predictor of his or her personality traits, activities, and behaviors (Halim & Ruble, 2010). Similarly, by the end of the school years, most children regard gender typing as socially rather than biologically influenced (Taylor, Rhodes, & Gelman, 2009).

But acknowledging that people *can* cross gender lines does not mean that children always *approve* of doing so. In one longitudinal study, between ages 7 and 13, children generally became more open-minded about girls being offered the same opportunities as boys (Crouter et al., 2007). But the change was less pronounced for boys than girls, and for children whose parents held more traditional gender attitudes.

Furthermore, many school-age children take a harsh view of certain violations—boys playing with dolls and wearing girls' clothing, girls acting noisily and roughly. They are especially intolerant when boys engage in these "cross-gender" acts, which children regard as nearly as bad as moral transgressions (Blakemore, 2003; Levy, Taylor, & Gelman, 1995). When asked for open-ended descriptions of boys and girls, children most often mention girls' physical appearance ("is pretty," "wears dresses") and boys' activities and personality traits ("likes trucks," "is rough") (Miller et al., 2009). The salience of these stereotypes helps explain why, when children of the other sex display the behaviors just mentioned, they are likely to experience severe peer disapproval.

Nevertheless, school-age children do extend more flexible gender attitudes to the peer context to some degree. As with ethnicity, the majority regard excluding an agemate from peer group activities on the basis of gender as unfair. But between fourth and seventh grades, more young people—again, especially boys—say it is OK to exclude on the basis of gender than ethnicity (see Figure 13.4). They

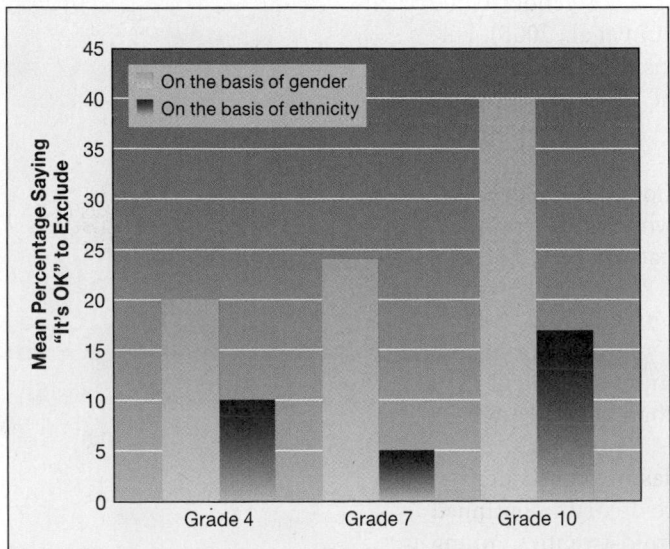

FIGURE 13.4 **Percentage of children and adolescents saying "It's OK" to exclude an agemate from a peer-group activity on the basis of gender and ethnicity.** When asked about excluding an other-sex or other-ethnicity peer from a peer-group activity (a music club in which members trade CDs), many more young people said that it is OK to do so on the basis of gender than on the basis of ethnicity. Willingness to exclude on the basis of gender increased with age, with many participants justifying their decision by pointing to sex differences in interests and communication styles. (Based on Killen et al., 2002.)

point to concerns about group functioning related to sex differences in interests and communication styles—boys' preference for active pursuits and commanding forceful behavior, girls' preference for quiet activities, politeness, and compromise (Killen et al., 2002, p. 56). Indeed, sex-segregated peer associations strengthen during middle childhood and continue to contribute powerfully to gender typing (see Chapter 10, page 386).

Gender Identity and Behavior

Children who were more strongly gender-typed relative to their agemates in early childhood usually remain so in middle childhood (Golombok et al., 2008). Nevertheless, overall changes do occur, with boys' and girls' gender identities following different paths.

From third to sixth grade, boys tend to strengthen their identification with "masculine" personality traits, whereas girls' identification with "feminine" traits declines. Girls often describe themselves as having some "other-gender" characteristics (Serbin, Powlishta, & Gulko, 1993). And whereas boys usually stick to "masculine" pursuits, many girls experiment with a wider range of options—from cooking and sewing to sports and science projects—and more often consider traditionally male future work roles, such as firefighter or astronomer (Liben & Bigler, 2002).

These changes reflect a mixture of cognitive and social forces. School-age children of both sexes are aware that society attaches greater prestige to "masculine" characteristics. For example, they rate "masculine" occupations as having higher status than "feminine" occupations, and an unfamiliar job as higher in status when portrayed with a male worker than a female worker (Liben, Bigler, & Krogh, 2001; Weisgram, Bigler, & Liben, 2010). Messages from adults and peers are also influential. In Chapter 10, we saw that parents (especially fathers) are especially disapproving when sons, as opposed to daughters, cross gender lines. Similarly, a tomboyish girl can interact with boys without losing the approval of her female peers, but a boy who hangs out with girls is likely to be ridiculed and rejected.

As school-age children make social comparisons and characterize themselves in terms of stable dispositions, their gender identity expands to include the following self-evaluations, which greatly affect their adjustment:

- *Gender typicality*—the degree to which the child feels similar to others of the same gender. Although children need not be highly gender typed to view themselves as gender-typical, their psychological well-being depends, to some degree, on feeling that they "fit in" with their same-sex peers.
- *Gender contentedness*—the degree to which the child feels comfortable with his or her gender assignment, which also promotes happiness.
- *Felt pressure to conform to gender roles*—the degree to which the child feels parents and peers disapprove of his or her gender-related traits. Because such pressure reduces the likelihood that children will explore options related to their interests and talents, children who feel strong gender-typed pressure are often distressed.

In a longitudinal study of third through seventh graders, *gender-typical* and *gender-contented* children gained in self-esteem over the following year. In contrast, children who were *gender-atypical* and *gender-discontented* declined in self-worth. Furthermore, gender-atypical children who reported *intense pressure to conform to gender roles* experienced serious difficulties—withdrawal, sadness, disappointment, and anxiety (Yunger, Carver, & Perry, 2004). Clearly, how children feel about themselves in relation to their gender group becomes vitally important in middle childhood and adolescence, and those who experience rejection because of their gender-atypical traits suffer profoundly.

Researchers and therapists are debating how best to help children who feel gender-atypical (Byne et al., 2012). Some favor providing therapy that reinforces traditional gender-role activities, to increase compatibility with same-sex peers (Zucker, 2006). Others oppose this approach on grounds that it is likely to heighten felt pressure to conform (which predicts maladjustment) and—for children who

An 8-year-old launches the rocket she made in her school's Young Astronaut Club. Whereas school-age boys usually stick to "masculine" pursuits, girls experiment with a wider range of options.

fail to change—may result in parental rejection. These experts advocate intervening with parents and peers to help them become more accepting of children's gender-atypical interests and behaviors (Bigler, 2007; Hill et al., 2010). **TAKE A MOMENT...** In view of what you have learned about the development of children's gender typing in Chapter 10 and this chapter, which approach do you think would be more successful, and why?

Ask Yourself

- **REVIEW** Return to page 389 in Chapter 10, and review the concept of *androgyny*. Which of the two sexes is more androygynous in middle childhood, and why?

- **CONNECT** Describe similarities in development of self-concept, attitudes toward racial and ethnic minorities, and gender-stereotyped beliefs in middle childhood.

- **APPLY** What changes in parent–child and teacher–child relationships are likely to help rejected children?

- **REFLECT** As a school-age child, did you have classmates you would classify as popular-antisocial? What were they like, and why do you think peers admired them?

13.8 How do parent–child communication and sibling relationships change in middle childhood?

13.9 How do children fare in lesbian and gay families and in never-married, single-parent families?

13.10 What factors influence children's adjustment to divorce and blended family arrangements?

13.11 How do maternal employment and life in dual-earner families affect children's development?

Family Influences

As children move into school, peer, and community contexts, the parent–child relationship changes. At the same time, children's well-being continues to depend on the quality of family interaction. In the following sections, we will see that contemporary diversity in family life—fewer births per family unit, more lesbian and gay parents who are open about their sexual orientation, more never-married parents, and continuing high rates of divorce, remarriage, and maternal employment—have reshaped the family system. **TAKE A MOMENT...** As you consider this array of family forms, note how children's well-being, in each instance, depends on the quality of family interaction, which is sustained by supportive ties to kin and community and by favorable public policies.

Parent–Child Relationships

In middle childhood, the amount of time children spend with parents declines dramatically. Children's growing independence means that parents must deal with new issues. "I've struggled with how many chores to assign, how much allowance to give, whether their friends are good influences, and what to do about problems at school," Rena remarked. "And then there's the challenge of keeping track of them when they're out—or even when they're home and I'm not there to see what's going on."

Despite these new concerns, child rearing becomes easier for parents who established an authoritative style during the early years. Reasoning is more effective with school-age children because of their greater capacity for logical thinking and their increased respect for parents' expert knowledge (Collins, Madsen, & Susman-Stillman, 2002). And children of parents who engage in joint decision making when possible are more likely to listen to parents' perspectives in situations where compliance is vital (Kuczynski & Lollis, 2002; Russell, Mize, & Bissaker, 2004).

As children demonstrate that they can manage daily activities and responsibilities, effective parents gradually shift control from adult to child. They do not let go entirely but, rather, engage in **coregulation,** a form of supervision in which they exercise general oversight while letting children take charge of moment-by-moment decision making (Maccoby, 1984). Coregulation grows out of a warm, cooperative relationship between parent and child based on give-and-take and mutual respect. Parents must guide and monitor from a distance and effectively communicate expectations when they are with their children. And children must inform parents of their whereabouts, activities, and problems so parents can intervene when necessary (Collins, Madsen, & Susman-Stillman, 2002). Coregulation supports and protects children while preparing them for adolescence, when they will make many important decisions themselves.

As at younger ages, mothers spend more time than fathers with school-age children and know more about children's everyday activities, although many fathers are highly involved (see page 271 in Chapter 7). Both parents, however, tend to devote more time to children of their own sex (Lam, McHale, & Crouter, 2012). In parents' separate activities with children, mothers are more concerned with caregiving and ensuring that children meet responsibilities for homework, after-school lessons, and chores. Fathers, especially those with sons, focus on achievement-related and recreational pursuits (Collins & Russell, 1991). But when both parents are present, fathers engage in as much caregiving as mothers.

Although children often press for greater independence, they also know how much they need their parents' support. In one study, fifth and sixth graders described parents as the most influential people in their lives, often turning to them for affection, advice, enhancement of self-worth, and assistance with everyday problems (Furman & Buhrmester, 1992). A strong sense of attachment security to at least one parent is positively related to school-age children's academic and social self-esteem and negatively related to depression (Diener et al., 2008; Kerns, Brumariu, & Seibert, 2011). And in a longitudinal survey of more than 13,000 nationally representative U.S. parents, those who were warm and involved, monitored their child's activities, and avoided coercive discipline were more likely to have academically and socially competent children. Using these authoritative strategies in middle childhood predicted reduced engagement in antisocial behavior when children reached adolescence (Amato & Fowler, 2002).

Siblings

In addition to parents and friends, siblings continue to be important sources of support. Yet sibling rivalry tends to increase in middle childhood. As children participate in a wider range of activities, parents often compare siblings' traits and accomplishments. The child who gets less parental affection, more disapproval, or fewer material resources is likely to be resentful and show poorer adjustment (Dunn, 2004; McHale, Updegraff, & Whiteman, 2012).

For same-sex siblings who are close in age, parental comparisons are more frequent, resulting in more quarreling and antagonism. This effect is particularly strong when parents are under stress as a result of financial worries, marital conflict, single parenthood, or child negativity (Jenkins, Rasbash, & O'Connor, 2003). Parents whose energies are drained become less careful about being fair. Perhaps because fathers, overall, spend less time with children than mothers, children react especially intensely when fathers prefer one child: Jealousy over attention from fathers predicts sibling conflict (Kolak & Volling, 2011).

To reduce rivalry, siblings often strive to be different from one another (McHale, Updegraff, & Whiteman, 2012). For example, two brothers we know deliberately selected different athletic pursuits and musical instruments. If the older one did especially well at an activity, the younger one did not want to try it. Parents can limit these effects by making an effort not to compare children, but some feedback about their competencies is inevitable. As siblings attempt to win recognition for their own uniqueness, they shape important aspects of each other's development.

Although conflict rises, many siblings continue to rely on each other for companionship, assistance, and emotional support (Siebert & Kerns, 2009). When researchers asked siblings about shared daily activities, children mentioned that older siblings often helped younger siblings with academic and peer challenges. And both offered each other help with family issues (Tucker, McHale, & Crouter, 2001). But for siblings to reap these benefits, parental encouragement of warm, considerate sibling ties is vital. Providing parents with training in mediation—how to get siblings to lay down ground rules, clarify their points of disagreement and common ground, and discuss possible solutions—increases siblings' awareness of each other's perspectives and reduces animosity (Smith & Ross, 2007).

An older sister helps her 6-year-old brother with homework. Although sibling rivalry tends to increase in middle childhood, siblings also provide each other with emotional support and help with difficult tasks

© SHEHZAD NOORANI/DRIK/MAJORITY WORLD/THE IMAGE WORKS

When siblings get along well, the older sibling's academic and social competence tends to "rub off on" the younger sibling, fostering more favorable achievement and peer relations (Brody & Murry, 2001; Lamarche et al., 2006). But destructive sibling conflict in middle childhood is associated with detrimental outcomes, including conflict-ridden peer relationships, anxiety, depressed mood, and later substance use and delinquency, even after other family-relationship factors are controlled (Kim et al., 2007; Ostrov, Crick, & Stauffacher, 2006).

Only Children

Although sibling relationships bring many benefits, they are not essential for normal development. Contrary to popular belief, only children are not spoiled, and, in some respects, they are advantaged. U.S. children growing up in one-child and multichild families do not differ in self-rated personality traits (Mottus, Indus, & Allik, 2008). And compared to children with siblings, only children are higher in self-esteem and achievement motivation, do better in school, and attain higher levels of education. One reason may be that only children have somewhat closer relationships with parents, who may exert more pressure for mastery and accomplishment and can invest more time in their child's educational experiences (Falbo, 2012). Furthermore, only children have just as many close, high-quality friends as children with siblings. However, they tend to be less well-accepted in the peer group, perhaps because they have not had opportunities to learn effective conflict-resolution strategies through sibling interaction (Kitzmann, Cohen, & Lockwood, 2002).

Favorable development also characterizes only children in China, where a one-child family policy was strictly enforced in densely populated urban areas for more than three decades to control population growth. (In 2013, China relaxed the policy, permitting couples to have two children if one parent is an only child.) Compared with agemates who have siblings, Chinese only children are advanced in cognitive development and academic achievement. They also feel more emotionally secure, perhaps because government disapproval promotes tension in families with more than one child (Falbo, 2012; Jiao, Ji, & Jing, 1996; Yang et al., 1995). Chinese mothers usually ensure that their children have regular contact with first cousins, who are considered siblings. Perhaps as a result, Chinese only children do not differ from agemates with siblings in social skills and peer acceptance (Hart, Newell, & Olsen, 2003).

Lesbian and Gay Families

According to recent estimates, about 20 to 35 percent of lesbian couples and 5 to 15 percent of gay couples are parents, most through previous heterosexual marriages, some through adoption, and a growing number through reproductive technologies (Brewster, Tillman, & Jokinen-Gordon, 2014; Gates, 2013). In the past, because of laws assuming that gay men and lesbians could not be adequate parents, those who divorced a heterosexual partner lost custody of their children. Today, the majority of U.S. states hold that sexual orientation is irrelevant to custody or adoption—a change likely spurred by the increasing acceptance of same-sex marriage, now legal in the majority of states. Custody and adoption by lesbian and gay parents are also legal in many other industrialized nations.

Most research on families headed by same-sex couples is limited to volunteer samples. Findings indicate that lesbian and gay parents are as committed to and effective at child rearing as heterosexual parents and sometimes more so (Bos, 2013). Also, whether born to or adopted by their parents or conceived through donor insemination, children in lesbian and gay families do not differ from the children of heterosexual parents in mental health, peer relations, gender-role behavior, or quality of life (Bos & Sandfort, 2010; Farr, Forssell, & Patterson, 2010; Goldberg, 2010; van Gelderen et al., 2012).

To surmount the potential bias associated with volunteer samples, some researchers take advantage of large, nationally representative

JENS KALAENE/PICTURE-ALLIANCE/DPA/AP IMAGES

Lesbian and gay parents are as committed to and as effective at child rearing as heterosexual parents. And their children do not differ in mental health, peer relations, gender-role behavior, or quality of life.

data banks to study lesbian and gay families. Findings confirm that children with same-sex and opposite-sex parents develop similarly, and that children's adjustment is linked to factors other than parental sexual orientation (Moore & Stambolis-Ruhstorfer, 2013). For example, close parent–child relationships predict better peer relations and a reduction in adolescent delinquency, whereas family transitions (such as parental divorce and remarriage) are related to academic difficulties, regardless of family form (Potter, 2012; Russell & Muraco, 2013).

The large majority of children of lesbian and gay parents identify as heterosexual (Patterson, 2013). But some evidence suggests that more adolescents from lesbian and gay families experiment for a time with partners of both sexes, perhaps as a result of being reared in families and communities especially tolerant of nonconformity and difference (Bos, van Balen, & van den Boom, 2004; Gartrell, Bos, & Goldberg, 2011). In support of this interpretation, a Dutch investigation found that 8- to 12-year-old children of lesbian parents felt slightly less parental pressure to conform to gender roles than did children of heterosexual parents. The two groups were similar in other aspects of gender identity (gender typicality and gender contentedness; see page 495). At the same time, the children of lesbian parents reported greater sexual questioning—less certainty about future heterosexual attractions and relationships, though the group difference was mild (see Figure 13.5) (Bos & Sandfort, 2010).

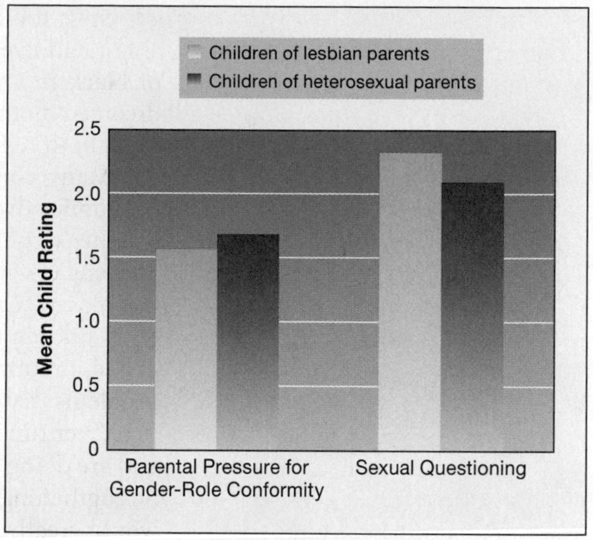

A major concern of lesbian and gay parents is that their children will be stigmatized by their parents' sexual orientation. Peer teasing and disapproval are problems for some children of same-sex parents, but close parent–child relationships, supportive school environments, and connections with other lesbian and gay families protect children from the negative effects of these experiences (Bos, 2013). Overall, children of lesbian and gay parents can be distinguished from other children mainly by issues related to living in discriminatory contexts.

FIGURE 13.5 **Reports of parental pressure for gender-role conformity and of sexual questioning by 8- to 12-year-olds of lesbian and heterosexual parents.** Compared with children of heterosexual parents, children of lesbian parents rated parental pressure slightly lower and sexual questioning higher. Neither group expressed strong parental pressure or sexual questioning (participants rated each on a 4-point scale, and mean ratings ranged from 1.5 to 2.3). (Based on Bos & Sandfort, 2010.)

Never-Married Single-Parent Families

Over the past several decades, births to unmarried mothers in industrialized nations have increased dramatically. Today, about 40 percent of U.S. births are to single mothers, more than double the percentage in 1980 (Martin et al., 2013). Whereas teenage parenthood has declined steadily since 1990, births to single adult women have increased, with a particularly sharp rise during the first decade of the twenty-first century (Curtin, Ventura, & Martinez, 2014).

A growing number of nonmarital births are planned and occur to cohabiting couples. But these relationships—common among young adults with low education—are often unstable (Cherlin, 2010; Gibson-Davis & Rackin, 2014). And despite this trend, more than 12 percent of U.S. children live with a single parent who has never married and does not have a partner. Of these parents, about 90 percent are mothers, 10 percent fathers (Curtin, Ventura, & Martinez, 2014; U.S. Census Bureau, 2014b).

Single motherhood is especially prevalent among African-American young women, who are considerably more likely than white women to give birth outside of marriage and less likely to live with the baby's father. As a result, more than half of births to black mothers in their twenties are to women without a partner, compared with about 14 percent of births to white women (Child Trends, 2014a; Hamilton et al., 2014). Job loss, persisting unemployment, and consequent inability of many black men to support a family have contributed to the number of African-American never-married, single-mother families.

Never-married African-American mothers often receive child-rearing support from extended family, especially their own mothers and sometimes male relatives (Anderson, 2012). Compared with their white counterparts, low-SES African-American women tend to marry later—within a decade after birth of the first child—but not necessarily to the child's biological father (Dixon, 2009; Wu, Bumpass, & Musick, 2001).

Still, for low-SES women, single parenthood generally increases financial hardship; about half live in poverty (Mather, 2010). Nearly 50 percent of white mothers and 60 percent of black mothers have a second child while unmarried. And they are far less likely than divorced mothers to receive paternal child support payments, although child support enforcement both reduces financial stress and increases father involvement (Huang, 2006).

Many children in single-mother homes display adjustment problems associated with economic adversity (Lamb, 2012). Furthermore, children of never-married mothers who lack a father's consistent warmth and involvement show less favorable cognitive development and engage in more antisocial behavior than children in low-SES, first-marriage families (Waldfogel, Craigie, & Brooks-Gunn, 2010). But marriage to the child's biological father benefits children only when the father is a reliable source of economic and emotional support. When a mother pairs up with an antisocial father, her child is at far greater risk for conduct problems than if she had reared the child alone (Jaffee et al., 2003).

Over time, most unmarried fathers—who usually have no more than a modest education and are doing poorly financially—spend less and less time with their children (Lerman, 2010). Strengthening social support, education, and employment opportunities for low-SES parents would greatly enhance the well-being of single mothers and their children.

Divorce

Children's interactions with parents and siblings are affected by other aspects of family life. Joey and Lizzie's relationship had been particularly negative only a few years before. Joey pushed, hit, taunted, and called Lizzie names. Although she tried to retaliate, Lizzie was no match for Joey's larger size. The arguments usually ended with Lizzie running in tears to her mother. Joey and Lizzie's fighting coincided with their parents' growing marital unhappiness. When Joey was 8 and Lizzie 5, their father, Drake, moved out.

Between 1960 and 1985, divorce rates in Western nations rose dramatically before stabilizing in most countries. The United States has experienced a decline in divorces over the past fifteen years, largely due to a rise in age at first marriage (couples marrying at older ages have a lower divorce rate). Nevertheless, the United States continues to have the highest divorce rate in the world (see Figure 13.6). Of the 45 percent of American marriages that end in divorce, half involve children. More than one-fourth of U.S. children live in divorced, single-parent households. Although most reside with their mothers, the percentage in father-headed households has increased steadily, to about 14 percent (U.S. Census Bureau, 2014b).

Children of divorce spend an average of five years in a single-parent home—almost a third of childhood. For many, divorce leads to new family relationships. About two-thirds of divorced parents marry again. Half their children eventually experience a third major change—the end of their parent's second marriage (Hetherington & Kelly, 2002).

These figures reveal that divorce is not a single event in the lives of parents and children. Instead, it is a transition that leads to a variety of new living arrangements, accompanied by changes in housing, income, and family roles and responsibilities. Although divorce is stressful for children and increases their risk of adjustment problems, most adjust favorably (Greene et al., 2012; Lamb, 2012). How well children fare depends on many factors: the custodial parent's psychological health, the child's characteristics, and social supports within the family and surrounding community.

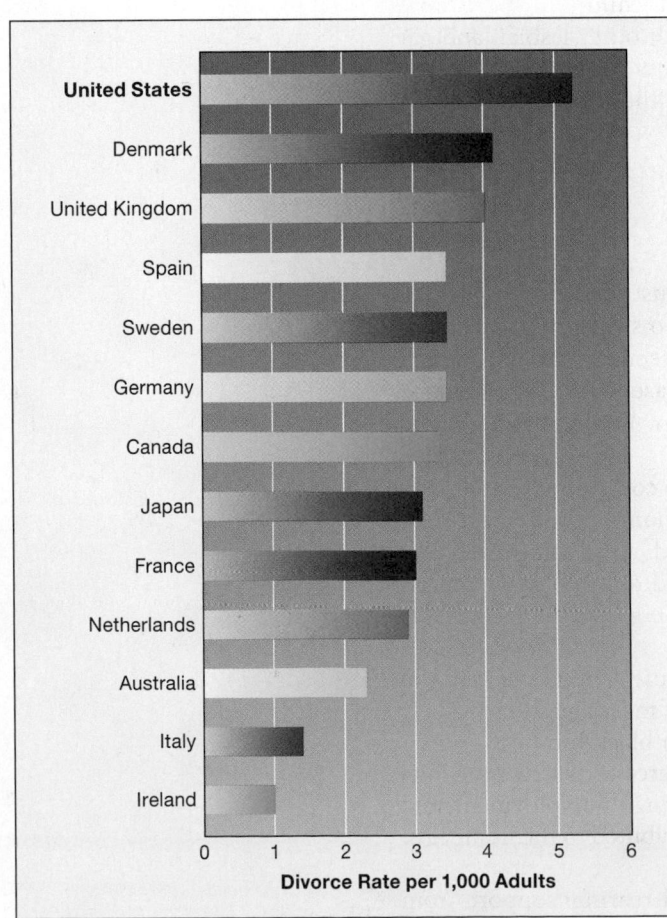

FIGURE 13.6   Divorce rates in 13 industrialized nations.
The U.S. divorce rate is the highest in the world, far exceeding divorce rates in other countries. (Based on U.S. Census Bureau, 2014b.)

IMMEDIATE CONSEQUENCES "Things were worst after Drake and I decided to separate," Rena reflected. "We fought over division of our belongings and custody of the children, and the kids suffered. Sobbing, Lizzie told me she was 'sorry she made Daddy go away.' Joey kicked and threw things at home and didn't do his work at school. In the midst of everything, I could hardly deal with their problems. We had to sell the house; I couldn't afford it alone. And I needed a better-paying job."

Family conflict often rises in newly divorced households as parents try to settle disputes over children and possessions. Once one parent moves out, additional events threaten supportive interactions between parents and children. Mother-headed households typically experience a sharp drop in income. In the United States, 28 percent of divorced mothers with young children live in poverty and many more are low-income, getting less than the full amount of child support from the absent father or none at all (U.S. Census Bureau, 2011). They often have to move to lower-cost housing, reducing supportive ties to neighbors and friends.

When parents divorce, young children often blame themselves and respond with both fear and anger. This father's soothing words help his daughter understand that she is not responsible for the marital breakup.

The transition from marriage to divorce typically leads to high maternal stress, depression, and anxiety and to a disorganized family life. Declines in well-being are greatest for mothers of young children (Williams & Dunne-Bryant, 2006). "Meals and bedtimes were at all hours, the house didn't get cleaned, and I stopped taking Joey and Lizzie on weekend outings," said Rena. As children react with distress and anger to their less secure home lives, discipline may become harsh and inconsistent. Over time, contact with noncustodial fathers—and the quality of the father–child relationship—often decreases, particularly when parental conflict is high (Troilo & Coleman, 2012). Fathers who see their children only occasionally are inclined to be permissive and indulgent, making the mother's task of managing the child even more difficult.

The more parents argue and fail to provide children with warmth, involvement, and consistent guidance, the poorer children's adjustment (Lamb, 2012). About 20 to 25 percent of children in divorced families display severe problems, compared with about 10 percent in nondivorced families (Greene et al., 2012; Lansford, 2009). At the same time, reactions vary with children's age, temperament, and sex.

Children's Age. Five-year-old Lizzie's fear that she had caused her father to leave home is not unusual. Preschool and young school-age children often blame themselves for a marital breakup and fear that both parents may abandon them (Lansford et al., 2006). Hence, they are more likely to display both anxious, fearful and angry, defiant reactions than older children and adolescents with the cognitive maturity to understand that they are not responsible for their parents' divorce.

Still, many school-age and adolescent youngsters also react strongly, experiencing depressed mood, declining in school performance, becoming unruly, and escaping into undesirable peer activities, such as running away, truancy, substance use, and early sexual activity, particularly when family conflict is high and parental supervision is low (Arkes, 2013; Kleinsorge & Covitz, 2012; Lansford et al., 2006). Some older children—especially the oldest child in the family—display more mature behavior, willingly taking on extra household tasks, care of younger siblings, and emotional support of a depressed, anxious mother. But if these demands are too great, these children may eventually become resentful, withdraw from the family, and engage in angry, acting-out behavior (Hetherington & Kelly, 2002).

Children's Temperament and Sex. Exposure to stressful life events and inadequate parenting magnifies the problems of temperamentally difficult children (see Chapter 7). In contrast, easy children are less often targets of parental anger and also cope more effectively with adversity.

These findings help explain sex differences in response to divorce. Girls sometimes respond as Lizzie did, with internalizing reactions such as crying, self-criticism, and withdrawal. More often, children of both sexes show demanding, attention-getting behavior. But in mother-custody families, boys are at slightly greater risk for serious adjustment problems (Amato, 2010). Recall from Chapter 10 that boys are more active and noncompliant—behaviors that increase with exposure to parental conflict and inconsistent discipline. Research reveals that long before the marital breakup, sons of divorcing couples display higher rates of impulsivity, defiance, and aggression—behaviors that may have been caused by their parents' marital problems while also contributing to them (Shaw, Winslow, & Flanagan, 1999; Strohschein, 2005). As a result, more boys enter the period of turmoil surrounding divorce with reduced capacity to cope with family stress.

Perhaps because their behavior is more unruly, boys of divorcing parents receive less emotional support from mothers, teachers, and peers. And as Joey's behavior toward Lizzie illustrates, the cycles of coercive interaction between distressed children and their divorced mothers soon spread to sibling relations (Sheehan et al., 2004). After divorce, children who are challenging to rear generally get worse.

LONG-TERM CONSEQUENCES Rena eventually found better-paying work and gained control over the daily operation of the household. Her own feelings of anger and rejection also declined. And after several meetings with a counselor, Rena and Drake realized the harmful impact of their quarreling on Joey and Lizzie. Drake visited regularly and handled Joey's disruptiveness with firmness and consistency. Soon Joey's school performance improved, his behavior problems subsided, and both children seemed calmer and happier.

Most children show improved adjustment by two years after divorce. Yet overall, children and adolescents of divorced parents continue to score slightly lower than children of continuously married parents in academic achievement, self-esteem, social competence, and emotional and behavioral adjustment (Lansford, 2009). Children with difficult temperaments are more likely to drop out of school, to be depressed, and to engage in antisocial behavior in adolescence. And divorce is linked to problems with adolescent sexuality and development of intimate ties. Young people who experienced parental divorce—especially more than once—display higher rates of early sexual activity and adolescent parenthood. Some experience other lasting difficulties—reduced educational attainment, troubled romantic relationships and marriages, divorce in adulthood, and unsatisfying parent–child relationships (Amato, 2006, 2010; Lansford, 2009). Thus, divorce can have consequences for subsequent generations.

The overriding factor in positive adjustment is effective parenting—how well the custodial parent handles stress and shields the child from family conflict, and the extent to which each parent uses authoritative child rearing (Lamb, 2012). Parent-training programs can help custodial parents support their children's development. For example, when researchers randomly assigned divorced mothers with children to parent training and control conditions, training improved mother–child relationships and increased children's coping skills, with effects persisting for six years (Velez et al., 2011).

Where the custodial parent is the mother, regular contact with fathers is also important. But only about one-third of children today experience at least weekly visits (Amato & Dorius, 2010). The more paternal contact and the warmer the relationship, the less children react with defiance and aggression (Dunn et al., 2004). For girls, a good father–child relationship protects against early sexual activity and unhappy romantic involvements. For boys, it seems to affect overall psychological well-being. In fact, some studies report that outcomes for sons are better when the father is the custodial parent (Clarke-Stewart & Hayward, 1996; McLanahan, 1999). Fathers' greater economic security and image of authority seem to help them engage in effective parenting with sons. And boys in father-custody families may benefit from greater involvement of both parents because noncustodial mothers participate more in their children's lives than noncustodial fathers.

Although divorce is painful for children, remaining in an intact but high-conflict family is much worse than making the transition to

Regular contact with both parents and effective coparenting—supporting each other in their child-rearing roles—greatly improve adjustment in children of divorce.

a low-conflict, single-parent household (Lamb, 2012; Strohschein, 2005). However, more parents today are divorcing because they are moderately (rather than extremely) dissatisfied with their relationship. Research suggests that children in these low-discord homes are especially puzzled and upset. Perhaps these youngsters' inability to understand the marital breakup and grief over the loss of a seemingly happy home life explain why the adjustment problems of children of divorce have intensified over time (Amato, 2001; Lansford, 2009).

Regardless of the extent of their friction, parents who set aside their disagreements and engage in effective coparenting (see page 69 in Chapter 2), supporting each other in their child-rearing roles, greatly improve their children's chances of growing up competent, stable, and happy (Lamb, 2012). Caring extended-family members, teachers, siblings, and friends also reduce the likelihood that divorce will result in long-term difficulties (Hetherington, 2003).

DIVORCE MEDIATION, JOINT CUSTODY, AND CHILD SUPPORT   Awareness that divorce is highly stressful for children and families has led to community-based services aimed at helping them through this difficult time. One such service is **divorce mediation,** a series of meetings between divorcing adults and a trained professional aimed at reducing family conflict, including legal battles over property division and child custody. Mediation increases out-of-court settlements, cooperation and involvement of both parents in child rearing, and parents' and children's feelings of well-being (Douglas, 2006; Emery, Sbarra, & Grover, 2005).

To further encourage parents to resolve their disputes, parent education programs are becoming common. During several sessions, professionals teach parents about the positive impact of constructive conflict resolution and of respectful, cooperative coparenting on children's well-being (Braver et al., 2005; Cookston et al., 2006; Wolchik et al., 2002). Because of the demonstrated impact of parent education on parental cooperation, courts in many U.S. states may require parents to attend a program.

Joint custody, which grants each parent an equal say in important decisions about the child's upbringing, is becoming increasingly common. Children usually reside with one parent and see the other on a fixed schedule, similar to the typical sole-custody situation. In other cases, parents share physical custody, and children move between homes and sometimes between schools and peer groups. These transitions can be especially hard on some children. Joint-custody parents usually report little conflict—fortunately so, since the success of the arrangement depends on effective coparenting (Bauserman, 2012). And their children, regardless of living arrangements, tend to be better-adjusted than children in sole-maternal-custody homes (Bauserman, 2002).

Finally, many single-parent families depend on child support from the absent parent to relieve financial strain. All U.S. states have procedures for withholding wages from parents who fail to make these payments. Although child support is usually not enough to lift a single-parent family out of poverty, it can ease its burdens substantially. Noncustodial fathers who have generous visitation schedules and see their children often are more likely to pay child support regularly (Amato & Sobolewski, 2004). And increases in contact with the child and in child support over time predict better coparenting relationships (Hofferth, Forry, & Peters, 2010). Applying What We Know on page 504 summarizes ways to help children adjust to their parents' divorce.

Blended Families

"If you get married to Wendell and Daddy gets married to Carol," Lizzie wondered aloud to Rena, "then I'll have two sisters and one more brother. And let's see, how many grandmothers and grandfathers? A lot!" exclaimed Lizzie.

About 60 percent of divorced parents remarry within a few years. Others *cohabit,* or share a sexual relationship and a residence with a partner outside of marriage. Parent, stepparent, and children form a new family structure called a **blended, or reconstituted, family.** For some children, this expanded family network is positive, bringing greater adult attention. But children in blended families usually have more adjustment problems—including internalizing and externalizing symptoms and poor school performance—than children in stable,

Applying What We Know

Helping Children Adjust to Their Parents' Divorce

SUGGESTION	EXPLANATION
Shield children from conflict.	Witnessing intense parental conflict is very damaging to children. If one parent insists on expressing hostility, children fare better if the other parent does not respond in kind.
Provide children with as much continuity, familiarity, and predictability as possible.	Children adjust better during the period surrounding divorce when their lives have some stability—for example, the same school, bedroom, babysitter, playmates, and daily schedule.
Explain the divorce and tell children what to expect.	Children may develop fears of abandonment if they are not prepared for their parents' separation. They should be told that their parents will not be living together anymore, which parent will be moving out, and when they will be able to see that parent. If possible, parents should explain the divorce together, providing a reason that each child can understand and assuring children that they are not to blame.
Emphasize the permanence of the divorce.	Fantasies of parents getting back together can prevent children from accepting the reality of their current life. Children should be told that the divorce is final and that they cannot change this fact.
Respond sympathetically to children's feelings.	Children need supportive, understanding responses to their feelings of sadness, fear, and anger. For children to adjust well, their painful emotions must be acknowledged, not denied or avoided.
Engage in authoritative parenting.	Parents who engage in authoritative parenting—providing affection and acceptance, reasonable demands for mature behavior, and consistent, rational discipline—greatly reduce their children's risk of maladjustment following divorce.
Promote continuing relationships with both parents.	When parents disentangle their lingering hostility toward the former spouse from the child's need for a continuing relationship with the other parent, children adjust well. Grandparents and other extended-family members can help by not taking sides.

Source: Teyber, 2001.

first-marriage families (Anderson & Greene, 2013; Pryor, 2014). Switching to stepparents' new rules and expectations can be stressful, and children often view steprelatives as intruders. How well they adapt is, again, related to the quality of family functioning (Hetherington & Kelly, 2002). This depends on which parent forms a new relationship, the child's age and sex, and the complexity of blended-family relationships. As we will see, older children and girls seem to have the hardest time.

MOTHER–STEPFATHER FAMILIES Because mothers generally retain custody of children, the most common form of blended family is a mother–stepfather arrangement. Boys tend to adjust quickly, welcoming a stepfather who is warm, who refrains from exerting his authority too quickly, and who offers relief from coercive cycles of mother–son interaction. Mothers' friction with sons also declines as a result of greater economic security, another adult to share household tasks, and an end to loneliness (Visher, Visher, & Pasley, 2003). Stepfathers who marry rather than cohabit are more involved in parenting, perhaps because men who choose to marry a mother with children are more interested in and skilled at child rearing (Hofferth & Anderson, 2003). Girls, however, often have difficulty with their custodial mother's remarriage. Stepfathers disrupt the close ties many girls have established with their mothers, and girls often react with sulky, resistant behavior (Pryor, 2014).

But age affects these findings. Older school-age children and adolescents of both sexes display more irresponsible, acting-out behavior than their peers not in stepfamilies (Hetherington & Stanley-Hagan, 2000; Robertson, 2008). If parents are warmer and more involved with their biological children than with their stepchildren, older children are more likely to notice and challenge unfair treatment. And adolescents often view the new stepparent as a threat to their freedom, especially

When stepparents move into their new roles gradually, first building warm relationships with stepchildren, they ease adjustment to life in a blended family.

© KAYTE DEIOMA/PHOTOEDIT

if they experienced little parental monitoring in the single-parent family. But when teenagers have affectionate, cooperative relationships with their mothers, many develop good relationships with stepfathers—a circumstance linked to more favorable adolescent well-being (King, 2009; Pryor, 2014).

FATHER–STEPMOTHER FAMILIES   Remarriage of noncustodial fathers often leads to reduced contact with their biological children, especially when fathers remarry quickly, before they have established postdivorce parent–child routines (Dunn, 2002; Juby et al., 2007). When fathers have custody, children typically react negatively to remarriage. One reason is that children living with fathers often start out with more problems. Perhaps the biological mother could no longer handle the difficult child (usually a boy), so the father and his new partner are faced with a youngster who has behavior problems. In other instances, the father has custody because of a very close relationship with the child, and his remarriage disrupts this bond (Buchanan, Maccoby, & Dornbusch, 1996).

Girls, especially, have a hard time getting along with their stepmothers, either because the remarriage threatens the girl's bond with her father or because she becomes entangled in loyalty conflicts between the two mother figures. But the longer children live in father–stepmother households, the closer they feel to their stepmothers and the more positive their interaction with them becomes (King, 2007). With time and patience, children of both genders benefit from the support of a second mother figure.

SUPPORT FOR BLENDED FAMILIES   Parenting education and couples counseling can help parents and children adapt to the complexities of blended families. Effective approaches encourage stepparents to move into their new roles gradually by first building a warm relationship with the child, which makes more active parenting possible (Pasley & Garneau, 2012; Pryor, 2014). Counselors can offer couples guidance in coparenting to limit loyalty conflicts and provide consistency in child rearing. And tempering parents' unrealistic expectations for children's rapid adjustment—by pointing out that building a unified blended family often takes years—makes it easier for families to endure the transition and succeed.

Unfortunately, the divorce rate for second marriages is even higher than for first marriages. Parents with antisocial tendencies and poor child-rearing skills are particularly likely to have several divorces and remarriages. The more marital transitions children experience, the greater their adjustment difficulties (Amato, 2010). These families usually require prolonged, intensive therapy.

Maternal Employment and Dual-Earner Families

Today, U.S. single and married mothers are in the labor market in nearly equal proportions, and more than three-fourths of those with school-age children are employed (U.S. Census Bureau, 2014b). In Chapter 7, we saw that the impact of maternal employment on early development depends on the quality of child care and the continuing parent–child relationship. The same is true in middle childhood.

MATERNAL EMPLOYMENT AND CHILD DEVELOPMENT   When mothers enjoy their work and remain committed to parenting, children show favorable adjustment—higher self-esteem, more positive family and peer relations, less gender-stereotyped beliefs, and better grades in school. Girls, especially, profit from the image of female competence. Regardless of SES, daughters of employed mothers perceive women's roles as involving more freedom of choice and satisfaction and are more achievement- and career-oriented (Hoffman, 2000).

Parenting practices contribute to these benefits. Employed mothers who value their parenting role are more likely to use authoritative child rearing and coregulation. Also, children in dual-earner households devote more daily hours to doing homework under parental guidance and participate more in household chores. And maternal employment often leads fathers—especially those who believe in the importance of the paternal role and who feel successful at parenting—to take on greater child-rearing responsibilities, with a small but

Employed mothers who enjoy their work while also valuing the parenting role tend to have children who show higher self-esteem, more positive family and peer relations, less gender-stereotyped beliefs, and better school performance.

increasing number staying home full-time (Gottfried, Gottfried, & Bathurst, 2002; Jacobs & Kelley, 2006). Paternal involvement is associated in childhood and adolescence with higher intelligence and achievement, more mature social behavior, and a flexible view of gender roles; and in adulthood with generally better mental health (Coltrane, 1996; Pleck & Masciadrelli, 2004).

But when employment places heavy demands on parents' schedules or is stressful for other reasons, children are at risk for ineffective parenting (Strazdins et al., 2013). Working many hours, working a nonstandard schedule (such as night or weekend shifts), or experiencing a negative workplace atmosphere is associated with lower quality parenting, fewer joint parent–child activities, poorer cognitive development, and increased behavior problems throughout childhood and adolescence (Li et al., 2014; Strazdins et al., 2006).

Negative consequences are magnified when low-SES mothers spend long days at low-paying, physically exhausting jobs—conditions linked to maternal depression and to harsh, inconsistent discipline (Raver, 2003). In contrast, part-time employment and flexible work schedules are associated with good child adjustment (Hill et al., 2006; Youn, Leon, & Lee, 2012). By preventing role overload, these arrangements help parents meet children's needs.

SUPPORT FOR EMPLOYED PARENTS AND THEIR FAMILIES In dual-earner families, the father's willingness to share responsibilities is crucial. If he helps little or not at all, the mother carries a double load, at home and at work, leading to fatigue, distress, and little time and energy for children. Fortunately, compared to three decades ago, today's U.S. fathers are far more involved in child care. But their increased participation has resulted in a growing number of fathers who also report role overload (Galinsky, Aumann, & Bond, 2009). In an Australian study, children (especially sons) of fathers who worked long hours were at higher risk for behavior problems (Johnson et al., 2013).

Employed parents need assistance from work settings and communities in their child-rearing roles. Part-time employment, flexible schedules, job sharing, on-site child care, and paid leave when children are ill help parents juggle the demands of work and child rearing (Butts, Casper, & Yang, 2013). Equal pay and employment opportunities for women are also important. Because these policies enhance financial status and morale, they improve the way parents feel and behave when they arrive home at the end of the working day.

CHILD CARE FOR SCHOOL-AGE CHILDREN High-quality child care is vital for parents' peace of mind and children's well-being, even during middle childhood. An estimated 4.5 million 5- to 14-year-olds in the United States are **self-care children,** who regularly look after themselves for some period of time during after-school hours (Laughlin, 2013). Self-care increases with age and also with SES, perhaps because of the greater safety of higher-income neighborhoods. But when lower-SES parents lack alternatives to self-care, their children spend more hours on their own (Casper & Smith, 2002).

The implications of self-care for development depend on children's maturity and the way they spend their time. Among younger school-age children, those who spend more hours alone have more adjustment difficulties (Vandell & Posner, 1999). As children become old enough to look after themselves, those who have a history of authoritative child rearing, are monitored by parental telephone calls, and have regular after-school chores appear responsible and well-adjusted. In contrast, children left to their own devices are more likely to bend to peer pressures and engage in antisocial behavior (Coley, Morris, & Hernandez, 2004; Vandell et al., 2006).

Before age 8 or 9, most children need supervision because they are not yet competent to handle emergencies (Galambos & Maggs, 1991). But

Attending high-quality after-school programs that include enrichment activities is linked to good school performance and emotional and social adjustment, particularly for low-SES children.

throughout middle childhood and early adolescence, attending after-school programs with well-trained and supportive staffs, generous adult–child ratios, and skill-building activities is linked to good school performance and emotional and social adjustment (Durlak, Weissberg, & Pachan, 2010; Kantaoka & Vandell, 2013). Low-SES children who participate in "after-care" programs offering academic assistance and enrichment activities (scouting, music and art lessons, clubs) show special benefits. They exceed their self-care counterparts in classroom work habits, academic achievement, and prosocial behavior and display fewer behavior problems (Lauer et al., 2006; Vandell et al., 2006).

Unfortunately, good after-care is in especially short supply in low-income neighborhoods. Ethnic minority children, immigrant children, and children from economically disadvantaged families are least likely to be enrolled (Greenberg, 2013). A special need exists for well-planned programs in poverty-stricken areas—ones that provide safe environments, warm relationships with adults, and enjoyable, goal-oriented activities.

LOOK and LISTEN

In your community, what school-based after-care programs are available, and how plentiful are they in low-income neighborhoods? If possible, visit a program, observing for supportive adult involvement, academic assistance, and enrichment activities.

Ask Yourself

- **REVIEW** Describe and explain changes in sibling relationships during middle childhood.

- **CONNECT** How does each level in Bronfenbrenner's ecological systems theory—microsystem, mesosystem, exosystem, and macrosystem—contribute to effects of parents' employment on children's development?

- **APPLY** Steve and Marissa are in the midst of an acrimonious divorce. Their 9-year-old son Dennis has become hostile and defiant. How can Steve and Marissa help Dennis adjust?

- **REFLECT** What after-school child-care arrangements did you experience in elementary school? How do you think they influenced your development?

Some Common Problems of Development

We have considered a variety of stressful experiences that place children at risk for future problems. Next, we address two more areas of concern: school-age children's fears and anxieties and the consequences of child sexual abuse. Finally, we sum up factors that help school-age children cope effectively with stress.

13.12 Cite common fears and anxieties in middle childhood.

13.13 Discuss factors related to child sexual abuse, its consequences for children's development, and its prevention and treatment.

13.14 Cite factors that foster resilience in middle childhood.

Fears and Anxieties

Although fears of the dark, thunder and lightning, and supernatural beings persist into middle childhood, older children's anxieties are also directed toward new concerns. As children begin to understand the realities of the wider world, the possibility of personal harm (being robbed, stabbed, or shot) and media events (war and disasters) often trouble them. Other common worries include academic failure, separation from parents, parents' health, physical injuries, the possibility of dying, and peer rejection (Muris & Field, 2011; Weems & Costa, 2005). Because children often mull over frightening thoughts at bedtime, nighttime fears actually increase between ages 7 and 9 (Muris et al., 2001).

As long as fears are not too intense, most children handle them constructively, using the more sophisticated emotional self-regulation strategies that develop in middle childhood. Consequently, overall number of fears declines with age, especially for girls, who express more fears than boys throughout childhood and adolescence (Gullone, 2000; Muris & Field, 2011). But about 5 percent of school-age children develop an intense, unmanageable fear, called a **phobia.** Children with inhibited temperaments are at high risk, displaying phobias five to six times as often as other children (Ollendick, King, & Muris, 2002).

Some children with phobias and other anxieties develop *school refusal*—severe apprehension about attending school, often accompanied by physical complaints such as dizziness, nausea, stomachaches, and vomiting (Wimmer, 2013). About one-third of children with school

Some children develop school refusal—severe apprehension about attending school. For many younger children, the real fear is maternal separation, often due to parental overprotection.

refusal are 5- to 7-year-olds for whom the real fear is maternal separation. Family therapy helps these children, whose difficulty can often be traced to parental overprotection (Elliott, 1999).

Most cases of school refusal appear around age 11 to 13, in children who usually find a particular aspect of school frightening—an overcritical teacher, a school bully, or too much parental pressure to achieve. A change in school environment or parenting practices may be needed. Firm insistence that the child return to school, along with training in how to manage anxiety and cope with difficult situations, is also helpful (Kearney, Spear, & Mihalas, 2014).

Severe childhood anxieties may also arise from harsh living conditions. In inner-city ghettos and in war-torn areas of the world, many children live in the midst of constant danger, chaos, and deprivation. As the Cultural Influences box on the following page reveals, they are at risk for long-term emotional distress and behavior problems. Finally, as we saw in our discussion of child abuse in Chapter 10, too often violence and other destructive acts become part of adult–child relationships. During middle childhood, child sexual abuse increases.

Child Sexual Abuse

Until recently, child sexual abuse was considered rare, and adults often dismissed children's claims of abuse. In the 1970s, efforts by professionals and media attention led to recognition of child sexual abuse as a serious and widespread problem. About 63,000 cases in the United States were confirmed in the most recently reported year (U.S. Department of Health and Human Services, 2013a). But this figure greatly underestimates the extent of sexual abuse, since most victims either delay disclosure for a long time or remain silent (Martin & Silverstone, 2013).

CHARACTERISTICS OF ABUSERS AND VICTIMS   Globally, an estimated 18 percent of girls and 8 percent of boys are sexually abused during childhood or adolescence (Stoltenborgh et al., 2011). Most cases are reported in middle childhood, but for some victims, abuse begins early in life and continues for many years (Collin-Vézina, Daigneault, & Hébert, 2013; Trickett, Noll, & Putnam, 2011).

In the vast majority of cases, the abuser is a male, often a parent or someone the parent knows well—a father, stepfather, live-in boyfriend, uncle, or older brother (Olafson, 2011). If the abuser is a nonrelative, the person is usually someone the child has come to know and trust, such as a teacher, caregiver, clergy member, or family friend (Sullivan et al., 2011). The Internet and mobile phones have become avenues through which some perpetrators commit sexual abuse—for example, by exposing children and adolescents to pornography and online sexual advances as a way of "grooming" them for sexual acts offline (Kloess, Beech, & Harkins, 2014). Sadly, a substantial number of abusers are themselves children or adolescents, many of whom are also victims of sexual abuse or other forms of maltreatment (Vizard, 2013).

Abusers make the child comply in a variety of distasteful ways, including deception, bribery, verbal intimidation, and physical force. You may wonder how any adult—especially a parent or close relative—could violate a child sexually. Many offenders deny their own responsibility, blaming the abuse on the willing participation of a seductive youngster. Yet children are not capable of making a deliberate, informed decision to enter into a sexual relationship! Even older children and adolescents are not free to say yes

Miami schoolchildren participate in a candlelight vigil sponsored by Amigos For Kids, a nonprofit organization dedicated to preventing child abuse and neglect. Adjustment problems resulting from child abuse, including sexual abuse, are often severe and persistent.

Cultural Influences

Impact of Ethnic and Political Violence on Children

Around the world, many children live with armed conflict, terrorism, and other acts of violence stemming from ethnic and political tensions. Some children participate in fighting, either because they are forced or because they want to please adults. Others are kidnapped, assaulted, and tortured. Child bystanders often come under direct fire and may be killed or physically maimed. And many watch in horror as family members, friends, and neighbors flee, are wounded, or die. In the past decade, wars have left 6 million children physically disabled, 20 million homeless, and more than 1 million separated from their parents (UNICEF, 2011).

When war and social crises are temporary, most children can be comforted and do not show long-term emotional difficulties. But chronic danger requires children to make substantial adjustments that can seriously impair their psychological functioning. Those who react with maladaptive thoughts about themselves ("I must be going crazy" or "I don't feel like myself anymore") and the world ("bad things always happen" or "other people cannot be trusted") are at heightened risk of experiencing posttraumatic stress symptoms—extreme fear and anxiety that persists, even after they are no longer in danger (Palosaari et al., 2013).

Many children of war lose their sense of safety, become desensitized to violence, are haunted by terrifying intrusive memories, display immature moral reasoning, and build a pessimistic view of the future. Anxiety and depression increase, as do aggression and antisocial behavior (Eisenberg & Silver, 2011; Klingman, 2006). These outcomes appear to be culturally universal, emerging among children in every war zone studied—from Bosnia, Rwanda, and the Sudan to the West Bank, Gaza, Iraq, Afghanistan, and Syria.

Parental affection and reassurance are the best protection against lasting problems. When parents offer security, discuss traumatic experiences with children sympathetically, and serve as role models of calm emotional strength, most children can withstand even extreme war-related violence (Gewirtz, Forgatch, & Wieling, 2008). Children who are separated from parents must rely on help from their communities. Orphans in Eritrea who were placed in residential settings where they could form close emotional ties with an adult showed less emotional stress five years later than orphans placed in impersonal settings (Wolff & Fesseha, 1999). Education and recreation programs are powerful safeguards, too, providing children with consistency in their lives along with teacher and peer supports.

With the September 11, 2001, terrorist attacks on the World Trade Center, some U.S. children experienced extreme wartime violence firsthand. Most children, however, learned about the attacks indirectly—from the media or from caregivers or peers. Both direct and indirect exposure triggered child and adolescent distress, but extended exposure—having a family member affected or repeatedly witnessing the attacks on TV—resulted in more severe symptoms (Agronick et al., 2007; Rosen & Cohen, 2010). During the following months, distress reactions declined, though more slowly for children with conflict-ridden parent–child relationships or preexisting adjustment problems.

Unlike many war-traumatized children in the developing world, students in New York's Public

At a refugee camp in Jordan, Syrian children wearing facemasks to protect against blowing sand play games with a caring adult. Most have witnessed violent atrocities and lost family members in Syria's civil war. Sensitive adult support can help them regain a sense of safety.

School 31, who watched from their classrooms as the towers collapsed, received immediate intervention—a "trauma curriculum" in which they expressed emotions through writing, drawing, and discussion and participated in experiences aimed at restoring trust and tolerance (Lagnado, 2001). Older children learned about the feelings of their Muslim classmates, the dire condition of children in Afghanistan, and ways to help victims as a means of overcoming a sense of helplessness.

When wartime drains families and communities of resources, international organizations must step in and help children. The Children and War Foundation, *www.childrenandwar.org*, offers programs and manuals that train local personnel in how to promote children's adaptive coping (Yule et al., 2013). Efforts to preserve children's physical, psychological, and educational well-being may be the best way to stop the transmission of violence to the next generation.

---

or no. Rather, the responsibility lies with abusers, who tend to have characteristics that predispose them toward sexual exploitation of children. They have great difficulty controlling their impulses and may suffer from psychological disorders, including alcohol and drug abuse. Often they pick out children who are unlikely to defend themselves or to be believed—those who are physically weak, emotionally deprived, socially isolated, or affected by disabilities (Collin-Vézina, Daigneault, & Hébert, 2013).

Reported cases of child sexual abuse are linked to poverty, marital instability, and resulting weakening of family ties. Children who live in homes with a constantly changing cast of characters—repeated marriages, separations, and new partners—are especially vulnerable. But children in economically advantaged, stable homes are also victims, although their abuse is more likely to escape detection (Murray, Nguyen, & Cohen, 2014).

No Secrets!

All secrets can be told.

We can tell a trusted adult about anything that makes us feel worried or unsafe.

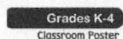

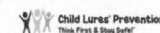

Teaching children to recognize inappropriate sexual advances and where to turn for help reduces the risk of abuse. Few schools include such programs, however, because any education about sex or sexual abuse is controversial.

CONSEQUENCES OF SEXUAL ABUSE The adjustment problems of child sexual abuse victims—including anxiety, depression, low self-esteem, mistrust of adults, and anger and hostility—are often severe and can persist for years after the abusive episodes. Younger children frequently react with sleep difficulties, loss of appetite, and generalized fearfulness. Adolescents may run away and show suicidal reactions, substance abuse, and delinquency. Longitudinal research suggests that rates of obesity and other physical and mental health problems are elevated among survivors of child sexual abuse. At all ages, persistent abuse accompanied by force, violence, and a close relationship to the perpetrator (incest) has a more severe impact. And sexual abuse, like physical abuse, is associated with central nervous system damage (Trickett, Noll, & Putnam, 2011; Wolfe, 2006).

Sexually abused children frequently display precocious sexual knowledge and behavior. In adolescence, abused young people often become promiscuous, increasing the risk of teenage pregnancy. As adults, they show elevated arrest rates for sex crimes (mostly against children) and prostitution. Furthermore, women who were sexually abused are likely to choose partners who abuse them and their children. As mothers, they often engage in irresponsible and coercive parenting, including child abuse and neglect (Collin-Vézina, Daigneault, & Hébert, 2013; Salter et al., 2003; Trickett, Noll, & Putnam, 2011). In these ways, the harmful impact of sexual abuse is transmitted to the next generation.

PREVENTION AND TREATMENT Treating child sexual abuse is difficult. The reactions of family members—anxiety about harm to the child, anger toward the abuser, and sometimes hostility toward the victim for telling—can increase children's distress. Because sexual abuse typically appears in the midst of other serious family problems, specialized trauma-focused therapy with both children and parents is usually needed (Olafson, 2011). The best way to reduce the suffering of victims is to prevent sexual abuse from continuing. Today, courts are prosecuting abusers more vigorously and taking children's testimony more seriously (see the Social Issues: Health box on the following page).

Educational programs that teach children to recognize inappropriate sexual advances and whom to turn to for help reduce the risk of abuse (Finkelhor, 2009). Yet because of controversies over educating children about sexual abuse, few schools offer these interventions. New Zealand is the only country with a national, school-based prevention program targeting sexual abuse. In Keeping Ourselves Safe, children and adolescents learn that abusers are rarely strangers. Parent involvement ensures that home and school collaborate in teaching children self-protection skills. Evaluations reveal that virtually all New Zealand parents and children support the program and that it has helped many children avoid or report abuse (Sanders, 2006).

Fostering Resilience in Middle Childhood

Throughout middle childhood—and other periods of development—children are confronted with challenging and sometimes threatening situations that require them to cope with psychological stress. In this trio of chapters, we have considered such topics as chronic illness, learning disabilities, achievement expectations, divorce, harsh living conditions and wartime trauma, and sexual abuse. Each taxes children's coping resources, creating serious risks for development.

Nevertheless, only a modest relationship exists between stressful life experiences and psychological disturbance in childhood (Masten, 2014). In our discussion in Chapter 4 of the long-term consequences of birth complications, we noted that some children manage to overcome the combined effects of birth trauma, poverty, and a troubled family life. The same is true for school difficulties, family transitions, the experience of war, and child maltreatment.

Social Issues: Health

Children's Eyewitness Testimony

Increasingly, children are being called on to testify in court cases involving child abuse and neglect, child custody, and other matters. The experience can be difficult and traumatic, requiring children to report on highly stressful events and sometimes to speak against a parent or other relative to whom they feel loyal. In some family disputes, they may fear punishment for telling the truth. In addition, child witnesses are faced with an unfamiliar situation—at the very least an interview in the judge's chambers and at most an open courtroom with judge, jury, spectators, and the possibility of unsympathetic cross-examination. Not surprisingly, these conditions can compromise the accuracy of children's recall.

Age Differences

Until recently, children younger than age 5 were rarely asked to testify, and not until age 10 were they assumed fully competent to do so. As a result of societal reactions to rising rates of child abuse and the difficulty of prosecuting perpetrators, legal requirements for child testimony have been relaxed in the United States (Brainerd & Reyna, 2012; Klemfuss & Ceci, 2012). Children as young as age 3 frequently serve as witnesses.

Compared with preschoolers, school-age children are better at giving accurate, detailed narrative accounts of past experiences and correctly inferring others' motives and intentions. Older children are also generally more resistant to misleading questions that attorneys may ask when probing for more information or, in cross-examination, trying to influence the child's response (Zajac, O'Neill, & Hayne, 2012). Inhibition (ability to suppress impulses and focus on a competing goal), which improves from early to middle childhood, predicts children's resistance to suggestion (Melinder, Endestad, & Magnussen, 2006).

Nevertheless, when properly questioned, even 3-year-olds can recall recent events accurately (Peterson & Rideout, 1998). And in the face of biased interviewing, adolescents and adults often form elaborate, false memories of events (Ceci et al., 2007).

Suggestibility

Court testimony often involves repeated questioning—a procedure that, by itself, negatively affects children's response consistency and accuracy (Krähenbühl, Blades, & Eiser, 2009). When adults lead witnesses by suggesting incorrect "facts," interrupt their denials, reinforce them for giving desired answers, ask complex and confusing questions, or use a confrontational style, they further increase the likelihood of incorrect reporting by children and adolescents alike (Sparling et al., 2011; Zajac, O'Neill, & Hayne, 2012).

In one study, 4- to 8-year-olds were asked to recall details about a visitor who had come to their classroom a week earlier. Half the children received a low-pressure interview containing leading questions that implied abuse ("He took your clothes off, didn't he?"). The other half received a high-pressure interview in which an adult told the child that her friends had said "yes" to the leading questions, praised the child for agreeing ("You're doing great"), and, if the child did not agree, repeated the question. Children were far more likely to give false information—even fabricating quite fantastic events—in the high-pressure condition (Finnilä et al., 2003).

By the time children appear in court, weeks, months, or even years have passed since the target events. When a long delay is combined with biased interviewing and with stereotyping of the accused ("He's in jail because he's been bad"), children can easily be misled into giving false information (Quas et al., 2007). The more distinctive and personally relevant an event is, the more likely children are to recall it accurately over time. For example, a year later, even when exposed to misleading information, children correctly reported details of an injury that required emergency room treatment (Peterson, Parsons, & Dean, 2004). Children's memories of these experiences remain remarkably intact for as long as five years (Peterson, 2012).

In many sexual abuse cases, anatomically correct dolls or body diagrams are used to prompt children's recall. Although these methods may help older children provide more detail, they increase the suggestibility of preschoolers, who report physical and sexual contact that never happened (Poole & Bruck, 2012). Props are confusing to very young witnesses because they require dual representation of the doll or drawing as both an object and a symbol—understandings that are still emerging during the preschool years (see Chapter 9, page 314).

School-age eyewitnesses are better able than preschoolers to give accurate, detailed descriptions and correctly infer others' motives and intentions. This juvenile court judge can promote accurate recall by using a warm, supportive tone and avoiding leading questions.

Interventions

Adults must prepare child witnesses so they understand the courtroom process and know what to expect. In some places, "court schools" take children through the setting and give them an opportunity to role-play court activities. Practice interviews—in which children learn to provide the most accurate, detailed information possible and to admit not knowing rather than agreeing or guessing—are helpful (Zajac, O'Neill & Hayne, 2012).

At the same time, legal professionals must use interviewing procedures that increase children's accurate reporting. Unbiased, open-ended questions that prompt children to disclose details—"Tell me what happened" or "You said there was a man; tell me about the man"—reduce suggestibility (Steele, 2012). Also, a warm, supportive interview tone fosters accurate recall, perhaps by easing children's anxiety so they feel freer to counter an interviewer's false suggestions (Ceci, Bruck, & Battin, 2000).

If children are likely to experience emotional trauma or later punishment (as in a family dispute), courtroom procedures are sometimes adapted to protect them. For example, children can testify over closed-circuit TV so they do not have to face an abuser. When it is not wise for a child to participate directly, impartial expert witnesses can provide testimony that reports on the child's psychological condition and includes important elements of the child's story.

Applying What We Know

Resources That Foster Resilience in Middle Childhood

TYPE OF RESOURCE	DESCRIPTION
Personal	• Easygoing, sociable temperament • Above-average intelligence • Favorable self-esteem • Persistence in the face of challenge and pleasure in mastery • Good emotional self-regulation and flexible coping strategies
Family	• Warm, trusting relationship with at least one parent • Authoritative child-rearing style • Positive discipline, avoidance of coercive tactics • Warm, supportive sibling relationships
School	• Teachers who are warm, helpful, and stimulating; who encourage students to collaborate; and who emphasize effort and self-improvement • Lessons in tolerance and respect and codes against bullying, which promote positive peer relationships and gratifying friendships • Extracurricular activities, including sports and social service pursuits, that strengthen physical, cognitive, and social skills
Community	• High-quality after-school programs that protect children's safety and offer stimulating, skill-building activities • An adult—such as an extended-family member, teacher, or neighbor—who provides warmth and social support and is a positive coping model • Stability of neighborhood residents and services—safe outdoor play areas, community centers, and religious organizations—that relieve parental stress and encourage families and neighbors to share leisure time • Youth groups—scouting, clubs, religious youth groups, and other organized activities—that promote positive peer relationships and prosocial behavior

Note: One or a few resources may be sufficient to foster resilience, since each resource strengthens others.
Sources: Commission on Children at Risk, 2008; Wright & Masten, 2005.

Refer to Applying What We Know above for an overview of factors that promote *resilience*—the capacity to overcome adversity—during middle childhood.

Often just one or a few of these ingredients account for why one child is "stress-resilient" and another is not. Usually, however, personal and environmental factors are interconnected: Each resource favoring resilience strengthens others in a *developmental cascade* (Masten & Cicchetti, 2010). For example, safe, stable neighborhoods with family-friendly community services reduce parents' daily hassles and stress, thereby promoting good parenting (Chen, Howard, & Brooks-Gunn, 2011). Unfavorable home and neighborhood experiences can also cascade, increasing the chances that children will act in ways that expose them to further hardship. When negative conditions pile up, such as marital discord, poverty, crowded living conditions, neighborhood violence, and abuse and neglect, the rate of maladjustment multiplies (Wright & Masten, 2005).

Of great concern are children's violent acts. Violence committed in schools and communities by U.S. children and adolescents with troubled lives has at times reached the level of atrocities—maimings and murders of adults and peers. Because children spend a great deal of time in school, the quality of their relationships with teachers and classmates strongly influences their development, academically and socially (Elias, Parker, & Rosenblatt, 2005; Hughes, 2011).

Several highly effective school-based *social and emotional learning programs* reduce violence (including bullying and gang involvement) and other antisocial acts and increase academic motivation by fostering social competence and supportive relationships (CASEL, 2013; Durlak et al., 2011). Among these is the 4Rs (Reading, Writing, Respect, and Resolution) Program, which provides elementary school students with weekly lessons in emotional and social understanding and skills (Aber et al., 2011). Topics include handling anger, developing empathy, being assertive, resolving social conflicts, cooperating, appreciating diversity, and identifying and standing up against prejudice and bullying. The program is integrated with language arts: High-quality children's literature, selected for relevance to program themes, complements each lesson. Discussion, writing, and role play of the stories deepen students' understanding of conflict, emotions, relationships, and community.

To evaluate the effectiveness of 4Rs, researchers randomly assigned 18 elementary schools in New York City to the program or a control condition. Teachers in 4Rs schools used more supportive instructional techniques—encouraging discussion, making concepts relevant to students' everyday lives, and providing feedback that acknowledges effort. And children who received 4Rs instruction became less depressed and less likely to misinterpret others' acts as hostile. After a second year of intervention, the benefits spread to other related outcomes: Teachers rated 4Rs children as less aggressive, more attentive, and more socially competent compared to children in control schools (Aber et al., 2011). In unsafe neighborhoods, 4Rs transforms schools into places of safety and mutual respect, where learning can occur.

Programs like 4Rs recognize that resilience is not a preexisting attribute but rather a capacity that *develops,* enabling children to use internal and external resources to cope with adversity (Dessel, 2010). Throughout our discussion, we have seen how families, schools, communities, and society as a whole can enhance or undermine the school-age child's developing sense of competence. As the following three chapters will reveal, young people whose childhood experiences helped them learn to control impulses, overcome obstacles, strive for self-direction, and respond considerately and sympathetically to others meet the challenges of the next period—adolescence—quite well.

Fifth graders in a social and emotional learning program role play stories emphasizing honesty, empathy, and resolving social conflicts. In the skit shown here, the two students on the left, after being caught shoplifting, are questioned by the store manager.

Ask Yourself

- **REVIEW** When children must testify in court cases, what factors increase the chances of accurate reporting?

- **CONNECT** Explain how results of the 4Rs program illustrate the concept of developmental cascade.

- **APPLY** Claire told her 6-year-old daughter to be very careful never to talk to or take candy from strangers. Why is Claire's warning unlikely to protect her daughter from sexual abuse?

- **REFLECT** Describe a challenging time during your childhood. What aspects of the experience increased stress? What resources helped you cope with adversity?

Summary

Erikson's Theory: Industry versus Inferiority (p. 473)

13.1 What personality changes take place during Erikson's stage of industry versus inferiority?

- According to Erikson, children who successfully resolve the psychological conflict of **industry versus inferiority** develop a sense of competence at useful skills and tasks, learn the value of division of labor, and develop a sense of moral commitment and responsibility.

Self-Understanding (p. 474)

13.2 Describe school-age children's self-concept and self-esteem, and discuss factors that affect their achievement-related attributions.

- During middle childhood, children's self-concepts include personality traits (both positive and negative), competencies, and **social comparisons.** Self-esteem differentiates further and becomes hierarchically organized and more realistic as children receive more competence-related feedback and compare their performance to that of others.

- Cultural forces and child-rearing practices affect self-esteem. Gender stereotypes contribute to sex differences in physical, academic, and social self-esteem. Warm extended families and strong ethnic pride may contribute to the slight self-esteem advantage of African-American over Caucasian children. The authoritative child-rearing style is linked to favorable self-esteem.

- Children with **mastery-oriented attributions** hold an incremental view of ability, believing that it can be improved by trying hard, and attribute failure to insufficient effort. In contrast, children with **learned helplessness** attribute success to external factors, such as luck, and hold a fixed view of ability. They believe their failures are due to low ability, which cannot be modified.

● Supportive parents and teachers and cultural valuing of effort increase the likelihood of a mastery-oriented approach. By teaching children that abilities are fixed, **person praise** promotes learned helplessness. In contrast, **process praise** by focusing on behavior and effort, fosters a mastery orientation. **Attribution retraining** encourages learned-helpless children to believe they can overcome failure by exerting more effort.

Emotional Development (p. 481)

13.3 Cite changes in the expression and understanding of emotion in middle childhood.

● Self-conscious emotions of pride and guilt become clearly governed by personal responsibility. Intense shame can shatter self-esteem.

● School-age children recognize that people can experience more than one emotion at a time and that emotional expressions may not reflect people's true feelings. They also reconcile contradictory cues in interpreting another's feelings. Empathy increases and includes sensitivity to people's immediate distress and their general life condition.

● By age 10, most children can shift adaptively between **problem-centered** and **emotion-centered coping** in regulating emotion. Emotionally well-regulated children develop a sense of emotional self-efficacy and are optimistic, prosocial, and well-liked by peers.

AP IMAGES/THE EVANSVILLE COURIER & PRESS, JASON CLARK

Moral Development (p. 483)

13.4 Describe changes in moral understanding during middle childhood, including children's understanding of diversity and inequality.

● During middle childhood, children construct a flexible appreciation of moral rules. They clarify and link moral imperatives and social conventions, considering the purpose of the rule; people's intentions, knowledge, and beliefs; and the context of their actions. They also better understand individual rights. When moral and personal concerns conflict, older school-age children typically emphasize fairness. Children in diverse cultures use similar criteria to reason about moral, social-conventional, and personal concerns.

● Children pick up prevailing societal attitudes about race and ethnicity. With age, school-age children understand that people who look different need not think, feel, or act differently and that prejudice violates widely held social standards. Consequently, explicit prejudice typically declines, although prejudice often continues to operate implicitly. Children most likely to hold racial and ethnic biases are those who believe that personality traits are fixed, who have overly high self-esteem, and who live among adults who highlight group differences. Long-term, intergroup contact may be most effective at reducing prejudice.

Peer Relations (p. 487)

13.5 How do peer sociability and friendship change in middle childhood?

● Peer interaction becomes more prosocial, and physical aggression declines. By the end of middle childhood, children organize themselves into **peer groups.**

● Friendships develop into mutual relationships based on trust and become more selective. Children tend to choose friends who resemble themselves in age, sex, race, ethnicity, SES, personality, popularity, academic achievement, and prosocial behavior. Girls form closer, more exclusive friendships than boys.

13.6 Describe major categories of peer acceptance and ways to help rejected children.

● On measures of **peer acceptance, popular children** are well-liked by many agemates; **rejected children** are mostly disliked; **controversial children** are both liked and disliked; **neglected children** arouse little reaction, positive or negative, but are usually well-adjusted; and **average children** receive average numbers of positive and negative reactions.

● **Popular-prosocial children** are academically and socially competent, while **popular-antisocial children** are aggressive but admired, perhaps for their athletic ability and sophisticated but devious social skills. Rejected children also divide into two subtypes: **rejected-aggressive children,** who are especially high in conflict and hostility, and **rejected-withdrawn children,** who are passive, socially awkward, and frequent targets of **peer victimization.**

● Coaching in social skills, academic tutoring, and training in perspective taking and social problem solving have been used to help rejected youngsters. To produce lasting change, intervening in parent–child interaction is often necessary.

Gender Typing (p. 493)

13.7 What changes in gender-stereotyped beliefs and gender identity occur during middle childhood?

● School-age children extend their awareness of gender stereotypes to personality traits and academic subjects. But they also develop **gender-stereotype flexibility**—a more open-minded view of what males and females can do.

● Boys strengthen their identification with the masculine role, whereas girls feel free to experiment with "cross-gender" activities. Gender identity includes self-evaluations of gender typicality, contentedness, and felt pressure to conform to gender roles—each of which affects adjustment.

Family Influences (p. 496)

13.8 How do parent–child communication and sibling relationships change in middle childhood?

● Despite declines in time spent with parents, **coregulation** allows parents to exercise general oversight of children, who increasingly make their own decisions.

● Sibling rivalry tends to increase with greater participation in diverse activities and more frequent parental comparisons. Siblings often try to reduce this rivalry by striving to be different from one another. Only children do not differ from children with siblings in self-rated personality traits and are higher in self-esteem, school performance, and educational attainment.

13.9 How do children fare in lesbian and gay families and in never-married, single-parent families?

● Lesbian and gay parents are as committed to and effective at child rearing as heterosexual parents. Their children do not differ from the children of heterosexual parents in adjustment and gender identity, except in feeling slightly less parental pressure to conform to gender roles.

© SHEHZAD NOORANI/DRIK/ MAJORITY WORLD/THE IMAGE WORKS

● Never-married parenthood generally increases financial hardship for low-SES mothers and their children. Children of never-married mothers who lack a father's warmth and involvement achieve less well in school and engage in more antisocial behavior than children in low-SES, first-marriage families.

13.10 What factors influence children's adjustment to divorce and blended family arrangements?

- Although marital breakup is stressful for children, individual differences exist based on parental psychological health, child characteristics (age, temperament, and sex), and social supports. Children with difficult temperaments are at greater risk for adjustment problems. In both sexes, divorce is linked to early sexual activity, adolescent parenthood, and long-term relationship difficulties.

- The overriding factor in positive adjustment following divorce is effective parenting. Positive father–child relationships have protective value, as do caring extended family members, teachers, siblings, and friends.

- **Divorce mediation** and parent education programs can foster parental conflict resolution and cooperation in the period surrounding divorce. The success of joint custody depends on effective coparenting.

- When divorced parents enter new relationships and form **blended, or reconstituted, families**, girls, older children, and children in father–stepmother families tend to have more adjustment problems. Stepparents can help children adjust by moving into their roles gradually.

13.11 How do maternal employment and life in dual-earner families affect children's development?

- When employed mothers enjoy their work and remain committed to parenting, their children benefit from higher self-esteem, more positive family and peer relations, less gender-stereotyped beliefs, and better school grades. In dual-earner families, the father's willingness to share household responsibilities is linked to many positive child outcomes. Workplace supports help parents meet the demands of work and child rearing.

- Authoritative child rearing, parental monitoring, and regular after-school chores lead **self-care children** to be responsible and well-adjusted. Good "after-care" programs also aid school performance and emotional and social adjustment, with low-SES children showing special benefits.

Some Common Problems of Development (p. 507)

13.12 Cite common fears and anxieties in middle childhood.

- School-age children's fears are directed toward new concerns, including personal harm, media events, academic failure, parents' health, and peer rejection. Children with inhibited temperaments are at high risk for developing **phobias.** Harsh living conditions, presenting constant danger, chaos, and deprivation, can result in long-term emotional stress and behavior problems.

13.13 Discuss factors related to child sexual abuse, its consequences for children's development, and its prevention and treatment.

- Child sexual abuse is generally committed by male family members, more often against girls than against boys. Abusers have characteristics that predispose them toward sexual exploitation of children. Reported cases are strongly associated with poverty and marital instability.

- Abused children often have severe, persisting adjustment problems. Treatment typically requires specialized trauma-focused therapy with both children and parents. Educational programs that teach children to recognize inappropriate sexual advances and whom to turn to for help reduce the risk of sexual abuse.

13.14 Cite factors that foster resilience in middle childhood.

- Only a modest relationship exists between stressful life experiences and psychological disturbance in childhood. Children's personal characteristics, a warm family life that includes authoritative parenting, and school and community resources predict resilience. Each resource favoring resilience usually strengthens others, in a developmental cascade.

Important Terms and Concepts

attribution retraining (p. 480)

average children (p. 490)

blended, or reconstituted, family (p. 503)

controversial children (p. 490)

coregulation (p. 496)

divorce mediation (p. 503)

emotion-centered coping (p. 482)

gender-stereotype flexibility (p. 494)

industry versus inferiority (p. 473)

learned helplessness (p. 478)

mastery-oriented attributions (p. 478)

neglected children (p. 490)

peer acceptance (p. 490)

peer groups (p. 488)

peer victimization (p. 492)

person praise (p. 479)

phobia (p. 507)

popular children (p. 490)

popular-antisocial children (p. 490)

popular-prosocial children (p. 490)

problem-centered coping (p. 482)

process praise (p. 479)

rejected children (p. 490)

rejected-aggressive children (p. 491)

rejected-withdrawn children (p. 491)

self-care children (p. 506)

social comparisons (p. 474)

MILESTONES
Development in Middle Childhood

6–8 YEARS

PHYSICAL

- Slow gains in height and weight continue until adolescent growth spurt. (405)
- Permanent teeth gradually replace primary teeth. (407)
- Legibility of writing increases. (421)
- Drawings become more organized and detailed and include some depth cues. (421)
- Games with rules and rough-and-tumble play become common. (422, 424)

COGNITIVE

- Thought becomes more logical, as shown by the ability to pass Piagetian conservation, class inclusion, and seriation problems. (429–430)

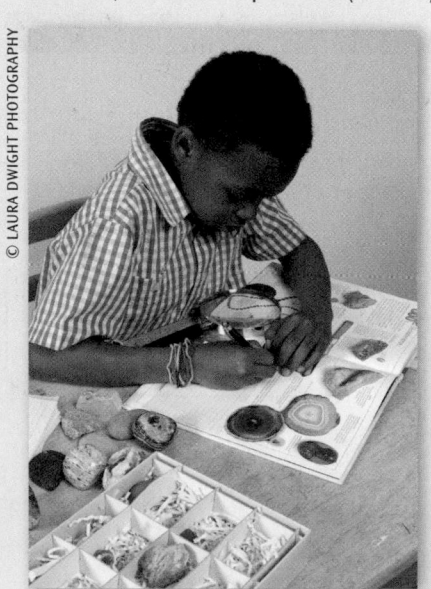

- Attention becomes more selective, flexible, and planful. (436–437)
- Uses memory strategies of rehearsal and then organization. (437)
- Awareness of mental activities, of the impact of psychological factors (such as applying memory strategies) on task performance, and of sources of knowledge (including mental inferences) expands. (440–441)
- Views situations from at least two perspectives, as indicated by appreciation of second-order false beliefs. (441)
- Uses informal knowledge of number concepts and counting to master more complex mathematical skills. (444–445)

LANGUAGE

- Vocabulary increases rapidly as children learn about 20 new words each day. (455)
- Word definitions are concrete, referring to functions and appearance. (455)
- Transitions from "learning to read" to "reading to learn." (444)

- Metalinguistic awareness improves. (455, 458)
- Communicates with increasing clarity, adapting to listeners' needs. (456)
- Grasps increasingly subtle, indirect expressions of language meaning, including irony and sarcasm. (456)
- Narratives increase in organization, detail, and expressiveness. (457)

EMOTIONAL/SOCIAL

- Self-concept includes personality traits and social comparisons. (474)
- Self-esteem differentiates, is hierarchically organized, and becomes more realistic. (475–476)
- Self-conscious emotions of pride and guilt are governed by personal responsibility. (481)
- Recognizes that people can experience more than one emotion at a time and that their expressions may not reflect their true feelings. (482)

- Empathy increases. (482)
- Reconciles contradictory facial and situational cues in understanding another's feelings. (482)
- Becomes more independent and trustworthy. (483)
- Constructs a flexible appreciation of moral rules, taking prosocial and antisocial intentions and the context of behavior into account. (484)
- Resolves conflicts more effectively; sharing, helping, and other prosocial acts increase. (488)
- Physical aggression declines; verbal and relational aggression continue. (487–488)

Note: Numbers in parentheses indicate the page or pages on which each milestone is discussed.

9–11 YEARS

PHYSICAL

- Adolescent growth spurt begins two years earlier in girls than in boys. (405)
- Executes gross motor skills of running, jumping, throwing, catching, kicking, batting, and dribbling more quickly and with better coordination. (420–421)

- Steady gains in attention and reaction time contribute to improved motor performance. (420–421)
- Representation of depth in drawings expands. (421)
- Dominance hierarchies become more stable, especially among boys. (424)

COGNITIVE

- Continues to master Piagetian tasks in a step-by-step fashion. (432)
- Spatial reasoning improves, as illustrated by more sophisticated map-reading and map-drawing skills, including an overall view of space and understanding of scale. (430–431)

- Selective attention and planning improve further. (436–437)
- Uses memory strategies of rehearsal and organization more effectively. (437)
- Applies several memory strategies simultaneously; begins to use elaboration. (437–438)
- Long-term knowledge base grows larger and becomes better organized. (438)
- Awareness of mental activities, including effective memory strategies and reasoning, becomes more elaborate and refined. (442)
- Cognitive self-regulation improves. (442)

LANGUAGE

- Thinks about and uses words more precisely; word definitions emphasize synonyms and categorical relations. (455)
- By the end of elementary school, has acquired a vocabulary of about 40,000 words. (455)
- Continues to master complex grammatical constructions, such as passive voice and infinitive phrases. (456)
- Continues to improve in understanding of subtle, indirect expressions of language meaning. (456)

- Narratives lengthen and increase in organization, detail, and expressiveness. (457)

EMOTIONAL/SOCIAL

- Continues to refine self-concept to include competencies, positive and negative personality traits, and more sophisticated social comparisons. (474)
- Distinguishes ability, effort, and luck in attributions for success and failure. (478–479)
- Empathic responding extends to general life conditions. (482)

- Shifts adaptively between problem-centered and emotion-centered strategies in regulating emotion. (482)
- Clarifies and links moral imperatives and social conventions. (484)
- Convictions about matters of personal choice strengthen, and understanding of individual rights expands. (484–485)
- Friendships become more selective and are based on mutual trust. (489)
- Peer groups emerge. (488)

- Becomes aware of a wider range of gender stereotypes, including personality traits and achievement areas, but has a flexible appreciation of what males and females can do. (493–494)
- Gender identity expands to include self-evaluations of typicality, contentedness, and pressure to conform. (494–495)
- Sibling rivalry tends to increase. (497)

Physical Development in Adolescence

"My Favorite Sport"
Yu Han Peng
14 years, Georgia, USA

These surfers seem exhilarated by their growing physical strength and competence. But as Chapter 14 reveals, adolescence can also be a time of apprehension and social difficulty as the body undergoes rapid change.

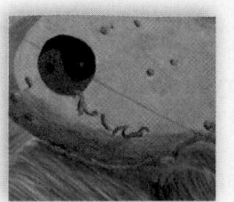

On Sabrina's eleventh birthday, her friend Joyce gave her a surprise party, but Sabrina seemed somber during the celebration. Although Sabrina and Joyce had been close friends since third grade, their relationship was faltering. Sabrina was a head taller and some 20 pounds heavier than most girls in her sixth-grade class. Her breasts were well-developed, her hips and thighs had broadened, and she had begun to menstruate. In contrast, Joyce still had the short, lean, flat-chested body of a school-age child.

Ducking into the bathroom while Joyce and the other girls put candles on the cake, Sabrina frowned at her image in the mirror. "I'm so big and heavy," she whispered. At church youth group on Sunday evenings, Sabrina broke away from Joyce and joined the eighth-grade girls. Around them, she didn't feel so large and awkward.

Once a month, parents gathered at Sabrina's and Joyce's school to discuss child-rearing concerns. Sabrina's parents, Franca and Antonio, attended whenever they could. "How you know they are becoming teenagers is this," volunteered Antonio. "The bedroom door is closed, and they want to be alone. Also, they contradict and disagree. I tell Sabrina, 'You have to go to Aunt Gina's on Saturday for dinner with the family.' The next thing I know, she's arguing with me."

Sabrina has entered **adolescence,** the transition between childhood and adulthood. In industrialized societies, the skills young people must master are so complex and the choices confronting them so diverse that adolescence is greatly extended. But around the world, the basic tasks of this period are much the same. Sabrina must accept her full-grown body, acquire adult ways of thinking, attain greater independence from her family, develop more mature ways of relating to peers of both sexes, and begin to construct an identity—a secure sense of who she is in terms of sexual, vocational, moral, ethnic, religious, and other life values and goals.

The beginning of adolescence is marked by **puberty,** a flood of biological events leading to an adult-sized body and sexual maturity. As Sabrina's reactions suggest, entry into adolescence can be an especially trying time for some young people. In this chapter, we trace the events of puberty and take up a variety of health concerns—physical exercise, nutrition, sexual activity, substance use and abuse, and other challenges that many teenagers encounter on the path to maturity. But first, let's consider how views of adolescence have changed over the past century. ■

Conceptions of Adolescence

Why is Sabrina self-conscious, argumentative, and in retreat from family activities? Historically, theorists explained the impact of puberty on psychological development by resorting to extremes—either a biological or a social explanation. Today, researchers realize that biological and social forces jointly contribute to adolescent psychological change.

The Biological Perspective

TAKE A MOMENT... Ask several parents of young children what they expect their sons and daughters to be like as teenagers. You will probably get answers like these: "Rebellious and irresponsible," "Full of rages and tempers" (Buchanan & Holmbeck,

14.1 How have conceptions of adolescence changed over the past century?

1998). This widespread view can be traced back to the ideas of eighteenth-century philosopher Jean-Jacques Rousseau (see Chapter 1), who believed that the biological upheaval of puberty triggered heightened emotionality, conflict, and defiance of adults.

In the early twentieth century, major theorists picked up this storm-and-stress perspective. The most influential, G. Stanley Hall, based his ideas about development on Darwin's theory of evolution. Hall (1904) described adolescence as a cascade of instinctual passions, a period so turbulent that it resembled the era in which humans evolved from savages into civilized beings. Similarly, Anna Freud (1969), who expanded the focus on adolescence of her father Sigmund Freud's theory, viewed the teenage years as a biologically based, universal "developmental disturbance." In Freud's *genital stage,* sexual impulses reawaken, triggering psychological conflict and volatile behavior. As adolescents find intimate partners, inner forces gradually achieve a new, more mature harmony, and the stage concludes with marriage, birth, and child rearing. In this way, young people fulfill their biological destiny: sexual reproduction and survival of the species.

The Social Perspective

Contemporary research suggests that the storm-and-stress notion of adolescence is greatly exaggerated. Certain problems, such as eating disorders, depression, suicide, and lawbreaking, do occur more often than earlier (Farrington, 2009; Graber, 2004). But the overall rate of serious psychological disturbance rises only slightly from childhood to adolescence, reaching 15 to 20 percent (Merikangas et al., 2010). Though much greater than the adulthood rate (about 6 percent), emotional turbulence is not a routine feature of the teenage years.

The first researcher to point out the wide variability in adolescent adjustment was anthropologist Margaret Mead (1928). She returned from the Pacific islands of Samoa with a startling conclusion: Because of the culture's relaxed social relationships and openness toward sexuality, adolescence "is perhaps the pleasantest time the Samoan girl (or boy) will ever know" (p. 308). In Mead's alternative view, the social environment is entirely responsible for the range of teenage experiences, from erratic and agitated to calm and stress-free. Later researchers found that Samoan adolescence was not as untroubled as Mead had assumed (Freeman, 1983). Still, she showed that to understand adolescent development, researchers must pay greater attention to social and cultural influences.

A Balanced Point of View

Today we know that biological, psychological, and social forces combine to influence adolescent development (Hollenstein & Lougheed, 2013). Biological changes are universal—found in all primates and all cultures. These internal stresses and the social expectations accompanying them—that the young person give up childish ways, develop new interpersonal relationships, and take on greater responsibility—are likely to prompt moments of uncertainty, self-doubt, and disappointment in all teenagers. Adolescents' prior and current experiences affect their success in surmounting these challenges.

At the same time, the length of adolescence and its demands and pressures vary substantially among cultures. Most tribal and village societies have only a brief intervening phase between childhood and full assumption of adult roles (Lancy, 2008). In industrialized nations, where successful participation in economic life requires many years of education, young people face prolonged dependence on parents and postponement of sexual gratification while they prepare for productive work roles. As a result, adolescence is greatly extended—so much so that researchers commonly divide it into three phases:

1. *Early adolescence* (11–12 to 14 years): This is a period of rapid pubertal change.
2. *Middle adolescence* (14 to 16 years): Pubertal changes are now nearly complete.
3. *Late adolescence* (16 to 18 years): The young person achieves full adult appearance and anticipates assumption of adult roles.

The more the social environment supports young people in achieving adult responsibilities, the better they adjust. For all the biological tensions and uncertainties about the future that teenagers feel, most negotiate this period successfully. With this in mind, let's look closely at puberty, the dawning of adolescent development.

Puberty: The Physical Transition to Adulthood

The changes of puberty are dramatic. Within a few years, the school-age child's body transforms into that of a full-grown adult. Genetically influenced hormonal processes regulate pubertal growth. Girls, who have been advanced in physical maturity since the prenatal period, reach puberty, on average, two years earlier than boys.

14.2 Describe body growth, motor performance, and sexual maturation during puberty.

14.3 What factors influence the timing of puberty?

14.4 Describe brain development and changes in the organization of sleep and wakefulness during adolescence.

Hormonal Changes

The complex hormonal changes that underlie puberty occur gradually and are under way during middle childhood. Recall from Chapter 8 that the *pituitary gland* releases *growth hormone (GH)* and stimulates other glands to produce hormones that act on body tissues, causing them to mature. Secretions of GH and *thyroxine* (a hormone released by the thyroid gland) increase, eventually leading to tremendous gains in body size and to attainment of skeletal maturity. As Figure 14.1 on page 522 shows, these hormonal changes are initiated and regulated by the *hypothalamus,* a structure located at the base of the brain near the pituitary gland.

Sexual maturation is controlled by the sex hormones. Although we think of *estrogens* as female hormones and *androgens* as male hormones, both types are present in each sex but in different amounts. Sex hormones begin to rise long before physical changes are visible, typically between ages 6 and 8, when the adrenal glands on top of each kidney start to release increasing levels of *adrenal androgens*—an event called **adrenarche** (from the Greek word *arche,* meaning "beginning"). By age 10, levels of adrenal androgens have increased tenfold, and some children experience their first feelings of sexual attraction (Best & Fortenberry, 2013).

Adrenal androgens influence girls' height spurt, and they stimulate growth of underarm and pubic hair. (Adrenal androgens have little visible impact on boys, whose physical characteristics are mainly influenced by androgen secretions from the testes.) Estrogens released by girls' maturing ovaries contribute to the height spurt by stimulating GH secretion, and they cause the breasts, uterus, and vagina to mature, the body to take on feminine proportions, and fat to accumulate. In addition, estrogens play a crucial role in regulation of the menstrual cycle.

Boys' maturing testes release large quantities of the androgen *testosterone,* which leads to muscle growth, body and facial hair, and other male sex characteristics. Androgens (especially testosterone) exert a GH-enhancing effect, contributing greatly to gains in body size. The testes secrete small amounts of estrogen as well, which add to the height spurt and lead many boys to experience temporary breast enlargement, lasting up to two years. In both sexes, estrogens in combination with androgens stimulate gains in bone density, which continue into early adulthood (Ambler, 2013; Cooper, Sayer, & Dennison, 2006).

As you can see, pubertal changes are of two broad types: (1) overall body growth and (2) maturation of sexual characteristics. We have seen that the hormones responsible for sexual maturity also affect body growth, making puberty the time of greatest sexual differentiation since prenatal life.

© MYRLEEN PEARSON/THE IMAGE WORKS

Sex differences in pubertal growth are obvious among these sixth graders. Although all are the same age, the girls are much taller and more mature looking than the boys.

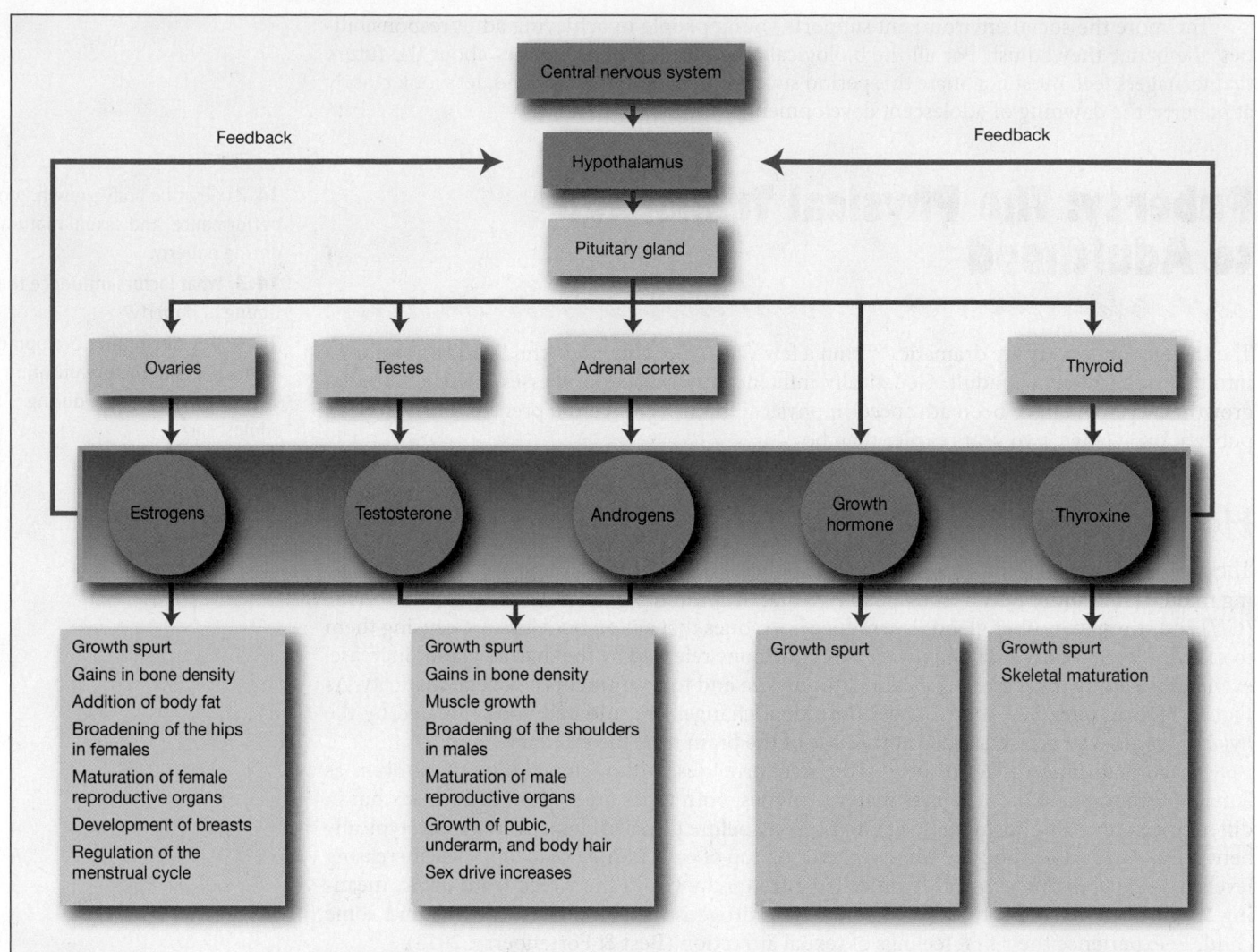

FIGURE 14.1 Hormonal influences on the body at puberty. The hypothalamus stimulates the pituitary gland to release hormones that either induce growth directly or stimulate other endocrine glands to release growth-inducing hormones (red lines). A highly sensitive feedback loop exists in which the hypothalamus detects hormone levels in the bloodstream and instructs the pituitary gland to increase or decrease the amount of each hormone accordingly (blue lines).

Body Growth

The first outward sign of puberty is the rapid gain in height and weight known as the **growth spurt.** On average, it is under way for North American and Western European girls shortly after age 10, for boys around age 12½. Because estrogens trigger and then restrain GH secretion more readily than androgens, the typical girl is taller and heavier during early adolescence (Archibald, Graber, & Brooks-Gunn, 2006; Bogin, 2001). By age 13½, however, she is surpassed by the typical boy, whose adolescent growth spurt has now started, whereas hers is almost finished (Ambler, 2013). Growth in body size is complete for most girls by age 16 and for boys by age 17½, when the epiphyses at the ends of the long bones close completely (see Chapter 8, page 287).

Altogether, adolescents add 10 to 11 inches in height and 50 to 75 pounds—nearly 50 percent of adult body weight. Even more striking is the swiftness of these changes. When growing at their peak, boys add more than 4 inches and 26 pounds in a single year, girls about 3.5 inches and 20 pounds (Rogol, Roemmich, & Clark, 2002). Figure 14.2 illustrates pubertal changes in general body growth.

Mariel at 18

Mariel at 11

Steven at 13

Mariel at 14

Steven at 16

Steven at 18

PHOTOS OF STEVEN: © ELLEN B. SENISI; PHOTOS OF MARIEL: © JIM WEST

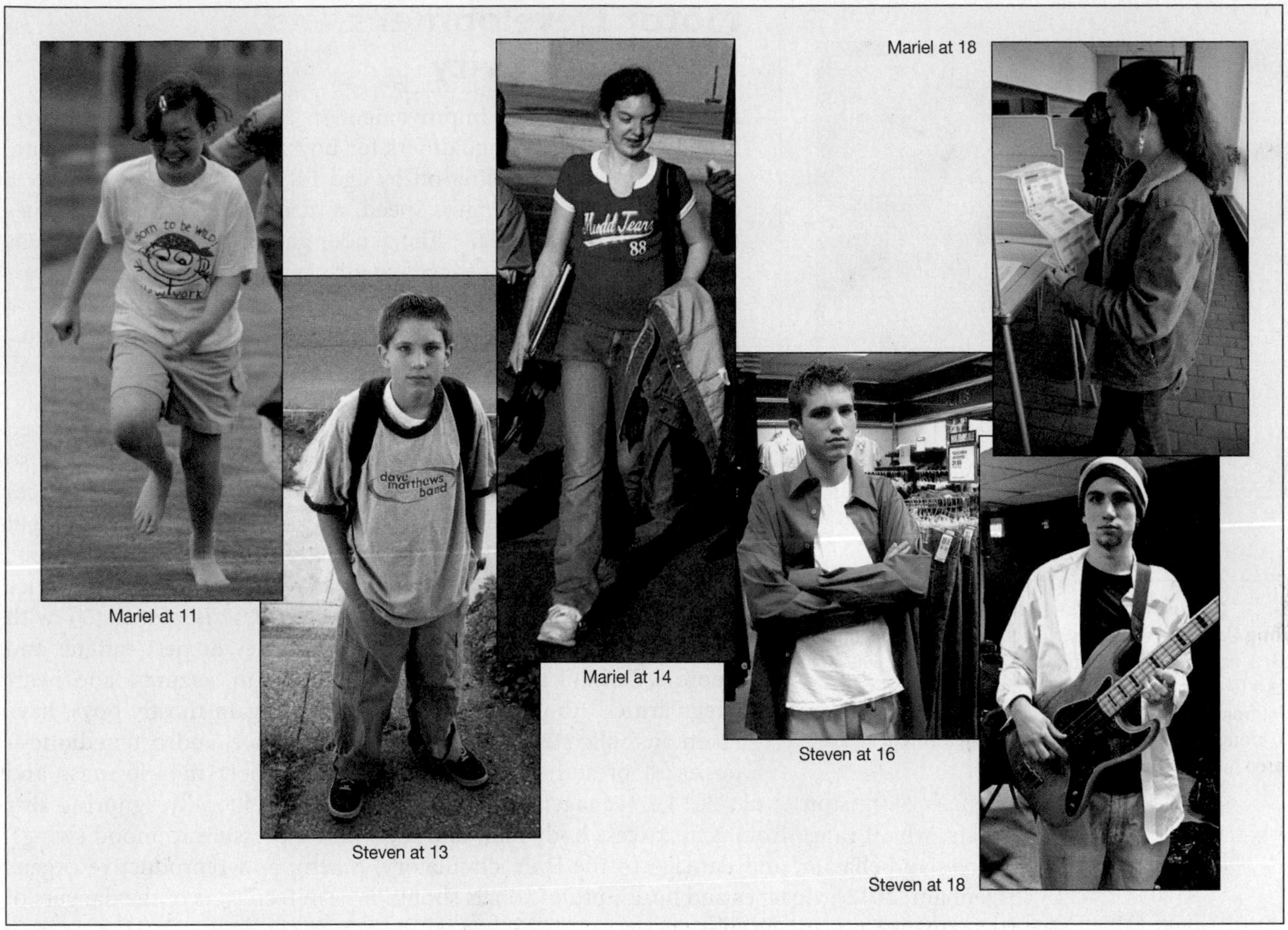

FIGURE 14.2 **Body growth during adolescence.** Because the pubertal growth spurt takes place earlier for girls than for boys, Mariel reached her adult body size earlier than Steven. Rapid pubertal growth is accompanied by large sex differences in body proportions that were not present in middle childhood (see Chapter 11, page 407).

BODY PROPORTIONS During puberty, the cephalocaudal trend of infancy and childhood reverses. The hands, legs, and feet accelerate first, followed by the torso, which accounts for most of the adolescent height gain (Sheehy et al., 1999). This pattern helps explain why early adolescents often appear awkward and out of proportion—long-legged and with giant feet and hands.

Large sex differences in body proportions also appear, caused by the action of sex hormones on the skeleton. Boys' shoulders broaden relative to the hips, whereas girls' hips broaden relative to the shoulders and waist. Of course, boys also end up considerably larger than girls, and their legs are longer in relation to the rest of the body. The major reason is that boys have two extra years of preadolescent growth, when the legs are growing the fastest.

MUSCLE–FAT MAKEUP AND OTHER INTERNAL CHANGES Sabrina worried about her weight because, compared with her later-developing girlfriends, she had accumulated much more fat. Around age 8, girls start to add more fat than boys on their arms, legs, and trunk, a trend that accelerates between ages 11 and 16. In contrast, arm and leg fat decreases in adolescent boys. Although both sexes gain in muscle, this increase is 150 percent greater in boys, who develop larger skeletal muscles, hearts, and lung capacity (Rogol, Roemmich, & Clark, 2002). Also, the number of red blood cells—and therefore the ability to carry oxygen from the lungs to the muscles—increases in boys but not in girls. Altogether, boys gain far more muscle strength than girls, a difference that contributes to boys' superior athletic performance during the teenage years (Greydanus, Omar, & Pratt, 2010).

LOOK and LISTEN

Observe 10- to 14-year-olds on school grounds or at another gathering place, noting changes in body size and proportions, along with sex differences in timing of the growth spurt.

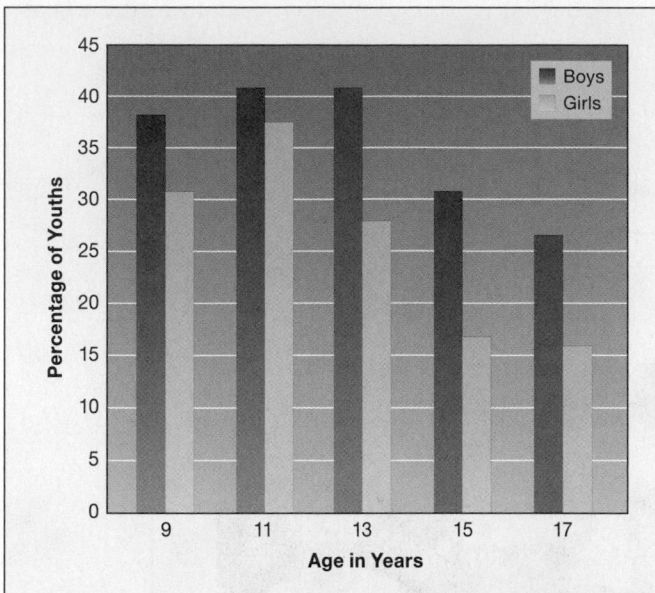

FIGURE 14.3   Decline in free-time physical activity from ages 9 to 17 among U.S. boys and girls. In a longitudinal-sequential investigation of a U.S. nationally representative sample of over 1,600 youths followed from ages 9 to 17, free-time daily exercise during the previous week declined from from 38 to 27 percent among boys and 31 to 16 percent among girls. Throughout adolescence, boys exceeded girls in regular daily exercise. (Based on Wall et al., 2011.)

Motor Development and Physical Activity

Puberty brings steady improvement in gross-motor performance, but the pattern of change differs for boys and girls. Girls' gains are slow and gradual, leveling off by age 14. In contrast, boys show a dramatic spurt in strength, speed, and endurance that continues through the teenage years. The gender gap in physical skill widens with age. By midadolescence, few girls perform as well as the average boy in running speed, broad jump, or throwing distance. And practically no boys score as low as the average girl (Greydanus, Omar, & Pratt, 2010; Haywood & Getchell, 2014; Malina & Bouchard, 1991).

Among adolescent boys, athletic competence is strongly related to peer admiration and self-esteem. Some adolescents become so obsessed with physical prowess that they turn to performance-enhancing drugs, with rates of use rising sharply with age. In recent large-scale surveys, more than 9 percent of U.S. high school seniors, mostly boys, reported using creatine, an over-the-counter substance that enhances short-term muscle power but is associated with muscle cramping, intestinal discomfort, rashes, anxiety, fatigue, and (more seriously) muscle tissue disease, brain seizures, and heart irregularities. About 2 percent of seniors, again mostly boys, have taken anabolic steroids or a related substance, androstenedione—powerful prescription medications that boost muscle mass and strength (Johnston et al., 2014). Teenagers usually obtain steroids illegally, ignoring side effects, which range from acne, excess body hair, and high blood pressure to mood swings, aggressive behavior, and damage to the liver, circulatory system, and reproductive organs (Denham, 2012). Coaches and health professionals should inform teenagers of the dangers of performance-enhancing substances.

In 1972, the U.S. federal government required schools receiving public funds to provide equal opportunities for males and females in all educational programs, including athletics. Since then, high school girls' sports participation has increased, although it still falls far short of boys'. According to a recent survey of all 50 U.S. state high school athletic associations, 42 percent of sports participants are girls, 58 percent boys (National Federation of State High School Associations, 2014). In Chapter 11, we saw that girls get less encouragement and recognition for athletic achievement, a pattern that starts early and clearly persists into the teenage years (see page 422).

Furthermore, when researchers followed a large, representative sample of U.S. youths from ages 9 to 17, daily free-time physical activity declined with age, more so for girls than boys. And at every age, only a minority of participants engaged in regular exercise outside of school hours (see Figure 14.3) (Wall et al., 2011). In high school, just 53 percent of U.S. boys and 43 percent of girls receive any physical education, with only 29 percent of all students experiencing a daily physical education class (Kann et al., 2014).

Besides improving motor performance, sports and exercise influence cognitive and social development. Interschool and intramural athletics provide important lessons in teamwork, problem solving, assertiveness, and competition. And regular, sustained physical activity—which mandatory physical education can ensure—is associated with lasting health benefits, including enhanced functioning of the immune system, cardiovascular health, better sleep quality, and improved psychological well-being (Brand et al., 2010).

High school students run in their school's cross country invitational. Adolescents who participate in endurance sports that do not require an organized team or special facilities are likely to continue being physically active into adulthood.

Adolescents vary in their enjoyment of sports and exercise, leading to differences in continued involvement. In one study, participating in team or individual sports at age 14 at least once a week for girls and twice a week for boys predicted high physical activity rates at age 31. Endurance sports, such as running and cycling—activities that do not require an organized team or special facilities—were especially likely to continue into adulthood (Tammelin et al., 2003). And adolescent exertion during exercise, defined as sweating and breathing heavily, is one of the best predictors of adult physical exercise, perhaps because it fosters high *physical self-efficacy*—belief in one's ability to sustain an exercise program (Motl et al., 2002; Telama et al., 2005).

Sexual Maturation

Accompanying rapid body growth are changes in physical features related to sexual functioning. Some, called **primary sexual characteristics,** involve the reproductive organs directly (ovaries, uterus, and vagina in females; penis, scrotum, and testes in males). Others, called **secondary sexual characteristics,** are visible on the outside of the body and serve as additional signs of sexual maturity (for example, breast development in females and the appearance of underarm and pubic hair in both sexes). As Table 14.1 shows, these characteristics develop in a fairly standard sequence, although the ages at which each begins and is completed vary greatly. Typically, pubertal development takes about four years, but some adolescents complete it in two years, whereas others take five to six years.

SEXUAL MATURATION IN GIRLS Female puberty usually begins with the budding of the breasts and the growth spurt. **Menarche,** or first menstruation, typically occurs relatively late in the sequence of pubertal events—around age 12½ for North American girls, 13 for Western Europeans. But the age range is wide, from 10½ to 15½ years. Following menarche, breast and pubic hair growth are completed, and underarm hair appears.

TABLE 14.1	Pubertal Development in North American Girls and Boys						
GIRLS	**AVERAGE AGE ATTAINED**	**AGE RANGE**		**BOYS**	**AVERAGE AGE ATTAINED**	**AGE RANGE**	
Breasts begin to "bud"	10	8–13		Testes begin to enlarge	11.5	9.5–13.5	
Height spurt begins	10	8–13		Pubic hair appears	12	10–15	
Pubic hair appears	10.5	8–14		Penis begins to enlarge	12	10.5–14.5	
Peak strength spurt	11.6	9.5–14		Height spurt begins	12.5	10.5–16	
Peak height spurt	11.7	10–13.5		Spermarche (first ejaculation) occurs	13.5	12–16	
Menarche (first menstruation) occurs	12.5	10.5–15.5		Peak height spurt	14	12.5–15.5	
Peak weight spurt	12.7	10–14		Peak weight spurt	14	12.5–15.5	
Adult stature reached	13	10–16		Facial hair begins to grow	14	12.5–15.5	
Pubic hair growth completed	14.5	14–15		Voice begins to deepen	14	12.5–15.5	
Breast growth completed	15	10–17		Penis and testes growth completed	14.5	12.5–16	
				Peak strength spurt	15.3	13–17	
				Adult stature reached	15.5	13.5–17.5	
				Pubic hair growth completed	15.5	14–17	

Sources: Chumlea et al., 2003; Herman-Giddens, 2006; Rogol, Roemmich, & Clark, 2002; Rubin et al., 2009; Wu, Mendola, & Buck, 2002.
Photos: (left) © Laura Dwight Photography; (right) © Bill Aron/PhotoEdit

Notice in Table 14.1 that nature delays sexual maturity until the girl's body is large enough for childbearing; menarche takes place after the peak of the height spurt. As an extra measure of security, for 12 to 18 months following menarche, the menstrual cycle often occurs without the release of an ovum from the ovaries (Fuqua & Rogol, 2013). But this temporary period of sterility does not occur in all girls, and it cannot be counted on for protection against pregnancy.

SEXUAL MATURATION IN BOYS   The first sign of puberty in boys is the enlargement of the testes (glands that manufacture sperm), accompanied by changes in the texture and color of the scrotum. Pubic hair emerges soon after, about the same time the penis begins to enlarge (Fuqua & Rogol, 2013).

As Table 14.1 reveals, the growth spurt occurs much later in the sequence of pubertal events for boys than for girls. Also, boys' height gain is more intense and longer lasting. When it reaches its peak around age 14, enlargement of the testes and penis is nearly complete, and underarm hair appears. Facial and body hair also emerge just after the peak in body growth and increase gradually for several years. Another landmark of male physical maturity is the deepening of the voice as the larynx enlarges and the vocal cords lengthen. (Girls' voices also deepen slightly.) Voice change usually takes place at the peak of the male growth spurt and often is not complete until puberty is over (Archibald, Graber, & Brooks-Gunn, 2006). When it first occurs, boys' newly acquired baritone occasionally breaks into a high-pitched sound.

While the penis is growing, the prostate gland and seminal vesicles (which together produce semen, the fluid containing sperm) enlarge. Then, around age 13½, **spermarche,** or first ejaculation, occurs (Rogol, Roemmich, & Clark, 2002). For a while, the semen contains few living sperm. So, like girls, boys have an initial period of reduced fertility.

Individual Differences in Pubertal Growth

Heredity contributes substantially to the timing of pubertal changes. Identical twins are more similar than fraternal twins in attainment of most pubertal milestones, including growth spurt, menarche, breast development, body hair, and voice change (Eaves et al., 2004; Jahanfar, Lye, & Krishnarajah, 2013).

Nutrition and exercise also make a difference. In females, a sharp rise in body weight and fat may trigger sexual maturation. Fat cells release a protein called *leptin,* which is believed to signal the brain that the girl's energy stores are sufficient for puberty—a likely reason that breast and pubic hair growth and menarche occur earlier for heavier and, especially, obese girls. In contrast, girls who begin rigorous athletic training at an early age or who eat very little (both of which reduce the percentage of body fat) usually experience later puberty (Kaplowitz, 2008; Rubin et al., 2009). Few studies, however, report a link between body fat and puberty in boys.

Variations in pubertal growth also exist between regions of the world and between SES and ethnic groups. Physical health plays a major role. In poverty-stricken regions where malnutrition and infectious disease are common, menarche is greatly delayed, occurring as late as age 14 to 16 in many parts of Africa. Within developing countries, girls from higher-income families typically reach menarche 6 to 18 months earlier than those living in economically disadvantaged homes (Parent et al., 2003).

But in industrialized nations where food is abundant, the joint roles of heredity and environment in pubertal growth are apparent. For example, breast and pubic hair growth begin, on average, around age 9 in African-American girls—a year earlier than in Caucasian-American girls. And African-American girls reach menarche about six months earlier, around age 12 (Ramnitz & Lodish, 2013). Although widespread overweight and obesity in the black population contribute, a genetically influenced faster rate of physical maturation is also involved. Black girls usually reach menarche before white girls of the same age and body weight (Herman-Giddens, 2006; Hillard, 2008; Webster et al., 2014).

Early family experiences may also affect pubertal timing. One theory suggests that humans have evolved to be sensitive to the emotional quality of their childhood environments. When children's safety and security are at risk, it is adaptive for them to reproduce early.

Research indicates that girls and (less consistently) boys with a history of family conflict, harsh parenting, or parental separation tend to reach puberty early. In contrast, those with warm, stable family ties reach puberty relatively late (Belsky et al., 2007a; Ellis & Essex, 2007; Ellis et al., 2011; Tremblay & Frigon, 2005). Critics offer an alternative explanation—that mothers who reached puberty early are more likely to bear children earlier, which increases the likelihood of marital conflict and separation (Mendle et al., 2006). But two longitudinal studies confirm the former chain of influence among girls: from adverse family environments in childhood to earlier pubertal timing to increased sexual risk taking in adolescence (Belsky et al., 2010; James et al., 2012).

The Secular Trend

In Chapter 11 we saw that children in industrialized nations grow faster and larger than in past generations. Similarly, age of menarche declined steadily—by about 3 to 4 months per decade—from 1900 to 1970, a period in which nutrition, health care, sanitation, and control of infectious disease improved greatly (see Figure 14.4). Boys, too, have reached puberty earlier in recent decades (Herman-Giddens et al., 2012). This *secular trend* in pubertal timing lends added support to the role of physical well-being in adolescent growth.

As noted in Chapter 11, the secular gain in height has slowed. And the trend toward earlier menarche has stopped or undergone a slight reversal in most industrialized nations. But in the United States and a few European countries, soaring rates of overweight and obesity are responsible for a modest, continuing trend toward earlier menarche (Kaplowitz, 2008). A worrisome consequence is that girls who reach sexual maturity at age 10 or 11 will feel pressure to act much older than they are. As we will see shortly, early-maturing girls are at risk for unfavorable peer involvements, including sexual activity.

Brain Development

The physical transformations of adolescence include major changes in the brain. In Chapter 11, we noted that during middle childhood and adolescence, *white matter* (myelinated nerve fibers) increases, especially in the prefrontal cortex, the parietal lobes, and the corpus callosum, while *gray matter* (neurons and supportive material) declines (see page 408 to review). Brain-imaging research reveals continued pruning of unused synapses in the cerebral cortex, especially the prefrontal cortex—the "governor" of thought and action. In addition, growth

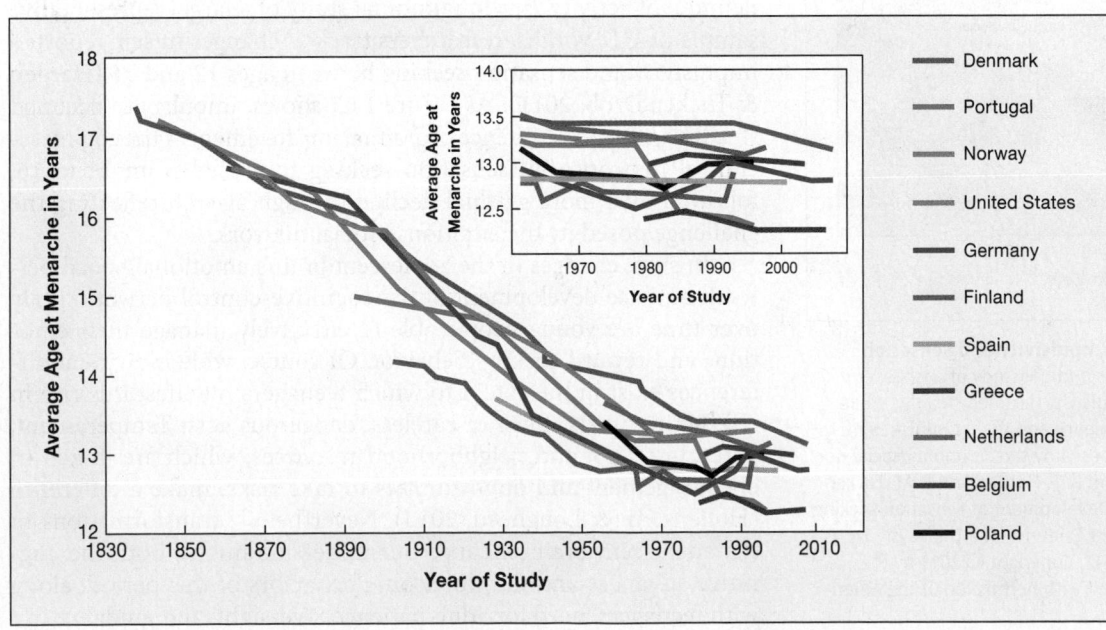

FIGURE 14.4 Secular trend in age at menarche in 11 industrialized nations. Age of menarche declined from 1830 to 1970. Thereafter, a few countries showed a modest, continuing decline due to rising rates of overweight and obesity. Others leveled off or underwent a slight reversal (see inset). (From K. Sørensen et al., 2012. "Recent Secular Trends in Pubertal Timing: Implications for Evaluation and Diagnosis of Precocious Puberty," *Hormone Research in Pædiatrics, 77,* p. 139. Copyright © 2012 Karger Publishers, Basel, Switzerland. Reprinted by permission.)

Changes in the brain's emotional/social network outpace development of the cognitive-control network, contributing to teenagers' drive for novel experiences, receptiveness to peer influence, and risk-taking behavior.

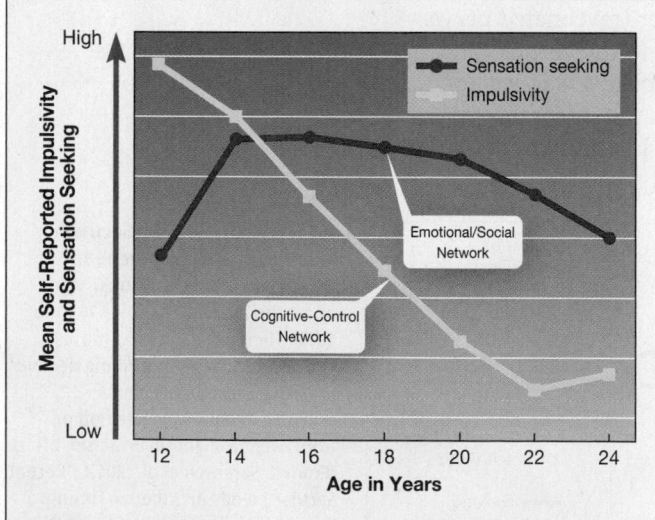

FIGURE 14.5 Development of impulsivity and sensation seeking from 12 to 24 years. In this longitudinal study of a large representative sample of 7,600 U.S. youths, impulsivity declined steadily, while sensation seeking increased in early adolescence and then diminished more gradually. Findings confirm the challenge posed by the emotional/social network to the cognitive control network. (From K. P. Harden and E. M. Tucker-Drob, 2011, "Individual Differences in the Development of Sensation Seeking and Impulsivity During Adolescence: Further Evidence of a Dual Systems Model," *Developmental Psychology, 47,* p. 742. Copyright © 2011 by the American Psychological Association. Adapted with permission of the American Psychological Association.)

and myelination of stimulated neural fibers accelerate, strengthening connections among various brain regions.

In particular, linkages between the two cerebral hemispheres through the corpus callosum, and between the prefrontal cortex and other areas in the cerebral cortex and the inner brain (including the amygdala), expand and attain rapid communication. As a result, the prefrontal cortex becomes a more effective "executive"—overseeing and managing the integrated functioning of various areas, yielding more complex, flexible, and adaptive thinking and behavior (Blakemore, 2012; Chavarria et al., 2014; Lenroot & Giedd, 2006). Consequently, adolescents gain in diverse cognitive skills, including processing speed and executive function.

But these advances in cognitive control occur gradually over the teenage years. fMRI evidence reveals that adolescents recruit the prefrontal cortex's network of connections with other brain areas less effectively than adults do. Because the *prefrontal cognitive-control network* still requires fine-tuning, teenagers' performance on executive function tasks requiring inhibition, planning, and future orientation (rejecting a smaller immediate reward in favor of a larger delayed reward) is not yet fully mature (Luna, Padmanabhan, & Geier, 2014; Smith, Xiao, & Bechara, 2012; Steinberg et al. 2009).

Adding to these self-regulation difficulties are changes in the brain's *emotional/social network.* As humans and other mammals become sexually mature, neurons become more responsive to excitatory neurotransmitters. As a result, adolescents react more strongly to stressful events and experience pleasurable stimuli more intensely. Changes in the emotional/social network also increase adolescents' sensitivity to social stimuli, making them highly reactive to peer evaluation (Somerville, 2013). During a simulated driving task, adolescents (but not adults) took more risks while being observed by peers than when alone—responses accompanied by increased activity in reward-sensitive brain regions (Albert, Chein, & Steinberg, 2013). When peers are present, adolescents' brains are especially receptive to cues associated with risk taking.

Because the cognitive-control network is not yet functioning optimally, most teenagers find it especially difficult to manage these powerful feelings and impulses (Albert, Chein, & Steinberg, 2013; Casey, Jones, & Somerville, 2011; Ernst & Spear, 2009). This imbalance contributes to adolescents' unchecked drive for novel experiences, including drug taking, reckless driving, unprotected sex, and delinquent activity. In a longitudinal study of a large, representative sample of U.S. youths, researchers tracked changes in self-reported impulsivity and sensation seeking between ages 12 and 24 (Harden & Tucker-Drob, 2011). As Figure 14.5 shows, impulsivity declined steadily with age—evidence of gradual improvement of the cognitive-control network. But sensation seeking increased from 12 to 16, followed by a more gradual decline through age 24, reflecting the challenge posed by the emotional/social network.

In sum, changes in the adolescent brain's emotional/social network outpace development of the cognitive-control network. Only over time are young people able to effectively manage their emotions and reward-seeking behavior. Of course, wide individual differences exist in the extent to which teenagers manifest this rise in risk taking in the form of careless, dangerous acts: Temperament, parenting, SES, and neighborhood resources, which are linked to encouragement and opportunities to take risks, make a difference (Hollenstein & Lougheed, 2013). Nevertheless, transformations in the adolescent brain enhance our understanding of both the cognitive advances and the worrisome behaviors of this period, along with teenagers' need for adult patience, oversight, and guidance.

Changing States of Arousal

At puberty, revisions occur in the way the brain regulates the timing of sleep, perhaps because of increased neural sensitivity to evening light. As a result, adolescents go to bed much later than they did as children. Yet they need almost as much sleep as they did in middle childhood—about nine hours. When the school day begins early, their sleep needs are not satisfied.

This sleep "phase delay" strengthens with pubertal growth. But today's teenagers—with more evening social activities, part-time jobs, and bedrooms equipped with screen media—get much less sleep than teenagers of previous generations. Sleep-deprived adolescents perform especially poorly on cognitive tasks during morning hours. And they are more likely to achieve less well in school; suffer from anxiety, irritability, and depressed mood; and engage in high-risk behaviors (Baum et al., 2014; Carskadon, 2011; Talbot et al., 2010). Sleep rebound on weekends sustains the pattern by leading to difficulty falling asleep on subsequent evenings (Laberge et al., 2001). Later school start times ease but do not eliminate sleep loss (Kirby, Maggi, & D'Angiulli, 2011). Educating teenagers about the importance of sleep is vital.

Ask Yourself

- **REVIEW** What changes in the brain contribute to cognitive advances during adolescence? What changes promote increased reward seeking along with high-risk behaviors?

- **CONNECT** Historically, theorists believed that the rising sexual passions of puberty make adolescents rebellious, volatile, and uncontrollable. Where did this view originate? Why is it incorrect?

- **APPLY** Jonah, age 16, routinely stays up until 2:00 A.M.—much later than he used to go to bed. He is often late for school and sometimes dozes in class. Why might Jonah's sleep habits have changed? What can his parents and his school do to help?

- **REFLECT** Do you currently engage in regular sports or exercise? If so, what activities do you enjoy, and why? How did your experiences during adolescence influence your current involvement in physical activity?

The Psychological Impact of Pubertal Events

14.5 Explain adolescents' reactions to the physical changes of puberty.
14.6 Describe the impact of pubertal timing on adolescent adjustment, noting sex differences.

TAKE A MOMENT... Think back to your late elementary and middle school days. As you reached puberty, how did your feelings about yourself and your relationships with others change? Research reveals that pubertal events affect the adolescent's self-image, mood, and interaction with parents and peers. Some outcomes are a response to dramatic physical change, whenever it occurs. Others have to do with pubertal timing.

Reactions to Pubertal Changes

Two generations ago, menarche was often traumatic. Today, girls commonly react with "surprise," undoubtedly due to the sudden onset of the event. Otherwise, they typically report a mixture of positive and negative emotions (Chang, Hayter, & Wu, 2010; DeRose & Brooks-Gunn, 2006). Yet research in wide-ranging nations, including the United States, India, and Taiwan, reveals large individual differences that depend on prior knowledge and support from family members, which in turn are influenced by cultural attitudes toward puberty and sexuality (Jackson & Falmagne, 2013; Kumar & Srivastava, 2011; Liu, Chen & Peng, 2012).

For girls who have no advance information, menarche can be shocking and disturbing (Marván & Alcalá-Herrera, 2014). Unlike 50 to 60 years ago, today few girls in developed countries are uninformed, a shift that is probably due to parents' greater willingness to discuss sexual matters and to the spread of health education classes (Omar, McElderry, & Zakharia, 2003).

In Hispanic communities, the quinceañera, celebrated at age 15, is a rite of passage honoring a girl's journey from childhood to maturity. However, the ceremony does not mark a meaningful change in social status in the larger society.

Almost all girls get some information from their mothers. And some evidence suggests that compared with Caucasian-American families, African-American families may better prepare girls for menarche, treat it as an important milestone, and express less conflict over girls reaching sexual maturity—factors that lead African-American girls to react more favorably (Martin, 1996).

Like girls' reactions to menarche, boys' responses to spermarche reflect mixed feelings. Virtually all boys know about ejaculation ahead of time, but many say that no one spoke to them prior to or during puberty about physical changes (Omar, McElderry, & Zakharia, 2003). Usually they get their information from reading material or websites. Even boys who had advance information often say that their first ejaculation occurred earlier than they expected and that they were unprepared for it. Whereas almost all girls eventually tell a friend that they are menstruating, far fewer boys tell anyone about spermarche (DeRose & Brooks-Gunn, 2006; Downs & Fuller, 1991). Overall, boys get much less social support than girls for the changes of puberty. They might benefit, especially, from opportunities to ask questions and discuss feelings with a sympathetic parent or health professional.

Many tribal and village societies celebrate the onset of puberty with an *initiation ceremony*, a ritualized announcement to the community that marks an important change in privilege and responsibility. Consequently, young people know that reaching puberty is a significant milestone in their culture. In contrast, Western societies grant little formal recognition to movement from childhood to adolescence or from adolescence to adulthood. Ceremonies such as the Jewish bar or bat mitzvah and the *quinceañera* in Hispanic communities (celebrating a 15-year-old girl's sexual maturity and marriage availability) resemble initiation ceremonies, but only within the ethnic or religious subculture. They do not mark a meaningful change in social status in the larger society.

Instead, Western adolescents are granted partial adult status at many different ages—for example, an age for starting employment, for driving, for leaving high school, for voting, and for drinking. And in some contexts (at home and at school), they may still be regarded as children. The absence of a widely accepted marker of physical and social maturity makes the process of becoming an adult more confusing.

Pubertal Change, Emotion, and Social Behavior

A common belief is that puberty has something to do with adolescent moodiness and the desire for greater physical and psychological separation from parents. Let's see what research says about these relationships.

ADOLESCENT MOODINESS   Higher pubertal hormone levels are linked to greater moodiness, but only modestly so (Graber, Brooks-Gunn, & Warren, 2006). What other factors might contribute? In several studies, the moods of children, adolescents, and adults were monitored by having them carry electronic pagers. Over a one-week period, they were beeped at random intervals and asked to write down what they were doing, whom they were with, and how they felt.

As expected, adolescents reported less favorable moods than school-age children and adults (Larson & Lampman-Petraitis, 1989; Larson et al., 2002). But negative moods were linked to a greater number of negative life events, such as difficulties with parents, disciplinary actions at school, and breaking up with a boyfriend or girlfriend. Negative events increased steadily from childhood to adolescence, and teenagers also reacted to them with greater emotion than children (Larson & Ham, 1993). (Recall that stress reactivity is heightened by changes in brain neurotransmitter activity during adolescence.)

Compared with the moods of older adolescents and adults, those of younger adolescents (ages 12 to 16) were less stable, often shifting from cheerful to sad and back again. These mood swings were strongly related to situational changes. High points of adolescents' days were times spent with friends and in self-chosen leisure activities. Low points tended to occur in adult-structured settings—class, job, and religious services. Furthermore, emotional highs coincided with Friday and Saturday evenings, especially in high school. Going out with friends and romantic partners increases so dramatically during adolescence that it becomes a "cultural script" for what is *supposed* to happen (Larson & Richards, 1998). Consequently teenagers who spend weekend evenings at home often feel profoundly lonely. Fortunately, frequent reports of negative mood level off in late adolescence (Natsuaki, Biehl, & Ge, 2009).

PARENT–CHILD RELATIONSHIPS Sabrina's father noticed that as his children entered adolescence, they kept their bedroom doors closed, resisted spending time with the family, and became more argumentative. Sabrina and her mother squabbled over Sabrina's messy room ("It's *my* room, Mom. You don't have to live in it!"). And Sabrina protested the family's regular weekend visits to Aunt Gina's ("Why do I have to go *every* week?"). Research in cultures as diverse as the United States and Turkey show that puberty is linked to a rise in intensity of parent–child conflict, which persists into middle adolescence (Gure, Ucanok, & Sayil, 2006; Laursen, Coy, & Collins, 1998; McGue et al., 2005).

Why should young teenagers' more adultlike appearance trigger these disputes? From an evolutionary perspective, the association may have adaptive value. Among nonhuman primates, the young typically leave the family group around the time of puberty. The same is true in many village and tribal cultures (Lancy, 2008; Schlegel & Barry, 1991). Departure of young people discourages sexual relations between close blood relatives. But adolescents in industrialized nations, who are still economically dependent on parents, cannot leave the family. Consequently, a modern substitute seems to have emerged: psychological distancing.

Puberty brings an increase in parent–child conflict—psychological distancing that may, in part, be a modern substitute for physical departure from the family. Parents and adolescents often argue over the young person's readiness for new responsibilities.

As children become physically mature, they demand to be treated in adultlike ways. And as we will see in later chapters, adolescents' new powers of reasoning may also contribute to a rise in family tensions. Parent–adolescent disagreements focus largely on everyday matters such as driving, dating partners, and curfews (Adams & Laursen, 2001). But beneath these disputes lie serious concerns: parental efforts to protect teenagers from substance use, auto accidents, and early sex. The larger the gap between parents' and adolescents' views of teenagers' readiness for new responsibilities, the more they quarrel (Deković, Noom, & Meeus, 1997).

Parent–daughter conflict tends to be more intense than conflict with sons, perhaps because girls reach puberty earlier and parents place more restrictions on girls (Allison & Schultz, 2004). But most disputes are mild, and by late adolescence, only a small minority of families experience continuing friction. In a longitudinal investigation of parent–child conflict-resolution strategies spanning early to late adolescence, after an initial increase, adolescents displayed fewer angry behaviors ("losing my temper," "saying things I don't mean"), while parents' angry responses declined steadily. At the same time, teenagers and their parents increasingly used positive problem solving, such as compromise and reasoning (Van Doorn, Branje, & Meeus, 2011). And throughout adolescence, positive problem solving greatly exceeded angry confrontation.

Although separation from parents is adaptive, both generations benefit from warm, protective family bonds throughout the lifespan. As the teenage years conclude, parent–adolescent interactions are less hierarchical, setting the stage for mutually supportive relationships in adulthood (Laursen & Collins, 2009).

LOOK *and* LISTEN

Interview several parents and/or 12- to 14-year-olds about recent changes in parent–child relationships. Has intensity of conflict increased? Over what issues?

Pubertal Timing

"All our children were early maturers," said Franca during the parents' discussion group. "The three boys were tall by age 12 or 13, but it was easier for them. They felt big and important. Sabrina was skinny as a little girl, but now she says she is too fat and needs to diet. She thinks about boys and doesn't concentrate on her schoolwork."

Findings of several studies match the experiences of Sabrina and her brothers. Both adults and peers viewed early-maturing boys as relaxed, independent, self-confident, and physically attractive. Popular with agemates, they tended to hold leadership positions in school and to be athletic stars. Late maturing boys often experienced transient emotional difficulties, until they caughtz up physically with their peers (Brooks-Gunn, 1988; Huddleston & Ge, 2003). But early-maturing boys, though viewed as well-adjusted, reported more psychological stress, depressed mood, and problem behaviors (sexual activity, smoking, drinking, aggression, delinquency) than both their on-time and later-maturing agemates (Natsuaki, Biehl, & Ge, 2009; Negriff, Susman, & Trickett, 2011; Susman & Dorn, 2009).

In contrast, early-maturing girls were unpopular, withdrawn, lacking in self-confidence, anxious, and prone to depression, and they held few leadership positions (Blumenthal et al., 2011; Galvao et al., 2014; Ge, Conger, & Elder, 1996; Graber, Brooks-Gunn, & Warren, 2006; Graber et al., 1997; Jones & Mussen, 1958). And like early-maturing boys, they were more involved in deviant behavior (smoking, drinking, early sexual activity, delinquency) (Arim et al., 2011; Ge et al., 2006; Mrug et al., 2014; Negriff, Susman, & Trickett, 2011). In contrast, their later-maturing counterparts were regarded as physically attractive, lively, sociable, and leaders at school.

Two factors largely account for these trends: (1) how closely the adolescent's body matches cultural ideals of physical attractiveness and (2) how well young people fit in physically with their agemates.

LOOK *and* LISTEN

Examine several magazines targeting teenage girls and several aimed at readers of diverse ages. What percentage of photos of females depict a thin body type?

THE ROLE OF PHYSICAL ATTRACTIVENESS   TAKE A MOMENT... Flip through your favorite popular magazine. You will see evidence of our society's view of an attractive female as thin and long-legged and of a good-looking male as tall, broad-shouldered, and muscular. The female image is a girlish shape that favors the late developer. The male image fits the early-maturing boy.

Consistent with these preferences, early-maturing Caucasian girls tend to report a less positive **body image**—conception of and attitude toward their physical appearance—than their on-time and late-maturing agemates. Compared with African-American and Hispanic girls, Caucasian girls are more likely to have internalized the cultural ideal of a thin female body (Rosen, 2003; Williams & Currie, 2000). Although boys are less consistent, early, rapid maturers are more likely to be satisfied with their physical characteristics (Alsaker, 1995; Sinkkonen, Anttila, & Siimes, 1998).

Body image is a strong predictor of young people's self-esteem (Harter, 2012a). But the negative effects of pubertal timing on body image and—as we will see next—emotional adjustment are greatly amplified when accompanied by other stressors (Stice, 2003).

THE IMPORTANCE OF FITTING IN WITH PEERS Because early-maturing adolescents of both sexes feel physically "out of place" when with their agemates, they often seek out older companions, who may encourage them into activities they are not yet ready to handle. And pubertal hormone influences on the brain's emotional/social network are stronger for early maturers, further magnifying their receptiveness to sexual activity, drug and alcohol use, and delinquent acts (Ge et al., 2002; Steinberg, 2008). For example, the eighth graders Sabrina met at church introduced her to several high school boys, who were unconcerned that she was only a sixth grader! And Sabrina welcomed their attentions, which gratified her desire to feel socially accepted and physically attractive. Perhaps because of involvements like these, early maturers of both sexes more often report feeling emotionally stressed and decline in academic performance (Mendle, Turkheimer, & Emery, 2007; Natsuaki, Biehl, & Ge, 2009).

At the same time, the young person's context greatly increases the likelihood that early pubertal timing will lead to negative outcomes. Early maturers in economically disadvantaged neighborhoods are especially vulnerable to establishing ties with deviant peers—associations that heighten defiant, hostile behavior (Obeidallah et al., 2004). And because families in such neighborhoods

Feeling "out of place" with same-age peers, an early maturing girl joins older teenagers at a shopping mall. Involvements with older companions risk drawing young teenagers into deviant activities.

© ADRIAN SHERRATT/ALAMY

tend to be exposed to chronic, severe stressors and to have few social supports, these early maturers are also more likely to experience harsh, inconsistent parenting (see page 75 in Chapter 2). Parental coercion, anger, and inconsistency, in turn, predict deviant peer associations as well as antisocial activity and depressive symptoms (Benoit, Lacourse, & Claes, 2013; Ge et al., 2002, 2011).

LONG-TERM CONSEQUENCES   Do the effects of pubertal timing persist? Follow-ups reveal that early-maturing girls, especially, are at risk for lasting difficulties. In one study, depression and frequently changing sexual partners persisted into early adulthood among early-maturing girls, with depression evident mainly in those who had displayed the severest adolescent conduct problems (Copeland et al., 2010). In another study, which followed young people from age 14 to 24, early-maturing boys showed good adjustment. But early-maturing girls reported poorer-quality relationships with family and friends, smaller social networks, and lower life satisfaction in early adulthood than did their on-time counterparts (Graber et al., 2004).

Recall that childhood family conflict and harsh parenting are linked to earlier pubertal timing, more so for girls than for boys (see page 527). Perhaps many early-maturing girls enter adolescence with emotional and social difficulties. As the stresses of puberty interfere with school performance and lead to unfavorable peer pressures, poor adjustment may extend and deepen (Graber, 2003).

Clearly, interventions that target at-risk early-maturing adolescents are needed. These include educating parents and teachers and providing adolescents with counseling and social supports so they will be better prepared to handle the emotional and social challenges of this transition.

Ask Yourself

- **REVIEW** Summarize the impact of pubertal timing on adolescent development.

- **CONNECT** How might adolescent moodiness contribute to psychological distancing between parents and adolescents? (*Hint:* Think about bidirectional influences in parent–child relationships.)

- **APPLY** As a school-age child, Chloe enjoyed leisure activities with her parents. Now, as a 14-year-old, she spends hours in her room and resists going on weekend family excursions. Explain Chloe's behavior.

- **REFLECT** Recall your own reactions to the physical changes of puberty. Are they consistent with research findings? Explain.

Health Issues

The arrival of puberty brings new health issues related to the young person's efforts to meet physical and psychological needs. As adolescents attain greater autonomy, their personal decision making becomes important, in health as well as other areas. Yet none of the health concerns we are about to discuss can be traced to a single cause. Rather, biological, psychological, family, peer, and cultural factors jointly contribute.

Nutritional Needs

When their sons reached puberty, Franca and Antonio reported a "vacuum cleaner effect" in the kitchen as the boys routinely emptied the refrigerator. Rapid body growth leads to a dramatic rise in food intake. During the growth spurt, boys require between 2,400 and 3,200 calories a day, girls between 1,800 and 2,400, depending on physical activity level (U.S. Department of Agriculture, 2010).

This increase in nutritional requirements comes at a time when the diets of many young people are the poorest. Of all age groups, adolescents are the most likely to skip breakfast

14.7 Describe nutritional needs, and cite factors related to eating disorders in adolescence.

14.8 Cite common unintentional injuries in adolescence.

14.9 Discuss social and cultural influences on adolescent sexual attitudes and behavior.

14.10 Describe factors involved in the development of homosexuality.

14.11 Discuss factors related to sexually transmitted infections and teenage pregnancy and parenthood.

14.12 What personal and social factors are related to adolescent substance use and abuse?

Although U.S. teenagers' diets have improved, many regularly consume unhealthy fast foods—choices that contribute to adolescent nutritional deficiencies and overweight and obesity.

(a practice linked to overweight and obesity), eat on the run, and consume empty calories rather than nutrient-rich fruits and vegetables (Piernas & Popkin, 2011; Ritchie et al., 2007).

Fortunately, recent efforts to improve young people's diets have resulted in positive changes. Among children and adolescents, consumption of popular items high in fat, sugar, and calories, such as pizza and soft drinks, declined from 2004 to 2010 (Slining, Mathias, & Popkin, 2013). Fast-food restaurants, where teenagers often gather, have begun to offer some healthy menu options, and many schools now offer more nutritious choices (French & Story, 2013). But adolescents need guidance in selecting these alternatives. Sweets, soft drinks, high-fat and sweetened milk, pizza, and French fries still figure prominently in many young people's diets (Poti, Slining, & Popkin, 2014).

One of the most common nutritional problems of adolescence is iron deficiency. Iron requirements increase to a maximum during the growth spurt and remain high among girls because of iron loss during menstruation. A tired, irritable teenager may be suffering from anemia rather than unhappiness and should have a medical checkup. Many adolescents—especially girls—do not get enough calcium and are also deficient in riboflavin (vitamin B_2) and magnesium, both of which support metabolism (Cavadini, Siega-Riz, & Popkin, 2000; Rozen, 2012).

Frequency of family meals is strongly associated with greater intake of fruits, vegetables, grains, and calcium-rich foods and reduced soft drink and fast-food consumption (Burgess-Champoux et al. 2009; Fiese & Schwartz, 2008). But compared to families with children, those with adolescents eat fewer meals together. In addition to their other benefits (see page 72 in Chapter 2 and page 457 in Chapter 12), family meals can greatly improve teenagers' diets.

Adolescents—especially girls concerned about their weight—tend to be attracted to fad diets. Unfortunately, most are too limited in nutrients and calories to be healthy for fast-growing, active teenagers (Donatelle, 2015). Adolescence is also a time when many young people choose to become vegetarians. As they formulate a philosophy of life, some find the killing of animals distasteful, while others claim that meats are sources of impurities and toxins. Vegetarian adolescents are far more likely than their nonvegetarian counterparts to have healthy eating habits (Amit, 2010). Still, because some vegetarian diets are deficient in certain nutrients, when a young person wants to try a special diet, parents should encourage consultation with a doctor or a dietitian.

Eating Disorders

Concerned about her daughter's desire to lose weight, Franca explained to Sabrina that she was really quite average in build for an adolescent girl and reminded her that her Italian ancestors had considered a plump female body more beautiful than a thin one. Girls who reach puberty early, who are very dissatisfied with their body image, and who grow up in homes where concern with weight and thinness is high are at risk for eating problems. Body dissatisfaction and severe dieting are strong predictors of the onset of an eating disorder in adolescence (Lock & Kirz, 2008; Rohde, Stice, & Marti, 2014). Disturbed eating is highest in Western societies, but as Western media and cultural values have spread to other parts of the world, Africa and Asia are becoming increasingly affected (Carr & Peebles, 2012). The three most serious eating disorders are anorexia nervosa, bulimia, and binge-eating disorder.

ANOREXIA NERVOSA　**Anorexia nervosa** is a tragic eating disorder in which young people starve themselves because of a compulsive fear of getting fat. About 1 percent of North American and Western European teenage girls are affected. During the past half-century, cases have increased sharply, fueled by cultural admiration of female thinness (Smink, van Hoeken, & Hoek, 2012).

In the United States, anorexia nervosa is observed less frequently among African Americans, Asian Americans, and Hispanics than among whites. African-American girls' greater satisfaction with their body image may offer some protection. Another possibility is that ethnic minorities less often access health services, yielding more undetected cases (American Psychiatric Association, 2013; Marques et al., 2011; Ozer & Irwin, 2009). Boys account for 10 to 15 percent of anorexia cases; up to half of these are gay or bisexual young people, who may be uncomfortable with a strong, bulky appearance or influenced by the cultural ideal of a lean but muscular male body (Darcy, 2012; Raevuori et al., 2009).

Individuals with anorexia have an extremely distorted body image. Even after becoming severely underweight, they see themselves as too heavy. Most go on self-imposed diets so strict that they struggle to avoid eating in response to hunger. To enhance weight loss, they exercise strenuously.

In their attempt to reach "perfect" slimness, individuals with anorexia lose 25 to 50 percent of their body weight. A normal menstrual cycle requires about 15 percent body fat, so many girls with anorexia experience delayed menarche or menstrual cycle disruptions. Malnutrition causes pale skin, brittle discolored nails, fine dark hairs all over the body, and extreme sensitivity to cold. If it continues, the heart muscle can shrink, the kidneys can fail, and irreversible brain damage and loss of bone mass can occur. About 5 percent of individuals with anorexia die of the disorder each decade, due to physical complications or suicide (American Psychiatric Association, 2013).

Aiva, age 16, an anorexia nervosa patient, is shown at left on the day she entered treatment. She weighed just 77 pounds—69 percent of her normal body weight. At right, Aiva appears 10 weeks later, on her last day of treatment. Less than 50 percent of young people with anorexia recover fully.

Forces within the person, the family, and the larger culture give rise to anorexia nervosa. Identical twins share the disorder more often than fraternal twins, indicating a genetic influence. Abnormalities in neurotransmitters in the brain, linked to anxiety and impulse control, may make some individuals more susceptible (Kaye, 2008; Lock & Kirz, 2008). And problem eating behavior in early childhood—persistently refusing to eat or eating very little—is linked to anorexia in adolescence (Nicholls & Viner, 2009). Many young people with anorexia have unrealistically high standards for their own behavior and performance, are emotionally inhibited, and avoid intimate ties outside the family. Consequently, they are often excellent students who are responsible and well-behaved. But as we have also seen, the societal image of "thin is beautiful" contributes to the poor body image of many girls—especially early-maturing girls, who are at greatest risk (Hoste & Le Grange, 2013).

In addition, parent–adolescent interactions reveal problems related to adolescent autonomy. Often the mothers of these girls have high expectations for physical appearance, achievement, and social acceptance and are overprotective and controlling. Fathers tend to be emotionally distant. These parental behaviors may contribute to affected girls' persistent anxiety and fierce pursuit of perfection in achievement, respectable behavior, and thinness (Kaye, 2008). Nevertheless, it remains unclear whether maladaptive parent–child relationships precede the disorder, emerge as a response to it, or both.

Because individuals with anorexia commonly deny or minimize the seriousness of their disorder, treating it is difficult. The complex family, psychological, and health concerns involved generally require a team of medical and mental health professionals collaborating with the patient's family (Hoste & Le Grange, 2013). Hospitalization is often necessary to prevent life-threatening malnutrition. The most successful treatment is family therapy and medication to reduce anxiety and neurotransmitter imbalances (Robin & Le Grange, 2010). As a supplementary approach, behavior modification—in which hospitalized patients are rewarded with praise, social contact, and opportunities for exercise when they eat and gain weight—is helpful.

Still, less than 50 percent of young people with anorexia recover fully. For many, eating problems continue in less extreme form. About 10 percent show signs of a less severe, but nevertheless debilitating, disorder: bulimia nervosa.

BULIMIA NERVOSA When Sabrina's 16-year-old brother, Louis, brought his girlfriend Cassie to the house, Sabrina admired her good figure. "What willpower!" Sabrina thought. "Cassie hardly touches food. But what's the matter with her teeth?"

Cassie's secret was not willpower. She actually had great difficulty controlling her appetite. Cassie suffered from **bulimia nervosa,** an eating disorder in which young people (again, mainly girls, but gay and bisexual boys are also vulnerable) engage in strict dieting and excessive exercise accompanied by binge eating, often followed by deliberate vomiting and purging with laxatives (Wichstrøm, 2006). When she was alone, Cassie often felt anxious and unhappy. She responded with eating rampages, consuming thousands of calories in an hour or two, followed by vomiting that eroded the enamel on her teeth. In some cases, bulimia can lead to life-threatening damage to the throat and stomach.

Bulimia is more common than anorexia nervosa, affecting about 2 to 4 percent of teenage girls, only 5 percent of whom previously suffered from anorexia. Twin studies show that bulimia, like anorexia, is influenced by heredity (Klump, Kaye, & Strober, 2001). Overweight and early menarche increase the risk. Some adolescents with bulimia, like those with anorexia, are perfectionists. But most are impulsive, sensation-seeking young people who lack self-control in many areas, engaging in petty shoplifting, alcohol abuse, and other risky behaviors (Kaye, 2008). And although girls with bulimia, like those with anorexia, are pathologically anxious about gaining weight, they may have experienced their parents as disengaged and emotionally unavailable rather than controlling (Fairburn & Harrison, 2003).

In contrast to young people with anorexia, those with bulimia usually feel depressed and guilty about their abnormal eating habits; many report suicidal thoughts (Bodell, Joiner, & Keel, 2013). Because affected individuals desperately want help, bulimia is usually easier to treat than anorexia, through support groups, nutrition education, training in changing eating habits, and anti-anxiety, antidepressant, and appetite-control medication (Hay & Bacaltchuk, 2004).

BINGE-EATING DISORDER Some adolescents repeatedly engage in out-of-control binge eating but do not purge afterward. Between 2 and 3 percent of adolescent girls and close to 1 percent of boys experience episodes of **binge-eating disorder**—binging at least once a week for three months or longer, without compensatory behavior (American Psychiatric Association, 2013; Smink et al., 2014).

Binge-eating disorder is equally prevalent among whites, African Americans, Asian Americans, and Hispanics, and it typically leads to weight gain and obesity. Some binge eaters try to lose weight by dieting, but they do not engage in the prolonged, restrictive dieting characteristic of anorexia and bulimia (American Psychiatric Association, 2013). Like other eating disorders, binge-eating disorder is associated with social adjustment difficulties, and similar to individuals with bulimia, many binge eaters experience heightened emotional distress and suicidal thoughts (Stice, Marti, & Rohde, 2013). Effective treatments resemble those used for bulimia (Vocks et al., 2010).

Injuries

As noted in Chapter 11, the rate of unintentional injuries increases during adolescence (see page 417), due to risk taking fueled by sensation seeking and a tendency to act without forethought. Automobile accidents are the leading killer of U.S. teenagers, accounting for more than 25 percent of deaths between ages 15 and 19 (Centers for Disease Control and Prevention, 2014d). Many result from driving at high speeds, using alcohol, not wearing seat belts, or texting while driving (Kann et al., 2014). Parents must set firm limits on their teenagers' car use, particularly with respect to drinking, using mobile devices, and fastening seat belts. These efforts are more likely to succeed in families with a history of good parent–child communication—a powerful preventive of adolescent injury (Sleet & Mercy, 2003).

U.S. adolescent automobile fatalities have declined steadily over the past 35 years, especially among boys, who account for the majority of these deaths (Child Trends, 2014b). Many states have adopted graduated licensing laws, aimed at keeping newly licensed teenagers from driving in high-risk situations—for example, by limiting the number of young passengers, imposing a lower speed limit, and setting a curfew to be off the roads. These laws greatly reduce adolescent fatalities (Williams, Teft, &, Grabowsky, 2012). The more restrictive the regulations, the more lives saved.

In the United States, firearms cause the majority of other fatal injuries. Although violence-related behaviors among high school students have declined in recent decades, nearly 18 percent report having carried a weapon within the past month—5 percent, a gun (Kann et al., 2014). The rate of disability and death resulting from firearms is especially high in poverty-stricken inner-city neighborhoods. In response, many schools have installed metal detectors and security guards—environmental changes that increase teenagers' fear of crime but have little impact on violence (Gagnon & Leone, 2002). School-based violence prevention programs (see Chapter 13, page 512) help reduce assaults. Banning handguns is an especially powerful tactic. In nations with strict gun registration, safety, and control policies, including prohibition of handguns, the firearm death rate among 15- to 19-year-olds is, on average, one-fourth the U.S. rate (see Figure 14.6).

A third type of adolescent injury is sports-related. Close to 2 million U.S. 10- to 19-year-olds with sports and recreational injuries visit hospital emergency departments each year (Centers for Disease Control and Prevention, 2011). Many sports injuries are muscle strains and bruises, but occasionally, severe injuries occur, generally from collision with others in basketball, football, ice hockey, and soccer and from physical fights between players.

Concussions, as noted in Chapter 11, are of particular concern, especially among football players. Once considered minor, concussions can have lasting effects on cognitive and emotional functioning, especially if an athlete returns to play too quickly. Compared to adults, adolescents require more recovery time (McCrory et al., 2013). Concussions among high school athletes have more than doubled during the past decade (Rosenthal et al., 2014). Some of this increase, however, may reflect greater awareness among coaches, parents, and players, leading to more accurate diagnoses.

The safest athletic activities during the pubertal growth period are limited-contact team sports, such as basketball and volleyball, and individual sports, such as track, swimming, and tennis. However, injuries—including concussions—can occur during any sports activity.

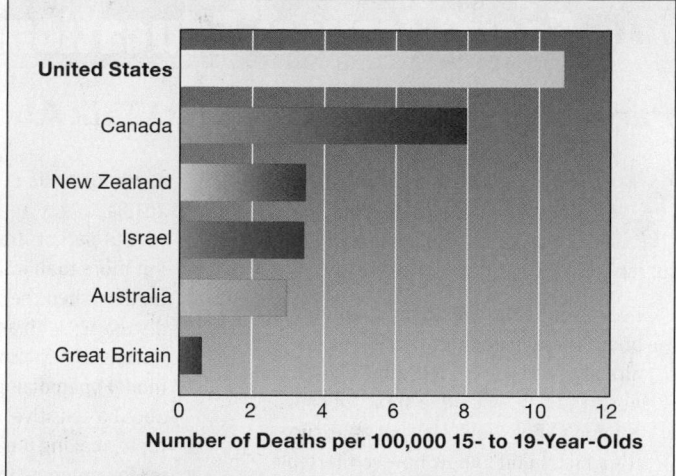

FIGURE 14.6 **Firearm death rates among 15- to 19-year-olds in six industrialized nations.** Death rates are far higher in the United States than in nations with strict gun control policies, including banning of handguns. (Based on Canadian Paediatric Society, 2005; Centers for Disease Control and Prevention, 2014d; Fingerhut & Christoffel, 2002.)

Sexual Activity

Louis and Cassie hadn't planned to have intercourse—it "just happened." After dating for three months, Cassie began to wonder, "Will Louis think I'm normal if I don't have sex with him? If he wants to and I say no, will I lose him?" Both young people knew their parents wouldn't approve. In fact, when Franca and Antonio noticed how attached Louis was to Cassie, they talked to him about the importance of waiting and the dangers of pregnancy. But that Friday evening, Louis and Cassie's feelings for each other seemed overwhelming. "If I don't make a move," Louis thought, "will she think I'm a wimp?"

Adolescence is an especially important time for the development of sexuality. But American teenagers receive contradictory and confusing messages about their readiness for sex.

Social Issues: Education

Parents and Teenagers (Don't) Talk About Sex

When a researcher asked a father of two girls and a boy to reflect on communication about sexual issues in his family, he replied,

> I've never had to talk to my children . . . about these issues because . . . my wife's already done it. . . . I feel almost guilty for not partaking. The other thing, of course, is I don't know how—it's not an excuse, it's a fact. I don't know how comfortable they would be, me trying to talk to them about these topics. . . . So I guess it's a bit of a coward's way out, to save embarrassment by both parties. (Kirkman, Rosenthal, & Feldman, 2002, p. 60)

In families varying widely in SES and ethnicity, warm communication, in which parents provide information on sex and contraception and convey their values, is associated with teenagers' adoption of parents' views and with reduced sexual risk taking (Commendador, 2010; Fasula & Miller, 2006; Usher-Seriki, Bynum, & Callands, 2008). But many parents fail to discuss sex, birth control, and negative consequences of pregnancy with their teenagers.

As this father's remarks suggest, parents often steer clear of meaningful discussions with teenagers about sex out of fear of embarrassment and uncertainty about how to address sexual issues (Wilson et al., 2010). They also express concern that the adolescent will not take them seriously. And parents frequently assume that talking about sex is unnecessary, believing that teenagers learn everything they need to know about the subject at school (Hyde et al., 2013).

But parents transmit more than information when they discuss sex with adolescents. They also model open dialogue about a sensitive topic, making it easier for young people to talk about sex with peers. In a study of middle school students, those who talked about sexual health with parents were more likely to discuss these topics with their dating partners (Widman et al., 2014). Through conversations with parents, teenagers practice communication skills that may help them refuse unwanted sexual advances, ensure that a sexual encounter is mutually consensual, and negotiate about birth control and protection against sexually transmitted infections.

When parents do initiate discussions, teenagers may be reluctant to participate. They complain that parents do not treat them as equals, know little about contemporary teenage lifestyles, and are not sufficiently open, supportive, and understanding. Perhaps because of their better communication skills, mothers talk to

By listening patiently and sympathetically, this mother encourages her daughter to ask questions and express opinions about sexual issues without feeling judged or uncomfortable. Warm communication about sexuality is associated with teenagers' adoption of parents' views and with reduced sexual risk taking.

adolescents about sex and birth control more than fathers do. But mothers more often dominate conversations about sexual than about everyday matters, especially when talking to sons. When parents dominate, teenagers withdraw, reporting fewer sexual discussions and less knowledge (Lefkowitz, Sigman, & Au, 2000; Lefkowitz et al., 2002). Overall, balanced, mutual interaction and thorough consideration of sexual topics occur more often with daughters than with sons (Raffaelli & Green, 2003).

Cultural variations exist in parental communication about sex. For example, when Hispanic women who had grown up in U.S. Spanish-

---

With the arrival of puberty, hormonal changes—in particular, the production of androgens in young people of both sexes—lead to an increase in sex drive (Best & Fortenberry, 2013). In response, adolescents become very concerned about managing sexuality in social relationships. New cognitive capacities involving perspective taking and self-reflection affect their efforts to do so. Yet like the eating behaviors we have just discussed, adolescent sexuality is heavily influenced by the young person's social context.

THE IMPACT OF CULTURE   TAKE A MOMENT... When did you first learn about sex, and how? Was sex discussed openly in your family, or was it treated with secrecy? Exposure to sex, education about it, and efforts to limit the sexual curiosity of children and adolescents vary widely around the world. At one extreme are a number of Middle Eastern peoples, who murder girls if they lose their virginity before marriage. At the other extreme are several Asian and Pacific Island groups with highly permissive sexual attitudes and practices. For example, among the Trobriand Islanders of Papua New Guinea, older companions provide children

speaking families were asked to recall what their parents had told them about sex as teenagers, only a minority recalled talking about physical changes, intercourse, and pregnancy. Rather, parental messages usually took the form of strict limits on dating. Teresa, from a Mexican-American family, said, "You would be outside the house [where you could be observed] . . . your parents would tell you . . . no kissing or holding hands or nothing, actually it was just talking . . . until you decided whether you wanted to get married and then . . . the guy would have to . . .

ask for your hand in marriage" (Raffaelli & Ontai, 2001, p. 301). The gap between parental expectations and U.S. cultural dating practices often became a source of conflict. Many women reported having engaged in "sneak dating," but they were ill-prepared to manage their own sexual behavior. Over half did not use birth control the first time they had sex, and nearly a third had an unplanned pregnancy.

In sum, parent-based sex education has many advantages. Parents can discuss topics in ways consistent with their own values and, unlike

school classes, can tailor their delivery of information to the adolescent's personality and current life circumstances. But parents need help communicating effectively. Parents who receive training in talking with teenagers about sex become more comfortable with the subject and have more frequent discussions (Akers, Holland, & Bost, 2011). Through training, parents can learn to engage in give-and-take, use open-ended questions, and avoid being judgmental. Refer to Applying What We Know below for qualities of successful communication.

Applying What We Know

Communicating with Adolescents About Sexual Issues

PARENTING STRATEGY	EXPLANATION
Foster open communication.	Let the teenager know you are a willing and trustworthy resource by stating that you are available when questions arise and will answer fully and accurately.
Use correct terms for body parts.	Correct vocabulary gives the young person a basis for future discussion and also indicates that sex is not a forbidden topic.
Use effective discussion techniques.	Listen, encourage the adolescent to participate, ask open-ended rather than yes/no questions, and give supportive responses. Avoid dominating and lecturing, which cause teenagers to withdraw.
Reflect before speaking.	When the adolescent asks questions or offers opinions about sex, remain nonjudgmental. If you differ with the teenager's views, convey your perspective in a nonthreatening manner, emphasizing that although you disagree, you are not attacking his or her character. Trying to dictate the young person's behavior generally results in alienation.
Keep conversations going.	Many parents think their job is finished once they have had the "big talk" in early adolescence. But young people are more likely to be influenced by an accumulation of smaller discussions. If open communication begins early and is sustained, the teenager is more likely to return with thoughts and questions and to discuss sexual health issues with dating partners.

Source: Berkowitz, 2004; Wilson et al., 2010.

with instruction in sexual practices, and adolescents are expected to engage in sexual experimentation with a variety of partners (Weiner, 1988).

Despite the prevailing image of a sexually free adolescent, sexual attitudes in North America are relatively restrictive. Typically, parents provide little or no information about sex, discourage sex play, and rarely talk about sex in children's presence. When young people become interested in sex, only about half report getting information from parents about intercourse, pregnancy prevention, and sexually transmitted infections (see the Social Issues: Education box above).

Rather, the majority learn about sex from friends, books, magazines, movies, TV, and the Internet (Jaccard, Dodge, & Dittus, 2002; Sprecher, Harris, & Meyers, 2008). Among TV shows that adolescents prefer, more than 80 percent contain sexual content (Wright, Malamuth, & Donnerstein, 2012). Most depict partners as spontaneous and passionate, taking no steps to avoid pregnancy or sexually transmitted infections, and experiencing no negative consequences. In several studies, teenagers' media exposure to sexual content predicted increased sexual activity, pregnancies, and sexual harassment behaviors (offensive name-calling or touching, pressuring a peer for a date), even after many other relevant factors were controlled (Brown & L'Engle, 2009; Roberts, Henriksen, & Foehr, 2009; Wright, Malamuth, & Donnerstein, 2012).

Not surprisingly, adolescents who are prone to early sexual activity choose to consume more sexualized media (Steinberg & Monahan, 2011; Vandenbosch & Eggermont, 2013). Still, the Internet is a hazardous "sex educator." In a survey of a large sample of U.S. 10- to 17-year-old Web users, 42 percent said they had viewed online pornographic websites (images of naked people or people having sex) while surfing the Internet in the past 12 months. Of these, 66 percent indicated they had encountered the images accidentally and did not want to view them. Most were 13- to 17-year-olds, but 16 percent of 10- to 11-year-olds experienced these unwanted encounters (Wolak, Mitchell, & Finkelhor, 2007). And youths who felt depressed, had been bullied by peers, or were involved in delinquent activities had more encounters with Internet pornography, which may have intensified their adjustment problems.

Consider the contradictory messages delivered by these sources. On one hand, adults emphasize that sex at a young age and outside marriage is wrong. On the other hand, the social environment extols sexual excitement, experimentation, and promiscuousness. American teenagers are left bewildered, poorly informed about sexual facts, and with little sound advice on how to conduct their sex lives responsibly.

ADOLESCENT SEXUAL ATTITUDES AND BEHAVIOR   Although differences between subcultural groups exist, sexual attitudes of U.S. adolescents and adults have become more liberal over the past half century. Compared with previous generations, more people approve of sexual intercourse before marriage (Elias, Fullerton, & Simpson, 2013; Rifkin, 2014). During the past 15 years, adolescents have swung slightly back toward more conservative sexual beliefs, largely in response to the risk of sexually transmitted infections, especially AIDS, and to teenage sexual abstinence programs sponsored by schools and religious organizations (Akers et al., 2011; Ali & Scelfo, 2002).

Trends in adolescents' sexual behavior are consistent with their attitudes. Rates of extramarital sex among U.S. young people rose for several decades but have recently declined (Kann et al., 2014; Martinez, Copen, & Abma, 2011). Nevertheless, as Figure 14.7 reveals, a substantial percentage of young people are sexually active quite early, by ninth grade (age 14 to 15).

The quality of adolescent sexual experiences varies, depending on circumstances. About 70 percent of sexually active teenagers report that they first had sex with a steady dating partner, and many have only one or two partners during high school (Martinez, Copen, & Abma, 2011). But 15 percent of high school students report having sexual relations with four or more partners in the past year (Kann et al., 2014). Mutually consensual sexual activity in the context of a stable, caring romantic relationship can be a positive and satisfying experience for older adolescents. But when teenagers engage in casual sex, or have sex when they have been drinking or using drugs, they often report negative feelings, including guilt and depression (Harden, 2014).

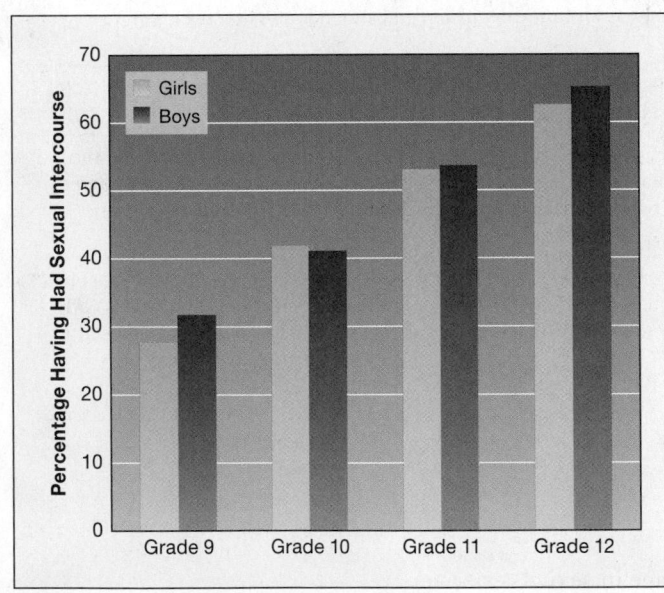

FIGURE 14.7 **U.S. adolescents who report ever having had sexual intercourse.** Most U.S. adolescents become sexually active during the high school years. Boys tend to have their first intercourse earlier than girls, but in general, rates of boys and girls having had sexual intercourse are similar. (Based on Kann et al., 2014.)

CHARACTERISTICS OF ADOLESCENTS WHO ENGAGE IN EARLY SEXUAL ACTIVITY
Although 74 percent of young people in the U.S. have sex before they turn 20, less than 10 percent do so before age 14. Compared to older adolescents, younger sexually experienced teenagers are less likely to be romantically involved with their partner or to use birth control. They are also more likely to report that their first sexual encounter was unwanted or forced (Finer & Philbin, 2013; Kaplan et al., 2013).

Early and frequent teenage sexual activity is linked to a variety of adverse personal, family, peer, and educational characteristics. These include childhood impulsivity, weak sense of personal control over life events, early pubertal timing, parental divorce, single-parent and stepfamily homes, large family size, little or no religious involvement, weak parental monitoring, disrupted parent–child communication, sexually active friends and older siblings, poor school performance, lower educational aspirations, and tendency to engage in norm-violating acts, including alcohol and drug use and delinquency (Coley, Votruba-Drzal, & Schindler, 2009; Siebenbruner, Zimmer-Gembeck, & Egeland, 2007; Zimmer-Gembeck & Helfand, 2008).

Because many of these factors are associated with growing up in a low-income family, it is not surprising that early sexual activity is more common among young people from economically disadvantaged homes. Living in a neighborhood high in physical deterioration, crime, and violence also increases the likelihood that teenagers will be sexually active early (Best & Fortenberry, 2013; Ge et al., 2002). In such neighborhoods, social ties are weak, adults exert little oversight and control over adolescents' activities, and negative peer influences are widespread. In fact, the high rate of early sexual activity among African-American teenagers— 14 percent report having had sexual intercourse before age 13, compared with 6 percent of all U.S. young people—may be largely explained by widespread poverty in the black population (Kann et al., 2014; Kaplan et al., 2013).

CONTRACEPTIVE USE Although adolescent contraceptive use has increased in recent years (see Figure 14.8), about 18 percent of sexually active teenagers in the United States are at risk for unintended pregnancy because they do not use contraception consistently (Jones, Mosher, & Daniels, 2012). Why do they fail to take precautions? Typically, teenagers respond, "I was waiting until I had a steady boyfriend," or "I wasn't planning to have sex."

As our discussion of adolescent cognitive development in Chapter 15 will reveal, although adolescents can consider many possibilities when faced with a problem, they often fail to apply this reasoning to everyday situations. We have seen that in the midst of everyday peer pressures, self-regulation is difficult for adolescents, who often overlook the consequences of engaging in risky behaviors. And many teenagers—especially those from troubled, low-SES families— do not have realistic expectations about the impact of early parenthood on their current and future lives (Stevens-Simon, Sheeder, & Harter, 2005).

In contrast, teenagers who report good relationships with parents and who talk openly with them about sex and contraception are more likely to use birth control (Henrich et al., 2006; Widman et al., 2014). But few adolescents believe their parents would be understanding and supportive. School sex education classes, as well, often leave teenagers with incomplete or incorrect knowledge. Some young people do not know where to get birth control counseling and devices. And those engaged in high-risk sexual behaviors are especially likely to worry that a doctor or family planning clinic might not keep their visits confidential (Lehrer et al., 2007). Most of these young people forgo essential health care but continue to have sex without contraception.

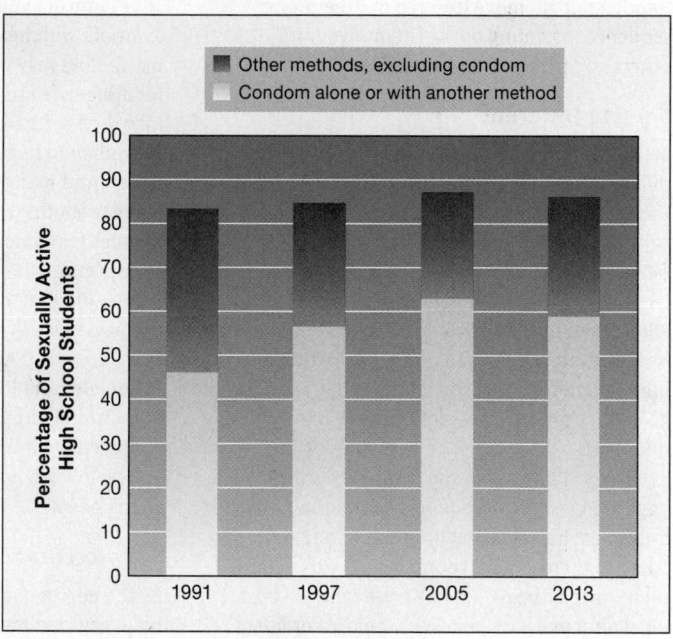

FIGURE 14.8 Contraceptive use at last intercourse among sexually active U.S. high school students, 1991 to 2013. Adolescents' use of contraceptives—especially condoms—increased throughout the 1990s and early 2000s. More recently, overall rates of contraceptive use stabilized, and condom use declined slightly. At the same time, adolescents increasingly chose other methods that are effective, most commonly hormonal options— the pill, patch, or vaginal ring. (Based on Centers for Disease Control and Prevention, 2014i; Kann et al., 2014.)

SEXUAL ORIENTATION So far, we have focused only on heterosexual behavior. About 5 percent of U.S. high school students identify as lesbian, gay, or bisexual, and another 2 to 3 percent report being unsure of their sexual orientation (Kann et al., 2011). An unknown number experience same-sex attraction but have not come out to friends or family (see the Biology and Environment box on page 542). Adolescence is an equally crucial time for the sexual development of these individuals, and societal attitudes, again, loom large in how well they fare.

Biology and Environment

Lesbian, Gay, and Bisexual Youths: Coming Out to Oneself and Others

Cultures vary as much in their acceptance of homosexuality as in their approval of extramarital sex. In the United States, societal attitudes toward lesbian, gay, and bisexual people are becoming more accepting, but anti-gay prejudice remains widespread (Pew Research Center, 2013b). This makes forming a sexual identity more challenging for sexual minority youths than for their heterosexual counterparts.

Wide variation in sexual identity formation exists, depending on personal, family, and community factors. Yet interviews with gay and lesbian adolescents and adults reveal that many (though not all) move through a three-phase sequence in coming out to themselves and others.

Feeling Different

Many gay men and lesbians say that they felt different from other children when they were young. Typically, this first sense of their biologically determined sexual orientation appears between ages 6 and 12, in play interests more like those of the other gender (Rahman & Wilson, 2003). Boys may find that they are less interested in sports, more drawn to quieter activities, and more emotionally sensitive than other boys; girls that they are more athletic and active than other girls.

By age 10, many of these children start to engage in *sexual questioning*—wondering why the typical heterosexual orientation does not apply to them. Often, young people experience their sense of being different as deeply distressing. Compared with children who are confident of their sexual orientation, sexual-questioning children report greater anxiety about peer relationships and greater dissatisfaction with their biological gender over time (Carver, Egan, & Perry, 2004).

Confusion

With the arrival of puberty, feeling different clearly encompasses feeling sexually different. Although wide variation exists, on average, boys begin to think they are gay at around age 10 and know for sure at around age 15 (Pew Research Center, 2013b). Awareness tends to emerge a few years later for girls, around 13 and 18, respectively, perhaps because adolescent social pressures toward heterosexuality are particularly intense for girls.

Realizing that same-sex attraction has personal relevance generally sparks additional confusion. A few adolescents resolve their discomfort by crystallizing a lesbian, gay, or bisexual identity quickly, with a flash of insight into their sense of being different. But most experience an inner struggle and deep sense of isolation—outcomes intensified by lack of role models and social support (Safren & Pantalone, 2006).

Some throw themselves into activities they associate with heterosexuality. Boys may go out for athletic teams; girls may drop softball and basketball in favor of dance. And many lesbian and gay youths (more females than males) try heterosexual dating, sometimes to hide their sexual orientation and at other times to develop intimacy skills that they later apply to same-sex relationships (D'Augelli, 2006). Those who are extremely troubled and guilt-ridden may escape into alcohol, drugs, and suicidal thinking. As Chapter 16 will reveal, suicide attempts are unusually high among lesbian, gay, and bisexual young people.

Self-Acceptance

By the end of adolescence, the majority of lesbian, gay, and bisexual teenagers accept their sexual identity. But they face another crossroad: whether to tell others. Powerful stigma against their sexual orientation leads some to decide that disclosure is impossible: While self-defining as gay, they otherwise "pass" as heterosexual. When they do come out, sexual minority youths often face intense peer hostility, including verbal abuse and physical attacks. These experiences trigger intense emotional distress, depression, school truancy, and drug use in victims (Dragowski et al., 2011; Rosario & Schrimshaw, 2013).

Nevertheless, many young people eventually acknowledge their sexual orientation publicly, usually by telling trusted friends first. Once teenagers establish a same-sex sexual or romantic relationship, many come out to parents. Few parents respond with severe rejection; most are either positive or slightly negative and disbelieving. Still, lesbian, gay, and bisexual young people report lower levels of family support than their

Lesbian, gay, bisexual, and transgender high school students and their allies participate in an annual Youth Pride Festival and March. When peers react with acceptance, coming out strengthens sexual identity formation among sexual minority youths.

heterosexual agemates (Needham & Austin, 2010). Yet parental understanding is a key predictor of favorable adjustment—including reduced *internalized homophobia,* or societal prejudice turned against the self (Bregman et al., 2013; Rothman et al., 2012).

When people react positively, coming out strengthens the young person's sexual identity as valid, meaningful, and fulfilling. Contact with lesbian, gay, and bisexual peers is important for reaching this phase, and changes in society permit many adolescents in urban areas to attain it earlier than their counterparts did a decade or two ago. Gay and lesbian communities exist in large cities, along with specialized interest groups, social clubs, religious groups, newspapers, and periodicals. But teenagers in small towns and rural areas may have difficulty meeting other sexual minority youths and finding a supportive environment. These adolescents have a special need for caring adults and peers who can help them find self- and social acceptance.

Lesbian, gay, and bisexual teenagers who succeed in coming out to themselves and others integrate their sexual orientation into a broader sense of identity, a process we will address in Chapter 16. As a result, they no longer need to focus so heavily on their sexual orientation, and energy is freed for other aspects of psychological growth. In sum, coming out can foster many aspects of adolescent development, including self-esteem, psychological well-being, and relationships with family and friends.

Heredity makes an important contribution to sexual orientation: Identical twins of both sexes are more likely than fraternal twins to share a homosexual orientation; so are biological (as opposed to adoptive) relatives (Kendler et al., 2000; Långström et al., 2010). Furthermore, male homosexuality tends to be more common on the maternal than on the paternal side of families, suggesting that it may be X-linked (see Chapter 2). Indeed, one gene-mapping study found that among 40 pairs of gay brothers, 33 (82 percent) had an identical segment of DNA on the X chromosome. One or several genes in that region might predispose males to develop same-sex attraction (Hamer et al., 1993).

How might heredity influence sexual orientation? According to some researchers, certain genes affect the level or impact of prenatal sex hormones, which modify brain structures in ways that induce homosexual feelings and behavior (Bailey et al., 1995; LeVay, 1993). In Chapter 10, we saw how prenatal androgen exposure influences children's gender-typical play behaviors (see page 386). Consistent with early hormonal influences, childhood gender non-conformity—boys' preference for quiet, "feminine" play and girls' preference for active, "masculine" pursuits—is strongly linked to homosexuality.

Keep in mind, however, that both genetic and environmental factors can alter prenatal hormones. Girls exposed prenatally to very high levels of androgens or estrogens—either because of a genetic defect or from drugs given to the mother to prevent miscarriage—are more likely to develop lesbian or bisexual orientations (Hines, 2011). Furthermore, gay men tend to be later in birth order and to have a higher-than-average number of older brothers (Bogaert & Skorska, 2011; VanderLaan et al., 2014). Perhaps mothers with several male children sometimes produce antibodies to androgens, which reduce the prenatal impact of male sex hormones on the brains of later-born boys.

Stereotypes and misconceptions about homosexuality and bisexuality continue to be widespread. For example, contrary to common belief, most sexual minority adolescents and adults are not "gender-deviant" in dress or behavior. Also, attraction to members of the same sex is not limited to lesbian, gay, and bisexual teenagers. In recent surveys, between 17 and 78 percent of teenagers who reported sexual experiences with same-sex partners identified as heterosexual (Kann et al., 2011). And a study of lesbian, bisexual, and "unlabeled" young women confirmed that bisexuality is not, as often assumed, a transient state (Diamond, 2008). Over a 10-year period, few bisexuals changed to a lesbian or heterosexual orientation, and most reported stable proportions of same-sex versus other-sex attractions over time.

The evidence to date indicates that genetic and prenatal biological influences are largely responsible for homosexuality; the origins of bisexuality are not yet known. In our evolutionary past, homosexuality may have served the adaptive function of reducing aggressive competition for other-sex mates (Rahman & Wilson, 2003).

Sexually Transmitted Infections

Sexually active adolescents, regardless of sexual orientation, are at risk for sexually transmitted infections (STIs) (see Table 14.2 on page 544). Young people age 15 to 24 have the highest rates of STIs of all age groups (Satterwhite et al., 2013). Despite a recent decline in STIs in the United States, one out of six sexually active teenagers contracts one of these illnesses each year—a rate three or more times that of Canada and Western Europe (Greydanus et al., 2012; Public Health Agency of Canada, 2014). Teenagers at greatest risk are the same ones most likely to engage in irresponsible sexual behavior: economically disadvantaged young people who feel a sense of hopelessness (Niccolai et al., 2004). Left untreated, STIs can lead to sterility and life-threatening complications.

By far the most serious STI is HIV/AIDS. In contrast to other Western nations, where the incidence of HIV infection among people under age 30 is low, one-fifth of U.S. HIV cases are young people between ages 13 and 24. Because AIDS symptoms typically do not emerge until 8 to 10 years after HIV infection, many young adults diagnosed with HIV or AIDS contracted the virus during adolescence. Male adolescents who have sex with HIV-positive same-sex partners account for most of these cases. But 18 percent are due to heterosexual spread of the disease—mostly through male to female transmission (Centers for Disease Control and

TABLE 14.2	Most Common Sexually Transmitted Infections of Adolescence			

INFECTION	CASES PER 100,000 U.S. 15- TO 19-YEAR-OLDS	CAUSE	SYMPTOMS AND CONSEQUENCES	TREATMENT
HIV	10.4	Virus	Fever, weight loss, severe fatigue, swollen glands, and diarrhea. As the immune system weakens, severe pneumonias and cancers, especially on the skin, appear. Death due to other diseases usually occurs.	No cure; experimental drugs prolong life
Chlamydia	2,001.7	Bacteria	Discharge from the penis in males; painful itching, burning vaginal discharge, and dull pelvic pain in females. Often no symptoms. If left untreated, can lead to inflammation of the pelvic region, infertility, and sterility.	Antibiotic drugs
Cytomegalovirus	Unknown[a]	Virus of the herpes family	No symptoms in most cases. Sometimes a mild flulike reaction. In pregnant women, can spread to the embryo or fetus and cause miscarriage or serious birth defects (see page 109).	None; symptoms usually disappear on their own
Gonorrhea	376.8	Bacteria	Discharge from the penis or vagina, painful urination. Sometimes no symptoms. If left untreated, can spread to other regions of the body, resulting in such complications as infertility, sterility, blood poisoning, arthritis, and inflammation of the heart.	Antibiotic drugs
Herpes simplex 2 (genital herpes)	820[b]	Virus	Fluid-filled blisters on the genitals, high fever, severe headache, and muscle aches and tenderness. No symptoms in a few people. In a pregnant woman, can spread to the embryo or fetus and cause miscarriage or serious birth defects (see page 109).	No cure; can be controlled with drug treatment
Human papillomavirus (HPV)	16,075[b]	Virus	Causes genital warts that typically grow near the vaginal opening in females, on the penis or scrotum in males, which may be accompanied by severe itching. Can cause cellular changes that lead to cervical, vaginal, anal, and less commonly penile and oral cancers. A vaccine that prevents the infection is recommended for adolescent girls and women age 11 to 26; its effectiveness for boys and men is not yet known.	Removal of warts, but virus persists
Syphilis	4.1	Bacteria	Painless chancre (sore) at site of entry of germ and swollen glands, followed by rash, patchy hair loss, and sore throat within 1 week to 6 months. These symptoms disappear without treatment. Latent syphilis varies from no symptoms to damage to the brain, heart, and other organs after 5 to 20 years. In pregnant women, can spread to the embryo and fetus and cause birth defects.	Antibiotic drugs
Trichomoniasis ("Trich")	345[b]	Parasite	No symptoms in most cases. When symptoms do occur, they include genital itching and burning, inflammation, and discharge. Inflammation due to trichomoniasis increases the risk of spreading or contracting other STIs, including HIV.	Antibiotic drugs

[a]Cytomegalovirus is the most common STI. Because there are no symptoms in most cases, its precise rate of occurrence is unknown. An estimated that 50 to 80 percent of the population contracts the virus by age 40.
[b]Reported rates are for 15- to 24-year-olds.
Sources: Centers for Disease Control and Prevention, 2013b; 2013d; Satterwhite et al., 2013; U.S. Department of Health and Human Services, 2013b.

Prevention, 2013b). It is at least twice as easy for a male to infect a female with any STI, including HIV, as for a female to infect a male.

As a result of school courses and media campaigns, about 60 percent of U.S. middle school students and 90 percent of high school students are aware of basic facts about HIV and AIDS. But most have limited understanding of other STIs and their consequences, underestimate their own susceptibility, and are poorly informed about how to protect themselves (Kann et al., 2014). Furthermore, high school students report engaging in oral sex much more often than intercourse, and with more partners. But few consistently use STI protection during

Applying What We Know

Preventing Sexually Transmitted Infections

STRATEGY	EXPLANATION
Know your partner well.	Take time to get to know your partner. Find out whether your partner has had sex with many people or has used injectable drugs.
Maintain mutual faithfulness.	This strategy works only when neither partner has an STI at the start of the relationship.
Do not use drugs.	Using a needle, syringe, or drug liquid previously used by others can spread STIs. Alcohol, marijuana, or other illegal substances impair judgment, reducing your capacity to think clearly about the consequences of behavior.
Always use a latex condom when having sex with a nonmarital partner.	Latex condoms give good (but not perfect) protection against STIs by reducing the passage of bacteria and viruses.
Do not have sex with a person you know has an STI.	Even if you are protected by a condom, you still risk contracting STIs. If either partner has engaged in behavior that might have risked HIV infection, a blood test to detect infection must be administered and repeated at least six months after that behavior, to allow for the time the body takes to develop antibodies.
If you get an STI, inform all recent sexual partners.	Notifying people you may have exposed to an STI permits them to get treatment before spreading the infection to others.
Immunization	A vaccine is available to protect against some forms of HPV. Ideally, young people should receive three doses before becoming sexually active, but sexually active youth who did not previously receive the HPV vaccine can still benefit.

oral sex, which is a significant mode of transmission of several STIs, including chlamydia, gonorrhea, herpes, and perhaps HIV (Vasilenko et al., 2014). Concerted efforts are needed to educate young people about the full range of STIs and risky sexual behaviors. Applying What We Know above lists strategies for STI prevention.

Adolescent Pregnancy and Parenthood

Cassie didn't get pregnant after having sex with Louis, but some of her high school classmates were less fortunate. Cassie had heard about Veronica, who missed several periods, pretended nothing was wrong, and didn't go to a doctor until a month before she gave birth. Veronica lived at home until she became pregnant a second time. When her parents told her they didn't have room for a second baby, Veronica dropped out of school and moved in with her 17-year-old boyfriend, Todd, who worked at a fast-food restaurant. A few months later, Todd—tired of being tied down with the babies—left Veronica, who had to apply for public aid to support herself and the two infants.

About 625,000 U.S. teenage girls (almost 11,000 of them younger than age 15)—an estimated 13 percent of those who had sexual intercourse—became pregnant in the most recently reported year (Kost & Henshaw, 2014). Despite a decline of more than 50 percent since 1990, the U.S. adolescent pregnancy rate remains higher than that of most other industrialized countries (see Figure 14.9) (Ventura et al. 2014; World Bank, 2014).

Because about one-fourth of U.S. adolescent pregnancies end in abortion, the number of American teenage births is considerably lower than it was 50 years ago (Kost & Henshaw, 2014). Still, it is up

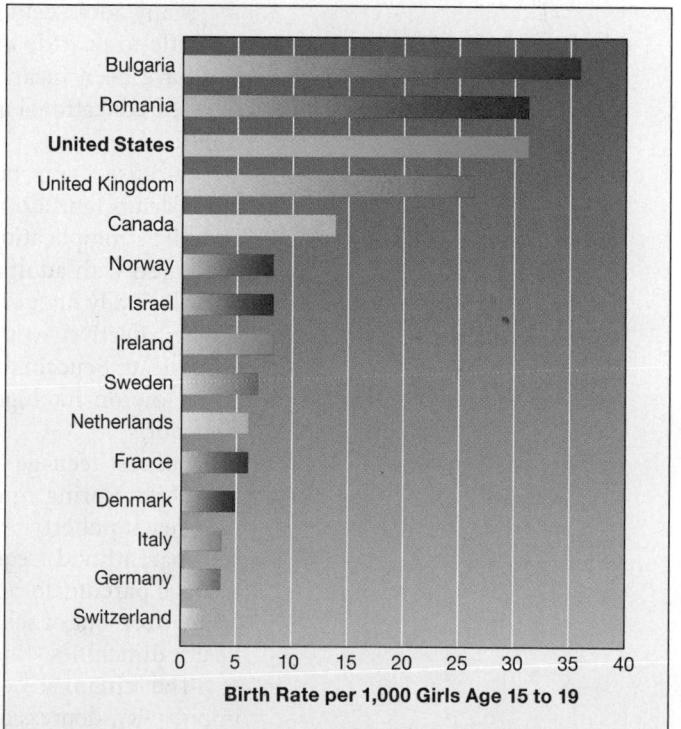

FIGURE 14.9 **Birth rates among 15- to 19-year-olds in 15 industrialized nations.** The U.S. adolescent birth rate greatly exceeds that of most other industrialized nations. (Based on World Bank, 2014.)

to five times higher than in many other developed nations (see Figure 14.9). But teenage parenthood remains a problem today because contemporary adolescents rarely marry before childbirth. In 1960, only 15 percent of teenage births were to unmarried females, compared with 89 percent today (Child Trends, 2014a). Increased social acceptance of single motherhood, along with the belief of many teenage girls that a baby might fill a void in their lives, means that very few girls give up their infants for adoption.

CORRELATES AND CONSEQUENCES OF ADOLESCENT PARENTHOOD Becoming a parent is especially challenging for adolescents, who have not yet established a clear sense of direction for their own lives. Life conditions and personal attributes jointly contribute to adolescent childbearing and also interfere with teenage mothers' capacity to parent effectively.

Teenage parents are far more likely to be poor than agemates who postpone parenthood. Their backgrounds often include low parental warmth and involvement, domestic violence, child abuse and neglect, repeated parental divorce and remarriage, adult models of unmarried parenthood, and residence in neighborhoods where other adolescents also display these risks. Girls at risk for early pregnancy also do poorly in school, use drugs and alcohol, have a childhood history of aggressive and antisocial behavior, associate with deviant peers, and experience high rates of depression (Hillis et al., 2004; Luster & Haddow, 2005; Noll & Shenck, 2013). A high percentage of births to single mothers occur among low-income ethnic minority teenagers. Many turn to early parenthood as a pathway to adulthood when educational and career avenues are unavailable.

The lives of expectant teenagers, already troubled in many ways, tend to worsen in several respects after the baby is born. Adolescent mothers are less likely than their peers to finish high school, get married, or secure employment. About 35 percent become pregnant again within two years, and of these, about half go on to deliver a second child (Child Trends, 2014c; Moore & Brooks-Gunn, 2002; Ruedinger & Cox, 2012). Teenage mothers who do marry are more likely to divorce and, consequently, spend more of their child-rearing years as single parents. Because of low educational attainment, marital instability, and poverty, many teenage mothers are on welfare. If they are employed, their limited education restricts them to unsatisfying, low-paid jobs.

Many adolescent fathers, too, are unemployed or work at unskilled jobs, usually earning too little to provide their children with basic necessities (Bunting & McAuley, 2004). About half have been incarcerated (Elfenbein & Felice, 2003). And for both mothers and fathers, reduced educational and occupational attainment often persists well into adulthood (Taylor, 2009).

Because many pregnant teenage girls have inadequate diets, smoke, use alcohol and other drugs, and do not receive early prenatal care, their babies often experience prenatal and birth complications—especially low birth weight (Khashan, Baker, & Kenny, 2010). And compared with adult mothers, adolescent mothers know less about child development, have unrealistically high expectations of their infants, perceive their babies as more difficult, interact less effectively with them, and more often engage in harsh or abusive parenting (Lee, 2013; Pomerleau, Scuccimarri, & Malcuit, 2003; Ruedinger & Cox, 2012). Their children typically score low on intelligence tests, achieve poorly in school, and engage in disruptive social behavior.

Because teenage parents tend to pass on their personal attributes as well as create unfavorable child-rearing conditions, their offspring are at risk for irresponsible sexual activity when they reach puberty. As the Social Issues: Health box on the following page indicates, adolescent parenthood frequently is repeated in the next generation. Even when children born to teenage parents do not become early childbearers, their development is often compromised: Many drop out of school, struggle financially, and experience long-term physical and mental health difficulties (Ruedinger & Cox, 2012).

The circumstances leading to adolescent parenthood—poverty, family dysfunction, impulsivity, depression, and school failure—are likely responsible for many of the negative consequences associated with it (Hawkes, 2010; Morinis, Carson, Quigley, 2013; Ruedinger & Cox, 2012). Young people from severely disadvantaged backgrounds tend to experience poor social, educational, and economic outcomes; to struggle with the challenges of child rearing;

Social Issues: Health

Like Parent, Like Child: Intergenerational Continuity in Adolescent Parenthood

Does adolescent parenthood increase the chances of teenage childbearing in the next generation? To find out, researchers conducted several unique studies of mothers (first generation)—some who gave birth as teenagers and some who postponed parenting—and their children (second generation), who were followed longitudinally (Campa & Eckenrode, 2006; Hardy et al., 1998; Meade, Kershaw, & Ickovics, 2008). Another investigation followed first-born children of teenage mothers, seeking to identify factors predicting which of these second-generation adolescents would become adolescent parents themselves (Wildsmith et al., 2012).

First-generation mothers' age at first childbirth strongly predicted the age at which second-generation young people—both daughters and sons—became parents. Yet becoming a second-generation teenage parent is not inevitable. Rather, adolescent parenthood is linked to a set of related, unfavorable family conditions and personal characteristics, which negatively influence development over an extended time and, therefore, often transfer to the next generation:

- *Home environmental quality and parenting skills.* The long-term poverty and unstable marital patterns linked to adolescent parenthood reduce the quality of the home environment—in terms of organization, play and learning materials, and parental warmth, encouragement, verbal stimulation, and acceptance of the child (as opposed to punitiveness and abuse) (Meade, Kershaw, & Ickovics, 2008; Wildsmith et al., 2012). Compared with daughters in other families, the daughters of unmarried adolescent mothers are far more likely to live in homes with negative features, even after mothers' prebirth SES is controlled (Campa & Eckenrode, 2006). Poor-quality home environments, as we saw in Chapter 9, are associated with lower language and IQ scores, which, in turn, contribute to the poor academic performance and decision making associated with early sexual activity, lax use of contraceptives, and adolescent childbearing.

- *Intelligence and education.* Younger mothers' cognitive deficits and reduced educational attainment increase the chances that their children will experience poor-quality home environments and, thus, in adolescence will engage in the maladaptive behaviors just mentioned (Hardy et al., 1998; Wildsmith et al., 2012).

- *Father absence.* In several studies, intergenerational continuity in adolescent parenthood—especially for daughters—was far greater when teenage mothers remained unmarried (Campa & Eckenrode, 2006; Meade, Kershaw, & Ickovics, 2008). Marriage may limit the negative impact of teenage childbearing on development by strengthening parental financial resources and

Will the child of this teenage couple also become an adolescent parent? Negative family conditions and personal characteristics associated with early childbearing increase the likelihood that teenage parenthood will recur in the next generation.

involvement and reducing family stress. It may be particularly protective for girls because unmarried fathers are less likely to remain in regular contact with daughters than with sons. Recall from Chapter 13 that a warm, involved noncustodial father is linked to reduced early sexual activity in girls (see page 502).

In sum, a life course of adversity—poverty, depleted and disorganized home environments, poor parenting, father absence, intellectual deficits, poor academic performance, and limited educational opportunities—contributes to intergenerational continuity in adolescent pregnancy and parenthood.

and to have children with cognitive, emotional, and behavior problems, whether they give birth as teenagers or delay parenthood until their twenties.

Still, outcomes vary widely. If a teenage mother finishes high school, secures gainful employment, avoids additional births, and finds a stable partner, long-term disruptions in her own and her child's development will be less severe.

PREVENTION STRATEGIES Preventing teenage pregnancy means addressing the many factors underlying early sexual activity and lack of contraceptive use. Too often, sex education courses are given late (after sexual activity has begun), last only a few sessions, and are limited to a catalog of facts about anatomy and reproduction. Sex education that goes beyond this minimum does not encourage early sex, as some opponents claim (Chin et al., 2012). It does improve awareness of sexual facts—knowledge that is necessary for responsible behavior.

Knowledge, however, is not enough. Sex education must also help teenagers build a bridge between what they know and what they do. Effective sex education programs combine several key elements:

- They teach techniques for handling sexual situations—including refusal skills for avoiding risky sexual behaviors and communication skills for improving contraceptive use—through role-playing and other activities in which young people practice those behaviors.
- They deliver clear, accurate messages that are appropriate in view of participating adolescents' culture and sexual experiences.
- They last long enough to have an impact.
- They provide specific information about contraceptives and ready access to them.

Many studies show that sex education that includes these components can delay the initiation of sexual activity, increase contraceptive use, and reduce pregnancy rates (Chin et al., 2012; Kirby, 2002, 2008).

Proposals to increase access to contraceptives are the most controversial aspect of U.S. adolescent pregnancy prevention efforts. Many adults argue that placing birth control pills or condoms in the hands of teenagers is equivalent to approving of early sex. Yet sex education programs focusing on abstinence have little or no impact on delaying teenage sexual activity or preventing pregnancy (Rosenbaum, 2009; Trenholm et al., 2008). In Canada and Western Europe, where community- and school-based clinics offer adolescents contraceptives and where universal health insurance helps pay for them, teenage sexual activity is no higher than in the United States—but pregnancy, childbirth, and abortion rates are much lower (Schalet, 2007).

Efforts to prevent adolescent pregnancy and parenthood must go beyond improving sex education and access to contraception to build academic and social competence (Allen, Seitz, & Apfel, 2007). In one study, researchers randomly assigned at-risk high school students to either a year-long community service class, called Teen Outreach, or to regular classroom experiences in health or social studies. In Teen Outreach, adolescents spent at least 20 hours per week in volunteer work tailored to their interests. They returned to school for discussions that focused on enhancing their community service skills and ability to cope with everyday challenges. At the end of the school year, pregnancy, school failure, and school suspension were substantially lower in the group enrolled in Teen Outreach, which fostered social skills, connection to community, and self-respect (Allen et al., 1997).

Teenagers work on a poster as part of a Teen Outreach lesson about healthy relationships. Volunteer work and related class discussions aimed at skill-building promote self-respect and community connection while reducing adolescent pregnancy, school failure, and school suspension.

Finally, school involvement is linked to delayed initiation of sexual activity and to reduced teenage pregnancy, perhaps because it increases interaction with and attachment to adults who discourage risk taking, and it strengthens belief in a promising future (Harris, 2008). We will take up factors that promote adolescents' commitment to school in Chapter 15.

INTERVENING WITH ADOLESCENT PARENTS The most difficult and costly way to deal with adolescent parenthood is to wait until it happens. Young parents need health care, encouragement to stay in school, job training, instruction in parenting and life-management skills, and high-quality, affordable child care. Schools that provide these services reduce the incidence of low-birth-weight babies, increase educational success, and prevent additional childbearing (Key et al., 2008; Seitz & Apfel, 2005).

Adolescent mothers also benefit from relationships with family members and other adults who are sensitive to their developmental needs. Those with more social support report reduced levels of depression during the year after giving birth (Brown et al., 2012). And in one study, African-American teenage mothers who had a long-term "mentor" relationship—an aunt, neighbor, or teacher who provided emotional support and guidance—were far more likely than those without a mentor to stay in school and graduate (Klaw, Rhodes, & Fitzgerald, 2003). Home visiting programs are also effective. Return to page 114 in Chapter 3 to review the Nurse–Family Partnership, which helps launch teenage mothers and their babies on a more favorable life course.

Programs focusing on fathers attempt to increase their financial and emotional commitment to the baby. Although nearly half of young fathers visit their children during the first few years, contact usually diminishes. By the time the child starts school, fewer than one-fourth have regular paternal contact. As with teenage mothers, support from family members helps fathers say involved (Bunting & McAuley, 2004). Teenage mothers who receive financial and child-care assistance and emotional support from the child's father are less distressed and more likely to sustain a relationship with him (Cutrona et al., 1998; Gee & Rhodes, 2003). And infants with lasting ties to their teenage fathers show better long-term adjustment (Martin, Brazil, & Brooks-Gunn, 2012).

Laws that enforce child support payments are aimed at increasing paternal responsibility. But unless these efforts are accompanied by assistance in finding adequate employment, teenage fathers may flee to evade arrest instead of becoming involved with their children (McLanahan & Carlson, 2002). Fatherhood interventions that begin early, before the relationship with the adolescent mother withers or terminates, are more likely to succeed.

Early parenthood imposes lasting hardships on adolescent parents and their newborn babies. But the involvement of a caring father and a stable partnership between the parents can improve outcomes for young families.

Substance Use and Abuse

At age 14, Louis waited until he was alone at home, took some cigarettes from his uncle's pack, and smoked them. At an unchaperoned party, he and Cassie drank several cans of beer and lit up marijuana joints. Louis got little physical charge out of these experiences. A good student, who was well-liked by peers and got along well with his parents, he did not need drugs as an escape valve. But he knew of other teenagers who started with alcohol and cigarettes, moved on to harder substances, and eventually were hooked.

Teenage alcohol and drug use is pervasive in industrialized nations. According to the most recent, nationally representative survey of U.S. high school students, 26 percent of tenth graders have tried smoking, 52 percent drinking, and 39 percent at least one illegal drug (usually marijuana). At the end of high school, 9 percent smoke cigarettes regularly, and 22 percent have engaged in heavy drinking during the past two weeks. About 25 percent have tried at least one highly addictive and toxic substance, such as amphetamines, cocaine, phencyclidine (PCP), Ecstasy (MDMA), inhalants, heroin, sedatives (including barbiturates), or OxyContin (a narcotic painkiller) (Johnston et al., 2014).

These figures represent a substantial decline since the mid-1990s, probably resulting from greater parent, school, and media focus on the hazards of drug taking. Although some illegal drugs made a comeback about a decade ago, teenagers' use of most sedatives, narcotics, amphetamines, and hallucinogens has declined or remained steady in recent years. But use of marijuana has risen gradually since the late 2000s. Many states have passed medical use laws, making it easier for young people to obtain marijuana. And compared to a decade ago, fewer adolescents today consider regular marijuana use to be risky (Johnston et al., 2014).

In part, drug taking reflects the sensation seeking of the teenage years. But adolescents also live in drug-dependent cultural contexts. They see adults relying on caffeine to stay alert, alcohol and cigarettes to cope with daily hassles, and other remedies to relieve stress,

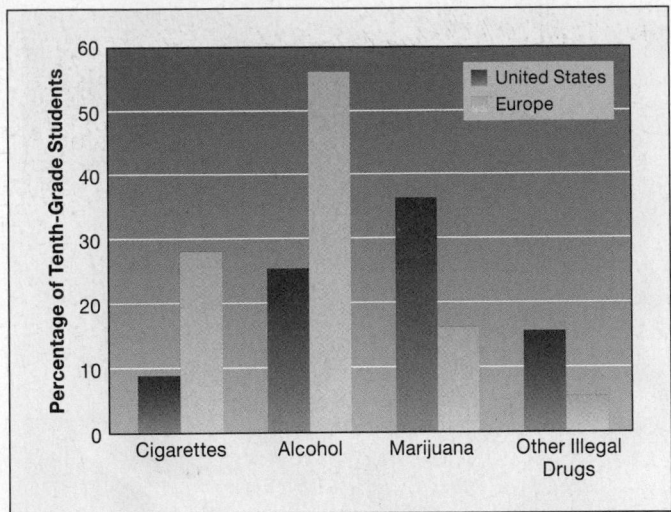

FIGURE 14.10 **Tenth-grade students in the United States and Europe who have used various substances.** Rates for tobacco and alcohol are based on any use in the past 30 days. Rates for marijuana and other illegal drugs are based on any lifetime use. Tobacco and alcohol use are greater for European adolescents, whereas illegal drug use is greater for U.S. adolescents. (Based on ESPAD, 2013; Johnston et al., 2014.)

depression, and physical discomfort. They also encounter high rates of cigarette, alcohol, and drug use in TV programs, music, movies, and advertisements (Strasburger, 2012). And compared to a decade or two ago, today doctors more often prescribe—and parents frequently seek—medication to treat children's problems (Olfman & Robbins, 2012). In adolescence, these young people may readily "self-medicate" when stressed.

Most teenagers who try alcohol, tobacco, or marijuana are not headed for a life of decadence and addiction. These *minimal experimenters* are usually psychologically healthy, sociable, curious young people (Shedler & Block, 1990). As Figure 14.10 shows, tobacco and alcohol use is somewhat greater among European than among U.S. adolescents, perhaps because European adults more often smoke and drink. But illegal drug use is far more prevalent among U.S. teenagers. A greater percentage of American young people live in poverty, which is linked to family and peer contexts that promote illegal drug use. At the same time, use of diverse drugs is lower among African Americans than among Hispanic and Caucasian Americans; Native-American youths rank highest in drug taking (Johnston et al., 2014; Swendsen et al., 2012; Wu et al., 2011). Researchers have yet to explain these variations.

Adolescent experimentation with any drug should not be taken lightly. Because most drugs impair perception and thought processes, a single heavy dose can lead to permanent injury or death. And a worrisome minority of teenagers move from substance *use* to *abuse*—taking drugs regularly, requiring increasing amounts to achieve the same effect, moving to harder substances, and using enough to impair their ability to meet daily responsibilities. More than 2 percent of high school seniors are daily drinkers, and 6 percent have used marijuana on a daily basis over the past month (Johnston et al., 2014).

Of all teenage drug habits, cigarette smoking has received the least attention because its short-term effects are minimal. Yet in the long run, it is one of the deadliest substances—an established cause of heart and lung disease and cancer. Habitual cigarette use usually begins in early adolescence; 4 percent of U.S. eighth graders say they smoked in the last month, and 2 percent report doing so daily. And more than 3 percent of twelfth graders smoke half a pack or more a day (Johnston et al., 2014).

CORRELATES AND CONSEQUENCES OF ADOLESCENT SUBSTANCE ABUSE Unlike experimenters, drug abusers are seriously troubled young people. Longitudinal evidence reveals that their impulsive, disruptive, hostile style is often evident in early childhood, and they engage in other high-risk behaviors and are inclined to express their unhappiness through antisocial acts. Compared with other young people, their substance use starts earlier and may have genetic roots (Dick, Prescott, & McGue, 2009; Patrick & Schulenberg, 2014).

Environmental factors also contribute. These include low SES, family mental health problems, parental and older sibling drug and alcohol abuse, lack of parental warmth and involvement, physical and sexual abuse, and poor school performance. Especially among teenagers with family difficulties, encouragement from friends who use and provide drugs increases substance abuse (Ohannessian & Hesselbrock, 2008; Patrick & Schulenberg, 2014).

Introducing drugs while the adolescent brain is still a work-in-progress can have profound, lasting consequences, impairing neurons and their connective networks. At the same time, teenagers who use substances to deal with daily stresses fail to learn responsible decision-making skills and alternative coping techniques. They show serious adjustment problems, including chronic anxiety, depression, and antisocial behavior, that are both cause and consequence of heavy drug taking (Kassel et al., 2005; Luciana et al., 2013). And they often enter into marriage, childbearing, and the work world prematurely and fail at these challenges—painful outcomes that further promote addictive behavior.

PREVENTION AND TREATMENT School and community programs that reduce drug experimentation typically combine several features:

- They promote effective parenting, including monitoring of teenagers' activities.
- They teach skills for resisting peer pressure.
- They reduce the social acceptability of drug taking by emphasizing health and safety risks (Stephens et al., 2009).

One intervention, the Strong African American Families (SAAF) program, teaches parents to monitor their youngsters' behavior, communicate and enforce clear expectations, and use cooperative problem solving to resolve disputes. Evaluations revealed that SAAF reduced substance use among African-American youths, and it was most effective for adolescents with the DRD4 7-repeat or the short 5-HTTLPR genes (see pages 258 and 268 in Chapter 7), which placed them at risk for self-regulation difficulties (Brody et al., 2009, 2014). Does this remind you of evidence discussed in previous chapters indicating that good parenting can protect the development of genetically vulnerable children?

Programs that teach at-risk teenagers effective strategies for handling life stressors and that build competence through community service reduce alcohol and drug use, just as they reduce teenage pregnancy. Providing appealing substitute activities, such as drug-free dances and sports activities, is also helpful. Physical activity works especially well as a substitute for cigarette smoking. In a program aimed at helping teenagers stop smoking, participants were most likely to cut back or quit if the intervention helped them exercise more (Horn et al., 2013).

When an adolescent becomes a drug abuser, family and individual therapy are generally needed to treat maladaptive parent–child relationships, impulsivity, low self-esteem, anxiety, and depression. Academic and vocational training to improve life success also helps. But even comprehensive programs have alarmingly high relapse rates—from 35 to 85 percent (Brown & Ramo, 2005; Sussman, Skara, & Ames, 2008).

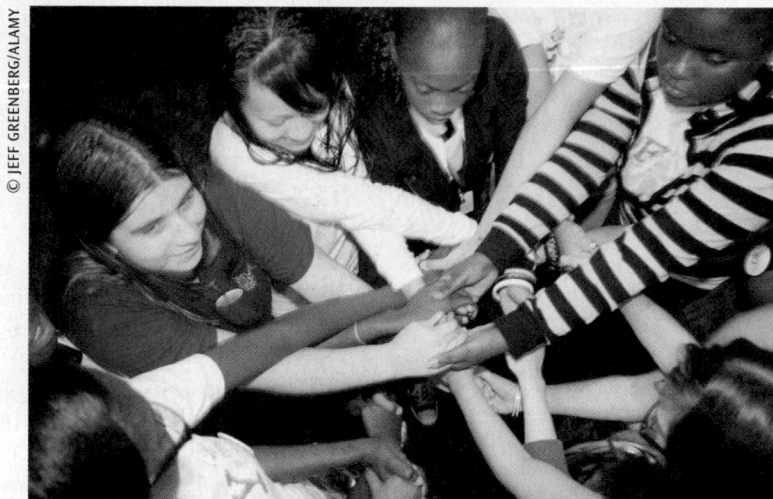

Teenagers participate in a leadership training conference sponsored by Drug Free Youth in Town (DFYIT), a youth substance abuse prevention program. DFYIT trains high school students as peer educators, who teach middle school students life skills and strategies for resisting peer pressure.

Adolescents who are motivated at the start of treatment have better outcomes (Joe et al., 2014). One recommendation is to initiate treatment gradually, through support-group sessions that focus on reducing drug taking. Modest improvements may boost the young person's sense of self-efficacy for behavior change and, as a result, increase motivation to make longer-lasting changes through intensive treatment.

Ask Yourself

- **REVIEW** What unfavorable life experiences do teenagers who engage in early and frequent sexual activity have in common with those who abuse drugs?

- **CONNECT** Some graduated licensing laws restrict the number of young passengers allowed in cars driven by other adolescents. According to research on adolescent brain development, how might these restrictions help reduce accidents?

- **APPLY** Return to page 545 to review Veronica's life circumstances after she became a teenage mother. Why are Veronica and her children likely to experience long-term hardships?

- **REFLECT** Describe your experiences with peer pressure to experiment with alcohol and drugs. What factors influenced your response?

Summary

Conceptions of Adolescence (p. 519)

14.1 How have conceptions of adolescence changed over the past century?

- **Adolescence** is the transition between childhood and adulthood. Early theorists viewed adolescence as either a biologically determined period of storm and stress or entirely influenced by the social and cultural environment.

- Contemporary research shows that adolescence is a joint product of biological, psychological, and social forces. In cultures that require many years of education for successful participation in work life, adolescence is greatly extended.

Puberty: The Physical Transition to Adulthood (p. 521)

14.2 Describe body growth, motor performance, and sexual maturation during puberty.

- Hormonal changes under way in middle childhood initiate **puberty,** on average, two years earlier for girls than for boys. Sex hormones begin to rise between ages 6 and 8, when, in **adrenarche,** levels of adrenal androgens increase. The first outward sign of puberty is the **growth spurt.** As the body enlarges, girls' hips and boys' shoulders broaden. Girls add more fat, boys more muscle.

- Puberty brings slow, gradual improvements in gross-motor performance for girls, dramatic gains for boys. Nevertheless, the number of U.S. adolescents participating in regular physical activity declines sharply with age.

- At puberty, changes in **primary** and **secondary sexual characteristics** accompany rapid body growth. **Menarche** occurs late in the girl's sequence of pubertal events, after the growth spurt peaks. After menarche, growth of the breasts and of pubic and underarm hair are completed. In boys, as the sex organs and body enlarge and pubic and underarm hair appear, **spermarche** takes place. This is followed by growth of facial and body hair and deepening of the voice.

14.3 What factors influence the timing of puberty?

- Heredity, nutrition, exercise, and overall health contribute to the timing of puberty. Young people in conflict-ridden families tend to reach puberty earlier, whereas those with warm, stable family ties do so relatively late.

- A secular trend toward earlier puberty has occurred in industrialized nations as physical well-being increased. In some countries, rising overweight and obesity rates have extended this trend.

14.4 Describe brain development and changes in the organization of sleep and wakefulness during adolescence.

- As synaptic pruning, myelination, and strengthening of connections among various brain regions continue, the prefrontal cortex becomes a more effective "executive," yielding more complex, flexible, and adaptive thinking. Because the cognitive-control network still needs fine-tuning, teenagers' performance on tasks requiring inhibition, planning, and future orientation is not fully mature

- With puberty, neurons become more responsive to excitatory neurotransmitters, contributing to adolescents' drive for novel experiences. These changes in the brain's emotional/social network outpace development of the cognitive-control network, resulting in heightened risk taking.

- Changes also occur in brain regulation of sleep timing, leading to a sleep "phase delay." Sleep deprivation increases, contributing to poorer achievement, depressed mood, and high-risk behaviors.

The Psychological Impact of Pubertal Events (p. 529)

14.5 Explain adolescents' reactions to the physical changes of puberty.

- Girls generally react to menarche with mixed emotions, although those who receive advance information and support from family members respond more positively. Boys also react to spermarche with mixed feelings but receive less social support for pubertal changes than girls.

- Besides higher hormone levels, negative life events and adult-structured situations are associated with adolescents' negative moods. In contrast, teenagers feel upbeat when with friends and in self-chosen leisure activities.

- Puberty is accompanied by psychological distancing between parent and child. The reaction may be a modern substitute for physical departure from the family, which typically occurs at sexual maturity in primate species. Parent–adolescent conflict also reflects parents' efforts to protect teenagers from such risks as substance use, auto accidents, and early sex.

14.6 Describe the impact of pubertal timing on adolescent adjustment, noting sex differences.

- Early maturing boys tend to be viewed as popular and well-adjusted, early maturing girls as unpopular. However, adolescents of both sexes who reach puberty early report more psychological stress and depressed mood than their on-time and late-maturing peers. They are also prone to deviant behavior, especially when exposed to other stressors.

- Early-maturing girls and late-maturing boys fit in least well physically with their peers. For girls, the adjustment problems accompanying early pubertal timing are likely to persist into early adulthood.

Health Issues (p. 533)

14.7 Describe nutritional needs, and cite factors related to eating disorders in adolescence.

● Nutritional requirements rise dramatically with rapid body growth. Poor eating habits lead to vitamin and mineral deficiencies in many adolescents. Frequency of family meals is associated with healthy eating.

● Girls who reach puberty early, who are dissatisfied with their body image, and who grow up in families where thinness is emphasized are at high risk for eating disorders. **Anorexia nervosa** typically affects girls with inhibited and perfectionist personalities, controlling mothers, and emotionally distant fathers. **Bulimia nervosa** is often associated with lack of self-control and disengaged parenting. Like other eating disorders, **binge-eating disorder** is linked to social adjustment difficulties.

14.8 Cite common unintentional injuries in adolescence.

● In the United States, automobile accidents are the leading cause of adolescent injury and death, with firearms causing the majority of other fatal injuries. Sports-related injuries, including concussions, are also common.

14.9 Discuss social and cultural influences on adolescent sexual attitudes and behavior.

● North American attitudes toward adolescent sex remain relatively restrictive, and the social environment—parents, schools, and mass media—delivers contradictory messages. Over the past half-century, sexual attitudes and behavior of adolescents have become more liberal.

● Early sexual activity is linked to a variety of adverse personal, family, peer, and educational characteristics, many of which are associated with economic disadvantage. A substantial minority of U.S. sexually active teenagers do not practice contraception consistently. Adolescent cognitive processes and weak social supports for responsible sexual behavior, including access to birth control, underlie this failure to take precautions against pregnancy.

14.10 Describe factors involved in the development of homosexuality.

● Biological factors, including heredity and prenatal hormone levels, play an important role in homosexuality. Lesbian, gay, and bisexual teenagers face special challenges in establishing a positive sexual identity.

14.11 Discuss factors related to sexually transmitted infections and teenage pregnancy and parenthood.

● Inconsistent contraceptive use results in high rates of sexually transmitted infections (STIs) among U.S. young people.

● The U.S. adolescent pregnancy rate is higher than that of most other industrialized nations. Life conditions linked to economic disadvantage, along with personal attributes, contribute to adolescent childbearing. Teenage parenthood is associated with school dropout, reduced chances of marriage, greater likelihood of divorce, and poverty—circumstances that jeopardize the well-being of both adolescent and newborn child.

● Effective sex education, access to contraceptives, and programs that build academic and social competence help prevent early pregnancy. Adolescent parents need school programs that provide job training, instruction in life-management skills, and child care. Young mothers benefit from relationships with family members and other adults who are sensitive to their developmental needs. When teenage fathers stay involved, children develop more favorably.

14.12 What personal and social factors are related to adolescent substance use and abuse?

● Teenage alcohol and drug use is pervasive in industrialized nations, reflecting the sensation seeking of adolescence as well as drug-dependent cultural contexts. The minority who move to substance abuse tend to start drug-taking early and have serious personal, family, school, and peer problems.

● Early drug taking can have lasting consequences, impairing brain functioning and opportunities to acquire alternative coping techniques. Effective prevention programs work with parents to improve parenting skills and with adolescents to teach effective strategies for handling life stressors and to build competence.

Important Terms and Concepts

adolescence (p. 519)
adrenarche (p. 521)
anorexia nervosa (p. 534)
binge-eating disorder (p. 536)

body image (p. 532)
bulimia nervosa (p. 536)
growth spurt (p. 522)
menarche (p. 525)

primary sexual characteristics (p. 525)
puberty (p. 519)
secondary sexual characteristics (p. 525)
spermarche (p. 526)

Cognitive Development in Adolescence

"Me in the New Millennium"
Ella Gordan-Latty
12 years, New Zealand

As she contemplates her changing world, this adolescent's increasingly effective thinking enables her to see herself and others in new ways. Chapter 15 delves into the complex reasoning powers of this transitional period between childhood and adulthood.

One mid-December evening, a knock at the front door announced the arrival of Franca and Antonio's oldest son, Jules, home for vacation after the fall semester of his sophomore year at college. The family gathered around the kitchen table. "How did it all go, Jules?" asked Antonio as he served pieces of apple pie.

"Well, physics and philosophy were awesome," Jules responded with enthusiasm. "The last few weeks, our physics prof introduced us to Einstein's theory of relativity. Boggles my mind, it's so incredibly counterintuitive."

"Counter-what?" asked 11-year-old Sabrina.

"Counterintuitive. Unlike what you'd normally expect," explained Jules. "Imagine you're on a train, going unbelievably fast, like 160,000 miles a second. The faster you go, approaching the speed of light, the slower time passes and the denser and heavier things get relative to on the ground. The theory revolutionized the way we think about time, space, matter—the entire universe."

Sabrina wrinkled her forehead, baffled by Jules's otherworldly reasoning. "Time slows down when I'm bored, like right now, not on a train when I'm going somewhere exciting. No speeding train ever made me heavier, but this apple pie will if I eat any more of it," Sabrina announced, leaving the table.

Sixteen-year-old Louis reacted differently. "Totally cool, Jules. If we could move at such extreme speeds, we'd age more slowly—imagine that! So what'd you do in philosophy?"

"It was a course in philosophy of technology. We studied the ethics of futuristic methods in human reproduction. For example, we argued the pros and cons of a world in which all embryos develop in artificial wombs."

"What do you mean?" asked Louis. "You order your kid at the lab?"

"That's right. I wrote my term paper on it. I had to evaluate it in terms of principles of justice and freedom. I can see some advantages but also lots of dangers. . . ."

As this conversation illustrates, adolescence brings with it vastly expanded powers of reasoning. At age 11, Sabrina finds it difficult to move beyond her own firsthand experiences to a world of possibilities. During the coming years, her thinking will take on the complex qualities that characterize the cognition of her older brothers. Jules and Louis consider multiple variables simultaneously and think about situations that are not easily detected in the real world or that do not exist at all. As a result, they can grasp advanced scientific and mathematical principles, grapple with social and political issues, and delve deeply into the meaning of a poem or story. Compared with school-age children's thinking, adolescent thought is more enlightened, imaginative, and rational.

The first part of this chapter traces these extraordinary changes. Systematic research on adolescent cognitive development began with testing of Piaget's ideas (Keating, 2012; Kuhn, 2009). Information-processing research has greatly enhanced our understanding. Next, we turn to research findings that have attracted a great deal of public attention: sex differences in mental abilities. We also discuss gains in language that reflect and also contribute to the advanced thinking of the teenage years. The middle portion of this chapter is devoted to the primary setting in which adolescent thought takes shape: the school. We conclude with a consideration of vocational development. ■

15.1 What are the major characteristics of formal operational thought?

15.2 Discuss follow-up research on formal operational thought and its implications for the accuracy of Piaget's formal operational stage.

Piaget's Theory: The Formal Operational Stage

According to Piaget, around age 11 young people enter the **formal operational stage,** in which they develop the capacity for abstract, systematic, scientific thinking. Whereas concrete operational children can "operate on reality," formal operational adolescents can "operate on operations." In other words, they no longer require concrete things or events as objects of thought. Instead, they can come up with new, more general logical rules through internal reflection (Inhelder & Piaget, 1955/1958). Let's look at two major features of the formal operational stage.

Hypothetico-Deductive Reasoning

Piaget believed that at adolescence, young people first become capable of **hypothetico-deductive reasoning.** When faced with a problem, they start with a *hypothesis,* or prediction about variables that might affect an outcome, from which they *deduce* logical, testable inferences. Then they systematically isolate and combine variables to see which of these inferences are confirmed in the real world. Notice how this form of problem solving begins with possibility and proceeds to reality. In contrast, concrete operational children start with reality—with the most obvious predictions about a situation. When these are not confirmed, they usually cannot think of alternatives and fail to solve the problem.

Adolescents' performance on Piaget's famous *pendulum problem* illustrates their new approach. Suppose we present several school-age children and adolescents with strings of different lengths, objects of different weights to attach to the strings, and a bar from which to hang the strings (see Figure 15.1). Then we ask each of them to figure out what influences the speed with which a pendulum swings through its arc.

Formal operational adolescents hypothesize that four variables might be influential: (1) the length of the string, (2) the weight of the object hung on it, (3) how high the object is raised before it is released, and (4) how forcefully the object is pushed. By varying one factor at a time while holding the other three constant, they test each variable separately and, if necessary, also in combination. Eventually they discover that only string length makes a difference.

In contrast, concrete operational children cannot separate the effects of each variable. They may test for the effect of string length without holding weight constant—comparing, for example, a short, light pendulum with a long, heavy one. Also, they typically fail to notice variables that are not immediately suggested by the concrete materials of the task—for example, how high the object is raised or how forcefully it is released.

FIGURE 15.1 Piaget's pendulum problem. Adolescents who engage in hypothetico-deductive reasoning think of variables that might possibly affect the speed with which a pendulum swings through its arc. Then they isolate and test each variable, as well as testing the variables in combination. Eventually they deduce that the weight of the object, the height from which it is released, and how forcefully it is pushed have no effect on the speed with which the pendulum swings through its arc. Only string length makes a difference.

Propositional Thought

A second important characteristic of Piaget's formal operational stage is **propositional thought**—adolescents' ability to evaluate the logic of propositions (verbal statements) without referring to real-world circumstances. In contrast, children can evaluate the logic of statements only by considering them against concrete evidence in the real world.

In a study of propositional reasoning, an adult showed children and adolescents a pile of poker chips and asked whether statements about the chips were true, false, or uncertain (Osherson & Markman, 1975). In one condition, the adult hid a chip in her hand and presented the following propositions:

"*Either* the chip in my hand is green *or* it is not green."
"The chip in my hand is green *and* it is not green."

In another condition, the adult made the same statements while holding either a red or a green chip in full view.

School-age children focused on the concrete properties of the poker chips. When the chip was hidden, they replied that they were uncertain about both statements. When it was visible, they judged both statements to be true if the chip was green and false if it was red. In contrast, most adolescents analyzed the logic of the statements. They understood that the "either–or" statement is always true and the "and" statement is always false, regardless of the chip's color.

Although Piaget did not view language as playing a central role in cognitive development (see Chapter 9), he acknowledged its importance in adolescence. Formal operations require language-based and other symbolic systems that do not stand for real things, such as those in higher mathematics. Secondary school students use such systems in algebra and geometry. Formal operational thought also involves verbal reasoning about abstract concepts. Jules was thinking in this way when he pondered relationships between time, space, and matter in physics and wondered about justice and freedom in philosophy.

In Piaget's formal operational stage, adolescents engage in propositional thought. As these students discuss problems in a social studies class, they show that they can reason logically with symbols that do not necessarily represent objects in the real world.

Follow-Up Research on Formal Operational Thought

Research on formal operational thought poses questions similar to those we discussed with respect to Piaget's earlier stages: Does formal operational thinking appear earlier than Piaget expected? Do all individuals reach formal operations during their teenage years?

ARE CHILDREN CAPABLE OF HYPOTHETICO-DEDUCTIVE AND PROPOSITIONAL THINKING? School-age children show the glimmerings of hypothetico-deductive reasoning, although they are less competent at it than adolescents. In simplified situations involving no more than two possible causal variables, 6-year-olds understand that hypotheses must be confirmed by appropriate evidence. They also realize that once a hypothesis is supported, it shapes predictions about what might happen in the future (Ruffman et al., 1993). But without direct instruction, school-age children cannot sort out evidence that bears on three or more variables at once (Lorch et al., 2010; Matlen & Klahr, 2013). And as we will see when we take up information-processing research on scientific reasoning, children have difficulty explaining why a pattern of observations supports a hypothesis, even when they recognize the connection between the two.

With respect to propositional thought, when a simple set of premises defies real-world knowledge ("All cats bark. Rex is a cat. Does Rex bark?"), 4- to 6-year-olds can reason logically in make-believe play. In justifying their answer, they are likely to say, "We can pretend cats bark!" (Dias & Harris, 1988, 1990). But in an entirely verbal mode, children have great difficulty reasoning from premises that contradict reality or their own beliefs.

Consider this set of statements: "If dogs are bigger than elephants, and elephants are bigger than mice, then dogs are bigger than mice." Children younger than 10 judge this reasoning to be false because some of the relations specified do not occur in real life (Moshman & Franks, 1986; Pillow, 2002). They automatically think of well-learned knowledge ("Elephants are larger than dogs") that casts doubt on the truthfulness of the premises. Children find it more difficult than adolescents to inhibit activation of such knowledge (Klaczynski, Schuneman, & Daniel, 2004; Simoneau & Markovits, 2003). Partly for this reason, they fail to grasp the **logical necessity** of propositional reasoning—that the accuracy of conclusions drawn from premises rests on the rules of logic, not on real-world confirmation.

Furthermore, in reasoning with propositions, school-age children rarely think carefully about the major premise and, therefore, violate the most basic rules of logic (Markovits, Schleifer, & Fortier, 1989). For example, when given the following problem, they almost always draw an incorrect conclusion:

Major premise: If Susan hits a tambourine, then she will make a noise.
Second premise: Suppose that Susan does not hit a tambourine.
Question: Did Susan make a noise?
Wrong conclusion: No, Susan did not make a noise.

Notice that the major premise did *not* state that Susan can make noise *if, and only if,* she hits a tambourine. School-age children perform better on tasks like this one when propositions are illustrated with concrete images and they are instructed to generate a wide range of alternative outcomes to similar scenarios (for example, "Imagine that the sidewalk is wet. How many different ways could this happen?") (Markovits & Brunet, 2012). In contrast, many adolescents solve these problems without such supports because they are better at reasoning on an entirely verbal plane and at searching their knowledge for examples that contradict wrong conclusions (Klaczynski, 2004; Markovits & Barrouillet, 2002).

With age, adolescents become better at analyzing the *logic* of a series of propositions, regardless of their *content.* And they handle problems requiring increasingly complex sets of mental operations. Further, in justifying their reasoning, they move from giving concrete examples ("She could have hit a drum instead of a tambourine") to explaining the logical rules on which it is based ("We can be certain that Susan did not hit a tambourine. But we cannot be certain that Susan did not make a noise; she might have done so in many other ways") (Müller, Overton, & Reene, 2001; Venet & Markovits, 2001). Nevertheless, these capacities do not appear suddenly at puberty. Rather, gains are gradual from childhood on—findings that call into question the emergence of a discrete new stage of cognitive development at adolescence (Kuhn, 2009; Moshman, 2005).

This adolescent lives in a small village in rural India, where she completed only a few years of elementary school. Although she would probably have difficulty with Piaget's formal operational tasks, she deftly builds woven bamboo stools, mentally coordinating multiple variables.

DO ALL INDIVIDUALS REACH THE FORMAL OPERATIONAL STAGE? TAKE A MOMENT... Try giving one or two of the formal operational tasks just described to your friends. How well do they do? Many well-educated adults fail hypothetico-deductive tasks and have trouble reasoning with sets of propositions that contradict real-world facts (Kuhn, 2009; Markovits & Vachon, 1990)!

Why are so many adults not fully formal operational? One reason is that people are most likely to think abstractly and systematically on tasks in which they have a history of extensive guidance and practice in using such reasoning (Kuhn, 2013). This conclusion is supported by evidence that taking college courses leads to improvements in formal reasoning related to course content. Math and science prompt gains in propositional thought, social science in methodological and statistical reasoning (Lehman & Nisbett, 1990). Like concrete reasoning in children, formal operations do not emerge in all contexts at once but are specific to situation and task (Keating, 2004, 2012).

Individuals in tribal and village societies rarely do well on tasks typically used to assess formal operational reasoning (Cole, 1990). For example, people in nonliterate societies often refuse requests to engage in propositional thought. Take this hypothetical proposition: "In the North, where there is snow, all bears are white. Novaya Zemlya is in the Far North, and it always has snow. What color are the bears there?" In response, a Central Asian peasant explains that he must see the event to discern its logical implications. Yet the peasant uses propositions to defend his point of view: "*If* a man . . . had seen a white bear and had told about it, [*then*] he could be believed, *but* I've never seen one and *hence* I can't say" (Luria 1976, pp. 108–109). Although he rarely displays it in everyday life, the peasant is clearly capable of formal operational thought!

Piaget acknowledged that without the opportunity to solve hypothetical problems, people in some societies might not display formal operations. Still, these findings raise further questions about Piaget's stage sequence. Does the formal operational stage result largely from children's and adolescents' independent efforts to make sense of their world, as Piaget claimed? Or is it a culturally transmitted way of thinking that is specific to literate societies and taught in school?

In an Israeli study of seventh to ninth graders, after controlling for participants' age, researchers found that years of schooling fully accounted for early adolescent gains in propositional thought (Artman, Cahan, & Avni-Babad, 2006). School tasks, the investigators speculated, provide crucial experience in setting aside the "if . . . then" logic of everyday conversations that is often used to convey intentions, promises, and threats ("If you don't do your chores, then you won't get your allowance") but that conflicts with the logic of academic reasoning. In school, then, adolescents encounter rich opportunities to realize their neurological potential to think more effectively.

An Information-Processing View of Adolescent Cognitive Development

15.3 How do information-processing researchers account for cognitive changes in adolescence?

Information-processing theorists refer to a variety of specific mechanisms, including diverse aspects of executive function—supported by brain development and experience—as underlying cognitive gains in adolescence (Keating, 2012; Kuhn, 2009, 2013; Kuhn & Franklin, 2006). Each was discussed in previous chapters. Now let's draw them together:

- *Attention* becomes more selective (focused on relevant information) and better-adapted to the changing demands of tasks, and *planning* improves.
- *Inhibition*—both of irrelevant stimuli and of well-learned responses in situations where they are inappropriate—improves, supporting gains in attention and reasoning.
- *Strategies* become more effective, improving storage, representation, and retrieval of information.
- *Knowledge* increases, easing strategy use.
- *Metacognition* (awareness of thought) expands, leading to new insights into effective strategies for acquiring information and solving problems.
- *Cognitive self-regulation* improves, yielding better moment-by-moment monitoring, evaluation, and redirection of thinking.
- *Working memory* increases, as speed of thinking and processing capacity increase. As a result, more information can be held in mind at once and combined into increasingly complex, efficient representations, "opening possibilities for growth" in the capacities just listed and also improving as a result of gains in those capacities (Demetriou et al., 2002, p. 97).

As we look at influential findings from an information-processing perspective, we will see some of these changes in action. And we will discover that researchers regard one of them—*metacognition*—as central to adolescent cognitive development.

Scientific Reasoning: Coordinating Theory with Evidence

During a free moment in physical education class, Sabrina wondered why more of her tennis serves and returns passed the net and dropped in her opponent's court when she used a particular brand of balls. "Is it something about their color or size?" she asked herself. "Hmm . . . or maybe it's their surface texture—that might affect their bounce."

According to Deanna Kuhn, the heart of scientific reasoning is coordinating theories with evidence. A scientist can clearly describe the theory he or she favors, knows what evidence is needed to support it and what would refute it, and can explain how pitting evidence against theories led to the acceptance of one theory as opposed to others. What evidence would Sabrina need to confirm her theory about the tennis balls?

FIGURE 15.2 **Which features of these sports balls—size, color, surface texture, or presence or absence of ridges—influence the quality of a player's serve?** This set of evidence suggests that color might be important, since light-colored balls are largely in the good-serve basket and dark-colored balls in the bad-serve basket. But the same is true for texture! The good-serve basket has mostly smooth balls, the bad-serve basket rough balls. Since all light-colored balls are smooth and all dark-colored balls are rough, we cannot tell whether color or texture makes a difference. But we can conclude that size and presence or absence of ridges are not important, because these features are equally represented in the good-serve and bad-serve baskets. (Adapted from Kuhn, Amsel, & O'Loughlin, 1988.)

LOOK and LISTEN

Describe one or more memorable experiences from your high school classes that helped you advance in scientific reasoning—pit theory against evidence and become receptive to disconfirming evidence, even for theories you favored.

Kuhn (2002) has conducted extensive research into the development of scientific reasoning, using problems that, like Piaget's tasks, involve several variables that might affect an outcome. In one series of studies, third, sixth, and ninth graders and adults were first given evidence—sometimes consistent and sometimes conflicting with theories—and then questioned about the accuracy of each theory.

For example, participants were given a problem much like Sabrina's: to theorize about which of several features of sports balls—size (large or small), color (light or dark), surface texture (rough or smooth), or presence or absence of ridges on the surface—influences the quality of a player's serve. Next, they were told about the theory of Mr. (or Ms.) S, who believes the ball's size is important, and the theory of Mr. (or Ms.) C, who thinks color matters. Finally, the interviewer presented evidence by placing balls with certain characteristics in two baskets labeled "good serve" and "bad serve" (see Figure 15.2).

Kuhn found that the capacity to reason like a scientist improved with age. The youngest participants often discounted obviously causal variables, ignored evidence conflicting with their own initial judgment, and distorted evidence in ways consistent with their theory. When one third grader, who judged that size was causal (with large balls producing good serves and small balls producing bad serves), was shown incomplete evidence (a single large, light-colored ball in the good-serve basket and no balls in the bad-serve basket), he insisted on the accuracy of Mr. S's theory (which was also his own). Asked to explain, he stated flatly, "Because this ball is big . . . the color doesn't really matter" (Kuhn, 1989, p. 677).

These findings, and others like them, reveal that on complex, multivariable tasks, children—instead of viewing evidence as separate from and bearing on a theory—often blend the two into a single representation of "the way things are." Children are especially likely to overlook evidence that does not match their prior beliefs when a causal variable is implausible (like color affecting the performance of a sports ball) and when task demands (number of variables to be evaluated) are high (Yang & Tsai, 2010; Zimmerman, 2007). The ability to distinguish theory from evidence and to use logical rules to examine their relationship in complex, multivariable situations improves steadily from childhood through adolescence, continuing into adulthood (Kuhn & Dean, 2004; Zimmerman & Croker, 2013).

How Scientific Reasoning Develops

What factors support adolescents' skill at coordinating theory with evidence? Greater working-memory capacity, permitting a theory and the effects of several variables to be compared at once, is vital. Adolescents also benefit from exposure to increasingly complex problems and to instruction that highlights critical features of scientific reasoning—for example, why a scientist's expectations in a particular situation are inconsistent with everyday beliefs and experiences (Chinn & Malhotra, 2002). This explains why scientific reasoning is strongly influenced by years of schooling, whether individuals grapple with traditional scientific tasks (like the sports-ball problem or Piaget's pendulum task) or engage in informal reasoning—for example, justifying a theory about what causes children to fail in school (Kuhn, 1993).

Sophisticated *metacognitive understanding* is vital for scientific reasoning (Kuhn, 2009, 2011, 2013). Microgenetic research (see Chapter 1, page 44) shows that when adolescents regularly pit theory against evidence over many weeks, they experiment with various strategies, reflect on and revise them, and gradually become aware of the nature of logic. Then they apply their appreciation of logic to an increasingly wide range of situations. The ability to think about theories, deliberately isolate and control variables, and inhibit an initial choice long enough to actively seek disconfirming evidence and weigh alternative possibilities is rarely present before adolescence (Kuhn, 2000; Kuhn et al., 2008; Moshman, 1998).

Though far more competent than children, adolescents and adults vary widely in scientific reasoning skills. Many continue to show a self-serving bias, applying logic more effectively to ideas they doubt than to ideas they favor (Klaczynski & Narasimham, 1998). Reasoning scientifically requires the metacognitive capacity to evaluate one's objectivity—to be fair-minded rather than self-serving (Moshman, 2011). As we will see in Chapter 16, this flexible, open-minded approach is not just a cognitive attainment but a personality trait—one that assists young people greatly in forming an identity and developing morally.

Adolescents develop scientific reasoning skills in a similar step-by-step fashion on different types of tasks. In a series of studies, 10- to 20-year olds were given sets of problems graded in difficulty. One set contained causal-experimental tasks like the sports ball problem in Figure 15.2, another contained quantitative-relational tasks like the pendulum problem in Figure 15.1, and still another consisted of verbal propositional tasks like the tambourine problem on page 558 (Demetriou et al., 1993, 1996, 2002).

In each type of task, adolescents mastered component skills in sequential order by expanding their metacognitive awareness. For example, on causal-experimental tasks, they first became aware of the many variables that—separately and in combination—could influence an outcome. This enabled them to formulate and test hypotheses. Over time, adolescents combined separate skills into a smoothly functioning system, constructing a general model that they could apply to many instances of a given type of problem. In the researchers' words, young people seem to form a "hypercognitive system," or supersystem, that understands, organizes, and influences other aspects of cognition (Demetriou & Kazi, 2001).

TAKE A MOMENT... Return to Chapter 12, page 433, and review Robbie Case's information-processing view of development during Piaget's concrete operational stage. Does Case's concept of *central conceptual structures* remind you of the metacognitive advances just described? Piaget also underscored the role of metacognition in formal operational thought when he spoke of "operating on operations" (see page 556). But information-processing findings confirm that scientific reasoning does not result from an abrupt, stagewise change, as Piaget believed. Instead, it develops gradually out of many specific experiences that require children and adolescents to match theories against evidence and reflect on and evaluate their thinking.

High school students work on a robotics project at a summer camp at Syracuse University. Extensive experience coordinating theory with evidence in complex problems results in gains in scientific reasoning as teenagers reflect on their strategies and revise them.

Consequences of Adolescent Cognitive Changes

15.4 Describe typical reactions of adolescents that result from their advancing cognition.

The development of increasingly complex, effective thinking leads to dramatic revisions in the way adolescents see themselves, others, and the world in general. But just as adolescents are occasionally awkward in the use of their transformed bodies, they initially falter in their abstract thinking. Teenagers' self-concern, idealism, criticism, and faulty decision making, though perplexing to adults, are usually beneficial in the long run. Applying What We Know on page 562 suggests ways to handle the everyday consequences of teenagers' newfound cognitive capacities.

Self-Consciousness and Self-Focusing

Adolescents' ability to reflect on their own thoughts, combined with physical and psychological changes, leads them to think more about themselves. Piaget believed that a new form of egocentrism arises, in which adolescents again have difficulty distinguishing their own and others' perspectives (Inhelder & Piaget, 1955/1958). Piaget's followers suggest that two distorted images of the relationship between self and other appear.

The first is called the **imaginary audience,** adolescents' belief that they are the focus of everyone else's attention and concern (Elkind & Bowen, 1979). As a result, they become extremely self-conscious, often going to great lengths to avoid embarrassment. When Sabrina woke up one Sunday morning with a large pimple on her chin, her first thought was, "I can't

Applying What We Know

Handling Consequences of Teenagers' New Cognitive Capacities

ABSTRACT THOUGHT EXPRESSED AS . . .	SUGGESTION
Sensitivity to public criticism	Avoid finding fault with the adolescent in front of others. If the matter is important, wait until you can speak to the teenager alone.
Exaggerated sense of personal uniqueness	Acknowledge the adolescent's unique characteristics. At opportune times, encourage a more balanced perspective by pointing out that you had similar feelings as a teenager.
Idealism and criticism	Respond patiently to the adolescent's grand expectations and critical remarks. Point out positive features of targets, helping the teenager see that all societies and people are blends of virtues and imperfections.
Difficulty making everyday decisions	Refrain from deciding for the adolescent. Model effective decision making, and offer diplomatic suggestions about the pros and cons of alternatives, the likelihood of various outcomes, and learning from poor choices.

possibly go to church! Everyone will notice how ugly I look." The imaginary audience helps explain the long hours adolescents spend inspecting every detail of their appearance and why they are so sensitive to public criticism. To teenagers, who believe that everyone is monitoring their performance, a critical remark from a parent or teacher can be mortifying.

A second cognitive distortion is the **personal fable.** Certain that others are observing and thinking about them, teenagers develop an inflated opinion of their own importance—a feeling that they are special and unique. Many adolescents view themselves as reaching great heights of omnipotence and also sinking to unusual depths of despair—experiences that others cannot possibly understand (Elkind, 1994). One teenager wrote in her diary, "My parents' lives are so ordinary, so stuck in a rut. Mine will be different. I'll realize my hopes and ambitions." Another, upset when a boyfriend failed to return her affections, rebuffed her mother's comforting words: "Mom, you don't know what it's like to be in love!"

Although imaginary-audience and personal-fable ideation is common in adolescence, these distorted visions of the self do not result from egocentrism, as Piaget suggested. Rather, they are partly an outgrowth of advances in perspective taking, which cause young teenagers to be more concerned with what others think (Vartanian & Powlishta, 1996). Recall, also, from Chapter 14 that changes in the brain's emotional/social network spark increased sensitivity to social feedback.

This teenager's swagger reflects self-confidence and delight that all eyes are on him. When the personal fable engenders a view of the self as highly capable and influential, it may help young people cope with the challenges of adolescence.

In fact, certain aspects of the imaginary audience may serve positive, protective functions. When asked why they worry about the views of others, adolescents responded that they do so because others' evaluations have important *real* consequences—for self-esteem, peer acceptance, and social support (Bell & Bromnick, 2003). The idea that others care about their appearance and behavior also has emotional value, helping teenagers hold onto important relationships as they struggle to separate from parents and establish an independent sense of self (Galanki & Christopoulos, 2011).

With respect to the personal fable, in a study of sixth through tenth graders, sense of omnipotence predicted self-esteem and overall positive adjustment. Viewing the self as highly capable and influential may help young people cope with challenges of adolescence. In contrast, sense of personal uniqueness was modestly associated with depression and suicidal thinking (Aalsma, Lapsley, & Flannery, 2006). Focusing on the distinctiveness of one's own experiences may interfere with forming close, rewarding relationships, which provide social support in stressful times. And when combined with a sensation-seeking personality, the personal fable seems to contribute to adolescent risk taking by reducing teenagers' sense of vulnerability (Alberts, Elkind, & Ginsberg, 2007). Young people with high personal-fable and sensation-seeking scores tend to take more sexual risks, more often use drugs, and commit more delinquent acts than their agemates (Greene et al., 2000).

Idealism and Criticism

Adolescents' capacity to think about possibilities opens up the world of the ideal. Teenagers can imagine alternative family, religious, political, and moral systems, and they want to explore them. They often construct grand visions of a world with no injustice, discrimination, or tasteless behavior. The disparity between teenagers' idealism and adults' greater realism creates tension between parent and child. Envisioning a perfect family against which their parents and siblings fall short, adolescents become fault-finding critics.

Overall, however, teenage idealism and criticism are advantageous. Once adolescents come to see other people as having both strengths and weaknesses, they have a much greater capacity to work constructively for social change and to form positive and lasting relationships (Elkind, 1994). Parents can help teenagers forge a better balance between the ideal and the real by tolerating their criticism while reminding them that all people are blends of virtues and imperfections.

Decision Making

Adolescents handle many cognitive tasks more effectively than they did when younger. But recall from Chapter 14 that changes in the brain's emotional/social network outpace development of the prefrontal cortex's cognitive control network. Consequently, teenagers perform less well than adults in planning and decision making, where they must inhibit emotion and impulses in favor of thinking rationally.

Good decision making involves: (1) recognizing the range of possible response options, (2) identifying pros and cons of each alternative, (3) assessing the likelihood of various outcomes, (4) evaluating one's choice in terms of whether one's goals were met, and, if not, (5) learning from the mistake and making a better future decision. When researchers modified a card game to trigger strong emotion by introducing immediate feedback about gains and losses after each choice, teenagers behaved more irrationally, taking far greater risks than adults in their twenties (Figner et al., 2009). In a second condition, in which players were merely asked what they would do at each step of the game but were not given feedback, adolescents and adults did not differ in quality of decision making. Additional evidence confirms that adolescents, relative to adults, are more influenced by the possibility of immediate reward—more willing to take risks and less likely to avoid potential losses (Albert & Steinberg, 2011; Cauffman et al., 2010; Christakou et al., 2013).

Nevertheless, other research indicates that teenagers are less effective than adults at decision making even under "cool," unemotional conditions (Huizenga, Crone, & Jansen, 2007). In one study, participants were given challenging real-world dilemmas—whether to have cosmetic surgery, whether to participate in an experimental study of a new acne medication, which parent to live with after a divorce—and were asked to explain how they would decide. Adults outperformed adolescents, especially the younger ones, more often considering alternatives, weighing benefits and risks, and suggesting advice seeking, especially in areas (such as medical decisions) where they had little experience (Halpern-Felsher & Cauffman, 2001).

Furthermore, in making decisions, adolescents, more often than adults (who also have difficulty), fall back on well-learned intuitive judgments (Jacobs & Klaczynski, 2002). Consider a hypothetical problem requiring a choice, on the basis of two arguments,

These high school students attending a college fair will face many important choices over the next few years. But in making decisions, teenagers are less effective than adults, who more often carefully weigh the pros and cons of each alternative.

between taking a traditional lecture class and taking a computer-based class. One argument contains large-sample information: course evaluations from 150 students, 85 percent of whom liked the computer class. The other argument contains small-sample personal reports: complaints of two honor-roll students who both hated the computer class and enjoyed the traditional class. Many adolescents, even those who knew that selecting the large-sample argument was "more intelligent," based their choice on the small-sample argument, which resembled the informal opinions they depend on in everyday life (Klaczynski, 2001).

In sum, in the heat of the moment, when making a good decision depends on inhibiting "feel-good" behavior and the possibility of immediate rewards, the brain's emotional/social network tends to prevail, and adolescents are far more likely than adults to emphasize short-term over long-term goals (Reyna & Farley, 2006; Steinberg et al., 2009). In Chapter 14, we also noted that processing skills governed by the prefrontal cognitive-control system develop gradually, into the early twenties. Like other aspects of brain development, the cognitive-control system is affected by experience (Kuhn, 2009). As "first-timers" in many situations, adolescents do not have sufficient knowledge to consider pros and cons and predict potential outcomes. And after engaging in risky behavior without negative consequences, teenagers rate its benefits higher and its risks lower than peers who have not tried it (Halpern-Felsher et al., 2004).

Furthermore, when teenagers were younger, adults usually limited the decisions they had to make. As adolescents, they face an increasing number of decisions and often feel overwhelmed by their expanding range of options—abundant choices of school courses, extracurricular activities, and social events. As a result, their efforts to choose frequently break down, and they resort to habit, act on impulse, or postpone decision making. Louis, for example, procrastinated over his college plans. When Franca mentioned that he was about to miss the deadline for taking entrance tests, he agonized over the forms, unable to decide when to take the exam.

Over time, young people learn from their successes and failures and gather information from others about factors that affect decision making (Reyna & Farley, 2006). School and community interventions that teach effective decision-making skills can help adolescents apply their capacity for metacognition, more often reflecting on and monitoring the decision process (Bruine de Bruin, 2012; Jacobs & Klaczynski, 2002). But because engaging in risk taking without experiencing harmful outcomes can heighten adolescents' sense of invulnerability, they also need supervision and protection from high-risk experiences until their decision making improves.

Ask Yourself

- **REVIEW** Describe research findings that challenge Piaget's view of a new, discrete stage of cognitive development at adolescence.

- **CONNECT** How does evidence on adolescent decision making help us understand teenagers' risk taking in sexual activity and drug use?

- **APPLY** Clarissa, age 14, is convinced that no one appreciates how hurt she feels at not being invited to the homecoming dance. Meanwhile, 15-year-old Justine, alone in her room, pantomimes being sworn in as student body president with her awestruck parents looking on. Which aspect of the personal fable is each displaying? Which adolescent is more likely to be well-adjusted, which poorly adjusted? Explain.

- **REFLECT** Cite examples of your own idealistic thinking or poor decision making as a teenager. How has your thinking changed?

15.5 What factors contribute to sex differences in mental abilities during adolescence?

Sex Differences in Mental Abilities

Sex differences in intellectual performance have sparked almost as much controversy as the ethnic and SES differences in IQ considered in Chapter 12. In most areas of cognitive functioning, including general intelligence, girls and boys are more similar than different (Hyde, 2014; Miller & Halpern, 2014). Still, they do vary in certain specific abilities, most notably reading, writing, and spatial skills.

Verbal Abilities

Throughout the school years, girls attain higher scores in reading and writing achievement and account for a lower percentage of children referred for remedial reading instruction. Girls continue to score slightly higher on tests of verbal ability in middle childhood and adolescence in every country in which assessments have been conducted (Reilly, 2012; Wai et al., 2010). And when verbal tests are heavily weighted with writing, girls' advantage is large (Halpern et al., 2007).

A special concern is that girls' advantage in reading and writing achievement increases in adolescence, with boys doing especially poorly in writing—trends evident in the United States and other industrialized nations (see Figure 15.3) (Stoet & Geary, 2013; U.S. Department of Education, 2012a, 2014b). These differences in literacy skills are believed to be major contributors to a widening gender gap in college enrollments. Whereas 40 years ago, males accounted for 60 percent of U.S. undergraduate students, today they are in the minority, at 43 percent (U.S. Department of Education, 2014b).

Recall from Chapter 6 that girls have a biological advantage in earlier development of the left hemisphere of the cerebral cortex, where language is usually localized. And fMRI research indicates that in tackling language tasks (such as deciding whether two spoken or written words rhyme), 9- to 15-year-old girls show concentrated activity in language-specific brain areas. Boys, in contrast, display more widespread activation—in addition to language areas, considerable activity in auditory and visual areas, depending on how words are presented (Burman, Bitan, & Booth, 2008). This suggests that girls are more efficient language processors than boys, who rely heavily on sensory brain regions and process spoken and written words differently.

But girls also receive more verbal stimulation from early childhood through adolescence, which may contribute to their more efficient processing (Peterson & Roberts, 2003). Furthermore, in Chapter 13 we noted that children view language arts as a "feminine" subject. And as a result of the high-stakes testing movement, students today spend more time at their desks being taught in a regimented way—an approach particularly at odds with boys' higher activity level, assertiveness, and incidence of learning problems.

Finally, high rates of divorce and out-of-wedlock births mean that more children today grow up without the continuous presence of a father who models and encourages good work habits and skill at reading and writing. Both maternal and paternal involvement influences the achievement and educational attainment of adolescents of both genders (Flouri & Buchanan, 2004). But some research suggests that high-achieving African-American boys are particularly likely to come from homes in which fathers are warm, verbally communicative, and demanding of achievement (Grief, Hrabowski, & Maton, 1998; Iruka, Winn, & Harradine, 2014). Clearly, reversing boys' weakening literacy skills is a high priority, requiring a concerted effort by families, schools, and communities.

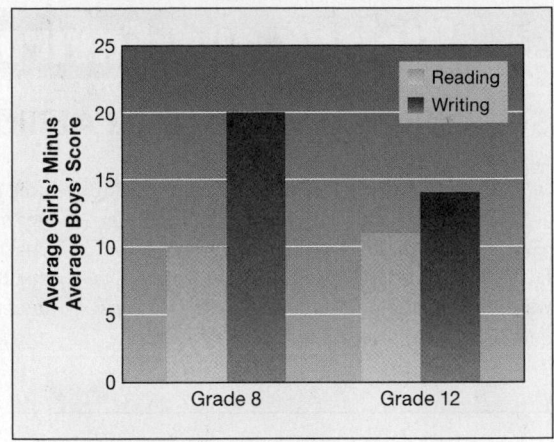

FIGURE 15.3 **Reading and writing achievement gaps favoring girls at grades 8 and 12.** Findings are based on the U.S. National Assessment of Educational Progress. The bars represent the average girls' score minus the average boys' score. Thus, the height of the bar indicates the extent to which girls outperform boys, a difference that increases in adolescence. By grades 8 and 12, girls have an especially large advantage in writing skill. Similar trends are evident in other industrialized nations. (Adapted from U.S. Department of Education, 2012b, 2014b.)

Mathematical Abilities

Studies of sex differences in mathematical abilities in the early school grades are inconsistent. Some find no disparities, others slight differences depending on the math skill assessed (Lachance & Mazzocco, 2006). Girls tend to be advantaged in counting, arithmetic computation, and mastery of basic concepts, perhaps because of their better verbal skills and more methodical approach to problem solving (Wei et al., 2012). But by late childhood and early adolescence, when math concepts become more abstract and spatial, boys outperform girls. The difference is especially evident on tests requiring complex reasoning (Gibbs, 2010b; Lindberg et al., 2010). In science achievement, too, boys' advantage increases as problems become more difficult (Penner, 2003).

This male advantage is evident in most countries where boys and girls have equal access to secondary education. But the gap is typically small, varies considerably across nations, and has diminished over the past 30 years (Aud et al., 2011; Else-Quest, Hyde, & Linn, 2010; Halpern, 2012; Reilly, 2012). Among the most capable, however, the gender gap is greater. In widely

Biology and Environment

Sex Differences in Spatial Abilities

Spatial skills are a key focus of researchers' efforts to explain sex differences in complex mathematical reasoning. The gender gap favoring males is large for *mental rotation tasks,* in which individuals must rotate a three-dimensional figure rapidly and accurately inside their heads (see Figure 15.4). Males also do considerably better on *spatial perception tasks,* in which people must determine spatial relationships by considering the orientation of the surrounding environment. Sex differences on *spatial visualization tasks,* involving analysis of complex visual forms, are weak or nonexistent. Because many strategies can be used to solve these tasks, both sexes may come up with effective procedures (Maeda & Yoon, 2013; Miller & Halpern, 2014).

Sex differences in spatial abilities emerge as early as the first few months of life, in male infants' superior ability to recognize a familiar object from a new perspective—a capacity requiring mental rotation (Moore & Johnson, 2011; Quinn & Liben, 2014). The male spatial advantage is present throughout childhood, adolescence, and adulthood in many cultures (Levine et al., 1999; Silverman, Choi, & Peters, 2007). The pattern is consistent enough to suggest a biological explanation. One hypothesis is that heredity, perhaps through prenatal exposure to androgen hormones, enhances right-hemispheric functioning, giving males a spatial advantage. (Recall that for most people, spatial

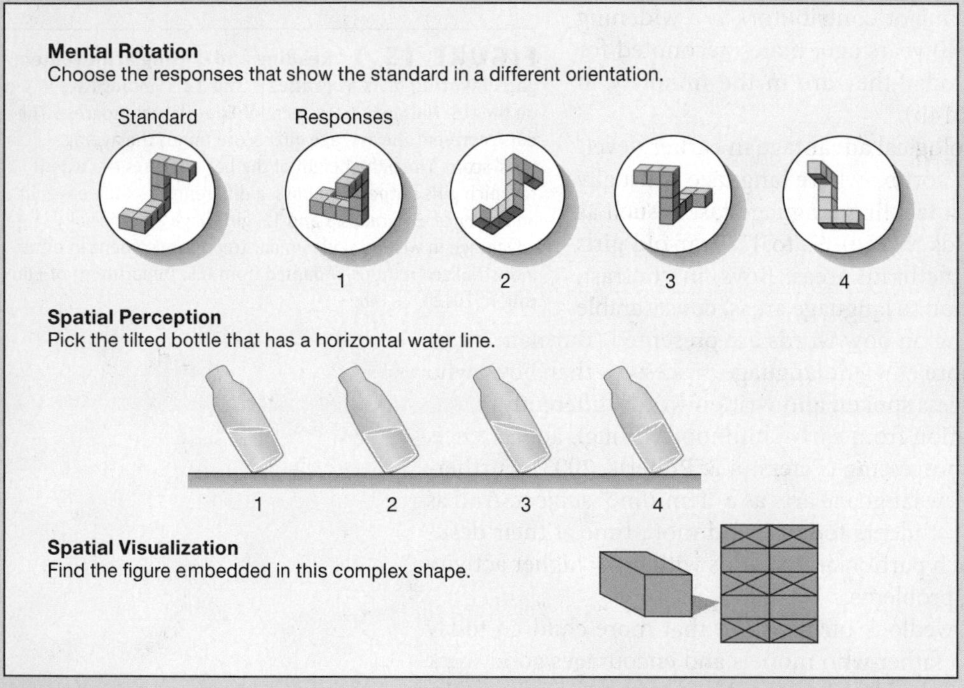

Mental Rotation
Choose the responses that show the standard in a different orientation.

Standard　　Responses

1　　2　　3　　4

Spatial Perception
Pick the tilted bottle that has a horizontal water line.

1　　2　　3　　4

Spatial Visualization
Find the figure embedded in this complex shape.

FIGURE 15.4 **Types of spatial tasks.** Large sex differences favoring males appear on mental rotation, and males do considerably better than females on spatial perception. In contrast, sex differences on spatial visualization are weak or nonexistent. (Adapted from M. C. Linn & A. C. Petersen, 1985, "Emergence and Characterization of Sex Differences in Spatial Ability: A Meta-Analysis," *Child Development, 56,* pp. 1482, 1483, 1485. © The Society for Research in Child Development. Reprinted by permission of John Wiley and Sons, Inc., conveyed through Copyright Clearance Center, Inc.)

publicized research on more than 100,000 bright seventh and eighth graders invited to take the Scholastic Assessment Test (SAT), boys outscored girls on the mathematics subtest year after year. Yet even this disparity has been shrinking. Thirty years ago, 13 times as many boys as girls scored over 700 (out of a possible 800) on the math portion of the SAT; today, the ratio is about 4 to 1 for seventh graders and 2 to 1 for high school students (Benbow & Stanley, 1983; Wai et al., 2010).

Some researchers believe that heredity contributes substantially to the gender gap in math, especially to the tendency for more boys to be extremely talented. Accumulating evidence indicates that boys' advantage originates in two skill areas: (1) their more rapid numerical memory, which permits them to devote more working-memory resources to complex mental operations; and (2) their superior spatial reasoning, which enhances their mathematical problem solving (Halpern et al., 2007). Indeed, 50 years of longitudinal evidence on nationally representative samples of U.S. high school students tracked for a decade or more reveals that consistently, high spatial ability in adolescence predicts subsequent advanced educational attainment in math-intensive fields and entry into science, technology, engineering, and math (STEM) careers, beyond the contributions of verbal and math ability (Wai, Lubinski, & Benbow, 2009). See the Biology and Environment box above for further consideration of this issue.

Social pressures are also influential. Long before sex differences in math achievement appear, many children view math as a "masculine" subject. Also, parents typically think boys

skills are housed in the right hemisphere of the cerebral cortex.) In support of this idea, girls and women whose prenatal androgen levels were abnormally high show superior performance on spatial rotation tasks (Puts et al., 2008). And women with a male twin brother, who are exposed to slightly higher levels of prenatal androgens, outperform women with a female twin sister in spatial rotation (Heil et al., 2011; Vuoksimaa et al., 2010).

Why might a biologically based sex difference in spatial abilities exist? Evolutionary theorists point out that mental rotation skill predicts rapid, accurate map drawing and interpretation, areas in which boys and men do better than girls and women. Over the course of human evolution, the cognitive abilities of males became adapted for hunting, which required generating mental representations of large-scale spaces to find one's way (Jones, Braithwaite, & Healy, 2003). But this explanation is controversial. Critics point out that female gatherers also needed to travel long distances to find fruits and vegetables that ripened in different seasons (Newcombe, 2007).

Experience also contributes to males' superior spatial performance. Children who engage in manipulative activities, such as block play, model building, and carpentry, do better on spatial tasks (Baenninger & Newcombe, 1995). Furthermore, playing action video games enhances many cognitive processes important for spatial skills, including visual discrimination, speed of thinking, attention shifting, tracking of multiple objects, mental rotation, and wayfinding—gains

that persist and generalize to diverse situations (Spence & Feng, 2010). Boys spend far more time than girls at these pursuits. Among low-SES children, sex differences in mental rotation and map-drawing skills are less pronounced (Levine et al., 2005). Perhaps boys from low SES families have fewer opportunities to engage in gender-typed activities that promote spatial skills.

Even during activities that are not gender-typed, adults may encourage spatial reasoning in boys more than girls. For example, when investigators observed preschoolers playing in their homes, boys and girls were equally likely to play with puzzles. But parents were more engaged and used more language referring to spatial concepts with sons, who more often tackled difficult puzzles (LeVine et al., 2012). Complex puzzle play predicted children's performance on a measure of spatial abilities several months later.

In studies of middle and high school students, *both* spatial abilities and self-efficacy at doing math were related to performance on complex math problems, with spatial skills being the stronger predictor (Casey, Nuttall, & Pezaris,

This 17-year-old science fair winner plans a career in physics. With supportive experiences, girls can excel in math and science.

1997, 2001). Boys are advantaged in both spatial abilities and math self-confidence. Still, spatial skills respond readily to training, with improvements often larger than the sex differences themselves. But because boys and girls usually show similar training effects, sex differences typically persist (Uttal et al., 2013). In one study of first graders, however, training in mental rotation strategies over several months—a more intensive approach than previously tried—led girls to reach the same performance level as boys (Tzuriel & Egozi, 2010). These findings suggest that the right kind of early intervention can override biologically based sex differences in spatial skills.

are better at it—an attitude that encourages girls to view themselves as having to work harder at math to do well, to blame their errors on lack of ability, and to consider math less useful for their future lives. These beliefs, in turn, reduce girls' confidence and interest in math, which undermines their performance and their willingness to consider STEM careers (Bhanot & Jovanovic, 2005; Ceci & Williams, 2010; Parker et al., 2012). Furthermore, *stereotype threat*—fear of being judged on the basis of a negative stereotype (see page 453 in Chapter 12)—causes females to do worse than their abilities allow on difficult math problems (Picho, Rodriguez, & Finnie, 2013). As a result of all these influences, even girls who are highly talented are less likely to develop effective math reasoning skills.

A positive sign is that today, American boys and girls reach advanced levels of high school math and science study in equal proportions—a crucial factor in reducing sex differences in knowledge and skill (Gallagher & Kaufman, 2005). But, as noted in Chapter 12, boys spend more time than girls with screen media, and boys tend to use them differently—more often playing video games, creating Web pages, writing computer programs, and using graphics programs (see page 465). As a result, boys acquire more specialized knowledge of screen-media technology.

Clearly, extra steps must be taken to promote girls' interest in and confidence at math and science. As Figure 15.5 on page 568 shows, in cultures that value gender equality, sex differences in math achievement are much smaller and, in two nations, reversed! Swedish and

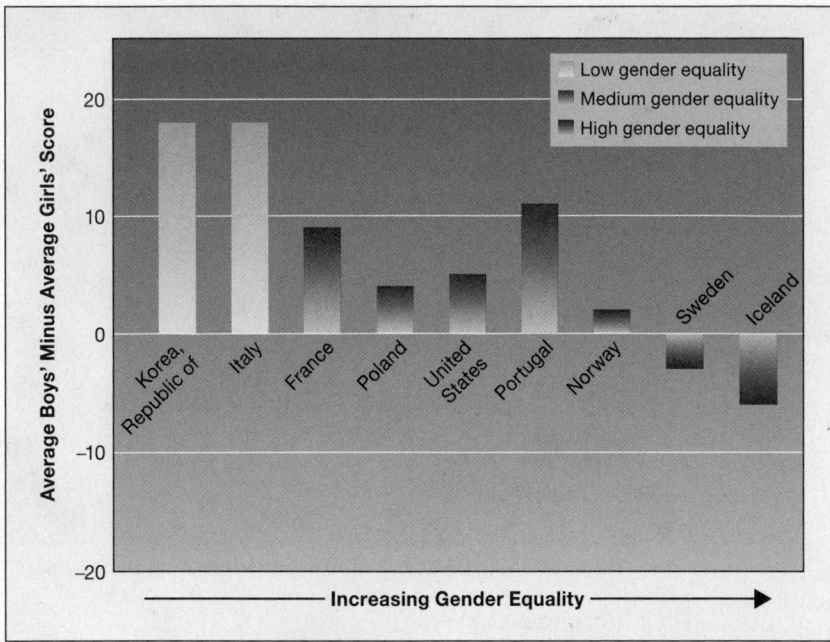

FIGURE 15.5 **Math achievement gender gaps in nine industrialized nations, arranged in order of increasing gender equality.** Math achievement scores are based on 15-year-olds' performance on an identical test in each country. Country gender equality is a composite measure that includes cultural attitudes toward women, women's participation in the labor force and in politics and government, and women's educational attainment and economic opportunities. As country gender equality increases, boys' advantage in math achievement tends to decline; in Sweden and Iceland, girls' math scores exceed boys'. (Adapted from Guiso et al., 2008; OECD, 2012).

Icelandic high school girls exceed boys in math scores (Guiso et al., 2008; OECD, 2012). Similarly, math and science achievement gaps are smaller in countries with higher proportions of women in research-related professions, and in countries where few individuals view science as "masculine" (Else-Quest, Hyde, & Linn, 2010; Nosek et al., 2009; Reilly, 2012). And in an intervention in which students in seventh grade (about the time the gender gap emerges) were taught that mental abilities are not fixed but can be improved, both boys and girls improved in math grades relative to a control group, with girls gaining more and nearly closing the gender gap (Blackwell, Trzesniewski, & Dweck, 2007; Dweck, 2007).

Finally, a math curriculum beginning in kindergarten that teaches children how to apply effective spatial strategies—drawing diagrams, mentally manipulating visual images, searching for numerical patterns, and graphing—is vital (Nuttall, Casey, & Pezaris, 2005). Because girls are biased toward verbal processing, they may not attain their math and science potential unless they are specifically taught how to think spatially. Exposure to successful women as role models is likely to improve girls' belief in their own capacity to succeed.

15.6 Describe changes in vocabulary, grammar, and pragmatics during adolescence.

Language Development

Although language development is largely complete by the end of childhood, subtle but important changes take place in adolescence. These gains are largely influenced by adolescents' improved capacity for reflective thought and abstraction, which enhances their *metalinguistic awareness,* or ability to think about language as a system.

Vocabulary and Grammar

In the conversation at the beginning of this chapter, note Jules's use of *counterintuitive, revolutionized, philosophy,* and *reproduction.* During adolescence, young people add a variety of abstract words to their vocabularies. In a comparison of autobiographical narratives written by 11-year-olds with those of 14- and 17-year-olds, older adolescents used more abstract nouns and metacognitive verbs, such as "realize," "conclude," and "hypothesize" (Sun & Nippold, 2012). Their use of sophisticated vocabulary was associated with production of grammatically more complex sentences. Furthermore, from high school to college, definitions of abstract words improve greatly in clarity and accuracy (Nippold, 1999). For example, in explaining the meaning of *burden,* Louis said, "It's like a heavy weight on your shoulders. You can also use it figuratively, to mean an unpleasant responsibility or a long-term problem."

As Louis's definition illustrates, grasp of figurative language improves greatly in adolescence. Proverbs—especially those that express subtle attitudes—are especially challenging. They can be used to comment ("Blood is thicker than water"), interpret ("His bark is worse than his bite"), advise ("Humility often gains more than pride"), warn ("Of idleness comes no goodness"), and encourage ("Every cloud has a silver lining") (Nippold, 2000). As with other aspects of semantic development, reading proficiency fosters understanding of proverbs (Nippold, Allen, & Kirsch, 2001). And a better grasp of figurative language enables teenagers to appreciate adult literary works.

Finally, teenagers more effectively analyze and correct their grammar. In U.S. schools, overt grammar instruction—out of favor since the 1970s—is making a comeback, prompted by the mediocre writing skills of many adolescents. In the most recent national assessment of educational progress, only about one-fourth of U.S. high school seniors scored at a "proficient" level or above in writing achievement (U.S. Department of Education, 2012b). But traditional grammar instruction (such as diagramming sentences) has no impact on students' writing skills (Graham & Perin, 2007). Rather, grammatically accurate written expression is best learned in the context of writing. And writing improves when teachers show students how to write for different purposes, give them many opportunities to write, and help them critique and improve their compositions.

Pragmatics

One obvious gain in adolescents' communication skills is an improved capacity to adapt language style to social context—in part because teenagers have opportunities to enter many more situations. To succeed on the debate team, Louis had to speak in a persuasive, well-organized, rapid-fire manner. In theater class, he worked on reciting memorized lines as if they were natural. At work, his boss expected him to respond to customers cheerfully and courteously. Greater skill at reflecting on the features of language and engaging in cognitive self-regulation also supports effective use of language styles (Obler, 2013). Teenagers are far more likely than school-age children to practice what they want to say in an expected situation, review what they did say, and figure out how they could say it better.

TAKE A MOMENT... Listen to adolescents conversing, and note their use of slang—another illustration of their mastery of language styles. Adolescents' electronic communication—especially text messaging and, increasingly, interaction on social networking sites—is also rich in slang. "Cyberslang," devised to facilitate communication while protecting its privacy, has become a familiar part of popular culture. Although many terms have become recognizable to adults, teenagers constantly invent new slang, some of which they also use in face-to-face communication—for example, "BAE" (before anyone else), "OTP" (one true pairing), "WAYN" (where are you now?), "PAW" (parents are watching). Adolescents use slang as a sign of group belonging and as a way to distinguish themselves from adults. Doing so is part of separating from parents and seeking a temporary self-definition in the peer group. We will discuss these developments in Chapter 16.

A student delivers a rebuttal for her high school debate team—an experience that greatly enhances her skill at persuasive speech. Opportunities to enter diverse situations contribute to adolescents' improved capacity to adapt language style to social context.

Learning in School

In complex societies, adolescence coincides with entry into secondary school. Most young people move into either a middle or a junior high school and then into a high school. With each change, academic achievement becomes more serious, affecting higher education options and job opportunities. In the following sections, we take up various aspects of secondary school life.

15.7 Discuss the impact of school transitions on adolescent adjustment.

15.8 Discuss family, peer, and school influences on academic achievement during adolescence.

15.9 What factors increase the risk of high school dropout?

School Transitions

When Sabrina started middle school, she left a small, intimate, self-contained sixth-grade classroom for a much larger school. "I don't know most of the kids in my classes, and my teachers don't know me," Sabrina complained to her mother at the end of the first week. "Besides, there's too much homework. I get assignments in all my classes at once. I can't do all this!" she shouted, bursting into tears.

On the first day of school, a teacher's caring attention helps this sixth grader deal with the stress of moving from a small self-contained elementary school classroom to a large middle school.

IMPACT OF SCHOOL TRANSITIONS As Sabrina's reactions suggest, school transitions can create adjustment problems. With each school change—from elementary to middle or junior high and then to high school—adolescents' grades decline (Benner, 2011; Ryan, Shim, & Makara, 2013). The drop is partly due to tighter academic standards, but school transitions are also associated with reductions in achievement test scores and in attendance—changes that cannot be explained by tougher grading (Benner & Wang, 2014; Schwerdt & West, 2013). The transition to secondary school often means less personal attention, more whole-class instruction, and less chance to participate in classroom decision making.

In view of these changes, it is not surprising that students often rate their middle- and high-school experiences less favorably than their elementary school experiences. They also report that their teachers care less about them, are less friendly, offer less support, grade less fairly, and stress competition more. Consequently, many young people feel less academically competent, and their liking for school and motivation decline (Barber & Olsen, 2004; De Wit et al., 2011; Otis, Grouzet, & Pelletier, 2005).

Adolescents facing added strains at either transition—family disruption, poverty, low parental involvement, high parental conflict, low social support, or learned helplessness on academic tasks—are at greatest risk for self-esteem and academic difficulties (de Bruyn, 2005; De Wit et al., 2011; Seidman et al., 2003). Furthermore, the high-school transition is particularly challenging for African-American and Hispanic students who move to a new school with substantially fewer same-ethnicity peers (Benner & Graham, 2009). Under these conditions, minority adolescents report decreased feelings of belonging and school liking, and they show steeper declines in grades.

Distressed youths whose school performance either remains low or drops sharply after school transition often show a persisting pattern of poor self-esteem, motivation, and achievement. In one study, researchers compared "multiple-problem" youths (those having both academic and mental health problems), youths having difficulties in just one area (either academic or mental health), and well-adjusted youths (those doing well in both areas) across the transition to high school. Although all groups declined in grade point average, well-adjusted students continued to get high marks and multiple-problem youths low marks, with the others falling in between. And as Figure 15.6 shows, the multiple-problem youths showed a far greater rise in truancy and out-of-school problem behaviors (Roeser, Eccles, & Freedman-Doan, 1999).

Adolescents with academic and emotional difficulties often turn to similarly alienated peers for the support they lack in other spheres of life (Rubin et al., 2013). For these vulnerable youths, the transition to high school may initiate a downward spiral in school involvement and performance that eventually leads to failure and dropping out.

HELPING ADOLESCENTS ADJUST TO SCHOOL TRANSITIONS As these findings reveal, school transitions often lead to environmental changes that fit poorly with adolescents' developmental needs (Eccles & Roeser, 2009). They disrupt close relationships with teachers at a time when adolescents need adult support. They emphasize competition during a period of heightened self-focusing. They reduce decision making and choice as the desire for autonomy is increasing. And they interfere with peer networks as young people become more concerned with peer acceptance.

Support from parents, teachers, and peers can ease these strains (Waters, Lester, & Cross, 2014). Parental involvement, monitoring, gradual autonomy granting, and emphasis on mastery rather than merely good grades are associated with better adjustment (Gutman,

FIGURE 15.6 **Increase in truancy and out-of-school problem behaviors across the transition to high school in four groups of students.** Well-adjusted students, students with only academic problems, and students with only mental health problems showed little change. (Good students with mental health problems actually declined in problem behaviors, so no yellow bar is shown for them.) In contrast, multiple-problem students—with both academic and mental health difficulties—increased sharply in truancy and problem behaviors after changing schools from eighth to ninth grade. (Adapted from Roeser, Eccles, & Freedman-Doan, 1999.)

Applying What We Know

Supporting High Achievement in Adolescence

FACTOR	DESCRIPTION
Child-rearing practices	Authoritative parenting
	Joint parent–adolescent decision making
	Parent involvement in the adolescent's education
Peer influences	Peer valuing of and support for high achievement
School characteristics	Warm, supportive teachers who develop personal relationships with parents and show them how to support their teenager's learning
	Learning activities that encourage high-level thinking
	Active student participation in learning activities and classroom decision making
Employment schedule	Job commitment limited to less than 15 hours per week
	High-quality vocational education for non-college-bound adolescents

2006). Adolescents with close friends are more likely to sustain these friendships across the transition, which increases social integration and academic motivation in the new school (Aikins, Bierman, & Parker, 2005).

Some school districts reduce the number of school transitions by combining elementary and middle school into K–8 buildings. Compared with agemates who transition to middle school, K–8 sixth and seventh graders score higher in achievement (Kleffer, 2013; Schwerdt & West, 2013). Furthermore, teachers and administrators in K–8 buildings report more positive social contexts—less chaos, fewer conduct problems, and better overall working conditions (Kim et al., 2014). These factors predict students' favorable school attitudes, academically and socially.

Other less extensive changes are also effective. Forming smaller units within large schools promotes closer relations with both teachers and peers along with greater extracurricular involvement (Seidman, Aber, & French, 2004). And a "critical mass" of same-ethnicity peers—according to one suggestion, at least 15 percent of the student body—helps teenagers feel socially accepted and reduces fear of out-group hostility (National Research Council, 2007). In the first year after a school transition, homerooms can be provided in which teachers offer academic and personal counseling and work closely with parents to promote favorable adjustment. Assigning students to classes with several familiar peers or a constant group of new peers also strengthens emotional security and social support. In schools that take these steps, students are less likely to decline in academic performance or display other adjustment problems, including low self-esteem, depression, substance abuse, delinquency, and dropping out (Felner et al., 2002).

LOOK and LISTEN

Ask several secondary school students to describe their experiences after school transition. What supports for easing the stress of transition did their teachers and school provide?

Academic Achievement

Adolescent achievement is the result of a long history of cumulative effects. Early on, positive educational environments, both family and school, lead to personal traits that support achievement—intelligence, confidence in one's own abilities, the desire to succeed, and high educational aspirations. Yet improving an unfavorable environment can foster resilience among poorly performing young people. See Applying What We Know above for a summary of environmental factors that enhance achievement during the teenage years.

CHILD-REARING STYLES Authoritative parenting is linked to higher grades in school among adolescents varying widely in SES, just as it predicts mastery-oriented behavior in childhood. In contrast, authoritarian and permissive styles are associated with lower grades (Collins & Steinberg, 2006; Vazsonyi, Hibbert, & Snider, 2003). Uninvolved parenting (low in both warmth and maturity demands) predicts the poorest grades and worsening school performance over time (Glasgow et al., 1997; Aunola, Stattin, & Nurmi, 2000).

The link between authoritative parenting and adolescents' academic competence has been confirmed in countries with diverse value systems, including Argentina, Australia, China, the Netherlands, Pakistan, and the United Kingdom (de Bruyn, Deković, & Meijnen, 2003; Chan & Koo, 2011; Steinberg, 2001). In Chapter 10, we noted that authoritative parents adjust their expectations to children's capacity to take responsibility for their own behavior. Adolescents whose parents engage in joint decision making, gradually permitting more autonomy with age, achieve especially well (Wang, Pomerantz, & Chen, 2007). Warmth, open discussion, firmness, and monitoring of adolescents' whereabouts and activities make young people feel cared about and valued, encourage reflective thinking and self-regulation, and increase awareness of the importance of doing well in school. These factors, in turn, are related to mastery-oriented attributions, effort, achievement, and high educational expectations (Gauvain, Perez, & Beebe, 2013; Gregory & Weinstein, 2004).

By attending parent–teacher conferences and keeping tabs on her son's progress in school, this mother sends her child a strong message about the importance of education and also builds a bridge between the worlds of home and school.

PARENT–SCHOOL PARTNERSHIPS   High-achieving students typically have parents who keep tabs on their child's progress, communicate with teachers, and make sure their child is enrolled in challenging, well-taught classes. These efforts are just as important during middle and high school as they were earlier (Hill & Taylor, 2004). In a large sample of adolescents, parent involvement in tenth grade predicted grade point average in eleventh grade, beyond the influence of SES and previous academic achievement. Students whose parents encouraged educational pursuits and conveyed the importance of academic achievement were more academically engaged (Wang & Sheikh-Khalil, 2014). Involved parents send a message to their child about the value of education, model constructive solutions to academic problems, and promote wise educational decisions—factors that induce in teenagers a sense of academic self-efficacy, of being able to handle academic challenges (Oyserman, 2007). Involved parents can also prevent school personnel from placing a bright student who is not working up to potential in unstimulating classes.

The daily stresses of living in low-income, high-risk neighborhoods reduce parents' energy for school involvement (Bunting et al., 2013). Yet stronger home–school links can relieve some of this stress. Schools can form parent–school partnerships by strengthening personal relationships between teachers and parents, building bridges between minority home cultures and the culture of the school, tapping parents' talents to improve the quality of school programs, and including parents in school governance so they remain invested in school goals.

PEER INFLUENCES   Peers play an important role in adolescent achievement, in a way that relates to both family and school. Teenagers whose parents value achievement not only tend to be academically motivated but generally choose friends who share those values (Kiuru et al., 2009; Rubin et al., 2013; Woolley, Kol, & Bowen, 2009). For example, when Sabrina began to make new friends in middle school, she often studied with her girlfriends. Each girl wanted to do well and reinforced this desire in the others. In an investigation that assessed a large sample of students at the beginning of seventh and again at the end of eighth grade, those with academically high-performing friends not only gained in school performance but were also more likely to avoid drugs, engage in responsible behavior, and participate in extracurricular activities (Cook, Deng, & Morgano, 2007). Of the diverse characteristics on which friends resemble each other, grade point average had the strongest association with future adjustment, predicting both academic and social outcomes.

Peer support for high achievement also depends on the overall climate of the peer culture, which, for ethnic minority youths, is powerfully affected by the surrounding social order. In one study, integration into the school peer network predicted higher grades among Caucasians and Hispanics but not among Asians and African Americans (Faircloth & Hamm, 2005). Asian cultural values stress respect for family and teacher expectations over close peer ties (Chao & Tseng, 2002; Chen, 2005). African-American minority adolescents may observe that

Social Issues: Education

Media Multitasking Disrupts Attention and Learning

"Mom, I'm going to study for my biology test now," called 16-year-old Ashley while shutting her bedroom door. Sitting down at her desk, she accessed a popular social-networking website on her laptop, donned headphones and began listening to a favorite song on her tablet, and placed her cell phone next to her elbow so she could hear it chime if any text messages arrived. Only then did she open her textbook and begin to read.

In a survey of a nationally representative sample of U.S. 8- to 18-year-olds, more than two-thirds reported engaging in two or more media activities at once, some or most of the time (Rideout, Foehr, & Roberts, 2010). Adolescents' most frequent type of media multitasking is listening to music while doing homework, but many also report watching TV or using the Internet while studying (Jeong & Fishbein, 2007). The presence of a television or computer in the young person's bedroom is a strong predictor of this behavior (Foehr, 2006). And it extends into classrooms, where students can be seen text-messaging under their desks or surfing the Internet on cell phones.

Research confirms that media multitasking fragments the attention span, greatly reducing learning. In one experiment, participants were given two tasks: learning to predict the weather in two different cities using colored shapes as cues and keeping a mental tally of how many high-pitched beeps they heard through headphones. Half the sample performed the tasks

simultaneously, the other half separately. Both groups learned to predict the weather in the two-city situation, but the multitaskers were unable to apply their learning to new weather problems (Foerde, Knowlton, & Poldrack, 2006).

fMRI evidence revealed that the participants working only on the weather task activated the hippocampus, which plays a vital role in *explicit memory*—conscious, strategic recall, which enables new information to be used flexibly and adaptively in contexts outside the original learning situation (see page 289 in Chapter 8). In contrast, the multitaskers activated subcortical areas involved in *implicit memory*—a shallower, automatic form of learning that takes place unconsciously.

As early as 1980, studies linked heavy media use with executive-function difficulties (Nunez-Smith et al., 2008). Frequent media multitaskers, who are accustomed to continuously shifting their attention from one task to another, have a harder time filtering out irrelevant stimuli when they are not multitasking (Ophir, Nass, & Wagner, 2009). Adolescents who often media multitask report multiple executive-function problems involving attention, impulse control, and flexible thinking in everyday life (Baumgartner et al., 2014).

Beyond superficial preparation for her biology test, Ashley is likely to have trouble concentrating and strategically processing new information after turning off her electronic devices. Experienced teachers often remark that compared to

© LAURA DWIGHT PHOTOGRAPHY

Media multitasking while doing homework fragments attention, yielding superficial learning. And frequent multitaskers are likely to have difficulty filtering out irrelevant stimuli even when they are not multitasking.

students of a generation ago, today's teenagers are more easily distracted and learn less thoroughly. One teacher reflected, "It's the way they've grown up—working short times on many different things at one time" (Clay, 2009, p. 40).

their ethnic group is worse off than the white majority in educational attainment, jobs, income, and housing. And discriminatory treatment by teachers and peers, often resulting from stereotypes that they are "not intelligent," triggers anger, anxiety, self-doubt, declines in achievement, association with peers who are not interested in school, and increases in problem behaviors (Wong, Eccles, & Sameroff, 2003).

Schools that build close networks of support between teachers and peers can prevent these negative outcomes. One high school with a largely low-income ethnic minority student body (65 percent African American) reorganized into "career academies"—learning communities within the school, each offering a different career-related curriculum (for example, one focused on health, medicine, and life sciences, another on computer technology). The smaller-school climate and focus on a common theme helped create caring teacher–student relationships and a peer culture that fostered valuing of school engagement, collaborating on projects, and academic success (Conchas, 2006). High school graduation and college enrollment rates rose from a small minority to over 90 percent.

Finally, teenagers' use of text messaging and e-mail to remain continuously in touch with peers—even during class and while working on homework—is an aspect of contemporary peer-group life that poses risks to achievement. See the Social Issues: Education box above to find out about the impact of "media multitasking" on attention and learning.

This high school teacher's warm, supportive way of relating to students leads to gains in motivation and achievement.

SCHOOL CHARACTERISTICS Adolescents need school environments that are responsive to their expanding powers of reasoning and their emotional and social needs. Without appropriate learning experiences, their cognitive potential is unlikely to be realized.

Classroom Learning Experiences. As noted earlier, in large, departmentalized secondary schools, many adolescents report that their classes lack warmth and supportiveness—a circumstance that dampens their motivation. One study tracked changes in students' academic orientation in math classes from seventh to eighth grade. Those who entered classrooms high in teacher support, encouragement of student interaction about academic work, and promotion of mutual respect among classmates gained in academic motivation and cognitive self-regulation (reflected in whether they understood concepts and in their willingness to check their work). But in classrooms emphasizing competition and public comparison of students, declines in motivation and self-regulation occurred (Ryan & Patrick, 2001). In other investigations, adolescents who perceived their relationships with teachers as warm, trusting, and cooperative and who viewed classroom control as shared between teacher and students showed better attendance and achievement (Eshel & Kohavi, 2003; McHugh et al., 2013).

Of course, an important benefit of separate classes in each subject is that adolescents can be taught by experts, who are more likely to encourage high-level thinking, teach effective learning strategies, and emphasize content relevant to students' experiences—factors that promote interest, effort, and achievement (Eccles, 2004). But many secondary school classrooms do not consistently provide stimulating, challenging teaching.

Wide variability in quality of instruction has contributed to increasing numbers of seniors who graduate from high school deficient in basic academic skills. Although the achievement gap separating African-American, Hispanic, and Native-American students from white students has declined since the 1970s, mastery of reading, writing, mathematics, and science by low-SES ethnic minority students remains disappointing (U.S. Department of Education, 2012a, 2012b, 2014b). Too often these young people attend underfunded schools with run-down buildings, outdated equipment, and textbook shortages. In some, crime and discipline problems receive more attention than teaching and learning.

To upgrade the academic achievement of poorly performing students, a *high-stakes testing* movement has arisen, which makes progress through the school system contingent on passing achievement tests. But as the Social Issues: Education box on the following page points out, high-stakes testing narrows the focus of classroom instruction to preparing for tests and, in some school districts, may widen group differences in educational attainment. Another source of educational inequity is the placement of many low-SES, minority students in low academic tracks, which compounds their learning difficulties.

Tracking. Ability grouping, as we saw in Chapter 12, is detrimental during the elementary school years. At least into middle school, mixed-ability classes are desirable. They support the motivation and achievement of students who vary widely in academic progress (Gillies, 2003a; Gillies & Ashman, 1996).

By high school, some grouping is unavoidable because certain aspects of education must dovetail with the young person's future educational and vocational plans. In the United States, high school students are counseled into college preparatory, vocational, or general education tracks. Unfortunately, low-SES minority students are assigned in large numbers to noncollege tracks, perpetuating educational inequalities of earlier years.

Longitudinal research following thousands of U.S. students from eighth to twelfth grade revealed that assignment to a college preparatory track accelerates academic progress, whereas assignment to a vocational or general education track decelerates it (Hallinan & Kubitschek, 1999). Even in secondary schools with no formal tracking program, low-SES minority students tend to be assigned to lower course levels in most or all of their academic subjects, resulting in *de facto* (unofficial) *tracking* (Kalogrides & Loeb, 2013).

LOOK and LISTEN

Ask a long-time high school teacher for his or her views on the impact of high-stakes testing on quality of classroom teaching. How successful, in the teacher's view, are such tests in improving student achievement?

Social Issues: Education

High-Stakes Testing

To better hold schools accountable for educating students, during the past two decades many U.S. states have mandated that students pass exams for high school graduation. Currently, about two-thirds of public high school students take exit exams (U.S. Department of Education, 2014b). As these high-stakes achievement tests spread, schools stepped up their testing programs, extending them downward to elementary school. Some states and school districts also made grade promotion (in New York City, as early as the third grade) and secondary-school academic course credits contingent on test scores (NYC Department of Education, 2014b).

The U.S. No Child Left Behind Act broadens high-stakes testing to the identification of "passing" and "failing" schools. The law mandates that each state evaluate every public school's performance through annual achievement testing and publicize the results. Schools that consistently perform poorly (have a high percentage of failing students) must give parents options for upgrading their children's education, such as transfers to nearby, higher-performing schools or enrollment in remedial classes. Some states offer schoolwide rewards for high scores, including official praise and financial bonuses to school staff. Penalties imposed for low scores include staff firing, withdrawal of accreditation, state takeover, closure, or other restructuring.

Proponents of high-stakes testing believe that it introduces greater rigor into classroom teaching, improves student motivation and achievement, and either turns around poor-performing schools or protects students from being trapped in them. But accumulating evidence indicates that high-stakes testing often undermines, rather than upgrades, the quality of education.

Research shows that high-stakes tests cause teachers to spend large amounts of time on activities that closely resemble test items—typically, drill-based exercises (Ravitch, 2010). Classroom experiences and assignments that require high-level reasoning, including extended writing and research projects, are de-emphasized, as are subjects not covered on the tests.

Because the main goal of high-stakes testing is to upgrade the performance of poorly achieving students, low-income and ethnic minority students are especially likely to be exposed to narrowly focused, regimented teaching (Darling-Hammond, 2010). Simultaneously, the educational needs of gifted and talented students are neglected (Scot, Callahan, & Urquhart, 2009).

An additional concern is that high-stakes testing promotes fear—a poor motivator for upgrading teaching and learning. Compared to other classroom testing, during high-stakes testing students report considerably greater test anxiety, which may negatively affect their performance (Segool et al., 2013). Principals and teachers worry about losing funding and their jobs if students do poorly—punishments that have sparked unprecedented levels of adult cheating and other educationally detrimental behaviors. These range from giving students answers, changing students' scores, and offering students rewards (including money and expensive toys) for earning high scores to suspending or expelling students likely to perform poorly just before test administration (Amrein-Beardsley, Berliner, & Rideau, 2010).

Furthermore, many students who get passing school grades, even high grades, fail high-stakes exams because a time-limited test can tap only a small sampling of the skills covered in the classroom (Plake, 2011). Students most likely to score poorly are minority youths living in poverty. When they are punished with course failure and grade retention, their self-esteem and motivation drop sharply. Research confirms that high school exit exam requirements have contributed to U.S. dropout rates (Baker & Lang, 2013).

The trend toward teaching to tests induced by high-stakes testing contrasts sharply with the

High-stakes testing often negatively affects educational quality and student learning. Pressure on teachers to "teach to the test" narrows the focus of the curriculum. And students who experience course failure or grade retention because of poor test performance are likely to decline in motivation and drop out of school.

emphasis on teaching for deeper understanding in countries that rank at the top in cross-cultural comparisons of academic achievement (see Chapter 12, pages 468–469). Even after hundreds of hours of class time devoted to test preparation, thousands of U.S. students fail school-exit exams and do not graduate. Although most retake these exams, some fail repeatedly, with potentially dire consequences for the course of their lives.

Clearly, serious issues remain for lawmakers and educators to resolve about the use of high-stakes tests. These include their questionable power to spark school reforms that make students better learners.

Breaking out of a low academic track is difficult. Track or course enrollment is generally based on past performance, which is limited by placement history. Interviews with African-American students in one high school revealed that many thought their previous performance did not reflect their ability. Yet teachers and counselors, overburdened with other responsibilities, had little time to reconsider individual cases (Ogbu, 2003). And compared to students in higher tracks, students in low tracks exert substantially less effort—a difference due in part to less stimulating classroom experiences (Worthy, Hungerford-Kresser, & Hampton, 2009).

This student is the child of migrant farmworkers in central California. Like many low-SES minority students, she is trapped in a low academic track, where her motivation and achievement almost certainly will decline. An estimated 90 percent of migrant workers' children drop out of high school.

High school students are separated into academic and vocational tracks in virtually all industrialized nations. In China, Japan, and most Western European countries, students' placement is determined by their performance on a national exam. The outcome usually establishes the young person's future possibilities. In the United States, students who are not assigned to a college preparatory track or who achieve poorly in high school can still attend college. Ultimately, however, many young people do not benefit from the more open U.S. system. By adolescence, SES differences in quality of education and academic achievement are greater in the United States than in most other industrialized countries (Marks, Cresswell, & Ainley, 2006). And the United States has a higher percentage of young people who see themselves as educational failures and drop out of high school (OECD, 2013a).

Dropping Out

Across the aisle from Louis in math class sat Norman, who daydreamed, crumpled his notes into his pocket after class, and rarely did his homework. On test days, he twirled a rabbit's foot for good luck but left most questions blank. Louis and Norman had been classmates since fourth grade, but they had little to do with each other. To Louis, who was quick at schoolwork, Norman seemed to live in another world. Once or twice each week, Norman cut class; then, one spring day, he stopped coming altogether.

Norman is one of about 7 percent of U.S. 16- to 24-year-olds who dropped out of high school and remain without a diploma or a GED (U.S. Department of Education, 2014b). The overall dropout rate has declined since the mid-2000s, largely due to substantial gains in Hispanic teenagers' graduation rates. Nevertheless, as Figure 15.7 shows, dropout rates remain elevated among low-SES ethnic minority youths, especially Hispanic and Native-American teenagers. Also, boys drop out at slightly higher rates than girls.

The decision to leave school has dire consequences. Youths without upper secondary education have much lower literacy scores than high school graduates, and they lack the skills valued by employers in today's knowledge-based economy. Consequently, dropouts have much lower employment rates than high school graduates. Even when employed, dropouts are far more likely to remain in menial, low-paid jobs and to be out of work from time to time.

FACTORS RELATED TO DROPPING OUT   Table 15.1 lists diverse factors related to leaving school early. The more that are present, the greater the risk of dropping out. Many dropouts show a persistent pattern of disruptive behavior combined with poor academic performance (Hawkins, Jaccard, & Needle, 2013). But others, like Norman, have few behavior problems; they simply experience academic difficulties and quietly disengage from school (Balfanz, Herzog, & MacIver, 2007). The pathway to dropping out starts early. Risk factors in first grade predict later dropout nearly as well as risk factors in secondary school (Entwisle, Alexander, & Olson, 2005).

Norman—like other dropouts—had a long history of marginal-to-failing school grades and low academic self-esteem (Wexler & Pyle, 2013). Faced with a challenging task, he gave up, relying on luck—his rabbit's foot—to get

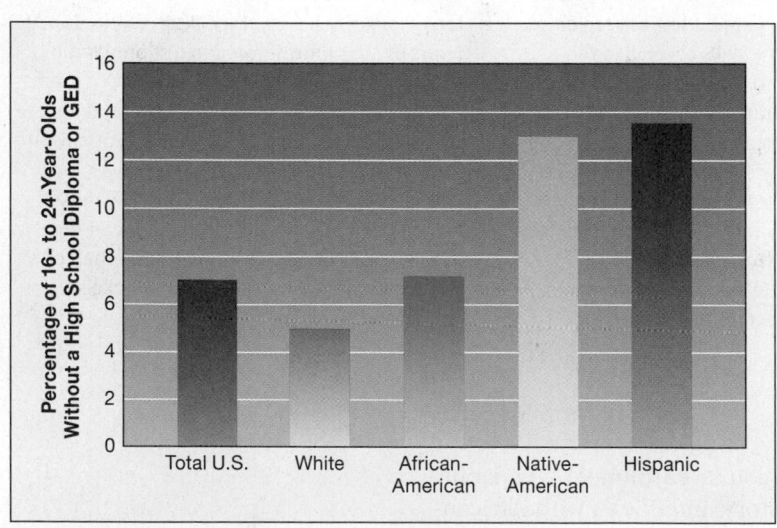

FIGURE 15.7   **U.S. high school dropout rates by ethnicity.** Because many African-American, Hispanic, and Native-American young people come from low-income and poverty-stricken families and attend underfunded, poor-quality schools, their dropout rates are above the national average. Rates for Native-American and Hispanic youths are especially high. (From DeVoe & Darling-Churchill, 2008; U.S. Department of Education, 2014b.)

TABLE 15.1   Factors Related to Dropping Out of High School

STUDENT CHARACTERISTICS	FAMILY CHARACTERISTICS	SCHOOL AND COMMUNITY CHARACTERISTICS
Poor school attendance	Parents who do not support or emphasize achievement	Large, unstimulating classes
Inattentiveness in class	Parents who were high school dropouts	Lack of opportunity to form personal relationships with teachers
School discipline problems, especially aggressive behavior	Parents who are uninvolved in the adolescent's education	Curriculum irrelevant to student interests and needs
Inability to get along with teachers	Parents who react with anger and punishment to the adolescent's low grades	School authority structure that emphasizes the teacher and discourages student input
1 to 2 years behind in grade level		
Poor school grades	Single-parent household	High rate of peer victimization at school
A sharp drop in academic performance after school transition	Parental divorce during high school	Large student body
Dislike of school	Low income	School located in low-SES racially or ethnically segregated neighborhood
Enrollment in a general education or vocational track	Frequent school changes	
Low educational aspirations		
Low self-esteem, especially academic self-esteem		High-poverty community
Friendships with peers who have left school		Availability of work that requires only on-the-job training
Low involvement in extracurricular activities		
Drug use		
Law-breaking behavior		
Early sexual activity and adolescent parenthood		

Sources: Hawkins, Jaccard, & Needle, 2013; Lee & Burkam, 2003; Peguero, 2011; Song, Benin, & Glick, 2012.

by. As Norman got older, he attended class less regularly, paid little attention when he was there, and rarely did his homework. He didn't join school clubs or participate in sports. As a result, few teachers or students got to know him well. By the day he left, Norman felt alienated from all aspects of school life.

As with other dropouts, Norman's family background contributed to his problems. Compared with other students, even those with the same grade profile, dropouts are more likely to have parents who are uninvolved in their teenager's education and engage in little monitoring of their youngster's daily activities. Many parents are single, never finished high school themselves, and are unemployed (Pagani et al., 2008; Song, Benin, & Glick, 2012).

Academically marginal students who drop out often have school experiences that undermine their chances for success: grade retention, which marks them as academic failures; large, impersonal schools; classes with unsupportive teachers and few opportunities for active participation; and frequent peer victimization (Lee & Burkam, 2003; Peguero, 2011). In such schools, rule breaking is common and often results in suspension, which—by excluding students from classes—contributes further to academic failure (Christie, Jolivette, & Nelson, 2007). Recent reports indicate that more than half of adolescents in some U.S. inner-city high schools do not graduate. Students in general education and vocational tracks, where teaching tends to be the least stimulating, are three times as likely to drop out as those in a college preparatory track (U.S. Department of Education, 2014b).

The high dropout rates among urban minority teenagers are also influenced by young people's observations and experiences of discrimination, which strengthen their conviction that finishing school will not bring them greater vocational and financial rewards (Harwood et al., 2002; Valdés, 1997). When work requiring only on-the-job training becomes available in their communities, these teenagers (more often boys), despite being within a year or two of graduating, often choose employment over school attendance (McNeal, 2011; Stearns & Glennie, 2006). And some ethnic-minority adolescents, especially girls, are more likely to be expected to take on family responsibilities, including care of siblings or aging adults, which may prompt school leaving.

LOOK and LISTEN

Contact an adult education program that sponsors GED classes, and interview one or more teachers about their students' unique academic and social needs. What factors, in the teacher's view, distinguish students who succeed in earning a GED from those who fail to do so?

A teenager receives additional academic support from a caring retired teacher—a successful way to prevent struggling students from dropping out of school.

PREVENTION STRATEGIES The most powerful way to prevent school dropout is to address the academic and social problems of at-risk students beginning in elementary school, and to involve their parents (Prevatt & Kelly, 2003). In addition, programs have been developed for adolescents. Among the diverse strategies available, several common themes are related to success:

- *Supplementary academic instruction and counseling that offer personalized attention.* Most potential dropouts need intensive remedial instruction in small classes that permit warm, caring teacher–student relationships to form. To overcome the negative psychological effects of repeated school failure, academic assistance must be combined with social support (Christenson & Thurlow, 2004; Wilson & Tanner-Smith, 2013). In one successful approach, at-risk students are matched with retired adults, who serve as tutors, mentors, and role models in addressing academic and vocational needs (Prevatt, 2003).
- *High-quality vocational education.* For many marginal students, the real-life nature of vocational education is more comfortable and effective than purely academic work (Levin, 2012). To work well, vocational training must carefully integrate academic and job-related instruction so students can see the relevance of what happens in the classroom to their future goals.
- *Efforts to address the many factors in students' lives related to leaving school early.* Programs that strengthen parent involvement, offer flexible work–study arrangements, and provide on-site child care for teenage parents can make staying in school easier for at-risk adolescents.
- *Participation in extracurricular activities.* Another way of helping marginal students is to draw them into the community life of the school (Mahoney & Stattin, 2000). The most powerful influence on extracurricular involvement is small school size (Crosnoe, Johnson, & Elder, 2004; Feldman & Matjasko, 2007). As high school student body size declines—dropping from 2,000 students to 500 to 700 students—at-risk youths are more likely to be needed to help staff activities. As a result, they feel more attached to their school. In large schools, creation of smaller "schools within schools" has the same effect.

Moderate (but not excessive) participation in arts, community service, or vocational development activities promotes diverse aspects of adjustment (Fredricks, 2012; Fredricks & Eccles, 2006). Among these are improved academic performance, reduced antisocial behavior, more favorable self-esteem and initiative, and increased peer acceptance.

As we conclude our discussion of academic achievement, let's place the school dropout problem in historical perspective. Over the second half of the twentieth century, the percentage of U.S. young people completing high school by age 24 increased steadily, from less than 50 percent to more than 90 percent. Although many dropouts get caught in a vicious cycle in which their lack of self-confidence and skills prevents them from seeking further education and training, of the 25 percent of high school freshman who do not graduate on time, more than two-thirds return to finish their secondary education by their mid-twenties (U.S. Department of Education, 2014b). And some extend their schooling further as they come to realize how essential education is for a rewarding job and a satisfying adult life.

Ask Yourself

- **REVIEW** List ways that parents can promote their adolescent's academic achievement. Explain why each is effective.

- **CONNECT** How are educational practices that prevent school dropout similar to those that improve learning for adolescents in general?

- **APPLY** Tanisha is finishing sixth grade. She can either continue in her current school through eighth grade or switch to a much larger seventh- to ninth-grade middle school. What choice would you suggest, and why?

- **REFLECT** Describe your own experiences in making the transition to middle school and then to high school. What did you find stressful? What helped you adjust?

Vocational Development

15.10 Trace the development of vocational choice, and cite factors that influence it.
15.11 What problems do U.S. non-college-bound youths face in preparing for a vocation?

As the end of adolescence approaches, young people face a major life decision: the choice of a suitable work role. As we will see in Chapters 16 and 17, selecting a vocation is central to the development of a solid, secure identity. This is not surprising, since economic independence and career progress are hallmarks of adulthood in industrialized societies.

Being a productive worker calls for many of the same qualities as being an active citizen and a nurturant family member—good judgment, responsibility, dedication, and cooperation. What influences young people's decisions about careers? What is the transition from school to work like, and what factors make it easy or difficult?

Selecting a Vocation

In societies with an abundance of career possibilities, occupational choice is a gradual process that begins long before adolescence and often extends into the mid-twenties. Major theorists view the young person as moving through several periods of vocational development (Gottfredson, 2005; Super, 1994):

1. The **fantasy period:** In early and middle childhood, children gain insight into career options by fantasizing about them (Howard & Walsh, 2010). Their preferences, guided largely by familiarity, glamour, and excitement, usually bear little relation to the decisions they will eventually make.

2. The **tentative period:** Between ages 11 and 16, adolescents think about careers in more complex ways, at first in terms of their *interests,* and soon—as they become more aware of personal and educational requirements for different vocations—in terms of their *abilities* and *values.* "I like business and selling things," 16-year-old Louis said as he neared high school graduation. "But I'm also good with people, and I'd like to do something to help others. So maybe counseling or social work would suit my needs."

3. The **realistic period:** By the late teens and early twenties, with the economic and practical realities of adulthood just around the corner, young people start to narrow their options. A first step is often further *exploration*—gathering more information about possibilities that blend with their personal characteristics. In the final phase, *crystallization,* they focus on a general vocational category and experiment for a time before settling on a single occupation (Stringer, Kerpelman, & Skorikov, 2011). As a college sophomore, Jules pursued his interest in science, but he is not sure whether he prefers chemistry, math, or physics. By the end of the academic year, he is likely to choose a major. Then he will consider whether he wants to work for a company following graduation or study further to become a doctor or research scientist.

Factors Influencing Vocational Choice

Most, but not all, young people follow this pattern of vocational development. A few know from an early age just what they want to be and follow a direct path to a career goal. Some decide and later change their minds, and still others remain undecided for an extended period. College students are granted added time to explore various options. In contrast, the life conditions of many low-SES youths restrict their range of choices.

Making an occupational choice is not just a rational process in which young people weigh abilities, interests, and values against career options. Like other developmental milestones, it is the result of a dynamic interaction between person and environment (Gottfredson & Duffy, 2008). A great many influences feed into the decision, including personality, family, teachers, and gender stereotypes, among others.

PERSONALITY People are attracted to occupations that complement their personalities. John Holland (1985, 1997) identified six personality types that affect vocational choice:

- The *investigative person,* who enjoys working with ideas, is likely to select a scientific occupation (for example, anthropologist, physicist, or engineer).
- The *social person,* who likes interacting with people, gravitates toward human services (counseling, social work, or teaching).
- The *realistic person,* who prefers real-world problems and work with objects, tends to choose a mechanical occupation (construction, plumbing, or surveying).
- The *artistic person,* who is emotional and high in need for individual expression, looks toward an artistic field (writing, music, or the visual arts).
- The *conventional person,* who likes well-structured tasks and values material possessions and social status, has traits well-suited to certain business fields (accounting, banking, or quality control).
- The *enterprising person,* who is adventurous, persuasive, and a strong leader, is drawn to sales and supervisory positions or to politics.

TAKE A MOMENT... Does one of these personality types describe you? Or do you have aspects of more than one type? Research confirms a relationship between personality and vocational choice in diverse cultures, but it is only moderate. Many people are blends of several personality types and can do well at more than one kind of occupation (Holland, 1997; Spokane & Cruza-Guet, 2005). Louis, for example, is both enterprising and social—dispositions that led him to consider both business and human services. Furthermore, career decisions are made in the context of family influences, educational opportunities, current life circumstances, and societal conditions.

FAMILY INFLUENCES Young people's vocational aspirations correlate strongly with their parents' jobs. Teenagers from higher-SES homes are more likely to select high-status, white-collar occupations, such as doctor, lawyer, scientist, or engineer. In contrast, those with lower-SES backgrounds tend to choose less prestigious, blue-collar careers—for example, plumber, construction worker, food service employee, or office worker. Parent–child vocational similarity is partly a function of similarity in personality, intellectual abilities, and—especially—educational attainment (Ellis & Bonin, 2003; Schoon & Parsons, 2002). Number of years of schooling completed is a powerful predictor of occupational status.

Other factors also promote family resemblance in occupational choice. Higher-SES parents are more likely to give their children important information about the worlds of education and work and to have connections with people who can help the young person obtain a high-status position. Although parents with limited education typically believe in the importance of supporting their children's career exploration, their knowledge of how to provide guidance is limited (Kalil, Levine, & Ziol-Guest, 2005; Levine & Sutherland, 2013). In a study of African-American mothers' influence on their adolescent daughters' academic and career goals, college-educated mothers engaged in a wider range of strategies to promote their daughters' progress, including gathering information on colleges and areas of study and identifying knowledgeable professionals who could help (Kerpelman, Shoffner, & Ross-Griffin, 2002).

Parenting practices also shape work-related preferences. Recall from Chapter 2 that higher-SES parents tend to promote curiosity and self-direction, which are required in many high-status careers. Still, all parents can foster higher aspirations. Parental guidance, pressure to doing well in school, and encouragement

© JUDY GRIESEDIECK/CORBIS

A 13-year-old helps in his parents' business—a lobster fishery in Maine. Because of similarity in personality, intellectual abilities, and—especially—educational attainment, adolescents' vocational aspirations frequently resemble the jobs of their parents.

toward high-status occupations predict confidence in career choice and vocational attainment beyond SES (Bryant, Zvonkovic, & Reynolds, 2006; Stringer & Kerpelman, 2010).

TEACHERS Jules regarded his high school chemistry teacher as the most important influence on his scientific career goal: "Mr. Garvin showed me how to think about chemistry—and science in general. If I hadn't taken his class my junior year, I probably wouldn't have considered a career in science." Young people preparing for or engaged in careers requiring extensive education often report that teachers influenced their choice (Bright et al., 2005). High school students who say that most of their teachers are caring and accessible, are interested in their future, and expect them to work hard feel more confident about choosing a personally suitable career and succeeding at it (Metheny, McWhirter, & O'Neil, 2008). College-bound adolescents tend to have closer relationships with teachers than do other students—relationships that are especially likely to foster high career aspirations in young women (Wigfield et al., 2002).

These findings provide yet another reason to promote positive teacher–student relations, especially for high school students from low-SES families. Teachers who offer encouragement and act as role models can serve as an important source of resilience for these young people.

GENDER STEREOTYPES Over the past few decades, young people of both genders have increasingly expressed interest in nontraditional occupations (Gati & Perez, 2014; Gottfredson, 2005). Nevertheless, gender differences in career choice persist, and women's progress in entering and excelling at male-dominated professions has been slow. As Table 15.2 shows, although the percentage of women engineers, lawyers, doctors, and business executives has risen in the United States over the past three decades, it still falls far short of equal representation. Women remain concentrated in less-well-paid, traditionally feminine professions such as writing, social work, education, and nursing (U.S. Census Bureau, 2014b). In virtually all fields, women's achievements lag behind those of men, who write more books, make more discoveries, hold more positions of leadership, and produce more works of art.

Ability cannot account for these dramatic sex differences. As we have seen, girls are advantaged in reading and writing achievement, and the gender gap favoring boys in math is small. Rather, gender-stereotyped messages play a key role. Although girls earn higher grades than boys, they reach secondary school less confident of their abilities, more likely to underestimate their achievement, and less likely to express interest in STEM careers (see page 567).

During high school and college, females' career aspirations decline further as many question their capacity and opportunities to succeed in male-dominated fields and worry about combining a highly demanding career with family responsibilities (Chhin, Bleeker, & Jacobs, 2008; Sadler et al., 2012). Many mathematically talented college women settle on nonscience majors. An investigation of science-oriented 15-year-olds in 50 nations revealed uniform findings: In every country, girls preferred careers in biology, agriculture, medicine, or another health profession, whereas boys favored computing, engineering, or math. And almost without exception, boys expressed greater confidence in their science ability than girls, even after science achievement test scores were controlled. This difference in sense of competence at science was considerably larger in industrialized than in developing nations (Sikora & Pokropek, 2012). In advanced countries, the researchers speculated, gender-typed beliefs about science ability had far greater opportunity to become deeply ingrained and widespread.

TABLE 15.2	Percentage of Women in Various Professions in the United States, 1983 and 2012	
PROFESSION	**1983**	**2012**
Engineer	5.8	12.9
Lawyer	15.8	31.5
Doctor	15.8	32.3
Business executive	32.4	38.2[a]
Author, artist, entertainer	42.7	46.2
Social worker	64.3	80.8
Elementary or middle school teacher	93.5	81.8
Secondary school teacher	62.2	57.0
College or university professor	36.3	45.9
Librarian	84.4	82.8
Registered nurse	95.8	91.1
Psychologist	57.1	66.7

Source: U.S. Census Bureau, 2014b.

[a]This percentage includes executives and managers at all levels. As of 2014, women made up only 5 percent of chief executive officers at Fortune 500 companies, although that figure represents a threefold increase over the past 10 years.

These findings reveal a pressing need for programs that sensitize parents, teachers, and school counselors to the special problems girls face in developing and maintaining high career aspirations and selecting nontraditional careers. Girls' aspirations rise in response to career guidance that encourages them to set goals that match their abilities and teachers who take steps to enhance girls' experiences in math and science courses. Contact with women scientists and engineers adds to female students' interest in and expectancies for success in STEM fields (Holdren & Lander, 2012). And it may help them see how altruistic values—which are particularly important to females—can be fulfilled within STEM occupations.

Vocational Preparation of Non-College-Bound Adolescents

Franca and Antonio's middle son, 18-year-old Martin—who is a year younger than Jules and two years older than Louis—graduated from high school in a vocational track. Like approximately one-third of U.S. young people with a high school diploma, he had no current plans to go to college. While in school, Martin held a part-time job selling candy at the local shopping mall. He hoped to work in data processing after graduation, but six months later he was still a part-time clerk at the candy store. Although Martin had filled out many job applications, he got no interviews or offers. He soon despaired of discovering any relationship between his schooling and a career.

Martin's inability to find a job other than the one he had held as a student is typical for U.S. non-college-bound high school graduates. Although they are more likely to find employment than youths who drop out, they have fewer work opportunities than high school graduates of several decades ago. With rising unemployment during the late-2000s recession, these conditions worsened as entry-level positions went to the large pool of available college graduates. About 30 percent of recent U.S. high school graduates who do not continue their education are unemployed (U.S. Department of Labor, 2014). When they do find work, most hold low-paid, unskilled jobs. In addition, they have few alternatives for vocational counseling and job placement as they transition from school to work.

American employers regard recent high school graduates as poorly prepared for skilled business and industrial occupations and manual trades. And there is some truth to this impression. In high school, nearly 30 percent of U.S. students age 16 and older are employed—a greater percentage than in other developed countries (Davis, 2012). But most are middle-SES youths in pursuit of spending money rather than vocational exploration and training. Low-income teenagers who need to contribute to family income or to support themselves find it harder to get jobs (U.S. Department of Education, 2014b).

Adolescents typically hold jobs that involve low-level, repetitive tasks and provide little contact with adult supervisors. A heavy commitment to such jobs is harmful. The more hours students work, the poorer their school attendance, the lower their grades, the less likely they are to participate in extracurricular activities, and the more likely they are to drop out (Marsh & Kleitman, 2005). Students who spend many hours at such jobs also report more drug and alcohol use and delinquent acts (Monahan, Lee, & Steinberg, 2011; Samuolis et al., 2013).

In contrast, participation in work–study programs or other jobs that provide academic and vocational learning opportunities is related to positive school and work attitudes, improved achievement, and reduced delinquency (Hamilton & Hamilton, 2000; Staff & Uggen, 2003). Yet high-quality vocational preparation for non-college-bound U.S. adolescents is

Teenagers' employment opportunities are generally limited to menial tasks that do little to extend their knowledge or skills. Students with a heavy time commitment to such jobs are less likely to participate in extracurricular activities and more likely to drop out of school.

© JEFF GREENBERG/ALAMY

scarce. Unlike some European nations, the United States has no widespread training system to prepare youths for skilled business and industrial occupations and manual trades. Although U.S. federal and state governments support some job-training programs, most are too brief to make a difference and serve only a small minority of young people who need assistance.

In Germany, adolescents who do not go to a Gymnasium (college-preparatory high school) have access to one of the world's most successful work–study apprenticeship systems for entering business and industry. About two-thirds of German youths participate. After completing full-time schooling at age 15 or 16, they spend the remaining two years of compulsory education in the Berufsschule, combining part-time vocational courses with an apprenticeship that is jointly planned by educators and employers. Students train in work settings for more than 350 blue- and white-collar occupations (Deissinger, 2007). Apprentices who complete the program and pass a qualifying examination are certified as skilled workers and earn union-set wages. Businesses provide financial

These students work on a three-dimensional design project in a video production class at their high school. High-quality vocational education, integrated with academic instruction, helps students at risk for dropping out see the relevance of school learning to their future goals.

support because they know that the program guarantees a competent, dedicated work force (Kerckhoff, 2002). Many apprentices are hired into well-paid jobs by the firms that trained them.

The success of the German system—and of similar systems in Austria, Denmark, Switzerland, and several Eastern European countries—suggests that a national apprenticeship program would improve the transition from high school to work for U.S. non-college-bound young people. The many benefits of bringing together the worlds of schooling and work include helping non-college-bound young people establish productive lives right after graduation, motivating at-risk youths to stay in school, and contributing to the nation's economic growth.

Nevertheless, implementing an apprenticeship system poses major challenges: overcoming the reluctance of employers to assume part of the responsibility for vocational training, ensuring cooperation between schools and businesses, and preventing low-SES youths from being concentrated in the lowest-skilled apprenticeship placements or from being unable to find any placement, an obstacle that Germany itself has not yet fully overcome (Lang, 2010). Currently, small-scale school-to-work projects in the United States are attempting to solve these problems and build bridges between learning and working.

Although vocational development is a lifelong process, adolescence is a crucial period for defining occupational goals. Young people who are well-prepared for an economically and personally satisfying work life are much more likely to become productive citizens, devoted family members, and contented adults. The support of families, schools, businesses, communities, and society as a whole can contribute greatly to a positive outcome.

Ask Yourself

- **REVIEW** What steps can schools take to help ensure that adolescents' occupational aspirations match their interests, personality dispositions, and abilities?

- **CONNECT** What have you learned in previous chapters about development of gender stereotypes that helps explain women's slow progress in entering and excelling at male-dominated professions? (*Hint:* See Chapter 13, pages 493–494.)

- **APPLY** Diane, a high school senior, knows that she wants to "work with people" but doesn't yet have a specific career in mind. Her father is a history professor, her mother a social worker. What can Diane's parents do to broaden her awareness of the world of work and help her focus on an occupational goal?

- **REFLECT** Describe personal and environmental influences on your progress in choosing a vocation.

Summary

Piaget's Theory: The Formal Operational Stage (p. 556)

15.1 What are the major characteristics of formal operational thought?

- During Piaget's **formal operational stage,** adolescents become capable of **hypothetico-deductive reasoning.** When faced with a problem, they start with a hypothesis about variables that might affect an outcome; deduce logical, testable inferences; and systematically isolate and combine variables to see which inferences are confirmed.

- **Propositional thought** also develops. Young people can evaluate the logic of verbal statements without referring to real-world circumstances.

15.2 Discuss follow-up research on formal operational thought and its implications for the accuracy of Piaget's formal operational stage.

- School-age children display the beginnings of hypothetico-deductive reasoning and propositional thought but are less competent than adolescents. Without direct instruction, school-age children cannot sort out evidence that bears on three or more variables at once. Also, they do not grasp the **logical necessity** of propositional reasoning. Adolescents are better at reasoning on an entirely verbal plane and at thinking of examples that contradict wrong conclusions.

© ALEX TREADWAY/NATIONAL GEOGRAPHIC SOCIETY/CORBIS

- Adolescents and adults are most likely to think abstractly and systematically in situations in which they have had a history of extensive guidance and practice in using such reasoning. Individuals in tribal and village societies rarely do well on tasks typically used to assess formal operational reasoning. Learning experiences in school provide adolescents with rich opportunities to acquire formal operations.

An Information-Processing View of Adolescent Cognitive Development (p. 559)

15.3 How do information-processing researchers account for cognitive changes in adolescence?

- Information-processing researchers believe that a variety of specific mechanisms, including diverse aspects of executive function, underlie adolescent cognitive development. These include gains in attention, planning, inhibition, and knowledge; more effective strategies; expansion of metacognition; and increases in cognitive self-regulation and working memory.

© SYRACUSE NEWSPAPERS/THE IMAGE WORKS

- Research on scientific reasoning reveals that the ability to coordinate theory with evidence improves as adolescents solve increasingly complex problems and reflect on their thinking, acquiring more sophisticated metacognitive understanding. Nevertheless, adolescents and adults continue to show a self-serving bias, applying logic more effectively to ideas they doubt than to ideas they favor.

- Adolescents develop scientific reasoning skills in a similar, step-by-step fashion on different types of tasks. Gradually, they combine separate skills, constructing general models that they can apply to many instances of a given type of problem.

Consequences of Adolescent Cognitive Changes (p. 561)

15.4 Describe typical reactions of adolescents that result from their advancing cognition.

- As adolescents reflect on their own thoughts, two distorted images of the relationship between self and other appear: the **imaginary audience** and the **personal fable.** Each is partly an outgrowth of gains in perspective taking and teenagers' concern with others' opinions of them.

- Adolescents' capacity to think about possibilities prompts idealistic visions at odds with everyday reality, and they often become fault-finding critics.

© JEFF GREENBERG/THE IMAGE WORKS

- Compared with adults, adolescents are less effective at decision making. In emotionally charged situations, they take greater risks, emphasizing short-term over long-term goals. Even under unemotional conditions, they less often consider alternatives and weigh benefits and risks, and more often fall back on intuitive judgments.

Sex Differences in Mental Abilities (p. 564)

15.5 What factors contribute to sex differences in mental abilities during adolescence?

- Girls score slightly better than boys on tests of verbal ability, and their advantage in reading and writing achievement increases in adolescence. Earlier development of the left hemisphere of the cerebral cortex, more efficient language processing, and greater verbal stimulation probably contribute to girls' better verbal performance. Also, gender stereotyping of language arts as "feminine" and regimented teaching may weaken boys' literacy skills.

- By late childhood and early adolescence, when math concepts become more abstract and spatial, boys outperform girls. Overall, the gender difference in math ability has declined over time and is small, but it is greater among the most capable students.

- Boys' biologically based more rapid numerical memory and superior spatial skills enhance their mathematical problem solving. Gender stereotyping of math as "masculine," self-confidence and interest in doing math, and specialized knowledge of screen-media technology contribute to boys' spatial and math advantages. The gender gap is reduced in countries that value gender equality.

Language Development (p. 568)

15.6 *Describe changes in vocabulary, grammar, and pragmatics during adolescence.*

- Adolescents add many abstract words to their vocabulary and define these words with greater clarity and accuracy. Their grasp of figurative language improves.

- Adolescents more effectively analyze and correct their grammar. They also show an improved capacity to adapt language style to social context—a change supported by opportunities to enter more situations, the ability to reflect on the features of language, and gains in cognitive self-regulation.

Learning in School (p. 569)

15.7 *Discuss the impact of school transitions on adolescent adjustment.*

- After middle- and high-school transitions, grades, achievement test scores, liking for school, and academic self-confidence often decline. Teenagers coping with added stressors, especially those with both academic and mental health difficulties, are at greatest risk for adjustment problems. Transitions are also particularly challenging for minority students who move to a new school with substantially fewer same-ethnicity peers.

- Reducing the number of transitions through K–8 schools results in improved achievement, more positive social contexts, and more favorable school attitudes. Forming smaller units within larger schools and assigning students to classes with familiar peers are also helpful.

15.8 *Discuss family, peer, and school influences on academic achievement during adolescence.*

- Authoritative parenting and parents' school involvement promote high achievement. Teenagers whose parents value achievement are likely to choose friends who share those values.

- Warm, supportive classroom environments that encourage student interaction about academic work, mutual respect among classmates, and high-level thinking enable adolescents to reach their academic potential. An emphasis on high stakes testing narrows the focus of instruction and may widen group differences in achievement.

- By high school, separate educational tracks that dovetail with adolescents' future plans are necessary. But high school tracking in the United States usually extends educational inequalities of earlier years. Low-SES students are at risk for unfair placement in noncollege tracks, less stimulating teaching, and resulting declines in school performance.

15.9 *What factors increase the risk of high school dropout?*

- About 7 percent of U.S. young people, many of them low-SES minority youths, leave high school and remain without a diploma or a GED. Family and school risk factors include lack of parental support for achievement, a history of poor school attendance and performance, grade retention, large impersonal schools, unsupportive teachers, unstimulating classes, and minority students' experiences with discrimination.

Vocational Development (p. 579)

15.10 *Trace the development of vocational choice, and cite factors that influence it.*

- Vocational development moves through a **fantasy period,** in which children explore career options by fantasizing about them; a **tentative period,** in which teenagers weigh careers against their interests, abilities, and values; and a **realistic period,** in which older adolescents and young adults settle on a vocational category and then a specific occupation.

- Vocational choice is influenced by personality; parents' provision of educational opportunities, vocational information, and encouragement; and close relationships with teachers.

- Women's progress in entering male-dominated professions has been slow, and their achievements lag behind those of men in virtually all fields. Gender-stereotyped messages play a key role. Girls' career aspirations rise in response to confidence-building messages from parents and teachers.

15.11 *What problems do U.S. non-college-bound youths face in preparing for a vocation?*

- U.S. non-college-bound high school graduates are poorly prepared for skilled business and industrial occupations and manual trades. Most are limited to low-paid, unskilled jobs, and too many are unemployed. Youth apprenticeships, like those widely available in European countries, would address the need for vocational training and improve the transition from school to work for these young people.

Important Terms and Concepts

fantasy period (p. 579)

formal operational stage (p. 556)

hypothetico-deductive reasoning (p. 556)

imaginary audience (p. 561)

logical necessity (p. 557)

personal fable (p. 562)

propositional thought (p. 556)

realistic period (p. 579)

tentative period (p. 579)

chapter 16

Emotional and Social Development in Adolescence

"My Friend"
Anastasiya Svivtunova
12 years, Ukraine

In adolescence, blossoming friendships become more deeply rooted in intimacy, mutual understanding, and loyalty. As Chapter 16 reveals, peer relationships become increasingly important, forming a crucial bridge between the family and adult social roles.

Louis sat on the grassy hillside overlooking the high school, waiting for his best friend, Darryl, to arrive. The two boys often had lunch together. Watching as hundreds of students poured onto the school grounds, Louis reflected on what he had learned in government class that day: "Suppose I *had* been born in the People's Republic of China. I'd be sitting here, speaking a different language, being called by a different name, and thinking about the world in different ways. Wow," Louis pondered. "I am who I am through some quirk of fate."

Louis awoke from his thoughts with a start to see Darryl standing in front of him. "Hey, dreamer! I've been shouting and waving from the bottom of the hill for five minutes. How come you're so spaced out lately, Louis?"

"Oh, just wondering about stuff—what I want, what I believe in. My older brother Jules—I envy him. He seems to know more about where he's going. I'm up in the air about it. You ever feel that way?"

"Yeah, a lot," Darryl admitted, looking at Louis seriously. "I wonder, what am I really like? Who will I become?"

Louis and Darryl's introspective remarks are signs of a major reorganization of the self at adolescence: the development of identity. Both young people are attempting to formulate who they are—their personal values and the directions they will pursue in life. The restructuring of the self that begins in adolescence is profound. Rapid physical changes prompt teenagers to reconsider what they are like as people. And the capacity to think hypothetically enables adolescents to project themselves into the distant future. They start to realize the significance of their choice of values, beliefs, and goals for their later lives.

We begin this chapter with Erikson's account of identity development and the research it has stimulated on teenagers' thoughts and feelings about themselves. The quest for identity extends to many aspects of development. We will see how a sense of cultural belonging, moral understanding, and masculine and feminine self-images are refined in adolescence. And as parent–child relationships are revised and young people become increasingly independent of the family, friendships and peer networks become crucial contexts for bridging the gap between childhood and adulthood. Our chapter concludes with a discussion of several serious adjustment problems of adolescence: depression, suicide, and delinquency. ■

Erikson's Theory: Identity versus Role Confusion

Erikson (1950, 1968) was the first to recognize **identity** as the major personality attainment of adolescence and as a crucial step toward becoming a productive, content adult. Constructing an identity involves defining who you are, what you value, and the directions you choose to pursue in life. One expert described it as an explicit theory of oneself as a rational agent—one who acts on the basis of reason, takes responsibility for those actions, and can explain them (Moshman, 2011). This search for what is true and real about the self drives many choices—vocation, interpersonal relationships, community involvement, ethnic-group membership, and expression of one's sexual orientation, as well as moral, political, and religious ideals.

16.1 According to Erikson, what is the major personality attainment of adolescence?

Although the seeds of identity formation are planted early, not until late adolescence and emerging adulthood do young people become absorbed in this task. According to Erikson, in complex societies, young people often experience an *identity crisis*—a temporary period of distress as they experiment with alternatives before settling on values and goals. They go through a process of inner soul-searching, sifting through characteristics that defined the self in childhood and combining them with emerging traits, capacities, and commitments. Then they mold these into a solid inner core that provides a mature identity—a sense of self-continuity as they move through various roles in daily life. Once formed, identity continues to be refined in adulthood as people reevaluate earlier commitments and choices.

Erikson called the psychological conflict of adolescence **identity versus role confusion.** He believed that successful psychosocial outcomes of infancy and childhood pave the way toward a positive resolution. Adolescents with a weak sense of *trust* have trouble finding ideals to have faith in. Those with little *autonomy* or *initiative* do not engage in the active exploration required to choose among alternatives. And those who lack a sense of *industry* fail to select a vocation that matches their interests and skills. In addition, if society limits young people's choices to ones that do not match their abilities and desires, they are likely to appear shallow and directionless.

Current theorists agree with Erikson that questioning of values, plans, and priorities is necessary for a mature identity, but they no longer describe this process as a "crisis." In fact, Erikson himself did not believe that the adolescent's inner struggle need be severe to form a clear, unified identity (Côté, 2009; Kroger, 2012). For most young people, identity development is not traumatic and disturbing but, rather, a process of *exploration* followed by *commitment*. As young people try out life possibilities, they gather important information about themselves and their environment and gradually move toward making enduring decisions (Moshman, 2011). In the following sections, we will see that young people go about the task of defining the self in ways that closely match Erikson's description.

At a community center, a teenager with a passion for music works with a teacher to understand how to compose using a computer beat machine. By exploring new activities, young people gather information about their interests and skills that contribute vitally to constructing a mature identity.

16.2 Describe changes in self-concept and self-esteem during adolescence.

16.3 Describe the four identity statuses, along with factors that promote identity development.

Self-Understanding

During adolescence, the young person's vision of the self becomes more complex, well-organized, and consistent. Compared with children, adolescents have more or less positive feelings about an increasing variety of aspects of the self. Over time, they construct a balanced, integrated representation of their strengths and limitations (Harter, 2012). Changes in self-concept and self-esteem set the stage for developing a unified personal identity.

Changes in Self-Concept

Recall from Chapter 13 that by the end of middle childhood, children describe themselves in terms of personality traits. In early adolescence, the self differentiates further. Teenagers mention a wider array of traits, which vary with social context—for example, self with mother, father, close friends, and romantic partner and as student, athlete, and employee. As one young teenager commented:

I'm an extrovert with my friends: I'm talkative, pretty rowdy, and funny. . . . With my parents, I'm more likely to be depressed. I feel sad as well as mad and also hopeless about ever pleasing them. . . . At school, I'm pretty intelligent. I know that because I'm smart when it comes to how I do in classes. I'm curious about learning new things, and I'm also creative when it comes to solving problems. . . . I can be a real introvert around people I don't know well. . . . I worry a lot about what others my age who are not my closest friends must think of me, probably that I'm a total dork. (Harter, 2012, p. 693)

Notice, also, that early adolescents unify separate traits ("smart" and "curious") into more abstract descriptors ("intelligent"). But these generalizations about the self are not interconnected and are often contradictory. For example, 12- to 14-year-olds might mention opposing traits—"intelligent" and "clueless," "extrovert" and "introvert." These disparities result from the expansion of adolescents' social world, which creates pressure to display different selves in different relationships. From early to midadolescence, traits mentioned for different social contexts become increasingly dissimilar. As adolescents' awareness of these inconsistencies grows, they frequently agonize over "which is the real me" (Harter, 2012).

By late adolescence, cognitive changes enable teenagers to combine their traits into an organized system. Their use of qualifiers ("I have a *fairly* quick temper," "I'm not *thoroughly* honest") reveals their awareness that psychological qualities can vary from one situation to the next. Older adolescents also add integrating principles that make sense of formerly troublesome contradictions. "I'm very adaptable," said one young person. "When I'm around my friends, who think what I say is important, I'm talkative; but around my family I'm quiet because they're never interested enough to really listen to me" (Damon, 1990, p. 88).

Compared with school-age children, teenagers place more emphasis on social virtues, such as being friendly, considerate, kind, and cooperative—traits that reflect adolescents' increasing concern with being viewed positively by others. Among older adolescents, personal and moral standards also appear as key themes. For example, here is how one 17-year-old described herself:

I'm a pretty conscientious person. . . . Eventually I want to go to law school, so developing good study habits and getting top grades are critical. . . . I'd like to be an ethical person who treats other people fairly, which is why I want to be a lawyer. Sometimes I'll do something that doesn't feel ethical. When that happens, I get a little depressed because I don't like myself as a person. But I tell myself that it's natural to make mistakes and the real me is a moral person. . . . While I am basically an introvert, especially on a date when I get pretty self-conscious, in the right social situation, like watching a ball game with my friends, I can be pretty extroverted. . . . I'm looking forward to leaving home and going to college, where I can be more independent, although I'm a little ambivalent. I love my parents, and really want to stay connected to them, plus, what they think about me is still important to how I feel about myself as a person. (Harter, 2012, pp. 705–706)

This well-integrated account of personal traits and values differs from the fragmented, listlike self-descriptions typical of children. As adolescents revise their views of themselves to include enduring beliefs and plans, they move toward the unity of self that is central to identity development.

Changes in Self-Esteem

Self-esteem, the evaluative side of self-concept, continues to differentiate in adolescence. Teenagers add several new dimensions of self-evaluation—close friendship, romantic appeal, and job competence—to those of middle childhood (see Chapter 13, page 476) (Harter, 2006).

Level of global self-esteem also changes. Though some adolescents experience temporary or persisting declines after school transitions (see Chapter 15, page 570), self-esteem rises from mid- to late adolescence for most young people, who report feeling especially good about their peer relationships, physical appearance, and athletic capabilities (Birkeland et al., 2012; Cole et al., 2001; Impett et al., 2008). Teenagers often assert that they have become more mature, capable, personable, and attractive than in the past. In longitudinal research on a nationally representative sample of U.S. youths, an increasing sense of mastery—feeling competent and

---

LOOK and LISTEN

Pose the following question to a 12- to 14-year-old and a 16- to 18-year-old: "What are you like as a person?" Do differences in their self-descriptions match research findings on development of self-concept?

During adolescence, self-esteem typically rises, fostered by pride in new competencies and growing self-confidence. This teenager beams as she displays the blue ribbon she won at an agricultural fair.

in control of one's life—strongly predicted this rise in self-esteem (Erol & Orth, 2011). With greater autonomy and opportunities to emphasize pursuits in which they experience success, older adolescents are better able to discount the importance of doing well in areas in which they feel inadequate.

At the same time, individual differences in self-esteem become increasingly stable in adolescence (Trzesniewski, Donnellan, & Robins, 2003). And positive relationships among self-esteem, valuing of various activities, and success at those activities strengthen. For example, academic self-esteem is a powerful predictor of teenagers' judgments of the importance and usefulness of school subjects, willingness to exert effort, achievement, and eventual career choice (Denissen, Zarrett, & Eccles, 2007; Di Giunta et al., 2013; Valentine, DuBois, & Cooper, 2004).

Across SES and ethnic groups, adolescents with mostly favorable self-esteem profiles tend to be well-adjusted, sociable, and conscientious. In contrast, low self-esteem in all areas is linked to adjustment difficulties (DuBois et al., 1999; Kim & Cicchetti, 2006). But certain self-esteem factors are more strongly related to adjustment. Adolescents with poor academic self-esteem tend to be anxious and unfocused, and those with negative peer relationships are likely to be anxious and depressed (Marsh, Parada, & Ayotte, 2004; Rudolph, Caldwell, & Conley, 2005). Let's take a closer look at factors that affect adolescents' self-esteem—both its level and its stability.

Factors That Affect Self-Esteem

In Chapters 14 and 15 we saw that adolescents who are off time in pubertal development, who are heavy drug users, and who fail in school feel poorly about themselves. And as in middle childhood, girls score lower than boys in overall sense of self-worth, though the difference remains slight. Nevertheless, of those young people whose self-esteem declines in adolescence, most are girls (Bachman et al., 2011; Birndorf et al., 2005; Shapka & Keating, 2005). Recall that teenage girls worry more than boys about their physical appearance and athletic skills, and they also feel less competent at math and science (see page 477 in Chapter 13). At the same time, girls continue to outscore boys on self-esteem dimensions of language arts, close friendship, and social acceptance.

But the contexts in which young people find themselves can modify these group differences. In adolescence as in childhood, authoritative parenting predicts stable, favorable self-esteem. Encouragement from teachers is associated with a positive self-image as well (Lindsey et al., 2008; McKinney, Donnelly, & Renk, 2008; Wilkinson, 2004). In contrast, teenagers whose parents are critical and insulting tend to have highly unstable and generally low self-esteem (Kernis, 2002). Feedback that is negative, inconsistent, or not contingent on performance triggers, at best, uncertainty about the self's capacities and, at worst, a sense of being incompetent and unloved. As a result, these young people's self-worth fluctuates in response to every evaluative remark by an adult or peer. Peer acceptance can have a protective effect on global self-esteem for teenagers experiencing low parental warmth and approval (Birkeland, Breivik, & Wold, 2014). But adolescents exposed to highly negative parental feedback tend to rely excessively on peers to affirm their self-worth—a risk factor for adjustment difficulties (DuBois et al., 1999, 2002a).

The larger social environment also influences self-esteem. Sustaining a middle-childhood trend, Caucasian-American adolescents' self-esteem is less positive than that of African-American and Hispanic teenagers, who benefit from warm, extended families and ethnic pride (Birndorf et al., 2005; Gray-Little & Hafdahl, 2000). And Asians score lower in self-esteem relative to Caucasians as adolescence progresses—a decline reflecting cultural valuing of modesty and disapproval of boastfulness rather than sense of personal competence (Bachman et al., 2011). Finally, teenagers who attend schools or live in neighborhoods where their SES or ethnic group is well-represented have fewer self-esteem problems (Gray-Little & Carels, 1997). Schools and communities that accept the young person's cultural heritage support a positive sense of self-worth as well as a solid and secure personal identity.

Paths to Identity

Adolescents' well-organized self-descriptions and differentiated sense of self-esteem provide the cognitive foundation for forming an identity. Using a clinical interviewing procedure devised by James Marcia (1980) or briefer questionnaire measures, researchers evaluate progress in identity development on two key criteria derived from Erikson's theory: *exploration* and *commitment*. Their various combinations yield four *identity statuses,* summarized in Table 16.1: **identity achievement,** commitment to values, beliefs, and goals following a period of exploration; **identity moratorium,** exploration without having reached commitment; **identity fore-closure,** commitment in the absence of exploration; and **identity diffusion,** an apathetic state characterized by lack of both exploration and commitment.

Identity development follows many paths. Some young people remain in one status, whereas others experience many status transitions. And the pattern often varies across *identity domains.* For example, in middle school, Louis accepted his parents' religious beliefs (foreclosure) and gave little thought to a vocational direction (diffusion). In his last two years of high school, he began exploring these issues. Like Louis, most adolescents change from "lower" statuses (foreclosure or diffusion) to "higher" statuses (moratorium or achievement) between their midteens and midtwenties, but nearly as many remain stable, and a few move in the reverse direction (Kroger, 2012; Kroger, Martinussen, & Marcia, 2010; Meeus, 2011). Also, the number of domains explored and the intensity with which they are examined vary widely, depending on the contexts young people enter and the importance they attach to them. Almost all grapple with work, close relationships, and family. Others add political, religious, community, and leisure-time commitments, some of which are more central to their identity than others.

Because attending college provides many opportunities to explore career options and life-styles, college students make more identity progress than they did in high school (Klimstra et al., 2010; Montgomery & Côté, 2003b). After college, as we will see in Chapter 17, many young people sample a broad range of life experiences before choosing a life course. Those who go to work immediately after high school graduation generally settle on a self-definition earlier. But if they encounter obstacles to realizing their occupational goals because of lack of training or vocational choices (see Chapter 15), they are at risk for long-term identity foreclosure or diffusion (Eccles et al., 2003).

TABLE 16.1 The Four Identity Statuses		
IDENTITY STATUS	**DESCRIPTION**	**EXAMPLE**
Identity achievement	Having already explored alternatives, identity-achieved individuals are committed to a clearly formulated set of self-chosen values and goals. They feel a sense of psychological well-being, of sameness through time, and of knowing where they are going.	When asked how willing she would be to give up going into her chosen occupation if something better came along, Lauren responded, "Well, I might, but I doubt it. I've thought long and hard about law as a career. I'm pretty certain it's for me."
Identity moratorium	*Moratorium* means "delay or holding pattern." These individuals have not yet made definite commitments. They are in the process of exploring—gathering information and trying out activities, with the desire to find values and goals to guide their lives.	When asked whether he had ever had doubts about his religious beliefs, Ramón said, "Yes, I guess I'm going through that right now. I just don't see how there can be a God and yet so much evil in the world."
Identity foreclosure	Identity-foreclosed individuals have committed themselves to values and goals without exploring alternatives. They accept a ready-made identity chosen for them by authority figures—usually parents but sometimes teachers, religious leaders, or romantic partners.	When asked if she had ever reconsidered her political beliefs, Emily answered, "No, not really, our family is pretty much in agreement on these things."
Identity diffusion	Identity-diffused individuals lack clear direction. They are not committed to values and goals, nor are they actively trying to reach them. They may never have explored alternatives or may have found the task too threatening and overwhelming.	When asked about his attitude toward nontraditional gender roles, Justin responded, "Oh, I don't know. It doesn't make much difference to me. I can take it or leave it."

With respect to gender, some girls show more sophisticated reasoning than boys in identity domains related to intimacy, such as sexuality and family versus career priorities. Otherwise, consistent with Erikson's psychosocial stages (see page 16 in Chapter 1), young people of both sexes typically make progress on identity concerns before experiencing genuine intimacy in romantic relationships (Arseth et al., 2009; Berman et al., 2006; Beyers & Seiffge-Krenke, 2010).

Identity Status and Psychological Well-Being

According to identity theorists, individuals who move away from foreclosure and diffusion toward moratorium and achievement experience a gratifying sense of personal continuity, competence, and social connection—of being the same person across time and contexts and of becoming a capable, respected member of the adult community (Luyckx et al., 2009; Schwartz et al., 2013). A wealth of research supports the conclusion that both identity achievement and moratorium are psychologically healthy routes to a mature self-definition, whereas long-term foreclosure and diffusion are maladaptive.

Although young people in moratorium are often anxious about the challenges they face, they resemble identity-achieved individuals in using an *active, information-gathering cognitive style* to make personal decisions and solve problems. They seek out relevant information, evaluate it carefully, and critically reflect on their views (Berzonsky, 2011). In Chapter 17, we will see that with age, the searching associated with moratorium becomes increasingly focused, involving in-depth consideration and reconsideration of potential commitments, which are often revised over time.

Young people who are identity-achieved or exploring tend to have higher self-esteem, are more open to alternative ideas and values, feel more in control of their own lives, are more likely to view school and work as feasible avenues for realizing their aspirations, and are more advanced in moral reasoning and more concerned with social justice (Berzonsky, 2011; Berzonsky et al., 2011; Crocetti et al., 2013). But an exception to these favorable outcomes exists: If exploration becomes *ruminative*—excessively concerned with making the right choice so the young person makes no choice at all—it is associated with distress and poor adjustment (Luyckx et al., 2008).

Adolescents stuck in either foreclosure or diffusion are passive in the face of identity concerns and have adjustment difficulties. Foreclosed individuals display a *dogmatic, inflexible cognitive style,* internalizing the values and beliefs of parents and others without deliberate evaluation and resisting information that threatens their position (Berzonsky, 2011; Berzonsky et al., 2011). Most fear rejection by people on whom they depend for affection and self-esteem. A few foreclosed teenagers who are alienated from their families and society may join cults or other extremist groups, uncritically adopting a way of life different from their past.

Long-term diffused teenagers are the least mature in identity development. They typically use a *diffuse-avoidant cognitive style* in which they avoid dealing with personal decisions and problems and, instead, allow current situational pressures to dictate their reactions (Berzonsky, 2011; Crocetti et al., 2013). Taking an "I don't care" attitude, they entrust themselves to luck or fate and tend to go along with the crowd. As a result, they often experience time-management and academic difficulties and, of all young people, are the most likely to commit antisocial acts and to use and abuse drugs (Berzonsky et al., 2011; Schwartz et al., 2005). Often at the heart of their apathy and impulsiveness is a sense of hopelessness about the future. Many are at risk for serious depression and suicide—problems we will address in the final section of this chapter.

Factors That Affect Identity Development

Adolescent identity formation begins a lifelong dynamic process in which a change in either the individual or the context opens up the possibility of reformulating identity (Kunnen & Bosma, 2003). A wide variety of factors influence identity development.

PERSONALITY   Identity status, as we saw in the previous section, is both cause and consequence of personality characteristics. Adolescents who are conformist and obedient and who assume that absolute truth is always attainable tend to be foreclosed, whereas those who are self-indulgent and who doubt they will ever feel certain about anything are more often identity-diffused. Young people who are curious, open-minded, and persistent in the face of obstacles, and who appreciate that they can use rational criteria to choose among alternatives, are likely to be in a state of moratorium or identity achievement (Berzonsky et al., 2011; Schwartz et al., 2013). This confident, flexible, self-reflective approach helps them greatly in identifying and pursuing educational, vocational, and other life goals.

FAMILY   Recall from Chapter 7 that toddlers with a healthy sense of self have parents who provide both emotional support and freedom to explore. Similarly, teenagers' identity development is enhanced when their families serve as a "secure base" from which they can confidently move out into the wider world. In families of diverse ethnicities, young people who feel attached to their parents but also free to voice their own opinions tend to have committed to values and goals and are on their way to identity achievement (Crocetti et al., 2014; Luyckx, Goossens, & Soenens, 2006; Schwartz et al., 2005). Foreclosed teenagers often have close bonds with parents but lack opportunities for healthy separation. And diffused young people report the lowest levels of parental support and of warm, open communication (Arseth et al., 2009; Reis & Youniss, 2004).

PEERS   Interaction with diverse peers through school and community activities encourages adolescents' to explore values and role possibilities (Barber et al., 2005). And close friends, like parents, can act as a secure base, providing emotional support, assistance, and models of identity development. In one study, 15-year-olds with warm, trusting peer ties were more involved in exploring relationship issues—for example, thinking about what they valued in close friends and in a life partner (Meeus, Oosterwegel, & Vollebergh, 2002). In another study, college students' attachment to friends predicted progress in choosing a career (Felsman & Blustein, 1999).

SCHOOL, COMMUNITY, AND CULTURE   Identity development also depends on schools and communities that offer rich and varied opportunities for exploration. Supportive experiences include classrooms that promote high-level thinking, teachers and counselors who encourage low-SES and ethnic minority students to go to college, elective classes and extracurricular and community activities that enable teenagers to pursue their interests and talents, and vocational training that immerses adolescents in the real world of adult work (Hardy et al., 2011; McIntosh, Metz, & Youniss, 2005; Sharp et al., 2007).

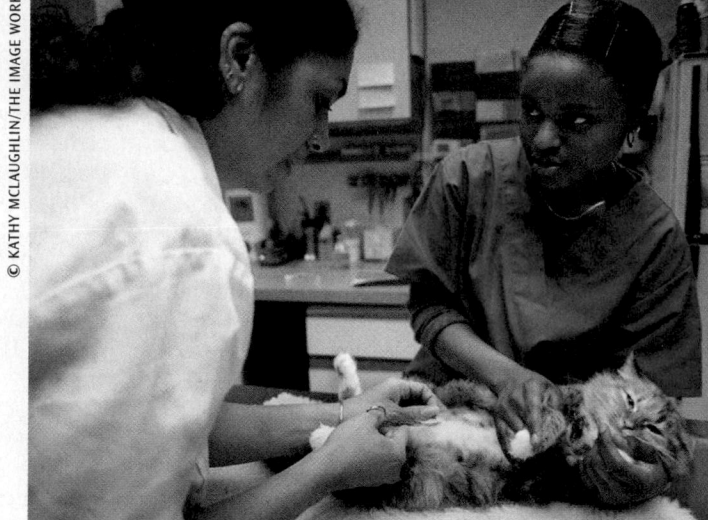

An internship in a veterinary office enables this adolescent to explore a real-world career related to her love of animals. Opportunities to take on responsible roles promote exploration and identity development.

Culture strongly influences an aspect of mature identity not captured by the identity-status approach: constructing a sense of self-continuity despite major personal changes. In one study, researchers asked Native Canadian and cultural-majority 12- to 20-year-olds to describe themselves in the past and in the present and then to justify why they regarded themselves as the same continuous person (Lalonde & Chandler, 2005). Both groups gave increasingly complex responses with age, but their strategies differed. Most cultural-majority adolescents used an individualistic approach: They described an *enduring personal essence,* a core self that remained the same despite change. In contrast, Native Canadian youths took an interdependent approach that emphasized a *constantly transforming self,* resulting from new roles and relationships. They typically constructed a *coherent narrative* in which they linked together various time slices of their life with a thread that explained how they had changed in meaningful ways.

Finally, societal forces are also responsible for the special challenges faced by lesbian, gay, and bisexual youths (see page 543 in Chapter 14) and by ethnic minority adolescents in forming a secure identity (see the Cultural Influences box on page 594). Applying What We Know on page 595 summarizes ways that adults can support adolescents in their quest for identity.

Cultural Influences

Identity Development Among Ethnic Minority Adolescents

Most adolescents are aware of their cultural ancestry but relatively unconcerned about it. However, for teenagers who are members of minority groups, **ethnic identity**—a sense of ethnic group membership and the attitudes, beliefs, and feelings associated with that membership—is central to the quest for identity. Research confirms that self-perceptions of ethnicity and race are interconnected and follow similar developmental paths (Umaña-Taylor et al., 2014). As minority youths develop cognitively and become more sensitive to feedback from the social environment, they become painfully aware of how their ethnicity and race compromise their life chances. These discoveries complicate their efforts to develop a sense of cultural belonging and a set of personally meaningful goals.

Minority youths often feel caught between the standards of the larger society and the traditions of their culture of origin. In many immigrant families from cultures that value interdependent qualities, adolescents' commitment to obeying their parents and fulfilling family obligations lessens the longer the family has been in the immigrant-receiving country. This circumstance induces **acculturative stress**—psychological distress resulting from conflict between the minority and the host culture (Phinney, Ong, & Madden, 2000). When immigrant parents tightly restrict their teenagers through fear that assimilation into the larger society will undermine their cultural traditions, their youngsters often rebel, rejecting aspects of their ethnic background.

At the same time, discrimination can interfere with the formation of a positive ethnic identity. In one study, Mexican-American youths who had experienced more discrimination were less likely to explore their ethnicity by seeking knowledge of their heritage and clarifying its positive meaning in their lives (Romero & Roberts, 2003). Those with low ethnic pride showed a sharp drop in self-esteem.

With age, some ethnic minority young people progress from ethnic-identity diffusion or foreclosure through moratorium to ethnic-identity achievement. But because the process of forging an ethnic identity can be painful and confusing, others show no change, and still others regress (Huang & Stormshak, 2011). Young people with parents of different ethnicities face extra challenges. In a large survey of high school students, part-black biracial teenagers reported as much discrimination as their monoracial black counterparts, yet they felt less positively about

their ethnicity. And compared with monoracial minorities, many biracials—including black–white, black–Asian, white–Asian, black–Hispanic, and white–Hispanic—regarded their ethnicity as less central to their identities (Herman, 2004). Perhaps these adolescents encountered fewer opportunities in their homes and communities to forge a strong sense of belonging to either culture.

Adolescents whose family members encourage them to disprove ethnic stereotypes of low achievement or antisocial behavior typically surmount the threat that discrimination poses to a favorable ethnic identity. These young people manage experiences of unfair treatment effectively, by seeking social support and engaging in direct problem solving (Scott, 2003). Also, minority adolescents whose families have taught them the history, traditions, values, and language of their ethnic group are more likely to explore and progress toward ethnic identity achievement (McHale et al., 2006; Umaña-Taylor, Zeiders, & Updegraff, 2013).

Interacting with same-ethnicity peers is also vital. Ethnic identity progress tends to be similar among same-ethnicity friends, and it can be predicted by the frequency with which they talk about ethnic and racial issues (Syed & Juan, 2012). At the same time, in a study of Asian-American adolescents, contact with other Asians strengthened positive feelings about their own ethnic group in a mostly white or a racially mixed school but not in a mostly Asian school (Yip, Douglass, & Shelton, 2013). Ethnic identity concerns become especially salient in ethnically and racially diverse settings.

How can society help minority adolescents resolve identity conflicts constructively? Here are some relevant approaches:

- Promote effective parenting, in which children and adolescents benefit from family ethnic pride yet are encouraged to explore the meaning of ethnicity in their own lives.
- Ensure that schools respect minority youths' native languages, unique learning styles, and right to a high-quality education.
- Foster contact with peers of the same ethnicity, along with respect between ethnic groups.

Adolescents of the Iroquois Tuscarora tribe perform a traditional dance at the New York State Fair. Minority youths whose cultural heritage is respected in their communities are more likely to incorporate ethnic values and customs into their identity.

A strong, secure ethnic identity is associated with higher self-esteem, optimism, and a sense of mastery over the environment (Umaña-Taylor & Updegraff, 2007; Worrell & Gardner-Kitt, 2006). For these reasons, adolescents with a positive connection to their ethnic group are better-adjusted. They cope more effectively with stress, report higher levels of daily happiness, show better achievement in school, and have fewer emotional and behavior problems than agemates who identify only weakly with their ethnicity (Ghavami et al., 2011; Seaton, Scottham, & Sellers, 2006; Umaña-Taylor & Alfaro, 2006). For teenagers faced with potential or actual adversity, ethnic identity is a powerful source of resilience.

Forming a **bicultural identity**—by exploring and adopting values from both the adolescent's subculture and the dominant culture—offers added benefits. Biculturally identified adolescents tend to be achieved in other areas of identity, to have a more secure ethnic identity, and to have especially positive relations with members of other ethnic groups (Basilio et al., 2014; Phinney, 2007). In sum, achievement of ethnic identity enhances many aspects of emotional and social development.

Applying What We Know

Supporting Healthy Identity Development

STRATEGY	EXPLANATION
Engage in warm, open communication.	Provides both emotional support and freedom to explore values and goals.
Initiate discussions that promote high-level thinking at home and at school.	Encourages rational, deliberate selection among competing beliefs and values.
Provide opportunities to participate in extracurricular activities and vocational training programs.	Permits young people to explore the real world of adult work.
Provide opportunities to talk with adults and peers who have worked through similar identity questions.	Offers models of identity achievement and advice on how to resolve identity concerns.
Provide opportunities to explore ethnic heritage and learn about other cultures in an atmosphere of respect.	Fosters identity achievement in all areas as well as ethnic tolerance, which supports the identity explorations of others.

Ask Yourself

- **REVIEW** List personal and contextual factors that promote identity development.

- **CONNECT** Explain the close link between adolescent identity development and cognitive processes.

- **APPLY** Return to the conversation between Louis and Darryl in the opening of this chapter. Which identity status best characterizes each of the two boys, and why?

- **REFLECT** Does your identity status vary across the domains of sexuality, close relationships, vocation, religious beliefs, and political values? Describe factors that may have influenced your identity development in an important domain.

Moral Development

16.4 Describe Kohlberg's theory of moral development, and evaluate its accuracy.

16.5 Describe influences on moral reasoning and its relationship to moral behavior.

16.6 Describe challenges to Kohlberg's theory.

Eleven-year-old Sabrina sat at the kitchen table reading the Sunday newspaper, her eyes wide with interest. "Look at this!" she said to 16-year-old Louis, who was munching cereal. Sabrina held up a page of large photos showing a 70-year-old woman standing in her home. The floor and furniture were piled with stacks of newspapers, cardboard boxes, tin cans, glass containers, food, and clothing. The accompanying article described crumbling plaster on the walls, frozen pipes, and nonfunctioning sinks, toilet, and furnace. The headline read: "Loretta Perry: My Life Is None of Their Business."

"Look what they're trying to do to this person," exclaimed Sabrina. "They're throwing her out of her house and tearing it down! Those city inspectors must not care about anyone. Here it says, 'Loretta Perry has devoted much of her life to doing favors for people.' Why doesn't someone help *her*?"

"Sabrina, you're missing the point," Louis responded. "She's violating 30 building code standards. The law says you're supposed to keep your house clean and in good repair."

"But Louis, she's old, and she needs help. She says her life will be over if they destroy her home."

"The building inspectors aren't being mean, Sabrina. Loretta Perry is stubborn. She's refusing to obey the law. And she's not just a threat to herself—she's a danger to her neighbors, too. Suppose her house caught on fire. You can't live around other people and say your life is nobody's business."

"You don't just knock someone's home down," Sabrina replied with exasperation. "Why aren't her friends and neighbors over there fixing up that house? You're just like those building inspectors, Louis. You've got no feelings!"

As Louis and Sabrina's discussion illustrates, cognitive development and expanding social experiences permit adolescents to better understand larger social structures—societal institutions and law-making systems—that govern moral responsibilities. As their grasp of social arrangements expands, adolescents construct new ideas about what ought to be done when the needs and desires of people conflict. As a result, they move toward increasingly just, fair, and balanced solutions to moral problems.

Kohlberg's Theory of Moral Development

Early work by Piaget (1932/1965) on the moral judgment of the child inspired Lawrence Kohlberg's more comprehensive cognitive-developmental theory of moral understanding. Kohlberg used a clinical interviewing procedure in which he presented a sample of 10- to 16-year-old boys with hypothetical *moral dilemmas*—stories presenting a conflict between two moral values—and asked them what the main actor should do and why. Then he followed the participants longitudinally, reinterviewing them at 3- to 4-year intervals over the next 20 years. The best known of Kohlberg's dilemmas, the "Heinz dilemma," pits the value of obeying the law (not stealing) against the value of human life (saving a dying person):

> In Europe a woman was near death from cancer. There was one drug the doctors thought might save her. A druggist in the same town had discovered it, but he was charging ten times what the drug cost him to make. The sick woman's husband, Heinz, went to everyone he knew to borrow the money, but he could only get together half of what it cost. The druggist refused to sell the drug for less or let Heinz pay later. So Heinz got desperate and broke into the man's store to steal the drug for his wife. Should Heinz have done that? Why or why not? (paraphrased from Colby et al., 1983, p. 77)

Kohlberg emphasized that it is *the way an individual reasons about the dilemma,* not *the content of the response* (whether or not to steal), that determines moral maturity. Individuals who believe that Heinz should steal the drug and those who think he should not can be found at each of Kohlberg's first four stages. Only at the two highest stages do moral reasoning and content come together in a coherent ethical system (Kohlberg, Levine, & Hewer, 1983). Given a choice between obeying the law and preserving individual rights, the most advanced moral thinkers support individual rights (in the Heinz dilemma, stealing the drug to save a life). **TAKE A MOMENT...** Does this remind you of adolescents' efforts to formulate a sound, well-organized set of personal values in constructing an identity? According to some theorists, the development of identity and moral understanding are part of the same process (Bergman, 2004; Blasi, 1994).

For more efficient gathering and scoring of moral reasoning, researchers have devised short-answer questionnaires. The most recent, the *Sociomoral Reflection Measure–Short Form* (SRM-SF), poses 11 questions that (like Kohlberg's clinical interview) ask individuals to evaluate the importance of moral values and to reason about them—for example: "Let's say a friend of yours needs help and may even die, and you're the only person who can save him or her. How important is it for a person (without losing his or her own life) to save the life of a friend?" For each question, participants rate the importance of the value it addresses (from "very important" to "not important") and write a brief explanation. Their explanations are coded according to a revised version of Kohlberg's stages. Scores on the SRM-SF correlate well with those obtained from Kohlberg's clinical interview but are far less time-consuming to obtain (Gibbs, Basinger, & Grime, 2003).

KOHLBERG'S STAGES OF MORAL UNDERSTANDING Kohlberg organized moral development into three levels, each with two stages, yielding six stages in all. He believed that moral understanding is promoted by the same factors Piaget thought were important for cognitive development: (1) actively grappling with moral issues and noticing weaknesses in one's current reasoning and (2) gains in perspective taking, which permit individuals to resolve moral conflicts in more effective ways. **TAKE A MOMENT...** As we examine Kohlberg's developmental sequence in light of possible responses to the Heinz dilemma, look for changes in perspective taking that each stage assumes.

The Preconventional Level. At the **preconventional level,** morality is externally controlled: Children accept the rules of authority figures and judge actions by their consequences. Behaviors that result in punishment are viewed as bad, those that lead to rewards as good.

- *Stage 1: The punishment and obedience orientation.* Children at this stage, while recognizing that others may have different thoughts and feelings, still find it difficult to consider two points of view in a moral dilemma. As a result, they overlook people's intentions. Instead, they focus on fear of authority and avoidance of punishment as reasons for behaving morally.

  Prostealing: "If you let your wife die, you will . . . be blamed for not spending the money to help her and there'll be an investigation of you and the druggist for your wife's death." (Kohlberg, 1969, p. 381)

  Antistealing: "You shouldn't steal the drug because you'll be caught and sent to jail if you do. If you do get away, [you'd be scared that] the police would catch up with you any minute." (Kohlberg, 1969, p. 381)

- *Stage 2: The instrumental purpose orientation.* Children at this stage realize that people can have different perspectives in a moral dilemma, but at first this understanding is concrete. They view right action as flowing from self-interest and understand reciprocity as equal exchange of favors: "You do this for me, and I'll do that for you."

  Prostealing: "[I]f Heinz decides to risk jail to save his wife, it's his life he's risking; he can do what he wants with it. And the same goes for the druggist; it's up to him to decide what he wants to do." (Rest, 1979, p. 26)

  Antistealing: "[Heinz] is running more risk than it's worth [to save a wife who is near death]." (Rest, 1979, p. 27)

The Conventional Level. At the **conventional level,** individuals continue to regard conformity to social rules as important, but not for reasons of self-interest. Rather, they believe that actively maintaining the current social system ensures positive human relationships and societal order.

- *Stage 3: The "good boy–good girl" orientation, or the morality of interpersonal cooperation.* The desire to obey rules because they promote social harmony first appears in the context of close personal ties. Stage 3 individuals want to maintain the affection and approval of friends and relatives by being a "good person"— trustworthy, loyal, respectful, helpful, and nice. The capacity to view a two-person relationship from the vantage point of an impartial, outside observer, which requires recursive thought (see page 441 in Chapter 12), supports this new approach to morality. At this stage, individuals understand *ideal reciprocity:* They express the same concern for the welfare of another as they do for themselves—a standard of fairness summed up by the Golden Rule: "Do unto others as you would have them do unto you."

  Prostealing: "No one will think you're bad if you steal the drug, but your family will think you're an inhuman husband if you don't. If you let your wife die, you'll never be able to look anyone in the face again." (Kohlberg, 1969, p. 381)

  Antistealing: "It isn't just the druggist who will think you're a criminal, everyone else will too. . . . [Y]ou'll feel bad thinking how you've brought dishonor on your family and yourself." (Kohlberg, 1969, p. 381)

- *Stage 4: The social-order-maintaining orientation.* At this stage, the individual takes into account a larger perspective—that of societal laws. Moral choices no longer depend on close ties to others. Instead, rules must be enforced in the same evenhanded fashion for everyone, and each member of society has a personal duty to uphold them. The Stage 4

© STEVE SKJOLD/ALAMY

If this teenager helps a preschooler climb an amusement park rope ladder because she expects a favor from someone in return, she is at Kohlberg's preconventional level. If she is guided by ideal reciprocity—"Do unto others as you would have them do unto you"—she has advanced to the conventional level.

individual believes that laws should be obeyed because they are vital for ensuring societal order and cooperation between people.

Prostealing: "Heinz has a duty to protect his wife's life; it's a vow he took in marriage. But it's wrong to steal, so he would have to take the drug with the idea of paying the druggist for it and accepting the penalty for breaking the law later."

Antistealing: "Even if his wife is dying, it's still [Heinz's] duty as a citizen to obey the law. . . . If everyone starts breaking the law in a jam, there'd be no civilization, just crime and violence." (Rest, 1979, p. 30)

The Postconventional or Principled Level. Individuals at the **postconventional level** move beyond unquestioning support for the laws and rules of their own society. They define morality in terms of abstract principles and values that apply to all situations and societies.

Boston young people demonstrate against rising public transportation fares and in favor of a discounted youth pass. Their actions reflect a belief that laws and policies are flexible instruments, open to change for the greater good—Kohlberg's social contract orientation.

- ***Stage 5: The social contract orientation.*** At Stage 5, individuals regard laws and rules as flexible instruments for furthering human purposes. They can imagine alternatives to their own social order, and they emphasize fair procedures for interpreting and changing the law. When laws are consistent with individual rights and the interests of the majority, each person follows them because of a *social contract orientation*—free and willing participation in the system because it brings about more good for people than if it did not exist.

  Prostealing: "Although there is a law against stealing, the law wasn't meant to violate a person's right to life. . . . If Heinz is prosecuted for stealing, the law needs to be reinterpreted to take into account situations in which it goes against people's natural right to keep on living."

  Antistealing: At this stage, there are no antistealing responses.

- ***Stage 6: The universal ethical principle orientation.*** At this highest stage, right action is defined by self-chosen ethical principles of conscience that are valid for all humanity, regardless of law and social agreement. Stage 6 individuals typically mention such abstract principles as respect for the worth and dignity of each person.

Prostealing: "It doesn't make sense to put respect for property above respect for life itself. [People] could live together without private property at all. Respect for human life and personality is absolute, and accordingly [people] have a mutual duty to save one another from dying." (Rest, 1979, p. 37)

Antistealing: At this stage, there are no antistealing responses.

RESEARCH ON KOHLBERG'S STAGE SEQUENCE   Kohlberg's original research and other longitudinal studies provide the most convincing evidence for his stage sequence. With few exceptions, individuals move through the first four stages in the predicted order (Boom, Wouters, & Keller, 2007; Colby et al., 1983; Dawson, 2002; Walker & Taylor, 1991b). Moral development is slow and gradual: Reasoning at Stages 1 and 2 decreases in early adolescence, while Stage 3 reasoning increases through midadolescence and then declines. Stage 4 reasoning rises over the teenage years until, among college-educated young adults, it is the typical response.

Few people move beyond Stage 4. In fact, postconventional morality is so rare that no clear evidence exists that Kohlberg's Stage 6 actually follows Stage 5. This poses a key challenge to Kohlberg's theory: If people must reach Stages 5 and 6 to be considered truly morally mature, few individuals anywhere would measure up! According to one reexamination of Kohlberg's stages, moral maturity can be found in a revised understanding of Stages 3 and 4 (Gibbs, 2014). These stages are not "conventional"—based on social conformity—as Kohlberg assumed. Rather, they require profound moral constructions—an understanding of ideal reciprocity as the basis for relationships (Stage 3) and for widely accepted moral standards, set forth in rules and laws (Stage 4). In this view, "postconventional" morality is a highly reflective endeavor limited to a handful of people who have attained advanced education, usually in philosophy.

TAKE A MOMENT... Think of an actual moral dilemma you faced recently. How did you solve it? Did your reasoning fall at the same stage as your thinking about Heinz? Real-life conflicts, such as whether to continue helping a friend who is taking advantage of you, often elicit moral reasoning below a person's actual capacity because they involve practical considerations and mix cognition with intense emotion (Carpendale, 2000). Although adolescents and adults still mention reasoning as their most frequent strategy for resolving these dilemmas, they also refer to other strategies—talking through issues with others, relying on intuition, and calling on religious and spiritual ideas. And they report feeling drained, confused, and torn by temptation—an emotional side of moral judgment not tapped by hypothetical situations (Walker, 2004). Hypothetical dilemmas evoke the upper limits of moral thought because they allow reflection without the interference of personal risk.

The influence of situational factors on moral judgments indicates that, like Piaget's cognitive stages, Kohlberg's moral stages are loosely organized and overlapping. Rather than developing in a neat, stepwise fashion, people draw on a range of moral responses that vary with context. With age, this range shifts upward as less mature moral reasoning is gradually replaced by more advanced moral thought.

Are There Sex Differences in Moral Reasoning?

As we have seen, real-life moral dilemmas often highlight the role of emotion in moral judgment. In the discussion at the beginning of this section, notice how Sabrina's moral argument focuses on caring and commitment to others. Carol Gilligan (1982) is the best-known of those who have argued that Kohlberg's theory does not adequately represent the morality of girls and women. Gilligan believes that feminine morality emphasizes an "ethic of care" that Kohlberg's system devalues. Sabrina's reasoning falls at Stage 3 because it is based on mutual trust and affection, whereas Louis's is at Stage 4 because he emphasizes following the law to ensure societal order. According to Gilligan, a concern for others is a *different* but no less valid basis for moral judgment than a focus on impersonal rights.

Many studies have tested Gilligan's claim that Kohlberg's approach underestimates the moral maturity of females, and most do not support it (Walker, 2006). On hypothetical dilemmas as well as everyday moral problems, adolescent and adult females display reasoning at the same stage as their male agemates, and often at a higher stage. Themes of justice and caring appear in the responses of both sexes, and when females do raise interpersonal concerns, they are not downgraded in Kohlberg's system (Jaffee & Hyde, 2000; Walker, 1995). Rather, girls shift from Stage 2 to Stage 3 reasoning earlier than boys (Gibbs et al., 2007). These findings suggest that although Kohlberg emphasized justice rather than caring as the highest moral ideal, his theory taps both sets of values.

Still, Gilligan makes a powerful claim that research on moral development has been limited by too much attention to rights and justice (a "masculine" ideal) and too little to caring and responsiveness (a "feminine" ideal). Some evidence indicates that although the morality of males and females taps both orientations, females do tend to emphasize care, or empathic perspective taking, whereas males either stress justice or focus equally on justice and care (Jaffee & Hyde, 2000; You, Maeda, & Bebeau, 2011). This difference in emphasis, which appears more often in real-life than in hypothetical dilemmas, may reflect women's greater involvement in daily activities involving care and concern for others.

Indeed, context profoundly affects use of a care orientation. In an Australian investigation, researchers presented 18- to 38-year-old university students with one of three versions of a moral dilemma, in which the main character varied in familiarity: (1) a close friend in class, (2) a person "known only vaguely" from class, or (3) a classmate whose relationship was unspecified (Ryan, David, & Reynolds, 2004). When asked whether they would permit the character, who was in danger of failing the course, to borrow a copy of their recently completed assignment despite risk of cheating, both males and females gave more care responses when considering a close friend than a socially distant classmate. Gender differences emerged only in the unspecified condition, where women—who tend to forge closer relationships and, thus, may have assumed greater familiarity—expressed more caring.

Coordinating Moral, Social-Conventional, and Personal Concerns

Adolescents' moral advances are also evident in their reasoning about situations that raise competing moral, social-conventional, and personal issues. In diverse Western and non-Western cultures, concern with matters of personal choice strengthens during the teenage years—a reflection of adolescents' quest for identity and strengthening independence (Neff & Helwig, 2002; Nucci, 2005). As young people firmly insist that parents not encroach on the personal arena (dress, hairstyle, diary records, friendships), disputes over these issues increase. In contrast, adolescents typically say that parents have a right to tell them what to do in moral and social-conventional situations. And when these issues spark disagreements, teenagers seldom challenge parental authority (Smetana & Daddis, 2002).

Teenagers in New York City prepare to march in favor of gun control. Adolescent moral development involves thinking intently about conflicts between personal choice and community obligation—for example, whether, and under what conditions, individuals' right to bear arms should be restricted.

As they enlarge the range of issues they regard as personal, adolescents think more intently about conflicts between personal choice and community obligations—for example, whether, and under what conditions, it is permissible to restrict speech, religion, marriage, childbearing, group membership, and other individual rights (Wainryb, 1997). Teenagers display more subtle thinking than school-age children on such issues. When asked if it is OK to exclude a child from a peer group on the basis of race or gender, fourth graders usually say exclusion is always unfair. But by tenth grade, young people, though increasingly mindful of fairness, indicate that under certain conditions—in intimate relationships (friendship) and private contexts (at home or in a small club), and on the basis of gender more often than race—exclusion is OK (Killen et al., 2002, 2007; Rutland, Killen, & Abrams, 2010). In explaining, they mention the right to personal choice as well as concerns about effective group functioning.

As adolescents integrate personal rights with ideal reciprocity, they demand that the protections they want for themselves extend to others. For example, with age, they are more likely to defend the government's right to limit individual freedom to engage in risky health behaviors such as smoking and drinking, in the interest of the larger public good (Flanagan, Stout, & Gallay, 2008).

Similarly, they are increasingly mindful of the overlap between moral imperatives and social conventions. Eventually they realize that violating strongly held conventions—showing up at a wedding in a T-shirt, talking out of turn at a student council meeting—can harm others, either by inducing distress or by undermining fair treatment. As their grasp of fairness deepens, young people realize that many social conventions have moral implications: They are vital for maintaining a just and peaceful society (Nucci, 2001). Notice how this understanding is central to Kohlberg's Stage 4, which is typically attained as adolescence draws to a close.

Influences on Moral Reasoning

Many factors affect maturity of moral reasoning, including the young person's personality and a wide range of social experiences—child-rearing practices, peer interaction, schooling, and aspects of culture. Growing evidence suggests that, as Kohlberg believed, these experiences work by presenting young people with cognitive challenges, which stimulate them to think about moral problems in more complex ways.

PERSONALITY A flexible, open-minded approach to new information and experiences is linked to gains in moral reasoning, just as it is to identity development (Matsuba & Walker, 1998). Because open-minded young people are more socially skilled, they have more opportunities for social participation. A richer social life enhances exposure to others' perspectives, and open-mindedness helps adolescents derive moral insights from that exposure. In contrast, adolescents who have difficulty adapting to new experiences are less likely to be interested in others' moral ideas and justifications.

CHILD-REARING PRACTICES As in childhood, parenting practices associated with moral maturity in adolescence combine warmth, exchange of ideas, and appropriate demands for maturity. Adolescents who gain most in moral understanding have parents who engage in moral discussions, encourage prosocial behavior, insist that others be treated respectfully and fairly, and create a supportive atmosphere by listening sensitively, asking clarifying questions, and presenting higher-level reasoning (Carlo et al., 2011; Pratt, Skoe, & Arnold, 2004). In one study, 11-year-olds were asked what they thought an adult would say to justify a moral rule, such as not lying, stealing, or breaking a promise. Those with warm, demanding, communicative parents were far more likely than their agemates to point to the importance of ideal reciprocity: "You wouldn't like it if I did it to you" (Leman, 2005). In contrast, when parents lecture, use threats, or make sarcastic remarks, adolescents show little or no change in moral reasoning over time (Walker & Taylor, 1991a).

In sum, parents who facilitate moral understanding use an authoritative approach that is affectionate, verbal, rational, and respectful and that promotes a cooperative style of family life. Notice that these are similar to the characteristics—discussed in Chapter 10—that promote moral internalization in young children.

SCHOOLING From late adolescence on, moral reasoning typically advances as long as a person remains in school (Gibbs et al., 2007). Higher education introduces young people to social issues that extend beyond personal relationships to entire political and cultural groups. Consistent with this idea, college students who report more perspective-taking opportunities (for example, classes that emphasize open discussion of opinions, friendships with others of different cultural backgrounds) and who indicate that they have become more aware of social diversity tend to be advanced in moral reasoning (Comunian & Gielan, 2006; Mason & Gibbs, 1993a, 1993b).

PEER INTERACTION Interaction among peers who present differing viewpoints promotes moral understanding. When young people negotiate and compromise with agemates, they realize that social life can be based on cooperation between equals (Killen & Nucci, 1995). Teenagers who report more close friendships and who more often participate in conversations with their friends are advanced in moral reasoning (Schonert-Reichl, 1999). The mutuality and intimacy of friendship, which foster decisions based on consensual agreement, may be particularly important for moral development. Furthermore, recall from Chapter 13 that intergroup contact—cross-race friendships and interactions in schools and communities—reduces racial and ethnic prejudice. It also affects both majority and minority adolescents morally, strengthening their conviction that race-based and other forms of peer exclusion are wrong (Crystal, Killen, & Ruck, 2008; Ruck et al., 2011).

Peer discussions and role playing of moral problems have provided the basis for interventions aimed at improving high school and college students' progress through Kohlberg's stage sequence. For these discussions to be effective, young people must be highly engaged—confronting, critiquing, and attempting to clarify one another's viewpoints, as Sabrina and Louis did when they argued over Mrs. Perry's plight (Berkowitz & Gibbs, 1983; Comunian & Gielen, 2006). And because moral development occurs gradually, many peer interaction sessions over weeks or months typically are needed to produce moral change.

CULTURE Individuals in industrialized nations move through Kohlberg's stages more quickly and advance to a higher level than individuals in village societies, who rarely move beyond Stage 3. One explanation for these cultural differences is that in village societies, moral

In Japan, a country that highly values interdependence, responses to moral dilemmas tend to emphasize caring as a communal responsibility. These high school students express their student body's collective empathy during a memorial visit to a school devastated by the 2011 tsunami.

cooperation is based on direct relations between people and does not allow for the development of advanced moral understanding (Stages 4 to 6), which depends on appreciating the role of larger social structures, such as laws and government institutions (Gibbs et al., 2007).

A second possible reason for cultural variation is that in both village societies and industrialized nations that highly value interdependence, responses to moral dilemmas are more other-directed than in North America and Western Europe (Miller, 2007). In one study, both male and female Japanese adolescents, who almost always integrated care- and justice-based reasoning, placed greater weight on caring, which they regarded as a communal responsibility. As one boy remarked, *yasashii* (kindness/gentleness) and *omoiyari* (empathy) are "something 'normal' that everyone shows" (Shimizu, 2001). Similarly, in research conducted in India, even highly educated people (expected to have attained Kohlberg's Stages 4 and 5) viewed solutions to moral dilemmas as the responsibility of the entire society, not of a single person (Miller & Bersoff, 1995).

These findings raise the question of whether Kohlberg's highest level represents a culturally specific way of thinking—one limited to Western societies that emphasize individualism and an appeal to an inner, private conscience. At the same time, a review of over 100 studies confirmed an age-related trend consistent with Kohlberg's Stages 1 to 4 across diverse societies (Gibbs et al., 2007). A common morality of justice is clearly evident in the dilemma responses of people from vastly different cultures.

Moral Reasoning and Behavior

A central assumption of the cognitive-developmental perspective is that moral understanding should affect moral action. According to Kohlberg, mature moral thinkers realize that behaving in line with their beliefs is vital for creating and maintaining a just social world (Gibbs, 2014). Consistent with this idea, higher-stage adolescents more often act prosocially by helping, sharing, and defending victims of injustice and by volunteering in their communities (Carlo et al., 2011; Comunian & Gielan, 2000, 2006). Also, they less often engage in cheating, aggression, and other antisocial behaviors (Raaijmakers, Engels, & Van Hoof, 2005; Stams et al., 2006).

Yet the connection between more mature moral reasoning and action is only modest. As we have seen in this and earlier chapters, moral behavior is influenced by many factors besides cognition, including the emotions of empathy, sympathy, and guilt; individual differences in temperament; and cultural experiences and intuitive beliefs that affect moral choice and decision making (Haidt & Kesebir, 2010). Compared with children, adolescents increasingly say they would feel negatively after committing a moral transgression and positively after they had acted morally (Krettenauer et al., 2014). Moral decisions and anticipated emotions become better coordinated over time, contributing to gains in teenagers' motivation to act morally.

Moral identity—the degree to which morality is central to self-concept—also affects moral behavior (Hardy & Carlo, 2011). In a study of low-SES African-American and Hispanic teenagers, those who emphasized moral traits and goals in their self-descriptions displayed exceptional levels of community service (Hart & Fegley, 1995). But they did not differ from their agemates in moral reasoning.

Researchers have begun to identify factors that strengthen moral identity in hopes of promoting moral commitment. Certain parenting practices—inductive discipline (see page 373 in Chapter 10) and clearly conveyed moral expectations—augment adolescents' moral identity (Patrick & Gibbs, 2011). And *just educational environments*—in which teachers model and guide students in democratic decision making and rule setting, resolving disputes civilly and fairly, and taking responsibility for others' welfare—are influential (Atkins, Hart, & Donnelly, 2004). In one study, tenth graders who reported fair teacher treatment were more likely than those who had experienced unjust treatment (an unfair detention or a lower grade than they

LOOK and LISTEN

Would you characterize the high school you attended as a *just educational environment?* Cite specific features and experiences that may have contributed to students' moral development and civic engagement.

KYODO/AP IMAGES

Social Issues: Education

Development of Civic Engagement

On Thanksgiving Day, Jules, Martin, Louis, and Sabrina joined their parents at a soup kitchen to serve a holiday dinner to poverty-stricken people. Throughout the year, Sabrina volunteered on Saturday mornings at a nursing home, conversing with bedridden elders. During a congressional election campaign, all four adolescents attended special youth meetings with candidates. At school, Louis and his girlfriend, Cassie, formed an organization devoted to promoting ethnic and racial tolerance.

These young people show a strong sense of *civic engagement*—a complex combination of cognition, emotion, and behavior. Civic engagement involves knowledge of social and political issues, commitment to making a difference in the community, and skills for achieving civic goals, such as how to resolve differing views fairly (Zaff et al., 2010).

When young people engage in community service that exposes them to people in need or to public issues, they are especially likely to express a commitment to future service. And youth volunteers—who tend to be advanced in moral reasoning—gain further in moral maturity as a result of participation (Gibbs et al., 2007; Hart, Atkins, & Donnelly, 2006). The power of family, school, and community to promote civic engagement stems from discussions, practices, and activities that jointly foster moral thought, emotion, and behavior.

Family Influences

Adolescents whose parents stress compassion for the less fortunate and engage in community service tend to hold socially responsible values. When asked what causes unemployment or poverty, for example, these teenagers more often mention situational and societal factors (lack of education, government policies, or the state of the economy) than individual factors (low intelligence or personal problems). Youths who endorse situational and societal causes, in turn, have more altruistic life goals, such as working to eradicate poverty or to preserve the earth for future generations (Flanagan & Tucker, 1999).

Parents' open communication, discussion of social problems, and own civic engagement carry over to their adolescent children's civic commitment and behavior (van Goethem et al., 2014). These young people not only volunteer but do so especially often.

School and Community Influences

A democratic climate at school, in which teachers promote discussion of controversial social issues while insisting that students listen to and respect one another, fosters knowledge and critical analysis of social and political concerns and participation in organizations with a civic purpose (Lenzi et al., 2012; Torney-Purta, Barber, & Wilkenfeld, 2007). Furthermore, high school students who view their community as one in which adults care about youths and work to make the community better report higher levels of civic participation (Kahne & Sporte, 2008). Participation in extracurricular activities whose primary objectives are to induce social change outside the organization itself is associated with civic commitment that persists into adulthood (Obradović & Masten, 2007; Zaff et al., 2003).

Two aspects of these involvements seem to account for their lasting impact. First, they introduce adolescents to the vision and skills required for mature civic engagement. Within student government, political and vocational clubs, service organizations, and student newspaper and yearbook staffs, young people see how their actions affect the wider school and community. They realize that collectively they can achieve results greater than any one person can accomplish alone. And they learn to work together, balancing strong convictions with compromise (Kirshner, 2009). Second, while engaged in these activities, young people explore political and moral ideals. Often they redefine their identities to include a responsibility to combat others' misfortunes, which further strengthens civic engagement (Crocetti, Jahromi, & Meeus, 2012).

UNIVERSALIMAGESGROUP/GETTY IMAGES

For this young teenager, planting a tree during an Earth Day celebration promotes civic engagement. When young people participate in community service that exposes them to public issues, they are likely to express a commitment to future service.

The majority of U.S. secondary schools provide students with community service opportunities. Many of these schools have *service-learning programs,* which integrate service activities into the academic curriculum. High school students who are required to serve their communities express as strong a desire to remain engaged as do students who volunteer. And when they reach early adulthood, they are equally likely to vote and participate in community organizations (Hart et al., 2007; Metz & Youniss, 2005).

Still, most U.S. schools offering service learning do not have policies encouraging or mandating enrollment in such programs. Furthermore, low-SES, inner-city youths attend schools and live in neighborhoods with fewer civic-training opportunities. And students without plans to go to college may be less motivated to enroll in service-learning programs. As a result, these youths score substantially lower than higher-SES and college-oriented youths in civic knowledge and participation (Lenzi et al., 2012; Syvertsen et al., 2011; Zaff et al., 2010). A broad societal commitment to fostering civic character must pay special attention to supportive school and community experiences for these young people.

deserved) to regard excluding a peer on the basis of race as a moral transgression (Crystal, Killen, & Ruck, 2010).

Schools can also foster students' moral identity by expanding opportunities to experience and explore moral emotions, thoughts, and actions through civic engagement. As the Social Issues: Education box above reveals, civic engagement can help young people see the connection between their personal interests and the public interest—an insight that may foster all aspects of morality.

Adolescents who are part of a religious community tend to be advantaged in moral values and behavior. The more activities they share with their religiously involved network of adults and peers, the higher they score in empathy and prosocial behavior.

Religious Involvement and Moral Development

Recall that in resolving real-life moral dilemmas, many people express religious and spiritual ideas. Religion is especially important in U.S. family life. In recent national polls, about 70 percent of Americans rated religion as very important in their lives, compared with 50 percent in Canada and Germany, 40 percent in Great Britain, and 30 percent in Sweden, making the United States the most religious Western nation (Pew Research Center, 2012; Pickel, 2013). People who regularly attend religious services include many parents with children. But as adolescents search for a personally meaningful identity, formal religious involvement declines—for U.S. youths, from 55 percent at ages 13 to 15 to 40 percent at ages 17 to 18 (Pew Research Center, 2010).

Nevertheless, teenagers who remain part of a religious community benefit in moral values and behavior. Compared with unaffiliated youths, they are more involved in community service activities aimed at helping the less fortunate (Kerestes, Youniss, & Metz, 2004). And religious involvement promotes responsible academic and social behavior and discourages misconduct (Dowling et al., 2004). It is associated with lower levels of drug and alcohol use, early sexual activity, and antisocial behavior (Good & Willoughby, 2014; Salas-Wright, Vaughn, & Maynard, 2014).

A variety of factors contribute to these favorable outcomes. In a study of inner-city high school students, religiously involved young people were more likely to report trusting relationships with parents, other adults, and friends who hold similar worldviews. The more activities they shared with this network, the higher they scored in empathy and prosocial behavior (King & Furrow, 2004). Furthermore, religious education and youth activities directly teach concern for others and provide opportunities for moral discussions and civic engagement. And adolescents who feel connected to a higher being may develop certain inner strengths, including prosocial values and a strong moral identity, that help them translate their thinking into action (Hardy & Carlo, 2005; Sherrod & Spiewak, 2008).

Because most teenagers, regardless of formal affiliation, identify with a religious denomination and say they believe in a higher being, religious institutions may be uniquely suited to foster moral and prosocial commitments and discourage risky behaviors. For youths in inner-city neighborhoods with few alternative sources of social support, outreach by religious institutions can lead to life-altering involvement (Jang & Johnson, 2001). An exception is seen in religious cults, where rigid indoctrination into the group's beliefs, suppression of individuality, and estrangement from society all work against moral maturity (Scarlett & Warren, 2010).

Further Challenges to Kohlberg's Theory

Although much evidence is consistent with the cognitive-developmental approach to morality, Kohlberg's theory has faced major challenges. The most radical opposition comes from researchers who—referring to wide variability in moral reasoning across situations—claim that Kohlberg's stage sequence inadequately accounts for morality in everyday life (Krebs & Denton, 2005). These investigators favor abandoning Kohlberg's stages for a *pragmatic approach to morality*. They assert that each person makes moral judgments at varying levels of maturity, depending on the individual's current context and motivations: Conflict over a business deal is likely to evoke Stage 2 (instrumental purpose) reasoning, a friendship or romantic dispute Stage 3 (ideal reciprocity) reasoning, and a breach of contract Stage 4 (social-order-maintaining) reasoning (Krebs, 2011).

According to the pragmatic view, everyday moral judgments—rather than being efforts to arrive at just solutions—are practical tools that people use to achieve their goals. To benefit personally, they often must advocate cooperation with others. But people often act first and then invoke moral judgments to rationalize their actions, regardless of whether their behavior is self-centered or prosocial (Haidt, 2001, 2013). And sometimes people use moral judgments for immoral purposes—for example, to excuse their transgressions.

Is the pragmatic approach correct that people strive to resolve moral conflicts fairly only when they themselves have nothing to lose? Supporters of the cognitive-developmental perspective point out that people frequently rise above self-interest to defend others' rights. For example, moral leaders in business—rather than resorting to Stage 2 reasoning—endorse trust, integrity, good faith, and just laws and codes of conduct (Damon, 2004; Gibbs, 2006). Also, when presented with moral justifications varying in maturity, adolescents and adults are well aware of the greater adequacy of higher-stage thinking, which some people act on despite highly corrupt environments. Furthermore, individuals who engage in sudden altruistic action may have previously considered relevant moral issues so thoroughly that their moral judgment activates automatically, triggering an immediate response (Gibbs, 2014; Gibbs et al., 2009). In these instances, people who appear to be engaging in after-the-fact moral justification are actually behaving with great forethought.

In sum, the cognitive-developmental approach to morality has done much to clarify our profound moral potential. And despite opposition, Kohlberg's central assumption—that with age, humans everywhere construct a deeper understanding of fairness and justice that guides moral action—remains powerfully influential.

Gender Typing

16.7 How does gender typing change in adolescence?

As Sabrina entered adolescence, she began to worry about walking, talking, eating, dressing, laughing, and competing in ways consistent with a feminine gender role. According to one hypothesis, the arrival of adolescence is typically accompanied by **gender intensification**—increased gender stereotyping of attitudes and behavior, and movement toward a more traditional gender identity. Research on gender intensification, however, is mixed, with some studies finding evidence for it and others reporting few instances (Basow & Rubin, 1999; Galambos, Berenbaum, & McHale, 2009; Huston & Alvarez, 1990; Priess, Lindberg, & Hyde, 2009). When gender intensification is evident, it seems to be stronger for adolescent girls. Although girls continue to be less gender-typed than boys, some may feel less free to experiment with "other-gender" activities and behaviors than they did in middle childhood.

In young people who do exhibit gender intensification, biological, social, and cognitive factors likely are involved. As puberty magnifies sex differences in appearance, teenagers spend more time thinking about themselves in gender-linked ways. Pubertal changes might also prompt gender-typed pressures from others. Parents with traditional gender-role beliefs may encourage "gender-appropriate" activities and behavior more than they did earlier (Crouter et al., 2007; Shanahan et al., 2007). And when adolescents start to date, they often become more gender-typed as a way of increasing their attractiveness (Maccoby, 1998). Finally, cognitive changes—in particular, greater concern with what others think—might make young teenagers more responsive to gender-role expectations.

Gender intensification typically declines by late adolescence, but not all affected young people move beyond it to the same degree. Some girls struggle with gender-typed social pressures to act in ways inconsistent with their actual beliefs, avoiding conflict by suppressing their honest thoughts and feelings (Tolman, 2002). In one study, eighth-grade girls who compromised their authenticity—by withholding their true opinions and feelings to avoid parental or peer disapproval—were less likely than their more authentic agemates to display the typical adolescent rise in self-esteem (Impett et al., 2008).

© JEFF GREENBERG/ALAMY

For some young people, early adolescence is a time of gender intensification. Pubertal changes in appearance, traditional gender-role expectations of parents, and increased concern with what others think can prompt teenagers to move toward a more traditional gender identity.

Teenagers who are encouraged to explore non-gender-typed options and to question the value of gender stereotypes for themselves and society are more likely to build an androgynous gender identity (see Chapter 10, page 389). Overall, androgynous adolescents, especially girls, tend to be psychologically healthier—more self-confident, more willing to speak their own mind, better-liked by peers, and identity-achieved (Bronstein, 2006; Dusek, 1987; Harter, 2012).

Ask Yourself

- **REVIEW** How does an understanding of ideal reciprocity contribute to moral development? Why are Kohlberg's Stages 3 and 4 morally mature constructions?

- **CONNECT** How might the exploration of values and goals associated with healthy identity development contribute to the eventual decline in adolescent gender intensification?

- **APPLY** Tam grew up in a small village culture, Lydia in a large industrial city. At age 15, Tam reasons at Kohlberg's Stage 3, Lydia at Stage 4. What factors might account for the difference?

- **REFLECT** Do you favor a cognitive-developmental or a pragmatic approach to morality, or both? Explain, drawing on both research evidence and personal experiences.

16.8 Discuss changes in parent–child and sibling relationships during adolescence.

The Family

Franca and Antonio remember their son Louis's freshman year of high school as a difficult time. Because of a demanding project at work, Franca was away from home many evenings and weekends. In her absence, Antonio took over, but when business declined and he had to cut costs at his hardware store, he, too, had less time for the family. That year, Louis and two friends used their computer know-how to gain entry to their classmates' systems to pirate video game software. Louis's grades fell, and he often left the house without saying where he was going. Franca and Antonio began to feel uncomfortable about the long hours Louis spent at his computer and their lack of contact with him. One day, when Franca and Antonio noticed the video-game icons covering Louis's computer desktop, they knew they had cause for concern.

Development at adolescence involves striving for **autonomy**—a sense of oneself as a separate, self-governing individual. Adolescent autonomy has two vital aspects: (1) an *emotional component*—relying more on oneself and less on parents for support and guidance, and (2) a *behavioral component*—making decisions by carefully weighing one's own judgment and the suggestions of others to arrive at a personally satisfying, well-reasoned course of action (Collins & Laursen, 2004; Steinberg & Silk, 2002). Typically, teenagers shift attention away from family to peers, with whom they explore new courses of action. Nevertheless, parent–child relationships remain vital for helping adolescents become autonomous, responsible individuals.

Parent–Child Relationships

A variety of changes within the adolescent support autonomy. In Chapter 14, we saw that puberty triggers psychological distancing from parents. In addition, as young people look more mature, parents give them more freedom to think and decide for themselves, more opportunities to regulate their own activities, and more responsibility (McElhaney et al., 2009). Cognitive development also paves the way toward autonomy: Gradually, adolescents solve problems and make decisions more effectively. And an improved ability to reason about social relationships leads teenagers to *deidealize* their parents, viewing them as "just people." Consequently, they

As adolescents strive for autonomy, they often disagree with parents over their readiness for certain privileges, such as going out with friends and dating. Effective parenting involves making appropriate demands for maturity while gradually granting increased freedom.

© ELLEN B. SENISI

Applying What We Know

Parenting Practices That Foster Adolescent Competence

PARENTING PRACTICE	ADOLESCENT OUTCOMES
Project warmth and acceptance.	Promotes high self-esteem, identity exploration and achievement, prosocial behavior, and more positive parent–adolescent communication.
Monitor activities.	Promotes high self-esteem and reduced likelihood of engaging in antisocial behavior. Most effective when parents have a cooperative relationship with the adolescent and modify their supervision to fit the young person's increasing competence.
Engage in democratic decision making and verbal give-and-take.	Promotes self-esteem and self-reliant, responsible behavior.
Establish firm control and consistent discipline.	When accompanied by warmth, explanations, and verbal give-and-take, promotes self-reliant, responsible behavior. (Firm control without explanations that clarify the legitimacy of parents' rules can undermine self-reliance and responsibility.)
Provide information and model effective skills.	Promotes competencies as diverse as academic achievement and conflict resolution; protects against high-risk behaviors, such as sex without contraception and substance use.

Sources: Collins & Steinberg, 2006.

no longer bend as easily to parental authority as they did when younger. Yet as Franca and Antonio's episode with Louis illustrates, teenagers still need guidance and, at times, protection from dangerous situations. (Recall from Chapter 14 our discussion of adolescent brain development, in which changes in the emotional/social network outpace gains in the cognitive-control network.)

EFFECTIVE PARENTING   TAKE A MOMENT... Think back to what we said earlier about the type of parenting that fosters academic achievement (Chapter 15), identity formation, and moral maturity. You will find a common theme: Effective parenting of adolescents strikes a balance between *connection* and *separation*. Warm, supportive parent–adolescent ties that make appropriate demands for maturity while permitting young people to explore ideas and social roles foster autonomy—in diverse ethnic groups, SES levels, nationalities, and family structures (including single-parent, two-parent, and stepparent). Autonomy, in turn, predicts high self-reliance, effortful control, academic achievement, positive work orientation, favorable self-esteem, and ease of separation in the transition to college (Bean, Barber, & Crane, 2007; Eisenberg et al., 2005; Supple et al., 2009; Vazsonyi, Hibbert, & Snider, 2003; Wang, Pomerantz, & Chen, 2007). Note that these are features of the authoritative style. See Applying What We Know above for a summary of practices emanating from authoritative parenting that promote adolescent cognitive and social development.

Conversely, parents who are coercive or psychologically controlling interfere with the development of autonomy. These tactics are linked to low self-esteem, depression, drug and alcohol use, and antisocial behavior—outcomes that often persist into early adulthood (Barber, Stolz, & Olsen, 2005; Bronte-Tinkew, Moore, & Carrano, 2006; Wissink, Deković, & Meijer, 2006).

In Chapter 2, we described the family as a *system* that must adapt to changes in its members. The rapid physical and psychological changes of adolescence trigger conflicting expectations in parent–child relationships—a major reason that many parents find rearing teenagers to be stressful. Earlier we noted that interest in making choices about personal matters strengthens in adolescence. Yet parents and teenagers—especially young teenagers—differ sharply on the appropriate age for granting certain privileges, such as control over clothing, school courses, going out with friends, and dating (Smetana, 2002). Consistent parental monitoring of the young person's daily activities, through a cooperative relationship in which the adolescent willingly discloses information, is linked to a variety of positive outcomes—prevention of delinquency, reduction in sexual activity, improved school performance, and positive psychological well-being (Crouter & Head, 2002; Jacobson & Crockett, 2000).

LOOK and LISTEN

Ask an early adolescent and his or her parent for their views on when the young person is mature enough to spend unsupervised evenings with friends, begin dating, own a cell phone, create a Facebook page, and be given other privileges. Do adolescent and parent perspectives differ?

Parents' own development can also lead to conflict with teenagers. While their children face a boundless future and a wide array of choices, middle-aged parents must accept the fact that their own possibilities are narrowing (Holmbeck, 1996). Often parents can't understand why the adolescent wants to skip family activities to be with peers. And teenagers fail to appreciate that parents want the family to spend as much time together as possible because an important period in their adult life—child rearing—will soon end.

CULTURE In cultures that place a high priority on interdependence, autonomy remains a central adolescent motive, but teenagers conceive of it differently than in Western nations. Rather than equating it with independent decision making, they view autonomy as *self-endorsed* decision making—engaging in actions that are consistent with authentic personal values. In an investigation of adolescents from both urban and rural regions of China, self-endorsed motives for both independent and "dependent" decision making (following parents' advice) were related to high self-esteem and a positive outlook (Chen et al., 2013). Chinese adolescents often accept their parents' decisions because they value parents' opinions, not because they feel pressured to comply.

Immigrant parents from cultures that emphasize obedience to authority have greater difficulty adapting to their teenagers' push for independent decision making, often reacting strongly to adolescent disagreement. And as adolescents acquire the Western host culture's language and are increasingly exposed to its individualistic values, immigrant parents may become even more critical, prompting teenagers to rely less on the family network for social support and to disclose less about personal feelings, peer relationships, and potentially risky activities (Yau, Tasopoulos-Chan, & Smetana, 2009). The resulting *acculturative stress* (see page 594) is associated with a decline in self-esteem and a rise in anxiety, depressive symptoms, and deviant behavior, including alcohol use and delinquency (Park, 2009; Suarez-Morales & Lopez, 2009; Warner et al., 2006).

A REORGANIZED RELATIONSHIP Throughout adolescence, the quality of the parent–child relationship is the single most consistent predictor of mental health. In well-functioning families, teenagers remain attached to parents and seek their advice, but they do so in a context of greater freedom (Collins & Steinberg, 2006). The mild conflict that typically arises facilitates adolescent identity and autonomy by helping family members learn to express and tolerate disagreement. Conflicts also inform parents of teenagers' changing needs and expectations, signaling a need for adjustments in the parent–child relationship.

By middle to late adolescence, most parents and children achieve this mature, mutual relationship, and harmonious interaction is on the rise. The reduced time that Western teenagers spend with their families—an estimated decline of 50 percent compared with middle childhood—has little to do with conflict. Rather, it results from the large amount of unstructured time available to teenagers in North America and Western Europe—on average, nearly half their waking hours (Larson, 2001; Larson et al., 1996). Young people tend to fill these free hours with activities that take them away from home—part-time jobs, a growing array of leisure and volunteer pursuits, and time with friends.

Compared with sheer amount of time spent together, type of shared parent–adolescent activities is more important. In an investigation of middle-SES white families, engaging in leisure pursuits and eating meals together (especially with both parents) enhanced teenagers' well-being (Offer, 2013). These contexts probably afford parents and adolescents greater opportunity to discuss important concerns in a relaxed atmosphere and to emphasize shared values (Fiese, Foley, & Spagnola, 2006). Turn back to page 73 in Chapter 2 to review evidence that family dinnertime promotes diverse aspects of adolescent adjustment, including improved mental health, fewer risky behaviors, and better school performance.

Finally, the drop in family time over the teenage years is not universal. In one study, urban low- and middle-SES African-American youths showed no decline in hours spent at home with family—a pattern typical in cultures stressing interdependence and family closeness (Larson et al., 2001). Furthermore, teenagers living in risky neighborhoods tend to have more trusting relationships with parents and adjust more favorably when parents maintain tighter control and pressure them not to engage in worrisome behaviors (McElhaney & Allen, 2001). In harsh surroundings, adolescents seem to interpret more measured granting of autonomy as a sign of parental caring.

Family Circumstances

As Franca and Antonio's experience with Louis reminds us, adult life stresses can interfere with warm, involved parenting and, in turn, with children's adjustment at any phase of development. But parents who are financially secure, not overloaded with job pressures, and content with their marriages usually find it easier to grant teenagers appropriate autonomy and experience less conflict with them (Cowan & Cowan, 2002). When Franca and Antonio's work stress eased and they recognized Louis's need for more involvement and guidance, his problems subsided.

Less than 10 percent of families with adolescents have seriously troubled relationships—chronic, escalating levels of conflict and repeated arguments over serious issues. Among these, most difficulties began in childhood (Collins & Laursen, 2004). Table 16.2 summarizes family conditions considered in earlier chapters that pose challenges for adolescents. Teenagers who develop well despite family stress continue to benefit from factors that fostered resilience in earlier years: an appealing, easygoing disposition; a parent who combines warmth with high expectations; and (especially if parental supports are lacking) bonds with prosocial adults outside the family who care deeply about the adolescent's well-being (Masten & Shaffer, 2006).

TABLE 16.2	Family Circumstances with Implications for Adolescent Adjustment
FAMILY CIRCUMSTANCE	**TO REVIEW, TURN TO . . .**
Type of Family	
Adoptive	Chapter 2, pages 66–67
Never-married, single parent	Chapter 13, pages 499–500
Divorced single-parent	Chapter 13, pages 500–503
Blended	Chapter 13, pages 503–505
Employed mother and dual-earner	Chapter 13, pages 505–506
Lesbian and gay	Chapter 13, pages 498–499
Family Conditions	
Economic hardship	Chapter 2, pages 73–75
Child maltreatment	Chapter 10, pages 396–398
	Chapter 13, pages 508–510
Adolescent parenthood	Chapter 14, pages 545–547

Siblings

Like parent–child relationships, sibling interactions adapt to development at adolescence. As younger siblings become more self-sufficient, they accept less direction from their older brothers and sisters, and sibling influence declines. Also, as teenagers become more involved in friendships and romantic relationships, they invest less time and energy in their siblings, who are part of the family from which they are trying to establish autonomy. As a result, sibling relationships often become less intense, in both positive and negative feelings (Hetherington, Henderson, & Reiss, 1999; Kim et al., 2006).

Despite a drop in companionship, attachment between siblings, like closeness to parents, remains strong for most young people. Overall, siblings who established a positive bond in childhood continue to display greater affection and caring, which contribute to favorable adolescent adjustment, including increased academic engagement, empathy, and prosocial behavior (Lam, Solmeyer, & McHale, 2012; McHale, Updegraff, & Whiteman, 2012; Samek & Rueter, 2011). Older siblings frequently offer useful advice as their younger teenage brothers and sisters face challenges in romantic relationships, schoolwork, and decisions about the future.

Adolescent sibling ties vary with gender and culture. Consistent with the high value girls place on emotional closeness, sisters report greater intimacy with their siblings than brothers do, and sister–sister pairings tend to be the closest (Kim et al., 2006). And in one study, Mexican-American adolescents who expressed a strong Mexican cultural orientation resolved sibling conflicts more cooperatively—compromising rather than controlling or confronting—than did those more oriented toward U.S. individualistic values (Killoren, Thayer, & Updegraff, 2008).

Sibling interaction at adolescence continues to be affected by other relationships, and vice versa. As at earlier ages, teenagers who have warm, supportive parents and a history of caring friendships report more positive sibling ties (Kramer & Kowal, 2005; Milevsky, Schlechter, & Machlev, 2011). And in bidirectional fashion, warm adolescent sibling relationships contribute to more gratifying friendships (Yeh & Lempers, 2004). Finally, mild sibling differences in perceived parental affection no longer trigger jealousy but, instead, predict greater sibling warmth (Feinberg et al., 2003). Perhaps adolescents interpret a unique relationship with parents, as long as it is generally accepting, as a gratifying sign of their own individuality.

16.9 Describe adolescent friendships, peer groups, and dating relationships and their consequences for development.

16.10 Discuss conformity to peer pressure in adolescence.

Peer Relations

As adolescents spend less time with family members, peers become increasingly important. In industrialized societies, young people spend most of each weekday with agemates in school. Teenagers also spend much out-of-class time together, more in some cultures than in others. For example, U.S. young people have an estimated 50 hours of free time per week, Europeans 45 hours, and East Asians 33 hours (Larson, 2001). A shorter school year and less demanding academic standards, which lead American youths to devote much less time to schoolwork, are responsible.

In the following sections, we will see that adolescent peer relations can be both positive and negative. At their best, peers serve as crucial bridges between the family and adult social roles.

Friendships

Number of "best friends" declines from about four to six in early adolescence to one or two in adulthood (Hartup & Stevens, 1999). At the same time, the nature of the relationship changes.

CHARACTERISTICS OF ADOLESCENT FRIENDSHIPS When asked about the meaning of friendship, teenagers stress three characteristics. The most important is *intimacy,* or psychological closeness, which is supported by *mutual understanding* of each other's values, beliefs, and feelings. In addition, more than younger children, teenagers want their friends to be *loyal*—to stick up for them and not leave them for somebody else (Collins & Madsen, 2006).

Teenagers' strong desire for friendship closeness likely explains why they say friends are their most important sources of social support (Brown & Larson, 2009). As frankness and faithfulness increase, *self-disclosure* (sharing of private thoughts and feelings) between friends rises steadily over the adolescent years (see Figure 16.1). As a result, teenage friends get to know each other better as personalities. Cooperation, mutual affirmation, and feelings of companionship and caring between friends also increase—changes that reflect greater effort and skill at preserving the relationship and sensitivity to a friend's needs and desires (De Goede, Branje, & Meeus, 2009). Adolescents also are less possessive of their friends than they were in childhood (Parker et al., 2005). Desiring a certain degree of autonomy for themselves, they recognize that friends need this, too.

In addition to the many characteristics that school-age friends share (see Chapter 13, page 489), adolescent friends tend to be alike in identity status, educational aspirations, political beliefs, and willingness to try drugs and engage in lawbreaking acts. Over time, they become increasingly similar in these ways, and the more similar they are, the greater the likelihood that their friendships will be long-lasting (Bagwell & Schmidt, 2011; Hafen et al., 2011). Friendship similarity partly reflects the way adolescents' social world is organized. Most teenagers live in neighborhoods segregated by income, ethnicity, and belief systems. Through tracking, schools sort them further. But teenagers also choose companions like themselves to increase the supportiveness of friendship. Occasionally, however, adolescents choose friends with differing attitudes and values, which permits them to explore new perspectives within the security of a compatible relationship.

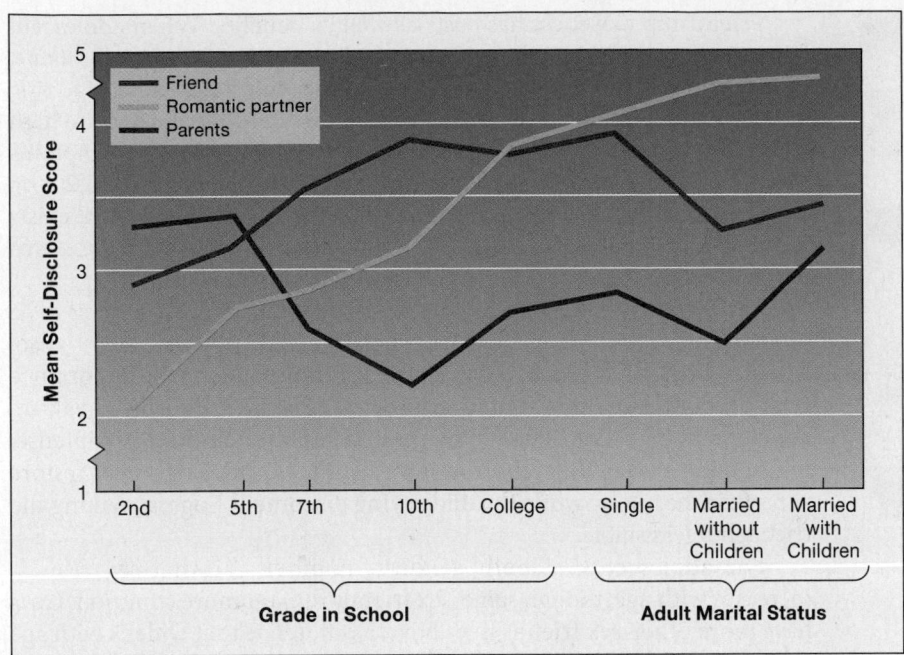

FIGURE 16.1 Age changes in reported self-disclosure to parents and peers, based on findings of several studies. Self-disclosure to friends increases steadily during adolescence, reflecting intimacy as a major basis of friendship. Self-disclosure to romantic partners also rises, but it does not surpass intimacy with friends until the college years. Self-disclosure to parents declines in early adolescence, a time of mild parent–child conflict. As family relationships readjust to the young person's increasing autonomy, self-disclosure to parents rises. (From D. Buhrmester, 1996, "Need Fulfillment, Interpersonal Competence, and the Developmental Contexts of Early Adolescent Friendship," in W. M. Bukowski, A. F. Newcomb, & W. W. Hartup, (Eds.), *The Company They Keep: Friendship in Childhood and Adolescence,* New York: Cambridge University Press, p. 168. Reprinted by permission of Cambridge University Press.)

Adolescent friendships—especially, best friendships—are fairly stable and become more so with age (Degirmencioglu et al., 1998). Nevertheless, the transition to middle school brings changes in friendships as teenagers encounter new peers and become interested in romantic relationships (Chan & Poulin, 2007; Hardy, Bukowski, & Sippola, 2002). And for a time, young teenagers often sacrifice similarity for admiration of superficial features—whether a potential friend is popular, physically attractive, athletically skilled, or defiant and aggressive (Bukowski, Sippola, & Newcomb, 2000).

With age, preference for friends who are prominent in the peer system subsides, and adolescents return to seeking friends whose traits, interests, and values resemble their own. Nevertheless, occasionally a friend's differing, positive traits have a favorable impact. In one study, low-achieving early adolescents who befriended a high-achieving classmate improved in academic performance (Altermatt & Pomerantz, 2005).

GENDER DIFFERENCES IN FRIENDSHIP QUALITY   TAKE A MOMENT... Ask several adolescent girls and boys to describe their close friendships. You are likely to find a consistent gender difference. Emotional closeness is more common between girls than boys (Hall, 2011; Markovits, Benenson, & Dolenszky, 2001). Girls frequently get together to "just talk," and their exchanges contain more self-disclosure and mutually supportive statements. In contrast, boys more often gather for an activity—usually sports and competitive games. Boys' discussions usually focus on accomplishments and mastery issues, such as attainments in sports and school, and involve more competition and conflict (Brendgen et al., 2001; Rubin, Bukowski, & Parker, 2006).

Because of gender-role expectations, girls' friendships typically focus on communal concerns, boys' on achievement and status. Boys, however, do form close friendship ties, but the quality of their friendships is more variable. When African-American, Asian-American, and Hispanic boys from low-income, urban families were asked to describe their friendships, they frequently mentioned closeness, mutual support, and self-disclosure—more often than their white counterparts. But as ethnic minority boys transitioned from mid- to late adolescence, many reported a decline in friendship closeness (Way, 2013; Way & Silverman, 2011). Though they continued to desire close male friends, their remarks revealed that masculine stereotypes—to be tough and unemotional—interfered with these bonds. Hispanic boys, however, were more likely than others to resist gender stereotypes (Way et al., 2014). They more often sustained intimate same-sex friendships.

Whereas girls tend to emphasize emotional closeness in their friendships, boys' more often gather for an activity—often sports or competitive games. This camper holds up a reward for catching the largest fish presented to him by his friends.

Friendship closeness has costs as well as benefits. When adolescent friends focus on deeper thoughts and feelings, they tend to *coruminate,* or repeatedly mull over problems and negative emotions, with girls doing so more often than boys. Corumination, while contributing to high friendship quality, also triggers anxiety and depression—symptoms more common in girls (Hankin, Stone, & Wright, 2010; Rose et al., 2014). And when conflict arises between intimate friends, more potential exists for one party to harm the other through relational aggression—for example, by divulging sensitive personal information to outsiders.

Partly for these reasons, girls' closest same-sex friendships tend to be of shorter duration than boys' (Benenson & Christakos, 2003). Also, whereas boys often resolve conflicts by minimizing their importance ("It's no big deal"), this strategy tends to result in friendship break-up among girls (Bowker, 2004). When friendships are emotionally intense, minimizing rather than confronting relationship tensions may restore superficial harmony while the underlying discontent lingers, making the friendship less stable.

For adolescents of both genders, number of other-sex friends increases with age, though same-sex friends remain more common. Girls have more other-sex friends than boys, a difference that widens with age as teenage girls form friendships with boys who are somewhat older (Poulin & Pedersen, 2007). Early-maturing girls have larger networks of other-sex friends, including older boys—relationships that can become contexts for antisocial behavior (see page 532 in Chapter 14).

Regardless of the gender make-up of friendships, adolescents report that girls provide more emotional support than boys (Poulin & Pedersen, 2007). Among boys without same-sex friends, having an other-sex friend is associated with feelings of competence. But girls with few or no same-sex friends and a greater number of other-sex friends report less positive psychological well-being and more antisocial behavior, such as drug and alcohol use (Bukowski, Sippola, & Hoza, 1999; Poulin & Denault, 2012). Perhaps these girls are especially likely to befriend boys with negative traits, such as disruptiveness and aggression.

FRIENDSHIPS, CELL PHONES, AND THE INTERNET Teenagers frequently use cell phones and the Internet to communicate with friends. About 77 percent of U.S. 12- to 17-year-olds have a cell phone. Texting has become the preferred means of electronic interaction between teenage friends, who send, on average, as many as 60 texts per day. Cell calling ranks second, followed by social networking sites and instant messaging (see Figure 16.2). Girls use cell phones to text and call their friends considerably more often than boys (Lenhart, 2012). These forms of online communication seem to support friendship closeness. In several studies, as amount of online messaging between preexisting friends increased, so did young people's perceptions of intimacy in the relationship and sense of well-being (Reich, Subrahmanyam, & Espinoza, 2012; Valkenburg & Peter, 2007a, 2007b, 2009). The effect is largely due to friends' online disclosure of personal information, such as worries, secrets, and romantic feelings.

Social networking sites such as Facebook—now used by more than 80 percent of U.S. teenagers—not only enable users to communicate with friends they know but to meet new people (Madden et al., 2013). The quality of adolescents' face-to-face relationships tends to be reproduced in this online medium. In a study of U.S. middle school students diverse in ethnicity and SES, those with positive face-to-face peer relationships had larger networks of webpage friends who frequently posted

FIGURE 16.2 **Percentage of U.S. 12- to 17-year-olds who use various communication channels daily to contact friends.** A nationally representative sample of 800 adolescents responded to a survey about their communication strategies with friends. Cell-phone texting was the preferred means of electronic communication, with nearly two-thirds reporting that they used it daily. (Based on Lenhart, 2012.)

supportive comments. Teenagers who reported engaging in delinquent acts tended to post hostile comments to their webpage "About Me" section. And those with depressive symptoms more often uploaded photos of themselves engaging in inappropriate behaviors (Mikami et al., 2010).

Adolescents are also frequent users of blogs, message boards, and chatrooms. Through these online associations, young people often explore central adolescent concerns—sexuality, challenges in parent and peer relationships, and identity issues, including attitudes and values—in contexts that may feel less threatening than similar conversations in the real world (Valkenburg & Peter, 2011). And teenagers suffering from eating disorders, depression, and other problems can access participants who provide mutual assistance, including a sense of group belonging and acceptance (Whitlock, Powers, & Eckenrode, 2006).

But online communication also poses dangers. In unmonitored chatrooms, teenagers are likely to encounter degrading racial and ethnic slurs and sexually obscene and harassing remarks (Subrahmanyam & Greenfield, 2008). And regardless of whether teen chatrooms are adult monitored, requests for romantic partners occur as frequently as two times per minute (Smahel & Subrahmanyam, 2007). Furthermore, although 60 percent of U.S. adolescent Facebook users keep their profiles private and 70 percent are friends with their parents, most are relatively unconcerned that information they share might be accessed by third parties without their knowledge. Over half post their e-mail address, and one-fifth their cell phone number. Adolescents are far more likely to describe their social media experiences as positive than negative, but about 17 percent report contact from strangers that made them feel scared or uncomfortable (Madden et al., 2013).

Finally, adolescent time devoted to social media is rising. For example, 30 percent of U.S. 12- to 17-year-olds send more than 100 texts per day, with half of these sending more than 200. And more than 70 percent use social networking sites for an average of 37 minutes per day. Some evidence suggests that very high social media use is linked to unsatisfying face-to-face social experiences, boredom, unhappiness, and Internet addiction (obsessive Internet use) (Madden et al., 2013; Pea et al., 2012; Smahel, Brown, & Blinka, 2012). Furthermore, high Internet consumers often engage in "face-to-face multitasking," such as texting at the dinner table or web surfing while chatting with friends (Abelson, Ledeen, & Lewis, 2008). These behaviors detract from high-quality face-to-face communication.

In sum, the Internet's value for enabling convenient and satisfying interaction among teenage friends must be weighed against its potential for facilitating harmful social consequences. Parents are wise to point out the risks of Internet communication, including excessive use, harassment, and exploitation, and to insist that teenagers follow Internet safety rules (see *www.safeteens.com*).

FRIENDSHIP AND ADJUSTMENT   As long as adolescent friendships are high in trust, intimate sharing, and support and not characterized by relational aggression or attraction to antisocial behavior, they contribute to many aspects of psychological health and competence into early adulthood (Bagwell & Schmidt, 2011; Waldrip, 2008), for several reasons:

- *Close friendships provide opportunities to explore the self and develop a deep understanding of another.* Through open, honest communication, friends become sensitive to each other's strengths and weaknesses, needs and desires—a process that supports the development of self-concept, perspective taking, and identity.
- *Close friendships provide a foundation for future intimate relationships.* Recall from Figure 16.1 that self-disclosure to friends precedes disclosure to romantic partners. Conversations with teenage friends about sexuality and romance, along with the intimacy of friendship itself, may help adolescents establish and work out problems in romantic partnerships (Connolly & Goldberg, 1999).
- *Close friendships help young people deal with the stresses of adolescence.* By enhancing sensitivity to and concern for another, supportive friendships promote empathy, sympathy, and prosocial behavior. As a result, they contribute to involvement in constructive youth activities, avoidance of antisocial acts, and psychological well-being (Lansford et al., 2003; Wentzel, Barry, & Caldwell, 2004).

LOOK *and* LISTEN

Interview several adolescents about qualities they value most in their best friends. Ask how friendships have helped them cope with stress and resulted in other personal benefits.

- *Close friendships can improve adolescents' attitudes toward and involvement in school.* Close friendships promote good school adjustment, academically and socially, in both middle- and low-SES students (Wentzel, Barry, & Caldwell, 2004). Teenagers who enjoy interacting with friends at school may begin to view all aspects of school life more positively.

Cliques and Crowds

In early adolescence, *peer groups* (see Chapter 13) become increasingly common and tightly knit. They are organized into **cliques**—groups of about five to eight members who are friends and, therefore, usually resemble one another in family background, attitudes, values, and interests (Brown & Dietz, 2009). At first, cliques are limited to same-sex members. Among girls but not boys, being in a clique predicts academic and social competence. Clique membership is more important to girls, who use it as a context for expressing emotional closeness (Henrich et al., 2000). By midadolescence, mixed-sex cliques become common.

Among adolescents attending high schools with complex social structures, often several cliques with similar values form a larger, more loosely organized group called a **crowd.** Unlike the more intimate clique, membership in a crowd is based on reputation and stereotype, granting the adolescent an identity within the larger social structure of the school.

Prominent crowds in typical North American and European high schools include "brains" (nonathletes who enjoy academics), "jocks" (who are very involved in sports), "populars" (class leaders with high peer acceptance), "partyers" (who value socializing but care little about schoolwork), "nonconformists" (who like unconventional clothing and music), "burnouts" (who frequently use alcohol and drugs, engage in sexual risk taking, and otherwise get into trouble), and "normals" (average to good students who get along with most other peers) (Stone & Brown, 1999; Sussman et al., 2007). In an investigation of high school crowds in Singapore, consistent with the country's high valuing of academic achievement, brains were more prominent and jocks less prominent than in Western high schools (Sim & Yeo, 2012). And a Singaporean popular crowd could not be identified.

What influences the assortment of teenagers into cliques and crowds? Crowd affiliations are linked to strengths in adolescents' self-concepts, which reflect their abilities and interests (Prinstein & La Greca, 2002). Ethnicity also plays a role. Minority teenagers who associate with an ethnically defined crowd, as opposed to a crowd reflecting their abilities and interests, sometimes are motivated by discrimination in their school or neighborhood. Alternatively, they may have joined the crowd as an expression of a strong ethnic identity (Brown et al., 2008). Family factors are important, too. In a study of 8,000 ninth to twelfth graders, adolescents who described their parents as authoritative were members of "brain," "jock," and "popular" groups that accepted both adult and peer reward systems. In contrast, boys with permissive parents aligned themselves with the "partyers" and "burnouts," suggesting lack of identification with conventional reward systems (Durbin et al., 1993).

These findings indicate that many peer-group values are extensions of values acquired at home. Once adolescents join a clique or crowd, it can modify their beliefs and behavior. In research on crowd affiliation and health-risk behaviors, brains were the lowest risk takers, populars and jocks were intermediate, and nonconformists and burnouts were the highest, often engaging in unhealthy eating, drug use, and unprotected sex and agreeing that they would "do anything on a dare" (La Greca, Prinstein, & Fetter, 2001; Mackey & La Greca, 2007). Furthermore, in a Dutch longitudinal study, membership in nonconventional crowds predicted a rise in internalizing and externalizing problems (Doornwaard et al., 2012). Perhaps nonconventional youths respond with anxiety and depressive symptoms to feeling disliked by members of higher-status crowds. And within their own crowds, they are more likely to experience peer modeling and encouragement for antisocial behavior.

© SYRACUSE NEWSPAPERS/PETER CHEN/THE IMAGE WORKS

These high school drama club members form a crowd, establishing relationships on the basis of shared interests. Crowd membership grants them an identity within the larger social structure of the school.

Although conventional-crowd memberships tend to be associated with better adjustment, the positive impact of having academically and socially skilled peers is greatest for teenagers whose own parents are authoritative. And the negative impact of having antisocial, drug-using friends is strongest for teenagers whose parents use less effective child-rearing styles (Mounts & Steinberg, 1995). In sum, family experiences affect the extent to which teenagers become like other group members over time.

As interest in dating increases, boys' and girls' cliques come together. Mixed-sex cliques provide boys and girls with models of how to interact and a chance to do so without having to be intimate (Connolly et al., 2004). Gradually, the larger group divides into couples, several of whom spend time going out together. By late adolescence, when boys and girls feel comfortable about approaching each other directly, the mixed-sex clique disappears (Connolly & Goldberg, 1999).

Crowds also decline in importance. As adolescents settle on personal values and goals, they no longer feel a need to broadcast, through dress, language, and preferred activities, who they are. From tenth to twelfth grade, many young people switch crowds, mostly in conventional directions (Doornwaard et al., 2012). Brains, popular, and normal crowds grow and deviant crowds lose members as teenagers focus more on their future.

Both cliques and crowds serve vital functions. The clique provides a context for acquiring social skills and experimenting with values and roles. The crowd offers the security of a temporary identity as adolescents separate from the family and construct a coherent sense of self (Newman & Newman, 2001).

Dating

The hormonal changes of puberty increase sexual interest (see Chapter 14), but cultural expectations determine when and how dating begins. Asian youths start dating later and have fewer dating partners than young people in Western societies, which tolerate and even encourage romantic involvements between teenagers from middle school on (see Figure 16.3). At age 12 to 14, these relationships are usually casual, lasting only briefly. By age 16, they have become steady relationships, continuing, on average, for one to two years, though breakups remain common for about one-third (Carver, Joyner, & Udry, 2003; Manning et al., 2014). Early adolescents tend to mention recreation and achieving peer status as reasons for dating. By late adolescence, as young people are ready for greater psychological intimacy, they look for dating partners who offer personal compatibility, companionship, affection, and social support (Collins & van Dulmen, 2006a; Meier & Allen, 2009).

The achievement of intimacy between dating partners typically lags behind that between friends. And positive relationships with parents and friends contribute to the development of warm romantic ties, whereas conflict-ridden parent–adolescent and peer relationships forecast hostile dating interactions (Furman & Collins, 2009; Linder & Collins, 2005). Recall from Chapter 7 that according to ethological theory, early attachment bonds lead to an *internal working model*, or set of expectations about attachment figures, that guides later close relationships. Consistent with this idea, secure attachment to parents in infancy and childhood—together with recollections of that security in adolescence—predicts quality of teenagers' and young adults' friendships and romantic ties (Collins & van Dulmen, 2006b; Collins, Welsh, & Furman, 2009). In a study of high school seniors, secure models of attachment and supportive interactions with parents predicted secure models of friendship, which, in turn, were related to the security of romantic relationships (Furman et al., 2002).

Perhaps because early adolescent dating relationships are shallow and stereotyped, early dating is related to drug use, delinquency, and poor academic achievement (Eaton et al., 2007; Miller et al., 2009). These factors, along with a history of uninvolved parenting and aggression in family and peer relationships, increase the likelihood

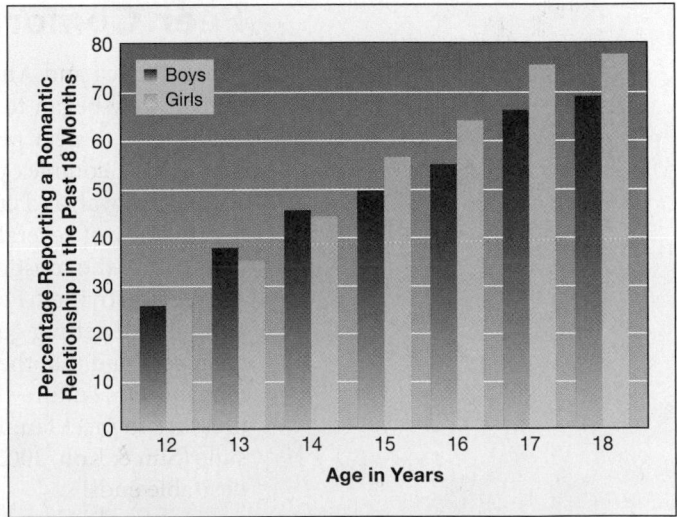

FIGURE 16.3 Increase in romantic relationships during adolescence. More than 16,000 U.S. youths responded to an interview in which they indicated whether they had been involved in a romantic relationship during the past 18 months. At age 12, about one-fourth of young people reported romantic involvement, a figure that rose to about three-fourths at age 18. (Based on Carver, Joyner, & Udry, 2003.)

© SCOTT HORTOP/ALAMY

As long as dating does not begin too soon, it extends the benefits of adolescent friendships, promoting sensitivity, empathy, and identity development.

of dating violence. About 10 to 20 percent of adolescents are physically or sexually abused by dating partners; boys and girls are equally likely to report being victims, and violence by one partner is often returned by the other (Narayan, Englund, & Egeland, 2013; Narayan et al., 2014; National Institute of Justice, 2014). Mental health consequences are severe, including increased anxiety, depression, alcohol and drug use, suicide attempts, risky sexual behavior, and—in girls—unhealthy weight control (vomiting and use of laxatives) (Exner-Cortens, Eckenrode, & Rothman, 2012; Silverman et al., 2001). Furthermore, whereas early adolescent boys who date gain in status among same-sex peers, girls often experience conflict due to competition and jealousy of other girls. For all these reasons, young teenagers are better off sticking with group activities, such as parties and dances, before becoming involved with a steady boyfriend or girlfriend.

Lesbian and gay youths face special challenges in initiating and maintaining visible romances. Recall from Chapter 14 that because of intense prejudice, sexual minority adolescents sometimes retreat into heterosexual dating. Although more adolescents are identifying their sexual orientation to others than in the past, many have difficulty finding a partner because their peers with same-sex romantic interests have not yet come out (Glover, Galliher, & Lamere, 2009). Often their first contacts with other sexual-minority youths occur in support groups, where they are free to date publicly and can discuss concerns about coming out.

As long as it does not begin too soon, dating provides lessons in cooperation, etiquette, and dealing with people in a wide range of situations. Among older teenagers, close romantic ties promote sensitivity, empathy, self-esteem, social support, and identity development. In addition, teenagers' increasing capacity for interdependence and compromise within dating enhances the quality of other peer relationships (Collins, Welsh, & Furman, 2009).

Still, many romances do not survive high school graduation, and those that do usually become less satisfying (Shaver, Furman, & Buhrmester, 1985). Because young people are still forming their identities, high school couples often find that they have little in common later. Nevertheless, warm, caring romantic ties in adolescence can have long-term implications. They are positively related to gratifying, committed relationships in early adulthood (Meier & Allen, 2009).

Peer Conformity

When Franca and Antonio discovered Louis's lawbreaking during his freshman year of high school, they began to worry about the negative side of adolescent peer networks. Although conformity to peer pressure is greater during adolescence than in childhood or early adulthood, it is a complex process, varying with the young person's age, current situation, need for social approval, and culture.

A study of several hundred U.S. youths revealed that adolescents felt greatest pressure to conform to the most obvious aspects of the peer culture—dress, grooming, and participation in social activities. Peer pressure to engage in proadult behavior, such as cooperating with parents and getting good grades, was also strong (Brown, Lohr, & McClenahan, 1986). Many teenagers said that their friends actively discouraged antisocial acts. In research conducted in Singapore, a culture that emphasizes family loyalty, outcomes were similar, except that peer pressure to meet family and school obligations exceeded pressure to join in peer-culture pursuits (Sim & Koh, 2003). As these findings reveal, adults and peers often act in concert, toward desirable ends!

As our discussion in Chapter 14 revealed, changes in the brain at puberty contribute to both increased reward-seeking and receptiveness to peer influence, which gradually decline with age. Still, wide individual differences exist (Sumter et al., 2009). Personal characteristics make a difference: Young people who feel competent and worthwhile, who score low in sensation-seeking, and who are more effective decision makers are less likely to fall in line with peer antisocial activity (Crockett, Raffaelli, & Shen, 2006; McIntyre & Platania, 2009). Authoritative child rearing is also influential. When parents are supportive and exert appropriate oversight, teenagers respect them—an attitude that acts as an antidote to unfavorable peer pressure (Dorius et al., 2004). In contrast, adolescents whose parents exert either too much or too little control tend to be highly peer-oriented. Youths who bend easily to peer influence display wide-ranging problems, including unstable friendships, aggression, delinquency, and declining peer acceptance and increasing depressive symptoms over time (Allen, Porter, & McFarland, 2006).

Ask Yourself

- **REVIEW** Describe the distinct positive functions of friendships, cliques, and crowds in adolescence. What factors lead some friendships and peer-group ties to be harmful?

- **CONNECT** How might gender intensification, discussed on page 605, contribute to the shallow quality of early adolescent dating relationships?

- **APPLY** Thirteen-year-old Mattie's parents are warm, firm in their expectations, and consistent in monitoring her activities. At school, Mattie met some girls who want her to tell her parents she's going to a friend's house and then, instead, join them at the beach for a party. Is Mattie likely to comply? Explain.

- **REFLECT** How did family experiences influence your crowd membership in high school? How did crowd membership influence your behavior?

Problems of Development

16.11 Describe factors related to adolescent depression and suicide.

16.12 Discuss factors related to delinquency.

Most young people move through adolescence with little disturbance. But as we have seen, some encounter major disruptions in development, such as early parenthood, substance abuse, and school failure. In each instance, biological and psychological changes, families, schools, peers, communities, and culture combine to yield particular outcomes. Serious difficulties rarely occur in isolation but are usually interrelated—as is apparent in three additional problems of the teenage years: depression, suicide, and delinquency.

Depression

Depression—feeling sad, frustrated, and hopeless about life, accompanied by loss of pleasure in most activities and disturbances in sleep, appetite, concentration, and energy—is the most common psychological problem of adolescence. Among U.S. teenagers, 20 to 50 percent experience mild to moderate feelings of depression, bouncing back after a short time. More worrisome are the 15 to 20 percent who have had one or more major depressive episodes, a rate comparable to that of adults. About 5 percent are chronically depressed—gloomy and self-critical for many months and sometimes years (American Psychiatric Association, 2013; Graber & Sontag, 2009).

Serious depression affects only 1 to 2 percent of children, who are far less likely than their adolescent counterparts to remain depressed when reassessed at older ages, including into adulthood (Carballo et al., 2011; Maughan, Collishaw, & Stringaris, 2012). In industrialized nations, depression increases sharply from ages 12 to 16. Teenage girls are twice as likely as boys to report persistent depressed mood—a difference sustained throughout the lifespan (Dekker et al., 2007; Hyde, Mezulis, & Abramson, 2008).

If allowed to continue, depression seriously impairs social, academic, and vocational functioning. Unfortunately, the stereotypical view of adolescence

RICHARD CLARK/GETTY IMAGES

Depression in teenagers should not be dismissed as just a passing phase. Without treatment, it can persist, leading to long-term adjustment problems.

as a period of storm and stress leads many adults to minimize the seriousness of adolescent depression, misinterpreting the despondency and irritability that accompany it as just a passing phase (Tharpar et al., 2012). As a result, the overwhelming majority of depressed teenagers do not receive treatment.

FACTORS RELATED TO ADOLESCENT DEPRESSION   The precise combination of biological and environmental factors leading to depression varies from one individual to the next. Twin studies indicate that depression is modestly heritable (see page 83 in Chapter 2). Furthermore, onset of depression in girls is more closely associated with the hormonal changes of puberty than with age (Angold et al., 1999). This suggests that the impact of estrogens on the adolescent brain is involved.

But pubertal hormone changes alone rarely trigger depression. Rather, genetic and hormonal risk factors seem to sensitize the brain to react more strongly to stressful experiences (Natsuaki, Samuels, & Leve, 2014). In support of this view, mounting evidence indicates that the short 5-HTTLPR gene (see page 258 in Chapter 7), which increases the likelihood of fear and self-regulation difficulties, is linked to adolescent depression, but only in the presence of negative life stressors (Karg et al., 2011; Li, Berk, & Lee, 2013; Uher & McGuffin, 2009). This gene–environment interaction operates more consistently in adolescent girls than in boys.

Although depression runs in families, recall from earlier chapters that depressed or otherwise stressed parents often engage in maladaptive parenting. As a result, their child's emotional self-regulation, attachment, and self-esteem may be impaired, with serious consequences for cognitive and social skills (Yap, Allen, & Ladouceur, 2008). In a vulnerable young person, numerous negative life events may spark depression—for example, failing at something important, parental divorce, the end of a close friendship or romantic partnership, victimization through bullying, or other abusive experiences.

GENDER DIFFERENCES   Why are girls more prone to depression than boys? Besides stressful life events, gender-typed coping styles seem to be involved. Early-maturing girls are especially prone to depression (see Chapter 14). Adolescent gender intensification may strengthen girls' passivity, dependency, and tendency to ruminate on (repetitively mull over) anxieties and problems—maladaptive approaches to tasks expected of teenagers in complex cultures. Consistent with this explanation, adolescents who identify strongly with "feminine" traits ruminate more and tend to be more depressed, regardless of their sex (Lopez, Driscoll, & Kistner, 2009; Papadakis et al., 2006). In contrast, girls with either an androgynous or a "masculine" gender identity show low rates of depressive symptoms (Priess, Lindberg, & Hyde, 2009).

In China, depression is more common in boys than in girls—a reversal of the sex difference typical in industrialized nations. Chinese boys report a higher level of stressful life events, including parental pressures and school performance expectations.

Having friends with depressive symptoms is linked to a rise in teenagers' own depressive symptoms, perhaps because corumination is high in such relationships (Conway et al., 2011). Girls who repeatedly feel overwhelmed by life challenges become even more physiologically reactive to stress and cope increasingly poorly (Hyde, Mezulis, & Abramson, 2008; Natsuaki, Samuels, & Leve, 2014). In this way, stressful experiences and stress reactivity feed on each other, sustaining depression.

An investigation of more than 17,000 urban youths in China underscores cultural variation in adolescent depression, along with the contributions of both stressors and ineffective coping. More Chinese boys than girls reported feeling depressed during the previous week. But boys also experienced a greater number of stressful life events, resulting from parental pressures, school performance expectations, health problems, and romantic involvements (Sun et al., 2010). Adaptive coping was linked to reduced depression in Chinese teenagers of both genders.

In Western youths as well, effective coping skills protect against depression. And good parenting—warmth, acceptance, and low coercive and psychological control—and supportive peer relationships promote resilience in adolescents at risk for depression, helping them manage stress successfully (Auerbach et al., 2011; Pargas et al., 2010).

Profound depression in adolescence predicts depression in adulthood and serious impairments in work, family life, and social life. And depression often leads to suicidal thoughts, which all too often are translated into action.

Suicide

Compared with his sister, who was an outstanding student, 17-year-old Brad couldn't measure up. With adulthood just around the corner, Brad's parents berated him for his lack of direction. "At your age, you oughta have a clue about where you're going!" Brad's father shouted. "Pick a college, get a trade—just stop sitting around!"

In high school, Brad had been a loner. He excelled in art class and spent hours in his room, sketching. Although Brad's parents worried that he seemed unhappy and didn't have many friends, they never showed much interest in his drawings, which were piled in a corner of his room. And they consoled themselves that at least he wasn't getting into trouble.

One day, Brad got up enough nerve to ask a girl out. His father, encouraged by Brad's interest in dating, gave him permission to use the family car. But when Brad arrived to pick up his date, she wasn't home. Several hours later, Brad's parents got a call from the police. He had been picked up for speeding, "driving under the influence," and evading the police. The chase through city streets ended when Brad drove into a ditch. Although he wasn't injured, the car was totaled. A terrible argument followed between Brad and his parents.

Over the next two days, Brad was somber and withdrawn. Then, after dinner one night, he seemed resolved to make things better. "I've taken care of things. I won't cause any more problems," he told his parents. Handing several of his favorite drawings to his sister, he said, "Here, I want you to have these—for keeps, to think of me." Early the next morning, Brad's parents found him hanging from a rope in his room.

FACTORS RELATED TO ADOLESCENT SUICIDE The suicide rate increases from childhood to late adulthood, but it jumps sharply at adolescence. Currently, suicide is the third-leading cause of death among American youths, after motor vehicle collisions and homicides. Perhaps because U.S. teenagers experience more stress and fewer supports than in the past, the adolescent suicide rate tripled between the mid-1960s and the mid-1990s. This was followed by a period of little change and, from the mid-2000s on, a slight increase (Centers for Disease Control and Prevention, 2014g). At the same time, rates of adolescent suicide vary widely among industrialized nations—low in Greece, Italy, and Spain; intermediate in Australia, Canada, Japan, and the United States; and high in Finland, Ireland, New Zealand, Norway, and Russia (Patton et al., 2012; Värnik et al., 2012). These international differences remain unexplained.

Striking gender differences in suicidal behavior exist. Despite girls' higher rates of depression, the number of boys who kill themselves exceeds the number of girls by a ratio of over 4 to 1. Boys have more risk factors for suicide, including substance abuse and aggression. Also, girls make more unsuccessful suicide attempts and use methods from which they are more likely to be revived, such as a sleeping pill overdose. In contrast, boys more often choose techniques that lead to instant death, such as firearms or hanging (Esposito-Smythers et al., 2014). Gender-role expectations may contribute; less tolerance exists for feelings of helplessness and failed efforts in males than in females.

Perhaps because of greater support from extended families, African Americans, Asian Americans, and Hispanics have slightly lower suicide rates than Caucasian Americans. Recently, however, suicide has risen among African-American adolescent males; the current rate approaches that

Compared to girls, boys have more risk factors for suicide and more often choose techniques for committing it that succeed.

of Caucasian-American males. And Native-American youths commit suicide at rates two to six times national averages (Centers for Disease Control and Prevention, 2014g). High rates of profound family poverty, school failure, alcohol and drug abuse, and depression probably underlie these trends—factors that also make homeless, runaway, and imprisoned youths prone to suicide (Spirito & Esposito-Smythers, 2006).

Lesbian, gay, and bisexual youths also are at high risk, attempting suicide three times as often as other adolescents. Those who have tried to kill themselves report more family conflict over their gender-atypical behavior, problems in romantic relationships, and peer victimization due to their sexual orientation (D'Augelli et al., 2005; Liu & Mustanski, 2012).

Suicide tends to occur in two types of young people. The first group includes adolescents much like Brad—highly intelligent but solitary, withdrawn, and unable to meet their own standards or those of important people in their lives. Members of a second, larger group show antisocial tendencies and express their unhappiness through bullying, fighting, stealing, increased risk taking, and drug abuse (Spirito et al., 2012). Besides being hostile and destructive toward others, they turn their anger and disappointment inward.

Suicidal adolescents often have a family history of emotional and antisocial disorders and suicide, and they typically suffer from chronic depression, anxiety, and unresolved anger. In addition, they are likely to have experienced multiple stressful life events, including economic disadvantage, parental divorce, frequent parent–child conflict, and abuse and neglect. Stressors typically increase during the period preceding a suicide attempt or completion (Kaminski et al., 2010). Triggering events include parental blaming of the teenager for family problems, the breakup of an important peer relationship, or the humiliation of having been caught engaging in antisocial acts.

Public policies resulting in cultural disintegration have amplified suicide rates among Native-American youths. From the late 1800s to the 1970s, Native-American families were forced to enroll their children in government-run residential boarding schools designed to erase tribal affiliations. In these repressive institutions, children were not allowed to "be Indian" in any way—culturally, linguistically, artistically, or spiritually (Goldston et al., 2008). The experience left many young people academically unprepared and emotionally scarred, contributing to family and community disorganization in current and succeeding generations (Barnes, Josefowitz, & Cole, 2006; Howell & Yuille, 2004). Consequently, alcohol abuse, youth crime, and suicide rates escalated.

Why does suicide increase in adolescence? In addition to the rise in depressed mood, teenagers' improved ability to plan ahead is a major factor. Although some act impulsively, many young people, like Brad, take purposeful steps toward killing themselves. Other cognitive changes also contribute. Belief in the personal fable (see Chapter 15) leads many depressed young people to conclude that no one could possibly understand their intense pain. As a result, despair, hopelessness, and isolation deepen. Suicidal behavior often recurs, with about 10 percent of attempters trying again within 6 months and more than 40 percent within 21 months (Hawton, Zahl, & Weatherall, 2003). A prior suicide attempt is the strongest predictor of suicide completion.

PREVENTION AND TREATMENT To prevent suicide, parents and teachers must be trained to pick up on the signals that a troubled teenager sends (see Table 16.3). Schools and community settings, such as recreational and religious organizations, can help by strengthening adolescents' connections with their cultural heritage and providing knowledgeable, approachable, and sympathetic adults, peer support groups, and information about telephone hot lines (Miller, 2011; Spirito et al., 2012). Once a teenager takes steps toward suicide, staying with the young person, listening, and expressing compassion and concern until professional help can be obtained are essential. Applying What We Know on the following page offers suggestions for how to respond to a young person who might be suicidal.

TABLE 16.3   **Warning Signs of Suicide**
Efforts to put personal affairs in order—smoothing over troubled relationships, giving away treasured possessions
Verbal cues—saying goodbye to family members and friends, making direct or indirect references to suicide ("I won't have to worry about these problems much longer"; "I wish I were dead")
Feelings of sadness, despondency, "not caring" anymore
Extreme fatigue, lack of energy, boredom
No desire to socialize; withdrawal from friends and family
Easily frustrated
Volatile mood swings—spells of crying or laughing, angry outbursts
Inability to concentrate, distractibility
Decline in grades, absence from school, discipline problems
Neglect of personal appearance
Sleep change—loss of sleep or excessive sleepiness
Obtaining a weapon or other means of self-harm, such as prescription medications

Applying What We Know

Ways to Respond to a Young Person Who Might Be Suicidal

STRATEGY	DESCRIPTION
Be psychologically and physically available.	Grant the young person your full attention, indicate when and where you can be located, and emphasize that you are always willing to talk.
Communicate a caring, capable attitude.	With such statements as "I'm concerned. I care about you," encourage the adolescent to discuss feelings of despair. Conveying a capable attitude helps redirect the young person away from a world of confusion toward psychological order.
Assess the immediacy of risk.	Gently inquire into the young person's motives: "Do you want to harm yourself? Do you want to die or kill yourself?" If the answer is yes, ask about the adolescent's plan. If it is specific (involving a method and a time), the risk of suicide is high.
Empathize with the young person's feelings.	Express empathy through such statements as "I understand your confusion and pain." Empathy increases your persuasive power and defuses the adolescent's negative emotion.
Oppose the suicidal intent.	Communicate sensitively but firmly that suicide is not an acceptable solution and that you want to help the adolescent explore other options.
Offer a plan for help.	Offer to assist the young person in finding professional help and in telling others, such as parents and school officials, who need to know about the problem.
Obtain a commitment.	Ask the adolescent to agree to the plan. If the young person refuses, negotiate a promise to contact you or another supportive person if and when suicidal thoughts return.

Source: National Center for Mental Health Promotion and Youth Violence Prevention, 2006.

Treatments for depressed and suicidal adolescents range from antidepressant medication to individual, family, and group therapy. Sometimes hospitalization is necessary to ensure the teenager's safety. Until the adolescent improves, removing weapons, knives, razors, scissors, and drugs from the home is vital. Strengthening social supports and training young people in effective strategies for coping with stress and depressed mood promote resilience and can prevent repeated suicide attempts (Goldney, 2013). On a broader scale, gun-control legislation that limits adolescents' access to the most frequent and deadly suicide method in the United States would greatly reduce both the number of suicides and the high teenage homicide rate (Lewiecki & Miller, 2013).

After a suicide, family and peer survivors need support to help them cope with grief, anger, and guilt over not having been able to help the victim. Teenage suicides often occur in clusters, with one death increasing the likelihood of others among depressed peers who knew the young person or heard about the death through the media (Feigelman & Gorman, 2008). In view of this trend, an especially watchful eye must be kept on vulnerable adolescents after a suicide happens. Restraint by journalists in publicizing teenage suicides also aids prevention.

Delinquency

Juvenile delinquents are children or adolescents who engage in illegal acts. Youth crime has declined in the United States since the mid-1990s. Nevertheless, 12- to 17-year-olds account for about 11 percent of police arrests, although they constitute only 8 percent of the population (U.S. Department of Justice, 2013). When asked directly and confidentially about lawbreaking, almost all teenagers admit to having committed some sort of offense—usually a minor crime, such as petty stealing or disorderly conduct (Flannery et al., 2003).

Both police arrests and self-reports show that delinquency rises over early and middle adolescence and then declines (Farrington, 2009; U.S. Department of Justice, 2013). Recall that antisocial behavior increases among teenagers as a result of heightened reward seeking and desire for peer approval. Over time, peers become

Delinquency rises over early and middle adolescence, mostly involving petty stealing, disorderly conduct, or occasional drug use. But a small percentage of young people engage in repeated serious offenses.

Biology and Environment

Two Routes to Adolescent Delinquency

Persistent adolescent delinquency follows two paths of development, one involving a small number of youths with an onset of conduct problems in childhood, the second a larger number with an onset in adolescence. The early-onset type is far more likely to lead to a life-course pattern of aggression and criminality (Moffitt, 2007). The late-onset type usually does not persist beyond the transition to early adulthood.

Both childhood-onset and adolescent-onset youths engage in serious offenses; associate with deviant peers; participate in substance abuse, unsafe sex, and dangerous driving; and spend time in correctional facilities. Why does antisocial activity more often continue and escalate into violence in the first group?

Longitudinal studies yield similar answers to this question. Most research has focused on boys, but several investigations report that girls who were physically aggressive in childhood are also at risk for later problems—occasionally violent delinquency but more often other norm-violating behaviors and psychological disorders (Broidy et al., 2003; Chamberlain, 2003). Early relational aggression is linked to adolescent conduct problems as well.

Early-Onset Type

Early-onset youngsters seem to inherit traits that predispose them to aggressiveness (Pettit, 2004). For example, violence-prone boys are emotionally negative, restless, willful, and physically aggressive as early as age 2. They also show subtle deficits in cognitive functioning that seem to contribute to disruptions in the development of language, memory, and cognitive and emotional self-regulation (Moffitt, 2007; Shaw et al., 2003). Some have attention-deficit hyperactivity disorder (ADHD), which compounds their learning and self-control problems (see Chapter 12, page 438).

Yet these biological risks are not sufficient to sustain antisocial behavior: Most early-onset boys decline in aggression over time. Among those who follow the life-course path, inept parenting transforms their undercontrolled style into defiance and persistent aggression (Brame, Nagin, & Tremblay, 2001; Broidy et al., 2003). As they fail academically and are rejected by peers, they befriend other deviant youths, who facilitate one another's violent behavior while relieving loneliness (see Figure 16.4) (Hughes, 2010; Lacourse et al., 2003). Limited cognitive and social skills result in high rates of school dropout

and unemployment, contributing further to antisocial involvements. Often these boys experience their first arrest before age 14—a good indicator that they will be chronic offenders by age 18 (Patterson & Yoerger, 2002).

Preschoolers high in relational aggression also tend to be hyperactive and frequently in conflict with peers and adults (Willoughby, Kupersmidt, & Bryant, 2001). As these behaviors trigger peer rejection, relationally aggressive girls befriend other girls high in relational hostility, and their relational aggression rises (Werner & Crick, 2004). Adolescents high in relational aggression are often angry, vengeful, and defiant of adult rules. Among teenagers who combine physical and relational hostility, these oppositional reactions intensify, increasing the likelihood of serious antisocial activity (Harachi et al., 2006; Prinstein, Boergers, & Vernberg, 2001).

Late-Onset Type

Other youths first display antisocial behavior around the time of puberty, gradually increasing their involvement. Their conduct problems arise from the peer context of early adolescence, not from biological deficits and a history of

less influential; decision making, emotional self-regulation, and moral reasoning improve; and young people enter social contexts (such as higher education, work, marriage, and career) that are less conducive to lawbreaking.

For most adolescents, a brush with the law does not forecast long-term antisocial behavior. But repeated arrests are cause for concern. Teenagers are responsible for 11 percent of violent offenses in the United States (U.S. Department of Justice, 2013). A small percentage become recurrent offenders, who commit most of these crimes, and some enter a life of crime. As the Biology and Environment box above reveals, childhood-onset conduct problems are far more likely to persist than conduct problems that first appear in adolescence.

FACTORS RELATED TO DELINQUENCY   Boys exceed girls in delinquent acts of all kinds, and in adolescence, the gender gap in physical aggression widens (Chesney-Lind, 2001; Gault-Sherman, 2013). Although girls account for about one in five adolescent arrests for violence, their offenses are largely limited to simple assault (such as pushing and spitting), the least serious category. Once labeled status offenses (noncriminal behavior), today these acts are more likely to lead to arrests, especially in physical exchanges with parents, who may report the youth's behavior to the police (Chesney-Lind & Belknap, 2004). Serious violent crime, however, is mostly the domain of boys (U.S. Department of Justice, 2013).

SES and ethnicity are strong predictors of arrests but only mildly related to teenagers' self-reports of antisocial acts. The difference is due to the tendency to arrest, charge, and punish low-SES ethnic minority youths more often than their higher-SES

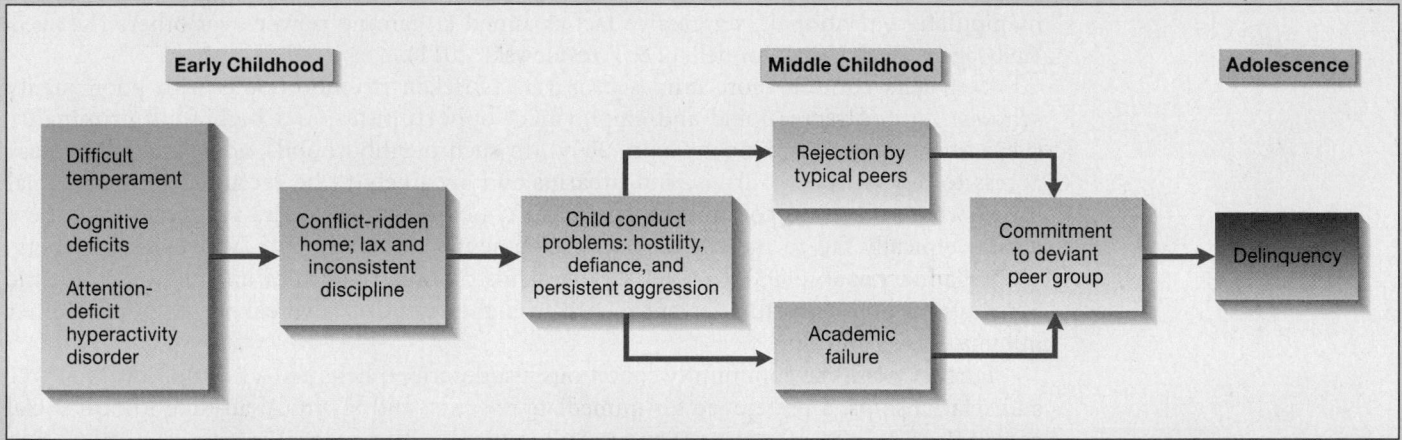

FIGURE 16.4 **Path to chronic delinquency for adolescents with childhood-onset antisocial behavior.** Difficult temperament and cognitive deficits characterize many of these youths in early childhood; some have attention-deficit hyperactivity disorder. Inept parenting transforms biologically based self-control difficulties into hostility and defiance.

unfavorable development. For some, quality of parenting may decline for a time, perhaps because of family stresses or the challenges of disciplining an unruly teenager (Moffitt, 2007). When age brings gratifying adult privileges, these youths draw on prosocial skills mastered before adolescence and abandon their antisocial ways.

A few late-onset youths do continue to engage in antisocial acts. The seriousness of their adolescent offenses seems to trap them in situations that close off opportunities for responsible behavior. Being employed or in school and forming positive, close relationships predict an end to criminal offending by age 20 to 25 (Farrington, Ttofi, & Coid, 2009). In contrast, the longer antisocial young people spend in prison, the more likely they are to sustain a life of crime.

These findings suggest a need for a fresh look at policies aimed at stopping youth crime. Keeping youth offenders locked up for many years disrupts their educational and vocational lives and access to positive, caring relationships with adults during a crucial period of development (Bernstein, 2014). In this way, juvenile incarceration condemns them to a bleak future.

white and Asian counterparts (Farrington, 2009; U.S. Department of Justice, 2013). In isolation from other life circumstances, ethnicity tells us little about youths' propensity to engage in violence and other lawbreaking acts.

Difficult temperament, low intelligence, poor school performance, peer rejection in childhood, and association with antisocial peers are linked to chronic delinquency (Laird et al., 2005). How do these factors fit together? One of the most consistent findings is that delinquent youths diverse in ethnicity and SES experience parenting that is low in warmth, high in conflict, and characterized by harsh, inconsistent discipline and weak control and monitoring (Deutsch et al., 2012; Harris-McKoy & Cui, 2013). Because marital transitions often contribute to family discord and disrupted parenting, boys who experience parental separation and divorce are especially prone to delinquency (Farrington, 2009). And youth crime peaks on weekdays between 2:00 and 8:00 p.m., when many teenagers are unsupervised (U.S. Department of Justice, 2013).

Our discussion on page 381 in Chapter 10 explained how ineffective parenting can promote and sustain children's aggression, with boys—who are more active and impulsive—more often targets of parental anger, physical punishment, and inconsistency. When these child temperamental traits combine with emotionally negative, inept parenting, aggression rises sharply during childhood, leads to violent offenses in adolescence, and persists into adulthood (again, see the Biology and Environment box).

Disruptive, peer-rejected children and adolescents whose parents are lax or ineffective in exerting control seek out antisocial friends, who facilitate one another's antisocial behavior (Deutsch et al., 2012; Lacourse et al., 2003). Delinquent youths seem to stick with these friends to avoid social isolation and to bolster their fragile self-esteem. Although low self-esteem is associated with conduct problems and delinquency, many aggressive youths report overly high self-esteem. When their arrogant, cocky behavior prompts others to challenge their inflated but vulnerable self-image, they lash out angrily (Orobio de Castro et al., 2007). Their narcissism is accompanied by a sense of personal entitlement, lack of empathy, and highly manipulative, relationally aggressive tactics aimed at gaining power over others (Kerig & Stellwagen, 2010; Witt, Donnellan, & Trzesniewski, 2011).

Teenagers commit more crimes in poverty-stricken neighborhoods with poor-quality schools, limited recreational and employment opportunities, and high adult criminality (Leventhal, Dupéré, & Brooks-Gunn, 2009). In such neighborhoods, adolescents have easy access to deviant peers, drugs, and firearms and are likely to be recruited into antisocial gangs, whose members commit the vast majority of violent delinquent acts. Schools in these locales typically fail to meet students' developmental needs (Chung, Mulvey, & Steinberg, 2011; Flannery et al., 2003). Large classes, weak instruction, rigid rules, and reduced academic expectations and opportunities are related to higher rates of lawbreaking, even after other influences are controlled.

Furthermore, the community conditions just described heighten a hostile view of people and relationships, a preference for immediate rewards, and a cynical attitude toward social conventions and moral norms (Simons & Burt, 2011). These social information-processing deficits increase the chances that adolescents will interpret situations in ways that legitimize antisocial behavior.

PREVENTION AND TREATMENT Because delinquency has roots in childhood and results from events in several contexts, prevention must start early and take place at multiple levels (Frey et al., 2009). Positive family relationships, authoritative parenting, high-quality teaching in schools, well-designed work–study vocational education programs, and communities with healthy economic and social conditions go a long way toward reducing adolescent antisocial acts.

Lacking resources for effective prevention, many U.S. schools have implemented *zero tolerance policies,* which severely punish all disruptive and threatening behavior, major and minor, usually with suspension or expulsion. Yet often these policies are implemented inconsistently: Low-SES minority students are two to three times as likely to be punished, especially for minor misbehaviors. No evidence exists that zero tolerance achieves its objective of reducing youth aggression and other forms of misconduct (Reppucci, Meyer, & Kostelnik, 2011; Teske, 2011). To the contrary, some studies find that by excluding students from school, zero tolerance heightens high school dropout and antisocial behavior.

Treating serious offenders requires an intensive, often lengthy approach that is also directed at the multiple determinants of delinquency. The most effective interventions include training parents in communication, monitoring, and discipline strategies and providing youths with experiences that improve cognitive and social skills, moral reasoning, anger management, and other aspects of emotional self-regulation (DiBiase et al., 2011; Heilbrun, Lee, & Cottle, 2005). Yet even these multidimensional treatments can fall short if adolescents remain embedded in hostile home lives, poor-quality schools, antisocial peer groups, and violent neighborhoods.

In a program called *multisystemic therapy,* counselors combined family intervention with integrating violent youths into positive school, work, and leisure activities and disengaging them from deviant peers. Compared with conventional services or individual therapy, random assignment to the intervention led to improved parent–adolescent relationships and school performance, a dramatic drop in number of arrests that persisted for two decades after treatment, and—when participants did commit crimes—a reduction in their severity (see Figure 16.5). Favorable outcomes extended to other family members: Closest-age siblings of intervention youths also showed large declines in criminality. Furthermore, multisystemic therapy helped limit family instability once youth offenders reached

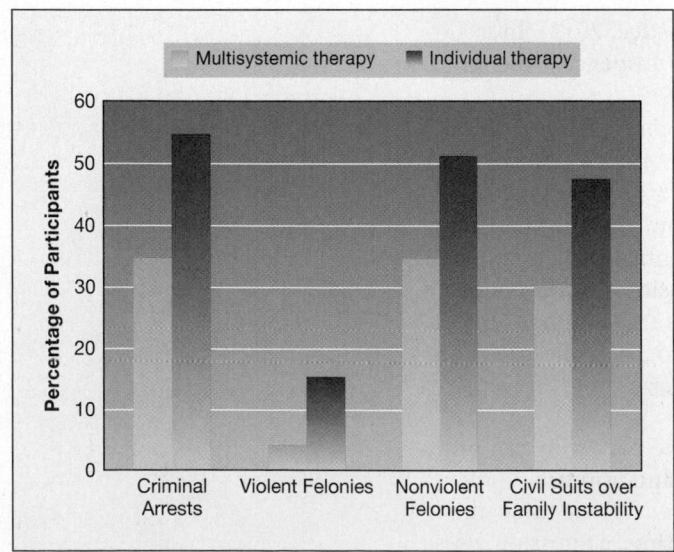

FIGURE 16.5 **Impact of multisystemic therapy on arrests and family-related civil suits 22 years after treatment.** A follow-up of violent youths two decades after treatment revealed that, compared to participants receiving individual therapy, those randomly assigned to multisystemic therapy had fewer criminal arrests overall, and the crimes they did commit were far less violent. Multisystemic therapy recipients also displayed reduced family instability—fewer civil suits over divorce, paternity, or child support, evidence of better adult adjustment. (Based on Sawyer & Borduin, 2011.)

adulthood, as measured by involvement in civil suits over divorce, paternity, or child support (Henggeler et al., 2009; Sawyer & Borduin, 2011; Wagner et al., 2014). Efforts to create non-aggressive environments—at the family, community, and cultural levels—are needed to help delinquent youths and to foster healthy development of all young people.

Ask Yourself

- **REVIEW** Why are adolescent girls at greater risk for depression and adolescent boys at greater risk for suicide?

- **CONNECT** Reread the sections on adolescent pregnancy and substance abuse in Chapter 14. What factors do these problems have in common with suicide and delinquency?

- **APPLY** Zeke had been well-behaved in elementary school, but at age 13 he started spending time with the "wrong crowd." At 16, he was arrested for property damage. Is Zeke likely to become a long-term offender? Why or why not?

- **REFLECT** During adolescence, did you or your friends engage in any lawbreaking acts? If so, at what ages? Were you motivated by a desire for excitement and/or peer approval?

At the Threshold

16.13 Review factors that foster resilience in adolescence.

The complex and rapid changes of development that occur during adolescence make teenagers vulnerable to certain problems. Most teenagers, however, do not show serious depression, suicidal tendencies, or persistent antisocial behavior. As we look back on the demands, expectations, dangers, and temptations of this period, the strength and vitality of young people are all the more remarkable. On a daily basis, adolescents must decide how vigorously to apply themselves in school, what kinds of friends to make, and whether to adopt risky behaviors. These short-term choices can profoundly affect the long-term paths they pursue.

Societies have good reason to treasure their youths as a rich national resource. Adolescents' ability to think seriously and deeply about possibilities, to commit themselves to idealistic causes, to be loyal to one another, and to experiment and take risks, while sometimes hazardous to themselves, energizes progress. But to realize their potential, they must have family, school, and community environments that nurture personal strengths while limiting exposure to adversity. To factors that foster resilience considered in earlier chapters (see Chapter 13, page 512) we can add the following resources, which are particularly beneficial in adolescence:

- A balance between family connection and separation
- Effective family problem solving that models and encourages rational decision making
- Parental monitoring and school involvement
- Close, supportive friendships
- High-quality vocational education
- A culturally sensitive school and community that foster a secure ethnic or bicultural identity
- Affiliation with a religious organization
- Opportunities to participate in extracurricular activities, youth organizations, and community service

As we turn now to the conclusion of our developmental journey, we will see that many young people in industrialized nations face even more complex choices today than several decades ago. Consequently, researchers have begun to investigate a new period that stands between adolescence and young adulthood. The support provided during the first 18 years is crucial for preparing young people to embrace the challenges of this transition. At no other time of life will the scope of possibilities and the freedom to experiment and make independent decisions be greater.

Summary

Erikson's Theory: Identity versus Role Confusion (p. 587)

16.1 According to Erikson, what is the major personality attainment of adolescence?

- Erikson's theory regards **identity** as the major personality attainment of adolescence. Young people who successfully resolve the psychological conflict of **identity versus role confusion** construct a solid self-definition consisting of self-chosen values and goals.

© SUSIE FITZHUGH/THE IMAGE WORKS

Self-Understanding (p. 588)

16.2 Describe changes in self-concept and self-esteem during adolescence.

- Cognitive changes lead adolescents' self-descriptions to become more organized and consistent. They place more emphasis on social virtues, and personal and moral values appear as key themes.
- Self-esteem differentiates further and, for most adolescents, rises. At the same time, individual differences in self-esteem become more stable. Authoritative parenting, encouragement from teachers, and schools and neighborhoods that accept the young person's cultural heritage support positive self-esteem.

16.3 Describe the four identity statuses, along with factors that promote identity development.

- Researchers evaluate progress in identity development on two criteria: exploration of alternatives and commitment to self-chosen values and goals. **Identity achievement** (exploration followed by commitment) and **identity moratorium** (exploration without having reached commitment) are psychologically routes to a mature self-definition. Ruminative exploration, however, is associated with poor adjustment. Long-term **identity foreclosure** (commitment without exploration) and **identity diffusion** (lack of both exploration and commitment) are related to adjustment difficulties.

- An information-gathering cognitive style, parental attachment along with freedom to explore, interaction with diverse peers, close friendships, and schools and communities that provide rich and varied opportunities promote healthy identity development. Similarly, supportive parents, peers, and schools can foster a strong, secure **ethnic identity** among minority adolescents. A **bicultural identity** offers additional emotional and social benefits.

Moral Development (p. 595)

16.4 Describe Kohlberg's theory of moral development, and evaluate its accuracy.

- According to Kohlberg, moral reasoning gradually develops through three levels, each containing two stages: At the **preconventional level,** morality is externally controlled by rewards, punishments, and authority figures; at the **conventional level,** conformity to laws and rules preserves positive interpersonal relationships and societal order; and at the **postconventional level,** morality is defined by abstract, universal principles of justice.
- A reexamination of Kohlberg's stages suggests that moral maturity can be found at Stages 3 and 4; few people move beyond the postconventional level. The influence of situational factors on moral judgment suggests that Kohlberg's stages are best viewed as loosely organized and overlapping.
- Contrary to Gilligan's claim, Kohlberg's theory does not underestimate the moral reasoning of females but instead taps both justice and caring moralities.
- Compared with children, teenagers display more subtle reasoning about conflicts between personal choice and community obligations. They are also increasingly mindful of the moral implications of following social conventions.

16.5 Describe influences on moral reasoning and its relationship to moral behavior.

- Experiences contributing to moral maturity include warm, rational parenting, extended schooling, and peer discussions of moral issues. In village societies, where moral cooperation is based on direct relations between people, moral reasoning rarely moves beyond Kohlberg's Stage 3. In both village cultures and industrialized societies that value interdependence, moral dilemma responses are more other-directed than in Western societies.

- Maturity of moral reasoning is only modestly related to moral behavior. Moral action is also influenced by the individual's empathy and guilt, temperament, cultural experiences and intuitive beliefs, and **moral identity.**
- Factors that strengthen moral identity include parenting practices, just educational environments, civic engagement, and religious involvement.

16.6 Describe challenges to Kohlberg's theory.

- Critics favoring a pragmatic approach to morality assert that individuals make moral judgments at varying levels of maturity, depending on their current context and motivations. Supporters of the cognitive-developmental perspective believe that people frequently rise above self-interest to defend others' rights.

Gender Typing (p. 605)

16.7 How does gender typing change in adolescence?

- Some research suggests that adolescence is a time of **gender intensification,** in which gender stereotyping of attitudes and behavior increases. Evidence, however, is mixed. In young people who exhibit gender intensification, pubertal changes, parental gender-role beliefs, and increased concern with others' opinions may be influential.

© JEFF GREENBERG/ALAMY

The Family (p. 606)

16.8 Discuss changes in parent–child and sibling relationships during adolescence.

- In their quest for **autonomy,** adolescents strive to rely more on themselves and less on parents for guidance and decision making. As teenagers deidealize their parents, they often question parental authority. During a time of major life transitions, adolescents and parents approach situations with conflicting expectations and from different perspectives. Warm, supportive parenting and consistent monitoring predict favorable adjustment, even in the face of reduced time spent with parents.

- Adolescents in cultures that value interdependence view autonomy as self-endorsed, rather than independent, decision making. Immigrant parents from cultures that emphasize obedience to authority often have difficulty adapting to their teenagers' striving for autonomy. The resulting **acculturative stress** is associated with adolescent adjustment problems.

- Sibling relationships become less intense as adolescents separate from the family and turn toward peers. Still, attachment to siblings remains strong for most young people.

Peer Relations (p. 610)

16.9 Describe adolescent friendships, peer groups, and dating relationships and their consequences for development.

- Adolescent friendships are based on greater intimacy, mutual understanding, and loyalty and contain more self-disclosure. With age, friendships become more stable. Girls' friendships place greater emphasis on emotional closeness, boys' on shared activities and accomplishments.

- Frequent electronic interaction, through texting, social networking sites, and instant messaging, supports friendship closeness. But online relationships may pose risks of harmful social experiences, including harassment and exploitation. Excessive use of online communication detracts from high-quality face-to-face communication.

- As long as they are not characterized by jealousy or aggression, adolescent friendships promote self-concept, identity, perspective taking, and the capacity for intimate relationships. They also help young people manage stress and can foster improved attitudes toward and involvement in school.

- Adolescent peer groups are organized into more intimate **cliques,** particularly important to girls, and **crowds,** which grant teenagers an identity within the larger social structure of the school. Adolescent self-concepts and ethnicity, as well as parenting styles, influence the assortment of teenagers into cliques and crowds. With interest in dating, mixed-sex cliques grow in importance and then decline. Crowds also diminish as teenagers settle on personal values and goals.

- Intimacy in dating relationships lags behind that of friendships. Positive relationships with parents and friends contribute to secure romantic ties, which enhance emotional and social development in older teenagers.

16.10 Discuss conformity to peer pressure in adolescence.

- Peer conformity is greater during adolescence than earlier or later. Most peer pressure is not in conflict with important adult values. Authoritative parenting is related to resistance to unfavorable peer pressure.

Problems of Development (p. 617)

16.11 Describe factors related to adolescent depression and suicide.

- In industrialized nations, depression rises sharply at adolescence and is the most common psychological problem of the teenage years, with girls at greater risk in industrialized nations. Various combinations of biological and environmental factors are implicated—heredity, pubertal hormone changes, maladaptive parenting, negative life events, "feminine" gender identity, and having friends with depressive symptoms.

- The suicide rate increases sharply at adolescence. Boys account for most teenage deaths by suicide, while girls make more unsuccessful suicide attempts. Teenagers at risk for suicide may be solitary and withdrawn, but more often, they are antisocial. They often have a family history of emotional and antisocial disorders and suicide, economic disadvantage, and family conflict.

16.12 Discuss factors related to delinquency.

- Although almost all teenagers engage in some delinquent activity, only a few are serious repeat offenders. Most are boys with a childhood history of conduct problems. Difficult temperament, cognitive deficits, inept parenting, and peer rejection are linked to chronic, violent delinquency. Teenagers commit more crimes in poverty-stricken neighborhoods with high crime rates and ineffective schools.

At the Threshold (p. 625)

16.13 Review factors that foster resilience in adolescence.

- In addition to factors mentioned in earlier chapters, the following resources foster resilience in adolescence: a balance between family connection and separation, effective family problem solving, parental monitoring and school involvement, close friendships, high-quality vocational education, culturally sensitive schools and communities, religious affiliation, and opportunities to participate in extracurricular activities, youth organizations, and community service.

Important Terms and Concepts

acculturative stress (p. 594)
autonomy (p. 606)
bicultural identity (p. 594)
clique (p. 614)
conventional level (p. 597)
crowd (p. 614)

ethnic identity (p. 594)
gender intensification (p. 605)
identity (p. 587)
identity achievement (p. 591)
identity diffusion (p. 591)
identity foreclosure (p. 591)

identity moratorium (p. 591)
identity versus role confusion (p. 588)
moral identity (p. 602)
postconventional level (p. 598)
preconventional level (p. 597)

MILESTONES
Development in Adolescence

EARLY ADOLESCENCE 11–14

PHYSICAL

- If a girl, reaches peak of growth spurt. (522)
- If a girl, adds more body fat than muscle. (523)
- If a girl, starts to menstruate. (525)
- If a boy, begins growth spurt. (522)
- If a boy, starts to ejaculate seminal fluid. (526)
- Is likely to be aware of sexual orientation. (542)
- If a girl, motor performance increases gradually, leveling off by age 14. (524)
- Reacts more strongly to stressful events; shows heightened sensation-seeking and risk-taking behavior. (528)
- Sleep "phase delay" strengthens. (529)

COGNITIVE

- Gains in hypothetico-deductive reasoning and propositional thought. (556–558)
- Gains in scientific reasoning—coordinating theory with evidence—on complex, multivariable tasks. (560–561)

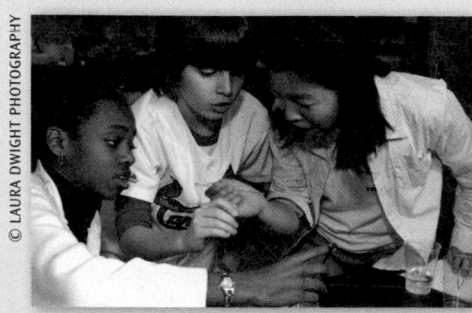

- Becomes more self-conscious and self-focused. (561–562)
- Becomes more idealistic and critical. (563)
- Improves in metacognition and self-regulation. (559)
- Evaluates vocational options in terms of interests. (579)

LANGUAGE

- Improves in metalinguistic awareness. (568)
- Adds many abstract words to vocabulary. (568)
- Gains in understanding of figurative language, such as proverbs. (579)
- Improves in understanding and use of complex grammatical constructions. (568)
- Gains in capacity to adapt speech style to social context. (569)

EMOTIONAL/SOCIAL

- Self-concept includes abstract descriptors unifying separate personality traits, but these are not interconnected and are often contradictory. (589)
- Moodiness and parent–child conflict tend to increase. (530–531, 606–608)
- In striving for autonomy, spends less time with parents and siblings and more time with peers. (608–610)

- Friendships decline in number and are based on intimacy, mutual understanding, and loyalty. (610)
- Peer groups become organized into same-sex cliques. (614)
- In high schools with complex social structures, cliques with similar values form crowds. (614)
- Conformity in response to peer pressure increases. (616)

MIDDLE ADOLESCENCE 14–16

PHYSICAL

- If a girl, completes growth spurt. (522)
- If a boy, reaches peak of growth spurt. (522)
- If a boy, voice deepens. (526)
- If a boy, adds muscle while body fat declines. (523)
- If a boy, motor performance improves dramatically. (524)
- May have had sexual intercourse. (540)

COGNITIVE

- Continues to gain in hypothetico-deductive reasoning and propositional thought. (556–557)

- Continues to gain in scientific reasoning, following a similar sequential order on different types of tasks. (560–561)
- Evaluates vocational options in terms of interests, abilities, and values. (579–580)

LANGUAGE

- Can read and interpret adult literary works. (568)

- More effectively analyzes and corrects grammar. (569)

Note: Numbers in parentheses indicate the page or pages on which each milestone is discussed.

EMOTIONAL/SOCIAL

- Combines features of the self into an organized self-concept. (588–589)
- Self-esteem differentiates further and tends to rise. (589)
- Begins to move from "lower" to "higher" identity statuses. (591)
- Increasingly emphasizes ideal reciprocity and societal laws as the basis for resolving moral dilemmas. (597)
- Engages in more subtle reasoning about conflicts between moral, social-conventional, and personal issues. (600)
- Mixed-sex cliques become common. (614)

- Has probably started dating. (615)
- Conformity to peer pressure may decline. (616)

LATE ADOLESCENCE 16–18

PHYSICAL

- If a boy, completes growth spurt. (522)
- If a boy, gains in motor performance continue. (524)

- Gradually declines in moodiness, reactivity to stressful events, and sensation-seeking. (528, 530)

COGNITIVE

- Continues to gain in metacognition and self-regulation. (559)
- Improves in decision making. (563–564)
- Narrows vocational options through exploration. (579)

EMOTIONAL/SOCIAL

- Self-concept emphasizes personal and moral standards. (589)
- Continues to construct an identity, likely moving to higher identity statuses. (591)
- Continues to advance in maturity of moral reasoning. (597–598, 600)
- Parent–child conflict declines, and harmonious interaction increases. (608)
- Cliques and crowds decline in importance. (615)
- Seeks psychological intimacy in romantic ties, which last longer. (615)

chapter 17

Emerging Adulthood

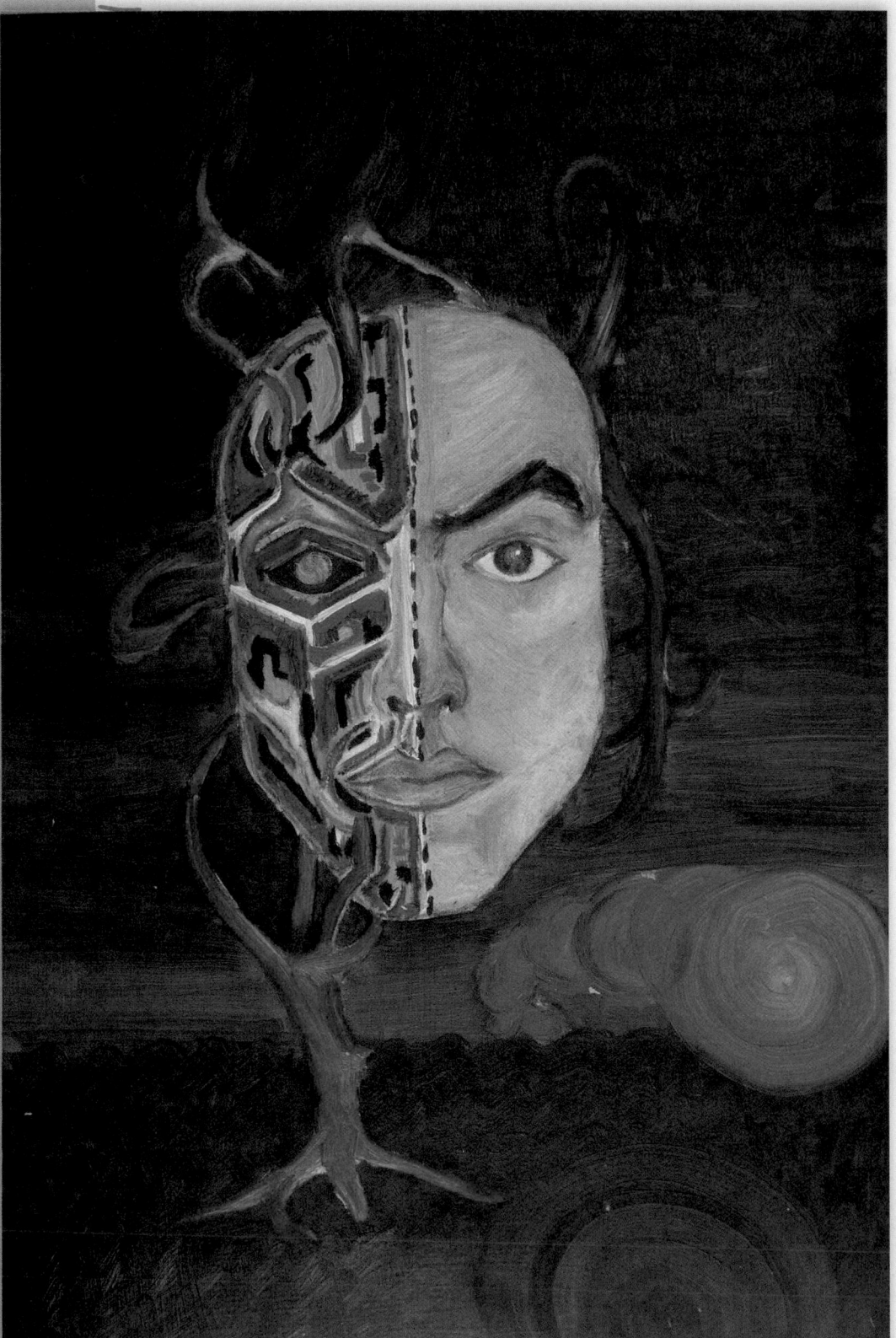

"Self-Portrait"
Cesar Bravo
17 years, Chile

A transitional period extending from the late teens to the mid-twenties, emerging adulthood is a time of intense exploration in education, work, personal values, and love. In this powerful painting, an emerging adult depicts himself as intimately connected to both his natural and industrial surroundings. He expresses a deep desire to confront environmental problems in his nation and world.

uring the café meeting that launched our collaboration in writing this textbook, Laura recalled an occasion in which her sons David and Peter, then in their early twenties, had asked how old she was when she got married, knew what she wanted to do for a career, and earnestly began to prepare for her life's work. To their surprise, she responded that she had attained all these widely accepted markers of adulthood by age 22—and that nearly all her friends had done so as well.

David and Peter's experiences were vastly different. Throughout college and for several years beyond, they explored possibilities. David, for example, completed a bachelor's degree in chemistry and pursued a master's degree in public health. Then he made another about-face. After volunteering for several months in an elementary school, at age 24 he returned to graduate school to become a teacher. Peter also vacillated after college about a vocational direction. Following a "year off" that included an internship, he settled on law school. Both young men deferred romance while they launched their work lives.

Similarly, few of David's and Peter's friends made lasting career or romantic commitments in their late teens and early twenties. To the contrary, their experimentation became more varied and deliberate. After graduating from college, one traveled the world for eight months, explaining that she wanted "to experience as much as possible." Another accepted a Peace Corps assignment in a remote region of Peru, forged a romance that she ended at the conclusion of her tour of duty, then returned to school to prepare for a career in international education. Each of these young people received financial and other forms of support from parents and other family members, which made possible their extended explorations.

TAKE A MOMENT... Think about your own development. Do you consider yourself to have reached adulthood? When a sample of 1,000 U.S. 18- to 29-year-olds diverse in SES and ethnicity was asked this question, the majority of those between 18 and 21 gave an ambiguous answer: "yes and no"—a proportion that declined with age as an increasing number replied with certainty, "yes" (see Figure 17.1) (Arnett & Schwab,

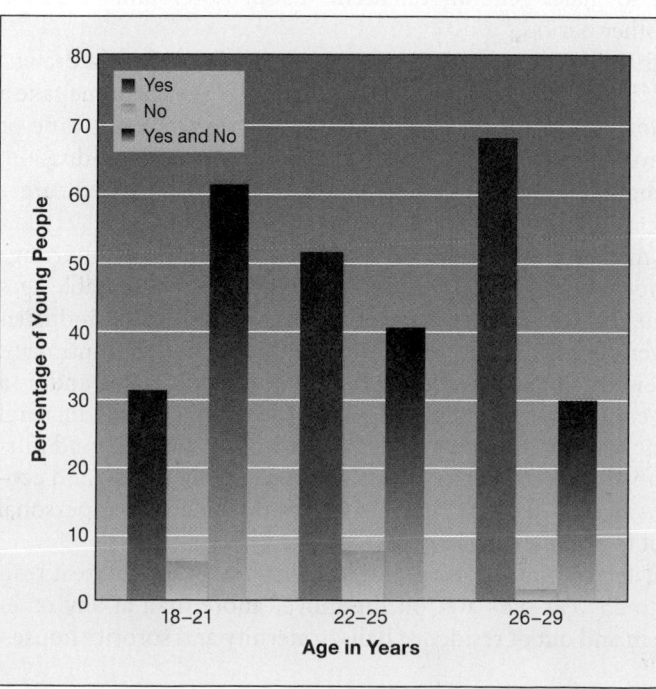

FIGURE 17.1
American young people's responses to the question, "Do you feel you have reached adulthood?" Between ages 18 and 21, the majority answered "yes and no." Even in their late twenties, 30 percent judged that they had not completed the transition to adulthood. (From J. J. Arnett & J. Schwab, 2013, *Clark University Poll of Emerging Adults, 2012: Thriving, Struggling, and Hopeful*, p. 7, Worcester, MA: Clark University. Adapted by permission of Jeffrey Jensen Arnett, Ph.D.)

2012). Similar findings are evident in a wide range of industrialized nations (Arnett, 2007; Buhl & Lanz, 2007; Nelson, 2009; Sirsch et al., 2009). The life pursuits and subjective judgments of many contemporary young people indicate that the transition to adult roles has become so delayed and prolonged that it has spawned a new transitional period extending from the late teens to the mid- to late-twenties, called **emerging adulthood.**

American psychologist Jeffrey Arnett (2011) is the leader of a movement that regards emerging adulthood as a distinct period of life—a new stage between adolescence and adulthood, defined by five features: *feeling in between* (neither adolescent nor adult), *identity exploration* (especially in love, work, and worldview), *self-focused* (not self-centered but lacking obligations to others), *instability* (frequent changes in living arrangements, relationships, education, and work), and *possibilities* (able to choose among multiple life directions). As Arnett explains, emerging adults have left adolescence but are still a considerable distance from taking on adult responsibilities.

Rather, young people who have the economic resources to do so explore alternatives more intensely than they did as teenagers. Many are earning advanced degrees and credentials—accumulating experiences and mastering practical skills so that they can land a personally and financially rewarding job in an ever-more-complex labor market. Those who are less economically privileged, however, often struggle to acquire the skills needed for work that will provide a decent standard of living for the family they desire—or may have already begun (see the discussion of non-college-bound youths on pages 582–583 in Chapter 15). ■

17.1 What is emerging adulthood?

Unprecedented Exploration

Emerging adulthood is a time of great challenge and uncertainty. During this period, many young people make frequent changes in educational paths, jobs, and love partners. Attaining adult milestones—finishing school, living on one's own, launching a career, and building a lasting intimate partnership—are highly diverse in timing and order across individuals (Côté, 2006). Consequently, it is harder to make general statements about development during emerging adulthood than for any other period.

Today, more college students than in past generations pursue their education in a drawn-out, nonlinear way. Only about half have earned their bachelor's degree by age 25. Some take a few courses while working part-time. Others leave school temporarily to work full-time or travel. Most change their majors several times as they try out career options. After graduation, about one-third enter graduate school, taking even longer to settle into their desired career track (U.S. Department of Education, 2014a).

Young people are postponing marriage as well. In 1950, the average age of first marriage in the United States was about 20 for women and 23 for men. Currently, the comparable ages are 27 and 29 (U.S. Census Bureau, 2014b). Similar delays have occurred in other industrialized nations, allowing for a longer period of experimentation with sexuality and intimacy. A half-century ago, Americans viewed marriage as a crucial marker of adult status and as a socially expected outcome of an enduring courtship. Although this view persists in rural America, the overwhelming majority of contemporary urban adults in their twenties and thirties say that marriage must be planned for, with personal goals for education, career, and economic security attained first (Kefalas et al., 2011). They also regard marriage as a personal choice, endorsing individuals' right to alternative lifestyles.

Together, extended education, delayed career entry, and later marriage lead to great residential instability. American 18- to 25-year-olds are "on the move," more than at any other time of life. About one-third move in and out of residence halls, fraternity and sorority houses, and apartments during college. And about half move in with a romantic partner, choosing *cohabitation* as their preferred way of entering into a committed intimate partnership (Copen, Daniels, & Mosher, 2013; U.S. Census Bureau, 2014b).

Furthermore, just over half of 18- to 25-year-olds return to their parents' home for brief periods after first leaving (U.S. Census Bureau, 2014b). Usually, role transitions, such as the end of college, bring young people back. But tight job markets, high housing costs, or failures in work or love can also prompt a temporary return home. As they encounter unexpected twists and turns on the road to adulthood, for many the parental home serves as a safety net and base of operations for launching adult life.

Economically well-off emerging adults are more likely to live independently than those from lower-SES and ethnic minority families. Among African-American, Hispanic, and Native-American groups, poverty and a cultural tradition of extended-family living lead to lower rates of leaving home and, when they do, higher rates of returning—among young people who are in college, have just graduated, or are working (Britton, 2013). Unmarried Asian emerging adults also tend to live with their parents, often exploring more hesitantly than their contemporaries as they reconcile their personal desires with the expectations of their parents, to whom they feel a strong sense of obligation (Fuligni, 2007). But the longer Asian families have lived in the United States, where they are exposed to individualistic values, the more likely young people are to move out before marriage (Lou, Lalonde, & Giguère, 2012).

Over the past several decades, financial strain has become more important in young peoples' decision to move back to the parental home. And whether or not they live with their parents, most emerging adults are financially dependent on them (Aquilino, 2006; Kahn, Goldscheider, & García-Manglano, 2013). Without parents' economic support, few emerging adults would be able to advance their education, explore career possibilities, or regroup when they encounter difficulties.

In Chapter 16, we noted that college students make more progress than high school students in constructing their identities (see page 591). Notice how emerging adulthood greatly prolongs identity development. And changes in reasoning capacity permit emerging adults to revise, and sometimes replace, their political and religious perspectives. Then, as they continue their explorations, they modify these philosophies further.

What explains the recent appearance of this rich, complex bridge between adolescence and assumption of adult responsibilities? Rapid cultural change seems to be the answer: Research suggests that emerging adulthood is a *cultural construction*.

The U.S. couple of the 1950s on the top married and became parents in their early twenties. In contrast, the Peace Corps volunteers on the bottom, who are teaching English to Cambodian villagers, are not yet considering marriage or parenthood. Typical of young people in industrialized nations today, they are taking time to explore career options and travel.

Cultural Change, Cultural Variation, and Emerging Adulthood

17.2 How has cultural change and variation contributed to emerging adulthood?

As the economies of industrialized nations have become more technical and information-based, the amount of education required to enter complex, well-paid careers has increased. In response, young people of the twenty-first century are pursuing higher education in record numbers. In 1950, only 14 percent of Americans enrolled in colleges and universities in the first year after graduating from high school; today, about two-thirds do so. And nearly half of the U.S. early-twenties population attend an educational institution full- or part-time (U.S. Department of Education, 2014a). This massive expansion of higher education has delayed financial independence and career commitment—trends that grant far more time for exploring options.

Dramatic gains in life expectancy in prosperous nations have also contributed to emerging adulthood. An American born in 1900 could expect to live to age 50. By 1950, life expectancy had increased to age 68. Today, it is 78.7 in the United States and even higher in most other industrialized countries (U.S. Census Bureau, 2014b). Nations with abundant wealth and longer-living populations have no pressing need for young people's labor, freeing those who are financially able for the extended moratorium of emerging adulthood.

Indeed, emerging adulthood is limited to cultures that postpone entry into adult roles until the twenties. In developing nations, only a privileged few—usually those from wealthier families who are admitted to universities—experience it, often for a shorter time span than their Western counterparts (Arnett, 2011; Nelson & Chen, 2007). Furthermore, the overwhelming majority of young people in traditional, non-Western countries—who have few economic resources or who remain in the rural regions where they grew up—have no emerging adulthood. With limited education, they typically enter marriage, parenthood, and lifelong work early (UNICEF, 2010).

In industrialized countries, where many experience these transitional years, young people nevertheless vary in their beliefs about what it means to become an adult. Reflecting the self-searching of these years, respondents from diverse cultures, ethnicities, and religious backgrounds emphasize psychological qualities, especially self-sufficiency—accepting responsibility for one's actions, deciding on personal beliefs and values, establishing an equal relationship with parents, and becoming financially independent. Forming mature relationships and complying with societal norms (such as avoiding drunk driving and committing petty crimes) are also frequently mentioned (Nelson, 2009; Swartz, Hartmann, & Mortimer, 2011).

Youths from collectivist cultures and subcultures attach especially high importance to becoming more considerate of others, to attaining certain roles, and to self-control. For example, Asian, African-American, and Hispanic young people point to supporting and caring for a family as a major marker of adulthood (Badger, Nelson, & Barry, 2006; Galambos & Martínez, 2007). And in a survey of Native Canadian and Métis (mixed Native-Canadian and European descent) college students, those who identified strongly with their cultural heritage regarded "good control over emotions" and "capable of supporting parents financially" as more important than did those with less cultural identification. Both groups of students placed greater weight on interdependent qualities (such as making lifelong commitments to others) than did Canadian white students (Cheah & Nelson, 2004).

Some non-college-bound young people may benefit from the extended transition of emerging adulthood, perhaps through trying out different types of work rather than college majors or travel (Tanner, Arnett, & Leis, 2009). Nevertheless, for low-SES young people in Western nations who are burdened by early parenthood, do not finish high school, are otherwise academically unprepared for college, or do not have access to vocational training, emerging adulthood is limited or nonexistent (see Chapters 14 and 15). Instead of excitement and personal expansion, these youths often alternate between unemployment and dead-end, low-paying jobs (Arnett & Tanner, 2011).

Because of its strong association with SES and higher education, some researchers reject Arnett's notion of emerging adulthood as a distinct life stage (see the Cultural Influences box

© THE STAR-LEDGER/ROBERT SCIARRINO/THE IMAGE WORKS

Massive expansion of higher education has led to delays in taking on adult roles, granting time for the extended exploration of emerging adulthood. Today, nearly two-thirds of Americans enroll in colleges and universities in the first year after graduating from high school.

LOOK and LISTEN

Ask several 18- to 29-year-olds for their beliefs about what it means to become an adult. Are their responses consistent with research findings on emerging adulthood?

Cultural Influences

Is Emerging Adulthood Really a Distinct Stage of Development?

Although broad consensus exists that cultural change has prolonged the transition to adult roles for many young people, disagreement exists over whether these years of "emergence" should be designated a new life stage (Kloep & Hendry, 2011). Critics of the concept of emerging adulthood offer the following arguments.

First, burgeoning higher education enrollment, delayed career entry, and later marriage and parenthood are cultural trends that began as early as the 1970s in industrialized nations, only gradually becoming more conspicuous. At no time has adulthood in complex societies been attained at a distinct moment (Côté & Bynner, 2008). Rather, young people in the past reached adult status earlier in some domains and later in others, just as they do today. They also may reverse direction—for example, move back to the parental home to get their bearings after finishing college or being laid off a job. Transitions occur during all periods of adult life, with societal conditions heavily influencing their timing, length, and complexity.

Second, the term *emerging adulthood* fails to describe the experiences of most of the world's youths (Galambos & Martínez, 2007). In developing countries, the majority of young people—particularly women—are limited in education and marry and have children early (see page 70 in Chapter 2). According to one estimate, over 1 billion individuals—nearly 70 percent of young people—follow this traditional route to adulthood (World Health Organization, 2011). We have also seen that many low-SES youths in industrialized nations lack the academic preparation and financial resources to experience an emerging adulthood.

Third, research on emerging adulthood largely emphasizes its personal benefits. But the extended exploration that defines this period might be largely a coping mechanism on the part of young people who cannot find rewarding jobs, even after college graduation. If satisfying work enabling financial independence were plentiful, perhaps emerging adults would not choose to postpone these responsibilities (Côté & Bynner, 2008). Furthermore, an extended emerging adulthood is risky for those who have not developed the personal agency (see page 638) to deal with the ambiguities and uncertainties of these years by making good choices and acquiring adult skills (Smith, 2011). These young people may remain uncommitted for too long—an outcome that would impede the focused learning required for a successful work life. A favorable emerging adulthood, then, depends on whether it is used to acquire competencies essential for contemporary living.

Finally, the financial upheaval of the late 2000s has left large numbers of bachelor's degree holders under age 25 with restricted options. In 2011, over 9 percent were unemployed, a figure that improved to 7 percent in 2014. However, about one-fourth are in jobs unrelated to their college major, many of whom are underemployed—in low-paid jobs not requiring a college degree (Staklis, Soldner, & Skomsvold, 2014; U.S. Department of Education, 2014a). Thus, they remain without work experiences necessary for advancing their professional skills. Rather than a period of unparalleled opportunities, these graduates' delayed leap into adult roles is filled with anxiety and frustration. One young person, who might have been high in personal agency in a stable economy, remarked, "It has been tough finding a job that keeps me wanting to stick with something" (Kotkin, 2012).

Proponents of emerging adulthood as a distinct stage respond that, though not universal, it applies to most young people in industrialized societies and is spreading in developing nations that play major roles in our global economy

© ELLEN B. SENISI

With few financial resources, this young woman in Burma already has adult responsibilities, caring for her baby while working as a food vendor. Like the majority of young people in developing countries, she has no emerging adulthood.

(Tanner & Arnett, 2011). But skeptics counter that emerging adulthood is unlikely to become prominent in developing countries with high concentrations of poverty or, in industrialized nations, among low-income youths or those not involved in higher education (Côté & Bynner, 2008; Kloep & Hendry, 2011). And for college graduates, societal conditions can readily restrict the prospects and rewards of this period.

Critics also emphasize that in developed nations, important milestones (such as marriage, career entry, parenthood, and retirement) have become less determined by age and more affected by social and economic conditions throughout adulthood (Hendry & Kloep, 2010). In their view, rather than being unique, emerging adults are part of a general trend toward blurring of age-related expectations, yielding multiple transitions and increased diversity in development across the adult years.

above). Others disagree, predicting that emerging adulthood will become increasingly common as *globalization*—the exchange of ideas, information, trade, and immigration among nations—accelerates. Contact between industrialized and developing countries fosters economic progress. It also heightens awareness of events, lifestyles, and practices in faraway places. As globalization proceeds, gains in financial security and higher education and the formation of a common "global identity" among young people may lead to the spread of emerging adulthood (Arnett, 2007, 2011).

Development in Emerging Adulthood

A wide array of demanding experiences and tasks await emerging adults. To make a successful transition to adulthood, they must acquire a wealth of new knowledge and skills.

Cognitive Changes

The cognitive gains of the late teens and early twenties are supported by further brain development, especially the prefrontal cortex and its connections with other brain regions. Pruning of synapses along with growth and myelination of stimulated neural fibers continue, though at a slower pace than in adolescence (Zelazo & Lee, 2010). These changes result in continued fine-tuning of the *prefrontal cognitive control network* (see page 528 in Chapter 14). Consequently, planning, reasoning, and decision making improve, supported by experiences, including higher education and entering a career. fMRI evidence reveals that as young people become increasingly proficient in a chosen field of endeavor, regions of the cerebral cortex specialized for those activities undergo further *experience-dependent brain growth* (see page 169 in Chapter 5). Besides more efficient functioning, structural changes occur as greater knowledge and refinement of skills results in more cortical tissue devoted to the task and, at times, reorganization of brain areas governing the activity (Lenroot & Giedd, 2006).

Piaget (1967) recognized that important advances in thinking follow the attainment of formal operations. He observed that adolescents prefer an idealistic, internally consistent perspective on the world to one that is vague, contradictory, and adapted to particular circumstances (see page 563 in Chapter 15). Research on **postformal thought**—cognitive development beyond Piaget's formal operational stage—reveals that college students make impressive strides in cognition. This is not surprising, since college serves as a "developmental testing ground," a time for devoting full attention to exploring alternative values, roles, and behaviors. To facilitate exploration, college exposes students to a form of culture shock—encounters with new ideas and beliefs, new freedoms and opportunities, and new academic and social demands. These experiences combine with personal effort to spark increasingly rational, flexible, and practical ways of thinking that accept uncertainties and vary across situations.

DEVELOPMENT OF EPISTEMIC COGNITION The work of William Perry (1981, 1970/1998) provided the starting point for an expanding research literature on the development of *epistemic cognition. Epistemic* means "of or about knowledge," and **epistemic cognition** refers to our reflections on how we arrived at facts, beliefs, and ideas. When mature, rational thinkers reach conclusions that differ from those of others, they consider the justifiability of these conclusions. When they cannot justify their approach, they revise it, seeking a more balanced, adequate route to acquiring knowledge.

Perry wondered why students respond in dramatically different ways to the diversity of ideas they encounter in college. To find out, he interviewed Harvard University undergraduates at the end of each of their four years, asking "what stood out" during the previous year. Responses indicated that students' reflections on knowing changed as they experienced the complexities of university life and moved closer to adult roles—findings confirmed in many subsequent studies (King & Kitchener, 2002; Magolda, Abes, & Torres, 2009; Magolda et al., 2012).

Younger students regarded knowledge as made up of separate units (beliefs and propositions), whose truth can be determined by comparing them to objective standards—standards that exist apart from the thinking person and his or her situation. As a result, they engaged in **dualistic thinking,** dividing information, values, and authority into right and wrong, good and bad, we and they. As one college freshman put it, "When I went to my first lecture, what the man said was just like God's word. I believe everything he said because he is a professor" (Perry, 1981, p. 81). When asked, "If two people disagree on the interpretation of a poem, how would you decide which one is right?" a sophomore replied, "You'd have to ask the poet. It's his poem" (Clinchy, 2002, p. 67). Dualistic thinkers approach learning by accepting what they are given.

Older students, in contrast, had moved toward **relativistic thinking,** viewing all knowledge as embedded in a framework of thought. Aware of a diversity of opinions on many topics, they gave up the possibility of absolute truth in favor of multiple truths, each relative to its context. As a result, their thinking became more flexible and tolerant. As one college senior put it, "Just seeing how [famous philosophers] fell short of an all-encompassing answer, [you realize] that ideas are really individualized. And you begin to have respect for how great their thought could be, without its being absolute" (Perry, 1970/1998, p. 90). Relativistic thinking leads to the realization that one's own beliefs are often subjective because several frameworks may satisfy the criterion of internal logical consistency (Sinnott, 2003). Thus, the relativistic thinker is acutely aware that each person, in arriving at a position, creates her own "truth."

Eventually, the most mature individuals progress to **commitment within relativistic thinking.** Instead of choosing between opposing views, they try to formulate a more satisfying perspective that synthesizes contradictions. When considering which of two theories studied in a college course is better or which of several movies most deserves an Oscar, the individual moves beyond the stance that everything is a matter of opinion and

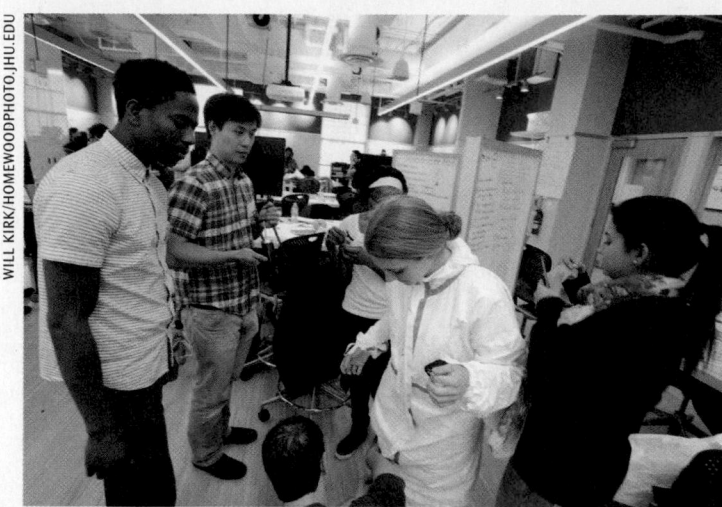

A team of university students participate in a global competition to design a more protective, lightweight, and comfortable suit for Ebola workers. Collaboratively tackling challenging, real-world problems leads to gains in epistemic cognition.

generates rational criteria against which options can be evaluated (Moshman, 2003, 2005). By the end of the college years, some students reach this extension of relativism. Those who do generally display a more sophisticated approach to learning, in which they actively seek differing perspectives to advance their knowledge and understanding. Attainment of commitment within relativism occurs more often among young people who pursue advanced graduate education (Greene, Torney-Purta, & Azevedo, 2010; King & Kitchener, 2002).

IMPORTANCE OF PEER INTERACTION AND REFLECTION   Advances in epistemic cognition depend on further gains in metacognition, which are likely to occur in situations that challenge young people's perspectives and induce them to consider the rationality of their thought processes (Magolda, Abes, & Torres, 2009). In a study of the college learning experiences of seniors scoring low and high in epistemic cognition, high-scoring students frequently reported activities that encouraged them to struggle with realistic but ambiguous problems in a supportive environment (Marra & Palmer, 2004). Their professors were committed to helping them understand how knowledge is constructed and why it must be subject to revision.

In tackling challenging, ill-structured problems, interaction among individuals who are roughly equal in knowledge and authority is beneficial because it prevents acceptance of another's reasoning simply because of greater power or expertise. When college students were asked to devise the most effective solution to a difficult logical problem, only 3 out of 32 students (9 percent) in a "work-alone" condition succeeded. But in an "interactive" condition, 15 out of 20 small groups (75 percent) arrived at the best answer following extensive discussion (Moshman & Geil, 1998). Whereas few students working alone reflected on their solution strategies, most groups engaged in a process of "collective rationality" in which members challenged one another to justify their reasoning and collaborated in working out the most effective strategy.

Of course, reflection on one's own thinking can also occur individually. But peer interaction fosters the necessary type of individual reflection: arguing with oneself over competing ideas and strategies and coordinating opposing perspectives into a new, more effective structure. As at earlier ages, peer collaboration remains a highly effective basis for education in emerging adulthood.

Emotional and Social Changes

During college, students' attitudes and values broaden. They express increased interest in literature, the performing arts, and philosophical and historical issues and greater tolerance for ethnic and cultural diversity. And as noted in Chapter 16, college leaves its mark on moral reasoning by fostering concern with individual rights and human welfare, sometimes expressed in political activism. Furthermore, exposure to multiple viewpoints encourages young people

Journalism students at Arizona State University conduct a live radio program in the campus studio. The experience helps them explore in depth—evaluating their existing career commitment—and advance in identity development.

to look more closely at themselves. As a result, they develop a more complex self-concept that includes awareness of their own changing traits and values over time, and self-esteem rises (Labouvie-Vief, 2006; Orth, Robins, & Widaman, 2012). Together, these developments contribute to advances in identity development. In emerging adulthood, young people refine their approach to constructing an identity. Besides exploring in *breadth* (weighing multiple possibilities), they also explore in *depth*—evaluating existing commitments (Luyckx et al., 2006; Schwartz et al., 2013). For example, if you have not yet selected your major, you may be taking classes in a broad array of disciplines. Once you choose a major, you are likely to embark on an in-depth evaluation of your choice—reflecting on your interest, motivation, and performance and on your career prospects as you take additional classes in that field. Depending on the outcome of your evaluation, either your commitment to your major strengthens, or you return to a broad exploration of options.

In a longitudinal study extending over the first two years of college, most students cycled between making commitments and evaluating commitments in various identity domains. Fluctuations in students' certainty about their commitments sparked movement between these two states (Luyckx, Goossens, & Soenens, 2006). **TAKE A MOMENT...** Think about your own identity progress. Does it fit this *dual-cycle model,* in which identity formation is a lengthy process of feedback loops? Notice how the model helps explain the movement between identity statuses displayed by many young people, described in Chapter 16. Emerging adults who move toward exploration in depth and certainty of commitment are higher in self-esteem, psychological well-being, and academic, emotional, and social adjustment. Those who spend much time exploring in breadth without making commitments tend to be poorly adjusted—anxious, depressed, and higher in alcohol and drug use, casual and unprotected sex, and other health-compromising behaviors (Kunnen et al., 2008; Schwartz et al., 2011).

Many aspects of the life course that were once socially structured—marriage, parenthood, religious beliefs, career paths—are increasingly left to individuals to decide on their own. As a result, emerging adults are required to "individualize" their identities—a process that requires a sense of self-efficacy, purpose, confidence in overcoming obstacles and responsibility for outcomes. Among young people of diverse ethnicities and SES levels, this set of qualities, termed *personal agency,* is positively related to an information-gathering cognitive style and identity exploration followed by commitment (Schwartz, Côté, & Arnett, 2005; Stringer & Kerpelman, 2010). Now let's turn to development in three main identity domains of this period: love, work, and worldview.

LOVE In Erikson's psychosocial theory (see Chapter 1, page 16), establishing an intimate love relationship is a major task of these years. As Erikson emphasized and research confirms, advanced identity development predicts involvement in a deep, committed love partnership or readiness to establish such a partnership (Beyers & Seiffge-Krenke, 2010).

With age, emerging adults' romantic ties typically last longer and involve greater trust, support, emotional closeness, and commitment. Also, conceptions of close relationships become more complex, expressing a wider array of desired qualities from others and from oneself—a trend that reflects both a more differentiated self-concept and increased experience with close peer bonds (Waldinger et al., 2002). One emerging adult described this change: "Now you know what it means to support your partner, to be with him, to understand him. Today it is deeper, we discuss matters, we negotiate" (Shulman & Kipnis, 2001, p. 342).

Emerging adults take their time about forging a committed relationship; many say they don't feel ready to make this choice and want to experience a variety of personal relationships before settling on a lifetime partner (Arnett & Schwab, 2012). At the end of high school, about 60 percent of U.S. young people are sexually active, but by age 25 nearly all have become so. Although emerging adults have more sexual partners than adults in their thirties, about 60 percent have had only one partner in the previous year (Lefkowitz & Gillen, 2006). Still, over half of young people in steady relationships at the beginning of emerging adulthood have moved on when followed up several years later (Meier & Allen, 2009).

Furthermore, for many, the college years are marked by an increase in uncommitted sexual encounters, including "hookups" (emotionally uninvolved, casual sex) and "friends with benefits" (casual sex as an add-on to an existing friendship). Estimates indicate that two-thirds or more of U.S college students have experienced at least one hookup during college, and as many as one-fourth 10 or more (Halpern & Kaestle, 2014). These emotionally indifferent sexual relationships tend be associated with other forms of risk-taking, including alcohol and drug abuse and unprotected sex. Although some young people report positive reactions, these encounters often have negative emotional consequences (more so for women), including lower self-esteem, regret, and depressed mood (Hamilton & Armstrong, 2009; Lewis et al., 2012). The prevalence of casual sex on college campuses suggests that emerging adults often use it to gratify sexual needs during a period in which they are not yet ready to invest in an intimate bond (Shulman & Connolly, 2013).

Finding a lifelong intimate partner is a major milestone with profound consequences for psychological well-being, and most emerging adults want to attain it eventually (Arnett & Schwab, 2012). On average, married couples are advantaged in physical and mental health and financial security. And committed partners, including emerging adults in ongoing relationships—and married couples even more so—report more frequent and satisfying sex than their single counterparts (McGuire & Barber, 2010; Paik, 2010).

Emerging adults who are religious or in a committed romantic relationship are more likely to want to marry (Halpern & Kaestle, 2014). Two interrelated factors increase the chances that an intimate bond forged in emerging adulthood will be mutually satisfying and last a lifetime: partner similarity and good communication.

Romantic ties in emerging adulthood last longer than those in adolescence and involve a deeper sense of emotional closeness. Still, many emerging adults say they don't feel ready to settle on a life partner.

Partner Similarity. Young people who establish happy, lasting intimate relationships often meet in conventional ways: Family members or friends introduce them, or they get to know each other at school, work, or social events where people similar to themselves congregate (Schmeeckle & Sprecher, 2004). Sustaining an intimate tie is easier when couples share interests and values and when people they know approve of the match.

Contrary to the popular belief that "opposites attract," lovers tend to resemble each other—in attitudes, personality, intelligence, educational plans, physical attractiveness, ethnicity, and (to a lesser extent) religious and political beliefs. The more alike two people are, the more satisfied they tend to be with their relationship, and the more likely they are to stay together (Blackwell & Lichter, 2004; Furnham, 2009).

Over the past decade, the Internet has become an increasingly popular way to initiate relationships: More than one-third of single adults go to dating websites or other online venues in search of romantic partners. In a survey of a nationally representative sample of 4,000 Americans, most of whom were in a committed relationship, 22 percent said they had met on the Internet, making it second most common way to meet a partner, just behind meeting through friends (Finkel et al., 2012). In fact, knowing someone who has successfully engaged in Internet dating strongly predicts single adults' willingness to look for a partner on dating websites (Sautter, Tippett, & Morgan, 2010; Sprecher, 2011). As reports of dating success spread through social networks, use of Internet dating services is likely to increase, despite widespread awareness that it poses risks.

Nevertheless, the services of online dating sites sometimes undermine the chances of forming a successful romantic relationship. Relying on Internet dating profiles and computer-mediated communication omits aspects of direct social interaction that are vital for assessing one's compatibility with a potential partner. Especially when computer mediated communication persists for a long time (six weeks or more), people form idealized impressions that often lead to disappointment at face-to-face meetings (Finkel et al., 2012). Furthermore, the techniques that matching sites claim to use to pair partners—sophisticated analyses of information that daters provide—have not demonstrated any greater success in bringing compatible partners together than conventional off-line means of introducing people.

Good Communication. Lasting romantic relationships are based on good communication. Couples who sustain warm, tender expressions of intimacy and who stay together, despite difficult moments, are more likely to express increased happiness over time. An important feature of their commitment is constructive conflict resolution—directly expressing wishes and needs, listening patiently, asking for clarification, compromising, accepting responsibility, and avoiding the escalation of negative emotion sparked by criticism, contempt, and defensiveness (Johnson et al., 2005).

As with best friendships and dating partners in adolescence (see page 616 in Chapter 16), a secure *internal working model* of attachment relationships fosters gratifying intimate ties in emerging adulthood. Young people who recall their attachment experiences with parents as warm and supportive tend to describe both their friendships and their romantic partnerships as trusting and happy (Cassidy, 2001; Collins & van Dulmen, 2006b). Their behaviors toward their partner are more supportive and their conflict resolution strategies more constructive than those of young people who describe their attachment histories as insecure. They are also more at ease in turning to their partner for comfort and assistance and report mutually initiated, enjoyable sexual activity (Collins et al., 2006; Holland & Roisman, 2010).

However, memories of early attachments are only one of several influences on the quality of emerging adults' romantic relationships. Characteristics of the partner and current life conditions also make a difference. When one partner feels secure and behaves considerately, the other is likely to respond in kind (Creasey & Jarvis, 2009). And young people who are content with progress in other aspects of their lives probably approach their love relationships with a more positive, relaxed state of mind.

Finally, among U.S. young couples, cohabitation is now the preferred mode of entry into a committed relationship, chosen by an estimated 70 percent of romantic partners age 30 and younger (Copen, Daniels, & Mosher, 2013). As in other Western nations, where cohabitation is even more common, U.S. emerging adults view living together as an integral part of the process of selecting a good spouse. When couples commit to getting married prior to cohabitation, their relationships are more stable. And once married, they are less prone to divorce than those who cohabit before they have made a commitment to each other (Jose, O'Leary, & Moyer, 2010; Manning & Cohen, 2012). U.S. young people who cohabit without commitment tend to have less conventional values. They have had more sexual partners and are more politically liberal and less religious. In addition, a larger number have parents who divorced (Kurdek, 2006). Perhaps the more open-ended nature of these partnerships reduces motivation to develop effective conflict-resolution skills. Consequently, these unions often dissolve when problems arise.

Among U.S. couples, committing to get married prior to cohabitation predicts an enduring marriage. U.S. young people who cohabit without commitment are at increased risk for divorce.

WORK Recall from Chapter 15 that U.S. teenagers rarely have access to meaningful paid work activities. Most view their part-time work merely as a way to obtain spending money. In emerging adulthood, work experiences increasingly focus on preparation for adult work roles. Young people eagerly seek apprenticeships with experts and internships in companies and community agencies to resolve vocational identity issues. They ask, What kind of work am I good at, and what will I find personally rewarding? Their selection of college courses also addresses these questions. They try out various possibilities, often changing majors several times. And graduate school permits them to switch directions again.

In his influential research on adult development, Daniel Levinson (1978, 1996) found that beginning in the late teens and early twenties, young people construct a *dream,* an image of oneself in the adult world that guides decision making. For men, the dream usually emphasized becoming an independent achiever in a career role. In contrast, most career-oriented women displayed "split dreams," in which both marriage and career were prominent—findings confirmed in subsequent investigations (Heppner, 2013).

To help realize their dream, young people often form relationships with *mentors*—people experienced in the career the young person wants to enter. Most of the time, professors and senior colleagues at work fill this role. Occasionally, knowledgeable friends or relatives provide mentoring. Mentors sometimes act as teachers who enhance the person's career-related skills. At other times, they serve as guides who acquaint the person with the values and customs of the work setting. Romantic partners can resemble mentors as well, believing in the other's capacity to succeed and facilitating the pursuit of each other's dreams (Shulman, Laursen, & Dickson, 2014). When emerging adults have varied mentors, each providing unique forms of assistance, they benefit more in terms of career-related learning (Hall & Las Heras, 2011).

Still, the overall quality of emerging adults' college education affects their chances of securing a desirable job. In research that tracked more than 1,600 U.S. students through their senior year at 25 four-year institutions, the likelihood of a favorable employment outcome two years after graduation varied with scores on a test of college learning assessment, which measured complex reasoning, critical thinking, and written communication. Graduates with better scores more often secured jobs requiring at least higher education and were more likely to go on to full-time graduate programs. In a typical semester, however, half the participants said they did not have any class that required more than twenty pages of writing, and one-third said no class required as much as forty pages of reading. During four years of college, 36 percent made no meaningful gains on the college learning test (Arum & Roksa, 2014). In accommodating to emerging adults' preferences, the researchers concluded, many colleges are not academically rigorous enough to support success in the work world.

Gender. Identity achievement in the vocational realm tends to be more challenging for women than for men. As indicated in Chapter 15, during college, women's career ambitions often decline, partly because of unresolved questions about their abilities and partly because of concerns about combining a highly demanding career with family responsibilities (Chhin, Bleeker, & Jacobs, 2008; Heppner & Jung, 2013). Low self-efficacy on the part of many college women about succeeding in male-dominated fields further limits their occupational choices. Recall that many mathematically talented college women settle on non-science majors or, if they remain in the sciences, enter one of the health professions rather than engineering, math, or physical science (see page 581).

Women who do pursue male-dominated careers usually have "masculine" traits—high achievement orientation, self-reliance, and a belief that their efforts will result in success. But even those with high self-efficacy are less certain than their male counterparts that they can overcome barriers to career success (Lindley, 2005). In fields dominated by men, women may have difficulty finding supportive mentors. In one study, science professors at a broad sample of U.S. universities were sent an undergraduate student's application for a lab manager position. For half, the application bore a male name; for the other half, a female name (Moss-Racusin et al., 2012). Professors of both genders viewed the female student as less competent, less deserving of mentoring, and meriting a lower salary, though her accomplishments were identical to those of the male.

Despite obstacles to success, most young women prefer to blend work and family, realizing that a rewarding career will increase psychological well-being and life satisfaction (Erdogan et al., 2012). Those who continue to achieve usually have four experiences in common:

- A college environment that values the accomplishments of women and that addresses women's historical and current experiences in its curriculum
- Frequent interaction with faculty and professionals in their chosen fields
- The opportunity to test their abilities in supportive extracurricular, internship, and work environments
- Models of accomplished women who have successfully dealt with family–career role conflict and who provide guidance on unique educational and workplace challenges that women encounter (Murphy, Steele, & Gross, 2007; Zeldin & Pajares, 2000)

Baylor University undergraduate students work with their forensic science professor to identify the remains of people who died on long, hot walks as they tried to enter the United States illegally. Young women pursuing high career achievement benefit from mentors, especially accomplished women, who serve as role models and guides in overcoming challenges.

Ethnic Minorities. Many ethnic minority young people from low-SES families also arrive at emerging adulthood with past experiences that compromise their self-confidence and academic preparedness for college and career success (see, for example, Chapter 15, pages 574–575). Consequently, they are at increased risk of dropping out of college, with most dropouts leaving during the first year and many within the first six weeks (ACT, 2014; Montgomery & Côté, 2003a). Reflecting this trend, U.S. graduation rates after five years of study are 35 percent for African Americans, 46 percent for Hispanics, and 32 percent for Native Americans compared with 52 percent for Caucasians (U.S. Department of Education, 2014a). Young people who leave college have few alternatives for successful entry into the workforce. They often end up in low-paid jobs or unemployed, with seriously compromised long-term work and earning prospects.

Preparing young people in childhood and adolescence with the necessary visions and skills can do much to improve college success. In a study that followed nearly 700 individuals from sixth grade until two years after high school graduation, a set of factors—grade point average, academic self-esteem, persistence in the face of challenge, parental SES and valuing of a college education, and the individual's plans to attend college—predicted college attendance at age 20 (Eccles, Vida, & Barber, 2004). Although parental SES is difficult to modify, improving parents' attitudes and behaviors and students' academic motivation and educational aspirations is within reach, through a wide array of strategies considered in Chapters 15 and 16.

Once emerging adults enroll in college, reaching out to them, especially in the early weeks and throughout the first year, is crucial. Programs that forge bonds between teachers and students and that generously fund student services—providing academic support, counseling to address academic and personal challenges, part-time work opportunities, and meaningful extracurricular roles—increase retention. Membership in campus-based social and religious organizations is especially helpful in strengthening minority students' sense of belonging (Chen, 2012; Kuh, Cruce, & Shoup, 2008). Young people who feel that they have entered a college community that is concerned about them as individuals are far more likely to graduate.

Despite laws guaranteeing equality of opportunity, racial and ethnic bias in career opportunities remains strong (Smith, Brief, & Colella, 2010). To investigate discrimination in hiring emerging adults into entry-level positions, researchers recruited two three-member teams consisting of a white, African-American, and Hispanic male job applicant, each 22 to 26 years old and matched on verbal ability, interpersonal skills, and physical attractiveness. The applicants were assigned identical fictitious résumés, with the exception that the résumé of the white member of the second team disclosed a criminal record. Then they were sent out to apply for 170 entry-level jobs in New York City (Pager, Western, & Bonikowski, 2009). The white applicant received callbacks or job offers from employers more often than the Hispanic applicant, with the African-American applicant trailing far behind. When the experiment was repeated with the second team, the white felon remained slightly preferred over both minority applicants, despite their clean records.

In another similar investigation, which varied applicant qualifications within résumés, whites with high-quality résumés received substantially more employer callbacks than those with low-quality résumés. In contrast, having a high-quality résumé made little difference for African Americans. As the researchers noted, "Discrimination appears to bite twice, making it harder for African Americans to find a job and to improve their employability" (Bertrand & Mullainathan, 2004, p. 3).

Ethnic minority women often must surmount combined gender and racial discrimination to realize their career potential. Those who succeed often develop an unusually high sense of self-efficacy, attacking problems head-on despite repeated obstacles to achievement. In interviews with African-American women who had become leaders in diverse fields, all reported intense persistence, fueled by supportive relationships with other women, including teachers and peers.

MICHELE MCDONALD/THE BOSTON GLOBE VIA GETTY IMAGES

A University of Massachusetts–Boston undergraduate student works full-time during the summer in a research lab at the Dana-Farber Cancer Institute. Close bonds with teachers and career-relevant employment enhance graduation rates among ethnic minorities.

Many described their mothers as inspiring role models who had set high standards for them. Others mentioned support from their African-American communities, stating that a deep sense of connection to their people had empowered them (Richie et al., 1997).

WORLDVIEW   Most emerging adults say that constructing a *worldview,* or set of beliefs and values to live by, is essential for attaining adult status (Arnett, 2007). Do today's young people forge self-centered worldviews, as the descriptor "generation me" suggests?

This issue has generated heated controversy. Analyses of large, nationally representative samples of U.S. young people, collected repeatedly over several decades, suggest that compared to past generations, the Millennial generation reports greater narcissism (egotistical self-admiration) and valuing of money and leisure and reduced empathy for the less fortunate and civic engagement (Gentile, Twenge, & Campbell, 2010; Twenge, 2013).

But other researchers claim that generational changes in egotism and other traits are so small as not to be meaningful. And gradual, age-related gains in self-esteem extending from adolescence through emerging adulthood and into midlife are similar across generations, with the average self-esteem of today's young people no higher than that of past cohorts (Orth, Robins, & Widaman, 2012; Orth, Trzesniewski, & Robins, 2010). Over these years, adults derive a greater sense of competence from making identity commitments, entering and succeeding at their careers, having families, and becoming involved in their communities.

Additional evidence indicates that the importance to college students of attaining material wealth has not risen over the past three decades (Arnett, Trzesniewski, & Donnellan, 2013). In one investigation, the overwhelming majority of a national sample of U.S. 18- to 29-year-olds indicated that enjoyment of their work would be more important than making a lot of money, and that it was important to have a career that "does some good in the world" (Arnett & Schwab, 2012). Emerging adults do rate highly certain individualistic goals, such as career success and finding purpose in life, but these are balanced by high valuing of relationship goals, such as a good marriage and strong friendships (Trzesniewski & Donnellan, 2010).

Civic and Political Commitments.   Additional evidence supports the view that many emerging adults want to improve their communities, nation, and world. In a survey of 165,000 first-year students enrolled in more than 200 U.S. colleges and universities, a record number expected to participate in community service, with nearly 35 percent saying that there is "a very good chance" they will do so—double the number 25 years ago (Eagan et al., 2013). Among those who expect to volunteer, the overwhelming majority actually do so within their first year (DeAngelo, Hurtado, & Pryor, 2010). Overall, emerging adults are about as likely as contemporary senior citizens to work with others on local projects in their communities and raise funds for charitable causes (Flanagan & Levine, 2010).

Furthermore, compared to young people in previous generations, today's emerging adults have a stronger *pluralistic orientation*—disposition for living in a diverse society that promotes individual respect and equality of opportunity, regardless of race, ethnicity, gender, and sexual orientation. They are also more concerned about addressing global problems (Arnett, 2013; Zogby, 2008). Overall, the intentions and behaviors of emerging adults reflect considerable caring and concern for others and civic commitment.

Finally, contemporary 18- to 29-year-olds have been labeled "apathetic no shows" when it comes to voting. After declining over the 1990s, their turnout rose in the 2000s, reaching 51

© JIM WEST/THE IMAGE WORKS

These University of Michigan students plant trees in an impoverished Detroit neighborhood. Today's emerging adults are as likely as senior citizens to volunteer in their communities.

LOOK and LISTEN

Ask a class of college students to answer the following question: What would you do if you had a million dollars? How often do respondents mention prosocial as opposed to self-centered acts?

© BLEND IMAGES/ALAMY

Unlike most of his contemporaries, this emerging adult decided to vote. Postponement of adult roles seems to reduce young people's stake in the political process

percent in 2008, then dropping to 45 percent in 2012. Throughout, participation remained below the 66 percent rate of 30-and-older citizens (Circle, 2013). Emerging adults' longer road to adulthood likely contributes to their low voting rates. Adult commitments and responsibilities—marriage, career progress, and financial stability—increase people's stake in the political process, strengthening voter participation (Flanagan & Levine, 2010). Young people vote in fewer numbers than older people in nearly all established democracies.

Religion and Spirituality. During the late teens and twenties, attendance at religious services drops to its lowest level throughout the lifespan, as departure from home reduces parental pressure to attend and as young people continue to question the beliefs they acquired in their families (Schwartz et al., 2011). One-third of U.S. 18- to 29-year-olds are unaffiliated with a particular faith—considerably more than in their parents' generation at the same age. Many express concern that religious institutions have become too judgmental, political, and concerned with money and power (Pew Research Center, 2014).

Yet about 50 percent of U.S. young people remain stable in their religious commitment (or lack thereof) from adolescence into emerging adulthood (Smith & Snell, 2009). And in certain ways, U.S. emerging adults are quite traditional in their religious beliefs and practices. Religion is more important in their lives than it is for young people in other developed countries. Similar to previous generations, most U.S. young people—even those who are religiously unaffiliated—say they believe in God and describe themselves as religious, spiritual, or both. Furthermore, more than one-third of those who are religiously affiliated say they are "strong" members of their faith—equivalent to same-age individuals who said so a decade earlier (Pew Research Center, 2010, 2014). Women and ethnic minorities tend to be more religious (Barry et al., 2010). Of the small number of young people who increase in religiosity during the late teens and early twenties, many are women, African American, or Hispanic.

Whether or not they are involved in organized religion, many young people begin to construct their own individualized faith and, if attending college, discuss religious and spiritual beliefs and experiences more often with friends than with parents or other adults. These peer dialogues promote spiritual development (Barry & Christofferson, 2014; Stoppa & Lefkowitz, 2010). Often emerging adults weave together beliefs and practices from diverse sources, including Eastern and Western religious traditions, science, and popular culture. They also grapple with reconciling religious or spiritual beliefs with scientific principles (Longest & Smith, 2011).

Emerging adults who view their parents as warm and accepting and as having used an authoritative child-rearing style are more likely to hold religious or spiritual beliefs and engage in religious practices similar to those of their parents (Nelson, 2014). The warmth, explanations, and autonomy granting of authoritative parenting seem to provide young people with a fuller understanding of their parents' religious ideology, as well as with greater freedom to evaluate it against alternatives. Consequently, they are more likely to integrate their parents' perspectives into their own worldview.

As with adolescents, emerging adults who are religious or spiritual tend to be better-adjusted. They are higher in self-esteem and psychological well-being; less often are anxious and depressed, engage in substance use and antisocial acts, and become involved in hookup and friends-with-benefits relationships; and more often engage in community service (Barry & Christofferson, 2014; Yonker, Schnabelruch, & DeHaan, 2012). But outcomes vary. Those experiencing profound religious and spiritual struggles are at risk for physical and mental health difficulties (Magyar-Russell, Deal, & Brown, 2014). And among sexual minority young people, religiosity is less protective against poor adjustment. A possible reason is that their religious communities often do not support (and sometimes condemn) their sexual orientation (Ream & Rodriguez, 2014). They benefit from religious affiliations where sexual minority status is valued as contributing to congregational diversity.

College students attend Sunday chapel services. Although religious participation declines to its lowest level in the late teens and twenties, U.S. young people more often engage in religious practice than do their agemates in other developed countries.

© MELANIE STETSON FREEMAN/CHRISTIAN SCIENCE MONITOR/THE IMAGE WORKS

LOOK and LISTEN

Interview several of your classmates about how their religious beliefs and practices have changed in emerging adulthood, along with factors they see as having influenced those changes.

For emerging adults who reap positive outcomes, religion and spirituality seem to serve as a reminder of social injustices and the importance of helping others in need. Also, as emerging adults seek their place in an increasingly complex, ever-changing world, religion helps anchor them (Kerestes & Youniss, 2003). It offers a link between the past and the present, a transcendent system through which they can view stressful, confusing events, and an image of an ideal future toward which they can strive.

Risk and Resilience in Emerging Adulthood

17.4 What risks do emerging adults face, and what factors foster a successful transition to adulthood?

Emerging adults play a more active role in their own development than at any earlier time (Arnett, 2006). They must choose and coordinate demanding life roles and refine the skills necessary to succeed in those roles.

As long as young people have access to the opportunities of this period, most experience it as a time of flourishing, in which they solidify beliefs and values, participate in prosocial activities, forge lasting friendships and romantic relationships, succeed educationally, and launch a career. But a sizable number flounder: Their lack of direction is evident in persisting low self-esteem; high anxiety, depression, and loneliness; poor academic performance; disengagement from their communities; and high levels of risky behaviors (Smith, 2011). For example, drug and alcohol use peak between ages 18 and 25, with U.S. emerging adults stating that their most frequent reasons for binge drinking are to relieve boredom and get away from problems (National Institute on Drug Abuse, 2014; Patrick & Schulenberg, 2013). And rates of sexual assault among 18- to 24-year-olds are more than twice those of older people. About 20 to 25 percent of women and 15 percent of men on college campuses have been victims (National Sexual Violence Resource Center, 2013). Most have had a prior intimate relationship with the attacker.

Clearly, emerging adults vary greatly in their adaptation. In an investigation of nearly 500 undergraduate students from five colleges and universities across the United States, 64 percent were well-adjusted; 28 percent displayed high levels of risk behaviors, including frequent drinking, drug use, violent video game play, and changes in sexual partners; and 8 percent were poorly adjusted, reporting low self-esteem, high anxiety and depression, and the highest levels of risk behaviors (Nelson & Padilla-Walker, 2013). What factors might differentiate emerging adults who flourish from those who flounder?

Longitudinal research indicates that the personal attributes and social supports listed in Applying What We Know on page 646 foster successful passage through this period, as indicated by completing a college education, forging a warm, stable intimate relationship, finding and keeping a well-paying job, and volunteering in one's community (Benson et al., 2006; Eccles & Gootman, 2002). Notice how the factors in the table overlap with ones discussed in earlier chapters that promote development through *resilience*, the capacity to overcome challenge and adversity. Emerging adults with more of these resources—and with resources in all three categories—probably make an especially smooth transition to adulthood. But some emerging adults with only a few resources also fare well.

As in childhood and adolescence, certain resources strengthen others. Relationships with parents have an especially wide-ranging influence. A secure, affectionate parent–emerging adult bond that extends the balance of connection and separation established in adolescence promotes many aspects of adaptive functioning: favorable self-esteem, identity progress, successful transition to college life, higher academic achievement, and more rewarding friendships and romantic ties. Autonomy-supportive parenting in particular—an empathic approach in which parents recognize the weighty decisions the young person faces and encourage personally valued choices—is linked to emerging adults' psychological well-being (Kins et al., 2009). As one reviewer of research summed up, "What seems advantageous for emerging adults' achievement

An incoming college freshman joins her mother in checking their respective orientation-week schedules before fall classes begin. Warm, autonomy-supportive parenting—encouraging the young person to make personally valued choices—promotes adaptive functioning in emerging adulthood.

EVELYN HOCKSTEIN/FOR THE WASHINGTON POST VIA GETTY IMAGES

Applying What We Know

Resources That Foster Resilience in Emerging Adulthood

TYPE OF RESOURCE	DESCRIPTION
Cognitive attributes	Effective planning and decision making
	Information-gathering cognitive style
	Good school performance
	Knowledge of vocational options and skills
Emotional and social attributes	Positive self-esteem
	Good emotional self-regulation and flexible coping strategies
	Good conflict-resolution skills
	Confidence in one's ability to reach one's goals
	Sense of personal responsibility for outcomes
	Persistence and good use of time
	Healthy identity development—movement toward exploration in depth and commitment certainty
	Strong moral character
	Sense of meaning and purpose in life, engendered by religion, spirituality, or other sources
	Desire to contribute meaningfully to one's community
Social supports	Positive relationships with parents, peers, teachers, and mentors
	Sense of connection to social institutions, such as school, religious institution, workplace, and community center

of independence is feeling connected, secure, understood, and loved in their families, and having the willingness to call on parental resources" (Aquilino, 2006, p. 201).

In contrast, parental overprotection, expressed through excessive contact and psychological control—including taking over when the young person encounters challenges—is linked to the indicators of poor adjustment we have just considered, including low self-esteem, inability to make commitments in identity formation, and increased anxiety, depression, and alcohol use (Luyckx et al., 2007; Patock-Peckam & Morgan-Lopez, 2009). And exposure to multiple negative life events—family conflict, abusive intimate relationships, repeated romantic breakups, academic or employment difficulties, and financial strain—undermines development, even in emerging adults whose childhood and adolescence prepared them well for this transition (Masten et al., 2004).

In sum, supportive family, school, and community environments are crucial, just as they were at earlier ages. The majority of young people with these resources are optimistic about their future (Arnett, 2006; Arnett & Schwab, 2012). As they grapple with momentous choices, they are convinced that they will someday arrive at where they want to be in life: secure enough financially and happy in work and close relationships.

Ask Yourself

● **REVIEW** What cultural changes have led to the appearance of emerging adulthood?

● **CONNECT** What family, school, and community experiences in adolescence increase the chances that emerging adults will engage in community service? (See Chapter 16, page 603.)

● **APPLY** List supports that your college environment offers emerging adults in its health and counseling services, academic advising, residential living, and extracurricular activities. How does each help young people master the challenges of this period?

● **REFLECT** Give an example of how your thinking has become more relativistic. Which college experiences probably contributed to this change?

Summary

Unprecedented Exploration (p. 632)

17.1 What is emerging adulthood?

- In **emerging adulthood,** many young people report that they do not yet view themselves as fully adult. Rather, from the late teens through the mid- to late-twenties, they feel in between adolescence and adulthood as they prolong identity development, exploring alternatives more intensely. Attaining adult milestones is highly diverse in timing and order across individuals.

Cultural Change, Cultural Variation, and Emerging Adulthood (p. 633)

17.2 How has cultural change and variation contributed to emerging adulthood?

- Increased education required for entry into complex, well-paid careers, gains in life expectancy, reduced need for young people's labor, and globalization have prompted the appearance and spread of emerging adulthood.

- The majority of young people in developing nations do not experience emerging adulthood. The same is true for low-SES youths in Western nations. In industrialized countries, wide variation exists in emerging adults' beliefs about the meaning of attaining adult status.

- Because it is strongly linked to SES and higher education, some researchers do not agree that emerging adulthood is a distinct life stage.

Development in Emerging Adulthood (p. 636)

17.3 What cognitive, emotional, and social changes take place during emerging adulthood?

- Cognitive gains of the late teens and early twenties are supported by further brain development, especially the prefrontal cortex and its connections with other brain regions.

- Research on **postformal thought** reveals that as college students explore new ideas and beliefs, their reasoning becomes more rational, flexible, and practical. As **epistemic cognition** advances, they move away from **dualistic thinking,** dividing information into right and wrong, toward **relativistic thinking,** awareness of multiple truths. Eventually, the most mature individuals arrive at **commitment within relativistic thinking,** a perspective that synthesizes contradictions.

- Opportunities to tackle challenging, ill-structured problems collaboratively with others who are equal in knowledge and authority promote reflection on one's own thinking and gains in epistemic cognition.

- College students' attitudes and values broaden, enhancing self-understanding and self-esteem. They refine their approach to constructing an identity, exploring not just in breadth but also in depth, cycling between making commitments and evaluating commitments in various identity domains.

- With age, emerging adults' romantic ties typically last longer and become more emotionally intimate and committed. Nevertheless, among U.S. college students, emotionally indifferent, uncommitted sexual encounters are widespread. Partner similarity and good communication predict happy, lasting relationships, as does a secure internal working model of attachment. In Western nations, cohabitation has become the preferred mode of entry into a committed relationship.

- Emerging adults' work experiences increasingly focus on preparation for adult work roles. Most construct a dream, typically emphasizing career for men and both marriage and career for women. Relationships with mentors, along with quality of higher education, contribute to emerging adults' realization of career goals.

- Identity achievement in the vocational realm tends to be more challenging for women, who often question their abilities and express concerns about combining work with family responsibilities. Ethnic minorities also face difficulties, as racial and ethnic bias in career opportunities remains strong.

- U.S. college students generally express both individualistic and relationship goals in their worldviews. Many emerging adults participate in community service and express a strong pluralistic orientation and desire to address global problems. Nevertheless, compared with older people, they vote in fewer numbers.

- During the late teens and twenties, attendance at religious services drops to its lowest level. Whether or not they remain involved in formal religious activities, many young people begin to construct their own individualized faith. Those who are religious or spiritual tend to be better adjusted.

Risk and Resilience in Emerging Adulthood (p. 645)

17.4 What risks do emerging adults face, and what factors foster a successful transition to adulthood?

- During this time of great change and challenge, a sizable number of emerging adults flounder, suffering from lack of direction and other problems. A wide array of personal attributes and social supports, especially secure, affectionate bonds with parents who support the young person's efforts to make personally valued choices, foster resilience and successful passage into adulthood.

Important Terms and Concepts

commitment within relativistic thinking (p. 637)	emerging adulthood (p. 632)	postformal thought (p. 636)
dualistic thinking (p. 636)	epistemic cognition (p. 636)	relativistic thinking (p. 636)

Glossary

A

academic programs Preschool and kindergarten programs in which teachers structure children's learning, teaching academic skills through formal lessons that often involve repetition and drill. Distinguished from *child-centered programs.* (p. 341)

accommodation In Piaget's theory, that part of adaptation in which new schemes are created and old ones adjusted to produce a better fit with the environment. Distinguished from *assimilation.* (p. 202)

acculturative stress Psychological distress resulting from conflict between an individual's minority culture and the host culture. (p. 594)

adaptation In Piaget's theory, the process of building schemes through direct interaction with the environment. Consists of two complementary activities: *assimilation* and *accommodation.* (p. 202)

adolescence The transition between childhood and adulthood that begins with puberty. It involves accepting one's full-grown body, acquiring adult ways of thinking, attaining greater independence from one's family, developing more mature ways of relating to peers of both sexes, and beginning to construct an identity. (p. 519)

adrenarche The rise in adrenal androgens long before physical changes of puberty are visible, typically between ages 6 and 8. (p. 521)

affordances The action possibilities that a situation offers an organism with certain motor capabilities. Discovering affordances plays a major role in perceptual differentiation. (p. 196)

age of viability The age at which the fetus can first survive if born early. Occurs sometime between 22 and 26 weeks. (p. 99)

alcohol-related neurodevelopmental disorder (ARND) The least severe form of fetal alcohol spectrum disorder, involving impairment in at least three areas of mental functioning but with typical physical growth and absence of facial abnormalities. Distinguished from *fetal alcohol syndrome (FAS)* and *partial fetal alcohol syndrome (p-FAS).* (p. 107)

allele Each of two or more forms of a gene, one inherited from the mother and one from the father, located at the same place on corresponding pairs of chromosomes. (p. 55)

amnion The inner membrane that forms a protective covering around the prenatal organism. (p. 97)

amniotic fluid The fluid that fills the amnion, which helps keep temperature constant and provides a cushion against jolts caused by the woman's movements. (p. 97)

amodal sensory properties Information that overlaps two or more sensory systems, such as rate, rhythm, duration, intensity, and temporal synchrony in visual and auditory input. (p. 195)

amygdala An inner-brain structure that plays a central role in processing of novelty and emotional information. (p. 290)

androgyny The gender identity held by individuals who score high on both traditionally masculine and traditionally feminine personality characteristics. (p. 389)

animistic thinking The belief that inanimate objects have lifelike qualities, such as thoughts, wishes, feelings, and intentions. (p. 315)

anorexia nervosa An eating disorder in which young people, mainly females, starve themselves because of a compulsive fear of getting fat and an extremely distorted body image. (p. 534)

A-not-B search error The error made by 8- to 12-month-olds who, after reaching several times for an object at one hiding place (A), then seeing it moved to second (B), still search for it in the first hiding place (A). (p. 204)

anoxia Inadequate oxygen supply. (p. 133)

Apgar Scale A rating system on each of five characteristics—heart rate, respiratory effort, reflex irritability, muscle tone, and color—used to assess the newborn baby's physical condition immediately after birth. (p. 126)

applied behavior analysis Observations of relationships between behavior and environmental events, followed by systematic changes in those events based on procedures of conditioning and modeling. The goal is to eliminate undesirable behaviors and increase desirable responses. (p. 18)

assimilation That part of adaptation in which the external world is interpreted in terms of current schemes. Distinguished from *accommodation.* (p. 202)

associative play A form of true social interaction in which children engage in separate activities but exchange toys and comment on one another's behavior. Distinguished from *nonsocial activity, parallel play,* and *cooperative play.* (p. 366)

attachment The strong affectionate tie that humans have with special people in their lives, which leads them to experience pleasure and joy when interacting with them and to be comforted by their nearness in times of stress. (p. 261)

Attachment Q-Sort A method of assessing attachment security, ranging from high to low, in children between 1 and 5 years of age through home observations of a variety of attachment-related behaviors. (p. 264)

attention-deficit hyperactivity disorder (ADHD) A disorder involving inattention, impulsivity, and excessive motor activity, resulting in academic and social problems. (p. 438)

attribution retraining An intervention that encourages learned-helpless children to believe they can overcome failure by exerting more effort and using more effective strategies. (p. 480)

authoritarian child-rearing style A child-rearing style that is low in acceptance and involvement, high in coercive and psychological control, and low in autonomy granting. Distinguished from *authoritative, permissive,* and *uninvolved child-rearing styles.* (p. 393)

authoritative child-rearing style A child-rearing style that is high in acceptance and involvement, adaptive control techniques, and appropriate autonomy granting. Distinguished from *authoritarian, permissive,* and *uninvolved child-rearing styles.* (p. 392)

autobiographical memory Long-lasting representations of personally meaningful one-time events from both the recent and the distant past. (p. 220)

automatic processes Cognitive activities that are so well-learned that they require no space in working memory and, therefore, permit an individual to focus on other information while performing them. (p. 216)

autonomy At adolescence, a sense of oneself as a separate, self-governing individual. Involves an emotional component—relying more on oneself and less on parents for support and guidance; and a behavioral component—engaging in careful, well-reasoned decision making. (p. 606)

autonomy versus shame and doubt In Erikson's theory, the psychological conflict of toddlerhood, which is resolved favorably when parents provide young children with suitable guidance and reasonable choices. (p. 246)

autosomes The 22 matching chromosome pairs in each human cell. (p. 53)

average children Children who receive average numbers of positive and negative votes on self-report measures of social preferences. Distinguished from *popular, rejected, controversial,* and *neglected children.* (p. 490)

B

babbling Repetition of consonant–vowel combinations in long strings, beginning around 6 months of age. (p. 235)

basic emotions Emotions such as happiness, interest, surprise, fear, anger, sadness, and disgust that are universal in humans and other primates and have a long evolutionary history of promoting survival. (p. 247)

basic trust versus mistrust In Erikson's theory, the psychological conflict of infancy, which is resolved positively when the balance of care is sympathetic and loving. (p. 246)

behavioral genetics A field devoted to uncovering the contributions of nature and nurture to the diversity in human traits and abilities. (p. 82)

behaviorism An approach that regards directly observable events—stimuli and responses—as the appropriate focus of study and views the development of behavior as taking place through classical and operant conditioning. (p. 17)

bicultural identity The identity constructed by individuals who explore and adopt values from both their family's subculture and the dominant culture. (p. 594)

binge-eating disorder An eating disorder in which young people engage in binge eating at least once a week for three months or longer but (unlike bulimia nervosa) do not purge afterward. (p. 536)

blastocyst The prenatal cell mass four days after fertilization, when 60 to 70 cells exist that form a hollow, fluid-filled ball. (p. 97)

blended, or **reconstituted, family** A family structure formed through cohabitation or remarriage that includes parent, stepparent, and children. (p. 503)

body image Conception of and attitude toward one's physical appearance. (p. 532)

bonding Parents' feelings of affection and concern for the newborn baby. (p. 141)

brain plasticity The capacity of various parts of the cerebral cortex to take over functions of damaged regions. Declines as hemispheres of the cerebral cortex lateralize. (p. 165)

breech position A position of the baby in the uterus that would cause the buttocks or feet to be delivered first. (p. 132)

bulimia nervosa An eating disorder in which young people, mainly females, engage in strict dieting and excessive exercise accompanied by binge eating, often followed by deliberate vomiting and purging with laxatives. (p. 536)

C

cardinality The mathematical principle stating that the last number in a counting sequence indicates the quantity of items in the set. (p. 338)

categorical self Classification of the self according to prominent ways in which people differ, such as age sex, physical characteristics, and goodness and badness. Develops between 18 and 30 months. (p. 278)

carrier A heterozygous individual who can pass a recessive trait to his or her children. (p. 55)

central executive In information processing, the conscious, reflective part of the mental system that directs the flow of information by deciding what to attend to, coordinating incoming information with information already in the system, and selecting, applying, and monitoring strategies that facilitate memory storage, comprehension, reasoning, and problem solving. (p. 216)

centration In Piaget's theory, the tendency of preoperational children to focus on one aspect of a situation while neglecting other important features. Distinguished from *decentration*. (p. 316)

cephalocaudal trend An organized pattern of physical growth in which the head develops more rapidly than the lower part of the body ("head to tail"). Distinguished from *proximodistal trend*. (p. 161)

cerebellum A structure at the rear and base of the brain that aids in balance and control of body movement. (p. 289)

cerebral cortex The largest, most complex structure of the human brain, containing the greatest number of neurons and synapses, which accounts for the highly developed intelligence of the human species. (p. 164)

cesarean delivery A surgical birth in which the doctor makes an incision in the mother's abdomen and lifts the baby out of the uterus. (p. 131)

child-centered programs Preschool and kindergarten programs in which teachers provide a variety of activities from which children select, and much learning takes place through play. Distinguished from *academic programs*. (p. 341)

child development An area of study devoted to understanding constancy and change from conception through adolescence. (p. 4)

child-rearing styles Combinations of parenting behaviors that occur over a wide range of situations, creating an enduring child-rearing climate. (p. 392)

chorion The outer membrane that forms a protective covering around the prenatal organism. It sends out tiny hairlike villi, from which the placenta begins to develop. (p. 97)

chromosomes Rodlike structures in the cell nucleus that store and transmit genetic information. (p. 51)

chronosystem In ecological systems theory, temporal changes in environments, either externally imposed or arising from within the child, that produce new conditions affecting development. Distinguished from *microsystem, mesosystem, exosystem,* and *macrosystem*. (p. 29)

circular reaction In Piaget's theory, a means of building schemes in which infants try to repeat a chance event caused by their own motor activity. (p. 203)

classical conditioning A form of learning that involves associating a neutral stimulus with a stimulus that leads to a reflexive response. Once the nervous system makes the connection between the two stimuli, the neutral stimulus produces the behavior by itself. (p. 176)

clinical interview An interview method in which the researcher uses a flexible, conversational style to probe for the participant's point of view. Distinguished from *structured interview*. (p. 34)

clinical, or **case study, method** A research method in which the aim is to obtain as complete a picture as possible of one individual's psychological functioning by bringing together a wide range of information, including interview data, observations, and sometimes test scores. (p. 35)

clique A group of about five to eight members who are good friends and, therefore, usually resemble one another in family background, attitudes, values, and interests. (p. 614)

cognitive-developmental theory An approach introduced by Piaget that views children as actively constructing knowledge as they manipulate and explore their world, and in which cognitive development takes place in stages. (p. 19)

cognitive maps Mental representations of spaces, such as classroom, school, or neighborhood. (p. 430)

cognitive self-regulation The process of continuously monitoring progress toward a goal, checking outcomes, and redirecting unsuccessful efforts. (p. 442)

cohort effects The effects of cultural-historical change on the accuracy of longitudinal and cross-sectional research findings. Results based on one cohort—individuals developing in the same time period, who are influenced by particular historical and cultural conditions—may not apply to other cohorts. (p. 41)

commitment within relativistic thinking The mature individual's formulation of a more satisfying perspective that synthesizes contradictions between opposing views, rather than choosing between them. (p. 637)

communities of learners An educational approach inspired by Vygotsky's theory, in which teachers guide the overall process of learning, but otherwise, no distinction is made between adult and child contributors: All participate in joint endeavors, and students have the authority to define and resolve problems as they work toward project goals, which often address complex real-world issues. (p. 462)

compliance Obedience to requests and commands. (p. 278)

comprehension In language development, the words and word combinations that children understand. Distinguished from *production*. (p. 238)

concrete operational stage Piaget's third stage, extending from about 7 to 11 years of age, during which thought becomes logical, flexible, and organized in its application to concrete information, but the capacity for abstract thinking is not yet present. (p. 429)

conditioned response (CR) In classical conditioning, a new response produced by a conditioned stimulus (CS) that is similar to the unconditioned, or reflexive, response (UCR). (p. 177)

conditioned stimulus (CS) In classical conditioning, a neutral stimulus that, through pairing with an unconditioned stimulus (UCS), leads to a new, conditioned response (CR). Distinguished from *unconditioned stimulus*. (p. 177)

conservation The understanding that certain physical characteristics of objects remain the same, even when their outward appearance changes. (p. 315)

constructivist classroom A classroom grounded in Piaget's view of children as active learners who construct their own knowledge. Features include richly equipped learning centers, small groups and individuals solving self-chosen problems, a teacher who guides and supports in response to children's needs, and evaluation based on individual students' progress in relation to their own prior development. Distinguished from *traditional classroom* and *social-constructivist classroom*. (p. 460)

contexts Unique combinations of personal and environmental circumstances that can result in different paths of development. (p. 8)

continuous development The view that development is a process of gradually adding more of the same types of skills that were there to begin with. Distinguished from *discontinuous development*. (p. 7)

contrast sensitivity A general principle accounting for early visual pattern preferences, which states that if babies can detect a difference in contrast between two patterns, they prefer the pattern with more contrast. (pp. 191–192)

controversial children Children who receive many votes, both positive and negative, on self-report measures of social preferences, indicating that they are both liked and disliked. Distinguished from *popular, rejected, neglected*, and *average children*. (p. 490)

conventional level Kohlberg's second level of moral development, in which moral understanding is based on conforming to social rules to ensure positive human relationships and maintain societal order. (p. 597)

convergent thinking The type of thinking emphasized on intelligence tests, which involves arriving at a single correct answer to a problem. Distinguished from *divergent thinking*. (p. 466)

cooing Pleasant vowel-like noises made by infants, beginning around 2 months of age. (p. 235)

cooperative learning Collaboration on a task by a small group of classmates who work toward common goals by considering one another's ideas, appropriately challenging one another, providing sufficient explanations to correct misunderstandings, and resolving differences of opinion on the basis of reasons and evidence. (p. 463)

cooperative play A form of social interaction in which children orient toward a common goal, such as acting out a make-believe theme. Distinguished from *nonsocial activity, parallel play*, and *associative play*. (p. 366)

coparenting The extent to which parents mutually support each other's parenting behaviors. (p. 69)

coregulation A form of supervision in which parents exercise general oversight while permitting children to take charge of moment-by-moment decision making. (p. 496)

core knowledge perspective A perspective that states that infants are born with a set of innate knowledge systems, or core domains of thought, each of which permits a ready grasp of new, related information and therefore supports early, rapid development of certain aspects of cognition. (p. 211)

corpus callosum The large bundle of fibers connecting the two hemispheres of the cerebral cortex. Supports smooth coordination of movements on both sides of the body and integration of many aspects of thinking. (p. 290)

correlational design A research design in which the investigator gathers information on individuals without altering their experiences and then examines relationships between participants' characteristics and their behavior or development. Does not permit inferences about cause and effect. (p. 38)

correlation coefficient A number, ranging from +1.00 to −1.00, that describes the strength and direction of the relationship between two variables. (p. 38)

creativity The ability to produce work that is original yet appropriate—something others have not thought of that is useful in some way. (p. 466)

cross-sectional design A research design in which groups of participants of different ages are studied at the same point in time. Distinguished from *longitudinal design*. (p. 42)

crowd A large, loosely organized social group consisting of several cliques with similar values. Membership is based on reputation and stereotype. (p. 614)

D

decentration In Piaget's theory, the capacity of concrete operational children to focus on several aspects of a problem and related them. Distinguished from *centration*. (p. 429)

deferred imitation The ability to remember and copy the behavior of models who are not present. (p. 205)

delay of gratification The ability to wait for an appropriate time and place to engage in a tempting act. (p. 279)

deoxyribonucleic acid (DNA) Long, double-stranded molecules that make up chromosomes. (p. 52)

dependent variable In an experiment, the variable the investigator expects to be influenced by the independent variable. Distinguished from *independent variable*. (pp. 38–39)

developmental cognitive neuroscience An area of investigation that brings together researchers from psychology, biology, neuroscience, and medicine to study the relationship between changes in the brain and the developing child's cognitive processing and behavior patterns. (p. 23)

developmental social neuroscience An area of investigation that brings together researchers from psychology, biology, neuroscience, and medicine to study the relationship between changes in the brain and emotional and social development. (p. 23)

developmentally appropriate practice A set of standards, devised by the U.S. National Association for the Education of Young Children, specifying program characteristics that meet young children's developmental and individual needs, based on current research and the consensus of experts. (p. 228)

developmental quotient (DQ) A score on an infant intelligence test, computed in the same manner as an IQ but labeled more conservatively because it does not tap the same dimensions of intelligence measured in older children. (p. 226)

developmental science An interdisciplinary field devoted to the study of all changes humans experience throughout the lifespan. (p. 4)

differentiation theory The view that perceptual development involves the detection of increasingly finer, invariant features in the environment. (p. 196)

difficult child A child whose temperament is characterized by irregular daily routines, slow acceptance of new experiences, and a tendency to react negatively and intensely. Distinguished from *easy child* and *slow-to-warm-up child*. (p. 254)

dilation and effacement of the cervix Widening and thinning of the cervix, as uterine contractions become more frequent and powerful, during the first stage of labor. (p. 125)

discontinuous development A view of development as a process in which new ways of understanding and responding to the world emerge at specific times. Distinguished from *continuous development*. (p. 8)

disorganized/disoriented attachment The attachment pattern reflecting the greatest insecurity, characterizing infants who show confused, contradictory behaviors when reunited with the parent after a separation. Distinguished from secure, *insecure–avoidant*, and *insecure–resistant attachment*. (p. 264)

displaced reference The realization that words can be used to cue mental images of things not physically present. (p. 209)

divergent thinking The type of thinking associated with creativity, which involves generating multiple and unusual possibilities when faced with a task or problem. Distinguished from *convergent thinking*. (p. 466)

divorce mediation A series of meetings between divorcing adults and a trained professional that are aimed at reducing family conflict, including legal battles over property division and child custody. (p. 503)

dominance hierarchy A stable ordering of group members that predicts who will win when conflict arises. (p. 424)

dominant cerebral hemisphere The hemisphere of the cerebral cortex responsible for skilled motor action and other important abilities. In right-handed individuals, the left hemisphere is dominant; in left-handed individuals, motor and language skills are often shared between the hemispheres. (p. 288)

dominant–recessive inheritance A pattern of inheritance in which, under heterozygous conditions, the influence of only one allele is apparent. (p. 55)

dualistic thinking The cognitive approach typical of younger college students, who divide information, values, and authority into right and wrong, good and bad, we and they. Distinguished from *relativistic thinking*. (p. 636)

dual representation The ability to view a symbolic object as both an object in its own right and a symbol. (p. 314)

dynamic assessment An innovative approach to testing consistent with Vygotsky's zone of proximal development, in which an adult introduces purposeful teaching into the testing situation to find out what the child can attain with social support. (p. 454)

dynamic systems perspective A view that regards the child's mind, body, and physical and social worlds as a dynamic, integrated system. A change in any part of the system leads the child to reorganize his or her behavior so the various components of the system work together again but in a more complex, effective way. (p. 29)

dynamic systems theory of motor development A theory that views new motor skills as reorganizations of previously mastered skills, which lead to more effective ways of exploring and controlling the environment. Each new skill is a joint product of central nervous system development, the body's movement capacities, the goals the child has in mind, and environmental supports for the skill. (p. 181)

E

easy child A child whose temperament is characterized by establishment of regular routines in infancy, general cheerfulness, and easy adaptation to new experiences. Distinguished from *difficult child* and *slow-to-warm-up child*. (p. 254)

ecological systems theory Bronfenbrenner's approach, which views the child as developing within a complex system of relationships affected by multiple levels of the surrounding environment, from immediate settings of family and school to broad cultural values, laws, customs, and resources. (p. 26)

educational self-fulfilling prophecies Teachers' positive or negative views of individual children, who tend to adopt and start to live up to those views. (p. 462)

effortful control The self-regulatory dimension of temperament, involving voluntary suppression of a dominant response in order to plan and execute a more adaptive response. (pp. 254–255)

egocentrism Failure to distinguish the symbolic viewpoints of others from one's own. (p. 315)

elaboration A memory strategy that involves creating a relationship, or shared meaning, between two or more items of information that are not members of the same category. (p. 438)

embryo The prenatal organism from 2 to 8 weeks after conception—the period when the groundwork is laid for all body structures and internal organs. (p. 98)

embryonic disk Cluster of cells on the inside of the blastocyst, from which the new organism will develop. (p. 97)

emergent literacy Children's active efforts to construct literacy knowledge through informal experiences. (p. 336)

emerging adulthood A new transitional period of development, extending from the late teens to the mid- to late-twenties, during which young people have left adolescence but have not yet assumed adult responsibilities. Rather, they continue to explore alternatives in love, work, and worldview. (p. 632)

emotional self-regulation Strategies for adjusting our emotional state to a comfortable level of intensity so we can accomplish our goals. (p. 252)

emotion-centered coping A strategy for managing emotion that is internal, private, and aimed at controlling distress when little can be done about an outcome. Distinguished from *problem-centered coping*. (p. 482)

empathy The ability to understand another's emotional state and to feel with that person, or respond emotionally in a similar way. (p. 278)

epigenesis Development resulting from ongoing, bidirectional exchanges between heredity and all levels of the environment. (p. 86)

episodic memory Memory for everyday experiences. (p. 329)

epistemic cognition Reflections on how one arrived at facts, beliefs, and ideas. (p. 636)

ethnic identity A sense of ethnic group membership and attitudes and feelings associated with that membership, as an enduring aspect of the self. (p. 594)

ethnography A research method in which an investigator attempts to understand the unique values and social processes of a culture or a distinct social group through participant observation—spending months and sometimes years in the cultural community, gathering field notes. (p. 36)

ethological theory of attachment Bowlby's theory, the most widely accepted view of attachment, which recognizes the infant's emotional tie to the caregiver as an evolved response that promotes survival. (p. 261)

ethology An approach concerned with the adaptive, or survival, value of behavior and its evolutionary history. (p. 24)

evolutionary developmental psychology An approach that seeks to understand the adaptive value of species-wide cognitive, emotional, and social competencies as those competencies change with age. (p. 25)

executive function The diverse cognitive operations and strategies that enable us to achieve our goals in cognitively challenging situations. Includes controlling attention, suppressing impulses, coordinating information in working memory, and flexibly directing and monitoring thought and behavior. (p. 216)

exosystem In ecological systems theory, social settings that do not contain children but nevertheless affect children's experiences—for example, parents' workplaces, their religious institutions, health and welfare services in the community, and parents' social networks. Distinguished from *microsystem, mesosystem, macrosystem,* and *chronosystem.* (p. 27)

expansions Adult responses that elaborate on children's speech, increasing its complexity. (p. 353)

experience-dependent brain growth Growth and refinement of established brain structures as a result of specific learning experiences that vary widely across individuals and cultures. Distinguished from *experience-expectant brain growth*. (p. 169)

experience-expectant brain growth The young brain's rapidly developing organization, which depends on ordinary experiences—opportunities to explore the environment, interact with people, and hear language and other sounds. Distinguished from *experience-dependent brain growth*. (p. 169)

experimental design A research design in which the investigator randomly assigns participants to two or more treatment conditions and studies the effect that manipulating an independent variable has on a dependent variable. Permits inferences about cause and effect. (p. 38)

expressive style A style of early language learning in which toddlers use language mainly to talk about people's feelings and needs, producing many social formulas and pronouns. Distinguished from *referential style*. (p. 239)

extended-family household A household in which parent and child live with one or more adult relatives. (p. 78)

F

fantasy period The period of vocational development in early and middle childhood, in which children gain insight into career options by fantasizing about them. Distinguished from *tentative period* and *realistic period*. (p. 579)

fast mapping Children's ability to connect new words with their underlying concepts after only a brief encounter. (p. 348)

fetal alcohol spectrum disorder (FASD) A range of physical, mental, and behavioral outcomes caused by prenatal alcohol exposure, including *fetal alcohol syndrome (FAS), partial fetal alcohol syndrome (p-FAS),* and *alcohol-related neurodevelopmental disorder (ARND).* (p. 106)

fetal alcohol syndrome (FAS) The most severe form of fetal alcohol spectrum disorder, distinguished by slow physical growth, facial abnormalities, and brain injury. Usually affects children whose mothers drank heavily throughout pregnancy. Distinguished from *partial fetal alcohol syndrome (p-FAS)* and *alcohol-related neurodevelopmental disorder (ARND).* (p. 106)

fetal monitors Electronic instruments that track the baby's heart rate during labor. (p. 130)

fetus The prenatal organism from the ninth week to the end of pregnancy—the period during which body structures are completed and rapid growth in size occurs. (p. 99)

formal operational stage Piaget's highest stage, beginning around 11 years of age, in which young people develop the capacity for abstract, systematic, scientific thinking. (p. 556)

Flynn effect The steady increase in IQ from one generation to the next. (p. 452)

fraternal, or dizygotic, twins Twins resulting from the release and fertilization of two ova. Genetically, they are no more alike than ordinary siblings. Distinguished from *identical, or monozygotic, twins.* (p. 53)

G

gametes Sex cells, or sperm and ova, which contain half as many chromosomes as regular body cells. (p. 53)

gender constancy A full understanding of the biologically based permanence of one's gender, including the realization that sex remains the same over time, even if clothing, hairstyle, and play activities change. (p. 390)

gender identity An image of oneself as relatively masculine or feminine in characteristics. (p. 389)

gender intensification Increased gender stereotyping of attitudes and behavior and movement toward a more traditional gender identity, sometimes evident in adolescence. (p. 605)

gender schema theory An information-processing approach to gender typing that explains how environmental pressures and children's cognitions work together to shape gender-role development. (p. 390)

gender-stereotype flexibility The belief that both males and females can display a gender-stereotyped personality trait or activity—that overlap exists in the characteristics of males and females. (p. 494)

gender typing Any association of objects, activities, roles, or traits with one sex or the other in ways that conform to cultural stereotypes. (p. 384)

gene A segment of a DNA molecule that contains instructions for producing various proteins that contribute to the body's growth and functioning. (p. 52)

genetic counseling A communication process designed to help couples assess their chances of giving birth to a baby with a hereditary disorder and choose the best course of action in view of risks and family goals. (p. 61)

gene–environment correlation The view that heredity influences the environments to which individuals are exposed. (p. 84)

gene–environment interaction The view that because of their genetic makeup, individuals differ in their responsiveness to qualities of the environment. (p. 83)

genomic imprinting A pattern of inheritance in which alleles are imprinted, or chemically marked, in such a way that one pair member is activated, regardless of its makeup. (p. 58)

genotype An individual's genetic makeup. Distinguished from *phenotype.* (p. 51)

gifted Displaying exceptional intellectual strengths, such as high IQ, creativity, or specialized talent. (p. 466)

glial cells Cells that are responsible for myelination of neural fibers, improving the efficiency of message transfer and, in certain instances, also participate directly in neural communication. (p. 162)

goodness-of-fit model A model that describes how favorable adjustment depends on an effective match, or good fit, between a child's temperament and child-rearing environment. (pp. 259–260)

growth faltering Failure of an infant to grow normally, characterized by weight, height, and head circumference substantially below age-related norms and by withdrawn, apathetic behavior, with a disturbed parent–infant relationship often a contributing factor. (p. 176)

growth hormone (GH) A pituitary hormone that affects the development of almost all body tissues. (p. 292)

growth spurt Rapid gain in height and weight that is the first outward sign of puberty. (p. 522)

guided participation Shared endeavors between more expert and less expert participants, without specifying the precise features of communication, thereby allowing for variations across situations and cultures. A broader concept than *scaffolding.* (p. 324)

H

habituation A gradual reduction in the strength of a response due to repetitive stimulation. (p. 178)

heritability estimate A measure of the extent to which individual differences in complex traits, such as intelligence or personality, in a specific population are due to genetic factors. (p. 82)

heterozygous Having two different alleles at the same place on a pair of chromosomes. Distinguished from *homozygous.* (p. 55)

hierarchical classification The organization of objects into classes and subclasses on the basis of similarities and differences. (p. 316)

hippocampus An inner-brain structure that plays a vital role in memory and in images of space we use to help us find our way. (p. 289)

Home Observation for Measurement of the Environment (HOME) A checklist for gathering information about the quality of children's home lives through observation and parental interview. (p. 226)

homozygous Having two identical alleles at the same place on a pair of chromosomes. Distinguished from *heterozygous.* (p. 55)

hypothetico-deductive reasoning A formal operational problem-solving strategy in which adolescents begin with a *hypothesis,* or prediction about variables that might affect an outcome, from which they *deduce* logical, testable inferences. Then they systematically isolate and combine variables to see which of those inferences are confirmed in the real world. (p. 556)

I

identical, or monozygotic, twins Twins that result when a zygote, during early cell duplication, separates into two clusters of cells that have the same genetic makeup. Distinguished from *fraternal, or dizygotic, twins.* (p. 54)

identity A well-organized conception of the self that defines who one is, what one values, and what directions one wants to pursue in life. (p. 587)

identity achievement The identity status of individuals who, after a period of exploration, have committed themselves to a clearly formulated set of self-chosen values and goals. Distinguished from *identity moratorium, identity foreclosure,* and *identity diffusion.* (p. 591)

identity diffusion The identity status of individuals who do not engage in exploration and are not committed to a set of values and goals. Distinguished from *identity achievement, identity moratorium,* and *identity foreclosure.* (p. 591)

identity foreclosure The identity status of individuals who do not engage in exploration but, instead, are committed to ready-made values and goals chosen for them by authority figures. Distinguished from *identity achievement, identity moratorium,* and *identity diffusion.* (p. 591)

identity moratorium The identity status of individuals who are exploring but not yet committed to self-chosen values and goals. Distinguished from *identity achievement, identity foreclosure,* and *identity diffusion.* (p. 591)

identity versus role confusion In Erikson's theory, the psychological conflict of adolescence, which is resolved positively when adolescents achieve an identity after a period of exploration and inner soul-searching. (p. 588)

imaginary audience Adolescents' belief that they are the focus of everyone else's attention and concern. (p. 561)

imitation Learning by copying the behavior of another person. Also known as *modeling* or *observational learning*. (p. 179)

implantation Attachment of the blastocyst to the uterine lining, which occurs 7 to 9 days after fertilization. (p. 97)

inclusive classrooms Classrooms in which students with learning difficulties learn alongside typical students in a regular educational setting for part or all of the school day. (p. 465)

incomplete dominance A pattern of inheritance in which both alleles are expressed in the phenotype, resulting in a combined trait, or one that is intermediate between the two. (p. 57)

independent variable In an experiment, the variable the researcher expects to cause changes in another variable and that the researcher manipulates by randomly assigning participants to treatment conditions. Distinguished from *dependent variable*. (p. 38)

induced labor A labor started artificially by breaking the amnion and giving the mother a hormone that stimulates contractions. (p. 131)

induction A type of discipline in which an adult helps the child notice feelings by pointing out the effects of the child's misbehavior on others. (p. 373)

industry versus inferiority In Erikson's theory, the psychological conflict of middle childhood, which is resolved positively when experiences lead children to develop a sense of competence at useful skills and tasks. (p. 473)

infantile amnesia The inability of most people to remember events that happened to them before age 3. (p. 220)

infant-directed speech (IDS) A form of communication used by adults to speak to infants and toddlers, consisting of short sentences with high-pitched, exaggerated expression, clear pronunciation, distinct pauses between speech segments, clear gestures to support verbal meaning, and repetition of new words in a variety of contexts. (p. 240)

infant mortality The number of deaths in the first year of life per 1,000 live births. An index used around the world to assess the overall health of a nation's children. (p. 138)

information processing An approach that views the human mind as a symbol-manipulating system through which information flows and that regards cognitive development as a continuous process. (p. 21)

inhibited, or shy, child A child whose temperament is such that he or she reacts negatively to and withdraws from novel stimuli. Distinguished from *uninhibited, or sociable, child*. (p. 255)

initiative versus guilt In Erikson's theory, the psychological conflict of early childhood, which is resolved positively through play experiences that foster a healthy sense of purposefulness and through development of a superego, or conscience, that is not overly strict or guilt-ridden. (p. 357)

insecure–avoidant attachment The attachment pattern characterizing infants who seem unresponsive to the parent when she is present, are usually not distressed by parental separation, and avoid or are slow to greet the parent when she returns. Distinguished from *secure, insecure–resistant*, and *disorganized/disoriented attachment*. (p. 264)

insecure–resistant attachment The attachment pattern characterizing infants who seek closeness to the parent before her departure, are usually distressed when she leaves, and combine clinginess with angry, resistive behavior or with an anxious focus on the parent when she returns. Distinguished from *secure, insecure–avoidant*, and *disorganized/disoriented attachment*. (p. 264)

intelligence quotient (IQ) A score that permits an individual's performance on an intelligence test to be compared to the performances of same-age individuals. (p. 225)

intentional, or goal-directed, behavior A sequence of actions in which schemes are deliberately coordinated to solve simple problems. (p. 204)

interactional synchrony A form of communication in which the caregiver responds to infant signals in a well-timed, rhythmic, appropriate fashion and both partners match emotional states, especially positive ones. (p. 266)

intermodal perception Perception that combines information from more than one modality, or sensory system, resulting in an integrated whole. (p. 195)

internal working model A set of expectations, derived from early caregiving experiences, about the availability of attachment figures, their likelihood of providing support during times of stress, and the self's interaction with those figures. Becomes a vital part of personality, serving as a guide for all future close relationships. (p. 262)

intersubjectivity The process by which two participants who begin a task with different understandings arrive at a shared understanding. (p. 324)

irreversibility The inability to mentally go through a series of steps in a problem and then reverse direction, returning to the starting point. Distinguished from *reversibility*. (p. 316)

J

joint attention A state in which the child and caregiver attend to the same object or event and the caregiver labels what the child sees. Contributes greatly to early language development. (p. 236)

K

kinship studies Studies comparing the characteristics of family members to determine the importance of heredity in complex human characteristics. (p. 82)

kwashiorkor A disease caused by an unbalanced diet very low in protein, which usually appears after weaning, between 1 and 3 years of age. Symptoms include an enlarged belly, swollen feet, hair loss, skin rash, and irritable, listless behavior. (p. 175)

L

language acquisition device (LAD) In Chomsky's theory, an innate system containing a universal grammar, or set of rules common to all languages, that enables children, no matter which language they hear, to understand and speak in a rule-oriented fashion as soon as they have learned enough words. (p. 231)

lanugo White, downy hair that covers the entire body of the fetus, helping the vernix stick to the skin. (p. 99)

lateralization Specialization of functions in the two hemispheres of the cerebral cortex. (p. 165)

learned helplessness Attribution of success to external factors such as luck, and failure to low ability, which cannot be improved through effort. Distinguished from *mastery-oriented attributions*. (p. 478)

learning disability Great difficulty with one or more aspects of learning, usually reading, resulting in achievement considerably behind what would be expected on the basis of a child's IQ. (p. 465)

logical necessity A basic property of propositional reasoning, which specifies that the accuracy of conclusions drawn from premises rests on the rules of logic, not on real-world confirmation. (p. 557)

longitudinal design A research design in which participants are studied repeatedly at different ages, and changes are noted as they get older. Distinguished from *cross-sectional design*. (p. 41)

long-term memory In information processing, the largest storage area in the mental system, containing our permanent knowledge base. (p. 216)

M

macrosystem In ecological systems theory, cultural values, laws, customs, and resources that influence experiences and interactions at inner levels of the environment. Distinguished from *microsystem, mesosystem, exosystem*, and *chronosystem*. (p. 27)

make-believe play A type of play in which children act out everyday and imaginary activities. (p. 205)

malocclusion A condition in which the upper and lower teeth do not meet properly. (p. 407)

marasmus A disease caused by a diet low in all essential nutrients that usually appears in the first year of life and leads to a wasted condition of the body. (p. 175)

mastery-oriented attributions Attributions that credit success to ability, which can be improved by trying hard, and failure to insufficient effort. Distinguished from *learned helplessness*. (p. 478)

matters of personal choice Concerns that do not violate the rights of others and, therefore, are up to each individual, such as choice of friends, hairstyle, and leisure activities. Distinguished from *moral imperatives* and *social conventions*. (p. 378)

maturation A genetically determined, naturally unfolding course of growth. (p. 13)

meiosis The process of cell division through which gametes are formed and in which the number of chromosomes in each cell is halved. (p. 53)

memory strategies Deliberate mental activities that improve the likelihood of remembering. (p. 329)

menarche First menstruation. (p. 525)

mental representation An internal depiction of information that the mind can manipulate. (p. 205)

mesosystem In ecological systems theory, connections between children's microsystems, or immediate settings. Distinguished from *microsystem, exosystem, macrosystem,* and *chronosystem*. (p. 27)

metacognition Thinking about thought; awareness of mental activities. (p. 332)

metalinguistic awareness The ability to think about language as a system. (p. 455)

methylation A biochemical process triggered by certain experiences, in which a set of chemical compounds (called a methyl group) lands on top of a gene and changes its impact, reducing or silencing its expression. (p. 86)

microgenetic design An adaptation of the longitudinal design, in which investigators present children with a novel task and follow their mastery over a series of closely spaced sessions to observe how change occurs. (p. 44)

microsystem In ecological systems theory, the innermost level of the environment, consisting of activities and interaction patterns in the child's immediate surroundings. Distinguished from *mesosystem, exosystem, macrosystem,* and *chronosystem*. (p. 26)

mirror neurons Specialized cells in many areas of the cerebral cortex in primates that underlie the ability to imitate by firing identically when a primate hears or sees an action and when it carries out that action on its own. (p. 180)

moral imperatives Rules and expectations that protect people's rights and welfare. Distinguished from *social conventions* and *matters of personal choice*. (p. 378)

moral identity The degree to which morality is central to an individual's self-concept. (p. 602)

mutation A sudden but permanent change in a segment of DNA. (p. 58)

mutual exclusivity bias Early in vocabulary growth, children's assumption that words refer to entirely separate (nonoverlapping) categories. (p. 349)

myelination The coating of neural fibers with *myelin,* an insulating fatty sheath that improves the efficiency of message transfer. (p. 162)

N

naturalistic observation A research method in which the researcher goes into the natural environment to observe the behavior of interest. Distinguished from *structured observation*. (p. 32)

natural, or **prepared, childbirth** A group of techniques aimed at reducing pain and medical intervention and making childbirth a rewarding experience. (p. 128)

nature–nurture controversy Debate among theorists about whether genetic or environmental factors are more important influences on development. (p. 9)

neglected children Children who are seldom mentioned, either positively or negatively, on self-report measures of social preferences. Distinguished from *popular, controversial, rejected,* and *average children*. (p. 490)

Neonatal Behavioral Assessment Scale (NBAS) A test developed to assess a newborn infant's behavior in terms of reflexes, muscle tone, state changes, responsiveness to physical and social stimuli, and other reactions. (p. 150)

neonatal mortality The number of deaths in the first month of life per 1,000 live births. (p. 138)

neural tube During the period of the embryo, the primitive spinal cord that develops from the ectoderm, the top of which swells to form the brain. (p. 98)

neurons Nerve cells that store and transmit information. (p. 161)

neurotransmitters Chemicals released by neurons that cross the synapse to send messages to other neurons. (p. 161)

niche-picking A type of gene–environment correlation in which individuals actively choose environments that complement their heredity. (p. 85)

nocturnal enuresis Bedwetting during the night. (p. 415)

non-rapid-eye-movement (NREM) sleep A regular sleep state in which the body is almost motionless and heart rate, breathing, and brain-wave activity are slow and even. Distinguished from *rapid-eye-movement (REM) sleep*. (p. 144)

nonsocial activity Unoccupied, onlooker behavior and solitary play. Distinguished from *parallel play, associative play,* and *cooperative play*. (pp. 365–366)

normal distribution The bell-shaped distribution that results when individual differences are measured in large samples. Most scores cluster around the mean, or average, with progressively fewer falling toward the extremes. (pp. 225–226)

normative approach An approach to development in which measures of behavior are taken on large numbers of individuals and age-related averages are computed to represent typical development. (pp. 13–14)

O

obesity A greater-than-20-percent increase over healthy weight, based on body mass index (BMI)—a ratio of weight to height associated with body fat. (p. 410)

object permanence The understanding that objects continue to exist when they are out of sight. (p. 204)

operant conditioning A form of learning in which a spontaneous behavior is followed by a stimulus that changes the probability that the behavior will occur again. (p. 178)

ordinality The mathematical principle specifying order relationships (more than and less than) between quantities. (p. 337)

organization In Piaget's theory, the internal rearrangement and linking together of schemes so that they form a strongly interconnected cognitive system. In information processing, a memory strategy that involves grouping related items together to improve recall. (pp. 202, 437)

overextension An early vocabulary error in which a word is applied to a wider collection of objects and events than is appropriate. Distinguished from *underextension*. (p. 237)

overlapping-waves theory A theory of problem solving, which states that when given challenging problems, children try out various strategies and gradually select those that are fastest and most accurate. (p. 331)

overregularization Extension of regular grammatical rules to words that are exceptions. (p. 351)

P

parallel play A limited form of social participation in which a child plays near other children with similar materials but does not interact with them. Distinguished from *nonsocial activity, associative play,* and *cooperative play*. (p. 366)

partial fetal alcohol syndrome (p-FAS) A form of fetal alcohol spectrum disorder characterized by facial abnormalities and brain injury, but less severe than fetal alcohol syndrome. Usually affects children whose mothers drank alcohol in smaller quantities during pregnancy. Distinguished from fetal alcohol syndrome (FAS) and alcohol-related neurodevelopmental disorder (ARND). (pp. 106–107)

peer acceptance Likability, or the extent to which a child is viewed by a group of agemates, such as classmates, as a worthy social partner. (p. 490)

peer groups Collectives of peers who generate unique values and standards for behavior and a social structure of leaders and followers. (p. 488)

peer victimization A destructive form of peer interaction in which particular children become targets of verbal and physical attacks or other forms of abuse. (p. 492)

perceptual narrowing effect Perceptual sensitivity that becomes increasingly attuned with age to information most often encountered. (p. 188)

permissive child-rearing style A child-rearing style that is high in acceptance but either overindulgent or inattentive, low in control, and inappropriately lenient in autonomy granting. Distinguished from *authoritative, authoritarian,* and *uninvolved child-rearing styles.* (p. 394)

person praise Praise from an adult that emphasizes the child's traits, as in "you're so smart"; "you're very artistic." Distinguished from *process praise.* (p. 479)

personal fable Adolescents' inflated opinion of their own importance—the belief that they are special and unique. (p. 562)

phenotype An individual's directly observable physical and behavioral characteristics, which are determined by both genetic and environmental factors. Distinguished from *genotype.* (p. 51)

phobia An intense, unmanageable fear. (p. 507)

phonics approach An approach to beginning reading instruction that emphasizes coaching children on phonics—the basic rules for translating written symbols into sounds—before exposing them to complex reading material. Distinguished from *whole-language approach.* (p. 443)

phonological awareness The ability to reflect on and manipulate the sound structures of spoken language, as indicated by sensitivity to changes in sounds within words, to rhyming, and to incorrect pronunciation. A strong predictor of emergent literacy. (p. 336)

physical aggression A form of aggression that harms others through physical injury to themselves or their property. Distinguished from *verbal aggression* and *relational aggression.* (p. 379)

pincer grasp The well-coordinated grasp that emerges at the end of the first year, involving thumb and index finger opposition. (p. 186)

pituitary gland A gland located at the base of the brain that releases hormones that induce physical growth. (p. 290)

placenta The organ that permits exchange of nutrients and waste products between the bloodstreams of the mother and the embryo, while also preventing the mother's and embryo's blood from mixing directly. (p. 97)

planning Thinking out a sequence of acts ahead of time and allocating attention accordingly to reach a goal. (p. 328)

plasticity Openness of human development to change in response to influential experiences. (p. 9)

polygenic inheritance A pattern of inheritance in which many genes affect the characteristic in question. (p. 59)

popular-antisocial children A subtype of popular children who are admired for their socially adept yet belligerent behavior. Includes "tough" boys who are athletically skilled but poor students who cause trouble and defy adult authority, and relationally aggressive boys and girls. Distinguished from *popular-prosocial children.* (p. 490)

popular children Children who receive many positive votes on self-report measures of social preferences, indicating they are well-liked. Distinguished from *rejected, controversial, neglected,* and *average children.* (p. 490)

popular-prosocial children A subtype of popular children who are both socially accepted and admired and who combine academic and social competence. Distinguished from *popular-antisocial children.* (p. 490)

postconventional level Kohlberg's highest level of moral development, in which individuals define morality in terms of abstract principles and values that apply to all situations and societies. (p. 598)

postformal thought Cognitive development beyond Piaget's formal operational stage. (p. 636)

pragmatics The practical, social side of language, concerned with how to engage in effective and appropriate communication. (p. 352)

preconventional level Kohlberg's first level of moral development, in which children accept the rules of authority figures and judge actions by their consequences, viewing behaviors that result in punishment as bad and those that lead to rewards as good. (p. 597)

prefrontal cortex The region of the cerebral cortex, lying in front of areas controlling body movement, that is responsible for thought—in particular, for consciousness, inhibition of impulses, integration of information, and use of memory, reasoning, planning, and problem-solving strategies. (p. 165)

prenatal diagnostic methods Medical procedures that permit detection of developmental problems before birth. (p. 64)

preoperational stage Piaget's second stage, extending from about 2 to 7 years of age, in which children undergo an extraordinary increase in representational, or symbolic, activity, although thought is not yet logical. (p. 311)

prereaching The poorly coordinated swipes toward objects of newborn babies. (p. 185)

preterm infants Infants born several weeks or more before their due date. (p. 135)

primary sexual characteristics Physical features of the reproductive organs—ovaries, uterus, and vagina in females; penis, scrotum, and testes in males. Distinguished from *secondary sexual characteristics.* (p. 525)

private speech Self-directed speech that children use to plan and guide their own behavior. (p. 323)

proactive aggression A type of aggression in which children act to fulfill a need or desire—to obtain an object, privilege, space, or social reward, such as adult or peer attention—and unemotionally attack a person to achieve their goal. Also called *instrumental aggression.* Distinguished from *reactive aggression.* (p. 379)

problem-centered coping A strategy for managing emotion in which the individual appraises the situation as changeable, identifies the difficulty, and decides what to do about it. Distinguished from *emotion-centered coping.* (p. 482)

process praise Praise from an adult that emphasizes the child's behavior and effort, such as "you worked really hard" or "you figured it out." Distinguished from *person praise.* (p. 479)

production In language development, the words and word combinations that children use. Distinguished from *comprehension.* (p. 238)

Project Head Start The most extensive U.S. federally funded preschool intervention program, which provides low-SES children with a year or two of preschool education, along with nutritional and health services, and encourages parent involvement in children's learning and development. (p. 342)

propositional thought A type of formal operational reasoning involving the ability to evaluate the logic of propositions (verbal statements) without referring to real-world circumstances. (p. 556)

prosocial, or **altruistic, behavior** Actions that benefit another person without any expected reward for the self. (p. 364)

protein-coding genes Genes that directly affect the body's characteristics. Distinguished from *regulator genes.* (p. 52)

proximodistal trend An organized pattern of physical growth that proceeds from the center of the body outward. Distinguished from *cephalocaudal trend.* (p. 161)

psychoanalytic perspective An approach to personality development introduced by Freud that assumes children move through a series of stages in which they confront conflicts between biological drives and social expectations. How these conflicts are resolved determines the person's ability to learn, to get along with others, and to cope with anxiety. (p. 15)

psychological control Parental control that attempts to take advantage of children's psychological needs by intruding on and manipulating children's verbal expressions, individuality, and attachments to parents. (p. 394)

psychosexual theory Freud's theory, which emphasizes that how parents manage children's sexual and aggressive drives in the first few years of life is crucial for healthy personality development. (p. 15)

psychosocial dwarfism A growth disorder, usually appearing between 2 and 15 years of age, caused by extreme emotional deprivation. It is characterized by decreased GH secretion, very short stature, immature skeletal age, and serious adjustment problems, which help distinguish it from normal shortness. (p. 292)

psychosocial theory Erikson's theory, which emphasizes that at each Freudian stage, individuals not only develop a unique personality but also acquire attitudes and skills that help them become active, contributing members of society. (p. 15)

puberty Biological changes that lead to an adult-sized body and sexual maturity. (p. 519)

public policies Laws and government programs designed to improve current conditions. (p. 79)

punishment In operant conditioning, removal of a desirable stimulus or presentation of an unpleasant stimulus, either of which decreases the occurrence of a response. (p. 178)

R

random assignment An unbiased procedure for assigning participants to treatment conditions in an experiment, such as drawing numbers out of a hat or flipping a coin. It increases the chances that participants' characteristics will be equally distributed across treatment groups. (p. 39)

rapid-eye-movement (REM) sleep An irregular sleep state in which brainwave activity is similar to that of the waking state. Distinguished from *non-rapid-eye-movement (NREM) sleep.* (p. 144)

reactive aggression An angry, defensive response to provocation or a blocked goal that is intended to hurt another person. Also called *hostile aggression.* Distinguished from *proactive aggression.* (p. 379)

realistic period The period of vocational development in which older adolescents and young adults focus on a general vocational category and, within it, experiment for a time before settling on a single occupation. Distinguished from *fantasy period* and *tentative period.* (p. 579)

recall The form of memory that involves remembering something not present, by generating a mental image of a past experience. Distinguished from *recognition.* (p. 218)

recasts Adult responses that restructure children's grammatically inaccurate speech into correct form. (p. 353)

reciprocal teaching A teaching method in which a teacher and two to four students form a cooperative group and take turns leading dialogues, creating a zone of proximal development in which children scaffold one another's progress. (p. 461)

recognition The form of memory that involves noticing whether a stimulus is identical or similar to one previously experienced. Distinguished from *recall.* (p. 218)

recovery Following habituation, an increase in responsiveness to a new stimulus. (p. 178)

recursive thought A form of perspective taking that requires the ability to view a situation from at least two perspectives—that is, to reason simultaneously about what two or more people are thinking. (p. 441)

referential style A style of early language learning in which toddlers use language mainly to label objects. Distinguished from *expressive style.* (p. 239)

reflex An inborn, automatic response to a particular form of stimulation. (p. 141)

regulator genes Genes that modify the instructions given by *protein coding genes,* greatly complicating their impact. (p. 52)

rehearsal A memory strategy that involves repeating information to oneself to improve recall. (p. 437)

reinforcer In operant conditioning, a stimulus that increases the occurrence of a response. (p. 178)

rejected-aggressive children A subtype of rejected children who show high rates of conflict, physical and relational aggression, and hyperactive, inattentive, and impulsive behavior. Distinguished from *rejected-withdrawn children.* (p. 491)

rejected children Children who receive many negative votes on self-report measures of social preferences, indicating they are disliked. Distinguished from *popular, controversial, neglected,* and *average children.* (p. 490)

rejected-withdrawn children A subtype of rejected children who are passive, socially awkward, and overwhelmed by social anxiety. Distinguished from *rejected-aggressive children.* (p. 491)

relational aggression A form of aggression that damages another's peer relationships through social exclusion, malicious gossip, or friendship manipulation. Distinguished from *physical aggression* and *verbal aggression.* (p. 380)

relativistic thinking The cognitive approach typical of older college students, who view all knowledge as embedded in a framework of thought and, therefore, give up the possibility of absolute truth in favor of multiple truths, each relative to its context. Distinguished from *dualistic thinking.* (p. 636)

resilience The ability to adapt effectively in the face of threats to development. (p. 10)

reticular formation A structure in the brain stem that maintains alertness and consciousness. (p. 289)

reversibility The capacity to think through a series of steps in a problem and then mentally reverse direction, returning to the starting point. Distinguished from *irreversibility.* (p. 429)

Rh factor incompatibility A condition that arises when the Rh protein is present in the fetus's blood but not in the mother's, causing the mother to build up antibodies to the foreign Rh protein. If these enter the fetus's system, they destroy red blood cells, reducing the oxygen supply to organs and tissues. (p. 113)

rooming in An arrangement in which the newborn baby stays in the mother's hospital room all or most of the time. (p. 141)

rough-and-tumble play A form of peer interaction involving friendly chasing and play-fighting that emerges in the preschool years and peaks in middle childhood. In our evolutionary past, it may have been important for the development of fighting skill. (p. 424)

S

scaffolding Adjusting the support offered during a teaching session to fit the child's current level of performance. As competence increases, the adult gradually and sensitively withdraws support, turning responsibility over to the child. (p. 324)

scale errors Toddlers' attempts to do things that their body size makes impossible, such as trying to put on dolls' clothes, sit in a doll-sized chair, or walk through a door too narrow to pass through. (p. 277)

scheme In Piaget's theory, a specific psychological structure, or organized way of making sense of experience, that changes with age. (p. 202)

scripts General descriptions of what occurs and when it occurs in a particular situation, used to organize, interpret, and predict everyday experiences. (p. 329)

secondary sexual characteristics Physical features visible on the outside of the body that serve as signs of sexual maturity but do not involve the reproductive organs—for example, breast development in females and the appearance of underarm and pubic hair in both sexes. Distinguished from *primary sexual characteristics.* (p. 525)

secular trends in physical growth Changes in body size from one generation to the next. (p. 406)

secure attachment The attachment pattern characterizing infants who use the parent as a secure base from which to explore and may be distressed by parental separation but actively seek contact and are easily comforted by the parent when she returns. Distinguished from *insecure–avoidant, insecure–resistant,* and *disorganized/disoriented attachment.* (p. 264)

secure base Role of the familiar caregiver as a point from which the infant explores, venturing into the environment and then returning for emotional support. (p. 250)

self-care children Children who regularly look after themselves for some period of time during after-school hours. (p. 506)

self-concept The set of attributes, abilities, attitudes, and values that an individual believes defines who he or she is. (p. 358)

self-conscious emotions Emotions involving injury to or enhancement of the sense of self, such as guilt, shame, embarrassment, envy, and pride. (p. 251)

self-esteem An aspect of self-concept that involves judgments about one's own worth and the feelings associated with those judgments. (p. 359)

semantic bootstrapping Using semantics, or word meanings, to figure out grammatical rules. (p. 351)

sensitive caregiving Caregiving that involves responding promptly, consistently, and appropriately to infants and holding them tenderly and carefully. (p. 266)

sensitive period A time that is biologically optimal for certain capacities to emerge because the individual is especially responsive to environmental influences. (p. 24)

sensorimotor stage Piaget's first stage, spanning the first two years of life, during which infants and toddlers "think" with their eyes, ears, hands, and other sensorimotor equipment. (p. 201)

sensory register In information processing, the part of the mental system in which sights and sounds are represented directly and stored briefly before they either decay or are transferred to working memory. (p. 215)

separation anxiety An infant's distressed reaction to the departure of their trusted caregiver. (p. 262)

sequential design A research design in which several similar cross-sectional or longitudinal studies (called sequences) are conducted at varying times. (p. 43)

seriation The ability to order items along a quantitative dimension, such as length or weight. (p. 430)

sex chromosomes The twenty-third pair of chromosomes—called XX in females, XY in males—which determines the sex of the individual. (p. 53)

shape constancy Perception of an object's shape as the same, despite changes in the shape projected on the retina. (p. 194)

short-term memory store That part of the mind in which attended-to information is retained briefly so that we can actively "work" on it to achieve our goals. (p. 215)

size constancy Perception of an object's size as the same, despite changes in the size of its retinal image. (p. 194)

slow-to-warm-up child A child whose temperament is characterized by inactivity; mild, low-key reactions to environmental stimuli; negative mood; and slow adjustment to new experiences. Distinguished from *easy child* and *difficult child*. (p. 254)

small-for-date infants Infants whose birth weight is below their expected weight considering length of the pregnancy. (p. 135)

social comparisons Judgments of one's own appearance, abilities, and behavior in relation to those of others. (p. 474)

social-constructivist classroom A classroom grounded in Vygotsky's sociocultural theory, in which children participate in a wide range of challenging activities with teachers and peers, with whom they jointly construct understandings. Distinguished from *traditional classroom* and *constructivist classroom*. (p. 461)

social conventions Customs determined by consensus, such as table manners and politeness rituals. Distinguished from *moral imperatives* and *matters of personal choice*. (p. 378)

social learning theory An approach that emphasizes the role of modeling, also known as imitation or observational learning, in the development of behavior. (p. 17)

social problem solving Generating and applying strategies that prevent or resolve disagreements, resulting in outcomes that are both acceptable to others and beneficial to the self. (p. 369)

social referencing Actively seeking emotional information from a trusted person in an uncertain situation. (p. 251)

social smile The infant's broad grin evoked by the parent's communication, first appearing between 6 and 10 weeks of age. (p. 248)

sociocultural theory Vygotsky's perspective, which focuses on how children acquire the ways of thinking and behaving that make up a community's culture through social interaction, especially cooperative dialogues with more knowledgeable members of society. (p. 25)

sociodramatic play The make-believe play with others that is under way by the end of the second year and that increases rapidly in complexity during early childhood. (p. 312)

socioeconomic status (SES) A measure of an individual's social position and economic well-being that combines three related variables: years of education, the prestige of one's job and the skill it requires, and income. (p. 70)

spermarche First ejaculation of seminal fluid. (p. 526)

stage A qualitative change in thinking, feeling, and behaving that characterizes a specific period of development. (p. 8)

standardization The practice of giving an intelligence test to a large, representative sample and using the results as the standard for interpreting individual scores. (p. 225)

states of arousal Degrees of sleep and wakefulness. (p. 143)

statistical learning capacity The capacity to analyze the speech stream for repeatedly occurring sequences of sounds, through which infants acquire a stock of speech structures for which they will later learn meanings. (p. 188)

stereotype threat The fear of being judged on the basis of a negative stereotype, which can trigger anxiety that interferes with performance. (p. 453)

stranger anxiety The infant's expression of fear in response to unfamiliar adults, which appears in many babies in the second half of the first year. (p. 249)

Strange Situation A laboratory procedure used to assess the quality of attachment between 1 and 2 years of age by observing the baby's responses to eight short episodes involving brief separations from and reunions with the caregiver in an unfamiliar playroom. (p. 263)

structured interview An interview method in which each participant is asked the same questions in the same way. Distinguished from *clinical interview*. (p. 35)

structured observation A research method in which the investigator sets up a laboratory situation that evokes the behavior of interest so that every participant has an equal opportunity to display the response. Distinguished from *naturalistic observation*. (p. 33)

subculture A group of people with beliefs and customs that differ from those of the larger culture. (p. 78)

sudden infant death syndrome (SIDS) The unexpected death, usually during the night, of an infant under 1 year of age that remains unexplained after thorough investigation. (p. 145)

sympathy Feelings of concern or sorrow for another's plight. (p. 364)

synapses The gaps between neurons, across which chemical messages are sent. (p. 161)

synaptic pruning Loss of synapses by seldom-stimulated neurons, a process that returns neurons not needed at the moment to an uncommitted state so they can support future development. (p. 162)

syntactic bootstrapping Figuring out word meanings by observing how words are used in syntax, or the structure of sentences. (p. 349)

T

talent Outstanding performance in a specific field. (p. 467)

telegraphic speech Toddlers' two-word utterances that, like a telegram, focus on high-content words while omitting smaller, less important ones. (p. 238)

temperament Early-appearing, stable individual differences in reactivity (quickness and intensity of emotional arousal, attention, and motor activity) and self-regulation (strategies that modify reactivity). (p. 253)

tentative period The period of vocational development in which adolescents begin to evaluate vocational options in terms of their interests, abilities, and values. Distinguished from *fantasy period* and *realistic period*. (p. 579)

teratogen Any environmental agent that causes damage during the prenatal period. (p. 101)

theory An orderly, integrated set of statements that describes, explains, and predicts behavior. (p. 7)

theory of multiple intelligences Gardner's theory, which proposes at least eight independent intelligences, defined in terms of distinct sets of processing operations that permit individuals to engage in a wide range of culturally valued activities. (p. 449)

thyroid-stimulating hormone (TSH) A pituitary hormone that stimulates the thyroid gland to release thyroxine, which is necessary for brain development and for growth hormone to have its full impact on body size. (p. 292)

time out A form of mild punishment in which children are removed from the immediate setting until they are ready to act appropriately. (p. 376)

traditional classroom A classroom in which the teacher is the sole authority for knowledge, rules, and decision making and students are relatively passive learners who are evaluated in relation to a uniform set of standards for their grade. Distinguished from *constructivist classroom* and *social-constructivist classroom*. (p. 460)

transition Climax of the first stage of labor, in which the frequency and strength of contractions are at their peak and the cervix opens completely. (p. 125)

transitive inference The ability to seriate, or order items along a quantitative dimension, mentally. (p. 430)

triarchic theory of successful intelligence Sternberg's theory, which identifies three broad, interacting intelligences—analytical, creative, and practical—that must be balanced to achieve success according to one's personal goals and the requirements of one's cultural community. (p. 448)

trimesters Three equal time periods, each lasting three months, into which prenatal development is divided. (p. 99)

trophoblast The thin outer ring of cells of the blastocyst, which will become the structures that provide protective covering and nourishment to the new organism. (p. 97)

U

ulnar grasp The clumsy grasp of the young infant, in which the fingers close against the palm. (p. 186)

umbilical cord The long cord connecting the prenatal organism to the placenta that delivers nutrients and removes waste products. (p. 98)

unconditioned response (UCR) In classical conditioning, a reflexive response that is produced by an unconditioned stimulus (UCS). Distinguished from *conditioned response*. (p. 177)

unconditioned stimulus (UCS) In classical conditioning, a stimulus that leads to a reflexive response. Distinguished from *conditioned stimulus*. (p. 177)

underextension An early vocabulary error in which young children apply a word too narrowly, to a smaller number of objects and events than is appropriate. Distinguished from *overextension*. (p. 237)

uninhibited, or sociable, child A child whose temperament is such that he or she displays positive emotion to and approaches novel stimuli. Distinguished from *inhibited, or shy, child*. (p. 255)

uninvolved child-rearing style A child-rearing style that combines low acceptance and involvement with little control and general indifference to issues of autonomy. Distinguished from *authoritative, authoritarian,* and *permissive child-rearing styles*. (p. 394)

V

verbal aggression A form of aggression that harms others through threats of physical aggression, name-calling, or hostile teasing. Distinguished from *physical* and *relational aggression*. (p. 379)

vernix A white, cheeselike substance that covers the fetus, protecting the skin from chapping due to constant exposure to amniotic fluid. (p. 99)

video deficit effect In toddlers, poorer performance on tasks after watching a video than a live demonstration. (p. 210)

violation-of-expectation method A method in which researchers show babies an expected event (one that is consistent with reality) and an unexpected event (a variation of the first event that violates reality). Heightened attention to the unexpected event suggests that the infant is "surprised" by a deviation from physical reality and, therefore, is aware of that aspect of the physical world. (p. 205)

visual acuity Fineness of visual discrimination. (p. 150)

W

whole-language approach An approach to beginning reading instruction in which children are exposed to text in its complete form, using reading materials that are whole and meaningful to promote appreciation of the communicative function of written language. Distinguished from *phonics approach*. (p. 443)

working memory The number of items that can be briefly held in mind while also engaging in some effort to monitor or manipulate those items—a "mental workspace" that we use to accomplish many activities in daily life. A contemporary view of the short-term memory store. (p. 215)

X

X-linked inheritance A pattern of inheritance in which a recessive gene is carried on the X chromosome, resulting in males being more likely than females to be affected because the male's sex chromosomes do not match. (p. 57)

Z

zone of proximal development In Vygotsky's theory, a range of tasks too difficult for a child to do alone but that the child can do with the help of more skilled partners. (p. 222)

zygote The newly fertilized cell formed by the union of sperm and ovum at conception. (p. 53)

References

A

Aalsma, M., Lapsley, D. K., & Flannery, D. J. (2006). Personal fables, narcissism, and adolescent adjustment. *Psychology in the Schools, 43,* 481–491.

Aarnoudse-Moens, C. S., Weisglas-Kuperus, N., & van Goudoever, J. B. (2009). Meta-analysis of neurobehavioral outcomes in very preterm and/or very low birth weight children. *Pediatrics, 124,* 717–728.

Abelson, H., Ledeen, K., & Lewis, H. R. (2008). *Blown to bits: Your life, liberty, and happiness after the digital explosion.* Upper Saddle River, NJ: Addison-Wesley.

Aber, L., Brown, J. L., Jones, S. M., Berg, J., & Torrente, C. (2011). School-based strategies to prevent violence, trauma, and psychopathology: The challenges of going to scale. *Development and Psychopathology, 23,* 411–421.

Abner, K. S., Gordon, R. A., Kaestner, R., & Korenman, S. (2013). Does child-care quality mediate associations between type of care and development? *Journal of Marriage and Family, 75,* 1203–1217.

Aboud, F. E. (2003). The formation of in-group favoritism and out-group prejudice in young children: Are they distinct attitudes? *Developmental Psychology, 39,* 48–60.

Aboud, F. E. (2008). A social-cognitive developmental theory of prejudice. In S. M. Quintana & C. McKown (Eds.), *Handbook of race, racism, and the developing child* (pp. 55–71). Hoboken, NJ: Wiley.

Aboud, F. E., & Doyle, A. (1996). Parental and peer influences on children's racial attitudes. *International Journal of Intercultural Relations, 20,* 371–383.

Abraham, M. M., & Kerns, K. A. (2013). Positive and negative emotions and coping as mediators of mother–child attachment and peer relationships. *Merrill-Palmer Quarterly, 59,* 399–425.

Achenbach, T. M., Howell C. T., & Aoki, M. F. (1993). Nine-year outcome of the Vermont Intervention Program for low-birthweight infants, *Pediatrics, 91,* 45–55.

Acker, M. M., & O'Leary, S. G. (1996). Inconsistency of mothers' feedback and toddlers' misbehavior and negative affect. *Journal of Abnormal Child Psychology, 24,* 703–714.

Ackerman, J. P., Riggins, T., & Black, M M. (2010). A review of the effects of prenatal cocaine exposure among school-aged children. *Pediatrics, 125,* 554–565.

ACT (2014). *2014 retention/completion summary tables.* Retrieved from www.act.org/research/policymakers/pdf/14retain_trends.pdf

Adam, E. K., Snell, E. K., & Pendry, P. (2007). Sleep timing and quantity in ecological and family context: A nationally representative time-diary study. *Journal of Family Psychology, 21,* 4–19.

Adams, M. J. (2002). Alphabetic anxiety and explicit, systemic phonics instruction. In S. B. Neuman & D. K. Dickinson (Eds.), *Handbook of early literacy research* (Vol. 1, pp. 66–80). New York: Guilford.

Adams, R., & Laursen, B. (2001). The organization and dynamics of adolescent conflict with parents and friends. *Journal of Marriage and the Family, 63,* 97–110.

Adolph, K. E. (2002). Learning to keep balance. In R. V. Kail (Ed.), *Advances in child development and behavior* (Vol. 30, pp. 1–40). Boston: Academic Press.

Adolph, K. E. (2008). Learning to move. *Current Directions in Psychological Science, 17,* 213–218.

Adolph, K. E., & Berger, S. E. (2006). Motor development. In D. Kuhn & R. Siegler (Eds.), *Handbook of child psychology: Vol. 2. Cognition, perception, and language* (6th ed., pp. 161–213). Hoboken, NJ: Wiley.

Adolph, K. E., Cole, W. G., Komati, M., Garciaguirre, J. S., Badaly, D., Lingeman, J. M., et al. (2012). How do you learn to walk? Thousands of steps and hundreds of falls per day. *Psychological Science, 23,* 1387–1394.

Adolph, K. E., Karasik, L. B., & Tamis-LeMonda, C. S. (2010). Motor skill. In M. H. Bornstein (Ed.), *Handbook of cultural developmental science* (pp. 61–88). New York: Psychology Press.

Adolph, K. E., & Kretch, K. S. (2012). Infants on the edge: Beyond the visual cliff. In A. Slater & P. Quinn (Eds.), *Developmental psychology: Revisiting the classic studies* (pp. 36–55). London: Sage.

Adolph, K. E., Kretch, K. S., & LoBue, V. (2014). Fear of heights in infants? *Current Directions in Psychological Science, 23,* 60–66.

Adolph, K. E., Tamis-LeMonda, C. S., Ishak, S., Karasik, L. B., & Lobo, S. A. (2008). Locomotor experience and use of social information are posture specific. *Developmental Psychology, 44,* 1705–1714.

Adolph, K. E., Vereijken, B., & Shrout, P. E. (2003). What changes in infant walking and why. *Child Development, 74,* 475–497.

Adolphs, R. (2010). What does the amygdala contribute to social cognition? *Annals of the New York Academy of Sciences, 119,* 42–61.

Adzick, N. S. (2013). Prospects for fetal surgery. *Early Human Development, 89,* 881–886.

Afifi, T. O., Brownridge, D. A., Cox, B. J., & Sareen J. (2006). Physical punishment, childhood abuse and psychiatric disorders. *Child Abuse and Neglect, 30,* 1093–1103.

Afifi, T. O., Mota, M., MacMillan, H. L., & Sareen, J. (2013). Harsh physical punishment in childhood and adult physical health. *Pediatrics, 132,* e333–e340.

Agronick, G., Stueve, A., Vargo, S., & O'Donnell, L. (2007). New York City young adults' psychological reactions to 9/11: Findings from the Reach for Health longitudinal study. *American Journal of Community Psychology, 39,* 79–90.

Aguiar, A., & Baillargeon, R. (2002). Developments in young infants' reasoning about occluded objects. *Cognitive Psychology, 45,* 267–336.

Ahmadlou, M., Gharib, M., Hemmti, S., Vameghi, R., & Sajedi, F. (2013). Disrupted small-world brain network in children with Down syndrome. *Clinical Neurophysiology, 124,* 1755–1764.

Aikens, J. W., Howes, C., & Hamilton, C. (2009). Attachment stability and the emergence of unresolved representations in adolescence. *Attachment and Human Development, 11,* 491–512.

Aikins, J. W., Bierman, K. L., & Parker, J. G. (2005). Navigating the transition to junior high school: The influence of pre-transition friendship and self-system characteristics. *Social Development, 14,* 42–60.

Ainsworth, M. D. S., Blehar, M. C., Waters, E., & Wall, S. (1978). *Patterns of attachment.* Hillsdale, NJ: Erlbaum.

Akers, A. Y., Gold, M. A., Bost, J. E., Adimore, A. A., Orr, D. P., & Fortenberry, J. D. (2011). Variation in sexual behaviors in a cohort of adolescent females: The role of personal, perceived peer, and perceived family attitudes. *Journal of Adolescent Health, 48,* 87–93.

Akers, A. Y., Holland, C. L., & Bost, J. (2011). Interventions to improve parental communication about sex: A systematic review. *Pediatrics, 127,* 494–510.

Akhtar, N., & Montague, L. (1999). Early lexical acquisition: The role of cross-situational learning. *First Language, 19,* 347–358.

Akimoto, S. A., & Sanbinmatsu, D. M. (1999). Differences in self-effacing behavior between European and Japanese Americans: Effect on competence evaluations. *Journal of Cross-Cultural Psychology, 30,* 159–177.

Aksan, N., & Kochanska, G. (2004). Heterogeneity of joy in infancy. *Infancy, 6,* 79–94.

Akutagava-Martins, G. C., Salatino-Liveira, A., Kieling, C. C., Rohde, A., & Hutz, M. H. (2013). Genetics of attention-deficit/hyperactivity disorder: Current findings and future directions. *Expert Review of Neurotherapeutics, 13,* 435–445.

Alati, R., Smith, G. D., Lewis, S. J., Sayal, K., Draper, E. S., Golding, J., et al. (2013). Effect of prenatal alcohol exposure on childhood academic outcomes: Contrasting maternal and paternal associations in the ALSPAC Study. *PLOS ONE, 8*(10), e74844.

Albareda-Castellot, B., Pons, F., & Sebastián-Gallés, N. (2010). The acquisition of phonetic categories in bilingual infants: New data from an anticipatory eye movement paradigm. *Developmental Science, 14,* 395–401.

Albers, C. A., & Grieve, A. J. (2007). Test review: Bayley, N. (2006). Bayley Scales of Infant and Toddler Development—Third Edition. San Antonio, TX: Harcourt Assessment. *Journal of Psychoeducational Assessment, 25,* 180–190.

Albert, D., Chein, J., & Steinberg, L. (2013). The teenage brain: Peer influences on adolescent decision making. *Current Directions in Psychological Science, 22,* 114–120.

Albert, D., & Steinberg, L. (2011). Judgment and decision making in adolescence. *Journal of Research on Adolescence, 21,* 211–224.

Alberts, A., Elkind, D., & Ginsberg, S. (2007). The personal fable and risk-taking in early adolescence. *Journal of Youth and Adolescence, 36,* 71–76.

Aldridge, M. A., Stillman, R. D., & Bower, T. G. R. (2001). Newborn categorization of vowel-like sounds. *Developmental Science, 4,* 220–232.

Alexander, J. M., Fabricius, W. V., Fleming, V. M., Zwahr, M., & Brown, S. A. (2003). The development of metacognitive causal explanations. *Learning and Individual Differences, 13,* 227–238.

Alhusen, J. L. (2008). A literature update on maternal–fetal attachment. *Journal of Obstetric, Gynecologic, and Neonatal Nursing, 37,* 315–328.

Ali, L., & Scelfo, J. (2002, December 9). Choosing virginity. *Newsweek,* pp. 60–65.

Alibali, M. W., Phillips, K. M. O., & Fischer, A. D. (2009). Learning new problem-solving strategies leads to changes in problem representation. *Cognitive Development, 24,* 89–101.

Aligne, C. A., Moss, M. E., Auinger, P., & Weitzman, M. (2003). Association of pediatric dental caries with passive smoking. *Journal of the American Medical Association, 289,* 1258–1264.

Alink, L. R. A., Mesman, J., van Zeijl, J., Stolk, M. N., Juffer, F., & Koot, H. M. (2006). The early childhood aggression curve: Development of physical aggression in 10- to 50-month-old children. *Child Development, 77,* 954–966.

Allely, C. S., Gillberg, C., & Wilson, P. (2014). Neurobiological abnormalities in the first few years of life in individuals later diagnosed with autism spectrum disorder: A review of recent data. *Behavioural Neurology.* Retrieved from www.hindawi.com/journals/bn/2014/210780/

Allen, J. P., Philliber, S., Herrling, S., & Kuperminc, G. P. (1997). Preventing teen pregnancy and academic failure: Experimental evaluation of a developmentally based approach. *Child Development, 64,* 729–742.

Allen, J. P., Porter, M. R., & McFarland, F. C. (2006). Leaders and followers in adolescent close friendships: Susceptibility to peer influence as a predictor of risky behavior, friendship instability, and depression. *Development and Psychopathology, 18,* 155–172.

Allen, J. P., Seitz, V., & Apfel, N. H. (2007). The sexually mature teen as a whole person. In J. L. Aber, S. J. Bishop-Josef, S. M. Jones, K. T. McLearn, & D. A. Phillips (Eds.), *New directions in prevention and intervention for teen pregnancy and parenthood* (pp. 185–199). Washington, DC: American Psychological Association.

Allen, K. A. (2014). Moderate hypothermia: Is selective head cooling or whole body cooling better? *Advances in Neonatal Care, 14,* 113–118.

Allen, S. E. M., & Crago, M. B. (1996). Early passive acquisition in Inuktitut. *Journal of Child Language, 23,* 129–156.

Allison, B. N., & Schultz, J. B. (2004). Parent–adolescent conflict in early adolescence. *Adolescence, 39,* 101–119.

Alloway, T. P. (2009). Working memory, but not IQ, predicts subsequent learning in children with learning difficulties. *European Journal of Psychological Assessment, 25,* 92–98.

Alloway, T. P., Bibile, V., & Lau, G. (2013). Computerized working memory training: Can it lead to gains in cognitive skills in students? *Computers in Human Behavior, 29,* 632–638.

Alloway, T. P., Gathercole, S. E., Kirkwood, H., & Elliott, J. (2009). The cognitive and behavioral characteristics of children with low working memory. *Child Development, 80,* 606–621.

Al-Namlah, A. S., Fernyhough, C., & Meins, E. (2006). Sociocultural influences on the development of verbal mediation: Private speech and phonological recoding in

Saudi Arabian and British samples. *Developmental Psychology, 42,* 117–131.

Alsaker, F. D. (1995). Timing of puberty and reactions to pubertal changes. In M. Rutter (Ed.), *Psychosocial disturbances in young people: Challenges for prevention* (pp. 37–82). New York: Cambridge University Press.

Altermatt, E. R., & Pomerantz, E. M. (2005). The implications of having high-achieving versus low-achieving friends: A longitudinal analysis. *Social Development, 14,* 61–81.

Amato, P. R. (2001). Children of divorce in the 1990s: An update of the Amato and Keith (1991) meta-analysis. *Journal of Family Psychology, 15,* 355–370.

Amato, P. R. (2006). Marital discord, divorce, and children's well-being: Results from a 20-year longitudinal study of two generation. In A. Clarke-Stewart & J. Dunn (Eds.), *Families count: Effects on child and adolescent development* (pp. 179–202). New York: Cambridge University Press.

Amato, P. R. (2010). Research on divorce: Continuing trends and new developments. *Journal of Marriage and Family, 72,* 650–666.

Amato, P. R., & Dorius, C. (2010). Fathers, children, and divorce. In M. E. Lamb (Ed.), *The role of the father in child development* (5th ed., pp. 177–200). Hoboken, NJ: Wiley.

Amato, P. R., & Fowler, F. (2002). Parenting practices, child adjustment, and family diversity. *Journal of Marriage and the Family, 64,* 703–716.

Amato, P. R., & Sobolewski, J. M. (2004). The effects of divorce on fathers and children: Nonresidential fathers and stepfathers. In M. E. Lamb (Ed.), *The role of the father in child development* (4th ed., pp. 341–367). Hoboken, NJ: Wiley.

Ambler, G. (2013). Normal physical development and growth at puberty. In K. Steinbeck & M. Kohn (Eds.), *A clinical handbook in adolescent medicine* (pp. 1–13). Hackensack, NJ: World Scientific Publishing.

American Academy of Pediatrics. (2001). Committee on Public Education: Children, adolescents, and television. *Pediatrics, 104,* 341–343.

American Academy of Pediatrics. (2012a). Breastfeeding and the use of human milk. *Pediatrics, 129,* e827–e841.

American Academy of Pediatrics. (2012b). SIDS and other sleep-related infant deaths: Expansion of recommendations for a safe sleep environment *Pediatrics, 128,* e1341.

American Academy of Pediatrics. (2013). The crucial role of recess in school. *Pediatrics, 131,* 183–188.

American Association of Birth Centers. (2014). *Position statement: Immersion in water during labor and birth.* Retrieved from www.birthcenters.org/webfm_send/145

American Diabetes Association. (2014). *Statistics about diabetes.* Retrieved from www.diabetes.org/diabetes-basics/statistics

American Psychiatric Association. (2013). *Diagnostic and statistical manual of mental disorders* (5th ed.). Arlington, VA: Author.

American Psychological Association. (2010). Ethical principles of psychologists and code of conduct. Retrieved from www.apa.org/ethics/code/index.aspx

Amit, M. (2010). Vegetarian diets in children and adolescents. *Paediatrics and Child Health, 15,* 303–308.

Amrein-Beardsley, A., Berliner, D. C., & Rideau, S. (2010). Cheating in the first, second, and third degree: Educators' responses to high-stakes testing. *Education Policy Analysis Archives, 18*(14), 1–31.

Amso, D., & Johnson, S. P. (2006). Learning by selection: Visual search and object perception in young infants. *Developmental Psychology, 42,* 1236–1245.

Amsterlaw, J. (2006). Children's beliefs about everyday reasoning. *Child Development, 77,* 443–464.

Ananth, C. V., Chauhan, S. P., Chen, H.-Y., & D'Alton, M. E. (2013). Electronic fetal monitoring in the United States: Temporal trends and adverse perinatal outcomes. *Obstetrics and Gynecology, 121,* 927–933.

Ananth, C. V., Friedman, A. M., & Gyamfi-Bannerman, C. (2013). Epidemiology of moderate preterm, late preterm and early term delivery. *Clinics in Perinatology, 40,* 601–610.

Anderman, E. M., Eccles, J. S., Yoon, K. S., Roeser, R., Wigfield, A., & Blumenfeld, P. (2001). Learning to value mathematics and reading: Relations to mastery and performance-oriented instructional practices. *Contemporary Educational Psychology, 26,* 76–95.

Andersen, E. (2000). Exploring register knowledge: The value of "controlled improvisation." In L. Menn & N. B. Ratner (Eds.), *Methods for studying language production* (pp. 225–248). Mahwah, NJ: Erlbaum.

Anderson, C. A., Berkowitz, L., Donnerstein, E., Huesmann, R., Johnson, J. D., Linz, D., Malamuth, N. M., & Wartella, E. (2003). The influence of media violence on youth. *Psychological Science in the Public Interest, 4*(3), 81–106.

Anderson, C. A., Shibuya, A., Ihori, N., Swing, E. L., Bushman, B. J., Sakamoto, A., et al. (2010). Violent video game effects on aggression, empathy, and prosocial behavior in Eastern and Western countries: A meta-analytic review. *Psychological Bulletin, 136,* 151–173.

Anderson, C. M. (2012). The diversity, strengths, and challenges of single-parent households. In F. Walsh (Ed.), *Normal family processes: Growing diversity and complexity* (4th ed., pp. 128–148). New York: Guilford.

Anderson, D. M., Huston, A. C., Schmitt, K. L., Linebarger, D. L., & Wright, J. C. (2001). Early childhood television viewing and adolescent behavior. *Monographs of the Society for Research in Child Development, 66*(1, Serial No. 264).

Anderson, E. R., & Greene, S. M. (2013). Beyond divorce: Research on children in repartnered and remarried families. *Family Court Review, 51,* 119–130.

Anderson, R. C., Wilson, P. T., & Fielding, L. G. (1988). Growth in reading and how children spend their time outside of school. *Reading Research Quarterly, 23,* 285–303.

Anderson, V., & Beauchamp, M. H. (2013). A theoretical model of developmental social neuroscience. In V. Anderson & M. H. Beauchamp (Eds.), *Developmental social neuroscience and childhood brain insult: Theory and practice* (pp. 3–20). New York: Guilford.

Anderson, V., Spencer-Smith, M., & Wood, A. (2011). Do children really recover better? Neurobehavioural plasticity after early brain insult. *Brain, 134,* 2197–2221.

Anderson, V. A., Catroppa, C., Dudgeon, P., Morse, S. A., Haritou, F., & Rosenfeld, J. V. (2006). Understanding predictors of functional recovery and outcome 30 months following early childhood head injury. *Neuropsychology, 20,* 42–57.

Andrews, G., & Halford, G. (2011). Recent advances in relational complexity theory and its application to cognitive development. In P. Barrouillet & V. Gaillard (Eds.), *Cognitive development and working memory* (pp. 47–68). Hove, UK: Psychology Press.

Andrews, G., & Halford, G. S. (2002). A cognitive complexity metric applied to cognitive development. *Cognitive Psychology, 45,* 475–506.

Ang, S., Rodgers, J. L., & Wänström, L. (2010). The Flynn effect within subgroups in the U.S.: Gender, race, income, education, and urbanization differences in the NLSY-Children data. *Intelligence, 38,* 367–384.

Angold, A., Costello, E. J., Erkanli, A., & Worthman, C. M. (1999). Pubertal changes in hormone levels and depression in girls. *Psychological Medicine, 29,* 1043–1053.

Anisfeld, M. (2005). No compelling evidence to dispute Piaget's timetable of the development of representational imitation in infancy. In S. Hurley & N. Chater (Eds.), *Perspectives on imitation: From neuroscience to social science: Vol. 2. Imitation, human development, and culture* (pp. 107–131). Cambridge, MA: MIT Press.

Annett, M. (2002). *Handedness and brain asymmetry: The right shift theory.* Hove, UK: Psychology Press.

Anzures, G., Quinn, P. C., Pascalis, O., Slater, A. M., Tanaka, J. W., & Lee, K. (2013). Developmental origins of the other-race effect. *Current Directions in Psychological Science, 22,* 173–178.

Apfelbaum, E. P., Pauker, K., Ambady, N., Sommers, S. R., & Norton, M. I. (2008). Learning (not) to talk about race: When older children underperform in social categorization. *Developmental Psychology, 44,* 1513–1518.

Apgar, V. (1953). A proposal for a new method of evaluation in the newborn infant. *Current Research in Anesthesia and Analgesia, 32,* 260–267.

Aquilino, W. S. (2006). Family relationships and support systems in emerging adulthood. In J. J. Arnett & J. L. Tanner (Eds.), *Emerging adults in America: Coming of age in the 21st century* (pp. 193–218). Washington, DC: American Psychological Association.

Aram, D., & Levin, I. (2011). Home support of children in the writing process. In S. B. Neuman & D. K. Dickinson (Eds.), *Handbook of early literacy research* (Vol. 3, pp. 189–199). New York: Guilford.

Archibald, A. B., Graber, J. A., & Brooks-Gunn, J. (2006). Pubertal processes and physiological growth in adolescence. In G. R. Adams & M. D. Berzonsky (Eds.), *Blackwell handbook of adolescence* (pp. 24–48). Malden, MA: Blackwell.

Arcus, D., & Chambers, P. (2008). Childhood risks associated with adoption. In T. P. Gullotta & G. M. Blau (Eds.), *Family influences on childhood behavior and development* (pp. 117–142). New York: Routledge.

Ardila-Rey, A., & Killen, M. (2001). Middle-class Colombian children's evaluations of personal, moral, and social–conventional interactions in the classroom. *International Journal of Behavioral Development, 25,* 246–255.

Arija, V., Esparó, G., Fernández-Ballart, J., Murphy, M. M., Biarnés, E., & Canals, J. (2006). Nutritional status and performance in test of verbal and nonverbal intelligence in 6 year old children. *Intelligence, 34,* 141–149.

Arim, R. G., Tamonte, L., Shapka, J. D., Dahinten, V. S., & Willms, J. D. (2011). The family antecedents and the subsequent outcomes of early puberty. *Journal of Youth and Adolescence, 40,* 1423–1435.

Arkes, J. (2013). The temporal effects of parental divorce on youth substance use. *Substance Use and Misuse, 48,* 290–297.

Armstrong, K. L., Quinn, R. A., & Dadds, M. R. (1994). The sleep patterns of normal children. *Medical Journal of Australia, 161,* 202–206.

Arnett, J. J. (2006). Emerging adulthood: Understanding the new way of coming of age. In J. J. Arnett & J. L. Tanner (Eds.), *Emerging adults in America: Coming of age in the 21st century* (pp. 3–19). Washington, DC: American Psychological Association.

Arnett, J. J. (2007). Emerging adulthood: What is it and what is it good for? *Child Development Perspectives, 1,* 68–73.

Arnett, J. J. (2011). Emerging adulthood(s): The cultural psychology of a new life stage. In L. E. Jensen (Ed.), *Bridging cultural and developmental approaches to psychology: New syntheses in theory, research, and policy* (pp. 255–275). New York: Oxford University Press.

Arnett, J. J. (2013). The evidence for Generation We and against Generation Me. *Emerging Adulthood, 1,* 5–10.

Arnett, J. J., & Schwab, J. (2012). *Clark University poll of emerging adults: Thriving, struggling, and hopeful.* Retrieved from clarku.edu/clarkpoll

Arnett, J. J., & Tanner, J. L. (2011). Themes and variations in emerging adulthood across social classes. In J. J. Arnett, M., Kloep, L. B. Hendry, & J. L. Tanner (Eds.), *Debating emerging adulthood: Stage or process?* (pp. 31–51). New York: Oxford University Press.

Arnett, J. J., Trzesniewski, K. H., & Donnellan, M. B. (2013). The dangers of generational myth-making: Rejoinder to Twenge. *Emerging Adulthood, 1,* 17–20.

Arnold, D. H., McWilliams, L., & Harvey-Arnold, E. (1998). Teacher discipline and child misbehavior in daycare: Untangling causality with correlational data. *Developmental Psychology, 34,* 276–287.

Arnon, S., Shapsa, A., Forman, L., Regev, R., Bauer, S., & Litmanovitz, I. (2006). Live music is beneficial to preterm infants in the neonatal intensive care unit. *Birth, 33,* 131–136.

Aronson, A. A., & Henderson, S. O. (2006). Pediatrics, otitis media. *eMedicine Specialties, Pediatrics.* Retrieved from www.emedicine.com/emerg/topic393.htm

Arsenio, W. F. (2010). Integrating emotion attributions, morality, and aggression: Research and theoretical foundations. In W. F. Arsenio & E. A. Lemerise (Eds.), *Emotions, aggression, and morality in children: Bridging development and psychopathology* (pp. 75–94). Washington, DC: American Psychological Association.

Arsenio, W. F., & Lemerise, E. A. (2001). Varieties of childhood bullying: Values, emotion processes, and social competence. *Social Development, 10,* 59–73.

Arseth, A. K., Kroger, J., Martinussen, M., & Marcia, J. E. (2009). Meta-analytic studies of identity status and the relational issues of attachment and intimacy. *Identity, 9,* 1–32.

Artman, L., & Cahan, S. (1993). Schooling and the development of transitive inference. *Developmental Psychology, 29,* 753–759.

Artman, L., Cahan, S., & Avni-Babad, D. (2006). Age, schooling, and conditional reasoning. *Cognitive Development, 21,* 131–145.

Arum, R., & Roksa, J. (2014). *Aspiring adults adrift: Tentative transitions of college graduates.* Chicago: University of Chicago Press.

Asbjornsen, A. E., Obrzut, J. E., Boliek, C. A., Myking, E., Holmefjord, A., & Reisaeter, S. (2005). Impaired auditory attention skills following middle-ear infections. *Child Neuropsychology, 11,* 121–133.

Asher, S. R., & Rose, A. J. (1997). Promoting children's social-emotional adjustment with peers. In P. Salovey & D. J. Sluyter (Eds.), *Emotional development and emotional intelligence* (pp. 193–195). New York: Basic Books.

Aslin, R. N., Jusczyk, P. W., & Pisoni, D. B. (1998). Speech and auditory processing during infancy: Constraints on and precursors to language. In D. Kuhn & R. S. Siegler (Eds.), *Handbook of child psychology: Vol. 2. Cognition, perception, and language* (5th ed., pp. 147–198). New York: Wiley.

Aslin, R. N., & Newport, E. L. (2012). Statistical learning: From acquiring specific items to forming general rules. *Psychological Science, 21,* 170–176.

Astington, J. W., & Hughes, C. (2013). Theory of mind: Self-reflection and social understanding. In S. M. Carlson, P. D. Zelazo, & S. Faja (Eds.), *Oxford handbook of developmental psychology: Vol. 2. Self and other* (pp. 398–424). New York: Oxford University Press.

Astington, J. W., & Jenkins, J. M. (1995). Theory of mind development and social understanding. *Cognition and Emotion, 9,* 151–165.

Astington, J. W., & Pelletier, J. (2005). Theory of mind, language, and learning in the early years: Developmental origins of school readiness. In B. D. Homer & C. S. Tamis-LeMonda (Eds.), *The development of social cognition and communication* (pp. 205–230). Mahwah, NJ: Erlbaum.

Astington, J. W., Pelletier, J., & Homer, B. (2002). Theory of mind and epistemological development: The relation between children's second-order false belief understanding and their ability to reason about evidence. *New Ideas in Psychology, 20,* 131–144.

Atance, C. M., & Meltzoff, A. N. (2005). My future self: Young children's ability to anticipate and explain future states. *Cognitive Development, 20,* 341–361.

Atkins, R., Hart, D., & Donnelly, T. M. (2004). Moral identity development and school attachment. In D. Narvaez & D. Lapsley (Eds.), *Moral development, self, and identity* (pp. 65–82). Mahwah, NJ: Erlbaum.

Au, T. K., Sidle, A. L., & Rollins, K. B. (1993). Developing an intuitive understanding of conservation and contamination: Invisible particles as a plausible mechanism. *Developmental Psychology, 29,* 286–299.

Aud, S., Hussar, W., Kena, G., Bianco, K., Frohlich, L., Kemp, F. J., & Tahan, K. (2011). *The condition of education 2011* (NCES 2011-033). U.S. Department of Education, National Center for Education Statistics. Washington, DC: U.S. Government Printing Office.

Auerbach, R. P., Bigda-Peyton, J. S., Eberhart, N. K., Webb, C. A., & Ho, M-H. R. (2011). Conceptualizing the prospective relationship between social support, stress, and depressive symptoms among adolescents. *Journal of Abnormal Child Psychology, 39,* 475–487.

Aunola, K., Stattin, H., & Nurmi, J.-E. (2000). Parenting styles and adolescents' achievement strategies. *Journal of Adolescence, 23,* 205–222.

Avis, J., & Harris, P. L. (1991). Belief–desire reasoning among Baka children: Evidence for a universal conception of mind. *Child Development, 62,* 460–467.

Axelin, A., Salantera, S., & Lehtonen, L. (2006). "Facilitated tucking by parents" in pain management of preterm infants—a randomized crossover trial. *Early Human Development, 82,* 241–247.

Azurmendi, A., Braza, F., Garcia, A., Braza, P., Munoz, J. M., & Sanchez-Martin, J. R. (2006). Aggression, dominance, and affiliation: Their relationships with androgen levels and intelligence in 5-year-old children. *Hormones and Behavior, 50,* 132–140.

B

Bacallao, M. L., & Smokowski, P. R. (2007). The costs of getting ahead: Mexican family system changes after immigration. *Family Relations, 56,* 52–66.

Bachman, J. G., O'Malley, P. M., Freedman-Doan, P., Trzesniewski, K. H., & Donnellan, M. B. (2011). Adolescent self-esteem: Differences by race/ethnicity, gender, and age. *Self and Identity, 10,* 445–473.

Badanes, L. S., Dmitrieva, J., & Watamura, S. E. (2012). Understanding cortisol reactivity across the day at child care: The potential buffering role of secure attachments to caregivers. *Early Childhood Research Quarterly, 27,* 156–165.

Badger, S., Nelson, L. J., & Barry, C. M. (2006). Perceptions of the transition to adulthood among Chinese and American emerging adults. *International Journal of Behavioral Development, 31,* 83–93.

Badiee, Z., Asghari, M., & Mohammadizadeh, M. (2013). The calming effect of maternal breast milk odor on premature infants. *Pediatrics and Neonatology, 54,* 322–325.

Baenninger, M., & Newcombe, N. (1995). Environmental input to the development of sex-related differences in spatial and mathematical ability. *Learning and Individual Differences, 7,* 363–379.

Baer, J. (2002). Is family cohesion a risk or protective factor during adolescent development? *Journal of Marriage and Family, 64,* 668–675.

Bagwell, C. L., & Coie, J. D. (2004). The best friendships of aggressive boys: Relationship quality, conflict management, and rule-breaking behavior. *Journal of Experimental Child Psychology, 88,* 5–24.

Bagwell, C. L., & Schmidt, M. E. (2011). *Friendships in childhood and adolescence.* New York: Guilford.

Bahrick, L. E. (2010). Intermodal perception and selective attention to intersensory redundancy: Implications for typical social development and autism. In G. Bremner & T. D. Wachs (Eds.), *Wiley-Blackwell handbook of infant development: Vol. 1* (2nd ed., pp. 120–166). Malden, MA: Blackwell.

Bahrick, L. E., Gogate, L. J., & Ruiz, I. (2002). Attention and memory for faces and actions in infancy: The salience of actions over faces in dynamic events. *Child Development, 73,* 1629–1643.

Bahrick, L. E., Hernandez-Reif, M., & Flom, R. (2005). The development of infant learning about specific face–voice relations. *Developmental Psychology, 41,* 541–552.

Bahrick, L. E., Hernandez-Reif, M., & Pickens, J. N. (1997). The effect of retrieval cues on visual preferences and memory in infancy: Evidence for a four-phase attention function. *Journal of Experimental Child Psychology, 67,* 1–20.

Bahrick, L. E., & Lickliter, R. (2012). The role of intersensory redundancy in early perceptual, cognitive, and social development. In A. J. Bremner, D. J. Lewkowicz, & C. Spence (Eds.), *Multisensory development* (183–206). Oxford, UK: Oxford University Press.

Bahrick, L. E., Lickliter, R., & Flom, R. (2004). Intersensory redundancy guides the development of selective attention, perception, and cognition in infancy. *Current Directions in Psychological Science, 13,* 99–102.

Bailar-Heath, M., & Valley-Gray, S. (2010). Accident prevention. In P. C. McCabe & S. R. Shaw (Eds.), *Pediatric disorders* (pp. 123–132). Thousand Oaks, CA; Corwin Press.

Bailey, J. M., Bobrow, D., Wolfe, M., & Mikach, S. (1995). Sexual orientation of adult sons of gay fathers. *Developmental Psychology, 31,* 124–129.

Baillargeon, R., & DeVos, J. (1991). Object permanence in young infants: Further evidence. *Child Development, 62,* 1227–1246.

Baillargeon, R., Li, J., Gertner, Y., & Wu, D. (2011). How do infants reason about physical events? In U. Goswami (Ed.), *Wiley-Blackwell handbook of childhood cognitive development* (2nd ed., pp. 11–48). Chichester, UK: Wiley-Blackwell.

Baillargeon, R., Li, J., Ng, W., & Yuan, S. (2009). An account of infants' physical reasoning. In A. Woodward & A. Needham (Eds.), *Learning and the infant mind* (pp. 66–116). New York: Oxford University Press.

Baillargeon, R., Scott, R. M., & He, Z. (2010). False-belief understanding in infants. *Trends in Cognitive Sciences, 14,* 110–118.

Baillargeon, R. H., Zoccolillo, M., Keenan, K., Côté, S., Pérusse, D., Wu, H.-X., & Boivin, M. (2007). Gender differences in physical aggression: A prospective population-based survey of children before and after 2 years of age. *Developmental Psychology, 43,* 13–26.

Baker, O., & Lang, K. (2013). The effect of high school exit exams on graduation, employment, wages, and incarceration. *National Bureau of Economic Research Working Paper,* No. 19182. Retrieved from www.nber.org/papers/w19182

Bakermans-Kranenberg, M. J., Steele, H., Zeanah, C. H., Muhamedrahimov, R, J, Vorria, P., & Dobrova-Krol, N. A. (2011). Attachment and emotional development in institutional care: Characteristics and catch up. In R. B. McCall, M. H. van IJzendoorn, F. Juffer, C. J. Groark, & V. K. Groza (Eds), Children without permanent parents: Research, practice, and policy. *Monographs of the Society for Research in Child Development, 76*(4, Serial No. 301), 62–91.

Bakermans-Kranenburg, M. J., & van IJzendoorn, M. H. (2011). Differential susceptibility to rearing environment depending on dopamine-related genes: New evidence and a meta-analysis. *Development and Psychopathology, 23,* 39–52.

Bakermans-Kranenburg, M. J., van IJzendoorn, M. H., & Juffer, F. (2003). Less is more: Meta-analyses of sensitivity and attachment interventions in early childhood. *Psychological Bulletin, 129,* 195–215.

Bakermans-Kranenburg, M. J., van IJzendoorn, M. H., Mesman, J., Alink, L. R. A., & Juffer, F. (2008a). Effects of an attachment-based intervention on daily cortisol moderated by dopamine receptor D4: A randomized control trial on 1-to 3-year-olds screened for externalizing behavior. *Development and Psychopathology, 20,* 805–820.

Bakermans-Kranenburg, M. J., van IJzendoorn, M. H., Pijlman, F. T. A., Mesman, J., & Juffer, F. (2008b). Experimental evidence for differential sensitivity: Dopamine D4 receptor polymorphism (DRD4 VNTR) moderates intervention effects on toddlers' externalizing behavior in a randomized control trial. *Developmental Psychology, 44,* 293–300.

Baker-Sennett, J., Matusov, E., & Rogoff, B. (2008). Children's planning of classroom plays with adult or child direction. *Social Development, 17,* 998–1018.

Balaban, M. T., & Waxman, S. R. (1997). Do words facilitate object categorization in 9-month-old infants? *Journal of Experimental Child Psychology, 64,* 3–26.

Balfanz, R., Herzog, L., & MacIver, D. J. (2007). Preventing student disengagement and keeping students on the graduation path in urban middle-grades schools: Early identification and effective interventions. *Educational Psychologist, 42,* 223–235.

Ball, H. (2006). Parent–infant bed-sharing behavior: Effects of feeding type and presence of father. *Human Nature, 17,* 301–318.

Ball, H. L., & Volpe, L. E. (2013). Sudden infant death syndrome (SIDS) risk reduction and infant sleep location—moving the discussion forward. *Social Science and Medicine, 79,* 84–91.

Baltes, P. B., Lindenberger, U., & Staudinger, U. M. (2006). Life span theory in developmental psychology. In R. M. Lerner & W. Damon (Eds.), *Handbook of child psychology: Vol. 1. Theoretical models of human development* (6th ed., pp. 569–664). Hoboken, N. J.: Wiley.

Bandstra, E. S., Morrow, C. E., Mansoor, E., & Accornero, V. H. (2010). Prenatal drug exposure: Infant and toddler outcomes. *Journal of Addictive Diseases, 29,* 245–258.

Bandura, A. (1977). *Social learning theory.* Englewood Cliffs, NJ: Prentice-Hall.

Bandura, A. (1992). Perceived self-efficacy in cognitive development and functioning. *Educational Psychologist, 28,* 117–118.

Bandura, A. (2001). Social cognitive theory: An agentic perspective. *Annual Review of Psychology, 52,* 1–26.

Bandura, A. (2011). Social cognitive theory. In P. A. M. Van Lange, A. W. Kruglanski, & E. T. Higgins (Eds.), *Handbook of theories of social psychology* (Vol. 1, pp. 349–373). Thousand Oaks, CA: Sage.

Bang, H. G. (2011). What makes it easy or hard for you to do your homework? An account of newcomer immigrant youths' afterschool academic lives. *Current Issues in Education, 14*(3), 1–26.

Banks, M. S. (1980). The development of visual accommodation during early infancy. *Child Development, 51,* 157–173.

Banks, M. S., & Ginsburg, A. P. (1985). Early visual preferences: A review and new theoretical treatment. In H. W. Reese (Ed.), *Advances in child development and behavior* (Vol. 19, pp. 207–246). New York: Academic Press.

Bannard, C., Lieven, E., & Tomasello, M. (2009). Modeling children's early grammatical knowledge. *Proceedings of the National Academy of Sciences, 106,* 17284–17289.

Banse, R., Gawronski, B., Rebetez, C., Gutt, H., & Morton, J. B. (2010). The development of spontaneous gender stereotyping in childhood: Relations to stereotype knowledge and stereotype flexibility. *Developmental Science, 13,* 298–306.

Barber, B. K., & Olsen, J. A. (1997). Socialization in context: Connection, regulation, and autonomy in the family, school, and neighborhood, and with peers. *Journal of Adolescent Research, 12,* 287–315.

Barber, B. K., & Olsen, J. A. (2004). Assessing the transitions to middle and high school. *Journal of Adolescent Research, 19,* 3–30.

Barber, B. K., Stolz, H. E., & Olsen, J. A. (2005). Parental support, psychological control, and behavioral control: Assessing relevance across time, culture, and method. *Monographs of the Society for Research in Child Development, 70*(4, Serial No. 282).

Barber, B. K., & Xia, M. (2013). The centrality of control to parenting and its effects. In R. E. Larzelere, A. S. Morris, & A. W. Harrist (Eds.), *Authoritative parenting: Synthesizing nurturance and discipline for optimal child development* (pp. 61–88). Washington, DC: American Psychological Association.

Barber, B. L., Stone, M. R., Hunt, J. E., & Eccles, J. S. (2005). Benefits of activity participation: The roles of identity affirmation and peer group norm sharing. In J. L. Mahoney, R. W. Larson, & J. S. Eccles (Eds.), *Organized activities as contexts of development: Extracurricular activities, after-school and community programs* (pp. 185–210). Mahwah, NJ: Erlbaum.

Bard, K. A., Todd, B. K., Bernier, C., Love, J., & Leavens, D. A. (2006). Self-awareness in human and chimpanzee infants: What is measured and what is meant by the mark and mirror test? *Infancy, 9,* 191–219.

Bar-Haim, Y., Ziv, T., Lamy, D., & Hodes, R. M. (2006). Nature and nurture in own-race face processing. *Psychological Science, 17,* 159–163.

Barker, D. J., Osmond, C., Thornburg, K. L., Kajantie, E., Forsen, T., & Eriksson, J. G. (2008). A possible link between the pubertal growth of girls and breast cancer in their daughters. *American Journal of Human Biology, 20,* 127–131.

Barker, D. J., & Thornberg, K. L. (2013). Placental programming of chronic diseases, cancer and lifespan: A review. *Placenta, 34,* 841–845.

Barker, D. J. P. (2009). Growth and chronic disease: Findings in the Helsinki Birth Cohort. *Annals of Human Biology, 36,* 445–458.

Barkley, R. A. (2003a). Attention-deficit/hyperactivity disorder. In E. J. Mash & R. A. Barkley (Eds.), *Child psychopathology* (2nd ed., pp. 75–143). New York: Guilford.

Barkley, R. A. (2003b). Issues in the diagnosis of attention-deficit hyperactivity disorder in children. *Brain and Development, 25,* 77–83.

Barkley, R. A. (2006). Attention-deficit/hyperactivity disorder. In R. A. Barkley, D. A. Wolfe, & E. J. Mash (Eds.), *Behavioral and emotional disorders in adolescents: Nature, assessment, and treatment* (pp. 91–152). New York: Guilford.

Barnes, G. M., Hoffman, J. H., Welte, J. W., Farrell, M. P., & Dintcheff, B. A. (2007). Adolescents' time use: Effects on substance use, delinquency and sexual activity. *Journal of Youth and Adolescence, 36,* 697–710.

Barnes, R., Josefowitz, N., & Cole, E. (2006). Residential schools: Impact on Aboriginal students' academic and cognitive development. *Canadian Journal of School Psychology, 21,* 18–32.

Barnett, D., & Vondra, J. I. (1999). Atypical patterns of early attachment: Theory, research, and current directions. In J. I. Vondra & D. Barnett (Eds.), *Atypical attachment in infancy and early childhood among children at developmental risk. Monographs of the Society for Research in Child Development, 64*(3, Serial No. 258), pp. 1–24.

Barnett, W. S. (2011). Effectiveness of early educational intervention. *Science, 333,* 975–978.

Barnett, W. S., Carolan, M. E., Squires, J. H., & Brown, K. C. (2013). *The state of preschool 2013.* Newark, NJ: National Institute for Early Education Research, Rutgers University.

Baron, I. S., & Rey-Casserly, C. (2010). Extremely preterm birth outcome: A review of four decades of cognitive research. *Neuropsychology Review, 20,* 430–452.

Baron-Cohen, S. (2011). What is theory of mind, and is it impaired in ASC? In S. Bolte & J. Hallmayer (Eds.). *Autism spectrum conditions: FAQs on autism, Asperger syndrome, and atypical autism answered by international experts* (pp. 136–138). Cambridge, MA: Hogrefe Publishing.

Baron-Cohen, S., & Belmonte, M. K. (2005). Autism: A window onto the development of the social and the analytic brain. *Annual Review of Neuroscience, 28,* 109–126.

Barr, H. M., Streissguth, A. P., Darby, B. L., & Sampson, P. D. (1990). Prenatal exposure to alcohol, caffeine, tobacco, and aspirin: Effects on fine and gross motor performance in 4-year-old children. *Developmental Psychology, 26,* 339–348.

Barr, R., & Hayne, H. (2003). It's not what you know, it's who you know: Older siblings facilitate imitation during infancy. *International Journal of Early Years Education, 11,* 7–21.

Barr, R., Marrott, H., & Rovee-Collier, C. (2003). The role of sensory preconditioning in memory retrieval by preverbal infants. *Learning and Behavior, 31,* 111–123.

Barr, R., Muentener, P., & Garcia, A. (2007). Age-related changes in deferred imitation from television by 6- to 18-month-olds. *Developmental Science, 10,* 910–921.

Barr, R. G. (2001). "Colic" is something infants do, rather than a condition they "have": A developmental approach to crying phenomena patterns, pacification and (patho) genesis. In R. G. Barr, I. St James-Roberts, & M. R. Keefe (Eds.), *New evidence on unexplained infant crying* (pp. 87–104). St. Louis: Johnson & Johnson Pediatric Institute.

Barr, R. G., Paterson, J. A., MacMartin, L. M., & Lehtonen, L. (2005). Prolonged and unsoothable crying bouts in infants with and without colic. *Journal of Developmental and Behavioral Pediatrics, 26,* 14–23.

Barrett, E. S., Redmon, J. B., Wang, C., Sparks, A., & Swan, S. H. (2014). Exposure to prenatal life events stress is associated with masculinized play behavior in girls. *NeuroToxicology, 41,* 20–27.

Barrett, K. C. (2005). The origins of social emotions and self-regulation in toddlerhood: New evidence. *Cognition and Emotion, 19,* 953–979.

Barros, R. M., Silver, E. J., & Stein, R. E. K. (2009). School recess and group classroom behavior. *Pediatrics, 123,* 431–436.

Barrouillet, P., & Gaillard, V. (2011a). Advances and issues: Some thoughts about controversial questions. In P. Barrouillet & V. Gaillard (Eds.), *Cognitive development and working memory* (pp. 263–271). Hove, UK: Psychology Press.

Barrouillet, P., & Gaillard, V. (2011b). (Eds.). *Cognitive development and working memory: A dialogue between neo-Piagetian and cognitive approaches.* Hove, UK: Psychology Press.

Bartgis, J., Lilly, A. R., & Thomas, D. G. (2003). Event-related potential and behavioral measures of attention in 5-, 7-, and 9-year-olds. *Journal of General Psychology, 130,* 311–335.

Barry, C., & Christofferson, J. L. (2014). The role of peer relationships in emerging adults' religiousness and spirituality. In C. M. Barry & M. M. Abo-Zena (Eds.), *Emerging adults' religiousness and spirituality* (pp. 76–92). New York: Oxford University Press.

Barry, C. M., Nelson, L., Davarya, S., & Urry, S. (2010). Religiosity and spirituality during the transition to adulthood. *International Journal of Behavioral Development, 34,* 311–324.

Barthell, J. E., & Mrozek, J. D. (2013). Neonatal drug withdrawal. *Minnesota Medicine, 96,* 48–50.

Bartocci, M., Berggvist, L. L., Lagercrantz, H., & Anand, K. J. (2006). Pain activates cortical areas in the preterm newborn brain. *Pain, 122,* 109–117.

Barton, M. E., & Strosberg, R. (1997). Conversational patterns of two-year-old twins in mother–twin–twin triads. *Journal of Child Language, 24,* 257–269.

Barton, M. E., & Tomasello, M. (1991). Joint attention and conversation in mother–infant–sibling triads. *Child Development, 62,* 517–529.

Bartrip, J., Morton, J., & de Schonen, S. (2001). Responses to mother's face in 3-week to 3-month-old infants. *British Journal of Developmental Psychology, 19,* 219–232.

Bartsch, K., London, K., & Campbell, M. D. (2007). Children's attention to beliefs in interactive persuasion tasks. *Developmental Psychology, 43,* 111–120.

Bartsch, K., & Wellman, H. M. (1995). *Children talk about the mind.* New York: Oxford University Press.

Basilio, C. D., Knight, G. P., O'Donnell, M., Roosa, M. W., Gonzales, N. A., Umaña-Taylor, A. J., & Torres, M. (2014). The Mexican American Biculturalism Scale: Bicultural comfort, facility, and advantages for adolescents and adults. *Psychological Assessment, 26,* 539–554.

Basinger, B. (2013). Low-income and minority children with asthma. In L. Rubin & J. Merrick (Eds.), *Environmental health disparities with children: Asthma, obesity and food* (pp. 61–72). Hauppauge, NY: Nova Science.

Basow, S. A., & Rubin, L. R. (1999). Gender influences on adolescent development. In N. G. Johnson & M. C. Roberts (Eds.), *Beyond appearance: A new look at adolescent girls* (pp. 25–52). Washington, DC: American Psychological Association.

Bass, J. L., Corwin, M., Gozal, D., Moore, C., Nishida, H., Parker, S., Schonwald, A., Wilker, R. E., Stehle, S., & Kinane, T. B. (2004). The effect of chronic or intermittent hypoxia on cognition in childhood: A review of the evidence. *Pediatrics, 114,* 805–816.

Bassok, D., & Reardon, S. F. (2013). "Academic redshirting" in kindergarten: Prevalence, patterns, and implications. *Educational Evaluation and Policy Analysis, 35,* 283–297.

Bass-Ringdahl, S. M. (2010). The relationship of audibility and the development of canonical babbling in young children with hearing impairment. *Journal of Deaf Studies and Deaf Education, 15,* 287–310.

Batchelor, J. (2008). "Failure to thrive" revisited. *Child Abuse Review, 17,* 147–159.

Bates, E. (2004). Explaining and interpreting deficits in language development across clinical groups: Where do we go from here? *Brain and Language, 88,* 248–253.

Bates, E., & MacWhinney, B. (1987). Competition, variation, and language learning. In B. MacWhinney (Ed.), *Mechanisms of language acquisition* (pp. 157–193). Hillsdale, NJ: Erlbaum.

Bates, E., Marchman, V., Thal, D., Fenson, L., Dale, P., Reznick, J. S., Reilly, J., & Hartung, J. (1994). Developmental and stylistic variation in the composition of early vocabulary. *Journal of Child Language, 21,* 85–123.

Bates, E., Wilson, S. M., Saygin, A. P., Dick, F., Sereno, M. I., Knight, R. T., & Dronkers, N. F. (2003). Voxel-based lesion-symptom mapping. *Nature Neuroscience, 6,* 448–450.

Bates, J. E., Wachs, T. D., & Emde, R. N. (1994). Toward practical uses for biological concepts. In J. E. Bates & T. D. Wachs (Eds.), *Temperament: Individual differences at the interface of biology and behavior* (pp. 275–306). Washington, DC: American Psychological Association.

Bathelt, J., O'Reilly, H., Clayden, J. D., Cross, J. H., & de Haan, M. (2013). Functional brain network organization of children between 2 and 5 years derived from reconstructed activity of cortical sources of high-density EEG recordings. *NeuroImage, 82,* 595–604.

Bauer, P. A. (2013). Memory. In S. M. Carlson, P. D. Zelazo, & S. Faja (Eds.), *Oxford handbook of developmental psychology: Vol. 1. Body and mind* (pp. 505–541). New York: Oxford University Press.

Bauer, P. J. (2002). Early memory development. In U. Goswami (Ed.), *Blackwell handbook of child cognitive development* (pp. 127–150). Malden, MA: Blackwell.

Bauer, P. J. (2006). Event memory. In D. Kuhn & R. Siegler (Eds.), *Handbook of child psychology: Vol. 2. Cognition, perception, and language* (6th ed., pp. 373–425). Hoboken, NJ: Wiley.

Bauer, P. J. (2007). Recall in infancy: A neurodevelopmental account. *Current Directions in Psychological Science, 16,* 142–146.

Bauer, P. J. (2009). Learning and memory: Like a horse and carriage. In A. Woodward & A. Needham (Eds.), *Learning and the infant mind* (pp. 3–28). New York: Oxford University Press.

Bauer, P. J., Bruch, M. M., Scholin, S. E., & Gulin, O. E. (2007). Using cue words to investigate the distribution of autobiographical memories in childhood. *Psychological Science, 18,* 910–916.

Bauer, P. J., Larkina, M., & Deocampo, J. (2011). Early memory development. In U. Goswami (Ed.), *Wiley-Blackwell handbook of childhood cognitive development* (2nd ed., pp. 153–179). Chichester, UK: Wiley-Blackwell.

Bauer, P. J., Wiebe, S. A., Carver, L. J., Lukowski, A. F., Haight, J. C., Waters, J. M., & Nelson, C. A. (2006). Electrophysiological indexes of encoding and behavioral indexes of recall: Examining relations and developmental change late in the first year of life. *Developmental Neuropsychology, 29,* 293–320.

Baum, K. T., Desai, A., Field, J., Miller, L. E., Rausch, J., & Beebe, D. W. (2014). Sleep restriction worsens mood and emotion regulation in adolescents. *Journal of Child Psychology and Psychiatry, 55,* 180–190.

Baumeister, R. F., Campbell, J. D., Krueger, J. I., & Vohs, K. D. (2003). Does high self-esteem cause better performance, interpersonal success, happiness, or healthier lifestyles? *Psychological Science in the Public Interest, 4*(1), 1–44.

Baumgartner, H. A., & Oakes, L. M. (2011). Infants' developing sensitivity to object function: Attention to features and feature correlations. *Journal of Cognition and Development, 12,* 275–298.

Baumgartner, S. E., Weeda, W. D., van der Heijden, L. L., & Huizinga, M. (2014). The relationship between media multitasking and executive function in early adolescence. *Journal of Early Adolescence, 34,* 1120–1144.

Baumrind, D. (1971). Current patterns of parental authority. *Developmental Psychology Monograph, 4* (No. 1, Pt. 2).

Baumrind, D. (2013). Authoritative parenting revisited: History and current status. In R. E. Larzelere, A. S. Morris, & A. W. Harrist (Eds.), *Authoritative parenting: Synthesizing nurturance and discipline for optimal child development* (pp. 11–34). Washington, DC: American Psychological Association.

Baumrind, D., Larzelere, R. E., & Owens, E. B. (2010). Effects of preschool parents' power assertive patterns and practices on adolescent development. *Parenting, 10,* 157–201.

Baumwell, L., Tamis-LeMonda, C. S., & Bornstein, M. H. (1997). Maternal verbal sensitivity and child language comprehension. *Infant Behavior and Development, 20,* 247–258.

Bauserman, R. (2002). Child adjustment in joint-custody versus sole-custody arrangements: A meta-analytic review. *Journal of Family Psychology, 16,* 91–102.

Bauserman, R. (2012). A meta-analysis of parental satisfaction, adjustment, and conflict in joint custody and sole custody following divorce. *Journal of Divorce & Remarriage, 53,* 464–488.

Bayley, N. (1969). *Bayley Scales of Infant Development.* New York: Psychological Corporation.

Bayley, N. (1993). *Bayley Scales of Infant Development* (2nd ed.). New York: Psychological Corporation.

Bayley, N. (2005). *Bayley Scales of Infant and Toddler Development* (3rd ed.). (Bayley III). San Antonio, TX: Harcourt Assessment.

Bean, R. A., Barber, B. K., & Crane, D. R. (2007). Parental support, behavioral control, and psychological control among African American youth: The relationships to academic grades, delinquency, and depression. *Journal of Family Issues, 27,* 1335–1355.

Beauchamp, G. K., & Mennella, J. A. (2011). Flavor perception in human infants: Development and functional significance. *Digestion, 83*(Suppl. 1), 1–6.

Bebko, J. M., McMorris, C. A., Metcalfe, A., Ricciuti, C., & Goldstein, G. (2014). Language proficiency and metacognition as predictors of spontaneous rehearsal in children. *Canadian Journal of Experimental Psychology, 68,* 46–58.

Becker, K., El-Faddagh, M., Schmidt, M. H., Esser, G., & Laucht, M. (2008). Interaction of dopamine transporter genotype with prenatal smoke exposure on ADHD symptoms. *Journal of Pediatrics, 152,* 263–269.

Becker, R. E. (2013). Nocturnal enuresis. In S. V. Kothare & A. Ivanenko (Eds.), *Parasomnias: Clinical characteristics and treatment* (pp. 293–301). New York: Springer Science + Media.

Beckett, C., Maughan, B., Rutter, M., Castle, J., Colvert, E., & Groothues, C. (2006). Do the effects of early severe deprivation on cognition persist into early adolescence? Findings from the English and Romanian adoptees study. *Child Development, 77,* 696–711.

Bédard, J., & Chi, M. T. (1992). Expertise. *Current Directions in Psychological Science, 1,* 135–139.

Bedard, K., & Dhuey, E. (2006). The persistence of early childhood maturity: International evidence of long-run age effects. *The Quarterly Journal of Economics, 121,* 1437–1472.

Bedi, K. S. (2003). Nutritional effects on neuron numbers. *Nutritional Neuroscience, 6,* 141–152.

Behm, I., Zubair, Connolly, G. N., & Alpert, H. R. (2012). Increasing prevalence of smoke-free homes and decreasing rates of sudden infant death syndrome in the United States: An ecological association study. *Tobacco Control, 21,* 6–11.

Behne, T., Liszkowski, U., Carpenter, M., & Tomasello, M. (2012). Twelve-month-olds' comprehension and production of pointing. *British Journal of Developmental Psychology, 30,* 359–375.

Behnke, M., & Smith, V. C. (2013). Prenatal substance abuse: Short- and long-term effects on the exposed fetus. *Pediatrics, 131,* e1009–e1024.

Behrens, K. Y., Hesse, E., & Main, M. (2007). Mothers' attachment status as determined by the Adult Attachment Interview predicts their 6-year-olds' reunion responses: A study conducted in Japan. *Developmental Psychology, 43*(6), 1553–1567.

Belcher, D., Lee, A., Solmon, M., & Harrison, L. (2003). The influence of gender-related beliefs and conceptions of ability on women learning the hockey wrist shot. *Research Quarterly for Exercise and Sport, 74,* 183–192.

Bell, J. H., & Bromnick, R. D. (2003). The social reality of the imaginary audience: A grounded theory approach. *Adolescence, 38,* 205–219.

Bell, M. A. (1998). Frontal lobe function during infancy: Implications for the development of cognition and attention. In J. E. Richards (Ed.), *Cognitive neuroscience of attention: A developmental perspective* (pp. 327–362). Mahwah, NJ: Erlbaum.

Bell, M. A., & Fox, N. A. (1996). Crawling experience is related to changes in cortical organization during infancy: Evidence from EEG coherence. *Developmental Psychobiology, 29,* 551–561.

Bellagamba, F., Camaioni, L., & Colonnesi, C. (2006). Change in children's understanding of others' intentional actions. *Developmental Science, 9,* 182–188.

Bellagamba, F., Laghi, F., Lonigro, A., & Pace, C. S. (2012). Re-enactment of intended acts from a video presentation by 18- and 24-month-old children. *Cognitive Processes, 13,* 381–386.

Bellinger, D. C., Leviton, A., & Sloman, J. (1990). Antecedents and correlates of improved cognitive performance in children exposed in utero to low levels of lead. *Environmental Health Perspectives, 89,* 5–11.

Belsky, J. (2001). Emanuel Miller Lecture: Developmental risks (still) associated with early child care. *Journal of Child Psychology and Psychiatry, 42,* 845–859.

Belsky, J. (2005). Attachment theory and research in ecological perspective: Insights from the Pennsylvania Infant and Family Development Project and the NICHD Study of Early Child Care. In K. E. Grossmann, K. Grossmann, & E. Waters (Eds.), *Attachment from infancy to adulthood: The major longitudinal studies* (pp. 71–97). New York: Guilford.

Belsky, J., & de Haan, M. (2011). Parenting and children's brain development: The end of the beginning. *Journal of Child Psychology and Psychiatry, 52,* 409–428.

Belsky, J., & Fearon, R. M. P. (2002). Early attachment security, subsequent maternal sensitivity, and later child development: Does continuity in development depend on caregiving? *Attachment and Human Development, 4,* 361–387.

Belsky, J., & Fearon, R. M. P. (2008). Precursors of attachment security. In J. Cassidy & P. R. Shaver (Eds.), *Handbook of attachment* (2nd ed., pp. 295–316). New York: Guilford.

Belsky, J., Schlomer, G. L., & Ellis, B. J. (2012). Beyond cumulative risk: Distinguishing harshness and unpredictability as determinants of parenting and early life history strategy. *Developmental Psychology, 48,* 662–673.

Belsky, J., Steinberg, L. D., Houts, R. M., Friedman, S. L., DeHart, G., Cauffman, E., et al. (2007a). Family rearing antecedents of pubertal timing. *Child Development, 78,* 1302–1321.

Belsky, J., Steinberg, L., Houts, R. M., & Halpern-Felsher, B. L. (2010). The development of reproductive strategy in females: Early maternal harshness → earlier menarche → increased sexual risk taking. *Developmental Psychology, 46,* 120–128.

Belsky, J., Vandell, D. L., Burchinal, M., Clarke-Stewart, K. A., McCartney, K., & Owen, M. T. (2007b). Are there long-term effects of early child care? *Child Development, 78,* 681–701.

Bemmels, H. R., Burt, A., Legrand, L. N., Iacono, W. G., & McGue, M. (2008). The heritability of life events: An adolescent twin and adoption study. *Twin Research and Human Genetics, 11,* 257–265.

Benbow, C. P., & Stanley, J. C. (1983). Sex differences in mathematical reasoning: More facts. *Science, 222,* 1029–1031.

Bender, H. L., Allen, J. P., McElhaney, K. B., Antonishak, J., Moore, C. M., Kelly, H. L., & Davis, S. M. (2007). Use of harsh physical discipline and developmental outcomes in adolescence. *Development and Psychopathology, 19,* 227–242.

Benenson, J. F., & Christakos, A. (2003). The greater fragility of females' versus males' closest same-sex friendships. *Child Development, 74,* 1123–1129.

Benigno, J. P., Byrd, D. L., McNamara, P. H., Berg, W. K., & Farrar, M. J. (2011). Talking through transitions: Microgenetic changes in preschoolers' private speech. *Child Language Teaching and Therapy, 27,* 269–285.

Benner, A. D. (2011). The transition to high school: Current knowledge, future directions. *Educational Psychology Review, 23,* 299–328.

Benner, A. D., & Graham, S. (2009). The transition to high school as a developmental process among multiethnic urban youth. *Child Development, 80,* 356–376.

Benner, A. D., & Wang, Y. (2014). Shifting attendance trajectories from middle to high school: Influences of school transitions and changing school contexts. *Developmental Psychology, 50,* 1288–1301.

Bennett, M., Barrett, M., Karakozov, R., Kipiani, G., Lyons, E., Pavlenko, V., & Riazanova, T. (2004). Young children's evaluations of the ingroup and outgroups: A multinational study. *Social Development, 13,* 124–141.

Benoit, A., Lacourse, E., & Claes, M. (2013). Pubertal timing and depressive symptoms in late adolescence: The moderating role of individual, peer, and parental factors. *Development and Psychopathology, 25,* 455–471.

Benson, J. E., Sabbagh, M. A., Carlson, S. M., & Zelazo, P. D. (2013). Individual differences in executive functioning predict preschoolers' improvement from theory-of-mind training. *Developmental Psychology, 49,* 1615–1627.

Benson, P. L., Scales, P. C., Hamilton, S. F., & Sesma, A., Jr. (2006). Positive youth development: Theory, research, and applications. In R. M. Lerner (Ed.), *Handbook of child psychology: Vol. 1. Theoretical models of human development* (6th ed., pp. 894–941). Hoboken, NJ: Wiley.

Bera, A., Ghosh, J., Singh, A. K., Hazra, A., Mukherjee, S., & Mukherjee, R. (2014). Effect of kangaroo mother care on growth and development of low birthweight babies up to 12 months of age: A controlled clinical trial. *Acta Paediatrica, 103,* 643–650.

Beratis, I. N., Rabavilas, A. D., Kyprianou, M., Papadimitriou, G. N., & Papageorgiou, C. (2013). Investigation of the link between higher order cognitive functions and handedness. *Journal of Clinical and Experimental Neuropsychology, 35,* 393–403.

Berenbaum, S. A., & Beltz, A. M. (2011). Sexual differentiation in human behavior: Effects of prenatal and pubertal organizational hormones. *Frontiers in Neuroendocrinology, 32,* 183–200.

Berger, A., Tzur, G., & Posner, M. I. (2006). Infant brains detect arithmetic errors. *Proceedings of the National Academy of Sciences, 103,* 12649–12653.

Berger, L. M., Paxson, C., & Waldfogel, J. (2009). Income and child development. *Children and Youth Services Review, 31,* 978–989.

Berger, S. E. (2010). Locomotor expertise predicts infants' perseverative errors. *Developmental Psychology, 46,* 326–336.

Berger, S. E., Theuring, C., & Adolph, K. E. (2007). How and when infants learn to climb stairs. *Infant Behavior and Development, 30,* 36–49.

Bergman, R. (2004). Identity as motivation. In D. K. Lapsley & D. Narvaez (Eds.), *Moral development, self, and identity* (pp. 21–46). Mahwah, NJ: Erlbaum.

Berk, L. E. (2001a). *Awakening children's minds: How parents and teachers can make a difference.* New York: Oxford University Press.

Berk, L. E. (2001b). Private speech and self-regulation in children with impulse-control difficulties: Implications for research and practice. *Journal of Cognitive Education and Psychology, 2*(1), 1–21.

Berk, L. E. (2006). Looking at kindergarten children. In D. Gullo (Ed.), *K today: Teaching and learning in the kindergarten year* (pp. 11–25). Washington, DC: National Association for the Education of Young Children.

Berk, L. E., & Harris, S. (2003). Vygotsky, Lev. In L. Nadel (Ed.), *Encyclopedia of cognitive science*. London: Macmillan.

Berk, L. E., & Meyers, A. M. (2013). The role of make-believe play in the development of executive function: Status of research and future directions. *American Journal of Play, 6,* 98–110.

Berk, L. E., & Spuhl, S. T. (1995). Maternal interaction, private speech, and task performance in preschool children. *Early Childhood Research Quarterly, 10,* 145–169.

Berkeley, S., Mastropieri, M. A., & Scruggs, T. E. (2011). Reading comprehension strategy instruction and attribution retraining for secondary students with learning and other mild disabilities. *Journal of Learning Disabilities, 44,* 18–31.

Berkowitz, C. M. (2004). *Talking to your kids about sex*. Somerville, NJ: Somerset Medical Center. Retrieved from www.somersetmedicalcenter.com/18417.cfm

Berkowitz, M. W., & Gibbs, J. C. (1983). Measuring the developmental features of moral discussion. *Merrill-Palmer Quarterly, 29,* 399–410.

Berkowitz, R. L., Roberts, J., & Minkoff, H. (2006). Challenging the strategy of maternal age-based prenatal genetic counseling. *Journal of the American Medical Association, 295,* 1446–1448.

Berman, R. A. (2007). Developing linguistic knowledge and language use across adolescence. In K. Hirsh-Pasek & R. M. Golinkoff (Eds.), *Action meets word: How children learn verbs* (pp. 347–367). New York: Oxford University Press.

Berman, S. L., Weems, C. F., Rodriguez, E. T., & Zamora, I. J. (2006). The relation between identity status and romantic attachment style in middle and late adolescence. *Journal of Adolescence, 29,* 737–748.

Berndt, T. J. (2004). Children's friendships: Shifts over a half-century in perspectives on their development and effects. *Merrill-Palmer Quarterly, 50,* 206–223.

Bernstein, N. (2014). *Burning down the house: The end of juvenile prison*. New York: New Press.

Bertenthal, B. I., Gredebäck, G., & Boyer, T. W. (2013). Differential contributions of development and learning to infants' knowledge of object continuity and discontinuity. *Child Development, 84,* 413–421.

Bertenthal, B. I., Longo, M. R., & Kenny, S. (2007). Phenomenal permanence and the development of predictive tracking in infancy. *Child Development, 78,* 350–363.

Bertrand, J., & Dang, E. P. (2012). Fetal alcohol spectrum disorders: Review of teratogenicity, diagnosis and treatment issues. In D. Hollar (Ed.), *Handbook of children with special health care needs* (pp. 231–258). New York: Springer Science + Business Media.

Bertrand, M., & Mullainathan, S. (2004). *Are Emily and Brendan more employable than Lakisha and Jamal? A field experiment on labor market discrimination*. Unpublished manuscript, University of Chicago.

Berzonsky, M. D. (2011). A social-cognitive perspective on identity construction. In S. J. Schwartz, K. Luyckx, & V. L. Vignoles (Eds.), *Handbook of identity theory and research* (Vol. 1, pp. 55–76). New York: Springer Science + Business Media.

Berzonsky, M. D., Cieciuch, J., Duriez, B., & Soenens, B. (2011). The how and what of identity formation: Associations between identity styles and value orientations. *Personality and Individual Differences, 50,* 295–299.

Best, C., & Fortenberry, J. D. (2013). Adolescent sexuality and sexual behavior. In W. T. O'Donohue, L. T. Benuto, & L. Woodward Tolle (Eds.), *Handbook of adolescent health psychology* (pp. 271–291). New York: Springer.

Best, D. (2009). From the American Academy of Pediatrics: Technical report—Secondhand and prenatal tobacco smoke exposure. *Pediatrics, 124,* e1017–1044.

Best, D. L. (2001). Gender concepts: Convergence in cross-cultural research and methodologies. *Cross-cultural Research: The Journal of Comparative Social Science, 35,* 23–43.

Beyers, J. M., Bates, J. E., Pettit, G. S., & Dodge, K. A. (2003). Neighborhood structure, parenting processes, and the development of youths' externalizing behaviors: A multilevel analysis. *American Journal of Community Psychology, 31,* 35–53.

Beyers, W., & Seiffge-Krenke, I. (2010). Does identity precede intimacy? Testing Erikson's theory on romantic development in emerging adults of the 21st century. *Journal of Adolescent Development, 25,* 387–415.

Bhanot, R., & Jovanovic, J. (2005). Parents' academic gender stereotypes influence whether they intrude on their children's work. *Sex Roles, 52,* 597–607.

Bhat, A., Heathcock, J., & Galloway, J. C. (2005). Toy-oriented changes in hand and joint kinematics during the emergence of purposeful reaching. *Infant Behavior and Development, 28,* 445–465.

Bhatt, R. M., & Bolonyai, A. (2011). Code-switching and the optimal grammar of bilingual language use. *Bilingualism: Language and Cognition, 14,* 522–546.

Bhatt, R. S., Rovee-Collier, C., & Weiner, S. (1994). Developmental changes in the interface between perception and memory retrieval. *Developmental Psychology, 30,* 151–162.

Bhatt, R. S., Wilk, A., Hill, D., & Rovee-Collier, C. (2004). Correlated attributes and categorization in the first half-year of life. *Developmental Psychobiology, 44,* 103–115.

Bialystok, E. (2011). Reshaping the mind: The benefits of bilingualism. *Canadian Journal of Experimental Psychology, 65,* 229–235.

Bialystok, E. (2013). The impact of bilingualism on language and literacy development. In T. K. Bhatia & W. C. Ritchie (Eds.), *Handbook of bilingualism and multilingualism* (pp. 624–648). Chichester, UK: Wiley-Blackwell.

Bialystok, E., Craik, F. I. M., & Luk, G. (2012). Bilingualism: Consequences for mind and brain. *Trends in Cognitive Sciences, 16,* 240–250.

Bialystok, E., & Martin, M. M. (2003). Notation to symbol: Development in children's understanding of print. *Journal of Experimental Child Psychology, 86,* 223–243.

Bianchi, D. W. (2012). From prenatal genomic diagnosis to fetal personalized medicine: Progress and challenges. *Nature Medicine, 18,* 1041–1051.

Bianchi, S. M., & Raley, S. B. (2005). Time allocation in families. In S. M. Bianchi, L. M. Casper, & R. B. King (Eds.), *Work, family, health, and well-being* (pp. 21–48). Mahwah, NJ: Erlbaum.

Bianco, A., Stone, J., Lynch, L., Lapinski, R., Berkowitz, G., & Berkowitz, R. L. (1996). Pregnancy outcome at age 40 and older. *Obstetrics and Gynecology, 87,* 917–922.

Bick, J., Dozier, M., Bernard, K., Grasso, D., & Simons, R. (2013). Foster mother–infant bonding: Associations between foster mothers' oxytocin production, electrophysiological brain activity, feelings of commitment, and caregiving quality. *Child Development, 84,* 826–840.

Biederman, J., Fried, R., Petty, C., Mahoney, L., & Faraone, S. V. (2012). An examination of the impact of attention-deficit hyperactivity disorder on IQ: A large controlled family-based analysis. *Canadian Journal of Psychiatry, 57,* 608–616.

Bielawska-Batorowicz, E., & Kossakowska-Petrycka, K. (2006). Depressive mood in men after the birth of their offspring in relation to a partner's depression, social support, fathers' personality and prenatal expectations. *Journal of Reproductive and Infant Psychology, 24,* 21–29.

Bierman, K. L., Domitrovich, C. E., Nix, R. L., Gest, S. D., Welsh, J. A., Greenberg, M. T., et al. (2008). Promoting academic and social-emotional school readiness: The Head Start REDI program. *Child Development, 79,* 1802–1817.

Bierman, K. L., Nix, R. L., Heinrichs, B. S., Domitrovich, C. E., Gest, S. D., Welsh, J. A., et al. (2014). Effects of Head Start REDI on children's outcomes 1 year later in different kindergarten contexts. *Child Development, 85,* 140–159.

Bierman, K. L., & Powers, C. J. (2009). Social skills training to improve peer relations. In K. H. Rubin, W. M. Bukowski, & B. Laursen (Eds.), *Handbook of peer interactions, relationships, and groups* (pp. 603–621). New York: Guilford.

Bifulco, R., Cobb, C. D., & Bell, C. (2009). Can interdistrict choice boost student achievement? The case of Connecticut's interdistrict magnet school program. *Educational Evaluation and Policy Analysis, 31,* 323–345.

Bigelow, A. E., MacLean, K., Proctor, J., Myatt, T., Gillis, R., & Power, M. (2010). Maternal sensitivity throughout infancy: Continuity and relation to attachment security. *Infant Behavior and Development, 33,* 50–60.

Bigler, R. S. (2007, June). Personal communication.

Bigler, R. S., Brown, C. S., & Markell, M. (2001). When groups are not created equal: Effects of group status on the formation of intergroup attitudes in children. *Child Development, 72,* 1151–1162.

Birch, E. E. (1993). Stereopsis in infants and its developmental relation to visual acuity. In K. Simons (Ed.), *Early visual development: Normal and abnormal* (pp. 224–236). New York: Oxford University Press.

Birch, L. L., & Fisher, J. A. (1995). Appetite and eating behavior in children. *Pediatric Clinics of North America, 42,* 931–953.

Birch, L. L., Fisher, J. O., & Davison, K. K. (2003). Learning to overeat: Maternal use of restrictive feeding practices promotes girls' eating in the absence of hunger. *American Journal of Clinical Nutrition, 78,* 215–220.

Birch, L. L., Zimmerman, S., & Hind, H. (1980). The influence of social-affective context on preschool children's food preferences. *Child Development, 51,* 856–861.

Birch, S. A. J., & Bloom, P. (2003). Children are cursed: An asymmetric bias in mental-state attribution. *Psychological Science, 14,* 283–285.

Bird, A., & Reese, E. (2006). Emotional reminiscing and the development of an autobiographical self. *Developmental Psychology, 42,* 613–626.

Biringen, Z., Altenhofen, S., Aberle, J., Baker, M., Brosal, A., Bennett, S., et al. (2012). Emotional availability, attachment, and intervention in center-based child care for infants and toddlers. *Development and Psychopathology, 24,* 23–34.

Biringen, Z., Emde, R. N., Campos, J. J., & Appelbaum, M. I. (1995). Affective reorganization in the infant, the mother, and the dyad: The role of upright locomotion and its timing. *Child Development, 66,* 499–514.

Birkeland, M. S., Breivik, K., & Wold, B. (2014). Peer acceptance protects global self-esteem from negative effects of low closeness to parents during adolescence and early adulthood. *Journal of Youth and Adolescence, 43,* 70–80.

Birkeland, M. S., Melkevik, O., Holsen, I., & Wold, B. (2012). Trajectories of global self-esteem development during adolescence. *Journal of Adolescence, 35,* 43–54.

Birken, C. S., Parkin, P. C., To, T., & Macarthur, C. (2006). Trends in rates of death from unintentional injury among Canadian children in urban areas: Influence of socioeconomic status. *Canadian Medical Association Journal, 175,* 867–868.

Birndorf, S., Ryan, S., Auinger, P., & Aten, M. (2005). High self-esteem among adolescents: Longitudinal trends, sex differences, and protective factors. *Journal of Adolescent Research, 37,* 194–201.

Birney, D. P., & Sternberg, R. J. (2011). The development of cognitive abilities. In M. H. Bornstein & M. E. Lamb (Eds.), *Developmental science: An advanced textbook* (6th ed., pp. 353–388). New York: Psychology Press.

Biro, F. M., & Wien, M. (2010). Childhood obesity and adult morbidities. *American Journal of Clinical Nutrition, 91,* 1499S–1505S.

Bjorklund, D. F. (2012). *Children's thinking* (5th ed.). Belmont, CA: Wadsworth Cengage Learning.

Bjorklund, D. F., Causey, K., & Periss, V. (2009). The evolution and development of human social cognition. In P. Kappeler & J. Silk (Eds.), *Mind the gap: Racing the origins of human universals* (pp. 351–371). Berlin: Springer Verlag.

Bjorklund, D. F., & Douglas, R. N. (1997). The development of memory strategies. In N. Cowan (Ed.), *The development of memory in childhood* (pp. 83–111). Hove, UK: Psychology Press.

Bjorklund, D. F., Schneider, W., Cassel, W. S., & Ashley, E. (1994). Training and extension of a memory strategy: Evidence for utilization deficiencies in high- and low-IQ children. *Child Development, 65,* 951–965.

Black, M. M. (2005). Failure to thrive. In M. C. Roberts (Ed.), *Handbook of pediatric psychology and psychiatry* (3rd ed., pp. 499–511). New York: Guilford.

Black, M. M., Dubowitz, H., Krishnakumar, A., & Starr, R. H., Jr. (2007). Early intervention and recovery among children with failure to thrive: Follow-up at age 8. *Pediatrics, 120,* 59–69.

Black, R. E., Victora, C. G., Walker, S. P., Bhutta, Z. A., Christian, P., de Onis, M. et al. (2013). Maternal and child undernutrition and overweight in low-income and middle-income countries. *Lancet, 382,* 427–451.

Black, R. E., Williams, S. M., Jones, I. E., & Goulding, A. (2002). Children who avoid drinking cow milk have low dietary calcium intakes and poor bone health. *American Journal of Clinical Nutrition, 76,* 675–680.

Blackwell, D. L., & Lichter, D. T. (2004). Homogamy among dating, cohabiting, and married couples. *Sociological Quarterly, 45,* 719–737.

Blackwell, L. S., Trzesniewski, K. H., & Dweck, C. S. (2007). Implicit theories of intelligence predict achievement across an adolescent transition: A longitudinal study and an intervention. *Child Development, 78,* 246–263.

Blair, B. L., Perry, N. B., O'Brien, M., Calkins, S. D., Keane, S. P., & Shanahan, L. (2014). The indirect effects of maternal emotion socialization on friendship quality in middle childhood. *Developmental Psychology, 50,* 566–576.

Blair, C. (2010). Stress and the development of self-regulation in context. *Child Development Perspectives, 4,* 181–188.

Blair, C., & Raver, C. C. (2012). Child development in the context of adversity: Experiential canalization of brain and behavior. *American Psychologist, 67,* 309–318.

Blair, C., & Razza, R. P. (2007). Relating effortful control, executive function, and false belief understanding to emerging math and literacy ability in kindergarten. *Developmental Psychology, 78,* 647–663.

Blake, J., & Boysson-Bardies, B. de (1992). Patterns in babbling: A cross-linguistic study. *Journal of Child Language, 19,* 51–74.

Blakemore, J. E. O. (2003). Children's beliefs about violating gender norms: Boys shouldn't look like girls, and girls shouldn't act like boys. *Sex Roles, 48,* 411–419.

Blakemore, J. E. O., Berenbaum, S. A., & Liben, L. S. (2009). *Gender development*. New York: Psychology Press.

Blakemore, J. E. O., & Hill, C. A. (2008). The Child Gender Socialization Scale: A measure to compare traditional and feminist parents. *Sex Roles, 58,* 192–207.

Blakemore, S.-J. (2012). Imaging brain development: The adolescent brain. *NeuroImage, 61,* 397–406.

Blakemore, S.-J., Dahl, R. E., Frith, U., & Pine, D. S. (2011). Developmental cognitive neuroscience. *Developmental Cognitive Neuroscience, 1,* 3–6.

Blasi, A. (1994). Moral identity: Its role in moral functioning. In B. Puka (Ed.), *Fundamental research in moral development: A compendium* (Vol. 2, pp. 123–167). New York: Garland.

Blasi, C. H., & Bjorklund, D. F. (2003). Evolutionary developmental psychology: A new tool for better understanding human ontogeny. *Human Development, 46,* 259–281.

Blass, E. M., Ganchrow, J. R., & Steiner, J. E. (1984). Classical conditioning in newborn humans 2–48 hours of age. *Infant Behavior and Development, 7,* 223–235.

Blatchford, P. (2012). Three generations of research on class-size effects. In K. R. Harris (Ed.), *APA educational psychology handbook: Vol. 2. Individual differences and cultural and contextual factors* (pp. 530–554). Washington, DC: American Psychological Association.

Blatchford, P., Bassett, P., & Brown, P. (2005). Teachers' and pupils' behavior in large and small classes: A systematic observation study of pupils aged 10 and 11 years. *Journal of Educational Psychology, 97,* 454–467.

Blatchford, P., Bassett, P., & Brown, P. (2011). Examining the effect of class size on classroom engagement and teacher–pupil interaction: Differences in relation to pupil prior attainment and primary vs. secondary schools. *Learning and Instruction, 21,* 715–730.

Bleeker, M. M., & Jacobs, J. E. (2004). Achievement in math and science: Do mothers' beliefs matter 12 years later? *Journal of Educational Psychology, 96,* 97–109.

Block, C. C. (2012). Proven and promising reading instruction. In J. S. Carlson & J. R. Levin (Eds.), *Instructional strategies for improving students' learning* (pp. 3–41). Charlotte, NC: Information Age Publishing.

Blood-Siegfried, J. (2009). The role of infection and inflammation in sudden infant death syndrome. *Immunopharmacology and Immunotoxicology, 31,* 516– 23.

Bloom, L. (2000). The intentionality model of language development: How to learn a word, any word. In R. Golinkoff, K. Hirsh-Pasek, N. Akhtar, L. Bloom, G. Hollich, L. Smith, M. Tomasello, & A. Woodward (Eds.), *Becoming a word learner: A debate on lexical acquisition.* New York: Oxford University Press.

Bloom, P. (1999). The role of semantics in solving the bootstrapping problem. In R. Jackendoff & P. Bloom (Eds.), *Language, logic, and concepts* (pp. 285–309). Cambridge, MA: MIT Press.

Bloom, T., Glass, N., Curry, M. A., Hernandez, R., & Houck, G. (2013). Maternal stress exposures, reactions, and priorities for stress reduction among low-income, urban women. *Journal of Midwifery and Women's Health, 58,* 167–174.

Blumenfeld, P. C., Marx, R. W., & Harris, C. J. (2006). Learning environments. In K. A. Renninger & I. E. Sigel (Eds.), *Handbook of child psychology: Vol. 4. Child psychology in practice* (6th ed., pp. 297–342). Hoboken, NJ: Wiley.

Blumenthal, H., Leen-Feldner, E. W., Babson, K. A., Gahr, J. L., Trainor, C. D., & Frala, J. L. (2011). Elevated social anxiety among early maturing girls. *Developmental Psychology, 47,* 1133–1140.

Bodell, L. P., Joiner, T. E., & Keel, P. K. (2013). Comorbidity-independent risk for suicidality increases with bulimia nervosa but not anorexia nervosa. *Journal of Psychiatric Research, 47,* 617–621.

Bodrova, E., & Leong, D. J. (2007). *Tools of the mind: The Vygotskian approach to early childhood education* (2nd ed.). Upper Saddle River, NJ: Merrill Prentice Hall.

Bogaert, A. F., & Skorska, M. (2011). Sexual orientation, fraternal birth order, and the maternal immune hypothesis: A review. *Frontiers in Neuroendocrinology, 32,* 247–254.

Bogin, B. (2001). *The growth of humanity*. New York: Wiley-Liss.

Bogin, B. (2013). Recent advances in growth research: Nutritional, molecular, and endocrine perspectives. In M. W. Gillman, P. D. Gluckman, & R. G. Rosenfeld (Eds.), *Recent advances in growth research: Nutritional, molecular and endocrine perspectives* (Vol. 71, pp. 115–126). Basel, Switzerland: Karger.

Bogin, B., Smith, P., Orden, A. B., Varela, S., & Loucky, J. (2002). Rapid change in height and body proportions of Maya American children. *American Journal of Human Biology, 14,* 753–761.

Bohannon, J. N., III, & Bonvillian, J. D. (2013). Theoretical approaches to language acquisition. In J. B. Gleason & N. B. Ratner (Eds.), *The development of language* (8th ed., pp. 190–240). Upper Saddle River, NJ: Pearson.

Bohannon, J. N., III, & Stanowicz, L. (1988). The issue of negative evidence: Adult responses to children's language errors. *Developmental Psychology, 24,* 684–689.

Boivin, M., Brendgen, M., Vitaro, F., Dionne, G., Girard, A., Pérusse, D., & Tremblay, R. E. (2013). Strong genetic contribution to peer relationship difficulties at school entry: Findings from a longitudinal twin study. *Child Development, 84,* 1098–1114.

Bolisetty, S., Bajuk, B., Me, A.-L., Vincent, T., Sutton, L., & Lui, K. (2006). Preterm outcome table (POT): A simple tool to aid counselling parents of very preterm infants. *Australian and New Zealand Journal of Obstetrics and Gynaecology, 46,* 189–192.

Bolzani, L. H., Messinger, D. S., Yale, M., & Dondi, M. (2002). Smiling in infancy. In M. H. Abel (Ed.), *An empirical reflection on the smile* (pp. 111–136). Lewiston, NY: Edwin Mellen Press.

Bono, K. E., & Bizri, R. (2014). The role of language and private speech in preschoolers' self-regulation. *Early Child Development and Care, 184,* 658–670.

Bono, M. A., & Stifter, C. A. (2003). Maternal attention-directing strategies and infant focused attention during problem solving. *Infancy, 4,* 235–250.

Boom, J., Wouters, H., & Keller, M. (2007). A cross-cultural validation of stage development: A Rasch reanalysis of longitudinal socio-moral reasoning data. *Cognitive Development, 22,* 213–229.

Booren, L. M., Downer, J. T., & Vitiello, V. E. (2012). Observations of children's interactions with teachers, peers, and tasks across preschool classroom activity settings. *Early Education and Development, 23,* 517–538.

Borchert, S., Lamm, B., Graf, F., & Knopf, M. (2013). Deferred imitation in 18-month-olds from two cultural contexts: The case of Cameroonian Nso farmer and German-middle class infants. *Infant Behavior and Development, 36,* 717–727.

Bornstein, M. H. (1989). Sensitive periods in development: Structural characteristics and causal interpretations. *Psychological Bulletin, 105,* 179–197.

Bornstein, M. H. (2006). Parenting science and practice. In K. Renninger & I. E. Sigel (Eds.), *Handbook of child psychology: Vol. 4. Child psychology in practice* (6th ed., pp. 893–949). Hoboken, NJ: Wiley.

Bornstein, M. H., & Arterberry, M. E. (1999). Perceptual development. In M. H. Bornstein & M. E. Lamb (Eds.), *Developmental psychology: An advanced textbook* (pp. 231–274). Mahwah, NJ: Erlbaum.

Bornstein, M. H., & Arterberry, M. E. (2003). Recognition, discrimination, and categorization of smiling by 5-month-old infants. *Developmental Science, 6,* 585–599.

Bornstein, M. H., Arterberry, M. E., & Mash, C. (2010). Infant object categorization transcends object–context relations. *Infant Behavior and Development, 33,* 7–15.

Bornstein, M. H., & Sawyer, J. (2006). Family systems. In K. McCartney & D. Phillips (Eds.), *Blackwell handbook of early childhood development* (pp. 381–398). Malden, MA: Blackwell.

Bornstein, M. H., Vibbert, M., Tal, J., & O'Donnell, K. (1992). Toddler language and play in the second year: Stability, covariation, and influences of parenting. *First Language, 12,* 323–338.

Borst, C. G. (1995). *Catching babies: The professionalization of childbirth, 1870–1920.* Cambridge, MA: Harvard University Press.

Borst, G., Poirel, N., Pineau, A., Cassotti, M., & Houdé, O. (2013). Inhibitory control efficiency in a Piaget-like class-inclusion task in school-age children and adults: A developmental negative priming study. *Developmental Psychology, 49,* 1366–1374.

Bos, H. (2013). Lesbian-mother families formed through donor insemination. In A. E. Goldberg & K. R. Allen (Eds.), *LGBT-parent families: Innovations in research and implications for practice* (pp. 21–37). New York: Springer.

Bos, H., & Sandfort, T. G. M. (2010). Children's gender identity in lesbian and heterosexual two-parent families. *Sex Roles, 62,* 114–126.

Bos, H. M. W., van Balen, F., & van den Boom, D. C. (2004). Experience of parenthood, couple relationship, social support, and child-rearing goals in planned lesbian mother families. *Journal of Child Psychology and Psychiatry, 25,* 755–764.

Bosacki, S. L., & Moore, C. (2004). Preschoolers' understanding of simple and complex emotions: Links with gender and language. *Sex Roles, 50,* 659–675.

Bost, K. K., Shin, N., McBride, B. A., Brown, G. L., Vaughn, B. E., & Coppola, G. (2006). Maternal secure base scripts, children's attachment security, and mother–child narrative styles. *Attachment and Human Development, 8,* 241–260.

Bouchard, G. (2011). The role of psychosocial variables in prenatal attachment: An examination of moderational effects. *Journal of Reproductive and Infant Psychology, 29,* 197–207.

Bouchard, T. J. (2004). Genetic influence on human psychological traits: A survey. *Current Directions in Psychological Science, 13,* 148–151.

Boucher, O., Bastien, C. H., Saint-Amour, D., Dewailly, E., Ayotte, P., Jacobson, J. L., Jacobson, et al. (2010). Prenatal exposure to methylmercury and PCBs affects distinct stages of information processing: An event-related potential study with Inuit children. *Neurotoxicology, 31,* 373–384.

Boucher, O., Muckle, G., & Bastien, C. H. (2009). Prenatal exposure to polychlorinated biphenyls: A neuropsychologic analysis. *Environmental Health Perspectives, 117,* 7–16.

Bouldin, P. (2006). An investigation of the fantasy predisposition and fantasy style of children with imaginary companions. *Journal of Genetic Psychology, 167,* 17–29.

Boutwell, B. B., Franklin, C. A., Barnes, J. C., & Beaver, K. M. (2011). Physical punishment and childhood aggression: The role of gender and gene–environment interplay. *Aggressive Behavior, 37,* 559–568.

Bowker, A. (2004). Predicting friendship stability during early adolescence. *Journal of Early Adolescence, 24,* 85–112.

Bowlby, J. (1969). *Attachment and loss: Vol. 1. Attachment.* New York: Basic Books.

Bowlby, J. (1980). *Attachment and loss: Vol. 3. Loss.* New York: Basic Books.

Bowman, L. C., Liu, D., Meltzoff, A. N., & Wellman, H. M. (2012). Neural correlates of belief–desire reasoning in

7- and 8-year-old children: An event-related potential study. *Developmental Science, 15,* 618–632.

Boyan, A., & Sherry, J. L. (2011). The challenge in creating games for education: Aligning mental models with game models. *Child Development Perspectives, 5,* 82–87.

Boyatzis, C. J. (2000). The artistic evolution of mommy: A longitudinal case study of symbolic and social processes. In C. J. Boyatzis & M. W. Watson (Eds.), *Symbolic and social constraints on the development of children's artistic style* (pp. 5–29). San Francisco: Jossey-Bass.

Boyd-Franklin, N. (2006). *Black families in therapy* (2nd ed.). New York: Guilford.

Boyle, M. H., & Lipman, E. L. (2002). Do places matter? Socioeconomic disadvantage and behavioral problems of children in Canada. *Journal of Consulting and Clinical Psychology, 70,* 378–389.

Boysson-Bardies, B. de, & Vihman, M. M. (1991). Adaptation to language: Evidence from babbling and first words in four languages. *Language, 67,* 297–319.

Bracken, B. A. (2000). *The psychoeducational assessment of preschool children.* Boston: Allyn and Bacon.

Brackett, M. A., Rivers, S. E., & Salovey, P. (2011). Emotional intelligence: Implications for personal, social, academic, and workplace success. *Social and Personality Compass, 5,* 88–103.

Bradley, R. H. (1994). The HOME Inventory: Review and reflections. In H. W. Reese (Ed.), *Advances in child development and behavior* (Vol. 25, pp. 241–288). San Diego: Academic Press.

Bradley, R. H., & Caldwell, B. M. (1982). The consistency of the home environment and its relation to child development. *International Journal of Behavioral Development, 5,* 445–465.

Bradley, R. H., & Corwyn, R. F. (2003). Age and ethnic variations in family process mediators of SES. In M. H. Bornstein & R. H. Bradley (Eds.), *Socioeconomic status, parenting, and child development* (pp. 161–188). Mahwah, NJ: Erlbaum.

Bradley, R. H., Corwyn, R. F., McAdoo, H. P., & García Coll, C. (2001). The home environments of children in the United States. Part I: Variations by age, ethnicity, and poverty status. *Child Development, 72,* 1844–1867.

Bradley, R. H., McKelvy, L. M., & Whiteside-Mansell, L. (2011). Does the quality of stimulation and support in the home environment moderate the effect of early education programs? *Child Development, 82,* 2110–2122.

Bradley, R. H., Whiteside, L., Mundfrom, D. J., Casey, P. H., Kelleher, K. J.,& Pope, S. K. (1994). Contribution of early intervention and early caregiving experiences to resilience in low-birthweight, premature children living in poverty. *Journal of Clinical Child Psychology, 23,* 425–434.

Brady, S. A. (2011). Efficacy of phonics teaching for reading outcomes: Indications from post-NRP research. In S. A. Brady, D. Braze, & C. A. Fowler (Eds.), *Explaining individual differences in reading: Theory and evidence* (pp. 69–96). New York: Psychology Press.

Braine, L. G., Schauble, L., Kugelmass, S., & Winter, A. (1993). Representation of depth by children: Spatial strategies and lateral biases. *Developmental Psychology, 29,* 466–479.

Braine, M. D. S. (1994). Is nativism sufficient? *Journal of Child Language, 21,* 1–23.

Brainerd, C. J. (2003). Jean Piaget, learning, research, and American education. In B. J. Zimmerman (Ed.), *Educational psychology: A century of contributions* (pp. 251–287). Mahwah, NJ: Erlbaum.

Brainerd, C. J., & Reyna, V. F. (2012). Reliability of children's testimony in the era of developmental reversals. *Developmental Review, 32,* 224–267.

Brame, B., Nagin, D. S., & Tremblay, R. E. (2001). Developmental trajectories of physical aggression from school entry to late adolescence. *Journal of Child Psychology and Psychiatry, 42,* 503–512.

Branca, F., & Ferrari, M. (2002). Impact of micronutrient deficiencies on growth: The stunting syndrome. *Annals of Nutrition and Metabolism, 46*(Suppl. 1), 8–17.

Brand, S., Gerber, M., Beck, J., Hatzinger, M., Puhse, U., & Holsboer-Trachsler, E. (2010). High exercise levels are related to favorable sleep and psychological functioning in adolescence: A comparison of athletes and controls. *Journal of Adolescent Health, 46,* 133–141.

Branje, S. J. T., van Lieshout, C. F. M., van Aken, M. A. G., & Haselager, G. J. T. (2004). Perceived support in sibling relationships and adolescent adjustment. *Journal of Child Psychology and Psychiatry, 45,* 1385–1396.

Braswell, G. S. (2006). Sociocultural contexts for the early development of semiotic production. *Psychological Bulletin, 132,* 877–894.

Braswell, G. S., & Callanan, M. A. (2003). Learning to draw recognizable graphic representations during mother–child interactions. *Merrill-Palmer Quarterly, 49,* 471–494.

Braungart-Rieker, J. M., Hill-Soderlund, A. L., & Karrass, J. (2010). Fear and anger reactivity trajectories from 4 to 16 months: The roles of temperament, regulation, and maternal sensitivity. *Developmental Psychology, 46,* 791–804.

Braver, S. L., Griffin, W. A., Cookston, J. T., Sandler, I. N., & Williams, J. (2005). Promoting better fathering among divorced non-resident fathers. In W. M. Pinsof & J. Lebow (Eds.), *Family psychology: The art of the science* (pp. 295–325). New York: Oxford University Press.

Bray, S., Dunkin, B., Hong, D. S., & Reiss, A. I. (2011). Reduced functional connectivity during working memory in Turner syndrome. *Cerebral Cortex, 21,* 2471–2481.

Brazelton, T. B., Koslowski, B., & Tronick, E. (1976). Neonatal behavior among urban Zambians and Americans. *Journal of the American Academy of Child Psychiatry, 15,* 97–107.

Brazelton, T. B., & Nugent, J. K. (2011). *Neonatal Behavioral Assessment Scale* (4th ed.). London: Mac Keith Press.

Brazelton, T. B., Nugent, J. K., & Lester, B. M. (1987). Neonatal Behavioral Assessment Scale. In J. D. Osofsky (Ed.), *Handbook of infant development* (2nd ed., pp. 780–817). New York: Wiley.

Bregman, H. R., Malik, N. M., Page, M. J. L., Makynen, E., & Lindahl, K. M. (2013). Identity profiles in lesbian, gay, and bisexual youth: The role of family influences. *Journal of Youth and Adolescence, 42,* 417–430.

Bremner, J. G. (2010). Cognitive development: Knowledge of the physical world. In J. G. Bremner & T. D. Wachs (Eds.), *Wiley-Blackwell handbook of infant development: Vol. 1. Basic research* (2nd ed., pp. 204–242). Oxford, UK: Wiley.

Bremner, J. G., Slater, A. M., Mason, U. C., Spring, J., & Johnson, S. P. (2013). Trajectory perception and object continuity: Effects of shape and color change on 4-month-olds' perception of object identity. *Developmental Psychology, 49,* 1021–1026.

Brendgen, M., Boivin, M., Dionne, G., Barker, E. D., Vitaro, F., Girard, A., Tremblay, R., & Pérusse, D. (2011). Gene-environment processes linking aggression, peer victimization, and the teacher–child relationship. *Child Development, 82,* 2021–2036.

Brendgen, M., Markiewicz, D., Doyle, A. B., & Bukowski, W. M. (2001). The relations between friendship quality, ranked-friendship preference, and adolescents' behavior with their friends. *Merrill-Palmer Quarterly, 47,* 395–415.a

Brennan, L. M., Shelleby, E. C., Shaw, D. S., Gardner, F., Dishion, T. J., & Wilson, M. (2013). Indirect effects of the family check-up on school-age academic achievement through improvements in parenting in early childhood. *Journal of Educational Psychology, 105,* 762–773.

Brennan, W. M., Ames, E. W., & Moore, R. W. (1966). Age differences in infants' attention to patterns of different complexities. *Science, 151,* 354–356.

Brenner, E., & Salovey, P. (1997). Emotional regulation during childhood: Developmental, interpersonal, and individual considerations. In P. Salovey & D. Sluyter (Eds.), *Emotional literacy and emotional development* (pp. 168–192). New York: Basic Books.

Bretherton, I., Fritz, J., Zahn-Waxler, C., & Ridgeway, D. (1986). Learning to talk about emotions: A functionalist perspective. *Child Development, 57,* 529–548.

Bretherton, I., & Munholland, K. A. (2008). Internal working models in attachment relationships. In J. Cassidy & P. R. Shaver (Eds.), *Handbook of attachment: Theory, research, and clinical applications* (2nd ed., pp. 102–127). New York: Guilford.

Brewster, K. L., Tillman, K. H., & Jokinen-Gordon, H. (2014). Demographic characteristics of lesbian parents in the United States. *Population Research and Policy Review, 33,* 485–502.

Bridgett, D. J., Gartstein, M. A., Putnam, S. P., McKay, T., Iddins, R., Robertson, C., et al. (2009). Maternal and contextual influences and the effect of temperament development during infancy on parenting in toddlerhood. *Infant Behavior and Development, 32,* 103–116.

Bright, G. M., Mendoza, J. R., & Rosenfeld, R. G. (2009). Recombinant human insulin-like growth factor-1 treatment: Ready for primetime. *Endocrinology and Metabolism Clinics of North America, 38,* 625–638.

Bright, J. E. H., Pryor, R. G. L., Wilkenfeld, S., & Earl, J. (2005). The role of social context and serendipitous events in career decision making. *International Journal for Educational and Vocational Guidance, 5,* 19–36.

Brisch, K. H., Bechinger, D., Betzler, S., Heineman, H., Kachele, H., Pohlandt, F., et al. (2005). Attachment quality in very low-birthweight premature infants in relation to maternal attachment representations and neurological development. *Parenting: Science and Practice, 5,* 11–32.

Britton, M. L. (2013). Race/ethnicity, attitudes, and living with parents during young adulthood. *Journal of Marriage and Family, 75,* 995–1013.

Brody, G. H., Beach, S. R. H., Philibert, R. A., Chen, Y., & Murry, V. M. (2009). Prevention effects moderate the association of 5-HTTLPR and youth risk behavior initiation: Gene x environment hypotheses tested via a randomized preventive design. *Child Development, 80,* 645–661.

Brody, G. H., Chen, Y., Beach, S. R. H., Kogan, S. M., Yu, T., DiClemente, R. J., et al. (2014). Differential sensitivity to prevention programming: A dopaminergic polymorphism-enhanced prevention effect on protective parenting and adolescent substance use. *Health Psychology, 33,* 182–191.

Brody, G. H., & Murry, V. M. (2001). Sibling socialization of competence in rural, single-parent African American families. *Journal of Marriage and the Family, 63,* 996–1008.

Brody, G. H., Stoneman, Z., & McCoy, J. K. (1994). Forecasting sibling relationships in early adolescence from child temperament and family processes in middle childhood. *Child Development, 65,* 771–784.

Brody, L. R. (1999). *Gender, emotion, and the family.* Cambridge, MA: Harvard University Press.

Brody, L. R. (1997). Gender and emotion: Beyond stereotypes. *Journal of Social Issues, 53,* 369–393.

Brody, N. (1997). Intelligence, schooling, and society. *American Psychologist, 52,* 1046–1050.

Brodzinsky, D. M. (2011). Children's understanding of adoption: Developmental and clinical implications. *Professional Psychology: Research and Practice, 42,* 200–207.

Broidy, L. M., Nagin, D. S., Tremblay, R. E., Bates, J. E., Brame, B., Dodge, K. A., Fergusson, D., Horwood, J. L., Loeber, R., Laird, R., Lynam, D. R., Moffitt, T. E., Pettit, G. S., & Vitaro, F. (2003). Developmental trajectories of childhood disruptive behaviors and adolescent delinquency: A six-site, cross-national study. *Developmental Psychology, 39,* 222–245.

Bronfenbrenner, U. (Ed.). (2005). *Making human beings human.* Thousand Oaks, CA: Sage.

Bronfenbrenner, U., & Morris, P. A. (2006). The bioecological model of human development. In R. M. Lerner (Ed.), *Handbook of child psychology: Vol. 1. Theoretical models of human development* (6th ed., pp. 793–828). Hoboken, NJ: Wiley.

Bronson, G. W. (1994). Infant's transitions toward adult-like scanning. *Child Development, 65,* 1243–1261.

Bronstein, P. (2006). The family environment: Where gender role socialization begins. In J. Worell & C. D. Goodheart (Eds.), *Handbook of girls' and women's psychological health: Gender and well-being across the life span* (pp. 262–271). New York: Oxford University Press.

Bronte-Tinkew, J., Moore, K. A., & Carrano, J. (2006). The father–child relationship, parenting styles, and adolescent risk behaviors in intact families. *Journal of Family Issues, 27,* 850–881.

Brooker, R. J., Buss, K. A., Lemery-Chalfant, K., Aksan, N., Davidson, R. J., & Goldsmith, H. H. (2013). The development of stranger fear in infancy and toddlerhood: Normative development, individual differences, antecedents, and outcomes. *Developmental Science, 16,* 864–878.

Brooks, K., Xu, X., Chen, W., Zhou, K., Neale, B., & Lowe, N. (2006). The analysis of 51 genes in DSM-IV combined type attention deficit hyperactivity disorder: Association signals in DRD4, DAT1, and 16 other genes. *Molecular Psychiatry, 11,* 935–953.

Brooks, P. J., Hanauere, J. B., Padowska, B., & Rosman, H. (2003). The role of selective attention in preschoolers' rule use in a novel dimensional card sort. *Cognitive Development, 18*, 195–215.

Brooks, R., & Meltzoff, A. N. (2005). The development of gaze following and its relation to language. *Developmental Science, 8*, 535–543.

Brooks, R., & Meltzoff, A. N. (2008). Infant gaze following and pointing predict accelerated vocabulary growth through two years of age: A longitudinal, growth curve modeling study. *Journal of Child Language, 35*, 207–220.

Brooks-Gunn, J. (1988). Antecedents and consequences of variations in girls' maturational timing. *Journal of Adolescent Health Care, 9*, 365–373.

Brooks-Gunn, J. (2003). Do you believe in magic? What we can expect from early childhood intervention programs. *Social Policy Report of the Society for Research in Child Development, 27*(1).

Brooks-Gunn, J. (2004). Intervention and policy as change agents for young children. In P. L. Chase-Lansdale, K. Kiernan, & R. J. Friedman (Eds.), *Human development across lives and generations: The potential for change* (pp. 293–340). New York: Cambridge University Press.

Brooks-Gunn, J., Han, W.-J., & Waldfogel, J. (2010). First-year maternal employment and child development in the first 7 years. *Monographs of the Society for Research in Child Development, 75*(No. 2, Serial No. 296).

Brooks-Gunn, J., Klebanov, P. K., Smith, J., Duncan, G. J., & Lee, K. (2003). The black–white test score gap in young children. Contributions of test and family characteristics. *Applied Developmental Science, 7*, 239–252.

Brown, A. L. (1997). Transforming schools into communities of thinking and learning about serious matters. *American Psychologist, 52*, 399–413.

Brown, A. M., & Miracle, J. A. (2003). Early binocular vision in human infants: Limitations on the generality of the Superposition Hypothesis. *Vision Research, 43*, 1563–1574.

Brown, B. B., Herman, M., Hamm, J. V., & Heck, D. (2008). Ethnicity and image: Correlates of minority adolescents' affiliation with individual-based versus ethnically defined peer crowds. *Child Development, 79*, 529–546.

Brown, B. B., & Larson, J. (2009). Peer relationships in adolescence. In R. M. Lerner & L. Steinberg (Eds.), *Handbook of adolescent psychology* (3rd ed., pp. 74–103). New York: Wiley.

Brown, B. B., Lohr, M. J., & McClenahan, E. L. (1986). Early adolescents' perceptions of peer pressure. *Journal of Early Adolescence, 6*, 139–154.

Brown, C. S., & Bigler, R. S. (2004). Children's perceptions of gender discrimination. *Developmental Psychology, 40*, 714–726.

Brown, G. L., Mangelsdorf, S. C., Agathen, J. M., & Ho, M.-H. (2008). Young children's psychological selves: Convergence with maternal reports of child personality. *Social Development, 17*, 161–182.

Brown, G. L., Mangelsdorf, S. C., & Neff, C. (2012). Father involvement, paternal sensitivity, and father–child attachment security in the first 3 years. *Journal of Family Psychology, 26*, 421–430.

Brown, G. L., Schoppe-Sullivan, S. J., Mangelsdorf, S. C., & Neff, C. (2010). Observed and reported supportive coparenting as predictors of infant–mother and infant–father attachment security. *Early Child Development and Care, 180*, 121–137.

Brown, J. D., Harris, S. K., Woods, E. R., Buman, M. P., & Cox, J. E. (2012). Longitudinal study of depressive symptoms and social support in adolescent mothers. *Maternal and Child Health Journal, 16*, 894–901.

Brown, J. D., & L'Engle, K. L. (2009). X-rated: Attitudes and behaviors associated with U.S. early adolescents' exposure to sexually explicit media. *Communication Research, 36*, 129–151.

Brown, R. B., & Dietz, E. L. (2009). Informal peer groups in middle childhood and adolescence. In K. H. Rubin, W. M. Bukowski, & B. Larsen (Eds.), *Handbook of peer interactions, relationships, and groups* (pp. 361–376). New York: Guilford.

Brown, R. W. (1973). *A first language: The early stages.* Cambridge, MA: Harvard University Press.

Brown, S. A., & Ramo, D. E. (2005). Clinical course of youth following treatment for alcohol and drug problems. In H. A. Liddle & C. L. Rowe (Eds.), *Adolescent substance abuse: Research and clinical advances* (pp. 79–103). Cambridge, UK: Cambridge University Press.

Brown, T. E. (2006). Executive functions and attention deficit hyperactivity disorder: Implications of two conflicting views. *International Journal of Disability, Development and Education, 53*, 35–46.

Browne, C. A., & Woolley, J. D. (2004). Preschoolers' magical explanations for violations of physical, social, and mental laws. *Journal of Cognition and Development, 5*, 239–260.

Browne, J. V., & Talmi, A. (2005). Family-based intervention to enhance infant–parent relationships in the neonatal intensive care unit. *Journal of Pediatric Psychology, 30*, 667–677.

Brownell, C. A., & Kopp, C. B. (2007). Transitions in toddler socioemotional development: Behavior, understanding, relationships. In C. A. Brownell & C. B. Kopp (Eds.), *Socioemotional development in the toddler years: Transitions and transformations* (pp. 1–40). New York: Guilford.

Brownell, C. A., Zerwas, S., & Ramani, G. B. (2007). "So big": The development of body self-awareness in toddlers. *Child Development, 78*, 1426–1440.

Bruer, J. T. (1999). *The myth of the first three years.* New York: Free Press.

Brühwiler, C., & Blatchford, P. (2011). Effects of class size and adaptive teaching competency on classroom processes and academic outcome. *Learning and Instruction, 21*, 95–108.

Bruine de Bruin, W. (2012). Judgment and decision making in adolescents. In M. Dhami, A. Schlottmann, & M. R. Waldmann (Eds.), *Judgment and decision-making as a skill: Learning, development, and evolution* (pp. 85–111). New York: Cambridge University Press.

Brummelman, E., Thomaes, S., Overbeek, G., Orobio de Castro, B., van den Hout, M. A., & Bushman, B. J. (2014). On feeding those hungry for praise: Person praise backfires in children with low self-esteem. *Journal of Experimental Psychology: General, 143*, 9–14.

Bruschweiler-Stern, N. (2004). A multifocal neonatal intervention. In A. J. Sameroff, S. C. McDonough, & K. L. Rosenblum (Eds.), *Treating parent–infant relationship problems* (pp. 188–212). New York: Guilford.

Bruzzese, J., & Fisher, C. B. (2003). Assessing and enhancing the research consent capacity of children and youth. *Applied Developmental Science, 7*, 13–26.

Bryan, A. E., & Dix, T. (2009). Mothers' emotions and behavioral support during interactions with toddlers: The role of child temperament. *Social Development, 18*, 647–670.

Bryant, B. K., Zvonkovic, A. M., & Reynolds, P. (2006). Parenting in relation to child and adolescent vocational development. *Journal of Vocational Behavior, 69*, 149–175.

Bryant, D. M., Hoeft, F., Lai, S., Lackey, J., Roeltgen, D., Ross, J., et al. (2012). Sex chromosomes and the brain: A study of neuroanatomy in XYY syndrome. *Developmental Medicine and Child Neurology, 54*, 1149–1156.

Bryant, P., & Nunes, T. (2002). Children's understanding of mathematics. In U. Goswami (Ed.), *Blackwell handbook of childhood cognitive development* (pp. 412–439). Malden, MA: Blackwell.

Brydges, C. R., Reid, C. L., Fox, A. M., & Anderson, M. (2012). A unitary executive function predicts intelligence in children. *Intelligence, 40*, 458–469.

Bryk, R. L., & Fisher, P. A. (2012). Training the brain: Practical applications of neural plasticity from the intersection of cognitive neuroscience, developmental psychology, and prevention science. *American Psychologist, 67*, 87–100.

Buchanan, C. M., & Holmbeck, G. N. (1998). Measuring beliefs about adolescent personality and behavior. *Journal of Youth and Adolescence, 27*, 609–629.

Buchanan, C. M., Maccoby, E. E., & Dornbusch, S. M. (1996). *Adolescents after divorce.* Cambridge, MA: Harvard University Press.

Buchanan-Barrow, E., & Barrett, M. (1998). Children's rule discrimination within the context of the school. *British Journal of Developmental Psychology, 16*, 539–551.

Buchsbaum, D., Dridgers, S., Weisberg, D. S., & Gopnik, A. (2012). The power of possibility: Causal learning, counterfactual reasoning, and pretend play. *Philosophical Transactions of the Royal Society B, 367*, 2202–2212.

Buckhalt, J. A., El-Sheikh, M., Keller, P. S., & Kelly, R. J. (2009). Concurrent and longitudinal relations between children's sleep and cognitive functioning: The moderating role of parent education. *Child Development, 80*, 875–892.

Buckingham-Howes, S., Berger, S., Shafer, S., Scaletti, L. A., & Black, M. M. (2013). Systematic review of prenatal cocaine exposure and adolescent development. *Pediatrics, 13*, e1917–e1936.

Bugental, D. B., Corpuz, R., & Schwartz, A. (2012). Preventing children's aggression: Outcomes of an early intervention. *Developmental Psychology, 48*, 1443–1449.

Bugental, D. B., Ellerson, P. C., Lin, E. K., Rainey, B., & Kokotovic, A. (2002). A cognitive approach to child abuse prevention. *Journal of Family Psychology, 16*, 243–258.

Bugental, D. B., & Happaney, K. (2004). Predicting infant maltreatment in low-income families: The interactive effects of maternal attributions and child status at birth. *Developmental Psychology, 40*, 234–243.

Buhl, H. M., & Lanz, M. (2007). Emerging adulthood in Europe: Common traits and variability across five European countries. *Journal of Adolescent Research, 22*, 439–443.

Buhrmester, D., & Furman, W. (1990). Perceptions of sibling relationships during middle childhood and adolescence. *Child Development, 61*, 1387–1398.

Buhs, E. S., Ladd, G. W., & Herald-Brown, S. L. (2010). Victimization and exclusion: Links to peer rejection, classroom engagement, and achievement. In S. R. Jimerson, S. M. Swearer, & D. L. Espelage (Eds.), *Handbook of bullying in schools: An international perspective* (pp. 163–172). New York: Routledge.

Bukacha, C. M., Gauthier, S., & Tarr, M. J. (2006). Beyond faces and modularity: The power of an expertise framework. *Trends in Cognitive Sciences, 10*, 159–166.

Bukowski, W. M., Sippola, L. K., & Hoza, B. (1999). Same and other: Interdependency between participation in same- and other-sex friendships. *Journal of Youth and Adolescence, 28*, 439–459.

Bukowski, W. M., Sippola, L. K., & Newcomb, A. F. (2000). Variations in patterns of attraction of same-and other-sex peers during early adolescence. *Developmental Psychology, 36*, 147–154.

Bullock, M., & Lutkenhaus, P. (1990). Who am I? The development of self-understanding in toddlers. *Merrill-Palmer Quarterly, 36*, 217–238.

Bulotsky-Shearer, R. J., Wen, X., Faria, A.-M., Hahs-Vaughn, D. L., & Korfmacher, J. (2012). National profiles of classroom quality and family involvement: A multilevel examination of proximal influences on Head Start children's school readiness. *Early Childhood Research Quarterly, 27*, 627–639.

Bunge, S. A., & Wright, S. B. (2007). Neurodevelopmental changes in working memory and cognitive control. *Current Opinion in Neurobiology, 17*, 243–250.

Bunting, H., Drew, H., Lasseigne, A., & Anderson-Butcher, D. (2013). Enhancing parental involvement and family resources. In C. Franklin, M. B. Harris, & P. Allen-Meares (Eds.), *School services sourcebook: A guide for school-based professionals* (2nd ed., pp. 633–643). New York: Oxford University Press.

Bunting, L., & McAuley, C. (2004). Teenage pregnancy and parenthood: The role of fathers. *Child and Family Social Work, 9*, 295–303.

Burchinal, M., Vandergrift, N., & Pianta, R. (2010). Threshold analysis of association between child care quality and child outcomes for low-income children in pre-kindergarten programs. *Early Childhood Research Quarterly, 25*, 166–176.

Burden, M. J., Jacobson, S. W., & Jacobson, J. L. (2005). Relation of prenatal alcohol exposure to cognitive processing speed and efficiency in childhood. *Alcoholism: Clinical and Experimental Research, 29*, 1473–1483.

Burgess-Champoux, T. L., Larson, N., Neumark-Sztainer, D., Hannan, P. J., & Story, M. (2009). Are family meal patterns associated with overall diet quality during the transition from early to middle adolescence? *Journal of Nutrition Education and Behavior, 41*, 79–86.

Burhans, K. K., & Dweck, C. S. (1995). Helplessness in early childhood: The role of contingent worth. *Child Development, 66*, 1719–1738.

Burkam, D. T., Ready, D. D., Lee, V. E., & LoGerfo, L. F. (2004). Social-class differences in summer learning between kindergarten and first grade: Model specification and estimation. *Sociology of Education, 77*, 1–31.

Burman, D. D., Bitan, T., & Booth, J. R. (2008). Sex differences in neural processing of language among children. *Neuropsychologia, 46,* 1349–1362.

Burns, C. E. (2000). *Pediatric primary care: A handbook for nurse practitioners.* Philadelphia: Saunders.

Burts, D. C., Hart, C. H., Charlesworth, R., Fleege, P. O., Mosley, J., & Thomasson, R. H. (1992). Observed activities and stress behaviors of children in developmentally appropriate and inappropriate kindergarten classrooms. *Early Childhood Research Quarterly, 7,* 297–318.

Bush, K. R., & Peterson, G. W. (2008). Family influences on child development. In T. P. Gullotta & G. M. Blau (Eds.), *Handbook of child behavioral issues: Evidence-based approaches to prevention and treatment* (pp. 43–67). New York: Routledge.

Bushman, B. J., & Huesmann, L. R. (2012). Effects of violent media on aggression. In Singer, D. G. & Singer, J. L. (Eds.), *Handbook of Children and the Media* (2nd ed., pp. 231–248). Thousand Oaks, CA: Sage.

Bushnell, E. W., & Boudreau, J. P. (1993). Motor development and the mind: The potential role of motor abilities as a determinant of aspects of perceptual development. *Child Development, 64,* 1005–1021.

Bussey, K. (1992). Lying and truthfulness: Children's definitions, standards, and evaluative reactions. *Child Development, 63,* 129–137.

Buswell, S. D., & Spatz, D. L. (2007). Parent–infant co-sleeping and its relationship to breastfeeding. *Journal of Pediatric Health Care, 21,* 22–28.

Butcher, L. M., Davis, O. S. P., Craig, I. W., & Plomin, R. (2008). Genome-wide quantitative trait locus association scan of general cognitive ability using pooled DNA and 500K single nucleotide polymorphism microarrays. *Genes, Brains and Behavior, 7,* 435–446.

Butler, M. G. (2009). Genomic imprinting disorders in humans: A mini-review. *Journal of Assisted Reproduction and Genetics, 26,* 477–486.

Butler, M. G., & Meaney, J. (Eds.). (2005). *Genetics of developmental disabilities.* Boca Raton, FL: Taylor & Francis.

Butler, R. (1998). Age trends in the use of social and temporal comparison for self-evaluation: Examination of a novel developmental hypothesis. *Child Development, 69,* 1054–1073.

Buttelmann, D., Over, H., Carpenter, M., & Tomasello, M. (2014). Eighteen-month-olds false beliefs in an unexpected-contents task. *Journal of Experimental Child Psychology, 119,* 120–126.

Butts, M. M., Casper, W. J., & Yang, T. S. (2013). How important are work–family support policies? A meta-analytic investigation of their effects on employee outcomes. *Journal of Applied Psychology, 98,* 1–25.

Bybee, J., Merisca, R., & Velasco, R. (1998). The development of reactions to guilt-producing events. In J. Bybee (Ed.), *Guilt and children* (pp. 185–213). San Diego: Academic Press.

Byne, W., Bradley, S. J., Coleman, E., Eyler, A. E., Green, R., Menvielle, E. J., et al. (2012). Report of the American Psychiatric Association Task Force on Treatment of Gender Identity Disorder. *Archives of Sexual Behavior, 41,* 759–796.

Byrnes, J. P., & Wasik, B. A. (2009). *Language and literacy development: What educators need to know.* New York: Guilford.

C

Cabrera, N. J., & Bradley, R. H. (2012). Latino fathers and their children. *Child Development Perspectives, 6,* 232–238.

Cabrera, N. J., & García Coll, C. (2004). Latino fathers: Uncharted territory in need of much exploration. In M. E. Lamb (Ed.), *The role of the father in child development* (4th ed., pp. 98–120). Hoboken, NJ: Wiley.

Cabrera, N. J., Fitzgerald, H. E., Bradley, R. H., & Roggman, L. (2007). Modeling the dynamics of paternal influence on children over the life course. *Applied Developmental Science, 11,* 185–189.

Cabrera, N. J., Shannon, J. D., & Tamis-LeMonda, C. (2007). Fathers' influence on their children's cognitive and emotional development: From toddlers to pre-K. *Applied Developmental Science, 11,* 208–213.

Cain, K., & Oakhill, J. (2011). Matthew effects in young readers: Reading comprehension and reading experience

aid vocabulary development. *Journal of Learning Disabilities, 44,* 431–443.

Cain, M. A., Bornick, P., & Whiteman, V. (2013). The maternal, fetal, and neonatal effects of cocaine exposure in pregnancy. *Clinical Obstetrics and Gynecology, 56,* 124–132.

Cairns, R. B., & Cairns, B. D. (2006). The making of developmental psychology. In R. M. Lerner (Ed.), *Handbook of child psychology: Vol. 1. Theoretical models of human development* (6th ed., pp. 89–165). Hoboken, NJ: Wiley.

Cairns, R. B., Xie, H., & Leung, M.-C. (1998). The popularity of friendship and the neglect of social networks: Toward a new balance. In W. M. Bukowski & A. H. Cillessen (Eds.), *Sociometry then and now: Building on six decades of measuring children's experiences with the peer group* (pp. 25–53). San Francisco: Jossey-Bass.

Calaff, K. P. (2008). Supportive schooling: Practices that support culturally and linguistically diverse students' preparation for college. *NASSP Bulletin, 92,* 95–110.

Caldera, Y. M., & Lindsey, E. W. (2006). Coparenting, mother–infant interaction, and infant–parent attachment relationships in two-parent families. *Journal of Family Psychology, 20,* 275–283.

Caldwell, B. M., & Bradley, R. H. (1994). Environmental issues in developmental follow-up research. In S. L. Friedman & H. C. Haywood (Eds.), *Developmental follow-up* (pp. 235–256). San Diego: Academic Press.

Callaghan, T. C. (1999). Early understanding and production of graphic symbols. *Child Development, 70,* 1314–1324.

Callaghan, T. C., Moll, H., Rakoczy, H., Warneken, F., Lizkowski, U., Behne, T., & Tomasello, M. (2011). Early social cognition in three cultural contexts. *Monographs of the Society for Research in Child Development, 76*(2, Serial No. 299).

Callaghan, T. C., & Rankin, M. P. (2002). Emergence of graphic symbol functioning and the question of domain specificity: A longitudinal training study. *Child Development, 73,* 359–376.

Callanan, M. A., & Oakes, L. M. (1992). Preschoolers' questions and parents' explanations: Causal thinking in everyday activity. *Cognitive Development, 7,* 213–233.

Callanan, M. A., & Sabbagh, M. A. (2004). Multiple labels for objects in conversations with young children: Parents' language and children's developing expectations about word meanings. *Developmental Psychology, 40,* 746–763.

Calvert, S. L., Strong, B. L., & Gallagher, L. (2005). Control as an engagement feature for young children's attention to, and learning of, computer content. *American Behavioral Scientist, 48,* 578–589.

Cameron, C. A., Lau, C., Fu, G., & Lee, K. (2012). Development of children's moral evaluations of modesty and self-promotion in diverse cultural settings. *Journal of Moral Education, 41,* 61–78.

Cameron, C. A., & Lee, K. (1997). The development of children's telephone communication. *Journal of Applied Developmental Psychology, 18,* 55–70.

Cameron, P. A., & Gallup, G. G. (1988). Shadow recognition in human infants. *Infant Behavior and Development, 11,* 465–471.

Cameron-Faulkner, T., Lieven, E., & Tomasello, M. (2003). A construction based analysis of child directed speech. *Cognitive Science, 27,* 843–873.

Campa, M. I., & Eckenrode, J. J. (2006). Pathways to intergenerational adolescent childbearing in a high-risk sample. *Journal of Marriage and Family, 68,* 558–572.

Campbell, A., Shirley, L., & Candy, J. (2004). A longitudinal study of gender-related cognition and behaviour. *Developmental Science, 7,* 1–9.

Campbell, D., Scott, K. D., Klaus, M. H., & Falk, M. (2007). Female relatives or friends trained as labor doulas: Outcomes at 6 to 8 weeks postpartum. *Birth, 34,* 220–227.

Campbell, D. A., Lake, M. F., Falk, M., & Backstrand, J. R. (2006). A randomized control trial of continuous support in labor by a lay doula. *Journal of Obstetrics and Gynecology and Neonatal Nursing, 35,* 456–464.

Campbell, F. A., Pungello, E. P., Miller-Johnson, S., Burchinal, M., & Ramey, C. T. (2001). The development of cognitive and academic abilities: Growth curves from an early childhood educational experiment. *Developmental Psychology, 37,* 231–242.

Campbell, F. A., & Ramey, C. T. (2010). Carolina Abecedarian Project. In A. Reynolds, A. J. Rolick, M. M. Englund, & J. A. Temple (Eds.), *Childhood programs and practices in the first decade of life: A human capital integration* (pp. 76–98). New York: Cambridge University Press.

Campbell, F. A., Ramey, C. T., Pungello, E., Sparling, J., & Miller-Johnson, S. (2002). Early childhood education: Young adult outcomes from the Abecedarian Project. *Applied Developmental Science, 6,* 42–57.

Campbell, S. B., Brownell, C. A., Hungerford, A., Spieker, S. J., Mohan, R., & Blessing, J. S. (2004). The course of maternal depressive symptoms and maternal sensitivity as predictors of attachment security at 36 months. *Development and Psychopathology, 16,* 231–252.

Campos, J. J., Anderson, D. I., Barbu-Roth, M. A., Hubbard, E. M., Hertenstein, J. J., & Witherington, D. (2000). Travel broadens the mind. *Infancy, 1,* 149–219.

Campos, J. J., Frankel, C. B., & Camras, L. (2004). On the nature of emotion regulation. *Child Development, 75,* 377–394.

Campos, J. J., Witherington, D., Anderson, D. I., Frankel, C. I., Uchiyama, I., & Barbu-Roth, M. (2008). Rediscovering development in infancy. *Child Development, 79,* 1625–1632.

Campos, R. G. (1989). Soothing pain-elicited distress in infants with swaddling and pacifiers. *Child Development, 60,* 781–792.

Camras, L. (2011). Differentiation, dynamical integration and functional emotional development. *Emotion Review, 3,* 138–146.

Camras, L., Kolmodin, K., & Chen, Y. (2008). Mothers' self-reported emotional expression in mainland Chinese, Chinese American and European American families. *International Journal of Behavioral Development, 32,* 459–463.

Camras, L. A. (1992). Expressive development and basic emotions. *Cognition and Emotion, 6,* 267–283.

Camras, L. A., Oster, H., Campos, J. J., & Bakeman, R. (2003). Emotional facial expressions in European-American, Japanese, and Chinese infants. *Annals of the New York Academy of Sciences, 1000,* 1–17.

Camras, L. A., Oster, H., Campos, J. J., Campos, R., Ujie, T., Miyake, K., Wang, L., & Meng, Z. (1998). Production of emotional and facial expressions in European-American, Japanese, and Chinese infants. *Developmental Psychology, 34,* 616–628.

Camras, L. A., Oster, H., Campos, J. J., Miyake, K., & Bradshaw, D. (1992). Japanese and American infants' responses to arm restraint. *Developmental Psychology, 28,* 578–583.

Camras, L. A., & Shutter, J. M. (2010). Emotional facial expressions in infancy. *Emotion Review, 2,* 120–129.

Canadian Paediatric Society. (2005). Youth and firearms in Canada. *Paediatric Child Health, 10,* 473–477.

Candelaria, M., Teti, D. M., & Black, M. M. (2011). Multi-risk infants: Predicting attachment security from sociodemographic, psychosocial, and health risk among African-American preterm infants. *Journal of Child Psychology and Psychiatry, 52,* 870–877.

Canfield, R., Henderson, C., Cory-Slechta, D., Cox, C., Jusko, T., & Lanphear, B. (2003). Intellectual impairment in children with blood lead concentrations below 10 µg per deciliter. *New England Journal of Medicine, 348,* 1517–1526.

Capirci, O., Contaldo, A., Caselli, M. C., & Volterra, V. (2005). From action to language through gesture. *Gesture, 5,* 155–177.

Carballo, J. J., Muñoz-Lornzo, L., Blasco-Fontecilla, H., Lopez-Castroman, J., García-Nieto, R., Dervic, K., et al. (2011). Continuity of depressive disorders from childhood and adolescence to adulthood: A naturalistic study in community mental health centers. *Primary Care Companion for CNS Disorders, 13,* PCC.11m01150.

Card, N. A., Stucky, B. D., Sawalani, G. M., & Little, T. D. (2008). Direct and indirect aggression during childhood and adolescence: A meta-analytic review of gender differences, intercorrelations, and relations to maladjustment. *Child Development, 79,* 1185–1229.

Carey, S., & Markman, E. M. (1999). Cognitive development. In B. M. Bly & D. E. Rumelhart (Eds.), *Cognitive science* (pp. 201–254). San Diego: Academic Press.

Carlo, G., Mestre, M. V., Samper, P., Tur, A., & Armenta, B. E. (2011). The longitudinal relations among dimensions of parenting styles, sympathy, prosocial moral reasoning, and prosocial behaviors. *International Journal of Behavioral Development, 35,* 116–124.

Carlson, S. M., & Meltzoff, A. N. (2008). Bilingual experience and executive functioning in young children. *Developmental Science, 11,* 282–298.

Carlson, S. M., Moses, L. J., & Claxton, S. J. (2004). Individual differences in executive functioning and theory of mind: An investigation of inhibitory control and planning ability. *Journal of Experimental Child Psychology, 87,* 299–319.

Carlson, S. M., & White, R. E. (2013). Executive function, pretend play, and imagination. In R. E. White & S. M. Carlson (Eds.), *Oxford handbook of the development of imagination* (pp. 161–174). New York: Oxford University Press.

Carlson, S. M., & Zelazo, P. D., & Faja, S. (2013). Executive function. In P. D. Zelazo (Ed.), *Oxford handbook of developmental psychology, Vol. 1: Body and mind* (pp. 706–743). New York: Oxford University Press.

Carlson, V. J., & Harwood, R. L. (2003). Attachment, culture, and the caregiving system: The cultural patterning of everyday experiences among Anglo and Puerto Rican mother–infant pairs. *Infant Mental Health Journal, 24,* 53–73.

Carpendale, J. I. M. (2000). Kohlberg and Piaget on stages and moral reasoning. *Developmental Review, 20,* 181–205.

Carpenter, M., Nagel, K., & Tomasello, M. (1998). Social cognition, joint attention, and communicative competence. *Monographs of the Society for Research in Child Development, 63*(4, Serial No. 255).

Carpenter, T. P., Fennema, E., Fuson, K., Hiebert, J., Human, P., & Murray, H. (1999). Learning basic number concepts and skills as problem solving. In E. Fennema & T. A. Romberg (Eds.), *Mathematics classrooms that promote understanding: Studies in mathematical thinking and learning series* (pp. 45–61). Mahwah, NJ: Erlbaum.

Carr, D., & Friedman, M. A. (2005). Is obesity stigmatizing? Body weight, perceived discrimination, and psychological well-being in the United States. *Journal of Health and Social Behavior, 46,* 244–256.

Carr, J. (2002). Down syndrome. In P. Howlin & O. Udwin (Eds.), *Outcomes in neurodevelopmental and genetic disorders* (pp. 169–197). New York: Cambridge University Press.

Carr, R., & Peebles, R. (2012). Developmental considerations of media exposure risk for eating disorders. In J. Lock (Ed.), *The Oxford handbook of child and adolescent eating disorders: Developmental perspectives* (pp. 56–66). New York: Oxford University Press.

Carroll, J. B. (2005). The three-stratum theory of cognitive abilities. In D. P. Flanagan & P. L. Harrison (Eds.), *Contemporary intellectual assessment: Theories, tests, and issues* (2nd ed., pp. 69–76). New York: Guilford.

Carskadon, M. A. (2011). Sleep in adolescents: The perfect storm. *Pediatric Clinics of North America, 58,* 637–647.

Carver, K., Joyner, K., & Udry, J. R. (2003). National estimates of adolescent romantic relationships. In P. Florsheim (Ed.), *Adolescent romantic relations and sexual behavior: Theory, research, and practical implications* (pp. 23–56). Mahwah, NJ: Erlbaum.

Carver, P. R., Egan, S. K., & Perry, D. G. (2004). Children who question their heterosexuality. *Developmental Psychology, 40,* 43–53.

CASA. (2006). *The importance of family dinners III.* New York: National Center on Addiction and Substance Abuse, Columbia University.

Casalin, S., Luyten, P., Vliegen, N., & Meurs, P. (2012). The structure and stability of temperament from infancy to toddlerhood: A one-year prospective study. *Infant Behavior and Development, 35,* 94–108.

Casalis, S., & Cole, P. (2009). On the relationship between morphological and phonological awareness: Effects of training in kindergarten and in first-grade reading. *First Language, 29,* 113–142.

Casasola, M., Bhagwat, J., & Burke, A. S. (2009). Learning to form a spatial category of tight-fit relations: How experience with a label can give a boost. *Developmental Psychology, 45,* 711–723.

Casasola, M., & Park, Y. (2013). Developmental changes in infant spatial categorization: When more is best and when less is enough. *Child Development, 84,* 1004–1019.

Case, R. (1996). Introduction: Reconceptualizing the nature of children's conceptual structures and their development in middle childhood. In R. Case & Y. Okamoto (Eds.), The role of central conceptual structures in the development of children's thought. *Monographs of the Society for Research in Child Development, 246*(61, Serial No. 246), pp. 1–26.

Case, R. (1998). The development of conceptual structures. In D. Kuhn & R. S. Siegler (Eds.), *Handbook of child psychology: Vol. 2. Cognition, perception, and language* (pp. 745–800). New York: Wiley.

Case, R., & Okamoto, Y. (Eds.). (1996). The role of central conceptual structures in the development of children's thought. *Monographs of the Society for Research in Child Development, 61*(1–2, Serial No. 246).

CASEL (Collaborative for Academic, Social, and Emotional Learning). (2013). *CASEL guide: Effective social and emotional learning programs (Preschool and elementary school edition).* Chicago, IL: Author.

Caserta, D., Graziano, A., Lo Monte, G., Bordi, G., & Moscarini, M. (2013). Heavy metals and placental fetal–maternal barrier: A mini-review on the major concerns. *European Review for Medical and Pharmacological Sciences, 17,* 2198–2206.

Casey, B. J., Jones, R. M., & Somerville, L. H. (2011). Braking and accelerating of the adolescent brain. *Journal of Research on Adolescence, 21,* 21–33.

Casey, B. M. (1986). Individual differences in selective attention among prereaders: A key to mirror-image confusions. *Developmental Psychology, 22,* 824–831.

Casey, B. M., Nuttall, R. L., & Pezaris, E. (1997). Mediators of gender differences in mathematics college entrance test scores: A comparison of spatial skills with internalized beliefs and anxieties. *Developmental Psychology, 33,* 669–680.

Casey, B. M., Nuttall, R. L., & Pezaris, E. (2001). Spatial-mechanical reasoning skills versus mathematics self-confidence as mediators of gender differences on mathematics subtests using cross-national gender-based items. *Journal for Research in Mathematics Education, 32,* 28–57.

Casper, L. M., & Smith, K. E. (2002). Dispelling the myths: Self-care, class, and race. *Journal of Family Issues, 23,* 716–727.

Caspi, A., Elder, G. H., Jr., & Bem, D. J. (1987). Moving against the world: Life-course patterns of explosive children. *Developmental Psychology, 23,* 308–313.

Caspi, A., Elder, G. H., Jr., & Bem, D. J. (1988). Moving away from the world: Life-course patterns of shy children. *Developmental Psychology, 24,* 824–831.

Caspi, A., Harrington, H., Milne, B., Amell, J. W., Theodore, R. F., & Moffitt, T. E. (2003). Children's behavioral styles at age 3 are linked to their adult personality traits at age 26. *Journal of Personality, 71,* 495–513.

Caspi, A., McClay, J., Moffitt, T. E., Mill, J., Martin, J., & Craig, I. W. (2002). Role of genotype in the cycle of violence in maltreated children. *Science, 297,* 851–854.

Caspi, A., Moffitt, T. E., Morgan, J., Rutter, M., Taylor, A., Kim-Cohen, J., & Polo-Tomas, M. (2004). Maternal expressed emotion predicts children's antisocial behavior problems: Using monozygotic-twin differences to identify environmental effects on behavioral development. *Developmental Psychology, 40,* 149–161.

Caspi, A., & Roberts, B. W. (2001). Personality development across the life course: The argument for change and continuity. *Psychological Inquiry, 12,* 49–66.

Caspi, A., & Shiner, L. (2006). Personality development. In N. Eisenberg (Ed.), *Handbook of child psychology: Vol. 3. Social, emotional, and personality development* (6th ed., pp. 300–365). Hoboken, NJ: Wiley.

Cassia, V. M., Turati, C., & Simion, F. (2004). Can a nonspecific bias toward top-heavy patterns explain newborns' face preference? *Psychological Science, 15,* 379–383.

Cassidy, J. (2001). Adult romantic attachments: A developmental perspective on individual differences. *Review of General Psychology, 4,* 111–131.

Cassidy, J., & Berlin, L. J. (1994). The insecure/ambivalent pattern of attachment: Theory and research. *Child Development, 65,* 971–991.

Catalano, R., Ahern, J., Bruckner, T., Anderson, E., & Saxton, K. (2009). Gender-specific selection in utero among contemporary human birth cohorts. *Paediatric and Perinatal Epidemiology, 23,* 273–278.

Catalano, R., Zilko, C. E., Saxton, K. B., & Bruckner, T. (2010). Selection in utero: A biological response to mass layoffs. *American Journal of Human Biology, 22,* 396–400.

Caton, D., Corry, M. P., Frigoletto, F. D., Hopkins, D. P., Liberman, E., & Mayberry, L. (2002). The nature and management of labor pain: Executive summary. *American Journal of Obstetrics and Gynecology, 186,* S1–S15.

Cauffman, E., Shulman, E. P., Steinberg, L., Claus, E., Banich, M. T., & Graham, S. (2010). Age differences in affective decision making as indexed by performance on the Iowa Gambling Task. *Developmental Psychology, 46,* 193–207.

Caughey, R. W., & Michels, K. B. (2009). Birth weight and childhood leukemia: A meta-analysis and review of the current evidence. *International Journal of Cancer, 124,* 2658–2670.

Cavadini, C., Siega-Riz, A. M., & Popkin, B. M. (2000). U.S. adolescent food intake trends from 1965 to 1996. *Archives of Diseases in Childhood, 83,* 18–24.

Ceci, S. J. (1999). Schooling and intelligence. In S. J. Ceci & W. M. Williams (Eds.), *The nature–nurture debate: The essential readings* (pp. 168–175). Oxford, UK: Blackwell.

Ceci, S. J., Bruck, M., & Battin, D. (2000). The suggestibility of children's testimony. In Bjorklund, D. (Ed), *False-memory creation in children and adults* (pp. 169–201). Mahwah, NJ: Erlbaum.

Ceci, S. J., Kulkofsky, S., Klemfuss, J. Z., Sweeney, C. D., & Bruck, M. (2007). Unwarranted assumptions about children's testimonial accuracy. *Annual Review of Clinical Psychology, 3,* 311–328.

Ceci, S. J., & Roazzi, A. (1994). The effects of context on cognition: Postcards from Brazil. In R. J. Sternberg (Ed.), *Mind in context* (pp. 74–101). New York: Cambridge University Press.

Ceci, S. J., Rosenblum, T. B., & Kumpf, M. (1998). The shrinking gap between high- and low-scoring groups: Current trends and possible causes. In U. Neisser (Ed.), *The rising curve: Long-term gains in IQ and related measures* (pp. 287–302). Washington, DC: American Psychological Association.

Ceci, S. J., & Williams, W. M. (2010). *The mathematics of sex: How biology and society conspire to limit talented women and girls.* New York: Oxford University Press.

Cecil, J. E., Watt, P., Murrie, I. S. L., Wrieden, W., Wallis, D. J., Hetherington, M. M., Bolton-Smith, C., & Palmer, C. N. A. (2005). Childhood obesity and socioeconomic status: A novel role for height growth limitation. *International Journal of Obesity, 29,* 1199–1203.

Center for Communication and Social Policy (Ed.). (1998). *National Television Violence Study* (Vol. 2). Newbury Park, CA: Sage.

Centers for Disease Control and Prevention. (2010). *The association between school-based physical activity, including physical education, and academic performance.* Retrieved from www.cdc.gov/healthyyouth/health_and_academics/pdf/pape_executive_summary.pdf

Centers for Disease Control and Prevention (2011). Nonfatal traumatic brain injuries related to sports and recreation activities among persons aged ≤19 Years—United States, 2001–2009. *Morbidity and Mortality Weekly Report, 60,* 1337–1342.

Centers for Disease Control and Prevention. (2012). *Trends in asthma prevalence, health care use, and mortality in the United States, 2001–2010.* Retrieved from www.cdc.gov/nchs/data/databriefs/db94.htm

Centers for Disease Control and Prevention. (2013a). Breastfeeding report card: United States 2013. Retrieved from www.cdc.gov/breastfeeding/pdf/2013breastfeedingreportcard.pdf

Centers for Disease Control and Prevention. (2013b, February). *HIV surveillance report, 2011. Vol. 23.* Retrieved from www.cdc.gov/hiv/topics/surveillance/resources/reports

Centers for Disease Control and Prevention. (2013c). *Results from the School Health Policies and Practices Study 2012.* Retrieved from www.cdc.gov/healthyyouth/shpps/2012/pdf/shpps-results_2012.pdf

Centers for Disease Control and Prevention. (2013d). *Sexually transmitted disease surveillance 2012.* Retrieved from www.cdc.gov/std/stats12/surv2012.pdf

Centers for Disease Control and Prevention. (2014a). Assisted reproductive technology (ART). Retrieved from www.cdc.gov/art/ARTReports.htm

Centers for Disease Control and Prevention. (2014b). *Bridging the Gap Research Program: Supporting recess in elementary schools.* Atlanta, GA: U.S. Department of Health and Human Services.

Centers for Disease Control and Prevention. (2014c). CDC's health homes and lead program: What do parents need to know to protect their children? Retrieved from www.cdc.gov/nceh/lead/acclpp/blood_lead_levels.htm

Centers for Disease Control and Prevention. (2014d). *CDC Wonder: About underlying cause of death 1999–2011.* Retrieved from wonder.cdc.gov/ucd-icd10.html

Centers for Disease Control and Prevention. (2014e). *Child maltreatment: Risk and protective factors.* Retrieved from www.cdc.gov/violenceprevention/childmaltreatment/riskprotectivefactors.html

Centers for Disease Control and Prevention. (2014f). National, state, and selected local area vaccination coverage among children aged 19–35 months—United States, 2013. *Morbidity and Mortality Weekly Report, 63,* 741–748.

Centers for Disease Control and Prevention. (2014g). *National suicide statistics at a glance.* Retrieved from www.cdc.gov/violenceprevention/suicide/statistics/mechanism01.html

Centers for Disease Control and Prevention. (2014h). Tobacco use and pregnancy. Retrieved from www.cdc.gov/Reproductivehealth/TobaccoUsePregnancy/index.htm

Centers for Disease Control and Prevention. (2014i). *Web-based Injury Statistics Query and Reporting System (WISQARS).* Retrieved from www.cdc.gov/injury/wisqars

Cernoch, J. M., & Porter, R. H. (1985). Recognition of maternal axillary odors by infants. *Child Development, 56,* 1593–1598.

Cetinkaya, M. B., Siano, L. J., & Benadiva, C. (2013). Reproductive outcome of women 43 years and beyond undergoing ART treatment with their own oocytes in two Connecticut university programs. *Journal of Assisted Reproductive Genetics, 30,* 673–678.

Chalabaev, A., Sarrazin, P., & Fontayne, P. (2009). Stereotype endorsement and perceived ability as mediators of the girls' gender orientation–soccer performance relationship. *Psychology of Sport and Exercise, 10,* 297–299.

Chall, J. S. (1983). *Stages of reading development.* New York: McGraw-Hill.

Chamberlain, P. (2003). Antisocial behavior and delinquency in girls. In P. Chamberlain (Ed.), *Treating chronic juvenile offenders* (pp. 109–127). Washington, DC: American Psychological Association.

Champion, T. B. (2003). "A matter of vocabulary": Performances of low-income African-American Head Start children on the Peabody Picture Vocabulary Test. *Communication Disorders Quarterly, 24,* 121–127.

Chan, A., Meints, K., Lieven, E., & Tomasello, M. (2010). Young children's comprehension of English SVO word order revisited: Testing the same children in act-out and intermodal preferential looking tasks. *Cognitive Development, 25,* 30–45.

Chan, A., & Poulin, F. (2007). Monthly changes in the composition of friendship networks in early adolescence. *Merrill-Palmer Quarterly, 53,* 578–602.

Chan, C. C. Y., Brandone, A. C., & Tardif, T. (2009). Culture, context, or behavioral control? English- and Mandarin-speaking mothers' use of nouns and verbs in joint book reading. *Journal of Cross-Cultural Psychology, 40,* 584–602.

Chan, C. C. Y., Tardif, T., Chen, J., Pulverman, R. B., Zhu, L., & Meng, X. (2011). English- and Chinese-learning infants map novel labels to objects and actions differently. *Developmental Psychology, 47,* 1459–1471.

Chan, S. M. (2010). Aggressive behaviour in early elementary school children: Relations to authoritarian parenting, children's negative emotionality and coping strategies. *Early Child Development and Care, 180,* 1253–1269.

Chan, T. W., & Koo, A. (2011). Parenting style and youth outcomes in the UK. *European Sociological Review, 27,* 385–399.

Chandra, A., Copen, C. E., & Stephen, E. H. (2013). *Infertility and impaired fecundity in the United States, 1982–2010: Data from the National Survey of Family Growth.* Hyattsville, MD: Centers for Disease Control and Prevention. Retrieved from www.cdc.gov/nchs/data/nhsr/nhsr067.pdf

Chandra, R. K. (1991). Interactions between early nutrition and the immune system. In *Ciba Foundation Symposium No. 156* (pp. 77–92). Chichester, UK: Wiley.

Chang, F., Dell, G. S., & Bock, K. (2006). Becoming syntactic. *Psychological Review, 113,* 234–272.

Chang, Y. T., Hayter, M., & Wu, S. C. (2010). A systematic review and meta-ethnography of the qualitative literature: Experiences of the menarche. *Journal of Clinical Nursing, 19,* 447–460.

Chao, R. K., & Tseng, V. (2002). Parenting of Asians. In M. H. Bornstein (Ed.), *Handbook of parenting: Vol. 4* (2nd ed., pp. 59–94). Mahwah, NJ: Erlbaum.

Chapman, R. S. (2006). Children's language learning: An interactionist perspective. In R. Paul (Ed.), *Language disorders from a developmental perspective* (pp. 1–53). Mahwah, NJ: Erlbaum.

Charity, A. H., Scarborough, H. S., & Griffin, D. M. (2004). Familiarity with school English in African American children and its relation to early reading achievement. *Child Development, 75,* 1340–1356.

Charman, T., Baron-Cohen, S., Swettenham, J., Baird, G., Cox, A., & Drew, A. (2001). Testing joint attention, imitation, and play as infancy precursors to language and theory of mind. *Cognitive Development, 15,* 481–49.

Chase-Lansdale, P. L., Gordon, R., Brooks-Gunn, J., & Klebanov, P. K. (1997). Neighborhood and family influences on the intellectual and behavioral competence of preschool and early school-age children. In J. Brooks-Gunn, G. Duncan, & J. L. Aber (Eds.), *Neighborhood poverty: Context and consequences for development* (pp. 79–118). New York: Russell Sage Foundation.

Chauhan, G. S., Shastri, J., & Mohite, P. (2005). Development of gender constancy in preschoolers. *Psychological Studies, 50,* 62–71.

Chavajay, P., & Rogoff, B. (1999). Cultural variation in management of attention by children and their caregivers. *Developmental Psychology, 35,* 1079–1090.

Chavajay, P., & Rogoff, B. (2002). Schooling and traditional collaborative social organization of problem solving by Mayan mothers and children. *Developmental Psychology, 38,* 55–66.

Chavarria, M. C., Sánchez, F. J., Chou, Y. Y., Thompson, P. M., & Luders, E. (2014). Puberty in the corpus callosum. *Neuroscience, 265,* 1–8.

Chawarska, K., Macari, S., & Shic, F. (2013). Decreased spontaneous attention to social scenes in 6-month-old infants later diagnosed with autism spectrum disorders. *Biological Psychiatry, 74,* 195–203.

Cheah, C. S. L., Leung, C. Y. Y., Tahseen, M., & Schultz, D. (2009). Authoritative parenting among immigrant Chinese mothers of preschoolers. *Journal of Family Psychology, 23,* 311–320.

Cheah, C. S. L. & Li, J. (2010). Parenting of young immigrant Chinese children: Challenges facing their social-emotional and intellectual development. In E. L. Grigorenko & R. Takanishi (Eds.), *Immigration, diversity, and education* (pp. 225–241). New York: Routledge.

Cheah, C. S. L., & Nelson, L. J. (2004). The role of acculturation in the emerging adulthood of aboriginal college students. *International Journal of Behavioral Development, 28,* 495–507.

Checkley, W., Epstein, L. D., Gilman, R. H., Cabrera, L., & Black, R. E. (2003). Effects of acute diarrhea on linear growth in Peruvian children. *American Journal of Epidemiology, 157,* 166–175.

Chen, B., Vansteenkiste, M., Beyers, W., Soenens, B., & Van Petegem, S. (2013). Autonomy in family decision making for Chinese adolescents: Disentangling the dual meaning of autonomy. *Journal of Cross-Cultural Psychology, 44,* 1184–1209.

Chen, E. S. L., & Rao, N. (2011). Gender socialization in Chinese kindergartens: Teachers' contributions. *Sex Roles, 64,* 103–116.

Chen, J. J. (2005). Relation of academic support from parents, teachers, and peers to Hong Kong adolescents' academic achievement: The mediating role of academic engagement. *Genetic, Social, and General Psychology Monographs, 131,* 77–127.

Chen, J. J., Howard, K. S., & Brooks-Gunn, J. (2011). How do neighborhoods matter across the life span? In K. L. Fingerman, C. A. Berg, J. Smith, & T. C. Antonucci (Eds.), *Handbook of life-span development* (pp. 805–836). New York: Springer.

Chen, L.-C., Metcalfe, J. S., Jeka, J. J., & Clark, J. E. (2007). Two steps forward and one back: Learning to walk affects infants' sitting posture. *Infant Behavior and Development, 30,* 16–25.

Chen, X. (2012). Culture, peer interaction, and socioemotional development. *Child Development Perspectives, 6,* 27–34.

Chen, X., Cen, G., Li, D., & He, Y. (2005). Social functioning and adjustment in Chinese children: The imprint of historical time. *Child Development, 76,* 182–195.

Chen, X., DeSouza, A. T., Chen, H., & Wang, L. (2006). Reticent behavior and experiences in peer interactions in Chinese and Canadian children. *Developmental Psychology, 42,* 656–665.

Chen, X., & Eisenberg, N. (2012). Understanding cultural issues in child development: Introduction. *Child Development Perspectives, 6,* 1–14.

Chen, X., Hastings, P. D., Rubin, K. H., Chen, H., Cen, G., & Stewart, S. L. (1998). Child-rearing attitudes and behavioral inhibition in Chinese and Canadian toddlers: A cross-cultural study. *Developmental Psychology, 34,* 677–686.

Chen, X., Rubin, K. H., & Li, Z. (1995). Social functioning and adjustment in Chinese children: A longitudinal study. *Developmental Psychology, 31,* 531–539.

Chen, X., Wang, L., & Cao, R. (2011). Shyness-sensitivity and unsociability in rural Chinese children: Relations with social, school, and psychological adjustment. *Child Development, 82,* 1531–1543.

Chen, X., Wang, L., & DeSouza, A. (2006). Temperament, socioemotional functioning, and peer relationships in Chinese and North American children. In X. Chen, D. C. French, & B. H. Schneider (Eds.), *Peer relationships in cultural context* (pp. 123–147). New York: Cambridge University Press.

Chen, Y., Li, H., & Meng, L. (2013). Prenatal sex selection and missing girls in China: Evidence from the diffusion of diagnostic ultrasound. *Journal of Human Resources, 48,* 36–70.

Chen, Y.-C., Yu, M.-L., Rogan, W., Gladen, B., & Hsu, C.-C. (1994). A 6-year follow-up of behavior and activity disorders in the Taiwan Yu-cheng children. *American Journal of Public Health, 84,* 415–421.

Chen, Y.-J., & Hsu, C.-C. (1994). Effects of prenatal exposure to PCBs on the neurological function of children: A neuropsychological and neuro-physiological study. *Developmental Medicine and Child Neurology, 36,* 312–320.

Chen, Z., Sanchez, R. P., & Campbell, T. (1997). From beyond to within their grasp: The rudiments of analogical problem solving in 10- to 13-month-olds. *Developmental Psychology, 33,* 790–801.

Cherlin, A. J. (2010). Demographic trends in the United States: A review of research in the 2000s. *Journal of Marriage and Family, 72*(3), 403–419.

Chesney-Lind, M. (2001). Girls, violence, and delinquency: Popular myths and persistent problems. In S. O. White (Ed.), *Handbook of youth and justice* (pp. 135–158). New York: Kluwer Academic.

Chesney-Lind, M., & Belknap, J. (2004). Trends in delinquent girls' aggression and violent behavior. In M. Putallaz & K. L. Bierman (Eds.), *Aggression, antisocial behavior, and violence among girls: A developmental perspective* (pp. 203–220). New York: Guilford.

Chess, S., & Thomas, A. (1984). *Origins and evolution of behavior disorders.* New York: Brunner/Mazel.

Chhin, C. S., Bleeker, M. M., & Jacobs, J. E. (2008). Gender-typed occupational choices: The long-term impact of parents' beliefs and expectations. In H. M. G. Watt & J. S. Eccles (Eds.), *Gender and occupational outcomes: Longitudinal assessments of individual, social, and cultural influences* (pp. 215–234). Washington, DC: American Psychological Association.

Chiang, T., Schultz, R. M., & Lampson, M. A. (2012). Meiotic origins of maternal age-related aneuploidy. *Biology of Reproduction, 86,* 1–7.

Child Care Aware. (2013). *Parents and the high cost of child care: 2013 report.* Arlington, VA: Author.

Child Health USA. (2013). *SIDS/SUID.* Retrieved from www.mchb.hrsa.gov/chusa13/perinatal-health-status-indicators/p/SIDS-SUID.html

Child Trends. (2013). *Full-day kindergarten: Indicators on children and youth.* Retrieved from www.childtrends.org/

wp-content/uploads/2013/06/102_Full-day-kindergarten.pdf

Child Trends. (2014a). *Births to unmarried women.* Retrieved from www.childtrends.org/?indicators=births-to-unmarried-women

Child Trends. (2014b). *Late or no prenatal care: Indicators on children and youth.* Retrieved from www.childtrends.org/wp-content/uploads/2012/11/25_Prenatal_Care.pdf

Child Trends. (2014c). *Motor vehicle deaths.* Retrieved from www.childtrends.org/?indicators=motor-vehicle-deaths

Child Trends. (2014d). *Teen births.* Retrieved from www.childtrends.org/wp-content/uploads/2012/11/13_Teen_Birth.pdf

Child Trends. (2014e). *Unintentional injuries: Indicators on children and youth.* Retrieved from www.childtrends.org/wp-content/uploads/2014/08/122_Unintentional_Injuries.pdf

Chin, H. B., Sipe, T. A., Elder, R., Mercer, S. L., Chattopadhyay, S. K., Jacob, V., et al. (2012). The effectiveness of group-based comprehensive risk-reduction and abstinence education interventions to prevent or reduce the risk of adolescent pregnancy, human immunodeficiency virus, and sexually transmitted infections: Two systematic reviews for the guide to community preventive services. *American Journal of Preventive Medicine, 42,* 272–294.

Chinn, C. A., & Malhotra, B. A. (2002). Children's responses to anomalous scientific data: How is conceptual change impeded? *Journal of Educational Psychology, 94,* 327–343.

Cho, S., Ryali, S., Geary, D. C., & Menon, V. (2011). How does a child solve 7 + 8? Decoding brain activity patterns associated with counting and retrieval strategies. *Developmental Science, 14,* 989–1001.

Choe, D. E., Olson, S. L., & Sameroff, A. J. (2013). The interplay of externalizing problems and physical discipline and inductive discipline during childhood. *Developmental Psychology, 49,* 2029–2039.

Choi, S., & Gopnik, A. (1995). Early acquisition of verbs in Korean: A cross-linguistic study. *Journal of Child Language, 22,* 497–529.

Choi, S., McDonough, L., Bowerman, M., & Mandler, J. M. (1999). Early sensitivity to language-specific spatial categories in English and Korean. *Cognitive Development, 14,* 241–268.

Chomsky, C. (1969). *The acquisition of syntax in children from five to ten.* Cambridge, MA: MIT Press.

Chomsky, N. (1957). *Syntactic structures.* The Hague: Mouton.

Chouinard, M. M. (2007). Children's questions: A mechanism for cognitive development. *Monographs of the Society for Research in Child Development, 72*(1, Serial No. 286).

Chouinard, M. M., & Clark, E. V. (2003). Adult reformulations of child errors as negative evidence. *Journal of Child Language, 30,* 637–669.

Christakis, D. A., Garrison, M. M., Herrenkohl, T., Haggerty, K, Rivara, F. P., Zhou, C., & Liekweg, K. (2013). Modifying media content for preschool children: A randomized controlled trial. *Pediatrics, 131,* 431–438.

Christakis, D. A., Zimmerman, F. J., DiGiuseppe, D. L., & McCarty, C. A. (2004). Early television exposure and subsequent attentional problems in children. *Pediatrics, 113,* 708–713.

Christakou, A., Gershman, S. J., Niv, Y., Simmons, A., Brammer, M., & Rubia, K. (2013). Neural and psychological maturation of decision-making in adolescence and young adulthood. *Journal of Cognitive Neuroscience, 25,* 1807–1823.

Christenson, S. L., & Thurlow, M. L. (2004). School dropouts: Prevention considerations, interventions, and challenges. *Current Directions in Psychological Science, 13,* 36–39.

Christiansen, M. H., & Chater, N. (2008). Language as shaped by the brain. *Behavioral and Brain Sciences, 31,* 489–558.

Christie, C. A., Jolivette, K., & Nelson, M. (2007). School characteristics related to high school dropout rates. *Remedial and Special Education, 28,* 325–339.

Christoffersen, M. N. (2012). A study of adopted children, their environment, and development: A systematic review. *Adoption Quarterly, 15,* 220–237.

Chumlea, W. C., Schubert, C. M., Roche, A. F., Kulin, H. E., Lee, P. A., Himes, J. H., & Sun, S. S. (2003). Age at menarche and racial comparisons in U.S. girls. *Pediatrics, 111,* 110–113.

Chung, H., Mulvey, E., & Steinberg, L. (2011). Understanding the school outcomes of juvenile offenders: An exploration of neighborhood influences and motivational resources. *Journal of Youth and Adolescence, 40,* 1025–1038.

Chung, H. H. (2006). Code switching as a communicative strategy: A case study of Korean–English bilinguals. *Bilingual Research Journal, 30,* 293–307.

Cicchetti, D. (2007). Intervention and policy implications of research on neurobiological functioning in maltreated children. In J. L. Aber, S. J. Bishop-Josef, S. M. Jones, K. T. McLearn, & D. A. Phillips (Eds.), *Child development and social policy* (pp. 167–184). Washington, DC: American Psychological Association.

Cicuto, N. A., Rocha, F., de Campos, A. C., & Silva, F. P. dos Santos. (2012). Adaptive actions of young infants in the task of reaching for objects. *Developmental Psychobiology, 55,* 275–282.

Cillessen, A. H. N. (2009). Sociometric methods. In K. H. Rubin & W. M. Bukowski (Eds.), *Handbook of peer interactions, relationships, and groups* (pp. 82–99). New York: Guilford.

Cillessen, A. H. N., & Bellmore, A. D. (2004). Social skills and interpersonal perception in early and middle childhood. In P. K. Smith & C. H. Hart (Eds.), *Blackwell handbook of childhood social development* (pp. 355–374). Malden, MA: Blackwell.

Cipriano, E. A., & Stifter, C. A. (2010). Predicting preschool effortful control from toddler temperament and parenting behavior. *Journal of Applied Developmental Psychology, 31,* 221–230.

Circle (Center for Information & Research on Civic Learning & Engagement). (2013). *Youth voting.* Retrieved from www.civicyouth.org/quick-facts/youth-voting

Clapp, J. F., III, Kim, H., Burciu, B., Schmidt, S., Petry, K., & Lopez, B. (2002). Continuing regular exercise during pregnancy: Effect of exercise volume on fetoplacental growth. *American Journal of Obstetrics and Gynecology, 186,* 142–147.

Clark, E. V. (2007). Young children's uptake of new words in conversation. *Language in Society, 36,* 157–182.

Clark, K. E., & Ladd, G. W. (2000). Connectedness and autonomy support in parent–child relationships: Links to children's socioemotional orientation and peer relationships. *Developmental Psychology, 36,* 485–498.

Clark, S. M., Ghulmiyyah, L. M., & Hankins, G. D. (2008). Antenatal antecedents and the impact of obstetric care in the etiology of cerebral palsy. *Clinical Obstetrics and Gynecology, 51,* 775–786.

Clarke-Stewart, K. A. (1998). Historical shifts and underlying themes in ideas about rearing young children in the United States: Where have we been? Where are we going? *Early Development and Parenting, 7,* 101–117.

Clarke-Stewart, K. A., & Hayward, C. (1996). Advantages of father custody and contact for the psychological well-being of school-age children. *Journal of Applied Developmental Psychology, 17,* 239–270.

Claxton, L. J., Keen, R., & McCarty, M. E. (2003). Evidence of motor planning in infant reaching behavior. *Psychological Science, 14,* 354–356.

Clay, R. A. (2009, Feb.). Mini-multitaskers. *Monitor on Psychology, 40*(2), 38–40.

Clearfield, M. W. (2011). Learning to walk changes infants' social interactions. *Infant Behavior and Development, 34,* 15–25.

Clearfield, M. W., & Nelson, N. M. (2006). Sex differences in mothers' speech and play behavior with 6-, 9-, and 14-month-old infants. *Sex Roles, 54,* 127–137.

Clements, D. H., & Sarama, J. (2003). Young children and technology: What does the research say? *Young Children, 58*(6), 34–40.

Clements, D. H., & Sarama, J. (2012). Learning and teaching early and elementary mathematics. In J. S. Carlson & J. R. Levin (Eds.), *Instructional strategies for improving students' learning* (pp. 205–212). Charlotte, NC: Information Age Publishing.

Clements, D. H., Sarama, J., Spitler, M. E., Lange, A. A., & Wolfe, C. B. (2011). Mathematics learned by young children in an intervention based on learning trajectories: A large-scale cluster randomized trial. *Journal for Research in Mathematics Education, 42,* 127–166.

Cleveland, E. S., & Reese, E. (2005). Maternal structure and autonomy support in conversations about the past: Contributions to children's autobiographical memory. *Developmental Psychology, 41,* 376–388.

Clifton, R. K., Rochat, P., Robin, D. J., & Berthier, N. E. (1994). Multimodal perception in the control of infant reaching. *Journal of Experimental Psychology: Human Perception and Performance, 20,* 876–886.

Clinchy, B. M. (2002). Revisiting women's ways of knowing. In B. K. Hofer & P. R. Pintrich (Eds.), *Personal epistemology: The psychological beliefs about knowledge and knowing* (pp. 63–87). Mahwah, NJ: Erlbaum.

Cluett, E. R., & Burns, E. (2013). Immersion in water in labour and birth. *São Paulo Medical Journal, 131,* 364.

Cnattingius, S., Lundberg, F., Sandin, S., Grönberg, H., & Iliadou, A. (2009). Birth characteristics and risk of prostate cancer: The contribution of genetic factors. *Cancer Epidemiology, 18,* 2422–2466.

Coene, M., Schauwers, K., Gillis, S., Rooryck, J., & Govaerts, P. J. (2011). Genetic predisposition and sensory experience in language development: Evidence from cochlear-implanted children. *Language and Cognitive Processes, 26,* 1083–1101.

Cohen, G. L., Garcia, J., & Master, A. (2006). Reducing the racial achievement gap: A social-psychological intervention. *Science, 313,* 1307–1310.

Cohen, L. B. (2003). Commentary on Part I: Unresolved issues in infant categorization. In D. H. Rakison & L. M. Oakes (Eds.), *Early category and concept development: Making sense of the blooming, buzzing confusion* (pp. 193–209). New York: Oxford University Press.

Cohen, L. B. (2009). The evolution of infant cognition: A personal account. *Infancy, 14,* 403–413.

Cohen, L. B. (2010). A bottom-up approach to infant perception and cognition: A summary of evidence and discussion of issues. In S. P. Johnson (Ed.), *Neoconstructivism: The new science of cognitive development* (pp. 335–346). New York: Oxford University Press.

Cohen, L. B., & Brunt, J. (2009). Early word learning and categorization: Methodological issues and recent empirical evidence. In J. Colombo, P. McCardle, & L. Freund (Eds.), *Infant pathways to language: Methods, models, and research disorders* (pp. 245–266). New York: Psychology Press.

Cohen, L. B., & Marks, K. S. (2002). How infants process addition and subtraction events. *Developmental Science, 5,* 186–201.

Cohen-Bendahan, C. C., van de Beek, C., & Berenbaum, S. A. (2005). Prenatal sex hormone effects on child and adult sex-typed behavior: Methods and findings. *Neuroscience and Biobehavioral Reviews, 29,* 353–384.

Cohn, N. (2014). Framing "I can't draw": The influence of cultural frames on the development of drawing. *Culture and Psychology, 20,* 102–117.

Colby, A., Kohlberg, L., Gibbs, J., & Lieberman, M. (1983). A longitudinal study of moral judgment. *Monographs of the Society for Research in Child Development, 48*(1–2, Serial No. 200).

Coldwell, J., Pike, A., & Dunn, J. (2008). Maternal differential treatment and child adjustment: A multi-informant approach. *Social Development, 17,* 596–612.

Cole, C., & Winsler, A. (2010). Protecting children from exposure to lead: Old problem, new data, and new policy needs. *Social Policy Report of the Society for Research in Child Development, 24*(1).

Cole, D. A., Maxwell, S. E., Martin, J. M., Peeke, L. G., Seroczynski, A. D., & Tram, J. M. (2001). The development of multiple domains of child and adolescent self-concept: A cohort sequential longitudinal design. *Child Development, 72,* 1723–1746.

Cole, M. (1990). Cognitive development and formal schooling: The evidence from cross-cultural research. In L. C. Moll (Ed.), *Vygotsky and education* (pp. 89–110). New York: Cambridge University Press.

Cole, M. (2006). Culture and cognitive development in phylogenetic, historical, and ontogenetic perspective. In D. Kuhn & R. S. Siegler (Eds.), *Handbook of child psychology: Vol. 2. Cognition, perception, and language* (6th ed., pp. 636–685). Hoboken, NJ: Wiley.

Cole, P. M., Armstrong, L. M., & Pemberton, C. K. (2010). The role of language in the development of emotion regulation. In S. D. Calkins & M. A. Bell (Eds.), *Child development at the intersection of emotion and cognition* (pp. 59–77). Washington, DC: American Psychological Association.

Cole, P. M., Bruschi, C. J., & Tamang, B. L. (2002). Cultural differences in children's emotional reactions to difficult situations. *Child Development, 73,* 983–996.

Cole, P. M., LeDonne, E. N., & Tan, P. Z. (2013). A longitudinal examination of maternal emotions in relation to young children's developing self-regulation. *Parenting: Science and Practice, 13,* 113–132.

Cole, P. M., & Tamang, B. L. (1998). Nepali children's ideas about emotional displays in hypothetical challenges. *Developmental Psychology, 34,* 640–648.

Cole, P. M., Tamang, B. L., & Shrestha, S. (2006). Cultural variations in the socialization of young children's anger and shame. *Child Development, 77,* 1237–1251.

Cole, T. J. (2000). Secular trends in growth. *Proceedings of the Nutrition Society, 59,* 317–324.

Coles, C. D., Goldstein, F. C., Lynch, M. E., Chen, X., Kable, J. A., Johnson, K. C., et al. (2011). Memory and brain volume in adults prenatally exposed to alcohol. *Brain and Cognition, 75,* 67–77.

Coley, R. L., Morris, J. E., & Hernandez, D. (2004). Out-of-school care and problem behavior trajectories among low-income adolescents: Individual, family, and neighborhood characteristics as added risks. *Child Development, 75,* 948–965.

Coley, R. L., Votruba-Drzal, E., & Schindler, H. S. (2009). Fathers' and mothers' parenting predicting and responding to adolescent sexual risk behaviors. *Child Development, 80,* 808–827.

Collins, J. W., Rankin, K. M., & David, R. J. (2011). Low birth weight across generations: The effect of economic environment. *Maternal and Child Health Journal, 15,* 438–445.

Collins, N. L., Guichard, A. C., Ford, M. B., & Feeney, B. C. (2006). Responding to need in intimate relationships: Normative processes and individual differences. In M. Mikulincer & G. S. Goodman (Eds.), *Dynamics of romantic love* (pp. 149–189). New York: Guilford.

Collins, W. A., & Hartup, W. W. (2013). History of research in developmental psychology. In P. D. Zelazo (Ed.), *Oxford handbook of developmental psychology* (pp. 13–34). New York: Oxford University Press.

Collins, W. A., & Laursen, B. (2004). Parent–adolescent relationships and influences. In R. M. Lerner & L. Steinberg (Eds.), *Handbook of adolescent psychology* (2nd ed., pp. 331–361). New York: Wiley.

Collins, W. A., & Madsen, S. D. (2006). Personal relationships in adolescence and early adulthood. In A. L. Vangelisti & D. Perlman (Eds.), *Cambridge handbook of personal relationships* (pp. 191–209). New York: Cambridge University Press.

Collins, W. A., Madsen, S. D., & Susman-Stillman, A. (2002). Parenting during middle childhood. In M. H. Bornstein (Ed.), *Handbook of parenting: Vol. 1. Children and parenting* (2nd ed., pp. 73–101). Mahwah, NJ: Erlbaum.

Collins, W. A., & Russell, G. (1991). Mother–child and father–child interactions in middle childhood and adolescence. *Developmental Review, 11,* 99–136.

Collins, W. A., & Steinberg, L. (2006). Adolescent development in interpersonal context. In N. Eisenberg (Ed.), *Handbook of child psychology: Vol. 3. Social, emotional, and personality development* (6th ed., pp. 1003–1067). Hoboken, NJ: Wiley.

Collins, W. A., & van Dulmen, M. (2006a). Friendships and romantic relationships in emerging adulthood: Continuities and discontinuities. In J. J. Arnett & J. Tanner (Eds.), *Emerging adults in America: Coming of age in the 21st century* (pp. 219–234). Washington, DC: American Psychological Association.

Collins, W. A., & van Dulmen, M. (2006b). "The course of true love(s) . . .": Origins and pathways in the development of romantic relationships. In A. Booth & A. Crouter (Eds.), *Romance and sex in adolescence and emerging adulthood: Risks and opportunities* (pp. 63–86). Mahwah, NJ: Erlbaum.

Collins, W. A., Welsh, D. P., & Furman, W. (2009). Adolescent romantic relationships. *Annual Review of Psychology, 60,* 631–652.

Collin-Vézina, D., Daigneault, I., & Hébert, M. (2013). Lessons learned from child sexual abuse research: Prevalence, outcomes, and preventive strategies. *Child and Adolescent Psychiatry and Mental Health, 7,* 1–9.

Colman, L. L., & Colman, A. D. (1991). *Pregnancy: The psychological experience.* New York: Noonday Press.

Colombo, J. (2002). Infant attention grows up: The emergence of a developmental cognitive neuroscience perspective. *Current Directions in Psychological Science, 11,* 196–199.

Colombo, J., Brez, C. C., & Curtindale, L. M. (2013). Infant perception and cognition. In R. M. Lerner, M. A. Easterbrooks, & J. Mistry (Eds.), *Handbook of psychology: Vol. 6. Developmental psychology* (pp. 61–89). Hoboken, NJ: Wiley.

Colombo, J., Kapa, L., & Curtindale, L. (2011). Varieties of attention in infancy. In L. M. Oakes, C. H. Cashon, M. Casasola, & D. Rakison (Eds.), *Infant perception and cognition* (3–25). New York: Oxford University Press.

Colombo, J., Shaddy, D. J., Richman, W. A., Maikranz, J. M., & Blaga, O. M. (2004). The developmental course of habituation in infancy and preschool outcome. *Infancy, 5,* 1–38.

Colson, E. R., Rybin, D. R., Smith, L. A., Colton, T., Lister, G., & Corwin, M. J. (2009). Trends and factors associated with infant sleeping position: The National Infant Sleep Position Study, 1993–2007. *Archives of Pediatric and Adolescent Medicine, 163,* 1122–1128.

Colson, E. R., Willinger, M., Rybin, D., Heeren, T., Smith, L. A., Lister, G., et al. (2013). Trends and factors associated with infant bed sharing, 1993–2010. The National Infant Sleep Position Study. *JAMA Pediatrics, 167,* 1032–1037.

Coltrane, S. (1996). *Family man.* New York: Oxford University Press.

Comeau, L., Genessee, F., & Mendelson, M. (2012). A comparison of bilingual and monolingual children's conversational repairs. *First Language, 30,* 354–374.

Commendador, K. A. (2010). Parental influences on adolescent decision-making and condom use. *Pediatric Nursing, 36,* 147–170.

Commission on Children at Risk. (2008). Hardwired to connect: The new scientific case for authoritative communities. In K. K. Kline (Ed.), *Authoritative communities: The scientific case for nurturing the whole child* (pp. 3–68). New York: Springer.

Common Core. (2010). *Common Core state standards for English language arts & literacy in history/social science, and technical subjects.* Retrieved from www.corestandards .org/ELA-Literacy

Common Sense Media. (2013). *Zero to eight: Children's media use in America 2013.* San Francisco, CA: Author. Retrieved from www.commonsensemedia.org/ research/zero-to-eight-childrens-media-use-in-america-2013

Compas, B. E., Jaser, S. S., Dunn, M. J., & Rodriguez, E. M. (2012). Coping with chronic illness in childhood and adolescence. *Annual Review of Clinical Psychology, 8,* 455–480.

Comstock, G., & Scharrer, E. (2006). Media and popular culture. In K. A. Renninger & I. E. Sigel (Eds.), *Handbook of child psychology: Vol. 4. Child psychology in practice* (6th ed., pp. 817–863). Hoboken, NJ: Wiley.

Comunian, A. L, & Gielen, U. P. (2000). Sociomoral reflection and prosocial and antisocial behavior: Two Italian studies. *Psychological Reports, 87,* 161–175.

Comunian, A. L., & Gielen, U. P. (2006). Promotion of moral judgment maturity through stimulation of social role-taking and social reflection: An Italian intervention study. *Journal of Moral Education, 35,* 51–69.

Conchas, G. Q. (2006). *The color of success: Race and high-achieving urban youth.* New York: Teachers College Press.

Conde-Agudelo, A., Belizan, J. M., & Diaz-Rossello, J. (2011). Kangaroo mother care to reduce morbidity and mortality in low birthweight infants. *Cochrane Database of Systematic Reviews, Issue 3*(Art. No. CD002771).

Condron, D. J. (2013). Affluence, inequality, and educational achievement: A structural analysis of 97 jurisdictions, across the globe. *Sociological Spectrum, 33,* 73–97.

Conger, R. D., & Donnellan, M. B. (2007). An interactionist perspective on the socioeconomic context of human development. *Annual Review of Psychology, 58,* 175–199.

Conner, D. B., & Cross, D. R. (2003). Longitudinal analysis of the presence, efficacy, and stability of maternal scaffolding during informal problemsolving interactions. *British Journal of Developmental Psychology, 21,* 315–334.

Connolly, J., Craig, W., Goldberg, A., & Pepler, D. (2004). Mixed-gender groups, dating, and romantic relationships in early adolescence. *Journal of Research on Adolescence, 14,* 185–207.

Connolly, J., & Goldberg, A. (1999). Romantic relationships in adolescence: The role of friends and peers in their emergence and development. In W. Furman, B. B. Brown, & C. Feiring (Eds.), *The development of romantic relationships in adolescence* (pp. 266–290). New York: Cambridge University Press.

Connor, J. M. (2003). Physical activity and well-being. In M. H. Bornstein, L. Davidson, C. L. M. Keyes, K. A. Moore, & the Center for Child Well-Being (Eds.), *Well-being: Positive development across the life course* (pp. 65–79). Mahwah, NJ: Erlbaum.

Conway, C. C., Rancourt, D., Adelman, C. B., Burk, W. J., & Prinstein, M. J. (2011). Depression socialization within friendship groups at the transition to adolescence: The roles of gender and group centrality as moderators of peer influence. *Journal of Abnormal Psychology, 120,* 857–867.

Cook, C. R., Williams, K. R., Guerra, N. G., & Kim, T. E. (2010). Variability in the prevalence of bullying and victimization: A cross-national and methodological analysis. In S. R. Jimerson, S. M. Swearer, & D. L. Espelage (Eds.), *Handbook of bullying in schools: An international perspective* (pp. 347–362). New York: Routledge.

Cook, T. D., Deng, Y., & Morgano, E. (2007). Friendship influences during early adolescence: The special role of friends' grade point average. *Journal of Research in Adolescence, 17,* 325–356.

Cookston, J. T., Braver, S. L., Griffin, W. A., De Lusé, S. R., & Miles, J. C. (2006). Effects of the Dads for Life intervention on interparental conflict and coparenting in the two years after divorce. *Family Process, 46,* 123–137.

Cooper, C., Sayer, A. A., & Dennison, E. M. (2006). The developmental environment: Clinical perspectives on effects on the musculoskeletal system. In P. Gluckman & M. Hanson (Eds.), *Developmental origins of health and disease* (pp. 392–405). Cambridge, UK: Cambridge University Press.

Cooper, H., Batts, A., Patall, E. A., & Dent, A. L. (2010). Effects of full-day kindergarten on academic achievement and social development. *Review of Educational Research, 80,* 54–70.

Cooper, R., & Huh, C. R. (2008). Improving academic possibilities of students of color during the middle school to high school transition: Conceptual and strategic considerations in a U.S. context. In J. K. Asamen, M. L. Ellis, & G. L. Berry (Eds.), *Sage handbook of child development, multiculturalism, and media* (pp. 143–162). Thousand Oaks, CA: Sage.

Copeland, W., Shanahan, L., Miller, S., Costello, E. J., Angold, A., & Maughan, B. (2010). Do the negative effects of early pubertal timing on adolescent girls continue into young adulthood? *American Journal of Psychiatry, 167,* 1218–1225.

Copen, C. E., Daniels, K., & Mosher, W. D. (2013). *First premarital cohabitation in the United States: 2006–2010 National Survey of Family Growth.* National Health Statistics Report, No. 64. Hyattsville, MD: National Center for Health Statistics.

Coplan, R. J., & Arbeau, K. A. (2008). The stresses of a "brave new world": Shyness and school adjustment in kindergarten. *Journal of Research in Childhood Education, 22,* 377–389.

Coplan, R. J., & Armer, M. (2007). A "multitude" of solitude: A closer look at social withdrawal and nonsocial play in early childhood. *Child Development Perspectives, 1,* 26–32.

Coplan, R. J., Gavinsky-Molina, M. H., Lagace-Seguin, D., & Wichmann, C. (2001). When girls versus boys play alone: Nonsocial play and adjustment in kindergarten. *Developmental Psychology, 37,* 464–474.

Coplan, R. J., & Ooi, L. (2014). The causes and consequences of "playing alone" in childhood. In R. J. Coplan & J. C. Bowker (Eds.), *The handbook of solitude: Psychological perspectives on social isolation, social withdrawal, and being alone* (pp. 111–128). Chichester, UK: Wiley- Blackwell.

Coplan, R. J., Prakash, K., O'Neil, K., & Armer, M. (2004). Do you "want" to play? Distinguishing between conflicted shyness and social disinterest in early childhood. *Developmental Psychology, 40,* 244–258.

Copple, C., & Bredekamp, S. (2009). *Developmentally appropriate practice in early childhood programs* (3rd ed.). Washington, DC: National Association for the Education of Young Children.

Corapci, F., Radan, A. E., & Lozoff, B. (2006). Iron deficiency in infancy and mother–child interaction at 5 years.

Journal of Developmental and Behavioral Pediatrics, 27, 371–378.

Corenblum, B. (2003). What children remember about ingroup and outgroup peers: Effects of stereotypes on children's processing of information about group members. *Journal of Experimental Child Psychology, 86,* 32–66.

Cornwell, A. C., & Feigenbaum, P. (2006). Sleep biological rhythms in normal infants and those at high risk for SIDS. *Chronobiology International, 23,* 935–961.

Correa-Chavez, M., Roberts, A. L. D., & Perez, M. M. (2011). Cultural patterns in children's learning through keen observation and participation in their communities. In J. B. Benson (Ed.), *Advances in child development and behavior* (Vol. 40, pp. 209–241). San Diego, CA: Elsevier Academic Press.

Costa, A., & Sebastián-Gallés, N. (2014). How does the bilingual experience sculpt the brain? *Nature Reviews Neuroscience, 15,* 336–345.

Costacurta, M., Sicuro, L., Di Renzo, L., & Condo, R. (2012). Childhood obesity and skeletal-dental maturity. *European Journal of Paediatric Dentistry, 13,* 128–132.

Côté, J. E. (2006). Emerging adulthood as an institutionalized moratorium: Risks and benefits to identity formation. In J. J. Arnett (Ed.), *Emerging adults in America: Coming of age in the 21st century* (pp. 85–116). Washington, DC: American Psychological Association.

Côté, J. E. (2009). Identity formation and self-development in adolescence. In R. M. Lerner & L. Steinberg (Eds.), *Handbook of adolescent psychology: Vol. 1. Individual bases of adolescent development* (3rd ed., pp. 266–304). Hoboken, NJ: Wiley.

Côté, J. E., & Bynner, J. M. (2008). Changes in the transition to adulthood in the UK and Canada: The role of structure and agency in emerging adulthood. *Journal of Youth Studies, 11,* 251–268.

Côté, S. M., Petitclerc, A., Raynault, M.-F., Falissard, B., Boivin, M., & Tremblay, R. E. (2010). Short- and long-term risk of infections as a function of group child care attendance: An 8-year population-based study. *Archives of Pediatric and Adolescent Medicine, 164,* 1132–1137.

Côté, S. M., Vaillancourt, T., Barker, E. D., Nagin, D., & Tremblay, R. E. (2007). The joint development of physical and indirect aggression: Predictors of continuity and change during childhood. *Development and Psychopathology, 19,* 37–55.

Coubart, A., Izard, V., Spelke, E. S., Marie, J., & Streri, A. (2014). Dissociation between small and large numerosities in newborn infants. *Developmental Science, 17,* 11–22.

Coulton, C. J., Crampton, D. S., Irwin, M., Spilsbury, J. C., & Korbin, J. E. (2007). How neighborhoods influence child maltreatment: A review of the literature and alternative pathways. *Child Abuse and Neglect, 31,* 1117–1142.

Courage, M. L., & Howe, M. L. (1998). The ebb and flow of infant attentional preferences: Evidence for longterm recognition memory in 3-month-olds. *Journal of Experimental Child Psychology, 18,* 98–106.

Courage, M. L., & Howe, M. L. (2010). To watch or not to watch: Infants and toddlers in a brave new electronic world. *Developmental Review, 30,* 101–115.

Courchesne, E., Mouton, P. R., Calhoun, M. E., Semendeferi, K., Ahrens-Barbeau, C., Hallet, M. J., et al. (2011). Neuron number and size in prefrontal cortex of children with autism. *Journal of the American Medical Association, 306,* 2001–2010.

Cowan, C. P., & Cowan, P. A. (1997). Working with couples during stressful transitions. In S. Dreman (Ed.), *The family on the threshold of the 21st century* (pp. 17–47). Mahwah, NJ: Erlbaum.

Cowan, N., & Alloway, T. (2009). Development of working memory in childhood. In M. L. Courage & N. Cowan (Eds.), *Development of memory in infancy and childhood* (pp. 303–342). Hove, UK: Psychology Press.

Cowan, N., Morey, C. C., AuBuchon, A. M., Zwilling, C. E., Gilchrist, A. L., & Saults, J. S. (2011). New insights into an old problem: Distinguishing storage from processing in the development of working memory. In P. Barrouillet & V. Gaillard (Eds.), *Cognitive development and working memory* (pp. 137–150). Hove, UK: Psychology Press.

Cowan, P. A., & Cowan, C. P. (2002). Interventions as tests of family systems theories: Marital and family relationships in children's development and psychopathology. *Development and Psychopathology, 14,* 731–759.

Cox, S. M., Hopkins, J., & Hans, S. L. (2000). Attachment in preterm infants and their mothers: Neonatal risk status and maternal representations. *Infant Mental Health Journal, 21,* 464–480.

Coyl, D. D., Newland, L. A., & Freeman, H. (2010). Predicting preschoolers' attachment security from parenting behaviours, parents' attachment relationships and their use of social support. *Early Child Development and Care, 180,* 499–512.

Coyle, T. R. (2013). Effects of processing speed on intelligence may be underestimated: Comment on Demetriou et al. (2013). *Intelligence, 41,* 732–734.

Coyne, S. M., Robinson, S. L., & Nelson, D. A. (2010). Does reality backbite? Verbal and relational aggression in reality television programs. *Journal of Broadcasting and Electronic Media, 54,* 282–298.

Crago, M. B., Annahatak, B., & Ningiuruvik, L. (1993). Changing patterns of language socialization in Inuit homes. *Anthropology and Education Quarterly, 24,* 205–223.

Craig, C. M., & Lee, D. N. (1999). Neonatal control of sucking pressure: Evidence for an intrinsic τ-guide. *Experimental Brain Research, 124,* 371–382.

Craig, H. K., & Washington, J. A. (2006). *Malik goes to school: Examining the language skills of African American students from preschool–5th grade.* Mahwah, NJ: Erlbaum.

Craig, W. M., Pepler, D., & Atlas, R. (2000). Observations of bullying in the playground and in the classroom. *School Psychology International, 21,* 22–36.

Crain, W. (2010). *Theories of development: Concepts and applications* (6th ed.). Upper Saddle River, NJ: Pearson.

Crair, M. C., Gillespie, D. C., & Stryker, M. P. (1998). The role of visual experience in the development of columns in the cat visual cortex. *Science, 279,* 566–570.

Cratty, B. J. (1986). *Perceptual and motor development in infants and children* (3rd ed.). Englewood Cliffs, NJ: Prentice-Hall.

Creasey, G., & Jarvis, P. (2009). Attachment and marriage. In M. C. Smith & N. DeFrates-Densch (Eds.), *Handbook of research on adult learning and development* (pp. 269–304). New York: Routledge.

Creasey, G. L., Jarvis, P. A., & Berk, L. E. (1998). Play and social competence. In O. N. Saracho & B. Spodek (Eds.), *Multiple perspectives on play in early childhood education* (pp. 116–143). Albany: State University of New York Press.

Crick, N. R., & Dodge, K. A. (1994). A review and reformulation of social information-processing mechanisms in children's social adjustment. *Psychological Bulletin, 115,* 74–101.

Crick, N. R., Ostrov, J. M., Burr, J. E., Cullerton-Sen, C., Jansen-Yeh, E., & Ralston, P. (2006). A longitudinal study of relational and physical aggression in preschool. *Journal of Applied Developmental Psychology, 27,* 254–268.

Crick, N. R., Ostrov, J. M., & Werner, N. E. (2006). A longitudinal study of relational aggression, physical aggression, and social-psychological adjustment. *Journal of Abnormal Child Psychology, 34,* 131–142.

Crocetti, E., Jahromi, P., & Meeus, W. (2012). Identity and civic engagement in adolescence. *Journal of Adolescence, 35,* 521–532.

Crocetti, E., Meeus, W. H. J., Ritchie, R. A., Meca, A., & Schwartz, S. J. (2014). Adolescent identity: Is this the key to unraveling associations between family relationships and problem behaviors? In L. M. Scheier & W. B. Hansen (Eds.), *Parenting and teen drug use: The most recent findings from research, prevention, and treatment* (pp. 92–109). New York: Oxford University Press.

Crocetti, E., Sica, L. S., Schwartz, S. J., Serafini, T., & Meeus, W. (2013). Identity styles, dimensions, statuses, and functions: Making connections among identity conceptualizations. *European Review of Applied Psychology, 63,* 1–13.

Crockenberg, S. C., & Leerkes, E. M. (2003). Parental acceptance, postpartum depression, and maternal sensitivity: Mediating and moderating processes. *Journal of Family Psychology, 17,* 80–93.

Crockenberg, S. C., & Leerkes, E. M. (2004). Infant and maternal behaviors regulate infant reactivity to novelty at 6 months. *Developmental Psychology, 40,* 1123–1132.

Crockett, L. J., Raffaelli, M., & Shen, Y.-L. (2006). Linking self-regulation and risk-proneness to risky sexual behavior: Pathways through peer pressure and early

substance use. *Journal of Research on Adolescence, 16,* 503–525.

Crookston, B. T., Schott, W., Cueto, S., Dearden, K. A., Engle, P., Georgiadis, A., et al. (2013). Postinfancy growth, schooling, and cognitive achievement: Young lives. *American Journal of Clinical Nutrition, 98,* 1555–1563.

Crosby, B., LeBourgeois, M. K., & Harsh, J. (2005). Racial differences in reported napping and nocturnal sleep in 2- to 8-year-old children. *Pediatrics, 115,* 225–232.

Crosnoe, R., Johnson, M. K., & Elder, G. H., Jr. (2004). School size and the interpersonal side of education: An examination of race/ethnicity and organizational context. *Social Science Quarterly, 85,* 1259–1274.

Crouch, J. L., Skowronski, J. J., Milner, J. S., & Harris, B. (2008). Parental responses to infant crying: The influence of child physical abuse risk and hostile priming. *Child Abuse and Neglect, 32,* 702–710.

Crouter, A. C., & Head, M. R. (2002). Parental monitoring and knowledge of children. In M. H. Bornstein (Ed.), *Handbook of parenting: Vol. 3. Being and becoming a parent* (2nd ed., pp. 461–483). Mahwah, NJ: Erlbaum.

Crouter, A. C., Whiteman, S. D., McHale, S. M., & Osgood, D. W. (2007). Development of gender attitude traditionality across middle childhood and adolescence. *Child Development, 78,* 911–926.

Cryer, D., Tietze, W., & Wessels, H. (2002). Parents' perceptions of their children's child care: A cross-national comparison. *Early Childhood Research Quarterly, 17,* 259–277.

Crystal, D. S., Killen, M., & Ruck, M. D. (2008). It is who you know that counts: Intergroup contact and judgments about race-based exclusion. *British Journal of Developmental Psychology, 26,* 51–70.

Crystal, D. S., Killen, M., & Ruck, M. D. (2010). Fair treatment by authorities is related to children's and adolescents' evaluations of interracial exclusion. *Applied Developmental Science, 14,* 125–136.

Csibra, G. (2010). Recognizing communicative intentions in infancy. *Mind and Language, 25,* 141–168.

Csibra, G., & Gergely, G. (2011). Natural pedagogy as evolutionary adaptation. *Philosophical Transactions of the Royal Society B, 366,* 1149–1157.

Cummings, E. M., & Davies, P. T. (2010). *Children, emotional security and marital conflict.* New York: Guilford.

Cummings, E. M., Goeke-Morey, M. C., & Papp, L. M. (2004). Everyday marital conflict and child aggression. *Journal of Abnormal Child Psychology, 32,* 191–202.

Curby, T. W., LoCasale-Crouch, J., Konold, T. R., Pianta, R. C., Howes, C., Burchinal, M., et al. (2009). The relations of observed pre-K classroom quality profiles to children's achievement and social competence. *Early Education and Development, 20,* 346–372.

Curran, M., Hazen, N., Jacobvitz, D., & Feldman, A. (2005). Representations of early family relationships predict marital maintenance during the transition to parenthood. *Journal of Family Psychology, 19,* 189–197.

Curtin, S., & Werker, J. F. (2007). The perceptual foundations of phonological development. In G. Gaskell (Ed.), *Oxford handbook of psycholinguistics* (pp. 579–599). Oxford, UK: Oxford University Press.

Curtin, S. C., Ventura, S. J., & Martinez, G. M. (2014). Recent declines in nonmarital childbearing in the United States. *NCHS data brief, no. 162.* Hyattsville, MD: National Center for Health Statistics. Retrieved from www.cdc.gov/nchs/data/databriefs/db162.pdf

Curtiss, S., & Schaeffer, J. (2005). Syntactic development in children with hemispherectomy: The I-, D-, and C-systems. *Brain and Language, 94,* 147–166.

Cutrona, C. E., Hessling, R. M., Bacon, P. L., & Russell, D. W. (1998). Predictors and correlates of continuing involvement with the baby's father among adolescent mothers. *Journal of Family Psychology, 12,* 369–387.

Cutuli, J. J., Herbers, J. E., Rinaldi, M., Masten, A. S., & Oberg, C. N. (2010). Asthma and behavior in homeless 4- to 7-year-olds. *Pediatrics, 125,* e145-e151.

Cvencek, D., Meltzoff, A. N., & Greenwald, A. G. (2011). Math-gender stereotypes in elementary school children. *Child Development, 82,* 766–779.

Cyr, C., Euser, E. M., Bakermans-Kranenburg, M. J., & van IJzendoorn, M. H. (2010). Attachment security and disorganization in maltreating and high-risk families: Implications for developmental theory. *Development and Psychopathology, 14,* 843–860.

D

Dabrowska, E. (2000). From formula to schema: The acquisition of English questions. *Cognitive Linguistics, 11,* 1–20.

Dakil, S. R., Cox, M., Lin, H., & Flores, G. (2012). Physical abuse in U.S. children: Risk factors and deficiencies in referrals to support services. *Journal of Aggression, Maltreatment, and Trauma, 21,* 555–569.

Daley, T. C., Whaley, S. E., Sigman, M. D., Espinosa, M. P., & Neumann, C. (2003). IQ on the rise: The Flynn effect in rural Kenyan children. *Psychological Science, 14,* 215–219.

Dallman, M. F., Pecoraro, N., Akana, S. F., la Fleur, S. E., Gomez, F., Houshyar, H., et al. (2003). Chronic stress and obesity: A new view of "comfort food." *Proceedings of the National Academy of Sciences, 100,* 11696–11701.

Damon, W. (1988). *The moral child.* New York: Free Press.

Damon, W. (1990). Self-concept, adolescent. In R. M. Lerner, A. C. Petersen, & J. Brooks-Gunn (Eds.), *Encyclopedia of adolescence* (Vol. 2, pp. 87–91). New York: Garland.

Damon, W. (2004). *The moral advantage: How to succeed in business by doing the right thing.* San Francisco: Berrett-Koehler.

Damon, W., & Hart, D. (1988). *Self-understanding in childhood and adolescence.* New York: Cambridge University Press.

Daniels, E., & Leaper, C. (2006). A longitudinal investigation of sport participation, peer acceptance, and self-esteem among adolescent girls and boys. *Sex Roles, 55,* 875–880.

Daniels, H. (2011). Vygotsky and psychology. In U. Goswami (Ed.), *The Wiley-Blackwell handbook of childhood cognitive development* (2nd ed., pp. 673–696). Malden, MA: Wiley-Blackwell.

Dannemiller, J. L., & Stephens, B. R. (1988). A critical test of infant pattern preference models. *Child Development, 59,* 210–216.

Danzer, E., & Johnson, M. P. (2014). Fetal surgery for neural tube defects. *Seminars in Fetal and Neonatal Medicine, 19,* 2–8.

Darcy, A. (2012). Gender issues in child and adolescent eating disorders. In J. Lock (Ed.), *Oxford handbook of child and adolescent eating disorders: Developmental perspectives* (pp. 88–105). New York: Oxford University Press.

Darling, N., & Steinberg, L. (1997). Community influences on adolescent achievement and deviance. In J. Brooks-Gunn, G. Duncan, & L. Aber (Eds.), *Neighborhood poverty: Context and consequences for children: Conceptual, ethological, and policy approaches to studying neighborhoods* (Vol. 2, pp. 120–131). New York: Russell Sage Foundation.

Darling-Hammond, L. (2010). *The flat world and education: How America's commitment to equity will determine our future.* New York: Teachers College Press.

Darwin, C. (2003). *The origin of species: 150th anniversary edition.* New York: Signet Classics. (Original work published 1859)

Das, D. A., Grimmer, D. A., Sparnon, A. L., McRae, S. E., & Thomas, B. H. (2005). The efficacy of playing a virtual reality game in modulating pain for children with acute burn injuries: A randomized controlled trial. *BMC Pediatrics, 5*(1), 1–10.

Datar, A., & Sturm, R. (2006). Childhood overweight and elementary school outcomes. *International Journal of Obesity, 30,* 1449–1460.

D'Augelli, A. R. (2006). Developmental and contextual factors and mental health among lesbian, gay, and bisexual youths. In A. M. Omoto & H. S. Howard (Eds.), *Sexual orientation and mental health: Examining identity and development in lesbian, gay, and bisexual people* (pp. 37–53). Washington, DC: American Psychological Association.

D'Augelli, A. R., Grossman, A. H., Salter, N. P., Vasey, J. J., Starks, M. T., & Sinclair, K. O. (2005). Predicting the suicide attempts of lesbian, gay, and bisexual youth. *Suicide and Life-Threatening Behavior, 35,* 646–660.

Davies, J. (2008). Differential teacher positive and negative interactions with male and female pupils in the primary school setting. *Educational and Child Psychology, 25,* 17–26.

Davies, P. T., & Cichetti, D. (2014). How and why does the 5-HTTLPR gender moderate associations between maternal unresponsiveness and children's disruptive problems? *Child Development, 85,* 484–500.

Davis, A. S., & Escobar, L. F. (2013). Early childhood disorders: Down syndrome. In A. S. Davis (Ed.), *Psychopathology of childhood and adolescence: A neuropsychological approach* (pp. 569–580). New York: Springer.

Davis, E. L., & Buss, K. A. (2012). Moderators of the relation between shyness and behavior with peers: Cortisol dysregulation and maternal emotion socialization. *Social Development, 21,* 801–820.

Davis, E. L., Levine, L. J., Lench, H. C., & Quas, J. A. (2010). Metacognitive emotion regulation: Children's awareness that changing thoughts and goals can alleviate negative emotions. *Emotion, 10,* 498–510.

Davis, J. (2012, October). School enrollment and work status: 2011. *American Community Survey Briefs.* Washington, DC: U.S. Department of Commerce. Retrieved from www.census.gov/prod/2013pubs/acsbr11-14.pdf

Davis, K. F., Parker, K. P., & Montgomery, G. L. (2004). Sleep in infants and young children. Part 1: Normal sleep. *Journal of Pediatric Health Care, 18,* 65–71.

Dawley, K., Loch, J., & Bindrich, I. (2007). The Nurse–Family Partnership. *American Journal of Nursing, 107,* 60–67.

Dawson, C., & Gerken, L. A. (2009). From domain-generality to domain-sensitivity: 4-month-olds learn an abstract repetition rule in music that 7-month-olds do not. *Cognition, 111,* 378–382.

Dawson, T. L. (2002). New tools, new insights: Kohlberg's moral judgment stages revisited. *International Journal of Behavioral Development, 26,* 154–166.

Deák, G. O., Ray, S. D., & Brenneman, K. (2003). Children's perseverative appearance–reality errors are related to emerging language skills. *Child Development, 74,* 944–964.

Deák, G. O., Yen, L., & Pettit, J. (2001). By any other name: When will preschoolers produce several labels for a reference? *Journal of Child Language, 28,* 787–804.

DeAngeleo, L., Hurtado, S., & Pryor, J. H. (2010). *Your first college year: National norms for the 2008 YFCY survey.* Los Angeles: Higher Education Research Institute, UCLA.

Dearing, E., McCartney, K., & Taylor, B. A. (2009). Does higher quality early child care promote low-income children's math and reading achievement in middle childhood? *Child Development, 80,* 1329–1349.

Dearing, E., Wimer, C., Simpkins, S. D., Lund, T., Bouffard, S. M., Caronongan, P., & Kreider, H. (2009). Do neighborhood and home contexts help explain why low-income children miss opportunities to participate in activities outside of school? *Developmental Psychology, 45,* 1545–1562.

Deary, I. J., Strand, S., Smith, P., & Fernandes, C. (2007). Intelligence and educational achievement. *Intelligence, 35,* 13–21.

Deater-Deckard, K., Lansford, J. E., Dodge, K. A., Pettit, G. S., & Bates, J. E. (2003). The development of attitudes about physical punishment: An 8-year longitudinal study. *Journal of Family Psychology, 17,* 351–360.

Debes, F., Budtz-Jorgensen, E., Weihe, P., White, R. F., & Grandjean, P. (2006). Impact of prenatal methylmercury exposure on neurobehavioral function at age 14 years. *Neurotoxicology and Teratology, 28*(3), 363–375.

DeBoer, T., Scott, L. S., & Nelson, C. A. (2007). Methods for acquiring and analyzing infant event-related potentials. In M. de Haan (Ed.), *Infant EEG and event-related potentials* (pp. 5–37). New York: Psychology Press.

Debrabant, J., Gheysen, F., Vingerhoets, G., & Van Waelvelde, H. (2012). Age-related differences in predictive response timing in children: Evidence from regularly relative to irregularly paced reaction time performance. *Human Movement Science, 31,* 801–810.

de Bruyn, E. H. (2005). Role strain, engagement and academic achievement in early adolescence. *Educational Studies, 31,* 15–27.

de Bruyn, E. H., & Cillessen, A. H. N. (2006). Popularity in early adolescence: Prosocial and antisocial subtypes. *Journal of Adolescent Research, 21,* 607–627.

de Bruyn, E. H., Deković, M., & Meijnen, G. W. (2003). Parenting, goal orientations, classroom behavior, and school success in early adolescence. *Journal of Applied Developmental Psychology, 24,* 393–412.

DeCasper, A. J., & Spence, M. J. (1986). Prenatal maternal speech influences newborns' perception of speech sounds. *Infant Behavior and Development, 9,* 133–150.

De Corte, E., & Verschaffel, L. (2006). Mathematical thinking and learning. In K. A. Renninger & I. E. Sigel (Eds.), *Handbook of child psychology: Vol. 4. Child psychology in practice* (6th ed., pp. 103–152). Hoboken, NJ: Wiley.

Degirmencioglu, S. M., Urberg, K. A., Tolson, J. M., & Richard, P. (1998). Adolescent friendship networks: Continuity and change over the school year. *Merrill-Palmer Quarterly, 44,* 313–337.

De Goede, I. H. A., Branje, S. J. T., & Meeus, W. H. J. (2009). Developmental changes and gender differences in adolescents' perceptions of friendships. *Journal of Adolescence, 32,* 1105–1123.

de Haan, M., & Gunnar, M. R. (2009). The brain in a social environment: Why study development? In M. de Haan & M. R. Gunnar (Eds.), *Handbook of developmental social neuroscience* (pp. 3–12). New York: Guilford.

de Haan, M., & Matheson, A. (2009). The development and neural bases of processing emotion in faces and voices. In M. de Haan & M. R. Gunnar (Eds.), *Handbook of developmental social science* (pp. 107–121). New York: Guilford.

Deissinger, T. (2007). "Making schools practical": Practice firms and their function in the full-time vocational school system in Germany. *Education + Training, 49,* 364–378.

de Jong, E., Visscher, T. L. S., HiraSing, R. A., Heymans, M. W., Seidell, J. C., & Renders, C. M. (2013). Association between TV viewing, computer use and overweight, determinants and competing activities of screen time in 4- to 13-year-old children. *International Journal of Obesity, 37,* 47–53.

Dekker, M. C., Ferdinand, R. F., van Lang, D. J., Bongers, I. L., van der Ende, J., & Verhulst, F. C. (2007). Developmental trajectories of depressive symptoms from early childhood to late adolescence: Gender differences and adult outcome. *Journal of Child Psychology and Psychiatry, 48,* 657–666.

Deković, M., Noom, M. J., & Meeus, W. (1997). Expectations regarding development during adolescence: Parent and adolescent perceptions. *Journal of Youth and Adolescence, 26,* 253–271.

De Laet, S. Doumen, S., Vervoort, E., Colpin, H., Van Leeuwen, K., Goossens, L., & Verschueren, K. (2014). Transactional links between teacher–child relationship quality and perceived versus sociometric popularity: A three-wave longitudinal study. *Child Development, 85,* 1647–1662.

Delahunty, K. M., McKay, D. W., Noseworthy, D. E., & Storey, A. E. (2007). Prolactin responses to infant cues in men and women: Effects of parental experience and recent infant contact. *Hormones and Behavior, 51,* 213–220.

De Lisi, R., & Gallagher, A. M. (1991). Understanding gender stability and constancy in Argentinean children. *Merrill-Palmer Quarterly, 37,* 483–502.

DeLoache, J. S. (1987). Rapid change in symbolic functioning of very young children. *Science, 238,* 1556–1557.

DeLoache, J. S. (2002). The symbol-mindedness of young children. In W. Hartup & R. A. Weinberg (Eds.), *Minnesota symposia on child psychology* (Vol. 32, pp. 73–101). Mahwah, NJ: Erlbaum.

DeLoache, J. S., Chiong, C., Sherman, K., Islam, N., Vanderborght, M., Troseth, G. L., et al. (2010). Do babies learn from baby media? *Psychological Science, 21,* 1570–1574.

DeLoache, J. S., & Ganea, P. A. (2009). Symbol-based learning in infancy. In A. Woodward & A. Needham (Eds.), *Learning and the infant mind* (pp. 263–285). New York: Oxford University Press.

DeLoache, J. S., Uttal, D., & Rosengren, K. (2004). Scale errors offer evidence for a perception–action dissociation early in life. *Science, 304,* 1027–1029.

Deltondo, J., Por, I., Hu, W., Merchenthaler, I., Semeniken, K., Jojart, J., & Dudas, B. (2008). Associations between the human growth hormone-releasing hormone and neuropeptide-Y-immunoreactive systems in the human diencephalons: A possible morphological substrate of the impact of stress on growth. *Neuroscience, 153,* 1146–1152.

DeMarie, D., & Lopez, L. M. (2014). Memory in schools. In P. J. Bauer & R. Fivush (Eds.), *Wiley handbook on the development of children's memory* (Vol. 2, pp. 836–864). Malden, MA: Wiley-Blackwell.

DeMarie, D., Miller, P. H., Ferron, J., & Cunningham, W. R. (2004). Path analysis tests of theoretical models of children's memory performance. *Journal of Cognition and Development, 5,* 461–492.

Demetriou, A., Christou, C., Spanoudis, G., & Platsidou, M. (2002). The development of mental processing: Efficiency, working memory, and thinking. *Monographs of the Society for Research in Child Development, 67*(1, Serial No. 268).

Demetriou, A., Efklides, A., Papadaki, M., Papantoniou, G., & Economou, A. (1993). Structure and development of causal–experimental thought: From early adolescence to youth. *Developmental Psychology, 29,* 480–497.

Demetriou, A., & Kazi, S. (2001). *Unity and modularity in the mind and the self: Studies on the relationships between self-awareness, personality, and intellectual development from childhood to adolescence.* London: Routledge.

Demetriou, A., Pachaury, A., Metallidou, Y., & Kazi, S. (1996). Universals and specificities in the structure and development of quantitative-relational thought: A cross-cultural study in Greece and India. *International Journal of Behavioral Development, 19,* 255–290.

DeNavas-Walt, C., Proctor, B. D., & Smith, J. C. (2011). Income, poverty, and health insurance coverage in the United States: 2010. *U.S. Census Bureau, Current Population Reports,* P60–P239. Washington, DC: U.S. Government Printing Office.

Denham, B. E. (2012). Anabolic-androgenic steroids and adolescents: Recent developments. *Journal of Addictions Nursing, 23,* 167–171.

Denham, S. (1998). *Emotional development in young children.* New York: Guilford.

Denham, S., Warren, H., von Salisch, M., Benga, O., Chin, J., & Geangu, E. (2011). Emotions and social development in childhood. In P. K. Smith & C. H. Hart (Eds.). *Wiley-Blackwell handbook of childhood social development* (2nd ed., pp. 413–433). Chichester, UK: Wiley-Blackwell.

Denissen, J. J. A., Zarrett, N. R., & Eccles, J. S. (2007). I like to do it, I'm able, and I know I am: Longitudinal couplings between domain-specific achievement, self-concept, and interest. *Child Development, 78,* 430–447.

Dennis, W. (1960). Causes of retardation among institutionalized children: Iran. *Journal of Genetic Psychology, 96,* 47–59.

Deprest, J. A., Devlieger, R., Srisupundit, K., Beck, V., Sandaite, I., Rusconi, S., et al. (2010). Fetal surgery is a clinical reality. *Seminars in Fetal & Neonatal Medicine, 15,* 58–67.

Der, G., Batty, G. D., & Deary, I. J. (2006). Effect of breastfeeding on intelligence in children: Prospective study, sibling pairs analysis, and meta-analysis. *British Medical Journal, 333,* 945.

DeRoche, K., & Welsh, M. (2008). Twenty-five years of research on neurocognitive outcomes in early-treated phenylketonuria: Intelligence and executive function. *Developmental Neuropsychology, 33,* 474–504.

Derom, C., Thiery, E., Vlietinck, R., Loos, R., & Derom, R. (1996). Handedness in twins according to zygosity and chorion type: A preliminary report. *Behavior Genetics, 26,* 407–408.

DeRose, L. M., & Brooks-Gunn, J. (2006). Transition into adolescence: The role of pubertal processes. In L. Balter & C. S. Tamis-LeMonda (Eds.), *Child psychology: A handbook of contemporary issues* (2nd ed., pp. 385–414). New York: Psychology Press.

DeRosier, M. E. (2007). Peer-rejected and bullied children: A safe schools initiative for elementary school students. In J. E. Zins, M. J. Elias, & C. A. Maher (Eds.), *Bullying, victimization, and peer harassment* (pp. 257–276). New York: Haworth.

de Rosnay, M., Copper, P. J., Tsigaras, N., & Murray, L. (2006). Transmission of social anxiety from mother to infant: An experimental study using a social referencing paradigm. *Behavior Research and Therapy, 44,* 1165–1175.

de Rosnay, M., & Hughes, C. (2006). Conversation and theory of mind: Do children talk their way to socio-cognitive understanding? *British Journal of Developmental Psychology, 24,* 7–37.

De Schipper, J. C., Tavecchio, L. W. C., van IJzendoorn, M. H., & van Zeijl, J. (2004). Goodness-of-fit in center day care: Relations of temperament, stability, and quality of care with the child's adjustment. *Early Childhood Research Quarterly, 19,* 257–272.

De Schipper, J. C., van IJzendoorn, M. H., & Tavecchio, L. W. C. (2004). Stability in center day care: Relations with children's well-being and problem behavior in day care. *Social Development, 13,* 531–550.

De Souza, E., Alberman, E., & Morris, J. K. (2009). Down syndrome and paternal age, a new analysis of case-control data collected in the 1960s. *American Journal of Medical Genetics, 149A,* 1205–1208.

Dessel, A. (2010). Prejudice in schools: Promotion of an inclusive culture and climate. *Education and Urban Society, 42,* 407–429.

Deutsch, A. R., Crockett, L. J., Wolff, J. M., & Russell, S. T. (2012). Parent and peer pathways to adolescent delinquency: Variations by ethnicity and neighborhood context. *Journal of Youth and Adolescence, 41,* 1078–1094.

Deutsch, F. M., Ruble, D. N., Fleming, A., Brooks-Gunn, J., & Stangor, C. (1988). Information-seeking and maternal self-definition during the transition to motherhood. *Journal of Personality and Social Psychology, 55,* 420–431.

Deutsch, W., & Pechmann, T. (1982). Social interaction and the development of definite descriptions. *Cognition, 11,* 159–184.

Devi, N. P. G., Shenbagvalli, R., Ramesh, K., & Rathinam, S. N. (2009). Rapid progression of HIV infection in infancy. *Indian Pediatrics, 46,* 53–56.

de Villiers, J. G., & de Villiers, P. A. (2000). Linguistic determinism and the understanding of false beliefs. In P. Mitchell & K. J. Riggs (Eds.), *Children's reasoning and the mind* (pp. 87–99). Hove, UK: Psychology Press.

Devlin, A. M., Brain, U., Austin, J., & Oberlander, T. F. (2010). Prenatal exposure to maternal depressed mood and the MTHFR C677T variant affect SLC6A4 methlation in infants at birth. *PLOS ONE, 5,* e12201.

DeVoe, J. F., & Darling-Churchill, K. E. (2008). *Status and trends in the education of American Indians and Alaska Natives: 2008* (NCES 2008–84). Washington, DC: U.S. Department of Education.

DeVries, R. (2001). Constructivist education in preschool and elementary school: The sociomoral atmosphere as the first educational goal. In S. L. Golbeck (Ed.), *Psychological perspectives on early childhood education* (pp. 153–180). Mahwah, NJ: Erlbaum.

de Waal, F. B. M. (1993). Sex differences in chimpanzee (and human) behavior: A matter of social values? In M. Hechter, L. Nadel, & R. E. Michod (Eds.), *The origin of values* (pp. 285–303). New York: Aldine de Gruyter.

de Waal, F. B. M. (2001). *Tree of origin.* Cambridge, MA: Harvard University Press.

de Weerd, A. W., & van den Bossche, A. S. (2003). The development of sleep during the first months of life. *Sleep Medicine Reviews, 7,* 179–191.

De Wit, D. J., Karioja, K., Rye, B. J., & Shain, M. (2011). Perceptions of declining classmate and teacher support following the transition to high school: Potential correlates of increasing student mental health difficulties. *Psychology in the Schools, 48,* 556–572.

De Wolff, M. S., & van IJzendoorn, M. H. (1997). Sensitivity and attachment: A meta-analysis on parental antecedents of infant attachment. *Child Development, 68,* 571–591.

Deynoot-Schaub, M. J. G., & Riksen-Walraven, J. M. (2006a). Peer contacts of 15-month-olds in childcare: Links with child temperament, parent—child interaction and quality of childcare. *Social Development 15,* 709–729.

Deynoot-Schaub, M. J. G., & Riksen-Walraven, J. M. (2006b). Peer interaction in child care centres at 15 and 23 months: Stability and links with children's socioemotional adjustment. *Infant Behavior and Development, 29,* 276–288.

Diamond, A. (2009). The interplay of biology and the environment broadly defined. *Developmental Psychology, 45,* 1–8.

Diamond, A., Cruttenden, L., & Neiderman, D. (1994). AB with multiple wells: 1. Why are multiple wells sometimes easier than two wells? 2. Memory or memory + inhibition. *Developmental Psychology, 30,* 192–205.

Diamond, L. M. (2008). Female bisexuality from adolescence to adulthood: Results from a 10-year longitudinal study. *Developmental Psychology, 44,* 5–14.

Dias, M. G., & Harris, P. (1988). The effect of make-believe play on deductive reasoning. *British Journal of Developmental Psychology, 6,* 207–221.

Dias, M. G., & Harris, P. (1990). The influence of the imagination on reasoning by young children. *British Journal of Developmental Psychology, 8,* 305–318.

Diav-Citrin, O. (2011). Prenatal exposures associated with neurodevelopmental delay and disabilities. *Developmental Disabilities, 17,* 71–84.

DiBiase, A.-M., Gibbs, J. C., Potter, G. B., & Blount, M. R. (2011). *Teaching adolescents to think and act responsibly: The EQUIP approach.* Champaign, IL: Research Press.

Dick, D. M., Prescott, C., & McGue, M. (2009). The genetics of substance use and substance use disorders. In Y.-K. Kim (Ed.), *Handbook of behavior genetics* (pp. 433–453). New York: Springer.

Dickinson, D. K., Golinkoff, R. M., & Hirsh-Pasek, K. (2010). Speaking out for language: Why language is central to reading development. *Educational Researcher, 39,* 305–310.

Dickinson, D. K., & McCabe, A. (2001). Bringing it all together: The multiple origins, skills, and environmental supports of early literacy. *Learning Disabilities Research and Practice, 16,* 186–202.

Dickinson, D. K., McCabe, A., Anastasopoulos, L., Peisner-Feinberg, E. S., & Poe, M. D. (2003). The comprehensive language approach to early literacy: The interrelationships among vocabulary, phonological sensitivity, and print knowledge among preschool-age children. *Journal of Educational Psychology, 95,* 465–481.

Dick-Read, G. (1959). *Childbirth without fear.* New York: Harper & Brothers.

DiDonato, M. D., & Berenbaum, S. A. (2011). The benefits and drawbacks of gender typing: How different dimensions are related to psychological adjustment. *Archives of Sexual Behavior, 40,* 457–463.

Diener, M. L., Isabella, R., Behunin, M. G., & Wong, M. S. (2008). Attachment to mothers and fathers during middle childhood: Associations with child gender, grade, and competence. *Social Development, 17,* 84–101.

Dietrich, K. N., Ware, J. H., Salganik, M., Radcliffe, J., Rogan, W. J., & Rhoads, G. C. (2004). Effect of chelation therapy on the neuropsychological and behavioral development of lead-exposed children after school entry. *Pediatrics, 114,* 19–26.

Di Giunta, L., Alessandri, G., Gerbino, M., Kanacri, P. L., Zuffiano, A., & Caprara, G. V. (2013). The determinants of scholastic achievement: The contribution of personality traits, self-esteem, and academic self-efficacy. *Learning and Individual Differences, 27,* 102–108.

Dildy, G. A., Jackson, G. M., Fowers, G. K., Oshiro, B. T., Varner, M. W., & Clark, S. L. (1996). Very advanced maternal age: Pregnancy after age 45. *American Journal of Obstetrics and Gynecology, 175,* 668–674.

DiPietro, J. A., Bornstein, M. H., Costigan, K. A., Pressman, E. K., Hahn, C.-S., & Painter, K. (2002). What does fetal movement predict about behavior during the first two years of life? *Developmental Psychobiology, 40,* 358–371.

DiPietro, J. A., Hodgson, D. M., Costigan, K. A., & Hilton, S. C. (1996). Fetal neurobehavioral development. *Child Development, 67,* 2553–2567.

DiPietro, J. A., Novak, M. F. S. X., Costigan, K. A., Atella, L. D., & Reusing, S. P. (2006). Maternal psychological distress during pregnancy in relation to child development at age two. *Child Development, 77,* 573–587.

Dishion, T. J., Shaw, D., Connell, A., Gardner, F., Weaver, C., & Wilson, M. (2008). The family checkup with high-risk indigent families: Preventing problem behavior by increasing parents' positive behavior support in early childhood. *Child Development, 79,* 1395–1414.

Dittmar, M., Abbot-Smith, K., Lieven, E., & Tomasello, M. (2014). Familiar verbs are not always easier than novel verbs: How German preschool children comprehend active and passive sentences. *Cognitive Science, 38,* 128–151.

Dix, T., Stewart, A. D., Gershoff, E. T., & Day, W. H. (2007). Atutonomy and children's reactions to being controlled: Evidence that both compliance and defiance may be positive markers in early development. *Child Development, 78,* 1204–1221.

Dixon, P. (2009). Marriage among African Americans: What does the research reveal? *Journal of African American Studies, 13,* 29–46.

Dodd, V. L. (2005). Implications of kangaroo care for growth and development in preterm infants. *JOGNN, 34,* 218–232.

Dodge, K. A., Coie, J. D., & Lynam, D. (2006). Aggression and antisocial behavior in youth. In N. Eisenberg (Ed.), *Handbook of child psychology: Vol. 3. Social, emotional, and personality development* (6th ed., pp. 719–788). Hoboken, NJ: Wiley.

Dodge, K. A., Lochman, J. E., Harnish, J. D., Bates, J. E., & Pettit, G. S. (1997). Reactive and proactive aggression in school children and psychiatrically impaired chronically assaultive youth. *Journal of Abnormal Psychology, 106,* 37–51.

Dodge, K. A., McLoyd, V. C., & Lansford, J. E. (2006). The cultural context of physically disciplining children. In V. C. McLoyd, N. E. Hill, & K. A. Dodge (Eds.), *African-American family life: Ecological and cultural diversity* (pp. 245–263). New York: Guilford.

Dodge, K. A., Pettit, G. S., McClaskey, C. L., & Brown, M. M. (1986). Social competence in children. *Monographs of the Society for Research in Child Development, 51*(2, Serial No. 213).

Dohnt, H., & Tiggemann, M. (2006). The contribution of peer and media influences to the development of body satisfaction and self-esteem in young girls: A prospective study. *Developmental Psychology, 42,* 929–936.

Domellöf, E., Johansson, A., & Rönnqvist, L. (2011). Handedness in preterm born children: A systematic review and meta-analysis. *Neuropsychologia, 49,* 2299–2310.

Domitrovich, C. E., Cortes, R. C., & Greenberg, M. T. (2007). Improving young children's social and emotional competence: A randomized trial of the preschool "PATHS" curriculum. *The Journal of Primary Prevention, 28,* 67–91.

Domitrovich, C. E., Gest, S. D., Gill, S., Bierman, K. L., Welsh, J. A., & Jones, D. (2009). Fostering high-quality teaching with an enriched curriculum and professional development support: The Head Start REDI program. *American Educational Research Journal, 46,* 567–597.

Donaldson, M., & Jones, J. (2013). Optimising outcome in congenital hypothyroidism: Current opinions on best practice in initial assessment and subsequent management. *Journal of Clinical Research in Pediatric Endocrinology, 5*(Suppl. 12), 13–22.

Donatelle, R. J. (2015). *Health: The basics* (11th ed.). San Francisco: Benjamin Cummings.

Dondi, M., Simion, F., & Caltran, G. (1999). Can newborns discriminate between their own cry and the cry of another newborn infant? *Developmental Psychology, 35,* 418–426.

Donnellan, M. B., Trzesniewski, K. H., Robins, R. W., Moffitt, T. E., & Caspi, A. (2005). Low self-esteem is related to aggression, antisocial behavior, and delinquency. *Psychological Science, 16,* 328–335.

Donnelly, J. E., Greene, J. L., Gibson, C. A., Smith, B. K., Washburn, R. A., Sullivan, D. K., DuBose, K., et al. (2009). Physical activity across the curriculum (PAAC): A randomized controlled trial to promote physical activity and diminish overweight and obesity in elementary school children. *Preventive Medicine, 49,* 336–341.

Doornwaard, S. M., Branje, S., Meeus, W. H. J., & ter Bogt, T. F. M. (2012). Development of adolescents' peer crowd identification in relation to changes in problem behaviors. *Developmental Psychology, 48,* 1366–1380.

Dorius, C. J., Bahr, S. J., Hoffman, J. P., & Harmon, E. L. (2004). Parenting practices as moderators of the relationship between peers and adolescent marijuana use. *Journal of Marriage and Family, 66,* 163–178.

Dorris, M. (1989). *The broken cord.* New York: Harper & Row.

Dorwie, F. M., & Pacquiao, D. F. (2014). Practices of traditional birth attendants in Sierra Leone and perceptions by mothers and health professionals familiar with their care. *Journal of Transcultural Nursing, 25,* 33–41.

Doss, B. D., Rhoades, G. K., Stanley, S. M., & Markman, H. J. (2009). The effect of the transition to parenthood on relationship quality: An 8-year prospective study. *Journal of Personality and Social Psychology, 96,* 601–619.

dos Santos Silva, I., De Stavola, B. L., Hardy, R. J., Kuh, D. J., McCormack, V. A., & Wadsworth, M. E. J. (2004). Is the association of birth weight with premenopausal breast cancer risk mediated through childhood growth? *British Journal of Cancer, 91,* 519–524.

Double, E. B., Mabuchi, K., Cullings, H. M., Preston, D. L., Kodama, K., Shimizu, Y., et al. (2011). Long-term radiation-related health effects in a unique human population: Lessons learned from the atomic bomb survivors of Hiroshima and Nagasaki. *Disaster Medicine and Public Health Preparedness, 5*(Suppl. 1), S122–S133.

Douglas, E. M. (2006). *Mending broken families: Social policies for divorced families.* Lanham, MD: Rowman & Littlefield.

Dowker, A. (2003). Younger children's estimates for addition: The zone of partial knowledge and understanding. In A. J. Baroody & A. Dowker (Eds.), *The development of arithmetic concepts and skills: Constructing adaptive expertise* (pp. 243–265). Mahwah, NJ: Erlbaum.

Dowling, E. M., Gestsdottir, S., Anderson, P. M., von Eye, A., Almerigi, J., & Lerner, R. M. (2004). Structural relations among spirituality, religiosity, and thriving in adolescence. *Applied Developmental Psychology, 8,* 7–16.

Downe, S., Finlayson, K., Walsh, D., & Lavender, T. (2009). "Weighing up and balancing out": A meta-synthesis of barriers to antenatal care for marginalized women in high-income countries. *BJOG, 116,* 518–529.

Downing, J. E. (2010). *Academic instruction for students with moderate and severe intellectual disabilities.* Thousand Oaks, CA: Corwin.

Downs, A. C., & Fuller, M. J. (1991). Recollections of spermarche: An exploratory investigation. *Current Psychology: Research and Reviews, 10,* 93–102.

Dozier, M., Stovall, K. C., Albus, K. E., & Bates, B. (2001). Attachment for infants in foster care: The role of caregiver state of mind. *Child Development, 72,* 1467–1477.

Dragowski, E. A., Halkitis, P. N., Grossman, A. H., & D'Augelli, A. R. (2011). Sexual orientation victimization and posttraumtic stress symptoms among lesbian, gay, and bisexual youth. *Journal of Gay and Lesbian Social Services, 23,* 226–249.

Drake, K., Belsky, J., & Fearon, R. M. P. (2014). From early attachment to engagement with learning in school: The role of self-regulation and persistence. *Developmental Psychology, 50,* 1350–1361.

Driscoll, M. C. (2007). Sickle cell disease. *Pediatrics in Review, 28,* 259–268.

Driver, J., Tabares, A., Shapiro, A. F., & Gottman, J. M. (2012). Couple interaction in happy and unhappy marriages: Gottman Laboratory studies. In F. Walsh (Ed.), *Normal family processes: Growing diversity and complexity* (pp. 57–77). New York: Guilford.

Druet, C., Stettler, N., Sharp, S., Simmons, R. K., Cooper, C., Smith, G. D., et al. (2012). Prediction of childhood obesity by infancy weight gain: An individual-level meta-analysis. *Paediatric and Perinatal Epidemiology, 26,* 19–26.

DuBois, D. L., Felner, R. D., Brand, S., & George, G. R. (1999). Profiles of self-esteem in early adolescence: Identification and investigation of adaptive correlates. *American Journal of Community Psychology, 27,* 899–932.

Duckworth, A. L., Quinn, P. D., & Tsukayama, E. (2012). What No Child Left Behind leaves behind: The roles of IQ and self-control in predicting standardized achievement test scores and report card grades. *Journal of Educational Psychology, 104,* 439–451.

Dudani, A., Macpherson, A., & Tamim, H. (2010). Childhood behavior problems and unintentional injury: A longitudinal, population-based study. *Journal of Developmental and Behavioral Pediatrics, 31,* 276–285.

Dueker, G. L., Modi, A., & Needham, A. (2003). 4.5-month-old infants' learning, retention and use of object boundary information. *Infant Behavior and Development, 26,* 588–605.

Duggan, A., McFarlane, E., Fuddy, L., Burrell, L., Higman, S. M., Windham, A., & Sia, C. (2004). Randomized trial of a statewide home visiting program: Impact in preventing child abuse and neglect. *Child Abuse and Neglect, 28,* 597–622.

Duncan, G. J., Dowsett, C. J., Claessens, A., Magnuson, K., Huston, A. C., Klebanov, P., et al. (2007). School readiness and later achievement. *Developmental Psychology, 43,* 1428–1446.

Duncan, G. J., & Magnuson, K. A. (2003). Off with Hollingshead: Socioeconomic resources, parenting, and child development. In M. H. Bornstein & R. H. Bradley (Eds.), *Socioeconomic status, parenting, and child development* (pp. 83–106). Mahwah, NJ: Erlbaum.

Duncan, L. E., Pollastri, A. R., & Smoller, J. W. (2014). Mind the gap: Why many geneticists and psychological scientists have discrepant views about gene–environment interaction (GXE) research. *American Psychologist, 69,* 249–268.

Duncan, S. R., Paterson, D. S., Hoffman, J. M., Mokler, D. J., et al. (2010). Brainstem serotonergic deficiency in sudden infant death syndrome. *Journal of the American Medical Association, 303,* 430–437.

Dundek, L. H. (2006) Establishment of a Somali doula program at a large metropolitan hospital. *Journal of Perinatal and Neonatal Nursing, 20,* 128–137.

Dunham, Y., Baron, A. S., & Banaji, M. R. (2006). From American city to Japanese village: A cross-cultural investigation of implicit race attitudes. *Child Development, 77,* 1129–1520.

Dunham, Y., Chen, E. E., & Banaji, M. R. (2013). Two signatures of implicit intergroup attitudes: Developmental invariance and early enculturation. *Psychological Science, 24,* 860–868.

Dunifon, R., Kalil, A., & Danziger, S. K. (2003). Maternal work behavior under welfare reform: How does the transition from welfare to work affect child development? *Children and Youth Services Review, 25,* 55–82.

Dunkel-Schetter, C. (2011). Psychological science on pregnancy: Stress processes, biopsychosocial models, and emerging research issues. *Annual Review of Psychology, 62,* 531–558.

Dunkel-Shetter, C., & Lobel, M. (2012). Pregnancy and birth: A multilevel analysis of stress and birth weight. In T. A. Revenson, A. Baum, & J., Singer (Eds.), *Handbook of Health Psychology* (2nd ed., pp. 431–463). London: Psychology Press.

Dunn, J. (1989). Siblings and the development of social understanding in early childhood. In P. G. Zukow (Ed.), *Sibling interaction across cultures* (pp. 106–116). New York: Springer-Verlag.

Dunn, J. (1994). Temperament, siblings, and the development of relationships. In W. B. Carey & S. C. McDevitt (Eds.), *Prevention and early intervention* (pp. 50–58). New York: Brunner/Mazel.

Dunn, J. (2002). The adjustment of children in stepfamilies: Lessons from community studies. *Child and Adolescent Mental Health, 7,* 154–161.

Dunn, J. (2004). Sibling relationships. In P. K. Smith & C. H. Hart (Eds.), *Handbook of childhood social development* (pp. 223–237). Malden, MA: Blackwell.

Dunn, J. (2005). Moral development in early childhood and social interaction in the family. In M. Killen & J. G. Smetana (Eds.), *Handbook of moral development* (pp. 331–350). Mahwah, NJ: Erlbaum.

Dunn, J., Cheng, H., O'Connor, T. G., & Bridges, L. (2004). Children's perspectives on their relationships with their nonresident fathers: Influences, outcomes and implications. *Journal of Child Psychology and Psychiatry, 45,* 553–566.

Durbin, D. L., Darling, N., Steinberg, L., & Brown, B. B. (1993). Parenting style and peer group membership among European-American adolescents. *Journal of Research on Adolescence, 3,* 87–100.

Durkin, M. S., Laraque, D., Lubman, I., & Barlow, B. (1999). Epidemiology and prevention of traffic injuries to urban children and adolescents. *Pediatrics, 103,* e74.

Durlak, J. A., Weissberg, R. P., Dymnicki, A. B., Taylor, R. D., & Schellinger, K. B. (2011). The impact of enhancing students' social and emotional learning: A meta-analysis of school-based universal interventions. *Child Development, 82,* 405–432.

Durlak, J. A., Weissberg, R. P., & Pachan, M. (2010). A meta-analysis of after-school programs that seek to promote personal and social skills in children and adolescents. *American Journal of Community Psychology, 45,* 294–309.

Durston, S., & Casey, B. J. (2006). What have we learned about cognitive development from neuroimaging? *Neuropsychologia, 44,* 2149–2157.

Dusek, J. B. (1987). Sex roles and adjustment. In D. B. Carter (Ed.), *Current conceptions of sex roles and sex typing* (pp. 211–222). New York: Praeger.

Duszak, R. S. (2009). Congenital rubella syndrome—major review. *Optometry, 80,* 36–43.

Dweck, C. (2007). Is math a gift? Beliefs that put females at risk. In S. J. Ceci & W. M. Williams (Eds.), *Why aren't more women in science? Top researchers debate the evidence* (pp. 47–55). Washington, DC: American Psychological Association.

Dweck, C. S. (2002). Messages that motivate: How praise molds students' beliefs, motivation, and performance (in surprising ways). In J. Aronson (Ed.), *Improving academic achievement: Impact of psychological factors on education* (pp. 37–60). San Diego, CA: Academic Press.

Dweck, C. S. (2009). Prejudice: How it develops and how it can be undone. *Human Development, 52,* 371–376.

Dweck, C. S., & Molden, D. C. (2013). Self-theories: Their impact on competence motivation and acquisition. In A. J. Elliott & C. J. Dweck (Eds.), *Handbook of confidence and motivation* (pp. 122–140). New York: Guilford.

Dynarski, M., James-Burdumy, S., Moore, M., Rosenberg, L., Deke, J., & Mansfield, W. (2004). *When schools stay open late: The national evaluation of the 21st Century Community Learning Centers Program: New findings.* Washington DC: U.S. Department of Education.

Dyrdal, G. M., & Lucas, R. E. (2013). Reaction and adaptation to the birth of a child: A couple-level analysis. *Developmental Psychology, 49,* 749–761.

Dzurova, D., & Pikhart, H. (2005). Down syndrome, paternal age and education: Comparison of California and the Czech Republic. *BMC Public Health, 5,* 69.

E

Eagan, K., Lozano, J. B., Hurtado, S., & Case, M. H. (2013). *The American freshman: National norms, Fall 2013.* Los Angeles: Higher Education Research Institute, UCLA.

Eaton, D. K., Davis, K. S., Barrios, L., Brener, N. D., & Noonan, R. K. (2007). Associations of dating violence victimization with lifetime participation, cooccurrence, and early initiation of risk behaviors among U.S. high school students. *Journal of Interpersonal Violence, 22,* 585–602.

Eaves, L., Silberg, J., Foley, D., Bulik, C., Maes, H., & Erkanli, A. (2004). Genetic and environmental influences on the relative timing of pubertal change. *Twin Research, 7,* 471–481.

Ebeling, K. S., & Gelman, S. A. (1994). Children's use of context in interpreting "big" and "little." *Child Development, 65,* 1178–1192.

Eccles, J. S. (2004). Schools, academic motivation, and stage–environment fit. In R. M. Lerner & L. Steinberg (Eds.), *Handbook of adolescent psychology* (2nd ed., pp. 125–154). Hoboken, NJ: Wiley.

Eccles, J. S., & Gootman, J. (Eds.). (2002). *Community programs to promote youth development.* Washington, DC: National Academy Press.

Eccles, J. S., Jacobs, J., & Harold, R. D. (1990). Gender-role stereotypes, expectancy effects, and parents' role in the socialization of gender differences in self-perceptions and skill acquisition. *Journal of Social Issues, 46,* 183–201.

Eccles, J. S., & Roeser, R. W. (2009). Schools, academic motivation, and stage– environment fit. In R. M. Lerner & L. Steinberg (Eds.), *Handbook of adolescent psychology* (Vol. 1, pp. 404–434). Hoboken, NJ: Wiley.

Eccles, J. S., Templeton, J., Barber, B., & Stone, M. (2003). Adolescence and emerging adulthood: The critical passage ways to adulthood. In M. H. Bornstein, L. Davidson, C. L. M. Keyes, K. A. Moore, & the Center for Child Well-Being (Eds.), *Well-being: Positive development across the life course* (pp. 383–406). Mahwah, NJ: Erlbaum.

Eccles, J. S., Vida, M. N., & Barber, B. (2004). The relation of early adolescents' college plans and both academic ability and task-value beliefs to subsequent college enrollment. *Journal of Early Adolescence, 24,* 63–77.

Eckerman, C. O., & Peterman, K. (2001). Peers and infant social/communicative development. In G. Bremner & A. Fogel (Eds.), *Blackwell handbook of infant development* (pp. 326–350). Malden, MA: Blackwell.

Eder, R. A., & Mangelsdorf, S. C. (1997). The emotional basis of early personality development: Implications for the emergent self-concept. In R. Hogan, J. Johnson, & S. Briggs (Eds.), *Handbook of personality psychology* (pp. 209–240). San Diego, CA: Academic Press.

Edwards, O. W., & Oakland, T. D. (2006). Factorial invariance of Woodcock-Johnson III scores for African Americans and Caucasian Americans. *Journal of Psychoeducational Assessment, 24,* 358–366.

Egeland, B., Jacobvitz, D., & Sroufe, L. A. (1988). Breaking the cycle of abuse. *Child Development, 59,* 1080–1088.

Ehri, L. C., & Roberts, T. (2006). The roots of learning to read and write: Acquisition of letters and phonemic awareness. In D. K. Dickinson & S. B. Neuman (Eds.), *Handbook of early literacy research* (Vol. 2, pp. 113–131). New York: Guilford.

Eichstedt, J. A., Serbin, L. A., Poulin-Dubois, D., & Sen, M. G. (2002). Of bears and men: Infants' knowledge of conventional and metaphorical gender stereotypes. *Infant Behavior and Development, 25,* 296–310.

Einspieler, C., Marschik, P. B., & Prechtl, H. F. R. (2008). Human motor behavior: Prenatal origin and early postnatal development. *Zeitschrift für Psychologie, 216,* 147–153.

Eisbach, A. O. (2004). Children's developing awareness of diversity in people's trains of thought. *Child Development, 75,* 1694–1707.

Eisenberg, N. (2003). Prosocial behavior, empathy, and sympathy. In M. H. Bornstein & L. Davidson (Eds.), *Well-being: Positive development across the life course* (pp. 253–265). Mahwah, NJ: Erlbaum.

Eisenberg, N. (2006). Emotion-related regulation. In H. E. Fitzgerald, B. M. Lester, & B. Zuckerman (Eds.), *The crisis in youth mental health: Critical issues and effective programs, Vol. 1: Childhood disorders* (pp. 133–155). Westport, CT: Praeger.

Eisenberg, N. (2010). Empathy-related responding: Links with self-regulation, moral judgment, and moral behavior. In M. Mikulincer & P. R. Shaver (Eds.), *Prosocial motives, emotions, and behavior: The better angels of our nature* (pp. 129–148). Washington, DC: American Psychological Association.

Eisenberg, N., Eggum, N. D., & Edwards, A. (2010). Empathy-related responding and moral development. In W. F. Arsenio & E. A. Lemerise (Eds.), *Emotions, aggression, and morality in children: Bridging development and psychopathology* (pp. 115–135). Washington, DC: American Psychological Association.

Eisenberg, N., Fabes, R. A., Shepard, S. A., Murphy, B. C., Jones, S., & Guthrie, I. K. (1998). Contemporaneous and longitudinal prediction of children's sympathy from dispositional regulation and emotionality. *Developmental Psychology, 34,* 910–924.

Eisenberg, N., Fabes, R. A., & Spinrad, T. L. (2006). Prosocial development. In N. Eisenberg (Ed.), *Handbook of child psychology: Vol. 3. Social, emotional, and personality development* (6th ed., pp. 646–718). Hoboken, NJ: Wiley.

Eisenberg, N., Sadovsky, A., Spinrad, T. L., Fabes, R. A., Losoya, S., & Valiente, C. (2005). The relations of problem behavior status to children's negative emotionality, effortful control, and impulsivity: Concurrent relations and prediction of change. *Developmental Psychology, 41,* 193–211.

Eisenberg, N., & Silver, R. C. (2011). Growing up in the shadow of terrorism. *American Psychologist, 66,* 468–481.

Eisenberg, N., Smith, C. L., & Spinrad, T. L. (2011). Effortful control: Relations with emotion regulation, adjustment, and socialization in childhood. In K. D. Vohs & R. F. Baumeister (Eds.), *Handbook of self-regulation: Research, theory, and applications,* (2nd ed., pp. 263–283). New York: Guilford.

Eisenberg, N., Spinrad, T., Fabes, R., Reiser, M., Cumberland, A., & Shepard, S. (2004). The relations of effortful control and impulsivity to children's resiliency and adjustment. *Child Development, 75,* 25–46.

Eisenberg, N., Spinrad, T. L., & Morris, A. S. (2013). Prosocial Development. In P. D. Zelazo (Ed.), *Oxford handbook of developmental psychology, Vol. 2: Self and other* (pp. 300–325). New York: Oxford University Press.

Eivers, A. R., Brendgen, M., Vitaro, F., & Borge, A. I. H. (2012). Concurrent and longitudinal links between children's and their friends' antisocial and prosocial behavior in preschool. *Early Childhood Research Quarterly, 27,* 137–146.

Ekéus, C., Christensson, K., & Hjern, A. (2003). Unintentional and violent injuries among preschool children of teenage mothers in Sweden: A national cohort study. *Journal of Epidemiology and Community Health, 58,* 680–685.

Ekéus, C., Högberg, U., & Norman, M. (2014). Vacuum assisted birth and risk for cerebral complications in term newborn infants: A population-based cohort study. *BMC Pregnancy and Childbirth, 14,* 36.

Ekman, P., & Friesen, W. (1972). Constants across culture in the face and emotion. *Journal of Personality and Social Psychology, 17,* 124–129.

Ekman, P., & Matsumoto, D. (2011). Reading faces: The universality of emotional expression. In M. A. Gernsbacher, R W. Pew, L. M. Hough, & J. R. Pomerantz (Eds.), *Psychology and the real world: Essays illustrating fundamental contributions to society* (pp. 140–146). New York: Worth.

Elfenbein, D. S., & Felice, M. E. (2003). Adolescent pregnancy. *Pediatric Clinics of North America, 50,* 781–800.

Elias, M. J., Parker, S., & Rosenblatt, J. L. (2005). Building educational opportunity. In S. Goldstein & R. B. Brooks (Eds.), *Handbook of resilience in children* (pp. 315–336). New York: Kluwer Academic.

Elias, V. L., Fullerton, A. S., & Simpson, J. M. (2013). Long-term changes in attitudes toward premarital sex in the United States: Reexamining the role of cohort replacement. *Journal of Sex Research.* Retrieved from www.tandfonline.com/doi/pdf/10.1080/00224499.2013 .798610#.VG49Z1fF9rE

Elicker, J., Englund, M., & Sroufe, L. A. (1992). Predicting peer competence and peer relationships in childhood from early parent–child relationships. In R. D. Parke & G. W. Ladd (Eds.), *Family–peer relationships: Modes of linkage* (pp. 77–106). Hillsdale, NJ: Erlbaum.

Elkind, D. (1994). *A sympathetic understanding of the child: Birth to sixteen* (3rd ed.). Boston: Allyn and Bacon.

Elkind, D., & Bowen, R. (1979). Imaginary audience behavior in children and adolescents. *Developmental Psychology, 15,* 33–44.

Elliott, J. G. (1999). School refusal: Issues of conceptualization, assessment, and treatment. *Journal of Child Psychology and Psychiatry and Allied Disciplines, 40,* 1001–1012.

Ellis, A. E., & Oakes, L. M. (2006). Infants flexibly use different dimensions to categorize objects. *Developmental Psychology, 42,* 1000–1011.

Ellis, B. J., & Essex, M. J. (2007). Family environments, adrenarche, and sexual maturation: A longitudinal test of a life history model. *Child Development, 78,* 1799–1817.

Ellis, B. J., Shirtcliff, E. A., Boyce, W. T., Deardorff, J., & Essex, M. J. (2011). Quality of early family relationships and the timing and tempo of puberty: Effects depend on biological sensitivity to context. *Development and Psychopathology, 23,* 85–99.

Ellis, L., & Bonin, S. L. (2003). Genetics and occupation-related preferences: Evidence from adoptive and non-adoptive families. *Personality and Individual Differences, 35,* 929–937.

Ellis, W. E., & Zarbatany, L. (2007). Explaining friendship formation and friendship stability: The role of children's and friends' aggression and victimization. *Merrill-Palmer Quarterly, 53,* 79–104.

Else-Quest, N. M. (2012). Gender differences in temperament. In M. Zentner & R. L. Shiner (Eds.), *Handbook of temperament* (pp. 479–496). New York: Guilford.

Else-Quest, N. M., Hyde, J. S., Goldsmith, H. H., & Van Hulle, C. A. (2006). Gender differences in temperament: A meta-analysis. *Psychological Bulletin, 132,* 33–72.

Else-Quest, N. M., Hyde, J. S., & Linn, M. C. (2010). Cross-national patterns of gender differences in mathematics: A meta-analysis. *Psychological Bulletin, 136,* 103–127.

El-Sheikh, M., Bub, K. L., Kelly, R. J., & Buckhalt, J. A. (2013). Children's sleep and adjustment: A residualized change analysis. *Developmental Psychology, 49,* 1591–1601.

El-Sheikh, M., Cummings, E. M., & Reiter, S. (1996). Preschoolers' responses to ongoing interadult conflict: The role of prior exposure to resolved versus unresolved arguments. *Journal of Abnormal Child Psychology, 24,* 665–679.

El-Sheikh, M., Kelly, R. J., Buckhalt, J. A., & Hinnant, B. (2010). Children's sleep and adjustment over time: The role of socioeconomic context. *Child Development, 81,* 870–883.

Eltzschig, H. K., Lieberman, E. S., & Camann, W. R. (2003). Regional anesthesia and analgesia for labor and delivery. *New England Journal of Medicine, 384,* 319–332.

Eluvathingal, T. J., Chugani, H. T., Behen, M. E., Juhasz, C., Muzik, O., Maqbook, M., et al. (2006). Abnormal brain connectivity in children after early severe socioemotional deprivation: A diffusion tensor imaging study. *Pediatrics, 117,* 2093–2100.

Emery, R. E., Sbarra, D., & Grover, T. (2005). Divorce mediation: Research and reflections. *Family Court Review, 43,* 22–37.

Ennemoser, M., & Schneider, W. (2007). Relations of television viewing and reading: Findings from a 4-year longitudinal study. *Journal of Educational Psychology, 99,* 349–368.

Entringer, S., Kumsta, R., Hellhammer, D. H., Wadhwa, P. D., & Wüst, S. (2009). Prenatal exposure to maternal psychosocial stress and HPA axis regulation in young adults. *Hormones and Behavior, 55,* 292–298.

Entwisle, D. R., Alexander, K. L., & Olson, L. S. (2005). First grade and educational attainment by age 22: A new story. *American Journal of Sociology, 110,* 1458–1502.

Epstein, L. H., Roemmich, J. N., & Raynor, H. A. (2001). Behavioral therapy in the treatment of pediatric obesity. *Pediatric Clinics of North America, 48,* 981–983.

Epstein, L. H., Saelens, B. E., Myers, M. D., & Vito, D. (1997). Effects of decreasing sedentary behaviors on activity choice in obese children. *Health Psychology, 16,* 107–113.

Erath, S. A., Bierman, K. L., & the Conduct Problems Prevention Research Group. (2006). Aggressive marital conflict, maternal harsh punishment, and child aggressive-disruptive behavior: Evidence for direct and mediate relations. *Journal of Family Psychology, 20,* 217–226.

Erdogan, B., Bauer, T. N., Truxillo, D. M., & Mansfield, L. R. (2012). Whistle while you work: A review of the life satisfaction literature. *Journal of Management, 38,* 1038–1083.

Erickson, J. D., Patterson, J. M., Wall, M., & Neumark-Sztainer, D. (2005). Risk behaviors and emotional well-being in youth with chronic health conditions. *Children's Health Care, 34,* 181–192.

Erikson, E. H. (1950). *Childhood and society*. New York: Norton.

Erikson, E. H. (1968). *Identity, youth, and crisis*. New York: Norton.

Ernst, M., Moolchan, E. T., & Robinson, M. L. (2001). Behavioral and neural consequences of prenatal exposure to nicotine. *Journal of the American Academy of Child and Adolescent Psychiatry, 40,* 630–641.

Ernst, M., & Spear, L. (2009). Reward systems. In M. de Haan & M. Gunnar (Eds.), *Handbook of developmental social neuroscience* (pp. 324–341). New York: Guilford.

Erol, R. Y., & Orth, U. (2011). Self-esteem development from age 14 to 30 years: A longitudinal study. *Journal of Personality and Social Psychology, 101,* 607–619.

Eshel, Y., & Kohavi, R. (2003). Perceived classroom control, self-regulated learning strategies, and academic achievement. *Educational Psychology, 23,* 249–260.

ESPAD (European School Project on Alcohol and Other Drugs). (2013). *A supplement to the 2011 ESPAD Report—Additional data from Bosnia and Herzegovina (Federation of Bosnia and Herzegovina), Kosovo (under UNSCR 1244) and the Netherlands.* Retrieved from www.espad.org/en/Reports--Documents/ESPAD-Reports

Esposito-Smythers, C., Weismoore, J., Zimmermann, R. P., & Spirito, A. (2014). Suicidal behaviors among children and adolescents. In M. Nock (Ed.), *Oxford handbook of suicide and self-injury* (pp. 61–81). New York: Oxford University Press.

Espy, K. A., Fang, H., Johnson, C., Stopp, C., & Wiebe, S. A. (2011). Prenatal tobacco exposure: Developmental outcomes in the neonatal period. *Developmental Psychology, 47,* 153–156.

Espy, K. A., Molfese, V. J., & DiLalla, L. F. (2001). Effects of environmental measures on intelligence in young children: Growth curve modeling of longitudinal data. *Merrill-Palmer Quarterly, 47,* 42–73.

Estourgie-van Burk, G. F., Bartels, M., van Beijsterveldt, T. C., Delemarre-van de Waal, H. A., & Boomsma, D. I. (2006). Body size in five-year-old twins: Heritability and comparison to singleton standards. *Twin Research and Human Genetics, 9,* 646–655.

Evanoo, G. (2007). Infant crying: A clinical conundrum. *Journal of Pediatric Health Care, 21,* 333–338.

Evans, G. W. (2003). A multimethodological analysis of cumulative risk and allostatic load among rural children. *Developmental Psychology, 39,* 924–933.

Evans, G. W. (2006). Child development and the physical environment. *Annual Review of Psychology, 57,* 424–451.

Evans, G. W., Fuller-Rowell, T. E., & Doan, S. N. (2012). Childhood cumulative risk and obesity: The mediating role of self-regulatory ability. *Pediatrics, 129,* e68–e73.

Evans, G. W., Gonnella, C., Marcynyszn, L. A. Gentile, L., & Slapekar, N. (2005). The role of chaos in poverty and children's socioemotional adjustment. *Psychological Science, 16,* 560–565.

Evans, G. W., & Schamberg, M. A. (2009). Childhood poverty, chronic stress, and adult working memory. *Proceedings of the National Academy of Sciences, 106,* 6545–6549.

Evans, N., & Levinson, S. C. (2009). The myth of language universals: Language diversity and its importance for cognitive science. *Behavioral and Brain Sciences, 32,* 429–492.

Exner-Cortens, D., Eckenrode, J., & Rothman, E. (2012). Longitudinal associations between teen dating violence victimization and adverse health outcomes. *Pediatrics, 131,* 71–78.

Eyler, L. T., Pierce, K., & Courchesne, E. (2012). A failure of left temporal cortex to specialize for language is an early emerging and fundamental property of autism. *Brain, 135,* 949–960.

F

Fabes, R. A., Eisenberg, N., Hanish, L. D., & Spinrad, T. L. (2001). Preschoolers' spontaneous emotion vocabulary: Relations to likability. *Early Education and Development, 12,* 11–27.

Fabes, R. A., Eisenberg, N., McCormick, S. E., & Wilson, M. S. (1988). Preschoolers' attributions of the situational determinants of others' naturally occurring emotions. *Developmental Psychology, 24,* 376–385.

Fabes, R. A., Martin, C. L., & Hanish, L. D. (2003). Young children's play qualities in same-, other-, and mixed-sex peer groups. *Child Development, 74,* 921–932.

Fagan, J. F., & Holland, C. R. (2007). Racial equality in intelligence: Predictions from a theory of intelligence as processing. *Intelligence, 35,* 319–334.

Fagan, J. F., Holland, C. R., & Wheeler, K. (2007). The prediction, from infancy, of adult IQ and achievement. *Intelligence, 35,* 225–231.

Fagan, J. F., III. (1973). Infants' delayed recognition memory and forgetting. *Journal of Experimental Child Psychology, 16,* 424–450.

Fagard, J., & Pezé, A. (1997). Age changes in interlimb coupling and the development of bimanual coordination. *Journal of Motor Behavior, 29,* 199–208.

Fagard, J., Spelke, E., & von Hofsten, C. (2009). Reaching and grasping a moving object in 6-, 8-, and 10-month-old infants: Laterality and performance. *Infant Behavior and Development, 32,* 137–146.

Fagot, B. I. (1985). Changes in thinking about early sex role development. *Developmental Review, 5,* 83–98.

Fagot, B. I., & Hagan, R. I. (1991). Observations of parent reactions to sex-stereotyped behaviors: Age and sex effects. *Child Development, 62,* 617–628.

Fahrmeier, E. D. (1978). The development of concrete operations among the Hausa. *Journal of Cross-Cultural Psychology, 9,* 23–44.

Fairburn, C. G., & Harrison, P. J. (2003). Eating disorders. *Lancet, 361,* 407–416.

Faircloth, B. S., & Hamm, J. V. (2005). Sense of belonging among high school students representing four ethnic groups. *Journal of Youth and Adolescence, 34,* 293–309.

Falagas, M. E., & Zarkadoulia, E. (2008). Factors associated with suboptimal compliance to vaccinations in children in developed countries: A systematic review. *Current Medical Research and Opinion, 24,* 1719–1741.

Falbo, T. (2012). Only children: An updated review. *Journal of Individual Psychology, 68,* 38–49.

Falbo, T., Poston, D. L., Jr., Triscari, R. S., & Zhang, X. (1997). Self-enhancing illusions among Chinese schoolchildren. *Journal of Cross-Cultural Psychology, 28,* 172–191.

Falk, D. (2005). Brain lateralization in primates and its evolution in hominids. *American Journal of Physical Anthropology, 30,* 107–125.

Fantz, R. L. (1961, May). The origin of form perception. *Scientific American, 204*(5), 66–72.

Faraone, S. V., Biederman, J., & Mick, E. (2006). The age-dependent decline of attention deficit hyperactivity disorder: A meta-analysis of follow-up studies. *Psychological Medicine, 36,* 159–165.

Farmer, T. W., Irvin, M. J., Leung, M.-C., Hall, C. M., Hutchins, B. C., & McDonough, E. (2010). Social preference, social prominence, and group membership in late elementary school: Homophilic concentration and peer affiliation configurations. *Social Psychology of Education, 13,* 271–293.

Farr, R. H., Forssell, S. L., & Patterson, C. J. (2010). Parenting and child development in adoptive families: Does parental sexual orientation matter? *Applied Developmental Science, 14,* 164–178.

Farrant, K., & Reese, E. (2000). Maternal style and children's participation in reminiscing: Stepping stones in children's autobiographical memory development. *Journal of Cognition and Development, 1,* 193–225.

Farrington, D. P. (2009). Conduct disorder, aggression and delinquency. In R. M. Lerner & L. Steinberg (Eds.), *Handbook of adolescent psychology: Vol. 1. Individual bases of adolescent development* (3rd ed., pp. 683–722). Hoboken, NJ: Wiley.

Farrington, D. P., Ttofi, M. M., & Coid, J. W. (2009). Development of adolescence-limited, late-onset, and persistent offenders from age 8 to age 48. *Aggressive Behavior, 35,* 150–163.

Farroni, T., Csibra, G., Simion, F., & Johnson, M. H. (2002). Eye contact detection in humans from birth. *Proceedings of the National Academy of Sciences, 99,* 9602–9605.

Farroni, T., Massaccesi, S., Menon, E., & Johnson, M. H. (2007). Direct gaze modulates face recognition in young infants. *Cognition, 102,* 396–404.

Farver, J. M., & Branstetter, W. H. (1994). Preschoolers' prosocial responses to their peers' distress. *Developmental Psychology, 30,* 334–341.

Fasula, A. M., & Miller, K. S. (2006). African-American and Hispanic adolescents' intentions to delay first intercourse: Parental communication as a buffer for sexually active peers. *Journal of Adolescent Health, 38,* 193–200.

Fearon, R. P., Bakermans-Kranenburg, M. J., Lapsley, A., & Roisman, G. I. (2010). The significance of insecure attachment and disorganization in the development of children's externalizing behavior: A meta-analystic study. *Child Development, 81,* 435–456.

Federal Interagency Forum on Child and Family Statistics. (2013). *America's children: Key national indicators of well-being.* Retrieved from www.childstats.gov/pdf/ac2013/ac_13.pdf

Feeney, J. A., Hohaus, L., Noller, P., & Alexander, R. P. (2001). *Becoming parents: Exploring the bonds between mothers, fathers, and their infants*. New York: Cambridge University Press.

Feigelman, W., & Gorman, B. S. (2008). Assessing the effects of peer suicide on youth suicide. *Suicide and Life-Threatening Behavior, 38,* 181–194.

Feinberg, M. E., McHale, S. M., Crouter, A. C., & Cumsille, P. (2003). Sibling differentiation: Sibling and parent relationship trajectories in adolescence. *Child Development, 74,* 1261–1274.

Feldman, A. F., & Matjasko, J. L. (2007). Profiles and portfolios of adolescent school-based extracurricular activity participation. *Journal of Adolescence, 30,* 313–332.

Feldman, R. (2003). Infant–mother and infant–father synchrony: The coregulation of positive arousal. *Infant Mental Health Journal, 24,* 1–23.

Feldman, R. (2006). From biological rhythms to social rhythms: Physiological precursors of mother–infant synchrony. *Developmental Psychology, 42,* 175–188.

Feldman, R. (2007a). Maternal–infant contact and child development: Insights from the kangaroo intervention. In L. L'Abate (Ed.), *Low-cost approaches to promote physical and mental health: Theory, research, and practice* (pp. 323–351). New York: Springer.

Feldman, R. (2007b). Maternal versus child risk and the development of parent–child and family relationships in five high-risk populations. *Development and Psychopathology, 19,* 293–312.

Feldman, R. (2007c). Parent–infant synchrony and the construction of shared timing: Physiological precursors, developmental outcomes, and risk conditions. *Journal of Child Psychology and Psychiatry, 48,* 329–354.

Feldman, R., Eidelman, A. I., & Rotenberg, N. (2004). Parenting stress, infant emotion regulation, maternal sensitivity, and the cognitive development of triplets: A model for parent and child influences in a unique ecology. *Child Development, 75,* 1774–1791.

Feldman, R., Gordon, I., Schneiderman, I., Weisman, O., & Zagoory-Sharon, O. (2010). Natural variations in maternal and paternal care are associated with systematic changes in oxytocin following parent–infant contact. *Psychoneuroendocrinology, 35,* 1133–1141.

Feldman, R., Granat, A., Pariente, C., Kanety, H., Kuint, J., & Gilboa-Schechtman, E. (2009). Maternal depression and anxiety across the postpartum year and infant social engagement, fear regulation, and stress reactivity. *Journal of the American Academy of Child and Adolescent Psychiatry, 48*, 919–927.

Feldman, R., & Klein, P. S. (2003). Toddlers' self-regulated compliance to mothers, caregivers, and fathers: Implications for theories of socialization. *Developmental Psychology, 39*, 680–692.

Feldman, R., Sussman, A. L., & Zigler, E. (2004). Parental leave and work adaptation at the transition to parenthood: Individual, marital, and social correlates. *Journal of Applied Developmental Psychology, 25*, 459–479.

Felner, R. D., Favazza, A., Shim, M., Brand, S., Gu, K., & Noonan, N. (2002). Whole school improvement and restructuring as prevention and promotion: Lessons from STEP and the Project on High Performance Learning Communities. *Journal of School Psychology, 39*, 177–202.

Felsman, D. E., & Blustein, D. L. (1999). The role of peer relatedness in late adolescent career development. *Journal of Vocational Behavior, 54*, 279–295.

Fenson, L., Dale, P. S., Reznick, J. S., Bates, E., Thal, D. J., & Pethick, S. J. (1994). Variability in early communicative development. *Monographs of the Society for Research in Child Development, 59*(5, Serial No. 242).

Ferguson, C. J. (2013). Spanking, corporal punishment and negative long-term outcomes: A meta-analytic review of longitudinal studies. *Clinical Psychology Review, 33*, 196–288.

Ferguson, T. J., Stegge, H., & Damhuis, I. (1991). Children's understanding of guilt and shame. *Child Development, 62*, 827–839.

Fernald, A., & Marchman, V. A. (2012). Individual differences in lexical processing at 18 months predict vocabulary growth in typically developing and late-talking toddlers. *Child Development, 82*, 203–222.

Fernald, A., Marchman, V. A., & Weisleder, A. (2013). SES differences in language processing skill and vocabulary are evident at 18 months. *Developmental Science, 16*, 234–248.

Fernald, A., & Morikawa, H. (1993). Common themes and cultural variations in Japanese and American mothers' speech to infants. *Child Development, 64*, 637–656.

Fernald, A., Perfors, A., & Marchman, V. A. (2006). Picking up speed in understanding: Speech processing efficiency and vocabulary growth across the 2nd year. *Developmental Psychology, 42*, 98–116.

Fernald, A., Taeschner, T., Dunn, J., Papousek, M, Boysson-Bardies, B., & Fukui, I. (1989). A cross-language study of prosodic modifications in mothers' and fathers' speech to preverbal infants. *Journal of Child Language, 16*, 477–502.

Fernald, L. C., & Grantham-McGregor, S. M. (1998). Stress response in school-age children who have been growth-retarded since early childhood. *American Journal of Clinical Nutrition, 68*, 691–698.

Fernyhough, C., & Fradley, E. (2005). Private speech on an executive task: Relations with task difficulty and task performance. *Cognitive Development, 20*, 103–120.

Ferrando, M., Prieto, M. D., Almeida, L. S., Ferándiz, C., Bermejo, R., López-Pina, J. A., et al. (2011). Trait emotional intelligence and academic performance: Controlling for the effects of IQ, personality, and self-concept. *Journal of Psychoeducational Assessment, 29*, 150–159.

Ferrari, P. F., & Coudé, G. (2011). Mirror neurons and imitation from a developmental and evolutionary perspective. In A. Vilain, C. Abry, J.-L. Schwartz, & J. Vauclair (Eds.), *Primate communication and human language* (pp. 121–138). Amsterdam, Netherlands: John Benjamins.

Ferrari, P. F., Tramacere, A., Simpson, E. A., & Iriki, A. (2013). Mirror neurons through the lens of epigenetics. *Trends in Cognitive Sciences, 17*, 450–457.

Ferrari, P. F., Visalberghi E., Paukner A., Fogassi L., Ruggiero A., Suomi, S. (2006). Neonatal imitation in rhesus macaques. *PLOS Biology, 4*, e302.

Ferry, A. L., Hespos, S. J., & Waxman, S. R. (2010). Categorization in 3- and 4-month-old infants: An advantage of words over tones. *Child Development, 81*, 472–479.

Ficca, G., Fagioli, I., Giganti, F., & Salzarulo, P. (1999). Spontaneous awakenings from sleep in the first year of life. *Early Human Development, 55*, 219–228.

Field, T. (2001). Massage therapy facilitates weight gain in preterm infants. *Current Directions in Psychological Science, 10*, 51–54.

Field, T. (2011). Prenatal depression effects on early development: A review. *Infant Behavior and Development, 34*, 1–14.

Field, T., Hernandez-Reif, M., & Freedman, J. (2004) Stimulation programs for preterm infants. *Social Policy Report of the Society for Research in Child Development, 18*(1).

Field, T. M. (1998). Massage therapy effects. *American Psychologist, 53*, 1270–1281.

Fiese, B. H., Foley, K. P., & Spagnola, M. (2006). Routine and ritual elements in family mealtimes: Contexts for child wellbeing and family identity. *New Directions for Child and Adolescent Development, 111*, 67–90.

Fiese, B. H., & Schwartz, M. (2008). Reclaiming the family table: Mealtimes and child health and well-being. *Social Policy Report of the Society for Research in Child Development, 22*(4), 3–18.

Fiese, B. H., & Winter, M. A. (2010). The dynamics of family chaos and its relation to children's socioemotional well-being. In G. W. Evans & T. D. Wachs (Eds.), *Chaos and its influence on children's development: An ecological perspective* (pp. 49–66). Washington, DC: American Psychological Association.

Fifer, W. P., Byrd, D. L., Kaku, M., Eigsti, I. M., Isler, J. R., Grose-Fifer, J., et al. (2010). Newborn infants learn during sleep. *Proceedings of the National Academy of Sciences, 107*, 10320–10323.

Figner, B., Mackinlay, R. J., Wilkening, F., & Weber, E. U. (2009). Affective and deliberative processes in risky choice: Age differences in risk taking in the Columbia Card Task. *Journal of Experimental Psychology: Learning, Memory, and Cognition, 35*, 709–770.

Findlay, L. C., & Coplan, R. J. (2008). Come out and play: Shyness in childhood and the benefits of organized sports participation. *Canadian Journal of Behavioural Science, 40*, 153–161.

Finer, L. B., & Philbin, J. M. (2013). Sexual initiation, contraceptive use, and pregnancy among young adolescents. *Pediatrics, 131*, 1–6.

Finger, B., Hans, S. L., Bernstein, V. J., & Cox, S. M. (2009). Parent relationship quality and infant–mother attachment. *Attachment and Human Development, 11*, 285–306.

Fingerhut, L. A., & Christoffel, K. K. (2002). Firearm-related death and injury among children and adolescents. *Future of Children, 12*, 25–37.

Finkel, E. J., Eastwick, P. W., Karney, B. R., Reis, H. T., & Sprecher, S. (2012). Online dating: A critical analysis from the perspective of psychological science. *Psychological Science in the Public Interest, 13*, 3–66.

Finkelhor, D. (2009). The prevention of childhood sexual abuse. *Future of Children, 19*, 169–194.

Finn, J. D., Gerber, S. B., & Boyd-Zaharias, J. (2005). Small classes in the early grades, academic achievement, and graduating from high school. *Journal of Educational Psychology, 97*, 214–233.

Finnilä, K., Mahlberga, N., Santtilia, P., & Niemib, P. (2003). Validity of a test of children's suggestibility for predicting responses to two interview situations differing in degree of suggestiveness. *Journal of Experimental Child Psychology, 85*, 32–49.

Fischer, K. W., & Bidell, T. (1991). Constraining nativisit inferences about cognitive capacities. In S. Carey & R. Gelman (Eds.), *The epigenesis of mind: Essays on biology and cognition* (pp. 199–235). Hillsdale, NJ: Erlbaum.

Fischer, K. W., & Bidell, T. R. (2006). Dynamic development of action and thought. In R. M. Lerner (Ed.), *Handbook of child psychology: Vol. 1. Theoretical models of human development* (6th ed., pp. 313–399). Hoboken, NJ: Wiley.

Fischman, M. G., Moore, J. B., & Steele, K. H. (1992). Children's one-hand catching as a function of age, gender, and ball location. *Research Quarterly for Exercise and Sport, 63*, 349–355.

Fish, M. (2004). Attachment in infancy and preschool in low socioeconomic status rural Appalachian children: Stability and change and relations to preschool and kindergarten competence. *Development and Psychopathology, 16*, 293–312.

Fisher, C. B. (1993, Winter). Integrating science and ethics in research with high-risk children and youth. *Social Policy Report of the Society for Research in Child Development, 4*(4).

Fisher, C. B., Hoagwood, K., Boyce, C., Duster, T., Frank, D. A., & Grisso, T. (2002). Research ethics for mental health science involving ethnic minority children and youths. *American Psychologist, 57*, 1024–1040.

Fisher, J. O., Mitchell, D. S., Smiciklas-Wright, H., & Birch, L. L. (2001). Maternal milk consumption predicts the tradeoff between milk and soft drinks in young girls' diets. *Journal of Nutrition, 131*, 246–250.

Fisher, J. O., Rolls, B. J., & Birch, L. L. (2003). Children's bite size and intake of an entrée are greater with large portions than with age-appropriate or self-selected portions. *American Journal of Clinical Nutrition, 77*, 1164–1170.

Fite, P. J., Stauffacher, K., Ostrov, J. M., & Colder, C. R. (2008). Replication and extension of Little et al.'s (2003) forms and functions of aggression measure. *International Journal of Behavioral Development, 32*, 238–242.

Fivush, R. (2001). Owning experience: Developing subjective perspective in autobiographical narratives. In C. Moore & K. Lemmon (Eds.), *The self in time: Developmental perspectives* (pp. 35–52). Mahwah, NJ: Erlbaum.

Fivush, R. (2009). Sociocultural perspectives on autobiographical memory. In M. L. Courage & N. Cowan (Eds.), *The development of memory in infancy and childhood* (pp. 283–301). Hove, UK: Psychology Press.

Fivush, R. (2011). The development of autobiographical memory. *Annual Review of Psychology, 62*, 559–582.

Fivush, R., & Haden, C. A. (2005). Parent–child reminiscing and the construction of a subjective self. In B. D. Homer & C. S. Tamis-LeMonda (Eds.), *The development of social cognition and communication* (pp. 315–336). Mahwah, NJ: Erlbaum.

Fivush, R., & Wang, Q. (2005). Emotion talk in mother–child conversations of the shared past: The effects of culture, gender, and event valence. *Journal of Cognition and Development, 6*, 489–506.

Flak, A. L., Su, S., Bertrand, J., Denny, C. H., Kesmodel, U. S., & Cogswell, M. E. (2014). The association of mild, moderate, and binge prenatal alcohol exposure and child neuropsychological outcomes: A meta-analysis. *Alcoholism: Clinical and Experimental Research, 38*, 214–226.

Flanagan, C., & Levine, P. (2010). Civic engagement and the transition to adulthood. *Future of Children, 20*, 159–179.

Flanagan, C. A., Stout, M., & Gallay, L. S. (2008). It's my body and none of your business: Developmental changes in adolescents' perceptions of rights concerning health. *Journal of Social Issues, 64*, 815–834.

Flanagan, C. A., & Tucker, C. J. (1999). Adolescents' explanations for political issues: Concordance with their views of self and society. *Developmental Psychology, 35*, 1198–1209.

Flannery, D. J., Hussey, D. L., Biebelhausen, L., & Wester, K. L. (2003). Crime, delinquency, and youth gangs. In G. R. Adams & M. D. Berzonsky (Eds.), *Blackwell handbook of adolescence* (pp. 502–522). Malden, MA: Blackwell.

Flavell, J. H., Flavell, E. R., & Green, F. L. (2001). Development of children's understanding of connections between thinking and feeling. *Psychological Science, 12*, 430–432.

Flavell, J. H., Green, F. L., & Flavell, E. R. (1987). Development of knowledge about the appearance–reality distinction. *Monographs of the Society for Research in Child Development, 51*(1, Serial No. 212).

Flavell, J. H., Green, F. L., & Flavell, E. R. (1995). Young children's knowledge about thinking. *Monographs of the Society for Research in Child Development, 60*(1, Serial No. 243).

Flavell, J. H., Green, F. L., Flavell, E. R., & Grossman, J. B. (1997). The development of children's knowledge about inner speech. *Child Development, 68*, 39–47.

Fletcher, A. C., Nickerson, P., & Wright, K. L. (2003). Structured leisure activities in middle childhood: Links to well-being. *Journal of Community Psychology, 31*, 641–659.

Fletcher, E. N., Whitaker, R. C., Marino, A. J., & Anderson, S. E. (2014). Screen time at home and school among low-income children attending Head Start. *Child Indicators Research, 7*, 421–436.

Floccia, C., Christophe, A., & Bertoncini, J. (1997). High-amplitude sucking and newborns: The quest for underlying mechanisms. *Journal of Experimental Child Psychology, 64*, 175–198.

Flom, R. (2013). Intersensory perception of faces and voices in infants. In P. Belin, S. Campanella, & T. Ethofer (Eds.),

Integrating face and voice in person perception (pp. 71–93). New York: Springer.

Flom, R., & Bahrick, L. E. (2007). The development of infant discrimination of affect in multimodal and unimodal stimulation: The role of intersensory redundancy. *Developmental Psychology, 43,* 238–252.

Flom, R., & Bahrick, L. E. (2010). The effects of intersensory redundancy on attention and memory: Infants' long-term memory for orientation in audiovisual events. *Developmental Psychology, 46,* 428–436.

Flom, R., & Pick, A. D. (2003). Verbal encouragement and joint attention in 18-month-old infants. *Infant Behavior and Development, 26,* 121–134.

Flouri, E., & Buchanan, A. (2004). Early father's and mother's involvement and child's later educational outcomes. *British Journal of Educational Psychology, 74,* 141–153.

Flynn, E., & Siegler, R. (2007). Measuring change: Current trends and future directions in microgenetic research. *Infant and Child Development, 16,* 135–149.

Flynn, J. R. (1999). Searching for justice: The discovery of IQ gains over time. *American Psychologist, 54,* 5–20.

Flynn, J. R. (2007). *What is intelligence? Beyond the Flynn effect.* New York: Cambridge University Press.

Flynn, J. R., & Rossi-Casé, L. (2011). Modern women match men on Raven's Progressive Matrices. *Personality and Individual Differences, 50,* 799–803.

Foehr, U. G. (2006). *Media multitasking among American youth: Prevalence, predictors, and pairings.* Menlo Park, CA: Kaiser Family Foundation.

Foerde, K., Knowlton, B. J., & Poldrack, R. A. (2006). Modulation of competing memory systems by distraction. *Proceedings of the National Academy of Sciences, 103,* 11778–11783.

Fogel, A., & Garvey, A. (2007). Alive communication. *Infant Behavior and Development, 30,* 251–257.

Fomon, S. J., & Nelson, S. E. (2002). Body composition of the male and female reference infants. *Annual Review of Nutrition, 22,* 1–17.

Fonnesbeck, C. J., McPheeters, M. L., Krishnaswami, S., Lindegren, M. L., & Reimschisel, T. (2013). Estimating the probability of IQ impairment from blood phenylalanine for phenylketonuria patients: A hierarchical meta-analysis. *Journal of Inherited Metabolic Disease, 36,* 757–766.

Forcada-Guex, M., Pierrehumbert, B., Borghini, A., Moessinger, A., & Muller-Nix, C. (2006). Early dyadic patterns of mother–infant interactions and outcomes of prematurity at 18 months. *Pediatrics, 118e,* 107–114.

Ford, D. Y. (2012). Gifted and talented education: History, issues, and recommendations. In K. R. Harris, S. Graham, T. Urdan, S. Graham, J. M. Royer, & M. Zeidner (Eds.), *APA educational psychology handbook: Vol. 2. Individual differences and cultural contextual factors* (pp. 83–110). Washington, DC: American Psychological Association.

Ford, L., Kozey, M. L., & Negreiros, J. (2012). Cognitive assessment in early childhood: Theoretical and practical perspectives. In D. P. Flanagan & P. L. Harrison (Eds.), *Contemporary intellectual assessment: Theories, tests, and issues* (pp. 585–622). New York: Guilford.

Fordham, K., & Stevenson-Hinde, J. (1999). Shyness, friendship quality, and adjustment during middle childhood. *Journal of Child Psychology and Psychiatry, 40,* 757–768.

Forman, D. R., Aksan, N., & Kochanska, G. (2004). Toddlers' responsive imitation predicts preschool-age conscience. *Psychological Science, 15,* 699–704.

Forman, D. R., O'Hara, M. W., Stuart, S., Gorman, L. L., Larsen, K. E., & Coy, K. C. (2007). Effective treatment for postpartum depression is not sufficient to improve the developing mother–child relationship. *Development and Psychopathology, 19,* 585–602.

Foster, W. A., & Miller, M. (2007). Development of the literacy achievement gap: A longitudinal study of kindergarten through third grade. *Language, Speech, and Hearing Services in Schools, 38,* 173–181.

Fox, C. L., & Boulton, M. J. (2006). Friendship as a moderator of the relationship between social skills problems and peer victimization. *Aggressive Behavior, 32,* 110–121.

Fox, N. A., & Davidson, R. J. (1986). Taste-elicited changes in facial signs of emotion and the asymmetry of brain electrical activity in newborn infants. *Neuropsychologia, 24,* 417–422.

Fox, N. A., Henderson, H. A., Pérez-Edgar, K., & White, L. K. (2008). The biology of temperament: An integrative approach. In C. A. Nelson & M. Luciana (Eds.), *Handbook of developmental cognitive neuroscience* (2nd ed., pp. 839–853). Cambridge, MA: MIT Press.

Fox, N. A., Nelson, C. A., III, & Zeanah, C. H. (2013). The effects of early severe psychosocial deprivation on children's cognitive and social development: Lessons from the Bucharest Early Intervention Project. In N. S. Landale, S. M. McHale, & A. Booth (Eds.), *Families and child health* (pp. 33–41). New York: Springer Science + Business Media.

Foy, J. G., & Mann, V. (2003). Home literacy environment and phonological awareness in preschool children: Differential effects for rhyme and phoneme awareness. *Applied Psycholinguistics, 24,* 59–88.

Fraiberg, S. (1971). *Insights from the blind.* New York: Basic Books.

Franchak, J. M., & Adolph, K. E. (2012). What infants know and what they do: Perceiving possibilities for walking through openings. *Developmental Psychology, 48,* 1254–1261.

Franco, P., Danias, A. P., Akamine, E. H., Kawamoto, E. M., Fortes, Z. B., Scavone, C., & Tostes, R. C. (2002). Enhanced oxidative stress as a potential mechanism underlying the programming of hypertension in utero. *Journal of Cardiovascular Pharmacology, 40,* 501–509.

Frank, J. B., Jarit, G. J., Bravman, J. T., & Rosen, J. E. (2007). Lower extremity injuries in the skeletally immature athlete. *Journal of the American Academy of Orthopaedic Surgeons, 15,* 356–366.

Franklin, V. P. (2012). "The teachers' unions strike back?" No need to wait for "Superman": Magnet schools have brought success to urban public school students for over 30 years. In D. T. Slaughter-Defoe, H. C. Stevenson, E. G. Arrington, & D. J. Johnson (Eds.), *Black educational choice: Assessing the private and public alternative to traditional K-12 public schools* (pp. 217–220). Santa Barbara, CA: Praeger.

Franks, P. W., Hanson, R. L., Knowler, W. C., Sievers, M. L., Bennett, P. H., & Looker, H. C. (2010). Childhood obesity, other cardiovascular risk factors, and premature death. *New England Journal of Medicine, 362,* 485–493.

Frazier, B. N., Gelman, S. A., & Welman, H. M. (2009). Preschoolers' search for explanatory information within adult–child conversation. *Child Development, 80,* 1592–1611.

Fredricks, J. A. (2012). Extracurricular participation and academic outcomes: Testing the overscheduling hypothesis. *Journal of Youth and Adolescence, 41,* 295–306.

Fredricks, J. A., & Eccles, J. S. (2002). Children's competence and value beliefs from childhood through adolescence: Growth trajectories in two male-sex-typed domains. *Developmental Psychology, 38,* 519–533.

Fredricks, J. A., & Eccles, J. S. (2006). Is extracurricular participation associated with beneficial outcomes? Concurrent and longitudinal relations. *Developmental Psychology, 42,* 698–713.

Freeman, D. (1983). *Margaret Mead and Samoa: The making and unmaking of an anthropological myth.* Cambridge, MA: Harvard University Press.

Freeman, H., & Newland, L. A. (2010). New directions in father attachment. *Early Child Development and Care, 180,* 1–8.

Freitag, C. M., Rohde, L. A., Lempp, T., & Romanos, M. (2010). Phenotypic and measurement influences on heritability estimates in childhood ADHD. *European Child and Adolescent Psychiatry, 19,* 311–323.

Frejka, T., Sobotka, T., Hoem, J. M., & Toulemon, L. (2008). Childbearing trends and policies in Europe. *Demographic Research, 19,* 5–14.

French, D. C., Chen, X., Chung, J., Li, M., Chen, H., & Li, D. (2011). Four children and one toy: Chinese and Canadian children faced with potential conflict over a limited resource. *Child Development, 82,* 830–841.

French, S. A., & Story, M. (2013). Commentary on nutrition standards in the national school lunch and breakfast programs. *The Journal of the American Medical Association Pediatrics, 167,* 8–9.

Freud, A. (1969). Adolescence as a developmental disturbance. In G. Caplan & S. Lebovici (Eds.), *Adolescence* (pp. 5–10). New York: Basic Books.

Freud, S. (1973). *An outline of psychoanalysis.* London: Hogarth. (Original work published 1938)

Frey, A., Ruchkin, V., Martin, A., & Schwab-Stone, M. (2009). Adolescents in transition: School and family characteristics in the development of violent behaviors entering high school. *Child Psychiatry and Human Development, 40,* 1–13.

Friedlmeier, W., Corapci, F., & Cole, P. M. (2011). Socialization of emotions in cross-cultural perspective. *Social and Personality Psychology Compass, 5,* 410–427.

Fries, A. B. W., & Pollak, S. D. (2004). Emotion understanding in postinstitutionalized Eastern European children. *Development and Psychopathology, 16,* 355–369.

Fries, A. B. W., Ziegler, T. E., Kurian, J. R., Jacoris, S., & Pollak, S. D. (2005). Early experience in humans is associated with changes in neuropeptides critical for regulating social behavior. *Proceedings of the National Academy of Sciences, 102,* 17237–17240.

Frontline. (2012). *Poor kids.* Retrieved from www.pbs.org/wgbh/pages/frontline/poor-kids

Fry, D. P. (2014). Environment of evolutionary adaptedness, rough-and-tumble play, and the selection of restraint in human aggression. In D. Narvaez, K. Valentino, A. Fuentes, J. J. McKenna, & P. Gray (Eds.), *Ancestral landscapes in human evolution: Culture, childrearing and social wellbeing* (pp. 169–188). New York: Oxford University Press.

Fryer, S. L., Crocker, N. A., & Mattson, S. N. (2008). Exposure to teratogenic agents as a risk factor for psychopathology. In T. P. Beauchaine & S. P. Hinshaw (Eds.), *Child and adolescent psychopathology* (pp. 180–207). Hoboken, NJ: Wiley.

Fu, G., Xu, F., Cameron, C. A., Heyman, G., & Lee, K. (2007). Cross-cultural differences in children's choices, categorizations, and evaluations of truths and lies. *Developmental Psychology, 43,* 278–293.

Fulcher, M., Sutfin, E. L., & Patterson, C. J. (2008). Individual differences in gender development: Associations with parental sexual orientation, attitudes, and division of labor. *Sex Roles, 58,* 330–341.

Fuligni, A. J. (1998). Authority, autonomy, and parent–adolescent conflict and cohesion: A study of adolescents from Mexican, Chinese, Filipino, and European backgrounds. *Developmental Psychology, 34,* 782–792.

Fuligni, A. J. (2004). The adaptation and acculturation of children from immigrant families. In U. P. Gielen & J. Roopnarine (Eds.), *Childhood and adolescence: Cross-cultural perspectives* (pp. 297–318). Westport, CT: Praeger.

Fuligni, A. J. (2007). Family obligation, college enrollment, and emerging adulthood in Asian and Latin American families. *Child Development Perspectives, 1,* 96–100.

Fuligni, A. S., Han, W.-J., & Brooks-Gunn, J. (2004). The Infant–Toddler HOME in the 2nd and 3rd years of life. *Parenting: Science and Practice, 4,* 139–159.

Fuller, C., Keller, L., Olson, J., Plymale, A., & Gottesman, M. (2005). Helping preschoolers become healthy eaters. *Journal of Pediatric Health Care, 19,* 178–182.

Fuller-Thomson, E., & Minkler, M. (2005). Native American grandparents raising grandchildren: Findings from the Census 2000 Supplementary Survey and implications for social work practice. *Social Work, 50,* 131–139.

Fuller-Thomson, E., & Minkler, M. (2007). Mexican American grandparents raising grandchildren: Findings from the Census 2000 American Community Survey. *Families in Society, 88,* 567–574.

Fullerton, J. T., Navarro, A. M., & Young, S. H. (2007). Outcomes of planned home birth: An integrative review. *Journal of Midwifery and Women's Health, 52,* 323–333.

Fuqua, J. S., & Rogol, A. D. (2013). Puberty: Its role in adolescent maturation. In W. T. O'Donohue, L. T. Benuto, & L. Woodword Tolle (Eds.), *Handbook of adolescent health psychology* (pp. 245–270). New York: Springer.

Furman, W., & Buhrmester, D. (1992). Age and sex differences in perceptions of networks of personal relationships. *Child Development, 63,* 103–115.

Furman, W., & Collins, W. A. (2009). Adolescent romantic relationships and experiences. In K. Rubin, W. M. Bukowski, & B. Laursen (Eds.), *Handbook of peer interactions, relationships, and groups* (pp. 341–360). New York: Guilford.

Furman, W., Simon, V. A., Shaffer, L., & Bouchey, H. A. (2002). Adolescents' working models and styles for relationships with parents, friends, and romantic partners. *Child Development, 73,* 241–255.

Furnham, A. (2009). Sex differences in mate selection preferences. *Personality and Individual Differences, 47,* 262–267.

Furusawa, T., Naka, I., Yamauchi, T., Natsuhara, K., Kimura, R., Nakazawa, M., et al. (2010). The Q223r polymorphism in LEPR is associated with obesity in Pacific Islanders. *Human Genetics, 127,* 287–294.

Fushiki, S. (2013). Radiation hazards in children—lessons from Chernobyl, Three Mile Island and Fukushima. *Brain & Development, 35,* 220–227.

Fuson, K. C. (2009). Avoiding misinterpretations of Piaget and Vygotsky: Mathematical teaching without learning, learning without teaching, or helpful learning-path teaching? *Cognitive Development, 24,* 343–361.

Fuson, K. C., & Burghard, B. H. (2003). Multidigit addition and subtraction methods invented in small groups and teacher support of problem solving and reflection. In A. J. Baroody & A. Dowker (Eds.), *The development of arithmetic concepts and skills* (pp. 267–304). Mahwah, NJ: Erlbaum.

G

Gagnon, J. C., & Leone, P. E. (2002). Alternative strategies for school violence prevention. In R. J. Skiba & G. G. Noam (Eds.), *Zero tolerance: Can suspension and expulsion keep school safe?* (pp. 101–125). San Francisco: Jossey-Bass.

Gakidou, E., Cowling, K., Lozano, R., & Murray, C. J. L. (2010). Increased educational attainment and its effect on child mortality in 175 countries between 1970 and 2009: A systematic analysis. *Lancet, 376,* 959–974.

Galambos, N. L., Berenbaum, S. A., & McHale, S. M. (2009). Gender development in adolescence. In R. M. Lerner & L. Steinberg (Eds.), *Handbook of adolescent psychology: Vol. 1. Individual bases of adolescent development* (3rd ed., pp. 305–357). Hoboken, NJ: Wiley.

Galambos, N. L., & Martínez, M. L. (2007). Poised for emerging adulthood in Latin America: A pleasure for the privileged. *Child Development Perspectives, 1,* 109–114.

Galambos, S. J., & Maggs, J. L. (1991). Children in self-care: Figures, facts and fiction. In J. V. Lerner & N. L. Galambos (Eds.), *Employed mothers and their children* (pp. 131–157). New York: Garland.

Galanki, E. P., & Christopoulos, A. (2011). The imaginary audience and the personal fable in relation to the separation-individuation process during adolescence. *Psychology, the Journal of the Hellenic Psychological Society, 18,* 85–103.

Galbally, M., Lewis, J., van IJzendoorn, M., & Permezel, M. (2011). The role of oxytocin in mother–infant relations: A systematic review of human studies. *Harvard Review of Psychiatry, 19,* 1–14.

Galinsky, E., Aumann, K., & Bond, J. T. (2009). *Times are changing: Gender and generation at work and at home.* New York: Families and Work Institute.

Gallagher, A. M., & Kaufman, J. C. (2005). Gender differences in mathematics: What we know and what we need to know. In A. M. Gallagher & J. C. Kaufman (Eds.), *Gender differences in mathematics: An integrative psychological approach* (pp. 316–331). New York: Cambridge University Press.

Galland, B. C., Taylor, B. J., Elder, D. E., & Herbison, P. (2012). Normal sleep patterns in infants and children: A systematic review. *Sleep Medicine Reviews, 16,* 213–222.

Galler, J. R., Bryce, C. P., Waber, D. P., Hock, R. S., Harrison, R., Eaglesfield, G. D., et al. (2012). Infant malnutrition predicts conduct problems in adolescents. *Nutritional Neuroscience, 15,* 186–192.

Galler, J. R., Ramsey, C. F., Morley, D. S., Archer, E., & Salt, P. (1990). The long-term effects of early kwashiorkor compared with marasmus. IV. Performance on the National High School Entrance Examination. *Pediatric Research, 28,* 235–239.

Galloway, J. C., & Thelen, E. (2004). Feet first. Object exploration in young infants. *Infant Behavior and Development, 27,* 107–112.

Gallup. (2013). *Desire for children still norm in U.S.* Retrieved from www.gallup.com/poll/164618/desire-children-norm .aspx

Galvao, T. F., Silva, M. T., Zimmermann, I. R., Souza, K. M., Martins, S. S., & Pereira, M. G. (2014). Pubertal timing in girls and depression: A systematic review. *Journal of Affective Disorders, 155,* 13–19.

Galvao, T. F., Thees, M. F., Pontes, R. F., Silva, M. T., & Pereira, M. G. (2013). Zinc supplementation for treating diarrhea in children: A systematic review and meta-analysis. *Pan American Journal of Public Health, 33,* 370–377.

Gambling, L., Kennedy, C., & McArdle, H. J. (2011). Iron and copper in fetal development. *Seminar in Cell Development Biology, 22,* 637–644.

Ganea, P. A., Allen, M. L., Butler, L., Carey, S., & DeLoache, J. S. (2009). Toddlers' referential understanding of pictures. *Journal of Experimental Child Psychology, 104,* 283–295.

Ganea, P. A., & Harris, P. A. (2010). Not doing what you are told: Early perseverative errors in updating mental representations via language. *Child Development, 81,* 457–463.

Ganea, P. A., Ma, L., & DeLoache, J. S. (2011). Young children's learning and transfer of biological information from picture books to real animals. *Child Development, 82,* 1421–1433.

Ganea, P. A., Shutts, K., Spelke, E., & DeLoache, J. S. (2007). Thinking of things unseen: Infants' use of language to update object representations. *Psychological Science, 8,* 734–739.

Ganger, J., & Brent, M. R. (2004). Reexamining the vocabulary spurt. *Developmental Psychology, 40,* 621–632.

Garcia, A. J., Koschnitzky, J. E., & Ramirez, J. M. (2013). The physiological determinants of sudden infant death syndrome. *Respiratory Physiology and Neurobiology, 189,* 288–300.

Garcia, M. M., Shaw, D. S., Winslow, E. B., & Yaggi, K. E. (2000). Destructive sibling conflict and the development of conduct problems in young boys. *Developmental Psychology, 36,* 44–53.

Garcia-Bournissen, F., Tsur, L., Goldstein, L. H., Staroselsky, A., Avner, M., & Asrar, F. (2008). Fetal exposure to isotretinoin—an international problem. *Reproductive Toxicology, 25,* 124–128.

García Coll, C., & Marks, A. K. (2009). *Immigrant stories: Ethnicity and academics in middle childhood.* New York: Basic Books.

Garde, J. B., Suryavanshi, R. K., Jawale, B. A., Deshmukh, V., Dadhe, D. P., & Suryavanshi, M. K. (2014). An epidemiological study to know the prevalence of deleterious oral habits among 6 to 12 year old children. *Journal of International Oral Health, 6,* 39–43.

Gardner, H. (1983). *Frames of mind: The theory of multiple intelligences.* New York: Basic Books.

Gardner, H. (1993). *Multiple intelligences: The theory in practice.* New York: Basic Books.

Gardner, H. (2000). *Intelligence reframed: Multiple intelligences for the twenty-first century.* New York: Basic Books.

Gardner, H. (2011). The theory of multiple intelligences. In M. A. Gernsbacher, R. W. Pew, L. M. Hough, & J. R. Pomerantz (Eds.), *Psychology and the real world: Essays illustrating fundamental contributions to society* (pp. 122–130). New York: Worth.

Gardner, M., & Sandberg, D. E. (2011). Growth hormone treatment for short stature: A review of psychosocial assumptions and empirical evidence. *Pediatric Endocrinology Reviews, 9,* 579–588.

Garner, P. W. (1996). The relations of emotional role taking, affective/moral attributions, and emotional display rule knowledge to low-income school-age children's social competence. *Journal of Applied Developmental Psychology, 17,* 19–36.

Garner, P. W. (2003). Child and family correlates of toddlers' emotional and behavioral responses to a mishap. *Infant Mental Health Journal, 24,* 580–596.

Garner, P. W., & Estep, K. (2001). Emotional competence, emotion socialization, and young children's peer-related social competence. *Early Education and Development, 12,* 29–48.

Gartrell, N. K., Bos, H. M. W., & Goldberg, N. G. (2011). Adolescents of the U.S. National Longitudinal Lesbian Family Study: Sexual orientation, sexual behavior, and sexual risk exposure. *Archives of Sexual Behavior, 40,* 1199–1209.

Gartstein, M. A., & Rothbart, M. K. (2003). Studying infant temperament via the revised infant behavior questionnaire. *Infant Behavior and Development, 26,* 64–86.

Gartstein, M. A., Slobodskaya, H. R., & Kinsht, I. A. (2003). Cross-cultural differences in temperament in the first year of life: United States of America (U.S.) and Russia. *International Journal of Behavioral Development, 27,* 316–328.

Gartstein, M. A., Slobodskaya, H. R., Zylicz, P. O., Gosztyla, D., & Nakagawa, A. (2010). A cross-cultural evaluation of temperament: Japan, USA, Poland and Russia. *International Journal of Psychology and Psychological Therapy, 10,* 55–75.

Gaskins, S. (1999). Children's daily lives in a Mayan village: A case study of culturally constructed roles and activities. In R. Göncü (Ed.), *Children's engagement in the world: Sociocultural perspectives* (pp. 25–61). Cambridge, UK: Cambridge University Press.

Gaskins, S. (2013). Pretend play as culturally constructed activity. In M. Taylor (Ed.), *Oxford handbook on the development of the imagination* (pp. 224–251). Oxford, UK: Oxford University Press.

Gaskins, S. (2014). Children's play as cultural activity. In L. Brooker, M. Blaise, & S. Edwards (Eds.), *Sage handbook of play and learning in early childhood* (pp. 31–42). London: Sage.

Gaskins, S., Haight, W., & Lancy, D. F. (2007). The cultural construction of play. In A. Göncü & S. Gaskins (Eds.), *Play and development: Evolutionary, sociocultural, and functional perspectives* (pp. 179–202). Mahwah, NJ: Erlbaum.

Gates, G. J. (2013). *LGBT parenting in the United States.* Los Angeles, CA: Williams Institute of the UCLA School of Law. Retrieved from http://williamsinstitute.law.ucla.edu/wp-content/uploads/LGBT-Parenting.pdf

Gathercole, S. E., Lamont, E., & Alloway, T. P. (2006). Working memory in the classroom. In S. Pickering (Ed.), *Working memory and education* (pp. 219–240). San Diego: Elsevier.

Gathercole, V., Sebastián, E., & Soto, P. (1999). The early acquisition of Spanish verbal morphology: Across-the-board or piecemeal knowledge? *International Journal of Bilingualism, 3,* 133–182.

Gati, I., & Perez, M. (2014). Gender differences in career preferences from 1990 to 2010: Gaps reduced but not eliminated. *Journal of Counseling Psychology, 61,* 63–80.

Gault-Sherman, M. (2013). The gender gap in delinquency: Does SES matter? *Deviant Behavior, 34,* 255–273.

Gauvain, M. (2004). Bringing culture into relief: Cultural contributions to the development of children's planning skills. In R. V. Kail (Ed.), *Advances in child development and behavior* (pp. 39–71). San Diego, CA: Elsevier.

Gauvain, M., de la Ossa, J. L., & Hurtado-Ortiz, M. T. (2001). Parental guidance as children learn to use cultural tools: The case of pictorial plans. *Cognitive Development, 16,* 551–575.

Gauvain, M., & Munroe, R. L. (2009). Contributions of societal modernity to cognitive development: A comparison of four cultures. *Child Development, 80,* 1628–1642.

Gauvain, M., Munroe, R. L., & Beebe, H. (2012). Children's questions in cross-cultural perspective: A four-culture study. *Journal of Cross-Cultural Psychology, 44,* 1148–1165.

Gauvain, M., Perez, S. M., & Beebe, H. (2013). Authoritative parenting and parental support for children's cognitive development. In R. E. Larzelere, A. S. Morris, & A. W. Harrist (Eds.), *Authoritative parenting: Synthesizing nurturance and discipline for optimal child development* (pp. 211–233). Washington, DC: American Psychological Association.

Gauvain, M., & Rogoff, B. (1989a). Collaborative problem solving and children's planning skills. *Developmental Psychology, 25,* 139–151.

Gauvain, M., & Rogoff, B. (1989b). Ways of speaking about space: The development of children's skill in communicating spatial knowledge. *Cognitive Development, 4,* 295–307.

Gaylor, E. E., Burnham, M. M., Goodlin-Jones, B. L., & Anders, T. (2005). A longitudinal follow-up study of young children's sleep patterns using a developmental classification system. *Behavioral Sleep Medicine, 3,* 44–61.

Ge, X., Brody, G. H., Conger, R. D., Simons, R. L., & Murry, V. (2002). Contextual amplification of the effects of pubertal transition on African American children's deviant peer affiliation and externalized behavioral problems. *Developmental Psychology, 38,* 42–54.

Ge, X., Conger, R. D., & Elder, G. H., Jr. (1996). Coming of age too early: Pubertal influences on girls' vulnerability to psychological distress. *Child Development, 67,* 3386–3400.

Ge, X., Jin, R., Natsuaki, M. N., Frederick, X., Brody, G. H., Cutrona, C. E., & Simons, R. L. (2006). Pubertal maturation and early substance use risks among African American children. *Psychology of Addictive Behaviors, 20,* 404–414.

Ge, X., Natsuaki, M. N., Jin, R., & Biehl, M. C. (2011). A contextual amplification hypothesis: Pubertal timing and girls' emotional and behavior problems. In M. Kerr, H. Stattin, R. C. M. E. Engels, G. Overbeek, & A.-K. Andershed (Eds.), *Understanding girls' problem behavior* (pp. 11–28). Chichester, UK: Wiley-Blackwell.

Geangu, E., Benga, O., Stahl, D., & Striano, T. (2010). Contagious crying beyond the first days of life. *Infant Behavior and Development, 33,* 279–288.

Geary, D. C. (2006). Development of mathematical understanding. In D. Kuhn & R. Siegler (Eds.), *Handbook of child psychology: Vol. 2. Cognition, perception, and language* (6th ed., pp. 777–810). Hoboken, NJ: Wiley.

Gee, C. B., & Rhodes, J. E. (2003). Adolescent mothers' relationship with their children's biological fathers: Social support, social strain, and relationship continuity. *Journal of Family Psychology, 17,* 370–383.

Geerts, C. C., Bots, M. L., van der Ent, C. K., Grobbee, D. E., & Uiterwaal, C. S. (2012). Parental smoking and vascular damage in their 5-year-old children. *Pediatrics, 129,* 45–54.

Gelman, R. (1972). Logical capacity of very young children: Number invariance rules. *Child Development, 43,* 75–90.

Gelman, R., & Shatz, M. (1978). Appropriate speech adjustments: The operation of conversational constraints on talk to two-year-olds. In M. Lewis & L. A. Rosenblum (Eds.), *Interaction, conversation, and the development of language* (pp. 27–61). New York: Wiley.

Gelman, S. A. (2003). *The essential child.* New York: Oxford University Press.

Gelman, S. A. (2006). Early conceptual development. In K. McCartney & D. Phillips (Eds.), *Blackwell handbook of early childhood development* (pp. 149–166). Malden, MA: Blackwell.

Gelman, S. A., & Kalish, C. W. (2006). Conceptual development. In D. Kuhn & R. Siegler (Eds.), *Handbook of child psychology: Vol. 2. Cognition, perception, and language* (6th ed., 687–733). New York: Wiley.

Gelman, S. A., Taylor, M. G., & Nguyen, S. P. (2004). Mother–child conversations about gender. *Monographs of the Society for Research in Child Development, 69*(1, Serial No. 275), pp. 1–127.

Gendler, M. N., Witherington, D. C., & Edwards, A. (2008). The development of affect specificity in infants' use of emotion cues. *Infancy, 13,* 456–468.

Genessee, F., & Jared, D. (2008). Literacy development in early French immersion programs. *Canadian Psychology, 49,* 140–147.

Gennetian, L. A., & Morris, P. A. (2003). The effects of time limits and make-work-pay strategies on the well-being of children: Experimental evidence from two welfare reform programs. *Children and Youth Services Review, 25,* 17–54.

Gentile, B., Grabe, S., Dolan-Pascoe, B., Twenge, J. M., Wells, B. E., & Maitino, A. (2009). Gender differences in domain-specific self-esteem: A meta-analysis. *Review of General Psychology, 13,* 34–45.

Gentile, B., Twenge, J. M., & Campbell, W. K. (2010). Birth cohort differences in self-esteem, 1988–2008: A cross-temporal meta-analysis. *Review of General Psychology, 14,* 261–268.

Gentile, D. A. (2011). The multiple dimensions of video game effects. *Child Development Perspectives, 5,* 75–81.

Geraci, A., & Surian, L. (2011). The developmental roots of fairness: Infants' reactions to equal and unequal distributions of resources. *Developmental Science, 14,* 1012–1020.

Gergely, G., & Watson, J. (1999). Early socio-emotional development: Contingency perception and the social-biofeedback model. In P. Rochat (Ed.), *Early social cognition: Understanding others in the first months of life* (pp. 101–136). Mahwah, NJ: Erlbaum.

Gershoff, E. T. (2002). Corporal punishment, physical abuse, and the burden of proof: Reply to Baumrind, Larzelere, and Cowan (2002), Holden (2002), and Parke (2002). *Psychological Bulletin, 128,* 602–611.

Gershoff, E. T., & Aber, J. L. (2006). Neighborhoods and schools: Contexts and consequences for the mental health and risk behaviors of children and youth. In L. Balter & C. S. Tamis-LeMonda (Eds.), *Child psychology: A handbook of contemporary issues* (2nd ed., pp. 611–645). New York: Psychology Press.

Gershoff, E. T., Grogan-Kaylor, A., Lansford, J. E., Chang, L., Zelli, A., Deater-Deckard, K., et al. (2010). Parent discipline practices in an international sample: Associations with child behaviors and moderation by perceived normativeness. *Child Development, 81,* 487–502.

Gershoff, E. T., Lansford, J. E., Sexton, H. R., Davis-Kean, P., & Sameroff, A. J. (2012). Longitudinal links between spanking and children's externalizing behaviors in a national sample of white, black, Hispanic, and Asian American families. *Child Development, 83,* 838–843.

Gershoff-Stowe, L., & Hahn, E. R. (2007). Fast mapping skills in the developing lexicon. *Journal of Speech, Language, and Hearing Research, 50,* 682–697.

Gershon, E. S., & Alliey-Rodriguez, N. (2013). New ethical issues for genetic counseling in common mental disorders. *American Journal of Psychiatry, 170,* 968–976.

Gerson, S., & Woodward, A. L. (2010). Building intentional action knowledge with one's hands. In S. P. Johnson (Ed.), *Neoconstructivism: The new science of cognitive development* (pp. 295–313). New York: Oxford University Press.

Gervai, J. (2009). Environmental and genetic influences on early attachment. *Child and Adolescent Psychiatry and Mental Health, 3,* 25. Retrieved from www.capmh.com/content/3/1/25

Gesell, A. (1933). Maturation and patterning of behavior. In C. Murchison (Ed.), *A handbook of child psychology.* Worcester, MA: Clark University Press.

Geuze, R. H., Schaafsma, S. M., Lust, J. M., Bouma, A., Schiefenhovel, W., Groothuis, T. G. G., et al. (2012). Plasticity of lateralization: Schooling predicts hand preference but not hand skill asymmetry in a non-industrial society. *Neuropsychologia, 50,* 612–620.

Gewirtz, A., Forgatch, M., & Wieling, E. (2008). Parenting practices as potential mechanisms for child adjustment following mass trauma. *Journal of Marital and Family Therapy, 34,* 177–192.

Ghavami, N., Fingerhut, A., Peplau, L. A., Grant, S. K., & Wittig, M. A. (2011). Testing a model of minority identity achievement, identity affirmation, and psychological well-being among ethnic minority and sexual minority individuals. *Cultural Diversity and Ethnic Minority Psychology, 17,* 79–88.

Ghim, H. R. (1990). Evidence for perceptual organization in infants: Perception of subjective contours by young infants. *Infant Behavior and Development, 13,* 221–248.

Gibbs, J. C. (2006). Should Kohlberg's cognitive developmental approach to morality be replaced with a more pragmatic approach? Comment on Krebs and Denton (2005). *Psychological Review, 113,* 666–671.

Gibbs, J. C. (2010a). Beyond the conventionally moral. *Journal of Applied Developmental Psychology, 31,* 106–108.

Gibbs, J. C. (2010b). *Moral development and reality: Beyond the theories of Kohlberg and Hoffman* (2nd ed.). Boston: Pearson Allyn & Bacon.

Gibbs, J. C. (2014). *Moral development and reality: Beyond the theories of Kohlberg, Hoffman, and Haidt* (3rd ed.). New York: Oxford University Press.

Gibbs, J. C., Basinger, K. S., & Grime, R. L. (2003). Moral judgment maturity: From clinical to standard measures. In S. J. Lopez & C. R. Snyder (Eds.), *Handbook of positive psychological assessment* (pp. 361–373). Washington, DC: American Psychological Association.

Gibbs, J. C., Basinger, K. S., Grime, R. L., & Snarey, J. R. (2007). Moral judgment development across cultures: Revisiting Kohlberg's universality claims. *Developmental Review, 24,* 443–500.

Gibbs, J. C., Moshman, D., Berkowitz, M. W., Basinger, K. S., & Grime, R. L. (2009). Taking development seriously: Critique of the 2008 JME special issue on moral functioning. *Journal of Moral Education, 38,* 271–282.

Gibson, E. J. (1970). The development of perception as an adaptive process. *American Scientist, 58,* 98–107.

Gibson, E. J. (2000). Perceptual learning in development: Some basic concepts. *Ecological Psychology, 12,* 295–302.

Gibson, E. J. (2003). The world is so full of a number of things: On specification and perceptual learning. *Ecological Psychology, 15,* 283–287.

Gibson, E. J., & Walk, R. D. (1960). The "visual cliff." *Scientific American, 202,* 64–71.

Gibson, J. J. (1979). *The ecological approach to visual perception.* Boston: Houghton Mifflin.

Gibson-Davis, C., & Rackin, H. (2014). Marriage or carriage? Trends in union context and birth type by education. *Journal of Marriage and Family, 76,* 506–519.

Giedd, J. N., Lalonde, F. M., Celano, M. J., White, S. L., Wallace, G. L., Lee, N. R., et al. (2009). Anatomical brain magnetic resonance imaging of typically developing children and adolescents. *Journal of the American Academy of Child and Adolescent Psychiatry, 48,* 465–470.

Giles, A., & Rovee-Collier, C. (2011). Infant long-term memory for associations formed during mere exposure. *Infant Behavior and Development, 34,* 327–338.

Giles, J. W., & Heyman, G. D. (2005). Young children's beliefs about the relationship between gender and aggressive behavior. *Child Development, 76,* 107–121.

Giles-Sims, J., Straus, M. A., & Sugarman, D. B. (1995). Child, maternal, and family characteristics associated with spanking. *Family Relations, 44,* 170–176.

Gill, M., Daly, G., Heron, S., Hawi, Z., & Fitzgerald, M. (1997). Confirmation of association between attention deficit hyperactivity disorder and a dopamine transporter polymorphism. *Molecular Psychiatry, 2,* 311–313.

Gill, S. V., Adolph, K. E., & Vereijken, B. (2009). Change in action: How infants learn to walk down slopes. *Developmental Science, 12,* 888–902.

Gillies, R. M. (2003a). The behaviors, interactions, and perceptions of junior high school students during small-group learning. *Journal of Educational Psychology, 95,* 137–147.

Gillies, R. M. (2003b). Structuring co-operative learning experiences in primary school. In R. M. Gillies & A. F. Ashman (Eds.), *Co-operative learning: The social and intellectual outcomes of learning in groups* (pp. 36–53). New York: Routledge.

Gillies, R. M., & Ashman, A. F. (1996). Teaching collaborative skills to primary school children in classroom-based workgroups. *Learning and Instruction, 6,* 187–200.

Gilligan, C. F. (1982). *In a different voice.* Cambridge, MA: Harvard University Press.

Gilliom, M., Shaw, D. S., Beck, J. E., Schonberg, M. A., & Lukon, J. L. (2002). Anger regulation in disadvantaged preschool boys: Strategies, antecedents, and the development of self-control. *Developmental Psychology, 38,* 222–235.

Gilmore, J. H., Shi, F., Woolson, S. L., Knickmeyer, R. C., Short, S. J., Lin, W., et al. (2012). Longitudinal development of cortical and subcortical gray matter from birth to 2 years. *Cerebral Cortex, 22,* 2478–2485.

Ginsburg, H. P., Lee, J. S., & Boyd, J. S. (2008). Mathematics education for young children: What it is and how to promote it. *Social Policy Report of the Society for Research in Child Development, 12*(1).

Giofré, D., Mammarella, I. C., & Cornoldi, C. (2013). The structure of working memory and how it relates to intelligence in children. *Intelligence, 41,* 396–406.

Giscombé, C. L., & Lobel, M. (2005). Explaining disproportionately high rates of adverse birth outcomes among African Americans: The impact of stress, racism and related factors in pregnancy. *Psychological Bulletin, 131,* 662–683.

Glade, A. C., Bean, R. A., & Vira, R. (2005). A prime time for marital/relational intervention: A review of the transition to parenthood literature with treatment recommendations. *American Journal of Family Therapy, 33,* 319–336.

Glasgow, K. L., Dornbusch, S. M., Troyer, L., Steinberg, L., & Ritter, P. L. (1997). Parenting styles, adolescents' attributions, and educational outcomes in nine heterogeneous high schools. *Child Development, 68,* 507–523.

Glazener, C. M., Evans, J. H., & Petro, R. E. (2005). Alarm interventions for nocturnal enuresis in children. *Cochrane Database of Systematic Reviews,* Issue 2. Art. No.: CD002911.

Gleason, J. B. (2013). The development of language: An overview and a preview. In J. B. Gleason & N. B. Ratner

(Eds.), *The development of language* (8th ed., pp. 1–29). Upper Saddle River, NJ: Pearson.

Gleason, T. R. (2013). Imaginary relationships. In M. Taylor (Ed.), *Oxford handbook of the development of imagination* (pp. 251–271). New York: Oxford University Press.

Gleason, T. R., & Hohmann, L. M. (2006). Concepts of real and imaginary friendships in early childhood. *Social Development, 15,* 128–144.

Gleason, T. R., Sebanc, A. M., & Hartup, W. W. (2000). Imaginary companions of preschool children. *Developmental Psychology, 36,* 419–428.

Gleitman, L. R., Cassidy, K., Nappa, R., Papfragou, A., & Trueswell, J. C. (2005). Hard words. *Language Learning and Development, 1,* 23–64.

Glenright, M., & Pexman, P. M. (2010). Development of children's ability to distinguish sarcasm and verbal irony. *Journal of Child Language, 37,* 429–451.

Glover, J. A., Galliher, R. V., & Lamere, T. G. (2009). Identity development and exploration among sexual minority adolescents: Examination of a multidimensional model. *Journal of Homosexuality, 56,* 77–101.

Gluckman, P. D., Sizonenko, S. V., & Bassett, N. S. (1999). The transition from fetus to neonate—an endocrine perspective. *Acta Paediatrica Supplement, 88*(428), 7–11.

Gnepp, J. (1983). Children's social sensitivity: Inferring emotions from conflicting cues. *Developmental Psychology, 19,* 805–814.

Gnoth, C., Maxrath, B., Skonieczny, T., Friol, K., Godehardt, E., & Tigges, J. (2011). Final ART success rates: A 10 years survey. *Human Reproduction, 26,* 2239–2246.

Goble, P. Martin, C. L., Hanish, L. D., & Fabes, R. A. (2012). Children's gender-typed activity choices across preschool social contexts. *Sex Roles, 67,* 435–451.

Godfrey, K. M., & Barker, D. J. (2000). Fetal nutrition and adult disease. *American Journal of Clinical Nutrition, 71,* 1344S–1352S.

Goeke-Morey, M. C., Papp, L. M., & Cummings, E. M. (2013). Changes in marital conflict and youths' responses across childhood and adolescence: A test of sensitization. *Development and Psychopathology, 25,* 241–251.

Goering, J. (Ed.). (2003). Choosing a better life? *How public housing tenants selected a HUD experiment to improve their lives and those of their children: The Moving to Opportunity Demonstration Program.* Washington, DC: Urban Institute Press.

Gogate, L. J., & Bahrick, L. E. (1998). Intersensory redundancy facilitates learning of arbitrary relations between vowel sounds and objects in seven-month-old infants. *Journal of Experimental Child Psychology, 69,* 133–149.

Gogate, L. J., & Bahrick, L. E. (2001). Intersensory redundancy and 7-month-old infants' memory for arbitrary syllable–object relations. *Infancy, 2,* 219–231.

Goh, Y. I., & Koren, G. (2008). Folic acid in pregnancy and fetal outcomes. *Journal of Obstetrics and Gynaecology, 28,* 3–13.

Goldberg, A. E. (2010). *Lesbian and gay parents and their children: Research on the family life cycle.* Washington, DC: American Psychological Association.

Goldberg, A. E., Kashy, D. A., & Smith, J. Z. (2012). Gender-typed play behavior in early childhood: Adopted children with lesbian, gay, and heterosexual parents. *Sex Roles, 67,* 503–513.

Goldberg, A. E., & Perry-Jenkins, M. (2003). Division of labor and working-class women's well-being across the transition to parenthood. *Journal of Family Psychology, 18,* 225–236.

Goldenberg, C., Gallimore, R., Reese, L., & Garnier, H. (2001). Cause or effect? Immigrant Latino parents' aspirations and expectations, and their children's school performance. *American Educational Research Journal, 38,* 547–582.

Goldfield, B. A. (1987). Contributions of child and caregiver to referential and expressive language. *Applied Psycholinguistics, 8,* 267–280.

Goldhaber, D. (2012). *The nature–nurture debates: Bridging the gaps.* New York: Cambridge University Press.

Goldin-Meadow, S. (2003). *The resilience of language.* New York: Psychology Press.

Goldin-Meadow, S. (2009). Using the hands to study how children learn language. In J. Colombo, P. McCardle, & L. Freund (Eds.), *Infant pathways to language: Methods,*

models, *and research directions* (pp. 195–210). New York: Psychology Press.

Goldin-Meadow, S., Gelman, S. A., & Mylander, C. (2005). Expressing generic concepts with and without a language model. *Cognition, 96,* 109–126.

Goldney, R. D. (2013). *Suicide prevention* (2nd ed.). Oxford, UK: Oxford University Press.

Goldschmidt, L., Richardson, G. A., Cornelius, M. D., & Day, N. L. (2004). Prenatal marijuana and alcohol exposure and academic achievement at age 10. *Neurotoxicology and Teratology, 26,* 521–532.

Goldstein, M. H., & Schwade, J. A. (2008). Social feedback to infants' babbling facilitates rapid phonological learning. *Psychological Science, 19,* 515–523.

Goldstein, S. (2011a). Attention-deficit/hyperactivity disorder. In S. Goldstein & C. R. Reynolds (Eds.), *Handbook of neurodevelopmental and genetic disorders in children* (2nd ed., pp. 131–150). New York: Guilford.

Goldstein, S. (2011b). Learning disabilities in childhood. In S. Goldstein, J. A. Naglieri, & M. DeVries (Eds.), *Learning and attention disorders in adolescence and adulthood: Assessment and treatment* (2nd ed., pp. 31–58). Hoboken, NJ: Wiley.

Goldstein, S. E., & Tisak, M. S. (2004). Adolescents' outcome expectancies about relational aggression within acquaintanceships, friendships, and dating relationships. *Journal of Adolescence, 27,* 283–302.

Goldston, D. B., Molock, S. D., Whitbeck, L. B., Murakami, J. L., Zayas, L. H., & Hall, G. C. N. (2008). Cultural considerations in adolescent suicide prevention and psychosocial treatment. *American Psychologist, 63,* 14–31.

Golinkoff, R. M., & Hirsh-Pasek, K. (2006). Baby wordsmith: From associationist to social sophisticate. *Current Directions in Psychological Science, 15,* 30–33.

Golinkoff, R. M., & Hirsh-Pasek, K. (2008). How toddlers begin to learn verbs. *Trends in Cognitive Sciences, 12,* 397–403.

Golomb, C. (2004). *The child's creation of a pictorial world* (2nd ed.). Mahwah, NJ: Erlbaum.

Golombok, S., Readings, J., Blake, L., Casey, P., Mellish, L., Marks, A., & Jadva, V. (2011). Children conceived by gamete donation: Psychological adjustment and mother–child relationships at age 7. *Journal of Family Psychology, 25,* 230–239.

Golombok, S., Rust, J., Zervoulis, K., Croudace, T., Golding, J., & Hines, M. (2008). Developmental trajectories of sex-typed behavior in boys and girls: A longitudinal general population study of children aged 2.5–8 years. *Child Development, 79,* 1583–1593.

Golombok, S., Rust, J., Zervoulis, K., Golding, J., & Hines, M. (2012). Continuity in sex-typed behavior from preschool to adolescence: A longitudinal population study of boys and girls aged 3–13 years. *Archives of Sexual Behavior, 41,* 591–597.

Gomez-Perez, E., & Ostrosky-Solis, F. (2006). Attention and memory evaluation across the life span: Heterogeneous effects of age and education. *Journal of Clinical and Experimental Neuropsychology, 28,* 477–494.

Gonzales, N. A., Cauce, A. M., Friedman, R. J., & Mason, C. A. (1996). Family, peer, and neighborhood influences on academic achievement among African-American adolescents: One-year prospective effects. *American Journal of Community Psychology, 24,* 365–387.

Gonzalez, A.-L., & Wolters, C. A. (2006). The relation between perceived parenting practices and achievement motivation in mathematics. *Journal of Research in Childhood Education, 21,* 203–217.

González-Rivera, M., & Bauermeister, J. A. (2007). Children's attitudes toward people with AIDS in Puerto Rico: Exploring stigma through drawings and stories. *Qualitative Health Research, 17,* 250–263.

Good, M., & Willoughby, T. (2014). Institutional and personal spirituality/religiosity and psychosocial adjustment in adolescence: Concurrent and longitudinal associations. *Journal of Youth and Adolescence, 43,* 757–774.

Good, T. L., & Brophy, J. (2003). *Looking in classrooms* (9th ed.). Boston: Allyn and Bacon.

Goodman, A., Schorge, J., & Greene, M. F. (2011). The long-term effects of in utero exposures—the DES story. *New England Journal of Medicine, 364,* 2083–2084.

Goodman, C., & Silverstein, M. (2006). Grandmothers raising grandchildren: Ethnic and racial differences in well-being among custodial and coparenting families. *Journal of Family Issues, 27,* 1605–1626.

Goodman, J., Dale, P., & Li, P. (2008). Does frequency count? Parental input and the acquisition of vocabulary. *Journal of Child Language, 35,* 515–531.

Goodman, K. S. (2005). *What's whole in whole language.* Berkeley, CA: RDR Books.

Goodman, S. H., Gravitt, G. W., Jr., & Kaslow, N. J. (1995). Social problem solving: A moderator of the relation between negative life stress and depression symptoms in children. *Journal of Abnormal Child Psychology, 23,* 473–485.

Goodnight, J. A., Bates, J. E., Staples, A. D., Pettit, G. S., & Dodge, K. A. (2007). Temperamental resistance to control increases the association between sleep problems and externalizing behavior development. *Journal of Family Psychology, 21,* 39–48.

Goodnow, J. J. (2010). Culture. In M. H. Bornstein (Ed.), *Handbook of cultural developmental science* (pp. 3–20). New York: Psychology Press.

Goodvin, R., Meyer, S., Thompson, R. A., & Hayes, R. (2008). Self-understanding in early childhood: Associations with child attachment security and maternal negative affect. *Attachment and Human Development, 10,* 433–450.

Goodvin, R., & Romdall, L. (2013). Associations of mother–child reminiscing about negative past events, coping, and self-concept in early childhood. *Infant and Child Development, 22,* 383–400.

Gooren, E. M. J. C., Pol, A. C., Stegge, H., Terwogt, M. M., & Koot, H. M. (2011). The development of conduct problems and depressive symptoms in early elementary school children: The role of peer rejection. *Journal of Clinical Child and Adolescent Psychology, 40,* 245–253.

Gopnik, A., & Choi, S. (1990). Do linguistic differences lead to cognitive differences? A cross-linguistic study of semantic and cognitive development. *First Language, 11,* 199–215.

Gopnik, A., & Nazzi, T. (2003). Words, kinds, and causal powers: A theory theory perspective on early naming and categorization. In D. H. Rakison & L. M. Oakes (Eds.), *Early category and concept development* (pp. 303–329). New York: Oxford University Press.

Gopnik, A., & Tenenbaum, J. B. (2007). Bayesian networks, Bayesian learning and cognitive development. *Developmental Science, 10,* 281–287.

Gordon, I., Zagoory-Sharon, O., Leckman, J. F., & Feldman, R. (2010). Oxytocin and the development of parenting in humans. *Biological Psychiatry, 68,* 377–382.

Gordon, R. A., Chase-Lansdale, P. L., & Brooks-Gunn, J. (2004). Extended households and the life course of young mothers: Understanding the associations using a sample of mothers with premature, low-birth-weight babies. *Child Development, 75,* 1013–1038.

Gormally, S., Barr, R. G., Wertheim, L., Alkawaf, R., Calinoiu, N., & Young, S. N. (2001). Contact and nutrient caregiving effects on newborn infant pain responses. *Developmental Medicine and Child Neurology, 43,* 28–38.

Gorman, B. K., Fiestas, C. E., Peña, E. D., & Clark, M. R. (2011). Creative and stylistic devices employed by children during a storybook narrative task: A cross-cultural study. *Language, Speech, and Hearing Services in Schools, 42,* 167–181.

Gormley, W. T., Jr., & Phillips, D. (2009). *The effects of pre-K on child development: Lessons from Oklahoma.* Washington, DC: National Summit on Early Childhood Education, Georgetown University.

Goswami, U. (1996). Analogical reasoning and cognitive development. In H. Reese (Ed.), *Advances in child development and behavior* (Vol. 26, pp. 91–138). New York: Academic Press.

Gottfredson, G. D., & Duffy, R. D. (2008). Using a theory of vocational personalities and work environments to explore subjective well-being. *Journal of Career Assessment, 16,* 44–59.

Gottfredson, L. S. (2005). Applying Gottfredson's theory of circumscription and compromise in career guidance and counseling. In S. D. Brown & R. W. Lent (Eds.), *Career development and counseling* (pp. 71–100). Hoboken, NJ: Wiley.

Gottfried, A. E., Gottfried, A. W., & Bathurst, K. (2002). Maternal and dual-earner employment status and parenting. In M. H. Bornstein (Ed.), *Handbook of parenting: Vol. 3. Being and becoming a parent* (2nd ed., pp. 207–230). Mahwah, NJ: Erlbaum.

Gottlieb, G. (1998). Normally occurring environmental and behavioral influences on gene activity: From central dogma to probabilistic epigenesis. *Psychological Review, 105,* 792–802.

Gottlieb, G. (2003). On making behavioral genetics truly developmental. *Human Development, 46,* 337–355.

Gottlieb, G. (2007). Probabilistic epigenesis. *Developmental Science, 10,* 1–11.

Gottlieb, G., Wahlsten, D., & Lickliter, R. (2006). The significance of biology for human development: A developmental psychobiological systems of view. In R. M. Lerner (Ed.), *Handbook of child psychology: Vol. 1. Theoretical models of human development* (6th ed., pp. 210–257). Hoboken, NJ: Wiley.

Gottman, J. M., Gottman, J. S., & Shapiro, A. (2010). A new couples approach to interventions for the transition to parenthood. In M. S. Schulz, M. K. Pruett, P. K. Kerig, & R. D. Parke (Eds.), *Strengthening couple relationships for optimal child development* (pp. 165–179). Washington, DC: American Psychological Association.

Gould, F., Clarke, J., Heim, C., Harvey, P. D., Majer, M., & Nemeroff, C. B. (2010). The effects of child abuse and neglect on cognitive functioning in adulthood. *Journal of Psychiatric Research, 46,* 500–506.

Gould, J. L., & Keeton, W. T. (1996). *Biological science* (6th ed.). New York: Norton.

Graber, J. A. (2003). Puberty in context. In C. Hayward (Ed.), *Gender differences at puberty* (pp. 307–325). New York: Cambridge University Press.

Graber, J. A. (2004). Internalizing problems during adolescence. In R. M. Lerner & L. Steinberg (Eds.), *Handbook of adolescent psychology* (2nd ed., pp. 587–626). Hoboken, NJ: Wiley.

Graber, J. A., Brooks-Gunn, J., & Warren, M. P. (2006). Pubertal effects on adjustment in girls: Moving from demonstrating effects to identifying pathways. *Journal of Youth and Adolescence, 35,* 413–423.

Graber, J. A., Lewinsohn, P. M., Seeley, J. R., & Brooks-Gunn, J. (1997). Is psychopathology associated with the timing of pubertal development? *Journal of the American Academy of Child and Adolescent Psychiatry, 36,* 1768–1776.

Graber, J. A., Nichols, T., Lynne, S. D., Brooks-Gunn, J., & Botwin, G. J. (2006). A longitudinal examination of family, friend, and media influences on competent versus problem behaviors among urban minority youth. *Applied Developmental Science, 10,* 75–85.

Graber, J. A., Seeley, J. R., Brooks-Gunn, J., & Lewinsohn, P. M. (2004). Is pubertal timing associated with psychopathology in young adulthood? *Journal of the American Academy of Child and Adolescent Psychiatry, 43,* 718–726.

Graber, J. A., & Sontag, L. M. (2009). Internalizing problems during adolescence. In R. M. Lerner & L. Steinberg (Eds.), *Handbook of adolescent psychology: Vol. 1. Individual bases of adolescent development* (3rd ed., pp. 642–682). Hoboken, NJ: Wiley.

Graham, S., & Perin, D. (2007). A meta-analysis of writing instruction for adolescent students. *Journal of Educational Psychology, 99,* 445–476.

Graham-Bermann, S. A., & Howell, K. H. (2011). Child maltreatment in the context of intimate partner violence. In J. E. B. Myers (Ed.), *Child maltreatment* (3rd ed., pp. 167–180). Thousand Oaks, CA: Sage.

Gralinski, J. H., & Kopp, C. B. (1993). Everyday rules for behavior: Mothers' requests to young children. *Developmental Psychology, 29,* 573–584.

Granic, I., Hollenstein, T., Dishion, T. J., & Patterson, G. R. (2003). Longitudinal analysis of flexibility and reorganization in early adolescence: A dynamic systems study of family interactions. *Developmental Psychology, 39,* 606–617.

Granier-Deferre, C., Bassereau, S., Ribeiro, A., Jacquet, A. Y., & Lecanuet, J.-P. (2003). *Cardiac "orienting" response in fetuses and babies following in utero melody-learning.* Paper presented at the 11th European Conference on Developmental Psychology, Milan, Italy.

Grant, K. B., & Ray, J. A. (2010). *Home, school, and community collaboration: Culturally responsive family involvement.* Thousand Oaks, CA: Sage Publications.

Grantham-McGregor, S., & Ani, C. (2001). A review of studies on the effect of iron deficiency on cognitive development in children. *Journal of Nutrition, 131,* 649S–668S.

Grantham-McGregor, S., Powell, C., Walker, S., Chang, S., & Fletcher, P. (1994). The long-term follow-up of severely malnourished children who participated in an intervention program. *Child Development, 65,* 428–439.

Grantham-McGregor, S., Schofield, W., & Powell, C. (1987). Development of severely malnourished children who received psychosocial stimulation: Six-year follow-up. *Pediatrics, 79,* 247–254.

Grantham-McGregor, S., Walker, S. P., & Chang, S. (2000). Nutritional deficiencies and later behavioral development. *Proceedings of the Nutrition Society, 59,* 47–54.

Gratier, M., & Devouche, E. (2011). Imitation and repetition of prosodic contour in vocal interaction at 3 months. *Developmental Psychology, 47,* 67–76.

Grattan, M. P., De Vos, E., Levy, J., & McClintock, M. K. (1992). Asymmetric action in the human newborn: Sex differences in patterns of organization. *Child Development, 63,* 273–289.

Gray, K. A., Day, N. L., Leech, S., & Richardson, G. A. (2005). Prenatal marijuana exposure: Effect on child depressive symptoms at ten years of age. *Neurotoxicology and Teratology, 27,* 439–448.

Gray, M. R., & Steinberg, L. (1999). Unpacking authoritative parenting: Reassessing a multidimensional construct. *Journal of Marriage and the Family, 61,* 574–587.

Gray-Little, B., & Carels, R. (1997). The effects of racial and socioeconomic consonance on self-esteem and achievement in elementary, junior high, and high school students. *Journal of Research on Adolescence, 7,* 109–131.

Gray-Little, B., & Hafdahl, A. R. (2000). Factors influencing racial comparisons of self-esteem: A quantitative review. *Psychological Bulletin, 126,* 26–54.

Green, G. E., Irwin, J. R., & Gustafson, G. E. (2000). Acoustic cry analysis, neonatal status and long-term developmental outcomes. In R. G. Barr, B. Hopkins, & J. A. Green (Eds.), *Crying as a sign, a symptom, and a signal* (pp. 137–156). Cambridge, UK: Cambridge University Press.

Greenberg, J. P. (2013). Determinants of after-school programming for school-age immigrant children. *Children and Schools, 35,* 101–111.

Greenberger, E., O'Neil, R., & Nagel, S. K. (1994). Linking workplace and homeplace: Relations between the nature of adults' work and their parenting behaviors. *Developmental Psychology, 30,* 990–1002.

Greendorfer, S. L., Lewko, J. H., & Rosengren, K. S. (1996). Family and gender-based socialization of children and adolescents. In F. L. Smoll & R. E. Smith (Eds.), *Children and youth in sport: A biopsychological perspective* (pp. 89–111). Dubuque, IA: Brown & Benchmark.

Greene, J. A., Torney-Purta, J., & Azevedo, R. (2010). Empirical evidence regarding relations among a model of epistemic and ontological cognition, academic performance, and educational level. *Journal of Educational Psychology, 102,* 234–255.

Greene, K., Krcmar, M., Walters, L. H., Rubin, D. L., Hale, J., & Hale, L. (2000). Targeting adolescent risk-taking behaviors: The contributions of egocentrism and sensationseeking. *Journal of Adolescence, 23,* 439–461.

Greene, S. M., Anderson, E. R., Forgatch, M. S., DeGarmo, D. S., & Hetherington, E. M. (2012). Risk and resilience after divorce. In F. Walsh (Ed.), *Normal family processes: Growing diversity and complexity* (4th ed., pp. 102–127). New York: Guilford.

Greenfield, P. M. (1992, June). *Notes and references for developmental psychology.* Conference on Making Basic Texts in Psychology More Culture-Inclusive and Culture-Sensitive, Western Washington University, Bellingham, WA.

Greenfield, P. M. (2004). *Weaving generations together: Evolving creativity in the Maya of Chiapas.* Santa Fe, NM: School of American Research.

Greenfield, P. M., Suzuki, L. K., & Rothstein-Fish, C. (2006). Cultural pathways through human development. In K. A. Renninger & I. E. Sigel (Eds.), *Handbook of child psychology: Vol. 4. Child psychology in practice* (6th ed., pp. 655–699). Hoboken, NJ: Wiley.

Greenhill, L. L., Halperin, J. M., & Abikoff, H. (1999). Stimulant medications. *Journal of the American Academy of Child and Adolescent Psychiatry, 38,* 503–512.

Greenough, W. T., & Black, J. E. (1992). Induction of brain structure by experience: Substrates for cognitive development. In M. Gunnar & C. A. Nelson (Eds.), *Minnesota symposia on child psychology* (pp. 155–200). Hillsdale, NJ: Erlbaum.

Greer, B. D., Neidert, P. L., Dozier, C. L., Payne, S. W., Zonneveld, K. L. M., & Harper, A. M. (2013). Functional analysis and treatment of problem behavior in early education classrooms. *Journal of Applied Behavior Analysis, 46,* 289–295.

Greer, T., & Lockman, J. J. (1998). Using writing instruments: Invariances in young children and adults. *Child Development, 69,* 888–902.

Gregory, A., & Weinstein, R. S. (2004). Connection and regulation at home and in school: predicting growth in achievement for adolescents. *Journal of Adolescent Research, 19,* 405–427.

Greydanus, D. E., Omar, H., & Pratt, H. D. (2010). The adolescent female athlete: Current concepts and conundrums. *Pediatric Clinics of North America, 57,* 697–718.

Greydanus, D. E., Seyler, J., Omar, H. A., & Dodich, C. B. (2012). Sexually transmitted diseases in adolescence. *International Journal of Child and Adolescent Health, 5,* 379–401.

Grief, G. L., Hrabowski, F. A., & Maton, K. I. (1998). African-American fathers of high-achieving sons: Using outstanding members of an at-risk population to guide intervention. *Families in Society, 79,* 45–52.

Groh, A. M., Fearon, R. M. P., Bakermans-Kranenburg, M. J., Van IJzendoorn, M. H., Steele, R. D., & Roisman, G. I. (2014). The significance of attachment security for children's social competence with peers: A meta-analytic study. *Attachment and Human Development, 16,* 103–136.

Groome, L. J., Swiber, M. J., Holland, S. B., Bentz, L. S., Atterbury, J. L., & Trimm, R. F., III. (1999). Spontaneous motor activity in the perinatal infant before and after birth: Stability in individual differences. *Developmental Psychobiology, 35,* 15–24.

Gropman, A. L., & Adams, D. R. (2007). Atypical patterns of inheritance. *Seminars in Pediatric Neurology, 14,* 34–45.

Grossmann, K., Grossmann, K. E., Fremmer-Bombik, E., Kindler, H., Scheuerer-Englisch, H., & Zimmermann, P. (2002). The uniqueness of the child–father attachment relationship: Fathers' sensitive and challenging play as a pivotal variable in a 16-year longitudinal study. *Social Development, 11,* 307–331.

Grossmann, K., Grossmann, K. E., Kindler, H., & Zimmermann, P. (2008). A wider view of attachment and exploration: The influence of mothers and fathers on the development of psychological security from infancy to young adulthood. In J. Cassidy & P. R. Shaver (Eds.), *Handbook of attachment: Theory, research, and clinical applications* (2nd ed., pp. 880–905). New York: Guilford.

Grossmann, K., Grossmann, K. E., Spangler, G., Suess, G., & Unzner, L. (1985). Maternal sensitivity and newborns' orientation responses as related to quality of attachment in Northern Germany. In I. Bretherton & E. Waters (Eds.), Growing points of attachment theory and research. *Monographs of the Society for Research in Child Development, 50*(1–2, Serial No. 209).

Grossmann, T., Striano, T., & Friederici, A. D. (2007). Developmental changes in infants' processing of happy and angry facial expressions: A neurobehavioral study. *Brain and Cognition, 64,* 30–41.

Grow-Maienza, J., Hahn, D.-D., & Joo, C.-A. (2001). Mathematics instruction in Korean primary schools: Structures, processes, and a linguistic analysis of questioning. *Journal of Educational Psychology, 93,* 363–376.

Gruendel, J., & Aber, J. L. (2007). Bridging the gap between research and child policy change: The role of strategic communications in policy advocacy. In J. L. Aber, S. J. Bishop-Josef, S. M. Jones, K. T. McLearn, & D. A. Phillips (Eds.), *Child development and social policy: Knowledge for action* (pp. 43–58). Washington, DC: American Psychological Association.

Grusec, J. E. (1988). *Social development: History, theory, and research.* New York: Springer-Verlag.

Grusec, J. E. (2006). The development of moral behavior and conscience from a socialization perspective. In M. Killen & J. Smetana (Eds.), *Handbook of moral development* (pp. 243–265). Philadelphia: Erlbaum.

Guedes, M., Pereira, M., Pires, R., Carvalho, P., & Canavarro, M. C. (2013). Childbearing motivations scale: Construction of a new measure and its preliminary psychometric properties. *Journal of Family Studies.* Retrieved from link.springer.com/article/10.1007% 2Fs10826-013-9824-0

Guerra, N. G., Graham, S. & Tolan, P. H., (2011). Raising healthy children: Translating child development research into practice. *Child Development, 82*, 7–16.

Guerra, N. G., Williams, K. R., & Sadek, S. (2011). Understanding bullying and victimization during childhood and adolescence: A mixed methods study. *Child Development, 82*, 295–310.

Guest, A. M. (2013). Cultures of play during middle childhood: Interpretive perspectives from two distinct marginalized communities. *Sport, Education and Society, 18*, 167–183.

Guglielmi, R. S. (2008). Native language proficiency, English literacy, academic achievement, and occupational attainment in limited-English-proficient students: A latent growth modeling perspective. *Journal of Educational Psychology, 100*, 322–342.

Guignard, J.-H., & Lubart, T. I. (2007). A comparative study of convergent and divergent thinking in intellectually gifted children. *Gifted and Talented International, 22*(1), 9–15.

Guilford, J. P. (1985). The structure-of-intellect model. In B. B. Wolman (Ed.), *Handbook of intelligence* (pp. 225–266). New York: Wiley.

Guilleminault, C., Palombini, L., Pelayo, R., & Chervin, R. D. (2003). Sleepwalking and sleep terrors in prepubertal children: What triggers them? *Pediatrics, 111*, e17–e25.

Guimond, F. A., Brendgen, M., Forget-Dubois, N., Dionne, G., Vitaro, F., Tremblay, R. E., & Boivin, M. (2012). Associations of mother's and father's parenting practices with children's observed social reticence in a competitive situation: A monozygotic twin difference study. *Journal of Abnormal Child Psychology, 40*, 391–402.

Guiso, L., Mont, F., Sapienza, P., & Zingales, L. (2008). Culture, gender, and math. *Science, 320*, 1164–1165.

Gullone, E. (2000). The development of normal fear: A century of research. *Clinical Psychology Review, 20*, 429–451.

Gulotta, T. P. (2008). How theory influences treatment and prevention practice within the family. In T. P. Gulotta (Ed.), *Family influences on child behavior and development: Evidence-based prevention and treatment approaches* (pp. 1–20). New York: Routledge.

Gunderson, E. A., Ramirez, G., Levine, S. C., & Beilock, S. L. (2012). The role of parents and teachers in the development of gender-related math attitudes. *Sex Roles, 66*, 153–166.

Gunnar, M. R., & Cheatham, C. L. (2003). Brain and behavior interfaces: Stress and the developing brain. *Infant Mental Health Journal, 24*, 195–211.

Gunnar, M. R., & de Haan, M. (2009). Methods in social neuroscience: Issues in studying development. In M. de Haan & M. R. Gunnar (Eds.), *Handbook of developmental social neuroscience* (pp. 13–37). New York: Guilford.

Gunnar, M. R., Morison, S. J., Chisholm, K., & Schuder, M. (2001). Salivary cortisol levels in children adopted from Romanian orphanages. *Development and Psychopathology, 13*, 611–628.

Gunnar, M. R., & Quevedo, K. (2007). The neurobiology of stress and development. *Annual Review of Psychology, 58*, 145–173.

Gunnarsdottir, I., Schack-Nielsen, L., Michaelson, K. F., Sørensen, T. I., & Thorsdottir, I. (2010). Infant weight gain, duration of exclusive breast-feeding, and childhood BMI—two similar follow-up cohorts. *Public Health Nutrition, 13*, 201–207.

Gupta, J. K., Hofmeyr, G. J., & Shehmar, M. (2012). Position in the second stage of labour for women without epidural anaesthesia. *Cochrane Database of Systematic Reviews, Issue 5*(Art. No. CD002006).

Guo, G., & VanWey, L. K. (1999). Sibship size and intellectual development: Is the relationship causal? *American Sociological Review, 64*, 169–187.

Guralnick, M. J. (2012). Preventive interventions for preterm children: Effectiveness and developmental mechanisms. *Journal of Developmental and Behavioral Pediatrics, 33*, 352–364.

Gure, A., Ucanok, Z., & Sayil, M. (2006). The associations among perceived pubertal timing, parental relations and self-perception in Turkish adolescents. *Journal of Youth and Adolescence, 35*, 541–550.

Gustafson, G. E., Green, J. A., & Cleland, J. W. (1994). Robustness of individual identity in the cries of human infants. *Developmental Psychobiology, 27*, 1–9.

Gustafson, G. E., Wood, R. M., & Green, J. A. (2000). Can we hear the causes of infants' crying? In R. G. Barr & B. Hopkins (Eds.), *Crying as a sign, a symptom, and a signal: Clinical, emotional, and developmental aspects of infant and toddler crying* (pp. 8–22). New York: Cambridge University Press.

Guterman, N. B., Lee, S. J., Taylor, C. A., & Rathouz, P. J. (2009). Parental perceptions of neighborhood processes, stress, personal control, and risk for physical child abuse and neglect. *Child Abuse and Neglect, 33*, 897–906.

Gutman, L. M. (2006). How student and parent goal orientations and classroom goal structures influence the math achievement of African Americans during the high school transition. *Contemporary Educational Psychology, 31*, 44–63.

Guttentag, R., & Ferrell, J. (2004). Reality compared with its alternatives: Age differences in judgments of regret and relief. *Developmental Psychology, 40*, 764–775.

Guttmacher Institute. (2013, December). *Unintended pregnancy in the United States*. Retrieved from www.guttmacher.org/pubs/FB-Unintended-Pregnancy-US.html

Gweon, H., Dodell-Feder, D., Bedney, M., & Saxe, R. (2012). Theory of mind performance in children correlates with functional specialization of a brain region for thinking about thoughts. *Child Development, 83*, 1853–1868.

Gwiazda, J., & Birch, E. E. (2001). Perceptual development: Vision. In E. B. Goldstein (Ed.), *Blackwell handbook of perception* (pp. 636–668). Oxford, UK: Blackwell.

H

Hack, M., & Klein, N. (2006). Young adult attainments of preterm infants. *Journal of the American Medical Association, 295*, 695–696.

Hafen, C. A., Laursen, B., Burk, W. J. Kerr, M., & Stattin, H. (2011). Homophily in stable and unstable adolescent friendships: Similarity breeds constancy. *Personality and Individual Differences, 51*, 607–612.

Hagerman, R. J., Berry-Kravis, E., Kaufmann, W. E., Ono, M. Y., Tartaglia, N., & Lachiewicz, A. (2009). Advances in the treatment of fragile X syndrome. *Pediatrics, 123*, 378–390.

Hahn, S., & Chitty, L. S. (2008). Noninvasive prenatal diagnosis: Current practice and future perspectives. *Current Opinion in Obstetrics and Gynecology, 20*, 146–151.

Haidt, J. (2001). The emotional dog and its rational tail: A social intuitionist approach to moral judgment. *Psychological Review, 108*, 814–834.

Haidt, J. (2013). Moral psychology for the twenty-first century. *Journal of Moral Education, 42*, 281–297.

Haidt, J., & Kesebir, S. (2010). Morality. In S. T. Fiske & D. Gilbert (Eds.), *Handbook of social psychology* (5th ed., pp. 797–832). Hoboken, NJ: Wiley.

Haight, W. L., & Miller, P. J. (1993). *Pretending at home: Early development in a sociocultural context*. Albany: State University of New York Press.

Hainline, L. (1998). The development of basic visual abilities. In A. Slater (Ed.), *Perceptual development: Visual, auditory, and speech perception in infancy* (pp. 37–44). Hove, UK: Psychology Press.

Hakuta, K., Bialystok, E., & Wiley, E. (2003). Critical evidence: A test of the critical period hypothesis for second-language acquisition. *Psychological Science, 14*, 31–38.

Hale, C. M., & Tager-Flusberg, H. (2003). The influence of language on theory of mind: A training study. *Developmental Science, 6*, 346–359.

Hales, V. N., & Ozanne, S. E. (2003). The dangerous road of catch-up growth. *Journal of Physiology, 547*, 5–10.

Halfon, N., & McLearn, K. T. (2002). Families with children under 3: What we know and implications for results and policy. In N. Halfon & K. T. McLearn (Eds.), *Child rearing in America: Challenges facing parents with young children* (pp. 367–412). New York: Cambridge University Press.

Halford, G. S., & Andrews, G. (2006). Reasoning and problem solving. In D. Kuhn & R. Siegler (Eds.), *Handbook of child psychology: Vol. 2. Cognition, perception, and language* (6th ed., pp. 557–608). Hoboken, NJ: Wiley.

Halford, G. S., & Andrews, G. (2010). Information-processing models of cognitive development. In J. G. Bremner & T. D. Wachs (Eds.), *Wiley-Blackwell handbook of infant development: Vol. 1. Basic research* (2nd ed., pp. 698–722). Oxford, UK: Wiley.

Halford, G. S., & Andrews, G. (2011). Information-processing models of cognitive development. In U. Goswami (Ed.), *Wiley-Blackwell handbook of childhood cognitive development* (2nd ed., pp. 697–722). Hoboken, NJ: Wiley-Blackwell.

Halgunseth, L. C., Ispa, J. M., & Rudy, D. (2006). Parental control in Latino families: An integrated review of the literature. *Child Development, 77*, 1282–1297.

Halim, M. L., & Ruble, D. (2010). Gender identity and stereotyping in early and middle childhood. In J. C. Chrisler & D. R. McCreary (Eds.), *Handbook of gender research in psychology* (pp. 495–525). New York: Springer.

Halim, M. L., Ruble, D. N., & Tamis-LeMonda, C. S. (2013). Four-year-olds' beliefs about how others regard males and females. *British Journal of Developmental Psychology, 2013*, 128–135.

Hall, D. G., Burns, T., & Pawluski, J. (2003). Input and word learning: Caregivers' sensitivity to lexical category distinctions. *Journal of Child Language, 30*, 711–729.

Hall, D. T., & Las Heras, M. (2011). Personal growth through career work: A positive approach to careers. In K. S. Cameron & G. M. Spreitzer (Eds.), *Oxford handbook of positive organizational scholarship* (pp. 507–518). New York: Oxford University Press.

Hall, G. S. (1904). *Adolescence*. New York: Appleton-Century-Crofts.

Hall, J. A. (2011). Sex differences in friendship expectations: A meta-analysis. *Journal of Personal and Social Relationships 28*, 723–747.

Halle, T. G. (2003). Emotional development and well-being. In M. H. Bornstein, L. Davidson, C. L. M. Keyes, K. A. Moore, & the Center for Child Well-Being (Eds.), *Well-being: Positive development across the life course* (pp. 125–138). Mahwah, NJ: Erlbaum.

Haller, J. (2005). Vitamins and brain function. In H. R. Lieberman, R. B. Kanarek, & C. Prasad (2005). *Nutritional neuroscience* (pp. 207–233). Philadelphia: Taylor & Francis.

Hallinan, M. T., & Kubitschek, W. N. (1999). Curriculum differentiation and high school achievement. *Social Psychology of Education, 3*, 41–62.

Halpern, C. T., & Kaestle, C. E. (2014). Sexuality in emerging adulthood. In D. L. Tolman & L. M. Diamond (Eds.), *APA handbook of sexuality and psychology* (pp. 487–522). Washington, DC: American Psychological Association.

Halpern, D. F. (2012). *Sex differences in cognitive abilities* (4th ed.). New York: Psychology Press.

Halpern, D. F., Benbow, C. P., Geary, D. C., Gur, R. C., Hyde, J. S., & Gernsbacher, M. A. (2007). The science of sex differences in science and mathematics. *Psychological Science in the Public Interest, 8*, 1–51.

Halpern-Felsher, B. L., Biehl, M., Kropp, R. Y., & Rubinstein, M. L. (2004). Perceived risks and benefits of smoking: Differences among adolescents with different smoking experiences and intentions. *Preventive Medicine, 39*, 559–567.

Halpern-Felsher, B. L., & Cauffman, E. (2001). Costs and benefits of a decision: Decision-making competence in adolescents and adults. *Journal of Applied Developmental Psychology, 22*, 257–273.

Hamer, D. H., Hu, S., Magnuson, V. L., Hu, N., & Pattatucci, A. M. L. (1993). A linkage between DNA markers on the X chromosome and male sexual orientation. *Science, 261*, 321–327.

Hamilton, B. E., Martin, J. A., Osterman, M. J. K., & Curtin, S. C. (2014). Births: Preliminary data for 2013. *National Vital Statistics Reports, 63*(2). Hyattsville, MD: National Center for Health Statistics. Retrieved from www.cdc.gov/nchs/data/nvsr/nvsr63/nvsr63_02.pdf

Hamilton, L., & Armstrong, E. A. (2009). Gendered sexuality in young adulthood: Double binds and flawed options. *Gender and Society, 23*, 589–616.

Hamilton, S. F., & Hamilton, M. A. (2000). Research, intervention, and social change: Improving adolescents' career opportunities. In L. J. Crockett & R. K. Silbereisen (Eds.), *Negotiating adolescence in times of social change* (pp. 267–283). New York: Cambridge University Press.

Hamlin, J. K., Hallinan, E. V., & Woodward, A. L. (2008). Do as I do: 7-month-old infants selectively reproduce others' goals. *Developmental Science, 11*, 487–494.

Hamlin, J. K., & Wynn, K. (2011). Young infants prefer prosocial to antisocial others. *Cognitive Development, 26*, 30–39.

Hammond, S. I., Müller, U., Carpendale, J. I. M., Bibok, M. B., & Lieberman-Finestone, D. (2012). The effects of parental scaffolding on preschoolers' executive function. *Developmental Psychology, 48*, 271–281.

Hammons, A. J., & Fiese, B. H. (2011). Is frequency of shared family meals related to the nutritional health of children and adolescents? *Pediatrics, 127*, e1565–e1574.

Hampton, T. (2014). Studies probe links between childhood asthma and obesity. *Journal of the American Medical Association, 311*, 1718–1719.

Hanawalt, B. A. (1993). *Growing up in medieval London: The experience of childhood in history*. New York: Oxford University Press.

Hanawalt, B. A. (2003). The child in the Middle Ages and the Renaissance. In W. Koops & M. Zuckerman (Eds.), *Beyond the century of childhood: Cultural history and developmental psychology*. Philadelphia: University of Pennsylvania Press.

Hanington, L., Heron, J., Stein, A., & Ramchandani, P. (2012). Parental depression and child outcomes—is marital conflict the missing link? *Child: Care, Health and Development, 38*, 520–529.

Hanioka, T., Ojima, M., Tanaka, K., & Yamamoto, M. (2011). Does secondhand smoke affect the development of dental caries in children? A systematic review. *International Journal of Environmental Research and Public Health, 8*, 1503–1509.

Hanish, L. D., Sallquist, J., DiDonato, M., Fabes, R. A., & Martin, C. L. (2012). Aggression by whom—aggression toward whom: Behavioral predictors of same- and other-gender aggression in early childhood. *Developmental Psychology, 48*, 1450–1462.

Hankin, B. L., Stone, L., & Wright, P. A. (2010). Corumination, interpersonal stress generation, and internalizing symptoms: Accumulating effects and transactional influences in a multiwave study of adolescents. *Development and Psychopathology, 22*, 217–235.

Hannon, E. E., & Johnson, S. P. (2004). Infants use meter to categorize rhythms and melodies: Implications for musical structure learning. *Cognitive Psychology, 50*, 354–377.

Hannon, E. E., & Trehub, S. E. (2005a). Metrical categories in infancy and adulthood. *Psychological Science, 16*, 48–55.

Hannon, E. E., & Trehub, S. E. (2005b). Tuning in to musical rhythms: Infants learn more readily than adults. *Proceedings of the National Academy of Sciences, 102*, 12639–12643.

Hans, S. L., & Jeremy, R. J. (2001). Postneonatal mental and motor development of infants exposed in utero to opiate drugs. *Infant Mental Health Journal, 22*, 300–315.

Hansell, N. K., Wright, M. J., Geffen, G. M., Geffen, L. B., Smith, G. A., & Martin, N. G. (2001). Genetic influence on ERP slow wave measures of working memory. *Behavioral Genetics, 31*, 603–614.

Hansen, M. B., & Markman, E. M. (2009). Children's use of mutual exclusivity to learn labels for parts of objects. *Developmental Psychology, 45*, 592–596.

Hao, L., & Woo, H. S. (2012). Distinct trajectories in the transition to adulthood: Are children of immigrants advantaged? *Child Development, 83*, 1623–1639.

Happé, F., & Frith, U. (2006). The weak coherence account: Detail-focused cognitive style in autism spectrum disorders. *Journal of Autism and Developmental Disorders, 1*, 1–21.

Harachi, T. W., Fleming, C. B., White, H. R., Ensminger, M. E., Abbott, R. D., Catalano, R. F., & Haggerty, K. P. (2006). Aggressive behavior among girls and boys during middle childhood: Predictors and sequelae of trajectory group membership. *Aggressive Behavior, 32*, 279–293.

Harden, K. P. (2014). A sex-positive framework for research on adolescent sexuality. *Perspectives on Psychological Science, 9*, 455–469.

Harden, K. P., & Tucker-Drob, E. M. (2011). Individual differences in the development of sensation seeking and impulsivity during adolescence: Further evidence for a dual systems model. *Developmental Psychology, 47*, 739–746.

Hardy, C. L., Bukowski, W. M., & Sippola, L. K. (2002). Stability and change in peer relationships during the transition to middle-level school. *Journal of Early Adolescence, 22*, 117–142.

Hardy, J. B., Astone, N. M., Brooks-Gunn, J., Shapiro, S., & Miller, T. L. (1998). Like mother, like child: Intergenerational patterns of age at first birth and associations with childhood and adolescent characteristics and adult outcomes in the second generation. *Developmental Psychology, 34*, 1220–1232.

Hardy, S. A., & Carlo, G. (2005). Religiosity and prosocial behaviours in adolescence: The mediating role of prosocial values. *Journal of Moral Education, 34*, 231–249.

Hardy, S. A., & Carlo, G. (2011). Moral identity: What is it, how does it develop, and is it linked to moral action? *Child Development Perspectives, 5*, 212–218.

Hardy, S. A., Pratt, M. W., Pancer, S. M., Olsen, J. A., & Lawford, H. L. (2011). Community and religious involvement as contexts of identity change across late adolescence and emerging adulthood. *International Journal of Behavioral Development, 35*, 125–135.

Harley, K., & Reese, E. (1999). Origins of autobiographical memory. *Developmental Psychology, 35*, 1338–1348.

Harlow, H. F., & Zimmerman, R. (1959). Affectional responses in the infant monkey. *Science, 130*, 421–432.

Harris, M. B. (2008). Primary prevention of pregnancy: Effective school-based programs. In C. Franklin, M. B. Harris, & P. Allen-Meares (Eds.), *The school practitioner's concise companion to preventing dropout and attendance problems* (pp. 89–100). New York: Oxford University Press.

Harris, Y. R., & Graham, J. A. (2007). *The African American child: Development and challenges*. New York: Springer.

Harris-McKoy, D., & Cui, M. (2013). Parental control, adolescent delinquency, and young adult criminal behavior. *Journal of Child and Family Studies, 22*, 836–843.

Harrison, A. O., Wilson, M. N., Pine, C. J., Chan, S. Q., & Buriel, R. (1994). Family ecologies of ethnic minority children. In G. Handel & G. G. Whitchurch (Eds.), *The psychosocial interior of the family* (pp. 187–210). New York: Aldine De Gruyter.

Hart, B. (2004). What toddlers talk about. *First Language, 24*, 91–106.

Hart, B., & Risley, T. R. (1995). *Meaningful differences in the everyday experience of young American children*. Baltimore: Paul H. Brookes.

Hart, C. H., Burts, D. C., Durland, M. A., Charlesworth, R., DeWolf, M., & Fleege, P. O. (1998). Stress behaviors and activity type participation of preschoolers in more and less developmentally appropriate classrooms: SES and sex differences. *Journal of Research in Childhood Education, 13*.

Hart, C. H., Newell, L. D., & Olsen, S. F. (2003). Parenting skills and social-communicative competence in childhood. In J. O. Greene & B. R. Burleson (Eds.), *Handbook of communication and social interaction skills* (pp. 753–797). Mahwah, NJ: Erlbaum.

Hart, C. H., Yang, C., Charlesworth, R., & Burts, D. C. (2003, April). *Kindergarten teaching practices: Associations with later child academic and social/emotional adjustment to school*. Paper presented at the biennial meeting of the Society for Research in Child Development, Tampa, FL.

Hart, C. H., Yang, C., Nelson, L. J., Robinson, C. C., Olsen, J. A., Nelson, D. A., et al. (2000). Peer acceptance in early childhood and subtypes of socially withdrawn behavior in China, Russia and the United States. *International Journal of Behavioral Development, 24*, 73–81.

Hart, D., Atkins, R., & Donnelly, T. M. (2006). Community service and moral development. In M. Killen & J. G. Smetana (Eds.), *Handbook of moral development* (pp. 633–656). Philadelphia: Erlbaum.

Hart, D., Atkins, R., & Matsuba, M. K. (2008). The association of neighborhood poverty with personality change in childhood. *Journal of Personality and Social Psychology, 94*, 1048–1061.

Hart, D., Donnelly, T. M., Youniss, J., & Atkins, R. (2007). High school community service as a predictor of adult voting and volunteering. *American Educational Research Journal, 44*, 197–219.

Hart, D., & Fegley, S. (1995). Prosocial behavior and caring in adolescence: Relations to self-understanding and social judgment. *Child Development, 66*, 1346–1359.

Hart, H., & Rubia, K. (2012). Neuroimaging of child abuse: A review. *Frontiers in Human Neuroscience, 6*, 52.

Harter, S. (1999). *The construction of self: A developmental perspective*. New York: Guilford.

Harter, S. (2006). The self. In N. Eisenberg (Ed.), *Handbook of child psychology: Vol. 3. Social, emotional, and personality development* (6th ed., pp. 505–570). Hoboken, NJ: Wiley.

Harter, S. (2012a). *The construction of the self: Developmental and sociocultural foundations* (2nd ed.). New York: Guilford.

Harter, S. (2012b). Emerging self-processes during childhood and adolescence. In M. R. Leary & J. P. Tangney (Eds.), *Handbook of self and identity* (2nd ed., pp. 680–715). New York: Guilford.

Hartshorn, K. (2003). Reinstatement maintains a memory in human infants for 1½ years. *Developmental Psychobiology, 42*, 269–282.

Hartshorn, K., Rovee-Collier, C., Gerhardstein, P., Bhatt, R. S., Klein, P. J., Aaron, F., Wondoloski, T. L., & Wurtzel, N. (1998a). Developmental changes in the specificity of memory over the first year of life. *Developmental Psychobiology, 33*, 61–78.

Hartshorn, K., Rovee-Collier, C., Gerhardstein, P., Bhatt, R. S., Wondoloski, T. L., Klein, P., Gilch, J., Wurtzel, N., & Campos-deCarvalho, M. (1998b). The ontogeny of long-term memory over the first year-and-a-half of life. *Developmental Psychobiology, 32*, 69–89.

Hartup, W. W. (2006). Relationships in early and middle childhood. In A. L. Vangelisti & D. Perlman (Eds.), *Cambridge handbook of personal relationships* (pp. 177–190). New York: Cambridge University Press.

Hartup, W. W., & Abecassis, M. (2004). Friends and enemies. In P. K. Smith & C. H. Hart (Eds.), *Blackwell handbook of childhood social development* (pp. 285–306). Malden, MA: Blackwell.

Hartup, W. W., & Stevens, N. (1999). Friendships and adaptation across the life span. *Current Directions in Psychological Science, 8*, 76–79.

Harwood, R., Leyendecker, B., Carlson, V., Asencio, M., & Miller, A. (2002). Parenting among Latino families in the U.S. In M. H. Bornstein (Ed.), *Handbook of Parenting: Vol. 4. Social conditions and applied parenting* (2nd ed., pp. 21–46). Mahwah, NJ: Lawrence Erlbaum Associates.

Hasebe, Y., Nucci, L., & Nucci, M. S. (2004). Parental control of the personal domain and adolescent symptoms of psychopathology: A cross-national study in the United States and Japan. *Child Development, 75*, 815–828.

Hau, K.-T., & Ho, I. T. (2010). Chinese students' motivation and achievement. In M. H. Bond (Ed.), *Oxford handbook of Chinese psychology* (pp. 187–204). New York: Oxford University Press.

Hauf, P., Aschersleben, G., & Prinz, W. (2007). Baby do–baby see! How action production influences action perception in infants. *Cognitive Development, 22*, 16–32.

Hauser-Cram, P., Warfield, M. E., Stadler, J., & Sirin, S. R. (2006). School environments and the diverging pathways of students living in poverty. In A. C. Huston & M. N. Ripke (Eds.), *Developmental contexts in middle childhood* (pp. 198–216). New York: Cambridge University Press.

Hauspie, R., & Roelants, M. (2012). Adolescent growth. In N. Cameron & R. Bogin (Eds.), *Human growth and development* (2nd ed., pp. 57–79). London: Elsevier.

Havstad, S. L., Johnson, D. D., Zoratti, E. M., Ezell, J. M., Woodcroft, K., Ownby, D. R., et al. (2012). Tobacco smoke exposure and allergic sensitization in children: A propensity score analysis. *Respirology, 17*, 1068–1072.

Hawkes, D. (2010). Just what difference does teenage motherhood make? Evidence from the millennium cohort study. In Duncan, S., Edwards, R., & Alexander, C. (Eds.), *Teenage parenthood: What's the problem?* (pp. 69–84). London: The Tufnell Press.

Hawkins, R. L., Jaccard, J., & Needle, E. (2013). Nonacademic factors associated with dropping out of high school: Adolescent problem behaviors. *Journal of the Society for Social Work and Research, 4*, 58–75.

Haws, R. A., Yakoob, M. Y., Soomro, T., Menezes, E. V., Darmstadt, G. L., & Bhutta, Z. A. (2009). Reducing stillbirths: Screening and monitoring during pregnancy and labour. *BMC Pregnancy and Childbirth, 9*(Suppl. S1).

Hawton, K., Zahl, D., & Weatherall, R. (2003). Suicide following deliberate self-harm: Long-term follow-up of patients who presented to a general hospital. *British Journal of Psychiatry, 182*, 537–542.

Hay, D. F., Pawlby, S., Waters, C. S., Perra, O., & Sharp, D. (2010). Mothers' antenatal depression and their children's antisocial outcomes. *Child Development, 81*, 149–165.

Hay, P., & Bacaltchuk, J. (2004). Bulimia nervosa. *Clinical Evidence, 12*, 1326–1347.

Hayne, H. (2002). Thoughts from the crib: Meltzoff and Moore (1994) alter our views of mental representation during infancy. *Infant Behavior and Development, 25,* 62–64.

Hayne, H. (2004). Infant memory development: Implications for childhood amnesia. *Developmental Review, 24,* 33–73.

Hayne, H., Herbert, J., & Simcock, G. (2003). Imitation from television by 24- and 30-month-olds. *Developmental Science, 6,* 254–261.

Hayne, H., Rovee-Collier, C., & Perris, E. E. (1987). Categorization and memory retrieval by three-month-olds. *Child Development, 58,* 750–767.

Hayslip, B., Jr., & Kaminski, P. L. (2005). Grandparents raising their grandchildren. *Marriage and Family Review, 37,* 147–169.

Haywood, H. C., & Lidz, C. (2007). *Dynamic assessment in practice.* New York: Cambridge University Press.

Haywood, K., & Getchell, N. (2014). *Life span motor development* (6th ed.). Champaign, IL: Human Kinetics.

Hazen, N. L., McFarland, L., Jacobvitz, D., & Boyd-Soisson, E. (2010). Fathers' frightening behavours and sensitivity with infants: Relations with fathers' attachment representations, father–infant attachment, and children's later outcomes. *Early Child Development and Care, 180,* 51–69.

Healthy Families America. (2011). *Healthy Families America FAQ.* Retrieved from www.healthyfamiliesamerica .org/about_us/faq.shtml

Heckman, J. J., Seong, H. M., Pinto, R., Savelyev, P., & Yavitz, A. (2010). A new cost-benefit and rate of return for the Perry Preschool Program: A summary. In A. J. Reynolds, A. J. Rolnick, M. M. Englund, & J. Temple (Eds.), *Childhood programs and practices in the first decade of life: A human capital integration* (pp. 199–213). New York: Cambridge University Press.

Heil, M., Kavsek, M., Rolke, B., Best, C., & Jansen, P. (2011). Mental rotation in female fraternal twins: Evidence for intrauterine hormone transfer? *Biological Psychology, 86,* 90–93.

Heilbrun, K., Lee, R., & Cottle, C. C. (2005). Risk factors and intervention outcomes: Meta-analyses of juvenile offending. In K. Heilbrun, N. E. S. Goldstein, & R. E. Redding (Eds.), *Juvenile delinquency: Prevention, assessment, and intervention* (pp. 111–133). New York: Oxford University Press.

Heinrich-Weltzien, R., Zorn, C., Monse, B., & Kromeyer-Hauschild, K. (2013). Relationship between malnutrition and the number of permanent teeth in Filipino 10- to 13-year-olds. *BioMed Research International, 2013,* Article ID 205950.

Hellemans, K. G., Sliwowska, J. H., Verma, P., & Weinberg, J. (2010). Prenatal alcohol exposure: Fetal programming and later life vulnerability to stress, expression and anxiety disorders. *Neuroscience and Biobehavioral Reviews, 34,* 791–807.

Helwig, C. C. (2006). Rights, civil liberties, and democracy across cultures. In M. Killen & J. G. Smetana (Eds.), *Handbook of moral development* (pp. 185–210). Philadelphia: Erlbaum.

Helwig, C. C., & Jasiobedzka, U. (2001). The relation between law and morality: Children's reasoning about socially beneficial and unjust laws. *Child Development, 72,* 1382–1393.

Helwig, C. C., & Prencipe, A. (1999). Children's judgments of flags and flag-burning. *Child Development, 70,* 132–143.

Helwig, C. C., & Turiel, E. (2004). Children's social and moral reasoning. In P. K. Smith & C. H. Hart (Eds.), *Blackwell handbook of childhood social development* (pp. 476–490). Malden, MA: Blackwell.

Helwig, C. C., & Turiel, E. (2011). Children's social and moral reasoning. In P. K. Smith & C. H. Hart (Eds.), *The Wiley-Blackwell handbook of childhood social development* (2nd ed., pp. 567–583). Chichester, UK: John Wiley & Sons.

Helwig, C. C., Zelazo, P. D., & Wilson, M. (2001). Children's judgments of psychological harm in normal and canonical situations. *Child Development, 72,* 66–81.

Hendry, L. B., & Kloep, M. (2010). How universal is emerging adulthood? An empirical example. *Journal of Youth Studies, 13,* 169–179.

Henggeler, S. W., Schoenwald, S. K., Borduin, C. M., Rowland, M. D., & Cunningham, P. B. (2009). *Multisystemic therapy for antisocial behavior in children and adolescents* (2nd ed.). New York: Guilford.

Henrich, C. C., Brookmeyer, K. A., Shrier, L. A., & Shahar, G. (2006). Supportive relationships and sexual risk behavior in adolescence: An ecological–transactional approach. *Journal of Pediatric Psychology, 31,* 286–297.

Henrich, C. C., Kuperminc, G. P., Sack, A., Blatt, S. J., & Leadbeater, B. J. (2000). Characteristics and homogeneity of early adolescent friendship groups: A comparison of male and female clique and nonclique members. *Applied Developmental Science, 4,* 15–26.

Henricsson, L., & Rydell, A.-M. (2004). Elementary school children with behavior problems: Teacher–child relations and self-perception. A prospective study. *Merrill-Palmer Quarterly, 50,* 111–138.

Hensley, E., & Briars, L. (2010). Closer look at autism and the measles-mumps-rubella vaccine. *Journal of the American Pharmacists Association, 50,* 736–741.

Hepper, P. G., Dornan, J., & Lynch, C. (2012). Sex differences in fetal habituation. *Developmental Science, 15,* 373–383.

Hepper, P. G., McCartney, G. R., & Shannon, E. A. (1998). Lateralised behaviour in first trimester human foetuses. *Neuropsychologia, 43,* 313–315.

Heppner, M. J. (2013). Women, men and work: The long road to gender equality. In S. D. Brown & R. W. Lent (Eds.), *Career development and counseling: Putting theory and research to work* (2nd ed., pp. 215–244). New York: Wiley.

Heppner, M. J., & Jung, A–K. (2013). Gender and social class: powerful predictors of a life journey. In W. B. Walsh, M. L. Savickas, & P. J. Hartung (Eds.), *Handbook of vocational psychology: Theory, research, and practice* (pp. 81–102). New York: Routledge.

Heraghty, J. L., Hilliard, T. N., Henderson, A. J., & Fleming, P. J. (2008). The physiology of sleep in infants. *Archives of Disease in Childhood, 93,* 982–985.

Herbert, J., Gross, J., & Hayne, H. (2007). Crawling is associated with more flexible memory retrieval by 9-month-old infants. *Developmental Science, 10,* 183–189.

Herman, M. (2004). Forced to choose: Some determinants of racial identification in multiracial adolescents. *Child Development, 75,* 730–748.

Herman-Giddens, M. E. (2006). Recent data on pubertal milestones in United States children: The secular trend toward earlier development. *International Journal of Andrology, 29,* 241–246.

Herman-Giddens, M. E., Steffes, J., Harris, D., Slora, E., Hussey, M., Dowshen, S. A., et al. (2012). Secondary sexual characteristics in boys: Data from the Pediatric Research in Office Settings Network. *Pediatrics, 130,* e1058–e1068.

Hernandez, D. J., Denton, N. A., & Blanchard, V. L. (2011). Children in the United States of America: A statistical portrait by race-ethnicity, immigrant origins, and language. *Annals of the American Academy of Political and Social Science, 633,* 102–127.

Hernandez, D. J., Denton, N. A., Macartney, S., & Blanchard, V. L. (2012). Children in immigrant families: Demography, policy, and evidence for the immigrant paradox. In C. García Coll & A. K. Marks (Eds.), *The Immigrant Paradox in Children and adolescents: Is becoming American a developmental risk?* (pp. 17–36). Washington, DC: American Psychological Association.

Hernando-Herraez, I., Prado-Martinez, J., Garg, P., Fernandez-Callejo, M., Heyn, H., Hvilsom, C., et al. (2013). Dynamics of DNA methyltion in recent human and great ape evolution. *PLOS Genetics, 9*(9), e1003763.

Heron, T. E., Hewar, W. L., & Cooper, J. O. (2013). *Applied behavior analysis.* Upper Saddle River, NJ: Pearson.

Heron-Delaney, M. Anzures, G., Herbert, J. S., Quinn, P. C., Slater, A. M., Tanaka, J. W., et al. (2011). Perceptual training prevents the emergence of the other race effect during infancy. *PLOS ONE, 6,* 231–255.

Herrnstein, R. J., & Murray, C. (1994). *The bell curve.* New York: Free Press.

Hespos, S. J., Ferry, A. L., Cannistraci, C. J., Gore, J., & Park, S. (2010). Using optical imaging to investigate functional cortical activity in human infants. In A. W. Roe (Ed.), *Imaging the brain with optical methods* (pp. 159–176). New York: Springer Science + Business Media.

Hesse, E., & Main, M. (2000). Disorganized infant, child, and adult attachment: Collapse in behavioral and attentional strategies. *Journal of the American Psychoanalytic Association, 48,* 1097–1127.

Hetherington, E. M. (2003). Social support and the adjustment of children in divorced and remarried families. *Childhood, 10,* 237–254.

Hetherington, E. M., Henderson, S. H., & Reiss, D. (1999). Adolescent siblings in stepfamilies: Family functioning and adolescent adjustment. *Monographs of the Society for Research in Child Development, 64*(4, Serial No. 259).

Hetherington, E. M., & Kelly, J. (2002). *For better or for worse: Divorce reconsidered.* New York: Norton.

Hetherington, E. M., & Stanley-Hagan, M. (2000). Diversity among stepfamilies. In D. H. Demo, K. R. Allen, & M. A. Fine (Eds.), *Handbook of family diversity* (pp. 173–196). New York: Oxford University Press.

Hewlett, B. S. (1992). Husband–wife reciprocity and the father–infant relationship among Aka pygmies. In B. S. Hewlett (Ed.), *Father–child relations: Cultural and biosocial contexts* (pp. 153–176). New York: Aldine De Gruyter.

Hewlett, B. S. (2004). Fathers in forager, farmer, and pastoral cultures. In M. E. Lamb (Ed.), *The role of the father in child development* (4th ed., pp. 182–195). Hoboken, NJ: Wiley.

Heyes, C. (2005). Imitation by association. In S. Hurley & N. Chater (Eds.), *Perspectives on imitation: From neuroscience to social science: Vol. 1. Mechanisms of imitation and imitation in animals* (pp. 157–177). Cambridge, MA: MIT Press.

Heyes, C. M. (2010). Where do mirror neurons come from? *Neuroscience and Biobehavioral Reviews, 34,* 575–583.

Heyman, G. D., Dweck, C. S., & Cain, K. M. (1992). Young children's vulnerability to self-blame and helplessness: Relationship to beliefs about goodness. *Child Development, 63,* 401–415.

Heyman, G. D., & Gelman, S. A. (1999). The use of trait labels in making psychological inferences. *Child Development, 70,* 604–619.

Heyman, G. D., & Gelman, S. A. (2000). Preschool children's use of trait labels to make inductive inferences. *Journal of Experimental Child Psychology, 77,* 1–19.

Heyman, G. D., & Legare, C. H. (2004). Children's beliefs about gender differences in the academic and social domains. *Sex Roles, 50,* 227–239.

Heywood, C. (2013). *A history of childhood: Children and childhood in the West from medieval to modern times.* Oxford, UK: Polity.

Hickling, A. K., & Wellman, H. M. (2001). The emergence of children's causal explanations and theories: Evidence from everyday conversation. *Developmental Psychology, 37,* 668–683.

Hicks, J. H., & Goedereis, E. A. (2009). The importance of context and the gain-loss dynamic for understanding grandparent caregivers. In K. Shifren (Ed.), *How caregiving affects development: Psychological implications for child, adolescent, and adult caregivers* (pp. 169–190). Washington, DC: American Psychological Association.

High, P. C., LaGasse, L., Becker, S., Ahlgren, I., & Gardner, A. (2000). Literacy promotion in primary care pediatrics: Can we make a difference? *Pediatrics, 105,* 927–934.

Hilbert, D. D., & Eis, S. D. (2014). Early intervention for emergent literacy development in a collaborative community pre-kindergarten. *Early Childhood Education Journal, 42,* 105–113.

Hildreth, K., & Rovee-Collier, C. (2002). Forgetting functions of reactivated memories over the first year of life. *Developmental Psychobiology, 41,* 277–288.

Hildreth, K., Sweeney, B., & Rovee-Collier, C. (2003). Differential memory-preserving effects of reminders at 6 months. *Journal of Experimental Child Psychology, 84,* 41–62.

Hill, A. L., Degnan, K. A., Calkins, S. D., & Keane, S. P. (2006). Profiles of externalizing behavior problems for boys and girls across preschool: The roles of emotion regulation and inattention. *Developmental Psychology, 42,* 913–928.

Hill, D. B., Menvielle, E., Sica, K. M., & Johnson, A. (2010). An affirmative intervention for families with gender variant children: Parental ratings of child mental health and gender. *Journal of Sex and Marital Therapy, 36,* 6–23.

Hill, E. J., Mead, N. T., Dean, L. R., Hafen, D. M., Gadd, R., Palmer, A. A., & Ferris, M. S. (2006). Researching the 60-hour dual-earner workweek: An alternative to the "opt-out revolution." *American Behavioral Scientist, 49,* 1184–1203.

Hill, J. L., Brooks-Gunn, J., & Waldfogel, J. (2003). Sustained effects of high participation in an early intervention for low-birth-weight premature infants. *Developmental Psychology, 39,* 730–744.

Hill, N. E., & Taylor, I. C. (2004). Parental school involvement and children's academic achievement: Pragmatics and issues. *Current Directions in Psychological Science, 13,* 161–164.

Hillard, P. J. A. (2008). Menstruation in adolescents: What's normal, what's not. *Annals of the New York Academy of Sciences, 1135,* 29–35.

Hillis, S. D., Anda, R. F., Dube, S. R., Felitti, V. J., Marchbanks, P. A., & Marks, J. S. (2004). The association between adverse childhood experiences and adolescent pregnancy, long-term psychosocial consequences, and fetal death. *Pediatrics, 113,* 320–327.

Hilt, L. M. (2004). Attribution retaining for therapeutic change: Theory, practice, and future directions. *Imagination, Cognition, and Personality, 23,* 289–307.

Hines, M. (2011). Prenatal endocrine influences on sexual orientation and on sexually differentiated childhood behavior. *Neuroendicronology, 32,* 170–182.

Hinojosa, T., Sheu, C.-F., & Michael, G. F. (2003). Infant hand-use preference for grasping objects contributes to the development of a hand-use preference for manipulating objects. *Developmental Psychobiology, 43,* 328–334.

Hipfner-Boucher, K., Milburn, T., Weitzman, E., Greenberg, J., Pelletier, J., & Girolametto, L. (2014). Relationships between preschoolers' oral language and phonological awareness. *First Language, 34,* 178–197.

Hirasawa, R., & Feil, R. (2010). Genomic imprinting and human disease. *Essays in Biochemistry, 48,* 187–200.

Hirsh-Pasek, K., & Burchinal, M. (2006). Mother and caregiver sensitivity over time: Predicting language and academic outcomes with variable- and person-centered approaches. *Merill-Palmer Quarterly, 52,* 449–485.

Hirsh-Pasek, K., & Golinkoff, R. M. (2003). *Einstein never used flash cards.* New York: Rodale.

Hobson, J. A., Hobson, R. P., Malik, S., Bargiota, K., & Calo, S. (2013). The relation between social engagement and pretend play in autism. *British Journal of Developmental Psychology, 31,* 114–127.

Hodges, J., & Tizard, B. (1989). Social and family relationships of ex-institutional adolescents. *Journal of Child Psychology and Psychiatry, 30,* 77–97.

Hodnett, E. D., Gates, S., Hofmeyr, G. J., & Sakala, C. (2012). Continuous support for women during childbirth. *Cochrane Database of Systematic Reviews, Issue 7*(Art. No. CD003766).

Hoehn, T., Hansmann, G., Bührer, C., Simbruner, G., Gunn, A. J., Yager, J., et al. (2008). Therapeutic hypothermia in neonates: Review of current clinical data, ILCOR recommendations and suggestions for implementation in neonatal intensive care units. *Resuscitation, 78,* 7–12.

Hoerr, T. (2004). How MI informs teaching at New City School. *Teachers College Record, 106,* 40–48.

Hoff, E. (2003). The specificity of environmental influence: Socioeconomic status affects early vocabulary development via maternal speech. *Child Development, 74,* 1368–1378.

Hoff, E. (2006). How social contexts support and shape language development. *Developmental Review, 26,* 55–88.

Hoff, E. (2013). Interpreting the early language trajectories of children from low-SES and language minority homes: Implications for closing achievement gaps. *Developmental Psychology, 49,* 4–14.

Hoff, E., Core, C., Place, S., Rumiche, R., Senor, M., & Parra, M. (2012). Dual language exposure and early bilingual development. *Journal of Child Language, 39,* 1–27.

Hoff, E., Laursen, B., & Tardif, T. (2002). Socioeconomic status and parenting. In M. H. Bornstein (Ed.), *Handbook of parenting: Vol. 2. Biology and ecology of parenting* (pp. 231–252). Mahwah, NJ: Erlbaum.

Hoff, E. V. (2005). A friend living inside me: The forms and functions of imaginary companions. *Imagination, Cognition and Personality, 24,* 151–189.

Hofferth, S. L. (2010). Home media and children's achievement and behavior. *Child Development, 81,* 1598–1610.

Hofferth, S. L., & Anderson, K. G. (2003). Are all dads equal? Biology versus marriage as a basis for paternal investment. *Journal of Marriage and the Family, 65,* 213–232.

Hofferth, S. L., Forry, N. D., & Peters, H. E. (2010). Child support, father–child contact, and preteens' involvement with nonresidential fathers: Racial/ethnic differences. *Journal of Family Economic Issues, 31,* 14–32.

Hoffman, L. W. (2000). Maternal employment: Effects of social context. In R. D. Taylor & M. C. Wang (Eds.), *Resilience across contexts: Family, work, culture, and community* (pp. 147–176). Mahwah, NJ: Erlbaum.

Hoffman, M. K., Vahratian, A., Sciscione, A. C., Troendle, J. F., & Zhang, J. (2006). Comparison of labor progression between induced and noninduced multiparous women. *Obstetrics and Gynecology, 107,* 1029–1034.

Hoffner, C., & Badzinski, D. M. (1989). Children's integration of facial and situational cues to emotion. *Child Development, 60,* 411–422.

Hokoda, A., & Fincham, F. D. (1995). Origins of children's helpless and mastery achievement patterns in the family. *Journal of Educational Psychology, 87,* 375–385.

Holditch-Davis, D., Belyea, M., & Edwards, L. J. (2005). Prediction of 3-year developmental outcomes from sleep development over the preterm period. *Infant Behavior and Development, 79,* 49–58.

Holdren, J. P., & Lander, E. (2012). *Engage to excel: Producing one million additional college graduates with degrees in science, technology, engineering, and mathematics.* Washington, DC: President's Council of Advisors on Science and Technology.

Holland, A. L. (2004). Plasticity and development. *Brain and Language, 88,* 254–255.

Holland, A. S., & Roisman, G. I. (2010). Adult attachment security and young adults' dating relationships over time: Self-reported, observational, and physiological evidence. *Developmental Psychology, 46,* 552–557.

Holland, J. L. (1985). *Making vocational choices: A theory of vocational personalities and work environments.* Englewood Cliffs, NJ; Prentice-Hall.

Holland, J. L. (1997). *Making vocational choices: A theory of vocational personalities and work environments* (3rd ed.). Odessa, FL: Psychological Assessment Resources.

Hollenstein, T., & Lougheed, J. P. (2013). Beyond storm and stress: Typicality, transactions, timing, and temperament to account for adolescent change. *American Psychologist, 68,* 444–454.

Hollich, G. J., Hirsh-Pasek, K., & Golinkoff, R. M. (2000). Breaking the language barrier: An emergentist coalition model for the origins of word learning. *Monographs of the Society for Research in Child Development, 65*(3, Serial No. 262).

Holmbeck, G. N. (1996). A model of family relational transformations during the transition to adolescence: Parent–adolescent conflict and adaptation. In J. A. Graber, J. Brooks-Gunn, & A. C. Petersen (Eds.), *Transitions through adolescence* (pp. 167–199). Mahwah, NJ: Erlbaum.

Holmes, J., Gathercole, S. E., & Dunning, D. L. (2010). Poor working memory: Impact and interventions. In P. Bauer (Ed.), *Advances in child development and behavior* (Vol. 39, pp. 1–43). London: Academic Press.

Hood, M., Conlon, E., & Andrews, G. (2008). Preschool home literacy practices and children's literacy development: A longitudinal analysis. *Journal of Educational Psychology, 100,* 252–271.

Hopf, L., Quraan, M. A., Cheung, M. J., Taylor, M. J., Ryan, J. D., & Moses, S. N. (2013). Hippocampal lateralization and memory in children. *Journal of the International Neuropsychological Society, 19,* 1042–1052.

Hopkins, B., & Westra, T. (1988). Maternal handling and motor development: An intracultural study. *Genetic, Social and General Psychology Monographs, 14,* 377–420.

Hopkins-Golightly, T., Raz, S., & Sander, C. J. (2003). Influence of slight to moderate risk for birth hypoxia on acquisition of cognitive and language function in the preterm infant: A cross-sectional comparison with preterm-birth controls. *Neuropsychology, 17,* 3–13.

Horn, K., Branstetter, S., Zhang, J., Jarett, T., Tompkins, N. O., Anesetti-Rothermel, A., et al. (2013). Understanding physical activity outcomes as a function of teen smoking cessation. *Journal of Adolescent Health, 53,* 125–131.

Horner, S. L., & Gaither, S. M. (2004). Attribution retraining instruction with a second-grade class. *Early Childhood Education Journal, 31,* 165–170.

Horner, T. M. (1980). Two methods of studying stranger reactivity in infants: A review. *Journal of Child Psychology and Psychiatry, 21,* 203–219.

Hoste, R. R., & Le Grange, D. (2013). Eating disorders in adolescence. In W. T. Donohue, L. T. Benuto, & L. Woodword Tolle (Eds.), *Handbook of Adolescent Health Psychology* (pp. 495–506). New York: Springer.

Houlihan, J., Kropp. T. Wiles, R., Gray, S., & Campbell, C. (2005). *Body burden: The pollution in newborns.* Washington, DC: Environmental Working Group.

Houts, R. M., Barnett-Walker, K. C., Paley, B., & Cox, M. J. (2008). Patterns of couple interaction during the transition to parenthood. *Personal Relationships, 15,* 103–122.

Hovdenak, N., & Haram, K. (2012). Influence of mineral and vitamin supplements on pregnancy outcome. *European Journal of Obstetrics & Gynecology and Reproductive Biology, 164,* 127–132.

Hoven, C. W., Duarte, C. S., Lucas, C. P., Wu, P., Mandell, D. J., Goodwin, R. D., et al. (2005). Psychopathology among New York City public school children 6 months after September 11. *Archives of General Psychiatry, 62,* 545–552.

Howard, K A. S., & Walsh, M. E. (2010). Conceptions of career choice and attainment: Developmental levels in how children think about careers. *Journal of Vocational Behavior, 76,* 143–152.

Howard, K. S., & Brooks-Gunn, J. (2009). The role of home-visiting programs in preventing child abuse and neglect. *Future of Children, 19,* 119–146.

Howe, M. L., Courage, M. L., & Rooksby, M. (2009). The genesis and development of autobiographical memory. In M. L. Courage & N. Cowan (Eds.), *The development of memory in infancy and childhood* (pp. 177–196). Hove, UK: Psychology Press.

Howe, N., Aquan-Assee, J., & Bukowski, W. M. (2001). Predicting sibling relations over time: Synchrony between maternal management styles and sibling relationship quality. *Merrill-Palmer Quarterly, 47,* 121–141.

Howell, K. K., Coles, C. D., & Kable, J. A. (2008). The medical and developmental consequences of prenatal drug exposure. In J. Brick (Ed.), *Handbook of the medical consequences of alcohol and drug abuse* (2nd ed., pp. 219–249). New York: Haworth Press.

Howell, S. R., & Becker, S. (2013). Grammar from the lexicon: Evidence from neural network simulations of language acquisition. In D. Bittner & N. Ruhlig (Eds.), *Lexical bootstrapping: The role of lexis and semantics in child language* (pp. 245–264). Berlin: Walter de Gruyter.

Howell, T. M., & Yuille, J. C. (2004). Healing and treatment of Aboriginal offenders: A Canadian example. *American Journal of Forensic Psychology, 22,* 53–76.

Howes, C., & Matheson, C. C. (1992). Sequences in the development of competent play with peers: Social and social pretend play. *Developmental Psychology, 28,* 961–974.

Hsu, A. S., Chater, N., & Vitányi, P. (2013). Language learning from positive evidence, reconsidered: A simplicity-based approach. *Topics in Cognitive Science, 5,* 35–55.

Huang, C.-C. (2006). Child support enforcement and father involvement for children in never-married mother families. *Fathering, 4,* 97–111.

Huang, C. Y., & Stormshak, E. A. (2011). A longitudinal examination of early adolescence ethnic identity trajectories. *Cultural Diversity and Ethnic Minority Psychology, 17,* 261–270.

Hubbs-Tait, L., Nation, J. R., Krebs, N. F., & Bellinger, D. C. (2005). Neurotoxicants, micronutrients, and social environments: Individual and combined effects on children's development. *Psychological Science in the Public Interest, 6,* 57–121.

Huddleston, J., & Ge, X. (2003). Boys at puberty: Psychosocial implications. In C. Hayward (Ed.), *Gender differences at puberty* (pp. 113–134). New York: Cambridge University Press.

Hudson, J. A., Fivush, R., & Kuebli, J. (1992). Scripts and episodes: The development of event memory. *Applied Cognitive Psychology, 6,* 483–505.

Hudson, J. A., & Mayhew, E. M. Y. (2009). The development of memory for recurring events. In M. L. Courage & N. Cowan (Eds.), *The development of memory in infancy and childhood* (pp. 69–91). Hove, UK: Psychology Press.

Hudziak, J. J., & Rettew, D. C. (2009). Genetics of ADHD. In T. E. Brown (Ed.), *ADHD comorbidities: Handbook for ADHD complications in children and adults* (pp. 23–36). Arlington, VA: American Psychiatric Publishing.

Huebner, C. E., & Payne, K. (2010). Home support for emergent literacy: Follow-up of a community-based implementation of dialogic reading. *Journal of Applied Developmental Psychology, 31,* 195–201.

Huesmann, L. R., Moise-Titus, J., Podolski, C., & Eron, L. D. (2003). Longitudinal relations between children's exposure to TV violence and their aggressive and violent behavior in young adulthood: 1977–1992. *Developmental Psychology, 39,* 201–221.

Hughes, C. (2010). Conduct disorder and antisocial behavior in the under-5s. In C. L. Cooper, J. Field, U. Goswami, R. Jenkins, & B. J. Sahakian (Eds.), *Mental capital and well-being* (pp. 821–827). Malden, MA: Wiley-Blackwell.

Hughes, C., & Dunn, J. (1998). Understanding mind and emotion: Longitudinal associations with mental-state talk between young friends. *Developmental Psychology, 34,* 1026–1037.

Hughes, C., & Ensor, R. (2007). Executive function and theory of mind: Predictive relations from ages 2 to 4. *Developmental Psychology, 43,* 1447–1459.

Hughes, C., & Ensor, R. (2010). Do early social cognition and executive function predict individual differences in preschoolers' prosocial and antisocial behavior? In B. W. Sokol, U. Müller, J. I. M. Carpendale, A. R. Young, & G. Iarocci (Eds.), *Social interaction and the development of social understanding and executive functions* (pp. 418–441). New York: Oxford University Press.

Hughes, C., Ensor, R., & Marks, A. (2010). Individual differences in false belief understanding are stable from 3 to 6 years of age and predict children's mental state talk with school friends. *Journal of Experimental Child Psychology, 108,* 96–112.

Hughes, C., Marks, A., Ensor, R., & Lecce, S. (2010). A longitudinal study of conflict and inner state talk in children's conversations with mothers and younger siblings. *Social Development, 19,* 822–837.

Hughes, J. N. (2011). Longitudinal effects of teacher and student perceptions of teacher–student relationship qualities on academic adjustment. *Elementary School Journal, 112,* 38–60.

Hughes, J. N., Cavell, T. A., & Grossman, P. B. (1997). A positive view of self: Risk or protection for aggressive children? *Development and Psychopathology, 9,* 75–94.

Hughes, J. N., & Kwok, O. (2006). Classroom engagement mediates the effect of teacher–student support on elementary students' peer acceptance. *Journal of School Psychology, 43,* 465–480.

Hughes, J. N., & Kwok, O. (2007). Influence of student–teacher and parent–teacher relationships on lower achieving readers' engagement and achievement in the primary grades. *Journal of Educational Psychology, 99,* 39–51.

Hughes, J. N., Wu, J.-Y., Kwok, O., Villarreal, V., & Johnson, A. Y. (2012). Indirect effects of child reports of teacher–student relationship on achievement. *Journal of Educational Psychology, 104,* 350–365.

Hughes, J. N., Zhang, D., & Hill, C. R. (2006). Peer assessments of normative and individual teacher–student support predict social acceptance and engagement among low-achieving children. *Journal of School Psychology, 43,* 447–463.

Huizenga, H., Crone, E. A., & Jansen, B. (2007). Decision making in healthy children and adults explained by the use of increased complex proportional reasoning rules. *Developmental Science, 10,* 814–825.

Humphrey, T. (1978). Function of the nervous system during prenatal life. In U. Stave (Ed.), *Perinatal physiology* (pp. 651–683). New York: Plenum.

Hunnius, S., & Geuze, R. H. (2004a). Developmental changes in visual scanning of dynamic faces and abstract stimuli in infants: A longitudinal study. *Infancy, 6,* 231–255.

Hunnius, S., & Geuze, R. H. (2004b). Gaze shifting in infancy: A longitudinal study using dynamic faces and abstract stimuli. *Infant Behavior and Development, 27,* 397–416.

Hunt, C. E., & Hauck, F. R. (2006). Sudden infant death syndrome. *Canadian Medical Association Journal, 174,* 1861–1869.

Hunt, E. (2011). *Human intelligence.* New York: Cambridge University Press.

Hunter, L. A. (2014). Vaginal breech birth: Can we move beyond the term breech trial? *Journal of Midwifery and Women's Health, 59,* 320–327.

Huntsinger, C., Jose, P. E., Krieg, D. B., & Luo, Z. (2011). Cultural differences in Chinese American and European American children's drawing skills over time. *Early Childhood Research Quarterly, 26,* 134–145.

Hurewitz, F., Brown-Schmidt, S., Thorpe, K., Gleitman, L. R., & Trueswell, J. C. (2000). One frog, two frog, red frog, blue frog: Factors affecting children's syntactic choices in production and comprehension. *Journal of Psycholinguistic Research, 29,* 597–626.

Hursti, U.-K. (1999). Factors influencing children's food choice. *Annals of Medicine, 31,* 26–32.

Hurt, H., Betancourt, L. M., Malmud, E. K., Shera, D. M., Giannetta, J. M., Brodsky, N. L., et al. (2009). Children with and without gestational cocaine exposure: A neurocognitive systems analysis. *Neurotoxicology and Teratology, 31,* 334–341.

Huston, A. C., & Alvarez, M. M. (1990). The socialization context of gender role development in early adolescence. In R. Montemayor, G. R. Adams, & T. P. Gullotta (Eds.), *From childhood to adolescence: A transitional period?* (pp. 156–179). Newbury Park, CA: Sage.

Huston, A. C., Wright, J. C., Marquis, J., & Green, S. B. (1999). How young children spend their time: Television and other activities. *Developmental Psychology, 35,* 912–925.

Hutchinson, E. A., De Luca, C. R., Doyle, L. W., Roberts, G., & Anderson, P. J. (2013). School-age outcomes of extremely preterm or extremely low birth weight children. *Pediatrics, 131,* e1053–e1061.

Huttenlocher, J., Waterfall, H., Veasilyeva, M., Vevea J., & Hedges, L. (2010). Sources of variability in children's language growth. *Cognitive Psychology, 61,* 343–365.

Huttenlocher, P. R. (2002). *Neural plasticity: The effects of environment on the development of the cerebral cortex.* Cambridge, MA: Harvard University Press.

Huyck, M. H. (1996). Continuities and discontinuities in gender identity in midlife. In V. L. Bengtson (Ed.), *Adulthood and aging* (pp. 98–121). New York: Springer-Verlag.

Hyde, A., Drennan, J., Butler, M., Howlett, E., Carney, M., & Lohan, M. (2013). Parents' constructions of communication with their children about safer sex. *Journal of Clinical Nursing, 22,* 3438–3446.

Hyde, D. C., & Spelke, E. S. (2011). Neural signatures of number processing in human infants: Evidence for two core systems underlying numerical cognition. *Developmental Science, 14,* 360–371.

Hyde, J. S. (2014). Gender similarities and differences. *Annual Review of Psychology, 65,* 373–398.

Hyde, J. S., Essex, M. J., Clark, R., & Klein, M. H. (2001). Maternity leave, women's employment, and marital incompatibility. *Journal of Family Psychology, 15,* 476–491.

Hyde, J. S., Mezulis, A. H., & Abramson, L. Y. (2008). The ABCs of depression: Integrating affective, biological, and cognitive models to explain the emergence of the gender difference in depression. *Psychological Review, 115,* 291–313.

Hymel, S., Schonert-Reichl, K. A., Bonanno, R. A., Vaillancourt, T., & Henderson, N. R. (2010). Bullying and morality: Understanding how good kids can behave badly. In S. Jimerson, S. M. Swearer, & D. L. Espelage (Eds.), *Handbook of bullying in schools: An international perspective* (pp. 101–118). New York: Routledge.

I

Iacoboni, M. (2009). Imitation, empathy, and mirror neurons. *Annual Review of Psychology, 60,* 653–670.

Imai, M., & Haryu, E. (2004). The nature of word-learning biases and their roles for lexical development: From a cross-linguistic perspective. In D. G. Hall & S. R. Waxman (Eds.), *Weaving a lexicon* (pp. 411–444). Cambridge, MA: MIT Press.

Imai, M., Li, L., Haryu, E., Okada, H., Hirsh-Pasek, K., Golinkoff, R. M., & Shigematsu, J. (2008). Novel noun and verb learning in Chinese-, English-, and Japanese-speaking children. *Child Development, 79,* 979–1000.

Impett, E. A., Sorsoli, L., Schooler, D., Henson, J. M., & Tolman, D. L. (2008). Girls' relationship authenticity and self-esteem across adolescence. *Developmental Psychology, 44,* 722–733.

Ingoldsby, E. M., Shelleby, E., Lane, T., & Shaw, D. S. (2012). Extrafamilial contexts and children's conduct problems. In V. Maholmes & R. B. King (Eds.), *Oxford handbook of poverty and child development* (pp. 404–422). New York: Oxford University Press.

Inhelder, B., & Piaget, J. (1958). *The growth of logical thinking from childhood to adolescence: An essay on the construction of formal operational structures.* New York: Basic Books. (Original work published 1955)

Insana, S. P., & Montgomery-Downs, H. E. (2012). Sleep and sleepiness among first-time postpartum parents: A field- and laboratory-based multimethod assessment. *Developmental Psychobiology, 55,* 361–372.

Ip, S., Chung, M., Raman, G. Trikalinos, T. A., & Lau, J. (2009). A summary of the Agency for Healthcare Research and Quality's evidence report on breastfeeding in developed countries. *Breastfeeding Medicine, 4*(Suppl. 1), S17–S30.

Iruka, I. U., Winn, D-M. C., & Harradine, C. (2014). High achieving African American boys: Factors that contribute to their excellence in the early years. In J. Moore, III, & C. Lewis (Eds.), *African American male students in preK-12 schools: Informing research, policy, and practice* (pp. 27–59). Bingley, UK: Emerald Group.

Isabella, R. (1993). Origins of attachment: Maternal interactive behavior across the first year. *Child Development, 64,* 605–621.

Isabella, R., & Belsky, J. (1991). Interactional synchrony and the origins of infant–mother attachment: A replication study. *Child Development, 62,* 373–384.

Ishihara, K., Warita, K., Tanida, T., Sugawara, T., Kitagawa, H., & Hoshi, N. (2007). Does paternal exposure to 2,3,7, 8-tetrachlorodibenzo-p-dioxin (TCDD) affect the sex ratio of offspring? *Journal of Veterinary Medical Science, 69,* 347–352.

Isles, A. R., & Wilkinson, L. S. (2011). Genomic imprinting effects on brain and behavior: Future directions. In A. Petronis & J. Mill (Eds.), *Brain, behavior and epigenetics* (pp. 169–184). New York: Springer.

Israel, M. Johnson, C., & Brooks, P. J. (2000). From states to events: The acquisition of English passive participles. *Cognitive Linguistics, 11,* 103–129.

Ivorra, J. L., Sanjuan, J., Jover, M., Carot, J. M., de Frutos, R., & Molto, M. D. (2010). Gene-environment interaction of child temperament. *Journal of Developmental and Behavioral Pediatrics, 31,* 545–554.

Izard, C. E., King, P. A., Trentacosta, C. J., Laurenceau, J. P., Morgan, J. K, Krauthamer-Ewing, E. S., & Finlon, K. J. (2008). Accelerating the development of emotion competence in Head Start children. *Development and Psychopathology, 20,* 369–397.

Izard, V., Dehaene-Lambertz, G., & Dehaene, S. (2008). Distinct cerebral pathways for object identity and number in human infants. *PLOS Biology, 6*(2), e11.

Izard, V., Sann, C., Spelke, E. S., & Streri, A. (2009). Newborn infants perceive abstract numbers. *Proceedings of the National Academy of Sciences, 106,* 10382–10385.

J

Jaccard, J., Dodge, T., & Dittus, P. (2002). Parent–adolescent communication about sex and birth control: A conceptual framework. In S. S. Feldman & D. A. Rosenthal (Eds.), *Talking sexuality: Parent–adolescent communication* (pp. 9–41). San Francisco: Jossey-Bass.

Jack, F., Simcock, G., & Hayne, G. (2012). Magic memories: Young children's verbal recall after a 6-year delay. *Child Development, 83,* 159–172.

Jackson, A. P., Bentler, P. M., & Franke, T. M. (2006). Employment and parenting among current and former welfare recipients. *Journal of Social Service Research, 33,* 13–25.

Jackson, L. A., von Eye, A., Witt, E. A., Zhao, Y., & Fitzgerald, H. E. (2011). A longitudinal study of the effects of Internet use and videogame playing on academic performance and the roles of gender, race and income in these relationships. *Computers in Human Behavior, 27,* 228–239.

Jackson, T. E., & Falmagne, R. J. (2013). Women wearing white: Discourses of menstruation and the experience of menarche. *Feminism and Psychology, 23,* 379–398.

Jacobs, J. E., & Klaczynski, P. A. (2002). The development of judgment and decision making during childhood and adolescence. *Current Directions in Psychological Science, 11,* 145–149.

Jacobs, J. E., Lanza, S., Osgood, D. W., Eccles, J. S., & Wigfield, A. (2002). Changes in children's self-competence and values: Gender and domain differences across grades one through twelve. *Child Development, 73,* 509–527.

Jacobs, J. N., & Kelley, M. L. (2006). Predictors of paternal involvement in childcare in dual-earner families with young children. *Fathering, 4,* 23–47.

Jacobson, J. L., & Jacobson, S. W. (2003). Prenatal exposure to polychlorinated biphenyls and attention at school age. *Journal of Pediatrics, 143,* 780–788.

Jacobson, K. C., & Crockett, L. J. (2000). Parental monitoring and adolescent adjustment: An ecological perspective. *Journal of Research on Adolescence, 10,* 65–97.

Jacquet, P. (2004). Sensitivity of germ cells and embryos to ionizing radiation. *Journal of Biological Regulators and Homeostatic Agents, 18,* 106–114.

Jadallah, M., Anderson, R. C., Nguyen-Jahiel, K., Miller, B. W., Kim, I-H., Kuo, L-J., et al. (2011). Influence of a teacher's scaffolding moves during child-led small-group discussions. *American Educational Research Journal, 48,* 194–230.

Jadva, V., Casey, P., & Golombok, S. (2012). Surrogacy families 10 years on: Relationship with the surrogate, decisions over disclosure and children's understanding of their surrogacy origins. *Human Reproduction, 27,* 3008–3014.

Jaffari-Bimmel, N., Juffer, F., van IJzendoorn, M. H., Bakermans-Kranenburg, M. J., & Mooijaart, A. (2006). Social development from infancy to adolescence: Longitudinal and concurrent factors in an adoption sample. *Developmental Psychology, 42,* 1143–1153.

Jaffee, S. R., Bowes, L., Ouellet-Morin, I., Fisher, H. L., Moffitt, T. E., Merrick, M. T., & Arseneault, L. (2013). Safe, stable, nurturing relationships break the intergenerational cycle of abuse: A prospective nationally representative cohort of children in the United Kingdom. *Journal of Adolescent Health, 53,* S4–S10.

Jaffee, S. R., Caspi, A., Moffitt, T. E., Belsky, J., & Silva, P. (2001). Why are children born to teen mothers at risk for adverse outcomes in young adulthood? *Development and Psychopathology, 13,* 377–397.

Jaffee, S. R., & Christian, C. W. (2014). The biological embedding of child abuse and neglect: Implications for policy and practice. *Society for Research in Child Development Social Policy Report, 28*(1).

Jaffee, S. R., & Hyde, J. S. (2000). Gender differences in moral orientation: A meta-analysis. *Psychological Bulletin, 126,* 703–706.

Jaffee, S. R., Moffitt, T. E., Caspi, A., & Taylor, A. (2003). Life with (or without) father: The benefits of living with two biological parents depend on the father's antisocial behavior. *Child Development, 74,* 109–126.

Jahanfar, S., Lye, M.-S., & Krishnarajah, I. S. (2013). Genetic and environmental effects on age at menarche, and its relationship with reproductive health in twins. *Indian Journal of Human Genetics, 19,* 245–250.

Jambon, M., & Smetana, J. G. (2014). Moral complexity in middle childhood: Children's evaluations of necessary harm. *Developmental Psychology, 50,* 22–33.

James, J., Ellis, B. J., Schlomer, G. L., & Garber, J. (2012). Sex-specific pathways to early puberty, sexual debut, and sexual risk taking: Tests of an integrated evolutionary–developmental model. *Developmental Psychology, 48,* 687–702.

Jang, S. J., & Johnson, B. R. (2001). Neighborhood disorder, individual religiosity, and adolescent use of illicit drugs: A test of multilevel hypotheses. *Criminology, 39,* 109–143.

Jansen, A., Theunissen, N., Slechten, K., Nederkoorn, C., Boon, B., Mulkens, S., & Roefs, A. (2003). Overweight children overeat after exposure to food cues. *Eating Behaviors, 4,* 197–209.

Jansen, J., de Weerth, C., & Riksen-Walraven, J. M. (2008). Breastfeeding and the mother–infant relationship. *Developmental Review, 28,* 503–521.

Jansen, P. W., Roza, S. J., Jaddoe, V. W. V., Mackenbach, J. D., Raat, H., Hofman, A., et al. (2012). Children's eating behavior, feeding practices of parents and weight problems in early childhood: Results from the population-based Generation R Study. *International Journal of Behavioral Nutrition and Physical Activity, 9,* 130–138.

Janssens, J. M. A. M., & Deković, M. (1997). Child rearing, prosocial moral reasoning, and prosocial behavior. *International Journal of Behavioral Development, 20,* 509–527.

Jaudes, P. K., & Mackey-Bilaver, L. (2008). Do chronic conditions increase young children's risk of being maltreated? *Child Abuse and Neglect, 32,* 671–681.

Jedrychowski, W., Perera, F. P., Jankowski, J., Mrozek-Budzyn, D., Mroz, E., Flak, E., et al. (2009). Very low prenatal exposure to lead and mental development of children in infancy and early childhood. *Neuroepidemiology, 32,* 270–278.

Jeffrey, J. (2004, November). Parents often blind to their kids' weight. *British Medical Journal Online.* Retrieved from content.health.msn.com/content/article/97/104292.htm

Jenkins, J. M., Rasbash, J., & O'Connor, T. G. (2003). The role of the shared family context in differential parenting. *Developmental Psychology, 39,* 99–113.

Jenni, O. G., & Carskadon, M. A. (2012). Sleep behavior and sleep regulation from infancy through adolescence: Normative aspects. *Sleep Medicine Clinics, 7,* 529–538.

Jennifer, D., & Cowie, H. (2009). Engaging children and young people actively in research. In K. Bryan (Ed.), *Communication in healthcare* (pp. 135–163). New York: Peter Lang.

Jensen, A. R. (1969). How much can we boost IQ and scholastic achievement? *Harvard Educational Review, 39,* 1–123.

Jensen, A. R. (1998). *The g factor: The science of mental ability.* New York: Praeger.

Jensen, A. R. (2001). Spearman's hypothesis. In J. M. Collis & S. Messick (Eds.), *Intelligence and personality: Bridging the gap in theory and measurement* (pp. 3–24). Mahwah, NJ: Erlbaum.

Jensen, A. R. (2002). Galton's legacy to research on intelligence. *Journal of Biosocial Science, 34,* 145–172.

Jeong, S.-H. & Fishbein, M. (2007). Predictors of multitasking with media: Media factors and audience factors. *Media Psychology, 10,* 364–384.

Jerome, E. M., Hamre, B. K., & Pianta, R. C. (2009). Teacher–child relationships from kindergarten to sixth grade: Early childhood predictors of teacher-perceived conflict and closeness. *Social Development, 18,* 915–945.

Jeynes, W. (2012). A meta-analysis of the efficacy of different types of parental involvement programs for urban students. *Urban Education, 47,* 706–742.

Ji, C. Y., & Chen, T. J. (2008). Secular changes in stature and body mass index for Chinese youth in sixteen major cities, 1950s–2005. *American Journal of Human Biology, 20,* 530–537.

Jiao, S., Ji, G., & Jing, Q. (1996). Cognitive development of Chinese urban only children and children with siblings. *Child Development, 67,* 387–395.

Jipson, J. L., & Gelman, S. A. (2007). Robots and rodents: Children's inferences about living and nonliving kinds. *Child Development, 78,* 1675–1688.

Joe, G. W., Kalling Knight, D., Becan, J. E., & Flynn, P. M. (2014). Recovery among adolescents: Models for post-treatment gains in drug abuse treatments. *Journal of Substance Abuse Treatment, 46,* 362–373.

Joh, A. S., & Adolph, K. E. (2006). Learning from falling. *Child Development, 77,* 89–102.

Johnson, A. D., Ryan, R. M., & Brooks-Gunn, J. (2012). Child-care subsidies: Do they impact the quality of care children experience? *Child Development, 83,* 1444–1461.

Johnson, C., & Mindell, J. A. (2011). Family-based interventions for sleep problems of infants. In M. El-Sheikh (Ed.), *Sleep and development: Familial and socio-cultural considerations* (pp. 375–402). New York: Oxford University Press.

Johnson, E. K., & Seidl, A. (2008). Clause segmentation by 6-month-old infants: A crosslinguistic perspective. *Infancy, 13,* 440–455.

Johnson, E. K., & Tyler, M. D. (2010). Testing the limits of statistical learning for word segmentation. *Developmental Science, 13,* 339–345.

Johnson, J. G., Cohen, P., Smailes, E. M., Kasen, S., & Brook, J. S. (2002). Television viewing and aggressive behavior during adolescence and adulthood. *Science, 295,* 2468–2471.

Johnson, M. D., Cohan, C. L., Davilla, J., Lawrence, E., Rogge, R. D., Karney, B. R., et al. (2005). Problem-solving skills and affective expressions as predictors of change in marital satisfaction. *Journal of Consulting and Clinical Psychology, 73,* 15–27.

Johnson, M. H. (1999). Ontogenetic constraints on neural and behavioral plasticity: Evidence from imprinting and face processing. *Canadian Journal of Experimental Psychology, 55,* 77–90.

Johnson, M. H. (2001). The development and neural basis of face recognition: Comment and speculation. *Infant and Child Development, 10,* 31–33.

Johnson, M. H. (2011). Developmental neuroscience, psychophysiology, and genetics. In M. H. Bornstein & M. E. Lamb (Eds.), *Developmental science: An advanced textbook* (6th ed., pp. 187–222). Mahwah, NJ: Erlbaum.

Johnson, M. H., & Mareschal, D. (2001). Cognitive and perceptual development during infancy. *Current Opinion in Neurobiology, 11,* 213–218.

Johnson, R. C., & Schoeni, R. F. (2011). Early-life origins of adult disease: National longitudinal population-based study of the United States. *American Journal of Public Health, 101,* 2317–2324.

Johnson, S., Li, J., Kendall, G., Strazdins, L., & Jacoby, P. (2013). Mothers' and fathers' work hours, child gender, and behavior in middle childhood. *Journal of Marriage and Family, 75,* 56–74.

Johnson, S. C., Dweck, C. S., & Chen, F. S. (2007). Evidence for infants' internal working models of attachment. *Psychological Science, 18,* 501–502.

Johnson, S. C., Dweck, C., Chen, F. S., Stern, H. L., Ok, S.-J., & Barth, M. (2010). At the intersection of social and cognitive development: Internal working models of attachment in infancy. *Cognitive Science, 34,* 807–825.

Johnson, S. L. (2000). Improving preschoolers' self-regulation of energy intake. *Pediatrics, 106,* 1429–1435.

Johnson, S. P. (1997). Young infants' perception of object unity: Implications for development of attentional and cognitive skills. *Current Directions in Psychological Science, 6,* 5–11.

Johnson, S. P. (2009). Developmental origins of object perception. In A. Woodward & A. Needham (Eds.), *Learning and the infant mind* (pp. 47–65). New York: Oxford University Press.

Johnson, S. P. (2010). How infants learn about the visual world. *Cognitive Science, 34,* 1158–1184.

Johnson, S. P. (2011). A constructivist view of object perception in infancy. In L. M. Oakes, C. H. Cashon, M. Casasola, & D. Rakison (Eds.), *Infant perception and cognition* (pp. 51–68). New York: Oxford University Press.

Johnson, S. P., Bremner, J. G., Slater, A., Mason, U., Foster, K., & Cheshire, A. (2003). Infants' perception of object trajectories. *Child Development, 74,* 94–108.

Johnson, S. P., Fernandes, K. J., Frank, M. C., Kirkham, N. Z., Marcus, G. F., et al. (2009). Abstract rule learning for visual sequences in 8- and 11-month-olds. *Infancy, 14,* 2–18.

Johnson, S. P., & Shuwairi, S. M. (2009). Learning and memory facilitate predictive tracking in 4-month-olds. *Journal of Experimental Child Psychology, 102,* 122–130.

Johnson, S. P., Slemmer, J. A., & Amso, D. (2004). Where infants look determines how they see: Eye movements and object perception performance in 3-month-olds. *Infancy, 6,* 185–201.

Johnston, L. D., O'Malley, P. M., Miech, R. A., Bachman, J. G., & Schulenberg, J. E. (2014). National survey results on drug use: 1975–2013. Key findings on adolescent drug use. Retrieved from www.monitoringthefuture.org/pubs/monographs/mtf-overview2013.pdf

Johnston, M. V., Nishimura, A., Harum, K., Pekar, J., & Blue, M. E. (2001). Sculpting the developing brain. *Advances in Pediatrics, 48,* 1–38.

Jokhi, R. P., & Whitby, E. H. (2011). Magnetic resonance imaging of the fetus. *Developmental Medicine and Child Neurology, 53,* 18–28.

Jones, A., Charles, P., & Benson, K. (2013). A model for supporting at-risk couples during the transition to parenthood. *Families in Society, 94,* 166–173.

Jones, C. M., Braithwaite, V. A., & Healy, S. D. (2003). The evolution of sex differences in spatial ability. *Behavioral Neuroscience, 117,* 403–411.

Jones, D. J., & Lindahl, K. M. (2011). Coparenting in extended kinship systems: African American, Hispanic, Asian heritage, and Native American families. In J. P. McHale & K. M. Lindahl (Eds.), *Coparenting* (pp. 61–79). Washington, DC: American Psychological Association.

Jones, H. E. (2006). Drug addiction during pregnancy: Advances in maternal treatment and understanding child outcomes. *Current Directions in Psychological Science, 15,* 126–130.

Jones, J., Lopez, A., & Wilson, M. (2003). Congenital toxoplasmosis. *American Family Physician, 67,* 2131–2137.

Jones, J., Mosher, W., & Daniels, K. (2012). Current contraceptive use in the United States 2006–2010, and changes in patterns of use since 1995. *National Health Statistics Reports, 60,* 1–26. Retrieved from www.cdc.gov/nchs/data/nhsr/nhsr060.pdf

Jones, M. C., & Mussen, P. H. (1958). Self-conceptions, motivations, and interpersonal attitudes of early- and late-maturing girls. *Child Development, 29,* 491–501.

Jones, S. (2009). The development of imitation in infancy. *Philosophical Transactions of the Royal Society B, 364,* 2325–2335.

Jordan, B. (1993). *Birth in four cultures.* Prospect Heights, IL: Waveland.

Jorgenson, L. A., Sun, M., O'Connor, M., & Georgieff, M. K. (2005). Fetal iron deficiency disrupts and maturation of synaptic function and efficacy in area CA1 of the developing rat hippocampus. *Hippocampus, 15,* 1094–1102.

Jose, A., O'Leary, D., & Moyer, A. (2010). Does premarital cohabitation predict subsequent marital stability and marital quality? A meta-analysis. *Journal of Marriage and Family, 72,* 105–116.

Joseph, R. M., & Tager-Flusberg, H. (2004). The relationship of theory of mind and executive functions to symptom type and severity in children with autism. *Development and Psychopathology, 16,* 137–155.

Josselyn, S. A., & Frankland, P. W. (2012). Infantile amnesia: A neurogenic hypothesis. *Learning and Memory, 19,* 423–433.

Juby, H., Billette, J.-M., Laplante, B., & Le Bourdais, C. (2007). Nonresident fathers and children: Parents' new unions and frequency of contact. *Journal of Family Issues, 28,* 1220–1245.

Judge, S., Puckett, K., & Bell, S. M. (2006). Closing the digital divide: Update from the Early Childhood Longitudinal Study. *Journal of Educational Research, 100,* 52–60.

Juffer, F., & van IJzendoorn, M. H. (2012). Review of meta-analytical studies on the physical, emotional, and cognitive outcomes of intercountry adoptees. In J. L. Gibbons & K. S. Rotabi (Eds.), *Intercountry adoption: Policies, practices, and outcomes* (pp. 175–186). Burlington, VT: Ashgate Publishing.

Junge, C., Kooijman, V., Hagoort, P., & Cutler, A. (2012). Rapid recognition at 10 months as a predictor of language development. *Developmental Science, 15,* 463–473.

Jürgensen, M., Hiort, O., Holterhus, P.-M., & Thyen, U. (2007). Gender role behavior in children with XY karyotype and disorders of sex development. *Hormones and Behavior, 51,* 443–453.

Jusczyk, P. W. (2002). Some critical developments in acquiring native language sound organization. *Annals of Otology, Rhinology and Laryngology, 189,* 11–15.

Jusczyk, P. W., Johnson, S. P., Spelke, E. S., & Kennedy, L. J. (1999). Synchronous change and perception of object unity: Evidence from adults and infants. *Cognition, 71,* 257–288.

Jusczyk, P. W., & Luce, P. A. (2002). Speech perception. In H. Pashler & S. Yantis (Eds.), *Steven's handbook of experimental psychology: Vol. 1. Sensation and perception* (3rd ed., pp. 493–536). New York: Wiley.

Justice, E. M. (1986). Developmental changes in judgments of relative strategy effectiveness. *British Journal of Developmental Psychology, 4,* 75–81.

Jutras-Aswad, D., DiNieri, J. A., Harkany, T., & Hurd, Y. L. (2009). Neurobiological consequences of maternal cannabis on human fetal development and its neuropsychiatric outcome. *European Archives of Psychiatry and Clinical Neuroscience, 259,* 395–412.

K

Kaffashi, F., Scher, M. S., Ludington-Hoe, S. M., & Loparo, K. A. (2013). An analysis of the kangaroo care intervention using neonatal EEG complexity: A preliminary study. *Clinical Neurophysiology, 124,* 238–246.

Kagan, J. (2003). Behavioral inhibition as a temperamental category. In R. J. Davidson, K. R. Scherer, & H. H. Goldsmith (Eds.), *Handbook of affective sciences* (pp. 320–331). New York: Oxford University Press.

Kagan, J. (2008). Behavioral inhibition as a risk factor for psychopathology. In T. P. Beauchaine & S. P. Hinshaw (Eds.), *Child and adolescent psychopathology* (pp. 157–179). Hoboken, NJ: Wiley.

Kagan, J. (2010). Emotions and temperament. In M. H. Bornstein (Ed.), *Handbook of cultural developmental science* (pp, 175–194). New York: Psychology Press.

Kagan, J. (2013a). Contextualizing experience. *Developmental Review, 33,* 273–278.

Kagan, J. (2013b). Equal time for psychological and biological contributions to human variation. *Review of General Psychology, 17,* 351–357.

Kagan, J. (2013c). *The human spark: The science of human development.* New York: Basic Books.

Kagan, J. (2013d). Temperamental contributions to inhibited and uninhibited profiles. In P. D. Zelazo (Ed.), *The Oxford handbook of developmental psychology* (142–164). New York: Oxford University Press.

Kagan, J., Snidman, N., Kahn, V., & Towsley, S. (2007). The preservation of two infant temperaments into adolescence. *Monographs of the Society for Research in Child Development, 72*(2, Serial No. 287).

Kagan, J., Snidman, N., Zentner, M., & Peterson, E. (1999). Infant temperament and anxious symptoms in school-age children. *Development and Psychopathology, 11,* 209–224.

Kahana-Kalman, R., & Walker-Andrews, A. S. (2001). The role of person familiarity in young infants' perception of emotional expressions. *Child Development, 72,* 352–362.

Kahn, J. R., Goldscheider, F., & García-Manglano, J. (2013). Growing parental economic power in parent–adult child households: Coresidence and financial dependency in the United States, 1960–2010. *Demography, 50,* 1449–1475.

Kahn, R. S., Khoury, J., Nichols, W. C., & Lanphear, B. M. (2003). Role of dopamine transporter genotype and maternal prenatal smoking in childhood hyperactive-impulsive, inattentive, and oppositional behaviors. *Journal of Pediatrics, 143,* 104–110.

Kahne, J. E., & Sporte, S. E. (2008). Developing citizens: The impact of civic learning opportunities on students' commitments to civic participation. *American Educational Research Journal, 45,* 738–766.

Kail, R. V. (2003). Information processing and memory. In M. H. Bornstein, L. Davidson, C. L. M. Keyes, K. A. Moore, and the Center for Child Well-Being (Eds.), *Well-being: Positive development across the life course* (pp. 269–280). Mahwah, NJ: Erlbaum.

Kail, R. V., & Ferrer, E. F. (2007). Processing speed in childhood and adolescence: Longitudinal models for examining developmental change. *Child Development, 78,* 1760–1770.

Kail, R. V., McBride-Chang, C., Ferrer, E., Cho, J.-R., & Shu, H. (2013). Cultural differences in the development of processing speed. *Developmental Science, 16,* 476–483.

Kaiser Family Foundation. (2014). *How will the uninsured fare under the Affordable Care Act?* Retrieved from kff.org/health-reform/fact-sheet/how-will-the-uninsured-fare-under-the-affordable-care-act

Kakihara, F., Tilton-Weaver, L., Kerr, M., & Stattin, H. (2010). The relationship of parental control to youth adjustment: Do youths' feelings about their parents play a role? *Journal of Youth and Adolescence, 39,* 1442–1456.

Kalil, A., Levine, J. A., & Ziol-Guest, K. M. (2005). Following in their parents' footsteps: How characteristics of parental work predict adolescents' interest in parents' jobs. In B. Schneider & L. J. Waite (Eds.), *Being together, working apart: Dual-career families and the work-life balance* (pp. 422–442). New York: Cambridge University Press.

Kalogrides, D., & Loeb, S. (2013). Different teachers, different peers: The magnitude of student sorting within schools. *Educational Researcher, 42,* 306–316.

Kalra, L., & Ratan, R. (2007). Recent advances in stroke rehabilitation. *Stroke, 38,* 235–237.

Kaminski, J. W., Puddy, R. W., Hall, D. M., Cashman, S. Y., Crosby, A. E., & Ortega, L. G. (2010). The relative influence of different domains of social connectedness on self-directed violence in adolescence. *Journal of Youth and Adolescence, 39,* 460–473.

Kaminsky, Z., Petronis, A., Wang, S–C., Levine, B., Ghaffar, O., Floden, D., et al. (2007). Epigenetics of personality traits: An illustrative study of identical twins discordant for risk-taking behavior. *Twin Research and Human Genetics, 11,* 1–11.

Kanazawa, S. (2012). Intelligence, birth order, and family size. *Personality and Social Psychology Bulletin, 38,* 1157–1164.

Kane, P., & Garber, J. (2004). The relations among depression in fathers, children's psychopathology, and father–child conflict: A meta-analysis. *Clinical Psychology Review, 24,* 339–360.

Kang, N. H., & Hong, M. (2008). Achieving excellence in teacher workforce and equity in learning opportunities in South Korea. *Educational Researcher, 37,* 200–207.

Kann, L., Kinchen, S., Shanklin, S. L., Flint, K. H., Hawkins, J., Harris, W. A., et al. (2014). Youth risk behavior surveillance—United States, 2013. *Morbidity and Mortality Weekly Report, 63*(4). Retrieved from www.cdc.gov/mmwr/pdf/ss/ss6304.pdf

Kann, L., Olsen, E. O., McManus, T., Kinchen, S., Chyen, D., Harris, W. A., et al. (2011). Sexual identity, sex of sexual contacts, and health-risk behaviors among students in grades 9–12.Youth Risk Behavior Surveillance, Selected Sites, United States, 2001–2009. *Morbidity and Mortality Weekly Report, 60,* 1–127.

Kantaoka, S., & Vandell, D. L. (2013). Quality of afterschool activities and relative change in adolescent functioning over two years. *Applied Developmental Science, 17*(3), 123–134.

Kanters, M. A., Bocarro, J. N., Edwards, M., Casper, J., & Floyd, M. F. (2013). School sport participation under two school sport policies: Comparisons by race/ethnicity, gender, and socioeconomic status. *Annals of Behavioral Medicine 45*(Suppl. 1), S113–S121.

Kaplan, D. L., Jones, E. J., Olson, E. C., & Yunzal-Butler, C. B. (2013). Early age of first sex and health risk in an urban adolescent population. *Journal of School Health, 83,* 350–356.

Kaplow, J. B., & Widom, C. S. (2007). Age of onset of child maltreatment predicts long-term mental health outcomes. *Journal of Abnormal Psychology, 116,* 176–187.

Kaplowitz, P. B. (2008). Link between body fat and timing of puberty. *Pediatrics, 121,* S208–S217.

Karafantis, D. M., & Levy, S. R. (2004). The role of children's lay theories about the malleability of human attributes in beliefs about and volunteering for disadvantaged groups. *Child Development, 75,* 236–250.

Karasik, L. B., Adolph, K., Tamis-LeMonda, C. S., & Zuckerman (2012). Carry on: Spontaneous object carrying in 13-month-old crawling and walking infants. *Developmental Psychology, 48,* 389–397.

Karasik, L. B., Tamis-LeMonda, C. S., & Adolph, K. E. (2011). Transition from crawling to walking and infants' actions with objects and people. *Child Development, 82,* 1199–1209.

Karemaker, A., Pitchford, N., & O'Malley, C. (2010). Enhanced recognition of written words and enjoyment of reading in struggling beginner readers through whole-word multimedia software. *Computers and Education, 54,* 199–208.

Karevold, E., Ystrom, E., Coplan, R. J., Sanson, A. V., & Mathiesen, K. S. (2012). A prospective longitudinal study of shyness from infancy to adolescence: Stability, age-related changes, and prediction of socio-emotional functioning. *Journal of Abnormal Child Psychology, 40,* 1167–1177.

Karg, K., Burmeister, M., Shedden, K., & Sen, S. (2011). The serotonin transporter promoter variant (5-HTTLPR), stress, and depression meta-analysis revisited: Evidence of genetic moderation. *Archives of General Psychiatry, 68,* 444–454.

Karkhaneh, M., Rowe, B. H., Saunders, L. D., Voaklander, D. C., & Hagel, B. E. (2013). Trends in head injuries associated with mandatory bicycle helmet legislation targeting children and adolescents. *Accident Analysis and Prevention, 59,* 206–212.

Karrass, J., & Braungart-Rieker, J. M. (2005). Effects of shared parent–infant book reading on early language acquisition. *Applied Developmental Psychology, 26,* 133–148.

Kärtner, J., Keller, H., Chaudhary, N., & Yovsi, R. D. (2012). The development of mirror self-recognition in different sociocultural contexts. *Monographs of the Society for Research in Child Development, 77*(4, Serial No. 305).

Kassel, J. D., Weinstein, S., Skitch, S. A., Veilleux, J., & Mermelstein, R. (2005). The development of substance abuse in adolescence: Correlates, causes, and consequences. In J. D. Kassel, S. Weinstein, S. A. Skitch, J. Veilleux, & R. Mermelstein (Eds.), *Development of psychopathology: A vulnerability-stress perspective* (pp. 355–384). Thousand Oaks, CA: Sage.

Kastens, K. A., & Liben, L. S. (2007). Eliciting self-explanations improves children's performance on a field-based map skills task. *Cognition and Instruction, 25,* 45–74.

Kataoka, S., & Vandell, D. L. (2013). Quality of afterschool activities and relative change in adolescent functioning over two years. *Applied Developmental Science, 17,* 123–134.

Katz, J., Lee, A. C. C., Lawn, J. E., Cousens, S., Blencowe, H., Ezzati, M., et al. (2013). Mortality risk in preterm and small-for-gestational-age infants in low-income and middle-income countries: A pooled country analysis. *Lancet, 382,* 417–425.

Katzmarzyk, P. T., & Leonard, W. R. (1998). Climatic influences on human body size and proportions: Ecological adaptations and secular trends. *American Journal of Physical Anthropology, 106,* 483–503.

Katz-Wise, S. L., Priess, H. A., & Hyde, J. S. (2010). Gender-role attitudes and behavior across the transition to parenthood. *Developmental Psychology, 46,* 18–28.

Kaufmann, K. B., Büning, H., Galy, A., Schambach, A., & Grez, M. (2013). Gene therapy on the move. *EMBO Molecular Medicine, 5,* 1642–1661.

Kavanaugh, R. D. (2006a). Pretend play. In B. Spodek & O. N. Saracho (Eds.), *Handbook of research on the education of young children* (2nd ed., pp. 269–278). Mahwah, NJ: Erlbaum.

Kavanaugh, R. D. (2006b). Pretend play and theory of mind. In L. Balter & C. S. Tamis-LeMonda (Eds.), *Child psychology: A handbook of contemporary issues* (2nd ed., pp. 153–166). New York: Psychology Press.

Kavšek, M. (2004). Predicting later IQ from infant visual habituation and dishabituation: A meta-analysis. *Journal of Applied Developmental Psychology, 25,* 369–393.

Kavšek, M., & Bornstein, M. H. (2010). Visual habituation and dishabituation in preterm infants: A review and meta-analysis. *Research in Developmental Disabilities, 31,* 951–975.

Kavšek, M., Yonas, A., & Granrud, C. E. (2012). Infants' sensitivity to pictorial depth cues: A review and meta-analysis. *Infant Behavior and Development, 35,* 109–128.

Kaye, W. (2008). Neurobiology of anorexia and bulimia nervosa. *Physiology and Behavior, 94,* 121–135.

Kearney, C. A., Spear, M., & Mihalas, S. (2014). School refusal behavior. In L. Grossman & S. Walfish (Eds.), *Translating psychological research into practice* (pp. 83–88). New York: Springer.

Keating, D. P. (2004). Cognitive and brain development. In R. M. Lerner & L. Steinberg (Eds.), *Handbook of adolescent psychology* (2nd ed., pp. 45–84). Hoboken, NJ: Wiley.

Keating, D. P. (2012). Cognitive and brain development in adolescence. *Enfance, 64,* 267–279.

Keating-Lefler, R., Hudson, D. B., Campbell-Grossman, C., Fleck, M. O., & Westfall, J. (2004). Needs, concerns, and social support of single, low-income mothers. *Issues in Mental Health Nursing, 25,* 381–401.

Keefe, M. R., Barbosa, G. A., Froese-Fretz, A., Kotzer, A. M., & Lobo, M. (2005). An intervention program for families with irritable infants. *American Journal of Maternal/Child Nursing, 30,* 230–236.

Keen, R. (2011). The development of problem solving in young children: A critical cognitive skill. *Annual Review of Psychology, 62,* 1–24.

Kefalas, M. J., Furstenberg, F. F., Carr, P. J., & Napolitano, L. (2011). "Marriage is more than being together": The meaning of marriage for young adults. *Journal of Family Issues, 32,* 845–875.

Keil, F. C. (1986). Conceptual domains and the acquisition of metaphor. *Cognitive Development, 1,* 72–96.

Keil, F. C., & Lockhart, K. L. (1999). Explanatory understanding in conceptual development. In E. K. Scholnick, K. Nelson, S. A. Gelman, & P. H. Miller (Eds.), *Conceptual development: Piaget's legacy* (pp. 103–130). Mahwah, NJ: Erlbaum.

Keller, H., Borke, Y. J., Kärtner, J., Jensen, H., & Papaligoura, Z. (2004). Developmental consequences of early parenting experiences: Self-recognition and self-regulation in three cultural communities. *Child Development, 75,* 1745–1760.

Keller, H., & Otto, H. (2009). The cultural socialization of emotion regulation during infancy. *Journal of Cross-Cultural Psychology, 40,* 996–1011.

Keller, S. S., Crow, T., Foundas, A., Amunts, K., & Roberts, N. (2009). Broca's area: Nomenclature, anatomy, typology and symmetry. *Brain and Language, 109,* 29–48.

Kelley, S. A., Brownell, C. A., & Campbell, S. B. (2000). Mastery motivation and self-evaluative affect in toddlers: Longitudinal relations with maternal behavior. *Child Development, 71,* 1061–1071.

Kellman, P. J., & Arterberry, M. E. (2006). Infant visual perception. In D. Kuhn & R. Siegler (Eds.), *Handbook of child psychology: Vol. 2. Cognition, perception, and language* (6th ed., pp. 109–160). Hoboken, NJ: Wiley.

Kelly, D. J., Liu, S., Ge, L., Quinn, P. C., Slater, A. M., Lee, K., et al. (2007). Cross-race preferences for same-race faces extend beyond the African versus Caucasian contrast in 3-month-old infants. *Infancy, 11,* 87–95.

Kelly, D. J., Quinn, P. C., Slater, A. M., Lee, K., Ge, L., & Pascalis, O. (2009). The other-race effect develops during infancy: Evidence of perceptual narrowing. *Psychological Science, 18,* 1084–1089.

Kelly, R., & Hammond, S. (2011). The relationship between symbolic play and executive function in young children. *Australasian Journal of Early Childhood, 36*(2), 21–27.

Kemeny, M. E. (2003). The psychobiology of stress. *Current Directions in Psychological Science, 12,* 124–129.

Kempe, C. H., Silverman, B. F., Steele, P. W., Droegemueller, P. W., & Silver, H. K. (1962). The battered-child syndrome. *Journal of the American Medical Association, 181,* 17–24.

Kendler, K. S., Thornton, L. M., Gilman, S. E., & Kessler, R. C. (2000). Sexual orientation in a U.S. national sample of twin and non-twin sibling pairs. *American Journal of Psychiatry, 157,* 1843–1846.

Kendrick, D., Barlow, J., Hampshire, A., Stewart-Brown, S., & Polnay, L. (2008). Parenting interventions and the prevention of unintentional injuries in childhood: Systematic review and meta-analysis. *Child: Care, Health and Development, 34,* 682–695.

Kennedy, A. M., & Gust, D. A. (2008). Measles outbreak associated with a church congregation: A study of immunization attitudes of congregation members. *Public Health Reports, 123,* 126–134.

Kennedy, B. S., Doniger, A. S., Painting, S., Houston, L., Slaunwhite, M, Mirabella, F., et al. (2014). Declines in elevated blood lead levels among children, 1997–2011. *American Journal of Preventive Medicine, 46,* 259–264.

Kennell, J. H., Klaus, M., McGrath, S., Robertson, S., & Hinkley, C. (1991). Continuous emotional support during labor in a U.S. hospital. *Journal of the American Medical Association, 265,* 2197–2201.

Kerckhoff, A. C. (2002). The transition from school to work. In J. T. Mortimer & R. Larson (Eds.), *The changing adolescent experience* (pp. 52–87). New York: Cambridge University Press.

Keren, M., Feldman, R., Namdari-Weinbaum, I., Spitzer, S., & Tyano, S. (2005). Relations between parents' interactive style in dyadic and triadic play and toddlers' symbolic capacity. *American Journal of Orthopsychiatry, 75,* 599–607.

Kerestes, M., & Youniss, J. E. (2003). Rediscovering the importance of religion in adolescent development. In R. M. Lerner, F. Jacobs, & D. Wertlieb (Eds.), *Handbook of applied developmental science* (Vol. 1, pp. 165–184). Thousand Oaks, CA: Sage.

Kerestes, M., Youniss, J., & Metz, E. (2004). Longitudinal patterns of religious perspective and civic integration. *Applied Developmental Science, 8,* 39–46.

Kerig, P. K., & Stellwagen, K. K. (2010). Roles of callous–unemotional traits, narcissism, and Machiavellianism in childhood aggression. *Journal of Psychopathology and Behavioral Assessment, 32,* 343–352.

Kernis, M. H. (2002). Self-esteem as a multifaceted construct. In T. M. Brinthaupt & R. P. Lipka (Eds.), *Understanding early adolescent self and identity* (pp. 57–88). Albany: State University of New York Press.

Kerns, K. A., Brumariu, L. E., & Seibert, A. (2011). Multi-method assessment of mother–child attachment: Links to parenting and child depressive symptoms in middle childhood. *Attachment and Human Development, 13,* 315–333.

Kerpelman, J. L., Shoffner, M. F., & Ross-Griffin, S. (2002). African American mothers' and daughters' beliefs about possible selves and their strategies for reaching the adolescents' future academic and career goals. *Journal of Youth and Adolescence, 31,* 289–302.

Kessen, W. (1967). Sucking and looking: Two organized congenital patterns of behavior in the human newborn. In H. W. Stevenson, E. H. Hess, & H. L. Rheingold (Eds.), *Early behavior: Comparative and developmental approaches* (pp. 147–179). New York: Wiley.

Kessler, R. C., Adler, L. A., Barkley, R., Biederman, J., Conners, C. K., & Demler, O. (2006). The prevalence and correlates of adult ADHD in the United States: Results from the National Comorbidity Survey Replication. *American Journal of Psychiatry, 163,* 716–723.

Kessler, R. C., Adler, L. A., Barkley, R., Biederman, J., Conners, C. K., & Faraone, S. V. (2005). Patterns and predictors of attention-deficit/hyperactivity disorder persistence into adulthood: Results from the National Comorbidity Survey Replication. *Biological Psychiatry, 57,* 1442–1451.

Kew, K., Ivory, G., Muniz, M. M., & Quiz, F. Z. (2012). No Child Left Behind as school reform: Intended and unintended consequences. In M. A. Acker-Hocevar, J. Ballenger, W. A. Place, & G. Ivory (Eds.), *Snapshots of school leadership in the 21st century: Perils and promises of leading for social justice, school improvement, and democratic community* (pp. 13–30). Charlotte, NC: IAP Information Age Publishing.

Key, J. D., Gebregziabher, M. G., Marsh, L. D., & O'Rourke, K. M. (2008). Effectiveness of an intensive, school-based intervention for teen mothers. *Journal of Adolescent Health, 42,* 394–400.

Khaleefa, O., Sulman, A., & Lynn, R. (2009). An increase of intelligence in Sudan, 1987–2007. *Journal of Biosocial Science, 41,* 279–283.

Khaleque, A., & Rohner, R. P. (2012). Pancultural associations between perceived parental acceptance and psychological adjustment of children and adults: A meta-analytic review of worldwide research. *Journal of Cross-Cultural Psychology, 43,* 784–800.

Khashan, A. S., Baker, P. N., & Kenny, L. C. (2010). Preterm birth and reduced birthweight in first and second teenage pregnancies: A register-based cohort study. *BMC Pregnancy and Childbirth, 10,* 36.

Kieras, J. E., Tobin, R. M., Graziano, W. G., & Rothbart, M. K. (2005). You can't always get what you want: Effortful control and children's responses to undesirable gifts. *Psychological Science, 16,* 391–396.

Killen, M., Crystal, D., & Watanabe, H. (2002). The individual and the group: Japanese and American children's evaluations of peer exclusion, tolerance of difference, and prescriptions for conformity. *Child Development, 73,* 1788–1802.

Killen, M., Henning, A., Kelly, M. C., Crystal, D., & Ruck, M. (2007). Evaluations of interracial peer encounters by majority and minority U.S. children and adolescents. *International Journal of Behavioral Development, 31,* 491–500.

Killen, M., Kelly, M. C., Richardson, C., Crystal, D., & Ruck, M. (2010). European American children's and adolescents' evaluations of interracial exclusion. *Group Processes and Intergroup Relations, 13,* 283–300.

Killen, M., Lee-Kim, J., McGlothlin, H., & Stangor, C. (2002). How children and adolescents evaluate gender and racial exclusion. *Monographs of the Society for Research in Child Development, 67*(4, Serial No. 271).

Killen, M., Margie, N. G., & Sinno, S. (2006). Morality in the context of intergroup relationships. In M. Killen & J. G. Smetana (Eds.), *Handbook of moral development* (pp. 155–183). Mahwah, NJ: Erlbaum.

Killen, M., Mulvey, K. L., Richardson, C., Jampol, N., & Woodward, A. (2011). The accidental transgressor: Morally relevant theory of mind. *Cognition, 119,* 197–215.

Killen, M., & Nucci, L. P. (1995). Morality, autonomy, and social conflict. In M. Killen & D. Hart (Eds.), *Morality in everyday life: Developmental perspectives* (pp. 52–86). Cambridge: Cambridge University Press.

Killen, M., Rutland, A., & Ruck, M. (2011). Promoting equity, tolerance, and justice in childhood. *Society for Research in Child Development Social Policy Report, 25*(4).

Killen, M., & Stangor, M. (2001). Children's social reasoning about inclusion and exclusion in gender and race peer group contexts. *Child Development, 72,* 174–186.

Killoren, S. E., Thayer, S. M., & Updegraff, K. A. (2008). Conflict resolution between Mexican origin adolescent siblings. *Journal of Marriage and Family, 70,* 1200–1212.

Kilmer, R. P., Cook, J. R., Crusto, C., Strater, K. P., & Haber, M. G. (2012). Understanding the ecology and development of children and families experiencing homelessness: Implications for practice, supportive services, and policy. *American Journal of Orthopsychiatry, 82,* 389–401.

Kim, G., Walden, T. A., & Knieps, L. J. (2010). Impact and characteristics of positive and fearful emotional messages during infant social referencing. *Infant Behavior and Development, 33,* 189–195.

Kim, H. Y., Schwartz, K., Cappella, E., & Seidman, E. (2014). Navigating middle grades: Role of social contexts in middle grade school climate. *American Journal of Community Psychology, 54,* 28–45.

Kim, J., & Cicchetti, D. (2006). Longitudinal trajectories of self-system processes and depressive symptoms among maltreated and nonmaltreated children. *Child Development, 77,* 624–639.

Kim, J. M. (1998). Korean children's concepts of adult and peer authority and moral reasoning. *Developmental Psychology, 34,* 947–955.

Kim, J.-Y., McHale, S. M., Crouter, A. C., & Osgood, D. W. (2007). Longitudinal linkages between sibling relationships and adjustment from middle childhood through adolescence. *Developmental Psychology, 43,* 960–973.

Kim, J.-Y., McHale, S. M., Osgood, D. W., & Crouter, A. C. (2006). Longitudinal course and family correlates of sibling relationships from childhood through adolescence. *Child Development, 77,* 1746–1761.

Kim, S., & Kochanska, G. (2012). Child temperament moderates effects of parent–child mutuality on self-regulation: A relationship-based path for emotionally negative infants. *Child Development, 83,* 1275–1289.

Kim, S., Kochanska, G., Boldt, L. J., Nordling, J. K., & O'Bleness, J. J. (2014). Developmental trajectory from early responses to transgressions to future antisocial behavior: Evidence for the role of the parent-child relationship from two longitudinal studies. *Development and Psychopathology, 26,* 93–103.

King, A. C., & Bjorklund, D. F. (2010). Evolutionary developmental psychology. *Psicothema, 22,* 22–27.

King, P. E., & Furrow, J. L. (2004). Religion as a resource for positive youth development: Religion, social capital, and moral outcomes. *Developmental Psychology, 40,* 703–713.

King, P. M., & Kitchener, K. S. (2002). The reflective judgment model: Twenty years of research on epistemic cognition. In B. K. Hofer & P. R. Pintrich (Eds.), *Personal epistemology: The psychological beliefs about knowledge and knowing* (pp. 37–61). Mahwah, NJ: Erlbaum.

King, V. (2007). When children have two mothers: Relationships with nonresident mothers, stepmothers, and fathers. *Journal of Marriage and Family, 69,* 1178–1193.

King, V. (2009). Stepfamily formation: Implications for adolescent ties to mothers, nonresident fathers, and stepfathers. *Journal of Marriage and Family, 71,* 954–968.

Kinney, H. C. (2009). Brainstem mechanisms underlying the sudden infant death syndrome: Evidence from human pathologic studies. *Developmental Psychobiology, 51,* 223–233.

Kinnunen, M.-L., Pietilainen, K., & Rissanen, A. (2006). Body size and overweight from birth to adulthood. In L. Pulkkinen & J. Kaprio (Eds.), *Socioemotional development and health from adolescence to adulthood* (pp. 95–107). New York: Cambridge University Press.

Kins, E., Beyers, W., Soenens, B., & Vansteenkiste, M. (2009). Patterns of home leaving and subjective well-being in emerging adulthood: The role of motivational processes and parental autonomy support. *Developmental Psychology, 45,* 1416–1429.

Kinsella, M. T., & Monk, C. (2009). Impact of maternal stress, depression and anxiety on fetal neurobehavioral development. *Clinical Obstetrics and Gynecology, 52,* 425–440.

Kirby, D. (2002). Effective approaches to reducing adolescent unprotected sex, pregnancy, and childbearing. *Journal of Sex Research, 39,* 51–57.

Kirby, D. B. (2008). The impact of abstinence and comprehensive sex and STD/HIV education programs on adolescent sexual behavior. *Sexuality Research and Social Policy, 5,* 18–27.

Kirby, M., Maggi, S., & D'Angiulli, A. (2011). School start times and the sleep–wake cycle of adolescents: A review and critical evaluation of available evidence. *Educational Researcher, 40,* 56–61.

Kiriakidis, S. P., & Kavoura, A. (2010). Cyberbullying: A review of the literature on harassment through the Internet and other electronic means. *Family and Community Health, 33,* 82–93.

Kirkham, N. Z., Cruess, L., & Diamond, A. (2003). Helping children apply their knowledge to their behavior on a dimension-switching task. *Developmental Science, 6,* 449–476.

Kirkman, M., Rosenthal, D. A., & Feldman, S. S. (2002). Talking to a tiger: Fathers reveal their difficulties in communicating about sexuality with adolescents. In S. S. Feldman & D. A. Rosenthal (Eds.), *Talking sexuality: Parent–adolescent communication* (pp. 57–74). San Francisco: Jossey-Bass.

Kirkorian, H. L., Pempek, T. A., Murphy, L. A., Schmidt, M. E., & Anderson, D. R. (2009). The impact of background television on parent–child interaction. *Child Development, 80,* 1350–1359.

Kirshner, B. (2009). "Power in numbers": Youth organizing as a context for exploring civic identity. *Journal of Research on Adolescence, 19,* 414–440.

Kisilevsky, B. S., & Hains, S. M. J. (2011). Onset and maturation of fetal heart rate response to the mother's voice over late gestation. *Developmental Science, 14,* 214–223.

Kisilevsky, B. S., Hains, S. M. J., Brown, C. A., Lee, C. T., Cowperthwaite, B., & Stutzman, S. S. (2009). Fetal sensitivity to properties of maternal speech and language. *Infant Behavior and Development, 32,* 59–71.

Kisilevsky, B. S., Hains, S. M. J., Lee, K., Muir, D. W., Xu, F., Fu, G., Zhao, Z. Y., & Yang, R. L. (1998). The still-face effect in Chinese and Canadian 3- to 6-month-old infants. *Developmental Psychology, 34,* 629–639.

Kisilevsky, B. S., & Low, J. A. (1998). Human fetal behavior: 100 years of study. *Developmental Review, 18,* 1–29.

Kit, B. K., Ogden, C. L., & Flegal, K. M. (2014). Epidemiology of obesity. In W. Ahrens & I. Pigeot (Eds.), *Handbook of Epidemiology* (2nd ed., pp. 2229–2262). New York: Springer Science + Business Media.

Kitsantas, P., Gaffney, K. F., & Cheema, J. (2012). Life stressors and barriers to timely prenatal care for women with high-risk pregnancies residing in rural and nonrural areas. *Women's Health Issues, 22,* e455–e460.

Kitzman, H. J., Olds, D. L., Cole, R. E., Hanks, C. A., Anson, E. A., Arcoleo, K. J., et al. (2010). Enduring effects of prenatal and infancy home visiting by nurses on children: Follow-up of a randomized trial among children at age 12 years. *Archives of Pediatric and Adolescent Medicine, 164,* 412–418.

Kitzmann, K. M., Cohen, R., & Lockwood, R. L. (2002). Are only children missing out? Comparison of the peer-related social competence of only children and siblings. *Journal of Social and Personal Relationships, 19,* 299–316.

Kiuru, N., Aunola, K., Vuori, J., & Nurmi, J.-E. (2009). The role of peer groups in adolescents' educational expectations and adjustment. *Journal of Youth and Adolescence, 36,* 995–1009.

Kjønniksen, L., Anderssen, N., & Wold, B. (2009). Organized youth sport as a predictor of physical activity in adulthood. *Scandinavian Journal of Medicine and Science in Sports, 19,* 646–654.

Kjønniksen, L., Torsheim, T., & Wold, B. (2008). Tracking of leisure-time physical activity during adolescence and young adulthood: A 10-year longitudinal study. *International Journal of Behavioral Nutrition and Physical Activity, 5,* 69.

Klaczynski, P. A. (2001). Analytic and heuristic processing influences on adolescent reasoning and decision-making. *Child Development, 72,* 844–861.

Klaczynski, P. A. (2004). A dual-process model of adolescent development: Implications for decision making, reasoning, and identity. In R. Kail (Ed.), *Advances in child development and behavior* (Vol. 31, pp. 73–123). San Diego, CA: Academic Press.

Klaczynski, P. A., & Narasimham, G. (1998). Development of scientific reasoning biases: Cognitive versus ego-protective explanations. *Developmental Psychology, 34,* 175–187.

Klaczynski, P. A., Schuneman, M. J., & Daniel, D. B. (2004). Theories of conditional reasoning: A developmental examination of competing hypotheses. *Developmental Psychology, 40,* 559–571.

Klahr, D., Matlen, B., & Jirout, J. (2013). Children as scientific thinkers. In G. J. Feist & M. E. Gorman (Eds.), *Handbook of the psychology of science* (pp. 223–247). New York: Springer.

Klaus, M. H., & Kennell, J. H. (1982). *Parent–infant bonding.* St. Louis: Mosby.

Klaw, E. L., Rhodes, J. E., & Fitzgerald, L. F. (2003). Natural mentors in the lives of African-American adolescent mothers: Tracking relationships over time. *Journal of Youth and Adolescence, 32,* 223–232.

Klebanov, P. K., Brooks-Gunn, J., McCarton, C., & McCormick, M. C. (1998). The contribution of neighborhood and family income to developmental test scores over the first three years of life. *Child Development, 69,* 1420–1436.

Kleffer, M. J. (2013). Development of reading and math skills in early adolescents: Do K–8 public schools make a difference? *Journal of Research on Educational Effectiveness, 6,* 361–379.

Kleinsorge, C., & Covitz, L. M. (2012). Impact of divorce on children: Developmental considerations. *Pediatrics in Review, 33,* 147–155.

Klemfuss, J. Z., & Ceci, S. J. (2012). Legal and psychological perspectives on children's competence to testify in court. *Developmental Review, 32,* 81–204.

Klemmensen, A.K., Tabor, A., Østerdal, M. L., Knudsen, V.K., Halldorsson, T. I., Mikkelsen, T. B., et al. (2009). Intake of vitamin C and E in pregnancy and risk of pre-eclampsia: Prospective study among 57,346 women. *BJOG, 116,* 964–974.

Kliegman, R. M., Behrman, R. E., Jenson, H. B., & Stanton, B. F. (Eds.). (2008). *Nelson textbook of pediatrics e-dition* (18th ed. text with continually updated online references.) Philadelphia: Saunders.

Kliewer, W., Fearnow, M. D., & Miller, P. A. (1996). Coping socialization in middle childhood: Tests of maternal and paternal influences. *Child Development, 67,* 2339–2357.

Klimes-Dougan, B., & Kistner, J. (1990). Physically abused preschoolers' responses to peers' distress. *Developmental Psychology, 26,* 599–602.

Klimstra, T. A., Hale, W. W., III., Raaijamkers, Q. A. W., Branje, S. J. T., & Meeus, W. H. J. (2010). Identity formation in adolescence: Change or stability? *Journal of Youth and Adolescence, 39,* 150–162.

Klingman, A. (2006). Children and war trauma. In K. A. Renninger & I. E. Sigel (Eds.), *Handbook of child psychology: Vol. 4. Child psychology in practice* (6th ed., pp. 619–652). Hoboken, NJ: Wiley.

Kloep, M., & Hendry, L. B. (2011). A systemic approach to the transitions to adulthood. In J. J. Arnett, M. Kloep, L. B. Hendry, & J. L. Tanner (Eds.), *Debating emerging adulthood: Stage or process?* (pp. 53–75). New York: Oxford University Press.

Kloess, J. A., Beech, A. R., & Harkins, L. (2014). Online child sexual exploitation: Prevalence, process, and offender characteristics. *Trauma, Violence, & Abuse, 15,* 126–139.

Klump, K. L., Kaye, W. H., & Strober, M. (2001). The evolving genetic foundations of eating disorders. *Psychiatric Clinics of North America, 24,* 215–225.

Kluwer, E. S., & Johnson, M. D. (2007). Conflict frequency and relationship quality across the transition to parenthood. *Journal of Marriage and Family, 69,* 1089–1106.

Knafo, A., & Plomin, R. (2006). Parental discipline and affection and children's prosocial behavior: Genetic and environmental links. *Journal of Personality and Social Psychology, 90,* 147–164.

Knafo, A., Zahn-Waxler, C., Davidov, M., Hulle, C. V., Robinson, J. L., & Rhee, S. H. (2009). Empathy in early childhood: Genetic, environmental, and affective contributions. In O. Vilarroya, S. Altran, A. Navarro, K. Ochsner, & A. Tobena (Eds.), *Values, empathy, and fairness across social barriers* (pp. 103–114). New York: New York Academy of Sciences.

Knickmeyer, R. C., Gouttard, S., Kang, C., Evans, D., Wilber, K., Smith, J. K., et al. (2008). A structural MRI study of human brain development from birth to 2 years. *Journal of Neuroscience, 28,* 12176–12182.

Knobloch, H., & Pasamanick, B. (Eds.). (1974). *Gesell and Amatruda's Developmental Diagnosis.* Hagerstown, MD: Harper & Row.

Knopf, M., Kraus, U., & Kressley-Mba, R. A. (2006). Relational information processing of novel unrelated actions by infants. *Infant Behavior and Development, 29,* 44–53.

Knudsen, E. I. (2004). Sensitive periods in the development of the brain and behavior. *Journal of Cognitive Neuroscience, 16,* 1412–1425.

Kobayashi, T., Hiraki, K., & Hasegawa, T. (2005). Auditory-visual intermodal matching of small numerosities in 6-month-old infants. *Developmental Science, 8,* 409–419.

Kobayashi, T., Kazuo, H., Ryoko, M., & Hasegawa, T. (2004). Baby arithmetic: One object plus one tone. *Cognition, 91,* B23–B34.

Kochanska, G. (1991). Socialization and temperament in the development of guilt and conscience. *Child Development, 62*, 1379–1392.

Kochanska, G., & Aksan, N. (2006). Children's conscience and self-regulation. *Journal of Personality, 74*, 1587–1617.

Kochanska, G., Aksan, N., & Carlson, J. J. (2005). Temperament, relationships, and young children's receptive cooperation with their parents. *Developmental Psychology, 41*, 648–660.

Kochanska, G., Aksan, N., & Nichols, K. E. (2003). Maternal power assertion in discipline and moral discourse contexts: Commonalities, differences, and implications for children's moral conduct and cognition. *Developmental Psychology, 39*, 949–963.

Kochanska, G., Aksan, N., Prisco, T. R., & Adams, E. E. (2008). Mother–child and father–child mutually responsive orientation in the first 2 years and children's outcomes at preschool age: Mechanisms of influence. *Child Development, 79*, 30–44.

Kochanska, G., Forman, D. R., Aksan, N., & Dunbar, S. B. (2005). Pathways to conscience: Early mother–child mutually responsive orientation and children's moral emotion, conduct, and cognition. *Journal of Child Psychology and Psychiatry, 46*, 19–34.

Kochanska, G., Gross, J. N., Lin, M.-H., & Nichols, K. E. (2002). Guilt in young children: Development, determinants, and relations with broader system standards. *Child Development, 73*, 461–482.

Kochanska, G., & Kim, S. (2012). Difficult temperament moderates links between maternal responsiveness and children's compliance and behavior problems in low-income families. *Journal of Child Psychology and Psychiatry, 54*, 323–332.

Kochanska, G., & Kim, S. (2014). A complex interplay among the parent–child relationship, effortful control, and internalized rule-compatible conduct in young children: Evidence from two studies. *Developmental Psychology, 50*, 8–21.

Kochanska, G., Kim, S., Barry, R. A., & Philibert, R. A. (2011). Children's genotypes interact with maternal responsive care in predicting children's competence: Diathesis-stress or differential susceptibility? *Development and Psychopathology, 23*, 605–616.

Kochanska, G., & Knaack, A. (2003). Effortful control as a personality characteristic of young children: Antecedents, correlates, and consequences. *Journal of Personality, 71*, 1087–1112.

Kochanska, G., Murray, K. T., & Harlan, E. T. (2000). Effortful control in early childhood: Continuity and change, antecedents, and implications for social development. *Developmental Psychology, 36*, 220–232.

Kochanska, G., Philibert, R. A., & Barry, R. A. (2009). Interplay of genes and early mother–child relationship in the development of self-regulation from toddler to preschool age. *Journal of Child Psychology and Psychiatry, 50*, 1331–1338.

Kochel, K. P., Ladd, G. W., & Rudolph, K. D. (2012). Longitudinal associations among youth depressive symptoms, peer victimization, and low peer acceptance: An interpersonal process perspective. *Child Development, 83*, 637–650.

Kohen, D. E., Leventhal, T., Dahinten, V. S., & McIntosh, C. N. (2008). Neighborhood disadvantage: Pathways of effects for young children. *Child Development, 79*, 156–169.

Kohlberg, L. (1966). A cognitive-developmental analysis of children's sex-role concepts and attitudes. In E. E. Maccoby (Ed.), *The development of sex differences* (pp. 82–173). Stanford, CA: Stanford University Press.

Kohlberg, L. (1969). Stage and sequence: The cognitive-developmental approach to socialization. In D. A. Goslin (Ed.), *Handbook of socialization theory and research* (pp. 347–480). Chicago: Rand McNally.

Kohlberg, L., Levine, C., & Hewer, A. (1983). *Moral stages: A current formulation and a response to critics.* Basel, Switzerland: Karger.

Kolak, A. M., & Volling, B. L. (2011). Sibling jealousy in early childhood: Longitudinal links to sibling relationship quality. *Infant and Child Development, 20*, 213–226.

Koletzko, B., Beyer, J., Brands, B., Demmelmair, H., Grote, V., Haile, G., et al. (2013). Early influences of nutrition on postnatal growth. *Nestlé Nutrition Institute Workshop Series, 71*, 11–27.

Kollmann, M., Haeusler, M., Haas, J., Csapo, B., Lang, U., & Klaritsch, P. (2013). Procedure-related complications after genetic amniocentesis and chorionic villus sampling. *Ultraschall in der Medizen, 34*, 345–348.

Konner, M. (2010). *The evolution of childhood: Relationships, emotion, mind.* Cambridge, MA: Harvard University Press.

Konner, M. J. (1977). Infancy among the Kalahari Desert San. In P. H. Leiderman, S. R. Tulkin, & A. Rosenfield (Eds.), *Culture and infancy: Variations in the human experience* (pp. 287–328). New York: Academic Press.

Kontos, A. P., Elbin, R. J., Fazio-Sumrock, V. C., Burkhart, S., Swindell, H., Maroon, J., et al. (2013). Incidence of sports-related concussion among youth football players aged 8–12 years. *Journal of Pediatrics, 163*, 717–720.

Kooijman, V., Hagoort, P., & Cutler, A. (2009). Prosodic structure in early word segmentation: ERP evidence from Dutch ten-month-olds. *Infancy, 14*, 591–612.

Kopp, C. B., & Neufeld, S. J. (2003). Emotional development during infancy. In R. Davidson, K. R. Scherer, & H. H. Goldsmith (Eds.), *Handbook of affective sciences* (pp. 347–374). Oxford, UK: Oxford University Press.

Kost, K., & Henshaw, S. (2014). *U. S. teenage pregnancies, births and abortions, 2010: National and state trends by age, race and ethnicity.* Alan Guttmacher Institute. Retrieved from www.guttmacher.org/pubs/ USTPtrends10.pdf

Kotkin, J. (2012, July 16). Are Millennials the screwed generation? *Newsweek.* Retrieved from www.thedailybeast .com/newsweek/2012/07/15/are-millennials-the-screwed-generation.html

Kowalski, R. M., & Limber, S. P. (2013). Psychological, physical, and academic correlates of cyberbullying and traditional bullying. *Journal of Adolescent Health, 53*, S13–S20.

Kowalski, R. M., Limber, S. P., & Agatston, P. W. (2008). *Cyber bullying: Bullying in the digital age.* Malden, MA: Blackwell.

Kozer, E., Costei, A. M., Boskovic, R., Nulman, I., Nikfar, S., & Koren, G. (2003). Effects of aspirin consumption during pregnancy on pregnancy outcomes: Meta-analysis. *Birth Defects Research: Part B, Developmental and Reproductive Toxicology, 68*, 70–84.

Kozulin, A. (Ed.). (2003). *Vygotsky's educational theory in cultural context.* Cambridge, UK: Cambridge University Press.

Kraebel, K. S. (2012). Redundant amodal properties facilitate operant learning in 3-month-old infants. *Infant Behavior and Development, 35*, 12–21.

Krafft, K., & Berk, L. E. (1998). Private speech in two preschools: Significance of open-ended activities and make-believe play for verbal self-regulation. *Early Childhood Research Quarterly, 13*, 637–658.

Krähenbühl, S., Blades, M., & Eiser, C. (2009). The effect of repeated questioning on children's accuracy and consistency in eyewitness testimony. *Legal and Criminological Psychology, 14*, 263–278.

Kral, T. V. E., & Faith, M. S. (2009). Influences on child eating and weight development from a behavioral genetics perspective. *Journal of Pediatric Psychology, 34*, 596–605.

Kramer, L., & Kowal, A. K. (2005). Sibling relationship quality from birth to adolescence: The enduring contributions of friends. *Journal of Family Psychology, 19*, 503–511.

Krcmar, M., Grela, B., & Lin, K. (2007). Can toddlers learn vocabulary from television? An experimental approach. *Media Psychology, 10*, 41–63.

Krebs, D. L. (2011). *The origins of morality: An evolutionary account.* New York: Oxford University Press.

Krebs, D. L., & Denton, K. (2005). Toward a more pragmatic approach to morality: A critical evaluation of Kohlberg's model. *Psychological Review, 112*, 629–649.

Kreppner, J., Kumsta, R., Rutter, M., Beckett, C., Castle, J., Stevens, S., et al. (2010). Developmental course of deprivation-specific psychological patterns: Early manifestations, persistence to age 15, and clinical features. *Monographs of the Society for Research in Child Development, 75*(1, Serial No. 295), 79–101.

Kreppner, J., Rutter, M., Beckett, C., Castle, J., Colvert, E., Groothues, C., et al. (2007). Normality and impairment following profound early institutional deprivation: A longitudinal follow-up into early adolescence. *Developmental Psychology, 43*, 931–946.

Kretch, K. S., & Adolph, K. E. (2013a). Cliff or step? Posture-specific learning at the edge of a drop-off. *Child Development, 84*, 226–240.

Kretch, K. S., & Adolph, K. E. (2013b). No bridge too high: Infants decide whether to cross based on the probability of falling not the severity of the potential fall. *Developmental Science, 16*, 336–351.

Krettenauer, T., Colasante, T., Buchmann, M., & Malti, T. (2014). The development of moral emotions and decision-making from adolescence to early adulthood: A 6-year longitudinal study. *Journal of Youth and Adolescence, 43*, 583–596.

Kroger, J. (2012). The status of identity: Developments in identity status research. In P. K. Kerig, M. S. Schulz, & S. T. Hauser (Eds.), *Adolescence and beyond: Family processes and development* (pp. 64–83). New York: Oxford University Press.

Kroger, J., Martinussen, M., & Marcia, J. E. (2010). Identity status change during adolescence and young adulthood: A meta-analysis. *Journal of Adolescence, 33*, 683–698.

Krueger, R. F., & Johnson, W. (2008). Behavior genetics and personality. In L. Q. Pervin, O. P. John, & R. W. Robins (Eds.), *Handbook of personality: Theory and research* (3rd ed., pp. 287–310). New York: Guilford.

Krumhansl, C. L., & Jusczyk, P. W. (1990). Infants' perception of phrase structure in music. *Psychological Science, 1*, 70–73.

Kuczynski, L. (1984). Socialization goals and mother–child interaction: Strategies for long-term and short-term compliance. *Developmental Psychology, 20*, 1061–1073.

Kuczynski, L., & Lollis, S. (2002). Four foundations for a dynamic model of parenting. In J. R. M. Gerris (Ed.), *Dynamics of parenting.* Hillsdale, NJ: Erlbaum.

Kuh, G. D., Cruce, T. M., & Shoup, R. (2008). Unmasking the effects of student engagement on first-year college grades and persistence. *Journal of Higher Education, 79*, 540–553.

Kuhl, P. K., Ramirez, R. R., Bosseler, A., Lin, J. L., & Imada, T. (2014). Infants' brain responses to speech suggest analysis by synthesis. *Proceedings of the National Academy of Sciences, 111*, 11238–11245.

Kuhl, P. K., Tsao, F.-M., & Liu, H.-M. (2003). Foreign-language experience in infancy: Effects of short-term exposure and social interaction on phonetic learning. *Proceedings of the National Academy of Sciences, 100*, 9096–9101.

Kuhn, D. (1989). Children and adults as intuitive scientists. *Psychological Review, 96*, 674–689.

Kuhn, D. (1993). Connecting scientific and informal reasoning. *Merrill-Palmer Quarterly, 39*, 74–103.

Kuhn, D. (1995). Microgenetic study of change: What has it told us? *Psychological Science, 6*, 133–139.

Kuhn, D. (2000). Why development does (and does not) occur: Evidence from the domain of inductive reasoning. In R. Siegler & J. McClelland (Eds.), *Mechanisms of cognitive development* (pp. 221–249). Mahwah, NJ: Erlbaum.

Kuhn, D. (2002). What is scientific thinking, and how does it develop? In U. Goswami (Ed.), *Blackwell handbook of childhood cognitive development* (pp. 371–393). Malden, MA: Blackwell.

Kuhn, D. (2009). Adolescent thinking. In R. M. Lerner & L. Steinberg (Eds.), *Handbook of adolescent psychology* (3rd ed., pp. 152–186). Hoboken, NJ: Wiley.

Kuhn, D. (2011). What is scientific reasoning and how does it develop? In U. Goswami (Ed.), *The Wiley-Blackwell handbook of childhood cognitive development* (2nd ed., pp. 497–523). Hoboken, NJ: Wiley-Blackwell.

Kuhn, D. (2013). Reasoning. In P. D. Zelazo (Ed.), *Oxford handbook of developmental psychology: Vol 1. Body and mind* (pp. 744–764). New York: Oxford University Press.

Kuhn, D., Amsel, E., & O'Loughlin, M. (1988). *The development of scientific thinking skills.* Orlando, FL: Academic Press.

Kuhn, D., & Dean, D. (2004). Connecting scientific reasoning and causal inference. *Journal of Cognition and Development, 5*, 261–288.

Kuhn, D., & Franklin, S. (2006). The second decade: What develops (and how)? In D. Kuhn & R. S. Siegler (Eds.), *Handbook of child psychology: Vol. 2. Cognition, perception, and language* (6th ed., pp. 953–994). Hoboken, NJ: Wiley.

Kuhn, D., Iordanou, K., Pease, M., & Wirkala, C. (2008). Beyond control of variables: What needs to develop to achieve skilled scientific thinking? *Cognitive Development, 23*, 435–451.

Kulkarni, A. D., Jamieson, D. J., Jones, H. W., Jr., Kissin, D. M., Gallo, M. F., Macaluso, M., et al. (2013). Fertility treatments and multiple births in the United States. *New England Journal of Medicine, 369,* 2218–2225.

Kumar, A., & Srivastava, K. (2011). Cultural and social practices regarding menstruation among adolescent girls. *Social Work in Public Health, 26,* 594–604.

Kumar, M., Chandra, S., Ijaz, Z., & Senthilselvan, A. (2014). Epidural analgesia in labour and neonatal respiratory distress: A case-control study. *Archives of Disease in Childhood—Fetal and Neonatal Edition, 99,* F116–F119.

Kunnen, E. S., & Bosma, H. A. (2003). Fischer's skill theory applied to identity development: A response to Kroger. *Identity, 3,* 247–270.

Kunnen, E. S., Sappa, V., van Geert, P. L. C., & Bonica, L. (2008). The shapes of commitment development in emerging adulthood. *Journal of Adult Development, 15,* 113–131.

Kunnen, S. E. (Ed.). (2012). *A dynamic systems approach to adolescent development.* London: Routledge.

Kuppens, S., Laurent, L., Heyvaert, M., & Onghena, P. (2013). Associations between parental control and relational aggression in children and adolescents: A multilevel and sequential meta-analysis. *Developmental Psychology, 49,* 1697–1712.

Kurdek, L. A. (2006). Differences between partners from heterosexual, gay, and lesbian cohabiting couples. *Journal of Marriage and Family, 68,* 509–528.

Kurdziel, L., Duclos, K., & Spencer, R. M. C. (2013). Sleep spindles in midday naps enhance learning in preschool children. *Proceedings of the National Academy of Sciences, 110,* 17267–17271.

Kurganskaya, M. E. (2011). Manual asymmetry in children is related to parameters of early development and familial sinistrality. *Human Physiology, 37,* 654–657.

Kurian, M. A., Gissen, P., Smith, M., Heales, S. J. R., & Clayton, P. T. (2011). The monoamine neurotransmitter disorders: An expanding range of neurological syndromes. *Lancet Neurology, 10,* 721–733.

Kurtz-Costes, B., Rowley, S. J., Harris-Britt, A., & Woods, T. A. (2008). Gender stereotypes about mathematics and science and self-perceptions of ability in late childhood and early adolescence. *Merrill-Palmer Quarterly, 54,* 386–409.

Kushnir, J., Kushnir, B., & Sadeh, A. (2013). Children treated for nocturnal enuresis: Characteristics and trends over a 15-year period. *Child and Youth Care Forum, 42,* 119–129.

Kwak, K. W., Lee, Y. S., Park, K. H., & Baek, M. (2010). Efficacy of desmopressin and enuresis alarm as first and second line treatment for primary monosymptomatic nocturnal enuresis: Prospective randomized crossover study. *Journal of Urology, 184,* 2521–2526.

L

Laberge, L., Petit, D., Simard, C., Vitaro, F., & Tremblay, R. E. (2001). Development of sleep patterns in early adolescence. *Journal of Sleep Research, 10,* 59–67.

Labouvie-Vief, G. (2006). Emerging structures of adult thought. In J. J. Arnett & J. L. Tanner (Eds.), *Emerging adults in America: Coming of age in the 21st century* (pp. 59–84). Washington, DC: American Psychological Association.

Lachance, J. A., & Mazzocco, M. M. M. (2006). A longitudinal analysis of sex differences in math and spatial skills in primary school age children. *Learning and Individual Differences, 16,* 195–216.

Lacourse, E., Nagin, D., Tremblay, R. E., Vitaro, F., & Claes, M. (2003). Developmental trajectories of boys' delinquent group membership and facilitation of violent behaviors during adolescence. *Development and Psychopathology, 15,* 183–197.

Ladd, G. W. (2005). *Children's peer relationships and social competence: A century of progress.* New Haven, CT: Yale University Press.

Ladd, G. W., Birch, S. H., & Buhs, E. S. (1999). Children's social and scholastic lives in kindergarten: Related spheres of influence? *Child Development, 70,* 1373–1400.

Ladd, G. W., Buhs, E. S., & Seid, M. (2000). Children's initial sentiments about kindergarten: Is school liking an antecedent of early classroom participation and achievement? *Merrill-Palmer Quarterly, 46,* 255–279.

Ladd, G. W., & Burgess, K. B. (1999). Charting the relationship trajectories of aggressive, withdrawn, and aggressive/withdrawn children during early grade school. *Child Development, 70,* 910–929.

Ladd, G. W., Kochenderfer-Ladd, B., Eggum, N. D., Kochel, K. P., & McConnell, E. M. (2011). Characterizing and comparing the friendships of anxious-solitary and unsociable preadolescents. *Child Development, 82,* 1434–1453.

Ladd, G. W., LeSieur, K., & Profilet, S. M. (1993). Direct parental influences on young children's peer relations. In S. Duck (Ed.), *Learning about relationships* (Vol. 2, pp. 152–183). London: Sage.

Lagattuta, K. H., Sayfan, L., & Blattman, A. J. (2010). Forgetting common ground: Six- to seven-year-olds have an overinterpretive theory of mind. *Developmental Psychology, 46,* 1417–1432.

Lagattuta, K. H., & Thompson, R. A. (2007). The development of self-conscious emotions: Cognitive processes and social influences. In J. L. Tracy, R. W. Robins, & J. P. Tangney (Eds.), *The self-conscious emotions: Theory and research* (pp. 91–113). New York: Guilford.

Lagattuta, K. H., Wellman, H. M., & Flavell, J. H. (1997). Preschoolers' understanding of the link between thinking and feeling: Cognitive cuing and emotional change. *Child Development, 68,* 1081–1104.

Lagnado, L. (2001, November 2). Kids confront Trade Center trauma. *Wall Street Journal,* pp. B1, B6.

La Greca, A. M., Prinstein, M. J., & Fetter, M. D. (2001). Adolescent peer crowd affiliation: Linkages with health-risk behaviors and close friendships. *Journal of Pediatric Psychology, 26,* 131–143.

Laible, D. (2007). Attachment with parents and peers in late adolescence: Links with emotional competence and social behavior. *Personality and Individual Differences, 43,* 1185–1197.

Laible, D. (2011). Does it matter if preschool children and mothers discuss positive vs. negative events during reminiscing? Links with mother-reported attachment, family emotional climate, and socioemotional development. *Social Development, 20,* 394–411.

Laible, D., & Song, J. (2006). Constructing emotional and relational understanding: The role of affect and mother–child discourse. *Merrill-Palmer Quarterly, 52,* 44–69.

Laible, D., & Thompson, R. A. (2002). Mother–child conflict in the toddler years: Lessons in emotion, morality, and relationships. *Child Development, 73,* 1187–1203.

Laird, R. D., Pettit, G. S., Dodge, K. A., & Bates, J. E. (2005). Peer relationship antecedents of delinquent behavior in late adolescence: Is there evidence of demographic group differences in developmental processes? *Development and Psychopathology, 17,* 127–144.

Lakshman, R., Elks, C. E., & Ong, K. K. (2012). Childhood obesity. *Circulation, 126,* 1770–1779.

Lalonde, C., & Chandler, M. (2005). Culture, selves, and time: Theories of personal persistence in native and non-native youth. In C. Lightfoot, C. Lalonde, & M. Chandler (Eds.), *Changing conceptions of psychological life* (pp. 207–229). Mahwah, NJ: Erlbaum.

Lalonde, C. E., & Chandler, M. J. (1995). False-belief understanding goes to school: On the social-emotional consequences of coming early or late to a first theory of mind. *Cognition and Emotion, 9,* 167–185.

Lalonde, C. E., & Chandler, M. J. (2002). Children's understanding of interpretation. *New Ideas in Psychology, 20,* 163–198.

Lam, C. B., McHale, S. M., & Crouter, A. C. (2012). Parent–child shared time from middle childhood to late adolescence: Developmental course and adjustment correlates. *Child Development, 83,* 2089–2103.

Lam, C. B., Solmeyer, A. R., & McHale, S. M. (2012). Sibling relationships and empathy across the transition to adolescence. *Journal of Youth and Adolescence, 41,* 1657–1670.

Lamarche, V., Brendgen, M., Boivin, M., Vitaro, F., Perusse, D., & Dionne, G. (2006). Do friendships and sibling relationships provide protection against peer victimization in a similar way? *Social Development, 15,* 373–393.

Lamaze, F. (1958). *Painless childbirth.* London: Burke.

Lamb, M. E. (2012). Mothers, fathers, families, and circumstances: Factors affecting children's adjustment. *Applied Developmental Science, 16,* 98–111.

Lamb, M. E., & Ahnert, L. (2006). Nonparental child care: Context, concepts, correlates, and consequences. In K. A. Renninger & I. E. Sigel (Eds.), *Handbook of child psychology: Vol. 4. Child psychology in practice* (6th ed., pp. 700–778). Hoboken, NJ: Wiley.

Lamb, M. E., & Lewis, C. (2004). The development and significance of father–child relationships in two-parent families. In M. E. Lamb (Ed.), *The role of the father in child development* (4th ed., pp. 272–306). Hoboken, NJ: Wiley.

Lamb, M. E., & Lewis, C. (2013). Father–child relationships. In N. J. Cabrera & C. S. Tamis-LeMonda (Eds.), *Handbook of father involvement* (2nd ed., pp. 119–134). New York: Routledge.

Lamb, M. E., Thompson, R. A., Gardner, W., Charnov, E. L., & Connell, J. P. (1985). Infant–mother attachment: The origins and developmental significance of individual differences in the Strange Situation: Its study and biological interpretation. *Behavioral and Brain Sciences, 7,* 127–147.

Lambert, S. M., Masson, P., & Fisch, H. (2006). The male biological clock. *World Journal of Urology, 24,* 611–617.

Lampl, M. (1993). Evidence of saltatory growth in infancy. *American Journal of Human Biology, 5,* 641–652.

Lampl, M., & Johnson, M. L. (2011). Infant growth in length follows prolonged sleep and increased naps. *Sleep, 34,* 641–650.

Lancy, D. F. (2008). *The anthropology of childhood.* Cambridge, UK: Cambridge University Press.

Lang, M. (2010). Can mentoring assist in the school-to-work transition? *Education + Training, 52,* 359–367.

Langer, J., Gillette, P., & Arriaga, R. I. (2003). Toddlers' cognition of adding and subtracting objects in action and in perception. *Cognitive Development, 18,* 233–246.

Langosch, D. (2012). Grandparents parenting again: Challenges, strengths, and implications for practice. *Psychoanalytic Inquiry, 32,* 163–170.

Långström, N., Rahman, Q., Carlström, E., & Lichtenstein, P. (2010). Genetic and environmental effects on same-sex sexual behavior: A population study of twins in Sweden. *Archives of Sexual Behavior, 39,* 75–80.

Lanphear, B., Hornung, R., Khoury, J., Yolton, K., Baghurst, P., Bellinger, D., et al. (2005). Low-level environmental lead exposure and children's intellectual function: An international pooled analysis. *Environmental Health Perspectives, 113,* 894–899.

Lansford, J. E. (2009). Parental divorce and children's adjustment. *Perspectives on Psychological Science, 4,* 140–152.

Lansford, J. E., Criss, M. M., Dodge, K. A., Shaw, D. S., Pettit, G. S., & Bates, J. E. (2009). Trajectories of physical discipline: Early childhood antecedents and developmental outcomes. *Child Development, 80,* 1385–1402.

Lansford, J. E., Criss, M. M., Laird, R. D., Shaw, D. S., Pettit, G. S., Bates, J. E., & Dodge, K. A. (2011). Reciprocal relations between parents' physical discipline and children's externalizing behavior during middle childhood and adolescence. *Development and Psychopathology, 23,* 225–238.

Lansford, J. E., Criss, M. M., Pettit, G. S., Dodge, K. A., & Bates, J. E. (2003). Friendship quality, peer group affiliation, and peer antisocial behavior as moderators of the link between negative parenting and adolescent externalizing behavior. *Journal of Research on Adolescence, 13,* 161–184.

Lansford, J. E., Malone, P. S., Castellino, D. R., Dodge, K. A., Pettit, G., & Bates, J. E. (2006). Trajectories of internalizing, externalizing, and grades for children who have and have not experienced their parents' divorce or separation. *Journal of Family Psychology, 20,* 292–301.

Lansford, J. E., Malone, P. S., Dodge, K. A., Pettit, G. S., & Bates, J. E. (2010). Developmental cascades of peer rejection, social information processing biases, and aggression during middle childhood. *Development and Psychopathology, 22,* 593–602.

Lansford, J. E., Wagner, L. B., Bates, J. E., Dodge, K. A., & Pettit, G. S. (2012). Parental reasoning, denying privileges, yelling, and spanking: Ethnic differences and associations with child externalizing behavior. *Parenting: Science and Practice, 12,* 42–56.

Lapierre, M. A., Piotrowski, J., & Klinebarger, D. L. (2012). Background television in the homes of U.S. children. *Pediatrics, 130,* 839–846.

Laranjo, J., Bernier, A., Meins, E., & Carlson, S. M. (2010). Early manifestations of children's theory of mind: The roles of maternal mind-mindedness and infant security of attachment. *Infancy, 15,* 300–323.

Larroque, B., Ancel, P.-Y., Marret, S., Marchand, L., André, M., Arnaud, C., et al. (2008). Neurodevelopmental disabilities and special care of 5-year-old children born before 33 weeks of gestation (the EPIPAGE study): A longitudinal cohort study. *Lancet, 371,* 813–820.

Larsen, J. A., & Nippold, M. A. (2007). Morphological analysis in school-age children: Dynamic assessment of a word learning strategy. *Language, Speech, and Hearing Services in Schools, 38,* 201–212.

Larson, R., & Ham, M. (1993). Stress and "storm and stress" in early adolescence: The relationship of negative events with dysphoric affect. *Developmental Psychology, 29,* 130–140.

Larson, R., & Lampman-Petraitis, C. (1989). Daily emotional states as reported by children and adolescents. *Child Development, 60,* 1250–1260.

Larson, R. W. (2001). How U.S. children and adolescents spend time: What it does (and doesn't) tell us about their development. *Current Directions in Psychological Science, 10,* 160–164.

Larson, R. W., Moneta, G., Richards, M. H., & Wilson, S. (2002). Continuity, stability, and change in daily emotional experience across adolescence. *Child Development, 73,* 1151–1165.

Larson, R. W., & Richards, M. (1998). Waiting for the weekend: Friday and Saturday night as the emotional climax of the week. In A. C. Crouter & R. Larson (Eds.), *Temporal rhythms in adolescence: Clocks, calendars, and the coordination of daily life* (pp. 37–51). San Francisco: Jossey-Bass.

Larson, R. W., Richards, M. H., Moneta, G., Holmbeck, G., & Duckett, E. (1996). Changes in adolescents' daily interactions with their families from ages 10 to 18: Disengagement and transformation. *Developmental Psychology, 32,* 744–754.

Larson, R. W., Richards, M. H., Sims, B., & Dworkin, J. (2001). How urban African-American young adolescents spend their time: Time budgets for locations, activities, and companionship. *American Journal of Community Psychology, 29,* 565–597.

Larzelere, R. E., Cox, R. B., Jr., & Mandara, J. (2013). Responding to misbehavior in young children: How authoritative parents enhance reasoning with firm control. In R. E. Larzelere, A. S. Morris, & A. W. Harrist (Eds.), *Authoritative parenting: Synthesizing nurturance and discipline for optimal child development* (pp. 89–111). Washington, DC: American Psychological Association.

Larzelere, R. E., Schneider, W. N., Larson, D. B., & Pike, P. L. (1996). The effects of discipline responses in delaying toddler misbehavior recurrences. *Child and Family Behavior Therapy, 18,* 35–7.

Lashley, F. R. (2007). *Essentials of clinical genetics in nursing practice.* New York: Springer.

Latendresse, G., & Ruiz, R. J. (2011). Maternal corticotropin-releasing hormone and the use of selective serotonin reuptake inhibitors independently predict the occurrence of preterm birth. *Journal of Midwifery and Women's Health, 56,* 118–126.

Latz, S., Wolf, A. W., & Lozoff, B. (1999). Sleep practices and problems in young children in Japan and the United States. *Archives of Pediatric and Adolescent Medicine, 153,* 339–346.

Lau, Y. L., Cameron, C. A., Chieh, K. M., O'Leary, J., Fu, G., & Lee, K. (2012). Cultural differences in moral justifications enhance understanding of Chinese and Canadian children's moral decisions. *Journal of Cross-Cultural Psychology, 44,* 461–477.

Lauer, P. A., Akiba, M., Wilkerson, S. B., Apthorp, H. S., Snow, D., & Martin-Glenn, M. (2006). Out-of-school time programs: A meta-analysis of effects for at-risk students. *Review of Educational Research, 76,* 275–313.

Laughlin, L. (2013). *Who's minding the kids? Child care arrangements: Spring 2011.* Current Population Reports, P70–135. Washington, DC: U.S. Census Bureau.

Laurent, H., Kim, H., & Capaldi, D. (2008). Prospective effects of interparental conflict on child attachment security and the moderating role of parents' romantic attachment. *Journal of Family Psychology, 22,* 377–388.

Lauricella, A. R., Gola, A. A H., & Calvert, S. L. (2011). Toddlers' learning from socially meaningful video characters. *Media Psychology, 14,* 216–232.

Laursen, B., Bukowski, W. M., Aunola, K., & Nurmi, J.-E. (2007). Friendship moderates prospective associations between social isolation and adjustment problems in young children. *Child Development, 78,* 1395–1404.

Laursen, B., & Collins, W. A. (2009). Parent–child relationships during adolescence. In R. M. Lerner (Ed.), *Handbook of adolescent psychology: Vol. 2. Contextual influences on adolescent development* (3rd ed., pp. 3–42). Hoboken, NJ: Wiley.

Laursen, B., Coy, K., & Collins, W. A. (1998). Reconsidering changes in parent–child conflict across adolescence: A meta-analysis. *Child Development, 69,* 817–832.

Lavelli, M., & Fogel, A. (2005). Developmental changes in the relationship between the infant's attention and emotion during early face-to-face communication: The 2-month transition. *Developmental Psychology, 41,* 265–280.

Law, E. C., Sideridis, G. D., Prock, L. A., & Sheridan, M. A. (2014). Attention-deficit/hyperactivity disorder in young children: Predictors of diagnostic stability. *Pediatrics, 133,* 659–667.

Law, K. L., Stroud, L. R., Niaura, R., LaGasse, L. L., Liu, J., & Lester, B. M. (2003). Smoking during pregnancy and newborn neurobehavior. *Pediatrics, 111,* 1318–1323.

Lawn, J. E., Mwansa-Kambafwile, J., Horta, B. L., Barros, F. C., & Cousens, S. (2010). "Kangaroo mother care" to prevent neonatal deaths due to preterm birth complications. *International Journal of Epidemiology, 39,* i144–i154.

Lawrence, E., Rothman, A., Cobb, R. J., & Bradbury, T. N. (2010). Marital satisfaction across the transition to parenthood. In M. S. Schulz, M. K. Pruett, P. K. Kerig, & R. D. Parke (Eds.), *Strengthening couple relationships for optimal child development* (pp. 97–114). Washington, DC: American Psychological Association.

Lawson, K. R., & Ruff, H. A. (2004). Early attention and negative emotionality predict later cognitive and behavioral function. *International Journal of Behavioral Development, 28,* 157–165.

Lazar, I., & Darlington, R. (1982). Lasting effects of early education: A report from the Consortium for Longitudinal Studies. *Monographs of the Society for Research in Child Development, 47*(2–3, Serial No. 195).

Lazarus, R. S., & Lazarus, B. N. (1994). *Passion and reason.* New York: Oxford University Press.

Lazinski, M. J., Shea, A. K., & Steiner, M. (2008). Effects of maternal prenatal stress on offspring development: A commentary. *Archives ofWomen's Mental Health, 11,* 363–375.

Leaper, C. (1994). Exploring the correlates and consequences of gender segregation: Social relationships in childhood, adolescence, and adulthood. In C. Leaper (Ed.), *New directions for child development* (No. 65, pp. 67–86). San Francisco: Jossey-Bass.

Leaper, C. (2000). Gender, affiliation, assertion, and the interactive context of parent—child play. *Developmental Psychology, 36,* 381–393.

Leaper, C. (2013). Gender development during childhood. In P. D. Zelazo (Ed.), *Oxford handbook of developmental psychology, Vol. 2: Self and other* (pp. 326–377). New York: Oxford University Press.

Leaper, C., Anderson, K. J., & Sanders, P. (1998). Moderators of gender effects on parents' talk to their children: A meta-analysis. *Developmental Psychology, 34,* 3–27.

Leaper, C., & Friedman, C. K. (2007). The socialization of gender. In J. E. Grusec & P. D. Hastings (Eds.), *Handbook of socialization: Theory and research* (pp. 561–587). New York: Guilford.

Learmonth, A. E., Lamberth, R., & Rovee-Collier, C. (2004). Generalization of deferred imitation during the first year of life. *Journal of Experimental Child Psychology, 88,* 297–318.

Leavell, A. S., Tamis-LeMonda, C. S., Ruble, D. N., Zosuls, K. M, & Cabrera, N. J. (2011). African American, White, and Latino fathers' activities with their sons and daughters in early childhood. *Sex Roles, 66,* 53–65.

Lebel, C., & Beaulieu, C. (2011). Longitudinal development of human brain wiring continues from childhood into adulthood. *Journal of Neuroscience, 31,* 10937–10947.

Lecanuet, J.-P., Granier-Deferre, C., & DeCasper, A. (2005). Are we expecting too much from prenatal sensory experiences? In B. Hopkins & S. P. Johnson (Eds.), *Prenatal development of postnatal functions* (pp. 31–49). Westport, CT: Praeger.

Lecanuet, J.-P., Granier-Deferre, C., Jacquet, A.-Y., Capponi, I., & Ledru, L. (1993). Prenatal discrimination of a male and female voice uttering the same sentence. *Early Development and Parenting, 2,* 217–228.

LeCuyer, E., & Houck, G. M. (2006). Maternal limitsetting in toddlerhood: Socialization strategies for the development of self-regulation. *Infant Mental Health Journal, 27,* 344–370.

LeCuyer, E. A., Christensen, J. J., Kearney, M. H., & Kitzman, H. J. (2011). African American mothers' self-described discipline strategies with young children. *Issues in Comprehensive Pediatric Nursing, 34,* 144–162.

Lee, C.-Y. S., & Doherty, W. J. (2007). Marital satisfaction and father involvement during the transition to parenthood. *Fathering, 5,* 75–96.

Lee, E. A., Torrance, N., & Olson, D. R. (2001). Young children and the say/mean distinction: Verbatim and paraphrase recognition in narrative and nursery rhyme contexts. *Journal of Child Language, 28,* 531–543.

Lee, E. H., Zhou, Q., Eisenberg, N., & Wang, Y. (2012). Bidirectional relations between temperament and parenting styles in Chinese children. *International Journal of Behavioral Development, 37,* 57–67.

Lee, G. Y., & Kisilevsky, B. S. (2013). Fetuses respond to father's voice but prefer mother's voice after birth. *Developmental Psychobiology, 56,* 1–11.

Lee, K., Xu, F., Fu, G., Cameron, C. A., & Chen, S. (2001). Taiwan and Mainland Chinese and Canadian children's categorization and evaluation of lie- and truth-telling: A modesty effect. *British Journal of Developmental Psychology, 19,* 525–542.

Lee, S. J., Ralston, H. J., Partridge, J. C., & Rosen, M. A. (2005). Fetal pain: A systematic multidisciplinary review of the evidence. *Journal of the American Medical Association, 294,* 947–954.

Lee, S. J., Taylor, C. A., Altschul, I., & Rice, J. C. (2013). Parental spanking and subsequent risk for child aggression in father-involved families of young children. *Children and Youth Services Review, 35,* 1476–1485.

Lee, V. E., & Burkam, D. T. (2002). *Inequality at the starting gate.* Washington, DC: Economic Policy Institute.

Lee, V. E., & Burkam, D. T. (2003). Dropping out of high school: The role of school organization and structure. *American Educational Research Journal, 40,* 353–393.

Lee, Y. (2013). Adolescent motherhood and capital: Interaction effects of race/ethnicity on harsh parenting. *Journal of Community Psychology, 41,* 102–116.

Leerkes, E. M. (2010). Predictors of maternal sensitivity to infant distress. *Parenting: Science and Practice, 10,* 219–239.

Leet, T., & Flick, L. (2003). Effect of exercise on birth weight. *Clinical Obstetrics and Gynecology, 46,* 423–431.

Lefkowitz, E. S., Boone, T. L., Sigman, M., & Au, T. K. (2002). He said, she said: Gender differences in mother–adolescent conversations about sexuality. *Journal of Research on Adolescence, 12,* 217–242.

Lefkowitz, E. S., & Gillen, M. M. (2006). "Sex is just a normal part of life": Sexuality in emerging adulthood. In J. J. Arnett & J. L. Tanner (Eds.), *Emerging adults in America* (pp. 235–256). Washington, DC: American Psychological Association.

Lefkowitz, E. S., Sigman, M., & Au, T. K. (2000). Helping mothers discuss sexuality and AIDS with adolescents. *Child Development, 71,* 1383–1394.

Legare, C. H., & Gelman, S. A. (2008). Bewitchment, biology, or both: The co-existence of natural and supernatural explanatory frameworks across development. *Cognitive Science, 32,* 607–642.

Legare, C. H., Zhu, L., & Wellman, H. (2013). Examining biological explanations in Chinese preschool children: A cross-cultural comparison. *Journal of Cognition and Culture, 13,* 67–93.

Legerstee, M., & Markova, G. (2007). Intentions make a difference: Infant responses to still-face and modified still-face conditions. *Infant Behavior and Development, 30,* 232–250.

Lehman, D. R., & Nisbett, R. E. (1990). A longitudinal study of the effects of undergraduate training on reasoning. *Developmental Psychology, 26,* 952–960.

Lehman, M., & Hasselhorn, M. (2007). Variable memory strategy use in children's adaptive intratask learning behavior: Developmental changes and working memory influences in free recall. *Child Development, 78,* 1068–1082.

Lehman, M., & Hasselhorn, M. (2012). Rehearsal dynamics in elementary school children. *Journal of Experimental Child Psychology, 111,* 552–560.

Lehnung, M., Leplow, B., Ekroll, V., Herzog, A., Mehdorn, M., & Ferstl, R. (2003). The role of locomotion in the acquisition and transfer of spatial knowledge in children. *Scandinavian Journal of Psychology, 44,* 79–86.

Lehr, V. T., Zeskind, P. S., Ofenstein, J. P., Cepeda, E., Warrier, I., & Aranda, J. V. (2007). Neonatal facial coding system scores and spectral characteristics of infant crying during newborn circumcision. *Clinical Journal of Pain, 23*, 417–424.

Lehrer, J. A., Pantell, R., Tebb, K., & Shafer, M. A. (2007). Forgone health care among U.S. adolescents: Associations between risk characteristics and confidentiality. *Journal of Adolescent Health, 40*, 57–75.

Lejeune, F., Marcus, L., Berne-Audeoud, F., Streri, A., Debillon, T., & Gentaz, E. (2012). Intermanual transfer of shapes in preterm human infants from 33 to 34 + 6 weeks postconceptional age. *Child Development, 83*, 794–800.

Leman, P. J. (2005). Authority and moral reasons: Parenting style and children's perceptions of adult rule justifications. *International Journal of Behavioral Development, 29*, 265–270.

Lemche, E., Lennertz, I., Orthmann, C., Ari, A., Grote, K., Hafker, J., & Klann-Delius, G. (2003). Emotion-regulatory process in evoked play narratives: Their relation with mental representations and family interactions. *Praxis der Kinderpsychologie und Kinderpsychiatrie, 52*, 156–171.

Lempert, H. (1989). Animacy constraints on preschoolers' acquisition of syntax. *Child Development, 60*, 237–245.

Lenhart, A. (2012). Teens, smartphones & texting. Washington, DC: Pew Research Center's Internet & American Life Project. Retrieved from pewinternet.org/Reports/2012/Teens-and-smartphones.aspx

Lenhart, A., Purcell, K, Smith, A., & Zickuhr, K. (2010). *Social media & mobile Internet use among teens and young adults*. Washington, DC: Pew Research Center.

Lenroot, R. K., & Giedd, J. N. (2006). Brain development in children and adolescents: Insights from anatomical magnetic resonance imaging. *Neuroscience and Biobehavioral Reviews, 30*, 718–729.

Lenzi, M., Vieno, A., Perkins, D. D., Santinello, M., Elgar, F. J., Morgan, A., et al. (2012). Family affluence, school and neighborhood contexts and adolescents' civic engagement: A cross-national study. *American Journal of Community Psychology, 50*, 197–210.

Lerman, R. I. (2010). Capabilities and contributions of unwed fathers. *Future of Children, 20*, 63–85.

Lerner, R. M., Leonard, K., Fay, K., & Issac, S. S. (2011). Continuity and discontinuity in development across the life span: A developmental systems perspective. In K. L. Fingerman, C. A. Berg, J. Smith, & T. C. Antonucci (Eds.), *Handbook of life-span development* (pp. 141–160). New York: Springer.

Lerner, R. M., & Overton, W. F. (2008). Exemplifying the integrations of the relational developmental system. *Journal of Adolescent Research, 23*, 245–255.

Lernout, T., Theeten, H., Hens, N., Braeckman, T., Roelants, M., Hoppenbrouwers, K., & Van Damme, P. (2013). Timeliness of infant vaccination and factors related with delay in Flanders, Belgium. *Vaccine, 32*, 284–289.

Leslie, A. M. (2004). Who's for learning? *Developmental Science, 7*, 417–419.

Lester, B. M., & Lagasse, L. L. (2010). Children of addicted women. *Journal of Addictive Diseases, 29*, 259–276.

Lett, D. (1997). *L'enfant des miracles: Enfance et société au Moyen Age (XIIe–XIIIe siecle)*. Paris: Aubier.

Leuner, B., Glasper, E. R., & Gould, E. (2010). Parenting and plasticity. *Trends in Neurosciences, 33*, 465–473.

LeVay, S. (1993). *The sexual brain*. Cambridge, MA: MIT Press.

Levendosky, A. A., Bogat, G. A., Huth-Bocks, A. C., Rosenblum, K., & von Eye, A. (2011). The effect of domestic violence on the stability of attachment from infancy to preschool. *Journal of Clinical Child and Adolescent Psychology, 40*, 398–410.

Leventhal, T., & Brooks-Gunn, J. (2003). Children and youth in neighborhood contexts. *Current Directions in Psychological Science, 12*, 27–31.

Leventhal, T., & Dupéré, V. (2011). Moving to opportunity: Does long-term exposure to "low-poverty" neighborhoods make a difference for adolescents? *Social Science and Medicine, 73*, 737–743.

Leventhal, T., Dupéré, V., & Brooks-Gunn, J. (2009). Neighborhood influences on adolescent development. In R. M. Lerner & L. Steinberg (Eds.), *Handbook of adolescent psychology, Vol. 2* (3rd ed., pp. 411–443). Hoboken, NJ: Wiley.

Levin, B. (2012). *More high school graduates: How schools can save students from dropping out*. Thousand Oaks, CA: Sage.

Levin, I., & Bus, A. G. (2003). How is emergent writing based on drawing? Analyses of children's products and their sorting by children and mothers. *Developmental Psychology, 39*, 891–905.

Levine, K. A., & Sutherland, D. (2013). History repeats itself: Parental involvement in children's career exploration. *Canadian Journal of Counselling and Psychotherapy, 47*, 239–255.

LeVine, R. A., Dixon, S., LeVine, S., Richman, A., Leiderman, P. H., Keefer, C. H., & Brazelton, T. B. (1994). *Child care and culture: Lessons from Africa*. New York: Cambridge University Press.

LeVine, R. A., LeVine, S., Schnell-Anzola, B., Rowe, M. L., & Dexter, E. (2012). *Literacy and mothering: How women's schooling changes the lives of the world's children*. New York: Oxford University Press.

LeVine, R. A., LeVine, S. E., Rowe, M. L., & Schnell-Anzola, B. (2004). Maternal literacy and health behavior: A Nepalese case study. *Social Science and Medicine, 58*, 863–877.

Levine, S. C., Huttenlocher, J., Taylor, A., & Langrock, A. (1999). Early sex differences in spatial skill. *Developmental Psychology, 35*, 940–949.

Levine, S. C., Ratliff, K. R., Huttenlocher, J., & Cannon, J. (2012). Early puzzle play: A predictor of preschoolers' spatial transformation skill. *Developmental Psychology, 48*, 530–542.

Levine, S. C., Vasilyeva, M., Lourenco, S. F., Newcombe, N. S., & Huttenlocher, J. (2005). Socioeconomic status modifies the sex difference in spatial skill. *Psychological Science, 16*, 841–845.

Levinson, D. J. (1978). *The seasons of a man's life*. New York: Knopf.

Levinson, D. J. (1996). *The seasons of a woman's life*. New York: Knopf.

Levy, G. D., Taylor, M. G., & Gelman, S. A. (1995). Traditional and evaluative aspects of flexibility in gender roles, social conventions, moral rules, and physical laws. *Child Development, 66*, 515–531.

Levy, S. R., & Dweck, C. S. (1999). The impact of children's static vs. dynamic conceptions of people on stereotype information. *Child Development, 70*, 1163–1180.

Lewiecki, E. M., & Miller, S. A. (2013). Suicide, guns, and public policy. *American Journal of Public Health, 103*, 27–31.

Lewis, M. (1992). *Shame: The exposed self*. New York: Free Press.

Lewis, M. (1995). Embarrassment: The emotion of self-exposure and evaluation. In J. P. Tangney & K. W. Fischer (Eds.), *Self-conscious emotions* (pp. 198–218). New York: Guilford.

Lewis, M. (1998). Emotional competence and development. In D. Pushkar, W. M. Bukowski, A. E. Schwartzman, E. M. Stack, & D. R. White (Eds.), *Improving competence across the lifespan* (pp. 27–36). New York: Plenum.

Lewis, M. (2014). *The rise of consciousness and the development of emotional life*. New York: Guilford.

Lewis, M., & Brooks-Gunn, J. (1979). *Social cognition and the acquisition of self*. New York: Plenum.

Lewis, M., & Ramsay, D. (2002). Cortisol response to embarrassment and shame. *Child Development, 73*, 1034–1045.

Lewis, M., & Ramsay, D. (2004). Development of self-recognition, personal pronoun use, and pretend play during the 2nd year. *Child Development, 75*, 1821–1831.

Lewis, M., Ramsay, D. S., & Kawakami, K. (1993). Differences between Japanese infants and Caucasian American infants in behavioral and cortisol response to inoculation. *Child Development, 64*, 1722–1731.

Lewis, M. A., Granato, H., Blayney, J. A., Lostutter, T. W., & Kilmer, J. R. (2012). Predictors of hooking up sexual behaviors and emotional reactions among U.S. college students. *Archives of Sexual Behavior, 41*, 1219–1229.

Lewis, M. D. (2008). Emotional habits in brain and behavior: A window on personality development. In A. Fogel, B. J. King, & S. G. Shanker (Eds.), *Human development in the twenty-first century* (pp. 72–80). New York: Cambridge University Press.

Lewis, T. L., & Maurer, D. (2005). Multiple sensitive periods in human visual development: Evidence from visually deprived children. *Developmental Psychobiology, 46*, 163–183.

Lew-Williams, C., Pelucchi, B., & Saffran, J. R. (2011). Isolated words enhance statistical language learning in infancy. *Developmental Science, 14*, 1323–1329.

Li, D.-K., Willinger, M., Petitti, D. B., Odouli, R., Liu, L., & Hoffman, H. J. (2006). Use of a dummy (pacifier) during sleep and risk of sudden infant death syndrome (SIDS): Population based case-control study. *British Medical Journal, 332*, 18–21.

Li, J., Johnson, S. E., Han, W., Andrews, S., Kendall, G., Strazdins, L. & Dockery, A. (2014). Parents' nonstandard work schedules and child well-being: A critical review of the literature. *Journal of Primary Prevention, 35*, 53–73.

Li, J. J., Berk, M. S., & Lee, S. S. (2013). Differential susceptibility in longitudinal models of gene–environment interaction for adolescent depression. *Developmental Psychopathology, 25*, 991–1003.

Li, K., Zhu, D., Guo, L., Li, Z., Lynch, M. E., Coles, C., et al. (2013). Connectomics signatures of prenatal cocaine exposure affected adolescent brains. *Human Brain Mapping, 34*, 2494–2510.

Li, S.-C., Lindenberger, U., Hommel, B., Aschersleben, G., Prinz, W., & Baltes, P. B. (2004). Transformation in the couplings among intellectual abilities and constituent cognitive processes across the life span. *Psychological Science, 15*, 155–163.

Li, W., Farkas, G., Duncan, G. J., Burchinal, M. R., & Vandell, D. L. (2013). Timing of high-quality child care and cognitive, language, and preacademic development. *Developmental Psychology, 49*, 1440–1451.

Li, X., Atkins, M. S., & Stanton, B. (2006). Effects of home and school computer use on school readiness and cognitive development among Head Start children: A randomized control trial. *Merrill-Palmer Quarterly, 52*, 239–263.

Li, X. Q., Zhu, P., Myatt, L., & Sun, K. (2014). Roles of glucocorticoids in human parturition: A controversial fact? *Placenta, 35*, 291–296.

Liben, L. S. (2006). Education for spatial thinking. In K. A. Renninger & I. E. Sigel (Eds.), *Handbook of child psychology: Vol. 4. Child psychology in practice* (6th ed., pp. 197–247). Hoboken, NJ: Wiley.

Liben, L. S. (2009). The road to understanding maps. *Current Directions in Psychological Science, 18*, 310–315.

Liben, L. S., & Bigler, R. S. (2002). The developmental course of gender differentiation: Conceptualizing, measuring, and evaluating constructs and pathways. *Monographs of the Society for Research in Child Development, 67*(2, Serial No. 269).

Liben, L. S., Bigler, R. S., & Krogh, H. R. (2001). Pink and blue collar jobs: Children's judgments of job status and job aspirations in relation to sex of worker. *Journal of Experimental Child Psychology, 79*, 346–363.

Liben, L. S., & Downs, R. M. (1993). Understanding person–space–map relations: Cartographic and developmental perspectives. *Developmental Psychology, 29*, 739–752.

Liben, L. S., Kastens, K. A., & Stevenson, L. M. (2002). Real-world knowledge through real-world maps: A developmental guide for navigating the educational terrain. *Developmental Review, 22*, 267–322.

Liben, L. S., Myers, L. J., Christensen, A. E., & Bower, C. A. (2013). Environmental-scale map use in middle childhood: Links to spatial skills, strategies, and gender. *Child Development, 84*, 2047–2063.

Lickliter, R., & Honeycutt, H. (2013). A developmental evolutionary framework for psychology. *Review of General Psychology, 17*, 184–189.

Lidstone, J. S. M., Meins, E., & Fernyhough, C. (2010). The roles of private speech and inner speech in planning during middle childhood: Evidence from a dual task paradigm. *Journal of Experimental Child Psychology, 107*, 438–451.

Lidz, C. S. (2001). Multicultural issues and dynamic assessment. In L. A. Suzuki & J. G. Ponterotto (Eds.), *Handbook of multicultural assessment: Clinical, psychological, and educational applications* (2nd ed., pp. 523–539). San Francisco: Jossey-Bass.

Lidz, J. (2007). The abstract nature of syntactic representations. In E. Hoff & M. Shatz (Eds.), *Blackwell handbook of language development* (pp. 277–303). Malden, MA: Blackwell.

Lidz, J., Gleitman, H., & Gleitman, L. (2004). Kidz in the 'hood: Syntactic bootstrapping and the mental lexicon. In

D. G. Hall & S. R. Waxman (Eds.), *Weaving a lexicon* (pp. 603–636). Cambridge, MA: MIT Press.

Liew, J., Eisenberg, N., Spinrad, T. L., Eggum, N. D., Haugen, R. G., Kupfer, A., et al. (2010). Physiological regulation and fearfulness as predictors of young children's empathy-related reactions. *Social Development, 20,* 111–134.

Li-Grining, C. P. (2007). Effortful control among low-income preschoolers in three cities: Stability, change, and individual differences. *Developmental Psychology, 43,* 208–221.

Lillard, A. (2007). *Montessori: The science behind the genius.* New York: Oxford University Press.

Lillard, A., & Else-Quest, N. (2006). Evaluating Montessori education. *Science, 313,* 1893–1894.

Lillard, A. S., Nishida, T., Massaro, D., Vaish, A., Ma, L., & McRoberts, G. (2007). Signs of pretense across age and scenario. *Infancy, 11,* 130.

Lillard, A. S., & Peterson, J. (2011). The immediate impact of different types of television on young children's executive function. *Pediatrics, 128,* 644–649.

Lillard, A. S., & Witherington, D. (2004). Mothers' behavior modifications during pretense snacks and their possible signal value for toddlers. *Developmental Psychology, 40,* 95–113.

Lin, T-J., Anderson, R. C., Hummel, J. E., Jadallah, M., Miller, B. W., Nguyen-Jahiel, K., et al. (2012). Children's use of analogy during collaborative reasoning. *Child Development, 83,* 1429–1443.

Lincove, J. A., & Painter, G. (2006). Does the age that children start kindergarten matter? Evidence of long-term educational and social outcomes. *Educational Evaluation and Policy Analysis, 28,* 153–179.

Lind, J. N., Li, R., Perrine, C. G., & Shieve, L. A. (2014). Breastfeeding and later psychosocial development of children at 6 years of age. *Pediatrics, 134,* S36–S41.

Lindberg, S. M., Hyde, J. S., Linn, M. C., & Petersen, J. L. (2010). New trends in gender and mathematics performance: A meta-analysis. *Psychological Bulletin, 136,* 1123–1135.

Lindblad, F., & Hjern, A. (2010). ADHD after fetal exposure to maternal smoking. *Nicotine and Tobacco Research, 12,* 408–415.

Linder, J. R., & Collins, W. A. (2005). Parent and peer predictors of physical aggression and conflict management in romantic relationships in early adulthood. *Journal of Family Psychology, 19,* 252–262.

Lindley, L. D. (2005). Perceived barriers to carreer development in the context of social-cognitive career theory. *Journal of Career Assessment, 13,* 271–287.

Lindsay-Hartz, J., de Rivera, J., & Mascolo, M. F. (1995). Differentiating guilt and shame and their effects on motivation. In J. P. Tangney & K. W. Fischer (Eds.), *Self-conscious emotions* (pp. 274–300). New York: Guilford.

Lindsey, E. W., & Colwell, M. J. (2013). Pretend and physical play: Links to preschoolers' affective social competence. *Merrill-Palmer Quarterly, 59,* 330–360.

Lindsey, E. W., Colwell, M. J., Frabutt, J. M., Chambers, J. C., & MacKinnon-Lewis, C. (2008). Mother–child dyadic synchrony in European-American and African-American families during early adolescence: Relations with self-esteem and prosocial behavior. *Merrill-Palmer Quarterly, 54,* 289–315.

Lindsey, E. W., & Mize, J. (2000). Parent–child physical and pretense play: Links to children's social competence. *Merrill-Palmer Quarterly, 46,* 565–591.

Linebarger, D. L., & Piotrowski, J. T. (2010). Structure and strategies in children's educational television: The roles of program type and learning strategies in children's learning. *Child Development, 81,* 1582–1597.

Linscheid, T. R., Budd, K. S., & Rasnake, L. K. (2005). Pediatric feeding problems. In M. C. Roberts (Ed.), *Handbook of pediatric psychology and psychiatry* (3rd ed., pp. 481–488). New York: Guilford.

Linver, M. R., Martin, A., & Brooks-Gunn, J. (2004). Measuring infants' home environment: The IT-HOME for infants between birth and 12 months in four national data sets. *Parenting: Science and Practice, 4,* 115–137.

Lipsitt, L. P. (2003). Crib death: A biobehavioral phenomenon? *Psychological Science, 12,* 164–170.

Lipton, J. S., & Spelke, E. S. (2003). Origins of number sense: Large-number discrimination in human infants. *Psychological Science, 14,* 396–401.

Liszkowski, U., Carpenter, M., & Tomasello, M. (2007). Pointing out new news, old news, and absent referents at 12 months of age. *Developmental Science, 10,* F1–F7.

Liszkowski, U., Carpenter, M., & Tomasello, M. (2008). Twelve-month-olds communicate helpfully and appropriately for knowledgeable and ignorant partners. *Cognition, 108,* 732–739.

Litovsky, R. Y., & Ashmead, D. H. (1997). Development of binaural and spatial hearing in infants and children. In R. H. Gilkey & T. R. Anderson (Eds.), *Binaural and spatial hearing in real and virtual environments* (pp. 571–592). Mahwah, NJ: Erlbaum.

Little, C., & Carter, A. S. (2005). Negative emotional reactivity and regulation in 12-month-olds following emotional challenge: Contributions of maternal—infant emotional availability in a low-income sample, *Infant Mental Health Journal, 26,* 354–368.

Liu, D., Sabbagh, M. A., Gehring, W. J., & Wellman, H. M. (2009). Neural correlates of children's theory of mind development. *Child Development, 80,* 318–326.

Liu, H.-L., Chen, K.-H., & Peng, N.-H. (2012). Cultural practices relating to menarche and menstruation among adolescent girls in Taiwan—qualitative investigation. *Journal of Adolescent and Pediatric Gynecology, 25,* 43–47.

Liu, J., Raine, A., Venables, P. H., Dalais, C., & Mednick, S. A. (2003). Malnutrition at age 3 years and lower cognitive ability at age 11 years. *Archives of Paediatric and Adolescent Medicine, 157,* 593–600.

Liu, J., Raine, A., Venables, P. H., & Mednick, S. A. (2004). Malnutrition at age 3 years and externalizing behavior problems at ages 8, 11, and 17 years. *American Journal of Psychiatry, 161,* 2005–2013.

Liu, R. T., & Mustanski, B. (2012). Suicidal ideation and self-harm in lesbian, gay, bisexual, and transgender youth. *American Journal of Preventive Medicine, 42,* 221–228.

Lleras, C., & Rangel, C. (2009). Ability grouping practices in elementary school and African American/Hispanic achievement. *American Journal of Education, 115,* 279–304.

Lloyd, M. E., Doydum, A. O., & Newcombe, N. S. (2009). Memory binding in early childhood: Evidence for a retrieval deficit. *Child Development, 80,* 1321–1328.

Lobo, M. A., & Galloway, J. C. (2013). The onset of reaching significantly impacts how infants explore both objects and their bodies. *Infant Behavior and Development, 36,* 14–24.

Lochman, J. E., & Dodge, K. A. (1998). Distorted perceptions in dyadic interactions of aggressive and nonaggressive boys: Effects of prior expectations, context, and boys' age. *Development and Psychopathology, 10,* 495–512.

Lock, J., & Kirz, N. (2008). Eating disorders: Anorexia nervosa. In W. E. Craighead, D. J. Miklowitz, & L. W. Craighead (Eds.), *Psychopathology: History, diagnosis, and empirical foundations* (pp. 467–494). Hoboken, NJ: Wiley.

Locke, J. (1892). Some thoughts concerning education. In R. H. Quick (Ed.), *Locke on education* (pp. 1–236). Cambridge, UK: Cambridge University Press. (Original work published 1690).

Lockhart, K. L., Chang, B., & Story, T. (2002). Young children's beliefs about the stability of traits: Protective optimism? *Child Development, 73,* 1408–1430.

Lockhart, K. L., Nakashima, N., Inagaki, K., & Keil, F. C. (2008). From ugly duckling to swan? Japanese and American beliefs about the stability and origins of traits. *Cognitive Development, 23,* 155–179.

Loehlin, J. C., Horn, J. M., & Willerman, L. (1997). Heredity, environment, and IQ in the Texas Adoption Project. In R. J. Sternberg & E. L. Grigorenko (Eds.), *Intelligence, heredity, and environment* (pp. 105–125). New York: Cambridge University Press.

Loganovskaja, T. K., & Loganovsky, K. N. (1999). EEG, cognitive and psychopathological abnormalities in children irradiated in utero. *International Journal of Psychophysiology, 34,* 213–224.

Loganovsky, K. N., Loganovskaja, T. K., Nechayev, S. Y., Antipchuk, Y. Y., & Bomko, M. A. (2008). Disrupted development of the dominant hemisphere following prenatal irradiation. *The Journal of Neuropsychiatry and Clinical Neurosciences, 20,* 274–291.

Lohman, D. F. (2000). Measures of intelligence: Cognitive theories. In A. E. Kazdin (Ed.), *Encyclopedia of psychology: Vol. 5* (pp. 147–150). Washington, DC: American Psychological Association.

Lohrmann, S., & Bambara, L. M. (2006). Elementary education teachers' beliefs about essential supports needed to successfully include students with developmental disabilities who engage in challenging behaviors. *Research and Practice for Persons with Severe Disabilities, 31,* 157–173.

Loman, M. M., & Gunnar, M. R. (2010). Early experience and the development of stress reactivity and regulation in children. *Neuroscience and Biobehavioral Reviews, 34,* 867–876.

Longest, K. C., & Smith, C. (2011). Conflicting or compatible: Beliefs about religion and science among emerging adults in the United States. *Sociological Forum, 26,* 846–869.

Longstaffe, S., Moffatt, M. E., & Whalen, J. C. (2000). Behavioral and self-concept changes after six months of enuresis treatment: A randomized, controlled trial. *Pediatrics, 105,* 935–940.

Lonigan, C. J., Purpura, D. J., Wilson, S. B., Walker, J., & Clancy-Menchetti, J. (2013). Evaluating the components of an emergent literacy intervention for preschool children at risk for reading difficulties. *Journal of Experimental Child Psychology, 114,* 111–130.

Looker, D., & Thiessen, V. (2003). *The digital divide in Canadian schools: Factors affecting student access to and use of information technology.* Ottawa: Statistics Canada, Catalogue no. 81-597-X. Retrieved from www.statcan.ca/bsolc/english/bsolc?catno=81-597-X

Loomans, E. M., Van der Stelt, O., van Eijsden, M., Gemke, R. J., Vrijkotte, T., & den Bergh, B. R. (2011). Antenatal maternal anxiety is associated with problem behaviour at age five. *Early Human Development, 87,* 565–570.

Lopez, C. M., Driscoll, K. A., & Kistner, J. A. (2009). Sex differences and response styles: Subtypes of rumination and associations with depressive symptoms. *Journal of Clinical Child and Adolescent Psychology, 38,* 27–35.

Lorch, R. F., Jr., Lorch, E. P., Calderhead, W. J., Dunlap, E. E., Hodell, E. C., & Freer, B. D. (2010). Learning the control of variables strategy in higher- and lower-achieving classrooms: Contributions of explicit instruction and experimentation. *Journal of Educational Psychology, 102,* 90–101.

Lorenz, K. Z. (1952). *King Solomon's ring.* New York: Crowell.

Lou, E., Lalonde, R. N., & Giguère, B. (2012). Making the decision to move out: Bicultural young adults and the negotiation of cultural demands and family relationships. *Journal of Cross-Cultural Psychology, 43,* 663–670.

Louie, V. (2001). Parents' aspirations and investment: The role of social class in the educational experiences of 1.5- and second-generation Chinese Americans. *Harvard Educational Review, 71,* 438–474.

Louis, J., Cannard, C., Bastuji, H., & Challamel, M.-J. (1997). Sleep ontogenesis revisited: A longitudinal 24-hour home polygraphic study on 15 normal infants during the first two years of life. *Sleep, 20,* 323–333.

Lourenço, O. (2003). Making sense of Turiel's dispute with Kohlberg: The case of the child's moral competence. *New Ideas in Psychology, 21,* 43–68.

Lourenço, O. (2012). Piaget and Vygotsky: Many resemblances, and a crucial difference. *New Ideas in Psychology, 30,* 281–295.

Love, J. M., Chazan-Cohen, R., & Raikes, H. (2007). Forty years of research knowledge and use: From Head Start to Early Head Start and beyond. In J. L. Aber, S. J. Bishop-Josef, S. M. Jones, K. T. McLearn, & D. Phillips (Eds.), *Child development and social policy: Knowledge for action* (pp. 79–95). Washington, DC: American Psychological Association.

Love, J. M., Harrison, L., Sagi-Schwartz, A., van IJzendoorn, M. H., Ross, C., & Ungerer, J. A. (2003). Child care quality matters: How conclusions may vary with context. *Child Development, 74,* 1021–1033.

Love, J. M., Kisker, E. E., Ross, C., Raikes, H., Constantine, J., Boller, K., & Brooks-Gunn, J. (2005). The effectiveness of early Head Start for 3-year-old children and their parents: Lessons for policy and programs. *Developmental Psychology, 41,* 885–901.

Low, M., Farrell, A., Biggs, B., & Pasricha, S. (2013). Effects of daily iron supplementation in primary-school-aged children: Systematic review and meta-analysis of randomized controlled trials. *Canadian Medical Association Journal, 185,* E791–E802.

Low, S. M., & Stocker, C. (2012). Family functioning and children's adjustment: Associations among parents' depressed mood, marital hostility, parent–child hostility, and children's adjustment. *Journal of Family Psychology, 19,* 394–403.

Lubart, T. I. (2003). In search of creative intelligence. In R. J. Sternberg, J. Lautrey, & T. I. Lubart (Eds.), *Models of intelligence: International perspectives* (pp. 279–292). Washington, DC: American Psychological Association.

Lubart, T. I., Georgsdottir, A., & Besançon, M. (2009). The nature of creative giftedness and talent. In T. Balchin, B. Hymer, & D. J. Matthews (Eds.), *The Routledge international companion to gifted education* (pp. 42–49). New York: Routledge.

Luby, J., Belden, A., Sullivan, J., Hayen, R., McCadney, A., & Spitznagel, E. (2009). Shame and guilt in preschool depression: Evidence for elevations in self-conscious emotions in depression as early as age 3. *Journal of Child Psychology and Psychiatry, 50,* 1156–1166.

Lucassen, N., Tharner, A., Van IJzendoorn, M. H., Bakermans-Kranenburg, M. J., Volling, B. L., Verhulst, F. C., et al. (2011). The association between paternal sensitivity and infant–father attachment security: A meta-analysis of three decades of research. *Journal of Family Psychology, 25,* 986–992.

Lucas-Thompson, R., & Clarke-Stewart, K. A. (2007). Forecasting friendship: How marital quality, maternal mood, and attachment security are linked to children's peer relationships. *Journal of Applied Developmental Psychology, 28,* 499–514.

Luciana, M., Collins, P. F., Muetzel, R. L., & Lim, K. O. (2013). Effects of alcohol use initiation on brain structure in typically developing adolescents. *The American Journal of Drug and Alcohol Abuse, 39,* 345–355.

Luecken, L. J., Lin, B., Coburn, S. S., MacKinnon, D. P., Gonzales, N. A., & Crnic, K. A. (2013). Prenatal stress, partner support, and infant cortisol reactivity in low-income Mexican American families. *Psychoneuroendocrinology, 38,* 3092–3101.

Lukowski, A. F., Koss, M., Burden, M. J., Jonides, J., Nelson, C. A., Kaciroti, N., et al. (2010). Iron deficiency in infancy and neurocognitive functioning at 19 years: Evidence of long-term deficits in executive function and recognition memory. *Nutritional Neuroscience, 13,* 54–70.

Luna, B., Padmanabhan, A., & Geier, C. (2014). The adolescent sensation-seeking period: Development of reward processing and its effects on cognitive control. In V. F. Reyna & V. Zayas (Eds.), *The neuroscience of risky decision making* (pp. 93–121). Washington, DC: American Psychological Association.

Luna, B., Thulborn, K. R., Monoz, D. P., Merriam, E. P., Garver, K. E., Minshew, N. J., et al. (2001). Maturation of widely distributed brain function subserves cognitive development. *Neuroimage, 13,* 786–793.

Lund, N., Pedersen, L. H., & Henriksen, T. B. (2009). Selective serotonin reuptake inhibitor exposure in utero and pregnancy outcomes. *Archives of Pediatrics and Adolescent Medicine, 163,* 949–954.

Lundy, B. L. (2002). Paternal socio-psychological factors and infant attachment: The mediating role of synchrony in father–infant interactions. *Infant Behavior and Development, 25,* 221–236.

Luo, L. Z., Li, H., & Lee, K. (2011). Are children's faces really more appealing than those of adults? Testing the baby schema hypothesis beyond infancy. *Journal of Experimental Child Psychology, 110,* 115–124.

Luria, A. R. (1976). *Cognitive development: Its cultural and social foundations.* Cambridge, MA: Harvard University Press.

Lussier, P., Corrado, R., & Tzoumakis, S. (2012). Gender differences in physical aggression and associated developmental correlates in a sample of Canadian preschoolers. *Behavioral Sciences and the Law, 30,* 643–671.

Luster, T., & Haddow, J. L. (2005). Adolescent mothers and their children: An ecological perspective. In T. Luster & J. L. Haddow (Eds.), *Parenting: An ecological perspective* (2nd ed., pp. 73–101). Mahwah, NJ: Erlbaum.

Luthar, S. S., & Barkin, S. H. (2012). Are affluent youth truly "at risk"? Vulnerability and resilience across diverse samples. *Development and Psychopathology, 24,* 429–449.

Luthar, S. S., & Goldstein, A. S. (2008). Substance use and related behaviors among suburban late adolescents:

The importance of perceived parent containment. *Development and Psychopathology, 20,* 591–614.

Luthar, S. S., & Latendresse, S. J. (2005a). Children of the affluent: Challenges to well-being. *Current Directions in Psychological Science, 14,* 49–53.

Luthar, S. S., & Latendresse, S. J. (2005b). Comparable "risks" at the socioeconomic status extremes: Preadolescents' perceptions of parenting. *Development and Psychopathology, 17,* 207–230.

Luthar, S. S., & Sexton, C. (2004). The high price of affluence. In R. V. Kail (Ed.), *Advances in child development* (Vol. 32, pp. 126–162). San Diego, CA: Academic Press.

Luyckx, K., Goossens, L., & Soenens, B. (2006). A developmental contextual perspective on identity construction in emerging adulthood: Change dynamics in commitment formation and commitment evaluation. *Developmental Psychology, 42,* 366–380.

Luyckx, K., Goossens, L., Soenens, B., & Beyers, W. (2006). Unpacking commitment and exploration: Preliminary validation of an integrative model of late adolescent identity formation. *Journal of Adolescence, 29,* 361–378.

Luyckx, K., Schwartz, S. J., Berzonsky, M. D., Soenens, B., Vansteenkiste, M., Smits, I., & Goosens, L. (2008). Capturing ruminative exploration: Extending the four-dimensional model of identity formation in late adolescence. *Journal of Research in Personality, 42,* 58–82.

Luyckx, K., Soenens, B., Vansteenkiste, M., Goossens, L., & Berzonsky, M. D. (2007). Parental psychological control and dimensions of identity formation in emerging adulthood. *Journal of Family Psychology, 21,* 546–550.

Luyckx, K., Vansteenkiste, M., Goossens, L., & Duriez, B. (2009). Basic need satisfaction and identity formation: Bridging self-determination theory and process-oriented identity research. *Journal of Counseling Psychology, 56,* 276–288.

Lynch, S. K., Turkheimer, E., D'Onofrio, B. M., Mendle, J., Emery, R. E., Slutske, W. S., & Martin, N. G. (2006). A genetically informed study of the association between harsh punishment and offspring behavioral problems. *Journal of Family Psychology, 20,* 190–198.

Lyon, T. D., & Flavell, J. H. (1994). Young children's understanding of "remember" and "forget." *Child Development, 65,* 1357–1371.

Lyons-Ruth, K., Bronfman, E., & Parsons, E. (1999). Maternal frightened, frightening, or aytpical behavior and disorganized infant attachment patterns. *Monographs of the Society for Research in Child Development, 64*(3, Serial No. 258), 67–96.

Lyster, R., & Genesee, F. (2012). Immersion education. In Carol A. Chapelle (Ed.), *Encyclopedia of Applied Linguistics* (pp. 2608–2614). Hoboken, NJ: Wiley.

Lytton, H., & Gallagher, L. (2002). Parenting twins and the genetics of parenting. In M. H. Bornstein (Ed.), *Handbook of parenting: Vol. 1. Children and parenting* (pp. 227–253). Mahwah, NJ: Erlbaum.

M

Ma, F., Xu, F., Heyman, G. D., & Lee, K. (2011). Chinese children's evaluations of white lies: Weighing the consequences for recipients. *Journal of Experimental Child Psychology, 108,* 308–321.

Ma, L., & Lillard, A. S. (2006). Where is the real cheese? Young children's ability to discriminate between real and pretend acts. *Child Development, 77,* 1762–1777.

Ma, W., Golinkoff, R. M., Hirsh-Pasek, K., McDonough, C., & Tardif, T. (2009). Imagine that! Imageability predicts the age of acquisition of verbs in Chinese children. *Journal of Child Language, 36,* 405–423.

Ma, W., Golinkoff, R. M., Houston, D., & Hirsh-Pasek, K. (2011). Word learning in infant- and adult-directed speech. *Language Learning and Development, 7,* 209–225.

Maas, F. K. (2008). Children's understanding of promising, lying, and false belief. *Journal of General Psychology, 13,* 301–321.

Maccoby, E. E. (1984). Middle childhood in the context of the family. In W. A. Collins (Ed.), *Development during middle childhood* (pp. 184–239). Washington, DC: National Academy Press.

Maccoby, E. E. (1998). *The two sexes: Growing up apart, coming together.* Cambridge, MA: Belknap/Harvard University Press.

Maccoby, E. E. (2002). Gender and group process: A developmental perspective. *Current Directions in Psychological Science, 11,* 54–58.

MacKenzie, M. J., Nicklas, E., Waldfogel, J., & Brooks-Gunn, J. (2013). Spanking and child development across the first decade of life. *Pediatrics, 132,* e1118–e1125. Retrieved from http://pediatrics.aappublications.org/content/132/5/e1118.full.html

Mackey, E. R., & La Greca, A. M. (2007). Adolescents' eating, exercise, and weight control behaviors: Does peer crowd affiliation play a role? *Journal of Pediatric Psychology, 32,* 13–23.

Mackey, K., Arnold, M. L., & Pratt, M. W. (2001). Adolescents' stories of decision making in more and less authoritative families: Representing the voices of parents in narrative. *Journal of Adolescent Research, 16,* 243–268.

Mackie, S., Show, P., Lenroot, R., Pierson, R., Greenstein, D. K., & Nugent, T. F., III. (2007). Cerebellar development and clinical outcome in attention deficit hyperactivity disorder. *American Journal of Psychiatry, 164,* 647–655.

MacLeod, J. (2009). *Ain't no makin' it: Aspirations and attainment in a low-income neighborhood.* Boulder, CO: Westview Press.

MacWhinney, B. (2005). Language development. In M. H. Bornstein & M. E. Lamb (Eds.), *Developmental science: An advanced textbook* (5th ed., pp. 359–387). Mahwah, NJ: Erlbaum.

Madden, M., Lenhart, A., Cortesi, S., Gasser, U., Duggan, M., Smith, A., et al. (2013). *Teens, social media, and privacy: Part 1. Teens and social media use.* Washington, DC: Pew Research Center's Internet and American Life Project. Retrieved from www.pewinternet.org/2013/05/21/part-1-teens-and-social-media-use

Madigan, S., Bakermans-Kranenburg, M. J., van IJzendoorn, M. H., Moran, G., Pederson, D. R., & Benoit, D. (2006). Unresolved states of mind, anomalous parental behavior, and disorganized attachment: A review and meta-analysis of a transmission gap. *Attachment and Human Development, 8,* 89–111.

Madole, K. L., Oakes, L. M., & Rakison, D. H. (2011). Information-processing approaches to infants' developing representation of dynamic features. In L. M. Oakes, C. H. Cashon, M. Casasola, & D. Rakison (Eds.), *Infant perception and cognition* (153–178). New York: Oxford University Press.

Madon, S., Willard, J., Guyll, M., & Scherr, K. C. (2011). Self-fulfilling prophecies: Mechanisms, power, and links to social problems. *Social and Personality Psychology Compass, 5/8,* 578–590.

Madsen, S. A., & Juhl, T. (2007). Paternal depression in the postnatal period assessed with traditional and male depression scales. *Journal of Men's Health and Gender, 4,* 26–31.

Maeda, Y., & Yoon, S. Y. (2013). A meta-analysis on gender differences in mental rotation ability measured by the Purdue Spatial Visualization Tests: Visualization of Rotations (PSV:R). *Educational Psychology Review, 25,* 69–94.

Magnuson, K., & Shager, H. (2010). Early education: Progress and promise for children from low-income families. *Children and Youth Services Review, 32,* 1186–1198.

Magolda, M. B., Abes, E., & Torres, V. (2009). Epistemological, intrapersonal, and interpersonal development in the college years and young adulthood. In M. C. Smith & N. DeFrates-Densch (Eds.), *Handbook of research on adult learning and development* (pp. 183–219). New York: Routledge.

Magolda, M. B. B., King, P. M., Taylor, K. B., & Wakefield, K. M. (2012). Decreasing authority dependence during the first year of college. *Journal of College Student Development, 53,* 418–435.

Magyar-Russell, G., Deal, P. J., & Brown, A. I. (2014). Potential benefits and detriments of religiousness and spirituality to emerging adults. In C. M. Barry & M. M. Abo-Zena (Eds.), *Emerging adults' religiousness and spirituality* (pp 21–38). New York: Oxford University Press.

Mahoney, J. L., & Stattin, H. (2000). Leisure activities and antisocial behavior: The role of structure and social context. *Journal of Adolescence, 23,* 113–127.

Main, M., & Goldwyn, R. (1998). *Adult attachment classification system.* London: University College.

Main, M., & Solomon, J. (1990). Procedures for identifying infants as disorganized/disoriented during the Ainsworth Strange Situation. In M. Greenberg, D. Cicchetti, & M. Cummings (Eds.), *Attachment in the preschool years:*

Theory, research, and intervention (pp. 121–160). Chicago: University of Chicago Press.

Majdandžić, M., & van den Boom, D. C. (2007). Multimethod longitudinal assessment of temperament in early childhood. *Journal of Personality, 75,* 121–167.

Malatesta, C. Z., Grigoryev, P., Lamb, C., Albin, M., & Culver, C. (1986). Emotion socialization and expressive development in preterm and full-term infants. *Child Development, 57,* 316–330.

Malina, R. M., & Bouchard, C. (1991). *Growth, maturation, and physical activity.* Champaign, IL: Human Kinetics.

Mandara, J., Varner, F., Greene, N., & Richman, S. (2009). Intergenerational family predictors of the black–white achievement gap. *Journal of Educational Psychology, 101,* 867–878.

Mandel, D. R., Jusczyk, P. W., & Pisoni, D. B. (1995). Infants' recognition of the sound patterns of their own names. *Psychological Science, 6,* 314–317.

Mandler, J. M. (2004). Thought before language. *Trends in Cognitive Sciences, 8,* 508–513.

Mandler, J. M., & McDonough, L. (1998). On developing a knowledge base in infancy. *Developmental Psychology, 34,* 1274–1288.

Mangelsdorf, S. C., Schoppe, S. J., & Buur, H. (2000). The meaning of parental reports: A contextual approach to the study of temperament and behavior problems. In V. J. Molfese & D. L. Molfese (Eds.), *Temperament and personality across the life span* (pp. 121–140). Mahwah, NJ: Erlbaum.

Manning, W. D., & Cohen, J. A. (2012). Premarital cohabitation and marital dissolution: An examination of recent marriages. *Journal of Marriage and Family, 74,* 377–387.

Manning, W. D., Longmore, M. A., Copp, J., & Giordano, P. C. (2014). The complexities of adolescent dating and sexual relationships: Fluidity, meaning(s), and implications for young adults' well-being. In E. S. Lefkowicz & S. A. Vasilenko (Eds.), *New directions for child and adolescent development* (Vol. 144, pp. 53–69). San Francisco: Jossey-Bass.

Mao, A., Burnham, M. M., Goodlin-Jones, B. L., Gaylor, E. E., & Anders, T. F. (2004). A comparison of the sleep–wake patterns of cosleeping and solitary-sleeping infants. *Child Psychiatry and Human Development, 35,* 95–105.

Maratsos, M. (2000). More overregularizations after all: New data and discussion on Marcus, Pinker, Ullman, Hollander, Rosen, & Xu. *Journal of Child Language, 27,* 183–212.

Marcia, J. E. (1980). Identity in adolescence. In J. Adelson (Ed.), *Handbook of adolescent psychology* (pp. 159–187). New York: Wiley.

Marcon, R. A. (1999). Positive relationships between parent–school involvement and public school innercity preschoolers' development and academic performance. *School Psychology Review, 28,* 395–412.

Marcus, G. F. (1995). Children's overregularization of English plurals: A quantitative analysis. *Journal of Child Language, 22,* 447–459.

Marcus, G. F., Vijayan, S., Rao, S. B., & Vishton, P. M. (1999). Rule learning by seven-month-old infants. *Science, 283,* 77–80.

Mares, M., & Acosta, E. E. (2010). Teaching inclusiveness via TV narratives in the US: Young viewers need help with the message. *Journal of Children and Media, 4,* 231–247.

Mares, M.-L., & Pan, Z. (2013). Effects of Sesame Street: A meta-analysis of children's learning in 15 countries. *Journal of Applied Developmental Psychology, 34,* 140–151.

Marian, V., Neisser, U., & Rochat, P. (1996). *Can 2-month-old infants distinguish live from videotaped interactions with their mothers* (Emory Cognition Project, Report #33). Atlanta, GA: Emory University.

Marin, T. J., Chen, E., Munch, T., & Miller, G. (2009). Double exposure to acute stress and chronic family stress is associated with immune changes in children with asthma. *Psychosomatic Medicine, 71,* 378–384.

Markant, J. C., & Thomas, K. M. (2013). Postnatal brain development. In P. D. Zelazo (Ed.), *Oxford handbook of developmental psychology: Vol. 1. Body and mind* (pp. 129–163). New York: Oxford University Press.

Markman, E. M. (1992). Constraints on word learning: Speculations about their nature, origins, and domain specificity. In M. R. Gunnar & M. P. Maratsos (Eds.),

Minnesota Symposia on Child Psychology (Vol. 25, pp. 59–101). Hillsdale, NJ: Erlbaum.

Markova, G., & Legerstee, M. (2006). Contingency, imitation, and affect sharing: Foundations of infants' social awareness. *Developmental Psychology, 42,* 132–141.

Markovits, H., & Barrouillet, P. (2002). The development of conditional reasoning: A Piagetian reformulation of mental models theory. *Merrill-Palmer Quarterly, 39,* 131–158.

Markovits, H., Benenson, J., & Dolenszky, E. (2001). Evidence that children and adolescents have internal models of peer interactions that are gender differentiated. *Child Development, 72,* 879–886.

Markovits, H., & Brunet, M.-L. (2012). Priming divergent thinking promotes logical reasoning in 6- to 8-year olds: But more for high than low SES students. *Journal of Cognitive Psychology, 24,* 991–1001.

Markovits, H., Schleifer, M., & Fortier, L. (1989). Development of elementary deductive reasoning in young children. *Developmental Psychology, 25,* 787–793.

Markovits, H., & Vachon, R. (1990). Conditional reasoning, representation, and level of abstraction. *Developmental Psychology, 26,* 942–951.

Marks, G. N., Cresswell, J., & Ainley, J. (2006). Explaining socioeconomic inequalities in student achievement: The role of home and school factors. *Educational Research and Evaluation, 12,* 105–128.

Marlier, L., & Schaal, B. (2005). Human newborns prefer human milk: Conspecific milk odor is attractive without postnatal exposure. *Child Development, 76,* 155–168.

Marques, L., Alegria, M., Becker, A. E., Chen, C. N., Fang, A., Chosak, A., et al. (2011). Comparative prevalence, correlates of impairment, and service utilization for eating disorders across U.S. ethnic groups: Implications for reducing ethnic disparities in health care access for eating disorders. *International Journal of Eating Disorders, 44,* 412–420.

Marra, R., & Palmer, B. (2004). Encouraging intellectual growth: Senior college student profiles. *Journal of Adult Development, 11,* 111–122.

Marsee, M. A., & Frick, P. J. (2010). Callous-unemotional traits and aggression in youth. In W. F. Arsenio & E. A. Lemerise (Eds.), *Emotions, aggression, and morality in children: Bridging development and psychopathology* (pp. 137–156). Washington, DC: American Psychological Association.

Marsh, H. W., & Kleitman, S. (2005). Consequences of employment during high school: Character building, subversion of academic goals, or a threshold? *American Educational Research Journal, 42,* 331–369.

Marsh, H. W. (1990). The structure of academic self-concept: The Marsh/Shavelson model. *Journal of Educational Psychology, 82,* 623–636.

Marsh, H. W., & Ayotte, V. (2003). Do multiple dimensions of self-concept become more differentiated with age? The differential distinctiveness hypothesis. *Journal of Educational Psychology, 95,* 687–706.

Marsh, H. W., Craven, R., & Debus, R. (1998). Structure, stability, and development of young children's self-concepts: A multicohort–multioccasion study. *Child Development, 69,* 1030–1053.

Marsh, H. W., Ellis, L. A., & Craven, R. G. (2002). How do preschool children feel about themselves? Unraveling measurement and multidimensional self-concept structure. *Developmental Psychology, 38,* 376–393.

Marsh, H. W., Gerlach, E., Trautwein, U., Lüdtke, O., & Brettschneider, W.-D. (2007). Longitudinal study of predadolescent sport self-concept and performance: Reciprocal effects and causal ordering. *Child Development, 78,* 1640–1656.

Marsh, H. W., Parada, R. H., & Ayotte, V. (2004). A multidimensional perspective of relations between self-concept (Self Description Questionnaire II) and adolescent mental health (Youth Self Report). *Psychological Assessment, 16,* 27–41.

Marsh, H. W., Trautwein, U., Lüdtke, O., Koller, O., & Baumert, J. (2005). Academic self-concept, interest, grades, and standardized test scores: Reciprocal effects models of causal ordering. *Child Development, 76,* 397–416.

Marshall, P. J., & Meltzoff, A. N. (2011). Neural mirroring systems: Exploring the EEG mu rhythm in human infancy. *Developmental Cognitive Neuroscience, 1,* 110–123.

Marshall-Baker, A., Lickliter, R., & Cooper, R. P. (1998). Prolonged exposure to a visual pattern may promote behavioral organization in preterm infants. *Journal of Perinatal and Neonatal Nursing, 12,* 50–62.

Martin, A., Brazil, A., & Brooks-Gunn, J. (2012). The socioemotional outcomes of young children of teenage mothers by paternal coresidence. *Journal of Family Issues, 34,* 1217–1237.

Martin, C. L., Eisenbud, L., & Rose, H. (1995). Children's gender-based reasoning about toys. *Child Development, 66,* 1453–1471.

Martin, C. L., & Fabes, R. A. (2001). The stability and consequences of young children's same-sex peer interactions. *Developmental Psychology, 37,* 431–446.

Martin, C. L., Fabes, R. A., Evans, S. M., & Wyman, H. (1999). Social cognition on the playground: Children's beliefs about playing with girls versus boys and their relations to sex segregated play. *Journal of Social and Personal Relationships, 16,* 751–771.

Martin, C. L., Fabes, R. A., Hanish, L., Leonard, S., & Dinella, L. M. (2011). Experienced and expected similarity to same-gender peers: Moving toward a comprehensive model of gender segregation. *Sex Roles, 65,* 421–434.

Martin, C. L., & Halverson, C. F. (1987). The role of cognition in sex role acquisition. In D. B. Carter (Ed.), *Current conceptions of sex roles and sex typing: Theory and research* (pp. 123–137). New York: Praeger.

Martin, C. L., Kornienko, O., Schaefer, D. R., Hanish, L. D., Fabes, R. A., & Goble, P. (2013). The role of sex of peers and gender-typed activities in young children's peer affiliative networks: A longitudinal analysis of selection and influence. *Child Development, 84,* 921–937.

Martin, C. L., & Ruble, D. (2004). Children's search for gender cues: Cognitive perspectives on gender development. *Current Directions in Psychological Science, 13,* 67–70.

Martin, C. L., Ruble, D. N., & Szkrybalo, J. (2002). Cognitive theories of early gender development. *Psychological Bulletin, 128,* 903–933.

Martin, E. K., & Silverstone, P. H. (2013). How much child sexual abuse is "below the surface," and how can we help adults identify it early? *Frontiers in Psychiatry, 4,* 1–10.

Martin, J. A., Hamilton, B. E., Osterman, J. K., Curtin, S. C., & Matthews, T. J. (2013). Births: Final data for 2012. *National Vital Statistics Reports, 62*(9). Hyattsville, MD: National Center for Health Statistics. Retrieved from www.cdc.gov/nchs/data/nvsr/nvsr62/nvsr62_09.pdf

Martin, K. A. (1996). *Puberty, sexuality and the self: Girls and boys at adolescence.* New York: Routledge.

Martinez, G., Copen, C. E., & Abma, J. C. (2011). Teenagers in the United States: Sexual activity, contraceptive use, and childbearing, 2006–2010 National Survey of Family Growth. *Vital and Health Statistics, 23.* Retrieved from www.cdc.gov/nchs/data/series/sr_23/sr23_031.pdf

Martinez-Frias, M. L., Bermejo, E., Rodríguez-Pinilla, E., & Frías, J. L. (2004). Risk for congenital anomalies associated with different sporadic and daily doses of alcohol consumption during pregnancy: A case-control study. *Birth Defects Research, Part A, Clinical and Molecular Teratology, 70,* 194–200.

Martinot, D., Bagès, C., & Désert, M. (2012). French children's awareness of gender stereotypes about mathematics and reading: When girls improve their reputation in math. *Sex Roles, 66,* 210–219.

Martinot, D., & Désert, M. (2007). Awareness of a gender stereotype, personal beliefs, and self-perceptions regarding math ability: When boys do not surpass girls. *Social Psychology of Education, 10,* 455–471.

Martins, N., & Harrison, K. (2012). Racial and gender differences in the relationship between children's television use and self-esteem: A longitudinal panel study. *Communication Research, 39,* 338–357.

Martinson, M. L., McLanahan, S., & Brooks-Gunn, J. (2012). Race/ethnic and nativity disparities in child overweight in the United States and England. *Annals of the American Association for the Psychological Study of Social Issues, 643,* 219–238.

Martlew, M., & Connolly, K. J. (1996). Human figure drawings by schooled and unschooled children in Papua New Guinea. *Child Development, 67,* 2743–2762.

Marván, M. L., & Alcalá-Herrera, V. (2014). Age at menarche, reactions to menarche and attitudes towards menstruation among Mexican adolescent girls. *Journal of Pediatric and Adolescent Gynecology, 27*, 61–66.

Marzolf, D. P., & DeLoache, J. S. (1994). Transfer in young children's understanding of spatial representations. *Child Development, 65*, 1–15.

Masataka, N. (1996). Perception of motherese in a signed language by 6-month-old deaf infants. *Developmental Psychology, 32*, 874–879.

Mascolo, M. F., & Fischer, K. W. (1995). Developmental transformations in appraisals for pride, shame, and guilt. In J. P. Tangney & K. W. Fischer (Eds.), *Self-conscious emotions* (pp. 114–139). New York: Guilford.

Mascolo, M. F., & Fischer, K. W. (2007). The codevelopment of self and sociomoral emotions during the toddler years. In C. A. Brownell & C. B. Kopp (Eds.), *Socioemotional development in the toddler years: Transitions and transformations* (pp. 66–99). New York: Guilford.

Mash, C., & Bornstein, M., H. (2012). 5-month-olds' categorization of novel objects: Task and measure dependence. *Infancy, 17*, 179–197.

Mashburn, A. J., Pianta, R. C., Hamre, B. K., Downer, J. T., Barbarin, O. A., Bryant, D., et al. (2008). Measures of classroom quality in prekindergarten and children's development of academic, language, and social skills. *Child Development, 79*, 732–749.

Mason, C. A., Walker-Barnes, C. J., Tu, S., Simons, J., & Martisez-Arrue, R. (2004). Ethnic differences in the affective meaning of parental control behaviors. *Journal of Primary Prevention, 25*, 601–631.

Mason, M. G., & Gibbs, J. C. (1993a). Role-taking opportunities and the transition to advanced moral judgment. *Moral Education Forum, 18*, 1–12.

Mason, M. G., & Gibbs, J. C. (1993b). Social perspective taking and moral judgment among college students. *Journal of Adolescent Research, 8*, 109–123.

Massey, Z., Rising, S. S., & Ickovics, J. (2006). CenteringPregnancy group prenatal care: Promoting relationship-centered care. *JOGNN, 35*, 286–294.

Masten, A. S. (2007). Resilience in developing systems: Progress and promise as the fourth wave rises. *Development and Psychopathology, 19*, 921–930.

Masten, A. S. (2011). Resilience in children threatened by extreme adversity: Frameworks for research, practice, and translational synergy. *Development and Psychopathology, 23*, 493–506.

Masten, A. S. (2014). Global perspectives on resilience in children and youth. *Child Development, 85*, 6–20.

Masten, A. S., Burt, K. B., Roisman, G. I., Obradović, J., Long, J. D., & Tellegen, A. (2004). Resources and resilience in the transition to adulthood: Continuity and change. *Development and Psychopathology, 16*, 1071–1094.

Masten, A. S., & Cicchetti, D. (2010). Developmental cascades. *Development and Psychopathology, 22*, 491–495.

Masten, A. S., & Reed, M. J. (2002). Resilience in development. In C. R. Snyder & S. J. Lopez (Eds.), *Handbook of positive psychology* (pp. 74–88). New York: Oxford University Press.

Masten, A. S., & Shaffer, A. (2006). How families matter in child development: Reflections from research on risk and resilience. In A. S. Masten & A. Shaffer (Eds.), *Families count: Effects on child and adolescent development* (pp. 5–25). New York: Cambridge University Press.

Mastropieri, D., & Turkewitz, G. (1999). Prenatal experience and neonatal responsiveness to vocal expressions of emotion. *Developmental Psychobiology, 35*, 204–214.

Mastropieri, M. A., Scruggs, T. E., Guckert, M., Thompson, C. C., & Weiss, M. P. (2013). Inclusion and learning disabilities: Will the past be prologue? In J. P. Bakken, F. E. Oblakor, & A. Rotatori (Eds.), *Advances in special education* (Vol. 25, pp. 1–17). Bingley, UK: Emerald Group Publishing.

Masur, E. F., & Rodemaker, J. E. (1999). Mothers' and infants' spontaneous vocal, verbal, and action imitation during the second year. *Merrill-Palmer Quarterly, 45*, 392–412.

Mather, M. (2010, May). *U.S. children in single-mother families* (PRB Data Brief). Washington, DC: Population Reference Bureau.

Matlen, B. J., & Klahr, D. (2013). Sequential effects of high and low instructional guidance on children's acquisition of experimentation skills: Is it all in the timing? *Instructional Science, 41*, 621–634.

Matsuba, M. K., & Walker, L. J. (1998). Moral reasoning in the context of ego functioning. *Merrill-Palmer Quarterly, 44*, 464–483.

Matthews, H. (2014, January 14). A billion dollar boost for child care and early learning. CLASP: Policy solutions that work for low-income people. Retrieved from www.clasp.org/issues/child-care-and-early-education/in-focus/a-billion-dollar-boost-for-child-care-and-early-learning

Mattson, S. N., Calarco, K. E., & Lang, A. R. (2006). Focused and shifting attention in children with heavy prenatal alcohol exposure. *Neuropsychology, 20*, 361–369.

Mattson, S. N., Crocker, N., & Nguyen, T. T. (2012). Fetal alcohol spectrum disorders: Neuropsychological and behavioral features. *Neuropsychological Review, 21*, 81–101.

Maughan, B., Collishaw, S., & Stringaris, A (2012). Depression in childhood and adolescence. *Journal of the Canadian Academy of Child and Adolescent Psychiatry, 22*, 35–40.

Maurer, D., & Lewis, T. (2013). Human visual plasticity: Lessons from children treated for congenital cataracts. In J. K. E. Steeves & L. R. Harris (Eds.), *Plasticity in sensory systems* (pp. 75–93). New York: Cambridge University Press.

Maurer, D., Mondloch, C. J., & Lewis, T. L. (2007). Sleeper effects. *Developmental Science, 10*, 40–47.

May, L. E., Glaros, A., Yeh, H., Clapp, J. E., & Gustafson, K. M. (2010). Aerobic exercise during pregnancy influences fetal cardiac autonomic control of heart rate and heart rate variability. *Early Human Development, 86*, 213–217.

Mayberry, R. I. (2010). Early language acquisition and adult language ability: What sign language reveals about the critical period for language. In M. Marshark & P. E. Spencer (Eds.), *Oxford handbook of deaf studies, language, and education* (Vol. 2, pp. 281–291). New York: Oxford University Press.

Mayes, L. C., & Zigler, E. (1992). An observational study of the affective concomitants of mastery in infants. *Journal of Child Psychology and Psychiatry, 33*, 659–667.

Mayeux, L., & Cillessen, A. H. N. (2003). Development of social problem solving in early childhood: Stability, change, and associations with social competence. *Journal of Genetic Psychology, 164*, 153–173.

Mayeux, L., Houser, J. J., & Dyches, K. D. (2011). Social acceptance and popularity: Two distinct forms of peer status. In A. H. N. Cillessen, D. Schwartz, & L. Mayeux (Eds.), *Popularity in the peer system* (pp. 79–102). New York: Guilford.

Maynard, A. E. (2002). Cultural teaching: The development of teaching skills in Maya sibling interactions. *Child Development, 73*, 969–982.

Maynard, A. E., & Greenfield, P. M. (2003). Implicit cognitive development in cultural tools and children: Lessons from Maya Mexico. *Cognitive Development, 18*, 489–510.

Mazumdar, M., Bellinger, D. C., Gregas, M., Abanilla, K., Bacic, J., & Needleman, H. L. (2011). Low-level environmental lead exposure in childhood and adult intellectual function: A follow-up study. *Environmental Health, 10*, 24.

McAdoo, H. P., & Younge, S. N. (2009). Black families. In H. A. Neville, B. M. Tynes, & S. O. Utsey (Eds.), *Handbook of African American psychology* (pp. 103–115). Thousand Oaks, CA: Sage.

McAlister, A., & Peterson, C. C. (2006). Mental playmates: Siblings, executive functioning and theory of mind. *British Journal of Developmental Psychology, 24*, 733–751.

McAlister, A., & Peterson, C. C. (2007). A longitudinal study of child siblings and theory of mind development. *Cognitive Development, 22*, 258–270.

McBride-Chang, C., Wagner, R. K., Muse, A., Chow, B. W.-Y., & Shu, H. (2005). The role of morphological awareness in children's English reading and vocabulary acquisition. *Applied Psycholinguistics, 26*, 415–435.

McCabe, A. (1997). Developmental and cross-cultural aspects of children's narration. In M. Bamberg (Ed.), *Narrative development: Six approaches* (pp. 137–174). Mahwah, NJ: Erlbaum.

McCabe, A., Tamis-LeMonda, C. S., Bornstein, M. H., Cates, C. B., Golinkoff, R., Guerra, A. W., et al. (2013). Multilingual children: Beyond myths and toward best practices. *Society for Research in Child Development Social Policy Report, 27*(4).

McCarter-Spaulding, D., Lucas, J., & Gore, R. (2011). Employment and breastfeeding outcomes in a sample of black women in the United States. *Journal of National Black Nurses' Association, 22*, 38–45.

McCartney, K., Dearing, E., Taylor, B., & Bub, K. (2007). Quality child care supports the achievement of low-income children: Direct and indirect pathways through caregiving and the home environment. *Journal of Applied Developmental Psychology, 28*, 411–426.

McCartney, K., Owen, M., Booth, C., Clarke-Stewart, A., & Vandell, D. (2004). Testing a maternal attachment model of behavior problems in early childhood. *Journal of Child Psychology and Psychiatry, 45*, 765–778.

McCarton, C. (1998). Behavioral outcomes in low birth weight infants. *Pediatrics, 102*, 1293–1297.

McCarty, M. E., & Ashmead, D. H. (1999). Visual control of reaching and grasping in infants. *Developmental Psychology, 35*, 620–631.

McCarty, M. E., & Keen, R. (2005). Facilitating problem-solving performance among 9- and 12-month-old infants. *Journal of Cognition and Development, 6*, 209–228.

McClelland, M. M., Cameron, C. E., Wanless, S. B., & Murray, A. (2007). Executive function, behavioral self-regulation, and social-emotional competence: Links to school readiness. In O. Saracho & B. Spodek (Eds.), *Contemporary perspectives on social learning in early childhood education* (pp. 83–107). Charlotte, NC: Information Age Publishing.

McColgan, K. L., & McCormack, T. (2008). Searching and planning: Young children's reasoning about past and future event sequences. *Child Development, 79*, 1477–1479.

McCormack, T., & Atance, C. M. (2011). Planning in young children: A review and synthesis. *Developmental Review, 31*, 1–31.

McCormack, V. A., dos Santos Silva, I., Koupil, I., Leon, D. A., & Lithell, H. O. (2005). Birth characteristics and adult cancer incidence: Swedish cohort of over 11,000 men and women. *International Journal of Cancer, 115*, 611–617.

McCormick, M. C., Brooks-Gunn, J., Buka, S. L., Goldman, J., Yu, J., Salganik, M., Scott, D. T., et al. (2006). Early intervention in low birth weight premature infants: Results at 18 years of age for the Infant Health and Development Program. *Pediatrics, 117*, 771–780.

McCrink, K., & Wynn, K. (2004). Large-number addition and subtraction by 9-month-old infants. *Psychological Science, 15*, 776–781.

McCrory, P., Meeuwisse, W. H., Aubry, M., Cantu, R. C., Dvorák, J., Echemendia, R. J., et al. (2013). Consensus statement on concussion in sport: The 4th International Conference on Concussion in Sport, Zurich, November 2012. *Journal of Athletic Training, 48*, 554–575.

McCune, L. (1993). The development of play as the development of consciousness. In M. H. Bornstein & A. O'Reilly (Eds.), *New directions for child development* (No. 59, pp. 67–79). San Francisco: Jossey-Bass.

McDonough, C., Song, L., Hirsh-Pasek, K., & Golinkoff, R. M. (2011). An image is worth a thousand words: Why nouns tend to dominate verbs in early word learning. *Developmental Science, 14*, 181–189.

McDonough, L. (1999). Early declarative memory for location. *British Journal of Developmental Psychology, 17*, 381–402.

McDowell, D. J., & Parke, R. D. (2000). Differential knowledge of display rules for positive and negative emotions: Influences from parents, influences on peers. *Social Development, 9*, 415–432.

McElhaney, K. B., & Allen, J. P. (2001). Autonomy and adolescent social functioning: The moderating effect of risk. *Child Development, 72*, 220–235.

McElhaney, K. B., Allen, J. P., Stephenson, J. C., & Hare, A. L. (2009). Attachment and autonomy during adolescence. In R. M. Lerner & L. Steinberg (Eds.), *Handbook of adolescent psychology: Vol. 1. Individual bases of adolescent development* (3rd ed., pp. 358–403). Hoboken, NJ: Wiley.

McElwain, N. L., & Booth-LaForce, C. (2006). Maternal sensitivity to infant distress and nondistress as predictors of infant–mother attachment security. *Journal of Family Psychology, 20*, 247–255.

McFarland-Piazza, L., Hazen, N., Jacobvitz, D., & Boyd-Soisson, E. (2012). The development of father–child attachment: Associations between adult attachment representations, recollections of childhood experiences and caregiving. *Early Child Development and Care, 182*, 701–721.

McGee, L. M., & Richgels, D. J. (2004). *Literacy's beginnings: Supporting young readers and writers* (4th ed.). Boston: Allyn and Bacon.

McGee, L. M., & Richgels, D. J. (2012). *Literacy's beginnings: Supporting young readers and writers* (6th ed.). Boston: Allyn and Bacon.

McGonigle-Chalmers, M., Slater, H., & Smith, A. (2014). Rethinking private speech in preschoolers: The effects of social presence. *Developmental Psychology, 50*, 829–836.

McGrath, S. K., & Kennell, J. H. (2008). A randomized controlled trial of continuous labor support for middle-class couples: Effect on cesarean delivery rates. *Birth: Issues in Perinatal Care, 35*, 9–97.

McGue, M., Elkins, I., Walden, B., & Iacono, W. G. (2005). Perceptions of the parent–adolescent relationship: A longitudinal investigation. *Developmental Psychology, 41*, 971–984.

McGuire, J. K., & Barber, B. L. (2010). A person-centered approach to the multifaceted nature of young adult sexual behavior. *Journal of Sex Research, 47*, 301–313.

McHale, J. P., Kazali, C., Rotman, T., Talbot, J., Carleton, M., & Lieberson, R. (2004). The transition to coparenthood: Parents' prebirth expectations and early coparental adjustment at 3 months postpartum. *Development and Psychopathology, 16*, 711–733.

McHale, J. P., & Rotman, T. (2007). Is seeing believing? Expectant parents' outlooks on coparenting and later coparenting solidarity. *Infant Behavior and Development, 30*, 63–81.

McHale, S. M., Crouter, A. C., Kim, J.-Y., Burton, L. M., Davis, K. D., Dotterer, A. M., & Swanson, D. P. (2006). Mothers' and fathers' racial socialization in African-American families: Implications for youth. *Child Development, 77*, 1387–1402.

McHale, S. M., Updegraff, K. A., Helms-Erikson, H., & Crouter, A. C. (2001). Sibling influences on gender development in middle childhood and early adolescence: A longitudinal study. *Developmental Psychology, 37*, 115–125.

McHale, S. M., Updegraff, K. A., & Whiteman, S. D. (2012). Sibling relationships and influences in childhood and adolescence. *Journal of Marriage and Family, 74*, 913–930.

McHugh, R. M., Horner, C. G., Colditz, J. B., & Wallace, T. L. (2013). Bridges and barriers: Adolescent perceptions of student–teacher relationships. *Urban Education, 48*, 9–43.

McIntosh, H., Metz, E., & Youniss, J. (2005). Community service and identity formation in adolescents. In J. S. Mahoney, R. W. Larson, & J. S. Eccles (Eds.), *Organized activities as contexts of development: Extracurricular activities, after-school and community programs* (pp. 331–351). Mahwah, NJ: Erlbaum.

McIntyre, K. A., & Platania, J. (2009). Giving in to group pressure: The impact of socialization risk on perceived outcomes. *Current Research in Social Psychology, 15*(1). Retrieved from www.uiowa.edu/~grpproc/crisp/crisp .html

McIntyre, S., Blair, E., Badawi, N., Keogh, J., & Nelson, K. B. (2013). Antecedents of cerebral palsy and perinatal death in term and late preterm singletons. *Obstetrics and Gynecology, 122*, 869–877.

McKenna, J. J. (2001). Why we never ask "Is it safe for infants to sleep alone?" *Academy of Breast Feeding Medicine News and Views, 7*(4), 32, 38.

McKenna, J. J. (2002, September/October). Breastfeeding and bedsharing: Still useful (and important) after all these years. *Mothering, 114*, 28–37.

McKenna, J. J., & McDade, T. (2005). Why babies should never sleep alone: A review of the co-sleeping controversy in relation to SIDS, bedsharing, and breastfeeding. *Paediatric Respiratory Reviews, 6*, 134–152.

McKenna, J. J., & Volpe, L. E. (2007). Sleeping with baby: An Internet-based sampling of parental experiences, choices, perceptions, and interpretations in a Western industrialized context. *Infant and Child Development, 16*, 359–385.

McKinney, C., Donnelly, R., & Renk, K. (2008). Perceived parenting, positive and negative perceptions of parents, and late adolescent emotional adjustment. *Child and Adolescent Mental health, 13*, 66–73.

McKown, C. (2013). Social equity theory and racial-ethnic achievement gaps. *Child Development, 84*, 1120–1136.

McKown, C., Gregory, A., & Weinstein, R. S. (2010). Expectations, stereotypes, and self-fulfilling prophecies in classroom and school life. In J. L. Meece & J. S. Eccles (Eds.), *Handbook of research on schools, schooling and human development* (pp. 256–274). New York: Routledge.

McKown, C., & Strambler, M. J. (2009). Developmental antecedents and social and academic consequences of stereotype-consciousness in middle childhood. *Child Development, 80*, 1643–1659.

McKown, C., & Weinstein, R. S. (2003). The development and consequences of stereotype consciousness in middle childhood. *Child Development, 74*, 498–515.

McKown, C., & Weinstein, R. S. (2008). Teacher expectations, classroom context, and the achievement gap. *Journal of School Psychology, 46*, 235–261.

McLanahan, S. (1999). Father absence and the welfare of children. In E. M. Hetherington (Ed.), *Coping with divorce, single parenting, and remarriage: A risk and resiliency perspective* (pp. 117–145). Mahwah, NJ: Erlbaum.

McLanahan, S. S., & Carlson, M. J. (2002). Welfare reform, fertility, and father involvement. *Future of Children, 12*, 111–115.

McLaughlin, K. A., Fox, N. A., Zeanah, C. H., & Nelson, C. A. (2011). Adverse rearing environments and neural development in children: The development of frontal electroencephalogram asymmetry. *Biological Psychiatry, 70*, 1008–1015.

McLeskey, J., & Waldron, N. L. (2011). Educational programs for elementary students with learning disabilities: Can they be both effective and inclusive? *Learning Disabilities: Research and Practice, 26*, 48–57.

McLoyd, V. C., Aikens, N. L., & Burton, L. M. (2006). Childhood poverty, policy, and practice. In K. A. Renninger & I. E. Sigel (Eds.), *Handbook of child psychology: Vol. 4. Child psychology in practice* (6th ed., pp. 700–778). Hoboken, NJ: Wiley.

McLoyd, V. C., Kaplan, R., Hardaway, C. R., & Wood, D. (2007). Does endorsement of physical discipline matter? Assessing moderating influences on the maternal and child psychological correlates of physical discipline in African-American families. *Journal of Family Psychology, 21*, 165–175.

McLoyd, V. C., & Smith, J. (2002). Physical discipline and behavior problems in African-American, European-American, and Hispanic children: Emotional support as a moderator. *Journal of Marriage and the Family, 64*, 40–53.

McMahon, C. A., Barnett, B., Kowalenko, N. M., & Tennant, C. C. (2006). Maternal attachment state of mind moderates the impact of postnatal depression on infant attachment. *Journal of Child Psychology and Psychiatry and Allied Disciplines, 47*, 660–669.

McNeal, R. B. (2011). Labor market effects on dropping out of high school: Variation by gender, race, and employment status. *Youth and Society, 43*, 305–332.

McNeil, D. G., Jr. (2014, March 5). Early treatment is found to clear H.I.V. in a 2nd baby. *New York Times*, p. A1.

Mead, G. H. (1934). *Mind, self, and society.* Chicago: University of Chicago Press.

Mead, M. (1928). *Coming of age in Samoa.* Ann Arbor, MI: Morrow.

Meade, C. S., Kershaw, T. S., & Ickovics, J. R. (2008). The intergenerational cycle of teenage motherhood: An ecological approach. *Health Psychology, 27*, 419–429.

Meazza, C., Pagani, S., & Bozzola, M. (2011). The Pygmy short stature enigma. *Pediatric Endocrinology Reviews, 8*, 394–399.

Meece, D. & Mize, J. (2011). Preschoolers' cognitive representations of peer relationships: Family origins and behavioural correlates. *Early Childhood Development and Care, 181*, 63–72.

Meeus, W. (2011). The study of adolescent identity formation 2000–2010: A review of longitudinal research. *Journal of Research on Adolescence, 21*, 75–94.

Meeus, W., Oosterwegel, A., & Vollebergh, W. (2002). Parental and peer attachment and identity development in adolescence. *Journal of Adolescence, 25*, 93–106.

Meier, A., & Allen, G. (2009). Romantic relationships from adolescence to young adulthood: Evidence from the National Longitudinal Study of Adolescent Health. *Sociological Quarterly, 50*, 308–335.

Meins, E., Fernyhough, C., Fradley, E., & Tuckey, M. (2001). Rethinking maternal sensitivity: Mothers' comments on infants' mental processes predict security of attachment at 12 months. *Journal of Child Psychology and Psychiatry and Allied Disciplines, 42*, 637–648.

Meins, E., Fernyhough, C., Wainwright, R., Clark-Carter, D., Gupta, M. D., Fradley, E., & Tucker, M. (2003). Pathways

to understanding mind: Construct validity and predictive validity of maternal mind-mindedness. *Child Development, 74*, 1194–1211.

Melby, J. N., Conger, R. D., Fang, S., Wichrama, K. A. S., & Conger, K. J. (2008). Adolescent family experiences and educational attainment during early adulthood. *Developmental Psychology, 44*, 1519–1536.

Melby-Lervag, M., & Hulme, C. (2010). Serial and free recall in children can be improved by training: Evidence for the importance of phonological and semantic representations in immediate memory tasks. *Psychological Science, 21*, 1694–1700.

Melinder, A., Endestad, T., & Magnussen, S. (2006). Relations between episodic memory, suggestibility, theory of mind, and cognitive inhibition in the preschool child. *Scandinavian Journal of Psychology, 47*, 485–495.

Meltzoff, A. N. (2007). "Like me": A foundation for social cognition. *Developmental Science, 10*, 126–134.

Meltzoff, A. (2013). Origins of social cognition: Bidirectional self-other mapping and the "like-me" hypothesis. In M. Banaji & S. A. Gelman (Eds.), *Navigating the social world: What infants, children, and other species can teach us* (pp. 139–144). New York: Oxford University Press.

Meltzoff, A. N., & Kuhl, P. K. (1994). Faces and speech: Intermodal processing of biologically relevant signals in infants and adults. In D. J. Lewkowicz & R. Lickliter (Eds.), *The development of intersensory perception: Comparative perspectives* (pp. 335–369). Hillsdale, NJ: Erlbaum.

Meltzoff, A. N., & Moore, M. K. (1977). Imitation of facial and manual gestures by human neonates. *Science, 198*, 75–78.

Meltzoff, A. N., & Moore, M. K. (1994). Imitation, memory, and the representation of persons. *Infant Behavior and Development, 17*, 83–99.

Meltzoff, A. N., & Moore, M. K. (1999). Persons and representation: Why infant imitation is important for theories of human development. In J. Nadel & G. Butterworth (Eds.), *Imitation in infancy* (pp. 9–35). Cambridge, UK: Cambridge University Press.

Meltzoff, A. N., & Williamson, R. A. (2010). The importance of imitation for theories of social-cognitive development. In J. G. Bremner & T. D. Wachs (Eds.), *Wiley-Blackwell handbook of infant development* (2nd ed., pp. 345–364). Oxford, UK: Wiley.

Melzi, G., & Schick, A. R. (2013). Language and literacy in the school years. In J. B. Gleason & N. B. Ratner (Eds.), *Development of language* (8th ed., pp. 329–365). Upper Saddle River, NJ: Pearson.

Memo, L., Gnoato, E., Caminiti, S., Pichini, S., & Tarani, L. (2013). Fetal alcohol spectrum disorders and fetal alcohol syndrome: The state of the art and new diagnostic tools. *Early Human Development, 89S1*, S40–S43.

Mendle, J., Turkheimer, E., D'Onofrio, B. M., Lynch, S., Emery, R. E., & Slutske, W. S. (2006). Family structure and age at menarche: A children-of-twins approach. *Developmental Psychology, 42*, 533–542.

Mendle, J., Turkheimer, E., & Emery, R. E. (2007). Detrimental psychological outcomes associated with early pubertal timing in adolescent girls. *Developmental Review, 27*, 151–171.

Menesini, E., Calussi, P., & Nocentini, A. (2012). Cyberbullying and traditional bullying: Unique, additive, and synergistic effects on psychological health symptoms. In Q. Li, D. Cross, & P. K. Smith (Eds.), *Cyberbullying in the global playground* (pp. 245–265). Malden, MA: Wiley-Blackwell.

Menesini, E., Nicocenti, A., & Calussi, P. (2011). The measurement of cyberbullying: Dimensional structure and relative item severity and discrimination. *Cyberspychology and Behavior, 14*, 267–274.

Menesini, E., & Spiel, C. (2012). Introduction: Cyberbullying: Development, consequences, risk and protective factors. *European Journal of Developmental Psychology, 9*, 163–167.

Mennella, J. A., & Beauchamp, G. K. (1998). Early flavor experiences: Research update. *Nutrition Reviews, 56*, 205–211.

Mennella, J. A., Jagnow, C. P., & Beauchamp, G. K. (2001). Prenatal and postnatal flavor learning by human infants. *Pediatrics, 107*, e88.

Ment, L. R., Vohr, B., Allan, W., Katz, K. H., Schneider, K. C., Westerveld, M., Cuncan, C. C., & Makuch, R. W. (2003). Change in cognitive function over time in very low-birth-weight infants. *Journal of the American Medical Association, 289,* 705–711.

Menyuk, P., Liebergott, J. W., & Schultz, M. C. (1995). *Early language development in full-term and premature infants.* Hillsdale, NJ: Erlbaum.

Meredith, N. V. (1978). *Human body growth in the first ten years of life.* Columbia, SC: State Printing.

Merikangas, K. R., He, J.-P., Burstein, M., Swanson, S. A., Avenevoli, S., Cui, L., et al. (2010). Lifetime prevalence of mental disorders in U.S. adolescents: Results from the National Comorbidity Survey Replication—Adolescent Supplement (NCS-A). *Journal of the American Academy of Child and Adolescent Psychiatry, 49,* 980–989.

Messinger, D. S., & Fogel, A. (2007). The interactive development of social smiling. In R. Kail (Ed.), *Advances in child development and behavior* (Vol. 35, pp. 327–366). Oxford, UK: Elsevier.

Metheny, J., McWhirter, E. H., & O'Neil, M. E. (2008). Measuring perceived teacher support and its influence on adolescent career development. *Journal of Career Assessment, 16,* 218–237.

Metz, E. C., & Youniss, J. (2005). Longitudinal gains in civic development through school-based required service. *Political Psychology, 26,* 413–437.

Meyer, R. (2009). Infant feeding in the first year. 1: Feeding practices in the first six months of life. *Journal of Family Health Care, 19,* 13–16.

Meyer, S., Raikes, H. A., Virmani, E. A., Waters, S., & Thompson, R. A. (2014). Parent emotion representations and the socialization of emotion regulation in the family. *International Journal of Behavioral Development, 38,* 164–173.

Meyers, A. B., & Berk, L. E. (2014). Make-believe play and self-regulation. In L. Brooker, M. Blaise, & S. Edwards (Eds.), *Sage handbook of play and learning in early childhood* (pp. 43–55). London: Sage.

Mezulis, A. H., Hyde, J. S., & Clark, R. (2004). Father involvement moderates the effect of maternal depression during a child's infancy on child behavior problems in kindergarten. *Journal of Family Psychology, 18,* 575–588.

Michalik, N. M., Eisenberg, N., Spinrad, T. L., Ladd, B., Thompson, M., & Valiente, C. (2007). Longitudinal relations among parental emotional expressivity and sympathy and prosocial behavior in adolescence. *Social Development, 16,* 286–309.

Michiels, D., Grietens, H., Onghena, P., & Kuppens, S. (2010). Perceptions of maternal and paternal attachment security in middle childhood: Links with positive parental affection and psychological adjustment. *Early Child Development and Care, 180,* 211–225.

Migliano, A. B., Vinicius, L., & Lahr, M. M. (2007). Life history trade-offs explain the evolution of human pygmies. *Proceedings of the National Academy of Sciences, 104,* 20216–20219.

Mikami, A. Y., Griggs, M. S., Lerner, M. D., Emeh, C. C., Reuland, M. M., Jack, A., & Anthony, M. R. (2013). A randomized trial of a classroom intervention to increase peers' social inclusion of children with attention-deficit/hyperactivity disorder. *Journal of Consulting and Clinical Psychology, 81,* 100–112.

Mikami, A. Y., Lerner, M. D., & Lun, J. (2010). Social context influences on children's rejection by their peers. *Child Development Perspectives, 4,* 123–130.

Mikami, A. Y., Szwedo, D. E., Allen, J. P., Evans, M. A., & Hare, A. L. (2010). Adolescent peer relationships and behavior problems predict young adults' communication on social networking websites. *Developmental Psychology, 46,* 46–56.

Milan, S., Snow, S., & Belay, S. (2007). The context of preschool children's sleep: Racial/ethnic differences in sleep locations, routines, and concerns. *Journal of Family Psychology, 21,* 20–28.

Milevsky, A., Schlechter, M., Netter, S., & Keehn, D. (2007). Maternal and paternal parenting styles in adolescents: Associations with self-esteem, depression, and life satisfaction. *Journal of Child and Family Studies, 16,* 39–47.

Milevsky, A., Schlechter, M. J., & Machlev, M. (2011). Effects of parenting style and involvement in sibling conflict on adolescent sibling relationships. *Journal of Social and Personal Relationships, 28,* 1130–1148.

Miller, C. F., Lurye, L. E., Zosuls, K. M., & Ruble, D. N. (2009). Accessibility of gender stereotype domains: Developmental and gender differences in children. *Sex Roles, 60,* 870–881.

Miller, D. I., & Halpern, D. F. (2014). The new science of cognitive sex differences. *Trends in Cognitive Sciences, 18,* 37–44.

Miller, D. N. (2011). *Child and adolescent suicidal behavior: School-based prevention, assessment, and intervention.* New York: Guilford.

Miller, G. E., Chen, E., Fok, A. K., Walker, H., Lim, A., Hiholls, E. F., et al. (2009). Low early-life social class leaves a biological residue manifested by decreased glucocorticoid and increased proinflammatory signaling. *Proceedings of the National Academy of Sciences, 106,* 14716–14721.

Miller, J. G. (2007). Cultural psychology of moral development. In S. Kitayama (Ed.), *Handbook of cultural psychology* (pp. 477–499). New York: Guilford.

Miller, J. G., & Bersoff, D. M. (1995). Development in the context of everyday family relationships: Culture, interpersonal morality, and adaptation. In M. Killen & D. Hart (Eds.), *Morality in everyday life: Developmental perspectives* (pp. 259–282). Cambridge, UK: Cambridge University Press.

Miller, L. E., Grabell, A., Thomas, A., Bermann, E., & Graham-Bermann, S. A. (2012). The associations between community violence, television violence, parent–child aggression, and aggression in sibling relationships of a sample of preschoolers. *Psychology of Violence, 2,* 165–178.

Miller, P. H. (2009). *Theories of developmental psychology* (5th ed.) New York: Worth.

Miller, P. H. (2011). Piaget's theory: Past, present, and future. In U. Goswami (Ed.), *Wiley-Blackwell handbook of childhood cognitive development* (2nd ed., pp. 649–672). Chicester, UK: Wiley-Blackwell.

Miller, P. J., Fung, H., & Koven, M. (2007). Narrative reverberations: How participation in narrative practices co-creates persons and cultures. In S. Kitayama & D. Cohen (Eds.), *Handbook of cultural psychology* (pp. 595–614). New York: Guilford.

Miller, P. J., Fung, H., Lin, S., Chen, E. C., & Boldt, B. R. (2012). How socialization happens on the ground: Narrative practices as alternate socializing pathways in Taiwanese and European-American families. *Monographs of the Society for Research in Child Development, 77*(1, Serial No. 302).

Miller, P. J., Fung, H., & Mintz, J. (1996). Self-construction through narrative practices: A Chinese and American comparison of early socialization. *Ethos, 24,* 1–44.

Miller, P. J., Hengst, J. A., & Wang, S. (2003). Ethnographic methods: Applications from developmental cultural psychology. In P. M. Camic & J. E. Rhodes (Eds.), *Qualitative research in psychology* (pp. 219–242). Washington, DC: American Psychological Association.

Miller, P. J., Wang, S., Sandel, T., & Cho, G. E. (2002). Self-esteem as folk theory: A comparison of European American and Taiwanese mothers' beliefs. *Parenting: Science and Practice, 2,* 209–239.

Miller, P. J., Wiley, A. R., Fung, H., & Liang, C.-H. (1997). Personal storytelling as a medium of socialization in Chinese and American families. *Child Development, 68,* 557–568.

Miller, S., Lansford, J. E., Costanzo, P., Malone, P. S., Golonka, M., & Killeya-Jones, L. A. (2009). Early adolescent romantic partner status, peer standing, and problem behaviors. *Journal of Early Adolescence, 29,* 839–861.

Miller, S. A., Hardin, C. A., & Montgomery, D. E. (2003). Young children's understanding of the conditions for knowledge acquisition. *Journal of Cognition and Development, 4,* 325–356.

Miller, W. B. (2009). The reasons people give for having children. In W. B. Miller (Ed.), *Why we have children: Building a unified theory of the reproductive mind* (pp. 1–19). Aptos, CA: Transnational Family Research Institute.

Milligan, K., Astington, J. W., & Dack, L. A. (2007). Language and theory of mind: Meta-analysis of the relation between language ability and false-belief understanding. *Child Development, 78,* 622–646.

Mills, C. M. (2013). Knowing when to doubt: Developing a critical stance when learning from others. *Developmental Psychology, 49,* 404–418.

Mills, D., & Conboy, B. T. (2005). Do changes in brain organization reflect shifts in symbolic functioning? In L. Namy (Ed.), *Symbol use and symbolic representation* (pp. 123–153). Mahwah, NJ: Erlbaum.

Mills, D., Plunkett, K., Prat, C., & Schafer, G. (2005). Watching the infant brain learn words: Effects of language and experience. *Cognitive Development, 20,* 19–31.

Mills, M., Rindfuss, R. R., McDonald, P., & te Velde, E. (2011). Why do people postpone parenthood? Reasons and social policy incentives. *Human Reproduction Update, 17,* 848–860.

Mills, R. S. L. (2005). Taking stock of the developmental literature on shame. *Developmental Review, 25,* 26–63.

Mills, R. S. L., & Grusec, J. E. (1989). Cognitive, affective, and behavioral consequences of praising altruism. *Merrill-Palmer Quarterly, 35,* 299–326.

Mills, T. L., Gomez-Smith, Z., & De Leon, J. M. (2005). Skipped generation families: Sources of psychological distress among grandmothers of grandchildren who live in homes where neither parent is present. *Marriage and Family Review, 37,* 191–212.

Mindell, J. A., Sadeh, A., Kwon, R., & Goh, D. Y. T. (2013). Cross-cultural differences in the sleep of preschool children. *Sleep Medicine, 14,* 1283–1289.

Minkler, M., & Fuller-Thomson, E. (2005). African American grandparents raising grandchildren: A national study using the Census 2000 American Community Survey. *Journal of Gerontology, 60B,* S82–S92.

Miranda, A., Presentacion, M. J., Siegenthaler, R., & Jara, P. (2013). Effects of a psychosocial intervention on the executive functioning in children with ADHD. *Journal of Learning Disabilities, 46,* 363–376.

Misailidi, P. (2006). Young children's display rule knowledge: Understanding the distinction between apparent and real emotions and the motives underlying the use of display rules. *Social Behavior and Personality, 34,* 1285–1296.

Mischel, W., & Liebert, R. M. (1966). Effects of discrepancies between observed and imposed reward criteria on their acquisition and transmission. *Journal of Personality and Social Psychology, 3,* 45–53.

Mistry, R. S., Biesanz, J. C., Chien, N., Howes, C., & Benner, A. D. (2008). Socioeconomic status, parental investments, and the cognitive and behavioral outcomes of low-income children from immigrant and native households. *Early Childhood Research Quarterly, 23,* 193–212.

Miura, I. T., & Okamoto, Y. (2003). Language supports for mathematics understanding and performance. In A. J. Baroody & A. Dowker (Eds.), *The development of arithmetic concepts and skills* (pp. 229–242). Mahwah, NJ: Erlbaum.

Mize, J., & Pettit, G. S. (2010). The mother–child playgroup as socialisation context: A short-term longitudinal study of mother–child–peer relationship dynamics. *Early Child Development and Care, 180,* 1271–1284.

Moffitt, T. E. (2007). Life-course-persistent vs. adolescence-limited antisocial behavior. In D. Cicchetti & D. J. Cohen (Eds.), *Developmental psychopathology* (2nd ed., pp. 570–598). Hoboken, NJ: Wiley.

Mok, M. M. C., Kennedy, K. J., & Moore, P. J. (2011). Academic attribution of secondary students: Gender, year level and achievement level. *Educational Psychology, 31,* 87–104.

Moll, H., & Meltzoff, A. N. (2011). How does it look? Level 2 perspective-taking at 36 months of age. *Child Development, 82,* 661–673.

Moll, H., & Tomasello, M. (2006). Level I perspective-taking at 24 months of age. *British Journal of Developmental Psychology, 24,* 603–613.

Moll, K., Ramus, F., Bartling, J., Bruder, J., Kunze, S., Neuhoff, N., et al. (2014). Cognitive mechanisms underlying reading and spelling development in five European orthographies. *Learning and Instruction, 29,* 65–77.

Moller, K., Hwang, C. P., & Wickberg, B. (2008). Couple relationship and transition to parenthood: Does workload at home matter? *Journal of Reproductive and Infant Psychology, 26,* 57–68.

Molloy, C. S., Wilson-Ching, M., Anderson, V. A., Roberts, G., Anderson, P. J., Doyle, L. W., et al. (2013). Visual processing in adolescents born extremely low birth weight and/or extremely preterm. *Pediatrics, 132,* e704–e712.

Molnar, D. S., Levitt, A., Eiden, R. D., & Schuetze, P. (2014). Prenatal cocaine exposure and trajectories of externalizing behavior problems in early childhood: Examining the role of maternal negative affect. *Development and Psychopathology, 26,* 515–528.

Monahan, K. C., Lee, J. M., & Steinberg, L. (2011). Revisiting the impact of part-time work on adolescent adjustment: Distinguishing between selection and socialization using propensity score matching. *Child Development, 82*, 96–112.

Mondloch, C. J., Lewis, T., Budreau, D. R., Maurer, D., Dannemillier, J. L., Stephens, B. R., & Kleiner-Gathercoal, K. A. (1999). Face perception during early infancy. *Psychological Science, 10*, 419–422.

Monk, C., Georgieff, M. K., & Osterholm, E. A. (2013). Research review: Maternal prenatal distress and poor nutrition—mutually influencing risk factors affecting infant neurocognitive development. *Journal of Child Psychology and Psychiatry, 54*, 115–130.

Monk, C. S., Weng, S.-J., Wiggins, J. L., Kurapati, N., Louro, H. M. C., Carrasco, M., et al. (2010). Neural circuitry of emotional face processing in autism spectrum disorders. *Journal of Psychiatry and Neuroscience, 35*, 105–114.

Montague, D. P. F., & Walker-Andrews, A. S. (2001). Peekaboo: A new look at infants' perception of emotion expressions. *Developmental Psychology, 37*, 826–838.

Montemayor, R., & Eisen, M. (1977). The development of self-conceptions from childhood to adolescence. *Developmental Psychology, 13*, 314–319.

Montgomery, M. J., & Côté, J. E. (2003a). College as a transition to adulthood. In G. R. Adams & M. D. Berzonsky (Eds.), *Blackwell handbook of adolescence* (pp. 150–172). Malden, MA: Blackwell.

Montgomery, M. J., & Côté, J. E. (2003b). The transition to college: Adjustment, development, and outcomes. In G. R. Adams & M. D. Berzonsky (Eds.), *Blackwell handbook of adolescence* (pp. 179–194). Malden, MA: Blackwell.

Moon, C., Cooper, R. P., & Fifer, W. P. (1993). Two-day-old infants prefer their native language. *Infant Behavior and Development, 16*, 495–500.

Moon, R. Y., Horne, R. S. C., & Hauck, F. R.(2007). Sudden infant death syndrome. *The Lancet, 370*, 1578–1587.

Moore, C., Mealiea, J., Garon, N., & Povinelli, D. (2007). The development of body self-awareness. *Infancy, 11*, 157–174.

Moore, D. S., & Johnson, S. P. (2011). Mental rotation of dynamic, three-dimensional stimuli by 3-month-old infants. *Infancy, 16*, 435–445.

Moore, E. G. J. (1986). Family socialization and the IQ test performance of traditionally and transracially adopted black children. *Developmental Psychology, 22*, 317–326.

Moore, G. A., Cohn, J. E., & Campbell, S. B. (2001). Infant affective responses to mother's still face at 6 months differentially predict externalizing and internalizing behaviors at 18 months. *Developmental Psychology, 37*, 706–714.

Moore, K. L., & Persaud, T. V. N. (2008). *Before we are born* (7th ed.). Philadelphia: Saunders.

Moore, K. L., Persaud, T. V. N., & Torchia, M. G. (2013). *Before we are born: Essentials of embryology and birth defects* (8th ed.). Philadelphia, PA: Saunders.

Moore, M., & Mindell, J. A. (2012). Sleep-related problems in childhood. In C. M. Morin & C. A. Espie (Eds.), *Oxford handbook of sleep and sleep disorders* (pp. 729–745). New York: Oxford University Press.

Moore, M. K., & Meltzoff, A. N. (1999). New findings on object permanence: A developmental difference between two types of occlusion. *British Journal of Developmental Psychology, 17*, 563–584.

Moore, M. K., & Meltzoff, A. N. (2004). Object permanence after a 24-hr delay and leaving the locale of disappearance: The role of memory, space, and identity. *Developmental Psychology, 40*, 606–620.

Moore, M. K., & Meltzoff, A. N. (2008). Factors affecting infants' manual search for occluded objects and the genesis of object permanence. *Infant Behavior and Development, 31*, 168–180.

Moore, M. R., & Brooks-Gunn, J. (2002). Adolescent parenthood. In M. H. Bornstein (Ed.), *Handbook of parenting: Vol. 3* (2nd ed., pp. 173–214). Mahwah, NJ: Erlbaum.

Moore, M. R., & Stambolis-Ruhstorfer, M. (2013). LGBT sexuality and families at the start of the twenty-first century. *Annual Review of Sociology, 39*, 491–507.

Moran, G., Forbes, L., Evans, E., Tarabulsy, G. M., & Madigan, S. (2008). Both maternal sensitivity and atypical maternal behavior independently predict attachment security and disorganization in adolescent mother–infant relationships. *Infant Behavior and Development, 31*, 321–325.

Moran, G. F., & Vinovskis, M. A. (1986). The great care of godly parents: Early childhood in Puritan New England. *Monographs of the Society for Research in Child Development, 50*(4–5, Serial No. 211).

Moran, S., & Gardner, H. (2006). Extraordinary achievements: A developmental and systems analysis. In D. Kuhn & R. S. Siegler (Eds.), *Handbook of child psychology: Vol. 2. Cognition, perception, and language* (6th ed., pp. 905–949). Hoboken, NJ: Wiley.

Morawska, A., & Sanders, M. (2011). Parental use of time out revisited: A useful or harmful parenting strategy? *Journal of Child and Family Studies, 20*, 1–8.

Morelli, G. A., Rogoff, B., & Angelillo, C. (2003). Cultural variation in young children's access to work or involvement in specialized child-focused activities. *International Journal of Behavioral Development, 27*, 264–274.

Morelli, G. A., Rogoff, B., Oppenheim, D., & Goldsmith, D. (1992). Cultural variation in infants' sleeping arrangements: Questions of independence. *Developmental Psychology, 28*, 604–613.

Moreno, A. J., Klute, M. M., & Robinson, J. L. (2008). Relational and individual resources as predictors of empathy in early childhood. *Social Development, 17*, 613–637.

Morgan, I. G., Ohno-Matsui, K., & Saw, S.-M. (2012). Myopia. *Lancet, 379*, 1739–1748.

Morgan, P. L., Farkas, G., Hillemeier, M. M., & Maczuga, S. (2009). Risk factors for learning-related behavior problems at 24 months of age: Population-based estimates. *Journal of Abnormal Child Psychology, 37*, 401–413.

Morinis, J., Carson, C., & Quigley, M. A. (2013). Effect of teenage motherhood on cognitive outcomes in children: A population-based cohort study. *Archives of Disease in Childhood, 98*, 959–964.

Morra, S., Gobbo, C., Marini, Z., & Sheese, R. (Eds.). (2008). *Cognitive development: Neo-Piagetian perspectives.* New York: Erlbaum.

Morrill, M. I., Hines, D. A., Mahmood, S., & Córdova, J. V. (2010). Pathways between marriage and parenting for wives and husbands: The role of coparenting. *Family Process, 49*, 59–73.

Morris, A. S., Silk, J. S., Morris, M. D. S., & Steinberg, L. (2011). The influence of mother–child emotion regulation strategies on children's expression of anger and sadness. *Developmental Psychology, 47*, 213–225.

Morris, A. S., Silk, J. S., Steinberg, L., Myers, S. S., & Robinson, L. R. (2007). The role of the family context in the development of emotion regulation. *Social Development, 16*, 362–388.

Morris, G., & Baker-Ward, L. (2007). Fragile but real: Children's capacity to use newly acquired words to convey preverbal memories. *Child Development, 78*, 448–458.

Morrissey, T., Dunifon, R. E., & Kalil, A. (2011). Maternal employment, work schedules, and children's body mass index. *Child Development, 82*, 66–81.

Morrissey, T. W. (2013). Multiple child care arrangements and common communicable illnesses in children aged 3 to 54 months. *Maternal and Child Health Journal, 17*, 1175–1184.

Morrongiello, B. A., Fenwick, K. D., & Chance, G. (1998). Crossmodal learning in newborn infants: Inferences about properties of auditory-visual events. *Infant Behavior and Development, 21*, 543–554.

Morrongiello, B. A., Kane, A., & Zdzieborski, D. (2011). "I think he is in his room playing a video game": Parental supervision of young elementary-school children at home. *Journal of Pediatric Psychology, 36*, 708–717.

Morrongiello, B. A., & Kiriakou, S. (2004). Mothers' home-safety practices for preventing six types of childhood injuries: What do they do, and why? *Journal of Pediatric Psychology, 29*, 285–297.

Morrongiello, B. A., Midgett, C., & Shields, R. (2001). Don't run with scissors: Young children's knowledge of home safety rules. *Journal of Pediatric Psychology, 26*, 105–115.

Morrongiello, B. A., Ondejko, L., & Littlejohn, A. (2004). Understanding toddlers' in-home injuries: I. Context, correlates, and determinants. *Journal of Pediatric Psychology, 29*, 415–431.

Morrongiello, B. A., & Rennie, H. (1998). Why do boys engage in more risk taking than girls? The role of attributions, beliefs, and risk appraisals. *Journal of Pediatric Psychology, 23*, 33–43.

Morrongiello, B. A., Widdifield, R., Munroe, K., & Zdzieborski, D. (2014). Parents teaching young children home safety rules: Implications for childhood injury risk. *Journal of Applied Developmental Psychology, 35*, 254–261.

Morse, S. B., Zheng, H., Tang, Y., & Roth, J., (2009). Early school-age outcomes of late preterm infants. *Pediatrics, 123*, e622–e629.

Mosby, L., Rawls, A. W., Meehan, A. J., Mays, E., & Pettinari, C. J. (1999). Troubles in interracial talk about discipline: An examination of African American child rearing narratives. *Journal of Comparative Family Studies, 30*, 489–521.

Mosely-Howard, G. S., & Evans, C. B. (2000). Relationships and contemporary experiences of the African-American family: An ethnographic case study. *Journal of Black Studies, 30*, 428–451.

Moses, L. J., Baldwin, D. A., Rosicky, J. G., & Tidball, G. (2001). Evidence for referential understanding in the emotions domain at twelve and eighteen months. *Child Development, 72*, 718–735.

Moshman, D. (1998). Cognitive development beyond childhood. In D. Kuhn & R. S. Siegler (Eds.), *Handbook of child psychology: Vol. 2. Cognition, perception, and language* (5th ed., pp. 947–978). New York: Wiley.

Moshman, D. (2003). Developmental change in adulthood. In J. Demick & C. Andreoletti (Eds.), *Handbook of adult development* (pp. 43–61). New York: Plenum.

Moshman, D. (2005). *Adolescent psychological development: Rationality, morality, and identity* (2nd ed.). Mahwah, NJ: Erlbaum.

Moshman, D. (2011). *Adolescent rationality and development: Cognition, morality, and identity* (3rd ed.). New York: Taylor and Francis.

Moshman, D., & Franks, B. A. (1986). Development of the concept of inferential validity. *Child Development, 57*, 153–165.

Moshman, D., & Geil, M. (1998). Collaborative reasoning: Evidence for collective rationality. *Thinking and Reasoning, 4*, 231–248.

Moss, E., Cyr, C., Bureau, J.-F., Tarabulsy, G. M., & Dubois-Comtois, K. (2005). Stability of attachment during the preschool period. *Developmental Psychology, 41*, 773–783.

Moss, E., Cyr, C., & Dubois-Comtois, K. (2004). Attachment at early school age and developmental risk: Examining family contexts and behavior problems of controlling-caregiving, controlling-punitive, and behaviorally disorganized children. *Developmental Psychology, 40*, 519–532.

Moss, E., Smolla, N., Guerra, I., Mazzarello, T., Chayer, D., & Berthiaume, C. (2006). Attachment and self-reported internalizing and externalizing behavior problems in a school period. *Canadian Journal of Behavioural Science, 38*, 142–157.

Mossey, P. A., Little, J., Munger, R. G., Dixon, M. J., & Shaw, W. C. (2009). Cleft lip and palate. *Lancet, 374*, 1773–1785.

Moss-Racusin, C. A., Dovidio, J. F., Brescoll, V. L., Graham, M. J., & Handelsman, J. (2012). Science faculty's subtle gender biases favor male students. *Proceedings of the National Academy of Sciences, 109*, 16474–16479.

Mosteller, F. (1995). The Tennessee Study of Class Size in the Early School Grades. *Future of Children, 5*(2), 113–127.

Mota, J., Silva, P., Santos, M. P., Ribeiro, J. C., Oliveira, J., & Duarte, J. A. (2005). Physical activity and school recess time: Differences between the sexes and the relationship between children's playground physical activity and habitual physical activity. *Journal of Sports Sciences, 23*, 269–275.

Motl, R. W., Dishman, R. K., Saunders, R. P., Dowda, M., Felton, G., Ward, D. S., & Pate, R. R. (2002). Examining social–cognitive determinants of intention and physical activity among black and white adolescent girls using structural equation modeling. *Health Psychology, 21*, 459–467.

Mottus, R., Indus, K., & Allik, J. (2008). Accuracy of only children stereotype. *Journal of Research in Personality, 42*, 1047–1052.

Mottweiler, C. M., & Taylor, M. (2014). Elaborated role play and creativity in preschool age children. *Psychology of Aesthetics, Creativity, and the Arts, 8*, 277–286.

Mounts, N. S., & Steinberg, L. (1995). An ecological analysis of peer influence on adolescent grade point average and drug use. *Developmental Psychology, 31*, 915–922.

Mounts, N. S., Valentiner, D. P., Anderson, K. L., & Boswell, M. K. (2006). Shyness, sociability, and parental support for the college transition: Relation to adolescents' adjustment. *Journal of Youth and Adolescence, 35*, 71–80.

Mrug, S., Elliott, M. N., Daies, S., Tortolero, S. R., Cuccaro, P., & Schuster, M. A. (2014). Early puberty, negative peer influence, and problem behaviors in adolescent girls. *Pediatrics, 133*, 7–14.

Mrug, S., Hoza, B., & Gerdes, A. C. (2001). Children with attention-deficit/hyperactivity disorder: Peer relationships and peer-oriented interventions. In D. W. Nangle & C. A. Erdley (Eds.), *The role of friendship in psychological adjustment* (pp. 51–77). San Francisco: Jossey-Bass.

Mu, Q., & Fehring, R. J. (2014). Efficacy of achieving pregnancy with fertility-focused intercourse. *American Journal of Maternal Child Nursing, 39*, 35–40.

Muenssinger, J., Matuz, T., Schleger, F., Kiefer-Schmidt, I., Goelz, R. Wacker-Gussmann, A., et al. (2013). Auditory habituation in the fetus and neonate: An fMEG study. *Developmental Science, 16*, 287–295.

Müller, O., & Krawinkel, M. (2005). Malnutrition and health in developing countries. *Canadian Medical Association Journal, 173*, 279–286.

Müller, U., Overton, W. F., & Reene, K. (2001). Development of conditional reasoning: A longitudinal study. *Journal of Cognition and Development, 2*, 27–49.

Mullett-Hume, E., Anshel, D., Guevara, V., & Cloitre, M. (2008). Cumulative trauma and posttraumatic stress disorder among children exposed to the 9/11 World Trade Center attack. *American Journal of Orthopsychiatry, 78*, 103–108.

Mulvaney, M. K., McCartney, K., Bub, K. L., & Marshall, N. L. (2006). Determinants of dyadic scaffolding and cognitive outcomes in first graders. *Parenting: Science and Practice, 6*, 297–310.

Mulvaney, M. K., & Mebert, C. J. (2007). Parental corporal punishment predicts behavior problems in early childhood. *Journal of Family Psychology, 21*, 389–397.

Mumme, D. L., Bushnell, E. W., DiCorcia, J. A., & Lariviere, L. A. (2007). Infants' use of gaze cues to interpret others' actions and emotional reactions. In R. Flom, K. Lee, & D. Muir (Eds.), *Gaze-following: Its development and significance* (pp. 143–170). Mahwah, NJ: Erlbaum.

Munakata, Y. (2001). Task-dependency in infant behavior: Toward an understanding of the processes underlying cognitive development. In F. Lacerda, C. von Hofsten, & M. Heimann (Eds.), *Emerging cognitive abilities in early infancy* (pp. 29–52). Mahwah, NJ: Erlbaum.

Munakata, Y. (2006). Information processing approaches to development. In D. Kuhn & R. S. Siegler (Eds.), *Handbook of child psychology: Vol. 2. Cognition, perception, and language* (6th ed., pp. 426–463). Hoboken, NJ: Wiley.

Muños-Hoyos, A., Molina-Carballo, A., Augustin-Morales, M., Contreras-Chova, F., Naranjo-Gómez, A., Justicia-Martínez, F., et al. (2011). Psychosocial dwarfism: Psychopathological aspects and putative neuroendocrine markers. *Psychiatry Research, 188*, 96–101.

Munroe, R. L., & Romney, A. K. (2006). Gender and age differences in same-sex aggregation and social behavior. *Journal of Cross-Cultural Psychology, 37*, 3–19.

Muret-Wagstaff, S., & Moore, S. G. (1989). The Hmong in America: Infant behavior and rearing practices. In J. K. Nugent, B. M. Lester, & T. B. Brazelton (Eds.), *Biology, culture, and development* (Vol. 1, pp. 319–339). Norwood, NJ: Ablex.

Muris, P., & Field, A. P. (2011). The "normal" development of fear. In W. K. Silverman, & A. P. Field (Eds.), *Anxiety disorders in children and adolescents* (2nd ed., pp. 76–89). Cambridge, UK: Cambridge University Press.

Muris, P., & Meesters, C. (2014). Small or big in the eyes of the other: On the developmental psychopathology of self-conscious emotions as shame, guilt, and pride. *Clinical Child and Family Psychology Review, 17*, 19–40.

Muris, P., Merckelbach, H., Ollendick, T. H., King, N. J., & Bogie, N. (2001). Children's nighttime fears: Parent–child ratings of frequency, content, origins, coping behaviors and severity. *Behaviour Research and Therapy, 39*, 13–28.

Murphy, J. B. (2013). Access to in vitro fertilization deserves increased regulation in the United States. *Journal of Sex and Marital Therapy, 39*, 85–92.

Murphy, M. C., Steele, C. M., & Gross, J. J. (2007). Signaling threat: How situational cues affect women in math, science, and engineering settings. *Psychological Science, 18*, 879–885.

Murphy, R. F., Penuel, W. R., Means, B., Korbak, C., Whaley, A., & Allen, J. E. (2002). *A review of recent evidence on the effectiveness of discrete educational software.* Washington, DC: U.S. Department of Education.

Murphy, T. H., & Corbett, D. (2009). Plasticity during recovery: From synapse to behaviour. *Nature Reviews Neuroscience, 10*, 861–872.

Murphy, T. P., & Laible, D. J. (2013). The influence of attachment security on preschool children's empathic concern. *International Journal of Behavioral Development, 37*, 436–440.

Murray, A. D. (1985). Aversiveness is in the mind of the beholder. In B. M. Lester & C. F. Z. Boukydis (Eds.), *Infant crying* (pp. 217–239). New York: Plenum.

Murray, L. K., Nguyen, A., & Cohen, J. A. (2014). Child sexual abuse. *Pediatric Clinics of North America, 23*, 321–337.

Mussen, P. H., & Eisenberg-Berg, N. (1977). *Roots of caring, sharing, and helping.* San Francisco: Freeman.

Mutchler, J. E., Baker, L. A., & Lee, S. (2007). Grandparents responsible for grandchildren in Native-American families. *Social Science Quarterly, 88*, 990–1009.

Myant, K. A., & Williams, J. M. (2005). Children's concepts of health and illness: Understanding of contagious illnesses, noncontagious illnesses and injuries. *Journal of Health Psychology, 10*, 805–819.

Myers, L. J., & Liben, L. S. (2008). The role of intentionality and iconicity in children's developing comprehension and production of cartographic symbols. *Child Development, 79*, 668–684.

Myowa-Yamakoshi, M., Tomonaga, M., Tanaka, M., & Matsuzawa, T. (2004). Imitation in neonatal chimpanzees *(Pan troglodytes). Developmental Science, 7*, 437–442.

N

Nadel, J., Prepin, K., & Okanda, M. (2005). Experiencing contingency and agency: First step toward self-understanding in making a mind? *Interaction Studies, 6*, 447–462.

Nader, P. R., O'Brien, M., Houts, R., Bradley, R., Belsky, J., Crosnoe, R., et al. (2006). Identifying risk for obesity in early childhood. *Pediatrics, 118*, e594–e601.

Nærde, A., Ogden, T., Janson, H., & Zachrisson, H. D. (2014). Normative development of physical aggression from 8 to 26 months. *Developmental Psychology, 6*, 1710–1720.

Nagy, E., Compagne, H., Orvos, H., Pal, A., Molnar, P., & Janszky, I. (2005). Index finger movement imitation by human neonates: Motivation, learning, and lefthand preference. *Pediatric Research, 58*, 749–753.

Naigles, L. R., & Swenson, L. D. (2007). Syntactic supports for word learning. In E. Hoff & M. Shatz (Eds.), *Blackwell handbook of language development* (pp. 212–231). Malden, MA: Blackwell.

Naito, M., & Seki, Y. (2009). The relationship between second-order false belief and display rules reasoning: Integration of cognitive and affective social understanding. *Developmental Science, 12*, 150–164.

Nánez, J., Sr., & Yonas, A. (1994). Effects of luminance and texture motion on infant defensive reactions to optical collision. *Infant Behavior and Development, 17*, 165–174.

Narayan, A. J., Englund, M. M., Carlson, E. A., & Egeland, B. (2014). Adolescent conflict as a developmental process in the prospective pathway from exposure to interparental violence to dating violence. *Journal of Abnormal Child Psychology, 42*, 239–250.

Narayan, A. J., Englund, M. M., & Egeland, B. (2013). Developmental timing and continuity of exposure to interparental violence and externalizing behavior as prospective predictors of dating violence. *Development and Psychopathology, 25*, 973–990.

Narr, K. L., Woods, R. P., Lin, J., Kim, J., Phillips, O. R., Del'Homme, M., et al. (2009). Widespread cortical thinning is a robust anatomical marker for attention-deficit/hyperactivity disorder. *Journal of the American Academy of Child and Adolescent Psychiatry, 48*, 1014–1022.

National Association for Sport and Physical Education. (2009). *Active start: A statement of physical activity guidelines for children from birth to age 5* (2nd ed.). Reston, VA: Author.

National Association for Sport and Physical Education. (2012). *Shape of the nation report: Status of physical education in the USA.* Retrieved from www.shapeamerica.org/advocacy/son/2012/upload/2012-Shape-of-Nation-full-report-web.pdf

National Center for Biotechnology Information. (2014). *Online Mendelian inheritance in man.* Retrieved from www.omim.org

National Center for Injury Prevention and Control. (2013). *WISQARS fatal injury reports, national and regional, 1999–2012.* Retrieved from webappa.cdc.gov/sasweb/ncipc/mortrate10_us.html

National Center for Mental Health Promotion and Youth Violence Prevention. (2006). *Recognizing and responding to the warning signs of suicide: A guide for teachers and school staff.* Retrieved from www.promoteprevent.org/recognizing-and-responding-warning-signs-suicide-guide-teachers-and-school-staff

National Coalition for the Homeless. (2009). How many people experience homelessness? Retrieved from www.nationalhomeless.org/factsheets/How_Many.html

National Council of Youth Sports. (2008). Report on trends and participation in organized youth sports. Stuart, FL: Author.

National Early Literacy Panel. (2008). *Developing early literacy: A scientific synthesis of early literacy development and implications for intervention.* Jessup, MD: National Institute for Literacy.

National Federation of State High School Associations. (2014). *2013–2014 High School Athletics Participation Survey.* Retrieved from www.nfhs.org

National Institute of Justice. (2014). *Prevalence of teen dating violence.* Retrieved from www.nij.gov/topics/crime/intimate-partner-violence/teen-dating-violence/Pages/prevalence.aspx

National Institute on Drug Abuse. (2014). *National survey of drug use and health.* Retrieved from www.drugabuse.gov/national-survey-drug-use-health

National Institutes of Health. (2011). *Dental caries (tooth decay) in children (age 2 to 11).* Retrieved from www.nidcr.nih.gov/DataStatistics/FindDataByTopic/DentalCaries/DentalCariesChildren2to11.htm

National Institutes of Health. (2014). *Genes and disease.* Retrieved from www.ncbi.nlm.nih.gov/books/NBK22183

National Research Council. (2007). *Race conscious policies for assigning students to schools: Social science research and the Supreme Court cases.* Washington, DC: National Academy Press.

National Sexual Violence Resource Center. (2013). *Statistics about sexual violence.* Encola, PA: Author.

National Survey of Children's Health. (2012). *Data Research Center for Child & Adolescent Health.* Retrieved from www.childhealthdata.org/learn/NSCH

Natsuaki, M. N., Biehl, M. C., & Ge, X. (2009). Trajectories of depressed mood from early adolescence to young adulthood: The effects of pubertal timing and adolescent dating. *Journal of Research on Adolescence, 19*, 47–74.

Natsuaki, M. N., Samuels, D., & Leve, L. D. (2014). Puberty, identity, and context: A biopsychosocial perspective on internalizing psychopathology in early adolescent girls. In K. C. McLean & M. Syed (Eds.), *Oxford handbook of identity development* (pp. 389–405). New York: Oxford University Press.

Nauta, J., van Mechelen, W., Otten, R. H. J., & Verhagen, E. A. L. M. (2014). A systematic review on the effectiveness of school and community-based injury prevention programmes on risk behaviour and injury risk in 8–12 year old children. *Journal of Science and Medicine in Sport, 17*, 165–172.

Needham, A. (2001). Object recognition in 4.5-month-old infants. *Journal of Experimental Child Psychology, 78*, 3–24.

Needham, B. L., & Austin, E. L. (2010). Sexual orientation, parental support, and health during the transition to young adulthood. *Journal of Youth and Adolescence, 39*, 1189–1198.

Needleman, H. L., MacFarland, C., Ness, R. B., Reinberg, S., & Tobin, M. J. (2002). Bone lead levels in adjudicated delinquents: A case control study. *Neurotoxicology and Teratology, 24*, 711–717.

Neff, K. D., & Helwig, C. C. (2002). A constructivist approach to understanding the development of reasoning about rights and authority within cultural contexts. *Cognitive Development, 17*, 1429–1450.

Negriff, S., Susman, E. J., & Trickett, P. K. (2011). The developmental pathway from pubertal timing to delinquency and sexual activity form early to late adolescence. *Journal of Youth and Adolescence, 40,* 1343–1356.

Neitzel, C., & Stright, A. D. (2003). Mothers' scaffolding of children's problem solving: Establishing a foundation of academic self-regulatory competence. *Journal of Family Psychology, 17,* 147–159.

Nelson, C. A. (2002). Neural development and lifelong plasticity. In R. M. Lerner, F. Jacobs, & D. Wertlieb (Eds.), *Handbook of applied developmental science* (Vol. 1, pp. 31–60). Thousand Oaks, CA: Sage.

Nelson, C. A. (2007a). A developmental cognitive neuroscience approach to the study of atypical development: A model system involving infants of diabetic mothers. In D. Coch, G. Dawson, & K. W. Fischer (Eds.), *Human behavior, learning, and the developing brain: Atypical development* (2nd ed., pp. 37–59). New York: Guilford.

Nelson, C. A. (2007b). A neurobiological perspective on early human deprivation. *Child Development Perspectives, 1,* 13–18.

Nelson, C. A., & Bosquet, M. (2000). Neurobiology of fetal and infant development: Implications for infant mental health. In C. H. Zeanah, Jr. (Ed.), *Handbook of infant mental health* (2nd ed., pp. 37–59). New York: Guilford.

Nelson, C. A., Fox, N. A., & Zeanah, C. H. (2014). *Romania's abandoned children: Deprivation, brain development, and the struggle for recovery.* Cambridge, MA: Harvard University Press.

Nelson, C. A., Thomas, K. M., & de Haan, M. (2006). Neural bases of cognitive development. In D. Kuhn & R. Siegler (Eds.), *Handbook of child psychology: Vol. 2. Cognition, perception, and language* (6th ed., pp. 3–57). Hoboken, NJ: Wiley.

Nelson, C. A., Wewerka, S., Borscheid, A. J., deRegnier, R., & Georgieff, M. K. (2003). Electrophysiologic evidence of impaired cross-modal recognition memory in 8-month-old infants of diabetic mothers. *Journal of Pediatrics, 142,* 575–582.

Nelson, C. A., Wewerka, S., Thomas, K. M., Tribby-Walbridge, S., deRegnier, R., & Georgieff, M. K. (2000). Neurocognitive sequelae of infants of diabetic mothers. *Behavioral Neuroscience, 114,* 950–956.

Nelson, C. A., III. (2011). Neural development and lifelong plasticity. In D. P. Keating (Ed.), *Nature and nurture in early child development* (pp. 45–69). New York: Cambridge University Press.

Nelson, D. A., & Coyne, S. M. (2009). Children's intent attributions and feelings of distress: Associations with maternal and paternal parenting practices. *Journal of Abnormal Child Psychology, 37,* 223–237.

Nelson, D. A., Nelson, L. J., Hart, C. H., Yang, C., & Jin, S. (2006). Parenting and peer-group behavior in cultural context. In X. Chen, D. French, & B. Schneider (Eds.), *Peer relations in cultural context* (pp. 213–246). New York: Cambridge University Press.

Nelson, D. A., Robinson, C. C., & Hart, C. H. (2005). Relational and physical aggression of preschool-age children: Peer status linkages across informants. *Early Education and Development, 16,* 115–139.

Nelson, D. A., Yang, C., Coyne, S. M., Olsen, J. A., & Hart, C. H. (2013). Parental psychological control dimensions: Connections with Russian preschoolers' physical and relational aggression. *Journal of Applied Developmental Psychology, 34,* 1–8.

Nelson, E. L., Campbell, J. M., & Michel, G. F. (2013). Unimanual to bimanual: Tracking the development of handedness from 6 to 24 months. *Infant Behavior and Development, 36,* 181–188.

Nelson, K. (1973). Structure and strategy in learning to talk. *Monographs of the Society for Research in Child Development, 38*(1–2, Serial No. 149).

Nelson, K. (2003). Narrative and the emergence of a consciousness of self. In G. D. Fireman & T. E. McVay, Jr. (Eds.), *Narrative and consciousness: Literature, psychology, and the brain* (pp. 17–36). London: Oxford University Press.

Nelson, L. J. (2009). An examination of emerging adulthood in Romanian college students. *International Journal of Behavioral Development, 33,* 402–411.

Nelson, L. J. (2014). The role of parents in the religious and spiritual development of emerging adults. In C. M. Barry & M. M. Abo-Zena (Eds.), *Emerging adults' religiousness and spirituality* (pp 59–75). New York: Oxford University Press.

Nelson, L. J., & Chen, X. (2007). Emerging adulthood in China: The role of social and cultural factors. *Child Development Perspectives, 1,* 86–91.

Nelson, L. J., & Padilla-Walker, L. M. (2013). Flourishing and floundering in emerging adult college students. *Emerging Adulthood, 1,* 67–78.

Nemet, D., Barkan, S., Epstein, Y., Friedland, O., Kowen, G., & Eliakim, A. (2005). Short- and long-term beneficial effects of a combined dietary–behavioural–physical activity intervention for the treatment of childhood obesity. *Pediatrics, 115,* e443–e449.

Nepomnyaschy, L., & Waldfogel, J. (2007). Paternity leave and fathers' involvement with their young children. *Community, Work and Family, 10,* 427–453.

Nesdale, D., Durkin, K., Maas, A., & Griffiths, J. (2004). Group status, outgroup ethnicity, and children's ethnic attitudes. *Applied Developmental Psychology, 25,* 237–251.

Nesdale, D., Durkin, K., Maas, A., & Griffiths, J. (2005). Threat, group identification, and children's ethnic prejudice. *Social Development, 14,* 189–205.

Neuman, S. B. (2003). From rhetoric to reality: The case for high-quality compensatory prekindergarten programs. *Phi Delta Kappan, 85*(4), 286–291.

Neuman, S. B. (2006). The knowledge gap: Implications for early education. In D. K. Dickinson & S. B. Neuman (Eds.), *Handbook of early literacy research* (Vol. 2, pp. 29–40). New York: Guilford.

Neuman, S. B., & Celano, D. (2001). Access to print in middle- and low-income communities: An ecological study of four neighborhoods. *Reading Research Quarterly, 36,* 8–26.

Neville, H. J., & Bavelier, D. (2002). Human brain plasticity: Evidence from sensory deprivation and altered language experience. In M. A. Hofman, G. J. Boer, A. J. G. D. Holtmaat, E. J. W. van Someren, J. Berhaagen, & D. F. Swaab (Eds.), *Plasticity in the adult brain: From genes to neurotherapy* (pp. 177–188). Amsterdam: Elsevier Science.

Neville, H. J., & Bruer, J. T. (2001). Language processing: How experience affects brain organization. In D. B. Bailey, Jr., J. T. Bruer, F. J. Symons, & J. W. Lichtman (Eds.), *Critical thinking about critical periods* (pp. 151–172). Baltimore: Paul H. Brookes.

Nevin, R. (2006). Understanding international crime trends: The legacy of preschool lead exposure. *Environmental Research, 104,* 315–316.

Newcombe, N. S. (2007). Taking science seriously: Straight thinking about spatial sex differences. In S. J. Ceci & W. M. Williams (Eds.), *Why aren't more women in science?* (pp. 69–77). Washington, DC: American Psychological Association.

Newcombe, N. S., Sluzenski, J., & Huttenlocher, J. (2005). Preexisting knowledge versus on-line learning: What do young infants really know about spatial location? *Psychological Science, 16,* 222–227.

Newheiser, A., Dunham, Y., Merrill, A., Hoosain, L., & Olson, K. R. (2014). Preference for high status predicts implicit outgroup bias among children from low-status groups. *Developmental Psychology, 50,* 1081–1090.

Newland, L. A., Coyl, D. D., & Freeman, H. (2008). Predicting preschoolers' attachment security from fathers' involvement, internal working models, and use of social support. *Early Child Development and Care, 178,* 785–801.

Newman, B. M., & Newman, P. R. (2001). Group identity and alienation: Giving the we its due. *Journal of Youth and Adolescence, 30,* 515–538.

Newnham, C. A., Milgrom, J., & Skouteris, H. (2009). Effectiveness of a modified mother–infant transaction program on outcomes for preterm infants from 3 to 24 months of age. *Infant Behavior and Development, 32,* 17–26.

Newson, J., & Newson, E. (1975). Intersubjectivity and the transmission of culture: On the social origins of symbolic functioning. *Bulletin of the British Psychological Society, 28,* 437–446.

Ng, F. F., Pomerantz, E. M., & Deng, C. (2014). Why are Chinese mothers more controlling than American mothers?: "My child is my report card." *Child Development, 85,* 355–369.

Ng, F. F., Pomerantz, E. M., & Lam, S. (2007). European-American and Chinese parents' responses to children's success and failure: Implications for children's responses. *Developmental Psychology, 43,* 1239–1255.

Ni, Y. (1998). Cognitive structure, content knowledge, and classificatory reasoning. *Journal of Genetic Psychology, 159,* 280–296.

NICHD (National Institute for Child Health and Human Development) Early Child Care Research Network. (1997). The effects of infant child care on infant–mother attachment security: Results of the NICHD Study of Early Child Care. *Child Development, 68,* 860–879.

NICHD (National Institute of Child Health and Human Development) Early Child Care Research Network. (1998). Relations between family predictors and child outcomes: Are they weaker for children in child care? *Developmental Psychology, 34,* 1119–1128.

NICHD (National Institute for Child Health and Human Development) Early Child Care Research Network. (1999). Child care and mother–child interaction in the first 3 years of life. *Developmental Psychology, 35,* 1399–1413.

NICHD (National Institute of Child Health and Human Development) Early Child Care Research Network. (2000a). Characteristics and quality of child care for toddlers and preschoolers. *Applied Developmental Science, 4,* 116–135.

NICHD (National Institute of Child Health and Human Development) Early Child Care Research Network. (2000b). The relation of child care to cognitive and language development. *Child Development, 71,* 960–980.

NICHD (National Institute of Child Health and Human Development) Early Child Care Research Network. (2001). Before Head Start: Income and ethnicity, family characteristics, child care experiences, and child development. *Early Education and Development, 12,* 545–575.

NICHD (National Institute of Child Health and Human Development) Early Child Care Research Network. (2002a). Child-care structure → process → outcome: Direct and indirect effects of child-care quality on young children's development. *Psychological Science, 13,* 199–206.

NICHD (National Institute of Child Health and Human Development) Early Child Care Research Network. (2002b). The interaction of child care and family risk in relation to child development at 24 and 36 months. *Applied Developmental Science, 6,* 144–156.

NICHD (National Institute of Child Health and Human Development) Early Child Care Research Network. (2003a). Does amount of time spent in child care predict socioemotional adjustment during the transition to kindergarten? *Child Development, 74,* 976–1005.

NICHD (National Institute of Child Health and Human Development) Early Child Care Research Network. (2003b). Does quality of child care affect child outcomes at age *Developmental Psychology, 39,* 451–469.

NICHD (National Institute of Child Health and Human Development) Early Child Care Research Network. (2004). Type of child care and children's development at 54 months. *Early Childhood Research Quarterly, 19,* 203–230.

NICHD (National Institute of Child Health and Development) Early Child Care Research Network. (2005). *Child care and development: Results from the NICHD Study of Early Child Care and Youth Development.* New York: Guilford.

NICHD (National Institute of Child Health and Human Development) Early Child Care Research Network. (2006). Child-care effect sizes for the NICHD Study of Early Child Care and Youth Development. *American Psychologist, 61,* 99–116.

Niccolai, L. M., Ethier, K. A., Kershaw, T. S., Lewis, J. B., Meade, C. S., & Ickovics, J. R. (2004). New sex partner acquisition and sexually transmitted disease risk among adolescent females. *Journal of Adolescent Health, 34,* 216–223.

Nicholls, A. L., & Kennedy, J. M. (1992). Drawing development: From similarity of features to direction. *Child Development, 63,* 227–241.

Nicholls, D. E., & Viner, R. M. (2009). Childhood risk factors for lifetime anorexia nervosa by age 30 in a national birth cohort. *Journal of the American Academy of Child and Adolescent Psychiatry, 48,* 791–799.

Nichols, K. E., Fox, N., & Mundy, P. (2005). Joint attention, self-recognition, and neurocognitive function in toddlers. *Infancy, 7,* 35–51.

Nickman, S. L., Rosenfeld, A. A., Fine, P., MacIntyre, J. C., Pilowsky, D. J., & Howe, R.-A. (2005). Children in adoptive families: Overview and update. *Journal of the American Academy of Child and Adolescent Psychiatry, 44,* 987–995.

Nicolopoulou, A., & Ilgaz, H. (2013). What do we know about pretend play and narrative development? A response to Lillard, Lerner, Hopkins, Dore, Smith, and Palmquist on "The impact of pretend play on children's development: A review of the evidence." *American Journal of Play, 6,* 55–81.

Niehaus, M. D., Moore, S. R., Patrick, P. D., Derr, L. L., Lorntz, B., Lima, A. A., & Gurerrant, R. L. (2002). Early childhood diarrhea is associated with diminished cognitive function 4 to 7 years later in children in a northeast Brazilian shantytown. *American Journal of Tropical Medicine and Hygiene, 66,* 590–593.

Nielsen, G. L., Andersen, E., & Lundbye-Christensen, S. (2010). Maternal blood glucose in diabetic pregnancies and cognitive performance in offspring in young adulthood: A Danish cohort study. *Diabetic Medicine, 27,* 786–790.

Nielsen, L. S., Danielsen, K. V., & Sørensen, T. I. (2011). Short sleep duration as a possible cause of obesity: Critical analysis of the epidemiological evidence. *Obesity Reviews, 12,* 78–92.

Nielsen, M. (2012). Imitation, pretend play, and childhood: Essential elements in the evolution of human culture? *Journal of Comparative Psychology, 126,* 170–181.

Nielsen, M., & Christie, T. (2008). Adult modeling facilitates young children's generation of novel pretend acts. *Infant and Child Development, 17,* 151–162.

Nielsen, N. M., Hansen, A. V., Simonsen, J., & Hviid, A. (2011). Prenatal stress and risk of infectious diseases in offspring. *American Journal of Epidemiology, 173,* 990–997.

Nievar, M. A., & Becker, B. J. (2008). Sensitivity as a privileged predictor of attachment: A second perspective on De Wolff & van IJzendoorn's meta-analysis. *Social Development, 17,* 102–114.

Nikulina, V., & Widom, C. S. (2013). Child maltreatment and executive functioning in middle adulthood: A prospective examination. *Neuropsychology, 27,* 417–427.

Nippold, M. A. (1999). Word definition in adolescents as a function of reading proficiency: A research note. *Child Language Teaching and Therapy, 15,* 171–176.

Nippold, M. A. (2000). Language development during the adolescent years: Aspects of pragmatics, syntax, and semantics. *Topics in Language Disorders, 20,* 15–28.

Nippold, M. A., Allen, M. M., & Kirsch, D. I. (2001). Proverb comprehension as a function of reading proficiency in preadolescents. *Language, Speech and Hearing Services in the Schools, 32,* 90–100.

Nippold, M. A., Taylor, C. L., & Baker, J. M. (1996). Idiom understanding in Australian youth: A cross-cultural comparison. *Journal of Speech and Hearing Research, 39,* 442–447.

Nisbett, R. E. (2009). *Intelligence and how to get it.* New York: Norton.

Nisbett, R. E., Aronson, J., Blair, C., Dickens, W., Flynn, J., Halpern, D. F., et al. (2012). Intelligence: New findings and theoretical developments. *American Psychologist, 67,* 130–159.

Nishitani, S., Miyamura, T., Tagawa, M., Sumi, M., Takase, R., Doi, H., Moriuchi, H., & Shinohara, K. (2009). The calming effect of a maternal breast milk odor on the human newborn infant. *Neuroscience Research, 63,* 66–71.

Noble, K. G., Fifer, W. P., Rauh, V. A., Nomura, Y., & Andrews, H. F. (2012). Academic achievement varies with gestational age among children born at term. *Pediatrics, 130,* e257–e264.

Noll, J. G., & Shenk, C. E. (2013). Teen birth rates in sexually abused and neglected females. *Pediatrics, 131,* e1181–e1187.

Noonan, C. W., Kathman, S. J., Sarasua, S. M., & White, M. C. (2003). Influence of environmental zinc on the association between environmental and biological measures of lead in children. *Journal of Exposure Analysis and Environmental Epidemiology, 13,* 318–323.

Noroozian, M., Shadloo, B., Shakiba, A., & Panahi, P. (2012). Educational achievement and other controversial issues in left-handedness: A neuropsychological and psychiatric view. In T. Dutta & M. K. Mandal (Eds.), *Bias in human behavior* (pp. 41–82). Hauppauge, NY: Nova Science.

Northstone, K., Joinson, C., Emmett, P., Ness, A., & Paus, T. (2012). Are dietary patterns in childhood associated with IQ at 8 years of age? A population-based cohort study. *Journal of Epidemiological Community Health, 66,* 624–628.

Norwitz, E. R. (2009). A blood test to predict preterm birth: Don't mess with maternal—fetal stress. *Journal of Clinical Endocrinology and Metabolism, 94,* 1886–1889.

Nosarti, C., Walsh, M., Rushe, T. M., Rifkin, L., Wyatt, J., Murray, R. M., et al. (2011). Neonatal ultrasound results following very preterm birth predict adolescent behavioral and cognitive outcome. *Developmental Neuropsychology, 36,* 118–135.

Nosek, B. A., Smyth, F. L., Siriram, N., Lindner, N. M., Devos, T., Ayala, A., et al. (2009). National differences in gender–science stereotypes predict national sex differences in science and math achievement. *Proceedings of the National Academy of Sciences, 106,* 10593–10597.

Noterdaeme, M., Mildenberger, K., Minow, F., & Amorosa, H. (2002). Evaluation of neuromotor deficits in children with autism and children with a specific speech and language disorder. *European Child and Adolescent Psychiatry, 11,* 219–225.

Nowicki, E. A., Brown, J., & Stepien, M. (2014). Children's thoughts on the social exclusion of peers with intellectual or learning disabilities. *Journal of Intellectual Disability Research, 58,* 346–357.

Nucci, L. (2001). *Education in the moral domain.* New York: Cambridge University Press.

Nucci, L. (2005). Culture, context, and the psychological sources of human rights concepts. In W. Edelstein & G. Nunner-Winkler (Eds.), *Morality in context* (pp. 365–394). Amsterdam: Elsevier.

Nucci, L. (2008). *Nice is not enough: Facilitating moral development.* Upper Saddle River, NJ: Prentice Hall.

Nucci, L. P., & Gingo, M. (2011). The development of moral reasoning. In U. Goswami (Ed.), *The Wiley-Blackwell handbook of childhood cognitive development* (2nd ed., pp. 420–444). Hoboken, NJ: Wiley.

Nunez-Smith, M., Wolf, E., Huang, H. M., Chen, P. G., Lee, L., Emanuel, E. J., et al. (2008). *The impact of media on child and adolescent health.* Retrieved from www.commonsensemedia.org.

Nuttall, R. L., Casey, M. B., & Pezaris, E. (2005). Spatial ability as a mediator of gender differences on mathematics tests: A biological–environmental framework. In A. M. Gallagher & C. J. Kaufman (Eds.), *Gender differences in mathematics: An integrated psychological approach* (pp. 121–142). New York: Cambridge University Press.

NYC (New York City) Department of Education. (2014). *Promotion standards.* Retrieved from schools.nyc.gov/RulesPolicies/default.htm

Nye, B., Hedges, L. V., & Konstantopoulos, S. (2001). Are effects of small classes cumulative? Evidence from a Tennessee experiment. *Journal of Educational Research, 94,* 336–345.

O

Oakes, L. M., Coppage, D. J., & Dingel, A. (1997). By land or by sea: The role of perceptual similarity in infants' categorization of animals. *Developmental Psychology, 33,* 396–407.

Obeidallah, D., Brennan, R. T., Brooks-Gunn, J., & Earls, F. (2004). Links between pubertal timing and neighborhood contexts: Implications for girls' violent behavior. *Journal of the American Academy of Child and Adolescent Psychiatry, 43,* 1460–1468.

Oberecker, R., & Friederici, A. D. (2006). Syntactic event-related potential components in 24-month-olds' sentence comprehension. *NeuroReport, 17,* 1017–1021.

Obler, L. K. (2013). Developments in the adult years. In J. B. Gleason (Ed.), *The development of language* (8th ed., pp. 366–392). Upper Saddle River, NJ: Pearson.

Obradović, J., Long, J. D., Cutuli, J. J., Chan, C.-K., Hinz, E., Heistad, D., & Masten, A. S. (2009). Academic achievement of homeless and highly mobile children in an urban school district: Longitudinal evidence on risk, growth, and resilience. *Development and Psychopathology, 21,* 493–518.

Obradović, J., & Masten, A. S. (2007). Developmental antecedents of young adult civic engagement. *Applied Developmental Science, 11,* 2–19.

O'Brien, M., Weaver, J. M., Nelson, J. A., Calkins, S. D., Leerkes, E. M., & Marcovitch, S. (2011). Longitudinal associations between children's understanding of emotions and theory of mind. *Cognition and Emotion, 25,* 1074–1086.

O'Connor, E., & McCartney, K. (2007). Examining teacher–child relationships and achievement as part of an ecological model of development. *American Educational Research Journal, 44,* 340–369.

O'Connor, T. G., & Croft, C. M. (2001). A twin study of attachment in preschool children. *Child Development, 72,* 1501–1511.

O'Connor, T. G., Marvin, R. S., Rutter, M., Olrich, J. T., Britner, P. A., & the English and Romanian Adoptees Study Team. (2003). Child–parent attachment following early institutional deprivation. *Development and Psychopathology, 15,* 19–38.

O'Connor, T. G., Rutter, M., Beckett, C., Keaveney, L., Dreppner, J. M., & the English and Romanian Adoptees Study Team. (2000). The effects of global severe privation on cognitive competence: Extension and longitudinal follow-up. *Child Development, 71,* 376–390.

O'Dea, J. A. (2003). Why do kids eat healthful food? Perceived benefits of and barriers to healthful eating and physical activity among children and adolescents. *Journal of the American Dietetic Association, 103,* 497–501.

O'Dea, J. A. (2012). Body image and self-esteem. In T. F. Cash (Ed.), *Encyclopedia of body image and human appearance* (pp. 141–147). London: Elsevier.

OECD (Organisation for Economic Cooperation and Development). (2012). *PISA 2012 results.* Retrieved from www.oecd.org/pisa/keyfindings/pisa-2012-results.htm

OECD (Organisation for Economic Cooperation and Development). (2013a). *Education at a Glance 2013: OECD Indicators.* Retrieved from www.oecd.org/edu/eag2013

OECD (Organisation for Economic Cooperation and Development). (2013b). *Health at a glance 2013: OECD indicators.* Retrieved from www.oecd.org/els/health-systems/Health-at-a-Glance-2013.pdf

OECD (Organisation for Economic Cooperation and Development). (2013c). *OECD health statistics 2013–Frequently requested data.* Retrieved from www.oecd.org/social/soc/oecdfamilydatabase.htm

OECD (Organisation for Economic Cooperation and Development). (2014). *OECD family data base.* Retrieved from www.oecd.org/social/soc/oecdfamilydatabase.htm

Offer, S. (2013). Family time activities and adolescents' emotional well-being. *Journal of Marriage and Family, 75,* 26–41.

Office of Head Start. (2014). *Head Start program facts: Fiscal year 2013.* Retrieved from eclkc.ohs.acf.hhs.gov/hslc/data/factsheets/2013-hs-program-factsheet.html

Ogan, A., & Berk, L. E. (2009, April). *Effects of two approaches to make-believe play training on self-regulation in Head Start children.* Paper presented at the biennial meeting of the Society for Research in Child Development, Denver, CO.

Ogbu, J. U. (2003). *Black American students in an affluent suburb: A study of academic disengagement.* Mahwah, NJ: Erlbaum.

Ogden, C. L., Carroll, M. D., Kit, B. K., & Flegal, K. M. (2014). Prevalence of childhood and adult obesity. *Journal of the American Medical Association, 311,* 806–814.

Ohannessian, C. M., & Hesselbrock, V. M. (2008). Paternal alcoholism and youth substance abuse: The indirect effects of negative affect, conduct problems, and risk taking. *Journal of Adolescent Health, 42,* 198–200.

Ohgi, S., Arisawa, K., Takahashi, T., Kusumoto, T., Goto, Y., Akiyama, T., & Saito, H. (2003a). Neonatal behavioral assessment scale as a predictor of later developmental disabilities of low-birth-weight and/or premature infants. *Brain and Development, 25,* 313–321.

Ohgi, S., Takahashi, T., Nugent, J. K., Arisawa, K., & Akiyama, T. (2003b). Neonatal behavioral characteristics and later behavioral problems. *Clinical Pediatrics, 42,* 679–686.

Ojha, S., Robinson, L., Symonds, M. E., & Budge, H. (2013). Suboptimal maternal nutrition affects offspring health in adult life. *Early Human Development, 89,* 909–913.

Okagaki, L., & Sternberg, R. J. (1993). Parental beliefs and children's school performance. *Child Development, 64,* 36–56.

Okami, P., Weisner, T., & Olmstead, R. (2002). Outcome correlates of parent–child bedsharing: An eighteen-year longitudinal study. *Developmental and Behavioral Pediatrics, 23,* 244–253.

Olafson, E. (2011). Child sexual abuse: Demography, impact, and interventions. *Journal of Child and Adolescent Trauma, 4,* 8–21.

Olds, D. L., Eckenrode, J., Henderson, C., Kitzman, H., Cole, R., Luckey, D., et al. (2009). Preventing child abuse and neglect with home visiting by nurses. In K. A. Dodge & D. L. Coleman (Eds.), *Preventing child maltreatment* (pp. 29–54). New York: Guilford.

Olds, D. L., Kitzman, H., Cole, R., Robinson, J., Sidora, K., Luckey, D. W., et al. (2004). Effects of nurse home-visiting on maternal life course and child development: Age 6 follow-up results of a randomized trial. *Pediatrics, 114,* 1550–1559.

Olds, D. L., Kitzman, H., Hanks, C., Cole, R., Anson, E., Sidora-Arcoleo, K., et al. (2007). Effects of nurse home visiting on maternal and child functioning: Age-9 follow-up of a randomized trial. *Pediatrics, 120,* e832–e845.

Olds, D. L., Robinson, J., O'Brien, R., Luckey, D. W., Pettitt, L. M., Henderson, C. R., Jr., et al. (2002). Home visiting by paraprofessionals and by nurses: A randomized, controlled trial. *Pediatrics, 110,* 486–496.

Olfman, S., & Robbins, B. D. (Eds.). (2012). *Drugging our children.* New York: Praeger.

Olineck, K. M., & Poulin-Dubois, D. (2009). Infants' understanding of intention from 10 to 14 months: Interrelations among violation of expectancy and imitation tasks. *Infant Behavior and Development, 32,* 404–415.

Ollendick, T. H., King, N. J., & Muris, P. (2002). Fears and phobias in children: Phenomenology, epidemiology, and aetiology. *Child and Adolescent Mental Health, 7,* 98–106.

Oller, D. K. (2000). *The emergence of the speech capacity.* Mahwah, NJ: Erlbaum.

Olson, D., Sikka, R. S., Hayman, J., Novak, M., & Stavig, C. (2009). Exercise in pregnancy. *Current Sports Medicine Reports, 8,* 147–153.

Olson, S. L., Lopez-Duran, N., Lunkenheimer, E. S., Chang, H., & Sameroff, A. J. (2011). Individual differences in the development of early peer aggression: Integrating contributions of self-regulation, theory of mind, and parenting. *Development and Psychopathology, 23,* 253–266.

Omar, H., McElderry, D., & Zakharia, R. (2003). Educating adolescents about puberty: What are we missing? *International Journal of Adolescent Medicine and Health, 15,* 79–83.

Ondrusek, N., Abramovitch, R., Pencharz, P., & Koren, G. (1998). Empirical examination of the ability of children to consent to clinical research. *Journal of Medical Ethics, 24,* 158–165.

O'Neil, R., Welsh, M., Parke, R. D., Wang, S., & Strand, C. (1997). A longitudinal assessment of the academic correlates of early peer acceptance and rejection. *Journal of Clinical Child Psychology, 26,* 290–303.

O'Neill, M., Bard, K. A., Kinnell, M., & Fluck, M. (2005). Maternal gestures with 20-month-old infants in two contexts. *Developmental Science, 8,* 352–359.

Ong, K. K., Ahmed, M. L., & Dunger, D. B. (2006). Lessons from large population studies on timing and tempo of puberty (secular trends and relation to body size): The European trend. *Molecular and Cellular Endocrinology, 254–255,* 8–12.

Ontai, L. L., & Thompson, R. A. (2008). Attachment, parent–child discourse and theory-of-mind development. *Social Development, 17,* 47–60.

Oosterwegel, A., & Openheimer, L. (1993). *The self-system: Developmental changes between and within self-concepts.* Hillsdale, NJ: Erlbaum.

Ophir, E., Nass, C., & Wagner, A. D. (2009). Cognitive control in media multitaskers. *Proceedings of the National Academy of Sciences, 106,* 15583–15587.

Opinion Research Corporation. (2009). *American teens say they want quality time with parents.* Retrieved from www.napsnet.com/pdf_archive/47/68753.pdf

Ordonana, J. R., Caspi, A., & Moffitt, T. E. (2008). Unintentional injuries in a twin study of preschool children: Environmental, not genetic risk factors. *Journal of Pediatric Psychology, 33,* 185–194.

O'Reilly, A. W. (1995). Using representations: Comprehension and production of actions with imagined objects. *Child Development, 66,* 999–1010.

Ornstein, P. A., Haden, C. A., & Elischberger, H. B. (2006). Children's memory development: Remembering the past and preparing for the future. In E. Bialystok & F. I. M. Craik (Eds.), *Lifespan cognition: Mechanisms of change* (pp. 143–161). New York: Oxford University Press.

Orobio de Castro, B., Brendgen, M., Van Boxtel, H., Vitaro, F., & Schaepers, L. (2007). "Accept me, or else . . .": Disputed overestimation of social competence predicts increases in proactive aggression. *Journal of Abnormal Child Psychology, 35,* 165–178.

Orobio de Castro, B., Veerman, J. W., Koops, W., Bosch, J. D., & Monshouwer, H. J. (2002). Hostile attribution of intent and aggressive behavior: A meta-analysis. *Child Development, 73,* 916–934.

Orth, U., Robins, R. W., & Widaman, K. F. (2012). Lifespan development of self-esteem and its effects on important life outcomes. *Personality Processes and Individual Differences, 102,* 1271–1288.

Orth, U., Trzesniewski, K. H., & Robins, R. W. (2010). Self-esteem development from young adulthood to old age: A cohort-sequential longitudinal study. *Journal of Personality and Social Psychology, 98,* 645–658.

Osherson, D. N., & Markman, E. M. (1975). Language and the ability to evaluate contradictions and tautologies. *Cognition, 2,* 213–226.

Oshima-Takane, Y., & Robbins, M. (2003). Linguistic environment of secondborn children. *First Language, 23,* 21–40.

Osterholm, E. A., Hostinar, C. E., & Gunnar, M. R. (2012). Alterations in stress responses of the hypothalamic-pituitary-adrenal axis in small for gestational age infants. *Psychoneuroendocrinology, 37,* 1719–1725.

Osterman M. J., & Martin J. A. (2011). Epidural and spinal anesthesia use during labor. *National Vital Statistics Report, 59*(5), 1–13.

Ostrov, J. M., Crick, N. R., & Stauffacher, K. (2006). Relational aggression in sibling and peer relationships during early childhood. *Applied Developmental Psychology, 27,* 241–253.

Ostrov, J. M., Gentile, D. A., & Mullins, A. D. (2013). Evaluating the effect of educational media exposure on aggression in early childhood. *Journal of Applied Developmental Psychology, 34,* 38–44.

Ostrov, J. M., Murray-Close, D., Godleski, S. A., & Hart, E. J. (2013). Prospective associations between forms and functions of aggression and social and affective processes during early childhood. *Journal of Experimental Child Psychology, 116,* 19–36.

Otis, N., Grouzet, F. M. E., & Pelletier, L. G. (2005). Latent motivational change in an academic setting: A three-year longitudinal study. *Journal of Educational Psychology, 97,* 170–183.

Otter, M., Schrander-Stempel, C. T. R. M., Didden, R., & Curfs, L. M. G. (2013). The psychiatric phenotype in triple X syndrome: New hypotheses illustrated in two cases. *Developmental Neurorehabilitation, 15,* 233–238.

Oude, L. H., Baur, L., Jansen, H., Shrewsbury, V. A., O'Malley, C., Stolk, R. P., & Summerbell, C. D. (2009). Interventions for treating obesity in children. *Cochrane Database of Systematic Reviews,* Issue 1, CD001872.

Ouko, L. A., Shantikumar, K., Knezovich, J., Haycock, P., Schnugh, D. J., & Ramsay, M. (2009). Effect of alcohol consumption on CpG methylation in the differentially methylated regions of H19 and IG-DMR in male gametes: Implications for fetal alcohol spectrum disorders. *Alcoholism, Clinical and Experimental Research, 33,* 1615–1627.

Overton, W. F. (2010). Life-span development: Concepts and issues. In W. F. Overton (Ed.), *Handbook of lifespan development: Cognition, biology, and methods* (pp. 1–29). Hoboken, NJ: Wiley.

Owen, C. G., Whincup, P. H., Kaye, S. J., Martin, R. M., Smith, G. D., Cook, D. G., et al. (2008). Does initial breastfeeding lead to lower blood cholesterol in adult life? A quantitative review of the evidence. *American Journal of Clinical Nutrition, 88,* 305–314.

Oyserman, D. (2007). Social identity and self-regulation. In A. Kruglanski & E. T. Higgins (Eds.), *Handbook of social psychology: Basic principles* (2nd ed., pp. 432–453). New York: Guilford.

Oyserman, D., Bybee, D., Mowbray, C., & Hart-Johnson, T. (2005). When mothers have serious mental health problems: Parenting as a proximal mediator. *Journal of Adolescence, 28,* 443–463.

Özçaliskan, S. (2005). On learning to draw the distinction between physical and metaphorical motion: Is metaphor an early emerging cognitive and linguistic capacity? *Journal of Child Language, 32,* 291–318.

Ozer, E. M., & Irwin, C. E., Jr. (2009). Adolescent and young adult health: From basic health status to clinical interventions. In R. M. Lerner & L. Steinberg (Eds.), *Handbook of adolescent psychology: Vol. 1. Individual bases of adolescent development* (pp. 618–641). Hoboken, NJ: Wiley.

P

Pacella, R., McLellan, M., Grice, K., Del Bono, E. A., Wiggs, J. L., & Gwiazda, J. E. (1999). Role of genetic factors in the etiology of juvenile-onset myopia based on a longitudinal study of refractive error. *Optometry and Vision Science, 76,* 381–386.

Padilla-Walker, L. M. (2008). "My mom makes me so angry!": Adolescent perceptions of mother–child interactions as correlates of adolescent emotions. *Social Development, 17,* 306–325.

Pagani, L. S., Japel, C., Vitaro, F., Tremblay, R. E., Larose, S., & McDuff, P. (2008). When predictions fail: The case of unexpected pathways toward high school dropout. *Journal of Social Issues, 64,* 175–193.

Pager, D., Western, B., & Bonikowski, B. (2009). Discrimination in a low-wage labor market: A field experiment. *American Sociological Review, 74,* 777–799.

Paik, A. (2010). "Hookups," dating, and relationship quality: Does the type of sexual involvement matter? *Social Science Research, 39,* 739–753.

Palacios, J., & Brodzinsky, D. M. (2010). Adoption research: Trends, topics, outcomes. *International Journal of Behavioral Development, 34,* 270–284.

Palincsar, A. S., & Herrenkohl, L. R. (1999). Designing collaborative contexts: Lessons from three research programs. In A. M. O'Donnell & A. King (Eds.), *Cognitive perspectives on peer learning. The Rutgers Invitational Symposium on Education Series* (pp. 151–177). Mahwah, NJ: Erlbaum.

Palosaari, E., Punamäki, R., Diab, M., & Qouta, A. (2013). Posttraumatic cognitions and posttraumatic stress symptoms among war-affected children: A cross-lagged analysis. *Journal of Abnormal Psychology, 122,* 656–661.

Pan, B. A., & Snow, C. E. (1999). The development of conversation and discourse skills. In M. Barrett (Ed.), *The development of language* (pp. 229–249). Hove, UK: Psychology Press.

Pan, C. W., Ramamurthy, D., & Saw, S. M. (2012). Worldwide prevalence and risk factors for myopia. *Ophthalmic and Physiological Optics, 32,* 3–16.

Pan, H. W. (1994). Children's play in Taiwan. In J. L. Roopnarine, J. E. Johnson, & F. H. Hooper (Eds.), *Children's play in diverse cultures* (pp. 31–50). Albany: SUNY Press.

Papadakis, A. A., Prince, R. P., Jones, N. P., & Strauman, T. J. (2006). Self-regulation, rumination, and vulnerability to depression in adolescent girls. *Development and Psychopathology, 18,* 815–829.

Papousek, M. (2007). Communication in early infancy: An arena of intersubjective learning. *Infant Behavior and Development, 30,* 258–266.

Paradis, J. (2007). Second language acquisition in childhood. In E. Hoff & M. Shatz (Eds.), *Blackwell handbook of language development* (pp. 387–405). Malden, MA: Blackwell.

Paradis, J., Genesee, F., & Crago, M. B. (2011). *Dual language development and disorders: A handbook on bilingualism and learning* (2nd ed.). Baltimore, MD: Brookes.

Paradise, R., & Rogoff, B. (2009). Side by side: Learning by observing and pitching in. *Ethos, 27,* 102–138.

Parameswaran, G. (2003). Experimenter instructions as a mediator in the effects of culture on mapping one's neighborhood. *Journal of Environmental Psychology, 23,* 409–417.

Parent, A., Teilmann, G., Juul, A., Skakkebaek, N. E., Toppari, J., & Bourguignon, J. (2003). The timing of normal puberty and the age limits of sexual precocity: Variations around the world, secular trends, and changes after migration. *Endocrine Reviews, 24,* 668–693.

Pargas, R. C., Brennan, P. A., Hammen, C., & Le Brocque, R. (2010). Resilience to maternal depression in young adulthood. *Developmental Psychology, 46,* 805–814.

Paris, S. G., & Paris, A. G. (2006). Assessments of early reading. In K. A. Renninger & I. E. Sigel (Eds.), *Handbook of child psychology: Vol. 4. Child psychology in practice* (6th ed., pp. 48–74). Hoboken, NJ: Wiley.

Parish-Morris, J., Golinkoff, R. M., & Hirsh-Pasek, K. (2013). From coo to code: A brief story of language development. In P. D. Zelazo (Ed.), *Oxford handbook of developmental psychology: Vol. 1. Body and mind* (pp. 867–908). New York: Oxford University Press.

Parish-Morris, J., Pruden, S., Ma, W., Hirsh-Pasek, K., & Golinkoff, R. M. (2010). A world of relations: Relational words. In B. Malt & P. Wolf (Eds.), *Words and the mind: How words capture human experience* (pp. 219–242). New York: Oxford University Press.

Park, W. (2009). Acculturative stress and mental health among Korean adolescents in the United States. *Journal of Human Behavior in the Social Environment, 19,* 626–634.

Parke, R. D. (2002). Fathers and families. In M. H. Bornstein (Ed.), *Handbook of parenting: Vol. 3* (2nd ed., pp. 27–73). Mahwah, NJ: Erlbaum.

Parke, R. D., & Buriel, R. (2006). Socialization in the family: Ethnic and ecological perspectives. In N. Eisenberg (Ed.), *Handbook of child psychology: Vol. 3. Social, emotional, and personality development* (6th ed., pp. 429–504). Hoboken, NJ: Wiley.

Parke, R. D., Coltrane, S., Fabricius, W., Powers, J., & Adams, M. (2004a). Assessing father involvement in Mexican-American families. In R. Day & M. E. Lamb (Eds.), *Conceptualizing and measuring paternal involvement* (pp. 17–38). Mahwah, NJ: Erlbaum.

Parke, R. D., Simpkins, S. D., McDowell, D. J., Kim, M., Killian, C., Dennis, J., Flyr, M. L., Wild, M., & Rah, Y. (2004b). Relative contributions of families and peers to children's social development. In P. K. Smith & C. H. Hart (Eds.), *Blackwell handbook of childhood social development* (pp. 156–177). Malden, MA: Blackwell.

Parker, J. G., Low, C. M., Walker, A. R., & Gamm, B. K. (2005). Friendship jealousy in young adolescents: Individual differences and links to sex, self-esteem, aggression, and social adjustment. *Developmental Psychology, 41,* 235–250.

Parker, P. D., Schoon, I., Tsai, Y-M., Nagy, G., Trautwein, U., & Eccles, J. (2012). Achievement, agency, gender, and socioeconomic background as predictors of postschool choices: A multicontext study. *Developmental Psychology, 48,* 1629–1642.

Parker, S. W., Nelson, C. A., & the Bucharest Early Intervention Project Core Group. (2005). The impact of early institutional rearing on the ability to discriminate facial expressions of emotion: An event-related potential study. *Child Development, 76,* 54–72.

Parten, M. (1932). Social participation among preschool children. *Journal of Abnormal and Social Psychology, 27,* 243–269.

Pascalis, O., de Haan, M., & Nelson, C. A. (1998). Long-term recognition memory for faces assessed by visual paired comparison in 3- and 6-month-old infants. *Journal of Experimental Psychology: Learning, Memory, and Cognition, 24,* 249–260.

Pascalis, O., de Haan, M., & Nelson, C. A. (2002). Is face processing species-specific during the first year of life? *Science, 296,* 1321–1323.

Pasley, K., & Garneau, C. (2012). Remarriage and stepfamily life. In F. Walsh (Ed.), *Normal family processes: Growing diversity and complexity* (4th ed., pp. 149–171). New York: Guilford.

Patel, S., Gaylord, S., & Fagen, J. (2013). Generalization of deferred imitation in 6-, 9-, and 12-month-old infants using visual and auditory contexts. *Infant Behavior and Development, 36,* 25–31.

Pathman, T., Larkina, M., Burch, M. M., & Bauer, P. J. (2013). Young children's memory for the times of personal past events. *Journal of Cognition and Development, 14,* 120–140.

Patock-Peckham, J. A., & Morgan-Lopez, A. A. (2009). Mediational links among parenting styles, perceptions of parental confidence, self-esteem, and depression on alcohol-related problems in emerging adulthood. *Journal of Studies on Alcohol and Drugs, 70,* 215–226.

Patrick, M. E., & Schulenberg, J. E. (2013). How trajectories of reasons for alcohol use related to trajectories of binge drinking: National panel data spanning late adolescence to early adulthood. *Developmental Psychology, 47,* 311–317.

Patrick, M. E., & Schulenberg, J. E. (2014). Prevalence and predictors of adolescent alcohol use and binge drinking in the United States. *Alcohol Research: Current Reviews, 35,* 193–200.

Patrick, R. B., & Gibbs, J. C. (2011). Inductive discipline, parental expression of disappointed expectations, and moral identity in adolescence. *Journal of Youth and Adolescence, 41,* 973–983.

Pattenden, S., Antova, T., Neuberger, M., Nikiforov, B., De Sario, M., Grize, L., & Heinrich, J. (2006). Parental smoking and children's respiratory health: Independent effects of prenatal and postnatal exposure. *Tobacco Control, 15,* 294–301.

Patterson, C. J. (2013). Children of lesbian and gay parents: Psychology, law, and policy. *Psychology of Sexual Orientation and Gender Diversity, 1*(S), 27–34.

Patterson, G. R., & Fisher, P. A. (2002). Recent developments in our understanding of parenting: Bidirectional effects, causal models, and the search for parsimony. In M. H. Bornstein (Ed.), *Handbook of parenting* (Vol. 5, pp. 59–88). Mahwah, NJ: Erlbaum.

Patterson, G. R., & Yoerger, K. (2002). A developmental model for early- and late-onset delinquency. In J. B. Reid & G. R. Patterson (Eds.), *Antisocial behavior in children and adolescents* (pp. 147–172). Washington, DC: American Psychological Association.

Patton, G. C., Coffey, C., Cappa, C., Currie, D., Riley, L., Gore, F., et al. (2012). Health of the world's adolescents: A synthesis of internationally comparable data. *Lancet, 379,* 1665–1675.

Patton, G. C., Coffey, C., Carlin, J. B., Sawyer, S. M., Williams, J., Olsson, C. A., et al. (2011). Overweight and obesity between adolescence and young adulthood: A 10-year prospective cohort study. *Journal of Adolescent Health, 48,* 275–280.

Paukner, A., Ferrari, P. F., & Suomi, S. J. (2011). Delayed imitation of lipsmacking gestures by infant rhesus macaques (*Macaca mulatta*). *PLOS ONE, 6*(12): e28848.

Paul, J. J., & Cillessen, A. H. N. (2003). Dynamics of peer victimization in early adolescence: Results from a four-year longitudinal study. *Journal of Applied School Psychology, 19,* 25–43.

Paulussen-Hoogeboom, M. C., Stams, G. J. J. M., Hermanns, J. M. A., & Peetsma, T. T. D. (2007). Child negative emotionality and parenting from infancy to preschool: A meta-analytic review. *Developmental Psychology, 43,* 438–453.

Pea, R., Nass, C., Meheula, L., Rance, M., Kumar, A., Bamford, H., et al. (2012). Media use, face-to-face communication, media multitasking, and social well-being among 8- to 12-year-old girls. *Developmental Psychology, 48,* 327–336.

Pearlman, D. N., Zierler, S., Meersman, S., Kim, H. K., Viner-Brown, & Caron, C. (2006). Race disparities in childhood asthma: Does where you live matter? *Journal of the National Medical Association, 98,* 239–247.

Pederson, D. R., & Moran, G. (1996). Expressions of the attachment relationship outside of the Strange Situation. *Child Development, 67,* 915–927.

Pedersen, S., Vitaro, F., Barker, E. D., & Anne, I. H. (2007). The timing of middle-childhood peer rejection and friendship: Linking early behavior to early adolescent adjustment. *Child Development, 78,* 1037–1051.

Peguero, A. A. (2011). Violence, schools, and dropping out: Racial and ethnic disparities in the educational consequence of student victimization. *Journal of Interpersonal Violence, 26,* 3753–3772.

Peirano, P., Algarin, C., & Uauy, R. (2003). Sleep–wake states and their regulatory mechanisms throughout early human development. *Journal of Pediatrics, 143,* S70–S79.

Pellegrini, A. D. (2003). Perceptions and functions of play and real fighting in early adolescence. *Child Development, 74,* 1522–1533.

Pellegrini, A. D. (2004). Rough-and-tumble play from childhood through adolescence: Development and possible functions. In P. K. Smith & C. H. Hart (Eds.), *Blackwell handbook of childhood social development* (pp. 438–453). Malden, MA: Blackwell.

Pellegrini, A. D., Huberty, P. D., & Jones, I. (1995). The effects of recess timing on children's playground and classroom behaviors. *American Educational Research Journal, 32,* 845–864.

Pellegrini, A. D., Kato, K., Blatchford, P., & Baines, E. (2002). A short-term longitudinal study of children's playground games across the first year of school: Implications for social competence and adjustment to school. *American Educational Research Journal, 39,* 991–1015.

Pellicano, E., Maybery, M., Durkin, K., & Maley, A. (2006). Multiple cognitive capabilities/deficits in children with an autism spectrum disorder: "Weak" central coherence and its relationship to theory of mind and executive control. *Development and Psychopathology, 18,* 77–98.

Penner, A. M. (2003). International gender item difficulty interactions in mathematics and science achievement tests. *Journal of Educational Psychology, 95,* 650–655.

Pennisi, E. (2012). ENCODE Project writes eulogy for junk DNA. *Science, 337,* 1160–1161.

Penny, H., & Haddock, G. (2007). Anti-fat prejudice among children: The "mere proximity" effect in 5–10 year olds. *Journal of Experimental Social Psychology, 43,* 678–683.

Peralta de Mendoza, O. A., & Salsa, A. M. (2003). Instruction in early comprehension and use of a symbol–referent relation. *Cognitive Development, 18,* 269–284.

Perlmutter, M. (1984). Continuities and discontinuities in early human memory: Paradigms, processes, and performances. In R. V. Kail, Jr., & N. R. Spear (Eds.), *Comparative perspectives on the development of memory* (pp. 253–287). Hillsdale, NJ: Erlbaum.

Perren, S., von Wyl, A., Burgin, D., Simoni, H., & von Klitzing, K. (2005). Depressive symptoms and psychosocial stress across the transition to parenthood: Associations with parental psychopathology and child difficulty. *Journal of Psychosomatic Obstetrics and Gynaecology, 26,* 173–183.

Perry, G. H., & Dominy, N. J. (2009). Evolution of the human pygmy phenotype. *Trends in Ecology and Evolution, 24,* 218–225.

Perry, W. G., Jr. (1998). *Forms of intellectual and ethical development in the college years: A scheme.* San Francisco: Jossey-Bass. (Originally published 1970.)

Perry, W. G., Jr. (1981). Cognitive and ethical growth. In A. Chickering (Ed.), *The modern American college* (pp. 76–116). San Francisco: Jossey-Bass.

Pesonen, A.-K., Räikkönen, K., Heinonen, K., & Komsi, N. (2008). A transactional model of temperamental development: Evidence of a relationship between child temperament and maternal stress over five years. *Social Development, 17,* 326–340.

Petch, J., & Halford, W. K. (2008). Psycho-education to enhance couples' transition to parenthood. *Clinical Psychology Review, 28,* 1125–1137.

Peters, R. D. (2005). A community-based approach to promoting resilience in young children, their families, and their neighborhoods. In R. D. Peters, B. Leadbeater, & R. J. McMahon (Eds.), *Resilience in children, families, and communities: Linking context to practice and policy* (pp. 157–176). New York: Kluwer Academic.

Peters, R. D., Bradshaw, A. J., Petrunka, K., Nelson, G., Herry, Y., Craig, W. M., et al. (2010). The Better Beginnings, Better Futures Project: Findings from grade 3 to grade 9. *Monographs of the Society for Research in Child Development, 75* (3, Serial No. 297).

Peters, R. D., Petrunka, K., & Arnold, R. (2003). The Better Beginnings, Better Futures Project: A universal, comprehensive, community-based prevention approach for primary school children and their families. *Journal of Clinical Child and Adolescent Psychology, 32,* 215–227.

Peterson, C. (2012). Children's autobiographical memories across the years: Forensic implications of childhood amnesia and eyewitness memory for stressful events. *Developmental Review, 32,* 287–306.

Peterson, C., Parsons, T., & Dean, M. (2004). Providing misleading and reinstatement information a year after it happened: Effects on long-term memory. *Memory, 12,* 1–13.

Peterson, C., & Rideout, R. (1998). Memory for medical emergencies experienced by 1- and 2-year-olds. *Developmental Psychology, 34,* 1059–1072.

Peterson, C., & Roberts, C. (2003). Like mother, like daughter: Similarities in narrative style. *Developmental Psychology, 39,* 551–562.

Peterson, C., Warren, K. L., & Short, M. M. (2011). Infantile amnesia across the years: A 2-year follow-up of children's earliest memories. *Child Development, 82*, 1092–1105.

Petitto, L. A., Holowka, S., Sergio, L. E., Levy, B., & Ostry, D. J. (2004). Baby hands that move to the rhythm of language: Hearing babies acquiring sign languages babble silently on the hands. *Cognition, 93*, 43–73.

Petitto, L. A., Holowka, S., Sergio, L. E., & Ostry, D. (2001). Language rhythms in babies' hand movements. *Nature, 413*, 35–36.

Petitto, L. A., & Marentette, P. F. (1991). Babbling in the manual mode: Evidence for the ontogeny of language. *Science, 251*, 1493–1496.

Petrill, S. A., & Deater-Deckard, K. (2004). The heritability of general cognitive ability: A within-family adoption design. *Intelligence, 32*, 403–409.

Pettigrew, T. F., & Tropp, L. R. (2006). A meta-analytic test of intergroup contact theory. *Journal of Personality and Social Psychology, 90*, 751–783.

Pettit, G. S. (2004). Violent children in developmental perspective. *Current Directions in Psychological Science, 13*, 194–197.

Pettit, G. S., Brown, E. G., Mize, J., & Lindsey, E. (1998). Mothers' and fathers' socializing behaviors in three contexts: Links with children's peer competence. *Merrill-Palmer Quarterly, 44*, 173–193.

Pew Research Center. (2010). *Religion among the millennials.* Washington, DC: Author.

Pew Research Center. (2012). *"Nones" on the rise: One-in-five adults have no religious affiliation.* Washington, DC: Author.

Pew Research Center. (2013a). *Among 38 nations, U.S. is the outlier when it comes to paid parental leave.* Retrieved from www.pewresearch.org/fact-tank/2013/12/12/among-38-nations-u-s-is-the-holdout-when-it-comes-to-offering-paid-parental-leave

Pew Research Center. (2013b). *A survey of LGBT Americans: Attitudes, experiences, and values in changing times.* Retrieved from www.pewsocialtrends.org/files/2013/06/SDT_LGBT-Americans_06-2013.pdf

Pew Research Center. (2014). *Millennials in adulthood: Detached from institutions, networked with friends.* Washington, DC: Author.

Pfeffer, C. R., Altemus, M., Heo, M., & Jiang, H. (2007). Salivary cortisol and psychopathology in children bereaved by the September 11, 2001 terror attacks. *Biological Psychiatry, 61*, 957–965.

Pfeifer, J. H., Ruble, D. N., Bachman, M. A., Alvarez, J. M., Cameron, J. A., & Fuligni, A. J. (2007). Social identities and intergroup bias in immigrant and nonimmigrant children. *Developmental Psychology, 43*, 496–507.

Pfeiffer, S. I., & Yermish, A. (2014). Gifted children. In L. Grossman & S. Walfish (Eds.), *Translating psychological research into practice* (pp. 57–64). New York: Springer.

Phillips, D. A., & Lowenstein, A. E. (2011). Early care, education, and child development. *Annual Review of Psychology, 62*, 483–500.

Phinney, J. S. (2007). Ethnic identity exploration in emerging adulthood. In J. J. Arnett & J. L. Tanner (Eds.), *Emerging adults in America: Coming of age in the 21st century* (pp. 117–134). Washington, DC: American Psychological Association.

Phinney, J. S., Ong, A., & Madden, T. (2000). Cultural values and intergenerational value discrepancies in immigrant and non-immigrant families. *Child Development, 71*, 528–539.

Piaget, J. (1926). *The language and thought of the child.* New York: Harcourt, Brace & World. (Original work published 1923)

Piaget, J. (1930). *The child's conception of the world.* New York: Harcourt, Brace, & World. (Original work published 1926)

Piaget, J. (1951). *Play, dreams, and imitation in childhood.* New York: Norton. (Original work published 1945)

Piaget, J. (1952). *The origins of intelligence in children.* New York: International Universities Press. (Original work published 1936)

Piaget, J. (1965). *The moral judgment of the child.* New York: Free Press. (Original work published 1932)

Piaget, J. (1967). *Six psychological studies.* New York: Vintage.

Piaget, J. (1971). *Biology and knowledge.* Chicago: University of Chicago Press.

Picho, K., Rodriguez. A., & Finnie, L. (2013). Exploring the moderating role of context on the mathematics performance of females under stereotype threat: A meta-analysis. *Journal of Social Psychology, 153*, 299–333.

Pickel, G. (2013). *Religion monitor: Understanding common ground. An international comparison of religious belief.* Gütersloh, Germany: Bertlsmann Foundation.

Pickens, J., Field, T., & Nawrocki, T. (2001). Frontal EEG asymmetry in response to emotional vignettes in preschool age children. *International Journal of Behavioral Development, 25*, 105–112.

Piernas, C., & Popkin, B. M. (2011). Increased portion sizes from energy-dense foods affect total energy intake at eating occasions in US children and adolescents: patterns and trends by age group and sociodemographic characteristics, 1977–2006. *American Journal of Clinical Nutrition, 94*, 1324–1332.

Pierroutsakos, S. L., & Troseth, G. L. (2003). Video verite: Infants' manual investigation of objects on video. *Infant Behavior and Development, 26*, 183–199.

Pierson, L. (1996). Hazards of noise exposure on fetal hearing. *Seminars in Perinatology, 20*, 21–29.

Piirto, J. (2007). *Talented children and adults* (3rd ed.). Waco, TX: Prufrock Press.

Pillow, B. (2002). Children's and adults' evaluation of the certainty of deductive inferences, inductive inferences, and guesses. *Child Development, 73*, 779–792.

Pine, J. M. (1995). Variation in vocabulary development as a function of birth order. *Child Development, 66*, 272–281.

Ping, R. M., & Goldin-Meadow, S. (2008). Hands in the air: Using ungrounded iconic gestures to teach children conservation of quantity. *Developmental Psychology, 44*, 1277–1287.

Pinker, S. (1999). *Words and rules: The ingredients of language.* New York: Basic Books.

Pinker, S., Lebeaux, D. S., & Frost, L. A. (1987). Productivity and constraints in the acquisition of the passive. *Cognition, 26*, 195–267.

Pipp, S., Easterbrooks, M. A., & Brown, S. R. (1993). Attachment status and complexity of infants' self- and other-knowledge when tested with mother and father. *Social Development, 2*, 1–14.

Pipp, S., Easterbrooks, M. A., & Harmon, R. J. (1992). The relation between attachment and knowledge of self and mother in one-year-old infants to three-year-old infants. *Child Development, 63*, 738–750.

Plake, B. S. (2011). Current state of high-stakes testing in education. In J. A. Bovaird, K. F. Geisinger, & C. Buckendahl (Eds.), *High-stakes testing in education: Science and practice in K–12 settings* (pp. 11–26). Washington, DC: American Psychological Association.

Plante, I., Théoret, M., & Favreau, O. E. (2009). Student gender stereotypes: Contrasting the perceived maleness and femaleness of mathematics and language. *Educational Psychology, 29*, 385–405.

Platt, M. P. W. (2014). Neonatology and obstetric anaesthesia. *Archives of Disease in Childhood—Fetal and Neonatal Edition, 99*, F98.

Pleck, J. H., & Masciadrelli, B. P. (2004). Paternal involvement by U.S. residential fathers: Levels, sources, and consequences. In M. E. Lamb (Ed.), *The role of the father in child development* (4th ed., pp. 222–271). Hoboken, NJ: Wiley

Plomin, R. (1994). *Genetics and experience: The interplay between nature and nurture.* Thousand Oaks, CA: Sage.

Plomin, R. (2009). The nature of nurture. In K. McCartney & R. A. Weinberg (Eds.), *Experience and development: A festschrift in honor of Sandra Wood Scarr* (pp. 61–80). New York: Psychology Press.

Plomin, R. (2013). Commentary: Missing heritability, polygenic scores, and gene–environment interactions. *Journal of Child Psychology and Psychiatry and Allied Disciplines, 54*, 1147–1149.

Plomin, R., DeFries, J. C., & Knopik, V. S. (2013). *Behavioral genetics* (6th ed.). New York: Worth.

Plomin, R., & Spinath, F. M. (2004). Intelligence: Genetics, genes, and genomics. *Journal of Personality and Social Psychology, 86*, 112–129.

Plucker, J. A., & Makel, M. C. (2010). Assessment of creativity. In J. C. Kaufman & R. J. Sternberg (Eds.), *Cambridge handbook of creativity* (pp. 48–73). New York: Cambridge University Press.

Pluess, M., & Belsky, J. (2011). Prenatal programming of postnatal plasticity? *Development and Psychopathology, 23*, 29–38.

Poehlmann, J. (2003). An attachment perspective on grandparents raising their very young grandchildren: Implications for intervention and research. *Infant Mental Health Journal, 24*, 149–173.

Poehlmann, J., Schwichtenberg, A. J. M., Shlafer, R. J., Hahn, E., Bianchi, J.-P., & Warner, R. (2011). Emerging self-regulation in toddlers born preterm or low birth weight: Differential susceptibility to parenting. *Developmental and Psychopathology, 23*, 177–193.

Polakowski L. L., Akinbami, L. J., & Mendola, P. (2009). Prenatal smoking cessation and the risk of delivering preterm and small-for-gestational-age newborns. *Obstetrics and Gynecology, 114*, 318–325.

Polderman, T. J. C., de Geus, J. C., Hoekstra, R. A., Bartels, M., van Leeuwen, M., Verhulst, F. C., et al. (2009). Attention problems, inhibitory control, and intelligence index overlapping genetic factors: A study in 9-, 12-, and 18-year-old twins. *Neuropsychology, 23*, 381–391.

Polka, L., & Rvachew, S. (2005). The impact of otitis media with effusion on infant phonetic perception. *Infancy, 8*, 101–117.

Pomerantz, E. M., & Dong, W. (2006). Effects of mothers' perceptions of children's competence: The moderating role of mothers' theories of competence. *Developmental Psychology, 42*, 950–961.

Pomerantz, E. M., & Eaton, M. M. (2000). Developmental differences in children's conceptions of parental control: "They love me, but they make me feel incompetent." *Merrill-Palmer Quarterly, 46*, 140–167.

Pomerantz, E. M., Grolnick, W. S., & Price, C. E. (2013). The role of parents in how children approach achievement: A dynamic process perspective. In A. J. Elliott & C. J. Dweck (Eds.), *Handbook of confidence and motivation* (pp. 259–278). New York: Guilford.

Pomerantz, E. M., & Kempner, S. G. (2013). Mothers' daily person and process praise: Implications for children's theory of intelligence and motivation. *Developmental Psychology, 13*, 2040–2046.

Pomerantz, E. M., Ng, F. F., & Wang, Q. (2008). Culture, parenting, and motivation: The case of East Asia and the United States. In M. L. Maehr, S. A., Karabenick, & T. C. Urdan (Eds.), *Advances in motivation and achievement: Social psychological perspectives* (Vol. 15, pp. 209–240). Bingley, UK: Emerald Group.

Pomerantz, E. M., & Ruble, D. N. (1998). The multidimensional nature of control: Implications for the development of sex differences in self-evaluation. In J. Heckhausen & C. S. Dweck (Eds.), *Motivation and self-regulation across the life span* (pp. 159–184). New York: Cambridge University Press.

Pomerantz, E. M., & Saxon, J. L. (2001). Conceptions of ability as stable and self-evaluative processes: A longitudinal examination. *Child Development, 72*, 152–173.

Pomerantz, E. M., & Wang, Q. (2009). The role of parental control in children's development in Western and East Asian countries. *Current Directions in Psychological Science, 18*, 285–289.

Pomerleau, A., Scuccimarri, C., & Malcuit, G. (2003). Mother–infant behavioral interactions in teenage and adult mothers during the first six months postpartum: Relations with infant development. *Infant Mental Health Journal, 24*, 495–509.

Pong, S., Johnston, J., & Chen, V. (2010). Authoritarian parenting and Asian adolescent school performance. *International Journal of Behavioral Development, 34*, 62–72.

Pong, S., & Landale, N. S. (2012). Academic achievement of legal immigrants' children: The roles of parents' pre- and postmigration characteristics in origin-group differences. *Child Development, 83*, 1543–1559.

Pons, F., Lawson, J., Harris, P. L., & de Rosnay, M. (2003). Individual differences in children's emotion understanding: Effects of age and language. *Scandinavian Journal of Psychology, 44*, 347–353.

Poole, D. A., & Bruck, M. (2012). Divining testimony? The impact of interviewing props on children's reports of touching. *Developmental Review, 32*, 165–180.

Poplinger, M., Talwar, V., & Crossman, A. (2011). Predictors of children's prosocial lie-telling: Motivation, socialization variables, and moral understanding. *Journal of Experimental Child Psychology, 110*, 373–392.

Portes, A., & Rumbaut, R. G. (2005), Introduction: The second generation and the Children of Immigrants

Longitudinal Study. *Ethnic and Racial Studies, 28,* 983–999.

Posner, M. I., & Rothbart, M. K. (2007a). *Educating the human brain.* Washington, DC: American Psychological Association.

Posner, M. I., & Rothbart, M. K. (2007b). Temperament and learning. In M. I. Posner & M. K. Rothbart (Eds.), *Educating the human brain* (pp. 121–146). Washington, DC: American Psychological Association.

Poti, J. M., Slining, M. M., & Popkin, B. M. (2014). Where are kids getting their empty calories? Stores, schools, and fast-food restaurants each played an important role in empty calorie intake among US children during 2009–2010. *Journal of the Academy of Nutrition and Dietetics, 114,* 908–917.

Potter, D. (2012). Same-sex parent families and children's academic achievement. *Journal of Marriage and Family, 74,* 556–571.

Poudevigne, M., & O'Connor, P. J. (2006). A review of physical activity patterns in pregnant women and their relationship to psychological health. *Sports Medicine, 36,* 19–38.

Poulin, F., & Denault, A.-S. (2012). Other-sex friendships as a mediator between parental monitoring and substance use in girls and boys. *Journal of Youth and Adolescence, 41,* 1488–1501.

Poulin, F., & Pedersen, S. (2007). Developmental changes in gender composition of friendship networks in adolescent girls and boys. *Developmental Psychology, 43,* 1484–1496.

Poulin-Dubois, D., Serbin, L. A., Eichstedt, J. A., Sen, M. G., & Beissel, C. F. (2002). Men don't put on make-up: Toddlers' knowledge of the gender stereotyping of household activities. *Social Development, 11,* 166–181.

Povinelli, D. J. (2001). The self—Elevated in consciousness and extended in time. In C. Moore & K. Lemmon (Eds.), *The self in time: Developmental perspectives* (pp. 75–95). Mahwah, NJ: Erlbaum.

Powell, M. P., & Schulte, T. (2011). Turner syndrome. In S. Goldstein & C. R. Reynolds (Eds.), *Handbook of neurodevelopmental and genetic disorders in children* (2nd ed.) (pp. 261–275). New York: Guilford.

Pratt, M. W., Skoe, E. E., & Arnold, M. L. (2004). Care reasoning development and family socialization patterns in later adolescence: A longitudinal analysis. *International Journal of Behavioral Development, 28,* 139–147.

Prechtl, H. F. R., & Beintema, D. (1965). *The neurological examination of the full-term newborn infant.* London: Heinemann Medical.

Pressley, M., & Hilden, D. (2006). Cognitive strategies. In D. Kuhn & R. Siegler (Eds.), *Handbook of child psychology: Vol. 2. Cognition, perception, and language* (6th ed., pp. 511–556). Hoboken, NJ: Wiley.

Pressley, M., Wharton-McDonald, R., Raphael, L. M., Bogner, K., & Roehrig, A. (2002). Exemplary first-grade teaching. In B. M. Taylor & P. D. Pearson (Eds.), *Teaching reading: Effective schools, accomplished teachers* (pp. 73–88). Mahwah, NJ: Erlbaum.

Preuss, T. M. (2012). Human brain evolution: From gene discovery to phenotype discovery. *Proceedings of the National Academy of Sciences, 109*(Suppl. 1), 10709–10716.

Prevatt, F. (2003). Dropping out of school: A review of intervention programs. *Journal of School Psychology, 41,* 377–399.

Prevatt, F., & Kelly, F. D. (2003). Dropping out of school: A review of intervention programs. *Journal of School Psychology, 41,* 377–395.

Previc, F. H. (1991). A general theory concerning the prenatal origins of cerebral lateralization. *Psychological Review, 98,* 299–334.

Priess, H. A., Lindberg, S. M., & Hyde, J. S. (2009). Adolescent gender-role identity and mental health: Gender intensification revisited. *Child Development, 80,* 1531–1544.

Principi, N., Baggi, E., & Esposito, S. (2012). Prevention of acute otitis media using currently available vaccines. *Future of Microbiology, 7,* 457–465.

Prinstein, M. J., Boergers, J., & Spirito, A. (2001). Adolescents' and their friends' health-risk behavior: Factors that alter or add to peer influence. *Journal of Pediatric Psychology, 26,* 287–298.

Prinstein, M. J., Boergers, J., & Vernberg, E. M. (2001). Overt and relational aggression in adolescents: Social–

psychological adjustment of aggressors and victims. *Journal of Clinical Child Psychology, 30,* 479–491.

Prinstein, M. J., & La Greca, A. M. (2002). Peer crowd affiliation and internalizing distress in childhood and adolescence: A longitudinal follow-back study. *Journal of Research on Adolescence, 12,* 325–351.

Proctor, M. H., Moore, L. L. Gao, D., Cupples, L. A., Bradlee, M. L., Hood, M. Y., & Ellison, R. C. (2003). Television viewing and change in body fat from preschool to early adolescence: The Framingham Children's Study. *International Journal of Obesity, 27,* 827–833.

Proffitt, D. R., & Bertenthal, B. I. (1990). Converging operations revisited: Assessing what infants perceive using discrimination measures. *Perception and Psychophysics, 47,* 1–11.

Programme for International Student Assessment. (2012). *PISA 2012 Results.* Retrieved from nces.ed.gov/surveys/pisa/pisa2012/index.asp

Proietti, E., Röösli, M., Frey, U., & Latzin, P. (2013). Air pollution during pregnancy and neonatal outcome: A review. *Journal of Aerosol Medicine and Pulmonary Drug Delivery, 26,* 9–23.

Proulx, M., & Poulin, F. (2013). Stability and change in kindergartners' friendships: Examination of links with social functioning. *Social Development, 22,* 111–125.

Pruden, S. M., Hirsh-Pasek, K., Golinkoff, R. M., & Hennon, E. A. (2006). The birth of words: Ten-month-olds learn words through perceptual salience. *Child Development, 77,* 266–280.

Pruett, M. K., & Donsky, T. (2011). Coparenting after divorce: Paving pathways for parental cooperation, conflict resolution, and redefined family roles. In J. P. McHale & K. M. Lindahl (Eds.), *Coparenting: A conceptual and clinical examination of family systems* (pp. 231–250). Washington, DC: American Psychological Association.

Pryor, J. (2014). *Stepfamilies: A global perspective on research, policy, and practice.* New York: Routledge.

Psychiatric Genomics Consortium. (2013). Identification of risk loci with shared effects of five major psychiatric disorders. *Lancet, 381,* 1371–1379.

Public Health Agency of Canada. (2014). Executive summary: Report on sexually transmitted infections in Canada: 2011. Retrieved from www.phac-aspc.gc.ca/sti-its-surv-epi/rep-rap-2011/index-eng.php

Puhl, R. M., Heuer, C. A., & Brownell, D. K. (2010). Stigma and social consequences of obesity. In P. G. Kopelman, I. D. Caterson, & W. H. Dietz (Eds.), *Clinical obesity in adults and children* (3rd ed., pp. 25–40). Hoboken, NJ: Wiley.

Puhl, R. M., & Latner, J. D. (2007). Stigma, obesity, and the health of the nation's children. *Psychological Bulletin, 133,* 557–580.

Pujol, J., Soriano-Mas, C., Ortiz, H., Sebastián-Gallés, N., Losilla, J. M., & Deus, J. (2006). Myelination of language-related areas in the developing brain. *Neurology, 66,* 339–343.

Puma, M., Bell, S., Cook, R., Heid, C., Broene, P., Jenkins, F., et al. (2012). *Third grade follow-up to the Head Start Impact Study final report.* OPRE Report #2012-45b. Washington, DC: U.S. Department of Health and Human Services.

Punamaki, R. L. (2006). Ante- and perinatal factors and child characteristics predicting parenting experience among formerly infertile couples during the child's first year: A controlled study. *Journal of Family Psychology, 20,* 670–679.

Purcell-Gates, V. (1996). Stories, coupons, and the TV guide: Relationships between home literacy experiences and emergent literacy knowledge. *Reading Research Quarterly, 31,* 406–428.

Putallaz, M., Grimes, C. L., Foster, K. J., Kupersmidt, J. B., Coie, J. D., & Dearing, K. (2007). Overt and relational aggression and victimization: Multiple perspectives within the school setting. *Journal of School Psychology, 45,* 523–547.

Putnam, S. P., Samson, A. V., & Rothbart, M. K. (2000). Child temperament and parenting. In V. J. Molfese & D. L. Molfese (Eds.), *Temperament and personality across the life span* (pp. 255–277). Mahwah, NJ: Erlbaum.

Puts, D. A., McDaniel, M. A., Jordan, C. L., & Breedlove, S. M. (2008). Spatial ability and prenatal androgens: Meta-analyses of CAH and digit ratio (2D:4D) studies. *Archives of Sexual Behavior, 37,* 100–111.

Q

Qin, L., and Pomerantz, E. M. (2013). Reciprocal pathways between American and Chinese early adolescents' sense of responsibility and disclosure to parents. *Child Development, 84,* 1887–1895.

Quas, J. A., Malloy, L. C., Melinder, A., Goodman, G. S., & D'Mello, M. (2007). Developmental differences in the effects of repeated interviews and interviewer bias on young children's event memory and false reports. *Developmental Psychology, 43,* 823–837.

Quinn, P. C. (2008). In defense of core competencies, quantitative change, and continuity. *Child Development, 79,* 1633–1638.

Quinn, P. C., & Intraub, H. (2007). Perceiving "outside the box" occurs early in development: Evidence for boundary extension in three- to seven-month-old infants. *Child Development, 78,* 324–334.

Quinn, P. C., Kelly, D. J., Lee, K., Pascalis, O., & Slater, A. (2008). Preference for attractive faces extends beyond conspecifics. *Developmental Science, 11,* 76–83.

Quinn, P. C., & Liben, L. S. (2014). A sex difference in mental rotation in infants: Convergent evidence. *Infancy, 19,* 103–116.

Quinn, P. C., Yahr, J., Kuhn, A., Slater, A. M., & Pascalis, O. (2002). Representation of the gender of human faces by infants: A preference for female. *Perception, 31,* 1109–1121.

R

Raabe, T., & Beelman, A. (2011). Development of ethnic, racial, and national prejudice in childhood and adolescence: A multinational meta-analysis of age differences. *Child Development, 82,* 1715–1737.

Raaijmakers, Q. A. W., Engels, R. C. M. E., & Van Hoof, A. (2005). Delinquency and moral reasoning in adolescence and young adulthood. *International Journal of Behavioral Development, 29,* 247–258.

Racanello, A., & McCabe, P. C. (2010). Role of otitis media in hearing loss and language deficits. In P. C. McCabe & S. R. Shaw (Eds.), *Pediatric disorders* (pp. 22–31). Washington, DC: Corwin Press

Racz, S. J., McMahon, R. J., & Luthar, S. S. (2011). Risky behavior in affluent youth: Examining the co-occurrence and consequences of multiple problem behaviors. *Journal of Child and Family Studies, 20,* 120–128.

Radesky, J. S., Kistin, C. J., Zuckerman, B., Nitzberg, K., Gross, J., Kaplan-Sanoff, M., et al. (2014). Patterns of mobile device use by caregivers and children during meals in fast food restaurants. *Pediatrics, 133,* e843–e849.

Raevuori, A., Hoek, H. W., Susser, E., Kaprio, J., Rissanen, A., & Keski-Rahkonen, A. (2009). Epidemiology of anorexia nervosa in men: A nationwide study of Finnish twins. *PLOS ONE, 4,* e4402.

Raffaelli, M., & Green, S. (2003). Parent–adolescent communication about sex: Retrospective reports by Latino college students. *Journal of Marriage and Family, 65,* 474–481.

Raffaelli, M., & Ontai, L. L. (2001). "She's 16 years old and there's boys calling over to the house": An exploratory study of sexual socialization in Latino families. *Culture, Health and Sexuality, 3,* 295–310.

Rahi, J. S., Cumberland, P. M., & Peckham, C. S. (2011). Myopia over the life course: Prevalence and early life influences in the 1958 British birth cohort. *Ophthalmology, 118,* 797–804.

Rahman, Q., & Wilson, G. D. (2003). Born gay? The psychobiology of human sexual orientation. *Personality and Individual Differences, 34,* 1337–1382.

Raikes, H. A., Robinson, J. L., Bradley, R. H., Raikes, H. H., & Ayoub, C. C. (2007). Developmental trends in self-regulation among low-income toddlers. *Social Development, 16,* 128–149.

Raikes, H. H., Chazan-Cohen, R., Love, J. M., & Brooks-Gunn, J. (2010). Early Head Start impacts at age 3 and a description of the age 5 follow-up study. In A. J. Reynolds, A. J. Rolnick, M. M. Englund, & J. Temple (Eds.), *Childhood programs and practices in the first decade of life: A human capital integration* (pp. 99–118). New York: Cambridge University Press.

Rakison, D. H. (2005). Developing knowledge of objects' motion properties in infancy. *Cognition, 96,* 183–214.

Rakison, D. H. (2010). Perceptual categorization and concepts. In J. G. Bremner & T. D. Wachs (Eds.), *Wiley-Blackwell handbook of infant development* (2nd ed., pp. 243–270). Oxford, UK: Wiley.

Rakison, D. H., & Lawson, C. A. (2013). Categorization. In P. D. Zelazo (Ed.), *Oxford handbook of developmental psychology: Vol. 1. Body and mind* (pp. 591–627). New York: Oxford University Press.

Rakoczy, H., Tomasello, M., & Striano, T. (2004). Young children know that trying is not pretending: A test of the "behaving-as-if" construal of children's early concept of pretense. *Developmental Psychology, 40*, 388–399.

Rakoczy, H., Tomasello, M., & Striano, T. (2005). How children turn objects into symbols: A cultural learning account. In L. Namy (Ed.), *Symbol use and symbol representation* (pp. 67–97). New York: Erlbaum.

Ramachandrappa, A., & Jain, L. (2008). Elective cesarean section: Its impact on neonatal respiratory outcome. *Clinics in Perinatology, 35*, 373–393.

Raman, L., & Gelman, S. A. (2004). A cross-cultural developmental analysis of children's and adults' understanding of illness in South Asia (India) and the United States. *Journal of Cognition and Culture, 4*, 293–317.

Ramchandani, P. G., Stein, A., O'Connor, T. G., Heron, J., Murray, L., & Evans, J. (2008). Depression in men in the postnatal period and later child psychopathology: A population cohort study. *Journal of the American Academy of Child and Adolescent Psychiatry, 47*, 390–398.

Ramey, C. T., Ramey, S. L., & Lanzi, R. G. (2006). Children's health and education. In K. A. Renninger & I. E. Sigel (Eds.), *Handbook of child psychology: Vol. 4. Child psychology in practice* (6th ed., pp. 864–892). Hoboken, NJ: Wiley.

Ramirez, M. M. (2011). Labor induction: A review of current methods. *Obstetrics and Gynecology Clinics of North America, 38*, 215–225.

Ramnitz, M. S., & Lodish, M. B. (2013). Racial disparities in pubertal development. *Seminars in Reproductive Medicine, 31*, 333–339.

Ramos, M. C., Guerin, D. W., Gottfried, A. W., Bathurst, K., & Oliver, P. H. (2005). Family conflict and children's behavior problems: The moderating role of child temperament. *Structural Equation Modeling, 12*, 278–298.

Ramsey-Rennels, J. L., & Langlois, J. H. (2006). Differential processing of female and male faces. *Current Directions in Psychological Science, 15*, 59–62.

Ramus, F. (2002). Language discrimination by newborns: Teasing apart phonotactic, rhythmic, and intonational cues. *Annual Review of Language Acquisition, 2*, 85–115.

Rasmussen, C., Ho, E., & Bisanz, J. (2003). Use of the mathematical principle of inversion in young children. *Journal of Experimental Child Psychology, 85*, 89–102.

Rasmussen, C., Neuman, R. J., Heath, A. C., Levy, F., Hay, D. A., & Todd, R. D. (2004). Familial clustering of latent class and DSM-IV defined attention-deficit hyperactivity disorder (ADHD) subtypes. *Journal of Child Psychology and Psychiatry, 45*, 589–598.

Rathunde, K., & Csikszentmihalyi, M. (2005). The social context of middle school: Teachers, friends, and activities in Montessori and traditional school environments. *Elementary School Journal, 106*, 59–79.

Rauber, M. (2006, May 18). Parents aren't sitting still as recess disappears. *Parents in Action.* Retrieved from www.parentsaction.org/news/parents-in-action/index.cfm?i=410

Rautava, L., Lempinen, A., Ojala, S., Parkkola, R., Rikalainen, H., Lapinleimu, H., et al. (2007). Acoustic quality of cry in very-low-birth weight infants at the age of 1½ years. *Early Human Development, 83*, 5–12.

Raver, C. C. (2003). Does work pay psychologically as well as economically? The role of employment in predicting depressive symptoms and parenting among low-income families. *Child Development, 74*, 1720–1736.

Ravid, D., & Tolchinsky, L. (2002). Developing linguistic literacy: A comprehensive model. *Journal of Child Language, 29*, 417–447.

Ravitch, D. (2010). *The death and life of the great American school system: How testing and choice are undermining education.* New York: Basic Books.

Ray, E., & Heyes, C. (2011). Imitation in infancy: The wealth of the stimulus. *Developmental Science, 14*, 92–105.

Ray, R., Gornick, J. C., & Schmitt, J. (2008). *Parental leave policies in 21 countries: Assessing generosity and gender equality.* Washington, DC: Center for Economic and Policy Research.

Ray, S., Reddy, P. J., Jain, R., Gollapalli, K., Moiyadi, A., & Srivastava, S. (2011). Proteomic technologies for the identification of disease biomarkers in serum: Advances and challenges ahead. *Proteomics, 11*, 2139–2161.

Rayner, K., Pollatsek, A., & Starr, M. S. (2003). Reading. In A. F. Healy & R. W. Proctor (Eds.), *Handbook of psychology: Experimental psychology* (Vol. 4, pp. 549–574). New York: Wiley.

Ream, G. L., & Rodriguez, E. M. (2014). Sexual minorities. In C. M. Barry & M. M. Abo-Zena (Eds.), *Emerging adults' religiousness and spirituality* (pp 204–219). New York: Oxford University Press.

Reed, C. E., & Fenton, S. E. (2013). Exposure to diethylstilbestrol during sensitive life stages: A legacy of heritable health effects. *Birth Defects Research. Part C, Embryo Today: Reviews, 99*, 134–146.

Reed, R. K. (2005). *Birthing fathers.* New Brunswick, NJ: Rutgers University Press.

Reese, E., & Newcombe, R. (2007). Training mothers in elaborative reminiscing enhances children's autobiographical memory and narrative. *Child Development, 78*, 1153–1170.

Reese, E., Newcombe, R., & Bird, G. M. (2006). The emergence of autobiographical memory: Cognitive, social, and emotional factors. In C. M. Flinn-Fletcher & G. M. Haberman (Eds.), *Cognition and language: Perspectives from New Zealand* (pp. 177–189). Bowen Hills, Australia: Australian Academic Press.

Reich, S. M., Subrahmanyam, K., & Espinoza, G. (2012). Friending, IMing, and hanging out face-to-face: Overlap in adolescents' online and offline social networks. *Developmental Psychology, 48*, 356–368.

Reilly, D. (2012). Gender, culture, and sex-typed cognitive abilities. *PLOS ONE, 7*, e39904.

Reis, O., & Youniss, J. (2004). Patterns in identity change and development in relationships with mothers and friends. *Journal of Adolescent Research, 19*, 31–44.

Reis, S. M. (2004). We can't change what we don't recognize: Understanding the special needs of gifted females. In S. Baum (Ed.), *Twice-exceptional and special populations of gifted students* (pp. 67–80). Thousand Oaks, CA: Corwin Press.

Reiss, D. (2003). Child effects on family systems: Behavioral genetic strategies. In A. C. Crouter & A. Booth (Eds.), *Children's influence on family dynamics* (pp. 3–36). Mahwah, NJ: Erlbaum.

Rentner, T. L., Dixon, L. D., & Lengel, L. (2012). Critiquing fetal alcohol syndrome health communication campaigns targeted to American Indians. *Journal of Health Communication, 17*, 6–21.

Repacholi, B. M., & Gopnik, A. (1997). Early reasoning about desires: Evidence from 14- and 18-month-olds. *Developmental Psychology, 33*, 12–21.

Repetti, R., & Wang, S. (2010). Parent employment and chaos in the family. In G. W. Evans & T. D. Wachs (Eds.), *Chaos and its influence on children's development: An ecological perspective* (pp. 191–208). Washington, DC: American Psychological Association.

Reppucci, N. D., Meyer, J. R., & Kostelnik, J. O. (2011). Tales of terror from juvenile justice and education. In M. S. Aber, K. I. Maton, & E. Seidman (Eds.), *Empowering settings and voices for social change* (pp. 155–172). New York: Oxford University Press.

Reschly, A. L., & Christenson, S. L. (2009). Parents as essential partners for fostering students' learning outcomes. In R. Gilman & E. Scott Huebner (Eds.), *Handbook of positive psychology in schools* (pp. 257–272). New York: Routledge.

Resnick, G. (2010). Project Head Start: Quality and links to child outcomes. In A. J. Reynolds, A. J. Rolnick, M. M. Englund, & J. Temple (Eds.), *Childhood programs and practices in the first decade of life: A human capital integration* (pp. 121–156). New York: Cambridge University Press.

Resnick, M., & Silverman, B. (2005). *Some reflections on designing construction kits for kids.* Proceedings of the Conference on Interaction Design and Children, Boulder, CO.

Rest, J. R. (1979). *Development in judging moral issues.* Minneapolis: University of Minnesota Press.

Resta, R., Biesecker, B. B., Bennett, R. L., Blum, S., Hahn, S. E., Strecker, M. N., & Williams, J. L. (2006). A new definition of genetic counseling: National Society of Genetic Counselors' Task Force Report. *Journal of Genetic Counseling, 15*, 77–83.

Reyna, V. F., & Farley, F. (2006). Risk and rationality in adolescent decision making: Implications for theory, practice, and public policy. *Psychological Science in the Public Interest, 7*, 1–44.

Reynolds, A. J., & Temple, J. A. (1998). Extended early childhood intervention and school achievement: Age thirteen findings from the Chicago Longitudinal Study. *Child Development, 69*, 231–246.

Rhoades, B. L., Greenberg, M. T., & Domitrovich, C. E. (2009). The contribution of inhibitory control to preschoolers' social-emotional competence. *Journal of Applied Developmental Psychology, 30*, 310–320.

Rhodes, M., Leslie, S.-J., & Tworek, C. M. (2012). Cultural transmission of social essentialism. *Proceedings of the National Academy of Sciences, 109*, 13526–13531.

Richardson, H. L., Walker, A. M., & Horne, R. S. C. (2008) Sleep position alters arousal processes maximally at the high-risk age for sudden infant death syndrome. *Journal of Sleep Research, 17*, 450–457.

Richie, B. S., Fassinger, R. E., Linn, S. G., Johnson, J., Prosser, J., & Robinson, S. (1997). Persistence, connection, and passion: A qualitative study of the career development of highly achieving African American black and white women. *Journal of Counseling Psychology, 44*, 133–148.

Richler, J., Luyster, R., Risi, S., Hsu, W.-L., Dawson, G., & Bernier, R. (2006). Is there a "regressive phenotype" of autism spectrum disorder associated with the measles-mumps-rubella vaccine? A CPEA study. *Journal of Autism and Developmental Disorders, 36*, 299–316.

Richmond, J., Colombo, M., & Hayne, H. (2007). Interpreting visual preferences in the visual paired-comparison task. *Journal of Experimental Psychology: Learning, Memory, and Cognition, 33*, 823–831.

Rideout, V., & Hamel, E. (2006). *The media family: Electronic media in the lives of infants, toddlers, preschoolers and their parents.* Menlo Park, CA: Henry J. Kaiser Family Foundation.

Rideout, V. J., Foehr, U. G., & Roberts, D. F. (2010). *Generation M²: Media in the lives of 8- to 18-year-olds.* Menlo Park, CA: Henry J. Kaiser Family Foundation.

Rieffe, C., Terwogt, M. M., & Cowan, R. (2005). Children's understanding of mental states as causes of emotions. *Infant and Child Development, 14*, 259–272.

Rifkin, R. (2014, May 30). *New record highs in moral acceptability: Premarital sex, embryonic stem cell research, euthanasia growing in acceptance.* Retrieved from www.gallup.com/poll/170789/new-record-highs-moral-acceptability.aspx

Riggins, T., Cheatham, C., Stark, E., & Bauer, P. J. (2013). Elicited imitation performance at 20 months predicts memory abilities in school age children. *Journal of Cognition and Development, 14*, 593–606.

Riggins, T., Miller, N. C., Bauer, P., Georgieff, M. K., & Nelson, C. A. (2009). Consequences of low neonatal iron status due to maternal diabetes mellitus on explicit memory performance in childhood. *Developmental Neuropsychology, 34*, 762–779.

Riggs, K. J., Jolley, R. P., & Simpson, A. (2013). The role of inhibitory control in the development of human figure drawing in young children. *Journal of Experimental Child Psychology, 114*, 537–542.

Rijlaarsdam, J., Stevens, G. W. J. M., van der Ende, J., Arends, L. R., Hofman, A., Jaddoe, V. W. V., et al. (2012). A brief observational instrument for the assessment of infant home environment: Development and psychometric testing. *International Journal of Methods in Psychiatric Research, 21*, 195–204.

Rijsdijk, F. V., & Boomsma, D. I. (1997). Genetic mediation of the correlation between peripheral nerve conduction velocity and IQ. *Behavior Genetics, 27*, 87–98.

Rindermann, H., & Ceci, S. J. (2008). Education policy and country outcomes in international cognitive competence studies. Graz, Austria: Institute of Psychology, Karl-Franzens-University Graz.

Ripley, A. (2013). *The smartest kids in the world: And how they got that way.* New York: Simon and Schuster.

Ripple, C. H., & Zigler, E. (2003). Research, policy, and the federal role in prevention initiatives for children. *American Psychologist, 58*, 482–490.

Ris, M. D., Dietrich, K. N., Succop, P. A., Berger, O. G., & Bornschein, R. L. (2004). Early exposure to lead and neuropsychological outcome in adolescence. *Journal of the International Neuropsychological Society, 10*, 261–270.

Ritchie, L. D., Spector, P., Stevens, M. J., Schmidt, M. M., Schreiber, G. B., Striegel-Moore, R. H., et al. (2007) Dietary patterns in adolescence are related to adiposity in young adulthood in black and white females. *Journal of Nutrition, 137,* 399–406.

Ritz, B., Oiu, J., Lee, P. C., Lurmann, F., Penfold, B., Erin Weiss, R., et al. (2014). Prenatal air pollution exposure and ultrasound measures of fetal growth in Los Angeles, California. *Environmental Research, 130,* 7–13.

Riva, D., & Giorgi, C. (2000). The cerebellum contributes to higher functions during development: Evidence from a series of children surgically treated for posterior fossa tumors. *Brain, 123,* 1051–1061.

Rivkees, S. A. (2003). Developing circadian rhythmicity in infants. *Pediatrics, 112,* 373–381.

Rizzolatti, G., & Craighero, L. (2004). The mirror-neuron system. *Annual Review of Neuroscience, 27,* 169–192.

Roben, C. K. P., Bass, A. J., Moore, G. A., Murray-Kolb, L., Tan, P. Z., Gilmore, R. O., et al. (2012). Let me go: The influences of crawling experience and temperament on the development of anger expression. *Infancy, 17,* 558–577.

Roberts, B. W., & DelVecchio, W. F. (2000). The rankorder consistency of personality traits from childhood to old age: A quantitative review of longitudinal studies. *Psychological Bulletin, 126,* 3–25.

Roberts, D. F., Foehr, U. G., & Rideout, V. (2005). *Generation M: Media in the lives of 8–18 year olds.* Menlo Park, CA: Henry J. Kaiser Family Foundation.

Roberts, D. F., Henriksen, L., & Foehr, U. G. (2009). Adolescence, adolescents, and media. In R. M. Lerner & L. Steinberg (Eds.), *Handbook of adolescent psychology: Vol. 2. Contextual influences on adolescent development* (3rd ed., pp. 314–344). Hoboken, NJ: Wiley

Roberts, J. E., Burchinal, M. R., & Durham, M. (1999). Parents' report of vocabulary and grammatical development of American preschoolers: Child and environment associations. *Child Development, 70,* 92–106.

Robertson, J. (2008). Stepfathers in families. In J. Pryor (Ed.), *International handbook of stepfamilies: Policy and practice in legal, research, and clinical environments* (pp. 125–150). Hoboken, NJ: Wiley.

Robila, M. (2012). Family policies in Eastern Europe: A focus on parental leave. *Journal of Child and Family Studies, 21,* 32–41.

Robin, A. L., & Le Grange, D. (2010). Family therapy for adolescents with anorexia nervosa. In J. R. Weisz & A. E. Kazdin (Eds.), *Evidence-based psychotherapies for children and adolescents* (2nd ed., pp. 359–374). New York: Guilford.

Robin, D. J., Berthier, N. E., & Clifton, R. K. (1996). Infants' predictive reaching for moving objects in the dark. *Developmental Psychology, 32,* 824–835.

Robins, R. W., Tracy, J. L., Trzesniewski, K., Potter, J., & Gosling, S. D. (2001). Personality correlates of self-esteem. *Journal of Research in Personality, 35,* 463–482.

Robinson, C. C., Anderson, G. T., Porter, C. L., Hart, C. H., & Wouden-Miller, M. (2003). Sequential transition patterns of preschoolers' social interactions during child-initiated play: Is parallel-aware play a bidirectional bridge to other play states? *Early Childhood Research Quarterly, 18,* 3–21.

Robinson, S., Goddard, L., Dritschel, B., Wisley, M., & Howlin, P. (2009). Executive functions in children with autism spectrum disorders. *Brain and Cognition, 71,* 362–368.

Robinson-Zañartu, C., & Carlson, J. (2013). Dynamic assessment. In K. F. Geisinger (Ed.), *APA handbook of testing and assessment in psychology: Vol. 3. Testing and assessment in school psychology and education* (pp. 149–168). Washington, DC: American Psychological Association.

Roca, A., Carcia-Esteve, L., Imaz, M. L., Torres, A., Hernández, S., & Botet, F. (2011). Obstetrical and neonatal outcomes after prenatal exposure to selective serotonin reuptake inhibitors: The relevance of dose. *Journal of Affective Disorders, 135,* 208–215.

Rochat, P. (1989). Object manipulation and exploration in 2- to 5-month-old infants. *Developmental Psychology, 25,* 871–884.

Rochat, P. (1998). Self-perception and action in infancy. *Experimental Brain Research, 123,* 102–109.

Rochat, P. (2001). *The infant's world.* Cambridge, MA: Harvard University Press.

Rochat, P. (2013). Self-conceptualizing in development. In P. Zelazo (Ed.), *Oxford handbook of developmental psychology* (Vol. 2, pp. 378–397). New York: Oxford University Press.

Rochat, P., & Goubet, N. (1995). Development of sitting and reaching in 5- to 6-month-old infants. *Infant Behavior and Development, 18,* 53–68.

Rochat, P., & Hespos, S. J. (1997). Differential rooting responses by neonates: Evidence for an early sense of self. *Early Development and Parenting, 6,* 105–112.

Rochat, P., & Striano, T. (2002). Who's in the mirror? Self–other discrimination in specular images by four- and nine-month-old infants. *Child Development, 73,* 35–46.

Rodgers, J. L., Cleveland, H. H., van den Oord, E., & Rowe, D. C. (2000). Resolving the debate over birth order, family size, and intelligence. *American Psychologist, 55,* 599–612.

Rodgers, J. L., & Wänström, L. (2007). Identification of a Flynn effect in the NLSY: Moving from the center to the boundaries. *Intelligence, 35,* 187–196.

Rodkin, P. C., Farmer, T. W., Pearl, R., & Van Acker, R. (2006). They're cool: Social status and peer group supports for aggressive boys and girls. *Social Development, 15,* 175–204.

Rodriguez, E. M., Dunn, M. J., & Compas, B. E. (2012). Cancer-related sources of stress for children with cancer and their parents. *Journal of Pediatric Psychology, 37,* 185–197.

Roelfsema, N. M., Hop, W. C., Boito, S. M., & Wladimiroff, J. W. (2004). Three-dimensional sonographic measurement of normal fetal brain volume during the second half of pregnancy. *American Journal of Obstetrics and Gynecology, 190,* 275–280.

Roeser, R. W., Eccles, J. S., & Freedman-Doan, C. (1999). Academic functioning and mental health in adolescence: Patterns, progressions, and routes from childhood. *Journal of Adolescent Research, 14,* 135–174.

Rogan, W. J., Dietrich, K. N., Ware, J. H., Dockery, D. W., Salganik, M., & Radcliffe, J. (2001). The effect of chelation therapy with succimer on neuropsychological development in children exposed to lead. *New England Journal of Medicine, 344,* 1421–1426.

Rogers, J. M. (2009). Tobacco and pregnancy. *Reproductive Toxicology, 28,* 152–160.

Rogoff, B. (1996). Developmental transitions in children's participation in sociocultural activities. In A. J. Sameroff & M. M. Haith (Eds.), *The five to seven year shift: The age of reason and responsibility* (pp. 273–294). Chicago: University of Chicago Press.

Rogoff, B. (1998). Cognition as a collaborative process. In D. Kuhn & R. S. Siegler (Eds.), *Handbook of child psychology: Vol. 2. Cognition, perception, and language* (5th ed., pp. 679–744). New York: Wiley.

Rogoff, B. (2003). *The cultural nature of human development.* New York: Oxford University Press.

Rogoff, B., Correa-Chavez, M., & Silva, K.G. (2011). Cultural variation in children's attention and learning. In M. A. Gernsbacher, R. W. Pew, L. M. Hough, & J. R. Pomerantz (Eds.), *Psychology and the real world: Essays illustrating fundamental contributions to society* (pp. 154–163). New York: Worth.

Rogoff, B., Malkin, C., & Gilbride, K. (1984). Interaction with babies as guidance in development. In B. Rogoff & J. V. Wertsch (Eds.), *Children's learning in the "zone of proximal development" (New directions for child development,* No. 23, pp. 31–44). San Francisco: Jossey-Bass.

Rogoff, B., & Waddell, K. J. (1982). Memory for information organized in a scene by children from two cultures. *Child Development, 53,* 1224–1228.

Rogol, A. D., Roemmich, J. N., & Clark, P. A. (2002). Growth at puberty. *Journal of Adolescent Health, 31,* 192–200.

Rohde, P., Stice, E., & Marti, C. N. (2014). Development and predictive effects of eating disorder risk factors during adolescence: Implications for prevention efforts. *International Journal of Eating Disorders, 47,* ISSN 1098-108X.

Rohner, R. P., & Veneziano, R. A. (2001). The importance of father love: History and contemporary evidence. *Review of General Psychology, 5,* 382–405.

Roid, G. (2003). *The Stanford-Binet Intelligence Scales, Fifth Edition, interpretive manual.* Itasca, IL: Riverside Publishing.

Roid, G. H., & Pomplun, M. (2012). The Stanford-Binet Intelligence Scales, Fifth Edition. In D. P. Flanagan & P. L. Harrison (Eds.), *Contemporary intellectual assessment: Theories, tests and issues* (pp. 249–268). New York: Guilford.

Roisman, G. I., & Fraley, R. C. (2008). Behavior-genetic study of parenting quality, infant-attachment security, and their covariation in a nationally representative sample. *Developmental Psychology, 44,* 831–839.

Roisman, R., & Fraley, C. (2006). The limits of genetic influence: A behavior-genetic analysis of infant–caregiver relationship quality and temperament. *Child Development, 77,* 1656–1667.

Romano, A. M., & Lothian, J. A. (2008). Promoting, protecting, and supporting normal birth: A look at the evidence. *Journal of Obstetric, Gynecologic, and Neonatal Nursing, 37,* 94–104.

Roman-Rodriguez, C. F., Toussaint, T., Sherlock, D. J., Fogel, J., & Hsu, C-D. (2014). Preemptive penile ring block with sucrose analgesia reduces pain response to neonatal circumcision. *Urology, 83,* 893–898.

Rome-Flanders, T., & Cronk, C. (1995). A longitudinal study of infant vocalizations during mother–infant games. *Journal of Child Language, 22,* 259–274.

Romero, A. J., & Roberts, R. E. (2003). The impact of multiple dimensions of ethnic identity on discrimination and adolescents' self-esteem. *Journal of Applied Social Psychology, 33,* 2288–2305.

Ronald, A., & Hoekstra, R. (2014). Progress in understanding the causes of autism spectrum disorders and autistic traits: Twin studies from 1977 to the present day. In S. H. Rhee & A. Ronald (Eds.), *Advances in Behavior Genetics* (Vol. 2, pp. 33–65). New York: Springer.

Rönnqvist, L., & Domellöf, E. (2006). Quantitative assessment of right and left reaching movements in infants: A longitudinal study from 6 to 36 months. *Developmental Psychobiology, 48,* 444–459.

Rönnqvist, L., & Hopkins, B. (1998). Head position preference in the human newborn: A new look. *Child Development, 69,* 13–23.

Roopnarine, J. L., & Evans, M. E. (2007). Family structural organization, mother–child and father–child relationships and psychological outcomes in English-speaking African Caribbean and Indo Caribbean families. In M. Sutherland (Ed.), *Psychology of development in the Caribbean.* Kingston, Jamaica: Ian Randle.

Roopnarine, J. L., Hossain, Z., Gill, P., & Brophy, H. (1994). Play in the East Indian context. In J. L. Roopnarine, J. E. Johnson, & F. H. Hooper (Eds.), *Children's play in diverse cultures* (pp. 9–30). Albany: SUNY Press.

Roopnarine, J. L., Krishnakumar, A., Metindogan, A., & Evans, M. (2006). Links between parenting styles, parent–child academic interaction, parent–school interaction, and early academic skills and social behaviors in young children of English-speaking Caribbean immigrants. *Early Childhood Research Quarterly, 21,* 238–252.

Roopnarine, J. L., Talukder, E., Jain, D., Joshi, P., & Srivastav, P. (1990). Characteristics of holding, patterns of play, and social behaviors between parents and infants in New Delhi, India. *Developmental Psychology, 26,* 667–673.

Rosander, K., & von Hofsten, C. (2004). Infants' emerging ability to represent occluded object motion. *Cognition, 91,* 1–22.

Rosander, K., & von Hofsten, C. (2011). Predictive gaze shifts elicited during observed and performed action in 10-month-old infants and adults. *Neuropsychologia, 49,* 2911–2917.

Rosario, M., & Schrimshaw, E. W. (2013). The sexual identity development and health of lesbian, gay, and bisexual adolescents: An ecological perspective. In C. J. Patterson & A. R. D'Augelli (Eds.), *Handbook of psychology and sexual orientation.* New York: Oxford University Press.

Rose, A. J., Schwartz-Mette, R. A., Glick, G. C., & Smith, R. (2014). An observational study of co-rumination in adolescent friendships. *Developmental Psychology, 50,* 2199–2209.

Rose, A. J., Swenson, L. P., & Waller, E. M. (2004). Overt and relational aggression and perceived popularity: Developmental differences in concurrent and prospective relations. *Developmental Psychology, 40,* 378–387.

Rose, L. (2000). Fathers of full-term infants. In N. Tracey (Ed.), *Parents of premature infants: Their emotional world* (pp. 105–116). London: Whurr.

Rose, S. A., Feldman, J. F., & Jankowski, J. J. (2001a). Attention and recognition memory in the 1st year of life:

A longitudinal study of preterm and full-term infants. *Developmental Psychology, 37,* 135–151.

Rose, S. A., Feldman, J. F., & Jankowski, J. J. (2001b). Visual short-term memory in the first year of life: Capacity and recency effects. *Developmental Psychology, 37,* 539–549.

Rose, S. A., Feldman, J. F., Jankowski, J. J., & Van Rossem, R. (2011). The structure of memory in infants and toddlers: An SEM study with full-terms and preterms. *Developmental Science, 14,* 83–91.

Rose, S. A., Jankowski, J. J., & Senior, G. J. (1997). Infants' recognition of contour-deleted figures. *Journal of Experimental Psychology: Human Perception and Performance, 23,* 1206–1216.

Roseberry, S., Hirsh-Pasek, K., & Golinkoff, R. M. (2014). Skype me! Socially contingent interactions help toddlers learn language. *Child Development, 85,* 956–970.

Roseberry, S., Hirsh-Pasek, K., Parish-Morris, J., & Golinkoff, R. M. (2009). Live action: Can young children learn verbs from video? *Child Development, 80,* 1360–1375.

Rosen, A. B., & Rozin, P. (1993). Now you see it, now you don't: The preschool child's conception of invisible particles in the context of dissolving. *Developmental Psychology, 29,* 300–311.

Rosen, C. S., & Cohen, M. (2010). Subgroups of New York City children at high risk of PTSD after the September 11 attacks: A signal detection analysis. *Psychiatric Services, 61,* 64–69.

Rosen, D. (2003). Eating disorders in children and young adolescents: Etiology, classification, clinical features, and treatment. *Adolescent Medicine: State of the Art Reviews, 14,* 49–59.

Rosenbaum, J. E. (2009). Patient teenagers? A comparison of the sexual behavior of virginity pledgers and matched nonpledgers. *Pediatrics, 123,* e110–e120.

Rosenbloom, A. L. (2009). Idiopathic short stature: Conundrums of definition and treatment. *International Journal of Pediatric Endocrinology,* Article ID 470378.

Rosenthal, J. A., Foraker, R. E., Collins, C. L., & Comstock, R. D. (2014). National high school athlete concussion rates from 2005–2006 to 2011–2012. *American Journal of Sports Medicine, 42,* 1710–1715.

Roseth, C. J., Pellegrini, A. D., Bohn, C. M., van Ryzin, M., & Vance, N. (2007). Preschoolers' aggression, affiliation, and social dominance relationships: An observational, longitudinal study. *Journal of School Psychology, 45,* 479–497.

Roskos, K. A., & Christie, J. F. (2013). Gaining ground in understanding the play–literacy relationship. *American Journal of Play, 6,* 82–97.

Ross, H. S., Conant, C., Cheyne, J. A., & Alevizos, E. (1992). Relationships and alliances in the social interactions of kibbutz toddlers. *Social Development, 1,* 1–17.

Ross, J. L., Roeltgen, D. P., Kushner, H., Zinn, A. R., Reiss, A., Bardsley, M. Z., et al. (2012). Behavioral and social phenotypes in boys with 47, XYY syndrome or 47, XXY Klinefelter syndrome. *Pediatrics, 129,* 769–778.

Ross, N., Medin, D. L., Coley, J. D., & Atran, S. (2003). Cultural and experiential differences in the development of folkbiological induction. *Cognitive Development, 18,* 25–47.

Rossi, B. V. (2014). Donor insemination. In J. M. Goldfarb (Ed.), *Third-party reproduction* (pp. 133–142). New York: Springer.

Ross-Sheehy, S., Oakes, L. M., & Luck, S. J. (2003). The development of visual short-term memory capacity in infants. *Child Development, 74,* 1807–1822.

Rothbart, M. K. (2003). Temperament and the pursuit of an integrated developmental psychology. *Merrill-Palmer Quarterly, 50,* 492–505.

Rothbart, M. K. (2011). *Becoming who we are: Temperament and personality in development.* New York: Guilford.

Rothbart, M. K., Ahadi, S. A., & Evans, D. E. (2000). Temperament and personality: Origins and outcome. *Journal of Personality and Social Psychology, 78,* 122–135.

Rothbart, M. K., & Bates, J. E. (2006). Temperament. In N. Eisenberg (Ed.), *Handbook of child psychology: Vol. 3. Social, emotional, and personality development* (6th ed., pp. 99–166). Hoboken, NJ: Wiley.

Rothbart, M. K., Posner, M. I., & Kieras, J. (2006). Temperament, attention, and the development of self-regulation. In K. McCartney & D. Phillips (Eds.),

Blackwell handbook of early childhood development (pp. 338–357). Malden, MA: Blackwell.

Rothbaum, F., Kakinuma, M., Nagaoka, R., & Azuma, H. (2007). Attachment and *amae:* Parent–child closeness in the United States and Japan. *Journal of Cross-Cultural Psychology, 38,* 465–486.

Rothbaum, F., Weisz, J., Pott, M., Miyake, K., & Morelli, G. (2000). Attachment and culture: Security in the United States and Japan. *American Psychologist, 55,* 1093–1104.

Rothman, E. F., Sullivan, M., Keyes, S., & Boehmer, U. (2012). Parents' supportive reactions to sexual orientation disclosure associated with better health: Results from a population-based survey of LGB adults in Massachusetts. *Journal of Homosexuality, 59,* 186–200.

Rouselle, L., Palmers, E., & Noël, M.-P. (2004). Magnitude comparison in preschoolers: What counts? Influence of perceptual variables. *Journal of Experimental Child Psychology, 87,* 57–84.

Rovee-Collier, C. (1999). The development of infant memory. *Current Directions in Psychological Science, 8,* 80–85.

Rovee-Collier, C., & Barr, R. (2001). Infant learning and memory. In G. Bremner & A. Fogel (Eds.), *Blackwell handbook of infant development* (pp. 139–168). Oxford, UK: Blackwell.

Rovee-Collier, C., & Bhatt, R. S. (1993). Evidence of long-term memory in infancy. *Annals of Child Development, 9,* 1–45.

Rovee-Collier, C., & Cuevas, K. (2009). Multiple memory systems are unnecessary to account for infant memory development: An ecological model. *Developmental Psychology, 45,* 160–174.

Rovers, M. M., Numans, M. E., Langenbach, E., Grobbee, D. E., et al. (2008). Is pacifier use a risk factor for acute otitis media? A dynamic cohort study. *Family Practice, 25,* 233–236.

Rowe, M. L. (2008). Child-directed speech: Relation to socioeconomic status, knowledge of child development and child vocabulary skill. *Journal of Child Language, 35,* 185–205.

Rowe, M. L., & Goldin-Meadow, S. (2009a). Differences in early gesture explain SES disparities in child vocabulary size at school entry. *Science, 323,* 951–953.

Rowe, M. L., & Goldin-Meadow, S. (2009b). Early gesture selectively predicts later language learning. *Developmental Science, 12,* 182–187.

Rowe, M. L., Raudenbush, S. W., & Goldin-Meadow, S. (2012). The pace of vocabulary growth helps predict later vocabulary skill. *Child Development, 83,* 508–525.

Rowe, R., Maughan, B., & Goodman, R. (2004). Childhood psychiatric disorder and unintentional injury: Findings from a national cohort study. *Journal of Pediatric Psychology, 29,* 119–130.

Rowland, C. F. (2007). Explaining errors in children's questions. *Cognition, 104,* 106–134.

Rowland, C. F., & Pine, J. M. (2000). Subject-auxiliary inversion errors and wh-question acquisition: "What children do know?" *Journal of Child Language, 27,* 157–181.

Rowley, S. J., Kurtz-Costes, B., Mistry, R., & Feagans, L. (2007). Social status as a predictor of race and gender stereotypes in late childhood and early adolescence. *Social Development, 16,* 150–168.

Rozen, G. S. (2012). Healthy eating among adolescents. In Y. Latzer & O. Tzischinsky (Eds.), *The dance of sleeping and eating among adolescents: Normal and pathological perspectives* (pp. 3–15). New York: Nova Science Publishers.

Rubin, C., Maisonet, M., Kieszak, S., Monteilh, C., Holmes A., Flanders, D., et al. (2009). Timing of maturation and predictors of menarche in girls enrolled in a contemporary British cohort. *Paediatric and Perinatal Epidemiology, 23,* 492–504.

Rubin, D. M., O'Reilly, A. L., Luan, X., Dai, D., Localio, A. R., et al. (2011). Variation in pregnancy outcomes following statewide implementation of a prenatal home visitation program. *Archives of Pediatrics and Adolescent Medicine, 165,* 198–204.

Rubin, K. H., Begle, A. S., & McDonald, K. L. (2012). Peer relations and social competence in childhood. In V. Anderson & M. H. Beauchamp (Eds.), *Developmental social neuroscience and childhood brain insult: Theory and practice* (pp. 23–44). New York: Guilford.

Rubin, K. H., Bowker, J. C., McDonald, K. L., & Menzer, M. (2013). Peer relationships in childhood. In P. D. Zelazo

(Ed.), *Oxford handbook of developmental psychology, Vol. 2: Self and other* (pp. 242–275). New York: Oxford University Press.

Rubin, K. H., Bukowski, W. M., & Parker, J. G. (2006). Peer interactions, relationships, and groups. In N. Eisenberg (Ed.), *Handbook of child psychology: Vol. 3. Social, emotional, and personality development* (6th ed., pp. 571–645). Hoboken, NJ: Wiley.

Rubin, K. H., & Burgess, K. (2002). Parents of aggressive and withdrawn children. In M. Bornstein (Ed.), *Handbook of parenting* (2nd ed., pp. 383–418). Hillsdale, NJ: Erlbaum.

Rubin, K. H., Burgess, K. B., & Hastings, P. D. (2002). Stability and social-behavioral consequences of toddlers' inhibited temperament and parenting behaviors. *Child Development, 73,* 483–495.

Rubin, K. H., Coplan, R., Chen, X., Bowker, J., & McDonald, K. L. (2011). Peer relationships in childhood. In M. E. Lamb & M. H. Bornstein (Eds.), *Social and personality development: An advanced textbook* (pp. 309–360). New York: Psychology Press.

Rubin, K. H., Fein, G. G., & Vandenberg, B. (1983). Play. In E. M. Hetherington (Ed.), *Handbook of child psychology: Vol. 4. Socialization, personality, and social development* (4th ed., pp. 693–744). New York: Wiley.

Rubin, K. H., Stewart, S. L., & Coplan, R. J. (1995). Social withdrawal in childhood: Conceptual and empirical perspectives. In T. H. Ollendick & R. J. Prinz (Eds.), *Advances in clinical child psychology* (Vol. 17, pp. 157–196). New York: Plenum.

Rubin, K. H., Watson, K. S., & Jambor, T. W. (1978). Free-play behaviors in preschool and kindergarten children. *Child Development, 49,* 539–536.

Ruble, D. N., Alvarez, J., Bachman, M., Cameron, J., Fuligni, A., Garcia Coll, C. T., & Rhee, E. (2004). The development of a sense of "we": The emergence and implications of children's collective identity. In M. Bennett & F. Sani (Eds.), *The development of the social self* (pp. 29–76). Hove, UK: Psychology Press.

Ruble, D. N., Martin, C. L., & Berenbaum, S. A. (2006). Gender development. In N. Eisenberg (Ed.), *Handbook of child psychology: Vol. 3. Social, emotional, and personality development* (6th ed., pp. 858–932). Hoboken, NJ: Wiley.

Ruble, D. N., Taylor, L. J., Cyphers, L., Greulich, F. K., Lurye, L. E., & Shrout, P. E. (2007). The role of gender constancy in early gender development. *Child Development, 78,* 1121–1136.

Ruck, M. D., Park, H., Killen, M., & Crystal, D. S. (2011). Intergroup contact and evaluations of race-based exclusion in urban minority children and adolescents. *Journal of Youth and Adolescence, 40,* 633–643.

Rudolph, K. D., Caldwell, M. S., & Conley, C. S. (2005). Need for approval and children's well-being. *Child Development, 76,* 309–323.

Ruedinger, E., & Cox, J. E. (2012). Adolescent childbearing: Consequences and interventions. *Current Opinions in Pediatrics, 24,* 446–452.

Ruff, C. (2002). Variation in human body size and shape. *Annual Review of Anthropology, 31,* 211–232.

Ruff, H. A., & Capozzoli, M. C. (2003). Development of attention and distractibility in the first 4 years of life. *Developmental Psychology, 39,* 877–890.

Ruffman, T., & Langman, L. (2002). Infants' reaching in a multi-well A not B task. *Infant Behavior and Development, 25,* 237–246.

Ruffman, T., Perner, J., Olson, D. R., & Doherty, M. (1993). Reflecting on scientific thinking: Children's understanding of the hypothesis–evidence relation. *Child Development, 64,* 1617–1636.

Ruffman, T., Slade, L., Devitt, K., & Crowe, E. (2006). What mothers say and what they do: The relation between parenting, theory of mind, language, and conflict/cooperation. *British Journal of Developmental Psychology, 24,* 105–124.

Runco, M. A. (1992). Children's divergent thinking and creative ideation. *Developmental Review, 12,* 233–264.

Rushton, J. P. (2012). No narrowing in mean black–white IQ differences—Predicted by heritable g. *American Psychologist, 67,* 500–501.

Rushton, J. P., & Jensen, A. R. (2006). The totality of available evidence shows the race IQ gap still remains. *Psychological Science, 17,* 921–922.

Rushton, J. P., & Jensen, A. R. (2010). The rise and fall of the Flynn effect as a reason to expect a narrowing of the black–white IQ gap. *Intelligence, 38,* 213–219.

Russell, A., Mize, J., & Bissaker, K. (2004). Parent–child relationships. In P. K. Smith & C. H. Hart (Eds.), *Blackwell handbook of childhood social development* (pp. 204–222). Malden, MA: Blackwell.

Russell, J., Alexis, D., & Clayton, N. S. (2010). Episodic future thinking in 3- to 5-year-old children: The ability to think of what will be needed from a different point of view. *Cognition, 114,* 56–71.

Russell, S. T., & Muraco, J. A. (2013). Representative data sets to study LGBT-parent families. In A. E. Goldberg & K. R. Allen (Eds.), *LGBT-parent families: Innovations in research and implications for practice* (pp. 343–356). New York: Springer.

Russo, A., Semeraro, F., Romano, M. R., Mastropasqua, R., Dell'Omo, R., & Costagliola, C. (2014). Myopia onset and progression: Can it be prevented? *International Ophthalmology, 34,* 693–705.

Rust, J., Golombok, S., Hines, M., Johnston, K., Golding, J., & the ALSPAC Study Team. (2000). The role of brothers and sisters in the gender development of preschool children. *Journal of Experimental Child Psychology, 77,* 292–303.

Ruthsatz, J., & Urbach, J. B. (2012). Child prodigy: A novel cognitive profile places elevated general intelligence, exceptional working memory and attention to detail at the root of prodigiousness. *Intelligence, 40,* 419–426.

Rutland, A., Killen, M., & Abrams, D. (2010). A new social-cognitive developmental perspective on prejudice: The interplay between morality and group identity. *Perspectives on Psychological Science, 5,* 279–291.

Rutter, M. (2007). Gene–environment interdependence. *Developmental Science, 10,* 12–18.

Rutter, M. (2011). Biological and experiential influences on psychological development. In D. P. Keating (Ed.), *Nature and nurture in early child development* (pp. 7–44). New York: Cambridge University Press.

Rutter, M., Colvert, E., Kreppner, J., Beckett, C., Castle, J., & Groothues, C. (2007). Early adolescent outcomes for institutionally deprived and non-deprived adoptees. I: Disinhibited attachment. *Journal of Child Psychology and Psychiatry, 48,* 17–30.

Rutter, M., & the English and Romanian Adoptees Study Team. (1998). Developmental catch-up, and deficit, following adoption after severe global early privation. *Journal of Child Psychology and Psychiatry, 39,* 465–476.

Rutter, M., O'Connor, T. G., & the English and Romanian Adoptees Study Team. (2004). Are there biological programming effects for psychological development? Findings from a study of Romanian adoptees. *Developmental Psychology, 40,* 81–94.

Rutter, M., Pickles, A., Murray, R., & Eaves, L. (2001). Testing hypotheses on specific environmental causal effects on behavior. *Psychological Bulletin, 127,* 291–324.

Rutter, M., Sonuga-Barke, E. J., Beckett, C., Castle, J., Kreppner, J., Kumsta, R., et al. (2010). Deprivation-specific psychological patterns: Effects of institutional deprivation. *Monographs of the Society for Research in Child Development, 75*(1, Serial No. 295).

Ryan, A. M., & Patrick, H. (2001). The classroom social environment and changes in adolescents' motivation and engagement during middle school. *American Educational Research Journal, 38,* 437–460.

Ryan, M. K., David, B., & Reynolds, K. J. (2004). Who cares? The effect of gender and context on the self and moral reasoning. *Psychology ofWomen Quarterly, 28,* 246–255.

Ryan, R. M., Fauth, R. C., & Brooks-Gunn, J. (2006). Childhood poverty: Implications for school readiness and early childhood education In B. Spodek & O. N. Saracho (Eds.), *Handbook of research on the education of young children* (2nd ed., pp. 323–346). Mahwah, NJ: Erlbaum.

Ryan, A. M., Shim, S. S., & Makara, K. A. (2013). Changes in academic adjustment and relational self-worth across the transition to middle school. *Journal of Youth and Adolescence, 42,* 1372–1384.

Ryding, M., Konradsson, K., Kalm, O., & Prellner, K. (2002). Auditory consequences of recurrent acute purulent otitis media. *Annals of Otology, Rhinology, and Laryngology, 111* (3, Pt. 1), 261–266.

S

Saarni, C. (2000). Emotional competence: A developmental perspective. In R. Bar-On & J. D. A. Parker (Eds.), *Handbook of emotional intelligence* (pp. 68–91). San Francisco: Jossey-Bass.

Saarni, C., Campos, J. J., Camras, L. A., & Witherington, D. (2006). Emotional development: Action, communication, and understanding. In N. Eisenberg (Ed.), *Handbook of child psychology: Vol. 3. Social, emotional, and personality development* (6th ed., pp. 226–299). Hoboken, NJ: Wiley.

Sabo, D. and Veliz, P. (2011). *Progress without equity: The provision of high school athletic opportunity in the United States, by gender 1993–94 through 2005–06.* East Meadow, NY: Women's Sports Foundation.

Sadeh, A. (1997). Sleep and melatonin in infants: A preliminary study. *Sleep, 20,* 185–191.

Sadeh, A., Flint-Ofir, E., Tirosh, T., & Tikotzky, L. (2007). Infant sleep and parental sleep-related cognitions. *Journal of Family Psychology, 21,* 74–87.

Sadler, P. M., Sonnert, G., Hazari, Z., & Tai, R. (2012). Stability and volatility of STEM career interest in high school: A gender study. *Science Education, 96,* 411–427.

Sadler, T. W. (2010). *Langman's medical embryology* (11th ed.). Baltimore, MD: Lippincott Williams & Wilkins.

Saenger, P. (2003). Dose effects of growth hormone during puberty. *Hormone Research, 60*(Suppl. 1), 52–57.

Safe Kids Worldwide. (2008). *Report to the nation: Trends in unintentional childhood injury mortality and parental views on child safety.* Retrieved from www.safekids.org/research-report/report-nation-trends-unintentional-childhood-injury-mortality-and-parental-views

Safe Kids Worldwide (2011). *A look inside American family vehicles: National study of 79,000 car seats, 2009–2010.* Retrieved from www.safekids.org/research-report/look-inside-american-family-vehicles-national-study-79000-car-seats-2009-2010

Safe Kids Worldwide. (2013). *Overview of childhood injury morbidity and mortality in the U.S.* Retrieved from www.safekids.org/fact-sheet/overview-childhood-injury-morbidity-and-mortality-us-fact-sheet-pdf

Saffran, J. R. (2009). What can statistical learning tell us about infant learning? In A. Woodward & A. Needham (Eds.), *Learning and the infant mind* (pp. 29–48). New York: Oxford University Press.

Saffran, J. R., Aslin, R. N., & Newport, E. L. (1996). Statistical learning by 8-month-old infants. *Science, 27,* 1926–1928.

Saffran, J. R., & Thiessen, E. D. (2003). Pattern induction by infant language learners. *Developmental Psychology, 39,* 484–494.

Saffran, J. R., Werker, J. F., & Werner, L. A. (2006). The infant's auditory world: Hearing, speech, and the beginnings of language. In D. Kuhn & R. Siegler (Eds.), *Handbook of child psychology: Vol. 2. Cognition, perception, and language* (6th ed., pp. 58–108). Hoboken, NJ: Wiley.

Safren, S. A., & Pantalone, D. W. (2006). Social anxiety and barriers to resilience among lesbian, gay, and bisexual adolescents. In A. M. Omoto & H. S. Kurtzman (Eds.), *Sexual orientation and mental health: Examining identity and development in lesbian, gay, and bisexual young people* (pp. 55–71). Washington, DC: American Psychological Association.

Saigal, S., Stoskopf, B., Streiner, D., Boyle, M., Pinelli, J., & Paneth, N. (2006). Transition of extremely low-birthweight infants from adolescence to young adulthood. *Journal of the American Medical Association, 295,* 667–675.

Saitta, S. C., & Zackai, E. H. (2005). Specific chromosome disorders in newborns. In H. W. Taeusch, R. A. Ballard, & C. A. Gleason (Eds.), *Avery's diseases of the newborn* (8th ed., pp. 204–215). Philadelphia: Saunders.

Salas-Wright, C. P., Vaughn, M. G., & Maynard, B. R. (2014). Religiosity and violence among adolescents in the United States: Findings from the National Survey on Drug Use and Health, 2006–2010. *Journal of Interpersonal Violence, 29,* 1178–1200.

Sale, A., Berardi, N., & Maffei, L. (2009). Enrich the environment to empower the brain. *Trends in Neurosciences, 32,* 233–239.

Salihu, H. M., Shumpert, M. N., Slay, M., Kirby, R. S., & Alexander, G. R. (2003). Childbearing beyond maternal age 50 and fetal outcomes in the United States. *Obstetrics and Gynecology, 102,* 1006–1014.

Salisbury, A. L., Ponder, K. L., Padbury, J. F., & Lester, B. M. (2009). Fetal effects of psychoactive drugs. *Clinics in Perinatology, 36,* 595–619.

Salley, B. J., & Dixon, W. E., Jr. (2007). Temperamental and joint attentional predictors of language development. *Merrill-Palmer Quarterly, 53,* 131–154.

Salmivalli, C., & Voeten, M. (2004). Connections between attitudes, group norms, and behaviour in bullying situations. *International Journal of Behavioral Development, 28,* 246–258.

Salomo, D., & Liszkowski, U. (2013). Sociocultural settings influence the emergence of prelinguistic deictic gestures. *Child Development, 84,* 1296–1307.

Salter, D., McMillan, D., Richards, M., Talbot, T., Hodges, J., Bentovim, A., & Hastings, R. (2003). Development of sexually abusive behavior in sexually victimized males: A longitudinal study. *Lancet, 361,* 471–476.

Samek, D. R., & Rueter, M. A. (2011). Considerations of elder sibling closeness in predicting younger sibling substance use: Social learning versus social bonding explanations. *Journal of Family Psychology, 25,*931–941.

Sameroff, A. (2006). Identifying risk and protective factors for healthy child development. In A. Clarke-Stewart & J. Dunn (Eds.), *Families count: Effects on child and adolescent development* (pp. 53–76). New York: Cambridge University Press.

Samuolis, J., Griffin, K. W., Williams, C., Cesario, B., & Botvin, G. J. (2013). Work intensity and substance use among adolescents employed part-time in entry-level jobs. In J. Merrick (Eds.), *Child and adolescent health yearbook, 2011* (pp. 81–88). Hauppauge, NY: Noval Biomedical Books.

Sanders, O. (2006). Evaluating the Keeping Ourselves Safe Programme. Wellington, NZ: Youth Education Service, New Zealand Police. Retrieved from www.nzfvc.org.nz/accan/papers-presentations/abstract11v.shtml

Sann, C., & Streri, A. (2007). Perception of object shape and texture in human newborns: Evidence from cross-modal transfer tasks. *Developmental Science, 10,* 399–410.

Sann, C., & Streri, A. (2008). The limits of newborn's grasping to detect texture in a cross-modal transfer task. *Infant Behavior and Development, 31,* 523–531.

Sansavini, A., Bertoncini, J., & Giovanelli, G. (1997). Newborns discriminate the rhythm of multisyllabic stressed words. *Developmental Psychology, 33,* 3–11.

Sarnecka, B. W., & Gelman, S. A. (2004). Six does not just mean a lot: Preschoolers see number words as specific. *Cognition, 92,* 329–352.

Sarnecka, B. W., & Wright, C. E. (2013). The idea of an exact number: Children's understanding of cardinality and equinumerosity. *Cognitive Science, 37,* 1493–1506.

Sato, T., Matsumoto, T., Kawano, H., Watanabe, T., Uematsu, Y., & Semine, K. (2004). Brain masculinization requires androgen receptor function. *Proceedings of the National Academy of Sciences, 101,* 1673–1678.

Satterwhite, C. L., Torrone, E., Meites, E., Dunne, E. F., Mahajan, R., Ocfemia, M. C. B., et al. (2013). Sexually transmitted infections among US women and men: Prevalence and incidence estimates, 2008. *Sexually Transmitted Diseases, 40,* 187–193.

Saucier, J. F., Sylvestre, R., Doucet, H., Lambert, J., Frappier, J. Y., Charbonneau, L., & Malus, M. (2002). Cultural identity and adaptation to adolescence in Montreal. In F. J. C. Azima & N. Grizenko (Eds.), *Immigrant and refugee children and their families: Clinical, research, and training issues* (pp. 133–154). Madison, WI: International Universities Press.

Saudino, K. J. (2003). Parent ratings of infant temperament: Lessons from twin studies. *Infant Behavior and Development, 26,* 100–107.

Saudino, K. J., & Plomin, R. (1997). Cognitive and temperamental mediators of genetic contributions to the home environment during infancy. *Merrill-Palmer Quarterly, 43,* 1–23.

Sautter, J. M., Tippett, R. M., & Morgan, S. P. (2010). The social demography of Internet dating in the United States. *Social Science Quarterly, 91,* 554–575.

Sawyer, A. M., & Borduin, C. M. (2011). Effects of multisystemic therapy through midlife: A 21.9-year follow-up to a randomized clinical trial with serious and violent juvenile offenders. *Journal of Consulting and Clinical Psychology, 79,* 643–652.

Saxe, G. B. (1988, August–September). Candy selling and math learning. *Educational Researcher, 17*(6), 14–21.

Saxton, M., Backley, P., & Gallaway, C. (2005). Negative input for grammatical errors: Effects after a lag of 12 weeks. *Journal of Child Language, 32,* 643–672.

Sayfan, L., & Lagatutta, K. H. (2009). Scaring the monster away: What children know about managing fears of real and imaginary creatures. *Child Development, 80,* 1756–1774.

Saygin, A. P., Leech, R., & Dick, F. (2010). Nonverbal auditory agnosia with lesion to Wernicke's area. *Neuropsychologia, 48,* 107–113.

Saygin, A. P., Wilson, S. M., Dronkers, N. F., & Bates, E. (2004). Action comprehension in aphasia: Linguistic and non-linguistic deficits and their lesion correlates. *Neuropsychologia, 42,* 1788–1804.

Saylor, M. M. (2004). Twelve- and 16-month-old infants recognize properties of mentioned absent things. *Developmental Science, 7,* 599–611.

Saylor, M. M., Sabbagh, M. A., & Baldwin, D. A. (2002). Children use whole–part juxtaposition as a pragmatic cue to word meaning. *Developmental Psychology, 38,* 993–1003.

Saylor, M. M., & Troseth, G. L. (2006). Preschoolers use information about speakers' desires to learn new words. *Cognitive Development, 21,* 214–231.

Scarlett, W. G., & Warren, A. E. A. (2010). Religious and spiritual development across the life span: A behavioral and social science perspective. In M. Lamb & A. Freund (Eds.), *Handbook of life-span development: Vol. 2. Social and emotional development* (pp. 631–682). Hoboken, NJ: Wiley.

Scarr, S., & McCartney, K. (1983). How people make their own environments: A theory of genotype–environment effects. *Child Development, 54,* 424–435.

Scarr, S., & Weinberg, R. A. (1983). The Minnesota adoption studies: Genetic differences and malleability. *Child Development, 54,* 260–267.

Schaal, B., Marlier, L., & Soussignan, R. (2000). Human fetuses learn odours from their pregnant mother's diet. *Chemical Senses, 25,* 729–737.

Schalet, A. (2007). Adolescent sexuality viewed through two different cultural lenses. In M. S. Tepper & A. F. Owens (Eds.), *Sexual health: Vol. 3. Moral and cultural foundations* (pp. 365–387). Westport, CT: Praeger.

Schauwers, K., Gillis, S., Daemers, K., De Beukelaer, C., De Ceulaer, G., Yperman, M., & Govaerts, P. J. (2004). Normal hearing and language development in a deaf-born child. *Otology and Neurotology, 25,* 924–929.

Scher, A., Epstein, R., & Tirosh, E. (2004). Stability and changes in sleep regulation: A longitudinal study from 3 months to 3 years. *International Journal of Behavioral Development, 28,* 268–274.

Scher, A., Tirosh, E., Jaffe, M., Rubin, L., Sadeh, A., & Lavie, P. (1995). Sleep patterns of infants and young children in Israel. *International Journal of Behavioral Development, 18,* 701–711.

Scherrer, J. L. (2012). The United Nations Convention on the Rights of the Child as policy and strategy for social work action in child welfare in the United States. *Social Work, 57,* 11–22.

Schlaggar, B. L., & Barnes, K. A. (2011). Developmental cognitive neuroscience: Infancy to young adulthood. In K. L. Fingerman, C. A. Berg, J. Smith, & T. C. Antonucci (Eds.), *Handbook of life-span development* (pp. 363–385). New York: Springer.

Schlagmüller, M., & Schneider, W. (2002). The development of organizational strategies in children: Evidence from a microgenetic longitudinal study. *Journal of Experimental Child Psychology, 81,* 298–319.

Schlegel, A., & Barry, H., III. (1991). *Adolescence: An anthropological inquiry.* New York: Free Press.

Schmeeckle, M., & Sprecher, S. (2004). Extended family and social networks. In A. Vangelisti (Ed.), *Handbook of family communication* (pp. 349–375). Mahwah, NJ: Erlbaum.

Schmid, R. G., Tirsch, W. S., & Scherb, H. (2002). Correlation between spectral EEG parameters and intelligence test variables in school-age children. *Clinical Neurophysiology, 113,* 1647–1656.

Schmidt, A. T., Waldow, K. J., Grove, W. M., Salinas, J. A., & Georgieff, M. K. (2007). Dissociating the long-term effects of fetal/neonatal iron deficiency on three types of learning in the rat. *Behavioral Neuroscience, 121,* 475–482.

Schmidt, L. A., Fox, N. A., Rubin, K. H., Sternberg, E. M., Gold, P. W., & Smith, C. C. (1997). Behavioral and neuroendocrine responses in shy children. *Developmental Psychobiology, 35,* 119–135.

Schmidt, L. A., Fox, N. A., Schulkin, J., & Gold, P. W. (1999). Behavioral and psychophysiological correlates of self-presentation in temperamentally shy children. *Developmental Psychobiology, 30,* 127–140.

Schmidt, M. E., Crawley-Davis, A. M., & Anderson, D. R. (2007). Two-year-olds' object retrieval based on television: Testing a perceptual account. *Media Psychology, 9,* 389–409.

Schmidt, S. (2013). *Early Head Start participants, programs, families and staff in 2012.* Washington, DC: CLASP. Retrieved from www.clasp.org/resources-and-publications/files/EHS-PIR-2012-Fact-Sheet.pdf

Schmitz, S., Fulker, D. W., Plomin, R., Zahn-Waxler, C., Emde, R. N., & DeFries, J. C. (1999). Temperament and problem behaviour during early childhood. *International Journal of Behavioral Development, 23,* 333–355.

Schneider, B. H., Atkinson, L., & Tardif, C. (2001). Child–parent attachment and children's peer relations: A quantitative review. *Developmental Psychology, 37,* 86–100.

Schneider, D. (2006). Smart as we can get? *American Scientist, 94,* 311–312.

Schneider, W. (1986). The role of conceptual knowledge and metamemory in the development of organizational processes in memory. *Journal of Experimental Child Psychology, 42,* 218–236.

Schneider, W. (2002). Memory development in childhood. In U. Goswami (Ed.), *Blackwell handbook of childhood cognitive development* (pp. 236–256). Malden, MA: Blackwell.

Schneider, W., & Bjorklund, D. F. (1992). Expertise, aptitude, and strategic remembering. *Child Development, 63,* 461–473.

Schneider, W., & Bjorklund, D. F. (1998). Memory. In D. Kuhn & R. S. Siegler (Eds.), *Handbook of child psychology: Vol. 2. Cognition, perception, and language* (5th ed., pp. 467–521). New York: Wiley.

Schneider, W., & Pressley, M. (1997). *Memory development between two and twenty* (2nd ed.). Mahwah, NJ: Erlbaum.

Schonberg, R. L., & Tifft, C. J. (2007). Birth defects and prenatal diagnosis. In M. L. Batshaw, L. Pellegrino, & N. J. Roizen (Eds.), *Children with disabilities* (6th ed., pp. 83–96). Baltimore: Paul H. Brookes.

Schöner, G., & Thelen, E. (2006). Using dynamic field theory to rethink infant habituation. *Psychological Review, 113,* 273–299.

Schonert-Reichl, K. A. (1999). Relations of peer acceptance, friendship adjustment, and social behavior to moral reasoning during early adolescence. *Journal of Early Adolescence, 19,* 249–279.

Schoon, I., Jones, E., Cheng, H., Maughan, B. (2012). Family hardship, family instability, and cognitive development. *Journal of Epidemiology and Community Health, 66,* 716–722.

Schoon, I., & Parsons, S. (2002). Teenage aspirations for future careers and occupational outcomes. *Journal of Vocational Behavior, 60,* 262–288.

Schoppe-Sullivan, S. J., Brown, G. L., Cannon, E. A., Mangelsdorf, S. C., & Sokolowski, M. S. (2008). Maternal gatekeeping, coparenting quality, and fathering behavior in families with infants. *Journal of Family Psychology, 22,* 389–398.

Schoppe-Sullivan, S. J., Mangelsdorf, S. C., Brown, G. L., & Sokolowski, M. S. (2007). Goodness-of-fit in family context: Infant temperament, marital quality, and early coparenting behavior. *Infant Behavior and Development, 30,* 82–96.

Schott, J. M., & Rossor, M. N. (2003). The grasp and other primitive reflexes. *Journal of Neurological and Neurosurgical Psychiatry, 74,* 558–560.

Schroeder, R. D., Bulanda, R. E., Giordano, P. C., & Cernkovich, S. A. (2010). Parenting and adult criminality: An examination of direct and indirect effects by race. *Journal of Adolescent Research, 25,* 64–98.

Schuetze, P., & Eiden, R. D. (2006). The association between maternal cocaine use during pregnancy and physiological regulation in 4- to 8-week-old infants: An examination of possible mediators and moderators. *Journal of Pediatric Psychology, 31,* 15–26.

Schull, W. J. (2003). The children of atomic bomb survivors: A synopsis. *Journal of Radiological Protection, 23,* 369–394.

Schulte-Ruther, M., Markowitsch, H. J., Fink, G. R., & Piefke, M. (2007). Mirror neuron and theory of mind mechanisms involved in face-to-face interactions: A functional magnetic resonance imaging approach to empathy. *Journal of Cognitive Neuroscience, 19,* 1354–1372.

Schultz, T. R. (2011). Computational modeling of infant concept learning: The developmental shift from features to correlations. In L. M. Oakes, C. H. Cashon, M. Casasola, & D. Rakison (Eds.), *Infant perception and cognition* (125–152). New York: Oxford University Press.

Schulz, M. S., Cowan, C. P., & Cowan, P. A. (2006). Promoting healthy beginnings: A randomized controlled trial of a preventive intervention to preserve marital quality during the transition to parenthood. *Journal of Consulting and Clinical Psychology, 74,* 20–31.

Schulze, C., Grassmann, S., & Tomasello, M. (2013). 3-year-old children make relevant inferences in indirect verbal communication. *Child Development, 84,* 2079–2093.

Schunemann, N., Sporer, N., & Brunstein, J. C. (2013). Integrating self-regulation in whole-class reciprocal teaching: A moderator–mediator analysis of incremental effects on fifth graders' reading comprehension. *Contemporary Educational Psychology, 38,* 289–305.

Schunk, D. H., & Pajares, F. (2005). Competence perceptions and academic functioning. In A. J. Andrew & C. S. Dweck (Eds.), *Handbook of competence and motivation* (pp. 85–104). New York: Guilford.

Schunk, D. H., & Zimmerman, B. J. (2013). Self-regulation and learning. In W. M. Reynolds, G. E. Miller, & I. B. Weiner (Eds.), *Handbook of psychology: Vol. 7. Educational psychology* (pp. 45–68). Hoboken, NJ: Wiley.

Schwanenflugel, P. J., Henderson, R. L., & Fabricius, W. V. (1998). Developing organization of mental verbs and theory of mind in middle childhood: Evidence from extensions. *Developmental Psychology, 34,* 512–524.

Schwartz, C. E., Kunwar, P. S., Greve, D. N., Kagan, J., Snidman, N. C., & Bloch, R. B. (2012). A phenotype of early infancy predicts reactivity of the amygdala in male adults. *Molecular Psychiatry, 17,* 1042–1050.

Schwartz, S. J., Beyers, W., Luyckx, K., Soenens, B. Zamboanga, B. L., Forthun, L. F., et al. (2011). Examining the light and dark sides of emerging adults' identity: A study of identity status differences in positive and negative psychosocial functioning. *Journal of Youth and Adolescence, 40*(7), 839–859.

Schwartz, S. J., Côté, J. E., & Arnett, J. J. (2005). Identity and agency in emerging adulthood: Two developmental routes in the individualization process. *Youth and Society, 37,* 201–229.

Schwartz, S. J., Donnellan, M. B., Ravert, R. D., Luyckx, K., & Zamboanga, B. L. (2013). Identity development, personality, and well-being in adolescence and emerging adulthood: Theory, research, and recent advances. In R. M. Lerner, M. A. Easterbrooks, & J. Mistry (Eds.), *Handbook of psychology: Vol. 6. Developmental psychology* (pp. 339–364). Hoboken, NJ: Wiley.

Schwartz, S. J., Pantin, H., Prado, G., Sullivan, S., & Szapocznik, J. (2005). Family functioning, identity, and problem behavior: Immigrant early adolescents. *Journal of Early Adolescence, 25,* 392–420.

Schwartz, S. J., Zamboanga, B. L., Luyckx, K., Meca, A., & Ritchie, R. A. (2013). Identity in emerging adulthood: Reviewing the field and looking forward. *Emerging Adulthood, 1,* 96–113.

Schwarz, N. (1999). Self-reports: How the questions shape the answers. *American Psychologist, 54,* 93–105.

Schwebel, D. C., & Bounds, M. L. (2003). The role of parents and temperament on children's estimation of physical ability: Links to unintentional injury prevention. *Journal of Pediatric Psychology, 28,* 505–516.

Schwebel, D. C., & Brezausek, C. M. (2007). Father transitions in the household and young children's injury risk. *Psychology of Men and Masculinity, 8,* 173–184.

Schwebel, D. C., Brezausek, C. M., Ramey, S. L., & Ramey, C. T. (2004). Interactions between child behavior patterns and parenting: Implications for children's unintentional injury risk. *Journal of Pediatric Psychology, 29,* 93–104.

Schwebel, D. C., & Gaines, J. (2007). Pediatric unintentional injury: Behavioral risk factors and implications for prevention. *Journal of Developmental and Behavioral Pediatrics, 28,* 245–254.

Schwebel, D. C., Roth, D. L., Elliott, M. N., Chien, A. T., Mrug, S., Shipp, E., et al. (2012). Marital conflict and fifth-graders' risk for injury. *Accident Analysis and Prevention, 47,* 30–35.

Schwebel, D. C., Roth, D. L., Elliott, M. N., Windle, M., Grunbaum, J. A., Low, B., et al. (2011). The association of activity level, parent mental distress, and parental involvement and monitoring with unintentional injury risk in fifth graders. *Accident Analysis and Prevention, 43,* 848–852.

Schweinhart, L. J. (2010). The challenge of the High/Scope Perry Preschool study. In A. J. Reynolds, A. J. Rolnick, M. M. Englund, & J. Temple (Eds.), *Childhood programs and practices in the first decade of life: A human capital integration* (pp. 199–213). New York: Cambridge University Press.

Schweinhart, L. J., Montie, J., Xiang, Z., Barnett, W. S., Belfield, C. R., & Nores, M. (2005). *Lifetime effects: The High/Scope Perry Preschool Study through age 40.* Ypsilanti, MI: High/Scope Press.

Schweizer, K., Moosbrugger, H., & Goldhammer, F. (2006). The structure of the relationship between attention and intelligence. *Intelligence, 33,* 589–611.

Schwenck, C., Bjorklund, D. F., & Schneider, W. (2007). Factors influencing the incidence of utilization deficiencies and other patterns of recall/strategy-use relations in a strategic memory task. *Child Development, 22,* 197–212.

Schwerdt, G., & West, M. R. (2013). The impact of alternative grade configurations on student outcomes through middle and high school. *Journal of Public Economics, 97,* 308–326.

Schwier, C., van Maanen, C., Carpenter, M., & Tomasello, M. (2006). Rational imitation in 12-month-old infants. *Infancy, 10,* 303–311.

Scot, T. P., Callahan, C. M., & Urquhart, J. (2009). Paint-by-number teachers and cookie-cutter students: The unintended effects of high-stakes testing on the education of gifted students. *Roeper Review, 31,* 40–52.

Scott, L. D. (2003). The relation of racial identity and racial socialization to coping with discrimination among African Americans. *Journal of Black Studies, 20,* 520–538.

Scott, L. S. (2009). *Two is enough.* Berkeley, CA: Seal Press.

Scott, L. S., & Monesson, A. (2009). The origin of biases in face perception. *Psychological Science, 20,* 676–680.

Scott, R. M., & Fisher, C. (2012). 2.5-year-olds use cross-situational consistency to learn verbs under referential uncertainty. *Cognition, 122,* 163–180.

Scrutton, D. (2005). Influence of supine sleeping positioning on early motor milestone acquisition. *Developmental Medicine and Child Neurology, 47,* 364.

Seaton, E. K., Scottham, K. M., & Sellers, R. M. (2006). The status model of racial identity development in African American adolescents: Evidence of structure, trajectories, and well-being. *Child Development, 77,* 1416–1426.

Seethaler, P. M., Fuchs, L. S., Fuchs, D., & Compton, D. L. (2012). Predicting first graders' development of calculation versus word-problem performance: The role of dynamic assessment. *Journal of Educational Psychology, 104,* 224–234.

Segool, N. K., Carlson, J. S., Goforth, A. N., von der Embse, N., & Barterian, J. A. (2013). Heightened test anxiety among young children: Elementary school students' anxious responses to high-stakes testing. *Psychology in the Schools, 50,* 489–499.

Seibert, A. C., & Kerns, K. A. (2009). Attachment figures in middle childhood. *International Journal of Behavioral Development, 33,* 347–355.

Seidl, A., Hollich, G., & Jusczyk, P. (2003). Early understanding of subject and object wh-questions. *Infancy, 4,* 423–436.

Seidman, E., Aber, J. L., & French, S. E. (2004). Assessing the transitions to middle and high school. *Journal of Adolescent Research, 19,* 3–30.

Seidman, E., Lambert, L. E., Allen, L., & Aber, J. L. (2003). Urban adolescents' transition to junior high school and protective family transactions. *Journal of Early Adolescence, 23,* 166–193.

Seitz, V., & Apfel, N. H. (2005). Creating effective school-based interventions for pregnant teenagers. In R. D. Peters, B. Leadbeater, & R. J. McMahon (Eds.), *Resilience in children, families, and communities: Linking context to practice and policy* (pp. 65–82). New York: Kluwer Academic.

Sekido, R., & Lovell-Badge, R. (2009). Sex determination and SRY: Down to a wink and a nudge? *Trends in Genetics, 25,* 19–29.

Senechal, M., & LeFevre, J. (2002). Parental involvement in the development of children's reading skill: A five-year longitudinal study. *Child Development, 73,* 445–460.

Senghas, R. J., Senghas, A., & Pyers, J. E. (2005). The emergence of Nicaraguan Sign Language: Questions of development, acquisition, and evolution. In J. Langer, S. T. parker, & C. Milbrath (Eds.), *Biology and knowledge revisited: From neurogenesis to psychogenesis* (pp. 287–306). Mahwah, NJ: Erlbaum.

Sengpiel, V., Elind, E., Bacelis, J., Nilsson, S., Grove, J., Myhre, R., et al. (2013). Maternal caffeine intake during pregnancy is associated with birth weight but not with gestational length: Results from a large prospective observational cohort study. *BMC Medicine, 11,* 42.

Senju, A., Csibra, G., & Johnson, M. H. (2008). Understanding the referential nature of looking: Infants' preference for object-directed gaze. *Cognition, 108,* 303–319.

Senn, T. E., Espy, K. A., & Kaufmann, P. M. (2004). Using path analysis to understand executive function organization in preschool children. *Developmental Neuropsychology, 26,* 445–464.

Serbin, L. A., Powlishta, K. K., & Gulko, J. (1993). The development of sex typing in middle childhood. *Monographs of the Society for Research in Child Development, 58*(2, Serial No. 232).

Sermon, K., Van Steirteghem, A., & Liebaers, I. (2004). Preimplantation genetic diagnosis. *Lancet, 363,* 1633–1641.

Serratrice, L. (2013). The bilingual child. In T. K. Bhatia & W. C. Ritchie (Eds.), *Handbook of bilingualism and multilingualism* (pp. 87–108). Chichester, UK: Wiley-Blackwell.

Sesame Workshop. (2014). *Where we work: All locations.* Retrieved from www.sesameworkshop.org/where-we-work/all-locations

Sevigny, P. R., & Loutzenhiser, L. (2010). Predictors of parenting self-efficacy in mothers and fathers of toddlers. *Child Care, Health and Development, 36,* 179–189.

Sewell, A., St George, A., & Cullen, J. (2013). The distinctive features of joint participation in a community of learners. *Teaching and Teacher Education, 31,* 46–55.

Seymour, S. C. (1999). *Women, family, and child care in India.* Cambridge, UK: Cambridge University Press.

SFIA (Sports & Fitness Industry Association). (2013). 2013 U.S. trends in team sports report. Retrieved from www.sfia.org/reports/305

Shah, T., Sullivan, K., & Carter, J. (2006). Sudden infant death syndrome and reported maternal smoking during pregnancy. *American Journal of Public Health, 96,* 1757–1759.

Shahaeian, A., Peterson, C. C., Slaughter, V., & Wellman, H. M. (2011). Culture and the sequence of steps in theory of mind development. *Developmental Psychology, 47,* 1239–1247.

Shanahan, L., McHale, S. M., Crouter, A. C., & Osgood, D. W. (2007). Warmth with mothers and fathers from middle childhood to late adolescence: Within- and between-families comparisions. *Developmental Psychology, 43,* 551–563.

Shapka, J. D., & Keating, D. P. (2005). Structure and change in self-concept during adolescence. *Canadian Journal of Behavioural Science, 37,* 83–96.

Sharp, E. H., Coatsworth, J. D., Darling, N., Cumsille, P., & Ranieri, S. (2007). Gender differences in the self-defining activities and identity experiences of adolescents and emerging adults. *Journal of Adolescence, 30,* 251–269.

Shaver, P., Furman, W., & Buhrmester, D. (1985). Transition to college: Network changes, social skills, and loneliness. In S. Duck & D. Perlman (Eds.), *Understanding personal relationships: An interdisciplinary approach* (pp. 193–219). London: Sage.

Shaw, D. S., Gilliom, M., Ingoldsby, E. M., & Nagin, D. S. (2003). Trajectories leading to school-age conduct problems. *Developmental Psychology, 39,* 189–200.

Shaw, D. S., Lacourse, E., & Nagin, D. S. (2005). Developmental trajectories of conduct problems and hyperactivity from ages 2 to 10. *Journal of Child Psychology and Psychiatry, 46,* 931–942.

Shaw, D. S., Winslow, E. B., & Flanagan, C. (1999). A prospective study of the effects of marital status and family relations on young children's adjustment among African-American and European-American families. *Child Development, 70,* 742–755.

Shaw, P., Brierley, B., & David, A. S. (2005). A critical period for the impact of amygdala damage on the emotional enhancement of memory? *Neurology, 65,* 326–328.

Shaw, P., Eckstrand, K., Sharp, W., Blumenthal, J., Lerch, J. P., & Greenstein, D. (2007, November 16). Attention-deficit/hyperactivity disorder is characterized by a delay in cortical maturation. *Proceedings of the National Academy of Sciences Online.* Retrieved from www.pnas.org/cgi/content/abstract/0707741104v1

Shedler, J., & Block, J. (1990). Adolescent drug use and psychological health: A longitudinal inquiry. *American Psychologist, 45,* 612–630.

Sheehan, G., Darlington, Y., Noller, P., & Feeney, J. (2004). Children's perceptions of their sibling relationships during parental separation and divorce. *Journal of Divorce and Remarriage, 41,* 69–94.

Sheehy, A., Gasser, T., Molinari, L., & Largo, R. H. (1999). An analysis of variance of the pubertal and midgrowth spurts for length and width. *Annals of Human Biology, 26,* 309–331.

Sherman, S. L., Freeman, S. B., Allen, E. G., & Lamb, N. E. (2005). Risk factors for nondisjunction of trisomy 21. *Cytogenetic Genome Research, 111,* 273–280.

Sherrod, L. R., & Spiewak, G. S. (2008). Possible interrelationships between civic engagement, positive youth development, and spirituality/religiosity. In R. M. Lerner, R. W. Roeser, & E. Phelps (Eds.), *Positive youth development and spirituality: From theory to research* (pp. 322–338). West Conshohocken, PA: Templeton Foundation Press.

Sherry, B., McDivitt, J., Brich, L. L., Cook, F. H., Sanders, S., Prish, J. L., Francis, L. A., & Scanlon, K. S. (2004). Attitudes, practices, and concerns about child feeding and child weight status among socioeconomically diverse white, Hispanic, and African-American mothers. *Journal of the American Dietetic Association, 104,* 215–221.

Shimada, S., & Hiraki, K. (2006). Infant's brain responses to live and televised action. *NeuroImage, 32,* 930–939.

Shimizu, H. (2001). Japanese adolescent boys' senses of empathy (*omoiyari*) and Carol Gilligan's perspectives on the morality of care: A phenomenological approach. *Culture and Psychology, 7,* 453–475.

Shipman, K. L., Zeman, J., Nesin, A. E., & Fitzgerald, M. (2003). Children's strategies for displaying anger and sadness: What works with whom? *Merrill-Palmer Quarterly, 49,* 100–122.

Shonkoff, J. P., & Bales, S. N. (2011). Science does not speak for itself: Translating child development research for the public and its policymakers. *Child Development, 82,* 17–32.

Shriver, L. H., Harrist, A. W., Page, M., Hubbs-Tait, L., Moulton, M., & Topham, G. (2013). Differences in body esteem by weight status, gender, and physical activity among young elementary school-aged children. *Body Image, 10,* 78–84.

Shulman, S., & Connolly, J. (2013). The challenge of romantic relationships in emerging adulthood: Reconceptualization of the field. *Emerging Adulthood, 1,* 27–39.

Shulman, S., & Kipnis, O. (2001). Adolescent romantic relationships: A look from the future. *Journal of Adolescence, 24,* 337–351.

Shulman, S., Laursen, B., & Dickson, D. J. (2014). Gender differences in the spillover between romantic experiences, work experiences, and individual adjustment across emerging adulthood. *Emerging Adulthood, 2,* 36–47.

Shuwairi, S. M., Albert, M. K., & Johnson, S. P. (2007). Discrimination of possible and impossible objects in infancy. *Psychological Science, 18,* 303–307.

Shwalb, D. W., Nakawaza, J., Yamamoto, T., & Hyun, J.-H. (2004). Fathering in Japanese, Chinese, and Korean cultures: A review of the research literature. In M. E. Lamb (Ed.), *The role of the father in child development* (4th ed., pp. 146–181). Hoboken, NJ: Wiley.

Shweder, R. A., Goodnow, J. J., Hatano, G., LeVine, R. A., Markus, H. R., & Miller, P. J. (2006). The cultural psychology of development: One mind, many mentalities. In R. M. Lerner (Ed.), *Handbook of child psychology: Vol. 1. Theoretical models of human development* (6th ed., pp. 716–792). Hoboken, NJ: Wiley.

Sidebotham, P., Heron, J., & the ALSPAC Study Team. (2003). Child maltreatment in the "children of the nineties": The role of the child. *Child Abuse and Neglect, 27,* 337–352.

Sidappa, A., Georgieff, M. K., Wewerka, S., Worwa, C., Nelson, C. A., & deRegnier, R. (2004). Iron deficiency

alters auditory recognition memory in newborn infants of diabetic mothers. *Pediatric Research, 55,* 1034–1041.
Siebenbruner, J., Zimmer-Gembeck, M. J., & Egeland, B. (2007). Sexual partners and contraceptive use: A 16- year prospective study predicting abstinence and risk behavior. *Journal of Research on Adolescence, 17,* 179–206.
Siebert, A. C., & Kerns, K. A. (2009). Attachment figures in middle childhood. *International Journal of Behavioral Development, 33,* 347–355.
Siegal, M., Iozzi, L., & Surian, L. (2009). Bilingualism and conversational understanding in young children. *Cognition, 110,* 115–122.
Siega-Riz, A. M., Deming, D. M., Reidy, K. C., Fox, M. K., Condon, E., & Briefel, R. R. (2010). Food consumption patterns of infants and toddlers: Where are we now? *Journal of the American Dietetic Association, 110,* S38–S51.
Siegler, R. S. (1996). *Emerging minds: The process of change in children's thinking*. New York: Oxford University Press.
Siegler, R. S. (2002). Microgenetic studies of self-explanation. In N. Granott & J. Parziale (Eds.), *Microdevelopment: Transition processes in development and learning* (pp. 31–58). New York: Cambridge University Press.
Siegler, R. S. (2006). Microgenetic analyses of learning. In D. Kuhn & R. Siegler (Eds.), *Handbook of child psychology: Vol. 2. Cognition, perception, and language* (6th ed., pp. 464–510). Hoboken, NJ: Wiley.
Siegler, R. S. (2009). Improving preschoolers' number sense using information-processing theory. In O. A. Barbarin & B. H. Wasik (Eds.), *Handbook of child development and early education: Research to practice* (pp. 429–454). New York: Guilford.
Siegler, R. S., & Crowley, K. (1991). The microgenetic method: A direct means for studying cognitive development. *American Psychologist, 46,* 606–620.
Siegler, R. S., & Mu, Y. (2008). Chinese children excel on novel mathematics problems even before elementary school. *Psychological Science, 19,* 759–763.
Siegler, R. S., & Svetina, M. (2006). What leads children to adopt new strategies? A microgenetic/cross-sectional study of class inclusion. *Child Development, 77,* 997–1015.
Sikora, J., & Pokropek, A. (2012). Gender segregation of adolescent science career plans in 50 countries. *Science Education, 96,* 234–264.
Silk, J. S., Sessa, F. M., Morris, A. S., Steinberg, L., & Avenevoli, S. (2004). Neighborhood cohesion as a buffer against hostile maternal parenting. *Journal of Family Psychology, 18,* 135–146.
Silk, T. J., & Wood, A. G. (2011). Lessons about neurodevelopment from anatomical magnetic resonance imaging. *Journal of Developmental and Behavioral Pediatrics, 32,* 158–168.
Silvén, M. (2001). Attention in very young infants predicts learning of first words. *Infant Behavior and Development, 24,* 229–237.
Silverman, I., Choi, J., & Peters, M. (2007). The hunter-gatherer theory of sex differences in spatial abilities. *Archives of Sexual Behavior, 36,* 261–268.
Silverman, J. G., Raj, A., Mucci, L. A., & Hathaway, J. E. (2001). Dating violence against adolescent girls and associated substance use, unhealthy weight control, sexual risk behavior, pregnancy, and suicidality. *Journal of the American Medical Association, 286,* 572–579.
Sim, T. N., & Koh, S. F. (2003). A domain conceptualization of adolescent susceptibility to peer pressure. *Journal of Research on Adolescence, 13,* 57–80.
Sim, T. N., & Yeo, G. H. (2012). Peer crowds in Singapore. *Youth and Society, 44,* 201–216.
Simcock, G., & DeLoache, J. (2006). Get the picture? The effects of iconicity on toddlers' reenactment from picture books. *Developmental Psychology, 42,* 1352–1357.
Simcock, G., Garrity, K., & Barr, R. (2011). The effect of narrative cues on infants' imitation from television and picture books. *Child Development, 82,* 1607–1619.
Simcock, G., & Hayne, H. (2003). Age-related changes in verbal and nonverbal memory during early childhood. *Developmental Psychology, 39,* 805–814.
Simion, F., Cassia, V. M., Turati, C., & Valenza, E. (2001). The origins of face perception: Specific versus nonspecific mechanisms. *Infant and Child Development, 10,* 59–65.
Simoneau, M., & Markovits, H. (2003). Reasoning with premises that are not empirically true: Evidence for the role of inhibition and retrieval. *Developmental Psychology, 39,* 964–975.
Simons, L. G., Chen, Y. F., Simons, R. L., Brody, G., & Cutrona, C. (2006). Parenting practices and child adjustment in different types of households: A study of African-American families. *Journal of Family Issues, 27,* 803–825.
Simons, L. G., Simons, R. L., & Su, X. (2013). Consequences of corporal punishment among African Americans: The importance of context and outcome. *Journal of Youth and Adolescence, 42,* 1273–1285.
Simons, R. L., & Burt, C. H. (2011). Learning to be bad: Adverse social conditions, social schemas, and crime. *Criminology, 49,* 553–597.
Simonton, D. K. (2009). Giftedness: The gift that keeps on giving. In T. Balchin, B. Hymer, & D. J. Matthews (Eds.), *The Routledge international companion to gifted education* (pp. 26–31). New York: Routledge.
Simpson, E. A., Varga, K., Frick, J. E., & Fragaszy, D. (2011). Infants experience perceptual narrowing for nonprimate faces. *Infancy, 16,* 318–328.
Simpson, J. A., Rholes, W. S., Campbell, L., Tran, S., & Wilson, C. L. (2003). Adult attachment, the transition to parenthood, and depressive symptoms. *Journal of Personality and Social Psychology, 84,* 1172–1187.
Simpson, K. R. (2011). Clinician's guide to the use of oxytocin for labor induction and augmentation. *Journal of Midwifery and Women's Health, 56,* 214–221.
Singer, D. G., & Singer, J. L. (2005). *Imagination and play in the electronic age*. Cambridge, MA: Harvard University Press.
Singleton, J. L., & Newport, E. L. (2004). When learners surpass their models: The acquisition of American Sign Language from inconsistent input. *Cognitive Psychology, 49,* 370–407.
Sinkkonen, J., Anttila, R., & Siimes, M. A. (1998). Pubertal maturation and changes in self-image in early adolescent Finnish boys. *Journal of Youth and Adolescence, 27,* 209–218.
Sinnott, J. D. (2003). Postformal thought and adult development: Living in balance. In J. Demic & C. Andreoletti (Eds.), *Handbook of adult development* (pp. 221–238). New York: Kluwer Academic.
Sirois, S., & Jackson, I. (2007). Social cognition in infancy: A critical review of research on higherorder abilities. *European Journal of Developmental Psychology, 4,* 46–64.
Sirois, S., & Jackson, I. R. (2012). Pupil dilation and object permanence in infants. *Infancy, 17,* 61–78.
Sirsch, U., Erher, E., Mayr, E., & Willinger, U. (2009). What does it take to be an adult in Austria? *Journal of Adolescent Research, 24,* 275–292.
Skinner, E. A., Zimmer-Gembeck, M. J., & Connell, J. P. (1998). Individual differences and the development of perceived control. *Monographs of the Society for Research in Child Development, 63*(2–3, Serial No. 254).
Skipper, Y., & Douglas, K. (2012). Is no praise good praise? Effects of positive feedback on children's and university students' responses to subsequent failures. *British Journal of Educational Psychology, 82,* 327–339.
Slack, K. S., & Yoo, J. (2005). Food hardship and child behavior problems among low-income children. *Social Service Review, 79,* 511–536.
Slater, A., & Johnson, S. P. (1999). Visual sensory and perceptual abilities of the newborn: Beyond the blooming, buzzing confusion. In A. Slater & S. P. Johnson (Eds.), *The development of sensory, motor and cognitive capacities in early infancy* (pp. 121–141). Hove, UK: Sussex Press.
Slater, A., Quinn, P. C., Kelly, D. J., Lee, K., Longmore, C. A., McDonald, P. R., & Pascalis, O. (2011). The shaping of the face space in early infancy: Becoming a native face processor. *Child Development Perspectives, 4,* 205–211.
Slater, A., Riddell, P., Quinn, P. C., Pascalis, O., Lee, K., & Kelly, D. J. (2010). Visual perception. In J. G. Bremner & T. D. Wachs (Eds.), *Wiley-Blackwell handbook of infant development: Vol. 1. Basic research* (2nd ed., pp. 40–80). Chichester, UK: Wiley-Blackwell.
Sleet, D. A., & Mercy, J. A. (2003). Promotion of safety, security, and well-being. In M. H. Bornstein, L. Davidson, C. M. M. Keyes, K. A. Moore, & the Center for Child Well-Being (Eds.), *Well-being: Positive development across the life course* (pp. 81–97). Mahwah, NJ: Erlbaum.
Slining, M. M., Mathias, K. C., & Popkin, B. M. (2013). Trends in food and beverage sources among U.S. children and adolescents: 1989–2010. *Journal of the Academy of Nutrition and Dietetics, 113,* 1683–1694.
Slonims, V., & McConachie, H. (2006). Analysis of mother–infant interaction in infants with Down syndrome and typically developing infants. *American Journal of Mental Retardation, 111,* 273–289.
Smahel, D., Brown, B. B., & Blinka, L. (2012). Associations between online friendship and Internet addiction among adolescents and emerging adults. *Developmental Psychology, 48,* 381–388.
Smahel, D., & Subrahmanyam, K. (2007). "Any girls want to chat press 911": Partner selection in monitored and unmonitored teen chat rooms. *Cyber Psychology and Behavior, 10,* 346–353.
Small, M. (1998). *Our babies, ourselves*. New York: Anchor.
Smart, J., & Hiscock, H. (2007). Early infant crying and sleeping problems: A pilot study of impact on parental well-being and parent-endorsed strategies for management. *Journal of Paediatrics and Child Health, 43,* 284–290.
Smetana, J. G. (2002). Culture, autonomy, and personal jurisdiction in adolescent–parent relationships. In R. V. Kail & H. W. Reese (Eds.), *Advances in child development and behavior* (Vol. 29, pp. 51–87). San Diego, CA: Academic Press.
Smetana, J. G. (2006). Social-cognitive domain theory: Consistencies and variations in children's moral and social judgments. In M. Killen & J. G. Smetana (Eds.), *Handbook of moral development* (pp. 119–154). Mahwah, NJ: Erlbaum.
Smetana, J. G., & Daddis, C. (2002). Domain-specific antecedents of parental psychological control and monitoring: The role of parenting beliefs and practices. *Child Development, 73,* 563–580.
Smetana, J. G., Rote, W. M., Jambon, M., Tasopoulos-Chan, M., Villalobos, M., & Comer, J. (2012). Developmental changes and individual differences in young children's moral judgments. *Child Development, 83,* 683–696.
Smink, R. F. E., van Hoeken, D., & Hoek, H. W. (2012). Epidemiology of eating disorders: Incidence, prevalence, and mortality rates. *Current Psychiatry Reports, 14,* 406–414.
Smink, R. F. E., van Hoeken, D., Oldehinkel, A. J., & Hoek, H. W. (2014). Prevalence and severity of DSM-5 eating disorders in a community cohort of adolescents. *International Journal of Eating Disorders, 47,* 610–619.
Smit, D. J. A., Boersma, M., Schnack, H. G., Micheloyannis, S., Doomsma, D. I., Pol, H. E. H., et al. (2012). The brain matures with stronger functional connectivity and decreased randomness of its network. *PLOS ONE, 7*(5), e36896.
Smith, A. N., Brief, A. P., & Colella, A. (2010). Bias in organizations. In J. F. Dovidio, M. Hewstone, P. Glick, & V. M. Esses (Eds.), *Sage handbook of prejudice, stereotyping, and discrimination* (pp. 441–456). Thousand Oaks, CA: Sage.
Smith, B. H., Barkley, R. A., & Shapiro, C. J. (2006). Attention-deficit/hyperactivity disorder. In E. J. Mash & R. A. Barkley (Eds.), *Treatment of childhood disorders* (3rd ed., pp. 65–136). New York: Guilford.
Smith, C. (2011). *Lost in transition: The dark side of emerging adulthood*. New York: Oxford University Press.
Smith, C., & Snell, P. (2009). *Souls in transition: The religious & spiritual lives of emerging adults*. New York: Oxford University Press.
Smith, C. L., Calkins, S. D., Keane, S. P., Anastopoulos, A. D., & Shelton, T. L. (2004). Predicting stability and change in toddler behavior problems: Contributions of maternal behavior and child gender. *Developmental Psychology, 40,* 29–42.
Smith, D. G., Xiao, L., & Bechara, A. (2012). Decision making in children and adolescents: Impaired Iowa gambling task performance in early adolescence. *Developmental Psychology, 48,* 1180–1187.
Smith, J., & Ross, H. (2007). Training parents to mediate sibling disputes affects children's negotiation and conflict understanding. *Child Development, 78,* 790–805.
Smith, J. P., & Forrester, R. (2013). Who pays for the health benefits of exclusive breastfeeding? An analysis of maternal time costs. *Journal of Human Lactation, 29,* 547–555.
Smith, J. R., Brooks-Gunn, J., Kohen, D., & McCarton, C. (2001). Transitions on and off AFDC: Implications for parenting and children's cognitive development. *Child Development, 72,* 1512–1533.

Smith, L. B., Jones, S. S., Landau, B., Gershkoff-Stowe, L., & Samuelson, L. (2002). Object name learning provides on-the-job training for attention. *Psychological Science, 13,* 13–19.

Smith, P. K., Mahdavi, J., Carvalho, M., Fisher, S., Russell, S., & Tippett, N. (2008). Cyberbullying: Its nature and impact in secondary school pupils. *Journal of Child Psychology and Psychiatry, 49,* 376–385.

Smith, R., Smith, J. I., Shen, X., Engel, P. J., Bowman, M. E., McGrath, S. A., et al. (2009). Patterns of plasma corticotrophin-releasing hormone, progesterone, estradiol and estriol change and the onset of human lablor. *Journal of Clinical Endocrinology and Metabolism, 94,* 2066–2074.

Smits, J., & Monden, C. (2011). Twinning across the developing world. *PLOS ONE, 6*(9), e25239.

Smyke, A. T., Zeanah, C. H., Fox, N. A., Nelson, C. A., & Guthrie, D. (2010). Placement in foster care enhances quality of attachment among young institutionalized children. *Child Development, 81,* 212–223.

Snell, E. K., Adam, E. K., & Duncan, G. J. (2007). Sleep and the body mass index and overweight status of children and adolescents. *Child Development, 78,* 309–323.

Snidman, N., Kagan, J., Riordan, L., & Shannon, D. C. (1995). Cardiac function and behavioral reactivity. *Psychophysiology, 32,* 199–207.

Snow, C. E., & Beals, D. E. (2006). Mealtime talk that supports literacy development. In R. W. Larson, A. R. Wiley, & K. R. Branscomb (Eds.), *Family mealtime as a context of development and socialization* (pp. 51–66). San Francisco: Jossey-Bass.

Snow, C. E., Pan, B. A., Imbens-Bailey, A., & Herman, J. (1996). Learning how to say what one means: A longitudinal study of children's speech act use. *Social Development, 5,* 56–84.

Snyder, J., Brooker, M., Patrick, M. R., Snyder, A., Schrepferman, L., & Stoolmiller, M. (2003). Observed peer victimization during early elementary school: Continuity, growth, and relation to risk for child antisocial and depressive behavior. *Child Development, 74,* 1881–1898.

Sobel, D. M. (2006). How fantasy benefits young children's understanding of pretense. *Developmental Science, 9,* 63–75.

Society for Research in Child Development. (2007). *SRCD ethical standards for research with children.* Retrieved from www.srcd.org/index.php?option=com_content&task=view&id=68&Itemid=110

Soderstrom, M. (2008). Early perception–late comprehension of grammar? The case of verbal –s: A response to de Villiers & Johnson (2007). *Journal of Child Language, 35,* 671–676.

Soderstrom, M., Seidl, A., Nelson, D. G. K., & Jusczyk, P. W. (2003). The prosodic bootstrapping of phrases: Evidence from prelinguistic infants. *Journal of Memory and Language, 49,* 249–267.

Solomon, G. B., & Bredemeier, B. J. L. (1999). Children's moral conceptions of gender stratification in sport. *International Journal of Sport Psychology, 30,* 350–368.

Solomon, J., & George, C. (2011). The disorganized attachment-caregiving system. In J. Solomon & C. George (Eds.), *Disorganized attachment and caregiving* (pp. 3–24). New York: Guilford.

Somerville, L. H. (2013). The teenage brain: Sensitivity to social evaluation. *Current Directions in Psychological Science, 22,* 121–127.

Song, C., Benin, M., & Glick, J. (2012). Dropping out of high school: The effects of family structure and family transitions. *Journal of Divorce and Remarriage, 53,* 18–33.

Sonuga-Barke, E. J., Schlotz, W., & Kreppner, J. (2010). Differentiating developmental trajectories for conduct, emotion, and peer problems following early deprivation. *Monographs of the Society for Research in Child Development, 75*(1, Serial No. 295), 102–124.

Sørensen, K., Mouritsen, A., Aksglaede, L., Hagen, C. P., Mogensen, S. S., & Juul, A. (2012). Recent secular trends in pubertal timing: Implications for evaluation and diagnosis of precocious puberty. *Hormone Research in Pædiatrics, 77,* 137–145.

Sorkhabi, N., & Mandara, J. (2013). Are the effects of Baumrind's parenting styles culturally specific or culturally equivalent? In R. E. Larzelere, A. S. Morris, &

A. W. Harrist (Eds.), *Authoritative parenting: Synthesizing nurturance and discipline for optimal child development* (pp. 113–135). Washington, DC: American Psychological Association.

Sosa, R., Kennell, J., Klaus, M., Robertson, S., & Urrutia, J. (1980). The effect of a supportive companion on perinatal problems, length of labor, and mother–infant interaction. *New England Journal of Medicine, 303,* 597–600.

Soska, K. C., Adolph, K. E., & Johnson, S. P. (2010). Systems in development: Motor skill acquisition facilitates three-dimensional object completion. *Developmental Psychology, 46,* 129–138.

South African Department of Health. (2009). *2008 National Antenatal Sentinel HIV and Syphilis Prevalence Survey.* Retrieved from www.doh.gov.za/docs/nassps-f.html

Sowell, E. R., Trauner, D. A., Camst, A., & Jernigan, T. (2002). Development of cortical and subcortical brain structures in childhood and adolescence: A structural MRI study. *Developmental Medicine and Child Neurology, 44,* 4–16.

Sowislo, J. F., & Orth, U. (2013). Does low self-esteem predict depression and anxiety? A meta-analysis of longitudinal studies. *Psychological Bulletin, 139,* 213–240.

Spangler, G., Fremmer-Bomik, E., & Grossmann, K. (1996). Social and individual determinants of attachment security and disorganization during the first year. *Infant Mental Health Journal, 17,* 127–139.

Spangler, G., Johann, M., Ronai, Z., & Zimmermann, P. (2009). Genetic and environmental influence on attachment disorganization. *Journal of Child Psychology and Psychiatry, 50,* 952–961.

Sparling, J., Wilder, D., Kondash, J., Boyle, M. & Compton, M. (2011). Effects of interviewer behavior on accuracy of children's responses. *Journal of Applied Behavior Analysis, 44,* 587–592.

Speece, D. L., Ritchey, K. D., Cooper, D. H., Roth, F. P., & Schatschneider, C. (2004). Growth in early reading skills from kindergarten to third grade. *Contemporary Educational Psychology, 29,* 312–332.

Spelke, E. S., & Hermer, L. (1996). Early cognitive development: Objects and space. In R. Gelman & T. K. Au (Eds.), *Perceptual and cognitive development* (pp. 71–114). San Diego: Academic Press.

Spelke, E. S., & Kinzler, K. D. (2007). Core knowledge. *Developmental Science, 10,* 89–96.

Spelke, E. S., Phillips, A., & Woodward, A. L. (1995). Infants' knowledge of object motion and human action. In D. Sperber, D. Premack, & A. J. Premack (Eds.), *Causal cognition: A multidisciplinary debate* (pp. 44–78). New York: Oxford University Press.

Spence, I., & Feng, J. (2010). Video games and spatial cognition. *Review of General Psychology, 14,* 92–104.

Spence, M. J., & DeCasper, A. J. (1987). Prenatal experience with low-frequency maternal voice sounds influences neonatal perception of maternal voice samples. *Infant Behavior and Development, 10,* 133–142.

Spencer, J. P., Perone, S., & Buss, A. T. (2011). Twenty years and going strong: A dynamic systems revolution in motor and cognitive development. *Child Development Perspectives, 5,* 260–266.

Spere, K. A., Schmidt, L. A., Theall-Honey, L. A., & Martin-Chang, S. (2004). Expressive and receptive language skills of temperamentally shy preschoolers. *Infant and Child Development, 13,* 123–133.

Spilt, J., Hughes, J. N., Wu, J-Y., & Kwok, O-M. (2012). Dynamics of teacher–student relationships: Stability and change across elementary school and the influence on children's academic success. *Child Development, 83,* 1180–1195.

Spinrad, T. L., & Eisenberg, N. (2009). Empathy, prosocial behavior, and positive development in schools. In R. Gilman, E. S. Huebner, & M. J. Furlong (Eds.), *Handbook of positive psychology in schools* (pp. 119–129). New York: Routledge.

Spirito, A., & Esposito-Smythers, C. (2006). Attempted and completed suicide. *Annual Review of Clinical Psychology, 2,* 237–266.

Spirito, A., Esposito-Smythers, C., Weismoore, J., & Miller, A. (2012). Adolescent suicide behavior. In P. C. Kendall (Ed.), *Child and adolescent therapy: Cognitive behavioral procedures* (4th ed., pp. 234–256). New York: Guilford.

Spock, B., & Needlman, R. (2012). *Dr. Spock's baby and child care* (9th ed.). New York: Gallery Books.

Spoelstra, M. N., Mari, A., Mendel, M., Senga, E., van Rheenen, P., van Dijk, T. H., et al. (2012). Kwashiorkor and marasmus are both associated with impaired glucose clearance related to pancreatic β-cell dysfunction. *Metabolism: Clinical and Experimental, 61,* 1224–1230.

Spokane, A. R., & Cruza-Guet, M. C. (2005). Holland's theory of vocational personalities in work environments. In S. D. Brown & R. W. Lent (Eds.), *Career development and counseling* (pp. 24–41). Hoboken, NJ: Wiley.

Sporer, N., Brunstein, J. C., & Kieschke, U. (2009). Improving students' reading comprehension skills: Effects of strategy instruction and reciprocal teaching. *Learning and Instruction, 19,* 272–286.

Sprecher, S. (2011). Internet matching services: The good, the bad, and the ugly (disguised as attractive). In W. R. Cupach & B. H. Spitzberg (Eds.), *The dark side of close relationships II* (pp. 119–143). New York: Routledge.

Sprecher, S., Harris, G., & Meyers, A. (2008). Perceptions of sources of sex education and targets of sex communication: Socio-demographic and cohort effects. *Journal of Sex Research, 45,* 17–26.

Sroufe, L. A. (2002). From infant attachment to promotion of adolescent autonomy: Prospective, longitudinal data on the role of parents in development. In J. G. Borkowski & S. L. Ramey (Eds.), *Parenting and the child's world* (pp. 187–202). Mahwah, NJ: Erlbaum.

Sroufe, L. A., Coffino, B., & Carlson, E. A. (2010). Conceptualizing the role of early experience: Lessons from the Minnesota Longitudinal Study. *Developmental Review, 30,* 36–51.

Sroufe, L. A., Egeland, B., Carlson, E., & Collins, W. (2005). *Minnesota Study of Risk and Adaptation from birth to maturity: The development of the person.* New York: Guilford.

Sroufe, L. A., & Waters, E. (1976). The ontogenesis of smiling and laughter: A perspective on the organization of development in infancy. *Psychological Review, 83,* 173–189.

Sroufe, L. A., & Wunsch, J. P. (1972). The development of laughter in the first year of life. *Child Development, 43,* 1324–1344.

St James-Roberts, I. (2007). Infant crying and sleeping: Helping parents to prevent and manage problems. *Sleep Medicine Clinics, 2,* 363–375.

St James-Roberts, I. (2012). *The origins, prevention and treatment of infant crying and sleep problems.* London: Routledge.

Staff, J., & Uggen, C. (2003). The fruits of good work: Early work experiences and adolescent deviance. *Journal of Research in Crime and Delinquency, 40,* 263–290.

Staklis, S., Soldner, M., & Skomsvold, P. (2014). *New college graduates at work: Employment among 1992–93, 1999–2000, and 2007–08 bachelor's degree recipients 1 year after graduation.* Washington, DC: U.S. Department of Education.

Stams, G. J. M., Brugman, D., Deković, M., van Rosmalen, L., van der Laan, P., & Gibbs, J. C. (2006). The moral judgment of juvenile delinquents: A meta-analysis. *Journal of Abnormal Child Psychology, 34,* 697–713.

Stams, G. J. M., Juffer, F., & van IJzendoorn, M. H. (2002). Maternal sensitivity, infant attachment, and temperament in early childhood predict adjustment in middle childhood: The case of adopted children and their biologically unrelated parents. *Developmental Psychology, 38,* 806–821.

Staniford, L. J., Breckon, J. D., & Copeland, R. J. (2012). Treatment of childhood obesity: A systematic review. *Journal of Child and Family Studies, 21,* 545–564.

Stanovich, K. E. (2013). *How to think straight about psychology* (10th ed.). Upper Saddle River, NJ: Pearson.

Staub, F. C., & Stern, E. (2002). The nature of teachers' pedagogical content beliefs matters for students' achievement gains: Quasi-experimental evidence from elementary mathematics. *Journal of Educational Psychology, 94,* 344–355.

Stearns, E., & Glennie, E. J. (2006). When and why dropouts leave high school. *Youth and Society, 38,* 29–57.

Steckel, R. H. (2012). Social and economic effects on growth. In N. Cameron & R. Bogin (Eds.), *Human growth and development* (2nd ed., pp. 225–244). London: Elsevier.

Steele, H., Steele, M., & Fonagy, P. (1996). Associations among attachment classifications of mothers, fathers, and their infants. *Child Development, 67,* 541–555.

Steele, L. C. (2012). The forensic interview: A challenging intervention. In P. Goodyear-Brown (Ed.), *Handbook of child sexual abuse: Identification, assessment, and treatment* (pp. 99–119). Hoboken, NJ: Wiley.

Steele, S., Joseph, R. M., & Tager-Flusberg, H. (2003). Developmental change in theory of mind abilities in children with autism. *Journal of Austism and Developmental Disorders, 33*, 461–467.

Stehr-Green, P., Tull, P., Stellfeld, M., Mortenson, P. B., & Simpson, D. (2003). Autism and thimerosal-containing vaccines: Lack of consistent evidence for an association. *American Journal of Preventive Medicine, 25*, 101–106.

Stein, Z., Susser, M., Saenger, G., & Marolla, F. (1975). *Famine and human development: The Dutch hunger winter of 1944–1945.* New York: Oxford.

Steinberg, L. (2001). We know some things: Parent–adolescent relationships in retrospect and prospect. *Journal of Research on Adolescence, 11*, 1–19.

Steinberg, L. (2008). A social neuroscience perspective on adolescent risk-taking. *Developmental Review, 28*, 78–106.

Steinberg, L., Blatt-Eisengart, I., & Cauffman, E. (2006). Patterns of competence and adjustment among adolescents from authoritative, authoritarian, indulgent, and neglectful homes: A replication in a sample of serious juvenile offenders. *Journal of Research on Adolescence, 16*, 47–58.

Steinberg, L., Darling, N. E., & Fletcher, A. C. (1995). Authoritative parenting and adolescent development: An ecological journey. In P. Moen, G. H. Elder, Jr., & K. Luscher (Eds.), *Examining lives in context* (pp. 423–466). Washington, DC: American Psychological Association.

Steinberg, L., Graham, S., O'Brien, L., Woolard, J., Cauffman, E., & Banich, M. (2009). Age differences in future orientation and delay discounting. *Child Development, 80*, 28–44.

Steinberg, L., & Monahan, K. C. (2011). Adolescents' exposure to sexy media does not hasten the initiation of sexual intercourse. *Developmental Psychology, 47*, 562–576.

Steinberg, L., & Silk, J. S. (2002). Parenting adolescents. In M. H. Bornstein (Ed.), *Handbook of parenting: Vol. 1. Children and parenting* (pp. 103–134). Mahwah, NJ: Erlbaum.

Steiner, J. E. (1979). Human facial expression in response to taste and smell stimulation. In H. W. Reese & L. P. Lipsitt (Eds.), *Advances in child development and behavior* (Vol. 13, pp. 257–295). New York: Academic Press.

Steiner, J. E., Glaser, D., Hawilo, M. E., & Berridge, D. C. (2001). Comparative expression of hedonic impact: Affective reactions to taste by human infants and other primates. *Neuroscience and Biobehavioral Reviews, 25*, 53–74.

Stenberg, C. R., & Campos, J. J. (1990). The development of anger expressions in infancy. In N. Stein, B. Leventhal, & T. Trabasso (Eds.), *Psychological and biological approaches to emotion* (pp. 247–282). Hillsdale, NJ: Erlbaum.

Stenberg, G. (2003). Effects of maternal inattentiveness on infant social referencing. *Infant and Child Development, 12*, 399–419.

Stephens, B. E., & Vohr, B. R. (2009). Neurodevelopmental outcome of the premature infant. *Pediatric Clinics of North America, 56*, 631–646.

Stephens, P. C., Sloboda, Z., Stephens, R. C., Teasdale, B., Grey, S. F., Hawthorne, R. D., & Williams, J. (2009). Universal school-based substance abuse prevention programs: Modeling targeted mediators and outcomes for adolescent cigarette, alcohol, and marijuana use. *Drug and Alcohol Dependence, 102*, 19–29.

Stern, D. (1985). *The interpersonal world of the infant.* New York: Basic Books.

Sternberg, R. J. (2005). The triarchic theory of successful intelligence. In D. P. Flanagan & P. L. Harrison (Eds.), *Contemporary intellectual assessment: Theories, tests, and issues* (pp. 103–119). New York: Guilford.

Sternberg, R. J. (2008). The triarchic theory of successful intelligence. In N. Salkind (Ed.), *Encyclopedia of educational psychology* (Vol. 2, pp. 988–994). Thousand Oaks, CA: Sage.

Sternberg, R. J. (2011). The theory of successful intelligence. In R. J. Sternberg & S. B. Kaufman (2011). *Cambridge handbook of intelligence* (pp. 504–527). New York: Cambridge University Press.

Sternberg, R. J. (2013). Contemporary theories of intelligence. In W. M. Reynolds & G. E. Miller (Eds.), *Handbook of psychology: Vol. 7. Educational psychology* (2nd ed., pp. 23–44). Hoboken, NJ: Wiley.

Sternberg, R. J., & Grigorenko, E. L. (2002). *Dynamic testing.* New York: Cambridge University Press.

Sternberg, R. J., & Jarvin, L. (2003). Alfred Binet's contributions as a paradigm for impact in psychology. In R. J. Sternberg (Ed.), *The anatomy of impact: What makes the great works of psychology great* (pp. 89–107). Washington, DC: American Psychological Association.

Stevenson, H. W., Lee, S., & Mu, X. (2000). Successful achievement in mathematics: China and the United States. In C. F. M. van Lieshout & P. G. Heymans (Eds.), *Developing talent across the lifespan* (pp. 167–183). Philadelphia: Psychology Press.

Stevenson, R., & Pollitt, C. (1987). The acquisition of temporal terms. *Journal of Child Language, 14*, 533–545.

Stevens-Simon, C., Sheeder, J., & Harter, S. (2005). Teen contraceptive decisions: Childbearing intentions are the tip of the iceberg. *Women and Health, 42*, 55–73.

Stewart, P. W., Lonky, E., Reihman, J., Pagano, J., Gump, B. B., & Darvill, T. (2008). The relationship between prenatal PCB exposure and intelligence (IQ). *Environmental Health Perspectives, 116*, 1416–1422.

Stewart, R. B., Jr. (1990). *The second child: Family transition and adjustment.* Newbury Park, CA: Sage.

Stice, E. (2003). Puberty and body image. In C. Hayward (Ed.), *Gender differences at puberty* (pp. 61–76). New York: Cambridge University Press.

Stice, E., Marti, C. N., & Rohde, P. (2013). Prevalence, incidence, impairment, and course of the proposed DSM-5 eating disorder diagnoses in an 8-year prospective community study of young women. *Journal of Abnormal Psychology, 122*, 455–457.

Stifter, C. A., & Braungart, J. M. (1995). The regulation of negative reactivity in infancy: Function and development. *Developmental Psychology, 31*, 448–455.

Stiles, J. (2008). *Fundamentals of brain development.* Cambridge, MA: Harvard University Press.

Stiles, J. (2012). The effects of injury to dynamic neural networks in the mature and developing brain. *Developmental Psychobiology, 54*, 343–349.

Stiles, J., Moses, P., Roe, K., Akshoomoff, N. A., Trauner, D., & Hesselink, J. (2003). Alternative brain organization after prenatal cerebral injury: Convergent fMRI and cognitive data. *Journal of the International Neuropsychological Society, 9*, 604–622.

Stiles, J., Nass, R. D., Levine, S. C., Moses, P., & Reilly, J. S. (2009). Perinatal stroke: Effects and outcomes. In K. O. Yeates, M. D. Ris, H. G. Taylor, & B. Pennington (Eds.), *Pediatric neuropsychology: Research, theory and practice* (2nd ed., pp. 181–210). New York: Guilford.

Stiles, J., Reilly, J. S., & Levine, S. C. (2012). *Neural plasticity and cognitive development.* New York: Oxford University Press.

Stiles, J., Reilly, J., Paul, B., & Moses, P. (2005). Cognitive development following early brain injury: Evidence for neural adaptation. *Trends in Cognitive Sciences, 9*, 136–143.

Stiles, J., Stern, C., Appelbaum, M., & Nass, R. (2008). Effects of early focal brain injury on memory for visuospatial patterns: Selective deficits of global–local processing. *Neuropsychology, 22*, 61–73.

Stipek, D. (2004). Teaching practices in kindergarten and first grade: Different strokes for different folks. *Early Childhood Research Quarterly, 19*, 548–568.

Stipek, D. (2011). Classroom practices and children's motivation to learn. In E. Zigler, W. S. Gilliam, & W. S. Barnett (Eds.), *The pre-K debates: Current controversies and issues* (pp. 98–103). Baltimore, MD: Paul H. Brookes.

Stipek, D. J., & Byler, P. (2001). Academic achievement and social behaviors associated with age of entry into kindergarten. *Journal of Applied Developmental Psychology, 22*, 175–189.

Stipek, D. J., Feiler, R., Daniels, D., & Milburn, S. (1995). Effects of different instructional approaches on young children's achievement and motivation. *Child Development, 66*, 209–223.

Stipek, D. J., Gralinski, J. H., & Kopp, C. B. (1990). Self-concept development in the toddler years. *Developmental Psychology, 26*, 972–977.

Stochholm, K., Bojesen, A., Jensen, A. S., Juul, S., & Grayholt, C. H. (2012). Criminality in men with Klinefelter's syndrome and XYY syndrome: A cohort study. *British Medical Journal, 2*, e000650.

Stoet, G., & Geary, D. C. (2013). Sex differences in mathematics and reading achievement are inversely related: Within- and across-nation assessment of 10 years of PISA data. *PLOS ONE, 8*, e57988.

Stoltenborgh, M., van IJzendoorn, M. H., Euser, E. M., & Bakermans-Kranenburg, M. J. (2011). A global perspective on child sexual abuse: Meta-analysis of prevalence around the world. *Child Maltreatment, 16*, 79–101.

Stone, M. R., & Brown, B. B. (1999). Identity claims and projections: Descriptions of self and crowds in secondary school. In J. A. McLellan & M. J. V. Pugh (Eds.), *The role of peer groups in adolescent social identity: Exploring the importance of stability and change* (pp. 7–20). San Francisco: Jossey-Bass.

Stone, R. (2005). *Best classroom management practices for reaching all learners: What award-winning classroom teachers do.* Thousand Oaks, CA: Corwin Press.

Stoner, R., Chow, M. L., Boyle, M. P., Sunkin, S. M., Mouton, P. R., Roy, S., et al. (2014). Patches of disorganization in the neocortex of children with autism. *New England Journal of Medicine, 370*, 1209–1219.

Stoppa, T. M., & Lefkowitz, E. S. (2010). Longitudinal changes in religiosity among emerging adult college students. *Journal of Research on Adolescence, 20*, 23–38.

Storch, S. A., & Whitehurst, G. J. (2001). The role of family and home in the literacy development of children from low-income backgrounds. In P. R. Britto & J. Brooks-Gunn (Eds.), *The role of family literacy environments in promoting young children's emerging literacy skills (New directions for child and adolescent development,* No. 92, pp. 53–71). San Francisco: Jossey-Bass.

Stormshak, E. A., Bierman, K. L., McMahon, R. J., Lengua, L. J., & the Conduct Problems Prevention Research Group. (2000). Parenting practices and child disruptive behavior problems in early elementary school. *Journal of Clinical Child Psychology, 29*, 17–29.

Strapp, C. M., & Federico, A. (2000). Imitations and repetitions: What do children say following recasts? *First Language, 20*, 273–290.

Strasburger, V. C. (2012). Children, adolescents, drugs, and the media. In D. G. Singer & J. L. Singer (Eds.), *Handbook of children and the media* (2nd ed., pp. 419–454). Thousand Oaks, CA: Sage.

Straus, M. A., & Stewart, J. H. (1999). Corporal punishment by American parents: National data on prevalence, chronicity, severity, and duration, in relation to child and family characteristics. *Clinical Child and Family Psychology Review, 2*, 55–70.

Strayer, L., & Roberts, W. (2004). Children's anger, emotional expressiveness, and empathy: Relations with parents' empathy, emotional expressiveness, and parenting practices. *Social Development, 13*, 229–254.

Strazdins, L., Clements, M. S., Korda, R. J., Broom, D. H., & D'Souza, R. M. (2006). Unsociable work? Nonstandard work schedules, family relationships, and children's well-being. *Journal of Marriage and the Family, 68*, 394–410.

Strazdins, L., O'Brien, L. V., Lucas, N., & Roders, B. (2013). Combining work and family: Rewards or risks for children's mental health? *Social Science and Medicine, 87*, 99–107.

Streissguth, A. P., Treder, R., Barr, H. M., Shepard, T., Bleyer, W. A., Sampson, P. D., & Martin, D. (1987). Aspirin and acetaminophen use by pregnant women and subsequent child IQ and attention decrements. *Teratology, 35*, 211–219.

Streri, A. (2005). Touching for knowing in infancy: The development of manual abilities in very young infants. *European Journal of Developmental Psychology, 2*, 325–343.

Stretesky, P., & Lynch, M. (2004). The relationship between lead and crime. *Journal of Health and Social Behavior, 45*, 214–229.

Striano, T., & Rochat, P. (2000). Emergence of selective social referencing in infancy. *Infancy, 1*, 253–264.

Striano, T., Tomasello, M., & Rochat, P. (2001). Social and object support for early symbolic play. *Developmental Science, 4*, 442–455.

Stright, A. D., Herr, M. Y., & Neitzel, C. (2009). Maternal scaffolding of children's problem solving and children's adjustment in kindergarten: Hmong families in the United States. *Journal of Educational Psychology, 101,* 207–218.

Stright, A. D., Neitzel, C., Sears, K. G., & Hoke-Sinex, L. (2002). Instruction begins in the home: Relations between parental instruction and children's self-regulation in the classroom. *Journal of Educational Psychology, 93,* 456–466.

Stringer, K., Kerpelman, J., & Skorikov, V. (2011). Career preparation: A longitudinal, process-oriented examination. *Journal of Vocational Behavior, 79,* 158–169.

Stringer, K. J., & Kerpelman, J. L. (2010). Career identity development in college students: Decision making, parental support, and work experience. *Identity, 10,* 181–200.

Strohschein, L. (2005). Parental divorce and child mental health trajectories. *Journal of Marriage and Family, 67,* 1286–1300.

Strohschein, L., Gauthier, A. H., Campbell, R., & Kleparchuk, C. (2008). Parenting as a dynamic process: A test of the resource dilution hypothesis. *Journal of Marriage and Family, 70,* 670–683.

Stromquist, N. P. (2007). Gender equity education globally. In S. S. Klein, B. Richardson, D. A. Grayson, L. H. Fox, & C. Kramarae (Eds.), *Handbook for achieving gender equity through education* (2nd ed., pp. 33–42). Mahwah, NJ: Erlbaum.

Stronach, E. P., Toth, S. L., Rogosch, F., Oshri, A., Manle, J. T., & Cicchetti, D. (2011). Child maltreatment, attachment security and internal representations of mother and mother–child relationships. *Child Maltreatment, 16,* 137–154.

Stroub, K. J., & Richards, M. P. (2013). From resegregation to reintegration: Trends in the racial/ethnic segregation of metropolitan public schools, 1993–2009. *American Educational Research Journal, 50,* 497–531

Stryer, B. K., Tofler, I. R., & Lapchick, R. (1998). A developmental overview of child and youth sports in society. *Child and Adolescent Psychiatric Clinics of North America, 7,* 697–719.

Sturge-Apple, M. L., Davies, P. T., Winter, M. A., Cummings, E. M., & Schermerhorn, A. (2008). Interparental conflict and children's school adjustment: The explanatory role of children's internal representations of interparental and parent–child relationships. *Developmental Psychology, 44,* 1678–1690.

Su, T. F., & Costigan, C. L. (2008). The development of children's ethnic identity in immigrant Chinese families in Canada: The role of parenting practices and children's perceptions of parental family obligation expectations. *Journal of Early Adolescence, 29,* 638–663.

Suarez-Morales, L., & Lopez, B. (2009). The impact of acculturative stress and daily hassles on preadolescent psychological adjustment: Examining anxiety symptoms. *Journal of Primary Prevention, 30,* 335–349.

Suárez-Orozco, C., Pimental, A., & Martin, M. (2009). The significance of relationships: Academic engagement and achievement among newcomer immigrant youth. *Teachers College Record, 111,* 712–749.

Subrahmanyam, K., Gelman, R., & Lafosse, A. (2002). Animate and other separably moveable things. In G. Humphreys (Ed.), *Category-specificity in brain and mind* (pp. 341–371). London: Psychology Press.

Subrahmanyam, K., & Greenfield, P. M. (2008). Online communication and adolescent relationships. *Future of Children, 18,* 119–146.

Subramanian, S. V., Perkins, J. M., Emre, O., & Smith, G. D. (2011). Weight of nations: A socioeconomic analysis of women in low- to middle-income countries. *American Journal of Clinical Nutrition, 93,* 232–233.

Substance Abuse and Mental Health Services Administration. (2013). *Results from the 2012 National Survey on Drug Use and Health: Summary of national findings.* Rockville, MD: Author.

Suddendorf, T., Simcock, G., & Nielsen, M. (2007). Visual self-recognition in mirrors and live videos: Evidence for a developmental asynchrony. *Cognitive Development, 22,* 185–196.

Sullivan, J., Beech, A. R., Craig, L. A., & Gannon, T. A. (2011). Comparing intra-familial and extra-familial child sexual abusers with professionals who have sexually abused children with whom they work. *International Journal of Offender Therapy and Comparative Criminology, 55,* 56–74.

Sullivan, M. C., McGrath, M. M. Hawes, K., & Lester, B. M. (2008). Growth trajectories of preterm infants: Birth to 12 years. *Journal of Pediatric Health Care, 22,* 83–93.

Sullivan, M. W., & Lewis, M. (2003). Contextual determinants of anger and other negative expressions in young infants. *Developmental Psychology, 39,* 693–705.

Sullivan, P. F., Daly, M. J., & O'Donovan, M. (2012). Genetic architectures of psychiatric disorders: The emerging picture and its implications. *Nature Reviews Genetics, 13,* 537–551.

Sullivan, S., & Glanz, J. (2006). *Building effective learning communities: Strategies for leadership, learning, and collaboration.* Thousand Oaks, CA: Corwin Press.

Sullivan, S. A., & Birch, L. L. (1990). Pass the sugar, pass the salt: Experience dictates preference. *Developmental Psychology, 26,* 546–551.

Sumter, S. R., Bokhorst, C. L., Steinberg, L., & Westenberg, P. M. (2009). The developmental pattern of resistance to peer influence in adolescence: Will the teenager ever be able to resist? *Journal of Adolescence, 32,* 1009–1021.

Sun, H., Ma, Y., Han, D., Pan, C. W., & Xu, Y. (2014). Prevalence and trends in obesity among China's children and adolescents, 1985–2010. *PLOS ONE, 9*(8), r105469j.

Sun, L., & Nippold, M. A. (2012). Narrative writing in children and adolescents: Examining the literate lexicon. *Language, Speech, and Hearing Services in Schools, 43,* 2–13.

Sun, Y., Tao, F., Hao, J., & Wan, Y. (2010). The mediating effects of stress and coping on depression among adolescents in China. *Journal of Child and Adolescent Psychiatric Nursing, 23,* 173–180.

Sunderam, S., Kissin, D. M., Crawford, S., Anderson, J. E., Folger, S. G., Jamieson, D. J., et al. (2013, December 6). Assisted reproductive technology surveillance—United States. *Morbidity and Mortality Weekly Report, 62*(9), 1–24.

Sundet, J. M., Barlaug, D. G., & Torjussen, T. M. (2004). The end of the Flynn effect? A study of secular trends in mean intelligence test scores of Norwegian conscripts during half a century. *Intelligence, 32,* 349–362.

Super, C. M. (1981). Behavioral development in infancy. In R. H. Monroe, R. L. Monroe, & B. B. Whiting (Eds.), *Handbook of cross-cultural human development* (pp. 181–270). New York: Garland.

Super, C. M., & Harkness, S. (2002). Culture structures the environment for development. *Human Development 45,* 270–274.

Super, C. M., & Harkness, S. (2009). The developmental niche of the newborn in rural Kenya. In J. K. Nugent, B. J. Petrauskas, & T. B. Brazelton (Eds.), *The newborn as a person: Enabling healthy development worldwide* (pp. 85–97). Hoboken, NJ: Wiley.

Super, C. M., & Harkness, S. (2010). Culture and infancy. In J. G. Bremner & T. D. Wachs (Eds.), *Wiley-Blackwell handbook of infant development: Vol. 1. Basic research* (2nd ed., pp. 623–649). Chichester, UK: Wiley-Blackwell.

Super, C. M., Harkness, S., van Tijen, N., van der Vlugt, E., Fintelman, M., & Dijkstra, J. (1996). The three R's of Dutch childrearing and the socialization of infant arousal. In S. Harkness & C. M. Super (Eds.), *Parents' cultural belief systems* (pp. 447–466). New York:

Super, D. E. (1994). A life span, life space perspective on convergence. In M. L. Savikas & R. W. Lent (Eds.), *Convergence in career development theories* (pp. 62–71). Palo Alto, CA: Consulting Psychologists Press.

Supple, A. J., Ghazarian, S. R., Peterson, G. W., & Bush, K. R. (2009). Assessing the cross-cultural validity of a parental autonomy granting measure: Comparing adolescents in the United States, China, Mexico, and India. *Journal of Cross-Cultural Psychology, 40,* 816–833.

Supple, A. J., & Small, S. A. (2006). The influence of parental support, knowledge, and authoritative parenting on Hmong and European American adolescent development. *Journal of Family Issues, 27,* 1214–1232.

Survey USA. (2005). *Disciplining a child.* Retrieved from www.surveyusa.com/50StateDisciplineChild0805Sortedby Teacher.htm

Susman, E. J., & Dorn, L. D. (2009). Puberty: Its role in development. In R. M. Lerner (Ed.), *Handbook of adolescent psychology: Vol. 1. Individual bases of adolescent development* (3rd ed., pp. 116–151). Hoboken, NJ: Wiley.

Sussman, S., Pokhrel, P., Ashmore, R. D., & Brown, B. B. (2007). Adolescent peer group identification and characteristics: A review of the literature. *Addictive Behaviors, 32,* 1602–1627.

Sussman, S., Skara, S., & Ames, S. L. (2008). Substance abuse among adolescents. *Substance Use and Misuse, 43,* 1802–1828.

Svirsky, M. A., Teoh, S. W., & Neuburger, H. (2004). Development of language and speech perception in congenitally profoundly deaf children as a function of age at cochlear implantation. *Audiology and Neuro-Otology, 9,* 224–233.

Swain, M. E. (2014). Surrogacy and gestational carrier arrangements: Legal aspects. In J. M. Goldfarb (Ed.), *Third-party reproduction* (pp. 133–142). New York: Springer.

Swan, S. H., Liu, F., Kruse, R. L., Wang, C., Redmon, J. B., Sparks, A., & Weiss, B. (2010). Prenatal phthalate exposure and reduced masculine play in boys. *International Journal of Andrology, 33,* 259–269.

Swanson, H., L. (2011). Intellectual growth in children as a function of domain specific and domain general working memory subgroups. *Intelligence, 39,* 209–219.

Swartz, T. T. Hartmann, D., & Mortimer, J. T. (2011). Transitions to adulthood in the land of Lake Woebegone. In M. C. Waters, P. J. Carr, M. J. Kefalas, & J. Holdaway (Eds.), *Coming of age in America: The transition to adulthood in the twenty-first century* (pp. 59–105). Berkeley, CA: University of California Press.

Sweet, M. A., & Appelbaum, M. L. (2004). Is home visiting an effective strategy? A meta-analytic review of home visiting programs for families with young children. *Child Development, 75,* 1435–1456.

Swendsen, J., Burstein, M., Case, B., Conway, K. P., Dierker, L., He, J., et al. (2012). Use and abuse of alcohol and illicit drugs in US adolescents: Results of the National Comorbidity Survey–Adolescent Supplement. *Archives of General Psychiatry, 69,* 390–398.

Swingley, D. (2005). Statistical clustering and the contents of the infant vocabulary. *Cognitive Psychology, 50,* 86–132.

Swinson, J., & Harrop, A. (2009). Teacher talk directed to boys and girls and its relationship to their behaviour. *Educational Studies, 35,* 515–524.

Syed, M., & Juan, M. J. D. (2012). Birds of an ethnic feather? Ethnic identity homophily among college-age friends. *Journal of Adolescence, 35,* 1505–1514.

Syvertsen, A. K., Wray-Lake, L., Flanagan, C. A., Osgood, D. W., & Briddell, L. (2011). Thirty-year trends in U.S. adolescents' civic engagement: A story of changing participation and educational differences. *Journal of Research on Adolescence, 21,* 586–594.

Szaflarski, J. P., Rajogopal, A., Altaye, M., Byars, A. W., Jacola, L., Schmithorst, V. J., et al. (2012). Left-handedness and language lateralization in children. *Brain Research, 1433,* 85–97.

Szepkouski, G. M., Gauvain, M., & Carberry, M. (1994). The development of planning skills in children with and without mental retardation. *Journal of Applied Developmental Psychology, 15,* 187–206.

T

Tabibi, Z., & Pfeffer, K. (2007). Finding a safe place to cross the road: The effect of distractors and the role of attention in children's identification of safe and dangerous road-crossing sites. *Infant and Child Development, 16,* 193–206.

Tacon, A., & Caldera, Y. (2001). Attachment and parental correlates in late adolescent Mexican American women. *Hispanic Journal of Behavioral Sciences, 23,* 71–88.

Takahashi, K. (1990). Are the key assumptions of the "Strange Situation" procedure universal? A view from Japanese research. *Human Development, 33,* 23–30.

Talaulikar, V. S., & Arulkumaran, S. (2011). Folic acid in obstetric review. *Obstetrics and Gynecological Survey, 66,* 240–247.

Talbot, L. S., McGlinchey, E. L., Kaplan, K. A., & Dahl, R. E. (2010). Sleep deprivation in adolescents and adults: Changes in affect. *Emotion, 10,* 831–841.

Tamis-LeMonda, C. S., & Bornstein, M. H. (1989). Habituation and maternal encouragement of attention in infancy as predictors of toddler language, play, and representational competence. *Child Development, 60,* 738–751.

Tamis-LeMonda, C. S., Shannon, J. D., Cabrera, N. J., & Lamb, M. E. (2004). Fathers and mothers at play with their 2- and 3-year-olds: Contributions to language and cognitive development. *Child Development, 75,* 1806–1820.

Tamm, L., Nakonezny, P. A., & Hughes, C. W. (2014). An open trial of metacognitive executive function training for young children with ADHD. *Journal of Attention Disorders, 18,* 551–559.

Tammelin, T., Näyhä, S., Hills, A. P., & Järvelin, M. (2003). Adolescent participation in sports and adult physical activity. *American Journal of Preventive Medicine, 24,* 22–28.

Tandon, S. D., Colon, L. Vega, P., Murphy, J., & Alonso, A. (2012). Birth outcomes associated with receipt of group prenatal care among low-income Hispanic women. *Journal of Midwifery & Women's Health, 57,* 476–481.

Tangney, J. P., Stuewig, J., & Mashek, D. J. (2007). Moral emotions and moral behavior. *Annual Review of Psychology, 58,* 345–372.

Tanimura, M., Takahashi, K., Kataoka, N., Tomita, K., Tanabe, I., Yasuda, M., et al. (2004). Proposal: Heavy television and video viewing poses a risk for infants and young children. *Nippon Shonika Gakkai Zasshi, 108,* 709–712 (in Japanese).

Tanner, J. L., & Arnett, J. J. (2011). Presenting "emerging adulthood": What makes it developmentally distinctive? In J. J. Arnett, M. Kloep, L. B. Hendry, & J. L. Tanner (Eds.), *Debating emerging adulthood: Stage or process?* (pp. 13–30). New York: Oxford University Press.

Tanner, J. L., Arnett, J. J., & Leis, J. A. (2009). Emerging adulthood: Learning and development during the first stage of adulthood. In M. C. Smith & N. DeFrates-Densch (Eds.), *Handbook of research on adult learning and development* (pp. 34–67). New York: Routledge.

Tanner, J. M., Healy, M., & Cameron, N. (2001). *Assessment of skeletal maturity and prediction of adult height* (3rd ed.). Philadelphia: Saunders.

Tanskanen, P., Valkama, M., Haapea, M., Barnes, A., Ridler, K., Miettunen, J., et al. (2011). Is prematurity associated with adult cognitive outcome and brain structure? *Pediatric Neurology, 44,* 12–20.

Taras, V., Sarala, R., Muchinsky, P., Kemmelmeier, M., Singelis, T. M., Avsec, A., et al. (2014). Opposite ends of the same stick? Multi-method test of the dimensionality of individualism and collectivism. *Journal of Cross-Cultural Psychology, 45,* 213–245.

Tardif, T. (2006). But are they really verbs? Chinese words for action. In K. Hirsh-Pasek & R. M. Golinkoff (Eds.), *Action meets word: How children learn verbs* (pp. 477–498). New York: Oxford University Press.

Tardif, T., Fletcher, P., Liang, W., Zhang, Z., Kaciroti, N., & Marchman, V. A. (2008). Baby's first 10 words. *Developmental Psychology, 44,* 929–938.

Tarren-Sweeney, M. (2006). Patterns of aberrant eating among preadolescent children in foster care. *Journal of Abnormal Child Psychology, 34,* 623–634.

Tarullo, A. R., Balsam, P. D., & Fifer, W. P. (2011). Sleep and infant learning. *Infant and Child Development, 20,* 35–46.

Tarullo, A. R., & Gunnar, M. R. (2006). Child maltreatment and the developing HPA axis. *Hormones and Behavior, 50,* 632–639.

Taumoepeau, M., & Ruffman, T. (2006). Mother and infant talk about mental states relates to desire language and emotion understanding. *Child Development, 77f* 465–481.

Taylor, C. A., Manganello, J. A., Lee, S. J., & Rice, J. C. (2010). Mothers' spanking of 3-year-old children and subsequent risk of children's aggressive behavior. *Pediatrics, 125,* e1057–e1065.

Taylor, J. L. (2009). Midlife impacts of adolescent parenthood. *Journal of Family Issues, 30,* 484–510.

Taylor, M., & Carlson, S. M. (1997). The relation between individual differences in fantasy and theory of mind. *Child Development, 68,* 436–455.

Taylor, M., & Carlson, S. M. (2000). The influence of religious beliefs on parental attitudes about children's fantasy behavior. In K. S. Rosengren, C. N. Johnson, & P. L. Harris (Eds.), *Imagining the impossible* (pp. 247–268). New York: Cambridge University Press.

Taylor, M., Carlson, S. M., Maring, B. L., Gerow, L., & Charley, C. M. (2004). The characteristics and correlates of fantasy in school-age children: Imaginary companions,

impersonation, and social understanding. *Developmental Psychology, 40,* 1173–1187.

Taylor, M., Esbensen, B. M., & Bennett, R. T. (1994). Children's understanding of knowledge acquisition: The tendency for children to report that they have always known what they have just learned. *Child Development, 65,* 1581–1604.

Taylor, M. C., & Hall, J. A. (1982). Psychological androgyny: Theories, methods, and conclusions. *Psychological Bulletin, 92,* 347–366.

Taylor, M. G., Rhodes, M., & Gelman, S. A. (2009). Boys will be boys; cows will be cows: Children's essentialist reasoning about gender categories and animal species. *Child Development, 80,* 461–481.

Taylor, R. D. (2010). Risk and resilience in low-income African American families: Moderating effects of kinship social support. *Cultural Diversity and Ethnic Minority Psychology, 16,* 344–351.

Taylor, R. L. (2000). Diversity within African-American families. In D. H. Demo & K. R. Allen (Eds.), *Handbook of family diversity* (pp. 232–251). New York: Oxford University Press.

Taylor, Z. E., Eisenberg, N., Spinrad, T. L., Eggum, N. D., & Sulik, M. J. (2013). The relations of ego-resiliency and emotion socialization to the development of empathy and prosocial behavior across early childhood. *Emotion, 15,* 822–831.

Team Up for Youth. (2014). *The perils of poverty: The health crisis facing our low-income girls . . . and the power of sports to help.* Retrieved from www.ussoccerfoundation .org/uploads/Health_of_Low_Income_Girls_Coaching_ Corps.pdf

Tecwyn, E. C., Thorpe, S. K. S., & Chappell, J. (2014). Development of planning in 4- to 10-year-old children: Reducing inhibitory demands does not improve performance. *Journal of Experimental Child Psychology, 125,* 85–101.

Telama, R., Yang, X., Viikari, J., Valimaki, I., Wanne, O., & Raitakari, O. (2005). Physical activity from childhood to adulthood: A 21-year tracking study. *American Journal of Preventive Medicine, 28,* 267–273.

Temple, C. M., & Shephard, E. E. (2012). Exceptional lexical skills but executive language deficits in school starters and young adults with Turner syndrome: Implications for X chromosome effects on brain function. *Brain and Language, 120,* 345–359.

Temple, J. L., Giacomelli, A. M., Roemmich, J. N., & Epstein, L. H. (2007). Overweight children habituate slower than nonoverweight children to food. *Physiology and Behavior, 9,* 250–254.

Tenenbaum, H. R., Hill, D., Joseph, N., & Roche, E. (2010). "It's a boy because he's painting a picture": Age differences in children's conventional and unconventional gender schemas. *British Journal of Psychology, 101,* 137–154.

Tenenbaum, H. R., & Leaper, C. (2002). Are parents' gender schemas related to their children's gender-related cognitions? A meta-analysis. *Developmental Psychology, 38,* 615–630.

Tenenbaum, H. R., & Leaper, C. (2003). Parent–child conversations about science: The socialization of gender inequities? *Developmental Psychology, 39,* 34–57.

Tenenbaum, H. R., Snow, C. E., Roach, K. A., & Kurland, B. (2005). Talking and reading science: Longitudinal data on sex differences in mother–child conversations in low-income families. *Journal of Applied Developmental Psychology, 26,* 1–19.

ten Tusscher, G. W., & Koppe, J. G. (2004). Perinatal dioxin exposure and later effects—A review. *Chemosphere, 54,* 1329–1336.

Teske, S. C. (2011). A study of zero tolerance policies in schools: A multi-integrated systems approach to improve outcomes for adolescents. *Journal of Child and Adolescent Psychiatric Nursing, 24,* 88–97.

Teti, D. M., Saken, J. W., Kucera, E., & Corns, K. M. (1996). And baby makes four: Predictors of attachment security among preschool-age firstborns during the transition to siblinghood. *Child Development, 67,* 579–596.

Teyber, E. (2001). *Helping children cope with divorce* (rev. ed.). San Francisco: Jossey-Bass.

Thakur, G. A., Sengupta, S. M., Grizenko, N., Schmitz, N., Pagé, V., & Joober, R. (2013). Maternal smoking during pregnancy and ADHD: A comprehensive clinical and neurocognitive characterization. *Nicotine & Tobacco Research, 15,* 149–157.

Tharpar, A., Collishaw, S., Pine, D. S., & Tharpar, A. K. (2012). Depression in adolescence. *Lancet, 379,* 1056–1066.

Thatcher, R. W., Walker, R. A., & Giudice, S. (1987). Human cerebral hemispheres develop at different rates and ages. *Science, 236,* 1110–1113.

Theil, S. (2006, September 4). Beyond babies. *Newsweek: International Edition.* Retrieved from www.msnbc.msn .com/id/14535863/site/newsweek

Thelen, E., & Adolph, K. E. (1992). Arnold Gesell: The paradox of nature and nurture. *Developmental Psychology, 28,* 368–380.

Thelen, E., & Corbetta, D. (2002). Microdevelopment and dynamic systems: Applications to infant motor development. In N. Granott & J. Parziale (Eds.), *Microdevelopment: Transition processes in development and learning* (pp. 59–79). New York: Cambridge University Press.

Thelen, E., Fisher, D. M., & Ridley-Johnson, R. (1984). The relationship between physical growth and a newborn reflex. *Infant Behavior and Development, 7,* 479–493.

Thelen, E., Schöner, G., Scheier, C., & Smith, L. B. (2001). The dynamics of embodiment: A field theory of infant perseverative reaching. *Behavioral and Brain Sciences, 24,* 1–34.

Thelen, E., & Smith, L. B. (1998). Dynamic systems theories. In R. M. Lerner (Ed.), *Handbook of child psychology: Vol. 1. Theoretical models of human development* (5th ed., pp. 563–634). New York: Wiley.

Thelen, E., & Smith, L. B. (2006). Dynamic systems theories. In R. M. Lerner (Ed.), *Handbook of child psychology: Vol. 1. Theoretical models of human development* (6th ed., pp. 258–312). Hoboken, NJ: Wiley.

Thiessen, E. D., Kronstein, A. T., & Hufnagle, D. G. (2012). The extraction and integration framework: A two-process account of statistical learning. *Psychological Bulletin, 139,* 792–814.

Thiessen, E. D., & Saffran, J. R. (2007). Learning to learn: Infants' acquisition of stress-based strategies for word segmentation. *Language Learning and Development, 3,* 75–102.

Thoermer, C., Woodward, A., Sodian, B., & Perst, H. (2013). To get the grasp: Seven-month-olds encode and selectively reproduce goal-directed grasping. *Journal of Experimental Child Psychology, 116,* 499–509.

Thomaes, S., Brummelman, E., Reijntjes, A., & Bushman, B. J. (2013). When Narcissus was a boy: Origins, nature, and consequences of childhood narcissism. *Child Developmental Perspectives, 7,* 22–26.

Thomaes, S., Stegge, H., Bushman, B. J., & Olthof, T. (2008). Trumping shame by blasts of noise: Narcissism, self-esteem, shame, and aggression in young adolescents. *Child Development, 79,* 1792–1801.

Thoman, E., & Ingersoll, E. W. (1993). Learning in premature infants. *Developmental Psychology, 29,* 692–700.

Thomas, A., & Chess, S. (1977). *Temperament and development.* New York: Brunner/Mazel.

Thomas, K. A., & Tessler, R. C. (2007). Bicultural socialization among adoptive families: Where there is a will, there is a way. *Journal of Family Issues, 28,* 1189–1219.

Thombs, B. D., Roseman, M., & Arthurs, E. (2010). Prenatal and postpartum depression in fathers and mothers. *Journal of the American Medical Association, 304,* 961.

Thompson, A., Hollis, C., & Richards, D. (2003). Authoritarian parenting attitudes as a risk for conduct problems: Results of a British national cohort study. *European Child and Adolescent Psychiatry, 12,* 84–91.

Thompson, A. L., & Bentley, M. E. (2013). The critical period of infant feeding for the development of early disparities in obesity. *Social Science and Medicine, 97,* 288–296.

Thompson, P. M., Giedd, J. N., Woods, R. P., MacDonald, D., Evans, A. C., & Toga, A. W. (2000). Growth patterns in the developing brain detected by using continuum mechanical tensor maps. *Nature, 404,* 190–192.

Thompson, R. A. (1990). Vulnerability in research: A developmental perspective on research risk. *Child Development, 61,* 1–16.

Thompson, R. A. (2006). The development of the person: Social understanding, relationships, conscience, self. In N. Eisenberg (Ed.), *Handbook of child psychology: Vol. 3. Social, emotional, and personality development* (6th ed., pp. 24–98). Hoboken, NJ: Wiley.

Thompson, R. A. (2008). Early attachment and later development: Familiar questions, new answers. In J. Cassidy & P. R. Shaver (Eds.), *Handbook of attachment* (2nd ed., pp. 348–365). New York: Guilford.

Thompson, R. A. (2009). Early foundations: Conscience and the development of moral character. In D. Narvaez & D. K. Lapsley (Eds.), *Personality, identity, and character: Explorations in moral psychology* (pp. 159–184). New York: Cambridge University Press.

Thompson, R. A. (2011). The emotionate child. In D. Cicchetti & G. I. Roisman (Eds.), *Minnesota symposium on child psychology: The origins and organization of adaptation and maladaptation* (pp. 13–53). Hoboken, NJ: Wiley.

Thompson, R. A. (2013). Attachment theory and research: Précis and prospect. In P. D. Zelazo (Ed.), *Oxford handbook of developmental psychology: Vol. 2. Self and other* (pp. 191–216). New York: Oxford University Press.

Thompson, R. A., & Goodman, M. (2010). Development of emotion regulation: More than meets the eye. In A. M. Kring & D. M. Sloan (Eds.), *Emotion regulation and psychopathology: A transdiagnostic approach to etiology and treatment* (pp. 38–58). New York: Guilford.

Thompson, R. A., & Goodvin, R. (2007). Taming the tempest in the teapot. In C. A. Brownell & C. B. Kopp (Eds.), *Socioemotional development in the toddler years: Transitions and transformations* (pp. 320–341). New York: Guilford.

Thompson, R. A., & Meyer, S. (2007). Socialization of emotion regulation in the family. In J. J. Gross (Ed.), *Handbook of emotion regulation* (pp. 249–268). New York: Guilford.

Thompson, R. A., Meyer, S., & McGinley, M. (2006). Understanding values in relationships: The development of conscience. In M. Killen & J. G. Smetana (Eds.), *Handbook of moral development* (pp. 267–298). Mahwah, NJ: Erlbaum.

Thompson, R. A., & Nelson, C. A. (2001). Developmental science and the media. *American Psychologist, 56,* 5–15.

Thompson, R. A., Winer, A. C., & Goodvin, R. (2011). The individual child: Temperament, emotion, self, and personality. In M. H. Bornstein & M. E. Lamb (Eds.), *Developmental science: An advanced textbook* (6th ed., pp. 427–468). Hoboken, NJ: Taylor & Francis.

Thompson, W. W., Price, C., Goodson, B., Shay, D. K., Benson, P., Hinrichsen, V. L., et al. (2007). Early thimerosal exposure and neuropsychological outcomes at 7 to 10 years. *New England Journal of Medicine, 357,* 1281–1292.

Thorne, B. (1993). *Gender play: Girls and boys in school.* New Brunswick, NJ: Rutgers University Press.

Thornton, S. (1999). Creating conditions for cognitive change: The interaction between task structures and specific strategies. *Child Development, 70,* 588–603.

Thorpe, K. (2006). Twin children's language development. *Early Human Development, 82,* 387–395.

Tien, A. (2013). Bootstrapping and the acquisition of Mandarin Chinese: A natural semantic metalanguage perspective. In D. Bittner & N. Ruhlig (Eds.), *Lexical bootstrapping: The role of lexis and semantics in child language* (pp. 39–72). Berlin: Walter de Gruyter.

Tienari, P., Wahlberg, K. E., & Wynne, L. C. (2006). Finnish adoption study of schizophrenia: Implications for family interventions. *Families, Systems, and Health, 24,* 442–451.

Tienari, P., Wynne, L. C., Laksy, K., Moring, J., Nieminen, P., Sorri, A., et al. (2003). Genetic boundaries of the schizophrenia spectrum: Evidence from the Finnish adoptive family study of schizophrenia. *The American Journal of Psychiatry, 160,* 1587–1594.

Tiet, Q. Q., Huizinga, D., & Byrnes, H. F. (2010). Predictors of resilience among inner city youths. *Journal of Child and Family Studies, 19,* 360–378.

Tiggemann, M., & Anesbury, T. (2000). Negative stereotyping of obesity in children: The role of controllability beliefs. *Journal of Applied Social Psychology, 30,* 1977–1993.

Tincoff, R., & Jusczyk, P. W. (1999). Some beginnings of word comprehension in 6-month-olds. *Psychological Science, 10,* 172–175.

Tinsley, B. J. (2003). *How children learn to be healthy.* Cambridge, UK: Cambridge University Press.

Tishkoff, S. A., & Kidd, K. K. (2004). Implications of biogeography of human populations for "race" and medicine. *Nature Genetics, 36* (11s): S21–7.

Tizard, B., & Rees, J. (1975). The effect of early institutional rearing on the behaviour problems and affectional relationships of four-year-old children. *Journal of Child Psychology and Psychiatry, 16,* 61–73.

Tolman, D. L. (2002). *Dilemmas of desire: Teenage girls talk about sexuality.* Cambridge, MA: Harvard University Press.

Tomasello, M. (2000). Do young children have adult syntactic competence? *Cognition, 74,* 209–253.

Tomasello, M. (2003). *Constructing a language: A usage-based theory of language acquisition.* Cambridge, MA: Harvard University Press.

Tomasello, M. (2006). Acquiring linguistic constructions. In D. Kuhn & R. Siegler (Eds.), *Handbook of child psychology: Vol. 2: Cognition, perception, and language* (6th ed., pp. 255–298). Hoboken, NJ: Wiley.

Tomasello, M. (2011). Language development. In U. Goswami (Ed.), *Wiley-Blackwell handbook of childhood cognitive development* (2nd ed., pp. 239–257). Malden, MA: Wiley-Blackwell.

Tomasello, M., & Akhtar, N. (1995). Two-year-olds use pragmatic cues to differentiate reference to objects and actions. *Cognitive Development, 10,* 201–224.

Tomasello, M., Akhtar, N., Dodson, K., & Rekau, L. (1997). Differential productivity in young children's use of nouns and verbs. *Journal of Child Language, 24,* 373–387.

Tomasello, M., & Brandt, S. (2009). Flexibility in the semantics and syntax of children's early verb use. *Monographs of the Society for Research in Child Development, 74*(2, Serial No. 293), 113–126.

Tomasello, M., Call, J., & Hare, B. (2003). Chimpanzees understand psychological states—the question is which ones and to what extent. *Trends in Cognitive Sciences, 7,* 153–156.

Tomasello, M., Carpenter, M., & Liszkowski, U. (2007). A new look at infant pointing. *Child Development, 78,* 705–722.

Tomasetto, C., Alparone, F. R., & Cadinu, M. (2011). Girls' math performance under stereotype threat: The moderating role of mothers' gender stereotypes. *Developmental Psychology, 47,* 943–949.

Tomyr, L., Ouimet, C., & Ugnat, A. (2012). A review of findings from the Canadian Incidence Study of reported child abuse and neglect (CIS). *Canadian Journal of Public Health, 103,* 103–112.

Tong, S., Baghurst, P., Vimpani, G., & McMichael, A. (2007). Socioeconomic position, maternal IQ, home environment, and cognitive development. *Journal of Pediatrics, 151,* 284–288.

Tong, S., McMichael, A. J., & Baghurst, P. A. (2000). Interactions between environmental lead exposure and sociodemographic factors on cognitive development. *Archives of Environmental Health, 55,* 330–335.

Toomela, A. (1999). Drawing development: Stages in the representation of a cube and a cylinder. *Child Development, 70,* 1141–1150.

Toomela, A. (2002). Drawing as a verbally mediated activity: A study of relationships between verbal, motor, visuospatial skills and drawing in children. *International Journal of Behavioral Development, 26,* 234–247.

Torney-Purta, J., Barber, C. H., & Wilkenfeld, B. (2007). Latino adolescents' civic development in the United States: Research results from the IEA Civic Education Study. *Journal of Youth and Adolescence, 36,* 111–125.

Torquati, J. C., Raikes, H. H., Huddleston-Casas, C. A., Bovaird, J. A., & Harris, B. A. (2011). Family income, parent education, and perceived constraints as predictors of observed program quality and parent rated program quality. *Early Childhood Research Quality, 26,* 453–464.

Torrance, E. P. (1988). The nature of creativity as manifest in its testing. In R. J. Sternberg (Ed.), *The nature of creativity: Contemporary psychological perspectives* (pp. 43–75). New York: Cambridge University Press.

Tottenham, N., Hare, T. A., & Casey, B. J. (2009). A developmental perspective on human amygdala function. In P. J. Whalen & E. A. Phelps (Eds.), *The human amygdala* (pp. 107–117). New York: Guilford.

Tottenham, N., Hare, T. A., Millner, A., Gilhooly, T., Zevin, J. D., & Casey, B. J. (2011). Elevated amygdala response to faces following early deprivation. *Developmental Science, 14,* 190–204.

Tough, S. C., Vekved, M., & Newburn-Cook, C. (2012). Do factors that influence pregnancy planning differ by maternal age? A population-based survey. *Journal of Obstetrics and Gynaecology Canada, 34,* 39–46.

Townsend, D. A., & Rovee-Collier, C. (2007). *The transitivity of 6-month-olds' preconditioned memories in deferred imitation.* Paper presented at the annual meeting of the Eastern Psychological Association, Philadelphia.

Tracy, J. L., Robins, R. W., & Lagattuta, K. H. (2005). Can children recognize pride? *Emotion, 5,* 251–257.

Tran, P., & Subrahmanyam, K. (2013). Evidence-based guidelines for informal use of computers by children to promote the development of academic, cognitive and social skills. *Ergonomics, 56,* 1349–1362.

Träuble, B., & Pauen, S. (2011). Cause or effect: What matters? How 12-month-old infants learn to categorize artifacts. *British Journal of Developmental Psychology, 29,* 357–374.

Traurig, M., Mack, J., Hanson, R. L., Ghoussaini, M., Meyre, D., Knowler, W., et al. (2009). Common variation in SIM1 is reproducibly associated with BMI in Pima Indians. *Diabetes, 58,* 1682–1689.

Trautner, H. M., Gervai, J., & Nemeth, R. (2003). Appearance–reality distinction and development of gender constancy understanding in children. *International Journal of Behavioral Development, 27,* 275–283.

Trautner, H. M., Ruble, D. N., Cyphers, L., Kirsten, B., Behrendt, R., & Hartman, P. (2005). Rigidity and flexibility of gender stereotypes in childhood: Developmental or differential? *Infant and Child Development, 14,* 365–381.

Trehub, S. E. (2001). Musical predispositions in infancy. *Annals of the New York Academy of Sciences, 930,* 1–16.

Tremblay, L., & Frigon, J.-Y. (2005). Precocious puberty in adolescent girls: A biomarker of later psychosocial adjustment problems. *Child Psychiatry and Human Development, 36,* 73–94.

Tremblay, R. E. (2000). The development of aggressive behavior during childhood: What have we learned in the past century? *International Journal of Behavioral Development, 24,* 129–141.

Trenholm, C., Devaney B., Fortson, K., Clark, M., Quay, L., & Wheeler, J. (2008). Impacts of abstinence education on teen sexual activity, risk of pregnancy, and risk of sexually transmitted diseases. *Journal of Policy Analysis and Management, 27,* 255–276.

Trenholm, C., Devaney, B., Fortson, K., Quay, L., Wheeler, J., & Clark, M. (2008). *Impacts of four, Title V, Section 510 abstinence education programs.* Princeton, NJ: Mathematics Policy Research, Inc.

Trentacosta, C. J., & Shaw, D. S. (2009). Emotional self-regulation, peer rejection, and antisocial behavior: Developmental associations from early childhood to early adolescence. *Journal of Applied Developmental Psychology, 30,* 356–365.

Trevarthen, C. (2003). Infant psychology is an evolving culture. *Human Development, 46,* 233–246.

Triandis, H. C. (2005). Issues in individualism and collectivism research. In R. M. Sorrentino, D. Cohen, J. M. Olson, & M. P. Zanna (Eds.), *Culture and social behavior: The Ontario Symposium* (Vol. 10, pp. 207–225). Mahwah, NJ: Erlbaum.

Triandis, H. C. (2007). Culture and psychology: A history of their relationship. In S. Kitahama (Ed.), *Handbook of cultural psychology* (pp. 59–76). New York: Guilford.

Triandis, H. C., & Gelfand, M. J. (2012). A theory of individualism and collectivism. In P. A. M. Van Lange, A. W. Kruglanski, & E. T. Higgins (Eds.), *Handbook of theories of social psychology* (Vol. 2, pp. 498–520). Thousand Oaks, CA: Sage.

Trickett, P. K., Noll, J. G., & Putnam, F. W. (2011). The impact of sexual abuse on female development: Lessons from a multigenerational, longitudinal research study. *Development and Psychopathology, 23,* 453–476.

Trionfi, G., & Reese, E. (2009). A good story: Children with imaginary companions create richer narratives. *Child Development, 80,* 1301–1313.

Trocmé, N., & Wolfe, D. (2002). *Child maltreatment in Canada: The Canadian Incidence Study of Reported Child Abuse and Neglect.* Retrieved from www.hcsc.gc.ca/pphb-dgspsp/cm-vee

Troilo, J., & Coleman, M. (2012). Full-time, part-time full-time, and part-time fathers: Father identities following divorce. *Family Relations, 61,* 601–614.

Tronick, E., & Lester, B. M. (2013). Grandchild of the NBAS: The NICU Network Neurobehavioral Scale (NNNS): A review of the research using the NNNS. *Journal of Child and Adolescent Psychiatric Nursing, 26,* 193–203.

Tronick, E. Z., Morelli, G., & Ivey, P. (1992). The Efe forager infant and toddler's pattern of social relationships: Multiple and simultaneous. *Developmental Psychology, 28,* 568–577.

Tronick, E. Z., Thomas, R. B., & Daltabuit, M. (1994). The Quechua manta pouch: A caretaking practice for buffering the Peruvian infant against the multiple stressors of high altitude. *Child Development, 65,* 1005–1013.

Trønnes, H., Wilcox, A. J., Lie, R. T., Markestad, T., & Moster, D. (2014). Risk of cerebral palsy in relation to pregnancy disorders and preterm birth: A national cohort study. *Developmental Medicine and Child Neurology, 56,* 779–785.

Troop-Gordon, W., & Asher, S. R. (2005). Modifications in children's goals when encountering obstacles to conflict resolution. *Child Development, 76,* 568–582.

Troseth, G. L. (2003). Getting a clear picture: Young children's understanding of a televised image. *Developmental Science, 6,* 247–253.

Troseth, G. L., & DeLoache, J. S. (1998). The medium can obscure the message: Young children's understanding of video. *Child Development, 69,* 950–965.

Troseth, G. L., Saylor, M. M., & Archer, A. H. (2006). Young children's use of video as a source of socially relevant information. *Child Development, 77,* 786–799.

Troutman, D. R., & Fletcher, A. C. (2010). Context and companionship in children's short-term versus long-term friendships. *Journal of Social and Personal Relationships, 27,* 1060–1074.

True, M. M., Pisani, L., & Oumar, F. (2001). Infant–mother attachment among the Dogon of Mali. *Child Development, 72,* 1451–1466.

Trzesniewski, K. H., & Donnellan, M. B. (2010). Rethinking "Generation Me": A study of cohort effects from 1976–2006. *Perspectives on Psychological Science, 5,* 58–75.

Trzesniewski, K. H., Donnellan, M. B., & Robins, R. W. (2003). Stability of self-esteem across the life span. *Journal of Personality and Social Psychology, 84,* 205–220.

Tsang, C. D., & Conrad, N. J. (2010). Does the message matter? The effect of song type on infants' pitch preferences for lullabies and playsongs. *Infant Behavior and Development, 33,* 96–100.

Tuchfarber, B. S., Zins, J. E., & Jason, L. A. (1997). Prevention and control of injuries. In R. Weissberg, T. P. Gullotta, R. L. Hampton, B. A. Ryan, & G. R. Adams (Eds.), *Enhancing children's wellness* (pp. 250–277). Thousand Oaks, CA: Sage.

Tucker, C. J., McHale, S. M., & Crouter, A. C. (2001). Conditions of sibling support in adolescence. *Journal of Family Psychology, 15,* 254–271.

Tudge, J. R. H., Hogan, D. M., Snezhkova, I. A., Kulakova, N. N., & Etz, K. E. (2000). Parents' child-rearing values and beliefs in the United States and Russia: The impact of culture and social class. *Infant and Child Development, 9,* 105–121.

Turati, C., Cassia, V. M., Simion, F., & Leo, I. (2006). Newborns' face recognition: Role of inner and outer facial features. *Child Development, 77,* 297–311.

Turiel, E., & Killen, M. (2010). Taking emotions seriously: The role of emotions in moral development. In W. F. Arsenio & E. A. Lemerise (Eds.), *Emotions, aggression, and morality in children: Bridging development and psychopathology* (pp. 33–52). Washington, DC: American Psychological Association.

Turnbull, K. P., Anthony, A. B., Justice, L., & Bowles, R. (2009). Preschoolers' exposure to language stimulation in classrooms serving at-risk children: The contribution of group size and activity context. *Early Education and Development, 20,* 53–79.

Turner, P. J., & Gervai, J. (1995). A multidimensional study of gender typing in preschool children and their parents: Personality, attitudes, preferences, behavior, and cultural differences. *Developmental Psychology, 31,* 759–772.

Turner, R. N., Hewstone, M., & Voci, A. (2007). Reducing explicit and implicit outgroup prejudice via direct and extended contact: The mediating role of self-disclosure and intergroup anxiety. *Journal of Personality and Social Psychology, 93,* 369–388.

Twenge, J. M. (2013). The evidence for Generation Me and against Generation We. *Emerging Adulthood, 1,* 11–16.

Twenge, J. M., & Campbell, W. K. (2001). Age and birth cohort differences in self-esteem: A cross-temporal meta-analysis. *Personality and Social Psychology Review, 5,* 321–344.

Twenge, J. M., & Crocker, J. (2002). Race and self-esteem: Meta-analyses comparing whites, blacks, Hispanics, Asians, and American Indians and comment on Gray-Little and Hafdahl (2000). *Psychological Bulletin, 128,* 371–408.

Tyano, S., Keren, M., Herrman, H., & Cox, J. (2010). *Parenthood and mental health.* Oxford, UK: Wiley-Blackwell.

Tzuriel, D., & Egozi, G. (2010). Gender differences in spatial ability of young children: The effects of training and processing strategies. *Child Development, 81,* 1417–1430.

U

Uccelli, P., & Pan, B. A. (2013). Semantic development. In J. B. Gleason & N. B. Ratner (Eds.), *Development of language* (8th ed., pp., 89–119). Upper Saddle River, NJ: Pearson.

Udechuku, A., Nguyen, T., Hill, R., & Szego, K. (2010). Antidepressants in pregnancy: A systematic review. *Australian and New Zealand Journal of Psychiatry, 44,* 978–996.

Uher, R., & McGuffin, P. (2010). The moderation by the serotonin transporter gene of environmental adversity in the etiology of depression: 2009 update. *Molecular Psychiatry, 15,* 18–22.

Ukrainetz, T. A., Justice, L. M., Kaderavek, J. N., Eisenberg, S. L., Gillam, R., & Harm, H. M. (2005). The development of expressive elaboration in fictional narratives. *Journal of Speech, Language, and Hearing Research, 48,* 1363–1377.

Ullrich-French, S., & Smith, A. L. (2006). Perceptions of relationships with parents and peers in youth sport: Independent and combined prediction of motivational outcomes. *Psychology of Sport and Exercise, 7,* 193–214.

Umaña-Taylor, A. J., & Alfaro, E. C. (2006). Ethnic identity among U.S. Latino adolescents: Measurement and implications for well-being. In F. A. Villarruel & T. Luster (Eds.), *The crisis in youth mental health: Critical issues and effective programs: Vol. 2. Disorders in adolescence* (pp. 195–211). Westport, CT: Praeger.

Umaña-Taylor, A. J., Quintana, S. M., Lee, R. M., Cross, Jr., W. E., Rivas-Drake, D., Schwartz, S. J. (2014). Ethnic and racial identity during adolescence and into young adulthood: An integrated conceptualization. *Child Development, 85,* 21–39.

Umaña-Taylor, A. J., & Updegraff, K. A. (2007). Latino adolescents' mental health: Exploring the interrelations among discrimination, ethnic identity, cultural orientation, self-esteem, and depressive symptoms. *Journal of Adolescence, 30,* 549–567.

Umaña-Taylor, A. J., Zeiders, K. H., & Updegraff, K. A. (2013). Family ethnic socialization and ethnic identity: A family-driven, youth-driven, or reciprocal process? *Journal of Family Psychology, 27,* 137–146.

Underwood, M. K. (2003). *Social aggression in girls.* New York: Guilford.

UNAIDS. (2012). *Global report: UNAIDS report on the global AIDS epidemic.* Retrieved from www.unaids.org/en/resources/publications/2012/name,76121,en.asp

Unger, C. C., Salam, S. S., Sarker, M. S. A., Black, R., Cravioto, A., & Arifeen, S. E. (2014). Treating diarrhoeal disease in children under five: The global picture. *Archives of Diseases of Childhood, 99,* 273–278.

UNICEF (United Nations Children's Fund). (2010). *The state of the world's children* (special edition). New York: Author.

UNICEF (United Nations Children's Fund). (2011). *Children in conflict and emergencies.* Retrieved from www.unicef.org/protection/armedconflict.html

UNICEF (United Nations Children's Fund). (2012). *Measuring child poverty: New league tables of child poverty in the world's richest countries* (Innocenti Report Card 10). Florence, Italy: UNICEF Innocenti Research Centre.

UNICEF (United Nations Children's Fund). (2013a). *Child info: Monitoring the situation of infants and children.* Retrieved from www.childinfo.org/statistical_tables.html

UNICEF (United Nations Children's Fund). (2013b). *Making education a priority in the post-2015 development agenda: Report of the Global Thematic Consultation on Education in the Post-2015 Development Agenda.* Retrieved from www.unicef.org/education/files/Education_Thematic_Report_FINAL_v7_EN.pdf

United Nations. (2012). *World population prospects: The 2012 revision. Population database.* Retrieved from esa.un.org/wpp/unpp/panel_population.htm

U.S. Census Bureau. (2011). *Marital events of Americans: 2009.* Retrieved from www.census.gov/prod/2011pubs/acs-13.pdf

U.S. Census Bureau. (2012). *School enrollment and work status: 2011.* Retrieved from www.census.gov/prod/2013pubs/acsbr11-14.pdf

U.S. Census Bureau. (2014a). International database. Retrieved from www.census.gov/population/international/data/idb/informationGateway.php

U.S. Census Bureau. (2014b). *Statistical abstract of the United States* (133rd ed.). Washington, DC: U.S. Government Printing Office.

U.S. Department of Agriculture. (2010). *Dietary Guidelines for Americans, 2010,* 7th Edition. Washington, DC: U.S.Government Printing Office. Retrieved from www.health.gov/dietaryguidelines/dga2010/DietaryGuidelines2010.pdf

U.S. Department of Agriculture. (2012). *WIC: The Special Supplemental Nutrition Program for Women, Infants, and Children.* Nutrition program facts. Retrieved from www.fns.usda.gov/sites/default/files/WIC-Fact-Sheet.pdf

U.S. Department of Agriculture. (2013a). *Expenditures on children by families, 2012.* Retrieved from www.cnpp.usda.gov/Publications/CRC/crc2012.pdf

U.S. Department of Agriculture. (2013b). *Household food security in the United States in 2013.* Retrieved from www.ers.usda.gov/publications/err-economic-research-report/err173.aspx#.VCGVHUg28dU

U.S. Department of Agriculture. (2014). *Fact sheet: WIC—The Special Supplemental Program for Women, Infants, and Children.* Retrieved from www.fns.usda.gov/wic/about-wic-wic-glance

U.S. Department of Education. (2006). *Calories in, calories, out: Food and exercise in public elementary schools, 2005.* Retrieved from nces.ed.gov/Pubs2006/ nutrition

U.S. Department of Education. (2012a). *The Nation's Report Card: Science 2011* (NCES 2012–465). Washington, DC: Institute of Education Sciences.

U.S. Department of Education. (2012b). *The Nation's Report Card: Writing 2011* (NCES 2012–470). Washington, DC: Institute of Education Sciences.

U.S. Department of Education. (2014a). *Digest of education statistics: 2012.* Washington, DC: U.S. Government Printing Office.

U.S. Department of Education. (2014b). *NAEP Data Explorer.* Retrieved from nces.ed.gov/nationsreportcard/naepdata/dataset.aspx

U.S. Department of Health and Human Services. (2006). *Research to practice: Preliminary findings from the Early Head Start Prekindergarten Follow-Up, Early Head Start Research and Evaluation Project.* Washington, DC: Author.

U.S. Department of Health and Human Services. (2010a). *Breastfeeding.* Retrieved from www.womenshealth.gov/breastfeeding/index.cfm

U.S. Department of Health and Human Services. (2010b). *Head Start Impact Study: Final report.* Washington, DC: U.S Government Printing Office.

U.S. Department of Health and Human Services. (2012). *Who is at risk for sickle cell anemia?* Retrieved from www.nhlbi.nih.gov/health/health-topics/topics/sca/atrisk.html

U.S. Department of Health and Human Services. (2013a). *Child Maltreatment 2012.* Retrieved from www.acf.hhs.gov/programs/cb/resource/child-maltreatment-2012

U.S. Department of Health and Human Services (2013b). *Women's health USA 2013.* Rockville, Maryland: U.S. Department of Health and Human Services. Retrieved from mchb.hrsa.gov/whusa13/

U.S. Department of Health and Human Services. (2014). *What causes Down syndrome?* Retrieved from www.nichd.nih.gov/health/topics/down/conditioninfo/Pages/causes.aspx

U.S. Department of Justice. (2013). *Crime in the United States 2012.* Retrieved from www.fbi.gov/about-us/cjis/ucr/crime-in-the-u.s/2012/crime-in-the-u.s.-2012

U.S. Department of Labor. (2014). *College enrollment and work activity of 2013 high school graduates.* Retrieved from www.bls.gov/news.release/hsgec.nr0.htm

Usher-Seriki, K. K., Bynum, M. S., & Callands, T. A. (2008). Mother–daughter communication about sex and sexual intercourse among middle- to upper-class African American girls. *Journal of Family Issues, 29,* 901–917.

Usta, I. M., & Nassar, A. H. (2008). Advanced maternal age. Part I: Obstetric complications. *American Journal of Perinatology, 25*, 521–534.

Uttal, D. H., Meadow, N. G., Tipton, E., Hand, L. L., Alden, A. R., Warren, C., & Newcombe, N. S. (2013). The malleability of spatial skills: A meta-analysis of training studies. *Psychological Bulletin, 139*, 352–402.

Uziel, Y., Chapnick, G., Oren-Ziv, A., Jaber, L., Nemet, D., & Hashkes, P. J. (2012). Bone strength in children with growing pains: Long-term follow-up. *Clinical and Experimental Rheumatology, 30*, 137–140.

V

Vaillancourt, T., Brittain, H., Bennett, L., Arnocky, S., McDougall, P., Hymel, S., et al. (2010a). Places to avoid: Population-based study of student reports of unsafe and high bullying areas at school. *Canadian Journal of School Psychology, 25*, 40–54.

Vaillancourt, T., Brittain, H. L., McDougall, P., & Duku, E. (2013). Longitudinal links between childhood peer victimization, internalizing and externalizing problems, and academic functioning: Developmental cascades. *Journal of Abnormal Child Psychology, 41*, 1203–1215.

Vaillancourt, T., & Hymel, S. (2006). Aggression and social status: The moderating roles of sex and peer-valued characteristics. *Aggressive Behavior, 32*, 396–408.

Vaillancourt, T., Hymel, S., & McDougall, P. (2013). The biological underpinnings of peer victimization: Understanding why and how the effects of bullying can last a lifetime. *Theory into Practice, 52*, 241–248.

Vaillancourt, T., McDougall, P., Hymel, S., & Sunderani, S. (2010b). Respect or fear? The relationship between power and bullying behavior. In S. R. Jimerson, S. M. Swearer, & D. L. Espelage (Eds.), *Handbook of bullying in schools: An international perspective* (pp. 211–222). New York: Routledge.

Vaillant-Molina, M., Bahrick, L. E., & Flom, R. (2013). Young infants match facial and vocal emotional expressions of other infants. *Infancy, 18*, E97–E111.

Vaish, A., Missana, M., & Tomasello, M. (2011). Three-year-old children intervene in third-party moral transgressions. *British Journal of Developmental Psychology, 29*, 124–130.

Vaish, A., & Striano, T. (2004). Is visual reference necessary? Contributions of facial versus vocal cues in 12-month-olds' social referencing behavior. *Developmental Science, 7*, 261–269.

Vakil, E., Blachstein, H., Sheinman, M., & Greenstein, Y. (2009). Developmental changes in attention tests norms: Implications for the structure of attention. *Child Neuropsychology, 15*, 21–39.

Valdés, G. (1997). Dual-language immersion programs: A cautionary note concerning the education of language-minority students. *Harvard Educational Review, 67*, 391–429.

Valdés, G. (1998). The world outside and inside schools: Language and immigrant children. *Educational Researcher, 27*(6), 4–18.

Valentine, J. C., DuBois, D. L., & Cooper, H. (2004). The relation between self-beliefs and academic achievement: A meta-analytic review. *Educational Psychologist, 39*, 111–133.

Valian, V. (1999). Input and language acquisition. In W. C. Ritchie & T. K. Bhatia (Eds.), *Handbook of child language acquisition* (pp. 497–530). San Diego: Academic Press.

Valiente, C., Eisenberg, N., Fabes, R. A., Shepard, S. A., Cumberland, A., & Losoya, S. H. (2004). Prediction of children's empathy-related responding from their effortful control and parents' expressivity. *Developmental Psychology, 40*, 911–926.

Valiente, C., Lemery-Chalfant, K., & Swanson, J. (2010). Prediction of kindergartners' academic achievement from their effortful control and emotionality: Evidence for direct and moderated relations. *Journal of Educational Psychology, 102*, 550–560.

Valkenburg, P. M., & Calvert, S. L. (2012). Media and the child's developing imagination. In D. G. Singer & J. L. Singer (Eds.), *Handbook of children and the media* (pp.157–170). Thousand Oaks, CA: Sage.

Valkenburg, P. M., & Peter, J. (2007a). Internet communication and its relation to well-being: Identifying some underlying mechanisms. *Media Psychology, 9*, 43–58.

Valkenburg, P. M., & Peter, J. (2007b). Preadolescents' and adolescents' online communication and their closeness to friends. *Developmental Psychology, 43*, 267–277.

Valkenburg, P. M., & Peter, J. (2009). Social consequences of the Internet for adolescents: A decade of research. *Current Directions in Psychological Science, 18*, 1–5.

Valkenburg, P. M., & Peter, J. (2011). Online communication among adolescents: An integrated model of its attraction, opportunities, and risks. *Journal of Adolescent Health, 48*, 121–127.

Valli, L., Croninger, R. G., & Buese, D. (2012). Studying high-quality teaching in a highly charged policy environment. *Teachers College Record, 114*(4), 1–33.

van Aken, C., Junger, M., Verhoeven, M., van Aken, M. A. G., & Deković, M. (2007). The interactive effects of temperament and maternal parenting on toddlers' externalizing behaviours. *Infant and Child Development, 16*, 553–572.

Vandell, D. L., Belsky, J., Burchinal, M., Steinberg, L., Vandergrift, N., & the NICHD Early Child Care Research Network. (2010). Do effects of early child care extend to age 15 years? Results from the NICHD Study of Early Child Care and Youth Development. *Child Development, 81*, 737–756.

Vandell, D. L., & Mueller, E. C. (1995). Peer play and friendships during the first two years. In H. C. Foot, A. J. Chapman, & J. R. Smith (Eds.), *Friendship and social relations in children* (pp. 181–208). New Brunswick, NJ: Transaction.

Vandell, D. L., & Posner, J. K. (1999). Conceptualization and measurement of children's after-school environments. In S. L. Friedman & T. D. Wachs (Eds.), *Measuring environment across the life span* (pp. 167–196). Washington, DC: American Psychological Association.

Vandell, D. L., Reisner, E. R., & Pierce, K. M. (2007). *Outcomes linked to high-quality after-school programs: Longitudinal findings from the Study of Promising After-School Programs.* Retrieved from www.gse.uci.edu/childcare/pdf/afterschool/PP%20Longitudinal%20Findings%20Final%20Report.pdf

Vandell, D. L., Reisner, E. R., Pierce, K. M., Brown, B. B., Lee, D., Bolt, D., & Pechman, E. M. (2006). *The study of promising after-school programs: Examination of longer term outcomes after two years of program experiences.* Madison, WI: University of Wisconsin. Retrieved from www.wcer.wisc.edu/childcare/statements.html

Vandell, D. L., & Shumow, L. (1999). After-school child care programs. *Future of Children, 9*(2), 64–80.

van den Akker, A. L. Deković, M., Prinzie, P., & Asscher, J. J. (2010). Toddlers' temperament profiles: Stability and relations to negative and positive parenting. *Journal of Abnormal Child Psychology, 38*, 485–495.

Van den Bergh, B. R. H., & De Rycke, L. (2003). Measuring the multidimensional self-concept and global self-worth of 6- to 8-year-olds. *Journal of Genetic Psychology, 164*, 201–225.

Van den Bergh, B. R. H., Van Calster, B., Smits, T., Van Huffel, S., & Lagae, L. (2008). Antenatal maternal anxiety is related to HPA-axis dysregulation and self-reported depressive symptoms in adolescence: A prospective study on the fetal origins of depressed mood. *Neuropsychopharmacology, 33*, 536–545.

Vandenbosch, L., & Eggermont, S. (2013). Sexually explicit websites and sexual initiation: Reciprocal relationships and the moderating role of pubertal status. *Journal of Research on Adolescence, 23*, 621–634.

van den Dries, L., Juffer, F., van IJzendoorn, M. H., & Bakermans-Kranenburg, M. J. (2009). Fostering security? A meta-analysis of attachment in adopted children. *Children and Youth Services Review, 31*, 410–421.

van den Eijnden, R., Vermulst, A., van Rooij, A. J., Scholte, R., & van de Mheen, D. (2014). The bidirectional relationships between online victimization and psychosocial problems in adolescents: A comparison with real-life victimization. *Journal of Youth and Adolescence, 43*, 790–802.

Vanderbilt, K. E., Liu, D., & Heyman, G. D. (2011). The development of distrust. *Child Development, 82*, 1372–1380.

Vanderbilt-Adriance, E., & Shaw, D. S. (2008). Protective factors and the development of resilience in the context of neighborhood disadvantage. *Journal of Abnormal Child Psychology, 36*, 887–901.

VanderLaan, D. P., Blanchard, R., Wood, H., & Zucker, K. J. (2014). Birth order and sibling sex ratio of children and adolescents referred to a gender identity service. *PLOS ONE, 9*, 1–9.

van der Meer, A. L. (1997). Keeping the arm in the limelight: Advanced visual control of arm movements in neonates. *European Journal of Paediatric Neurology, 4*, 103–108.

van de Vijver, F. J. R. (2011). Bias and real difference in cross-cultural differences: Neither friends nor foes. In F. J. R. van de Vijver, A. Chasiotis, & H. F. Byrnes (Eds.), *Fundamental questions in cross-cultural psychology* (pp. 235–258). Cambridge, UK: Cambridge University Press.

Vandewater, E. A., Bickham, D. S., Lee, J. H., Cummings, H. M., Wartella, E. A., & Rideout, V. J. (2005). When the television is always on: Heavy television exposure and young children's development. *American Behavioral Scientist, 48*, 562–577.

Van Doorn, M. D., Branje, S. J. T., & Meeus, W. H. J. (2011). Developmental changes in conflict resolution styles in parent–adolescent relationships: A four-wave longitudinal study. *Journal of Youth and Adolescence, 40*, 97–107.

van Geel, M., & Vedder, P. (2011). The role of family obligations and school adjustment in explaining the immigrant paradox. *Journal of Youth and Adolescence, 40*, 187–196.

van Gelderen, L., Bos, H. M. W., Gartrell, N., Hermanns, J., & Perrin, E. C. (2012). Quality of life of adolescents raised from birth by lesbian mothers: The U.S. National Longitudinal Family Study. *Journal of Developmental and Behavioral Pediatrics, 33*, 17–23.

van Goethem, A. A. J., van Hoof, A., van Aken, M. A. G., de Castro, B. O., & Raaijmakers, Q. A. W. (2014). Socialising adolescent volunteering: How important are parents and friends? Age-dependent effects of parents and friends on adolescents' volunteering behaviours. *Journal of Applied Developmental Psychology, 35*, 94–101.

van Grieken, A., Renders, C. M., Wijtzes, A. I., Hirasing, R. A., & Raat, H. (2013). Overweight, obesity and underweight is associated with adverse psychosocial and physical health outcomes among 7-year-old children: The "Be Active, Eat Right" Study. *PLOS ONE, 8*, e67383.

Van Hulle, C. A., Goldsmith, H. H., & Lemery, K. S. (2004). Genetic, environmental, and gender effects on individual differences in toddler expressive language. *Journal of Speech, Language, and Hearing Research, 47*, 904–912.

van IJzendoorn, M. H., & Bakermans-Kranenburg, M. J. (2006). DRD4 7-repeat polymorphism moderates the association between maternal unresolved loss or trauma and infant disorganization. *Attachment and Human Development, 8*, 291–307.

van IJzendoorn, M. H., Bakermans-Kranenburg, M. J., & Ebstein, R. P. (2011). Methylation matters in child development: Toward developmental behavioral epigenetics. *Child Development Perspectives, 5*, 305–310.

van IJzendoorn, M. H., Belsky, J., & Bakermans-Kranenburg, M. J. (2012). Serotonin transporter genotype 5-HTTLPR as a marker of differential susceptibility: A meta-analysis of child and adolescent gene-by-environment studies. *Translational Psychiatry, 2*, e147.

van IJzendoorn, M. H., Juffer, F., & Poelhuis, C. W. K. (2005). Adoption and cognitive development: A meta-analytic comparison of adopted and nonadopted children's IQ and school performance. *Psychological Bulletin, 131*, 301–316.

van IJzendoorn, M. H., & Kroonenberg, P. M. (1988). Cross-cultural patterns of attachment: A meta-analysis of the Strange Situation. *Child Development, 59*, 147–156.

van IJzendoorn, M. H., & Sagi, A. (1999). Cross-cultural patterns of attachment. In J. Cassidy & P. R. Shaver (Eds.), *Handbook of attachment: Theory, research, and clinical applications* (pp. 713–734). New York: Guilford.

van IJzendoorn, M. H., & Sagi-Schwartz, A. (2008). Cross-cultural patterns of attachment: Universal and contextual dimensions. In J. Cassidy & P. R. Shaver (Eds.), *Handbook of attachment* (2nd ed., pp. 880–905). New York: Guilford.

van IJzendoorn, M. H., Vereijken, C. M. J. L., Bakermans-Kranenburg, M. J., & Riksen-Walraven, J. M. (2004). Assessing attachment security with the Attachment Q Sort: Meta-analytic evidence for the validity of the Observer AQS. *Child Development, 75*, 1188–1213.

Varela-Silva, M. I., Frisancho, A. R., Bogin, B., Chatkoff, D., Smith, P. K., Dickinson, F., & Winham, D. (2007). Behavioral, environmental, metabolic, and

intergenerational components of early life undernutrition leading to later obesity in developing nations and in minority groups in the U.S.A. *Collegium Antropologicum, 31,* 39–46.
Varnhagen, C. (2007). Children and the Internet. In J. Gackenbach (Ed.), *Psychology and the Internet* (2nd ed., pp. 37–54). Amsterdam: Elsevier.
Värnik, P., Sisask, M., Värnik, A., Arensman, E., Van Audenhove, C., van deer Feltz-Cornelis, C. M., et al. (2012). Validity of suicide statistics in Europe in relation to undetermined deaths: Developing the 2–20 benchmark. *Injury Prevention, 18,* 321–325.
Vartanian, L. R., & Powlishta, K. K. (1996). A longitudinal examination of the social-cognitive foundations of adolescent egocentrism. *Journal of Early Adolescence, 16,* 157–178.
Vasilenko, S. A., Kugler, K. C., Butera, N. M., & Lanza, S. T. (2014). Patterns of adolescent sexual behavior predicting young adult sexually transmitted infections: A latent class analysis approach. *Archives of Sexual Behavior, 43,* ISSN 1573-2800.
Vaughn, B. E., Bost, K. K., & van IJzendoorn, M. H. (2008). Attachment and temperament. In J. Cassidy & P. R. Shaver (Eds.), *Handbook of attachment: Theory, research, and clinical applications* (2nd ed., pp. 192–216). New York: Guilford.
Vaughn, B. E., Colvin, T. N., Azria, M. R., Caya, L., & Krzysik, L. (2001). Dyadic analyses of friendship in a sample of preschool-age children attending Head Start: Correspondence between measures and implications for social competence. *Child Development, 72,* 862–878.
Vaughn, B. E., Kopp, C. B., & Krakow, J. B. (1984). The emergence and consolidation of self-control from eighteen to thirty months of age: Normative trends and individual differences. *Child Development, 55,* 990–1004.
Vaughn, B. E., Vollenweider, M., Bost, K. K., Azria-Evans, M. R., & Snider, J. B. (2003). Negative interactions and social competence for preschool children in two samples: Reconsidering the interpretation of aggressive behavior for young children. *Merrill-Palmer Quarterly, 49,* 245–278.
Vazsonyi, A. T., Hibbert, J. R., & Snider, J. B. (2003). Exotic enterprise no more? Adolescent reports of family and parenting processes from youth in four countries. *Journal of Research on Adolescence, 13,* 129–160.
Veenstra, R., Lindenberg, S., Munniksma, A., & Dijkstra, J. K. (2010). The complex relation between bullying, victimization, acceptance, and rejection: Giving special attention to status, affection, and sex differences. *Child Development, 81,* 480–486.
Velderman, M. K., Bakermans-Kranenburg, M. J., Juffer, F., & van IJzendoorn, M. H. (2006). Effects of attachment-based interventions on maternal sensitivity and infant attachment: Differential susceptibility of highly reactive infants. *Journal of Family Psychology, 20,* 266–274.
Velez, C. E., Wolchik, S. A., Tien, J., & Sandler, I. (2011). Protecting children from the consequences of divorce: A longitudinal study of the effects of parenting on children's coping processes. *Child Development, 82,* 244–257.
Venet, M., & Markovits, H. (2001). Understanding uncertainty with abstract conditional premises. *Merrill-Palmer Quarterly, 47,* 74–99.
Venezia, M., Messinger, D. S., Thorp, D., & Mundy, P. (2004). The development of anticipatory smiling. *Infancy, 6,* 397–406.
Veneziano, R. A. (2003). The importance of paternal warmth. *Cross-Cultural Research, 37,* 265–281.
Ventura, S. J., Hamilton, B. E., & Mathews, T. J. (2014). National and state patterns of teen births in the United States, 1940–2013. *National Vital Statistics Reports, 63.* Retrieved from www.cdc.gov/nchs/data/nvsr/nvsr63/nvsr63_04.pdf
Verhulst, F. C. (2008). International adoption and mental health: Long-term behavioral outcome. In M. E. Garralda & J.-P. Raynaud (Eds.), *Culture and conflict in adolescent mental health* (pp. 83–105). Lanham, MD: Jason Aronson.
Verissimo, M., & Salvaterra, F. (2006). Maternal secure-base scripts and children's attachment security in an adopted sample. *Attachment and Human Development, 8,* 261–273.
Vernon-Feagans, L., & Cox, M. (2013). The Family Life Project: An epidemiological and developmental study of young children living in poor rural families. *Monographs of the Society for Research in Child Development, 78*(5, Serial No. 310).
Vernon-Feagans, L., Hurley, M. M., Yont, K. M., Wamboldt, P. M., & Kolak, A. (2007). Quality of childcare and otitis media: Relationship to children's language during naturalistic interactions at 18, 24, and 36 months. *Journal of Applied Developmental Psychology, 28,* 115–133.
Vernon-Feagans, L., Pancsofar, N., Willoughby, M., Odom, E., Quade, A., & Cox, M. (2008). Predictors of maternal language to infants during a picture book task in the home: Family SES, child characteristics and the parenting environment. *Journal of Applied Developmental Psychology, 29,* 213–226.
Vest, A. R., & Cho, L. S. (2012). Hypertension in pregnancy. *Cardiology Clinics, 30,* 407–423.
Vinden, P. G. (1996). Jun'n Quechua children's understanding of mind. *Child Development, 67,* 1707–1716.
Vinden, P. G. (2002). Understanding minds and evidence for belief: A study of Mofu children in Cameroon. *International Journal of Behavioral Development, 26,* 445–452.
Vinik, J., Almas, A., & Grusec, J. (2011). Mothers' knowledge of what distresses and what comforts their children predicts children's coping, empathy, and prosocial behavior. *Parenting: Science and Practice, 11,* 56–71.
Visher, E. B., Visher, J. S., & Pasley, K. (2003). Remarriage families and stepparenting. In F. Walsh (Ed.), *Normal family processes: Growing diversity and complexity* (pp. 153–175). New York: Guilford.
Vistad, I., Cvancarova, M., Hustad, B. L., & Henriksen, T. (2013). Vaginal breech delivery: Results of a prospective registration study. *BMC Pregnancy and Children, 13,* 153.
Vitaro, F., Boivin, M., Brendgen, M., Girard, A., & Dionner, G. (2012). Social experiences in kindergarten and academic achievement in grade 1: A monozygotic twin difference study. *Journal of Educational Psychology, 2,* 366–380.
Vitaro, F., & Brendgen, M. (2012). Subtypes of aggressive behaviors: Etiologies, development, and consequences. In T. Bliesner, A. Beelmann, & M. Stemmler (Eds.), *Antisocial behavior and crime: Contributions of developmental and evaluation research to prevention and intervention* (pp. 17–38). Cambridge, MA: Hogrefe.
Vitrup, B., & Holden, G. W. (2010). Children's assessments of corporal punishment and other disciplinary practices: The role of age, race, SES, and exposure to spanking. *Journal of Applied Developmental Psychology, 31,* 211–220.
Vivanti, G., Nadig, A., Ozonoff, S., & Rogers, S. J. (2008). What do children with autism attend to during imitation tasks? *Journal of Experimental Psychology, 101,* 186–205.
Vizard, E. (2013). Practitioner review: The victims and juvenile perpetrators of child sexual abuse—assessment and intervention. *The Journal of Child Psychology and Psychiatry, 54,* 503–515.
Vocks, S., Tuschen-Caffier, B., Pietrowsky, R., Rustenbach, S. J., Kersting, A., & Herpertz, S. (2010). Meta-analysis of the effectiveness of psychological and pharmacological treatments for binge eating disorder. *International Journal of Eating Disorders, 43,* 205–217.
Voegtline, K. M., Costigan, K. A., Pater, H. A., & DiPietro, J. A. (2013). Near-term fetal response to maternal spoken voice. *Infant Behavior and Development, 36,* 526–533.
Vogel, C. A., Xue, Y., Maiduddin, E. M., Carlson, B. L., & Kisker, E. E. (2010). *Early Head Start children in grade 5: Long-term follow-up of the Early Head Start Research and Evaluation Study sample* (OPRE Report No. 2011-8). Washington, DC: U.S. Department of Health and Human Services.
Vohr, B. R., Stephens, B. E., McDonald, S. A., Ehrenkranz, R. A., Laptook, A. R., Pappas, A., et al. (2013). Cerebral palsy and growth failure at 6 to 7 years. *Pediatrics, 132,* e905–e914.
Volling, B. L. (2001). Early attachment relationships as predictors of preschool children's emotion regulation with a distressed sibling. *Early Education and Development, 12,* 185–207.
Volling, B. L. (2012). Family transitions following the birth of a sibling: An empirical review of changes in the firstborn's adjustment. *Psychological Bulletin, 138,* 497–528.
Volling, B. L., & Belsky, J. (1992). Contribution of mother–child and father–child relationships to the quality of sibling interaction: A longitudinal study. *Child Development, 63,* 1209–1222.
Volling, B. L., Mahoney, A., & Rauer, A. J. (2009). Sanctification of parenting, moral socialization, and young children's conscience development. *Psychology of Religion and Spirituality, 1,* 53–68.
Volling, B. L., McElwain, N. L., & Miller, A. L. (2002). Emotion regulation in context: The jealousy complex between young siblings and its relations with child and family characteristics. *Child Development, 73,* 581–600.
Vondra, J. I., Shaw, D. S., Searingen, L., Cohen, M., & Owens, E. B. (2001). Attachment stability and emotional and behavioral regulation from infancy to preschool age. *Development and Psychopathology, 13,* 13–33.
von Gontard, A., Heron, J., & Joinson, C. (2011). Family history of nocturnal enuresis and urinary incontinence: Results from a large epidemiological study. *Journal of Urology, 185,* 2303–2306.
von Hofsten, C. (1993). Prospective control: A basic aspect of action development. *Human Development, 36,* 253–270.
von Hofsten, C. (2004). An action perspective on motor development. *Trends in Cognitive Sciences, 8,* 266–272.
von Hofsten, C., & Rosander, K. (1998). The establishment of gaze control in early infancy. In S. Simion & G. Butterworth (Eds.), *The development of sensory, motor and cognitive capacities in early infancy* (pp. 49–66). Hove, UK: Psychology Press.
Vouloumanos, A. (2010). Three-month-olds prefer speech to other naturally occurring signals. *Language Learning and Development, 6,* 241–257.
Vuoksimaa, E., Kaprio, J., Kremen, W. S., Hokkanen, L., Viken, R. J., Tuulio- Henriksson, A., et al. (2010). Having a male co-twin masculinizes mental rotation performance in females. *Psychological Science, 21,* 1069–1071.
Vuoksimaa, E., Koskenvuo, M., Rose, R. J., & Kaprio, J. (2009). Origins of handedness: A nationwide study of 30,1671 adults. *Neuropsychologia, 47,* 1294–1301.
Vygotsky, L. S. (1978). *Mind in society: The development of higher psychological processes.* Cambridge, MA: Harvard University Press. (Original works published 1930, 1933, and 1935)
Vygotsky, L. S. (1987). Thinking and speech. In R. W. Rieber, A. S. Carton (Eds.), & N. Minick (Trans.), *The collected works of L. S. Vygotsky: Vol. 1. Problems of general psychology* (pp. 37–285). New York: Plenum. (Original work published 1934)

W

Waber, D. P. (2010). *Rethinking learning disabilities.* New York: Guilford.
Waber, D. P., Bryce, C. P., Girard, J. M., Zichlin, M., Fitzmaurice, G. M., & Galler, J. R. (2014). Impaired IQ and academic skills in adults who experienced moderate to severe infantile malnutrition: A 40-year study. *Nutritional Neuroscience, 17,* 58–64.
Wadell, P. M., Hagerman, R. J., & Hessl, D. R. (2013). Fragile X syndrome: Psychiatric manifestations, assessment and emerging therapies. *Current Psychiatry Reviews, 9,* 53–58.
Wadsworth, M. E., Rindlaub, L., Hurwich-Reiss, E., Rienks, S., Bianco, H., & Markman, H. J. (2013). A longitudinal examination of the adaptation to poverty-related stress model: Predicting child and adolescent adjustment over time. *Journal of Clinical Child and Adolescent Psychology, 42,* 713–725.
Wagenaar, K., van Wessenbruch, M. M., van Leeuwen, F. E., Cohen-Kettenis, P. T., Delemarre-van de Waal, H. A., Schats, R., et al. (2011). Self-reported behavioral and socioemotional functioning of 11- to 18-year-old adolescents conceived by in vitro fertilization. *Fertility and Sterility, 95,* 611–616.
Wagner, D. V., Borduin, C. M., Sawyer, A. M., & Dopp, A. R. (2014). Long-term prevention of criminality in siblings of serious and violent juvenile offenders: A 25-year follow-up to a randomized clinical trial of multisystemic therapy. *Journal of Consulting and Clinical Psychology, 82,* 492–499.
Wai, J., Cacchio, M., Putallaz, M., & Makel, M. C. (2010). Sex differences in the right tail of cognitive abilities: A 30-year examination. *Intelligence, 38,* 412–423.
Wai, J., Lubinski, D., & Benbow, C. P. (2009). Spatial ability for STEM domains: Aligning over 50 years of cumulative psychological knowledge solidifies its importance. *Journal of Educational Psychology, 101,* 817–835.
Wainryb, C. (1997). The mismeasure of diversity: Reflections on the study of cross-cultural differences. In

H. D. Saltzstein (Ed.), *New directions for child development* (No. 76, pp. 51–65). San Francisco: Jossey-Bass.
Wainryb, C., & Ford, S. (1998). Young children's evaluations of acts based on beliefs different from their own. *Merrill-Palmer Quarterly, 44,* 484–503.
Walberg, H. J. (1986). Synthesis of research on teaching. In M. C. Wittrock (Ed.), *Handbook of research on teaching* (3rd ed., pp. 214–229). New York: Macmillan.
Waldfogel, J., Craigie, T.-A., & Brooks-Gunn, J. (2010). Fragile families and child wellbeing. *Future of Children, 20,* 87–112.
Waldfogel, J., & Zhai, F. (2008). Effects of public preschool expenditures on the test scores of fourth graders: Evidence from TIMMS. *Educational Research and Evaluation, 14,* 9–28.
Waldinger, R. J., Diguer, L., Guastella, F., Lefebvre, R., Allen, J. P., & Luborsky, L. (2002). The same old song? Stability and change in relationship schemas from adolescence to young adulthood. *Journal of Youth and Adolescence, 31,* 17–44.
Waldman, I. D., Rowe, D. C., Abramowitz, A., Kozel, S. T., Mohr, J. H., & Sherman, S. L. (1998). Association and linkage of the dopamine transporter gene and attention-deficit hyperactivity disorder in children: Heterogeneity owing to diagnostic subtype and severity. *American Journal of Human Genetics, 63,* 1767–1776.
Waldorf, K. M. A., & McAdams, R. M. (2013). Influence of infection during pregnancy on fetal development. *Reproduction, 146,* R151–R162.
Waldrip, A. M. (2008). With a little help from your friends: The importance of high-quality friendships on early adolescent adjustment. *Social Development, 17,* 832–852.
Walenski, M., Tager-Flusberg, H., & Ullman, M. T. (2006). Language in autism. In S. O. Moldin & J. L. R. Rubenstein (Eds.), *Understanding autism: From basic neuroscience to treatment* (pp. 175–203). Boca Raton, FL: CRC Press.
Walker, C. M., Walker, L. B., & Ganea, P. A. (2012). The role of symbol-based experience in early learning and transfer from pictures: Evidence from Tanzania. *Developmental Psychology, 49,* 1315–1324.
Walker, L. J. (1995). Sexism in Kohlberg's moral psychology? In W. M. Kurtines & J. L. Gewirtz (Eds.), *Moral development: An introduction* (pp. 83–107). Boston: Allyn and Bacon.
Walker, L. J. (2004). Progress and prospects in the psychology of moral development. *Merrill-Palmer Quarterly, 50,* 546–557.
Walker, L. J. (2006). Gender and morality. In M. Killen & J. G. Smetana (Eds.), *Handbook of moral development* (pp. 93–118). Philadelphia: Erlbaum.
Walker, L. J., & Taylor, J. H. (1991a). Family interactions and the development of moral reasoning. *Child Development, 62,* 264–283.
Walker, L. J., & Taylor, J. H. (1991b). Stage transitions in moral reasoning: A longitudinal study of developmental processes. *Developmental Psychology, 27,* 330–337.
Walker, O. L., Degnan, K. A., Fox, N. A., & Henderson, H. A. (2013). Social problem solving in early childhood: Developmental change and the influence of shyness. *Journal of Applied Developmental Psychology, 34,* 185–193.
Walker, O. L., & Henderson, H. A. (2012). Temperament and social problem solving competence in preschool: Influences on academic skills in early elementary school. *Social Development, 21,* 761–779.
Walker, S. M. (2013). Biological and neurodevelopmental implications of neonatal pain. *Clinics in Perinatology, 40,* 471–491.
Wall, M., & Côté, J. (2007). Developmental activities that lead to dropout and investment in sport. *Physical Education and Sport Pedagogy, 12,* 77–87.
Wall, M. I., Carlson, S. A., Stein, A. D., Lee, S. M., & Fulton, J. E. (2011). Trends by age in youth physical activity: Youth Media Campaign Longitudinal Survey. *Medicine and Science in Sports and Exercise, 40,* 2140–2147.
Walton, G. E., Armstrong, E. S., & Bower, T. G. R. (1998). Newborns learn to identify a face in eight-tenths of a second? *Developmental Science, 1,* 79–84.
Wang, M.-T., & Sheikh-Khalil, S. (2014). Does parental involvement matter for student achievement and mental health in high school? *Child Development, 85,* 610–625.
Wang, Q. (2004). The emergence of cultural self-constructs: Autobiographical memory and self-description in European American and Chinese children. *Developmental Psychology, 40,* 3–15.
Wang, Q. (2006a). Earliest recollections of self and others in European American and Taiwanese young adults. *Psychological Science, 17,* 708–714.
Wang, Q. (2006b). Relations of maternal style and child self-concept to autobiographical memories in Chinese, Chinese immigrant, and European American 3-year-olds. *Child Development, 77,* 1794–1809.
Wang, Q. (2008). Emotion knowledge and autobiographical memory across the preschool years: A cross-cultural longitudinal investigation. *Cognition, 108,* 117–135.
Wang, Q., Doan, S. N., & Song, Q. (2010). Talking about internal states in mother–child reminiscing influences children's self-representations: A cross-cultural study. *Cognitive Development, 25,* 380–393.
Wang, Q., Pomerantz, E. M., & Chen, H. (2007). The role of parents' control in early adolescents' psychological functioning: A longitudinal investigation in the United States and China. *Child Development, 78,* 1592–1610.
Wang, Q., Shao, Y., & Li, Y. J. (2010). "My way or mom's way?" The bilingual and bicultural self in Hong Kong Chinese children and adolescents. *Child Development, 81,* 555–567.
Wang, S., Baillargeon, R., & Paterson, S. (2005). Detecting continuity violations in infancy: A new account and new evidence from covering and tube effects. *Cognition, 95,* 129–173.
Wang, Z., & Deater-Deckard, K. (2013). Resilience in gene–environment transactions. In S. Goldstein & R. B. Brooks (Eds.), *Handbook of resilience in children* (2nd ed., pp. 57–72). New York: Springer Science + Business Media.
Warner, L. A., Valdez, A., Vega, W. A., de la Rosa, M., Turner, R. J., & Canino, G. (2006). Hispanic drug abuse in an evolving cultural context: An agenda for research. *Drug and Alcohol Dependence, 84*(Suppl. 1), S8–S16.
Warnock, F., & Sandrin, D. (2004). Comprehensive description of newborn distress behavior in response to acute pain (newborn male circumcision). *Pain, 107,* 242–255.
Warren, A. R., & Tate, C. S. (1992). Egocentrism in children's telephone conversations. In R. M. Diaz & L. E. Berk (Eds.), *Private speech: From social interaction to self-regulation* (pp. 245–264). Hillsdale, NJ: Erlbaum.
Warren, S. L., & Simmens, S. J. (2005). Predicting toddler anxiety/depressive symptoms: Effects of caregiver sensitivity on temperamentally vulnerable children. *Infant Mental Health Journal, 26,* 40–55.
Washington, J. A., & Thomas-Tate, S. (2009). How research informs cultural-linguistic differences in the classroom: The bi-dialectal African American child. In S. Rosenfield & V. Berninger (Eds.), *Implementing evidence-based academic interventions in school settings* (pp. 147–164). New York: Oxford University Press.
Washington, T., Gleeson, J. P., & Rulison, K. L. (2013). Competence and African American children in informal kinship care: The role of family. *Children and Youth Services Review, 35,* 1305–1312.
Wasik, B. A., & Bond, M. A. (2001). Beyond the pages of a book: Interactive book reading and language development in preschool classrooms. *Journal of Educational Psychology, 93,* 243–250.
Wasserman, E. A., & Rovee-Collier, C. (2001). Pick the flowers and mind your As and 2s! Categorization by pigeons and infants. In M. E. Carroll & J. B. Overmier (Eds.), *Animal research and human health: Advancing human welfare through behavioral science* (pp. 263–279). Washington, DC: American Psychological Association.
Watamura, S. E., Donzella, B., Alwin, J., & Gunnar, M. R. (2003). Morning-to-afternoon increases in cortisol concentrations for infants and toddlers at child care: Age differences and behavioral correlates. *Child Development, 74,* 1006–1020.
Watamura, S. E., Phillips, D., Morrissey, T. W., McCartney, K., & Bub, K. (2011). Double jeopardy: Poorer social–emotional outcomes for children in the NICHD SECCYD experiencing home and child-care environments that confer risk. *Child Development, 82,* 48–65.
Waters, E., de Silva-Sanigorski, A., Brown, T., Campbell, K. J., Goa, Y., Armstrong, R., et al. (2011). Interventions for preventing obesity in children. *Cochrane Database of Systematic Reviews,* Issue 12. Art. No.: CD0011871.
Waters, E., Merrick, S., Treboux, D., Crowell, J., & Albersheim, L. (2000). Attachment security in infancy and early adulthood: A twenty-year longitudinal study. *Child Development, 71,* 684–689.
Waters, E., Vaughn, B. E., Posada, G., & Kondo-Ikemura, K. (Eds.). (1995). Caregiving, cultural, and cognitive perspectives on secure-base behavior and working models: New growing points of attachment theory and research. *Monographs of the Society for Research in Child Development, 60*(2–3, Serial No. 244).
Waters, S., Lester, L., & Cross, D. (2014). How does support from peers compare with support from adults as students transition to secondary school? *Journal of Adolescent Health, 54,* 543–549.
Waters, S. F., & Thompson, R. A. (2014). Children's perceptions of the effectiveness of strategies for regulating anger and sadness. *International Journal of Behavioral Development, 38,* 174–181.
Watrin, J. P., & Darwich, R. (2012). On behaviorism in the cognitive revolution: Myth and reactions. *Review of General Psychology, 16,* 269–282.
Watson, J. B., & Raynor, R. (1920). Conditioned emotional reactions. *Journal of Experimental Psychology, 3,* 1–14.
Watson, M. (1990). Aspects of self development as reflected in children's role playing. In D. Cicchetti & M. Beeghly (Eds.), *The self in transition: Infancy to childhood* (pp. 281–307). Chicago: University of Chicago Press.
Wax, J. R., Pinette, M. G., & Cartin, A. (2010). Home versus hospital birth—process and outcome. *Obstetric and Gynecological Survey, 65,* 132–140.
Waxman, S. R., & Lidz, J. L. (2006). Early word learning. In D. Kuhn & R. Siegler (Eds.), *Handbook of child psychology: Vol. 2. Cognition, perception, and language* (6th ed., pp. 464–510). Hoboken, NJ: Wiley.
Waxman, S. R., & Senghas, A. (1992). Relations among word meanings in early lexical development. *Developmental Psychology, 28,* 862–873.
Way, N. (2013). Boys' friendships during adolescence: Intimacy, desire, and loss. *Journal of Research on Adolescence, 23,* 201–213.
Way, N., Cressen, J., Bodian, S., Preston, J., Nelson, J., & Hughes, D. (2014). "It might be nice to be a girl . . . then you wouldn't have to be emotionless": Boys' resistance to norms of masculinity during adolescence. *Psychology of Men and Masculinity, 15,* 241–252.
Way, N., & Silverman, L. R. (2011). The quality of friendships during adolescence. In P. K. Kerig, M. S. Schulz, & S. T. Hauser (Eds.), *Adolescence and beyond: Family processes and development* (pp. 91–112). New York: Oxford University Press.
Webb, N. M., Franke, M. L., Ing, M., Chan, A., De, T., Freund, D., & Battey, D. (2008). The role of teacher instructional practices in student collaboration. *Contemporary Educational Psychology, 33,* 360–381.
Webb, N. M., Nemer, K. M., & Chizhik, A. W. (1998). Equity issues in collaborative group assessment: Group composition and performance. *American Educational Research Journal, 35,* 607–651.
Webb, S. J., Monk, C. S, & Nelson, C. A. (2001). Mechanisms of postnatal neurobiological development: Implications for human development. *Developmental Neuropsychology, 19,* 147–171.
Weber, C., Hahne, A., Friedrich, M., & Friederici, A. (2004). Discrimination of word stress in early infant perception: Electrophysiological evidence. *Cognitive Brain Research, 18,* 149–161.
Webster, G. D., Graber, J. A., Gesselman, A. N., Crosier, B. J., & Schember, T. O. (2014). A life history theory of father absence and menarche: A meta-analysis. *Evolutionary Psychology, 12,* 273–294.
Webster-Stratton, C., & Reid, M. J. (2010). The Incredible Years Parents, Teachers, and Children Training Series: A multifaceted treatment approach for young children with conduct disorders. In J. R. Weisz & A. E. Kazdin (Eds.), *Evidence-based psychotherapies for children and adolescents* (2nd ed., pp. 194–210). New York: Guilford.
Webster-Stratton, C., Rinaldi, J., & Reid, J. M. (2011). Long-term outcomes of Incredible Years parenting program: Predictors of adolescent adjustment. *Child and Adolescent Mental Health, 16,* 38–46.
Wechsler, D. (2002). *WPPSI-III: Wechsler Preschool and Primary Scale of Intelligence* (3rd ed.). San Antonio, TX: Psychological Corporation.
Wechsler, D. (2003). *WISC-IV: Wechsler Intelligence Scale for Children* (4th ed.). San Antonio, TX: Psychological Corporation.
Weems, C. F., & Costa, N. M. (2005). Developmental differences in the expression of childhood anxiety

symptoms and fears. *Journal of the American Academy of Child and Adolescent Psychiatry, 44,* 656–663.

Wehren, A., DeLisi, R., & Arnold, M. (1981). The development of noun definition. *Journal of Child Language, 8,* 165–175.

Wei, W., Lu, H., Zhao, H., Chen, C., Dong, Q., & Zhou, X. (2012). Gender differences in children's arithmetic performance are accounted for by gender differences in language abilities. *Psychological science, 23,* 320–330.

Weikart, D. P. (1998). Changing early childhood development through educational intervention. *Preventive Medicine, 27,* 233–237.

Weikum, W. M., Vouloumanos, A., Navarra, J., Soto-Faraco, S., Sebastián-Gallés, N., & Werker, J. F. (2007). Visual language discrimination in infancy. *Science, 316,* 1159.

Weiland, C., & Yoshikawa, H. (2013). Impacts of a prekindergarten program on children's mathematics, language, literacy, executive function, and emotional skills. *Child Development, 84,* 2112–2130.

Weinberg, M. K., & Tronick, E. Z. (1994). Beyond the face: An empirical study of infant affective configurations of facial, vocal, gestural, and regulatory behaviors. *Child Development, 65,* 1503–1515.

Weiner, A. (1988). *The Trobrianders of Papua New Guinea.* New York: Holt.

Weinfield, N. S., Sroufe, L. A., & Egeland, B. (2000). Attachment from infancy to early adulthood in a high-risk sample: Continuity, discontinuity, and their correlates. *Child Development, 71,* 695–702.

Weinfield, N. S., Whaley, G. J. L., & Egeland, B. (2004). Continuity, discontinuity, and coherence in attachment from infancy to late adolescence: Sequelae of organization and disorganization. *Attachment and Human Development, 6,* 73–97.

Weinstein, R. S. (2002). *Reaching higher: The power of expectations in schooling.* Cambridge, MA: Harvard University Press.

Weinstock, M. (2008). The long-term behavioural consequences of prenatal stress. *Neuroscience and Biobehavioral Reviews, 32,* 1073–1086.

Weisberg, D. S., Zosh, J. M., Hirsh-Pasek, K., & Golinkoff, R. M. (2013). Talking it up: Play, language development, and the role of adult support. *American Journal of Play, 6,* 39–54.

Weisgram, E. S., Bigler, R. S., & Liben, L. S. (2010). Gender, values, and occupational interests among children, adolescents, and adults. *Child Development, 81,* 778–796.

Weisman, O., Magori-Cohen, R., Louzoun, Y., Eidelman, A. I., & Feldman, R. (2011). Sleep–wake transitions in premature neonates predict early development. *Pediatrics, 128,* 706–714.

Weiss, K. M. (2005). Cryptic causation of human disease: Reading between the germ lines. *Trends in Genetics, 21,* 82–88.

Weizman, Z. O., & Snow, C. E. (2001). Lexical output as related to children's vocabulary acquisition: Effects of sophisticated exposure and support for meaning. *Developmental Psychology, 37,* 265–279.

Wekerle, C., & Wolfe, D. A. (2003). Child maltreatment. In E. J. Mash & R. A. Barkley (Eds.), *Child psychopathology* (2nd ed., pp. 632–684). New York: Guilford.

Weller, E. B., Kloos, A. L., & Weller, R. A. (2006). Mood disorders. M. K. Dulcan & J. M. Wiener (Eds.), *Essentials of child and adolescent psychiatry* (pp. 267–320). Washington, DC: American Psychiatric Association.

Wellman, H. M. (2002). Understanding the psychological world: Developing a theory of mind. In U. Goswami (Ed.), *Blackwell handbook of child cognitive development* (pp. 167–187). Malden, MA: Blackwell.

Wellman, H. M. (2011). Developing a theory of mind. In U. Goswami (Ed.), *Wiley-Blackwell handbook of childhood cognitive development* (2nd ed., pp. 258–284). Malden, MA: Wiley-Blackwell.

Wellman, H. M. (2012). Theory of mind: Better methods, clearer findings, more development. European *Journal of Developmental Psychology, 9,* 313–330.

Wellman, H. M., Fang, F., Liu, D., Zhu, L., & Liu, G. (2006). Scaling of theory-of-mind understandings in Chinese children. *Psychological Science, 17,* 1075–1081.

Wellman, H. M., & Hickling, A. K. (1994). The mind's "I": Children's conception of the mind as an active agent. *Child Development, 65,* 1564–1580.

Wellman, H. M., Lopez-Duran, S., LaBounty, J., & Hamilton, B. (2008). Infant attention to intentional action predicts

preschool theory of mind. *Developmental Psychology, 44,* 618–623.

Weng, S. F., Redsell, S. A., Swift, J. A., Yang, M., & Glazebrook, C. P. (2012). Systematic review and meta-analyses of risk factors for childhood overweight identifiable during infancy. *Archives of Disease in Childhood, 97,* 1019–1026.

Wentworth, N., Benson, J. B., & Haith, M. M. (2000). The development of infants' reaches for stationary and moving targets. *Child Development, 71,* 576–601.

Wentzel, K. R., Barry, C. M., & Caldwell, K. A. (2004). Friendships in middle school: Influences on motivation and school adjustment. *Journal of Educational Psychology, 96,* 195–203.

Wentzel, K. R., & Brophy, J. E. (2014). *Motivating students to learn.* Hoboken, NJ: Taylor & Francis.

Werner, E. E. (1989, April). Children of the garden island. *Scientific American, 260(4),* 106–111.

Werner, E. E. (2001). *Journeys from childhood to midlife: Risk, resilience, and recovery.* Ithaca, NY: Cornell University Press.

Werner, E. E. (2013). What can we learn about resilience from large-scale longitudinal studies? In S. Goldstein & R. Brooks (Eds.), *Handbook of resilience in children* (2nd ed., pp. 87–102). New York: Springer Science + Business Media.

Werner, E. E., & Smith, R. S. (1982). *Vulnerable but invincible: A study of resilient children.* New York: McGraw-Hill.

Werner, E. E., & Smith, R. S. (1992). *Overcoming the odds: High risk children from birth to adulthood.* Ithaca, NY: Cornell University Press.

Werner, N. E., & Crick, N. R. (2004). Maladaptive peer relationships and the development of relational and physical aggression during middle childhood. *Social Development, 13,* 495–514.

Westermann, G., Sirois, S., Shultz, T. R., & Mareschal, D. (2006). Modeling developmental cognitive neuroscience. *Trends in Cognitive Sciences, 10,* 227–232.

Wexler, J., & Pyle, N. (2013). Effective approaches to increase student engagement. In C. Franklin, M. B. Harris, & P. Allen-Meares (Eds.), *School services sourcebook: A guide for school-based professionals* (2nd ed., pp. 381–394). New York: Oxford University Press.

Whaley, S. E., Koleilat, M., & Jiang, L. (2012). WIC infant food package issuance data are a valid measure of infant feeding practices. *Journal of Human Lactation, 28,* 134–138.

Whaley, S. E., Koleilat, M., Whaley, M., Gomez, J., Meehan, K., & Saluja, K. (2012). Impact of policy changes on infant feeding decisions among low-income women participating in the Special Supplemental Nutrition Program for Women, Infants, and Children. *American Journal of Public Health, 102,* 2269–2273.

Whipple, E. E. (2006). Child abuse and neglect: Consequences of physical, sexual, and emotional abuse of children. In H. E. Fitzgerald, B. M. Lester, & B. Zuckerman (Eds.), *The crisis in youth mental health: Vol 1. Childhood disorders* (pp. 205–229). Westport, CT: Praeger.

Whipple, N., Bernier, A., & Mageau, G. A. (2011). Broadening the study of infant security of attachment: Maternal autonomy-support in the context of infant exploration. *Social Development, 20,* 17–32.

White, B., & Held, R. (1966). Plasticity of sensorimotor development in the human infant. In J. F. Rosenblith & W. Allinsmith (Eds.), *The causes of behavior* (pp. 60–70). Boston: Allyn and Bacon.

White, M. A., Wilson, M. E., Elander, G., & Persson, B. (1999). The Swedish family: Transition to parenthood. *Scandinavian Journal of Caring Sciences, 13,* 171–176.

White, Y. A., Woods, D. C., Takai, Y., Ishihara, O., Seki, H., & Tilly, J. L. (2012). Oocyte formation by mitotically active germ cells purified from ovaries of reproductive-age women. *Nature Medicine, 18,* 413–421.

Whitehurst, G. J., & Lonigan, C. J. (1998). Child development and emergent literacy. *Child Development, 69,* 848–872.

Whiteman, S. D., & Loken, E. (2006). Comparing analytic techniques to classify dyadic relationships: An example using siblings. *Journal of Marriage and Family, 68,* 1370–1382.

Whitesell, N. R., Mitchell, C. M., Spicer, P., and the Voices of Indian Teens Project Team. (2009). A longitudinal study of self-esteem, cultural identity, and academic

success among American Indian adolescents. *Cultural Diversity and Ethnic Minority Psychology, 15,* 38–50.

Whiteside-Mansell, L., Bradley, R. H., Owen, M. T., Randolph, S. M., & Cauce, A. M. (2003). Parenting and children's behavior at 36 months: Equivalence between African-American and European-American mother–child dyads. *Parenting: Science and Practice, 3,* 197–234.

Whiting, B., & Edwards, C. P. (1988). *Children in different worlds.* Cambridge, MA: Harvard University Press.

Whitlock, J. L., Powers, J. L., & Eckenrode, J. (2006). The virtual cutting edge: The Internet and adolescent self-injury. *Developmental Psychology, 42,* 407–417.

Whitney, C. G., Zhou, F., Singleton, J., & Schuchat, A. (2014). Benefits from immunization during the Vaccines for Children Program Era—United States, 1994–2013. *Morbidity and Mortality Weekly Report, 63,* 352–355.

Wichman, A. L., Rodgers, J. L., & MacCallum, R. C. (2007). Birth order has no effect on intelligence: A reply and extension of previous findings. *Personality and Social Psychology Bulletin, 33,* 1195–1200.

Wichmann, C., Coplan, R. J., & Daniels, T. (2004). The social cognitions of socially withdrawn children. *Social Development, 13,* 377–392.

Wichstrøm, L. (2006). Sexual orientation as a risk factor for bulimic symptoms. *International Journal of Eating Disorders, 39,* 448–453.

Widen, S. C., & Russell, J. A. (2011). In building a script for an emotion do preschoolers add its cause before its behavior consequence? *Social Development, 20,* 471–485.

Widman, L., Choukas-Bradley, S., Helms, S. W., Golin, C. E., & Prinstein, M. J. (2014). Sexual communication between early adolescents and their dating partners, parents, and best friends. *Journal of Sex Research, 51,* 731–741.

Wigfield, A., Battle, A., Keller, L. B., & Eccles, J. S. (2002). Sex differences in motivation, self-concept, career aspiration, and career choice: Implications for cognitive development. In A. McGillicudy-De Lisi & R. De Lisi (Eds.), *Biology, society, and behavior: The development of sex differences in cognition* (pp. 93–124). Westport, CT: Ablex.

Wigfield, A., Eccles, J. S., Schiefele, U., Roeser, R. W., & Davis-Kean, P. (2006). Development of achievement motivation. In N. Eisenberg (Ed.), *Handbook of child psychology: Vol. 3. Social, emotional, and personality development* (6th ed., pp. 933–1002). Hoboken, NJ: Wiley.

Wigfield, A., Eccles, J. S., Yoon, K. S., Harold, R. D., Arbreton, A. J., Freedman-Doan, C., & Blumenfeld, P. C. (1997). Changes in children's competence beliefs and subjective task values across the elementary school years: A three-year study. *Journal of Educational Psychology, 89,* 451–469.

Wilcox, T., & Woods, R. (2009). Experience primes infants to individuate objects. In A. Woodward & A. Needham (Eds.), *Learning and the infant mind* (pp. 117–143). New York: Oxford University Press.

Wildsmith, E., Manlove, J., Jekielek, S., Moore, K. A., & Mincieli, L. (2012). Teenage childbearing among youth born to teenage mothers. *Youth and Society, 44,* 258–283.

Wilkinson, R. B. (2004). The role of parental and peer attachment in the psychological health and self-esteem of adolescents. *Journal of Youth and Adolescence, 33,* 479–493.

Willatts, P. (1999). Development of means—end behavior in young infants: Pulling a support to retrieve a distant object. *Developmental Psychology, 35,* 651–667.

Williams, A. F., Tefft, B. C., & Grabowski, J. G. (2012). Graduated driver licensing research, 2010–present. *Journal of Safety Research, 43,* 195–203.

Williams, G. R. (2008). Neurodevelopmental and neurophysiological actions of thyroid hormone. *Journal of Neuroendocrinology, 20,* 784–794.

Williams, J. M., & Currie, C. (2000). Self-esteem and physical development in early adolescence: Pubertal timing and body image. *Journal of Early Adolescence, 20,* 129–149.

Williams, K., & Dunne-Bryant, A. (2006). Divorce and adult psychological well-being: Clarifying the role of gender and age. *Journal of Marriage and Family, 68,* 1178–1196.

Williams, K., Haywood, K. I., & Painter, M. (1996). Environmental versus biological influences on gender differences in the overarm throw for force: Dominant and nondominant arm throws. *Women in Sport and Physical Activity Journal, 5,* 29–48.

Williams, P. E., Weiss, L. G., & Rolfhus, E. (2003). *WISC-IV: Theoretical model and test blueprint*. San Antonio, TX: Psychological Corporation.

Williams, S. C., Lochman, J. E., Phillips, N. C., & Barry, T. D. (2003). Aggressive and nonaggressive boys' physiological and cognitive processes in response to peer provocations. *Journal of Clinical Child and Adolescent Psychology, 32*, 568–576.

Williams, S. T., Mastergeorge, A. M., & Ontai, L. L. (2010). Caregiver involvement in infant peer interactions: Scaffolding in a social context. *Early Childhood Research Quarterly, 25*, 251–266.

Williamson, J., Softas-Nall, B., & Miller, J. (2003). Grandmothers raising grandchildren: An exploration of their experiences and emotions. *Counseling and Therapy for Couples with Families, 11*, 23–32.

Willoughby, J., Kupersmidt, J. B., & Bryant, D. (2001). Overt and covert dimensions of antisocial behavior. *Journal of Abnormal Child Psychology, 29*, 177–187.

Wilson, E. K., Dalberth, B. T., Koo, H. P., & Gard, J. C. (2010). Parents' perspectives on talking to preteenage children about sex. *Perspectives on Sexual and Reproductive Health, 42*, 56–63.

Wilson, S. J., & Tanner-Smith, E. E. (2013). Dropout prevention and intervention programs for improving school completion among school-aged children and youth: A systematic review. *Journal of the Society for Social Work and Research, 4*, 357–372.

Wilson-Ching, M., Molloy, C. S., Anderson, V. A., Burnett, A., Roberts, G., Cheong, J. L., et al. (2013). Attention difficulties in a contemporary geographic cohort of adolescents born extremely preterm/extremely low birth weight. *Journal of the International Neuropsychological Society, 19*, 1097–1108.

Wimmer, M. B. (2013). *Evidence-based practices for school refusal and truancy*. Bethesda, MD: NASP.

Winkler, I., Háden, G. P., Ladinig, O., Sziller, I., & Honing, H. (2009). Newborn infants detect the beat in music. *Proceedings of the National Academy of Sciences, 106*, 2468–2471.

Winner, E. (1986, August). Where pelicans kiss seals. *Psychology Today, 20*(8), 25–35.

Winner, E. (1988). *The point of words: Children's understanding of metaphor and irony*. Cambridge, MA: Harvard University Press.

Winner, E. (2000). The origins and ends of giftedness. *American Psychologist, 55*, 159–169.

Winsler, A. (2009). Still talking to ourselves after all these years: A review of current research on private speech. In A. Winsler, C. Fernyhough, & I. Montero (Eds.), *Private speech, executive functioning, and the development of self-regulation*. New York: Cambridge University Press.

Winsler, A., Abar, B., Feder, M. A., Rubio, D. A., & Schunn, C. D. (2007). Private speech and executive functioning among high functioning children with autism spectrum disorders. *Journal of Autism and Developmental Disorders, Online First*™.

Winsler, A., Fernyhough, C., & Montero, I. (2009). *Private speech, executive functioning, and the development of verbal self-regulation*. New York: Cambridge University Press.

Wissink, I. B., Deković, M., & Meijer, A. M. (2006). Parenting behavior, quality of the parent–adolescent relationship, and adolescent functioning in four ethnic groups. *Journal of Early Adolescence, 26*, 133–159.

Witherington, D. C. (2005). The development of prospective grasping control between 5 and 7 months: A longitudinal study. *Infancy, 7*, 143–161.

Witherington, D. C., Campos, J. J., Harriger, J. A., Bryan, C., & Margett, T. E. (2010). Emotion and its development in infancy. In G. Bremner & T. D. Wachs (Eds.), *Wiley-Blackwell handbook of infant development: Vol. 1. Basic research* (2nd ed., pp. 568–591). Hoboken, NJ: Wiley-Blackwell.

Witt, E. A., Donnellan, M. B., & Trzesniewski, K. H. (2011). Self-esteem, narcissism, and Machiavellianism: Implications for understanding antisocial behavior in adolescents and young adults. In C. T. Barry, P. K. Kerig, K. K. Stellwagen, & T. D. Barry (Eds.), *Narcissism and Machiavellianism in youth* (pp. 47–68). Washington, DC: American Psychological Association.

Wolak, J., Mitchell, K., & Finkelhor, D. (2007). Unwanted and wanted exposure to online pornography in a national sample of youth Internet users. *Pediatrics, 119*, 247–257.

Wolchik, S. A., Sandler, I. N., Millsap, R. E., Plummer, B. A., Greene, S. M., Anderson, E. R., et al. (2002). Six-year follow-up of preventive interventions for children of divorce: A randomized controlled trial. *Journal of the American Medical Association, 288*, 1874–1881.

Wolf, A. W., Jimenez, E., & Lozoff, B. (2003). Effects of iron therapy on infant blood lead levels. *Journal of Pediatrics, 143*, 789–795.

Wolfberg, A. J. (2012). The future of fetal monitoring. *Reviews in Obstetrics and Gynecology, 5*, e132–e136.

Wolfe, D. A. (2005). *Child abuse* (2nd ed.) Thousand Oaks, CA: Sage.

Wolfe, V. V. (2006). Child sexual abuse. In E. J. Mash & R. A. Barkley (Eds.), *Treatment of childhood disorders* (3rd ed., pp. 647–727). New York: Guilford.

Wolff, P. H. (1966). The causes, controls and organization of behavior in the neonate. *Psychological Issues, 5*(1, Serial No. 17).

Wolff, P. H., & Fesseha, G. (1999). The orphans of Eritrea: A five-year follow-up study. *Journal of Child Psychology and Psychiatry and Allied Disciplines, 40*, 1231–1237.

Wong, C. A., Eccles, J. S., & Sameroff, A. (2003). The influence of ethnic discrimination and ethnic identification on African American adolescents' school and socioemotional adjustment. *Journal of Personality, 71*, 1197–1232.

Wood, E., Desmarais, S., & Gugula, S. (2002). The impact of parenting experience on gender stereotyped toy play of children. *Sex Roles, 47*, 39–49.

Wood, J. J., Emmerson, N. A., & Cowan, P. A. (2004). Is early attachment security carried forward into relationships with preschool peers? *British Journal of Developmental Psychology, 22*, 245–253.

Wood, J. N., Kouider, S., & Carey, S. (2009). Acquisition of singular-plural morphology. *Developmental Psychology, 45*, 202–206.

Wood, R. M. (2009). Changes in cry acoustics and distress ratings while the infant is crying. *Infant and Child Development, 18*, 163–177.

Woodward, A. (2009). Infants' grasp of others' intentions. *Current Directions in Psychological Science, 18*, 53–57.

Woodward, J., & Ono, Y. (2004). Mathematics and academic diversity in Japan. *Journal of Learning Disabilities, 37*, 74–82.

Woolley, J. D. (1997). Thinking about fantasy: Are children fundamentally different thinkers and believers from adults? *Child Development, 68*, 991–1011.

Woolley, J. D. (2000). The development of beliefs about direct mental–physical causality in imagination, magic, and religion. In K. S. Rosengren, C. N. Johnson, & P. L. Harris (Eds.), *Imagining the impossible* (pp. 99–129). New York: Cambridge University Press.

Woolley, J. D., Browne, C. A., & Boerger, E. A. (2006). Constraints on children's judgments of magical causality. *Journal of Cognition and Development, 7*, 253–277.

Woolley, J. D., & Cornelius, C. A. (2013). Beliefs in magical beings and cultural myths. In M. Taylor (Ed.), *Oxford handbook of the development of imagination* (pp. 61–74). New York: Oxford University Press.

Woolley, J. D., Cornelius, C. A., & Lacy, W. (2011). Developmental changes in the use of supernatural explanations for unusual events. *Journal of Cognition and Culture, 11*, 311–337.

Woolley, J. D., & Cox, V. (2007). Development of beliefs about storybook reality. *Developmental Science, 10*, 681–693.

Woolley, M. E., Kol, K. L., & Bowen, G. L. (2009). The social context of school success for Latino middle school students: Direct and indirect influences of teachers, family, and friends. *Journal of Early Adolescence, 29*, 43–70.

World Bank. (2014). *World Development Indicators: Reproductive Health*. Retrieved from wdi.worldbank.org/table/2.17

World Health Organization. (2008). *World report on child injury prevention*. Geneva, Switzerland: Author.

World Health Organization. (2011). *The world's women 2010: Trends and statistics*. Retrieved from unstats.un.org/unsd/demographic/products/Worldswomen/Executive%20summary.htm

World Health Organization. (2012a). *Countdown to 2015: Building a future for women and children*. Geneva, Switzerland: Author.

World Health Organization. (2012b). *The World Health Organization's infant feeding recommendation*. Retrieved from www.who.int/nutrition/topics/infantfeeding_recommendation/en/index.html

World Health Organization. (2013a). *Levels and trends in child mortality: Report 2013*. Geneva, Switzerland: Author.

World Health Organization. (2013b). *World health statistics 2013*. Retrieved from apps.who.int/iris/bitstream/10665/81965/1/9789241564588_eng.pdf?ua=1

World Health Organization. (2014a). *Immunization, vaccines, and biologicals: Data, statistics and graphics*. Retrieved from www.who.int/immunization/monitoring_surveillance/data/en/

World Health Organization. (2014b). Rubella. Fact Sheet No. 367. Retrieved from www.who.int/mediacentre/factsheets/fs367/en

World Health Organization. (2014c). *WHO global infobase*. Retrieved from apps.who.int/infobase/Comparisons.aspx

World Health Organization. (2014d). *World health statistics 2014*. Retrieved from www.who.int/gho/publications/world_health_statistics/2014/en

Wörmann, V., Holodynski, M., Kärtner, J., & Keller, H. (2012). A cross-cultural comparison of the development of the social smile: A longitudinal study of maternal and infant imitation in 6 and 12-week-old infants. *Infant Behavior and Development, 35*, 335–347.

Worrell, F. C., & Gardner-Kitt, D. L. (2006). The relationship between racial and ethnic identity in black adolescents: The cross-racial identity scale and the multigroup ethnic identity measure. *Identity, 6*, 293–315.

Worthman, C. M. (2011). Developmental cultural ecology of sleep. In M. El-Sheikh (Ed.), *Sleep and development: Familial and socio-cultural considerations* (pp. 167–194). New York: Oxford University Press.

Worthy, J., Hungerford-Kresser, H., & Hampton, A. (2009). Tracking and ability grouping. In L. Christenbury, R. Bomer, & P. Smargorinsky (Eds.), *Handbook of adolescent literacy research* (pp. 220–235). New York: Guilford.

Wright, B. C. (2006). On the emergence of the discriminative mode for transitive inference. *European Journal of Cognitive Psychology, 18*, 776–800.

Wright, B. C., Robertson, S., & Hadfield, L. (2011). Transitivity for height versus speed: To what extent do the under-7s really have a transitive capacity? *Thinking and Reasoning, 17*, 57–81.

Wright, J. C., Huston, A. C., Murphy, K. C., St. Peters, M., Pinon, M., Scantlin, R., & Kotler, J. (2001). The relations of early television viewing to school readiness and vocabulary of children from low-income families: The Early Window Project. *Child Development, 72*, 1347–1366.

Wright, J. P., Dietrich, K., Ris, M., Hornung, R., Wessel, S., Lanphear, B., et al. (2008). Association of prenatal and childhood blood lead concentrations with criminal arrests in early adulthood. *PLOS Medicine, 5*, e101.

Wright, M. O., & Masten, A. S. (2005). Resilience processes in development. In S. Goldstein & R. B. Brooks (Eds.), *Handbook of resilience in children* (pp. 17–37). New York: Springer.

Wright, P. J., Malamuth, N. M., & Donnerstein, E. (2012). Research on sex in the media: What do we know about effects on children and adolescents? In D. G. Singer & J. L. Singer (Eds.), *Handbook of children and the media* (2nd ed., pp. 273–302). Thousand Oaks, CA: Sage.

Wright, R. O., Tsaih, S. W., Schwartz, J., Wright, R. J., & Hu, H. (2003). Associations between iron deficiency and blood lead level in a longitudinal analysis of children followed in an urban primary care clinic. *Journal of Pediatrics, 142*, 9–14.

Wright, W. E. (2013). Bilingual education. In T. K. Bhatia & W. C. Ritchie (Eds.), *Handbook of bilingualism and multilingualism* (pp. 598–623). Chichester, UK: Wiley-Blackwell.

Wrotniak, B. H., Epstein, L. H., Raluch, R. A., & Roemmich, J. N. (2004). Parent weight change as a predictor of child weight change in family-based behavioral obesity treatment. *Archives of Pediatric and Adolescent Medicine, 158*, 342–347.

Wu, G., Bazer, F. W., Cudd, T. A., Meininger, C. J., & Spencer, T. E. (2004). Maternal nutrition and fetal development. *Journal of Nutrition, 134*, 2169–2172.

Wu, L. L., Bumpass, L. L., & Musick, K. (2001). Historical and life course trajectories of nonmarital childbearing. In L. L. Wu & B. Wolfe (Eds.), *Out of wedlock: Causes and consequences of nonmarital fertility* (pp. 3–48). New York: Russell Sage Foundation.

Wu, L.-T., Woody, G. E., Yang, C., Pan, J.-J., & Blazer, D. G. (2011). Racial/ethnic variations in substance-related disorders among adolescents in the United States. *Archives of General Psychiatry, 68*, 1176–1185.

Wu, T., Mendola, P., & Buck, G. M. (2002). Ethnic differences in the presence of secondary sex characteristics and menarche among U.S. girls: The Third National Health and Nutrition Examination Survey, 1988–1994. *Pediatrics, 110*, 752–757.

Wulczyn, F. (2009). Epidemiological perspectives on maltreatment prevention. *Future of Children, 19*, 39–66.

Wyman, E., Rakoczy, H., & Tomasello, M. (2009). Normativity and context in young children's pretend play. *Cognitive Development, 24*, 146–155.

Wynn, K. (1992). Addition and subtraction by human infants. *Nature, 358*, 749–750.

Wynn, K., Bloom, P., & Chiang, W.-C. (2002). Enumeration of collective entities by 5-month-old infants. *Cognition, 83*, B55–B62.

Wynne-Edwards, K. E. (2001). Hormonal changes in mammalian fathers. *Hormones and Behavior, 40*, 139–145.

X

Xu, F., Han, Y., Sabbagh, M. A., Wang, T., Ren, X., & Li, C. (2013). Developmental differences in the structure of executive function in middle childhood and adolescence. *PLOS ONE, 8*, e77770.

Xu, F., Spelke, E., & Goddard, S. (2005). Number sense in human infants. *Developmental Science, 8*, 88–101.

Y

Yamada, T., Yamada, T., Morikawa, M., & Minakami, H. (2012). Clinical features of abruptio placentae as a prominent cause of cerebral palsy. *Early Human Development, 88*, 861–864.

Yang, B., Ollendick, T. H., Dong, Q., Xia, Y., & Lin, L. (1995). Only children and children with siblings in the People's Republic of China: Levels of fear, anxiety, and depression. *Child Development, 66*, 1301–1311.

Yang, C.-K., & Hahn, H.-M. (2002). Cosleeping in young Korean children. Developmental and Behavioral Pediatrics, 23, 151–157.

Yang, F.-Y., & Tsai, C.-C. (2010). Reasoning about science-related uncertain issues and epistemological perspectives among children. *Instructional Science, 38*, 325–354.

Yap, M. B. H., Allen, N. B., & Ladouceur, C. D. (2008). Maternal socialization of positive affect: The impact of invalidation on adolescent emotion regulation and depressive symptomatology. *Child Development, 79*, 1415–1431.

Yarrow, M. R., Scott, P. M., & Waxler, C. Z. (1973). Learning concern for others. *Developmental Psychology, 8*, 240–260.

Yau, J. P., Tasopoulos-Chan, M., & Smetana, J. G. (2009). Disclosure to parents about everyday activities among American adolescents from Mexican, Chinese, and European backgrounds. *Child Development, 80*, 1481–1498.

Yeates, K. O., Schultz, L. H., & Selman, R. L. (1991). The development of interpersonal negotiation strategies in thought and action: A social-cognitive link to behavioral adjustment and social status. *Merrill-Palmer Quarterly, 37*, 369–405.

Yeh, C. J., Kim, A. B., Pituc, S. T., & Atkins, M. (2008). Poverty, loss, and resilience: The story of Chinese immigrant youth. *Journal of Counseling Psychology, 55*, 34–48.

Yeh, H.-C., & Lempers, J. D. (2004). Perceived sibling relationships and adolescent development. *Journal of Youth and Adolescence, 33*, 133–147.

Yip, T., Douglass, S., & Shelton, J. N. (2013). Daily intragroup contact in diverse settings: Implications for Asian adolescents' ethnic identity. *Child Development, 84*, 1425–1441.

Yirmiya, N., Erel, O., Shaked, M., & Solomonica-Levi, D. (1998). Meta-analyses comparing theory of mind abilities of individuals with autism, individuals with mental retardation, and normally developing individuals. *Psychological Bulletin, 124*, 283–307.

Yonker, J. E., Schnabelrauch, C. A., & DeHaan, L. G. (2012). The relationship between spirituality and religiosity on psychological outcomes in adolescents and emerging adults: A meta-analytic review. *Journal of Adolescence, 35*, 299–314.

Yook, J.-H., Han, J.-Y., Choi, J.-S., Ahn, H.-K., Lee, S.-W., Kim, M.-Y., et al. (2012). Pregnancy outcomes and factors associated with voluntary pregnancy termination in women who had been treated for acne with isotretinoin. *Clinical Toxicology, 50*, 896–901.

Yoshida, H., & Smith, L. B. (2003). Known and novel noun extensions: Attention at two levels of abstraction. *Child Development, 74*, 564–577.

Yoshikawa, H., Aber, J. L., & Beardslee, W. R. (2012). The effects of poverty on the mental, emotional, and behavioral health of children and youth: Implications for prevention. *American Psychologist, 67*, 272–284.

Yoshikawa, H., Weiland, C., Brooks-Gunn, J., Burchinal, M. R., Espinosa, L. M., Gormley, W. T., et al. (2013). *Investing in our future: The evidence base on preschool education.* Ann Arbor, MI: Society for Research in Child Development. Retrieved from fcd-us.org/resources/evidence-base-preschool

You, D., Maeda, Y., & Bebeau, M. J. (2011). Gender differences in moral sensitivity: A meta-analysis. *Ethics and Behavior, 21*, 263–282.

Youn, M. J., Leon, J., & Lee, K. J. (2012). The influence of maternal employment on children's learning growth and the role of parental involvement. *Early Child Development and Care, 182*, 1227–1246.

Young, S. E., Friedman, N. P., Miyake, A., Willcutt, E. G., Corley, R. P., Haberstick, B. C., et al. (2009). Behavioral disinhibition: Liability for externalizing spectrum disorders and its genetic and environmental relation to response inhibition across adolescence. *Journal of Abnormal Psychology, 118*, 117–130.

Young-Hyman, D., Tanofsky-Kraff, M., Yanovski, S. Z., Keil, M., Cohen, M. L., & Peyrot, M. (2006). Psychological status and weight-related distress in overweight or at-risk-for-overweight children. *Obesity, 14*, 2249–2258.

Yousafzai, A. K., Yakoob, M. Y., & Bhutta, Z. A. (2013). Nutrition-based approaches to early childhood development. In P. R. Britto, P. L. Engle, & C. M. Super (Eds.), *Handbook of early childhood development research and its impact on global policy* (pp. 202–226). New York: Oxford University Press.

Yu, R. (2002). On the reform of elementary school education in China. *Educational Exploration, 129*, 56–57.

Yuill, N., & Pearson, A. (1998). The developmental bases for trait attribution: Children's understanding of traits as causal mechanisms based on desire. *Developmental Psychology, 34*, 574–586.

Yule, W., Dyregov, A., Raundalen, M., & Smith, P. (2013). Children and war: The work of the Children and War Foundation. *European Journal of Psychotraumatology, 4*, 1–8.

Yumoto, C., Jacobson, S. W., & Jacobson, J. L. (2008). Fetal substance exposure and cumulative environmental risk in an African-American cohort. *Child Development, 79*, 1761–1776.

Yunger, J. L., Carver, P. R., & Perry, D. G. (2004). Does gender identity influence children's psychological well-being? *Developmental Psychology, 40*, 572–582.

Z

Zachrisson, H. D., Dearing, E., Lekhal, R., & Toppelberg, C. O. (2013). Little evidence that time in child care causes externalizing problems during early childhood in Norway. *Child Development, 84*, 1152–1170.

Zadjel, R. T., Bloom, J. M., Fireman, G., & Larsen, J. T. (2013). Children's understanding and experience of mixed emotions: The roles of age, gender, and empathy. *The Journal of Genetic Psychology, 174*, 582–603.

Zafeiriou, D. I. (2000). Plantar grasp reflex in high-risk infants during the first year of life. *Pediatric Neurology, 22*, 75–76.

Zaff, J. F., Hart, D., Flanagan, C. A., Youniss, J., & Levine, P. (2010). Developing civic engagement within a civic context. In M. Lamb & A. Freund (Eds.), *Handbook of life-span development: Vol. 2. Social and emotional development* (pp. 590–630). Hoboken, NJ: Wiley.

Zaff, J. F., Moore, K. A., Papillo, A. R., & Williams, S. (2003). Implications of extracurricular activity participation during adolescence on positive outcomes. *Journal of Adolescent Research, 18*, 599–630.

Zahn-Waxler, C., Kochanska, G., Krupnick, J., & McKnew, D. (1990). Patterns of guilt in children of depressed and well mothers. *Developmental Psychology, 26*, 51–59.

Zajac, R., O'Neill, S., & Hayne, H. (2012). Disorder in the courtroom? Child witnesses under cross-examination. *Developmental Review, 32*, 181–204.

Zalewski, M., Lengua, L. J., Wilson, A. C., Trancik, A., & Bazinet, A. (2011). Emotion regulation profiles, temperament, and adjustment problems in preadolescents. *Child Development, 82*, 951–966.

Zaslow, M. J., Weinfield, N. S., Gallagher, M., Hair, E. C., Ogawa, J. R., Egeland, B., Tabors, P. O., & De Temple, J. M. (2006). Longitudinal prediction of child outcomes from differing measures of parenting in a low-income sample. *Developmental Psychology, 42*, 27–37.

Zeanah, C. H. (2000). Disturbances of attachment in young children adopted from institutions. *Journal of Developmental and Behavioral Pediatrics, 21*, 230–236.

Zeifman, D. M. (2003). Predicting adult responses to infant distress: Adult characteristics associated with perceptions, emotional reactions, and timing of intervention. *Infant Mental Health Journal, 24*, 597–612.

Zelazo, N. A., Zelazo, P. R., Cohen, K. M., & Zelazo, P. D. (1993). Specificity of practice effects on elementary neuromotor patterns. *Developmental Psychology, 29*, 686–691.

Zelazo, P., & Paus, T. (2010). Developmental social neuroscience: An introduction. In M. K. Underwood & L. H. Rosen (Eds.), *Social development: Relationships in infancy, childhood, and adolescence* (pp. 29–43). New York: Guilford.

Zelazo, P. D., & Carlson, S. M. (2012). Hot and cool executive function in childhood and adolescence: Development and plasticity. *Child Development Perspectives, 6*, 354–360.

Zelazo, P. D., Carlson, S. M., & Kesek, A. (2008). The development of executive function in childhood. In C. A. Nelson & M. Luciana (Eds.), *Handbook of cognitive developmental neuroscience* (2nd ed., pp. 553–574). Cambridge, MA: MIT Press.

Zelazo, P. D., & Lee, W. S. C. (2010). Brain development: An overview. In W. Overton & R. M. Lerner (Eds.), *Handbook of life-span development: Vol. 1. Cognition biology, and methods* (pp. 89–114). Hoboken, NJ: Wiley.

Zelazo, P. D., Muller, U., Frye, D., & Marcovitch, S. (2003). The development of executive function: Cognitive complexity and control—revised. *Monographs of the Society for Research in Child Development, 68*(3), 93–119.

Zeldin, A. L., & Pajares, F. (2000). Against the odds: Self-efficacy beliefs of women in mathematical, scientific, and technological careers. *American Educational Research Journal, 37*, 215–246.

Zeller, M. H., & Modi, A. C. (2006). Predictors of health-related quality of life in obese youth. *Obesity Research, 14*, 122–130.

Zellner, D. A., Loaiza, S., Gonzales, Z., Pita, J., Morales, J., et al. (2006). Food selection changes under stress. *Physiology & Behavior, 87*, 789–793.

Zeskind, P. S., & Barr, R. G. (1997). Acoustic characteristics of naturally occurring cries of infants with "colic." *Child Development, 68*, 394–403.

Zhang, T.-Y., & Meaney, M. J. (2010). Epigenetics and the environmental regulation of the genome and its function. *Annual Review of Psychology, 61*, 439–466.

Zhou, Q., Lengua, L. J., & Wang, Y. (2009). The relations of temperament reactivity and effortful control to children's adjustment problems in China and the United States. *Developmental Psychology, 45*, 724–739.

Zhou, X., Huang, J., Wang, Z., Wang, B., Zhao, Z., Yang, L., & Zheng-zheng, Y. (2006). Parent–child interaction and children's number learning. *Early Child Development and Care, 176*, 763–775.

Ziemer, C. J., Plumert, J. M., & Pick, A. D. (2012). To grasp or not to grasp: Infants' actions toward objects and pictures. *Infancy, 17*, 479–497.

Zimmer-Gembeck, M., & Helfand, M. J. (2008). Ten years of longitudinal research on U.S. adolescent sexual behavior: Developmental correlates of sexual intercourse, and the importance of age, gender and ethnic background. *Developmental Review, 28*, 153–224.

Zimmer-Gembeck, M. J., & Skinner, E. A. (2011). The development of coping across childhood and adolescence: An integrative review and critique of research. *International Journal of Behavioral Development, 35*, 1–17.

Zimmerman, B. J., & Labuhn, A. S. (2012). Self-regulation of learning: Process approaches to personal development. In K. R. Harris, S. Graham, T. Urdan, C. B. McCormick, G. M. Sinatra, & J. Sweller (Eds.), *APA educational psychology handbook: Vol. 1. Theories, constructs, and critical issues* (pp. 399–425). Washington, DC: American Psychological Association.

Zimmerman, C. (2007). The development of scientific thinking skills in elementary and middle school. *Developmental Review, 27,* 172–223.

Zimmerman, C., & Croker, S. (2013). In G. J. Feist & M. E. Gorman (Eds.), *Handbook of the psychology of science* (pp. 49–70). New York: Springer.

Zimmerman, F. J., & Christakis, D. A. (2005). Children's television viewing and cognitive outcomes. *Archives of Pediatrics and Adolescent Medicine, 159,* 619–625.

Zimmerman, F. J., Christakis, D. A., & Meltzoff, A. N. (2007). Television and DVD/video viewing in children younger than 2 years. *Archives of Pediatrics and Adolescent Medicine, 161,* 473–479.

Zimmermann, L. K., & Stansbury, K. (2004). The influence of emotion regulation, level of shyness, and habituation on the neuroendocrine response of three-year-old children. *Psychoneuroendocrinology, 29,* 973–982.

Zitzmann, M. (2013). Effects of age on male fertility. *Best Practice & Research Clinical Endocrinology and Metabolism, 27,* 617–628.

Ziv, Y. (2013). Social information processing patterns, social skills, and school readiness in preschool children. *Journal of Experimental Child Psychology, 114,* 306–320.

Zoëga, H., Rothman, K. J., Huybrechts, K. F., Olafsson, O., Baldursson, G., Almarsdottir, A. B., et al. (2012). A population-based study of stimulant drug treatment of ADHD and academic progress in children. *Pediatrics, 130,* e53–e62.

Zogby, J. (2008). *The way we'll be: The Zogby Report on the transformation of the American dream.* New York: Random House.

Zolotor, A. J., & Puzia, M. E. (2010). Bans against corporal punishment: A systematic review of the laws, changes in attitudes and behaviours. *Child Abuse Review, 19,* 229–247.

Zolotor, A. J., Theodore, A. D., Runyan, D. K., Chang, J. J., & Laskey, A. L. (2011). Corporal punishment and physical abuse: Population-based trends for three-to-11-year-old children in the United States. *Child Abuse Review, 20,* 57–66.

Zosuls, K. M., Ruble, D. N., Tamis-LeMonda, C. S., Shrout, P. E., Bornstein, M. H., & Greulich, F. K. (2009). The acquisition of gender labels in infancy: Implications for gender-typed play. *Developmental Psychology, 45,* 688–701.

Zucker, K. J. (2006). "I'm half-boy, half-girl": Play psychotherapy and parent counseling for gender identity disorder. In R. L. Spitzer, M. B. First, J. B. W. Williams, & M. Gibbon (Eds.), *DSM-IVTR Casebook: Vol. 2. Experts tell how they treated their own patients* (pp. 322–334). Washington, DC: American Psychiatric Publishing.

Zukow-Goldring, P. (2002). Sibling caregiving. In M. H. Bornstein (Ed.), *Handbook of parenting: Vol. 3* (2nd ed., pp. 253–286). Hillsdale, NJ: Erlbaum.

Zukowski, A. (2013). Putting words together. In J. B. Gleason & N. B. Ratner (Eds.), *The development of language* (pp. 120–162). Upper Saddle River, NJ: Pearson.

Zur, O., & Gelman, R. (2004). Young children can add and subtract by predicting and checking. *Early Childhood Research Quarterly, 19,* 121–137.

Zwart, M. (2007). The Dutch system of perinatal care. *Midwifery Today with International Midwife, 81*(Spring), 46.

Name Index

Italic *n* following page numbers indicates source note accompanying an illustration, figure, or table.

Subject Index

Figures and tables are indicated by *f* and *t* following page numbers.

ENCYCLOPEDIA OF AESTHETICS

ENCYCLOPEDIA OF

AESTHETICS

MICHAEL KELLY

Editor in Chief

Volume 4

OXFORD UNIVERSITY PRESS

New York   1998   Oxford

OXFORD UNIVERSITY PRESS

Oxford   New York
Athens   Auckland   Bangkok   Bogotá
Buenos Aires   Calcutta   Cape Town   Chennai
Dar es Salaam   Delhi   Florence   Hong Kong   Istanbul
Karachi   Kuala Lumpur   Madrid   Melbourne   Mexico City
Mumbai   Nairobi   Paris   São Paulo   Singapore
Taipei   Tokyo   Toronto   Warsaw

and associated companies in
Berlin   Ibadan

Published by Oxford University Press, Inc.,
198 Madison Avenue, New York, New York 10016
http://www.oup-usa.org

Library of Congress Cataloging-in-Publication Data
Encyclopedia of aesthetics / editor in chief, Michael Kelly.
p.   cm.
Includes bibliographical references and index.
1. Aesthetics—Encyclopedias.   I. Kelly, Michael, 1953–.
BH56.E53   1998   111′.85′03—dc21   98-18741 CIP
ISBN 0-19-511307-1 (set)
ISBN 0-19-512648-3 (vol. 4)

Printing (last digit): 9 8 7 6 5 4 3 2 1

Printed in the United States of America
on acid-free paper

PLEASURE. The concept of pleasure is fundamental to aesthetics as it arose in the eighteenth century as a specific style of philosophical meditation on the nature of art and beauty. Having decided that taste is the central category under which the aesthetic is be thought, taste is in turn conceived of as the capacity for a special and rarefied kind of pleasure taken in the sensuous encounter with—indifferently—art and nature. Eighteenth-century theories that enfranchise the aesthetic as the central category of experience and value in terms of which art and beauty are to be thought, do so in part by attempting to specify what is distinctive about "aesthetic" pleasure. Highly sublimated and even "contemplative" in character, largely (in the case of Immanuel Kant completely) drained of desire and interest, such pleasure does not function to impel a person to get up and act but serves instead as a form of enjoyment that occurs "for its own sake." Self-justifying in essence, the autonomous character of such enjoyment from the stream of life in which it is set is in fact just what serves to justify it. For in accord with the great eighteenth-century idea that persons are autonomous beings who are by natural capacity and right able to form their own "pursuits of happiness," to follow through on their own life plans in accord with their tastes and desires, the exercise of taste (i.e., of this species of pleasure) is conceived of as part of this exercise of personal autonomy, and indeed as a celebration of it. In aesthetic enjoyment—in enjoyment for its own sake—is thus contained the promise of human happiness.

Eighteenth-century aesthetic theory quickly comes to see, however, that it cannot succeed in getting remotely clear on, much less define, taste purely by reference to the kind of pleasure that pertains to it. It must take a dual approach: at once attempting to mark out aesthetic pleasure as a distinctive psychological or metaphysical kind, and attempting to mark out the objects of taste in terms of what is distinctive about them. For pleasure is too diffuse a kind of thing—its domain, range, and vicissitudes are too opaque, its intermediate cases too many—for any definition of the aesthetic to rest entirely on it. We cannot beyond a certain point know what pleasure (or enjoyment or delight) is apart from speaking about the kinds of objects toward which it directs its gaze and which occasion or cause it. Aesthetic pleasure must therefore be characterized not merely in terms of its psychological or "metaphysical" kind but also in terms of the kinds of objects, events, or forms (the sunsets, paintings, performances, colors, shapes, timbres) toward which the "aesthetic attitude" is directed.

Eighteenth-century aesthetic theory may be glossed as having its origins in the writings of David Hume and Kant, who set the two conceptual poles in terms of which taste is thought. Each philosopher takes this dual approach. According to Hume, taste involves the capacity to detect the subtle parts of objects (Hume calls this "delicacy of passion") as it operates in conjunction with the ability to respond vividly to their material and formal qualities (he calls this "strong sense"). Insofar as one is defective in these (and other) characteristics, one's taste is lacking. The pleasure caused by this act of vivid yet delicate perception is of a refined sort (relatively distant from the powerful desires that lead directly to action). Similarly, the unpleasure caused by an equally intense survey of "distasteful" objects is of a refined sort that does not lead to the violent feelings felt about truly repugnant things. Feeling such pleasure (or unpleasure) is itself the judgment of taste (the act of feeling says, "I like it" or "It does not appeal to me"). Therefore, taste is both the capacity to detect properties of objects (their delicate colors, shapes, expressive nuances, narrative intensities, brilliant chiaroscuros, floral aromas) and the actual pleasure caused by this attitude of perception. While pleasure or displeasure (the judgment of taste) is described as a causal effect of the object, it is easy to see that pleasure (in the sense of enjoyment) is also (along with modes of tension and attention) the attitude under which vivid and delicate parts of the object are perceived. Pleasure is a "sliding signifier": it is both a causal state and an attitude of enjoyment directed toward its object. Pleasure suffuses the entire aesthetic event.

By contrast, Kant begins by specifying taste as a metaphysical kind: it is a noncognitive, disinterested (read: free of all interest) delight taken in an "object." Being free of all interest this type of delight does not involve any ordinary experience of psychological "satisfaction." (Similarly, it is unrelated in kind to the unpleasure of dissatisfaction or the frustration felt at the interruption of satisfaction.) This in turn means that the delight is in no way conditioned on properties of the object itself. For were the delight directed toward and caused by the specific properties of the objects of taste, these properties would excite our interest (by virtue of their pleasurable effects), and the perception of them would provide us with "satisfaction." It thus follows, somewhat astoundingly, from the disinterested condition of taste that delight must be unconditioned by the object. What, then, is it directed toward? It can only be directed toward the subject herself. The Kantian twist is that the objects, events, natural scenes, or performances we perceive are the mere occasions for the imagination to construct from them a harmonious play of forms. Kant describes this free play of forms as the "harmonization" of the subject's "faculties." Perhaps the deepest theorist of autonomy in the entire history of aesthetics, Kant is therefore saying that taste is the subject's means of taking pleasure in herself: in her own capacities for autonomous harmonization. Note that even Kant cannot avoid saying something about the "object" of pleasure, and he tells us that the free play of harmonization that is the "object" of delight is characterized by "purposiveness without purpose." All the forms seem to conspire to produce some end, even though they have in actuality no end at all and are "for their own sake." This is important for Kant because it shows that in her experience of delight, the subject is celebrating her own capacity for free and purposive activity: for moral activity. Taste is the celebration of autonomy, not merely (as in Hume) its exercise. [See Hume; and Kant.]

In the history of aesthetics since the eighteenth century, the concept of pleasure has gone through a number of reconceptualizations that have partly freed it from its connection with taste. Two in particular will be noted here, and a third, of special importance, will be noted below. All are part of the legacy of present thinking on pleasure, making our current approaches multiperspectival and highly fragmented. The first major changes in the concept occur in the late nineteenth and early twentieth centuries with the vitalist writing of George Santayana and John Dewey. Writing as they are in the whirl of a modernity whose rhythm and energy appear indomitable, writing also in response to biological theory that preaches the organismic "energy" of the species, these thinkers conceive of art and the aesthetic as experience writ large, experience intensified in all of its energies, vitalized to the point of ecstasy, and characterized by the pleasures of memory, repetition, crisscrossing between art and life, and the transmogrification of fragments into wholes. For Dewey, "having an experience" becomes a theoretical ideal and practical achievement defined by its robustness and wholeness. In a noted phrase, he now thinks of the opposite of the aesthetic not as a state of displeasure but as the an-aesthetic: an "aenesthecized" state in which experience is diminished, habitual to the point of catatonia or anhedonia. In the rich liveliness of "experience," form and content merge organically since form is nothing other than the way content unravels and comes to completion (in a thrust of formal mastery). The distinctiveness of art (its formal pleasure associated with timbres, colors, modeling,

carving, representation, song, and the like) pales into oblivion; what is stressed are the crisscrossings between the arts and the energies of life generally. Everything that happens in art happens because it also happens elsewhere, and vice versa. Simultaneity and interpenetration, two of John Cage's basic ideas for avant-garde art, find their origin here. It is not fortuitous that Dewey is writing out of direct experience of early avant-garde art (the canvases of Henri Matisse, Pablo Picasso, Paul Cézanne, and others that he is privileged to see in the collection of his friend Albert Barnes). [See Dewey; and Santayana.]

It is worth noting that this American immersion of aesthetics into the whirl of modernity has its counterpart in the writing of Charles Baudelaire (who famously inaugurates the aesthetics of modernity with his concept of "the pleasure of the present" half a century earlier than Dewey). Baudelaire is keener to stress the pleasures of the fragmentary than Dewey, who is obsessed with the way the embodied person formulates wholeness out of the blooming, buzzing confusion of experience. Baudelaire's *flâneur* resists the imposition of wholeness, preferring to sample, taste (taste is still important), watch, wait, and purchase from the contingent and modulating spectacle that is Parisian modernity. It is the impression as such, not simply its transmutation into an eternalized form of wholeness (in art); it is the transience of things, not simply their eternalization in Impressionist painting, that counts. What is at stake is reverie as much as formulation.

With Baudelaire pleasure is reconceptualized in another new way: as a poetic mood of the subject that must always be thought in relation to states of pain or "spleen" that give pleasure meaning and shape and that are themselves part of the aesthetic as such. Pleasure is a mode of apprehending the world, a mood of abandonment to its details of transience and reverie at its details, yet this mood is always counterbalanced by attitudes of resentment, anxiety, boredom, and disenchantment that are at once essential to the subject and directed to the "disenchantment" produced by modernity itself. (Again, pleasure and pain are characterized in part in terms of their quality and in part in terms of the object—modernity and the self's being in it—to which they are directed.) If the aesthetic is about the proprioceptive and emotional embodiment of the subject in the world, then pain is now thought to be a fundamental part of the aesthetic rather than the mere interruption or negation of it. [See Baudelaire.]

This second change in how pleasure is thought in relation to the aesthetic is immensely deepened by Sigmund Freud and psychoanalysis. Pleasure (in art and life) is now rethought in terms of a locus of concepts: the unconscious, the principles of association, overdetermination, the ideas of fantasy, wish fulfillment, symptom, and working through, but also in terms of the idea of unconscious conflicts, repressions, anxieties, and, finally, death wishes, that engender the structure of fantasy, repetition, and working through. Freud thinks of pleasure in art in various interrelated ways, and together these provide a rich picture of the complexity of pleasure. The pleasures of art consist in a repetition of earlier pleasures taken in childhood play. Reading across his writings freely, we can see that Freud thinks of childhood games as occurring for a number of reasons, any or all of which may be repeated in the work of art. Games may serve the mere purpose of spontaneous fun. They may have cognitive purposes. Or they may be symbolic ways in which the child acts out, expresses in symptomatic form, or works through unconscious conflict—as in Freud's famous description of his grandchild's game of sending a ball out and uttering "fort!" ("gone!"; "out there!") and then bringing it back and uttering "da!" ("here!"; "here again!"; Freud, 1957). Freud tells us that through this repetitive game the child is symbolically working through the dislocation and anxiety surrounding his separation from the mother. He goes on to tell us that this rhythm of sending the self (the ball) out and then pulling it back in is also the rhythm of mourning: the mourning process repeats the childhood process of separation. In the work of art this and many other such games may be repeated: the pleasure in art (as well as its pain) consisting of the pleasures in this symbolic act of working through unconscious conflicts and requirements of all kinds.

Freud also assimilates the pleasure in art to the (often unconscious) wish fulfillments encoded in fantasies and dreams. In the work of art, formal pleasures "seduce" the viewer to take up an identification with the artist's own unconscious fantasies, which therefore spread the pleasure associated with them from artist to viewer. In art we should find exhibited the wish to be loved, to dominate, to possess the phallic grandiosity of a Don Giovanni or the Oedipal victory of an Electra, and the panoply of pleasures associated with the fulfillment of these desires through the mechanism of fantasy. Indeed, both Freud and the character of Giovanni have shown that the artist (be he a painter or a *Lebenskunstler*) may "win through his art what the neurotic merely wins in fantasy (and, we may add, the viewer wins only through identification with the artist): fame, fortune and the love of beautiful women." This highly gendered remark (which views women as prizes to be won like money or travel) is spoken by Freud but responds to the romanticization of the artist as a person capable of bringing about special pleasures through his sacred and seductive instrument (read: phallus). (Of course, if Giovanni is an example, he will die by the hand of the law of the father in the end. The "Oedipal victory" is short-lived.)

Finally, Freud speaks of the pleasures of art in connection with those of sublimation. Leonardo da Vinci's art is said to allow that painter the pleasure of sublimating his symptomatic "compromise formations" into a new and vital domain where "talent and genius" subsume the neurotic impulse and give it transformed form. That is, the artwork may be understood as itself a symptom: an arena of representation in which desire and its negation are simultaneously expressed, a "compromise formation" in Freud's own language. Again, Freud will tell us that it is the beauty of the work of art's form that will "seduce" the viewer into accepting and even enjoying this symptomatic "content." (We may assume that it is through the sublimation of symptom into form that the fantasy of wish fulfillment is likewise expressed by the artist and "accepted" by the audience, on Freud's account.) Note that Freud's own account of sublimation in art is not adequate to the complexity of the concept he actually introduced, since the pleasures of sublimation will, if deep enough, pass far beyond the mere exhibition of symptoms into a realm of elevation in which desire is given space to be born. No doubt this elevation of desire will also involve the anxieties of the sublime, since an expressive act in which unrepresentable desire is brought to presentation must bring forth terror as well as joy: the fear of obliteration by "the I that is elsewhere [than in myself]," as Jacques Lacan, the deepest theorist of *jouissance* (the sublime), will say. It is well known that the art of the twentieth century contains these depths of expression, making important regions of it an occasion for terror and self-obliteration (whose generic name is "pain"), as well as for the raising up of conflict into its revelatory and communicable forms. It is not by accident that Jackson Pollock was deeply influenced by the field of psychoanalysis.

Nor is Freud's account adequate to ideas that he breached at the end of his life about the "death instinct," alternately phrased as the desire on the part of the organism to attain a total state of null excitation (Dewey's "anaesthetic") and as a masochistic desire for the pleasure inflicted through painful excitations. Whether or not the death instinct is an instinct, or is even coherent as a singular concept (see Laplanche, 1976), it is certain that human "self-destructive" desires do give rise to repetition/compulsion in art, especially in twentieth-century Modernist art, which expresses a planet on the brink of self-annihilation and, more particularly, art on the brink of self-annihilation (see Foster, 1993, and Herwitz, 1995). [*See* Freud.]

Lacan's complex "writing through" of Freud has engendered in his followers a picture of the poetic as an existential and indeed metaphysical state in which the symbolic rule of the father is partly "suspended." Through an amalgamation of psychoanalysis and avant-garde culture, Lacanians associate the poetically amniotic and disruptive values of modernist writing with the capacity for the subject's desire to break through the bounds of law, which have been imposed on it during the moment of the Oedipal conflict. In that psychological moment, "desire is castrated," and law in its most general form (moral, cultural, linguistic, legal, even stylistic) is imposed on the body and person of the subject, thus making him or her into a "person." To be a person is therefore to lack wholeness, which means that the fantasy of wholeness is fundamental to the human condition. The work of art can represent a breakthrough of *jouissance:* the sublime, unrepresentable flow of primordial desire known only by its lack, in which erotic joy, amniotic oneness, and reverie merge and spontaneously recur, thus affording a unique and untranslatable form of enjoyment and renewal (the roots of Lacan in Baudelaire's poetics of reverie are also clear).

The work of Lacan has also given rise to a mode of critiquing practices of enjoyment as they are psychologically constituted. The fantasy of wholeness can lead to regression to the famous "mirror phase," in which the young, childlike Narcissus misrecognizes his own reflection and takes himself to be perfect. This desire for the return to the illusion of perfection, the desire to defeat the recognition that one is forever incomplete, tends, according to Lacan, to be played out visually, since in the earlier mirror phase the sense of perfection is engendered visually (through the "scopophilic" drive). In the light of Lacan's work, visual and plastic art—especially cinema—have undergone a generation of interrogation regarding the extent to which these media inculcate the scopophilic pleasures associated with this fantasy. [*See* Lacan.]

It is a great insight of the twentieth century that the cultivation of practices of enjoyment—like the theorization of enjoyment that arises in conjunction with those practices—can serve to inculcate scopophilic fantasies, forms of fetishization, and, ultimately, styles of domination. One can call this insight the twentieth century's response to the great eighteenth-century Enlightenment thought (again due to Kant but deepened by Friedrich von Schiller) that a culture may achieve a route toward moral perfectionism by developing shared forms of pleasure ("delight"). Kant believes in the need to cultivate a *sensus communis:* a community of taste in which persons will share objects in which delight is taken, thus at once taking pleasure in their shared moral capacities and taking pleasure in the fact that all other members of the community are taking the same pleasure as themselves. This idea finds its first and most trenchant criticisms in the 1880s in the writings of Friedrich Nietzsche, the third and perhaps most overarching innovator in the thinking about pleasure. Nietzsche formulated the thought that enjoyment taken in the moral self must be understood as a cultural construction—the construction of the entire history of the West—which represses the genuine pleasure an individualized and empowered subject might take in the contours of his own life, mortifies the subject into believing that he is guilty (which for Nietzsche means nothing else than that he believes that he has a soul that can "speak the truth about life"), and thus constructs him as a person displaced from his own potential sources of power. The pleasure this disempowered subject is now brought to take in the kind of highly sublimated art, nature, and religion that

Kant praised is for Nietzsche a form of compensatory enjoyment, a form of pleasure in the ascetic rather than the genuine aesthetic. Indeed, for Nietzsche the history of eighteenth-century aesthetics is really part of the history of the ascetic—part of the history by which the subject is mortified. For Kant's delight in the moral is in effect a symptom of the power of desire blocked from its own expression. Kantian delight is an aspirin that makes the subject feel better about her dispossessed (read: moralized) self but in the end does her no more good than Karl Marx's "opiate of the masses" does. Thus, aesthetic enjoyment for Nietzsche, and after him for Michel Foucault, is always to be understood in terms of its modality of power: in terms of how it empowers women, cultures, selves, and the like, or disempowers them through hegemonic practices or symptomatic displacements of desire into "delight."

Indeed, it is not by chance that the category of autonomous aesthetic enjoyment arose historically in conjunction with the institution of the museum in the European capitals of the eighteenth century. For the modern museum also displaces works of art from the sites of their making and the streams of life in which they are set and places them in ordered relations (chronological, regional, by media, and so on) with other artworks—some of which would seem quite unrelated to each other when viewed in situ. Having been displaced from the sites of their enmeshment and turned into sights to be viewed in abstraction by the fascinated and absorbed viewer, artworks are now relegated to the realm of autonomous enjoyment (read: enjoyment abstracted from and oblivious of context, which means of the otherness of the work). This removal of art from the world of its locality, tradition, social commerce, and distinctive cultural conceptualization, this orphaning, prepares the category of the aesthetic by assimilating art to the category of abstract natural beauty, with a work of art "meaning" little more than a sunset or a waterfall. Autonomous enjoyment was for Europeans in part the power to turn the art and culture of the other into a museumized sign, an abstracted, naturalized form for their own gaze. Not to overstate this point, but even Kant's theory of aesthetic autonomy must be understood to arise in conjunction with (and play some role in articulating) practices of enjoyment that license this abstracted gaze: a gaze disinterested in the otherness of colonial art and culture. In this specific sense, eighteenth-century theories of taste license domination through styles of (abstracted) enjoyment. Herein resides the Foucauldian interrogation of enjoyment and its theorization by eighteenth-century aesthetics.

We are now in a position to draw three general consequences about the history of "aesthetic" pleasure.

1. The realm of "aesthetic pleasure" is always conceptualized as a cross section between art and something else. Whether the pleasures of art are assimilated to the realm of taste (which goes beyond art to include nature and, in

Hume's case, whatever we ordinarily have taste in), to the realm of the vitalist (which is everywhere and nowhere), to the realm of fantasies, dreams, and sublimations (which inform all representations), or to the poststructuralist realm of that place where desire is freed from the domination of law (linguistic, Oedipal, moral, cultural, legal), enjoyment in art will always be thought in relation to a set of models, examples or regions of life with which it is seen to have essential relations. As the conceptualization of pleasure changes, so the other regions of life with which enjoyment in art is thought to be essentially connected also change. We thus have a history of these realignments between art and whatever else that is the history of writing about pleasure in art. It is the history of the aesthetic—that always amorphous, always partly articulated, always shifting domain.

2. Pleasure must always be thought of in relation to its opposite (distaste, anhedonia, masochism), which changes and whose aesthetic relevance changes.

3. The history of these theories of pleasure (and unpleasure) must be contextualized in relation to two other histories. It must be understood in relation to the history of art and culture. As the history of art evolves, so modernity brings its changes to the practices of cultural enjoyment, changing their dimension, their quality, and their centrality. The theory of pleasure must thus change accordingly to keep pace. (No doubt the history of art and culture evolves in part by absorbing new concepts of pleasure, making the exchange between these semiautonomous histories a two-way one.) In short, art practices have changed since the eighteenth century from an art of delight (Jean-Antoine Watteau, Joshua Reynolds, the Rococo) and absorption (Jean-Baptiste Greuze, Jean-Baptiste-Siméon Chardin) to an art of twentieth-century avant-garde practices no longer concerned with pleasure primarily but instead with increasingly deep and painful expression (which finds its theoretical voice in the theories of R. G. Collingwood and Benedetto Croce), cultural interruption, the construction of radical futures, with the interrogation of cultural rationality, the defamiliarization of ordinary belief, the destruction of past aesthetics, especially of nature and naturalism, and with the sublime in all of its forms. This history of art has also inaugurated its own critique of pleasure, and this history, from Édouard Manet to contemporary postmodern practices via the route of Marcel Duchamp, is well known and is evidently in alliance with the history of theory. Some would call it a history of theory, although this is to forget that the medium of writing theory (mostly in the academy) is substantially different from that of making it arise through an experimental practice with plastic forms.

The history of pleasure must also be understood in relation to the history of institutions (the growth of the concert hall, the museum, the academy of art, the gallery system), of technologies (mass media and so on), and to the larger socioeconomic setting (the growth of commodity capitalism, etc.) in which art is played out. It is the crisscrossing intersections of these histories that together characterize the history of enjoyment from its inception in the eighteenth century to the present. But in thinking through these crisscrossings, let us not assume that each notion of pleasure renders its predecessor wholly obsolete. No doubt we should not dehistoricize the history of pleasure to the point where we believe that every concept of pleasure applies to every work of art. That would simply be to project onto art a postmodern attitude according to which theories of enjoyment are tried on objects like clothes in a department store. New notions of pleasure do arise historically (for example, in the context of late modernity) that are to some degree irrelevant to past art. New art arises that renders past notions to a degree out of date. But we also need the entire range of what has been thought and practiced in the history of pleasure to stand as potentially available for the interpretation of any art object. We need, for example, the concept of taste to interpret Cézanne's choices of his motifs and even Duchamp's composition of parts into wholes. Similarly, we need the concepts of fantasy, reverie, and "working through" to speak to the elegant and playful art of Watteau with its whiffs of psychologically dark chiaroscuro. Pleasure never comes simple, even if it is spontaneous. Pleasure is overdetermined and must be approached from various perspectives. What pleasure in art does is to confirm for both the artist and the viewer that to be embodied in the world is to participate in this spontaneity of feeling, without which one is not human.

[*See also* Emotions; *and* Taste.]

BIBLIOGRAPHY

Baudelaire, Charles. "The Painter of Modern Life." In *The Painter of Modern Life and Other Essays,* translated by Jonathan Mayne, pp. 1–41. London, 1964.

Collingwood, R. G. *The Principles of Art.* Oxford, 1938.

Croce, Benedetto. *Aesthetic* (1902). Translated by Douglas Ainslie. Rev. ed. Reprint, Boston, 1978.

Croce, Benedetto. *Guide to Aesthetics* (1913). Translated by Patrick Romanell (1965). Indianapolis, 1995.

Dewey, John. *Art as Experience* (1934). Reprint, New York, 1979.

Foster, Hal. *Compulsive Beauty.* Cambridge, Mass., 1993.

Foucault, Michel. *The Order of Things: An Archaeology of the Human Sciences.* New York, 1970.

Freud, Sigmund. "The Relation of the Poet to Day-Dreaming" (1908). Translated by Grant Duff. In *Character and Culture,* edited by Philip Reiff, pp. 34–43. New York, 1963.

Freud, Sigmund. *Leonardo da Vinci and a Memory of His Childhood* (1910). Translated by Alan Tyson. New York, 1964.

Freud, Sigmund. "Mourning and Melancholia" (1917). Translated by Joan Riviere. In *The Standard Edition of the Complete Psychological Works of Sigmund Freud,* edited by James Strachey, vol. 14, pp. 237–258.

Herwitz, Daniel. "Review of Hal Foster, *Compulsive Beauty." Journal of Aesthetics and Art Criticism* 53.4 (Fall 1995): 433–435.

Hume, David. "Of the Standard of Taste." In *Essays: Moral, Political, Literary,* rev. ed., edited by Eugene F. Miller, pp 226–249. Indianapolis, 1987.

Kant, Immanuel. *Critique of Judgment.* Translated by Werner S. Pluhar. Indianapolis, 1987.

Kristeva, Julia. *The Kristeva Reader.* Edited by Toril Moi. New York, 1986.

Lacan, Jacques. *Ecrits: A Selection.* Translated by Alan Sheridan. New York, 1977.

Laplanche, Jean. *Life and Death in Psychoanalysis.* Translated by Jeffrey Mehlman. Baltimore, 1976.

Melville, Stephen. "Psychoanalysis and the Place of *Jouissance.*" *Critical Inquiry* 13.2 (Winter 1987): 349–370.

Mulvey, Laura. "Visual Pleasure and Narrative Cinema." In *Narrative, Apparatus, Ideology,* edited by Philip Rosen, pp. 198–209. New York, 1986.

Nietzsche, Friedrich. *The Genealogy of Morals* (with *The Birth of Tragedy*). Translated by Francis Golffing. Garden City, N.Y., 1956.

Santayana, George. *The Sense of Beauty.* New York, 1896.

Santayana, George. *Reason in Art.* New York, 1905.

Wollheim, Richard. *Painting as an Art.* Princeton, N.J., 1987.

Wollheim, Richard. "Freud and the Understanding of Art." In *The Cambridge Companion to Freud,* edited by Jerome Neu, pp. 249–266 Cambridge and New York, 1992.

DANIEL HERWITZ

PLOTINUS (205–270 CE), Roman Neoplatonic philosopher. Art, in the modern sense of fine art, is not a central notion in Plotinus, although it does come up for consideration in his writings. Beauty, however, is a central focus of two treatises: treatise 1.6, and treatise 5.8. In these, Plotinus accounts for beauty within the context of his understanding of the nature of soul and its progress from ignorance to self-knowledge. This larger account of the nature of the soul, its place in the universe, and the course of its development is the subject especially of his treatises 5.1, 4.8, 6.9, 3.8, 5.2, and 2.9. In order to understand Plotinus's doctrine of beauty one must first understand his account of the condition of the soul and, especially, the soul's relationship to intelligence.

According to Plotinus, souls are lost. We find ourselves involved in a changing world without a clear sense of our bearings, which especially means without a clear sense of ourselves. Although involved in this world we remain in a sense alien, strangers. We seek an understanding of ourselves and our situation, and we want to find our proper place, our home. To be a person—to be a soul—is, according to Plotinus, to be in this situation of disorientation and desire to get home.

This desire we have is not a self-conscious wish but is a constitutive drive, more like the innate impulse a plant has to turn and open itself toward the sun. This desire to get to its metaphysical home is experienced by the soul as a longing. Initially, this longing is immature and the object toward which it is directed will not give the soul all of what it wants, but will only advance the soul a single step. Taking this step, however, is the beginning of the soul's education, because from this point the soul's longing can develop to a more sophisticated state. The objects toward which this longing is directed, the things that are immediately attractive to the

soul's constitutive drive, are beauties. Objects that are beautiful, *kalon,* act as beacons for the soul, and the soul feels for these beauties a passionate longing, an *erōs.* The development of the soul on its path homeward, the education of its *erōs,* is equally a journey along a path of recognizing progressively more sophisticated—and progressively more beautiful—beauties.

The list of the beauties through which we must advance according to Plotinus is basically taken over from Diotima's speech in Plato's *Symposium.* Plotinus accepts from Diotima that we must develop from initially seeing beauty in body to seeing beauty in soul to seeing beauty in laws and knowledge and ultimately to seeing real beauty itself, that is, the Platonic Form, which is the cause of the beauty in all the particular sensible beauties. In its search for its home, then, the soul must go from lusting after beautiful bodies to engaging in virtuous relations with other souls, and ultimately to understanding its own true nature. Its true nature is that it is a being that participates in the world of intellect and the eternal intelligible truths while struggling to realize and embrace the unity and goodness that govern all reality. On most interpretations of Plotinus, the intelligible vision of beauty itself is the stepping-stone to a mystical experience of "the One," the ultimate principle of Plotinus's universe. It is within the context of this understanding of the condition of the soul that Plotinus's technical doctrines concerning beauty can be understood and his place in the history of philosophy can be delineated.

The specific condition that makes a thing beautiful is the mastering of that thing by its own immanent form: to be beautiful, the thing must exist in a way that supports the full flowering of its defining essence without impediment or intrusion of anything foreign. Form, reality, beauty, and intelligibility are various ways of describing the same thing, according to Plotinus. Consequently, the extent to which a thing is mastered by its form is the extent to which it is real, which is equally the extent to which it is intelligible, the extent to which its existence is given over to the manifestation and realization of the rational principle that is its generative ground. A dwarf corn plant is not as beautiful as a corn plant whose perfected growth has fully expressed its guiding reason. A cancerous body is not as beautiful as a healthy body because the cancerous growth is a material existence acting independently of the definitive organic form. A hedonistic, uneducated criminal is not as beautiful as a soul that has perfected its nature in a virtuous life. A painting that still shows itself to be paint and canvas is not as beautiful as a painting that immediately conveys us to an embrace with the intelligibility it communicates by concealing its own existence as a painting and allowing us to be directly absorbed in its subject matter. Beauty exists when the matter as which a thing is realized is wholly given over to the resistance-free expression of form: beauty is intelligence displaying itself.

It is because beauty is thus the show of intelligence in a thing that beauty can play the role of stimulating the soul's development to self-knowledge. Beauty is attractive to the soul because it is itself like the soul, and because in seeing beauty the soul sees a mirror of its own inner essence as intelligent. It is the soul's inherent kinship to the beautiful that allows beauty to be the privileged route for the soul's ascent.

An understanding of beauty is itself something that can come only through the experience of beauty and cannot be explained to those who have not had the experience, in the same way that one cannot explain color to a blind person. The experience of beauty is thus irreducible to any other form of experience. This experience is also necessary to the soul's experience of intelligence, for it is the recognition of and attraction to beauty that is our most immediate way of acknowledging the presence and value of intelligence. Finally, the experience of beauty itself takes the form of a desire to create something in the presence of the beauty to which one is attracted. This erotic pursuit of beauty thus equally amounts to an activity of self-expression.

Plotinus's philosophy in general is marked by an ambivalence toward the body, and this can also be seen in his account of beauty. In many places throughout his writings, Plotinus seems to regard the body as inherently good, and he interprets embodiment as the soul's natural self-expression. On other occasions he treats the body in a more dualistic way as an alien vessel used by the soul. Although this ambivalence is present in his account of the ascent of the soul through beauty, the dualistic emphasis is the more prevalent tone, and the soul's ascent is described more as a purification of the soul from any alien materiality than as an attraction to the immanent rationality of its own embodiment. This dualistic attitude toward the body is perhaps also visible in Plotinus's claim that beauty is something added to bodies, whereas the beauty in the higher steps on Diotima's ladders is not added to, but is the substance of, the beautiful objects themselves.

Plotinus's philosophy in general and his doctrine of beauty in particular stand at an interesting and ambiguous border between ancient Greek philosophy and medieval Christian philosophy. Plotinus's doctrine of beauty as the route to mystical union with the One became for Saint Augustine a model for the turning of the soul to God. At the hands of Augustine, Plotinus's understanding of the soul's return to its true home simultaneously received legitimacy and was transformed from a pagan, possibly pantheistic, possibly nontheistic metaphysics of the soul into a Christian journey toward personal salvation by God. It is a matter of debate whether Plotinus should be read as a latent Christian or whether Augustine should be read as a misguided Neoplatonist. Analogous questions can be asked regarding the relation of Plato and Plotinus. Plotinus's doctrines clearly synthesize the doctrines of Plato with those of Aristotle and the Stoics, and it is not clear whether this is a development

or a confusion of the Platonic doctrines. With respect to beauty in particular, Plotinus may reveal a Stoic (or generally Hellenistic) inclination toward the self-sufficiency of the single individual that seems at odds with Plato's (and Aristotle's) insistence on the inherently political nature of human existence. Although Plotinus repeats from Diotima the need for the soul's *erōs* to develop to the love of beautiful laws and institutions, Plotinus's writings (and life) as a whole evince no serious interest in politics, and, indeed, he pays no attention to Plato's extensive discussion of the political ambivalence of art.

Plotinus's Neoplatonic doctrine of beauty was extremely influential for artists and art theoreticians of the Italian Renaissance in particular. Much of the debate between competing artistic movements of this period turned on such questions as whether beauty was to be found in intelligible design or sensible color, in idealization of subject matter or in realistic portrayal of earthly things, whether art was an end in itself, or whether its goal was the elevation of the soul, and so on. For artists like Michelangelo and writers like Giovanni Bellori, the Neoplatonic doctrines of the mastery of matter by form and of the soul's striving for intellect provided the basis for their preferred artistic program.

[*See also* Beauty, *article on* Classical Concepts; *and* Plato.]

BIBLIOGRAPHY

Work by Plotinus

Enneads. 7 vols. Translated by A. H. Armstrong. Loeb Classical Library. Cambridge, Mass., 1966–1988. Contains complete Greek text and English translation of Plotinus's writings.

Other Sources

Anton, J. "Plotinus' Refutation of Beauty and Symmetry." *Journal of Aesthetics and Art Criticism* 23 (1964–1965): 273–284.

Anton, J. "Plotinus' Conception of the Functions of the Artist." *Journal of Aesthetics and Art Criticism* 26 (1967–1968): 91–101.

Armstrong, A. H. "Plotinus." In *The Cambridge History of Later Greek and Early Medieval Philosophy,* Corr. ed. Cambridge, 1970.

Armstrong, A. H. "Beauty and the Discovery of Divinity in the Thought of Plotinus." In *Kephalaion: Studies in Greek Philosophy and Its Continuation,* edited by J. Mansfield and L. M. de Rijk. Assen, 1975.

Armstrong, A. H. "The Divine Enhancement of Earthly Beauties: The Hellenic and Platonic Tradition." *Eranos Jahrbuch* 53 (1984): 49–81.

Brown, Jonathan, and Robert Enggass. *Italy and Spain, 1600–1750: Sources and Documents.* Englewood Cliffs, N.J., 1970.

Moreau, J. "Origine et expressions du beau suivant Plotin." In *Neoplatonisme: Mélanges offerts à Jean Trouillard,* pp. 249–263. Cahiers de Fontenay. Fontenay, 1981.

Panofsky, Erwin. *Idea: A Concept in Art Theory.* Translated by Joseph J. S. Peake. Columbia, S. C., 1968.

Rich, Audrey N. M. "Plotinus and the Theory of Artistic Imitation." *Mnemosyne* 13 (1960): 233–250.

Rist, John M. *Plotinus: The Road to Reality.* Cambridge, 1967.

Schwyzer, H.-R. "Plotinos." *Paulys Realencyclopäedie der klassischen Altertumswissenschaft* 21 (1951): 471–592.

JOHN RUSSON

POETICS. In a comment that does not even refer explicitly to poetry, in a book concerned primarily with linguistics and psychology rather than aesthetics, Ludwig Wittgenstein not only succinctly formulates the basic aesthetic question regarding poetry, but also expresses the perpetual fascination with poetry that gives the question its force: "Can anything be more remarkable than this, that the *rhythm* of a sentence should be important for exact understanding of it?" (Wittgenstein, 1980).

Poetics, the attempt to understand, appreciate, explain, and evaluate poetry, asks many questions: What is poetry? What distinguishes poetry from prose? What makes some poetry more beautiful than other poetry? What does poetry do? What social and political value does poetry have? Does poetry convey truth? All those questions, however, bear some relation to the question why the rhythm of a sentence (or, more narrowly, the sounds of words or, more broadly, the poetic elements in an utterance) matters to its meaning.

The first substantial statement of a poetics in the traditional literature of Western philosophy comes from Plato, who in several dialogues, especially the *Ion* and *Republic,* puts into Socrates' mouth negative evaluations of poetry. Many later commentators have attempted to construe Plato's view of poetry as less condemnatory than it appears, on the assumption that no well-intentioned lover of wisdom can reject poetry, least of all Plato, whose writings are themselves so poetic. With or without mitigation, Plato's condemnation of poetry exposes the centrality of the Wittgensteinian question about the importance of the rhythm of a sentence. Plato's poetics centers on the question about poetry's social and political value. He answers the question by excluding poetry from his ideal republic, but he justifies that exclusion on the basis of his answer to a different question, the one about what poetry does: poetry, he says, destroys the rational part of the soul. In turn, that answer depends on his answer to the question about what poetry is: Plato sees it as *mimēsis,* a copying that substitutes a mendacious appearance for a veracious reality. But how does poetry fool its hearers into accepting the pastiche? Plato says that the rhythm of a sentence seduces the *thumos,* the basest part of the soul and the adversary of reason: it "awakens and nourishes this part of the soul, and by strengthening it impairs the reason." Poetry intoxicates, Plato charges, and its musical elements are the inebriants.

Aristotle does not deny Plato's contention that poetry intoxicates, but he does assert, against Plato, that the intoxication has salubrious effects. At least as tragedy, the one type of poetry for which we have extant Aristotle's full exposition, poetry does stimulate irrational states of the soul (pity and fear), but rather than strengthening their grip on the soul, as Plato believes, poetry actually releases us from their domination. Tragedy, Aristotle says, purges us of pity and fear. Because Aristotle disagrees with Plato about what poetry does, he also disagrees about poetry's social and politi-

cal value, but those two questions, central to Plato's poetics, are secondary in Aristotle's, where the accent falls heavily on clarifying what poetry is.

Following his usual method of investigation, Aristotle first identifies the genus into which poetry fits. Like Plato, Aristotle considers all poetry a mode of imitation, but unlike Plato, who sees imitation as necessarily meretricious, Aristotle considers imitation a healthy part of human nature. We delight actively in imitating, and passively in works produced by imitation; the *Nicomachean Ethics* even makes imitation one of the ways we acquire virtue. After identifying the genus of poetry, Aristotle distinguishes its species: epic, tragedy, comedy, dithyrambic and nomic poetry, and even flute and lyre playing. These species, he notes, differ in their means (the particular combination of rhythm, language, and harmony employed), their objects (what kind of characters they portray), and their manner of imitation (narrative, dramatic, or mixed form).

Aristotle finds in tragedy six formative elements: spectacle, character, plot, diction, melody, and thought. Identifying these elements enables Aristotle to offer more subtle answers than those Plato gives to the various aesthetic questions about poetry. For instance, to the question of what distinguishes poetry from prose, Aristotle specifically discounts the easiest answer, that poetry employs verse. Putting the work of Herodotus into verse, says Aristotle, would not make it poetry. Instead, poetry differs from prose in the nature of its plot. The historian, Aristotle's exemplar of prose writing, narrates what has happened, but the poet narrates "what may happen,—what is possible according to the law of probability or necessity" (Poetics).

Enumeration of poetry's elements grounds not only Aristotle's answers to descriptive questions like what distinguishes poetry from prose, but also his answers to normative questions. The same thing that makes poetry different from prose also makes it better than prose: according to Aristotle, narrating what might be instead of what has been makes poetry's statements universals, unlike the merely singular statements of prose. The historian records, but the poet exemplifies. Pericles is Pericles, but Oedipus is all of us. The elements disclose what makes some poetry better than other poetry. All tragedies produce pity and fear, but one that does so primarily by use of spectacle is inferior to one that does so through its plot. The plot of a good play would arouse pity and fear simply by being told, even without the events being shown; to arouse pity and fear "by the mere spectacle is a less artistic method." Similarly, characters should be good, appropriate, realistic, and consistent; ceteris paribus, a poem with inconsistent characters is weaker than a poem with consistent characters.

Under the influence of Christianity, poetics in and around Europe took as its primary object biblical texts. No figure stands as more representative of this practice than Saint Augustine, who says Scripture does what Aristotle says tragedy does: remove the soul's flaws. But the mechanism Augustine posits differs from Aristotle's. Tragedy, according to Aristotle, cures by catharsis, purging the offending states, pity and fear; Scripture, according to Augustine, cures by displacement, substituting the love of God for the offending state, sin. Whatever the character of its tropes (the poetic elements with which Augustine is preoccupied), a scriptural passage always signifies the love of God. Whoever

> thinks that he understands the divine Scriptures or any part of them so that it does not build the double love of God and our neighbor does not understand it at all. Whoever finds a lesson there useful to the building of charity, even though he has not said what the author may be shown to have intended in that place, has not been deceived, nor is he lying in any way.
>
> (Augustine, 1958)

In spite of (or because of) Christianity, Aristotle's *Poetics* remained for centuries the definitive anatomy of those poetic elements for which the rhythm of a sentence stands as synecdoche in Wittgenstein's remark, as can be seen by the Aristotelian influence on figures as disparate as Saint Thomas Aquinas and Alexander Pope. Still, the esteem accorded Aristotle's descriptions could not forever prevent others from questioning his evaluations, as the British Romantic poets did at the beginning of the nineteenth century. In his preface to the *Lyrical Ballads,* William Wordsworth contradicts Aristotle on many points. For instance, one part of Aristotle's answer to what makes one poem better than another has to do with the element of character: on his view, tragedy is better than comedy in part because it depicts "persons who are above the common level," or to use Northrop Frye's later Neo-Aristotelian terminology, because it is written in the "high mimetic" mode. To purge us of pity and fear, says Aristotle, a poem needs to depict an unusually good person enduring unusually bad circumstances. In contrast, Wordsworth advocates what Frye would call "low mimetic" poetry, preferring to portray persons who are on the common level, not above it. He depicts "humble and rustic life" in the *Lyrical Ballads* "because, in that condition, the essential passions of the heart find a better soil in which they can attain their maturity, are less under restraint, and speak a plainer and more emphatic language." Could they agree for the sake of argument on Horace's observation that poetry serves a dual function, to delight and to teach, Aristotle and Wordsworth might go on to agree that poetry instructs through the example of its characters; but they would still disagree about what kind of characters provide the best exemplars. Aristotle asks for kings, the men most nearly gods; Wordsworth wants carls, boors, those nearest nature: "such men hourly communicate with the best objects from which the best part of language is originally derived."

Wordsworth shares Aristotle's disdain for spectacle, asserting the inferiority not only of spectacular poems but even of people who demand spectacle: "one being is elevated above another, in proportion as he possesses" the capability "of being excited without the application of gross and violent stimulants." But Wordsworth disagrees with the primacy Aristotle grants to plot. Wordsworth answers the question of what poetry is by calling it "the spontaneous overflow of powerful feelings." By making feeling definitive of poetry, he also gives it precedence over plot: "the feeling therein developed gives importance to the action and situation, and not the action and situation to the feeling."

In Wordsworth, as in Plato and Aristotle, the foregrounded question betrays its immediate connection to the Wittgensteinian question about the importance of the musical elements to understanding. The poet's possession of a larger capacity for feeling than ordinary mortals leads poetry "to produce excitement in co-existence with an overbalance of pleasure." Wordsworth thus agrees with Plato that poetry produces "an unusual and irregular state of the mind; ideas and feelings do not, in that state, succeed each other in accustomed order." But the rhythm of the sentence alleviates the danger of this overstimulated state of mind: "the co-presence of something regular"—namely, the meter of the poem—"cannot but have great efficacy in tempering and restraining the passion."

Less than a quarter century after Wordsworth disputed Aristotle's views on plot and character, Percy Bysshe Shelley in *A Defence of Poetry* seconded Aristotle's asseverations of poetry's truth against Plato's accusations of its falsity. "A poem," Shelley says, "is the image of life expressed in its eternal truth." As with other theorists, Shelley's answer to the question that preoccupies him (whether poetry conveys truth) connects with his answers to the other questions of poetics, in particular the question about the importance of the rhythm of a sentence. Like Aristotle, Shelley refuses as oversimplified the most obvious answer to the question about what distinguishes poetry from prose. Shelley contends that "the popular division into prose and verse is inadmissible in accurate philosophy," and should be replaced by "the distinction between measured and unmeasured language." Doing so, he claims, would clarify that the rhythm of a sentence invokes truth.

Unlike Aristotle, who asserts only a greater potential for truth in the universal statements of poetry than in the singular statements of prose, Shelley insists on the necessity of truth in poetry. For Aristotle, poetry's truth telling is a matter of degree: a poem is capable of more truth than is prose, and presumably capable of more falsehood as well. But for Shelley, poetry's truth is absolute: if it is poetry, it tells the truth. "All the authors of revolutions in opinion" are necessarily poets partly because they are inventors whose "words unveil the permanent analogy of things by images which participate in the life of truth," but mostly because "their periods are harmonious and rhythmical, and contain in themselves the elements of verse; being the echo of the eternal music."

The question about the relation of sound and sense remains central in contemporary poetics, informing all of its various preoccupations. For example, both the philosopher Hans-Georg Gadamer and the poet Louise Glück cite "the rhythm of a sentence" in their own answers to the question whether poetry conveys truth.

That the relation between sound and meaning stands as the crux of poetry's truthfulness appears in Gadamer's writing when he announces that he considers "incontrovertible" the "particular and unique relationship to truth" enjoyed by what he names not poetry but, more specifically, "poetic language." Gadamer argues for poetry's truth-telling character by a genus-and-species definition. Poetry belongs to the genus of "autonomous" texts, along with two other species, religious texts and legal texts. The religious text is a pledge, which can be called on and relied on as binding in ways that mere communication cannot, but only when "acknowledged on the part of the believer" (Gadamer, 1986). The legal text, too, is binding, but only becomes so by declaration and promulgation throughout a community.

Poetry belongs in the category of autonomous texts because, like religious and legal texts, it claims completeness. It "expresses fully what the given state of affairs is." Poetry's specific difference from religious and legal texts, however, lies in its being "self-fulfilling." Religious and legal texts effect their aims only through the complicity of their audience, but poetry "bears witness to itself and does not admit anything that might verify it." Gadamer illustrates his point by appeal to the staircase down which Smerdyakov falls in *The Brothers Karamazov*: every reader knows exactly—and correctly—what the staircase looks like, even though Dostoyevsky himself could not adjudicate an argument between a reader who contends the staircase turns to the right and one who contends it turns to the left. The poet, Gadamer says, "manages to conjure up the self-fulfillment of language." Poetry resembles less an assertion of empirical fact than a performative utterance. It *does* something, and the doing subjects it to coherence rather than correspondence as the criterion for its truth.

But how does poetry assume this disposition? Gadamer's answer should by now be predictable: "in the language of poetry, the dimensions of sound and sense are inextricably interwoven." Because of the sound of its words, the rhythm of its sentences, "the poetic creation does not intend something, but rather is the existence of what it intends." Sound and rhythm, Gadamer says, raise the poem above the need for confirmation by the world, giving it a necessary rather than a contingent connection to truth. A poem is no more subject to empirical validation or invalidation than is a symphony. Or, to use a sentence from Wittgenstein as another avatar of Gadamer's idea, "Do not forget that a poem, even though it is composed in the language of information, is not used in the language game of giving information" (Wittgenstein).

The question whether poetry conveys truth Gadamer answers in one way, by an answer to the question what poetry is; Glück answers the same question in a different way, by an answer to what makes one poem better than another. Glück argues that an artist's success "depends on conscious willingness to distinguish truth from honesty or sincerity" (Glück, 1994). Our customary association of honesty with truth, Glück calls "a form of anxiety." She defines truth as "the embodied vision, illumination, or enduring discovery which is the ideal of art."

Glück argues that honest speech is merely a relief, but true speech a discovery. Like Gadamer, she subjects poetry to a coherence rather than a correspondence standard of truth: "Any attempt to evaluate the honesty of a text must always lead away from that text, and toward intention," but any attempt to evaluate the truth of a text leads into the text, and it does so through the rhythm of the sentences. When Glück sets out to elucidate the truth of her three illustrative works, poems by John Keats, John Milton, and John Berryman, she does so by studying the musical elements of the poems. She connects truth to "distinctive voice," itself inseparable from rhythm. An informed reader can recognize the voice of Keats in the rhythm of his poems no less certainly than one recognizes the voice of a friend or lover by its rhythms. Truth, on Glück's view, is elemental, incapable of change in form without change in substance, and that elementalness derives from and is manifested in the musical elements of the poem.

Like Gadamer's and Glück's accounts of poetry's truth, recent attempts to answer other questions in poetics touch on the relation of sound and sense. The last quarter of the twentieth century saw heated debates over what should be included in the poetic canon (one form of the question what makes one poem better than another). Albert Cook's entry in that debate argues that the criterion for including a poem or body of poetry in the canon should be its wisdom. Wise poetry should be included, unwise poetry excluded. Cook states explicitly his intention not to consider rhythm. "Wisdom," he says, "comes about through a strategic combination of features," namely, thought, image, and story. Cook alludes to Ezra Pound's list of relevant features, melopoeia (charging the words "with some musical property" that directs the "bearing" of their meaning), phanopoeia (imagery), logopoeia ("the dance of the intellect among words"), but what Pound placed first, rhythm, Cook eliminates—or tries to eliminate.

Cook makes wisdom his criterion for canon formation, but rhythm proves to be a component of wisdom. Explaining why *Leaves of Grass* should be canonized, but *Hiawatha* should not, Cook calls Whitman's wisdom "far more complex" than Longfellow's, and attributes that complexity in large part to "the rhythms of *Leaves of Grass*." Not all wisdom is complex, though: some resides "in a radiant simplicity." Still, Cook argues for the generality of the connection between poetry's musical elements and its wisdom, contending that *any* explication of the superiority of one poem's wisdom to that of another poem will appeal to "the particular arrangement of language that brings about so penetrating an utterance."

Even in the apparently paradoxical preoccupation with silence in recent poetics, the Wittgensteinian question about the relation of sound and sense has a place. No ingredient appears more frequently in recent *ars poetica* poems than silence. Archibald MacLeish's "Ars Poetica" avers that a poem should be

> mute
> As a globed fruit,
>
> Dumb
> As old medallions to the thumb,
>
> Silent as the sleeve-worn stone
> Of casement ledges where the moss has grown –
>
> A poem should be wordless
> As the flight of birds.

Heather McHugh begins her volume of selected poems with "What He Thought," in which one of the characters recounts the execution of Giordano Bruno on charges of heresy. Fearing his eloquence, "his captors / placed upon his face / an iron mask," in which they burned him. "That is how / he died," the speaker says, "without a word, in front / of everyone. // And poetry . . . is what // he thought, but did not say." W. S. Merwin describes poetry as "what passes between // us now in a silence / on this side of the flames."

The relation between the silence so often alluded to by poets and "the rhythm of a sentence" receives its explicit formulation in T. S. Eliot's "Four Quartets." After saying that "Words, after speech, reach / Into the silence," Eliot explains how: "Only by the form, the pattern, / Can words or music reach / The stillness." Poets' frequent recourse to silence in their own poetics expresses the fact that a poem cannot be reduced to its propositional content, as if (returning now to Wittgenstein) to modify the Tractarian maxim that "What can be shown, cannot be said," not by reducing language to pictures but by insisting that neither sound nor sense can be separated from the totality that is the poem. The sense of a poem cannot be *ex*tracted because the form cannot be *sub*tracted. In Eliot's formulation, "the sound of a poem is as much an abstraction from the poem as is the sense."

Silence has become a stock poetic metaphor for the inseparability of sound and sense, the untranslatability of poetry, the inevitability of the poem that prevents it from being restated. Sound and sense generate a totality greater than its parts, and that totality prohibits adding anything to the poem by further speech. Thus, contemporary poets make a virtue of the vice Socrates in the *Phaedrus* attributes to writing: writing fails, he says, because, unlike speech, it

cannot defend itself from misinterpretation and will not respond when queried. It speaks once, but cannot speak again. Poetry, like Giordano Bruno in Heather McHugh's poem, refuses to defend itself. The frequent appeal to silence in the statements of poetics offered by recent poets means not that poems do not speak, but that they do not speak twice.

To assert the centrality to any poetics of the question of why the rhythm of a sentence should be important for understanding is not to accept the doctrine of formalism, a particular poetics with its roots in Kant and its flowering in critics like Eliot and Cleanth Brooks, but to acknowledge that any question about poetry will include within itself a question about form. "The rhythm of a sentence," the formal aspects of a poem, will not be the entirety of any attempt to understand poetry, but will be a part of every attempt.

[*See also* Aristotle; Baudelaire; Coleridge; Collage, *article on* Collage and Poetry; Dryden; Haiku; Hölderlin; Ibn Rushd; Ibn Sīnā; Mallarmé; Plato; Postmodernism *article on* Postmodern Poetry; Russian Aesthetics, *article on* Russian Formalism; Stein; Symbolism; *and* Wordsworth.]

BIBLIOGRAPHY

Aristotle. *Poetics.* Translated by Stephen Halliwell. Chapel Hill, N.C., 1987.

Augustine. *On Christian Doctrine.* Translated by D. W. Robertson, Jr. Indianapolis, 1958.

Cook, Albert. "The Canon of Poetry and the Wisdom of Poetry." *Journal of Aesthetics and Art Criticism* 49:4 (Fall 1991): 317–329.

Eliot, T. S. "Four Quartets." In *Collected Poems 1909–1962,* pp. 173–209. New York, 1963.

Eliot, T. S. "The Music of Poetry." In *Selected Prose of T. S. Eliot,* edited by Frank Kermode, pp. 107–114. New York, 1975.

Frye, Northrop. *Anatomy of Criticism: Four Essays.* Princeton, N.J., 1957.

Gadamer, Hans-Georg. "On the Contribution of Poetry to the Search for Truth." In *The Relevance of the Beautiful and Other Essays,* edited by Robert Bernasconi, translated by Nicholas Walker, pp. 105–115. Cambridge and New York, 1986.

Glück, Louise. "Against Sincerity." In *Proofs and Theories: Essays on Poetry,* pp. 33–51. Hopewell, N.J., 1994.

Hall, Donald, ed. *Claims for Poetry.* Ann Arbor, 1982.

Handy, William J., and Max Westbrook, eds. *Twentieth Century Criticism: The Major Statements.* New York, 1974.

Kaplan, Charles, ed. *Criticism: The Major Statements.* 2d ed. New York, 1986.

Lilburn, Tim. *Poetry and Knowing: Speculative Essays and Interviews.* Kingston, Ontario, 1995.

MacLeish, Archibald. "Ars Poetica." In *Collected Poems: 1917–1952,* pp. 40–41. Boston, 1952.

McHugh, Heather. "What He Thought." In *Hinge and Sign: Poems, 1968–1993,* pp. 3–4. Hanover, N.H., 1994.

Merwin, W. S. "Cover Note." In *Travels* pp. ix–x. New York, 1992.

Pound, Ezra. "How to Read." In *Literary Essays of Ezra Pound,* edited by T. S. Eliot, pp. 15–40. Reprint, New York, 1968.

Wittgenstein, Ludwig. *Remarks on the Philosophy of Psychology,* vol. 1. Edited by G. E. M. Anscombe and G. H. von Wright, translated by G. E. M. Anscombe. Chicago, 1980.

HARVEY HIX

POLITICS AND AESTHETICS. *To clarify both the politics of art and the ways in which aesthetics has embraced or excluded politics, this entry comprises six essays:*

Historical and Conceptual Overview
Culture and Political Theory
Difference and Culture
Politicized Art
Aestheticized Politics
AIDS, Aesthetics, and Activism

The first essay is an overview of the many ways art and politics have supported or opposed one another in the history of aesthetics from Plato to the present. The second essay analyzes the role of the concept of culture in debates between liberalism and communitarianism in contemporary political theory. The third essay critically examines how art history and criticism have treated various forms of difference—race, gender, and sexual preference—in contemporary American and European culture. The fourth essay discusses examples of twentieth-century art that have been the subject of political controversy. The fifth essay shifts the focus from politicized art to the aestheticization of politics that occurs under fascism. The final essay analyzes the debate between aestheticism and activism in the contemporary discussions about art and AIDS (Acquired Immune Deficiency Syndrome). For related discussion, see Iconoclasm and Iconophobia; Ideology; Law and Art; Monuments, *article on* Twentieth-Century Countermonuments; Morality and Aesthetics; National Endowment for the Arts; Nietzsche, *article on* Nietzsche on Art and Politics; Obscenity; Post-colonialism; *and* Sociology of Art.]

Historical and Conceptual Overview

Historically, art and politics have been linked for almost as long as there have been political entities. Throughout the civilizations of antiquity, we find poems, statues, and structures commemorating the rulers, warriors, and battles that past peoples believed contributed to the course of history. Moreover, that art still has this practical function for politics can be seen in evidence ranging from lowly postal stamps to the Vietnam War Memorial in Washington, D.C., and to structures projecting the aura of state power, such as the Pentagon. Likewise, philosophically, the nexus between art and politics is long-standing. In Plato's *Republic*—the earliest sustained theoretical treatment of art in the Western tradition—political censorship of the arts is defended for reasons of state.

Because the practical as well as the theoretical linkage between art and politics has been perennial, it should come as no surprise that the range of relationships between art and politics is quite diverse. For the purpose of giving some order to this collection of functions, we can organize our thinking around two primary relationships, namely, support and opposition. This yields four basic (nonexhaustive and not mutually exclusive) categories: art in support of poli-

tics, art in opposition to politics, politics in support of art, and politics in opposition to art. Using these categories, it is possible to organize the most fundamental functional relationships between art and politics.

Art in Support of Politics. If we begin by taking the extension of *politics* narrowly—that is, as pertaining to formal political entities, such as the state, and political organizations, such as political parties—then the first role of art with respect to politics is that of service. Under this category, art explicitly advances the cause of the state, the ruling monarchy, and class or political factions. Art that celebrates military prowess, such as the monuments on Freedom Square in Budapest, is political art in the service of the state. Triumphal arches; victory steles; the paintings of historic lawgivers, generals, civic founders, battle scenes; and epic poems all commemorate the past of a people, often linking present regimes with fondly remembered ones. The imagery on stamps and currency functions this way as well, whereas governments use architecture to erect an appropriate vision of themselves—such as august courthouses and suitably solid, central banking offices. Art can make government buildings feel creditable.

Art in the service of the state often has a legitimating function. Artistic images may correlate a contemporary government with a past regime in order to claim the authority of history for the present. Such was Benito Mussolini's appropriation of the sign of the fasces. For this reason, art in the service of government often trades in idealizations. That is why the workers are so much more muscular in Socialist Realist paintings than they are in actual factories. Artists can also endorse specific political programs, as did those depression artists in the United States who portrayed social welfare as justifiable.

Political regimes and movements require commitments from their citizens and followers. Customarily, art provides the symbols around which solidarity can take root and flourish. Even liberal democracies require allegiance to certain core values, such as equal respect and tolerance. Thus, liberal art generally aspires to promote and to rhapsodize the sentiments of equality.

In the twentieth century, attempts have been made to transform art in the service of politics into a quasi science. This endeavor is called propaganda. The notion of propaganda itself has at least two senses—a pejorative sense and a nonpejorative one. The pejorative sense of propaganda construes propaganda as always a matter of deception. On this account, propaganda is the dissemination of what its creators know to be lies for the purpose of intentionally misleading the public for political ends. Falsely depicting enemy aircraft allegedly strafing civilian populations would be an example here.

Alternatively, the notion of propaganda may simply apply to any explicit attempt to persuade by means of artful rhetoric. Thus the opening shots of Leni Riefenstahl's *Tri-*

umph of the Will, portraying Adolf Hitler as a demigod and savior alighting from the clouds, would count as propaganda in the nonpejorative sense so long as Riefenstahl believed this to be a fair account of Hitler. But, if Riefenstahl thought otherwise and was merely cynically manipulating her audience, then the sequence would count as propaganda in the pejorative sense. Although it is hard to be certain in this matter, nowadays "propaganda" appears to be used most frequently in the pejorative sense.

So far we have been concerned with art in the service of politics narrowly construed. Some critics and theorists, however, think of "politics" more broadly—not in terms of specific political formations (regimes, factions), but in terms of society at large. Art performs a service to society at large, of course, inasmuch as it acts as a conduit for social values and beliefs. Call this the reflection theory of art.

Art presupposes many of the beliefs and values of the society from which it emerges, and readers, listeners, and viewers must fill in these presuppositions in the process of assimilating the artworks in question. In this way, artworks may come not only to reflect but also to reinforce the beliefs and values of the larger culture. Art, for example, may reflect and reinforce prevailing social ideals of leadership even in fictions and pictures not expressly concerned with politics. Many critics, especially since the 1960s, have come to regard the role of art in the transmission of culture as a political function.

Of course, one can take a more circumscribed view than this. One may not find it advisable to suppose that every aspect of art is involved in politics. One might want to focus one's attention on only those artworks that are concerned with disseminating false (or otherwise epistemically defective) thoughts, beliefs, attitudes, emotions, and desires for the purpose of sustaining some practice of social domination. This is to be concerned with the *ideological* function of art.

This approach tracks the service of art to political formations less formally individuated than regimes and parties. It allows one to speak of racist, homophobic, and patriarchal ideologies. At the same time, this approach is more specific than the reflection theory of art, since it does not regard every topic as politically significant. The ideologue also differs from the propagandist (in the pejorative sense) because, although both traffic in deceptions, the propagandist does so intentionally and in the service of an overt political institution, whereas the ideologue need not meet either of these conditions. In this respect, it may be profitable to regard propaganda (in the pejorative sense) as a subcategory of ideology.

Our discussion of the services art performs for politics has emphasized content rather than form. In the twentieth century, however, questions have arisen, not only about the use of art's content to promote political ideas and emotions, but also about the means that art employs to do so. Revolu-

tionary movements, such as Soviet Marxism, have spawned artistic fellow travelers who aspire to create new revolutionary forms in order to express appropriately and to emblematize heralded transformations of revolutionary consciousness—hence, Soviet Constructivism. Nevertheless, at the same time, such endeavors have often been denounced as formalist by other political radicals, who defend realism as the proper form of socialist art on the grounds that, though it is admittedly bourgeois in origin, it is what the people understand and, therefore, the politically appropriate means of serving them. Bertolt Brecht and Sergei Eisenstein are famous representatives of the formalist line. György Lukács is a leading theorist of Socialist Realism. In dance, for example, this contrast can be marked by Nikolai Foregger's machine dances, on the one hand, and ballets like *White Haired Girl* and *Red Detachment of Women,* on the other.

Art in Opposition to Politics. Of course, art can oppose foreign regimes and factions, although in this sense of political opposition, opposition to one regime can just as easily be reconceived as political service to another regime. Thus, in considering art in opposition to politics, it is most useful to focus on art's opposition to the political unit with which it is affiliated, as is the case with Bill T. Jones's *Last Supper at Uncle Tom's Cabin/The Promised Land.* In this light, Francisco José de Goya's *Execution of May 3, 1808* is primarily in the service of Spanish patriotism, while Erich Maria Remarque's *All Quiet on the Western Front* opposes war as a political instrument in general, including the German war machine. Art in opposition to politics can also be referred to as protest art, subversive art, or social criticism.

Art as social criticism may be explicit or implicit, and it may be targeted broadly or narrowly. Social criticism is narrowly targeted where its domain of concern comprises formally individuated entities like states and political parties. It is broadly targeted where it is directed at society or culture at large (or, at least, at substantial portions thereof, such as bourgeoisie culture or patriarchal ideology).

An example of explicit social criticism, targeted narrowly, is a film like *El Norte,* which focuses expressly on U.S. immigration policy and makes its concern with the injustice of that policy evident. Similarly, John Steinbeck's *Grapes of Wrath* explicitly addresses an identifiable social problem. Honoré Daumier's drawing "The Third Class Carriage," on the other hand, while clearly critical, does seems critical, not of isolable social practices, but of the treatment of the poor in general. In a similar vein, the choreographer Kurt Jooss's *Green Table* criticizes war throughout the ages. Likewise, much German Expressionist painting appears to be critical of the existing social world as such rather than of this or that policy of any specific political regime.

Indeed, throughout the twentieth century, many avant-garde artists have come to conceive of art as a form of social criticism. Dada is overtly critical, but of everything (or

POLITICS AND AESTHETICS: Overview. Francisco Goya, *Execution of May 3* (1808), oil on canvas, 266 × 345 cm; Prado Gallery, Madrid. (Courtesy of Alinari/Art Resource, New York.)

everything bourgeois), rather than of anything in particular. Much contemporary art commentary—as well as practice—presumes that art, or, at least, ambitious art, is always subversive social criticism of such large-scale social phenomena as capitalism, racism, sexism, and homophobia. This is not to say that contemporary artists may not focus on criticizing specific policies and identifiable official regimes, but that their conception of the political is frequently much broader than one restricted to particular governments and self-conscious parties. Sometimes artists will attack Senator Jesse Helms—as in Paul Schmidt's play *The Bathtub*—but "Amerika" is a more likely, explicit target for most of them.

Social criticism may also be implicit in art. An artist may reveal the machinations of a society while being unaware that he or she is doing so. Lukács maintains that the conservative Honoré de Balzac actually portrayed French society in his *Comédie humaine* in a way congenial to socialism. Certain structuralist theorists, such as Pierre Macherey and Louis Althusser, perhaps imitating Claude Lévi-Strauss's analysis of myth, have even argued that it is the role of art to reflect social contradictions, as if art were essentially a Marxist social critic.

Some theorists, like Herbert Marcuse, argue that art itself is essentially (rather than contingently) a form of progressive social criticism, since the artwork, by means of such core art-making structures as fiction and representation, provides alternatives to what exists and, thereby, effectively argues for the possibility of social change (although this argument appears to overlook the possibility that certain artworks may at the same time be in the service of ignoble social alternatives).

Similarly, Theodor W. Adorno allegorizes Modernist art's quest for autonomy as an implied criticism of the tendency in capitalist society to reduce all value to market or instrumental value. Modernist art does not succeed in this quest, but its honorable defeat shows us in microcosm—from a critical perspective—the operation of capitalist society writ large. For Adorno, this is only true for Modernist art. Mass art, on the other hand, is complicit with the marketplace and functions to sustain the political domination of the population by capitalism.

Arguments that suppose that it is of the nature of art to belong to the general species of social criticism err either by being too loose in what they think of as social criticism (e.g., Marcuse) or by speaking of art in an honorific rather than in a classificatory or descriptive sense of the term (Adorno). Art is not essentially social criticism. Too much of it is either critically mute politically or involved in uncritical political advocacy. Nevertheless, social criticism and protest represent one avenue of art, an avenue increasingly traveled since the eighteenth century (as art came to be more independent of religious and political patronage) and one especially popular toward the end of the twentieth century.

Politics in Support of Art. As we have already seen, art making itself can be a form of political activity. Governments hire artists to design stamps, currency, monuments, and uniforms; to compose music; to sing anthems; to play marches; to organize parades and spectacles; and so on. Where governments or official parties pay the bills or otherwise support artistic activity, politics plays the role of employer with respect to art. In the past and across different cultures, many artists were employed by sovereigns, nobles, and churches in this manner. Nevertheless, even in modern times in the industrial world, artists are employed to secure political ends.

Despite being a source of revenue for artists, government commissions can also result in a conflict between the claims of artistic autonomy and claims about the common good. This happened with respect to the publicly financed monument titled *Tilted Arc*, by Richard Serra. Serra's claim to a right to express freely his belief in the oppressiveness of modern life by means of a sculpture that oppressed spectators was challenged by citizens who claimed the right not to be oppressed by a public edifice. After extended court hearings, a judge ordered that *Tilted Arc* be dismantled, indicating that political backing of the arts, insofar as it is political, can be a risky source of support.

Artists are employed by political units when they are commissioned or salaried to produce specifiable artworks for use by political entities (narrowly construed). There is another form of government support of the arts, however. We might call this "patronage" (where this means that artists are given government support to pursue their own ends, rather than the ends of the commonwealth). That is, whereas government employment involves hiring artists to produce specifiable artworks for public use—such as a mayoral seal—patronage involves extending money or benefits, directly or indirectly, to artists so that they can carry out their own aims. Indirect support for the arts involves things like tax benefits to museums, nonprofit accreditation of arts organizations, and federal grants to art schools. Direct support for the arts involves outright cash payments or benefits in kind (land, buildings, etc.) to artists or to arts organizations to produce their own work.

Government patronage of the arts is widespread throughout the industrial world. It is, however, a practice that has recently become controversial in the United States. A particular source of debate concerns monies granted by government organizations, like the National Endowment for the Arts, to individual artists in order to produce original art. The recent furor began over federally funded artworks—like *Piss Christ* by Andres Serrano—that offended the sensibilities of many taxpayers, especially those of a religious and right-wing bent. Nevertheless, the theoretical concerns here are not simply conservative, they cut to the heart of liberalism as well. For if liberalism is the doctrine that the state should be neutral between competing conceptions of the good life, and if there are significant numbers of citizens who doubt whether the pursuit of art is anything but a sectarian perspective on the good, then the question arises whether a liberal state can, on its own terms, legitimately extract taxation on behalf of the art world from nonconsenting citizens.

Political entities, like governments, may also benefit the arts through their licensing and regulatory activities by creating venues for artistic creativity. Government regulatory activities can also, however, impede the autonomous development of art in a number of ways.

Politics in Opposition to Art. Political bodies, whether formally constituted or informal, may oppose the arts through criticism. Public officials, party leaders, and the representatives of social movements may speak out against the political content, putative cultural repercussions, social significance, and alleged moral consequences of artworks. Political entities, such as states, typically, however, have even more powerful levers than criticism for opposing art. They standardly have the prerogative to regulate and, ultimately, to prohibit artworks. That is, formal political entities, like states, have the capacity to censor art. The theoretical grounds for censorship were established long ago by Plato. Censorship rests on the presumption that the function of art is to serve the political ends of the state. Where art fails to advance those ends, or where it even appears to subvert those ends, censorship is apposite.

From the eighteenth century until quite recently, a typical Western response to the Platonic viewpoint was that art is autonomous—it is not an instrument of politics or of anything else. Art, so the story went, has its own ends and functions, irrespective of and independent from those of politics. Art, that is to say, is disinterested. This position, however, has come to sound rather empty by the end of the twentieth century, which is perhaps why the case against political censorship seems more embattled now than at any other time since the 1960s.

Political censorship can be motivated by opposition to the political content of the relevant artworks. Artworks containing explicit or implied criticism of certain sets of political arrangements or of regnant philosophies may be suppressed—as they were in the former Soviet Union. But political censorship can also be motivated by fear of the behavioral consequences of certain types of artworks. This seems to be the direction that movements in favor of censorship have taken recently in the United States.

Violent programming on television and in the movies as well as aggressive song lyrics are opposed on the grounds that they will lead to violent behavior. Pornographic art, likewise, is condemned, and banning it is advocated because it is said to lead to rape or to other sex crimes. These allegations are extremely difficult to test. One obvious reason for this is that any experiments that possessed the potential of causing criminal activity would probably themselves be illegal and would certainly be immoral.

The emphasis on behavioral consequences in American debates about censorship undoubtedly signals a commitment in the United States to the liberal notion of the harm principle. That is, for government censorship to be legitimate, certain burdens of proof must be met. Specifically, the state must show that the artworks in question are likely to cause harm to innocent, nonconsenting bystanders. This desideratum can be met—at least in principle—by claiming that the artworks in question are likely to bring about untoward consequences to the interests of third parties. Whether they do so, however, is in the end an empirical question, one to which no one has yet found a conclusive answer.

BIBLIOGRAPHY

Adorno, Theodor W., and Max Horkheimer. *Dialectic of Enlightenment.* Translated by John Cumming. New York, 1972.
Adorno, Theodor W. *Aesthetic Theory.* Edited by Gretel Adorno and Rolf Tiedemann, translated by Robert Hullot-Kentor. Minneapolis, 1997.
Althusser, Louis. *Lenin and Philosophy and Other Essays.* Translated by Ben Brewster. London, 1971.
Barrell, John. *The Political Theory of Painting from Reynolds to Hazlitt: "The Body of the Public."* New Haven, 1986.
Brecht, Bertolt. *Brecht on Theatre: The Development of an Aesthetic.* Edited and translated by John Willett. New York, 1964.
Carroll, Noël. "Can Government Funding of the Arts Be Justified Theoretically?" *Journal of Aesthetic Education* 21.1 (Spring 1987): 21–35.
Carroll, Noël. *Philosophical Problems of Mass Art.* New York and Oxford, 1998.
Copp, David, and Susan Wendell, eds. *Pornography and Censorship.* Buffalo, N.Y., 1983.
Eagleton, Terry. *Criticism and Ideology: A Study in Marxist Literary Theory.* Atlantic Highlands, N.J., 1976.
Edelman, Murray. *From Art to Politics: How Artistic Creations Shape Political Conceptions.* Chicago, 1995.
Johnson, Pauline. *Marxist Aesthetics: The Foundations within Everyday Life for an Emancipated Consciousness.* London and Boston, 1984.
Lukács, Georg. *Realism in Our Time: Literature and the Class Struggle.* Translated by John Mander and Necke Mander. New York, 1964.
Macherey, Pierre. *A Theory of Literary Production.* Translated by Geoffrey Wall. London and Boston, 1978.
Marcuse, Herbert. *The Aesthetic Dimension: Toward a Critique of Marxist Aesthetics.* Boston, 1978.
National Television Violence Study: Scientific Papers, 1994–1995. Studio City, Calif., 1995.
Plato. *Republic.* Translated by G. M. A. Grube. Indianapolis, 1974.
Sorrell, Tom. "Art, Society and Morality." In *Philosophical Aesthetics,* edited by Oswald Hanfling, pp. 297–347. Oxford and Cambridge, Mass., 1992.
Williams, Raymond. *Marxism and Literature.* Oxford and New York, 1977.

NOËL CARROLL

Culture and Political Theory

Liberal political philosophers have often been charged with failing to recognize the importance of culture in the design of social and political policies and institutions. While the basic liberties guarantee citizens the freedom to pursue their own cultural aims and conceptions of the good, liberalism's advocacy of state neutrality with regard to the value of different ways of life is said to undermine political support for cultural values, encourage an atomistic conception of society, and disregard the role of cultural mechanisms in generating ideological distortions of citizens' preferences.

It has been thought by some that the conception of justice proposed in John Rawls's *Theory of Justice* excludes state support for culture. Rawls develops a "political" or (as he says in more recent publications) "freestanding" conception of justice for what he calls a nearly just, democratic, well-ordered society. Such a society is viewed as a fair system of cooperation between citizens (rather than an involuntary scheme coordinated from above), and principles of justice are to specify the fair terms of cooperation between citizens viewed as free and equal persons. A conception of justice is said to be justified if it would be agreed to by citizens themselves in a suitably specified initial situation.

The original position (Rawls, 1971, section 4) is Rawls's favored interpretation of such an initial situation. Rawls describes the original position as a "device of representation" intended to help us model and introduce order into our considered judgments about justice. Rational individuals are thought of as coming together to choose principles for the basic structure of society, which Rawls describes as "the way in which the major social institutions distribute fundamental rights and duties and determine the division of advantages from social cooperation" (section 2). The basic structure of society is the first subject of justice, and its importance derives in part from the profound and pervasive role it plays in shaping citizens' expectations over a complete lifetime.

The original position represents the parties to this choice of principles as free, equal, mutually disinterested, and rational. In order to rule out the effects of social and natural contingencies on their choice of principles, and in order to exclude unfair bargaining advantages and threats of force, coercion, and fraud, Rawls specifies that the parties are situated behind a veil of ignorance that excludes knowledge of particular contingencies such as their place in society, their class and wealth, gender or race, strength, intelligence, cultural sophistication, talents, or conceptions of the good. In this way, bargaining advantages that normally arise as a result of cumulative historic, social, and natural processes cannot influence the choice of principles.

Rawls argues that, deprived of this knowledge, but rational and aware that they possess two basic powers of moral personality (the capacities for a sense of justice and for a conception of the good), the parties in the original position would vote unanimously for a social scheme that would secure them an adequate share of certain all-purpose primary social goods ("rights and liberties, powers and opportunities, income and wealth and the social bases of self respect") needed for the realization of any plan of life or, as he later emphasizes, for the exercise and development of the basic powers of moral personality. No matter what their eventual starting place in society, they hope, by making their choice of principles under the guidance of this thin theory of the good, to guarantee themselves the basic resources necessary to the pursuit and successful realization of any foreseeable plan of life.

Rawls maintains that in this choice situation the parties would rank his own two principles of justice higher than other well-known conceptions of social justice (including classical and average utilitarianism). Rawls's first principle of justice, which is lexically prior to (i.e., must be satisfied before) his second principle, entitles each citizen to a fully adequate scheme of equal basic liberties compatible with a similar scheme for all (the principle of liberty). The second principle is designed to ensure a roughly equal distribution of primary social goods, with the modification that inequalities are to be permitted to the extent that they improve the position of the least well off representative group in society (the difference principle) and subject to the further condition that opportunities must be open on a fair basis to all (the principle of fair equality of opportunity).

Because they are situated behind a veil of ignorance, the parties to the agreement made in the original position are compelled to avoid choosing principles of justice that might require them to sacrifice their as yet unknown particular conceptions of the good to all-embracing social and cultural ideals such as the maximization of utility or human excellence. In section 50 of *A Theory of Justice*, Rawls argues that the principle of perfection, in both pure and mixed ("as but one standard among several in an intuitionist theory") forms, and other principles advocating a teleologically motivated design of the basic structure of society would therefore be rejected. At the same time, he insists that, in the

well-ordered society of what he calls justice as fairness, the human excellences and perfections could still be pursued by individuals or groups at their own initiative, without government support, within the limits of the principle of free association. Further support for associations dedicated to advancing the arts, sciences, and culture generally would have to come from voluntary contributions or as a "fair return for services rendered" rather than from the state.

Rawls's apparent readiness to abandon support for culture to the "private" sphere and to the activities of individual associations within society has provoked a variety of criticisms. Joseph Raz, for example, has argued that such a policy would undermine the chances of survival of "many cherished aspects of our culture" (Raz, 1986). According to Raz, society as a whole must shoulder the burden of preserving certain basic perfectionistic ideals or risk total cultural impoverishment. Amy Gutmann has argued, in an extensive study of the social and philosophical foundations of democratic education, that the citizens of the well-ordered society paired with Rawls's two principles of justice would be compelled to forgo collective political support for the cultural heritage. She proposes, instead, a form of democratic perfectionism that would secure the place of the most widely accepted cultural values within society while also equalizing the cultural influence of equally interested and able citizens.

Communitarians such as Michael J. Sandel argue that Rawls fails to make allowance for the morally significant role of a common cultural life in enabling individuals to develop values and discover and shape their own identity. Rawls is said to conceive the human self without regard for the constitutive aims and deep human attachments that are bound up with existence in a community founded on solidarity and a shared sense of obligation. Another philosopher sometimes described as a communitarian, Charles Taylor, argues that free and autonomous moral agents can only achieve and maintain their identities in the context of certain institutional "bearers of culture" such as museums, symphony orchestras, universities, laboratories, political parties, courts of law, newspapers, publishing houses, and television stations, which require "stability and continuity and frequently also support from society as a whole" (Taylor, 1985).

But although Rawls rejects perfectionistic justifications for the support of specific cultural associations and enterprises, his theory does allow for culture to be treated as a public good that government may promote in those cases in which, as with the defense of a nation in time of war or the maintenance of public health, the market mechanism breaks down because the desired benefits are indivisible, and must hence be enjoyed by all or none. In such cases, Rawls foresees among the background institutions of government an "exchange branch" (1971, section 43), which is an arrangement designed to discover the most efficient method for providing society with indivisible goods of the kind everyone is likely to want. Where there is a de facto social consensus concerning the desirability of certain cultural goods, Rawls sees no difficulty in making their provision and administration the task of background institutions of government.

Furthermore, Rawls states at the end of section 50 of *A Theory of Justice* that a well-ordered society may devote substantial resources to support "social conditions that secure the equal liberties or advance the long-term interests of the least advantaged." Goods secured or provided by cultural institutions may well figure (although not for perfectionistic reasons) among the primary goods to be distributed under the principles of justice. The equal liberties, inasfar as they are essential conditions for the adequate development and full realization of the moral powers, will play an important role in the protection and promotion of culture. Fair equality of opportunity requires that citizens have equal opportunities of education, and that chances to acquire cultural knowledge and skills not depend on one's class position. Rawls also states, in section 17, that resources for education would be allocated under the difference principle, not merely in the interests of economic efficiency and social welfare but to enable "a person to enjoy the culture of his society and to take part in its affairs." It is thus evident that support for culture and access to cultural resources will indeed play a significant role in the well-ordered society associated with Rawls's two principles of justice.

Although some criticisms of Rawls's views on culture may be accommodated in this way, it might still be argued that he attaches too low a value to the role, character, and significance of cultural institutions in society. To treat culture as a public or primary good is to disregard the fact it is in their noninstrumental character that the real significance of cultural values resides. It is perhaps skepticism in this respect that makes Rawls's perfectionistic and communitarian critics argue that government must take a more active role in determining the character and quality of a society's culture. But such proposals, rarely elaborated in detail, also conjure up the specter of a state perfectionism that liberalism is bound to regard as unworkable in a society of free and autonomous individuals.

One alternative for liberals, therefore, is to look in the direction of primary goods and the thin theory of the good for a deeper understanding of cultural values that is compatible with the basic premises of liberalism, but does not ignore what might be regarded as the distinctive character of cultural values. The concept of culture can be understood in a variety of ways. Traditionally, it has often identified it with a realm of "higher," authentic values and self-contained ends in opposition to a practical and "lower" world of social utility. Social scientists and economists, by contrast, often seek to resolve questions about cultural preferences in the context of the theory of rational choice. According to such

views, no qualitative distinction ought to be made between preferences for "higher" cultural values and other preferences, wants, or needs. What counts is not what people want but how much they want of it.

But the term *culture* may also refer to a more basic kind of context within which value judgments and aesthetic preferences are possible. In this sense, it may be regarded as a background structure that gives meaning to individual choices, rather than as a set of foreground options or alternatives. Considerations such as these have led Ronald Dworkin to distinguish "two kinds of consequences our culture has for us: on the one hand particular paintings, performances, novels . . . and on the other, the structural framework which makes aesthetic values of that sort possible" (Dworkin, 1985).

According to Dworkin, the "cultural structure" of a society is not a particular conception of value or set of values to be secured by direct political intervention in specific cultural transactions, but rather a basic framework within which citizens are able to form and pursue their own cultural preferences. In this sense culture may be compared to a language. Just as a language presents us with the opportunity to say many different things, so the cultural structure of society furnishes the basic context of choice within which individuals can pursue diverse conceptions of the good. The center of the cultural structure of a community, according to Dworkin, is its language, together with "a shared vocabulary of tradition and convention, and the conceptual equipment to find aesthetic value in historical and cultural continuity."

A rich and diverse cultural structure is needed if citizens are to be able to entertain a diversity of different models and ways of life. Since the existence of a cultural structure rich in opportunities must be presupposed if citizens are to be able to pursue any values whatsoever, and since in promoting such a structure it would not be permissible to create or oppose any individual's specific preferences, a government may promote and protect the cultural structure of a society without paternalism or perfectionism.

But what would it mean to protect the cultural structure of a society? If the cultural structure resembles a language, can it be subjected to political influence? How can a government enhance a basic context of choice without promoting or favoring particular kinds of cultural choice? Moreover, what justification is there for thinking that there is just one cultural structure rather than many?

Such considerations have led Will Kymlicka to argue that while Rawls and Dworkin recognize the importance of the cultural structure, they mistakenly assume the political community to be culturally homogeneous and hence take cultural membership to be "a kind of public good, equally available to all." In fact, a modern political community embraces many different cultures, and the good of cultural membership may be enjoyed by different citizens to different degrees. Since participation in a culture, viewed as a context of choice, is essential if the representative citizen is to be able to pursue a meaningful plan of life, access to a cultural community may be a relevant criterion for distributing the burdens and benefits of social cooperation. Hence, there is a strong case for regarding cultural membership as a primary good, an individual's claim to which may be balanced against other primary goods, including the basic liberties.

But while liberal regimes may have good reason to want to protect the existence of specific, perhaps threatened, cultural structures within the larger political community, it remains unclear whether treating membership of a specific culture as a primary good is the most reasonable way of achieving that goal. An alternative view, not so far considered, is that it is not so much access to specific cultural contexts of choice as the ability to develop a relationship to and master different contexts of choice that should be the focus of liberal concern.

Dworkin's and Kymlicka's accounts of the cultural structure might be deepened by invoking the idea of a basic cultural competence. On this view, suggested by applications of Noam Chomsky's linguistic competence theory to a variety of specific areas of culture such as art theory, music, and literature, citizens' capacities to choose and revise particular conceptions of the good and to take advantage of different contexts of choice presuppose a more fundamental mastery of the basic framework within which cultural choices can be made. Like any specific aesthetic or cultural competence, such a basic cultural competence may be assumed to be extremely complex in character, including a variety of temporal, linguistic, cognitive, and aesthetic components.

Unlike a specific competence, however, this more fundamental kind of cultural competence may be taken to involve the basic capacity to have a relation to linguistic, cultural, and historical continuity as such, and not merely to particular kinds of representation, value, tradition, or cultural continuity. On this view, it is not in protecting the cultural structure, or guaranteeing citizens membership of a specific culture, but in the provision of the primary goods necessary to the development of a more basic capacity to have value that the fundamental cultural task of a liberal political regime consists.

[See also Cultural Studies.]

BIBLIOGRAPHY

Chomsky, Noam. *Aspects of the Theory of Syntax.* Cambridge, Mass., 1965.
Dworkin, Ronald. "Can a Liberal State Support Art?" In *A Matter of Principle,* pp. 221–233. Cambridge, Mass., 1985.
Gutmann, Amy. *Democratic Education.* Princeton, N.J., 1987.
Kymlicka, Will. *Liberalism, Community, and Culture.* Oxford, 1989.
Kymlicka, Will. *Contemporary Political Philosophy.* Oxford, 1990.
MacIntyre, Alisdair. *After Virtue: A Study in Moral Theory.* 2d ed. Notre Dame, Ind., 1984.
Rawls, John. *A Theory of Justice.* Cambridge, Mass., 1971.
Rawls, John. "The Basic Liberties and Their Priority." In *The Tanner Lectures on Human Values,* edited by S. MacMurrin, vol. 3, pp. 3–87. Salt Lake City, 1982.
Rawls, John. *Political Liberalism.* New York, 1993. Includes revised version of "The Basic Liberties and Their Priority."
Raz, Joseph. *The Morality of Freedom.* Oxford, 1986.
Sandel, Michael J. *Liberalism and the Limits of Justice.* Cambridge and New York, 1982.
Taylor, Charles. *Philosophical Papers,* vol. 2, *Philosophy and the Human Sciences.* Cambridge and New York, 1985.

JOHN STOPFORD

Difference and Culture

In the epilogue to his *Mythologies,* a treatise on modern-day myth, representation, and ideology that helped shape an entire generation of critical thinkers, Roland Barthes wrote about a chance encounter with the image of a black youth in the racially charged Paris of the late 1950s. While waiting in a barbershop for a haircut, Barthes was offered a copy of *Paris-Match.* On the cover was the photograph of a young man of African descent dressed in a French military uniform. His hand was raised to his head in a gesture of salute. His uplifted eyes were fixed on the tricolor, that great symbol of French militarism and civility. The image intrigued Barthes: he searched for the political meaning that lay just below its glossy surface; he speculated on the ideological demands that would sanction its presence on the cover of one of France's leading picture magazines; he analyzed the various semiotic systems that conspired to produce its multiple meanings. While the cover's signifier—a black soldier saluting the French flag—yielded its literal meaning, Barthes argued that it was in the realm of secondary signification, the signified, that one could decipher its intended ideological message: "that France is a great Empire, that all her sons, without any color discrimination, faithfully serve under her flag, and that there is no better answer to the detractors of an alleged colonialism than the zeal shown by this Negro in serving his so-called oppressors" (Barthes, 1972).

Not satisfied with merely articulating the message, Barthes journeyed deeper into interpretation, arriving at the image's purest, and paradoxically most sinister, level of meaning—that plane of content he would refer to as myth. Within the realm of public speech, myth existed to conceal the undesirable, to make bearable the unbearable, to whitewash the contradictions and dissonance that threatened to disrupt the social order. Contemporary myths, Barthes argued, served "not to deny things" but to take the problematic representations of everyday life, depictions fraught with our fears, our intolerance, our bigotry, and make "them innocent . . . give . . . them a natural and eternal justification." It was this "duplicity of the signifier" that determined the special character of myth, allowing it to "henceforth appear . . . both like a notification and like a statement of fact." Following through on this logic, Barthes concluded that *Paris-Match*'s mythic notification—that colonialism was a fiction—existed to assuage anxiety and guilt at a time when France was coming to terms with its own history of brutal racism. Thus, the image further oppressed the black subject even as it offered its bourgeois audience a reassuring alternative to the historically encoded presence of the angry, colonized black body.

More than thirty-five years after Barthes first directed his uncompromising and rigorous eye toward society's myths, social institutions, in an atmosphere of little or no critical resistance, continue to freely perpetuate lies and deceptions. Despite the supposed vigilance of a media-oriented culture that bombards us daily with political exposés and instant polling results, the vast majority of American and European cultural commentators remain blissfully ignorant of the duplicity of visual representation: while critical methodologies have come a long way since the 1950s—one thinks of the advances of a whole range of new critical and historical studies—most writers, out of naïveté, cowardice, or even malice, ignore these mechanisms for exposing our intolerance. Even when such methodologies are employed, there is no guarantee that theoretical critics and historians, who are themselves often lacking the self-awareness that might allow them to see their own bigotry, will not avert their eyes from what they would rather not see.

This map of misreadings and distortions is perhaps most pronounced in the severe methodological deficit of American and European art-historical, museological, and critical practices in the second half of the twentieth century. While the disciplines of art history and art criticism are not interchangeable, either in their methods or motives, they both share a direct relationship to the ideological hierarchies of the art world and, as such, can be understood to embrace similar attitudes toward the issue of art and politics. Ruled by the interests of upper-class white patrons, the art world has long accepted the mythology of its own social removal. The Baudelairean dandy, a hallmark of early modernist conceptions of the role of the artist in society, celebrated his distance from the grimy reality of a new, urbanized Paris by refusing to identify with a specific economic class.

For the critic Clement Greenberg a century later, formalism could serve as a way out of the harsh realities of late industrial society, but only as a negation of social reality—as a metaphysical transcendence from politics and mass culture (or what he called "kitsch"). More recently, art history and criticism rooted in structuralist and poststructuralist methodologies—while considerably more sophisticated than formalism in its analyses of visual representation—most often assume formalism's apolitical stance by refusing to consider cultural artifacts in their broader socioeconomic context. The rise of neo-Marxist methodologies in the 1980s has not been without problems: frequently lacking a rigorous theory of representation, such writing has often settled on a simplistic iconographic approach. All of these methods have preserved a fundamentally conservative and restrictive definition of high culture, one that inevitably embraces the interests of white, upper-class people at the exclusion of others. Greenberg's racist and classist definition of high culture ironically continues to resonate in most art-historical and curatorial circles: "There has always been on one side the minority of the powerful—and therefore the cultivated—and on the other the great mass of the exploited and the poor—and therefore the ignorant," he wrote in 1939. "Formal culture has always belonged to the first, while the last have had to content themselves with folk or rudimentary culture, or kitsch" (Greenberg, 1961).

The world of the art museum is no less politically isolated. In the work of the curator, which fastens on objects, conservation, and elegant installation, a resistance to the flux and chafe of the social sphere (and, most particularly, issues of marginality) may be the path of least resistance. Despite a range of ideologically grounded art-historical methodologies, contemporary curatorial method continually returns to principles established more than half a century ago by Alfred H. Barr, Jr., the first director of the Museum of Modern Art in New York and incontestably the father of Modernist curatorial studies. In many ways, Barr was an extraordinarily innovative curator, sanctioning groundbreaking exhibitions of Latin American modernism or reexamining the physical nature of the exhibition itself and the role of the catalog in elucidating issues beyond the formal. It was his ambition, for example, to provide analyses of modern art that were as scholarly as academic studies of earlier work. But despite his exposure to debates on the nature of social cause in art (particularly during his travels to Soviet Russia), his writing largely overlooked this particular kind of historical specificity. By attending to stylistic concerns above all others, Barr produced what is now commonplace in catalog essays—a curatorial history constructed outside political or social issues. In effect, he retrospectively validated certain sectors of the Modernist aesthetic at the expense of others. While he read the abstract symbolism of Paul Gauguin, for example, as a progenitor of German Expressionism, he omitted from his historical equation the activist realism of Gustave Courbet and Honoré Daumier.

The dualistic modern art that Barr proposed—an art predicated either on abstract, rationalist tendencies or on dreamlike, romantic sensibilities—virtually forced contradictory elements into agreement in broadly defined and vigorously defended dialectical categories and movements. Barr's reading was fundamentally motivated by his belief in the exhaustion of "representational" art and, consequently, in the autonomy of art from social conditions. Ultimately, his hermetic style of organizing exhibitions preempted the notion that one purpose of the art exhibition could be to analyze the relationship between society and the cultural artifacts it produces and sanctions. What is most problematic about Barr's still-prevalent model is that it rarely considers the audience or the social imperatives for art; it presumes that such issues as patronage and the social temperature at both the art's creation and reception are somehow irrelevant to the institutional interests of the art world. But the museum is not just a place to preserve beautiful objects; it is also a space where the relics and events of history can be juxtaposed in order to allow access to a range of social and cultural meanings.

Over the past decade, the narrow ideological basis of art history, criticism, and curatorial practice has shown definite signs of expanding. For one, the nature of history writing itself, the historiography of art history and history in general, has come under intense scrutiny. Such interrogations into the discipline of history—from the French historian Michel Foucault's influential analysis of the relationship between knowledge, ideology, and power to the emergence in the United States of community or identity-based history projects—have served as important catalysts in the transgression of traditional historical methodologies. The colonized, the working classes, people of color, women, gay men, and lesbians are now writing their own histories, more or less independently of the hierarchies of the academic patrimony. Such enterprises as subalternist, gay and lesbian, race, and feminist studies, the history workshop movement in Europe and the United States (which sponsors the publication of local history pamphlets and workshops on the oral history of working-class people), have brought together academics, activists, and workers to change the social agenda of history. Indeed, as Barbara Kruger and Phil Mariani have pointed out, it is these projects that have cogently demonstrated the inability of "conventional methods of historical analysis—which create polarities or tend to choose the most 'dramatic' movement or end in the typical trajectory of linearity—[to] . . . excavate and disentangle all the voices" that constitute any historical moment (Kruger and Mariani, 1989).

The strides made by these critical reevaluations of the historian's practice have, to one degree or another, trickled down to art history. Since the mid-1970s in the United States and Europe, a number of influential cultural journals (e.g., *Block, October, Representations,* and *Screen*) have challenged, mostly through poststructural theoretical methods, the conception of art history and art, film, and literary criticism as ideologically neutral disciplines. Yet, the question of difference and who was entitled to speak for whom was less rigorously examined. Building on the innovations and consciousness-raising of feminism and the civil rights movement, however, other art historians and critics (such as Gerald Davis, Ann Gibson, Lucy R. Lippard, Eugene Metcalf, Linda Nochlin, Griselda Pollock, Richard Powell, Abigail Solomon-Godeau, Lisa Tickner, Jonathan Wein-

berg, and Judith Wilson) have attempted over the past three decades to include the possibility of difference—to allow those voices marginalized by official history to speak, to be analyzed, and to be heard.

Visual artists have also helped to create an art-world environment conducive to recent theoretical advances in feminist, gay and lesbian, and race studies. Looking to these theoretical models as well as to the aesthetic innovations of the 1960s and 1970s—including Pop art, Minimalism, conceptual art, post-Minimalism, and 1970s feminist art—socially minded conceptual artists such as Hans Haacke, Jenny Holzer, Kruger, Adrian Piper, Carrie Mae Weems, and Fred Wilson have produced radical and theoretically rigorous work that has examined the relationship between culture, politics, and the institutions of culture. Their work has engaged questions and strategies central to the recent revisionist debates around art-historical, critical, and museological practices: the relationship between representation and ideology and representation and power; the appropriation of mass-media strategies; the challenging of the white, male, upper-class hegemony of art and art history; the role of community; the validation of gender, sexuality, and race as legitimate issues in art; the deconstruction of patronage; and the conservative institutional values of the museum.

The area of identity politics, in particular, has pushed the envelope of art-historical revisionism. The politics of identity—a subject central to much so-called political art of the past two decades—both magnifies the methodological limitations of art history and suggests important models for transcending these limitations. Because the issue of racial, ethnic, national, and sexual identities stirs up a torrent of emotions about difference, power, and entitlement, questions concerning identity are often charged with feelings of resistance, anxiety, and even outright bigotry. The issue of race is a significant case in point. It is clear that certain aspects of deconstructive theory have played an important role in elucidating the mechanisms and effects of racism. The recent critiques of "essentialism," for example, have been useful for African-American intellectuals and others concerned with challenging outmoded notions of identity that have imposed, from both the inside and the outside, what bell hooks has called "a narrow, constricting notion of blackness" (hooks, 1990).

But many of prejudices that beset African Americans in the cultural "mainstream," for example, also plague the various disciplines of critical theory: the tendency to ignore cultural producers of color, the impulse to reduce racist behavior or representations to intellectual abstractions, and most important, the inability to engage in any substantive degree of self-inquiry or to question one's own absolute authority to speak. As hooks has observed, in order for "radical postmodernist thinking" to have a transformative impact, it must make a critical break with the notion of "'authority' as 'mastery over.'" This break must not simply be a rhetorical device, she argues, but must be reflected in the "habits of being," including styles of writing as well as chosen subject matter. "Third world nationals, elites, and white critics who passively absorb white supremacist thinking," she concludes, "are not likely to produce liberatory theory that will challenge racist domination, or promote a breakdown in traditional ways of seeing and thinking about reality, ways of constructing aesthetic theory and practice."

The art historian and the curator, driven as they are by the ideological and disciplinary need to construct tidy categories and movements, face a significant challenge in meeting this goal of refashioning an aesthetic theory motivated by difference rather than unity and bias. Few curators or art historians challenge the "mythic" nature, to reinscribe Barthes, of their disciplines—the unquestioned ease by which the messy paradoxes of our lives and of our culture are repressed within the art-historical, critical, or curatorial narrative. It is precisely these parodoxes and differences that need to be foregrounded—a methodological exchange, to paraphrase Cornel West, of the monolithic with the diverse, the abstract with the concrete, the universal with the specific—if new and more socially responsible interpretive practices are to emerge. While the need to systematize and homogenize diverse and often disparate objects and ideas can appear to enhance the didactic role of the museum, the art journal, and the art-history professor, such avoidance of difference also distorts meaning, fosters stereotypes, and engenders a false sense of aesthetic and intellectual unity. In an increasingly diverse and global society, it is the challenge of the art historian, critic, and curator to be self-critical as well as to find or create methodologies for exposing the myths of our time and for exploring the meaningful variances that resonate in the interaction between people and culture and culture and politics.

BIBLIOGRAPHY

Barthes, Roland. *Mythologies.* Translated by Annette Lavers. New York, 1972.

Berger, Maurice, ed. *Modern Art and Society: An Anthology of Social and Multicultural Readings.* New York, 1994.

Bhabha, Homi K. *The Location of Culture.* London and New York, 1994.

The Block Reader in Visual Culture. London and New York, 1996.

Clark, T. J. "Clement Greenberg's Theory of Art." In *Pollock and After: The Critical Debate,* edited by Francis Frascina. New York, 1985.

Ferguson, Russell, Martha Gever, Trinh T. Minh-ha, and Cornel West, eds. *Out There: Marginalization and Contemporary Cultures.* Cambridge, Mass., 1990.

Foucault, Michel. *The Archaeology of Knowledge.* Translated by A. M. Sheridan Smith. New York, 1972.

Greenberg, Clement. "Avant-Garde and Kitsch." In *Art and Culture: Critical Essays,* pp. 3–21. Boston, 1961.

hooks, bell. *Yearning: Race, Gender, and Cultural Politics,* Boston, 1990.

Kruger, Barbara, and Phil Mariani, eds. *Remaking History.* Seattle, 1989.

Lippard, Lucy R. *Mixed Blessings: New Art in a Multicultural America.* New York, 1990.

Owens, Craig. *Beyond Recognition: Representation, Power, and Culture.* Edited by Scott Bryson, Barbara Kruger, Lynne Tillman, and Jane Weinstock. Berkeley, 1993.

Rutherford, Jonathan, ed. *Identity: Community, Culture, Difference.* London, 1990.

Wallis, Brian, ed. *Art after Modernism: Rethinking Representation.* New York, 1984.

West, Cornel. "A Matter of Life and Death." *October* 61 (Summer 1992): 20–27.

MAURICE BERGER

Politicized Art

The French public savored a bumper crop of pears throughout the 1830s. The artist and publisher Charles Philipon was largely responsible for this fecundity, through the innumerable caricatures he presented of King Louis-Philippe as a dowdy fruit in the pages of *La caricature* and *Le charivari.* Philipon's most famous spoof appeared in 1831: in a series of four drawings titled *Les Poires,* he metamorphosed the sovereign's face from a solemn, jowly chap into a ridiculous, scowling pear. It was a brilliant artistic turn, and an ingenious linguistic one, too: the appellation was also slang for "simpleton."

This image was an instant hit on the streets, and Philipon's journals kept refining the idea: the persona French liberty sits and frets, her foot clenched in a chain attached to a massive pear; pear trees are irrigated by blood; typographic pears spell out the terms of repressive government edicts; pears are symbolically castrated or guillotined. A particularly robust sign, these permutations considerably rankled the powers that be. Not surprisingly, Philipon was prosecuted six times for publishing various caricatures, and twice convicted.

Philipon was part of an elaborate minuet of regulation and transgression performed between French governmental functionaries on the one hand, and artists and their publishers on the other. Such pas de deux regularly took place from 1820 until 1881—the number of participants overall was immense, including Philipon's renowned colleague Honoré Daumier—because drawings were subject to official censorship at various junctures during this period, whereas words were not. In a largely illiterate society, the power of images was thus duly acknowledged. While the specific partners may change over time and space, the following general principle pertains: whenever and wherever the realms of art and politics intersect, a *danse macabre* of some sort frequently plays out.

In the past, artists' dependence on the patronage of leaders of church and state sometimes led to even more subtle forms of resistance. Consider *Don Manuel Osorio Manrique de Zuñiga* by the court painter Francisco José de Goya (ca.1788). At first glance, it is the tender portrait of a young boy, the embodiment of innocence. But it contains an ominous quality as well: the boy holds a string that tethers the leg of a magpie, while three wide-eyed cats lurk close by. The child may appear to be guileless, but he is, in fact, complicit. Moreover, the bird holds a card in its beak that bears Goya's name, dramatizing the risks and restrictions of his professional life.

Artists in our own time, at least those in the West, are seldom so indirect. They have adopted a more "in-your-face" attitude as the twentieth century has unfolded, often frankly confronting their leaders and directly addressing political and social issues. The resulting disputes confirm Michel Foucault's observation about "perpetual spirals of power and pleasure" (Foucault, 1980, p. 45): there are thrills to be had both in challenging and in exercising authority, in being either a provocateur or a police officer.

The following discussion will focus primarily on the late nineteenth and the twentieth century. *Art* and *artists* will be construed in the widest possible sense, and examples will be drawn from a variety of creative fields. In many instances, the material in question self-consciously confronts significant social and political questions. But artists' intentions are merely one factor in a complex equation of critical response that includes aspects of production as well as reception. Even those artists who aim to stay above the fray are sometimes swept along with the tide of controversy.

It is not uncommon for contemporary artists to transgress boundaries. They dissipate the distinctions between time-honored categories, melding together what cultural prescriptions traditionally have kept apart. Since the advent of modernism, artists have been blending what anthropologist Mary Douglas designates as "natural categories," binary classifications of experience such as masculine and feminine, public and private, sacred and profane, which every society sustains in some form. In this regard, many artists no longer fit the Marxian view of them as handmaidens of the ruling class, transmitting dominant ideologies and perpetuating systems of economic (or even gender or racial) stratification; they instead commonly disturb the presumptions of everyday life.

When an artist fiddles with revered taxonomies, there is often hell to pay. Jean-Baptiste Carpeaux discovered this when he produced a sculptural group for the facade of the new Paris Opéra. *La Danse* (1865–1869) featured a cluster of frenzied female dancers surrounding a *génie de la danse*. The central figure is sexually ambiguous, bearing the slim body of a male youth capped by a female face. S/he became the lightning rod for a heated controversy that included extensive debate in periodicals of the day, defacement with a bottle of ink, and even an order of banishment issued by Napoleon III.

The sculptor Constantin Brancusi precipitated something similar with *Princess X* (1916). In one respect it resembles the classic pose of a madonna, her enshrouded head tilted reverentially. But it also unmistakably resembles a set of male genitalia, the penis gracefully arched over the scrotum. The salon president had it removed from the Salon des Indépendants in 1920, preempting the possibility of adverse public response or even police action.

All the cast members, along with the producer of the play *The God of Vengeance* (penned by Sholem Asch, 1910), were arrested and charged with obscenity, immorality, and indecency after a New York production in 1922. This is the tale of Yankel, who operates a brothel in the basement while he maintains a "wholesome" atmosphere for his wife and chaste daughter, Rivkele, upstairs. Sacred and profane, public and private are strictly segregated—until Rivkele falls in love with the prostitute Manke.

Today, many artists blur the distinctions between natural categories. The photographer Andres Serrano's notoriety was established by *Piss Christ* (1987), when he placed a plastic crucifix in a jar of his own urine. Whereas many people were repulsed by the idea of mixing sacred and profane, one canny reviewer shifted the figure/ground perspective: instead of the crucifix being despoiled, perhaps more importantly the urine was being sanctified. Nevertheless, politicians condemned Serrano on the floor of the U.S. Congress, he received death threats, and others claimed his work was an example of the inappropriate use of taxpayers' money, channeled through the National Endowment for the Arts (NEA).

The widespread protests against Martin Scorsese's film *The Last Temptation of Christ* (1988) and Salman Rushdie's novel *The Satanic Verses* (1988) have similar origins. In both, major religious figures were demystified by focusing on their humanity alongside their divinity. But to the fundamentalist mind, this was an unbearable assault on received wisdom.

Protection of natural categories, and intolerance of their combination or violation, are at the base of a significant portion of modern-day controversies about art. Feminist performance artists Karen Finley and Annie Sprinkle transgress social expectations of femininity, the self, and the proper display of the body in public: they use "earthy" language, vault from persona to persona, and reveal intimate parts of their bodies and their functions. Each has been roundly condemned, as have many gay and lesbian artists: they elicit criticism by candidly including who they are in their creations, for the mere fact of their choice of partners automatically unnerves people wedded to conventional notions of what is appropriately masculine and feminine. Art makes homosexuality visible and tangible, as with the homoerotic photographs of Robert Mapplethorpe.

An artwork that demonstrates the hazards of boundary crossings was a 1988 portrait of the late Chicago mayor Harold Washington, created by School of the Art Institute of Chicago (SAIC) student David Nelson. Nelson unflatteringly presented Washington seminude, outfitted only in women's underwear. This white art student symbolically emasculated a revered African-American politician, recalling archaic measures of controlling "uppity niggers" such as lynching. In one of the most sensational contemporary bids to quash expression, several Chicago aldermen marched to SAIC and, with the support of police, "arrested" the painting.

Beyond the adverse response to what is, in essence, coloring outside of approved lines, it is clear that addressing certain hot-button issues in practically any manner can provoke controversy. The most important of these topics are race, religion, patriotism, gender, and sex. Because the United States is a complex, heterogeneous society—and one that experiences a great deal of social change—people hold a wide range of opinions on these subjects. Many works of art incorporating them are therefore destined to offend someone.

Race remains, in Gunnar Myrdal's notable 1944 phrase, "an American dilemma," and artistic representations of it an important flash point. Religious depictions also easily inflame passions, as Serrano, Scorsese, Rushdie, and many others can attest. Indeed, religion and politics become the warp and woof of many public conflicts, so that when either spiritual or secular officials feel threatened by what they view or hear, they pull out all the stops to protect both their doctrines and their institutions.

Patriotism may seem passé in many quarters at present, but it can be quickly mobilized when central social values appear to be threatened. Self-named artist-provocateur Dread Scott discovered this when he displayed his mixed-media installation *What Is the Proper Way to Display a U.S. Flag?* in *A/Part of the Whole*, an SAIC-sponsored exhibition showcasing the work of minority students in 1989. The work consisted of three parts: a photocollage of students burning the U.S. flag in various parts of the world; a shelf with a blank book for comments; and a flag on the floor. The piece seemed to invite viewers to step on the flag, although the book could in fact be reached without doing so.

Many people were scandalized and expressed their outrage in a variety of ways. Some entered the gallery, removed the flag from the floor, ceremoniously folded it, and placed it on the shelf, turning this into a truly interactive piece (gallery personnel or supporters of the artist would then restore it to its original position). Thousands more turned out for public rallies, and political opportunists at every level—local, state, and national—sensed the opening to polish up their nationalistic credentials and to enhance their own positions. There was also considerable congressional support for a constitutional amendment to safeguard this symbol. Artworks seldom generate fireworks of such magnitude and luster. But whenever artists skewer the performance or integrity of politicians, they are likely to find their work tossed around in a political game where they are up against more powerful, much more savvy opponents.

Sex and gender are the final hot-button issues. In fact, some observers claim that they are the most important ones, arguing that a "sex panic" has commenced in the late twentieth century. While there is truth to this assertion, it masks several important points. First, the anxiety over candid depictions of sexuality is long-standing and broadly expressed, from the papal decree that Michelangelo's nudes on the ceiling of the Sistine Chapel be covered with loincloths soon after they were completed, to the similar alterations ordered by cemetery administrators in Paris regarding the male genitalia on Jacob Epstein's sphinxlike memorial to Oscar Wilde (1909–1912).

Second, as we have seen, other issues commonly kindle controversy as well. It is myopic and exclusionary to focus solely on gender and sex. Finally, many of the disputes over culture can only artificially be confined to one category of event. Rushdie was condemned because of his religious transgression, yes, but an additional consideration was that he fictionally characterized the wives of Muḥammad as prostitutes. Nelson's portrait of Harold Washington drew charges of racism, certainly, but some of the monikers attached to the work—including "the African Queen"—also recognize its allusions to transvestism and homosexuality. Few "pure cases" of violation exist.

Having said this, once critics started to sound the alarm over the depiction of sexual issues in the late 1980s, they indeed found it difficult to remove their fingers from the panic button. Feminist, gay, and lesbian artists have become particular targets, especially as they reflect the current debate over sex roles in the United States and elsewhere.

Although the primary emphasis up to this point has been on the artistic content of artworks that have become controversial, more specific attention must be paid to their denouncers. A 1957 study by philosopher Richard McKeon and his associates clarifies a key point: in order for constraints to be placed on expression, not only must there be the sense that values have been violated, but power must also be mobilized to do something about it. Outrage that is not backed up by action subsides into undirected anger; power that is not guided by principles disintegrates into diffuse and arbitrary force.

The concept of moral entrepreneurs, which was developed by sociologist Howard S. Becker to describe individuals who are profoundly unsettled by something and contrive to stamp it out—by legislative measures or other restrictive means—is obviously relevant here. Girolamo Savonarola, who staged "Bonfires of Vanities" in late fifteenth-century Florence, "antifilth" campaigner Anthony Comstock, who attempted to regulate everything from fine-art reproductions to birth control information in late nineteenth-century New York, and a panoply of contemporary crusaders are all examples of ideologues or absolutists who inflexibly embrace conventional rules and understandings, and are unable to abide ideas and representations that challenge them. Those moral crusaders who establish a lasting name for themselves are those who successfully couple values with power in a distinctive fashion.

Donald Wildmon, leader of the American Family Association, has done just that. He has parlayed his anxieties over what he perceives to be "anti-Christian biases" in contemporary culture into a multimillion-dollar industry sustaining radio shows, publications, and direct action. Yet, it is important to note that absolutists exist on the other end of the political spectrum as well. With the evolution of identity politics—people united on the basis of common ancestry or other ascribed characteristics, behaviors, or shared interests—so-called progressive individuals and groups on the political left sometimes also act in a heavy-handed, dictatorial way against cultural forms they feel compromise their sense of themselves and the world. For example, a female writing instructor successfully pressured administrators at a branch of Penn State University in 1991 to remove a reproduction of Goya's classic painting *Naked Maja* from the classroom wall where it had hung for years; she found teaching in the room a form of "sexual harassment."

In many instances such actions are aimed at influencing market or curatorial decisions, not legislation. These groups are typically so disenfranchised, or distrustful of governmental regulation, that they are less likely to view the government as an ally than are some groups on the right. The political waters have recently become so murky, however, that classifications such as "left" and "right" have been drained of much of their meaning. For example, how to classify law professor Catharine MacKinnon and writer Andrea Dworkin? They claim to be working for women's rights, but many other feminists distance themselves from the pair because of their puritanical notions and their attempts to enact laws restricting sexual expression. Rather than a horizontal continuum of political sentiments ranging from right to left, perhaps the measure we should use now is more horseshoe-shaped: the ends contain the absolutists of either stripe, the rounded middle admits of flexible plurality with a greater threshold for difference and change.

Those who hold elected offices have become important players in these battles. The Republican Jesse Helms of North Carolina, one of the most tireless critics of contemporary culture in the U.S. Senate, is clearly an accomplished practitioner of the politics of diversion. Helms targets symbolic issues while his constituents languish under the burden of tangible problems such as high infant mortality rates, low wages, and a seriously deficient educational system.

A related issue is the social construction of acceptability. In other words, work that is tolerated or even venerated in one time and place can be vilified in another. The work itself does not change. But audiences, and the values, experiences, and beliefs they carry with them, vary widely. The range of reactions accorded the Mapplethorpe retrospective *The Perfect Moment*, which toured the United States from 1988 through 1990, is a prime example.

The exhibit was a critical and popular success when it was mounted in Philadelphia and Chicago. It ran aground, however, when it was scheduled to open at Washington, D.C.'s Corcoran Gallery: the director canceled it, fearing that the conjunction of sexually charged images and an overheated congressional debate regarding public support of the arts had made it too hot to handle. It traveled to Hartford and Berkeley with little commotion, but encountered a substantial challenge when it reached Cincinnati. There, long-established moral entrepreneurs and their governmental allies tried to draw a moral line in the sand: in a uniquely vigorous alliance of values and power, they brought obscenity charges against the Cincinnati Contemporary Arts Center and its director (both were subsequently acquitted).

By the time the show reached its conclusion in Boston, public sentiment had changed—or at the very least, its supporters had learned how to become proactive. Neighboring institutions installed a number of "solidarity shows" on the body and censorship; the local public television affiliate broadcast some of Mapplethorpe's most controversial images; and gay and arts activists far outnumbered opposing demonstrators at the opening. Supporters had significantly transformed the context of reception.

In fact, we can talk of cycles of reception: work may fall in and out of favor as social attitudes shift. This lies at the heart of the *Naked Maja* controversy: peering through a late twentieth-century feminist lens, the college instructor shifted the work out of the canon and into the realm of sexist, degrading portrayals of women.

In conclusion, three important preconditions heighten the likelihood for art to become politicized and controversy to erupt. First, controversy is more likely when a community has already become fractured by conflict, public morale is low, and polarization and alienation are high. At these times, art can crystallize problems and present a visible target for people to vent their frustrations on. Second, the probability of conflict over art is enlarged when the legitimacy or effectiveness of governmental leaders is being questioned. Emotions are closer to the surface then, and defenses more likely to be rallied. Third, controversy is common when art is presented in public places or when it is publicly funded. Public display widens the audience and therefore the likelihood that divergent points of view will clash. Government monies always come with the string of accountability attached to them—just ask Goya.

[*See also* Law *and* Art, *article on* Censorship.]

BIBLIOGRAPHY

Becker, Howard S. *Outsiders: Studies in the Sociology of Deviance.* New York, 1963.

Childs, Elizabeth, ed. *Suspended Licenses: Essays in the History of Censorship and the Visual Arts.* Seattle, 1997.

de Grazia, Edward. *Girls Lean Back Everywhere: The Law of Obscenity and the Assault on Genius.* New York, 1992.

Douglas, Mary. *Natural Symbols: Explorations in Cosmology.* New York, 1973.

Dubin, Steven C. *Bureaucratizing the Muse: Public Funds and the Cultural Worker.* Chicago, 1987.

Dubin, Steven C. *Arresting Images: Impolitic Art and Uncivil Actions.* London and New York, 1992.

Dubin, Steven C. "Art's Enemies: Censors to the Right of Me, Censors to the Left of Me." *New Art Examiner* 21 (March 1994): 26–31.

Foucault, Michel. *The History of Sexuality,* vol. 1, *An Introduction.* Translated by Robert Hurley. New York, 1980.

Goldstein, Robert Justin. *Censorship of Political Caricature in Nineteenth-Century France.* Kent, Ohio, 1989.

Jansen, Sue Curry. *Censorship: The Knot That Binds Power and Knowledge.* New York and Oxford, 1991.

MacKinnon, Catharine A. *Only Words.* Cambridge, Mass., 1993.

McKeon, Richard, Robert K. Merton, and Walter Gellhorn. *The Freedom to Read: Perspective and Program.* New York, 1957.

Shikes, Ralph E. *The Indignant Eye: The Artist as Social Critic in Prints and Drawings from the Fifteenth Century to Picasso.* Boston, 1969.

Strossen, Nadine. *Defending Pornography: Free Speech, Sex, and the Fight for Women's Rights.* New York, 1995.

STEVEN C. DUBIN

Aestheticized Politics

Culture can be conceived as a dynamic in modern political systems, and in the case of fascism this relation is magnified. Fascism, which came to dominate Italy following Benito Mussolini's rise to power in 1922, and engulfed Germany with Adolf Hitler's seizure of power in 1933, is a form of politics in which aesthetic issues permeate all aspects of society. Thus, the political, economic, and cultural realms cannot be considered separately when discussing fascist societies. Analyzing the "palingenetic" dimension of fascism, the historian Roger Griffin has demonstrated that fascism's

> thrust towards a *new* type of society means that it builds rhetorically on the cultural achievements attributed to former, more "glorious" or healthy eras in national history only to invoke the regenerative ethos which is the prerequisite for national rebirth, and not to suggest socio-political models to be duplicated in a literal minded restoration of the past.   (Griffin, 1991, p. 47)

The historian Emilio Gentile has reached similar conclusions, claiming that references to ancient Rome in Italian fascist discourses were

> reconciled, without notable contradiction, with other elements of fascism that were more strictly futurist, such as its activism, its cult of youth and sport, the heroic ideal of adventure, and above all the will to experience the new continuity in action projected toward the future, without reactionary nostalgia for an ideal of past perfection to be restored.   (Gentile, 1994)

Thus, fascism's palingenetic, totalitarian, and nationalist aspirations allowed this ideology to address both the past and the future by proclaiming the present to be decadent and therefore in need of regenerative cultural renewal (Sternhell, 1994).

Both Griffin and the historian George L. Mosse (Mosse, 1988) have analyzed fascism's restriction of its critique of modernism to those elements considered to be degenerative, and its palingenetic drive to create a new (hence modern) type of society. Griffin has drawn on this theory to critique those who would describe Nazi ideology and its aesthetics as ultraconservative, restorationist, and antimodern. Indeed, in the period before Hitler's coming to power the Nazi leadership remained divided over whether avant-garde art should be condemned as antithetical to fascism's racial ideals or considered revelatory of an emerging National Socialist ethos. Before Joseph Goebbels took up his position as Reich Minister for Public Enlightenment and Propaganda in 1933, he and Nazi ideologue Alfred Rosenberg waged a pitched battle over the relative merits of the Expressionist painter (and party member) Emile Nolde, the Expressionist sculptor Ernst Barlach, and the architecture of such figures as Walter Gropius. Thus, Goebbels, in his semiautobiographical novel *Michael: Diary of a German Destiny* (1931), condemned the Jews as an "anti-race" and "poisonous bacillus" on the body of the German *Volk* even as he proclaimed the Expressionism of Vincent van Gogh an embodiment of the "Christian Socialist" ideals of "a new Germany" (Goebbels, cited in Griffin, 1995, pp. 119–120). After the Nazi rise to power, Goebbels signaled his continued support of Expressionism by appointing the young Expressionist painter Hans Weidemann as one of his chief aides in the propaganda ministry (Lane, 1968, p. 177). For Goebbels, Weidemann, and their followers, Nolde's art supposedly combined references to Nordic regionalism with an expressive style reflective of the youthful vigor of the new Germany; by contrast, Rosenberg, in the *Völkischer Beobachter* (July 1933), declared Nolde's Expressionist technique "negroid, impious, raw, and lacking in any genuine inner power" (Rosenberg, cited in Berman, 1992, p. 58). To successively overcome contemporary decadence, Rosenberg instructed artists to emulate the "ideal of beauty" created by the Greeks and such "Nordic" artists as Sandro Botticelli and Hans Holbein.

This debate was settled in 1934 when Hitler, speaking at a Nazi party congress, indicated that he did not consider Expressionism in keeping with Nazi ideals; in response, Goebbels initiated the suppression of modern painting that culminated in the inaugural *Entartete Kunst* (Degenerate Art) exhibition in July 1937 (the exhibition circulated throughout Germany and Austria between 1937 and 1941). Organized into nine groups that were listed in the *Guide to the Exhibition of Degenerate Art,* works by Nolde dominated a section representing the art promoted by "Jewish art dealers" to falsely symbolize "German religiosity"; other sections focused on themes of political and artistic "anarchy" (represented by George Grosz and Otto Dix), social decay, loss of "racial consciousness" through endorsement of "Negro" art (Expressionist sculpture), art that celebrated physical and mental deformity, and "the endless supply of Jewish trash" as a prelude to the "height of degeneracy," namely, the nonobjective art of Cubists and German Constructivists (Hinz, 1979, p. 40). The Nazi association of avant-garde art with spiritual and biological degeneracy was indebted to the writings of the architect and racial theorist Paul Schultze-Naumburg, whose 1928 volume *Kunst und Rasse* (Art and Race) juxtaposed examples of Expressionist art with photographs of diseased and deformed people to suggest the models for such pictorial innovations. In short, German Expressionism was now identified with a state of degenerative decay to be overcome by the palingenetic turn to other art forms.

The *Entartete Kunst* exhibit was counterbalanced by the July 1937 opening of the first *Great German Art* exhibition in the newly opened House of German Art, co-designed in a modernized, neoclassical style by architect Paul Ludwig Troost and Hitler. This exhibition—the first of a series of exhibitions from 1937 to 1941—celebrated painting and sculpture patterned after Greek sculpture, eighteenth-century neoclassicism, and nineteenth-century realism. The Nazi counterpart to degenerate avant-gardism was an aestheticized conception of the human body, patterned after those societies and cultures deemed to be morally, hence physically, regenerative (Mosse, 1988, 1991). Sculptural images of the ideal male, such as Arno Breker's *Readiness* (1937), were modeled after works of Greek classical sculpture such as Polykleitos's *Spear Bearer* (450–420 BCE; Mosse, 1991). Whereas the political role of the male as national symbol required dynamic images of nude warriors and contemporaneous soldiers, woman's role as childbearer was emphasized in images of peasant fecundity such as Jürgen Wegener's *Thanksgiving* (*Great German Art* exhibition, 1943; Adam, 1992, pp. 140–155). Resolutely heterosexual, such imagery captured what Mosse has termed the bourgeois ideal of "beauty without sensuality," conducive to the Nazi official emphasis on marriage, the family, chastity, and self-discipline (Mosse, 1991). In the realm of architecture the Nazi aesthetic was much more eclectic, however; every building type alluded to an idealized "Nordic" or "Aryan" past in order to reconnect German society to a healthy cultural precedent that would point the way to a regenerated future. Thus, the modernized neoclassicism of Albert Speer's party congress buildings in Nuremberg, like Clemens Klotz's neo-Romanesque, quasi-military schools at Ordensburgen, or the thatched-roof buildings that served as hotels along the ultramodern autobahn, were meant to suggest the continuity uniting a racially pure German past to modern society under the Nazi dictatorship (Lane, pp. 185–200).

The concept of palingenesis, furthermore, is also germane to the study of Italian fascist aesthetics, and this is especially evident in critical reassessments of Walter Benjamin's evaluation of the relation of Italian Futurism to fascism, as developed in his important essay "The Work of Art in the Age of Mechanical Reproduction" (1936). In this

POLITICS AND AESTHETICS: Fascism. David Alfaro Siqueiros, *Echo of a Scream* (1937), enamel on wood, 48 × 36 in. (121.9 × 91.4 cm); Museum of Modern Art, New York (Gift of Edward M. M. Warburg). (Photograph copyright 1998 by the Museum of Modern Art; used by permission.)

text, Benjamin highlights the fascist championing of the retrograde aesthetics of *l'art pour l'art*, and contrasts that aesthetic model with the emancipatory role signaled by new aesthetic forms such as cinema and montage. By cloaking politics in auratic rituals and aestheticized rhetoric, fascism sought to impose passivity on the working class and simultaneously uphold the bourgeois order that was threatened by the class-based politics of the newly created urban proletariat. Aesthetic notions of an unchanging, organic unity, whose self-referential value transcends the historical circumstances from which it emerged, were transferred to the political realm to justify fascism. Thus, in Benjamin's view, fascism sought to overcome sociopolitical dissension under capitalism by imposing an aestheticized ideology on the fragmented and pluralistic flux of contemporary society. To quote the historian Russell Berman, Benjamin regarded "the closed order of the organic work of art," as "a deception that imposes an enervated passivity on the bourgeois recipient"; in contrast, Benjamin valorized "fragmentary, open genres: the German Trauerspiel of the baroque as well as the avant-gardist valorisation of montage," whose negation of aesthetic closure precluded any passive response on the part of what was invariably a collective audience. "In place of the auratic art work, with its isolated and pacified recipient lost in contemplation," asserts Berman, Benjamin proposed "a postauratic model that would convene a collective recipient (the 'masses') endowed with an active and critical character" (Berman, 1989, pp. 38–39). Thus, Benjamin valorized those art movements—Dada and Surrealism—that consciously attacked bourgeois notions of artistic autonomy, while aligning Futurism with the aestheticized discourse of the Italian fascists (Benjamin, 1969, p. 254).

Benjamin's analysis of fascist aesthetics has inspired contemporary scholars not only to explore the implications of his model for an analysis of literary texts written by fascism's apologists, but also to counter that the aestheticization of politics can serve a variety of political positions, and to question Benjamin's restriction of fascist aestheticization to nostalgic models of organic unity and completion (Jay, 1993, pp. 71–83). In this regard, fascism's relation to Futurism has undergone revision, for a number of historians have argued that Futurist aesthetics embraced the very fragmentary, dynamic, and collage-based aesthetic that Benjamin would associate with antifascism and proletarian emancipation. Thus, the literary historian Andrew Hewitt claims that Benjamin's relation of fascism's politics to "falsified principles of harmony, organic totality, and unity," serving to mask a society typified by class conflict and social fragmentation, cannot explain the fascist embrace of Futurism, because that movement trumpeted the very conflict fascism supposedly sought to cover up (Hewitt, 1993, pp. 134–137). Turning Benjamin's construct on its head, Hewitt argues that Futurist proponents of fascism thought contemporary society was in a condition of ossification, organic closure, and stasis, and thus in need of rejuvenation through violence. By calling for "the ontologization of struggle as both an aesthetic and a political principle," the Futurist wished to reinvigorate a culture subsumed in the very organicist metaphors Benjamin would identify with the fascist project. "Whereas a more traditional analysis might stress the occultation and aesthetic resolution of class struggle under fascism," states Hewitt, "it might be more valuable to speak instead of the generation of depotentialized areas of struggle within the aesthetic," that is, the transference of the dynamism of class conflict to a realm of avant-gardism.

Hewitt's critique of more "traditional" analyses, which, like Benjamin's, would relate Futurism to "the classical aesthetic of harmonization" and "the false reconciliation of social conflict," finds an echo in Mosse's essay "The Political Culture of Futurism" (Mosse, 1993, pp. 91–105). Here, Mosse analyzes two forms of nationalism, one that "apparently slowed down change and restrained the onslaught of modernity" by "condemning all that was rootless and that refused to pay respect to ancient and medieval traditions" and "another kind of nationalism, exemplified by the futurists in their acceptance of modernity." Paradoxically, "while most twentieth-century nationalism retained its role as an immutable and unchanging force, the repository of eternal and unchanging truth," Futurism exemplified a "different nationalism" that exalted violence, condemned the past, and declared modern technology to be "a vital symbol" of renewed national energies. The human correlate to this cult of violence and technological dynamism was the "so-called new man—symbolic both of modernity and the power of the nation." Thus, for Mosse, fascism in Italy embraced two aesthetics, one dynamic and fully accepting of technology, the other more traditional in its desire to anchor nationalism in the organicist and auratic aestheticism outlined by Benjamin.

Here, Mosse raises a key issue, that is, whether fascism, though resolutely modern in its aim to create a new society, nevertheless subsumed the auratic vestiges of past traditions within its aesthetic. In this manner, the organic and dynamic could coexist within a political aesthetic premised on regeneration. This Janus-faced aesthetic serves to confirm the palingenetic model developed by Griffin. It also bears directly on Italian fascist and Nazi approaches to architecture, both of which sought to impose an "auratic" and "theatrical" experience on the beholder. For instance, Hitler's favorite architect, Albert Speer, created architectural spaces designed for theatrical events on a scale that consciously evoked the sublime (Mosse, 1975). "We must build as large as today's technical possibilities permit," declared Hitler in 1939, for "we must build for eternity" (cited in Lane, pp. 189–190). To meet Hitler's demands, Speer constructed a gigantic *Zeppelinfeld* at Nuremberg, designed to accommodate more than one hundred thousand people at mass rallies and parades. In order to build for eternity, Speer developed a "theory of ruin value": the buildings of the Third Reich were designed so as to ensure that they would resemble Greek and Roman models after centuries or even thousands of years had passed (Hinz, p. 197). In effect, Hitler and Speer collapsed the past, present, and future life of Germany under the Nazis into an image of the monumental and sublime, modeled after their aestheticized experience of the ruins of ancient Rome and Athens.

In Italy itself, Mussolini's aestheticized politics led him to employ his favorite architect, Marcello Piacentini, in the creation of a modern Imperial Rome. In his 31 December 1925 address, "La nuòva Róma," Mussolini declared that Rome must appear "vast, ordered, mighty, as it was in the days of the first empire of Augustus"; to achieve that goal he would "open space around the Augusteo [the mausoleum of Augustus], the Theatre Marcellus, the Campidoglio, the Pantheon." "Everything from the periods of decadence must disappear," Mussolini declared, and "the majestic temples of Christian Rome" would likewise be liberated from "parasitic and profane constructions," for "the millenary monuments of our history must tower like giants in a necessary solitude" (Mussolini, cited in Etlin, 1991, pp. 391–392). In short, Mussolini wished to convert architecture into a form of monumental sculpture, isolated for veneration by the masses; moreover, through the creation in 1932 of the vast Vìa dell'Impèro, which connected the Colosseum to the monument to Victor Emmanuel II, Mussolini drew a symbolic connection between Roman imperial glory, the nineteenth-century unification of Italy, and fascism's imperial aspirations.

The use of historical references also has relevance for an evaluation of modernist architecture of the Italian rationalists or Gruppo Sette, composed of architects Adalberto Libera, Luigi Figini, Guido Frette, Sebastiano Larco, Gino Pollini, Carlo Enrico Rava, and Guiseppe Terragni. The historians Diane Ghirardo and Richard Etlin have attributed the conflation of traditionalist and modernist themes in the architecture of the Italian rationalists to Gruppo Sette's wholesale endorsement of fascist ideology. Thus, in contrast to Italian architectural historians who would cite the rationalists' embrace of the modernism of the French architect Le Corbusier as proof of their distance from fascist political aims, Ghirardo and Etlin demonstrate the integral relation of Italian rationalism to a fascist ideology that, in Ghirardo's words, vacillated "between an apparently adventurous modernism and a recalcitrant traditionalism" (Ghirardo, 1989). This conflation of modernist forms with references to Italy's past is even evident in the ground plan for Terragni's Casa del Fàscio in Como (1932–1936), which, according to Ghirardo, resembles that of the Palazzo Farnese in Rome. Ghirardo has also noted the rationalists' assimilation of Le Corbusier's authoritarian pronouncements in *Vers une architecture* (1923) to the fascist imposition of a corporate hierarchy *(gerarchìa)* on Italian society, while Etlin has charted Gruppo Sette's relation of Le Corbusier's stated interest in Greek classicism to the fascist doctrine of *mediterraneità*. By arguing that Le Corbusier was a modernist wedded to Mediterranean culture, the rationalists effectively countered claims that they favored internationalism over an indigenous Italian tradition, reflective of a "Latin" and imperial past. In this manner the rationalists could take their place alongside architectural advocates of *Romanità* and *latinità* in supporting an ideology that laid claim to the cultural legacy of Imperial Rome as a springboard to colonial conquest in Africa. "The cult of Romanness," to quote Emilio Gentile, served to justify "political action" and as such "was celebrated modernistically as a myth of action for the future" (Gentile, 1994).

In Italy, in contrast to the German situation after 1934, fascist aesthetics was heterogeneous in nature; that is, the messages of fascism were articulated across a spectrum of sensibility that ranged from various abstract trends through many versions of historicist and traditionalizing figuration. Nevertheless, a fascist aesthetics can be effectively defined, at a formal level, through the same characteristic structure of polarization that informs our study of fascist ideology. That is to say, fascist aesthetics, although revolutionary and modernist, comprised progressive and traditionalizing currents, and was both elitist and populist in its logic. It is important to note, furthermore, that fascist aesthetics brought together these opposed terms in such a way as to challenge, on the theoretical level, any simple parallelism between progressive aesthetics and utopian and revolutionary ideologies, on the one hand, and reactionary art and authoritarian politics, on the other. Indeed, the study of fascist aesthetics has helped to call into question a central precept in the theory of the avant-garde, according to which the concepts of modernism and fascism were generally seen as mutually exclusive.

BIBLIOGRAPHY

Adam, Peter. *Art of the Third Reich.* New York, 1992.

Adamson, Walter L. *Avant-Garde Florence: From Modernism to Fascism.* Cambridge, Mass., 1993.

Benjamin, Walter. "The Work of Art in the Age of Mechanical Reproduction." In *Illuminations,* edited by Hannah Arendt, translated by Harry Zohn, pp. 219–254. New York, 1969.

Berman, Russell A. *Modern Culture and Critical Theory: Art, Politics, and the Legacy of the Frankfurt School.* Madison, Wis., 1989.

Berman, Russell A. "German Primitivism/Primitive Germany." In *Fascism, Aesthetics, and Culture,* edited by Richard J. Golsan, pp. 56–66. Hanover, N.H., 1992.

Carroll, David. *French Literary Fascism: Nationalism, Anti-Semitism, and the Ideology of Culture.* Princeton, N.J., 1995.

Etlin, Richard A. *Modernism in Italian Architecture, 1890–1940.* Cambridge, Mass., 1991.

Gentile, Emilio. *Il culto del littorio: La sacrilizzazione délla politica nell'Itàlia fascista.* Rome, 1993.

Gentile, Emilio. "The Conquest of Modernity: From Modernist Nationalism to Fascism." *Modernism/Modernity* 1.3 (September 1994): 55–87.

Ghirardo, Diane. *Building New Communities: New Deal America and Fascist Italy.* Princeton, N.J., 1989.

Griffin, Roger. *The Nature of Fascism.* New York, 1991.

Griffin, Roger, ed. *Fascism.* New York and Oxford, 1995.

Hewitt, Andrew. *Fascist Modernism: Aesthetics, Politics, and the Avant-Garde.* Stanford, Calif., 1993.

Hinz, Berthold. *Art in the Third Reich.* Translated by Robert Kimber and Rita Kimber. New York, 1979.

Jay, Martin. *Force Fields: Between Intellectual History and Cultural Critique.* London and New York, 1993.

Lane, Barbara Miller. *Architecture and Politics in Germany, 1918–1945.* Cambridge, Mass., 1968.

Mosse, George L. *The Nationalization of the Masses.* New York, 1975.

Mosse, George L. *Nationalism and Sexuality: Middle-Class Morality and Sexual Norms in Modern Europe* (1985). 2d ed. Madison, Wis., 1988.

Mosse, George L. "Beauty without Sensuality/The Exhibition *Entertete Kunst.*" In *"Degenerate Art": The Fate of the Avant-Garde in Nazi Germany,* edited by Stephanie Barron, pp. 25–31. New York, 1991.

Mosse, George L. *Confronting the Nation: Jewish and Western Nationalism.* Hanover, N.H., 1993.

Sternhell, Zeev. *The Birth of Fascist Ideology: From Cultural Rebellion to Political Revolution* (1989). 2d ed. Translated by David Maisel. Princeton, N.J., 1994.

MARK ANTLIFF

AIDS, Aesthetics, and Activism

In the late 1980s, before the AIDS crisis was a decade old, a debate broke out over the uncertain role of the arts in the mobilization of cultural forces against the epidemic. It was never a formal scholarly debate: its participants were far too engaged (as many still are) in life-and-death struggles with the disease itself to simplify their dialectical moves into an intellectual game. Nevertheless, for the purposes of provocation, a critical distinction was drawn in 1987 between two movements emerging out of the conflicting cultural reactions to the epidemic. The authors of the distinction, gay art critics Douglas Crimp and Simon Watney, defined their movement as "cultural activism" by opposing it to "aestheticism." Cultural activism was not opposed to "aesthetics," however, because Crimp and Watney strove to defend certain philosophical views about the social function of art in accordance with their political theorization of the epidemic as a "crisis of representation." Whereas cultural activism with its revolutionary fervor looked forward to a radical reinvention of art as a social healing force, aestheticism with its transcendental impulse harked back to the "art-for-art's-sake" movement of the Wildean Belle Époque.

Background. In 1987, when the AIDS Coalition to Unleash Power (ACT UP) was formed in New York City, the militant objectives of the activists seemed momentously at odds with the memorializing projects of the aesthetes. Many gay artists and authors "acted up" at the time by producing AIDS-related works that addressed the crisis of representation in terms or images directly influenced by the debate. The debate itself became a subject for artistic meditation in the provocative installation "Let the Record Show . . ." (1987) at New York's New Museum of Contemporary Art. So aggressively did this work attack the political apathy behind the elegiac posturing of America in the "Age of AIDS" that its critical repercussions were soon felt beyond New York. By 1989, similar works were challenging gallerygoers in San Francisco, Los Angeles, Toronto, Montreal, London, Paris, and Berlin.

As the cultural vistas of the epidemic broaden with the increasing incidence of HIV-infection among heterosexual "risk groups"—for example, Hispanic, Asian, and African-American women—the aestheticism-activism debate is bound to resurface in communities far beyond the New York art world and in terms that complicate the oppositions originally experienced by white gay men (for whom the epidemic has tended to sink, of late, into the background of ordinary life). When AIDS educators in Thailand advertise the importance of safer sex to villagers by painting brightly colored condoms on the sides of elephants, is this an example of activist art practice? Should it be judged by the same aesthetic criteria as the cartoon-style condoms painted by New York graffiti artist Keith Haring? Although specific issues raised by the aestheticism-activism debate may not be relevant to all art produced in response to the epidemic, perhaps the international efforts to redefine and resolve the debate as its cultural implications expand will reveal its universal applicability to the problem of defining the social value of art.

Media pronouncements of an "AIDS Apocalypse" provided the background noise to the activism-aestheticism debate, stirring the activists especially to take aggressive stands on basic aesthetic issues ignored or glossed over in journalistic accounts of the epidemic as a "special crisis for the arts." The prejudicial representation of people with AIDS (PWAs) in the mainstream media generated heated discussions on the obligation of artists to become activists. The ancient issue of the truthfulness of images surfaced in an urgent new guise in the critical years 1985–87 when the politics of representation became a major concern for radicalized PWAs who strongly objected to being cast in the passive and intensely moralized role of "AIDS victims."

Certain ethical and epistemological issues long debated in university circles were now raised by plague anxiety to a level of more than academic interest. Is the pedagogical function of art more important than its "purely" aesthetic role? Does any clear criterion exist for distinguishing truthful images of reality from delusional misrepresentations? Can artists know what AIDS really is apart from its cultural metaphors or artistic signs? Should art be valued solely on the basis of its social impact? These were some of the questions that demanded to be addressed whenever the arts were recruited to join the war against AIDS or to create the "AIDS Renaissance" prophesied by the media.

Aestheticism. With the consoling notion of an artistic renaissance resulting from the epidemic came a renewed focus on artist-centered aesthetic issues. "The artist's choice to produce representational work always affects more than a single artist's career, going beyond . . . the walls on which an artist's work is displayed," proclaimed an activist flyer handed out to protest the opening of photographer Nicholas Nixon's "Pictures of People" exhibition at New York's Museum of Modern Art in 1988. The time-lapse design of Nixon's black-and-white portrait series seemed to critics to have the disquieting effect of turning people still living with AIDS into studies for a Still Life with AIDS. Much to his dismay, Nixon found himself figuring in activist diatribes as the archaesthete who had haughtily ignored his critics' counteraesthetic dictum: "Ultimately, representations affect those represented."

Many artists and authors sympathetic with Nixon's memorializing aims preferred not to engage in public disputes over the politics of representation. Their introspective focus was fixed primarily on the agonies of the creative process: how the task of representing AIDS affects those struggling to represent it. Were Nixon's images a painful documentary record of the artist's brave examination of the impact of the virus on the human body? Or was his show simply a high-art version of the "Before and After" diptych endlessly repeated in the media? The Wildean design of the diptych remains all too familiar: a beautiful face or figure on the nostalgic pre-AIDS side helplessly confronts its wrinkled and withered double on the postdiagnostic side—like Oscar Wilde's Dorian Gray confronting the image of his decadent inner self.

No artist-centered issue in the Western aesthetic tradition has provoked more agonized reflection during the AIDS crisis than the difficulty of reconciling two indispensable truisms concerning beauty. The first and no doubt more ancient of these, an idealistic promise that the combined beauties of nature and art may console the living in grievous times, has traditionally justified the creation of beautiful memorials for the dead. The second, its cynical counterdictum, thwarts the desire to memorialize by insisting that art can neither soften nor stop the relentless blows of death because all beauties in this world inevitably "come to dust."

Reflected in the design of the "Before and After" diptych is the teasing opposition of aesthetic idealism and apathetic cynicism always latent in elegy. Why offer beautiful words and music to the dead when death itself cannot hear "what vain art can reply"? This is an issue for all mourners, regardless of race, gender, sexuality, or serostatus. If frail memorials and frantic laments cannot stop death, might they not at least save lives? Should elegiac art not ally itself with epidemiology on the educational front? Or should it act as a polemical fuse, exploding the medical construct of the syndrome as a battle between faceless pathogens and failed immune systems? Medical knowledge has long been subject to aesthetic critique. "Physic himself must fade," as the English elegist Thomas Nashe lamented in 1592, for "All things to end are made."

The elegists of the new plague are haunted by an old Renaissance question: why should a ruinous disease prompt its sufferers (both the infected and the affected) to contemplate beautiful scenes, capture beautiful moments, construct beautiful monuments? To some, aesthetic compensation for loss seems too fragile an explanation for the prodigal expense of artistic spirit that has been lavished on memorializing the AIDS dead—who are no more lost, after all, than those who die of other causes. Even frailer, to others, is the classic pedagogical rationale for elegiac art: its usefulness as a moralizing mirror held up to the vanities of mortal corporeality. However earnestly Nixon may have conceived his photo series as a memento mori for people without AIDS, his critics were quick to point out that the sick and the stricken need no reminding from him (or from his romantic forerunner John Keats) that we all live in a bad ugly world where "Youth grows pale, and spectre-thin, and dies."

Adrienne Rich, in her 1987 elegy "In Memoriam," explains the aestheticization of AIDS as a therapeutic antidote to cynical despair. A PWA of her acquaintance was losing his lifelong delight in flowers, poetry, and music. To him, and to herself as his soul mate, she poses a devastating question about art as therapy: "How will culture cure you?" Despite the difficulty, if not failure, of elegists' efforts to transcend the ugliness and meanness of death, the aestheticizing drive that AIDS simultaneously frustrates and sustains must be gratefully acknowledged by the living as a prophetic yearning for the miraculous. Elegies such as "In Memoriam" ensure at least the preservation (if not the realization) of the dream of a *locus amoenus* where ancient fantasies of purgation and regeneration are mythically recollected.

Countering the cynical attitudes litanized by the media is a transcendental impulse that few AIDS elegists on the aesthetic side of the debate have resisted in their efforts to justify the momentous outpouring of literature and art concerned with the epidemic. Andrew Holleran, for instance, has shown how swiftly the gay male gaze can transform scenes of erotic dejection into visions of ecstatic joy through aesthetic refigurations of memory. Haunted by the shades of men who reveled in the lost world of 1971, he hails their successors at a bathhouse in 1983:

> They were as improbable and beautiful lying in their rooms in their Jockey shorts and towels as the gods Michael [a recently deceased PWA] had painted on his ceiling on Seventh Street—a burst of beauty, fantasy, art—in the midst of a nightmare reality. The thrill of homosexuality is finally an aesthetic thrill.   (1988)

More than an aesthetic thrill in the jaded Dorian Gray sense, this burst of beauty is a prophetic transport beyond the here and now into a Sistine Chapel afterlife where Michael (replacing Michelangelo) has endured martyrdom for the Religion of Art. However ironic its setting, the mystical intensity of Holleran's vision contrasts sharply with the media-hallowed mundanity of another aesthetic thrill: the dubious pleasure afforded by the Silver Lining fantasy that the arts are currently enjoying a miraculous rebirth because of the AIDS crisis.

Even if artists were to declare an end to the AIDS Renaissance, the hope of aesthetic transcendence would surely persist along with the fantasy of resurrection because of the clinical manifestations of the syndrome itself. AIDS does not simply debilitate. It disfigures. Despite the pharmaceutical industry's promise to restore the look of health to PWAs who drink the right "cocktail" of protease inhibitors, the epidemic still stirs up deep-seated religious wishes about the preservation and transfiguration of the flesh.

"The body becomes central," reflected Holleran's friend and fellow apologist for aestheticism, Edmund White, in 1987. "If art is to confront AIDS more honestly than the media have done," he argued, "it must begin in tact, avoid humor, and end in anger." Thus condensed into an Horatian epigram was the neoclassical argument for artistic truthfulness, high seriousness, creative self-restraint, tragic decorum, sensitivity to social proprieties. Horace could not have argued the case more succinctly—even if he had had White's pressing medical motive for doing so. Like the Stoic hero in a Roman tragedy who must face the predicted consequences of his fatal flaw but not give way to unseemly grief or rage, White grimly confessed to feeling "very alone with the disease": the isolation that it imposed on him because of its infectious character (or that he imposed on himself because of his good manners) was consolingly similar to the leave he had long ago taken from ordinary social life to follow the Parnassian route of the "solitary high arts."

It is hard not to hear an epitaph in his epigram. Here lies a gay outsider who began his literary career by turning closety tact into an exquisite prose style; avoided queeny humor and low camp in his lofty pursuit of artistic fame; and would inevitably end his life in anger at the vulgar misrepresentation of himself as just another poor plague victim. A decorous beginning, a serious middle, and a furious end: it is also hard not hear Aristotle's classic formula for the perfect tragic plot behind White's triple prescription for a dignified life with AIDS. Because this formula is also his aesthetic cure for AIDS hysteria, it seems to offer the diminishing arts community he addresses a nobly rational, perhaps even cathartic, way out of the AIDS tragedy chorally lamented by the media. The solitary high arts alone can purge the irrationality clogging up the channels of the popular mind.

In a spiritual sense, the muddle of the plague ceases for the oracular aesthete who can impose a tragic form on its maddening incertitudes. By bravely facing the terrible facts of the plague, White can give the lie to the simplistic myth of divine judgment that "explains" its origin to the masses; then, by heroically rising above his own sufferings, he can see with transfiguring (if not transcendent) clarity the whole design of the crisis from its hidden causes to its catastrophic effects. AIDS truly becomes for him a crisis in a neoclassical sense: a disastrous turning point in the hero's career when his rising action begins to fall, as fall it must, through righteous anger, desperate fury, and helpless rage, down to dusty death.

There is no humor in this solemn patterning of otherwise random agonies. Its form has to be clear because its function is moral clarification. Its appeal to Stoic fatalism has to be strong because its therapeutic strength lies in its demand for aesthetic detachment. But there also lies the tragic dilemma for White: his artistic prescription for a more honest (i.e., honorable as well as true-to-life) representation of AIDS compels him to organize its confusing vastness into a mimetic design that is surely no less fictional—despite tragedy's higher claims to aesthetic sophistication—than the vulgar mythologizations of the epidemic in the media. This design may well help White feel less alone with the disease by granting him the luxury of identification with tragic heroes: but how does it connect him to the multitudes of un-

heroic PWAs? Perhaps a shared appreciation of the moral truths revealed in the terrible beauty born of his tragic engagement with AIDS will bind the prophetic aesthete to the community of artists who share his anagnorisis. Perhaps, if pushed, they would attempt some philosophical defense of Keats's tautology about truth and beauty.

Activism. The activists scorned the neoclassical attitude of Stoic grief. If art is really to confront AIDS more honestly than the media have done, they rejoined, it must begin in anger—not end in it. "What will it take to make you angry?" was playwright Larry Kramer's incendiary refrain after the recitation of Centers for Disease Control statistics at the early meetings of ACT UP. His incessant questioning of the fantasy of the AIDS Renaissance ushered in what might be called the "Activist Reformation," a period of skeptical attack on the prevailing orthodoxies (medical, political, aesthetic) of the official AIDS world that climaxed in 1989 when ACT UP stormed the podium at the opening ceremonies of the Montreal International AIDS Conference. The activist demonstrations and art exhibitions at this critical collision of the AIDS establishment with its unorthodox opponents endeavored to shift concern away from artist-centered aesthetic issues toward the complex system of economic and political power relations in which the epidemic was being constructed to profit the institutions supposedly responsible for controlling or containing it.

The iconography of rage crackled with the satiric humor of ACT UP's graphic arts collective Gran Fury, which took its name not only from the driving emotion behind activist polemics but also from the make of car favored by the New York Police Department. The symbolic engine of heterosexism was wittily "queered" to drive home ACT UP's main political point that AIDS phobia was fueled by homophobia. Gran Fury's wit was a discordant concord of critical theory and street-level politics. "AID$ Now" proclaimed a poster from their 1988 campaign. Behind its forthright demand for more AIDS research funding lies a sly reference to Michel Foucault's theorization of disease as a "discourse" constructed by the financially empowered institutions of dominant culture.

The furiously comic work of Gran Fury ran counter to White's solemn decree that humor should be avoided because it "seems grotesquely inappropriate to the occasion." Why avoid humor when it can be used as a weapon against the false prophets and fascist profiteers of the official AIDS world? As for tact, that was merely a face-saving rhetorical strategy for presidents and belletrists. How could tact spark a revolution against the massive institutional forces mustered by the dominant culture to blame the crisis on already stigmatized minorities? Tact was just another word for closetry, complacency, self-censorship. Its consequences were spelled out in the activist slogan "Silence = Death." Fortified with desperate certainties and defiant rallying cries, ACT UP threw tact to the winds as it brashly picketed art openings, stopped rush-hour traffic, "zapped" television stations with surprise on-air protests, and rioted in savvy political overstatement.

If aestheticism was in bad odor among the activists, aesthetics was not. Far from ignoring or downplaying the aesthetic issues raised by their punchy poster campaigns ("demo graphics") or by their militant mourning rites ("die-ins"), the strategists of ACT UP advanced and articulated a counteraesthetics that justified their aggressive reaction to the AIDS Renaissance—which they saw as the self-congratulatory flip side of the AIDS Apocalypse.

Two basic principles of activist art theory may be inferred from the balanced negatives and affirmatives of Crimp's 1987 manifesto: "We don't need a cultural renaissance; we need cultural practices actively participating in the struggle against AIDS. We don't need to transcend the epidemic; we need to end it" (1988). First, the transcendental impulse of aestheticism must be countered by a practical focus on specific medical and social justice issues affecting those who struggle against AIDS in the here and now. Second, the process of activist art making must become primarily collective if it is to meet the enormous social and political challenges of the epidemic: in other words, a demanding "we" must replace the "I" hallowed by the Renaissance tradition of the lone creative genius, even as the preemptive "we" of the official AIDS world (like the "general public" of the media) must defer to the emerging authority of the sick. Implicit in these principles is a recommendation that the value of any AIDS-related cultural work be judged chiefly on the basis of its effectiveness in addressing the urgent needs of PWAs and their caregivers.

A stringent utilitarianism underlies the activist struggle to replace the production of passive "cultural commodities" (e.g., paintings auctioned at a benefit) with vital "cultural practices" that might alter the status quo to benefit the sick (e.g., protesting placebo trials). Activist insistence on "cultural interventions" to help the infected springs from moral outrage at the injustices of a culture hierarchically ordered by race, class, gender, sexuality, and health.

Aesthetic issues, from the activist viewpoint, cannot be divorced from the ethics of civil disobedience or the morality of holy warfare. Like their mortal foes, the televangelists, AIDS activists are inveterate moralists to whom notions such as aesthetic distance or transcendence make no sense. The street is their original pulpit, and the small screen their happy zapping ground. By reversing the homophobic messages of their doctrinal opponents, activist icon makers effectively define their mission as preaching to the perverted, the ritually shamed, the socially excluded. Thus, while activist art is designed to take on the immediate task of saving lives, its ultimate goal is the frankly apocalyptic telos of deliverance from evil. Considered from this angle, the activist critique of aestheticism has an intellectual history that predates the AIDS crisis: its philosophical origins surely lie in the schism between formalism and contextualism that has deeply divided artists, critics, and aesthetic theorists through much of the twentieth century.

According to the activists, art stored in museums is a passive bourgeois commodity, whereas art storming the battlements of public health is an active force for saving lives and salvaging society. The institutional theory of art expounded by Crimp in his activist manifesto reveals his allegiance to contextualism as a corrective approach to the formalist dismissal of ideological contents and social constraints in the definition and evaluation of art. If the activist drive to champion art or literature that strategically represents PWAs as an oppressed class ripe for insurgency (at least within the panoptical constraints of what Watney has called "the spectacle of AIDS") owes something to the decades-old momentum of the Marxist aesthetic tradition, a brisk current of which surfaced in the "Black is Beautiful" movement of the 1960s before flowing into the gay and women's liberation movements of the 1970s and thence into the angry turbulence of ACT UP. A Marxist contempt for the worship of religious or commercial icons must surely underlie the activist reflex to criticize to the point of excoriation the "ars longa, vita brevis" line spouted by the black-tie organizers of AIDS benefits.

If the Marxist critical impulse to dissolve art objects into the conflictual fluidity of their social contexts had any counterpart on the creative side in the 1980s, it might be found in the subversive disposability of Gran Fury's agitprop—words and images deliberately designed to work only within specific "zaps" or "actions"; to have no meaning apart from their ideological frameworks and political frays; and to mock by their very disappearance after the events that called them into being the formalist admiration for the immutability and autonomy of the artistic masterpiece. Marxist art practices must hasten the revolution. Activist art practices must advance the cure.

Aestheticism and Activism. Are advocates for the aesthetic transcendence of AIDS necessarily noncontextualists in their evaluation of art? Or do they only seem so from the polarizing standpoint of the activists? Have aestheticism and activism been falsely dichotomized in the debates over detachment and engagement? Or have they been pushed toward synthesis by the metamorphic pressures of the epidemic on the medical front? Has the fire of dialectical urgency cleared a middle ground for activists with aesthetic leanings and aesthetes with activist links?

Questions of this sort were left hanging at the end of the first decade of the epidemic. Now, as the possibility of a "magic bullet" cure seems increasingly tenuous, they are being asked again with fresh urgency by artists and critics whose works on AIDS are assessing the progress made on the cultural front following the decline of ACT UP and related groups in the early 1990s. Whether that decline is irreversible remains to be seen: it may be the result of the permanent thinning of the activist ranks as "the plague full swift runs by," or merely to a temporary exhaustion of their reserves of energizing anger.

In any case, the muting of the activist voice in the political arena does not mean that the aesthetes have won the day (or the debate) in the philosophical forum. Although art production on the activist side has noticeably dropped off since the heyday of Gran Fury, the contextualist principles of cultural activism have not been discarded: their academic promulgation has ensured that the repercussions of ACT UP are now felt in cultural contexts far broader and more diverse than the New York art circles that polemically equated silence with death.

Philosophical debates conducted over many years tend to lapse into the silence that equals tedium. So where is the activism-aestheticism debate headed if it is to remain vital and engaging? Will the aesthetes launch a kind of counter-reformation against the activists? Indications from the volatile worlds of the gallery and the theater suggest that aestheticism is indeed returning in the aftermath of ACT UP's war against the indulgences of the AIDS establishment. But it is no longer a simple "et in Arcadia ego" effort to meditate on death in the presence of beauty. The aestheticism of the 1990s has fortified itself against critical attack by absorbing and redeploying activist anger into a new elegiac project: the invention of queer anagoges. Like the saints of the Catholic Counter-Reformation, who float heavenward on clouds of glory in Baroque painting and sculpture, the martyrs of the Aesthetic Counter-Reformation are finding their way up into strange new heavens in dirigible-size AZT capsules, through magic video portals, and on libidinous angel's wings.

If the arts have hitherto failed to synthesize activist fire with aesthetic form, it has not been for lack of trying. The results have been bewildering, at times contradictory. Compare, for instance, the bleakly menacing poster "Enjoy AZT" by Vincent Gagliostro and Avram Finkelstein (1990) with the brightly monumental installation "One Day of AZT" by General Idea (1991). Both works gesture toward the same controversial subject, the therapeutic value of the antiviral drug zidovudine. Both are parodic in design: the poster copies the white wave image of the "Enjoy Coke" logo with the deadpan humor of Andy Warhol; the installation recalls the outsize objects of Pop art in the style of Claes Oldenburg. An academic taste for postmodern archness mixed with political cheek would certainly find satisfaction in both.

Yet, how differently their respective artists treat the same unlikely material—as if they were setting up a textbook contrast between activist engagement and aesthetic detachment. Whereas the poster was published anonymously for distribution at demos during the San Francisco AIDS conference, the installation was launched on a widely publicized tour of major contemporary art galleries in Europe and North America. Whereas the poster shouted its sarcas-

tic slogan ("We Volunteer—They Profiteer") against an enemy establishment, the ruefully ironic installation celebrated the promise of pharmaceutical magic bulletry by displaying five giant AZT capsules on the gallery floor. Once the poster had zapped out its ideological critique, it was stapled over or torn down and trashed. Once the installation had finished its tour, it was bought by the National Gallery of Canada and permanently displayed in a white alcovelike space for meditating on the impact of the epidemic on the arts. Now that two members of General Idea have died of AIDS, their giant capsules look like space-age sarcophagi launched on a shuttle mission to paradise.

No art has been more engaged in the ecumenical project to link the solace of the AIDS Renaissance with the zeal of the ACT UP Reformation than drama, which was also the first art to envision the birth of activism as a mythical rupturing of gay aesthetic culture. That was in 1984, when Larry Kramer's political antimasque *The Normal Heart* opened at the Public Theater in New York. Nine years later, with audiences still reeling from the steady blows of Kramer's rhetoric, the masque of heavenly beauty bursts onto the scene at the climactic end of *Millennium Approaches*, part 1 of Tony Kushner's two-part mystery play *Angels in America*. Along with its sequel, *Perestroika*, which opened on Broadway in 1994, this "Gay Fantasia on National Themes" is at once an aesthete's vast elaboration of the "Before and After" diptych and an activist's visionary explosion of the media fantasy of the AIDS Apocalypse.

The aesthete's urge to impose a unifying structure on the confusing vastness of the plague is expressed early in part 1 by Lou, a burned-out leftie who seeks solace in aesthetic meditation after his lover Prior is diagnosed with AIDS. To Lou's Edmund Whitish argument that "it should be the questions and shape of a life, its total complexity gathered, arranged, and considered, which matters in the end," Prior responds with a sardonic putdown: "I like this; very Zen; it's . . . reassuringly incomprehensible and useless. We who are about to die salute you."

Just when the split between the lovers threatens to divide the play's restless philosophical current into a repudiation of aesthetic solace on Lou's side, and a drift toward activist martyrdom on Prior's, Kushner sends an angel—the ultimate embodiment of the Aesthetic Counter-Reformation—crashing through the ceiling of their old bedroom into the confusion of their debate. The angel comes "with a great blaze of triumphal music" to celebrate what looks like the imminent victory of transcendental aestheticism over the ugliness of the plague. Surely, now the discord between aestheticism and activism will be resolved through divine intervention.

In part 2, however, Prior discovers that the angel cannot cure him with illuminated books, Baroque trumpet concerti, or flaming Michelangelesque tableaux. Ironically, it is the PWA who is summoned into heaven to save the angelic hierarchs from the plague of mortality, the "Virus of Time." By firing Prior up with prophetic zeal, restoring his defunct libido, and liberating him from the mundane prison of the status quo, the angel reveals herself as the driving force behind the sexual revolution in America. Far from floating above the action as a decorative image in a traditional elegiac allegory, she plunges into it with ferocious energy as if she were an ACT UP zapper with wings. She knows how to fan the flames of rage. Prior must wrestle with her (literally) as a flying contradiction *in actu* as well as *in verbo*—a beautiful yet terrible synthesis of activist spunk and aesthetic spirituality—as we must too, it seems, unflinchingly, as long as the old debate over form and context renews itself in our prayers and protests.

[*See also* Gay Aesthetics.]

BIBLIOGRAPHY

Crimp, Douglas. "AIDS: Cultural Analysis/Cultural Activism." In *AIDS: Cultural Analysis/Cultural Activism,* edited by Douglas Crimp, pp. 3–16. Cambridge, Mass., 1988.

Crimp, Douglas. "Mourning and Militancy." *October* 51 (Winter 1989): 3–18.

Crimp, Douglas, and Adam Rolston. *AIDS demo graphics.* Seattle, 1990.

Holleran, Andrew. *Ground Zero.* New York, 1988.

Kramer, Larry. *The Normal Heart.* New York, 1985.

Kramer, Larry. *Reports from the Holocaust.* New York, 1989.

Kushner, Tony. *Angels in America,* part 1, *Millennium Approaches.* London, 1992.

Miller, James, ed. *Fluid Exchanges: Artists and Critics in the AIDS Crisis.* Toronto, 1992.

Miller, James. "Raising Spirits: The Arts Transfigure the AIDS Crisis." In *1995 Medical and Health Annual: Encyclopaedia Britiannica,* pp. 124–149. Chicago, 1995.

Murphy, Timothy, and Suzanne Poirier, eds. *Writing AIDS: Gay Literature, Language, and Analysis.* New York, 1993.

Rich, Adrienne. "In Memoriam." In *Poets for Life: Seventy-Six Poets Respond to AIDS,* edited by Michael Klein, p. 202. New York, 1989.

Watney, Simon. *Policing Desire: Pornography, AIDS, and the Media.* Minneapolis, 1987.

White, Edmund. "Esthetics and Loss." *Artforum* 25.5 (January 1987): 68–71.

JAMES MILLER

POP ART. [*To explore the twentieth-century art movement known as Pop art, this entry comprises two essays:*
An Overview
Aesthetics of Andy Warhol
The first essay explains the general history and legacy of Pop art. The second essay, although focused exclusively on Warhol, examines the philosophical and aesthetic significance of Pop art. For related discussion, see Comics; *and* Popular Culture.]

An Overview

For thirty years scholars have asked, "What is Pop art?" Art historians and theorists pose the question in different voices while addressing many of the same issues. The historian wants to know how the art world initially received Pop art, how Pop artists responded to or rejected the artists who preceded them, what historiographic shape emerged in subsequent years. The theorist conceptualizes Pop as implicated in a larger cultural condition—for many theorists, that of late capitalism. While these two strategies are not mutually exclusive, they are distinct: historians emphasize details of artistic careers and critical responses, whereas theoretical practitioners draw out broad synthetic structures.

One of the shared beliefs of those who identify with modernism is that the public fails to understand the avant-garde of its time; true to form, bewilderment was the primary reaction to Pop art. In 1962, Peter Selz hosted "A Symposium on Pop Art" at the Museum of Modern Art in New York. Selz did not ask his five invited critics "to come up with a definition of Pop art at this stage," but simply "to present prepared papers and engage in a lively discussion." Nonetheless, almost every one of the participants began with the question, "Is it art?," taking the rhetorical opportunity to define art themselves. Curator Henry Geldzahler found the question ridiculous, asserting that Marcel Duchamp had demonstrated that artists define what art is by their actions. Hilton Kramer answered that Pop is art, but only by default, by virtue of not being anything else. Leo Steinberg too answered in the affirmative, reserving the right to adjust his assessment of Pop art in time, but provisionally defining art as whatever produces "a new shudder" in the audience; he determined that Pop art met this requirement.

If Pop art followed certain patterns of Modernist art's introduction to the art world and, eventually, the art-historical canon, it also notably disappointed these expectations, breaking from Modernist art history. In a new twist on the avant-garde posture of the traditional rejection of new objects and forms of expression, the question for these critics was not quite "Is it *good* art?" but "Is it art at all?" This new question centered on Pop's "realism"—not whether artists had ineffectually or insufficiently aestheticized the real object, but whether they had aestheticized it at all. An earlier avant-garde realist painter, such as Gustave Courbet, might be accused of making ugly paintings, but because he took his subjects from live models and natural scenes, there was no possibility of avoiding some kind of translation from three dimensions into two. Pop artists such as Roy Lichtenstein, however, chose two-dimensional subjects from the mass media and depicted them two-dimensionally, often using a technique seemingly borrowed from those same media and from commercial art. The question becomes not good or bad, or beautiful or ugly, but art object or mass-culture object. That is, had the Pop artist failed to adequately "transform" the model? Once the viewers of Pop art decide that even Lichtenstein's paintings of comic book subjects are high art, and not the low culture they superfi-

POP ART: Overview. Jasper Johns, *Painting with Two Balls* (1960), encaustic and collage on canvas with objects (three panels), 65 × 54 in. (165.1 × 137.2 cm); collection of the artist. (Copyright by Jasper Johns/Licensed by VAGA, New York; photograph courtesy of Leo Castelli Gallery, New York; used by permission.)

cially resemble, the question "Is it art?" seemed to be (at least provisionally) answered.

Despite the fact that Pop art holds its own relationship with high and low as constantly shifting, critics and public agreed they could, indeed, exchange the one question for another: "What is Pop art?" The inquiry seemed so pressing in the 1960s that G. H. Swenson used it as the title of the two important interviews he conducted with the leading Pop artists. Seen against contemporary art history, this posing of the question appears ironic. When, in the 1940s, artists such as Willem de Kooning, Jackson Pollock, and Mark Rothko began to work in their well-known styles, art critics immediately recognized that they were making a new kind of art, one that furthered rather than imitated the achievements of European abstraction. Critics basically agreed which artists belonged to this group (although not necessarily who was major or minor) and what they were doing, but not what to call them. In response to a 1945 exhibit, *A Problem for Critics,* prominent art critics were invited to suggest a variety of names for this new American art (one of them being "the New American Art"). But whereas Abstract Expressionism's problem was always to name properly a recognizable artistic phenomenon, the

problem with Pop art was to define the strange thing with a familiar name. It was immediately understood who was a Pop artist, which artworks were Pop; but today one can still look directly at this uncannily familiar art, and yet remain unsure of its meaning: "What is it?" Here, then, is a double irony. Abstract Expressionism, superficially so turgid and murky, so personal and idiosyncratic, has become clearly legible for us—in both form and content, and even in its sociopolitical "subtext." Pop art, almost always crisp and clean formally, apparently public or common in its meaning, so literally legible, is enduringly difficult to read.

The term *Pop art* was invented by an English critic in the late 1950s. Although we commonly think of this movement as emerging around 1962 under the supervision of American artists such as Andy Warhol, the term was first used by Lawrence Alloway in 1957. Alloway initially conceived of Pop art, not as the latest avant-garde art movement, but as a shorthand reference to increasingly dominant modes and monuments of popular culture—television, magazines, film, advertising. He characterized this early usage as Pop's "anthropological" phase. In the hands of British artists such as those in the Independent Group, which met at London's Institute for Contemporary Art in the mid-1950s, *Pop art* came to indicate their art practice as well as their source material. Most notably, the artist Richard Hamilton, who worked in collage and painting, created art with a startlingly banal content: British and American consumer life. His famous collage *What Is It That Makes Today's Homes So Different, So Appealing?* was shocking not only for the images it used—vacuum cleaners, swimsuits, bomb blasts—but also for its cut-and-paste aesthetic, which underlined the art's parodic, rather than sublime, aspirations.

Between 1960 and 1962, in New York City, several young artists seemed to find their signature styles within a few short months of each other, initially appearing in group exhibitions, then having their first solo exhibitions one after the other. The key word for these early group exhibitions of Pop art was *new,* in exhibitions such as *New Forms, New Media* of 1960, and *New Realists* of 1962. Critics were initially shocked by the subject matter of these paintings—in fact, by the fact that they *had* a subject matter. Appearing after approximately fifteen years during which all "serious" American painting was abstract, this new way of painting was defiantly referential, if not representational—hence, their tentative descriptions as the "New Realists." Looking more closely, the content of that newness made itself felt almost immediately: comic books, consumer products, canned soup, hamburgers. Finally, however, the style of the newness came into its own: Pop art took consumer, image-based culture not only as its subject but also as its style. Benday dots, billboard airbrushing, and multiple, collectively produced silkscreens constituted the form as well as the content of Pop art. According to Harold Rosenberg, the public debut of the Pop artists, creating a break in both content and form, hit New York and particularly the Abstract Expressionists "like an earthquake."

By the end of 1962, all of the major Pop figures had held solo exhibitions and begun to establish their positions publicly and in the art world. While it has been debated to what extent the artists were aware of each other's work, it seemed clear from the beginning that their art held something in common. Who were these artists? Retrospectively, the first histories of Pop art in the late 1960s and 1970s used differing criteria to determine membership. Lucy R. Lippard admits to only five truly "hard-core" Pop artists: Warhol, Lichtenstein, Claes Oldenburg, James Rosenquist, and Tom Wesselman. She identifies these artists as sharing a hard-edge, commercial style (with exceptions made for Oldenburg's sensual idiosyncrasies). But this kind of formal approach to Pop art (also taken by Robert Rosenblum) seems primarily designed to insert Pop smoothly into the historical chain of contemporary art, linking Pop art to hard-edge abstraction before and minimalism afterward. As with any approach that places the art-historical end before the individual art object, this feels forced. More commonly, the list of Pop artists included not only the most successful figures listed above, but lesser-known artists from both New York and California ("West Coast Pop") such as Jim Dine, Mel Ramos, George Segal, Robert Indiana, Billy Al Bengston, Ed Ruscha, Joe Goode, Wayne Thiebaud, and Marisol. The list could easily be longer still.

Pop art hit the ground running. During 1960–1962, not only did the major figures find their signature styles and appear in their first gallery shows, they were introduced to a broader public in magazines like *Time* and *Life*. From that point forward, critics and historians have debated endlessly the attitude of Pop art toward popular culture: does high art critique or celebrate mass culture? Regardless of the position one takes, it is clear that Pop art turned the attention of high art (and its audience) toward popular culture. The nature of that attention—aesthetic appreciation, semiotic game playing, or social investigation—often shifted. Conversely, Pop art turned the attention of the mass audience toward high art. That is, Pop art took popular culture as its subject matter, but also engaged the popular more directly in drawing attention from a mass audience, appearing to be predicated, in fact, on notions of career, commercialism, success, attention, fame, celebrity. Two new figures, each a topic of critical debate, were created in the 1960s: the mass audience as art audience and the artist as a combination of movie star and professional.

A 1963 article in *Time* magazine, "Pop Art: Cult of the Commonplace," designed to introduce its broad national readership to Pop art, described its viewers as "decorous teenage girls" from prestigious private schools giggling at the Guggenheim Museum. Similarly, the art critic Max Kozloff, in an early review of Pop art, referred to its supporters as "vulgarians" and "bobby soxers." Obviously, there was

something new about this audience, something at least as seemingly popular as the art. This new audience of high schoolers and bobby soxers was young, much like the audience for movies, Top 40 music, and comic books—the products of popular culture. It was also an audience that cut across class boundaries, including traditional art audiences, the nouveaux riches, and average American consumers. Lichtenstein, Oldenburg, and Warhol discussed this issue in a 1964 interview with Bruce Glaser. The artists disagreed whether Pop appeals to a larger audience—it comes as no surprise that Warhol insisted that it does. Oldenburg argued that the audience, having heard that the art was about Coca-Cola, was often disappointed to find it so much like traditional art. Warhol, in a rare assertive moment, stated that people loved it because the subject matter was familiar: "it looks like something they know and see every day." This contrast reflects a difference in the two artists' work. Although Oldenburg's art is often humorous, his artistic engagement with paint and issues of material sensuality is much less ironic than Warhol's seemingly affectless recreation of flat, commercial art appearances.

In 1965 the critic Sidney Tillim went so far as to characterize the whole of Pop art by its relationship with its audience. Rather than falsely credit the artists with a ponderous social critique, Tillim located the importance of Pop art in its reception. The entire American culture here adheres to the model of the rebellious and perhaps fun-loving adolescent, rather than the more sophisticated adult or the more innocent child: "We are witnessing . . . a release from the conventions, values and consciousness of a culture. . . . grown men and women have thrown off the trappings of 'respectability,' i.e., the serious side of culture, auctioned off their collections of Abstract Expressionism and rolled out the American flag" (Tillim, 1965). Tillim describes a change in a certain group of established art collectors who, together with the "bobby soxers," formed "the new audience."

As Pop art has become the object of art history, by simple virtue of historical distance, a line of inquiry related to the sociologically based criticism of Kozloff, William Seitz, and Tillim has appeared. Economic and social histories by scholars such as Christin J. Mamiya detail not only the reception of Pop art but its context of American consumer society. Mamiya in particular finds that changes in the way the United States did business between 1959 and 1964—the new pervasiveness of mass marketing and a corporate mentality—established a "climate" conducive to the inventions and interests of Pop art. Subsequent art-historical accounts have developed more specific topics, such as the gendered role of the consumer as woman in the 1950s.

The historian William Seitz had made a similar point in 1963, saying of Pop art, "New manifestations now appear with such regularity and rapidity that the professional or collector who wants to remain in style must switch quickly"

(Seitz, 1963). Seitz concentrated on the effects on the rhythm of artistic creation itself rather than on its audience. Even in comparing the relatively recent career development of artist Jasper Johns during the mid-1950s to that of the Pop artists during the early 1960s, Seitz found a tremendous acceleration in both the success and the obsolescence of artists. He was concerned that the notion of the avant-garde or newness itself had been co-opted by advertising and thus rendered invalid for the art world (to which it is nevertheless returned, tainted with the language and expectations of the commercial world). The artist becomes a celebrity marketing a commodity. As Robert Indiana said in 1964, "It isn't the Popster's fault that the A-Ers [Abstract Expressionists] fought and won the bloody Battle of the Public-Press-Pantheon."

Indiana's seemingly flippant statement reveals an important change in American art that began with Abstract Expressionism and was completely realized by Pop art. Many critics noted at the end of the 1950s that the recent market success and public acceptance of Abstract Expressionism invalidated its avant-garde status. As "advanced" art gained critical and public acceptance more and more quickly (almost immediately in the case of Pop art), the time during which it was possible to consider an art movement avant-garde grew shorter and shorter, placing the future viability of any avant-garde in doubt. This concept of the "death of the avant-garde" responds to a change in art's social position. By altering the artist's traditional relationship to society, this "death" creates uncertainty as to the very nature of artists: if they are no longer to act as figures of passionate alienation, what is their new role?

For some, the answer was for the artist to act as a professional. Warhol, Rosenquist, and others were successful commercial artists before becoming fine artists. Warhol claimed he made the switch in part because he realized he could make more money in the latter role; he thus brought his commercial motivation to an area where it had previously been taboo. Although fine artists had often worked in illustration and other fields, for the first time these "day jobs" were not merely despised necessities for artists, but in fact clearly influenced their artistic practices. In a subtle way, Warhol serves as a model for the contemporary artist Barbara Kruger, who proudly displays rather than hides her credential of years spent working at *Mademoiselle* magazine.

If popular culture fascinated the Pop artists, they were equally absorbed by and equally ambivalent toward high art and its history. Most of the Pop artists struggled with and often rejected the very concept of artistic expression, as embodied primarily in Abstract Expressionism, the dominant mode of American painting during the 1940s and 1950s. In large part they addressed the exhausted, even debased, version on public offer toward the end of the 1950s—thousands of second-rate, second-generation Abstract Expressionist "expressive" but unoriginal paintings. Allan

Kaprow, who taught with Lichtenstein and was much admired by him, said of these painters that they all threw their inner beings onto the white canvas, but unfortunately the canvases (and by extension their inner beings) appeared to be almost identical. As Warhol facetiously asked Swenson, "How many painters are there? Millions of painters and all pretty good." Warhol may have been alluding to a Stanford Research Institute study (cited by Stanley Kunitz in the 1962 Pop symposium) that found that there were "as many painters in this country as hunters," 50 million altogether (counting the "do it yourself practitioners," as Kunitz calls them). These comments reflect a certain careerist bent, the concept of newly professional artists pressured by a flooding of the market. But they also bespeak another function for art in contemporary America: that of avocation, or even hobby, and a concomitant disgust with the reality of the ideal of individual expression for all, including the most unimaginative.

The Pop artists also critique the possibility of a sustained use of any kind of Expressionist mark, in the sense that it cannot be performed both consistently *and* authentically. Lichtenstein's representations of heroically scaled abstract brushstrokes, carefully crafted from benday dots, make this point. Warhol also developed a critique of the authenticity of expression in his work, as well as in these often-cited remarks: "I think everybody should be a machine . . . you do the same thing every time. You do it over and over again. . . . You should be able to be an Abstract-Expressionist next week, or a Pop artist, or a realist, without feeling that you've given up something." Given a painter's ability to switch from style to style, Warhol questions the need to "mean" even a style of painting that appears to be extremely expressive. Existential anguish becomes simply another pose to adopt and discard. Warhol most famously, but the other Pop artists as well, has the ironic sense that the artist is motivated by self-interest and exterior concerns, rather than helplessly impelled by the need to reveal a coherent, interior identity.

Pop art was heralded as the quintessentially American art, as was Abstract Expressionism only years before: how to reconcile these two positions? A social historian would assert that the difference between the two practices is only the facet of American life that they choose to represent or express. The point can be made that to communicate the idea of impersonality or uniformity, so prevalent in the United States of the 1960s, one must paint in that way, just as to convey the idea of expressive individuality, the hallmark of the 1950s, one must paint in a different way. The counterintuitive swerves into the ridiculous only when we insist that Abstract Expressionism and Pop art are equally expressive. Yet, we would do well to remember that both Lichtenstein and Oldenburg state that their styles merely *seem* impersonal, that what they are painting in fact, is their own "fantasies"—a word that indicates that they work from their private imaginations as much as from parodied stereotypes.

Both of these facets of Pop art—its involvement in popular culture and with the traditional aspirations of high art—share a common ground in the manipulation of a preexisting discourse. We have seen that Pop art plays with the difference between popular culture and fine art, as well as the difference between the sincere, original, or expressive mark, and that which is calculated, imitative, or constructed. Beginning in the early 1970s, a new approach to art history, semiotics, addressed both of these concerns. Semiotics, initially theorized by Charles Sanders Peirce and Ferdinand de Saussure, is a method of understanding the process of representation through linguistic terms such as *signifier* (the representational symbol), *referent* (the thing represented), and *signified* (the meaning, or contextual interpretation).

In the book accompanying his 1974 retrospective of Pop art at the Whitney Museum, Alloway defined the concerns and message of Pop art as lying in four directions. Primary among these concerns is Pop art's function as a sign. This point had first appeared in Swenson's "The New American 'Sign Painters'" (1962). At that time, semiotics was not prevalent as an art-historical method of interpretation; and Swenson, for the most part, speaks of signs in the literal, material sense, largely in reference to Indiana, who painted words and numbers within bold, geometric designs. Nevertheless, Swenson does argue that many Pop art paintings recreate the tension between handmade and mass-produced signs and symbols, an issue previously recognized by earlier twentieth-century artists. Selz also made reference to this tradition by including photographs of gas stations and roadside stores by Walker Evans in the slides shown at the Pop art symposium.

The Culture of Consumption (1970) stands as one of the first works to use semiotic theory deliberately in order to understand Pop art. Jean Baudrillard asserts that by painting numbers, symbols, and labels the Pop artists realize what is important about consumer culture: not the objects, but their trademarks or signs. We are not interested in the Brillo pad inside the Brillo box any more than we are interested in what is "inside" Marilyn Monroe. The traditional hierarchy of signifier and signified is leveled into a play of simulation. Baudrillard takes the familiar idea of resemblance (present in early commentary on Pop art) to an extreme, depicting a complex (yet shallow) culture composed solely of images, or "simulacra"—Guy Debord's famous "society of the spectacle."

Baudrillard's Pop artist (who most resembles Warhol) performs a Duchampian trick: he acts like an artist and therefore he is an artist. He copies or simulates a cultural type—the artist (or, as suggested earlier, the movie star or professional)—rather than occupying the role naturally and without any attendant irony, "feeling" it like earlier avant-garde artists. The artist of late capitalism, like the manufacturer of late capitalism, is not satisfying needs but creating them, producing objects that seemingly answer a new demand, the demand created by the object itself. In a parody of early capitalism and early modernism, these new objects appear to improve an older, obsolescent objects. But for most theorists, the notion of modernist progress lies moribund at this point in history, and Pop art is no more a genuine improvement on Abstract Expressionism than a white telephone is on a black one, or an old detergent (or scouring pad) packaged in a new box. Clement Greenberg, champion of Modernist painting, suggested that despite its rapid canonization, Pop art was at best frivolous, at worst simply bad art; the Pop artists themselves leave us room to wonder, not only about their own status, but about the very logic of modernism itself.

The semiotician and cultural critic Umberto Eco began his 1971 commentary on Pop art with the standard question: "What is pop art?" Eco's argument focuses on the shifting nature of the messages and references running between high and low culture. He asserts that Pop artists borrow from mass-media sources, while the mass media in turn borrow back, and are inflected by both the formal conventions and the knowing tenor of Pop art itself. Eco also touches on an anxiety present in the very earliest commentary on Pop art: the reverse of the implication that Pop art may not be art is that things we do not consider to be art may indeed be Pop art (such as a can of soup). Once Pop imagery begins to circulate between realms of high and low culture, the divisions seem to disappear. In fact, in Alloway's chronology of Pop art, the third and final phase is the co-optation of "Pop art" by common language, and our commensurate ability to see horror movies and romance comics as already being Pop art, or kitsch. Eco ends his essay not by answering his original question but by obviating it, in a sense. He concludes that there is no such thing as purely highbrow or lowbrow culture: all are equally part of the metadiscourse of bourgeois society.

In a 1980 essay, the critic Roland Barthes ends by asking his own particular question: "What do you mean?" Much like Eco, Barthes emphasizes that Pop art upsets the relationship between the signifier (in this case, the art object), the referent (the mass-culture source object), and the signified (the meaning, what is inside or behind). It is the last, he maintains, that Pop art at least pretends to destroy. According to Barthes, Pop art critiques the social and cultural world through the simultaneous "banal conformity" of the image to the thing represented, and a cold distance lying between them. By flatly posing the object to the viewer, Pop art returns the spectator—clueless—to the perennial question of meaning in art.

The closeness between the interpretations of Baudrillard, a sociologist, and Eco and Barthes, language theorists, shows that Pop, more than any other kind of art, has the ca-

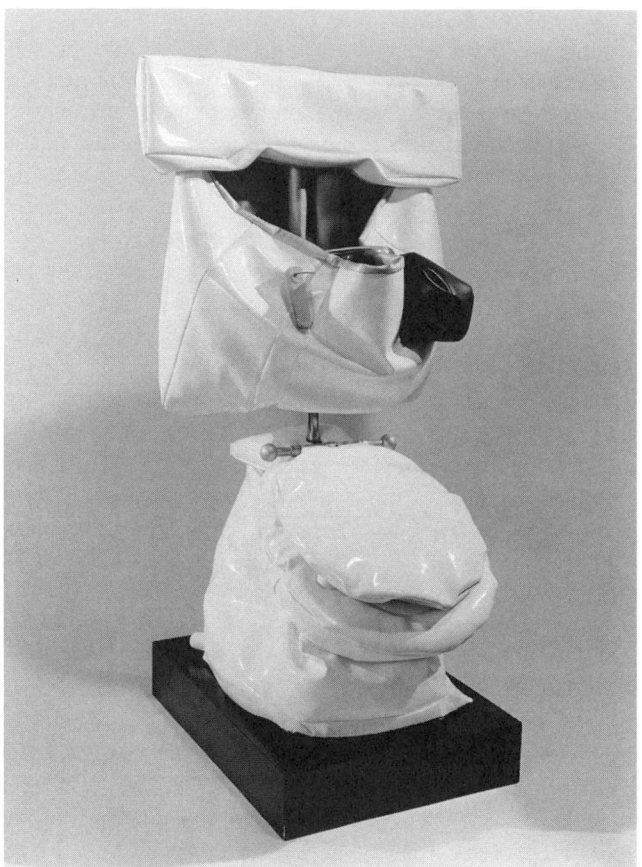

POP ART: Overview. Claes Oldenburg, *Soft Toilet* (1966), vinyl, plexiglass, and kapok on painted wood, overall: 57 1/16 × 27 5/8 × 28 1/16 in. (144.9 × 70.2 × 56.7 cm.); Whitney Museum of American Art, New York (Purchase, with funds from the Howard and Jean Lipman Foundation, Inc. [69.6a-b]). (Copyright 1997 by the Whitney Museum of American Art; used by permission.)

pacity to mediate semiotics and social history, two methodologies usually seen as distant, if not oppositional. Baudrillard is explicit: the logic of consumption can be defined as the manipulation of signs. Looking back from the 1990s, it appears that both semiotics and cultural and social history have defined our approach to Pop more definitively than have other methods.

At the same time artists were inventing Pop art, philosophically inclined academics were moving away from aesthetics and toward ideas about art based on semiotics, general theories of representation, and the study of cultural context. These concerns, as much as the advent of Pop art, gave rise to conclusions about changes in art that went beyond the moment of Pop art itself. In the 1980s a general consensus developed among historians and critics that Pop art marked the beginning of a new kind of art, perhaps even a new period in art history, in which image and idea superseded formal values and authorial presence. Hal Foster in *The Anti-Aesthetic* (Port Townsend, Wash., 1983), and Paul Taylor in

his *Post-Pop Art* (Cambridge, Mass., 1989), premised their anthologies on the given that, beginning with Pop, we have moved toward an art form that cannot be explained by considerations of beauty or even artistic expression; instead, this art develops interpretive strategies, cultural critiques, and finely drawn theoretical points. This shift has often been characterized as the advent of postmodernism.

The philosopher Arthur C. Danto's interest in Pop art intersects at certain points with those of the theorists discussed above. Like Foster, Danto reaches the conclusion that works such as Warhol's *Brillo Boxes* changed the very way we see art, perhaps effecting a break in art history. But unlike proponents of the postmodern, Danto believes that Pop art has revealed the fullest nature of art itself, rather than merely reflecting a historical shift in its social production. Like Baudrillard, Eco, and Barthes, he is concerned with the close relationship between the products of Pop art and the common objects that serve as its models. But Danto eschews specialized, theoretical language, citing John L. Austin's ideas on ordinary language usage rather than semiotic theory. He has long maintained a simple, literal lack of a perceptible difference between art and the commonplace as the center of his argument. Danto's inference is that the status of artworks does not depend on beauty, or appeal to the senses, or visual information of any dimension.

Nevertheless, the Pop artists themselves have often insisted on the unique physical presence of their artwork, its final difference from other objects. Even if one finds that Danto has elided the material and visual differences between a Brillo box and a *Brillo Box* (between the mass-produced household product and the mass-produced art product), it is possible to see that this is beside the point. The 1964 exhibition of Warhol's *Brillo Boxes,* a revelatory experience for Danto, marks an event in his own thinking that ends his career as an aesthetician and begins his career as an art critic. Concomitantly, although Danto believes that Pop represents the end of art (as a visual form of high culture), he also believes that it functions as a new beginning. Rather than closing down the debate on Pop art, or assigning a particular methodological lesson to Pop, he opens up its possible meanings, and the larger possibilities for the nature of art. For Danto, Pop art is fundamentally philosophical in that it not only asks "Is it art?," "What does it mean?," and "What is Pop art?," but returns the viewer to the initial and ultimate question, "What is art?"

Curiously, despite at least twenty years of committed theoretical work on Pop art, the sophistication of the statements by the artists themselves has not been surpassed. (Does Pop level the playing field of intellectuals as well as objects?) The early interviews conducted by Swenson and Glaser with Warhol, Lichtenstein, Oldenburg, and others provide humorous, but also profound, insights into the individual characters of the artists. Additionally, they provide unusually clear but also complex discussions of the relations between individual style, mass culture, personal expression, and artistic technique. If these artists are equal to their critics, they are no less but also no more illuminating on the question of Pop art:

> OLDENBURG: I think we have made a deliberate attempt to explore this area [the line between fine art and popular culture]. . . . But still the motives are not too clear to me as to why I do this.

> LICHTENSTEIN: Nor with me either, nor even why I say I do it.

For the Pop artists, to do and to "say," or to represent that doing, are equal, and equally opaque.

[*See also* Baudrillard; Danto; *and* Eco.]

BIBLIOGRAPHY

Alloway, Lawrence. *American Pop Art.* New York, 1974. Exhibition catalog, Whitney Museum of Art, New York.

Battcock, Gregory, ed. *The New Art: A Critical Anthology.* New rev. ed. New York, 1973.

Baudrillard, Jean. *La societé de consommation.* Paris, 1970.

Coplans, John. "The New Painting of Common Objects." *Artforum* 1.6 (December 1962): 26–29.

Danto, Arthur C. *The Transfiguration of the Commonplace.* Cambridge, Mass., 1981.

Glaser, Bruce. "Oldenburg, Lichtenstein, Warhol: A Discussion." *Artforum* 4.6 (February 1966): 20–24.

Kozloff, Max. "Pop Art, Metaphysical Disgust, and the New Vulgarians." *Art International* 6.2 (1962): 34–36.

Lippard, Lucy R. *Pop Art.* New York, 1966.

Mahsun, Carol Ann. *Pop Art and the Critics.* Ann Arbor, 1987.

Mamiya, Christin J. *Pop Art and Consumer Culture: American Super Market.* Austin, Tex., 1992.

McShine, Kynaston, ed. *Andy Warhol: A Retrospective.* New York, 1989. Exhibition catalog, Museum of Modern Art, New York.

The New Realists. New York, 1962. Exhibition Catalog, Sidney Janis Gallery.

Rose, Barbara. *Claes Oldenburg.* New York, 1970. Exhibition catalog, Museum of Modern Art, New York.

Seitz, William. *What's Happened to Art? An Interview with Marcel Duchamp on Present Consequences of New York's Armory Show.* New York, 1963.

Selz, Peter, et al. "A Symposium on Pop Art." *Arts* 37.7 (April 1963): 36–45.

Swenson, G. H. "The New American 'Sign Painters'." *ArtNews* 61.5 (September 1962): 44–47, 60–62.

Swenson, G. H. "What Is Pop Art? Part I." *ArtNews* 62.7 (November 1963): 24–27, 60–65.

Swenson, G. H. "What Is Pop Art? Part II." *ArtNews* 62.10 (February 1964): 40–43, 62–67.

Taylor, Paul. *Post-Pop Art.* Cambridge, Mass., 1989.

Tillim, Sidney. "Further Observations on the Pop Phenomenon." *Artforum* 4.3 (December 1965): 7.

KATY SIEGEL

Aesthetics of Andy Warhol

Since at least Andy Warhol's exhibition in the spring of 1964 of Brillo (and other) cartons at the Stable Gallery on East Seventy-fourth Street in Manhattan, it is arguable that he possessed a philosophical intelligence of an intoxicatingly high order. He could not touch anything without at the same time touching the very boundaries of thought, at the very least thought about art. The 1975 text *The Philosophy of Andy Warhol: From A to B and Back Again,* and its pendant volume, *POPism: The Warhol 1960s,* sparkle with conceptual observations and wit, put forth in the most piquant aphoristic language ("So full of thorns and secret spices, that you made me sneeze and laugh," Friedrich Nietzsche says of his own "written and painted thoughts" in *Beyond Good and Evil*). But one could refer to the very art that Warhol's critics saw as mindless and meretricious. Indeed, it was among Warhol's chief contributions to the history of art that he brought artistic practice to a level of philosophical self-consciousness never before attained. G. W. F. Hegel had proposed that art and philosophy are two "moments," as he put it, of Absolute Spirit (religion was the third). In a certain sense, if he is right, there must be a basic identity between the two, and Hegel believed that art fulfills its historical and spiritual destiny when its practice is disclosed as a kind of philosophy in action.

That someone as astute as Warhol should have chosen to disguise his depth by what passed as motley in the 1960s has, in its own right, a certain allegorical appropriateness. In any case, we can identify some fragments of the philosophical structure of Warhol's art, while also relating it to certain of its art-historical as well as cultural circumstances. But this interpretation differs from the standard art-historical exercise in that it seeks to identify the importance of Warhol not in terms of the art he influenced (or by which he was influenced) but in terms of the thought he brought to our awareness. Whatever he did, "he did it as a philosopher might," wrote Edmund White in a memorial tribute. Warhol violated every condition thought necessary to something being an artwork, but in so doing he disclosed the essence of art. As White goes on to say, all this was "performed under the guise of humor and self-advancing cynicism, as though a chemist were conducting the most delicate experiments at the target end of a shooting gallery" (see McShine, 1989, p. 441).

These claims about Warhol can be illustrated with an initial example drawn from Warhol's films, which, whatever their standing in the history of cinema may prove to be, have an unparalleled contribution to make in our philosophical understanding of the concept of film. The example is his *Empire* of 1964, which someone might just wander into under the misapprehension that its title promises one of those sagas of colonization or business in which a nation, or a mogul, builds up an empire. It is indeed of epic length, but it is marked by a total absence of incident, and its title is a pun on the Empire State Building, which is its only actor, doing what it always does, namely, nothing.

Imagine that someone, inspired by Warhol, were to make a film titled *Either/Or* "based," as the title promises, on the masterpiece of the celebrated Danish philosopher Søren Kierkegaard. Let the film be just as long as *Empire* (or longer, if you wish), and let it consist of nothing but the title page of the book, because the producer thinks that there might be an internal joke here for someone who is familiar with Kierkegaard's sly aphorisms. These aphorisms allow us to ponder the ambiguity in the concept of books, which exist as physical objects, of a certain color and size and weight, and as objects of meaning, which have a certain content and are in a certain language, and capable, as makes no sense with physical objects, of translation. That ambiguity immediately is transferred to the concept of being based on. Here is one of the aphorisms: "What the philosophers have to say about reality is often as disappointing as a sign you see in a shop window, which reads Pressing Done Here. If you brought your clothes in to be pressed, you would be fooled: for the sign is only for sale."

The two modes of being of a sign, as one might portentously say, are as a rectangle of plywood with paint and ink on its surface, which costs so many kroner at the store where signs are made and sold; and also as an emblem that gives information to potential customers—information, for example, that they can have their clothes pressed in the place where the sign, by convention, means that that is the business of the place where the sign is.

These are also the two modes of being of a book—as something that takes up space and as something dense with wisdom. It is this that makes the film *Either/Or* a kind of joke, or for that matter, makes *Empire* a kind of joke. The ambiguity that generates them, in fact, generates certain of Warhol's paradigmatic works of art such as, for signal example, the *Brillo Box* sculptures, which as works of art have all sorts of rights and privileges mere cartons of Brillo systematically lack, not being art. Here might be two Kierkegaardian-Warholian jokes:

> A man sees what looks like an ordinary soap-pad carton in a shop window and, needing to ship some books, asks the shopkeeper whether he can have it. The shop turns out to be an art gallery and the shopkeeper a dealer who says: "That is a work of art, just now worth thirty thousand dollars."

> A man sees what looks like Warhol's *Brillo Box* in what looks like an art gallery, and asks the dealer, who turns out to be a shopkeeper, how much it is. The latter says the man can have it, he was going to throw it away anyway, it was placed in the window temporarily after it was unpacked.

Perhaps half the visitors to the Stable Gallery were angry that something could be put forward as art that so verged on reality that no interesting perceptual difference distinguished them. Perhaps the other half were exultant that something could be put forward as art that so verged on reality that it was distinguished by no interesting perceptual difference. In the early 1960s it was universally assumed that art must be something exalted and arcane, which put one in touch with a reality no less arcane and exalted. The reality on which Warhol's art verged was neither arcane nor exalted: it was banal. This was perceived as intoxicating or degrading, depending on where one stood on a number of issues having to do with American commercial reality, the values and virtues of the commonplace, the role and calling of the artist, the point and purpose of art. For me, the interesting feature of the *Brillo Box* was that it appropriated the philosophical question of the relationship between art and reality and incorporated it into the *Brillo Box* and in effect asks why, if it is art, the boxes of Brillo in the supermarket, which differ from it in no interesting perceptual way, are not. At the very least the *Brillo Box* made plain that one cannot any longer think of distinguishing art from reality on perceptual grounds, for those grounds have been cut away.

The *Brillo Box* example helps to explain what makes *Empire* finally so philosophical a film. Philosophers from ancient times down have been concerned with framing definitions—definitions of justice, of truth, of knowledge, of art. This means in effect identifying the essential conditions for something to be an instance of art, of knowledge, of truth, of justice. The first thing that might occur to anyone as obvious in framing a distinction between moving and still pictures is that the former do and the latter do not show things in motion. A still picture (let us restrict ourselves to photography) can show us things we know must be moving, as in a famous image by Henri Cartier-Bresson of a man leaping over a puddle. But it cannot show them in motion. A motion picture of the same scene would show the trajectory the leaping man describes, and with this the hopeful philosopher of film might suppose something had been nailed down. What *Empire* demonstrates is that something can be a moving picture and not show movement. Nothing much in the film changes at all, in fact, even though, since the film was taken over an eight-hour stretch, something did change: a light in a window went on or off, a plane could have passed, the dusk in fact fell. But none of this is essential to the thought that the entire film could have been made in which nothing whatever changed or moved. At once it must become clear that only moving pictures can show stillness, as well as motion.

A photograph by Ansel Adams of the Rockies, paradigmatically immobile to the point of being natural symbols for eternity, is a still picture of a still object. But even so, the photograph, we now realize, no more shows the stillness than Cartier-Bresson's shows the motion. Still pictures show neither stillness nor motion. Think, for comparison, of the difference between black-and-white photography and color photography. A black-and-white photograph may be taken of a black-and-white object—a zebra, say. But it does not show the blackness and the whiteness of that object, it merely shows the difference. For all we can tell from the photograph, what registers as black could be red and what registers as white could be pink. A color photograph of a black-and-white object actually shows the black and the white of the object. Black-and-white photography, like still photography, is essentially more abstract than its counterpart.

Warhol subtracted everything from the moving picture that might be mistaken for an essential property of film. What was left was pure film. What we learn is that in a moving picture it is the film itself that moves and not necessarily its object, which may remain still. Warhol's art, in film and elsewhere, goes immediately to the defining boundaries of the medium, and brings these boundaries to conceptual awareness. What makes him an artist, however, is that he actually makes the art and is not content with imagining it, after the manner of my *Either/Or*. To sit through an entire seance of *Empire*, all eight or so hours of it, in which nothing essentially happens but nothing, may have the collateral effect of making the experience of time palpable, almost as if in a sensory deprivation experiment. We do not become aware of time in ordinary cinema, because too much takes place in time for time itself to become the object of consciousness. Time ordinarily lies outside the experiences with which, as we say, we kill time, seeking distraction. Time is not killed but restored to awareness in *Empire*. Usually, in the ordinary moving picture, the time in the film is a kind of narrative time, so that a century may pass in the course of watching a two-hour film. In *Empire*, narrative time and real time are one. The time in and the time of the film are the same. There is, as with the *Brillo Box* and the cartons of Brillo, no interesting perceptual difference.

Finally, with *Empire*, we become aware of the material properties of film, of the scratches, the grain, the accidental luminosities, and above all the passing before our eyes of the monotonous band. Warhol had an almost mystical attitude toward the world: everything in it had equal weight, it was all equally interesting. Or perhaps it says something about the human mind that under conditions of sensory deprivation it will find interest in the most marginal and unpromising differences. The film is made with the barest equipment, the zero degree of intervention, the null degree of editing. It was concerned, rather, with meaning, material, and, finally, mystery. That the film, like the *Brillo Box* itself—like almost everything to which Warhol put his hand—should have the form of a philosophical joke bears out a conjecture of Ludwig Wittgenstein's that it is conceivable that a philosophical work could be composed consisting solely of jokes. They have to be the right kinds, of course. For one thing, Warhol's jokes are not funny. There was, in my recollection of the Stable Gallery nearly thirty years ago, a spirit of play. But the boxes on display were not made in the spirit of play, Nor was Warhol capable of play. His seriousness seems almost otherworldly.

The deep philosophical bearing of Warhol's central achievement is part of the classical phase of Pop art in the early 1960s. A great many questions must be answered before we have a full historical understanding of this extraordinary movement, and in particular of what it meant that imagery was appropriated from all across the face of commercial and mass culture. It was often suggested, even by some of the Pop artists themselves at the time, that their intentions were to blur, if not obliterate, the boundaries between high and low art, challenging, with commercial logos or panels from comic strips or advertisements from newspapers and magazines, distinctions assumed and reinforced by the institutions of the art world—the gallery, with especially its decor and the affected styles of its personnel; the collection; the carved and gilded frame; the romanticized myth of the artist.

Even then, differences among Pop artists must be made. In 1962, for example, Roy Lichtenstein painted a work that looked like a monumentalized composition book of the most familiar kind, with black-and-white mottling on the cover, and a label that says "Compositions." Iconographically, it looks as if it goes with the soup cans and the like that Warhol used, but in fact it has a really different meaning altogether. The word *compositions* is something of a pun, for it of course refers to the ways artists arrange forms in pictorial space. And the black-and-white mottling looks like the allover composition for which Jackson Pollock earned high critical praise. The whole work makes a number of sly artworld allusions, and is in every sense a piece of "art about art," as such work came to be known. It is like the painting of large brushstrokes Lichtenstein made, lampooning the veneration of the heavy, looped swirl of paint that emblemized Abstract Expressionism. Mockery is one of the armaments of civilized aggression, and Lichtenstein's work is filled with internal art-world barbs.

Warhol's jokes were of another order altogether and had little to do with insider attacks on the pretensions of the art world. Rather, he was asking where the distinction is to be sited between art high or low on the one side, and reality on the other. This in a way was a question that had driven philosophy from Plato onward, and while it would be preposterous to pretend that Warhol generated the kind of systematic metaphysics that seeks to define the place of art in the totality of things, he did, in a way that one could say had never before been achieved, demonstrate what the form of the philosophical question must be. In doing this he invalidated some two millennia of misdirected investigation. It is the imagery of Pop that enabled him to do this.

There is a famous section of the *Philosophical Investigations* in which Wittgenstein seeks to call into question the idea of philosophical definitions, asking whether they can be achieved and whether there is any point in achieving them. Wittgenstein uses the example of games and asks us to try to imagine what a definition of *game* would look like. He asks us to "look and see," and then, when we have complied, we will see that there are no overarching properties shared by all the games and only the games. Rather, games form a kind of "family," the members of which share some but by no means all properties. Yet, Wittgenstein says, we all know what a game is and have no difficulty in recognizing something as one without benefit of a definition. So what is the point of pursuing it? His followers not long afterward applied this strategy to art, where similar reasoning suggested that artworks form a family rather than a homogeneous class, that there are thus no properties common and peculiar to works of arts, and that anyway we all know which are the works of art without benefit of such a definition. The upshot, these philosophers argued, is that the long search for definitions was misguided.

It is against this background that Warhol's *Brillo Box* seems to have something significant to say. A photograph of Warhol among his boxes looks indiscernible from a photograph of a stockroom clerk among the boxes in the supermarket. With what license can we pretend to tell the work of art from the mere utilitarian object? One is made of plywood, the other of cardboard, but can the difference between art and reality rest on a difference that could have gone the other way? In the end, there seems to be a "family resemblance" far more marked between *Brillo Box* and a Brillo box than between the former and, say, any paradigm work of art you choose—the *Night Watch*, say—which in fact seems to have exactly as many resemblances to the Brillo carton as to *Brillo Box*. After all, experts in the art world at the time were quite ready to consign Warhol's Brillo boxes to some less exalted category than sculpture, making them subject to customs duties when a gallery sought to import them into Canada. The point is that the difference between art and reality is not like the difference between camels and dromedaries, where we can count humps. Something cannot be a camel that looks like a dromedary, but something can be an artwork that looks just like a real thing. What makes the one art may be something quite invisible, perhaps how it arrived in the world and what someone intended it to be.

Brillo Box does for art what *Empire* does for film. It forces reflection on what makes it art, when that is not something that is obvious, just as the film demonstrates how little is required for something to be a film. To see *Empire* as film is to shelve as inessential a lot of what theorists have supposed central to film, all of which Warhol unerringly subtracted.

To be sure, Warhol made his point in a clearly negative way. He did not tell us what art was. But by his framing the question, those whose business it is to provide positive philosophical theories could at last address the subject. It is difficult to pretend that Warhol's intention was to clear the underbrush and make room for a finally adequate theory of art. In some ways it is perhaps inscrutable what his intentions ever were. Warhol's name is associated with frivolity, glamour, publicity, and making it big. The awesomeness of his achievement is that under the guise of the simple son of the fairy tale, seemingly no match for his daunting siblings,

Warhol made the most profound conceptual discoveries, and produced examples of pure art that appear uncannily to look like examples of pure reality.

BIBLIOGRAPHY

Works by Warhol

The Philosophy of Andy Warhol: From A to B and Back Again. New York, 1975.
POPism: The Warhol '60s. In collaboration with Pat Hackett. New York, 1980.

Other Sources

Angell, Callie, et al. *The Andy Warhol Museum.* Pittsburgh, 1994.
Bourdon, David. *Warhol.* New York, 1989.
Colacello, Bob. *Holy Terror: Andy Warhol Close Up.* New York, 1990.
Crow, Thomas. "Saturday Disasters: Trace and Reference in Early Warhol." In *Modern Art in the Common Culture,* pp. 49–65. New Haven, 1996.
Danto, Arthur C. "The Abstract-Expressionist Coca-Cola Bottle." In *Beyond the Brillo Box: The Visual Arts in Post-Historical Perspective,* pp. 131–145. New York, 1992.
Foucault, Michel. *This Is Not a Pipe.* Translated by James Harkness. Berkeley, 1983.
Herwitz, Daniel. "Andy Warhol without Theory." In *Making Theory/Constructing Art: On the Authority of the Avant-Garde,* pp. 232–268. Chicago, 1993.
Krauss, Rosalind. *The Optical Unconscious.* Cambridge, Mass., 1993. See chap. 6.
McShine, Kynaston, ed. *Andy Warhol: A Retrospective.* New York, 1989. Contains a tribute by Edmund White in "A Collective Portrait of Andy Warhol," pp. 423–455, on p. 441.
Swenson, G. R. "What Is Pop Art? Answers from 8 Painters." *ArtNews* 62 (November 1963): 24–27, 60–65; 62 (February 1964): 40–43, 62–67.
Yau, John. *In the Realm of Appearances: The Art of Andy Warhol.* Hopewell, N.J., 1993.

ARTHUR C. DANTO

POPULAR CULTURE. The term *popular culture* can refer broadly to common aesthetic or life practices, in both the statistical and qualitative senses. But theorists have used the term more precisely to designate a particular form of common culture that arises only in the modern period. Popular culture in this account is distinct from both folk culture and high culture: unlike the former, it is mass-produced; unlike the latter, it is mass-consumed.

Throughout the eighteenth and nineteenth centuries, western European societies experienced a particularly intense social reorganization. Vast numbers of the former peasantry now concentrated in dense cities to work in newly developing mass-production industries. Industrialization and the rise of organized capitalism restructured virtually every sphere of life: new concepts of uniform time, the mixing of previously dispersed local cultures, and the dehumanizing life of factory work all contributed to a homogenization of experience, producing a sense of shared fate across wide territories. At the same time, mounting social density and the vastly higher division of labor in capitalism increased social differentiation, giving rise particularly to vibrant middle classes. The demands of complex administration in capitalist industry and in the state contributed to widespread literacy in these new groups. These changes had profound implications for political as well as cultural life.

A decisive shift in the sources of power occurred with the simultaneous concentration and differentiation of society. The notion of the popular as distinct from the folk and elite implies not just large numbers of ordinary people, but large numbers organized as the people. The French Revolution marks the people's emergence as a political and cultural force. Earlier, power flowed down from the heavens through the monarch and its agent, the feudal aristocracy. The French Revolution challenged this ancient order, relocating power in the Third Estate, that protoparliamentary body representing and, for the first time, conceptualizing the people as possessing "interests" that differed from those of the old regime. Where Louis XIV had declared he was the state, the Third Estate declared they were the nation. Modern politics was thus born, in which legitimacy flows from the people, and "citizens" demanded the right to participate in their own governance.

Throughout this period, culture industries arose to meet the aesthetic desires of the newly emerged middle classes just as these groups developed new administrative and governmental forms to represent their political interests. As the ever-growing middle classes became more and more literate, as the efficiencies of mass industry produced often stupendous economies, and as social differentiation gave more people a sense of their own lives as projects filled with possibility, the western European bourgeoisie sought to "cultivate" themselves as more than mere interchangeable workers laboring for existence. The novel, for instance, rose as an expression of and reflection on modern life and its central figure, the subjective individual. The "news" was invented by as well as spread through new media, documenting the accelerated occurrence of history. Entertainment and leisure emerged as new categories of experience and possibility, at first restricted to the high middle classes, later accessible to virtually everyone.

These new cultural interests and practices contributed to, as well as grew from, changes in the social organization of aesthetic production. A court-based system of arts sponsorship in Europe before the nineteenth century had supported a "high" culture not available to ordinary people. Such a system provided necessary insulation for an artistic conception of aesthetic production, allowing producers to pursue aesthetic impulses in the abstract; while they depended on the understanding and support of an elite audience, that audience was cultivated and trained, with the time and energy to contemplate aesthetic products as a separate category of existence. Artists were thus free from the uncultivated judgments of the masses, while through their association with the centers of power they and their work enjoyed high status and official sanction.

With the rise of industrial society, however, these conditions of aesthetic production changed dramatically. The resources and prestige of court patrons declined precipitously at the same time that less insulated and exalted forms of culture began to occupy the public stage. Industry produced culture and leisure products on a mass scale just as it manufactured durable goods. Creators of high culture thus faced the choice of appealing to wider publics by subjecting their work to popular criteria, working in the culture industries as hired hands, or retreating to specialized—often countercultural—settings, contexts in which they produced only for themselves in ever more esoteric forms, creating as well the contemporary ideal of the devoted artist who renounces all worldly goods.

A clear-cut distinction between popular culture and high culture, however, depended not just on the middle classes generally or on the situation of aesthetic production from the point of view of the artist, but on the active work of the upper classes in response to these changed circumstances. Qualitative distinctions do not come only from the intrinsic qualities of works—that is, from their level of abstraction and degree of esotericism—but from the ways various social groups use culture to distinguish themselves socially. In his own time, for instance, William Shakespeare's plays were common entertainment, and the Globe theater included room for all sorts of people, though each group in its separate place. In the mid-nineteenth century, roving theater troupes performed Shakespeare all over the American countryside as popular distraction, and lines from the plays were at the hands not only of specially educated elites but of wide numbers of ordinary people as well, perhaps more so. Music performances included all varieties of composition in one long evening, ranging from what we now call the "classics" to dance and folk music.

In the realm of culture, threatened elites developed qualitative distinctions to dramatize and defend their exalted status. Although the newly emerging middle classes might achieve material equality, there was to be no doubt that they were not true equals of the older establishment, who distinguished themselves through their level of aesthetic and intellectual cultivation. Old elites engaged in processes of cultural entrepreneurship, founding art museums and symphony societies in which to entrench their cultural values and, thereby, defend their social position. In the process, they created conditions for the autonomy of high cultural values, even leading initiatives to educate and enrich the masses; but in practice these arrangements led to even further separation of high art from popular culture, and elites gained even more status from their association with the arts since the criteria of excellence were now objectified in purportedly impartial institutions.

Similar processes were at work in politics as well as culture, and arguments in the two fields are in fact intricately connected. Through the French Revolution, aristocratic elites articulated a political theory to shore up their declining fortunes: democracy—the rule of the people—was inherently debased, nothing more than submission to an undifferentiated and unknowing mob. Early on, this critique focused on the danger *from* the masses, who had no idea of what was good for themselves and whose unfettered passions threatened stability and the proper order of things; later, elite theorists highlighted the dangers *to* the masses, whose essential formlessness left them gullible and susceptible to demagogic manipulation, especially through new media.

As popular culture developed into a powerful category of aesthetic and life practice, there thus arose as well a vibrant tradition of commentary on it. Within such discourse, the concept of popular culture is Janus-faced: with it, we either celebrate or revile the ordinary people. Popular culture refers democratically to the capacities of all human beings, no matter what their social position or level of "cultivation," to produce and consume symbolic products, indeed, to entertain ideas worth attention at all. It refers as well to the baseness of common thinking, the homogenized incapacity of the masses, their danger to the life of aesthetic refinement, their irrelevance, even threat, to thoughtful governance. In politics, we simultaneously embrace democracy and lament its low level. In culture, we encourage general aesthetic expression and bemoan its poverty.

A basic line of division is thus between those who identify popular culture negatively as mass culture—undifferentiated and low—and those who reject the association. The so-called mass culture critics, nevertheless, come from both left and right. Among the most famous of right-wing mass-culture critiques is Matthew Arnold's *Culture and Anarchy*. Arnold argued that the middle classes were uncultured "Philistines," wealthy but lacking proper appreciation of what he called "the best that has been thought and known in the world." Later, Van Wyck Brooks drew a distinction between "highbrow" and "lowbrow" culture. Critics in this tradition saw the battle lines clearly: on the one side, the invading hordes, on the other, that small cultivated elite who alone were able to discern what is of value, on whose judgment and leadership alone the future depends. They often employed analogies to the decline of the Roman Empire, though now the enemy was within—it was the people itself.

Defense of "high" culture against the masses, however, was by no means limited to the right. Theorists in the Western Marxist tradition worried about the effects of mass production and mass media on political as well as cultural life. Members of the so-called Frankfurt School argued that popular culture was "industrial" insofar as it shared the debased features of capitalist society more generally, which included rampant individualism, superficiality, and instru-

mentalism. Given the unique capacities of mass production in all spheres of life, popular culture destroys the foundations for critical reflection, pervading leisure time with entertainment commodities that have a narcotizing effect on the masses. These cultural commodities, like capitalist commodities generally, helped maintain the alienated condition of contemporary society, creating out of atomized individuals a shapeless mass incapable of recognizing its own situation. In contrast, the aesthetic dimension of a "pure" high culture provided a last refuge of critical thinking. Insofar as commodification is an ever-expanding scourge, however, mass culture threatened to extinguish even that remaining realm of hope and critical potential.

In contrast, however, there have been varieties of popular culture theory that reject the identification of popularity with massification and commodification. Theories of this variety criticize mass-culture theorists for objectifying ordinary people, for denigrating their enduring capacities for reflection and subjectivity even in a mass-mediated surround. Herbert J. Gans, for instance, argues for a populist position that appreciates the aesthetic (and, by extension, political) capacities of all people, no matter what their level of "cultivation." Gans argues that differences between high culture and popular culture have been exaggerated, that they are similar in their abilities to express the needs of different people: for every "taste public" there corresponds a "taste culture." Moreover, Gans argues that all taste cultures are of equal value, to be judged not one against the other but in relation to the groups they serve.

Additionally, writers from widely divergent political positions saw some redemptive possibilities in popular culture. Walter Benjamin, for instance, while wary of many aspects of culture in the age of mechanical reproduction, also saw in it a liberating potential: mass-produced works were no longer enthralled to the "aura" of the original, thereby providing an escape from the jargon of authenticity that defined so much work in aesthetic theory. It also allowed more people to approach the "great" works, although such works did face the risk of becoming clichéd and debased through repetition. Edward Shils, as well, argued that the spread of classical music and art through mass production had to some degree "improved" the tastes of the people, though the condescending tone of this argument is apparent.

In the second half of the twentieth century, a new line of (often British) cultural theory known as Cultural Studies has emerged from the tradition of Western Marxism, critically appropriating that school's understanding of commodification, but avoiding its implied low opinion of the people. Cultural Studies theorists agree with the Frankfurt School that the industrial commodification of culture inculcates the masses into a hegemonic ideology that saps them of some critical potential. But writers in this tradition disagree with the Frankfurt School about the totality of ideological domination: ordinary people bring to bear sometimes significant critical capacities in their reception of culture, and oppositional readings are always inscribed in mass-culture texts, even if only through their exclusion.

Theorists in the Cultural Studies tradition redefine popular culture—the culture of the people—in terms of reading and reception as a realm of resistance to dominant culture: popular culture is the culture that arises out of the experiences of ordinary people, experiences that include consuming mass-produced culture but only within contexts that are always more complex than can be controlled by such over-generalized, mass-produced images. Cultural Studies thus involves a shift from a focus on production to a focus on reception.

Writers like E. P. Thompson, Raymond Williams, and Richard Hoggart emphasize the ways in which people use mass-produced culture within the contexts of their everyday lives, pointing out especially the ways in which ordinary people resist the implied messages of that culture. Through continuous selection and interpretation, people resist the totality of mass culture: they act as gatekeepers, rejecting the majority of what is produced; they "read" what is offered through the sometimes quite critical lenses of their own experiences, which are often not those addressed by the products (women, for instance, filter male-addressed media through their lives, as working-class youths respond to middle-class utopias not always in the inscribed manner); consumers often create hidden—and sometimes not-so-hidden—practices of resistance or appropriate images and commodities contrarily to the ways in which these are sold. An important implication of this approach, then, is that meanings are not transcendent, to be uncovered through expert strategies, but are products of social contestation, the result of negotiation among producers, texts, and readers. Pure aesthetics has thus fallen, and sociology replaces philosophy. Distinctions among kinds of culture are matters of social relations, not intrinsic aspects of the works themselves.

Artists as well as cultural theorists have also participated in this "deconstruction" of pure aesthetic distinctions. In the 1960s, Pop art blurred and eventually demolished distinctions between high and low, exalted and ordinary, pure and prosaic. Supportive theorists of this movement dismissed the possibility of distinguishing between highbrow and lowbrow, attacking those who maintain such distinctions as elitist. This so-called new sensibility sought to explode the "canon" of Western civilization's great works, embracing film as well as painting, the Beatles as well as J. S. Bach and Ludwig van Beethoven. Later, this rejection of boundaries contributed to an attack on traditional reading lists in American universities as inscribing an exclusionary program meant to support the dominance of a Eurocentric worldview. Critics sought to make reading lists more "inclusive," reflecting the experiences of people (mainly women and minorities) traditionally excluded from analysis and participation in academic and political discourse. In the wider political context, we refer now to the "culture wars," where the parties argue about the political implications of social and cultural distinctions and about the very possibility of drawing them innocently or objectively.

[*See also* Comics; Cultural Studies; Fashion; Folk Art; Kitsch; Pop Art; Rock Music; *and* Television.]

BIBLIOGRAPHY

Arnold, Matthew. *Culture and Anarchy.* Edited by J. Dover Wilson. Reprint, Cambridge, 1963.

Benjamin, Walter. "The Work of Art in the Age of Mechanical Reproduction." In *Illuminations,* edited by Hannah Arendt, translated by Harry Zohn, pp. 217–251. New York, 1969.

Bourdieu, Pierre. *Distinction: A Social Critique of The Judgement of Taste.* Translated by Richard Nice. Cambridge, Mass., 1984.

Burke, Peter. *Popular Culture in Early Modern Europe.* New York, 1978.

Fiske, John. "British Cultural Studies and Television." In *Channels of Discourse,* edited by Robert C. Allen, pp. 254–289. Chapel Hill, N.C., 1987.

Gans, Herbert J. *Popular Culture and High Culture: An Analysis and Evaluation of Taste.* New York, 1974.

Hall, Stuart. "Cultural Studies: Two Paradigms." In *Media, Culture and Society: A Critical Reader,* edited by Richard Collins. Beverly Hills, Calif., 1986.

Hoggart, Richard. *The Uses of Literacy.* London, 1957.

Horkheimer, Max, and Theodor W. Adorno. "The Culture Industry: Enlightenment as Mass Deception." In *Dialectic of Enlightenment,* translated by John Cumming. New York, 1972.

Mukerji, Chandra, and Michael Schudson, eds. *Rethinking Popular Culture: Contemporary Perspectives in Cultural Studies.* Berkeley, 1991.

Rosenberg, Bernard, and David Manning White, eds. *Mass Culture: The Popular Arts in America.* New York, 1957.

Thompson, E. P. *The Making of the English Working Class.* London, 1963.

Williams, Raymond. *The Long Revolution.* London, 1961.

Williams, Raymond. *Keywords.* Rev. ed. New York, 1985.

JEFFREY K. OLICK

PORNOGRAPHY. *See* Obscenity.

PORTRAITURE. The terms *portraiture,* conventionally defined as "the action or art of portraying," and *to portray* as "to make a picture, image, or figure of" are familiar terms in everyday language. They move between the poles of descriptive delineation in the literal sense and a much more generalized concept of representation, where depiction has a tenuous connection with a palpable object of reference to which some name, some specific identification can be given. In either case, there is an operative assumption that the portrait, the product of portrayal, bears a significant relationship with some being, or entity, in the world that has, or had, both actual existence and some degree of singularity, sufficient for identification. However difficult it may be to portray a specific person, the exclusive subject of "por-

PORTRAITURE. Man Ray, *Gertrude Stein Sitting in Front of Picasso's Portrait of Her* (1922), photograph. (Copyright 1998 by Artists Rights Society, New York/ADAGP/Man Ray Trust, Paris; photograph courtesy of Man Ray Trust; used by permission.)

traiture," however unrecognizable to all but a chosen few, portraying "the face" of someone is an infinitely simpler task than portraying, to quote Christopher Marlowe, the "personage of a wondrous man." The former seemingly provides a tangible, material point of reference, the object of verifiable description, even if disputed by readers, viewers, and other respondents. The latter requires a complex process of interpretive analysis whose goal is to manifest the intangibles of personality, spirit, character, "soul," and the self, the very qualities that, allegedly, fill the corporeal envelope with "being" and make its portrayal of value and interest to others.

Still, visualizing or otherwise representing the self is a task beset with serious obstacles. In his discussion of concepts of identity and their uncertain reliance on the posited continuity of permanence of some defining essence of being, David

Hume observed that he had never seen a self and, by implication, that he was rather skeptical of its existence. Others have challenged the very notion of selfhood, alleging its fictional character as a particular cultural artifact of the now discredited ideology of individualism, the latter deemed a manifestation, perhaps, of the sin of pride, or at the very least of an anticommunitarian sensibility. There are many, moreover, who argue that terms such as *personality, character,* and *self* are themselves transitory concepts, constantly subjected to redefinition and incapable of being indissolubly associated with anyone. Indeed, these very terms, with or without a psychological or philosophical gloss, are ultimately imposed from the outside—by an artist, by a viewer-reader, by all who participate in the social order and are concerned about their place in it—and they serve to establish an effective frame of reference for simplifying the encounter with another. Even self-portraiture may be understood as a form of representation, couched in terms either formulated by others or based knowingly on their expectations: to wit, "I am the person you think I am, or I'm not."

Putting aside the ongoing dispute about the nature of the existence of selfhood, portraiture may be considered a well-tested instrument for differentiating among persons, past and present, and for preserving that difference over time through the medium of art. Portraiture should also be construed as an operative construct, asserting a particular predicate (fictional or not), as a propositional statement of the subject portrayed, in the form, "This is XYZ, who . . ." The act of portrayal can then be compared with the use of personal pronouns in ordinary speech—especially in the third person—but with a permanence that neither speech nor the corporeal being possesses. In this way, portraits serve to extricate individuals from the mass of humanity and provide a lens to focus on the defining "idiosyncracies" of various persons; they also fix such persons in time but are limited neither in their affective authority nor in their reception to the time and conditions of making. Above all, portraits are the products of a conscious intent to portray and of a strong interest in such portrayals. Without this reciprocity, portraits not only fail to function but will be unrecognizable for what they are or purport to be, a "picture, image, or figure of" a particular someone.

But does that someone of whom the portrait is an image have to exist? All of us can recall fictional characters in novels, so completely realized by an author that they leap off the page into our minds and there form vivid mental images of the individuals portrayed. Charles Dickens and many other novelists of the nineteenth and early twentieth centuries created such characters, whose very existence seemed an intrinsic part of life, certainly less circumscribed in their apparent nature and appearance than the depiction of these selfsame characters in the movies. The novelist's art creates such characters from life, but the world they inhabit is fictional, and the only access to them is through the medium of their depiction by an imaginative writer.

Absent the requisite intention to portray an actual figure, the genre of the novel itself categorically stands in the way of the reader taking the author's characters as portraits, however lifelike they may appear. On the other hand, artistic invention alone does not necessarily impugn the claim of these fictional characters to be thought of as "portraits." Visual access to the long dead may exist only through the medium of preserved portraits, whose legitimacy or authenticity has been established by convention rather than by any rational method of historical verification. We readily accept sculpted and painted portraits as being "true" likenesses of actual, living persons, even without identifying labels and, often, in the absence of corroborating evidence. An example of our willingness to suspend doubt, to accept the propositional truth presented by the work of visual art,

occurs in the case of the sculpted busts of Homer, acknowledged to be posthumous inventions, at best. Since antiquity, they have been accepted as portraits of the poet because they satisfied preconceived notions of Homer, the blind master of epic. All Greek portraits of Homer must be considered historical fictions on two counts: as portraits they are pure inventions because Homer preceded the development of portraiture in Greek art, and "Homer" himself may never have existed. The classical "Homer" can be differentiated from Dickens's Fagin, who existed only in fictive time, but they do share many features of inventive characterization. More closely, perhaps, the fictive image of "Homer" resembles those actual personages whose participatory appearance in historical novels imparts an air of veracity, or authenticity, especially in the figures of Napoleon and the Russian generals in Leo Tolstoy's *War and Peace*, Walter Scott's medieval English kings and nobles, and Gore Vidal's nineteenth-century American politicians.

Indeed, such personage-punctuated historical novels occupy an intermediate position between the wholly fictive presentation of lifelike characters and the biographical treatment of historical figures in works ostensibly devoted to that sole purpose. The genre of literary portraiture notoriously tends to blur distinctions between an objective depiction of the subject and the highly confected forms of self-representation assumed, consciously or not, by the same subject, just like portraits painted on commission. Literary portraiture traditionally combines the description of places, persons, and circumstances with the interpretive analysis of behavior patterns and their reception in an attempt to define the whole subject; literary models, narrative conventions, and the codified language of psychological insight offer a much broader repertory to the biographer than is available to the visual artist, although both rely heavily on typologically determined forms to portray the person "in context." Biography establishes its own justification for being in human curiosity, in the desire to explain the actions of distinguished persons as part of something greater than their momentary instantiation. The autobiographer is further preoccupied with self-justification, whether expressed in a confessional mode or with pseudo–third person distance, but has the great advantage of speaking in his or her own voice, however contrived.

What, of course, separates the literary from the visual portrait is the space and time available to the writer, permitting the establishment of the changing contours of the subject's presence over the years and revealing the transformation of body and spirit. In this regard, the literary portrait is surely more rounded, the multivalent interaction between the subject and his or her contemporaries more fully revealed, the author's analysis both grander and more detailed than in the visual portrait. As a result, although the biography may be full of literary symbols and motifs, the visual portrait functions more immediately as a comprehensive sign, collapsing biographical dilation into a single, all-incorporating image, closer then to the actual experience available to us all in the course of an encounter with another.

Alterity energizes the visual and psychological transaction between the beholder and the portrait image, especially when the portrait is presented at human scale, so direct eye contact takes place. This *simulacrum* of the person portrayed thus functions as a surrogate presence, and the intensity of the relationship engages all those faculties that are brought into play in social encounters with friends, relatives, and strangers, sometimes to such a degree of rapport that the artwork becomes invisible. The resulting triumph of the person-sign, materialized in the art object and existing in the viewer's space and in his or her field of vision, may account for the appearance of the visual portrait before the textual, at least in the Western cultural tradition. It is much easier to empathize with the portrait when confronting the visual image of another, even if the viewer is restricted to the immediate perception of the moment. Histories are written in faces, bodies, poses, costumes, settings, and in the conventions of portraiture itself.

Considerations of the visual portrait as an effective surrogate for the original inevitably bring up the question of *likeness,* that much used, or abused, term, imposed for centuries as the standard of achievement by which the success of the portrait was measured. Achieving a good likeness guaranteed continued employment, because verisimilitude was the normative goal of the portraitist, or at least a close approximation to it, subject, of course, to such improvements of the original deemed necessary. The invention of photography in the nineteenth century seemed to preempt the field, because with the photograph it seemed possible to attain such a truthful likeness whose verifiable objectivity denied to the portraitist the opportunity to impose his or her interpretation on the portrait image. The new technology appeared to nullify the distortions, the departures from objective truth that made painted and sculpted portraits so defective as likenesses—even if the photograph itself was small and lacked the color of nature. This illusion of photographic objectivity still informs the documentary use of photographs for purposes of identification, an index of one's existence. It has little to do with portraiture, fundamentally an interpretive art that through depiction reveals the individuality of the subject; and a portrait, whatever its value as a surrogate, does not reproduce the original but, rather, stands apart from that subject, linked to it forever like cause and effect.

Most twentieth-century portraits still resemble the physical appearance of their subjects because recognition/identification remains a desideratum of the genre, and so too its practice of representing the social dimensions of a life, implicit in the depiction of someone as "a someone." Photography, however, liberated modern portraiture from the tyranny of likeness; the authority of an illusory objectiv-

ity, derived from the world, weakened before the growing sensitivity to the perceiver's subjectivity as the only authentic source of knowledge about the world and its human inhabitants. The mimetic function of traditional portraiture thus gave way to interpretive strategies, expressed in a formal language of symbolic abstraction, that seek to visualize the particular, salient aspects of the subject's interior life—to go beneath the skin, that accident of nature, to reach the heretofore unrepresented "self" within. Evidently, the modern portraitist's investigative, reactive approach to the subject demonstrates a preference for characterization over description, for the dynamic of response over the stability of presence, sometimes at the price of recognizability. When that happens, the portrait's very reason to exist is compromised, and the fundamental connection between *image* and *of,* essential to portraiture, has been severed.

[*See also* Photography; Realism; *and* Representation.]

BIBLIOGRAPHY

Borgatti, Jean M., and Richard Brilliant. *Likeness and Beyond: Portraits from Africa and the World.* New York, 1990.

Breckenridge, James D. *Likeness: A Conceptual History of Ancient Portraiture.* Evanston, Ill., 1968.

Brilliant, Richard. *Portraiture.* Cambridge, Mass., 1991.

Feldman, Melissa E., and Benjamin H. D. Buchloh. *Face-Off: The Portrait in Recent Art.* Philadelphia, 1994.

Freedman, Luba. *Titian's Portraits through Aretino's Lens.* University Park, Pa., 1995.

Koerner, Joseph Leo. *The Moment of Self-Portraiture in German Renaissance Art.* Chicago, 1993.

Marin, Louis. *Le portrait du roi.* Paris, 1981.

Parfit, Derek. *Reasons and Persons.* Oxford, 1984. See esp. pp. 199–347.

Spiro, Audrey. *Contemplating the Ancients: Aesthetic and Social Issues in Early Chinese Portraiture.* Berkeley, 1990.

Taylor, Charles. *The Sources of the Self: The Making of the Modern Identity.* Cambridge, Mass., 1989.

Wendorf, Richard. *The Elements of Life: Biography and Portrait-Painting in Stuart and Georgian England.* Oxford, 1990.

Zanker, Paul. *Die Maske des Sokrates: Das Bild des Intellektuellen in der antiken Kunst.* Munich, 1995.

RICHARD BRILLIANT

POSTCOLONIALISM. During the 1980s, the term *postcolonialism* emerged as a popular rubric for a certain terrain of discussion within the fields of literary criticism, culture studies, and the humanities in general. There is no simple bundle of theories or ideas that, packaged together, constitute a single, unified entity of postcolonial thought; rather, postcolonial theory is a hotly debated set of conflicting beliefs and interests, with scholars, artists, authors, and critics fiercely advancing and defending opposing views on what postcoloniality is, whether and where it exists, and who is best fit to understand and explain it. In order to provide a framework to make some sense of these debates, this essay will (1) stake out the boundaries of the field's terrain—the frame that sets up a space for coherent discourse between the various voices who speak in these debates; (2) discuss and explain some of the critical terms commonly used by participants in this field; and (3) chart a brief history of the ideas advanced by a small selection of some of the more influential figures in the field: Frantz Fanon, Edward W. Said, Gayatri Chakravorty Spivak, and Homi K. Bhabha.

At the most basic level, postcolonial studies are investigations into the cultural situations of nations or peoples who have formerly been subject to imperialist colonizing territorial control. The field includes critical analyses of the processes of colonization and decolonization, and discussions of how those historical processes are responsible for the present cultural contexts and cultural products of the formerly colonized.

Postcolonial studies are generally based on the idea that the material conditions of colonization and decolonization are determinative elements in shaping the makeup of a culture, and thus in defining the subject identities of all those peoples who are constructed within that cultural system. Postcolonial theory is a response to an interest in the way concrete political and historical cultural interrelations have affected various cultures' internal systems. Within this approach, a culture's aesthetics must be seen both as a tool used in furthering its specific intercultural agenda and as a product of its own political past.

The *post* in *postcolonialism* might seem to imply that the effective period of colonial impact on colonized cultures ends once territorial control has been returned from the imperialistic powers to the indigenous peoples. *Colonialism,* however, is seen as the social assertion of a national identity whose perceived uniqueness and special value justify that nation's acts of interference and control in regards to the peoples and nations outside its own self-designated boundaries. These acts of interference may include political, economic, and cultural dominance as well as raw territorial domination. With this broadened understanding of colonialism, theorists can justify their concern with the ways in which postcolonial societies remain subject to forms of neocolonial domination, despite putative political independence.

In the same way, the seeming polar oppositionality of the terms *colonial* and *postcolonial* might appear to suggest that historical periods of overt territorial colonialism are typified by monolithic one-sided domination of colonized peoples by their colonizers. While the profound inequity of the colonizer-colonized relationships should never be downplayed, colonial discourse theory argues that the domination of the colonizers always calls forth a response of resistance from the colonized. The ways in which colonized subjects subvert their colonizers' tools of cultural control and counter their domination with secret defiance constitute a major topic for analysis in postcolonial studies.

The field is primarily concerned with the cultural history and situation of territories and peoples made "marginal" by the self-positioning of Western societies and cultures as "the center" of the civilized world. At the same time, the field's very privileging of these so-called marginal territories and their cultural products is a tacit acknowledgment of the real historical and present-day power wielded by this Western center. The complex and intricate dynamics of the relationships between marginal and central societies are discussed by many postcolonial theorists.

Postcolonial analysis comes out of an awareness of cultural borders—the imagined separating spaces from which people project the beginnings and endings of their own identities and the identities of those they call Other (the imaginary oppositional subjects whose invention supports the definition of the self). The postcolonial project addresses the construction and projection of identities—of the processes of conformation and repudiation that allow people to position themselves within the realm of the social.

This general interest in the problem of identity is related to other contemporary theories that focus on the difficulties in discussing human agency and subjecthood. Postcolonial theorists, like scholars in other branches of contemporary studies, investigate the ways in which ideology and cultural discourse—specifically the ideologies and discourses of colonialist relations—are responsible for determining individual positions within social systems. The place from which the colonized subject speaks, writes, or projects himself into the social realm is of great interest to postcolonial theorists. Solutions to this problem are widely divergent, ranging from positions that emphasize a need to recover or invent essential discrete cultural or ethnic identities to positions that suggest that colonized subjects can ever project their voices into the common territory of global discourse (see discussions of Fanon and Spivak, below).

The postmodern, poststructural emphasis on text and on the textuality of social discourse has had enormous influence on the approaches used by many postcolonial theorists. As a result, there have been far more investigations of the literary text as a means of cultural domination than of the impact of other forms of aesthetic production. The literary text is often seen as the site within which the identity of the "native" is constructed and affixed by the colonizing culture. Contemporary literary theories have also led postcolonial theorists to emphasize the lapses, omissions, and contradictions that reveal the agenda beneath colonialist literary formulae (see discussion of Said, below).

In addition, the major academic disciplinary ancestor of the postcolonial field is "Commonwealth literature," a subset of British literary studies that took on the (primarily English-language) literary production of the Commonwealth's outlying territories. This has led to much debate over the meaning and consequence of language usage itself. Questions have been raised as to whether the continued use of the colonizers' language in postcolonial culture is a politically justified and forward-looking aesthetic choice, or whether it merely demonstrates a continued submission to one of the major forms of colonial domination.

The ways in which the texts of colonized and formerly colonized peoples "write back" at their colonizers, subverting the cultural forms of their oppressors to create a mode of resistance, are another significant area of postcolonial interest. This area of literary analysis highlights the ways in which a text achieves some sort of double meaning, seeming on the surface to bow to the standards of the dominant culture, yet finding ways to project secondary, oppositional meanings from the same space. Rhetorical forms such as irony, which simultaneously work within an existent discourse and also contest that discourse, are of particular interest here.

Finally, the strangely intimate relationship that exists between colonizing and colonized cultures has led to extensive discussion of the notion of hybridity. A dialectical relationship between cultures is theorized that involves two-way receptions and resistances. The idea of syncretism is often raised, positing a pluralistic notion of cross-cultural interpenetration. Working out the nuances of these sorts of interactions within the grid of the primary relationship of oppression that exists between the two cultures occupies a significant portion of contemporary postcolonial theoretical discussion (see discussion of Bhabha, below).

The scope of postcolonial theory is too broad and too multidisciplinary (spanning sociology, anthropology, philosophy, literary studies, and even mathematics) to condense its major lines of research into a discussion of a few representative theorists. Within the general scope of the field, however, a few writers have had such impact on the thinking of their fellows that their work requires a more specific treatment. Although the case could be made that there are others whose work deserves such treatment, there is no doubt that the works and influence of Fanon, Said, Spivak, and Bhabha justify their inclusion in this category. The following discussions treat only their works that have been broadly influential on the field at large; it would be impossible adequately to treat the full scope of any of these authors' works within the limitations of this space.

Fanon. Frantz Fanon, a French West Indian psychiatrist who trained in France after World War II, came to global prominence through his best-selling texts *Black Skin, White Masks* (1952) and *The Wretched of the Earth* (1961), both of which were originally published in French. Based on his observation of French colonial practices and their consequences for their colonized subjects, Fanon promoted an ideology of resistance through a strategy of national identification.

Although his death in 1961 situates his theories into a historical period preceding the articulated development of postcolonial theory, he has taken a place as a sort of ancestor figure to present-day theorists. His work, which theorizes the enormous complexity of colonial subjectivities, has

been particularly influential in considerations of the psychological relations between colonizers and colonized. His focus on the states of marginality and Otherness that are forced on the colonized subject and his prescriptions for resistance prefigure many of the major threads of contemporary postcolonial discussion. In addition, his analysis of the role of nationalism and national cultures in helping to effect the transition from the colonial to postcolonial states has had significant impact on later thinkers and writers.

Fanon's ideas regarding the importance of the ways that the combined forces of nationalism and local culture can act to provide an organizational framework for mounting indigenous opposition to a colonial presence are best articulated in *The Wretched of the Earth*. In the chapter titled "On National Culture," he suggests that the search for a valorous and authentic precolonial local culture is the first necessary step in breaking through a colonized state's psychological dependence on the colonizer.

The intellectual and upper classes in a colonized state have the greatest access to the cultural, economic, and militaristic tools of resistance, and yet, because these groups have achieved their elite positions through successful negotiations of the colonizer's educational and economic systems, they are also the people who have been most thoroughly ideologically formed in the colonizer's mold of the "good native." In order even to contemplate resistance against the colonizing presence, the colonized must find a way to value a heritage separate from that of the colonizer.

Fanon tells us that "for these [cultured] individuals, the demand for a national culture and the affirmation of the existence of such a culture represent a special battle-field. While the politicians situate their action in present-day events, men of culture take their stand in the field of history" (Fanon, 1967, p. 168). For Fanon, one of the primary psychological violences visited on colonized subjects is the mutilation of their past. "By a kind of perverted logic, [colonization] turns to the past of oppressed people, and distorts, disfigures and destroys it" (p. 169). Restoring that sense of past becomes a means by which native intellectuals gather the strength and self-conviction that will enable them to actively oppose their oppressors.

Fanon argues that colonized subjects begin from a state in which they accept the cultural standards of the colonizers as transparent (what is "good writing"? It is writing like a Westerner, in the Western tradition). From this starting point, he theorizes an evolutionary model of rising opposition.

Fanon suggests that the first attempts at countering the cultural domination of the oppressor will come in the form of paeans to a romanticized version of a mythically splendid native past, which still demonstrate formal obedience to the conventions of the oppressor's cultural categories. For example, instead of trying to write novels with Western characters moving through Western scenes, the writer will now produce novels with native character in native scenes—yet the product, a *novel,* will still be judged according to the traditions of the novel, as developed in the West.

The nationalist phase of cultural development comes next, and it is also the first phase of active resistance to the oppressor. This phase is typified by shift in intended audience for a native intellectual's work. No longer written to be read by the oppressors, either in order to please them or to castigate them, the native intellectual's writings are now constructed for consumption by a local readership.

It is at this point, when native writers begin addressing their own people with their texts, that Fanon tells us we can truly speak of a national literature. This is the point when the national culture will become vital and meaningful to the local audience. Cultural products will no longer be met with disinterest, but will become the means of a cohesion among society, coalescing them against their oppressors.

Fanon warns of the dangerous potential contained within the rise of a national consciousness (see "The Pitfalls of National Consciousness" in *The Wretched of the Earth*), as the nationalized middle class who wrest power from the colonial regimes can easily assume the roles held by their former oppressors, creating a state whose class-based system replicates the injustices of the colonial past.

Fanon's influence has led to certain theoretical investments in essentialized ideas of national or racial identity as useful tools for effecting political change. Concepts like ncgritude (which theorized a discrete cultural identity for black peoples) and movements like the Pan-African political project (which attempted to promote a sense of meta-African shared identity) have roots in Fanon's cultural prescriptions and his pragmatic politics.

Said. Edward W. Said's 1978 text, *Orientalism,* essentially laid the groundwork for postcolonial thinking, introducing an entirely new territory for academic study. This text provides a rigorous analysis of the binary opposition between West and East, or Occident and Orient. Said attacks the white Western ways of thinking about the peoples that they term "Oriental." The basic goal of his text is to demonstrate that the idea—the organizing category—of the "Orient" is a Western invention that, among other things, serves as an Other for the West's construction of its own sense of identity. Crucial to his argument is his insistence that this invented Orient is not purely a thing of the West's imagination: it is an integral part of Western material culture, embedded in Western images, literature, and language. For Said, the aesthetic is essentially a sphere of invented stereotypes that permit one culture to define and thus control another.

Said uses a Foucauldian-based analysis to identify Orientalism as a discourse of domination, allowing and asserting a Western network of power to repress and dominate the peoples and cultures it purports to describe. Following this Foucauldian line, he asserts that, during its period of hege-

mony, the overarching discourse of Orientalism has controlled the products of every Western person writing about, thinking about, or otherwise representing the Orient. At the same time, unlike Michel Foucault, he does acknowledge some "determining imprint of individual writers upon the otherwise anonymous collective body of texts constituting a discursive formation like Orientalism" (Said, 1978, p. 23). His goal in the text is to make some beginning toward unraveling the many interrelated strands of this network of power—to see how they function to determine what the West can (and does) say about the Orient.

This task is one that has subsequently been carried out by many postcolonialist theorists. Said's ideas regarding the manner in which Western discourse has represented the "Orient" in a manner aimed at furthering covert political goals and his desire to uncover the imperialist agenda behind the West's manufacturing of powered knowledge have served as a blueprint for further analyses, most often of literary texts, but also of the visual arts (see Nochlin, 1989).

A significant part of Said's strategic effort to dismantle these modes of Orientalist discourse, however, is to suggest not only that the discourse is flawed insofar as it is a means of oppression, but also that it is flawed because it does not match up to the "brute reality" of the East. This insistent suggestion that the West, in its construction of the "Orient," is failing to see the true cultures and peoples that occupy the nations and spaces of the East becomes the most troubling aspect of his work. How this "truer" vision might be achieved is never spelled out, but its potential existence lurks within the text, serving as an additional justification for condemning the Orientalist construct that Said deplores. Nonetheless, his discussions of the myriad ways in which the West has constructed its relationships with the East, always maintaining the upper hand, are compelling and continue to be useful. In his isolation of the rhetoric and behavior of Western scientific, scholastic, militaristic, religious, and mercantile activities, Said is able to reveal significant patterns of conceptual control.

Said's project is an overtly political one, aimed at undermining what he sees as the West's continuing modes of repressive representation of the East. For Said, following Foucault, knowledge is power, and thus the primary role of the academic, that of accumulating and legitimizing knowledges, is one of secret power. In his essay "Criticism between Culture and System," he contrasts the value of the reading theories advanced by Foucault and Jacques Derrida, in terms of their usefulness for his project.

He describes Foucault and Derrida as having a similar reactions to text, insofar as both see text as duplicitous, as containing more than it makes visible. Derrida, however, Said views as content simply to make these lacks in the text his business—content to show that texts have no link to reality or to meaning. Foucault, on the other hand, identifies texts (and knowledge) with power, and he attacks the invisible, or hidden, moments in the text as a part of his larger scheme to attack and make visible the secret modes of power and repression that control all of social discourse. Said, in essence, prefers Foucault to Derrida because he perceives Foucault as providing a linguistic/critical model that is useful for motivated political activity, whereas he thinks Derrida is too esoteric; he finds that Derrida's linguistic strategy cannot be applied in any larger context. It becomes a general question of power: Said finds the Derridean method useful only for baring the ultimate powerlessness of all textual (social) effort, while he sees Foucault's ideas as having more potential for use in a directed, strategic effort to strip power from the empowered and transfer it to the (currently) powerless.

Ultimately, Said's quarrel with Derrida boils down to Said's impatience with what he sees as Derrida's insistent attack on the hope of making meaning. Said's own agenda is bound up in the need to make knowledge and, indeed, to make that knowledge intentionally, through the application of will and reason. Said believes that Derrida disallows such a possibility, and thus Said finds his method useless. Said wants to target and dismantle "Western thought," and feels this cannot be done so long as "Western thought" remains the abstraction it must be for Derrida.

Because Said sees Foucault as using textual analysis to identify the links between institutional power and textual assumption, he believes Foucault's method will allow him to reveal and thus agitate against this monolithic Western social discourse. Where Derrida concerns himself with texts as locations where the impotence of the writer is constantly revealed, Foucault concerns himself with texts as locations where the potence of social discourse is constantly concealed. Said's project becomes the locating and mapping of these strategies of control as they manifest themselves in text.

Spivak. Gayatri Chakravorty Spivak's greatest influence on postcolonial theory comes out of her various writings that theorize the position of the colonized subject within the cultural space created by their colonizers. She has brought particular attention to bear on the position of the postcolonial female, whose double marginalization within the spheres of patriarchy and colonial control makes her case both particularly difficult and particularly valuable to address.

Spivak's essay "Can the Subaltern Speak?" focused attention on the role of the "subaltern"—the insurgent colonized subject—asking whether the subaltern can inject her voice into the master discourse of dominant culture. Spivak's conclusion is that, in fact, there is no possibility for the subaltern's voice to be heard in this way. In "Subaltern Studies: Deconstructing Historiography," Spivak asserts that "the subaltern is necessarily the absolute limit of the place where history is narrativized into logic" (Spivak, 1987). This conclusion has provoked strong disagreement,

including Benita Parry's criticism that Spivak's work serves to valorize the theorist and silence the colonized subjects, perpetuating the very conditions of colonialism that postcolonial theorists are supposed to be committed to dismantling.

Spivak bases her argument on a combined rejection of the theories proposed by Foucault and an alignment with the work of Derrida. Spivak's criticism of Foucault is based on her belief that later stages of his work claim to grant an expressive subjectivity to the oppressed—a notion that is criticized in earlier stages of his logical construct. In addition, she sees Foucault as having a complicit relationship with Western culture's imperialistic domination of the colonized subject-states. She accuses him of ignoring the international division of labor that locates bourgeois-capitalist control in the industrialist hands of the West and has them exploiting the labor of the colonized non-Western nations. Indeed, she suggests that Foucault's emphasis on the repressed of the West—the mad, children, prisoners—serves as a mask that reemphasizes a Western-centric vision of the world, hiding the greater power relation of repression and domination that ultimately connects West to non-West.

She is especially troubled by what she reads as Foucault's (and also Gilles Deleuze's) expectation that the dominant networks of power/desire/interest can be revealed in the narratives or histories constructed by intellectuals, and further by his belief that the intellectual can (and should) identify and disclose the discourse of society's Other. She feels that Foucault's work supposes that these oppressed subjects know their condition and can speak their condition if permitted. In contrast, she suggests that through the ideological power of the dominant culture, the masses are brought to participate in the imagination of and maintenance of the very system that represses them. Spivak argues that the networks of power/desire/interest are so heterogeneous that they cannot be reduced to useful narrative or text. Further, she sees no possibility for the intellectual, either Western or Eastern, ever to be genuinely able to know and speak (for) the marginalized Other.

Instead, Spivak proposes a political agenda for the intellectual: "the difficult task of rewriting . . . conditions of impossibility as the conditions of its possibility" (Spivak, 1988). Representation, although impossible, is advocated as necessary and useful. She anchors this approach in the methodology of Derrida, seeing his critique of Western humanism's quest for origin as the means that invalidates Foucault's efforts. Derrida having, in her eyes, cleared the field of the obstacles represented by the Western tradition that she sees culminating in the work of Foucault, Spivak sees herself free to proceed with her own project, which is the critique of imperialism.

Her politically motivated interest in representing the status of the subaltern, despite the ultimate impossibility of that task, is made more clear in her discussion of the Subaltern Studies writers, a group of revisionary theorists of India's colonial history and postcolonial state.

While she disagrees with the group's positivistic efforts at providing an account of the "true" Indian subject, she suggests that the group's work uncovers the limits of the poststructuralist critique of humanism. "The radical intellectual in the West is either caught in a deliberate choice of subalternity, granting to the oppressed either that very expressive subjectivity which s/he criticizes or, instead, a total unrepresentability" (1987).

She suggests that (unbeknownst to them) the work of the Subaltern Studies group rests on the idea of the subject consciousness as a moment of individuation constituted on the great semiotic chain of the socius (or the essentially textual web that links people into a social group). Because all historians attempting to discuss such a subject consciousness must themselves also be positioned in the same semiotic chain, their work will always be incontrovertibly compromised. All of the group's works, therefore, are and must be failures.

Spivak suggests, however, that the methodology of deconstruction (specifically of Derrida) can be used to reassess these failures as a practice that denotes its success in the action of disruption rather than in the possibility of making meaning.

The failure inherent in the work of the Subaltern Studies group, as she sees it, would be the failure inherent in making their work of investigating and establishing the subaltern consciousness a positivistic project—making it a project that assumes it can, in fact, uncover or discover some actual, objectively true narrative of reality. She offers this justification for such a seemingly positivistic project, however: it becomes valuable not as an actual project of truth revealing or knowledge making, but instead as a strategic project with a political object. The "truth" or "knowledge" that is found or made should be weighed not against an objective, positive standard of actuality, but instead against the political standard of effectivity. If the knowledge that is "found" or made is useful for achieving the political goals of the group, it does not have to live up to its own professed goal of verity.

She discusses the importance of the group's work in revealing the inadequacy of Western categories of identity for locating the subaltern. Neither the Marxist category of preindustrial (and thus lacking class consciousness) nor the Marxist category of "working class" fits the communal identity asserted by the group for the subaltern. For Spivak, the value to be found in the practices of history writing and literary critique is in the power of such activities to take away the ability of Western master narratives (such as Marxism) to define and thus control their subaltern states and subjects.

Spivak's work has been especially influential in focusing critical attention on the significance of the concept-

metaphor of woman for the practice of postcolonial theory. For Spivak, women become the ultimate subalterns—wholly unvoiced, wholly displaced, stripped of identity within and without. As such, her (woman's) position is one of extreme discursive usefulness. Spivak's construction of histories for such displaced subaltern women has constituted a significant portion of her contribution to the field.

Said and Spivak are tied together, despite their very different reactions to and uses of the work of Derrida and Foucault, by the desire to effect a political goal through their scholarly work. Both Said and Spivak assert overt political agendas, and both evaluate available critical approaches in terms of their usefulness for furthering those political ends.

Bhabha. Homi K. Bhabha's essays, collected in *The Location of Culture,* return to some of the questions raised by Fanon in the 1950s, looking again at the issue of the subjectivity formation of the colonized person. Bhabha's project focuses on an attempt to theorize the ways in which colonized and colonizing subjects are determined by their colonial relationships, and to challenge any notion of simple polar dissimilarity between the two groups. Identity formation and the ways in which it is manifested through representations of Self and Other are his major interests, leading him to question practices of image making and imaginary spatial positioning. This approach incorporates an understanding of the aesthetic as a means of creating identities within social space.

In "Of Mimicry and Man," included in *The Location of Culture,* Bhabha sets out to describe some of the ways that colonial cultures imagine an identity for the cultures that they dominate. Unlike Said and Spivak, whose methods of analysis are essentially textual, Bhabha provides a descriptive narrative highly reliant on the ideas of psychoanalysis, especially those of Jacques Lacan. He sets up the idea of mimicry as one of the fundamental ways in which the colonizer invents a colonial subject who is always both controllable and in need of control. The colonized is put into an identity construct that mimics the colonizer's own identity: the colonized subject is always *almost* but *not quite* like the colonizer.

This complex relationship of sameness and difference informs Bhabha's notion of the essential hybridity of colonized identities. In "Signs Taken for Wonders" (also included in *The Location of Culture*), Bhabha tells us that

> produced through the strategy of disavowal, the *reference* of discrimination is always to a process of splitting as the condition of subjugation: a discrimination between the mother culture and its bastards, the self and its doubles, where the trace of what is disavowed is not repressed but repeated as something *different*—a mutation, a hybrid.

For Bhabha, this ambivalence becomes the heart of the relationship constructed by the colonizer. It provides the ground for colonial control: the colonial subject, insofar as she or he is never precisely like (never as good as, as able as, as civilized as) the colonizer, is in need of the colonizer's guidance and aid. Insofar as the colonized is almost like the colonizer, the colonized can be controlled, which means that she or he is fertile ground for the colonizer's efforts at civilization and social control.

Bhabha suggests that within the constructed thinking of the colonial mind, the native is fixed at the boundaries of civilization, the liminal space from which the white person feels her own presence begin. The colonizer projects the native as almost like (but not quite like) herself. This double (k)not (not different, not the same) that binds the relationship is presented by the colonizer as transparent: yet in order to keep it fixed, it must be constantly repeated. The terms of the colonizer's stereotype threaten one another: "almost" implies the possibility of the native becoming the same as the white man, whereas "not quite" implies that the native could become so wholly Other that the white person might lose the ability to know and thus to control the native. Neither of these changes would permit the continuation of the colonial situation. Thus, the representation of the colonized is couched in terms of eternity—terms that insist on the fundamentally static nature of the colonized culture.

Bhabha's Lacanian foundation becomes apparent in his discussion of the colonizer's controlling gaze. Gaze, which is linked to the exertion of control, is also linked to desire. It is here that the colonizer's construction of a colonized subject elides into a threat. Desire and gaze are associated with lack as well as with control. Bhabha suggests that because the colonizer has imagined a colonized that is not quite like himself, he has constructed for himself a lack that can never be made up: the colonizer will never be able to gaze on this invisible face of the colonized. This unredressable lack threatens the colonizer's feelings of control and well-being.

Bhabha theorizes that the colonizer makes the native an alien in her own land. The realm of the construction of the relationship between colonial and colonized is, in Bhabha's thinking, essentially spatial. Who owns this space? The colonial eye/I makes a representation of the colonized in order to define the space of control. The eye/I that makes this space delights in its control: the eye/I sees the colonized, but the colonized cannot return that gaze. The I/eye surmises that the colonized is unaware of being watched, too innocent, too foolish to feel the eyes on her back. But even as the colonizer asserts dominance over the space of the colonized, with the gaze of secret surveillance, secret fears tear at the core of this construct. The colonizer's fantasy of control, of possession itself, produces a phobia of impotence. The ability to make a representation—to make an image—hinges on the ability of the colonizer to know, to define, to see the colonized.

It is that very need to represent, and to anxiously rehearse and repeat the terms of the representation, that demon-strates the colonizer's suppressed awareness of the limits of that knowing/defining/seeing. The colonizer's image construct is a product both of power and of lack of power. The colonial construct of the native further complicates this situation. As the native is almost (but not quite) of the same nature as the colonizer, so the native can almost (but not quite) be represented within the framework of the colonial mind. The impossibility of representing the truly other, the wholly alien, eats away at the colonial vision.

The delight that the colonial eye/I took in its illicit possession of the native village/body is tainted by limits imposed by its fixed position. This static viewing position is written into all representations of the colonized—into the stereotypes of the enigmatic Oriental, the lying Indian, the primitive African. The colonizer's paradox goes like this: the only thing more dangerous than a native who lies is one who tells the truth: the only thing more dangerous than the native who cannot be seen is the native who can.

Within the pleasure taken in the colonial eye/I's scopic surveillance of the native, there lives the fear that the native will respond with some scopic surveillance of his/her own. There exists always the fear/the threat of the returned gaze. The colonizing eye prefers to construct an uncomfortably incomplete representation of the native, rather than to construct a representation that would allow the native access to this power. Hence the native is turned away from the gaze of the colonizing eye/I. The colonizer cannot see him or her (or it?)—but only in this way is the colonizing gaze assured of safety from the reciprocal desires manifested in the colonized subject's own gaze.

In Bhabha's work, the making of the colonial representation constructs two subjects: the colonized and the colonizer. The representation exists only in the colonist's mind. In the ambivalent shifting of desire, fear, possession, and lack, the categories of Self and Other are constantly under formation and re-formation. The existence of the two categories depends on their relation and response to one another. In the colonial construction, ultimately both self and other belong within the colonizing consciousness. As the eye/I constructs its oppositional they, the eye/I disappears; and as the eye/I reasserts itself, the they fades away. Ultimately, both eye/I and they must inhabit a tenuous relation of partial presencing in order to allow for and account for the Other.

Modes of analysis such as the ones sketched here are ultimately appealing because, within the sphere of cultural and aesthetic analysis, they enable a recognition of the significant conditions that peculiarly inform postcolonial societies and cultures. The postcolonial condition includes a particularly vital present-day relationship to history: the postcolonial identity is simultaneously constituted by its history and by a need to break with that history and become something entirely new and distinct. For the theorist of culture and cultural products, an understanding of this relationship is crucial.

The very popularity of postcolonial studies breeds a new set of problems, however. The steady broadening of the term's usage threatens to eliminate its specific relation to the historical condition of prior colonization and, instead, generally to assign it a catchall meaning aligned with any condition of marginality. While widening the possibilities for employing the term's attendant theories, this must inevitably weaken the potency of both term and theories, decreasing their usefulness for unraveling specific modes of social discourse.

At the same time, it is worth remembering that postcolonialist theory is predicated on the existence of difference and the dangers of essentialism, or subscribing to monolithic understanding of entire cultures or peoples. Formulations that rely on the existence of some monolithic "postcolonial condition," "postcolonial subject," or "postcolonial discourse" threaten to recreate the colonial situation, in which the postcolonial intellectual's academic discourse serves simply to reconstitute the West-East knowledge/power relationship of ownership and domination. The discussion of postcolonial women is especially problematic, with certain formulations threatening to create an essentialized "third-world Woman" who serves only as a foil for Western feminist intervention.

In other words, as many theorists at work in the field acknowledge, postcolonial theory threatens, at worst, to erase the various, singular words and actions of actual postcolonial peoples in favor of the ideas of an intellectual elite located within the Western academic system. The lived experiences of the colonized and formerly colonized become raw data to be fed into the machinery of postcolonial theory. Once again, East becomes mere fodder for the global theory knowledge-making activities of the West. The theorist becomes the hero of the piece, the one capable of explaining the postcolonial past and present to the very players who lived out that history. As postcolonial theorists square off against one another, debating variations of their conceptual constructs, postcolonial subjects become pawns whose location matters only in terms of institutional one-upmanship.

This leaves Western scholars in the following situation: we can either discuss the postcolonial situation and in doing so, potentially perpetuate it, or we can ignore it entirely, thereby *certainly* perpetuating it. Said's and Spivak's preoccupation with the motivated political aspects of their work must be recognized as crucial to this dilemma. Perhaps it is only when postcolonial theory is deliberately wielded as a political tool, aimed at unsettling the dominant power relationships linking the cultures of center and margin, that it might hope to escape becoming simply another excuse for the production of academic symposia, panel discussions, journal articles, and encyclopedia entries.

[See also African Aesthetics; Caribbean Aesthetics; Cultural Studies; Indian Aesthetics; Orientalism; Politics and Aesthetics; and Primitivism.]

BIBLIOGRAPHY

Adam, Ian, and Helen Tiffin, eds. *Past the Last Post: Theorizing Post-colonialism and Post-modernism.* Calgary, 1990.

Appiah, Kwame Anthony. "Is the Post- in Postmodern the Post- in Postcolonial?" *Critical Inquiry* 17.2 (Winter 1991): 336–357.

Ashcroft, Bill, Gareth Griffiths, and Helen Tiffin. *The Empire Writes Back: Theory and Practice in Post-colonial Literatures.* London and New York, 1989.

Ashcroft, Bill, Gareth Griffiths, and Helen Tiffin, eds. *The Post-colonial Studies Reader.* London and New York, 1995.

Bhabha, Homi K., ed. *Nation and Narration.* London and New York, 1990.

Bhabha, Homi K. *The Location of Culture.* London and New York, 1994.

Fanon, Frantz. *The Wretched of the Earth.* Translated by Constance Farrington. New York, 1963.

Fanon, Frantz. *Black Skin, White Masks.* Translated by Charles Lam Markmann. New York, 1967.

Hutcheon, Linda. "Circling the Downspout of Empire: Postcolonialism and Postmodernism." *Ariel* 20.4 (October 1989): 149–175.

Mercer, Kobena. "Diaspora Culture and the Dialogic Imagination." In *Blackframes: Critical Perspectives on Black Independent Cinema,* edited by Mbye B. Cham and Claire Andrade-Watkins, pp. 50–61. Cambridge, Mass., 1988.

Nochlin, Linda. "The Imaginary Orient." In *The Politics of Vision: Essays on Nineteenth-Century Art and Society,* pp. 33–59. New York, 1989.

Parry, Benita. "Problems in Current Theories of Colonial Discourse." *Oxford Literary Review* 9.1–2 (1987): 27–58.

Said, Edward W. *Orientalism.* New York, 1978.

Said, Edward W. *The World, the Text, and the Critic.* Cambridge, Mass., 1983.

Said, Edward W. *Culture and Imperialism.* New York, 1993.

Spivak, Gayatri Chakravorty. "Subaltern Studies: Deconstructing Historiography." In *In Other Worlds: Essays in Cultural Politics,* pp. 197–221. New York and London, 1987.

Spivak, Gayatri Chakravorty. "Can the Subaltern Speak?" In *Marxism and the Interpretation of Culture,* edited by Cary Nelson and Lawrence Grossberg, pp. 271–313. Urbana, Ill., 1988.

Spivak, Gayatri Chakravorty. *The Post-colonial Critic: Interviews, Strategies, Dialogues.* Edited by Sarah Harasym. New York and London, 1990.

Tiffin, Chris, and Alan Lawson, eds. *De-scribing Empire: Post-colonialism and Textuality.* London and New York, 1994.

Williams, Patrick, and Laura Chrisman, eds. *Colonial Discourse and Post-colonial Theory: A Reader.* New York, 1994.

Young, Robert. *White Mythologies: Writing History and the West.* London and New York, 1990.

Young, Robert. *Colonial Desire: Hybridity in Theory, Culture, and Race.* London and New York, 1995.

ELIZABETH CORNWELL

POSTMODERNISM. [*To clarify the phenomenon of postmodernism, this entry comprises three essays:*

    Historical and Conceptual Overview

    Postmodern Dance

    Postmodern Poetry

The first essay is examines the meaning, history, and current status of postmodernism as both a historical and an aesthetic concept. This overview is followed by essays that explain what postmodernism has meant in the specific arts of dance and poetry—two areas where postmodernism has been particularly important. While the focus in both essays is on the American context of postmodernism, the broader, international context is also discussed. For a discussion of postmodern architecture, see Architecture; *for postmodern art, see* Contemporary Art. *For related discussion, see* Appropriation; Modernism; *and* Poststructuralism.]

Historical and Conceptual Overview

The more one begins to fathom the plethora of discourses, theories, sociocultural conditions, art objects, stylistic traits and historical events that are called, envisioned, stigmatized, or theorized as postmodern, the less it is clear that there is any clear and coherent object of study to be encompassed by the encyclopedic imagination. Thus at issue in an overview of postmodernism is the question of what an overview ought to look like, granted the diffuse, fragmentary, multi-dimensional, and contestable character of the object of study. The problem is not insuperable, but is indeed one at the very origin of postmodernism itself, which is why we begin with a statement of it. For the epistemological difficulties raised about 1) the coherence of an object of study (here: "postmodernism"), 2) the capacity of a genre (here: the encyclopedia) to provide a coherent narrative of that object of study, and 3) the socio-politics of the "archive" (the storehouse of texts, the fabric of research, the social attitudes) out of which the narrative is composed, are issues at the heart of the postmodern debate. Certain postmodernists throw their hands up in glee over the supposed collapse of the project of rendering the world comprehensible at all—even in "overview" terms, while others seek to expand our sense of how the world is composed (the unity of the object, the structure of the subject), and how our languages capture it: making these terms more elastic, multi-perspective, and contextual. We should be obliged to keep this issue in mind in what follows.

History of Postmodernism. The history of the postmodern—that is, of a collection of events with roots in modern life, modernism in the arts, and post-war economics and politics,—events which are, some will say, still occurring—is straightforward enough. The term *postmodernism* was first made popular by Ihab Hassan, who used it to characterize emerging trends in the literature in the 1960s. Such writers as John Barth, Donald Barthelme, and, later, Thomas Pynchon, responding to the great stylistic and conceptual breakthrough of James Joyce's *Finnegans Wake* and the work of Samuel Beckett, began to write novels that played with the very idea of the novel—novels whose twists of language, contortions of plot, multiple narrative voices, unclarities of narrative resolution, and stylistic games called into question the claims of the novel to objectivity and authority in characterizing, explaining, and, in

general, picturing its subject. Whereas the classic vision of the novel as articulated by Stendhal described the novel as a mirror being carried along a road, as if the novelistic form were nothing but a transparent recording device that presented reality in its deepest form, these novels called attention to their lack of transparent connection to reality—to the fact that they are acts of creative writing that arise out of literary genres. By extension they called attention to the prismatic nature of reality itself. The epistemological self-suspicions voiced by the postmodern novel (suspicions no doubt already present in nascent form in such great modernist works as Joseph Conrad's) may also be found in the early poststructuralist writings of the 1960s. It is as if the postmodern novel were written in tandem with the writing of Jacques Derrida, whose critique of subjectivity, authorship, and truth, whose attention to the artifices, complexities of dissemination, and intertextual nature of writing, whose exposure of the contradictions in its conceptual organization, and whose play with language, are of a piece with these novels. Roland Barthes also spoke of the exhaustion of the novel as a genre, and raised the question in his work of what it means to write in an exhausted art form (the question of the one who comes too late).

These attitudes shared by postmodern novelists and certain poststructuralist writers prepared a later interweaving between postmodernism and poststructuralism. Many theoretical pictures or definitions of the postmodern are provided by poststructuralism, and these definitions—whether adequate or not—enter the fabric of postmodern arts. Postmodern art has continually relied on poststructuralist ideas (about the critique of the unity of the subject, the failure of discourse to contain the world through its conceptual "laws," about the implication of language in the history of power, about the collapse of traditions of philosophical objectivity and historical progress), and in its later phases on feminist and multicultural ideas, in articulating to itself its own concerns and investing its art with theoretical power and perspicuity. This infusion of theory into the practice of the arts is itself a legacy from modern art, which had already relied on its own theories and the theories of others in investing its art with meaning and force, in articulating its artistic experiments and lending it a theoretical and a political voice. Through theory conjoined with artistic experimentalism, art claims to make a statement to the world about life, art, the institutions of art, to speak in a political voice. In turn, poststructuralism formulates its theories partially in response to modern and postmodern art (Marcel Duchamp, René Magritte, Valerio Adami, John Cage, Dada, Surrealism, and so on).

Postmodernism then comes into play in architecture in the late 1960s and early 1970s. It is roughly datable to the writings and architecture of Robert Venturi, whose book *Learning from Las Vegas* claimed that the urges of modern architecture—to impose utopian changes on the lives of

POSTMODERNISM: Overview. Charles Moore, *Piazza d'Italia* (1978). New Orleans. (Photograph courtesy of Michael Kelly.)

everybody through an architecture whose purist principles could be elaborated prior to all actual building contexts—were almost totally wrong. Turning from the high to the low, Venturi stated with admirable cheek that the buildings of Las Vegas could serve as worthy architectural models for the United States in virtue of their intelligent adaptation to the context of the automobile, their inventiveness, and their dramatic elaborations of architectural space. His early buildings from that time sent up modernism by interpolating "wrong" architectural details into essentially modernist structures (cf. his Guild House). (More profoundly disturbational to the concept of art were Cage's riotous interpolations of the sounds of everyday life into the space of music and Merce Cunningham's recasting of dance forms into vernacular [everyday] movements produced in part by chance operations. Cage and Cunningham aimed to overrule those hierarchies according to which art is distinguished from the flow of life itself.)

Architecture could hardly survive indefinitely on a joking style, and it tended to move in a variety of directions in accord with Venturi's injunctions: (1) to build contextually in terms of local vernaculars, in terms of the desires of local patrons, the specific needs of cities, towns, and distinctive populations; (2) to play the game of stylistic juxtaposition and pluralism; and (3) to retain the game of high modernist send up (turning it into a somewhat stale joke). Architecture also continued modernist stylistics in a number of ways, retaining modular construction, open plans, and (in some domains) theory-based architecture.

Architectural pluralism began as free and wonderful aesthetic innovation but all too often degenerated into mere consumerism, with the architect treating the variety of extant styles as mere consumer products locatable in a huge cultural department store called "the global museum" and juxtaposing these for no other reason than to come up with the latest architecturally new "look" for the client to consume. As buildings turned into consumer products, attention to the complex issues surrounding stylistic appropriation and pluralistic context diminished. This degeneration of the artist or architect into a mere consumer and the artwork into something to be valued by its audience as little more than a commodity is a general postmodern tendency, one theorized as the result of late capitalism's colonization of the cultural sphere by Fredric Jameson, David Harvey, and others. Other strands of architecture continued avant-garde norms of theory-based design. Thus, for example, the deconstructionist architecture of Peter Eisenman aims to speak philosophically against architectural totality and determinacy and for the idea of architecture as an event through its "deconstructionist" look. The claim of the postmodern to speak through its spectacular look or theatrical event—itself a legacy of avant-garde shock values—places postmodern art securely within the space of the "society of the spectacle" (Debord, 1967).

Visual arts exhibit a similar trajectory to that of architecture in the 1970s and 1980s. What Arthur C. Danto has called the creative pluralism of the 1970s (in which visual art, like architecture, freed itself from minimalist/modernist canons of purity and discovered the norms of free expression and juxtaposition) gave way (especially in New York) to "the painting of importance" (Danto). This painting arrived with a size, inscrutability, and suggestion of depth guaranteed to impress the viewer who enjoyed being seduced into the illusion of meaningfulness, and who wished to consume and collect greatness as if it were a glamour product available with the immediacy by which television delivers the news. The concept of meaningfulness became replaced by its simulacrum (Jean Baudrillard), as "you invest[ed] in the divinity of the masterpiece" (Barbara Kruger). Paintings by David Salle, Rodney Allen Greenblatt, and Julian Schnabel are often mentioned in this regard, although each of these artists may also be given a counterreading.

Other regions of postmodern art have aimed to voice their suspicions of this commodification of art (even if these artists have sometimes ended up generating their own commodification in the process). These regions have also voiced suspicions about the history of representation and their place in this history. They have done so by theatricalizing art and its history in the manner of Duchamp, creating games played in and around art that aim to expose the practices of art as veils that silently encode attitudes of omnipotence, ideology, gender, and degradation—art practices ironically played out under the guise of the beautiful, the natural, and the sublime. (Again, poststructuralist ideas have informed this art.) At its best, postmodern art also comprehends that power is produced and conveyed (in part) through "visualities": by turning words into white hot images and images into spectacles (Debord, Michel Foucault). Such artists (Hans Haacke, Kruger, Jenny Holzer, Cindy Sherman) simulate the guise of the media (photos, newsprint, ads, signage, etc.) in order to symbolically harness its power and subvert this power to the purpose of critique.

Even those regions of art that cannot bear to live in a state bereft of the artistic voices of their past (Anselm Kiefer) are also deeply suspicious of their inheritances, believing the representational schemes of the past can be resurrected only through a rigorous interrogation of their bleak interconnections with social and political life (as in Kiefer's interrogation—as far as it goes—of connections between the grandiose German Romantic voice and the Nazi atrocity).

Postmodernism and Modern Life. *Postmodernism* quickly came into use as a term in sociology, political science, and other academic disciplines as way of characterizing alterations in the structure not only of the arts but also of the greater processes of life in which the arts are set. If postmodernism in the arts has stood in some ambivalent position toward modernism—on the one hand, desiring clear separation from some region of modern art, while on the other, working within the aesthetic legacies that modernism had set up—postmodernism as an academic philosophical position directs its ambivalence toward modernity (the structures, processes, and myths of modern life). Postmodernism in the academy is thus a debate about the dissolution of modernity or its preservation in transformed form (a debate also extending to the role of art in this). This debate is complicated, however, by the difficulty in producing a clear (much less a complete) list of the elements comprising modern life. Different theorists claim that different aspects of modernity (philosophical, cultural, political, economic, geographical, etc.) have broken up just as different artists write the epitaph for different regions of modern art (and, by extension, modern life).

The locus classicus of the theory of modernity is G. W. F. Hegel, who posited as the central structures of modern life those of the state (the nation), with its three modes of absolute spirit (art, religion, and philosophy), its connections to science, its vision of itself as existing within history, and its boundless capacity for self-reflection, self-reflection that could and had produced, in Hegel's self-adulating idea, continuous historical progress. At the basis of this vision is that of humanity as a singular, universal entity capable of being seen and exemplified in the actions of the particular man, a vision which has allowed the West to claim that its men (above all, Hegel himself) speak in the name of everybody. It is this grandiose self-conception held by the West that Gianni Vattimo takes to be the underlying myth that has characterized its modernity. According to Vattimo, the dissolution of this cultural myth and its powerful employment in the history of the West has in turn prepared the West for a multicultural liberation in which history may be written and society understood as multiplex tapestries inclusive of the stories and concerns of everybody, rather than as singular stories that silence the voices of this multitude. Jean-François Lyotard's vision of justice as the free forging of dialogue between different persons (such that none will be consigned to indignity) imposes on art and culture the goal of witnessing differences between persons, thereby searching (in the absence of pregiven rules) to find and invent ways of their speaking and listening to one another. On this view, those regions of postmodern art that attempt to witness how representational schemes are implicated in processes of victimization (Kiefer) and those that remake representational schemes to articulate the identities of persons not yet listened to by society (Sherman, Nancy Spero) are paramount.

By contrast, Harvey believes the conditions of modern life to be defined in terms of economics and geography. For him, modern Fordist capitalism (the production line) has given way to late or "flexible" capitalism in a world of postmodern "space-time compression," with the results that (1) cultural life is commodified as information processes (computers, global markets, telecommunications, etc.) become the locus of capitalism; and (2) we live in Marshall McLuhan's global village, in a state of overstimulation by the flow of information. For Baudrillard it is the media that have engendered the current "age," a desultory age in which we can no longer tell simulacrum from reality, in which reality has become the object of scopophilic interest, and the autonomy of the self is obliterated by the ecstatic pressures of media(tion).

Theories of the Postmodern. The most famous and influential theory of postmodern (and therefore modern) life is Lyotard's. His *The Postmodern Condition: A Report on Knowledge* assumes that three factors jointly define the postmodern. First and foremost, the postmodern is defined by our age's incredulity toward metanarratives—stories that claim to determine the relations between the subject, humanity, objectivity, and the sociocultural or historical spheres—the stories of Hegel, Karl Marx, Christianity, the avant-gardes, and the like. Old metanarratives of legitimation are no longer viable, granted the pressures of late-capitalist production (which turns information into capital), our suspicions of what our totalizing ideas have wrought in this century, and the vague and multiplex dispersion of language games played over forms of knowledge in our contemporary interglobal world. The world is interdisciplinary, multiperspectival, and shifting, thus denying all the old repertoire of justifications for the forms of knowledge. Nor are any new large-scale pictures of legitimation adequate to the terms of the age. Thus, we are skeptical about all general concepts of legitimation. The contemporary instability of knowledge practices to shift and realign themselves also has, according to Lyotard, its positive side; it provides for the possibility of new and creative modes of knowledge in which disciplines converge and social institutions realign. These new sources of knowledge can only be legitimated contextually: in terms of their specific modes of application.

Lyotard's picture of knowledge as a contextual and pluralistic mode of combining old ideas and conceptual styles in new ways can easily be seen to picture trends in the literature, art, and architecture of the 1970s. Indeed, Lyotard believes that avant-garde art is in fact the underlying model for authentic knowledge in general today, with its experimentalism and its capacity (in Lyotard's rosy picture of it) for resisting bourgeois sedimentation through its free experimentalism. Moreover, the postmodern task of witnessing those who are different and forging dialogue between such persons also cannot rest assured by previous acts of legitimation, since the point is to find and invent modes of listening, speaking, and connection that are, by Lyotard's definition, not captured by existing rules.

In general, the postmodern will look very different depending on whether it is pictured as a moment of new opportunity for the West or (primarily) as a moment of loss, breakdown, and corruption. Thus, on the one hand, one has Baudrillard's bleak vision and, on the other, Vattimo's and Lyotard's rosier one.

Each of these theoretical perspectives relies on some favored set of examples that paradigmatically illustrate (and prove the truth of) its analytic categories. Each of these theories therefore may be read to contain an implicit Hegelian (i.e., modern) assumption that the postmodern is a univocal zeitgeist with an underlying shape capable of being explained in terms of that single analytic category that the theory provides. Thus, Baudrillard's vision of the postmodern as a vast simulacrum depends on the choice of television, the media, and the half-real and half-mythical America of his *America* as definitive (Baudrillard, Kiefer, and Sherman would be old modernists). Jameson's vision of the commodification of art, the loss of the "semi-autonomous cultural sphere," and the empty tiredness of this age of stylistic "pastiche" relies on regions of art and architecture already discussed, and on high-concept Hollywood films. Lyotard's vision adulates Duchamp and Cage and nicely characterizes Kiefer. Note also that all these theorists fall into the Eurocentric mode of theorizing the postmodern (and the modern) to the exclusion of most of the world. Little attention is given to the diversity of (plausibly) postmodern cultures. Indeed, even the various cultures of the United States and Europe exhibit distinctive postmodernist features. For example, Italian postmodern art is closer to traditional aesthetic features of the beautiful and the expressive than its counterparts from New York.

Finally, different theories (and different works of art) negotiate the *post* in *postmodern* differently. Some wish to, hope to, intend to, or claim to produce or theorize a radical break with whatever came before the "post" (the avant-garde, modernism, modern life, the nation-state as the paradigmatic modern institution, modernity as a systematic arrangement of concepts including those of objectivity, subjectivity, historical progress, justice, etc.). Others view their *post* phase as a continuation of the past in a modified form, as a pause from it, or even a sublation of it. There is no one way in which the past is received, negotiated, or theorized, but rather many.

Postmodernism and the Classical Concepts of Aesthetics. The discourses of aesthetics arose in the eighteenth century in conjunction with the culture of the museum, and postmodern art is typically suspicious of both, while also remaining unwilling and unable to pry itself away from its dependence on the museum. Postmodern art, when concerned to expose the dark underside of artistic practices, focuses not only on the social codes inscribed in works of art but also on the modes of voyeuristic omnipotence cultivated in art making and art viewing, and the museum is seen to play a central role in the cultivation of what postmodern art history has called (if not fetishized as) "the gaze." When Édouard Manet and, later, Duchamp attack the gaze, they thereby attack the museum (Manet implicitly and Duchamp explicitly), along with those related institutions of art that have participated in its construction and been a crucial condition of its possibility. The museum (and the museumizing imagination associated with it) fixes the art object independently of its original site and turns it into a sight: an object known independently of its enmeshment in the stream of life and redefined through its artificial placement in the visual space and narrative arrangement. It has traditionally served to rewrite the history of art as part of its national patrimony (Benedict Anderson), thus encoding viewers as agents of the nation who are symbolically allowed to revel in their ownership of these objects and this story. Furthermore, by turning the entire colonial world into a museum without walls—into a timeless space of exotic objects (Edward Said) and endlessly repeated calcifications of life—colonialism bridged the museum and the colonial world, laying claim to unbridled possession of and unchallenged epistemic access to both. Were one to speak in a Foucauldian way about the museum, one would refer to it as an institution whose genealogy derives in part from a heterogeneous pattern of power—national, colonizing, and male—that partially brought it about, and that it serves to articulate. This is to speak in a postmodern way, the other side of the equation being the museum's recent contributions to fostering multicultural presentations of art.

Seen from Foucault's perspective, the eighteenth-century discourses of aesthetics—ironically and in spite of their explicit intentions—also played a role in the articulation of this power. In spite of their emphases on the ideals of artistic autonomy, on art's capacity to engender a free play of the human imagination and its role in inculcating a moral community of persons, aesthetic discourses have served the interests of the museumizing imagination by defining fine art and the beautiful in abstraction from art's role in the stream of cultural life. Thus, these discourses helped to legitimate the transposition of art from specific cultural context to museum, and the sedimentation of the museumizing gaze, a gaze now believed to be "aesthetic" because it is abstracted from particular interests, desires, beliefs, and forms of cultural life. The claim of aesthetics that art is there to give pleasure and delight of a sensuous and formal kind was, moreover, precisely what the museum required when it feminized the object before the prideful and possessive gaze of the nationalist, Western, male viewer. No epistemic (or moral) problem could therefore arise in the viewing and interpretation of artworks since they were meant to be viewed "aesthetically" in abstraction from their streams of life—no question about the viewer's own capacity to know, understand, cognize, perceive, or fathom them, no question about their subjectivity. Therefore, a postmodern approach to the history of aesthetics would render these discourses objects of ambivalence: on the one hand, the propounder of thoughts about art we cannot do without and, on the other, deeply implicated in the history of power. Feminist critiques of aesthetic discourses are of this sort.

A postmodern approach to aesthetics would also abjure universal definitions of art and instead stress the diversity of art objects, the contextual nature of artistic construction and definition, the role of art in the stream of life generally, and the opacities of artistic interpretation. It would also, following the thought of Foucault, find the aesthetic to be a basic dimension of the social construction of bodies, whose systems of pleasure and taste are in part products of the history of power. A corollary would be the retrieval of ancient ideas linking the aesthetic to the erotics of pleasure.

Postmodern Explanation of the Postmodern. We may grant both the failure of modern styles of (Hegelian) explanation to place the complex and diffuse set of events that fall under the name of the postmodern into a single procrustean explanatory framework, and of the extreme postmodernist position that gleefully exclaims that neither object of study nor discourse of analysis can therefore allow for any coherent account or "overview." Perhaps the best sketch of the kind of overview we have indeed given is provided by the work of the philosopher Ludwig Wittgenstein. Wittgenstein's work pictures the identity and integrity of concepts in terms of strands of crisscrossing similarities and organic interconnections that hold them together. A Wittgensteinian approach to the postmodern would think of it as a family of related discourses and events (including events in the history of theory), related not in one way but in myriad ways, the myriad of interrelationships defining the concept of the postmodern—or, the postmodern "world." Postmodernism is an interlocking set of language games, related in numerous ways: nothing more and nothing less. Let us further appropriate a thought from Wittgenstein and state that in different contexts of discussion, different conceptions of the postmodern (and different representative examples of it) will be useful or required. Since we give up the Hegelian assumption that there is an age called the postmodern with a single historical shape that can be theorized in accord with a single analytic category, we are thereby freed to use all theories, to test each for its domain, its range, its contexts of use. All will have some use or other. (The key is to avoid becoming a consumer of theories like the artist or architect who consumes rather than recasts styles, something all too rampant in the academy.) Finally Wittgenstein's contextualist thought that our concepts depend for their integrity and use on a broad and interwoven background context will open us up to the right range of explanatory sources for the postmodern—namely, everything. In this sense, Wittgenstein's monumental writings, like Joyce's in literature, inaugurate the postmodern approach to explanation in philosophy.

[*See also* Baudrillard; *and* Lyotard.]

BIBLIOGRAPHY

Anderson, Benedict. *Imagined Communities: Reflections on the Origin and Spread of Nationalism.* Rev. ed. London and New York, 1991.

Baudrillard, Jean. *Simulations.* Translated by Paul Foss, Paul Patton, and Philip Beitchman. New York, 1983.

Baudrillard, Jean. *America.* Translated by Chris Turner. London and New York, 1988.

Danto, Arthur C. *The Transfiguration of the Commonplace: A Philosophy of Art.* Cambridge, Mass., 1981.

Danto, Arthur C. *Beyond the Brillo Box: The Visual Arts in Post-Historical Perspective.* New York, 1992.

Debord, Guy. *La société du spectacle.* Paris, 1967.

Derrida, Jacques. *Dissemination.* Translated by Barbara Johnson. Chicago, 1981.

Docherty, Thomas, ed. *Postmodernism: A Reader.* New York, 1993.

Ferguson, Russell, et al., eds. *Discourses: Conversations in Postmodern Art and Culture.* Cambridge, Mass., 1990.

Foucault, Michel. *The Order of Things: An Archaeology of the Human Sciences.* New York, 1970.

Foster, Hal, ed. *The Anti-Aesthetic: Essays on Postmodern Culture.* Port Townsend, Wash., 1983.

Harvey, David. *The Condition of Postmodernity: An Enquiry into the Origins of Cultural Change.* Oxford and Cambridge, Mass., 1989.

Hassan, Ihab. *The Postmodern Turn: Essays in Postmodern Theory and Culture.* Columbus, Ohio, 1987.

Jameson, Fredric. *Postmodernism: or, The Cultural Logic of Late Capitalism.* Durham, N.C., 1991.

Jencks, Charles A. *The Language of Post-Modern Architecture.* 6th ed. New York, 1991.

Jencks, Charles. *Post-Modernism: The New Classicism in Art and Architecture.* New York, 1987.

Lyotard, Jean-François. *The Postmodern Condition: A Report on Knowledge.* Translated by Geoff Bennington and Brian Massumi. Minneapolis, 1984.

Lyotard, Jean-François. *The Postmodern Explained: Correspondence, 1982–1985.* Translation edited by Julian Pefanis and Morgan Thomas, translations by Don Barry et al. Minneapolis, 1992.

Perloff, Marjorie, ed. *Postmodern Genres.* Norman, Okla., 1988.

Rorty, Richard. *Contingency, Irony, and Solidarity.* Cambridge and New York, 1989.

Said, Edward W. *Orientalism.* New York, 1978.

Vattimo, Gianni. *The End of Modernity: Nihilism and Hermeneutics in Post Modern Culture.* Translated by Jon R. Snyder. Baltimore, 1988.

Vattimo, Gianni. *The Transparent Society.* Translated by David Webb. Baltimore, 1992.

Venturi, Robert. *Complexity and Contradiction in Architecture.* 2d ed. New York, 1977.

Venturi, Robert, Denise Scott Brown, and Stephen Izenour. *Learning from Las Vegas: The Forgotten Symbolism of Architectural Form.* Rev. ed. Cambridge, Mass., 1977.

Wellmer, Albrecht. *The Persistence of Modernity: Essays on Aesthetics, Ethics, and Postmodernism.* Translated by David Midgley. Cambridge, Mass., 1991.

Wittgenstein, Ludwig. *Philosophical Investigations.* 3d ed. Translated by G. E. M. Anscombe. New York, 1968.

DANIEL HERWITZ

Postmodern Dance

In dance, the term *postmodern* is used differently from its application in the other arts. In the other arts, especially architecture, the visual arts, and literature, the term *postmodern* is used to refer to art that sets itself in opposition to high modernism in various ways: by making allusions to the history of the art form; by eliding "high" and "low" culture in the self-conscious fusion of modernism with the vernacular; and by embracing pleasure and rejecting austerity. Postmodern artworks are thus said to challenge values of originality, authenticity, and the masterpiece by copying, commenting on, or otherwise "deconstructing" modernist artworks, perhaps thereby offering political resistance to dominant Western culture. They reintroduce representation, but by making representations of representations.

Yet, often it has been in the arena of postmodern dance that issues of modernism in the other arts have arisen: for example, the acknowledgment of the medium's materials, the revealing of dance's essential qualities as an art form, the separation of formal elements, the abstraction of forms, and the elimination of external references as subjects. Certain aspects of postmodern dance also fit, however, with current notions of postmodern culture: irony, playfulness, historical reference, the use of vernacular materials, the breakdown of boundaries between art forms and between art and life. Charles Jencks has argued that in architecture, postmodern style has a doubly coded aesthetic that appeals to both popular, untutored audiences and to esoteric specialists (Jencks, 1986). In dance, this definition could be used to categorize the work of such crossover choreographers, straddling modern dance and ballet, as Mark Morris and Twyla Tharp. But to do so would be to ignore the term's use since the 1960s to mean something quite different. That is, there is an ambiguity in the use of the term *postmodern dance*. Using it as a historical term has a certain temporal and geographic specificity. In this sense, it is a historical style marker, like the term *German Expressionism*. But there is also an analogical use of the term that is transhistorical and transgeographic. This article will primarily be concerned with the historical use of the term, since that is the way it was introduced into dance-historical and theoretical discourse and that is its primary reference. The analogical uses of the term will also be briefly discussed.

Yvonne Rainer first used the label "postmodern dance" in the 1960s in a strictly chronological sense, referring to her own generation of American dancers as that which came after historical modern dance. In the modern dance of Martha Graham, Doris Humphrey, José Limón, and others, stylized movements and energy levels, organized in legible (usually musical) structures (such as theme and variations, ABA, and so on) conveyed feeling tones and social messages. With the publication of the postmodern dance issue of the *Drama Review* (1975), the term gained wide currency and began to be used to classify what had by then emerged as a style.

Although postmodern dance continued into the 1980s and 1990s and spread from New York to other parts of the United States and internationally, the term is generally used to refer to the values of the 1960s and 1970s, rooted in the origins of the movement in the work of dancers associated with the Judson Dance Theater in New York City, which had by then become recognized as the world center for modern dance. Sally Banes has referred to the 1960s and 1970s as encompassing two phases of postmodern dance: "breakaway" postmodern dance and "analytic" postmodern dance (Banes, 1987). These two phases are discussed here, tracing the history of the genre in terms of its aesthetic and moral commitments.

The early postmodern choreographers saw as their task the purging and amelioration of historical modern dance, which they felt had made unfulfilled promises in regard to the use of the body and the social and artistic functions of dance. The radical departures of Merce Cunningham's dances and John Cage's theories of music and performance formed an important base from which many of the ideas and actions of the postmodern choreographers sprang, either in opposition or in a spirit of extension.

Perhaps the most important principle, for the dancers of the breakaway years, was the Cageian idea that boundaries between art and life should be broken down. This led them away from Cunningham's virtuosic technique as well as from the theatricality of modern dancers like Graham. Perhaps the most important break with the past was their use of the ordinary body and workaday, nondance actions (parallel to Cage's opening up of music to ordinary, nonmusical sounds). For some, this was simply an aesthetic issue—a way to refresh the exploration of movement qualities by using bodies that were not already constrained by a given dance technique. But for many, this—along with the cooperative structure of the Judson Dance Theater group—stemmed from a political commitment to the democratic ideals of equality and freedom. It was meant to embody equal rights, to level the playing field so that even the non-specialist could perform, and so that all members of the audience might find something familiar (or at least doable) in the dance spectacle they beheld. Out of this perspective, a communitarian ethos emerged in many of the works.

Thus, in Rainer's *We Shall Run* (1963), a group of twelve adults—dancers and nondancers, in work clothes ranging from suits to sweatpants—runs steadily in shifting patterns that cause them to group and regroup for seven minutes to music by Hector Berlioz. There are no permanent leaders; every time someone seems to head the group for a time, the changing floor plan guarantees that a new facing will produce a new leader—from the back of the flock this time. The temporary leaders are sometimes men, sometimes women; the large group is not factionalized, but harmoniously and with a purposeful mien constantly divides in random groups and then reunites. The image is one of a serious, even heroic, egalitarian collective.

But the incorporation of the ordinary into choreography extended not only to including the nondancers' bodies onstage. It framed ordinary movements and quotidian gestures, even by trained dancers, as worthy of notice in a dance. This was an aspect of democratic leveling that celebrated the mundane, the awkward, and other aspects of movement that, it was felt, had previously been overlooked in both ballet and modern dance, which had privileged special, heightened, theatrical movements.

As well, the postmodern dancers showed that any space could be an appropriate stage. As the dance critics raised their eyebrows, the postmoderns danced in church sanctuaries, gymnasiums, lofts, galleries, outdoors in fields, and in all sorts of other buildings and nontheatrical sites.

Arthur Danto has argued that 1964 was the key year in the history of modern art, because in that year Andy Warhol's *Brillo Boxes* confronted the art world with the possibility that something indiscernible from an ordinary object could be an artwork. In 1963, however, at Judson Dance Theater concerts, postmodern choreographers had already anticipated Warhol's breakthrough in dances like *We Shall Run* and Judith Dunn's *Acapulco*, which included a woman ironing a dress and combing another woman's hair and two women playing cards. These dances raised the question of the difference between dance and ordinary movement. If Warhol leveled the perceptible distance between artworks and real things, Rainer, Dunn, Steve Paxton, and others attempted to put dance on a par with everyday gesture. Undoubtedly, an aspect of this leveling was not merely an exercise in aesthetic experimentation, but political symbolism as well.

And the demotic ideal focused not only on issues of equality but also on aspirations to freedom. In this, the body—with its complex social meanings—served as a potent medium. An unabashed examination of the body and its functions and powers threaded through early postmodern dance. One form it took was relaxation, a deliberate letting go of the tight control that has characterized much Western dance technique (both in ballet and modern dance). This loosening of the body's boundaries metaphorically stood for liberation from cultural restrictions, foreshadowing the many modes of bodily freedom practiced in the late 1960s. Basing dances on children's games and free play also served as a model for escaping adult bodily strictures. Simone Forti explored these in dances such as *See-Saw* (1960) and *Huddle* (1961). Another form of searching for the emancipated body was the use of nudity, as in Robert Morris's *Waterman Switch* (1965), in which he and Rainer appeared totally nude, walking slowly while clinched in an embrace. Many dances espoused liberation from bourgeois codes of propriety by celebrating erotic pleasure, as in Carolee Schneemann's *Meat Joy* (1964), an orgiastic performance in which men and women undressed one another, painted one another's bodies, cavorted with raw fish, chicken, and hot dogs, and generally indulged in making a mess with paper, paint, and other objects. Yet another aspect of the body and its open boundaries was various references to bodily processes, from eating to digestion, as in Paxton's works involving food and plastic inflatable tunnels, reminiscent of digestive tracts.

The years 1968 through 1973 saw more political themes and contexts emerge in postmodern dance, which, like the experimental theater movement, participated in the heightened political activism around the country. Active audience engagement extended the democratic values of the early 1960s even in ostensibly nonpolitical dances, for instance, Trisha Brown's *Rummage Sale and the Floor of the Forest* (1971), in which old clothes were threaded through a rope grid and two dancers worked their way through it, while the audience had to choose between watching them and participating in a genuine rummage sale taking place below. In a gesture of democratic leveling, Brown seemed to put the "special" theater event—the dance performance—on a par with a perfectly ordinary event.

The rise of improvisational groups like the Grand Union advanced the theme of liberation through methods that stood metaphorically for freedom. Many dances, such as Deborah Hay's *Deborah Hay with a Large Group Outdoors* (1969), mobilized large groups as if inspired by the political movements of the late 1960s.

But other dances were more explicitly engaged in anti–Vietnam War, black liberation, or feminist politics. This, too, was part of the democratic project of this generation, for although undemocratic countries also fight wars, these choreographers exercised their right to protest the war, just as millions of demonstrators did. Dances that supported the liberation of African Americans and women fitted with democratic ideals of freedom as well as equal rights. In 1970, Rainer choreographed *WAR* as well as a street protest, and she contributed a dance to the Judson Flag Show, supporting the rights of artists to use the flag in their works. In 1971, the Grand Union gave a benefit performance for the Black Panthers, and a women's improvisation collective, the Natural History of the American Dancer, was formed. Paxton's *Intravenous Lecture* (1970) protested censorship, and his *Collaboration with Wintersoldier* (1971) was an antiwar piece done in collaboration with a Vietnam veterans group. Contact improvisation evolved,

beginning in 1972, as an alternative social network as well as an alternative dance technique and performance format (Novack, 1990).

Although many of the white dancers supported civil rights for African Americans or even the Black Power movement, for complex historical reasons, very few African Americans were involved in the early postmodern dance movement. The aesthetic and political objectives of the black dance movement in the 1960s diverged sharply from the predominantly white postmodern dance. Although at times the broad political goals of the two groups may have coincided, the paths toward those goals were quite separate (with one notable exception in Gus Solomons, Jr.) until the 1980s, when a younger group of African-American choreographers identified themselves as "bicultural" artists—both black and postmodern.

By 1973, a wide range of basic questions about dance had been raised in the arena of postmodern choreography. A new phase of consolidation and analysis began, building on the issues that the experiments of the breakaway years had unearthed. Michael Kirby has defined the genre at this stage:

> In the theory of postmodern dance, the choreographer does not apply visual standards to the work. The view is an interior one: movement is not pre-selected for its characteristics but results from certain decisions, goals, plans, schemes, rules, concepts, or problems. Whatever actual movement occurs during the performance is acceptable as long as the limiting and controlling principles are adhered to. . . . In the discussion of their work, the post-modern dancers do not mention such things as meaning, characterization, mood, or atmosphere. (Kirby, 1975)

Although Kirby does not refer to stylistic features, in fact, the conceptual basis of analytic postmodern dance and its systematic attention to the essential features of dance had given rise to an identifiable style. It was casual, dispassionate, and ascetic. If the watchword of the early 1960s was *play*, that of the seventies was *work*. Postmodern dance no longer participated in an unruly, carnivalesque disruption of social boundaries, or in a mass political movement, but rather, moved into a laboratory to carry out serious investigations into dance, attempting to strip the art form down to its quintessence.

In order to do this, choreographers did away with extra theatrical trappings like music, special lighting, costumes, and props, as well as what Kirby has elsewhere called the theatrical "matrices" of character and place (Kirby, 1969). Or, if they used them, it was to disrupt theatrical illusion and "bare the devices" of the dance. Choreographers used simple movements, often performed with a low-energy, uninflected phrasing, in structures of comparison and contrast that would allow for reflection on the medium of dance itself.

In analytic postmodern dance, movement became objective as it was distanced from personal expression through the use of scores, bodily attitudes that suggested—in a democratic spirit—work and other ordinary daily movements, verbal commentaries, and tasks. These dances called attention to the workings of the body in an almost scientific way. The anti-illusionist approach demanded close viewing and clarified the smallest unit of dance, shifting the emphasis from the phrase to the step or gesture. For instance, in Lucinda Childs's *Particular Reel* (1973), the choreographer walks along twenty-one parallel lines, making her way in silence from one corner of the space to the opposite corner, while rotating and reeling her arms in a three-minute phrase that then reverses and finally repeats in its original order.

Esoteric as these research projects may sound, they nevertheless partook of the democratic project, for as they immersed themselves in the exploration of the dance medium, the postmodern choreographers did so by rejecting virtuosity as well as the specialized symbols and conventions of theatrical dancing. One of the most obvious divergences from modern dance and ballet was the rejection of musicality and rhythmic organization. But also, postmodern choreographers retained the 1960s renunciation of refined bodily techniques. They were no longer necessarily committed to a project of audience accessibility—perhaps they had come to realize that popular audiences found art that broke down boundaries between art and life less, rather than more, accessible than conventional high-art masterpieces—but they nevertheless subscribed to a democratic aesthetic of the ordinary, insisting on the evidence of the senses and getting back to basics.

Although the analytic mode of postmodern dance dominated the mid-1970s, another strand developed out of related sources. The spiritual aspect of the same asceticism that led to the clarification of simple movements led in another way to devotional expression. The appreciation of non-Western dance as an alternative to Western dance techniques led to an interest in the spiritual, religious, healing, and social functions of dance in other cultures. The disciplines of the martial arts forms led to new metaphysical as well as physical techniques. The spinning dances of Laura Dean and Andy deGroat, recalling Sufi dances, fell somewhere between images of private and communal devotion. Related to this metaphysical strand of postmodern dance was a metaphoric style, for instance, in the mythic, theatrical works of Meredith Monk and in Kenneth King's uses of dance as a metaphor for technology, information and power systems, and the mind itself. Metaphoric postmodern dance included the expressive theatrical means and representations analytic postmodern dance had eschewed. But it still differed from modern dance in significant ways. These dances drew on the processes and techniques of postmodern choreography, especially that of radical juxtaposition. They also used ordinary movements and objects; they proposed new relationships between the performer and spectator; they employed pronounced stillness and marked repetition; and they participated in the distribution system—the lofts, galleries, and downtown theaters—that had become the venues for postmodern dance. Harking back to Cage's zen tenets, the metaphysical and metaphoric postmodern dancers united the quotidian with the spiritual.

For several reasons—among them New York's dominance in the international art world generally after World War II, that city's centrality to the development of American modern dance, and the quiescence of postwar German modern dance—New York was the site where postmodern dance emerged in the 1960s and 1970s. By the 1970s, however, postmodern dance spread throughout the United States and began to be exported abroad through tours of American postmodern dancers as well as an influx of European, Canadian, and Japanese dancers studying and performing in New York. The situation in dance internal to various countries, partly influenced by American postmodern dance, resulted in distinctive national avant-garde movements, including the New Dance movement in Great Britain, *danse actuelle* in Montreal, and *Tanztheater* in Germany. These movements often paralleled, but did not necessarily imitate, the American experience of the 1960s and 1970s. In Japan, the movement known as *butoh,* which correlates in some ways to American postmodern dance, arose during the 1960s and 1970s in reaction to both Japanese traditional dance forms and Western modern dance.

Also, in the 1980s and 1990s, a new movement arose in dance, perhaps most appropriately called postmodern*ist* dance, that was akin to postmodernism in gallery art and architecture. Choreographers of this generation were not necessarily concerned with ordinary movement but, rather, often used virtuosic movement, engaged in theatricality and narrative, made allusions to popular culture, mixed genres of dance from high- and low-art traditions, and raised questions about identity politics, while still taking a critical approach to dance traditions.

[*See also* Dance.]

BIBLIOGRAPHY

Banes, Sally. *Terpsichore in Sneakers: Post-Modern Dance.* 2d ed. Middletown, Conn., 1987.

Banes, Sally. *Democracy's Body: Judson Dance Theater, 1962–1964.* 2d ed. Durham, N.C. 1993.

Banes, Sally. *Greenwich Village 1963: Avant-Garde Performance and the Effervescent Body.* Durham, N.C., 1993.

Carroll, Noël. "Post-Modern Dance and Expression." In *Philosophical Essays on Dance,* edited by Gordon Fancher and Gerald Myers, pp. 95–104. Brooklyn, N.Y., 1981.

Carroll, Noël, and Sally Banes. "Working and Dancing: A Response to Monroe Beardsley's 'What Is Going On in a Dance?'" *Dance Research Journal* 15 (Fall 1982): 37–41.

Copeland, Roger. "Postmodern Dance/Postmodern Architecture/Postmodernism." *Performing Arts Journal* 19 (1983): 27–43.

Danto, Arthur. *After the End of Art: Contemporary Art and the Pale of History.* Princeton, N.J., 1997.

Drama Review 19 (March 1975; T65). Postmodern dance issue.

Febvre, Michèle, ed. *La danse au défi.* Montreal, 1987.

Hoghe, Raimund. *Pina Bausch: Tanztheatergeschichten.* Frankfurt am Main, 1986.

Jencks, Charles. *What Is Post-Modernism?* London and New York, 1986.

Johnston, Jill. "The New American Modern Dance." In *The New American Arts,* edited by Richard Kostelanetz, pp. 162–193. New York, 1965.

Jordan, Stephanie. *Striding Out: Aspects of Contemporary and New Dance in Britain.* London, 1992.

Jowitt, Deborah. *Time and the Dancing Image.* New York, 1988.

Kirby, Michael. Introduction. *Drama Review* 19 (March 1975; T65): 3–4.

Kirby, Michael. "The New Theatre." In *The Art of Time: Essays on the Avant-Garde,* pp. 75–102. New York, 1969.

Kuniyoshi, Kazuko. "Butoh Chronology, 1959–1984." *Drama Review* 30 (Summer 1986): 127–41.

Livet, Anne, ed. *Contemporary Dance.* New York, 1978.

Novack, Cynthia J. *Sharing the Dance: Contact Improvisation and American Culture.* Madison, Wis., 1990.

Rainer, Yvonne. *Work, 1961–1973.* Halifax, 1974.

SALLY BANES

Postmodern Poetry

Describing any aspect of postmodernism is, to a postmodernist, inseparable from enacting it, and hence from partially undoing any truth-value in the description. How can one capture self-reflexively where one actually stands, or what one actually performs, while also trying to bracket one's involvement so as to make testable claims? Problems compound when we turn to contemporary American poetry, since there was a substantial "postmodernism" in the 1950s that is in many ways sharply opposed to contemporary versions, and yet continues to wield considerable influence. There also seem to be in the genre itself certain orientations difficult to reconcile with the versions of postmodernism that now prevail in the art world and in social theory: poetry tends to impose emotional pressures not compatible with relying on the play of simulacra; there is no significant marketplace that poets can ironically manipulate; and poetry makes demands on its audience for close attention to precise articulation and structural intricacy not well suited to immediate consumption and pastiche. Perhaps the only fully postmodern mode for poetry is the poetry slam. Nonetheless, postmodernism remains an important issue for many poets because it provides a rubric for setting "experimental" poetic work in opposition to traditional romantic versions of lyric expression. These oppositions are difficult to fix in any abstract formula, in part because these experiments destabilize the very notion of lyric poetry. It is possible, however, to offer a general definition of contemporary postmodern poetry as a range of efforts to make the condensed space of poetic language responsive to themes and dispositions developed within postmodern theory, such as the celebration of contradiction and heterogeneity, the foregrounding of surfaces, commitments to transgression and marginality, and treatments of the person stressing unstable, decentered, and multiple selves.

The tale of two postmodernisms in poetry begins with the widespread rebellion in the late 1950s against a New Critical establishment that had reduced modernism to a cult of dry, impersonal meditative lyrics intricately balancing passion with ironic distance and suffusing its concern for worldly particulars with an overwhelming sense of mortality. Most of the work that emerged could not be considered postmodern, largely because it turned away from theoretical models of any kind to concentrate on the personal intensities exemplified by Robert Lowell and Sylvia Plath. But Donald Allen's anthology *The New American Poetry, 1945–1960* (1960) would popularize three loose communities of poets that did set themselves the task of directly addressing what seemed changing notions of self, world, and society requiring a distinctively postmodern sensibility. The earliest and most theoretically sophisticated of these emerged from Black Mountain College—preeminently in Charles Olson's writings on poetics and in the poetry of Robert Duncan and Robert Creeley. Olson insisted that the then-dominant concerns for formal balance and closure tied poets to an outmoded metaphysics and psychology: "to take on the post-modern" poets would have to pursue "continuous inquiries into what ways ideality no longer fit modern reality in a form proper to its content." Ideality was problematic because it located the basic values made available by art in the work of formal composition. Hence, the work becomes abstract, something to interpret in terms of how the artist imposed form on experience. This orientation separates the work from the immediate processes of thinking, feeling, and selecting in which the artist's full creative energy might take direct concrete expression. To "restate man" so as to "repossess him of his dynamic," verse had to become "projective": it had to restore a sense of spirit as inseparable from the poet's control of breath as the basis for a rhythm not tied to fixed measure, and it had to make the syllable its cutting edge for the display of intelligence, since there could be no more elemental unit by which to display a selecting intelligence at work. Finally, such unmediated intelligence could establish form in terms of how it gathered "the objects which occur at every given moment of composition (of recognition we can call it)" (ibid.) into a field defined simply by the internal tensions responsible for its intensity. Relying on projective energies does not allow for hypotheses about mysterious inwardness or meditative comprehensiveness. No longer bound to the "lyrical interference of the subject as ego," this poetry could establish "a seriousness" sufficient to cause the thing the poet makes to "take its place alongside the things of nature" (ibid.).

Olson's own poetry has few advocates now, probably because it seems dangerously flat, impersonal, and abstract in its efforts to make concrete descriptions bear large cultural ideals. But Duncan and Creeley opened other possible uses of projectivist concerns for breath and syllable taken up by numerous poets. Duncan transformed Olson's concern for myth into an intricate psychology sustained by a remarkable ear for how syllables might dance together. Creeley used the sense of breath units to bring within the psyche the objectivist techniques of William Carlos Williams, so that his poetry seemed excruciatingly exact and direct in its renderings of personal states. Creeley showed how poetry could build dense lyrical presence by an intelligence at the level of the syllable's refusing any of the trappings of well-made representational artifice.

By the mid-1950s this suspicion of artifice had also become central for the New York art world and the poets who worked within the sense of excitement the art created—first in the action painting of Jackson Pollock, then in the flatbed openness of Robert Rauschenberg and the paradoxical doubling of mediating surfaces in Jasper Johns, and later in the influence of John Cage's elaborate structural ways of freeing the imagination from cultural indoctrination. These models influenced work ranging from the black arts aesthetics of Amiri Baraka to Jackson MacLow's chance operations to the talk poems of David Antin. But for contemporaries, Frank O'Hara's work seems to best represent what that art world made possible for a poetry in rebellion against modernist values. Like the confessional poets, O'Hara is completely personal, but his is a version of the personal thinkable only in relation to the fascination with surfaces and folds emerging in the art world of the 1950s; and his is a mode of taking things lightly sadly lacking in poets who continue to sing the tribulations of the romantic ego. O'Hara's "Steps," for example, offers a love poem based entirely on being able to feel "foolish and free" as he celebrates the simple details of wandering through New York. Rather than offer ideas and idealizations of love, O'Hara defines it simply in terms of the atmosphere it creates and the expansiveness it releases:

> oh god it's wonderful
> to get out of bed
> and drink too much coffee
> and smoke too many cigarettes
> and love you so much.

This love, in fact, can be measured precisely by its capacity to free the self from any need to take itself more seriously, and thereby to lose its openness to its environment. Here O'Hara's fluid urban world finds a corresponding subjectivity capable of thriving on contingency and multiplicity.

On the other coast, in San Francisco, quite different formal experiments seemed necessary for freeing postmodern subjectivities. At the center of the revolution was the New Yorker Allen Ginsberg's *Howl* (1956), with its ecstatic refusal of all decorums and its insistence that poetry had to find ways of addressing public life and popular culture

without losing either a critical edge or a commitment to soul making as still a viable lyrical ideal. But West Coast writers had their own versions of the postmodern to elaborate, ranging from Gary Snyder's efforts to recast Western experiences of nature in terms compatible with Zen Buddhist models of attention to Jack Spicer's self-hating internalization of Zen emptiness.

As various discursive versions of postmodernism proliferated, each of these modes of writing underwent severe transformations, but without surrendering the two basic demands distinguishing postmodernist ambitions from more traditional lyric work—its resistance to the formal and thematic closure basic to an ideal of well-made artifacts and its foregrounding aspects of experience that emerge within the very processes of writing and hence cannot be captured as aspects of some illusionistic drama. The most elaborate transformations took place as Olson's projectivism came ultimately to serve as one sponsor for the work published in the $L=A=N=G=U=A=G=E$ anthology edited by Charles Bernstein and Bruce Andrews (1978). Olson himself was far too resolutely a New Englander to satisfy the needs that poets conscious of immigrant traditions like Bernstein had as basic to their sense of America. So these language poets crossed projectivism with the objectivist tradition and with the disjunctive work of Gertrude Stein and Louis Zukofsky, in the process providing radically new understandings of how breath and syllable might address postmodern realities.

This is Bernstein's "Use No Flukes":

> Close to stand
> Glitter with edge
> Clouds, what's but
> Weather of devoid
> Uses unwrapping
> Lower the second
> Gravity for allowing, but
> Slowly, as if
> Backward, falling
> Folded

It would be foolish to attempt to interpret this poem in any traditional way. Rather than postulate an imaginative situation that it portrays or that underlies its speaking, we are better off treating it as a painterly exploration of the texture, weight, and possible harmony among verbal elements, each bearing a range of semantic echoes. Notice first how the sounds actually do fall folded into two basic patterns—one characterized by versions of a long *o*, the other by versions of *a*, with "allowing" bringing both melodies into harmony. This flow of echoes then provides a key for approaching what the poem does semantically. Its opening lines can be read as either imperatives or descriptions, so that the play of possibility between noun and verb in the composition of a visual field becomes a literal "grammar for allowing." What this grammar affords is best defined by the closing lines as they bind the work of words to the drifting clouds. If we let ourselves seem to move backward, by analogy to the clouds, we find ourselves as viewers and as readers reaching through our confusions to a glimpse of harmonious reconciliation in the folds that the scene composes, even though, or perhaps because, the language too drifts and will not allow us to confine it to any one representation. We have enough structure to see how there emerges a kind of stability within passing time and loss, if only we can learn to conform our own reading habits to a world in which there is no need to impose specific determinate structures as mirrors of a will to order.

For Bernstein, Olson's emphasis on breath needs to be redirected: the primary energy within the poem is to be attributed not to the writer but to the readers' coming to a grasp of what occurs as their participation deepens within the sets of forces potential within the poem. Olson's emphasis on syllable now provides a means of understanding how a composing intelligence can find satisfactions while it resists the structure of demands inherent in more imposing syntactic and semantic units. As Cage loved to demonstrate, simple depersonalized structure can develop a "gravity for allowing" that is a worthy antagonist to the will to power—a lesson central to Language poets' experiments in form that extend to Ron Silliman's using a Fibonacci series as the framework for his long poem *Tjanting*.

In their more recent work these Language writers have let cogent syntax and some sense of referentiality return, primarily because they have discovered that their purposes are best served by foregrounding a range of voices, as if voices themselves were the actual building blocks of our semantic universe because they most intensively embody a postmodern sense of how social grammars carry embedded emotions and habits and political orientations. Their elemental approach to language then turns out to be a feasible way of making good on Olson's dreams that poetry could become a means of social research because it could make vital America's most fundamental imaginative orientations. Thus, we find Rosemary Waldrop bringing the voices of Puritan Connecticut into conjunction with contemporary life, and we find Susan Howe teaching us to hear both how women came to bear their oppression and how fully writers like Herman Melville and Rowlandson made that resistance the basis for modes of expression valorizing much of what had to remain marginal in relation to the dominant imperial culture.

Language poetry engages postmodern culture by treating poets' encounters with silences and gaps not as openings into some metaphysical site beyond the powers of understanding but as conditions generated by the overlap and discontinuity among language practices within society. Thus, it lends itself not only to the concerns about gender in Howe and Waldrop, but also to various ways that the logic of what Jean-François Lyotard calls "différends" plays out in all cultural domains. Nathanial Mackey, for example, manages to extend Baraka's insistence on immediate political speech into a concern for "discrepant awarenesses" and dissonances through which we gain access to "an unlikely Other whose inconceivable occupancy glimpses of ocean beg access to." Understanding race in America is largely a matter of what we can hear in what is not said or said obliquely or projected beyond seeing. More generally, the same set of poetic resources provides crucial means for keeping cultural diversity in the foreground without collapsing into an identity politics that claims as new the very idealizations of the romantic expressive ego that postmodern poets have been trying to overcome. In the work of Alfred Arteaga and Myung Mi Kim, ethnicity is less a matter of seeking individual identity than of learning to recognize the constraints on lives and the corollary experience of potential powers that emerge for those living in bilingual societies: the more finely poetry attunes us to the social embeddings carried in our senses of voice and linguistic expression, the better it prepares us for appreciating forces and dangers within a multicultural society that extend far beyond the quite limited languages we have for projecting personal and ethnic identities.

The New York school has followed a very different trajectory, keeping issues of contradiction and multiplicity confined primarily to quasi-philosophical reflection. Yet it has in the person of John Ashbery the contemporary poet most fully connectable to postmodern theoretical discourses (perhaps especially when he is in fact indulging his own version of late nineteenth-century decadence). Ashbery retains Olson's and O'Hara's antiartifactual immediacy of the speaking voice alive to its own compositional activity, but for him this sense of presence finds itself wound into an impenetrable set of social echoes that poetry gets us to hear within our language. If there is to be any satisfying sense of personal speech, it will emerge only in and as the quality of play that the poet sets up within a constant process of displacement:

The clarity of the rules dawned on you for the first time.
They were the players, and we who had struggled at the game
Were merely spectators, though subject to its vicissitudes
And moving with it out of the tearful stadium, born on shoulders,
    at last.

The last line here so fully takes on the space of public fantasy that it allows a strange sense of emotional release. In other poems Ashbery asks us to see how "Underneath the talk lies / the moving and not wanting to be moved, the loose / meaning, untidy and simple like a threshing floor." So while the lyric ego is forced to surrender the sense of "permanent tug that used to be its notion of home," it reemerges in an astonishing range of registers leading us from the sliding functions of the *you*s that the imagination invokes to a sense of something driving desire that resists all our efforts to represent it within a cogent language of motives. Multiple, fragmented, contradictory, and evanescent states of self become his lyric version of O'Hara's habitable urban space.

This Ashberyian poetic space has proved a fertile field for younger poets who only now are fully finding their own ways to develop his interplay of floating surfaces with enigmatic resistance to all our interpretive efforts. Where Kenneth Koch emphasizes the comic side of a flip urban imagination, David Shapiro's latest book, *After a Lost Original*, beautifully brings the resources of lyric intensity to the work of furthering that enigmatic psychology:

> We are the sculptors now making our own doors
> The words remain, but the gods are gone for good

The idea remains but the words are gone like gods. In work that increasingly opens itself to highly charged visible fragments evoking and displacing an intense personal pressure, Ann Lauterbach restores to this painterly poetics some of the sharp edges and collagist formal dignity evocative of modernism at its most ambitious, without losing an Ashberyian commitment to the constant slippage among surfaces that may be the only available locus for imaginative life.

The heritage of the San Francisco Renaissance and Beats is now far more diffuse, perhaps because so much of what the Beats created got consumed by and as popular culture. One still hears in recent work echoes of the most intense, least playful poets from that Renaissance, like Spicer and Duncan, especially in the ways that Robin Blaser has brought their ways of approaching myth and discursivity to the lively writing scene in British Columbia. But Beat values have not had much to offer those contemporary cultures where alienation is just bad economics. The interest in Zen fostered by Snyder and Philip Whalen still has considerable currency, however, although often in ways that adapt it to urban Western lifestyles. One might say that Zen provides for these younger West Coast poets a mode of strangeness analogous to what New York poets get from Surrealism and Rousselian enigma. Leslie Scalapino's work provides the purest example of Zen fused with postmodernist versions of the absences that haunt our efforts to make experience articulate, and Michael Palmer's fascination with echoes and mirrors and traces manages to thicken Zen concerns for emptiness by combining that with a profound engagement in the negative dialectics Palmer finds in French modernist writing. Finally, perhaps the most original of Bay area poets, Lynn Hejinian, adapts this strangeness to distinctively Western intricacies of self-consciousness by always positioning her lyrical intelligence on the margins of anything that counts as knowledge. For her the basic quest of poetry is making palpable the "experiencing of experience." In place of pursuing knowledge and its idealities, she tries to decompose "the unity / of the subjective mind by / dint of

its own introspection." Quotation is necessary here because valuing Hejinian's thinking depends on our registering its capacity both to coexist with and to transform the denotative ambitions basic to received ideals of knowledge. Each line break calls attention to the disruption of habitual unities, and the ensemble defines the powers of mind by its capacity to register complex echoes and variations on pacing and weighing of phrases, so that rhyme becomes something a good deal more than a formal device. In Hejinian's poetry this mind is able to maintain the dignity Olson sought by denying itself any of our typical representational fantasies that serve as mirrors facilitating our struggles to establish stable egos.

Now that postmodernist theory seems no longer capable of producing fresh ideas, and hence rests on the verge of becoming one more layer of history's junk heap, young poets have the task of determining what they can make of this heritage. It may be the case that as the contradictions within the theory become more evident, the poetry discussed here will emerge as more fully contemporary because of how it tried to negotiate what in the theory became forced into dichotomies. But even if this distinction between the poetry and the theoretical environment proves impossible, the past three decades will make it extremely difficult for serious poetry to celebrate those struggles by the romantic ego, unless the egos involved manage to coexist with the various bodies afforded it by its own listening to the language that is its dwelling.

BIBLIOGRAPHY

Primary Sources

Allen, Donald, ed. *The New American Poetry, 1945–1960*. New York, 1960.

Hoover, Paul, ed. *Postmodern American Poetry*. New York, 1994.

Lehman, David, ed. *Ecstatic Occasions, Expedient Forms: Sixty-five Leading Contemporary Poets Select and Comment on Their Own Poems*. New York, 1987.

Messerli, Douglas, ed. *From the Other Side of the Century: A New American Poetry, 1960–1990*. Los Angeles, 1994.

Other Sources

Altieri, Charles. *Enlarging the Temple: New Directions in American Poetry during the 1960's*. Lewisburg, Pa., 1979.

Altieri, Charles. *Self and Sensibility in Contemporary American Poetry*. Cambridge and New York, 1984.

Breslin, James E. B. *From Modern to Contemporary: American Poetry, 1945–1965*. Chicago, 1984.

Conte, Joseph M. *Unending Design: The Forms of Postmodern Poetry*. Ithaca, N.Y., 1991.

DuPlessis, Rachel Blau. *The Pink Guitar: Writing as Feminist Practice*. New York and London, 1990.

Easthope, Antony, and John O. Thompson, eds. *Contemporary Poetry Meets Modern Theory*. New York and London, 1991.

Gardiner, Thomas, ed. *American Poetry of the 1980s*. Special issue of *Contemporary Literature* 33.2 (Summer 1992): 177–413.

Hartley, George. *Textual Politics and the Language Poets*. Bloomington, Ind., 1989.

McGann, Jerome. *Black Riders: The Visible Language of Modernism.* Princeton, N.J., 1993.

Nelson, Cary. *Our Last First Poets: Vision and History in Contemporary American Poetry.* Urbana, 1981.

Perloff, Marjorie. *Poetic License: Essays on Modernist and Postmodernist Lyric.* Evanston, Ill., 1990.

Perloff, Marjorie. *Radical Artifice: Writing Poetry in the Age of Media.* Chicago, 1991.

Quartermain, Peter. *Disjunctive Poetics: From Gertrude Stein and Louis Zukofsky to Susan Howe.* Cambridge and New York, 1992.

Schultz, Susan M., ed. *The Tribe of John: Ashbery and Contemporary Poetry.* Tuscaloosa, Ala., 1995.

Shoptaw, John. *On the Outside Looking Out: John Ashbery's Poetry.* Cambridge, Mass., 1994.

CHARLES ALTIERI

POSTSTRUCTURALISM. Poststructuralism is aptly characterized by Roland Barthes in his 1977 "Inaugural Lecture to the Chair of Literary Semiology at the Collège de France" as "a certain *individual* labor, the adventure of a certain subject," one of whose aims is to bring about a forgetting that "imposes unforeseeable change . . . on the sedimentation of the knowledges, cultures, and beliefs we have traversed." Arising in the mid-1960s and centering on the radical conception of language advanced by Ferdinand de Saussure early in the century, poststructuralism has wrought various changes on the tenets of what is known as structuralism. Saussure developed linguistics as an ahistorical science at a time when the study of language consisted of phonology, the history of the sounds of language. He deemed the proper study of linguistics to be language and language to be a system of signs that signify by virtue of their difference from other signs in the system rather than by their connection with any kind of language-independent meaning. A sign is defined as the indissoluble union of a sound image (signifier) and concept (signified), where concepts are language dependent in being constituted by the same cut in the "ribbon of thought" that breaks the "ribbon of sound" into identifiable units. The arbitrariness of language lies in there being nothing in the flow of sound or thought that necessitates the constituting cuts being made in one place rather than another. Pragmatic criteria, and chance, reign.

The model of language developed by Saussure proved to be a powerful explanatory tool and was responsible for the spread of structuralism across the human sciences. Starting in the 1950s the model was extended to art, film, and literature (Roman Jakobson), kinship systems (Claude Lévi-Strauss), the unconscious mind (Jacques Lacan), the history of knowledge (Michel Foucault), and contemporary culture and its myths (Roland Barthes). It was taken to yield knowledge of the unobservable structure that underlay and determined the nature of the observable world. The original model consisted of two axes, a horizontal string (syntagma) broken into units of signification identified as such by the possibility of their being occupied by various other units taken from a vertical list (paradigm). For example, the paradigm for "___" in "The ___ is on the mat" has as members *cat, pet, dog, feline creature,* or *feather* if the membership condition is sense or grammaticality, but not if it is truth. If the membership condition is truth and, for example, "The cat is on the mat" is true, then *pet* and *feline creature* belong to the paradigm, while *dog* and *feather* do not.

Two changes made in Saussurean linguistics paved the way for the inauguration of poststructuralism. The first undercut Saussure's belief that language exists for the sake of speech and that, therefore, only signs uttered are present in language, while the indefinitely many signs exchangeable for any sign in an utterance are present only in the minds of the language users but absent from language itself. At a conference in 1956 celebrating the fortieth anniversary of the publication of Saussure's *Course in General Linguistics,* Jakobson argued that members of paradigms of the model of language are fully as much in language as are spoken syntagmas. He went on to assert that it is the resonance in signs actually used of the presence of all the signs exchangeable with them that gives language its peculiar power. Since the primacy accorded to speech by Saussure gave weight to the role of the speaker's intention in selecting signs from among all the possible occupants of a position, once language is thought of as having all the possible occupants already within it, the importance of the choice of the signs actually used fades along with the importance of the distinction between actual and possible occupants of given positions.

Moreover, possible occupants are precisely what the Freudian unconscious has at hand to use as disguises to dupe the conscious mind into letting unconscious contents slip past its censor. This gives rise to the thought that what has been repressed by any mental faculty or social institution or what has simply settled out from everything might return in a guise other than that under which it fell or was pushed out of mind or present time. This in turn gives rise to the thought that the concept of the unconscious can be extended to language and other signifying systems, whose unconscious is what is latent in the manifest system of signs, namely, the signs substitutable for other signs in the system, where this unconscious contributes causally to the system's having developed as it has and being operated as it is. Finally, the idea of the unconscious can be extended as well to social systems and their practice of constituting themselves by excluding myriad others, where the unconscious consists of those put out of sight and hearing but nonetheless there, an energy and a force.

Poststructuralism theorizes not only the ways in which Saussure's linguistic paradigm contributes to the production of meaning but also the ways in which what is repressed by social and cultural institutions contributes to their constitution and functioning. In undermining the sovereignty of the sign (what actually occupies a given site that could be filled by other members of a paradigm), poststructuralism undermines the social institutions whose signs are agents of repression. It does so by disrupting the founding oppositions of such institutions, governed as they are by the law of excluded middle. With this change worked on Saussure, poststructuralism becomes a critique of culture, especially of its modernist conceit that certain things, the visual and narrative arts among them, have finally been got right because "What is X?" has been unflinchingly asked and "X is . . ." increasingly refined. Poststructuralism contests the modernist belief that the subject can be determined by excluding from its concept whatever is not essential to it. For what particular predicates are essential to X is a function of those that are accidental. The accidental turn out to be necessary and cannot have been excluded, but only repressed, whereas X is determined precisely by its difference from them.

The second enabling moment of poststructuralism questioned Saussure's prediction of the creation of a science of signs in general, semiology, where a sign is any kind of element that signifies by virtue of its difference from other elements within a system and linguistics is but part of the general science. In the *Elements of Semiology*, published in France in 1965, Barthes reversed the envisioned relation between linguistics and semiology. He noted that nearly fifty years after its existence was predicted there was still no science of semiology because there are only trivial nonlinguistic signifying systems like the highway code. The reason for this, he argued, is that collections of objects or images and instances of behavior are significant only when admixed with language, which "extracts their signifiers (in the form of nomenclature) and names their signifieds (in the forms of usages or reasons)." Semiology needs language both as a model and as a component. The science of language is, then, not part of semiology, but semiology is part of it.

Thanks to this reversal, semiology need not be a science to assure that linguistics is, and indeed semiology ceased to be a science as structuralism ran its course, branching off into poststructuralism. Since science is a social rather than an individual labor that seeks to explain rather than to "impose unforeseeable change" on the status quo formed in part from the deposits of our collective past, the semiology heralded by Barthes is not a science but a playing of signs, albeit an utterly serious play. To the extent that the status quo valorized by the science of signs is determined by such deposits and to the extent that their contribution is unknown, evaluation of the object of the science cannot be objective. Nor can the science itself be objective, for it too is influenced by what Barthes refers to as the residue of "what we have traversed." Semiology as it is practiced by poststructuralism is an art, not a science: it reveals the individual subject's operating the signs of the world, as does the artist in producing and the audience in receiving a work of art.

With this second change, poststructuralism becomes a performance of the deconstruction of the various oppositions between art and its others, a disruption. [*See* Barthes.]

French structuralism was introduced into the United States at a conference in Baltimore in 1966. Even as it arrived in the English-speaking world, however, changes that would issue in poststructuralism were being wrought by such as Foucault's *The Order of Things: An Archaeology of the Human Sciences* and Lacan's *Ecrits: A Selection,* which appeared in 1966 to be followed in 1967 by the first books of Derrida: *Of Grammatology, Writing and Difference,* and *Speech and Phenomena.* May 1968 saw the uprisings in Paris by factor workers and students for whom the political and intellectual status quo was unsatisfactory. They wanted its transformation, not a science of its signs. The idea grew that what was to be sought was not knowledge of the structure of what underlay the manifest world but knowledge of its workings, of what had to have been excluded for the world to be as it is, of what happened to have settled out from the restless workings of instinct, desire, intention, mind, of the myriad overlappings of instincts and intentions, of chance. Barthes, Derrida, Foucault, and Lacan nourished this idea by directing their inquiries to what was murmuring underground. Those engaged in such inquiry must silence the music of the world in order to be able to hear its underground: and what will be heard cannot be foreseen.

Poststructuralism's discoveries are unforeseeable because of the large element of arbitrariness in its objects. While Saussure located the arbitrariness of language in the fact that its units could have been other than they are, poststructuralism locates it in how values get assigned to variables or how signs get selected for positions on either axis of the linguistic model. Because a sign carries with it all the other signs difference from which enables it to signify, what particular sign gets foregrounded barely matters. But to read anything in a productive way, a way that unsettles assignments of meanings that have become fixed, it is necessary to know what are the various series of signs whose difference gives significance to the present manifest signs. Each sign present in a text is a path out of the text to other signs, and there are at least two ways to recover the others and to enter the intertext, the vast open network of language of which a particular work is but a fragment. One way is to make the kind of totally uncensored association of given signs with others that the analysand is called on to make in psychoanalysis. Such associations yield a very small subset of all the possible associations that can be made with any fragment. That there are indefinitely many of them can be seen by thinking of a computer running, for example, through all the items in the six paradigms that intersect each of the positions in "The cat is on the mat," then running through all the syntagmas in which each item in each paradigm can occur, then through all the paradigms in each of these syntagmas, and so on. This strategy is licensed by the belief that there is no principled way to close (to totalize) the set and its corollary that there is no principled way to exclude anything from the set.

The other way to recover signs whose difference from present signs gives them significance is to cruise the past to recover associations of which present signs were or could have been a part. The privilege of the present having waned with the waning of the privilege that structuralism accorded speech, poststructuralism takes the present to be combinations and permutations of the already written and the past to be there in the present as the elements combined and permutated. Where structuralism makes a science of language, poststructuralism makes language the scene of a performance in which the performer is working with the already written or inscribed, combining and permutating readymade signs. Tradition has held that the present and the spoken are privileged because of their presence to consciousness, but the intuition of poststructuralism is precisely that presence and speech are mediated by and constructed out of the past and the written, respectively, as consciousness is constructed out of the unconscious. The potential is prior to the actual, and the actual is the unstable product of the performance of language, of acts of speaking, hearing, writing, reading. Here, as in any performance, the individual and the imaginary reign. Association of sign with sign is limited only by the imagination of the individual language user in so associating them as to make some sort of sense in and for the moment at which the user makes the assignment.

Poststructuralism risks contradiction and radical relativism in order to reconceive certain concepts centering on that of the human subject. The intuition is that both the electronic revolution and breakthroughs in the life sciences have had the effect that extant conceptions of the human subject as the only or primary source of meaning do not do justice to what is already written in the material world, instructions and inscriptions that are not mere records of speech. Should poststructuralism fail, it will stand convicted of having contradicted and relativized the tradition. Should it succeed, it will have imposed an "unforeseeable change . . . on the sedimentation of the knowledges, cultures, and beliefs we have traversed," through its refusal to allow what has been wrought to stay still.

[*See also* Postmodernism; Semiotics; *and* Structuralism.]

BIBLIOGRAPHY

Barthes, Roland. *S/Z.* Translated by Richard Miller. New York, 1974.
Barthes, Roland. *The Responsibility of Forms: Critical Essays on Music, Art, and Representation.* Translated by Richard Howard. New York, 1985.
Barthes, Roland. *Elements of Semiology.* Translated by Annette Lavers and Colin Smith. New York, 1967.
Derrida, Jacques. *Of Grammatology.* Translated by Gayatri Chakravorty Spivak. Baltimore, 1976.
Derrida, Jacques. *The Truth in Painting.* Translated by Geoff Bennington and Ian McLeod. Chicago, 1987.
Foucault, Michel. *The Order of Things: An Archaeology of the Human Sciences.* New York, 1970.
Jakobson, Roman, and Morris Halle. *Fundamentals of Language.* The Hague, 1956.
Kristeva, Julia. *Desire in Language: A Semiotic Approach to Literature and Art.* Edited by Leon S. Roudiez, translated by Thomas Gora, Alice Jardine, and Leon S. Roudiez. New York, 1980.
Lacan, Jacques. *Ecrits: A Selection.* Translated by Alan Sheridan. New York, 1977.
Lévi-Strauss, Claude. *Structural Anthropology.* Translated by Claire Jacobson and Brooke Grundfest Schoepf. New York, 1963.
Saussure, Ferdinand de. *Course in General Linguistics.* Edited by Charles Bally and Albert Sechehaye, translated by Wade Baskin. New York, 1959.
Wiseman, Mary Bittner. *The Ecstasies of Roland Barthes.* London and New York, 1989.

MARY WISEMAN

POUSSIN, NICOLAS (1594–1665), French painter. Nicolas Poussin stands at the center of several important turning points in early modern European art. He was born in France, but he worked primarily in Italy, in the Baroque Rome that was the artistic capital of Europe in the seventeenth century. Steeped in the austere classicism of both Roman antiquities and the High Renaissance, Poussin's paintings came to be seen as the foundation of a new French school of painting. French neoclassicism, partly based on the model of Poussin's works, would then dominate the European art world for the next two centuries. Poussin's career thus marks an important shift from the artistic hegemony of Italy to that of France, and from a Renaissance model of classicism to the academic neoclassicism that is the gateway to modernism in the nineteenth century.

The two most important early biographies of the artist—by Giovanni Pietro Bellori and André Félibien—are also important texts in establishing the later theory and practice of neoclassicism. They tell us that Poussin was born in the rural village of Les Andelys in Normandy. Little is said of his early training with provincial painters, nor of his work in Paris before he departed for Rome sometime in 1624. But the biographies document an apparently crucial friendship in Paris, between Poussin and the great Italian poet Giambattista Marino. Bellori's biography notes that Poussin provided drawings to illustrate one of Marino's most famous poems, the *Adone*. However, a set of extant drawings from this early period now in Royal Library at Windsor Castle, known as the Marino drawings, show that the text Poussin illustrated was Ovid's *Metamorphoses*. These rapidly executed, vivid line and wash drawings show an expressive force not previously found in Ovid illustrations, and reveal Poussin's affinity for classical texts and mythology in particular. Marino encouraged the artist to leave the artistic backwater of Paris and travel to Rome.

On Poussin's arrival in Italy, the poet introduced him to the powerful circle around the Barberini pope, Urban VIII.

Eventually it was Cassiano dal Pozzo, the learned secretary to the pope's nephew Francesco Barberini, who championed Poussin and gave him work. Poussin provided drawings for Cassiano's *musèo cartàceo,* or paper museum of antiquities, which gathered together images of all known fragments of ancient Roman arts. His paintings for Cassiano and others at this time were relatively small in scale, many representing subjects from classical mythology and ancient history, often in a highly poetic mode: a representative example from this period would be his *Diana and Endymion,* now in the Detroit Institute of Arts. For Cassiano he painted a series of seven paintings depicting the *Seven Sacraments,* each ritual set in a painstaking re-creation of early Christian antiquity. Poussin thus settled into the rarefied world of erudition and antiquarianism that flourished among intellectuals under the Barberini papacy. For the rest of his career, he would shun the exuberant public art of the Baroque, working instead for a small group of private patrons in Italy and France.

In 1640 the French king Louis XIII called the now prominent Poussin back to Paris to serve as *premier peintre du roi.* The artist reluctantly complied, spending two unhappy years battling court intrigue in Paris and working on the kind of public, decorative projects that he had hitherto avoided. His work on the decoration of the Louvre has since been lost except for drawings. Letters from Paris show that Poussin found some refuge with a few intellectual friends of Cassiano dal Pozzo's who now also found themselves in Paris. These were men like Gabriel Naudé, who later became the librarian of the prime minister Cardinal Mazarin, or Pierre Gassendi, a prominent opponent of Jules René Descartes's, who wrote on natural science and Epicurean philosophy. But Naude and Gassendi are now also well known as the core of the secret group of religious and political skeptics known as *libertins* or *libertins érudits.* Poussin may have shared some of their attitudes, as his later painted allegories seem to be based on *libertin* texts and ideas about the relation between history, natural history, and human morality.

After Poussin fled back to Rome in 1642 he never again traveled. But increasingly his paintings were bought by French patrons, particularly by Paul Fréart de Chantelou, whose friendship and patronage eclipsed the artist's earlier relationship with Cassiano dal Pozzo. For Chantelou, Poussin painted a second set of *Seven Sacraments.* Like the first set done for Cassiano, it depicts each Christian ritual in careful historical context. But the Chantelou version also shows the artist's evolving concern for the play of light and deep shadows, as well as the overall unification of light with pictorial space and action. This series, painted between 1639 and 1647, shows Poussin at the peak of his powers as a history painter.

After 1647, Poussin turned increasingly to landscape painting in addition to historical or religious subjects. Works such as the *Landscape with Diogenes* or the *Landscape with Orpheus,* both from around 1650 and both now in the Louvre, show how the artist transformed the classical landscape format he inherited from earlier artists such as the Carraccis or Domenichino. The landscape is still an idealized, symmetrical container for human narratives. But Poussin found a more perfect union between the portrayal of nature and the depiction of dramatic action. He also explored ways of uniting landscape with the communication of rather abstract ideas, as in his late *Landscape with the Blind Orion,* which E. H. Gombrich showed was an allegorical depiction of a stormcloud's birth.

Poussin's mature paintings were acclaimed as models for serious painting in the following generations. When the Académie Royale de Peinture et de Sculpture was founded in Paris in 1648, it was to foster the ideal of a learned artist after the manner of Poussin, as well as to break with the older guild traditions of training artists in the manner of craftsmen. In the 1660s, when the minister Jean-Baptiste Colbert sponsored official monthly discourses on individual paintings, several of Poussin's works from the royal collection were among the first to be selected. Poussin himself kept his distance from the Académie and never joined forces with it in any way. But the reception of his works by the Académie was crucial to that institution's formation as well as to Poussin's later reputation. Charles Le Brun, the driving force behind the Académie, derived his tenets about the centrality of design over color, and the clear articulation of human expression as the basis of painted narrative, from his discourses on Poussin's *Israelites Gathering Manna* and *Saint Paul in Ecstasy.* Similarly from outside the *Académie,* the critic Roger de Piles grounded his opposition to Le Brun in an opposition to Poussin, holding up the colorism of Peter Paul Rubens against Poussin's emphasis on line. The ensuing quarrel over *dessein* versus *coloris* was also about many other issues—institutional politics, of course, but also the notion of a temporal versus an instantaneous perception of pictures, and the definition of painting as primarily concerned with visual illusion or with the exposition of ideas. The highly simplified understanding of both Rubens and Poussin as they were employed in this battle was only partly based in reality: Rubens was a consummate master of design as well as color, and Poussin's use of color is far richer than this view would allow. But the reception of Poussin in the late seventeenth-century Académie brought about a remarkable reversal in the significance of both painters' works. As Svetlana Alpers has recently remarked, the emphasis on his color transformed the public diplomacy of Rubens's art into a model for private and intimate painting—as in the works of Antoine Watteau. The private, almost arcane art of Poussin became the model for public, state-sponsored history painting, an understanding of his works that would later influence Jacques-Louis David.

POUSSIN. Nicolas Poussin, *The Shepherds in Arcadia* (1650, after restoration), oil on canvas, 85 × 121 cm; Musée du Louvre, Paris. (Photograph courtesy of Giraudon/Art Resource, New York.)

The critical and public reception of Poussin from the eighteenth century to the present has, however, consistently focused on an aspect of his art that would indeed seem to have been crucial to the artist himself: the relation of the painted image to written texts. In a letter, Poussin admonished a patron to "read the story and read the painting." In a conversation recorded by Félibien, the artist spoke of the letters of the alphabet forming words as the depicted expressions in a painting form the story. Poussin's remarks come from the Renaissance tradition of *ut pictura poesis*, or the parallel of painting and poetry. Later generations of critics, even while questioning the validity of the analogy, would turn to Poussin as the best example of its application.

In a 1719 text that forms a prehistory to Gotthold Ephraim Lessing's more famous *Laocoön,* in which the sister arts of painting and poetry are similarly driven apart, the abbé Jean-Baptiste Du Bos would cite Poussin's *Death of Germanicus* as the most extraordinary visualization of a scene of heroic death, in which the painting's vividness would far surpass the ability of a writer to convey the same scene. But not even Poussin, Dubos claimed, could make a painting that would reveal the interior workings of the soul with the same force as the poet and playwright.

Some of the finest and most important twentieth-century interpretations of Poussin have also focused on word and image in his art. Perhaps the most famous is Erwin Panofsky's seminal essay on Poussin's painting *Et in Arcadia Ego,* also called *The Shepherds in Arcadia,* Panofsky's essay pioneered the study of pastoral literature and art, providing the first cultural history of Arcadia from antiquity through the Renaissance. But the core of the essay is his attempt to link Poussin's image of shepherds encountering a tomb in the midst of a landscape with the textual motto shown engraved on the tomb's side: *et in Arcadia ego.* Later generations understood the motto as Johann Wolfgang van Goethe translated it: "Auch ich in Arkadien," in the nostalgic sense of "I, too, was once in Arcadia." But Panofsky believed the phrase could only be translated accurately as "Even in Arcadia am I," an ominous phrase spoken by an invisible personified Death. In an early version of the painting, the motto seems to emerge, metaphorically, from a death's-head atop the tomb, and the mood of moral urgency is carried through in the diagonal surge of the composition. The calm, planar stability of the later painting seems to mistranslate the warning words on the tomb, but in a way that was peculiarly resonant for later viewers. Panofsky did not dwell on the mismatch between the text and the painting, finding Poussin's image an appropriate expression of pastoral reverie. But perhaps now we can see more in it: from an accurate use of classical Latin in a more Baroque painting, to an incorrect Latin in a consummately classical composition, Poussin's two works show the trajectory of a new "classicism" in the making—one whose genesis begins with a rift between word and image.

More recently, the later *Et in Arcadia Ego* also inspired the critic Louis Marin, in various essays that form the core of Marin's writing on French painting in the "classical age." Marin relied on the linguist Émile Benveniste's distinction between *discours* and *récit*, discourse and narration, to analyze the structure of Poussin's painting. He focused not only on the absent verb in the inscription—so appropriate in painted narration, where there is no equivalent to the temporal marker of a verb—but also on the absent, undefined "ego" who speaks the phrase. The eclipse of the speaker is then the hallmark of this painting's narrative structure, just as the turn to *récit* in writing makes the narrated events seem to emerge as if by their own volition on the horizon of the reader's consciousness. This structure of *récit* then allows Marin to situate Poussin's work as a prime example of what Michel Foucault defined as "the classical sign."

After the post–World War II burst of scholarship on Poussin, much of which was iconographic in nature, a new wave of Poussin scholarship seems to be emerging in the wake of Marin's writings. The Poussin who was *peintre-philosophe* or painter-philosopher in the French academic tradition may take on a similar role for our own fin de siècle, as the representation of history and the functions of representation itself remain important critical concerns that link us to the art of this pivotal figure.

[*See also* Classicism; *and* Ut Pictura Poesis.]

BIBLIOGRAPHY

Work by Poussin

Poussin, Nicolas. *La correspondance de Nicolas Poussin.* Edited by C. Jouanny. Archives de l'art français, vol. 5. Paris, 1911; reprint, Paris, 1968.

Other Sources

Batschmann, Oskar. *Nicolas Poussin: Dialectics of Painting.* London, 1990.

Blunt, Anthony. "The Heroic and the Ideal Landscape in the Work of Nicolas Poussin." *Journal of the Warburg and Courtauld Institutes* 2 (1938–1939): 271–276.

Blunt, Anthony. *Nicolas Poussin.* 2 vols. New York, 1967; reprint, London, 1995.

Carrier, David. *Poussin's Paintings: A Study in Art-Historical Methodology.* University Park, Pa., 1993.

Cropper, Elizabeth, and Charles Dempsey. *Nicolas Poussin: Friendship and the Love of Painting.* Princeton, N.J., 1996.

Gombrich, E. H. "The Subject of Poussin's *Orion*." In *Studies in the Art of the Renaissance,* vol. 2, *Symbolic Images,* pp. 119–22. London, 1972.

Marin, Louis. *Détruire la peinture.* Paris, 1977.

McTighe, Sheila. *Nicolas Poussin's Landscape Allegories.* Cambridge and New York, 1996.

Pace, Claire. *Félibien's Life of Poussin.* London, 1981.

Panofsky, Erwin. "Et in Arcadia Ego: Poussin and the Elegiac Tradition." In *Meaning in the Visual Arts,* pp. 295–320. Garden City, N.Y., 1955; reprint, Chicago, 1982.

Rosenberg, Pierre, and Louis-Antoine Prat. *Nicolas Poussin, 1594–1665.* Paris, 1994.

Teyssèdre, Bernard. *Roger de Piles et les débats sur le coloris au siècle de Louis XIV.* Paris, 1957.

Verdi, R. "Poussin's *Eudamidas:* Eighteenth Century Criticism and Copies." *Burlington Magazine* 124 (November 1982): 681–685.

Thuillier, Jacques. *Nicolas Poussin.* Paris, 1988.

SHEILA McTIGHE

PRAGUE SCHOOL. The Prague school is the established name for the international group of scholars in linguistics, literature, theater, folklore, and general aesthetics institutionalized as the Prague Linguistic Circle (1926–1948). In its origins, the Prague school was in part indebted to Russian Formalism, especially the Moscow branch (the Moscow Linguistic Circle) with whom it shared its name as well as some members (Petr Bogatyrev, Roman Jakobson). At the same time, the Prague school had roots in the Czech aesthetic tradition: the nineteenth-century Herbartian Formalism (Josef Durdík, Otakar Hostinský), which conceived of the artistic work as a set of formal relations, and in some post-Herbartian developments in poetics and theater (Otakar Zich). Among other schools of thought the Prague school was influenced by Saussurean linguistics, Edmund Husserl's phenomenology, and Gestalt psychology. Such intellectual affinities were welcomed by the members of the Prague school because they perceived their enterprise as the crystallization of the new scholarly paradigm for the humanities and social sciences that Jakobson in 1929 christened structuralism.

The history of the Prague school can be conveniently divided into three periods. The first begins with the establishment of the circle in 1926 and extends to 1934. During this time, the research of the structuralists was oriented toward the internal organization of poetic works, especially their sound stratum. Jakobson's and Jan Mukařovský's histories of old and modern Czech metrics are the most representative works of this phase.

The subsequent period (1934–1939) opens with Mukařovský's study of a little-known Czech poet of the early nineteenth century, Milota Zdirad Polák, which sparked an extensive and thoroughgoing discussion about the fundamentals of criticism, and ends with the circle's collective volume devoted to the leading Czech Romantic, Karel Hynek

Mácha. In this period, the Prague school transcended its immanent orientation toward literary history: the semiotic concept of a literary work rendered it a collective entity (i.e., a sign understood by the members of a given society), and, furthermore, it enabled the structuralists to relate the developmental changes in literary history to all other aspects of human culture. Consequently, Prague school scholars extended poetics into aesthetics, shifting from a concern with verbal art alone to a concern with all the arts and with extra-artistic aesthetics as well. Mukařovský's *Aesthetic Function, Norm, and Value as Social Facts* (1936) exemplifies this theoretical shift.

The last period, roughly from 1938 to 1948, is delimited by external interventions. The German invasion forced some members of the group to leave Czechoslovakia (Bogatyrev, Jakobson, René Wellek) and severed the international contacts of the circle; the Communist takeover a decade later effectively banned the structuralist study of art and eventually led to the disbanding of the circle. The first blow, however, was mitigated by an influx of junior members into the group: the literary historian Felix Vodička, the student of dramatic art Jiří Veltruský, and the musicologist Antonín Sychra, among others. During this final stage the research of the Prague school moved toward the subjects involved in artistic process (both the author and the perceiver). Vodička's systematic attempt to elaborate the history of literary reception is among the most promising developments of this last stage.

In the postwar years the intellectual heritage of the group was disseminated around the globe by those members who left Prague. The structuralist revolution of the 1960s in France and the United States was to a considerable degree stimulated by Jakobson, who in the 1940s helped to establish the Linguistic Circle of New York, of which the French anthropologist Claude Lévi-Strauss was a member. Petr Bogatyrev, who returned to the Soviet Union at the outbreak of the war, performed a similar role there. A group of young literary scholars (Miroslav Červenka, Lubomír Doležel, Mojmír Grygar) attempted a resurrection of the school in Czechoslovakia in the 1960s, but the Soviet invasion of 1968 dealt it a final blow.

For the Prague school, structuralism was a dialectic synthesis of the two global paradigms dominating European thought in the nineteenth century: Romanticism and Positivism. "European Romantic scholarship, Jakobson observed in 1935, "was an attempt at a general, *global* conception of the universe. The antithesis of Romantic scholarship was the sacrifice of unity for the opportunity to collect the richest factual material, to gain the most varied *partial truth.*" Structuralism, the Prague scholars argued, would avoid the one-sidedness of its predecessors by being neither a totalizing philosophical system nor a narrow concrete science. As Mukařovský put it in 1941,

Structuralism is a scholarly attitude that proceeds from the knowledge of the unceasing interaction of science and philosophy. I say "attitude" in order to avoid terms such as "theory" or "method." "Theory" suggests a fixed body of knowledge, "method" an equally homogenized and unchangeable set of working rules. Structuralism is neither—it is an epistemological stance from which particular working rules and knowledge follow, to be sure, but which exists independently of them and is, therefore, capable of development in both these aspects.

(Steiner, ed., 1982)

What characterizes Prague structuralism is its conceptual frame formed by the interplay of three complementary notions—structure, function, and sign.

Structure. The concept of structure, which gave this intellectual matrix its name, requires special attention. In the parlance of the Prague school it referred to what might be seen as two distinct entities. On the one hand, it denoted the holistic organization of a single work as a hierarchical system of dominant and subordinated elements. But in the same way as Ferdinand de Saussure recognized that every concrete utterance *(parole)* is meaningful only against the background of the collectively shared linguistic code *(langue),* the Prague scholars saw every individual work as an implementation of a particular aesthetic code—a set of artistic norms. These they also termed a structure.

There were, however, important differences in how the Swiss linguist and the Prague group conceived of the code (whether linguistic or aesthetic). For Saussure it was a harmonious system, synchronic by its very essence and incapable of changing. Once affected by an external intervention the code was destroyed and replaced by another one. From this perspective the history of language was a random succession of disconnected momentary codes. For the Prague group, on the other hand, the system was a priori diachronic. Its present state, they believed, contained not only the traces of the past but also the seeds of the future. Concerned with literary history, the structuralists advanced three different models accounting for the code's development. The earliest emulated to a considerable degree the immanent orientation of Russian Formalism according to which the literary series develops because of its intrinsic need for deautomatization *(aktualisace).* But the limits of this approach soon became apparent. Poetry does not exist in a social vacuum Mukařovský recognized in 1934: "The developmental series of individual structures changing in time (e.g., political, economic, ideological, literary) do not run parallel to each other without contact. On the contrary, they are elements of a structure of a higher order and this structure of structures has its hierarchy and its dominant (prevailing) series." The immanent study of literary change was thus supplemented by consideration of its external context. The historical trajectory of any art was seen as determined simultaneously by the purely artistic needs and the external impulses stemming from social developments.

Despite their differences, the immanent and extrinsic models of literary change describe history from the same vantage point: that of production. But it is clearly insufficient to explain the becoming of a text solely as a function of the context that generated it, as Vodička observed in 1942: "Only if read does the work achieve its aesthetic realization [and] become an aesthetic object in the reader's consciousness" (Vodička). The history of literary reception proposed by Vodička relativizes significantly the bond between the text and the underlying literary code against the background of which it was written and which allegedly provides it with its identity. Any work can potentially be reconstituted according to reading conventions that did not exist during its inception and, in this way, assume new and unprecedented appearances.

Function. The second key concept and the trademark of Prague structuralism was function. Rooted in a purposive view of human behavior, it designated in Mukařovský's parlance "the active relation between an object and the goal for which this object is used." The Prague group always stressed the social dimension of functionality, the necessary consensus among the members of a collectivity concerning the purpose that an object serves and its utility for such a purpose. From the functional perspective, every individual structure mentioned above (political, economic, artistic, etc.) appeared as a set of social norms regulating the attainment of values in these cultural spheres.

Within the functional typology proposed by the structuralists, the aesthetic function played a special role. Whereas in "practical" functions the telos lies outside the object used, in the aesthetic function the telos is this object. That is to say, in extra-artistic activities functional objects are instruments whose value stems from their suitability for particular purposes. Works of art, on the other hand, as objects of aesthetic function, do not serve any particular goal directly and thus constitute ultimate values in and of themselves.

The structuralists, however, did not believe that an artistic work is completely severed from its social context. The Prague group conceived of an object's functionality in terms of hierarchy rather than mutual exclusivity: the dominance of the aesthetic function does not preclude the presence of other functions. Although unrealized, practical functions do not vanish from the work; they remain there in all their potentiality, merely shifting their corresponding values to a different level. The transformation that extra-aesthetic values undergo in art depends on another component of the structuralist frame of reference—the sign.

Sign. "The problem of the sign," the members of the circle declared in their joint statement inaugurating their new journal, *Slovo a slovesnost*, in 1935, "is one of the most urgent philosophical problems of the cultural re-birth of our time," because, "all of reality, from sensory perception to the most abstract mental constructs, appears to modern man as a vast and complex realm of signs." As mentioned above, the Prague group classified all artifacts according to

the functions they serve. Humanmade objects do not, however, merely carry out their functions (i.e., a house protecting us from weather) but also signify them (i.e., a house as a sign of civilization). A conjunction of material vehicle and immaterial meaning, the sign reinscribes in different terms the dual nature of structure—its physical embodiment in individual artifacts and its mental, socially shared existence as a normative code. From a semiotic perspective, then, culture appears as a complex interaction of signs mediating among the members of a particular collectivity.

At this point we might return to extra-aesthetic functions in art whose appurtenant values are not realized because of a dominant aesthetic function. But since an artistic work is also a sign, these unrealized values are transferred from an empirical to a semantic plane. They become partial meanings that contribute to the total semantic structure of the work. Thus, "from the most abstract point of view," Mukařovský concluded in 1936,

> the work of art is nothing but a particular set of extra-aesthetic values. The material components of the artistic artifact and the way they are exploited as formal devices are mere conductors of energy represented by extra-aesthetic values. If at this point we ask ourselves where aesthetic value lies, we find that it has dissolved into individual extra-aesthetic values and is nothing but a general term for the dynamic totality of their interrelations.
> (Mukařovský, 1970)

Poetic Language. Despite the breadth of their research interests, the members of the Prague school devoted most of their attention to the study of literature. Following the path charted by the Russian formalists, they approached verbal art from a linguistic perspective, treating it as a particular functional dialect—poetic language. The circle's "Theses" of 1929 presented such dialects as a series of binary oppositions: internal versus external, intellectual versus emotional, poetic versus communicative (the latter subdivided into practical versus theoretical), and so on. Although in subsequent years the structuralists further elaborated, augmented, and terminologically modified this typology, the basic characteristics of poetic dialect remained the same. As a realization of the aesthetic function in linguistic material, it transforms the verbal sign from an instrument for signifying other, extra-linguistic realities to a self-centered composition.

The most obvious manifestation of the aesthetic function in language is the hypertrophy of the signifier—the striking organization of linguistic sound, especially in poetry. The entire range of phonic features, which in messages governed by other functions serve as an automatized vehicle of meaning, are arranged in poetic language so as to call attention to themselves, turning thus from a means toward something else into their own ends. Consequently, the Prague group investigated closely the problems of sound orchestration, prosody, and intonation in poetic compositions. The distinctive feature of these inquiries was their phonological basis. That is, for the Prague structuralists only those phonic elements of language capable of differentiating cognitive meanings could be exploited poetically. By the same token, they regarded the sound configurations permeating the poetic work (including meter) not as mere formal clusters but as partial semantic structures comprising the overall meaning of the text.

The foregrounding of the *phonē* in a poetic composition disrupts the process of linguistic designation, the matching of signifiers with signifieds to produce meaning, and results in the heightened polysemy of verbal art. To explain this point, we can turn to the Prague model of linguistic designation advanced in 1929 by one of Saussure's students, Sergej Karcevskij.

According to this model, every language use is a struggle between the "psychological" meaning the speaker wishes to express and the "ideological" meaning imposed by the code. Linguistic designation, then, involves two antithetical tendencies. The signifier and the signified can be matched in a way the speaker sees as adequate to the particular context or as adequate to socially shared linguistic conventions. The tension between these two tendencies results in the homonymic/synonymic extension of the word: the asymmetrical dualism of sound and meaning. That is to say, every application of a linguistic sign necessarily implies other possible applications of the same sign in different contexts (homonymity) as well as the existence of applicable, but in this case not applied, alternative signs (synonymity). In Karcevskij's words:

> The signifier (sound) and the signified (function) slide continually on the "slope of reality." Each "overflows" the boundaries assigned to it by the other: the signifier tries to have functions other than its own; the signified tries to be expressed by means other than its sign. They are asymmetrical; coupled, they exist in a state of unstable equilibrium.

The aesthetic manipulation of sound in verbal art intensifies the semantic slippage of linguistic signs. The dissolution of the signifier into its constitutive elements and their regrouping according to a particular phonic prescript (e.g., meter) provide language with a new network of signifying possibilities: a different ground on which sound and meaning can meet. Yet, by problematizing the process of verbal representation, according to the Prague group, poetic language performs a signal role in the linguistic system. In contrast to some other functional accounts that stress the maximal adequacy of signs to what they stand for and strive to obliterate their difference, poetic language underscores the reciprocal inadequacy of the two, their deepseated nonidentity. But, "why is it necessary to point out that the sign does not merge with the object [it signifies]?" Jakobson asked in 1934 in his probing essay, "What Is Poetry?":

> Because besides the immediate awareness of the identity between the sign and object (A is A₁) we need the immediate awareness of the lack of this identity (A is not A₁). This antinomy is necessary for without contradictions there is no mobility of concepts, no mobility of signs, and the relationship between concept and sign becomes automatized. Activity stops and the awareness of reality dies out.   (Jakobson, 1987)

The extreme extension of signs in verbal art, however, was still an insufficient criterion by which to distinguish poetic language from other functional dialects. Emotive designations (curses, endearments), Mukařovský insisted, demonstrate an equal if not higher tendency toward semantic novelty; yet, their purpose is clearly not aesthetic. The specificity of poetic language vis-à-vis its emotive counterpart, therefore, cannot be sought in the act of designation but in another fundamental linguistic operation: the process of combining signs into higher linguistic units.

The difference between linguistic designation and combination corresponds to another basic semiotic dichotomy discussed by the Prague group, between arbitrary and motivated signs. "Language," Karcevskij paraphrased Saussure in 1927, "always offers the spectacle of battle between lexicology (the tendency toward the arbitrary and phonological sign) and syntagmatics (the tendency toward the 'motivated' and morphological sign)." The possibility of homonymic/synonymic slippage is predicated on the essential arbitrariness of the link between the signifier and signified; anything can be designated by any word, and vice versa. The conventionality of the linguistic system provides this flux with social limits, but in itself is incapable of stopping it because the individual sign users may always violate these limits in the name of "psychological adequacy." Given this fact, it is not surprising that emotive language charged with the task of expressing a speaker's immediate mental state strives toward the pole of lexicological arbitrariness.

Although poetic and emotive languages share a propensity for semantic shifts, they differ in regard to arbitrariness. For the Prague school, verbal art was the prime example of syntagmatically motivated signs. Since the aesthetic function transforms language from an instrument for signifying something else into a self-centered sign, the meaning of poetic designation is a function not of the external context but of the internal contexture of the utterance. This fact results from the complexity and systematic organization of the poetic text at all levels. The series of phonological, morphological, and syntactic parallelism, and the hierarchical correlations among partial signs create what the structuralists termed the work's "semantic gesture"—the grid of formal possibilities that motivates the overall meaning of the literary sign. It is the relational properties of the signifier, the interactions among its partial constituents that create the structure of its signified, the work's semantic universe. Therefore, in transgressing linguistic conventionality, poetic language does not slide toward the pole of arbitrariness. Instead, each work generates from within its own textual conventions, a paradigm of intersubjective expectations that suggest its interpretation.

[*See also* Formalism; Poetics; Russian Aesthetics, *article on* Russian Formalism; Semiotics; *and* Structuralism.]

BIBLIOGRAPHY

Galan, Frank W. *Historic Structures: The Prague School Project, 1928–1946.* Austin, 1985.

Garvin, Paul L., ed., *A Prague School Reader on Esthetics, Literary Structure, and Style.* Washington, D.C., 1964.

Havránek, Bohuslav, and Jan Mukařovský, eds. *Čtení o jazyce a poesii.* Prague, 1942.

Jakobson, Roman. *Verbal Art, Verbal Sign, Verbal Time.* Edited by Krystyna Pomorska and Stephen Rudy. Minneapolis, 1985.

Jakobson, Roman. *Language in Literature.* Edited by Krystyna Pomorska and Stephen Rudy. Cambridge, Mass., 1987.

Matejka, Ladislav, and Irwin R. Titunik, eds. *Semiotics of Art: Prague School Contributions.* Cambridge, Mass., 1976.

Mukařovský, Jan. "Polákova *Vznešenost přírody:* Pokus o rozbor a vývojové zařazení básnické struktury." *Sborník filologický* 10 (1934–1935): 1–68.

Mukařovský, Jan. ed. *Torso a tajemství Máchova díla.* Prague, 1938.

Mukařovský, Jan. *Aesthetic Function, Norm and Value as Social Facts.* Translated by Mark E. Suino. Ann Arbor, 1970.

Mukařovský, Jan. *The Word and Verbal Art.* Edited and translated by John Burbank and Peter Steiner. New Haven, 1977.

Mukařovský, Jan. *Structure, Sign, and Function.* Edited and translated by John Burbank and Peter Steiner. New Haven, 1977.

Rudy, Stephen. *Roman Jakobson, 1896–1982: A Complete Bibliography of His Writings.* Berlin, 1990.

Steiner, Peter, ed. *The Prague School: Selected Writings, 1929–1946.* Translated by John Burbank et al. Austin, 1982.

Striedter, Jurij. *Literary Structure, Evolution, and Value: Russian Formalism and Czech Structuralism Reconsidered.* Cambridge, Mass., 1989.

Vodička, Felix. *Počátky krásné prózy novočeské.* Prague, 1948.

PETER STEINER

PRE-COLUMBIAN AESTHETICS.

It has often been said that in archaic societies art is the handmaiden of religion. Concomitant with that is the fact that in such societies there is no word for "art." Yet, these societies have a remarkable amount of formally sophisticated objects that appear to fit the concept of art of those societies that have it. Moreover, despite the apparent emphasis on religion, some of the most sacred objects in archaic societies are not formally exquisite works of art but simple, rough-hewn, or even found objects, like pebbles and feathers in bundles or rock outcrops, indicating that the relationship of art and sacredness is not a simple matter. Artistry is clearly lavished on the dresses, badges, crests, palaces, temples, and images of the social and political world. Although its subjects are often religious, art is, more correctly, the handmaiden of society.

Pre-Columbian concepts of art are coded into the works of art themselves and, hence, implicit. We collectors, curators, scholars, and tourists tease an aesthetic philosophy out of the works, the texts, and other data. It is our creation. The aesthetic does not reside in the object nor in the mind of the viewer, but is a complex relation of the two. Reconstructing the mind of the pre-Columbian viewer in the absence of texts and informants is nearly impossible. Nevertheless, pre-Columbian cultures are particularly instructive for the Western intellectual quest to understand the nature of art. In at least one pre-Columbian society, the Classic Maya (317–889 CE), art appears to have been a somewhat self-conscious enterprise with a glorification of the artist that is closer to the concept of art and artist in the West. Having emerged outside of the Old World traditions, the cultures of ancient America are a fruitful testing ground for theories derived from the development of Western art.

Before attempting a reconstruction of the pre-Columbian concept of art it is useful to note how the West had come to see it as "art" and how it has been fitted into Western schemata of aesthetics. In the sixteenth century, when the Americas were conquered, the only art admired was that of architecture and engineering. The bridges, causeways, and temples of the Aztec and the Inca aroused the admiration of Europeans used to living with monumental architecture. It was a sign of high civilization. The other arts were seen as either heathen images and works of the devil that had to be destroyed or merely as quaint curiosities. There is a famous passage in Albrecht Dürer's notebooks in which he merely admired the Mexican objects taken to the court of Charles V in Brussels for their ingenuity and strangeness, in the same way that he was fascinated by all other oddities he came across on his trip. His language in describing them is not the one he uses for Western art. No one in the sixteenth century admired the "art" of the goldwork enough not to melt it down for the value of the metal. It can be said quite categorically that in Renaissance times, pre-Columbian things were wonderful curiosities, but not "art." Moreover, despite the interest in local European styles, northern and southern, Florentine and Venetian, there is much less a sense that for them exotic objects had a "style" of their own other than a generic strangeness, crudeness, or grotesqueness. (The one foreign artistic tradition the West saw and understood to some extent was that of the Islamic Arab countries, because of their closeness and long intertwined history with the West.) So it is not surprising that in the many books engraved by Théodore de Bry on the Americas there is often no precise knowledge of, or apparent desire for, accurate stylistic depiction. Roman arches form the buildings, and European pitchers and trays are put in the hands of the Inca. Naked Caribbean Indians greet Christopher Columbus with similar Renaissance gold vessels in another de Bry engraving. Such stylistic vagueness is generally true of early illustrated books, such as the *Nuremberg Chronicle* (1493), in which all dress and constructions of various places and epochs are seen as if they were contemporary or purely imaginary.

Recognizably exotic styles emerge in the illustrations of the middle of the seventeenth century as, for example, in the monumental treatise on Egypt written by Athanasius Kircher. Egypt plays the role of the exotic ancient "other" to classical European civilization. Kircher compared Egyptian to all exotic world art known to him, including Chinese, Hindu, and pre-Columbian, and the illustrations indicate a sense of the style of each of these. Their spirit, however, is scientific rather than artistic or aesthetic. To Kircher's mind, all these styles were similar to one another and to the Egyptian and different from that of the West. This attitude in various guises has remained in force until the first half of the twentieth century.

The late eighteenth and early nineteenth centuries were the great sorting ground of the arts and civilizations in Western thought. While on the one hand this is the era of Lord Elgin and the museum enshrinement of the marbles of the Parthenon, of Johann Joachim Winckelmann's glorification of Greek art as the supreme creation of Western man, it is also the time of the creation of the exotic, the non-Western, the archaic and the primitive. The fascination with Greece coincides in time with Napoleon's colossal scientific project regarding the antiquities of Egypt, visits to the ruins of the ancient Near East, and the beginning of the exploration and recording of Maya ruins. The apotheosis of the classical and the delectation of the exotic go hand in hand, and, in fact, define each other. John Lloyd Stevens and Frederick Catherwood both traveled in Greece, Egypt, and the Near East looking at ruins before joining forces and setting out in search of the Maya. Their attitude was thoroughly comparative.

None of this could have been possible without a philosophical concept of aesthetics. It is precisely the separation of the aesthetic aspect of works of art from their functional, social, and religious aspects that made it possible to see alien arts as nonthreatening and nonheretical. While the sixteenth century saw the art of the Americas in religious terms, the eighteenth could see it in two new ways: scientific and aesthetic. These indicate a major change in attitude to which the Kantian concepts of disinterest, detachment, and universal judgment of taste are crucial. Whereas the scientific attitude is detachment for the sake of knowledge, the aesthetic attitude is detachment for the sake of appreciation. The foreign can now be understood and enjoyed without its having to be the same as one's own. There is no heresy involved. The eighteenth-century concept of the sublime also allowed for exotic beauty and grandeur that was not within the canons of Western art, but could include that which was strange, violent, disturbing, or perhaps even ugly. The only element alien to the aesthetic, for Immanuel Kant, was the disgusting.

The Western measure of exotic art was, and to a large extent remains, classical art, and especially the art of the Greeks—what in the mid-twentieth century E. H. Gom-

PRE-COLUMBIAN AESTHETICS. *Mayan Figurine of a Woman Writing* (seventh to tenth century CE), terra cotta, Island of Jaina; Museo Nacional de Antropologia, Mexico City. (Photograph courtesy of Werner Forman/Art Resource, New York.)

brich still considered unique and a "miracle" ("The Miracle of the Greeks"). Idealistic naturalism, characteristic of Greek art, is still therefore the favorite style of the West. Maya sculptures, first brought to Western attention in the late eighteenth century, were immediately fascinating precisely because such "idealistic naturalism" is their hallmark. (Eventually the Maya would be considered the "Greeks of the New World.") When Jean-Frederic Waldeck, the self-proclaimed pupil of the neoclassic painters Jacques-Louis David, Joseph-Marie Vien, and Pierre-Paul Prud'hon depicted the images of Palenque with some enthusiastic inaccuracy, he saw them as approximating neoclassic forms. Actually, Waldeck's original drawings were in the "scientific tradition," much like his sketches of fish and flowers, and quite "exact" in that sense. As he elaborated them into paintings, however, the Maya forms began to look more and more Western and classical, in order to become "beautiful," at the same time that their grotesque features were exaggerated in order to become "sublime." In his finished paintings he enlarged them next to small human figures so as to increase the sense of their awesomeness. (Giambattista Piranesi had already used such changes in scale to make his views of Roman ruins more exotic.) Many modern collectors still appreciate Maya art for the same reasons Waldeck did: because its ideals of beauty are close to that of the classical while it has the added excitement of the exotic features, mysterious hieroglyphics, and barbaric (i.e., violent or sexual) elements that to the West signify the "other." At the end of the twentieth century the most accessible and favorite pre-Columbian style remains that of the Maya.

Most other pre-Columbian styles had to wait for the twentieth-century language of modernism and the appreciation of abstraction and conventionalization to be seen as works of art. While the art of the Maya is lauded for its elegance and naturalism, the arts of Mezcala, Teotihuacán, or Tiahuanaco, are appreciated for their abstraction and compared to Constantin Brancusi, Georges Braque, or Pablo Picasso. Modernism set itself up in opposition to classical values of representation and sought as "authorities" and precursors various "primitive," "archaic," and "medieval" styles. There is no question, however, that Western modes of art wag the tail of pre-Columbian appreciation. Minimalist Earth art of the 1960s, for example, has kindled interest in the famous lines in the desert of the Nazca plateau in Peru. The very language of the appreciation of these pre-Columbian arts is borrowed directly from the formal analysis of modern art, with its preoccupation with lines and shapes and the invention of ingenious abstractions. While modern art in the West has a sizable following, it is still an acquired taste for most people whose preference is for classical forms. There is thus a clear ranking of pre-Columbian arts in the minds of both scholars and the public. These tastes determine the valuation and language of (and even prices paid for) pre-Columbian arts. The rise of any new Western artistic movement may potentially rescue some so far obscure pre-Columbian artistic tradition.

Because of the preference for classical art, since the nineteenth century evolutionist theories generally imagined art to have a stylistic progression from abstraction, which seemed to be "crude and easy," to naturalism, which was seen as "sophisticated and difficult." These concepts derive from a parallel of art and technology, the acquisition of naturalism being compared to the slow accumulation of technical and scientific knowledge. In most of his work, Gombrich is still a proponent of this idea on the basis of the type of "vision" required for naturalism, which, in his view, is a detached, scientific vision in which an attempt is made to match images to the real world rather than to create, through abstractions, alternative worlds. Abstraction is thus associated with "magical" as opposed to "scientific" thinking. His terms for these "visions" are the "conceptual" and the "perceptual." According to the prevalent nineteenth-century art-historical paradigm, the Greeks created a "perceptual" art out of the rigid "conceptual" canons of Egyptian art by gradually "matching" the image to reality. Nineteenth-century anthropologists studying ornament debated endlessly whether designs began in naturalistic forms

and became more abstract as time went on, or the opposite. Such evolutionist theories presupposed gradual, incremental evolution in a single direction (even though neither medieval nor modern art fitted into that schema particularly well). Non-Western arts were condemned often for not fitting into linear evolutionary sequences and thus lacking proper "development" and in any case remaining at a primitive, nonnaturalistic level.

Pre-Columbian art history, as we know it so far through archaeology, does not support the Western evolutionary paradigm of naturalism rising out of abstraction. The earliest art in Mesoamerica, that of the Olmecs, is one of the most naturalistic, three-dimensional, and free in movement (1300–900 BCE). Thereafter the arts are in many ways more constricted in form. Olmec art does not appear to have emerged out of an older more "abstract" tradition, but to have been invented fully in that form. Some centuries later, Classic Maya art undergoes a seven-hundred-year-long history in which for about a hundred and fifty years there is remarkable naturalism in style (650–800 CE). Andean art has its idealized/naturalistic cameo appearance in the Moche style (200 BCE–600 CE), but then becomes progressively more abstract and minimal. Idealized naturalism occurs at various points in pre-Columbian history, but it is more episodic than developmentally determined.

Because the arts of pre-Columbian America emerged entirely separately from the arts of the Old World, they are crucial to the understanding of the evolution of art and of the roles of naturalism and abstraction. It is clear that naturalism and abstraction are cultural choices and potentially always possible, not steps on a ladder, or end points on a scale. Naturalism is neither a specific "vision" nor a technological skill belonging to a particular stage of culture. It has most to do with the social and political requirements of a given context. Moreover, it is also clear that there is not, necessarily, a grand overall development in the arts of an area. Development is restricted largely to the art of individual cultures, such as Olmec, Moche, or Maya. Within individual cultures there are developments that can be described as "formative," "classical," or "baroque," and tendencies either toward or away from naturalism. But, the disjunctions between cultures are great enough to redirect art into any new directions, depending on the given social conditions. The developments of Western art seemed so compelling to art historians such as Heinrich Wölfflin precisely because they were part of a single cultural tradition.

In order to reconstruct pre-Columbian aesthetics one is forced to deal with the context as defined anthropologically. The most immediate issue is the function of art, which is said to be "utilitarian" in traditional societies and "free" in the modern West. Although we can say that as the embodiment of value, status, taste, and intellect, art of all periods has a similar function, there is indeed a difference between implicit and explicit concepts of aesthetics. Pre-Columbian cultures whose arts survived in permanent media were complex hierarchical societies defined as chiefdoms and states. Because these cultures had limited systems of writing, artworks were the most important communicating media. While their means were aesthetic, these were as implicit as the good design of cars or rockets is implicit—indeed, it is not their primary function. (We usually do not ask who designed the lines of a space shuttle.) Any perusal of the few texts available on the arts or the artists of the Aztec, Inca, and Maya indicates a high regard for skill, the ability to understand a commission in terms of the genre required, the imagination to invent something new and different. Curiously, traditional non-Western arts are considered conservative and unchanging (the Egyptian example is usually quoted) and yet extremely varied and ingenious (the vast variety of non-Western styles). The variety of styles existing worldwide and archaeologically makes sense only if the notion of sticking to tradition had to have been very loosely understood in most of these cultures.

Every culture has its concept of the beautiful. Frequently that is evident in an idealized or stylized human figure or face, or in elaborate ornament. Both from contexts and from texts we know that the beautiful, the good, and the powerful were often equated with one another. Characteristic of preindustrial arts of states is a high valuation of technical skill, virtuosity of craft, labor, and time intensiveness—the use of stone tools to carve jade and basalt in Mexico, the painstaking textile techniques of the Andes. There is also evidence that the artist is seen to have a mysterious creative power akin to the supernatural and that some of that power also resides in the work the artist creates.

What most pre-Columbian art did not share with Western art since the Renaissance is a "cult of the aesthetic" and a "cult of the artist." Artists did not sign their works or make images of themselves. The aesthetic features of their works may have been discussed as "better" or "worse" than others, but there was no philosophy of art. This does not make such art "anonymous," since it is likely that these artists were known in their day. But the lack of the glorification of the artist affects the nature of the art created. It gives it a straightforward, self-assured and unself-conscious quality sometimes much admired by aesthetically self-conscious cultures such as ours. Mannerist strivings for effect—or a kind of visual "signature"—are usually lacking.

The Maya are a partial exception to this in the Americas because they appear to have had a cult of the aesthetic. The evidence that the Maya focused specifically on the "aesthetic" as a facet of experience comes from the nature of their art and the inscriptions. Aestheticism among the Maya is generally an aspect of the emphasis on individual rulers and aristocrats. The glorification of individual achievement characterizes much of Maya art, which is concerned with dynastic matters such as accessions and conquest. Rulers are sometimes individualized by portraiture and by inscrip-

tions giving their names, proofs of legitimacy, and exploits. It is this climate of the celebration of individual achievement that appears to be behind the development of individual polity styles in art. Within the short span of Classic Maya art there is a wide variety of regional styles, as each Maya city, like the cities of Renaissance Italy, has its own genres and forms.

Tatiana Proskouriakoff has shown that temporal changes in style affect the art of all the Maya cities, indicating high levels of interaction. As she conceptualizes them, these phases are comparable to the European developmental notions of the formative, classical, and Baroque. It is relatively easy within a given site, like Yaxchilan, to select the work of an individual carver on the basis of style. Advances in hieroglyphic inscriptions have made it possible to see the styles favored and patronized by individual rulers.

Aesthetic preoccupation is also evident in the design of individual monuments in which the elegance of forms and exquisiteness of detail suggest patrons interested in aesthetic matters, and especially clever refinements. All these elements can be read out of the works of art just with a cross-cultural knowledge of art. Recent excavations and finds have brought to light more specific proofs of this aesthetic interest in the form of the sculpture of a deity represented as an artist with a brush in his hands from Copán, and names on pottery that are interpreted by some as the names of the artists who painted them. Most dramatic of all is a carved bone from Tikal that represents the hand of an artist with a brush emerging from the maw of a supernatural creature, in the same way that deities are often shown emerging from supernatural maws. It does not take much imagination to interpret the hand and brush as representing the divine aspect of artistic creation. Various pre-Columbian sources indicate that younger sons of aristocratic families were involved in different sorts of artistic activity and that artistic activity was an integral part of court life, especially among the Maya.

Besides idealistic naturalism, self-conscious aestheticism brings the Maya close to the Western classical ideal of high art. The really interesting question is why explicit aestheticism developed among the Maya only for that relatively brief period of time. One possible answer is that, like the Balinese or Louis XIV, the Maya lords ruled through a form of theatricality of which aesthetics was a significant and distinct component. Aesthetics was separated out because it was in some ways socially useful. As Clifford Geertz noted for Bali, theatrical aesthetic activity may be one way for a state to pretend to have and thus acquire power it is not able to amass in more practical ways. Another possible answer is that with the high development of hieroglyphic writing, images were freed from the necessity of conveying certain sorts of information and were available to communicate ideas about art itself. This does not, however, explain why writing was so much more elaborate among the Maya than

PRE-COLUMBIAN AESTHETICS. *Sculpture of Quetzalcoatl, God of Life and Death* (fourteenth to sixteenth century), Aztec; Museo Nacional de Anthropologia, Mexico City. (Photograph courtesy of Giraudon/Art Resource, New York.)

among their neighbors. Writing seems to have been invested with an artistic interest similar to that of calligraphy in Asia. Regardless of cause and effect, the Maya were clearly separating image and text, and it is partly within that separation that explicit aestheticism emerged.

The aesthetic attitude assumes that the raison d'être of art objects is to be visual. That is, they can be examined, decoded, enjoyed, perhaps even feared or hated, but the sensory experience of vision and the intentionality of some visual effect are presumed to be primary. This is indeed the case in Western art since the Renaissance: an invisible work of art is meaningless. (Market value and aesthetic delight assume a human audience. Twentieth-century art has tried to invert this value by creating nonvisual or noncollectible arts.) Archaic societies are neither "visual" nor "antivisual" in this sense. The Aztecs carved the bottom of colossal sculptures with intricate images of the earth, presumably for the visual appreciation of a supernatural audience with human tastes. Many Maya reliefs, such as lintels, were originally embedded in badly lit and difficult-to-see architectural contexts accessible only to the elite. The designs of Nazca lines are mainly visible from the air or partially from

a nearby hill but were invisible to their makers and users the way we see them now. Aestheticism assumes display—in a church, museum, palace, or home in which a work can be present either as "background" ornament or as the focus of attention.

Astheticism emerges in a continuum and not as an absolute stage. It is always involved with display, however, and thus with secular, political power or the pomp and circumstance of religious power. The most sacred objects of many cultures are either natural objects not fashioned by man, such as the rocks of Mecca and Jerusalem, or crude and overtly nonaesthetic objects, such as the boli of the Bamana. In many cultures artworks are destroyed in the process of their use. The "oracle" in the Andean temple of Chavín de Huantar was a crudely carved natural stone, much less finished and "beautiful" than the carvings in the anteroom courtyards. The Aztec patron god Huitzilopochtli had no images and was perhaps a collection of powerful charms in a bundle, or a dough image. The really sacred statue of Athena on the Acropolis was an old wooden one and not the colossal ivory-and-gold masterpiece of Phidias in the Parthenon. In many cultures, natural, crude, or old objects are more venerated than elaborately made new ones.

Magnificent objects buried with the dead in many past cultures also illustrate the point that availability for use and the visibility of an object for the living were not always its main essence in the past. The beautiful and elaborate, when it is meant to be visual, is intended to communicate with a human audience in some social context. In a spectacular funeral there is at least one, final, grand display. Subsequently, the objects communicated functionally and aesthetically with the dead and the gods. Aesthetics in this sense is an immanent rather than transcendent social value. The ultimate powers of the unseen are often felt to be inexpressible, invisible, and unrealizable—beyond the province of the visual arts.

The transcendent aspects of aesthetics, art turned into the expression of the divine in human beings, emerges fully in eighteenth-century European thought, associated with the decline of religious faith. Since the eighteenth century, aesthetics has become a sort of religion, a substitute for the forms of worship of the past, with the museum as its temple. This is not, however, a sudden and total change, nor is it restricted to the West. Various forms of aestheticism existed in Asia and Africa, as well as in pre-Columbian America. Paradoxically, although the aesthetic has always been felt to have something supernatural about it, it is mostly secular and worldly in its manifestations: this, too, it has in common with aspects of religion.

One of the most striking aspects of archaic and exotic arts is the ease with which we recognize them as "arts" and the extent to which we can understand their formal "message," even if their precise cultural meanings are unknown. One of Immanuel Kant's most important observations about aesthetic judgment is that it is "universal"—even if we disagree, the mere fact that we can quarrel about taste means that we have grounds in common. We need not have the same opinions, but we have a similar ability to form judgments. Kant's own taste seems to have run to classical allegories and English gardens, but Maori tattoos, Sumatran pepper gardens, mathematics, and tulips are among the broad range of things that inform his thinking. This eighteenth-century concept of a shared, universal ability to make aesthetic judgments is related to the new ability to see and valorize exotic arts as desirable and pleasurable. Many eighteenth-century scholars and travelers routinely used charts to compare the arts of all of these peoples. The aim of these comparisons was to show the similarities despite the apparent differences between Egyptian, Hindu, Mayan, and other styles. While this attempt seems naive to those of us who are attuned to differences, it underlines the universalizing tendency of the previous century and the process by which the foreign was made available as "art" in Western terms. In the sixteenth century, Huitzilopochtli was represented in European prints as a devil with hooves. To the eighteenth century, pre-Columbian art looks more like Greek art. For the twentieth century, pre-Columbian art outdoes Cubism in abstraction and complexity.

Nevertheless, while pre-Columbian art reveals a great richness and variety of traditions and implicit aesthetics, and while it has been and will be used to justify and authorize Western experiments in art, as Henry Moore once used it, it is a passive body of material on which aesthetic theory can play its games and test its various ideas. Although these aesthetic games have been suspect in the eyes of anthropologically oriented scholars in the business of serious cultural reconstruction, would we expend the energy on excavation and analysis of the Maya if it were not for the great body of extant Maya art and what it means to us? We claim that reason, science, and technology are more central to our culture than art, but we define the peoples and cultures of the past through their art. It matters a great deal who has art and what kind of art it is.

[See also Caribbean Aesthetics; and Latin American Aesthetics.]

BIBLIOGRAPHY

Baudez, Claude-François. *Jean-Frederic Waldeck, peintre: Le premier explorateur des ruines mayas.* Paris, 1993.
Bennett, Tony. *The Birth of the Museum.* London and New York, 1995.
Boone, Elizabeth H. "Incarnations of the Aztec Supernatural: The Image of Huitzilopochtli in Mexico and Europe." In *Transactions of the American Philosophical Society.* vol. 79, pt. 2. Philadelphia, 1989.
Braun, Barbara. *Pre-Columbian Art and the Post-Columbian World.* New York, 1993.
Burger, Richard L. *Chavin and the Origins of Andean Civilization.* New York, 1992.
Burke, Edmund. *A Philosophical Enquiry into the Origin of Our Ideas of the Sublime and Beautiful* (1757). 2d ed. Edited by James T. Boulton. Notre Dame, Ind., 1968.
Coe, Michael D. *The Maya.* (1966). 5th rev. exp. ed. London, 1993.
Cohodas, Marvin. "The Identification of Workshops, Schools and Hands at Yaxchilan, a Classic Maya Site in Mexico." In *Proceedings of the 42nd International Congress of Americanists,* vol. 7, pp. 301–313. Paris, 1976.
Demarest, Arthur A. "Ideology in Ancient Maya Cultural Evolution: The Dynamics of Galactic Polities." In *Ideology and Pre-Columbian Civilizations,* edited by Arthur A. Demarest and Geoffrey W. Conrad, pp. 135–158. Santa Fe, N. Mex., 1992.
Fash, William L. *Scribes, Warriors and Kings: The City of Copan and the Ancient Maya.* London, 1991.
Geertz, Clifford. *Negara: The Theatre State in Nineteenth-Century Bali.* Princeton, N.J., 1980.
Gombrich, E. H. *The Story of Art.* (1950). 16th exp. ed. London, 1995.
Gombrich, E. H. *Art and Illusion: A Study in the Psychology of Pictoral Representation.* (1960). 2d ed. Reprint, Princeton, N.J., 1969.
Heidegger, Martin. "The Origin of a Work of Art." In *Philosophies of Art and Beauty: Selected Readings in Aesthetics from Plato to Heidegger,* edited by Albert Hofstader and Richard Kuhns, pp. 650–703. Reprint, Chicago, 1976.
Kant, Immanuel. *Critique of Judgment* (1790). Translated by Werner S. Pluhar. Indianapolis, 1987.
Kircher, Athanasius. *Oedipus Aegipticus.* 3 vols. 1652–1655.
Kubler, George. *Studies in Classic Maya Iconography.* New Haven, 1969.
Leon-Portilla, Miguel. *Aztec Thought and Culture.* Norman, Okla., 1963.
Pasztory, Esther. "Shamanism and North American Indian Art." In *Native North American Art History: Selected Readings,* edited by Aldona Jonaitis and Zena Pearlstone Mathews, pp. 7–30. Palo Alto, Calif., 1982.
Pasztory, Esther. *Aztec Art.* New York, 1983.
Pasztory, Esther. "The Function of Art in Mesoamerica." *Archaeology* 37.1 (1984): 18–25.
Pasztory, Esther. "Still Invisible: The Problems of the Aesthetics of Abstraction in Pre-Columbian Art and Its Implications for Other Traditions." *RES* 19/20 (1990–1991): 105–136.
Proskouriakoff, Tatiana. "The Study of Classic Maya Sculpture." *Carnegie Institution of Washington Publication,* no. 593. Washington, D.C., 1950.
Reents-Budet, Dorie. *Painting the Maya Universe: Royal Ceramics of the Classic Period.* Durham, N.C., 1994.
Tate, Carolyn E. *Yaxchilan: The Design of a Maya Ceremonial City.* Austin, Tex., 1992.

ESTHER PASZTORY

PRICE, UVEDALE (1747–1829), English landscape designer. Uvedale Price contributed to the development of the Picturesque way of seeing from 1794 until his death. He did so in theoretical terms, in *Essays on the Picturesque, as compared with the Sublime and the Beautiful; and on the Use of Studying Pictures for the Purpose of Improving Real Landscape* (1794–1801, reprinted in three volumes in 1810), *A Letter to Humphry Repton, Esq., on the Application of the Practice as well as Principles of Landscape-Painting to Landscape-Gardening* (1795), and *A Dialogue on the Distinct Characters of the Picturesque and the Beautiful* (1801). Price argues that the Picturesque is a visual property of landscape that takes its independent place alongside Edmund Burke's categories of the Sublime and the Beautiful; but as the lengthy titles of his works reveal, for Price, much more than for the other major Picturesque theorist, William Gilpin, the Picturesque was a property that could be given practical expression (that could, in short, be designed). Price's main contributions on the practical level were made at his own estate of Foxley (approximately 3,800 acres) in Herefordshire, although he also advised some friends or relations about their estates at Cassiobury Park, Bentley Priory, Beckett, Mongewell, Coleorton Hall, Whitfield, Eywood, Packington Hall, and Guy's Cliffe. Another of his achievements was his enthusiastic recommendation of William Sawrey Gilpin (nephew of William Gilpin) as a garden designer. William Sawrey Gilpin's published ideas on landscape gardening were strongly influenced by Price, and his major work, the garden at Scotney Castle, survives in a very recognizably Picturesque state. The house became the home of Christopher Hussey, whose book *The Picturesque: Studies in a Point of View* (1927) contributed to the twentieth-century resurgence of interest in the Picturesque. Other landscape gardeners, notably J. C. Loudon in Britain and Andrew Jackson Downing in the United States, avowed Price's influence. That the Picturesque idea had become so largely naturalized and widespread in thinking about gardens by the 1840s is in part due to Price: especially in his changing the emphasis away from Picturesque tourism toward active intervention in the landscape.

While the categories Burke was interested in arose from the biological imperatives of self-preservation and reproduction, Price advanced explanations for the Picturesque of a more practical and material kind: he explained the delight we get from Picturesque stimuli (which are greatly characterized by roughness and variety—expressible in the visual texture of foliage, for example) in terms of the "irritation" of the optic nerve, which we experience as a pleasure, and which Price links to "curiosity." Landscapes that displayed smoothness and sameness were therefore less pleasing than rugged and intricate ones, and Price decided that the landscape gardens of Lancelot "Capability" Brown and Repton exemplified the former. With a resonant clashing of military similes, he condemned Brown's work as a "levelling" system that produced boring landscapes of "solitary grandeur."

For Price, picturesqueness is a quality innate in certain scenes and things. His love for broken and textured surfaces led him to celebrate a range of objects, from old mills, shattered oaks, and worn-out cart horses to gypsies and beggars. In contrast to these he rejected the "arts of industry," stating that "in a moral view, the industrious mechanic is a more pleasing object, than the loitering peasant. But in a picturesque light, it is otherwise." His preference for dilapidation often had a historical sense. He explained the joy derived from ruins in national and historically specific terms. Referring to the castles and abbeys that occur frequently in the English countryside, he urged that they should be seen as the nation's pride: "we may glory that the abodes of

tyranny and superstition are in ruin." While metaphysical concerns might underlie this attitude, they are buried some levels beneath the surface. Price's vision of landscape rarely reaches a purely formal level devoid of associations. Indeed, one of his chief criteria for a pleasing countryside was a sense of "connection" between social classes. The desire of parvenu landowners to isolate themselves from poorer classes met with disapproval from Price's brand of Toryism. Interest in "connection" led him to embrace farming as able to contribute to picturesqueness, and his own forest management at Foxley became of great importance to him. In his composition of views there, foreground details (gnarled trees, bushes, banks of lanes) became as important as long vistas. For Price, studying paintings was a guide "in our search for the numberless and untouched varieties and beauties of nature."

[*See also* Landscape; *and* Picturesque.]

BIBLIOGRAPHY

Work by Price

Essays on the Picturesque. 3 vols. London, 1810. This contains the *Letter to H. Repton* and the *Dialogue*.

Other Sources

Andrews, Malcolm. *The Search for the Picturesque: Landscape Aesthetics and Tourism in Britain, 1760–1800.* Stanford, Calif., 1989.
Andrews, Malcolm. *The Picturesque: Literary Sources and Documents.* Robertsbridge, Sussex, 1994.
Daniels, Stephen, and Charles Watkins. "Picturesque Landscaping and Estate Management: Uvedale Price and Nathaniel Kent at Foxley." In *The Politics of the Picturesque: Literature, Landscape and Aesthetics since 1770,* edited by Stephen Copley and Peter Garside, pp. 13–41. Cambridge and New York, 1994.
Downing, Andrew Jackson. *A Treatise on the Theory and Practice of Landscape Gardening.* New York, 1841.
Everett, Nigel. *The Tory View of Landscape.* New Haven, 1994.
Gilpin, William Sawrey. *Practical Hints on Landscape Gardening.* London, 1832.
Hunt, John Dixon. *Gardens and the Picturesque: Studies in the History of Landscape Architecture.* Cambridge, Mass., 1992.
Hussey, Christopher. *The Picturesque: Studies in a Point of View.* London, 1927.
Lambin, Denis. "Foxley: The Prices' Estate in Herefordshire." *Journal of Garden History* 7 (1987): 244–270.
Loudon, J. C. *Observations on the Formation and Management of Useful and Ornamental Plantations: On the Theory and Practice of Landscape Gardening; and on Gaining and Embanking Land from Rivers or the Sea.* Edinburgh, 1804.
Repton, Humphrey. *Observations on the Theory and Practice of Landscape Gardening.* London, 1803.

MICHAEL CHARLESWORTH

PRIESTLEY, JOSEPH

PRIESTLEY, JOSEPH (1733–1804), English clergyman, chemist, and polymath. In particular, Joseph Priestley was known for sermons and theological writings in defense of a tolerant, Socinian (Unitarian), and rational form of Nonconformist religion. He also had a substantial influence in experimental science; for example, his experiments on the nature of gases and combustion led him to identify oxygen as a separate gas from air. He may have been even more important as a historian of the contemporary scientific movements. At the behest of Benjamin Franklin, Priestley wrote a history of electricity that helped to popularize and codify scientific practice. He followed its success with a later history of theories of vision. Finally, Priestley entered into the philosophical debates of his day, defending associationism and a Lockean view of ideas against the theories of Thomas Reid (1710–1796), James Beattie (1735–1802), James Oswald (d. 1793), and others and taking the side of toleration in ethical and political theory as well as in religious matters. He was honored by the revolutionary movement in France and eventually immigrated to the new United States, where he died in western Pennsylvania.

Priestley wrote his *Lectures on Oratory and Criticism* in 1762 as part of his duties at the Warrenton Academy, one of the dissenting schools that provided an alternative to Anglican and Calvinist education, although the *Lectures* were not published until 1777. Priestly was less concerned with originality than with providing practical advice to potential preachers. He drew heavily on the recently published work of Henry Home (Lord Kames; 1696–1782) and illustrated his points copiously and practically. But Priestley had come under the influence of David Hartley (1705–1757), whose *Observations on Man* established associationist psychology. According to Hartley, simple atomistic ideas combine by association into complex ideas, and that process of associationist combination can be controlled by education and skill. Thus, Priestley's practical and theoretical concerns came together in the areas of rhetoric and criticism and extended the Lockean program along associationist lines.

Priestley advocated a Lockean version of beauty and criticism interpreted in terms of Hartley's associationist mechanics. Priestley explicitly claimed that he wrote to extend and promote Hartley's work. But Priestley's approach was his own, and, perhaps because he saw theories of beauty in relatively pragmatic terms, he gave to them a straightforwardness that they lacked elsewhere. Hartley had a very Newtonian, mechanical interpretation of association, complete with undetectable vibrations in the nervous fluid that served to account for the similarity of ideas. Priestley abandoned that microscopic theory in favor of a more ordinary grouping of ideas that come together as the result of education and accumulated experience. In the process, he also departed from Locke, for whom complex ideas were the passive result of accumulated experience or the reflexive product of the mind's reflection on its own activity. Priestley took the activity of the mind to be combinatory and built his theory on the ways that mental activity may be influenced.

According to Priestley, taste and judgment are both the product of acquiring experience. The operative principles are all traceable to the ways that the mind is acted on by ideas and in turn is actively engaged. The pleasure and effectiveness of oratory and taste arise from mental activity. Thus, there can be no standard of taste independent of one's situation in life (Priestley, 1968, p. 134). Beauty has two sources: it may arise directly from the exercise of the mind, or it may arise from association. The former attributes pleasure, and thus beauty, not to qualities in objects but to the kind of mental activity in which the mind is engaged. The extremes of mental activity are torpor and hyperactivity. Both produce discomfort. But a moderate exercise of one's faculties is experienced as pleasurable and thus as beautiful. Once such expectations have been established either for objects or situations, association also produces pleasure even in the absence of the mental activity itself. Thus, a speech that is too short and easy or too long and confusing will not be beautiful. But one that engages the minds of an audience actively without overwhelming them will be pleasant and a just object of taste. By association, one may then also take pleasure in contemplating such a speech, in anticipating it, and in preparing to give it. A person of taste will have acquired many such associations and will be an able judge of what is good and what is not. Those who have no such extended experience are excluded as fit judges of taste.

Priestley treats the mind as a faculty with an appetite for exercise. For him, no special sense or attitude is required. Arts and sciences alike may exercise the mind. Aesthetic pleasure is no different from the pleasure of a theorem or experiment. Instead, association does the work of sorting ideas and combining them anew. Novelty and the sublime are instances of how mechanical operations of the brain plus associations combine to change simple pleasures into more complex wholes by providing new stimulation and mental activity. Priestley's aesthetic predicates are not expressive metaphors such as *force* and *elegance* but predicates like *novel* that imply degrees of mental activity. Thus, he is eventually led back into his practical discussion of tropes and their effects.

Priestley should not be made into too much of an innovator. Most of his ideas are to be found in other, more theoretically minded writers on taste and the beauty and pleasure of imagination. Had Priestley published his defense of Hartley's associationism in the realm of taste when it was written, it might have had more influence. But even then, it would have been secondary to David Hume's "Of the Standard of Taste" and Edmund Burke's *On the Sublime*. Priestley's efforts in the theory of taste are interesting primarily for their Lockean overtones and their simplification of Hartley. Priestley was a supreme optimist. He believed in the perfectibility of human beings through education and scientific discovery. He carried that optimism over to matters of taste. He was tolerant, hopeful, and rather limited in his vision. After 1762, Priestley turned his attention to what to him were more important matters in science, religion, and politics. His aesthetics remains interesting nevertheless.

[*See also* Beauty; *and* Taste.]

BIBLIOGRAPHY

Works by Priestley

A Course of Lectures on Oratory and Criticism (1777). Menston, England, 1968.
Selections from His Writings. Edited by Ira Brown. University Park, Pa., 1962.
The Scientific Works. 10 vols. Hildesheim, n.d. Facsimile editions prepared by Bernhard Fabian.

Other Sources

McEvoy, J. G., and J. E. McGuire. "God and Nature: Priestley's Way of Rational Dissent." In *Historical Studies in the Physical Sciences: Sixth Annual Volume,* edited by Russell McCormmach, pp. 325–404. Princeton, N.J., 1975.
Schwartz, A. Truman, and John G. McEvoy, eds. *Motion toward Perfection: The Achievement of Joseph Priestley.* Boston, 1990.
Townsend, Dabney. "The Aesthetics of Joseph Priestley." *Journal of Aesthetics and Art Criticism* 51.4 (Fall 1993): 561–571.

DABNEY TOWNSEND

PRIMITIVISM. A particularly succinct definition for the polymorphous and multivalent phenomenon in modern culture known as primitivism might be deliberate regression. Primitivism always involves a going back, a return to, a recovery of some early state of being that is perceived to be simpler or more vital or more innocent; for primitivism always has at its core a sense of loss. Emerging as a cultural force in the Enlightenment and dominating the arts of the twentieth century primitivism was one of the principal directions taken by modern European culture. It was not simply the emulation of so-called primitive or early visual expression; rather it was a search for origins and an attempt to escape the inexorable progress of historical time. Yet, the linkage of *deliberate* with *regression* describes the powerful contradiction within primitivism. Regress is not a simple antonym of progress, but a negative-to-positive relation as well. Regress implies a backward movement that is (unlike progressive movement) without intention.

Conjoined with the contradictions within primitivism is its self-reflexivity, always playing against the insurmountable distance between that which is perceived to be "primitive" and its contemporary emulation. Two phrases coined by Émile Zola (from his daring essay "Une nouvelle manière en peinture: Édouard Manet," 1867): "elegant awkwardness" *(raideurs élégantes)* and "sweet brutality" *(brutalité douce)* offer further critical insight into this phenomenon. *Elegant awkwardness* captures the persistent irony that runs through much of the primitivist aesthetic. Zola is describing qualities in Manet's paintings that were not only objectionable to the general public, but were consistently linked to folk and "primitive" expressions, including brutality or crudeness, awkwardness, rudeness, naïveté. He qualifies each, however, to indicate not only that the brutality and awkwardness are intentional, but that they are pleasurable

to the viewer who understands them as such, as a deliberate regression.

In this way, primitivism corresponds closely to the root definition of irony, *eirōnia,* "to dissemble, or to simulate ignorance." Self-aware and ironic are quite the opposite of what primitivism purports to be: instinctive and spontaneous, or raw, physical, even transgressive expression. Irony exists in relationships, one of the most common being when the literal meaning of the thing expressed is the exact contrary of the actual meaning intended. But the intended meaning is only discernible (or visible) to those who know better, those who have the memory or experience that provides the broader context necessary to discern irony in a situation. For example, Paul Gauguin's *Soyez Amoureuses et Vous Serez Heureuses* (1889), a carved and painted wooden relief, exhibits both brutality and awkwardness. The sophisticated discourse of the piece is contradictory to its literal patois and apparent only to the viewer aware of the relationship between academic classicism and Gauguin's deliberate inversion of it. A viewer unaware of this relationship would simply think this was a folk carving. For even the naive viewer, however, context is everything. If the relief were found in an antique or curiosity shop, it would seem indeed to be a folk carving; but if it were exhibited with contemporaneous paintings and sculptures, even an untutored eye would perceive the contradiction held in balance by this image. Someone like Zola, however, would appreciate the Gauguin relief precisely for its ironic relationship to the fine-art tradition. To the naïf, it is brutal. To Zola, it is a sweet brutality, for he understands that Gauguin's regression is deliberate, that while he appears to be falling backward, he is actually moving forward into the vanguard of modern art.

These linkages do not simply illustrate that deliberate regression often creates ironic situations. The relationship is more fundamental: primitivism is irony in a historical and cultural matrix. Put another way, the manifestations of primitivism, however diffuse and various, all draw on the conditions and relations of irony. The inverse: only in reconstructing the historical and cultural contexts of a given example of primitivism does the irony of the relationship become apparent. Yet surprisingly, little research has been done on the eighteenth-century origins and development of primitivism, despite its impact on both modern and contemporary art. Art-historical discussions of primitivism, notably Robert Goldwater's *Primitivism in Modern Art* (1938) and the 1984 Museum of Modern Art exhibition and catalog organized by William Rubin, have until recently been primarily formalist inquiries, defining primitivism as a twentieth-century phenomenon. In this line of thought, primitivism is characterized as stylistic influence from so-called primitive styles, particularly African and Oceanic, leading to the overthrow of the classical hegemony in Western art.

Recent challenges to this view of primitivism, all drawing on the seminal work of Edward W. Said (1978), point out the ethnocentricity and one-sidedness of these histories. These critiques redefine primitivism on what might be described as ideological grounds, challenging the formalist, apolitical representations. Arguing that primitivism encompasses far more than the assimilation of stylistic elements, the postmodern critiques describe this phenomenon in terms of complex cultural exchanges, issues of representation and appropriation, and link visual culture in Europe to imperialist, colonialist political culture. Neither the modernist story nor its postmodern critique attempts to reconstruct the formation of the primitivist aesthetic, although this process began almost two hundred years prior to Pablo Picasso's *Demoiselles d'Avignon* (1907). As a consequence, two of the most vexing problems concerning primitivism remain: (1) identifying what "primitive" art is or was, and (2) explaining why, since primitivism emulates the "primitive," there are so few examples of direct influence.

One of the difficulties facing any study of primitivism is the bewildering array of styles identified and emulated by modern artists as "primitive." In the work of Gauguin alone, the "primitive" encompasses Italian Gothic, Javanese Buddhist, Marquesan, pre-Columbian, Japanese, Egyptian, Tahitian, and medieval. Folk arts and popular arts were frequently included in this mix, although artists in this category, like Henri Rousseau or Grandma Moses, differ from those in Gothic Italy, Benin, or the Marquesas Islands in that they have not been trained in the image tradition of their culture, and therefore might be more accurately described as naive. Compounding the confusion concerning what is "primitive" is the proliferation of primitivisms (consider, for example, the distance between the primitivizing of Dominique Ingres, Paul Klee, and Joseph Beuys). European artists used the term *primitive* loosely and often. Even more problematic than the shifting identity of "primitive" art are the derogatory connotations of the word when it is applied to culture. To identify something as "primitive" is to place it in an early stage of development, an entirely appropriate use of the term when applied to technology: a hoe, a typewriter, a wristwatch. To describe a culture and its symbolic expression as "primitive" assumes a single path of progression and a single definition of civilization, branding that culture as infantile and undeveloped. It is in the latter half of the eighteenth century that archaic Greek and Gothic images were first described as "primitive," and throughout the nineteenth century, other art traditions were included under this rubric. Some historians have drawn a distinction between historical "primitives," the archaic or "court" styles that influenced nineteenth-century artists, and living "primitives," or tribal styles that exerted their full impact only in the twentieth century, in order to claim precedence for Picasso as the fountainhead of primitivism in modern art. The tacit claim made here, however, is that

African, Native American, and Oceanic arts are indeed "primitive," whereas nineteenth-century references to Egyptian, pre-Columbian, or Italian Gothic arts as "primitive" are simply incorrect. The historical sources show that these distinctions were not made by Picasso, Gauguin, or other primitivizing artists. Rather, the interest in "primitive" art began with styles of the historical past that were more readily assimilated and progressed ever outward to the more distant and alien.

Rejecting the idea that any actual tradition is "primitive," the postmodern critique corroborated Said's thesis by arguing that the "primitive," like the "Orient," was located in the eye of the European beholder, and reflects more on the viewer than the object of his or her gaze. This puts us far closer to understanding the relationships involved in primitivism, but this critical stance needs more historical grounding. Without considering the limitations and contingencies of actual, historical circumstances, the beholder's-eye argument implies that definitions of the "primitive" are completely individual and arbitrary, or that cultural constructions are more fantasy than reality. It does not confront the historical reality that European artists and intellectuals of the nineteenth and twentieth centuries consistently used terms like *primitive, savage,* and *art nègre* to identify a wide range of imagery, including African and Oceanic arts as well as Western traditions like Romanesque and archaic Greek. "Primitive" art cannot be defined as either objective reality or subjective eye-of-the beholder; it exists in the relationship between the two.

Another rather surprising aspect of primitivism confronting art historians is that a remarkably small percentage of modern paintings or sculptures contain documentable examples of direct visual borrowing, despite the obvious impact of "primitive" art. Picasso's *Demoiselles d'Avignon,* a pivotal image in any history of primitivism, quotes no specific "primitive" source directly. At the same time, however, this painting is consistent with other primitivizing imagery, demonstrating that there was some agreement as to what "primitive" art was assimilated. [*See* Picasso.] This problem is particularly troublesome to art historians because it poses a real challenge concerning historical process and creative exchange. In fact, one of the principal tasks undertaken by the 1984 Museum of Modern Art exhibition was to attempt to historically ground the phenomenon of primitivism by documenting these "primitive" sources. Goldwater argued that European artists were influenced more by an idea of "primitive" art than by specific visual images. Defining primitivism as an "attitude productive of art," Goldwater reasoned that "primitive art only served as a kind of stimulating focus, a catalytic which, though not in itself used or borrowed from, still helped the artists to formulate their own aims because they could attribute to it the qualities they themselves sought to attain." It is possible to find a common framework of ideas concerning "primitive" expression through a careful reading of period sources from the eighteenth and nineteenth centuries, including voyage accounts, ethnographic studies, missionary reports, and art criticism. It is important to recognize that the ideas concerning the nature of "primitive" expression were established well before "artificial curiosities" were brought back from the South Seas by Captain James Cook or the Comte de Bougainville (c.1770s), Egyptian artifacts were carted from Egypt for display in the Musée Napoléon (c.1800), or African masks and sculptures were featured in the colonial sections of world's fairs (c.1890s).

In the first decades of the eighteenth century the efforts to reconstruct the origins of culture began in earnest; the earliest such enterprise was Giambattista Vico's landmark treatise of 1725, *La sciènza nuòva*, which used as evidence biblical accounts, Homeric poetry, Roman descriptions of ancient Germans, Gauls, and Picts, as well as contemporary reports of New World peoples. The notion of "primitivity" as an infant state of development through which all cultures passed was an invention of Enlightenment universalism (and paradoxically, this universalist notion opened the door for the assimilation of particular ethnic traditions). Through these early cultural studies a diverse collection of art traditions was redefined as "primitive" art. It is not coincidental that art history emerged as a discipline concurrently with these studies of cultural development. Johann Joachim Winckelmann's *Reflections on the Imitation of Greek Works in Painting and Sculpture* (1755) and *History of Ancient Art* (1764) were extremely effective in promoting his conception of classical art as the standard against which all other artistic expressions were measured. Classicism was already established as the official "fine art" taught in the art academies (following the influential French model). Winckelmann's polemical writings elevated the classical tradition to a master narrative, transforming the elements of classical style into universal principles. In the same era that Winckelmann codified an idealist and intellectual classicism as "fine art," an odd grouping of nonclassical styles was categorized as "primitive" art through scholarly debate and ethnographic collections. If "fine art" exemplified the culmination of artistic progress, "primitive art" represented its earliest stages. Classicism functioned as both end point and as center. Not surprisingly, the characteristics of "primitive" art, also thought to be universal, were comprised of visual elements that already existed on the periphery of the classical tradition.

Period sources, including voyage accounts, art criticism, and popular literature, reveal that debates about the nature of "primitive" art were less concerned with specific styles than with these "universal" attributes that Europeans identified and later assimilated as *Urformen*. Although a great deal of nonclassical imagery was routinely identified as "primitive," "savage," "art nègre," and "carib," with little if any care or consistency for actual provenance or use, there was surprising consistency in the visual characteristics ascribed to "primitive" expression. Understanding "primitive" art as a collection of visual attributes goes some distance toward explaining the comparisons made between radically different art traditions. It corroborates Goldwater's observation that the avant-garde emulated the idea of "primitive" imagery more often than specific styles, but goes further to demonstrate that this idea of "primitive" art was far more consistent and complex than previously thought. Although eighteenth- and nineteenth-century characterizations of "primitive" imagery are ethnocentric and inaccurate as descriptions of actual styles, it does not follow that they are without meaning or system. To the contrary, these terms carried specific aesthetic meanings within the classical tradition and fit into a consistent European construction of "primitive" art, however derogatory and misapplied they were as descriptions of actual traditions. The negative connotations of the term *primitive art* have provoked efforts to find neutral substitutes, or to condemn the term altogether, but historical sources show that "primitive art" was an amalgam of visual traits, completely a European construction that had only vague associations with actual styles. The characteristics ascribed to "primitive" art point directly to the classical tradition as the principal framework through which certain images could be assimilated into European verbal and visual discourse as "primitive." These terms, *naive, grotesque, ornament, hieroglyph*, defined "primitive" art by its opposition to classical norms and determined the directions primitivism could and could not take.

These terms also link "primitive" art to visual traits associated with excessive imagination and lack of reason, setting it in contrast to the excessively rational classicism taught in the academies. Without the tools of rationality, "primitives" were immersed in an immediate, physical world, with no way to mediate this experience. They could not impose the abstract systems of illusion and narrative, idealized form and action, that were the foundations of European fine art. Imagine any figure from the Parthenon frieze next to the elaborate carvings of a Maori canoe prow. To the European observer, this "primitive" carving provided indisputable evidence that its maker lacked the rational faculties necessary to impose abstract ideals on random experience. Unlike the slab of Parthenon marble, carved so that the figures seem to have volume and the slab seems to be an illusionistic space continuous with our own, the "primitive" image manipulates line and pattern on a flat two-dimensional surface. Narrative was just as much an abstraction as illusion, isolating a significant moment, such as the Panathenaic procession, and composing it for maximum dramatic and didactic effect. The Maori's submersion of figures within the pattern and the determination of its form by an ornamental scheme seemed to echo the "primitive's" own submersion in unreflective experience. It is also important to recognize the extent to which idealized beauty was synonymous with intellectual rigor and moral purity in Winckelmann's theory and in academic pedagogy. Framed by this standard, a great deal of nonclassical imagery was categorized as caricatured, or if more horrific, as grotesque, and these visual traits carried associations with unreason, passion, and superstition, as well as profane or bestial behavior.

If the classical tradition constructed "primitive" art as its inferior opposite, what then is the relationship of modernism to the classical tradition? The story modernism wrote for itself was that the encounter with "primitive" art was an epiphany, inspiring avant-garde artists to break free from the past, not simply from academic convention but from their cultural patrimony. The assimilation of the "primitive" led to the overthrow of academic classicism.

Or so we are led to believe. This Oedipal drama, like the original, is not what it seems. The historical sources tell quite the opposite story. They show that the "primitive" existed in a dialectical relationship with the classical tradition. If the classical tradition determined the initial construction of "primitive" art, it follows that it also defined the shape of primitivism. Although modernist appropriations of "primitive" art have been heralded as a precocious appreciation of non-Western imagery, historical sources show that the avant-garde borrowed only those elements already identified through the classical tradition as "primitive." Consequently, their primitivism might better be understood as the construction of an anticlassical aesthetic, the antithesis of the classical thesis. The avant-garde did not so much break from the aesthetic norms as turn them upside down, because the center of academic classicism determined the ways in which they rebelled against it. Primitivizing artists did not reinterpret the nature of "primitive" art, nor did they describe "primitive" art with terminology that was in any way different. The critical distinction lay in their embrace of the attributes of the "primitive." Gauguin clearly associated a love of ornament with "primitive" expression, but this was turned to a positive attribute. He observed in *Avant et après* that "one does not seem to suspect in Europe that there exists, among the Maoris of New Zealand, as with the Marquesans, a very advanced decorative art." He characterized his own work as decorative, fully aware that this would offend the sensibilities of his European readers and viewers as much as his stated desire to become a savage. In short, the reasons for admiring "primitive" art were just as culture bound as the reasons for rejecting it. Gauguin, like other primitivizing artists seeking to overthrow academic classicism, nevertheless operated within its system. Another look at his panel, *Soyez amoureuses,* reveals a thorough inversion of the classical standards: with grotesque, crude, and crudely rendered figures, the male (self-portrait?) profile willfully disfigured; with hieroglyphic or emblematic segmentation of the picture plane and inclusion of lettering and seemingly symbolic imagery; and with increased orna-

mentation and pattern at the expense of illusionistic form and space; but, significantly, there is no direct quote from any specific nonclassical tradition. Picasso's *Demoiselles d'Avignon* presents a similar case in which the inversion of the classical/rational is systematic and explains far more about the meaning of this image than attempts to describe its possible affinities with Iberian, Oceanic, or African traditions. Goldwater's argument that borrowing from styles outside the Western tradition signals a breakthrough because it "frees the individual and so makes his desired return to a single underlying intensity that much easier" now reads as the height of irony.

Primitivism is the ultimate in dissembling, then, for it is only within the larger frame of a self-defined "civilized" and "rational" culture that artists can be "primitive" and "irrational." The crude and grotesque figures of Picasso or Jean Dubuffet are frightening yet pleasurable because they, like the primitivism they embody, are framed and controlled by the broader aesthetic norms of "fine art." Herein lies their "sweet brutality." While the driving force behind primitivism was a desire to return art to its vital origins, to reembody it by eschewing the rational and verbal, it is no small irony that these increasingly mute and physical images have generated an extremely sophisticated critical theory to frame them. As Goldwater observed, the more childlike the image, the more subtle and esoteric the argument necessary to distinguish it from the art of a child. Primitivism's progress was as inexorable as it was voracious, moving from those "primitives" close to the classical center to those ever more distant and other, until that which was strange was now familiar. No longer a screen for the projections of a dominant culture, the other now has a voice and a presence that look back at us, like Olympia's gaze. By the 1930s the search for the primal began turning inward, toward the exploration of the subconscious. In the last quarter of the twentieth century, deliberate regression has turned toward Earth art and the environment.

Modernism was so successful in its struggle against a dominant classical tradition that, like all victors, it rewrote its own history. Only when we resituate modernism into its own history are we able to confront its complex and conflicting relationships with non-Western arts and with the classical tradition. It is telling that Westerners have only been able to see the irony in the modernist "discovery" of "primitive" art in recent decades when the voices of those whose cultural expressions were partially assimilated began to be heard in intellectual and artistic discourse.

Examining the course taken by primitivizing artists from the late nineteenth through the twentieth century reveals a fascinating reversal of identities as well. The desire to recover cultural memories and expressions that Europeans presumed to be "universal" led to the rapid assimilation of an extremely diverse range of non-Western styles. This process resulted in a modern style that superseded classicism as the international style. The modern styles shaped by the assimilation of non-Western arts have become (through the dominance of Western culture) the global, universal definition of fine art in the twentieth century, taught in academies around the world and displacing traditional expressions. But whose universal style is it? As we have seen, these "universal" attributes constructed a kind of transcultural style that first obliterated the identity of its influences, stripped away their cultural moorings, and then incorporated them into a new lexicon as "primitive," rude, grotesque, ornamental. In the late twentieth century, the quest for identity has shifted: the concern now is to find ways for postcolonial peoples to recover or retain their identities. In Europe, artists such as Anselm Kiefer have crafted a progressive strategy for the legitimate primitivist desire to reject the dehumanizing elements of modern culture. Kiefer's images reach back into the mythic traditions of Germany, Egypt, and Judaism, but they do so in an attempt to recover historical memory, and in order to confront modern Western history rather than to escape it.

[*See also* Cubism; Modernism, *overview article;* Orientalism; Postcolonialism; *and* Romanticism.]

BIBLIOGRAPHY

Antliff, Mark, and Patricia Leighten. "Primitivism." In *Critical Terms for Art History,* edited by Robert S. Nelson and Richard Shiff, pp. 170–184. Chicago, 1996.

Bhabha, Homi. "Of Mimicry and Man: The Ambivalence of Colonial Discourse." *October* 28 (Spring 1984): 125–133.

Boas, George, and Arthur O. Lovejoy. *Primitivism and Related Ideas in Antiquity.* A Documentary History of Primitivism and Related Ideas, vol. 1. Baltimore, 1935.

Clifford, James. *The Predicament of Culture: Twentieth-Century Ethnography, Literature, and Art.* Cambridge, Mass., 1988.

Connelly, Frances. *The Sleep of Reason: Primitivism in Modern European Art and Aesthetics, 1725–1907.* University Park, Pa., 1995.

Foster, Hal. *Recodings: Art, Spectacle, Cultural Politics.* Port Townsend, Wash., 1985.

Goldwater, Robert. *Primitivism in Modern Art* (1938). Enl. ed. Cambridge, Mass., 1986.

Harbison, Robert. *Deliberate Regression.* New York, 1980.

Hiller, Susan, ed. *The Myth of Primitivism: Perspectives on Art.* London and New York, 1991.

Laude, Jean. *La peinture française, 1905–1914, et l'art nègre.* Paris, 1968.

Leighten, Patricia. "The White Peril and l'Art Nègre: Picasso, Primitivism, and Anticolonialism." *Art Bulletin* 72 (December 1990): 609–630.

Previtali, Giovanni. *La fortuna dei primitivi dal Vasari ai neoclassici.* Turin, 1964.

Rhodes, Colin. *Primitivism and Modern Art.* London and New York, 1994.

Rosenblum, Robert. *Transformations in Late Eighteenth-Century Art.* Princeton, N.J., 1967.

Rubin, William, ed. *Primitivism in 20th Century Art: Affinity of the Tribal and the Modern.* 2 vols. New York, 1984. Exhibition catalog, Museum of Modern Art.

Said, Edward W. *Orientalism.* New York, 1978.

Todorov, Tzvetan. *The Conquest of America: The Question of the Other.* Translated by Richard Howard. New York, 1984.

Torgovnick, Marianna. *Gone Primitive: Savage Intellects, Modern Lives.* Chicago, 1990.

FRANCES S. CONNELLY

PSYCHICAL DISTANCE. *See* Bullough.

PSYCHOANALYTIC THEORIES OF ART. *See* Bachelard; Freud; Irigaray; Klein; Lacan; Marcuse; *and* Winnicott.

PSYCHOLOGY OF ART.

All aspects of the human mind have applications to the arts. These aspects can be described under the three main headings of motivation, cognition, and emotion.

Motivation refers to the mind's strivings, the dynamic straining toward certain goals. The most general problem facing the psychologist of art in regard to motivation concerns the question of why art exists. What are the impulses that make human beings create performances and works of art, and what makes people all over the world so eager to receive art? The oldest answer to these questions has asserted that art exists universally because it gives pleasure. The hedonistic approach to motivation derives in Western culture from the Cyrenaic school of Greek philosophy and has been favored as an easy answer through the ages to the present. Psychologists have used it in experimental aesthetics when they confronted their subjects with sets of objects, such as shapes and colors, and asked, "Which one do you like best?" The answers to such questions, however, served at most to ascertain preferences, for instance, in market research; they did not discover the causes of motivational pleasure, and only those causes tell us why art exists.

The most general answer to this question relates the aesthetic impulse to a more general human striving. It is the desire to unfold all potential abilities of mind and body to the fullest extent. The ability to discover, to enjoy, to think, to construct makes for the strong wish to do so. In their more specific realm, artists feel impelled to explore the entire range of human experiences and to clarify their nature by describing and representing them. In particular, the puzzles, the mysteries, and the imperfections of reality challenge not only the philosopher, the scientist, the ruler, and the reformer, but equally the artist, who endeavors to wrestle with the tasks of life in his or her own way. To be sure, to undertake and carry out such tasks generates pleasure, but pleasure is merely the symptom of the motives bringing it about.

One of the most attractive motives of artistic creation is that of conjuring up an ideal state of being. To give shape to perfection, artists use their imagination with all degrees of realism, depending on how well they adapt human wishes to the actual conditions of existence. The fancies of wish fulfillment operate at their least responsible level in cheap literature depicting total fulfillment at the price of neglecting the actual obstacles to be faced in the world. Similar purposes are met by the kitsch images of painting or sculpture, offering embodiments of perfection and harmony. Their lack of realism, however, makes more thoughtful persons ridicule and reject them. Emotional indulgence in music reduces artistic quality by reducing music's more arduous concerns with building structures, dealing with counterforces, and so on that make better music portray the more serious and mature mind facing the tasks of life.

Such differences in artistic value modify the prime products of artistic motivation, which embody beauty and ideals. When traditional theory of aesthetics limits the definition of beauty to perfection and harmony, it really reduces itself to the inferior category of kitsch. Ideals defined in a similarly limited fashion produce—for example, in the literary depictions of utopias—pictures of tedious societies where nobody would care to live. Such one-sided definitions of the most desirable conditions and products imply also an inferior conception of human motivation.

Psychologists have confirmed the harmful consequences of such one-sided motivation. The "Bovary effect" of cheap novels or movies deflects their users from effectively dealing with the problems and offerings of life and from realistically accepting responsibility. The opposite one-sidedness of artistic motivation leads to a similar reduction of quality by limiting itself to the negative aspects of human existence. It distinguishes the depiction of human depravity and inferiority, say, in the etchings of a William Hogarth from the satires of an Honoré Daumier, whose figures display their frailties and distortions to make viewers laugh without depriving them of a melancholy compassion for the human condition.

In the field of social psychology, the position and function of art and artists in society make for a great variety of motivational relations. In early societies, performers and art makers are so closely integrated in the community that their motivational objectives coincide with those of the group. At first, there may be no distinction between those who supply the arts and those who consume them. Performances of dances and other ceremonies are shared by all for a common purpose, and craft work is contributed by everybody. Even when the arts become specialities reserved for certain individuals, there is in early societies no noticeable distinction between the objectives of the artists and those of the community. Only in ages of individualism such as that of the Renaissance in the Western world do artists cease to be employed artisans like bricklayers or shoemakers and develop their own aesthetic values, which must try to cope with those of monarchal and ecclesiastical princes using their services. By the time of Michelangelo, motivational conflicts between providers and customers in the arts re-

flect simply the interplay of antagonistic forces in a modern economy. In the nineteenth century, the artist, detached from the give-and-take of well-functioning social relations, is typified by isolated loners pursuing their own standard and taste, which more often than not are not shared by the public.

In particular, the narrative media of literature or painting mirror the social conditions of the time. They vary from period to period and depict the differences between totalitarian regimes and liberal democracies. Hence the psychological and sociological content analyses of the narrative media, whose ideologies are extracted and theoretically formulated. A world of difference emerges between, say, Voltaire's *Candide* of 1750 and Bertolt Brecht's biting satire of modern society in his *Three Penny Opera* of 1934.

When the discussion moves from motivation to cognition, psychologists ask more generally what the arts contribute to the knowledge and understanding of the world facing the mind. Sensory perception is our only access to that world, and among the senses vision, hearing, and the sensations of touch and kinesthesia are the principal contributors. Only one of the sense modalities, namely, vision, is truly an exteroceptive distance sense in that it provides images of the outer world; and only two are truly proprioceptive: kinesthesia and touch provide information by sensations of the perceiver's body. The others, such as hearing or smell, are intermediate in that they generate experiences not clearly separating the outer from the inner world. These basic differences of the sensory modalities influence their applications to the arts. They determine the ways in which the various media select and represent aspects of reality.

While the sense of vision provides images of the physical world, it is limited to doing so by projections of three-dimensional space on a two-dimensional receptor surface in the eyes. This means that at any moment of time the visual image records the way the world is seen from a particular vantage point; but because the viewer synthesizes a multitude of these momentary perceptions, the resulting image of the world can greatly compensate for the one-sidedness of optical projections. This makes for a basic difference between media such as painting, which must commit themselves to single projections or their combinations, and media that move in time, such as the film. Sculpture and architecture dwell in physical space and allow viewers freely to move around the art objects they are looking at.

Nevertheless, although vision is limited optically to projection, the visual images of painting hardly ever proclaim their worldview as one determined by the individual observer. Object-bound rather than subjective, pictorial images of the three-dimensional world present the world as a hierarchy of powers differing in weight and distinguishing the dominance of what is close and large from what is distant and small. This is particularly obvious in styles ignoring central perspective, such as Western pre-Renaissance paintings or those of classical China. But even central perspective is mostly perceived as offering particular ways of how the world *is*, rather than how it appears to someone's momentary vision.

When a visual medium uses the time dimension, as do the dance or film, it is able to show the interaction of motion and stillness. The world of becoming and changing is presented in counterpoint with that of being, and depending on the mental attitude of the artist, the more fundamental state of the world appears to be either that of timeless persistence or that of restless flux. Visual representation, however, profits not only from naturalistic completeness but equally from a partial selection of perceptual aspects. Architecture, painting, and sculpture use timelessness as an indispensable virtue.

Similarly, the omission of color makes for monochromatic images in which all surface values are fitted to a unitary gray scale. This enhances the compositional unity and simplicity of the image and lets the powerful contrast of light and darkness rule undisturbed. The use of color, while increasing the wealth of complexity and allowing for more naturalistic representation, greatly complicates the artist's task. It increases the number of parameters to be dealt with, dominant among them being the compositional primaries of red, blue, and yellow. Psychologists have studied the number and selection of colors referred to in the languages of various cultures.

Music, like nonrepresentational painting, combines abstractness with strong concreteness. It is abstract by disregarding the world of objects, which is so prominent in representational painting; but it strikes the ears with the unmatched immediacy of auditory expression. It limits itself to describing reality as action, motion, and change, and it thereby serves admirably to accompany and interpret visual events, such as social ceremonies. In the opera, the happenings on the stage and the dynamics of the music complement each other. Film music supplies the action on the screen with all levels of emotion, from the serenity of idylls to the highest pitch of excitement. Experiments have demonstrated how the character of what the eyes see in a film can be changed when a different music accompanies it.

Music takes place essentially in the two dimensions of progression in time and the simultaneity of what may be called musical space. Pure percussion on a single drum limits the performance to the differences of rhythm, from the regular beat to its endless deviations of speed or syncopations. To such rhythmical play, monophonic music adds the variations of high and low tones, of rising and falling in a single melodic line. The mere progression of monophony is enriched, under certain cultural conditions, by polyphony. Here a basic psychological difference is observed between antagonistic actions, as in the voices of counterpoint, and the rich unity of consonant or dissonant chords.

In spite of the differences between the various musical systems, most of them, and perhaps all, rely on some of the basic intervals, such as the octave, the fifth, and the fourth. Their universality has been derived in several theories from physical and physiological factors, reflected in aural experience. The diatonic system of traditional Western music relies on the interplay between the attractive powers of the basic intervals, especially those serving as the tonic, and the gravitational weight governing high and low pitch. The absence of bases of reference in modern atonal or serial music has deprived the system of its clearly centered stability and replaced it with the mutual relations of the individual tones—a symbolical reflection of a social situation devoid of a dominant central power.

Literature, the aesthetic medium of language, differs from the other media by not basing its references to the outer world on the direct perception of either sight or sound. Language is a referential medium, meaning that it has to rely strongly on memory images. Here it needs to be said that, in a much more general sense, memory images are the indirect medium of the mind. Even in the absence of language, memory images are an indispensable component of cognitive behavior. They enable animals or persons to connect past experiences with present ones, to compare and distinguish them. What is more, they also strengthen perceptual concepts, which generalize perceptual experience. All perception is tied to generalization. For example, the knowledge of trees begins with "treeness" in general and is specified only gradually to, say, oaks. From there, perception may be individualized to one's recognizing the oak in one's garden, different from all others.

Perceptual concepts make verbal language possible because language consists of tokens for concepts. Language strengthens the system of concepts most powerfully by naming concepts at all levels of abstraction, from the individual to the general. Because language consists explicitly of concepts, it refers to any percept by calling it by its name: "I am seeing an oak!"

Hence the unique range of the verbal medium. Not only can it rely on the mental images of all sensory modalities in any combination, talking of smell and sound and vision in the same sentence, it also combines all levels of abstraction. When Emily Dickinson writes, "past the houses, past the headlands, into deep eternity," she connects the most concrete with the most abstract concepts, thereby raising her poem to a philosophical level of thought without abandoning concrete presence. This unique virtue of the verbal medium is evident in metaphors, which relate experiences from different realms and thereby raise the comparison to a higher level of abstractness.

Literature, however, is limited like the other media to a selection from the experiential aspects of reality. It is limited to sequences in time, which strengthen its emphasis on action, but make it difficult to describe events occurring simultaneously or objects dwelling in the same space. It must resort to translating synchrony into diachrony.

Even so, psychologists see literature as the most comprehensive of all aesthetic media. It compensates for its remoteness from direct perceptual experience by its unrivaled range of perceptual references at all levels of abstraction. It unites experience and thought in a uniquely human fashion.

Finally, a reference is needed to the third aspect of the human mind, namely, emotion. Emotion is the level of tension or excitement accompanying all acts of motivation and cognition. All motivational strivings for a goal or the escaping from a threat are tinged by the nervous system with some degree of excitement. Similarly, any cognitive recognition or discovery makes for an arousal of tension, which may be slight or powerful. This is as true for the making of art and responses to art as it is for any other human behavior. It adds a particular quality of warmth and involvement to what, by comparison, may be described as the mere functions of existence—the functions of striving toward goals as well as identifying and understanding the world. Emotion is no privilege of the arts, but they would feel dead without it.

[*See also* Arnheim; Color, *article on* Color Science; Creativity; Freud; Gombrich; Imagery; Imagination; Klein; Lacan; Perception, *article on* Psychology of Perception; Perspective; Synaesthesia; *and* Winnicott.]

BIBLIOGRAPHY

Arnheim, Rudolf. *Art and Visual Perception* (1954). New exp. rev. ed. Berkeley, 1974.

Arnheim, Rudolf. *Visual Thinking.* Berkeley, 1969.

Berlin, Brent, and Paul Kay. *Basic Color Terms: Their Universality and Evolution.* Berkeley, 1969.

Berlyne, D. E. *Aesthetics and Psychobiology.* New York, 1971.

De la Motte-Haber, Helga. *Handbuch der Musikpsychologie.* Laaber, 1985.

Freud, Sigmund. *Creativity and the Unconscious.* New York, 1958.

Kobbert, Max J. *Kunstpsychologie.* Darmstadt, 1986.

Kreitler, Hans, and Shulamith Kreitler. *Psychology of the Arts.* Durham, N.C., 1972.

Langfeld, Herbert Sidney. *The Aesthetic Attitude* (1920). Port Washington, N.Y., 1967.

Mitchell, W. J. T. *Iconology: Image, Text, Ideology.* Chicago, 1986.

RUDOLF ARNHEIM

Q-R

QUALITIES, AESTHETIC. Whether a painting has a black square in the middle, or a particular poem is written in French or Italian, is seldom the subject of controversy. If any two people were to disagree over this, the issue could be settled quickly by persons without aesthetic taste; the contested statements are intersubjectively testable by fairly uncontroversial methods. But whether a painting or poem is graceful, unified, melancholic, harmonious, clumsy, or disorganized is something that is often debated. When critics and others disagree over this, it would seem that the issue can only be settled by people with some aesthetic taste; and it is far from obvious that the contested statements are testable by uncontroversial methods. The notions of "aesthetic taste" and "ability to make aesthetic discriminations" are difficult to apply in an uncontroversial way, however; alleged counterexamples may be defined away by arguing that the critic has no aesthetic taste or no ability to make aesthetic discriminations. They are also notoriously difficult to analyze in a coherent and convincing way, and without ending up in a vicious circle or an infinite regress. They are probably as obscure as the notion of an aesthetic quality. Thus, the question arises as to whether there are any alternative but roughly equivalent ways of demarcating and characterizing aesthetic qualities or concepts.

Many theoretical problems are raised by such qualities and the attribution of them to artworks and other objects. The starting point of the discussion can be the terms used to characterize the aesthetic qualities of artworks and other objects. The focus can then be on these terms, or on certain uses of them, or on the qualities they refer to, or on the act of attributing these qualities to objects and actions of different kinds. If focus is on the terms, the methods used are often semantic analyses of how these terms are used by certain critics in a specified context, possibly combined with philosophical analysis and criticism of such uses. If, however, focus is on the qualities, a phenomenological approach suggests itself.

The problems include the relation of aesthetic qualities to qualities and properties of other kinds, the further characterization and definition of these qualities, what methods, if any, could be used to check such attributions, the relativity or objectivity of aesthetic attributions, and the truth claims of aesthetic judgments.

Historical Background. How are aesthetic qualities related to qualities and properties of other kinds? The history of the problems raised by aesthetic qualities can be traced back to the ancient distinction between primary and secondary qualities discussed by Democritus (c.469–370 BCE), a distinction also commented on by Galileo Galilei (1564–1642), René Descartes (1596–1650), and Robert Boyle (1627–1691). But the classical starting point of the contemporary discussion of the distinction between primary qualities (such as solidity and extension) and secondary qualities (such as color and taste) is to be found in John Locke's *Essay concerning Human Understanding* (1690). Locke states the distinction in several ways, and argues for it in several different ways. These passages have been the subject of widely different interpretations and also criticized. The precise way to state the distinction between primary and secondary qualities is still controversial, though there is growing agreement that the distinction is basically sound.

The contemporary discussion of the nature of aesthetic qualities started with Frank Sibley's seminal essay "Aesthetic Concepts" (1959), which gave rise to a lively and intensive exchange of ideas that lasted for decades. It concerned semantic and phenomenological as well as ontological and epistemological issues. For example, is it true, as Peter Kivy (1968) has suggested, that "X is graceful" is synonymous with "Look how graceful X is!"? If so, in what contexts? This semantic problem is clearly different from the ontological question of whether qualities such as "graceful" are part of the fabric of the world, as well as from the epistemic problem of what can be known about such qualities. These problems are not identical with the phenomenological question of how such qualities are experienced, and if, for instance, they are experienced as qualities of objects or as responses in us to objects.

The Characterization of Aesthetic Qualities. Because "aesthetic taste" is probably just as obscure as "aesthetic quality," it is hardly astonishing that attempts have been made to identify a number of conditions, each of which is necessary and jointly sufficient, for qualities to be aesthetic.

The following characteristics, among others, have been proposed as elements of a three-part conjunction:

1. that aesthetic qualities are perceived or perceivable;
2. that aesthetic qualities are value-relevant, that is, relevant as reasons for positive and negative judgments about the aesthetic (but not artistic) value of objects; and

3. that aesthetic qualities are tertiary, supervenient, or emergent, that is, dependent on primary and secondary qualities.

The precise interpretation of these conditions has been much discussed. The second requirement presupposes an analysis of the notion of aesthetic value, which is just as problematic as the notion of aesthetic quality. Also, the analysis of the dependence requirement—(3) above—has been debated in the literature.

Do "This movie is obscene" or "That picture is sacrilegious" attribute or ascribe aesthetic qualities to the works referred to? If not, why not? It seems clear that here the notion of "aesthetic value" plays a crucial role in arguments over answers to these questions. Given a narrow, formalistic conception of artistic value, the answer to the first question will be no. But given a wider notion of aesthetic value, where no sharp distinction between aesthetic and ethical concerns is maintained, the answer will be different. The basic idea underlying the above characterization is that aesthetic qualities (e.g., "is unified") resemble secondary qualities (e.g., "is red") in that both are phenomenal, that is, perceivable and perceived. But they differ from secondary qualities in that they are value-relevant and tertiary.

To say that a particular painting has a blue spot in the upper right corner is not to say or suggest anything about the value of the painting; such a statement is clearly not relevant as grounds for aesthetic praise or blame of that painting. Moreover, one can easily imagine two objects x and y that differ qualitatively only in that one of them is red, the other not—for example, a red and a black billiard ball. But it is not possible for two paintings or sculptures x and y to differ *only* in that one of them is unified, but the other is not. If x is unified but y is not, there must also be other differences between these two works of art, concerning, for example, how the parts are related to the whole or the way colors are spread on the canvas.

The Variety of Aesthetic Qualities. Examples of aesthetic qualities include garishness, tenseness, grace, harmony, gaiety, nervousness, sadness, excitement, somberness, sereneness, solemnity, joy, cheerfulness, boldness, vitality, restraint, sublimity, monumentality, coherence, picturesqueness, mysteriousness, and beauty.

An important obstacle to progress in the discussion of the nature of aesthetic qualities has been the implicit or explicit assumption that these qualities form a homogeneous class. This assumption needs to be examined critically. In other words, it is important to recognize that within the class of qualities thus demarcated, there is a variety of aesthetic qualities that cannot be analyzed in quite the same way. Thus, attempts have been made to distinguish between aesthetic qualities along a number of dimensions: (complexity) simple, complex; (location) internal, external; (value) descriptive, evaluative; (sense) literal, metaphoric. Thus, "sad-

ness" is a simple quality, but "unity" is a complex one in that it presupposes that the parts of the work are related to the whole in a particular way. The quality "melancholy" is internal in that it is experienced as a quality in the work, whereas "excitement" is different. Some aesthetic qualities are more obviously tied to value judgments than are others. For example, to say that a work is disorganized or clumsy is to give an argument for a negative value judgment. (But it does not prove that the work is bad: the work can be good, though it is disorganized or clumsy.) To say that a work is "powerful," that a tune is "cheerful," or that a line is "nervous" is clearly to use these terms in a metaphoric way; living as well as dead metaphors are among the terms used in aesthetic characterizations.

Moreover, some aesthetic qualities ("unity," "balance") behave like gestalt qualities in that the parts of the work are related to each other in such a way that the work would look unified (or balanced, respectively) to anyone contemplating the work under standard conditions and noticing the relation between these parts. Other aesthetic qualities ("joyfulness," "sadness," "melancholy") are perceived emotional qualities in objects, and still others (such as being intriguing, moving, or exciting) are tied to the reactions or responses of the beholders in a way that the previous ones are not. To put some of these differences in a nutshell: a work of art cannot be moving if nobody is moved by it. But a work can be unified or harmonious even if nobody is unified or rendered harmonious by it.

The Relativity of Aesthetic Qualities. Are aesthetic qualities in the objects themselves or in the eye of the beholder? In the latter case, aesthetic attributions could be relative to many things. The basic idea is then simply that an object does not have a particular aesthetic quality A per se, but only relative to a certain tradition, upbringing, culture, frame of reference, and so forth.

In view of the obvious differences between aesthetic characterizations in different cultures, and disagreements between critics in the same culture, relativism would seem to be a tempting and rational choice. But it could also be argued that one needs to distinguish not only between different kinds of relativism (e.g., perceptual, descriptive, normative) but also between whether a particular object x has the (aesthetic or nonaesthetic) quality A and whether, as a matter of fact, certain people discern or discover that x has A.

If it is true that certain people do *not* discern this quality, this may be the result of their upbringing, lack of training, cultural frame of reference, and so forth; but the fact that they do not notice that x has A does not prove that x does not have the quality A. On the contrary, the statement that a particular person does not notice that x has A is clearly compatible with the statement that x has A.

The Existence of Qualities in General. The statement that there are qualities of a certain kind can be interpreted in several ways. To say that there are qualities of a certain sort—let us call them Q's—can be to say or imply that a statement such as "x is Q" is meaningful, can have truth-value, or that one can distinguish between objects exemplifying or having Q and those that do not, or that there are reliable methods by means of which such discriminations can, on the whole, be made.

More important than a general discussion about conditions for the existence of qualities is probably whether there are rational methods, or generally accepted methods, in disciplines such as art history or musicology, by means of which it is possible for art historians and critics to settle conflicting claims concerning aesthetic attributions in particular cases. Such methods are based on some of the arguments below.

A number of arguments have been raised for and against the existence and objectivity of aesthetic qualities. The most important arguments against the existence and objectivity of aesthetic qualities are probably various versions of the arguments of variation and simplicity. According to the former, aesthetic attributions vary with individuals, time, upbringing, and culture. Because there is no unprejudiced way of deciding which of two incompatible qualities attributed to an object is indeed a quality of that object, aesthetic qualities are not qualities of objects. They are, rather, in the eye of the beholder. According to the latter argument, there is no need to introduce aesthetic qualities when one wants to describe, interpret, and explain works of art and one's responses to them; to assume the existence of aesthetic qualities introduces unnecessary complications and violates Occam's razor (that is, the commitment not to introduce unnecessary entities).

The most important arguments for the existence and objectivity of aesthetic qualities are probably the causal, the phenomenological, and public language arguments. According to the core of the causal argument, aesthetic qualities are dependent qualities: if a work of art x has the aesthetic quality A, then it has A because of the presence of the primary or secondary qualities B in x. If A is caused by B, then: if B exists, A also exists. According to the phenomenological argument, there is no fundamental difference between our experiences of a line as red and as graceful; hence, it would be arbitrary to say that in one case but not in the other we are dealing with a quality of an object. Finally, according to the public language argument, critical disagreement presupposes that the contested terms are understood by the disagreeing critics; the terms are mutually understood only if the critics agree on the general conditions of application of these terms—and these conditions define in principle the truth conditions (or the correctness conditions) of aesthetic attributions.

[*See also* Attitude, *article on* Aesthetic Attitude; Beauty; *and* Realism.]

BIBLIOGRAPHY

Beardsley, Monroe C. "What Is an Aesthetic Quality?" *Theoria* 39. 1–3 (1973): 50–70.

Beardsley, Monroe C. "The Descriptivist Account of Aesthetic Attributions." *Revue Internationale de Philosophie* 109.3 (1974): 336–352.

Halldén, Sören. *Emotive propositions.* Stockholm, 1954.

Hermerén, Göran. *The Nature of Aesthetic Qualities.* Lund, 1988.

Hermerén, Göran. "Emotive Properties: The Role of Abstraction, Introspection and Projection." *Theoria* 51 (1993): 80–112.

Kivy, Peter. "Aesthetic Appraisals and Aesthetic Qualities." *Journal of Philosophy* 65.4 (22 February 1968): 85–93.

Kivy, Peter. *Speaking of Art.* The Hague, 1973.

Levinson, Jerrold. "Aesthetic Supervenience." *Southern Journal of Philosophy* suppl. vol. 22 (1983): 93–110.

Margolis, Joseph. *Pragmatism without Foundations: Reconciling Realism and Relativism.* Oxford and New York, 1986.

Mitias, Michael H., ed. *Aesthetic Quality and Aesthetic Experience.* Amsterdam, 1988.

Sibley, Frank. "Objectivity and Aesthetics." *Proceedings of the Aristotelian Society* suppl. vol. 42 (1968): 31–54.

Sibley, Frank. "Aesthetic Concepts." *Philosophical Review* 68.4 (October 1959): 421–450. Reprinted in *Philosophy Looks at the Arts,* edited by Joseph Margolis, 3d ed. (Philadelphia, 1987).

Tormey, Alan. *The Concept of Expression: A Study in Philosophical Psychology and Aesthetics.* Princeton, N.J., 1971.

GÖRAN HERMERÉN

QUINCY, ANTOINE CHRYSOSTOME QUATREMÈRE DE. *See* Originality.

QUINTILIAN, MARCUS FABIUS QUINTILIANUS. *See* Rhetoric; Roman Aesthetics; Sublime, *article on* The Sublime from Longinus to Montesquieu; *and* Text.

RACE AND AESTHETICS. *See* Black Aesthetic; Harlem Renaissance; *and* Locke.

RAPHAEL, MAX (1889–1952), German aesthetician.

Max Raphael was born in Schönlanke (West Prussia) and studied art history, philosophy, and political economy at the universities of Berlin and Munich with Heinrich Wölfflin, Georg Simmel, and Gustav von Schmoller. While in Munich he became acquainted with the artistic founders of Expressionism: Paul Klee, Franz Marc, August Macke, and Max Pechstein, who had founded the groups Der Blaue Reiter and Die Brücke. In the course of his encounter with these Expressionists, Raphael developed an interest in French painting. He moved to Paris to study philosophy, where he attended the lectures of Henri Bergson, studied the work of Henri Matisse, and met the young Pablo Picasso. Out of these experiences came his first book, *Von Monet zu Picasso,* based on lectures he gave on Picasso in Munich in 1913.

Raphael moved to Switzerland around the end of 1913, where he studied sociology with the idea of applying sociological theory to art history. There he remained until the outbreak of World War I, in which he served a brief period in the German army. After the war, he returned to Switzerland, where he again became deeply immersed in the world of art. Here he wrote *Idee und Gestalt* in 1919, published in Munich in 1921. More books followed: *Der dorische Tempel* (1930), *Proudhon, Marx, Picasso* (1933), *Zur Erkenntnistheorie der konkreten Dialektik* (1934).

In 1941, during the Nazi occupation of France, he was temporarily detained in the concentration camps at Gurs and Les Milles. After many difficulties, he was able to leave France and emigrate, via Lisbon, to the United States. After he arrived in New York, he studied and wrote on neolithic Egyptian paintings and prehistorical cave art. These studies resulted in the publication of *Prehistoric Cave Paintings* (1945) and *Prehistoric Pottery and Civilization in Egypt* (1947). After the posthumous publication of *The Demands of Art* (1969), there followed the publication in German editions of his unpublished manuscripts in the 1980s and 1990s (see bibliography). Raphael continued to write while in the United States until his death.

Raphael's Method. It was in 1921 that Raphael began to develop his distinctive method. This method he characterized as the taking up of an objective attitude. The "objective attitude," which is preliminary to a more complete analysis, involves taking the artwork as a singular datum and analyzing its constituent elements. This was not meant as a formalist deviation from Marxist social-historical analysis, but a new way, a more dialectical way, toward its fulfillment. It takes "pure" aesthetic inquiry to be prior to the historical sociology of art. Raphael insists that an adequate formal analysis of a work of art will reveal not only the laws of construction of the work itself, but also the causal connections between aesthetic form and the social conditions that give rise to it. This method can be called "inside-out" dialectics. But Raphael's point is that if one deduces the meaning and compositional components of a work of art from social theory, then one has abandoned dialectics for a mechanical method of positivistic sociological description; one has lost the inner dynamic of the work.

Raphael's method was highly original in that he believed that one must know the nature of the object itself before its history and content can be reconstructed and written. His analysis applies the Marxist dialectic to the sociology of art, thus uniting sociology, political economy, art history, and philosophical aesthetics.

In his book *Prehistoric Cave Paintings,* unappreciated by most Marxist aestheticians of the period, Raphael's grasp of the internal compositional elements and total structure of Paleolithic cave drawings allowed him to establish a direct correlation between the mode of production in Paleolithic communities and their artistic production. And as he was to write later, his method

involves the comparative study of works of art from all epochs in the history of all peoples. From this comparative study are ab-

stracted the most general elements, relationships, totalities, and domains of concretization. In this manner, the ideal work of art in its most typical aspects is constituted. . . . Moreover, the laws for the construction of form in the work of art, as well as the laws of connection among various kinds of art, are at the same time the laws of relation and association of production.

Even though the process of mediation between art and material society in modern times is far more complex than in Paleolithic communities, an understanding of this relationship is still possible. Establishing such an understanding was to become Raphael's life's work.

Major Works. *The Demands of Art*, Raphael's most important book, consists of five highly concentrated analyses of individual works of art. These studies are supplemented by an introductory chapter titled "The Struggle to Understand Art" and an extract from Raphael's essay on method, "Toward an Empirical Theory of Art." In these analyses, Raphael seems primarily concerned with understanding the work of art only as a work of art, as a specific aesthetic datum, as autonomous—not as a reflection, not as mediating the relations of production. But these are not purely formal studies. Raphael himself warns in this text against excluding those social and historical conditions that inform the painting. A purely aesthetic and structural analysis leads to empty formalism. On close analysis, however, we can discover Raphael's penetrating dialectical technique at its best; for the historical and social conditions are perceptible in each work, even though contextual detail is absent—the social and the historical impregnate each painting. This is especially true of the chapter on *Guernica*, the sociological details of which were already set out earlier in *Proudhon, Marx, Picasso*. In this work, Raphael begins with an attack on the utopian tendencies of some currents of modernism, specifically the Abstractionist and Surrealist movements. By means of this critique, he is able to show how art functions to mediate contradictions in the forces and relations of production, through an explication of the internal dialectical interaction of form and content in actual works of art.

In demonstrating the manner in which the laws of dialectical materialism operate in art history, Raphael opposes the view attributed to "crude Marxist sociology" that art is a direct reflection of the economic basis of society and that art develops in correspondence with stages of economic development. Here, of course, he can refer to Karl Marx's own, and presumably very similar position, in the introduction to the *Contribution to the Critique of Political Economy:* "certain periods of the highest development of art stand in no direct connection with the general development of society."

Both in this work and in *Arbeiter, Kunst, und Kunstler* (1975), Raphael examines the role of myth in the artistic mediation of material anxiety. With regard to the mediating function of myth, he writes that Marx expressed a view that is usually associated with that form of bourgeois aesthetics found in the art of Richard Wagner, Arnold Böcklin, and Paul Gauguin. The differences are as follows:

1. For Marx, only an indigenous mythology was capable of constructively mediating art, that is, a mythology with the same origins, the same people, the same cultural outlook, and the same economic organization of society that produced the work of art.

2. For Marx, mythology was a cultural product *(Volksprodukt)*. For the (Romantic) artist and aesthetician of the nineteenth century, its attraction lay directly in the personal (and objective) transformation of its *(völkisch)* content.

3. The bourgeois and reactionary artist necessarily sought in mythology—because he wanted to escape the real conditions of his own time and place—an idealistic, metaphysical, symbolic mode with which to conceal the fragmentation and truncated nature of his own composition and construction.

4. For Marx, mythology was a historically conditioned connection or link that would disappear with the ascendancy of natural understanding, so that a demythologized art would be possible in the nineteenth and twentieth centuries.

Myth, he concludes, is a crucial element in the mediation of material society through art. By grasping the role of myth, one is able to specify the lack of proportion between the economic and ideological developments of a society and to account for the attribution of normative status to certain arts whose economic foundations have long since disappeared. Raphael is now in a position to show that only certain ages have been capable of producing works of art that are organically and "naturally" coordinated to prevailing developments in the forces and relations of production. He assumes that communism will represent a stage in which such an integration becomes possible.

In these explications of mediation and organic unity, Raphael believed that he had discovered the key to understanding artistic efflorescence and how the normative values expressed in art are related to material society. Thus, he began to apply his assumptions and methodology to specific problems of modern art. The best statement of his methodology is to be found in "Toward an Empirical Theory of Art," which was published as an appendix to *The Demands of Art*. By *empirical*, Raphael means an approach that makes art an object of scientific cognition. Such a theory would involve empirical analyses of works of art from all periods and all nations. Subjective experiences of works should be eliminated whenever possible and replaced with mathematical techniques. For example, Raphael writes in his studies of Giotto di Bondone:

Unlike the *Lamentation*, the scheme of the *Death of Saint Francis* is fitted into a rectangular format in the ratio 3:2, i.e., the golden section, the proportion that most closely links the whole with its parts . . . there is no tension between format and compositional scheme, for the verticals at the left and right extend nearly to the top of the picture.

Raphael was opposed to the traditional analytic procedure in which knowledge is built up from elementary units with no reference to any concept of the whole. Rather, he believed that

it is more in keeping with the facts of art to start with a more highly structured element whose components are variable . . . I should like to replace an abstract system of concepts, each designating a simple thing with a simple term, with a system of variable elements and variable functions.

In the domain of art, he argues that one must pair the concept of particularity with the concept of totality. A totality that "combines the . . . factors of form, content, and method at a higher level."

It is assumed in this theory that there are laws governing human creative activity and that these laws can be studied theoretically. Such study will show that a composition is rendered in such a way that it makes it possible to discover that universal in the particular. Raphael's approach is, perhaps, best exemplified in studies of Paul Cézanne, Edgar Degas, Giotto, Rembrandt van Rijn, and Picasso in *The Demands of Art*. The comments that follow focus on his study of Picasso, in whose work he had a long-standing fascination.

To criticize Picasso's art, and particularly the political effort that *Guernica* represented, was to go in the face of most, if not all, progressive criticism of the time. Nevertheless, Raphael was compelled by the dialectical logic of his own system to come to grips with this great artist and his work. In the analysis of *Guernica*, Raphael traces the exact relationship between the social, material, and ideological conditions, on the one hand, and the forms in the painting, on the other. He describes Picasso's art as being conditioned by capitalist society. Picasso's fundamental individualism is in conflict with his mathematical, generalized means of composition. In his work, Picasso has resorted to an abstract idealism—this is most evident in *Guernica*.

To say that the painting is antifascist is no more than to reiterate its political purpose. No gain has been made toward an understanding of those forces that mediate the subject and the expressive means employed. Nor is it enough to invoke the political view that capitalism, its technology, and its ideology dominate society and the individual, alienating man from himself and his community, and that his condition is reflected in the work. Indeed, Raphael maintains, the painting shows Picasso's own continued alienation and his inability to abandon bourgeois values. But how does one come to this in the painting? Raphael argues that it is reflected in the composition. Raphael's task is to show that this personal failure is discoverable in the work, and his thesis is that even though Picasso sought a new pictorial form, the form he achieves fails utterly. *Guernica* is a striking contradiction between form and content.

A compact account of Raphael's treatment of the painting exhibits both his political attitude and his analytic approach to most modernist art: The immediate objective of the painting is shock. The assault on the visual senses gives rise to feelings of uncertainty and irritation. Thus, both the visual and the emotional assimilation of expressive elements are precluded. Feelings of isolation and destruction are intensified. Yet, the artist is the only one who knows the road to the picture's inner allegorical and symbolic truth. Still, it is apparent that the painting constitutes the annihilation of traditional expressive forms, just as the bombing signifies the destruction of impotent pleas for peace. Yet, nothing in this picture is synthesized: form and content remain irreconcilable.

> The local movement of lines scans the emotion which has become affect, the end effect, divorced both from its cause and from the process of its emergence. And it is by this choice of the emotional end effect that Picasso brings the line of movement closest to the effect of color [in which the picture is virtually lacking]—the torment of the finite, frozen in its explosion, in the face of an absolutely silent conscious-being, none of whose potentialities are realized. This is a world without hope of salvation; mankind is reduced to a scream.   (1968)

What is the pictorial solution to this desperate clash? According to Raphael, the horror and anguish of the psychological content of the work suggest no answer. Perhaps this is the key to an understanding of the fundamental discord between form and content. This discord exhibits a collapse of affect in the painting that corresponds to the rampant violence and destruction in the real world. Here Raphael shows that Picasso has attempted to overcome the horror and panic (which are pictorially superficial precisely because they are restricted to the subjects) by means of a serene execution of colorless lines: "these lines are born of emotion, [but] they are not themselves emotional; rather, they are aloof to the point of academic coolness" (ibid.)

In this work, the total construction is sundered by a contradiction—the willingness to radically destroy established tradition pictorially in opposition to a refusal to come to grips with the brutalization of social reality. For Raphael, this last was an intellectual failure characteristic of the bourgeois, liberal mentality. Hence, all of the elements of content are visually brought to materialization in the work, but they fail to achieve form within the whole. Form is separated from content as bourgeois theory is separated from practice. The possibility of achieving essential artistic unity is foreclosed.

The contradiction is reinforced again, for even though Picasso portrays a historical event in *Guernica* (which none of his other paintings do), he fails to grasp the event pictorially in its historical significance. It appears as an ahistorical historical event, a puzzle, to be illuminated only through that impotent mentality that invokes a plea for reason (reasonableness) symbolized in the lamp questing after lost truth.

But, as Raphael points out, bourgeois appeals to reason and nonintervention were exactly what the fascist barbarization of capitalism thrived on. Reasonableness at this juncture of history was complicity. Picasso imposes his personal allegory of reason, which in turn sanctions and sustains the values of that class that "needs it because it can only talk and talk cannot act, and therefore thinks it understands Picasso, although it misunderstands him" (ibid.). Raphael insists that understanding resides in the contradiction, not in an uncritical acceptance of the impotent ideology that informs the work. Picasso has, in this sense, a limited appeal to literati who dwell in a dreamworld in which his art serves as a fetish for those dreams. The work is politically constrained, naive. It fails to transcend the immediate sense of events. As bourgeois ideology, it cannot resolve the present into a possible future. Helplessly, it appeals to reason.

This ideology in its vacuity was unable to stem the fascist tide. In its false consciousness" we glimpse one of the reasons for the split between line and color and between empirical emotion and [a metaphysical and nonhistorical solution that uses] signs and allegories to bridge the gap" (ibid.).

Against the trend of leftist criticism, Raphael insisted that *Guernica* was a contrived painting and therefore arbitrary. Yet, it is important to recognize the admiration in which Raphael held Picasso. The conclusion reached was the result of a most detailed analysis of the work itself—and this is true of all of Raphael's studies of individual paintings.

What was at stake in the struggle to understand Picasso's art was not whether he was a gifted painter—that must be acknowledged in any event. Rather, it was, in Raphael's words, "the historical fate of the European bourgeoisie" (ibid.). Raphael saw in this study, and also in his analyses of classical art undertaken in his period of American emigration, a continuing struggle against all forms of irrationalism and subjectivism: phenomenology, existentialism, Expressionism, and Surrealism.

Raphael's Legacy. What, then, was Raphael's paradigm for good art? The answer is that it is those works of art that are autonomous, dialectical, and organic in nature. Agreeing with Marx, he concludes that this kind of art is most typically characteristic of classical Greece. Genuine classical art, he says, is dialectical and that is why Marx and many others have remarked on its timeless quality. It is this dialectical and timeless quality that artists must grasp if the art of the future is to be great. Such an art will bear a resemblance to the society that conditions and informs it. In the aesthetic sphere, its dialectical characteristics will be increased integration of form and content. In the social field, it will be a reflection of increased integration of social institutions and individuals, a free and yet collective society devoid of exploitation, that is, a socialist society. Raphael believed that only art that is created in the environment of socialism is capable of overcoming the contradictions inherent in modern art.

Although Raphael's contributions to Marxist aesthetics still remain somewhat unrecognized, it is likely that a Marxist theory of the visual arts must begin with his work, for in this field he has not been surpassed. Before Raphael, many approaches to art had been empirical in the sense that they were limited to a history of artifacts or a "scientific" analysis of the structure of individual artworks (formalism) or philosophical generalizations based on the interpreter's personal sensibility (subjectivism). Raphael's originality lies in an approach to empirical facts that employs a complete theory of the psychology of creative activity within a Marxist framework.

Raphael's influence in the fields of aesthetics, art history, and criticism has been modest at best. There are several reasons for this. Among them, his works were virtually ignored in the socialist countries because they were not compatible with official Socialist Realism. He was read widely in Poland and Bulgaria in the 1970s and 1980s, but no publications appear to have resulted.

In the United States, at the time of the posthumous publication of his major book, *The Demands of Art,* grand systematic theories of art were looked on with suspicion as a result of the analytic movement in aesthetics that followed Morris Weitz's dismissal of theory in "The Role of Theory in Aesthetics" in 1956. Raphael's method was adopted, however, by the art historian Hanna Deinhard in her *Meaning and Expression* (1970).

[*See also* Marxism.]

BIBLIOGRAPHY

Works by Raphael

Von Monet zu Picasso: Grundzüge einer Ästhetik und Entwicklung der modernen Malerei. Munich, 1913.
"Die Wertung des Kunstwerkes." *Deutsche-Französische Rundschau* 36.2 (May 1915): 144–155.
Idee und Gestalt: Ein Führer zum Wesen der Kunst. Munich, 1921.
Der dorische Tempel, dargestellt am Poseidontempel zu Paestum. Augsburg, 1930.
"Zur Kunst Theorie des dialektischen Materialismus." *Philosophische Hefte* 3.3–4 (1932): 313–329.
"C. G. Jung Vergreift sich an Picasso." *Information* 6 (December 1932): 11–18.
Proudhon, Marx, Picasso: Trois études sur la sociologie de l'art. Paris, 1933.
Zur Erkenntnistheorie der konkreten Dialektik. Paris, 1934.
Prehistoric Cave Paintings. Translated by Norbert Guterman. New York, 1945.
Prehistoric Pottery and Civilization in Egypt. Translated by Norbert Guterman. New York, 1947.
The Demands of Art. Translated by Norbert Guterman. Princeton, N.J., 1968.
Arbeiter, Kunst und Kunstler. Frankfurt am Main, 1975.
Marx, Picasso: Die Renaissance des Mythos in der bürgerlichen Gesellschaft. Edited by Klaus Binder. Frankfurt am Main, 1983.
Lebens-Erinnerungen: Briefe, Tagebucher, Skizzen, Essays. Edited by Hans-Jürgen Heinrichs. Frankfurt am Main, 1989.
Das schöpferische Auge, oder, Die Geburt des Expressionismus. Vienna, 1993.

Other Sources

Barrett, Michele. "Max Raphael and the Question of Aesthetics." In *The Politics of Pleasure: Aesthetics and Cultural Theory,* edited by Stephan Regan, pp. 33–58. Buckingham, 1992.
Deinhard, Hanna. *Meaning and Expression: Toward a Sociology of Art.* Boston, 1970.
Heinrichs, H. J. "The Empirical Aesthetics of Max Raphael." *Merkur-Deutsche Zeitschrift für Europäisches Denken* 40.9–10 (1986): 844–851.
Pazura, Stanislaw. "The Concept of Art in the Aesthetics of Max Raphael." *Dialectics and Humanism* 15 (Winter–Spring 1988): 133–136.
Truitt, Willis. "A Marxist Theory of Aesthetic Inquiry: The Contribution of Max Raphael." *Journal of Aesthetic Education* 5.1 (January 1971): 151–161.
Truitt, Willis. "Towards an Empirical Theory of Art: A Retrospective Comment on Max Raphael's Contribution to Marxian Aesthetics." *British Journal of Aesthetics* 11.3 (Summer 1971): 227–236.
Truitt, Willis. "Ideology, Expression, and Mediation." In *For Dirk Struik,* edited by Robert S. Cohen et al., pp. 435–463. Dordrecht, 1974.
Truitt, Willis. *Mainstreams in American Aesthetics: A Marxist Analysis.* New York, 1991. See chap. 3.

WILLIS TRUITT

RASA. An emotive theory of aesthetics first formulated by Bharata in his *Nāṭyaśāstra* (c. second century BCE–second century CE), primarily in the context of the theater, *rasa* later developed into a general poetic principle by Ānandavardhana (ninth century) in his *Dhvanyāloka* and by Abhinavagupta (tenth to eleventh century) in his commentary on Bharata, "Abhinavabhāratī," and on *Dhvanyāloka,* "Locana." Its influence is also seen on the theories of dance, music, painting, and sculpture. Literally, "savor," *rasa* has come to mean "aesthetic relish" generally, and it comprehends two related ideas: the relishable quality of the work, that is, its emotional content, and the relishable experience produced by the work in the reader/spectator—the *rasa* experience, which, for Bharata, was the essence of stage drama. Again, because emotions are many and every work will exhibit a different emotional quality, one may also speak of *rasa*s in the plural and categorize works generically, each according to its *rasa.*

The Sanskrit word for "emotion" is *bhāva,* meaning a mental state. No differentiation is made between emotions, feelings, moods, and other cognate terms, as they are all mental states or affects, ranging from simple sensations to the most complex emotional attitudes, dispositions, and inner tensions of varying intensity and duration. A distinction is made, however, between *bhāva*s or "life emotions" described as undergone by the persons in the poem and *rasa*s or the aesthetically excited emotions that are generalized or departicularized in the reader's apprehension owing to the pressure of the literary context, namely, its phenomenological remoteness from the personal concerns of the reader. But still, these (the *rasa*s) are qualitatively the same as the ordinary emotions, not some anonymous "aesthetic" emotions.

Rasa is generally taken to be a theory of emotional response to artworks. True, but it is equally a theory of the art object. Notwithstanding the spiritualized accounts of *rasa* experience by Abhinavagupta and others, the overriding concern of the *Nātyaśāstra* and other critical texts is with objective criteria for identifying and interpreting emotions and with the formal means for presenting them in art; for only the emotions expressed in the work as its meanings are fit for comment. Whether in life or in art, emotions are identified by their (intentional) objects or causes (which may be any emotion-producing object, thought, or event) and by their overt expressions (speech and voluntary and involuntary behavioral reactions). But these situational factors must appear in conjunction, because of the contingent connection between emotion objects and emotion expressions. There can be no objectless emotion—one that cannot be specified in terms of its criteria.

Bharata works out an elaborate typology of emotions, of nearly all the commonly recognized varieties, each with its distinct criteria. Of these, nine—erotic love, humor, grief, rage, heroism, fear, disgust, wonder, and serenity—are the major generic categories and are called the basic emotions (*sthāyin*s), and thirty-three others, such as joy, longing, and agitation, are the transient type (*vyabhicārin*s) because they have no fixed identity of their own and they become meaningful only in the context of one or other of the basic emotions (e.g., the "joy" of victory, of sexual fulfillment). A poem is conceived of as an orchestration of several emotions. But, as a unified discourse, it will establish a single dominant tone—that of a basic emotion. This dominant tone, which colors the whole composition and stamps it as tragic, comic, erotic, and so on, is the focalized mood of the poem, its basic emotion or emergent *rasa*. The *rasa*s, in this sense, are phenomenally objective because they are anchored in the meanings of the work and are not merely qualities ascribed to the work paronymously. They are delivered by the words of the poem. *Rasa*, as a commentator puts it, is the purport of the poetic statement.

The *rasa* theory further holds that the primary end of poetry is "evocation"—not, however, in the perlocutionary sense, but in the sense that the presentation of the emotions in terms of their objects and situational contexts will have the illocutionary act potential of prompting *(bhāvanā)* the reader to contemplate it for its emotional significance, not for its "propositional sense" alone, but for the "propositional attitudes" expressed via the sense. This being the case, the purely cognitive or heuristic values of poetry, although they may still coexist with the evocative value, are subordinated to the primary end of aesthetic gratification.

There were three other, rival theories of poetry in Sanskrit poetics: poetry as figuration or deviant speech *(alaṃkāra, vakrokti)*, poetry as style or structured expression *(rīti)*, and poetry as suggestion or implied meaning *(dhvani)*. The critics of the *dhvani* school, Ānandavardhana and Abhinavagupta, argued for a special poetic semantics, but they were also responsible for restoring Bharata's concept of *rasa* to its former status of essentiality, after its comparative neglect by the figurationists, by assimilating it into the doctrine of suggestion. They maintained that the emotive purport of the sentence describing the objects and expressions is not its literal meaning but another meaning flowing from it through the power of implication. The admissibility of this claim was questioned by other schools of thought. The *dhvani* critics must be given credit, however, for giving the *rasa* concept a firm semantic footing and for establishing the primacy of emotive meaning over figuration and style in determining the aesthetic character of a poem.

Bharata's theater was a composite theater and included not only speech and physical action, but dance and music too as enhancing devices. He uses the term *rasa* to describe the total experience of the stage spectacle. But the question of how *rasa*, understood as a kind of meaning or thematic content, may be applied to dance and music is left ambiguous. On the one hand, Bharata and, following him, Abhinavagupta, maintain that dance as pure rhythmic movement of the limbs of the body serves no expressive need, even when it occurs in the context of the stage drama; it is simply an ornamental addition to drama. Whereas nonrhythmic movements of legs, hands, face, and so on are naturally meaningful as symptomatic expressions of the characters' emotional states, dance steps and dance figures do not stand in any such expresser-expressed relation to the emotive meanings of the literary text or of the action situation of the drama. There is no direct apprehension of a content in them.

But, on the other hand, both Bharata and Abhinavagupta seem to recognize tacitly that there can be an infusion of gestic meaning even in abstract dance when it is introduced in an expression context. Bharata mentions that Śiva's dances were called forth by certain specific emotional situations—which suggests that they were behavioral acts on Śiva's part, performed through dance. Further, Bharata's distinction between the forceful *(tāṇḍava)* and graceful *(lāsya)* modes of dancing—the former being suitable for expressing heroic fervor, ecstasy, and wrath, and the latter for expressing amorous sentiment—is based on the quality of feeling. It implies that even noncontextualized dance movements are capable of exhibiting not only "regional" or "volitional" qualities, such as languidness, grace, and energy, but more specific emotive attitudes, such as amorous, heroic, and angry, associated with those qualities, and (at least some of them) are isomorphically related to expressive human behavior. They do so especially in conjunction with facial expressions that invariably accompany bodily movements and that Bharata regards as vital to stage action. Again, following a long tradition of dance theory, post-Bharata writers, including Abhinavagupta, assign to the various dance actions, movement patterns, group formations, gaits, jumps, pirouettes, and stances, and to rhythm patterns and tempi, described by Bharata, their appropriate expressive uses. The formal distinction between pure dance (nrtta) and expressive action (nātya, abhinaya) established by Bharata is still maintained in the texts on dance written after Abhinavagupta, but a distinction is set up between pure dance (nrtta) and expressive dance (nrtya), and greater value attached to the latter. One gathers from Abhinavagupta's account of dance drama varieties that even in the ancient theater pure dance was fused, in varying degrees, with expression. Even in current practice, in its pan-Indian format, one may notice the same fusion: as when expression itself is rendered rhythmically in dance step, or when a rhythmic number is employed to reinforce or prolong the emotive import of a text or action situation, or when it is presented as part of a ritual or some other performance context, thereby giving it a gestic or mimetic import and dramatic motivation. At any rate, it is apparent that Indian dance is heavily influenced by the rasa concept.

The relation of rasa to music is more problematic. No doubt, Bharata assigns specific emotional or evocative values to musical notes (svaras) and melody patterns or tunes (jātis or rāgas) when they are used in stage presentation for heightening purposes. To each note or tune is assigned its use in the evocation of specific moods, such as love, sorrow, and fear. But neither Bharata nor his commentator, Abhinavagupta, explains how precisely musical sounds are related to the moods and how they can even evoke any definite emotional responses. Sometimes specific musical notes or tunes may seem more fitted than others to the expression of certain moods. But this relation may be purely associational or subjective, not something constant and invariable; for, in practice it can be seen that the same rāga or choice of notes may be adapted to different emotional contexts, and it is not always possible to tell the emotion from the rāga without a meaning-giving context, such as that of a verbal text or the action situation of a play. Again, Ānandavardhana and Abhinavaguta credit musical sounds with a suggestive property even though they recognize that they have no denotative value. But they do not clarify how a semantic function, which suggestion is claimed to be, can be attributed to sounds that are not meaning-bearing signs. The texts on music too do not clarify the matter. But, following Bharata, they tacitly assume a vague connection between music and emotion. The musical notes, as well as the rāgas, are defined affectively, in terms of the delight they cause to the listener's ears.

On the other hand, the application of the rasa concept to the theory of portrait painting and sculpture is well established in the Vāstu and Āgama texts. Expressiveness was considered to be the very essence of image making. Portrayal of feelings (bhāva-vyakti) and faithful representation of human and animal attitudes, conditions, and actions (avasthānukrti) were among the guiding principles of image making, as they were of dancing and stage acting. The Visnudharmottara says that image making is an extension of dance pantomime in the sense that both arts seek to depict human actions and feelings, and employ the same expressive devices—eye expressions (rasa-drstis), hand gestures (mudrās), and body postures (āsanas and sthānas). Even as one speaks of dramatic emotions (nātya-rasas), one can also speak of the rasas expressed in painting and sculpture (citra-rasas).

As for temple architecture, the chief concerns of the Āgama and Vāstu texts are either utilitarian or metaphysical. Temples were designed according to certain metaphysical/symbolic formulas and for various ritual and practical uses. There is no suggestion in the texts that the temple structure as such—barring, of course, the reliefs and sculptured images on it—is expressive of any emotion. There is no mention of rasa in this connection at all.

Emotive theories run into difficulties when they are applied to all art forms irrespective of the differences in their mediums, as may be seen from discussions in Western aesthetics. For the expression of emotions in art, in terms of rasa, two conditions must be presupposed: first, a well-defined emotional situation or attitude, involving sentient beings who are capable of expressing emotions; and second, a medium that is inherently meaningful or self-expressive—that is, either speech (vācika) or physical gestures (āngika), including involuntary reactions (sāttvika). These two are, according to Bharata, the most essential modes of expression (abinayss) in stage action. By these criteria, only literature (where expression is effected solely through the verbal medium) and some forms of the visual and performing arts (which use physical gesture in one way or another to express feelings) would be amenable to an explanation in terms of rasa. Nonsentient, nonexpressive (avācaka) objects—buildings, landscapes, musical sounds—can only be objects of emotion to people, not expressers of it. Hence, emotive characterizations of such objects are necessarily metaphoric, in the sense that the quality of the effect is extended to the cause, as a maxim in Sanskrit has it.

The rasa concept cannot therefore serve as a basis for a global theory of art. In fact, the Sanskrit critics do not essay a general philosophy of art in terms of this or any other concept. They are, wisely enough, content to treat the arts separately, each according to its mode of existence, although their mutual affinities and interdependence are also recognized.

[See also Abhinavagupta; Indian Aesthetics; Music, historical overview article; Poetics; Taste; and Theater.]

BIBLIOGRAPHY

Ānandavardhana. *Dhvanyāloka of Ānandavardhana with the Locana of Abhinavagupta.* Translated and edited by Daniel H. H. Ingalls et al. Cambridge, Mass., 1990.

Bharata Muni. *The Nāṭyaśāstra.* 2d rev. ed. 2 vols. Translated by Manomohan Ghosh. Calcutta, 1961–1967.

Chari, V. K. *Sanskrit Criticism.* Honolulu, 1990.

Deutsch, Eliot. "Reflections on Some Aspects of the Theory of *Rasa.*" In *Sanskrit Drama in Performance,* edited by Rachel Van M. Baumer and James R. Brandon, pp. 214–225. Honolulu, 1981.

Gerow, Edwin. "Rasa as a Category of Literary Criticism: What Are the Limits of Its Application?" In *Sanskrit Drama in Performance,* edited by Rachel Van M. Baumer and James R. Brandon, pp. 226–257. Honolulu, 1981.

Gnoli, Raniero, ed. *The Aesthetic Experience according to Abhinavagupta.* 2d rev. enl. ed. Varanasi, 1968.

Masson, J. L., and M. V. Patwardhan. *Aesthetic Rapture: The Rasādhyāya of the Nāṭyaśāstra,* vol. 1, *Text.* Poona, 1970.

Rowland, Benjamin. *The Art and Architecture of India.* Harmondsworth, England, 1953.

Śārṅgadeva. *Saṅgītaratnākara of Śārṅgadeva,* vol. 4, *Chapter on Dancing.* Translated by K. Kunjunni Raja and Radha Burnier. Madras, 1976.

Śārṅgadeva. *Saṅgītaratnākara of Śārṅgadeva* vol. 1. *Text and Translation.* Translated by R. K. Shringy and Prem Lata Sharma. Delhi, 1978.

The Viṣṇudharmottaram (Pt. III): A Treatise on Indian Painting and Image-Making. 2d rev. enl. ed. Translated and edited by Stella Kramrisch. Calcutta, 1928.

V. K. CHARI

READING. *See* Imagery; *and* Reception Aesthetics.

READYMADE. *See* Duchamp.

REALISM. [*To analyze the multiple meanings of the concept of realism, this entry comprises two essays:*

Realism and Aesthetics
Pictorial Realism

The first essay explains the meaning of realism in aesthetics, namely, the belief that aesthetic qualities, such as beauty, are independent of those making judgments about them; it also discusses the views of antirealists who critique this belief. The second essay explains what realism has meant in art history, where it represents a particular type of art as well as an aesthetic concept tied to many art types. For related discussion, see Fiction; Mimesis; Photography, *article on* Catachresis; Qualities, Aesthetic; Representation; *and* Russian Aesthetics, *article on* Socialist Realism.]

Realism and Aesthetics

Realism in aesthetics is the thesis that properties such as grace, beauty, power, unity, or sadness are instantiated in artworks independently of judgments ascribing them and of the values and perceptions underlying these judgments. Such properties are held to ground and explain aesthetic perceptions and judgments. Realism requires a distinction between the ways artworks appear to various audiences and the properties they really have. According to the antirealist, by contrast, aesthetic properties can be analyzed as ways of appearing to perceivers with different aesthetic sensibilities. Realism allows for a broader class of errors in aesthetic judgments.

Realists will generally defend their view on explanatory grounds. According to them, critics will agree that Wolfgang Amadeus Mozart's concertos are graceful and Ludwig van Beethoven's powerful because these judgments are true in the ordinary correspondence sense. These works instantiate grace and power. This explains the perceptions and judgments that they do so, and contrary judgments must result from faulty or nonoptimal perceptions. Realists offer more particular explanations and predictions as well, which include appeal to particular tastes. A certain critic prefers grace to power; hence, she appreciates Mozart more than Beethoven. A certain artist paints as he does in order to create a delicate poignancy in his works; the property aimed at, but not always achieved, explains his technique. Realists will argue that their opponents cannot offer equally plausible explanations for such phenomena.

Antirealists in response will point to disagreements among even educated tastes for which the realist seems to lack an explanation. What one critic finds powerful, another finds strident, grating, or raucous; what one judges to be delicate and poignant, another finds mawkish or maudlin. In both cases, both critics are knowledgeable of the traditions from which the works emerge, and both perceive all the formal properties of the works that prompt these opposing judgments. Antirealists will argue that there is no fact of the matter in such cases as to which property the work has; it is instead simply a matter of different taste or sensibility. The opponent who holds that one of the parties to such a dispute must be mistaken has no non–question begging way to defend that claim.

Can each side to these arguments respond to its opponents? Antirealists will attempt to offer rival explanations for the phenomena to which realists appeal. They will explain agreements in aesthetic judgments by appeal to common aesthetic educations and resultant tastes and sensibilities. Such common training or upbringing will result in similar responses to the same works, hence in agreed judgments. To the other cases cited by the realist, the response will be slightly more complex. Instead of aiming at a real aesthetic property, an artist will actually aim at a certain response from an audience that shares her taste (in a transparent sense of "aim"). This goal will explain the artist's technique. Instead of preferring real grace to real power, a critic will prefer works (or formal properties of them) that prompt ascriptions of grace from those with his sensibility to works that other critics call powerful (but he probably finds raucous or strident). This more complex preference (again, not normally conceived as such) will explain the more particular preference for Mozart over Beethoven.

On the other side, realists, like antirealists, will explain seemingly intractable disagreements in terms of different backgrounds and training. But for realists, training in a particular tradition or style may lead to insensitivity to properties typical of opposed or very different styles. This will in turn explain why certain critics who are otherwise well educated will fail to perceive those properties in certain sorts of works.

This dispute can be brought into sharper focus by examining what both sides can agree on in regard to the nature of aesthetic properties. Both realists and their opponents must admit that ascribing such properties to works expresses a reaction on the part of the subject to the objective structural properties of the works. This reaction typically includes an evaluative component. To call a work powerful or unified is normally to praise it; to call it raucous or monotonous is normally to condemn it. There are nevertheless exceptions: to call a musical work sad may not be to evaluate it one way or the other. But the ascription of sadness still involves a perceptual and normally an affective response to the music (not necessarily the feeling of sadness itself). One can therefore largely assimilate the structure of aesthetic properties to that of secondary qualities of objects. The latter are analyzed in terms of objects being such as to appear certain ways to certain observers, where reference to the appearance or perceptual response is essential to the analysis. Aesthetic properties seem also to be relations of this sort, although they involve higher-order responses, in many cases responses to the secondary qualities and formal relations among them within artworks.

That aesthetic properties are relational in this way and include a subjective component does not in itself defeat the realist, although it might seem otherwise. The analogy to secondary qualities shows this, because debates occur between realists and antirealists regarding them, even though both sides accept the sort of analysis suggested above. In the case of colors, the realist's position depends on our being able to specify a class of ideal or normal perceivers and conditions relative to which colors appear as they are. The perceptions of others in other conditions then prompt errors in regard to real colors, as these conditions directly reveal only misleading appearances. Realists then have the distinction they need. Similarly, if the analogy is sound, an aesthetic realist would need to specify a class of ideal critics and conditions of judgment such that they perceive real aesthetic properties as they are, while others err in their judgments or are misled by false appearances.

The task of isolating such a class is more difficult in the case of aesthetics. To begin with, one cannot find physical defects in those whose aesthetic judgments differ from others whom one might take to set the standards for art criticism at a given time, whereas one can find such defects in those whose color vision deviates sharply from the norm. In the absence of physical differences, one can nevertheless demand that ideal critics, whose judgments in the face of disagreements refer to real aesthetic properties, be educated in the type of work being judged, be capable of perceiving all its relevant formal properties and relations, and be knowledgeable of the tradition from which the work emerges. Thus, one does not trust those who listen mainly to rock music and are untrained in the classical traditions to judge the aesthetic properties of classical works.

But who is to judge the aesthetic properties of rock songs? One answer is those who know and love rock, instead of classical devotees who hear only grating noise when rock lovers hear driving force. The problem with this answer is that further subdivisions can be made within rock music—heavy metal versus disco versus rap, and so on. If one specifies only lovers of each subgenre (who will also tend to be most knowledgeable of each) as critics ideal for perceiving the real aesthetic properties of songs within that style, the outcome of this narrowing process would be that virtually every piece has mainly positive evaluative aesthetic properties (because each will have its devotees). The criterion is too lenient.

The alternative answer is that the perceptions of those with the best overall taste in music, presumably devotees of serious classical music, are to be the gauge of the real aesthetic properties of musical works. (This answer, of course, still requires divisions among arts, because no one has best taste across all the arts. Thus, one would have to justify divisions across but not within artistic media.) This alternative might be held justified by the best overall explanatory theory, in terms of which realism for aesthetic properties is itself justified. But finding the required explanatory asymmetries is not so easy. The claim that the failure of rock lovers to discern positively evaluative and subtle aesthetic properties in classical works can be explained by their lack of musical education can be matched by the claim that most classical devotees lack detailed knowledge of the current rock repertoire. Ultimately, the realist who seeks to identify ideal perceivers of aesthetic properties across styles and genres must defend the thesis that taste can be compared across styles and genres, and that better taste indicates greater ability to discern real aesthetic properties and to distinguish them from mere appearances. Perhaps this can be accomplished by isolating better works (by consensus) within each genre and then showing that the better works in the inferior genres are distinguished by properties (e.g., complexity, subtle nuance, variety) that works in the better genres have to a higher degree.

Even if they can successfully make this case, realists are not yet out of the water. The equally difficult problem for the realist account being considered is that disagreements seem to persist among fully qualified critics within each suitably broadly defined genre. For one music critic, the triumphant final movement of Camille Saint-Saëns's organ symphony is powerfully moving and uplifting; for a second, it is bombastic, banal, and overblown. When such disputes occur, the realist's proposed criterion seems to require assigning incompatible properties to the same works, properties that they cannot simultaneously have. It becomes inconsistent.

In order to avoid this inconsistency, the realist who accepts the relational account of aesthetic properties must find some way to explain away such disagreement. Two options are available, but neither seems very promising. The first is to find some reason why an apparently well-educated and qualified critic would nevertheless err in aesthetic perception in the case at hand. Perhaps some hidden bias deriving from past experience might be postulated. The second option is to maintain that these disagreements among qualified critics occur mainly at the borders of aesthetic concepts or properties. Just as red and orange might be real properties despite vagueness at their borders, so might higher-order aesthetic properties. This option is problematic, however, because disputes do not seem to be confined to the border areas in the case of aesthetic properties. What is a paradigm of a triumphant, uplifting quality to one critic might be a central case of bombastic prententiousness to another.

It might be argued that nonevaluative aesthetic properties on which critics can agree underlie these opposed evaluative judgments and properties. But the two critics mentioned above will appeal only to the objective formal properties of the piece in defending their opposed aesthetic judgments; and this makes it doubtful that there exists a layer of aesthetic properties between the evaluative properties ascribed and the objective properties that prompt those ascriptions. As noted earlier, not all aesthetic properties include an evaluative component. Sadness as ascribed to music or paintings normally does not. But even here, when one attempts to specify more narrowly the property as instantiated in particular works, disagreements will arise. Is the slow movement of Gustav Mahler's Fifth Symphony melancholy, wistful, or tragic?

It might also be objected that the relational account of aesthetic properties is the problem for the realist in the face of educated disagreement. But it is difficult to see how realists can avoid some such account. If secondary qualities must be analyzed in terms of objective properties causing objects to appear in certain ways, or causing certain perceptual responses, then the same must be true of aesthetic properties. The latter are akin to higher-order perceptual properties, often including also affective and evaluative response components.

If realists could give a plausible account of educated disagreement in ascriptions of aesthetic properties, then realism would be the more attractive metaphysical position. This is because realists can offer other explanations that are deeper and/or more economical than their nonrealist counterparts. Whereas nonrealist explanations for aesthetic judgments end in appeals to aesthetic sensibilities that at bottom only summarize sets of such judgments, realists explain these judgments more deeply by appealing to aesthetic properties that prompt them. As noted earlier, the antirealist can appeal to the objective properties on which, according to the realist, the aesthetic properties supervene, but then the realist's explanations are more economical. If different works prompt similar judgments, the antirealist will have to refer to different objective properties in each case. But the realist can unify many such explanations by appealing to the same aesthetic properties as causes of the same judgments. Different formal relations among musical elements in different symphonies will prompt judgments that the works are powerful, but for realists the same property prompts all these judgments. If their framework is not inconsistent, such explanations may be preferable.

In the end, a compromise position might be best. In order to avoid inconsistency in the face of disagreement among ideal critics, one might have to relativize aesthetic judgments to critics who share taste. That the truth of these judgments should be relative in this way contradicts full-blooded realism. But this would not imply that aesthetic properties reduce to the ways artworks appear to whoever happens to be viewing them. Errors in ascribing such properties remain possible. If one is uneducated in the relevant tradition, or inattentive, or biased (on nonaesthetic grounds), then one is likely to miss the aesthetic properties of a work, to ascribe properties that an ideal critic who otherwise shares one's taste would not ascribe. The suggested account also allows for the fact that taste can improve. Those with undeveloped tastes may judge as no ideal critic would.

The conclusion is that aesthetic realism, that is, independence of aesthetic properties from appearances and beliefs about them, is a matter of degree. There may be several viable positions between the extremes of full-blooded realism and antirealism.

[*See also* Qualities, Aesthetic; *and* Representation.]

BIBLIOGRAPHY

Goldman, Alan H. "Realism about Aesthetic Properties." *Journal of Aesthetics and Art Criticism* 51.1 (Winter 1993): 31–37.

Levinson, Jerrold. "Aesthetic Supervenience." In *Music, Art, and Metaphysics: Essays in Philosophical Aesthetics.* Ithaca, N.Y., 1990.

McDowell, John. "Aesthetic Value, Objectivity, and the Fabric of the World." In *Pleasure, Preference and Value: Studies in Philosophical Aesthetics,* edited by Eva Shaper. Cambridge and New York, 1983.

Pettit, Philip. "The Possibility of Aesthetic Realism." In *Pleasure, Preference and Value: Studies in Philosophical Aesthetics,* edited by Eva Shaper. Cambridge and New York, 1983.

Scruton, Roger. *Art and Imagination: A Study in the Philosophy of Mind.* London, 1974.

Sibley, Frank. "Aesthetic Concepts." *Philosophical Review* 68.4 (October 1959): 421–450.

Zangwill, Nick. "Metaphor and Realism in Aesthetics." *Journal of Aesthetics and Art Criticism* 49.1 (Winter 1991): 57–62.

Zemach, Eddy. "Real Beauty." *Midwest Studies in Philosophy* 16 (1991): 249–265.

ALAN GOLDMAN

Pictorial Realism

From Zeuxis's painting of grapes and the dubiously naive birds of which aestheticians are so fond to today's debates about pictorial perception and the politics of representation, the concept of pictorial realism has been central to reflection on the nature of art and its history. What pictorial realism is, however, is not easily answered.

Jean-Baptiste-Siméon Chardin's still-life paintings, James Abbott McNeill Whistler's portraits, and John Constable's landscapes are paradigms of realistic painting. A natural way of explaining this realism—call it a theory of realism as resemblance—is to say that a painting is realistic in virtue of looking like what it is a painting of. A natural objection to this explanation is that even the most realistic painting looks very little like what it depicts: paintings typically have a flat surface, exhibit brushstrokes, and possess edges, whereas subjects of paintings typically do not. Nelson Goodman (1976) argues that the concept of resemblance does not explain any relation among natural objects in the world, and, a fortiori, it does not explain the relation between pictures and the natural objects they depict. He puts the objection stated above this way: a realistic painting resembles another realistic painting more than it resembles what it depicts, thus resemblance cannot be the relevant relation between a realistic work of art and what it represents. Although concise, this seems a weak way of describing the objection because the resemblance view need only be committed to describing a relation in virtue of not all, but only certain, features of a depiction and what it depicts, such as color, shape, and scale, but not felt texture or absolute size. One should add, moreover, that if two pictures resemble each other, it may be in virtue of each painting being the kind of thing that resembles what it depicts.

What does threaten to undermine the resemblance view is the suspicion that there is a circularity involved in the appeal to resemblance as an explanation of realism, that is, a suspicion that the concept of resemblance employed in explaining realism may be itself explicable only with reference to the concept of realism, or concepts that stand in for it, such as verisimilitude, likeness, and so on.

A second kind of theory of pictorial realism—realism as illusionism—dispenses with the need to define the notion of resemblance, and holds that a painting is realistic if, and to the extent that, under appropriate conditions, a viewer of the painting would have a tendency to mistake it for actually being what it only depicts. Richard Wollheim rejects this theory because, he says, no such tendency in a viewer exists: "It is surely quite untrue to suggest that, in looking at the masterpieces of Constable or [Claude] Monet, we have any temptation, even a partial or inhibited temptation, to react towards them in a way similar to that in which we would to the objects they represent" (Wollheim, 1973, p. 277). Wollheim is right in saying that we have no tendency to respond to realistic works as if they succeeded as illusions, but it may be that we have no such tendency to be deceived *in spite of* their potential for illusionistic depiction, say, because we know upon approaching them that they are only representations. Certainly, some kinds of painting, most notably trompe l'oeil, have an illusionistic effect, and this illusionistic effect is affected in great measure by what spectators believe in viewing the paintings; that is, whatever measure of success such works have in appearing to display, for example, real playing cards and dollar bills, that success is immediately diminished when one learns that such paintings belong to a genre of which illusionism is a defining goal. Such illusionism may be strengthened, by contrast, if one comes to believe that the painting in question belongs to a painter who, like a Cubist painter, routinely used the methods of collage in his work. Thus, it is not a strong argument against the view of realism as illusionism to say that a realistic work by Constable or Monet may not be illusionistic to most or all spectators, because this may not be a difference in kind, but only in degree, from such works as trompe l'oeil that do tempt one to respond as one responds to what they depict. Nonetheless, there is still a question as to why one should assume that the tendency of a painting to deceive its viewers is an explanation of the painting's realism; that is, what justifies the assumption that the illusionism of a painting should be identified with its realism? One can know with certainty that a painting is nothing more than a representation and still judge it realistic. If illusionism were essential to, or identical with, realism, this absence of any possibility of a painting's illusionism should not leave its realism uncompromised.

A third account of pictorial realism, often attributed to E. H. Gombrich, is that the realism of a painting is a matter of how much true information can be derived from the painting about what it depicts. Described in this general way, the account is intuitively plausible. It allows one to say that a painting of a bowl of apples is realistic because one can derive from it facts such as that apples are red, somewhat spherical, look like they weigh less than automobiles but more than raisins, and so on; and, in comparing two paintings of apples, one might say that the more realistic painting gives more true information about those apples. The problem with this view is that different paintings can yield different information about an object by representing it in different ways. Information about the shape or color of an apple can be supplied by one painting, information about molecular structure by another. The amount of information in each case could be identical, but only one painting would possess realism in the sense that it is being discussed here. That realism is not a matter of how much true information is supplied by a painting is also suggested by the fact that sometimes the way in which an image offers *false* information can support its realism. In, for example, Andrea Mantegna's foreshortened depiction of the dead Christ laid out on a slab, the feet are reduced in scale compared to the rest of the body. This deliberate distortion in foreshortening is necessary to avoid having the feet seem impossibly large, as they would in "correct" depiction. In this case, the realistic image is a poor guide to the nature of things independent of how they appear. As it happens, the truth or falsity of the information one could derive from a painting is of little consequence in whether the painting appears realistic. Jan Vermeer's *View of Delft* supplies a great amount of information about the place it depicts: the shapes and relative heights of the buildings, the geography of the harbor, the construction of the ships, and so on. But how unimportant it is for this information to be true is demonstrated when one reverses, say, with a slide projector, a reproduction of the painting such that everything that was on the left is now on the right and vice versa. Now, someone else who did not know the proper orientation of the image could derive information about the same kinds of things in the same fashion; but whereas much of this information would be false, it seems to be at no cost to the image's realism.

Returning to the theory of realism as resemblance, Wollheim and other commentators have stressed that the perception of pictures has a twofold nature. One can both attend to the brushstrokes, colors, and surface of a painting and see these aspects of a painting as an image. This capacity to "see in," rather than explaining how a painting can resemble what it depicts, takes it for granted that such resemblance is possible. Still, because one can "see in" a painting, one need not be troubled by the objection to the resemblance theory that features of a painting seen when viewing the painting—the texture of its brushstrokes, the flat array of patches of colors—do not look like whatever object in the world the painting depicts. One refers not to those material features of the work, but to what one "sees in" those features, what image one sees those material features as.

Finally, support for the resemblance view, although not an explanation of pictorial resemblance per se, is found in studies such as Julian Hochberg's demonstration that a child raised to nineteen months in a picture-free environment was able, when confronted with pictures for the first time, to recognize and speak of the objects in the pictures in the same way that he recognized and spoke of the objects themselves. This kind of experiment—and those with chimpanzees, that, after being taught to communicate with objects, are able, without further training, to use pictures of the objects for the same functions—suggest that however

one explains pictorial resemblance, it exists in a form that is not exclusively, although perhaps extensively, a conventional phenomenon.

[*See also* Perception.]

BIBLIOGRAPHY

Bryson, Norman. *Vision and Painting: The Logic of the Gaze.* New Haven, 1983.
Danto, Arthur C. *The Transfiguration of the Commonplace: A Philosophy of Art.* Cambridge, Mass., 1981.
Gombrich, E. H., Julian Hochberg, and Max Black. *Art, Perception, and Reality.* Baltimore, 1972.
Goodman, Nelson. *Languages of Art: An Approach to a Theory of Symbols.* 2d ed. Indianapolis, 1976.
Wollheim, Richard. *On Art and the Mind: Essays and Lectures.* London, 1973; reprint, Cambridge, Mass., 1974.
Wollheim, Richard. *Art and Its Objects* 2d ed. with six supplementary essays. Cambridge and New York, 1980.

JONATHAN GILMORE

REALITY, VIRTUAL. *See* Virtual Reality.

RECEPTION AESTHETICS. Sometimes known as "reception theory," reception aesthetics is commonly used to designate a direction in literary criticism developed by scholars in West Germany, particularly at the University of Constance, during the late 1960s and early 1970s. In general, the members of the "Constance school" advocated turning to the reading and reception of literary texts instead of to traditional methods that emphasize the production of texts or a close examination of texts themselves. Their approach is therefore related to reader-response criticism in the United States, although reception aesthetics for a time was more homogeneous in its theoretical presuppositions and general outlook than its American counterpart. Informed by the Continental traditions of hermeneutics and phenomenology, reception aesthetics dominated literary theory in Germany for about a decade. It was virtually unknown in the English-speaking world until around 1980, when it was made more readily accessible by a number of translations of the most seminal works. Hans Robert Jauss and Wolfgang Iser are the two most original theorists, although several of Jauss's students, among them Rainer Warning, Hans Ulrich Gumbrecht, and Karlheinz Stierle, also made important contributions to this branch of theory. In response to the writings of Jauss and Iser, scholars from the German Democratic Republic such as Robert Weimann, Manfred Naumann, and Rita Schober raised objections to some propositions and suggested Marxist alternatives, and the most productive East–West postwar dialogue in literary theory involved issues of reception and response.

Reception aesthetics arose at a time of great turbulence in West German society. At universities throughout the country, the student movement agitated for educational reform and advocated a basic questioning of traditional methods and educational standards. The impact on literary studies was substantial. During much of the postwar era, criticism had been dominated by close textual analysis, existentially based theory, and other ahistorical methods. Only in the 1960s did the climate gradually change when students, together with younger professors, demanded a reexamination of the canon and insisted on relevance in literary scholarship. The experimental University of Constance, founded in 1967, was at the forefront of general educational reform. Thus, it is not surprising that it fostered an atmosphere in which novel ideas about literary theory and aesthetics flourished as well.

An inaugural address at the University of Constance in April 1967 marked the beginning of reception aesthetics. This lecture was delivered by the newly appointed scholar of Romance languages, Hans Robert Jauss, and the title echoed another famous inaugural essay, one held on the eve of the French Revolution at the University of Jena by the playwright, theorist, and historian Friedrich von Schiller. Schiller had spoken on the topic "What Is and for What Purpose Does One Study Universal History?" Jauss modified this title by substituting the word *literary* for *universal,* but this slight alteration did not diminish the impact in the least. Jauss suggested, as Schiller had in 1789, that the present age needed to restore vital links between the artifacts of the past and the concerns of the present. For literary scholarship and instruction, such a connection could be established only if literary history were no longer relegated to the periphery of the discipline, Jauss maintained. He therefore sought to prod his colleagues into a new era of historical criticism, and the revised title to this lecture, "Literary History as a Provocation to Literary Scholarship," captured the innovative challenge that Jauss sought.

The approach to literary texts that Jauss outlined in his lecture became known as reception aesthetics. It is best understood as an attempt to overcome what Jauss viewed as limitations in two important and putatively opposed literary theories: Russian Formalism and Marxist criticism. In general, Marxism represents for him an outmoded approach to literature, related to an older positivist paradigm. Yet, Jauss also recognizes in this body of criticism, especially in the writings of less orthodox Marxists such as Werner Krauss, Roger Garaudy, and Karel Kosík, a fundamentally correct concern with the historicity of literature. The Formalists, on the other hand, are credited with introducing aesthetic perception as a theoretical tool for exploring literary works. Yet, Jauss also detects in their works the tendency to isolate art from its historical context, a *l'art pour l'art* aesthetics that valorizes the synchronic over the diachronic. The task for a new literary history, therefore, becomes to merge successfully the best qualities of Marxism and Formalism. This can be accomplished by satisfying the Marxist demand for his-

torical mediation while retaining the Formalist advances in the realm of aesthetic perception.

Reception aesthetics proposes to do this by altering the perspective from which literary texts are normally interpreted. Traditional literary histories were composed from the perspective of the producers of texts; Jauss proposes that one can truly understand literature as a process by recognizing the constitutive role of the consuming or reading subject. The interaction between author and public replaces literary biography as the basis for literary historiography. Thus, Jauss meets the Marxist demand for historical mediations by situating literature in the larger continuum of events; he retains the Formalist achievements by placing the perceiving consciousness at the center of his concerns. History and aesthetics, which seemed to be irreconcilable, are united in his theory. The historical significance of a work is not established by qualities of the work or by the genius of its author, but by the chain of receptions from generation to generation. In terms of literary history, Jauss thus envisions a historiography that will play a conscious, mediating role between past and present. The historian of literary reception is called on to rethink continuously the works of the canon in light of how they have affected, and are affected by, current conditions and events. Past meanings are understood as part of the prehistory of present experiencing.

The integration of history and aesthetics is to be accomplished largely by examining what Jauss refers to as the horizon of expectation (*Erwartungshorizont*). This methodological centerpiece of Jauss's theory is an obvious adaptation of the notion of horizon (*Horizont*) found most prominently in the hermeneutic theory of Jauss's teacher Hans-Georg Gadamer. For Gadamer, the horizon is a fundamental tenet for the hermeneutical situation. It refers primarily to our situatedness in the world, our necessarily perspectival and limited purview. [*See* Gadamer.] Jauss's use of the term is slightly different. For him, the horizon denotes an intersubjective system or structure of expectations, a system of references, or a mind-set that a hypothetical individual brings to a given text. All works are read against some horizon of expectation; indeed, certain types of texts—parody, for example—intentionally foreground this horizon. The task of the literary scholar, Jauss suggests, is to "objectify" the horizon, so that one may evaluate the artistic character of the work of art. This is most readily accomplished when the work in question thematizes its horizon. But even works whose horizon is less obvious can be examined with this method. Generic, literary, and linguistic aspects of the work in question can be used to construct a probable horizon of expectation.

After establishing the horizon of expectation, the critic can then proceed to determine the artistic merit of a given work by measuring the distance between the work and the horizon. Basically, Jauss employs a deviationist model: the aesthetic value of a text is seen as a function of its deviation from a given norm. If the expectations of a reader are not "disappointed" or violated, then the text will approach the culinary; if, on the other hand, it breaks through the horizon, then it will be a work of high art. Sometimes a work may break its horizon of expectation and yet remain unrecognized as a great work of art. This case poses no problems for Jauss's theory. The first experience of disrupted expectations will almost invariably evoke strong negative responses from its initial audience, but the original negativity will disappear for later readers. The reason for this is that in a later age the horizon has changed, so that the work in question no longer ruptures expectations. Instead, it may be recognized as a classic, that is, as a work that itself has contributed in an essential way to the establishment of a new horizon of expectation.

Jauss modified his deviationist position in the 1970s, when he reexamined the viability of a model based exclusively on an aesthetics of negativity. Reacting in particular to the posthumous publication of Theodor Adorno's *Aesthetic Theory* (1997), as well as to the aesthetics of the *Tel Quel* group in France, Jauss reconsiders the implications of his own theoretical provocation of the late 1960s. What bothers Jauss about Adorno's view is that it allows a positive social function for art only when the artwork negates the specific society in which it is produced. It therefore leaves no room for an affirmative *and* progressive literature, because literature in general is defined by its opposition to social practices, by its "ascetic" character. Such a theory tends to valorize modernist directions, promoting an elitist, avant-garde concept of art, and scorning communication in literature as anathema to genuine cultural achievement. Jauss therefore recognizes the weakness in his earlier work when he admits the partial nature of his former depiction of aesthetic experience. By excluding a primary and positive aesthetic experience, the reception aesthetics shared an artistic asceticism with other contemplative and self-reflexive modes of speculation; and, by orienting itself on autonomous art, it ignored not only the important role of preautonomous art (pre-Romantic), but also the great variety of functions that art has historically possessed and potentially still possesses. Eventually, Jauss expanded his purview, developing a theory that encompasses a great variety of aesthetic responses, from uncritical identification to critical reflection against ironic negation.

Jauss's historical approach to understanding literary works was complemented by Wolfgang Iser's examination of the interaction between reader and text. Like Jauss, Iser attracted a great deal of attention with his inaugural lecture at Constance, but his theory is perhaps best represented in his book *The Act of Reading* (1976). What has interested Iser from the outset is the question of how and under what conditions a text has meaning for a reader. In contrast to traditional interpretation, which has sought to elucidate a hidden meaning in the text, he wants to see meaning as the result of an interaction between text and reader, as an effect that is experienced, not an objection that must be found. Roman Ingarden's conception of the literary work of art thus provided him with a useful framework for his investigation. According to Ingarden, the aesthetic object is constituted only through an act of cognition on the part of the reader. Adopting this fundamental precept from Ingarden, Iser thus switches focus from the text as an object to the text as a potential, from the results of a reading to the act of reading itself. [*See* Ingarden.]

To examine the interaction between text and reader, Iser looks at those qualities in the text that make it readable or that influence one's reading, and at those features of the reading process that are essential for understanding the text. Particularly in his early work, he adopts the term *implied reader* to encompass both of these functions; it is at once textual structure and structured act. Later, depending more heavily on Ingarden's terminology, he distinguishes between the text, its concretization, and the work of art. The first is the artistic aspect, what is placed there by the author to be read, and it may be conceived best as a potential waiting to be realized. Concretization, by contrast, refers to the product of the reader's own productive activity; it is the realization of the text in the mind of the reader, accomplished by the filling in of blanks or gaps (*Leerstellen*) to eliminate indeterminacy. Finally, the work of art is neither text nor concretization, but something in between. It occurs at the point of convergence of text and reader, a point that can never be completely defined.

The work of art is characterized by its virtual nature and is constituted by various overlapping procedures. One of these involves the dialectic of protention and retention, two terms borrowed from the phenomenological theory of Edmund Husserl. Iser applies them to our activity in reading successive sentences. In confronting a text, we continuously project expectations that may be fulfilled or disappointed; at the same time, our reading is conditioned by preceding sentences and concretizations. Because our reading is determined by this dialectic, it acquires the status of an event and can give us the impression of a real occurrence. If this is so, however, our interaction with texts must compel us to endow our concretizations with a degree of consistency—or at least as much consistency as we admit to reality. This involvement with the text is seen as a type of entanglement in which the foreign is grasped and assimilated. Iser's point is that the reader's activity is similar to actual experience. Although Iser distinguishes between perception (*Wahrnehmung*) and ideation (*Vorstellung*), structurally these two processes are identical. According to Iser, reading therefore temporarily eliminates the traditional subject-object dichotomy. At the same time, however, the subject is compelled to be split into two parts, one that undertakes the concretization and another that merges with the author, or at least the constructed image of the author. Ultimately, the reading process involves a dialectical process of self-realization and change: by filling in the gaps in the text, we simultaneously reconstruct ourselves. Our encounters with literature are part of an enlightenment process in which we come to understand others and ourselves more completely.

Iser's model of reading has been productively supplemented in the work of Karlheinz Stierle, the most incisive second-generation theorist from the Constance school during the 1970s. Stierle proceeds from Iser's contention that the formation of illusions and images is essential for the reading process, and labels this level of reading "quasi-pragmatic," a designation that distinguishes it from the reception of nonfictional texts ("pragmatic reception"). Although Iser seems to remain on this plane in his studies, Stierle suggests that a quasi-pragmatic reading must be supplemented with higher forms of reception capable of doing justice to the peculiarities of fiction. He argues for a pseudoreferential use of language, an application located between its usage in simple reference and its autoreferential function. What distinguishes narrative fiction is this pseudoreferentiality, which may be considered autoreferentiality in the guise of referential forms. Fiction is self-referential, although it appears to be referential. What Stierle suggests, therefore, is an additional reflexive level of understanding in our encounter with literary texts.

The critics of reception aesthetics from the former German Democratic Republic approach its accomplishments from a somewhat different stance. Robert Weimann and Manfred Naumann are not as interested in the reading process outlined by Iser and Stierle as they are in the literary historiography developed by Jauss. Their objections to his theory are threefold. First, they complain of one-sidedness, claiming that reception theory has gone too far in emphasizing the response to a work of art. Although they admit that this is an important aspect—and one that has been downplayed somewhat in the Marxist tradition—Jauss and his colleagues, in positing reception as the sole criterion for a revitalization of literary history, destroy the dialectic of production and reception. Second, Marxist critics detect a danger in the totally subjective apprehension of art and the resultant relativizing of literary history. The problem here is that if one follows Jauss (and Gadamer) in relinquishing all objective notions of the work of art, then one's access to history would seem to be completely arbitrary, because it is ceaselessly changing. Third, these critics argue that reception aesthetics provides scant sociological grounding for the reader, who supposedly stands at the center of its concerns. Scholars from the former German Democratic Republic find a general failure to link literary history with larger concerns. The reader in the reception aesthetics of Jauss and Iser, they claim, is conceived as an idealized individual rather than as a social entity with political and ideological, as well as aesthetic, dimensions.

In the United States, where reception theory had comparatively little impact until the 1980s, the work of Iser provoked the most controversy. Stanley Fish (1981) argued that Iser's theoretical apparatus, when applied to literary works, produces comprehensible interpretations of texts. He denies, however, that Iser's theory identifies elements in a literary work; rather, he asserts that it creates them. The issue for Fish is thus really one of epistemology. Perception, for him, is always a mediated activity; it is never innocent of assumptions. For Iser, on the other hand, there are some things that simply exist and must be grasped by all rational perceivers.

Jauss and Iser defended their positions against these and other objections in polemical rejoinders during the 1970s. They have also corrected and refined theoretical positions based on criticism. But the cost of these modifications has been a loss of the original excitement that surrounded the emergence of reception theory in the late 1960s and early 1970s. Both Jauss and Iser subsequently took directions that depart somewhat from their most influential work. Increasingly, Iser has concerned himself with the notions of the imaginary in fiction and with literary anthropology. Jauss's magnum opus, *Aesthetic Experience and Literary Hermeneutics* (1982), in which he articulated a more differentiated notion of response, was no longer perceived as a provocation to literary scholarship, but as a differentiated scholarly treatise. For this reason, this work evidenced a comparatively smaller impact on critical circles in Germany, and one could argue that reception aesthetics as a coherent and innovative approach to literature had exhausted itself by the early 1980s. Activity around literary theory at Constance, on the other hand, has survived the demise of its most important theoretical product by virtue of the personalities of its members and the biannual scholarly colloquiums held there. The meetings of the group Poetics and Hermeneutics, so important for the advent of reception theory, continue to produce some of the most exciting contributions to literary, cultural, and philosophical criticism in Germany.

[*See also* Hermeneutics; *and* Literature, *article on* Literary Aesthetics.]

BIBLIOGRAPHY

Primary Sources

Adorno, Theodor W. *Ästhetische Theorie*. Edited by Gretel Adorno and Rolf Tiedemann. Frankfurt am Main, 1970. Translated by Robert Hullot-Kentor as *Aesthetic Theory* (Minneapolis, 1997).

Gumbrecht, Hans Ulrich. "Konsequenzen der Rezeptionsästhetik oder Literaturwissenschaft als Kommunikationssoziologie." *Poetica* 7 (1975): 388–413.

Iser, Wolfgang. *Die Appellstruktur der Texte: Unbestimmtheit als Wirkungsbedingung literarischer Prosa*. Constance, 1970. In English as "Indeterminacy and the Reader's Response in Prose Fiction," in *Aspects of Narrative: Selected Papers from the English Institute,* edited by J. Hillis Miller (New York, 1971), pp. 1–45.

Iser, Wolfgang. *Der implizite Leser: Kommunikationsformen des Romans von Bunyan bis Beckett.* Munich, 1972. In English as *The Implied Reader: Patterns of Communication in Prose Fiction from Bunyan to Beckett* (Baltimore, 1974).

Iser, Wolfgang. *Der Akt des Lesens: Theorie ästhetischer Wirkung.* Munich, 1976. In English as *The Act of Reading: A Theory of Aesthetic Response* (Baltimore, 1978).

Iser, Wolfgang. "The Current Situation of Literary Theory: Key Concepts and the Imaginary." *New Literary History* 11 (1979): 1–20.

Jauss, Hans Robert. "Paradigmawechsel in der Literaturwissenschaft." *Linguistische Berichte* 3 (1969): 44–56.

Jauss, Hans Robert. *Literaturgeschichte als Provokation.* Frankfurt am Main, 1970.

Jauss, Hans Robert. *Kleine Apologie der ästhetischer Erfahrung.* Constance, 1972.

Jauss, Hans Robert. *Ästhetische Erfahrung und literarische Hermeneutik.* Frankfurt am Main, 1982.

Jauss, Hans Robert. *Aesthetic Experience and Literary Hermeneutics.* Translated by Michael Shaw. Minneapolis, 1982.

Jauss, Hans Robert. *Toward an Aesthetic of Reception.* Translated by Timothy Bahti. Minneapolis, 1982.

Naumann, Manfred, et al. *Gesellschaft, Literatur, Lesen: Literaturrezeption in theoretischer Sicht.* Weimar, 1973.

Naumann, Manfred. "Das Dilemma der 'Rezeptionsästhetik.'" *Poetica* 8 (1976): 451–466.

Schober, Rita. *Abbild, Sinnbild, Wertung: Aufsätze zur Theorie und Praxis literarischer Kommunikation.* Berlin, 1982.

Stierle, Karlheinz. *Text als Handlung: Perspektiven einer systematischen Literaturwissenschaft.* Munich, 1975.

Stierle, Karlheinz. "Was heisst Rezeption bei fiktionalen Texten?" *Poetica* 7 (1975): 345–387. Abbreviated version in English as "The Reading of Fictional Texts," in *The Reader in the Text: Essays on Audience and Interpretation,* edited by Susan R. Suleiman and Inge Crosman (Princeton, N.J., 1980), pp. 83–105.

Warning, Rainer, ed. *Rezeptionsästhetik: Theorie und Praxis.* Munich, 1975.

Weimann, Robert. "'Rezeptionsästhetik' und die Krise der Literaturgeschichte: Zur Kritik einer neuen Strömung in der bürgerlichen Literaturwissenschaft." *Weimarer Beiträge* 19.8 (1973): 5–33. In English as "'Reception Aesthetics' and the Crisis of Literary History," *Clio* 5 (1975): 3–33.

Weimann, Robert. "'Rezeptionsästhetik' oder das Ungenügen an der bürgerlichen Bildung: Zur Kritik einer Theorie literarischer Kommunikation." In *Kunstensemble und Öffentlichkeit,* edited by Robert Weimann, pp. 85–133. Halle, Germany, 1982.

Weinrich, Harald. "Für eine Literaturgeschichte des Lesers." *Merkur* 21 (1967): 1026–1038.

Other Sources

Bürger, Peter. "Probleme der Rezeptionsforschung." *Poetica* 9 (1977): 446–471.

Fish, Stanley. "Why No One's Afraid of Wolfgang Iser." *Diacritics* 11.1 (1981): 2–13.

Fokkema, D. W., and Elrud Kunne-Ibsch. "The Reception of Literature: Theory and Practice of 'Rezeptionsästhetik.'" In *Theories of Literature in the Twentieth Century,* pp. 136–164. New York, 1977.

Grimm, Gunter. *Rezeptionsgeschichte: Grundlegung einer Theorie.* Munich, 1977.

Hohendahl, Peter Uwe, ed. *Sozialgeschichte und Wirkungsästhetik: Dokumente zur empirischen und marxistischen Rezeptionsforschung.* Frankfurt am Main, 1974.

Holub, Robert C. *Reception Theory: A Critical Introduction.* London and New York, 1984.

Holub, Robert C. *Crossing Borders: Reception Theory, Poststructuralism, Deconstruction.* Madison, Wis., 1992.

Link, Hannelore. "'Die Appellstruktur der Texte' und 'ein Paradigmawechsel in der Literaturwissenschaft.'" *Jahrbuch der deutschen Schillergesellschaft* 17 (1973): 532–583.

Solms, Wilhelm, and Norbert Schöll. "Rezeptionsästhetik." In *Literaturwissenschaft heute,* edited by Friedrich Nemec and Wilhlem Solms, pp. 154–196. Munich, 1979.

Zimmermann, Bernhard. *Literturrezeption im historischen Prozess: Zur Theorie einer Rezeptionsgeschichte der Literatur.* Munich, 1977.

ROBERT C. HOLUB

REFERENCE. *See* Perception, *article on* Music Perception; Realism; *and* Representation.

REID, THOMAS (1710–1796), Scottish philosopher and founder of the "commonsense" school of philosophy. Reid was born into a distinguished family of clerics and intellectuals and received his education in theology and philosophy at Marischal College, Aberdeen. From 1736 to 1750, he served as minister of New Machar, where he first read David Hume's *A Treatise of Human Nature.* This work was to have a profound impact on Reid's own philosophy, which is by and large an attempt to refute some of Hume's basic assumptions and thus to avoid the "skeptical" conclusions that he believed Hume was forced to draw concerning humankind's relation to the world. From 1751 to 1764, Reid was professor of philosophy at King's College, Aberdeen, where he wrote his first work, *Inquiry into the Human Mind on the Principles of Common Sense* (1764). In 1764, he succeeded Adam Smith in the chair of moral philosophy at Glasgow, where in 1774 he delivered his *Lectures on the Fine Arts.* He gave up lecturing in 1780 in order to work on the *Essays on the Intellectual Powers of Man,* which was published in 1785. He remained at Glasgow for the next ten years, during which he wrote a number of philosophical papers and the *Essays on the Active Powers of Man* (1788), in which he defends a rationalist theory of ethics.

Reid's "commonsense" philosophy gives an account of the basic powers (practical and intellectual) of the human mind. The account is driven by a conviction that the most universal aspects of human language and practice mirror the basic structures of thought—the first principles of truth and judgment that he takes to be embodied in a "common sense" universal to mankind.

The three following claims capture the most essential and most distinctive features of Reid's aesthetics:

1. Theories that analyze beauty in terms of a subjective state are inadequate because they misdescribe our aesthetic practices.
2. There are intersubjective criteria for justifying claims of taste, and these criteria are based on objective perfections.

3. There are different kinds of beauty and sublimity (e.g., original or derived, natural or artistic) that must be analyzed in different ways.

The most striking feature of Reid's aesthetics is perhaps his claim that objects that are beautiful or sublime must either possess or signify some real perfection. Reid is here reacting to a tendency among empiricist aestheticians "to resolve everything into feelings," to think of beauty as a feeling in our minds rather than a property of objects (Reid, 1973, p. 35). Francis Hutcheson, for example, identifies beauty with a sensible "idea raised in us"—an idea that may, for all we know, carry no resemblance to what caused it—and has to conclude that "were there no mind with a sense of beauty to contemplate these objects, I see not how they could be called beautiful" (An Inquiry Concerning Beauty, Order, Harmony, Design, 1973). Reid thinks people like Hutcheson confuse our response to beauty with that *to which* we are responding. This leads them to misrepresent what we take ourselves to be doing when we make aesthetic judgments—namely, to be making claims about *objects* and not about the mental states they evoke in us (Reid, 1969, pp. 755, 759, 783). In order to capture this fact about our aesthetic experience, Reid insists that objects are beautiful or sublime in virtue of either possessing or expressing some perfection—more specifically, some perfection of mind and its active powers (ibid., 791; 1973, pp. 43–51). In what follows, this claim will be referred to as the "objectivity thesis."

Reid puts forward the objectivity thesis in order to identify a source of value for objects of taste. He thinks that the falsity of locating their value in our affective response to them becomes apparent when we examine our own aesthetic practices and modes of judgment. The structure of our claims of taste shows that "in every operation of taste, there is a judgment implied" (1965, p. 759)—a judgment that does not refer to the mental state of the subject, but rather involves the belief that the object we deem beautiful or sublime has some real value (ibid., p. 807; cf. pp. 759–760). Our aesthetic judgments, in other words, indicate that favorable responses do not supply the source of value that merits those very responses. Because our claims of taste refer to something else than a subjective state, it is misguided to think that the fact that we favor objects of taste is our only basis for deeming them valuable.

Reid thinks that not only our common sense but also our use of language attest to the objectivity thesis. When we argue about matters of taste, we strive to justify our love or admiration for certain objects. In other words, we take the object to have some real merit stemming from a source of value to which we can refer in justifying our aesthetic judgments (ibid., pp. 807–808; cf. p. 758). Because we do dispute about taste, Reid thinks that there exist public criteria—both affective and rational—for defending our claims of taste and that these criteria are veridical (guide us to the truth) in the sense that they pick out real perfections in the world.

The problem with this argument is that the existence of intersubjective criteria for justifying claims of taste does not imply their veridicality, does not imply that they refer to real (perceiver-independent) perfections in the world. It is possible that the things we deem excellent have no value in themselves but are instead valuable only with regard to our own contingent purposes or to our historically conditioned social and moral codes. If that is the case, it is hard to see how a beautiful or sublime object can have "its excellence from its own constitution, and not from ours" (ibid., p. 770), because its value would then stem entirely from the fact that we (or other perceivers) approve of that particular quality.

Here we need to remind ourselves that Reid's location of beauty in real excellence is a move against empiricist aestheticians' tendency to explain beauty in terms of utility, which in turn reduces to an object's tendency to produce pleasure. Reid believes that the mere fact that we take pleasure in aesthetic objects cannot explain why we value them. Our sentiments must themselves be well grounded, and it is in order to justify those responses that Reid insists that beauty and sublimity must be sought in "the scale of perfection and real excellence"—in particular, in the perfections of mind and its active powers.

All the beauty and sublimity in the material world are then said to "derive" from mental perfection: material objects are beautiful or sublime insofar as they bear the signs or effects of mental excellence—that is, either insofar as they express amiable or admirable mental qualities by resembling the physical expressions or "natural signs" of those qualities, or else insofar as they show a high degree of "design, art, and wise contrivance" by being well adapted to their specific end (ibid., pp. 791–792; 1973, pp. 41–42, 47). Aesthetic objects in the material world are thus connected to mental perfection through expression, and that is what gives them the value that "merits" our favorable response.

Reid emphasizes that there are different kinds of beauty in the world. Because only intelligent creatures can properly be said to possess mental and active perfections, they become the primary objects of taste in Reid's theory—the bearers of what he calls "original" beauty and sublimity. His account of "derived" beauty divides into the following categories:

1. the beauty of organisms and machines (attributable to their adaptedness to a natural end or function);
2. the beauty of things that express or bear the signs of mental excellence (a birch swaying in the breeze is beautiful because it "beckons," reminding us of hospitality);
3. the beauty of things that are analogous to certain kinds of mental excellence (musical harmony and soft colors or shapes are analogous to mental balance and concord).

By connecting aesthetic merit to mental excellence, Reid explains how certain inanimate objects can justly inspire the feelings of love and admiration that we normally think of as reserved for our fellow human beings.

[*See also* Hume; Hutcheson; *and* Taste.]

BIBLIOGRAPHY

Works by Reid

Essays on the Intellectual Powers of Man (1785). Cambridge, Mass., 1969.

Lectures on the Fine Arts. In *Thomas Reid's Lectures on the Fine Arts*, edited by Peter Kivy. The Hague, 1973. An unpublished manuscript transcribed and edited by Kivy.

Other Sources

Cummings, Phillip D. "Reid's Realism." *Journal of the History of Philosophy* 12.4 (October 1974): 317–340.

Dalgarno, Melvin, and Eric Matthews, eds. *The Philosophy of Thomas Reid*. Dordrecht and Boston, 1989.

DeRose, Keith. "Reid's Anti-Sensationalism and His Realism." *Philosophical Review* 158.3 (July 1989): 313–348.

Ferreira, M. Jamie. *Skepticism and Reasonable Doubt: The British Naturalist Tradition in Wilkins, Hume, Reid, Newman*. Oxford, 1986.

Gallie, Roger D. *Thomas Reid and "The Way of Ideas."* Dordrecht and Boston, 1989.

Gracyk, Theodore A. "The Failure of Thomas Reid's Aesthetics." *Monist* 70.4 (October 1987): 465–482.

Jones, Peter. *The "Science of Man" in the Scottish Enlightenment: Hume, Reid and Their Contemporaries*. Edinburgh, 1989.

Kivy, Peter. "Introduction." In *Thomas Reid's Lectures on the Fine Arts*, pp. 1–17. The Hague, 1973.

Kivy, Peter. "The Logic of Taste: Reid and the Second Fifty Years." In *Thomas Reid: Critical Interpretations*, edited by Stephen F. Barker and Tom L. Beauchamp, pp. 118–132.

Lehrer, Keith. "Reid on Primary and Secondary Qualities." *Monist* 61.2 (April 1978): 184–191, esp. pp. 188–189.

Lehrer, Keith. *Thomas Reid*. London and New York, 1989.

Lobkowicz, Erich. *Common Sense und Skeptizismus: Studien zur Philosophie von Thomas Reid und David Hume*. Weinheim, 1986.

Manns, James. "Beauty and Objectivity in Thomas Reid." *British Journal of Aesthetics* 28.2 (Spring 1988): 115–131.

Nauckhoff, Josefine C. "Objectivity and Expression in Thomas Reid's Aesthetics." *Journal of Aesthetics and Art Criticism* 52.2 (Spring 1994): 183–191.

Robbins, D. O. "The Aesthetics of Thomas Reid." *Journal of Aesthetics and Art Criticism* 5 (1942): 37–38.

JOSEFINE NAUCKHOFF

REINHARDT, AD (1913–1967), American painter, critic, and art activist. Coming of age in the United States in the 1930s, Reinhardt saw himself not as an innovator but rather as the uncompromising militant in defense of the "timeless" tradition of radical modern avant-garde art. Abstraction is an ethos that with Reinhardt assumed the standing of a ideological cause. In paintings that at last approached, yet never quite reached, the absolute condition of black, Reinhardt remained an idealist in both his art and his politics, resisting any popular or ingratiating form. His car-toons of aesthetic and art-political "isms," published from college on into maturity, show Reinhardt early on to have been criticizing the sociologically distracted ideology of abstraction from within.

Reinhardt's assimilation, synthesis, and deliberate reduction of radical abstraction antecedent to his era, and the significance of this artistic process, are symptomatic of the ethos that attaches to abstraction immediately after World War II. If viewed historically, Reinhardt came to be known as the most extreme of those New York school painters whose color field reductions of formal and symbolic content enabled an abstract painting of aesthetic rectitude.

A chronology that Reinhardt himself compiled of his life-world in 1966 reveals the narrative the artist wished for himself and art. The year 1913 is miraculous on this account: Reinhardt's birth, coinciding with the fact that "Malevich paints first geometric-abstract painting," announces an implicit design for Reinhardt's future development as an artist. In 1914, Henri Matisse paints *Porte-Fenêtre, Collioure* appears, and "Mondrian begins 'plus-minus' paintings." Reinhardt will later cite Piet Mondrian and Matisse, together with the Cubists, as indispensable to art history.

The significance of this is that, in Reinhardt's constructed narration of his career after the fact, he acknowledged his historical antecedent in the Suprematist icon of nonobjectivity, Kasimir Malevich's *Black Square* of 1913. Liberated from resemblances, the *Black Square* is a radical expression of something like the highest level of mind, an absolute mind in art to which Reinhardt refers in mature work, culminating in his reconceiving the notion of black on black in paintings achieved during the last decade of his life.

Aesthetically, Suprematism and Neoplasticism attain to idealist explanations of a concrete reality, and the concrete realizations of idealist syntheses informing Suprematism and Neoplasticism will in turn inform Reinhardt's aesthetic vocabulary. Malevich's own polemic reflects the changing lexicon of the avant-garde in Soviet Russia. Initially, Malevich speaks of the pure plasticity of Suprematist art as achieving a compound of "utilitarian reason and intuitive reason"; by 1920, he speaks of plastic relationships among lines and planes forming a dynamic "system." The idealist and utopian construal of concrete form similarly holds true in Mondrian's scheme of things, for, having penetrated nature, abstraction has achieved the "expression of relationships" exclusively. Perpendicularity expresses the "one permanent relationship," attaining, as it does, an equilibrium of spirit with matter, active with passive, male with female, truth with beauty. Reinhardt will assume the mantle of this aesthetic. By the late 1940s, he will have adapted a version of Mondrian's late Neoplasticism to a contrapuntal horizontality of planes within a vertical format.

More like annals that pick events of historical significance highly selectively and leave conspicuous gaps, Reinhardt's chronology displays its partisan view of world-historical events as though providing the relevant context for the artist's own life: "1917 October Revolution in Russia. Lenin replaces Kerensky. 1921 Abstract painters have trouble in Russia. 1922 Mexican painters issue anti 'art for art's sake' manifesto. Joyce completes *Ulysses*. 1923 Duchamp gives up painting."

Sampling this chronology brings into focus further cultural constellations of personal significance to Reinhardt. "1929 Museum of Modern Art opens. Stock market crashes. Georgia O'Keeffe paints 'Black Cross, New Mexico'." A nexus of events in Reinhardt's life-world that indicates not only themes but the content of these themes, and the value invested in them.

"1931 Enters Columbia College. 1932 Paints studies of Michelangelo's Sistine Ceiling figures for literature class of Raymond Weaver, who suggests courses with Meyer Schapiro, who suggests joining radical campus groups." This notation is symptomatic of the relation of art to politics and social action in Reinhardt's understanding of things. Schematically put, for Reinhardt there is no contradiction in the phrase "political artist," if it means that an artist is radical in art, and radical in politics without appeasement to the public taste in either activity. One can be a political artist without doing what is popularly construed as political art, the subject matter of which is overtly about politics. Finally, one can be a political artist insofar as commerce is resisted and materialistic values are disdained.

"1943 Tries to talk Thomas Merton out of becoming a Trappist. Refuses to help Arshile Gorky start a camouflage school. Wonders what Adolph Gottlieb and Mark Rothko are up to when they announce, 'There is no such thing as good painting about nothing.' Continues making paintings about nothing." The axiological aetheticism of Reinhardt is in place. It comes in part to his having subscribed to Clive Bell's notion that "all uncompromising belief is religious" (not that Bell urged subscription to religion as such). Reinhardt also responds to Bell's notion that, pictorial content having been dispensed with, certain combinatory relations appear as significant form (Bell, 1914). An aesthetic "disinterestedness" capable of sparking ironies and paradoxes characterizes Reinhardt's attitude toward art. Although Reinhardt had read Søren Kierkegaard and Friedrich Nietzsche in his German literature seminar at Columbia University, the renunciations he professes are those expendable to abstraction in art, including marks of individuality and variety. As Reinhardt sees it, the renunciations are positive choices for the integrity of abstraction. Ethical resistance to journalism and commerce, because they encourage easy choices in art, does not imply withdrawal from the world.

"1944 Liberation of Paris." Reinhardt notes the first show in an art gallery, and in this year and those following World War II other professional events interleave notices of peace, wars, and independence.

The late 1940s brings a crisis of competing modes of abstraction. Alternating between hard-edge and painterly facture, Reinhardt's compositions chromatically calibrate fragmented labyrinthine elements dispersed throughout the visual field. In some works from around 1946 to 1949, small calligraphic gestures disperse across a monochromatic field even as, in other paintings, contrasting or close-valued tesserae of color assume modular form. Then, too, taking into account later Neoplasticism (owing in part to Carl Holty's intervening introduction to Mondrian), by 1951 Reinhardt's restatement will come to systematize a few large tesserae by relating them symmetrically.

Reinhardt's mature style announces itself through entries beginning in 1953: "Gives up principles of asymmetry and irregularity in painting" and "Paints last paintings in bright colors." From 1950 to 1953, Reinhardt concentrates on a counterpoint of optically keyed planes, oriented horizontally within a vertical field. A state of dynamism through "certain magnetic interrelations" of planes in Malevich, or equilibrium in Mondrian (especially those canvases of 1917 in which tonal pinks and tinted blues align with gray in a gridded field), has assumed a singular opticality once Reinhardt, graying his colors, brings close-valued chromatism into privileged cohesiveness (see Bois, 1991).

In the next decade, pictorial dynamism will come to be expressed in forces at rest in the perfect symmetry of Reinhardt's off-black cruciform composition, "at rest yet no less binding after all," as Hermann Weyl puts it when lecturing on symmetry. Meanwhile, however, one observes Reinhardt's concern to establish formal cohesion, and through cohesion, necessity.

A concern with form's structural entailment is culturally pervasive as well. Beyond Weyl's celebrated book *Symmetry*, deriving from a 1951 lecture series, the events and publications that aggregate in evidence also include "Aspects of Form"—a symposium held in conjunction with the exhibition "On Growth and Form" at the Institute of Contemporary Art, London, and published in book form 1951, in homage to D'Arcy Thompson's classic work *On Growth and Form* (1924)—to provide an instance of the reinvigoration of logical and scientific thought after the cataclysmic interruption of World War II. These publications are indicative of cultural concerns for congruent arrangements (a definition of geometry employed by Weyl) in the artistic milieu that Reinhardt found compatible.

The collective wish for stable structures developing into form language are revealed through Reinhardt's own words. Participating in the three-day symposium on art published in *Modern Artists in America* (1951), Reinhardt, at odds with Willem de Kooning, assumes synonymy between geometry and intellectual clarity and is particularly keen on distinguishing geometry in other ways: "An emphasis on geometry is an emphasis on the 'known,' on order and knowledge." He inquires of Hedda Sterne whether her art is, as it suggests, "planned and preconceived." By these comments, Reinhardt reveals his own concern for an abstraction that signifies structure rather than expression. He insists on an art that is "classic" in form.

"1953 Visits Greece. Daughter born. 1954 Cambodia, Laos, Vietnam achieve independence. Macdonald Wright returns to Abstract Art. 1955 Listed in *Fortune* magazine as one of top twelve investments in art market. 1956 Borrows money from bank to travel. Suez crisis. Makes last cartoon, a mandala." From travels to Greece in 1953 and travels to Japan, India, Persia, and Egypt in 1958, and to Turkey, Syria, and Jordan in 1961, there accumulated "hundreds of color slides" (Wittman, 1992). These he presented at the Artists' Club on 10 October 1958 and 23 January 1959, in a two-thousand-slide lecture titled "An Evening of Slides: The Moslem World and India." The lecture, as well as an album of photographs from travels aggregating architectural detail by structural theme, indicate Reinhardt's intentions for an imaginary museum of world art. Clustered by formal motif or structural function are pyramids, arches, windows, lattice ornaments, and crosses, among many forms. Predominantly architectural, the album also collates painting in this personal "museum without walls." The implicit intention would be to derive a universal language of form implicative of necessity in painting.

Ultimately significant is Reinhardt's very choice of travel destinations: traditional and ancient civilizations, the form languages of which are utterly antithetical to the premium on novelty in the West. But this only substantiates Reinhardt's commitment to the tradition of abstraction and gives credence to his belief that form is an expression of thought within art, thought re-created throughout historical time—hence timeless. Notions of progress in art were, therefore, ill conceived in Reinhardt's view of things, and held no sway against the notion of stylistic recurrence. Reinhardt found this attitude shored up through the writing of Henri Focillon, whose *The Life of Form*, originally published in France in 1934 (and translated by George Kubler in 1948), became a "classic" for students of art and literature soon after, and provided the direct inspiration for Kubler's equally revered argument for "a linked succession of prime works with replications," in *The Shape of Time*, published in 1962 and reviewed favorably by Reinhardt.

Meanwhile, Reinhardt has given up publishing cartoons, for instance, those on art-historical lineage whereby the modern trunk is all that remains once the representational limb snaps (1948), and the abstract limb, weighed down by ideology and commerce, comes crashing down (1960). As Lucy Lippard (1981) remarks, Reinhardt engaged in political activity throughout his life, and civil liberties were always very much on his mind; indeed, as his notebooks say, "Painting cannot be the only activity of a mature artist." But by announcing the end of cartooning with a mandala that brings a phase of public chastisement of the art world to a close, Reinhardt renounces a certain form of applied polemic for an argument conveyed through the internalized polemic of fine art alone. In 1959, he sends a Black Painting to be the hermetic companion of the Trappist Thomas Merton, who already had taken a vow of silence.

"Black as Symbol and Concept," written in 1967, the year of his death, shows Reinhardt continuing to contemplate the meaning of the term to which he had devoted himself since 1955:

> I once organized a talk on black, and I started with black as a symbol, black as a color, and the connotation of black in our culture where our whole system is imposed on us in terms of darkness, lightness, blackness, whiteness. Goodness and badness are associated with black. As an artist I would like to eliminate the symbolic pretty much, for black is interesting not as a color but as a non-color and as the absence of color.

If intentions matter, then this statement reveals Reinhardt's own shift in the nature of "meaningless" art for art's sake over the years. If anything, Reinhardt now chooses to reinforce the positive sense of the once derogatory Stalinist use of meaningless formalism by declaring the irrelevancy of even the traditional symbolic meanings of black in art history and culture. Yet, throughout this talk, Reinhardt in fact continues to accrete, in effect, shades of the symbolism he has just forsworn.

The Black Paintings, then, may be said to embody the conventional cultural symbolism of black newly aestheticized and designated as such. Pragmatically, the Black Paintings remain as they were once for him, a "free, unmanipulated and unmanipulatable, useless, unmarketable, irreducible, unphotographable, unreproducible, inexplicable icon." Epistemologically, the Black Paintings are meant to stand for the epitome of painting even as they resist every Western satisfaction with things identifiably known as paintings. Sometimes considered icons without iconography, these Black Paintings take their (paradoxically) replete meaninglessness from known ideas of spirituality informing traditional religion and culture. Presupposed by Reinhardt is fulfillment of these traditions in the art, art history, and the endless cycle of universally renewed aesthetic ideas that bring forth art through time.

Metaphysically, the spiritual content of traditional cultures informs Reinhardt's own, whether the artist legislates against this meaning or not (Masheck, 1978; Inboden and Kellein, 1985). This includes Christianity, if not its institutions. Friends with Thomas Merton since their days at Columbia, Reinhardt retained respect for religion as being better than any business, for the value placed in principled integrity and the resistance to worldliness. In a postwar ecumenical spirit, Reinhardt further prized the "negative theology" of Buddhism as well as the likes of Meister Eckehart in the West. "The tao is dim and dark," Reinhardt quotes Laozi in his talk "Black as Symbol and Concept." The posi-

REINHARDT. Ad Reinhardt, *Black Paintings* (23 December 1966–15 January 1967), photograph of Ad Reinhardt room; Jewish Museum Exhibition, New York. (Copyright by the Artists Rights Society, New York; photograph courtesy of the Jewish Museum/Art Resource, New York; used by permission.)

tive value of black as a signifier of receptivity may complement the Pietist equilibrium achieved through union of dualistic spiritualist principles.

He was confident in the universal and lawlike nature of painting, and largely impervious to the cultivation of doubt in his humanist contemporaries, insofar as the affirmation of belief also coincides with his assertion of negation set forth in contemporary modes of thought. Yet, a phenomenological existentialism may also be said to inform Reinhardt's writing on art, and in notes to himself, the concept of black as "absence" or "negative presence" coexists alongside "dematerialization, nonbeing" and "the dark of absolute freedom." Thus, by the time Reinhardt delivered his seminar talk "Black as Symbol and Concept," he was intent on emphasizing the entirety of cultural content of black: "I want to emphasize the idea of black as intellectuality and conventionality."

Finally, however, black conventionally signifies the radical principle itself. If, in Alexei Kruchenikh's *Victory over the Sun* (1913), the eclipse of the sun supersedes the world as it is in everyday life, Malevich's blackening square done in backdrop shows—to the extent it symbolizes anything—the sun in eclipse, a metonomy for nature in eclipse. An eclipse of objective for nonobjective art expresses the aesthetic principle in extremis. It is a principle of radical commit-

ment to art as art. Eclipsing nature for culture informs the Black Paintings by Reinhardt, and ultimately identifies painting as a sign for itself.

That black absorbs all pigmented color may be a material fact that Reinhardt exploits to make a point about painting at the limits of its own enterprise, and the synonymy of painting with self-reflexivity. In this sense, Reinhardt's aesthetic meaning differs from that proposed by Malevich in his famous 1918 white-on-white canvas. Reinhardt's messianic utopianism proffers no "futurism." Instead, it signifies an eternal present. Contemplative rather than active, Reinhardt's darkly hued blacks would seek to manifest a certain antithesis of Suprematism in a steady-state dialectic.

"Art-as-art" in Reinhardt's lexicon would then fulfill its prescription for art. The tincture of color that renders black "almost" black is suggestive of an articulation of the absolute situation for painting; or, it is suggestive of the articulation of final painting. Whether art-as-art does not finally suggest the limit of painting (Bois, 1991) rather than nature's extinction is an issue still under discussion.

"1966 One hundred twenty paintings at Jewish Museum." The significance of Reinhardt's art, as with Reinhardt himself, lies with an idea of artistic integrity and purpose. In a more immediate historical sense, it inspired a younger generation of artists (arguably named Minimalists) to imitate an aesthetic of formalism even as it provoked a materialism in reaction. Surface and support determining the quantification of aesthetic result appear in the work of Frank Stella, Robert Ryman, and others, to substantiate through constitutive means the physical nature of painting as object. Despite the competition offered by Pop Art on the one hand, and varieties of conceptual art on the other, the sort of dematerialization embodied in Reinhardt's art remains substantially unchanged in the formal grammar developed from the principles and methods of structuralism emerging thereafter.

At the same time, the consummation of a tradition also implies an exhaustion of that tradition. Cued by Reinhardt's statement that his are the "last paintings one can make," critics have found the work to intend a minimal expressivity and a minimal content (Wollheim, 1965). On this account, not only has the pictorial subject matter been vacated, but the canvas appears vacant, owing to the elimination of only the most necessary differentiation made to render the artifact a work of art.

On other accounts, Reinhardt's art announces a postformalist era, insofar as composition and other creative choices are deemed to be expendable to abstraction as a sign of itself. Whether in Ellsworth Kelly's or Gerhard Richter's canvases showing a mechanistically charted color series in modular extension, or, for that matter, in Andy Warhol's replication of the commercial image and object, the so-called exhaustion of form has been said to emerge in part from the grid that Reinhardt eventually preconceived in lieu of composition. Further rationalizing painting's exhaustion is the metaphor of entropy, as a metaphor derived from the science of natural systems popular in the 1950s and 1960s. Art discourse would then find form exhaustion implicative of some Minimalism and/or dematerialized conceptual art, especially such as that of James Turrell, for which (in analogy with Reinhardt) actual emanating light or its palpable absence tests the limits of phenomenal visibility.

Reinhardt's art has continued to remain paradoxical in the meaning and significance imputed to it. Replete with meaning, yet also meaninglessness; symbolist yet concrete, it has contributed to a history of art in which recurrence rather than progress of formal language is the norm, while bringing art to the point of, if not extinction, then objectlessness.

[See also Abstraction; Malevich; Modernism; and Mondrian.]

BIBLIOGRAPHY

Works by Reinhardt

Art-as-Art: The Selected Writings of Ad Reinhardt. Edited by Barbara Rose. New York, 1975; reprint, Berkeley, 1991.
Modern Artists in America. Edited by Ad Reinhardt, Robert Motherwell, and Bernard Karpel. New York, 1951.

Other Sources

Arnason, H. H. "The Quest for Art-Is-Art." In Ad Reinhardt: Black Paintings, 1951–1967. New York, 1970.
Bell, Clive. Art. New York, 1914.
Bois, Yve-Alain. "The Limit of Almost." In Ad Reinhardt. New York, 1991.
Inboden, Gudrun, and Thomas Kellein. Ad Reinhardt. Stuttgart, 1985.
Kubler, George. The Shape of Time: Remarks on the History of Things. New Haven, 1962.
Lippard, Lucy R. Ad Reinhardt. New York, 1981.
Malevich, Kasimir S. Essays on Art, 1915–1933. 2d ed. Translated by Xenia Glowacki-Prus and Arnold McMillan, edited by Troels Andersen. New York, 1971.
Mascheck, Joseph. "Two Sorts of Monk: Reinhardt and Merton." Artforum (December 1978). Reprinted in Historical Present: Essays of the 1970s (Ann Arbor, 1984).
Mondrian, Piet. Natural Reality and Abstract Reality. Translated by Martin S. James. New York, 1995.
Rowell, Margit. Ad Reinhardt and Color. New York, 1986.
Weyl, Hermann. Symmetry. Princeton, N.J., 1952.
Wittman, Walter T. "Ad Reinhardt Collection." Museum of Modern Art Library Bulletin 85 (Fall 1992).
Wollheim, Richard. "Minimal Art." Arts Magazine (January 1965).

MARJORIE WELISH

RELATIVISM. Relativists standardly make two claims: first, with regard to some subject matter, they claim that there is no universal standard for understanding or evaluating it; second, they claim that the correctness of an understanding or evaluation always depends on something local, such as a conceptual scheme, conventions or norms shared within a community, or the reactions of a group or an individual. There are two main subject matters for relativism in aesthetics: relativism about aesthetic value judgments (e.g., "William Shakespeare's Hamlet is a great tragedy") and relativism about interpretative judgments or claims ("It is Hamlet's Oedipus complex that causes him to hesitate").

One can be a relativist about the truth of these judgments by claiming that this varies with a variation in conceptual scheme, in community norms or conventions, or simply in the actual or hypothetical reactions pro or con of individuals or groups. Such a relativism implies that these judgments are true or false, but not true or false simpliciter. Rather, their truth-value is relative to scheme, convention, or individual or group reaction. Hence, not all conjunctions of (nonrelativized) true judgment preserve truth.

One might instead be a relativist about the justification of such judgments, claiming that what would justify them for one group differs from what would justify them for another, depending again on variation in scheme, convention/norm, reaction, or, alternatively, differences in histories or practices. A relativist regarding justification might not be one regarding truth. This might be because one believes these judgments to lack truth-value or because one believes that their truth-value is nonrelative.

Finally (for the purposes of this survey), one may be a relativist about the very meaning of such judgments. Thus, if one believes that one's procedures of justification enter into the meaning of one's aesthetic value judgments, and these procedures vary from group to group, then the meaning of these judgments would also vary from group to group. Two individuals from different groups might say, "Pablo Picasso's *Guernica* is a great painting," but they would be making different statements. An individual from a third group might at first appearance deny the first two judgments by claiming that *Guernica* is not great. But if her standards of justification were different in nature than those of the others, and the assumption holds that these standards enter into the meaning of her judgment, then she says something different from, but not strictly inconsistent with, the others.

Motivations for Relativism. What makes a relativistic position attractive? One of the strongest and most widespread reasons for embracing relativism is the existence of seemingly irresolvable disagreements with regard to both judgments of value (in aesthetics as well as ethics) and interpretative claims. Such disputes appear to continue without closure, and often without mutual agreement on the evidence or considerations that would produce closure. This motivation is epistemic in nature, based on a problem of establishing value judgments and interpretative claims to everyone's satisfaction.

A second reason to accept some form of relativism derives from a sociological or political conception of the origin of aesthetic value judgments and interpretative claims. It is sometimes suggested that these judgments and claims have their basis in supporting the hegemony or legitimacy of a particular class, or group, whether a large social class such as the bourgeoisie or a small academic subdiscipline. Given such a view, it might seem plausible to suppose that such judgments and claims have validity only within the relevant group. If, as suggested in the preceding paragraph, there really were no generally accepted evidential criteria for accepting or rejecting the statements in question, that fact might bolster this view of them.

A third motivation for accepting relativism is that there is a way of conceiving of the world that can provide a reason for doing so. There is no easy way to state this conception, but a simple rendering would be that the world is in part constructed by human cognitive activity (by perceiving, conceiving, theorizing, and interpreting). What is meant is not merely that among the things that exist are artifacts that are in part the result of the cognitive activity of their makers. What is meant is that even "natural objects" are at least in part constructed, and artifacts reconstructed, by our ways of thinking about them. Add now to this idea that this construction of the world varies according to historical period, tradition, society and culture, and language or conceptual scheme, and one has a basis for believing that the truth,

justification, and even the meaning of our statements would also vary and be relative. The basis of this relativism, however, is itself a kind of ontological relativism that would be in need of independent justification.

A final motivation is based on an understanding of the appreciation appropriate to art and the role of interpretation in bringing about this appreciation. One appreciates many works of art by interpreting them, and if one can come to interpret them in more than one way, perhaps in many ways, then the possibilities and opportunities for appreciation are enhanced. Hence, the practice of interpretation ought to, and in fact does, allow for multiple interpretations of artworks, even interpretations that often seem to clash. This has suggested to many that some sort of relativism is required by the very nature of art, or the very point of art appreciation, in order to explain how clashing interpretations can all be acceptable. This relativism would carry over to aesthetic value judgments insofar as they are based on interpretations of artworks.

Relativism about Aesthetic Value Judgments. Although all of the motivations just mentioned are influential, it is the first that has been most important in discussions of aesthetic value, whereas the final one has been dominant in discussions of interpretive claims.

The crucial issue regarding aesthetic value judgments was concisely set out by David Hume in his brief but much-discussed essay "Of the Standard of Taste." Everyone recognizes the great variety of tastes that inform evaluative judgments and that creates the disagreements noted earlier. A painting that seems vibrant to one spectator may seem gaudy to another. An avant-garde gesture that seems profound to one spectator may seem respectively gratuitous, banal, and superficial to three others. Some of this diversity in judgment results from defects in the spectator, who may be biased, uninformed, or insufficiently sensitive to the nuances of an art form. Even after judgments defective in these and other ways are disqualified, it is plausible that differences in taste—that is, differences in the way individuals perceive and react to artworks—will result in different evaluations of the same work. This suggest that evaluations are relative to taste, however "taste" is ultimately defined. [*See* Hume.]

Whether one accepts such a relativism depends on at least two issues. The first issue concerns the nature of artistic value. What are the properties that make works valuable as artworks? The relativist claims that these properties are to be defined in part in terms of potentially variable reactions (tastes). Second, even if the relativist is right on this matter, are some tastes (possibly a single taste) better than others? For example, perhaps there are some tendencies to react to artworks that are more likely to deliver more valuable experiences and other things of value than other tendencies. These issues are only beginning to receive the attention they deserve and remain largely unresolved.

Relativism about Interpretation. An obsessive concern with the interpretability of art and literature, along with many other phenomena, has been characteristic of the thought of the twentieth century. To get a proper perspective on the nature and plausibility of a relativistic position about interpretation, it should be distinguished from another doctrine with which it is easily confused. The doctrine is critical pluralism, which claims that, for many works of art and literature, there are multiple, acceptable interpretations that cannot be combined into a single acceptable interpretation. The doctrine with which critical pluralism is usually thought to directly compete is critical monism, the view that there is a single true interpretation of each work of art and literature that captures the meaning of those works. Critical pluralism is widely, though not universally, accepted. The acceptance of critical pluralism is not, however, tantamount to the acceptance of relativism. Relativists are pluralists, but not all pluralists are relativists.

Relativism provides one explanation for the truth of critical pluralism. The standard relativist explanation is that the correctness of an interpretation is not determined simply by its adequacy to the work under interpretation, but by the conventions, assumptions, or norms of a community of interpreters. Correctness is relative to such a community. The correctness of interpretation i of a work w in community c_1 does not imply correctness in any other interpretive community, and hence there is no valid inference from the fact that i is correct in c_1, and j is correct in c_2, to the conclusion that the conjunction of i and j gives a correct interpretation of w. Because this implies that there are acceptable, noncombinable interpretations of w, the truth of critical pluralism is secured by this route.

One of the clearest examples of this standard version of relativism in contemporary thought is provided by the writings of Stanley Fish. Fish not only holds that interpretations of a given work are true only relative to the assumptions of an interpretive community, but that this is so because works acquire meaning only when these assumptions are applied to them. Hence, the very meaning that works possess and the justification for ascribing such meaning to them are also relative to such communities.

An alternative view is advanced by Joseph Margolis under the label "robust relativism." Margolis rejects the standard relativist approach of indexing the truth or warrant of an interpretation, or the meaning of an object of interpretation, to a community. His alternative is to claim that interpretive claims are to be understood within a many-valued logic. On such a logic, interpretative claims can be false, but are never true. Instead, they are affirmed by "truthlike" predicates such as "plausible," "reasonable," and "apt." According to Margolis, this view permits one to affirm (as plausible, reasonable, or apt) interpretations that would be logically inconsistent, that is, incapable of being true together, in a bivalent logic. Such interpretations nevertheless remain "nonconverging" even within the many-valued logical framework. If Margolis is right about all of this, then he offers an alternative route to critical pluralism, because on his view too there are acceptable, noncombinable interpretations.

Robust relativism resembles standard relativism in claiming that the appearance of logical inconsistency between interpretative claims that we accept is illusory, because, when properly understood, both claims make true (or truthlike) claims that nevertheless cannot be conjoined. Hence, although they offer different routes to critical pluralism, they are routes that share a somewhat similar strategy.

There are nonrelativistic ways of establishing pluralism, however. One is to take matters a step further than Margolis and deny that interpretations make claims that are true, false, or even truthlike. On this view, an interpretation's acceptability is determined in other ways, such as its ability to heighten appreciation of a work. Clearly, there can be interpretations that are acceptable because they accomplish this, but are noncombinable because, when yoked together, they fail to enhance appreciation.

There are more conservative strategies that suffice to establish critical pluralism. Suppose one holds the view that interpretations of a work are to be constrained by the conventions in place when it is created (not conventions in place when it is being interpreted, as relativists tend to hold), and only by such conventions. Such a constraint provides a standard of acceptability that applies to all interpretations, but may permit several noncombinable interpretations of the same work. Or suppose one holds the view that interpretations of a work are acceptable if one is justified in believing that they were intended by the creator of the work (whether or not they were really so intended). Again, several different interpretations may satisfy this requirement.

Finally, one can arrive at critical pluralism by recognizing that one interprets with different aims. Sometimes one aims at understanding a work as the product of the historically situated artist. Sometimes one merely looks for *an* understanding of a work, one that makes plausible sense of it in a way that promotes appreciation. Sometimes one aims at maximizing the aesthetic value or intelligibility of a work. Sometimes one is trying to make a work relevant to a particular audience by finding a significance in the work especially appropriate to that group. In the process of pursuing these different aims, one sometimes will offer interpretations that genuinely contradict each other, and hence cannot both be true. Even in this case, both may be acceptable relative to the evidence on hand, which is insufficient to eliminate one of the interpretations. Given the different aims with which one interprets, however, it will often happen that apparently inconsistent interpretations are in fact logically compatible. The assertion that a work can be understood as representing an F is compatible with the assertion that it can be understood as representing not F, but G.

(Grant Wood's *American Gothic* is usually understood as representing a man and his wife, though there is some evidence that it was meant to represent a man and his daughter. It is at least true that it can also be understood in this way.) Although such interpretations are strictly compatible, there may be no point in combining interpretation pursued with different aims (or sometimes the same aim, as in the case just cited).

The last approach also renders compatible critical pluralism with its supposed rival, critical monism. If one interprets with different aims, it is possible that only one of these aims seeks to discover the meaning or core content of a work. It is also possible that there is only one correct interpretation that gives a comprehensive statement of this meaning. This still permits many other acceptable interpretations that aim at something other than identifying work meaning and do not sensibly combine with such a statement. This is not to say that monism is actually true. To establish that would require a great deal of further argument.

Evaluation of Relativism about Interpretation. Sometimes *relativism* is a term used to dismiss a view as being beyond the pale of reason. A universal relativism (e.g., the view that all truth is relative) is sometimes said to be self-refuting because its very assertion implies that at least one truth is not relative (that is, that *all* is relative). The relativisms being examined here, however,—about the interpretation of artworks and aesthetic value judgments—are local rather than universal, and thus could not be criticized in this way.

A limited relativism is not an intrinsically unreasonable doctrine. The question that should be asked is whether the motives for adopting relativism provide sufficient reason to accept it.

It must be said that most of the motivations offered for a relativism about interpretation fail to do this. Of the four reasons for accepting relativism discussed earlier, the first is the apparent irresolvability of interpretative disagreements. Standard relativism explains some of this irresolvability by claiming that many of the disagreements are not real when relativized to different communities. Irresolvability results from the different standards underlying the apparently conflicting interpretative claims. Proponents of this view, however, fail to show that real disagreements within an interpretative community are any more resolvable—as they should be—than merely apparent disagreements among different communities. Robust relativists would claim that interpretations are evaluated as more or less plausible, apt, or reasonable. This process would eliminate some interpretations, while leaving a plurality of others in the field. What a robust relativist is not so clear about is why disagreements should persist beyond this point.

Other approaches offer as good, or better, explanations of interpretative disagreement. The approach that claims that one interprets with different aims would suggest that a certain amount of apparent disagreement arises through unclarity about interpretative aim, through talking at cross-purposes, as it were. The remaining real disagreements have to be handled piecemeal, for resolvability turns on what is actually asserted by an interpretation, and this will vary with aim. Once again, the problem does not require a relativist solution.

A second motivation for relativism is the view that interpretative claims have an underlying social or political basis. Whether or not such a view has plausibility, it supplies the weakest reason to accept relativism—a view about the truth, justification, or meaning of interpretive claims. A political basis for such claims—such as a tendency to help sustain the power of a group—says nothing about the meaning of those claims or whether they are true or justified even within a particular group. Hence, they do not provide a good reason to accept relativism.

A third reason to accept a relativism about interpretive claims derives from an ontological relativism—the idea that what exists is constructed by human cognitive activity and the practices and institutions in which this activity is embedded. This view itself is not easy to understand, and its implications are far from clear. Suppose that it implies that groups with different institutions and practices are interpreting different *Guernica*s and different *Hamlet*s, which are, in part at least, constructed by the cognitive activity of individuals within the respective groups. It would then be true that they would be interpreting objects with different meanings, which would make appropriate different truth claims, but this would be no more surprising than that *Hamlet* and *Twelfth Night* or *Guernica* and *The Man with a Violin* (Picasso, 1912) have different meanings. If one has already established a difference in object of interpretation, one does not need a relativism about meaning or truth to explain differences in interpretative claims.

A final reason for accepting relativism is that the nature of artistic appreciation encourages—perhaps requires—one to accept multiple interpretations of artworks. That, however, merely points to the truth of critical pluralism, and relativism is only one of numerous routes to that doctrine. Hence, this motive provides no compelling argument for relativism.

One can conclude that none of the reasons for accepting relativism about interpretative claims provides compelling reasons to do so. There is a another sort of relativism, however, that does seem compelling. This relativism derives from the view, mentioned earlier, that one interprets works of art with different aims. When one evaluates interpretations, it is plausible that one should bring different standards of acceptability to interpretations with different aims. Thus, it would be wrong to apply the same standard to an interpretation that attempts to recover the intention of the artist and an interpretation that attempts to find significance in a work that would make it relevant to a particular contemporary audience. Success in these two cases involves very different things. Thus, it appears to be true that the acceptability of an interpretation is relative to its aim.

[*See also* Essentialism; Goodman; Historicism; Interpretation; Truth; *and* Universals.]

BIBLIOGRAPHY

Relativism about Aesthetic Value Judgments

Budd, Malcom. *Values of Art: Pictures, Poetry, and Music.* London, 1995.
Goldman, Alan H. *Aesthetic Value.* Boulder, Colo., 1995.
Hume, David. "Of the Standard of Taste." In *Essays: Moral, Political, and Literary,* edited by John W. Lenz, pp. 226–249. Indianapolis, 1987.
Hutcheson, Francis. *An Inquiry into the Original of Our Ideas of Beauty and Virtue* (1725). New York, 1971.
Kant, Immanuel. *Critique of Judgement.* Translated by James Creed Meredith. Oxford, 1952.

Relativism about Interpretation

Carrier, David. *Principles of Art History Writing.* University Park, Pa., 1991.
Fish, Stanley. *Is There a Text in This Class: The Authority of Interpretive Communities.* Cambridge, Mass., 1980.
Iseminger, Gary ed. *Intention and Interpretation.* Philadelphia, 1992.
Krausz, Michael. *Rightness and Reasons: Interpretation in Cultural Practices.* Ithaca, N.Y., 1993.
Margolis, Joseph. *The Truth about Relativism.* Oxford and Cambridge, Mass., 1991.
Margolis, Joseph. "Plain Talk about Interpretation on a Relativistic Model." *Journal of Aesthetics and Art Criticism* 53.2 (Spring 1995): 1–7.
Stecker, Robert. *Artworks: Definition, Meaning, Value.* University Park, Pa., 1997.

ROBERT STECKER

RELIGION AND AESTHETICS. [*To examine the relationship between religion and aesthetics, this entry comprises two essays:*

An Overview
Religion and Art

The first essay explains the relationships between religion and art in the history of aesthetics. The second concerns the relationships between religion and art in the histories of religion and art. For related discussion, see Byzantine Aesthetics; *and* Russian Aesthetic, *article on* Religious Aesthetics.]

An Overview

The religions of humanity and the art of humanity have always been intertwined; neither can be understood without attending to the other. Most religions use music in their rituals and liturgies, and develop architecture to house the performance of their liturgies. Most use poeticized language in their address to God. Most use visual art to keep alive the memory of their founding and defining narrative, and to represent or symbolize the holy and the divine. For these reasons, and many more, the religions call forth art. Then, subsequently, the art shapes the religion—shapes the affections, the emotions, the beliefs, the memories, the actions, of the religious participant and believer. It all happens so naturally that, even in literate cultures, relatively little about art and religion was written down before the modern era. Abbot Suger wrote down some of his thoughts concerning the church of Saint Denis in Paris, whose construction he supervised; Procopius wrote a bit about Hagia Sophia in Constantinople; the church fathers wrote a bit about iconography; Augustine made some comments about the power of liturgical music; and so forth. But in the West, at least, altogether it does not come to much—no substantial reflections on the positive relation of religion to art.

Things do not always go smoothly between religion and art, however. Religions not only evoke art, they reprimand artists, and try to dismiss and exclude certain forms of art; and artists, rather than laboring faithfully in the cause of one or another religion, sometimes rebel and act subversively. In the Occident, the most substantial writing that exists from the premodern era about the relation of religion and art is polemical writing, evoked by points of tension. The most articulate of such polemical writing is that which emerged from the Byzantine iconoclast controversy that raged from around 725 CE until about 840 CE.

Controversies concerning images have erupted repeatedly in the history of Christendom. The biblical proscription of idols has always played a role in these, often up front, sometimes in the background. In the biblical Book of Exodus the second of the Ten Commandments given by God through Moses to Israel states: "You shall not make for yourself an idol, whether in the form of anything that is in heaven above, or that is on the earth beneath, or that is in the water under the earth. You shall not bow down to them or worship them." But although controversies over images have been common, the Byzantines conducted the debate with a level of sophistication never elsewhere equaled. [*See* Icon.] Let it suffice to say here that though a major point of contention throughout the controversy pertained to the appropriate mode of interacting with an image of a holy person—is it appropriate to kneel before such an image and kiss it—there were also debates concerning the worth, and even the legitimacy, of such images. Quite astonishingly, the Byzantine emperor Leo III developed the argument that images of Christ violated the Christological formulas agreed on in earlier councils, and were accordingly heretical. Whereas the councils had declared that Christ's humanity and divinity are inseparable, an image of Christ is only capable of representing him as human, not as divine.

Although the most substantial body of writing about art and religion from the premodern West is polemical in character, that is not true for the closely related topic of beauty. The topic was placed on the intellectual agenda of the West by the Neoplatonists, Plotinus in particular, with Plato's

Symposium in the background. It was generally agreed that beauty is that which pleases upon being contemplated; and a question regularly considered was which features of entities evoke such delight. The answers given varied somewhat: unity, due proportion, clarity, brightness, perfection. But it was agreed by all parties that there is beauty in things because, and insofar as, those things reflect God. God is primordially beautiful.

To understand modern Western discussions about religion and the arts—of which there are a multitude—one must recall the dramatic changes in the arts, and our characteristic way of thinking about them, that took place in eighteenth-century Europe. A number of related things happened more or less simultaneously. First, and perhaps most important, the concept of the aesthetic emerged. Though the concept was related to the older concept of beauty, it was nonetheless significantly different. Beauty had been understood as a property, or "transcendental"; the aesthetic, by contrast, was understood as a distinct sphere of value. Although the eighteenth-century theorists borrowed from the traditional discussions of beauty by defining "aesthetic delight" as delight in contemplating, they added two important qualifications not found in the medieval discussions of beauty: delight in contemplating, to be aesthetic delight, must be *universal,* in the sense that it is grounded in our shared human nature rather than in particularities of makeup or training; and, even more important, it must be *disinterested.* That is to say, it must be independent of delight experienced in the achievement of purposes or the satisfaction of desires. Second, the conviction emerged that art, along with wilderness, is peculiarly apt for evoking such delight. Third, increasingly it became the case that works of art were created, and made available to the bourgeois public in performance and display, for exactly this purpose. Such works and such performances constitute the "high art" of the modern Western world. Fourth, as Paul Oskar Kristeller argues in his well-known article "The Modern System of the Arts" (1965), the conviction solidified that music, poetry, fiction, painting, and sculpture are to be grouped together as paradigmatically "fine" arts. Finally, the conviction emerged that commerce with the arts and wilderness that is aesthetic in its orientation—thus, contemplative and disinterested—is essential to becoming a member of what Joseph Addison, in a pair of articles in *The Spectator* (19 and 21 June 1712), called "polite people," by which he meant, in present-day vocabulary, cultured people. Aesthetic commerce with the arts is essential to the acquisition of what the Germans came to call *Bildung.*

Almost all modern Western discussions of religion and the arts take for granted the coherence and legitimacy of these developments. For example, they focus their attention on the high art of the modern West, and ask what that art has to do with religion. Liturgical art seldom comes into view; when it does, it is regularly dismissed as art that has not yet come into its own. So too for memorial art—art meant to keep alive in a religious community the memory of central events and persons in its founding and defining narrative.

The views on art and religion that have been articulated in the modern West do not appear to fall into any natural classification. One theme that emerged already in the eighteenth century was that of the sublime. When discussing art, wilderness, contemplation, and imagination (imaging), the eighteenth-century theorists spoke regularly not only of beauty but also of sublimity—by which they meant the grand, the majestic, the awesome, to which correspond feelings of being overpowered and being overwhelmed. Writers reported experiencing such feelings in the presence of mountains and oceans, but also, early in the nineteenth century, when listening to the music of Ludwig van Beethoven or reading the poetry of William Wordsworth. Feelings of sublimity were, as one might expect, also regarded as prominent among the religious affections. Friedrich Schleiermacher located the origin of religion in one's primordial feeling of dependence; and that feeling, if not exactly the same as what the eighteenth-century theorists had in mind by feelings of sublimity, certainly incorporated such feelings. Thus, sublimity and its feelings were regularly regarded as connecting art and religion. As to the precise mode of connection, there was little consensus, and often not much clarity. The feelings of sublimity that one sometimes experiences when contemplating wilderness or art—are these merely one species of the genus, feelings of sublimity, with another species being the feelings one has when one senses oneself in the presence of God? Or is the connection closer than that? Are the former feelings themselves somehow religious in character? When one contemplates oceans and mountains, when one listens to Beethoven and reads Wordsworth, are the feelings of sublimity experienced themselves *religious* affections? Is one somehow in the presence of the divine? Is the feeling of sublimity, regardless of its phenomenal object, a religious emotion—perhaps the *primordial* religious emotion?

Somewhere in the latter part of the nineteenth century, sublimity fell from fashion, with the consequence that, since then, beauty has more often been seen as the connector between art and religion than sublimity. The book by the bishop of Oxford, Richard Harries, *Art and the Beauty of God* (1993), is a good example of this approach. Harries argues, in classic neo-Plotinian fashion, and with the assistance of a good many neo-Plotinian references, that beauty in "earthly" things is a reflection of the beauty of God. All beauty is, in that way, of "spiritual" significance. Accordingly, Harries calls the religious person to be sensitive to the beauty in earthly things (lack of such sensitivity indicates a deficiency of spirituality), and he calls the person concerned with the arts to ascend from "earthly" to "heavenly" beauty (lack of sensitivity to "heavenly" beauty indicates a deficiency of openness to the full range of beauty).

This same theme, of art as reflecting God, is found in the essays of Dorothy Sayers and a number of her Anglo-Catholic cohorts. Rather than singling out beauty as the point of connection, however, Sayers and her group focus on artistic creation: the religious believer, she argues, and especially the Christian believer, should see in artistic creation a rich and articulate reflection of the creative activity of the Triune God.

In a line of thought articulated with extraordinary eloquence by Clive Bell in his *Art* (1914), it is not sublimity or beauty but the aesthetic attitude itself that is the fundamental connection between art and the aesthetic. Some writers, such as Frank Burch Brown, have argued that the aesthetic attitude is always an informed attitude, and that part of what enters into its formation, for many people anyway, is their religious convictions. What Bell singles out instead is the supposed disinterestedness of the aesthetic attitude. Definitive of art, Bell argues, is that art has "significant form"—by which he means form that evokes aesthetic emotion. He goes on to ask why it is that human beings are moved by the contemplation of pure form. The answer he proposes is that when it is the pure form of an object that evokes emotion, one has set off to the side all of one's purposes and come face to face with reality itself—Reality. Whether it is called God, says Bell, is a matter of indifference. Disinterested contemplation pierces the veil of human purposes and intentions and puts one in touch with the Ultimate—hence the deep feelings.

Quite a different approach from any of these emerged in the early years of Romanticism. The Romantics were the first great critics of modernity. Their fundamental critique—whether of the new science on which they had their eye, or capitalism, or institutional Protestantism, or French revolutionary politics—was that modernity dissolves the organic unities in society, self, and culture that previously characterized human life. In the words of John Keats, it "unweaves the rainbow." It was also the conviction of the Romantics, however, that the genuine work of art constitutes a true, organic unity. Thus, the work of art provides an image of what society and culture would be like if the dynamics of division and alienation were overcome. Some writers have gone farther and suggested that art not only provides an imagistic symbol of a healed humanity, but is itself an agent for bringing about renewal in society and culture. Repeatedly in the modern period, salvific potential has been ascribed to art. The major aesthetician of the Frankfurt School, Theodor Adorno, was on many points a biting critic of Romanticism. On this point, however, he shared their hopes, albeit guardedly; art, and perhaps art alone, has the potential of casting a "messianic light" on a fractured society.

Finally, the enormously influential line of thought that G. W. F. Hegel initiated should be mentioned. It was Hegel's conviction that art, religion, and philosophy represent alternative ways of giving expression to the mentality, the spirit, the *Geist*, of an age. Art does so in a sensuous medium; religion does so imagistically, though without a sensuous medium; philosophy does so neither imagistically nor in a sensuous medium. Hegel clearly regarded philosophy as the most advanced expression of *Geist*. Yet, he did not regard art and religion as simply outmoded. In any case, he regarded all three—art, religion, and philosophy—as fundamentally united in being cultural expressions of the mentality of an age. The writings on art of the Protestant theologian Paul Tillich are a twentieth-century variant on the Hegelian approach.

As these observations suggest, modern discussions on religion and art have been diffuse. In the eighteenth century, something of extraordinary importance happened to Western art, and to Western ways of thinking about art. A form of high art emerged that has nothing directly to do with the church or any other form of institutional religion. Many theologians and theorists of the arts have nonetheless been convinced that this development did not mean a separation of art from religion, nor of religion from art. Surely, they are right about that. The connections are subtle, however; the multiplicity of lines of attack are witness to that.

It should be mentioned, in conclusion, that a few authors have refused, in their reflections on art and religion, to go along with the majority in focusing all attention on the modern Western institution of high art, and have insisted that an accurate understanding of the interaction between art and religion requires the recognition that the modern Western institution of high art represents an idiosyncratic development within the history of humanity's art. It is true that the high art of the modern West has religious significance, and that this art continues to interact in various ways with religion; but the full story of religion and art cannot be told if one focuses just on this high art. The story of religion and art in earlier ages cannot be told; witness the Byzantine iconoclast controversy mentioned earlier. But neither can the full story of religion and art today. Alongside high art, for example, liturgical and memorial art continue to thrive.

[*See also* Beauty; Iconoclasm and Iconophobia; *and* Sublime.]

BIBLIOGRAPHY

Abrams, M. H. *The Mirror and the Lamp: Romantic Theory and the Critical Tradition.* New York and Oxford, 1953.

Abrams, M. H. *Natural Supernaturalism: Tradition and Revolution in Romantic Literature.* New York, 1971.

Adorno, Theodor W. *Minima Moralia: Reflections from Damaged Life.* Translated by E. F. N. Jephcott. London, 1974.

Adorno, Theodor W. *Aesthetic Theory.* Edited by Gretel Adorno and Rolf Tiedemann, translated by Robert Hullot-Kentor. Minneapolis, 1997.

Balthasar, Hans Urs von. *The Glory of the Lord: A Theological Aesthetics.* 7 vols. Various translators. San Francisco, 1982–1989.

Bell, Clive. *Art.* London, 1914.

Brown, Frank Burch. *Religious Aesthetics: A Theological Study of Making and Meaning.* Princeton, N.J., 1989.

Burke, Edmund. *A Philosophical Inquiry into the Origin of Our Ideas of the Sublime and the Beautiful.* London, 1757.

Dillenberger, John. *A Theology of Artistic Sensibilities: The Visual Arts and the Church.* New York, 1986.

Eco, Umberto. *Art and Beauty in the Middle Ages.* Translated by Hugh Bredin. New Haven, 1986.

Eire, Carlos M. N. *War against the Idols: The Reformation of Worship from Erasmus to Calvin.* Cambridge and New York, 1986.

Harries, Richard. *Art and the Beauty of God.* London, 1993.

Hegel, Georg Wilhelm Friedrich. *Aesthetics: Lectures on Fine Art.* 2 vols. Translated by T. M. Knox. Oxford, 1975.

Kant, Immanuel. *Critique of Judgment.* Translated by Werner S. Pluhar. Indianapolis, 1987.

Kristeller, Paul Oskar. "The Modern System of the Arts." In *Renaissance Thought II: Papers on Humanism and the Arts,* pp. 163–227. New York, 1965.

Van der Leeuw, Gerardus. *Sacred and Profane Beauty: The Holy in Art.* Translated by David E. Green. New York, 1963.

Maritain, Jacques. *Art and Scholasticism.* Translated by Joseph W. Evans. New York, 1962.

Maritain, Jacques. *Creative Intuition in Art and Poetry.* Reprint, Princeton, N.J., 1978.

Pelikan, Jaroslav. *Imago Dei: The Byzantine Apologia for Icons.* Princeton, N.J., 1990.

Sayers, Dorothy. *The Mind of the Maker.* London, 1941.

Sayers, Dorothy. *Christian Letters to a Post-Christian World.* Edited by Roderick Jellema. Grand Rapids, Mich., 1969.

Tatarkiewicz, Wladyslaw. *A History of Six Ideas.* Translated by Christopher Kasparek. The Hague, 1980.

Tillich, Paul. *On Art and Architecture.* Edited by John Dillenberger and Jane Dillenberger, translated by Robert P. Scharlemann. New York, 1987.

Wandel, Lee Palmer. *Voracious Idols and Violent Hands: Iconoclasm in Reformation Zurich, Strasbourg, and Basel.* Cambridge and New York, 1995.

Wolterstorff, Nicholas. *Art in Action: Toward a Christian Aesthetic.* Grand Rapids, Mich., 1980.

NICHOLAS WOLTERSTORFF

Religion and Art

The question of the relations between art and religion can be analyzed according to four complementary approaches, at once thematic and chronological:

1. the role of art and the controversies surrounding it in the definition of religious identities;
2. the functions and practices—private and public, orthodox and heterodox, liturgical and devotional—of the religious image;
3. the substitution of the work of art for the cultual (or cultic) image and the modern emergence of an aesthetic posture;
4. the religion of art.

Such an analysis is comprehensive, yet it avoids being a general synthesis and does not privilege an ahistorical history of ideas.

Art and the Definition of Religious Identities. May one see in the place conceded to art a satisfactory criterion for distinguishing different cultures and the forms of religious experience they favor? There is a general consensus here (Baaren, 1962) to oppose, in this respect, magic and religion. In the case of magic, cultual objects are generally realized by those who use them, are not destined to be viewed permanently by a large public, and are tied to the manipulation of natural forces. In the case of religion, the objects refer to supernatural forces and to the acquired distinctions among professional clerics and producers and spectators of artworks, and thus, ultimately, to the need to legitimize these last and to define their usages within the church—that is, to elaborate a theology, a liturgy, and a discipline of images. If one limits oneself to Europe and the figurative arts, one can only note that the attitude of great religions of the Book with regard to images has served to accentuate religious borders and differences.

Even if it is necessary to give up the cliché of radical Jewish and Muslim aniconism (that is, absolute renunciation of religious imagery), as recent works (Sed-Rajna, in Boespflug and Lossky, 1987) and archaeological discoveries (the synagogue of Dura-Europos) show, there is no doubt that in the interval between late antiquity and the Middle Ages, the gap in facts, and above all in mental outlooks, became more pronounced between a Christianity unified by the use of images and by the pilgrimages (Wirth, 1989) and other religions. Countless examples of such a divergence are provided by the religious controversies among Jews, Christians, and Muslims; by the direct confrontations at the time of the Crusades; and by more or less legendary accounts (Jean-Claude Schmitt, in Boespflug and Lossky, 1987).

The parallel history of Greek and Latin Christianities is a testimony as well to the role played by the question of the image in the definition of religious orthodoxies. The iconoclastic crisis of the eighth century and the final success of iconodules had lasting consequences. Not only did the fathers of the Second Council of Nicaea (787) confirm the legitimacy of figurative and anthropomorphic representation, but they made the practice of icon worship obligatory as well. For a long time, they delineated the position of the Greek church in affirming that the icon is the imprint of the prototype, which is, as it were, present in it; it thus takes part in the nature of the prototype and establishes a direct connection between humans and God. John of Damascus affirms also: "I do not venerate matter, but rather the Creator of matter who became matter for me and who deigned to live in matter and perform the work of salvation by matter." The icon is thus a theology of presence, indissociable from the Incarnation. Closely linked with the liturgy that it intensifies and clarifies, the icon will thus be a gospel (Nikephoros). In the preparation of the icon, the artist is only an agent whose conformity with the rules is expected above all. The Frankish church rejected the conclusions of the Second Council of Nicaea and established, notably in the *Libri Carolini*, a via media destined to a long posterity in the West. The Frankish bishops recognized only the pedagogical, memorial, and ornamental functions of images, refusing the idea of the passage of the image to the prototype in religious practices, the notion of an access to the invisible world by visible objects, and above all the idea of the presence of the prototype in the image drawing veneration. The opposition between the Orient, which develops a rich and complex theology of the image, and the Occident, which sustains above all a practice and an aesthetics, is thus shaped since the iconoclastic controversy.

Certainly, from the fifth century onward, the East and the West assumed convergent paths, and the worship of images took on similar aspects on both sides. Despite this rapprochement and the considerable success of the Byzantine icons that flooded the Occident beginning with the Fourth Crusade and the fall of Constantinople—such as the icon of Suffering Christ represented in mosaics around 1300 and transferred from Rome to Santa Croce in Jerusalem in 1380 (Belting, 1990; Os, 1994)—the gap has never been closed. Moreover, as a form of creative liberation, the Renaissance made an effort to break with the techniques and the iconography of the icon. Giorgio Vasari thus recalled the meaning of the innovations of Cimabue, who knew how to surpass his masters who worked not in the Greek manner of Antiquity, but in that of the modern Greeks.

Within the very interior of Latin Christianity, the quarrel over images precipitated the confessional explosion of the sixteenth century and played a decisive role in the makeup of religious boundaries between Catholics, Lutherans, Calvinists, and dissidents. The break between Martin Luther and the radical reform of Andreas Bodenstein von Carlstadt and Thomas Münzer took place in the winter of 1521–1522 in large part as a result of this quarrel. In England and the Netherlands, the internal disputes over Protestant confessions were as lively as those between Protestants and Catholics. The Lutheran via media (the condemnation of idolatry as well as iconoclasm, the retention of certain images for noncultual ends, a simplification of the themes and a predilection for the episodes of the Passion represented with a didactic care) led then to a combat on two fronts between Catholic iconoduly, confirmed by the Tridentine decree of December 1563 concerning the relics of saints and images and Calvinist iconophobia. The efforts to establish a reconciliation between Protestants and Orthodox stumbled as well over the image, following the example of the discussions (1574–1581) between the theologians of Tübingen and the patriarch of Constantinople (Michalski, 1993).

The problem of adaptation partially complicates the analysis with regard to architecture: the utilization in Christian churches of architectural elements taken or copied from Roman monuments, the conversion of churches into mosques or of mosques into churches, and the transformations of Catholic churches into Protestant temples suggest a greater flexibility. In a general manner, art, including music, seemed to have constituted, and to constitute still, an effective religious marker. The scandal raised in autumn 1995 by the destruction of the image of the Virgin of Brazil, relayed by the world press, bears a supplementary proof.

Functions and Practices of the Religious Image. The question of the relationships between art and religion covers three interdependent but distinct problems:

1. the artistic treatment of themes, dogmas, and religious personages: choice and diffusion of subjects, evolution of styles and techniques, innovations and iconographic repetitions
2. the functions of religious art and the immense diversity of usages—orthodox and heterodox, private and public—of the image (Baxandall 1972, 1980)
3. the position of the churches and clerics in regard to figurative arts, architecture, or music

Concerning images in particular, it is not impossible to identify the dominant and recurring arguments. Since the sixth century in the East and the West, one encounters arguments of a didactic type: for example, in a famous letter by Gregory the Great, for whom paintings are the reading of the illiterate. Arguments of a memorial and emotional type also certainly play a role, as in a sermon that appeared in 1492 according to which images were introduced "firstly because of the lack of education of simple peoples; secondly because of our emotional inertia; thirdly because of the precariousness of our memory" (Baxandall, 1972). Most important are the Christological arguments and considerations on the Incarnation as putting an end to the Old Testament taboo on images (Exodus 20), along with arguments indirectly inspired by the Neoplatonic philosophy of Pseudo-Dionysius the Areopagite, in particular in the East, and by anagogic reasoning, which all consider the icon a receptacle of a constant presence of the divine. Theodore of Studious concludes that once that Christ is born of a describable Mother, he naturally has an image corresponding to that of his Mother; and if he could not be represented in art, it would mean that he was born solely of his Father and was thus not incarnate.

Here, it is only a question of an analytic division, which is impossible to retain in the course of the inquiry because the historical phenomena across the three areas can be understood only in their interaction and intersection. The example of the sixteenth-century quarrel over images, familiarity with which was profoundly revived, suffices to illustrate the point. It quickly proves deceptive to confine oneself to theological controversies to explain the conflicts surrounding the image in the sixteenth century and the iconoclasm that affects the greatest part of Europe. The overwhelming majority of the arguments employed by the adversaries were already found in the quarrel of the eighth century and in the thought of Carolingian theologians (Scavizzi, 1992). In a significant manner, Theodore of Studious, John Damascus, the canons of Nicaea II, and the *Libri Carolini* were edited and often translated during the strongest conflicts of the sixteenth century. Iconoclasm itself did not constitute in any way a radical novelty in the Europe of the 1520s: the medieval precedents in the Lollard and Hussite uprisings (Bredekamp, 1975), as well as in the banal situations of the coercion of saints are countless.

The quarrel over images and the iconoclasm of the sixteenth century can be understood, then, as a conjunction of complex and partially autonomous processes:

1. The quantitative and qualitative explosion of images at the end of the Middle Ages, in part under the effect of the activity of mendicant orders, brotherhoods, and certain devout circles, in part also as a function of the technical ease offered by the printing press and wood engraving, which allowed for the reproduction of images at the slightest cost.

2. The concomitant diversification of usages and the expansion of images of devotion *(Andachtsbilder)* next to images invested with liturgical functions (Os, 1994). The question remains controversial, both concerning the existence of a particular type of image linked to the new culture of prayer that established itself at the end of the Middle Ages and concerning what touches on the interpretation of the complex symbolism of art in this epoch of transformation. How, for example, can one distinguish in the Flemish retables of the fourteenth to fifteenth centuries the elements that refer to the strong times of the liturgy from those that attest rather to the personal piety of the donors, to their spiritual experiences, their visions? Does the painting of the Arnolfini couple illustrate the debates about the sacrament of marriage or a precise marriage contract? In a good many cases, we are reduced to hypotheses by the lack of sufficient sources. There is no doubt, however, that between the fourteenth and sixteenth centuries, art expressed more and more the aspirations and personal religious experiences of donors and patrons, religious, and laity, and that, in turn, it played a growing role in their devotions in supporting their prayers and meditations. Of this change, the *Livres d'Heures* bear proof.

3. The stylistic, thematic, and iconographic transformations of the end of the Middle Ages and of the sixteenth century reveal at the same time an affirmation of new genres (portraits, landscapes), the emergence of novel subjects linked to the evolution of religious practices (the interest in the humanity of Christ leads artists and religious people to accord more importance to Joseph, Anne, and the Holy Family), and the increasing use of illusionist or realist processes. These transformations provoked the suspicion of numerous theologians and prelates who were concerned about the confusion that could result for believers between the image and its prototype, the propagation of superstitions linked to the excessive cult of images (notably in the works of Desiderius Erasmus with regard to the cult of Saint Christopher), or the diffusion of indecent apocryphal or heretic subjects (for example, in Saint Anthony of Florence, who condemns the three-headed Trinities.

4. The crisis of the theology of the image and the erosion of the Thomist position—which affirmed that one owes the same veneration to the image of Christ and to Christ himself *(Summa Theologiae,* IIIa, 25, a3)—under the double critique of heterodox movements and the internal dispute of the church. In 1542 again, in the middle of confessional confrontations of the Reform, the theologians Matthew Ory, Ambroglio Catarino, and Martin Perez de Ayala, having remained loyal to the Roman church, could only state their disagreement on the question, however central, of adoration and keep a prudent distance with regard to the Thomist thesis. Until the Council of Trent, Catholicism did not present a united front before Protestant disputes.

In Byzantium, as in the medieval Occident or modern Europe, the legitimacy and function of religious art depends on the interactions between the three aspects distinguished at the beginning of this section in the interest of clarity and on the historically changing configuration of the relationship between artists, patrons/buyers, believers/spectators, clergy, and political authorities. Its status itself thus predisposes the image to be at the same time the stakes, the terrain, and the means of struggle (Bredekamp) for confrontations and complex compromises in which political preoccupations, social aspirations, economic conflicts, and religious rivalries are inextricably intertwined (Cormack, 1985; Warnke, 1973). Lacking consistent works, it is difficult to bring a similar judgment on architecture and music, even if the quarrels of the sixteenth century surrounding religious music, organ music, and canticles in the vernacular provide convincing elements.

Substitution of Art for the Cultural Image. The problem of the transformation of the status and function of the image and of the autonomization of the artistic field around the end of the Middle Ages has become the object of new debates, the stakes of which can be reviewed.

The emergence of collectionism (Groote, 1994) and the aesthetic posture that constitutes the image as a work of art whose value resides above all in its formal qualities opened the way to the transformation of the gaze and the forms of judgment made on artistic creations: "A picture is no longer to be understood in terms of its theme, but as a contribution to the development of art" (Belting, 1994). It leads as well to the formation of places consecrated only for aesthetic pleasure and to the exercise of a judgment of taste: cabinets, galleries (of sovereigns, princes, cardinals, or dealers), salons, and museums. The works that were collected there were invested with a new value, which was largely independent of the political, dynastic, or liturgical functions formerly imparted to the image. In the modern collection, the icon became a work of art, as Victor I. Stoichita shows concerning the garland Madonnas in the cabinets of Antwerp amateurs (in Groote, 1994). Ultimately, the religion of art for art, with its own rites, substituted for Christian practices. Is it any wonder, then, that the traditionalist Pope John Paul II concluded that "art for art's sake which only refers to its author, without establishing a rapport with the divine world, has no place in the Christian conception of the icon" (*Duodecimum Saeculum,* 1987)?

The thesis calls for a few nuances. Allowing for exceptions, the adoption of an aesthetic posture and the new type of relationship to the work of art that it implies was found at first in a limited number of intellectual and social elites and did not touch the immense majority of believers, who continued to maintain more traditional relationships with their images, relationships in which artistic judgment played only a very secondary role. It is in this sense that one can understand the refusal in March 1794 of the Museum of Arts opened by the revolutionary French government to accept a Saint Jerome from Gaspand De Crayer into its collections, for fear that such paintings "would serve only to feed the fanaticism further."

Moreover, certain images produced for precise liturgical, pastoral, or spiritual ends (paintings of missions, popular engravings, ex-votos) lent themselves very badly to the new discourse of aesthetic celebration because they did not comply with the criteria of excellence decreed by the academies. Moreover, the officiants of the new cult of the beautiful did not have strict enough terms to censure the processes and works that seemed to them to be incompatible with the rules in use in the modern artistic field and especially everything that recalled the ancient bonds between the artist, the religious person, and the patron: Charles Perrault at the end of the seventeenth century *(Parallèle des Anciens et des Modernes)* and Stendhal at the beginning of the nineteenth century *(Voyages en Italie)* thus took an ironic stance toward the habits and moral prejudices that called for donors to be present in the paintings that they had done. The discredit that struck the religious images that could not be reduced to aesthetic discourse beginning with the seventeenth century bore proof *a contrario* of their survival and of the permanence of the religious sentiments that they continued to inspire in certain categories of the population at least, as one observes in the scornful judgment passed on the ex-voto in the *Encyclopédie* of Denis Diderot and Jean Le Rond d'Alembert. Finally, the too clear-cut distinction made between the epoch of images-objects of veneration and that of the art object of admiration and pleasure undoubtedly underestimates the medieval aesthetic and the long heritage of Neoplatonic philosophy, from Pseudo-Dionysius to Michelangelo, which favored the development of the arts within Christianity.

From the sixteenth century onward—earlier here, later there—art in the service of religion loses the preponderant place it had held since late antiquity or the High Middle Ages. The rather strict control over images introduced by the Tridentine decree (1563) certainly did not condemn medieval art to a rapid disappearance, as has been at times suggested, but it ultimately drove the church to adopt a position of extreme prudence—indeed, of suspicion—regarding stylistic or iconographic innovations. The attempts that were more or less aimed at the revival of sacred art (pre-Raphaelites, German Nazarenes, the Sacred Art of Father Couturier) did not succeed in reversing this process; it was thereafter outside of the institutional orders of the church, its liturgy, and its dogmas that the most brilliant artistic careers were made and that the modern artistic field was formed.

The appearance of matters of artistic blasphemy (in literature Théophile de Viau and Molière, in painting Gustave Courbet for *The Burial at Ornans,* George Grosz for his *Crucifixion with Gas Mask* at the origin of a series of trials between 1928 and 1931) attests as well to this reciprocal distancing between the religious and artistic fields.

The Religion of Art. The autonomy claimed for the field of art, the affirmation of the aesthetic position with the eighteenth and nineteenth centuries, and Kantian criticism led to new theoretical formalizations and new experiences of the relations between and art and religion that go well beyond the simple substitution of one for the other. One might seek to annul the respective distance between the areas of religion and art, as Father Couturier and the initiators of Sacred Art attempted, by trying to make religious art the site of an avant-garde at once spiritual and aesthetic. Or one might work to invest art with a new sacrality that owes nothing to the institution of the church, or the liturgy, or even the religious subject, strictly speaking, of the artwork. Finally, one might try to escape the strict limits of Christianity to reconcile an intense religious sentiment, enthusiasm for Greco-Roman antiquity, and admiration for Islam.

It is thus that from Gotthold Ephraim Lessing to August Wilhelm von Schlegel and Friedrich Schlegel, and via Johann Wolfgang von Goethe, there is affirmed a will to go beyond Christianity and to find an art acceptable to the three great religions. Despite their divergences and their hesitations, these efforts favor the creation of religious works of which the subject matter is not Christian, and they anticipate the formation, in the nineteenth century, of a secular religion of art, which would have Albrecht Dürer and Raphael for its patron saints. Goethe goes so far as to venture that whoever has science and art, has religion as well; whoever has neither of those two has no religion either.

Inspired originally by Novalis, but taken up and developed by Georg Wilhelm Friedrich Hegel and the Jena Romantics, the concept of art-religion *(Kunstreligion)* defines art as a divine service that is not conceived of as a service rendered to God, for the absolute resides in the person who is capable of the sublime: art itself—at least Greek art—is in itself a religion. The beautiful is an intuition of absolute Spirit; art is invested with an ontological function of revealing transcendental truths in a way inaccessible to profane cognitive activity. From the circles of German Romanticism, these theories, which make art into the privileged place of knowledge, are disseminated in all of Europe, including artistic milieus.

Finally, how is one not to see in the reflection of von Ramdohr about Caspar David Friedrich's *Cross in the Mountains (Tetschen Altar)*—from now on landscape painting wants to climb onto the altars—a penetrating definition of the ambitions of nineteenth-century art?

BIBLIOGRAPHY

Baaren, Theodorus Petrus van. *Bezielend Beelden: Inleiding tot de beeldende Kunst der primitieve Volken.* Amsterdam, 1962.

Baxandall, Michael. *Painting and Experience in Fifteenth Century Italy: A Primer in the Social History of Pictorial Style.* Oxford, 1972.

Baxandall, Michael. *The Limewood Sculptors of Renaissance Germany.* New Haven, 1980.

Belting, Hans. *Bild und Kult: Eine Geschichte des Bildes vor dem Zeitalter der Kunst.* Munich, 1990. Translated by Edmund Jephcott as *Likeness and Presence: A History of the Image before the Era of Art* (Chicago, 1994).

Boespflug, François, and Nicolas Lossky, eds. *Nicée II, 787–1987: douze siècles d'images religieuses.* Paris, 1987.

Bredekamp, Horst. *Kunst als Medium sozialer Konflikte. Bilderkämpfe von der Spätantike bis zur Hussitenrevolution.* Frankfurt am Main, 1975.

Christin, Olivier. *Une révolution symbolique: l'iconoclasme huguenot et la reconstruction catholique.* Paris, 1991.

Cormack, Robin S. *Writing in Gold: Byzantine Society and Its Icons.* London, 1985.

Foucart, Bruno. *Le renouveau de la peinture religieuse en France, 1800–1860.* Paris, 1987.

Freedberg, David. *The Power of Images: Studies in the History and Theory of Response.* Chicago, 1989.

Groote, Andreas, ed. *Macrocosmos in Microcosmo: Die Welt in der Stube: Zur Geschichte des Sammelns, 1450 bis 1800.* Opladen, 1994.

Hofmann, Werner, ed. *Luther und die Folgen für die Kunst.* Munich, 1983.

Michalski, Sergiusz. *The Reformation and the Visual Arts: The Protestant Image Question in Western and Eastern Europe.* London and New York, 1993.

Os, Henk van. *The Art of Devotion in the Late Middle Ages in Europe, 1300–1500.* With Eugene Honee, Hans Niewdorp, Bernhard Ridderbos. Translated by Michael Hoyle. London, 1994.

Scavizzi, Giuseppe. *Arte e architettura sacra.* Rome, 1981.

Scavizzi, Giuseppe. *The Controversy on Images from Calvin to Baronius.* New York, 1992.

Warnke, Martin, ed. *Bildersturm: die Zerstörung des Kunstwerks.* Munich, 1973.

Wirth, Jean. *L'image médiévale: Naissance et développement, VIᵉ–XVᵉ siècles.* Paris, 1989.

OLIVIER CHRISTIN
Translated from French by Terri Gordon

RENAISSANCE ITALIAN AESTHETICS.

It is difficult to speak of Renaissance aesthetics in general terms, as if there were an established doctrine representative of all re-flection on art in that period. The large number of works dedicated to artistic topics from the fourteenth to the late sixteenth century actually suggests that attempts to codify principles of artistic creation are as manifold as Renaissance art itself. There is, indeed, a variety of different, more or less elaborated views on art written in Latin or in the vernacular. They take the shape of scientific treatises making much use of perspective studies, or else align themselves in the tradition of erudite humanist dialogues and letters. Both genres, the "scientific" and the humanist, are sometimes united in one and the same text, revealing the writer's competence in both fields. Among the earliest authors of treatises exploring topics devoted to the nature of art are Italian poets of the late thirteenth century. They are soon followed by fourteenth-century humanists who elevated poetry to the rank of liberal art. A new phenomenon appears in fifteenth-century Italy with the artists breaking out of the realm of mere craftsmanship (which medieval culture had assigned to them) and addressing their own reflections on art to fellow artists as well as to the learned public. Finally, philosophers made rich contributions to the Renaissance discussion of art. Although they were initially relegated to the role of observers passively witnessing the discovery of perspective by mathematicians and artists, they soon gave thought to how the geometrization of space and bodies in the arts might affect the perceptual theories of their time and developed concepts supportive of theories of artistic creation. Moreover, they emphasized human inventiveness to the extent that "creativity" became a central theme in their philosophies.

The distinction between poets, humanists, artists, and philosophers is not a strict one, because Renaissance authors typically excelled in more than just one field. In addition, Renaissance dialogues that examine topics related to art offer a vivid picture of intensive discussions across disciplines that were differently demarcated in those days. The philosopher Marsilio Ficino, for instance, appears in Cristoforo Landino's *Disputationes Camaldulenses* (1475), and Landino is himself one of the representatives of humanism in Ficino's *Commentary on Plato's Symposium* (1469). A generation later, the poet Torquato Tasso wrote a dialogue, *Il Ficino, o vero dell'arte*, in which both Landino and Ficino converse on art. Although Ficino occupied a unique position in the intellectual life of the early Renaissance, other examples could be cited to show how freely similar views, opinions, and theories circulated in different fields—making it in some cases difficult to determine precisely the authorship of a single idea or a concept.

Poets and Humanists. The poets' reflections on art—whether incorporated in the classical form of a "poetic" or laid down in treatises, dialogues, or letters—are an indispensable source for an overall appreciation of the Renaissance discussion of art. The poets' theories of inspiration and, more specifically, their claim to truth (and not just

RENAISSANCE ITALIAN AESTHETICS. Jacopo de Barbari, *Portrait of Luca Pacioli* (1495), oil on wood, 99 × 120 cm; Museo Nazionale die Capodimonte, Naples. (Photograph courtesy of Alinari/Art Resource, New York.)

verisimilitude) paved the way for the humanist emancipation of poetry from grammar and rhetoric. Already Albertino Mussato (1261–1329) had conceived of the poet as a *poeta doctus* and an enunciator of "truth," whether dealing with fictional or historical events. As to the poet's relationship to history, Mussato announced proudly that he, for instance, was in ancient Troy "before" the city's founder himself appeared there—implying that his knowledge of past events was rooted in a historical memory accessible to divinely inspired poets like himself. Although Mussato found a severe critic in the Dominican Giovanni di Mantua, who defended the Thomist position according to which truth needs to be anchored ontologically, many later poets and humanists followed in his footsteps. His conviction that poetry represented a *theologia mundi* is echoed in Francesco

Petrarca's and Giovanni Boccaccio's writings with their assertion that the poet's fables have the same origin as the stories of Scripture and therefore harbor a divine message. In line with this view is Pico della Mirandola's (1463–1494) project of a "poetical theology" that aimed at unifying ancient and biblical traditions. Asked about the sense of the *poetica figmenta* that "veil" the true nucleus of their fables, poets and humanists answered that divine wisdom needed to be "protected" from profanation. More significantly, they also pointed out that figurative speech bears the mark of "inventiveness." Authors such as Leonardo Bruni (1377–1444) and Juan Luis Vives (1492–1540) attributed poetic figures to a creative natural disposition, called by Roman poets *ingenium*. This natural disposition uncovers similarities between objects and between words that cannot be detected by reason alone and it translates them, in the field of poetry, into figurative language. Landino (1424–1498) therefore suggested that poetry, being the art of vesting truth with the beauty of metaphoric garments, occupied an intermediary position between unreflected myth and rational philosophy. Other humanists such as Coluccio Salutati (1331–1406) argued, with Mussato, Dante Alighieri, and Petrarca, that poetry, insofar as it embraces all of the liberal arts, is itself philosophy. Salutati also justified poetic speech by emphasizing the salutary effect it has on the recipient, to whom it transmits not only the poet's encyclopedic knowledge but also his inspired state of mind. Salutati is alluding to the Platonic doctrine of *furors*, which was discussed by poets and humanists long before Ficino offered his elaborate version of it. The concept of poetry as an activity unto itself added to the "nobility" of poetical production and provided a basis for the notion of the poet as a creator and as an *alter deus*. Variations on the creator-poet theme can be found in almost all works that emphasize the inventive nature of poetry, most importantly in Pierre de Ronsard's *Abrégé de l'art poétique* (1565), Sir Philip Sidney's *A Defence of Poetry* (1595), and Lope de Vega's *Arte nueva de hacer comedias* (1607). A particularly striking passage is offered in "A Defence of Poetry": "Onely the poet disdeining to be tied to any such subjection, lifted up with the vigor of his own invention, doth grow in effect into *another nature*: a making things either better then nature bringeth foorth, or quite a new, . . . so as he goeth hand in hand with nature" (Sidney, 1973, p. 78).

The other powerful doctrine of the time was Aristotle's theory of imitation and whose *Poetics* became available in the original in the fifteenth century. Although Latin translations followed, it is only after Francesco Robortello's *In librum Aristotelis de Arte Poetica Explicationes* (1548) that many other commentaries began to appear (not all of which promoted an Aristotelian stand). Robortello himself worked within the limits of the ancient author's philosophy, for instance, by conceiving poetry as the product of a natural process of intellection. In a similar vein, Julius Caesar Scaliger, in his *Poetice* (1561), connected poetical theory with Aristotle's psychology when he reflected on the effect of pleasure on the soul.

The Artists. A fruitful connection between humanist studies and art theory is found in the works of Leon Battista Alberti (1404–1472), the only Renaissance artist whose systematic studies included perspective as well as painting, sculpture, architecture, and theory of inspiration. In the dedication of *Della pittura*, Alberti stated to his fellow artist Filippo Brunelleschi that mathematics revealed the emerging of art "from roots within Nature itself" (Alberti, 1972, p. 32), implying that the measures used by painters have their origin in nature's creations. Central to this understanding is the concept of "proportion," which is derived from the observation of physical objects and their relations

to other objects and is then transmitted to works of art through the use of perspective. Related to the notion of proportion are comparisons as a means of accuracy: "There is in comparison a power which enables us to recognize the presence of more or less or just the same" (ibid., p. 53). This power *(vis)* is also needed for conceiving the outlines of a painting, especially if the painting is a *storia* involving many figures whose spatial relations have to be carefully designed. Most remarkably, the theory of composition that Alberti developed in that context also serves as a basis for artistic creativity, which earlier artists such as Cennino Cennini did not think of stimulating. The humanistically well trained Alberti sought help to that effect from two established disciplines, rhetoric and poetry. Although he recommended the reading of poetical works as an essential source for developing the *storia* (a step that in rhetoric corresponds to *inventio*), he used rhetorical schemes as a way to systematize the sequence and variation of figures (equivalent to *ordo*). The strength of his theory of composition lies in his idea of figures that are not to be understood abstractly but always in connection with the *storia* they represent (Kuhn, 1984, p. 163). Composition thus exerts a "double" visual impact on the artist's creative disposition, through the cohesion of narrative and figurative elements and through the mutual correspondence between these elements.

Unlike Alberti, Leonardo da Vinci (1452–1519) rigorously opposed the idea of "ennobling" art by linking it with humanist studies. Although Leonardo owed many insights to his predecessor, he legitimated the high status of painting not by borrowing from liberal arts but by understanding it as a science. As a consequence, he demolished the humanist opposition between "imitators" and "creators" by stating that all who deal solely with "words" condemn themselves to futile mimetic production. For him, a "discoverer" bases himself on "experience" mediating between "artful nature" and humankind (Vinci, 1970, C.A. 85a). The other prerequisite is mathematics, a tool that confers "certitude" on the scientific investigation of nature (W. An. III 241a; G 95b). There has been much debate concerning Leonardo's understanding of mathematics. It appears that for him the real power of mathematics does not lie in its ability to trace back reality to abstract laws, but, on the contrary, in its being instrumental in rendering nature's laws visible. This explains, for instance, the high status of mechanics as "the paradise" in which the fruits of mathematics can be found (E, 8b), or why water currents are being called "visible science" (ibid, 54b). Painting as the discipline par excellence that captures the visible world by the use of mathematics (perspective and geometry) is therefore a science and at the same time an art in that it is creative. Theory of science parallels theory of art, and both disciplines are considered "second creations." Nevertheless, it is only of the painter that Leonardo says that he is the perfecter of nature. The scientist's (i.e., the engineer's) inventions can never compare to nature's creations, "because in her inventions nothing is lacking and nothing is superfluous, and she does not use counterweights, but places there the soul, the composer of the body" (*Leonardo da Vinci: Engineer and Architect,* 1987, p. 109). Not so the painter's work, which, born of nature, as the source of all visible things, can even surpass her finite basic creations by producing infinite new compounds of natural forms. As a consequence, the art of painting is a "grandchild" of nature and also related with God (Ash. I, 15b; 16a).

Most of Michelangelo Buonarroti's (1475–1564) aesthetic views are dispersed throughout his *Rime*—beauty in visual arts being, as it were, expressible through the veil of poetry only. A distinctive feature of his artistic understanding is the rejection of the mathematical expression of reality, particularly in respect to the human body, although he did admit that proportions "please" the eye (and also applied them to the buildings he designed). In contrast to his contemporary Albrecht Dürer (1471–1528), who was aware that beauty ultimately escapes mathematical formulation but still recommended the use of proportions, Michelangelo did not view beauty as a calculable harmonious concord of lines and colors. The actual measure is not performed by the compass in the artist's hand, but by his *intelletto,* a term that for Michelangelo translated Plotinus's *voûs noûs* (reason, intuition) and also had features typically associated with the *ingegno.* Warren Cheney aptly coined the notion of "creative proportion" to characterize Michelangelo's art (Clements, 1961, p. 33). The possession of *intelletto,* however, does not dispense with the process—and torment—of artistic creation. The beauty discerned by the "external eye," explained Michelangelo, penetrates the artist's soul and "grows" therein to a new "shape." Through the artist's technical skills, that new shape (the terms used are *concetto, immagine,* and *idea*) will eventually outlive nature's creations. In this respect, "Cause to effect bows and gives way, whence nature is bested by art" (ibid., p. 12). This also justifies why, even though all forms preexist in nature (another Plotinian notion), the sculpted stone is worthier than the untouched rock. Nevertheless, art is ultimately not superior to nature, because it is nature herself that gives art the power to overcome her. This is in harmony with Michelangelo's ideal of an effortlessness, or spontaneous creation, that is modeled after nature's own mode of creation—requiring no preparatory studies, no instruments, and no measurements.

The Philosophers. The advancement of fine arts accompanied by the enhancement of technical skills suggested to many Renaissance philosophers the return of the golden age. They did not, however, develop an actual aesthetics—something that emerged as an independent philosophical discipline only in the eighteenth century. They nevertheless worked with concepts that clearly reveal the impact of artistic themes and procedures. The most visible

expressions of that impact are the many terms they used associated with notions of order, symmetry, and harmony: *ordo, numerus, modus, mensura (immensurabilitas), commensuratio, commensurabilitas, convenientia partium, consonantia, concordia, dispositio, harmonia, proportio, proportionabilitas, forma, species, figura, figuratio, adaequatio, congruitas, pulchritudo, formositas, venustas, elegantia, gratia.* Although not all of these terms refer necessarily to a reflection on art, the concentration of some of them does indicate an interest in aesthetic categories. More significant, of course, are concepts clearly reminiscent of artistic topics or philosophical problems that are encoded in aesthetic terms. Nicholas of Cusa, or Cusanus (1401–1464), for instance, not only employed almost all of the terms above, but also elaborated the philosophical foundation of "proportion," the use of which he strongly recommended for the fine arts. Moreover, the notion of proportion was of major importance because "every inquiry is comparative and uses the means of comparative relation [*proportio*]" (*On Learned Ignorance,* 1981, I, I, p. 50). This is a lesson one can learn also from Alberti, with whom Nicholas of Cusa shared some of his mathematical studies. He focused his attention, however, on the presuppositions of a comparative relation. Such a relation does not equalize the terms it relates, but only opens up a perspective under which similarity can be established. On the one hand, because similitude requires a notion of dissimilitude, proportion must be understood as a derivative of sameness and otherness. On the other hand, its substantiation requires that the opposite terms, from which it stems metaphysically, be unified. This is effected by the famous doctrine of the *coincidentia oppositorum,* which, translated into modern terms, represents the condition of the possibility of any opposition. There is only one opposition for which no adequate proportion can be found, and that is the distance between the finite and the infinite. Nicholas of Cusa offered a brilliant solution to this problem in *The Vision of God,* a work that employs a recently discovered technique in portraiture that makes the face appear to be watching observers independently of the position they take. To him, this exemplified the absolute seeing of God as an unmovable "omnivoyant" who "encompasses at one and the same time each and every mode of seeing" (*The Vision of God,* 1985, vol. 2, p. 121), and is thereby present to every individual visual act. Whereas human seeing is "contracted," that is, perspectively determined and thus finite, divine vision is integral and infinite. Although "uncontractible" in itself, absolute vision functions as the "contraction of contractions," meaning the totality of all perspective sights. Whether this subtle speculation on vision has had an impact on the actual practice of painting is difficult to establish, although Leonardo, for instance, was apparently acquainted with Nicholas of Cusa's works, which were discussed in learned Milanese circles (Cassirer, 1963, pp. 48ff.). He could certainly have drawn on the philosopher's view that man is a *secundus deus* be-

RENAISSANCE ITALIAN AESTHETICS. Sandro Botticelli, *Calumny of Apelles* (1495), tempera on wood, 62 × 91 cm; Uffizi, Florence. (Photograph courtesy of Alinari/Art Resource, New York.)

cause he is himself a creator whose mind produces mathematical and rational notions that measure God's creation.

Renaissance scholars are sometimes disappointed to find that Marsilio Ficino (1433–1499), the Florentine friend of Alberti and the brothers Antonio and Piero Pollaiuolo and inspirer of Sandro Botticcelli (Cheney, 1985), did not himself attempt to codify principles of aesthetics. But in fact, as André Chastel's (1975) study on the Florentine philosopher shows, Ficino took a deep interest in optics and perspective, reflected on the applicability of the Vitruvian canon, and even developed a scale of colors—not to mention his studies on musical theory. It is true that Ficino did not analyze single works of art. The primary object of his aesthetic investigation was beauty in natural bodies, and in that his approach was no different from an artist's point of view. Ficino distinguished between shape *(figura)* and beauty *(pulchritudo)* of bodies, in terms that echo Vitruvius's definition of *symmetry* and *eurythmy* and also some aspects of Alberti's aesthetic categories *pulchritudo* and *concinnitas* (Alberti, 1988, 9, 5, pp. 302ff.). Whereas shape can be described in terms of agreeable arrangements of parts and

colors, beauty is "act, vitality, and a certain grace shining in itself through the influence of its own Idea" (Ficino, 1985, 5, 6, p. 93). Because beauty is related to vitality, the soul, which gives life to the body, is defined as the artist *(artifex corporis)* fashioning the body from inside. To that effect, the soul predisposes the body for its final shaping by introducing three intelligible components: disposition *(ordo)*, measure *(modus)*, and aspect *(speties)*. Disposition has to do with the distance between the body parts; measure is responsible for the shaping of the parts by using the scale of geometric progression (surface–line–point); aspect provides the accord of light, shadows, and lines (ibid., p. 93f.). Ficino's description of the soul's operations on the body as an artistic process is one that can easily be applied to his understanding of the artist's work. More significantly, it exemplifies a Renaissance mentality that was not content with adorning living space, but also strived to "aestheticize" the world of thought (to the extent that psychology was also conceived in aesthetic terms). The human soul in Ficino's metaphysics eventually "re-forms," that is, reshapes, the face of the universe in the soul's effort to understand it (Albertini, 1997, pp. 130–147)—intellectualizing thus becoming an equivalent of beautifying.

Many more Renaissance authors have aestheticized their philosophies or used features of artistic creation as paradigms for epistemological and metaphysical notions. Charles de Bovelles (1479–1567), Francesco Patrizi (1529–1597), Giordano Bruno (1548–1600), and Tommaso Campanella (1568–1639), for instance, made abundant use of these conceptual transformations. Patrizi, whose work bridges fourteenth-century humanism and early modern science, not only wrote on various humanistic disciplines and the philosophy of nature, but also managed to link the two divergent study fields through the use of geometry. He applied the methodical rigor of geometry to history and rhetoric and took its spatial quality as a basis for the studying of physical bodies. Reflecting on the presuppositions of corporeity, he discovered that space—being at the same time corporeal (three-dimensional) and incorporeal (without the bodily quality of resistance)—is prior to the world of bodies. In *Nova de Universis Philosophia* (1591), Patrizi defines space as what "communicates to them [bodies] all of its points, lines, surfaces, and depths, . . . so that they possess those things that it retains for itself" (Patrizi, 1943, p. 239). He insisted that geometric bodies are not abstracted from physical bodies but are to be thought of as being actualized in nature as their primary space. Interpreted in the context of sixteenth-century art theory, this concept of (absolute) space can be understood as a response to the mathematically constructed space in the artist's shop that still rested on the Aristotelian assumption that space is what is being occupied by a body. The aesthetic dimension of Patrizi's theory of space becomes evident if one considers that space is related to light—also an "incorporeal body"—and that light is the first to "fill" physical space (ibid., p. 244). This dimension has been acknowledged by artists, in particular by El Greco (1541–1614), who held Patrizi's metaphysics in high esteem.

Looking at how artistic categories have been employed in the works of Renaissance philosophers, one understands why no independent aesthetic discipline emerged from their reflections on art. More appealing than the examination of the ontological status of an artistic object, more significant than the analysis of pleasure derived from harmonies and proportions found in artworks, and certainly more urgent than questions related to taste, was the global quest for harmony. It was that quest that gave rise to new metaphysics and new cosmologies, in which the universe itself was considered as an object of "beautification." Not content with mere symmetry and regularity in the planetary order, Johannes Kepler (1571–1630), for instance, searched for the divine *disegno* in the way the cosmos is structured, a scheme that he considered to be governed by rules of artistic disposition. As is well known, Kepler embodied his aesthetically determined vision of the heavenly order in a model of nesting polyhedrons—which has been recently interpreted as an arrangement of "cosmopoetic" figures (Hallyn, 1993, p. 182). The demands of Renaissance art theory, with its ideal of harmonious disposition, which could be codified in many different ways, pervaded philosophical discourse and eventually reached the threshold of modern science.

The contribution of Renaissance philosophers to the refinement of aesthetic categories lies in their elaboration of notions that were basic to the artistic discussions of their time. Their interest in aesthetic principles was, in a sense, an extension of their desire to make their own intellectual work conform to the highest standards of art and beauty.

[*See also* Alberti; Architecture, *article on* Italian Renaissance Aesthetics; Artist; Origins of Aesthetics; Perspective; Rhetoric; *and* Vasari.]

BIBLIOGRAPHY

Primary Sources

Alberti, Leon Battista. *On Painting and On Sculpture*. Edited and translated by Cecil Grayson. London, 1972.

Alberti, Leon Battista. *On the Art of Building in Ten Books*. Translated by Joseph Rykwert, Neil Leach, and Robert Tavernor. Cambridge, Mass., 1988.

Buonarroti, Michelangelo. *Complete Poems and Selected Letters*. Translated by Creighton Gilbert, edited by Robert N. Linscott. Reprint, Princeton, N.J., 1980.

Ficino, Marsilio. *Commentary on Plato's Symposium on Love*. 2d rev. ed. Translated by Sears Jayne. Dallas, 1985.

Hopkins, Jasper. *Nicholas of Cusa on Learned Ignorance: A Translation and an Appraisal of De docta ignorantia*. Minneapolis, 1981.

Hopkins, Jasper. *Nicholas of Cusa's Dialectical Mysticism: Text, Translation, and Interpretative Study of De Visione Dei*. Minneapolis, 1985.

Patrizi, Francesco. "On Physical Space." Translated by Benjamin Brickman. *Journal of the History of Ideas* 4 (1943): 224–245.

Sidney, Philip. "A Defence of Poetry." In *Miscellaneous Prose of Sir Philip Sidney,* edited by Katherine Duncan-Jones and Jan van Dorsten. Oxford, 1973.

Vinci, Leonardo da. *The Notebooks of Leonardo da Vinci*. Compiled and edited by Jean Paul Richter. 2 vols. New York, 1970.

Other Sources

Albertini, Tamara. *Marsilio Ficino. Die Vermittlung von Denken und Welt in einer Metaphysik der Einfachheit*. Munich, 1997.

Barasch, Mosche. *Light and Color in the Italian Renaissance Theory of Art*. New York, 1978.

Baxandall, Michael. *Painting and Experience in Fifteenth Century Italy: A Primer in the Social History of Pictorial Style*. 2d ed. Oxford and New York, 1988.

Burke, Peter. *Culture and Society in Renaissance Italy, 1420–1540*. New York, 1972.

Cassirer, Ernst. *The Individual and the Cosmos in Renaissance Philosophy*. Translated by Mario Domandi. New York, 1963. Originally published as *Individuum und Kosmos in der Philosophie der Renaissance* (Leipzig, 1927).

Chastel, André. *Marsile Ficin et l'art*. 2d ed. Geneva, 1975.

Cheney, Liana. *Quattrocento Neoplatonism and Medici Humanism in Botticelli's Mythological Paintings*. Lanham, Md., 1985.

Clements, Robert John. *Michelangelo's Theory of Art*. New York, 1961.

Elkins, James. *The Poetics of Perspective*. Ithaca, N.Y., 1994.

Greenfield, Concetta Carestia. *Humanist and Scholastic Poetics, 1250–1500.* Lewisburg, Pa., 1981.

Hallyn, Fernand. *The Poetic Structure of the World: Copernicus and Kepler.* Translated by Donald M. Leslie. New York, 1993. Originally published as *La structure poétique du monde: Copernic, Kepler* (Paris, 1987).

Kristeller, Paul Oskar. *Renaissance Thought and the Arts: Collected Essays.* Exp. ed. Princeton, N.J., 1990.

Kuhn, Rudolf. "Alberti's Lehre über die *Komposition* als die Kunst in der Malerei." *Archiv für Begriffsgeschichte* 28 (1984): 123–178.

Leonardo da Vinci: Engineer and Architect. Montreal, 1987.

Panovsky, Erwin. *Studies in Iconology: Humanistic Themes in the Art of the Renaissance.* Reprint, New York, 1962.

Tigerstedt, F. N. "The Poet as Creator. Origins of a Metaphor." *Comparative Literature Studies* 5 (1968).

Weinberg, Bernard. *A History of Literary Criticism in the Italian Renaissance.* 2 vols. Chicago, 1961.

Wind, Edgar. *Pagan Mysteries in the Renaissance.* New Haven, 1958.

TAMARA ALBERTINI

REPRESENTATION. [*To clarify the role of the concept of representation in aesthetics, this entry comprises three essays:*

Conceptual and Historical Overview
Depiction
Resemblance

The first essay is an overview of the general topic of representation as it has been treated in the history of aesthetics. The second essay analyzes two of the main theoretical accounts of pictoral depiction: perceptual theories and symbol theories. The third essay, on resemblance, discusses a topic that has been important in the history of aesthetics but that has been marginalized by various critiques of it since the 1960s. For related discussion, see Fiction; Goodman; Gombrich; Imagery; Mimesis; Perception; Photography, *article on* Catachresis; Portraiture; *and* Realism.]

Conceptual and Historical Overview

Plato gave birth to aesthetics when Socrates claims in book 10 (598b) of *The Republic* that a painting is a representation that aims to reproduce only the appearance or image of an object. In this brief passage, Plato both suggests a criterion for a painting's representing a certain object and begins to raise deep skeptical questions about the value of such representation. The criterion, properly spelled out, stands up remarkably well despite much criticism and many proposals of alternatives in the contemporary literature of aesthetics, and the skeptical questions have proved remarkably difficult to answer.

The criterion for a painting's representing an object, which Plato describes as aiming to reproduce its appearance, might be spelled out as follows: a painting represents a certain object if and only if its artist intends by marking the canvas with paint to create visual experience in viewers that resembles the visual experience they would have of the object. One might add that the intention must be successful

in the sense that the following conditional is true: if the painting is seen in normal conditions, then it will produce visual experience similar to that of the object, such that the intention is recoverable from this experience.

The idea that resemblance could be sufficient for representation has been attacked by Nelson Goodman (1976). Borrowing freely, his counterexamples to this claim are as follows: twins resemble but do not represent each other; reprints of a painting resemble the painting more than it resembles what it represents, yet both the painting and its reprints represent the objects seen in them and not each other; a fabric sample both resembles the fabric and (in a sense broader than that intended to be captured by our criterion) represents it, but it is not a pictorial representation (depiction) of it. Our criterion as spelled out refers to resemblance between visual experiences of a painting and an object and not to resemblance between the objects themselves, but the Goodman's counterexamples are not affected by this difference, because the objects in question will generate similar visual experiences.

The other clauses of the criterion do eliminate such counterexamples, however. These clauses include reference to the intention of the artist and to her marking a canvas with paint as the manner of fulfilling that intention. Twins, fabric samples, and reprints are not created in that way with those intentions behind them. Goodman's counterexamples do show that resemblance is not sufficient for representation, but Plato's criterion does not claim that it is.

Goodman held that resemblance is not necessary and is not an important factor in pictorial representation either. According to him, depiction depends on a conventional symbolic system similar to language in its referential functions but different in the formal structure of its symbolic system. Aesthetic symbols are, for example, syntactically and semantically dense, that is, small differences in them make for different symbols and they pick out small differences in their objects. They typically refer by exemplification, that is, by referring to some of their own properties. These are interesting features of aesthetic representation, but Goodman's main thesis that such representation depends on conventional symbols has been successfully attacked, most notably by Flint Schier (1986).

Schier points out that, in order to recognize represented objects in a painting, one does not require semantic rules to relate its parts to their referents or syntactic rules to relate these parts to each other. Recognition of represented objects normally depends only on one's ability to recognize the real objects represented. One simply assimilates the perceptual experiences of painting and object. Schier proposes a criterion of pictorial representation based on this point. Roughly, something is a picture of an object if one can naturally interpret it visually as such, if this interpretation depends only on one's being able to recognize the object.

This proposal again appears to be an alternative to that which appeals to the intentional creation of resemblances between experienced visual properties. But it also seems upon reflection that the recognitional capacity triggered by a picture of an object can itself be explained by the similarities between visual experiences of picture and object. Thus, Plato's criterion is not only compatible with Schier's, but it seems to be the more deeply explanatory of the two. Furthermore, Schier's criterion fails just when the relevant intention of the artist is not recoverable on the basis of resemblances between experiences alone. If an artist paints a biblical figure that he has never seen, then one's ability to recognize the real person in the closest possible world in which one saw him might not suffice to interpret the painting correctly. The artist here relies on his image of what the figure looked like (or would look like), and viewers might need to rely on knowledge of certain conventional ways of representing the figure in paintings. This example shows that Plato's criterion needs some filling out to cover such cases, but it also shows once more that Schier's criterion depends for its application on the applicability of Plato's. One's interpretation of a picture as being a representation of an object O will be based on ability to recognize O only if there is a resemblance between visual experience of the picture and visual experience of the object.

Another alternative has been advocated by Kendall Walton (1990). He holds that a painting is a representation of an object if it prescribes that one imagine that the experience of looking at it is visual experience of that object. If one is indeed to react to paintings in this way, one remains suspicious that the aptness of this prescription would depend on an antecedent similarity between the visual experience of the painting and that of the object. Without this similarity, the prescription (if it could be communicated in some other way) would be useless and, in any case, would not render the painting a representation of the object. Thus, once more, Plato's criterion seems to be more fundamental.

To complete properly the account implicit in Plato's criterion would require spelling out the ways in which visual experience of a painting must resemble that of its object if the intention of its artist is to be successful. Similarity of shape in the visual field is usually crucial, but not always so. A child's depiction of a leaf may depend more for its success on its bright green color, for example. If this criterion is correct, however, then, because resemblance comes in degrees, being a successful representation falls in a scale somewhere between failure and perfect true-to-lifeness. In addition, a painting will be more true to life the more visual experience of it resembles that of its object.

The question of value raised by Plato—how a representation, an imitation of an appearance of an object, could have value approaching that of the object itself (let alone its Platonic form)—has been addressed far less often in contemporary philosophy. One might imagine three standard sorts of answers, all problematic, to the question of the value of representation in painting. The first would appeal to knowledge of an object gained through perceiving its painted representation, at best knowledge normally not gained by perceiving the object itself. The second appeals to the way that viewing paintings is supposed to alter one's visual experience of objects in the real world. The third emphasizes the exercise of imagination that pictorial representation prompts.

The claim about representation as a source of knowledge of its objects might be most plausible in the cases of portraiture and historical and religious paintings. A good portrait might be claimed to reveal deep or hidden facets of its subject's personality or to reveal her true personal identity. But in fact, most portraits, even very good ones, reveal rather wooden poses, designed to project a certain dignity and social status instead of true inner states. Other genres, such as still life, afford no (propositional) knowledge of their objects worth having at all. Historical and religious paintings might bring to life episodes of which there is prior knowledge, but they cannot teach anything about those events not available in far more detail in written texts.

The latter two examples suggest the second and third answers to the question of value. Still lifes might be said to retrain one's vision, to invite one to appreciate aesthetic qualities of everyday objects that are normally overlooked in everyday practical concerns. This sort of answer—the effect of representational art on ways of perceiving outside the context of art—is again associated with Goodman. Many still lifes provide evidence for it in the way that they distribute sharp focus evenly across the canvas, seemingly directing attention at otherwise unnoticed qualities that they exemplify or refer to. But this thesis assumes a plasticity in viewers' visual systems that they may not have. That visual perception remains normally in the service of practical behavior may be evolutionarily hardwired and therefore not subject to such facile readjustment. It is more plausible that viewing art changes the ways one looks at other art, where practical concerns are suspended, than that they have major effects on one's perceptions in more pressing everyday contexts.

In bringing to life episodes from religious or mythological texts or from history, narrative paintings may have the sort of value suggested by Walton's theory of representation, the value of exercising imagination in fictional games. According to him, representations function as props in games of make-believe. By prescribing certain complex imaginings in common, they prompt viewers to enter imaginatively the worlds of fictional texts and paintings. They therefore allow others to share in the imaginative genius of artists, to enter artists' imaginary worlds, thereby expanding their own emotional capacities, envisaging new possibilities of experience, and sharing these vicarious experiences with others. But does one typically imagine oneself to be in the fictional world of a painting? The thesis seems more at home in the context of literature, but even there it is more likely that one imagines the narrated events occurring than that one imagines oneself witness to them, or even to their narration. Some paintings may encourage the viewer to enter their fictional worlds, as when a subject in a portrait averts her gaze, but others—for example, those that strongly emphasize formal balance or unity—discourage it. The thesis therefore at best provides a very partial answer to Plato's question (Walton never intends otherwise).

An approach at least as promising as any of the three canvased above would focus on the way that representation contributes to or enhances other acknowledged sources of value in painting. It is obvious that representation functions as a means of expression. Despite the somewhat misnomered movement of Abstract Expressionism, there can be little doubt that human events, demeanors, and (not surprisingly) expressions, as well as natural scenes as depicted in paintings, are more expressive than abstract forms and colors. Perhaps less appreciated is the fact that representation enhances the pure sensuous beauty of many paintings and affords the possibility of levels of formal structure beyond those achievable in purely abstract forms. The flesh tones of a Titian or a Renoir are far more sensuously beautiful for being just that—representations of flesh tones.

In regard to form, representations naturally group formal elements into larger units, which can unify otherwise diverse or incomprehensible spaces and can relate into higher-level formal structures. In addition, they create new formal elements: increased depth, movement, weight, and human mental aspects that can create tensions, harmonies, contrasts, unities, and so on. All this can greatly enrich the formal possibilities available to artists beyond those derivable from line and color alone. In a representational painting, such material forms can reinforce expressive aspects or tensions and harmonies on the psychological level, for example, or they can generate new contrasts and tensions.

Thinking thus of the interactions between representation and other sources of aesthetic value makes it easier to answer Plato's question. Returning to the genre of still life, if one thinks of how perceptual and cognitive capacities are challenged and satisfied in grasping the ways that formal elements in the paint create content, which in turn creates and enhances formal structure in a painting, it seems easy to see why such rich perceptual experience is of more value than the visual experience of ordinary real fruit. That the former must resemble the latter in order for representation to succeed at all does not imply, as Plato seemed to think, that it must remain subordinate in value. That we appreciate this more easily when we relate representation to expression and form does not imply that there is not some truth in each of the approaches indicated to answering Plato's challenge.

[*See also* Plato.]

BIBLIOGRAPHY

Gombrich, E. H. *Art and Illusion: A Study in the Psychology of Pictorial Representation* (1960). 2d rev. ed. New York, 1961; reprint, Princeton, N.J., 1969.
Goodman, Nelson. *Languages of Art: An Approach to a Theory of Symbols.* 2d ed. Indianapolis, 1976.
Neander, Karen. "Pictorial Representation: A Matter of Resemblance." *British Journal of Aesthetics* 27.3 (Summer 1987): 213–226.
Peacocke, Christopher. "Depiction." *Philosophical Review* 96.3 (July 1987): 383–410.
Plato. *The Republic.* Translated by Allan Bloom. New York, 1968.
Sartwell, Crispin. "Natural Generativity and Imitation." *British Journal of Aesthetics* 31.1 (January 1991): 58–67.
Schier, Flint. *Deeper into Pictures: An Essay on Pictorial Representation.* Cambridge and New York, 1986.
Walton, Kendall L. *Mimesis as Make-Believe: On the Foundations of the Representational Arts.* Cambridge, Mass., 1990.
Wollheim, Richard. *Painting as an Art.* Princeton, N.J., 1987.

ALAN GOLDMAN

Depiction

Our visual world is awash with pictures representing all kinds of objects and scenes. The ease with which we interpret these pictures, using what seem to be ordinary visual skills, might make it seem as though there can be little mystery to pictorial representation. But three facts about pictures seem to be in conflict and prove difficult to reconcile.

The first fact is that we understand what pictures represent almost without effort. Unlike languages, for example, little or no learning is needed to interpret pictures. This a fact about our *competence* with pictures. The second fact is that when we look at pictures, we seem to see the objects and scenes they represent or purport to represent. All pictures inform us about things by causing us to have visual experiences "as of" those things. This fact about the *phenomenology* of pictures also sets them apart from other representational media such as language. The third fact is that pictures represent their subjects in a remarkable variety of ways. Consider, for example, how a Cubist, a Haida printmaker, and a Byzantine icon painter would portray a face. As already acknowledged, each portrait will evoke an experience as of the face, yet none of these experiences will be much like looking at the face itself. (Picasso's portrait of Kahnweiler evokes an experience that is not at all like looking at the art dealer in the flesh.) This *diversity* gives pictures a history, an anthropology, and a sociology, for how the world is portrayed varies with time, place, and purpose. It suggests that pictures are like languages in their reliance on social conventions.

These three facts are puzzling when taken together. Our competence with pictures and our experiences of them lend support to the widely endorsed view that pictures are perceptual representations. But some philosophers, notably Nelson Goodman, have been so impressed by the fact of pictorial diversity that they have argued that pictures are not perceptual representations but function as symbols whose meaning is determined by social conventions.

Perceptual Theories. The central tenet of perceptual theories is that depiction is applied seeing: the processes employed in interpreting pictures depend on the very processes involved in seeing the real-world objects that are their subjects. Of course, this claim can be, and has been, elaborated in different ways. Different conceptions of vision are apt to inspire different views of the way it figures in depiction.

Mimesis or resemblance. According to one version of the perceptual theory, a picture represents either because it is objectively similar to its subject, sharing visual properties with it, or because it evokes visual experiences that are similar to visual experiences of its subject. Thus, we interpret *Wivenhoe Park,* the painting, by noticing that it looks like Wivenhoe Park, the place. But "looking like" can mean just about anything, so the challenge is to state in some detail what features pictures (or our experiences of them) share with their subjects (or our experiences of them).

Surprisingly, the resemblance theory wins little support from the phenomenology of pictures, provided certain elementary distinctions are drawn. In particular, one must not confuse the marks, shapes, colors, and textures on a picture's surfaces in virtue of which it represents its subject with the visual properties (including properties of shape, color, and texture) it represents its subject as having. Call the former a picture's "design," and the latter its representational "content." It is undeniable that the fact that we experience pictures as of their subjects means that their contents resemble properties of their subjects. But this lends no support to the resemblance theory because it is precisely this content-subject resemblance that we are seeking to explain. The resemblance theory must therefore explain how pictures acquire their contents in terms of similarities between their designs (or experiences of them) and properties of their subjects (or experiences of them).

The resemblance theory loses much of its appeal once it is acknowledged that it posits similarities between a picture's designed but flat surface and the scene it represents. After all, a picture's designed surface usually looks more like the designed surfaces of other pictures than like its typically three-dimensional, animate subject. Moreover, it is doubtful that the kinds of similarities in virtue of which pictures are alleged to represent things are uniform across the spectrum of pictorial styles. The design-subject similarities that obtain in *Wivenhoe Park* and its subject are not of the same kind as those that obtain between Marcel Duchamp's *Nude Descending a Staircase* and its subject. Finally, the resemblance theory must come to terms with pictures that represent things that do not exist. How can a picture of a unicorn resemble a unicorn when there are no unicorns?

Illusion and seeing-in. One might maintain that depiction depends in some way on vision, but without invoking the notion of resemblance. In his groundbreaking discussion of depiction, *Art and Illusion* (1960), E. H. Gombrich explains that pictures exploit "illusion devices," designs that take advantage of the possibility of visual ambiguities and failures in visual discrimination, so as to trigger false or "illusionistic" visual experiences as of objects that are really not there. *Wivenhoe Park* tricks viewers, as it were, into experiencing it as if it were Wivenhoe Park. Likewise, Richard Wollheim (1987), taking a hint from Leonardo da Vinci's notebook on painting, suggests that viewers *see* things *in* pictorial designs, just as they see horses in clouds or landscapes in certain water-stained walls. Both the illusion and seeing-in theories are ultimately concerned with the network of relations between the experience of a picture's designed surface, its content, and the actual objects or scenes that it represents.

As his use of the concept of illusion would suggest, Gombrich claims that an experience of a picture is the kind of experience one might actually have of its subject. An experience of *Wivenhoe Park* is illusionistic because it is the kind of experience one might have while looking at the place itself. This does not mean, as some object, that pictures are necessarily deceptive in the sense of engendering false beliefs ("oh, there is Wivenhoe Park!") but merely that they have the potential to deceive.

Yet, it seems unlikely that the illusion theory either accommodates the diversity of pictures or correctly characterizes all pictorial experiences. Surely, there is little if any chance that Cubist collages, or even line drawings, for instance, cause experiences that might be confused with experiences caused by their subjects themselves. Moreover, the illusion theory implies that when one looks at a picture, one experiences either its designed surface or the scene it represents, but not both at the same time. If an experience of a picture is an experience that its (three-dimensional) subject might cause, then it is not simultaneously an experience as of a flat, designed, inanimate surface. But surely one can simultaneously experience a picture as a flat, colored surface and as representing its subject.

The seeing-in theory takes seriously the possibility—indeed, the desirability—of simultaneous experience of a picture's designed surface and an experience as of its represented subject. Wollheim argues that the distinctive phenomenology of pictorial experience lies in its "twofoldness." Unlike experiences its subject itself might cause, an experience of a picture is always both an experience as of its subject and an experience of a flat, designed surface. This suggests that the seeing-in theory can embrace pictorial diversity. Indeed, line drawings and Cubist collages might deliberately draw attention to their surface features and the way those features support a particular content. If pictorial experience is distinct from ordinary visual experience, however, and if seeing-in is a distinctive kind of seeing, then we need an account of the relationship between seeing-in and just plain seeing. Wollheim speculates that seeing-in comes down to resemblance, but what rules out the possibility that seeing-in depends not on seeing visual resemblances, but on a mastery of symbols, as the symbol theorist claims?

Symbol Theories. Goodman is the most prominent champion of the symbol theory of depiction. Pictures, he argues, do not depict because we first see scenes and objects in them; on the contrary, what we see in pictures is determined by our beliefs, imaginings, or knowledge about what they represent. The notoriety of Goodman's repudiation of perceptual theories of depiction has, unfortunately, overshadowed his more abiding insight that an analysis of pictures can usefully be modeled on an analysis of linguistic expressions and other symbols with which they share certain logical properties. It is useful to separate Goodman's observations about the logic of pictures from his assault on perceptualism.

The logic of pictures. Goodman offers a semantic theory of depiction: pictorial representation involves denotation and predication in a symbol system. Just as a word or sentence in a language refers to an object or a state of affairs, a picture belongs to a pictorial symbol system in which it refers to objects and scenes; and just as some words or phrases in a language function as predicates, pictures in a pictorial symbol system represent what they denote as having properties. The *Mona Lisa* portrays a woman as smiling enigmatically because it belongs to a system in which it denotes a certain person and predicates of her the property "is enigmatic." With predication comes the possibility of misrepresentation and the phenomenon of representation-as. A drawing that represents Winston Churchill as a lion denotes Churchill and predicates a property of him that he does not literally have. The distinctions that Goodman draws among the various representational functions that a picture can perform enable us to rigorously analyze the complex structure of its content.

Denotation and predication always take place in the context of a system whose function is to lay down what any given design denotes or predicates. The systematicity of pictures accommodates their diversity. As already noted, pictures belong to diverse styles or systems, each sufficiently different from the others to frustrate the resemblance theory. These styles have an internal coherence because pictorial competence is system-relative; that is, an ability to interpret some pictures in a style or system entails an ability to interpret readily and correctly other pictures in the same system, but not necessarily an ability to interpret readily and correctly pictures in other styles or systems. Someone versed in the system popularized by Leon Battista Alberti can interpret any number of academic landscapes but may need to learn how to "read" Cubist pictures because they belong to an unfamiliar system.

What systems are familiar varies from one social setting to another. Pictorial systems, like languages, gain footholds in communities whose members have developed the requisite picture-reading skills. The hypothesis that the competence of makers and users of pictures is a social phenomenon is a powerful analytic tool, useful to anybody who studies pictures, for investigating why pictures are made in certain styles at certain times and places.

Although picture systems have the same semantic structure of denotation and predication as linguistic systems, the two media are obviously different. Goodman ascribes this to the formal properties of pictorial symbol systems. Pictures are "analogue," because any difference in a design property makes a difference in what symbol the picture is and what content it has; and pictures are "relatively replete," because more surface properties have representational significance in pictures than in other kinds of symbols.

Antiperceptualism. None of Goodman's observations about the logic of pictures entails antiperceptualism. Assuming a sufficiently fluid conception of vision, there is no reason why the mechanisms of pictorial denotation and predication and the organization of pictures into systems might not turn out to depend on facts about vision. Despite this, Goodman insists that pictorial representation is arbitrary. *Wivenhoe Park*, he proclaims, could represent a pink elephant—it could denote an elephant and attribute to it the property of being pink. The arguments for this are unconvincing. Goodman proceeds with remarkable insouciance from a refutation of the resemblance theory and the observation that pictures denote and predicate to a repudiation of perceptualism. To admit that pictures belong to diverse systems is not to say that any picture may depict any object as having any property.

Moreover, the antiperceptualist version of the symbol theory neglects the obvious candidate for distinguishing pictorial symbol systems from others, namely, their visual phenomenology. This is implicit in the principle that what a picture represents does not depend simply on the look of the individual picture, but on what pictorial symbol system the picture is part of.

The symbol theorist might attribute the distinctive phenomenology of pictures to the way they are embedded in social contexts. In a particular social setting, pictures in familiar symbol systems will typically be taken as setting the standard for what things look like. As Goodman puts it, pictures do not look like nature, they look the way nature is usually painted. The trouble with this, however, is that even a picture in a wholly unfamiliar system is experienced as looking like its subject in some way (though perhaps not in the preferred way). *Nude Descending a Staircase* belongs to an unfamiliar system, yet it looks like its subject (though not in the same way as would a portrayal employing a more familiar system). All pictures are experienced as of their subjects, not just pictures in familiar systems.

Hybrid Theories. One response to the impasse between symbol and perceptual theories is to cobble them together.

According to Gombrich, for example, there is a continuum of pictorial styles, with illusionistic pictures employing purely perceptual means of representation at one extreme and "conceptual" pictures that represent by convention at the other. Like too many attempts at compromise, however, Gombrich's pictorial dualism avoids the disadvantages of neither theory. By separating conceptual pictures (Cubism, the split style) from illusionistic ones (Constable and Company), it privileges the latter as most closely approaching an absolute ideal of visual experience that is insulated from social factors, while simultaneously relinquishing perceptual accounts of so-called conceptual pictures.

A better, nondualistic, hybrid recognizes the contribution that both symbol and perceptual theories can make to a unified theory for all pictures. The symbol theory stresses the advantages of sensitivity to the diversity and systematic organization of pictorial styles, and reminds us that what system of depiction is used depends on who uses it and where it is used. Enjoying these advantages does not commit one to antiperceptualism. The advantage of perceptual theories is that they promise to explain the obvious phenomenological affinities between seeing things in pictures and seeing them in the flesh.

Most perceptual theories are unstable because they rest on too narrow conceptions of vision. Pictorial diversity does not call perceptualism into question, provided one tolerates a fluid and flexible conception of visual processes. It is useful perhaps to think of pictorial diversity as stretching the boundaries of the visual in a number of directions.

Recent years have seen a growing appreciation among philosophers and psychologists of the dynamism of vision. For example, such processes as object recognition cannot be reduced to noticing resemblances, for we are able to recognize objects despite changes in the way they look. We can recognize objects from novel points of view, in distorting mirrors, or when changed over time. We can also recognize objects as they appear in pictures belonging to different styles or systems of representation. These new recognition abilities are learned, though in a special way: once we have learned to recognize some objects whose appearance changed in a particular way, we can recognize any object changed in the same way. Once we can recognize some things upside down, we can recognize anything upside down; once we have learned to recognize a Cubist mandolin, we can recognize a Cubist art dealer. This might explain why there are many styles of depiction, why new ones are acquired as a system following a moderate amount of learning, and why pictures can evoke experiences of objects that do not appear as they do in the flesh.

Hybrid theories have the happy side effect of illuminating the aesthetics of pictures. Not all pictures are works of art, of course, but if aesthetic engagement with pictorial art differs from engagement with other kinds of art, then a theory of depiction should provide a foundation for explanations of this distinctive pictorial aesthetic. Both the view that pictures merely imitate reality and the view that pictures are merely conventional symbols assimilate experience of pictorial art to a generic aesthetic. One should acknowledge that pictures extend the kinds of visual experiences one can have in novel ways that are responsive to social practices, for herein lies the importance of picture-making not only as a form of communication but also as a medium for artistic expression unlike any other.

BIBLIOGRAPHY

Black, Max. "How Do Pictures Represent?" In *Art, Perception, and Reality*, by E. H. Gombrich, Julian Hochberg, and Max Black, edited by Maurice Mandelbaum. Baltimore, 1972.

Bryson, Norman. "Semiology and Visual Interpretation." In *Visual Theory*, edited by Norman Bryson, Michael Ann Holly, and Keith Moxey. New York, 1991.

Gombrich, E. H. *Art and Illusion: A Study in the Psychology of Pictorial Representation* (1960). 2d rev. ed. Reprint, Princeton, N.J., 1969.

Gombrich, E. H. *The Image and the Eye: Further Studies in the Psychology of Pictorial Representation.* Oxford, 1982.

Goodman, Nelson. *Languages of Art: An Approach to a Theory of Symbols.* 2d ed. Indianapolis, 1976.

Hagen, Margaret A., ed. *The Perception of Pictures.* 2 vols. New York and London, 1980.

Hagen, Margaret A. *Varieties of Realism: Geometries of Representational Art.* Cambridge and New York, 1986.

Lopes, Dominic. *Understanding Pictures.* Oxford, 1996.

Maynard, Patrick. "Depiction, Vision, and Convention." *American Philosophical Quarterly* 9.3 (July 1972): 243–250.

Neander, Karen. "Pictorial Representation: A Matter of Resemblance." *British Journal of Aesthetics* 27.3 (Summer 1987): 213–226.

Novitz, David. "Picturing." *Journal of Aesthetics and Art Criticism* 34.2 (Winter 1975): 144–155.

Peacocke, Christopher. "Depiction." *Philosophical Review* 96.3 (July 1987): 383–410.

Podro, Michael. "Depiction and the Golden Calf." In *Visual Theory*, edited by Norman Bryson, Michael Ann Holly, and Keith Moxey. New York, 1991.

Schier, Flint. *Deeper into Pictures: An Essay on Pictorial Representation.* Cambridge and New York, 1986.

Walton, Kendall L. *Mimesis as Make-Believe: On the Foundations of the Representational Arts.* Cambridge, Mass., 1990.

Wollheim, Richard. "Seeing-As, Seeing-In, and Pictorial Representation." In *Art and Its Objects.* 2d ed., with six supplementary essays. Cambridge and New York, 1980.

Wollheim, Richard. *Painting as an Art.* Princeton, N.J., 1987.

DOMINIC M. MCIVER LOPES

Resemblance

One often talks about works of art as resembling what they represent in some respects and to some degree. Paintings, photographs, and sculptures are said to look like the objects they stand for. Some pieces of music are said to sound like their subjects. Actors are sometimes said to move like the people they portray. The issue of interest to philosophers of art is whether these resemblances are significant. Does an artwork represent or refer to an object by virtue of resembling it? Is an artwork a better or more realistic or more pleasing representation the more it resembles the object it stands for? Can one distinguish different forms of representation by the fact that some forms necessarily resemble what they represent and some do not?

Although these are questions about the general relationship between artworks and their subjects, the notion of resemblance in aesthetics is most often introduced in theorizing about the pictorial arts. Most people are inclined to believe that pictures bear some resemblance or likeness to the objects that they depict, and this intuition has led many theorists to claim that it is just this relation of resemblance between a picture and its referent that is the condition of pictorial significance; it is by virtue of a resemblance between pictures and objects in the world that pictures make sense, that one can tell what a picture is of. Thus, a picture of Winston Churchill represents or refers to Churchill and not Napoleon Bonaparte because it resembles or looks like the former and not the latter. In the so-called copy theory of representation, one of the least complicated models adopting this ontological approach, resemblance is taken as natural relation between a picture and referent where the referent is "reality" or "the way things are" or "the way things look." A belief in this privileged relation accounts for the way many art historians and theorists explain elements of realistic depiction. Pictures can be said to be more "realistic" in proportion to the completeness of the resemblance relation. The more the picture of Churchill resembles that man, the more realistic or perhaps more accurate a representation of Churchill it is.

The view that representational works, especially pictures, resemble or mirror or look like things in the world has been a predominant one in Western aesthetics. Its influence is often traced to the development of naturalistic representation in Greek visual art from the sixth and fourth centuries BCE. Historically, Greek naturalism is believed to be important for two reasons: first, because it is believed to have determined the main character of European art in antiquity, and second because the naturalistic tradition was revived in the Renaissance and has retained its influence until this century. The main concern of aesthetic naturalism is to produce convincing facsimiles of the visible appearances of things; the more an artwork looks like the object being represented, the more successful it is as a naturalistic representation of that object. A considerable fund of popular stories about the Greek artists has been preserved, mainly by Pliny, attesting to their fascination with the creation of illusions of nature. Apelles was supposed to have painted a horse so realistically that live horses were deceived and neighed. In a painting competition between Parrhius and Zeuxis, Zeuxis painted grapes so lifelike that birds pecked at them. Parrhius was supposed to have countered by painting a curtain that deceived even Zeuxis into asking to have the curtain drawn so that he could see the picture. Similar stories appear during the Renaissance. Giorgio Vasari, for example, recounts that Bernazzone painted strawberries that were pecked at by peacocks. Giotto painted a fly on the nose of a portrait that Giovanni Cimabue was working on that was so lifelike that Cimabue took it for a real fly and tried to brush it away.

The conception of artworks as illusions or replicas of reality encourages the view that representational art involves the copying of the external appearances of things. To a great extent, this view was largely taken for granted by many philosophers and historians prior to the twentieth century, and this had a profound effect on the kinds of theoretical questions raised about the arts. One question that concerned both Plato and Aristotle is whether or not artworks have any cognitive value. If one assumes, as both these thinkers do, that the primary purpose of the arts is to duplicate the way the world looks, then one might wonder whether they can teach us anything about the objects that they represent. In the now famous passages of the *Republic* dealing with the mimetic arts, Plato concludes that they cannot. His attack is largely influenced by his ontological commitment to a unique and unvarying realm of Forms. For Plato, any particular sensible object is not wholly a real thing because it comes into being and perishes and is perpetually changing. Sensible objects do embody, however, albeit imperfectly, their respective essential Forms. A picture, because it is merely a two-dimensional representation of the appearance of a solid object seen at a certain angle, is, so to speak, as far as possible from the realm of Forms. One cannot, in other words, gain any knowledge of reality, the Forms, through pictures. Aristotle also assumes that pictorial art is imitative, although he believes that the enjoyment of recognizing likenesses in pictures is specifically the intellectual pleasure involved in learning something new about the objects represented.

The adoption of the resemblance model led to an increasing emphasis being placed on the representational content of artworks and on the skills of the artist in reproducing those likenesses. The work of art becomes, as it were, transparent and one looks through it at what it represents. One does not see a beautiful picture so much as a beautiful body skillfully imitated. Thus, in much of Western art criticism, attention is focused on the scenes and the stories represented as opposed to the artworks themselves, and if the quality of the artwork is to be evaluated, it is usually in respect to how accurately or how cleverly it achieves a semblance of reality. For example, for many theorists, including Aristotle, it is the artist's craftsmanship that explains why one enjoys looking at pictures of ugly or disturbing subjects. The notion of accuracy or craftsmanship of representation is also at the heart of a dominant view in art history that the development of new representational styles and techniques is connected with the progression toward greater and greater verisimilitude.

Clearly, if one assumes that artworks visually resemble the world in some way, then the problem arises about how to deal with works that purport to represent something that cannot be seen. For Plato, the Forms are the kinds of things that could not be understood or approached through the appearances of things. Pictures and poetry, he believes, are misleading or dangerous precisely because they give the impression of reality without affording any access to it. This idea is echoed in the religious debates on idolatry and in the biblical injunction against the production of likenesses of God. Again, the assumption at work here is that certain representations, specifically pictures and sculptures, resemble what they represent. One of the fears with similarity-based representation is that there is the possibility of substitutive error in which the symbol, the idol, ceases to be a representation of God and comes to be seen as God himself or as part of him. If one assumes that God has no image or that no person has ever seen it, then any likeness created of God must necessarily be mistaken. The error involved is in the very act of making a likeness of something that either has no image or of which one has no visual experience.

The ban against the production of likenesses of God is interpreted as a ban specifically on the visual arts and is not typically extended to linguistic descriptions of deities. Representations of the latter sort are not considered prone to the same kind of representational or substitutive errors because they do not purport to resemble the objects they stand for. The idea that pictures and words can be distinguished by the way in which representations or symbols refer gains greater prominence at the start of the twentieth century with the development of semiotics. Charles Sanders Peirce, for example, divided the various kinds of representations into three categories. The first is representation based on resemblance; the second is causal representation; and the third is conventional-based representation. Representation based on similarity means that one thing represents or refers to another in virtue of its being similar to it. In causal representation, the relation between the symbol and the thing symbolized is not a relation of similarity; other relations are involved, such as metonymy, in which a part represents the whole. In conventional representation, the symbol is associated with a thing by conventions or rules. This is taken not to be true of representations based on similarity, where the representation is natural and obvious and not controlled by special rules that must be learned. [*See* Peirce.]

Although Peirce's taxonomy does not necessarily commit him to placing pictures in one class over another, he nevertheless puts pictures squarely in the class of similarity-based symbols and words in the class of symbols determined by conventions. Like many before him, he assumes that this is the way that pictures work. In the later part of the twentieth century, this assumption comes under greater and greater scrutiny. Partly this is the result of increasing interest in

both philosophy and psychology with understanding the formal nature of the relation and the nature of similarity judgments. Also, during this time, there is growing skepticism of the ontological and epistemological assumptions inherent in naturalism that there is one way that the world is or is given to us. In fact, some of the most thorough accounts of pictorial representation in the twentieth century are all predicated on a rejection of a natural connection between pictures and the objects they depict. There is a group of art historians and philosophers who argue that various sorts of resemblance, or naturalist accounts of pictorial representation, cannot be correct. According to these so-called conventionalists, there is no special sort of similarity between a picture and its subject. Instead, one is habituated to certain styles of picturing the world and it is in only virtue of this familiarity that such styles seem so well suited to their representational tasks. For a conventionalist, it is habit that favors or constrains the choice of pictorial styles and the way pictures work within those styles. For the naturalist, on the other hand, there is a real resemblance between picture and pictured. There are facts about us as human beings, and facts about the world, that prompt us to recognize the world in pictures.

The art historian E. H. Gombrich (1960) argues that there is no "innocent eye," no way of perceiving objects free of experience and knowledge, and thus no way to determine the way these objects "really are." Although he does not want to deny that visual skills are perhaps at some deep level automatic and programmed to seek out certain features of the world, Gombrich stresses that perception itself is the product of habit. Elicited by certain clues in the environment, vision is a process of making judgments about meaning or expectations. One does not passively receive information from the world. Instead, one is motivated by specific purposes to look for and find significant features of the world. Representational practices are conventional in that the artist has to invent rules or schemata for laying down clues that can substitute for the information sought when looking at nature. The recent history of art, for Gombrich, is a progressive history in which the artist has sought to invent artificial methods of eliciting these responses. Pictures are realistic not because they mirror or look like the objects they depict but because they can be read or interpreted in the same terms as natural objects. The similarity of a picture with natural objects is not like the relation of a copy to an original but of the kind of mental or visual activities both can arouse. Although Gombrich shifts the relation of resemblance away from the representation and the object to the judgments of viewers and denies the naturalist's epistemological and ontological assumptions that one can get at the way the world actually is, he manages only to postpone and recast the question of a natural or privileged relation between pictures and the world. If a judgment that two things are similar is based on similar uses of visual skills, and if ultimately these skills are anchored in a natural mechanism, then there remains the possibility of explaining depictive practices in terms of this natural basis.

A more radical conventionalist analysis of representation is put forward by Nelson Goodman. According to Goodman, descriptions and pictures are semantically analogous. Both kinds of symbols denote what they represent and denotation is independent of resemblance. That pictures seem to function symbolically is quite important for Goodman. If pictorial systems are symbolic systems, then he thinks that he can fully explain the relation between a picture and what it pictures merely by detailing the formal conditions of these systems. Outlining what these formal conditions are for representational systems makes up a large part of his project in *Languages of Art* (1976). Although Goodman likes to stress the analogy between picturing and describing, he does maintain that pictorial and discursive systems are different. Nevertheless, because both picturing and describing are species of the same mode of symbolization, Goodman believes that the difference between them is not found in the way that symbols are correlated with their referents (as in Peirce's analysis), but in the structure of the systems themselves. In order to know whether or not something is a picture and in order to determine what a picture is of, one need only know the lexicon and formal rules of the actual representational system that the symbol belongs to. Whether a picture depicts Napoleon depends on the rules correlating the picture with that French emperor, in the same way that a series of sentences in French describing the emperor is a function of the rules or the linguistic system of French. Just as one could choose another language—for example, English—to describe the world, one could choose another pictorial system to depict it. Pictures are just as conventional as language.

It should be noted that Goodman's claim that many systems of representation can be constructed does not by itself constitute a threat to the resemblance model of depiction. The possibility of there being many systems may lead one to ask which is the more correct. Proponents of resemblance need not deny the possibility of there being a system of representation in which the symbols stand for objects they in no way resemble. What they do deny is that all systems accurately or truthfully describe the world. Resemblance, therefore, works as a kind a standard of realism or accuracy or truthfulness. The system of representation employed in the Renaissance, for example, can be said to be more realistic than that employed by the Cubists because the pictures produced in accordance with that system more resemble the objects and scenes that they stand for. Given Goodman's own analysis of the pictorial, it should not be surprising that he is committed to showing that resemblance is not a condition for pictorial representation. Much of Goodman's critique of this relation, however, is motivated by doubts of a more general, and perhaps more damning, nature. Goodman thinks that the notions of resemblance and similarity can play no explanatory role in philosophical analysis. Moreover, and more importantly in his specific attacks against the role of resemblance in the pictorial arts, he thinks that any account that appeals to these relations either to explain the relationship of pictures to the world or to explain their accuracy does so because of what he believes to be misguided ontological assumptions.

One of the major problems that Goodman finds with the notion of similarity is that it cannot be formally defined in a way that can do any explanatory work. If one takes similarity as an unrelativized primitive holding between objects and measured in terms of possession of common features, then one option might be to say that two things are similar if they have only one property in common. The problem with this definition is that any two things have some property in common: any two objects, regardless of what they are, are similar. We advance no further if one specifies that the objects must share all their properties, because no two distinct things have all their properties in common. Defined in this way, the relation turns out to be either vacuous (the claim that an object resembles itself) or false (the claim that there exist no two distinct objects that are similar). This problem is only complicated when one tries to define similarity as a comparative rather than an absolute relation—objects x and y are more similar to one another than objects a and b—for any two things have as many properties in common as any other two. If there are three things in the universe, then any two of them belong exactly in two classes and have exactly two properties in common: the property of belonging to the class of two things and the property of belonging to the class of three things. As the universe gets bigger, the number of shared properties—the classes they belong to—will be larger, but will remain the same for any two things. Every two things will be as similar as any other two things. If resemblance is going to do any explanatory work—for example, if it is to distinguish resembling pairs from nonresembling ones—it has to be defined in a nonvacuous way. As Goodman has shown, a definition of resemblance in terms of quantity of properties shared will not suffice. This puts the burden of proof on the proponent of resemblance to come up with another definition, and most importantly, a definition that functions as a fixed standard for measuring likenesses in all cases.

One might object that, in saying that two objects resemble each other, one has not established any significant relationship between these objects until one specifies the respect in which they are similar, that is, until one specifies what the properties shared are. Goodman argues, however, that once one defines similarity in terms of specified respects, the resemblance relation turns out to be epistemically superfluous, for it is the respects and not some abstract principle of resemblance that conveys the meaning of the relation. Put another way, to say that a set of things is similar in respect to be being green is just to say that all those things are green, and to know this is to undermine the need to ask why they are similar in the first place. Resemblance in terms of respects, for Goodman, is highly dependent on the conceptual systems used to classify features of the world: to say that someone resemble her grandmother in one respect and not in another is a matter of the task, the conceptual system employed, and the appropriateness under that system of applying that predicate to that person and not to her grandmother. It is these conceptual systems (or, in Gombrich's terminology, schemata), that are the force in determining which respects are a relevant or significant feature of an object, not nature. Like Gombrich, Goodman is opposed to the idea that knowledge of the world can be built up of conceptually free perception. All knowledge and perception involves classification and selection for specific purposes. The world does not come ready-made.

As Goodman sees it, the resemblance view of representation is committed both to the idea that pictures mirror the world and to the idea that the world is structured in only one way. It is this latter ontological commitment that Goodman takes to be at the heart of the naturalist's belief that pictures are more or less true, or more or less realistic, in virtue of how well or how poorly they resemble this world. Given this commitment, Goodman argues, the naturalist cannot be satisfied with resemblance in respects because this kind of resemblance is not independent of the representational systems we are accustomed to. What the naturalist needs is a kind of resemblance that will allow her to judge degrees of correlation with reality across representational systems, a kind of similarity that has some sort of epistemically privileged status outside any particular way of conceptualizing the world.

Another common line of attack aimed specifically against resemblance as a requirement of depiction, and one used both by Goodman and Max Black, is that resemblance cannot be a sufficient condition for representation. The claim that resemblance is a sufficient condition for representation amounts to the claim that every case of resemblance is a case of representation, and both Goodman and Black believe that this is fairly easy to disprove. They point out that, unlike representation, resemblance is reflexive. Particular objects resemble themselves to a maximum degree, but rarely represent themselves. Also unlike representation, resemblance is symmetrical. If a portrait resembles its sitter, then it follows that the sitter resembles her portrait. The sitter, however, does not represent her portrait. Many pairs of objects resemble each other to various degrees—a twin looks like his twin and a car of a certain make and model resembles another car of the same make and model—yet not every like pair exhibits a symbolic relation. The success of this attack is dependent on it being the case that resemblance and not representation is both reflexive and symmetrical. Neither Goodman nor Black substantiates this claim.

Nevertheless, it is not hard to see why they believe it to be true. In many cases, what one means when one says that two objects resemble one another is that the objects share properties.

Against this line of argument, critics have replied that when one says that a portrait looks like its sitter, one rarely means that the sitter looks like her picture. The formal properties of the relation are not reflected in the way one makes similarity judgments. Several studies in psychology support this view. Amos Tversky (1977) concludes that resemblance statements are in fact highly directional and never constant. For Tversky, this shows that similarity should not be understood as the matching of properties between two objects but as a process in which a subject, in a particular context, determines which predicates apply to two objects once the choice of primary subject and reference—which variable position the objects fill in the statement "a is similar to b"—has already been given. Similarity judgments are highly dependent on context and tasks. Although Tversky's analysis of similarity judgments takes a lot of the power out of Goodman's and Black's counterexamples, his conclusions do support Goodman's contention that similarity judgments are highly relative to one's purposes. If one assumes that determinations of similarity in pictorial cases are dependent on the systems of representation one is accustomed to, then it is the systems that constrain the fact that a picture looks like its subject. Claiming this is not to deny that pictures resemble their referents, but to deny that they look like them in any fixed or independent way.

Because Goodman's attack on resemblance is primarily an attack on a certain metaphysical picture, it works well against theories of depiction that assume that the relation between pictures and the world is direct and neutral and that measure fidelity in terms of a fixed standard of correspondence between the two. The problem is that Goodman assumes that any account of depiction asserting a correspondence between pictures and objects, be it through the notions of imitation or illusion or "looking like," is guilty of these assumptions. He takes all as saying that there is only one correct way that a picture can look or be like its referent. He rules out the possibility that when one talks about likenesses between pictures and natural objects, one can be employing a notion of resemblance for which standards vary from cases to case.

One of the fundamental problems in saying that a picture represents its subject by virtue of resembling it is that it confuses the problem of how pictures are about their referents with how they are like them. To say that something represents something else is to say that it is about or refers to that object. What is it that gives one the status of a signifier and the other the status of something signified? Suppose one has two Brillo boxes, one by the artist Andy Warhol and the other a "real" Brillo box; one wants to say that the former is a representation of the latter. Apart from the fact that one seems to enter into the history of the other, however, there is no observational criterion for saying that one is the "real" Brillo box and the other a representation of the box. Resemblance cannot establish reference in this case, yet it is clear nonetheless that one signifies the other. One cannot reduce the question of what a picture is about to the question of how it is like what it refers to. The former is one of which objects have semantic significance, and this representational significance has to be determined by the appropriate conventions. On at least this point Goodman seems to be correct.

The question of what it means for pictures to look like or resemble what they depict remains open. The problem is that, as they stand, these notions are too loose to bear any weight. Just what does it mean for a picture to look like its subject? One way of trying to spell out these relations is in terms of shared properties. The weakness with this approach is that resemblance is a matter of degree. Even if one assumes that both Pablo Picasso's portrait of his daughter Paloma and Jacques-Louis David's portrait of Napoleon resemble the people they depict in this way, it does not appear that the properties that the latter shares with the French emperor are exactly the same as those shared by Paloma and her portrait. Nor do the portraits and their sitters seem to share the same number of properties. The likenesses between pictures and their subjects will be have to be accounted for on a case-by-case basis.

Many people have pointed out that the intuition that resemblance is involved in depiction does not amount to the claim that there is similarity of substance. No one expects the physical object that is the painting to resemble the physical object that is its subject. One does think, however, that the picture visually resembles the appearance of its subject. Thus, rather than searching for resemblances between things perceived, perhaps one should search for whether there are significant similarities between the experience or act of seeing a picture and the experience or act of seeing things. One of the benefits of understanding resemblance in this way is that it does not appear, at least initially, to fall prey to the kind of formal critique of the similarity relationship leveled by Goodman and Black, because their attacks are aimed primarily against resemblance theories adopting a shared-property relation explaining the relationship between pictures and their subjects. To say that one should understand the seeming correspondence between pictures and their subjects in terms of a correspondence between kinds of visual experiences, however, is merely the start of an analysis of depiction. The primary work that needs to be done is in characterizing the kind of experience involved in seeing representational pictures as well as in specifying how this particular kind of experience is similar to, as well as different from, visual experiences of natural objects.

One of the earliest proponents for understanding pictorial representation as a kind of perceptual capacity, Richard Wollheim (1980), proposed that there is a specific kind of visual experience of a picture—what he calls "seeing-in"—that is analogous to seeing the object pictured and that accounts for the picture's representational effects. Christopher Peacocke (1987) has taken this kind of approach one step further by arguing that depiction can be understood as a "purely perceptual phenomenon" and can thus be defined exclusively in perceptual terms. For Peacocke, a picture of a cat is related to a cat in that it is presented in a region of the visual field experienced as similar in shape to that in which that cat could be presented. Peacocke's account stands in stark opposition to conventionalist analyses of representation, for, on his view, depiction will turn out to be independent of any representational or referential practices that one might learn and employ: the only thing that makes something a picture of a cat and not of anything else is the special perceptual relation of experienced similarity. Not all theorists ascribing to the idea that the relationship between pictures and their subjects should be understood in terms of a correspondence between seeing a picture and seeing a thing take an anticonventionalist stance. In Kendall Walton's (1985) theory of depiction, pictures are props in games of visual make-believe. Make-believe games are governed by conventions that determine which propositions or activities are fictionally true within that game. According to Walton, in the make-believe game played when looking at pictures, fictional truths about the viewer's visual activities are generated by the viewer's actual visual activities, and it is this correspondence that makes the act of looking at pictures similar to the act of looking at things. Joel Snyder (1980), on the other hand, argues that both representing and seeing are conventional practices governed by constructional rules. One learns to see the "natural" world just as one learns to make pictures, and what explains belief in a special relationship between pictures and their subjects is that the same rules of construction apply to both the seeing of an object and the seeing of a representation of that object.

Although these attempts to understand the relationship between pictures and their subjects come to very different conclusions, all of them suggest that depiction is integrally and importantly connected to certain visual practices or experiences. Moreover, it is just this connection that may be at the heart of the deeply entrenched belief in the arts that pictures, unlike other representations, bear a significant and privileged relationship to objects in the world. Whether this is a relationship of resemblance of some kind, or whether it is natural or conventional, is still a matter of debate.

BIBLIOGRAPHY

Gombrich, E. H. *Art and Illusion: A Study in the Psychology of Pictorial Representation* (1960). 2d. rev. ed. New York, 1961; reprint, Princeton, N.J., 1969.
Gombrich, E. H., Julian Hochberg, and Max Black. *Art, Perception and Reality.* Baltimore, 1972.

Goodman, Nelson. "Seven Strictures on Similarity." In *Problems and Projects,* pp. 437–446. Indianapolis, 1972.

Goodman, Nelson. *Languages of Art: An Approach to a Theory of Symbols.* 2d ed. Indianapolis, 1976.

Goodrich, R. A. "Plato on Poetry and Painting." *British Journal of Aesthetics* 22.1 (Winter 1982): 126–137.

Maynard, Patrick. "Depiction, Vision and Convention." *American Philosophical Quarterly* 9.3 (July 1972): 243–250.

Peacocke, Christopher. "Depiction." *Philosophical Review* 96.3 (July 1987): 383–410.

Podro, Michael. "Depiction and the Golden Calf." In *Visual Theory: Painting and Interpretation,* edited by Norman Bryson, Michael Ann Holly, and Keith Moxey, pp. 163–189. New York, 1991.

Pole, David. "Goodman and the 'Naive' View of Representation." *British Journal of Aesthetics* 14.1 (Winter 1974): 68–80.

Schier, Flint. *Deeper into Pictures: An Essay on Pictorial Representation.* Cambridge and New York, 1986.

Snyder, Joel. "Picturing Vision." In *The Language of Images,* edited by W. J. T. Mitchell, pp. 219–246. Chicago, 1980.

Tversky, Amos. "Features of Similarity." *Psychological Review* 84.3 (July 1977): 322–352.

Walton, Kendall L. "Looking at Pictures and Looking at Things." In *Philosophy and the Visual Arts: Seeing and Abstracting,* edited by Andrew Harrison, pp. 277–300. Dordrecht and Boston, 1985.

Wollheim, Richard. *Art and Its Objects.* 2d ed., with six supplementary essays. Cambridge and New York, 1980.

GABRIELA SAKAMOTO

REYNOLDS, JOSHUA (1723–1792), a British portrait painter and aesthetic theorist. A native of Plympton, Devon, Reynolds trained under the portraitist Thomas Hudson, before embarking on a journey to Italy in 1749. Upon returning in 1752, Reynolds painted his first significant work—a dramatic full-length portrait of his companion on the continental journey, Commodore Augustus Keppel (c.1753–1754; London, National Maritime Museum). Reynolds established his home and studio in Leicester Fields, London, and developed an extraordinarily lucrative portrait practice, with a wide range of patrons that included royalty, writers, actors, nobility, and the gentry. He moved in a variety of social circles, and was a member of the Literary Club and the Society of Dilettanti. When the Royal Academy was established in December 1768, King George III appointed Reynolds the institution's first president. His first of fifteen discourses on art was given at the academy's inaugural annual exhibition of paintings on 2 January 1769 and, three months later, he was knighted. Reynolds's grand style is best typified by the portraits of *Sarah Siddons as the Tragic Muse* (exh. RA 1784; San Marino, Huntington Library and Art Gallery) and *Lord Heathfield* (exh. RA 1788; London, Royal Academy), and the subject pictures *The Infant Hercules* (exh. RA 1788; Saint Petersburg, Hermitage) and *Cymon and Iphigenia* (exh. RA 1789; Royal Collection). Reynolds died having established himself as the most successful portraitist of the era and an artist who attempted to enlarge the subject, scope, and quality of English art, in addition to elevating the status of artists in society, through his pictures, publications, and teaching.

It was to *The Idler* that Reynolds first offered his ideas on art in the form of three letters published in 1759. These initially appeared in the *Universal Chronicle* on 29 September, 20 October, and 10 November of that year, and were later republished together as "A Letter on Painting" in the 12–14 May 1761 edition of the *London Chronicle.* The letters represent the first indication of the range of Reynolds's literary aspirations prior to the *Discourses,* serving as a prelude to some of the directions he would later pursue. *The Idler* was published by his close friend Dr. Samuel Johnson, an immense presence in English literary society and a man whom Reynolds clearly emulated. Along with Oliver Goldsmith and Edmund Burke, Johnson was a founding member of Reynolds's The Club (later the Literary Club) in 1764, and encouraged the artist's literary pursuits.

The first letter both attacked and challenged wayward critics of painting and connoisseurs who slavishly adhered to restrictive rules. The second letter presented Reynolds's initial concept of the grand style with respect to the art of Italian painters, contrasting their manner to the fine detail and empirical approach of Dutch artists, which Reynolds saw as mechanical simulation—an idea reprised in his later writings: "Painters should go to the Dutch school to learn the art of painting, as they would go to a grammar school to learn languages. They must go to Italy to learn the higher branches of knowledge" (Reynolds, 1851, vol. 2, pp. 205–206). The final letter provides a recognition of beauty, identifying it with the concept of the "central form" as it emerges from nature and as it is relevant in specific cultures. The issue of beauty defined as the "central form" would be an integral aspect of his aesthetic theory as it later emerged in the *Discourses on Art.*

In 1765, five of Reynolds's scholarly notes were published in the final volume of Johnson's edition of Shakespeare. Two other notes were subsequently included in the edition of 1780. Although these works were largely reprises of arguments by Johnson and earlier authors, they also were indicative of the range of Reynolds's interests across the arts and his aspirations as a writer and critic. There is evidence that he preferred his reputation to rest on his scholarly writings, at times over his profession as a painter, as seen in a number of self-portraits (mid-1770s, London, Royal Academy of Arts) and in portraits of him by his friends and peers, such as Angelica Kauffmann's of 1767 (Saltram, The National Trust).

The *Discourses,* which Reynolds referred to as "some instructive observations on the arts" (1975, no. 15), were a series of fifteen lectures delivered from 1769 to 1790 at the Royal Academy's annual distribution of prizes to students. The first seven discourses were published in 1778, and in 1797 the entire series appeared in Edmond Malone's posthumous compilation of Reynolds's works. Reynolds's general aim was to provide words of guidance for a very specific audience consisting primarily of aspiring art students, and ultimately to develop a theory of painting and aesthetics that would promote painting as one of the liberal arts, on a par with poetry, and thus elevate the status of the painter in society. The *Discourses* functioned as the guidelines for the newly formed Royal Academy. After the publication of the first seven lectures in 1778, Reynolds seems to have recognized the expanding audience for his ideas and responded by widening the appeal of his themes. Thus, the early lectures tell students how to go about creating art via a step-by-step process in which the student begins by acquiring a mechanical facility in drawing and using artistic implements. This is followed by a call for rigorous study of the approved forms of past art, including the old masters as typified by sculpture from antiquity, the painters of the High Renaissance, and the Baroque painters of France and Italy. The final stage of artistic learning allows the advanced student to make his own compositions and to begin his professional career by creating works that draw on the knowledge gleaned in the first two stages and attain perfection through the application of the student's intellect and imagination. The later *Discourses* are concerned with what is appropriate for the artist to then attempt in his work.

In Reynolds's theory, the object of art was beauty of a general and intellectual nature, which is an idea derived from the mind itself, and thus dependent on the imagination of the artist. It is the painter's role to objectify this beauty, in order to "raise the thoughts, and extend the views of the spectator," and to become the "means of bestowing on whole nations refinement of taste" (ibid., no. 9). Ultimately, by adhering to this process, art will result in forms of "virtue" that are at once ethical and moral. This forms the end of art. It is a truth not meant to enhance the artist's professional profile, nor the pleasure of art's audience, but for the edification, in a broad moral sense, of the human mind.

Beauty, for Reynolds, was initially derived from the natural world, but throughout the *Discourses* there is a distinction between an artistic approach to nature based on description and specificity, and one that implies generality. "Deception, which is so often recommended by writers on the theory of painting, instead of advancing the art, is in reality carrying it back to its infant state" (Du Fresnoy annotations, in Reynolds, 1851, vol. 2, p. 350). Accordingly, beauty must be attained through a distillation of nature and a thorough grounding in the achievements of past artists, to the extent that the artist is encouraged to look at past art for inspiration and models, and also for specific forms that one may subtly borrow. This theory of beauty "as an idea in the mind abstracted from the bedrock of experience" (Mahoney, 1978, p. 127) is very much of its era, a firm part of the tradition of neoclassical theory dating back to the previous century. Essential in this conception is the importance of experience via study and awareness. It is this experience that must then be accessed by the artist to inspire his or her creative productions, and then to touch the audience.

Reynolds also presents a simplistic form of reception theory by isolating the importance of the viewer's imagination and response in aesthetic creation, but it is an approach steeped in the rhetoric of association of ideas that was prevalent in the eighteenth century. "The great end of the art is to strike the imagination. . . . the spectator is only to feel the result in his bosom" (*Discourses,* no. 5). This is combined with his concepts of custom and habit, which influence the perception of beauty and essentially the viewer's culturally formed taste. For Reynolds, taste was something aesthetically intuitive and objective—a response to the very nature of an object—yet it also had a spontaneous or subjective dimension, as considered most fully in the seventh discourse. This is just one of the many instances in which Reynolds appears to be presaging the concerns of the next generation of artists in Romanticism, while remaining tethered to the prevailing tradition of the eighteenth century. Implicit and important in these writings is the distinction between art as a mechanical trade and the fine artist, a gentleman schooled in higher knowledge, who pursues one of the liberal arts rather than a craft.

The inspiration for the *Discourses* and Reynolds's other writings on art appears to come from a variety of sources. These include the French and Italian literary traditions arising out of the works of Plato and Aristotle such as the writings of Roland Fréart, whose treatise on painting, *L'idée de la perfection de la peinture* (1662), Reynolds had with him in Italy. Reynolds was also well versed in British writings of the seventeenth and eighteenth centuries, including his contemporaries Johnson, Burke, Goldsmith, and David Hume. In total, the *Discourses* represent "the most eloquent, as well as the last, presentations of the ideas that dominated European art criticism and theory from the mid-fifteenth to the mid-eighteenth century" (Robert R. Wark, in Reynolds, 1959, p. xxiii).

In *A Journey to Flanders and Holland*, the notes of a voyage undertaken in 1781, Reynolds rarely strayed from descriptions of individual pictures and largely confirmed his thoughts in the early *Discourses*. But he occasionally delivered broad pronouncements on general themes, such as the death of history painting (1851, vol. 2, pp. 188–190), its relationship to religious changes, and its exclusion from the productions in English art. This should be seen as part of a continuing protest over Reynolds's failed proposal, together with the artists Benjamin West, Kauffmann, James Barry, and others, to decorate the interior of St. Paul's cathedral, which had been vetoed by the Bishop of London in 1773.

Subsequent publications of Reynolds's theories include annotations added to William Mason's publication of Charles Alphonse du Fresnoy's *The Art of Painting*, appearing in 1783, and his *Ironical Discourse*, published in the *Gen-*

tleman's Magazine of July 1791. In the annotations to du Fresnoy, he reiterates many of his ideas regarding the painting of particulars and generalities in approaches to nature but also acknowledges the limitation of restrictive rules, much as he did in his first letter to *The Idler:*

> What relates to the mind or imagination, such as invention, character, expression, grace, or grandeur, certainly cannot be taught by rules; little more can be done than pointing out where they are to be found; it is a part which belongs to general education, and will operate in proportion to the cultivation of the mind of the artist. (Du Fresnoy annotations, in ibid., p. 353)

It is also in these annotations that Reynolds writes very practically and usefully about technique, composition, and individual artists. The *Ironical Discourse* largely reprises his previous conceptions in a sarcastic manner. Reynolds's aesthetic theories set the standard for academic artistic practice in England and the Royal Academy through the nineteenth century. His ideas on education were critiqued by Barry in the 1770s, however, although his aesthetic perspectives remained essential. The most sustained and aggressive attack on his pedagogy remains William Blake's notes in the margin of his copy of the *Discourses* that had been published in 1798, providing a Romantic perspective on Reynolds's teachings. Taken individually, Blake's comments read as fiery outbursts focused on individual points, but, when considered comprehensively, they reveal Blake's objections to the substance of Reynolds's ideas. For Blake, who began his marginalia with "This Man was Hired to Depress Art," Reynolds was a paradox who did not practice his prescriptions in his own art, and Blake's own wellspring of creativity—his private visions and imagination, which combined with an awareness of past art to result in minutely realized imagery in watercolors, prints, and tempera on a small and symbolic scale—stood in direct opposition to Reynolds's preaching, the grand style, and use of an oil-based medium. Additionally, Blake's insistence on the workings of genius and the appeal to reason allowed him little sympathy for Reynolds, a man who appeared to stand for the age of reaction, the patronage of the upper classes, and an earlier generation.

The vituperative nature of Blake's criticisms would be picked up in the 1840s by the Pre-Raphaelites, whose pejorative nomenclature for Reynolds, "Sir Sloshua," not only drew attention to the slathering manner of the grand style that they found so repulsive but also to Reynolds's high social position and overarching influence in academic circles. They also clearly deplored his taste in art in their fundamental antipathy toward the post–High Renaissance painters. A more level assessment was provided consistently over the whole of his career by John Ruskin, the most important art critic and theorist of the era. Ruskin found himself moved by Reynolds's art from a young age, and repeatedly cited Reynolds as one of the seven or eight most important artists in history, as well as the artist most representative of the English school. Nonetheless, Ruskin disagreed intensely with Reynolds's denial of empirical accuracy and detail in painting, an essential aspect of Ruskin's own writings and the preferred Pre-Raphaelite practice. Ruskin also was completely opposed to Reynolds's appeal for generality and conception of beauty as the effect of custom. Despite the fact that Ruskin found the artist's teaching fundamentally flawed, he encouraged students to look at Reynolds's paintings for inspiration. He wrote that Reynolds "seems to have been born to teach all error by his precept; but that is because the only errors that were to be found in his precept, were seized upon as its essence by scholars determined to err" (Ruskin, Oxford Lectures 1875, *Works*, vol. 22, p. 494). Later Victorian critics are typified by Frederic George Stephens, formerly a member of the Pre-Raphaelite Brotherhood and later lead critic for the *Athenaeum*, who agreed with Ruskin in recognizing that Reynolds did not practice what he preached, labeling his mythological and subject pictures "laborious mistakes," but still remained enamored of the portraits and the artist's skillful brushwork and composition. Victorian interest in the artist was confirmed by an exhibition of his works at the Grosvenor Gallery in 1883–1884.

Many twentieth-century critics have been attracted to Reynolds's art and theories. Roger Fry republished the *Discourses* in 1905 with an introduction and notes that served to reintroduce the artist to the modern public. Of particular relevance for Fry were Reynolds's practical approach and applied aesthetics, his hands-on manner, and his artist's point of view. He also perceived Reynolds's later writings, especially *A Journey to Flanders and Holland,* as indicative of Reynolds's cutting-edge taste in past art such as Flemish primitives—a predilection for the kind of art that would gain adherents and acclaim in the nineteenth century. Finally, Fry, who was reflecting back on the revolt and individualism of the tumultuous nineteenth century and was ushering in the twentieth century with an eye toward stability and a hope for the resurgence of English art, was drawn by Reynolds's call for an adherence to tradition and an implicitly national community of artists formed around solid principles of instruction.

Scholars of the postwar era have consistently delved into Reynolds's writings and found relevance for his traditional approach in the twentieth century. Wark's republication of the *Discourses* in 1959 and its subsequent reprinting introduced the artist's theories to the second half of the twentieth century. There remains a continuing interest in his art, as demonstrated by the retrospective exhibition of 1986 at the Royal Academy of Arts in London and the Grand Palais in Paris. Moreover, Reynolds's theories figured heavily in John Barrell's *The Political Theory of Painting from Reynolds to Hazlitt* (1986), in which the author interpreted Reynolds's call for a public painting that would create a specific audience for art as part of a pancultural move toward defining a political public in the late eighteenth century. Barrell has been followed by David Solkin, who, in *Painting for Money* (1993), establishes connections between Reynolds's writings in *The Idler* and the *Discourses* and those of Anthony Ashley Cooper, earl of Shaftesbury, and explores Reynolds's conception of the grand style in the construction of a public for art.

The continued importance and relevance of Reynolds's writings are evidenced by a small allegorical portrait by him of "Theory" on the ceiling of the foyer of the Royal Academy of Arts in Burlington House. She is imaged with a pair of dividers symbolizing order, proportion, reason, and judgment—and holding a scroll in her left hand that reads "THEORY is the Knowledge of what is truly NATURE." The portrait is a succinct assessment of Reynolds's ideas, placed for posterity in the institution to which he devoted much of his intellectual and artistic life. He was, however, an artist well aware of the place of his particular theories in history:

> Rules are to be considered . . . as fences placed only where trespass is expected; and are particularly enforced in proportion as peculiar faults or defects are prevalent at the time, or age, in which they are delivered; for what may be proper strongly to recommend or enforce in one age, may not with equal propriety be so much laboured in another, when it may be the fashion for artists to run into the contrary extreme, proceeding from prejudice to a manner adopted by some favorite painter then in vogue.
>
> (Du Fresnoy annotations, in Reynolds, 1851, vol. 2, pp. 353–354)

[*See also* Beauty; Ruskin; *and* Taste.]

BIBLIOGRAPHY

Works by Reynolds

Discourses. Edited by Roger Fry. London, 1905. Edited by Robert R. Wark as *Discourses on Art* (San Marino, Calif., 1959); reprinted including Blake's marginalia (New Haven, 1975).
Letters of Sir Joshua Reynolds. Edited by Frederick Whiley Hilles. Cambridge, 1929.
The Literary Works of Sir Joshua Reynolds. 2 vols. Edited by Henry William Beechey. London, 1851.
Portraits. Edited by Frederick Whiley Hilles. New York, 1952.

Other Sources

Barrell, John. *The Political Theory of Painting from Reynolds to Hazlitt.* New Haven, 1986.
Hilles, Frederick Whiley. *The Literary Career of Sir Joshua Reynolds.* Cambridge, 1936.
Hipple, Walter John, Jr. "General and Particular in the Discourses of Sir Joshua Reynolds: A Study in Method." *Journal of Aesthetics and Art Criticism* 11 (1953): 231–247. Revised in *The Beautiful, and the Sublime, and the Picturesque in Eighteenth-Century British Aesthetic Theory* (Carbondale, Ill., 1957), pp. 133–148.
Mahoney, John L. "Reynolds's 'Discourses on Art': The Delicate Balance of Neoclassic Aesthetics." *British Journal of Aesthetics* 18 (1978): 126–136.
Mitchell, Charles. "Three Phases of Reynolds's Pictorial Method." *Burlington Magazine* 80 (1942): 35–42.
Murray, Roger. "Working Sir Joshua: Blake's Marginalia in Reynolds." *British Journal of Aesthetics* 17 (1977): 82–91.
Olson, Elder. Introduction to *Longinus' On the Sublime and Sir Joshua Reynolds' Discourses on Art.* Chicago, 1945.
Penny, Nicholas, ed. *Reynolds.* London, 1986.
Perini, Giovanna. "Sir Joshua Reynolds and Italian Art and Literature." *Journal of the Warburg and Courtauld Institutes* 51 (1988): 141–168.
Postle, Martin. *Sir Joshua Reynolds: The Subject Pictures.* Cambridge and New York, 1995.
Solkin, David H. *Painting for Money: The Visual Arts and the Public Sphere in Eighteenth-Century England.* New Haven, 1993.
Will, Frederic. "Blake's Quarrel with Reynolds." *Journal of Aesthetics and Art Criticism* 15 (1956–1957): 340–349.

JASON M. ROSENFELD

RHETORIC. [*To treat the relation between rhetoric and aesthetics, this entry comprises two essays:*
Historical and Conceptual Overview
Exemplarity
The first essay explains the tradition of rhetoric and its relationship to aesthetics. The second essay explores the topic of exemplarity, that is, the use of examples to persuade somebody of an aesthetic point or to illustrate that same point; exemplarity also serves to mediate between aesthetic theory and practice. For related discussion, see Poetics; *and* Renaissance Italian Aesthetics.]

Historical and Conceptual Overview

The connection of rhetoric and *aisthēsis* (sensation) is originary and strong. Classical rhetoric depended on a classical psychology that predicated a continuum, a series of interactive human faculties and actions, including sensation or *aisthēsis,* imagination *(phantasia),* memory, reason, and the acts of perceiving, self-movement, desire *(orexis),* choice, judgment *(krisis).* This dependence is stipulated by the nature of the rhetorical task. Turning to Aristotle, as compendious of early Greek rhetorical moments and the opposition they generated, one finds rhetoric defined as the art *(technē)* that masters the available means of persuasion in a specific problematic (1991, 1355b). Cicero and Quintilian, who dominated the Latin tradition, divided rhetorical persuasion into three tasks—instructing *(docere),* delighting *(delectare),* and moving *(movere)* (Cicero, *Brutus,* 1952, p. 185). The practice of rhetoric, in short, requires a base in psychological theory, because its focus is not simply on discourse and discursive techniques but on discursive effect on an audience, on doing things with words. Whether one chooses the civic, Aristotelian notion of persuasion or Quintilian's more inclusive claim that rhetoric is the art/science of speaking well ("ars/scientia bene dicendi"; 1921, II,xiv,5;xvii,38), one notes two heavy constraints. First, because the speaker, the audience, and the issue inhabit a domain of the probable, uncertain, the rhetor must always specify (Aristotle, 1991, 1357a). Variety is basic parameter of both issue and mode. Second, the rhetor is obliged to appeal to the entire range of human faculties. To put it briefly, where the Platonic philosopher prefers to address and develop the disembodied mind, the rhetor may not exclude any function of the incarnate soul in his practice.

Thus *aisthēsis*, sensation, which is inevitably accompanied by pleasure and pain, gives rise to desire or avoidance. The rhetor as orator must connect virtue with pleasure and vice with pain in his primary public task of seeking adhesion of spirits to the shared beliefs *(doxa)* of a community. Rhetorical address assumes the centrality of the passions *(pathos* or *adfectus)*. The passions are situated in the map of body *(soma)* and soul *(psyche)* relations, which account for human motive and motion. But because the actions of sensation are enchained with the actions of the imagination in producing, and the memory in storing images, a primary mode of engaging the passions is through vivid imagery *(enargeia* or *illustratio)* (Quintilian, VI,ii.29–32). Quintilian claims that of the three tasks, moving the affects is the quintessential rhetorical competence (ibid., VI,ii,4). The rhetorician, unlike the philosopher, does not have the luxury of dealing only with an educated elite within a rationally delimited discourse. On the contrary, he must at times perturb the audience's feelings, and drag them away from the truth in order to make truth and justice prevail (ibid., V,xiv, 29). The emphasis is on motion: the affects are, and cause, motions of the soul, *(motus animi)*. The passions, according to Aristotle, are the elements that cause changes, movements; in judgment, they are responsible for differences in beliefs (Aristotle, 1991, 1378a). Quintilian's strategic division of affects into mild *(ethos)* and perturbing *(pathos)* is a strong tactic of insisting on emotion as both substance and mode (vol. VI,ii,8f.). The orator functions within a domain of the ethical and pathetic, where he must confront the distances and differences within the community by means of a range of strategies of conciliation and perturbation; the passions, then, are constitutive of politics as the practice of vital negotiations of differences in a community. Thus *aisthēsis* and imagination, pleasure and passion ground rhetoric as a political as well as simply a literary competence. Strong classical theory presumes and presents continuities: between reason and emotions, between argumentation and appeal to affect, and between topic and mode, substance and expression, *res* and *verba;* and there are continuities within the classical and medieval curriculum of the seven liberal arts, where rhetoric shares interests and strategies with grammar and dialectic, the other elements of the liberal trivium, the arts of language.

Canons and Techniques. The premise of psychological continuum grounds the very rich elaboration of canons and techniques in the rhetorical tradition. The tidiness and clarity, and often the brevity and simplicity, of instruction in the wealth of pedagogical manuals of this very long development should not obscure the enduring complexity of the rhetorical project; because the mechanisms of human motive are so various and interconnected, so must be the skills of appeal, of engagement with motive. It is a mistake to stipulate too strong an opposition between, for example, style and argument, between frivolous ornamentation and serious reasoning. If there is a continuous range of faculties, there is, necessarily, a continuous range of modes of appeal to these faculties, a range that includes subtle changes of mood, as well as the coercion of dialectical argument, or passionate arousal.

Yet, there is a single, comprehensive rule: because the rhetor functions in the realm of the probable *(eikos)*, not the certain, the hegemonic canon for argument as well as style is decorum: the orator must at all times seek the appropriate *(to prepon, quid decet)* to time, place, audience. In Greek rhetoric, decorum rules in three genres of oratory: the deliberative, which deals with the politically expedient or useful, the juridical, which defines the just, and epideictic, which engages in praise of the honorable, in blame of the shameful or vicious (Aristotle, 1991, 1358b); to be sure, any one genre may employ a mixture of appeals. The injunction of decorum also gives rise to Cicero's lengthy treatment of *genera dicendi,* types that persist in the tradition: they specify a high style for grave, serious topics, a middle style for quotidian affairs, and a low style for popular use and reception. Decorum requires that of the three sources of skill, exercise *(exercitatio)* is more important than nature *(ingenium)* or art *(doctrina);* imitation *(imitatio)* is the necessary exercise in the appropriation from authoritative texts of the decorous. Even the late-antique development by Longinus of the canon of the sublime as value simply specifies a necessary surpassing of decorum as goal; it delimits a domain of excess as edification.

Although decorum should invest every aspect of rhetorical performance, Cicero's specification of five distinct rhetorical competences endures in the Western textual tradition of rhetoric manuals, and offers an organizational frame for the extraordinary diversity of their technical instructions. Cicero's faculties of invention *(inventio,* the finding of arguments) and disposition *(dispositio,* the arrangement into parts of the—usually juridical—text) address tasks of instruction, *docere.* Yet, disposition, into preface *(exordium),* narration *(narratio,* or setting out of the case), confirmation and disputation *(confirmatio* and *disputatio,* the positive and negative arguments for the case), and peroration *(peroratio,* conclusion) makes a place for *movere* as well; the *exordium* and *peroratio* offer the great opportunities for moving the affects. In the long tradition, invention and judgment *(judicium)* encompass the skills of finding arguments and critically establishing them as valid. Here Aristotle reveals an archetypical rhetorical complexity. Although it is possible to see Aristotle, in making rhetoric the counterpart *(antistrophe)* of dialectic (1354a), as providing a rationalist account of rhetoric as argument, it is more accurate to see him as proffering a continuum of modes of suasion, ranging from the most rigorous to the most relaxed. He claims that there are three sorts of "proof" or means of establishing belief *(pistis): ethos,* those establishing the speaker's character; *pathos,* those appealing to the audience's deeply held convictions or affects; and *logos,* those establishing the veridical in the text. But, Aristotle calls the *enthymeme,* or rhetorical syllogism, the body *(soma)* of all three proofs; and the concern with audience dominates. Both Quintilian and Aristotle call the enthymeme a defective, because only two-part, syllogism; the enthymeme constrains the audience to supply the defect, the third part, either major or minor premise, or conclusion. Thus, the enthymeme is more powerfully audience-oriented than the logical syllogism because it draws the audience into participation and pleasure (Aristotle, 1991, 1400b). Further, the Aristotelian commonplaces *(koinoi topoi)* have a rich historical development in rhetorical and dialectical manuals. These both map and give access to the intersubjectively held beliefs of audience and speaker. The topics are both the bins or spaces that contain lines of argument ("the more and the less") and the contents (the precepts contained—"virtue exceeds pleasure as goal"). The maxims as content require the example *(paradigma* or *exemplum)* as illustration or instantiation in the rhetorician's inductive appeal to a particular audience. There is a strong relation between rhetorical invention and skeptical inquiry, brought out in Cicero's *Academica.* The argument on both sides of the question *(in utramque partem)* is both primary skeptical tactic, according to Sextus Empiricus, and basic to rhetoric, where it is, again, audience-oriented. In rhetorical training, argument on both sides, deemed immoral by the philosophers, is an exercise in anticipating, countering, and replacing audience beliefs.

Under Cicero's competence of elocution *(elocutio)* are gathered all the skills and elements of what is called style. In modern rhetoric, elocution *is* rhetoric: the prolix lists of tropes and figures of premodernity now constitute a rhetorical epistemology as well as rhetorical technique, heavily elaborated in the *Rhétorique générale* of the Groupe Mu. *Elocutio* is associated with the task of *delectare* and *movere* in Roman rhetoric, but, again, the concept of continuum must be evoked; Quintilian, in his masterly accounts of books 8 and 9, distinguishes between trope and figure, and then between figures of speech and figures of thought. This account, with its plethora of terms, maps in great detail an area of connections and disjunctions, parallelisms and contrasts, that enable the rhetorician to use language in innovative, powerful, and pleasing ways. Repetitions and contrasts of sounds and rhythm, as well as the conjunctions and distinctions of metaphor, metonymy, synecdoche, and irony, and the distinctions and connections of argument, enforce

eloquential power. In a seventeenth-century text, amplification *(amplificatio)* is the rubric for moving the affects, yet it is defined simply as an extension or intensification of argument. The same criterion controls the employment of argumentative example and of stylistic figure: both require vividness, lifelikeness.

Cicero's pronunciation *(pronuntiatio)* is the competence of bodily gesture *(gestus, actio)* as well as oral delivery, and is strongly associated with the goal of *movere.* Once again, psychological continuum motivates: the body represents the soul of the orator, the visage bespeaks his mind. The rhetorical program requires here, too, a discipline of decorum, lest extremes of pride or humility in external signs subvert the verbal performance. In the Renaissance and early modernity, very elaborate treatises detail every minute adjustment of the body and voice; every posture or sound is assigned oratorical meaning, and decorum of gesture and voice is a primary value.

Cicero's skill of memory *(memoria)* is a competence most pertinent to an oral culture, which requires spontaneity and quickness of argumentative and stylistic invention and response. The Renaissance, again, proffers a rich development of treatises on the arts of memory. Excellence in memory is psychologically defined, visually stipulated in the early Latin treatise the *Rhetorica ad Herrenium.* Memory stores and makes available the phantasmata of the imagination, which may be the product of external sensation. Sensible pictures, the visual images of buildings and landscapes, provide the organizational frame for this storage and retrieval.

Rhetoric, Poetics, Criticism. Of course, the figures of rhetoric are important in poetry as well as in prose, and the figures of sound, of repetition and rhythmic emphasis are essential. Quintilian offers a merely technical distinction between poetry and prose: prose is freer, less constrained by patterns of sound and rhythm. Quintilian's metaphor is that of prose eloquence as a broad, free-flowing river, poetry as a channeled stream, controlled by sharply formed banks (V,xiv,33). In Quintilian's encyclopedic education, the early, grammatical stages of the orator's formation include training in *enarratio,* in the critical reading of the great poetic, historical, and moral works in order to distinguish and internalize aesthetic as well as moral value. Indeed, his book 10 prescribes a continuous task of reading and rereading as necessary to the development of a sense of value and goal in private as well as public discursive performance. Rhetoric is an enduring source of moral-aesthetic formulas in criticism; Quintilian's definition of the orator as a good man experienced in speaking ("vir bonus dicendi peritus") (ibid., XII,i,1) roots eloquence, speaking well, in virtuous posture. Most important, however, rhetorical canons and values furnish the basic vocabulary for poetics and for criticism and appreciation of literature and the fine arts through early modernity. Thus, the goal of *enargeia, illustratio,* or vividness in representation, informs visual as well as verbal arts. This rhetorical vocabulary—such as seriousness *(gravitas)*, charm *(venustas)*, copiousness *(copia)*—persists beyond the Renaissance in treatises on art. It must be stressed that many of these canons of beauty and excellence—harmony *(harmonia)*, accord *(convenientia)*, the golden mean or moderation *(mediocritas)*—derive from the hegemonic rhetorical canon of decorum.

Continuity and Change in the Rhetorical Tradition. The history of rhetoric is marked not simply by the continuous development of formulas, but by the enduring contestation of its claims to value by philosophy. Whether one follows Cicero's and Aristotle's account of the origins of rhetoric in the instruction in legal pleading of Corax and Tisias after the fall of the Sicilian tyrants or agrees with modern historical narratives that stipulate the advent of Athenian democracy and the ensuing activity in legislative and legal arenas as creating a demand for Sophistic instruction in public discursive performance, the connection between rhetorical competence and civic identity defines rhetoric against philosophy. For Jacqueline de Romilly (1992), Sophistic rhetoric and Plato's antagonist Gorgias are exemplary, engaged in the task of forming civic theory as well as practice; similarly, Eugene Garver (1994) argues that Aristotle's *Rhetoric* is primarily a handbook on discursive action for politicians. This emphasis coheres with Cicero's account in the *Brutus,* which maps the decline of eloquence onto the decline of the Roman republic, and with Quintilian's project, which assumes the absence of political possibility, and designs an encyclopedic education for a Roman elite, still engaged in the public domain of the law but engaged as well, or primarily, in a lifelong task of moral-aesthetic formation and self-fulfillment in discursive as well as intellectual performance. Quintilian illustrates one of the important, but elided, continuities of rhetoric, for the generation of texts and the analysis of texts are not two separate roles, but two sides of a single competence; there is no disjunction between criticism and performance in the rhetorical student or the finished orator. Yet, modern critics must note a nonreciprocity: one may analyze the rhetoric of any text but need not presuppose conscious rhetorical program in generation.

In the Middle Ages, the early patristic, preeminently Augustinian, appropriation of rhetoric for biblical exegesis and ecclesiastical homiletics and apologetics was a striking innovation. John O. Ward (1995) argues that, contrary to modern notions of medieval impoverishment, the Middle Ages was a time of enlargement and elaboration of rhetorical technical instruction in a very wide range of functions: in arts of bureaucratic and commercial communication *(ars dictaminis)*, in arts of preaching *(ars predicandi)*, in arts of praying *(ars precandi)*, and in arts of poetry *(ars poetria)*. Because rhetorical theory and practice are organized in specific handbooks for these functions, there is a general diffusion of rhetorical canons and values through a wide range of cultural practices.

In the Renaissance, the Italian humanists of the fourteenth and fifteenth centuries are the first to return to the task of elaborating a Ciceronian and Quintilianesque adult rhetorical formation. In part, this is a strong reaction against the dysfunction of a scholastic formation, an assemblage of university discursive genres and of topics, a formation that the humanists see as ignoring, or impertinent to, both the familiar, intimate moral domain and the political needs of the new Renaissance elites. There is, then, a general revival of rhetoric as the art dominating grammar and dialectic in the trivium, a strong rhetorical defense of poetry, a reconnection of rhetoric and politics in civic humanism, and a rhetorical contribution to the hermeneutical skills of philology. In the sixteenth century, there are strong pedagogical developments for these new elites that consist, by and large, in the rearranging of the relations of dialectic and rhetoric in instructive and investigative modes. A major strategy is to collapse rhetorical and dialectical interests in argument into dialectic, as a simple technical formation; this has the effect of splitting off *elocutio* or style as the primary, even only, rhetorical interest.

In early modernity, this reduction of rhetoric to a concern with style considered as "mere" ornament is abetted by the Cartesian innovations in psychology. The strong intrusion of rationalist and mechanist models, the power of the new psychology that purveys a dualism of mind and body, subverts the classical psychology of continuum, and thus disallows the claims of rhetorical engagement across the board and relegates rhetoric to an inferior, impure realm of frivolous activity. This subversion endures in the modernist account that stipulates rhetoric as a subordinate, merely complicitous, skill.

In part as a continuation of Friedrich Nietzsche's revisionist approach to the classics, however, there are, in the twentieth century, a variety of modes of revival of rhetorical interests and values. The "new rehabilitation of the Sophists" in classical scholarship functions as well as a rehabilitation of rhetoric as competence in civil theory and practice. To some extent, all positive modern initiatives can be seen as acts of retrieval of classical rhetorical problematic. They are not simply retrievals, however. The anti-Cartesianism that informs recent philosophical revision informs rhetorical revision as well, for the new rhetorical theory does not simply restate classical continuum, but is sharply, polemically, antidualist. Thus, Chaim Perelman (1969) attempts to undo the Cartesian subversion of rhetoric, by focusing on epideictic as the central genre, with a task of creating through praise and blame "adhesion of spirits" to the intersubjectively held values that form political and social identity, a goal that transcends mere referential translucence. This moment contests, then, another modern revisionism, that of the Groupe Mu or of Paul de

Man as first, an acceptance and systematization of the late-Renaissance reduction of rhetoric to style, and, indeed, to metaphor, and second, as complicitous with a Cartesian solipsism in epistemology, subversively apolitical. Further, the new rhetorical hermeneutics is more than a Foucauldian effort to restore to the text its character as event, to reconstruct the vital speaker–text–audience relation. Claims for the importance of recognizing rhetorical argumentative and figurative strategies in the texts of inquiry in general are based on the pervasiveness and inclusiveness of rhetorical modes of appeal. When Michel Meyer (1993), a paradigmatic contemporary theorist, asserts that rhetoric flourishes where ideologies fail, he argues that the rhetorical concern with audience reveals a deep commitment to question/response formations as more fundamental than concepts of referentiality in discursive exchange, a commitment that structures political rhetoric. Meyer refers to Martin Heidegger's lectures on Aristotle's *Rhetoric* of 1924, where Heidegger argues that the emotions constitute the social, and passions ground politics. Because the passions constitute difference, the preoccupation with the passions distinguishes rhetorical from philosophical formation; where philosophy seeks identity, intellectual closure in its arguments, rhetoric, committed to movement, emotion, deals with difference. This insistence on rhetoric as preeminently a political skill recalls the originary classical position, but also marks in rhetoric a resistance to systemic closure; rhetoric aims at specific victories, perhaps, but not closure. Finally, Meyer, like all strong rhetorical theorists, explicates and insists on continuities. There is a vital, self-conscious engagement of bodily, sensitive capacities; *aisthēsis* is folded into the account of rhetorical competence. Or, command of the range of discursive techniques associated with rhetoric requires mastery of what Klaus Dockhorn (1966) calls *pathosanthropologie,* an anthropology of the passions.

BIBLIOGRAPHY

Aristotle. *On Rhetoric: A Theory of Civic Discourse.* Translated by George A. Kennedy. New York and Oxford, 1991.
Augustine. *On Christian Doctrine.* Translated by D. W. Robertson, Jr. New York, 1958.
Cicero. *De oratore.* 3 vols. Translated by E. W. Sutton and H. Rackham. Loeb Classical Library. Cambridge, Mass., 1942.
Cicero. *Brutus.* Translated by G. L. Hendrickson. *Orator.* Translated by H. M. Hubbell. Loeb Classical Library. Cambridge, Mass., 1952.
Conley, Thomas M. *Rhetoric in the European Tradition.* Reprint, Chicago, 1994.
Dockhorn, Klaus. Review of Hans-Georg Gadamer, *Wahrheit und Methode. Göttingische Gelehrte Anzeigen* 218.3–4 (1966): 169–206.
Garver, Eugene. *Aristotle's Rhetoric: An Art of Character.* Chicago, 1994.
Groupe Mu. *Rhétorique générale.* Paris, 1970.
Meyer, Michel. *Questions de rhétorique: langage, raison et séduction.* Paris, 1993.
Nietzsche, Friedrich. *Friedrich Nietzsche on Rhetoric and Language.* Edited and translated by Sander L. Gilman, Carole Blair, and David J. Parent. New York and Oxford, 1989.
Ong, Walter J. *Ramus, Method and the Decay of Dialogue: From the Art of Discourse to the Art of Reason.* Cambridge, Mass., 1958.
Perelman, Chaim, and L. Olbrechts-Tyteca. *The New Rhetoric: A Treatise on Argumentation.* Translated by John Wilkinson and Purcell Weaver. Notre Dame, Ind., 1969.
[Pseudo-Cicero]. *Rhetorica ad Herennium.* Translated by Harry Caplan. Loeb Classical Library. Cambridge, Mass., 1989.
Quintilian. *Institutio oratoria.* 4 vols. Translated by H. E. Butler. Loeb Classical Library. Cambridge, Mass., 1921–1922.
Romilly, Jacqueline de. *The Great Sophists in Periclean Athens.* Translated by Janet Lloyd. Oxford, 1992.
Ward, John O. *Ciceronian Rhetoric in Treatise, Scholion, and Commentary.* Turnhout, Belgium, 1995.

NANCY S. STRUEVER

Exemplarity

Exemplarity may be defined as a form of argument and persuasion where a particular instance supports a general conclusion. Although the instance is typically narrative (historical or fictive), it need not be explicitly rendered: allusion to a name or a relevant feature suffices. What constitutes exemplarity is not the case or instance as such but a feature extracted from it, a feature "drawing its meaning from the controlling generality" (Lyons, 1989). In this sense, exemplarity involves not so much a discursive entity to be studied analytically as a hermeneutical practice, a practice that is integral to many kinds of discourse—literary, ethical, juridical, political. In the context of literature, example is not itself a genre but serves as a central component of genres where an aesthetic appeal is interwoven with a pragmatic—parable, fable, novella, *roman à thèse,* essay, sermon.

In rhetorical terms, the goal of example is not proof but persuasion and illustration, the latter in the sense of making visible, showing forth (cf. Latin *evidentia, ex + videre*). The persuasive or didactic use of example is often designed to mask its contingent status by invoking some basis in authority or tradition. But, in another sense, it is this very contingency, the irreducible particularity of example, that contributes to its cognitive capacity. Its intermediate status—both inside and outside the rule or truth exemplified—allows it to serve as a discovery tool, a means of testing the applicability of truth claims.

Whatever is designated as example functions as a nexus for convergent interrogations: What is it an example of? To whom is the example directed? What makes it "exemplary"? Consistent with its etymology (Latin *eximere*), example implies an excision, a sampling cut out of an entity. There is a vector back to a source, the whole from which the example derives. In this sense, example operates in a heuristic manner, opening up a generality and extracting constitutive features. But there is also a vector in the other direction—to an addressee, an agency for whom the example has been prepared. The pragmatic force of the example—its didactic or prescriptive function—has traditionally been associated not so much with the enunciation of truths or rules as with the construction of models to be imitated. Example thus turns into exemplar. One can appreciate from this why, in the system of ancient rhetoric, the function of pictorial realization, *imago*, was closely linked to the structure of exemplum (Barthes, 1985).

From early Greek thought, the offering of examples has been both approved of and disdained. A primary goal of Homeric epic was to provide exemplars, paradigms of experience and judgment, for aristocratic education and culture. Such models from the mythic tradition may have served as a basis for the Ideas or absolute forms of Platonic philosophy, as Werner Jaeger (1945) has suggested, but in the process the status of the exemplar was subject to change. In Plato's *Euthyphro*, Socrates challenges his interlocutor not to list particular cases but "to tell me what is the essential form *[paradeigma]* of holiness which makes all holy actions holy." Aristotle, however, in both his ethics and his rhetorical theory, stressed the inductive function of example, how the gathering and linking of particular instances can bring about a conclusion, whether in the context of judgment or of persuasion. The practical wisdom at the heart of Aristotelian ethics, Martha C. Nussbaum (1990) has argued, involves the distillation of an immensely complex fabric of particulars, a fabric that could not be derived from any rule or generality. In this sense, moral choice requires the kind of "attentiveness to particulars in all their contextual embededness" (Nussbaum, 1990) that, in the modern era, can be found in certain novels, biographies, and other narrative forms.

Whenever an example is invoked as support for a general proposition, what is claimed implicitly is that its validity, its "exemplarity," will be self-evident. But just how is this validation realized? If by way of the example, then it can hardly serve as conclusive support for the general proposition, because the example would be taken primarily on its own terms, as an isolate, singular instance. If, on the other hand, the validation is to be achieved at the level of the generality, this would require an act of stipulation or imposition, which exceeds the logical framework, because the general proposition has not yet been authenticated. "Can any example ever truly fit a general proposition?" Paul de Man asks. "Is not its particularity, to which it owes the illusion of its intelligibility, necessarily a betrayal of the general truth it is supposed to support and convey?" (1984).

Within a relatively homogeneous culture such as that of medieval Christianity, the illustrative function of example will typically tend toward the performative. What might seem to be simply a demonstration of a principle or truth assumes, in such a context, the force of a directive. The medieval exemplum, Larry Scanlon writes,

illustrates a moral because what it recounts is the enactment of that moral. . . . [It] is not a purely textual exchange between two discursive genres, the narrative and the interpretive, in which the narrative supports some proverb-like interpretation. In its narrative the exemplum reenacts the actual, historical embodiment of communal value in a protagonist or an event, and then, in its moral, effects the value's reemergence with the obligatory force of moral law.   (1994)

But this does not mean that the form of exemplum in medieval usage followed a single pattern. The invocation of great individuals and notable occurrences *(exempla maiorum)* characteristic of classical (Ciceronian) rhetoric coexisted with a more popular sermonizing style that featured instances typical of the quotidian experience of the congregation. This latter type, labeled "paraestenic Everyman-exemplum" by Peter von Moos, was the staple of diverse kinds of popular predication and religious instruction. At the same time, "historical-inductive exempla were always a basic constituent of the culture of aristocratic courts: as a form of diversion, of dynastic self-legitimation, of ethical training for rulers and functionaries, or as pragmatic initiation into worldly practices and strategies" (Moos, 1988).

The authority of historical models in ancient and medieval culture, as expressed in the Ciceronian motto "historia magistra vitae," was based on a conception of history in which criteria of age and established authority far outweighed a modern sense of probability and verifiability.

In the daily life of the Middle Ages, the past was clearly more directly present and operative than in the modern era; but knowledge about the past was not yet governed, as is the case now, by an underlying conception of evolution and change. The first point can help us understand the extraordinarily vast range of applicability granted to the *historical* example; the second explains why it is so difficult to separate, in terms of a pragmatic perspective, the historical example from the *fictional*.
                        (Gumbrecht, 1986)

Within the institution of literature, the example is most readily associated with the fable, the novella, and certain forms of the novel. In the fable, the example is intended to support something like a general truth, often expressed as maxim or *sententia*, whereas in more elaborated genres, such as the novel, one often finds mutually reflective narrative elements where one might be posited as providing the truth factor, the signified, and others then serve as illustrative instances.

The proximity of exemplum to fable—already noted by Aristotle—is instructive. Both fable and exemplum orient a narrative core in terms of a larger, systematic whole. But, as Karlheinz Stierle notes, fable does so by presenting the general *as* a singular instance, thus in a sense allegorizing the instance. In the exemplum, on the other hand, the moral is, as it were, implied *in* the particular, and for this the narrative instance is required. Thus, exemplum

is a form of expansion and reduction all in one—expansion as regards its underlying maxim, reduction as regards a story from which is extracted and isolated that which the speech action of the exemplum needs in order to take on a concrete form. . . . [U]nderlying the unity of the whole is the "purpose" of the exemplum, the moral precept. (Stierle, 1979)

Insofar as the exemplum is in the service of doctrine or ideology, the congruence of narrative and moral conclusion is anticipated and unchallenged. But a narrative may be taken in ways that exceed any single conclusion. "The example, it seems to me," says a character in Johann Wolfgang Goethe's *Die Wahlverwandtschaften* (The Elective Affinities), "doesn't exactly fit our case," and this could be said of any example. The fit of an example is dependent on the mode of extraction or, to draw on the terminology of speech-act theory, its performative force is a function of the uptake.

When the joining of an example with a rule or general principle proves to be questionable, the example, far from serving as validation or illustration, becomes a means of testing or challenging the applicability of any truth claim. This can be evidenced in the uses of *mashal* (signifying both example and parable in the Jewish tradition of midrash [see Boyarin, 1995]) or in various types of fable. In Jean de La Fontaine's *Fables,* one reads:

L'exemple est un dangereux leurre:
Tous les mangeurs de gens ne sont pas grands seigneurs;
Où la guêpe a passé, le moucheron demeure. (Book 2, no. 16)

[The example can be a dangerous bait: Those who would be man-eaters may not be such great personages; where the wasp has slipped through, the flea gets caught.]

In the postmedieval period, the exemplum gives way to diverse forms of exemplarity—in the Renaissance tale and novella (Geoffrey Chaucer, Giovanni Boccaccio, Marguerite de Navarre), in the essay (Michel de Montaigne), in political philosophy (Niccolò Machiavelli). What is common to all these is a problematization of the exemplum model whereby the narrative element comes to occupy an oblique relation to a stated or implied precept.

Machiavelli, Nancy S. Struever writes, "compels the sharing of unwanted knowledge." The reader is drawn into "a hypothetical exchange of dialogic counters, tokens. . . . Each exchange implicates, making the reader complicitous in the handling of the tokens" (1992). For Montaigne, "Le Dire est autre chose que le faire" (saying is quite another thing from doing), and it is in this gap, "the *écart,* or disjunction between the model and recognized norms of human behavior" (Nichols, 1995), that Montaigne engages in the work of exemplification in the *Essays.*

What comes to the fore in these instances is the way that example is capable of entangling the reader, engaging him to account for the discrepancy, the bad fit between particular and universal. Montaigne's "Tout exemple cloche" (Every example limps) is evoked by Thomas Keenan when he writes: "Responsibility begins in the bad example: one could even say that the only good example, the only one worthy of the imitation, interiorization, and identification that the example calls for, is the bad example" (1995). The "bad example" has the effect of foregrounding the mode of address, of interpellation, that inheres in the form. Commenting on Horace's dictum, "mutato nomine de te fabula narratur" (with a change of names, the fable is told about you), Keenan writes, "We are addressed in the fable under what can only be a pseudonym. . . . And the other is, among others, you" (ibid.)

Although exemplarity was conceived primarily in rhetorical terms from antiquity to the Renaissance, in the modern era it has been incorporated in various theoretical constructs, for example, of aesthetics, logic, and language. This is well illustrated in Immanuel Kant's philosophy, which both devalues and revalues exemplarity.

The issue emerges at various points in Kant's philosophy. In the *Critique of Pure Reason,* he distinguishes between the understanding, as the faculty concerned with formulating and grasping rules or principles, and judgment *(Urteilskraft),* whose special function consists in the application of rules, or more precisely, of *subsuming* particular cases under a rule in order to determine "whether a case falls under it in concreto." This is "a particular talent that cannot be studied but only practiced *[geübt]*" (Kant, 1956, p. A133). Kant likens it to a native, ingrained wit, *Mutterwitz.* In a theoretical sense, the status of examples is accessory, prosthetic. Kant refers to them as training wheels, a child's walker for the judgment ("Gängelwagen der Urteilskraft"). A given example in its particularity is replaceable. But it is only by way of examples that general principles can be activated and applied. Examples are thus both secondary and, for heuristic purposes, necessary. There can be no rules for the application of rules, and thus the "singular and great use of examples [is] that they sharpen the judgment" (ibid., p. A134).

In the *Critique of Judgment,* examples assume a primary and irreducible function in justifying the basis of evaluation, of judgment itself. What is at issue is the capacity of judgment "to think the particular as contained under the universal." The realization of the universal rule by way of example does not lead to an abstract, reified sense of a universal, but rather to "the means whereby the rule regulates diverse instances within a circle of possible applications" (Buck, 1967).

Kant's analysis of the work of art—more properly, of the *experience* of art—proceeds by way of a revision of key concepts such as taste, beauty, pleasure *(Wohlgefallen),* and common sense *(sensus communis).* Kant's approach was not to focus on *what* evokes an aesthetic response, but rather to inquire why it cannot be objectified or conceptualized independent of the experience itself. Aesthetic judgment takes its point of departure in the particular case and then needs to find a more general basis for assigning value. The analysis of what makes the judgment reflective—turned on itself and drawing its standard of judgment from the example of its own operation—is designed to demonstrate an outgoing, creative facet of the mind's "response."

This subjective experience, which may at the same time serve as the basis of an act of judgment, is curious: it is not altogether "cognitive" in that it does not operate on the basis of a *theoretical cognition* related to a priori concepts of nature (Kant, 1987, Introduction). Yet, it does "cognize" what it itself feels. This form of cognition operates not in terms of the a priori of nature, but by deriving validation from its own pleasure or displeasure.

Kant conceived the reflective judgment as a way of establishing a form of generality or finality that is neither apodictic (derived from a rule) nor empirical (based on experience), but "only *exemplary*," defining it as "the necessity of the agreement of *all* [men] in a judgment that can be considered as example for a general rule that cannot be stated" (ibid., section 18). Exemplarity here involves a principle of universal validity *(Gemeinsinn)* that serves as a basis for the communicability of cognitive data. The "general rule that cannot be stated" signifies not a hidden or inaccessible truth but the *positing* of such a generality as the condition for predication and communicability. Although the standard invoked here may be "a merely ideal norm" (ibid., section 22), it serves as the necessary bridge between subjective judgments of taste and any general standard of aesthetic value.

This *projection* of a (universal) principle that cannot be stated but only postulated is predicated on "a formalization of the particular" (Lloyd, 1995) Thus, an appeal to common sense is an appeal to example not only specifically (to an instantiation) but generically, to the very structure that underwrites common sense. "This paradoxical demand is rooted in the first place in the problem of a common sense that is at once the a priori foundation of taste *and* its product" (ibid.).

Kant's focus on the structure of judgment is designed to underwrite the continual need to judge even in light of the relative indeterminacy of available criteria, whether at the level of aesthetics ("Is it beautiful?") or of ethics ("Is it right?"). Far from being unconsidered or merely intuitive, the Kantian reflective judgment operates in terms of a projective-reflexive loop, invoking a "general rule that cannot be stated." Exemplarity here assumes a quite different valence than it had in a rhetorical context. In Kant, as in other modern thinkers, the focus is not so much on the modeling function, the example as exemplar, but rather on its paradoxical but indispensable role in an evaluative praxis.

Although the rule or law as such resists formulation, its point (or *pointing*) may be deduced from what has been termed a "symbolization . . . through permutations of instances" (Lyotard, 1991). It is in Ludwig Wittgenstein's *Philosophical Investigations* that one finds a sustained reflection on the effect of a series, the tendency or "drift" that multiple instances set into motion. "You give him examples,—but he has to guess their drift" (Wittgenstein, 1958). Wittgenstein focuses on practices rather than foundations, rules being taken primarily as "signposts" along a path. They may be limiting but are not mandatory or prohibitive in any absolute sense. One can always not follow a rule, though one may pay for it. At the same time, any instance of a rule in practice can raise questions as to how it is to be taken, what application it has in a given case.

The true test of a rule, for Wittgenstein, is how it is acted on, what practice it gives rise to, but our need to supply cognitive validation, to *know* what the rule means, draws us repeatedly into a mode of interpretation, an effort to formulate how the rule fits the case at hand. What Wittgenstein stresses is the sense of the indetermination of rule in relation to the act of judgment. Example brings together a model and a directive. Nothing guarantees that a reception, an "uptake" in J. L. Austin's (1975) sense, will come out right. Nor need the form of the uptake be precisely calibrated. But as example, the particular is projected beyond itself, not so much toward a formulable rule, a universal, as toward what Wittgenstein termed "a form of life"; and in the process, rules of a kind are repeatedly invoked and displaced.

Lyotard has put forward a conception of postmodern art under the aegis of the sublime that derives from a dialectization of exemplarity in the sense of Theodor W. Adorno's negative dialectics. In order to rescue the example from the universalizing drift of the concept, of speculative thought, Adorno envisaged a kind of "micrological activity" that would give voice to what lay immanent in objects:

> Only a philosophy in fragment form would give their proper place to the monads, those illusory idealistic drafts. They would be conceptions, in the particular, of the totality that is inconceivable as such. . . . The call for binding statements without a system is a call for thought-models *[Denkmodellen]*, and these are not merely monadological in kind. A model covers the specific, and more than the specific, without letting it evaporate in its more general covering concept.   (1973)

Lyotard's postmodern sublime represents an application of Adorno's call for a fragmented, "micrological" mode of thought. What Edmund Burke and Kant identified as the sublime may now be understood, according to Lyotard, as an adumbration of the avant-garde's terror of the void, of the insistent and unanswerable "Is it happening?" ("Arrive-t-il?") that denotes a response to art no longer guided by the aesthetic norms of beauty or taste. What Enlightenment thinkers diagnosed as a breach of those norms, the sublime, "outlined a world of possibilities for artistic experiments in which the avant-gardes would later trace out their paths. . . . The art-object no longer bends itself to models, but tries to present the fact that there is an unpresentable" (Lyotard, 1991).

Lyotard's "presentation of an unpresentable" as a distinguishing feature of postmodern art parallels what Kant analyzed as the failure of the imagination in relation to the sublime, its incapacity to realize by way of representation or figuration experiences of overwhelming magnitude or power, of the sublime. Although for Kant this incapacity served as a kind of negative warrant of an Absolute, Lyotard's "Is it happening?" may be taken as emblematic of the exemplarity of postmodern art, of its insistent, ongoing interrogation of the very possibility of art.

The difficulty of defining or circumscribing the topic of exemplarity is that it is not a formal entity, like a trope or a genre, but rather a constituent of a variety of rhetorical and hermeneutical practices, part of the back-and-forth between part and whole, though never simply an instance of a universal or the application of a rule. It lies not in the particular instance nor in any governing principle but in the oscillation that puts into question, that *imposes* the question of their mutual determination. As illustration, the example is like the *illustrandum* (that which is illustrated), but not altogether, because a sign cannot exemplify itself. Thus, there always needs to be another feature, distinct from illustration, that marks the example, singles it out as emblem of something sought. Exemplarity constitutes a breach in discourse, an opening that exposes an inside to an outside, a particular to a universal, but always with the possibility that the particular will be inassimilable to any universality of meaning.

[*See also* Kant.]

BIBLIOGRAPHY

Adorno, Theodor W. *Negative Dialectics.* Translated by E. B. Ashton. New York, 1973.

Aristotle. *On Rhetoric: A Theory of Civic Discourse.* Translated by George A. Kennedy. New York and Oxford, 1991.

Austin, J. L. *How to Do Things with Words.* Cambridge, Mass., 1975.

Barthes, Roland. "L'ancienne rhétorique." In *L'Aventure sémiologique,* pp. 85–165. Paris, 1985.

Boyarin, Daniel. "Take the Bible for Example: Midrash as Literary Theory." In *Unruly Examples: On the Rhetoric of Exemplarity,* edited by Alexander Gelley, pp. 27–47. Stanford, Calif., 1995.

Buck, Günther. *Lernen und Erfahrung: Zum Begriff der didaktischen Induktion.* Stuttgart, 1967.

de Man, Paul. "Aesthetic Formalization: Kleist's *Über das Marionettentheater.*" In *The Rhetoric of Romanticism,* pp. 263–290. New York, 1984.

Derrida, Jacques. "Parergon." In *The Truth in Painting,* translated by Geoff Bennington and Ian McLeod, pp. 15–147. Chicago, 1987.

Gelley, Alexander. "The Pragmatics of Exemplary Narrative." In *Unruly Examples: On the Rhetoric of Exemplarity,* edited by Alexander Gelley, pp. 142–161. Stanford, Calif., 1995.

Gumbrecht, Hans-Ulrich. "Menschliches Handeln und göttliche Kosmologie: Geschichte als Exempel." In *La littérature historiographique des origines à 1500,* edited by Hans Ulrich Gumbrecht et al., Grundriss der Romanischen Literaturen des Mittelalters, pp. 869–950. Heidelberg, 1986.

Hampton, Timothy. *Writing from History: The Rhetoric of Exemplarity in Renaissance Literature.* Ithaca, N.Y., 1990.

Harvey, Irene. "Derrida and the Issues of Exemplarity." In *Derrida: A Critical Reader,* edited by David Wood, pp. 193–217. Oxford and Cambridge, Mass., 1992.

Jaeger, Werner. *Paideia: The Ideals of Greek Culture.* 3 vols. Translated by Gilbert Highet. 2d ed. New York and Oxford, 1945.

Kant, Immanuel. *Critique of Pure Reason* (1781). Translated by Norman Kemp Smith. Reprint, London, 1956.

Kant, Immanuel. *Critique of Judgment* (1790). Translated by Werner S. Pluhar. Indianapolis, 1987.

Keenan, Thomas. "Fables of Responsibility." In *Unruly Examples: On the Rhetoric of Exemplarity,* edited by Alexander Gelley pp. 121–141. Stanford, Calif., 1995.

Koselleck, Reinhart. "*Historia Magistra Vitae:* The Dissolution of the Topos into the Perspective of a Modernized Historical Process." In *Futures Past: On the Semantics of Historical Time,* translated by Keith Tribe, pp. 21–38. Cambridge, Mass., 1985.

Lloyd, David. "Kant's Examples." In *Unruly Examples on the Rhetoric of Exemplarity* edited by Alexander Gelley pp. 255–276. Stanford, Calif., 1995.

Lyons, John D. *Exemplum: The Rhetoric of Example in Early Modern France and Italy.* Princeton, N.J., 1989.

Lyotard, Jean-François. *The Postmodern Condition: A Report on Knowledge.* Translated by Geoff Bennington and Brian Massumi. Minneapolis, 1984.

Lyotard, Jean-François. *The Inhuman: Reflections on Time.* Translated by Geoffrey Bennington and Rachel Bowlby. Stanford, Calif., 1991.

Nichols, Stephen G. "Example versus *Historia:* Montaigne, Erigena, and Dante." In *Unruly Examples on the Rhetoric of Exemplarity,* edited by Alexander Gelley, pp. 48–85. Stanford, Calif., 1995.

Nussbaum, Martha C. "The Discernment of Perception: An Aristotelian Conception of Private and Public Rationality." In *Love's Knowledge: Essays on Philosophy and Literature,* pp. 54–105. New York and Oxford, 1990.

"Paradigma." In *Historisches Wörterbuch der Philosophie,* edited by Joachim Ritter et al., vol. 7, col. 74–76. Basel, 1989.

Plato *Euthyphro.* In *The Collected Dialogues,* edited by Edith Hamilton and Huntington Cairns, pp. 170–185. New York, 1961.

Scanlon, Larry. *Narrative, Authority, and Power: The Medieval Exemplum and the Chaucerian Tradition.* Cambridge and New York, 1994.

Stierle, Karlheinz. "Story as Exemplum—Exemplum as Story: On the Pragmatics and Poetics of Narrative Texts." In *New Perspectives in German Literary Criticism,* edited by Richard E. Amacher and Victor Lange, pp. 389–417. Princeton, N.J., 1979.

Struever, Nancy S. *Theory as Practice: Ethical Inquiry in the Renaissance.* Chicago, 1992.

Moos, Peter. *Geschichte als Topik: Das rhetorische Exemplum von der Antike zur Neuzeit und die historiae im "Policraticus" Johanns von Salisbury.* Hildesheim and New York, 1988.

Suleiman, Susan Rubin. "'Exemplary' Narratives." In *Authoritarian Fictions: The Ideological Novel as a Literary Genre,* pp. 25–61. New York, 1983.

Warminski, Andrzej. "Reading for Example: 'Sense-Certainty' in Hegel's *Phenomenology of Spirit.*" In *Readings in Interpretation: Hölderlin, Hegel, Heidegger,* pp. 163–179. Minneapolis, 1987.

Wittgenstein, Ludwig. *Philosophical Investigations.* Translated by G. E. M. Anscombe. 3d ed. New York, 1958.

ALEXANDER GELLEY

RICHARDS, IVOR ARMSTRONG (1893–1979),

one of the founders of modern literary criticism. Richards contributed to aesthetics, semantics, literary criticism, the theory of metaphor and translation, elementary reading and second-language training, and world literacy. In the decade following World War, I he published a series of works that ushered the age of analysis into the study of literature.

The third son of a Welsh chemical engineer, Richards was born in Sandbach, Cheshire. He entered Magdalene College, Cambridge, in 1911 and studied moral sciences under J. M. E. McTaggart, W. E. Johnson, and G. E. Moore, who exerted the strongest influence. After winning first-class honors in 1915 Richards succumbed to tuberculosis and spent the war years recuperating in the mountains of Wales, where he took up what became a lifelong sport, high mountaineering. In 1919 he began teaching the theory of criticism and contemporary novels in the new English School at Cambridge. He was appointed Lecturer in English and Moral Science by Magdalene in 1922 and Fellow in 1926, the year in which he was married to Dorothy Eleanor Pilley.

At the outset of his career, Richards rejected nineteenth-century historicism and biography, fin-de-siècle aesthetics, and abstract formalism. He attacked Roger Fry and Benedetto Croce, the one for blurring the distinction between aesthetic and scientific theory and for positing a specifically aesthetic emotion, the other for his idealist premises and his reduction of art to expression. Instead, Richards argued that truth is the "decisive notion" for both art and science, however differing are their modes of verification, and he defined six ways in which emotion enters art. *The Foundations of Aesthetics* (1922; coauthored by C. K. Ogden and James Wood) outlines sixteen theories of beauty ranging from objectivism and imitation to social usefulness and psychological wholeness. His preferred theory is "synaesthesis," which involves a full, disciplined engagement of the self, without a tendency to action. He distinguishes between an end state of equilibrium and harmony (where, in a state of heightened tension, the mind experiences the varied attitudes before it) and a mere oscillation of just two sides, or a deadlock, or an inflexible order.

A vast and many-sided project, *The Meaning of Meaning* (1923; coauthored by Ogden), has been called the best-known book on semantics ever written. Again, Richards performs a "multiple definition," analyzing twenty-two meanings of "meaning" (Richards's favorite book was the dictionary and 250 "multiple definitions" of key words can be found across his writings). Abstractions, universals, and concepts are taken as so much symbolic machinery—some useful as heuristic tools, the rest, verbiage or "word magic." Combining American pragmatism and behaviorism with British philosophical psychology, his corrective theory begins with a Triangle of Interpretation, which subsequently became a common item in linguistics textbooks: symbol (e.g., a noun), reference (or thought), and referent. Words carry out jobs or functions; no utterance has its meaning alone, but only in a context, described in physical and psychological terms. One function is referential, the pointing to objective reality; a second is emotive, the conveyance of

feeling; a third, the expression of a sense of relation to an audience; a fourth, the attitude of the speaker to the object under discussion; a fifth, the overall intention of the utterance. Richards later enumerated seven functions, each more or less simultaneously present in a given utterance. At times, however, he spoke simply of two broad uses of language: "referential," exemplified by strict scientific or expository prose; and "emotive," conveying or stimulating feeling and attitude. His early emphasis on the emotive function and poetic form stemmed from his effort to counter an excessively message-oriented approach to literature, but, as the battle was won, his attention went increasingly to referential factors. His semantic theory anticipated developments in logical positivism.

Principles of Literary Criticism (1924) applies a psychological model and theories of value and communication to the analysis of literature. The poet's mind (and its representative, the poem) "outwits the force of habit" and presents "conciliations of impulses which in most minds are still confused, intertrammelled, and conflicting"; it has gone furthest in temporary conciliations—temporary because a fresh reading might result in a newly balanced poise—and exemplifies a central principle: a "growing order is the principle of the mind." In the lesser "poetry of exclusion," a writer eliminates the heterogeneous elements for the sake of a more easily won wholeness and closure. The highly valued "poetry of inclusion" wins its unity by embracing the broadest oppositions within its formal boundaries; contrary attitudes are not scarecrows but menacing alternatives. The poem creates an "equilibrium of opposed impulses." Irony is prized for widening the scope of a poem; it "consists in the bringing in of the opposite, the complementary impulses." Tragedy, greatest of the poetries of inclusion, is Richards's paradigmatic genre because it is "perhaps the most general, all-accepting, all-ordering experience known" and can "take anything into its organisation, modifying it so that it finds a place." Through the mid-1920s, Richards explored the nature of poetic ambiguity, which opens up linguistic complexities in a poem and prevents premature closure.

Often considered his masterpiece, *Practical Criticism* (1929) presents the results of an experiment in which Richards enlisted hundreds of students to interpret thirteen poems of varying quality. Four hundred responses (many as shocking as they are revealing) are examined and ten main obstacles in reading are identified: stock responses, irrelevant associations, doctrinal adhesion, inhibition, sentimentality, and so on. A poem is a blend of many meanings and linguistic functions, categorized under "sense," "feeling," "tone," and "intention." Tone, for example, includes the author and the narrator, their separate attitudes toward each other, toward the audience (real or fictitious), and toward the subject matter. Linguistic structures are broken down into smaller and smaller units, which can then be studied in relation to one another and to the whole. The poem allows for variant readings, while defending itself from misreading by contextual checks and controls. "Close reading" or contextualism, as the method also came to be known, had its precursors, but no one had ever proceeded so systematically with a micrological approach to language, nor endowed the method with such incisive theoretical depth, nor applied it so broadly and with such revolutionary results. One proof of the method was that it could deal with high modernist texts, some of the most difficult literature ever written. In the lecture hall—Richards was a spellbinding lecturer—he championed high modernism, and his influence hastened its acceptance by the academy. William Empson, Richards's pupil at Magdalene, employed the method in his epoch-making *Seven Types of Ambiguity* (1930). Richards also exerted a powerful impact on American New Criticism, of which he is the acknowledged "father," and which dominated the academic study of literature from the 1940s to the 1960s.

Practical Criticism is also concerned with the effects of literature on behavior, as well as the deleterious effects of the new communications media, propaganda, and "bad" art, a strong theme throughout Richards's career. In studies on "doctrine in poetry" and "sincerity," he questions how readers "translate" the import of writers whose beliefs and systems of thought have passed into history. One should not, he argues, suppress the problem by concentrating attention solely on formalist matters or historical reconstruction. Neither is suspension of belief (as commonly understood) a solution—pretending, say, to believe for a moment in Dante's angels, then to drop the belief. What great writers communicate ought to be assimilated by and modify the structure of the mind. Acceptance of the artistic import depends not on the object of belief, which may be disproved or superseded, but on the value of the feelings and attitudes associated with the belief. Although Richards expects preparatory work of "unremitting research and reflection" on a work of art, which in itself may settle the question of value, there remains the "technique" or "ritual" of sincerity and a pragmatic "backwash" effect of the poem over the long term. A supreme virtue of the critic and reader, "sincerity" is the feeling that comes from accepting and speaking truth, the deepening sense of inner coherence and stability.

In the 1930s, Richards elaborated on his theories. *Mencius on the Mind* (1932) contains multiple definitions of key words in Mencius's psychological vocabulary. *Coleridge on Imagination* (1934), reinterpreting a Romantic transcendental metaphysics in terms of applied psychology, refounds studies of Samuel Taylor Coleridge in the modern era. *Interpretation in Teaching* (1938) attempts for expository prose what *Practical Criticism* did for poetry. The most significant and influential work of this period lay in an original theory of metaphor propounded in *The Philosophy of Rhetoric* (1936). Traditionally, the two halves of a metaphor (the "image" and the "idea") were given unequal value: one side was treated as ornamental (often called the "metaphor"); the other contained "the meaning." By contrast, Richards grants parity to the two halves of the metaphoric copula; the metaphor is the whole double unit whose meaning is generated by the interactive process of a *tenor* ("underlying idea" or "principal subject") and a *vehicle* (what the principal subject is compared to, the "figure"); the *ground* is what they share in common. Tenor and vehicle bring their own contexts, not all parts of which become active, to the process that creates a metaphor; more often, what is *not* shared in common determines its effectiveness; and neither tenor nor vehicle go through the process unchanged. Metaphor is "a transaction between contexts."

In 1939, Richards left Cambridge to accept a position at Harvard and the task of developing methods for English language instruction. Teaching in China had convinced him of the potential benefits of audiovisual aids in the teaching of Basic English, an 850-word version of normal English designed by Ogden as an international auxiliary language. With Basic and expanded versions of it, he experimented for two decades applying the media to learning to read a first or second language, beginning with stick-figure drawings, filmstrip, record, tape, and moving on to television, video, cassette, and computer, as they became available. Devised in collaboration with Christine M. Gibson, his *Language through Pictures* series went into seven languages. He also translated such works as Homer's *Iliad* and Plato's *Republic* into expanded Basic so that learners could have invaluable works to read upon entering the new language.

Richards was University Professor at Harvard from 1944 to 1963. In his sixtieth year, he turned to writing poetry and published four collections as well as three verse plays. His humanist testament, *Beyond* (1974), explores relations between central human figures and their gods, from Homer, Plato, and the Book of Job to Dante and Percy Bysshe Shelley.

In 1974, Richards returned to Cambridge, England. In spring 1979, he was lecturing in China on the teaching of English as a second language when he fell seriously ill. He was taken back to Cambridge, where he died on 7 September.

[*See also* Literature, *article on* Literary Aesthetics; New Criticism; *and* Rhetoric.]

BIBLIOGRAPHY

Works by Richards

The Foundations of Aesthetics. Coauthored by C. K. Ogden and James Wood. London, 1922.
The Meaning of Meaning. Coauthored by C. K. Ogden. London, 1923.
Principles of Literary Criticism. London, 1924.
Science and Poetry. London, 1926.
Practical Criticism: A Study of Literary Judgment. London, 1929.

Mencius on the Mind: Experiments in Multiple Definition. London, 1932.
Coleridge on Imagination. London, 1934.
The Philosophy of Rhetoric. New York and Oxford, 1936.
Interpretation in Teaching. New York, 1938.
How to Read a Page. New York, 1942.
The Pocket Book of Basic English: A Self-Teaching Way into English. Coauthored by Christine M. Gibson. New York, 1945.
Speculative Instruments. Chicago, 1955.
So Much Nearer: Essays toward a World English. New York, 1968.
Internal Colloquies: Poems and Plays. New York, 1971.
Beyond. New York, 1973.
Complementarities: Uncollected Essays. Edited by John Paul Russo. Cambridge, Mass., 1976.
New and Selected Poems. Manchester, 1978.

Other Sources

Collini, Stefan. "On Highest Authority: The Literary Critic and Other Aviators in Early Twentieth-Century Britain." In *Modernist Impulses in the Human Sciences, 1870–1930,* edited by Dorothy Ross, pp. 152–169. Baltimore, 1995.
Hotopf, W. H. N. *Language, Thought, and Comprehension: A Case Study of the Writings of I. A. Richards.* London, 1965.
McCallum, Pamela. *Literature and Method: Towards a Critique of I. A. Richards, T. S. Eliot, and F. R. Leavis.* Dublin, 1983.
Needham, John. *"The Completest Mode": I. A. Richards and the Continuity of English Criticism.* Edinburgh, 1982.
Russo, John Paul. "A Bibliography (1919–1973)." In *I. A. Richards: Essays in His Honor,* edited by Reuben A. Brower, Helen Vendler, and John Hollander. New York, 1973.
Russo, John Paul. *I. A. Richards: His Life and Work.* Baltimore, 1989.
Schiller, Jerome P. *I. A. Richards' Theory of Literature.* New Haven, 1969.
Shusterman, Ronald. *Critique et poésie selon I. A. Richards: De la confiance au relativisme naissant.* Bordeaux, 1988.

JOHN PAUL RUSSO

RICHTER, FRIEDRICH. *See* Paul.

RICOEUR, PAUL (b. 1913), French philosopher. The tradition of phenomenological hermeneutics has had two principal representatives: Hans-Georg Gadamer (b. 1900), whose *Truth and Method* (1960) first defined the tradition, and Paul Ricoeur, author of major works extending the scope of the tradition, most notably *Freud and Philosophy: An Essay on Interpretation* (1965), *The Symbolism of Evil* (1960), *The Conflict of Interpretations* (1969), *The Rule of Metaphor* (1975), the three-volume *Time and Narrative* (1983–1985), and *Oneself as Another* (1990). Because the development of Ricoeur's thought has been unusually complex, driven at various points by the powerful influence of a wide array of thinkers—in addition to Gadamer and Martin Heidegger, Gabriel Marcel, Jacques Lacan, Claude Lévi-Strauss, and Jacques Derrida—this article will confine itself to a presentation of a summary account of Ricoeur's theory of interpretation as developed especially in the work of the 1970s and 1980s.

Gadamer's key hermeneutical insight, which distinguishes his position from that of the Romantic hermeneutic tradition, is that all interpretation involves of necessity an act of appropriation in which the object of interpretation is made "one's own" through the reader's endeavor to make sense of the text in the light of her personal experience. Thus, Gadamer insists on the autonomy of the text's meaning—on its freedom from the dictates of the author's intention and its perpetual availability for reinterpretation by new readers—and, by implication, on the legitimacy of varied readings of the same text. Although Ricoeur endorses Gadamer's claim that appropriation is an integral component of the interpretive act, he contends as well that Gadamer, in his eagerness to apply Heidegger's phenomenological insights to the interpretive problems of the human sciences, does not attend seriously enough to the *actual practices* of those disciplines. Thus, in trying to complete Gadamer's project, Ricoeur vows to "keep in contact with the disciplines which seek to practice interpretation in a methodical manner, and . . . resist the temptation to separate *truth,* characteristic of understanding, from the *method* put into operation by [the] disciplines which have sprung from exegesis" (1974, p. 11).

The problem that Ricoeur takes as central, then, is how to reintroduce the possibility of critically distinguishing between correct and incorrect interpretations of a text without sacrificing the Gadamerian insight that interpretation is essentially a matter of making the text "one's own." The first thing to be recognized, Ricoeur claims, is that certain important consequences follow from the text's independent existence as a written communication. Although it is true that the text belongs to us in the sense that it is addressed to us and must be appropriated, it is also true that the text is not ours—that it inevitably stands at a distance from us by virtue of its having a verbal structure that we (as readers) did not produce. This verbal structure establishes, Ricoeur claims, borrowing his terminology from J. L. Austin, the locutionary (or propositional) dimension of the text's meaning. Insofar as the text can be said to have a stable and re-identifiable sense, it is to be found here. But the meaning of the text has dimensions extending beyond the locutionary. These concern the author's intention and the effect that the text produces on its readers, and constitute, respectively, the illocutionary and perlocutionary dimensions of the text's meaning.

These three distinct dimensions of the text's meaning must still be seen as interrelated. What we take to be the author's intention must be consistent with the words that are actually on the page, for these were chosen by the author specifically in order to fulfill her intention. So too, only those personal appropriations—those perlocutions—can be considered correct that do justice to the actual propositional (locutionary) sense of the text; for, as an interpretation of the text in question, the implicit claims made about its meaning in our appropriation of it can be either correct or incorrect.

Corresponding to the three dimensions of textual meaning are three separate stages in the process of interpretation: explanation, understanding, and appropriation. Explanation is concerned with elucidating textual structure, understanding with the clarification of meaning (understood as the author's intention), and appropriation with the establishment of the text's significance for a particular reader. These three stages are passed through in succession, and the success of each depends on the correctness of what has been determined in the earlier stages. Only on the basis of an accurate explanation of textual structure can one hope to arrive at a proper understanding of the author's intention, and only when the author's intention has been correctly identified can one meaningfully appropriate the significance of the text for one's own life.

Given Gadamer's critique of the attempt to re-create the mind of the author, this may seem like a strange position for Ricoeur to adopt. But, in speaking of the "author's intention," he does not mean (quite) the flesh-and-blood author of the work in question. Rather, what he has in mind is, in a sense, the text itself understood as the product of an author. As he explains,

> rhetoric can escape the objection of falling back into the "intentional fallacy" . . . inasmuch as what it emphasizes is not the alleged creation process of the work but the techniques by means of which a work is made communicable. These techniques can be discerned in the work itself. The result is that the only type of author whose authority is in question here is not the real author, the object of biography, but the implied author.
>
> (1988, vol. 3, p. 160)

The author *is* the architect of the work in question, then, and the intention that interests us *did* govern the creation of the text, but that intention is to be discovered, not through psychological intuition, but through a painstaking stylistic examination of the text's structure.

Explanation appeals to the laws of grammar and the lexical values attached to the words of the text in establishing the prima facie legitimacy of some readings and simultaneously ruling out as illegitimate a great many others. But structural explanation cannot constitute the whole of interpretation, for, in restricting its focus to the self-enclosed system of differences and oppositions that is language, it fails to engage with the subject matter of the work. Understanding, in Ricoeur's estimation, as in Gadamer's, is a matter of entering into a dialogue with the text concerning its subject matter. What makes this dialogue possible, freeing the interpreter from the tyranny (the monologue) of a strictly univocal reading, is the surplus of meaning that attaches to all linguistic expressions word-length or longer.

Considered in isolation, individual words and expressions are sheer potential—mere sets of possible usages. Placed in juxtaposition within a sentence, however, individual words can no longer lay equal claim to all of their potential meanings; for, contextualized within the sentence, words screen out as inapplicable many of the potential meanings associated with their neighbors. Thus, the syntactic dimension of the sentence constricts for each and every word in the sentence the semantic dimension belonging to it, until eventually there emerges, out of an array of initially open-ended possibilities, a more or less determinate meaning. In addition to the denotations attaching to individual words, however, there are also connotations and emotional colorings. These too are subjected to the process of sifting caused by the juxtaposition of words in the sentence. But because these associations are often highly subjective, and also because of their comparative imprecision, connotations are not as susceptible as denotations to definitive screening. As a result, room for disagreement always arises with respect to the nuances and emotional coloring of a sentence or work, even if there is virtually no disagreement possible with respect to its explicit propositional content. This lack of closure with respect to the screening of connotations guarantees the perpetual openness of literary works to reinterpretation.

According to Ricoeur, it is the initial surplus of meaning that necessitates our speaking "of semantic regulation by the content and not simply of structural regulation" (1974, p. 48). In other words, given the capacity of a text to be taken in many different ways, the reader must turn to the subject matter of the text—which is to say, to his own experience of the subject matter of the text—in order to decide finally between the various readings that are possible. Thus, the text provides, for each new reader, an occasion for reflection on its subject matter.

An important parallel exists between the language-discourse relationship and the tradition-interpretation relationship. Our tradition constitutes what is given to us before we begin to formulate in discourse the interpretations we arrive at on the basis of our personal experience. Thus, tradition, like language, is a system or structure that embodies and makes available interpretations, just as language is the system that embodies and makes available discourse. In each case, moreover, the system in question is in essence nothing more than sedimented function—that is, the possibility of repeating what has already been done, already been intended. But if system (either language or tradition) is sedimented function (either discourse or interpretation), it follows that neither of these systems is static in any permanent sense, for sedimentation is itself an ongoing process. Thus, innovation in discourse and interpretation, grounded in the particularity of the individual's lived experience, holds open the possibility of change and renewal for both language and tradition.

Ricoeur's most important and original contributions to interpretation theory are the fruits of his penetrating investigations into the workings of the actual "points of exchange" where the givenness of language and tradition first shape, and then in turn are shaped by, discourse and interpretation. Three of these crucial "points of exchange"—the metaphor, the symbol, and the narrative—particularly attracted his attention, and each became the subject of a book-length study.

On the subject of metaphor, Ricoeur embraces the interaction theory of I. A. Richards, which stresses that a metaphor is always composed of two parts: tenor and vehicle. When these are brought together, there is an illuminating irruption of one context upon another. A metaphor has cognitive significance—it *shows* us something—because the interaction of contexts that it brings about will only make sense if we can find some point of resemblance that makes the vehicle *fit* against the background established by the tenor. The recognition of this resemblance, which guides the creation of metaphor, is the same recognition of resemblance that underlies concept formation (and that thus governs all language use). Whereas in concept formation the recognition of similarity is all-important, however, in metaphor a disturbing tension arises: the tenor and vehicle, by virtue of their similarity, draw together and seem inclined to lose themselves in a single identity; at the same time, by virtue of the "inappropriateness" of their conjunction, they want to fly apart. This tension at the very heart of metaphor is, Ricoeur contends, something that we must take care to respect; for it is only while this tension persists that metaphor is alive and able to challenge us to see further than we have.

The symbol, like the metaphor, "invites us to think." It "calls for an interpretation, precisely because it says more than it says and because it never ceases to speak to us" (ibid., p. 28). To say, as Ricoeur is inclined to, that symbol is *opaque* is to say that it never gives up its whole store of meaning. This is because, in the analogy that the symbol essentially is, only one term—the material symbol itself—is clearly defined. In other words, in contrast to the situation where we recognize that an analogy can be drawn between two terms that are already thoroughly known, in our dealings with symbol we always arrive on the scene *after* the analogy is ensconced and *before* the second or symbolized term is thoroughly grasped. Thus, "a meditation on symbols starts from the fullness of language and of meaning already there; it begins from within language which has already taken place and in which everything in a certain sense has already been said" (ibid. 287–288). The symbol itself is indicated, and so too is the fact that, as symbol, it stands in an analogical relationship to some aspect of our situation. Interpreting the symbol, then, consists in clarifying what that second, and only incompletely specified, term in the analogy must amount to, given that an analogical relationship is known to exist.

According to Ricoeur, this interpretive meditation involves an interplay of speculation and reflection: speculation that begins from our preunderstanding of the signifi-

cance of the symbol in question, but that is then drawn in new directions by the material nature of the symbol itself, and reflection that takes what is uncovered by such speculation and reintegrates it into the coherent body of our beliefs. This process, however, is fraught with danger in both directions, because reflective and speculative thought conflict. Reflection, which is by nature demythologizing, would, if given free rein, transform symbolism into allegory; and "allegory implies that the true meaning, the philosophical meaning, preceded the [symbol], which was only a second guise, a veil deliberately thrown over the truth to mislead the simple" (ibid., p. 299). Reflection, then, seeks the domination of the symbol by whatever spiritual doctrine is already in place. Speculation, on the other hand, left to itself, is prone to "rationalizing symbols as such, and thereby fixing them on the imaginative plane where they are born and take shape" (ibid.). This is the temptation of "dogmatic mythology" or gnosis—the temptation to allow the material symbol to carry thought wherever it will, unchecked by any need to remain consistent with an initial core of spiritual belief. These two dangers are to be avoided only by firmly yoking reflection and speculation together. Properly constrained, speculation, guided by the nature of the material symbol, extends and fleshes out the initial spiritual insight underlying the symbol, while reflection guards that original insight against the danger of heresy. Thus, when speculation and reflection are properly yoked, we can pursue a line of thought that is "at once *bound* and *free*" in the process of arriving at "an interpretation that would respect the original enigma of symbols, let itself be taught by this enigma, but, with that as a start, bring out the meaning, give it form, in the full responsibility of an autonomous systematized thought" (ibid., p. 300).

The symbol's capacity to carry thought in new and valuable directions even as it recovers insights to which we have a long-standing precommitment illustrates

> the double dependence of the self on the unconscious and on the sacred, . . . [which] is manifested only in a symbolic mode. In order to elucidate this double dependence, reflection must reduce the status of consciousness and interpret it in terms of the symbolic meanings that approach it from behind and ahead, from above and below. In short, reflection must embrace both an archaeology and an eschatology. (Ibid., p. 333)

The form of "archaeology" that Ricoeur has in mind here is the psychoanalytic interpretation of religious symbolism, in the light of which religion is seen as "a projection of an ancient destiny, both ancestral and infantile" (ibid.). It is not necessary, however, to tie this claim too tightly to a specifically psychoanalytic interpretation of our symbols. In a broader sense, what is being suggested is that, in our efforts to come to know ourselves, we must reflect on both the past that has determined what we now are and the possibilities of new meaning that lie perpetually open before us. According to Ricoeur, this is the very essence of the hermeneutic task: to understand what might be on the basis of what is already given.

Not all expressions lend themselves equally well to the pursuit of this task. The symbol, in its opacity, and living metaphor, with its clash of contexts, each open up for us valuable avenues of understanding. But worthwhile as metaphor and symbol are in this regard, narrative offers still richer possibilities of understanding and self-discovery.

In "The Model of the Text," Ricoeur remarks that an action, like a text, can be understood only if it is meaningful and if it is given "a kind of objectification which is equivalent to the fixation of a discourse by writing" (1981, p. 203). Moreover, the action, like the text, possesses locutionary, illocutionary, and perlocutionary dimensions. These features found in both the text and human action—the fixation of meaning in structural form, the dissociation of this meaning (as a result of its fixation) from the intention of the author, the openness of the text or action to interpretation by anyone who takes an interest in it, and finally, the fact that the meaning of the text or action is something about which we are qualified (as inhabitants of the shared world of experience) to shape an opinion—are precisely the features that guarantee the possibility of objectivity in interpretation. To say that textual and historical interpretation are thus guaranteed a kind of objectivity, however, is to say only that the objectified form of the text or action must be done justice by any serious interpretation, and thus that a restriction is placed on possible readings. But again, because the meaning of a text or action does not reside exclusively within the fixed form, because meaning in its broader sense encompasses the three dimensions of locution, illocution, and perlocution (or significance), there are inevitably grounds for disagreement in the interpretation of human actions as well as of texts.

As humans, we are fascinated with narratives because they illustrate the possibilities of our nature—possibilities that cannot be known a priori, but that can be discovered by attending to what others have done. (What human nature has already demonstrated itself capable of, it obviously remains capable of.) Important as this recognition of more or less abstract possibilities is, it constitutes only a necessary preliminary to self-understanding, which entails, over and above this, the appropriation of what are specifically *one's own* possibilities of being—that is, those that speak to one's nature and open up new avenues of self-definition. According to Ricoeur, because one does define oneself, choosing to embrace some of the modes of being that one has uncovered and rejecting others, "the positing of the self is not a given, it is a *task*" (1974, p. 329).

Although each of the various "expressions in which life objectifies itself" has something to show us about the possibilities that are open to us as human beings, literature tends to have a unique advantage in this respect—the advantage of having been created for no other purpose than the imaginative exploration of possible ways of being human. The task of the playwright and the novelist "is to render as perfectly as possible the vision of the world that inspires [him]" (1988, vol. 3, p. 177) through the persuasive handling of plot and characterization. The corresponding task of the reader is to explicate and appropriate the type of being-in-the-world that the author has unfolded. This proposed world, moreover, "is not *behind* the text, as a hidden intention would be, but *in front* of it, as that which the work unfolds, discovers, reveals. Henceforth, to understand is *to understand oneself in front of the text*" (1981, p. 143).

What does it mean to say that the text opens up a "world"? When we read a novel, play, or historical narrative, we find ourselves called on to flesh out the actual account of events given in the text with our own sense of what is implied about how these explicit details of the narrative might relate to other circumstances and events that could be considered. Because the whole point of a fictional account is to persuade us that the events described might actually have occurred, it is implied that the sort of further information that is always, at least in principle, available in an account of real events is also available here. This additional information, however, is provided not by the author, but by the reader, who, under the guidance of what is explicitly given in the text, "fleshes it out" in her imagination. This fleshing out constitutes the world of the text—a world whose existence the text implies, but that is realized only by virtue of the reader's interpretation of the text (and that therefore, considered in its particulars, will differ somewhat from reader to reader).

In opening up these new worlds, literature invites the reader to consider alternative modes of being. As Ricoeur observes, "to understand is . . . to expose oneself to [the text]; it is to receive a self enlarged by the appropriation of the proposed worlds which interpretation unfolds" (ibid., p. 94). The reader, through projective identification with the characters of a novel or play, steps into—temporarily and "hypothetically"—an alien viewpoint, and in so doing achieves a certain measure of freedom from the circumstances of her own situation. This in turn affords the reader the sort of distance from herself that makes it possible for her to criticize her own nature and her own illusions:

> In the idea of the "imaginative variation of the ego," I see the most fundamental possibility for a critique of the illusions of the subject. . . . [T]he appropriation of the proposed worlds offered by the text passes through the disappropriation of the self. The critique of *false consciousness* can thus become an integral part of hermeneutics. (Ibid., p. 94)

In Ricoeur's estimation, this constitutes an answer of sorts to those critics of hermeneutics—such as Jürgen Habermas—who contend that too great a concern for appropriating the insights of one's tradition can only reinforce current ideologies and power structures. If exposure to the literary masterpieces of one's tradition increases the flexibility of one's outlook, surely this implies that one's commitments to institutions and practices already in place must become more thoughtful and more carefully qualified. In other words, literature has ethical significance. It shapes our understanding of what is right and wrong, valuable and insignificant, and thus determines in no small measure how we choose to live our lives. As Ricoeur puts it, "literature is a vast laboratory in which we experiment with estimations, evaluations, and judgments of approval and condemnation through which narrativity serves as a propaedeutic to ethics" (1992, p. 115).

Yet another way in which the reading of narratives contributes to the shape of one's self-understanding is in enabling one to see one's life as possessing narrative unity. This matters because "if [one's] life cannot be grasped as a singular totality, [one] could never hope it to be successful [or] complete" (ibid., p. 160). The successful life, after all, is one in which various projects are brought to fruition. But the completion of projects can itself only be understood in terms of a narrative structure—in terms of the initiation of action, followed by a sequence of intermediary events in which particular means are brought to bear for the sake of desired ends, which lead, finally, to the arrival of a conclusion.

This sense of the narrative unity of one's life, moreover, helps one to assimilate and make sense of those arbitrary and contingent aspects of experience that tend to disrupt and frustrate one's intentions. All narrative exhibits a "dialectic of concordance and discordance" (ibid., p. 147), by which Ricoeur means that any *interesting* story tells us how some intention was fixed upon, how its achievement was frustrated in various ways, and how these impediments were eventually surmounted and the goal in question was reached. What this implies is that the unexpected hindrance and, for that matter, the unexpected deliverance or benefit are essential elements of the narrative in which they appear. Beyond these contingencies, in fact, the narrative is constituted of only one other element—the character of the hero, which finds *its* expression in the hero's choice of goals and in the ways in which he responds to the various impediments and strokes of good fortune that come his way. But, according to Ricoeur, "it is the identity of the story that makes the identity of the character" (ibid., p. 148). "The contingency of the event contributes to the necessity, retroactive so to speak, of the history of a life. . . . The person, understood as a character in a story, is not an entity distinct from his or her 'experiences'" (ibid., p. 147). We come to recognize this, in particular, through the reading of literature; and insofar as our familiarity with literature enables us to grasp the narrative unity in our own lives, to see *ourselves* as characters in a story, our reading of literature paves the way to a proper appreciation of the significance of those arbitrary and contingent events that help to define us.

[*See also* Gadamer; Hermeneutics; Narrative; *and* Phenomenology.]

BIBLIOGRAPHY

Works by Ricoeur

La symbolique du mal. In *Philosophie de la volonté: Finitude et culpabilité,* vol. 2. Paris, 1960. Translated by Emerson Buchanan as *The Symbolism of Evil* (Boston, 1967).

De l'interprétation. Paris, 1965. Translated by Denis Savage as *Freud and Philosophy: An Essay on Interpretation* (New Haven, 1970).

Le conflit des interprétations. Paris, 1969. Translated as *The Conflict of Interpretations,* edited by Don Ihde (Evanston, Ill., 1974).

La métaphore vive. Paris, 1975. Translated by Robert Czerny, Kathleen McLaughlin, and John Costello as *The Rule of Metaphor* (Toronto, 1977).

Hermeneutics and the Human Sciences. Translated and edited by John B. Thompson. Cambridge and New York, 1981.

Temps et récit. 3 vols. Paris, 1983–1985. Translated by Kathleen Blamey and David Pellauer as *Time and Narrative,* 3 vols. (Chicago, 1984–1988).

Du texte à l'action. Paris, 1986.

Soi-même comme un autre. Paris, 1990. Translated by Kathleen Blamey as *Oneself as Another* (Chicago, 1992).

Other Sources

Ihde, Don. *Hermeneutic Phenomenology: The Philosophy of Paul Ricoeur.* Evanston, Ill., 1971.

Wood, David, ed. *On Paul Ricoeur: Narrative and Interpretation.* London and New York, 1991.

RON BONTEKOE

RIEGL, ALOIS (1858–1905), professor of art history at the University of Vienna at the turn of the century, pioneer of modern formal analysis, and spokesperson for a relativistic theory of artistic value. Both the latter endeavors were crystallized in Riegl's theory of a formally analyzable "artistic volition" *(Kunstwollen),* which develops throughout history, informs all artistic manifestations of a given period, and relates artistic form to a wider cultural context. One can judge art faithfully, Riegl thought, only in relation to its own *Kunstwollen,* not according to universal standards, and only in terms of form, not content.

The development of his theory of formal analysis is an illuminating example of a conservative revolution. In his studies and early scholarly work, Riegl's academic pursuits were in accord with the then current enthusiasm for realist artistic styles inspired by positivist intellectual trends. He sought to trace an evolutionary development toward realism throughout the centuries. From his perspective, artistic realism had a scholarly cast, as though art were a quasi-scientific method of gathering and analyzing data. This view was modeled on the empiricist education he received from his teachers at the University of Vienna in the 1870s and 1880s. Thus, while his Habilitationsschrift on the illustration of medieval calendars established the persistence of the Hellenistic tradition into the Middle Ages, it did so only to pinpoint the moment in the Middle Ages when artists departed from conventional models in order to study nature. He sought to preserve his quasi-scholarly view of art as, in following years, it encountered successive challenges both by philosophical developments with which he came in contact and by the artistic material with which he found himself confronted. By the end of his career, his attempt to preserve a representational theory of art based on realism led him to back into a nonrepresentational stance inspiring to Expressionist artists who created revolutionary abstract art early in the twentieth century.

The first challenge to Riegl's interpretation of the development of art in terms of realism alone came from the subject matter of his studies. His first professional position was as curator of textiles at the Austrian Museum of Art and Industry. Through it, Riegl moved out of necessity into the field of ornament. With ammunition in part provided by theories of the contemporary Arts and Crafts movement, he developed, in *Altorientalische Teppiche* (1891) and *Stilfragen* (1893), a complex theory of surface ornamentation. He kept this theory compatible with his quasi-scientific theory of realism by arguing that whereas representational art sought to approach a naturalistic rendering of the external world, ornamental art represented its own material, symbolizing the structure of the surface it covered through the construction and articulation of ornamental motifs. Riegl traced an evolutionary development in this type of "structural symbolism." His primary example was the Egyptian lotus ornament, whose fortunes he traced through its inception in Egypt to its transformations in Assyrian, Greek, Roman, and finally medieval Islamic ornament. According to Riegl, decorative motifs began as relatively simple parts, linked straightforwardly in rows. Through creative adaptation of the laws of (primarily vegetal) nature, however, they gradually developed more sophisticated methods of linkage. Ultimately, decorative motifs became extremely sophisticated representational tools with multilevel means for making a surface cohere visually and demonstrate flatness while maintaining visual interest. The makers of ornament, like Realist painters, studied and applied the laws of nature.

As close as the formal application of Riegl's theory may seem to mid-twentieth-century formalism, it remained a two-tiered notion of representation that left the role of artistic realism unquestioned. During the mid-1890s, however, Riegl's optimistic view of the ever-advancing discovery of the laws of reality through empirical study and classification faced serious challenges by subjectivist philosophies and art movements. Riegl reacted to this epistemological crisis by struggling to reveal and substantiate the element of physical reality and ultimately standards of value that he thought ensured the validity of the visual arts and all cultural endeavors. In so doing, he tried to incorporate into his theories elements of current subjective theories that threatened to undermine his attempts to preserve objectivity. The result-

ing synthesis, some of which can be seen in process in his posthumously published manuscript *Historische Grammatik der bildenden Künste* (1966), produced the impressive and puzzling work on which depends his historical significance. It led him to seek to reconcile the scientific model of art as the pursuit of knowledge with which he started with a voluntaristic, subjective model; to transform structural symbolism into perceptual psychology; to shift the locus of his endeavor from the work of art to the beholder; and ultimately to leave the field of art proper, and dwell on the ethical development of the beholder's system of values.

The concept of the *Kunstwollen*, which suggests subjectivity, came out of this endeavor. Riegl had employed the term loosely in *Stilfragen* as a symbol of artistic freedom to enlist creative artists in the struggle against "materialistic" theories of art based on the primacy of technique. In *Spätrömische Kunstindustrie* (1901) he canonized the *Kunstwollen*, and the "will" to which it refers, as the sole determinant of artistic form, expressly linked to the historically determined desire for a particular configuration of the visible world. At the same time, Riegl abandoned the distinction between the tasks of the fine and applied arts as incompatible with the notion of a singular *Kunstwollen*. The all-embracing *Kunstwollen* developed historically, and made itself known in the formal signs of outline, color, spatial and planar configurations. Tracing the development of the *Kunstwollen* through stages, Riegl developed a vocabulary that showed how a representational figure and an ornamental pattern play identical roles against their backgrounds, and allowed the central nave of a church to be perceived as acting similarly as a pattern against the background of its apse and side aisles. Using this concept, he could analyze all art in purely formal terms.

Although the *Kunstwollen* manifested itself only in formal relationships, however, Riegl was not ready to abandon art's relation to reality altogether. He used a widespread perceptual theory that allied objective reality with palpability to defend art's ability to represent material reality. According to Riegl's interpretation of the theory, the sense of touch isolated objects in order to validate their separate material existence, whereas the more intellectual optical sense united objects in large abstractions. The viewer who feels capable of touching an object is convinced that it exists. Riegl sought to harness this verifiability for artistic representation. Without claiming that the work of art represented external objects directly, he nevertheless thought that art could represent the impressions they made on the senses. Art could validate its representation within perception itself, through reference to the most objectively valid sense.

Historically, Riegl thought art began with the tactile, and increasingly admitted optical elements. In order to show how art could represent touch, Riegl developed a formal iconography of palpability based on the theories of the Arts and Crafts movement, translating the theory of representation articulated in *Stilfragen* into perceptual terms. He identified as signs of touch the elements that in *Stilfragen* he had thought symbolized the solidity and flatness of surfaces, among them hard outlines, flat planes of color, repetition, and symmetry. What he had seen as representations of (external) material became representations of the (internal) tactile sense. Such representational devices characterize surfaces as flat whether they are or not. Similarly, the artistic signs of visibility, the well-known artistic devices of Impressionism, could be used to characterize any surface as optical and ephemeral. Riegl, along with other German critics, regarded Impressionism as a movement concerned primarily with ephemeral qualities of light.

Formal relationships represented only perceptions, not the external world. Nevertheless, they had an important volitional tie to the external world. Using perceptual theory that conceived the optical sense as connecting objects within a single visual field, whereas touch separates objects from one another, Riegl defined the *Kunstwollen* as a demand that art visually reflect the relationships desirable in all domains of life at a particular moment. Art had an intellectual and a political significance, therefore. Opticality came to stand for connectives that are emotional, political, and even causal, whereas touch stood for separation, individuality, and power. Thus, the ornamental designs of buckles and pins acted out relations of both causality and might. In this respect, the historical development that Riegl postulated toward greater opticality articulated a theory of political and intellectual historical development, because greater opticality meant greater power to make connections conceptually as well as greater social cohesion with a looser hierarchy.

Through the mediation of art critics and essayists such as Wilhelm Worringer, the concepts of opticality, palpability, their formal components, and their meanings found echoes in the writings of Expressionist artists as they groped their way toward abstract art. Although their concerns differ widely from those of Riegl, traces of Riegl's spatial and perceptual terminology can also be found in formalist art historians and even in modernist critics, such as Clement Greenberg, in the mid-twentieth century. Thus, for decades Riegl was known chiefly for his system of formal analysis, and *Spätrömische Kunstindustrie* remained his most well known work. But far more significant for the present day are the works of his last few years, when he expanded the implications for the representation of relationships that preoccupied him in his study of late-antique ornament. *Das holländische Gruppenporträt* (1902) concerns seventeenth-century Dutch group portraits whose subjects look at the beholder. In it, Riegl developed a theory of "attentiveness" that addressed the issue of the relationship between the beholder and the work of art in formal and ethical terms. The desired relationship to the world is not simply reflected in the relationship between parts of the work of art, but in the

relationship it performs with the beholder. Art that looks back, for example, depends on the viewer to give the work formal coherence, but it can also, as does a Dutch group portrait, claim a right to its own existence and demand respect for itself. Thus, mutual regard involves a relationship of respect between art and beholder. In works of art contemporary to Riegl (genre paintings, for example), figures do not acknowledge the viewer. They allow themselves to be subsumed into the viewer's imagination, feeding the viewer's own subjectivity. A developmental theory informs Riegl's work on Dutch art, just as it does *Spätrömische Kunstindustrie*, but Riegl has to struggle to identify as progressive the demise of the later period, because it means the loss of the mutual respect exemplified in the Dutch paintings.

Both *Spätrömische Kunstindustrie* and *Das holländische Gruppenporträt* deliberately chose works of art undervalued by Riegl's contemporaries. He hoped to make the alien *Kunstwollen* known through an exploration of its differences from that of his own culture. The knowledge of alien values depended on an understanding of one's own in a form of hermeneutics that might today be called dialogic. Thus, Riegl's work, though it relied on developmental theories, had a relativistic edge, and has had the effect of encouraging research in minor or undervalued media and historical periods. The acceptance of historical changes in values is central to his important late theoretical essays on the subject of monuments, which stemmed from his work, from 1902 on, as conservator general of the Austrian Commission on Historical Monuments. These essays carried his ruminations on the ethical basis of the relation between beholder and object beyond the world of art. In the essay "Der moderne Denkmalkultus, sein Wesen, seine Entstehung" (in *Gesammelte Aufsätze*), he traced a hierarchy of values themselves, conceived in terms of the relation between man and the environment, and projected into a developmental history. A tendency to merge with the environment is conceived in optical, subjective terms and connected with the appreciation of aged objects, whose outlines become less defined, while the objective, crisp outlines of palpability suggest newness. As humanity becomes more subjective and optical, it is increasingly able to accept the ravages of time. Again, however, Riegl finds it difficult to embrace subjectivity wholeheartedly. In this essay, he historicizes the writing of history itself, attributing to the historian the tactile respect for the individual of the past. Although historical studies prepare humanity for the spiritual revolution signaled by the cult of age, the historian's respect for detail also comes across as the necessary antidote to the unchecked submission to the cult of subjectivity.

Because so much of it attempted to rescue the highly valued notion of representation from the onslaught of modern challengers, Riegl's work occupies a precarious position between the values he upheld and the antirepresentational theories that it would later help others to support. His work both exemplifies and signals the demise of the representational theory of art. Its pivotal character explains the resistance to easy appropriation by any one point of view that has contributed to its continuing significance. It has been given a variety of different readings, within and outside of the field of art history, that keep it useful and challenging from a formal, structuralist, or poststructuralist point of view. Early on, controversies over Riegl's significance centered on his work's political potential. Hans Sedlmayr's enthusiastic 1929 reading of the *Kunstwollen* as a totalizing concept that united a people, an era, and a country helped lead others, such as E. H. Gombrich and Ernst Bloch, writing in the postwar era, to condemn the concept of the *Kunstwollen* as protofascist. Marxist thinkers, however, had already begun to appropriate Riegl's ideas for their own, very different, aims. The notion of the near and the distant, for example, appealed to Walter Benjamin, who used it as the basis of his own idea of the "aura," which he developed in his essay "The Work of Art in the Age of Mechanical Reproduction" in 1937. Mikhail Bakhtin, although he was unaware of Riegl's protodialogic investigations into the relation between the beholder and the work of art, which he might have found of interest, appreciated Riegl's work for the content that he inscribed into his formalism. Bakhtin alluded to Riegl as a foil against the sterility of the Russian Formalists.

Although Riegl has never been neglected by scholars, his works were not translated into English for decades. The notorious difficulty of Riegl's German is usually given as the reason. Thus, the translation of several of his works into English suggests a renewed interest in Riegl. This new interest seems to be the result of the possibility of regarding Riegl from new points of view, some of them shaped by postmodernism. Interest in the conceptual foundations of art history, for example, has led to examinations of his historiographical methods in the context of Hegelian and Kantian ideas as part of the enterprise of a "critical history of art." The notion of the gaze, articulated in *Das holländische Gruppenporträt*, has attracted renewed attention in relation to recent theories of beholding. The eclecticism of postmodern architecture has encouraged an interest in his concept of the historical career of monuments, which he saw as eclectic because they belonged not only to the historical period that created them, but also to those that preserved, renovated, and modified them. Several signs, including the publication of Riegl's collected writings on historical preservation, attest to this current interest. But more broadly, the upsurge in interest in Riegl attests to the significance for the present, poststructural climate of arttheoretical and -historical practice, of Riegl's protodialogic hermeneutic investigation into the relationship between the beholder and the work of art and, more broadly, between our own values and those of the past.

BIBLIOGRAPHY

Works by Riegl

"Die mittelalterliche Kalendarillustration." *Mitteilungen des Instituts für österreichische Geschichtsforschung* 10 (1889): 1–74.
Altorientalische Teppiche (1891). Reprint, Mittenwald, 1979.
Stilfragen: Grundlegungen zu einer Geschichte der Ornamentik (1893). 2d ed. Berlin, 1923.
Spätrömische Kunstindustrie (1901; 2d ed., 1927). Reprint, Darmstadt, 1973.
Das holländische Gruppenporträt (1902). 2d ed. 2 vols. Edited by Karl M. Swoboda. Vienna, 1931.
Gesammelte Aufsätze (1929). Edited by Karl M. Swoboda. Berlin, 1995.
Historische Grammatik der bildenden Künste. Edited by Karl M. Swoboda and Otto Pächt. Graz, 1966.
Kunstwerk oder Denkmal? Alois Riegls Schriften zur Denkmalpflege. Edited by Ernst Bacher. Vienna, 1995.

English Translations of Riegl

"The Modern Cult of Monuments: Its Character and Its Origin." Translated by Kurt W. Forster and Diane Ghirardo. *Oppositions* 25 (1982): 21–50. Translation of "Der moderne Denkmalkultus, sein Wesen, seine Entstehung," in *Gesammelte Aufsätze,* edited by Karl M. Swoboda (Berlin, 1995), pp. 144–194.
Problems of Style: Foundations for a History of Ornament. Translated by Evelyn Kain. Princeton, N.J., 1992.
"Excerpts from *The Dutch Group Portrait.*" Translated by Benjamin Binstock. *October* 74 (1995): 3–35.

Other Sources

Bacher, Ernst. Introduction to Alois Riegl, *Kunstwerk oder Denkmal?* pp. 11–48. Vienna, 1995.
Binstock, Benjamin. "Alois Riegl in the Presence of *The Nightwatch.*" *October* 74 (1995): 36–44.
Forster, Kurt. "Monument/Memory and the Mortality of Architecture." *Oppositions* 25 (1982): 2–19.
Iversen, Margaret. *Alois Riegl: Art History and Theory.* Cambridge, Mass., 1993.
Kemp, Wolfgang. "Alois Riegl (1858–1905)". In *Altmeister moderner Kunstgeschichte,* edited by Heinrich Dilly, pp. 37–62. Berlin, 1990.
Kemp, Wolfgang. "Nachwort." In Alois Riegl, *Gesammelte Aufsätze,* pp. 207–222. Berlin, 1995.
Olin, Margaret. *Forms of Representation in Alois Riegl's Theory of Art.* University Park, Pa., 1992.
Pächt, Otto. "Alois Riegl" (1963). In *Methodisches zur kunsthistorischen Praxis: Ausgewählte Schriften,* edited by Jörg Oberhaidacher, Artur Rosenauer, and Gertraut Schikola, pp. 141–152. Munich, 1977.
Panofsky, Erwin. "Der Begriff des Kunstwollens." In *Aufsätze zu Grundfragen der Kunstwissenschaft,* 2d rev ed., edited by Hariolf Oberer and Egon Verheyen, pp. 29–43. Berlin, 1974. Translated by Kenneth J. Northcott and Joel Snyder as "The Concept of Artistic Volition," *Critical Inquiry* 8 (Autumn 1981): 7–34.
Podro, Michael. "Riegl." In *The Critical Historians of Art,* pp. 71–97. New Haven, 1982.
Sauerländer, Willibald. "Alois Riegl und die Entstehung der autonomen Kunstgeschichte am Fin de Siècle." In *Fin de Siècle: Zur Literatur und Kunst der Jahrhunderwende,* edited by Roger Bauer et al., pp. 125–139. Frankfurt am Main, 1978.
Scarrocchia, Sandro. "'Al tempo la sua arte, all'arte la sua libertà': il Denkmalkultus di Riegl." In Alois Riegl, *Il Culto Moderno dei monumenti: Il suo carättere e I suoi inizi,* translated by Sandro Scarrocchia and Renate Trost, pp. 9–23. Bologna, 1985.

Scarrocchia, Sandro. *Studi su Alois Riegl*. Ricerche dell'Instituto per i beni artistici culturali naturali della Regione Emilia-Romagna, no. 12. Bologna, 1986.

Scarrocchia, Sandro, ed. *Alois Riegl: Teoria e Prassi Della Conservazione Dei Monumenti: Antologia di scritti, discorsi, rapporti, 1898–1905, con una scelta di saggi critici*. Bologna, 1995.

Sedlmayr, Hans. "Die Quintessenz des Lehren Riegl." In Alois Riegl, *Gesammelte Aufsätze*, edited by Karl M. Swoboda, pp. xii–xxxiv. Augsburg and Vienna, 1929.

Worringer, Wilhelm. *Abstraction and Empathy: A Contribution to the Psychology of Style* (1909). Translated by Michael Bullock. New York, 1953.

Zerner, Henri. "Alois Riegl: Art, Value, and Historicism." *Daedalus* 105 (Winter 1976): 177–189.

MARGARET OLIN

ROCK MUSIC. Rock music has its own standards of evaluation, which differ in significant ways from those of traditional musical aesthetics. Rock musicians and serious listeners to rock music know and understand these criteria, which derive from the history and practices of rock music and its antecedents. The traditions from which rock arose (folk, blues, and country) emphasize performance rather than composition, and value the communication of feeling and emotion much more highly than either the formal complexity of the composition or the technical accuracy of the performance. Consequently, rock music is judged more by its effects on the listener's body than by a "disinterested" appreciation of its formal properties. The three principal criteria by which rock is judged are authenticity of voice, rhythm, and loudness. These categories do not exhaust what is important in rock music, but they point to its most obviously significant aspects.

Authenticity of Voice. Rock music succeeds where there is a direct emotional connection with the listener. The most important vehicle for expressing emotion in rock was originally the human voice, and this voice was judged by the conviction and intensity of the singing, because this was a sign of the authenticity or "truth" of the singer, a sign that the singer is singing from experience, and not simply "faking" emotions the singer has never felt. As is also the case with the blues, which is the basis for much of rock music, what matters is the singer's involvement in the material, as revealed by the amount of emotion and feeling in how the tones are sung. Whether the "correct" tones are sung, or sung at the "correct" time, is very much a secondary consideration, especially because the melody, rhythm, and even structure of the "same" song can vary so much from performance to performance that the very notion of a single "correct" tone is nearly meaningless. In rock and blues music, the "right" note is the one that is right for that performance, and depends on what has preceded the singing of that tone, and on what the performers are moving toward later in the performance. This is true, of course, of any performance-based and improvisational form of music, includ-ing jazz. In such music, the "song" is merely the framework for a performance, and it is the performance or the singer that is paramount, not the composition. As for the performance, what counts is whether the singer "tells the truth," that is, whether the expression of feeling is judged to be genuine. The criteria for determining authenticity are not formalizable rules but the effect of the voice on the body of the listener: the voice "rings true" or sounds "fake" depending on the complicated visceral response it arouses. This response is hard to describe, and it is unlikely that anyone could determine a set of "objective" criteria that could determine whether the response indicated a good or bad vocal performance, but it is immediately recognizable to the experienced listener.

These criteria of vocal expressiveness gradually were taken up by other instruments, and by the guitar in particular. Again, rock followed the lead of the blues, where artists such as Muddy Waters and B. B. King had made the electric guitar into a second "voice," rather than the mere accompaniment to the human voice that the guitar had been. Not surprisingly, the rock musicians who made the guitar into a vehicle of emotional expression were themselves strongly influenced by the blues, and the legacy of such pioneers as Eric Clapton and Jimi Hendrix is that, for succeeding generations of rock musicians, it is how the tones are played, and not the tones themselves or whether they are the "right" ones, that makes a rock performance successful. Occasionally, this emphasis on performance can degenerate into virtuosity for its own sake or "showboating." Sheer speed and flashiness will always have their place as part of rock's brazenness and rebelliousness, but discerning listeners value these less than the ability to convey feeling, which at times requires constraint, in much the same way as good rock singing is not all shouting, because on occasion more meaning is conveyed in a whisper than by a holler or a yell.

Rock's concern with emotional expressiveness rather than technical accuracy or faithfulness to a score should not be confused with lack of technique. There is a world of difference between someone who is trying to master the growling and howling of blues singing and someone, such as Muddy Waters or Janis Joplin, who is able to focus on what is being expressed rather than on the technique used to express it. A good rock musician is also sufficiently immersed in the forms and traditions of rock music to understand what can and cannot be given adequate expression in that idiom. Sometimes, a simple combination of exposure to the idiom and raw, inborn talent is enough; Elvis Presley was at his best when his singing was unschooled by anything other than an appreciation for blues and country music. In cases like these, the acquisition of "proper" technique serves only to obscure and distort a technique that had been acquired "naturally," which is to say, by a combination of innate gifts and lucky circumstances. Such "natural" technique might be confused with no technique at all, but these techniques are not easy; if they were, everyone could be an Elvis.

On the other hand, there is a significant body of rock music that claims to disdain technique altogether. This was notably the case with "punk rock," which arose in the 1970s in part as a protest against notions of technique and virtuosity. Many punk rockers could barely play their instruments, but were intent rather on creating an effect through sheer loudness, rhythmic intensity, and shrieking vocals. Nevertheless, punk rock was highly expressive, although the predominant emotions expressed were anger and aggression. Punk aficionados distinguished between authentic expressions of anger, such as Johnny Rotten's performances with the Sex Pistols, and inferior versions that were less capable of communicating significant emotion, or that did so less persuasively, or were seen as having nothing to say (the same Johnny Rotten, now John Lydon, in P.I.L.). It would be a mistake, then, to think that punk rock lacks technique. Rather, its technique relies on aggressive guitar chording and rapid tempo drumming, combined with aggressive vocals. It is a technique entirely opposed to the "art rock" of the period, the latter consisting of a technical mastery of an instrument that is not dissimilar from the virtuousity of a classical musician, and highly involved musical compositions that sometimes took on Wagnerian dimensions (the album by Yes, *Tales from Topographic Oceans,* is representative). Punk uses its instruments as aids in a dramatic enactment of emotions, rather than for their musical capabilities alone. This element, always present in rock music, became explicit in performances by The Who in the 1960s, which involved the drummer and guitarist physically destroying their instruments as an expression of pure rage. Punk took this element of rock performance and made it into nearly the entire content.

Given that punk rock strips rock to its bare essentials, and produces an antitechnical technique, the question arises as to whether the value of rock music is in any way based on its expressive capabilities or "authenticity of voice." In numerous publications, Simon Frith argues for a more sociological analysis of musical value. Popular music, including rock music, has value for a particular group if its style of performance embodies or expresses values with which the group identifies or toward which it feels an allegiance, and not all of these values need be "musical." This determines whether a certain kind of music will be popular with a certain social group, and the value of the music consists simply in its thus being valued by a social group. Values such as "authenticity" are no more than disguised expressions of the subjective preferences of the critic.

It could be argued, however, that criteria of "authenticity" are not those of a critic but those of a social group. Criteria of "authenticity" arise from the practices of musicians and listeners. These will vary according to the subcategories of rock music involved, each of which has its own norms and its own following. There is an enormous spectrum in rock music, from punk, grunge, thrash, and heavy metal at one extreme, to more balladic and lyrical folk rock and "adult-oriented" rock forms that verge into country and pop music. Within any of those subcategories, there are knowledgeable listeners capable of distinguishing between music of high quality, judged according to fairly objective and practice-based criteria, and music that they happen to enjoy for other reasons, such as political—the association of a piece of music with personal memories or with nonmusical symbols and values—or some other "subjective" criteria.

Rhythm. Rhythm is perhaps the most obvious and frequently remarked upon aspect of rock music. Rock music, like blues and country, was originally for dancing, and in dance the connection between the music and the listener's body is felt and enacted, rather than merely contemplated. A good rock song is one that makes the listener's body want to move, and this cannot be done simply by observing the correct tempo and time signature: good rock musicians will sometimes deliberately vary the tempo in order to create a certain effect (speeding up the tempo to build excitement, or slowly building up and slowing down the tempo in order to build up tension in the body that is later released with explosive energy), and play behind, in front of, and around the beat, rather than right on it. Timing—knowing whether to play ahead of or behind or on the beat—is more important than tempo, and the "rightness" of the timing, tempo, and rhythm is judged by whether the music inspires the body to dance. Good rock musicians enter into a dialogue with the dancers, adjusting their performance according to the dancers' responses, which is something that requires a great deal of practice and training, but not the sort of thing that could be captured in a score or some other set of formalized instructions. For the musicians as well as the dancers, the body and its feelings reveal whether or not the performance is successful.

The importance of rhythm varies in the different genres of pop music. In rhythm and blues, soul, funk, and rap, rhythm is often the most important element. In some of the more intellectualized rock forms, such as psychedelia, "progressive rock," and some types of heavy metal, rhythm is sometimes of little consequence, because these are forms of rock that have departed from the constraints of dance-oriented music in order to give more free play to the voice of the instruments. But even when rock is not meant for dancing, the rhythmical element remains, in the tempo shifts, the repetitive figures (or "riffs"), and the impact of the drums and electric bass, both of which resonate in the body core and convey a feeling of movement, even if the movement is not expressed as dance.

Loudness. Rock music is notorious for being loud, but the sheer volume or loudness adds to its intensity and can be effectively used as a vehicle of expression. Loud music vibrates in the chest cavity and the body core, and this feature can be used to create feelings of being lifted up, let down, or driven backwards. Music that is uniformly loud can be simply exhausting, which sometimes is deliberate, as with some punk rock, but otherwise is a sign of ineptitude. Most of the better rock performances make extensive use of dynamics, utilizing the loudness made possible by electrical amplification as a means of expression, and not simply as a technological given. Amplification and loudness also enter into the authenticity of voice in rock music. Some passages of rock music do not sound right unless they are played loud, and amplification gives the musician a whole new register of possibilities, something rock discovered as early as the pioneering "Rocket 88" (sometimes called the first rock-and-roll record because of its use of the distorted electric guitar accompanying the boogie-woogie piano) and exploited to great effect in Hendrix's guitar playing. Distortion and feedback can give guitar either a very dense and "fat" sound (as in the Kinks' "You Really Got Me") or a high, wailing sound (for example, the guitar on the choruses of The Who's "I Can See for Miles"). Reverb, echo, and tape delays, developed in conjunction with amplification, have added to the sound of rock music since Elvis's recording of "Mystery Train" for Sun Records in the mid-1950s, and reverb in particular has been used to create a haunting, bluesy sound in the harmonica playing of blues artist Little Walter Jacobs and some of Clapton's early guitar playing (with John Mayall and Cream). Bad rock musicians take a mechanical, rule-based approach to dynamics (or eschew dynamic variation altogether), and tend to be dominated by the technology of amplification, treating the technology as an end rather than a means. But for good rock musicians, loudness creates further expressive possibilities.

Rock and Pop. Like other forms of popular music, rock can be characterized by its relative accessibility to listeners and musicians with little formal or academic training; and, like pop music, the basic form of rock music is the song, which results in an emphasis on qualities of vocal expressiveness. Much of popular music is meant for dancing, and hence has regular rhythms and meters. All of these elements in both popular and rock music speak directly to the bodily responses of the listener.

Rock diverges from other forms of popular music, however, in much the way its antecedents do, and in particular, blues and jazz. Early jazz is a form of blues, and, in its "hot" variety, remains close to the vocal expressiveness and rhythmic intensity of blues music. Like blues and some jazz, rock has a more intense and aggressive feel than other popular music. In some cases, this is because the rhythms are more aggressive, marked by strong downbeats and syncopation; it can also be a result of allowing more free play in the playing or singing of a tone, so that the sound rises and falls in microtones that would be controlled and smoothed into a more unified sound in pop music; and it is also the result of

a greater tolerance for dissonance (the use of overtones such as those in the blues harmonica or blues harp, seventh and ninth chords, feedback effects, and so on). The contrast between rock and the pop music of its period is similar to that between the Benny Goodman Orchestra's recording of "Sing Sing Sing" and the "sweet" dance music of the 1930s. Pop tends to be "easy listening," that is, more melodious, less dissonant, with more lilting rhythms and a gentler "swing." Although rhythm is always a component in rock, it can disdain "swing" altogether; Led Zeppelin's "Dazed and Confused" is exemplary in that regard. Although both pop rock and soft rock exist, rock is, in virtue of its origins, "hard."

For that reason, rock music has often been associated with aggression: with anger and rebellion (as in early rock and roll, and in punk rock) and with an aggressive form of sexuality (in the blues and its derivatives). Even in its gentlest moments, there is an undercurrent of tension and even violence in much rock music. The effect, then, is not of calm so much as of violent passions held in check. The violence of some forms of rock music, such as heavy metal, have tended to make them into exclusively male enclaves. On the other hand, there have been a number of female punk rock groups (Siouxie and the Banshees, the Slits), and the role of aggressive rocker has more recently been taken up by Courtney Love's grunge-rock group, Hole. In addition, in rock and soul music, a number of female vocalists, such as Aretha Franklin and Etta James, have used a very aggressive and "hard" vocal style with considerable success. The aggressiveness of rock has made it in many ways "a man's world," but it is also a world where assertive women have made themselves heard. Assertiveness or outright aggression, however, whether expressed through rhythm or through the intensity and unguardedness of vocal and instrumental expression, is the primary means of distinguishing rock from other forms of popular music. Even so, many of these characteristics of rock music can now be found elsewhere, particularly in the "new country" music that has developed since the 1980s.

Conclusion. Authenticity of voice, rhythm, and loudness are perhaps the principal characteristics of rock music. All three elements have a direct effect on the body, and their proper use is judged by how the body responds to them, rather than by any formal criteria. All three come from the performance-oriented tradition, in which listeners bodily participate in the music (whether through dance or more visceral responses), and there is a direct emotional connection between the musician and the listener that allows the listener to judge whether the musical expression of emotion is true to the listener's experience. Not that either the musician or the listener lives in a realm of pure immediacy; that is a fiction of antirock theorists, who would like to reduce rock music to the "animal" level. The listener's response and the musician's performance are both mediated by a history of practices, forms, and conventions. But when the music rings true, it is the body that tells us so. This is something that has to be experienced to be understood. As the song says, "I'd tell you 'bout the music that can free your soul, but it's like trying to tell a stranger about rock and roll."

[*See also* Music, *historical overview article; and* Popular Culture.]

BIBLIOGRAPHY

Eisen, Jonathan, ed. *The Age of Rock: Sounds of the American Cultural Revolution.* New York, 1969.

Escott, Colin, and Martin Hawkins. *Good Rockin' Tonight: Sun Records and the Birth of Rock 'n' Roll.* New York, 1991.

Frith, Simon. *The Sociology of Rock.* London, 1978.

Frith, Simon. *Sound Effects: Youth, Leisure and the Politics of Rock.* New York, 1981.

Frith, Simon. *Music for Pleasure: Essays in the Sociology of Pop.* Cambridge, 1988.

Frith, Simon. *Performing Rites: On the Value of Popular Music.* Oxford and New York, 1996.

Gaar, Gillian G. *She's a Rebel: The History of Women in Rock and Roll.* Seattle, 1992.

Gracyk, Theodore, *Rhythm and Noise: An Aesthetics of Rock.* Durham N.C., 1996.

Marcus, Greil. *Mystery Train: Images of America in Rock 'n' Roll Music* (1975). 3rd rev. ed., New York, 1990.

Marcus, Greil. *Lipstick Traces: A Secret History of the Twentieth Century.* Cambridge, Mass., 1989.

Miller, Jim. *The Rolling Stone Illustrated History of Rock and Roll.* Rev. upd. ed. New York, 1980.

O'Brien, Lucy. *She-Bop: The Definitive History of Women in Rock, Pop, and Soul.* Harmondsworth, England, 1995.

Palmer, Robert. *Deep Blues.* New York, 1981.

BRUCE BAUGH

ROMAN AESTHETICS. "And Rome was taken captive by its captives." Such was the opinion of the Romans themselves about their debt to Greek art and artists, and it has been the conventional view of Greek art—but not architecture—from Johann Joachim Winckelmann through generations of grecophilic German art historians and aestheticians until the present. But Roman art, the principles governing its generation and production, the objectives of its patrons, both public and private, and the nature of its reception are not so easily defined by this alleged self-determining dependency on the artistic culture of an "other." After all, works of Roman art were produced in unprecedented number for centuries—third century BCE to fourth century CE—over a very wide area, encompassing ethnically diverse populations and varied belief systems, all within a society that was sharply divided by class, by distinctions between "Romans" and "provincials," yet was also dominated by an urban culture that was remarkably consistent throughout the Roman Empire. Simplistic or reductive definitions of Roman aesthetics, aesthetic attitudes, or the exercise of Roman taste, whether expressed in terms of relative servitude to Greek artistic norms or in response to and/or rejection of them, fail to do justice to the complexity of this first world art, the foundation of European art itself. To complicate matters further, not only is there no modern consensus about the essential character of Roman art, but the ancient Romans rarely exhibited self-conscious pursuit of "beauty," so essential to the conventional formulation of an aesthetic attitude.

To a considerable degree, Roman aesthetic attitudes were overtly impoverished by a studied indifference to the matter of "beauty" and to its embodiments and creators. Artists in Roman society were déclassé, deemed unworthy of specific mention among the members of the Roman cultural elite who left few verbal statements of their views but who repeatedly made informed, deliberate, if often eclectic choices among competing artistic traditions, or styles, and their masters. Roman attitudes must be extracted from the extensive evidence of the exercise of Roman taste in action and from the highly selective, programmatic patterns of patronage. Furthermore, there can be no question that the language and topics of critical, aesthetic discourse had been previously established by Greek philosophers and scholar-critics, from Plato and Aristotle to Xenokrates of Athens and Longinus—almost exclusively with reference to drama, epic, rhetoric, and poetics, and rarely applied to works of fine art and architecture. Some Greek artists and architects wrote treatises recounting the history of their art and its current practice, expressing inter alia their views about the relative merits of its practitioners, and many of these treatises were known to the Romans. Among the most important of them was a five-volume treatise, written by the neoclassical sculptor Pasiteles in the first century BCE as a guide to the arts and to good taste for the benefit of eager, unsophisticated, would-be Roman patrons and collectors.

These treatises, now unfortunately lost, entered Latin literature in epitomized form, most notably in the writings of Vitruvius, Cicero, Quintilian, and Pliny the Elder. In his *Ten Books on Architecture,* Vitruvius, a practicing architect in the early Augustan Age, composed a conservative treatise on contemporary architectural design and urban planning that included a canned history of Greek architecture and a highly schematic system of values, or proprieties, dependent on Greek precedents, especially on the late-Hellenistic architect-critic Hermogenes of Alabanda. About a century later, Pliny the Elder, a distinguished Roman politician and encyclopedist who died in the eruption of Vesuvius in 79 CE, prosaically inserted the most complete, if very condensed, history of Greek sculpture and painting that survived classical antiquity in books 34–37 of his compendium of practical knowledge, the *Natural History.*

Even Pliny's views about artworks and artists, if one can so dignify them, were shaped by Greek classicizing standards with little reference to past or present Roman artistic practice or taste beyond the most banal comments or annal-istic remarks. He even repeated the received dogma that artistic creativity ended in the late second century BCE *(deinde cessavit ars)*, although the creative energy of contemporary Roman art and architecture in the Flavian period would seem to belie such an assertion. Clearly, Pliny either had no eye for the present or was unable or unwilling to judge its qualities. Throughout its history, Roman aesthetic education would seem to have been blindly insensitive to Roman artistic achievement and stultified in its judgments, were one restricted to the passages of description, ekphrastic imagery, and the repetition of the stale criteria of value preserved, here and there, in Roman literature. But there are the monuments, and they tell a different story.

The principal Roman writers on aesthetic topics—Cicero, Horace, and Quintilian—clearly responded to their Greek sources but in their own terms, especially with regard to the importance of style as a value-laden construct, carrying familiar, associative meanings, deemed appropriate for particular situations. These authors emphasized the rhetorical power of art to elicit desired responses from an audience that has its place in the persistent Roman effort to use art instrumentally to further the psychological conditioning of well-prepared viewers. Rhetorical effectiveness can be rightly considered the objective of much Roman artistic activity; conversely, because it is so result-oriented, the degree to which that objective is reached, as measured by the receptivity of the viewing public, would qualify artistic achievement. Romans never quite articulate this cost-benefit relationship, perhaps because it would have been too crass, too undignified, but they were always interested in creating a favorable impression by whatever means.

This endeavor to reach the heart and mind of Romans through the eye impelled artists and architects toward splendid visual effects, increasingly evident in later Roman Imperial art. It is symptomatic of the desire of those in power to exert their control over the spectating audience, as if that audience could be made ever more visually sensitive to the theatrical potential of monuments. In the process, the audience's great thirst for spectacular presentations was further stimulated: thus, the extravagant public ceremonies—the triumph in the bedecked Forum, the bloody games and battles in the stadia, the vicious gladiatorial contests in the arena, the wild chariot races in the circus, the ornamented luxury of public bathing—all participate in creating the urban culture of spectacle. This intensely visual Roman culture responds to a manifest preference for optical effects in painting, mosaic, and sculpture and for dematerialized forms, even in architecture, that substitute the *simulacrum* and the *signum* for the physical presence of solid things. This visual approach to the aesthetic experience constitutes the Roman opposition to the characteristically Greek exploitation of the physical reality of plastic forms that appeals directly to the sense of touch, the appreciation

of mass. This distinction between so-called Greek haptic naturalism and Roman optical abstraction was never absolute, nor were the differences ever fully resolved in the course of Roman art, although a progressive move toward abstraction informs late-antique art.

In its formative phase from the Middle Republic to the Early Empire, Roman art exhibited two very distinct tendencies, both developing under the liberating mantle of Greek artistic culture. One, characterized by modesty *(modestia)* of means and gravity *(gravitas)* of manner, is consistent with the old Roman tradition that stressed self-restraint as a virtue and with the cool, clarified idealism associated with neoclassical art, principally derived from Attic fifth-century models. Cicero and Augustus, in their own ways, clearly preferred this classicizing manner, or style, as the proper vehicle for the noble expression of Roman thought and art. This classicizing style retained its elevated image-value well into late antiquity, most especially during the reign of the philhellene Hadrian, and as a statement of cultural politics in the opposition of the "old Romans" to the newly Christianized Empire in the fourth century. But the doctrine of artistic restraint with a Republican and Stoic gloss also underlies the Vitruvian concepts of *decor* (beauty) and *proprietas* (fitness, suitability); these aesthetic propositions contribute to a moral attitude about the arts, *austeritas*, as a means of avoiding the excesses typical of Hellenistic art/architecture and of the Roman nouveaux riches. Paradoxically, this notion of austerity also advanced the claim of indigenous *Italian* art—unadorned, matter-of-fact, "realistic" but often inorganic, in sum, plain—to be truly representative of native Roman culture and society, unaffected, it was asserted, by Greek pretensions. This nativist tendency, sometimes erroneously termed "plebian," has its own long history, its relative importance waxing and waning as urban and provincial subcultures challenged the hegemony of the Roman elite. The plain style is especially prominent under Trajan and from the Severan emperors to the Tetrarchs, when Roman absolutism was fully established.

The other tendency, loosely called "baroque," is no less a combination of Greek and indigenous elements, but it looked to the Hellenistic world for inspiration. This rich, sumptuous manner emphasized extravagant effects, lavish combinations of colorful materials, heightened expression, and a taste for ostentatious splendor and conspicuous consumption. Romans associated these qualities with *luxuria*, whose active, if costly, pursuit soon became one of the operative principles of Roman aesthetics. *Luxus* (splendor or magnificence) is deeply implicated in the Roman ideology of display. Perhaps because *luxus-luxuria* carried some residue of moral opprobrium or the taint of decadence—a view offered by Cato, that dour defender of Roman virtue—this lavish mode was categorized as "Asiatic" in the rhetorical tradition or "Pergamene" in art and architecture, after that major center of Hellenistic art and architecture inherited by Rome in 133 BCE. This negative terminology, laden with adverse political and moral significance in the Late Republic, if much less so in the empire, sharply differentiated ostentatious opulence from the allegedly purified Attic of neoclassicism, although both modes derived their effectiveness as tendentious bearers of meaning from the creative *interpretatio romana* of the Greek artistic legacy—Roman literature was similarly bifurcated. A certain luxurious ambition in design and affect informs a number of Late Republican architectural projects (e.g., Palestrina), comes into prominence again under the Flavians, especially Domitian, and bursts into exuberant complexities of light, color, and aggressive affect under the Antonine emperors and in the Eastern Provinces.

These polar categories, separating the "neoclassical" from the "baroque," tend to be as much modern historiographical fictions as ancient value judgments, especially when one considers the combination of neoclassical, idealized forms with visual splendor so characteristic of Augustus, who found Rome a city of brick and left it one of marble. Yet, behind these subsets of "style," or modalities of artistic performance, lurk the tensions of an incomplete hybridization of the indigenous Italian and the imported Greek tradition. From this difficult situation arises the historiographic problem of isolating "Roman art" as a discrete entity and of characterizing its distinctive features. Clearly, a self-conscious, even deliberate eclecticism pervades Roman art throughout its history, a history punctuated as well by the constant revival of past "styles," always slightly different from their previous instantiation yet charged with "pure" and "impure" connotations, depending on the perceived motives of their patrons. This oscillation between a re-created past and a nostalgic present seems deeply embedded in Roman culture; it constitutes a framework of social and political action that ever renews itself through calculated self-reference as an artistic metaphor for the historical continuity of the state. Thus, the styles that together comprise Roman art and define its aesthetic horizon bespeak an attitude that prizes tradition—or traditions—much as the *pax romana* relied on Roman law to bind together the disparate elements of a world state.

The Column of Trajan in Rome, that most classic if not classical of all Roman monuments, epitomizes the fundamental reliance on an externalized, highly visible field of signs—principally the helical relief—imposed on a simple, organizing structure (the column) that provides order, stability, and coherence to the ensemble. The column itself functions as a purified architectural symbol, recalling the Greek Orders from which it is derived as well as the Roman practice of using these Orders in a manner that robs them of their load-bearing, architectural role in favor of their ornamental prestige as noble elements of the classical tradition. Hadrian's Pantheon exemplifies this practice, juxtaposing the Greek temple front, dressed in marble, and the

ROMAN AESTHETICS. *Augustus of Prima Porta* (early first century), marble sculpture, h. 204 cm; Vatican Museums, Vatican State. (Photograph courtesy of Alinari/Art Resource, New York.)

great cylindrical volume of the vaulted interior, a triumph of space over mass, of surface over substance. Roman sculpture, too, may be considered a heavily freighted vehicle for the display of carefully confected sign systems; Roman togati, cuirassed emperors, modest matrons, mythological sarcophagi, triumphal arches, replicas of Greek "masterpieces," all instantiate the impulse to address the spectating audience with important messages for its consumption, messages displayed on the surfaces of the forms, often subsumed for this purpose. This is no less true with respect to large-scale Roman architecture—the Imperial Fora, the great baths—where perceptible axiality and bilateral symmetry provide the abstract armature that supports and frames space, the immaterial but basic constituent of this architecture.

If Roman art retains its rhetorical purpose over the centuries, there is a discernible movement from materialist values toward a greater dependence on the transcendent sign, the transparency of surfaces, and the immateriality of space—all characteristic of late-antique art. Perhaps one can extract from this phenomenological change a basic premise of Roman aesthetics: that the purpose of art is to convince the spectator of the truth of the proposition presented to his eye. In the third century, Plotinus might have asserted that the realities of prime forms lie behind the surface of things, only dimly perceptible through art, but the contemporary Roman artist would have argued, on the contrary, that such realities come into being before these surfaces in the mind's eye.

[*See also* Classicism.]

BIBLIOGRAPHY

Becatti, Giovanni. *Arte e Gusto negli Scrittori Latini.* Florence 1951.
Hölscher, Tonio. *Römische Bildsprache als semantisches System.* Heidelberg, 1987.
Jucker, Hans. *Vom Verhältnis der Römer zur bildenden Kunst der Griechen.* Frankfurt am Main, 1950.
Keyser, Eugénie De. *La signification de l'art dans les Ennéades de Plotin.* Louvain, 1955.
Pelikán, Oldrich. *Vom antiken Realismus zur spätantiken Expressivität.* Prague, 1965.
Pollitt, Jerome J. *The Ancient View of Greek Art: Criticism, History, and Terminology.* New Haven, 1974. See pp. 1–111.
Riegl, Alois. *Spätrömische Kunstindustrie.* 2d ed. Vienna, 1927.

RICHARD BRILLIANT

ROMANTICISM. [*To analyze the meaning and history of Romanticism both as a distinct period of art and as a general aesthetic category, this entry comprises three essays:*
  Philosophy and Literature
  Visual Arts
  Music
The first essay examines the philosophical roots of Romanticism and the development of Romantic literature. Because Romanticism has had different histories in the various arts, there are separate essays on the visual arts and music. For related discussion, see Aestheticism; Autonomy, *historical overview article;* Difficulty, Aesthetics of; Hegel; Kant; Novalis; Originality; Primitivism; Schiller; A. von Schlegel; *and* F. von Schlegel.]

Philosophy and Literature

Romanticism begins in an experience of anxiety at one's possible human unreality, an anxiety that is strongly voiced by Immanuel Kant in the *Critique of Judgment* and closely associated with him by his philosophical and literary successors. "How," Kant asks, "can I express my freedom and rationality, somehow lodged deep within me noumenally, in a phenomenal world ordered under physical causal laws?" "The concept of freedom is meant to actualize in the sensible world the end proposed by its laws" (*Critique of Judgment*). How? And if I can't thus actualize my freedom and rationality, what then am I? Perhaps I am capable of nothing more than the "almost savage torpor" that William Wordsworth saw in his urban countrymen ("Preface to *Lyrical Ballads,*" 1801). The achievement of expressive freedom, in writing and in life, is then seen as the task of humanity, as it seeks to raise itself out of mere naturalness.

As Philippe Lacoue-Labarthe and Jean-Luc Nancy cogently observe, Kant's "weakening of the subject" ontologically as a being no longer present to itself in inner intuition "is accompanied by an apparently compensatory 'promotion' of the *moral subject* which . . . launches a variety of philosophical 'careers'" (1988). In German Idealist philosophy, the effort is to overcome various forms of division—subject/object, value/fact, freedom/nature, consciousness/the unconscious, self/other—by systematically describing a developing metaphysical order that undergirds both nature and humanity, explains the present existence of those divisions, and secures the possibility of overcoming them to achieve expressive freedom.

Romanticism, in contrast, is more self-critical in pursuing this same ambition. Romantics are characteristically more aware that their efforts at expression arise out of and remain marked by the divisions that they wish to escape. They remain in anxiety about their receptions by their audiences. Their best works—in a generalization that holds true for Wordsworth, Samuel Taylor Coleridge, Percy Bysshe Shelley, John Keats, Lord Byron, Friedrich von Schiller, and Friedrich Schlegel—are characteristically either incomplete, or fragmentary, or self-critical, or finally ironic. This had led Lacoue-Labarthe and Nancy to speak of a "literary absolute" that is sought and imperfectly, infinitely, enacted in their works, and it has similarly led Jerome McGann (1983) to distinguish between a doctrinal "Romantic ideology" of the overcoming of dualisms and the more troubling, more self-critical work of "Romantic poetry" that never quite accomplishes its longed-for transformations.

The wish for achieving full humanity through expressiveness, coupled with an enduring anxiety about the possibility of success, while arguably simply part of human consciousness of temporality, also arises with special intensity around 1790 in part out of occasioning social-political and scientific circumstances. The development of a widespread commercial and early industrial economy, particularly in England, in the sixty or so years before 1790, led to increased division of labor and social mobility. Writers and other artists began to make their livings, when they could, through publication, performance, and sales, rather than through patronage. The necessities of doing this, and the uncertainties of reception in a divided economy, led to increased anxiety about both the specific offices of art and the possibility of expressing humanity generally. Rather than seeing humanity expressed collectively in the partial conformity of social structures to a divinely ordained archetype, individuals began to worry about how to win their particular places in the market. As the conditions for the expression and ratification of rationality, humanity, and freedom become more uncertain and tenuous, Schiller notes the "negative results of divided labor" ("On the Aesthetic Education of Man,"), and

Wordsworth alludes to "a multitude of causes, unknown to former times" ("Preface") that are acting to degrade the fitness of social life for humanity.

At the same time, human beings, as a result of the seventeenth-century revolution in mathematical physics and its associated achievements in engineering, are now beginning to possess greater powers to free themselves from natural misery, and hence more scope for the expression of individual personality. There is, in 1790, no going back to any ruder, premodern state without the benefits of technology. The effort is instead to blend modern achievements with more stable simplicities, to blend what Schiller called "the naive"—the pastoral, where mind and nature are one, often identified with the pre-Socratic Greeks—with "the sentimental," the modern realm of dividedness and self-consciousness. The movement of the imagination on the whole is forward toward synthesis, toward "something evermore about to be" (Wordsworth, *Prelude)*, not backward. The French Revolution, with its ideals of liberty, equality, and fraternity, is seen as an especially promising, but then desperately failed, response to these modern social conditions and plights of mind. After the September Massacres of 1792, the Terror of 1793–1794, and the growing domination of Napoleon from 1795 onward, writers increasingly turn inward in attempting to take up the Revolution's ambitions and to avoid its failures. The transfiguration of humanity comes to be posited or announced proleptically, in art or within the subject, not immediately in politics, though the difficulties of proclaiming a message that requires a new audience in order to be received lead such proclamations typically to be crossed by despair, self-doubt, or irony.

Romanticism's aims for humanity thus contrast powerfully with the ancient world's pursuit of naturalness and *eudaimonia*, with medieval Christianity's ideals of obedience, continence, and beatitude, and with the Enlightenment's commitment to scientific understanding, material improvement, and satisfaction. Instead of any of these, expressiveness, or what Wordsworth and Ralph Waldo Emerson call Power, is the aim, wherein subjective personality and social reciprocity support one another, rather than being locked in conflict. Social peace is to be won without sacrificing individuality and spontaneity.

A number of thematic and stylistic features distinguish the Romantic writing that pursues this aim from its predecessors.

1. There is a prominent retrospective stance that expresses a consciousness of fallenness or dividedness. "Was it for this . . .?" Wordsworth asks about his present impotent state in the *Prelude* in undertaking to review his life; "That time is past, / And all its aching joys are now no more, / And all its dizzy raptures," he laments in "Tintern Abbey." In his 1808 "Lectures on Dramatic Art and Literature"—the principal critical document on Jena Romanticism for both Madame de Staël and Coleridge, who transmitted its analyses to France and England, respectively—August Wilhelm

von Schlegel remarks that "The Grecian ideal of human nature was perfect unison and proportion between all the powers—a natural harmony. The moderns, on the contrary, have arrived at the consciousness of an internal discord which renders such an ideal impossible." This consciousness of discord and division traces back to Schiller's essay "On Naive and Sentimental Poetry," and before that to Kant's remarks in his historical and anthropological essays on humanity's fitful progress through alienation. In France, it is expressed in Jean-Jacques Rousseau's opposition to the idea that the arts and civilization have led to an improvement in manners; in England, in the mythologies of loss of William Blake, Keats, and Shelley, and in Wordsworth's complaints about modern urban life.

2. In opposition to the neoclassical ideal of decorum in style aiming at pleasure, Romanticism reconceives the work of art as flowing from imagination, *poesis,* or genius, in relative freedom from rules. Wordsworth condemns "false refinement" and "what is usually called poetic diction," and he urges the merits of "prosaisms" ("Preface"). Taste is stigmatized as "a passive faculty" unable to engage with "the profound and exquisite in feeling, the lofty and universal in thought and imagination" (Wordsworth, "Essay, Supplementary," 1815). Instead, "Imagination . . . / Like an unfathered vapour that enwraps, at once, some lonely traveller" (Wordsworth, *Prelude*), is to move us, in art and in life. "Internal authority alone is decisive" in the arts, August Wilhelm von Schlegel observes, and we ought not to accord "an unlimited authority" to the ancients ("Lectures"). A marked emphasis on originality—according to Kant the "primary property" of genius *(Critique of Judgment)*—issues in a pervasive antimoralistic, antinomian stance that has led some twentieth-century critics to accuse Romantics of sentimentality, vapidity, and a cult of idle sincerity in homage to nothing. Yet, the Romantic animus against borrowing and imitativeness—"even what we borrow from others, to assume a true poetical shape, must as it were be born again within us" (August Wilhelm von Schlegel, "Lectures")—also powerfully undermines dogma and complacency, in politics, art, religion, and life. In opposition to formalisms, the decorous, and the hierarchical, Romanticism's direction of thought is generally democratic-individualist. Wordsworth's "Muse," William Hazlitt observes, "is a levelling one" ("The Spirit of the Age").

3. Seeking to avoid both materialistic-oriented naturalisms and abstract moral or religious formulas, Romanticism moves epistemologically between empiricism and rationalism. The mind is typically pictured as quickened or awakened to autonomy and self-productive power in and through its engagements with certain natural scenes, numinous places, or genius loci of sublimity or beauty. "The sentimental poet" of modernity, as Schiller puts it, "*reflects* upon the impression that objects make upon him, and only in that reflection is the emotion grounded which he himself experiences and which he excites in us" ("On Naive and Sentimental Poetry"). The mind is both receptive and active, in its engagements with nature. Ordinary experience, figured by Wordsworth as "humble and rustic life" ("Preface"), reveals itself as uncanny—both in need of and in admitting of the unleashing of as yet muted powers.

4. Where medieval Christianity sought to locate humanity cosmologically within an exterior order, Romanticism tends to find either our home or the route toward our transformation in a descent within the psyche, so much so that it is possible to speak, with Northrop Frye, of the "internalizing of reality in Romanticism proper" (1963) or the internalization of quest romance. As Geoffrey Hartman puts it, the effort is "to draw the antidote to self-consciousness," in its present alienation and dividedness, "from consciousness itself," through a movement of descent. ". . . in such strength / Of usurpation, when the light of sense / Goes out, but with a flash that has revealed / The invisible world, doth greatness made abode, / There harbours whether we be young or old. / Our destiny, our being's heart and home, / Is with infinitude, and only there" (Wordsworth, *Prelude*).

5. As a result of its political and religious antinomianism and its emphasis on the transfiguration of our condition, Romanticism reintroduces anticlassical, Augustinian themes of the existence of standing struggles within the person, between the person and society, and between opposed sectors within society. Charles Taylor notes the Romantics' "resistance to a one-dimensional picture of the human will and their recovery of the sense that good and evil are in conflict in the human breast" (1989). Instead of knowing what we want, individually or collectively, we find that our impulses are divided, polymorphous, in need of a kind of harmonization that is never wholly achieved.

6. The typical protagonist of a Romantic text is more or less a solitary—from Wordsworth's *Prelude* persona, to Shelley's Prometheus, Keats's Hyperion, and Friedrich Schlegel's Julius. Often this protagonist is locked in a struggle with chthonic forces, internal and external, in an effort to achieve free expressiveness. Often the implied author-protagonist stands somewhat outside the fragmentary work as the locus of a hazy power of assemblage and vision. Even when others are presented in Romantic narratives, they typically appear as potential members of a small band, a company apart or an intellectual-political-artistic coterie, that has lifted itself out of generalized humanity's more vulgar commercial self-stultifications. For example, some of Jane Austen's happily married pairs self-consciously stand apart in this way in her endings, at home in higher tastes and manners that are supported by economic privilege. The ordinary travails of finding a job and earning a wage are rarely presented as providing opportunities for the development of identity. The action of identity development tends to take place in mythic arenas, or in pastoral seclusion, or in conditions of economic privilege. This has led some readers to regard Romantic impulses toward rebirth in retreat as a politically escapist bourgeois indulgence. Whether this is so depends in large measure on what one makes of the presence of problems of expressiveness within many or most human lives, and on the resources for addressing those problems that one sees in the arts and in internal descent, in contrast with class- or group-based political organization.

7. In seeking to retreat from commercial, public life, and ultimately to transfigure it, Romantics often turn to various forms of the vernacular or the exotic, against the public high culture of the neoclassical period. Figures from the Arab world or the Orient appear in works of Wordsworth, Novalis, and Coleridge and are associated with archaic-visionary alternatives to Western public culture; or the Greek gods are treated as such figures of human possibility, as in Keats and Shelley. Medieval Christianity is sometimes seen as an alluring time of social harmony and meaningfulness, especially in Novalis's "Christianity or Europe." Older quest romance literary forms and figures are reconsidered and rewritten. Interest in the North and in the medieval competes with and jostles attraction to the ancients and to Latin. William Shakespeare, Aristo, and Ossian are seen as significant predecessors, Ovid much less so. As August Wilhelm von Schlegel notes,

> the word [*romantic*] is derived from *romance*—the name originally given to the languages which were formed from the mixture of the Latin and the old Teutonic dialects, in the same manner as modern civilization is the fruit of the heterogeneous union of the peculiarities of the northern nations and the fragments of antiquity; whereas the civilization of the ancients was much more of a piece. ("Lectures")

A sense of the artistic attractiveness of mixtures and liminal figures, rather than smoothness of finish, predominates. "No one," Friedrich Schlegel remarks, "can be the direct mediator for even his own spirit" ("Ideas").

8. Crossed with self-consciousness and opposed to neoclassical ideals of formal completion, many of the most important Romantic works are either unfinished or continually self-revising, including Wordsworth's *Prelude* and *The Excursion,* Coleridge's *Kubla Khan,* Keats's Hyperion poems, Shelley's "The Triumph of Life," Blake's *The Four Zoas,* and Friedrich Schlegel's *Lucinde* and "Critical Fragments," "Athenaeum Fragments," and "Ideas," among many others. In their fragmentariness or their self-revisions, these works often seek indirectly to suggest the persistence of a poetic, self-formative power beyond or outside the work. As Friedrich Schlegel puts it:

> The romantic kind of poetry is still in a state of becoming; that, in fact, is its real essence: that it should forever be becoming and never be perfected. It can be exhausted by no theory and only a divinatory criticism would dare to try to characterize its ideal. It alone is infinite, just as it alone is free.
>
> ("Athenaeum Fragments")

Likewise Novalis: "The great mind would make of every acquaintance, every incident, the first item in an infinite series—the beginning of a never ending romance" ("Miscellaneous Writings"). Movement is all. Romantic doctrinal conclusions, when they occur, are often forced and unconvincing, unless they arrive at either irony, as in Byron, or despair, as in Coleridge.

The extent to which Romanticism has been supplanted as a form of sensibility, aspiration, and artistic expression by realism or modernism or postmodernism remains in dispute. Each of these movements takes up some aspects of the Romantic style and often in one way or another continues its tropes of rebirth and its emphasis on the movement of becoming. The social conditions of commerce, industry, and public life that influenced Romanticism have intensified, not disappeared, and human consciousness of temporality and wishes for rebirth and recognition have not altered structurally, even while the continuing deferral of the satisfaction of Romantic aspirations—itself noted in Romantic writing—has furthered our sense of being trapped in complexities and divided against ourselves.

[*See also* Classicism; Coleridge; Emotions; Genius, *conceptual and historical overview article;* Goethe; Irony; *and* Wordsworth.]

BIBLIOGRAPHY

Abrams, M. H. *The Mirror and the Lamp: Romantic Theory and the Critical Tradition.* New York and Oxford, 1953.

Abrams, M. H. *Natural Supernaturalism: Tradition and Revolution in Romantic Literature.* New York, 1971.

Abrams, M. H. "Neoclassic and Romantic." In *A Glossary of Literary Terms,* 6th ed., pp. 125–129. Fort Worth, Tex., 1993.

Frye, Northrop, ed. *Romanticism Reconsidered.* New York, 1963.

Gaull, Marilyn. *English Romanticism: The Human Context.* New York, 1988.

Lacoue-Labarthe, Philippe, and Jean-Luc Nancy. *The Literary Absolute: The Theory of Literature in German Romanticism.* Translated by Philip Barnard and Cheryl Lester. Albany, N.Y., 1988.

Lockridge, Laurence S. *The Ethics of Romanticism.* Cambridge and New York, 1989.

Lovejoy, Arthur O. "The Meaning of 'Romantic' in Early German Romanticism" (1916) and "On the Discrimination of Romanticisms" (1934). In *Essays in the History of Ideas,* pp. 185–206 and 228–253. Baltimore, 1948.

McFarland, Thomas. *Romanticism and the Forms of Ruin: Wordsworth, Coleridge, and Modalities of Fragmentation.* Princeton, N.J., 1981.

McGann, Jerome J. *The Romantic Ideology.* Chicago, 1983.

Mellor, Anne K. *English Romantic Irony.* Cambridge, Mass., 1980.

Seyhan, Azade. *Representation and Its Discontents: The Critical Legacy of German Romanticism.* Berkeley, 1992.

Taylor, Charles. *Sources of the Self: The Making of the Modern Identity.* Cambridge, Mass., 1989.

Wellek, René. "The Concept of Romanticism in Literary History" (1949) and "Romanticism Re-examined." In *Concepts of Criticism,* edited by Stephen G. Nichols, Jr., pp. 128–198 and 199–221. New Haven, 1963.

RICHARD ELDRIDGE

Visual Arts

Books on Romanticism—even when the term's application is restricted, as here, to a European movement of around 1790 to 1850—begin by stressing its sprawling nature and the consequent difficulty even of approximate definition. When attention is focused on Romantic art, in all its variety, matters seem hardly more tractable, so that one can sympathize with Stendhal's verdict that Romantic art is what pleases people "in the present state of their customs," classical art what pleased their grandfathers. To take just the case of painting, Romantic works, unlike those of Dutch genre painting or French Impressionism, are not to be grouped by a distinctive subject matter, style, or technique. Gallery visitors ignorant of intellectual history would have no reason to gather, under a single "ism," the geometrical drawings of William Blake, the somber crucifixions of Caspar David Friedrich, the "misty" works of Joseph Mallord William Turner, and the "exotic" canvases of Eugène Delacroix.

It is tempting to conclude that the only common factor among such artists is the very individualism that also separates them, that the "essential distinguishing characteristic of Romantic art" is the artist's personal "authenticity" (Honour, 1991, p. 20). A better conclusion is that Romantic art is identifiable only in relation to Romantic aesthetics. Crudely, artworks are Romantic to the extent that they are informed by, or manifest tenets of, Romantic aesthetic thought—"crudely," because not all Romantic artists were self-consciously executing a particular aesthetic, and in the case of those who were, it is not always obvious how their works relate to their program. Philipp Otto Runge proclaimed the familiar Romantic idea that "art should be the expression of . . . religious mysticism," but specialized in static portrayals of fat children.

Efforts to articulate the aesthetic that informed Romantic art range from locating some overarching tenet (the supreme value of the creative imagination, the achievement of the unity of spirit and matter, or whatever) from which more particular artistic ambitions might flow, to drawing up a long list of Romantic predilections (for emotion, spontaneity, movement, expression, individuality, and so on), some sufficient set of which the Romantic artwork must reflect. The danger in the former attempt is that of Procrusteanism; in the latter, that of failure to lend any order and coherence to the ideas informing the artworks.

A way of bringing into relief the Romantic aesthetic in its bearing on the visual arts, which steers between those two dangers, is to attend to several hierarchical classifications typically subscribed to by Romantic thinkers:

1. the superiority of the artist over the scientist, even over the philosopher, and certainly over everyone else;
2. the superiority, among the arts, of music and literature over the visual arts;

3. the superiority, within the visual arts, of painting over sculpture and architecture.

These hierarchical orderings are themselves ordered. Not only do they become increasingly specific, but the reasons for a later ordering stem from an earlier one. The predilection for painting—and, within that art, for landscape—ultimately stems from reasons for elevating the artist's calling over any other.

Before addressing the three hierarchies, a word is needed on the famous distinction between Romantic and neoclassical attitudes. Modern scholarship is apt to soften the impression of agonistic dichotomy that once prevailed. It is true that August Wilhelm von Schlegel, the first seriously to elaborate the distinction, recognizes in both tendencies a similar ambition, the expression of a sense of harmony, albeit one that in the classicist is "natural," in the Romantic striven for in the teeth of an initial "awareness of inner dissension" between "the intellectual and the sensual" (quoted in Willson, 1982, p. 183f.). It is true as well that artworks of the period do not all fit unambiguously under one or other label. The "neoclassicist" Jacques-Louis David's *The Death of Marat* is as expressive and moving as anything by Delacroix, although the latter portrayed classical figures, such as Medea, as often as David. Still, it is grossly exaggerated to write that "neoclassicism . . . is no more than an aspect of Romanticism" on the grounds, apparently, that the Romantics, too, often looked back to and "revived" earlier styles, such as the Gothic (Janson, 1986, p. 575). Hence, it is a constraint on any framework for elucidating Romantic aesthetics that it bring out the contrasts between Romantic and neoclassical aspirations, even if these are more blurred than older histories of art suggest.

Artists, Scientists, Philosophers. A constant lament of Romantic thinkers is that Enlightenment science has disastrously misrepresented nature, ourselves, and the relation between the two. "The world must be romanticized" again, wrote Novalis, after its "disenchantment" at the hands of science. At least three charges were leveled against science. First, it is atomistic and hence divisive, portraying the world as so many discrete items instead of the organic whole we sense it to be. In particular, as Friedrich Hölderlin complained, it teaches people to feel separate from—at best as interacting with—what surrounds them, nature. Second, it offers a completely mechanistic account of the world, thereby dismissing the testimony both of those "dark feelings" that for Wilhelm Wackenroder, evoke an "invisible" realm (in Schmitt, 1980, pp. 84ff.), and of experiences of "sublime" nature, replete with processes not captured under discoverable laws of cause and effect. Third, it treats the world as something objective, awaiting discovery: but this is to ignore, as Blake put it, that "this world is all one . . . vision of . . . imagination," that imagination which, in Samuel Taylor Coleridge's famous phrase, is the "prime

agent" in forging the world as we can ever encounter it (in Wu, 1994, pp. 108 and 574).

Therefore, it cannot be science that is the epitome of human activity. For some idealist philosophers, notably George Wilhelm Friedrich Hegel, it was philosophical reason that would demonstrate the unity and character of reality that science is incapable of doing. But, for the Romantics among them, philosophy was too much in cahoots with science to achieve this, thus leaving art as the only possible vehicle. First, as Friedrich Schlegel explains, "the Highest" cannot be "reached . . . by reflection." It is "unrepresentable," for reflection and representation employ concepts that are at once limited in their scope and divisive of what they are applied to (Bowie, 1990, chap. 2). Art, of course, cannot *represent* "the Highest," the Absolute, but it can exhibit that "longing" for something unlimited that philosophy pretends to delimit. Moreover, in the "play-drive" that Friedrich von Schiller postulated, art can embody those unities—notably between the intellectual and the sensual—that reason cannot explain. It is for such reasons that Friedrich Wilhelm von Schelling pronounced art the "organ of philosophy" (1988, p. 695).

Second, if nature is a whole of which we are integral parts, then it is something that "courses through" each of us: hence, the most promising strategy for insight into nature is not that of disengaged spectating but "espousing the inner élan . . . or impulse" of nature within us, and by "expressing" this to "make what was hidden manifest both for myself and others" (Taylor, 1989, p. 375). The person supremely fitted to do that is the artist.

Finally, if in a sense the world is a creature of the imagination, then the best place to turn if one is to explore those passing "worlds" so created is, as Schelling and Johann Gottfried von Herder insisted, to those self-consciously imaginative myths, allegories, and artworks through which human beings have, over the ages, expressed their visions.

The Romantic elevation of artists over everyone else affords them a very different status and role from the (neo)classically envisaged ones. In particular, the artist's function is not the relatively modest one of mimesis or representation. For Nicolas Poussin and Sir Joshua Reynolds, admittedly, the artist should not represent what is superficially before him but, in the "grand manner," capture ideal forms, "representing in every one of his figures the character of its species." But this ambition reflects just that assumption of an objectively ordered nature, awaiting rational discovery, whose rejection entailed a new conception of art as imaginative expression of a vision whose full articulation we can only ever "long" for.

Music, Poetry, and Visual Art. It is a striking feature of Romantic aesthetics that, in quantity at least, the literature on visual art pales in comparison to that on poetry and music. We have Wackenroder's and Runge's ruminations on painting, Charles Baudelaire's essays on Delacroix, and

ROMANTICISM: Visual Arts. Joseph Mallord William Turner, *Moonlight, A Study at Millbank* (c. 1797), oil on canvas, 314 × 403 cm; Tate Gallery, London. (Copyright by Clore Collection, Tate Gallery, London; photograph courtesy of Art Resource, New York.)

John Ruskin's celebration of Turner in *Modern Painters,* but little else of note to compare with the voluminous theorizing on the nonvisual arts by the Schlegel brothers, Coleridge, E. T. A. Hoffmann, and many others. This discrepancy reflects the conviction that the visual arts come in third after music and literature. (Opinions differed as to which came in first.) Influenced, doubtless, by the prevalence of neoclassical or "academic" painting and sculpture, the common impression was that visual artworks were too static, mimetic, or limited to be the ideal media for giving full expression to the creative imagination, the inchoate sense of the unity of everything, and the "dark feelings" of an organic nature coursing through the veins.

Reversing Immanuel Kant's judgment, music gets praised precisely because it is nonconceptual. Unencumbered by representational, conceptual devices, music ad-

dresses us as "spirit speaking directly to spirit." It is because he "leaves behind" what is "determinable by concepts" that Ludwig van Beethoven, according to Hoffmann, can "devote himself to the unsayable," the Absolute (quoted in Bowie, 1990, p. 184). Music, moreover, as Hegel observed, is better placed than painting to express the "inward" life that was the special concern of the Romantics—and this because it, like the life of mind and will, moves in time. (Arthur Schopenhauer was to claim that music is an immediate "copy" of the Will, the ineffable principle of reality in itself.) If Hegel's point alludes to the melodic aspect of music, other writers, exploiting Kant's remark that music is suited to express the "idea of a connected whole," stressed the harmonic dimension. The rich chord is the perfect "sensuous," yet nonconventional, symbol of that unity-in-difference that, for Romantics, reality is. Finally, the composer is more free than the visual artist, able to give vent to his imagination by combining notes with a spontaneity and élan that, emulated by the painter, would result in a mere mess.

It is the freedom enjoyed that is also a reason for placing the poet above the painter. Language, Percy Bysshe Shelley argues, permits "more various and delicate combinations, than colour [and] form," and hence is more "obedient" to the "arbitrary" imagination than the materials of the visual artist, which "limit" and "interpose between conception and expression" (quoted in Wu, 1994, p. 958). Poetry, moreover, is the ideal vehicle for that "romantic irony," of which the Schlegels made so much, through which the artist draws attention to his own creative procedure, thereby driving home the Romantic message that we stand to things not as reflective mirrors but imaginative producers. (Here, of course, is a significant affinity with those latter-day critics of the "Enlightenment project," the postmodernists.)

The subordination of painting and sculpture, and the lessons that were drawn for the practice of these arts, would have been impossible for neoclassicists to accept. In their canon, still echoed in Kant's remarks on music, the merely "sensuous," nonconceptual character of music made it the Cinderella of the arts; and although the visual arts could claim no superiority over poetry, they were no less capable of portraying the ideal types and "noble and serious actions" that, for Poussin, were every artist's true calling.

Painting, Sculpture, and Architecture. Schelling's aphorism "architecture is frozen music" is only the best known of many statements attesting to the Romantics' idea that the visual arts should emulate music or poetry. Baudelaire, for example, was to demand that painters should use their colors as "epic poets" do their words (1992, p. 59). (Emulation was sometimes taken rather literally, as when the Hudson River school painter Thomas Cole tried to construct a "piano" that produced colors instead of sounds.) Artists were often judged according to their success in such emulation. Delacroix, for Baudelaire, was the "true painter" of the nineteenth century because he was "a poet in painting," whereas, for Ruskin, it was Turner who deserved that title, not least because, as in a "choral harmony," each element in his paintings "helps" every other element, with nothing "fortuitous" (Ruskin, 1987, pp. 492ff.). Other Romantic painters, such as Friedrich and Runge, saw themselves engaged in an essentially literary exercise, deploying symbols in original combinations, rather as the poet juxtaposes metaphors.

Unsurprisingly, the visual arts were typically ranked according to their assumed capacity to emulate music or literature—the usual order being painting, sculpture, and architecture. Painting, it was argued, was clearly better placed to achieve such characteristically Romantic ambitions as expressing a vision of nature and rendering visible aspects of the "inward" life. Sculpture, after all, was preeminently representation of the human form, and no one could sculpt the sky or sea. As Hegel observed, mere "shape as such" is not the medium for communicating the "grief, agony, . . . deep feeling, and emotion" that are the "proper content of the . . . romantic imagination" (Hegel, 1975, p. 788). One reason he gives is that such communication requires greater and more subtle contrasts between light and dark than sculpture affords. This illustrates the emphasis on the central role of color, as against line and form, that became familiar in Romantic criticism. It was mainly in his depiction of color that the "truth" of Turner resided, according to Ruskin, whereas, for Baudelaire, too keen an eye for line is a positive hindrance to the expression of "atmosphere," "spirituality, . . . [and] yearning for the infinite," in all their indefiniteness, to which Romantic art aspires (1992, pp. 53 and 58). Still less could sculpture vie with painting in expressing the "spontaneous," "arbitrary" feelings of the artist. A "spontaneously" carved statue, after all, is likely to fall down. It is no accident that the most striking Romantic sculptures were not free-standing works, but the almost flat reliefs of Auguste Préault. His critics might have endorsed August Wilhelm von Schlegel's remark that "modern sculptors are too much painters" (quoted in Willson, 1982, p. 180).

With painting favored as closest to music and literature, architecture suffered even more than sculpture in comparison, sometimes being denied the title of "art" at all. More typical was Schopenhauer's verdict that architecture is the lowest grade of art, because the solid matter and forces of gravity it explores are at a far remove from the processes of organic life and human behavior that are the "higher" embodiments of the Will (1969, pp. 214ff.). There were several reasons, doubtless, why it was Gothic architecture that most appealed to the Romantic imagination—a phenomenon paralleled to some degree by the German Nazarene and British Pre-Raphaelite enthusiasm for medieval painting. The great cathedrals, after all, belonged to an age when, supposedly, humans still experienced the world about them as the Book of God. But an important reason was the alleged affinities between Gothic architecture and music or literature. The sheer complexity and copious use of symbols in a medieval church made it more akin than a simple Greek temple to a literary work. And Walter Pater was echoing a familiar analogy of the time in contrasting the "mere *melody*" of a temple with the "harmony" and hence "richer music generated by opposition of sounds" of Notre-Dame d'Amiens (quoted in Honour, 1991, p. 148).

The elevation of painting, and the consequent demands made on the other visual arts, strikingly conflict with neoclassical convictions. Indeed, sculpture and architecture suffered in the Romantic period from their status as the paradigmatically classical arts, ideal conveyors of Johann Joachim Winckelmann's "noble simplicity and calm grandeur." For August Wilhelm von Schlegel, "the spirit of all the art . . . of antiquity is plastic, just as that of modernity is picturesque" (quoted in Willson, 1982, p. 180). For Hegel, classical sculpture necessarily belongs to the past, because it perfectly expressed just that "immediate" unity of spirit and body that is no longer recognized, as the Romantics' obsession with the "inward" all too clearly exhibits.

Romanticism was indeed a broad tendency and there are aspects—a taste for the "exotic," say, or the idea of a *Volksgeist* as a source of inspiration—that have not been touched on in this essay. In the case of the visual arts, at least, these aspects did not play a vital role in shaping the best work of the period—Delacroix's "Arab" paintings being an outstanding exception—although it is not too difficult perhaps to appreciate their appeal to some Romantics. For example, an interest in the different ways that different peoples have envisioned the world is a natural corollary to abandonment of the idea of a single, universally valid representation of reality. To the extent, however, that Romantic visual art reflected an aesthetic, the debt was to the *idées mères*—such as holism and the centrality of the imagination—of the response to radical Enlightenment.

[*See also* Hölderlin.]

BIBLIOGRAPHY

Baudelaire, Charles. *Selected Writings on Art and Artists* (1972). Translated and edited by P. E. Charvet. Harmondsworth, England, 1992.
Bowie, Andrew. *Aesthetics and Subjectivity: From Kant to Nietzsche.* Manchester, 1990.
Hegel, G. W. F. *Aesthetics: Lectures on Fine Art.* 2 vols. Translated and edited by T. M. Knox. Oxford, 1975.
Honour, Hugh. *Romanticism* (1979). Harmondsworth, England, 1991.
Janson, H. W. *History of Art.* 3d ed. Revised and expanded by Anthony F. Janson. New York, 1986.
Kant, Immanuel. *Critique of Judgement.* Translated by James Creed Meredith. Oxford, 1952.
Ruskin, John. *Modern Painters.* Abridged in one volume by David Barrie. London, 1987.
Schelling, Friedrich Wilhelm von. *System of Transcendental Idealism* (1800). Translated by Peter Heath. Charlottesville, Va., 1978.
Schmitt, Hans-Jürgen, ed. *Romantik,* vol. 1. Stuttgart, 1980.
Schopenhauer, Arthur. *The World as Will and Representation.* 2 vols. Translated by E. J. F. Payne (1958). New York, 1969.
Taylor, Charles. *Sources of the Self: The Making of the Modern Identity.* Cambridge, Mass., 1989.
Willson, A. Leslie, ed. *German Romantic Criticism.* New York, 1982.
Wu, Duncan, ed. *Romanticism: An Anthology,* Oxford and Cambridge, Mass., 1994.

DAVID E. COOPER

Music

A powerful mythology connects music and Romanticism, defining each in terms of the other. "Music is the most romantic of the arts," declared E. T. A. Hoffmann in 1814; and Friedrich Nietzsche wrote, in 1888: "I fear I am too much of a musician not to be a romantic." These pronouncements have little to do, on the surface, with Romantic music as an artistic category roughly bounded by their two dates. In the history of European music, Romanticism generally designates the period between the classical and the modern, or a set of compositional practices and attitudes relatively independent of chronology, or a canon of names (usually including Franz Schubert, Carl Maria von Weber, Frédéric Chopin, Hector Berlioz, Robert Schumann, Felix Mendelssohn, Franz Liszt, Richard Wagner, and Johannes Brahms) within the wider range of nineteenth-century music. None of these categories applies to Hoffmann's remark, which alludes to composers now regarded as classical: Josef Haydn, Wolfgang Amadeus Mozart, and Ludwig van Beethoven. (Nietzsche was thinking of Wagner.) A symphony by Mozart or Beethoven was Romantic, for Hoffmann, in that it seemed to represent a separate, ineffable domain—an "Orphic world," he called it—complete in itself, free from human contingency or social purpose, independent of language yet coherent as the most rigorous grammatical logic. It was music in its purest and highest sense, music in its very essence—music itself. Revolutionary when first propounded at the close of the eighteenth century by the early German Romantics, this idea of music as a pure, "absolute" art gained rapid and long-lived ascendancy. In the classical-music sphere, it determines to this day most people's idea of what music is, and as a result scarcely any Western musical practice, theory, custom, or institution can be fully understood apart from it.

One practice that the twentieth century inherited from the nineteenth is a sharp distinction between classical and popular music, for the aesthetics of pure music implies an opposition between high and low cultures, between the elite few and the philistine crowd. Class distinctions swept away by the French and industrial revolutions were reborn not only in a hierarchy of talents, according to the Napoleonic creed, but in a new aristocracy of artists and a cult of high art. Music had a leading role to play in that cult: it promised accession to a truth beyond reason and language, the now-discredited foundations of the old order, and it rested that promise in "great" works that could be prized as timeless "classics." Whereas literature and the fine arts possessed canons of great works reaching back to antiquity, music outside the church had tended to vanish with its time; a concert-hall canon, in the modern sense, emerged only with Hoffmann's trio of Viennese classics, and with the late eighteenth century's new historical consciousness, cult of individual genius, and helpful developments in music printing. What is often called the "Romantic rebellion" was highly selective in its rebelliousness: it rejected, from the past, neoclassical models of good taste and correctness, while reviving artists of power (William Shakespeare being the prime example) spurned by the neoclassics. The cult of Johann Sebastian Bach, the enthusiasm for early music in general, the primacy of German music, the establishment of a standard concert repertoire based on that primacy, the idea of the musical work as a unified whole intended for performance "as written," all date from the Romantic period.

Hoffmann's "romantic" epithet must consequently be understood, in part, as polemical: it claimed a new dignity for music against its detractors of long standing; and it set "great" music apart from the trivial and the mediocre. The existence of incontrovertible masterpieces in the art of music, such as Beethoven's Fifth Symphony (1807), made it possible to argue a demonstrable permanence about an art traditionally disparaged as ephemeral by the very nature of its medium. In his *Critique of Judgment* of 1790, Immanuel Kant concedes that music "moves the mind in a greater variety of ways and more intensely" than poetry, but objects that it does so only "transitorily." With Kant, as with the neoclassics, music's very intensity of effect remains cause for suspicion: as an art of performance in sound, music has the power to act directly on the senses and thus to undermine the faculty of reason essential to the social order. But if philosophers since Plato had feared music for its sensual power, they had attacked it chiefly for its lack of conceptual content. Music was the least amenable of the arts to the neoclassical principle, inherited from Aristotle, whereby art's chief task was the imitation of a moral, ideal nature: as "mere sensations without concepts," according to Kant, music was of "less worth than any other of the fine arts." From this lowly position, music could redeem itself only in conjunction with the voice, capable of articulating "concepts" that could explain and "motivate" the music. Instrumental music had little place in such an aesthetic, which summoned music to remember its place as handmaiden of the word, and instruments to remain servants of the voice. It was a veritable declaration of independence—and evidence of a sweeping reversal of values—when Hoffmann not only claimed for music supreme status among the arts, but did so on the basis of instrumental music, the most denigrated of its manifestations. For Hoffmann, as for Johann Gottfried von Herder who, in 1800, directly responded to Kant's aspersions, music's evanescence, its action on the imagination and the senses, its "vagueness" of content were the very secret of its power and the foundation of its supremacy among the arts.

In a general sense, Hoffmann's "romantic" epithet served to decree a separate province for art, symbolized by the self-contained world of the masterpiece, safe from the intrusions of the everyday. During the 1830s, Schumann, Berlioz, and Liszt used the word *poetic* for similar purposes in fighting engulfment by a bourgeois *prose*. The threat to the "poetic," as they perceived it, came from both without and within: from a callous society concerned only with business and profit; and from musicians (such as virtuosos) who turned their art into a business, or from their old-guard teachers at the Paris Conservatoire, who, in the name of rules, forms, and formulas—including the formulas of commercial success—opposed anything that smacked of innovation. In response, rebel adepts of the new creed become educators and campaigners, priests of the religion of Art, defenders of music as equal to the greatest literature or philosophy. They found a forum for their efforts in the first music journals, where they subjected the objects of their devotion to the new practices of musical analysis and interpretation. In these writings, Beethoven was the supreme model—first inspiring, later inhibiting—against whom all other composers were judged. Among those who did not quite measure up were Gioacchino Rossini and Giacomo Meyerbeer, the two most-adulated composers of the first half of the nineteenth century. Others were Daniel Auber, Adolphe Adam, Ferdinand Hérold, Jacques-François Halévy, Gaetano Donizetti, and Vincenzo Bellini, or virtuosos such as Liszt himself, whose conversion to "high art" in the 1830s ultimately led him to renounce his pianistic career, incompatible with his role as purveyor of the new cult. That cult has stood squarely in the way of appreciating an entire "other" nineteenth-century repertoire, which derives from an earlier, performance-based aesthetic vigorously opposed but never fully supplanted by the "Romantic" one.

Set against the background of French military and cultural hegemony, and the resistance to both by the German Romantics, Hoffmann's aspiration to transcendence through art suggests a conservative withdrawal and retreat, at best an inner liberation through art. As such, it prefigures the art-for-art's-sake philosophy formulated in the 1820s and 1830s, and, at the end of the century, the Symbolist movement, explicit in its reverence for music and its wish to make of poetry a kind of music. It was also in tune with the rise of German idealism, a succession of philosophies that gave music an importance (especially with Georg Wilhelm Friedrich Hegel and Arthur Schopenhauer) it had not had since Plato. Rather than Plato, to be sure, Hoffmann's idea of music recalls the esoteric Pythagorean tradition, gone underground with modern science but kept alive in Gottfried Wilhelm Leibniz's description of music as "an unconscious exercise in mathematics" and in Jean-Philippe Rameau's elegantly rationalist system of chordal harmony. In the last decades of the eighteenth century, a more precise link was forged through the teachings of Karl Philipp Moritz, professor of "the fine arts and the relevant science of mathematics" at the University of Berlin, whose lectures on artistic autonomy were followed by Ludwig Tieck and Wilhelm Heinrich Wackenroder, Hoffmann's fellow adepts of the musical sublime. In the second half of the nineteenth century, this early Romantic musical aesthetics brought forth both idealist and formalist offshoots in musical theory, the latter associated with the name of Eduard Hanslick. Twentieth-century formalism derives from this lineage, with the ironic result that Romantic musical aesthetics, divested of its metaphysics, is the precursor of a modernist aesthetic established in scornful opposition to Romanticism.

What modernism has scorned in Romanticism is in fact a very different set of qualities from those of Hoffmann's Orphic world: qualities—sometimes extreme—of individual and social expression. Far from offering a retreat, Romantic art most often exposes and engages in all levels of the real, summoning up the widest possible range of inward and outward experience. If classical art seeks the general, Romantic art explores the particular. As such, it requires a capacity for expressiveness that Hoffmann's conception of music, read in formalist terms, would seem to exclude. Indeed, the question whether music could express or evoke anything outside itself was the central issue of nineteenth-century musical aesthetics, a question aired especially in the polemics over program music. When Berlioz's *Symphonie fantastique,* subtitled "Episode in the Life of an Artist" and accompanied by a programmatic story, was first performed in 1830, the critic François-Joseph Fétis condemned the genre with the help of Hoffmann, whose essay on Beethoven had ridiculed program music as exhibiting a woefully trivial conception of the art. In the 1850s, Liszt defended his programmatic conception of the symphonic poem (and, subsequently, the aesthetic of Wagner's music dramas) in the face of similar attacks from Hanslick, whose influential tract *On the Beautiful in Music* appeared in 1854. Yet, Berlioz and Liszt had no quarrel with the rejection of narrowly imitative views of music. They claimed kinship with Beethoven, as a model neither of imitation nor abstraction but of expression—the expression of human energies and emotion. Hoffmann himself maintained that the symphony had become "the opera of the instruments." More specifically, later critics understood the instrumental "opera" or drama as lyrical in content, distinguished by the direct or indirect revelation of an author's inner self. Symphonic music after Beethoven was conceived in large measure as episodes in the lives of its composers, though with little need, after Berlioz, for explicit programs. Those programs could be found in abundance elsewhere, such as in Schumann's song cycles, to many the quintessential Romantic music.

Among the implications for musical aesthetics of this implicit or explicit narrative of the "self" was an unprecedented freedom of form and emphasis on individual style. While denouncing conventional genres and procedures, Romantic composers made free use of any and all of them, assimilating styles and techniques from earlier periods, other cultures, and various social settings with an appetite that prefigures the postmodern. In Chopin's preludes, études, mazurkas, and waltzes, genres divested of their earlier functions supply color and character in a style so original it is best labeled "Chopinesque." In Schubert's "Moments musicaux," Mendelssohn's "Songs without Words," or Schumann's *Phantasiestücke* or *Nachtstücke,* the imaginative titles (the last two borrowed from Hoffmann's tales of the fantastic) suggest both independence and rivalry with respect to words, and a notion of genre limited only by the composer's imagination. Liberated from the classical hierarchy, vocal and instrumental textures contribute as equals to melodrama, *Lieder* and *mélodies,* and venturesome forms of opera and oratorio: Berlioz's *Damnation of Faust* blends opera, oratorio, and symphony to produce a work illustrating no genre but its own. Liszt, with the symphonic poem, attempted to create a genre bearing the prestige of the symphony without the strictures of its form. Even works designated as "symphony" or "sonata" in the nineteenth century, make such independent use of harmony, timbre, and rhetorical gesture as to blur or erase the classical implications of the labels.

Musical expression after the French Revolution meant not only individual expression, with its potential for difficulty and alienation, but also a force for communal utterance and social purpose, as in the Revolution's mass festivals. In the political chanson, popular melodrama, choral societies and their music, French grand opera with its political themes and crowd scenes, religious music, and efforts toward mass musical education, the Romantic period displays strong convictions of music's power to affect society. Like Beethoven, the composer of the popular "Ode to Joy" as well as the late quartets, Berlioz the uncompromising innovator spoke also to the masses in broadly conceived works for national occasions. Giuseppe Verdi and Wagner drew from the same tradition, from French grand opera, and from Berlioz in works designed to guide and inspire a nationalist spirit. Influenced by Schopenhauer, Wagner strove to sublimate that purpose and transcend spectacle in a music drama incorporating the early Romantic ideal of "pure" music. Nietzsche understood that ideal but questioned its motives. Critics today face a similar need to question motive and assumption in the aesthetic debates of musical Romanticism, in the current debates that issue from them, and even in the books that best help understand them.

[*See also* Music, *overview article; and* Wagner.]

BIBLIOGRAPHY

Barzun, Jacques. *Berlioz and the Romantic Century* (1950). 3d ed. New York, 1969.

Blume, Friedrich. *Classic and Romantic Music* (1958). Translated by M. D. Herter Norton. New York, 1970.

Brown, Marshall. Review of John Daverio, *Nineteenth-Century Music and the German Romantic Ideology. Nineteenth-Century Music* 18.3 (Spring 1995): 290–303.

Dahlhaus, Carl. *The Idea of Absolute Music* (1978). Translated by Roger Lustig. Chicago, 1989.

Dahlhaus, Carl. *Nineteenth-Century Music* (1980). Translated by J. Bradford Robinson. Berkeley, 1989.

Daverio, John. *Nineteenth-Century Music and the German Romantic Ideology.* New York, 1993.

Kramer, Lawrence. *Music as Cultural Practice, 1800–1900.* Berkeley, 1990.

Le Huray, Peter, and James Day. *Music and Aesthetics in the Eighteenth and Early-Nineteenth Centuries.* 2 vols. Cambridge and New York, 1981.

Lippman, Edward, ed. *Musical Aesthetics: A Historical Reader*, vol. 2, *The Nineteenth Century*. New York, 1988.

Lippman, Edward. *A History of Western Musical Aesthetics*. Lincoln, Nebr., 1992.

Neubauer, John. *The Emancipation of Music from Language: Departure from Mimesis in Eighteenth-Century Aesthetics*. New Haven, 1986.

Rosen, Charles. *The Classical Style*. New York, 1972.

Subotnik, Rose Rosengard. *Developing Variations: Style and Ideology in Western Music*. Minneapolis, 1991.

KATHERINE KOLB

ROUSSEAU, JEAN-JACQUES (1712–1778), Swiss-French philosopher, political theorist, writer, and composer. Rousseau made his name among the philosophes of Paris as the musician and playwright who condemned the artistic and intellectual achievements of the Enlightenment for having destructive effects on social life. Rousseau's aesthetic theory, therefore, is both informed by his experience as an artist and serves to advance his broader philosophical analysis of society.

Music was the art to which Rousseau remained closest throughout his life. He became a musician as a young man, and his *Confessions* describe his misadventures as an aspiring music teacher in provincial France. He arrived in Paris with a proposal to reform musical notation, which he presented to the French Academy of Sciences in 1742. While in Paris he presented several works, including his great success, *The Village Soothsayer* (1752), which was presented at court and remained in the repertory of the Opera for half a century. During this time, and indeed until his death, he earned money as a music copyist. The success of *The Village Soothsayer* led to the staging of a one-act comedy, *Narcissus*, written many years before, which, however, received only a handful of performances. Rousseau worked on several other plays in the 1740s and 1750s—but none was presented publicly, and some remained unfinished. In 1760, he published *Julie, or the New Héloïse*, which became perhaps the best-selling novel of the eighteenth century.

At its core, Rousseau's aesthetic theory is quite traditional: he holds that the fundamental principle of the fine arts is imitation. This definition of art as essentially mimetic is directed against the view that it is a matter of creating pleasing sensations. Rousseau links these two opposing conceptions of art to two opposing conceptions of human nature. He associates the sensationalist view with the materialism espoused by Enlightenment thinkers, according to which human beings are nothing more than complex physical systems. Rousseau argues, however, that human freedom—that is, the ability to choose whether or not to obey natural impulses—reveals a "spiritual" dimension of human nature. This possibility of freedom is what gives human life its moral potential, and Rousseau uses the term *moral* to describe the features of experience that are distinctively human.

It follows for Rousseau that in the human being sensations have two aspects: they are physical events, but they also have meaning:

> Whoever wishes to philosophize about the power of sensations must therefore begin by distinguishing between exclusively sensory impressions and the intellectual and moral impressions which we receive by way of the senses but of which the senses are merely the occasional causes. . . . Colors and sounds can do much as representations and signs, and little as simple objects of sensation.   (*Essay on the Origin of Languages* [1781], chap. 15)

As signs, sensations can have what Rousseau calls moral effects, that is, effects concerning our status as conscious, choosing beings. Rousseau's mimeticism rests on this understanding of sensation: artists exploit the full power of their media, and address their audiences as fully moral beings, when the sensations caused by their works function as more than sources of sensory pleasure, that is, serve to represent things other than themselves.

Rousseau illustrates his view of the centrality of imitation with a discussion of the art of painting. The lovely colors of a painting in and of themselves might offer a pleasurable visual stimulation, but that stimulus has no effect beyond the pleasure it yields; it cannot generate an emotional or cognitive response. Thus, Rousseau's view is hostile to abstraction: he would say that a painter who worked merely with swaths of color would be limited to eliciting merely physical responses from viewers, rather than responses that spring from the viewers' full mental lives. What truly involves us in a painting, Rousseau argues, is its figurative aspect, that is, its status as an imitation, for we are able to grasp what the painting is of by interpreting the outlines of the figures as signs representing the subject. Only then can we respond to that subject in human terms.

Rousseau's remarks on painting serve largely as an analogy, to explain his view that music is a mimetic art. He argues that while harmony plays the role of color, providing mere physical stimulation, melody plays the role of figuration, enabling sounds to become signs. Melody, he holds, is intrinsically related to speech, because music and language both emerge out of the primitive vocalizations by which early human beings expressed their various passions. Rousseau does not argue that music is mimetic in the same way as language, that is, in virtue of a conventionalized semantics. Rather, it imitates a subject indirectly, by expressing the passion one feels in the subject's presence. Thus, for example, a melody directly imitates the inflections of a voice expressing an emotional response to a majestic forest, and thereby indirectly serves as a sign for the forest itself. Because the essence of fine art is imitation, it follows that melody is the essential element of music.

Rousseau insisted on the preeminence of melody in music in the face of the leading musical theorist of the day, the noted composer Jean-Philippe Rameau. Rameau held that harmony was the fundamental feature of music, and indeed that he had discovered universally valid principles of musical expression, based in the nature of sound and of human perception, that specified the proper harmonic structure for any composition. Although Rousseau initially accepted Rameau's views, which he incorporated in articles on music he wrote for Denis Diderot's *Encyclopedia,* he later came to reject them.

This rejection was announced in Rousseau's contributions to the "Querelle des Bouffons," a dispute over the relative merits of French and Italian opera sparked by the performances of Italian comic opera (opera buffa) in Paris in the early 1750s. He restated his position in his *Dictionary of Music* (1768). The Italian style contrasted strongly with French opera: the latter was formal and aristocratic, emphasizing elaborate music; the former was simpler and more popular, emphasizing melodic arias. Rousseau defended the Italians, arguing that because their language is itself melodic, musical settings of Italian could preserve the musical power of melody. By contrast, because French is an unmelodious language, composers are forced to compensate by devising elaborate harmonies to produce any musical effect.

In his *Essay on the Origin of Languages* (1781), Rousseau generalizes this criticism of French into a conjectural account of the degeneration of music. He argues that, in the earliest times, the ease of life afforded by warm southern climates led to the creation of sonorous languages well suited to the poetic expression of passion. By contrast, the harshness of the North forced people to speak harshly: with greater clarity, but less expressiveness. The barbaric invasions at the close of the Roman Empire spread the rough languages of the North across Europe. Because Northerners' singing could not, in virtue of their language, be melodic, they learned to create pleasant effects with harmony. Gradually, musicians developed complex theories of harmony, which now dominate musical practice. The music that results is now the product of rules and conventions, rather than a direct expression of natural passions.

This conjectural "fall" of music parallels the accounts of the "fall" of humanity that Rousseau offers in his *Discourse on the Sciences and Arts,* or *First Discourse* (1750), and his *Discourse on the Origin of Inequality,* or *Second Discourse* (1755). In the former, Rousseau argued that Enlightenment culture in general has a corrupting effect on social life. Whereas in primitive society, people's behavior reveals their thoughts directly, in contemporary society the arts contribute to strict rules of decorum that enable people to conceal their true thoughts behind masks of politeness. In a corresponding fashion, Rousseau elevates melody, in which passion finds a direct expression, over harmony, in which feeling is lost in a web of artificial conventions. In the latter discourse, Rousseau describes the progression of humanity from an original state of nature, through a golden age of

primitive communities, to the unjust, inequitable bourgeois society of the present. Again, his views on music reflect his general valorization of the original, natural condition of human life over the artificial condition that human beings have constructed for themselves.

In addition to his extensive writings on music, Rousseau published an important work on theater. The *Letter to d'Alembert* (1758) is an extended argument against Jean Le Rond d'Alembert's suggestion, offered in his article on Geneva in the *Encyclopedia,* that the city drop its Calvinist prohibition of performances of plays. Rousseau's views owe much to book 10 of Plato's *Republic,* which he paraphrased in preparation for writing the *Letter.* Like Plato, Rousseau discusses theater less from a purely aesthetic standpoint than a moral—and ultimately political—one.

Rousseau frames his argument by asking about the usefulness of a theater to its city. Will the presence of a playhouse make the citizens' way of life better or worse? Rousseau examines this question from two perspectives. First, he considers theater's status as a mimetic art, noting that it represents the working out of human passions, allowing the audience to see itself on the stage. But he notes that the spectators must respond favorably to the characters in a play or the play will fail. Thus, in order to succeed, authors will depict the passions in a way that accords with the audience's preexisting values. It follows that plays tend to reinforce the audience's attitudes and way of life. Where these are good, theater will make them better; where these are bad, it will make them worse.

Rousseau's argument leads him to deny the neoclassical account of catharsis, whereby the dangerous passions of characters are countered by appropriate passions in the spectators. Following Plato, Rousseau worries that exposure to characters' passions in the theater—in particular erotic passions, identified with women—makes spectators more vulnerable to their own, which they will be unable to control at all. If anything is likely to be purged in the theater, it is the spectators' sense of responsibility, for they might feel satisfied with their own consciences because they have taken pleasure in the imaginary moral actions performed on stage, without meeting the challenge of acting morally in their actual lives.

The second perspective that Rousseau adopts toward theater is to consider it as an institutional presence in society. From this perspective, because time spent at the theater is time spent away from other pursuits, the value of theater is inversely related to the value of other activities available to the citizens. In the degraded culture of contemporary Europe, exemplified for Rousseau by Paris, theater serves a useful function, because it keeps its audience out of worse trouble. Here again, Rousseau pursues the attack on Enlightenment culture that he announced in his *First Discourse* and elaborated in the series of replies to various critiques of his views. Indeed, in the *Preface* to his play *Narcisse* (1753), the critic of theater declared: "I would count myself most happy to have a Play a day hissed, if at that price I could keep the evil intentions of but a single one of its Spectators in check for two hours."

But if the institution of theater has a salutary effect in Paris, it would be a disaster for Geneva. Geneva was Rousseau's native city, and in his writings he represents it as a preserve of cultural purity. He notes that its citizens entertain themselves by participating in small social clubs called circles, and argues that the circles inculcate values and habits that support the city's republican political regime. A theater would distract the Genevans from their circles, leading to the corruption of their way of life. Not least of the damaging consequences would be the mixing of the sexes—men and women had their own circles—which in turn would result in the feminization of men. Following the tradition of civic republicanism, Rousseau construes feminization as a danger to republican political institutions.

Rousseau concludes that the effects of theater as an institutional presence outweigh the effects resulting from its mimetic content. Thus, on balance, although theater is acceptable in Paris, it is to be kept out of Geneva. But Rousseau is quick to emphasize that cities such as Geneva ought to stage appropriate spectacles to serve as entertainments. He concludes the *Letter to d'Alembert* with a call for "republican festivals," in which "the spectators become an entertainment to themselves." His suggestions range from contests of skill that honor socially useful activities, to a series of balls for the marriageable young.

Rousseau clearly suggested these participatory spectacles as alternatives to the traditionally accepted fine arts. Indeed, they appear to invert his criterion for the fine arts: they appear to be nonmimetic, because the participants present themselves to each other as themselves, not as fictional characters. It should be noted, however, that, at a deeper level, the festivals are indeed mimetic; for, through their participation in the festivals, the participants experience a representation of the structure of their social relations.

From a purely aesthetic point of view, Rousseau's theory—with its insistence on the centrality of mimesis—may today seem outmoded, if not somewhat quaint. One must bear in mind, however, that this insistence stems from his subordination of purely aesthetic considerations to moral concerns. Rousseau is less interested in artworks in and of themselves than he is in their status as elements in the cultural life of society. Perhaps the central topic in his political theory is the role of culture in the maintenance of just political regimes. Rousseau firmly agrees with the ancients that it is the function of culture to mold citizens, and this moral responsibility outweighs any other value that artworks might have. The appalling totalitarian implications of Rousseau's conception of art are today abundantly clear. (Indeed, these implications emerged shortly after Rousseau's death, when the French revolutionaries made

use of his views on art in their spectacular popular festivals, designed by the painter Jacques-Louis David.) It is therefore quite possible to criticize Rousseau's aesthetic theory as a whole on the moral ground that he himself prefers.

Nonetheless, by raising the issues of the moral function of culture, Rousseau's theory of art certainly speaks to questions that continue to be relevant today. For example, the *Letter to d'Alembert* is in large part an inquiry into whether popular culture merely reflects or actively changes public opinion. The current debate over the role of mass media is often pursued in precisely these terms. Thus, in an obvious instance, it is suggested both that television eroded public support for the Vietnam War and that it only broadcast criticisms of U.S. policy after the mood of the public had already turned against the war effort. On another front, in the debate over advertising as an element of popular culture, Stuart Ewen has argued that advertising generates new consumer demand for previously unwanted products, whereas Michael Schudson has responded that advertisers merely detect and exploit already existing trends. These and other current discussions pick up threads of a long-standing debate, in which Rousseau took a strong and influential stand.

[*See also* Theater.]

BIBLIOGRAPHY

Works by Rousseau

The First and Second Discourses Together with the Replies to Critics and Essay on the Origin of Languages. Translated by Victor Gourevitch. New York, 1986.

Politics and the Arts: Letter to M. d'Alembert on the Theatre. Translated by Allan Bloom. Reprint, Ithaca, N.Y., 1968.

Œuvres complètes. 5 vols. Edited by Bernard Gagnebin and Marcel Raymond. Paris, 1964–1995.

Other Sources

Barber, Benjamin R. "Rousseau and Brecht: Political Virtue and the Tragic Imagination." In *The Artist and Political Vision,* edited by Benjamin R. Barber and Michael J. Gargas McGrath, pp. 1–30. New Brunswick, N.J., 1982.

Cranston, Maurice. *Jean-Jacques: The Early Life and Work of Jean-Jacques Rousseau, 1712–1754.* New York, 1983.

Dent, N. J. H. *A Rousseau Dictionary.* Oxford and Cambridge, Mass., 1992.

Hamilton, James F. *Rousseau's Theory of Literature: The Poetics of Nature.* York, S.C., 1979.

O'Dea, Michael. *Jean-Jacques Rousseau: Music, Illusion, and Desire.* London and New York, 1995.

Trachtenberg, Zev M. *Making Citizens: Rousseau's Political Theory of Culture.* London and New York, 1993.

Verba, Cynthia. "Jean-Jacques Rousseau: Radical and Traditional Views in his *Dictionnaire de musique.*" *Journal of Musicology* 7.3 (1989): 308–326.

Wokler, Robert. *Rousseau on Society, Politics, Music and Language: An Historical Interpretation of His Early Writings.* New York, 1987.

Woodward, Servanne. *Diderot and Rousseau's Contributions to Aesthetics.* New York, 1991.

ZEV TRACHTENBERG

RUSKIN, JOHN (1819–1900),   English art critic and social theorist known especially for his four-volume *Modern Painters*. Ruskin is significant historically as the first English writer on art with a national and international audience. His themes are so wide-ranging as to be a compendium of cultural and social ingredients of the nineteenth century. The ways in which Ruskin shook up and recombined these themes opened up new possibilities for thought and action across several arts. He inducted diverse audiences into existence as a new sort of public gathered around his persona. Over five decades, this public evoked from Ruskin streams of jumbled, yet somehow coherent, communications. Ruskin also targeted more particular audiences during his self-shaped career of fifty years: evangelical religionists and tourists during its first half, and the civic-minded throughout. Early on he listened to writers, later to architects, always to painters. Ruskin stimulated considerable interaction across such groups, often serving as a catalyst.

Learning to See. What had begun in Ruskin's *Modern Painters* as a way of comparing Joseph Mallord William Turner's presentation of nature in painting with the "truth" of nature as observed became a general way to help others learn to see. Initially, Ruskin described this as sheer attentiveness without previous schemata, without preconceptions. Rejecting classical idealist inventories for looking, he addressed not simply the artist or the aristocratic connoisseur, but all of an emerging public willing to read and to look for itself. In "Of the Truth of Skies" (*Modern Painters,* vol. 1, section 3), for example, Ruskin took to task those who fail to look up at the part of creation that is accessible to every creature, who thus get along with secondhand images of skies and clouds.

Ruskin directed readers to look for themselves like scientific observers, to explore their visual perceptions. He often interspersed directions for visual experiments. These prescriptions derive from and appeal to the interest in optics, carried on from the eighteenth century, and to a popular fondness for amateur scientific experiments in books and lecture demonstrations. Even if his readers did not actually carry out the experiments, the possibility of "doing" could draw them into the ideas he was presenting. To engage the reader or hearer, to bring them into the center of the action, were his continual strategies.

With *The Elements of Drawing* (1857), Ruskin invited his reader pupils to share his experience of drawing to see. Writing with clarity and directness, he rejected the notion of drawing as polite accomplishment, even though he was addressing amateurs:

> . . . if you wish to learn drawing that you may be able to set down more clearly . . . records of such things as cannot be described in words . . . to obtain quicker perceptions of the natural world . . .

This was a serious endeavor; but it required no previous training, education, or "taste."

Ruskin's style in his drawing manual was conversational; there were both benevolent dictates and supportive, empathetic comments. He addressed the reader as "you" throughout. This personal rhetoric of teaching is a mode that Ruskin used frequently and effectively, especially in his lectures. His drawing exercises were easy to follow, although they demanded meticulous, patient care—which was his own way of working in his lifelong, daily pursuit of drawing. He again provided experiments in optics and perception, bringing his students back to the truth of their own eyes and hands.

Ruskin's teaching methods were based on a knowledge of the visual process from his own experience and from his reading. That the eyes explore and scan across a visual field, fixating on many points in succession, was confirmed by the then current knowledge about the structure and function of the eye's focusing capacity. Addressing the question of depth of field, Ruskin was especially interested in the boundary points of distance from the viewer, at which recognition and processing of detail changes over to a more generalized sense of light and dark masses and textual quality and infinite complexity. In painting, this "truth" is represented by the artist's fine-tuning of these transitions and by faithful and ingenious presentation of the "mystery" inherent in our close-up or faraway view of nature, "never distinct and never vacant." Ruskin points out that the "mystery" is always there, hovering on the bounds of seeing, and it is part of literal, visual truth. Thus, the artist is charged with mimicking what the eyes would see clearly—and suggesting what they could not see—in looking at an actual landscape. But it is clear too that the artist (especially if he is Turner) is editing, manipulating, arranging the elements of that scene to lead and convince the spectator's eyes and perceptions.

Having placed the viewer before the painted landscape with plenty of visual incentives to form conceptions of what is there, the artist has fulfilled the first "great end." The beholder's work is to practice the kind of visual awareness, the curiosity, and the readiness to meet the artist's imagination that Ruskin has modeled in his own writing. The beholder must be "both watchful of [the work's] every hint, and capable of understanding and carrying it out." This "power of continuing or accepting the direction of feeling given" is, Ruskin thought, "less a peculiar gift . . . than a faculty dependent on attention and improvable by cultivation." The beholder's effort must be earnest and he must take time to know the work of art.

Ruskin's rhetoric called on the beholder much as a preacher might call on the believer: be vigilant, be alert, watch and pray! Clearly, from Ruskin's viewpoint, and from the beginning, this is spiritual work. The habit of approaching art with a worshipful attitude was to develop during

Ruskin's century and become an element in cultural and social class attitudes about cultural tourism and museum going.

Thus, Ruskin brought together the maker and the beholder of art:

> Between the painter and the beholder, each doing his proper part, the reality should be sustained; and after the beholding one should be able to say, I feel as if I were at the real place, or seeing the real incident.

This is a moral activity, not only in the messages and values expressed, but in the making and apprehension of the work of art. The artist produces the truest work he can, and it is the beholder's obligation to interact with it, to participate with his truth and integrity as well. Beauty happens in that process.

Moving to See. The other basic method that Ruskin offered for learning to see was more social and historical. It was to take his readers (or listeners) along on a guided visual tour. The invitation to participate in a journey of the eyes and perceptions came of Ruskin's own experiences as a sightseer. On such a tour, the audience is meant to see with Ruskin's eyes, as enhanced by his descriptive power. This is a crucial area on the Ruskinian map. Here are found connections and concordances with thought and practice of the Romantic tradition, with natural science, and with cultural, social, and economic developments.

Early on, illustrated books of travel narratives were a fixture in Ruskin's parlor. Many of the engraved pictures in these books were by topological artists and were "open composition" scenes in which, rather than a single, contrived focus, there were many areas of detail to be discovered. Ruskin used his experiential knowledge of visual perception in an authoritative and convincing way, scanning a natural landscape much like a painting.

Truly, the eyes can see only part of a rushing stream or a copse of trees at a time, but the observer can learn to chain together the sequence of discrete visual experiences, to go search out structure of movement, growth, and relation. This linking of perceptions to build a dramatic sequence was one of Ruskin's main stylistic tools: skillfully he manipulated phrase rhythms, making a narrative of visual images. It was at once a prose work of art and a model for viewing art and nature, and indeed it fits well into the modern ecological theory of viewing enunciated by perceptual psychologist James Jerome Gibson (1979).

Ruskin's way of presenting ideas is similarly sequential, narrative, and accumulative. Beginning in childhood journeys with his parents, Ruskin spent much of his lifetime traveling. Travel was for him a stimulus, an occasion for intense study and acquisition of material; at other times, it was a period of convalescence from physical or psychological illness (this latter use of travel was common with other Victorians of his class as well). Many of the key events of

Ruskin's life and art took place in travel, especially those that are, as Wolfgang Kemp notes, "conversion experiences."

For example, in Turin, before a painting by Paolo Veronese, Ruskin experienced a revelation signaling loss of his Protestant evangelical faith around 1858, an "unconversion" through which a positive belief in the glorious nature of man began to inform his thinking and writing. Documentary scholarship has concluded, however, that Ruskin created some of the "conversion scenes" in various versions and at later dates. Nonetheless, they are significant as "types" in his understanding and representation of his life's progress and, in turn, as factors in his developing aesthetic and social ideas. Tied to a sense of historical change and a cultural preoccupation with autobiography, these cognitive and aesthetic changes are associated with being away in a different space, where new self-definitions might occur.

Just as the Ruskin family extended its travel beyond Britain to Germany, the Alps, and Italy, so others like them ventured further afield. Their mode was very different from that of the aristocrat on the road. Destinations were often different, less well known, not conventional stations of the upper-class grand tour. Of the nouveaux travelers, Kemp says: "In a sense, they filled in the gaps between other people's destinations" (1990). Kemp sees this typical middle-class traveler as often alone, "free," looking at nature—or at a public art collection—as an individual experience.

These habits of travel may be seen as a kind of symbolic expansion for those who were in the process of defining themselves socially and culturally. They were staking out their own territory as cultured travelers. As the range of travel destinations widened, so did the range of what was considered aesthetically significant, or worth looking at. Old guidebooks registering a few "sublime" spots gave way to more detailed and practical handbooks that included geological information and natural history lists. The Ruskin family, and throughout his life John himself, returned again and again to "their" places. For him, it was a reconnection with the earlier experiences in which he had scanned and studied. In a sense, it was a returning home.

Ruskin's most widely known book, *The Stones of Venice,* asks the reader to participate in the narrative reconstruction of a city, to be led into the stone-yard with the author to find out, from the very cutting of the stones, how Venice was built in both architectural and human, historical terms.

The first volume includes descriptions of stonecutting and the laws of structural dynamics as he understands them. Throughout the work, he introduces consideration of structural necessities, as well as "laws" that fit a particular style or specific materials. As he states in an 1853 lecture, he believes that everyone can—and ought to—learn architecture, "because all are concerned with it."

At the close of the introductory volume, the reader is finally conveyed to a gondola, and, in a stirring word voyage,

Venice—decaying Venice of the 1850s—comes into view. Ruskin uses imaginative descriptions to introduce places, to highlight comparisons, to underscore ideas. Most often, these employ movement in space. His comparative scenarios of the approach to an English cathedral close and the approach to the Venetian Church of San Marco are alike classics. They are satisfying to the armchair traveler as well as the British tourist who goes to Venice, Ruskin's book in hand.

Reaching His Audiences. Ruskin reached out and seized his readers with passionate weavings of insights ever more diverse and yet each keyed to himself. One of the Ruskinian paradoxes is that although he had, increasingly, little trust that his audiences would heed or even understand what he was saying, his ideas continued to be formed in the heat and heart of his styles of communication. From having been the observer who once wished to lose himself in observation, to be unobserved, Ruskin went on to become the observer who as artist and critic moves outward seeking relations, whether joyful or painful. His message— that his audiences must read the signs well and endeavor to change their environment in order that art may survive and beauty flourish—became the impetus for his work as lecturer and for his most direct and interactive communication with his audiences, his serial "journal" *Fors Clavigera* (1871–1884).

Ruskin worked in many genres, however: the guidebook to landscapes or cities or art collections or exhibitions; the travel essay; the popular science handbook; the polemical pamphlet; the texts of lectures; serialized essays; books on art history and theory. Frequently, he even mixed styles within a single presentation, as George Landow (1971) described in his analysis of Ruskin as Victorian sage. Ruskin could move from relaxed and humorous commentary to a detailed analysis of art, to topical events, to a lashing satirical harangue, and, finally, to an inspiring biblical close, all in the course of one lecture.

When Ruskin began writing, critical discussions of artists' interpretations of nature had been largely in terms of literature. The "rules" for viewing pictures in a classical literary sense put the viewer at some remove from both the work of art and its creator. This was true socially: a sense of aristocratic patronage, connoisseur's taste, and socially separated knowledge clung about painting and sculpture long after it had ceased to be relevant to the art being produced. The visual artist was in an anomalous position: no longer a servant but not quite accepted as a professional, a learned man yet also an entrepreneur. (Turner is an example of just such a mixture.)

There had also been distancing visually that Ruskin was to override. His description of Turner's painting *Coventry* (*Modern Painters,* vol. 1) is a beautiful example of Ruskin's way of pulling the viewer into the picture, linking detailed observations into a visual narrative, increasing the pace of his language, building to a climax, and then providing, as

the painter has done, a quiet close. During this period, Romantic poetry and novels also beckoned the growing English reading public to new ways of regarding both nature and the writer, and Ruskin set out to communicate his correspondingly intense experiences in viewing paintings. Even though he used analysis of literary works to illuminate processes of perception and imagination in the visual arts, he was intent on "reading" pictures and poems differently, beyond the classical framework. He created not so much narratives about the work of art, but rather, stories of a visual and kinesthetic journey round about a landscape painting or into an Italian sixteenth-century work, or into a medieval city. Similarly, when Ruskin discussed a poem or a play, he was inside the text, moving about among images and characters, tasting and testing the validity of the work.

Ruskin believed that his audiences, whoever they might be, had the potential to learn how to see art and nature well. Ruskin was aware, as lecturer and preacher, of the character and possibilities of audiences. With his writing of the late volumes of *Modern Painters* and completion of the magnificent *Stones of Venice,* he brought the reader even more explicitly into the story, dramatizing this participation in visual and spatial, and finally, social, terms.

Ruskin's styles as a verbal artist always predicate interaction with his audiences, as they teach interaction with the visible world, the work of art, and the artist. He spoke to the consumers he assumed were "out there." Sometimes these are straw men—or women—delineated to prove a point. He spoke also to the ideal consumers whom he wanted to create. He challenged them continually—sometimes gently, as in his manual *The Elements of Drawing,* sometimes sharply, as in his huge public lectures to industrialists and townsfolk, of Midlands cities and of Edinburgh—to participate actively in the seeing and understanding of art, and to make that activity part of their own self-determination.

He made some assumptions about his audience. There are occasions when he addresses women directly, as in his preface to his published lectures, *Sesame and Lilies* (1871). In fact, many women corresponded with him, as amateurs using his drawing manual. Sometimes they are regular correspondents seeking information and guidance on collecting art. Often they are responders to his challenging and frequently outrageous comments in his serial journal *Fors Clavigera.*

In speaking to his "beholder," Ruskin was clearly looking for people who were ready to be active in their looking at art. Writing of "finish" in art, Ruskin advanced the argument that overdone finish deprives beholders of any share in completing the suggestions of the artist. He hoped for readers who have an interest in the natural world, ready to plunge into the study of water, clouds, or stones as "diligent amateurs."

An artist may be merely the viewer's "conveyance, not his companion." But then, says Ruskin, if the artist "talks to [the viewer], makes him a sharer in his own strong feelings and quick thoughts; hurries him away in his own enthusiasms, guides him to all that is beautiful; snatches him from all that is base" then the viewer experiences "the sense of having not only beheld a new scene, but of . . . having been endowed for a time with the keen perception and impetuous emotions of a nobler and more penetrating intelligence" (*Modern Painters,* vol. 1, chap. 1).

Ruskin's initial ideas on the collaborative nature of the artist and viewer relationship partake of this image of the artist as a sort of demigod "endowing" the viewer. Such a connection with the "highest art" can probably only be attained by those who are themselves of superior intellect and imagination, he said. As he moved on to look more closely, however, he began to form ideas of imagination as a creative process infusing many human activities. He began to describe and define imagination more carefully, moving away from a high-Romantic description and closer to his own experience as a draftsman and painter, and also, interestingly, toward scientific modes of analogies.

In what form did Ruskin's theories and high visions about art reach those consumers most active in the contemporary English art world, in particular those attending the increasingly crowded and mundane annual exhibition in London of the Royal Academy of Art? In 1855, Ruskin began writing an annual critique of the Royal Academy Exhibition, which he called "Academy Notes," an outgrowth, he says in his Preface, of the circular letter he had been writing in response to the requests of friends, "to mark for them the pictures in the exhibitions that appear to me the most interesting, either in their good qualities or in their failure." Ruskin's pamphlet proved to be hugely successful, going into many additional printings. The "Notes," expanded to include the Watercolour Societies' exhibitions and also the occasional exhibition of French paintings, were then published in book form in 1859, and once more in 1875.

Aesthetics. A good deal of the first two volumes of *Modern Painters* is devoted to attempts to articulate formal philosophical and theological frameworks for what was becoming a vastly expanded work. Ruskin continued to use some older specialized categories for aesthetic content and experience, in particular from the Romantics—"sublime" and "grotesque," for example—but he is in fact demonstrating a way of seeing that can be applied to anything under the sun, in nature or in art: cliffs, rocks, cathedral walls, clouds, tree branches, waterfalls, whether Turner's or Tintoretto's or a Pre-Raphaelite's painting. This initial structuring did provide a kind of order for Ruskin's flood of observations, images, and polemics, and parts of it remained as keynotes throughout all five volumes of *Modern Painters.* It served also as an offering of intellectual credentials from a still-young author.

Ruskin's most consistent purpose in aesthetics was to describe and analyze the creative process. He was writing amid an environment of ideas in which empiricist psychologies and philosophies of perception made the viewer the main focus, not the object, and much less the continuing interaction among viewer and object and creator. Ruskin was familiar with works on the physiology of vision and with writings of John Locke and many of his later interpreters, among them, Archibald Alison, author of a widely read work titled *Essays on the Nature of Principles of Taste* (1790, with many nineteenth-century editions). Alison's theory of "associationism" held that the key to perception and the literary aesthetic experience is the triggering, by a sensory event, of a sequence of emotion and associated ideas. Ruskin was uncomfortable with this theory on the grounds of its relativism and its implication of a sort of passivity in the aesthetic response. Nevertheless, he came to include associationism by modifying it to suit his purposes. [*See* Alison.]

What Ruskin really knew with authority was his own experience as an intense observer of nature, a collector and recorder of visual experience; and he wrote as an artist who had "been there," struggling with the process of making a painting or a poem. At the close of volume 1 of *Modern Painters,* he talks of the critic's role:

> to tell us whether we are making our best painter do his best . . . none are capable of doing this but those whose principles of judgment are based on thorough practical knowledge of art, and on broad general ideas of what is true and right, without reference to what has been done . . . in one school or another. . . . such references to former excellence are the . . . refuge and resource of persons endeavoring to be critics without being artists.

Clearly, Ruskin believed that he had the necessary artistic qualifications.

In a delightful passage that rings true to personal experience, Ruskin described the "unimaginative painter." He traced a series of missteps by the unfortunate artist, who begins with a carelessly routine form of a tree, proceeds to follow "rules" about drawing trees, gets into all sorts of trouble as each element he adds forces a change in the other elements, and ends in a shambles.

The "imaginative painter," in contrast, knows the laws of nature but follows no rules; he goes out on his own to discover, and he moves boldly. He begins with an overall, holistic vision: "He saw his tree, trunk, boughs, foliage and all, from the first moment; not only the tree, but the sky behind it." All the elements fit together and all are essential to the whole conception. Ruskin introduced the idea that within this unity of the imaginative conception each part is imperfect, but each is "corrected by the presence of the other." The result is "a whole, an organized body with dependent members." This process of creation is, "as far as I can see, absolutely inexplicable." But Ruskin went on to liken it to a chemical change in which the elements are not seen to react in sequence but rather to interact simultaneously. This kind of near-mystical leap—"the possession-taking power of the imagination," he called it, is what he saw in Turner's work.

The artist's sense of the whole conception, for Ruskin, should inform the compilation of truths that include associated ideas, a "garland of thoughts." Ruskin made it clear that this is not merely "composition," which he valued and described in some of his fine analyses of Turner's drawings; rather, it is an overall process in which all the artist's activities operate by means of the "law of help," Ruskin's image for a kind of coordination and life-enhancing energy that runs through the whole creation. Indeed, Ruskin's model of the maker's work seems to be a vision of the unity he longed for in his own life and in his society.

How, then, might the viewer participate in this seemingly separate and rather godlike process? The assumption that Ruskin made was that perception can be trained to an open-ended awareness toward a work of art. He always stressed the active nature of the aesthetic experience: not only did he think, with Locke, that we do not really see until that sensory input has been registered and stored in organized structure in the mind, but he also described the perceptual activity as having a "bodily sensibility" that is clearly physical and also emotional, "both loving and moral," as he put it.

The essentially moral relation between the artist and the beholder that Ruskin advocates differentiates him from theories and practices of the later movement called Aestheticism. Walter Pater, its purest exponent, was a follower of Ruskin; but his ideas and prose departed from those of the master. For Pater, the beholder's effort was an intense focus on an experience snatched from physical and mental flux, an isolated activity in which each individual might find his or her spiritual "abiding place" in the cosmos. Although Pater wrote with great sensitivity and eloquence about individual artists, the moment in time of seeing their art is separated from them and belongs to the viewer only. Ruskin was wary of loading that sort of expectation onto the viewers' perception and, as he called it, the "weariable imagination." [See Pater.]

Seeing well and plainly is, in the end, worth more to Ruskin than is ecstasy, because the viewer may thus participate more nearly in the artist's work and in the Creation. This religious sense is always a ground base for Ruskin, even though its variations are multiple in the course of his life. Marcel Proust, also profoundly influenced by Ruskin and a first translator of many of his works, pointed this out when he wrote to refute other French works that placed Ruskin as the founder of Aestheticism. [See Aestheticism.]

Of Architects and Painters. Ruskin's verbal and pictorial descriptions of Gothic buildings in Venice, together with his theories of architecture, as in *The Seven Lamps of Architecture* (1855), helped change the face of British cities. This happened in the way in which many of Ruskin's artistic practices and values were disseminated. He intensified the interest in and discussion of architecture that had already begun around issues of religious practice and urban development.

A Ruskin-inspired building would most likely have hallmarks of massiveness, a certain squareness and solidity of form that made it intelligible, with nothing hidden and no materials masquerading as something else. Above all, the building should be decorated, preferably in color, using the natural color inherent in the material. A building should reach the beholder emotionally, should engage the creative imagination just as surely as a painting might. Architects agreed and disagreed with Ruskin, picked and chose, sometimes being quite literally Ruskinian, and often negotiating compromises with the institutions for which they were building. Ruskin was often involved in this, he and the architect frequently playing off against one another with ideas, support, encouragement, and discouragement.

It was with architects that Ruskin came closest to collaborative work, despite massive limits to the practicality of Ruskin's themes for architects. He was against the use of iron and steel, against the very idea of progress, and yet, through his opposition to modular design, at the same time against much of the classical Roman tradition in architecture. But some of his social utopian themes that might seem merely naive today struck a strong note in the era, and architects learned to be selectively practical. Perhaps painting had too much of plumbing, of a practical trade unmixed with speculation, to respond as readily.

The Americans seemed particularly adept at picking and choosing among Ruskin's strictures, meant though they were to be taken as a whole. Andrew Jackson Downing, the best-known American landscape architect of mid-century, was an admirer of Ruskin and a proselytizer for his ideas, but did not blush to build his own mansion in stucco against Ruskin's strongest stricture to build only in materials true to their appearance and function. Downing and his associate, the architect Arthur J. Davis, seemed to have come rather independently to some of the same themes as Ruskin, in the same decade.

There remain questions about Ruskin's great impact on architecture. For all his focus on the creative process, Ruskin's central concern, speaking in political economy terms, was consumption, not production. Ruskin was against machines, against steam, indeed, against working professionals. Producer of superb drawings, he could not abide diagrams—like machines, they spoke of mechanistic reproduction rather than imaginative creation. Ruskin had little concern even with the "production" of daily living, urging that no decoration be bestowed on chimneys, which were merely utilitarian. Ruskin focused on the decorative pattern, the colors and masses of buildings seen as rocks, rocks with rich but solid interiors. He indeed was obsessed with the problematics of roof design, going so far as to say, in his lectures as the first Slade Professor of Art in Oxford, that building design was just roofs (roofs over the interiors that Ruskin wished to disdain as being mere building, not architecture).

One answer to the puzzle is just this texture and color that Ruskin treated together and gave first place in importance for buildings, just as for paintings and landscapes. One generation after another of young architects felt liberated by this positive emphasis and took up structural polychromy. Another answer is Ruskin's enunciation of themes that played into the emerging desire for more beautiful, planned cities and neighborhoods. After all, Ruskin saw buildings primarily as elements in a landscape to be judged in the overall design. These account for the greater reception given to *The Seven Lamps of Architecture* than to almost any book on architecture perhaps before or since.

Ruskin's influence on the actual practice of painting was much more muted. He began with the study of paintings, and he drew every day of his life, whereas he had no such direct connection with building. Ruskin saw considerably more of painters than of architects, even later after his turn toward issues of social welfare and justice.

Evidence for Ruskin's impact on actual practices of painters is sparse. The clearest example is William Holman Hunt's acting on Ruskin's encouragement to take up the evangelical themes that most interested Hunt. Ruskin certainly tried to direct and shape style as well as content in other painters, but to little effect except in commissioned portraits.

Ruskin was coming into his own as a public figure during the emergence of the Pre-Raphaelites. During the course of his annual "Notes" on Royal Academy shows, Ruskin had discussed not only the works of the three artists in the original core of the Pre-Raphaelite group, but also works of the many who clustered around the group stylistically. He was, if anything, more discriminating in praising this sort of painting than any other. He noted that, with each year, Pre-Raphaelitism was becoming more a norm than an aberration. "Animosity has become emulation," he commented, and in 1858 he announced that "Pre-Raphaelitism has entirely prevailed (as I stated five years ago that it would)."

Then he made another prediction: the many rather ordinary followers of Pre-Raphaelitism will come to be disappointed at no longer being noticed, because they are no longer considered sensational. But, he said, beyond the comfort of "being right," there is this:

> The kind of painting they now practice is capable of far more extended appeal to the popular mind. The old art of trick and tradition had no language but for the connoisseur; this natural art speaks to all men . . . pictures will become gradually as necessary to domestic life as books; they will be largely bought.

This observation was partly true, perhaps, but offered little specific guidance to painters and in no way affected the continuing current of banal and sentimental genre scenes in the established Academic patterns.

It was a publicist, as mentor, and as patron that Ruskin constructed his relationships with the various Pre-Raphaelite artists. The content and context were quite different from his connection to Turner. When he came to write about them, he often used their work as a jumping-off point for more generalized history and theory, as, for example, the decline of religious belief and the corresponding decline of art, post-Raphael. He praised much of their work for its observant study and rendering of natural form, but he made it clear that this was only to be considered a beginning.

It was other artists, such as William Dyce, who first had recognized merit in the Pre-Raphaelite Brotherhood and literally tugged at Ruskin's sleeve to make him pay real attention to Millais's famous and infamous work *Christ in the House of His Parents* at the 1850 Royal Academy exhibition. Then, in 1851, the poet Coventry Patmore, a recent acquaintance of Ruskin's and a friend of Millais, wrote to Ruskin (at Millais's request) asking the critic to write in defense of the Brotherhood's works. Ruskin's first letter was quite moderate in its praise but did include the key statement that the artists were at "a turning point in their career from which they may either sink into nothingness or rise to very real greatness." In a second letter, he recorded hopes for the "foundations of a new school of art nobler than the world has seen for three hundred years." Millais and Holman Hunt then wrote Ruskin directly, thanking him, and Ruskin's more personal relationship with the Pre-Raphaelites, and their followers, began. With the third member of the original Pre-Raphaelite Brotherhood, Dante Gabriel Rossetti, Ruskin was more directly a patron. He bought Rossetti's work and helped finance his living expenses and art trips to the continent. He attempted to be the painter's mentor, a role in which he was largely ignored by Rossetti.

There was a close relationship between Ruskin's lessons in basic drawing at the Working Men's College in London and his understanding and support of the Pre-Raphaelite group (some of whom he recruited to teach there also). The kind of truthful observation and meticulous rendering that were characteristic of the Pre-Raphaelite Brotherhood and its followers coincided with the approach that Ruskin taught in *The Elements of Drawing*.

Conclusion. Ruskin's writing and scholarship, sometimes diffuse and overdone, often purposeful and powerful, transformed the discussion of art: he pointed his audiences toward empirical experience of art, emphasizing its accessibility; he linked the practice, the consumption, and the economics of art; he insisted on correlations between images and the societies in which they were born; and he continually crossed boundaries among art, architecture, natural history, religious practice, mythology, social behavior, labor, capital, and ethics. His painterly, descriptive style blurred the boundaries between artist and critic to provide a new literary form for writers on art and architecture.

[*See also* Landscape, *article on* Landscape from the Eighteenth Century to the Present.]

BIBLIOGRAPHY

Works by Ruskin

The Works of John Ruskin. 39 vols. Edited by E. T. Cook and Alexander Wedderburn. London, 1903–1912.
The Elements of Drawing. Edited by Bernard Dunstan. London, 1991.

Other Sources

Altholz, Joseph L., ed. *The Mind and Art of Victorian England.* Minneapolis, 1976.
Ball, Patricia M. *The Science of Aspects: The Changing Role of Fact in the Work of Coleridge, Ruskin, and Hopkins.* London, 1971.
Baxandall, Michael. *Patterns of Intention: On the Historical Explanation of Pictures.* New Haven, 1985.
Brooks, Michael W. *John Ruskin and Victorian Architecture.* New Brunswick, N.J., 1987.
Gibson, James Jerome *The Ecological Approach to Visual Perception.* Boston, 1979.
Gillet, Paula. *Worlds of Art: Painters in Victorian Society.* New Brunswick, N.J., 1990.
Helsinger, Elizabeth. *Ruskin and the Art of the Beholder.* Cambridge, Mass., 1982.
Hewison, Robert, ed. *New Approaches to Ruskin.* London and Boston, 1981.
Hilton, Timothy. *John Ruskin,* vol. 1, *The Early Years, 1819–1859.* New Haven, 1985.
Hunt, John Dixon. *The Wider Sea: A Life of John Ruskin.* London, 1982.
Kemp, Wolfgang. *The Desire of My Eyes: The Life and Work of John Ruskin.* Translated by Jan van Heurck. New York, 1990.
Landow, George P. *The Aesthetic and Critical Theories of John Ruskin.* Princeton, N.J., 1971.
Pater, Walter. *Selected Writings of Walter Pater.* Edited by Harold Bloom. New York, 1974.
Rosenberg, John D. *The Darkening Glass: A Portrait of Ruskin's Genius.* New York, 1986.
Schuyler, David. *Apostle of Taste: Andrew J. Downing, 1815–1852.* Baltimore, 1996.
Walton, Paul H. *The Drawings of John Ruskin.* Oxford, 1972.
White, Harrison C. *Careers and Creativity: Social Forces in the Arts.* Boulder, Colo., 1993.

HARRISON COLYAR WHITE and CYNTHIA WHITE

RUSSIAN AESTHETICS.

[*To examine the relationship between Russian art and aesthetics, this entry comprises three essays:*

Religious Aesthetics
Russian Formalism
Socialist Realism

The first essay pays particular attention to religious aesthetics because it played a dominant role in the history of Russian art and aesthetics. The other essays address two distinct and influential twentieth-century Russian aesthetic movements. See also Bakhtin; Constructivism; Eisenstein; Stravinsky; *and* Suprematism.]

Religious Aesthetics

Russian religious aesthetics is the oldest and most peculiar trend in Russian aesthetics that has continued to exist within Orthodox culture from the eleventh to the twentieth century. The history of Russian religious aesthetics can be divided into four periods: medieval (or Old Russian; c.1000–1650); transitional (c.1650–1700); conservative or preservative (c.1700–1900); and neo-Orthodox (c.1900–1950).

Medieval Period. The first period, Old Russian aesthetics, is marked by an implicit type of aesthetic consciousness that finds its most adequate expressive forms in art, liturgy, and religious (in particular, monastic) life, and not in theories and concepts that are set in writing. Even on the conceptual level, however, a variety of texts of diverse genres (chronicles, saints' lives, religious polemics, rulings of church councils) reveal a rather complete picture of aesthetic ideas of medieval Russians.

Old Russian aesthetics has two main sources: the artistic culture and mythological consciousness of pre-Christian Eastern Slavs, and Byzantine aesthetics, whose influence in Rus began at the end of the tenth century. The Eastern Slavic (inner, archetypal) element of Old Russian aesthetic consciousness is characterized by tendencies to perceive spiritual phenomena as concrete, material, and palpable; to view nature as sacred; to visualize the world beyond and perceive it as "documented" and determinate; and to experience a feeling of mutual magical connection of all things. The Orthodox Byzantine culture and aesthetics that arrived in Rus with the Christianization of the Slavs are superimposed on this substrate—already rich, wholesome, and self-sufficient in its own way—and both reshape it and receive strong influences from it. The written sources of about 1000–1350 well reflect the process of formation of Christianized aesthetic ideas. The *Slovo o polku Igoreve,* the "Story of the Bygone Years" *(Povest' vremennykh let),* as well as the writings of Illarion, Kirill Turovsky, Hegumen Daniil, and other learned writers reflect the views of medieval Russians on beauty (natural, spiritual, artistic), art, the sublime, and the heroic, which combine the elements of both pagan and Christian Weltanschauungen. Books, as the main carriers of spiritual values, inspire particular reverence in medieval Rus. Together with them, all that belongs to the sphere of spirituality is apprehended primarily aesthetically—as leading man toward God and bringing spiritual pleasure and joy—and is designated as beautiful. The characteristic features of Old Russian aesthetics are paying particular attention to the sensibly apprehended realizations of spiritual beauty; endowing the beautiful with palpable thingness; thinking of beauty as an expression of the true and the essential; developing specific sensibility to the beauty of artistic activity; having an increased emotionality and positive mind-set; and thinking of light (primarily visible light) as an important modification of the beautiful. In arts (architecture, painting, applied arts), Old Russian aesthetics values artistic wroughtness, grandeur, colorfulness, luminosity, brightness, and the presence of precious materials. The church building is apprehended, first of all, as an immense luxurious work of jeweler's art. The sacred apprehension of nature by Eastern Slavs is replaced by the understanding of nature as a beautiful work of the supreme artist. They now see in it a beautiful order *(stroj)* that delights the human soul. The main characteristics of natural beauty are magnitude, height, roundness, "artistic wroughtness," a particular ability to stand out in space. Toward the middle of the sixteenth century, moral beauty gains a prominent position in the aesthetic consciousness of Russians.

The period from about 1400 to 1600 is the time of growth and consolidation of a united and mighty Russian state— the Muscovite Rus—which is headed by the Great Prince whose powers rival those of the Byzantine emperor. Russian political thought advances the idea of Great Russia as the direct successor of the Byzantine Empire in spiritual and political matters. Sixteenth-century Russia sees the rise of the popular theory of "Moscow as the third Rome." Orthodoxy forms the spiritual and ideological foundation of the new "empire." Hence, religious mentality during this period is actively developed, and church art, literature, and aesthetics thrive. The aesthetic consciousness of this period includes a number of principles that are most adequately realized in art but only partly acknowledged by the medieval Russians themselves. In Russian religious aesthetics, they do not become the subject of literary discussion until much later—in the nineteenth and twentieth centuries. These are such principles as the *sobornost'* of aesthetic consciousness, the *sophiynost'* of art and artistic activity in general, the systematic character (or certain synthetism) of church art, its increased artistic symbolism, its high spirituality, and its canonicity.

Sobornost' signifies the essentially extrapersonal (suprapersonal) and atemporal nature of aesthetic consciousness. This is the consciousness of a community *(sobor)* of people, akin in spirit, who, in the process of communal liturgical life, have reached a spiritual unity both with each other and with the higher spiritual levels, ideally with God, that is, a people who receive gracious help from above. For this reason, medieval Russian art and other products of the spirit are essentially anonymous. The medieval Russian learned writer, icon painter, or architect does not consider himself personally as the author or creator of his own work, but only as a voluntary executor of the supreme will that acts through him, a middleman in artistic activity, or an instrument guided by the communal *(sobornoe)* consciousness of the Orthodox church. The communal *(sobornoe)* consciousness not only inspires creative activity in medieval artists, but also preserves carefully the forms, schemes, and methods that have been worked out in the process of this activity,

and that are considered to be the most capacious and adequate carriers and expressions of the Orthodox spirit.

It is for this reason that canonicity becomes the main principle of medieval creative activity. The artistic canon reflects and embodies the spiritual and aesthetic ideals of the epoch and establishes the system of representational and expressive methods that is most adequate to those ideals. In particular, the iconographic canon of Old Russian art, which goes back to its Byzantine prototype, determines the ideal visual structures that contain the ultimate graphic expression, for the Orthodox Middle Ages, of the essence of the portrayed phenomenon (a personage or an event from sacred history).

Faith in the divine origin of artistic activity leads to the understanding of a work of art (icon, church building, literary text) as a carrier of a certain supreme union of wisdom, beauty, and art. It is not until the twentieth century that this trait of Old Russian art receives the name *sophiynost'* (Florensky, 1993; Bulgakov, 1917) and a rather detailed theoretical elaboration in the Orthodox culture, resulting in the high spirituality of this art, for nothing transient, material, or base can penetrate into the sphere of *sophiynost'*. The artistic aim to express supreme spiritual values of culture leads to the raising of the level of abstraction of the language of art, as well as to the deepening of the degree of conventionality of artistic expressive means, that is, to artistic symbolism.

The system of these principles achieves its highest perfection and expressive completeness in the art of Andrei Rublev (around 1400), the most prominent painter of medieval Rus. Epiphanij Premudry, the most gifted hagiographer of that epoch, together with his literary colleagues, devise and put into practice the principles of a highly aestheticized literary style, which they call "word weaving" *(pleteniye sloves)* and which consists in infinite multiplication of metaphors and exquisite and complicated epithets around one thought.

The period around 1500–1600 is marked by a more pronounced literary expression of aesthetic views in medieval Russia. The leader of the ascetically oriented monks, Nil Sorsky, works out a Russian variant of "asceticist aesthetics," and Iosif Volotsky, his opponent in regard to the organization of monastic life, is occupied with the rethinking of liturgical aesthetics. It is he who, for the first time in Rus, expounds, in a rather detailed way, the Orthodox theory of the icon and the iconographical program for icon painters.

In the sixteenth century, a contribution to the consolidation of medieval aesthetic views is made by such thinkers as Maxim Grek, Vassian Patrikeyev, Zinovij Otensky, the monk Artemij, Prince Andrei Kurbsky, and the church councils of 1551 (the so-called *Stoglav*) and 1554. During this period, the sphere of the aesthetic—primarily literature and church art—is closely intertwined with the political, ecclesiastical, and ideological struggle between various church and state factions. Canonicity and traditionalism are acknowledged as the most important principles of art, but at the same time artistic practice gradually departs from them—a fact that foreshadows the beginning of the crisis of the medieval type of artistic thinking that comes to completion around 1700. A sharp polemic is initiated concerning complex religious allegorical representations that appear in church icon painting, as a result of which the symbolic theology of Pseudo-Dionysius the Areopagite, and in particular his concept of "unlike likenesses," is being interpreted, for the first time in the Orthodox aesthetics, as the theoretical foundation of religious painting.

Transitional Period. The characteristic feature of the second period of Russian religious aesthetics—the transition from the Middle Ages to modern times—is the spirit of sharp polemic between traditionalists and innovators regarding the main aesthetic problems and the gradual departure from the medieval style in art under the influence of sixteenth- and seventeenth-century western European art. The seventeenth century sees the appearance of manuals of grammar, rhetoric, and arithmetic in Russian, the creation of special treatises on music and painting, regulative handbooks (chinovnik, from Russian chin, "order") on ceremonial aesthetics ("The Chinovnik of Archpriestly Service," "The Order [chin] of the Blessing of Water," "The Order of Anointing for Kingship," "The Wedding Order," "The Order [uryadnik] of Falconry," etc.), where the aesthetic problematic holds a prominent place. The characteristic tendency of the specific treatises on art that are written between about 1650 and 1700—as a rule, promoting new methods and styles in religious art that differ from the medieval—is an attempt to prove that their methods do not contradict the medieval (and even the patristic) tradition, but, on the contrary, realize it more profoundly than the earlier ones.

Thus, Simeon Polotsky, the most prominent court poet, playwright, and theoretician of art in this period, undertakes to replace the traditional prose Slavonic translation of the Book of Psalms with a free poetic interpretation. He justifies his efforts not so much by the fact that the Hebrew original was also in verse, as by an observation that poetic text allows for a more laconic expression of thoughts, while it also emphasizes and interprets their inner meaning. According to him, poetic form (meter and rhyme) brings spiritual delight to the reader and thus facilitates the process of penetrating the spiritual depths of the text.

Nikolai Diletsky and Ivan Korenev, the authors of *Musikijskaya grammatika,* the first treatise on music, published in 1679 in Moscow, defend the advantages of the new polyphonic ecclesiastical chant against the old unison one and believe that, far from denying the medieval tradition, the new chant continues it on a higher level. A similar tendency manifests itself in treatises on painting. The treatise of Iosif Vladimirov, a "new" icon painter *(ikono-pisets)* and *zhivo-*

RUSSIAN AESTHETICS: Religious Aesthetics. *Nicholas the Wonderworker* (third quarter of the sixteenth century), Russian (attributed to Tver'); Ikonen-Museum Recklinghausen, Germany. (Photograph courtesy of Ikonen-Museum Recklinghausen; used by permission.)

pisets (Russian for *painter,* literally, the *painter of life,* this term not being in use before the second half of the seventeenth century), is especially noteworthy for its fullness and depth. Consistently defending the advantages of the new "lifelike" *(zhivo-podobnaya,* i.e., tending first of all toward an illusionist and naturalistic representation of man) painting against the icons of the older style, he supports his claim by the arguments of Byzantine iconodules in defense of mimetic images (which only existed in Byzantium at an early stage)—in particular, the legend of the "made without hands" *(acheiropoietos)* image of Christ (i.e., the image-imprint of the ideal face of Christ on a piece of cloth that was imprinted by Christ himself). In the seventeenth century, such "made without hands" images were painted with great technical skill by Simon Ushakov, a friend of Vladimirov. The seventeenth- and eighteenth-century traditionalists (first of all the so-called *staroobryadtsy*—the "Old Believers"—but not only them) fight frantically against all those Westernizing (and, in their understanding, heretical) innovations in church art and its theory, but they find little support from their mainstream contemporaries. The artistic culture of Russia relentlessly departs from the medieval Weltanschauung and artistic language in all genres of art. Within Russian religious art itself, new tendencies take shape: toward the secularization of art, aesthetics, and culture, and a departure from medieval mentality. They become dominant in Russia in the eighteenth and nineteenth centuries.

Conservative or Preservative Period. In the eighteenth century, the cultural and political reforms of Peter I actively contribute to the process of secularization of culture. From Byzantium, Peter inherits the tendency toward the consolidation of monarchical empire, in which even the church is fully subject to the monarch. Thus, it is Peter who abolishes the highest ecclesiastical rank of "Patriarch of All Russia." In matters of culture, he abandons the course of national and religious isolation of Russia from the West and starts to develop actively a variety of Western trends in culture and art (often alien to the Russian mentality) on Russian soil. Beginning with Feofan Prokopovitch (1681–1736)—a priest of the new orientation and a devoted follower of Peter I, who writes *Poetics* and *Rhetoric* according to the spirit of similar ancient and western European treatises—Russian thinkers, writers, and art critics of the eighteenth and nineteenth centuries actively rework and introduce the ideas of ancient (Greco-Roman) and modern European aesthetics into Russian culture. The views and teachings of the Enlightenment, classicism, Romanticism, sentimentalism, and classical German aesthetics receive wide circulation during these centuries, especially as part of university courses on aesthetics.

The nineteenth century sees a rapid formation, under the influence of Western ideas, of democratic views and sentiments among the Russian intelligentsia in areas ranging from science to literature and art. These views also hold sway in the areas of artistic creation and aesthetic thought. A new democratic trend in aesthetics is formed, represented by such prominent figures as Alexander I. Herzen, Nikolai A. Dobrolyubov, Vissarion G. Belinsky, Nikolai G. Chernyshevsky, and Vladimir V. Stasov. In this situation, Russian religious aesthetics is pushed to the far background of culture and survives only in part among the Old Believers, in the monasteries, and in the minds of certain thinkers and writers.

Among the latter is one of the most prominent Russian writers Nicolai Gogol (1809–1852), who realizes, from his own experience as a writer, the absolute futility of the tendency—very popular at that time—of "aesthetic humanism," or an attempt to introduce morals into society by means of secularized art. He reserves the power to overcome the tragic dissonance between aesthetic and moral principles only for the sphere of religion, and points out the importance of the problem of a relationship between the church and culture, as well as of a Christian metamorphosis of secular culture. He is the first among Russian thinkers to

introduce conscientiously the notion of "Orthodox culture." He sees the mission of the artist only as awakening souls for the encounter with God, in their moral purification, and in the theurgical experience of a realization of divine justice *(pravda)* on Earth.

The movement of "Slavophiles" *(slavyanofily)*, and in particular the activities of Alexei S. Khomyakov (1804–1860) and Ivan V. Kireevsky (1806–1856), becomes another noteworthy phenomenon in Russian religious aesthetics. Their aesthetics is based on a peculiar mixture of ideas from German Romanticism and Orthodox aesthetics. It is Khomyakov who, for the first time in Orthodox culture, finally gives a definition of *sobornost'*: according to him, it is a mystical "unity of God and man," or a certain ideal spirit of the people enlightened by the Christian faith. He understands art as an expression of this spirit on the basis of divine love, or as an artistic "self-consciousness of life" through the mediation of the artist.

Alexander M. Bukharev (monastic name Archimandrite Feodor; 1824–1871)—a prominent figure in nineteenth-century religious culture—attempts to overcome the narrow ecclesiastical rigorism and present all contemporary culture and art (including nonecclesiastical) as imbued with the "light of Christ" and cherished by the "secret warmth" of the church. By that, he tries to overthrow the (in his opinion) unnatural idea of secularism in culture. According to him, any creative activity is an act of divine grace, even if it has no clear external indications of its religious or ecclesiastical character. Bukharev's conception thus removes the tragic character of the situation that overwhelms Gogol in the late period of his life and forces him to destroy the second volume of *Dead Souls* as belonging, in his opinion, to secular rather than to Orthodox culture.

After Gogol, the relationship and interaction between the aesthetic element and Christian ethics in culture becomes one of the most important problems in Russian religious aesthetics. This problem becomes particularly acute for the great nineteenth-century Russian writers. Like Gogol, Konstantin N. Leontyev (1831–1891)—a prophet of pure aestheticism—toward the end of his life resolves this problem in favor of Christian ethics. Fyodor Dostoyevsky centers his literary activity on his attempts to resolve the tragic conflict between the ethical and the aesthetic. As a result, the Russian writer chooses the ideal of early Christian ethics—the highest beauty that will "save the world," or Jesus Christ himself in his eschatological aspect—over against the modernized (or diabolic, in Dostoyevsky's interpretation) Roman Catholic "rationalistic" ethics of the Great Inquisitor. The great Russian writer Leo Nicolaevich Tolstoy (1828–1910) is also among those trying to find a clue to the complex dialectic of the ethical and the aesthetic. Toward the end of his literary activity, he turns to the Christianity of the early church fathers and severs his ties with secular culture, which he served for decades in his writings, with the official church, and with aesthetics as such. He experiences a tragic inner discord between his personal mystical experience and western European rationalism that has been acquired from the outside. As a result, both his manifesto *What Is Art?* and his other works are subject to a strict dictate of panmoralism. Beauty has nothing in common with the good. It follows that art based on aesthetic principles is an empty amusement that leads humanity away from goodness: "aesthetic pleasure is a pleasure of a lower rank." In the late period of his life, Tolstoy rejects almost all famous names in art (Eurypides, Dante, William Shakespeare, Rafael, Michelangelo, Ludwig van Beethoven) and accepts only art that contains "truth" in a simplified religious form that is accessible to people.

Neo-Orthodox Period. The new stage in Russian religious aesthetics begins with the philosopher Vladimir S. Solovyov (1853–1900) and reaches its apogee in the writings of his followers: the philosopher Nikolai A. Berdyaev (1874–1948) and especially the theoreticians of neo-Orthodoxy Florensky (1882–1937) and Bulgakov (1871–1944). This period coincides with tempestous social and political commotions in Russia and world culture in general, the latter undergoing essential changes under the influence of a positivist and materialist world outlook and the rise of scientific and technological progress. Russia is not left behind in this process. The Russian monarchy is on the verge of a crisis, and many democratic and progressive-minded figures in early twentieth-century culture actively contribute to its downfall. The representatives of the avant-garde in contemporary art and aesthetics—especially the Futurists and the Constructivists—support all revolutionary movements in Russia, including the Communist revolution. The representatives of Russian religious aesthetics, however, maintain their traditional conservative attitude in politics, although the general atmosphere of a mighty shift in culture has some influence even on their views. The "Russian religious renaissance" of the beginning of the twentieth century is largely an attempt of the most educated and creatively minded Orthodox thinkers to bring Orthodoxy into some degree of correspondence with the contemporary zeitgeist.

The aesthetics of Soloviev—the founder of "neo-Orthodoxy"—whose thought is based on Neoplatonism, German classical philosophy (mainly Friedrich Wilhelm von Schelling), and many ideas of nineteenth-century Russian aesthetics, is much broader than religious, let alone Orthodox, aesthetics as such. His philosophical concept of universal unity (*vseyedinstvo*), his understanding of art as mystical "free theourgy" that transforms the world on the way to its spiritual perfection, his concept of the symbol, and the mystical intuition of Sophia as a cosmic and artistic creative principle (his sophiology) have a strong influence on aesthetic theories at the beginning of the twentieth century, in particular on the theorists of Russian Symbolism and neo-Orthodox aesthetics.

The aesthetic views of Berdyaev, which follow from his personalist philosophy, are of a mystical and romantic orientation. One of the main themes in his philosophy is the concept of creative activity that brings to their logical completion the ideas of theourgy (in art, culture, life, and being as a whole) that are present in Russian aesthetics since the time of Gogol and are partly developed by Solovyov and Vyatcheslav I. Ivanov. Berdyaev sees the meaning of human life in creative activity, for it is only in it that man can truly assimilate himself to God the creator and the supreme artist, and achieve, with his help, a breakthrough from the "ugly" earthly life to the supreme cosmic "life in beauty." To this point in history, creative activity realizes itself most fully in art. Art is tragic, however, for it has not been able to fulfill its main—theourgical—goal and has remained stuck in earthly reality, instead of rising to the level of cosmic being. Berdyaev distinguishes between Christian and pagan art. Pagan (Greco-Roman) art reaches the classical completeness of its forms in this earthly immanent world. It knows of no other higher world and does not long for it. Christian art, on the contrary, is the art of "transcendental longing" for another world, of "transcendental breakthrough" into that world. This is why it is essentially incomplete, in its highest sense, for it does not reach the other world in reality, but only points at it in its symbols.

Berdyaev distinguishes between the two main types of artistic activity: realism and symbolism. He sees realism as the ultimate form of adaptation of art to "this world," which in its foundation is ugly. Therefore, realism is the "least creative form of art." True art—especially Christian art (in a broad sense, the art of Christian regions in general)—is always symbolic to a certain degree, for it creates the symbols of the other world. It follows that art attains its highest state in Symbolism as an artistic trend from about 1850 to 1900. It is also in Symbolism, however, that it reaches the limit of its own capacities, or its own crisis. Symbolism reveals the tragic character of artistic activity in a particularly acute manner. The symbol is a "bridge crossing over from the creative act to the hidden, ultimate reality" and hanging over empty space with its other end. In Symbolism, artistic activity outgrows itself and goes beyond the limits of art in its traditional understanding: it leaves the sphere of culture and flows into being itself. It is Berdyaev who gives, finally, a clear definition of theourgy, to which the aesthetic consciousness of Orthodoxy is constantly drawn throughout almost all of its history: "It is not culture that theourgy creates, but new being; theourgy is above culture. Theourgy is art that creates a different world, different being, different life, beauty as being. . . . Theourgy is man's acting together with God: acting in a divine way, joint creative activity of God and man" (Berdyaev, 1916). In addition to this, Berdyaev considers the problem of art as theourgy mainly as a Russian problem, and it is with theourgy that he connects the future "Slavo-Russian renaissance."

Florensky—one of the most prominent Orthodox theologians and a scholar of encyclopedic knowledge and universal orientation who draws on all previous experience and achievements of human culture—pays particularly close attention to aesthetics and art. For him, it is God who is the supreme beauty, through the participation in which all becomes beautiful. Hence, the aesthetic, according to his definition, is not some particular section of being or consciousness, but a force, or energy, that penetrates all layers of being. Beauty and (spiritual, divine) light are important ontological and epistemological factors in his system. It is in them and through their mediation that man "cognizes" the trihypostatical truth in the mystical acts of liturgy, contemplation of icons, and, above all, monastic feats, which fills him with ineffable spiritual joy. In Florensky's understanding, then, the main aesthetic subjects are monks who devote their whole life to the contemplation of spiritual light. On the other hand, asceticism is, in the full sense of these terms, aesthetics and art. Ascetics themselves, Florensky stresses, call their activity the "art of arts," and the goal of their activity—"contemplative knowledge"—the "love of beauty" (this is how Florensky translates *philokalia,* in opposition to the traditional ecclesiastical translation "love of goodness"), as distinct from the rational "love of wisdom" *(philosophia).* Moreover, this activity does not limit itself only to contemplation, but even—ideally—has a goal of real transformation of the flesh of an ascetic into a more spiritual and luminous substance already in his lifetime, that is, a real crossing of the border between the material and spiritual worlds. On the level of cosmogony, it is sophia the wisdom of God who dwells at this border: a certain unknowable person and the creative principle of God, his creating energy, the spiritual foundation of the world and man who makes them beautiful. Hence, the sphere of the aesthetic and beauty, in its most intricate forms, is the transitional sphere between the heavenly and earthly worlds. The supreme beauty, however, in its pure form, is revealed only to select monk-ascetics, and therefore its real carriers in the world are symbols in liturgy and art (in its purest form—the icon).

Florensky understands the symbol not only as a semiotic unit but also as an ontological entity. Not only does it signify something else, but it also manifests it in reality, possesses its energy, and appears as a "living mutual interpenetration of two entities." Florensky extends the ancient Jewish understanding of the symbol (or name) as a bearer of the essence, together with the Byzantine notion of the liturgical symbol, to the general concept of the symbol. Among such symbols he includes, first of all, the icon, which he considers to be the highest achievement of the art of painting of all times and nations. When he considers in detail the peculiarities of the artistic language of the icon—including its canonicity, "reversed perspective," particular ways of organizing space, symbolism of color, and conventional character of forms—and compares all this with the language of modern European painting ("Renaissance-type," in his terminology), he comes to the conclusion that it is with the "great" masters of the Renaissance who had rejected the medieval Weltanschauung and artistic language that the decline of representational art begins. Florensky is convinced that the essence of art is not the conveyance of visible forms of the material world, or of psychological states of man, but symbolic expression and the ascent, with the help of conventional images of art, to the everlasting spiritual world, and ultimately to God. Florensky pays much attention to the question of the synthesis of arts in liturgy, as well as to the philosophy and aesthetics of the ritual, the problems of the canon, and the organization of the space-time continuum in art.

Bulgakov largely continues Florensky's tradition in aesthetics. The cornerstone of his teaching is sophiology: the essentially antinomical teaching about sophia, which appears to him as "impossible" for the intellect, as an alogical mediator between God and the world, as a "round square," as a "square root of minus one," and, at the same time, as the original aggregation of all ideas of the creation—a neo-Orthodox rethinking of the (Neo) platonic theory of preexistent ideas—and as a creative principle of being and art. In fact, his sophiology can rightly be called neo-Orthodox aesthetics in the full sense of the word. At the center of it, Bulgakov, like Florensky, places the teaching about the icon, which he sees as an essentially antinomical phenomenon (because of its ability to represent the nonrepresentable God) ideally embodying the *sophijnost'* of the creation because of its canonicity. Under *sophijnost',* Bulgakov understands the expression of the primordial ideality of the material world in this world itself. The main criterion and indicator of the level of *sophijnost'* of a thing or a work of art is beauty, which is at the same time understood as the "revelation of the Holy Spirit" in matter, as the "sacred, without sin, palpability and perceptibility of the idea," that is, as "spiritual, sacred corporeity." Bulgakov draws particular attention to the category of corporeity in its ideal understanding, or "spiritual corporeity," for it forms the foundation of art. The artist "intuits beauty as the realized sacred corporeity" and strives to express it in his own art. In Bulgakov's opinion, the ancient Greeks perfectly succeed in this task in their sculpture (especially in nude figures), as do the medieval Orthodox artists in their icons. Hence, he defines the work of art as an "erotic encounter of matter and form, their enamored confluence, the idea that has been felt and has become beauty: it is the shining of the ray of *sophijnost'* in our world" (1917). Bulgakov makes no essential distinction between beauty in art and nature. The latter he understands as a "great and wondrous artist," and art he understands very broadly, as is customary for the Orthodox tradition in general. It is man, in all his "spiritual corporeity" and ideal "life in beauty," who is the main work of art. This "life in beauty" for the human being is difficult and tempting, however, for here—Bulgakov recalls Dostoyevsky—is the field of battle between the devil and God. "Earthly beauty is enigmatic and ominous, like Gioconda's smile. . . . Longing for beauty, torments through beauty, is the scream of all the universe" (ibid.). It is possible to overcome this tragic character of beauty in the world (an idea common to the whole of neo-Orthodox aesthetics) with the help of the theurgical function of art, which would then cross the boundaries of its proper works and in reality transform the world and man on their way of eschatological *sophijno-aesthetic* transfiguration, or the uplifting of the created world to its preexistent beauty, or sophia.

One more significant theme in aesthetics—the relationship between culture and civilization—is taken up by Russian religious aesthetics in the twentieth century. Vladimir V. Weidle (1895–1979), a prominent religious art critic and thinker who left Russia after the October Revolution, perceives a well-pronounced crisis and even "dying" in contemporary art (cf. his principal work, *The Dying of Art,* 1937). The causes of the latter he sees in the domination of rationalism and mechanistic principles, in the rift between the humanity and nature (these principles he defines as the traits of civilization, which is taken in opposition to culture), and ultimately in the loss of religious faith and religious *Weltanschauung.* True sound art, he believes, is always closely connected to religion and is religious in its foundation (whether the artist recognizes himself as a believer or not), "for artistic experience is in its very depth religious, because no creative act can exclude an expression of faith, and because the world that harbors art is ultimately transparent only to religion" (Weidle, 1996). Even the basic notions lying at the foundation of the interpretation of art, according to Weidle, are rooted in religious thought. Among these notions are transfiguration, incarnation, sacrament, antinomical wholeness, and miracle. The phenomena described by these notions belong as much to art as they do to religion, although art and religion as a rule are not identical. Art and religion are "con-natural" in their essence, and the "logic of art is the logic of religion." They do not, however, substitute, but supplement and strengthen, each other in culture. Certainly, even in modern times not all artists of genius have been religious in a narrow ecclesiastical sense. Yet, they were creating in a world that was still penetrated with "secret religion," a world that was "truly human, guided by conscience." Contemporary art is dying not because the artist ceased to be a believer but because he stopped acknowledging his creative act as a sacrament.

From about 1900 to 1930, Russian religious aesthetics had a strong influence on Russian culture in general and affected the views of many artists, writers, and thinkers. It is this aesthetics, for example, that, together with other spiritual trends, serves as a foundation for the main theoretical treatise—*Concerning the Spiritual in Art*—and the deeply mystical artistic activity of Vassily V. Kandinsky, a founder of abstract art. The founder of Suprematism, Kazimir Malevich, who is otherwise removed from any particular religious tradition, sees his *Black Square* as the new icon of the twentieth century. One of the most prominent twentieth-century Russian poets, Aleksandr Aleksandrovich Blok, receives the Russian Revolution of the 1917 in a mystico-Christian light. The image of Christ plays a prominent role in the art of Mark Z. Shagall, a Russian Hasidic Jew. One also finds echoes of Russian religious aestheticism in the aesthetic system of Alexei F. Losev (1893–1988), a prominent Russian aesthetician, philologist, and philosopher, one of the followers of Soloviev, who was secretly consecrated as a monk in the Soviet era. In his book *The Dialectic of Artistic Form* (1927), he outlines a system of aesthetic categories—in a rigorous dialectical form that is characteristic for him—relying on Neoplatonism, phenomenology, and Orthodox aesthetics. This system includes successive categories that generate (express) each other, such as eidos, myth, symbol, person (art belongs to this level), the energy of the essence, and the name of the essence. A strong influence of neo-Orthodox aesthetics can be felt in the way Losev develops such categories as symbol, person, energy, and name, as well as in his consciously acknowledged principle of antinomies, although as a whole his aesthetic system transcends the boundaries of Russian religious aesthetics as such.

The destiny of the last representatives of Russian religious aesthetics, like that of most of the Russian intelligentsia of the beginning of this century, is tragic. After the establishment of Communist rule, many were deported or forced to emigrate. The ones who stayed in Russia fell victim to repression (e.g., Florensky, who was executed in a Stalinist concentration camp) or were forced to change their occupation (e.g., Losev who devoted himself mainly to the study of antiquity after serving his term in a labor camp).

[*See also* Byzantine Aesthetics; Icon; Religion and Aesthetics; *and* Tolstoy.]

BIBLIOGRAPHY

Berdyaev, Nikolaj A. *Smysl tvorchestva, Opyt opravdaniya cheloveka* (The Meaning of Creative Activity, the Experience of Justification of Man). Moscow, 1916.

Bulgakov, Sergij N. *Svet nevecherniy, Sozertsaniya i umozreniya* (Contemplations and Meditations). Moscow, 1917.

Bychkov, Victor V. "Schönheit verweist auf Transzendenz, Maxim Grek: Zur Entwicklung des philosophisch-aesthetischen Gedankens in der Alten Rus." *Zeitschrift für Ästhetik und allgemeine Kunstwissenschaft* 34.1 (1989): 73–81.

Bychkov, Victor V. "L'esthétique internationale en Russie au 17ème siècle, Juraj Krizanic et Nicolai Milescu Spatarul." *Syntesis Philosophica* 9 (1990): 161–182.

Bychkov, Victor V. *Russkaya srednevekovaya estetika, XI–XVII veka* (Medieval Russian Aesthetics). Moscow, 1992.

Bychkov, Victor V. *The Aesthetic Face of Being: Art in the Theology of Pavel Florensky.* Translated by Richard Pevear and Larissa Volokhonsky. Crestwood, N.Y., 1993.

Bychkov, Victor V. "Künstlerische und ästhetische Aspekte in der Sophiologie Vater Sergi Bulgakows." *Stimme der Orthodoxie* 4 (1994): 26–30.

Florensky, Pavel A. "Statyi po iskusstvu." In *Sobraniye sochineniy,* vol. 1 (Essays on Art. in Complete Works), edited by N. A. Struve. Paris, 1985.

Florensky, Pavel A. *Analiz prostranstvennosti i vremeni v hudozhestvenno izobrazitelnykh proizvedeniyakh* (The Analysis of Spatiality and Time in the Works of Representational Arts). Moscow, 1993.

Likhachyov, Dmitrij S. *Poetika drevnerusskoj literatury* (Poetics of Old Russian Literature). Moscow, 1979.

Rozanov, Vasilij V. *Religiya i kul'tura* (Religion and Culture). Saint Petersburg, 1899.

Rupnik, Marko I. *L'arte memoria della comunione. Il significato teologico missionario dell'arte nella saggistica di Vjaceslav Ivanovic Ivanov.* Rome, 1994.

Spidlik, Tomas. *L'idée russe: Une autre vision de l'homme.* Troyes, France, 1994.

Weidle, Vladimir V. *Umiraniye iskusstva, Razmyshleniya o sud'be literaturnogo i hudozhestvennogo tvorchestva* (The Dying of Art, Meditations on the Destiny of Literary and Artistic Activity, 1937). 2d ed. Moscow, 1996.

Zernov, Nicolas. *The Russian Religious Renaissance of the Twentieth Century.* London, 1963.

VICTOR V. BYCHKOV and OLEG V. BYCHKOV
Translated from Russian by Oleg V. Bychkov

Russian Formalism

Russian Formalism comprises a group of literary and aesthetic doctrines held by a number of early twentieth-century Moscow and Saint Petersburg linguistic and literary scholars and theoreticians. They founded the Society for the Study of Poetic Language, known by the Russian acronym OPOYAZ, in 1916. OPOYAZ was dedicated to the premise that literary language was autonomous in its function (the "self-sufficient word"), and operated against the background of a nonrepresentational aesthetics. As a discrete movement, Formalism came to an end in 1930, after which time it was denounced as "Western" and "bourgeois" (the term *Formalist* itself was later destined to become one of the strongest pejorative terms in the Soviet critical vocabulary). The later characterization of "bourgeois" seems ironic in view of the fact that the Formalists were leftists in the context of Soviet politics of the 1920s.

Still, a certain amount of clandestine Formalism continued to survive in the Soviet Union after 1930, more in literary theory than in actual criticism of specific literary works; with the reappearance of greater freedom of expression in the 1970s, Formalism became the chief literary approach followed by Soviet theoreticians, now blended with more recent Western trends in literary theory such as semiotics (though this use in literary theory and criticism developed to a degree out of Formalism and was only indirectly "Western").

Formalism is vaguely Kantian in its philosophical foundations, especially in its epistemology and its faith in art

as displaying "purposiveness without purpose," but in the Russian context it sprang more directly from a number of positivist philosophers such as Alexander Potebnja (1835–1891), who was influenced in part by Alexander von Humboldt. But the most powerful intellectual influence on Formalism was its close contact with linguistic theory and the Formalists' insistence that literature was the "art of the word" and not the "art of images," as certain nineteenth-century German aestheticians and their Russian followers had insisted.

The Russian Formalists were particularly unhappy with the prevailing eclecticism in literary theory and criticism, tending to follow biographical (biography of the writer), psychological, sociological, philosophical, cultural-historical, and other approaches, and often intermingling them without any precise methodological plan. The Formalists sought to create a "science of literature" (they used the term *poetry* more often than *literature,* not in order to exclude prose, but to emphasize that kind of literature in which verbal play had its fullest effect). The Formalists rejected the traditional duality of form and content; this dualistic concept was much too crude: it implied that content was poured into a kind of mold called form, which gave it a literary "shaping." Indeed, they rejected all external use of devices in literature: rhyme and rhythm were not mere ornaments but an intrinsic part of the organic work of art.

Instead of form and content, the Formalists postulated a new duality, that of material and device. Words are the "material" of literature, to be given shape by the application of devices.

"Device" was probably the basic concept in the Formalist arsenal. It was introduced by Viktor Shklovsky (1893–1984), a philosophically grounded Formalist. In a seminal article published in 1917, Shklovskij introduced his famous slogan "Literature as Device." Device makes it possible to bring fresh perspectives to the word, which is thus freed of its banal ties to everyday life. Besides purely poetic devices such as rhyme and rhythm, the concept includes distortion, both of meaning and syntax, and the insertion of the word in new, previously unused contexts, both semantic and syntactic. Shklovskij likened the thus renewed perceptions of the word to viewing a landscape through a pair of colored spectacles, which serve to revive its freshness.

The central poetic device that Shklovskij postulates is "defamiliarization" or "making strange" (Russian *ostranenie*). Banal words are introduced into strange, often distorted contexts (e.g., the illicit use of the verb *overcome* as intransitive in the civil-rights hymn), a use that gives it greater effect than the correct transitive use would permit. Defamiliarization is intended to revive words and impart to them a new vividness and freshness, especially in a revivified literary context. But, though literary satire shows a great deal of defamiliarization (e.g., *Gulliver's Travels*) in the form of distortions of ordinary reality, it would be difficult to apply this device to the language of all literature (e.g., in the Russian tradition, to Leo Nicolaevich Tolstoy's realistic novels, though Shklovskij strove, partly in vain, to accomplish this).

A second major device for Shklovskij is that of "making difficult" *(zatrudnenie):* writers deliberately make their writings difficult, partly in order to stimulate readers to make a greater effort to enter into the literary work and to comprehend it. This seems acceptable, but radical simplicity may seem to be an equally effective and compelling device. Another weakness in Shklovskij's thought is his frequent failure to differentiate verbal devices from nonverbal ones, as the other Formalists usually did. The distortions that Shklovskij finds in *Gulliver's Travels* more often concern descriptions of people and their stature than they do the use of language as such.

The force and the partial validity of the notion of defamiliarization proceed chiefly from the Formalists' insistence that the work of art is an artifact, a construct. But because it also has semiotic significance in works of satire, where the revivified words and images take on satiric effect, there is a considerable confusion here, restricted principally to Shklovskij's brand of Formalism. In his confusion on this point, Shklovskij attempted to show that much of Tolstoy's realism was actually satire.

The most radical and extreme Formalist was no doubt Roman Jakobson (1896–1982), later prominent as a Prague structuralist (both literary and linguistic), and still later active in the United States. Rather than defining rhythm as a condition of the lexicon and syntax of the poet's language, Jakobson declared it to be "organized violence perpetrated by the poetic form on the language." He began with the dictum, "Poetry is indifferent to the object of expression." The first dictum happened to fit well into Shklovskij's views, but the second goes far beyond them. Jakobson insisted that a poet who writes a love poem is not necessarily in love, and a poet who writes a religious poem is not necessarily religious. Later, Jakobson partly recanted the latter view, because it might have been difficult to take literature seriously if it was viewed as having no relevant content whatsoever. None of the other Formalists went so far: while denying the importance, or even the relevance, of content, they would dismiss these by the door in order to admit them again through the window.

Jakobson introduced the concept of "laying bare the device" *(obnazhenie priema),* familiar in parody, burlesque, travesty, and commonly occurring in advertising. Laying bare the device means exposing the techniques of the author, stripped from their message or content, and so displacing or "defamiliarizing" that message or content. Laying bare the device was the favorite technique of the Formalists' beloved Laurence Sterne in *Tristram Shandy* (1760–1767).

Formalism supplied a useful critical method for analyzing short poems and short stories, giving rise to literary studies not unlike those of the later Anglo-American critics (who were not aware of the Formalists). But the Formalists rarely tackled larger literary forms, and no Formalist ever attempted a history of literature. Shklovskij did suggest a most important dialectic force motivating the historical progress of literature: parody. The Formalists broadened the notion of parody beyond the humorous: parody was the opposition, through distorted imitation, of the younger generation to the older one. What is often viewed as the peaceful inheritance of literary forms by a younger generation is in fact the dialectical thrust of parody, which liberates the young writer from the tyranny of the older one, and makes it possible for him to advance literarily. Thus, the young Fyodor Dostoevsky parodies Nikolai Gogol in his first novel, *Poor Folk* (1846), but later finds his own independent path. In Sterne's celebrated novel *Tristram Shandy,* Shklovskij found a perfect parody of the developing novel form and its devices, verbal and imagistic.

Another dialectical notion popularized by Shklovskij is his theory that higher prose forms often represent the canonization of inferior genres. Thus, Dostoevsky employs the devices of the French boulevard novel, as Giovanni Boccaccio had the bawdy jokes of his day. These theories are interesting, but it is easy to see why Shklovskij could not construct a coherent history of literature based on them. Another manifest difficulty in Formalist historical theory, one observed by Viktor Zhirmunskij (1881–1971), is the fact that periods in the development of world literature often correspond to periods in the other arts, such as music, painting, and architecture.

In their analysis of narrative, the Formalists made another fundamental dialectical distinction between "fable" *(fabula)* and "plot" *(suzhet).* "Fable" denoted the basic narrative stuff that the author employs as raw material, which for fiction may be a "true" story; "plot" designates that material as rearranged or restructured by the application of devices. Such devices include repetition of episodes, alterations in temporal sequence, including flashbacks, retardation and acceleration, parallelism of episodes, and so on. Both stages are creatively essential to the work, though "plot" of course achieves the status of artifact and is closer to the finished work of art.

Although the Formalists wrote relatively little about other arts, one, Vladimir Propp (1895–1970), did apply Formalist analysis to the structure of the fairy tale: his *Morphology of the Folktale* (1928) attempted to reduce the structure of fairy tales to a limited number of functions; other criteria of classification, such as the identity of the characters, were shown to be irrelevant: for example, the character who plays the role of villain may be a sorcerer, a dragon, or even a bear without affecting the basic nature of a tale; in other words, it is the villain's role or function in the tale that is important, not his superficial characterization.

Formalism had a powerful influence on creative writing in Russia, particularly on such writers as Evgenii Zamyatin

(1884–1937), Veniamin Kaverin (b. 1902), and Jurii Olesha (1899–1960). This did not survive the school itself, but abroad, Formalism had an enormous shaping effect on all the branches of literary and linguistic structuralism that subsequently emerged: on Polish integralism and Czech structuralism of the prewar period; on French and Bulgarian structuralism of the postwar era and their international impact, as, for instance, in the United States, and on a kind of homegrown structuralism in the Soviet Union (the so-called Tartu School of Juri Lotman). Structuralism even finds earlier precursors in the Soviet Union, as in the work of the Formalists Jurii Tynjanov (1894–1943) and Mikhail Bakhtin (1896–1975) in the 1930s, though Bakhtin in particular worked under great constraints. In its insistence on the autonomy of artistic language, Formalism shows itself as a kind of literary criticism that has clearly risen to a higher *étape* of an accepted set of generalizations that scarcely can be rejected any longer from the literary critical arsenal, at least not in toto.

Formalism, in its stress on semiotics, provides a model for the French structuralist notion of "deconstruction," though some of the deconstructionists employed their new technique for political and social purposes, which the Russian Formalists always eschewed, in spite of their leftist political orientation.

[*See also* Formalism; Poetics; Semiotics; *and* Structuralism.]

BIBLIOGRAPHY

Erlich, Victor. *Russian Formalism: History, Doctrine.* 4th ed. The Hague, 1980.

Harkins, William. "Slavic Formalist Theories in Literary Scholarship." *Word* 7.2 (1951): 177–185.

Matejka, Ladislav, ed. *Readings in Russian Poetics.* 2 vols. Michigan Slavic Materials, nos. 2, 5. Ann Arbor, 1962–1964.

Medvedev, Pavel N., and Mikhail M. Bakhtin. *The Formal Method in Literary Scholarship: A Critical Introduction to Sociological Poetics.* Translated by Albert J. Wehrle. Baltimore, 1978; reprint, Cambridge, Mass., 1985.

Pomorska, Krystyna. *Russian Formalist Theory and Its Poetic Ambiance.* The Hague, 1968.

Steiner, Peter. *Russian Formalism: A Metapoetics.* Ithaca, N.Y. 1984.

Striedter, Jurij, ed. *Texte der russischen Formalisten.* 2 vols. Munich, 1969–1972.

Terras, Victor, ed. *Handbook of Russian Literature.* New Haven, 1985. See "Formalism," pp. 154–155.

Thompson, Ewa M. *Russian Formalism and Anglo-American New Criticism: A Comparative Study.* The Hague, 1971.

WILLIAM E. HARKINS

Socialist Realism

Socialist Realism is a twentieth-century prescriptive doctrine aimed at defining and delimiting the content and, to an extent, the form of works of literature and art in the Soviet Union and in other socialist countries. Socialist Realism is sometimes claimed by its advocates to be an aesthetic, but at best it is a *politically correct* aesthetic. The elaboration of the doctrine of Socialist Realism did not prevent Soviet philosophers from developing unrelated systems of aesthetic theory, generally imagistic and deriving from Plato, G. W. F. Hegel, and other philosophers.

The sources of Socialist Realism are not obvious. The concept clearly does not derive from the teachings of Karl Marx, Friedrich Engels, or Vladimir Ilich Lenin, none of whom had very much that was specific to say about literature or art. The Soviet writer Maxim Gorky has generally been credited with providing at least models for the doctrine, and he did play a leading role in providing models for its formulation. But, though the doctrine seems to be ideological in nature, it is increasingly clear that it was created as a method aimed at restricting and focusing works of literature and the other arts. Its introduction forms one of the changes introduced by Joseph Stalin and his followers in Soviet ideology during the early 1930s, which served to put an end to the "class struggle" and introduce (at least in principle), a more conservative, classless society.

The doctrine of Socialist Realism was ratified in 1932 by a decision of the Seventeenth Congress of the Soviet Communist Party. The decision was set into the context of a thoroughgoing reorganization of the Union of Soviet Writers, and this union was entrusted with the enforcement of the new doctrine. As promulgated, Socialist Realism had relatively little content, but it did point to a few works of literature, notably Gorky's early revolutionary novel *The Mother* (1906), as models for writers to follow. Stalin's dictum that "Writers are engineers of human souls" was also taken as a key leitmotif of the new doctrine, though its actual meaning is not entirely clear.

The effect of this paucity of sources was to leave very great power to officials of the Union of Soviet Writers and to Soviet critics, and in effect to overweigh the balance normally obtaining between authors and their critics. Critics became umpires enforcing the "rules" of Socialist Realism, though in effect such rules had hardly been laid down. Only with time and the interplay of creative writing, critical stricture, and theoretical writing could it become clear what Socialist Realism meant. Paradoxically, definitions were more readily reached outside the Soviet Union than inside it, for outside the Soviet Union it could often be given real meaning and real social pathos by Marxist writers and critics who wrote in greater freedom.

Socialist Realism had been preceded by the proletarian movement, vested with authority in literature in the Russian Association of Proletarian Writers (RAPP), which dominated the literary scene at the end of the 1920s. The RAPP and its literary controls were based on a theory of class adherence and class cultural values; this theory would no longer be relevant when the Soviet Union proclaimed itself a "classless society" in the early 1930s. The prevalent Communist Party cultural ideology in the 1920s had favored "proletarianism," a view according to which the Communist proletariat would create a new socialist culture based on its own class values and its role in the Marxist class struggle. But Stalin was seeking to construct a new society and a new state order, for which an effort to sharpen the dialectical division of Soviet people into proletarians and others would have been counterproductive. A monolithic, "classless" writers' union seemed to point to greater freedom, when in fact the system under Socialist Realism would become even tighter.

Socialist Realism is a compound term, and this is both an advantage and a disadvantage in seeking a definition. *Socialist* might seem obvious, except that its use might seem to imply the elimination of a great deal of literature dealing with individual human life and with "eternal themes" such as love, fulfillment, ambition, family, and freedom that evidently evade the category of "socialist." *Socialist* implies that all literature should deal with the building of socialism and socialist society. This is true even in the past, where Marxist historical categories, such as bourgeois versus feudal, can be used as part of a system of historical *étapes* leading up and pointing forward to socialism. Even love and individual existence can be subsumed in such a way under the great theme of the building of socialism, though clearly always as secondary themes.

Historical fiction was largely discouraged in this light, but not totally excluded: "progressive" forces working toward the eventual order of socialist society could carry the heroic burden in a historical novel. Similarly, novels or dramas (these were the preferred forms of Socialist Realism) could be set in foreign countries where members of the local Communist Party or other "progressives" could play the heroic role.

The term *realism* is equally vexed. In part, its use stems from a desire to legalize a style current, popular, and acceptable to the Soviet rulers. Additionally, its use derives, no doubt, from the apparent truth implications of the word. One controversy (subsequently lost by the rebels) sought to find greater freedom in "Socialist Romanticism," but this concept survived only as a minor and nonobligatory subtype of Socialist Realism.

Realism in part corroborates the term *socialist:* the building of socialism is the great "truth" of our times; but "realism" is also an artistic method—only "realism" can give us any truth. In its application to painting, this was even clearer and simpler: distortion and abstraction were condemned totally.

In historical perspective, this meant that literature must not advance beyond the stylistic means of portrayal used by writers such as Tolstoy, Ivan Sergeevich Turgenev, or Anton

RUSSIAN AESTHETICS: Socialist Realism. Vitaly Komar and Alexander Melamid, *The Origin of Socialist Realism* (1982–1983), oil on canvas, 72 × 48 in.; Private Collection, Chappaqua, New York. (Photograph by D. James Dee; courtesy of the artists and Ronald Feldman Fine Arts, New York; used by permission.)

Pavlovich Chekhov. Again, Gorky (though there is a certain amount of Expressionism in his work) could serve as a model. This view hardly follows a priori from the doctrine itself, but it does seem to follow from a need not to complicate aesthetic means beyond the intellectual capacities or tastes of uneducated or semieducated persons of Stalin's generation, who were cultural parvenus. Curiously, in music this implied a *romantic* taste (Pyotr Ilich Tchaikovsky rather than Sergei Prokofiev or Dmitri Shostakovich) instead of a "realist" one ("realism" scarcely exists in music).

A facile application to literature was the factory novel, in which the building of a factory or the accomplishment of its assigned task could be equated both metonymically and metaphorically with the building of socialism. Secondary themes, such as love affairs, could readily be integrated into the woof of the whole without great risk. Valentin Kataev's

Five-Year Plan novel, *Time Forward!* (1932), about the construction of the Magnitogorsk chemical combine, was appropriated to serve as a model for this type of socialist novel.

Although Socialist Realism provided a method for dealing with the past, it did not resolve the problems and contradictions raised by the literature of the past. The term "bourgeois realism" was created by the critics for "bourgeois" realists such as Turgenev and Tolstoy, whom they were loath to discard completely; such writers, it was claimed, had pointed out many of the social problems and contradictions inherent in past Russian society, though without showing the way to the socialism of the future. But still, "bourgeois realism" could not extend back very far into the past: what does one do with a writer such as Aleksandr Sergeevich Pushkin, for instance, a poet of aristocratic origins and tastes, but still a Soviet favorite? He too was salvaged as a "realist," though hardly a "bourgeois" one. There were even attempts to label medieval Russian literature as "realist."

Although Socialist Realism arose as a literary doctrine, one enforced by the Union of Soviet Writers, it soon spread to the other arts. In painting, it had perhaps its greatest success, and tended to reduce Soviet painting to the level of mere copying. Abstraction was ruled out totally. Curiously, because the doctrine had little implication for the technique of Soviet painting (unlike literature), technique did not always suffer, at least not directly. What did suffer was the thematic poverty and the tendency to sentimentality of the great bulk of new Soviet painting.

Soviet film was largely a reflection of literature; films were either directly based on works of literature or on scripts that could be analyzed according to the criteria of Socialist Realism. The Soviet film, which had been created by such greats as Sergei Eisenstein, Vsevolod Ilarionovich Pudovkin, and Aleksandr Dovzhenko, was impoverished as much as literature or painting.

In music, the concepts of Socialist Realism could be applied readily to opera, ballet, and program music, and were so employed; attempts to apply them to more abstract music were largely abortive, as might have been expected; sometimes such works were dealt with as music with implicit programs, drawn from the life of the composer or the circumstances or period of composition. The popularity of nineteenth-century Russian opera and ballet, as of Tchaikovsky, for instance, made it impossible to circumscribe the older repertoire (this had not always succeeded in literature either), so that many compromises and exceptions had to be made where the popularity of older works was concerned. But new operas and ballets, such as Aram Khatchaturian's *Spartacus,* were created according to the formulas of Socialist Realism.

Literature produced for children (as well as other art) partly escaped the constraints of Socialist Realism. Of course, Socialist Realist works were created for children, but there was also a large repertoire of fairy tales and other imaginative writing. Russian folklore, venerated by Soviet critics as "progressive," also escaped proscription, though new Soviet works in a "folklore spirit" were also created in the mold of Socialist Realism.

Three fundamental corollaries were subsequently added to the basic doctrine of Socialist Realism. *Partiinost* ("Party orientation") implied making clear the role of the Communist Party in leading socialist progress. Non-Party factory workers in a work of fiction had either to be converted to the Party or act under the Party's mentorship. *Ideinost* ("ideological attitude") was in fact an older romantic notion of the need for ideology in political and cultural thought; the term now implied Communist ideology. *Narodnost* is the most difficult of the three concepts; the term implies not only "nationality," but also "folk" or "popular quality." What it should mean in literature was unclear; some critics equated it with the use or influence of popular folk forms such as proverbs or folk songs, while others argued that it meant the achievement of a good Russian style, an idea that was largely redundant.

The excesses of the doctrine brought a parodying reaction in the plays of Nikolai Virta (b.1906), who, in the late 1950s, wrote "conflictless" dramas. Virta argued, obviously tongue in cheek, that, because there were no more vestiges of bourgeois attitudes in the Soviet Union, there could no longer be any impedance to the building of socialism, at least not inside the Soviet Union, and hence dramas could no longer have conflicts, but only pseudoconflicts, based on faulty communication or temporary misunderstandings. Virta's ironic logic did not long deceive his critics, however, and they denounced him as someone who had strayed from the true path.

After Nikita Khrushchev (1960s to date), the doctrine of Socialist Realism fell largely into abeyance and writers no longer took the categories of the doctrine very seriously. Still, until about 1985, a good deal of lip service was paid by critics to the idea, probably because criticism lagged behind original creation.

In the Soviet satellite countries—especially Poland, Czechoslovakia, and Hungary—the doctrine was accepted as official and unilateral, less so perhaps in art and music. Even in literature, however, there was a certain tendency to pay lip service to Socialist Realism and then write as one wished—without, of course, attacking the idea of socialism itself.

Outside the Soviet Union, the doctrine had considerable influence on Marxist writers and critics, though lack of a firm definition coming from the Soviet homeland meant that it was taken more as an enthusiastic slogan than as a doctrine. Still, a number of writers, prominent among whom are the French Communist Louis Aragon (1897–1982) and the Hungarian Communist György Lukács (1885–1971), did employ both the term and the concept in their literary theory and criticism. Aragon had the difficult and probably thankless task of reconciling it with his Dadaism and Surrealism. Lukács had taken up residence in the Soviet Union for some fifteen years beginning in 1929, and was there during the early years of development of the doctrine. But he broadened the concept into that of "socialist humanism," and later was reproached by his fellow Hungarian Communists for his apparent preference for "bourgeois realism" to "Socialist Realism."

In linking literary (and artistic) quality to a political base, Socialist Realism may be viewed as one (though of course not the only) source for the present widespread notion of "politically correct."

[*See also* Ideology; Lukács; Marxism; *and* Realism.]

BIBLIOGRAPHY

Ermolaev, Herman. *Soviet Literary Theories, 1917–1934: The Genesis of Socialist Realism.* Berkeley, 1963.

Hayward, Max. "The Decline of Socialist Realism." *Survey* 18.1 (1972): 73–97.

James, Caradog Vaughan. *Soviet Socialist Realism: Origins and Theory.* London, 1973.

Mozejko, Edvard. *Der sozialistische Realismus.* Leipzig, 1977.

Ovcharenko, Aleksandr I. *Sotsialisticheskii realizm i sovremenny i literaturnyi protsess.* Moscow, 1968.

Terras, Victor, ed. *Handbook of Russian Literature.* New Haven, 1985. See "Socialist Realism," pp. 429–431.

Tertz, Abram [Andrej Sinyavsky]. *On Socialist Realism* (with *The Trial Begins*). Translated by Max Hayward and George Demis. Berkeley, 1960.

WILLIAM E. HARKINS

S

SAID, EDWARD WILLIAM. *See* Orientalism; *and* Postcolonialism.

SANTAYANA, GEORGE (1863–1952), Spanish-born philosopher and poet who was educated and later taught in the United States, and who wrote in English. Santayana's life and writings are punctuated with irony, including his place in the study of aesthetics. Although considered a principal figure in the development of aesthetic inquiry, Santayana abandoned efforts to delineate or discuss the nature of aesthetics shortly after his first book, *The Sense of Beauty* (1896). Nevertheless, the impact of his first major work is significant, marking a turning point in the theory of art and discussions of the sense of beauty. Santayana's later comments on aesthetics foreshadow modern discussions.

Philip Blair Rice wrote in the foreword to the 1955 Modern Library edition:

> To say that aesthetic theory in America reached maturity with *The Sense of Beauty* is in no way an overstatement. Only John Dewey's *Art as Experience* has competed with it in the esteem of philosophical students of aesthetics and has approached its suggestiveness for artists, critics and the public which takes a thoughtful interest in the arts.
> (p. ix)

Santayana's clear influence on aesthetic inquiry results largely from his method of analysis, which differs sharply from the preceding intellectualist traditions of aesthetics. This radical approach is emphasized in Arthur C. Danto's "Introduction" to the 1988 critical edition in which he says that Santayana brings "beauty down to earth" by treating it as a subject for science and giving it a central role in human conduct (p. xxviii).

The argumentative force of *The Sense of Beauty* lies in its dramatic and epigrammatic thesis: beauty is pleasure objectified. Why is this a daring thesis? In the nineteenth century, aesthetics and morals were considered by many as distinctive characteristics setting human beings apart from other animals and from scientific investigation. The sense of beauty was considered central to human experience, informing action as well as reflection. Beauty was not an abstract point of discussion related to art in museums or music in concert halls, but was an integral part of quotidian life, which was both elevated and evaluated by the sense of beauty. In 1928, Santayana wrote to the aesthetician Thomas Munro:

> You must remember that we were not very much later than Ruskin, Pater, Swinburne, and Matthew Arnold: our atmosphere was that of poets and persons touched with religious enthusiasm or religious sadness. Beauty (which mustn't be mentioned now) was then a living presence, or an aching absence, day and night.
> (Letters, pp. 238–239)

Santayana assumes the centrality of the sense of beauty, but instead of being a distinctly human characteristic and beyond scientific investigation, Santayana squarely places the sense of beauty in the pleasurable, in the satisfaction of individual desires that occur in particular settings. The satisfaction of a desire indicates as much about the nature of the person or animal having the desire as it does about the desired object. Furthermore, desires are not uniquely distinctive of human beings; they are a part of all animal experience. If one says that a sunset or an opera is beautiful, one is objectifying one's own pleasure as if it were characteristic of the sunset or the opera. By assuming that one's pleasure characterizes an existing object, one is projecting beauty as an objectified quality, as if beauty were a physical property rather than an objectified pleasure. This projection is natural but, if taken literally, is false. Hence, Santayana concludes that the sense of beauty is a reflection of the individual, not of an existing property in the world; it is a projection of one's pleasures on objects in the world. If this is true, then careful analysis conducted by able scientists may discern the origin of the sense of beauty, although the qualities projected on the object, according to Santayana, cannot become the subject of empirical research because they are individual, both in their origin and in their being. In his mature outlook, Santayana refers to the objects of consciousness as essences, universals that have no existence in the physical world but are the terms of consciousness, and he sometimes refers to the consciousness of aesthetic qualities as supervening on the physical relations.

Although the basic naturalism of Santayana's later philosophy is incipient in *The Sense of Beauty*, this work relies too heavily on the subjective experience of beauty to be fully in line with his more mature naturalism. There are some obvious problems with characterizing beauty as objectified pleasure. Does not the beautiful sometimes come without pleasure? Hence, it would appear that any rigid identification of beauty with objectified pleasure will not hold in all cases. Is beauty the only form of objectified pleasure? If there are other forms, then what is their relationship to the sense of beauty? These questions, and others, may have caused Santayana to pause in reconsidering his epigrammatic analysis of beauty and pleasure, but his assessment was more fundamental. There was something basically wrong with the approach he had taken.

He later characterizes his early philosophical method as relying too heavily on literary psychology, being neither true philosophy nor reliable psychology. Literary psychology is the analysis of experience without a full appreciation of the role of imagination or of the physical and social circumstances of that analysis and of the experience itself. "My whole little book *The Sense of Beauty* was written from a subjective point of view" (Santayana, 1967, 421 n. 2). A focus on radical empiricism, on experience alone, may become art if raised by imagination to the level of poetry and literature, but it is neither good philosophy nor good science. Hence, the role of the imagination, of possible meanings, is taken to be fundamental in aesthetics and other value-laden aspects of human existence. In *Interpretations of Poetry and Religion* (1900), Santayana maintains that imagination makes religion and poetry celebrations of life, but, if either is taken for science and not as rich imaginative works, the art of life is lost along with the beauty of poetry and religion. At their best, poetry and religion are identical; then "poetry loses its frivolity and ceases to demoralise, while religion surrenders its illusions and ceases to deceive" (1990, p. 172). This conclusion is found in his early correspondence with his father and appears as late as 1946 in *The Idea of Christ in the Gospels,* where Santayana presents the idea of Christ as poetic and imaginative, contrasted with a reading of the Gospels as historical events.

For Santayana, aesthetic experience is infused throughout everyday life. It is not uncommon, and, as a result, it is difficult or impossible to discern a particular field of experiences that can be isolated as subject to aesthetic analysis or to designate a particular set of characteristics that are definitive of the sense of beauty. To understand beauty, one must look beyond the experience of beauty and of pleasure objectified. Although Santayana abandons his definition of the sense of beauty as pleasure objectified, the basic direction of Santayana's aesthetics is clear even in *The Sense of Beauty:* the experience of beauty is more important than understanding it, and an understanding of it cannot rest solely on the experience.

Santayana wrote *The Sense of Beauty* as counterpoint to Josiah Royce's idealism and William James's radical empiricism, believing both of these to be literary and psychological without acknowledging it. Plato, Aristotle, and Immanuel Kant influence Santayana's account of beauty, and other intellectual influences include Rudolf Hermann Lotze's aesthetic metaphysics, Hermann Ebbinghaus's physiological psychology, Georg Simmel's critical account of abstract concepts, Herbert Spencer's evolutionary theories, and Friedrich Paulsen's account of Greek ethics. Prominent among the historical influences is Arthur Schopenhauer's *The World as Will and Idea* with its focus on objectification. "The world is my idea" is Schopenhauer's central notion in his system of the world as will objectified. Although owing much to Schopenhauer, Santayana's objectification is not a metaphysical necessity. It is a natural, evolutionary accident that, if understood, leads to a better understanding of the nature of the sense of beauty and of its origins in the physiology and social settings of the individual. This perspective is reminiscent of Simmel's account of abstract conceptions originating in the physical base of impulse and habit.

Being a product of the late nineteenth century, Santayana's outlook was shaped in part by his account of evolution and tempered by his view of Greek rational ethics. For Santayana, evolution is directionless and without goals, but from the perspective of the individual organism the ideal goal is a vital equilibrium between individual and the environment. Conscious experience is an accidental occurrence in a world of material forces and is incidental to any explanatory account of events in the world. Aesthetic experience is not lessened by this discovery, however; rather, it is the lyric cry in the wilderness of unconscious physical forces. The experience of beauty gives life meaning and significance when there is no meaning or significance in the world apart from that projected on it by individuals, but this is true not only for the sense of beauty but for any value projected on material events or objects. Santayana's view of evolution, supported by his reading of Spencer and coupled with his respect for Greek rational ethics, enabled him to account for the sense of beauty as originating in an organism that is at momentary harmony with the environment, whose pleasure is in the moment, and who revels in that fleeting delight in a world of conflicting and unthinking forces. Such passing harmonies may result in a sense of beauty, but they may also result in emergence of other moral values that reflect animal interests in an uninterested world. As a result, Santayana found it difficult to designate aesthetics as a discrete discipline, let alone designate specific characteristics of the beautiful or of art in general.

As early as 1904, Santayana abandons the notion that aesthetics is a separable field of inquiry: "Now the word 'aesthetics' is nothing but a loose term lately applied in academic circles to everything that has to do with works of art or with the sense of beauty" (1936, p. 32). He goes on to say:

Aesthetic good is accordingly no separable value; it is not realizable by itself in a set of objects not otherwise interesting. Anything which is to entertain the imagination must first have exercised the senses; it must first have stimulated some animal reaction, engaged attention, and intertwined itself in the vital process; and later this aesthetic good, with animal and sensuous values imbedded in it and making its very substance, must be swallowed up in a rational life; for reason will immediately feel itself called upon to synthesize those imaginative activities with whatever else is valuable. (Ibid.)

In a 1927 reappraisal of *The Sense of Beauty,* Santayana writes:

Nor was the phrase "objectified pleasure" a definition of beauty, a visionary essence utterly indefinable: it was an indication of the conditions and manner in which the momentary apparition of beauty arose and vanished. If I tried now to give such an indication I might perhaps say that beauty was a vital harmony felt and fused into an image under the form of eternity.

(Santayana, 1967, p. 422 n. 2)

In brief, Santayana's mature view of aesthetic experience is as an accidental feature of evolutionary nature, rooted in the unique physiological and environmental circumstances of the individual and enveloped in a complex system of interests and values that find their expression in momentary vital harmonies. His account of aesthetics, as with his account of morals, is remarkably individualistic and creates difficulties in understanding how artistic criticism and a sense of community among artists are possible. Moments of aesthetic consciousness, taken collectively, would appear to be an anarchy of values, each legitimate in its origin and being. Yet, Santayana is a major cultural and art critic of his day, and he clearly had a sense of community among artists. How is this possible? Primarily, the answer lies in his naturalism. The growth of aesthetic experience is based on the physiological development of the individual and the environment, and, once this is clear, appraisal and community can be understood as natural outgrowths of the material world, fleeting and momentary though they may be.

One of Santayana's best appraisals of twentieth-century art is found in "Penitent Art" (reprinted in *Obiter Scripta*), an essay representing his approach to art criticism. He sustains an evolutionary approach to painting (although he maintains the criticism applies to other arts as well), which he describes as developing in three stages: blooming, flowering, and desiccating. Penitent art is in the last stage when art, having had its initial stages of innocence and then self-consciousness and sophistication, employs elaborate contrivances to retain its former status. When these contrivances dissolve and more genuine forms appear, art is penitent, rightly giving up its previous glory and accepting its present state. Santayana goes on to give an account of pure color and caricature in modern art, which many critics viewed as primitive. But for Santayana such penitent art is highly refined, revealing and enveloping its previous history in simplicity and suggestion. It is the integrity of the art to its heritage and present culture that determines its role in human history. Holding to the past without the spontaneity requisite for the present is a characteristic of dying art. Penitent art delights in the present, responding to the world in an imaginative and spontaneous manner while respecting artistic heritage.

Santayana's sense of community is the subject of "An Aesthetic Soviet." Published in 1927 and reprinted in *Obiter Scripta,* his allusion to the Soviet Union is clear, but by *soviet* Santayana means a "caucus of comrades." A central question is how can there be a community of artists if aesthetic experience is radically individual and momentary. Fundamental to the aesthetic soviet is valuing an image for its pure immediacy. Setting aside personal gain, practical consequences, and patronage to industry or custom, the aesthetic soviet revels in the spontaneous acts and intuitions that are not subject to institutional control. The basis for the community is, as one might suspect, animal motivation and natural circumstances that generate intuition, or consciousness, and enable an individual, and those of a similar nature, to be a part of the aesthetic community. By analogy, Santayana argues that fish swim in schools even though the water has no paths, and just as naturally those with an artistic physical base will be a part of each other's company.

To say that Santayana abandons aesthetics in his later philosophy is not fully accurate. He expanded the notion of aesthetics and subsumed it under a more complete notion of consciousness. Based on delighting in a present image, Santayana develops the idea of a spiritual life—a life that generates consciousness or intuition of images and delights in their presence without projecting one's own interest on them or taking them for anything other than as they appear. Hence, the spiritual life, for Santayana, is not a religious life necessarily; rather, it is a life of aesthetic enjoyment of the present, an enjoyment that is spontaneous and not forced. Individuals who have and cultivate the constitution and environment for such a life are the fortunate ones, and their spiritual life is not bounded by religion, art, or museums. It is, rather, a spontaneous celebration found in everyday living.

[*See also* Beauty; *and* Poetics.]

BIBLIOGRAPHY

Works by Santayana

The Sense of Beauty: Being the Outlines of Aesthetic Theory (1896). In *The Works of George Santayana,* edited by William G. Holzberger and Herman J. Saatkamp, Jr., vol. 2. Cambridge, Mass., 1988.

Interpretations of Poetry and Religion (1900). In *The Works of George Santayana,* edited by William G. Holzberger and Herman J. Saatkamp, Jr., vol. 3. Cambridge, Mass., 1990.

Reason in Art. In *The Life of Reason; or, The Phases of Human Progress,* vol. 4. New York, 1905.

Obiter Scripta: Lectures, Essays and Reviews. Edited by Justus Buchler and Benjamin Schwartz. New York, 1936.

The Idea of Christ in the Gospels: or, God in Man. New York, 1946.

Animal Faith and Spiritual Life. Previously Unpublished and Uncollected Writings by George Santayana with Critical Essays on His Thought. Edited by John Lachs. New York, 1967.

Other Sources

Arnett, Willard E. *Santayana and the Sense of Beauty*. Bloomington, Ind., 1955.

Ashmore, Jerome. *Santayana, Art and Aesthetics*. Cleveland, Ohio, 1966.

Cory, Daniel, ed. *The Letters of George Santayana*. New York, 1955.

Jones, John, and Herman J. Saatkamp, Jr. *George Santayana: A Bibliographical Checklist, 1880–1980*. Bowling Green, Ohio, 1982.

Levinson, Henry Samuel. *Santayana, Pragmatism, and the Spiritual Life*. Chapel Hill, N.C., 1992.

McCormick, John. *George Santayana: A Biography*. New York, 1987.

Rice, Philip Blair. "Foreword." In *The Sense of Beauty* (Modern Library Edition), pp. ix–xii. New York, 1955.

Schilpp, Paul Arthur, ed. *The Philosophy of George Santayana*. Library of Living Philosophers, vol. 2. Evanston, Ill., 1940.

Sprigge, Timothy L. S. *Santayana: An Examination of His Philosophy*. Rev. enl. ed. London and New York, 1995.

HERMAN SAATKAMP, JR.

SARTRE, JEAN-PAUL (1905–1980), French philosopher, playwright, novelist, and political activist. Perhaps no philosopher in the twentieth century has so typified the union of philosophy, politics, and art as Sartre. The presence of these often mutually conflicting interests gives a richness as well as a tension to his aesthetics that surfaced in his famous theory of committed literature. But the speculative source of these concerns lies in his conviction that imaging consciousness is the paradigm of consciousness in general. This explains his ready adoption of Edmund Husserl's phenomenology, with its use of "eidetic reduction" or the free imaginative variation of examples to yield an insight into the essence or intelligible contour of any object in question. Sartre's seminal *The Psychology of Imagination* (1940) employs such a method to reveal the essence of the image. The image, in turn, is the key to his aesthetic theory and practice.

Elements of a Sartrean Aesthetic. Although Sartre never wrote a treatise on aesthetics, one can glean the basic principles of such a theory from his ontology and philosophical psychology with significant additions drawn from his numerous essays on individual artists and interviews regarding his own literary works. Ontologically, he defended a dualism of spontaneity/inertia throughout his career. The spontaneous is usually described as "being-for-itself," though later as "praxis," and the inert is denoted as "being-in-itself" and later as the "practico-inert." The human individual is an ambiguous mixture of both dimensions and so, in Sartre's famous phrase, "is what it is not and is not what it is." This lack of self-coincidence, this inner distance, that we bring to every situation is the source of our freedom and of our creativity. As Sartre summarizes: "Human Reality is free because it is not a self but a presence to self." This ontological freedom is best exhibited in our imaginative creations that invite others to exercise their recreative freedom as they accept the artist's gift and respond to her appeal.

Imaging consciousness. Sartre's phenomenological description warrants the following definition: "The image is an act that intends [literally, "aims at" *(vise)*] an absent or nonexistent object in its corporeality by means of a physical or psychical content which is given not for its own sake but only as an 'analogical representative' [*analogon*] of the intended object." The image is not a thing but a conscious act. As conscious, it "intends" an other-than-consciousness (Husserl's thesis that all consciousness is intentional or *of* an other). Both imaging consciousness and perceptual consciousness intend their objects in their concrete individuality, not as mere simulacra. The object imaginatively presented is one we would perceive, were it a matter of perceptual awareness. But unlike perception, which grasps its object simply as present, imaging attains its object as *present-absent* or, as Sartre will sometimes say, as "derealized."

The analogon. The pivotal term for Sartre's aesthetics is the "analogon" or "intellectual representative." Introduced in *The Psychology of Imagination*, Sartre continued to defend his theory of the analogon throughout his career, eventually applying it to historiography as well, where the historian's narrative it taken as the analogon of the past event. The term denotes the *function* of the medium (the physical or mental content) as rendering the object present-absent, that is, present in the imaginary mode. The written words are the physical medium that serves as the "analogical representative" of the novel, just as the organized pigment on canvas does for the painting, the spoken words and gestures for the theater, or the eye movements for hypnagogic images. Although external images have a sensible residue aside from their function as analogues, Sartre believes that mental images do not. In any case, the physical artifact is the material component of the aesthetic object that appears when and so long as one intends the artifact in the aesthetic manner. Unfortunately, Sartre never provides a theory of analogy to support this pivotal concept, nor does he clearly distinguish between aesthetic and other forms of imaging. His increasing criticism of art for art's sake, however, reflects both his opposition to aestheticism and the correlative presence of the political dimension in his aesthetic theory. The imaginary comes to pervade his entire work. It appears in the "image" of the kind of person one thinks we all should be when one makes a moral choice and it emerges in the ideal of the "city of ends" that directs one's political commitments. Late in life, Sartre would insist that "everything is aesthetic," which should not be taken to imply that nothing is real. Rather, the relation between the imaginary and the real was one of his lifelong concerns. His multivolume study of Gustave Flaubert turns on it, as do his other "biographies" of Charles Baudelaire, Jean Genet, and Stéphane Mallarmé.

Presence. If Sartre's aesthetics is "representational," it is not mimetic. His use of Husserlian intentionality precludes the latter. But the concept of *presence* emerges as a basic aesthetic value for Sartre. Several examples support this claim. In his description of a woman doing an impersonation of Maurice Chevalier, we are led by various signs, such as the announcement that an impersonation is about to occur and the straw hat (cognitive elements), and by the actions of the impersonator herself (the physical analogue), to overlook the incongruity of the situation—for example, a woman of small stature (adoption of the imaginative attitude)—as we make present-absent Chevalier. But what "brings the performance off" is her ability to elicit from us an effective reaction similar to what we would feel in the presence of Chevalier himself. Correlative to this affective consciousness is the affective meaning of Chevalier's face, "a certain indefinable quality which we could call its 'meaning' [*sens*]." This *sens* synthesizes the various signs and gestures, animating them, as it were, with Chevalier's *presence*. Similarly, he distinguishes Francesco Guardi's paintings of Venice from those of Canaletto (Giovanni Antonio Canal) in that the latter are simply reproductive views of the city, "mere identity cards," whereas "Venice is *present* in each of [Guardi's] canvases, as we have all *experienced* but as no one has seen." Again, it is the *sens* of Guardi's work that the other lacks. Suggesting the overlap of aesthetics and historiography in his thought, Sartre argues that the entire Renaissance is present in Michelangelo Buonarroti's *David* and in the *Mona Lisa*'s smile as the German Baroque age is present in a Brandenburg Concerto. *Sens* always denotes a totality achieved through the artist's style.

Sens and signification. Sartre draws a sharp distinction between meaning *(sens)* and signification precisely to account for "meaning" in the nonsignifying arts. *Sens* is correlative to imaging consciousness, signification to signs. Thus, he can claim that music has a *sens* but no signification, which is why he has trouble with the political commitment of "pure music." This is the root of his well-known distinction between "poetry" and prose. "The poetic attitude," he explains, "considers words as things and not as signs. . . . Rather than using it as a *sign* of an aspect of the world, [the poet] sees in the word the image of one of these aspects." And again: "One does not paint significations; one does not put them to music." He concludes that "the empire of signs is prose." But he warns that prose is primarily an attitude of mind, one that uses language for utilitarian purposes. Hence, it is more the *use* to which one places art than its essential character that grounds his distinction between poetry and prose. Sartre only gradually came to acknowledge that at least some "poetry" could be politically committed.

Freedom. Sartre insists that whatever aesthetic principles he may have developed stem from the idea of freedom and not from that of commitment, which is more the byproduct of freedom. The evolution of his understanding of freedom was echoed in his aesthetic theory. Just as Sartrean freedom in the mid-1940s broadened to include that of all people (one cannot be free unless all are free) and thickened to include socioeconomic freedom (freedom in the concrete sense), so the political dimension of artistic creation grew accordingly. Although it is an exaggeration to claim that Sartre abandoned art for political action, it is true that later in life he moved from writing plays and art criticism to devoting himself to the massive study of Flaubert's life and times, *The Family Idiot*. But even this he described as "a novel that is true" and characterized it as a sequel to *The Psychology of Imagination*. What he hoped would be a model of "socialist biography," this complex and prolix work stands as the crowning synthesis of those philosophical, political, and aesthetic interests that marked Sartre's lifework.

The work of art is an invitation from one freedom (the artist's) to another (the viewer's) in a manner that neither forces nor alienates. As such, the artwork is the model of nonalienating communication. But what it communicates is neither information nor emotive values. It invites a free agent to realize itself and thereby "reveal" Being. Human reality is a "revealer," that is, "man is the means by which things are manifested." But if we are inessential to the things revealed (through perceptual consciousness), we are correspondingly essential to the revelation of being in imaging consciousness. Art both as created and as *re*-created by the audience is a revelation of our freedom as revealers of being. Thus, the atheistic Sartre joins more theistic aestheticians in claiming that aesthetic experience is an image of Creation itself. But its source, like that of our freedom, is our consciousness: "the same insufficiency enables man to form images and prevents him from creating being."

The aesthetic event. It follows that, for Sartre, the aesthetic object is more an event than a "thing." Even immobile and spatial objects such as sculpture, for which Sartre showed little appreciation (with the exception of Alberto Giacometti, David Hare, and Alexander Calder), can be seen as aesthetic "events" when the viewer "derealizes" them into analogues for aesthetic enjoyment. This phenomenological aspect of Sartre's theory is buttressed by an existentialist dimension of freedom and its corresponding moral responsibility. Art, when it succeeds, increases our freedom and responsibility. Not that Sartre would subscribe to moralizing or censorship of any kind. In fact, he warned: "Beauty is a value which is only applicable to the imaginary and which requires the negation of the world in its essential structure. That is why it is stupid to confuse the moral with the aesthetic." But his linking of imaging consciousness and freedom makes it impossible, in his words, to produce an authentic work of art that proposes to enslave people or undermine their freedom. Hence, his animus against anti-Semitic "literature" and propagandistic "art."

Sartre and the Genres. As a creative artist in his own right (he was awarded but refused the Nobel prize for literature in 1964), Sartre could claim both the studio and the gallery views of the artwork. Given his ontological commitments, it was natural that his theory should focus on the nature of the artwork and the contrast between representation and imitation.

Literature. Sartre's most influential contribution to literary theory is the set of essays published as *What Is Literature?* in which he draws the prose/poetry distinction and introduces the concept of committed literature. Despite attacks from proponents of the *nouveau roman* among others, he continued to defend this distinction, albeit in a somewhat nuanced form, for the rest of his career.

True to his theory of the imagination, he claims that reading, like the apprehension of any work of art, is a synthesis of perception and creation. But the literary work of art, "though realized *through* language [the *analogon*], is never given *in* language." In fact, the appearance of a work of art is "a new event which cannot *be explained* by anterior data." It is a "directed creation" that, as an absolute beginning, is brought about by the freedom of the reader. He concludes that the writer "appeals to the reader's freedom to collaborate in the production of his work." Sartre's ontology and politics converge in the constitution of the work of art when he writes:

> One cannot address oneself to freedom as such by means of constraint, fascination, or entreaties. There is only one way of attaining it; first by recognizing it, then having confidence in it, and finally, requiring of it an act, an act in its own name, that is, in the name of the confidence that one brings to it.   (1988)

This is what he calls, in his posthumously published *Notebooks for an Ethics* (1992), the "gift-appeal" relationship. He takes it as the paradigm of all nonalienating interpersonal relations. But he does not recognize this gift-appeal phenomenon in nature, so he insists that "our freedom is never called forth by natural beauty."

But *The Family Idiot* reminds us of the role of criticism in Sartre's work, for it constitutes, among other things, a major study of French literary history in the nineteenth century. Although his critical essays on William Faulkner, Albert Camus, Francis Ponge, and others continue to be of interest and his "existential psychoanalyses" of Charles Baudelaire, Jean Genet, and Stéphane Mallarmé remain both insightful and controversial, except for a few occasional pieces, Sartre seems to have abandoned explicit art and literary criticism for political writing in the late 1960s.

Theater. Although his first novel, *Nausea*, made his name in literary circles, he is best known as a playwright. In addition to having written such plays as *The Flies, No Exit, Dirty Hands, The Condemned of Altona,* and *The Devil and the Good Lord,* Sartre reflected at length on the theater as a literary genre in essays and interviews over the years. His ethical and political concerns conspired to produce what has been called "a theater of situations," where the emphasis is on action (intention) and character rather than on the "pessimistic naturalism" of bourgeois deterministic behavior.

Here too his themes reflect his evolving understanding of "freedom" and "responsibility." They echo the political theater of Bertolt Brecht and others. But he appeals to understanding (the *Verstehen* of German social theory) over Brechtian explanation when he recommends that we combine the strengths of dramatic and epic theater, the subjective and the objective, in a postbourgeois theater where the play is presented to the audience as an image in which the spectators sympathetically participate rather than as an object that they view.

Painting. Sartre wrote essays on Jacopo Tintoretto and Titian (Tiziano Vecellio), and on several twentieth-century artists. His phenomenological method is especially apt to describe the absence of imitation in favor of "presentation." Appealing to his basic distinction between signification and *sens,* he remarks that the painter does not wish to trace signs on his canvas, that he wishes to create a thing; and if he gathers together some red, yellow, and green, it is not to give the ensemble a definable signification, that is, so as to refer to another object. He notes that "Tintoretto did not choose that yellow rent in the sky above Golgotha in order to 'signify' anguish or to 'provoke' it; it 'is' anguish and yellow sky at the same time." The "directed creation" of our response takes its cue from the suggestive power of the *analogon.*

But what of abstract painting? How does the theory of the *analogon* fare in this approach? It fares in a manner similar to that of music and other nonrepresentational art. The physical object becomes an *analogon* of itself; in other words, it invites the "presence" of any successful aesthetic object. To claim that such art is "meaningless" is to confuse signification with *sens.* Abstract art has meaning without necessarily carrying any signification. In fact, most "poetic" art will be of this sort. Of course, the emotive and informational components of any *analogon* cannot be discounted. They help to "direct" the re-creative act of the viewer. But these do not point "beyond" themselves as signs of an external object. Rather, they are ingredients in the synthetic "derealizing" act that constitutes the aesthetic object itself.

Sculpture. Given Sartre's valuing of dynamic being-for-itself over inert being-in-itself, it is not surprising that he favored sculptors such as Calder and Giacometti who attempted to overcome the limitations of their medium by appeal to motion and to bidimensionality, respectively. Whereas "for three thousand years sculptors have been carving only cadavers," in Sartre's view, Calder's mobiles exist "halfway between matter and life," while Giacometti confers "absolute distance on his [sculptured] images just as a painter confers absolute distance on the inhabitants of his canvas." True to his concept of the *analogon,* Sartre insists that "a statue truly resembles neither what the model *is* nor what the sculptor *sees.*" As Sartre explains it, Giacometti, for example, has recourse to elongation "to give perceptible expression to pure presence." What gives sculpture aesthetic value in Sartre's eyes is its ability to be what it is not and to not be what it is—like the human subject for which it exists.

Music. Although an amateur pianist himself, Sartre wrote little about music or musicians. Appealing to his *sens*/signification distinction, he claims that the eighteenth century is "present" in the sounds of a Brandenburg Concerto "just as the Renaissance smiles on the lips of the *Mona Lisa.*" But music cannot be "committed" as can prose, for it is a nonsignifying art. Rather, its revolutionary power is a function of the freedom inherent in every work of art as constituting a gift-appeal relationship: "Bach furnished the image of a freedom which, though seeming to remain within a traditional framework, transcended tradition toward a new creation." What Sartre says of the composer expresses his view of any artist: "the artist reflects *by anticipation*" of possibilities not realized in the present state of art or in the society that sustains it. In a pair of interviews on modern music given two years before his death, Sartre reflected on the works of Arnold Schoenberg, Krzysztof Penderecki, Luigi Nono, Iannis Xenakis, and others. Admitting his preference for music as "the art of sounds," he questioned what place is left for beauty in much contemporary "art of noise *(bruit).*" His remarks on Duke Ellington and John Coltrane remind us that he was an aficionado of jazz since his early years.

Art and Life. As the foregoing indicates, Sartre's existentialist aesthetic is a valorization of freedom in its many dimensions. None of these is a flight from reality, which he conceives as the realm of purposive action and dialectical counterfinality. Although his first novel, *Nausea,* seemed to defend art as a kind of salvation, his subsequent theory of "committed" literature in the 1940s placed art at the service of social justice, and his much-publicized abandonment of imaginative literature for political action in the 1960s was more apparent than real. Sartre's continued work on his "true novel" of the life and times of Flaubert was both a labor of creative imagination and an act of political and social critique. He never abandoned his conviction formed in the immediate postwar years that the artist has a social responsibility inherent in the freedom of the human condition not to pander to those who would deny this freedom but to foster it by the risk of artistic creativity, which is an act of confidence in the other's freedom. For Sartre, the moral, the political, and the aesthetic coalesce in the authentic work of art.

[*See also* Imagination; Literature, *article on* Literary Aesthetics; Marxism; Phenomenology; *and* Theater.]

BIBLIOGRAPHY

Works by Sartre

Essays in Aesthetics. Edited and translated by Wade Baskin. New York, 1963.
Literary and Philosophical Essays. Translated by Annette Michelson. New York, 1955.
Œuvres romanesques. Edited by Michel Contat and Michel Rybalka. Paris, 1981.
Sartre on Theater. Edited by Michel Contat and Michel Rybalka, translated by Frank Jellinek. New York, 1976.
The Family Idiot: Gustave Flaubert, 1821–1857. 5 vols. Translated by Carol Cosman. Chicago, 1981–1993.
The Psychology of Imagination (1940). New York, 1948.
What Is Literature? and Other Essays. Cambridge, Mass., 1988.

Other Sources

Barnes, Hazel E. *Sartre and Flaubert.* Chicago, 1981.
Bauer, George H. *Sartre and the Artist.* Chicago, 1969.
Flynn, Thomas R. "The Role of the Image in Sartre's Aesthetic." *Journal of Aesthetics and Art Criticism* 33.4 (Summer 1975): 431–442.
Goldthorpe, Rhiannon. *Sartre: Literature and Theory.* Cambridge and New York, 1984.
Hollier, Denis. *The Politics of Prose: Essay on Sartre.* Translated by Jeffrey Mehlman. Minneapolis, 1986.
Howells, Christina. *Sartre's Theory of Literature.* London, 1979.
Jameson, Fredric. *Marxism and Form: Twentieth-Century Dialectical Theories of Literature.* Princeton, N.J., 1971.
Jameson, Fredric. *Sartre: The Origins of a Style.* 2d ed. New York, 1984.
Kaelin, Eugene F. *An Existentialist Aesthetic: The Theories of Sartre and Merleau-Ponty.* Madison, 1962.
Kaelin, Eugene F. "On *Meaning* in Sartre's Aesthetic Theory." In *Jean-Paul Sartre: Contemporary Approaches to His Philosophy,* edited by Hugh J. Silverman and Frederick A. Elliston, pp. 124–140. Pittsburgh, 1980.
Sicard, Michel. *Essais sur Sartre, Entretiens avec Sartre, 1975–1979.* Paris, 1989.
Tenney, Charles D. "Aesthetics in the Philosophy of Jean-Paul Sartre." In *The Philosophy of Jean-Paul Sartre,* edited by Paul Arthur Schilpp, pp. 112–138. LaSalle, Ill., 1981.

THOMAS R. FLYNN

SAUSSURE, FERDINAND DE. *See* Metonymy; Semiotics, *article on* Semiotics as a Theory of Art; *and* Structuralism.

SCHAPIRO, MEYER (1904–1996), Lithuanian-born American art historian. Raised in Brooklyn, he was first exposed to art in evening classes at the Hebrew Education Society Settlement House, Schapiro continued his studio training at the art school of the Brooklyn Museum. His membership in the Young Peoples Socialist League expanded the political and ideological dimensions of his early education. Schapiro entered Columbia College in 1920 at the age of sixteen; his course of studies was broad, including Latin, modern languages, ancient and modern literature, anthropology, philosophy, mathematics, and art history—a range that was to inform and characterize his work throughout his career. He continued his graduate studies at Columbia—where, he confessed, his classes with Franz Boas and John Dewey were more important than any in art history. In 1929, he submitted his dissertation for the Ph.D., the first in fine arts and archaeology awarded by Columbia. "The Romanesque Sculpture of Moissac," parts of which were published in the *Art Bulletin* of 1931, opened entirely new critical perspectives for the study of medieval art (*Selected Papers*, vol. 1).

Schapiro traveled widely in Europe and the Near East in 1926–1927, viewing a vast range of art, preparing the foundations for his subsequent work, and leaving behind a trail of anecdotal legends that continued to be recounted long afterward by those who met the brilliant young graduate student—including Bernard Berenson, who compared the perceptive eloquence of the "very handsome youth" to the sweetness of Solomon's discourse on the hyssop in the wall.

Schapiro began his teaching career at Columbia in 1928 and rose through the academic ranks, becoming full professor in 1952; he was named University Professor in 1965 and became University Professor Emeritus upon his retirement in 1973. Elected a member of the National Institute of Arts and Letters in 1976, he was awarded a five-year MacArthur Foundation Fellowship in 1987.

Throughout his career, Schapiro moved between the Columbia campus on Morningside Heights and his home neighborhood in Greenwich Village, between the university and the city at large. From the late 1930s and through the 1940s, he lectured as well at the New School for Social Research, thereby reaching the wider community of the New York art world, especially the artists, in the years when New York was becoming the dynamic center of contemporary art. An engaged intellectual and a painter himself, Schapiro was as comfortable in the studios of the artists as in the realms of ideas and politics. Such a complex reach of experience was an essential component of the dialectics of his critical achievement.

Between Past and Present: The Reclamation of the Artist. As an art historian, Schapiro moved between the medieval and the modern, in full awareness of the reciprocal dynamics of his dual focus. His experience of developments in modern art opened him to phenomena in older art that had hitherto been ignored or uncomprehended by a too generalized or limited art historiography. Qualities of "perfection, coherence, and unity of form and content"—the subject of a later essay (1966; *Selected Papers*, vol. 4)—he recognized in the Romanesque sculpture of Moissac as well as in the paintings of the modern era. To each he brought a searching precision of analysis. He was attentive to the nuanced decisions, conscious and unconscious, of the sculptors of Moissac, Souillac (1939; *Selected Papers*, vol. 1), and Silos (1939; *Selected Papers*, vol. 1); that same close critical attention allowed him to articulate the creating brush strokes and constructive color choices of the Impressionists and Henri Matisse (1932).

The larger aim of Schapiro's project might be termed the reclamation of the artist in and from history. From the beginning his method involved effectively reconstructing the creative process; through close and sympathetic stylistic de-

scription he discovered unsuspected sources of vital expression in art. From the expressive physiognomy of the work of art, discerned in accordance with what he termed "general psychological laws," there emerged a persona of its creator. Behind the style, Schapiro sought and found the artist. To support his search for the explicitly "artistic character" of works of medieval art, he enlisted as unlikely allies from the medieval past harsh but sensitive critics such as Saint Bernard of Clairvaux. Reading Bernard's diatribe against the Cluniac art of his time in positive terms, Schapiro discovered a powerful voice on behalf of his own radical thesis "On the Aesthetic Attitude in Romanesque Art" (1947; *Selected Papers*, vol. 1): namely, that within church art there had emerged "a new sphere of artistic creation . . . imbued with values of spontaneity, individual fantasy, delight in color and movement, and the expression of feeling that anticipate modern art." This creativity was to be found, significantly, on the margins of the religious work, and it inspired a new appreciation for the beauty of the materials and craft of art distinct from its religious meaning. Invoking the "aestheticism" of troubadour poetry, Schapiro set out, in effect, to secularize the achievements of the medieval artist, to isolate his professional ambition and skill.

The marginal figures of jongleurs at Silos, he argued, affirmed "the self-consciousness of an independent artistic virtuosity." In contrast to the traditional, exclusively religious interpretation of this art, he emphasized the significance of these

lay artists, free, uninstitutionalized entertainers whose performance is valued directly for its sensuous and artisan qualities; just as in modern art, which is wholly secular, painters so often represent figures from the studio or from an analogous world of entertainment—acrobats, musicians, and harlequins—consciously or unconsciously affirming their own autonomy as performers and their conception of art as a spectacle for the senses." (Ibid.)

The Dialectics of Marginality: The Social Bases of Art. Even as he sought the individual personality of the artist in the anonymous creations of the Middle Ages, Schapiro knew well that "individuality is a social fact." The artists he discovered in history were embedded in and conditioned by larger realities, material and ideological; their prospects were hardly unlimited. It was precisely the tense dialectic between the individual and the social that attracted him. That tension reflected the complexities of his own personal conflicts and commitments, including his Jewish background and his socialist beliefs. If, in his personal life, he deliberately rejected religion as a barrier to intellectual freedom, he remained committed to the ideals of socialism; he assumed a leading position for his moral principles in the political debates of the radical left in the late 1930s.

At the first American Artists' Congress against War and Fascism in 1936, Schapiro delivered a paper titled "The Social Bases of Art." Possibly against expectation, he opened by denying that his intention was "to reduce art to economics or sociology or politics." Art, he insisted, "has its own conditions which distinguish it from other activities. It operates with its own special materials and according to general psychological laws." He went on to define the marginal situation of the artist in modern society, his professional isolation: "Yet helpless as he is to act on the world, he shows in his art an astonishing ingenuity and joy in transforming the shapes of familiar things." Not unlike his medieval predecessors, then, the modern artist liberates himself from oppressive social constraint through the aesthetic, the free operations of his art. Schapiro's was a dialectics of marginality.

In the *Marxist Quarterly* of January–March 1937, he published a paper titled "The Nature of Abstract Art" (*Selected Papers,* vol. 2). Responding to the pioneering exhibition Cubism and Abstract Art organized by Alfred H. Barr, Jr., at the Museum of Modern Art, Schapiro countered the essentially formalist schema of Barr's art history and its assumption of the autonomy of art, its presumption of the independence of modern abstract art from modern historical realities. Schapiro insisted instead on the moral dimensions of that art, its intimate, if complex, rapport with the values of modern bourgeois life.

The shifting, unconventional, unregulated vision of early Impressionism offered "an implicit criticism of symbolic social and domestic formalities." Schapiro isolated the "informal and spontaneous sociability" of Impressionist imagery, the urban idylls of bourgeois recreation. Where others had celebrated the presumed insignificance of subject matter in this art *pour l'art*, he saw the very choice of subjects as integral to the new aesthetic devices of the art. Impressionist touch and broken color found their social base in Schapiro's criticism:

> In enjoying realistic pictures of his surroundings as a spectacle of traffic and changing atmospheres, the cultivated rentier was experiencing in its phenomenal aspect that mobility of the environment, the market and of industry to which he owed his income and his freedom. And in the new Impressionist techniques which broke things up into finely discriminated points of color, as well as in the "accidental" momentary vision, he found, in a degree hitherto unknown in art, conditions of sensibility closely related to those of the urban promenader and the refined consumer of luxury goods.

With a critical sensibility that joined the aesthetic perception of the studio—as a student he had been inspired by the writings of Roger Fry, and he himself continued to draw and paint—with a Marxist vision grounded in social and material reality, Schapiro's essay established an entirely new basis for the understanding of modern art, one that acknowledged it as part of a larger social life. He made the visual delights of the bourgeois art of Impressionism more intelligible and much more interesting, and he demonstrated the complexity of values, "the burden of contemporary experience," inherent in more recent abstract art, which "bears within itself at almost every point the mark of the changing material and psychological conditions surrounding modern culture." Yet, these were the conditions, ultimately, of personal expression: "there is a burden of feeling underlying this 'geometrical' art," he declared of the *White on White* of Kazimir Malevich.

The Correlation of Form and Meaning. In the essay "On Perfection, Coherence, and Unity of Form and Content" (1966; *Selected Papers,* vol. 4), Schapiro addressed the "ascription of certain qualities to the work of art as a whole . . . , which are regarded as conditions of beauty." It was the last of the three that most engaged his attention, for the dynamic relationship between content and form and the distinction between content and subject constituted core issues for him. "Content and form," he wrote, "are plural concepts that comprise many regions and many orders within the same work." The essay epitomizes many aspects of Schapiro's larger effort. Early in his career he had argued the perfection and coherence of the Romanesque monuments, and his critical focus had always remained on the relation of part to whole. Now, considering Michelangelo's Sistine Chapel ceiling, he again felt compelled to acknowledge the content of form, the "pictorial meaning of each figure as a form" in its "unmistakable physiognomy." Like the anonymous Romanesque carver, the celebrated Renaissance master was to be reclaimed for art:

> Here the forms have become for us the main content of the work in a literal sense; they speak to us powerfully and we feel that we have perceived through them the force of the artist's creative powers, his imagination and conception of man, his style as a living person.

Seeking to explain stylistic change in "From Mozarabic to Romanesque in Silos" (1939; *Selected Papers,* vol. 1), Schapiro defined his method as the "critical correlation of the forms and meanings in the images with historical conditions of the same period and region." That method, with its essentially Marxist assumptions, proved more tractable and fruitful in confronting problems in nineteenth-century art, as demonstrated in "Courbet and Popular Imagery: An Essay on Realism and Naïveté" (1940–1941; *Selected Papers,* vol. 2). Woven into this study of the origins of realism in a "consciousness of the community," awakened by the Revolution of 1848, were themes that Schapiro found central to the values of modern art: a direct engagement of reality, a rejection of authority, an appreciation of the primitive and the naive—especially in the drawings of children.

The assumed correlation of form and meaning is what allowed Schapiro to move so easily between the large and small dimensions of style, between the work of art as a manifestation of shared social values and as the most personal expression; it is what permitted him to identify the work so intimately with its maker. In "The Still Life as a Personal Object" (1968; *Selected Papers,* vol. 4), Schapiro rejected Heidegger's reading of a pair of shoes painted by Vincent van Gogh as those of a peasant woman, and therefore redolent of the earth and symbolic of the world of the peasant. Instead, he identified them as the artist's own and argued the meaning of such identity, as "a memorable piece of his own life, a sacred relic." In "Further Notes on Heidegger and van Gogh" (1994; *Selected Papers,* vol. 4), he wrote of the painting as a "picture of objects seen and felt by the artist as a significant part of himself—he faces himself like a mirrored image—chosen, isolated, carefully arranged, and addressed to himself."

Precisely that identity, of image and maker, charged Schapiro's most sustained essay on the subject, "The Apples of Cézanne: An Essay on the Meaning of Still-Life" (1968; *Selected Papers,* vol. 2). Establishing the special place of apples in Cézanne's biography—in his study of literature and his own poetic efforts and in his early friendship with Émile Zola—Schapiro proceeded to demonstrate the significance of choice of subject matter to meaning in the genre itself and of the very act of depicting such objects. Acknowledging that in Cézanne's "habitual representation of the apples as a theme by itself there is a latent erotic sense, an unconscious symbolizing of repressed desire," Schapiro nonetheless admitted that such a formulation leaves much unexplained. Although responsive to the possibilities of psychoanalytic theory, he had severely criticized Sigmund Freud's interpretive essay on Leonardo da Vinci for the a priori limitations of its focus, its failure to recognize the contributing conditions of a larger social world, and its cultural conventions ("Leonardo and Freud: An Art-Historical Study" [1956; *Selected Papers,* vol. 4]). In considering Cézanne's apples, he expanded the discussion to engage that larger world and to explore the more general implications of the painter's activity and choice of subject, the synaesthesia of its appeal, especially to touch and taste. The apples are the "themes par excellence of an empirical standpoint wherein our knowledge of proximate objects, and especially of the instrumental, is the model or ground of all knowledge." He goes on to quote George Herbert Mead: "The reality of what we see is what we can handle."

The personal world of the tabletop, with its idiosyncratic selection of assembled objects, became for modern artists, the Cubists especially, the "plane of our active traversal of the world, into an intimate vertical surface and field of random manipulation," Schapiro wrote in "The Social Bases of Art" (1936). Schapiro's phenomenology was built from the full range of his own experience, as a viewer, a reader, and a painter. But it was particularly on his deep understanding of the creative choices of the artist, the formal decisions and marking gestures, that his vision was based.

The Operations of Art: Frame and Field. Schapiro's criticism was essentially empirical, a direct encounter with the work. On a larger scale, he was involved in a search for the operational principles that distinguished art, and his main concern as a scholar was with those periods in the history of art when the basic elements of image making were subject to the most fundamental pressures and reevaluation. In the dialectical conflict between frame and field, he located the tension between the artist and the determining social order; this was the arena of creative challenge, latent with possibilities. In Impressionism, as in Hiberno-Saxon and Romanesque art, the picture plane itself is viewed as a dynamic field of conflicting energies and ambiguous relationships, the resolution of which resides in the inventive act of design—and in the responsive act of interpretation.

Those elements and principles of pictorial representation that concerned Schapiro throughout his studies he most succinctly and systematically enumerated in a paper titled "On Some Problems in the Semiotics of Visual Art: Field and Vehicle in Image-Signs" (1969; *Selected Papers,* vol. 4). The issues themselves go directly to the heart of image making in its several dimensions—historical, cultural, psychological. Schapiro begins his discussion with the invention of the smooth prepared surface, reminding the reader that "such a field corresponds to nothing in nature or mental imagery." Related to this prepared ground is the concept of its boundaries: "we tend to take for granted the regular margin and frame as essential features of the image," but we are then reminded that the frame itself is a relatively late invention. Taking nothing for granted in the mechanics of picture making, Schapiro continues by isolating still further "non-mimetic elements of the image-sign and their role in constituting the sign." He isolates position and direction within the context of the field, the relative values of high and low, right and left, and the format of the field itself.

Finally, he turns to the sign-bearing matter of the picture, the "image-substance of inked or painted lines and spots." These are nonmimetic elements that have properties different from the objects they represent. The line that bounds a depicted face may be thick or thin, continuous or broken, and, whereas those qualities may lend a particular character to the face rendered, the line itself remains "an artificial mark with properties of its own." The ambivalence of the alternating function of the mark, mimetically referring to the face it denotes or graphically declaring its own independent existence, epitomizes the situation of the surface as a basic locus of tension and conflict. These contradictions constitute a crucial part of the aesthetic experience. "The artist and the sensitive viewer of the work of art are characterized by their ability to shift attention freely from one aspect to the other, but above all, to discriminate and judge the qualities of the picture substance itself." (Schapiro developed this theme in the essay "Eugène Fromentin as Critic" [1949; *Selected Papers,* vol. 4], which may be read as a highly personal credo.)

Schapiro quite naturally adduced as his example Impressionist painting, "in which the parts have been freed from the rule of detailed correspondence to the parts of an object." Throughout, in his lectures and in his writing, he consistently presented this art as central to any view of the art of the twentieth century, for in it the terms of the debate between the mimetic and the nonmimetic, between image-sign and image-substance, were fully articulated. If abstract art has capitalized on the liberation of the mark in representational art, the independent stroke nonetheless retains an indelibly physiognomic character, determined by "many of the qualities and formal relationships of the preceding mimetic art."

The Physiognomics of Expression. "The picture-sign seems to be through and through mimetic." This declaration may stand as key to Schapiro's own aesthetic values. In a different art-historical context, criticizing the polarities of another scholar who had posited in Romanesque monumental art a "contradiction" between architecture and sculpture, a contrast of order and disorder, Schapiro suggested instead a distinction between "constructive and physiognomic forms" ("On Geometrical Schematism in Romanesque Art" [1932; *Selected Papers*, vol. 1]). His selection of terms here implicates a system of values that extends beyond merely formal distinctions, for in Schapiro's usage, whether in regard to medieval or modern art, "physiognomic" properties suggest the deliberately expressive, the willfully inventive, the projection of human feeling and freedom. He himself responded to the "exuberant fantasy which delights us in Romanesque art," in the variety of capitals in an arcade, the individualization of the parts regardless of their functional identity, in the "wild involvement of monstrous aggressive beasts and human figures" in a Cistercian manuscript, and which he found "astoundingly modern in their freedom of conception" ("On the Aesthetic Attitude in Romanesque Art" [1947; *Selected Papers*, vol. 1]).

It is in the perception and analysis of such freedom and inventiveness that Schapiro consistently made reference to the concept and function of the frame, the "constructive" context within which he gauged the operations of the "physiognomic" element. In his vision, the two elements interact, creating that dynamic interplay that will define the field itself and its special properties, an arena projected by, even as it hosts, the forces of creative freedom.

What might be termed the humanism of Schapiro's critical attitude can be further gauged in his discussions of another set of basic options in pictorial representation: the alternative between frontal and profile. In *Words and Pictures: On the Literal and the Symbolic in the Illustration of a Text* (1973), this distinction informs a discussion of aspects of narration. Schapiro builds on a linguistic model: The profile is like the grammatical form of the third person, "the impersonal 'he' or 'she' with its concordantly inflected verb," whereas the frontal view of the face "corresponds to the role of the 'I' in speech with its complementary 'you'." Such grammatical analogies, however, retain their full social phenomenology: The profile face "is detached from the viewer and belongs with the body in action (or in an intransitive state) in a space shared with other profiles on the surface of the image" (ibid.). The frontal face enters into a dialogic relationship with the viewer, seeming to "exist both for us and for itself in a space virtually continuous with our own" (ibid.). Schapiro is ultimately less concerned with the generalized rule than with the individual case, and he carries this concern directly to the level of affect and response.

Too keenly aware of the variety, the alternatives and inflections, available within any determining context—and especially to the vigorously inventive artist—Schapiro stops short of the definition of laws:

> The plurality of meaning in each of these two appearances of the head would seem to exclude a consistent explanation based on inherent qualities of the profile and the frontal or full-face view. It is like the difficulty of finding in colors a universal, culturally unconditioned ground for their symbolic use, though we experience colors as strongly charged with feeling.   (Ibid.)

Schapiro's critical language is characterized by a special candor, a clarity of thought and directness—even simplicity—of expression. The markers of his argument are references to the essentials of the art: frame and field, figure and ground, mimetic and nonmimetic. Such basic terms, however, are never presented as abstractions or as absolute values. He refused to subordinate the artist's freedom to the laws of art; he insisted on that freedom, even if it be latent rather than actual.

Questions of Style. It was this attitude that made it difficult for Schapiro to accept the great descriptive and explanatory models of the earlier generation of theorists he so admired for their intellectual ambition. His earliest published paper (1925) was a discussion of Emanuel Löwy's *Rendering of Nature in Early Greek Art*, which analyzed the development from archaism to realism in seven stages. Here Schapiro first confronted the concept of the archaic, including its analogies to other primitive arts and to the drawings of children; it is a concept that was to prove central to his own investigations of Romanesque art. As important, the young Schapiro, uncomfortable with the traditional valorization of realism, began his own search for fundamental principles, asking the questions that were to challenge him throughout his career, the search for "a comprehensive study of the 'forms' of art." In the magisterial article "Style" (1953; *Selected Papers*, vol. 4), he reviewed the efforts of the earlier theorists: the stylistic polarities postulated by Heinrich Wölfflin, the cyclical pattern conceived by Paul Frankl, the phenomenological duality of Alois Riegl, as well as Löwy's progressive stages. Each is found wanting, as is the crude application of Marx to the explanation of style by the forms of social life.

"A theory of style adequate to the psychological and historical problems has still to be created," Schapiro concludes, somewhat wistfully. "It waits for a deeper knowledge of the principles of form construction and expression and for a unified theory of the processes of social life in which the practical means of life as well as emotional behavior are comprised."

Through his teaching, public lectures, and publications, as well his direct impact on several generations of practicing artists, Schapiro offered a model of engaged criticism. By the example of his own involvement and the nature of his inquiry, he affirmed the value of art as an essential unifying quality of humanity.

[*See also* Marxism; *and* Style.]

BIBLIOGRAPHY

Works by Schapiro

Words and Pictures: On the Literal and the Symbolic in the Illustration of a Text. The Hague, 1973.

Selected Works, vol. 1, *Romanesque Art.* New York, 1977.

Selected Works, vol. 2, *Modern Art, 19th and 20th Centuries.* New York, 1978.

Selected Works, vol. 3, *Late Antique, Early Christian and Mediaeval Art.* New York, 1979.

Selected Works, vol. 4, *Theory and Philosophy of Art: Style, Artist, and Society.* New York, 1994.

Essays Cited

"On Emanuel Löwy's *Rendering of Nature in Early Greek Art.*" *The Arts* 8 (September 1925): 170–172.

"The Romanesque Sculpture of Moissac." *Art Bulletin* 13.3 (September 1931): 249–352; 13.4 (December 1931): 464–531. Reprinted in *Selected Papers,* vol. 1, pp. 131–264.

"Matisse and Impressionism." *Androcles* 1.1 (February 1932): 21–36.

"Über den Schematismus in der Romanischen Kunst." *Kritische Berichte zu kunstgeschichtlichen Literatur* 1 (1932–1933): 1–21. Reprinted as "On Geometrical Schematism in Romanesque Art," in *Selected Papers,* vol. 1, pp. 265–284.

"The Social Bases of Art." In *First American Artists' Congress,* pp. 31–37. New York, 1936.

"The Nature of Abstract Art." *Marxist Quarterly* 1.1 (January–March 1937): 77–98. Reprinted in *Selected Papers,* vol. 2, pp. 185–211.

"From Mozarabic to Romanesque in Silos." *Art Bulletin* 21.4 (December 1939): 313–374. Reprinted in *Selected Papers,* vol. 1, pp. 28–101.

"The Sculptures of Souillac." In *Medieval Studies in Memory of A. Kingsley Porter,* edited by Wilhelm R. W. Koehler, pp. 359–387. Cambridge, Mass., 1939. Reprinted in *Selected Papers,* vol. 1, pp. 102–130.

"Courbet and Popular Imagery: An Essay on Realism and Naïveté." *Journal of the Warburg and Courtauld Institutes* 4.3–4 (1940–1941): 164–191. Reprinted in *Selected Papers,* vol. 2, pp. 47–85.

"On the Aesthetic Attitude in Romanesque Art." In *Art and Thought: Issued in Honour of Dr. Ananda K. Coomaraswamy,* pp. 130–150. London, 1947. Reprinted in *Selected Papers,* vol. 1, pp. 1–27.

"Fromentin as a Critic." *Partisan Review* 16.1 (January 1949): 25–51. Reprinted in *Selected Papers,* vol. 4, pp. 103–134.

"Style." In *Anthropology Today,* edited by Alfred Kroeber, pp. 287–312. Chicago, 1953. Reprinted in *Selected Papers,* vol. 4, pp. 51–102.

"Leonardo and Freud: An Art-Historical Study." *Journal of the History of Ideas* 17.2 (April 1956): 147–178. Reprinted in *Selected Papers,* vol. 4, pp. 153–300.

"On Perfection, Coherence, and Unity of Form and Content." In *Art and Philosophy: A Symposium,* edited by Sidney Hook, pp. 3–15. New York, 1966. Reprinted in *Selected Papers,* vol. 4, pp. 33–50.

"The Apples of Cézanne: An Essay on the Meaning of Still-Life." *Art News Annual* 34 (1968): 35–53. Reprinted in *Selected Papers,* vol. 2, pp. 1–38.

"The Still Life as a Personal Object: A Note on Heidegger and van Gogh." In *The Reach of Mind: Essays in Memory of Kurt Goldstein,* edited by Marianne L. Simmel, pp. 203–209. New York, 1968. Reprinted in *Selected Papers,* vol. 4, pp. 135–142.

"On Some Problems in the Semiotics of Visual Art: Field and Vehicle in Image-Signs." *Semiotica* 1.3 (1969): 223–242. Reprinted in *Selected Papers,* vol. 4, pp. 1–32.

Other Sources

Epstein, Helen. "Meyer Schapiro: A Passion to Know and Make Known." *Artnews* 82.5 (May 1983): 60–85; 82.6 (Summer 1983): 84–95.

Special issue "On the Work of Meyer Schapiro." *Social Research* 45.1 (Spring 1978).

Oxford Art Journal 17.1 (1994). Special issue devoted to Meyer Schapiro.

Schapiro, Lillian Milgram. *Meyer Schapiro: The Bibliography.* New York, 1995.

DAVID ROSAND

SCHELLING, FRIEDRICH WILHELM JOSEPH VON

(1775–1854), German idealist philosopher. Schelling contributed to aesthetics early in his career, especially in 1798–1803, years spent in Jena with the Romantic critics Karl Wilhelm Friedrich von Schlegel, and August Wilhelm von Schlegel, but close to the classicist Weimar of Friedrich von Schiller and Johann Wolfgang von Goethe. His work in aesthetics was theoretical rather than critical, exploring the interfaces between epistemology, psychology, and hermeneutics or philosophy of language. On the formal side, he followed Immanuel Kant in treating aesthetics as a quasi-cognitive domain, but deepened the theory of "aesthetic genius" by adding an account, inspired by Baruch Spinoza and Goethe, of unconscious knowing and producing in the artist. By focusing on the dialectic of conscious and unconscious intention in the artist's psyche, Schelling shifted the inquiry from the cognitive processes of the artist to the work of art itself, to its multiply determined (or "symbolic") meaning inside the public world of cultural objects. Implicit in his treatment of aesthetic production as the function of imagination (*Einbildungskraft*) was a general theory of semiotics (or "schematism"). Schelling found symbolism or schematism at work in all artistic domains: formative, plastic, and literary arts; in this he differed from August Schlegel, who thought the medium of language necessary for the highest arts.

On the side of content, Schelling's originality lay in his identification of the content of fine art with that of religion, with Greek mythology serving as the world-historical center of gravity for both art and religion. Rather than preferring classical to Romantic art, or the reverse, Schelling argued for a necessary unity of objective and subjective modes of symbolic communication. Modern art—Romantic, Christian, optimistic, embodying the poetics (and politics) of freedom—is meaningful only in contrast to the structured form and necessity embodied in classic art and pre-Christian religions. In his critical remarks on specific works, Schelling generally followed Schiller's in the formative and plastic arts and August Schlegel's in the literary arts, but he defined himself as a systematic philosopher, not a practicing critic. Whatever the thematic thread that shaped his total systematic view—identity philosophy (1800–1806), or philosophy of history (1809–1815), or philosophy of God (1821–1846)—he always viewed philosophy of art as one specialized but culturally accessible form of philosophical metatheory.

In his early years (1794–1800), Schelling worked alongside Johann Gottlieb Fichte to develop a self-standing philosophical system based on Kant's critical writings. Fichte brought Kant's three forms of reason—intellect, will, and judgment—under the umbrella of practical reason. The I is in essence act or self-deed. Affected by a vanishing but irremovable not-I, the I's act is intelligence. Expressed within the natural and social worlds, it becomes the various forms of will: biological drive, emotive striving, arbitrary choice, submission to social and moral laws. The watchword of Fichte's Kantianism was the "primacy of praxis." It left a deep imprint on Goethe's *Faust*, on Friedrich Hölderlin's poetry, and on the critical theories of the Schlegel brothers.

While Schelling supported the program of Fichte's *Wissenschaftslehre* as the logical ground for any transcendental philosophy, his early essays of 1794–1800 search for an alternate real ground for systematic philosophy. The 1797 *Ideas for a Philosophy of Nature* supplements Fichte's account of consciousness with a philosophy of nature inspired by Kant's *Metaphysical Foundations for Natural Philosophy*. Schelling argued that the same opposed activities that transcendental philosophy postulates to explain the "I think" of consciousness also explain the ladder of natural phenomena, from matter up to the animated body that is the platform of consciousness. Just as the I is "constructed" (i.e., explained) as a dynamic interplay of two activities, one unbounded, another limiting, so matter's basic property of filling space is explained as a dynamic balance between expansive and contractive forces.

A second attempt to systematize Kant's philosophy is found in the 1800 *System of Transcendental Idealism*. Following the clue of Schiller's *Letters on the Aesthetic Education of Humanity*, Schelling makes aesthetics the region that unites theoretical and practical philosophy, not the passive experience of viewer, auditor, or reader, but the peculiar productive activity of the artist: "aesthetic intuition." In Kant's language, an intuition of *x* is both my representation of *x* and the production of the *x* represented. In producing the work of art, the "intuitive" creator performs a knowing-as-doing that is more fundamental than the nonproductive knowing

and the noncognitive production that differentiate "knowing" and "doing" in other phenomenal contexts. Also, conscious and unconscious productivity, the forces constructive of the natural and social worlds, merge here in the artist's psyche as the interplay of conscious and unconscious intention. In the very independence of the finished work of art from the material and psychological sources of its production is proof that the artist produces more than she literally knows.

How can artistic production ground a philosophical system or serve as the capstone for a series of other philosophical inquiries? Schelling argued that because the artist's activity—aesthetic intuition—taps into the primary divided energy that first produces an objective world for the I and then ceaselessly conquers its objectivity by the I's knowledge and action, it is not a case of ordinary activity but a laying bare of foundations. What kinship can there be between the ground of being and the artist's activity?

In the 1800 *System*, Schelling utilized a vocabulary given currency by Kant and Fichte for naming the ultimate active ground of being. Kant had defined sensible intuition in opposition to a hypothetical intellectual intuition where, for example, God knowing *y* would also mean God realizes *y* or causes it to exist; Kant first noted in 1770 that artists seem to have some faculty analogous to this conceptually defined divine creativity. Fichte had used the term to designate the immediate certainty of agency involved in self-consciousness, the *doing* involved in the thinking of "I think." Schelling now uses *intellectual intuition* to indicate at the start of the system a pure (thus empirically unavailable) act of spontaneity that transcendental philosophy must postulate to explain self-consciousness: the analytical I = I that mutates into the synthetic I = ~I. The philosopher imitates this primal act by a freely undertaken conscious exercise—mediated by language, hence by imagination and by time, the primary schematism. The philosophical narrative that results is a "construction of consciousness"; in it the original synthesis of the I, which would be both conceptually clear and empirically there if the philosopher *had* the (merely) postulated intellectual intuition, is unpacked into epochs of the "history" of understanding and will. Schelling is clear that this "history of consciousness" is just an explanatory device; his work as a philosopher is primarily imaginative in Kant's sense: it translates the all-at-once of the I's self-constituting act (the fundamental synthesis that cannot be understood) into a series of acts that are at once objective and subjective (and that explain each other, at least minimally, in their succession). These acts form a "pragmatic history" of consciousness—not an empirical history, but a heuristic construction that shows how the features of self-consciousness and of objective nature nest inside the original synthetic act like Chinese boxes.

Despite the brilliance of these initial moves, Schelling was unable to close the story of the unfolding consciousness with a return to original identity. The inability rested on a logical prohibition. Because transcendental philosophy aimed at establishing the conditions for the possibility of experience, what explains and what is to be explained must be of different orders, one hypothetical, the other empirical. If the transcendental philosopher posits spontaneous self-realizing activity as the nonempirical explanatory element, and meanwhile uses analysis of that activity to explain the structure of both natural and social phenomenal worlds, he must in the end bring forward some empirical *explanandum* that is obviously *a case* of spontaneous self-realizing activity. If the tie-down to experience is lacking, there is no explanation, and a metaphysical fantasy has been perpetrated. Schelling was able to argue to the case of spontaneously self-realizing activity ("aesthetic intuition") only from the ambiguous status of the work of art once it is detached from the process of its production. Because a work—say, Goethe's *Faust*—has different meanings to various actors, directors, and critics, Schelling maintained that the work carried an unanalyzable multitude of meanings, and that the artist, consciously and unconsciously, endowed the play with all these meanings. He thus thought that the work displayed the existence of the infinite (at least the indefinitely multiple) in the finite and that, therefore, the artist's aesthetic intuition was an empirical case of the postulated intellectual intuition, everywhere informing but factually missing in the philosopher's activity. Schelling thus surmised that aesthetic intuition was the phenomenal analogue of the (empirically absent) intellectual intuition claimed by the philosopher.

Although the transcendental stance of Schelling's early philosophy and the prominence he accorded aesthetic intuition in the 1800 *System* were not permanent features of his philosophy, they captured the political, moral, and religious yearning of the Romantic poets and literary critics who were first Fichte's, then Schelling's, fellows at the University of Jena. These features of Schelling's thought found their way into Samuel Taylor Coleridge's *Biographia Literaria,* and from there into English Romantic literature and American Transcendental philosophy. That Coleridge assembled its twelfth chapter on productive imagination from various early texts of Schelling occasioned the charges and countercharges about plagiarism that have followed that author and his editors.

Schelling's preference for aesthetic intuition over discursive reasoning as the philosopher's tool in the 1800 *System* threatened to dissolve philosophy itself into literary theory (or *Poesie* as it was then called). In 1801, Schelling pulled back from this radical aestheticism and, in a third phase of philosophical innovation, announced an absolute system, which he casually called "Identity Philosophy." In *Presentation of My System of Philosophy,* (*Darstellung meines System der Philosophie,* 1927) Schelling claimed that the philosopher not merely presupposes but possesses intellectual intuition, the synoptic faculty that Kant called "pure reason." If

the philosopher distances himself from what is arbitrary and subjective in his thought the way the artist distances himself from his personality, he can move in and with reason and so with purely logical means construct a theory of the absolute. The philosopher posits a logical domain of pure identity on the basis of concrete identities seen within the items of experience. Because these identities are combinatory, fashioned from differences, their mode of being is identity-in-difference; their conceptualization demands not a logic of bare identity but one that integrates universals and particulars, concepts and intuitions. These integrative structures motivate the philosopher's postulation of a ground of explanation whose logic is not that of abstract identity as opposed to difference, but of *in*difference or the identity of opposites. This absolute is a transcendental (or heuristic) posit, a noumenal unity of everything that phenomenally manifests itself as connected by difference.

Because this move is made with the necessity and universality of thought, Schelling felt that philosophy had become methodologically self-sufficient and no longer needed to appeal to the artist's aesthetic intuition as an empirical correlate of intellectual intuition. The 1802 dialogue *Bruno* demoted the artist to an unconscious collaborator of the philosopher. The artist, it is now said, produces an infinite fund of meaning in the work of art not by conscious agency, but by an unconscious outworking of a reality contained in the absolute as an "idea." This idea is the "soul" of the artist, but it comes to expression only partially and in distorted form in the artist's psyche and in the bodily movements that produce the separate artifact. This explains why there is so much bad art that is "personal," and so little grand art that is universal: most artists have small "souls" or limited empirical personalities. *Bruno* thus demoted artistic creativity from a transcendent to a robotic activity. What Schelling viewed as the conscious *and* unconscious character of aesthetic intuition in the 1800 *System* is viewed as merely unconscious production in 1802.

In 1802–1803 and 1804–1805, Schelling lectured on *the philosophy of art.* He did not publish these lectures in his lifetime, perhaps because of his dependence on August Wilhelm von Schlegel's Berlin lectures *On Dramatic Art and Literature* (1801–1803) for critical evaluation of particular literary artists and their achievements, for example, of Dante Alighieri's poetry and the plays of Pedro Calderón de la Barca and William Shakespeare. The lectures stand, nonetheless, as Schelling's most important contribution to aesthetic theory. In the general parts of the lectures, the topics of imagination, language, and symbolism are used to present the metaphysics of identity. The treatment of symbolism as a general function of expression stands on its own outside the metaphysical theory and is of interest to contemporary readers because Schelling used language itself as his primary example of a "symbol" or materially expressed meaning.

Once he had subjugated the arts to philosophy as inferior domains of cognition, as he had in 1802, Schelling could approach *philosophy* of art as a suitable vehicle for presenting metaphysics. If one can mix—as the later Schelling frequently did—abstract talk of "the absolute" with talk of the object of religion, the fine arts are the place where "God-talk" and metaphysics overlap. Not only are the contents of the highest visual and literary forms of fine art religious, but all the arts come to be in activities of expression or *informing—Einbildung*, as in *Einbildungskraft*, imagination. The absolute, or "God" in the language of these lectures, has an autopoetic or imaginative form of being; its essence is to express or affirm itself, to translate its reality from unarticulated identity into a differentiated world of form. As the essential identity of universality and particularity, or ideality and reality, God is the source of the various projections of one factor upon the other that make the phenomenal world a series of images *(Einbildungen)* of the absolute. God's perfect self-affirmation is the identification *(Ineinsbildung)* or equal informing of universality and particularity into perfect particulars or "ideas."

With these general metaphysical structures in place—God as expressive, informing universality and particularity into ideas in the absolute, and occasioning "reflected" imagings of ideas in the two phenomenal domains of nature and human culture—Schelling is able to generate a philosophical model of the cultural world as detailed and compelling as the model of nature he constructed in the two editions of *Ideas for a Philosophy of Nature*. The ideal phenomenal universe—which Georg Wilhelm Friedrich Hegel calls "spirit"—is structurally the reflection of reality (or particularity) into ideality (or universality). The root identity (of real and ideal) is expressed in three stages or under three *powers:* on the objective level as knowledge, on the subjective as action, and on the highest level as art, where the two factors are posited as equal. The realm of art is thus the place where ideality is realized in perfect, crystalline form as ideas or perfect particulars and where subjectivity is perfectly manifested in objective shape, as in the bodies the Greeks gave to their gods and goddesses in ancient sculpture. Schelling did not think it was accidental that the most penetrating naive art portrayed ideas as individual gods. Although he was aware of the mythologies of other cultures and keenly interested in the phenomena of comparative religion, Schelling asserted that the world of the Greek Olympians was the paradigmatic content of all art. The love of all things Greek fostered by German classicism and the unconscious Eurocentrism fostered by Christianity conspired in Schelling to shape the narrow view that art can have only two sorts of contents: the realistic mythology of Greece with its poetics of eternity and the idealistic mythology of Christianity's attempts to display the workings of providence in history.

Schelling's remarks on the formal side of art expanded on the idea of "expression" that ties God to the universe or phenomenal worlds; they also build on August Schlegel's discussions of original language as part of *Naturpoesie*. All art is symbolic in a general sense, because it is at once the purest expression of the absolute's ideality, but in an objectified form, under the guise of pure sensuous objectivity. Language is the basic symbol because it is idea materialized, its first conceptual expression. There are three specialized sorts of symbolism: schematism, where the particular is intended by the universal (as in painting or generally in language); allegory, where the universal is intended by the particular (as in music); and symbolism proper, where universal and particular are one (as in the plastic arts). The subjugation of all fine arts to language and of the metaphysics of art to symbolic expression makes it clear that Schelling assimilated art to cognition, and that his theory could comprehend art only insofar as it served a cognitive or informational function. There is little discussion of the sensuous in his lectures on the *Philosophy of Art* and no hint of the possibilities that later art forms explore of manipulating the sensuous media themselves to produce nonrepresentative content.

Schelling made a final contribution to aesthetic theory in an 1807 essay, "Concerning the Relationship of the Plastic Arts to Nature." This essay repeats themes familiar from the Identity Philosophy, for example, the way good art strikes a balance between naturalism and formalism, exhibited perfectly in the concreteness whereby the "ideas" of mythology and religion are shown in painting and sculpture. New to Schelling's theory as he advanced toward the Philosophy of Freedom of 1809 and thereafter are the ideas that art redeems a nature intrinsically frustrated and sorrowful and that, in artistic creator and spectator alike, the agent that unifies form and matter and that perceives their essence is "spirit" *(Geist)*. After 1807, Schelling's interests in the arts and in philosophy of language fade as he gravitates toward philosophy of history and philosophy of religion. The aesthetic vehicle is discarded as the philosopher becomes confident of a historical-anthropological access to God.

BIBLIOGRAPHY

Works by Schelling

Bruno; or, On the Natural and Divine Principle of Things (1802). Edited and translated by Michael G. Vater. Albany, N.Y., 1984.

Concerning the Relationship of the Plastic Arts to Nature. Translated by Michael Bullock. In *The True Voice of Feeling: Studies in English Romantic Poetry*, edited by Herbert Read. London, 1953.

Darstellung meines Systems der Philosophie. In *Sämtliche Werke*, Jubilee Edition, vol. 3. Munich, 1927. Reprint of original edition in 14 vols. by K. F. A. Schelling (Stuttgart, 1856–1861).

Ideas for a Philosophy of Nature (1797). Translated by Errol E. Harris and Peter Heath. Cambridge and New York, 1988.

On the History of Modern Philosophy. Edited and translated by Andrew Bowie. Cambridge and New York, 1994.

On University Studies. Translated by E. S. Morgan, edited by Norbert Guterman. Athens, Ohio, 1966.

System of Transcendental Idealism (1800). Translated by Peter Heath. Charlottesville, Va., 1978.

Other Sources

Burwick, Frederick. "Perception and 'the Heaven-Descended Know-Thyself'." In *Coleridge's Biographia Literaria,* edited by Frederick Burwick. Columbus, Ohio, 1989.

Coleridge, Samuel Taylor. *Biographia Literaria; or, Biographical Sketches of My Literary Life and Opinions.* In *The Collected Works of Samuel Taylor Coleridge,* edited by James Engell and W. Jackson Bate, vol. 7. Princeton, N.J., 1983.

Fackenheim, Emil L. "Schelling's Philosophy of the Literary Arts." *Philosophical Quarterly* (St. Andrews) 4 (1954): 310–326.

Jähnig, Dieter. *Schelling: Die Kunst in der Philosophie.* 2 vols. Pfüllingen, 1966–1969.

Lawrence, Joseph. "Art and Philosophy in Schelling." *Owl of Minerva* 20 (1988): 5–19.

Marx, Werner. *The Philosophy of F. W. J. Schelling: History, System, and Freedom.* Translated by Thomas Nenon. Bloomington, Ind., 1984.

Seidel, George J. "Creativity in the Aesthetics of Schelling." *Idealistic Studies* 4 (1974): 170–180.

Snow, Dale. "The Role of the Unconscious in Schelling's System of Transcendental Idealism." *Idealistic Studies* 19 (1989): 231–250.

MICHAEL G. VATER

SCHILLER, JOHANN CHRISTOPH FRIEDRICH VON

(1759–1805), a poet, playwright, and aesthetician of the classical age of German literature, the so-called age of Goethe *(Goethezeit),* which began toward the close of the eighteenth century. Schiller was born in Marback on the Neckar, Germany. He attended the Duke of Württemberg's military academy, and in 1780 he qualified as a surgeon. Although Schiller seemed to adapt well to military life, he began reading, and eventually writing, Sturm und Drang (verse and plays). In 1783, Schiller worked as a dramatist for the Mannheim theater, and the next year, he began publishing a theatrical journal, *Die rheinische Thalia.* In 1785, he moved first to Leipzig, then to Dresden, where he joined Karl Theodor Körner's literary circle. In 1787, he moved to Weimar; the next year he was appointed honorary professor of history at Jena. Schiller was ennobled in 1802.

Schiller's aesthetic writings consist in four major treatises and many smaller essays, most of them written between 1791 and 1795. Each of the treatises has been influential in the history of aesthetics, and so they deserve separate analysis here.

Much admired by Friedrich Schlegel, Friedrich Wilhelm von Schelling, Friedrich Hölderlin, and Georg Wilhelm Friedrich Hegel, Schiller's aesthetic writings played a formative role in the development of German Idealism and Romanticism. Schiller was indeed the central spokesman for the aestheticism of the age of Goethe, the founder of its faith in the redemptive value of art. Schiller's aestheticism consisted in his belief that the perfect person, society, and state is a work of art, and that one should strive to make them aesthetic wholes. The main theme of his aesthetic writings is that a person, society, or state achieves excellence only through beauty. It is the task of the arts, Schiller also believed, to make people aware of their highest moral aspiration: the longing to recover their lost harmony with themselves, nature, and society.

The central influence behind the formation of Schiller's aesthetics was Immanuel Kant, whom Schiller began to study in 1791. His aesthetics is scarcely comprehensible without some understanding of Kant's doctrines, because Schiller began from the same problems, adopted the same vocabulary, and applied the same ideas to new fields. Nevertheless, it is a mistake to consider Schiller a Kantian or to measure his work only in Kantian terms, for Schiller criticized Kant as much as he borrowed from him. Precisely how and why Schiller differs from Kant is a complex and controversial issue, which this essay will attempt to unravel.

Although Kant was the central figure in the development of Schiller's aesthetics, Schiller was also influenced by other writers. He was steeped in most classical and eighteenth-century sources. In the winter of 1792–1793 alone, the formative period for the development of his mature aesthetic view, he read Johann Georg Sulzer, Henry Home, Moses Mendelssohn, Edmund Burke, Raphael Mengs, Johann Joachim Winckelmann, and Charles de Batteux. Schiller's early *Philosophische Briefe* (Philosophical Letters; 1786) reveals the influence of Anthony Ashley Cooper, earl of Shaftesbury, whose doctrine of the unity of beauty, truth, and goodness continues to color his mature views.

It is also important to recognize that Schiller's philosophy antedates his acquaintance with Kant. In the early 1780s, Schiller became preoccupied with the question of the role of the artist in society, and his early essays on the German theater, *Über das gegenwärtige deutsche Theater* (On the Present German Theater; 1782) and *Die Schaubühne als eine moralische Anstalt betrachtet* (The Stage as a Moral Institution; 1784), laid the foundation for much of his later work. Schiller also sketched the rudiments of his metaphysics and ethics in the *Philosophie der Physiologie* (Philosophy of Physiology; 1779), the doctoral dissertation "Versuch über den Zusammenhang der tierischen Natur des Menschen mit seiner geistigen" (Essay on the Connection between Our Animal and Spiritual Nature; 1780), and the *Philosophical Letters* (1786). All these early writings are important for the problematic of Schiller's later aesthetics. In them, Schiller poses the questions that his later works will attempt to answer: "How is it possible to explain the unity of human nature?" "How is it possible to reconcile enlightened criticism with religious belief?" and "What is the role of the artist in the modern world?"

The Analysis of Beauty. Schiller laid the foundation for his mature aesthetic views in a series of letters to Gottfried Körner, which he wrote from the end of January to the end of February 1793. He intended to publish these letters under the title *Kallias oder über die Schönheit* (Kallias, or on Beauty), but the planned work never appeared. Although they are virtually complete and polished in substance and style, they are usually available only in collected editions of Schiller's correspondence.

In the first letter, Schiller outlines his own position vis-à-vis the prevailing views of his day, specifically those of Burke, the Wolffians (Alexander Gottlieb Baumgarten, Sulzer, and Mendelssohn), and, above all, Kant. There are, Schiller explains, four possible ways to explain the beautiful: the objective or the subjective, according to whether beauty exists in things or only in our perception of them; and the sensible or the rational, according to whether it is an empirical or an intellectual property, one determined by the senses or reason. Burke's theory is subjective and sensible; the Wolffians' is objective and rational; Kant's is subjective and rational. The fourth possibility is Schiller's own: that beauty is objective and sensible. In other words, Schiller thinks that beauty is an empirical and objective characteristic inhering in objects themselves.

The main problem with the Burkean theory, in Schiller's view, is that it regards beauty as simply a kind of sensation, so that aesthetic judgment must forfeit all claim to universality. The Wolffians rightly see that beauty must be a quality of objects themselves; but they go astray in placing it entirely in its purely rational or formal properties, especially perfection or unity in multiplicity. Schiller gives two reasons why beauty cannot consist in such properties alone. First, they are characteristic of mathematical regularity, which is not beautiful; and, second, they can be imposed on the object, so that they distort its real nature.

What, then, is wrong with Kant's position? According to Schiller, Kant had demoted beauty to a subjective quality, to the feeling of pleasure involved in the free play of our cognitive faculties, which has no reference to objects themselves (even as appearances). Schiller maintained, however, that beauty must be based on at least one characteristic inherent in the object itself: namely, whether the object is *self-determining*, that is, whether it is free from external influences and acts according to its own inherent nature alone. We cannot have an experience of beauty, Schiller argues, if what we perceive does not express its inner nature, if it is somehow subject to constraint, whether moral or physical. Here Schiller was developing a point made by Kant himself, who stressed that a work of fine art is beautiful only if it appears like nature and does not seem to conform to the rules of art (*Critique of Judgment*, section 45).

The *Kallias Letters* are essentially a defense and elaboration of Schiller's definition of beauty: freedom in appearance *(Freiheit in der Erscheinung)*. This definition recurs as a leitmotif throughout Schiller's aesthetic writings. Some analysis of each of its terms—*freedom* and *appearance*—is therefore necessary.

The "freedom" of beauty means that an object is autonomous, not subject to foreign ends or influences. Following Kant, Schiller insists that an aesthetic object must be an end in itself and not a means to physical or moral ends. To be subject to such ends would be a form of constraint, and so they would distort the inner nature of an object. This autonomy or self-determination does not mean, Schiller is quick to add, that an aesthetic object is completely free from necessity and acts in a totally arbitrary manner. On the contrary, it is subject to rules or laws. Nevertheless, these are compatible with, and indeed necessary to, freedom, because they are *self-imposed* or follow from its inner and characteristic nature. Like Kant, Schiller thinks that freedom consists not in the absence of law, but in autonomy, the self-imposition or consent to law.

Schiller gives several reasons why beauty is freedom *in appearance*. First, the aesthetic object, though it is subject to rules and thus necessity, must *seem* or *appear* to be free. Second, the freedom of an aesthetic object, which must appear to the senses, is not the same as moral freedom itself, which is purely intelligible or transcendental, and so not given in the realm of appearances. The aesthetic object must therefore simply appear to be free, because it cannot really be free in the moral sense. In other words, aesthetic freedom is only an analogue to or symbol of moral freedom.

Ultimately, for all its sophistication, the *Kallias Letters* is a flawed work, suffering from inner tensions, mainly because of Schiller's ambivalent relationship to Kant. Although Schiller wants to establish an objective concept of beauty in opposition to Kant, his other Kantian premises undermine him. According to Kant, freedom cannot be a property of objects themselves in the natural world. Although we sometimes read the ideas of practical reason into objects in the sensible world, we have no right to assume that they really do act for ends; we can at most think of nature *as if* it were free (*Critique of Judgment*, sections 15, 58). Schiller himself adopts this Kantian point when he insists that we can regard appearances as only analogues of freedom. Yet, it is a doctrine that is scarcely compatible with his attempt to provide an objective concept of beauty.

This hardly means, however, that Schiller's theory, when consistent, collapses into Kant's. One of its more striking and novel characteristics is Schiller's subsumption of aesthetic judgment under the domain of practical reason, his placing of beauty within the domain of morality. Schiller maintains that aesthetic judgment is a form of moral judgment, because, when we see an object as beautiful, we subsume it under the concept of freedom, the fundamental concept of morality. Kant held that aesthetic judgments are distinct from moral judgments because each kind of judgment has a distinct subject matter or object: whereas aesthetic judgments appraise appearances in the sensible world, moral judgments assess moral intentions in the rational world. Yet, Kant failed to see, Schiller thinks, that there is an aesthetic use of moral judgment, because, in determining beauty, we have to apply moral concepts. Ironically, toward the close of the first part of the *Critique of Judgment* (section 59), Kant himself had prepared the ground for this doctrine. Here he argued that beauty is a symbol of the ideas of morality, and he even suggested that the demand for universal agreement in aesthetic judgments depends on it. Nevertheless, the main thrust of his teaching was that art belongs to a sui generis domain apart from science and morality, so that the beautiful is distinct from both truth and the good. It was the aim of Schiller to reunite the realms of the good and the beautiful that had been so sharply separated by Kant.

Grace and Dignity. Schiller's treatise *Über Anmut und Würde* (On Grace and Dignity), written in spring 1793, is not a work in aesthetics in the narrow sense. Although it attempts to provide precise definitions of the concepts of grace and dignity, which were common fare of eighteenth-century aesthetics, its central aim is to explain the fundamental role of these concepts in moral philosophy. Schiller's argument is primarily directed against Kant's ethics of duty, which he criticized for its narrow conception of human perfection.

Schiller's analysis of grace and dignity must be placed firmly in its eighteenth-century context. His work was influenced by Home, Christoph Martin Wieland, Sulzer, Lord Shaftesbury, and Mendelssohn, who all analyzed these concepts. Like most of his contemporaries, Schiller maintains that grace is a specific form of beauty: the beauty of human action and movement. He also agrees with his contemporaries about some of the defining characteristics of a graceful action: that it is performed naturally and spontaneously, without effort or compulsion, and that it complies with rules without acting because of them or for their sake alone. These characteristics also follow, of course, from the definition of beauty in the *Kallias Letters*.

Schiller's analysis of grace stresses, however, its moral rather than its aesthetic characteristics. In other words, grace involves less the beauty of an action—whether it is pleasing to the senses—and more the motives and personality behind it. Thus, Schiller stresses that graceful actions must be voluntary, having their source in personality or character rather than any physical or inherited characteristics. He therefore distinguishes the *architechtonic* beauty of human action and form, which is simply a gift of nature, from its *rational* beauty, which depends on the will alone. The architechtonic beauty comprises anatomy, posture, and complexion, whereas rational beauty consists in the motives or spirit behind an action. A person possesses grace, Schiller further explains, when his moral education has become "second nature" to him. According to this account, then, the aesthetic dimension of grace virtually disappears, because a person could possess grace even if his actions appeared awkward and ungainly to the senses.

The most controversial feature of Schiller's treatise is his application of the concept of grace to Kant's moral philosophy. To many of his contemporaries, Kant's moral philosophy seemed unduly rigoristic because it gave a too strict analysis of moral worth. Kant had maintained that the only actions having moral value are those done for the sake of duty or because of moral principle. Apparently paradoxically, he excluded actions done from benevolent as well as selfish inclinations; but Kant's reasoning was plausible enough: generous impulses stem from nature no less than selfish ones, so they too do not depend on the will, the ultimate source of all moral value.

The source of Schiller's quarrel with Kant has often been misunderstood. Schiller did not wish to defend the moral worth of benevolent impulses or a good heart, which have their source in nature alone. Furthermore, he expressed his agreement with Kant's analysis of moral action: to have a moral worth, an action must be done for the sake of duty, and its value must stem from the will. Wishing to minimize his differences with Schiller, Kant himself stressed these common points in a footnote to his *Religion innerhalb der Grenzen der blossen Vernunft* (Religion within the Limits of Reason Alone, 1793). Schiller was delighted with Kant's remarks.

Nevertheless, such apparent agreement should not obscure the deeper differences between Schiller and Kant. The main point of friction between them concerns not the analysis of moral action but human excellence or perfection; in other words, they differ over the conditions for becoming a good person, not the conditions for performing a morally good action. Schiller argued that Kant had given a much too narrow account of human perfection. The sole excellence of a human being could not be simply the execution of moral duty, for this failed to cultivate a person's sensibility, to develop his feelings and desires, which are as distinctively human as reason. If doing duty for its own sake is made into the sole or chief human virtue, Schiller contended, then Kant's ethic degenerates into a moral tyranny where reason dominates and eventually represses human sensibility. An excellent or perfect human being is, for Schiller, someone who acts as a whole, someone whose reason and sensibility are in perfect harmony, so that the demands of duty and inclination never conflict.

It is in this context that Schiller applies his concept of grace. A graceful action is one that stems from a person's whole character, from his reason and sensibility acting in harmony. It is not done simply from natural desire or inclination, and still less from a sense of duty alone. Rather, the person does his duty from desire and with feeling. These desires and feelings are not, however, simply those given by nature, which are still raw and selfish, but those created by moral education. In a graceful action, then, desires and feelings are neither repressed nor indulged. Rather, they are refined and ennobled, or, to use a more modern term, "sublimated."

For Schiller, dignity is the complement of grace. Although the graceful or "beautiful" soul acts in harmony with his feelings and desires, the dignified soul has full mastery over them in those extreme cases where duty demands sacrifice. Dignity is more self-possession than self-renunciation, however. Like grace, it shows no signs of external compulsion or effort, and no trace of righteousness or zealotry.

In stressing the value of dignity, Schiller recognized that there are some cases where duty and desire, moral principle and inclination, conflict. In an ideal world, people would need only grace; but in the real world they must also sometimes act with dignity. Schiller stressed that the ideal person has both grace and dignity. These virtues are, indeed, necessary to each other: a person acts with grace rather than simply a good heart if he can act according to dignity; and he acts according to dignity if his actions show grace rather than severity and punctiliousness.

Aesthetic Education. Schiller's most influential work on aesthetics was his *Über die ästhetische Erziehung des Menschen, in einer Reihe von Briefen* (On the Aesthetic Education of Mankind, in a Series of Letters), which he wrote in the summer and autumn of 1794. This work can be seen as a reply to Plato's and Jean-Jacques Rousseau's strictures against the arts. Schiller does not banish the arts but celebrates them. They are the chief instrument of political education and enlightenment in his republic. The arts, he contends, do not corrupt us with pleasant illusions but inspire us to live according to the laws.

The context of the *Aesthetic Letters* was the reception of the French Revolution in Germany. Like many of his contemporaries, Schiller admired the goals of the Revolution—liberty, equality, fraternity, and the rights of man—but disapproved of its violent methods. The bloodshed, strife, and anarchy in France seemed to show that the people were not ready for the high ideals of a republic. The key to political reform and stability, Schiller believed, was the enlightenment and education of the people. This task, however, demanded more than moral preaching, simply propagating the principles of reason. Most people already knew these principles; the problem was to make them act according to them. The most effective means of encouraging the people to do so was to educate their sensibility, to transform their hearts and feelings. The chief impulses for human action, Schiller explained, lay not in the cold reasoning of the intellect but in the desires and feelings of the human heart.

Schiller therefore saw art as the key to the education of the people. It was art, and art alone, that could address desire and sentiment. It alone could appeal to a person's feelings and imagination, and so inspire him to act according to the principles of reason. Hence, art had none of the limitations of philosophy or religion. Whereas philosophy could at best address a person's intellect, religion had lost its credibility in the Age of Reason.

In stressing the value of art in addressing the passions, Schiller was, in effect, attacking one of the weakest points in Plato's criticism of the arts: his failure to understand *akra-*

sia, that we can know the good but have no desire to live according to it. If Plato only fully admitted this point, Schiller seemed to be saying, then he would have seen the important role of the arts in his republic; for, if philosophy is necessary to know the good, art alone inspires and motivates to act according to it.

Schiller's faith in the redemptive powers of art in the *Aesthetic Letters* reflects, in part, the argument of his earlier work *The Stage as a Moral Institution*. Here Schiller argued that the theater is "a school of practical wisdom, a guide through civil life, an infallible key to the most secret passages of the human soul." Although the theater does not preach a new morals or religion, it holds up a mirror to human life and action, making us more aware of moral issues and so creating a greater civic consciousness. By directly appealing to our imagination and feelings, it provides a more effective sanction for the laws than religion or philosophy.

It would be a mistake, however, to see the argument of the *Aesthetic Letters* from the perspective of this earlier work alone. Schiller does not rest his case against Plato and Rousseau on his belief in the moral effects of the arts, and he even concedes that history shows the arts to flourish only when morals and the state decline. In the tenth letter, he explains that his main argument lies elsewhere: that he wants to prove the value of the arts a priori, by showing how beauty is "a necessary condition of humanity."

The heart of Schiller's tract is his argument from the eleventh to the fifteenth letters that beauty alone unifies the two fundamental drives of human nature, the intellectual and the sensible, the formal and the material. Whereas the formal drive attempts to give form to matter, to universalize the particular, or to internalize the external, the material drive tries to give content to form, to particularize the universal, or to externalize the internal. Each drive, Schiller explains, has its characteristic limit or constraint: the formal drive stands under the constraint of moral laws, whereas the material drive is subject to physical needs. What unites these two drives is beauty, the unity of form and content, of the universal and the particular, or of structure and life. This unity comes into existence through a third drive, what Schiller calls the "play drive." He chooses this term because the creation of beauty is like a form of play, in that we are no longer subject to the constraints of moral duty or physical need.

The dense and difficult argument in behalf of beauty in the *Aesthetic Letters* becomes clearer when we recall some of Schiller's early works. Schiller presupposes the definition of beauty in the *Kallias Letters*. If beauty is the appearance of freedom, then the play drive must create beauty, because it is only in play, Schiller argues, that we become free, liberated from the constraints of physical need and moral duty. Schiller also assumes the analysis of grace and dignity in *On Grace and Dignity*. The unity of the formal and material drives will be a form of beauty also because it consists in grace, those actions where we act from our whole nature.

Although Schiller's *Aesthetic Letters* have been ridiculed for their idealism and naïveté, these criticisms do not come to terms with its main argument. Schiller's case does not rest on the good effects of the arts—watching plays, reading poems, or listening to music—but on his anthropology, his belief that human beings are complete and fulfilled only as aesthetic wholes. The argument is, then, that if we were self-realized as human beings, we would become like works of art ourselves. This point alone, Schiller believes, and not any case for the good effects of the fine arts, means that we should recognize the significance of the aesthetic dimension in our lives.

The Naive and Sentimental. The last of Schiller's major works on aesthetics is his *Über naive und sentimentalische Dichtung* (On Naive and Sentimental Poetry), which appeared in Schiller's journal *Die Horen* from November 1795 to January 1796. This work is important in the history of aesthetics because of its influence on the development of Romanticism. The young Friedrich Schlegel's ideal of Romantic poetry was inspired by Schiller's concept of the sentimental.

Schiller's tract begins with an observation of Kant's: that sometimes we are pleased with objects simply because they are natural (*Critique of Judgment*, section 42). If something apparently natural turns out to be artificial (for example, a flower), then we lose our pleasure in it. This shows, Schiller thinks, that our pleasure is not really aesthetic. Both the artificial and the natural flower are beautiful, possessing the same formal characteristics; yet we still prefer the natural one. Therefore, the question arises: Why do we prefer the natural over the artificial? In what does our pleasure in natural objects consist?

Schiller's answer is that our pleasure in nature has more a moral than an aesthetic source. What we enjoy is not so much the objects themselves as the moral ideas we read into them. We project into natural objects the ideas of "quiet creative life, of acting from within oneself, of existence according to one's own laws, of inner necessity, and of eternal unity with oneself." In short, nature represents a state of complete independence, of total self-sufficiency, the absence of need and constraint.

When we observe natural objects, Schiller explains, we are moved because they represent something we have lost and to which we long to return. We once lived in a state of complete independence because we were in harmony with ourselves, with others, and with the external world. This is the state enjoyed by children and primitive man. But it has been lost with the development of civilization. The growth of bureaucratic government, of the division of labor, and of the arts and sciences has divided man from himself, from nature, and from others. Still, we hope to restore what we have lost, to re-create what was once given to us. The civi-

lization that has destroyed nature for us should also become the means for our return to it. Through the development of the arts and sciences, we will once again achieve that harmony with others, ourselves, and the external world.

Schiller's distinction between naive and sentimental poetry derives from this utopian philosophy of history. According to it, we stand in two possible relations with nature: either we are part of nature and it is given to us; or we have lost nature and desire to return to it. Naive poetry is the imitation of a nature that is given to us; sentimental poetry is the idealization of a nature that we have lost and to which we long to return. Schiller maintains that naive poetry is characteristic of the poetry of classical antiquity, when people lived more in harmony with nature, whereas sentimental poetry is characteristic of the modern age, which has fallen from its unity with nature.

Against the hidebound classicists, Schiller argues that each kind of poetry is valid in its own right, and that we should not attempt to measure modern poetry by classical standards. To be sure, classical poetry attained a high degree of perfection, but that was only because its aim was simply to describe its object; having such a limited goal, it had little trouble in achieving it. Modern poetry does not achieve such perfection, yet it has the great merit of aspiring to an infinite ideal—the expression of complete independence, of our harmony with nature, ourselves, and others. This means that modern poetry enjoys more freedom and flexibility: whereas ancient poetry stuck to a definite genre, one manner of seeing and feeling things, modern poetry reflects on its object in all kinds of ways, approaching it from many different angles.

Schiller's defense of modern or sentimental poetry stimulated the young Friedrich Schlegel, who had been a convinced classicist before reading Schiller's tract. Schiller's concept of sentimental poetry indeed anticipates Schlegel's own ideal of Romantic poetry in some striking respects: like Romantic poetry, sentimental poetry mixes genres, idealizes its object, and expresses the longing for an infinite ideal. In these respects, Schlegel's Romantic aesthetic simply canonized the virtues of Schiller's sentimental poetry.

Aesthetic Autonomy and Morality. How can Schiller insist on both the autonomy of art and its beneficial moral effects? It would seem that the arts benefit society and the state only by serving moral or political ends, and thus by forfeiting their autonomy.

This was a problem that Schiller himself addressed on several occasions, and to which he had various solutions. He discussed it most explicitly in his 1792 essay "Über den Grund des Vergnügens an tragischen Gegenstände" (On the Basis of Our Pleasure in Tragic Objects). Here, under the influence of Kant, Schiller seems to distance himself from his earlier views on the mission of German theater. Now he states that the purpose of art is to give pleasure, and that it should not submit to moral ends. He criticizes the old aesthetics of the Gottschedian school, which made art the servant of morality. The attempt to make art conform to moral ends, he insists, had led all too often to bad art. Nevertheless, Schiller immediately adds that this does not imply that the aim of art is merely entertainment, and that it cannot serve higher ends. The enjoyment of art, he explains, is a "free pleasure," and as such is opposed to the physical pleasures of our sensibility, which are subject to natural laws. The free pleasure of art rests on moral conditions, because it consists in the self-awareness of our freedom, the recognition that we are moral beings who stand above the causality of the natural world. According to Schiller, then, morality is only a means to the end of art—free pleasure—and we should never confuse means with ends by making art the servant of morality.

Schiller addressed the paradox from another angle in letters twenty-two and twenty-three of the *Aesthetic Letters*. He explains that a good work of art acts on a person as a whole and not on any faculty in particular. Art imparts energy and power to all of our capacities, but it does not determine how any one of them is applied. It does not, then, attempt to make us more moral because it does not prescribe any specific principles or action. Still, by acting on our whole nature, it stimulates all of our faculties, and so allows each of them to perform its specific function more effectively.

In the end, Schiller's belief in the moral value of art rests on an apparent paradox. The great value of art, he argues in most of his work, is that it helps us to achieve freedom. If art only does this, then it has promoted the highest moral value of all, namely, freedom. Yet, the paradox is that this great moral value can be attained only if art helps us to transcend the constraints of morality, which demand the suppression of our desires and so limit the expression of our whole nature. Hence, ironically, art achieves its greatest moral end only in virtue of its autonomy, its freedom from all moral constraint.

[*See also* Beauty; Education, Aesthetic; Kant; *and* Romanticism, *article on* Philosophy and Literature.]

BIBLIOGRAPHY

Works by Schiller

Schillers Werke: Nationalausgabe. 44 vols. Edited by L. Blumenthal and B. von Wiese. Weimar, 1943. This is now the standard edition of Schiller. For the aesthetics, see volumes 20 and 21. For Schiller's correspondence with Gottfried Körner, see volume 26, pp. 174–229.

Translations of Works by Schiller

The Aesthetic Letters, Essays and *the Philosophical Letters of Schiller.* Translated by J. Weiss. Boston, 1845.
Naive and Sentimental Poetry, and *On the Sublime: Two Essays by Friedrich von Schiller.* Translated by Julius A. Elias. New York, 1966.
On the Aesthetic Education of Man in a Series of Letters. Edited and translated by Elizabeth M. Wilkinson and L. A. Willoughby. Oxford, 1967.
On the Naive and Sentimental in Literature. Translated by Helen Watanabe-O'Kelly. Manchester, 1981.

Aesthetic Reconstructions: The Seminal Writings of Lessing, Kant and Schiller. Translation by Anthony Savile. Aristotelian Society Series, vol. 8. Oxford and New York, 1987.

Other Sources

Berger, Karl. *Die Entwicklung von Schillers Ästhetik.* Weimar, 1894.
Borcherdt, Hans Heinrich, ed. *Schiller und die Romantiker: Briefe und Dokumente.* Stuttgart, 1948.
Cassirer, Ernst. "Die Methodik des Idealismus in Schillers philosophischen Schriften." In *Idee und Gestalt: Goethe, Schiller, Hölderlin, Kleist,* pp. 79–108. Berlin, 1921.
Ellis, J. M. *Schiller's Kalliasbriefe and the Study of His Aesthetic Theory.* The Hague, 1969.
Hell, Victor. *Schiller: Théories esthétiques et structures dramatiques* Paris, 1974. On the aesthetics, see part 2, chap. 2, pp. 146–251.
Heuer, Fritz. *Darstellung der Freiheit: Schillers transzendentale Frage nach der Kunst.* Cologne, 1970.
Janz, Rolf-Peter. *Autonomie und soziale Funktion der Kunst: Studien zur Ästhetik von Schiller und Novalis.* Stuttgart, 1973.
Kerry, S. S. *Schiller's Writings on Aesthetics.* Manchester, 1961.
Kühnemann, Eugen. *Kants und Schillers Begründung der Ästhetik.* Munich, 1895.
Miller, R. D. *Schiller and the Ideal of Freedom.* Oxford, 1970.
Norton, Robert E. *The Beautiful Soul: Aesthetic Morality in the Eighteenth Century.* Ithaca, N.Y., 1995.
Reed, T. J. *Schiller.* Oxford and New York, 1991.
Sychrava, Juliet. *Schiller to Derrida: Idealism in Aesthetics.* Cambridge and New York, 1989.

FREDERICK BEISER

SCHLEGEL, AUGUST WILHELM VON

(1767–1845), German literary critic. Along with his brother Karl Wilhelm Friedrich von Schlegel (1772–1829), he inaugurated the project of early German Romanticism (known as the *Frühromantik*), a project that established the foundation of modern literary history and criticism. The emergence of this new movement at the end of the eighteenth century in the German university town of Jena proved to be a turning point in the history of criticism. Influenced by the critical insights and writings of their literary forebears Gotthold Ephraim Lessing and Johann Gottfried von Herder, and drawing on the intellectual fruits of the philosophical revolution in Germany, the early Romantics relieved modern poetry from its burden of allegiance to an exemplary classical past and recognized it as the decisive and enduring aesthetic expression of modern consciousness. The Romantic paradigm of literary criticism was formulated in the pages of the journal *Athenäum*, founded by the Schlegel brothers and published during the years 1798–1800 in Jena. The journal represented one of the most fruitful literary and editorial collaborations of the age and counted among its contributors the greatest critical talents of the time, including Ludwig Tieck, the poet-philosopher Novalis (Friedrich von Hardenberg), the theologian Friedrich Schleiermacher, Caroline Schlegel-Schelling, and Dorothea Schlegel.

Schlegel was born in Hannover into a family known for its scholarly accomplishments. His father, Johann Adolf

Schlegel, and his uncle, Elias Schlegel, were prominent critics. He studied classical philology at the University of Göttingen with the renowned Hellenist Christian Gottlob Heyne and matriculated on 3 May 1786. Between 1787 and 1792, Schlegel wrote extensively for several literary journals, among them the *Göttinger Musenalmanach,* and contributed many articles to Friedrich von Schiller's *Horen* and *Musenalmanach* from 1795 until the poet and the Schlegel brothers had a final falling out in 1799. In 1798, Schlegel was offered a teaching position *(Extraordinariat)* at the University of Jena. Thus, the Romantic literary movement, whose critical gaze was trained on an unprecedented universality of literary representation, gained legitimate entry into the university. In 1818, Schlegel was invited to teach at the University of Berlin. He chose to go to the University of Bonn, however, where he was professor of Indology from 1819 to his death in 1845. During his tenure at Bonn, he served as the rector of the university from 1824 to 1825.

Schlegel was a prodigious man of letters, linguist, classicist, Orientalist, and one of the most accomplished translators of all times. In addition to the members of the Romantic school and Schiller, he was acquainted with the leading literary figures of Germany, including Johann Wolfgang von Goethe and Tieck, author of the quintessential German Romantic novel, *Franz Sternbald's Wanderungen* (Franz Sternbald's Travels). He was a devoted friend of the French writer Mme Germaine de Staël, who, under his tutorship, became an ardent student of modern German letters and published the widely reviewed and popularly received book *De l'Allemagne,* which introduced the modern German literary scene to French readers. Between 1797 and 1810, Schlegel translated most of William Shakespeare's plays into German, and to this day his translations are considered the best rendering of the bard's work in German. He also translated numerous works from French, Spanish, and Portuguese. During the latter part of his literary career, Schlegel became a highly regarded scholar of Sanskrit. Between the years 1820 and 1830, he published the journal *Indische Bibliothek* (Indian Library) and made available critical editions of the *Bhagavadgītā* in 1823 and the *Rāmāyaṇa* during the years 1829–1831.

Friedrich Schlegel and Novalis, the two major theorists of the Romantic school, are credited with translating the Kantian notions of critique and the autonomy of the work of art and Johann Gottlieb Fichte's philosophy of reflection, respectively, into usable terms of Romantic criticism. Although the theoretical strength of Schlegel's aesthetics was questioned by later critics, it is generally acknowledged that his comprehensive treatment of literature through history, language theory, and criticism is the most impressive trait of his oeuvre. Schlegel undertook the steady and laborious task of recovering and contextualizing, in the frameworks of modern poesy, a long history of forgotten, lost, and occulted literary traditions and histories. The desire to make accessible a significant but often misunderstood past, the past as a foreign territory, informed all of Schlegel's work. This work saw the light of day in a comprehensive array of formal vehicles, including translations, letters, essays, reviews, critical editions, fragments, and perhaps most significant, lectures. In their printed form, these lectures were widely read. Schlegel's vast knowledge of the history of world literatures and his reading of individual works of antiquity, the Middle Ages, and ancient India in a hermeneutically informed context reevoked a fast-receding and fading literary history in the imaginary universal library of German Romanticism.

Romantic poetry is defined as "progressive universal poesy" in the oft-cited *Athenäum* fragment 116. In the early Romantic lexicon, the word *Poesie* (poesy) referred to both literary arts and poetics. This fragment, considered an early manifesto of the Romantic project, equates modern poetry with the Romantic. The aim of Romantic poesy is to reintegrate separated domains of human knowledge, combining philosophy with rhetoric, poetry with prose, inspiration with criticism, and poeticizing life as well as infusing poetry with life. Romantic poesy strives to embrace all forms of poetic expression, from the greatest systems of art to the artless song of a child. Although other forms of poetry have come full circle and are complete, Romantic poesy is in a state of becoming, which is its essential characteristic. It reflects on itself and sees this reflection in an infinite series of mirrors. Thus, in the Romantic idiom, modern poetry expresses a progressive striving.

In Schlegel's university lectures, the critical agenda of German Romanticism, which was partially articulated in the *Athenäum* fragments, finds its comprehensive and elaborate format of expression. The lecture series, starting with the Berlin *Vorlesungen über schöne Literatur und Kunst* (Lectures on Beautiful Literature and Art; 1801–1804) after the dissolution of the *Athenäum* group and including the 1808 Vienna *Vorlesungen über dramatische Kunst und Literatur* (Lectures on Dramatic Art and Literature), delineate against a vast panoroma of literary historical detail the particular artistic destiny of modern Romantic poesy. To a certain extent, Romanticism's poetic paradigm owes its inception to an earlier controversy of literary history known as the Quarrel of the Ancients and the Moderns, the confrontation between the proponents of classical antiquity and those of aesthetic modernity. In the seventeenth and eighteenth centuries, French and English critics began to advocate the freedom of modern art from its subordination to classical models. Toward the end of the eighteenth century, the debate had penetrated German literary territory and became a formative impetus in the historical self-understanding of early Romanticism. Romanticism moderated this debate by acknowledging the mutability of genres, the emergence of novel forms, and the role of creative imagination in ordering these in new configurations. Romantic literary criticism gained its formative critical position from the famous distinction between Romanticism and classicism articulated by the Schlegels and developed to precision in Schlegel's *Lectures on Dramatic Art and Literature*. Unlike the Quarrel of the Ancients and the Moderns, the Romantic versus the classical distinction is not a strictly oppositional one. Rather, as Schlegel demonstrates in his many formulations, it is complementary, for the Romantic incorporates the memory of past forms and myths into the present moment of poetic self-reflexivity and reevaluation. Thus, Romantic criticism becomes a completion and complementation of its subject, the work of art, both ancient and modern.

In the *Lectures on Dramatic Art and Literature,* Schlegel sees the function of the history of art forms as recording what has happened and that of theory as teaching what ought to be accomplished by art. Without an intermediate link, however, history and theory alone cannot elucidate their respective concerns and remain inadequate forms of inquiry. Criticism is the mediating term between the history of art forms and the theory that furnishes their cognitive map. It illuminates the conditions for the production of the work of art. Like Romantic poetry, Romantic criticism is a generative field duplicating the gestures of its object of study and cannot operate as a closed system. Nations and individuals who are fettered by educational conventions, dictates of taste, and habits of mind lack the capacity for genuine criticism. Schlegel concludes that no person can be a true critic or connoisseur without a universality of mind and an understanding of other times, places, and systems of art and thought. He applies this notion of universality to the history of fine arts and observes that the reverent reception of antiquity had been fatally misguided and undermined the true appreciation of modern art by judging it only in terms of its imitation of ancient models. Finally, in the recent past, several critical minds, mostly Germans—here Schlegel is implicitly referring to the *Frühromantik* circle—attempted to redress this poverty of judgment by giving the moderns their due without detracting from the value of the ancients. They named the modern spirit of art *romantic* as opposed to the ancient and classical. Schlegel finds this a fitting description, because the word derives from *romance*, a name given to languages derived from a mixture of Latin and Teutonic dialects. As a reconfiguration of the characteristics of northern peoples and fragments of classical cultures, the modern age represents a heterogeneity in contrast to antiquity, whose culture was much more homogeneous and unified. Furthermore, drawing on Dutch philosopher and aesthetician Frans Hemsterhuis's critical observation that the ancient painters were too much sculptors and the modern sculptors too much painters, Schlegel sees the formal character of classical art and poetry as plastic and that of the modern or romantic as picturesque.

Schlegel's lectures set the terms of difference between the historical impulse of Greek antiquity and that of Romantic modernity. Classical art represents a finished product, a closed cycle. Romantic art, on the other hand, is always a state of becoming and characterized by the ethos of infinite perfectibility. The poetry of the Greeks, Schlegel argues in his Vienna lectures, marked a final settlement. It was housed in tropes of rest, arrest, and closure, whereas modern poetry needs continually to negotiate between remembrance and anticipation. There was a clear dichotomy between dissimilars in antiquity. In Romantic modernity, however, there is an intimate link between opposites such as nature and culture, poetry and prose, remembrance and anticipation, and the mortal and the divine. The classical and the modern represent different modes of the world of human experience. The Grecian ideal of human nature assumes perfect accord and harmony between all faculties. No gap separates fantasy and understanding, and the world exists as a coherent mythos. The modern age, however, is marked by a consciousness of internal discord where impression and reflection are divided. Thus, modern poetry strives to heal this breach in its construction of a "new mythology" that can recreate the internal coherence of the mythical condition in the contemporary world.

Every chapter of Schlegel's scholarly writing is marked by a vast comparative understanding of literary histories and the contingencies of historical modes of evaluation, and a universal acuity of aesthetic appreciation. This expanded historical consciousness of literary pasts led the Romantic critics to the retrieval of neglected and erased cultural forms that did not necessarily conform to the perceived superiority of classical standards. The Romantic recovery of fairy tales, the literature of the troubadours, the culture of the European Middle Ages and of ancient India, and the enthusiastic reappraisal of Dante Alighieri, Giovanni Boccaccio, Miguel de Cervantes, Pedro Calderón de la Barca, and Shakespeare, all more or less eclipsed by the sun of antiquity, marked a new appreciation of the diversity of literary forms, histories, and mythologies.

Whereas Schlegel's Vienna lectures historicized the ideas of early Romanticism and summarized in retrospect its broad range of literary activity, his earlier lectures in Berlin are characterized by highly original formulations. They register the critical impulse of early Romanticism in a nuanced fashion. *Poesie*, Schlegel argues, is neither bound to things and concepts nor generated by them. Rather, it is a self-creation, an "aesthetic invention," that transforms the nature it touches. Schlegel maintains that ultimately all poetry *(Poesie)* is indisputably poetry of poetry *(Poesie der Poesie)*. This felicitous phrase coined by Friedrich Schlegel refers in the first instance to the Romantic notion that poetry is always a reflection or commentary on poetry, on the coming into being of poetry, in other words, metapoetry. Borrowing from Immanuel Kant's philosophical lexicon, Friedrich Schlegel also called this metapoetic character of modern poetry *Transzendentalpoesie*. August Wilhelm von Schlegel appropriates the phrase to further elucidate the intimate chain of signification between language and poetry and to underscore the self-generative and autonomous nature of poetry.

Poetry presupposes language, which in turn is an invention of poetic sensibility, and the latter is the constantly self-transforming and never-ending poem of humanity. The transcendental view of poesy allows Schlegel to maintain that language itself is poetry and the literary work is poetry raised to a higher power, poetry of poetry. Schlegel sees a reciprocal and unbroken chain of signification between all things. This signification process is grounded in the symbolizing capacity of language, which, in the process of self-recreation, produces poetry. Poetry is born of language and builds on mythology, which itself is a "potentiated" language of the representation of nature. Poetry uses the material of mythology to carry it to a higher level of aesthetic expression. In this way, poetry constantly regenerates itself and never leaves humanity, accompanying it through the first words of childhood to the highest peaks of speculative thought and back to the ocean of its birth. Here, Schlegel makes the radical claim that poetry reproduces itself out of its own resources. Poetry constitutes a world with its own internal laws, measures, and relations.

The Berlin lectures also redefine mythology in a Viconian sense. Very much in the spirit of Giambattista Vico's understanding of myths as a cognitive approach to the world of experience, Schlegel sees in the human need to mythologize not merely an allegorical expression of complicated ideas or the replacement of an abstract concept with an image. Rather, mythology takes into its purview the complete field of intuitions that transcend the limits of understanding and lends them a sensible form. Like language, myth forms a structural system of human cognition. Certain mythologies, such as those of ancient Greeks, go through different stages of development and may become obsolete as belief systems of a particular people. Even after the demise of myth as religion, however, the poetic essence of myth remains. Artists and poets of later ages have continued to re-create ancient myths, albeit in selective, fragmentary, or reconfigured fashion. But quite apart from this conscious and deliberate reproduction of myths, our experience of the world is informed by a tendency to mythologize that manifests itself in the metaphorical transformation of everything we come in contact with. In his critique of Enlightenment ideals, Schlegel reimagines the relation between understanding and imagination as the dialectic of light and darkness. In the sunshine of reason we see the conditions of reality, but these are suspended at night, gently concealed, in order to highlight a new realm of possibilities. Reason and imagination are the common forces of our lives, and whereas reason insists on unequivocality, imagination validates the free play of ideas in unbound diversity. It is in the dark recesses of imagination, so to speak, that the magic of life and the spirit of poetry reside.

The understanding of the dialectical relation of language, poetry, and mythology requires a genuinely critical vision.

After a historically informed presentation of Romantic poetry, Schlegel formulates a hermeneutic approach to the reading of texts, which he names a "synthetic" procedure. Friedrich Schlegel's and Novalis's critique of Kantian and Fichtean idealistic philosophies took issue with the highly analytic nature of their systems. Novalis argued that true criticism had to take "both the analytic and the synthetic road" to understanding and knowledge. In a lesser philosophical vein, August Wilhelm von Schlegel argues that mere explanations of words or accidental characteristics of a work of art do not contribute to our understanding of language and art. In order to analyze poetry, we need to look at the poetic whole. Here, the true method of criticism is synthetic and hermeneutic, whereby individual poetic forms need to be understood in the larger context of *Poesie* and the theory of *Poesie* is derived or synthesized from the particularities of poetic forms. Ultimately, Schlegel's work on Romantic aesthetics enacts this synthesizing process that he advocates in the practice of criticism.

[*See also* Novalis; Poetics; *and* Romanticism, *article on* Philosophy and Literature.]

BIBLIOGRAPHY

Works by Schlegel

A. W. Schlegel's Lectures on German Literature from Gottsched to Goethe, Given at the University of Bonn and Taken Down by George Toynbee in 1933. Edited by H. G. Fidler. Oxford, 1944.

Course of Lectures on Dramatic Art and Literature. Translated by John Black. Revised by A. J. W. Morrison. London, 1846; reprint, New York, 1973.

Kritische Schriften und Briefe. 7 vols. Edited by Edgar Lohner. Stuttgart, 1962–1974.

Other Sources

Behler, Ernst. *Die Zeitschriften der Brüder Schlegel.* Darmstadt, 1983.

Behler, Ernst. *Frühromantik.* Berlin and New York, 1992.

Ewton, Ralph W. *The Literary Theories of August Wilhelm Schlegel.* The Hague, 1971.

Haym, Rudolf. *Die romantische Schule.* 3d ed. 2 vols. Berlin, 1914.

Lohner, Edgar. "August Wilhelm Schlegel." In *Deutsche Dichter der Romantik: Ihr Leben und Werk,* edited by Benno von Wiese, pp. 135–162. Berlin, 1971.

Sauer, Thomas G. *A. W. Schlegel's Shakespearean Criticism in England, 1811–1846.* Bonn, 1982.

Schenk-Lenzen, Ulrike. *Das ungleiche Verhältnis von Kunst und Kritik: Zur Literaturkritik August Wilhelm Schlegels.* Würzburg, 1991.

Schirmer, Ruth. *August Wilhelm Schlegel und seine Zeit: Ein Bonner Leben.* Bonn, 1986.

Schirmer, Walter F. *Kleine Schriften.* Tübingen, 1950.

Schlegel, Friedrich. "Athenäums Fragmente." In *Kritische Ausgabe,* edited by Ernst Behler et al., vol. 2, pp. 165–255. 35 vols. to date. Paderborn, 1959–.

Thalman, Marianne. *August Wilhelm Schlegel: Gedenkschrift zum 200. Geburtstag.* Bad Godesberg, 1967.

Wellek, René. *A History of Modern Criticism, 1750–1950,* vol. 2, *The Romantic Age.* New Haven, 1955.

AZADE SEYHAN

SCHLEGEL, KARL WILHELM FRIEDRICH VON (1772–1829), German aesthetician during the early formative phase of Romanticism, the period known as *Frühromantik,* which flourished from 1797 to 1802. Born in Hannover, he was educated at Göttingen and Leipzig. He later moved to Jena, where he developed his influential concept of Romantic poetry, formulated his famous idea of literary irony, and, together with his brother August Wilhelm, edited the journal of the early Romantic circle, *Athenäum.*

What did Schlegel mean by "romantic poetry" *(romantische Poesie)?* Obviously, that is the crucial question regarding the aesthetics of German Romanticism. But it is not easy to answer, partly because Schlegel's explanations are obscure and fragmentary, and partly because his meaning heavily depends on his intellectual context. "I cannot send you my explanation of the word 'romantic,' " he wrote his brother in December 1797, "because it would be two thousand pages long." With that in mind, this essay will only sketch an explanation here, beginning with a few basic points about Schlegel's use of the term *romantische Poesie.*

First, Schlegel began by using the term not only in a normative or stylistic sense, but also in a descriptive or historical one to refer to a specific period of literature. Romantic poetry denoted early modern in contrast to classical literature. More specifically, it signified the literature of the late Middle Ages and the Renaissance written in the Romance languages and in the countries of the former Roman Empire. This historical use of the term was common in the eighteenth century. Schlegel probably acquired it from Johann Gottfried von Herder, who, in his *Briefe zur Beförderung der Humanität* (1793–1794; Letters toward the Promotion of Humanity), used it to distinguish early modern from classical literature. The great authors of early modern literature were, in Herder's view, Miguel de Cervantes, Petrarch, Dante Alighieri, and William Shakespeare. What was characteristic of their work, he explained, is that it mixes all kinds of genres, portrays the spirit of its age, and expresses a spirit of love and adventure. Schlegel first used the term virtually in the same sense as Herder.

Second, Schlegel gradually stopped using the term in a historical sense and eventually defined it only in a normative one. As early as 1798, he stated that Romantic poetry is the ideal of *all* poetry, so that even forms of classical poetry were romantic. Schlegel combined and confused the historical and normative senses for many years, and only started using the term in a fully normative sense in his 1812 lectures *Geschichte der alten und neuen Literatur* (History of Old and New Literature).

Third, Schlegel never used the term *romantische Poesie* to refer to a specific kind or genre of poetry. It is not necessarily poetry in the sense of verse—speech with rhyme or meter—because it can also be prose. But it is not even a kind or genre of literature—poetry, drama, or novel—because one of its essential characteristics is that it is a *mixture* of genres.

In his *Brief über den Roman* (Letter on the Novel), Schlegel insisted that Romantic poetry was not a genre but an element or quality that could be applied to any genre. What was characteristic of the Romantic was "a spirit of love," "a sentimental material in a fantastic form," qualities that could be attributed to novels, plays, or poems.

Fourth, the term *romantic poetry* is indeed connected with *der Roman,* but more in the older sense of a romance than in the modern sense of a novel. This connection has been the subject of some dispute. In 1870, Rudolf Haym, in his monumental *Die romantische Schule* (The Romantic School), maintained that Schlegel's *romantische Poesie* essentially meant *romanartig* (like a novel). This point was strongly denied in 1916 by Arthur Lovejoy, who argued that the connection was accidental and negligible. In the 1950s, Haym's point was rehabilitated by Hans Eichner (1956), who argued that the terms *romantische Poesie, Romanpoesie,* and *Roman* were virtual synonyms. Eichner demonstrated that Schlegel used *der Roman* in the eighteenth-century sense to refer to the romances of early modern literature, the works that were the precursors of the modern novel (namely, Shakespeare and Cervantes). It is important to recognize, however, that Schlegel himself wanted to disassociate Romantic poetry from the verse stories of Samuel Richardson or Henry Fielding, which are closer to the novel in the modern sense.

Obviously, these basic points do not take us very far. We still do not know the specific characteristics of Schlegel's Romantic poetry, and still less why he advocated them. The most straightforward answer to these questions is to turn to Schlegel's intellectual development. Schlegel's ideal of Romantic poetry was essentially, but not entirely, a reaction against his own earlier classicism. One can understand what Schlegel meant by *Romanticism,* and why he championed it, only if one examines his classicism and why he rejected it.

Schlegel began his career as a classical philologist. His main aim was to do for the history of Greek poetry what Johann Joachim Winckelmann had done for Greek sculpture. The motives for Schlegel's classicism were, of course, more aesthetic than antiquarian. Like Winckelmann, Schlegel believed that German culture could revive only on a classical foundation through the imitation of Greek models. He regarded the Greeks as the very model of civilization, contrasting their purity, simplicity, and harmony with the corruption, complexity, and discord of modern life.

The main work of Schlegel's neoclassical period, *Ueber das Studium der griechischen Poesie* (1795; On the Study of Greek Poetry), is a sustained argument in behalf of the virtues of ancient poetry. Schlegel makes a sharp distinction between ancient and modern poetry that is heavily slanted in favor of the classical form. According to his distinction, the fundamental value of ancient poetry is beauty. Beauty means (1) that a work is complete in itself, not depending on moral and political ends; (2) that it conforms to the laws of a definite genre, so that it is an ode, an epic, or a satire but nothing more; and (3) that it is objective, imitating nature, and not subjective, expressing the sentiment of the artist. Modern poetry is the antithesis of ancient. Its aim is not to attain beauty but to be "interesting," to catch the reader's attention with novel and striking effects. It violates the basic law of aesthetic autonomy by pandering to public taste and attempting to express the spirit of the age; and, rather than conforming to the rules of a definite genre, it mixes all genres. Modern poetry is indeed so corrupt, Schlegel thinks, that its only law is to be lawless. Schlegel maintained that modern poetry is bankrupt because its quest for effects would eventually exhaust itself. Only the perception of beauty, provided by classical art, gives complete satisfaction.

Schlegel soon began to have serious doubts about his neoclassicism, however. He already had the idea of Romantic poetry in the *Studium*, and in his 1797 notebooks he began to elaborate it. In his 1797 *Lyceum Fragments* he formally repudiated his earlier classicism, dismissing the whole idea of imitation and ridiculing the belief that the ancients had a monopoly on good art. Then, in his famous 1798 *Athenäum* fragment 116, Schlegel finally revealed his new ideal of Romantic poetry.

In some respects, Schlegel's ideal is a synthesis of his earlier concepts of classical and modern poetry. Romantic poetry, he says, should be both subjective and objective, expressing sentiment (like modern poetry) and portraying its object (like classical). But, in other respects, Romantic poetry simply absorbs the characteristics of the earlier modern poetry, and so is still conceived in opposition to classical poetry. To an important extent, then, Schlegel reverses his old position, celebrating and embracing the modern poetry he once condemned. Although recent research has tended to emphasize the continuities in Schlegel's development—that he already had the idea of Romantic poetry and doubts about classical literature in the *Studium*—there is still an indisputable rupture, an indubitable volte-face, which is apparent from the many contradictions between the *Lyceum Fragments* and the *Studium*. The problem of Schlegel scholarship is to explain this reversal, not to smooth it over or deny it.

In the *Athenäum Fragments*, Schlegel attributes at least four characteristics to Romantic poetry that are at odds with classical poetry. First, whereas classical poetry strives for completion, Romantic poetry is *progressive,* constantly in a process of becoming. Second, if classical poetry sticks to a genre, Romantic poetry is a *mélange des genres,* mixing and fusing together all kinds of literary styles. Third, Romantic poetry, unlike classical, aspires to be the portrait of an age, not to create ageless beauty. Fourth, whereas classical poetry adheres to rules, Romantic poetry knows none except the caprice of the author.

To reconstruct the reasons behind Schlegel's romantic conversion, at least three factors should be emphasized:

First, Schlegel admitted even in the *Studium* that the classical aesthetic is no longer attainable in, or appropriate to, the modern age. The poetry of the Greeks arose from their immediate relationship to nature, which allowed them to imitate its objects. This relationship had disappeared in modern life, however, with the growth of individual freedom and self-consciousness. The more modern man grew in his powers of self-reflection, the more he separated himself from the natural world. Second, Schlegel had always recognized that modern culture has its own unique values, and that they are equal to those of ancient culture. If the chief principle behind ancient culture is the law of nature or instinct, that of modern culture is the law of freedom or understanding. Like Friedrich von Schiller and Johann Gottlieb Fichte, Schlegel admired modern culture for its striving for freedom, its progressive tendency. The distinction between these cultures raised the question, however, why each should not have its own distinctive art form. Why should the moderns imitate the ancients if their culture is governed by different principles? Third, under Schiller's influence, Schlegel recognized that modern poetry has its own distinctive worth. Just as classical poetry expressed the ethos of ancient culture, so modern poetry did the same for its culture.

Schlegel was converted to Romantic poetry, then, because he eventually recognized that it is more appropriate for modern culture, that it alone expresses its free, progressive, and intellectual spirit. The concept of Romantic poetry had acquired an ethical quality that modern poetry did not have in the *Studium* essay. Romantic poetry no longer stemmed from the quest for interesting effects, as modern poetry, but from a deeper moral purpose, the need to express the characteristic strivings of modern man.

Ultimately, the foundation for Schlegel's belief in Romantic poetry was his philosophy of history, which he inherited from Immanuel Kant, Fichte, and Schiller. This philosophy is essentially a secularized version of the biblical drama of paradise–Fall–redemption. There are three main stages to history, as in the biblical fable. In the first stage, man lives in harmony with nature and society. This period is best represented by the classical scholar's equivalent of the Garden of Eden: Greek civilization in the Periclean Age. In the second stage, this primitive harmony is destroyed with the growth of individuality, freedom, and self-consciousness. This period is best represented by the decline in the classical polis and the growth of the Middle Ages. The rise of Christianity expresses a longing to return to mankind's original unity and harmony; but because this is impossible on Earth, it is projected onto an imaginary heaven. In the third or final stage, the modern era, mankind strives to regain its lost unity with nature and the community. What had been given to the Greeks, and what the Christians had held on faith, it is now the task of modern man to create through his own efforts. The kingdom of God will be realized on Earth through endless struggle and striving. Of course, it is not possible to attain this ideal; but we have a duty at least to approach it.

The task of Schlegel's Romantic poetry was to express, and ultimately to promote, the striving of modern man to achieve his lost ideal. The starting point of modern culture, Schlegel wrote in his *Athenäum Fragments,* is the revolutionary wish to realize the kingdom of God on earth; but the end of every romantic work, he said in his *Lyceum Fragments,* is the *Vaterunser,* the wish that God's kingdom would come. But just as this ideal could be approached but never achieved, so Romantic art would be progressive but incomplete, the expression of a struggle to attain the unattainable.

It is in this context that Schlegel's famous concept of irony should be placed. Irony was the artist's recognition that his ultimate goal is unattainable, that he can approach it but never achieve it. If the artist fully understood this point, Schlegel believed, then he would be able to distance himself from any one of his productions, for each would be only finite and imperfect, and therefore inadequate to express his infinite and perfect ideal. In number 108 of his *Lyceum Fragments,* Schlegel wrote of irony: "It contains and excites the feeling of the irresolvable conflict between the unconditioned and condition, the impossibility and necessity of complete communication." Complete communication is impossible because any creation is finite and imperfect; but it is also necessary because it is only through striving and creating anew that we approach our ideal. Irony was thus, as Schlegel also put it in *Athenäum* fragment 51, the "constant change from self-creation to self-negation."

It should be clear from this general analysis of Schlegel's Romantic aesthetic that it does not conform to the common stereotype of Romanticism as escapism, a flight from a grim reality into an imaginary heaven. Rather, the aim of Romantic art was to *transform* reality, to bring humans closer to heaven on Earth. Its aim was to re-create the lost magic, beauty, and mystery of the world, so that humans could once again feel at home in it. If they could only achieve the final goal, then all of nature, society, and the state would become works of art. Romanticism was thus the aesthetics of modern utopianism.

[*See also* Irony; Poetics; *and* Romanticism, *article on* Philosophy and Literature.]

BIBLIOGRAPHY

Works by Schlegel

Dialogue on Poetry and Literary Aphorisms. Edited and translated by Ernst Behler and Roman Struc. University Park, Pa., 1968.
Friedrich Schlegel's Lucinde and the Fragments. Edited and translated by Peter Firchow. Minneapolis, 1971.
Kritische Friedrich-Schlegel-Ausgabe. 35 vols. Edited by Ernst Behler et al. Paderborn, 1958. The standard edition.
Literary Notebooks, 1791–1801. Edited by Hans Eichner. Toronto, 1957.

Other Sources

Ayrault, Roger. *La genèse du romantisme allemand.* 4 vols. Paris, 1961–1976.
Behler, Ernst. *Frühromantik.* Berlin and New York, 1992.
Belgardt, Raimund. "Romantische Poesie in Friedrich Schlegels Aufsatz über das Studium der griechischen Poesie." *German Quarterly* 40 (1967): 165–185.
Brinkmann, Richard. "Romantische Dichtungstheorie in Friedrich Schlegels Frühschriften und Schillers Begriffe des Naiven und Sentimentalischen." *Deutsche Vierteljahrschrift für Literaturwissenschaft und Geistesgeschichte* 32 (1958): 344–371.
Eichner, Hans. "Friedrich Schlegel's Theory of Romantic Poetry." *Publications of the Modern Language Association* 71 (1956): 1018–1041.
Haym, Rudolf. *Die romantische Schule.* Berlin, 1870.
Kluckhohn, Paul. *Das Ideengut der deutschen Romantik.* Tübingen, 1941.
Lovejoy, Arthur. "On the Meaning of 'Romantic' in Early German Romanticism." *Modern Language Notes* 31 (1916): 385–396; 32 (1917): 65–77.
Pikulik, Lothar. *Frühromantik: Epoche, Werke, Wirkung.* Munich, 1992.

FREDERICK BEISER

SCHLEIERMACHER, FRIEDRICH DANIEL ERNST

(1768–1834), a systematic theologian of nineteenth-century Protestantism. He achieved sudden public reknown with the appearance of his first book, *Reden über die Religion* (On Religion: Speeches to Its Cultured Despisers), in 1799. This was followed in short order by two works on ethics, *Monologen* and *Grundlinien einer Kritik der bisherigen Sittenlehre.* His major theological work, *Der christliche Glaube* (The Christian Faith), was published in 1821–1822. Among his other accomplishments was a three-volume translation of Plato's dialogues into German.

Schleiermacher's relevance for contemporary aesthetics stems primarily from his position as the first major theorist of the modern hermeneutical tradition. During his lifetime he published nothing on hermeneutics, but among his posthumous papers were three sets of lecture notes on the subject. The importance of these (published as *Hermeneutics: The Handwritten Manuscript* [1977]) was first made clear by Wilhelm Dilthey, who saw himself as continuing and extending into the sphere of historical interpretation Schleiermacher's methodology of textual interpretation.

Before Schleiermacher, inquiry into the problems of interpretation tended to take the form of discipline-specific rules of thumb. Historians, philologists, and scriptural exegetes would leave their colleagues advice on how to discern the meanings of texts within their own fields without paying any significant attention to how scholars in other fields dealt with their parallel problems. What was lacking was any systematic approach to the problem of interpreting written texts in general. Schleiermacher changed this situation, establishing textual interpretation as a single clearly defined subject of inquiry, by drawing out the implications of the principle of the hermeneutic circle—a principle "of such consequence for hermeneutics . . . that one cannot even begin to interpret without using it" (Schleiermacher, 1977, p. 196). The basic idea is that a whole can be understood only in terms of its parts, which in their turn can be understood only in terms of the whole to which they belong. This deceptively simple principle operates on a multiplicity of levels. Thus, words are the parts of which sentences are the wholes, sentences are the parts of which texts are the wholes, texts are the parts of which an author's total literary output is the whole, and the lifework of a given author is itself, considered as a unit, merely one part of the whole of a culture's literary tradition. Similarly, a word or expression is a part of language, a text belongs to, and is thus a part of, a particular literary genre, and a genre in turn is a part of the whole of literature. In each case, the parts and the whole in question must be understood reciprocally.

The idea that the applicability of hermeneutical rules of thumb would vary substantially from discipline to discipline was based, in Schleiermacher's opinion, on the mistaken conviction that "understanding occurs as a matter of course," and thus that the methods of hermeneutics need only be applied to difficult cases of interpretation. Schleiermacher's contention, in contrast, is that the "more rigorous practice of the art of interpretation . . . is based on the assumption that misunderstanding occurs as a matter of course, and so understanding must be . . . sought at every point" (ibid., p. 110). "This more rigourous practice," he explains, "presupposes that the speaker and hearer differ in their use of language and in their ways of formulating thoughts, although to be sure there is an underlying unity between them" (ibid.).

Without the "underlying unity" of a shared language, there would be no possibility of a hearer's coming to understand a speaker. But the degree to which speaker and hearer possess a *genuinely* shared language is easily exaggerated. Because a given word acquires its meanings only by virtue of the various contexts within which it is encountered, and these contextual encounters with a given word are always encounters on the part of some particular speaker, whose track through the social forum of linguistic communication will not be exactly the same as anyone else's, it follows that the connotations attached to a word will necessarily vary from speaker to speaker. What this means, Schleiermacher contends, is that interpreters must be aware that the seemingly unproblematic utterance, expressed in familiar terms, may in fact have a meaning quite other than that which they attribute to it. Because even contemporaries "differ in their use of language and in their ways of formulating thoughts," the task of interpretation "is not limited to what is fixed in writing, but arises whenever we have to understand a . . . series of thoughts expressed in words" (ibid., p. 182). Thus, rather than a science dedicated to the deciphering of texts distantly removed from the reader by period or culture,

hermeneutics is, for Schleiermacher, simply the art of understanding language. In every case of interpretation, moreover, the task confronting one is the same, although it consists of two clearly distinguishable parts: on the one hand, to determine the manner in which the speaker is inclined to formulate his thoughts and, on the other, to discover the speaker's personal style in his use of language.

The two-sidedness of interpretation—the fact that it consists of what Schleiermacher calls a "grammatical" and a "technical" (or "psychological") side—is grounded in the fact that speech is intimately related both to the language in which it is presented and to the thoughts of the speaker. Thus, grammatical interpretation is based on a mastery of such things as vocabulary, punctuation, sentence structure, and genre—including an understanding of how these features of language have changed historically—as well as a sensitivity to the nuances of style. Technical or psychological interpretation, by contrast, is concerned with establishing how the text in question fits into the context of its author's intellectual life. This requires an investigation of the author's biography, an examination of the social conditions of the time and place in which she lived, and a consideration of how one text should be read in the light of the author's other texts.

Schleiermacher describes the aim of technical interpretation as the complete understanding of an author's personal style. This way of putting the matter alerts us to the interdependence of the two sides of interpretation, for "we are accustomed to restrict the term 'style' to the way language is handled" (ibid., p. 148), and yet, because thoughts and language are intertwined, the way in which an author reveals her character in the organization and development of her ideas is also a matter of style. Thus, the technical and grammatical sides of interpretation involve two different ways of trying to bring the same object into view. Given this common target of the two sides of interpretation, the task of understanding "is finally resolved when either side could be replaced by the other, though both must be treated, that is to say, when each side is treated in such a way that the treatment of the other side produces no change in the result" (ibid., p. 100). The task is finished, in other words, when what we have learned about the meaning of a text by reconstructing the author's character and way of thinking (through an investigation of her life and times) serves only to confirm, and no longer to augment, what we have learned about the meaning of the text by examining the way in which it is presented in language, and vice versa.

The task of interpretation *would* be resolved if that point were reached, but according to Schleiermacher, it is in principle unreachable. "The goal of technical interpretation," he writes, "can only be approximated. . . . Not only do we never understand an individual view exhaustively, but what we do understand is always subject to correction" (ibid., p. 149). Indeed, it is precisely because neither side of interpretation can ever be brought to genuine completion that the two sides of interpretation have to be pursued in tandem. It is necessary to move back and forth between the grammatical and technical sides of interpretation because, when we are confronted, on the grammatical side, with two possible readings of a passage and there is nothing that we can discern in the author's use of language that enables us to choose between them, it is often the case that insights concerning the author's character and way of thinking—insights gathered, in other words, on the technical side of interpretation—will help us decide which of the possible readings is probably correct. On the other hand, what is learned about an author on the technical side invariably leaves open a number of directions in which her thinking might have turned at a given point, and an examination of the way in which she actually chose to express herself is of course the best way to determine what the author had in mind.

Each of the two sides of interpretation is an art, Schleiermacher contends, because it "constructs something finite and definite from something infinite and indefinite" (the clues to be found in the language of the text and in the life of the author) without the benefit of "rules which may be applied with self-evident certainty" (ibid., p. 100). The language of a text is "infinite" in that the meaning of an expression is a function of the countless relations in which its individual components stand to all the other elements of language. So, too, the nuances of individual thought processes, the ways in which they come to be affected by prior events, the ways in which ideas are interrelated within those processes, and the ways in which those processes in turn influence the thinking of others and events in the world generally, are also infinitely variable.

The art of interpretation depends, then, on the reader's possession of two separate talents: a command of language and a knowledge of human nature. According to Schleiermacher, "to the extent that a person is deficient in one of these talents, he is hampered [in his capacity to grasp the text], and the other gift can do no more than help him choose wisely from the suggestions made by others" (ibid., p. 101). Again, because both sides of interpretation have to be pursued simultaneously, so that each can be used as a check on the other, an interpreter who, for example, has a fine ear for language but little insight into human nature is not, on that basis, excused from pursuing the technical side of interpretation. On the contrary, given his handicap, he will have to be especially circumspect in his approach to the psychological side.

Schleiermacher speaks, with respect to each of the two different sides of interpretation, of two methods—divination and comparison—that are to be employed by turns. In technical interpretation, divination involves a projection of oneself into the position of the author and an attempt to anticipate on this basis what the author intended in her work.

One cannot, of course, project oneself into the position of the author without first having ascertained, at least in general terms, what the author's position actually was, and that requires a certain amount of research. On the other hand, one can never expect to re-create completely the circumstances of a person's life merely by means of research. Indeed, if one *could* perfectly re-create the author's position in this way, divination would be unnecessary, for divination is employed to compensate for the fact that what we can learn through research alone is inevitably limited with respect to detail and lacking in discriminations of significance. In the process of divination, we appeal to our shared humanity in order to get a sense of what must have seemed trivial and what important to the author, given her interests and circumstances. Thus, divination is based "on the assumption that each person is not only a unique individual in his own right, but that he has a receptivity to the uniqueness of every other person" (ibid., p. 150). Because the interpreter's act of projection is always grounded in (potentially inadequate) prior research, however, the conclusions arrived at by means of divination are always at first merely hypothetical, and become certain only when they are corroborated through the process of comparison.

According to Schleiermacher, each conclusion arrived at through divination can be thought of as "subsuming the author under a general type" (ibid.); that is to say, anything we might feel inclined to suggest on the basis of our immediate intuition of the author's intent—that the text is ironic, tragic, lyrical, and so on—can be represented as a claim about what *sort* of author she is. Whenever such a claim is advanced, moreover, it needs to be confirmed through a comparison of this author and her work (*as* an ironist, a tragedian, or a lyricist, etc.) with the work of others of the same type, the same period, and the same culture. This process of comparison establishes the range of literary possibilities available to the author in her own day. Establishing these boundaries is significant because, although it is always conceivable that the author in question has creatively extended the range of literary possibilities, if *as* an ironist, a tragedian, a lyricist, and so on she seems to have written in entirely unprecedented ways, there is good reason to believe that one's first intuitions about the text are mistaken.

The point of research carried out on the technical side of interpretation is to enable the reader to put himself in the position of the author. This is not an end in itself, but rather a mere preliminary to the reader's interpretive re-creation of the text. The relationship that is assumed here, between occupying the position of the author and understanding the text, gives rise to the best-known and most contentious of Schleiermacher's remarks on hermeneutics: that the task of interpretation is "to understand the text at first as well as and then even better than its author" (ibid., p. 112). The idea that the reader of a text should be in a position to understand it *better* than the person who actually selected each word that it contains and whose intention was realized in the writing of it has been criticized by many theorists of interpretation on the obvious grounds that the interpreter comes to the text, after all, as a stranger who cannot possibly recover, through any amount of research, the privileged relationship to the work that authorship confers. Most of these same theorists argue, however, that as interpreters we should take no special notice of the privileged position the author enjoys. What *we* make of the text is presumed to be what counts. Today, then, the tendency is to follow Hans-Georg Gadamer in celebrating the fact that each of us "understands in a different way, if we understand at all."

But, given what Schleiermacher actually means by suggesting that the aim of interpretation is to understand the text better than the author did, the objection of those who follow Gadamer rather misses the mark; for it is not especially controversial to suggest that an author might have been unaware on a conscious level of some of the reasons for her constructing a text as she did, and that nonetheless an interpreter might manage to bring those reasons to light. The author, after all, need not be aware of her own psychological predispositions, motivations, and personal prejudices in order for these things to have an effect on her work. In the process of interpretation, however, the reader must first recognize *that* these determining factors have played a role in the production of the text and then must establish *what* that role is.

To understand a text better than its author did is thus neither a meaningless nor an altogether unachievable goal. Schleiermacher, however, sees the attainment of this goal as nothing more than a by-product of the interpreter's pursuit of the proper—and genuinely unattainable—goal of interpretation; for the stronger, more accurate formulation of the task of hermeneutics is the "historical and divinatory, objective and subjective reconstruction of a given statement" (ibid., p. 111). This task has four parts to it:

1. "objective-historical" reconstruction, which involves "consider[ing] the statement in [its] relation to the language as a whole, and consider[ing] the knowledge it contains as a product of language";
2. "objective-prophetic" reconstruction, which involves "sens[ing] how the statement itself will stimulate further developments in the language";
3. "subjective-historical" reconstruction, which involves determining "how the statement, as a fact in the person's mind, has emerged"; and
4. "subjective-prophetic" reconstruction, which involves "sens[ing] how the thoughts contained in the statement will exercise further influence on and in the author." (Ibid., p. 112)

According to this more stringent formulation of the task of hermeneutics, the interpreter is to concern himself not only with establishing (in its entirety) the history of the text's creation as the product of a particular language and the product of a particular person embedded within the social fabric of her time, but also with anticipating the impact that the text will have, first, on the author's own future work, and second, on the future of the language in which it was written. "So formulated," Schleiermacher writes, "the task is infinite, because in a statement we want to trace a past and a future which stretch into infinity" (ibid.).

In his pursuit of this ideal interpretation of a text—one that correctly situates it in the web of historical and linguistic influences acting on and emanating from the text—the interpreter is necessarily drawn into a number of different fields of inquiry. He becomes, of necessity, a biographer, a psychologist, a historian, and a linguist, as well as a literary critic. Each of these fields, however, is another interpretive discipline, dominated in its turn by the open-endedness of the hermeneutic circle relating (discipline-specific) parts to their correspondent wholes. Thus, in each of the various disciplines that the interpreter finds himself having to traverse in pursuit of a correct and thorough reading of a text, the interpreter is confronted with yet another in principle incompletable task. The nature of the author's character, the nature of the social world in which she lived, the nature of the language in which she wrote, the nature of the text's genre—the comprehension of each of these things is an adjunct to the interpretation of the text itself, and yet none of these can ever be fully comprehended. The task of textual interpretation, then, is in principle incompletable for any number of reasons. The one finally correct and true interpretation of a text *is* approachable, through the application of the divinatory-comparative method on both the grammatical and technical sides of interpretation, but approachable only asymptotically. In the real world of time constraints, limited resources, and personal motives, Schleiermacher observes, "the question of how far and in which directions interpretation will be pressed must be decided . . . on practical grounds" (ibid.).

[*See also* Hermeneutics.]

BIBLIOGRAPHY

Works by Schleiermacher

Der christliche Glaube. 2 vols. Edited by Martin Redeker. Berlin, 1960. Translated as *The Christian Faith* by H. R. Mackintosh and J. S. Stewart (Edinburgh, 1928).

Hermeneutics: The Handwritten Manuscripts. Translated by James Duke and Jack Forstman, edited by Heinz Kimmerle. Missoula, Mont., 1977.

Monologen. Edited by Friedrich Michael Schiele and Hermann Mulert. Leipzig, 1914. Translated as *Soliloquies* by Horace Leland Friess (Chicago, 1926).

Reden über die Religion. Edited by G. C. B. Pünjer. Braunschweig, 1879. Translated as *On Religion: Speeches to Its Cultured Despisers* by Richard Crouter (Cambridge and New York, 1988).

Sämtliche Werke, 1835–1864. Published in three divisions: I, theological; II, sermons; III, philosophical and related subjects.

Schleiermacher's Introductions to the Dialogues of Plato. Translated by William Dobson. New York, 1973.
Vorlesungen über die Ästhetik aus Schleiermacher's handschriftlichem Nachlasse und aus nachgeschriebenen Heften. Edited by Carl Lommatzsch. Berlin, 1974.

Other Sources

Brandt, Richard B. *The Philosophy of Friedrich Schleiermacher.* New York, 1941.
Dilthey, Wilhelm. *Leben Schleiermachers.* Berlin, 1870.
Scholtz, Gunter. *Die Philosophie Schleiermachers.* Darmstadt, 1984.

RON BONTEKOE

SCHMARSOW, AUGUST (1853–1936), German educator and art theoretician. Schmarsow was born in Mecklenburg and died in Baden-Baden. As a student, after abandoning his original plan to study cultural history with Jacob Burckhardt in Basel, Schmarsow attended courses in art history with Rudolf Jahn (Zurich) and Carl Justi (Bonn); classical archaeology with Adolf Michaelis (Strasbourg); history with Julius Weizsäcker and Hermann Baumgarten (Strasbourg); German literature and philosophy with Wilhelm Scherer (Strasbourg), Karl Simrock, and Alexander Reifferscheid (Bonn); and philosophy with Ernst Laas (Strasbourg). His doctoral dissertation was in German philology on the grammarian Georg Schottelius, published in part in 1877 under the title "Leibniz und Schottelius." Schmarsow started his professional career as an assistant at the Berlin *Kupferstichkabinett* (Copper Engraving Department), moved to the directorship of the Göttingen museum in 1881, and then on to an academic career that took him from Göttingen to Breslau and Leipzig (1893), where he taught for twenty-six years. This brief summary indicates that, in his studies as well as his subsequent teaching and writing, Schmarsow had founded his theories on a broad basis, with an emphasis on cultural sciences *(Kulturwissenschaft)* rather than on any specific discipline. Although Schmarsow's academic work is today almost totally neglected, he was without doubt one of the most influential figures of his time, both as a teacher and as a theoretician. His theory of architecture had the most far-reaching effects.

Schmarsow's published work shows that his interest followed two directions. The first phase of his academic career was marked by in-depth research that resulted in monographs on a number of artists as well as detailed analysis of individual works of art. Upon taking up the chair in Leipzig, a second tendency gained prominence. His interest was now primarily in establishing general principles *(Grundbegriffe)* for the newly emerging *Kunstwissenschaft* (science of art). His intention to combine aesthetics and historic analysis of art resulted in the establishment of the foundation of a systematic science of art based on psychological and philosophical principles.

Schmarsow's inaugural lecture at Leipzig, titled *Das Wesen der architektonischen Schöpfung* (The Essence of Architectural Creation), was to prove programmatic for most of his major writings over the next quarter of a century. Schmarsow diagnosed the position of architecture within the context of a science of art as one between two extreme positions, neither of which can do it justice. For aestheticians, architecture cannot be regarded as an art per se, but as an "unfree art" indistinguishable from tectonics and handicrafts. On the other hand, "thinking architects" regard architecture as *Bekleidungskunst* (art of cladding) and therefore view their activity as scarcely anything other than an external composition of a purely technical and decorative nature, a pasting of inherited styles onto the frame of a functional structure. For Schmarsow, Gottfried Semper's notion of architecture as the "art of cladding" lent itself only too readily to an interpretation that gave undue prominence to the outside appearance of a building, that is, the way in which the building "presents" itself, externally, its facade. This (mis)interpretation, however, was all the more convincing because it seemed to reflect the actual state of architecture throughout much of the nineteenth century, which was marked by an unprecedented historical eclecticism and by a growing preoccupation with new, industrially produced materials and techniques of construction (e.g., Karl Friedrich Schinkel, Henri Labrouste). An architect might then, indeed, choose from among a number of readily available "styles" while placing increasing emphasis on the functional aspects of building.

To overcome the deplorable "aesthetics from without," Schmarsow demanded an "aesthetic from within." In doing this, he alluded to Gustav Theodor Fechner's contrasting pair of "aesthetics from above" and "aesthetics from below." Fechner, in his psychophysics, had sought to replace the speculative, idealist "aesthetics from above," whose main aim was to define the principles of beauty. In its place he advocated an "aesthetics from below," a purely experimental science of beauty, based on direct observation. With his "aesthetics from within," however, Schmarsow evoked an internal psychological point as opposed to an "external" one that concentrated on form and formal changes. Yet, as it emerged in his lecture of 1893, it was also meant in the very concrete sense of "interior space" as opposed to the prevalent formal preoccupation with the exterior of architectural creation. Schmarsow's double claim to an "aesthetics from within" set his theory apart from a number of contemporary theories that concentrated almost exclusively on the effect of the exterior of architectural constructs. Thus, he avoided viewing the essence of architecture as a purely physical response to the relation of load and force or as an art of corporeal masses. Rejecting Semper's categorical distinction between the "Caribbean hut" and architecture as an "unhistorical and unphilosophical" art, Schmarsow argued that notwithstanding the differences in material and technics of construction, both the Caribbean hut and the most sophisticated building shared a common denominator that determined their status as architecture, namely, that every human-made structure is a spatial construct.

Schmarsow was one of the first scholars to develop and employ simultaneously methods of the recently established science of art. Greatly influenced by both the physiological and psychological theories of Hermann Lotze and Wilhelm Wundt, but also by the scientific genetic methodology of the historian Karl Lamprecht, Schmarsow was a firm advocate of a genetic approach, which placed him in marked contrast to Semper's establishment of a classificatory-taxonomical system. Because the creating and/or appreciating individual is at the center of all artistic manifestations, Schmarsow concluded logically that the enclosing of a subject is the crucial criterion in the human understanding of space and consequently in the creation of space, that is, architecture.

Schmarsow's premise, based mainly on Wundt's and Lotze's theories that human perception of space is a psychological synthesis between sensory experience and spatial intuitions *(Vorstellungen)* originating in the human body, was shared by many of his contemporaries. These intuitions were rooted in a similar part of the psyche where mathematical thinking, the psychological basis of the science of space, is to be found. The only difference between the *Raumwissenschaft* (science of space) and the *Raumkunst* (art of space) lies in the fact that architecture as an art of space strives to transform inner intuition into external appearance and concrete representation, whereas science on the contrary operates only in the abstract without a concrete product. History shows the two to be inseparable in the evolution of human culture. The ideal is always pure intentional form, the laws of which are investigated by the science of space, whereas the *Baukunst,* which executes its creation in the physical world, has to come to terms with circumstances of setting and physical laws. Both are ruled by basic intellectual laws, however, which constitute the basis of the order that humans perceive in the external world. This ideal form was, for Schmarsow, evident in the tendency inherent in human nature toward regularity, repeatability of parts, and purity of forms exhibited by all human interventions in the environment. The organization of the human body affects unconsciously all products of human creation, tools as well as the decoration of the environment and the body (tattooing). In the next step, and as a continuation of his argument, Schmarsow analyzed human experience of three-dimensional space by relating each dimension to the human subject, who—as postulated—is at the center of this space, whose directional axes intersect in us.

Schmarsow developed his theory of architecture by focusing on interior space (domestic space and the basilica). It was, indeed, the crucial postulate of his theory. The experience of the exterior of an architectural construct is fundamentally and conceptually different as we experience the architectural construct as another object or body *(Körper)* external to and opposite to our own body in space. In viewing the exterior, humans arrange their own meridians as middle axes, thereby enforcing their inherent law of symmetry and proportion.

Schmarsow further elaborated his theory of architecture into a full-fledged theory of the arts that connects all of them in a coherent system of basic principles. In 1896, at a public meeting of the Royal Saxonian Society of Sciences, Schmarsow delivered a lecture titled "Über den Werth der Dimensionen im menschlichen Raumgebilde" (On the Importance of Dimensions in Human Spatial Creation) that contained most of the ideas that were further established in his *Grundbegriffe der Kunstwissenschaft am Übergang vom Altertum zum Mittelalter* (Basic Principles of the Science of Art at the Transition from Antiquity to the Middle Ages) of 1905. Schmarsow's definition of art as our creative coming to terms with the world into which we have been placed presupposed two poles: the human being and the external world. Our creative coming to terms with the world is determined by our physical and psychic organization and constitution. Elaborating on his theory as presented in the 1893 lecture, Schmarsow distinguished three essential constituents of the human anatomy that are of crucial importance in our experiencing of the world and consequently make their mark in any aesthetic creation: our erect position, which distinguishes us from animals; our physical organization in pairs, such as two eyes, arms, ears, hands, breasts, legs, feet; and our pronounced frontal orientation (face, directional axis of the arms, legs, and feet).

Our coming to terms with the world follows the three-dimensionality of the intuited category that we call space. In a psychophysiological interpretation, Schmarsow identified the three peculiarities of the human anatomy as decisive in the experience of the three dimensions. Thus, height, as the dominant first dimension, is deduced from a human's vertical axis; width, the second dimension, is primordially experienced as a correlate of the extension of our shoulders, emphasized by our outstretched arms; the third dimension, depth, is correlated to our pronounced frontality, which determines our forward looking and moving. The location of the different organs, the peculiarity of their positioning, the degree of their mobility, their dependence on the torso, their degree of cooperation—all these determine not only our orientation in space but even our understanding of it and our rendering of space in the arts.

Schmarsow then established each of the three dimensions or axes as the generating force for one of the fine arts. It is with perfect inner logic that Schmarsow spoke in his 1896 lecture of *Raumgebilde* (creation in and of space), referring to all three fine arts. According to his elaborate system, the first dimension or vertical axis predominates in sculpture, the *Körperbilderin* (shaper of bodies); the second dimension or axis of width in painting, the *Flächengestalterin* (creatress of surfaces); and the third dimension or axis of depth in architecture, the actual *Raumgestalterin* (creatress of space). Following Semper's tripartite classification, Schmarsow arrives at the three principles of proportionality, symmetry, and rhythm, the latter replacing Semper's term *direction*. The principle of proportionality follows the different segmentations along our own vertical axis and is the determining principle for sculpture. Our own "symmetrical" organization (eyes, ears, breasts, arms, legs) requires a demand for symmetry that is established as a decisive principle for painting. The principle of rhythm, according to Schmarsow, is the natural outcome of our own breathing and heartbeat as well as our rhythmical moving forward. Consequently, rhythm is the decisive principle for architecture.

Schmarsow's complex construct can be represented in the following schema:

Human body	Dimensions	Fine art	Creative principle
Vertical axis	1st dimension	Sculpture	Proportion
Horizontal axis	2d dimension	Painting	Symmetry
Direction (depth)	3d dimension	Architecture	Rhythm

In establishing his system of basic principles of art, Schmarsow placed overriding emphasis on the human body and its particular organization in the experience of space. Yet, in doing so, he did not rely on an exclusively physiological or psychological position, nor did his theory conform to Robert Vischer's *Einfühlung* (empathy). Already in his *Grundbegriffe* he explicitly distanced himself from the "scientific or more specifically physiological basis" that he, like many others—including Alois Riegl and Adolf von Hildebrand—had thought essential, "from which we originally expected the highest triumph of exact science." Schmarsow now called it an *Abweg* (the wrong track) that "has to be renounced if we want to proceed."

Comparing the different stages in the development of Schmarsow's theories, an evident, increasing tendency toward phenomenological thinking emerged. Throughout his work there are increasing indications of implicit affinities between his theories and those of the early phenomenologists. It is, however, only in his 1919 essay "Kunstwissenschaft und Kulturphilosophie mit gemeinsamen Grundbegriffen" (The Basic Concepts Underlying a Science of Art and Cultural Philosophy) that he referred openly to phenomenology and especially to Max Scheler's *Der Formalismus in der Ethik und die materielle Weltethik* (Formalism in Ethics and Material World Ethics). In this essay, Schmarsow took up Scheler's distinction of the human body as *Körper* and *Leib*. For Scheler, the term *Leib* refers to the consciousness of our having a body that transcends our experience of our body as a *Körper,* that is, the sum of internal and external sensations.

Schmarsow used this distinction already in his *Grundbegriffe*, without, however, providing a reference for it. There he stated that the human subject's coming to terms with the external world begins with his own *Leib,* and, a few lines later, that the condition of the organic creature that finds itself *Körper* determines its relation to the world. Schmarsow's insistence on the determining factor of movement regarding the third dimension, of space, shows affinities to Edmund Husserl's theory of kinesthesia as being constitutive for the notion of space. Furthermore, the relevance of the "ground," the *Grund und Boden,* for man's experience of the world is emphasized on several occasions in the *Grundbegriffe*. Out of this relation to the common "ground" that we share with all other bodies arises also the basic condition for all artistic creation.

Thus, although it would be exaggerated to classify Schmarsow as a phenomenologist, numerous references throughout his theories clearly indicate a development away from positivistic psychology into a phenomenology of the visual arts.

[*See also* Architecture.]

BIBLIOGRAPHY

Works by Schmarsow

"Leibniz und Schottelius: Die 'unvorgreiflichen Gedanken'." Strasbourg, 1877. Reprinted in *Quellen und Forschungen zur Sprach- und Culturgeschichte der Germanischen Völker* 23 (1877): 1–43 (doctoral dissertation).

Das Wesen der architektonischen Schöpfung. Leipzig, 1994. Inaugural lecture given at the University of Leipzig on 8 November, 1893.

"Über den Werth der Dimensionen im menschlichen Raumgebilde." *Berichte über die Verhandlungen der königlich Sächsischen Gesellschaft der Wissenschaften zu Leipzig, Philologisch-historische Klasse* 48 (1896): 44–61. Address delivered to the society on 23 April 1896.

Beiträge zur Ästhetik der bildenden Künste. 3 vols. Leipzig, 1896–1899.

Barock und Rokoko: Eine kritische Auseinandersetzung über das Malerische in der Architektur. Leipzig, 1897.

Plastik, Malerei und Reliefkunst in ihrem gegenseitigen Verhältnis. Leipzig, 1899.

Grundbegriffe der Kunstwissenschaft am Übergang vom Altertum zum Mittelalter, kritisch erörtert und in systematischen Zusammenhänge dargestellt. Leipzig, 1905.

"Kunstwissenschaft und Völkerpsychologie: Ein Versuch zur Verständigung." *Zeitschrift für Ästhetik und allgemeine Kunstwissenschaft* 2 (1907), part 1: 305–339; part 2: 469–500.

"Raumgestaltung als Wesen der architektonischen Schöpfung." In *Kongress für Ästhetik und allgemeine Kunstwissenschaft, Berlin 9–10 Oktober 1913,* pp. 246–250. Stuttgart, 1914.

"Kunstwissenschaft und Kulturphilosophie mit gemeinsamen Grundbegriffen." *Zeitschrift für Ästhetik und allgemeine Kunstwissenschaft* 13 (1919), part 1: 165–190; part 2: 225–258.

"Rhythmus in menschlichen Raumgebilden." *Zeitschrift für Ästhetik und allgemeine Kunstwissenschaft* 14 (1920): 171–187.

"Zur Lehre vom Rhythmus." *Zeitschrift für Ästhetik und allgemeine Kunstwissenschaft* 16 (1922): 109–118.

"August Schmarsow: Rückschau beim Eintritt ins siebzigste Lebensjahr." In *Die Kunstwissenschaft der Gegenwart in Selbstdarstellungen,* edited by Johannes Jahn, pp. 135–156. Leipzig, 1924.

Other Sources

Mallgrave, Harry Francis, and Eleftherios Ikonomou, eds. *Empathy, Form and Space: Problems in German Aesthetics, 1873–1893*. Santa Monica, Calif., 1994.

Schwarzer, Mitchell. "The Emergence of Architectural Space: August Schmarsow's Theory of Raumgestaltung." *Assemblance* 15 (1991): 48–61.

ELEFTHERIOS IKONOMOU

SCHOENBERG, ARNOLD FRANZ WALTER

(1874–1951), composer and music theorist. Born in Vienna, Schoenberg (or Schönberg) came of age within the cultural and artistic traditions of the late nineteenth century, and he remained deeply committed to preserving and extending these. But he was also caught up in the revolutionary transformations that took place in his native city during the early years of the twentieth century; and balancing traditional and innovative elements, he forged from these circumstances a new compositional language with profound consequences for twentieth-century music and musical thought.

Most of Schoenberg's first fifty years were spent in Vienna, punctuated by two periods in Berlin (1901–1903 and 1911–1915). Dominated by conservative musical institutions, the city took little note of his work; often beset by extreme financial hardships, Schoenberg departed willingly and permanently in 1925 when offered the prestigious chair in composition at the Prussian Academy of Arts, Berlin, recently vacated by Ferruccio Busoni. With Adolf Hitler's rise to power in 1933, however, Schoenberg lost his position and, recognizing the implications for himself and his music, soon emigrated. After a brief period in Paris, he came to the United States, settling in California in 1934, where he spent the remainder of his life.

Schoenberg's musical aesthetic is inseparable from his compositional development. Largely self-taught, in the first years of the twentieth century he produced a remarkable series of compositions in a late-Romantic manner, motivated by both Wagnerian and Brahmsian influences and thereby synthesizing the "programmatic" and "absolute-music" lines of the Germanic tradition. In these works, Schoenberg pushed the boundaries of traditional tonal language to their breaking point. What distinguished him from others (Gustav Mahler, Claude Debussy, and Richard Strauss, for example), was his taking the final step toward "atonality" in fully abandoning the two primary attributes of traditional musical grammar: triadically constructed harmony and the privileging of a single, hierarchically elevated tone to which all others were subordinated. Tied to this was what Schoenberg called the "emancipation of dissonance": the treatment of dissonance not as the opposite of consonances, but as different only in degree. This move completely redefined the boundaries of what might be considered musically possible; and thereafter, no younger composer could approach musical material in quite the same way as before.

The final rupture with tonality occurred in 1907, initiating a period of intense creative activity for Schoenberg. Within a short period he composed a stream of new works, written as if improvised without conscious controls, and including several seminal works of musical modernism (most famously *Pierrot Lunaire*, a 1912 song cycle for soprano—employing *Sprechstimme*, a manner midway between speech and song—and five instrumentalists). To some extent, the atonal works can be viewed as extending developments initiated in the preceding ones. If there tonal definition was pushed to the breaking point, here it was annihilated; and if there traditional phrase structures and formal balances achieved ever more complex realizations, here they were abandoned entirely. The "last straw" effect produced by these developments was shattering, giving birth to a music of unprecedented formal fragmentation and expressive schism.

Following this initial explosive release, Schoenberg's work quickly approached a crisis point. Already between 1909 and 1916 fewer compositions appeared, and complete silence set in from 1916 until 1923. Far from being inactive in these years, Schoenberg experimented ceaselessly, attempting to develop a new compositional grammar to replace the traditional one that he had discarded. A move toward more conscious formulation is already evident in the works of 1909 to 1916 and can be traced in the gestation of a single composition, the one-act opera *Die glückliche Hand*, composed intermittently between 1909 and 1913, acquiring a significantly more rigorous complexion as it neared completion. During the period of silence, Schoenberg continued to work on numerous unfinished pieces, exploring new constructive principles designed to order and contain the highly chromatic musical material he felt to be the inevitable outcome of the dissolution of tonality.

In 1923, having completed his search, Schoenberg published the first works written according to a procedure he called the "method of composing with twelve tones which are related only with one another," subsequently known as the "twelve-tone system." (The tonal system, by contrast, uses seven primary tones, the remaining five being treated as departures.) Taking a particular ordering of all twelve pitches as a norm, uniquely chosen for each particular work, this "row," or "series," is placed within a larger configuration of symmetrical reflections: inversion, retrograde, and retrograde-inversion forms of the same row. This configuration then forms the basis for the pitch material used in the work, providing a basis for determining pitch choices within a fully chromatic, twelve-tone context while allowing for complete freedom in the determination of rhythm, texture, form, and other matters. (In this latter respect, Schoenberg's system differs fundamentally from the so-called integral serialism of the 1950s, where not only pitches are serialized but other compositional parameters as well, most notably rhythm.) Schoenberg stated that his system was based on the "principle of the absolute and unitary perception of musical space," putting it in marked contrast to the asymmetrical, unidirectional musical space of traditional tonality.

After 1923, Schoenberg again composed with relative ease, working primarily with his new method and exploring and extending its possibilities until his death in 1951. Once again he adopted traditional formal types, such as sonata and variation, discarded when he first abandoned tonality, bringing him back full circle to his initial formal presuppositions. Due to his persisting posttonal orientation, however, Schoenberg at this time was frequently paired and contrasted with Igor Stravinsky, who remained resolutely committed to tonality during these years (rethought by him as a more generalized play of "polar attractions"), the two becoming the leading representatives of what were considered the two principal compositional directions of the first half of the twentieth century. Theodor W. Adorno's *Philosophie der neuen Musik* (1948), for example, one of the most important early studies of musical modernism, is framed exclusively in terms of their divergent developments:

> It is . . . not in the illusion of grand personality that only these two composers—Schoenberg and Stravinsky—are to be discussed. For if the total product of new music—as defined by its inner qualities rather than by chronology—were to be scrutinized in its entirety, including all transitions and compromises, these same extremes would again be encountered.
>
> (Adorno, 1973, pp. 3–4)

Although Schoenberg thought of himself primarily as a composer, he was one of the major music theorists of his time, and an important teacher of composition. Always intensely self-aware, he expressed himself publicly on all aspects of his art. Unlike such nineteenth-century writer-composers as Robert Schumann, Hector Berlioz, and Richard Wagner, he did not limit himself to general critical and philosophical matters but addressed the mechanics of his craft. (In the preface to his *Theory of Harmony*, published in 1911, the first of several technical monographs, he states that his intent is to provide "a good practical theory," not "a bad aesthetic.") Among a number of major younger composers taught by Schoenberg (including such unlikely figures as Hanns Eisler and John Cage), the most closely—and famously—associated with him were his fellow Austrians Alban Berg and Anton Webern, the three eventually coming to be designated as the "second Viennese school."

Schoenberg was also a profoundly original amateur painter, the librettist for his three operas, and an inventor and designer of great skill. His intensely expressionistic, idiosyncratic paintings date almost entirely from one brief period, not coincidentally the years immediately following his liberation from traditional tonality, when his amateur status as artist accorded well with his then commitment to unmediated personal expression. The painter Wassily Kandinsky, with whom Schoenberg was in close contact at the time, thought highly enough of his work to include two of his paintings in his almanac *Der blaue Reiter*. In an article he contributed for a 1912 *Festschrift*, Kandinsky commented:

> We see *at once* that Schoenberg paints, not in order to produce "beautiful," "nice," etc. pictures; rather, while painting he does not even think about the picture itself. Ignoring the objective result, he seeks only to pin down his subjective "sensation," and in doing so, employs only those resources that appear to him at that moment indispensable. Not even all professional painters can boast of this manner of painting!
>
> (Quoted in Hahl-Koch, 1984, p. 126)

Schoenberg's multiple talents were most fully united in *Die glückliche Hand*, for which he supplied the music and libretto, choreographed gestures and movements, painted the sets, and designed the lighting—a totality that he characterized as "making music with the media of the stage."

Despite his stress on technical matters, Schoenberg wrote eloquently on the aesthetic foundations of his art. His early creative evolution was shaped by Romantic—primarily Schopenhauerian—ideals of transcendental expression, which in his hands took on a distinctly expressionistic cast, encouraging rejection of inherited conventions in search of a unique inner vision and private compositional language. The idea that each work should define its own standards, independent of acquired rules or other restrictions, colors all of Schoenberg's early output. He articulated the position most emphatically in a series of letters written to Busoni in 1909: "My only intention is to have *no* intentions! . . . to place nothing inhibiting in the stream of my unconscious sensations. But to allow anything to infiltrate which may be invoked either by intelligence or consciousness." Two years later he wrote to Kandinsky:

> Every formal procedure which aspires to traditional effects is not completely free from conscious motivation. But art belongs to the *unconscious!* One must express *oneself!* Express oneself *directly!* Not one's taste, or one's upbringing, or one's intelligence, knowledge or skill. Not all these *acquired* characteristics, but that which is *inborn, instinctive*. (Quoted in Hahl-Koch, 1984, p. 23)

Although this intuitive aesthetic was essential to Schoenberg's renunciation of tonality, it eventually raised issues in his own mind concerning the comprehensibility of his music. After the initial two years of intense activity, as his output declined, he began to question the advisability of composing in such a seemingly improvisatory manner. Whereas the final compositions of 1909, such as the violently eruptive psychological monodrama *Erwartung* (twenty minutes in length, and composed in a mere seventeen days), were not only "atonal" but also "athematic," without fixed, recurring melodic substance (Adorno writes of *Erwartung's* "seismographic registration of traumatic shock"), subsequent pieces began to reveal more explicit melodic correspondences and even such traditional structural devices as canonic imitation. Having reached the extremes of unfettered expressivity, Schoenberg evidently questioned the possibility of sustaining such a high-wire act of creative intensity and began to introduce more conscious constraints. Looking back from 1941, he observed:

> From the very beginning such [atonal] compositions differed from all preceding music, not only harmonically but also melodically, thematically, and motivically. But the foremost characteristics of these pieces *in statu nascendi* were their extreme expressiveness and their extraordinary brevity. At that time, neither I nor my pupils were conscious of the reasons for these features. Later I discovered that our sense of form was right when it forced us to counterbalance extreme emotionality with extraordinary shortness. Thus, subconsciously, consequences were drawn from an innovation which, like every innovation, destroys while it produces. New colourful harmony was offered, but much was lost. . . . Whether one calls oneself conservative or revolutionary, . . . one must be convinced of the infallibility of one's own fantasy and one must believe in one's own inspiration. Nevertheless, the desire for a conscious control of the new means and forms will arise in every artist's mind; and he will wish to know *consciously* the laws and rules which govern the forms which he has conceived "as in a dream." Strongly convincing as this dream may have been, the conviction that these new sounds obey the laws of nature and of our manner of thinking—the conviction that order, logic, comprehensibility and form cannot be present without obedience to such laws—forces the composer along the road of exploration. He must find, if not laws or rules, at least ways to justify the dissonant character of these harmonies and their successions. After many unsuccessful attempts during a period of approximately twelve years I laid the foundations for a new procedure in musical construction which seemed fitted to replace those structural differentiations provided formerly by tonal harmonies.
>
> (Schoenberg, 1975, pp. 217–218)

This "new procedure" was the twelve-tone system. Although its formalist orientation, as well as its coupling with traditional formal types, was consistent with the general anti-Romantic retrenchment and turn toward "sobriety" evident throughout European art in the years following World War I, the overtly systematic Constructivism of the new system assured that it attained considerable notoriety. Schoenberg was widely attacked for having turned music into a sort of mathematical game, and for the rest of his life he was considered by many to be little more than a modernist musical engineer. Yet, as his own words make clear, Schoenberg considered his path not in opposition to the Western musical tradition but as leading logically out of it. It is in this context that he remarked to one of his students in 1921 that the twelve-tone system would "insure the supremacy of German music for the next one hundred years."

With regard to historical process, Schoenberg was fundamentally traditionalist: he viewed his own work from the perspective of nineteenth-century notions of historical evolution and progress, as a logical and indeed necessary continuation of lines deeply anchored in the past. It was his belief that these lines traced a development toward ever greater concision and comprehensibility, the ornamental and unnecessary being progressively discarded so as to allow composers to say the "most important things in the most concentrated manner in every fraction of time." (In his earlier years, Schoenberg had confessed to Karl Kraus, inveterate opponent of all linguistic cant and imprecision: "I have learned more from you, perhaps, than a man should learn, if he wants to remain independent.") "This is why," Schoenberg noted, "when composers have acquired the technique of filling one direction with content to the utmost capacity, they must do the same in the next direction, and finally in all the directions in which music expands" (Schoenberg, 1975, p. 116). Through this process, music moved ever closer to its true nature. Schoenberg always emphasized, therefore, the close links between his own work and that of his forerunners, and stressed that any valid compositional technique had to be rooted in the past. He denied that he was a "revolutionary," convinced that everything he did "grew out of a necessity," servicing "progress in the direction toward an unrestricted musical language."

Schoenberg thus increasingly saw himself as an artistic prophet whose mission it was to chart music's path out of the modern wasteland—an idea powerfully brought to symbolic realization in the opera *Moses und Aron* (which remained, significantly, unfinished). Composing took on the aura of a responsibility, undertaken in response to an order from God (characterized as the "Supreme Commander"): "I knew I had to fulfill a task: I had to express what was necessary to be expressed and I knew I had the duty of developing my ideas for the sake of progress in music, whether I liked it or not" (ibid., p. 53)

This sense of duty made Schoenberg's journey both burdensome and lonely. In a 1910 aphorism, published in the periodical *Die Musik*, he stated: "Art is the cry of despair of those who experience within themselves the fate of all mankind." Indeed, pain and isolation are evident both in the difficulty of Schoenberg's music and in his belief that great art can only be for the few ("If it is art, it is not for all, and if it is for all, it is not art"). This acquired concrete expression in Schoenberg's formation of the Society for Private Musical Performances in Vienna in 1918, conceived so that performances of new works could be heard under carefully controlled conditions, divorced from normal concert life. Schoenberg's sense of alienation was also closely linked to his experience as an Austrian Jew, increasingly forced to see himself as an artistic, cultural, and racial outsider. Whether compelled or by choice, Schoenberg was always "in opposition."

The idea of "destiny," of taking "decisive steps" in response to historical necessity, cuts across the lines separating Schoenberg's tonal, free atonal, and twelve-tone compositions. It even informs his unexpected return to traditional tonality in several works written intermittently during the final two decades of his life. Typically, Schoenberg explained this move as an effort to close a lacuna in his own historical evolution: the Organ Variations, op. 48 of 1941, for example, were written to "fill out the gap" between the still-tonal Chamber Symphony (1907) and the immediately following atonal works. Similarly, a concerto by Georg Matthias Monn (1717–1750) was reworked in 1933 to lend it "true substance" by removing the "principal deficiencies of the Handel style" (Monn thereby being elevated to the "true" tradition).

Today, when such ideas have come to epitomize the hubris and masculine aggressiveness said to characterize the modernist endeavor in general, Schoenberg's aesthetic may appear hopelessly dated. Yet the composer's quasi-theological belief in artistic necessity must be measured against his overall artistic persona, with its profound contradictions in compositional output and aesthetic attitude. There is an almost schizophrenic split between Schoenberg's early position of unmediated expression and his later formalism and Constructivism; or between his deep distrust of all calculation, exact sequential repetition, and balanced proportioning in tonal music and his enthusiastic acceptance of the mirror symmetries underlying the twelve-tone system. There is also, though rarely acknowledged, the fact that Schoenberg's artistic self-consciousness and eclectic pluralism anticipate qualities now associated with musical postmodernism. The fundamental uncertainty reflected in Schoenberg's aesthetic and compositional shifts, along with the very extremity with which he espoused historical determinism, bespeak a tradition already in the throes of dissolution. Perhaps this helps explain one of the more perplexing features of music scholarship today: that this much-disputed composer, whose music remains almost as rarely performed today as during his own lifetime, retains such a defiant hold on contemporary musical consciousness.

[*See also* Modernism, *article on* Modern Music; *and* Music, *historical overview article.*]

BIBLIOGRAPHY

Works by Schoenberg

Letters. Edited by Erwin Stein, translated by Eithne Wilkins and Ernst Kaiser. London, 1964; reprint, Berkeley, 1987.
Style and Idea: Selected Writings of Arnold Schoenberg. Edited by Leonard Stein, translated by Leo Black. London, 1975; reprint, Berkeley, 1985.
Theory of Harmony (1911). Translated by Roy E. Carter. Berkeley, 1978.

Other Sources

Adorno, Theodor W. *Philosophy of Modern Music* (1948). Translated by Anne G. Mitchell and Wesley V. Blomster. New York, 1973.
Auner, Joseph H. "Schoenberg's Handel Concerto and the Ruins of Tradition." *Journal of the American Musicological Society* 49.2 (Summer 1996): 264–313.
Dahlhaus, Carl. *Schoenberg and the New Music.* Translated by Derrick Puffett and Alfred Clayton. Cambridge and New York, 1987.
Hahl-Koch, Jelena, ed. *Arnold Schoenberg/Wassily Kandinsky: Letters, Pictures and Documents.* Translated by John C. Crawford. London and Boston, 1984.
Kallir, Jane. *Arnold Schoenberg's Vienna.* New York, 1984. See on Schoenberg's paintings.
Morgan, Robert P. "Secret Languages: The Roots of Musical Modernism." *Critical Inquiry* 10.3 (March 1984): 442–461.
Ringer, Alexander L. *Arnold Schoenberg: The Composer as Jew.* Oxford, 1990.
Rosen, Charles. *Arnold Schoenberg.* 2d ed. Chicago, 1996.
Rufer, Joseph. *The Works of Arnold Schoenberg: A Catalogue of His Compositions, Writings, and Paintings.* Translated by Dika Newlin. London, 1962.
Schorske, Carl E. *Fin-de-Siècle Vienna: Politics and Culture.* New York, 1980. See chap. 7: "Explosion in the Garden: Kokoschka and Schoenberg."
Smith, Joan Allen. *Schoenberg and His Circle: A Viennese Portrait.* New York, 1986.
Stuckenschmidt, H. H. *Arnold Schoenberg: His Life, World and Work.* Translated by Edith Temple Roberts and Humphrey Searle. Reprint, New York, 1977.

ROBERT P. MORGAN

SCHOPENHAUER, ARTHUR (1788–1860), German philosopher who was an archrival of G. W. F. Hegel and who considered himself Immanuel Kant's only true heir in philosophy. Schopenhauer's aesthetics has arguably been more widely influential than that of any other philosopher of the past two centuries. Not only have subsequent philosophers, notably Friedrich Nietzsche, Henri Bergson, Ludwig Wittgenstein, and Susanne Knauth Langer, been much affected by his vision of the place and power of art, but a wide array of writers, composers, and intellectuals have testified, either explicitly or in their own works, to the power of that vision and of the metaphysics in which it is embedded: Richard Wagner, Gustav Mahler, Stendhal, Leo Tolstoy, Rainer Maria Rilke, Thomas Mann, Sigmund Freud, Marcel Proust, Thomas Hardy, Joseph Conrad. It would be fair to say that Schopenhauer's aesthetics has been, in the twentieth century, the artist's favored philosophy of art.

One cannot understand Schopenhauer's aesthetics without some understanding of Schopenhauer's metaphysics, and it is impossible to understand Schopenhauer's metaphysics without at least a passing grasp of the metaphysics of Kant, Schopenhauer's great predecessor and chief mentor among philosophers. Fortunately, however, it is possible to understand Schopenhauer's aesthetics without understanding Kant's aesthetics—though here too, naturally, influences and similarities can be noted. Thus, for the purposes of this essay, we can make do with thumbnail sketches of Kant's and Schopenhauer's metaphysics, and then proceed to the main topic, Schopenhauer's aesthetics.

The Metaphysical Background. The central notion in Kant's philosophy, the philosophy of transcendental idealism, is that the empirical world, the world known in perception, is in significant part a product of the mind's active structuring of the raw data of experience. This structuring is in terms of the forms of sensory intuition, namely, space and time, and the categories of the understanding, such as substance, causality, and relation. This structuring, furthermore, has a necessary or a priori status; without it, coherent experience of an objective world would not be possible, nor would knowledge of the sort represented by arithmetic, geometry, and pure physics. Hence, the world as it is known to us cannot, in virtue of such extensive and ineluctable structuring by the knowing mind, be identified with the world as it is in itself. The former has features that, because they are contributed by our very mode of knowing, cannot be features of the latter. The world as it is in itself must thus be granted—at least negatively, as a limiting condition of the world of experience—while evidently remaining beyond the possibility of being known as such. The known, or phenomenal, world is not all there is to reality: there is an unknowable, noumenal world, in some way underlying the appearances constituting the phenomenal one, and in unfathomable correspondence with it.

Schopenhauer takes over Kant's transcendental idealism wholesale, but with certain simplifications. Although he accepts space and time as primary modes of perceptual structuring, Schopenhauer reduces Kant's twelve categories of the understanding to one, causality, and regards space, time, and causality as in fact all forms of the Principle of Sufficient Reason, that everything must have a reason or ground for existing in just the way it does, which applies to all appearances or representations. The Principle of Sufficient Reason is valid only for the world of phenomena, including human action, and has no application beyond it. As we shall see, Schopenhauer ultimately entertains a notion of knowing "outside of" the Principle of Sufficient Reason, a knowing that finds its clearest exemplification in art, but this remains confined to the phenomenal realm, because still participating in and thus affected by the fundamental condition of knowledge in general, namely, the distinction of subject and object, or knower and known. For Schopenhauer, "subject" and "object" are correlative terms: all objects are inherently objects for a subject, and all subjects are inherently subjects cognizing objects; moreover, the characters of subjects and objects so correlated are always themselves importantly parallel.

Schopenhauer refers to space, time, and causality collectively as the *principium individuationis*. The existence of a plurality of distinct individuals and the existence of a framework of spatial, temporal, and causal relations are, for Schopenhauer, inseparable. But because space, time, and causality are aspects of the human way of knowing, individuality and plurality are themselves artifacts of that way of knowing, and cannot bear on the world as it is in itself. Noumenal reality must be nonplural, or nondivided, in nature. But can anything more be said, in a more positive vein, about that reality?

This is where the most distinctive part of Schopenhauer's metaphysics emerges. Although Schopenhauer, as a Kantian, holds throughout that the in-itself can, in the nature of things, never be known as such, there are still experiences available at the phenomenal level that give some insight into the nature of noumenal reality, and that ground a certain kind of extrapolation to its character. The key to this knowledge, albeit relative, of the thing-in-itself, of the inner nature of the world, is one's own person, and more particularly, one's own body. As Schopenhauer puts it, "we ourselves are the thing-in-itself" (1958, vol. 2, p. 195).

All other objects one knows only from the outside, as items in space and time enmeshed in a web of causes and effects. One's own body, on the other hand, is known also from within, introspectively and noninferentially. The purposeful movements of this body, observable to all externally, are known at the same time by the agent, internally, as acts of will. My body and my will are one: what manifests itself outwardly as matter moving through space manifests itself inwardly as agency or volition. What is more—and this is the crucial step in Schopenhauer's metaphysical argument—in knowing my body from the inside, I am knowing it in a way that gives some indication (the most it is possible for me to have, from this side of the phenomenal fence) of what it is like in and of itself, because certain of the forms of structuring that operate to generate phenomenal appearances are absent. In particular, the appearance of bodily action from within is freed of the filter of space, and, to some extent, causality, even though such an appearance is still in time, that is, apprehensible only successively, and still reflects, as an appearance, the essential division of knower and known.

Thus, Schopenhauer proclaims, my entire inner nature is willing—desiring, striving, urging—and all varieties of affect and emotion, pleasure and pain, that conduce to or inhibit action. Furthermore, one must take this as the best indication one has been vouchsafed as to the noumenal character of one's self: since when the distorting forms of phenomenal appearance are partially removed, the in-itself reveals itself as essentially conative, we can only assume that were they to be all removed, the in-itself would display a character somehow further along in that direction. (Schopenhauer is careful to caution, though, that we can have no assurance that this would be so; what the world is in itself absolutely, apart from all knowing, remains for him, as for Kant, unknowable.) Finally, by a second extrapolation, relying in part on the previously established nonplurality of noumenal reality, Schopenhauer draws the conclusion that the inner nature or noumenal character of everything is, again, to our best approximation, on the order of will as well. "If all other phenomena could be known by us just as immediately and intimately [as our own actions], we should be obliged to regard them precisely as that which the will is in us" (ibid., p. 197). All natural phenomena, including physical forces, are to be understood as forms of the sort of willing or agency with which we are familiar in our own cases, and the phenomenal world as a whole as the manifestation of a single, undifferentiated, so to speak cosmic, Will. In fact, and serving as a kind of empirical confirmation of this metaphysical deduction, the whole of nature, organic and inorganic, according to Schopenhauer, shows itself when suitably viewed as nothing other than a theater in which the universal will manifests itself in innumerable ways, and in the playing out of which conflict, frustration, and suffering are ubiquitous and inevitable.

This brings us, naturally, to Schopenhauer's famous pessimism. Human nature is at its core essentially striving or desire. But desire is a state of lack—of not having—and is thus an inherently unpleasant and disagreeable condition. Furthermore, the needs and wants of a given individual are generally both internally in conflict and externally in conflict with those of others; thus, as might be expected, the unclouded satisfaction of desire only infrequently occurs. Finally, such satisfaction as occurs is a very minor good, for three reasons. First, it has an entirely negative character, being just the pleasure of momentary cessation of desiring. Second, any desire actually fulfilled, and so extinguished, is as a rule quickly replaced by a multitude of others, whose noisy demands soon drown out the sensation of relief just noted. Third, in the odd event that new desires do not immediately surge up to take the place of those that have been quelled, what one has is nothing more than a state of perfect boredom or ennui, no more pleasant than the more usual state of constant unfulfilledness. It should be borne in mind that the foregoing diagnosis, which might seem to be based simply on a somewhat jaundiced observation of human psychology, together with some conceptual analysis, is, for Schopenhauer, undergirded by the metaphysical conviction that persons, and indeed the whole of existence, have willing as their essential and thus inescapable nature. Thus, insofar as one remains anchored in willing as a spatiotemporally bound individual—a bundle of strivings and cravings—suffering is virtually guaranteed.

Schopenhauer's Aesthetics. There is, however, a means of temporary escape from this sorry condition. It is afforded by aesthetic experience. Aesthetic experience, unlike ordinary perception, is focused not on material particulars in space and time, but on the perceivable essences or universals that such particulars embody, and that Schopenhauer, following Plato, calls Ideas. In the course of focusing on such objects, the perceiver is in effect transmuted: spatiotemporally rooted, practically oriented individuality gives

way, and what Schopenhauer calls the "pure subject of knowing," the same in everyone, takes its place. In aesthetic experience, one knows the world independently of the Principle of Sufficient Reason, grasping not the "why" or "how" of things, but only the "what": the knowledge faculty, ordinarily the servant of the will, becomes merely the mirrorer of Ideas, which are not "interesting" to the individual in which this faculty resides.

There are thus two sides to aesthetic experience, an objective and a subjective. On the objective side, there are the Ideas embodied in concrete particulars, on which attention now rests, and whose natures are grasped in contemplation; the aesthetic experience is thus centrally a cognitive one. On the subjective side, there is the transformation of the perceiver from an interested bundle of willing, concerned with objects only insofar as they are related, spatiotemporally and causally, to the satisfaction of needs and desires, into a disinterested beholder of Ideas, with which individual willing can have nothing to do. The disengagement of the subject's will and the shift in focus from one sort of object to another are two sides of the same coin; as noted earlier, subject and object for Schopenhauer are always correlated.

Schopenhauer thinks of the Ideas as grades of objectification of will, or thing-in-itself, on the phenomenal level. Ideas are intermediary between the nonplural will and the plurality of spatiotemporal individuals, but an Idea is still a representation for a subject, and thus not a thing-in-itself. Ideas are the most direct of the will's objectifications, or manifestations for a knowing mind, logically prior to the plurality of individuals that Schopenhauer conceived as in effect arising from the refraction of the Ideas through the lenses of space, time, and causality. The Ideas are something like the fundamental kinds of the phenomenal world, or the essences of them. There are Ideas corresponding to the species of living things, the varieties of natural forces, and the innumerable individual human characters, conceived of by Schopenhauer as virtually each a species unto itself. Unlike abstract concepts, however, Ideas are intuitively apprehensible; they are grasped in perception, and not through reason or language. (But how the Ideas of living things, say, can be both perceptually graspable, and yet entirely nonspatial, is not something for which Schopenhauer ever gives a satisfying explanation.)

The artist or man of genius, according to Schopenhauer, is one who is particularly gifted in two respects. First, through an excess of intellect beyond what is required for the practical purposes of daily living, the artist is enabled to perceive the Ideas in things more readily, more widely, and more sustainedly than the ordinary man, who as a rule has just enough understanding to grasp things in their spatiotemporal-causal, and thus will-relevant, relationship to him. "Whereas to the ordinary man his faculty of knowledge is a lamp that lights his path, to the man of genius it is the sun that reveals the world" (1958, vol. 1, p. 188). Second, the artist has the ability to embody this apprehension of Ideas in an artwork, a perceivable object in which the Idea has been made more vivid, more striking, more easily discerned than it was in nature, and so capable of triggering in the ordinary perceiver the sort of will-less contemplation that the artist had before nature unassisted. Yet, Schopenhauer stresses that the "power of recognizing in things their Ideas, of divesting themselves for a moment of their personality . . . must be present in all men in a lesser and different degree, as otherwise they would be just as incapable of enjoying works of art as of producing them" (ibid., p. 194). Schopenhauer can be viewed as taking up Plotinus's response to Plato's notorious charge against art of merely copying the ontologically already inferior, by stressing that the artist embodies in his work not the mundane, imperfect, and atypical object—even when this serves as model or ostensible subject—but rather its Idea or essence, and in such fashion that others are enabled to experience the sort of transcendence of self in viewing it that the artist achieved unaided in his interaction with the world.

So far, this essay has highlighted the cognitive dimension of aesthetic awareness more than the hedonic, but Schopenhauer's conception certainly includes the latter. The pleasure of aesthetic experience on his account would seem to be twofold. One part, that most stressed by him, is purely negative: temporary relief from the pain of constant striving, through transcendence of the standpoint of the individual willer. But a second part, less stressed though no less important, is of more positive character, and connects the hedonic aspect with the cognitive: satisfaction in contemplation of the given Idea and in the insight thus afforded into the timeless manifestations of Will. In effect, this is a delight in knowing, such as Aristotle and Kant, in different ways, posit as well. The negative pleasure of relief from the cycle of want and desire is provided equally, it seems, by any object offering an Idea for will-less contemplation; the positive pleasure from knowledge of an Idea, though, rather varies with the significance of the Idea involved.

Appreciation of beauty in nature and appreciation of beauty in art are both founded in contemplation of Ideas. In the one case, Ideas, or visible essences of willing, are simply strikingly evident in the world itself, in its unmodified state; in the other case, Ideas grasped in the world through the extraordinary perceptions of genius are embodied in a created object—the distilled experience of the genius—so as to be available to those of only modest powers of perception. At one point, Schopenhauer remarks that "everything is beautiful." What he means is that because everything embodies Ideas, if only those of the simplest sort, everything can in principle be made the object of disinterested contemplation. But, on the other hand, as he also remarks, "some things are more beautiful than others." This is because, in virtue of their forms, whether natural or human-made, or in virtue of the value of the Ideas they offer to contemplation,

objects will differ in the readiness with which they prompt such contemplation and in the worth of the contemplation they so prompt. Schopenhauer, with Kant, is thus one of the important sources of the idea of the aesthetic attitude as disinterested attention that can theoretically be brought to bear on anything, whatever its nature or degree of fashioning, thus potentially "aestheticizing" the world. Schopenhauer's emphasis on the nonspatiotemporal Idea rather than the concrete particular as the object of aesthetic attention might also be seen as cousin to Kant's notion of the disinterestedness of aesthetic judgment as rooted in the disconnectedness from "real existence" of the object so judged.

Schopenhauer, like Kant, distinguishes the sublime from the beautiful, and the account he offers is more convincing than Kant's. The difference between beauty and sublimity for Schopenhauer resides in the differing relation of the Ideas embodied to the human will, and a concomitant difference in the mode of engagement with the object that embodies them. "What distinguishes the feeling of the sublime from that of the beautiful is that, with the beautiful, pure knowledge has gained the upper hand without a struggle" (ibid., p. 202). In the case of the beautiful, the Ideas presented by an object are either agreeable or else neutral with respect to human nature, thus enabling the shift from interested perception to pure contemplation to occur passively, with a purely pleasurable upshot. In the case of the sublime, the Ideas presented by an object are inimical or threatening to the human mode of being, and so a shift to contemplation of them occurs only with the active participation of the subject, in a partly willful manner, resulting in pleasure with a painful undercurrent. Contemplation in the case of the sublime requires a forcible disengagement of the will, consciously and effortfully maintained, a free exaltation beyond the relations of the object recognized as unfavorable to human existence. The subject experiencing the sublime focuses on the fearful aspect of the object, while at the same time inhibiting the practical responses that the will would ordinarily have toward such hostile forces. Such a subject is aware of the antagonistic relationship of the object—for example, a maelstrom or thunderstorm—to human existence generally, but suspends, through an effort of will, the sense of threat to his personal well-being. The reward is the peculiarly mixed exhilaration known as the sublime.

Schopenhauer provides a categorization of the different arts, according to the grade of Ideas embodied and the quality of cognition thus afforded. On this scheme, the arts run from the lowest, architecture (whose objects manifest primarily the simple Ideas of gravity and rigidity), through landscape painting, animal painting, sculpture, historical painting (whose objects manifest, respectively, Ideas of vegetal nature, animal life, human body, and human character), to the highest, tragedy, for Schopenhauer a species of dramatic poetry. Tragedy deals with the conflict of human wills at the highest level, epitomizing the inevitability of suffering, the futility of aspiration, and the inexorability of fate, and thus ultimately teaching—what Schopenhauer endorses in his ethics—resignation and denial of the will.

The only art with no place in this scheme is music, and yet, for Schopenhauer, it is perhaps the greatest art of all. It lacks a place in that scheme because, as Schopenhauer was well aware, being nonrepresentational, it presents for contemplation no Ideas, no perceivable objectifications of willing, and thus seemingly provides no occasion for the transformation of the individual into a momentarily will-less pure subject of knowledge.

Two signs, for Schopenhauer, that music has an especially intimate relation with the deep nature of things are, first, that its effect on us is so profound, and second, that it is immediately understood by all. Thus, music does not copy or present Ideas, concludes Schopenhauer, but rather Will itself. Music, in all its forms, is willing made audible, in all its inner variety. Music and the phenomenal world are in fact parallel—complete, though different, expressions of the nature of Will. Confirmation of this is the fact that structural similarities between the two abound, and Schopenhauer is quite resourceful in suggesting analogies between aspects of the natural world and such musical features as melody, bass, fixed-scale positions, major and minor modes, cadences, modulations, and the impossibility of equal temperament.

There may appear to be a difficulty in the thesis that music is a complete alternate expression of Will, namely, that of music's itself being phenomenal, that is, bunches of sounds or sound waves. What this suggests is that it is music as repeatable pattern or succession, rather than as concrete event, that is meant here, or alternatively, sticking with music as concrete sonic phenomenon, that such a phenomenon is to be regarded as a microcosm of Will, in contrast with the phenomenal world as a whole, inclusive of music, taken as a macrocosm of Will.

Whether or not Schopenhauer's grounds for postulating this parallelism between music and world are fully adequate, there is a more pressing problem for his philosophy of music, one that might be labeled the "paradox of music's appeal." Music confronts a listener most directly with the awful inner nature of the world, being in effect a direct copy of the cosmic Will, the source of universal suffering, while at the same time offering no Ideas with which to engage objective contemplation and thus afford the subject momentary relief from willing. How, then, can music be even tolerable to us, much less immensely appealing? How can music gratify us, if what it centrally offers is the unfiltered spectacle of the root of all evil?

Schopenhauer provides a number of hints as to how this paradox might be resolved, and others can be offered on his behalf. First, although music by hypothesis confronts one directly with willing, the bane of existence, in a pure form, it is will-in-general, rather than some particular manifestation

of willing, that thus serves to divert attention from one's own situation and its incessant demands; contemplation of the universal will thus puts one's individual will in abeyance. Even though, in auditing music, the subject is not presented with any Ideas, disengaging practical concern in virtue of their utter unrelatedness to the subject in spatiotemporal terms, there supervenes a similar attitude of effectively selfless absorption in an image—that of Will itself—that has nothing to do with the phenomenally situated self and its materially tethered needs and desires. Second, music is still a representation of willing—even of the most immediate sort—rather than willing itself, and is furthermore divested of the particulars, spatial and causal, that characterize any real instance of willing; thus, emotions, even violent ones, may be reflected in musical flow, but being stripped of their concrete motivations and targets, they are not found personally distressing. Third, there is cognitive satisfaction in knowing will more completely by confronting it in its most transparent manifestation, that of music. Fourth, there is in contemplating music a kind of elation in grasping one's ultimate identity with and nonseparateness from the world, if in fact everything is at bottom the same blind will or life energy. Finally, it can be suggested that music models the vicissitudes of willing in ways that, however misleadingly, give impressions from time to time of purposefulness, rightness, or closure, which thus provide real if transient satisfactions, offsetting the distress that the naked image of Will might induce.

Schopenhauer's general view of the arts other than music as vehicles for contemplation of Ideas, affording temporary release from willful strife, is certainly not above criticism. First, much art seems very much concerned with unique particulars, with getting us to relish distinctive features of the concretely real, rather than allowing us to break free of such particularity. Second, much art appears designed to engage, rather than detach, our passionate or willing natures, even if still preserving some distance between art and life. Third, much art appears aimed at an active consumer, rather than one in whom the will is to be passively neutralized, through the presentation of objects supremely uninteresting to it, that is, ones that can only be contemplated. Finally, much art seems capable of providing a portion of positive, outgoing, and unadulterated pleasure much greater than that which Schopenhauer's view is able to accommodate, with its emphasis on the negative, crabbed pleasure of relief, however seconded by satisfactions of a cognitive sort. Underlying this, of course, is Schopenhauer's metaphysically driven overestimation of the degree to which people are indeed the suffering slaves of their willing natures, awash in a sea of dissatisfactions broken up only by islands of boredom.

Some of the ideas in Schopenhauer's aesthetics that are of lasting importance, ideas largely detachable from their metaphysical moorings, are the following: aesthetic attention as in principle capable of being brought to anything; art as a means of transcending the self and overcoming the narrow bounds of individuality; art's reward as lying partly in the cognitive insight it affords into the nature of things; the artist's essential power, that of heightened perception, as continuous with that of appreciators of art; an art form's value as bearing a strong relation to its range of concerns or subject matter; and music as fundamentally different from, and more immediately affecting than, the other arts.

[*See also* Disinterestedness; Kant; Music, *historical overview article; and* Nietzsche, *article on* Nietzsche, Schopenhauer, and Disinterestedness.]

BIBLIOGRAPHY

Works by Schopenhauer

Parerga and Paralipomena. 2 vols. Translated by E. F. J. Payne. Oxford, 1974.
The Fourfold Root of the Principle of Sufficient Reason. Translated by E. F. J. Payne. La Salle, Ill., 1974.
The World as Will and Representation. 2 vols. Translated by E. F. J. Payne. Indian Hills, Colo., 1958; reprint, New York, 1969.

Other Sources

Alperson, Philip. "Schopenhauer and Musical Revelation." *Journal of Aesthetics and Art Criticism* 40.2 (Winter 1981): 155–166.
Budd, Malcolm. *Music and the Emotions.* London and Boston, 1986. See chap. 5.
Diffey, T. J. "Schopenhauer's Account of Aesthetic Experience." *British Journal of Aesthetics* 30.2 (April 1990): 132–142.
Hamlyn, D. W. *Schopenhauer.* London and Boston, 1980.
Jacquette, Dale, ed. *Schopenhauer, Philosophy, and the Arts.* Cambridge and New York, 1995.
Janaway, Christopher. *Self and World in Schopenhauer's Philosophy.* Oxford, 1989.
Janaway, Christopher, ed. *The Cambridge Companion to Schopenhauer.* Cambridge and New York, forthcoming.
Knox, Israel. "Schopenhauer's Aesthetic Theory." In *Schopenhauer: His Philosophical Achievement,* edited by Michael Fox, pp. 132–146. Brighton, 1980.
Krukowski, Lucian. *Aesthetic Legacies.* Philadelphia, 1992. See chap. 3.
Magee, Bryan. *The Philosophy of Schopenhauer.* Oxford, 1983.
Young, Julian. *Willing and Unwilling: A Study in the Philosophy of Arthur Schopenhauer.* Dordrecht and Boston, 1987.

JERROLD LEVINSON

SCIENCE AND AESTHETICS. [*To treat the relationship between science and aesthetics, this entry comprises two essays:*

Conceptual and Historical Overview
Contemporary Thought

The first essay is an overview of the aesthetics in and of science, especially during two major transformations of science in the seventeenth and twentieth centuries. The second essay is a critique of common misconceptions about science and art that have, it is argued, unduly influenced aesthetics in ways that this critique may help to reverse. For related discussion, see Bachelard; Color; Mathematics and Aesthetics; Sensibilité; *and* Synaesthesia.]

Conceptual and Historical Overview

From Johannes Kepler to Albert Einstein and beyond, the aesthetics of science was governed by mathematical aesthetics. "A physical law must possess mathematical beauty," Paul Dirac famously said in 1956. The statement itself defines his views and practice of physics from the 1930s onward. By that time, both the question of the relationships between mathematical objects, beautiful or not, and physical law (or among mathematics, physics, and nature in general) and the question of the ontological and epistemological status of mathematical objects themselves acquired extraordinary complexity. Several radical developments in mathematics and science (in particular quantum physics, to which Dirac made an extraordinary contribution), philosophy, and the arts were responsible for transforming thinking concerning all these issues. By so doing, they also introduced new dimensions and complexities into the mathematical aesthetics of science, or into the aesthetics of mathematics itself, although one can trace some of these complexities (aesthetic or epistemological) to much earlier events and, in a certain sense, to the known origins of mathematics and science, or philosophy. As a result, the very concept of mathematical beauty has become increasingly ambiguous and problematic. The role of aesthetic considerations, however, especially those of a mathematical nature, both in the practice of science itself and in our understanding of this practice, has been extraordinary throughout Western intellectual history.

It is true, of course, that in mathematics and science, consistency and rigor, agreement with experimental data, and other (as they might be called) logico-epistemological factors are ultimately more significant than and take priority over aesthetic considerations, to the point (it has been argued) of making the latter irrelevant. This last claim requires much qualification, even if one leaves aside the complexity of the constitution of such nonaesthetic factors (including whether, or to what degree, they are independent from aesthetics), which have been the subject of powerful critical scrutiny. At the very least, aesthetic considerations have always played a major role in establishing directions for the development of mathematics and science—local (selecting one venue or another in approaching a given problem) or global (that of a given field or even discipline as a whole). One of the main reasons for this role is their prominence in the work of key scientists, who have given a primary or, sometimes (as in the case of Dirac), even *the* primary significance to the aesthetic dimensions of their work or their view of mathematics and science, or of nature itself. It may be that this aesthetic ideology—that is, the significance and implications (scientific, philosophical, or political) of certain aesthetic principles and ideas—defines the work of a small minority of major practitioners, such as Kepler, Einstein, and Dirac. Their aesthetic choices, however, and their aesthetic ideology as a whole often shaped the direction of modern mathematics and science at key points and crossroads of their development, and limited (sometimes severely) other venues of mathematical and scientific pursuit.

As a—or even *the*—paradigmatic example of this ideology of mathematical aesthetics, one might consider Kepler's famous "longing for harmonies" and "noble proportions," and his grand vision of the "harmony of the world." Following the Pythagoreans, Kepler's theory of planetary motion connects arithmetic and geometric harmonies—the harmony of numbers and of figures. The connections established by Kepler are elegant and beautiful by most classical criteria but complex in structure, especially in view of the elliptical (rather than circular) character and, one might say, the elliptical harmony of planetary motion around the sun, discovered by Kepler. Kepler "saved" the principle of harmony by introducing a more complex harmony into nature, or claiming this harmony for nature, which may well have been his greatest achievement. Ever since Kepler, this strategy has defined much of the history of mathematics and science, and of their aesthetics, as part of the aesthetic ideology of modern science. More generally, in all of their aspects, Kepler's aesthetics and aesthetic ideology have been decisive for developing modern mathematics, physics, and astronomy, no less—and sometimes more—than the scientific or explanatory aspects of his discoveries. As (along with astronomy) the earliest scientific discipline in the modern sense, mathematics was a natural prototype for Kepler's, and then post-Keplerian, science. This science, as Martin Heidegger argues, is not only mathematical, but is also experimental because it is mathematical, in view of the connections it establishes between measurement and its representation of natural objects by means of mathematical objects, a kind of reduction of natural objects to mathematical objects. Galileo Galilei's work is, arguably, most crucial in this respect, although his aesthetics and his understanding of the project of science were, ideologically, quite different from both Kepler's and Isaac Newton's. In spite of such differences between different projects and views of science (or indeed aesthetics), however, the aesthetics of science has been powerfully shaped by this mathematico-experimental determination of modern science and by reflecting and interconnecting the aesthetics of mathematics and the aesthetics of experimentation.

Kepler both mathematized and mathematically aestheticized Tycho Brahe's experimental data, and by so doing he established a paradigmatic model of modern mathematical science. Both his science and its aesthetics are Pythagorean in the sense that a mathematical "harmony" also "shapes" the data, unless one believes that reality (material or spiri-

tual) already possesses this harmony. From the modern perspective, there may not be any data that would be "unshaped"—that is, not conditioned by theoretical, cultural, political, and other forces acting within situations where these data are generated. In any given situation, this shaping may also be aesthetic to one degree or another. Brahe's data, too, possessed a complex organization, some of which may be seen as aesthetic, and Kepler's own reorganization and re-aestheticization of these data is a complex issue. A full mathematization of planetary motion in the sense of modern physics—that of mathematical equations defining physical laws—came essentially with Newton (and took its modern form even later, with Joseph-Louis Lagrange and Sir William Rowan Hamilton), although in terms of aesthetics Kepler's contribution has been the greatest since Pythagoras. Newtonian and post-Newtonian physics also extended the mathematical aesthetics of science by complementing Kepler's geometric harmonies with those of algebra and the emerging calculus, following the mathematics of René Descartes (whose analytic geometry connected algebra and geometry) and Pierre de Fermat. Copernican and Ptolemaic systems had their own harmonies, mathematical and other. The choice between them in Kepler's (or Galileo's) case had complex aesthetic (or, of course, scientific, theological, philosophical, and political) determinations. As indicated earlier, however, Kepler's theory both enabled a better fit and introduced the aesthetics of complex harmonies into science, which finds its contemporary manifestations in the Riemannian geometry of Einstein's relativity or in the broken symmetries of quantum physics.

In general, although it entails a certain—beautiful—"simplicity," mathematical beauty should not be identified with mathematical simplicity. As Dirac argued, Einstein's theory of gravity (general relativity), while more complex than Newton's, is also more beautiful. First, the relationship to the experimental evidence, which classical physics can no longer account for, affects aesthetic considerations. Second, from Pythagoras and Plato onward, the mathematical harmony reflects the relationships—or a kind of harmony—of complexity (for example, the complexity of the parts) and simplicity (for example, that of connecting the parts into the whole). The same would refer to most economy principles, such as Occam's razor, which reflect a similar complexity—or, again, economy—of the relationships between parsimony and excess. These considerations apply at both levels—that of specific configurations and that of broader theoretical matrices or fields. Most grand programs in mathematics, physics, and other sciences are based on this double economy relating simplicity and complexity. The programs of unification of fundamental forces in modern physics offer arguably the best-known example in this respect. The search for mathematically and otherwise harmonious theories, and in particular unifying and unified theories, has shaped much of modern science. The concept of the One that would unify the diversity of immense and perhaps infinite richness (as in Gottfried Wilhelm Leibniz and Georg Wilhelm Friedrich Hegel), or an undifferentiated One lurking behind the diversities (as in Plotinus), has long governed much of the aesthetics of mathematics and science. Obviously, the significance of these concepts is much broader. They have also exerted immense philosophical, ideological, and political force throughout their history in mathematics and science. These nonaesthetic dimensions of their functioning in mathematics and science have powerfully affected and, reciprocally, have been affected by the aesthetic ones. This reciprocity is a manifestation of a more general fact that, whatever form it might take, the aesthetics of mathematics and science inevitably acquires a complex constitution that requires and has received, especially in recent years, an equally complex critical analysis—scientific, philosophical, historical, political, and, of course, aesthetic.

Much of the preceding discussion would apply to the aesthetics of nonmathematical science. Without considering the latter separately, several key examples of scientific discoveries and their aesthetics may be offered here in order, first, to illustrate key points and, second, to show the complexity of the relationships between mathematical and nonmathematical science and their respective aesthetics.

Dmitri Ivanovich Mendeleev's periodical table of the elements—a sort of Kepler's system of chemistry—is one of the greatest examples of scientific classification. The harmonies of Mendeleev's arrangement may or may not be seen as mathematical, although it would be hard to deny their mathematical dimensions. Obviously, chemistry in general has its own aesthetics, mathematical and other—the aesthetics of molecular arrangements, chemical equations, experiments, and so forth. As it happens, Mendeleev's table reflects the underlying mathematical harmony of atomic structures, which, once discovered (by Niels Bohr), added to both its scientific and its aesthetic significance.

Spectrography offers an analogous example. It never quite found its Mendeleyev's table, although the so-called Balmer's formulas and Rydberg's constant for the hydrogen spectrum played a somewhat similar role on a limited scale. It is only with Bohr's 1913 theory of atomic structure, in the wake of Max Planck's and Einstein's discoveries concerning the quantum nature of radiation, that spectra received their Mendeleev's system. It was, of course, the same system that explained the order that Mendeleev discovered. Jointly, these discoveries produced an extraordinary example of a complex harmony in nature and implied a still more complex one, which was eventually discovered by the (new) quantum mechanics of Werner Heisenberg and Erwin Schrödinger and subsequent developments in quantum physics, and which enabled a full theoretical understanding of atomic spectra. Bohr's explanation of Balmer's formulas and Rydberg's constant have been compared to Kepler's laws and the harmony of the world they represented, or,

again, to Pythagoras. The key elements of spectrographic analysis, based on the so-called Fourier analysis, are, fundamentally, the same, or rather offer a rigorous mathematical rendition of the numerical principles of musical harmony discovered by Pythagoras. Analogous harmonies and harmonics describe both musical chords and the music of the world, cosmic or atomic—the mathematical-aesthetic unity or, again, harmony of the world, which Bohr both enriched and undermined by his discoveries and his philosophy of science. By so doing, Bohr made major contributions to both old and new quantum theory, and he may be seen as the central figure who moved from Keplerian to more radical epistemology and aesthetics, combining old and new harmonies and dissonances.

In crystallography, overtly the most aesthetic of scientific disciplines, the geometric structure and symmetry of crystals is mathematically described by means of group theory, the most general mathematical embodiment of the principle of symmetry. Here, too, the underlying (micro)physics responsible for the (macro)harmony of crystals proved to be atomic and, ultimately, quantum (micro)physics, defined by its own complex symmetries. Louis Pasteur's work on the polarization of crystals would be another example of the discovery of the broken symmetry in nature. "L'univers est dissymmétrique," Pasteur proclaimed. The handedness of the so-called weak interactions and other broken symmetries of quantum physics tell us that Pasteur might have been more right than he thought, although a better maxim might be: the universe is both symmetrical and asymmetrical.

Finally, in biology, Charles Darwin's theory of evolution offers an example of what might be called the dynamic (temporal or historical) organization of the data it considers. The complex aesthetic planes of Darwin's theory and of subsequent biology and genetics emerge at many levels—in their classification, structures, experiments, and so forth. Preceding (and subsequent) investigations in botany, zoology, and other fields that were concerned with morphology and gestalt have shaped the history of aesthetics in biology and elsewhere. The nature of the processes responsible for the phenomena at issue in Darwin's theory have not yet emerged. The discovery of the genetic mechanisms responsible for evolutionary processes was a crucial step, which may be compared to Newton's more systematic rethinking of Kepler's laws. The explosion of biology and genetics in the twentieth century has established complex networks of connections between physics, chemistry, and biology, and various levels of mathematization of biological processes. The aesthetics in/of biology has been extended accordingly. At this point, however, only God knows how this mechanism really works, and, as in quantum physics, this God, contrary to Einstein's belief, appears to be playing dice. As a result, modern biology has significantly affected developments in the epistemology and aesthetics of science. It is quite clear already that its mathematization involved some among the most complex—structurally and aesthetically—areas of mathematics. Many key aspects of the systems involved conform to mathematics and the mathematical aesthetics of such theories as probability and statistics, the so-called dynamic system, and more recently chaos theory and complexity theory, and hence to the theories and aesthetics of the interaction of chaos and order. It may well be that modern biology will reveal as yet unheard-of harmonies and dissonances—scientific, philosophical, and aesthetic.

[*See also* Helmholtz.]

BIBLIOGRAPHY

Cartier, Pierre. "Kepler et la musique du monde." *La Recherche* 278.26 (1995).

Chandrasekhar, S. *Truth and Beauty: Aesthetics and Motivations in Science.* Chicago, 1987.

Curtin, Deane W., ed. *The Aesthetic Dimension of Science.* New York, 1982.

Dirac, Paul. "The Relation between Mathematics and Physics." *Proceedings of the Royal Society* (Edinburgh) 59 (1938–1939): 122–129.

Feynman, Richard. *The Character of Physical Law.* Cambridge, Mass., 1967.

Heisenberg, Werner. *Across the Frontiers.* Translated by Peter Heath. Reprint, Woodbridge, Conn., 1990.

Kragh, Helge. "The Principle of Mathematical Beauty." In *Dirac: A Scientific Biography.* Cambridge and New York, 1990.

Lyotard, Jean-François. *The Postmodern Condition: A Report on Knowledge.* Translated by Geoff Bennington and Brian Massumi. Minneapolis, 1984.

Poincaré, Henri. *Science and Method.* Translated by Francis Maitland. Reprint, New York, 1952.

Weyl, Hermann. *Symmetry.* Princeton, N.J., 1952.

Wigner, Eugene P. *Symmetries and Reflections: Scientific Essays.* Bloomington, Ind., 1967.

ARKADY PLOTNITSKY

Contemporary Thought

Pernicious stereotypes underwrite the opposition of art and science. Art, it is said, seeks beauty, science seeks truth; art induces pleasure, science discloses facts; unfettered inspiration makes for art, slavish adherence to methodological canons, for science; art is subjective, science objective. Such stereotypes consign art and science to hostile camps. In so doing, they misrepresent both. By dispelling such stereotypes, we gain a better understanding of the relations between the two disciplines.

Counterexamples are legion. Michelangelo Buonarroti's *Last Judgment,* Joseph Conrad's *Heart of Darkness,* and Gustav Mahler's Ninth Symphony are dark, disconcerting, even horrific works. They are not beautiful. But we do not and should not consider them defective on that account.

To preserve the stereotype, we could revise our assessments, exiling such works from the aesthetic realm for their lack of beauty. But as the list of exclusions lengthens, the plausibility of such a strategy wanes. Alternatively, we might contend that the beauty relevant to aesthetics is distinct from being pretty, attractive, pleasing to the senses or the sensibilities. Aesthetic beauty, so construed, would be compatible with ugliness, hideousness, and so on. We retain the term *beauty,* then, by leaching out its content. What remains is just a label for whatever makes for artistic excellence. That art seeks whatever makes for artistic excellence may be true, but it is hardly informative. It seems best, then, to retain our familiar notion of beauty and admit that beauty is not always art's objective.

Equally vulnerable is the contention that science singlemindedly seeks truth. Science is riddled with approximations, idealizations, and simplifying assumptions that make no pretense of being true. The ideal gas law, for example, is a fundamental principle of thermodynamics. It is not true. Nothing in the world displays the features the law ascribes to the ideal gas. To construe such an express untruth as true would, of course, be an error. We would misunderstand both the phenomenon and the science if we took the ideal gas law to state a truth. But untruths, *acknowledged as such,* are often vehicles of scientific understanding.

So is beauty. Concern for beauty explains the appeal of symmetry principles, and the aversion to ad hoc excrescences. Concern for truth does not. Theories incorporating symmetry principles are no more likely to be true than theories that exclude them, nor are theories that make ad hoc assumptions more likely to be false than theories that eschew them.

Sometimes art induces pleasure. Sometimes it does not. Its effect depends on the audience as well as the art. The orchestra continued to play while the *Titanic* went down. But regardless of its merits, the listeners probably did not enjoy the performance. That a besotted swain delights in his beloved's braying monotone is no evidence that she is a talented singer. Kitsch that pleases philistines displeases connoisseurs. Atonal music that pleases sophisticated audiences displeases the hoi polloi. Evidently not all pleasure or displeasure occasioned by works of art is a measure of aesthetic merit.

Perhaps a distinctive sort of pleasure—aesthetic pleasure—is a measure of aesthetic merit. Because only people with refined sensibilities have the capacity for such pleasure, the reactions of the masses are aesthetically irrelevant. The difficulty is that connoisseurs do not always agree. Nor do they always enjoy the works whose merits they acknowledge. Only a sadist would take pleasure in Francisco de Goya's *Disasters of War,* or Sophocles' *Oedipus Rex.* Even if the responses of suitably sensitive, suitably receptive audiences afford evidence of aesthetic merit, no single response functions as a merit monitor.

Science often discloses facts. But it need not do so. A cosmology that acceptably accounted for currently known facts would be counted a success, whether or not it disclosed any new ones. A science strives to produce a systematic, integrated understanding of diverse phenomena. Disclosure of particular facts is far from its central concern.

A science does not, in any case, accept an antecedent demarcation of what constitutes the facts it studies. It contrives a conceptual framework that fixes its facts. Chemistry organizes its domain in terms of discrete chemical elements. Until it has done so, there is no fact of the matter as to whether copper is lighter than zinc; for until the two are recognized as distinct sorts of substances, the issue of their respective weights does not arise.

Science, moreover, devises methods—not just for disclosing facts, but also for making approximations, calculations, models, and so on. A powerful method may constitute a greater scientific advance than any particular finding of fact it facilitates.

Art also discloses facts. In seventeenth-century Dutch still lifes, for example, the juxtaposition of opulent materials with decaying fruit and dying flowers reveals the Calvinist burghers' ambivalence about worldly success. Toni Morrison's *Beloved* spells out the enormity of the psychological price slaves had to pay in order to survive. Science has no monopoly on facts, then, nor has art a monopoly on pleasure.

The widespread conviction that scientific inquiry consists in mechanical application of prescribed methods cannot do justice to the conceptual and methodological innovation crucial to scientific progress. It cannot, for example, explain the development of the theory of relativity, which involved reconceptions of space, time, mass, and other physical magnitudes. Nor can it account for the ingenuity needed to apply even well-established methods and concepts in recalcitrant cases. Science, like art, is a creative enterprise.

And art, like science, is conditioned by constraints. Some are formal—the requirements on linear perspective or counterpoint or iambic pentameter, for example. Others derive from medium, method, motif, or style. A poem need not, of course, be seventeen syllables long. But unless it is, it is not haiku. Nor need a sample respect the requirement of variety of evidence. But unless it does, it is not statistically significant. Of course, science and art have resources for challenging, revising, even repudiating accepted constraints. Both are open to innovation. But to recognize this is not to deny that constraints—sometimes quite severe ones—frame the activities of artists and scientists alike.

Art and science deploy symbols of many kinds. One mode of symbolization operative in both is exemplification, whereby a symbol exhibits and refers to some of its own features. A Piet Mondrian painting, for example, exemplifies squareness. It not only contains squares, it refers to and focuses attention on the squares it contains. A positive litmus test exemplifies the presence of acid. Because litmus paper turns pink only when acid is present, its turning pink serves as a symbol that points up the presence of acid. By highlighting particular features, an exemplar affords epistemic access to them. The features in question may be elusive. Elaborate contrivance is sometimes necessary to bring them to light. Thus, a complex experiment is mounted to exemplify subtle differences between closely related viruses; and intricate stage setting is devised to exemplify the differences between very similar moods—nostalgia and melancholy, for example. Exemplification, moreover, need not be literal. Constantin Brancusi's *Bird in Flight* metaphorically exemplifies soaring, and a computer simulation of the behavior of electrons at absolute zero metaphorically exemplifies the disappearance of resistance.

Fiction is a staple of art. That their protagonists do not exist is no criticism of *Faust,* or *Madame Bovary,* or *The Birth of Venus.* Perhaps surprisingly, fictions are common in science too. Thought experiments are among the most obvious examples. Even though no one ever rode on a light wave, Albert Einstein was able to elaborate implications of the theory of relativity by considering what someone riding on a light wave would see. Nor is the role of scientific thought experiments merely heuristic. Erwin Schrödinger's cat and the two-slit experiment are integral to quantum mechanics. The conviction that fiction is antithetical to serious science is false.

We have seen that science, like art, can be beautiful, creative, pleasurable, and that art, like science, can disclose facts, respect rigorous constraints, engage reason. Both make use of fictions, exemplars, and metaphors. Both advance understanding. Is there, then, no difference between science and art?

Such differences as there are derive from the sorts of symbols the disciplines favor; and their rationales for favoring the sorts of symbols they do stem from their cognitive values and priorities.

Science values repeatable results and intersubjective accord, for it is a collaborative enterprise in which independent investigators build on one another's findings. Science thus places a premium on being able to tell just what results it reaches. If every difference in a magnitude constituted a distinct finding, one could never tell that two samples were the same, for identical readings might obscure differences beyond the threshold of measurement. Science, then, has reason to partition its domain into discrete, disjoint alternatives, and set a lower bound on the precision of its computations. It restricts its parameters, regiments its units of measure, and counts its measurements accurate only up to a specifiable number of significant figures. Finer-grained differences are ignored. Far from being more precise than art, science sacrifices precision to achieve accord.

As far as possible, it eschews vagueness, ambiguity, and other forms of semantic indeterminacy on the same ground, for such symbols invite divergent interpretations. If disagreements in interpretation are irresolvable, science cannot safely build on its results.

Art's priorities are different. It values delicacy of discrimination more highly than accord and aspires to irreproducible results. It thus favors dense, replete symbols, where the finest differences in certain respects matter and where a symbol may symbolize along indefinitely many dimensions at once. In a scientific graph, for example, only the shape of the line and its distance from the axes are significant. In a drawing, not just the line's shape and position, but also its precise shade, thickness, and texture at every point may be significant, as may the color, texture, and weave of the paper, the contrast between figure and ground, and so on. What the graph symbolizes is readily determined. What the drawing symbolizes may be permanently in dispute.

There are, of course, differences within the arts. Symbols in the visual arts are syntactically dense. The finest differences in shape, color, position, and the like affect their identity. But *Middlemarch* is *Middlemarch* regardless of the typeface, ink, or paper on which it is printed. All that matters is spelling. Literary works, then, are syntactically differentiated, their symbols being constructed from the finite list of alternatives that an alphabet supplies. Such works are, however, semantically dense. A natural language has the resources for drawing the finest distinctions among items in its field of reference. Literature makes use of these resources. In a scientific study of, say, the responses of commuters to traffic delays, the choice between *grumble* and *grouse* would probably make no difference. In a literary work, it can carry enormous weight.

Literary symbols are, moreover, relatively replete. That Ernest Hemingway avoided polysyllabic prose is no accident. The austerity of his language reflects the austerity of the world his characters confront. Sentence structure, cadence, juxtapositions, omissions, literal and metaphoric resonances, both within and beyond a work, may be aesthetically significant. One paraphrases at one's peril. Although substituting *one-half gallon* for *two quarts* would be unobjectionable in a scientific context, in a literary context such a substitution is impermissible, for some significance may attach to the fact that the volume is characterized as twice another, or that the expression *two quarts* contains exactly two, equally stressed syllables, or that the letter *q* appears. Debate about which, and how many, of these features are significant and about what they signify may be endless.

Ambiguity, vagueness, and indeterminacy are aesthetic virtues. They foster multiple, often incompatible, interpretations of a single work. There is no hope of deciding once and for all whether Hamlet was genuinely mad. Nor should we want to. Much of the power of the work derives from the interplay of divergent interpretations.

Art's susceptibility to multiple interpretations is perhaps the source of the final stereotype—that art is subjective, science objective. But such susceptibility does not ordinarily make for subjectivity. An ambiguous term such as *bank* admits of different readings. But we cannot ordinarily choose to take it to refer to whatever we like—a flock of geese, for example. Nor can we simply opt for the accepted interpretation we prefer, regardless of context and operative presuppositions. In the context of an agreement to repay an auto loan, for example, we cannot elect to construe it as pertaining to the river's edge.

Interpretation of works of art is, of course, more difficult than interpretation of ordinary language. But in neither sort of interpretation is it the case that just anything goes. Under no acceptable interpretation is *Medea* a comedy of manners or Rembrandt van Rijn's *Sacrifice of Isaac* a joke.

Interpretation in the arts is subject to constraints. Because several sets of constraints may apply, and a given set of constraints may be multiply satisfiable, a given work can admit of several acceptable interpretations. Still, reasons can be adduced to support or undermine a proposed interpretation and consensus on its acceptability often is reached. Availability of constraints, support by reasons, and the prospect of consensus are hallmarks of objectivity. Granted, the constraints are debatable, the reasons less than conclusive, and the consensus far from assured. But these weaknesses are not peculiar to art. Science holds out the promise that physics will eventually settle on a unique interpretation of quantum mechanics, but cannot guarantee that the promise will be kept. Art is objective if science is.

[*See also* Goodman.]

BIBLIOGRAPHY

Einstein, Albert. *Relativity: The Special and the General Theory: A Popular Exposition.* Translated by Robert W. Lawson. Reprint, New York, 1961.

Elgin, Catherine Z. "Understanding: Art and Science." In *Philosophy and the Arts,* edited by Peter A. French, Theodore E. Uehling, Jr., and Howard Wettstein, pp. 196–208. Midwest Studies in Philosophy, vol. 16. Notre Dame, Ind., 1991.

Elgin, Catherine Z. "Relocating Aesthetics." *Revue Internationale de Philosophie* 46 (1993): 171–186.

Elgin, Catherine Z. *Considered Judgment.* Princeton, N.J., 1997.

Elgin, Catherine Z., ed. *The Philosophy of Nelson Goodman.* 4 vols. New York, 1997.

Goodman, Nelson. *Languages of Art: An Approach to a Theory of Symbols.* 2d ed. Indianapolis, 1976.

Goodman, Nelson. *Ways of Worldmaking.* Indianapolis, 1978.

Goodman, Nelson, and Catherine Z. Elgin. *Reconceptions in Philosophy and Other Arts and Sciences.* Indianapolis, 1988.

Gombrich, E. H. *Art and Illusion: A Study in the Psychology of Pictorial Representation* (1960). 2d rev. ed. Reprint, Princeton, N.J., 1969.

McAllister, James W. *Beauty and Revolution in Science.* Ithaca, N.Y., 1996.

Wollheim, Richard. *Painting as an Art.* Princeton, N.J., 1987.

van Fraassen, Bas, and Jill Sigman. "Interpretation in Science and in the Arts." In *Realism and Representation,* edited by George Levine, pp. 73–99. Madison, Wis., 1993.

CATHERINE Z. ELGIN

SCULPTURE. Attempts to establish a specific sculptural aesthetics have rarely been undertaken in the history of philosophical reflection on the visual arts. Fundamental issues such as the essence of visual arts, the ontological status of the work of art, aesthetic experience, or art as expression have mainly been explored with regard to the painted image, which was taken as *pars pro toto* for the visual arts. In fact, it has been widely held that there are no essential differences between the visual problems and values of painting and sculpture. From the late Renaissance until after the middle of the twentieth century, painting was regarded as the superior art practice on the assumption that art represents (that is, imitates, simulates, or even re-creates) reality, and that the painted image is most suited to fulfill this task and to carry transcendental meaning. The bias toward painting is also rooted in a dominant anthropocentric view of the world that is inextricably linked to the preference of a single viewpoint, and thus to the picture plane and a central perspective as respective modes of representation. The sculptural object, being a three-dimensional body with potentially an indefinite number of aspects, does not fit comfortably into this conception of the world.

Although numerous philosophical works deal with the specific forms, developments, and functions of sculpture and its technical peculiarities from antiquity to the present day, consistent theories of sculptural aesthetics are mostly of fairly recent origin. Historically, the generic debates from the eighteenth to the twentieth century played a crucial part in establishing modern sculpture as an aesthetic form and practice distinct from painting.

From Antiquity to the Nineteenth Century. Plato and Aristotle regarded mimetic representation of nature as the goal of art. According to Aristotle, beauty is an inherent law of nature and determinated by order, symmetry, and definiteness (*Poetics*, 1078b). He distinguishes between an internal morphology (order and symmetry) and an external structure (definiteness) of beauty through which a work of art stands out from the accidental, arbitrary, incoherent, and conflicting features of the world. For him, size matters as an important aspect of definiteness:

> Beauty is a matter of size and order, and therefore impossible either . . . in a very minute creature, since our perception becomes indistinct as it approaches instantaneity; or . . . in a creature of vast size . . . as in that case, instead of the object being seen at once, the unity and wholeness of it is lost to the beholder.
> (Ibid., 1450b)

Rooted in Aristotle's definition of beauty as symmetry, order, and definiteness is an Occidental tradition that restricted the ideal of beauty to these categories, particularly in the Middle Ages. Yet, the understanding of beauty changed from an integrated "organic" unity to a "unity in variety" as manifest in Galen's summary of the canon of beauty: "Beauty does not consist in the elements, but in the harmonious proportion of the parts, the proportion of one finger to the other, of all fingers to the rest of the hand . . . of all parts to all others, as it is written in the canon of Poli-

clitus" (quoted in Eco, 1986, p. 29). Before Galen, Vitruvius, who in his treatise *De architectura* focused on the aesthetic structures of the plastic arts, defines harmony as "arising out of the details of the work itself; the correspondence of each given detail among the separate details to the form of the design as a whole" (ibid.). The relational, quantitative conception of beauty as either inherent in all things, or only in the human body, yet not as a specific quality of human artifice, explains why, on the whole, medieval thinkers were above all concerned with the internal conditions of beautiful things rather than their "edifice." Wholeness being achieved by "coherence" (that is, mathematical proportions) potentially pointed toward infiniteness rather than definiteness.

Concepts of physical beauty in the Renaissance, which dealt with an ideal canon of measured proportions, also took up an Aristotelian stance by generally emphasizing that beauty lies not only in the shape of an object but also in its intended function. Based on an analogy between nature and art, the work of art became equated with an organism in which every part plays its part within a whole, as put forward by Leon Battista Alberti, who defines perfect beauty as "a Harmony of all the Parts, in whatever Subject it appears, fitted together with such Proportion and Connection, that nothing could be added, diminished or altered, but for the Worse" (quoted in Beardsley, 1966, p. 125). Until the late Renaissance, considerations of sculptural form and practice had their place mainly in technology, and found articulation as rules in treatises, because sculpture was treated as a mechanical art, that is, a craft that relied on skill and manual labor, and fulfilled, above all, material and practical needs rather than intellectual and spiritual ones. The amount of physical labor involved in sculpture provides Leonardo da Vinci with a crucial argument for the "Paragone" at the beginning of his *Treatise on Painting*, which stimulated a dispute over the precedence of art among many Renaissance artists and thinkers. Sculpture, because it involves a great amount of physical effort, remains essentially a craft inferior to the liberal art of painting. In contrast, Benvenuto Cellini, along with Michelangelo Buonarotti and others, argues that this very aspect redounds to the privilege of sculpture, and that the skill and craftsmanship involved elevate the sculptor over the painter. To prove the latter point, Cellini brings up the multifaceted nature of sculpture whereby only a truly dedicated artist can achieve eight views of equal quality (Wittkower, 1991, p. 144).

When, during the Renaissance, sculpture became gradually emancipated from its existence as visual design bound to architecture as its matrix, interest began to shift toward aspects and modes of representation in the arts that were interrelated with changing ideals of beauty but still firmly grounded in a normative approach. Influenced by René Descartes's rationalism, thoughts on the arts in the seventeenth and early eighteenth centuries concentrated on establishing rules and systems, hierarchical canons of styles, and genres governed by the principle of art as imitation of beautiful nature.

Generic definitions of sculpture, which arose mainly in the second half of the eighteenth century and the early nineteenth century, took the classical Greek tradition as a paradigm. In the neoclassical spirit of his time, Johann Joachim Winckelmann revived the concept of the *beau ideal* based on an early sixteenth-century Italian scheme of *divinia proporzione*. In his *Geschichte der Kunst des Altertums*, published in 1764, Winckelmann demands for sculpture "noble simplicity and quiet grandeur." He justifies a strong predilection for immaculate white marble with the argument that "a body is all the more beautiful the whiter it is." A high degree of unity, firm contours, and simple proportions within the human figure are emphasized through the whiteness of the stone, thus sublimating beauty (Winckelmann, 1966, p. 148). This notion, based on the assumption that Greek sculpture originally existed in "pure" substance, remained unchallenged until well into the nineteenth century, despite mounting evidence undermining its very foundation, and a sculptural practice of the past (from antiquity to the Renaissance) that had indulged in color without hesitation. [*See* Winckelmann.] Saint Augustine, for instance, claims that the beauty of the body lies in a "harmony of its parts with a certain pleasing colour" (Eco, 1986, p. 28).

The controversial debate about whether color is an intrinsic property of sculpture sheds light on complex aesthetic inquiries into the question of the nature of truth in the work of art. Reservations against the use of color in sculpture reach back to antiquity. Although Plato, for instance, acknowledged the use of color in the sculptural practice of his time, he did not think of it as an essential criterion of beauty. His argument—that color above all serves an imitation of reality, that is, that color is potentially deceptive or mendacious— returns in the debate of the eighteenth and nineteenth centuries—in the writings of Denis Diderot and Johann Gottfried von Herder, for instance, who share a concern for the rules of art insofar as they are not mere external application but inscribed in the structure of the work. Their writing is symptomatic insofar as it signaled a general shift from an interest in a normative canon of forms to the effect the work of art has on the viewer. Both equate sculpture with truth on the basis of its materiality. Hegel, in positing that the aim of sculpture lies in the representation of "an abstract side of the human body," emphasizes: "The spirit which sculpture presents is spirit compact in itself, not variously splintered into the play of accidents and passions" (1985, p. 85). Color in sculpture could only mean detraction from the "real existence of the spirit" by bringing the object too close to the "singularity" and "particularity" of real phenomena—the equation of color with naturalism is not far removed from Georg Wilhelm Friedrich Hegel's argument (Drost, 1996,

p. 64). A growing minority of Hegel's contemporaries, on the other hand, thought of color as perfection of the plastic work; but polychromatic concepts only began to gain currency in the second half of the nineteenth century, particularly in Symbolist and Art Nouveau sculpture. Throughout these debates about color there were two crucial issues: Is there a single truth in the visual arts and, if so, where does it emanate from? Is it possible to operate with two seemingly incompatible sets of truths: truth to color (i.e., illusion) and truth to material (i.e., real substance)?

Because of its specific material qualities, such as solidity, stability, and durability, sculpture was held to preserve and hand down images with "ideal significance," that is, the stone or the bronze as the embodiment of seemingly permanent and universal values. Its authoritative status was not least generated from the costs, effort, and time involved in the making of the object. For centuries, from Polykleitos to Michelangelo, from Gianlorenzo Bernini to Henry Moore, this aspect had helped to determine both its public character, scale, and format (as statue and monument) and the range of its respective functions (commemorative, celebrative, votive, etc.).

In his influential essay "Laokoön" published in 1766, Gotthold Ephraim Lessing, writing in the rationalist tradition, compares painting as *pars pro toto* (and ideal) for the visual arts with poetry. According to Lessing, the visual arts are concerned with bodies in space, and imitate physical beauty. This separates them from poetry as an art that represents action—that is, exists in time. The visual work of art as an interplay between formal elements is perceived all at once. The simultaneous nature of perception stands at the core of the instantaneous presence of a statue or painting. Although, Lessing adds, bodies exist in time, too, he points out that a visual objet d'art can suggest action—that is, time—only as a fixed moment in time through the specific relationship between coexisting bodies (Lessing, 1910, p. 102). Simultaneity of vision takes the picture plane as ideal for the visual arts. Thus, Lessing's comparison is oriented toward a recurrent notion of sculpture in proximity to the relief, a sculpture that champions a principal view rather than a sculpture in the round. [*See* Lessing.]

Attempts to develop a systematic approach to the arts reached their zenith in Hegel's lectures on the philosophy of art written between 1820 and 1829. His thoughts proved instrumental in shifting the emphasis from a concern for beauty toward the "cognitive significance" of art. Hegel's systematic description of the arts is based on the exploration of the specific character of the relationship between the "Idea" and formal properties in individual art forms. Summing up a notion of the essence and function of sculpture that had prevailed in Western art since the Renaissance, he assigned sculpture to the classical art form, to which an equilibrium between the meaningful content of the object and its material form is fundamental. "For through sculpture the spirit should stand before us in blissful tranquility in its bodily form in an immediate unity therewith, and the form should be brought to life by a content of spiritual individuality" (Hegel, 1975, p. 85). Sculpture as a self-contained, bodily object generates its potential meaning in and through the image of the human body as the "real existence of the spirit." This individuality of the human figure is to be represented in "abstract spatiality and the totality of its dimensions" (ibid.).

Sculpture as a three-dimensional body in space exists as part of the object-reality and, therefore, its external and internal structure has been regarded as important, in order for it to maintain a reality and significance of its own; hence the centrality of the categories of unity and wholeness in aesthetic debates. "The compact unity in itself which the god has in sculpture disperses into the plurality of the inner lives of individuals whose unity is not sensuous but purely ideal" (ibid., p. 86). The firm attachment of aesthetic values such as beauty and truth to formal unity and structured wholeness based on the representation of the human (and animal) body can be traced backward to antiquity and forward into the nineteenth century and beyond. [See Hegel.]

Hegel, among others, acknowledges the multifaceted aspect of sculpture and draws attention to the nature of its perception as a process of successive vision, that is, of taking in, comparing, and synthesizing the different aspects of a sculptural object to acquire an overall view while circumnavigating it. In practice, a type of sculpture had been cultivated that enabled the viewer to gain a "synoptic grasp" at once, as in the work of Antonio Canova. Thus, frontality—as the principal view that contained all information vital for the recognition, reading, and appreciation of the sculptural object—went along with a preference for formal principles, such as clear contours, and conventionalized narrative subjects through which a high degree of unity and wholeness could be achieved. The focus on perception as an integral part of an aesthetic experience provided arguments for a restrictive use of materials, against (or for) the application of color, and for championing the single figure in moderate movement, as they facilitate a clear identification of the object as art and its contemplation. A fixed subject-object relationship is implied a priori, however, when contemplation is taken as the appropriate mode of aesthetic reception.

Adolf von Hildebrand's influential work *Das Problem der Form in der bildenden Kunst* (The Problem of Form in Painting and Sculpture), published in 1893, rekindled a controversial debate on the formal properties of sculpture in relation to the process of perception that they induce in the viewer. On similar grounds as some of his predecessors, he suggested that a three-dimensional object ought to fit into a two-dimensional picture plane of "perceptual space," that is, a space exclusively created for the eye. Therefore, he took the relief as the ideal form of sculpture. His approach tried to overcome the prevailing disdain for the sculpted work by bringing it into proximity with the picture plane and the central perspective at a time when "plastic art" had already degenerated into an empty and pompous phrase.

Sculptural Aesthetics in the Twentieth Century. Innovative generic forms and aesthetic practices indicated a growing crisis of representation toward the end of the nineteenth century. Two intertwined developments in sculpture, most apparent in the work of Auguste Rodin, seem of particular significance. First, the body fragment (i.e., the torso) as a genre in its own right—distinguished from the archaeological fragment, the Michelangelesque *non finito*, and conventionalized entities such as the portrait bust—threw into question the traditional concepts of completeness and wholeness based on the human form. Second, the appearance of the body fragment as a genre cannot be conceived of without a process in which the common concept of a linear translation of a figure's anatomical facts into meaning was already abandoned, and with it the traditional notion of narrative structures as being literally embodied. The surface, constituted by interior and exterior forces, by the object's internal "life" and the external process of its making, has become the "locus of meaning" (Krauss, 1981, p. 28). Phenomenological ideas, expressed particularly in Edmund Husserl's thoughts on "intersubjectivity and the intersubjective world," that is, on the relationship between the self, consciousness, and experience of the life-world, may provide a rationale for early modernist sculpture and its rupture between surface, volume, and representational content. Taking the "paradox of the alter ego" as a point of departure, Husserl argues that the self is not a hermetic entity, sealed from direct access from the outside, but formed at the juncture of consciousness and the surface of the body. From there derives the ability to think of a synchronous interrelation of the "surface configuration" of the sculpture and its unpremeditated experience (ibid.). Experience is understood as unpremeditated and immediate through a sensuous grasp of formal relations.

In the visual arts, the relationship between extrinsic and intrinsic values became an issue of discussion with the emergence of abstract painting. Roger Fry and Clive Bell, among others, divorced formal qualities from any representational aspect and claimed that the essence of aesthetic values lay in "purely formal relations"—that is, form is the only intrinsic quality of a work of art and thus the "one constant quality of art" (Fry, 1926, p. 197). A representational content of the object awakes an aesthetic interest only as form, because only form produces "aesthetic" emotions. Representation is regarded as either "irrelevant" or merely "descriptive," that is, as an extrinsic element, for it potentially detracts from both the creation of a work of art and its appreciation. In this way, formalist theories helped to free the debate on sculpture from its tight focus on the depiction of the human and animal body, and subsequently raised awareness of its specific formal condition and expressive potential. Through the sculptural work of artists such as

Constantin Brancusi, Henry Laurens, and Pablo Picasso, the relationship between expressive values of volume and space became reappraised in practice and in theory.

Until the early twentieth century, aesthetic analyses concentrated on the body, while the space in which it existed was considered as merely necessary, passive surrounding. Herbert Read, among others, elaborates on the concept of "touch-space" and emphasizes the essentially palpable character of the plastic object. In *The Art of Sculpture* (1941), he argues that the established convention of making sculpture accessible only for the visual sense is a violation of its true haptic nature (that is, vision mediated through touch), which demonstrates the hegemony of vision in Western culture. Taking up Alois Riegl's notion of "space-shyness," Read reinvestigates the historical development of sculpture and comes to the conclusion that the truly free-standing sculpture with a multiplicity of viewpoints is a recent achievement and heavily indebted to *Kleinplastik* (small statues). Only the small-scale entity can warrant an analysis by the sense of touch as well as by sight, in a processual character of perception in which the multiple aspects are synthesized into an overall sensation.

Susanne Knauth Langer, whose work is founded on developments in logic and linguistics, describes the nature of sculpture as haptic; yet she argues that "the business of sculpture is to translate its data into entirely visual terms, i.e. to make tactual space visible" (1953, p. 89). She considers form in sculpture to be the abstract presentation of a virtual object that is apparent only to sensory perception. Volume and space are engaged in a synthetic relationship, in which space actively participates in the constitution of form, as the void that possesses expressive qualities. In *Feeling and Form,* published in 1953, she writes:

> The volume, however, is not a cubic measure, like the space in a box. . . . it is space made visible, and it is more than the area which the figure virtually occupies. The tangible form has a complement of empty space that it absolutely commands, that is given with it and only with it, and is, in fact, part of the sculptural volume. The figure itself seems to have a sort of continuum with the emptiness around it, however much its solid masses may assert themselves as such. The void enfolds it, and the enfolding space has vital forms as a continuation of the figure.
>
> (Ibid., p. 88)

Langer's concept of sculpture projects a fixed object-subject positioning [*see* Langer]:

> Sculpture is literally the image of kinetic volume in sensory space. . . . Though a statue is, actually, an object, we do not treat it as such; we see it as a center of a space all of its own; but its kinetic volume and the environment it creates are illusory—they exist for our vision alone, a semblance of the self and its world.
>
> (Ibid., p. 91)

Maurice Merleau-Ponty's phenomenological investigations abandon the dichotomy between subject and object by ren-

SCULPTURE. Eva Hesse, *Untitled (3 Nets)* (1966), three net bags with painted papier mache weights, 42 1/2 × 11 1/2 × 6 in. (Copyright by the Estate of Eva Hesse; photograph courtesy of Robert Miller Gallery, New York; used by permission.)

dering fixed centers such as self and world nonexistent. The human body is subject and object in one. For Merleau-Ponty, it is the perceiving body that forms the intersection between the world and consciousness, because consciousness is necessarily embodied. From there emanates art—that is, sculpture transcends the human experience of existing as body in the world.

> I see things, each one in its place, precisely because they eclipse one another, and . . . they are rivals before my sight precisely because each one is in its own place. Their exteriority is known in their envelopment and their mutual dependence in their autonomy. Once depth is understood in this way, we no longer call it a third dimension. . . . Depth thus understood is, rather, the experience of the reversibility of dimensions, of a global "locality"—everything in the same place at the same time, a locality from which height, width, and depth are abstracted, of a voluminosity we express in a word when we say that a thing is there.
>
> (Merleau-Ponty, 1994, p. 290)

SCULPTURE. Sol LeWitt, *Tower* (1990), painted cinder block, 24 × 10.8 × 10.8 ft.; Commissioned by the Wexner Center for the Arts, Ohio State University; collection of the artist. (Photograph by Kevin Fitzsimons; copyright 1998 by Sol LeWitt/Artists Rights Society, New York; courtesy of Wexner Center for the Arts; used by permission.)

Merleau-Ponty, extrapolating his position in respect to painting, turns against the notion of spatiality as a third dimension altogether and puts into place a synchronous, relational time-space concept; he thus provides a tool to disentangle the internal principles of sculpture from an anthropocentric bias. [*See* Merleau-Ponty.]

Merleau-Ponty's idea of voluminosity as an expression for a certain quality of presence is echoed in Adrian Stokes's and Kurt Badt's Platonistic reference to "plasticity" as the metaphysical presence of a tangible idea, a surge of energy from the center of a work of art, notwithstanding the medium in which the idea is embodied. Initially, the distinction between sculpture and plastic art is rooted in the difference between two basic generic practices: carving and modeling. Sculpture is derived from the Latin verb *sculpere* and implies a process that works from the outside to the inside of resistant material. The other term, *plastic,* derived from the Greek *plastikos,* is associated with modeling and malleable materials, that is, a process in which material is added from the inside to the outside. Through a historically extended use of the term *sculpture,* it came to be accepted to cover both practices.

Addressing the inherent contradiction of surface and spatial morphology, of flatness and volume as inherent to sculptural practice, Stokes and Badt establish the fundamental structure of sculpture as an interrelation between the organic (i.e., plastic) form and geometry as the ordering and regulative principle. Their position implies the equation of a work of art with an organism and the view that "life" is the telos of art, a position that also motivates Langer's "virtual kinetic volume that is created by—and with—the semblance of living form" (Langer, 1953, p. 89). Stokes's and Badt's concepts, however, embrace a notion of unity and wholeness that potentially allows for open structures and constructed form based on geometry as the unifying principle through which a sense of definiteness is achieved in the object. Their theory provides a rationale for constructive sculpture, as a new generic practice and the apparent "descent" of modeling in the twentieth century. Artists such as Vladimir Tatlin, Aleksandr Rodchenko, and Naum Gabo, and later David Smith and Anthony Caro, employed the "tools and techniques" of the engineer as well as the natural properties of new materials and thus freed the sculptural volume from its mass, weight, and self-contained character. Their objects—often resonant of architectural engineering or machine design—explore the conditions of the physical world in a concrete mode.

Unlike Gabo's and Antoine Pevsner's expansion of sculpture into the fourth dimension of time (as proclaimed in their "Realist Manifesto" of 1920), neither Stokes's and Badt's elaboration on "plasticity" nor Langer's "kinetic volume" implies that time might constitute an inherent property of sculptural structure and provide a necessary and sufficient criterion for its definition. In a traditional way, they consider time to be an external element of perception rather than an internal structural component of the object. In contrast, artists such as Umberto Boccioni, Alexander Calder, László Moholy-Nagy, and Jean Tinguely used "real" movement as an integral part of their sculpture.

Artists' and art critics' concerns were central to the recurrence of generic debates from the 1950s to the 1970s. They grew out of an increasing diversity of creative strategies and pluralistic styles, which went hand in hand with a collapse of traditional generic practices. Approaches from that direction concentrate on a reconsideration of sculpture's goal, explore the relationship between sculpture as object and as representation of reality, or focus on the genesis of specific morphologies in an evaluative way. Jack Burnham's *Beyond Modern Sculpture* (1968) or William Tucker's *The Language of Sculpture* (1974) might serve as examples for the rich literature of this kind. Burnham draws a link between kinetic sculpture, technological progress, and the human craving to re-create life in order to extrapolate sculpture's ability ultimately to bridge the gap between art and life by replacing the human organism. Tucker, on the other hand, reconsiders the sculptural tradition through a focus on the object's earthbound character, its existence in the round, and its close relation to a perception that is mediated through bodily experience.

In his influential essay "Art and Objecthood," Michael Fried links purity of form with value. He writes: "The concept of quality and value—and to the extent that these are central to art, the concept of art itself—are meaningful, or wholly meaningful, only within the individual arts. What lies within is theatre" (1969, p. 142). Sculpture that enfolds not only in space but in time, sculpture as a performative act, poses a threat to its representational function by "theatricalizing" the space, and, ultimately, blurring clear-cut object-subject positionings. Its essence also comes under attack for an overbearing scale and repetitive pattern. Fried turns against the increasing anonymity of Minimalist sculpture because of its impersonal composition and the fact that, with the use of industrial materials and the aestheticization of technology, traces of the creative process were completely eliminated by artists such as Robert Morris and Donald Judd during the 1960s. With reference to Constructivism and in opposition to the highly emotionally and psychologically charged subjective gesture in art, artists such as Dan Flavin, Carl Andre, and Frank Stella imposed the clarity of mathematical formulas onto their works. By operating with series of similar objects, they accentuated both the arrangement of the parts into a simple rational order and the whole of the composition, rather than its individual elements, in order to achieve a high degree of immediacy.

This attitude is intertwined with a break between the "language" of sculpture and an "extraneous" content. According to Fried, these artists put in jeopardy sculpture's essential qualities such as "presentness and instantaneousness." Insisting on a tight-knit unity and wholeness as essential qualities of the sculptural object based on the instantaneous nature of its perception, he writes:

> It is this continuous and entire presentness, amounting, as it were, to the perpetual creation of itself, that one experiences as a kind of instantaneousness; as though if only one were infinitely more acute, a single infinitely brief instance would be long enough to see everything, to experience the work in all its depth and fullness, to be forever convinced by it. (Ibid., p. 146)

Fried's conception of sculpture as constancy that grows out of its perception comes close to Hildebrand's demand of sculpture having to submit to a "perceptual space." In addition, Fried's derogatory use of the term *theater* excludes those visual forms from the concerns of sculpture that reach out for the dimension of time, such as the kinetic object, installation, and performance.

Different strategies employed from different perspectives have oscillated between a dissolution or an expansion of generic boundaries. Of great influence were structuralist and semiotic theories that regarded art in general as text with a vocabulary of symbolic forms, and a system of syntactic and semantic codes that provided unifying principles. As early as the beginning of the twentieth century, Benedetto Croce developed the view that aesthetic expression necessarily entails embodiment in a material form but is founded in the artist's intuition. The notion of wholeness and unity is replaced as a criterion by intuition as a coherent, self-contained idea formulated in the mind of the artist that completes the work of art. In order to grasp the work, the artist's intuition has to be re-created in the viewer's own imagination. This concept has been of utmost importance for the many strands of conceptual art in which the process of conceiving an idea takes precedence over the realization and existence of the actual (material) object.

Umberto Eco's (1989) theory of the *opera aperta*, the open work of art, comes as a response to the problem of an ever-greater diversity of complex and contradicting aesthetic practices, from, on the one hand, Marcel Duchamp's conceptual approach to Sol LeWitt's Minimalist concept, from Alberto Giacometti's figurations to the Fluxus movement, and, on the other hand, the exclusive nature of necessarily confining generic boundaries. Eco draws on information theory and phenomenology in his linkage between "formal innovation," "ambiguity," and "information." The modern work of art is defined as an ambiguous one that breaks with the codes of practice, whereas the traditional work is based on conventions through which it remains potentially unambiguous, and therefore closed. Ambiguity evolves from formal innovation and generates information. Eco sees information in contrast to meaning. The former points toward unpredictability, toward infiniteness and incompleteness, and thus potentially opens up the work of art in terms of its material structure and its readings, whereas the latter ultimately means fixture and closure. The work of art operates at the center of a complex and multidirectional field of possibilities. This field interacts with the viewer and revokes the traditional notion of a polarization between subject and object on the basis of stable identities. [*See* Eco.]

Whereas Eco's approach potentially dissolves generic terms in an open field of innovative cultural practice, other approaches, such as Rosalind E. Krauss's analysis in "Sculpture in the Expanded Field," aim at keeping generic terms that are traditionally marked by a specific aesthetic practice. Krauss expands the field in which this practice is suspended, in order to turn away from a situation in which modernist sculpture only exists as "ontological absence," as *negativum*, neither constructed nor natural. The binary opposition of nonarchitecture and nonsculpture is opened up into a "quaternary field" by adding their positive terms through inversion: "Sculpture is no longer the privileged middle term between two things that it isn't. Sculpture is rather only one term on the periphery of a field in which

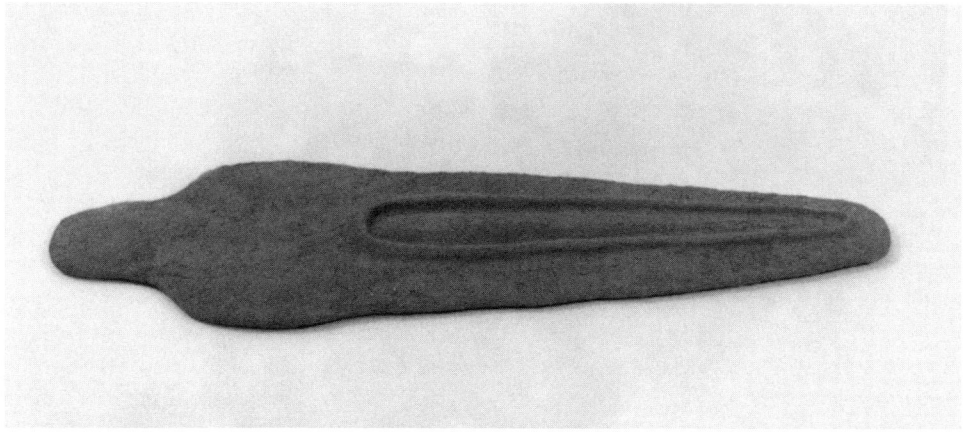

SCULPTURE. Ana Mendieta, *Nile Born (Nacido del Nilo)* (1984), sand and binder on wood, 2 3/4 × 19 1/4 × 16 1/2 in. (7 × 48.9 × 156.2 cm); Museum of Modern Art, New York (Gift of Agnes Gund). (Photograph copyright 1998 by the Museum of Modern Art; used by permission.)

there are other, differently structured possibilities" (Krauss, 1985, p. 284).

The flood of new labels for an increasing pluralism of innovative aesthetic practices in the twentieth century has highlighted the problems involved in defining an objet d'art in terms of classified groups of artifacts. Addressing the changed nature of the objet d'art and Duchamp's ready-mades in particular, Arthur C. Danto (1992) and George Dickie (1992) argue that neither intrinsic formal properties nor aesthetic values constitute the essence of art according to which it could be independently classified and appreciated. Rather, art's "not exhibited properties"—that is, the institutional framework in which art is presented, the "art-world"—define what is aesthetically appreciated. An artifact aquires the status of "candidate for appreciation" when it is put forward as such by a "person acting on behalf of the artworld." "The only difference between the appreciation of art and the appreciation of non-art is that they have different objects" (Dickie, 1992, p. 439). Therefore, a work of art achieves its meaning through the context of the institutions and its potentially indefinite number of "subsystems," such as sculpture. The subsystem's rules impose the terms and conditions of the reception of the object. This approach ultimately regards the question of inherent aesthetic qualities and their link to generic considerations as irrelevant for philosophical investigations into the nature of contemporary art.

[*See also* Bourgeois; Constructivism; Judd; Minimalism; *and* Monuments.]

BIBLIOGRAPHY

Aristotle. *The Poetics of Aristotle.* Translation and commentary by Stephen Halliwell. London, 1987.

Badt, Kurt. *Raumphantasien and Raumillusionen: Wesen der Plastischen.* Cologne, 1963.

Beardsley, Monroe C. *Aesthetics from Classical Greece to the Present: A Short History.* New York, 1966.

Bell, Clive. *Art.* London, 1914.

Burnham, Jack. *Beyond Modern Sculpture: The Effects of Science and Technology on the Sculpture of This Century.* New York, 1968.

Croce, Benedetto. *Aesthetic as Science of Expression and General Linguistic.* Translated by Douglas Ainslie. 2d ed. London, 1922.

Danto, Arthur C. "The Artworld." In *The Philosophy of the Visual Arts,* edited by Philip Alperson, pp. 426–433. New York and Oxford, 1992.

Dickie, George. "What Is Art? An Institutional Analysis." In *The Philosophy of the Visual Arts,* edited by Philip Alperson, pp. 434–444. New York and Oxford, 1992.

Drost, Wolfgang. "Colour, Sculpture, Mimesis: A 19th Century Debate." In *The Colour of Sculpture, 1840–1910,* pp. 61–73. Amsterdam, 1996.

Eco, Umberto. *Art and Beauty in the Middle Ages.* Translated by Hugh Bredin. New Haven, 1986.

Eco, Umberto. *The Open Work.* Translated by Anna Cancogni. Cambridge, Mass., 1989.

Fried, Michael. "Art and Objecthood." In *Minimal Art: A Critical Anthology,* edited by Gregory Battock, pp. 116–147. London, 1969.

Fry, Roger. *Art and Design.* London, 1926.

Hegel, Georg Wilhelm Friedrich. *Aesthetics: Lectures on Fine Art.* 2 vols. Translated by T. M. Knox. Oxford, 1975.

Herder, Johann von Gottfried. *Plastik: Einige Wahrnehmungen über Form und Gestalt aus Pygmalions bildendem Traume.* Berlin, 1964.

Hildebrand, Adolf von. *The Problem of Form in Painting and Sculpture* (1893). Translated by Max Meyer and Robert Morris Ogden. Reprint, New York, 1945.

Husserl, Edmund. *Formal and Transcendental Logic.* Translated by Dorion Cairns. The Hague, 1969.

Krauss, Rosalind E. *Passages in Modern Sculpture.* New York, 1977; reprint, Cambridge, Mass., 1981.

Krauss, Rosalind E. "Sculpture in the Expanded Field." In *The Originality of the Avant-Garde and Other Modernist Myths,* pp. 276–290. Cambridge, Mass., 1985.

Langer, Susanne K. *Feeling and Form.* London, 1953.

Lessing, Gotthold Ephraim. "Laokoön." In *Laokoön: Lessing, Herder, Goethe* (1766), edited by William Guild Howard, pp. 19–154. New York, 1910.

Merleau-Ponty, Maurice. "Eye and Mind." In *Art and Its Significance: An Anthology of Aesthetic Theory*, 3d ed., edited by Stephen David Ross, pp. 282–298. Albany, N.Y., 1994.

Plato. *The Dialogues of Plato*. 3d rev. corr. ed. 5 vols. Translated by Benjamin Jowett. Oxford, 1892.

Read, Herbert. *The Art of Sculpture* (1941). New York, 1956; reprint, Princeton, N.J., 1977.

Stokes, Adrian. "The Stones of Rimini." In *The Critical Writings of Adrian Stokes*, vol. 1, pp. 181–302. London, 1978.

Tucker, William. *The Language of Sculpture*. London, 1974.

Winckelmann, Johann Joachim. *Geschichte der Kunst des Altertums* (1764). Facs. ed. Baden-Baden, 1966.

Wittkower, Rudolf. *Sculpture: Processes and Principles* (1977). Reprint, London, 1991.

KERSTIN MEY

SEMIOTICS. [*To clarify the meaning of semiotics, a theory of signs, this entry comprises three essays:*

Semiotics as a Theory of Art
Semiology of Music
Semiotics and Architecture

The first explains the development of semiotics in general and in contemporary art history. The other two essays treat semiotics as it has been practiced in connection with music and architecture, two other arts wherein a semiotic or linguistic turn has taken place. For related discussion, see Barthes; Eco; Kristeva; Peirce; Structuralism; Theater; *and* Theories of Art.]

Semiotics as a Theory of Art

The basic tenet of semiotics, the theory of signs and sign use, is an antirealist one. Human culture is made up of signs, each of which stands for something other than itself, and the people inhabiting culture busy themselves making sense of those signs. The core of semiotic theory is the definition of the factors involved in this permanent process of sign making and interpreting, and the development of conceptual tools that help to grasp that process as it goes on in various arenas of cultural activity. Art is one such arena.

Semiotic debates focus on such issues as the polysemy of meaning; the problematics of authorship, context and reception; the implications of the study of narrative for the study of images; the issue of sexual difference in relation to verbal and visual signs; and the truth claims of interpretation. This essay is limited to the first two, and focuses on the critique of disciplinary tenets. In all these areas, semiotics challenges the positivist view of knowledge.

Context. The problem here lies in the term *context* itself. Precisely because it has the root *text* while its prefix distinguishes it from the latter, *context* seems comfortably out of reach of the pervasive need for interpretation that affects all texts. Yet, this is an illusion. As Jonathan Culler (1988) has argued, the opposition between an act and its context seems to presume that the context is given and determines the meaning of the act. Context, however, is not given but produced; what belongs to a context is determined by interpretive strategies; contexts are just as much in need of elucidation as events; and the meaning of a context is determined by events.

Context, in other words, is a text itself, and thus consists of signs that require interpretation. What we take to be positive knowledge is the product of interpretive choices. The art historian or critic is always present in the construction she or he produces. In order to endorse the consequences of this insight, Culler proposes to speak not of context but of "framing": "Since the phenomena criticism deal with are signs, forms with socially constituted meanings, one might try to think not of context but of the framing of signs: how are signs constituted (framed) by various discursive practices, institutional arrangements, systems of value, semiotic mechanisms?" (1988, p. xiv).

This proposal does not mean to abandon the examination of "context" altogether, but to do justice to the interpretive status of the insights thus gained. Not only is this more truthful, but it also advances the search for social history itself; for, by examining the social factors that frame the signs, it is possible to analyze simultaneously the practices of the past and our own interaction with them, an interaction that is otherwise in danger of passing unnoticed. What art historians are bound to examine, whether they like it or not, is the work as effect and affect, not only as a neatly remote product of an age long gone.

Semiotics, following the structuralist phase of its evolution, has had to examine the conceptual relations between *text* and *context* in detail, in order to ascertain the fundamental dynamics of socially operated signs. When a particular work of art is placed "in context," it is usually the case that a body of material is assembled and juxtaposed against the work in question in the hope that such contextual material will reveal the determinants that make the work of art what it is. But, from a semiotic point of view, it cannot be taken for granted that the evidence that makes up *context* is any simpler or more legible than the text or image upon which such evidence is to operate. The observation is directed against any assumption of opposition, or asymmetry, between *context* and *text*, such that here lies the work of art, waiting for context to order its uncertainties, and over there is the context, as that which will act upon the work of art and transfer to the latter its own certainties and determination. The idea of "context" invites us to step back from the uncertainties of text to context, posited as platform or foundation. But once this step is taken, it is by no means clear why it may not be taken again; that is, *context* implies from its first moment a *mise-en-abîme*, a potential regression "without brakes."

Semiotics has been obliged to confront this problem head-on, and how it did so has shaped the history of its own development. In its "structuralist" era semiotics (Ferdinand de Saussure) frequently operated on the assumption that the meanings of signs were determined by sets of internal oppositions and differences mapped out within a static system. In order to discover the meanings of the words in a particular language, for example, the interpreter turned to the global set of rules (the *langue*) simultaneously governing the language as whole, outside and away from actual utterances *(parole)*. The crucial move was to invoke and isolate the synchronic system, putting its diachronic aspects to one side; what was sought, in a word, was structure. The critique launched against this theoretical immobility of sign systems pointed out that a fundamental component of sign systems is their aspects of ongoing semiosis, of dynamism. The changeover from theorizing semiosis as the product of static and immobile systems to thinking of semiosis as unfolding in time is indeed one of the points at which structuralist semiotics gave way to poststructuralism.

From this perspective, *context* appears to have strong resemblances to the Saussurean signified. Against such a notion, poststructuralist semiotics argues that *context* is in fact unable to arrest the fundamental mobility of semiosis for the reason that it harbors exactly the same principle of interminability within itself. J. L. Austin's remark concerning speech act theory is a case in point: "the total speech act in the total speech situation is the *only actual* phenomenon which, in the last resort, we are engaged in elucidating" (1975). Semiotics' objection to such an enterprise focuses primarily on the idea of mastering a totality, together with the notion that such a totality is "actual," that is, that it can be known as a present experience.

The problem concerns the stroke or bar (/) between the terms *text* and *context*. That mark of separation presupposes that one can, in fact, separate the two, that they are truly *independent* terms. Yet, the relation between *context* and *text* (or *artwork*) that these terms often take for granted implies that history stands prior to artifact; that context generates, produces, gives rise to text, in the same way that a cause gives rise to an effect. But often the sequence (from context to text) is actually inferred from its end point, leading to the kind of metalepsis that Friedrich Nietzsche called "chronological reversal."

Elements of (visual) texts migrate from text to context and back, but recognition of such circulation is prevented by the primary cut of text-stroke-context. The operation of the stroke consists in the creation of what, for semiotics, is a phantasmic cleavage between text and context, followed by an equally uncanny drawing together of the two sides that had been separated. The stroke dividing *text* from *context* is a move that semiotic analysis would criticize as a rhetorical operation.

Semiotics is averse neither to the idea of history nor even to the idea of historical determination. But meanings are always determined in specific sites in a historical and material world. Semiotics does not work to avoid the concept of historicity; rather, its reservations concern forms of historiog-

raphy that would present themselves in an exclusively aoristic or constative mode, eliding the determinations of historiography as a performative discourse active in the present. The same historiographic scruple that requires us to draw a distinguishing line between "us" and the historical "them"—in order to see how they are different from us—should, in the semiotic view, by the same token urge us to see how "we" are different from "them," and to use *context* not as a legislative idea but as a means that helps "us" to locate ourselves instead of bracketing out our own positionalities from the accounts we make.

Senders. No less problematic is the status of the concept of "artist" (painter, photographer, sculptor, here "author"). It might seem at first that the idea of the author is, again, a natural term in the order of explanation, and one that is now much more substantial and tangible than "context." The author of a work of art is surely someone we can indeed point to, a living (or once living), flesh-and-blood personage with a palpable presence in the world. Yet, as Michel Foucault points out, the relation between an individual and his or her proper name is quite different from the relation that obtains between a proper name and the function of authorship. The name of an author or artist oscillates between designation and description: when we speak of Homer, we do not designate a particular individual, we refer to the author of the *Iliad* or the *Odyssey*, of the body of texts performed by the rhapsodists at the Panathenaic Festivals, or we intend a whole range of qualities, "Homeric" qualities that can be applied to any number of cases (epics, epithets, heroes, types of diction, of poetic rhythm—the list is open-ended). A "J. Bloggs" is in the world, but an "author" is in the works, in a body of artifacts and in the complex operations performed on them. Like "context," "authorship" is a work of framing, something we elaborately produce rather than something we simply find.

Some of the processes of this enframement can be seen at work in the strategies of attribution. Perhaps the first procedure in attribution is to secure clear evidence of the material traces of the author in the work, metonymic contiguities that move in a series from the author in the world, the flesh-and-blood J. Bloggs, into the artifact in question. The traces may be directly autographic—evidence of a particular hand at work in the artifact's shaping; they may be more indirect—perhaps documents pertaining to the work, or the physical traces of a milieu (as when an artifact is assigned to the category "Athenian, c.700 BCE"). Attribution in art history involves further operations that lead away from science and technology into subtler, and more ideologically motivated, considerations concerning quality and stylistic standardization. Before, the "author" referred to a physical agent in the world, but now it refers to the putative creative subject. In the drastic changeover from scientific procedures built on measurement and experimental knowledge, to the highly subjective and volatile appraisals of quality and stylistic uniformity, one already sees how multifarious are the principles that "authorship" bring into play.

A further and quite different range of the arbitrary is found in the procedures for "setting limits" to what counts within authorship. The author, under the forensic principle, is the origin of all the physical traces that point to her presence in the world. But "authorship" is an exclusionary concept. On one side, it works to circumscribe the artistic corpus, and on the other it works to circumscribe the archive. As a concept, "authorship" turns out after all to entail the same regressions and *mise-en-abîme* involved in "context"; and, as it operates in practice, "authorship" manages these receding vistas through many variations on the theme of nonadmission.

The forces of authorship must also include the protocols of writing and the rules governing what is to count as a correct mode of narration. For instance, a catalogue raisonné would be breaking those rules if it wandered into the realm of an author's doodles and napkin sketches, just as a biography of the author would be breaking them if it widened the aperture of relevance to the proportions of a *Tristram Shandy*. That such deviant narratives are rarely encountered is proof of the efficiency of the "authorship" operation. By a rule of correct narration or "emplotment," only those aspects of an author's innumerable wanderings through the world that may be harmonized with the corpus of works will count as relevant, whereas, on the other side, only a certain number of an author's traces will count as elements of the authorized corpus. The exclusionary moves are mutually supportive, and "correct" narration will set up further conventions concerning exactly how much latitude may be permitted in describing the perimeters.

Authorship, then, is no more a natural ground of explanation than is context. The moment of narrative closure, when all the metonymic chains draw to a convergent close, can also be read as a denial of the actual continuation of the contiguities in which the narrator stands. The movement of contiguities in fact passes on from the artwork into the (art) historian's own situation; the work of art is also contiguous with her or him. But the modernist discourses, which foreclose metonymic movement by getting the chain to end with the artwork, can work to deny this, making "contiguity then" eclipse and elide "contiguity now." The draining of hagiographic qualities from the "author" in the past can also be said to justify a corresponding emptying out of the qualities of positionality, motivation, and investment present in the author of the historical narrative.

Semiotics assumes that not only artworks, but the accounts we fashion for them, are works of the sign. From the viewpoint of semiotics, the modernist no less than the humanist discourses are constructed in such a way as to prevent realization that when we confront works of art we enter the field of the sign and of semiosis, of potentially infinite regressions and expansions, and that we deal with this situ-

ation by delimiting it from the place where we stand "now." In this process of concealing where we stand, the concept of "author" plays a crucial role, if as a result of its operation "author then" comes to mask—and to mask the masking of—"author now."

Receivers. Semiotics is centrally concerned with reception. It will describe the logic according to which meanings are engendered. Semiotic analysis of visual art does not set out in the first place to produce interpretations of works of art, but rather to investigate how works of art are intelligible to those who view them, the processes by which viewers make sense of what they see. Standing somewhat to one side of the work of interpretation, its object is to describe the conventions and conceptual operations that shape what viewers or readers do.

Reception semiotics usually draws a distinction between "ideal" and "empirical" spectators. "Ideal" refers to the various roles ascribed to viewers by the paintings they see, the set of positions or functions proposed and assumed by each of the images on display. Within modern art history, for example, the ideal spectator has been a continuing focus of interest, from Alois Riegl's *Dutch Group Portraiture* through the reception studies of Wolfgang Kemp to Michael Fried's *Absorption and Theatricality*. Bringing empirical spectatorship into sharper focus has been the goal of a far more materialist analysis which begins by investigating the actual traces left by actual encounters between viewers and works of art. This project and its approach accord closely with semiotics' own understanding of the concreteness, materiality, and sociality of sign-events.

But if analysis of reception discloses particular social groups, whose visual responses to particular works of art vary in semiotic terms; if different groups possess different codes for viewing even the same work, the idea of *possession* of codes of viewing cannot be taken for granted. If one is really going to address reception, it must be recognized that possession of codes of viewing is a process, not a given, and that members of groups acquire their familiarity with codes of viewing, and their ability to operate those codes, to varying degrees. Access to the codes is a matter of unevenness: codes have to be learned and their distribution varies (and changes) within a group. The danger here is that the term *group* may function as an unacknowledged, and undetectable, synecdoche: in fact, members of the group have different levels of access to the group's codes, varying degrees of competence and expertise; but the condition of expertise is generalized to all of them.

What semiotic analysis draws attention to is the plurality and unpredictability at work in contexts of reception. Surrounding those forms of looking that have given rise to discursive configurations that actually figure in the archive are other, submerged series of procedures that addressed other needs, procedures whose traces can still be derived from the forcefulness of the attempts to repress them. Such series will include codes of viewing that represent residual practices edged out by the rise of those later codes that come to replace them, and, conversely, codes that are hardly yet formed, emergent ways of seeing whose coherence has not yet been established and whose energies have not yet taken root, still tentative and faltering configurations that still have to find each other and lock together to form a configuration that may be seen emerging into the historical record. In a separate category are complete idiolects of viewing, private languages of memory and habit that reorder the dominant codes into secret configurations of desire and identity, codes that may or may not be revealed to another human being, whose nature may or may not be consciously recognized.

A semiotic analysis of reception seeks to add a question and to shift the claim. The better question to ask would be: from where, from what position, is the reconstruction being made? Discussions of reception seem to move between two poles: the plural, dispersed, often submerged "polytheism" of actual, empirical reception; and the delimitations of a discourse on viewing that produces out of this plurality a cast of viewers whose responses are said to follow the most determinable contours. Out of the welter of concrete reception is distilled a character, "the viewer" whose attributes vary from one narration to another. But however this figure is defined, the viewer is essentially a character, a personification, in stories of viewing written in the first place according to the disciplinary norms of the narratives they work within.

History and the Status of Meaning. But what about history? Three issues complicate the historical search: intertextuality, polysemy, and the location of meaning. The term *intertextuality* was introduced by the Soviet philosopher of language Mikhail Bakhtin. It refers to the ready-made quality of linguistic—and, one can add, visual—signs, that a writer or image maker finds available in the earlier texts that a culture has produced. This concept does not quite overlap with iconographic precedent. Iconographic analysis tends to take the historical precedent as the source that virtually dictated to the later artist what forms can be used. But one may consider the work of the later artist as an active intervention into the material handed down to her. This reversal, which also amounts to a deconstruction of the relation between cause and effect, already challenges the idea of precedent as origin, and thereby makes the claim of historical reconstruction problematic.

A second difference is the place of meaning. Iconographic analysis frequently avoids statements about the meaning of the borrowed motifs. To borrow a motif is not a priori also to borrow a meaning. The concept of intertextuality, in contrast, implies precisely that: the sign taken over, because it is a sign, comes with a meaning. This is not to say that the later artist necessarily endorses that meaning; but she will inevitably have to deal with it: reject or reverse it,

ironize it, or simply, often unawares, insert it in the new text. Thus, referring to Albrecht Dürer's *Melencolia I* in the pose of the aggressive elder in his *Susanna* in Berlin, Rembrandt van Rijn cannot help bringing in the quite unsettling meaning of that precedent, suggesting that illegitimate and abusive looking paralyses the transgressor.

A third difference resides in the *textual* character of intertextual allusion. By reusing forms taken from earlier works, an artist also takes along the text out of which the borrowed element is broken away, while constructing a new text with the debris. Reusing a pose used earlier in a self-portrait, Rembrandt inserts the discourse of self-portraiture into his *Bellona* of 1633 (New York, Metropolitan Museum). The new text, say, a mythography, is contaminated by the discourse of the precedent, and thereby fractured, so to speak, ready at any time to fall apart again. The fragility of the objectifying, distancing device of mythography is displayed by this taint of "first person" subjectivity. The historical narrative is infected by subjective discourse. Such a view obviously has consequences for the interpretation of this painting in terms of gender.

One can push this reflection of the implications of intertextuality further, in the direction of the kind of self-reflection advocated by Jürgen Habermas; for the reader cannot help but bring to the pictures her own legacy of discursive precedents, and reading texts or images entails the inevitable mixture of these signs with those perceived in the work. The allusion to *Melencolia*, for example, occurred to us for reasons that Habermas would wish us to explore further, and of which it is obvious that they have to do with contemporary gender issues. This input from the present is emphatically not to be taken as a flaw in our historical awareness, or a failure to distance ourselves from our own time, but as an absolutely inevitable proof of the presence of the cultural position of the analyst within the analysis. To take that presence into account makes the analysis, in fact, more rather than less historically responsible.

This leads to the second issue, that of *polysemy*. Because readers and viewers bring to the images their own cultural baggage, there can be no such thing as a fixed, predetermined, or unified meaning. Attempts to fix meaning provide the most convincing evidence for this view. The field in which struggles over meanings are fought is a social arena where power is at stake. A good example of this mechanism is allegory, the interpretation of, say, a mythical story and all its representations as referring to something outside itself. On the one hand, allegory demonstrates the fundamental polysemous nature of signs. If stories can mean something entirely outside of themselves, then there is no constraint. But take the allegorical interpretations of mythical stories of rape as "really" dealing with tyranny and the establishment of democracy. Intertextual analysis will bluntly refuse such abdication of the meaning imported by the sign: if rape means political tyranny, then the bodily, subjective experience of the woman raped cannot be divorced from the politics at stake. The myth of Lucretia, then, is allegorical, but with a vengeance. The *allos* of allegory is, after all, not only "other," but also "within."

This problem with allegory is, in turn, allegorical for a larger problem implied by polysemy; for the dynamism of signs implied in this view might be mistaken as an abdication of the scholarly position altogether. In spite of the attraction of this idea, especially as a corrective to the remants of positivism still pervasive in the humanities, it needs emphasis that the play of interpretation is surely not entirely free, or else there would be no cause for chagrin about power relations and exclusions in academic practice. In agreement with Ludwig Wittgenstein's concept of the language game, semiotics proposes to see signs as active, and requires them to be both deployed according to rules and public. A sign, then, is not a thing but an event. Sign-events take place in specific circumstances and according to a finite number of culturally valid, conventional, yet not unalterable rules that semiotics calls codes. The selection of those rules and their combination leads to specific interpretive behavior. That behavior is socially framed, and any semiotic view that is to be socially relevant will have to deal with this framing, precisely on the basis of the fundamental polysemy of signs and the subsequent possibility of dissemination.

[*See also* Art History.]

BIBLIOGRAPHY

Austin, J. L. *How to Do Things with Words.* 2d ed. Edited by J. O. Urmson and Marina Sbisa. Cambridge, Mass., 1975.

Bal, Mieke. *Reading Rembrandt: Beyond the Word-Image Opposition.* Cambridge and New York, 1991.

Bal, Mieke, and Norman Bryson. "Semiotics and Art History." *Art Bulletin* 73.2 (June 1991): 174–208.

Bryson, Norman. "Art in Context." In *The Point of Theory: Practices of Cultural Analysis,* edited by Mieke Bal and Inge E. Boer, pp. 66–78. New York, 1994.

Culler, Jonathan. *Framing the Sign: Criticism and Its Institutions.* Norman, Okla., 1988.

Derrida, Jacques. "Living On: Border Lines." In *Deconstruction and Criticism,* by Harold Bloom et al., pp. 75–176. New York, 1979.

Derrida, Jacques. *Dissemination.* Translated by Barbara Johnson. Chicago, 1981.

Derrida, Jacques. *The Truth in Painting.* Translated by Geoff Bennington and Ian McLeod. Chicago, 1987.

Eco, Umberto. *The Role of the Reader: Explorations in the Semiotics of Texts.* Bloomington, Ind., 1979.

Eco, Umberto. *Semiotics and the Philosophy of Language.* Bloomington, Ind., 1984.

Fried, Michael. *Absorption and Theatricality: Painting and Beholder in the Age of Diderot.* Berkeley, 1980.

Goodman, Nelson. *Languages of Art: An Approach to a Theory of Symbols.* 2d ed. Indianapolis, 1976.

Holly, Michael Ann. "Past Looking." *Critical Inquiry* 16 (Winter 1990): 371–396.

Shapiro, Meyer. "On Some Problems in the Semiotics of Visual Art: Field and Vehicle in Image-Signs." *Semiotica* 1.3 (1969): 223–242.

MIEKE BAL and NORMAN BRYSON

Semiology of Music

If one accepts the minimal idea that the sign is, as Saint Augustine said, something that *refers* to something else for someone, then music is a semiological phenomenon in two ways: (1) The musical sign refers to other musical signs. This is the intrinsic or formalist conception of musical meaning: music is a language that signifies itself. (2) The musical sign refers to the experienced, affective, imaging, cultural, ideological world.

If this is so, then one can see in the semiology of music, if not a discipline, in any case an activity or a point of view (1) according to which one can question the symbolic possibilities of music: in this sense, a project of musical semiology has an ontological dimension (which makes a philosophical and aesthetic investigation of interest); and (2) according to which one analyzes music: musical semiology is thus one of the possible forms of musical analysis, and as such, it already has its place, as is evidenced in the *New Grove Dictionary of Music and Musicians,* in the history of analysis and musicology (Bent, 1980).

Even if it has rarely been formulated in these terms, the question of the semiological status of music is at the heart of the millennial aesthetic reflection on music (Fubini, 1983). When Plato assigned distinct ethical values to different modes in the *Republic,* considering some of them dangerous for society, he recognized in music a power of influence *exterior* to sonorous structures themselves. When Eduard Hanslick opened the way to the modern aesthetic of music in 1854 by making the claim that one must not look for musical *thought* anywhere but in the sounds themselves—and in this, he was to be followed by Igor Stravinsky, Anton Webern, and Pierre Boulez—he acknowledged that music possessed a semiological dimension, but on an intrinsic level. In truth, one could compile a history of the musical aesthetic that would show how the semiological pendulum has oscillated between the extrinsic pole and the formalist pole. In the seventeenth century, when instrumental music got the upper hand over the vocal music of the Renaissance, Bernard Le Bovier de Fontenelle exclaimed, "Sonata, what do you want from me?" ("Sonate, que me veux-tu?"). Once instrumental music had acquired its autonomy, Richard Wagner swung the pendulum back in the other direction by making music the servant of drama, whereas Franz Liszt invented the symphonic poem. Johannes Brahms never wrote one, leaning on classical forms in his symphonies and chamber music. When an innovator such as Claude Debussy wrote *La Mer,* some conductors made it their objective to render present the play of the waves and the ringing of the Tritons (Ernest Ansermet), while others stressed above all the modernity of the construction and sonority (Boulez). It soon becomes clear that the semiological status of music (does it refer to itself or to the lived world?) not only runs through aesthetic reflection but implicates the composers and performers as well.

It seems unnecessary to choose between the two options and among the intermediary positions that Leonard B. Meyer (1956) has brilliantly distinguished—the pure formalists, the absolutist expressionists, the referentialist expressionists, and the pure referentalists. One can certainly adopt a normative semiologico-aesthetic position, but the day will come when it will be necessary to violate it. Because the most intransigent formalist will never be able to prevent descriptive music from existing (without mentioning opera music), the most expressionist of musicians will never be able to deny that a work exists first as an ensemble of sonorous configurations. Therefore, one can hear more expressions and indeed more sentiments in a Webern piece than he wanted to put in it; one can be more interested in the rhythmic structures of *Le Sacre du Printemps* than in seeing a pagan ritual in it. This is because another, more fundamental distinction characterizes the semiological functioning of music beyond the opposition between referentialism and formalism. The perceptive strategies, relative as much to forms as to sentiments expressed, do not necessarily correspond to compositional strategies, even if there exists something between the two that is at once the point of departure and the end point: a constellation of sonorous combinations.

SEMIOTICS: Semiology of Music. *Microstructure and macrostructure in the first fifteen bars of "Le Cathédrale Engloutie, Préludes" by Claude Debussy.* (Courtesy of Jean-Jacques Nattiez.)

Following the model proposed by J. Molino (1990), and which, in fact, can be applied to every form of work or human practice, one can call the "semiology of music" every area of reflection or every kind of musical analysis that, as much from the standpoint of form as from that of expression, endeavors to distinguish what Molino denotes as the *poietic* (compositional strategies), the *neutral level* (immanent structures), and the *aesthesic* (perceptive strategies) and to study the modalities of their articulation (Nattiez, 1976, 1987, 1990).

Before presenting a few instances of this semiological conception of musical aesthetics, its relevance may be illustrated with the example of a tripartite musical analysis. To this end, particular aspects of the first fifteen bars of Debussy's *La Cathédrale Engloutie* will be examined (see Figure 1).

An analysis of neutral level (an immanent one) may, among many other characteristics of this piece, note in the opening of the text the following phenomenon of repetition and variation. The motif D-E-B in bar one is taken up again an octave higher in the same bar, but without the B. This group is found again in bars 3 and 5. In bars 14 and 15, the motif D-E-B reappears, again repeated an octave higher, but this time with a high B. The whole forms a descending mirror form at bar 15. One finds a transformation of this motif of a second plus a fifth in the theme, in bars 7 and 8: C#-D#-G# also presents the intervallic succession of second and fifth. The same motif is transformed in bars 9 and 10 and 11–12 (G#-A#-D#). The motif D-E-B is also present in these first fifteen bars on a macroscopic level: the first chord of bars 1, 3, and 5 displays a high D; the E of the motif is present, in the form of an ostinato, from bar 5 to bar 13; and the B intervenes as the top note of the first chord in bar 14.

One speaks here of a neutral type of analysis, for it has been content with noting the recurrence of a motif with its variations without asking questions of poetic and aesthetic relevance.

The poetic question occurs when one asks if these repetitions and transformations form part of Debussy's compositional strategies. The answer is unhesitatingly yes. The specificity of the intervallic configuration of second and fifth and the identity of the motif D-E-B in bar 1 with the larger macroscopically stretched motif can hardly be the product of mere chance.

On the other hand, it is not evident that, when one hears this piece in real time, the ear should be able to establish all these connections that musicology may find in its laboratory analysis. Is the high B of bar 15 perceived as the complement to that which was left in suspense at the end of bars 1, 3, and 5? Can the listener establish a link between the motif D-E-B and its stretching out over fifteen bars? Research following the lines of experimental psychology (which will be dealt with elsewhere in detail) shows that the repetition of the motif in bars 1, 3, and 5 is noticed by the majority of listeners. The motif's transformation in the theme, however, is perceived by a much smaller group. The two other phenomena (completion at bars 14–15 of the expectation created at the beginning, and correspondence between the micro- and macrostructure) are not perceived by anyone.

This example well illustrates the necessity of distinguishing, in musical analysis, between immanent, poetic, and aesthetic points of view. How do things lie in the aesthetic domain?

A good number of musicians and musicologists have difficulty accepting the pertinence of this tripartite distinction, and here, many different configurations are possible. There are those for whom music is nothing other than a formal game (described by Molino as the analysis of the neutral level). What is the point, then, in worrying about the poietic and the aesthesic? For others, music would not exist without the gesture of the composer. For others still, it is made above all to be heard. Few theories have attempted to embrace the relationship between these three levels, either because theorists do not recognize the necessity of a level of immanent description of music or because they do not acknowledge the "discrepancy" between the poietic and the aesthesic.

Why is this so? First of all because of the bias, conveyed by certain semiologists (Roman Jakobson, Umberto Eco), but shared by many, according to which a musical work (or a film, a poem, a sentence) is supposed to be a phenomenon of communication: a *common code* to the sender and the receiver is supposed to make communication possible, and the task of the semiologist is to make an inventory of these codes. Unfortunately, one quickly discovers that there are an infinite number of "codes" implied in "communication." It appears theoretically and empirically more appropriate, if not easier, to examine which *interpretants* (in Charles Sanders Peirce's sense) intervene in musical production and musical perception, that is, which traits or aspects of lived, musical, semantic, expressive, and ideological experience are connected to sonorous structures, and this, for the composer, performer, or listener.

Second, a large majority of musicians consider harmony to be equally constitutive of the foundation of the tonal system. For them, the other parameters are subordinated to it, and the principles of harmonic functioning have remained unvaried from Johann Sebastian Bach to Wagner. How could one acknowledge the slightest gap between the poietic and the aesthesic before such stability? Even if the cycle of fifths seems quite constant during the entire period of so-called common practice, and even though the cycle of thirds are strongly present in the nineteenth century, it is necessary all the same to wonder why a treatise of melody (Anton Reicha) considered independently of harmony appears at the beginning of the nineteenth century; why Hec-

tor Berlioz, in composing one of the first treatises of orchestration, sanctions a new autonomy of timbre that will lead to electro-acoustic music; why modern theorists such as Fred Lerdahl and Ray Jackendoff (1983), all the while acknowledging the fundamental ideas of harmony according to Heinrich Schenker, base their analytic approach on a metrico-rhythmic cadre.

Confining our discussion to the West, tonal music is far from constituting a harmonious hierarchized group. The diverse parameters that constitute it—melody, rhythm, meter, harmony, timbre—have, to use the terminology of Étienne Gilson, a specific physical mode of existence. To put it roughly, the melodic line extends over the duration; harmony is constituted by vertical entities; and rhythm is what remains when the pitches, and so on, have been removed. In short, it is possible to distinguish them, and thus, the parameters and their components have experienced different rhythms of historical evolution for more than three centuries. Consequently, it is difficult to decide if Ludwig van Beethoven is a classicist or a Romantic in the *Periodisierung* of German musicology. Harmony and phraseology are still considered classical in it, but in Beethoven there is already a thematic construction based on the cell that will become fundamental for Brahms and that will appear again at the root of the Schoenbergian series.

The relative equilibrium between the poietic and the aesthesic seems only to characterize the brief classical period. The works of experimental psychology have confirmed that the series was not made to be perceived, having opportunely recalled that, during an audition, a talented conservatory student could not differentiate the subject, the countersubject, and the answer of a fugue of Bach (Francès, 1958). This is because of the fact that one finds in the musical phenomenon what could be called purely poietic instruments that are far from having authority over communication. Conversely, the act of musical perception is not a phenomenon of reception, but of construction. It suffices to read the diverse descriptions of Debussy's style, for example, to realize that although characteristic traits such as parallel fifths or the tonal scale (which was already picked up because of its novelty by Marcel Proust, who was not a musician) are cited by everybody, as soon as one enters into details, the corpus of more detailed traits that are specific to Debussy vary according to the perception of the individual. Is this to say that the description of style is eminently subjective? No. This means simply that style, like every other aspect of the musical phenomenon, is a symbolic reality with three dimensions: it is not only a phenomenon of perception, but a poietic phenomenon (from which musical tradition—Frédéric Chopin, the Russians, Emmanuel Chabrier, André Messager—did Debussy develop his own style?) and a phenomenon of structure: there are harmonies and melodic phrases that are found nowhere else except in Debussy.

It soon becomes clear that, starting from an aesthetic and ontological reflection on the semiological nature of music, we have imperceptibly moved toward musical *analysis*. Do specifically semiological analytic approaches exist?

At first, as we have just seen concerning the example of style, the semiological tripartition makes it possible to classify the diverse types of musical analysis—an undertaking that is pedagogically of cardinal importance, because each inventor of an analytic paradigm is evidently convinced of having proposed the best and the last one. When Boulez analyzes rhythm in *Le Sacre du Printemps,* he deliberately proposes an *immanent analysis.* When Rudolph Réti draws the hypothesis, based on text of *La Cathédrale Engloutie,* that Debussy used the third and the fourth as "generative intervals," he proceeds from what can be called an *inductive poietic.* If, on the contrary, one projects onto the text a piece of information exterior to the work such as the preliminary studies of Beethoven or Wagner, one undertakes an *external poietic.* The situation is symmetrical on the side of perception: Meyer and Lerdahl and Jackendoff practice an *inductive aesthesic* in drawing the hypothesis of perceptive behavior from the musical text on the basis of general rules of perception. Conversely, experimental psychologists (Robert Francès, Michel Imberty) and cognitivists today construct an *external aesthesic* in interrogating subjects about what they have effectively perceived and then projecting their responses onto the text subject to inquiry. Finally, there are theorists such as Schenker for whom the analysis of harmonic structures is poietically pertinent and normatively determines how the work should be perceived. If it were systematically put into practice, this classification of analyses would facilitate discussion between specialists, because there is no point in accusing an author of neglecting an aspect of a work if it is clear that he or she tackled a single side of its symbolic dimension that is incompatible with the others.

Can one say that there are musical analyses that are specifically semiological? This is the qualifier that has often been given to the technique of paradigmatic decomposition of the musical syntagma proposed by Nicolas Ruwet (1972, 1987) and inspired by the structuralism of Jakobson and Claude Lévi-Strauss. Paradigmatic analysis is an effective instrument in the analysis of immanent structures because of two aspects: the systematic rewriting of open units and the rendering explicit of procedures utilized. The paradigmatic technique lends itself to a large number of uses: the hierarchization of the formal unities of a piece; the analysis of processes of variation throughout a work; the reconstruction of protomelodies; the establishment of scales; and the assessment of recurrent harmonic schemata. This method is specifically semiological if one considers music an "introversive" semiological system, as Jakobson (1973) indicated when he specifically cited the paradigmatic technique as a means to describe the play of signs between musical units.

But even from the immanent point of view, the paradigmatic model is not the only appropriate one. The intramusical semiological sign does not only exist between taxonomic units. One must also take into account the prolongational phenomena so well demonstrated by Schenker on the harmonic level and of which Meyer seems to have shown the specific semiological dimension in analyzing melodic phenomena in detail. Finally, these two forms of immanent description—taxonomic and prolongational—only constitute a first step toward bringing together poietic strategies at the origin of the sonorous with aesthesic strategies that reconstruct it with semantic associations that link it to the lived universe of the composer or listener.

The musical semantic without a doubt provides the most concrete example of the difficulty that one encounters in establishing links between musical structures and that to which they refer. Insofar as it is prudent to understand musical significance as referring to every kind of intra- and extramusical sign, if one does not want to fall into the frequent trap of taking language as a model of all symbolic functioning, the term *semantic* must be reserved for the part of musical semiology that treats verbal associations that are conceptualized by means of music. On the poietic side, it has been the object of a certain tradition in the history of music, notably in the theories described in the eighteenth century as *Affektenlehre,* which were essentially elaborated in the Baroque era. On the aesthesic side, experimental psychology has constructed many often statistically sophisticated tools to obtain and classify the data obtained from subjects listening to music. Contrary to the widespread idea that these experiments have discovered what was already known, they have made it apparent that beyond the central tendencies, networks of associations existed that were not less real for being a minority. They have equally allowed "semantic maps" of style to come to light: for example, the works of Imberty (1979, 1981) reveal the interweaving of diverse types of water in Debussy: waters that are clear and demonstrated; waters that are cascading, transparent, torrential, flowing, undulating, heavy, despairing, majestic, weighty, or imposing; waters that allow listeners to link the musical phenomenon to the most profound in their imaginary.

One will be able to speak about musical semiology, strictly speaking, when one has succeeded in putting one's finger on the intermediary symbolic behaviors between verbal associations and sonorous structures and in clarifying the nature of the connection between the two. Despite the fact that the enormous cultural interferences probably constitute one of the deepest mysteries of musicology—indeed, of the human sciences—Imberty managed to establish a patent connection between the type of response obtained and the degree of heterogeneity in the musical form calculated according to the frequency of melodic intervals and the duration of metrical intervals. C. Boilès, for his part, demonstrated (1967, 1969) that, in the civilizations he studied (the Otomi and the Tepehua in Mexico), one could make precise meanings correspond to stable musical figures in a ritual context. Undoubtedly, more civilizations than is generally realized possess a system of semantic association: the evidence of Geneviève Calame-Grialue (1965) drawn from the Dogan people, and the work of Nicole Beaudry (1983) on the music of Haitian vodun and of Monique Desroches (1980) on that of the Hindus of Martinique would seem to confirm this.

Semiological research on music must allow music to be situated among the other symbolic forms, while avoiding the pitfall of taking human language as the standard. Music and language certainly have two common traits: linearity and organization in discrete units. It has been said often enough that music is *lacking* a first articulation, without, however, examining if it does not have something "more" as well. In any case, it could well be that, on the basis of the information furnished by the history of music and ethnomusicology, without having the status of a substitute for spoken language, the immersion of music in limiting contexts, notably religious ones, has given it a power of semantic expression that is stronger than what one is often ready to recognize in it today.

[*See also* Music, *historical overview article*.]

BIBLIOGRAPHY

Beaudry, Nicole. "Le langage des tambours dans la cérémonie vaudou haïtienne." *Revue de musique des universités canadiennes* 4 (1983): 125–140.

Bent, Ian. "Analysis." In *New Grove Dictionary of Music and Musicians,* edited by Stanley Sadie, vol. 1. London, 1980.

Boilès, C. "Tepehua Thought-Song: A Case of Semantic Signaling." *Ethnomusicology* 11.3 (1967): 267–292.

Boilès, C. "Otomi Cult Music." Ph.D. diss., Tulane University, 1969.

Calame-Griaule, Geneviève. *Ethnologie et langage: la parole chez les Dogon.* Paris, 1965.

Desroches, Monique. "Validation empirique de la méthode sémiologique en musique: le cas des indicatifs de tambour dans les cérémonies indiennes en Martinique." *Yearbook of the International Folk Music Council* 12 (1980): 67–76.

Francès, Robert. *La perception de la musique.* Paris, 1958.

Fubini, Enrico. *Les philosophes et la musique.* Translated by Daniele Pistone. Paris, 1983.

Hanslick, Edvard. *On the Musically Beautiful: A Contribution towards the Revision of the Aesthetics of Music.* Translated and edited by Geoffrey Payzant. Indianapolis, 1986.

Imberty, Michel. *Entendre la musique.* Paris, 1979.

Imberty, Michel. *Les écritures du temps.* Paris, 1981.

Jakobson, Roman. "Le langage en relation avec les autres systèmes de communication." In *Essais de linguistique générale,* translated by Nicolas Ruwet, vol. 2, pp. 91–103. Paris, 1973.

Lerdahl, Fred, and Ray Jackendoff. *A Generative Theory of Tonal Music.* Cambridge, Mass., 1983.

Meyer, Leonard B. *Emotion and Meaning in Music.* Chicago, 1956.

Meyer, Leonard B. *Explaining Music.* Berkeley, 1973.

Molino, J. "Fait musical et sémiologie de la musique." *Musique en Jeu* 17 (1975): 37–62. Translated into English as "Musical Fact and the Semiology of Music," *Music Analysis* 9.2 (1990): 105–156.

Musique en Jeu 1–33 (November 1970–November 1978). See nos. 5, 10, 12, and 17.

Nattiez, Jean-Jacques. *Fondements d'une sémiologie de la musique.* Paris, 1976.

Nattiez, Jean-Jacques. *Musicologie générale et sémiologie.* Paris, 1987. English translation by Carolyn Abbate published as *Music and Discourse: Toward a Semiology of Music* (Princeton, N.J., 1990).

Ruwet, Nicolas. *Langage, musique, poésie.* Paris, 1972. English translation of chap. 4 published as "Methods of Analysis in Musicology," *Music Analysis* 6.1–2 (1987): 3–36.

Stefani, Gino. *Introduzione alla semiotica della musica.* Palermo, 1976.

JEAN-JACQUES NATTIEZ
Translated from French by Terri Gordon
and Larsen Powell

Semiotics and Architecture

By the mid-1950s, confidence in the principles of modernism in architecture had reached a point of crisis—if not for architectural practitioners at large, then certainly for its most thoughtful historians and critics. Mainstream modernism's "functionalist" design methods had come to seem prosaic, and its long-accepted aesthetics of abstraction increasingly vacuous. In historical retrospect, it is evident that there were two particular bodies of theory outside architecture to which revisionist thinkers predominantly turned at that time, to seek intellectual reinvigoration for their discipline. These were "operations research," on the one hand, and theories of "perception" and of "reception," on the other. By means of a retheorization of "functionalism" in architecture, "operations research" led eventually to what came to be known as "systematic design methodology." The various theories of "perception" and "reception," on the other hand, through an intensified consideration of architecture's audience, led to an effort to apply semiotics to architecture.

One key venue at which both of these lines of inquiry were explored early on was the Hochschule für Gestaltung in Ulm, founded as a sort of "new Bauhaus" in 1955. Not a school of architecture in the usual sense, the Ulm Hochschule combined industrial and building design with visual communication and information—encompassing press, films, broadcasting, television, and advertising. At Ulm, all these design disciplines were intended to be explored from the perspective of what one of the school's notable early pedagogues, Gui Bonsiepe, named "technological rationalism." Tomás Maldonado—another of the leading figures at Ulm—eventually concluded that "operations research" alone could not adequately address the significance of form in architecture; as a result, like many of his colleagues, he found himself exploring theories of perception and reception as well. One important source was Max Bense, whose approach to communications was first outlined in his *Aesthetica* of 1954, and another one was the early American semiotician, Charles Morris, whose works had first appeared in the 1930s. Kenneth Frampton observed, in an essay on the Ulm school, that "operation" and "communication" were the two poles that were to "play major roles in the evolution of *Hochschule* theory" (1973). The school's commitment to technological rationalism meant that both these poles were being explored from a predominantly positivist philosophical vantage point.

The fact that this was so was not lost on an early visitor to Ulm, who was later to become one of the most committed critics of its "scientistic" intellectual orientation. This was Joseph Rykwert, whose 1958 lectures at the school eventually took the form of an essay (to be discussed later) titled "The Sitting Position: A Question of Method." Rykwert had already published the previous year an essay; "Meaning in Building," in which he lamented what he saw as the vulgar and banal consequences of a "preoccupation with rational criteria" for the design process, and called instead for architects to "acknowledge the emotional power of their work," insisting further that such an acknowledgment would depend on "investigations of a content, even of a referential content in architecture" (1982). In choosing to employ a term such as "referential content," Rykwert challenged the supposedly transparent abstract aesthetics of mainstream modernism head-on, and opened the way to the explicit consideration of the semiological "signifier" and "signified" in architecture, which was to commence some years later. "The Sitting Position," moreover, emphasized the anthropological—as opposed to the functional—aspects even of such an "operational" discipline as ergonomics. (Both of Rykwert's prescient essays of the late 1950s were later compiled in a collection titled *The Necessity of Artifice* [1982].)

As it happens, the first publication of Rykwert's "Meaning" essay was in the Italian magazine *Zodiac*, no. 6, and Italy became the home of the next notable series of efforts to apply semiotics to architecture. For example, in 1964, Giovanni Klaus Koenig published his *Analisi del linguaggio architettonico,* the first extended text devoted explicitly to the study of the possible application of the models of semiotics to architecture along parallel lines to those that had been explored at Ulm. (Appropriately enough, Koenig's text was preceded by an introduction by Maldonado.) In 1967, Koenig's book was followed by Renato de Fusco's *Architettura come mass medium* of 1967—this being a text whose very title foregrounded what was coming to be known as "reception theory"—in particular, the influence of the celebrated Canadian media theorist Marshall McLuhan. Then, in 1968, the rapidly evolving Italian perspective on semiotics was put into a definitively sharp focus with the publication of Umberto Eco's *La struttura assente.* Eco's comprehensive text not only summarized the whole earlier history of the various intellectual strands that made up the theory of semiotics up to that date; it put into context the contributions of Koenig and de Fusco to a possible semiotics of ar-

chitecture, and went on to set out the clearest, most detailed, and most broadly based application of the such principles to architecture that had appeared up to that time. (Eco made a number of efforts to translate this text into English, but eventually abandoned the effort, instead folding its arguments into a later book, which he wrote in English, *A Theory of Semiotics* (1976), and incorporating its architectural contents, translated into English, in a 1980 anthology discussed later in this essay.)

In a stream of thinking parallel in many ways to that of the Ulm thinkers and the Italians, a group of French scholars had begun to make their own significant contribution to the emerging field. From 1954 to 1957 had appeared the now-famous series of feuilletons of Roland Barthes that were compiled in French under the title *Mythologies* (1957). The following year, Barthes's text was joined by the French edition of Claude Lévi-Strauss's equally influential *Structural Anthropology.* Like most of the "structuralist" French texts of that period, both of these were more heavily dependent on their respective authors' debts to the linguistic theory of the Swiss pioneer Ferdinand de Saussure than on the work of either Charles Morris or Charles Sanders Pierce, even though the French scholars, like Eco, acknowledged the significant role played in the early development of semiotic theory by such figures. As a result of the rapid rise to prominence of Barthes's and Lévi-Strauss's typical methods of cultural interpretation, their works rapidly achieved considerable intellectual influence in an increasing number of nonliterary cultural fields—painting, photography, and cinema no less than architecture itself. With the French publication of Barthes's *Elements of Semiology* in 1964, this growing influence reached a definitive first culmination.

Among the revisionist theoreticians of architecture who eagerly read Lévi-Strauss's and Barthes's arguments of the early 1960s was the present author, who was engaged during the mid-1960s in the preparation of a doctoral dissertation in architecture at University College London. The professor of architecture there at that time was Richard Llewellyn-Davies, and he had made his school a British center of a revisionist architectural tendency known in those years in the English-speaking world as "systematic design methodology." Like their intellectual fellow travelers at the Ulm school, the British methodologists were engaged in an intellectual project intended to devise a new mode of designing that would possess the authority of science, and that would eschew any preoccupation with subjectivity, intuition, or myth.

It is difficult from the vantage point of three decades later to recall just how powerful this tendency appeared to be in the mid-1960s—especially in Britain, given how little influence it has managed to sustain in the years since. At the time, the advocates of this tendency bid fair to succeed in their project, at least insofar as they did manage to supplant the rapidly fading pieties of "orthodox" modernism, in numerous schools of architecture throughout the world, especially those of the former British Empire. Probably the first culmination of their project of revisionism was the publication in 1964 of *Notes on the Synthesis of Form* by Christopher Alexander. In this first of his many influential books, Alexander employed the concept of "fit" within the design process to devise a sort of utterly frictionless end point by which the ultimate appropriateness of any finally designed "form" could, as he saw it, be dispassionately assessed.

Revisionist theoreticians, who wished to see architecture regain a securer social role than mainstream modernism had been able to achieve for it, but who also believed that such a role needed to be one that was not limited to "functionality"—even to the sophisticated new versions of functionality that the design methodologists were claiming to find in applications of architecture of "operations research"—found highly promising the potential alternative applications of semiotics, particularly in the structuralist semiotics associated which the French intellectual lineage stretching back to de Saussure.

Among the intellectual efforts to realize that promise was a 1967 issue of *ARENA,* the journal of the Architectural Association School of Architecture in London, England, edited by the present author and devoted to the theme "Meaning in Architecture." Among the texts included in this issue that have proved to have some historical influence were "Typology and Design Method" by Alan Colquhoun, "The Sitting Position: A Question of Method" by Rykwert (the first English-language publication of the essay that had been first published in Italian in 1965 in *Edilizia Moderna*), and "*La Dimension Amoureuse* in Architecture" by George Baird. Colquhoun's essay was one of the first attempts to challenge the methodologies that had been developed at Ulm and at University College London, and was even framed as an explicit reply to Maldonado, whom Colquhoun had met when they were simultaneously visiting faculty at Princeton University. Baird's "*La Dimension Amoureuse* in Architecture" was one of the first published in English to set out a systematic exposition of the Saussurean concepts of *langue* and *parole,* of the "signifier" and the "signified," and of "system" and "syntax," as they might be employed to interpret architecture as a social field of meaning. In 1968, the journal publication was followed by a book of the same title, edited by Charles Jencks and Baird, and substantially expanded to include a number of additional texts on related topics by authors such as Françoise Choay, Gillo Dorfles, Kenneth Frampton, and Charles Jencks. In subsequent years, the book *Meaning in Architecture* went on to play a role in the dissemination of Saussurean semiotics as applied to architecture, first in the English-speaking world, and then also in Spain and in France, where foreign-language editions appeared.

In 1972, it became possible for the first time to discern the impact of the project of semiotics in architecture on an already established generation of thinkers, for in that year a still-controversial text was published that was much more directly oriented to the design of actual buildings than *Meaning in Architecture* had been, and was thereby more influential—at least in the English-speaking world. This was *Learning from Las Vegas,* by Robert Venturi, Denise Scott Brown, and Steven Izenour. Of this trio of authors, Venturi had already made himself famous as the author of the seminal revisionist text of 1966 *Complexity and Contradiction in Architecture*—probably the single most important of the critiques of the principles of "orthodox modern architecture," to use Venturi's sardonic term, that had preceded the historic application to architecture of the methods of semiotics. But the *Las Vegas* text went much farther down a revisionist road than Venturi's earlier text had done. Where *Complexity* had mounted a formalist critique of the compositional principles of modernism, *Las Vegas* went on to make a much more "sociological" and "populist" disparagement of modernism, and the precepts of semiotics formed a supportive methodological backdrop to it. For that matter, the choice by Venturi and his coauthors of Las Vegas itself as the putative exemplar of an identifiably distinctive—and popular—American urbanism was deliberately polemical.

It is interesting to note that the authors of this inflammatory book cited arguments from *Meaning in Architecture,* in particular Colquhoun's increasingly influential essay "Typology and Design Method." Indeed, during the early 1970s, the concept of "type" that had been so compellingly employed by Colquhoun in his 1967 essay merged with a body of ideas that had been being developed in Europe during those same years, and that revolved around the paired concepts of building "typology" and urban "morphology." Associated in the first instance with an Italian architectural lineage from Ernesto Rogers to Saverio Muratori and Aldo Rossi, the body of ideas comprising "typology/morphology" established a conceptual relationship of architecture to urban form that, like semiotics, was deeply embedded in the "social."

Five years after Venturi's *Las Vegas* came what is still probably the most influential English-language text on semiotics in architecture, Jencks's *The Language of Post-Modern Architecture* (1977). Where *Meaning in Architecture* set out a theoretical apparatus for consideration, and *Las Vegas* oriented this apparatus to "popular culture," Jencks's book not only recapitulated and extended both of these intellectual trajectories, but it also went on to illustrate a number of actual built examples, and explicitly linked the analogy of "language" in architecture, based on semiotics, with the specific architectural tendency then coming to be known as "postmodernism." For the next decade, the postmodernist tendency rapidly took over the practice of architecture throughout the English-speaking world, now intellectually sanctioned by the apparatus of "semiotics." In the United States, architects who became very prominent celebrities—

such as Michael Graves, Charles Moore, and Robert A. M. Stern—all did so as perceived practitioners of the new "postmodernist" style, and they in turn were followed in the world of more commercial architecture by practitioners in large corporate firms.

In 1980, a shift from popularizing texts back to more scholarly ones occurred in the English-speaking world with the publication of a follow-up volume to *Meaning in Architecture,* edited by one of that book's coeditors, Jencks, this time joined by Geoffrey Broadbent and Richard Bunt. *Signs, Symbols and Architecture* brought together a revised version (and English translation) of the portion of Eco's *La struttura assente* that had been devoted to architecture, with various texts by other authors. These included specific, detailed applications of semiological analysis to specific building elements (by Eco and Jencks, as well as by Mario Gandelsonas and David Morton), texts of a more sociological character (by Judith Blau and Maria Luisa Scalvini), and even certain expressions of skepticism in respect to the whole project of semiotics in architecture (by Xavier Rubert de Ventos and Bunt).

Historically speaking, the contribution to this book by Gandelsonas and Morton (a reprint of an essay that was first published in 1972) is particularly interesting, because it was devoted to semiological interpretations of the work of a number of American architects, including Peter Eisenman. Eisenman was soon to become part of a polemical backlash against the influence of semiotics in architecture. As of 1980, it was still politically possible for his work to be discussed in a volume of essays largely oriented to it affirmatively. It is true, of course, that at an earlier point in his career, Eisenman had been interested in a loose linguistic analogy with architecture, based on the concept of "deep structure" that had been framed by the American linguist Noam Chomsky. By 1980, Eisenman had abandoned the influence of Chomsky, but this did not prevent Gandelsonas and Morton from reprinting in that year an earlier text that discussed his work in terms primarily in terms of its "syntactics."

As the 1980s proceeded, and as the populist and popular phenomenon of "postmodernism" in architecture grew ever more ubiquitous throughout the world, it became increasingly uncommon to emphasize the "syntactic" aspects of the application of semiotics to architecture. Instead, the overwhelming bias of postmodern architecture toward the "semantic" utterly overwhelmed mainstream architectural practice. At the same time, the parallel urban ideas that had been framed in Europe in relation to the concepts of "typology" and "morphology" similarly lost their former sharp focus. Worst of all, other related aspects of this bias became strikingly evident as well. Instances were, on the one hand, the increasingly reactionary polemics in favor of a historicist, populist urbanism propounded by Britain's Prince of Wales and, on the other, the newly systematic appropriation of the techniques of "postmodern" architecture then being undertaken by the Disney Corporation for its proliferating theme parks.

An undercurrent of dissent also became increasingly visible among leading theorists and critics in those years. The increasingly "scenographic" character of postmodernist architecture—in both its historicist and its more commercial theme-park modes—precipitated stronger and stronger objections among its critics, who pointed to its increasingly evident loss of cultural authenticity. What is more, some of these identified the application of semiotics to architecture as a cause of the perceived undesirable direction of architecture that had become so widespread. Polemical counterattacks on postmodernism—and at least implicitly on semiotics—grew increasingly vociferous in the late 1980s and early 1990s, and most of them derived from two distinct, but related, cultural/intellectual positions. The first was a resurgent architectural neo-avant-gardism, and Eisenman was a prominent representative of it. He had, of course, from the very beginning of his career had avant-gardist leanings, and the accommodationist political success of postmodern architecture offended him. Its historicist iconography, its mainstream popularity, and its corporate acceptability—all these eventually made postmodernism anathema for such American neo-avant-gardists as himself. His turning away from the ideas of Chomsky, and toward those of Jacques Derrida, only speeded up his neo-avant-gardist antipathy to "pomo," as he famously labeled it.

But perhaps equally as important in the backlash against postmodernism—as well as against typology/morphology studies—in intellectual circles was a distinct new commitment by a younger generation of critics to a phenomenological philosophical stance that was hostile not only to postmodern architecture, but to structuralist theory itself. Appropriately representing this position is Alberto Perez-Gomez, whose Gadamerian, hermeneutical *Architecture and the Crisis of Modern Science* had appeared in 1983. For the phenomenological position as represented by Perez-Gomez, the entire intellectual project of structuralism, including semiotics and typology, had to be rejected as "preconstituted" and thereby as inauthentic knowledge. Occupying an intermediate position between Eisenman and Perez-Gomez was Daniel Libeskind, who rose to fame during the period of the loss of credibility of postmodernism, effectively combining the charisma of the neo-avant-gardist designer with the moral indignation of the phenomenological critic of inauthenticity. By the mid-1990s, the impact of the combination of neo-avant-gardist and phenomenological attacks on postmodernism—and by implication on semiotics and structuralism as well—was effective enough to largely destroy the intellectual legitimacy that architecture and urban design had inherited from those bodies of theory two decades previously.

As a result, during the decade of the 1990s, a bifurcation of orientations to architecture split the intelligentsia of the profession off from its mainstream practitioners more se-verely than at any time since the early part of the twentieth century. On the one side, the popular project of postmod-ernism, launched in the 1970s, in large part in the name of semiotics, continues to dominate commercial architectural practice and popular taste. On the other, architectural edu-cation in leading schools, following on from the avant-gardist, phenomenological attack, has completely rejected postmodernism, committing itself instead to an architecture of critique and to an at least hypothetical tectonic integrity, which defines itself precisely in opposition to current main-stream practices.

If it can be said at the present time that the project of semiotics in architecture is to have any chance of intellec-tual rediscovery, it may well be as follows. It has become ap-parent that the architecture of critique is now a largely ex-hausted trope and cannot any longer sustain substantial new design creativity—even in predominantly academic ar-chitectural circles. At the same time, the inability of the neo-avant-gardism promulgated by figures such as Peter Eisen-man and Libeskind to come compellingly to terms with the "social" and with the urban is evidently troubling to an in-creasing number of contemporary observers. The revision-ist theory of the 1960s and 1970s—now so long in disrepute as to have been forgotten—appears to be becoming a topic of increasing interest to a younger generation of architec-tural historians and theorists. Perhaps the combination of the inadequacies of the once-ascendant avant-gardist proj-ect, combined with the aura of historical rediscovery, will yet reinvigorate the historic project of semiotics and archi-tecture.

[*See also* Architecture; *and* Postmodernism.]

BIBLIOGRAPHY

Alexander, Christopher. *Notes on the Synthesis of Form.* Cambridge, Mass., 1964.

Barthes, Roland. *Mythologies.* Paris, 1957.

Barthes, Roland. *Elements of Semiology.* Translated by Annette Lavers and Colin Smith. London, 1967.

Broadbent, Geoffrey, Richard Bunt, and Charles Jencks, eds. *Signs, Symbols and Architecture.* Chichester and New York, 1980.

Eco, Umberto. *La struttura assente: Introduzione alla ricerca semiologica.* Milan, 1968.

Eco, Umberto. *A Theory of Semiotics.* Bloomington, Ind. 1976.

Frampton, Kenneth. "*Apropos Ulm.*" *Oppositions* (New York) 3 (1973): 17–36.

de Fusco, Renato. *Architettura come mass medium.* Bari, 1967.

Jencks, Charles A. *The Language of Post-Modern Architecture.* 6th ed. New York, 1991.

Jencks, Charles, and George Baird, eds. *Meaning in Architecture.* London, 1969.

Koenig, Giovanni Klaus. *Analisi del linguaggio architettonico.* Florence, 1964.

Lévi-Strauss, Claude. *Structural Anthropology.* Translated by Claire Ja-cobson and Brooke Grundfest Schoepf. New York, 1963.

Perez-Gomez, Alberto. *Architecture and the Crisis of Modern Science.* Cambridge, Mass., 1983.

Rossi, Aldo. *The Architecture of the City.* Translated by Diane Ghirardo and Joan Ockman, revised by Aldo Rossi and Peter Eisenman. Cam-bridge, Mass., 1982.

Rykwert, Joseph. *The Necessity of Artifice: Ideas in Architecture.* New York, 1982.

Venturi, Robert. *Complexity and Contradiction in Architecture.* 2d ed. New York, 1977.

Venturi, Robert, Denise Scott Brown, and Steven Izenour. *Learning from Las Vegas: The Forgotten Symbolism of Architectural Form.* Rev. ed. Cambridge, Mass., 1977.

GEORGE BAIRD

SEMPER, GOTTFRIED (1803–1879), German archi-tect and theorist. Born in Hamburg, Semper first studied mathematics at Göttingen University before attending briefly the Munich Academy of Fine Arts. He next traveled to Paris, where he learned architecture at a private school. From Paris he embarked on a three-year tour of Italy, Sicily, and Greece, during which time he developed an interest in classical polychromy. In 1834, Semper received a chair at the Dresden Academy of Fine Arts. In that city he built a major architectural practice with notable designs for the Hoftheater and Art Gallery. This promising career as a monumental builder was rudely halted by the political up-rising of 1849, in which Semper and Richard Wagner par-ticipated; their involvement led to their political exile. Sem-per lived first in Paris but then crossed the English Channel to London, where he eventually taught at Henry Cole's De-partment of Practical Art (later Victoria and Albert Mu-seum). In 1855, Semper moved to Zurich to head the archi-tecture department of the newly created federal Polytechnikum (now ETH). Eventually, he returned to practice; counted among his late works are the Winterthur town hall (1864–1870), the second Dresden Hoftheater (1869–1878), the Vienna Art History and Natural History Museums (1869–1891), and the Hofburg Theater (1871–1888).

The formative impulse to Semper's architectural and aes-thetic theories was his trip to Greece in 1833. He had left Paris in 1830 on the heels of Jacques-Ignaz Hittorff's ad-dress to the Académie des Beaux-Arts, at which the noted architect displayed his brilliantly colored reconstruction of a Sicilian monument. In Athens, Semper recorded patches of paint on the Hephaesteum and Parthenon on both the inte-rior and exterior walls. In the preliminary publication of his findings in 1834, he responded to the inadequacy of Johann Joachim Winckelmann's "white" vision of the past and in-sisted that color was not only essential to Greek plastic works but also held the key to their conception of art. Tem-ples were painted for artistic and environmental reasons (the sunny climate, the variegated landscape) as well as for symbolic ones. The hanging of flowers, branches, imple-ments, shields, and other emblems on early temples initi-ated a process whereby these motifs were later incorporated into monuments plastically. What gave these elements a higher artistic calling, however, was the addition of paint, gilding, draperies, baldachins, spectators, priests, choruses, and processions—all of which elevated the temple to the center point of elaborate communal rituals. These dramatic *Gesamtkunstwerken,* as it were, functioned more theatrically than religiously in their sentiments; their development paralleled the perfection of the classical Greek stage.

Semper's busy Dresden practice prevented the completion of his planned folio on polychromy, but his beliefs remained firm and were enriched in the 1840s by new archaeological and ethnological findings. Another force affecting his intellectual development was the arrival in Dresden in 1842 of the young Richard Wagner. The latter's first operas were performed in the theater that Semper had designed and the two men became close friends. Their spirited artistic debates, during which Wagner also came to form his view of a classical synthesis of the arts, became a focal point of Dresden's lively artistic culture.

The Dresden uprising of May 1849 ended this happy period and Semper suffered greatly as a result of his exile. With his career in ruins, he turned his attention to writing. His plans for a major work of theory faltered, but in 1851 he published a short work titled *The Four Elements of Architecture.* The first few chapters were a defense of his earlier views on polychromy; in the second half of the study, however, he developed the theme of architecture's conceptual origins.

Drawing on Gustav Klemm's cultural history and the Assyrian findings of Sir Austin Henry Layard and Paul Émile Botta, Semper proposed that architectural forms were generated by four primal motives or ideas: walling, roofing, mounding, and hearth gathering. The last was the social motive for civilization; tribes gathered around the fire after the chase. The other three motives appeared to protect the hearth against inclement weather: the mound raised the fire off the damp earth; the roof shielded it overhead; the wall protected it from wind. Each motive developed formally in different ways in different cultures. Each motive also spawned its own art industries. The hearth gave rise to the ceramic and metal arts. From the roof came the idea of carpentry or the concept of a fixed framework. The notion of mounding was developed in earthworks and waterworks, later evolving into terracing and masonry.

The fourth element, the vertical enclosure or wall, was the most significant in Semper's theory. He was struck by ethnological descriptions of aboriginal abodes in which crude mats were hung vertically from timber frames, the mats serving as walls. These hangings, Semper reasoned, gave rise to the art of textiles, but just as importantly to the spatial motive of architecture: the separation of an inner world distinct from the outer. Later, as more durable walls were erected, textile fabrics continued to be hung inside solid walls as symbolic reminders of their primordial past.

Still later, these dressings give rise to other types of sheathing or paneling, whose decorative motifs and stylistic details often alluded to their textile forerunners. This was a stage exemplified for Semper by the Assyrian bas-reliefs in alabaster. The Greeks inherited this "dressing principle" *(Bekleidungprinzip)* from the East, which they exploited in their polychrome temples.

In 1851, Semper became involved in laying out some of the national exhibits for the Great London Exhibition. The commissions in themselves were insignificant, but they allowed him access to the one million square feet of wares on display. He was able to examine artifacts from the so-called primitive nations as well as the latest implements of industrialized technology. At the close of the event, he wrote a lengthy review of its significance, *Wissenschaft, Industrie, und Kunst* (Science, Industry, and Art).

This book, presaging ideas of Walter Benjamin, is a masterful analysis of industrialization and its effect on traditional conceptions of art. If the art of the past was based on handicraft methods of fabrication, new industrial forces and the division of labor were quickly rendering this approach obsolete. Machines now sew, knit, embroider, paint, carve, encroach deeply on the field of human art, and put to shame every human skill. This devaluation of labor results in a devaluation of meaning, as art made in the traditional way comes to be seen as eccentric. This abundance of means, moreover, is aided by the speculative forces of capitalism, which has insinuated itself into the marketplace with its values of fashion and consumption. If artistic forms produced for the masses worked well with some items such as carriages or musical instruments, this process was having a stultifying effect on the traditional arts. High art, in particular, was being mortally hit.

After Semper moved to Zurich in 1855, he began in earnest his major work of theory: *Style in the Technical and Tectonic Arts, or Practical Aesthetics.* It appeared in two lengthy volumes between 1860 and 1863. A planned third volume devoted to architecture was never started.

Semper's masterwork carried forward many of his earlier ideas, but it also expanded greatly the scope and depth of interests. In essence, he conceived the book as a general theory of artistic forms—a study of the ornamental and formal development of motifs from their origin in the four industrial motives of textiles, ceramics, tectonics, and stereotomy. Semper now placed more emphasis on the symbolic values of forms and their evolution, for instance, how a simple wreath might signify the notion of eurythmic binding or how an ornamental pattern might derive from the art of tattooing. In parts of his study, he undertook psychological analyses of the formal significance of certain artistic paradigms, such as his cultural interpretation Egyptian *situla* and Greek *hydria.* In other parts, he showed how a basket weave in textiles or the specific curvature of a ceramic vase might be transposed to a column capital or entablature molding. Even linguistic analysis played a prominent role in his method. The German word for "hem" or "border" *(Saum),* for instance, shares a linguistic similarity with the German word for "hedge" *(Zaum).* Both also have the additional meanings of "fillet" and "fence." Again, the word for "clothing" *(Gewand)* is related to the word for "partition wall" *(Wand).*

The heart of his aesthetic theory, however, lay in those passages dealing with the "masking of reality" in the arts. Drawing on Romantic themes going back to Friedrich von Schiller, Semper cited the improvised and brilliantly endowed festival stage of antiquity as the motive for the permanent monument—an event that makes its Dionysian entry in Attic times. Now the polychrome "dressing" that was inherited from the East becomes a dissimulating fabric, a conscious masking of the material reality and thematic content of artistic forms. If Greek drama with its chorus and masked actors sought to represent life's tragic and comic underpinnings, he argued, so monumental Greek art strove to become a symbolic masking of life's ennobling cultural forms. He identifies the "haze of carnival candles" as the "true atmosphere" for all high art—from the "stone dramas" of Phidias to the "carnival sentiment" of William Shakespeare.

Semper joined with Wagner in Munich in the 1860s to put these ideas into practice in the design of a colossal opera house, a building intended to stage the nearly completed *Ring* cycle. The glorious design, the forerunner to the less-ambitious theater at Bayreuth, was never realized—in part a result of Ludwig II's tenuous grasp of reality, in part of Wagner's scandalous behavior. But it was significant in other respects.

Friedrich Nietzsche began reading Semper in the summer of 1869 and took notes of those passages dealing with the Greek stage and its connection with monumental architecture. The following winter, Nietzsche delivered two lectures that dealt with Greek drama. Their leading theme was that the known works of Aeschylus and Sophocles are only stripped-down librettos of far more complex choral works. If modern man were somehow transposed back into Attic times, he would find these more satiric performances both foreign and barbaric in their emotional display. Nietzsche expanded this theme in his first book, *The Birth of Tragedy* (1872), in which he argued that Greek tragedy was born out of the union of Apollonian and Dionysian elements—a union in which, however, the Dionysian tendency dominated. This union effectively ended at the height of classical Greek culture when the rational tendencies of Euripides and Socrates purged the Dionysian component.

This theme gains additional relevance because, during these same months, Semper was preparing the iconographic scheme for his second Hoftheater in Dresden, in which he too paid homage to the "return of Dionysus" at the expense of more traditional Apollonian motifs. He saw

his theater in emotional terms as a frenzied realm of a Dionysian dithyramb, as a dramatic *Gesamtkunstwerk* in which reality should be masked.

By the time of his death in 1879 Semper dominated the German architectural world and his ideas continued to assert themselves across Europe and North America for the next two decades. But his thought was equally influential in such areas as archaeology, anthropology, art history, and aesthetics.

Semper's impact on aesthetics was long-standing. In Zurich he was close to Friedrich Theodor Vischer, and the latter's "Kritik meiner Aesthetik" (Critique of My Aesthetics, 1866) almost certainly owes much to Semper's criticisms of Hegelian notions. Conrad Fiedler's essay "Observations on the Nature and History of Architecture" (1878) was written as a commentary to Semper's book on style, and in it Fiedler lauded the idealism of Semper for its many revelations. Heinrich Wölfflin's dissertation, "Prolegomena to a Psychology of Architecture" (1886), also owes a large debt to Semper's thought. August Schmarsow's inaugural address at the University of Leipzig, "The Essence of Architectural Creation" (1893), is entirely Semperian in its conception. One can measure Semper's importance at this time by Wilhelm Dilthey's contemporaneous characterization of him as the "real successor to Goethe."

Perhaps the most devout Semperian was the Viennese art historian Alois Riegl. As curator of textiles at the Austrian Museum for Art and Industry in the late 1880s, Riegl was intellectually raised on Semper's body of thought. In his early writings, he followed Semper's lead closely and his book *Stilfragen* (Questions of Style, 1893) is driven by his spirited defense of Semper's idealism against the materialist excesses of latter-day Semperians. Ironically, it was Riegl's subsequent and inexplicable reversal of this argument in 1901 that confused critics and art historians for more than three-quarters of a century.

[*See also* Architecture; *and* Riegl.]

BIBLIOGRAPHY

Works by Semper

Gottfried Semper: Ein Bild seines Lebens und Wirkens. Berlin, 1880.
The Four Elements of Architecture and Other Writings. Translated by Harry Francis Mallgrave and Wolfgang Herrmann. Cambridge and New York, 1989.

Other Sources

Bayer, Josef. "Gottfried Semper." *Zeitschrift für Bildende Kunst,* vol. 14. Leipzig, 1879. Also in *Baustudien und Baubilder: Schriften zur Kunst,* edited by Robert Stiassny (Jena, 1919).
Berry, J. Duncan. "The Legacy of Gottfried Semper: Studies in Späthistorismus." Ph.D. diss., Brown University, 1991.
Bletter, Rosmarie Haag. "Gottfried Semper." In *Macmillan Encyclopedia of Architects,* edited by Adolf K. Placzek, vol. 4 pp. 25–33. London, 1982.
Ettlinger, Leopold. *Gottfried Semper und die Antike: Beiträge zur Kunstanschauung des deutschen Klassizismus.* Halle, Germany, 1937.

Fröhlich, Martin. *Gottfried Semper: Zeichnerischer Nachlass an der ETH Zürich.* Basel, 1974.

Herrmann, Wolfgang. *Gottfried Semper: Theoretischer Nachlass an der ETH Zürich: Katalog und Kommentare.* Basel, 1981.

Herrmann, Wolfgang. *Gottfried Semper: In Search of Architecture.* Cambridge, Mass., 1984.

Laudel, Heidrun. *Gottfried Semper: Architektur und Stil.* Dresden, 1991.

Lipsius, Constantin. *Gottfried Semper in seiner Bedeutung als Architekt.* Berlin, 1880.

Magirius, Heinrich. *Gottfried Sempers zweites dresdner Hoftheater: Entstehung, künstlerische Ausstattung, Ikonographie.* Vienna, 1985.

Magirius, Heinrich. "Die Gemäldegalerie in Dresden: Ein Bau von Gottfried Semper." In *Gemäldegalerie Dresden.* Leipzig, 1992.

Mallgrave, Harry Francis. *Gottfried Semper: Architect of the Nineteenth Century.* New Haven, 1996.

Quitzsch, Heinz. *Die ästhetischen Anschauungen Gottfried Sempers.* Berlin, 1962.

Staatliche Kunstsammlungen Dresden. *Gottfried Semper, 1803–1879: Baumeister zwischen Revolution und Historismus.* Dresden, 1979; 2d ed., Munich, 1980.

Stockmeyer, Ernst. *Gottfried Sempers Kunsttheorie.* Zurich, 1939.

Technische Universität Dresden. *Gottfried Semper, 1803–1879: Sein Wirken als Architekt, Theoretiker und revolutionärer Demokrat und die schöpferische Aneignung seines progressiven Erbes.* Dresden, 1979.

HARRY F. MALLGRAVE

SENSIBILITÉ. Of all the major concepts of the French Enlightenment, none is quite so difficult to pinpoint as *sensibilité*. Etymologically, this term belonged to the same family of words as *sens, sensation, sentiment, sentimental,* and *sensiblerie*. Also associated with the term's moral and social vocabulary were notions such as sympathy, virtue, pity, benevolence, and various expressions for tender feeling and compassion. Yet, *sensibilité* was also central to physiological terminology beginning in the 1740s, when it edged out *irritabilité* as the word most commonly used to describe the innate capacity to react to stimuli that was held to underlie all the phenomena of life in the human body. The concept of *sensibilité* was thus invested with enormous connotative power in mid- to late eighteenth-century France, and figured prominently in fields as diverse as the philosophy of the mind, ethics and social theory, biomedical science, aesthetics, and literature—all of which belonged to the loose confederation of naturalistic discourses then known as the "sciences of man."

In fact, the various meanings attached to sensibility at this time tended to be mutually permeable, because the philosophes used the word as a bridging concept, a means of establishing causal connections between the physical and moral realms. From sensationalist philosophers of the intellect such as Étienne Bonnot de Condillac, Charles Bonnet, and Georges-Louis Leclerc de Buffon, to aestheticians such as Abbé Jean-Baptiste Dubos and Denis Diderot, to moralists such as Charles Duclos and Jean-Jacques Rousseau, to the vitalist theorists of the Montpellier medical school, French Enlightenment thinkers subscribed to the idea that sensibility was the essential link between the human body and the psychological, intellectual, and ethical faculties of humankind. Sensibility was thus fundamental to this period's understanding of human nature: it was seen as the root of all human perceptions and reflections (G. S. Rousseau, 1976; Figlio, 1975); as the innate and active principle of sociability that gave rise to human society (Baasner, 1986); as a kind of sixth sense whose special affective energy was essential both to virtue and to art (Spink, 1977); and finally, as the paradigmatic vital force, whose actions could be detected in every bodily function, be it healthful or morbid (Williams, 1994). Sensibility was consequently far more than a fashionable cult of high-minded feeling or histrionic emotionalism, as some literary critics and historians have characterized it (Wilson, 1931). It was also the object of a unique culture: a "constellation of ideas, feelings, and events" that developed around the concept of sensibility throughout eighteenth-century Europe, albeit with often striking national differences (Barker-Benfield, 1992).

Three major traits distinguished the eighteenth-century French culture of sensibility from the ideas that surrounded the term elsewhere in Europe. First, sensibility and sentimentalism were closely associated in France with the process of secularization that the philosophes were intent on advancing (Denby, 1994). Second, French writers did not polarize sensibility in relation to sex and gender nearly as much as did their British counterparts (Barker-Benfield, 1992; Jones, 1993), at least not until the last few decades of the century; rather, even the most hard-boiled philosophes prided themselves on their sensibility, and saw nothing unmanly about cultivating this quality (Ridgeway, 1973). Third, sensibility was often imbued by French writers with a pronounced physicalist or materialist undertone, without provoking any major outcry from the defenders of morality and religion. One factor underlying the greater French tolerance for such approaches to sensibility was the unusual appeal that medicine held for this nation's intellectual and social elite (Coleman, 1974). To see just how physicalized the concept of sensibility became during the French Enlightenment, one need only consult the *Encyclopédie,* whose fifteenth volume contained two entries on the property: first, a lengthy medical article that affirmed sensibility's primacy in human physiology and pathology and described how it varied according to age, sex, temperament, the passions, and external factors such as climate; and second, a one-paragraph article on sensibility's extraordinary capacity to inspire virtue, to reinforce the intellectual faculties, and to persuade by appealing to the heart. The juxtaposition of these two articles is revealing, because it shows both the proximity of sensibility's physical and moral meanings and the prestige that was accorded to the physicians who rallied to the cause of sensibility during the second half of the century.

Chief among the theoretical inventions of eighteenth-century France was this working assumption: before one could assess an individual's moral disposition, one first had to determine how he or she reacted and interacted with the world as an organically sensitive being. Inspired by this assumption, a particular group of medical theorists set out at mid-century to develop a comprehensive and authoritative explanation of sensibility. These vitalistic-leaning theorists, based in Montpellier, called themselves *médecins philosophes;* their leader was Théophile de Bordeu, who was later cast in a somewhat caricatural form as an interlocutor in the *Rêve de d'Alembert,* Diderot's fictional dialogue on the origins of life. Bordeu and his followers seized on the landmark experimental studies of sensibility and irritability that the Swiss physiologist Albrecht von Haller had recently published and used them to refute the iatromechanistic doctrines that had dominated seventeenth- and early eighteenth-century European medicine (Moravia, 1978). Like Haller and contemporary English physicians such as Robert Whytt, the French medical vitalists believed that sensibility was conveyed via a system of natural, interorganic "sympathetic" coordination; they did not, however, perceive that system as limited exclusively to the nervous apparatus. Rather, using a metaphor that would soon reappear in other discursive contexts (such as Diderot's writings), they compared the sensible body to a beehive—a federation of semiautonomous parts, each of which followed rhythms determined by its particular dose of local sensibility. What held this "beehive" together, as Bordeu described it, was not the soul but rather a triumvirate of major vital centers (the brain, chest, and lower abdomen) whose influence over the local parts maintained the harmony of the general animal economy. The *médecins philosophes* then extrapolated this model of the animal economy onto the social economy, and concluded that it, too, was driven by sensibility and thus subject to medical intervention. In short, they saw the principle of sensibility as the key to forging not only new ways of diagnosing and treating the human body, but also a new, global understanding of the human race.

The *médecins philosophes* thus sought to catapult their field to the forefront of the Enlightenment movement by making physical sensibility the primary factor in the crusade to illuminate and improve humanity. They were, however, hardly alone in their efforts to use the notion of vital sensibility as a means of explaining the nonphysical phenomena of human life. A similar idea also resounded through the literature of the period—most particularly, the novel of sensibility. To be sure, sensibility was also central to eighteenth-century theater, especially to the hybrid dramatic genre known as the *drame bourgeois.* Yet, the literary genre in which sensibility's expanded meanings were most provocatively deployed was, without question, the novel. Prior to 1750, sensibility in the French novel was largely a worldly affair: upper-class sociability, as represented in fiction, was a mode of social intercourse that revolved around the acts of manifesting and deciphering such phenomena as

"delicacy" and "tender emotion" in oneself and in others (Marivaux, 1731–1741). After 1750, by contrast, the novel of sensibility became a fertile testing ground for exploring the medico-philosophical idea that all manifestations of sensibility were ultimately rooted in its organic foundations. Diderot, for example, created fictional works that both echoed and exploited Bordeu's conception of the body as a dynamically resonating sensible network. Rousseau, in turn, used his novel *La nouvelle Héloïse* to carry out the hygienically based *morale sensitive* that he, along with the Swiss physician Samuel-Auguste-André-David Tissot, envisioned as a means of containing sensibility within wholesome, moderate bounds. Later in the century, Choderlos de Laclos and Donatien-Alphonse-François de Sade produced libertine novels that ironically mimicked both the conventions of literary sentimentalism and the sexually bimorphic model of sensible constitution that emerged in the 1770s.

With its heavy emphasis on visualizing the invisible interior of the body—most particularly that of woman—the physiophilosophy of sensibility was not without a certain aesthetic dimension in its own right (Jordanova, 1989; Stafford, 1991). Equally intriguing, however, were the theories of fiction put forth in order to account for the ambiguous effects of sensibility, sentiment, and sympathy on aesthetic response (Marshall, 1988). Diderot, for example, argued vehemently in favor of creating literary works that would engage the reader-spectator intensely and involuntarily in touching scenes from the drama of everyday experience. His reflections on the aesthetic and ethical dimensions of fiction making are contained in a series of texts composed during the 1750s and 1760s: the *Entretiens sur le fils naturel* and *De la poésie dramatique,* where he set forth the principles underlying the new genre of *drame* with which he wanted to reform and update French theater; the *Éloge de Richardson,* where he described the epiphanic experience of reading Samuel Richardson's intimately absorbing novels; and *La religieuse,* where he explored the connections between the sympathy to which the novel of sensibility explicitly appealed and its implicit capacity to seduce its readers. As in his art criticism, Diderot called for the development of "detheatricalized modes of beholding" in theater and in the novel (Fried, 1988): he urged playwrights and novelists to forgo the contrived coups de théâtre typical of traditional French comedy, tragedy, and novels, and instead to present moving visual tableaux of sympathetic characters caught up in a moral crisis or a moment of strong emotion. Only then, Diderot maintained, would fiction truly stir the sensibility of its audience and give it the profound vision of moral and physical nature that great art should provide. To appreciate the austere pleasures of serious fiction, one had, in Diderot's view, to possess a pure and refined taste, a tender and honest soul, a good deal of experience in life, a noble mind, a slightly melancholic temperament, and "delicate organs" (Diderot, 1757). One had, in other words, to be a philosophe as he defined the figure: Diderot's ideal beholder was a venerable, paternal bourgeois who, by being moved to tears before a dramatic tableau, would not only demonstrate his own sensitivity to the moral turmoil being represented, but also prompt his fellow reader-spectators to respond in kind (Caplan, 1985).

Although their literary works often revolved around the spectacle of a virtuous heroine in distress, Diderot and the numerous writers he inspired (these included Pierre-Augustin Caron de Beaumarchais, Louis-Sébastien Mercier, and the Marquis de Sade) promoted an aesthetic of sensibility that was not so much "feminized" or even sentimental as philosophical: by infusing their fictions with maximum intensity of dramatic effect, they hoped to put their audiences into direct, visceral contact with the great but often terrible energies of nature and the passions. One finds a similar effort to promote a more serious and emotional kind of fiction in the writings of Rousseau, but with an important difference: Rousseau was so deeply suspicious of the seductive powers of conventional French novels and theater that he deemed both to be beyond redemption. He thus took a dim view of contemporary efforts to transform these literary genres into forums for activating sensibility in the name of moral edification and sympathetic sociability, because he maintained that those virtues could only flourish beyond the boundaries of the existing social world. At the same time, Rousseau's phenomenally successful *La nouvelle Héloïse* was instrumental in popularizing the sentimentalist conception of fiction as an intensely affecting and potentially life-changing experience (Brooks, 1969).

In his emphasis on the problematic relationship between sensibility and society, Rousseau was closer to the other theorists of sensibility than he might have admitted. Although sensibility was largely seen as a gloriously harmonious and life-expanding force when held in the proper degree, it also seemed to lead people into physical disorder and moral decay when misdirected. Many medical theorists of the day perceived excessive sensibility to be a rising problem in the contemporary population, most particularly among their wealthy, idle, urban patients; hence, the peculiar mid-eighteenth-century fear that an epidemic of nervous maladies or "vapors" was overtaking France's cities—the very places where sympathy seemed most important, because of the complexity of the social interactions that took place there. The specter of vapors thus introduced an unsettling note into the theory of sensibility, a property that had once seemed to be the unequivocally positive mark of an ungendered moral elite, but was now increasingly associated with the debilitated, effeminate members of the leisure class (Foucault, 1961).

One response to this dilemma was semantic: new terms such as *sensiblerie* were coined during the 1770s and 1780s to differentiate positive from negative kinds of sensibility (Trahard, 1931–1933; Brissenden, 1974). Yet, there were also some interesting theoretical responses, as, for example, in Pierre Roussel's *Système physique et moral de la femme* (1775). Roussel's method of differentiating between types of sensibility was overtly anthropological: he divided the attributes of sensibility into complementary but incommensurate sets—feminine versus masculine, yielding versus resistant, womb-based versus cerebral. In other words, Roussel masculinized the noblest qualities of sensibility while feminizing those that he deemed primitive or less evolved, thus transforming the contemporary view of human nature into two perspectives: a progressive, meliorist perspective on man's nature, and a biologically deterministic perspective on woman's nature (Vila, 1995).

Roussel's bimorphic model of sensibility not only took so-called philosophical medicine in a new and troubling direction, but also demonstrated a growing tendency, both in medicine and beyond, to split sensibility into modes of expression that were often radically different. This conceptual movement, which became increasingly pronounced during the aftermath of the Enlightenment movement (the 1790s to 1830s), ran directly counter to the philosophes' efforts to devise a unified vision of humankind in which everything human could be seen as linked together in a seamless natural continuum. Sensibility and the jointly sentimentalist and vitalist ideas related to it remained popular even at the violent heights of the French Revolution (Trahard, 1936), and continued to be endowed with great explicative power in the biomedical sciences, philosophy, aesthetics, and literature. Yet, as nineteenth-century thinkers refined the meaning of sensibility for their particular fields, the old "enlightened" consensus over the property's integrated physico-moral-intellectual nature not only weakened, but was, in some cases, rejected outright.

In early nineteenth-century physiology, Xavier Bichat developed a new, more empirically grounded system for conceptualizing vitality in which sensibility was subdivided into two distinct modes: the inferior, involuntary mode characteristic of the organic or passional life, versus the highly developed, voluntary kind associated with the animal or intellectual life. Thanks in part to the greater precision that Bichat brought to vitalism, the monistic vision of sensibility persisted in medical theory well into the 1830s (Cabanis, 1802; Broussais, 1828). This concept of sensibility, however, encountered stiff opposition from rival biomedical theories of a dualist and politically conservative bent, which emerged after 1800 (Williams, 1994). A similar spiritualist, antimaterialist reinterpretation of sensibility was undertaken by philosophers such as Marie François Pierre Maine de Biran, who demoted it to an essentially passive role in the operations of cognitive perception and moral consciousness. And in literature, the antirevolutionary and generally antiphilosophe authors who launched the fledgling Romantic movement took pains to redefine the notions of sensibility and artistic genius in terms that were more restrictive, moralizing, and private, such that sensibility became endowed with religious and antisocial overtones that it had not had in the previous century outside of Rousseau's writings (Baasner, 1988).

The old unitary conception of sensibility thus fell victim after the end of the ancien régime to social upheaval, politics, new theoretical developments, and a pervasive urge to resacralize many of the aspects of human experience that had been desacralized during the Enlightenment: consciousness, personality, ethical imperatives, and the living process itself. *Sensibilité* did not disappear in the nineteenth century, but it did take a distinctly different form, most particularly in literature, philosophy, and aesthetics, where it became associated not with the rational and sociable qualities of humankind, but rather with imagination, mysticism, and the idiosyncracies of artistic temperament; hence, the emergence of a new dichotomy between sensibility and reason—a dichotomy that has since been misapplied to eighteenth-century France. That dichotomy does not, however, suffice to explain sensibility's complexity during the French Enlightenment, the era when *sensibilité* truly flourished and enjoyed a conceptual dynamism and breadth of meaning that have since been lost.

[*See also* French Aesthetics, *article on* Eighteenth-Century French Aesthetics; Science and Aesthetics; *and* Taste.]

BIBLIOGRAPHY

Primary Sources

Beaumarchais, Pierre-Augustin Caron de. "Essai sur le genre dramatique sérieux" (1757). In *Œuvres,* edited by Pierre Larthomas. Paris, 1988.
Bichat, Xavier. *Recherches physiologiques sur la vie et la mort* (1800). Paris, 1955.
Bonnet, Charles. *Essai analytique sur les facultés de l'âme* (1759). Reprint, Geneva, 1970.
Bordeu, Théophile de. *Recherches anatomiques sur la position des glandes, et sur leur action* (1752). In *Œuvres complètes,* vol. 2. Paris, 1818.
Broussais, François-Joseph-Victor. *De l'irritation et de la folie, ouvrage dans lequel les rapports du physique et du moral sont établis sur les bases de la médecine physiologique* (1828). Paris, 1986.
Cabanis, Pierre-Jean-Georges. *Rapports du physique et du moral de l'homme* (1802). Reprint, Geneva, 1980.
Diderot, Denis. *Entretiens sur le fils naturel* (1757). In *Le paradoxe sur le comédien, précédé des Entretiens sur le fils naturel.* Paris, 1981.
Diderot, Denis. *Discours sur la poésie dramatique* (1758). In *Œuvres complètes,* vol. 10. Paris, 1975.
Diderot, Denis. *La religieuse* (1760/1780–1782). Translated by Francis Birrell as *Memoirs of a Nun.* London, 1959.
Diderot, Denis. *Éloge de Richardson* (1761). Translated by Beatrix L. Tollemache as "An Eulogy of Richardson." In *Diderot's Thoughts on Art and Style.* London, 1896.
Diderot, Denis. *Le rêve de d'Alembert* (1769). In *Œuvres complètes,* vol. 17. Paris, 1975.
Fouquet, Henri. "Sensibilité, Sentiment (Médecine)" (1765). In *Encyclopédie, ou Dictionnaire raisonné des sciences, des arts et des métiers,* vol. XV. Reprint, New York, 1969.
Haller, Albrecht von. *Dissertation on the Sensible and Irritable Parts of Animals* (1755). Reprint, Baltimore, 1936.

Jaucourt, Louis de. "Sensibilité" (1765). In *Encyclopédie, ou Dictionnaire raisonné des sciences, des arts et des métiers,* vol. 3. 15. Reprint, New York, 1969.
Laclos, Choderlos de. *Les liaisons dangereuses* (1782). Translated and edited by Douglas Parmée. Oxford and New York, 1995.
Maine de Biran, Marie François Pierre. *Mémoire sur la décomposition de la pensée* (1805). In *Œuvres,* edited by François Azouvi, vol. 3. Paris, 1984.
Marivaux, Pierre Carlet de Chamblain de. *La vie de Marianne* (1731–1741). Translated Mary Mitchell Collyer as *The Virtuous Orphan.* Edited by William Harlin McBurney and Michael Francis Shugrve. Carbondale, Ill., 1965.
Mercier, Louis-Sébastien. *Du théâtre, ou Nouvel essai sur l'art dramatique* (1773). Reprint, Geneva, 1970.
Rousseau, Jean-Jacques. *Lettre à d'Alembert sur les spectacles* (1758). Paris, 1987.
Rousseau, Jean-Jacques. *La Nouvelle Héloïse* (1758). Translated by Judith H. McDowell as *Julie, or The New Eloise.* University Park, Pa., 1968.
Roussel, Pierre. *Système physique et moral de la femme, ou tableau philosophique de la constitution, de l'état organique, du tempérament, des mœurs et des fonctions propres au sexe* (1775). 7th ed. Paris, 1820.
Sade, Donatien-Alphonse-François de. *Justine, ou Les malheurs de la vertu* (1791). Translated and edited by Richard Seaver and Austryn Wainhouse as "Justine, or Good Conduct Well Chastised." In *The Complete Justine, Philosophy in the Bedroom, and Other Writings.* New York, 1965.
Sade, Donatien-Alphonse-François de. "Idée sur les romans" (1800). Translated by Austryn Wainhouse and Richard Seaver as "Reflections on the Novel." In *The 120 Days of Sodom and Other Writings.* New York, 1966.
Tissot, Samuel-André-Auguste-David. *Essai sur les maladies des gens du monde* (1770). In *Œuvres de M. Tissot,* vol. 4. Lausanne, 1788.

Other Sources

Baasner, Frank. "The Changing Meaning of 'Sensibilité': 1654 till 1704." *Studies in Eighteenth-Century Culture* 15 (1986): 77–96.
Baasner, Frank. *Der Begriff "sensibilité" im 18. Jahrhundert. Aufstieg und Niedergang eines Ideals.* Heidelberg, 1988.
Barker-Benfield, G. J. *The Culture of Sensibility: Sex and Society in Eighteenth-Century Britain.* Chicago, 1992.
Brissenden, R. F. *Virtue in Distress: Studies in the Novel of Sentiment from Richardson to Sade.* London, 1974.
Brooks, Peter. *The Novel of Worldliness.* Princeton, N.J., 1969.
Caplan, Jay. *Framed Narratives: Diderot's Genealogy of the Beholder.* Minneapolis, 1985.
Coleman, William. "Health and Hygiene in the Encyclopédie: A Medical Doctrine for the Bourgeoisie." *Journal of the History of Medicine* 29 (1974): 399–421.
Denby, David J. *Sentimental Narrative and the Social Order in France, 1760–1820.* Cambridge and New York, 1994.
Figlio, Karl M. "Theories of Perception and the Physiology of Mind in the Late Eighteenth Century." *History of Science* 12 (1975): 177–212.
Foucault, Michel. *Histoire de la folie à l'âge classique.* Paris, 1961. Translated by Richard Howard as *Madness and Civilization: A History of Insanity in the Age of Reason* (New York, 1965).
Fried, Michael. *Absorption and Theatricality: Painting and Beholder in the Age of Diderot.* Reprint, Chicago, 1988.
Jones, Chris. *Radical Sensibility: Literature and Ideas in the 1790s.* London and New York, 1993.
Jordanova, Ludmilla. "Natural Facts: An Historical Perspective on Science and Sexuality." In *Sexual Visions: Images of Gender in Science and Medicine between the Eighteenth and Twentieth Centuries.* Madison, Wis., 1989.

Marshall, David. *The Surprising Effects of Sympathy.* Chicago, 1988.

Moravia, Sergio. "From *homme machine* to *homme sensible:* Changing Eighteenth-Century Models of Man's Image." *Journal of the History of Ideas* 39.1 (1978): 45–60.

Ridgeway, R. S. *Voltaire and Sensibility.* Montreal, 1973.

Rousseau, G. S. "Nerves, Spirits, and Fibres: Towards Defining the Origins of Sensibility." In *Studies in the Eighteenth Century,* vol. 3, edited by R. F. Brissenden and J. Eade. Toronto, 1976.

Spink, John S. "'Sentiment', 'sensible', 'sensibilité': Les mots, les idées, d'après les 'moralistes' français et britanniques du début du dix-huitième siècle." *Zagadnienia Rodzajów Literackich* 20 (1977): 33–47.

Stafford, Barbara Maria. *Body Criticism: Imaging the Unseen in Enlightenment Art and Medicine.* Cambridge, Mass., 1991.

Trahard, Pierre. *Les maîtres de la sensibilité française au XVIIIe siècle, 1715–1789.* 4 vols. Paris, 1931–1933.

Trahard, Pierre. *La sensibilité révolutionnaire, 1789–1794.* Paris, 1936.

Vila, Anne C. "Sex and Sensibility: Pierre Roussel's *Système physique et moral de la femme.*" *Representations* 51 (1995): 54–71.

Vila, Anne C. *Between Enlightenment and Pathology: Sensibility in the Literature and Medicine of Eighteenth-Century France.* Baltimore, 1997.

Williams, Elizabeth A. *The Physical and the Moral: Anthropology, Physiology, and Philosophical Medicine in France, 1750–1850.* Cambridge and New York, 1994.

Wilson, Arthur M., Jr. "Sensibility in France in the Eighteenth Century: A Study in Word History." *French Quarterly* 13 (1931): 35–46.

ANNE VILA

SEXUALITY. In present-day theoretical and critical usage in philosophy and the humanities, the term *sexuality* refers to an individual's historically determined and psychologically meaningful selection of erotic objects—not necessarily limited to partners of the opposite sex in genital intercourse—with the aim of satisfying sexual desire, understood to be an irreducible drive for pleasure in erotic activity. It is possible to classify social groups in terms of such selections, often described as an "orientation" or a "preference" when they seem endogenous and persistent; hence, different sociologically real sexualities can be defined. In the early part of the nineteenth century, however, "sexuality" referred to the teleological organization of human generation. In common usage as well as in modern biology, it generally denotes the possession and exercise of the reproductive functions as such. In aesthetics, sexuality can be broadly defined as the eroticism—even the pleasurableness—of art in its personal and intersubjective origins and significance. But it would also be possible to conceive it as the reproductive rationale of art (if any), for example, in its evolutionary emergence as a mode of human adaptation.

Eighteenth- and early nineteenth-century thinkers recognized different modes of personal eroticism and different institutions of sex and sexual feeling in society (for example, the "pederasty" of the ancient Greeks). But a systematic theory of erotic variability, including a typology of sexual "perversion," did not emerge until the second half of the nineteenth century. Psychiatric nosology, clinical observations of "contrary sexual feeling," suggestion therapy, and

sexual and criminal anthropology were coordinated in the many editions of Richard von Krafft-Ebing's *Psychopathia sexualis* (1st ed., 1886; 9th ed., 1894), a major reference until well into the twentieth century. Krafft-Ebing's work reflected its wider juridical-legal and social context. It investigated the relations between—and the balance of—the reflexive (or "irresponsible") and the volitional or ("ethical") dimensions of human sexual behavior and erotic feeling, an interest also expressed in the prepsychoanalytic work of Sigmund Freud (for example, in an 1888 essay, "The Brain"). *Psychopathia sexualis* was still implicitly taken up with the definition, punishment, or absolution of sodomy—nonprocreative and/or adulterous practices—as it had been treated in established canon law. It was also strongly influenced by contemporary and earlier antimasturbation movements (represented, for instance, in Heinrich Kaan's *Psychopathia sexualis* of 1844, an exclusively antionanism tract).

The modern theory of "sexuality" attempted to detach Krafft-Ebing's and similar "clinical forensics" of *psychopathia sexualis* from their traditional moralizing foundations and confusing typologies based on superficial patterns of behavior. Several thinkers sought to develop an empirically grounded or at least conceptually coherent concept of the sexual reflex in its long-term organization, beginning with its earliest observable manifestations in the human organism well before puberty. Ultimately, some "perversions" recognized by Krafft-Ebing, such as kleptomania, became less interesting to the newer approach, which saw them as offshoots of more fundamental structures; by the same token, the new approach recognized structures not distinguished in the earlier clinical forensics. The most influential version of the updated approach was the psychoanalytic sexology of Freud, stated in his *Three Essays on the Theory of Sexuality* (1st ed., 1905; 3d ed., 1915). Other thinkers, such as Magnus Hirschfeld, believed that sexual variation resulted from embryonic differentiation or mutation. These theories often appealed to reformers concerned to assert the criminal irresponsibility of alleged sexual perverts. But they lacked convincing empirical foundation until the endocrinological studies of the latter half of the twentieth century. Thus, it is with psychoanalysis that much of the literature on sexuality and the arts has been most closely connected.

Freud tracked the vicissitudes of the sexual drives from infancy through adulthood in relation to the habits of thought, speech, and behavior, psychosomatic symptoms, and imaginative constructions (whether private fantasy or conventionalized works of creative art), which serve, he believed, as relays in the transmission of the drive-energy ("libido") in its long-term arc from original stimulation to final discharge. Freud stressed both the archaic endogeny of sexual reflex—so-called infantile sexuality—and its "polymorphous" quality, the apparent fact that sexual stimulation can be obtained or desire directed at almost all parts or zones of the human body and in relation to almost any conceivable object of interest, including people of the same sex or inanimate objects. Such observations had been made before, but they had not been well integrated with a psychology as general as Freud's theories of the unconscious, of psychic defense ("repression"), and of dreams and parapraxes. Freud's approach was compatible with many forms of the biographical and historical analysis of persons and their imaginative productions; indeed, Freud's sexological theories were in part a response to certain traditions of art and literary production not only as they had been studied by Freud himself but also as they had been inherited by patients in Freud's client pool. Freud himself and a number of early followers produced pathographies of artists and writers, studies of works of art, and speculative anthropologies. Often criticized by art and literary historians, these endeavors nonetheless had an enormous impact on twentieth-century scholarship. They addressed aspects of aesthetic experience and of the history of the arts that other methods have barely broached. Not surprisingly, many twentieth-century artists became involved with Freudianism. Hence, twentieth-century art itself has made sexuality both one of its materials and one of its subjects. For this reason alone, sexuality is (or should be) a crucial analytic concern of aesthetics or of the history and criticism of the arts.

Psychoanalysis treats sexuality as a temporal process: it is both a cognitive history and a development, even a normative maturation, from an initial stimulation of the organism, whether innocuous or traumatic, to a satisfaction of the feelings created, sometimes retrospectively, by the stimulation and its analogues. Freud developed a complex account of the typical situations and thresholds of stimulation, trauma, and defense that organize a person—in or as his or her "sexuality"—from earliest childhood into adulthood. Each phase both retains and replaces elements of the earlier ones. In general, Freud saw much of emergent sexuality as a *Reizschutz*, a "shield against stimuli," in which a person protects and attempts to reproduce and augment what provides or has provided pleasure. In theory, then, one can work backward from a particular work of art—conceived as a relay of sexual reflex—toward earlier and possibly more defining conditions of the maker's "sexuality." By the same token, one can work forward from a work toward possible conditions of its reception—considering the ways, for example, in which it will or might stimulate an audience. Finally, one can work outward from a work to analogous or associated objects, persons, or situations in the artist's or the audience's life history. The work of art can be said to have—to express or to reflect—a "sexuality" in all of these directions just to the extent that it really is a node in the personal and social networks that transmit and organize eroticism.

But this is precisely the problem. Although the theories of sexuality have been widely embraced, methodology remains unclear. To what extent can a work of art relay sexuality when it must be conventionalized—responding to technical limits, stylistic norms, and social functions? Moreover, if completing the work requires active "repression" of motivating sexuality, as might be the case, to what extent can one rediscover sexuality *in* the work? Freud regarded the psychoanalysis itself as a manifestation of the patient's sexuality (brought into relation with the sexuality of the analyst). For this reason, the analysis is a platform from which a reconstructive archaeology can be launched. But in the case of art produced outside psychoanalysis, other means must be found to locate it in the historical web of a sexuality, presuming that sexuality itself is taken to be an intrapsychic and intersubjective reality. (An alternative—that sexuality is essentially a "textual" or aesthetic reality—will be considered momentarily, but it has less empirical and theoretical support.) For example, what an artist might offer as meaningful associations to an image within a psychoanalysis could be inferred by a historian from a pattern of stylistic or iconographic similarities among works of art. To take a similar example, what the analyst might interpret as a significant repeated symptom within a psychoanalysis could be inferred by the critic from a pattern of conventions—or seeming violations of convention—characteristic of a particular artistic canon.

In general, an archaeology of sexuality in the history and criticism of the arts requires properly clarified data in two domains. First, the temporal sequence of the production and reception of works of art must be charted comprehensively. This history supports analysis of sexual desire continuously represented and relayed in cognition and maturation. (In particular, long-term patterns of revision, erasure, and preservation should be studied; these might index a history of "repression.") Second, the relation of works of art to other constructions and activities of life must be mapped. This anthropology supports analysis of sexual desire continuously stimulated by and attached to situations, people, or objects. A substantial criticism of art can be conducted in the absence of this research, but it is unlikely to reveal much about sexuality (unless it is the sexuality of the critic). Of course, these topographies have little theoretical interest in themselves; they might conform to ordinary presentations of stylistic development or social history. The key will be provided by historically identifying or critically interpreting some aspect of style or history to be the satisfactory analogue of a symptom, parapraxis, or association—thus connected with stimulation, trauma, and defense—in the psychoanalytic sense. At this point, a stylistic or social history can be rewritten as a history of sexuality.

Influenced by linguistic and structuralist models in psychoanalysis, associated largely with the work of Jacques Lacan, many writers have urged that patterns of critical response to or social discourse about the arts can reveal the relay and pressure points of sexuality. For example, if popular response systematically avoided the homoerotic dimension of iconography, one could suspect that the images in question evoked forbidden or unspoken feelings of homosexual desire and anxiety. Although self-fulfilling to some extent, such accounts make sense if artistic languages and response systems as a whole—their points of articulation and slippage—are comprehensively understood: we need to know that a gap is, in fact, not *just* a gap but a silence or suppression. But although it is theoretically required, such a structural(ist) overview is rarely available.

More convincing have been a series of more strictly Freudian and Lacanian studies of the "letter" of artistic significance—that is, of the actual material structures of linguistic or imagistic usage in creative production, requiring painstaking attention to the temporality and rhythms of sexual desire charted by Freudian theories of defense, maturation (chiefly organized in the Oedipal complexes), and object relations, processes often called "subjectivity." Because Lacan considered subjectivity to be a basic "gap" in the person's relationship to language and other forms of representation (although this is not the place to review his several formulas), his students and followers could readily transform his psychoanalysis into a textual—or pictorial or cinematic—codicology and criticism, related to established philological as well as to phenomenological and deconstructive aesthetics. Like traditional Freudian pathographies, however, these inquiries risk implausible interpretations—for example, finding intricately coded but hidden features of a linguistic or visual structure. More troubling, they can readily lose sight of the human person and of the erotic status of aesthetic production for him or her; Lacanian criticism is highly formalistic.

Paradoxically, many recent students of sexuality in the arts oppose psychoanalysis, at least in part; they wish to reject the primacy it allegedly accords heterosexual male erotic experience and history. Feminists approach sexuality in relation to—sometimes even as a function of—the differences (biological, social, or experiential) between historically variable gender identities, histories, or positions. Gay and lesbian studies takes homosexuality as its central topic. In the 1990s, a broad "antihomophobia" movement arose out of contemporary feminism and gay and lesbian studies and an associated body of "queer theory." Like Krafft-Ebing, queer theory considers *all* nonstandard or "queer" sociosexual formations, such as transvestism or fetishism; like psychoanalysis, it treats normative sexuality (i.e., genital heterosexuality) as peculiar—that is, as a specific formation of the sexual reflex requiring cognitive and developmental analysis like any other. But, like feminism and gay studies, queer theory is substantially different in its intellectual foundation and direction from established sexological and psychoanalytic approaches. Three areas of divergence between established and newer approaches can be noted.

First, in feminism, gay and lesbian studies, and queer theory, Michel Foucault's historicist theories of discourse and subjectivity have provided attractive substitutes for the psychophysical and neurological platforms that Krafft-Ebing and Freud assumed. The *Introduction* to Foucault's *History of Sexuality* (1976) stressed that whatever its biopsychological matrix, homosexuality was and is the product of a social process of cultivation—namely, the formation of subjects in relation to classifications of sexual behavior, the chief effect, if not the sole cause, of which is to secure the purity, intelligibility, and reproducibility of the social order. Foucault's proposals about the actual history of this process in Western society were incomplete. But, as he intended, his deft blend of Freudian, Marxist, and structuralist insights offered a model for—if not quite a method for—a sociocultural history of sexuality. It is not clear what a Foucauldian art-critical perspective, or an aesthetics, strictly speaking, would look like. On the one hand, Foucault's historicism (his doctrine of the subject as slave) suggests that works of art might be vehicles for the social classification and management of sexual desire—as it were, creating or "calling into being" the sexuality of their makers and users. On the other hand, Foucault's strongly ethicist and libertarian views (his doctrine of the subject as ascetic), prominent in his later writing, might imply that art sustains a person's essential freedom to constitute himself or herself in a domain reserved from the surveillance and management of others. (Here Foucault's account of the human ego differs sharply from Lacan's account of the human subject.) Probably both of these aesthetic and art-critical perspectives could legitimately claim Foucault as godfather.

Second, the Freudian legacy has been reassessed. The research of social and cultural historians, many of them influenced by Foucault, tends to conceive Freud's sexology as a powerful interpretation—but also as a generalization—of specific erotic practices, social relations, and cultural traditions in the client pool Freud surveyed. This finding does not vitiate Freudian concepts of the unconscious, repression, identification, or anxiety; these remain central to all views of sexuality, including Foucault's. But Freud's model of infantile eroticism—what he called "bisexuality," a supposed lack of gender and other differentiation in sexual object choice—has come under strong pressure. Some scholars see it as Freud's ideological, albeit innovative, effort metaphysically to describe sexual variation in terms of latent or immanent potentials in order to satisfy the needs of his own commercial therapy of personal postnatal development. At the moment, quasi-psychoanalytic theories of primary undifferentiated sexuality and of a developmental history of erotic identifications and anxieties remain a touchstone for much feminism, gay and lesbian studies, and queer theory in aesthetics, histories of the arts, and cultural criticism. But some philosophers and critics of the arts have begun to explore (or, more exactly, to re-explore) the possibilities that sexuality, though it is surely constructed socially as a mosaic of intersubjectives and object relations, cannot be mapped as the history of the vicissitudes of a single sexual drive. This view—it ignores or opposes the founding doctrine of the sexual reflex with which psychoanalysis attempted to clarify sexological forensics—has remained popular in belles-lettres and nonacademic aesthetics and criticism since the end of the nineteenth century. There it tended to be connected with cultural conservatisms. Today, however, the deconstruction of the sexual reflex—and emerging ethical and aesthetic models of sexuality—tends to be connected with more radical, or at least libertarian, social and cultural philosophies.

Third, the history and anthropology of sexuality, on a worldwide and transhistorical scale, have been greatly enlarged. For the first time, evidence drawn from the arts has come to play a major role in the very theory of sexuality itself. Aesthetics has stressed the construction of fluid eroticisms in the specifically imagistic (i.e., visual, acoustic, tactile, kinesthetic) dimensions of sensation and thought and in the fields of gestural, sartorial, and interpersonal activity. Some theorists propose that, irrespective of the biopsychological nature of sexuality, it must always be presented or performed in a social arena using the cultural forms and aesthetic strategies available to or devised by the performers. This concept, trading on the close philosophical connection between erotics and aesthetics, probably generalizes from the social histories of specifically performative sexualities, such as transvestism. It certainly embodies familiar Wildean and Dadaist conceptions of the supposedly transgressive roles of art, theater, dress, and so on in private and public life. But, for this reason, it has helped aesthetics to grasp influential artistic movements of recent decades—from Duchamp to performance art—and to interpret historical practices of body ornamentation, cross-dressing, masquerading, interior design, and the like. Moreover, there are substantial overlaps, if not identities, between judgments of desire and desirability rendered in sexual and in aesthetic categories.

In the hands of some historians and critics of the arts, the performative theory of gender and sexuality often ascribes a high degree of self-conscious agency and creativity not only to the technical process of aesthetic construction itself, but also to the management of erotic identity—the supposed basis and aim of much artistic production. But the orthodox Freudian theory of sexuality and offshoots such as the Lacanian theory of subjectivity consider the infantile and longer-term aspects of eroticism, personal and intersubjective, to be largely outside the reach of such individual technical creation and recreation. Art might be repetition, revision, or symptom, and it could be therapy, but it is not sexuality as such. Moreover, some feminist and gay/lesbian critics have objected on ethical and political grounds to the idea that sexualities might be constructed and recon-

structed like works of art, even though it might be true that works of art are constructed and reconstructed in sexualities. Finally, the real theoretical difference, if any, between a "performative"-aesthetic theory of gender and sexuality and a standard philosophical model of intentionality in its complex—layered, nested, and reflexive—structures remains to be clarified.

At the present time, the theory, history, and criticism of sexuality in the arts find themselves at a complex crossroads; intellectually, they are positioned midway between Krafft-Ebing's *Psychopathia sexualis* and Oscar Wilde's "Decay of Lying." Freud's *Three Essays on the Theory of Sexuality* and Foucault's *History of Sexuality* remain indispensable points of reference, but neither offered an explicit perspective on the relation between sexuality and aesthetics. Many writers work from expectations based on a formal theory of sexuality, such as Freud's or Foucault's, to particular studies of individual works of art or aesthetic problems. But a formal aesthetic theory should also generate expectations guiding research into the most elementary data of sexual behavior and feeling. Some of the most compelling treatments of sexuality in the arts assume both of these analytic possibilities; they make about equal contributions, for instance, to psychoanalysis and to narratology, or to the history of painting and to the history of homosexuality. Any forced or limited choice between the options is likely to be unproductive.

[*See also* Foucault; Freud; Gay Aesthetics; Lacan; *and* Lesbian Aesthetics.]

BIBLIOGRAPHY

Bersani, Leo. *The Freudian Body: Psychoanalysis and Art.* New York, 1986.

Davis, Whitney. *Replications: Archaeology, Art History, Psychoanalysis.* University Park, Pa., 1996.

Foucault, Michel. *The History of Sexuality,* vol. 1, *An Introduction* (1976). Translated by Robert Hurley. New York, 1978.

Freud, Sigmund. *Drei Abhandlungen zur Sexualtheorie.* Vienna, 1905. Translated as *Three Essays on the Theory of Sexuality,* in *The Standard Edition of the Complete Psychological Works of Sigmund Freud,* edited James Strachey, vol. 7 (London, 1953), pp. 125–245.

Freud, Sigmund. *Eine Kindheitserinnerung des Leonardo da Vinci.* Vienna, 1910. Translated as *Leonardo da Vinci and a Memory of His Childhood,* in *The Standard Edition of the Complete Psychological Works of Sigmund Freud,* edited by James Strachey, vol. 11 (London, 1957), pp. 59–137.

Krafft-Ebing, Richard von. *Psychopathia Sexualis: Mit besonderer Berücksichtigung der conträren Sexualempfindung: Eine klinisch-forensische Studie.* 9th ed. Stuttgart, 1894.

Lacan, Jacques. *Écrits: A Selection* (1966). Translated by Alan Sheridan. New York, 1977.

Potts, Alex. *Flesh and the Ideal: Winckelmann and the Origins of Art History.* New Haven, 1994.

Rose, Jacqueline. *Sexuality in the Field of Vision.* London, 1986.

Sedgwick, Eve Kosofsky. *Epistemology of the Closet.* Berkeley, 1990.

Weeks, Jeffrey. *Sexuality and Its Discontents: Meanings, Myths, and Modern Sexualities.* London and Boston, 1985.

Wilde, Oscar. "The Decay of Lying." In *The Complete Works of Oscar Wilde*, edited by Robert Ross, vol. 4, pp. 3–57. New York, 1905.
Wollheim, Richard. *Painting as an Art.* Princeton, N.J., 1987.

WHITNEY DAVIS

SHAFTESBURY, EARL OF. *See* Cooper.

SIDNEY, PHILIP (1554–1586), a poet of the English Renaissance, who suffered an early death, from a battle wound. Sidney's *A Defence of Poetry,* published posthumously in 1595, is widely regarded as the most significant work of aesthetics in the Elizabethan era. Yet, Sidney did not live to witness the apex of Elizabethan drama and poetry—William Shakespeare was only twenty-two when Sidney died, and John Donne was fourteen. This may explain Sidney's disrespect for the contemporary theater, which he criticized for violating the Aristotelian unities and for the vulgarity of the public playhouses (though Shakespeare himself would soon be reproved on similar grounds). Indeed, Sidney is curiously ambivalent in his defense of both his own métiers, drama and the love poem. Although Sidney's production of courtly spectacles won him fame as an upscale "Master of the Revels," his enduring reputation as a poet rests on his amorous verse. Because Sidney's influence on aesthetics is owing almost solely to the *Defence,* however, this essay will focus exclusively on that work, which is a rich source of eloquently expressed ideas, both new and received.

Sidney's characterization of poetry as an art of imitation appeals explicitly to Aristotle, but the influence of Horace and Julius Caesar Scaliger can be seen in his gloss of poetic imitation as "a speaking picture—with this end, to teach and delight" (Sidney, 1966, p. 25). Similarly, although the *Defence* is clearly meant to answer the Platonic indictment of poetry, Sidney's Plato is always seen through the eyes of contemporary Puritanism. Sidney was particularly influenced by Stephen Gosson, whose *The School of Abuse* is the most famous tract in the Puritan sermon and pamphlet campaign against the theater, which culminated in the suppression of stage plays in 1642 by an edict of the Long Parliament. Sidney sought wherever possible to appease his opponents, even granting their complaint that poetry can be morally corrupting. Yet, because it can also serve as a powerful force for virtue, Sidney insists that the admitted "abuses" of poetry do not infect its proper use. He thus embraced a form of humanist aesthetics, which claims an ethical function for art. Yet, Sidney's humanism was less a moralistic constraint on poetry than an expression of his faith in the Horatian ideal, that the poet mingle the useful and the sweet, which elides any tension between moral and aesthetic demands.

Sidney expressly defends poetry against four charges: that poetry is a waste of time, that poets are liars, that poems indulge "sinful fancies," and that Plato banished the poet from his ideal republic. This last charge is dismissed with the dubious claim that Plato too disparaged only bad poetry. More authentically Platonic is Sidney's quick rejection of the triviality charge, on the grounds of poetry's ability to move us in morally significant ways, by giving us attractive pictures of virtue (although, of course, Sidney was far more sanguine about the effects of poetry than was Plato). But the bulk of Sidney's argument is directed against the charges of deception and sin. Although antecedents of both accusations can be found in Plato, their metaphysical and religious baggage was lost in the translation from antiquity. It has been questioned whether Plato actually held that poetry is inevitably misleading, but this reading was long standard. Cast in the Puritan idiom, it was expressed as the idea that poets are liars by nature. Plato's most serious charge, that poetry encourages emotional incontinence, was sexualized in the Puritan imagination. Thus, whereas Plato was primarily concerned with tragedy's power to induce such unmanly emotions as sorrow and fear, Sidney focuses on the idea that poetry encourages "wanton sinfulness and lustful love" (ibid., p. 54).

But there is a more profound difference between the burden of Sidney's defense of poetry and Aristotle's. Because Plato took pleasure to be intrinsically good, it follows that any argument against a form of pleasure must rest on the adverse consequences of its indulgence. In contrast, Sidney's Puritan opponents were innately suspicious of pleasure. Therefore, in defending poetry, Sidney had both a positive and a negative task: he needed to locate a suitably nonhedonic value of poetry, and to acquit the poet of the charges of deception and incitement. He found the positive value of poetry in its ability to teach virtue. Although Sidney develops this idea in a rather scattershot manner, his most distinctive humanist thesis is that "the poets' persons and doings are but pictures what should be, and not stories what have been" (ibid., p. 53). The two significant negative charges against poetry are handled quite differently. Sidney grants that the abuse of poetry can be an incitement to sin, but he denies that poets are even capable of lying. Thus, the *Defence* responds to both the positive and the negative challenge; but there is a tension at the center of Sidney's thought, which foreshadows his deeply conflicted legacy to aesthetics.

Sidney is perhaps best remembered for his uncompromising response to the deception charge. Although poets traffic in the depiction of imaginary scenarios, we are not asked to believe in them, nor do we. Rather, Sidney famously insists that "the poet, he nothing affirms, and therefore never lieth" (ibid., p. 52). This slogan was taken up by a variety of twentieth-century literary critics and philosophers, who wanted to claim that fiction can involve only the pretense of assertion, never the genuine article. Their motives for denying poetic assertion are diverse. It is a central tenet of modernism that aesthetic value is radically autonomous from the values of truth and goodness; and the New Critics in particular feared that to consider poetry as a vehicle for assertion inevitably leads to its being judged on adventitious criteria. Some postmodern successors of the New Critics, while rejecting their conception of aesthetic value, have embraced the related idea that literature can speak only of itself, and not of the world. One major philosophical theory attempts to ground fictionality on the speech act of pretended assertion.

It is much easier, however, to hold that we are not expected to believe in the poet's scenarios, or that some flimsy stage prop is the gate of Thebes, than it is to claim that a fable does not actually assert its moral. There is good reason to think that Sidney never meant to make this stronger claim, or to hold that poets literally assert nothing. The poet can be acquitted of being a liar by nature once we see that we are not being asked to believe in the fictitious persons and doings he depicts. Any more thoroughgoing denial of poetic assertion is deeply problematic, and typically rests on a faulty theory of assertion or a tendentious view of fiction. Moreover, it would belie the distinctive aspect of Sidney's humanism: his idea that the poet shows us what should, or should not, be. If the poet makes moral claims, then he does assert something rather than nothing; and he is therefore capable of error and deceit, after all. There are several ways one might seek to reconcile Sidney's humanism with his claim that poets never lie; but the route most in keeping with the gist of Sidney's view retreats somewhat from his most famous dictum. Although poets are capable of moral deception, by putting forward pernicious views of what should be, we are not in danger of being taken in, because though moral motivation is lamentably scarce, moral knowledge is easily had.

However Sidney might have resolved this tension, had he recognized it, two aspects of his view cannot be doubted: first, he pays poetry the Platonic compliment of thinking it powerful enough to be dangerous; and, second, his commitment to humanist aesthetics is undaunted by poetry's acknowledged dangers. Although Sidney allows that "by the reason of his sweet charming force, [poetry] can do more hurt than any other army of words" (ibid., p. 55), he nevertheless insists that, when properly used, it can also do the most good. Even so, unless we can be convinced that the "proper use" of poetry accommodates both moral and aesthetic demands, Sidney's position seems vulnerable to charges of moralism. Perhaps Plato was right, and it is just when poetry is most charming that it is also most treacherous.

[*See also* Literature, *article on* Literary Aesthetics; *and* Poetics.]

BIBLIOGRAPHY

Work by Sidney

A Defence of Poetry (1595). Edited by Jan A. Van Dorsten. New York and Oxford, 1966.

Antecedents of Sidney's *Defence*

Aristotle. *Poetics*. Edited by D. W. Lucas. Oxford, 1968.
Gosson, Stephen. *The School of Abuse*. London, 1841.
Horace. *The Art of Poetry*. In *Horace on the Art of Poetry*, edited by Edward Henry Blakeney. London, 1928.
Plato. *Republic*. Translated by G. M. A. Grube. Indianapolis, 1974.
Scaliger, Julius Caesar. *Poetics*. In *Select Translations from Scaliger's Poetics*, edited by Frederick Morgan Padelford. New York, 1905.

Other Sources

Abrams, M. H. *The Mirror and the Lamp: Romantic Theory and the Critical Tradition*. New York and Oxford, 1953.
Buxton, John. *Sir Philip Sidney and the English Renaissance*. 2d ed. London, 1964.
Frye, Northrop. *The Anatomy of Criticism: Four Essays*. Princeton, N.J., 1957.
Graff, Gerald. *Poetic Statement and Critical Dogma*. Evanston, Ill., 1970.
Heninger, S. K., Jr. "Sidney's Speaking Pictures and the Theater." *Style* 23.3 (Fall 1989).
Jacobson, Daniel. "Sir Philip Sidney's Dilemma: On the Ethical Function of Narrative Art." *Journal of Aesthetics and Art Criticism* 54 (Fall 1996): 327–336.
Wimsatt, W. K., and Cleanth Brooks. *Literary Criticism: A Short History*. New York, 1957.

DANIEL JACOBSON

SIGN. *See* Prague School; Semiotics; *and* Structuralism.

SIMMEL, GEORG (1858–1918), German sociologist who explored the different facets of culture. Besides history, religion, ethics, and economics, Simmel also examined the arts and the lives of various artists as illustrations of his cultural theory. He did not, however, develop a systematic philosophy or sociology of art. Writings on art include articles about artists such as Michelangelo, Stefan George, Auguste Rodin, and Rembrandt van Rijn, to whom he also devoted an entire book in 1917, *Rembrandt: A Philosophical Essay on Art*, after already publishing a book on *Goethe* (1913). In other essays, he analyzed aesthetic phenomena such as the picture frame, the handle, the face, the portrait, and the caricature. Simmel also drew attention to the aesthetic dimensions of cities, ruins, and landscapes. In his book *The Philosophy of Money* (1900), he applied an aesthetic perspective to the analysis of money and its symbolic function in society. In his late articles on realism, style, naturalism, and art ("L'art pour l'art," 1914), Simmel introduced criteria concerning the ontological status of artworks and their specific properties. Overall, his widespread deliberations about the arts stand in a systematic relationship with his other studies on history and on the development and effects of culture.

Background. Simmel was born in Berlin, the youngest child of a converted Jewish merchant family. He studied history, ethnopsychology, philosophy, Italian, and the history of art at the University of Berlin, where he encountered the historicist and the neo-Kantian movement. His dissertation on ethnomusicology was rejected in 1881. It was considered too aphoristic and unscientific, a criticism that Simmel would be confronted with throughout his life. He finally earned his doctorate with a treatise on Immanuel Kant. Although the department accepted his Habilitationsschrift, he initially failed the oral defense, where he openly criticized the views of his mentor Eduard Zeller. Simmel subsequently taught in Berlin as Privatdozent without attaining a full professorship until 1914, when he finally received a call to Strasbourg.

Artists such as Rodin and Max Liebermann and the poets Rainer Maria Rilke and George were among Simmel's acquaintances. He also held weekly private meetings in his house where issues of art were discussed. Like Wilhelm Dilthey and Max Weber, Simmel was among those turn-of-the-century intellectuals who responded to the challenge posed by modernity: the need for the humanities *(Geisteswissenschaften)* to rethink their theoretical foundation given the success of modern industrialization and rationalization. Simmel's scope from early on was to understand the origin of culture, and how its change could be explained. The analysis of different artists lies at the core of his theory of understanding culture and his concept of modern history as the development of individualization. The arts are seen as a resort from the process of alienation, harmonizing the tension between subjective creativity and objective culture. In response to Henri Bergson's work Simmel turned to a philosophy of life *(Lebensphilosophie),* which manifested itself in his essay collection *Philosophical Culture* (1911), his studies on Goethe (1913) and Rembrandt (1916), and his last book, *Views of Life* (1918). During the last part of his life, he increasingly devoted himself to aesthetic questions and deliberations on a philosophy of art.

The Theory of Culture. Simmel's theory of culture is crucial to his philosophy of art, because he analyzes art in light of its reflection of a cultural form. In his essay "Personal and Objective Culture" (1900), he stipulates that in modern times the cleavage between subjective culture—that is, the intellectual work of an individual—and the objective culture as the totality of cultural products of a society has increased as a result of the division of labor. We are alienated from the objective culture, because we feel surrounded by an increasing number of anonymous objects and thus retreat into individual isolation, Simmel maintains in "The Future of Our Culture" (1909). Only the artist is able to combine objective culture with his own subjective culture by achieving a harmony between the reception of the objective culture and his own creative production.

At the same time, the objective culture, Simmel states in "On the Essence of Culture" (1908), is also the result of the individual's attributing value to it. In "On the Concept and Tragedy of Culture" (1911), he calls it the tragedy of culture that subjective life—being a continuous flow—cannot achieve its own end from within itself, but only via the objectified and flowless form of culture. Only for the genius is the development of his subjective spirit the same as selfless devotion to the objective task; he succeeds in harmonizing the subjective life and the objective culture by giving objective form to his own life. Particularly in his later work, Simmel refers to the dualism between cultural subject and object as a dualism between life and form ("Change of Cultural Forms" [1916]). In "The Conflict in Modern Culture" (1918), he applies his philosophy of history to a theory of conflict between life and form. History is examined as the change of cultural forms whereby life—constantly changing—opposes the objective validity of its own forms and products. The conflict of modern culture is that life can only realize itself in forms that limit its liberty. Simmel's analysis of various artists serves to show that they can overcome that conflict.

As one of the first gender theorists, Simmel also analyzes culture in the light of gender difference. In "Female Culture" (1902), he claims that culture is not gender-neutral but male, because it is defined by male forms of productivity. The lack of female cultural products is the result of the fact that female creativity does not match the existing male cultural forms. In most of women's cultural products Simmel sees friction between the content derived from female experience and the form pertinent to a male world. In cases where women found their authentic means of expression, such as Käthe Kollwitz, they appear to communicate a holistic understanding of the world alien to a man's cultural production.

Sociological Aesthetics—Aesthetic Sociology. Simmel not only analyzed the arts as illustrations of his cultural analysis, he also applied aesthetics as a method to examine sociological phenomena, which brought him the reputation of being an aestheticist. He aestheticizes in the following ways: (1) he chooses and examines his objects of analysis (e.g., sociological phenomena) with respect to their aesthetic qualities, such as purposiveness, symmetry, formal relations between parts and whole, and/or symbolic features; and (2) he relates attitudes that individuals take toward society and/or the objective culture to aesthetic categories such as distance and self-sufficiency.

In his article "Sociological Aesthetics" (1896), Simmel had already introduced his aesthetic perspective to sociology. He focuses on the sense behind the appearance, on the examination of rules and symmetries behind the outer senselessness. Society as a whole can become a work of art when one can attribute sense and meaning to each of its parts by virtue of their contribution to the whole. The social organization itself is aesthetic to the extent that it develops a purposiveness to the functioning of its parts and their interrelationship.

In his *The Philosophy of Money* (1900), Simmel claims that any object can be examined aesthetically. This aesthetic quality of perception should be used for an analysis of society. Money is only a symbol for the interrelationship of objects, exemplifying the aesthetic category of analogy by making objects analogous with regard to their monetary value. As a symbol of exchange, money represents the interrelation between culture and its form, just like a work of art. Money thus becomes objectified culture similar to the arts, religion, or law. At the same time, Simmel values the autonomy of means from any purpose as a condition for aesthetic pleasure. In money, as a means without content, this aesthetic pleasure must reach its peak.

According to Simmel, our attitude toward society is also aesthetic in that we try to distance ourselves from our surroundings as a reaction to the obtrusiveness of the modern world.

In "Fragments from a Psychology of Women" (1904), as well as in "On Psychology of Women" (1890), Simmel compares the female psyche to the character of artworks with respect to their self-sufficiency and autonomy. The close relation between world and individual experience is inherent to the inner self of women so that—similar to artworks—their inner life gains universality only by the expression of its very personal form.

Artists Expressing Their Age. Simmel analyzed different artists and their work as an illustration of the history of cultural forms developing to an increased individualization. Each age, however, evolves a specific idea about the interrelation between the subjective expression and the objective form, the analysis of which is the task of a philosophical sociology.

The central idea of the Renaissance is embodied in "Michelangelo" (1911). Michelangelo's figures do not show the individual but the classical ideal, that is, the unity of life above all individual forms. The tragedy of his work is that, at the same time, it also represents melancholy deriving from the actual dualism of life and form that Michelangelo only forced into a synthesis. Similarly, Leonardo da Vinci—as Simmel pointed out in "Leonardo da Vinci's Last Supper" (1905)—created an ideal space that allows the simultaneity of temporally different events, thereby condemning us to recognize our own powerlessness with respect to our finiteness.

Rembrandt—as Simmel tried to show in his *Rembrandt Studies* (1914), as well as in his 1917 book on the artist—finally overcame the dualism between life and form inherent to the Renaissance. In his portraits, he captured the individual's development as rooted in a life history, thus depicting the stream of life in one form, and expressing what Simmel called the individual law. Form in Rembrandt's baroque art appears to be a part of life, whereas Michelangelo's work uses life to lend content to a given form. Michelangelo's figures, therefore, seem unfree, despite their formal perfectionism.

Rodin, as Simmel pointed out in articles on the artist in 1902 and 1911, succeeded in expressing modernity. The unity of life and form is realized in such a way that its elements are explicitly shown as separate. By deliberately leaving his sculptures unfinished, Rodin satisfies the modern desire to have as much autonomy as possible in interpreting the work. His statues express movement, which makes the liveliness of the whole human being visible, and which is able to combine form and content. Similarly, George's poems express movement through their musicality, thus giving an adequate form to the subjective experience. The entire fate of life becomes apparent, not as a general idea as in Michelangelo, but in its immediacy. In three essays on George from 1898, 1901, and 1909 ("The Seventh Ring"), Simmel describes George's poetry as going beyond the individual feeling by making feelings art. George's interest does not lie in the content but in the artistic form. The content has become the means for sheer aesthetic values expressing the inner life.

Cities and Landscapes. Simmel also analyzed the aesthetic role of cities and landscapes with regard to his sociology of forms and his philosophy of life. As Simmel pointed out in an article on his contemporary Arnold Böcklin in 1895, landscapes, like works of art, are self-sufficient, enabling us to look beyond our momentary fate. In "Philosophy of the Landscape" (1913), Simmel claims that the concept of landscape also implies the idea of individualization as opposed to nature. Thus, the objectivity of landscapes is actually forged as unity, that is, subjective form by the artist. In this way, landscapes are a human construction. In his article "The Alps" (1911), Simmel maintains that the Alps in their monumentality serve as a symbol of the transcendent, which compels us to realize that there is something higher and purer than our life. Thus, Simmel illustrates his idea of cultural development as a process of increasing individualization that involves the acknowledgment of a higher force. His essays on three cities—"Rome, an Aesthetic Analysis" (1898), "Florence" (1906), and "Venice" (1907), serve similar purposes. Whereas Rome expresses the simultaneity of different time periods, Florence unites nature and spirit by forming its surrounding nature—Tuscany—through culture. Whereas the Roman unity is still a tension between ancient and modern culture, the synthesis of Florence is from within life and culture itself. Venice, on the other hand, shows a unity that is just a mask, disguising life so that the appearance of the city can only offer artificiality.

Aesthetic Phenomena. In "Picture Frame" (1902), "Handle" (1911), and "Ruin" (1911), Simmel discovers phenomena that are aesthetically pertinent because of their status at the border between art and reality, art and usefulness, and art and nature. The picture frame keeps art at a distance from the outer world, thus enhancing aesthetic pleasure. It emphasizes the unity of art against the observer and the world, and, at the same time, mediates between the two. Similarly, the handle of a vase represents the interrelation between art and the world of purposes. The handle presents art and usefulness as unity, thus pointing to a higher beauty where idea and life find their synthesis. Simmel sees this function of the handle reflected in the fate of the human soul, which, on the one hand, is self-sufficient and part of our being, and, on the other, has to reach out to the world and its purposes. The ruin, finally represents nature regaining power over a cultural form, which results in a new unity between nature and art, deriving its new purpose from the secret harmony of the unintended. The tension between purpose and chance, nature and culture, past and present reaches an outer unity in the form of the ruin.

In "The Aesthetic Significance of the Face" (1901), Simmel finally examines the face as a synthesis of body and soul, of symmetry and individuality. It is the bodily and geometric space where the inner personality can express itself. This is the reason why Simmel, in his 1918 essay on the portrait, regards it as the most important object of painting. The challenge for the painter is to attribute an inner necessity to the outer visibility. The artistic form of the portrait proves anew the unity of body and soul. By showing this unity in a portrait, the work of art is guided by the soul, which functions as a law of singular traits.

Toward a Philosophy of Art. In his late work, Simmel introduces criteria to determine what art is as opposed to nonart. In his essay "On the Third Dimension of Art" (1906), he maintains that the artwork has to legitimize its quality by offering meaning beyond what can be seen. The meaning has to be experienced in the perception of the artwork, however: it is the "third dimension" that adds to the actual sensual properties of the artwork a quality that spells itself out as enrichment and reinforcement of the two-dimensional content. It derives its force from the artist's ability to organize imagination, thus adding a specific nuance to the perceptual properties. The third dimension is the form that the artist gives to the relationship between himself and the world. In his "Fragments from a Philosophy of Art" (1916), Simmel elaborates his concept of the third dimension as the sensibility immanent in a work of art. In his posthumously published piece "Lawfulness in the Work of Art," he describes art as an objective form whose reality is idea and law: the artistic criterion is an individual law that arises from the creation of art itself, and whose own ideal necessity serves as its guideline. The work of art at the same time creates the problem it wants to address. This is the reason why style receives a rather negative connotation in Simmel's concept of art. He claims that style is a general principle that limits the individuality of an artwork. A great artwork derives its power from the individual law, unlike crafts, which follow a general principle of style ("The Problem of Style" [1908]).

Finally, the realism of an artwork has nothing to do with the imitation of reality. First, without imitating reality, the artwork can provoke the same psychological reactions with different means. Second, the artist sees in reality only what he intends to create. Receptivity and activity are the same in the artist. Third, art does not even gain its specific aesthetic quality from its outer appearance as it compares to reality. It derives its force from the third dimension, where things are independent of appearance ("On Realism in Art" [1908]). Simmel rejects naturalism precisely for its claim that one should find the given in art. Art is not supposed to reach out to the world, but to lead the world into art. Truth in art does not refer to a correspondent relationship between art and reality, but to the truthful expression of the artist ("The Problem of Naturalism" [posthumous]). In "On the Philosophy of an Actor" (1908), Simmel points out that the actor as much as the painter creates a new world that shares some of its properties with the "real" world because their contents both stem from all being. It is only art, however, if this content is artistically experienced, thus not realizing a certain content, but making it sensual. A work of art has a double character in that it excludes the world and our lives, but at the same time is part of our life. Art is self-sufficient only because behind its self-sufficiency there lies the deeper dimension of its relationship with life ("L'art pour l'art" [1914]).

[*See also* Sociology of Art.]

BIBLIOGRAPHY

Works by Simmel

Philosophische Kultur: Über das Abenteuer, die Geschlechter und die Krise der Moderne (1911). 3d ed. Berlin, 1983. Contains "The Alps," "Handle," "Ruin," "On the Concept and Tragedy of Culture," "Michelangelo," and "Auguste Rodin."

Goethe. Leipzig, 1913.

Rembrandtstudien (1914). Basel, 1954.

Rembrandt: Ein kunstphilosophischer Versuch (1917). Edited by Beat Wyss. Munich, 1985.

Zur Philosophie der Kunst: Philosophische und kunstphilosophische Aufsätze von Georg Simmel. Edited by Gertrud Simmel. Potsdam, 1922. Contains "Rome, an Aesthetic Analysis," "Florence," "Venice," "Picture Frame," "The Portrait," "L'art pour l'art," "Leonardo da Vinci's Last Supper," "Stefan George," "The Seventh Ring," and "Arnold Böcklin."

Fragmente und Aufsätze aus dem Nachlass und Veröffentlichungen der letzten Jahre. Edited by Gertrud Kantorowicz. Munich, 1923. Contains "Lawfulness in the Work of Art," "On the Philosophy of an Actor," and "The Problem of Naturalism."

Das Individuum und die Freiheit (1957). Berlin, 1984. Contains "Philosophy of the Landscape," "The Aesthetic Significance of the Face," "The Future of Our Culture," "On the Essence of Culture," "Change of Cultural Forms," and "Sociological Aesthetics."

George Simmel, 1858–1918: A Collection of Essays. Edited and translated by Kurt H. Wolff et al. Columbus, Ohio, 1959. Contains "The Handle," "Ruin," and "The Aesthetic Significance of the Face."

The Conflict in Modern Culture and Other Essays. Translated by K. Peter Etzkorn. New York, 1967. Contains "The Conflict in Modern Culture," "Sociological Aesthetics," "On the Concept and Tragedy of Culture," and "On the Third Dimension of Art."

Das individuelle Gesetz: Philosophische Exkurse (1968). Edited by Michael Landmann. Frankfurt am Main, 1989. Contains "Handle," "Fragments from a Philosophy of Art," "On the Concept and

Tragedy of Culture," "The Conflict in Modern Culture," and "Sociological Aesthetics."

On Individuality and Social Forms. Edited by Donald N. Levine, translated by Donald N. Levine and Kurt H. Wolff. Chicago, 1971. Contains "The Conflict in Modern Culture."

The Philosophy of Money. Translated by Tom Bottomore and David Frisby. London and Boston, 1978.

Essays on Interpretation in Social Science. Edited and translated by Guy Oakes. Totowa, N.J., 1980.

Gesamtausgabe. 20 vols. Edited by Otthein Rammstedt. Frankfurt am Main, 1989–.

Vom Wesen der Moderne: Essays zur Philosophie und Ästhetik. Edited by Werner Jung. Hamburg, 1990. Contains "The Problem of Style," "On Realism in Art," "Rome, an Aesthetic Analysis," "Florence," "Venice," "Picture Frame," "The Portrait," "L'art pour l'art," "Stefan George," "The Seventh Ring," and "Auguste Rodin."

Other Sources

Böhringer, Hannes, and Karlfried Gründer, eds. *Ästhetik und Soziologie um die Jahrhundertwende: Georg Simmel.* Frankfurt am Main, 1976.

Dahme, Heinz-Jürgen, and Otthein Rammstedt, editors. *Georg Simmel und die Moderne.* Frankfurt am Main, 1984.

Dörr, Felicitas. *Die Kunst als Gegenstand der Kulturanalyse im Werk Georg Simmels.* Berlin, 1993.

Frisby, David. *Sociological Impressionism: A Reassessment of Georg Simmel's Social Theory.* London, 1981.

Frisby, David. *Simmel and Since: Essays on Georg Simmel's Social Theory.* London and New York, 1992.

Jung, Werner. *Georg Simmel zur Einführung.* Hamburg, 1990.

Levine, Donald N. *The Flight from Ambiguity: Essays in Social and Cultural Theory.* Chicago, 1985.

Liebersohn, Harry. *Fate and Utopia in German Sociology, 1870–1923.* Cambridge, Mass., 1988.

Utitz, Emil. "Georg Simmel und die Philosophie der Kunst." *Zeitschrift für Ästhetik und allgemeine Kunstwissenschaft* 14 (1920): 1–41.

Weingartner, Rudolph H. *Experience and Culture: The Philosophy of Georg Simmel.* Middleton, Conn., 1962.

MONIKA BETZLER

SIMULACRUM. *See* Baudrillard; *and* Deleuze.

SITUATIONIST AESTHETICS. There is no such thing as Situationism, there are only Situationists—those who construct situations. This makes it difficult to ascribe a general aesthetic to Situationists as a whole, because the principal characters involved were too individually creative to be generalized. The problem is exacerbated by deep fractures within the movement—if movement it is—and made worse still because the notion of a Situationist aesthetic would be anathema to Situationist philosophy: by definition, situations are conceived as the opposite of works of art.

At their origin, the different strains of Situationist agreed only that the political and technical progress that marked the twentieth century had invaded individual creativity, colonizing and enclosing a territory in which the imagination was supposed to run free. United against passive submission to the "society of the spectacle"—as articulated by Guy Debord, their foremost philosopher, Situationists formed a caucus of opposition to the mediated experience of life under capitalism. They issued a call for the simultaneous dissolution and transcendence of art, for a return to pleasure, to spontaneity, to instinct and prelogical creativity. As Raoul Vaneigem—a leading theorist of situations—argued: "men live in a state of creativity twenty-four hours a day. Once that's clear, power's scheming use of freedom forces to birth the idea of lived freedom, inseparable from individual creativity" (1972). The situation to which they collectively aspired was one in which the imagination was freed, in and by an environment that allowed and encouraged liberated expression. Clearly, such a move would reduce the validity of, and necessity for, a discrete concept of "Art," and, indeed, various Situationist tendencies relegated Art to an inspirational historical entity at best, and at worst to a reactionary impediment to freedom. In general, Situationists understood that even the radical cultural alternatives offered by Dada and Surrealism had been "emasculated" by bourgeois culture. Combining a Surrealist admiration for the marvelous and the subconscious with Dada's anarchic adventure, they sought, in very varied ways, to recapture the anti-art fervor of their predecessors, and to continue the revolutionary program.

The immediate progenitors of the Situationist International included Lettrisme, an obscure and extremist group dedicated to the reinvention and reempowerment of languages, led by Isidore Isou; and the philosophy of Henri Lefebvre, a Marxist academic whose *Critique de la vie quotidienne* was published in 1947. Lefebvre introduced the notion of everyday life into political science, and his definitions are, if not the source of Situationist theory, clearly allied to it.

> Let us simply say about daily life that it has always existed, but permeated with values, with myths. The word "everyday" designates the entry of this daily life into modernity: the everyday as an object of programming, whose unfolding is imposed by the market, by the system of equivalences, by marketing and advertisements. (1991)

Lefebvre contemporaneously taught Jean Baudrillard, whose concept of the hyperreal reveals a shared influence, and he was at one time close to Debord and other leading members of the Paris-based Situationist International.

Other European Situationists were made up of members of the Movement for an Imaginist Bauhaus (IMIB), and CoBrA, this latter being a well-known group of expressive, abstract, and gestural painters founded in 1948 by Asger Jorn, Christian Dotremont, and Constant (Niewenhuis). Articulating the frustrations that these disparate groups shared, Constant wrote in a 1948 manifesto: "this culture, unable to make artistic expression possible, can only make it impossible." A multifaceted artist, architect, and theorist,

Constant was—paradoxically—later excluded from the Situationist International, in part because of ideological failures discerned in his designs for a utopian city, "New Babylon."

Both Constant and Jorn were involved with IMIB, a small international coterie whose members also included painter/collagist Enrico Baj and Debord. Apparently in agreement with the early aims of the Weimar Bauhaus, they saw its descent into Formalism as a clear sign of the degenerate effects of technology on cultural thought and action. They proposed a fresh attempt to integrate art and society, this time avoiding the commercially driven rationalism of the German original.

Situationist groups operated as a network rather than a movement—a shifting association of artists and activists who agreed simply on the derelict state of culture, on the imprisoned condition of the collective imagination, and on the harmful alienation that scientific progress and capitalism had combined to induce in the nuclear world. Their history can only be dimly discerned in an almost parodic succession of schisms and factions, coalescing and dividing around a number of conferences spread across Europe through the 1950s and early 1960s. Their fundamentally anarchic ambition provided fuel for many disparate versions of Situationist argument and activity, including publication of at least two periodicals: the *International Situationist* and the *Situationist Times*. There were also numerous exhibitions, conferences, articles, brochures, films, books, and tracts; and, of course, innumerable situations were constructed.

The First Conference of International Situationists took place in 1957, in Alba, Italy, a site that had in other years seen the formation of similarly polysyllabic organizations such as the First World Congress of Liberated Artists (1956) and the International Movement for an Imaginist Bauhaus (1953). Many of these groups were composed of the same people, presumably summering at the artists' colony known from 1956 onward as the Experimental Laboratory, under the directorship of Dr. Giuseppe Pinot-Gallizio, a sometime Situationist who produced an astonishing hybrid between painting and architecture: pseudoindustrially produced rolls of paint-splattered canvas that could be used as wall and furniture covers.

Jorn appears to have been a constant presence at these gatherings. An artist who, by the early 1950s, had garnered an international reputation as a painter of wild, weird, and colorful nightmares, often produced automatically or through chance processes, Jorn's works exemplify the Situationist concept of *détournement*—an adaptation of collage as developed by Dada—particularly his 1959 exhibit of junk-store paintings, crudely overpainted to pervert their original status and deliberately confuse their message. An avid discussant and theorist, Jorn believed that color was capable of provoking immediate and indescribable meaning.

He initiated, participated in, and financially or morally supported a number of artist groups, each sharing internationalist, revolutionary, and essentially playful characteristics, and once proposed, for example, a "Scandinavian Institute for Comparative Vandalism." One Situationist authority has detected among Jorn's personal influences such disparate concepts as "happy Christianity," Johan Huizinga's concept of *homo ludens,* and, of course, Dada. Jorn's expansive and restless nature caused him to consider founding another Nordic Situationist Bauhaus in 1960 and led him to closer connections with Gruppe SPUR, a Munich-based group of expressive painters whom he first encountered in 1953. Grafted onto the Situationist International after 1959, the Gruppe SPUR was "officially" excluded from the group in 1961, shortly after the Fifth Congress in Gothenburg.

Constant had conceived of "an architecture of situation" in 1953, and architecture—or at least, human reaction to the built environment—was a common concern, particularly the insidious but accelerating effects of industrial culture. According to Debord, their original desire had been for a city that would incite and deploy unbounded new passions. In the rapidly expanding cities of postwar Europe, however, where bomb-blasted historic centers were being overrun and overshadowed by massive and depersonalized development, life was, in Situationist terms, becoming a visual and virtual embodiment of aggressive capitalism. New conceptual tools were required to identify, experiment with, or oppose these phenomena, and these devices included, most famously, the spectacle and the *dérive*.

Debord, whose career had begun with Lettrisme, and whose activities included filmmaking in addition to cultural criticism, did most to develop the concept of the spectacle. He argued that the perceptible world was being transformed into a very effective illusion, in the way that media stars become mere representations of living human beings, surrendering their "real" life to the collective fantasy of their alienated audiences. Life had become pseudolife, lived in spectacular time, by virtue of having been turned into an endless succession of commodities through the inevitable machinations of capitalism. More than an imposition of values, and more abstract even than money, the spectacle is "not just the servant of pseudo-use—it is already in itself the pseudo-use of life" (Debord, 1994). Debord's provocative condemnation, increasingly persuasive with the passage of time, is perhaps one reason for the continued pertinence of Situationist thought.

The *dérive*, although translated as a "drift," was originally an active urban exploration of environmental effects—showing its roots in Surrealist automatism. Drifting across Amsterdam, London, or Rome in small select groups, directed only by the psychic topography, and occasionally aided by walkie-talkie, the *dérive* fulfilled useful research functions for the architectural, theoretical, and political arguments being developed by Debord and others, particularly the notion of unitary urbanism. A form of "living criticism" that linked areas of the city psychogeographically, unitary urbanism operated on the level of a subversive activity. As an International Situationist editorial made clear; 'all space is occupied by the enemy. We are living under a permanent curfew. Not just the cops—the geometry. True urbanism will start by causing the occupying forces to disappear."

Ultimately, Situationists were appealing for liberty, believing that this both entailed and would bring about complete and creative human expression. Such a state is generally antithetical to classification and categories, and in turn makes a coherent Situationist style unlikely. "Nothing could have been wider off the mark," wrote Gordon Fazakerly, sometime editor of the *Situationist Times,* "had some cretin stood forth with a pictorial belief" (1992). It is not surprising, therefore, that Situationist production varies enormously in style, medium, and quality, from hermetic drifting in groups, to Hardy Strid's biting Pop collages, to publicity-grabbing guerrilla pranks. Although pavement graffiti might seem to be at odds with, for instance, Debord's disruptively challenging films, both clearly aim at a joint societal target, and both offer, in the words of Bjørn Rosendahl, "playful revelations of society's absurdity" based on the premise that life could be viewed as one gigantic "happening" (Rosendahl, 1992). Similarly, although there are considerable formal differences between complex architectural theory and the *co-ritus*—free-form multimedia community actions instigated by Jorgen Nash—both looked toward a defined moment of life concretely and deliberately constructed by the collective organization of a unitary ambiance and a game of events.

All Situationist works attempted to tamper with the conventional relationship between individual and society, and to render explicit the implied assumptions therein. Without regard to normal aesthetic considerations, their intent was effected in any way that seemed appropriate—by deflecting and subverting intended meaning through *détournement,* by an insistence on artistic collaboration, or in the form of direct intervention.

Cultural terrorism was widely practiced by Situationists, sometimes in an arena directly connected to the visual arts, as in an outrageous anti-Documenta assemblage-cum-happening inflicted on the fifth Documenta (an international art show in Kassel, Germany held about every five years); and at other times connected to ideological targets, such as the Lettriste's famous proto-Situationist assault on the Cathedral of Notre-Dame, in which a fake Dominican priest read Serge Berna's antitheist, anti-Catholic tract to a horrified and hostile congregation. Probably the most notorious scandal surrounded the 1964 decapitation of Copenhagen's well-known bronze symbol, the Little Mermaid, and the subsequent disappearance of her head. The police were led to suspect members of the Movement for a Scan-

dinavian Bauhaus Situationniste (MSBS), after Nash hinted to journalists that he knew the identity of the culprit. As a prank at the expense of the spectacle-hungry mass media, it leads a field that includes a Lettriste attack on Charlie Chaplin, Nash's dissonant disruption of the Copenhagen Opera, and, in a slightly different vein, the diversion of student funds to publish an excoriating critique of student life. Having gained control of the University's Student Union in 1966, Strasbourg Situationists used their newly acquired budget to print and distribute Mustapha Khayati's pamphlet *De la misère en milieu étudiant;* conventional authority was suitably scandalized, and the widely disseminated text became—ironically, perhaps—an instant classic.

Since the early 1960s, Situationists had been divided both by geography and, increasingly, by ideology. The conventional distinction between "artistic" northerners and "political" Parisians only foregrounds two rather conventional artist groupings at the expense of more obscure cells—particularly as, in an unofficial census published in 1974, Christopher Grey lists seventy individual Situationists from more than a dozen countries, collected into eight sections. There is evidence, however, of a predilection for theory from France contrasting with action and exhibition centered on Sweden. Calling themselves the Movement for a Scandinavian Bauhaus Situationniste, and based around a rambling farmhouse known as "Drakkabygget," which was also the title of their publication, three or four members of the "original" Situationist International, including some from Gruppe SPUR, were joined by various self-styled Situationists, who continued to produce paintings, collages, films, actions, and scandals until their 1972 attempts to overthrow the official Documenta. After a short lull, a continuously changing group including Yoshio Nakajima continued the anarchist, activist heritage of the Situationists through a proliferation of correspondence art, outrageous performance, and Jean Sellem's heroically unpopular exhibitions in the university town of Lund.

The Paris-based "Central Council," including Michélé Bernstein, Attila Kotányi, and Guy Debord, had always operated on the perimeters of the far left, and had, during the 1960s, been involved with the producers of the radical journal *Socialisme ou Barbarie.* They created an impressive legacy, largely based on their critical social theories and increasingly political philosophy, which eventually provided the inspiration for some involved in the 1968 uprisings in Paris. There is dispute about the exact nature of their connections with the worker-student riots, but there is no doubt that some aspects of the failed revolution were influenced and encouraged by their ideas, if only as upholders of an imaginative contrarian tradition. Certainly, a number of the famous Situationist slogans seen on the streets of Paris are as much distillations of William Godwin or Pierre-Joseph Proudhon as they are Surrealist imprecation: "The passion for destruction is a creative passion," wrote Mikhail

Bakunin; "Beneath the cobblestones, the beach!" answered the mob.

Along with Debord's *The Society of the Spectacle*, the most well known text from the Parisian Situationists is Vaneigem's *The Revolution of Everyday Life*. Each text acts as a critique of bourgeois consciousness, and each essays a wide variety of subject areas; from the proletariat as subject and representation, through time and history, to the decline and fall of work. Both were published in 1967, and both had been translated and freely republished in English by the early 1970s, although Debord's text is better known, and his concept of the spectacle has been subsequently popularized almost to the point of parody.

This text-based Situationism has been widely dispersed and has spawned a number of progeny on the radical fringes of cultural theory and architectural or artistic practice. It is argued that Malcolm McLaren's manipulation of the Sex Pistols, and the early moments of Punk, are natural heirs to this activism: the inherent aggression and nihilist leanings, combined with a slash-and-paste approach to production, give credence to this idea and thus place Punk in the widening wake of anti-art.

The legacy of the Situationists is as anti-aesthetic as the original, and even more diffracted. In the 1970s and 1980s, their ideas were spread largely through the blossoming of live art forms; through small press publications—often without copyright; and through international correspondence art circuits, which operated as a kind of World Wide Web using kitchen-table technology. Situationist activities continue to diversify into—among other things—direct political activism, legally questionable performance, postmodern projects to attack conventional culture, poetic terrorism, fiction, and, increasingly, academies, where the "crime" of categorizing the revolution is undertaken with sardonic humor.

Situationists might be seen as among the last heroes of modernity, cast into the paradoxical role of the antihero. Disrupting and distorting the comfortable hierarchy of the spectacle, and unmasking the "natural" order of culture, they have, despite—or because of—their apparent authenticity, assumed the mantle of the romantic rebel, a symbol whose value as entertainment is in inverse proportion to its revolutionary significance. On the other hand, when viewed as standard-bearers of the ancient impulse to refuse authority, to disobey, to turn, turn, and turn again, Situationists should not be dismissed. Despite naive, 1960s assumptions, despite turgid nit-picking tracts and petty personality contests magnified into ideological tirades, the construction of situations remains as a valuable step toward individuality, spontaneity, and finally, freedom.

[*See also* Anti-Art; *and* Installation Art.]

BIBLIOGRAPHY

Bernstein, Michéle. "In Praise of Pinot Gallizio" (1958). Translated by John Shepley. In *Guy Debord and the Internationale Situationniste*, special issue edited by Thomas F. McDonough. *October* 79 (Winter 1997): 93–94.

Debord, Guy. *La société du spectacle*. Paris, 1967. Translated by Donald Nicholson-Smith as *The Society of the Spectacle* (New York, 1994).

Fazakerly, Gordon. "The Ferry Boat." In *Bauhaus Situationist*, special issue edited by Jean Sellem. *Lund Art Press* 2.3 (1992): 131–133.

Gray, John. *Action Art: A Bibliography of Artists' Performance from Futurism to Fluxus and Beyond*. Westport, Conn., 1993.

Home, Stewart. *The Assault on Culture: Utopian Currents from Lettrisme to Class War*. London, 1988.

Knabb, Ken, ed. *Situationist International Anthology*. Berkeley, 1981.

Kotányi, Attila, and Raoul Vaneigem. "Unitary Urbanism." Translated by Christopher Grey in *Leaving the Twentieth Century: The Incomplete Work of the Situationist International*. London, 1974.

Lefebvre, Henri. *Critique de la vie quotidienne*. 3 vols. Paris, 1947–1981. Volume 1 translated by John Moore as *Critique of Everyday Life* (London and New York, 1991).

Marcus, Greil. *Lipstick Traces: A Secret History of the Twentieth Century*. Cambridge, Mass., 1989.

Rosendahl, Bjorn. "Bauhaus Situationist in Sweden: A Retrospective." In *Bauhaus Situationist*, special issue edited by Jean Sellem. *Lund Art Press* 2.3 (1992): 23–27.

Sellem, Jean. *Hardy Strid's Work and Swedish Modernism in Art from 1935 to 1980*. Munich, 1981.

Stokvis, Willemijn. *Cobra: An International Movement in Art after the Second World War*. Translated by J. C. T. Voorthuis. New York, 1988.

Vaneigem, Raoul. *Traité de savoir-vivre à l'usage des jeunes générations*. Paris 1967. Translated by John Fullerton and Paul Sieverking as *The Revolution of Everyday Life* (London, 1972). Also translated by Donald Nicholson-Smith (2d ed., Seattle, 1994).

SIMON ANDERSON

SMITH, ADAM (1723–1790), Scottish economist. Smith was born in Kirkcaldy, Scotland, and educated at the Universities of Glasgow and Oxford. In 1751, he became professor, first of logic and then of moral philosophy, at Glasgow. He resigned in 1764 to travel abroad as a private tutor to the young Duke of Buccleuch, and he returned to Scotland in 1767. Between 1773 and 1776, he advised the government in London on economic matters, and returned to Edinburgh in 1778 as a commissioner for customers. The two major books he published during his lifetime were *The Theory of Moral Sentiments* (1759), and *An Inquiry into the Nature and Causes of the Wealth of Nations* (1776). His collected works and correspondence were published only in 1976, and include lectures on rhetoric and jurisprudence, and various essays on philosophical subjects.

Smith wrote no comprehensive theory of aesthetics, or "criticism," as it was typically called, and most of his remarks are incidental to some other discussion, such as those on morality or effective communication. But Smith himself read widely, even by the standards of the day, took part in a number of literary and artistic activities, and wrote one, probably late, essay on imitation. It has to be conceded that Smith's remarks on the arts had almost no influence on later writers.

Like his close friend David Hume, he was much influenced by the writings of the abbé Jean-Baptiste Du Bos, whose *Réflexions critiques sur la poésie et sur la peinture* first appeared in 1719. Smith agreed with the view that poetry is the first form of human discourse, although both dancing and primitive music may predate it as pleasurable social activities. The "fine arts" develop later, on the basis of the leisure, wealth, and political stability of self-sufficient communities.

Smith said little about the three aesthetic issues that most occupied his contemporaries: the nature of beauty, taste, and critical judgment. But, in his lectures on rhetoric, he wrote at length on kinds of effective communication, and elsewhere on ways in which works of art represent their "subjects" and convey their meaning to audiences. Smith developed Hume's emphasis on the need to identify the proper contexts for critical judgment, by arguing that the overriding concern is with the meaning of works; hence, the very high intellectual pleasure that accompanies sensual pleasure in the arts. Like Hume, Smith derives his views mainly from reflection on literature, and his observations on painting and the "decorative arts" ignore the special character of the medium. He does, however, recognize the unique expressive and nonrepresentational character of music.

For Smith, if the main purpose of history is instruction, that of epic or romance is entertainment; but the fundamental difference between them lies in the fictionality of the latter's stories. Moral instruction requires that narrated facts be real, because the moral worth of actions depends on the worth of the agent's motives; the worth of art depends crucially on its effects. Poetic license is allowed to poets only because their task is to amuse. Smith agrees with Hume that utility is one of the main sources of beauty, but it is usually a derivative rather than a fundamental source. In the field of morality, as elsewhere, the aesthetic dimension can be accorded illicit priority.

In the 1750s, the nature of taste was extensively discussed in Edinburgh by philosophers such as Smith, Hume, Alexander Gerard, Lord Kames, and the painter Allan Ramsay. In *The Theory of Moral Sentiments* (part 5), Smith argued that two related principles, fashion and custom, influence all judgments concerning beauty. Poetry, music, and architecture are just as subject to their influence as dress and furniture. Smith implicitly links such views with the notions of style and tradition, emphasized by later theorists. He holds that however dominant a fashion becomes, it is entirely contingent which styles become accepted as fitting and appropriate.

Smith's most sustained thinking about problems in aesthetics occurs in an incomplete essay on "imitation," much of which was probably written in the 1780s (in Smith, *Essays on Philosophical Subjects*, 1980). He is mainly interested in how both expressive and cognitive meaning are conveyed and recognized in the different mediums of the various arts. Like most of his contemporaries, he used the term *imitation* to cover any kind of what might be called "representation,"

whether natural or symbolic; and he explicitly linked the notions of imitation, representation, resemblance, correspondence, and expression, sometimes using them interchangeably.

Some of the viewer's pleasure in the imitative arts may derive from the skills exercised in the medium, but admiration for difficulties overcome ought not to be carried over into admiration of a work's content; meaning should always be clear, however recalcitrant the medium in which it is expressed. The primary burden is on the artist to be perspicuous, and spectators, for Smith, carry less responsibility for effort and attention than they do for Hume. In urging that even inexpert spectators derive pleasure from, and achieve modest understanding of, at least the best works, Smith forgets to mention his earlier insight that everyone has to learn a repertoire of responses in a familiar tradition and culture. He also reflects on the mutual advantages of juxtaposing arts in different media, such as painting and sculpture. He here conflates two issues, however, namely, the overall harmony of different works in a setting, where judgment focuses on the whole effect, and the influence of one work on another when each is considered singly.

Music and dancing are the most natural pleasures, Smith holds, but, in its power to express a meaning with clarity and distinctness, dancing is superior to music, and poetry to dancing. He moves toward a distinction between the transitive and intransitive sense of expression; that is, between a view that music elicits response because it both expresses emotion and implants it, possibly in a reduced and transformed state, in a listener, and the view that the expressive character of unaccompanied instrumental music is in the music itself. Such music implants its moods by virtue of one's mental capacity to attend to, and remember, the sequence and character of its sounds.

BIBLIOGRAPHY

Works by Smith

The Glasgow Edition of the Works and Correspondence of Adam Smith. 6 vols. Oxford, 1976–1983. Consists of vol. 1, *The Theory of Moral Sentiments*; vol. 2, *An Inquiry into the Nature and Causes of the Wealth of Nations*; vol. 3, *Essays on Philosophical Subjects*; vol. 4, *Lectures on Rhetoric and Belles Lettres*; vol. 5, *Lectures on Jurisprudence*; vol. 6, *Correspondence.*

Other Sources

Avison, Charles. *An Essay on Musical Expression.* London, 1752.
Bonar, James. *A Catalogue of the Library of Adam Smith.* 2d ed. London, 1932.
Dubos, Jean-Baptiste. *Réflexions critiques sur la poésie et sur la peinture.* Paris, 1719.
Gerard, Alexander. *An Essay on Taste.* Edinburgh, 1759.
Hume, David. "Of the Standard of Taste." In *Four Dissertations,* pp. 203–240. London, 1757.
Jones, Peter. *Hume's Sentiments: Their Ciceronian and French Context.* Edinburgh, 1982.

Jones, Peter. "The Aesthetics of Adam Smith." In *Adam Smith Reviewed,* edited by Peter Jones and Andrew Skinner, pp. 56–78. Edinburgh, 1992.

Jones, Peter. "Hume's Literary and Aesthetic Theory." In *The Cambridge Companion to Hume,* edited by David Fate Norton. Cambridge and New York, 1993.

Ramsay, Allan, Jr. "A Dialogue on Taste." In *The Investigator,* 2d ed., pp. 1–77. London, 1762.

Richardson, Jonathan. *An Essay on the Theory of Painting.* London, 1715.

Ross, Ian Simpson. *The Life of Adam Smith.* Oxford, 1995.

PETER JONES

SOCIOLOGY OF ART. Only a few decades ago, a survey of the sociology of art would have begun and ended with contentiously worded assertions about the relations of the arts and society. A number of scholars would have affirmed that art mirrors society, but there consensus would end. Whereas some have insisted that art reflects societal production relationships, serving as an ideological tool to support dominant groups, others, equally positively, would have maintained that art—at least great art, the rest not being worthy of attention—is an autonomous sphere, capable of surmounting material constraints, that reaches for higher values, or presages cultural and societal trends. Deriving from the materialist orientation of Karl Marx, who actually wrote little about art, it provides the foundation of Arnold Hauser's massive analysis of artistic creativity through the ages, *The Social History of Art.* Of the many anti-Marxist variants on the idea that art mirrors society, the one elaborated by Pitirim Sorokin in an equally massive work viewed art as representative of the spirit of its age.

Other social theorists, such as Émile Durkheim, have thought of art as a substitute religion, a secularized spirituality of emotional support or constraint for individuals, which helps to hold society together. For Max Weber, on the contrary, in an increasingly rationalized modern world the aesthetic sphere may, under certain conditions, foster a discourse that competes with the ethical sphere of society (Weber, 1946, pp. 340–342).

As different as they are, these interpretations of the relations of the arts and society aim to unearth hidden postulates of art in relation to broad social structural processes. Whether from the standpoint of Marxist macrostructural analysis, anti-Marxist idealist perspectives, or those that look on art as a quasi religion, these universalizing conceptions of art represent a western European, hierarchicizing scheme of cultural classification. In particular, its presumption of an aesthetic domain analytically divorced from society is questionable and, in any case, idiosyncratic. Work by anthropologists, who see art as a cultural system that needs to be understood according to its cultural context, shows the inadequacy of such assumptions (Geertz, 1983).

Even though these perspectives continue to underlie some of the current analyses of the arts, in practice they have given way to different concerns and questions. Regardless of the political or intellectual stance of individual scholars today, their ambitions are far more modest. Sorokin embraced twenty-five hundred years of civilization, and Hauser's study starts from the even earlier point of prehistoric cave painting, and both extended their discussion to include contemporary artists. Today's social analysts rarely undertake to encompass such magisterial breadth. This does not necessarily entail a narrowing of vision, however, because the types of art that contemporary researchers consider worthy of analysis are far more varied than what their predecessors documented. Neither Hauser nor Sorokin paid much attention to non-Western civilizations, and barely any at all to primitive and folk forms and, except disparagingly, commercial art and entertainment (Hauser, 1982). Neither considered the absence of women artists as a question to be examined. Even within the domain of fine art, both shared a largely unexamined, but generally unfavorable, opinion of avant-garde art. Finally, like most of their more aesthetically oriented peers, although they dealt with changing genres and stylistic modes, they accepted extant categories of art as unproblematic givens, without considering that other forms of expression might be contenders for inclusion in the aesthetic field. Yet, beyond their ambitious reach, what is remarkable about the Hauser and Sorokin studies is that they were exceptional: on the whole, social scientists gave short shrift to the subject of art.

More recently, however, culture and the arts have become increasingly visible in sociological publications (Peterson, 1976; Becker, 1982; Crane, 1987; Balfe, 1993), disciplinary recognition, and professional organizations, both in the United States and elsewhere (Zolberg, 1990). This essay begins by considering the place that this field has occupied in sociology, and suggesting why it has changed. It examines developments within sociology itself, and trends exogenous to it that impinge on its composition. Work in the sociology of art today is characterized by four trends. First, sociologists elaborate the roles of the institutions and processes that give rise to or constrain the emergence of artworks. Second, they analyze the artistic practice of creators, and patterns of appreciation and acquisition of patrons and collectors. Third, they investigate degrees of access of new and different publics to the arts, and the role of the arts in status reproduction. Fourth, most radically, some scholars call into question the very nature of the arts, arguing that their definition as art needs to be understood not as self-evident, but as a social construction that requires analysis.

Art: In the Periphery of Sociology. Aside from literary and aesthetic scholars who touched lightly on the social contexts or cultural history surrounding the arts, in the first half of the twentieth century the sociology of art was largely the concern of a few European, and even fewer American, scholars. Among Europeans, a single major work by Weber (1958) dealt directly with a specific art form—music—as a case of his theory concerning the cultural rationalization in the West. Durkheim placed what he termed aesthetic sociology into the matrix of the sociology that he was trying to establish, but only under the residual rubric *divers,* and did no study of it himself (Zolberg, 1990, p. 38). Only Georg Simmel wrote frequently about the arts, though less as a social scientist than as a literary and art critic, philosopher, or fashionable essayist (Coser, 1965).

Even though American sociology had its origins in, and continued to look toward, European theoretical formulations, by the end of World War II, with the destruction or undermining of much European scholarship by totalitarian regimes, or under their military occupation, American sociology, along with American science more generally, had become the most dynamic and expansive in the world. This growth was a counterpart to the prominence of the United States on the international scene as the champion of Western humanist values during the war and defender of freedom during the cold war.

American social-scientific scholarship, however, had hardly acknowledged the arts as a legitimate object of study. This stance had its nearly symmetrical correlative in the opposing and equally intransigent stance on the part of humanist scholarship, including literature, aesthetics, art theory, musicology, cultural history, toward what seemed the threat of the social sciences. The foundations for this antagonism are situated at least as much in scholarly, institutionally strategic, and political domains as in intellectual considerations. The increasing preeminence of the exact sciences during and after the war had drawn many social scientists to adopt the presuppositions, techniques, and methodologies of these disciplines, an orientation that cast a shadow over humanist subjects and qualitative interpretive methods. Still, as higher education was expanded, despite official emphasis on the exact sciences, the social sciences and the humanities were expanded as well. Far from being only an American phenomenon, universities swelled in most European countries as well, providing structural conditions in which both scientific and humanist fields might flourish. Although the legacy of earlier misgiving persists, it has become considerably muted because of changes in both sets of disciplines that have produced convergences in their orientations (Zolberg, 1990).

In the United States, that the arts were studied at all had been largely the result of émigré scholars, especially members of the Frankfurt School such as Theodor Adorno (1976). Straddling the intersection of the humanities and social science, these exiles remained marginal to the mainstream, were treated as outsiders, and saw themselves in that light (Wilson, 1964, p. v). This marginality was enhanced by the Marxist orientation to which some adhered, combined more generally with their critical views on American sociology's scientistic empiricism and, in many cases, contempt for what they took to be its intellectual shallowness (Zolberg, 1990, p. 72). They deplored the development of mass society and culture and its impact on individuals and intellectual life. Their insistence on a value-laden stance and rejection of what they regarded as a fictive scientific objectivity reinforced their exclusion from the academic mainstream of sociology. Nevertheless, some of them attracted a following of American scholars, intrigued by their inquiry, in the spheres of both high culture and commercial culture.

Foundations for a New Social Study of the Arts. Although in many countries a considerable body of scholarship was devoted to aesthetics, it was only in the post–World War II period that an autonomous field of sociology of art distinct from philosophy, history, or criticism materialized. This was the case in France, as Raymonde Moulin (1986, p. xiv) has observed, where, through the efforts of Pierre Bourdieu and his associates (1990; 1984) and of Moulin herself (1986; 1992), intellectual leadership and institutional support led to the development of new perspectives. German philosophical, musicological, and art-historical scholarship continued to straddle the social domain, as successors to the Frankfurt School tradition for whom the arts, both fine and commercial, were foci of study. English literary and historical scholarship infused Raymond Williams's (1981) social analysis of what he saw as the hegemonic role of the arts, and underpinned the development of British culture studies. In the United States, the multifaceted challenge to the university as an agent of government policy, especially the Vietnam War, and "normal" sociology in particular, challenged what was seen as scientistic biases of the social sciences.

Simultaneously, the art world itself was undergoing transformations that included an enormous increase of the numbers of aspiring artists, a shift to New York as the center of the international art market, initiation by the national government of public subsidies for the arts, and growth of private foundation support (Crane, 1987). The arts themselves exploded their boundaries, as artists introduced new media, broke the barriers separating genres, and reversed conventional hierarchical arrangements. The process, begun earlier in the century when Marcel Duchamp gathered (or invented) "found objects"—ceramic urinals, snow shovels, bicycle wheels—"assisted" them to the status of art by supplying them with titles and an (alleged) artist's signature, had shaken standard conceptions. With renewed interest in his (and other Dadaists') innovations, artists and composers began routinely to wreak havoc with artistic tradition.

John Cage serves as archetype of this revival in the post–World War II period. Cage composed music on the basis of throwing *Yi jing* sticks, thus creating aleatory music—music by chance. He organized open-air concerts to which the audience was invited to bring transistor radios and turn them on as loudly as possible to any station they wished, thus producing the "music." In this way, he extended to new media the innovations of the literary Dadaist Tristan Tzara, who wrote poetry by tossing about printed words that he had clipped from newspapers, and which he then pasted together in whatever way they fell (Zolberg, 1990).

It may be argued that this mayhem developed in response to the magnified consumerism of late-capitalist society. This is not a trivial idea—economics rarely is trivial—but it does not explain everything, either in sociology or in the arts. The entry of large numbers of aspiring artists into the avant-garde art world, and the growth of foundation, corporate, and government support for the arts, must be included in the economic expansion (Crane, 1987). The United States during this period offered an unprecedented hospitable environment for social scientists interested in culture and the arts—in relation to consumerism, as a right of citizenship, and in creative innovation. Aside from a few articles, no major sociological works had increased the small pre-1950 bookshelf. On the basis of what had become "normal sociology" of the 1950s and 1960s, it would have been difficult to predict that an efflorescence in the sociology of art was in the offing.

An indication of this trend appeared in the exploratory work *The Arts in Society* (1964) by Robert Wilson, who wrote and compiled a number of essays on aspects of the arts in society. Justifying his choices by taking as his point of departure the fairly orthodox idea that artists could "often see what is going on in the society or the psyche a good bit earlier than other men do" (1964, p. vi), and unabashedly "concerned with the products and producers of high culture," Wilson's own selections analyze the role of the artist, poet, composer, and dancer. Essays by others included in the book focus on artworks, writers, and literary personages as exemplars of their social milieus (Lowenthal; Speier). Still others analyze the effects of institutional arrangements on artistic practice (White and White; Graña). Opting for high culture, the essayists pay little attention to popular or mass culture. In what must be seen as a paean to democratic pluralism, and a riposte to the Frankfurt School (and other) attacks on mass society, Edward Shils's essay "The High Culture of the Age" argues that far from deteriorating (ibid., p. 321), high culture is enriched by expanding education to make increasingly sophisticated publics, that enlarging the markets for art liberates the artist from the trammels of private patronage.

Only a few years later, another collection of essays heralded an "institutional" approach that examines the functions of the arts in meeting human needs, and maintaining social stability (Albrecht, Barnett, and Griff, 1970). The editors included studies on the relationship of forms and styles to various social institutions; artists' careers and their interactions in a variety of artistic milieus; distribution and reward systems; the roles of critics, dealers, and the public in recognizing artists and works. Despite its structural-functionalist orientation, dominated by the idea of art as an integrative force to maintain the social system and meet emotional needs, the editors were generously open to divergent views that encompassed even Marxian analysts such as Lucien Goldmann (pp. 582–609). Yet, these essays also demonstrated the infancy of the field: of the authors represented, only one fourth were actually sociologists, whereas the rest were in anthropology, comparative literature, history, and art history, or were practicing artists, painters, dancers, and writers. The happy result of this *omnium gatherum* was that Albrecht and his coauthors created an American field that integrated European contributions and was strongly cross-disciplinary, ranging over the fine arts, classical and contemporary, as well as folk art, music, dance, and literature, and their corresponding institutional grounding.

A Sociological Space for Art—Current Trends. Ever-greater diversity has become the hallmark of the sociological study of culture and the arts today. Methodological approaches range from empiricism that relies on quantitative tools to analyze masses of available data, such as the degree of access to cultural resources (Blau, 1988), to survey data of art-world practices and audience studies (Gans, 1975). Equally empirical, but based on microscopic observation and qualitative analysis of cultural practices, is the ethnography of Howard S. Becker's *Art Worlds* (1982). Historical and semiotic perspectives have been imported from literary analysis into the social studies. Even more striking is that the range of works and art forms investigated has burgeoned and includes the commercial domain. But, rather than seconding Shils's triumphalism, sociologists have recognized that the arts may be a means to exclude certain classes of aspiring artists, such as women and racial minorities, from what were defined as the most distinguishing and distinguished art forms (Bourdieu, 1984).

The most distinctive American school of sociology has been a synthesis of scattered approaches to the social study of science, religion, and work, brought together under the rubric of the "production of culture" (Peterson, 1976). Defining culture in a broad sense that allied it to anthropology—comprising art, popular culture, science, religion, and symbols, Richard Peterson urges that the questions broached should themselves determine the use of synchronic or diachronic modes according to their appropriateness. Proponents of this approach considered how cultural products were constituted, accentuating the effects of institutional and structural arrangements, both as facilitators of or impediments to creation. Characteristically, they reject macrosociological ambitions in favor of granting priority to middle-range and microscopic levels of analysis that, they believe, more effectively reveal the impact of laws, culture industry practices, and gatekeepers on the form and content of artworks.

Peterson also championed a "genetic" perspective, which treats culture as the "code by which social structures reproduce themselves" as the foundation for understanding how culture is "received" by individuals bearing different social characteristics. This involves a focus on the role of family, education, media, and other enculturating institutions and agencies that, at the time, was not being actively pursued by most American sociologists in relation to the arts. Their approach was considerably expanded through their intermingling with European and non-Western scholarship.

Institutions and processes. The role of certain institutions, such as official academies and government agencies or ministries, in providing support for artistic creation or, conversely, foiling it has been decried by critics and artists since their establishment. However, the pioneering sociological study by Harrison White and Cynthia White of the French painting world in the nineteenth century (1965) was one of the first to analyze systematically the changing structure of opportunity that the French Academy provided for artists. The Whites reconstructed quantitative data to show how the Academy's recruitment, educational, and marketing functions succeeded in drawing an increasing number of applicants to what was an honorable and lucrative profession. But the Academy's very success caused it to be overwhelmed by aspirants, to the point that both would-be artists and even already successful academicians had to turn to art dealers who had been cultivating a new middle-class clientele in order to sell their works. As this market expanded, new art styles, such as Impressionism, came to a prominence that the Academy's conservatism had begrudged them.

A more recent study of how academies selected among those allowed entry, and the implications for artists, was carried out by Gladys Engel Lang and Kurt Lang (1990). Focusing on the revival of etching as an art form in the nineteenth century, they show how the exclusion, or severe limitation, of women as students and members by most European academies impeded their entry into the highly regarded world of oil painting. Diverted to other, lesser media, such as etching and watercolor, whose professional organizations were newer and less restrictive, aspiring women artists were able to gain entry, and a measure of status and recognition.

Research on French art institutions has continued to thrive with the work of Moulin (1992) on the interplay among art museums, the art market, and government policy in providing official recognition for innovative art. In the United States, a system in which the national government's support for the arts is far more limited, and declining, the study of the effect of institutions on the arts has advanced under the leadership of Paul DiMaggio (1986). In fact, with the postwar growth of government subsidies in many countries, the effects of governmental policies are being investigated in other countries as well. Following the lead of Bour-

dieu and his associates (Bourdieu et al., 1990), English researchers have examined changing cultural institutions, especially museums, in representing the arts to new publics (Lumley, 1988), as have Dutch sociologists (Gubbels and Van Hemel, 1993).

Artistic practices and worlds of art. Inside the creative processes themselves, a major contribution to understanding how the arts are constituted was Becker's *Art Worlds* (1982). By adapting a "sociology of work" approach to study what is customarily viewed as unique creations of individual geniuses, Becker starts from the premise that making art is not qualitatively different from other social activities. Controversially, he sets out the convincing argument that, far from being an individual act, the making of art needs to be understood as a collective process, in which interactions among participants, of whom the named artist is only one, result in in the production of "artworks." The other participants—support personnel—may range from assistants to servants, to managers or agents, critics, buyers, and organizations.

Taking into account the size and complexity of modern societies, Becker does not reduce the arts to a single art world. Instead, he argues that art making is constituted in four principal art worlds, each characterized by a particular style of working, as based on its own conventions. Thus, the Integrated Professional artist is trained according to the conventions of an art form such as music, painting, and dance, within the domain of either high culture or commercial culture. The Maverick is also trained according to those conventions, but refuses to abide by them, preferring risk of isolation and failure in order to innovate and go his own way. The Folk Artist works within conventions traditional in his community's lore. Finally, outside of actual constituted art worlds, the least integrated is the Naive artist, untrained in art and following an internal urging, whose works represent idiosyncratic experiences that may include religious symbolism, representations of personal remembrances, or even aberrations and madness. Whereas the other art worlds have ties to regular art-world institutions or practitioners, or make it their goal to develop ties to them, Naive artists must be "discovered" by others, or else remain unknown.

Internal structures among informal groups of creative artists (or scientists) and their ties to their societal context have been analyzed by Charles Kadushin (in Peterson, 1976, pp. 107–122). His framework highlights circles within, and networks of, communications to external supporters. In his inquiry into the rise of the New York school of Abstract Expressionism, he shows how the circles of adherents promoted creativity *against* conventional forms, providing mutual support in the face of rejection by established art-world gatekeepers. Lacking channels for entrée to galleries or prestigious institutions, these mavericks and their supporters initiated networks of relationships to important external agents, media, and organizations, through which they eventually achieved recognition. In their turn, however, they became increasingly reserved about accepting newcomers into their midst, thus provoking the creation of competing circles.

Art and its publics: Status reproduction and taste. One of the most misleading adages of all time must be "de gustibus non disputandum est." In fact, taste is always being disputed. Thorstein Veblen was one of the first social scientists to interpret the symbolic meanings of expressed taste in his analysis of leisure class behavior during the Gilded Age (Veblen, 1899). Approximately a half century later, Russell Lynes published his classification of high-, middle-, and lowbrow taste preferences, in which artworks and fashion are taken as status markers (Lynes, 1954). On the basis of writings by these and other astute spectators, a number of sociologists have noted that taste, in art, design, and fashion, may be revealing of one's social standing. Far from viewing taste as trivial, purely personal, and difficult to fathom because it is nonrational, sociologists such as Bourdieu contend that taste is social in its formation, symbolic in its expression, and has social consequences for individuals and social institutions.

In his pioneering work on the taste cultures of American consumers, Herbert Gans (1974) treated the arts as a right of democratic choice. Contrary to the derision heaped on those of low educational level, living in rural areas or in relative poverty, for preferring popular, commercial art forms (pop music, country and western, gospel), Gans challenged both the government and commercial media to educate people to appreciate high cultural forms, and make them accessible, either directly or through radio or other media. If these institutions, agencies, and firms do not provide these cultural forms, he argued, they should abandon the judgmental manner that turns the "wrong" taste into a weapon of scorn against the culturally deprived.

Going beyond the idea of taste as a "right" of consumerism, Bourdieu (1984) takes observations of social differences in artistic taste to a more complex level of analysis. He shows the linkages among taste, symbolic status, and the mechanisms by which they tend to reproduce existing status hierarchies in society at large, from generation to generation. Treating taste as an aspect of the individual's cultural baggage, a durably structured behavioral orientation whose origin stems from early childhood and schooling, Bourdieu employs a variety of methods, quantitative and ethnographic, to show how taste functions as a form of capital to crystallize inequalities based on economic and social advantages or disadvantages. In this way, taste becomes a badge of social honor or scorn, signaling to influential groups that some are more acceptable than others.

English sociologists of culture have been pursuing cultural reproduction from a comparable standpoint. Although not as a rule using large surveys of taste, many have analyzed the content and uses of aesthetic culture, both high

and popular. Williams (1981), beginning from a Marxian perspective, and moving between literary or film criticism and academic life, was a major influence on what became the field of Culture Studies. Beyond the simple base-superstructure correspondence of Marxism, in which culture is conceived as merely epiphenomenal to existing production relationships, Williams and his followers, including Stuart Hall (1980) and Janet Wolff (1993), among many others, conceived of culture as a constitutive practice in the construction of social meanings. They have tried to overcome the prevailing, decontextualized, literary-critical mode of analysis by elucidating the relations between, on the one hand, cultural images, objects, and practices, and, on the other, social institutions and processes. Scholars associated with the Birmingham Centre for Contemporary Cultural Studies analyzed many aspects of British youth subcultures and their relationship to new artistic styles.

Is taste a simple offshoot of socioeconomic status, a device of social reproduction? Or is the connection more complex? It would be misleading to suggest that there is complete agreement among sociologists about how taste and status are related, and with what consequences. Many find it essential to take into account observable changes in social stratification patterns, and the conditions of their expression. Whereas Bourdieu attributes expertise in manipulating symbolic capital through complex codes available in the lore of dominant class fractions, David Halle (1994), who has studied the collection and display of art *inside* of people's homes, argues differently. His interviews with elite collectors of abstract art reveal that they have little understanding of the works in their own homes, which are nearly as esoteric for them as for nonelites. In fact, Halle finds widespread sharing of taste across status lines, especially noting a nearly universal and, it appears, similar mode of appreciation of the landscape genre. Moreover, although educational level is an important enabler of high-culture taste, ethnicity and race play important roles in how people select works for the home, in contrast to their responses to questionnaires administered in public spaces.

Beyond the linkage established by Bourdieu, Gans, Lynes, and other investigators between social status and social class, or educational attainment, others find that our conception of social status needs to incorporate gender, race, and ethnicity in order to take into account both the volume and the variety of preferences that appear to vary among social classes. In studies of how musical tastes are related to occupational status, Peterson and Simkus (1992) suggest that although classical music continues to be a status marker for high-status occupational groups, more striking is the great breadth of their preference for a variety of musics. Thus, whereas fewer than a third of holders of prestigious occupations say that they like classical music best, surprisingly, a somewhat larger proportion of such respondents prefer country-and-western music to grand opera. What is more distinguishing is that high-status individuals participate in more cultural activities and enjoy a wider range of music than do those of lesser status. As Peterson and Simkus put it, they are "omnivores," as opposed to less elite groups, whose limited range of taste in music makes them "univores" (1992, pp. 152–186).

But what is art? In the past, scholars investigating the place of the arts in society have taken for granted the categories of art conventionally agreed to by art-world participants, but in recent times certain sociologists have turned their attention to how art classifications are constructed. Like the sociologist of science, Bruno Latour (1987), who questions the processes by which certain frameworks of analysis, categories, and findings come to be incorporated into the scientific canon, some see even more plausible reasons for interrogating how artistic canons are established. Art is a stake in the arena of competition that pervades much of social life, as Bourdieu contends, not only for artists themselves, but for their supporters, patrons, collectors, and dealers, and for the writers and scholars who compose the art worlds in which they exist.

Under pressure from potential publics, market forces, including collectors, and political action, and in light of the openness of the fine arts to new media, existing cultural institutions, such as art museums, are exhibiting works previously excluded from consideration as art. Whereas previously, for example, African carvings were largely consigned to ethnological collections, their entry into art museums has taken the form of an upward spiral; art of the insane has attained high market value (Anne E. Bowler, in Zolberg and Cherbo, 1997); and women artists are gaining a level of recognition that had routinely been denied them (Zolberg and Cherbo, 1997). In the worlds of culture industry as well, new musical forms such as rock-and-roll and rap have emerged from the interplay of business developments, technological innovations, and enacted statutes in such fields as copyright law, which set the parameters for works to come to public attention (Ennis, 1992, pp. 5–7).

Prospects. By now the study of culture and the arts has become a lively sociological arena in the United States, as it had already been in much of Europe. No longer a stepchild of the *serious* business of sociologists, the arts are, if not central, then at least a legitimate, as opposed to a frivolous, subject. This flowering has come about despite a traditional anti-aesthetic orientation in American social science, and, until recently, relative retarded development of much contemporary European social science. Despite this change, the position of the arts in the social-science disciplines is likely to remain tenuous, and requires renewed justification as an intellectual enterprise. The reasons for this have to do with both the intellectual outlooks that have become embedded in understandings of the arts and the social structures of their creation—or "production."

First, the crux of the arts since the Renaissance has been the artist as an individual, a tradition of several centuries that emphasizes the uniqueness of the actor and the work he (rarely, she) created. Although the notion of such an individual agent is relatively compatible with the discipline of psychology, it is less easily reconciled with the collectivist understanding of behavior by sociology. This perception underlies the view of art as a collective process (Becker, 1982) and sociologists' emphasis on the production, rather than creation of culture. Retaining or reinserting the individual artist as agent has both ethical importance, because it implies respect for the autonomy of the individual, and intellectual validity in a discipline that would easily reduce art to an outcome of overly general structures and processes.

A second reason, and one related to this disciplinary tradition, surrounds that of aesthetic judgment. This presents even more arduous barriers for sociologists, for whom scientific objectivity pervades their disciplinary orientation. But aesthetic judgment is problematic for literary and humanist scholars, many of whom avoid it. In part, this is because of the objective and scientific turn that humanist studies have taken, one of whose consequences is that categories of value are too deeply embedded in society to be disaggregated from it. Sociologists are only too aware of how contaminated our judgments of most things are, and the expanded notion of art today does not render evaluation any easier.

Finally, the extraordinary transformation of the international arena in recent years requires that scholarship move more explicitly outside of the scholarly world and into the domain of artists and policymakers. Knowledge of their functioning is essential if we are to grasp the future relationships of the arts and society in a world that brings together what had been largely national concerns. The arts are no longer understandable in terms of one society alone (if that was ever the case), because few societies are either homogeneous or sealed off from other geographic, national, or societal units. Thus, whereas it may still be possible to study such issues as arts censorship in the context of a single society, it is more likely that political transformations open the door to new conflicts, as a global phenomenon.

Related to globalization, a second set of factors that militates against retaining the single society as the primary unit of analysis stems from the opportunities offered by technological innovations such as developments in cyberspace and computer technology. Not only do they permit new forms of artistic expression, but they also enhance attempts to evade control over art content. Providing new avenues for artistic dissemination, they also substitute for direct contact with the storehouses of art, museums. These developments suggest that this contextual metamorphosis will set the parameters of the next phase of studies in the sociology of the arts.

[*See also* Art Market; Art World; Artist; Bourdieu; Cultural Studies; Institutional Theory of Art; Mannheim; Marxism; Museums; Politics and Aesthetics; Popular Culture; Simmel; *and* Taste.]

BIBLIOGRAPHY

Adorno, Theodor W. *Introduction to the Sociology of Music* (1962). Translated by E. B. Ashton. New York, 1976.

Albrecht, Milton C., James H. Barnett, and Mason Griff, eds. *The Sociology of Art and Literature: A Reader.* New York, 1970.

Balfe, Judith Huggins, ed. *Paying the Piper: Causes and Consequences of Art Patronage.* Urbana, 1993.

Becker, Howard S. *Art Worlds.* Berkeley, 1982.

Blau, Judith R. *The Shape of Culture.* Cambridge and New York, 1988.

Bourdieu, Pierre. *Distinction: A Social Critique of the Judgement of Taste* (1979). Translated by Richard Nice. Cambridge, Mass., 1984.

Bourdieu, Pierre, Alain Darbel, and Dominique Schnapper. *The Love of Art: European Art Museums and Their Public* (1969). Translated by Caroline Beattie and Nick Merriman. Stanford, Calif., 1990.

Coser, Lewis, ed. *Georg Simmel.* Englewood Cliffs, N.J., 1965.

Crane, Diana. *The Transformation of the Avant-Garde: The New York Art World, 1940–1985.* Chicago, 1987.

DiMaggio, Paul J. *Nonprofit Enterprise in the Arts: Studies in Mission and Constraint.* New York and Oxford, 1986.

Durkheim, Émile. *The Elementary Forms of the Religious Life* (1912). Translated by Joseph Ward Swain. New York, 1965.

Ennis, Philip H. *The Seventh Stream: The Emergence of Rocknroll in American Popular Music.* Hanover, N.H., 1992.

Gans, Herbert J. *Popular Culture and High Culture: An Analysis and Evaluation of Taste.* New York, 1975.

Geertz, Clifford. *Local Knowledge: Further Essays in Interpretive Anthropology.* New York, 1983.

Gubbels, Truus, and Annemoon Van Hemel, eds. *Art Museums and the Price of Success.* Amsterdam, 1993.

Hall, Stuart. "Cultural Studies and the Centre: Some Problematics and Problems." In *Culture, Media, Language: Working Papers in Cultural Studies, 1972–1979,* edited by Stuart Hall et al., pp. 15–47. London, 1980.

Halle, David. *Inside Culture: Art and Class in the American Home.* Chicago, 1994.

Hauser, Arnold. *The Social History of Art.* 4 vols. Translated in collaboration with the author by Stanley Godman. New York, 1951; reprint, New York, 1957–1958.

Hauser, Arnold. *The Sociology of Art* (1974). Translated by Kenneth J. Northcott. Chicago, 1982.

Lang, Gladys Engel, and Kurt Lang. *Etched in Memory: The Building and Survival of Artistic Reputations.* Chapel Hill, N.C., 1990.

Latour, Bruno. *Science in Action: How to Follow Scientists and Engineers through Society.* Cambridge, Mass., 1987.

Lumley, Robert, ed. *The Museum Time Machine: Putting Cultures on Display.* London and New York, 1988.

Lynes, Russell. *The Tastemakers: The Shaping of American Popular Taste* (1954). New York, 1980.

Moulin, Raymonde, ed. *Sociologie de l'art.* Paris, 1986.

Moulin, Raymonde, with Pascaline Costa. *L'artiste, l'institution et le marché.* Paris, 1992.

Peterson, Richard A. ed. *The Production of Culture.* Beverly Hills, Calif., 1976.

Peterson, Richard A., and Albert Simkus. "How Musical Tastes Mark Occupational Status Groups." In *Cultivating Differences: Symbolic Boundaries and the Making of Inequality,* edited by Michele Lamont and Marcel Fournier, pp. 152–186. Chicago, 1992.

Sorokin, Pitirim. *Social and Cultural Dynamics,* vol. 1, *Fluctuations of Forms of Art.* New York, 1937.

Veblen, Thorstein. *The Theory of the Leisure Class* (1899). New York, 1934.

Weber, Max. *From Max Weber: Essays in Sociology.* Translated and edited by Hans H. Gerth and C. Wright Mills. New York and Oxford, 1946.

Weber, Max. *The Rational and Social Foundations of Music.* Translated and edited by Don Martindale et al. Carbondale, Ill., 1958.

White, Harrison C., and Cynthia A. White. *Canvases and Careers: Institutional Change in the French Painting World.* New York, 1965; reprint, Chicago, 1993.

Williams, Raymond. *The Sociology of Culture.* (1981). Reprint, Chicago, 1995.

Wilson, Robert N., ed. *The Arts in Society.* Englewood Cliffs, N.J., 1964.

Wolff, Janet. *The Social Production of Art.* 2d ed. New York, 1993.

Zolberg, Vera L. *Constructing a Sociology of the Arts.* Cambridge and New York, 1990.

Zolberg, Vera L., and Joni M. Cherbo, eds. *Outsider Art: Contesting Boundaries in Contemporary Culture.* Cambridge and New York, 1997.

VERA ZOLBERG

SONTAG, SUSAN. *See* Camp; *and* Photography.

SOREL, CHARLES (c. 1600–1674), prolific author who engaged in fields as varied as science, historiography, moral theory, philosophy, fiction, and literary history. Although Sorel himself expressed a keen preference for his encyclopedic work *La science universelle* at the end of his career, he would be recognized by posterity for his novelistic creations above all. For example, in his masterly study *Le roman jusqu'à la Révolution,* Henri Coulet calls Sorel "the greatest comic novelist of the Baroque age" (1967). Sorel's importance in the evolution of fiction, and the definition of his aesthetics, are most evident in the conception of a genre in which he both experimented and served as main critic: the *histoire comique* (comic novel). In 1623 appeared the first part of the work with which his name is still associated by many readers: *Histoire comique de Francion.* The huge success of this text is attested by the numerous editions and translations it underwent over the course of the seventeenth century. *Francion* established a tradition that would include the *histoires comiques* of Scarron and Furetière, whose works also testify to the crisis in the aesthetics of fiction that occurred in France during the *grand siècle.*

Throughout his career as a writer, and particularly in his works of literary criticism (*La bibliothèque française* [1664] and *De la connaissance des bons livres* [1671]), Sorel tirelessly invoked "verisimilitude" as a criterion for judgment and a principle of evolution in fiction. Having elaborated, in *Francion,* the model of a novel designed to present "as realistically as possible the temperaments, actions, and ordinary conversations" of men, Sorel undertook in *Le berger extravagant* (1627) a systematic attack on the "absurdities" of the kind of fiction that was then in fashion (most particularly pastoral novels such as *L'astrée*). While imitating the formula of novelistic madness that was initiated by *Don Quixote*, Sorel went further: the parodical target of his text was explained in lengthy *remarques* in which he commented on the ineptitude of the existing models. *Le berger extravagant* (retitled *L'anti-roman* in the edition of 1633) was thus conceived essentially as the "tomb of fiction." With *Polyandre* (1648), Sorel attempted once again to bring the novel closer to everyday life, by breaking with the picaresque framework that he had in part followed in *Francion*, and embracing *bienséance* (decorum) that had become essential with the advent of classicism. Through the social milieu it presented, this third *histoire comique* (which inspired Molière) directly paved the way for Furetière's *Roman bourgeois* (1666).

The *histoire comique* as Sorel conceived of it was, therefore, above all a reaction against traditional fiction (the tale of chivalry, the pastoral, or the heroic novel). "Farcical heroes" and "chimerical adventures," which "incite all sorts of vices," should, according to Sorel, be abandoned in favor of "natural tableaux of human life" in which moral lessons could be artfully insinuated. "Verisimilitude" implied, moreover, "mixing conditions" and "temperaments." A novel's plot should, therefore, no longer focus on the idealized representation of love, or depict the torments of two young heroes of noble birth and spirit who often lived in a time and place that distanced them even further from the reader. It is even questionable whether one should use the term *hero* to refer to the protagonists of *histoires comiques*, who were generally bourgeois and more preoccupied with their social position than with the quest for pure love. Through its depiction of persons of "mediocre" social standing and its satiric intent, the *histoire comique* can be compared to comedy. Just like the tableaux of social mores created by Molière and other comic playwrights of the period, these novels resort to grotesque deformation as a means of presenting the vices of human nature via the portrayal of types or *caractères*—a term that Sorel used (well before Jean de La Bruyère) in *Polyandre*.

The critical works of Sorel and the preface to *Polyandre* underscore the importance of assuming a "natural" style that strikes a *juste milieu* (happy medium) between coarseness and affectation, in order to reinforce the effect of verisimilitude. From the very beginning of his career, Sorel decried exaggerated style and metaphorical abuses that undermine truthfulness. The most revealing emblem of his aesthetic principles is undoubtedly the "metaphoric" portrait of Charite in *Le berger extravagant*, which was illustrated by the famous engraver Crispin de Passe and thoroughly critiqued in the text. In this work, the painter entrusted with representing Charite transposes quite literally the "extravagant descriptions of poets" that the shepherd Lysis uses to describe his beloved. When he composed this "monstrous" portrait, Sorel sought to denounce the disparity between figurative language and what it is supposed to translate, and allowed the reader to appreciate visually the absurdity that resulted from that gap.

The aesthetic principles that Sorel brought into play in his conception of the *histoire comique* cannot be separated from his freethinking philosophy, which he voiced most openly in *Francion*. Indeed, this text both contested traditional literary forms and questioned the social and moral conventions of the day. By virtue of its lack of fixed conventions, the *histoire comique* seemed to be the ideal format for expressing audacious ideas; libertine authors such as Théophile de Viau *(Première journée)* or Cyrano de Bergerac *(L'autre monde)* would exploit the genre's potential in this regard by also expounding "things that no one has ever been bold enough to say" *(Francion)*.

In the last analysis, beyond his contribution to the development of a genre that has been considered the "avant-garde of novelistic creation" (Serroy, 1981) and that contributed significantly to the expansion of this field, Sorel's entire body of works—including fiction, science, and history—came down to a single, essential principle: the defense of and quest for truth. When, in the novel bearing his name, Francion declares that his goal is to rid his mind of "vulgar opinions" so that he might seek to understand the "natural reason for all things," he expresses the objective that would guide *La science universelle*, where Sorel also refuted the "old authorities" and touched on the project of demystification that informed *Le berger extravagant*. Because it championed the improvement of reason over the course of time, along with the need for innovation in the field of literature, Sorel's thought was closely akin to the proclamations of those who belonged to the "moderns"; and, thanks to the longevity of the author, it presented an important reflection on—and of—the progression of seventeenth-century aesthetics toward classicism.

BIBLIOGRAPHY

Works by Sorel

Histoire comique de Francion. Paris, 1623; 3d ed., Paris, 1933. Reprinted in *Romanciers du XVIIe siècle*, edited by Antoine Adam. Paris, 1958.

Le berger extravagant. Paris, 1627; 2d ed., Paris, 1928; reprint, Geneva, 1972.

Polyandre, histoire comique. Paris, 1648; reprint, Geneva, 1972–1974.

La bibliothèque françoise. Paris, 1664; 2d ed., Paris, 1667; reprint, Geneva, 1970.

La science universelle: dernière édition revue et augmentée. Paris, 1668.

De la connaissance des bons livres, ou examen de plusieurs autheurs. Paris, 1671. Critical edition, edited by Luoia Moretti Cenerini (Rome, 1974).

Other Sources

Coulet, Henri. *Le roman jusqu'à la Révolution*. 2 vols. Paris, 1967–1968.

Debaisieux, Martine. *Le procès du roman: écriture et contrefaçon chez Charles Sorel*. Saratoga, 1989.

DeJean, Joan. *Libertine Strategies: Freedom and the Novel in Seventeenth-Century France*. Columbus, Ohio, 1981.

DiPiero, Thomas. *Dangerous Truths and Criminal Passions: The Evolution of the French Novel, 1569–1791.* Stanford, Calif., 1992.

Howells, Robin. *Carnival to Classicism: The Comic Novels of Charles Sorel.* Biblio 17. Paris and Seattle, 1989.

Showalter, English. *The Evolution of the French Novel, 1641–1782.* Princeton, N.J., 1972.

Suozzo, Andrew G., Jr. *The Comic Novels of Charles Sorel: A Study of Structure, Characterization, and Disguise.* Lexington, Ky., 1982.

Sutcliffe, F. E. *Le réalisme de Charles Sorel: problèmes humains du XVIIᵉ siècle.* Paris, 1965.

Verdier, Gabrielle. *Charles Sorel.* Boston, 1984.

MARTINE DEBAISIEUX

SPORTS are an obvious topic for philosophical reflection. There are connections between a conceptual interest in sports and moral philosophy, the theory of mind, and the theory of action, to name but a few relevant areas of philosophy. This essay, however, is confined to mentioning a few respects in which sports are of interest in the philosophy of art.

One salient characteristic shared by sport and art is that they are among the most conspicuous of those human undertakings done for no obvious external reason. That human beings do such things ought to be of interest in many areas of philosophy, and it is of special interest in aesthetics. Sport and art are things we do that we do not have to do, at least not in the way in which we have to build shelters (in order to survive the elements and other degradations) and have to cultivate food (in order to eat). When it is possible for us to live indoors without building, then we do not build, and when we can get food without growing it, we do not grow it. Even if one thinks that there is some end for the sake of which art and sport are engaged, it is not "detachable" in the sense that we can suppose that if that end were otherwise available, we would forgo the actual art and sport. This is not to say that art and sports satisfy no need, but it is to say that whatever satisfaction they provide, that satisfaction is not available without the sport and the art themselves, and this seems to be true both of those who engage in these activities as participants and of those who observe. Nor, of course, is it to deny that some artists and athletes may well do what they do only because they are paid to do it, and if they could secure income otherwise, they would leave off making art and playing sports. It is to say only that, at their cores, both activities are carried on—and sustained in human history—because engagement in them seems to satisfy some human need that knows no other satisfaction. Finally, moreover, it is not to say that art and sport satisfy the same human need, nor that they are the only human enterprises thus irreplaceable ("social" conversation, experiencing nature, and engaging in religious ritual may be some among many other examples). But perhaps they both satisfy the same generic need. Is it, perhaps, that those things we do that are not things we have to do are precisely the things we do to "express ourselves"? These are things we are free not to do, and so when we do them, we do them freely, therein showing what we truly are as we do what we truly want.

There are several topics of interest in aesthetics when one looks to sports. The first is simply the interest in sporting activities as objects of what might be called "aesthetic appreciation," and the others take sports as a kind of parallel to art and inquire into just how appreciation of sports differs (or does not) from the appreciation of art.

Athletic performances are obvious occasions for the display of grace, elegance, beauty, and so on, and as such they are occasions for the appreciation of these features, just as works of art and their performances are. In some cases, there seems to be a kind of means/end distinction to be made in the case of sports but not in the case of art, whereas in other cases the distinction virtually is absent in the appreciation of sports. In the first case, the gracefulness of, say, a basketball player shooting a ball, or a third baseman fielding a hard ground ball in baseball, or a cricket batsman executing a perfectly stroked swing at a downward diving ball might be compared with the gracefulness of a ballet dancer executing a particular sequence—with this difference: the admirability of the athlete is understood at least in large part in terms of his scoring a basket, cleanly picking up the baseball, or knocking for six; that is, the gracefulness is exhibited in the service of something, of some end, whereas the gracefulness of the dancer seems to be just that, and it seems to be an object of appreciation, so to speak, in itself. In other cases—for instance, those of a gymnast or a figure skater—although there may be certain specific requirements built into the routine done by the athlete, the judgment of the athlete's exhibition seems very like that of the dancer, a judgment simply of the performance itself without reference to any specific end.

Sports players are, typically, appreciated for doing things that are *difficult.* So are artists. Why is this? Why is it admirable to do something difficult, and just what does it mean for something to be difficult to do? Does the difficulty consist simply in the fact that most other people could not do this thing? Is that why a performance by Sviatoslav Richter and a century struck (in cricket) by Hobbs are admirable, because almost no one else can play the piano like that or bat so successfully as that?

If both sports and art are of interest, at least in part and at least sometimes, because difficult things are done, why do some difficult things support extensive interest and appreciation whereas other equally difficult things do not? Why are tumbling (in gymnastics) and tennis playing substantially successful "spectator sports," whereas walking on one's hands and speed-typing are not? Why does figure painting have the status of high art and command substantial attention from the art-minded public, whereas dress designing does not?

When the difficulty being overcome is significant, and its apprehension is a matter of intense and deep appreciation, so that the performer (sports player or artist) may even be considered a virtuoso, how is it that the audience is aware of this difficulty? Is the difficulty of a task, so to speak, exhibited in the doing of the task itself, or does a competent appreciator need some independent experience in order to be able to gauge the level of difficulty? Must one have tried playing the piano or the violin to appreciate the virtuosity of an Alfred Brendel or a Itzhak Perlman? Must one have tried playing basketball to appreciate the stunning performance of Michael Jordan? It might be enough to have seen and heard enough people attempting to play the piano or the violin or basketball to begin to have an idea of just how difficult it is to do those things. Perhaps it varies, and some human endeavors are near enough to things we all do for us to infer just how difficult they are, and others are sufficiently arcane to contain a difficulty that novice observers will be unaware of. The matter is complicated by the fact that a mark of certain exhibitions of virtuosity is that the difficulty being overcome is concealed. Thus, some genuine virtuosos are complimented, as it is said, for making the difficult look easy. In such a case, genuine appreciation requires that we know the task is not easy despite the fact that it "looks" as if it were. If it does indeed look easy, then we will take it to *be* easy unless we have something to go on besides how it looks.

These matters seem well worth looking into, if only because they illustrate that "appreciation" is not only not confined to engagements with works of art, but that it might not even have its primary exhibition there. The matters are all related to the topic of spectator or audience "identification," and it is here, perhaps, that one can see most clearly that the phenomenon of aesthetic appreciation is linked closely to the phenomenon of the appreciation of sports. It is a commonplace that the appreciation of many works of art requires that an appreciator "identify himself with" someone else. Often the identification is to be with a fictional character, as in the appreciation of novels, stories, operas, plays, and movies. Sometimes the identification is to be with the artist. A common way of explaining both the emotional and the intellectual content of certain paintings and pieces of music is to say that the appreciator must come to understand that he himself would execute these brush strokes or write these harmonies if he were possessed of certain convictions or feelings, and were able to create these things. This requires somehow imagining oneself to be the painter of this painting, or the composer of this music. It is very difficult to give such an explanation clearly, and one of the immediate complexities is that what seems to be required is not identification with the painter or composer as such, but with the painter or composer insofar as this painting or this musical work is concerned; that is, for instance, it is not required that Igor Stravinsky have felt playful when he composed this section in one of his works, but that Stravinsky himself had to understand what a person feeling playful composing music of this kind might have done in this section; and the audience is required to achieve the same understanding.

There is an astonishing similarity to be found in the full appreciation of sports. To appreciate fully the achievement of some sportsman, it is necessary, frequently, to be able to do something that might be called imagining oneself to be doing what the sportsman does. How is this done if in fact one knows absolutely that one could not do that? Can one still imagine oneself doing it? Can one identify with the athlete? It seems that one can do something like this, however difficult it is to describe the achievement. That is why when one is pleased by a sporting achievement in which, say, the sportsman wins his game or scores his point, besides being pleased that the person or team the fan wanted to succeed has indeed succeeded, there is an additional, perhaps different, satisfaction that comes with feeling, virtually, that one has done the winning oneself. Many art theorists and artists have claimed something similar for the appreciation of art. Both R. G. Collingwood and Paul Hindemith, for instance, argue that the full appreciation of a work is achieved only by those who can feel themselves, and think of themselves, as creating the work.

If we think of sportsmen in this way, as people whose activities we appreciate in much the way that we appreciate the work of artists, then we must ask what kind of artists they resemble. Are they like authors, painters, and composers, or are they more like performers, typically those who perform works initially created by others? Perhaps the nearest analogy is with performers, but performers engaged in improvisation, such as certain kinds of jazz musicians and improvisatory actors. There is a background score or script to be performed *from* in nonimprovisatory cases, but in cases of genuine improvisation there is only something like a given melody or a topic or a situation. The sports player has the background of whatever sport or game he is engaged in, with its rules and their specification of what is allowable to him, but after that the sportsman, like the improvising artist, is to find his own way within whatever confines have been established. There remains the difference that, in typical sporting endeavors, there is in place an overall, controlling requirement that whatever one does be aimed at *winning*. In art, success is gauged in some other way. It is worth considerable thought to try to explain this artistic success, and in particular how it is, in some respects, rather like winning, but in other respects it is not like winning just because it does not require in any clear sense that anyone lose.

The philosophy of art has two main insights waiting to be gained in time spent considering sports. The first is the discovery that what is customarily thought of as "aesthetic appreciation," in all its complexity and subtlety, is to be found in the rich appreciation of sports, and therefore that aesthetic appreciation may not be linked essentially to art, but may have only a special provenance there. The second insight is a realization that the characteristic of art that it is pursued "for its own sake" does not by itself set art apart from other human endeavors. Both insights hold the promise of underwriting a deeper understanding of art by way of a precise formulation of just how art differs from sports, its surprisingly close cousin.

[*See also* Appreciation.]

BIBLIOGRAPHY

Andre, Judith, and David N. James, eds. *Rethinking College Athletics.* Philadelphia, 1991.

Journal of the Philosophy of Sport 1– (1974–). See especially no. 14 (1987), which contains an extensive bibliography.

Morgan, William, and Klaus Meier, eds. *Philosophic Inquiry in Sport.* Champaign, Ill., 1988.

Vanderwerken, David L., and Spencer K. Wertz, eds. *Sport Inside Out: Readings in Literature and Philosophy.* Fort Worth, Tex., 1985.

TED COHEN

STEIN, GERTRUDE (1874–1946), American poet and writer. For most of the twentieth century, Stein was considered the great eccentric of modern letters, a fascinating "character," more read about than read, the subject of memoir, biography, portraiture (from Pablo Picasso to Man Ray), and seemingly endless gossip. As someone who wrote no formal criticism, Stein the theorist is only now beginning to be recognized as one of the foundational modernist thinkers.

Stein's career is full of paradoxes. She lived most of her life in France; French was the language spoken in her salon but she boasted of never reading or writing in it. A writer of German-Jewish origins, she had as little taste for German culture as for the Jewish religion, always insisting that she belonged to the Anglo-American tradition, as it came down to her from William Shakespeare to George Eliot and Henry James. A writer who was lesbian, she expressed no interest in or enthusiasm for the work of other lesbian writers—or of women writers in general, unless, as in the case of Edith Sitwell, they played the role of disciple. Indeed, to the company of literary women or literary men she preferred the company of male artists, especially the artist who was in many ways her opposite, being a Catholic-born Spaniard, violent and volatile, with an enormous (heterosexual) libido and, at least later in life, a marked taste for radical left politics. The only critical monograph Stein ever wrote was an homage to this artist: her *Picasso* (1938), written, in violation of her own principles, in French.

There is the further difficulty of distinguishing between the official and the unofficial Stein discourse on literature. Her first invited public lecture, "Composition as Explanation," given at Cambridge in June 1926 and published the following year by the Hogarth Press, was written to impress an audience that was quite unfamiliar with her major works, few of which had been published. Consequently, Stein exhibits a certain coy defensiveness that becomes even more pervasive in *Lectures in America* (written in 1935), written by the now best-selling author of *The Autobiography of Alice B. Toklas* (written in 1933), a sixty-year-old smiling public woman who has finally been invited to lecture in her native land in what turned out to be a grand coast-to-coast tour. *Lectures in America* creates the Stein persona most people still mistake for the actual Stein: a kind of female Douanier Rousseau, charmingly naive and "primitive," who is given to locutions such as the following in the lecture "Pictures":

> Having thus become familiar with oil paintings I looked at any and all of them and I looked at thousands and thousands of them. Any year in Paris if you want to look at any and all paintings you can look at thousands and thousands of them, you can look at them any day and everywhere. There are a great great many oil paintings in Paris.

This is by way of leading up to the recognition that "there is a relation between anything that is painted and the painting of it." Stein makes similar statements elsewhere, but in her more "unofficial" writings these are repeatedly revised, qualified, complicated, and recharged. Indeed, we do not have, in Stein's case, a corpus of critical writings detachable from a corpus of "primary" works, as is the case with T. S. Eliot or Virginia Woolf. Some of Stein's most profound theoretical speculation is found in her poems, her "portraits," her autobiographies, and in the various unclassifiable prose texts of the 1920s, beginning with "An Elucidation" (written in 1923) and culminating in the pieces collected in *How to Write* (written in 1931). For Stein, in short, writing, whatever the genre, is theory.

Consider, for starters, the opening piece of *Tender Buttons* (written in 1914), which is called "A Carafe, That is a Blind Glass":

> A kind in glass and a cousin, a spectacle and nothing strange a single hurt color and an arrangement in a system to pointing. All this and not ordinary, not unordered in not resembling. The difference is spreading.

Stein herself insisted that *Tender Buttons* was entirely "realistic" in the tradition of Gustave Flaubert. "I used to take objects on a table, like a tumbler or any kind of object and try to get the picture of it clear and separate in my mind and create a *word relationship between the word and the things seen,*" she recalls in "A Transatlantic Interview—1946)" with Robert Bartlett Haas. What she no doubt means is that *reference* remains central to her project even if *representation* does not. Unlike Eliot or Ezra Pound, unlike, for that matter, the Cubist Picasso, she does not give us an *image,* however fractured, of a carafe on a table; rather, she forces us to reconsider what the objects in question are and how they function.

A carafe is, of course, "A kind in glass"—a kind of object belonging to the glass family, which includes its "cousins": bottles, pitchers, jugs, tumblers, wineglasses, and so on. A carafe is a "blind glass" because it is filled with wine, presumably red wine, and so one cannot see through it. It is also a blind glass in that it does not mirror the spectator. Nor can it be used, like a pair of glasses, to look at anything. One looks at it and through it ("a spectacle") but it does not improve our vision in any way. "Nothing strange" about this: one does not expect a carafe to be otherwise.

"A single hurt color": This carafe is evidently filled with red wine and one associate red with hurt. But "hurt" may also refer to some sort of contamination; something has bled into that single color (perhaps soda water) and changed it. At the same time, the carafe participates in what Stein calls "an arrangement in a system to pointing." Here "realism" meets Cubism: like the distorted, fragmented carafes of Picasso or Juan Gris, Stein's is part of a larger compositional arrangement, a grammar in which every verbal unit points to all the others. The carafe is "not ordinary" (i.e., not just a pitcher), "not unordered in not resembling" (it is distinct from all its "cousins," but they are all part of the compositional system). Stein concludes with the seemingly Derridean assertion "The difference is spreading." The more one studies such an "arrangement in a system to pointing," in other words, the more one becomes aware of the subtle differences between seemingly similar things. In this sense, Stein no doubt felt that she had established, as closely or "realistically" as possible, the relation between the word and the thing seen.

"A Carafe, That Is a Blind Glass" thus asks the reader to rethink the function of language in literature. There is no use, Stein implies, in giving minute verbal renditions of visual objects; words can never fully reproduce the thing seen anyway, and besides, a photograph can do the job much better. In the age of mechanical reproduction, she suggests, ostensive definition has become quite pointless. Accordingly, the aesthetic of *Tender Buttons* stands opposed to Pound's Imagist demand for "direct treatment of the thing, whether subject or object," and to William Carlos Williams's "No ideas but in things!" On the contrary, the conviction is that there are no "things" outside language to be "treated," whether directly or indirectly; there are only words. Poetic language, Stein implies, though she makes no overt statement on the subject, is not the verbal transcription of a preexistent content, nor does it provide us with what Eliot termed the "objective correlative"—"a set of objects, a situation, a chain of events which shall be the formula of [a] *particular* emotion"—for nothing can be the "formula" for anything else. But—and this is the paradox—the primacy of language does not mean that the literary text is autonomous, that it is a verbal artifact isolated from the real

world. On the contrary—and here Stein's "fine new kind of realism," as her mentor William James called it, again comes into play—literature is always directly related to life.

We can see the same process at work in the "tender button" called "Custard":

> Custard is this. It has aches, aches when. Not to be. Not to be narrowly. This makes a whole little hill.
> It is better than a little thing that has mellow real mellow. It is better than lakes whole lakes, it is better than seeding.

Again, Stein avoids actual description. She gives us neither the recipe for making custard nor a visual image of a custard cup. Yet, consider the generative force of her words. Custard does not "ache" but it does shake or quiver. When we see something or someone shake, the inference that the movement is produced by the rhyming "ache" is reasonable. Custard quivers (aches) in a delicate way: overcook it and it turns solid—a hard lump. Conversely, beat the eggs insufficiently and it becomes runny, liquid—a lake. Thus, success depends on precision: "Not to be narrowly" and you get a "whole little hill"—"better than a little thing that has mellow real mellow." "Mellow" rhymes with "yellow"—custard color, a whole little hill of it.

But the last line is puzzling: what does "seeding" have to do with this custard? It is at this point that the sexual allusions, latent throughout the poem in the references to "custard," "aches when," "not to be narrowly," and "better than a little thing" come together. The "ache" of "custard" is "better than seeding": lesbian loving is more enjoyable than heterosexual sex. Like most of the poems in "Tender Buttons," "Custard" celebrates Stein's newfound erotic happiness with Alice B. Toklas, and feminist critics have been quick to read this and related texts as veiled sexual allegories in which each word or phrase really means something else. But such translation has a way of flattening out the work. The wit of "Custard" is that nothing is ever just one thing: for all we know, custard is, well, just custard, even as Marcel Duchamp's erotically charged readymade *Why Not Sneeze, Rrose Sélavy?* is, after all, a birdcage containing sugar cubes, a cuttle bone, and a thermometer. The main thing to note is that Stein's little poem is deeply ambiguous, but that its ambiguity is the function less of its figurative language, as would be the case in its Symbolist counterparts, than of its morphology and syntax.

"A Grammar," we read in "Arthur a Grammar," relates to "not liking to see again those you used to know" *(How to Write)*. "Those you used to know" are, in Stein's lexicon, nouns and adjectives. In "Poetry and Grammar," Stein declares:

> A noun is a name of anything, why after a thing is named write about it. A name is adequate or it is not. If it is adequate then why go on calling it, if it is not then calling it by its name does no good. . . . just naming names is alright when you want to call a roll but is it any good for anything else.

And on the next page:

> . . . nouns as I say even by definition are completely not interesting, the same is true for adjectives. In a way anybody can know always has known that, because after all adjectives affect nouns and as nouns are not really interesting the thing that affects a not too interesting thing is of necessity not interesting.
>
> *(Lectures in America)*

Here Stein's rejection of the naming function recalls Ludwig Wittgenstein's critique in the *Philosophical Investigations* (1953; a work Stein could not possibly have known although it was drafted, like *Lectures in America,* in the mid-1930s) of the Augustinian theory of language, the notion that, in Wittgenstein's summary, "Every word has a meaning. This meaning is correlated with the word. It is the object for which the word stands." But what about words such as *is* or *but* or *five* that have no such object equivalent? What about nouns such as *game* or verbs such as *read,* whose specific meaning is determined only by its *use* in a specific context?

Stein was thus something of a Wittgensteinian *avant la lettre.* She was fascinated by the little words—articles, pronouns, prepositions—whose meanings necessarily depend on context. Pronouns, for example, "in not being his or its or her name . . . already have a greater possibility of being something" ("Poetry and Grammar"). "Arthur A Grammar" contains the following passage:

> What is it. Who was it. . . .
> He merely feels.
> Does he.
> Does it.
> He merely feels does it.
> He merely feels does he.
> Makes.
> In prints it.
> Prints prints it
> Forgotten.
> He has forgotten to count.
> He has forgotten how to count.

Here the slightest adjustment of preposition or pronoun *(in/on; does it/does he)* alters the meaning, reminding us of the strangeness of ordinary language. "He has forgotten to count": it is clear what that means. But when "how" is inserted before *to, count* can be construed as an intransitive verb and the sentence may thus mean "He has forgotten how to make his presence felt."

"When a sentence is called senseless," we read in the *Philosophical Investigations,* "it is not as it were its sense that is senseless. But a combination of words is being excluded from the language, withdrawn from circulation" (no. 500). The real question is then: why is this particular combination withdrawn? In her writings, Stein makes a similar case for a radical deconstruction of language and its function in culture. Why can we not say "Grammar will" or "Grammar an

angel"? Why can one not be "worried hours aloud" or refer to "our last hourglass"? How is it that we communicate as adequately as we do in daily life, when we must discriminate between phrases such as

> Two next
> To be next to it
> To be annexed
> To be annexed to it.   ("An Elucidation")

Think of the possibilities for writing varied and vivid sentences. "A sentence is an interval in which there is a finally forward and back." It follows that a real writer is someone who puts before us not intricate narrative, or the complex psychological interaction between characters, or subtly charged images, or even elegant sound structures, but rather someone who reinvents the language itself so as to make manifest the possibilities that have been there all along. "I am a grammarian," Stein declares in *How to Write,* and again, "Grammar. Fills me with delight. / I am having it as a habit"—which again recalls a Wittgenstein phrase, this time from his Cambridge *Lectures 1930–1932:* "In philosophy all that is not gas is grammar." Or, in what sounds like a Steinian aphorism, "There are no gaps in grammar; grammar is always complete."

If, then, as Stein insists, the writer's unit is not the image or the symbolic construct but the smallest grammatical unit that is the sentence, it follows that composition in the larger sense will depend on what Stein calls "using everything." In "Composition as Explanation" (1926), "using everything" is related to "beginning again and again" and the "continuous present"; these three compositional principles, Stein explains, first make their appearance in the early fictions generated by repetition and permutation: *Melanctha, The Making of Americans,* and *A Long Gay Book.* In his introduction to the paperback reprint of *The Geographical History of America* (written in 1935), William Gass has an excellent discussion of this aspect of Stein's work:

> Life is repetition, and in a dozen different ways Gertrude Stein set out to render it. We have only to think how we pass our days: the doorbell rings, the telephone, sirens in the street, steps on the stairs, the recurrent sounds of buzzers, birds, and vacuum cleaners. . . . Life is rearrangement, and in a dozen different ways Gertrude Stein set out to render it. We are not clocks, designed to repeat without remainder, to mean nothing by a tick, not even the coming tock, and so we must distinguish between merely mechanical repetition, in which there is no progress of idea, no advance or piling up of wealth, and that which seriously defines our nature, describes the central rhythms of our lives.
>
> Almost at once [Stein] realized that language itself is a complete analogue of experience because it, too, is made of a large but finite number of relatively fixed terms which are then allowed to occur in a limited number of clearly specified relations, so that it is not the appearance of a word that matters but *the manner of its reappearance.*
>
> (1973)

Not appearance but reappearance: this is what Stein has in mind when she speaks of "beginning again and again" and the "continuous present"; for repetition only becomes meaningful when the word or phrase or even whole sentence is repeated often enough—and repeated, of course, with the most delicate variations—to make a difference. But the third principle in the triad, "using everything," has implications for writers and artists whose mode and style may otherwise have little to do with Stein's. In the "Transatlantic Interview," she makes her meaning clearer:

> Everything I have done has been influenced by Flaubert and Cézanne, and this gave me a new feeling about composition. Up to that time composition had consisted of a central idea, to which everything else was an accompaniment and separate but was not an end in itself, and Cézanne conceived the idea that in composition one thing was as important as another thing. Each part is as important as the whole, and that impressed me enormously.

Here Stein is referring, however elliptically, to one of the cornerstones of modernist aesthetics. From the Renaissance to the late nineteenth century, painting distinguished between figure and ground, foreground and background, and Stein rightly (if somewhat schematically) attributes the breakdown of that basic distinction to Paul Cézanne—or, so far as literature is concerned, to Flaubert, especially the Flaubert of the *Éducation sentimentale*, whose canvas depends precisely on the conviction that "each thing is as important as every other thing." James, Stein goes on to say, still discriminates between figure and ground: he bathes his characters in an "atmosphere" that assumes great importance, but it is still atmosphere, against which a Maggie Verver or Lambert Strether is silhouetted. But in Stein's world, as in Picasso's or, for that matter, in Dada, "using everything" means that no part of the canvas (or, in her case, the poem or narrative) is more important than any other part. What this means in practice is that the writer does not begin with a central image or ruling myth or dominant symbol and then gather his or her materials around it, as, for example, William Butler Yeats does in his Byzantium poems. Rather, the process of writing is itself the "hero" of the work.

In art discourse, the notion of "using everything," of getting rid of the figure/ground distinction, has been taken as a given from Cubism and Futurism on down, but in literary theory, it remains a radical concept. It is interesting to compare Stein to Pound in this regard. Such well-known Pound theorems as "Use no word that does not contribute to the presentation," or his definition of the Vortex as a "radiant node or cluster . . . from which, and through which, and into which, ideas are constantly rushing," are based on precisely the premise that there is a focal point, a "radiant node" or "figure" to which everything else in the composition is subordinated. "Use no word that does not contribute to the presentation" makes no sense from a Steinian perspective because it implies that there are more and less important words—images that are central and "filler" words that connect those images. For Stein, by contrast, there are no filler words, no phrases such as "Petals on a wet black bough" that subordinate the preposition and the article to nouns and adjectives. Each thing is as important as every other thing.

The theory of "using everything," eccentric as it was taken to be in the poetics of the early twentieth century, has, ironically enough, become one of the important precepts of postmodern poetics. From the Objectivists and French Oulipo writers to such younger poet-theorists as Lyn Hejinian, Susan Howe, Steve McCaffery, Joan Retallack, Tom Raworth, and Charles Bernstein, the Stein injunction to "Act so there is no use in a centre" has become an article of faith. Accordingly, Stein is now hailed as the precursor of contemporary avant-garde movements.

Yet, one must be careful not to overdo such analogies. Despite Stein's radical critique of conventional theories of signification, she did not hold, as did Jacques Derrida, that language is no more than trace structure, the infinite regress whereby "words and concepts receive meaning only in sequences of differences" (Derrida, 1976). The notion that the signified (say, the mental image of a sugar bowl on the table, to which one points when one says, "Please pass the sugar") is "originally and essentially . . . trace, that it is *always already in the position of the signifier*," and that accordingly no word can have "full presence," would have been quite alien to Stein's pragmatist way of thinking. She would have scoffed that of course a sugar bowl is a sugar bowl (no more, no less), the question being, as in "Marry Nettie," how it functions in the text.

Here, as already suggested, the apposite figure is not Derrida (or any other poststructuralist theorist) but Stein's contemporary, Wittgenstein, for whom the meaning of a word is its use in the language. If you and I function within the same language community and I say to you, as we sit at the breakfast table, "Pass the sugar, please," you know exactly what I mean. The signifier *sugar* does not participate in the play of *significance*, the oscillation of presence and absence. But difficulties arise when you are not sure what language game I am playing:

> When I say that the orders "Bring me sugar" and "Bring me milk" make sense, but not the combination "Milk me sugar", that does not mean that the utterance of this combination of words has no effect. And if its effect is that the other person stares at me and gapes, I don't on that account call it the order to stare and gape, even if that was precisely the effect that I wanted to produce.
>
> To say that "This combination of words makes no sense" excludes it from the sphere of language and thereby bounds the domain of language. But when one draws a boundary it may be for various kinds of reason. . . . So if I draw a boundary line that is not yet to say what I am drawing it for.
>
> (Wittgenstein, 1968, nos. 498–499)

There may, in short, be a good reason to say "Milk me sugar." Stein, for that matter, wrote a poem called "Milk" that begins: "A white egg and a colored pan and a cabbage showing settlement, a constant increase." At first this sentence seems perverse: what is the resemblance between milk and egg or milk and cabbage? But if one consider what the "boundary lines" here might be, one soon notices that the poem describes quite accurately the process of boiling milk. Poured into one of those colored enamel pans, milk does look like an oval egg and, as it rises to the boil ("a constant increase") it settles into the hilly form of a cauliflower (a member of the cabbage family). If one takes the language game in question to be a cooking lesson, it all makes perfectly good sense.

Such defamiliarization—what Pound called "Make It New!"—was, of course, a central tenet of modernism. Where Stein's form of defamiliarization differs from that of most of her contemporaries (though not from such avant-gardists as Duchamp) is in her rejection of poetry (or fiction) as the representation of a particular subjectivity, as revelation of self. Or rather: she understood, long before it was fashionable to do so, that the self is at least partially a cultural construction, that context makes all the difference. "Arthur," in her scheme of things, is only "a grammar," and even in her more conventional works, such as *The Autobiography of Alice B. Toklas,* the principals—Picasso, his mistress Fernande, Guillaume Apollinaire, Marie Laurencin, Constance Fletcher—are seen as functions in a "system of pointing" rather than as individual characters. " 'I,' " she might have said with Wittgenstein, "is a word like any other." It is in this respect that Stein seems very much our contemporary.

[*See also* Aleatoric Processes; Feminism; Modernism, *article on* Modern Literature; *and* Poetics.]

BIBLIOGRAPHY

Note: There is to date no collected or definitive edition of Gertrude Stein's works, and the published texts are by no means reliable, as Ulla E. Dydo points out in her excellent *A Stein Reader* (see below). In the Stein items listed, I therefore supply the original date of publication (often much later than the year of composition cited in the text), where relevant.

Works by Stein

Tender Buttons (1914). In *Selected Writings of Gertrude Stein,* edited by Carl Van Vechten, pp. 460–509. New York, 1990.
How To Write (1931). Los Angeles, 1995.
The Autobiography of Alice B. Toklas (1933). New York, 1990.
"An Elucidation" (1934). In *A Stein Reader,* edited by Ulla E. Dydo, pp. 429–442. Evanston, Ill., 1993.
The Geographical History of America (1935). New York, 1973.
Lectures in America (1935). Boston, 1985.
Selected Writings of Gertrude Stein (1946). Edited by Carl Van Vechten. New York, 1990.
"A Transatlantic Interview—1946." In *A Primer for the Gradual Understanding of Gertrude Stein,* edited by Robert Bartlett Haas, pp. 15–35. Los Angeles, 1971.
A Stein Reader. Edited by Ulla E. Dydo. Evanston, Ill., 1993.

Other Sources

Bridgman, Richard. *Gertrude Stein in Pieces.* New York and Oxford, 1970.
Derrida, Jacques. *Of Grammatology.* Translated by Gayatri Chakravorty Spivak. Baltimore, 1976.
Perloff, Marjorie. *The Poetics of Indeterminacy: Rimbaud to Cage.* Princeton, N.J., 1981.
Perloff, Marjorie. *Wittgenstein's Ladder: Poetic Language and the Strangeness of the Ordinary.* Chicago, 1996.
Pound, Ezra. *Literary Essays.* Edited by T. S. Eliot. New York, 1954.
Wittgenstein, Ludwig. *Philosophical Investigations* (1953). 3d ed. Translated by G. E. M. Anscombe. New York, 1968.
Wittgenstein, Ludwig. *Wittgenstein's Lectures, Cambridge, 1930–1932* (1980). From the Notes of John King and Desmond Lee, edited by Desmond Lee. Chicago, 1989.
White, Ray Lewis. *Gertrude Stein and Alice B. Toklas: A Reference Guide.* Boston, 1984.

MARJORIE PERLOFF

STOICISM. See Hellenistic Aesthetics.

STOKES, ADRIAN DURHAM (1902–1972), critic, heir to the nineteenth-century tradition of Walter Pater and John Ruskin. Stokes wrote about old master art as if it were part of a living cultural tradition. His greatest books, *Quattro Cento* (1932) and *Stones of Venice* (1935)—both reprinted in Stokes, 1978—presented a theoretical conception, modified but never abandoned in his later writing. What he calls "Quattro Cento" art—he turns the Italian *quattrocento* (fourteenth century) into a descriptive phrase—appears essentially atemporal. To these Quattro Cento carved works, the most visual kind of visual art, he contrasts that lesser painting and sculpture which, in its musical-like play with temporality, uses modeling. The familiar contrast between the carver's cutting into his medium and the modeler's building up a form thus is reinterpreted.

Stokes's early books, which aided the revival of interest in quattrocento sculpture, employ ways of thought that are alien to the modern art historian. Charles Seymour's scholarly account (1966, pp. 129–134) identifies the ideas that may have influenced Agostino di Duccio, the sculptor of the Tempio Malatestiano, Rimini. Stokes's deeply felt belief was that these relief sculptures express fantasies about the history of their materials. "Agostino's root preoccupation was with water forms and water movement" (Stokes, 1978, vol. 1, p. 229). Within modern art history, there is a broad division between iconographers' study of the literary sources of artworks and connoisseurs' concern with qualities that are immediately knowable visually. Like a connoisseur, Stokes is interested in what is directly knowable; but, unlike most connoisseurs, he is not concerned with attributions. Stokes believes that, in carving the stone, the artist entertained fantasies that can be intuited by an attentive observer.

Some art historians admire the "poetic" qualities of Stokes's writing, but even his admirers are unlikely to adopt his way of thinking, which today seems highly speculative. His ways of thinking about visual art deserve attention from aestheticians, both because of the intrinsically valuable literary qualities of his writing and for the challenge it poses to "normal" art history. It provides a highly original model of what can be done with that much-discussed topic psychoanalytic aesthetics. Stokes was primarily concerned with the materials of art, not with art as a vehicle for personal fantasy. Because his way of thought differs so radically from that of both traditional art historians and those revisionist historians concerned with poststructuralism, his work provides a valuable critical perspective.

The most important philosopher of art influenced by Stokes is Richard Wollheim, whose "Adrian Stokes" (1972) remains the best introduction to the thought of his friend.

BIBLIOGRAPHY

Works by Stokes

The Critical Writings of Adrian Stokes. Edited by Lawrence Gowling. London, 1978.

Other Sources

Carrier, David. *Artwriting.* Amherst, Mass., 1987. See chap. 3.
Seymour, Charles, Jr. *Sculpture in Italy, 1400–1500.* Baltimore, 1966.
Wollheim, Richard. "Adrian Stokes" (1972). In *On Art and the Mind: Essays and Lectures,* pp. 315–335. London, 1973; reprint, Cambridge, Mass., 1974.

DAVID CARRIER

STRAVINSKY, IGOR FEDOROVICH (1882–1971), Russian composer. As a prominent representative of musical modernism and advocate of an aesthetic of musical objectivity, Stravinsky had enormous influence on musical developments in Europe in the first half of the twentieth century. His artistic development, like that of many of his contemporaries, was shaped by political circumstances, which forced him onto a cosmopolitan compositional trajectory: born in Russia in 1982, he went to Paris in 1911, moved to Switzerland in 1914, to Paris again in 1920, to California in 1940, and lived in New York after 1969 until his death in 1971. His compositional oeuvre divides logically into three stylistic periods, which coincide with major geographic dislocations: the works of his early years (1903–1917) reflect Russian cultural traditions and evince the composer's attraction to primitivist aesthetics, which are most evident in the three ballets that Sergei Diaghilev commissioned for the Parisian programs of the Ballets Russes: *The Firebird, Petrouchka,* and *Le Sacre du Printemps.* His second stylistic period (1914 or 1922, depending on interpretation, to 1951) corresponds with his emigration to western Europe and gradual rejection of his Russian musical heritage in favor of a French-influenced "objective" style that his critics subsequently labeled neoclassical. This new approach to composition characterizes works ranging from the *Three Pieces for String Quartet* through the Concerto for Piano and Winds to *The Rake's Progress.* In his third, "late" stylistic period (1952–1963), Stravinsky surprised some of his followers by adopting and transforming the twelve-tone method of a composer whom critics since the 1920s had considered his nemesis: Arnold Schoenberg.

Stravinsky outlines his aesthetics most comprehensively in "Some Ideas about My Octuor" (1924), his autobiographical *Chronique de ma vie* (1935), and his *Poétique musicale* (1942), a publication resulting from the six Charles Eliot Norton lectures he gave in French at Harvard University from October 1939 to May 1940. It would be erroneous to consider these texts either as a comprehensive aesthetic or as a systematic explanation of the composer's thoughts on art throughout his life. They do, however, provide the most explicit account of Stravinsky's highly influential aesthetic of musical objectivity. Ideas presented here also reappeared later, with variations, in the numerous published conversations with Robert Craft.

Perhaps Stravinsky's most significant yet most misunderstood statement on musical aesthetics is contained in his *Chronique de ma vie:*

> I consider music, by its very essence, incapable of expressing anything at all, whether it be a feeling, an attitude, a psychological state, or a phenomenon of nature, and so on. Expression has never been the immanent property of music and in no way defines its essence. If, as is usually always the case, music seems to express something, it is only an illusion and not a reality. Expression is simply an additional element that we, because of some tacit or inflexible convention, have lent to or imposed on music like a name tag, a report, or, in sum, a posture, and that we have come to confuse with music's essence whether unconsciously or by habit.   (1935)

In denying music the ability to express anything whatsoever, Stravinsky explicitly rejects nineteenth-century aesthetics of feeling, musical Expressionism, and the psychology of the individual subject. In their place, he envisions music as "a type of speculation formed in terms of sound and time" or conscious organization of tones. The musical work becomes an "artifice" or abstract order that is neither mimetic (i.e., representative of an outside reality) nor a vehicle for expressing human feeling. Rather, it reveals and justifies itself in the "free play of its functions" and is most analogous to an architectural structure.

Stravinsky solves the problem of how listeners can still perceive emotions in music even when the composer has not invested it with any by attributing to form the ability to present emotions independently of human agency. Form is defined as the "only emotive subject of composition"; and the means of composition become "emotive in themselves."

His description of emotions in music as the "heterogeneous play of movements and volumes" reveals that he understands emotion as universal and impersonal, and has so accepted the meanings music had acquired in Western culture that he had come to understand them as natural, or intrinsic to the notes. Largely uninterested in the sociocultural construction of musical meaning, Stravinsky was willing to deny that human subjects had originally invested such emotional content in music.

In Stravinsky's nonexpressive universe, the human subject and musical object are linked primarily through their existence in time: "the phenomenon of music is given to us with the sole aim of establishing order among things, especially between *man* and *time*." Following Pierre Souvtchinsky, Stravinsky distinguishes between two kinds of music: one parallel to the course of psychological time, the other following ontological time. In the first type, music is subject to the composer's emotive impulses. Such music emphasizes contrast and variation, is most likely tonal, and is best exemplified by Richard Wagner's works. Stravinsky rejects this music in favor of the second type, or what Souvtchinsky calls "chronometric music," in which the musical process is in equilibrium with real time, or the beat becomes the identity of the subject. Stravinsky favors this type of music because he believes that "music is the only domain where man realizes the present. Because of the imperfection of his nature, man is forced to succumb to the passing of time—of the categories of past and future—without ever rendering real, in other words stable, the category of the present" (ibid.). In his *Poétique musicale,* Stravinsky encourages composers to link their music to ontological time by emphasizing the evident or hidden similarities between musical materials. In his music, he evokes the metaphor of ontological time by returning to the steady beat of Baroque music, echoing the effects of mechanical performance media, and encouraging a *perpetuum mobile*-style continuity that caused critics to compare his music to a "sewing machine." Wary of the hierarchy of tonal functions that characterize psychological time, Stravinsky advocates a harmony based on poles of attraction.

Stravinsky's aesthetic of an objective music based on ontological time is best revealed in practice in the so-called neoclassical works of his second period. First applied to Stravinsky's music by Boris de Schloezer in 1923, the term *neoclassical* originally served the function of distinguishing Stravinsky's work from that of Schoenberg, and of accentuating its affinity to classical as opposed to Romantic musical aesthetics. "Neoclassicism" is most useful as a means of defining the new relationship to musical materials that Stravinsky developed around the time he emigrated to western Europe and was exposed to the music and thought of Erik Satie and Jean Cocteau. Influenced also by the nonexpressive, kinetic choreography of Diaghilev's Ballets Russes and Vsevolod Meyerhold's revival of commedia dell'arte,

Stravinsky developed a compositional approach in his second period in which sounds involved the listener directly in an aural ritual, rather than acting as symbols or signs denoting emotional or expressive psychological content. By transferring the practice of juxtaposing and superimposing motivic cells that he had established in Russian ballets such as *Le Sacre du Printemps* to instrumental works such as *Three Pieces for String Quartet* and *Symphonies des Instruments à Vent,* Stravinsky objectified a practice of simultaneity originally associated with the violent rhythms of primitivist dance. These pieces evince ontological time as a metaphor for a musical practice in which the beat becomes the unit of measurement over metric accent. Surface discontinuities confuse the listener's sense of the beat, forcing him or her to concentrate on the passage of time, or the present. Using register, timbre, nonexpressive, experimental instrumental techniques, tempo, harmony, and silence to alienate highly differentiated cellular materials, Stravinsky focuses the listener's attention on isolated musical events and their formal development. Drawing on his experiences as a student of Nikolai Rimsky-Korsakov and on his knowledge of Aleksandr Scriabin's music, from which he developed an understanding of the octatonic system, and building on the polarized harmonic organization that he had established in *Petrouchka,* he developed a harmonic technique based on the interaction between diatonic and octatonic systems. Devoid of tonal hierarchies and marked by severe temporal discontinuity, this music could no longer communicate expressive and emotional content in the manner of Western art music.

Stravinsky broke most dramatically with nineteenth-century aesthetics of expression by alienating the musical material of his compositions in multiple ways. In *L'histoire du soldat,* for example, he used the visual scenario of a marionette theater, the instrumental colors and combinations of the fairground, and non-Western phrase structure and repetition in order to create a distanced, seemingly mechanical music. Inspired by the notion of abstract types as opposed to the more personally expressive individual, Stravinsky evoked the universal in this work by parodying characteristic genres such as the march and incorporating general, stylized allusions to other genres such as the tango and ragtime. Parody became for Stravinsky a vehicle for distancing listeners from musical materials in a nonjudgmental—that is, objective—way. In the commedia dell'arte ballet *Pulcinella,* he made listeners conscious of their emotional response to the original music by Giambattista Pergolesi and Domenico Gallo by recomposing the accompaniment of melodies, destabilizing the meter, distorting harmonies, shortening phrases, reorchestrating passages, and confusing the focus of the music by introducing unusual timbres and accents. In contrast to other classicists such as Ferruccio Busoni, Stravinsky did not manipulate these materials in order to comment on them, but rather, in the spirit of Aleksandr Benois's ballet scenario, to free them by liberating them from their conventional meanings. In the opera *Mavra,* begun a year later, he expanded his manipulation of musical artifacts by exploring within a modernist framework materials as diverse as the tonality of Western music, Mikhail Glinka's and Pyotr Ilich Tchaikovsky's styles, rudimentary jazz rhythms, and elements of Russian variety shows.

After the fiasco of *Mavra,* Stravinsky turned to instrumental works based on textbook, stereotypical classical forms such as the sonata, variations, and rondo. He did not intend to reconstruct these historical forms with all their compositional implications, but rather only to allude to them as a means of signaling to his audience that they should enter the formalist mode of listening. Even when tonality reappears, it is often drained of its goal-directed force and forced into a quasi inertia. In works such as the *Octet,* he evoked the style and classical sonata form of Franz Joseph Haydn and Ludwig van Beethoven, for example, only in order to undermine them with contradicting formal and stylistic strategies, like those of Johann Sebastian Bach. Styles, genres, and forms serve less as a compositional foundation than as neutral material that the composer mixed and matched at will. This practice is most clear in *Oedipus Rex,* in which Stravinsky fused a wide range of styles, among them those of George Frideric Handel, Giuseppe Verdi, Bach, and even the Folies Bergères, in order to destabilize the denotative meaning of the music and thereby achieve an extreme objectivity accentuated by the unidiomatic use of Latin and inclusion of a speaker satirizing the action. *Oedipus Rex* realizes objectivity by referencing past artistic achievements in an impersonal way. "Resolutely negating all individualism," Stravinsky's colleague Arthur Lourié wrote in 1927, Stravinsky, "revives impersonal yet solidly constructed forms of the culture of past centuries, making them serve new needs and aims" (1927).

Lourié's statement demonstrates that the emotional objectivity commonly associated with Stravinsky's neoclassical works results only partially from their inherent compositional features. To a large extent, the composer and his supporters created an aura of objectivity around these works through the words they used to describe them and the polemics surrounding their composition. In his writings, Stravinsky emphasizes his lack of emotional involvement in these works, for example, by referring to himself not as their composer but as their craftsman; he does not express himself, but rather *makes* this music in a productive process that follows controlled, rational principles to impose on the materials a form that he has consciously conceived. Avoiding the spiritual and psychological implications of the notion of inspiration by delegating it to the insignificant role of an "emotive disturbance," Stravinsky solidifies his theory of the artist as craftsman by seeking the source of his creative work in a less mystical "appetite for discovery" that, for the

composer, was a "natural need." The composer does not make ethical or aesthetic choices, but rather "ensures the rightness of [his/her] operation" by acquiring certain methods through experience, inventiveness, and apprenticeship. This experience is not personal, but rather "objective" and linked to "concrete values." Composers can make such proper aesthetic judgments because they have culture and inner taste—the necessary basis for being able to observe and thus compose. They have to deny their personalities, however, in order to recognize true principles of organization and realize them objectively in music.

Stravinsky is able to minimize the role of the composer and subjective expression in composition because he has reinstated a classical belief in transcendental rules of art and metaphysical values in his aesthetic system. He has accepted the metaphysical theory of the substantially unified human subject, for example: music "emanates from the integral man. I mean from a man armed with all the resources of his senses, his psychological faculties, and his intellectual capacities." He has also accepted without questioning the unity of the autonomous artwork, which is suprapersonal and superreal, coherent and sufficient in itself. Finally, his entire poetic is based on the existence of a set of rules or dogmas that are "demanded by the very organization of the spiritual being" and resemble spiritual truths or religious laws. This dichotomy between a materialist or formalist approach to composition and a belief in metaphysical values led Enrico Fubini to label Stravinsky's aesthetic a "metaphysical formalism."

By evoking the authority of transcendental truths, Stravinsky absolves himself from the task of addressing the thorny issue of the moral obligation of the artist. From a liberal perspective, Stravinsky appears to be blindly accepting authority and refusing ethical responsibility for his work. His approach to ethics becomes clearer, however, in light of Jacques Maritain's Neo-Thomist philosophy of art, which Stravinsky came to know through Lourié in the 1920s and which strongly influenced his thought. In *Art et scolastique,* Maritain had proposed that art was not self-expression, but rather a virtue of the "practical intellect" whose goal was the goodness of the thing made. Art was distinct from moral virtue because it was "outside the human sphere; it had an end, rules, values, which were not those of man, but those of the work to be produced. The work was everything for Art; there was for Art but one law—the exigencies and the good of the work" (Maritain, 1965). Thus, the capacity of the artist to produce good artifacts was independent of his moral condition. Maritain could distinguish the artist's morality from his art because he believed in transcendent truth, as did Stravinsky. This faith in metaphysical values has been the subject of the most skeptical critical attacks on Stravinsky by postmodern critics.

Stravinsky's aesthetics had a wide influence throughout the twentieth century, creating disciples and provoking vivid critical response. Perhaps the most influential and incriminating critique came from Theodor W. Adorno, who rejected Stravinsky's goal of objectivity as the attempt to evoke a nonexistent "objective" society and to deny the reality of sociopolitical relations in his time. Adorno equated objectivity with an absence of meaning and the commercialization of art, and defined it as representative of the alienated state of consciousness of the modern subject. Dedicated to the project of ideology critique and sociological analysis of the Frankfurt School, Adorno necessarily rejected Stravinsky's attempts to create a nonmimetic art, which he interpreted as an escape into an "illusory realism." In his highly influential *Philosophie der neuen Musik* (1975), Adorno attacked the very backbone of Stravinsky's aesthetic approach: his interpretation of musical time. For Adorno, Stravinsky's ontological time was equivalent to a rejection of subjectivity and a reduction of humanity to a thing. Because he interpreted art as the encounter between the conscious compositional subject and socially established material, Adorno could hardly have had less sympathy for Stravinsky's Neo-Thomist notions of craftsmanship. He likewise rejected Stravinsky's neoclassicism as the impossible attempt to reconstitute styles of the past that reflected the society of their time and could thus only appear false in the present.

Adorno's writings had an overwhelming influence on how Stravinsky's aesthetics were received in Europe, particularly in Germany. The German musicologist Rudolf Stephan has reinterpreted Stravinsky's aesthetics within the context of Russian Formalism. Although Stravinsky and Russian Formalists pursued radically different objectives, Stephan and others have noted their affinity in terms of the alienation of musical material through parody. This technique enables the composer to objectify material and enter into a dialogue with the musical past, and offers a new means of understanding a nonexpressive form of composition.

More recently, Stravinsky's aesthetics have come under attack from the American musicologist Richard Taruskin. In the tradition of Adorno, Taruskin condemns the reactionary ideology that allowed Stravinsky to submit to rules and deny human subjectivity. Taruskin pinpoints the fundamental problem of Stravinsky's aesthetics: namely, how do we assure the moral responsibility of the artist if we accept rules and orders uncritically as eternal and given? Taruskin's writings are representative of the postmodern trend toward rejecting the aesthetic postulates of modernism.

[*See also* Modernism, *article on* Modern Music; Music, *historical overview article; and* Russian Aesthetics.]

BIBLIOGRAPHY

Works by Stravinsky

"Some Ideas about My Octuor." *The Arts* (January 1924). Reprinted in Eric W. White, *Stravinsky: The Composer and his Works* (London, 1966), pp. 528–531.

Chronique de ma vie. Paris, 1935.
Poetics of Music in the Form of Six Lessons. Bilingual Edition. Translated by Arthur Knodel and Ingolf Dahl. Cambridge, Mass., 1947.
Conversations with Igor Stravinsky. With Robert Craft. London, 1958.
Memories and Commentaries. With Robert Craft. London, 1959.
Expositions and Developments. With Robert Craft. Garden City, N.Y., 1962.
Dialogues and a Diary. With Robert Craft. London, 1968.
Retrospectives and Conclusion. With Robert Craft. New York, 1969.
Themes and Conclusions. With Robert Craft. London, 1972.
Selected Correspondence. 3 vols. New York, 1985.

Other Sources

Adorno, Theodor W. *Philosophie der neuen Musik.* Edited by Rolf Tiedemann. Frankfurt am Main, 1975.
Druskin, Mikhail. *Igor Stravinsky: His Life, Works, and Views.* Translated by Martin Cooper. Cambridge and New York, 1983.
Fubini, Enrico. "L'estetica di Stravinskij." In *Stravinskij Oggi: Convegno internazionale, Milano, 28–30 Maggio 1982,* edited by Anna Maria Morazzoni, Quaderni di Musica/Realta 10, pp. 32–45. Milan, 1986.
Griffiths, Paul. *Stravinsky.* New York, 1992.
Lourié, Arthur. "Oedipus-Rex." *La revue musicale* 8.8 (April–October 1927): 240–253.
Maritain, Jacques. *Art et scolastique.* 4th ed. Paris, 1965.
Messing, Scott. *Neoclassicism in Music: From the Genesis of the Concept through the Schoenberg/Stravinsky Polemic.* Ann Arbor, 1988.
Pusler, Jann, ed. *Confronting Stravinsky: Man, Musician, and Modernist.* Berkeley, 1986.
Schloezer, Boris de. *Igor Stravinsky.* Paris, 1929.
Souvtchinsky, Pierre. "La notion du temps et la musique." *La revue musicale* (1939): 310–320.
Stephan, Rudolf. "Zur Deutung von Strawinskys Neoklassizismus." In *Igor Stravinsky,* Musikkonzepte 34/35, pp. 80–88. Stuttgart, 1984.
Stravinsky, Vera, and Robert Craft. *Stravinsky in Pictures and Documents.* New York, 1978.
Taruskin, Richard. "The Pastness of the Present and the Presence of the Past." In *Authenticity and Early Music,* edited by Nicholas Kenyon, pp. 137–210. Oxford and New York, 1988.
Taruskin, Richard. "Back to Whom? Neoclassicism as Ideology." *19th-Century Music* 16.3 (Spring 1993): 286–302.
Taruskin, Richard. *Stravinsky and the Russian Traditions: A Biography of the Works through Mavra.* 2 vols. Berkeley, 1996.
Walsh, Stephen. *The Music of Stravinsky.* Reprint, Oxford, 1993.
Walsh, Stephen. *Stravinsky: Oedipus Rex.* Cambridge and New York, 1993.
Watkins, Glenn. *Pyramids at the Louvre: Music, Culture and Collage from Stravinsky to the Postmodernists.* Cambridge, Mass., 1994.
White, Eric Walter. *Stravinsky: The Composer and His Works.* 2d ed. London, 1979.

TAMARA LEVITZ

STRUCTURALISM. One might sum up structuralism by saying that it is a theory that conceives of all cultural phenomena, including artistic artifacts, as sign systems, and those systems as operating according to the dictates of a deep structure (one might think of the latter as being analogous to a genetic program). Its roots lie mainly in the linguistic theories of the Swiss linguist Ferdinand de Saussure, although the work of the early Soviet school of literary theorists, the Russian Formalists (plus those connected with them in their brief heyday following the Russian Revolution), also played a part in structuralism's development. Structuralism has had an impact on many areas of intellectual endeavor in the twentieth century—aesthetic theory and criticism, anthropology, and psychoanalysis, to name some of the most prominent.

Saussure's linguistic theories, as expounded in his *Course in General Linguistics* (put together, after his death in 1913, by his students from their notes of his lecture program at the University of Geneva), are based in the first instance on the principle that language (that is, the whole family of human languages) is a self-contained system with its own rules and regulations governing its internal operations—in other words, that there is an underlying grammar to all human language. The "linguistic model" that resulted from Saussure's research was put forward as a model for how all systems operated, and structuralism as it has developed since Saussure's death relies heavily on this original model as the basis for its analyses of cultural phenomena. Language, for Saussure, was to be divided into two main parts: *langue* and *parole*. The former referred to language as a system, the latter to the body of individual utterances made by human beings within that system. *Langue* was where Saussure's interest was almost exclusively concentrated, that is, with language as a system, its grammar, and its methods (*parole* being more a matter of behavior than of rules). In his favorite analogy, language was like a game of chess, in that it was self-contained, self-regulating, and bound by rules as to how the pieces could be used. The grammar of chess dictated that pawns could make certain moves only, knights others again, and so on with castles, bishops, queens, and kings. The consequence of this conception of systems was that the elements of the system (the chess pieces, for example) were to be defined by their function: to ask the meaning of a pawn was to be told its function within a game of chess, and equally, of a linguistic unit (such as a verb) its role within the grammar of the linguistic system. Individual elements were, in fact, to be defined by their difference from other elements within the given system; thus, to be a pawn was to have a function different from a bishop (etc.), and to stand in a clearly defined relationship to that figure within the confines of the game.

Language was taken to be a system of signs to which we respond in a more or less predictable way (as, to use an example of a rudimentary sign system with a very restricted grammar, we would to traffic lights). Signs were made up of a signifier and a signified (basically, a word and its mental concept), which combined together in the mind, in an act of understanding, to form the sign: the union of the word *cat* and the mental concept "cat," for example, signaled the object being referred to. The bond between signifier and signified was described as arbitrary, meaning that any word at all, in theory, could be used to signify a given object; all that was needed was a consensus among a linguistic community at any given time as to the particular word being used to refer to a particular object. Proof of the arbitrariness of the bond could be found in the fact that different words were used to describe the same object across the family of human languages: *cat* in English, *chat* in French, *gatto* in Italian, and so on. There was nothing intrinsic to the word *cat* itself that required that it be associated with that particular animal. For Saussure, language was dominated by this principle of arbitrariness, although in practice the need for consensus meant that any changes in the meanings of words tended to happen gradually. He argued, therefore, that the arbitrariness was relative only, and that systems displayed order rather than disorder. Finding order within systems has remained a primary preoccupation of structuralist analysis.

Saussure saw language as operating according to a series of binary oppositions (such as the *langue/parole* distinction). The relations between words could be either syntagmatic or associative. In a sentence constructed according to the rules of, say, English grammar (subject-verb-object, "The book is on the desk"), the words were joined together in a linear sequence (or "syntagma"). Associative (later also called "paradigmatic") relations depended on looser connections, in effect, something more like association of ideas: teaching/education/apprenticeship being one example of such a sequence given by Saussure. Language was also to be seen in either synchronic or diachronic perspective, the former being a case of observing the system as a whole, the latter in one of its dynamic phases (the difference between the game of chess as a totality, with a set of rules governing its operation, and a particular move in a game initiating a change in the state of play). The diachronic perspective enables structuralist analysts to scrutinize selected aspects of the whole against the background of the total system, thus communicating a sense of historical change.

Saussure is also famous for predicting the development of a "science of signs," or "semiology," as he called it (now more generally referred to as "semiotics"). This discipline is effectively coterminous with structuralism, and language is only one of many systems that it studies, although arguably the most important, in that it provides the basic model for semiotic inquiry (for the psychoanalyst Jacques Lacan, for example, even the unconscious is a sign system structured like a language). The promise that semiology held out was that ultimately we could come to understand the workings of all cultural phenomena. Structuralism appeared to offer a key to unlock the secrets of the myriad sign systems in human experience, a way of coming to terms with the complexity of the world. When applied to aesthetic matters, structuralism enabled us to see how works of art could be read as sign systems designed to elicit certain responses from their audiences, and to grasp how those responses were generated. Not the least of the virtues of structuralism is that it is a relatively easy method to assimilate, and it very quickly enables the practitioner to amass large amounts of data about works of art—the details of the internal grammar, the relations between its various elements, and how these compare to the grammar and elements of other works. Comparative analysis, and the wider understanding that is engendered by it, are a logical outcome of the structuralist approach. Structuralism also aspires to universal applicability, and, by ranging over so many fields, it has helped to foster interdisciplinary inquiry, which in itself has helped to give a broader picture of the world by cutting across intellectual specialization.

Russian Formalism prefigured structuralism's systematic approach to the study of narratives. In *The Morphology of the Folktale,* for example, Vladimir Propp broke down folktales into a series of narrative functions (or conventions), which appeared each time around but in subtly different forms across a range of tales (the concept later known as "transformation," and in that guise a key element in Claude Lévi-Strauss's methodology). Roman Jakobson, another theorist from the Formalist milieu, emphasized the role of linguistics in literary analysis and helped to influence the direction of Lévi-Strauss's thinking when they were colleagues together in New York during World War II.

Of the many practitioners working in what can be called the "high structuralist" tradition (the 1950s and 1960s, when the theory was at the height of its popularity, particularly in France), arguably the two most important are Lévi-Strauss and Roland Barthes—although the latter eventually moved away from structuralism to a certain extent, and is even considered poststructuralist in his later career by many commentators. The emphasis in the work of each thinker is on the notion of unity. All narratives are considered to contain common features, or codes, and to share a common sense of structure. In Lévi-Strauss's case, this led him to conclude that groups of myths were all variants of a central myth ("variations on a theme," to use his musical analogy), and that it was the task of the analyst to chart the variety of ways (the transformations) in which the same set of narrative conventions were deployed over a range of narratives. These transformations signaled that, although the surface details might be different, the underlying structure remained in force. If a myth demanded the intervention of the gods as one of its structural elements (or "functions"), then that intervention might be accomplished by various means: the gods might take human form, or animal form, even insect form, or work through natural phenomena such as the weather (storms, for example, having a long tradition of being read as evidence of the gods' wrath being expressed against humankind). Barthes similarly insisted, in his high structuralist phase, on the unity of narratives, treating them as linked by their deep structural elements, and arguing against the possibility of there being any chance elements involved: everything had to be accounted for in terms of the overall pattern. In each and every case, there was a deep

structural grammar to be identified, and it was the analyst's role to reveal this. Barthes applied this principle over a wide-ranging series of analyses of cultural phenomena (all of which he treated in the manner of a narrative), such as advertising, the fashion industry, and cultural politics, in each instance being concerned to notate the underlying grammar (that is, sense of order) involved.

Structuralism even reached into Marxism, with the "structural Marxism" of Louis Althusser and his followers having a considerable vogue from the 1950s to the 1970s. Althusser posited the existence of large-scale institutional structures within an ideology that worked to control the thought and behavior of individual human beings (thus functioning like the deep structure of ideology). These structures were Ideological State Apparatuses (ISAs for short) and the Repressive State Apparatus (RSA). The former category included such phenomena as the legal and educational systems and the media, the latter the government, police, and army. Collectively, these entities worked to prevent questioning of the dominant ideology of a society, as well as to hide the contradictions that were encoded within that ideology (it being part of Althusser's definition of ideology that it contained contradictions that it was in the interest of the ruling class to conceal). Althusser's theories were adapted to the field of literary theory by his disciple Pierre Macherey, in the highly influential study *A Theory of Literary Production,* which advocated "reading against the grain" of texts in order to uncover the ideological contradictions hidden within narratives. The point of this technique was to reveal the ways in which ISAs and the RSA were controlling the thought processes of a society, even down to the level of artistic activity. Literary texts, to Macherey, were first and foremost productions of ideology, and, by an act of critical "interrogation," they could be made to yield up the secrets of that ideology.

Barthes's *S/Z* represents a desire to escape from what many were beginning to regard by the 1970s as the rigidity of structuralist methodology, with its demand that all cultural phenomena conform to the workings of the linguistic model and display an underlying sense of order. *S/Z* approached texts as inexhaustible sources of meaning and interpretation (a text being a "galaxy of signifiers"), and demonstrated, by a reading of Honoré de Balzac's novella *Sarrasine,* how the narrative was a complex sequence of overlapping codes (five in number in this case). Barthes's interest had now switched to narratives that invited multiple interpretations ("writerly," as he called them), such as the open-ended texts of the modernist tradition, which, he maintained, encouraged active participation on the part of the reader. These "writerly" texts were to be compared to "readerly" texts, which required a passive response only from the reader. In later Barthes, the reader becomes an increasingly important figure in the literary process, with Barthes announcing the "death of the author" as an authority figure controlling the reception of a text's meaning, and upgrading the reader's role accordingly.

Similar moves to Barthes can be seen in the work of the semiotic theorists Umberto Eco and Julia Kristeva, who provide some of the most important developments in later structuralism. Kristeva put together a hybrid of semiotic, Marxist, and Freudian theory that she called "semanalysis," and that was designed to break away from the linguistic model inherited from Saussure. By the time Kristeva entered onto the French intellectual scene, structuralism was under attack from a new wave of poststructuralist thinkers such as Jacques Derrida, and semanalysis was an attempt to reconstitute semiotics on a more scientific basis than hitherto (mathematics and logic were where Kristeva drew her inspiration from at this stage). An important contribution of Kristeva's to semiotic discourse was the notion of intertextuality. For Kristeva, every text was intertextual, that is, a signifying system made up of a "mosaic of quotations" drawn from other signifying systems. Texts were, therefore, plural, and incapable of being reduced to a single meaning or interpretation. Eco's answer to the apparent restrictiveness of the interpretive model of high structuralism was the notion of the "labyrinth," which also allowed for multiple interpretations of a given text. The labyrinth was to be considered as a form of net, such that any one point on its surface could be joined to any other point. In Eco's words, the net was "an unlimited territory." This meant that there was an infinite number of routes through the territory in question, with a different collection of connected points being possible on each and every occasion. Eco gives as an example the fact that one is not compelled to pass through Saint Louis on a trip from New York to Dallas, and that one could never exhaust the possible routes between the two points. There is no prescribed interpretation of a text using semiotic theory, therefore, although there is an overall framework within which the analysis has to take place. Like Kristeva, Eco takes issue with the primacy accorded the Saussurean linguistic model in semiotic analysis, complaining that it is arguable that all sign systems are comparable in nature, as the high structuralists, taking their lead from Saussure, had assumed.

The notion of a deep structure, or underlying program, determining how systems operate, and ultimately how human beings behave, has come in for considerable criticism. Critics of humanist bent have objected that it leaves little scope for the exercise of individual free will and reduces individuals to the status of mere puppets for the working out of amorphous forces. Ideas such as the "death of man" (announced by Michel Foucault in *The Order of Things*), and the "dissolution" of man (Lévi-Strauss, *The Savage Mind*) are also at odds with the humanist ideals of modern Western culture, which emphasize the improvability of humankind and the importance of the individual in the cultural scheme of things. Structuralism's emphasis on the system at the expense of the individual (and that individual's assumed freedom of action) has led to it being described on occasion as antihumanist in orientation.

Even more trenchant criticisms of the structuralist project have come from within the poststructuralist movement, with Derrida in particular being very harsh on what for him is structuralism's teleological bias and interpretive rigidity. For Derrida, it is a case of structuralists knowing beforehand what they will find in their analysis, because it is in the nature of their theory to impose a sense of structure on any work or discourse. Derrida considers this method to be authoritarian in that it closes off the creation of new meanings and new interpretations of texts. It is also argued to be essentialist because it assumes that the deep structure is the essence of each text, and can only envisage texts as expressions of that deep structure.

Another criticism of the structuralist enterprise has been that it has turned Saussure into something like an idealist philosopher, when in real terms he was a linguist pure and simple. This is the criticism voiced by Leonard Jackson (1991), who has also remarked scathingly of the system-building side of structuralism that it amounts to little more than "cultural meccano." Certainly, there is a sense in which structuralist analysis can become highly predictable (identify the grammar, specify how it works in the particular instance in question, and your analytic inquiry is all but complete), and it is also open to the charge that it does not actually say a great deal about the meaning, or value, of texts, or of cultural phenomena in general. What it *does* say a great deal about is function, but ultimately, it could be argued, this provides a somewhat impoverished view of texts, no less than of cultural phenomena. To be told how the various parts of a text relate to each other reveals very little about the nature of its emotional impact on its audience, or why some texts have a greater resonance over time than others.

Despite such criticisms, structuralism has made enormous contributions to twentieth-century thought. It remains a superb basis for comparative analysis (between cultures or literary genres, for example), and it has had many notable successes in this regard, with the work of Barthes in particular still finding an audience and informing current critical practice and debate. Few methods of cultural or aesthetic inquiry have not adopted something from structuralism, and many of its techniques have now become absorbed to the point where they are simply taken for granted by critics and teachers alike.

[*See also* Barthes; Formalism; Kristeva; Poststructuralism; Prague School; Russian Aesthetics, *article on* Russian Formalism; *and* Semiotics.]

BIBLIOGRAPHY

Althusser, Louis. *Lenin and Philosophy and Other Essays.* Translated by Ben Brewster. New York, 1971.

Barthes, Roland. *S/Z.* Translated by Richard Miller. New York, 1974.

Barthes, Roland. *Image-Music-Text.* Translated and edited by Stephen Heath. New York, 1977.

Culler, Jonathan. *Structuralist Poetics: Structuralism, Linguistics, and the Study of Literature.* Ithaca, N.Y., 1975.

Culler, Jonathan. *Saussure.* London, 1976.

Derrida, Jacques. *Writing and Difference.* Translated by Alan Bass. Chicago, 1978.

Eco, Umberto. *Semiotics and the Philosophy of Language.* Bloomington, Ind., 1984.

Foucault, Michel. *The Order of Things: An Archaeology of the Human Sciences.* New York, 1970.

Jackson, Leonard. *The Poverty of Structuralism: Literature and Structuralist Theory.* London and New York, 1991.

Kristeva, Julia. *The Kristeva Reader.* Edited by Toril Moi. New York, 1986.

Lévi-Strauss, Claude. *The Savage Mind.* Chicago, 1966.

Lévi-Strauss, Claude. *Mythologies I: The Raw and the Cooked.* Translated by John Weightman and Doreen Weightman. New York, 1970.

Macherey, Pierre. *A Theory of Literary Production.* Translated by Geoffrey Wall. London and Boston, 1978.

Propp, Vladimir. *The Morphology of the Folktale.* Translated by Laurence Scott. Austin, Tex., 1958.

Saussure, Ferdinand de. *Course in General Linguistics.* Edited by Charles Bally, Albert Sechehaye, and Albert Reidlinger. Translated by Wade Baskin. New York, 1959.

STUART SIM

STYLE. The word style has produced more than its share of definitions and descriptions; the *Oxford English Dictionary* finds twenty-eight variants for the term, with even the common elements among them inviting as many questions as they resolve. Because of the central place of artistic style in this broader history, the analysis of its structure has been equally complex. Closely tied to the concept of art as such, discussions of artistic style have, furthermore, constantly faced the question of whether and how art and style are to be distinguished. The common view of style as a "way" or manner implies the existence of an act that the manner qualifies; the difficulty of determining where these two elements of art diverge is at once a clue to their relationship and an important factor in the analysis of style.

The etymology of *style* reverts to the Latin, appearing there as a metonymy in which the *stilus,* used for inscribing wax tablets, represented the manner or quality of writing in contrast to its content. The claim has been made as well of an earlier source in the Greek *stylos* ("column") based on the several orders of entablature, but the evidence for this reference is less clear. In any event, the Greek commentators (e.g., Theophrastus, *On Style*) also associated style almost exclusively with rhetoric, relating it to the latter's persuasive function and using its categories to distinguish among various rhetorical means and effects in contrast to the substantive assertions communicated.

This instrumental origin influenced subsequent discussions of style, which, continuing to the present, have emphasized the "how" of stylistic expression as distinguished from its presumably non- or extrastylistic "what"—for example, the threefold distinction in Latin rhetoric among the grand, the mixed or middle, and the plain styles, a distinction based on the "levels" of language used, as these took account of the audience addressed and the specific purpose intended, with the combined effect of these then judged to be the "decorum" of the speech made. Quintilian summarized the art of rhetoric as "speaking well," and again in this phrase, it is the adverbial "how" that makes style an issue.

These early accounts, however, also recognized the importance of the relation between the rhetorical means and the subject articulated by it—beginning with the contingent character of that relation (as in Aristotle's criticism of those who speak "casually about weighty matters or solemnly about trivial ones"), but then moving on to suggest a stronger, intrinsic connection, the "form" of a work then reciprocally affecting and affected by its "content." The latter conceptualization of style has come increasingly to the fore since the shift of stylistic analysis to a focus on the arts that gains strength in the Renaissance; it has been the source at once of the most important advances and of the most troublesome issues in the analysis of style.

Almost without exception, modern accounts of style have ascribed to it a characteristic regularity or reiteration—in Meyer Schapiro's (1961) phrase, a "constant form"—which must also, however, be expressive (or, in related terms that are sometimes used, exemplary or symbolic). *Natural* regularities—the shape of an oak leaf or the pattern of an EKG—are not ordinarily held to be pertinent to style, although Nelson Goodman (1975) cites a "sunrise in Mandalay style" as one of what would then be many exceptions. On most accounts, even "human-made" regularities are not features or instances of style unless they are also integral to the works in which they appear: the sequential page numbers of a novel are not relevant to its style, although their total number may well be (i.e., in contrast to the characteristic length of the short story). For the purpose of making attributions, "connoisseurship" in the visual arts has at times relied on physical elements so limited as to be nonexpressive—ranging from characteristics of the parts of figures represented (ears, eyes) to the texture of brush strokes; but such elements seem in themselves no more relevant to style than the artist's fingerprints would be as identified on a canvas.

Viewed historically, both the categories of style and individual stylistic features appear not as "natural kinds" but as conventions varying among cultures, developmentally *within* cultures, and in and sometimes across specific arts. This contingent status argues against the possibility of determining universal categories of style or even of specifying stylistic properties in contrast to those that count aesthetically but nonstylistically in the individual artwork. There seems no part of a work (even its "grammar," insofar as violations of syntactic norms may reflect stylistic intention) that cannot in principle function as an element of style—an openness so broad that commentators such as Monroe Beardsley have regarded it as diminishing the usefulness of style in critical or aesthetic discourse. But the continued referral to categories of style in interpretation and evaluation suggests their relevance notwithstanding this disadvantage; the histories of art criticism and critical theory would be unrecognizable without reference to stylistic elements such as patterns of figurative discourse, distinctions among genres, or the classification of artworks by school or group.

A leading example of the conceptual tension affecting the analysis of style has been the issue of synonymy—the claim that two expressions can be identical in meaning yet differ in form. Theorists such as E. D. Hirsch (1975) have held synonymy to be a necessary condition of style; others, such as Goodman, have denied the possibility of synonymy (in style or elsewhere) and advanced a conception of style without it. The pertinence to style of synonymy (if it *were* possible) is unmistakable, because it would provide a systematic basis for the distinction between the way something is formulated and its "what" or substance. Even if synonymy is ruled out strictly speaking, the fact that certain locutions come closer than others to realizing that condition may be all that is necessary for grounding stylistic categories in the form-content distinction. In any event, the claim that the content and the expressive form of a work's style are intrinsically connected, with their relationship then varying contextually, does not mean that differences asserted between the two must be arbitrary; the shifting line would reflect the functional status of style—resembling in this respect the work's nonstylistic features (some aesthetic, some not) from which its own are distinguished.

The stakes in applying categories of style in interpretation and evaluation become progressively higher as those applications have shifted from their early focus on rhetorical distinctions to the more diverse and less immediately utilitarian arts. The modern typology of the arts coincided with the increasing recognition accorded individual artists in the Renaissance. The new emphasis on "self" in and outside art, together with the growing professionalization of the arts and artists, led the analysis of style to consider more closely the individual character (and identity) of its creator—that is, the artist's "signature." This use of the categories of style as a means of reaching back to the artist continues to have a place (on some accounts, a central one) among the definitions of style, but it seems even here subordinate systematically to the conception of style as generally expressive; that is, as going beyond the person or history of the individual artist. The emphasis on style as signature, furthermore, is problematic in its own terms, insofar as some identifying markers (such as a painter's *literal* signature) have nothing to do with style, and some typical features of style are only marginal indicators of the individual artist's or even group identity (as in the use of broadly accepted artistic conventions such as those governing perspective or tonality).

It has been claimed of style (e.g., by Richard Wollheim [1993]) that its attribution to groups or schools—the "Post-Impressionist" painters, the "metaphysical" poets—is no more than an ad hoc shorthand that, for external reasons, brings together independent instances of individual style. This view of group style as essentially derivative has been contested, however; not only is the emphasis on style as expressing the artist's individual "physiognomy" (in Arthur Schopenhauer's term) relatively recent in art's own history, but even a recognizably personal style does not preclude indebtedness to other styles (of individuals *or* groups). One need not, moreover, posit a collective mind to acknowledge the social origins of much, or aspects of all, individual expression. Features of a group style are sometimes more notable than those of individual styles, and there is sufficient historical evidence of reciprocity between the two to speak noninvidiously of style in both connections. The question of priority between individual and group style seems as much open to dispute—and similarly, more than only a historical or an empirical question—as the question of priority, in theories of human nature, between a socially constituted self and a private, autonomous one. It has often been noted that the most radical stylistic innovations are typically *not* found in artists who are the most celebrated individually.

To attribute to style an expressive or representational role underscores the question of what it is that style expresses or represents. This question impinges on the general issue of artistic representation, and although the analysis of style is not alone accountable for resolving that issue, one element of style in particular—the factor of choice—bears directly on it. No more for style than for art in general can accident or nature by themselves explain its development or varieties; deliberation or choice are thus in some sense implicated (leaving Goodman's reference to "natural style" as metaphoric at best). The intentional character of style is pertinent to the practical and historical analysis of art as well as to its ontology; Leonard Meyer (1989), for example, traces specific changes and genre distinctions in the history of musical style to the contrast between options rejected by various composers and those that they selected and then elaborated. Ascribing a role to choice in style supports the view of artistic representation and meaning that has been charged with the "intentional fallacy"—although even agreement on a role for intentions in the formation of style leaves open the question of what the specific relation is between intentions and artistic meaning.

It is evident in any case that stylistic "choice" is not only a matter of deciding among determinate options, like choosing among different dishes on a restaurant menu. Some stylistic choices may be of this sort, but others involve the creation of the options among which choice is then made. This does not imply that style is even here free of historical constraint (thus, Heinrich Wölfflin's statement that, stylistically, "Not everything is possible at any [particular] time" [1951]); it leaves room for originality in individual or group style while insisting that it occurs always within a historical context. (The objection against linking style to choice because the artist's "character" to which style is related will then also have been "chosen" seems to argue for rather than against the connection.)

The problem of synonymy also bears on the contingency of the categories of style insofar as attempts to determine common or universal categories have failed; there is, and arguably can be, no fixed list of stylistic predicates or categories either within the individual arts or across them. Franz Kafka's use of the preposition *aber* ("but") two or three times more frequently than the norm among German writers may or may not be stylistically significant; a connection would have to be shown between it and the characteristic expression of his works (the relevance to style of the general property of word-use frequency would also have to be tested by such particular instances). Similarly, the curve of a painted or sculpted or dancer's arm may or may not be stylistically significant—as would be the case for the gracefulness (or grace*lessness*) of the same curve. Stylistic categories or their instantiations, like the connection between style and expression on which they depend, can thus be validated (or rejected) only contextually, that is, by the other aesthetic categories or properties with which they stand in contrast in the artwork. This circularity in identifying what is stylistically significant has been a central factor historically in the instability of stylistic categories—as these have evolved in relation to changes and decisions within or among the arts as well as in relation to history external to art. It is not only that individual styles develop in these ways, but that accounts and appreciation of the "same" style or the "same" stage of a style also change; the history of the reception of painting in the twentieth century provides numerous examples of such alteration—as does the varied reception over time of many of the now-canonical figures in all the arts. Whatever style is style *of,* furthermore, discloses a similarly labile character, evoking Roland Barthes's metaphoric description of style as an onion: peeling away its layers in the hope of reaching a "core," the viewer of style has to settle in the end for the layers themselves. For these same reasons, the identification of stylistic features in art requires imagination in the critic comparable if not identical to the artist's in constituting them.

The categories of style, moreover, are typically conceived after the fact: Pyotr Ilich Tchaikovsky did not set out to be a "Romantic" composer or Pierre Corneille a "neoclassical" dramatist. This retrospective feature of style strengthens the resemblance between style and art; neither is prescriptive or rule-governed. Certainly, the development of particular styles does not seem to be dictated by formula or entailed by the stylistic past—although, as for other questions related to style, the opposing view on this question of origins has had its advocates. Thus, stylistic "explanation" has at times claimed to enumerate the sufficient conditions for particular styles, basing this on an internal logic and full-scale determinism. The best-known instance of the latter is Georg Wilhelm Friedrich Hegel's view of the history of art as moving necessarily from the "symbolic" to the "classical" to the "romantic" stages. Beyond this progression, Hegel conceived the phenomenon of art itself as a stylistic "moment"—one that he claims has ended and been superseded in the life of "Spirit" first by religion and (that) then by philosophy.

Numerous more limited efforts than Hegel's have been made to identify a developmental logic in the history of particular styles (as in Early, High, and Late Renaissance art). Such attempts have often identified useful categories (as in Wölfflin's five-paired distinction between Renaissance and Baroque art), although these categories do not justify the claim sometimes made for them as reflecting a *necessary* progression. Common or analogous stylistic patterns may appear in different media (as in the related features of Baroque music and Baroque architecture), and such likenesses may extend beyond the arts as well. But the assertion of a *Weltgeist* that, on the Hegelian concept, imparts a common style to all contemporary modes of expression seems more than the evidence supports, if it is verifiable at all.

Style is sometimes invoked as itself a positive attribute, as when a person "has style" or acts "with style" (or *is* "stylish")—although, on the other hand, something designedly "in" a style may by that fact be presented as less than the real thing (as a "Georgian-style" building would not be *quite* Georgian). Furthermore, individual categories may have positive connotations; it would be as unlikely to find a "unified" theme cited in evidence of a work's failure as it would be for "incoherence" to be a positive feature. Often, however, stylistic terms are neutral in evaluative connotation, as they mark differences between one work and others of a kind, or between the one kind and others, or call attention to particular aspects of the work that subsequently affect its evaluation. Whether stylistic features are executed well or badly in a given work is a separate question from that of their presence or identity; even an unusually distinctive style provides no more assurance of aesthetic quality—kitsch is an example of this—than would less distinctive ones, although to find that a work is *without* style would ordinarily be a negative and probably decisive judgment.

Many standard stylistic categories now applied descriptively and neutrally originally had evaluative connotations (as *Baroque* denoted the bizarre or absurd and *Mannerist* an affected or exaggerated quality). The claim that all stylistic categories were initially evaluative, as E. H. Gombrich (1968) asserts for those of art history, is debatable; it seems clear, in any event, that not all terms evaluative of art are style terms, beginning with "beauty" itself. Insofar as an expressive function is intrinsic to style, the categories of style *would* be closely associated with the intensity of an audience's reaction to corresponding features of the artwork itself.

Categories employed in descriptive stylistics may affect critical evaluation internal to the category (as in distinguishing between a good and a bad instance of Gothic) or by external comparison (the Gothic as judged superior or inferior to the Romanesque). An individual work may be judged a failure or a success in its style, but such judgment implies an independent stylistic baseline. Even if the distinction is at some points indeterminate, the difference between a work of "bad" style and one with no style seems worth preserving (even for an evaluative relativism that refuses to judge among styles, the absence of all style would be noteworthy). To the extent that stylistic features are distinguished from other aesthetic features, it follows that a "bad" style may be outweighed by other features, and that a "good" style (necessarily more than only *being* a style) would not be sufficient for similarly judging the whole. Not all aesthetically relevant or even all "good-making" features of a work are features of style; the "thought" ingredient in literature, for example—as noted in Aristotle's *Poetics* among the six elements of tragedy—extends beyond style (as in respect to judgment of its truth or importance) even though it also may also appear as an aspect of individual or group style.

Style can be imitated or forged, with the latter's most successful examples no doubt hanging undetected in museums or wrongly attributed in library catalogs. The claim that forgeries too are stylistically identifiable in relation to their creator has been made for many that have been discovered, but this is no more compelling a basis for assuming that all forgeries are in principle detectable than for inferring that all forgeries *will* be detected. This constraint suggests that a forger's style might succeed in *being* that of the original artist, although an objection to that possibility registers in Cardinal John Newman's contention that somebody could "as well say that one man's shadow is another's as that the style of a really gifted mind can belong to any but himself." Such emphasis on the uniqueness of individual style—a still-recurrent theme inherited from Romanticism—narrows what style does in art to the function of representing the artist's persona or emotional state; Jonathan Swift's brief tribute to style that places expression in a broader, more impersonal framework—"Proper words in proper places"—offers an instructive contrast.

In recent aesthetic theory and art criticism, the role of style and its categories has been attacked from various directions; at an extreme, style, whether as phenomenon or concept, is denied all warrant. Some objections to this effect come from antiformalist theories that, committed to psychological, cultural, or material bases of interpretation, dispute the usefulness or even the possibility of translating those grounds into stylistic categories. A different source of opposition appears in the objections of postmodernist or poststructuralist theory to the reification it finds in interpretations of style where the artist appears as its source or embodiment, or to what it claims is the imposition of an "essentialist" unity of style on disparate aesthetic features. The latter assumptions are attacked as tendentious: if style is an epiphenomenon, aesthetic analysis should see through it; and if the self is not unified, styles that are described as unified expressions of the artist's self would have had that unity imposed by the "stylist" (for reasons that may have little to do with art). Such objections have not, however, prevented the use of *postmodernist* itself as a stylistic category, applied first to architecture but then to other arts as well, as traditional norms of style in them are subverted—replaced, however, by what turn out to be almost "constant forms" like the pastiche or (in Fredric Jameson's [1994] categorization) "dirty realism."

Coincident with attacks on style from this direction has been an extension of the concept to forms of expression not previously associated with it, as in "styles" of historical, philosophical, or scientific discourse, and in the still more inclusive "lifestyles." The proposed extension to these areas conflicts with the more traditional ideal of truth or cognitive content as unaffected by its means (or styles) of presentation. This conflict calls attention to an often unnoticed condition of style as a pluralistic and, to that extent, skeptical concept that presupposes alternate possibilities—no one style, in other words, without (at least) two. The denial of this condition implies a view of the content of art or of other discourses as supralinguistic and, still more clearly, suprastylistic—a recurrent theme of rationalism that is epitomized in Baruch Spinoza's statement that "God has no particular style in speaking." Situated in this way between denials of the existence of style, on the one hand, and proposals to find it everywhere, on the other, the present status of style promises a future hardly less unsettled than its past.

[See also Baroque Aesthetics; Benjamin, *article on* Benjamin's Writing Style; Japanese Aesthetics, *article on* Kire and Iki; Literature, *article on* Literary Aesthetics; Narrative; Nietzsche, *article on* Nietzsche's Literary Style; Schapiro; *and* Wölfflin.]

BIBLIOGRAPHY

Ackerman, James. "A Theory of Style." *Journal of Aesthetics and Art Criticism* 20 (1962): 227–237.

Chatman, Seymour, ed. *Literary Style: A Symposium.* New York and Oxford, 1971.

Clifford, James, and George E. Marcus, eds. *Writing Culture: The Poetics and Politics of Ethnography.* Berkeley, 1986.

Danto, Arthur C. *The Transfiguration of the Commonplace.* Cambridge, Mass., 1981.

Foucault, Michel. "What Is an Author?" In *Language, Counter-Memory, Practice: Selected Essays and Interviews,* translated by Donald F. Bouchard and Sherry Simon, pp. 113–138. Ithaca, N.Y., 1977.

Gombrich, E. H. "Style." In *International Encyclopedia of the Social Sciences*, vol. 15, edited by David L. Sills, pp. 353–361. New York, 1968.

Gombrich, E. H. *Norm and Form* (1966). 4th ed. London, 1985.

Goodman, Nelson. *Problems and Projects.* Indianapolis, 1972.

Goodman, Nelson. "The Status of Style." *Critical Inquiry* 1.4 (June 1975): 799–811.

Gross, Alan G. *The Rhetoric of Science.* Cambridge, Mass., 1990.

Hegel, Georg Wilhelm Friedrich. *Aesthetics: Lectures on Fine Art.* 2 vols. Translated by T. M. Knox. Oxford, 1975.

Hirsch, E. D. "Stylistics and Synonymy." *Critical Inquiry* 1.3 (March 1975): 559–579.

Hough, Graham. *Style and Stylistics.* London, 1969.

Jameson, Fredric. *The Seeds of Time.* New York, 1994.

Kennedy, George. *The Art of Rhetoric in the Roman World.* Princeton, N.J., 1972.

Kristeller, Paul Oskar. "The Modern System of the Arts." *Journal of the History of Ideas* 12.4 (October 1951): 496–527; 13.1 (January 1952): 17–46.

Lang, Berel, ed. *The Concept of Style.* Rev. exp. ed. Ithaca, N.Y., 1987.

Lang, Berel. *The Anatomy of Philosophical Style: Literary Philosophy and the Philosophy of Literature.* Oxford and Cambridge, Mass., 1990.

Meyer, Leonard B. *Style and Music: Theory, History, and Ideology.* Philadelphia, 1989.

Schapiro, Meyer. "Style." In *Aesthetics Today*, edited by Morris Philipson, pp. 91–113. Cleveland, Ohio, 1961.

van Eck, Caroline, James McAllister, and Renee van de Vall, eds. *The Question of Style in Philosophy and the Arts.* Cambridge and New York, 1995.

White, Hayden. *Metahistory: The Historical Imagination in Nineteenth-Century Europe.* Baltimore, 1973.

Wölfflin, Heinrich. *Principles of Art History: The Problem of the Development of Style in Later Art.* Translated by M. D. Hottinger (1932). New York, 1951.

Wollheim, Richard. *The Mind and Its Depths.* Cambridge, Mass., 1993.

BEREL LANG

SUBLIME. [*To analyze the role of the concept of the sublime in aesthetics, this entry comprises three essays:*

The Sublime from Longinus to Montesquieu
The Sublime from Burke to the Present
Feminine Sublime

The first essay traces the early history of the concept of the sublime before and up to the birth of aesthetics. The second essay continues this history from that period up through contemporary theories of the sublime. The final essay introduces the notion of the feminine sublime, which serves as a critical challenge to the traditional understanding of the sublime. For related discussion, see Beauty; *and* Nature.]

The Sublime from Longinus to Montesquieu

Belonging to an old Greek and Latin tradition, the concept of the sublime experienced two main "renaissances": the first began not in the Romantic age, but at the height of classicism; the second appeared in the late twentieth century along with the rise of postmodernism. In order to understand the grounds for such resurgences, one has to consider the first writings on the sublime, and the various points of view they represented.

Adjective or Noun? First of all, the absence of homogeneity between a long literary tradition and a philosophical one must be stressed. In the former, *sublime* is not infrequently an adjective, synonymous with *grave, elevated, strongly conceived,* or *impressive.* In the latter, on the contrary, *sublime* designates a category opposed to the beautiful, both aesthetic and trans-aesthetic, the theoretization of which in the mid-eighteenth century accompanies the birth of the aesthetic problematically: does it confirm the closure of aesthetics, or, to the contrary, demonstrate the impossibility of such closure?

In fact, a profound duality of origin is hidden under the current uniformity in the vocabulary of the sublime: whereas the same term, pronounced differently, is used in English, French, Italian, and Spanish, as a simple or substantivized adjective, reflection on the sublime has developed historically from Greek and Latin terms of dissimilar grammatical and etymological nature. The Greek *hypsous* is a noun, belonging to a rich and well-constructed family of terms all derived from the adverb *hypsi. Hypsous* commonly means "height," conceived as a spatial dimension and opposed to width and length, and takes on the figurative meaning of a climax. On the contrary, the Latin *sublimis* is an adjective, and indeed an unusual one, with a problematic meaning. It is derived from *sub,* which marks the displacement toward the high, and from *limis* or *limus* (oblique, askew), which characterize a certain direction of gaze, such as that of cross-eyed Athena, or a certain type of ascension nonorthogonal to the ground. Quintilian sanctions this use in the expression "sublime type of speech" *(genus sublime dicendi).* In fact, it is impossible to substantivize adjectives in Latin—a language lacking articles. As for the term *sublimity (sublimitas),* it is certainly not correctly rendered as *hypsous,* because it does not designate the full range of things that are sublime, but the simple fact of being sublime.

In theorizing about the sublime, this leads to considerable divergences of evaluation. On the one hand, it is the idea of the sublime that commands attention and one endeavors to elucidate its genesis and status. On the other hand, one is concerned more with styles or levels of discourse, in order to try to determine one or several sublime traits. Thus, two conceptions of invention come face-to-face: one defining its object according to the theory of stylistic genres and the other locating the force of the conception in its nascent state, in its creative virtue.

But between an adjective, conceived as a simple descriptive and evaluative tool, and a substantive, which refers to an essence, a gap appears that seems essential. Indeed, the real problem is to understand the sublime as simultaneously being (1) in its more or less contingent vehicles; (2) in its effects, which cannot be reduced to the strict combination of admiration and pleasure; and (3) in its principles, which appear bound to the constitution of the subject as self-transcending. On this single condition it would be possible to avoid not only the uncontrolled usage of the concept, which seems bound up with the generalization of adjectival employment, but also its dogmatic use, based on a specific theory. Having avoided the radical dispersal of the sublime in the sensible world, the difficulty lies in not hypostatizing the idea of the sublime. One must preserve absolutely the operational and critical sense of the concept historically attributed to it. The sublime remains a question that is always subdividing, for one can discriminate certain modes of "entry" or angles from which an artwork, a deed, or even a life might be considered sublime.

Accordingly, it is important to investigate by which type of variation—spontaneous, or more or less voluntary—one privileges certain values in a given field or space. Only a certain selection allows the sublime to emerge in its entirety. Now, is not the desire to encourage one type of redistribution and develop the appreciation of the sublime the basis for a truly educating education?

Longinus and the Founding of the Sublime. Such is the case in the sole treatise on the sublime that antiquity has bequeathed to us, under the name of *Peri Hypsous* (On the Sublime) and whose orientation is presented from the very start as practical. *On the Sublime* does not concern itself with defining the sublime theoretically for a public assumed to be unaware of it, but rather with finding "by what means" we might be able to lead "our natural gifts to a certain degree of elevation." This work, baptized the "golden book" by Isaac Casaubon (1605), nearly disappeared in antiquity and was revived in the Renaissance, broken off in seven places and attributed to a fictional author. It is reasonable to assume at present that this anonymous or pseudoauthor, who we still call Longinus, lived during the reigns of Claudius and Nero, perhaps in Alexandria. His culture was principally Hellenistic, he quotes Genesis once, and he presents his treatise as a missive to a Roman friend. Accordingly, *On the Sublime* is situated at the crossroads of three great traditions and it is quite significant that the category of the sublime was elaborated in a time of unprecedented change: one in which Christian monotheism asserted its authority, while the power of Rome grew greater out of the wreckage of the Republic. In a period of crisis affecting all values, does not the sublime correspond to a will to recapture what dazzles and deserves to dazzle?

Longinus essentially studies the sublime immanent in discourse. He excludes the idea of a sublime transcending all manifestation, but not that of a natural sublime. True to the anthropocentric tendency in Greek philosophy, he concentrates on humankind more than on the external world. Nevertheless, under his aegis, although only in an incidental clause of chapter 35, the sublime acquires a body, a hydrography, and a cosmography: on the one hand, the vast and indefinite, on the other, the unpredictable and terrible. No mere rivers inspire astonishment, but great ones and, even more, the ocean; it is not the burst of a slight flame that sears, but the lights tearing through the celestial darkness and rivers of fire pouring down from Mount Etna.

Prevalent in the rhetorical and poetic spheres, the sublime is defined as "a certain distinction and excellence in discourse." It aims neither at persuading nor pleasing; it is neither useful nor agreeable. Rather, it causes rapture or ecstasy by storm. The violence is indeed accepted, but it is violence all the same—attesting to the properly "irresistible" character of the sublime. The dazzled witness then tends to identify with the source, acting as if the constraint emanated not from without, but from within himself, "for, as if instinctively, our soul is uplifted by the true sublime; it takes a proud flight, and is filled with joy and vaunting, as though it had itself produced what it has heard" (Longinus, 1899).

Analyzing the sources of the sublime, Longinus insists on the reversibility of art and nature. Art does nothing but reveal nature, whereas nature itself cannot act without art. As for nature, the power of conception and the vehement and inspired character of passion constitute the sources of the sublime. As for art, on the contrary, we distinguish the due formation of figures, nobility of expression, and, lastly, the dignity and elevation of the composition. But the redundancy of the expression clearly shows the circle in which we are caught: the sublime arises out of what is already sublime. Its character is to require itself. If we vacillate then in the interpretation, opting at times for a hierarchization of the sources that puts greatness of mind at the forefront, at other times for equal dignity for each source, this really results from an inability to think the unity. The sublime is not one among many other possible qualities. It radiates from all sides at once, like what is achieved in the singular melding of genius with its instruments. One must say of sublime discourse, then, not that it possesses sublimity, but that it *is* the sublime in nascent state.

The Sublime and Genus Dicendi. One Latin translation played a large role in the history of the resurrection of Longinus's treatise even before the principal edition of the Greek text. Gustavo Costa has attributed it to Fulvio Orsini and has demonstrated its influence, from the outset of the cinquecento, on the intellectual environment of the Farnese and, particularly, on Michelangelo. Apart from this exception and the first Italian version of 1639, all later editions use the expression *sublime genus dicendi* in their titles. We must try therefore to analyze on what basis the junction of sublime style and the Longinian *hypsous* can have been brought about.

The theory of types of speech *(genera dicendi)* begins with Theophrastus in the fourth century BCE. The meager *(ischnos)* and mean *(mesos)* styles, corresponding to the Latin terms *gracilis* and *mediocris,* respectively, were opposed by the Greeks to the muscular or robust *(adros)* style. The *Rhetorica ad Herennium* (c.86–83 BCE), which is the oldest

Latin source, distinguishes between three genres: grave or imposing *(gravis),* intermediate *(mediocris),* and diminished *(extenuatus* or *attentuatus).* Cicero picks up on this triad in one of his last works, *The Orator* (46 BCE), and coins the adjective *grandiloquent,* to which he gives a laudatory sense lost today. The grand style is characterized by the abundance of gravity, but Cicero adds three new criteria: vehemence, variety, and impressiveness. Choice of style is made according to the criterion of appropriateness: "to prove is proper to necessity, to charm proper to agreement, to yield proper to victory." Nevertheless, the grave style overshadows the other criteria because, concentrating on the greatest power, it arouses the wonder of peoples and dominates them. Thus, Quintilian awards the palm cleanly to the sublime style, acknowledging that it leaves the audience defenseless. "Delivered to the disorder of his senses, beyond himself, the judge gives himself entirely over to the orator without concerning himself with the matter of the case." In fact, the sublime of Quintilian has in common with the Longinian *hypsous* the "fascinating splendor" that plunges the discussion of facts into shadow and that, far from soberly persuading the audience, ravishes it in ecstasy, even against its will; and so the handling of it should be reserved to honest men.

Moreover, we have at our disposal Demetrius's treatise *On Style,* dating back to the first century BCE or perhaps earlier. Demetrius contrasts the elevated style *(megaloprepēs)* to the vehement style *(deinos),* in order to set both over against simple style. Elevated style, exemplified by Thucydides, is characterized by a solemn gravity and already eludes ordinary language, whose clarity makes emotive power disappear. Vehement style, illustrated by Demosthenes, evokes combatants dealing blows at close quarters and goes so far as to seek darkness, in the belief that what is suggested by allusion has more value than what is flatly exposed.

Although Demetrius treats a question of style, and not the sublime properly speaking, he has the merit of introducing a remarkable tension: should we seek the sublime more in terms of the force of conception, or more in terms of that of passion? Morpurgo Tagliabue (1980) believes it possible to show that Edmund Burke's sublime of the terrible is closer to the *deinos* of Demetrius than the *hypsous* of Longinus. But, if Longinus makes the sublime first and foremost "the echo of a great spirit," and if he affirms that *pathos* is not absolutely necessary to the sublime, he nevertheless recognizes that "there is no tone so lofty as that of genuine passion, in its right place."

Nicolas Boileau and the Revision of Rhetoric. Boileau was the first to uproot the sublime explicitly from the categories of rhetoric and to use the substantivized adjective in the title of his translation of Longinus, *A Treatise on the Sublime; or, on the Marvelous in Discourse* (1674): "We must therefore know that by 'sublime' Longinus does not understand what orators call sublime style. . . . A thing can be in the sublime style yet fail to be sublime, that is, fail to have anything extraordinary or astonishing." The Longinian revolution consists in suppressing the opposition between the simple and sublime styles at the heart of the theory of the *genera dicendi*—put another way, it was to rehabilitate the simple and make it consubstantial with the sublime.

Boileau no doubt ends up making a caricature of Longinus's thought by projecting onto it his own rationalist and normative conception of art in which clarity of expression follows from excellence of conception, which, in turn, follows from a single, universal precept: "to please at length and never to make weary." Such is Boileau's aim, where Longinus found, above all else, ecstasy.

That Boileau bestowed a dignity on the English sublime is nevertheless implicitly acknowledged by Samuel Johnson when he declares that "'the sublime' is a Gallicism, but now naturalized." But the translation of *hypsous* as "sublime," which in itself seems suitable in Romance languages, continues to pose problems in English. According to W. Rhys Roberts, who nevertheless adopts the term in 1899, "a misconception has been the result, a misconception which the existence of Burke's homonymous treatise *On the Sublime and the Beautiful* has done much to increase" (Longinus, 1899).

The Invention of New Landscapes: From the Rhetorical to the Natural Sublime. However powerful the impulse of Boileau to reconsider the sublime, the decisive fact derives less from deliberated theoretical change than from a radical change in sensibility. Under the influence of new *practica* with nature and of new scientific and technical discoveries, attention was no longer directed just toward the inhabited earth, but to the mountain, the littoral, the sea, and the desert. On the one hand, the custom of the grand tour, mountaineering, medicinal sea baths; on the other, the challenge to geocentrism and geostatism, as well as the discovery of the richness of nature viewed with the new optical apparatuses (the microscope and telescope)— all contributed to shape a new way of looking at the phenomenal world that the "natural sublime" perfectly symbolizes. If Samuel Monk (1960) could maintain that, in the eighteenth century, the history of the sublime generally coincides with interpretations of Longinus, that is doubtless primarily because the new sensibility could think itself prefigured in chapter 35 of his work, mentioned earlier as involving the sublime of great rivers, oceans, and volcanoes.

It is striking that all the traits that Charles de Marguetel de Saint-Denis de Saint-Évremond, for example, negatively emphasizes in his *Dissertation on the Word "Vast"* (1685) might easily be called on to characterize the sublime. Stigmatizing inordinate and excessive grandeur, kindred to the ugly and horrible, and sign of the impermeability to culture or of a destruction just exerted, Saint-Évremond defines in a premonitory way what will become the natural sublime:

> vast things do not suit things that make an agreeable impression upon us. . . . Vast forests frighten us. The view dissipates and disappears in looking upon vast fields. . . . Rivers that are too large, overwhelming things, and floods displease us by their unrest and our eyes are unable to endure their vast extent. . . . *Vasius quasi vastatus*, vast. It is nearly the same as decayed and ruined.

The first writer who, far from disapproving of it, expresses a fascination with physical grandeur is Thomas Burnet, to whom we owe a "novel" about the earth compatible with biblical teaching and illustrated with engravings designed to excite the imagination: the *Telluris Theoria Sacra*, which appeared in 1681, with an English translation by 1684. Burnet praises, in an entirely new way, the magnificence of the ocean and of mountain ranges: "The greatest objects of Nature are, methinks, the most pleasing to behold; and next to the great Concave of the Heavens, and those boundless Regions where the stars inhabit, there is nothing that I look upon with more pleasure than the wide Sea and the Mountains of the Earth." Quite impressed by Burnet's theory, John Dennis in 1693 describes the "delightful horror" in which he is plunged by the contemplation of the Alps: "we may well say [of nature] what some affirm of great Wits, that her careless, irregular and boldest Strokes are most admirable. For the Alps are works which she seems to have design'd, and executed too in Fury" (1693).

Anthony Ashley Cooper, earl of Shaftesbury, will powerfully echo these themes in *The Moralists* of 1709, more precisely in part 3, which praises the beauty of wild places and deserts: "The wildness pleases," declares Theocles, "we seem to live alone with Nature. We view her in her inmost recesses, and contemplate her with more delight in these original wilds than in the artificial labyrinths and feigned wilderness of the palace." [*See* Cooper.] But the text that exercises the most influence is undoubtedly Joseph Addison's famous series "On the Pleasures of Imagination," which appeared in *The Spectator* in 1712. Addison, who had been Burnet's student, focuses his analysis on the great, an aesthetic category that he sets over against both the uncommon and the beautiful: "By greatness, I do not only mean the bulk of any single object, but the largeness of a whole view, considered as one entire piece. . . . Our imagination loves to be filled with an object, or grasp at anything that is too big for its capacity" (1712). Thus, Addison glorifies Longinus as being one of the few critics able to take into consideration "something more essential, to the art, something that elevates and astonishes the fancy, and gives a greatness of mind to the reader" (ibid.).

Of an Overwhelming Principle Grasped in Astonishment. What was the status accorded to the constitutive experiences of the new landscapes? How can one explain that the vacillation caused by the awareness of new phenomena and by the progression of our faculties beyond their accustomed bounds can be converted into delight? A peculiar form of reality arises along with the sublime, which questions us while it dazzles us. But the odd thing is that we would be able to draw from this experience a form of pleasure.

It is with Giambattisa Vico that we encounter, in the first half of the eighteenth century, the most extraordinary attempt to grasp in *uncivilized* humankind the wondering that permits the constitution of a properly human world. The metaphysics of the first humans—neither rational nor abstract, but felt and imagined—will allow us to understand how imagination and thought were set in motion and how a similar stimulation can be renewed in our own time in the experience of the sublime, conceived as a conversion in the poetic order of an originary impact. Recall the cardinal experience of a shock that it is the property of the sublime to restore in its values of actualization: one hundred years after the Flood, when the earth was finally dry, the sky hurled bolts of lightning and terrifying claps of thunder. "Thereupon a few giants, who must have been the most robust . . . were frightened and astonished by the great effect whose cause they did not know, and raised their eyes and became aware of the sky" (Vico, 1968). From this followed a belief in a god, search for shelter in caverns, and, by degrees, divination, marriage, and agriculture. Therefore, one would have to show how in Vico's work man becomes everything, not by understanding the world, but by *not* understanding it *(homo, non intelligendo, fit omnia)*. Man feels himself confronted by irreducible alterity, whose marvelous halo, paradoxically, it attains in the most trying of circumstances. The progress of civilization provides extraordinary testimony of this awareness.

In another register—no longer involved with converting an emotion, but rather with an emotion already converted by the agency of art—recall the eulogy of continual surprise that one finds in Montesquieu's *Essay on Taste*, translated by Burke in 1759: surprise is born of the contrast between what we know and what we see; above all, it springs out of the consideration of an almost unbearable spectacle. "In the Passion in the gallery in Florence, Michelangelo has painted the Virgin upright, looking upon her crucified son without sadness, pity, regret, or weeping. He assumes her aware of this great mystery and therefore makes her bear the sight of this death with grandeur" (1759). Does the horror of death yield to the sublime of consent? The witness remains placed before the door of the mystery, where what appears immediately slips away and where the imminence of the inaccessible is felt. View and review the object as we might, "our suspension and, I dare say, our ignorance, still remains" (ibid.). The essential is no doubt of a different order than positive knowledge; the experience of the sublime is fundamental in that it brings about a relativization of knowledge. Thus Montesquieu assigns the disappearance of the sublime to "that new philosophy which only talks of general laws and which removes from the mind all particular thoughts of divinity" (ibid.)—in short, to the philosophy that Vico principally opposed as built on a misunderstanding of the power of the imagination and the nature of language in its poetic mode of constitution.

Thus, everything seems now in place for Burke to systematically oppose the sublime to the beautiful: the beautiful settles us in the world, the sublime dazzles and bewilders by transgressing form and confusing reference. Burkean astonishment will upset the subject in his intimacy, thanks to the revelation of a radical principle of dispossession, which Burke's originality is to apprehend independently of any religious or moral consideration. Moreover, looking for the sources of the sublime in the phenomenal world, Burke tries to define the qualities belonging not only to single objects, but to atmospheres, as we would say today. "When danger or pain press too nearly, they are incapable of giving any delight, and are simply terrible; but at certain distances, and with certain modifications, they may be, and they are delightful, as we every day experience." Thus, the problem will be to understand the "distance" and the "modifications" that allow the terrifying principle to be converted into the sublime principle, and the effect of fright into that of astonishment.

But how to distinguish the true mystery from the seeming mystery and the deepest awe from superficial dread? One can see how easily the sublime could arouse suspicion and be changed into its contrary. If we want to avoid the misunderstandings caused by Demetrius's and Burke's theory, we must state that the sublime is not only an immediate overwhelming power, but also a lasting incitement to critical reflection.

[*See also* Longinus.]

BIBLIOGRAPHY

Addison, Joseph. "On the Pleasures of Imagination." *The Spectator* (June–July, 1712).

Boileau-Despréaux, Nicolas. Preface to translation of Longinus, *Traité du sublime.* Paris, 1674.

Burnet, Thomas. *Telluris Theoria Sacra.* Londini, 1681.

Cooper, Anthony Ashley, Earl of Shaftesbury. *Characteristics of Men, Manners, Opinions, Times.* London, 1711.

Demetrius. *Demetrius on Style: The Greek Text of Demetrius, "De Elocutione," Edited after the Paris Manuscript.* Edited and translated by W. Rhys Roberts. Cambridge, 1902.

Dennis, John. *Miscellanies in Verse and Prose.* London, 1693.

Longinus. *Longinus on the Sublime: The Greek Text Edited after the Paris Manuscript.* Edited and translated by W. Rhys Roberts. Cambridge, 1899.

Monk, Samuel H. *The Sublime: A Study of Critical Theories in Eighteenth-Century England.* New York, 1935; reprint, Ann Arbor, 1960.

Montesquieu, Charles de Secondat, Baron de. *Essai sur le goût.* Paris, 1757.

Saint Girons, Baldine. *Fiat lux: Une philosophie du sublime.* Paris, 1993.

Vico, Giambattista. *The New Science of Giambattista Vico* (1744). Rev. ed. Translated by Thomas Goddard Bergin and Max Harold Fisch from the 3d ed. of 1774. Ithaca, N.Y., 1968.

BALDINE SAINT GIRONS
Translated from French by Fred L. Rush, Jr.

The Sublime from Burke to the Present

The modern history of the notion of the sublime begins with the discovery of the fragments of the classical text *Peri Hypsous* (rendered as *On Elevation, On Greatness,* or *On the Sublime*). This text is now attributed to Longinus or Pseudo-Longinus who lived in the first century CE. Formerly it was attributed to Cassius Longinus, a rhetorician and teacher of rhetoric taken to have lived in the third century CE. This text had a profound impact on the world of modern European letters from the time of Nicolas Boileau's translation into French in 1672. The treatise's basic contribution was to reanalyze the stylistic hierarchy of speech—the high, middle, and low styles—to argue that rhetoric involved not merely the capacity for recognizing and deploying a style appropriate to one's subject matter but also included a judgment on a rhetorical performance or a literary work. For the moderns, it came to be seen as a central statement of the view that art involved the achievement of a previously unanticipated success, what would later be known as the "je ne sais quoi" or the "grace beyond the reach of art" that made successful works of art seem not just successful but surprisingly so. As a registration of the difficulties of resolving artistic accomplishment or greatness into prescriptive formulas that artists might simply follow, the classical text came to be the modern pretext for insisting on the aesthetic as an arena of the surprising, the unexpected—a position that seemed only to have been enhanced by the fact that the treatise's rediscovery made it look like an intriguing interruption of literary tradition, a kind of classical novelty.

Longinus's fragmentary treatise had posed a significant challenge to the very tradition that it participated in. If the rhetorician had most frequently seen himself as teaching others how to be rhetorically effective, Longinus, by contrast, stressed the limitations of conventions and formulas and instead appealed to the significance of audience reaction as evidence of those limitations. What would once have been described as correct came to be seen as "merely correct." Although Longinus's remarks, particularly because of their imperfect state of preservation, constituted something more like practical criticism than a full-blown theory of rhetoric, their general tendency became especially important for the examination of the sublime under the auspices of a formalist aesthetics, in which neither the original intention of the author nor the originary context of a work was seen as particularly important in justifying a claim about the aesthetic power of that object.

The clearest version of that argument would, however, only emerge with Immanuel Kant's *Critique of Judgment* (1790). Initially, the rediscovery of the sublime took the form of investigating the impact of both objects of experience and literary works on observers. The sublime was routinely coupled with the beautiful to produce a classificatory system for judgments about experience. In Edmund Burke's empiricist treatment, the analysis of the beautiful and the sublime was simply a way of noticing the physiological effects of objects on individuals. Thus, his *A Philosophical Enquiry into the Origin of Our Ideas of the Sublime and Beautiful* (1757) insisted first on the reliability and universality of the testimony of the senses, and tried to uncover large patterns in that testimony by organizing it under the categories of the beautiful and the sublime. The beautiful, which Burke continually related to the social emotions of companionability, encompassed a range of qualities that all shared familiarity and comprehensibility; the sublime, which Burke linked with the more strenuous purposes of heroism, he associated with the sense of exertion brought on by a confrontation with the surprising or unfamiliar, with objects of experience extending beyond an individual's reach. In keeping with this general division, things that were diminutive and smooth were conceived as beautiful because they seemed to conform especially well with the human sensory organs, and things that were novel, obscure, and terrible were conceived as sublime because they seemed to challenge those organs. Thus, Burke saw himself as demonstrating, for example, the aptness of sweetness for the tongue by describing how sugars, as versions of several "perfect globes," move on the taste buds in such a way as to confirm the taste in its own conformation. Analogously, he described the ways in which such things as darkness or excessive light would seem sublime on account of the difficulty that the senses had in working with them.

Especially in the most insistently physiological discussions, Burke's *Enquiry* suggested that beauty and sublimity were properties of objects, persistent attributes that could be discovered by experience. The judgment of taste, from this standpoint, appeared merely a way of categorizing experiences of that were unequivocal. Yet, even as he pursued that claim, he was also simultaneously advancing another somewhat different view, one in which the purpose of aesthetic experience was not so much to reveal the stable and intrinsic properties of objects as to draw attention to the various aspects under which they might be considered. Thus, he made it clear that the same object might be viewed in various "distinct lights": "The description of the wild ass, in Job, is worked up into no small sublimity, merely by insisting on his freedom, and his setting mankind at defiance; otherwise the description of such an animal could have had nothing noble in it" (II, v).

What Burke had accomplished in his *Enquiry*, then, was both to suggest that rhetoric had traditionally been credited with power inasmuch as it dealt in obscure connections between understanding and affect and to argue that not only language provided instances of such difficulties. Although his introduction on taste had implied that he was merely cataloging the uniformity of reactions that all people would have to objects of experience, he had ended by discovering the extent to which representation itself produced a new set of elements to be responded to. Memory and anticipation began to complicate the testimony that he developed about the sensory experience of objects, and the specific words and images of a speech from Homer or a passage from Job came to appear less like testimony about physiological regularity than like an occasion for new sensations.

Yet, if Burke's attention could be said to shift in the *Enquiry* from the objects of experience to the various senses through which they were represented—and, indeed, to various representational systems such as poetry or language—Kant's *Critique of Judgment* (1790) reoriented the project of the sublime. Turning away from the more nearly Burkean perspective that he had adopted in his earlier *Observations on the Feeling of the Beautiful and Sublime* (1763), in which he had tried to scan the collections of objects that he identified as beautiful or sublime and to talk about their common properties, he foregrounded the differences between aesthetic judgments and both epistemological claims and moral judgments. This project involved him in dividing the beautiful and the sublime in a novel way. While most commentators on the sublime proceeded, as Burke had, by treating both natural objects and human artifacts as beautiful or sublime, Kant restricted the sublime—or what he termed the "sublime properly so-called" (section 23)—to judgments on *natural* objects alone. His purpose in making such a restriction was not to argue that one could not see stirring and thus sublime themes or effects in art or in other human productions. Rather, he isolated the sublime in cases that demonstrated natural might or infinitude because he wanted to call attention to the ways in which judgments on the sublime were no less important for not being objective, for not being readily resolved into claims about the nature of the object under scrutiny or about the conditions under which it was viewed. The natural sublime thus provided a clear instance of an individual judgment that could appeal to no evidence outside itself: one could neither solicit confirmation from other people nor appeal to the conventions and conditions under which the object had been produced. Sublime aesthetic experience was important because it involved treating what was not produced to be meaningful to us as if it were meaningful, or what he called, in one of the *Critique*'s most significant phrases, "purposiveness without purpose." What the experience of the sublime contributed, over and above the experience of the beautiful, was restlessness as opposed to satisfaction, a drive toward the as yet unapprehended, that would come to be associated with the claim that sublime aesthetic experience contained within it a commitment to avant-gardism.

Kant identified two different kinds of sublimity: (1) the mathematical, in which the reflective judgment is occupied not with measuring an object but with recognizing "in our imagination a striving toward infinite progress and in our reason a claim for absolute totality" that surpasses "every standard of sense"; and (2) the dynamical, in which one confronts the difference between human limitations as natural creatures and the nonsensuous standard of reason that enables us to find "in our mind . . . a superiority to nature even in its immensity." In the sublime, Kant sought to identify the curious pleasure that an individual might have in the experience of a negative; that is, he argued that we do not subscribe to the conventions that underwrite a mathematical series or acknowledge natural might out of a sense of necessity, or from the conviction that human society or nature require us to accept them. Rather, both human conventions and natural necessity become supportable, and indeed interesting, because sublime experience enables us to imagine them as reflection allows, so that reflection seems to allow for choice in relation to even the least elective aspects of experience. If the beautiful seemed to Kant to present particular difficulties and particular richness because it raised the question of how one might perceive new aspects of previously identified objects (the beauty of objects that had been made to be serviceable, for instance), the sublime, by contrast, involved a claim that the judgment needed to use an encounter with a *presentation* in the external world to discover the inadequacy of the presentation: "We must seek a ground external to ourselves for the beautiful in nature, but seek it for the sublime merely in ourselves and in our attitude of thought, which introduces sublimity into the representation of nature" (section 23).

The sublime in nature thus becomes a particularly pure instance of aesthetic judgment, because it is peculiarly unavailable to epistemological claims both about objects and about the nature of representational systems or the conditions of perception. Although judgments about beauty may well overlap with judgments about a particular concept (so that it becomes difficult to say how far one appreciates a flower, say, because it is beautiful, and how far one appreciates it because it is a good example of a flower), Kant attempted to describe the sublime independent of conceptual categories. Although he acknowledged the plausibility of describing a whole range of experiences and artifacts with the adjective *sublime,* he was not committed to identifying a general field of associations for the term or properties of objects that could be said to be sublime. Instead, he foregrounded the way in which nature might represent sublimity to humans, because he wanted to stress that nature harbored no views for or about persons. (It is a particularly important implicit theme of Kant's Third Critique that he is not describing nature as a book on which a divinity has en-

rolled a statement of its will.) Moreover, the ventriloquism that was involved in imagining that nature might speak to humans as they took it to be sublime made it possible to imagine what Kant meant in talking about the disinterestedness of the aesthetic judgment; an aesthetic judgment about sublime nature could not, by its nature, involve a claim about what a human agent had meant in making it a particular way. Because the significance of a sublime object existed in reception rather than in production, it would be especially difficult to describe sublime interest in any ordinary lexicon of motivation.

It may have been partially in reaction to Burke's affectivism, which Kant characterized as his capacity for penetrating observations from empirical psychology, that Kant introduced into the notion of the sublime a distinction between the mathematical and the dynamical sublime. His account of the dynamical sublime resembled Burke's account of the sublime generally; it involved a staged process of representing an object as exciting fear, recognizing that one "can regard an object as *fearful* without being afraid of it," and feeling pleasure that "in our rational faculty we find a different, nonsensuous standard" that reminds us of our own powers. The consciousness of nature's power over the sensuous aspect of human beings yields to the consciousness that "nature is here called sublime merely because it elevates the imagination to a presentation of those cases in which the mind can make felt the proper sublimity of its destination, in comparison with nature itself" (section 28). The mathematical sublime involved a less contestatory rhetoric. It enabled Kant to register the point that all standards (whether they have a tree, an English mile, or the human body as their unit) are themselves aesthetic, that "we can never have a first or fundamental measure" (section 26), and to suggest that this recognition could lead not simply to skepticism about the usefulness of measurement but to a pleasure in the mind's production of its own insatiable demand for a measure that could be enlarged to achieve a totality.

Friedrich von Schiller's brief essay *On the Sublime* (1801) extends an essentially Kantian position about the significance of the supersensible aspects of aesthetic experience. What Schiller draws from Kant's *Critique of Judgment* is the basic sense that the significance of aesthetic experience is its subjective character. Thus, whereas a figure like Burke had seen it as a limitation in aesthetic experience that it might be so subjective and variable as to be unavailable as knowledge, Schiller echoes Kant's distinction between cognitive statements and aesthetic judgments. Aesthetic objects therefore come to have less interest because of what they might teach us about the things they depict and greater interest because of what they lead us to recognize about human capacities. Opening his discussion by quoting from Gotthold Ephraim Lessing's *Nathan the Wise,* "No man must 'must,'" Schiller focuses his discussion on the support that he takes aesthetic judgments to lend to the will. For Schiller, human beings are, above all else, characterized by the capacity to will. This capacity manifests itself in what might, from Burke's perspective, look like a failure in aesthetic judgment. Whereas it might seem like a deficiency in the aesthetic judgment that one might not be able to communicate one's particular judgments to other people and that one might not be able to replicate one's particular judgments even for oneself, Schiller argued forcefully that this apparent weakness was not a failure in human understanding. It was, he thought, instead an indication that "the will is the genetic characteristic of man as species, and even reason is only its external rule" (Schiller, 1966).

If Burke had stressed the importance of natural might that reminded human beings of the comparative insignificance of their own powers and had argued that a consciousness of having escaped annihilation produced energizing emotions, Schiller proceeded from a diametrically opposed position. For him, the experience of the sublime involved the affirmation of human identity as the refusal to suffer violence from any of the "countless forces" that are superior to man's own and wield physical mastery over him. In an intensification of the Kantian view that what is termed "sublimity" can only be applied to external objects through a "subreption" of a descriptive language that ought, properly speaking, to be applied only to human consciousness, Schiller devotes his attention almost exclusively to that consciousness. He argues that "Man can no longer be the being that wills if there is even a *single* case in which he simply must do what he does not will" (ibid.), developing in the process a defense of "aesthetic education" as the process of enhancing the natural human powers with the kind of artificial enhancement that they can gain as they develop their consciousness of the importance of their wills in altering what might look like necessity. With the emphasis on aesthetic education as the development of character and the consolidation of a subjective technology, the sublime comes scarcely to seem attributable to external objects, which are significant largely as a series of obstacles that human consciousness seeks to overcome.

In Georg Wilhelm Friedrich Hegel's view, as he set it forth in his Berlin lectures on aesthetics of the 1820s, Schiller's opposition between natural necessity and the freedom of the human will only dramatized what he took to be a fatal weakness in Kantianism—that it tended to make the phenomenal world look merely conjectural. Hegel's criticism of Kant would operate on a number of different philosophical fronts; he would characteristically hold that Kant continually condemns experience to seeming possible rather than actual. With relation to aesthetic judgments, he criticized Kant's willingness to sacrifice objective knowledge to what he took to be the requirements of subjectivity, and to insist on the postulate that aesthetic experience might not be unified but that we had to treat it as if it were.

Thus, Hegel replies to Kant's statement that "the faculty of judgment must assume as a principle for its own use that what is contingent for us contains a unity, which for us indeed is not knowable, but yet thinkable, in the connection of the manifold with an implicitly possible experience" with the charge that this fixes "Being-in-itself" "once for all . . . outside of self-consciousness" and conceives the "Understanding . . . only in the form of the self-conscious, not in its becoming another."

The term *sublime* comes under considerable pressure in the substantial disagreement between Kant and Hegel. Kant had isolated the sublime from the beautiful along lines that were radically different from those of most commentators; that is, he had argued that the sublime was an interesting category precisely because it included no human artifacts, because its objects were identifiable as objects only through an individual subjective act of judgment. In so doing, he had made it seem merely metaphoric to speak of "sublime poetry" or "sublime painting," because those arts obviously had to have been made by someone and thus already had an objective existence that was independent of a particular viewer's experience of them. In Hegel's account, this Kantian notion of "purposiveness without purpose," with its emphasis on the *look* of intentional significance, comes under particular attack. Kant's account of the sublime had revolved around what Hegel singled out as objects with only "external adaption to end," and had thus pointed to the way in which Kant had defined the sublime not as an attribute of existing objects, but instead as a statement made on behalf of the human faculty of reason. From the perspective of Hegelian phenomenology, Kant's account of the sublime was thus unacceptable in its simultaneous suggestion and refusal of illusion. Hegel thus occupies himself exclusively with the fine arts insofar as they instantiate a unity of content and its presentation, and he tends to locate the sublime as one of the three basic relations of the Idea to its configuration. Arguing that "art begins" when "the Idea, still in its indeterminacy and obscurity, or in bad and untrue determinacy, is made the content of artistic shapes," he identifies sublimity as an an insufficiently individualized version of symbolic form, one in which "abstraction and one-sidedness leave its shapes externally defective and arbitrary." In the sublime mode, which he associates with the earliest stages of the historical unfolding of art, "the first form of art is . . . rather a *mere search* for portrayal than a capacity for true presentation; the Idea has not found the form even in itself and therefore remains struggling and striving after it" (ibid). Whereas Kant had spoken of the sublime as providing an understanding of the motives for art that always lies beyond the reach of actual art, Hegel's effort is to identify the sublime as an aspect of art with specific limitations that can be, and are, overcome. Thus, he instances the incompatibility of the relationship between the Idea and natural objects that are thoroughly determinate in their shape as an instance of the sublime, and describes the incompatibility as "a *negative* one," because "the Idea, as something inward, is itself unsatisfied by such externality, and, as the inner universal substance thereof, it persists *sublime* above all this multiplicity of shapes which do not correspond with it."

If Hegel had revived the notion of representational strain in his account of the symbolic mode of sublime art, Theodor W. Adorno, in his *Aesthetic Theory* (1997), identified Hegel's determination to viewing "spirit as a defining characteristic of works of art" as a significant weakness, one that hypostatized spirit's "objectivity as a kind of absolute identity," a simple epiphenomenon of the Hegelian system. In so doing, he revived interest in Kantian aesthetics for its principled ambiguity in "beginning with a sense of necessity and at the same time denying necessity's existence" (1997). He thus adapts Kant's account of the sublime, treating it as the prototype of contradictory experiences of the same object, and describing it as particularly well instanced in the "kind of art that vibrates and quakes by suspending itself for the sake of a non-illusory truth content, while simultaneously being unable to slough off its illusory quality as an art" (ibid.). For Adorno, then, the sublime does not remain outside of art (as it had in the Kantian account). Indeed, Kant's recognition of the sublime in a feeling for nature is simply a historical fact, evidence of the fact that Kant "had not yet experienced great subjective art." And if Adorno comes to aver that it "might be better to stop talking about the sublime completely," because "the term has been corrupted beyond recognition by the mumbo jumbo of the high priests of art religion" (ibid.), he retains a commitment to seeing the sublime as an essentially oppositional structure. Although the Kantian depiction of the sublime in terms of "the resistance that spirit marshals against the prepotence of nature" may have a limited purchase on an aesthetic practice that has thoroughly incorporated subjectivity into itself, Adorno's commitment to the critical function of art continually holds aesthetic experience up as staging just such a resistance. The targets of this resistance may shift from the prepotence of nature to the prepotence of authoritarian government and, indeed, to the prepotence of subjective art itself, and the resistance need not have any direct political consequence. Yet, Adorno is clearly interested in recuperating from Kantian aesthetics an image of the sublime that serves to provide an explanation of modernity's relentless search for novelty and, moreover, to depict it as a spiritual restlessness. In his view, Hegel's major contribution is to have acknowledged art in terms of the human consciousness of need, and his interest in sublimity is in interrogating that need in such a way as to distinguish the "objectively spiritual" aspect of works of art from their materials, to identify what separates works of art "in principle from food and drink."

Against just such a repudiation of the materiality of works of art, Jacques Derrida was interested in examining the sublime to locate the importance of the notion of the limit in philosophical thought and in language and to argue that the sublime only apparently involves a movement beyond its material presentation toward the supersensible. Thus, in *The Truth in Painting,* he takes up the question of the relationship between a beautiful painting and its frame to prepare the way for a discussion of the sublime. Arguing for the importance of the material features of the presentation of an aesthetic object, Derrida advances the view that the frame around a painting should not be thought of as merely an accessory, a parergon or hors d'oeuvre that comes in physical contact with the "work itself" but has no significant relationship to it. Rather, the parergon, "this supplement outside the work," establishes itself as what Derrida calls a "transcendent exteriority" that presses "against the limit itself" and intervenes "in the inside only to the extent that the inside is lacking" (1987). In other words, the encounter with beautiful paintings suggests that the constant distinction between frame and painting, what is an accessory and what is the real work, would not be necessary if works of art established their own boundaries in the terms that have seemed available in accounts of internal coherence, harmonious balance, and imitative adequacy. By contrast with the beautiful painting, the sublime cannot have a "parergon." As an infinite, the sublime has no obvious physical limit; it is not, Derrida says, "bordered" or bounded. For Derrida, the sublime epitomizes the process of establishing limits for the illimitable, a process that he sees as omnipresent in ordinary linguistic operations in which individuals delimit the significance of linguistic signs that are, by virtue of what he terms "iterability," always potentially repeatable with a difference and, he argues, infinite. In making this suggestion, Derrida obviously rejects the distinction between the understanding and the imagination on which the Kantian account had turned. Kant had affirmed, in his discussion of the mathematical sublime, that the understanding frequently rests content with something less than concrete comprehension of an absolute and infinite whole. Indeed, the interest of the sublime for him lay in its imposing a new demand—a demand that imagination comprehend all the elements of an infinite series in just such an absolute whole—that marked off aesthetic experience as distinctive. Derrida's account aims at suggesting that we might want to extend the claims made for aesthetic judgment in the Third Critique to our more general understanding of language, which Derrida wants to detach from the Kantian emphasis on intentionality in the process of arguing that written language does not so much produce evidence of the existence of a conscious author as militate toward a sense of the superfluousness of such an author (as a written message implies for him the disposability of its maker).

For Jean-François Lyotard, the sublime was a topic that opened on a variety of social and ethical problems. Although he published lectures exclusively devoted to Kant's Analytic of the Sublime (1991), Lyotard was less concerned with identifying an exclusively aesthetic domain than with examining the implications that aesthetic experience has for knowledge more generally. By contrast with Derrida, he was less concerned with identifying the material conditions of judgment and instead emphasized the importance of the Kantian notion of the sublime for directing attention to the tension between logical descriptions and individual intention. In such an account, the importance of the sublime lies less in the notion of challenging or transcending conventions than in designating the possibility of movement from one set of rules or conventions to another. The sublime thus becomes a way of designating a passage to a new perception. He shrewdly recognized that Kant may have departed from Burke in most respects but that he "ransacked" Burke's aesthetic for its "major gambit—to show that the sublime is kindled by the threat that nothing further might happen" (1991). Thus, in *The Postmodern Condition: A Report on Knowledge* (1984), Lyotard examines the sublime as an index to the importance of the avant-garde. What he calls "modern" in art is an art committed to the sublime, which he characterizes, following Kant, as taking place "when the imagination fails to present an object which might, if only in principle, come to match a concept." Insofar as sublime ideas—ideas of the infinitely great, the infinitely powerful, and the like—are "unpresentable," they "impart no knowledge about reality" and interfere with the free union of the faculties that occurs in the response to the beautiful. Instancing figures such as Kazimir Malevich, Paul Klee, and Barnett Newman as artists of "negative presentation," he argues for an art that dedicates its "'little technical expertise'" to "present the fact that the unpresentable exists" (ibid.). By contrast with what he characterizes as Jürgen Habermas's commitment to consensus as an appropriate goal, Lyotard attacks the "task which academicism had assigned to realism: to preserve various consciousnesses from doubt," and instead defends the project of a sublime avant-garde art that is "perpetually flushing out artifices of presentation which make it possible to subordinate thought to the gaze and to turn it away from the unpresentable" (ibid.).

With the work of Adorno and Lyotard, the sublime recovers the social function that Longinus had attributed to it: it becomes the arena for a recognition of the force of the unanticipated, the success that seemed not to have been predicted. If the notion of "negative presentation" does not entirely seem to convey the nature of the shock of recognition that the sublime produces, it registers the increasingly strong claim that commentators on the sublime have made for its significance in altering the usually tacit rules of the games of social interchange.

[*See also* Burke; Kant, *article on* Kant on the Sublime; *and* Lyotard.]

BIBLIOGRAPHY

Adorno, Theodor W. *Aesthetic Theory.* Edited by Gretel Adorno and Rolf Tiedemann, translated by Robert Hullot-Kentor. Minneapolis, 1997.

Bourdieu, Pierre. *Distinction: critique sociale du jugement.* Paris, 1979. Translated as *Distinction: A Social Critique of the Judgement of Taste* by Richard Nice (Cambridge, Mass., 1984).

Burke, Edmund. *A Philosophical Enquiry into the Origin of Our Ideas of the Sublime and Beautiful.* Edited by James T. Boulton. Oxford, 1987.

Crowther, Paul. *The Kantian Sublime: From Morality to Art.* Oxford, 1989.

de Man, Paul. "Phenomenality and Materiality in Kant." In *Hermeneutics: Questions and Prospects,* edited by Gary Shapiro and Alan Sica. Amherst, Mass., 1984.

Derrida, Jacques. "Economimesis." In *Mimesis: des articulations.* Paris, 1975.

Derrida, Jacques. *La vérité en peinture.* Paris, 1978. Translated as *The Truth in Painting* by Geoff Bennington and Ian MacLeod (Chicago, 1987).

Ferguson, Frances. *Solitude and the Sublime: Romanticism and the Aesthetics of Individuation.* New York and London, 1992.

Ginsborg, Hannah. *The Role of Taste in Kant's Theory of Cognition.* New York, 1990.

Guyer, Paul. *Kant and the Experience of Freedom: Essays on Aesthetics and Morality.* Cambridge and New York, 1993.

Hegel, Georg Wilhelm Friedrich. *Aesthetics: Lectures on Fine Art.* 2 vols. Translated by T. M. Knox. Oxford, 1975.

Hegel, Georg Wilhelm Friedrich. *Hegel's Introduction to Aesthetics: Being the Introduction to the Berlin Aesthetics Lectures of the 1820s.* Translated by T. M. Knox. Oxford, 1979.

Kant, Immanuel. *Critique of Judgment.* Translated by Werner S. Pluhar. Indianapolis, 1987.

Lyotard, Jean-François. *Le différend.* Paris, 1983. Translated as *The Differend: Phrases in Dispute.* by Georges Van Den Abbeele (Minneapolis, 1988).

Lyotard, Jean-François. *Leçons sur l'analytique du sublime.* Paris, 1991. Translated as *Lessons on the Analytic of the Sublime* by Elizabeth Rottenberg (Stanford, Calif., 1994).

Lyotard, Jean-François. *The Postmodern Condition: A Report on Knowledge.* Translated by Geoff Bennington and Brian Massumi. Minneapolis, 1984.

Nancy, Jean-Luc. "L'offrande sublime." *Poésie* 30 (1984): 76–116.

Schiller, Friedrich von. *Naive and Sentimental Poetry and On the Sublime.* Translated by Julius A. Elias. New York, 1966.

Weiskel, Thomas. *The Romantic Sublime: Studies in the Structure and Psychology of Transcendence.* Baltimore, 1976.

Žižek, Slavoj. *The Sublime Object of Ideology.* London and New York, 1989.

Žižek, Slavoj. *Tarrying with the Negative: Kant, Hegel, and the Critique of Ideology.* Durham, N.C., 1993.

FRANCES FERGUSON

Feminine Sublime

From Longinus's day until today, writers have viewed the sublime as a more or less explicit mode of domination. The vast majority of theorists conceptualize it as a struggle for mastery between opposing powers, as the self's attempt to appropriate and contain whatever would exceed, and thereby undermine, it. Within the tradition of Romantic aesthetics that sees the sublime as the elevation of the self over an object or experience that threatens it, the sublime becomes a strategy of appropriation. For Immanuel Kant, its most authoritative and influential theorist, the sublime moment entails the elevation of reason over an order of experience that cannot be represented. Typically, the sublime involves a moment of blockage followed by one of heightened lucidity in which reason resists the blocking source by representing its very inability to represent the sublime "object"; it thereby achieves supremacy over an excess that resists its powers. Thus, the central moment of the sublime marks the self's newly enhanced sense of identity; a will to power drives its style, a mode that establishes and maintains the self's domination over its objects of rapture. Without domesticating the sublime by defusing its profound and important connections to the realms of power, conflict, and agency, or suggesting that the feminine sublime is merely another, more intense version of the beautiful, it is important to emphasize that, rather than represent the object of rapture as a way of incorporating it, as does the traditional sublime, the feminine sublime does not attempt to master or dominate its objects of rapture.

The feminine sublime is neither a rhetorical mode nor an aesthetic category but a domain of experience that resists categorization, in which the subject enters into relation with an otherness—social, aesthetic, political, ethical, erotic—that is excessive and unrepresentable. The feminine sublime is not a discursive strategy, technique, or literary style that the female writer invents, but rather a crisis in relation to language and representation that a certain subject undergoes. As such it is the site both of women's affective experiences and of their encounters with the gendered mechanisms of power from the mid-eighteenth century (when the theory of the sublime first came to prominence) to the present, for it responds specifically to the diverse cultural configurations of women's oppression, passion, and resistance.

The sublime is a theoretical discourse, with its unique history, canon, and conventions, about the subject's diverse responses to that which occurs at the very limits of symbolization, and gender plays a crucial yet unexamined role in the history of this theory. The theory of the sublime not only describes the subject's encounters with excess but also defines the ways in which excess may or may not be conceptualized. Theories that seem merely to explain the sublime also evaluate, domesticate, and ultimately exclude an otherness that, almost without exception, is gendered as feminine. The texts that form the canon of the sublime—Longinus's *Peri Hypsous* (On the Sublime), Edmund Burke's *A Philosophical Enquiry into the Origin of Our Ideas of the Sublime and Beautiful* (1757), Kant's Third Critique—are able to represent the sublime only through recourse to metaphors of sexual difference; moreover, the structure of the sublime depends on (and results from) a preexisting construction of "the feminine." What appears to be a theory of how excess works actually functions to keep it at bay.

The notion of spectatorship as the site of sublime experience is one of the principal strategies through which such a neutralization occurs. Joseph Addison's "Essay on the Pleasures of the Imagination," from the *Spectator* papers of 21 June through 3 July 1712 (nos. 409, 411–421), emphasizes sublime experience as that of the spectator of an overwhelming event, landscape, or text, and thereby suggests a principal avenue of inquiry that Burke and Kant were to explore more thoroughly. Why, he asks, do we "take delight in being terrified or dejected by a Description, when we find so much Uneasiness in the Fear or Grief which we receive from any other Occasion?" Addison explains that such pleasures depend on a comparison between our own state of safety and the danger or terror we contemplate:

> When we look on such hideous Objects, we are not a little pleased to think we are in no Danger of them. We consider them at the same time, as Dreadful and Harmless; so that the more frightful Appearance they make the greater is the Pleasure we receive from the sense of our own Safety. . . . In the like manner, when we read of Torments, Wounds, Deaths, and like dismal Accidents, our Pleasure does not flow so properly from the Grief which such melancholy Descriptions give us, as from the secret Comparison which we make between ourselves and the Person who suffers.

The distinguishing features of the sublime, however, unsettle the very notion of spectatorship on which Addison and subsequent theorists rely. [*See* Addison.] Although Addison, Burke, and Kant regularly posit a subject who observes pain or terror without partaking of or being directly affected by it, the very hallmark of sublime experience is an identification between auditor and orator or between reader and text in which, as Longinus was the first to observe, "we come to believe that we have created what we have only heard" (7.2). Such a moment, in which the subject, whether in thought or in fact, merges with that which she perceives distinguishes sublime discourse from language that, in Longinus's words, is merely "persuasive and pleasant" (1.4). It is important to emphasize that the very nature of the sublime—its ability to blur distinctions between observer and observed, reader and text, or spectator and event—undercuts the claim on which its theorists rely to explain and defuse its peculiar force. The internal contradiction so central to the history of the sublime is that its theorists regularly claim for the spectator a state of detachment that, were it to exist, would nullify the very features of rapture, merger, and identification that characterize and define the sublime, for the sublime event is precisely one in which what happens to "the other" also happens to the subject who perceives it.

The sublime of William Wordsworth, Samuel Taylor Coleridge, John Keats, and Percy Bysshe Shelley finds its most typical expression in epic or narrative (rather than lyric) poetry, yet there is nothing inherent in the genre of poetry that makes it uniquely suited to or evocative of the sublime. The genre of sublime poetry was effectively closed to women. Dorothy Wordsworth, or any woman of her period, could not have written a poem such as "Tintern Abbey," with its celebration of "A presence that disturbs me with the joy / of elevated thoughts; a sense sublime / Of something far more deeply interfused" and abiding faith in the poet's infinite ability to "revive again." Wordsworth, the poet of the "egotistical sublime" that so provoked Keats, inherits as his birthright a self-assurance, entitlement, and confidence in his right to speak and be heard that no woman of his era could share. The moment of conversion that Wordsworth experiences in *The Prelude* when he encounters a blind beggar in the streets of London—"My mind did at this spectacle turn round / As with the might of waters" (VII, lines 643–644)—is a paradigm of Romantic transcendence and celebrates a kind of power that was forbidden to women. It also privileges a subject who subsumes all experience into an infinitely expanding "I," as if the goal of the Wordsworthian sublime were to consume the very otherness it appears to bespeak and demonstrate mastery over an experience that had seemed overwhelming.

Keats criticizes the "Wordsworthian or egotistical sublime" as "a thing per se" that "stands alone." Unlike Wordsworth, he views the sublime as residing in the extinction and not the enhancement of identity: "poetical Character," he observes, "is not itself—it has no self—it is every thing and nothing—it has no character": to be sublime is to have "no Identity . . . no self." As with Keats, Coleridge's sublime also depends on the self's awareness of its own absence. His comments on the sublimity of a Gothic cathedral provide a striking contrast to Wordsworth's response to the craggy peaks in the Mount Snowdon passage of *The Prelude* or Shelley's rhapsodic identification with Mont Blanc:

> But Gothic art is sublime. On entering a cathedral, I am filled with devotion and with awe; I am lost to the actualities that surround me, and my whole being expands into the infinite; earth and air, nature and art, all swell up into eternity, and the only sensible expression left is, "That I am nothing!"

Whereas Wordsworth's sublime culminates in what Thomas Weiskel describes as "an infinitely repeatable 'I am'" (1976), in the sublime of Keats and Coleridge individual consciousness is subsumed by the eternal. The grandeur of the Gothic church suspends Coleridge's self-awareness; all the self can know of itself is that is "nothing." [*See* Coleridge *and* Wordsworth.]

In contrast to Wordsworth's "I am every thing" and Coleridge's "I am nothing," the feminine sublime neither celebrates self-presence and the self's capacity to master the other nor consecrates the immediacy of its absence. If Coleridge's identity is diminished by the sublime, whereas Wordsworth's expands, the feminine sublime contests the logic of identity that conceives of the self in exclusive terms

of presence or absence. Here, one might envision a sublime in which the self neither possesses nor merges with the other but attests to a relation with it.

No innate femininity or unique style of women's writing accompanies the feminine sublime. Indeed, the very search for an essential difference that would function outside any specific context to fix, determine, guarantee, and control meaning is precisely what the sublime contests. At stake in the notion of the feminine sublime is the refusal to define the feminine as a specific set of qualities or attributes that might be called irreducible and unchanging. Here the term *feminine* functions as a synonym for textual and/or political practices that contest binaries, including a rigid notion of sexual difference that would insist on separate male and female selves. The appeal to a "feminine sublime" is not to a specifically feminine subjectivity or mode of expression, but rather to that which calls such categories into question. It is one name for what cannot be grasped in established systems of ideas or articulate within the current framework in which the term *woman* has meaning.

To investigate the feminine sublime is not to embark on a search for an autonomous female voice, realm of experience, or language, although these categories may be valuable as a dimension of the strategic interventions of feminist practice. What is specifically feminine about the feminine sublime is not an assertion of innate sexual difference, but a radical rearticulation of the role that gender plays in producing the history of discourse on the sublime and the formulation of an alternative position with respect to excess and the possibilities of its figuration. To assert the importance of the feminine in this context is not to reinscribe normative gender categories, but to offer a critique of a tradition that has functioned historically to reassert masculine privilege. In this sense, the notion of the feminine does not refer to a particular affinity group, gender, or class, but rather to a putting in question of the master discourse that perpetuates the material and psychological oppression of actual women.

The word *feminine* refers to the socially constructed category of woman that has endured universal and transhistorical oppression and thus underscores the reality of women's patriarchal order, whether it is perpetuated and sustained by biological women or by men. Here, the term does not so much refer to actual women as designate a position of critique with respect to the masculinist systems of thought that contribute to women's subjugation. Although such a conception of the feminine does not suspend reference to existing women, it does suspend the notion of an ultimate feminine identity that could function as the ground of sexual difference. Rather, it becomes one name for a residue that disrupts the oppositional structure male/female and thereby calls for a radical rearticulation of the symbolic order:

> If we had a keen vision and a feeling for all ordinary human life, it would be like hearing the grass grow and the squirrel's heart

beat, and we should die of that roar which lies on the other side of silence.　　　　　　　　(George Eliot, *Middlemarch*)

The Borderlands are physically present wherever two or more cultures edge each other, where people of different races occupy the same territory, where under, lower, middle and upper classes touch, where space between two individuals shrinks with intimacy. . . . A border is a dividing line, a narrow strip along a steep edge. A borderland is a vague and undetermined place created by the emotional residue of an unnatural boundary. It is in a constant state of transition. The prohibited and forbidden are its inhabitants.　　　(Gloria Anzaldúa, *Borderlands/La Frontera*)

She listened, but it was all very still; cricket was over; the children were in their baths; there was only the sound of the sea. She stopped knitting; she held the long reddish-brown stocking dangling in her hands a moment. She saw the light again. With some irony in her interrogation, for when one woke at all, one's relations changed, she looked at the steady light, the pitiless, the remorseless, which was so much her, yet so little her, which had her at its beck and call (she woke in the night and saw it bent across their bed, stroking the floor), but for all that she thought, watching it with fascination, hypnotized, as if it were stroking with its silver fingers some sealed vessel in her brain whose bursting would flood her with delight, she had known happiness, exquisite happiness, intense happiness, and it silvered the rough waves a little more brightly, as daylight faded and the blue went out of the sea and it rolled in waves of pure lemon which curved and swelled and broke upon the beach and the ecstasy burst in her eyes and waves of pure delight traced over the floor of her mind and she felt, It is enough! It is enough!
　　　　　　　　　　　　　(Virginia Woolf, *To the Lighthouse*)

Woman is not to be related to any simple designatable being, subject, or entity. Nor is the whole group (called) women. One woman + one woman + one woman will never add up to some generic entity: woman. (The/a) woman refers to what cannot be defined, enumerated, formulated or formalized. Woman is a common noun for which no identity can be defined. (The/a) woman does not obey the principle of self-identity, however the variable x for self is defined. She is identified with every x variable, not in any specific way. Presupposed is an excess of all identification to/of self. But this excess is no-thing: it is vacancy of form, gap in form, the return to another edge where she retouches herself with the help of—nothing. Lips of the same form—but of a form that is never simply defined—ripple outwards as they touch and send one another on a course that is never fixed into a single configuration.
　　　　　　　　　　(Luce Irigaray, *Speculum of the Other Woman*)

To hear the roar that lies within silence, and write it; inhabit a borderland (not a wasteland) in which boundaries overlap and differences of race, class, sexuality, and geography collide; to see waves of light breaking upon the beach as a movement in which otherness appears; or to define *woman* not as a shared fantasy of sexual identity, but in a way that contests any notion of essence, feminine or otherwise—across different trajectories Eliot, Anzaldúa, Woolf, and

Irigaray articulate crucial aspects of the feminine sublime, for each makes explicit the subject's encounter with and response to an alterity that exceeds, limits, and defines her.
　　[*See also* Feminism.]

BIBLIOGRAPHY

de Bolla, Peter. *The Discourse of the Sublime: Readings in History, Aesthetics, and the Subject.* Oxford and New York, 1989.

Burke, Edmund. *A Philosophical Enquiry into the Origin of Our Ideas of the Sublime and Beautiful* (1757). Edited by Adam Phillips. Oxford and New York, 1990.

Ferguson, Frances. *Solitude and the Sublime: Romanticism and the Aesthetics of Individuation.* New York and London, 1992.

Freeman, Barbara Claire. *The Feminine Sublime: Gender and Excess in Women's Fiction.* Berkeley, 1995.

Guerlac, Suzanne. *The Impersonal Sublime: Hugo, Baudelaire, Lautréamont.* Stanford, Calif., 1990.

Hertz, Neil. *The End of the Line: Essays on Psychoanalysis and the Sublime.* New York, 1985.

Kant, Immanuel. *Critique of Judgment.* Translated by Werner S. Pluhar. Indianapolis, 1987.

Longinus. *"Longinus" on Sublimity.* Translated by D. A. Russell. Oxford, 1965.

Lyotard, Jean-François. *The Postmodern Condition: A Report on Knowledge.* Translated by Geoff Bennington and Brian Massumi. Minneapolis, 1984.

Lyotard, Jean-François. *The Differend: Phrases in Dispute.* Translated by Georges Van Den Abbeele. Minneapolis, 1988.

Monk, Samuel Holt. *The Sublime: A Study of Critical Theories in Eighteenth-Century England.* New York, 1935; reprint, Ann Arbor, 1960.

Weiskel, Thomas. *The Romantic Sublime: Studies in the Structure and Psychology of Transcendence.* Baltimore, 1976.

Yaeger, Patricia. "Toward a Female Sublime." In *Gender and Theory: Dialogues on Feminist Criticism,* edited by Linda Kauffman, pp. 191–212. Oxford and New York, 1989.

　　　　　　　　　　　　　BARBARA CLAIRE FREEMAN

SUGER (Abbé of Saint-Denis.) *See* Gothic Aesthetics.

SULZER, JOHANN GEORG (1720–1779), Swiss aesthetician and philosopher. Born in Winterthur, the son of a Protestant minister, Sulzer studied theology, philosophy, mathematics, and botany and was greatly influenced by the critic Johann Jakob Bodmer. In Germany, he became friends with the representatives of the Berlin Aufklärung. In 1750, he was elected to the Royal Academy of Arts and Sciences of Berlin, and from 1775 onward he presided over its speculative philosophy class. He contributed to keeping the influence of Christian Wolff's philosophy alive. In 1755, he translated David Hume's *Inquiry concerning Human Understanding.* Written within the framework of the physicotheological movement of the interpretation of nature, his first essays on aesthetics are devoted to natural beauty and to its moral use. His major work, the *Allgemeine Theorie der schö-*

nen Künste (General Theory of Fine Arts), is truly an encyclopedic synthesis of the aesthetics of the period.

The aesthetic thought of Sulzer, whose best work can be found in various essays written between 1750 and 1770 and in his *Allgemeine Theorie,* reflects both the theoretical eclecticism and the refusal to develop a philosophical system that characterized the "popular philosophy" of the German Aufklärung. Even if he remained largely within the intellectual scope of later rationalism and of the aesthetics of perfection elaborated by Wolff, Alexander Gottlieb Baumgarten, Georg Friedrich Meier and Moses Mendelssohn, Sulzer approached aesthetic and philosophical problems from a highly psychological perspective. Thus, he played an important mediating role by combining the new themes of the French and English aesthetics of sentiment (Anthony Ashley Cooper, earl of Shaftesbury, Joseph Addison, Abbé Jean-Baptiste and Dubos) with a subjectivist interpretation of Leibnizian monadology. Sulzer's psychology, in particular his analysis of pleasure, rests on a Leibnizian interpretation of the fundamental tendency of the soul to produce continuously new representations for itself. In opposition to Baumgarten, who accentuated the "logic of sensual knowledge" (*cognitio sensitiva*), Sulzer approached aesthetics from the point of view of the perceiving subject's feeling of pleasure. He insisted on the mediating dimension of the fine arts, whose main task is to awaken the moral feeling of the good, thus preparing the subject for moral action. Although the subordination of the beautiful to the good and the moral orientation of aesthetics remain a constant of later rationalist aesthetics, Sulzer's originality was to have limited both moral sense and the faculty of desire to the sphere of feeling. In all likelihood, this stemmed from the influence of English and Scottish aesthetics and moral thought. Thereafter, Sulzer assigned an almost instrumental function to aesthetic sensibility.

Sulzer's strict aesthetic moralism is accompanied by a real sense of aesthetic problems. Sulzer identified two primary faculties of the soul: the faculty of representation, or apperception, through which the soul is absorbed in the object; and the faculty of sentiment or feeling, through which the soul is absorbed in its own state of being. Between the state of distinct perception, where one feels nothing, and the state of strong sensation, where one sees nothing, Sulzer distinguished an intermediary state of "contemplation." This latter state, which acts as mediator between the two other states, and which also serves to mediate between speculative ideas (which are clear but inert) and practical ideas, is equated with taste. Taste is defined as the ability to perceive the beautiful, the latter being the result of the simple subjective perfection of the form of the object: this perfection is said to be subjective because it consists in the free and effortless representational activity of the imagination, the outcome of which is a pleasant sensation. Thus, the notion of "aesthetic form" developed by Sulzer may be placed in the overall process of

subjectivization of the "aesthetic of perfection" initiated by Baumgarten (article "Schön" of the *Allgemeine Theorie*). Although at times Sulzer seems to develop the theoretical tools that would enable him to give a more complex explanation of the specificity of the aesthetic sphere and its relation to both understanding and moral sensibility, the moral instrumentalism that governs his aesthetics tends to undermine the most original ideas contained in his theory of taste and art. Thus, beauty is simply formal and must be completed by a beauty of a superior order, "which is born from the union of the perfect, the beautiful, and the good" (article "Schön"); only "thinking sensations" render the soul "sensitive to moral goodness," and it is "in this that the highest end of the fine arts resides" (article "Sinnlich").

Regarding questions about the intermediary position of taste, the critique of the rationalist notion of "perfection," and the relationship between taste and morality, Sulzer paved the way for Immanuel Kant's aesthetics and foreshadowed the theory of the tripartite faculties of the soul (Johann Nikolaus Tetens, Mendelssohn, Kant). Although Sulzer was severely attacked by the representatives of the Sturm und Drang, who rejected both his morals and his encyclopedism, his aesthetics advanced certain themes later developed by them. For example, like the Sturm und Drang, his conception of genius conceives of art not as an imitation of nature, but rather as the imitation of the creative process of nature itself. Moreover, genius is a state of enthusiasm, an intensification of the representational activity of the entire soul that spreads itself throughout the work of art by a radically original representation.

BIBLIOGRAPHY

Works by Sulzer

Versuch einiger moralischer Betrachtungen über die Werke der Natur. Berlin, 1745.

Unterredungen über die Schönheit der Natur. Berlin, 1750; new ed., Berlin, 1770; reprint, Frankfurt am Main, 1971.

Allgemeine Theorie der schönen Künste. 5 vols. Leipzig, 1771–1774; reprint, Hildesheim and New York, 1967–1970.

Vermischte philosophische Schriften. 2 vols. Leipzig, 1773–1781.

Other Sources

Baker, Nancy Kovaleff, and Thomas Christensen, eds. *Aesthetics and the Art of Musical Composition in the German Enlightenment: Selected Writings of Johann Georg Sulzer and Heinrich Christoph Koch.* Cambridge and New York, 1995.

Dobai, Johannes. *Die bildenden Künste in J. G. Sulzers Ästhetik, seine Allgemeine Theorie der schönen Künste.* Winterthur, 1978.

Gross, Karl Josef. *Sulzers Allgemeine Theorie der schönen Künste.* Berlin, 1905.

Heym, L. M. *Darstellung und Kritik der ästhetischen Ansichten J. G. Sulzers.* Leipzig, 1894.

Leo, Johannes Hermann. *Zur Entstehungsgeschichte der "Allgemeinen Theorie der schönen Künste" J. G. Sulzers.* Heidelberg, 1906.

Nivelle, Armand. *Les théories esthétiques en Allemagne de Baumgarten à Kant.* Paris, 1955. German translation published as *Kunst- und Dichtungstheorien zwischen Aufklärung und Klassik.* 2d ed. (Berlin, 1971).

Palme, Anton. *J. G. Sulzer Psychologie und die Anfänge der Dreivermögenslehre*. Berlin, 1905.

Sommer, Robert. *Grundzüge einer Geschichte der deutschen Psychologie und Ästhetik Von Wolff-Baumgarten bis Kant-Schiller.* Würzburg, 1892.

Tumarkin, Anna. *Der Ästhetiker Johann Georg Sulzer.* Die Schweiz im deutschen Geistesleben, vols. 79–80. Leipzig, 1933.

DANIEL DUMOUCHEL

SUPREMATISM. Exemplified and defined by the iconic work *Black Square* (1915), Suprematism is a direction in early twentieth-century abstract painting that was launched in December 1915 by Kazimir Malevich (1878–1935). The movement was inaugurated in Petrograd as a cohesive artistic orientation with the display of thirty-nine paintings shown at "0.10: The Last Futurist Exhibition." The term *Suprematism* was coined by Malevich, a key figure of the Russian and Ukrainian artistic avant-gardes of the 1910s and 1920s, to define not only an artistic style, but also a philosophical stance propounding the revelatory and transformative power of art. Suprematism consummated this power by negating conventional form. Malevich's concept of "zero-form" brought to a close the disjunctive rendering of three-dimensional objects and ushered in new categories of interpreting reality.

As an aesthetic of nonfigurative art, Suprematism put an end to the formalist manipulation of the painted surface through the convention of static collage and countered the subversion of represented images by resorting to an overt and unadulterated pure nonobjectivity. By abandoning the heterogeneity of collage that separates form from subject, Suprematism reestablished form and its content on the same ontological level of meaning. It explored new concepts of relief and weight based on the deliberate and calculated arrangement of autonomous, monochromatic geometric shapes floating homogeneously on a white, seamless background in a vast, undetermined space. Leaving behind the materialist illusionism of observed reality, Suprematism was instead guided by a philosophical imperative that put forth a transcendent, rather than empirical, order for art. Suprematism, as implied by its name, was to be a new and prophetic kind of painting, representing a world to be, rather than one that is.

To the degree that Malevich abandoned the mimetic tradition of Western art, he also embraced ever more profoundly the canon of Orthodox iconographic practice. The Iconoclastic Controversy did not lead to an absolute refusal of the image but challenged the precepts by which the iconographer could express man's supernatural nature and his rise toward eternity. Under the influence of Hellenism, the iconographer overcame illusionistic figuration (and the risk of idolatry) through the use of abstract planimetric modules to relay key theological and spiritual meaning via a monumental, but flexible, format. In the Orthodox icon, various elements of the subject are organized along curved planes confined within rectangular areas. Archetypal paradigms for the various iconographic subjects were made available in guidebooks called *podlinnyky*. In them, the depiction of sacred figures overlay substructures of squares inscribed within circles, or along diagonals determined by arcs and single curved lines extending from the top to the bottom of the icon panel. Such prescriptions prevented the iconographer from transgressing canonic form and bespoiling the content, which was to remain whole and unchangeable within a fixed framework.

Malevich's *Black Square* is the iconic template of Suprematist painting. The square within a square format derives from the geometric structure of traditional icons, while the seriality of Suprematist paintings parallels the devolution of icons from a single archetype. That the *Black Square,* the seminal piece of "0.10: The Last Futurist Exhibition," hung strategically at the juncture of the walls and ceiling planes in the corner of the "Suprematist" room in the Dobychina Gallery, gives further evidence of its iconic function, for the installation appropriates the sacred or "beautiful" corner of a typical peasant home where the patron icon was ordinarily situated.

The tension between Suprematism as a painting style and its transcendental or spiritual dimensions is enacted in the production of the 1913 Futurist opera *Victory over the Sun*. Although the opera predates Suprematism's official and public birth, its production provided a laboratory where Malevich was able to formulate his theory of painting. The opera spawned Malevich's venture into a sphere that surpassed the material and rational world. The action outlined in a libretto written by the Futurist poet Alexei Kruchenikh, aspired to a "Tenth Land"—a utopian realm that bore no resemblance to a present physical world constrained by materiality. The key ideas of the opera were presented reductively in two acts, demonstrating at once opposition and progression, as well as opposition to (technological) progress. Act 1 marks the end of a present world, an experience of the "here and now" that is connected to a delusive and inert realm of appearances, filled with unease caused by the invasive influx of technology. Act 2 defines a new land, dimensionally removed by a passing from zero to ten, a measured and metaphoric distance from the chimeric field of illusion, and is characterized by the cataclysmic destruction of an old cultural order. Here, new technologies are neutralized (a plane crashes to the earth) and, in their place, a new conception of art (and life) is put forth. It is ensconced in a box of concrete, shielded against space, time, and history. Two years hence, when Suprematism would be introduced to the world for the first time, the black square on a white background would dare not be referred to as an empty flat space, void of meaning.

The genesis of Suprematist content can be traced to the absolute darkness brought about by the dramatic eclipse in

SUPREMATISM. *Last Futuristic Exhibition 0.10* (1915), Petrograd (Saint Petersburg), Russia. (Photograph courtesy of Avery Architectural and Fine Arts Library, Columbia University, New York; used by permission.)

Victory over the Sun. This was the point of transition between the acts (and two distinct realms of experience) in the opera, occurring at the instant that the sun is vanquished. The iconology of the play is connected to its place in the perspective of Russian culture of the time, a culture profoundly affected by the feeling of the death of a civilization explored by the Symbolists. Yet, the violent gesture of destroying the sun opens up possibilities of a new and unstifling reality experienced without the inhibitions of time and restrictions of space. This crossing over barriers from one realm into another creates a new sphere of understanding, a dimension of perception unhampered by the mimetic limits of representionalism. The physical and materialist world is thus liberated by an ethereal and transcendental reality—a New Realism. The sun, as a symbol of tired conventions (cf. the Apollonian myth, enlightenment, rationalism, materialism, and the use of chiaroscuro for the palpable rendering of form), can no longer obstruct or interfere with the trans-

migration of experience into unknown, numinous territories.

As part of the current dialogue concerning the expansion of consciousness about the world and new states of awareness, discussions regarding the "fourth dimension" surfaced in Russia by 1911, when *Tertium Organum* was published by the Russian philosopher on hyperspace Peter Demianovich Ouspensky. Ouspensky had a popular influence on the reception of the fourth dimension, largely because of the efforts of Mikhail Matiushin, composer of the opera *Victory over the Sun*. In 1911, Matiushin had begun to write on the subject and, during winter 1912–1913, he composed an essay with Ouspenskian overtones titled "The Sensation of the Fourth Dimension." When, in 1913, Matiushin translated excerpts from Albert Gleizes and Jean Metzinger's *Du cubisme* (1912) into Russian, he included among the passages quotations from Ouspensky's books *The Fourth Dimension* (1909) and *Tertium Organum*. Later,

Matiushin, through the concept of *zorved* (see-know), would develop ideas on broadened vision that related color to space and time. Under such influences, Malevich began to refer to his colors as "real colors"—making visible the pure sensation of color not of this world, but in another reality of a different dimension—a new, "painterly realism."

References such as "Color Masses in the Fourth Dimension" in the subtitles of Malevich's Suprematist paintings were mechanistic devices that disclosed his intuitive understanding of the concept. Indeed, the inauguration of Suprematism, coinciding with the end of Futurism, marked the institution of a new kind of reason in the visual arts. The annihilation of the sun in the Futurist opera meant the destruction of old and worn devices in art, but it also enfeebled a worn vocabulary no longer capable of defining a reality beyond this world. Kruchenikh's "transrational" language *(zaum)* obfuscated a lexicon of crude utterances that could not contain the emphatic iconographic "logos"—the coherent, complete, and compact message contained in icons. With the old notion of "style" presupposing a manipulation of discrete painterly elements suddenly obliterated, style and its vocabulary began to assume one and the same form where only the laws of pure form presided. Thus, Suprematism is not a subjectless art. It divines the conquest of chaos through the power and mystique of a vast and absolute nothingness—the ultimate reality.

The visionary interpretation of nature as it undergoes physical demise is a theme explored by the Symbolists and lies at the base of Suprematism. For Malevich, it stemmed, in part, from the mystical (and occult) inclinations of the Blue Rose painters, a small group of Moscow Symbolist artists who were engaged in an intense and persistent quest for eternal truth as espoused by the Russian philosopher Vladimir Soloviev. Malevich's early Symbolist paintings of around 1905–1907 focus Soloviev's apocalyptic metaphors as the artist seeks to reconcile inner subjective impulses with the contemplation of immutable cosmic energies. A series of frescoes from this period, exhibited by Malevich at the Golden Fleece exhibitions, explore Symbolist content by dwelling on themes of transfiguration of life by way of a Promethean regenerative wholesomeness. To the degree that Symbolism had outlined its own search for a new contemporary language through the metaphoric value of color, it opened up the possibility for a transition from the real world to one that was more meaningful. Blue Rose painting emphasized the immateriality of physical experience by submitting its workings to the expressive forces of music defined by such abstract features as rhythm, movement, texture, and *gama* (color). With it came a process of depiction that strove toward simplicity and restraint to preserve the tremulous feeling of nature. As in the ambiguous, twilight world of the Blue Rose, where the color blue transcends and fructifies the literal references to the sky and water, so Malevich, in his 1916 booklet *From Cubism and Futurism to Suprematism,* describes the forms of Suprematism as a "construction of forms out of nothing"—the fertile stimulus or starting point of an artistic image that permits one to soar above reality.

Part of this redirection was rooted in Malevich's concurrent interest in the chaste values of indigenous folk art traditions embodied in Russian Neo-Primitivism (c.1905–1913), which inspired the work of Natalia Goncharova, Mikhail Larionov, David Burliuk, and others and could be found in the harmonious rhythms and compositional unities unveiled by a fluid calligraphic handling of icons. It is at this point that Malevich turned to the simple graphite pencil as a way of releasing in a work of art direct but meaningful expression, free of all affectation. Fellow Neo-Primitivist Alexander Gritchenko, in his 1913 essay "On the Relationship between Russian Painting with Byzantium and the West from the Thirteenth to the Twentieth Century," traced the legitimate role of the icon as a formal inspiration for contemporary painting. He claimed that the foundations of the "new painting" (which included all the Picassos dutifully studied by the members of the Russian avant-garde in the collections of the Moscow magnates Ivan Morozov and Sergei Shchukin) go back to the Byzantine iconographic tradition. Thus, in response to philosopher Nikolai Berdyaev's warnings about the contemporary "crisis of art," Gritchenko countered that the crisis only exists in our not knowing how to approach contemporary painting, namely, through pure form and pure color.

Suprematism manifested an end to formalist experimentation. As an abstract style, it was given impetus by contemporary Cubist and Futurist positions about visual representation that found resonance in Malevich's works just prior to Suprematism's debut. Hence, the Futurist breaking up of kineticized elements into repetitious compositional units aggressively penetrating space and form alike, as in Malevich's *Knife Grinder* (c.1913), and the Cubist exploration of relativity, both in the process of observing objects and in recording them as temporal and visual shifts of overlapping planes, as translated by Malevich in a series of paintings from 1914 (e.g., *Lady at the Advertisement Pillar, Private of the First Division,* and *An Englishman in Moscow*), established what Malevich called an "alogical realism"—a play between illusionistic reality and its tactile materiality *(faktura)* that blurred over shifts of time and space. Displayed at exhibitions of the Union of Youth, a society that sponsored many events to publicize the aims of the avant-garde in Saint Petersburg and Moscow, these works of alogical (or transrational) realism, rendered in painting by visual cleavages and ruptures of logical syntax and meaning, served as Malevich's springboard to Suprematism.

It was only in the 1920s that Malevich began to incorporate references to "relativity" and the fourth dimension in his writings. By that time, the inability of Malevich's contemporaries to reconcile the style with his personal philosophy resulted in Suprematism's evolving into a one-man movement. Suprematism would have been a logical construct for Russian post-Revolution society seeking, through political ideology, to build a new world and a new humanity. Even Malevich entertained brief interludes for implementing Suprematism into potentially functional habitats *(arkhitektony)* and "space stations" *(planity)*, and, under the aegis of Unovis, the organization that sprang up after the Russian Revolution for the Advocacy of the New in Art, he designed proletarian tea services and published pamphlets with a Suprematist New Art logo, a square within a square, inscribed by a circle. But except for El Lissitzky's *Prouns,* which had their starting point in Suprematism, Malevich's conception of Suprematism's being an art for a new transformed reality had no true followers, even though his theories on art prevailed until the late 1920s. Two distinct generations benefited from Malevich's efforts. The first, known as the Supremus Circle, extolled Malevich's system by planning a journal in 1916 under the name *Supremus* (a plan that never materialized) and included artists such as Ivan Kliun, Liubov Popova, and Olga Rozanova who successfully employed Suprematist forms in their paintings and found equally (but differently) provocative resolutions to the objectives of the wartime avant-garde. A second generation of adherents included a group who, connected through Unovis, responded to post-Revolution demands and made of Suprematism an applied art form. These included design artists such as Nikolai Suetin and Ilya Chashnik, both of whom studied with Malevich in Vitebsk.

Ultimately, Suprematism's intuitive and subconscious premises were translated, and only temporarily at that, into cognitive functions of art that laid the way for Constructivists such as Aleksandr Rodchenko to address the immediate concerns of the artist's role as engineer in making art that was socially meaningful. Suprematism's universal system for the reshaping of life as a whole thus gave way to the reforming of the physical attributes of an earthly environment alone.

[*See also* Bauhaus; Constructivism; Malevich; Modernism, *overview article; and* Russian Aesthetics.]

BIBLIOGRAPHY

Andersen, Troels. *Malevich: Catalogue Raisonné of the Berlin Exhibition 1927, Including the Collection in the Stedelijk Museum.* Amsterdam, 1970.

Andersen, Troels, ed. *K. S. Malevich: The World as Non-Objectivity; Unpublished Writings, 1922–1925.* Translated by Xenia Glowacki-Prus and Edmund T. Little. Copenhagen, 1976.

Andersen, Troels, ed. *K. S. Malevich: The Artist, Infinity, Suprematism; Unpublished Writings, 1913–1933.* Translated by Xenia Hoffmann. Copenhagen, 1978.

Bowlt, John E., ed. and trans. *Russian Art of the Avant-Garde: Theory and Criticism, 1902–1934* (1976). Rev. enl. ed. London and New York, 1988.

Bowlt, John E., and Charlotte Douglas, eds. *Kazimir Malevich, 1878–1935–1978.* Special issue of *Soviet Union/Union Soviétique* 5.2 (1978).

Douglas, Charlotte. *Swans of Other Worlds: Kazimir Malevich and the Origins of Abstraction in Russia.* Ann Arbor, 1980.

Douglas, Charlotte. *Kazimir Malevich.* New York, 1994.

Gray, Camilla. *The Russian Experiment in Art, 1863–1922* (1962). Rev. ed. by Marian Burleigh-Motley. London and New York, 1986.

Groys, Boris. *The Total Art of Stalinism: Avant-Garde, Aesthetic Dictatorship, and Beyond.* Translated by Charles Rougle. Princeton, N.J., 1992.

Henderson, Linda Dalrymple. "Transcending the Present: The Fourth Dimension in the Philosophy of Ouspensky and in Russian Futurism and Suprematism." In *The Fourth Dimension and Non-Euclidean Geometry in Modern Art,* pp. 238–299. Princeton, N.J., 1983.

Kasimir Malewitsch zum 100. Geburtstag. Cologne, 1978. Exhibition catalog, Galerie Gmurzynska.

Kazimir Malevich, 1878–1935. Amsterdam, 1988. Exhibition catalog, Leningrad, Russian Museum; Moscow, Tretyakov Gallery; Amsterdam, Stedelijk Museum.

Kazimir Malevich 1878–1935. Los Angeles, 1990. Exhibition catalog, Armand Hammer Museum of Art and Cultural Center.

Marcadé, Valentine. *Le renouveau de l'art pictural russe, 1863–1914.* Lausanne, 1971.

Nakov, Andrei B. *Kasimir Malevich.* London, 1976. Exhibition catalog, Tate Gallery.

Simmons, W. Sherwin. *Kasimir Malevich's Black Square and the Genesis of Suprematism, 1907–1915.* New York, 1981.

Zhadova, Larissa A. *Malevich: Suprematism and Revolution in Russian Art, 1910–1930.* Translated by Alexander Lieven. London, 1982.

MYROSLAVA M. MUDRAK

SURREALISM. [*To explain the aesthetics of Surrealism, an early twentieth-century art movement, as well as the impact of Surrealism on aesthetics, this entry comprises two essays:*
Surrealism and the Visual Arts
Surrealism and Literature
Because Surrealism emerged and developed separately in the visual arts and literature, the first essay treats the visual arts and the second deals with literature. For related discussion, see Avant-Garde; Bataille; Breton; *and* Modernism, *overview article.*]

Surrealism and the Visual Arts

Surrealism proper—literary Surrealism, or a less genre-specific aesthetic project of fusing life and art, dream and reality, conscious and unconscious experience—was a highly theorized entity, full of self-conscious manifestos. Yet there was no mention in these earliest declarations of how the visual arts specifically could be Surrealist, partly because the movement's main theoreticians were not even convinced that a properly Surrealist art could exist. A challenge by Pierre Naville in the pages of *La révolution surréaliste* in 1924 and 1925 started the debate. Naville argued that painting would always fail to represent adequately the pure psychic automatism unfettered by the control of reason sought by Surrealists, because painting was quite simply too mediated a technique—it had neither the speed of execution nor the apparent immediacy and transparency of written or spoken language. Naville's stance clearly illustrates the hegemonic status enjoyed by automatic writing in Surrealism's early history; its privileged position put all other techniques—and all other artistic mediums—out of reach for orthodox Surrealists.

André Breton was thus forced to defend the possibility of Surrealist art: his response to Naville, *Surrealism and Painting,* was published as a series of articles between 1925 and 1927. Breton pointed out that the works already being produced by artists associated with the movement were valuable contributions to the investigation of the surreal, and he went on to discuss these artistic practices in terms of their formal strategies. In Breton's essays, Surrealist art is defined according only to its proficiency in serving the larger goals of revealing the unconscious in representation, dismantling the opposition between the real and the imaginary, and expressing pure thought. From Pablo Picasso's Cubism, which was interpreted as a demonstration of the "treacherous nature of tangible entities," to Max Ernst's collage with its poetic juxtapositions of outmoded banalities, from Man Ray's photography, which blurred the boundaries between real and unreal, animate and inanimate, to André Masson's automatic paintings with their speed of execution and lack of aesthetic concern, Breton identified the different and varied formal solutions employed by these artists as routes to the surreal without ever defining what *surreal* could be for the visual arts.

Breton expressed contempt for those who would reduce Surrealism to style or technique, although he would, in his later writings on Surrealism, divide Surrealist art practice into two categories, automatism and dream transcription. At the time of his earliest writings, however, Breton avoided a stylistic definition of Surrealism in the face of what would seem to be an unreconcilable variety in Surrealist aesthetic procedures. Later historians of the movements who treated *form* or *style* as the central term to their definitions of Surrealist aesthetics would face this problem as well: how to find the common stylistic terms in which to describe work that ranged from painting and sculpture to collage and photography, and in which activities that fell outside of traditional aesthetic categories (for example, the Surrealist object or wanderings through Paris), were difficult to separate from other, more traditionally bound, practices?

If Breton avoids providing a definition of Surrealist art or aesthetics in his essay on the subject, one can turn to other writings, notably the First Manifesto of Surrealism (1924), *Nadja* (1928), *Les vases communicants* (1932), and *L'amour fou* (1937), for concepts that prove more fruitful in the analysis of Surrealist visual art production: the marvelous, and its subcategories or cognates, convulsive beauty and objective chance. These three concepts can be understood as organizing principles of Surrealist production, in both the literary and the visual arts.

The marvelous provides the most complete manifestation of a Surrealist aesthetic philosophy, because, Breton states

in the First Manifesto, "the marvelous is always beautiful, anything marvelous is beautiful, and in fact only the marvelous is beautiful." Signifying an almost miraculous rupture in the natural order, the marvelous was essentially a challenge to rational causality. Louis Aragon, in his important text "La peinture au défi" (1930), is even more emphatic in his attitude toward the marvelous; he defines it as the "refusal of *one* reality, but also of the development of a new relationship, a new reality liberated by that refusal," and declares that "it is Surrealism's *duty* [which he characterizes in specifically ethical terms] to make the point of the marvelous" (1970). It is only in the miraculous negation of the real that a synthesis or conciliation of the real and the marvelous can—and must—occur.

According to Breton, the marvelous, in the form of convulsive beauty, was produced in the confusion of animate and inanimate (veiled-erotic), or in the sudden stop of something that ought to be in motion, something that has been taken out of its normal flow of existence, or the arrested motion of a body become image (fixed-explosive). Its effects were also produced by the found object or found verbal fragment that, though part of the external, material world, carries a message informing the recipient of his own desire, and thus acts as a sign of that desire—the marvelous, in other words, is also an effect of the Surrealist notion of objective chance.

These notions—the marvelous, objective chance, and convulsive beauty—held in common their capacity to provide access to the unconscious. It is, indeed, the unconscious and its mechanisms that most interested Surrealists: Breton alleged in *Surrealism and Painting* that art would refer to a "purely interior model" or would cease to exist. Defining Surrealist *visual* art according to an understanding of the poetic image, and thus as a hypnogogic vision or upwelling of the unconscious in the mind's eye, he insisted that the job of the Surrealist artist was to reproduce faithfully that image, whether by automatism or dream transcription, making all attempts to bypass the rationalizing structures of thought. To a certain degree, Breton was resuscitating the premises of an outmoded realism, in which painting was understood to be a window onto a parallel reality, and in which the image is thought to exist a priori. At the same time, however, he declared perception to be wholly subjective and recognized the role of the unconscious in molding an individual's perception of reality according to secret desires and buried memories, and by doing so effectively critiqued the premises of realism.

It must be made clear, however, that the Surrealists' interest in psychoanalysis, and especially Sigmund Freud's version of it, was not simply on the level of the motif; rather than a superficial metaphorization of Freudian thought, what the Surrealists sought—and, for the most part, achieved through its various techniques—was a way of structuring representation according to psychic operations of dreaming, a poetic understanding of the *operations* and not just the content of the unconscious. In order to explore the mechanisms at work in the unconscious, the Surrealists explored the language of dreams and the process of dream work; however, Surrealism's use of psychoanalysis was not diagnostic but poetic, focusing rather on the aesthetic and critical potential of this new psychology.

Of these psychic processes, the one that seems to explain much Surrealist practice—artistic and extra-artistic—is that of the uncanny. Freud's concept of the uncanny (translated from the German *unheimlich*) is all that is not "homely" or "familiar"; it is the return of a familiar phenomenon (image or object, person or event) made strange by repression. Its primary effects are threefold: first, an indistinction between the real and the imagined; second, a confusion between animate and inanimate; and third, a replacement of physical reality by psychic reality. All three effects are basic to the Surrealist project—the Freudian uncanny is simply another way of thinking or describing the Surrealist idea of the marvelous.

In this understanding of the psychoanalytic structure of Surrealist practice, explored most extensively by the art historian Hal Foster (1993), the marvelous as convulsive beauty is seen as the uncanny confusion between animate and inanimate states, and the marvelous as objective chance is seen as an uncanny reminder of the compulsion to repeat. Brassaï's untitled photograph of 1933, in which a woman's torso is seen from behind and cropped such that it could be mistaken for a phallus, or Man Ray's photograph *Explosante-fixe* (1934), in which a dancer in the throes of a rhythmic frenzy is stopped, crystallized, by the click of the photographer's shutter in an unnatural state of limbo between life and death, are both examples of the uncanny logic of convulsive beauty. In these cases, the animate approaches the inanimate, and, in Foster's words, "not only natural form and cultural sign but also life and death become blurred" (1993).

It would be a mistake, however, to concentrate solely on the structural conditions of the Surrealist work of art in one's analysis of Surrealism, for this interest in psychoanalysis and the operations of dreaming also played a role in determining the artist's approach to—or moral stance toward—the marvelous. In other words, there was an interest on the part of many Surrealists, including artists, in speaking from the place of the unconscious, and in inhabiting madness, rationalism's ultimate destabilizer. Even the notions of convulsive beauty and objective chance can be seen in this light, for the ultimate goal of both these phenomena was to produce shock, a route to the unconscious related to hysteria, and thus a simulation of madness itself.

Max Ernst's description of his discovery of collage ("One rainy day in 1919, . . . I was struck by the obsession which held under my gaze the pages of an illustrated catalogue" [1948]) makes clear that the operations of the uncanny not only structure the collages themselves, but played a part in Ernst's own obsessional fascination with the catalog of outmoded illustrations that provoked a succession of hallucinatory visions in him. In Ernst's description of his discovery of frottage, there is an uncanny sense of the compulsion to repeat, because this memory is almost identical to his memory of the birth of collage:

> On the tenth of August, 1925, an insupportable visual obsession caused me to discover the technical means which have brought a clear realization of this lesson of Leonardo. . . . I was struck by the obsession that showed to my excited gaze the floor-boards upon which a thousand scrubbings had deepened the grooves.
> (Ibid.)

In both descriptions, Ernst refers to a childhood memory of his father on the occasion of Ernst's own conception; one sees the eruption of the past in the present as Ernst returns (compulsively?) to an unresolved, disturbing, and clearly sexually charged experience of his childhood—a primal fantasy—which he has contained and repressed, and presents it as the starting point of his creative activities.

Perhaps no other artist better exemplifies this desire to speak from the place of not merely the unconscious but of madness itself than Salvador Dalí. Dalí's paranoiac-critical method of painting took Breton's and Paul Éluard's experiment in *The Immaculate Conception,* in which the poets attempted to simulate various states of madness in order to demonstrate the fluid boundaries between sanity (rationality) and insanity (irrationality), one step further. Paranoiac-criticism attempted to reproduce paranoiacs' ability to systematically interpret the world through the imposition of their own desires and to make other people believe in the reality of their impressions. The double image of Dalí's paranoiac-critical paintings was described by him as "a representation of an object that is also, without the slightest physical or anatomic change, the representation of another entirely different object, the second representation being equally devoid of any deformation or abnormality betraying arrangement" (1930). The number of images that could be projected onto a single form was limited only by the degree of paranoiac capacity. Using this method, Dalí actively sought "to systematize confusion and thus to help discredit completely the world of reality" (ibid.) because it allowed the artist continually to call into question the stability and intransitory nature of images in the external world.

Ernst's canvas *Surrealism and Painting* (1942) introduces a final problematic into this discussion of Surrealist aesthetics. It represents a fantastic, many-headed bird of monstrous proportions and uncertain anatomy, working on a small automatist canvas, paintbrush in hand. What is striking about Ernst's canvas, which promises through its title to make clear the uneasy relation between painting and Surrealism, is that the canvas on which Ernst's bird works is the least interesting aspect of the image. Ernst's work points out

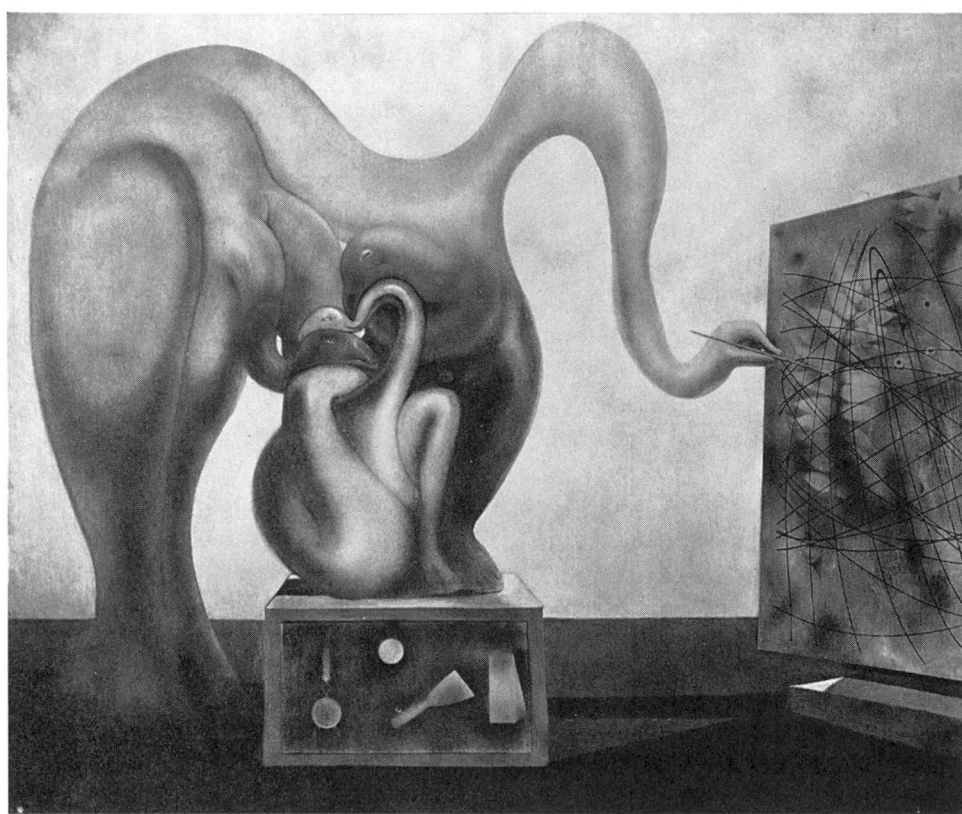

SURREALISM: Surrealism and the Visual Arts. Max Ernst, *Le Surrealisme et la Peinture* (1942), oil on canvas, 76 3/4 × 91 3/4 in.; private collection. (Copyright 1998 by the Artists Rights Society, New York/ADAGP, Paris; photograph courtesy of Avery Architectural and Fine Arts Library, Columbia University, New York; used by permission.)

the element of Surrealism that makes all traditional categories of formalism, connoisseurship, style, or perhaps even aesthetics, inappropriate for an effective understanding of the movement: in Surrealist art, the art object is not the end but the beginning of the Surrealist experience. The Surrealist work of art was not just the record or reproduction of the artist's contact with his or her unconscious; it was evidence of the artist's psychic state, which could be analyzed after the fact to reveal deep desires, and a tool by which the viewer could also experience that sublime state of pure thought, unfettered by rationalizing controls of perception.

Ultimately, however, one must return to Breton's Manifesto of 1924, in which he declares Surrealism outside any moral or aesthetic consideration, and to Naville's original objection to the idea of a Surrealist visual art, which claims the inadequacy of painting to capture "the street, kiosks, automobiles, screeching doors, lamps bursting the sky . . .": in both cases, the authors declare aesthetics to be obsolete—Breton because of his objection to Enlightenment thought, Naville because of his insistence on the synthesis of life and art in the face of twentieth-century spectacle culture. How, then, to map an aesthetic program for a movement whose most radical potential was found in its understanding of the

inseparability of life and art rather than in a removal of art into an aesthetic realm, and which was, despite its claims, highly aestheticized?

BIBLIOGRAPHY

Aragon, Louis. "Challenge to Painting." In *Surrealists on Art*, edited by Lucy R. Lippard, pp. 36–50. Englewood Cliffs, N.J., 1970. Originally published in March 1930 as "La peinture au défi."

Breton, André. *Surrealism and Painting*. Translated by Simon Watson Taylor. New York, 1972. Originally published in 1965 as *Le surréalisme et la peinture*.

Dalí, Salvador. "L'âne pourri." *Le surréalisme au service de la révolution* 1 (1930): 9–12.

Ernst, Max. *Max Ernst: Beyond Painting; and Other Writings by the Artist and His Friends*. New York, 1948.

Fer, Briony. "Surrealism, Myth and Psychoanalysis." In *Realism, Rationalism, Surrealism: Art between the Wars*, edited by Briony Fer et al., pp. 170–249. New Haven, 1993.

Foster, Hal. *Compulsive Beauty*. Cambridge, Mass., 1993.

Greenberg, Clement. "Surrealist Painting." In *Clement Greenberg: The Collected Essays and Criticism*, vol. 1, edited by John O'Brian, pp. 225–231. Chicago, 1986. Originally published in *The Nation*, nos. 12 and 19 (August 1944).

Krauss, Rosalind E. "The Photographic Conditions of Surrealism." In *The Originality of the Avant-Garde and Other Modernist Myths*, pp. 87–118. Cambridge, Mass., 1985.

Krauss, Rosalind E. *The Optical Unconscious.* Cambridge, Mass., 1993.

Krauss, Rosalind E. and June Livingston. *L'amour fou: Surrealism and Photography.* New York, 1985.

Kuspit, Donald. "Surrealism's Re-vision of Psychoanalysis." In *Psychoanalytic Perspectives on Art,* vol. 3, edited by Mary Mathews Gedo, pp. 197–209. Hillsdale, N.J., 1985.

Lippard, Lucy R., ed. *Surrealists on Art.* Englewood Cliffs, N.J., 1970.

Mundy, Jennifer. "Surrealism and Painting: Describing the Imaginary." *Art History* 10.4 (December 1987): 492–508.

Nadeau, Maurice. *The History of Surrealism.* Translated by Richard Howard. New York, 1965; reprint, Cambridge, Mass., 1989.

Rubin, William S. *Dada and Surrealist Art.* New York, 1968.

Rubin, William S. *Dada, Surrealism, and Their Heritage.* New York, 1968. Exhibition catalog, Museum of Modern Art.

Spitz, Ellen Handler. *Museums of the Mind: Magritte's Labyrinth and Other Essays in the Arts.* New Haven, 1994.

ARUNA D'SOUZA

Surrealism and Literature

The question is probably *not* whether Surrealism occupies, in the literature of the twentieth century, the central place held in the visual arts of the twentieth century, according to most critics, by Cubism; for that can be, and generally is, answered in the positive. The question is, rather, the more meaningful one about why this should be so.

The easy answer is that automatism, the freeing of the mind by the unthinking tracing of a text or a drawing, has itself to be examined. As it is, the history of automatism, even within Surrealism, is not untroubled. At one point, even Surrealism's leader, André Breton, will allege automatic writing to have been a catastrophe. (For those who have played the games associated with it, even the deservedly celebrated Exquisite Corpse, they can find themselves full of repetition, triviality, and—worst of all—fakery. Each human mind has its obsessions and its limited vocabulary: it is these drawbacks that tend to dominate, in the long run, the material that the "unguided" and unthinking mind is supposed so freely to pour forth.) It is not this technique or any other that in the long run accounts for the tremendous impact that Surrealism has had, and continues to have, on the contemporary mind and its productions. Rather, it is a basic and remarkably *serious* optimism.

It is often said that Dada, the movement that originated in 1917 in Zurich, was based in the Cabaret Voltaire, and spread to Berlin and Hannover before coming to Paris with some of its adherents, is generally negative and anarchic, and that Surrealism is its more organized and more positive side. It is certainly true that Tristan Tzara, Hugo Ball, and Richard Huelsenbeck, the papas of Dada, were ecstatically negative, reacting to the militaristic endeavors around them with mockery and to everything organized with scorn, all of them being presidents of Dada, for example. It is true that Tzara called on the Dadas and those who would join them in their poetics and politics to befoul all the embassies and places of authority, shitting in bright colors on everything everywhere. He and his cohorts chose to race down the mountains of built-up sentimentality like a vivid poison, purging the veins of all the slow-moving emotions that would, like so much chocolate, block the clarity of the dynamic nay-saying Dada intellect. All his notes on art and on poetry confirm this rapidity and this joyous destruction. His notes on Negro art and his importation into his poetry and thought of the "primitive" impulse and of the particular sophistication of African art play the same role for Dada and, subsequently, for Surrealism as does African art for Cubism.

It is equally true that Tzara's image of the yes and the no meeting on street corners like grasshoppers is taken over in Breton's formulation of the contraries meeting and communicating—as in the famous image of and theorization of communicating vessels in the book by the same name. That particular meeting of contraries has a double origin, for it appears also in the contemporaneous writings of the "Cubist" Pierre Reverdy, in the article "The Image," appearing in both French and English in Reverdy's 1917 publication *Nord-Sud,* North-South like directions of the subway line. The two elements of the image, says Reverdy, must be taken from different and opposing realms in order for an illumination or shock to take place. Breton will develop this seed into a full-blown theory of the meeting of day and night, of life and death, of up and down, so that reality and dream combine in a kind of Hegelian synthesis of thesis and antithesis.

Guillaume Apollinaire, a great poet and terminologist, who himself wanted to be called a Futurist, but who, when he was discouraged by Filippo Tommaso Marinetti in this endeavor, called his movement Orphism, coined the term *Surrealism* in his make-more-babies satire *The Breasts of Tiresias.* It stuck to what was originally to be called superrealism, but ended up as Surrealism, because the former term grazed too closely on the land of the spiritual. Surrealism, as it finally develops, is authentically antireligious: at one point, the "truest" gesture of a Surrealist was not to go down into the street and shoot the first passerby—a sentiment briefly flirted with—but to spit at passing priests. There was even a hero of this heroic gesture, and Benjamin Péret, Breton's most loyal and long-enduring sidekick, is photographed in such a heroic stance. In any case, superrealism turns into Surrealism, and Surrealism, influenced by German Romanticism and by French poets such as Charles Baudelaire and Arthur Rimbaud, and the odd Uruguayan Lautréamont—author of the image of the sewing machine and the umbrella meeting on the dissection table and a proponent of collective writing—defined at the start as having to do with this automatism of writing and drawing and speaking, gradually deepens.

In the beginning, a sentence was heard tapping on the window of Breton's brain. With Philippe Soupault, he wrote out a series of these automatic givens and called them *Les champs magnétiques* (1919; Magnetic Fields), and he imagined, superbly, how humans are soluble in their own thought: an odd version of idealism, touching also on the material world, which undergoes a "crisis of the object." The *Surrealist Manifesto* of 1924 formulates the idea of automatism and the freeing of the spirit. The initial enthusiasm was great, in all the endeavors: automatic writing, hypnotic sleep and texts, dream transcriptions, public performances. The major Surrealists, along with Breton, their leader with the mane of hair, the serious stance, and the charismatic personality, abounded in dramatic gestures and undertakings, desirous of changing the mental world the way Marxism was to change the political world and the world of the mind in the way Rimbaud wanted to—in a sense, especially the latter sense, it did so.

Under the political impulse, the journal of the Surrealists, *La révolution surréaliste,* changes its name to *Le surréalisme au service de la révolution,* and there is a period of association with the Communist Party. Then Surrealism as such separates from the party as such, and affiliates with Leon Trotsky in Mexico, where Breton and his wife Jacqueline Lamba the painter, visit and where Breton and Trotsky write a *Manifesto for an Independent Art* (although, for political reasons, the manifesto is signed by Breton and Diego Rivera). As the years go on, there are dissociations (Louis Aragon and Paul Éluard remain with the Communist Party), banishments (Robert Desnos for having a job), disillusions and uncertainties, as with all movements. The *Second Surrealist Manifesto* of 1930 speaks of all this, and has a sermonizing air about it. By the time Breton writes *Prolegomena to a Third Surrealist Manifesto,* the movement has hardened and become both less flexible and less interesting. When Breton and others go to Marseille for shelter during the war, with the aid of Varian Fry, and then to New York, where they start the journal VVV, after a brief association with the journal *View,* the movement changes character. Breton was never to learn English, and so his relation to the non-French world has a flavor of otherness to it; when he returns to France after the war, Tzara lectures against him in the Sorbonne; the group has a coterie of younger members, and gradually becomes more aesthetic, even mystical, than revolutionary.

But always, and more than most groups, during the early or heroic period of the 1920s, and even later, to its end, Surrealism really grouped. In the various cafés the group patronized, they would assemble every day in the late afternoon, Breton with his Mandarin curaçao, most of the others following in his wake, and undertake organized discussions. The *ordering* Breton favored is what springs to the eye: the games played were played to a purpose. From the Game of Truth, aimed at releasing all prudery about sexual matters by questions of the most intimate sort (when, how often, what position, etc.), to the game of the Exquisite Corpse, play was aimed at release, but also at serious construction

by the collective of something that would reveal what social and intellectual habit could not. Thus, in the Exquisite Corpse, the first player writes a noun on a piece of paper and folds the paper so that the subsequent entries will be only attached by a hidden and not an obvious logic. The second player places an adjective on the folded paper, folds it again, the third puts down a verb, the fourth another noun, and the fifth an adjective again, so that a French sentence emerges fresh and of a kind unlikely to be available to the waking deliberate mind: the name comes from the first game played—"The Exquisite Corpse Will Drink the New Wine." The results in the visual realm were oddly delightful: three, four, or five players would construct a whole by folding the paper over, leaving just a connecting line for the next part, defined in advance: a head, a neck, a middle, legs, and feet, depending on the number of players, or then an umbrella, a trunk, and various other elements, with ribbons stringing it all out: variations are endless. The point, of course, is the illogical and marvelous connection made without the working mind. This is the ludic equivalent of the marvelous in everyday life, in which an object in the outside world responds to a question one did not know one had.

Part of the particular fascination of Surrealism for present readers has to do with moral and political issues related to aesthetics. For example: in a restaurant, a waiter drops his purse. Should the Surrealist group return it, or is that a bourgeois gesture? How does a group react to a chance event? Another example: with Claude Lévi-Strauss and Roger Caillois, Breton examines a Mexican jumping bean. What makes it jump? Do they open it, do they leave it closed and simply speculate about it, or do they, as Breton later says he suggested, use their wits at speculating about it and then open it at the end? What should be, in short, the attitude of the artist or the writer toward the chance event and the marvelous? What is certain is that the high points of emotion and imagination are to be cherished above deadening daily happenings and customs.

What survives from Surrealism, apart from the visual art (generally agreed to be less powerful than the written), is a kind of group spirit and group vibrancy, as well as some remarkable writings. Heavily influenced by Sigmund Freud, whom Breton disappointingly visited, with neither quite understanding the other (see the texts at the end of *Communicating Vessels*), the various endeavors of the Surrealist imagination—from the short-lived Office of Surrealist Dream Research, staffed by Antonin Artaud among others, to the novels of Aragon and Desnos, to the lyric essays of Breton and the great poems of Éluard, and the aesthetic writings of Aragon, Georges Limbour, and others—are often masterpieces. One of the most mind-blowing is the attempt by Aragon and Éluard to simulate the writing of various mental derangements: *The Immaculate Conception,* these texts are called. Another is the collective three-person poetry of Breton, René Char, and Éluard, called *Slow Down*, or *Ralentir travaux*. Among the more remarkable speculative texts by Breton, *Communicating Vessels* stands out, together with his lyric meditations on love (*Nadja* and *L'amour fou* [Mad Love]). In *Nadja*, the fact that the author of so many invocations to madness should have been, as he avows himself, "unable to love Nadja," the madwoman, remains as valuable and disturbing evidence of how the mind and reality do not always fit. In *L'amour fou*, Breton's madly loved wife leaves him after the glorious early days, so that the final pages, a letter to his small daughter, express both the hope that she will be "madly loved" and the sad certainty that sublime love and the "sublime point" in which, so famously, all the contraries were to meet could be pointed out but not lived in, any more than the "crystal house" of complete transparent truth that Breton had believed for a moment he could inhabit. *Arcane 17*, the written account of the finding of a new love and a new kind of peaceful accord between desire and actuality, is a lyric evocation of the Gaspé Peninsula in Canada, and of what Surrealism in its late period can do, more calmly, in the mind. It is here that Breton invokes Mélusine the mermaid, the power of the woman-child singing forever in the imagination of man, the power of the irrational and the unmilitary that could, were it given a chance, undo the warring instinct in the heart of man.

Aragon's early novels are nothing short of brilliant: *Anicet ou le Panorama;* (1936; Anicet or the Panorama), a spoof on the art world, leads to the famous invocation of the architectural and mental glassed-in wandering place or *passage* dwelled on by Baudelaire and Walter Benjamin, in Aragon's unforgettable *Paysan de Paris;* (1926; The Peasant of Paris). The strange and compelling prose of Desnos in *Deuil pour deuil* (Grief for Grief) and *La liberté ou l'amour!;* (1993; Freedom or Love!) remains as testimony to a moment, lasting, and promising still.

[*See also* Benjamin, *article on* Benjamin and Surrealism; Dadaism; *and* Play.]

BIBLIOGRAPHY

Primary Sources

Aragon, Louis. *The Peasant of Paris*. Translated by Simon Watson Taylor. London, 1971; reprint, Boston, 1994.
Breton, André. *Nadja* (1928). Translated by Richard Howard. New York, 1960.
Breton, André. *Communicating Vessels* (1932). Translated by Mary Ann Caws and Geoffrey Harris. Lincoln, Nebr., 1990.
Breton, André. *Mad Love* (1937). Translated by Mary Ann Caws. Lincoln, Nebr., 1987.
Breton, André. *Conversations: The Autobiography of Surrealism* (1952). Translated by Mark Polizzotti. New York, 1993.
Breton, André. *Manifestoes of Surrealism* (1962). Translated by Richard Seaver and Helen R. Lane. Ann Arbor, 1969.
Breton, André. *Poems of André Breton: A Bilingual Anthology*. Translated and edited by Jean-Pierre Cauvin and Mary Ann Caws. Austin, 1982.
Breton, André. *Œuvres complètes*. 2 vols. Edited by Marguerite Bonnet, Étienne-Alain Hubert, José Pierre, Marie-Claire Dumas, and Philippe Bernier. Paris, 1988–1992.

Works on Breton

Balakian, Anna. *André Breton: Magus of Surrealism*. New York and Oxford, 1971.
Balakian, Anna, and Rudolf Kuenzli, eds. *André Breton Today*. Iowa City, 1989.
Caws, Mary Ann. *André Breton*. Rev. ed. New York, 1996.
Polizzotti, Mark. *Revolution of the Mind: The Life of André Breton*. New York, 1995.

Other Sources

Balakian, Anna. *Surrealism: The Road to the Absolute*. Rev. enl. ed. New York, 1970.
Caws, Mary Ann. *A Metapoetics of the Passage: Architextures in Surrealism and After*. Hanover, N.H., 1981.
Caws, Mary Ann. *The Surrealist Look: An Erotics of Encounter*. Cambridge, Mass., 1997.
Caws, Mary Ann. *The Surrealist Painters and Poets*. Cambridge, Mass., 1997.
Chénieux-Gendron, Jacqueline. *Surrealism*. Translated by Vivian Folkenflik. New York, 1990.
Gershman, Herbert S. *The Surrealist Revolution in France*. Ann Arbor, 1969.
Matthews, J. H. *Surrealism and the Novel*. Ann Arbor, 1966.
Nadeau, Maurice. *The History of Surrealism*. Translated by Richard Howard. New York, 1965; reprint, Cambridge, Mass., 1989.
Philbrick, Jane, ed. *Return of the Cadavre Exquis*. New York, 1993.

MARY ANN CAWS

SYMBOL. See Cassirer; Goodman; Langer; Metaphor; Semiotics; *and* Symbolism.

SYMBOLISM. By evoking a forest of symbols in a sonnet, "Les Correspondances," Charles Baudelaire launched a poetic terminology of which he never suspected the consequences. It was a simple sonnet on relationships between mental states and the world of nature; but in the last six lines, a shift occurs. Baudelaire initiated a language that integrated the spiritual and the material into single images that appealed to several of the senses in a synaesthetic manner. Although principally a Romantic poet, in his major work, *Les fleurs du mal*, Baudelaire left a number of poems that create the conjunction of the mind and the senses that, without recourse to the supernatural, expand the enjoyment and range of sensual realities ad infinitum. Some of his symbols were to become a springboard for the poets of the later decades of the nineteenth century.

Literary historians and critics recognize Symbolism as a literary movement that creates a cenacle in France around 1885–1886. Its theories are illustrated in a flurry of poems appearing in special journals such as *La revue wagnerienne, La plume, La vogue, Vers et prose*, and *Décadance*. Paul Verlaine and Stéphane Mallarmé form the axis of Symbolist direction. A decade earlier, Verlaine had written a manifesto-poem, "L'art poétique," in praise of ambiguity and musicality. But Mallarmé's theories had more precise aesthetic principles: a poem must not narrate or describe but evoke little by little an unnamed object or mood. He proposed two ways of arriving at relationships between the poet's inner world and the objective exterior world. One sprang from an inner mood, undefined, which was projected onto an object, figure, or landscape; the other direction emanated from a concrete object whose effect on the poet gradually penetrated him and aroused an inner state of being. Synaesthesia was no longer a promise of supernal experience but a strictly human possibility dependent on verbal achievement. Mallarmé became the mentor of the group, which gathered at his home every Tuesday between 1885 and 1895. Mallarmé's disciples were a generation younger than he and have become less prominent with the passage of time than in their own era. Those poets and novelists in the group who did not reach beyond the decadent ambience of the "Belle Époque" remained representative of a limited cultural moment rather than emerging as avant-garde innovators. But they elaborated on Verlaine's and Mallarmé's precepts and gave the movement aesthetic dimensions. In the coterie were Gustave Kahn, who liberated French poetry from the alexandrine, which had dominated it for four centuries; René Ghil, who tried to establish a correlation between instrumental sounds and associable combinations in poetic language; the Greek Jean Moréas, who proliferated classical settings for Symbolist poetry; and two Americans, Francis Vielé-Griffin and Stuart Merrill, both brought up in France, who became strong proponents of free verse in French poetry. Rubén Darío passed through the experimental climate of Parisian Symbolism and took it back to Latin America to incorporate its concepts into Hispanic modernism. The first generation of Symbolists explored synaesthetic effects, tried to strengthen the bonds between literature and music, and used the language of ambiguity to suggest the indeterminism of meaning that music has. The Symbolists adopted Richard Wagner as their patron saint because he had promoted the alliance of music and art, and subsequently the coordination of all the arts into closer unity. In the waning years of the nineteenth century, Symbolism spread to international proportions in both its philosophical and its literary dimensions. It crystallized the post-Darwinian existential shake-up relating to questions of origin and destiny, human necessity and objective chance. As the uncertainties of the human condition were compounded and human values ceased to be *givens*, the poet searched through the use of certain tropes for a language to express the uncertainties and concern over the evanescence of human life and over the survival of its imprint through the permanence of the arm forms; Symbolist writing became recognizable globally and outlived its emblematic messages. It also found structures that spread from poetry to the other genres. Proceeding from a nonnational

grouping in Paris, the movement spread all over Europe and into the Western Hemisphere. It had its apogee in the first three decades of the twentieth century. Symbolist literature became a body of writings integral to a profound philosophical crisis in which poesis became a conduit to a substitute universe.

Although French literary historians mark the end of the Symbolist movement in the 1890s, in the long view Mallarmé's theories had their aesthetic and philosophical impact on the major poets and dramatists of the early part of the twentieth century both in Europe and in other parts of the world.

Beyond these specific historical boundaries, there occurs an aesthetic evolution that has wider scope. Symbolism's more permanent permeation contradicts the general notion that it is the tail end of Romanticism. The basic problem for Mallarmé was how to suppress the overt "I" from poetry, so dominant in Romanticism, and yet to filter the subjectivity of the poet into the poem. Symbolism also reflects an entirely different ontology and its ontology creates a new function for poetic discourse. Although through Baudelaire, the Symbolists made use of Swedenborgian language, their perspective was totally different. Emanuel Swedenborg said: "Everything that springs from the spiritual world is called 'correspondences.'" Romanticism, which espoused this Christian sense of duality, made of poetry the reflector both of the subjectivity of the writer, expressed through the personal "I," and the image of a supernal world. It developed the Swedenborgian forest of symbols, such as flowers, soaring birds, meaningful gardens, boats, veils, fountains, and Promethean figures in search of the divine. The symbols on earth had direct meanings (correspondences) in heaven. The Symbolists often used the same symbols in totally opposite contexts. Their correspondences eliminated the sacred and emphasized relationships between human states and nature.

In the distortion of the Romantic image, the Symbolists developed an internationally recognizable series of key images of their own. The obvious similarities that arose from the interchange among poets created a linguistic code intended to suggest the ephemeral quality of being, the purity toward which humans aspire, and the putrefaction that awaits them. The swan, beautiful in its solitude and state of exile, had been previously evoked by Baudelaire in a famous poem by that name, a figure identified as an inhabitant of land, sea, and sky, but a stranger on all three planes, representative of the poet's uncomfortable position on all the common spaces of existence. Mallarmé's swan poem describes the swan metonymically and does not name it until the end of his poem, "Le vierge, le vivace et le bel aujour-d'hui"; the image of the creature's wings trapped in an ice-cold lake is not overtly associated with classical references of alienation, and refers more implicitly to the poet without direct self-identification.

Other flying creatures, from seagulls to fireflies, images of solitary parks, vacant mansions, a wide range of musical instruments, pale virgins fearful of life, all contribute to suggest the "daily tragic," the precarious human condition in the process of losing confidence in divine assistance. Poets searched not for the blue flower of Romanticism but for Mallarmé's "absent" one "from all bouquets," boats run into dry dock, lakes become stagnant pools, green valleys become glaciers, the wasteland that T. S. Eliot was eventually to use as the title of his major poem.

The cult of imagery had a direct effect on a coterie of American poets who called themselves "imagists," but it left a much more important mark in aesthetics in its evolution among the major poets of the twentieth century, such as William Butler Yeats, Paul Valéry, Rainer Maria Rilke, Federico García Lorca, Jorge Gillen, Hugo von Hofmannsthal, Endre Ady, Aleksandr Blok, Andrei Bely, Eliot, and Wallace Stevens. Symbolism in its broader sense developed its ontological dimension, derived principally from Mallarmé, and reflecting, as Stevens said, the "age of inconstancy." It faced the philosophically renewed problem of the artist in society, his position between the subjective and objective worlds, a reexamination of long-fatigued concepts such as reality, representation, and communication. Indeed, it probed the nature of nature itself. Those who saw beyond the mere technical innovations of Symbolism confronted an ever-widening sense of reality that linked the inner dream with outer phenomena; they experimented with alternatives to representation that introduced interference into mimetic reflection so that Narcissus saw not his own image in the water but another, and communication no longer aimed to convey information or even a mood from the writer to the reader or respondent in direct discourse but to instigate in indirect discourse a bond from the writer's perception to the reader's capability to connect the poem with his own mental or moral state or associations. As Eliot remarked, "The ambiguities may be due to the fact that the poem means more, not less, than ordinary speech can communicate."

The symbol became a mediator between the writer and his readers. Symbolist poetry developed a selective system of communication that identifies, without any intention of clarifying, the domains of human perplexity in respect to time and place; it extended its domain beyond the "interpreted universe," in Rilke's words, and it suggested the discontinuity of events and the perceived reality of an indifferent universe. Poets who followed in the path of Mallarmé expressed the disjunction between the cosmos and the human world, by demolishing the relationship in normal linguistic expression between the signifier and the signified. Words absolved of previous relationships to one another were stripped of congealed codes. Mystery was moved from what was "behind the veil" into language itself. The poet generated his symbols but left the responsibility of interpre-

tation to his readers. This kind of occultism differs from traditional gnosticism and hermeticism; it is not a palimpsest, eventually decipherable, but a communication containing multiple, simultaneous connotations.

The hermetic character of Symbolism was intended to create a breach between literature and journalism. Verlaine had ended his "Art poétique" with the line "Et tout le reste est littérature," using *literature* in a derogatory sense to mean *reportage* and to create a cleavage between Symbolist writing and popular literature.

Verlaine's other theories that were adopted by "Symbolist" poetry—ambiguity and musicality—were to be modified in meaning as time went by. When he gave instances of the ambiguous, he used images of vagueness and veiled objects. The words themselves were vague. Later practitioners of Symbolist *écriture* followed Mallarmé's rather than Verlaine's perception of aesthetics and use of language: the words were no longer veiled but very clear and concrete. Ambiguity consisted of a conscious search for an idiom of polyvalences. The enigma was created by the freeing of signifiers from their usual significations, the destruction of clichés, the return from heavy and congealed connotations to original denotation, to etymological meanings, the play between several meanings contained in a single word; their range of substitution of words, principally by projecting the subjectivity of the "poet" into images of other artists and performers such as painters, acrobats, dancers, clowns, weavers. The aesthetic course taken in poetics leading to the most sophisticated forms of Symbolist *écriture* went from analogy to metaphor, from metaphor to metonymy, which opened up the meaning of closed symbols, and finally to the use of single words that could assume the prismatic character of multiple and simultaneous evocations. Valéry remarked that the power of the single word is "limitless." The association of words with one another was not necessarily through meaning but through semantic contagion and phonemic contamination.

The references to the divine and the sacred changed in signification. They passed from a dualistic vision of existence to a monistic one bringing exterior physical nature into complicity with a fictitious cyberspace of the artist's own creation. Language tried to convey archaeological or discontinuous time, which Mallarmé had illustrated in his enigmatic poem *Hérodiade,* the suspension of time or static time best illustrated in the plays of Maurice-Polydore-Marie-Bernard Maeterlinck and coming all the way down to the writings of Samuel Beckett.

Musicality, explicit in Verlaine's "Music above all things", turned from its function as imitation of the sound of music, *la chanson grise,* to that of the process of musical composition. Mallarmé's understanding of the parallel was not confined to the creation of a mood but in making poetry that is "architectural and premeditated," the result not of vague inspiration but conscious strategy, composed of specific, calculated annotation like musical composition, which avoids explicit meaning but challenges the receiver's imagination and elicits various interpretations of the uncertainty of meaning that it carries.

Mallarmé's major poetry was not simply musical, it contained an episteme. Between more and more awareness of the perishable character of human existence and the unreliability of the material world of uncontrollable phenomena, the work of the artist looms as the only immutable refuge. The artist withdraws into his own shell and into the product of his own mind, which carries him into total introspection. Edmund Wilson grouped the generation after that of the coterie of Symbolists under the title *Axel's Castle*. Axel was a character in a play written by a contemporary of the Symbolists, Auguste, comte de Villiers de l'Isle-Adam, who preferred annihilation to the life of ordinary man. "Live?" asked Axel. "Let my servants do that for me."

Eventually, the linguistic devices created new associations that in their turn became congealed into codes that could be decoded because of the frequency of imitative referents, robbing Symbolism of its mystery. Eliot's "objective correlative," evolving from Symbolist correspondences, returned poetry to the demon of allegory. Poetic language became stylized, produced new conventions, the range of interpretations waned, narration returned to poetry, the philosophical elements were no longer self-contained but reverted from verbal alchemy to versified philosophy expressed in direct discourse. Symbolist writing became a signature. It also got confused with *decadent* literature, which identifies with the Symbolists' philosophy but is a direct and overt expression of it.

It took another movement, Surrealism, to make an even more invasive attack on language and establish a deeper association between the inside world of the subconscious and an ever-expanding external universe. Surrealist poets also confronted chance and chaos, but they attempted to show how man could transform his own existence and the work of his imagination if, instead of avoiding the natural hazards, he capitalized on them, making of chance a necessity, replacing a nihilistic philosophy with a more positive view of the challenges of human life. Elsewhere, the subjective "I" returned even more vigorous and overtly collective and universal, particularly in American poetry under the increasing impact of Walt Whitman. By the end of the twentieth century, most poets preferred the descriptive style of ecological expression and the direct confessional discourse of psychiatry.

[See also Baudelaire; Mallarmé; *and* Poetics.]

BIBLIOGRAPHY

Abastado, Claude. *Expérience et théorie de la création poétique chez Mallarmé.* Paris, 1970.
Balakian, Anna. *The Symbolist Movement: A Critical Appraisal* (1967). New York, 1977.
Balakian, Anna. ed. *The Symbolist Movement in the Literature of European Languages.* Budapest, 1982.
Balakian, Anna. *The Fiction of the Poet: From Mallarmé to the Post-Symbolist Mode.* Princeton, N.J., 1992.
Bertocci, Angelo Philip. *From Symbolism to Baudelaire.* Carbondale, Ill., 1964.
Boon, James A. *From Symbolism to Structuralism: Lévi-Strauss in a Literary Tradition.* New York, 1972.
Bowie, Malcolm. *Mallarmé and the Art of Being Difficult.* Cambridge and New York, 1978.
Bowra, C. M. *The Heritage of Symbolism.* 3 vols. London, 1943.
Cornell, Kenneth. *The Symbolist Movement.* New Haven, 1951.
Cornell, Kenneth. *The Post-Symbolist Period: French Poetic Currents, 1400–1920.* New Haven, 1958.
Decaudin, Michel. *La crise des valeurs symbolistes.* Toulouse, 1960.
Hertz, David Michael. *The Tuning of the Word: The Musico-Literary Poetics of the Symbolist Movement.* Carbondale, Ill., 1987.
Houston, John Porter. *French Symbolism and the Modernist Movement.* Baton Rouge, La., 1980.
Lawler, James R. *The Language of French Symbolism.* Princeton, N.J., 1969.
Michaud, Guy. *Message poétique du symbolisme.* 3 vols. Paris, 1947.
Porter, Lawrence M. *The Crisis of French Symbolism.* Ithaca, N.Y., 1990.
Symons, Arthur. *The Symbolist Movement in Literature.* London, 1899; reprint, New York, 1958.
Weinberg, Bernard. *The Limits of Symbolism.* Chicago, 1966.
Wilson, Edmund. *Axel's Castle: A Study in the Imaginative Literature of 1870–1930.* New York, 1931.

ANNA BALAKIAN

SYNAESTHESIA. The classic view that each of the five senses—touch, sight, hearing, taste, and smell—has its proper and distinct sphere of activity was first formulated by Aristotle (*De anima* II, 6 [418a]; III, 1 [425a–b]), and was reinforced in the early nineteenth century by Johannes Müller's influential physiological law of the "specific nerve energies." But during Müller's own lifetime (1801–1858), several cases of individuals who had the capacity to experience involuntarily two sensations simultaneously as the result of a single stimulus were reported. The phenomenon, which was identified by the adjective *synesthétique* for the first time in a French dictionary in 1872, attracted the attention of many psychologists, especially at first in Germany, Switzerland, and England (Fechner, 1876–1877; Bleuler and Lehmann, 1881; Galton, 1883); the number of identified cases had increased so much by 1890 that the Congrès International de Psychologie Physiologique decided to sponsor a thorough investigation in that year. The heyday of the scientific study of synaesthesia was between about 1880 and 1930; it has only recently become accessible and interesting to neurologists and experimental psychologists again because of the development of more exact and sophisticated techniques of monitoring the activity of parts of the brain (Cytowic, 1993; Harrison and Baron-Cohen, 1994).

It can be no accident that the earliest phase of intense scientific interest in synaesthesia coincides with the European

Symbolist movement for, although there have been reported instances of the synaesthetic operation of taste, smell, and touch, by far the majority of recorded cases have involved sight and hearing, and have therefore been especially accessible to visual and aural art. The most commonly experienced variety of synaesthesia has been colored hearing—originally, it seems, an English term, but more often referred to in its French form, *audition colorée,* in which a particular musical or spoken sound evokes a particular color. Two artists closely associated with Symbolism, the French poet Arthur Rimbaud and the Russian composer Aleksandr Scriabin, provided some of the best-known cases of synaesthetic perception; the Russian nonrepresentational painter Wassily Kandinsky also appears to have possessed the faculty of synaesthesia, and to have been notably sympathetic toward its aesthetic potential. From the point of view of aesthetics, synaesthesia may be seen as having provided a positivist inflection for the ancient and still-persistent concern to engage several senses simultaneously, usually in the context of theater or religious ritual (Schrader, 1969), a concern that, again in the period of Symbolism, involved the demands of coherence implicit in the *Gesamtkunstwerk.* In practice, even the nineteenth-century total artwork was scarcely able to give equality to each of the senses, and its founding father, Richard Wagner, was insistent that his music dramas could best be appreciated with closed eyes. Scriabin's *Prometheus Symphony* (op. 60, 1910/11) was performed in its earliest years without the light accompaniment *(tastiera per luce)* that the composer had written into it, but that, for technical reasons, proved very difficult to supply (Peacock, 1985). Yet, the investigation of the phenomenon of synaesthesia offered the possibility of basing aesthetic coherence on physiology.

Although Aristotle had supposed that it was the function of the various senses to keep the perceptions of the sensible properties of natural objects distinct, he also posited some "common sensibles" that might be perceived simultaneously by more than one sense. The examples he gave were movement, magnitude, and number; but, in the event, he was only able to instance movement, as perceptible to sight and to touch. Conversely, he only gave a single example, yellow bile, of objects whose multiple characteristics were more or less simultaneously apprehended by more than one sense, in this case sight and taste. He was above all anxious to preserve a clear demarcation between subject and object, and this was equally so in his influential suggestion (*De sensu et sensili,* 439b) that the unknown principles of color harmony might be inferred from the known mathematical principles of musical harmony, by assuming that the intermediate colors were all composed of exact numerical proportions of white and black. The many theories of the relationship of colors to musical sounds (for example Immanuel Kant's in the *Critique of Judgment,* sections 14, 51), and the many instruments devised to exemplify this relationship before the late nineteenth century, all started

from this "objective" proportional analogy. The best-known of these instruments, the *clavecin oculaire* of the French Jesuit Louis-Bertrand Castel, which he developed between about 1725 and 1755, but perhaps never made fully operable, became the focus of interest for the debate on the relationship between visual and aural harmonies for more than a century (Franssen, 1991).

The ancient tradition (Vitruvius, *Ten Books on Architecture,* I,i,3) that music was an essential study for the architect because of the geometric proportionality common to both arts had a particularly vital revival in the Italian Renaissance (Wittkower, 1962, Onians, 1984); and it was still capable of elaboration in the Romantic period in England, when Francis Webb extended the fragmentary ideas of the painter Giles Hussey (1710–1788) into a comprehensive theory of the universal relationship of geometric proportion in form and color, in his *Panharmonikon* of 1814 (Gage, 1993). As late as 1888, Georges Seurat's polymathic friend Charles Henry, drawing on the unpublished notes of Leonardo da Vinci, issued his *rapporteur esthétique* (aesthetic protractor), in which all measurable proportions were interiorized as psychological perceptions. It is striking that Seurat's late compositions, painted under the influence of Henry's ideas—*La Parade, Le Chahut,* and *Le Cirque*—unite carefully calibrated line and color with the imagery of music. Another symptom of the period of Symbolism, indeed, in which synaesthetic research was seen to flourish, was that the color-music analogy moved from common proportions to the subjective ground of instrumental color: musical sound was now seen as akin to color not by virtue of their similar harmonic structure but because of its perceived quality, its *timbre,* in German, its *Klangfarbe.* This related the old color-sound analogy far more closely to the newer *audition colorée.*

Rather more common than the evocation of color sensations by pitched (i.e., musical) sounds has been the synaesthetic experience of colored speech. Although whole words, such as numbers and days of the week or months of the year, and even historical periods, have been seen to evoke colors, most reported cases have involved single discrete sounds: consonants or, more frequently, vowels. Rimbaud's sonnet "Voyelles" (1871), with its opening line "A noir, E blanc, I rouge, U vert, O bleu: voyelles" (which should be spoken in the original French, because it is the sound rather than the visual form of the letter that is in question), was introduced into the scientific literature very shortly after its first publication, by Verlaine, in 1883 (Rochas, 1885). But in a note to the poem in "Une saison en enfer" (1873), Rimbaud claimed that he had invented these correspondences in order to open the poetic word to all the senses; and, in "Voyelles," he did indeed introduce metaphors of touch and smell as well as of color.

The early literature on colored hearing tended to treat it as neurologically based and even as pathological, but the most recent investigations, including those by neurologists themselves (Cuddy, 1985, Cytowic, 1993), have emphasized the structural links with the processes of language formation, to which metaphor is intrinsic. This has helped to modify the apparently irreducible lack of agreement about color-sound equivalents among various synaesthetes, which has seemed to some investigators to place it beyond the scope of scientific investigation. As Francis Galton wrote as early as 1883:

> Persons who have colour associations are unsparingly critical. To ordinary individuals one of these accounts seems just as wild and lunatic as another, but when the account of one seer is submitted to another seer, who is sure to see the colours in a different way, the latter is scandalized and almost angry at the heresy of the former.

This understanding of synaesthesia as a particularly vivid and compelling kind of metaphoric structure has brought it closer to the more expansive rhetorical activity of symbolizing, an activity that has similarly—for example, in Jungian psychology—been seen to function at a profound and quasi-biological level.

One of the obstacles to treating color-hearing synaesthesia as a function of rhetoric is that it is commonly found more frequently in children than in adults (Vernon, 1930; Reichard, Jakobson, and Werth, 1949; Marks, 1978). This may be related to the earliest formation of phonemes in infancy, and the perception of letters in early reading (Harrison and Baron-Cohen, 1994); and it is true that a good deal of interest has been shown in the phenomenon of colored hearing by structural phonologists such as Roman Jakobson (Jakobson, 1968). One of the most fascinating cases to be investigated to date has been that of a young multilingual female subject studied by Jakobson in the 1940s (Reichard, Jakobson, and Werth, 1949), who gave one of the most extended accounts of the acquisition of sound-colors:

> As time went on words became simply sounds differently colored, and the more outstanding one color was the better it remained in my memory. That is why, on the other hand, I have great difficulty with short English words like *jut, jug, lie, lag* etc.: their colors simply run together and are obscured by the longer words that stand near them.
>
> I like to play with words. I like to listen to new sound combinations and to arrange them in color patterns. For example, Russian has a lot of long, black and brown words, like Serbian words; in both these languages the combinations of *ya* or *yu* are little sparkling stars. The German scientific expressions are accompanied by a strange, dull yellowish glimmer, the word *English* and many English words are steel blue to my mind. Hungarian with its frequent *cs, zs, cz, sz* twinkles in violet and dark green, while French, the language I love most, is richest in colors, colors that at the same time carry a tone: hence a vivid mental picture when I listen to French.

The investigation of a phonetic basis for colored hearing goes back to Jakobson's association with the Moscow Linguistic Circle in the 1910s, and especially to the writing of Velimir Khlebnikov who, unusually, regarded the correspondence of verbal sounds and colors as a universally understandable language. It can thus be closely related to that search for a universal language of visual form and color by such early nonrepresentational artists as Kandinsky and another associate of Jakobson and Khlebnikov, Kazimir Malevich.

If children have been more prone to synaesthetic experiences than adults, there also seems to be a perceptual asymmetry between the sexes. Although the first substantial collection of case histories of colored hearing, published in 1890, recorded only thirty-nine female subjects among the 134 investigated (Suarez de Mendoza, 1890), modern research has reversed that proportion, finding that in some tests females were two or three times more susceptible to synaesthetic perception than males (Shanon, 1982). It has been suggested that this unbalance may reflect an underlying sex-linked genetic factor (Baron-Cohen et al., 1993), just as color-deficient vision is identifiable in about 2 percent of the male white population, but in less than .03 percent of females.

Rimbaud's Symbolist "derangement of all the senses" had been understood by the previous generation of writers in France as the creation of "correspondences," where, in Baudelaire's sonnet of that title, "Les parfums, les couleurs et les sons se répondent" (Perfumes, colors, and sounds (cor)respond to one another). These sublime and apparently involuntary metaphors had often, in Théophile Gautier, in Baudelaire, and perhaps in Rimbaud himself, been a by-product of experiments with drugs. Depressants such as alcohol and hashish *(cannabis indica)* are well-known stimulants to synaesthetic experiences, just as stimulants such as caffeine inhibit them. These antithetical and characteristic effects of drugs have been interpreted as the result of shifting the emphasis of brain activity from the cortex (the rational brain) to the limbic system (the emotional brain) (Cytowic, 1993). Yet, just as Baudelaire maintained that hashish could only enhance what is already present in the mind, so the increased activity of the limbic brain does not seem to create synaesthetic perception, but simply to facilitate it.

It remains that, although synaesthesia, in its looser sense of metaphor and association (sometimes called "pseudo-synaesthesia"), is very widely experienced in Western societies, in its stricter sense of a wholly involuntary multisensual response to a single stimulus, it seems to be rather rare. One estimate suggests that there may be only a single synaesthete in a hundred thousand of the population (as already noted, synaesthesia is far more common among children than among adults, and among females than among males). This, together with the almost wholly individual character of synaesthetic perceptions—as opposed to a possibly common neurological process lying behind them—makes it at present unlikely to be available to aesthetics conceived as a potentially universal system, even though this seemed to be a distinct possibility when the topic was first introduced into Gustav Theodor Fechner's experimental aesthetics in the mid-nineteenth century, and it remained so until at least the early years of the twentieth.

[*See also* Perception; Psychology of Art; Science and Aesthetics; *and* Symbolism.]

BIBLIOGRAPHY

Baron-Cohen, Simon, John Harrison, Laura H. Goldstein, and Maria Wyke. "Coloured Speech Perception: Is Synaesthesia What Happens When Modularity Breaks Down?" *Perception* 22.4 (1993): 419–426.

Bleuler, Eugen, and K. Lehmann. *Zwangsmässige Lichtempfindungen durch Schall und verwandte Erscheinungen auf dem Gebiete der andern Sinnesempfindungen.* Leipzig, 1881.

Cuddy, L. L. "The Color of Melody." *Music Perception* 2 (1985): 345–360.

Cytowic, Richard E. *The Man Who Tasted Shapes: A Bizarre Medical Mystery Offers Revolutionary Insights into Emotions, Reasoning, and Consciousness.* New York, 1993.

Fechner, Gustav Theodor. *Vorschule der Ästhetik.* 2 vols. Leipzig, 1876–1877.

Franssen, M. "The Ocular Harpsichord of Louis-Bertrand Castel: The Science and Aesthetics of an Eighteenth-Century *Cause Célèbre*." *Tractrix: Yearbook for the History of Science, Medicine, Technology, and Mathematics* 3 (1991): 15–77.

Gage, John. *Color and Culture: Practice and Meaning from Antiquity to Abstraction.* Boston, 1993.

Galton, Francis. *Inquiries into Human Faculty and Its Development.* London, 1883.

Harrison, John, and Simon Baron-Cohen. "Synaesthesia: An Account of Coloured Hearing." *Leonardo* 27.4 (1994): 343–346.

Jakobson, Roman. *Child Language, Aphasia, and Phonological Universals.* The Hague, 1968.

Marks, Lawrence E. *The Unity of the Senses: Interrelations among the Modalities.* New York, 1978.

Onians, John. "On How to Listen to High Renaissance Art." *Art History* 7.4 (December 1984): 411–437.

Peacock, K. "Synaesthetic Perception: Alexander Scriabin's Color Hearing." *Music Perception* 2 (1985): 483–506.

Reichard, G. A., R. Jakobson, and E. Werth. "Language and Synesthesia." *Word* 5 (1949): 224–233.

Rochas, A. de. "L'audition colorée." *La Nature* 1 (1885); 2 (1885).

Schrader, Ludwig. *Sinne und Sinnesverknüpfungen: Studien und Materialien zur Vorgeschichte der Synästhesie und zur Bewertung der Sinne in der italienischen, spanischen und französischen Literatur.* Heidelberg, 1969.

Shanon, Benny. "Color Associates to Semantic Linear Orders." *Psychological Research* 44.1 (May 1982): 75–83.

Suarez de Mendoza, F. *L'audition colorée: étude sur les fausses sensations secondaires physiologiques et particulièrement sur les pseudo-sensations de couleurs associées aux perceptions objectives des sons.* Paris, 1890.

Tornitore, Tonino. *Scambi di Sensi: Preistorie delle Sinestesie.* Turin, 1988.

Vernon, P. E. "Synaesthesia in Music." *Psyche* 10 (1930): 22–40.

Wittkower, Rudolf. *Architectural Principles in the Age of Humanism.* 3d rev. ed. London, 1962.

JOHN GAGE

T

TAINE, HIPPOLYTE ADOLPHE (1828–1893), French philosopher, historian, and critic. Taine is known as the historian who, immediately after the Paris Commune (1871), started to write the *Origines de la France contemporaine* (1876–1896). He wrote in the most important journals of the time, such as *Le journal de l'instruction publique* and *La revue des deux mondes,* and he published extensively in both philosophy and literary criticism. *Les philosophes classiques du XIXe siècle en France* (1857), and especially *Essais de critique et d'histoire* (1858) and *Histoire de la littérature anglaise* (1863–1864), made him one of the most visible critics in France, and situated him in the camp of the Positivists, as a follower of Auguste Comte. In addition, Taine had an important role in aesthetics, as the author of *Philosophie de l'art* (1865). His position within aesthetics was both the logical extension of his general interest in philosophical systems and history and the result of his first academic position, as professor of aesthetics and art history at the École des Beaux-Arts. What is probably most interesting about Taine today is the contradiction between the classical aim of his whole philosophy of art and the influence of his style on the Symbolist generation of art critics at the end of the century.

Taine was new to the field of art when, in 1864, he was appointed as professor at the École des Beaux-Arts, a position previously held by the architect Eugène-Emmanuel Viollet-le-Duc. It is impossible to separate his aesthetic vision from his whole system in philosophy, literature, and history, where he was perceived as a controversial figure, and a dangerously modern one: his theoretical motto was *race, milieu, moment* (race, social milieu, historical moment), the phrase that gave its deterministic impulse to his monumental *Histoire de la littérature anglaise,* published just before he was appointed to the Beaux-Arts, where he would lecture for twenty years in front of large crowds. Some contemporaries—such as the literary critic Charles-Augustin Sainte-Beuve and the art critic Ludovic Vitet—commented on the paradox that somebody so modern in criticism would embody the classical trend. Vitet was not wrong in considering him as a scholar who could be "a real friend of the Parthenon." In fact, since his opening lecture, the critic, who was, together with Ernest Renan and Émile Littré, the initiator of the new scientific approach to research, insisted on the perfection of Greek sculpture and of Italian Renaissance painting. Taine was obsessed by questions of Positivist method, and hardly commented on the most discussed artistic topics of the time: his appreciation of Eugène Delacroix comes up once in May 1854 in his correspondence, and once in 1867 in his article "Les beaux-arts en France." This essay is a short fiction envisioning a conversation between Taine himself and an elegant Italian tourist sensitive to the beauty of Renaissance art, and Delacroix is considered as an example of how the moderns are inferior to the ancients for their style; but Taine acknowledged that the Romantic painter powerfully expressed the anguish of the present.

Taine's aesthetics was the result of translating his philosophical and historical framework into the field of art. It placed the ideal of classical beauty within the modern scientific ambition suggested by nineteenth-century physiology, founded on factual and experimental truth, and capable of classifying events according to their "degree of importance." Taine was influenced by Georg Wilhelm Friedrich Hegel's vision of Greek sculpture, but his method was mainly informed by Comte's *Cours de philosophie positive.* Already in 1856, Taine expressed his enthusiasm for Théodore Jouffroys's *Cours d'esthétique,* which he defined in *Les philosophes français du XIXe siècle* as the only book that one could read after Hegel's *Aesthetics.* His vision of Italian Renaissance art and history was indebted to Stendhal's *Histoire de la peinture en Italie.*

Taine's whole aesthetic enterprise, as expressed in his lectures at the Beaux-Arts, first published in his *Philosophie de l'art* in 1865, aimed to "understand the precise conditions and the fixed laws" of the making of art, to define its nature and object, its role and character. Here Taine declared his ambition to consider nothing but *facts* and their causes, to constitute a truly "modern" aesthetics that would be "historical and not dogmatic, capable of reporting laws rather than imposing precepts." That historical approach encompassed a division in chronological periods and national characteristics that structured also his *Voyage en Italie* (1866). Taine adopted the historicist idea that flourishing periods are followed by decay, and therefore that there are periods of great art and of decline. Sculpture in ancient Greece and the art of the Italian Renaissance were the highest artistic productions in human history (two large sections of the *Philosophie de l'art* explore those periods): they both represented the beauty of the human body. The Middle

Ages, on the contrary, is presented as a dark Christian and feudal epoch, when plague, hunger, "universal misery and filth" reigned together with the terror of God. No wonder, for Taine, that its art was sad and gloomy.

Taine was not interested in the philological study of a work's attribution, and his formula was quite simple: history of art depends on history itself, and on the identification of historical periods with economic, political, and cultural characteristics. His conception simplified the Hegelian identity between aesthetics and art history, while his Positivist explanatory system lacked the dynamics of Hegelian dialectics (as has been pointed out by his detractors, such as Péladan in 1906). Taine's aesthetics is the example of a critical model that is rooted outside the medium itself: structural phenomena are considered as the sources of art, which seems, among human activities, the most erratic. The evidence on which he built his sociological system in the fine arts was the same on which, following Comte and Sainte-Beuve, he established his literary history and criticism, centered on the author's biography. A simple chain of causal relations ties an element to another, which Taine called "the larger whole": one work of art is linked to the other works of the same artist; one artist is linked to the school or group of artists in the same country and historical period to which he belongs; and, finally, the group of artists depends on the world surrounding them, which is the same as for the audience.

Works of art and artists are not isolated phenomena. It would be a mistake, for example, to consider Peter Paul Rubens as a unique case, because it would suffice to go to Belgium, and visit the churches of Ghent, Brussels, Bruges, or Antwerp in order to realize that there was a whole group of painters whose talents were similar to his. Dealing with painting in Holland, Taine showed that artists such as Albrecht Dürer, Jan van Eyck, and Hans Holbein existed because of the spirit and the habits of the German race, and because of the national character of Flemish and Dutch art. Taine founded his idea of race on a whole theory of climate, completely in tune with the conceptions of the time, which are also present in aesthetic conceptions very different from Taine's, such as those of Delacroix and Charles Baudelaire. Taine argued that the northern people did not tend toward the ideal but tried to reproduce what existed in nature; they did not concentrate on the sole nude, but, without fear of being trivial, looked for the real in all its aspects, and liked all its elements, such as buildings, landscapes, animals, and costumes.

The idea of nation and national character was shaped from within the historical vision: Taine's history represents fully and exactly what today's conceptions are departing from. In typical nineteenth-century overtones, similar to the narratives of historians such as Augustin Thierry and Jules Michelet, Taine describes the genealogy of races and geographic settlements, together with the physical and mental effects of climate, as preceding any artistic production, which then becomes the visible expression of those elements. Taine's aesthetics is not important today as a set of rules that could inform contemporary research, but as evidence of the historicist-national vision prevailing at the moment it asserted itself and claimed its own modernity within the institution of the École des Beaux-Arts and of the publishing market (namely, Hachette), totally open to the new generation.

Taine's aesthetics is especially interesting to see within the network of contradictions within a supposedly coherent ideology. The "real friend of the Parthenon," who, in a period of intense artistic debates, appreciated the realistic paintings of Constant Troyon, and, as a traveler in London, was suspicious of the enthusiasm for Joseph Mallord William Turner, was unsuspectedly tending to a vision of classicism that had little to do with historical truth. The second chapter of his *Philosophie de l'art*, whose title is "De la production de l'œuvre d'art" (On the Production of the Work of Art), contains this law: "The work of art is determined by the general state of mind and surrounding habits." One of the cases illustrating this theory is Greek art. But the deterministic perspective did not have the dryness of a statistical study: Taine ended up constructing a wonderful fantasy, close to Hegel's judgment on Greek sculpture, and already sketching the classical myth typical of decadent painters and Symbolist art critics. The fable started more or less three thousand years ago, in the unique milieu that was the Greek city-state, in the unique harmony between mind and body that characterized everyday life as well as gods, who had a human physical presence: sculptors could produce such perfect human forms because in the world in which they lived, they could constantly admire beautiful bodies. Page after page, description after description, Taine seems to forget his Positivist distance, and almost sounds like the fin de siècle critic Walter Pater writing on Johann Joachim Winckelmann's vision of ancient Greece: the whole ideal of the nude in art seemed to derive from the beauty of naked young and healthy people freely showing their bodies in athletic exercise and everyday life.

Paradoxically, Taine's aesthetics influenced the Symbolist generation. His teaching, more than confirming his sociology of art, touched those who looked for a type of art criticism completely separated from art history and any historical concern. This astonishing reversal was possible because of Taine's accuracy as a historian who was dutifully presenting periods of decadence as well as periods of splendor, and also because of an inner contradiction within his work where the project of a "philosophy of art" was doubled by another literary genre devoted to the pleasure of describing works of art: voyage literature. Taine's contradiction can be seen as a continuous temptation of blending in his colorful descriptions what his scientific criticism wanted to keep separate: facts of knowledge and facts of feeling. Having identified the Middle Ages as one of the four epochs of European civilization from Greek and Roman antiquity to contemporary industrial democracy, he extensively described art in that period, as well as the beginning of the Renaissance. He therefore emphasized those periods that were not valuable for the classicists, but would matter highly for the decadents and the Symbolists. In *L'art moderne* (1883), Joris-Karl Huysmans attacked Taine's systematic approach, and reversed it in order to establish his own passion for modern painters, the Primitifs, and Gothic cathedrals. Beyond the question of art and history, Taine's taste for descriptions favored the *écriture artiste*, the descriptive talents of such writers and art critics as the brothers Edmond and Jules Huot de Goncourt, Huysmans himself, or Jules Laforgue, who audited Taine's lectures at the Beaux-Arts and was enthusiastic about his presentation of Beato Angelico. Thanks to his descriptions, Taine the art historian produced the rich and ornate prose that would characterize art criticism in favor of Impressionist art. Taine himself, coherent with his abstract historical and philosophical stand, never commented on an Impressionist painter. Nevertheless, in 1889, discussing the Realist painter Édouard Bertin, he contrasted at length the differences between the optical performances of the painters aiming at the precision of design, and those sensitive to the infinite vibrations of color. If the masters of design are judged as achieving the most splendid artistic results, the most intense descriptions are displayed for the Impressionist technique and its nervous sensitivity. The Positivist thinker, who endlessly described the perception of light and color in his psychology masterpiece *De l'intelligence,* offered the model of the physiological explanation of Impressionism that became fashionable among its critics and historians.

[*See also* Symbolism.]

BIBLIOGRAPHY

Works by Taine

Les philosophes français du XIXe siècle. Paris, 1857.
Histoire de la littérature anglaise. 4 vols. Paris, 1863–1864.
Philosophie de l'art. Paris, 1865. After 2d ed. of 1872, 2 vols.
Voyage en Italie. 2 vols. Paris, 1866.
De l'idéal dans l'art. Paris, 1867. After 1882, included in *Philosophie de l'art.*
De l'intelligence. Paris, 1870.
Notes sur l'Angleterre. Paris, 1872.
"Les beaux-arts en France" and "Édouard Bertin." In *Les derniers essais de critique et d'histoire.* Paris, 1894.
H. Taine: sa vie et sa correspondance. 4 vols. Edited by Victor Giraud. Paris, 1902–1907.

Other Sources

Delacroix, Eugène. "Des variations du beau." *La revue des deux mondes* 9 (March 1857): 908–914.
Huysmans, Joris-Karl. *L'art moderne.* Paris, 1883.
Laforgue, Jules. *Œuvres complètes,* vol. 3, *Mélanges posthumes.* Paris, 1903.
Péladan. *Réfutation esthétique de Taine.* Paris, 1906.
Sainte-Beuve, Charles-Augustin. "Entretiens sur l'architecture par Viollet-le-Duc." In *Nouveaux Lundis,* vol. 7. Paris, 1867.
Vitet, Ludovic. "Les arts du dessin en France." *La revue des deux mondes* 54 (November 1864): 92–99.

PATRIZIA LOMBARDO

TAOIST AESTHETICS. *See* Daoist Aesthetics.

TASTE. [*In tracing the history of the concept of taste and its development in aesthetics since the concept first emerged (even before aesthetics itself), this entry comprises two essays:*

    Early History
    Modern and Recent History

The first essay explains the origins of taste and its history up to the eighteenth century, when it becomes a main aesthetic concept, especially in the British tradition. The second essay offers a critique of the concept of taste and at the same time explains the rise and fall of taste in aesthetic theory up through the twentieth century. See also Beauty; Disinterestedness; Food; Perception; Pleasure; Rasa; *and* Sensibilité.]

Early History

The centrality of "taste" as a theoretical concept is part of the rise of modern aesthetics in the eighteenth century. "Taste" extended the empiricist paradigm based on sense to critical practice and aesthetic appreciation. It provided a way to account for the subjective immediacy of aesthetic response in the context of judgment and discrimination. The prominence of the concept in the eighteenth century makes its origins of special interest. Conventional histories of aesthetics trace the concept to seventeenth-century Mannerism. It has classical roots, however, and Renaissance writers on art and art theory anticipate and develop the concept in its modern form.

Aristotle assigned to sense an important position as a starting point for judgment and wisdom. Sense is the immediate element, which in turn leads to memory. Memory makes possible experience, and experience leads to judgment. In the *Metaphysics*, sight is the primary sense, but in *De Anima,* a different priority is given to touch, which is a necessary condition for sentient beings. Aristotle also considers touch as the basis for taste because one can only taste what the tongue can touch. It is possible on these Aristotelian grounds, therefore, for taste to become the most immediate and discriminating sense.

Taste can only become a fully theoretical aesthetic term when the universals of Plato and Aristotle are replaced by the empiricism of the seventeenth and eighteenth centuries. Prior to that point, however, many of the elements were in place. Umberto Eco (1986, p. 110) points out the increasing empiricism of the later Middle Ages, citing Thomas Aquinas (*Summa theologiae*, I,78,4; Comm. *De anima*, III,4,633). Medieval art continued to subordinate sense to transcendent forms represented in traditional iconography, however. One must look to the Renaissance for the expressive emergence of the artist, and with that expression, the increasing dependence on personal factors that ultimately led to a theory of taste.

Among the first to use the metaphor of taste in connection with judgment was Leon Battista Alberti (1404–1472). Alberti regarded taste as a negative concept that undermined rules, however. Leonardo da Vinci (1452–1519) is similarly ambivalent on how the senses are related to judgment. Sense and experiment are important, but they are a means to imitation, not an independent source of knowledge. Much of the High Renaissance reference to sense is still within the Aristotelian mode in that it subordinates the senses to a judgment that operates at a higher level.

Taste comes to be linked directly to judgment and wit in later sixteenth-century Italian writers on art and painting. As the individuality and expressiveness of the artist became central, taste took its place as an indicator of the makeup of the artist and the means of transforming the artist's sense into a form of expression. This appeal to sense moves beyond the reliance of Alberti and Leonardo on sense as a means for artistic imitation. One place that this can be seen is in the shifting importance of illusion. In classical art, illusion had something of the quality of a forbidden fruit. It fascinates, but it also shows the fundamental unreliability of the senses. In the sixteenth century, a fascination with illusion and skill takes a different direction. The classical appeal is to the ability to fool the audience. One has anecdotes such as Zeuxis birds that are deceived and peck the painted fruit. The Renaissance appeal is to sense itself. One is not fooled; the pleasure depends on recognizing the illusion. For example, Sabba di Castiglione (1485–1554) connects decorative illusion with judgment. Theory is moving in the direction of a connoisseurship that connects taste and desire. Desire is a physical appetite, a lack that seeks to be satisfied. What is desired is a product of taste. Individual desire finds its expression in one of the marks of Mannerism, design, which is understood as satisfying an appetite. All of the elements of a theory of taste except the explicit application of the metaphor are present at this point.

The Venetian Paolo Pino's *Dialogue on Painting* (1548) offers an interesting distinction in the way that sense is being promoted by linking color and style as individual expression. Pino's idea was that color should reflect the skill of the artist, bringing honor to those who master its use. This judgment provides the basis for comparing individual painters. Pino's definition of charm as relish made this a matter of taste. The medieval *claritas* as it is found in Aquinas's threefold definition of beauty (integrity, harmony, clarity) is transformed into individual expression.

The emphasis on style as a reflection of individuality is a necessary step in the construction of taste as a critical term. Lodovico Dolce, in the *Dialogo della pittura intitolato l'Aretino* (Venice, 1557) provides an interesting example of how this individuality of expression is incorporated into critical judgments. In defending Raphael's superiority to Michelangelo, Dolce assigned it to a "je ne sais quoi" that fills the mind of the spectator with delight. This "je ne sais quoi" requires an immediacy of sense because it cannot be given a principled formulation. It gives pleasure without depending on anything other than direct contact. Critically, that poses a problem for a classical theory that looked to rules and rational forms. The only principle at work is pleasure, and the "je ne sais quoi" is accessible only to sense. Both source and critical means are sensibles. One is once again led back to contact, touch, and the analogy of taste.

Dolce also provides a link to *maniera*—"manner"—which is important. Dolce regards "manner" as negative—a stylization that subordinates the subject to the artist's manner. But the root of *maniera* is *some* individuality. If it is not the artist's, it is the subject's. The alternative, positive sense stresses the free play that the artist indulges in by his manner, thus developing his own style that exhibits his good taste. The positive sense of "manner" can be illustrated from Giorgio Vasari's *Lives of the Painters* (Florence, 1550). Vasari lists five achievements that advance painting beyond its earlier stage: rule, order, proportion, design, and manner *(regola, ordine, misura, designo, maniera)*. He goes on to define manner as a choice of parts. Although this definition represents manner as a stylized idealization, it also identifies it with a style that cedes the authority for the process to the artist. Without the ability to select, there is no manner, no beautiful figure. Thus, artists compete to develop a style that exhibits more and more detail, more and more of the ideal in concrete form. More is better. Elaboration is a positive move. Above all, the artificial is a product of the judgment of advanced artists. Vasari specifically sees this new style as a move beyond the simplicity of Giotto.

Taste corresponds to the essentially personal nature of a new form of judgment. A striking example is provided by Vasari's description of Jacopo Pontormo. Pontormo painted what he pleased for whom he pleased. Behavior that nowadays seems merely stereotypical of artists struck Vasari as exceptional, and in fact it could only occur in an eccentric such as Pontormo, who shut himself up with a work for years only to produce something so singular that it baffled his contemporaries (the fresco in the Temple of San Lorenzo). Vasari's estimation of that work (which was covered over in the eighteenth century) is thrown back on individual judgment. Something so singular can only be judged directly by the response of each person who sees it. To lose oneself in this way still appears to a Renaissance critic as madness (as it may well have been in Pontormo's case).

Mannerism retained the classical ordering of sense but shifted the emphasis. One of the tenets of Mannerism was that the combination of forms that presented beauty must go beyond mere imitation of nature and even beyond the earlier reliance on idealization. What now appears as elaboration and even distortion was central to the Mannerist desire to exhibit a beauty that could not be found naturally. In his *Dei veri precetti della pittura* (1586 or 1587), Giovanni Battista Armenini added one additional factor to the traditional theories of imitation and illusion: "If Zeuxis had not possessed a unique personal style [*singolar maniera*] in addition to his great diligence, he would never have been able to harmonize the beautiful individual parts he copied from so many virgins" (1977, p. 160). Armenini effectively connects Mannerist theory and taste by linking style and person. One who has a singular manner—a manner that is unique, individualistic, and not imitative—can unite elements and go beyond imitation, just as one who has a common sense can unite the five senses into a single sensory impression. Armenini's singular manner makes manner into a kind of sense. Style plays the same structural role as a common sense. Because taste is the analogy that worked best for the classical writers, it is a natural move to identify having taste with having the Mannerist style. If such a style, or a response to it, is instinctive, then not only are manner and taste linked, but taste can operate immediately and take on even more of the sense characteristics of its empirical origin.

The primary function of such judgment was productive. The final move to an explicitly metaphoric use of taste as a critical and aesthetic term can be located in the Mannerist writers who make explicit the connection between judgment and taste. Federico Zuccaro writes in his *L'idea de' pittori, scultori et architetti* (1607), "Grace is . . . a soft and sweet accompaniment which attracts the eye and contents the taste . . . ; it depends entirely on good judgment and good taste [*gusto*]" (quoted in Blunt, 1940, p. 146). The essentially aesthetic property "grace" is linked to the eye, and good judgment is explicitly identified with a second sense, taste. Zuccaro effectively unites the Aristotelian sense theories in a new way.

Renaissance and seventeenth-century writers evidently found grounds for the metaphoric extension of "taste" not directly in Aristotle but in the classical rhetorical tradition. Both Ernest Robert Curtius and Benedetto Croce cite Cicero and Quintilian as sources for seventeenth-century authors who use *taste* as a critical term (Curtius, 1953, p. 296; Croce, 1922 p. 193). Quintilian says, for example, that "It is no more possible to teach it [judgment/*iudicium*] than it is to instruct the powers of taste and smell" (VI, v, 1–2). But in context, although the analogy is suggested, taste and smell remain just what they were for Aristotle—senses that are lower on the scale of mental operations than the imagination, memory, and reason. It is not clear that either Cicero or Quintilian would be able to import a direct sensible element in the way that it came to be applied later. Only when *taste* became critically reflective did it become the dominant critical term that is at once normative and individual.

The final critical assimilation of taste and *maniera* came in the seventeenth century. Balthasar Gracian (1601–1658) is widely acknowledged as the principal source of this critical transformation, but clearly taste was already being used in the necessary sense by earlier Mannerist writers such as Zuccaro and Armenini. Gracian treated taste as something that could be acquired and imitated independently of intellect. In this regard, its character as sense is taken for granted. Metaphorically, taste is a form of judgment and discrimination. It relates directly to Gracian's concept of *agudeza*, "acuteness," which is an essentially prudential principle. Prudentially, the variability of taste leaves the critic or the would-be connoisseur exposed. Knowledge in this case is not Aristotle's higher form but simply knowing what is going to be accepted. Gracian does not mean that vulgar taste will win, but clearly one does not want to be the one who is different. Bad taste is just eccentric taste.

Thomas Hobbes (1588–1679) is roughly contemporary with Gracian and uses *taste* in the same way, though he is much less happy with the moral consequences of such use. Speaking of those who ignore science and retain the philosophy of the schools, Hobbes accuses them of being dependent only on their own taste:

> They make the rules of good and bad, by their own liking and disliking: by which means, in so great diversity of taste, there is nothing generally agreed on; but every one doth (as far as he dares) whatsoever seemeth good in his own eyes, to the subversion of commonwealth.   (Hobbes, 1994, part 4, chap. 46)

Both Hobbes and Gracian take for granted the importance of taste as a sense. In becoming a critical term, sense was transformed into a normative judgment. Good and bad taste are ways of praising and blaming.

Taste was rapidly assimilated into the critical vocabulary of Europe in the later seventeenth century, particularly in France and England. It retains a substantial element of the prudential, personal quality that it had in the Mannerists. For example, Dominique Bouhours, in "The Conversations of Aristo and Eugene" (1671), uses taste with regard to men, who have a certain "je ne sais quoi." The concept of taste finds a particular use in empiricist philosophy after John Locke (1632–1704). Both Anthony Ashley Cooper, earl of Shaftesbury (1671–1713) and Francis Hutcheson (1694–1746) draw on Locke's limitation of knowledge to ideas to locate aesthetic and moral judgment within the individual. If knowledge is conceived of as wholly dependent on ideas and ideas are the product of individual experience, then, they reason, the source of aesthetic ideas must be an aesthetic sense on the model of physical taste. Beauty may remain the nominal object of those ideas, but taste is the sense that alone can make aesthetic judgments.

Taste is also a feeling. Lord Shaftesbury, Hutcheson, and David Hume (1711–1776), most prominently, develop the sentiment of taste into a dominant aesthetic. A taste for something just is the subjective pleasure that one takes in it. Lord Shaftesbury's *Characteristics of Men, Manners, Opinions, Times* (1711) and the *Critical Reflections on Poetry and Painting* of Abbé Jean-Baptiste Du Bos (1719) begin with the indisputable nature of that pleasure and seek to cultivate and explain it. The primary datum is the pleasure itself. Its source is something that operates like an empirical sense to the extent that its operation is natural and automatic. "Internal sense" in the sentimental line is never simply a sixth or seventh sense without qualification, but the pressure of the empiricist model makes it much closer to the external senses than the Aristotelian common sense or the Augustinian and medieval internal sense that acted as a unifying and judging faculty. The sentimentalist line thus takes taste as a hedonistic principle of human nature.

For the sentimentalists, taste alone cannot be trusted. For Lord Shaftesbury, aesthetics becomes the problem of educating and restricting taste. This is a genuine dilemma, because the analogy of taste suggests that although one's taste may change, it is, in its immediate occurrence, beyond dispute. The solutions offered turn on increasing delicacy and discrimination. A more discriminating palate and a finer and more subtle perception are the goals of taste, but in the last analysis, a preference for such refined pleasures is difficult to justify. Lord Shaftesbury clings to classical values and justifies refined taste because it ultimately leads back to and coincides with virtue. Hutcheson is more empirically rigorous and finds the justification in taste's perception of order and purpose. Both also believe that taste is allied to benevolence and offers quantitatively more pleasure when the social and communal virtues are perceived. Lower tastes and selfish tastes are neither as perceptive nor as naturally satisfying according to these forms of sentimentalism as those attested to by classical virtues and benevolence.

Du Bos and Hume are more willing than Lord Shaftesbury and Hutcheson to grant a complete independence to taste. For Du Bos, the audience cannot be wrong. The problems for Du Bos are how to explain and predict taste so that one can be both prudentially with the majority and constructively productive. His explanations include elaborate comparisons on national and even climatic causes. Hume goes much deeper than Du Bos in granting to emotion, passion, and sentiment an epistemological authority. Taste is one element in a thoroughgoing empirical reliance on impressions and ideas. As such, taste is evidential. It discloses regularities in aesthetic and moral responses. Hume looked back to Lord Shaftesbury to link taste with character, but, for Hume, character has no existence apart from its expression in stable forms of moral and aesthetic behavior. When we judge taste, as we inevitably do, we are judging the stable identity that virtue and aesthetic preferences exhibit. Hume

thus founds an aesthetic and moral personhood on sentiment and taste.

The sentimentalist line appeared much too subjective and hedonistic for other empiricists as well as for most neoclassical critics and theologically influenced philosophers. Lord Shaftesbury and Hume tended to be grouped with Bernard Mandeville, whose *Fable of the Bees* (1714–1729) was seen as defending the hedonistic utility of vice. Nevertheless, taste became the dominant term for the more conservative aesthetic philosophers as well. Experience, on its new scientific and empiricist models, displaced Neoplatonic forms of beauty. Taste was either good taste or bad taste, depending on whether it conformed to or differed from the naturally founded artistic rules. Thus, Joshua Reynolds (1723–1792) expects painting to conform to rules that are discovered by painters through experimentation and learned through time and history by study of the masters. Beauty may be what is felt, but the whole aesthetic apparatus has become a quasi-scientific empirical exploration of the applicable rules of art to which taste conforms. Taste becomes a sign of an educated patron, a connoisseur. As Hume's cousin, Henry Home, Lord Kames, explained in *Elements of Criticism* (1762), "Do we not talk of a good and bad taste? . . . What is universal, must have a foundation in nature. If we can reach that foundation, the standard of taste will no longer be a secret" (vol. 2, p. 383).

Both main lines of development of the concept of taste in the eighteenth century are empiricist in their origins, therefore. Rationalist aesthetics in the tradition of Alexander Baumgarten (1714–1762) had little use for the concept of taste. Voltaire (1694–1778) summed up both lines in his *Philosophical Dictionary*. On the one hand, he defined taste as a sense. On the other hand, it is only an analogy. Good taste perceives actual beauties. In the last analysis, taste is a kind of national or cultural trait to be developed over time by nature. "Is there not a good and a bad taste? Without doubt; although men differ in opinions, manners, and customs. The best taste in every species of cultivation is to imitate nature with the highest fidelity, energy, and grace" (Voltaire, 1901, pp. 48–49). Denis Diderot (1713–1784) concurred: "What, then, is taste?" he asks. "A facility, acquired by repeated experiences, for grasping the true or the good, as well as those circumstances that render either of them beautiful, and for being promptly and keenly affected by them" (1966, p. 167). The empiricism of Hume is far more radical than this language, but its spirit is similar.

Two problems dominate discussions of taste in the later eighteenth century. The first is how to move beyond the "je ne sais quoi" of early taste theories. In order to give taste coherence and order, it needs to be traced to some more fundamental psychological principles. The dominant psychology is associationist. Taste is understood as a response to associations provided by the external senses. Alexander Gerard, in his *Essay on Taste* (1759), attributes the operations of taste to the imagination. This is a significant move because it leads in the direction of treating taste as a form of expression rather than a passive sensory response. Ultimately, taste takes its place in the *Critique of Judgment* (1790) of Immanuel Kant (1724–1804) as a response to pure intuition based on the free play of the imagination.

The second persistent problem concerning taste is how to establish a standard of taste. Hume, famously, juxtaposed two equally obvious alternatives: there is no disputing about taste, but it is absurd to say that someone who prefers Ogilby to John Milton is right. Kant turned this paradox into the antinomy of taste: taste is subjective, but it judges universally. Hume sought the standard in the character of the judges rather than in taste itself. Others, such as Lord Kames and Gerard, maintained, somewhat inconsistently, that taste was subject to rules if they could just be discovered. Kant ultimately moved the dispute onto new ground by arguing that a disinterested intuition was at once both universal and subjective. This displaced taste as it had been understood and replaced it in the course of the nineteenth century with a form of attention. Then, instead of a standard of taste, what one needed was a different way of experiencing that was uniquely aesthetic and beyond (rather than the subject of) critical disputes.

A number of factors tended to reduce the importance of taste toward the end of the eighteenth century. Aesthetic senses tended to multiply. By the time that Archibald Alison wrote his *Essays on the Nature and Principles of Taste* (1790), every aesthetic predicate could be regarded as requiring a separate sense: the sense of grace, of elegance, and so on. The passive, immediate receptivity of Lockean sense has been replaced by the actively associationist and imaginative operations of a mind that is expressing its own powers in its aesthetic activities and takes pleasure in those activities primarily because that is the way that it comes to know itself.

Kant, whose *Critique of Judgment* sums up theories of taste, also displaces them by shifting aesthetic perception to a form of intuition that underlies not just beauty but all theoretical and practical judgment as well. Taste achieved its centrality in aesthetics by uniting judgment and perception. Kant separates judgment into interested and disinterested forms. Disinterested judgment is independent of practical and theoretical considerations that belong to science and morality. Practical criticism is effectively moved out of aesthetics. In its place, disinterestedness, which had gradually assumed aesthetic importance in the eighteenth century, takes its place. Taste is the means of responding aesthetically and disinterestedly, but genius is the ability to produce aesthetically. Gerard and others had already begun to use *genius* in this sense. In effect, imagination and genius explain the two functions of taste. The imagination creates and re-creates. Genius exercises a primary form of imagination, as Samuel Taylor Coleridge argued, and then what genius has created can be re-created by imaginative reproduction in audiences and other, lesser artists.

After Kant, idealist aesthetics had other ways of explaining what is aesthetic. The unification of taste with judgment is pulled apart again. In *Modern Painters* (1843), John Ruskin distinguishes taste from judgment. Taste is the ability to take pleasure in true works of art; judgment is a separate activity. The determination of what is a true work no longer depends on taste, which is reduced to the role of refined sensibility. In the mid-twentieth century, taste reappears briefly as a matter of concern just because it is understood not to be rule-governed and plays no theoretical role. It is contrasted to attempts to define art that are under attack by philosophers influenced by Ludwig Wittgenstein. Their notions of taste are far more limited, however, than the central sense of taste that shaped seventeenth- and eighteenth-century empiricist aesthetics.

[*See also* Alberti; Cooper; Du Bos; Hume; Hutcheson; Kant; *and* Vasari.]

BIBLIOGRAPHY

Aristotle. *The Basic Works of Aristotle.* Edited by Richard McKeon. New York, 1941.

Armenini, Giovanni Battista. *On the True Precepts of the Art of Painting.* Edited and translated by Edward J. Olszewski. New York, 1977.

Blunt, Anthony. *Artistic Theory in Italy, 1450–1600.* Oxford, 1940.

Cooper, Anthony Ashley, Earl of Shaftesbury. *Characteristics of Men, Manners, Opinions, Times.* Edited by John M. Robertson. Indianapolis, 1964.

Croce, Benedetto. *Aesthetic.* Translated by Douglas Ainslie. 2d ed. New York, 1922.

Curtius, Ernest Robert. *European Literature and the Latin Middle Ages.* Translated by Willard R. Trask. New York, 1953.

Diderot, Denis. "Essay on Painting" (1765). In *Diderot's Selected Writings,* edited by Lester G. Crocker, translated by Derek Coltman, pp. 161–168. New York, 1966.

Du Bos, Jean-Baptiste. *Réflexions critiques sur la poésie et sur la peinture* (1719). Paris, 1993.

Eco, Umberto. *Art and Beauty in the Middle Ages.* Translated by Hugh Bredin. New Haven, 1986.

Gerard, Alexander. *An Essay on Taste* (1759). Facsimilie of 3d ed (1780). Gainesville, Fla., 1963.

Gracian, Balthasar. *The Art of Worldly Wisdom.* Translated by Joseph Jacobs. New York, 1945.

Hobbes, Thomas. *Leviathan.* Edited by Edwin Curley. Indianapolis, 1994.

Home, Henry, Lord Kames. *Elements of Criticism* (1762). 2 vols. in 1. Boston, 1796. First American from the seventh London edition reprinted from the edition of 1763.

Hume, David. "Of the Standard of Taste." In *Essays, Moral, Political, and Literary,* rev. ed., edited by Eugene F. Miller, pp. 226–249. Indianapolis, 1987.

Hutcheson, Francis. *An Inquiry into the Original of Our Ideas of Beauty and Virtue.* London, 1725.

Kant, Immanuel. *The Critique of Judgment.* Translated by Werner S. Pluhar. Indianapolis, 1987.

Klein, Robert. "Judgment and Taste in Cinquecento Art Theory." In *Form and Meaning: Essays on the Renaissance and Modern Art,* translated by Madeline Jay and Leon Wieseltier, pp. 161–169. New York, 1979.

Klein, Robert, and Henri Zerner, eds. *Italian Art, 1500–1600: Sources and Documents.* Englewood Cliffs, N.J., 1966.

Quintilian. *Institutio Oratoria.* 4 vols. Translated by H. E. Butler. Loeb Classical Library. Cambridge, Mass., 1958–1960.

Voltaire. *A Philosophical Dictionary. In The Works of Voltaire.* vol. 7, part 2, translated by William F. Fleming. New York, 1901.

DABNEY TOWNSEND

Modern and Recent History

Philosophies of taste were developed in the eighteenth century in response to two questions: What is the nature of beauty and other aesthetic qualities? What kind of perception enables one to find an object beautiful? Aesthetic evaluations were termed "judgments of taste," and a "man of taste" was viewed as someone sensitive to beauties of both nature and art.

Issues of taste became urgent in the philosophical climate of the Enlightenment, because under the influence of empiricism it was widely agreed that "beauty" names no objective quality but signals the pleasure of the perceiver. To identify beauty with pleasure, however, runs the risk of dismissing it as merely a matter of idiosyncratic enjoyment, but judgments of beauty are at the center of important disputes and thus are not merely matters of personal preference. Therefore, eighteenth-century theorists searched for a standard of taste that would reconcile subjective aesthetic pleasure and a shared way to evaluate objects of that pleasure.

Taste has been employed since about the sixteenth century as the metaphor of choice for aesthetic evaluation, because it captures the sense of immediacy of aesthetic pleasures and of the phenomenon of savoring and enjoying experienced qualities. But although the pleasures of eating are comparable to aesthetic pleasures in that both demand intimate, firsthand experience to assess, they are importantly different. Disagreement about tasty foods is seen as a matter of individual preference with no pressing need to adjust to a standard; pleasures of beauty and art are as important as ethical evaluations and require mutual agreement. Indeed, many Enlightenment thinkers regarded moral and aesthetic sensibilities as close kin and beauty as the countenance of goodness.

Philosophers such as Francis Hutcheson, David Hume, and Immanuel Kant developed theories of taste that rely on a concept of common human nature, such that judgments of aesthetic value signal a special sort of pleasure that is in principle sharable with all human perceivers. Although their philosophies are very different, they agree that it is important to recognize a pleasure that is free from desire, a condition that has become known as "disinterestedness." Interest, or, more precisely, self-interest, hinders agreement on aesthetic matters because it is concerned with personal desires and advantages. The absence of personal interest in a judgment of taste is thus philosophically important because it permits evaluations that tap into a source of pleasure common to all human beings. For similar reasons, it is important to stipulate that aesthetic approval is distinct from other sorts of evaluations, including practical or instrumental assessments, because these vary with cultural and individual contexts. A "pure" judgment of taste is pleasure in an object presented to the senses or to the imagination, freed from special individual desire. Taste so understood is a particularly developed ability to discern the fine qualities of art and nature. Thus, good taste both describes individuals of particular refinement and is based on a disposition common to all people. Eighteenth-century philosophies of taste laid the foundation for the development of the modern discipline of aesthetics. Assumptions about the need to refer to a special sensitivity to explain the perception of aesthetic qualities persist well into the twentieth century, as is evident in the influential essay by Frank Sibley, "A Contemporary Theory of Aesthetic Qualities: Aesthetic Concepts" (1959).

The latter part of the twentieth century saw a mounting criticism of the concept of taste and skepticism about the notion of a common human nature that underlies these philosophies. Several probing questions have served as avenues for the deconstruction of the concept of taste: What sort of "perceiver" is envisioned in theories of human nature presumed by philosophies of taste? What social context prompts the development of taste? What is the relationship between the perceiving subject and the aesthetic object? Critics of Enlightenment theories call attention to what they see as a conservatism built into the concept of taste: A person with good taste all too frequently comes to appreciate the very artifacts that have been appreciated for centuries. He thus enters an elite company of people with good taste, who are suspiciously coincident with people of wealth and social standing within a select group of European nations. Thus, it is argued, the notion of a standard of taste universal to all is covertly an imposition of national and class-based preferences.

Sociologically minded scholars have analyzed philosophies of taste by calling attention to the historical context of their development. The eighteenth century saw the rise of bourgeois social influence in Europe and the spread of democratic ideals. In this climate, the newly powerful middle classes conceived of themselves as active subjects who could regulate themselves politically and morally without the imposition of governing authorities. Philosophies of taste were appealing to many because they claim a universal ability to appreciate art that expands the privileges of good taste beyond a small elite; yet, at the same time, the exercise of taste is effectively limited to a class of people who have the leisure to develop the refinement of their perceptions. The universality of taste by this account is a fiction; taste really describes appreciation for the accepted canon of art that perpetuates the cultural hegemony of an elite. This phenomenon is disguised by the fact that so many people willingly subscribe to the aesthetic ideas of their times. Michel Foucault demonstrated that power is not only exercised by some central social authority but is most effective when values are absorbed by a population and enacted in daily social practice. So it is with taste: what appears to be an exercise of common dispositions is the acceptance of values as one's own that mimic and thereby confirm social privilege. The concept of the aesthetic, with taste preferences supposedly reflecting the proclivities of common human nature, crystallizes the self-regulation of this class of citizens. Scholars such as Terry Eagleton (1990) and Janet Wolff (1993) have offered analyses of theories of taste that translate philosophical concerns into the social exigencies of modern Europe. Approaching the subject by emphasizing the historical context within which aesthetics developed, taste appears to concern common human nature less than the power of certain classes and nations to select cultural artifacts for special attention, and to denigrate as base or savage the artifacts both of popular, nonelite provenance and of alien cultures.

Sociologist Pierre Bourdieu offers another trenchant criticism of taste in *Distinction: A Social Critique of the Judgement of Taste* (1984). Bourdieu also assails early modern defenses of a uniform standard of taste as disguised class hegemony that regulates values of domination and submission in European societies. He particularly takes issue with Kant, who most stringently purified aesthetic pleasures from practical contexts. Rather than providing the grounds for universal aesthetic pleasures that transcend the differences of individuals, Bourdieu argues, Kant's disinterested pleasure is a product of history that prescribes a contemplative, detached attitude only possible among people wealthy enough for leisure.

Bourdieu amassed data from different strata of French society, and concluded that "good taste" in art, fashion, or food is only that which is preferred by the bourgeois classes; it rarely matches the actual preferences of the working classes. Although eighteenth-century theory insisted on the distinction between aesthetic taste, about which it is important to have common judgments, and gustatory taste, about which individual preferences reign, Bourdieu argues that the two kinds of taste are comparable. A diet full of meat and heavy food is considered healthy and tasty for one who labors with his body, yet this food does not achieve the ranks of "gourmet" taste. Similarly, enjoyment of classical music describes the taste of a cultural elite that is socially powerful enough to determine what is "good" taste. Values are intrinsic to the habitus within which one lives, the subtle material and cultural influences that operate more or less below the level of awareness and shape one's pleasures. The concept of a standard of taste is an illusion rooted in the attempt to make class distinctions irrelevant to contemplative ideals of aesthetics; far from being irrelevant, they were only rendered invisible.

Collapsing the distinction between gustatory tastes and the aesthetic sense of taste is philosophically provocative, for it redirects attention to the traditional assumption that although taste for food is not of great importance beyond the nourishment of an individual, taste for cultural artifacts such as artworks is important enough to be a matter for public debate and resolution. Food has not figured importantly in aesthetic theories or philosophies of art in part because the sense of taste is a "bodily" sense rather than a "distance" sense such as sight or hearing. According to long philosophical tradition, only the distance senses detach the observer sufficiently from the state of his own body to yield "objective" knowledge. Bodily senses such as taste, smell, and to some degree touch are understood to be merely more subjective and to direct attention inward to one's own body; they also yield pleasures that are "merely animal" and run the risk of overindulgence, a point emphasized by the Aristotelian ethical tradition. The late twentieth-century philosophical turn to the body and interest in its role in cognition and evaluation opens up opportunities to consider food and the sense of taste more seriously as philosophical subjects.

Not only class but also gender enters into the construction of an ideal consumer of art. The "man of taste" is a person positioned with a degree of social power manifest in his confident survey of the world for his aesthetic enjoyment. Theoretically, a woman of taste is also in this position. Yet, at the same time, women's social position differs from that of men. The bodies and faces of women are regularly conceived as representative objects of beauty, and, when this is the case, women occupy the positions of both perceiver and perceived. Feminist writers have reexamined the "disinterested attitude" of the person of taste and argued that the aesthetic distance prescribed for the exercise of taste is an objectifying, controlling distance that is apt to pinion women as aesthetic objects. This is especially evident if one considers certain works of visual art. What position of viewing is presumed to appreciate aesthetically a painting such as the Rokeby Venus (one of many European paintings of nude females in erotic poses)? Certainly, sexual desire needs to be distanced to permit aesthetic assessment, traditionally understood. But the appreciative position, however disinterested, is still a masculine one from which a heterosexual male views and savors the form of a beautiful female body. "Disinterestedness" thus does not free the perceiver from gender, for any viewer is positioned by such art traditions in the masculine role of surveyor. Similar analyses have been articulated to probe the appreciation of foreign, primitive, or exotic subjects of art.

There is much at stake philosophically in the dispute between traditional philosophies of taste and social deconstructions of the concept of taste; and feminist critics have raised deep issues about the psychology of perception and the social construction of aesthetic points of view. Even if one is persuaded that traditional concepts of taste fall prey to gender, class, or national biases disguised as universalism, the questions that originally prompted philosophies of taste are not answered by cultural analysis alone. In assessing all these matters, several questions need to be kept distinct. What historical conditions fostered the development of theories of taste, and how important are these conditions for the formulation of philosophical problems and standards of taste? To what degree is appreciation of art constructed by gender, class, and national determinants, and do such influences exhaust the freedom of the imagination to appreciate disinterestedly? Finally, what philosophical problems do theories of taste continue to address? One may grant the salience of historical context and the near impossibility of true disinterested appreciation, and yet acknowledge that there are questions about aesthetic qualities and standards for judgments still to be answered.

[*See also* Bourdieu; *and* Food.]

BIBLIOGRAPHY

Bourdieu, Pierre. *Distinction: A Social Critique of the Judgement of Taste.* Translated by Richard Nice. Cambridge, Mass., 1984.

Dickie, George. *The Century of Taste: The Philosophical Odyssey of Taste in the Eighteenth Century.* New York and Oxford, 1996.

Eagleton, Terry. *The Ideology of the Aesthetic.* Oxford and Cambridge, Mass., 1990.

Kivy, Peter, "Recent Scholarship and the British Tradition: A Logic of Taste—the First Fifty Years." In *Aesthetics: A Critical Introduction,* edited by George Dickie, Richard Sclafani, and Ronald Roblin, pp. 254–268. 2d ed. New York, 1989.

Mattick, Paul, Jr., ed. *Eighteenth-Century Aesthetics and the Reconstruction of Art.* Cambridge and New York, 1993.

Pollock, Griselda. *Avant-Garde Gambits, 1888–1893: Gender and the Color of Art History.* London and New York, 1993.

Sibley, Frank. "A Contemporary Theory of Aesthetic Qualities: Aesthetic Concepts." *Philosophical Review* 68.4 (1959): 421–450.

Wolff, Janet. *The Social Production of Art.* 2d ed. New York, 1993.

Woodmansee, Martha. *The Author, Art, and the Market: Rereading the History of Aesthetics.* New York, 1994.

CAROLYN KORSMEYER

TEA CEREMONY. *See* Japanese Aesthetics.

TELEVISION. [*To treat the modern, global social-aesthetic phenomenon of television, this entry comprises two essays:*

An Overview

Contemporary Thought

The first essay explains the history of television and explores the various ways it has been studied culturally. The second essay examines the relevance of television (and, specifically, television series) to the philosophy of art. For related discussion, see Cultural Studies; Popular Culture; *and* Video.]

An Overview

As an object of study, television is a confounding concept. It calls for attention from the sciences, social sciences, and humanities, but requires each to acknowledge ways in which the others might alter or challenge basic and originating assumptions. It is experienced in the most common and off-hand fashion, yet it synthesizes complex technological, economic, regulatory, aesthetic, psychological, and cultural categories. It is, in many respects, a global phenomenon, while remaining in most instances the strongest indigenous example of a "cultural industry," far more powerful and direct than cinema in addressing national audiences, preserving linguistic distinction, and developing or maintaining local and regional identities.

In spite of these multiple connections and relations, however, television is still most often approached from single perspectives. Those perspectives, and attendant methods of analysis or argument, generally reflect deep interests directed toward specific agendas. Thus, for the social psychologist concerned with the welfare of children, any study of television must gather data of a certain sort, capable of securing a voice in the arena of public policy, or at least in the attendant bodies of academic literature that might be cited in public debate. For the political economist focused on international flows of media, however, children's programming might be examined as a relatively inexpensive commodity best understood with "public good" economic theory. Programming thus cited might be considered an example of why certain producing entities or nations have come to have particular influence in world markets. Yet, for the critic interested in the history of fictional forms, the same body of programs might be "read" as versions of expressive culture, works that rely on familiar forms of narration, stories that can be placed within a very long tradition of "representation."

But by far the most interesting questions begin to emerge when the critic suggests to the social psychologist that it is impossible to study children's responses without some sophisticated notion of narrative theory, or when the political economist argues that the relatively limited number of story forms is the result of powerful interests in control of "storytelling" in all cultural and social contexts. What these interactions suggest is that television can best be understood not as an entity—economic, technological, social, psychological, or cultural—but as a site, the point at which numerous questions and approaches intersect and inflect one another. For this reason, television should also be thought of as "television," somehow "marked" to remind that no single definition or set of terms can gather or control the power and significance of this most ubiquitous entity. Indeed, in this tendency to complicate singly focused approaches, television has also become the site at which various theories and methods—not to say larger systemic constructions such as "the social sciences" or "the humanities" or "critical theory"—have been forced to recognize shortcomings and attempt conversation, if not always conjunction, with others.

Moreover, the difficulties posed by television's complexities are further greatly perplexed by variations among national contexts. Any discussion of critical approaches to television must acknowledge these distinctions, even as it recognizes the enormous international influence of U.S. television. An analysis of the crime genre in British television, for example, must establish connections with British literary and cinematic traditions, but must also deal with the ways in which imported U.S. programming, growing from its own traditions, influenced British program development. Yet, to make such a comparison fully applicable, the analysis must also deal with the intersecting problems facing the study of television as outlined earlier, and deal with them in terms of the basic facts of two very different television systems:

- Britain's public service system versus the U.S. system of advertiser-supported, commercially oriented television;
- Resulting from this basic distinction, Britain's much more highly regulated programming procedures versus a virtually unregulated U.S. system;
- Resulting from these regulatory differences, one possible explanation for generic distinctions regarding the representation of violence, power, and authority;
- Finally, the recognition that these distinctions bear direct relation to concerns for the monitoring and regulating of social behavior in the two societies, concerns often addressed and processed in crime fiction in many media.

Such an example could be easily multiplied—and greatly entangled by comparing cultural and social contexts even more distinct from one another than the Anglo-American case. Yet, even within a single national-cultural context, this recognition of multiple interrelated questions and issues must inform a growing body of work grounded in critical, theoretical, and historical approaches best defined as "television studies." The development of these complex approaches grew, in a relatively short period, from more narrowly focused projects, often tentative, but perhaps necessary as foundational efforts to understand the medium. This growth of "television studies," however, hardly occurred in a vacuum. Much to the contrary, these approaches had to make their way into or adjacent to a massive existing discourse guided by the notion of "television as a social problem."

Following World War II, the shattered infrastructures of broadcasting throughout Europe began to rebuild at varying speeds, most often in accordance with other elements of economic and material redevelopment. From that period until the present, television growth in postcolonial, nonaligned, developing nations has also continued as part of technological and economic development. In the postwar United States, however, the widespread implementation of television at national and local levels exploded, so rapidly in fact that the Federal Communications Commission imposed a "freeze" on the allocation of new television frequencies in 1948. Originally planned as a brief interlude, the freeze lasted until 1952, and during this period competing interests struggled for control of various aspects of the medium. When the freeze was lifted, "television" in the United States was configured in a pattern that remained in place until the mid-1980s, when new technologies and newly organized older technologies brought an end to what might be called television's "network era."

From the late 1940s through the mid-1970s, almost all serious attention to television was filtered through a model of American social science designed to explore and determine the "effects" of the medium. Serious attention was focused on the effects of television on children, on political processes, and on general problems related to the representation of violence on television. Much of this work is cited or referenced in a series of summary studies published in the mid- to late 1970s (e.g., George Comstock and Marilyn Fisher, *Television and Human Behavior: A Guide to Pertinent Scientific Literature*, Santa Monica, Calif. 1975). Often conducted with substantial funding from government sources, the studies conducted from this general epistemological model were instrumental in establishing certain forms of American social science that, when applied in the construction of a growing number of departments of communications studies, educated generations of faculty, forged curricula, and filled academic journals.

Humanistic approaches to television were fugitive in nature, often appearing in general readership magazines such as the *Nation* or *Saturday Review*. Critical, analytic work focused on textual analysis, aesthetic evaluation, or interpretive studies did not appear in academic journals, even in the increasingly available venues devoted to the study of film. Film studies had begun to find a place in academic settings during this same period, largely because "film as art" focused on European and other national cinemas rather than "Hollywood film." This term, with its connotations of "commercial," "superficial," "popular," or "mass," was synonymous with "inferior" or "unworthy," and prohibited "serious" study of these forms of expression. (Early in the history of television in the United States, live broadcasts of original single plays had been conceived by journalists as a new art form, honored with serious attention. When the economic configuration of the medium pushed production to Hollywood and filmed series, this early period was immediately identified as the "golden age" of American television and discussed with reverence and awe. In some circles, this remains a dominant perspective.)

In the mid-1970s, a number of influences led to the development of new approaches to the study of television. In the United States, the study of popular culture grew out of departments of English, history, and sociology. Scholars paid serious attention to popular genres such as the western, mysteries, and science fiction in literature and film, and to the "auteurs" who created these works. Often ridiculed in the popular press itself, and battled in academic settings, interest in such endeavors nevertheless continued to spread. Recognition of the pleasures and complexities of popular music (the Beatles' influence) and some forms of visual representation (Pop art) suggested that lines between "popular culture" and "high culture" could be blurred—despite ongoing and often rancorous debates in scholarly journals. Television, however, remained the latest and most despised of debased forms.

But other perspectives, other voices, were at work. A major influence in the growth of attention to television came from serious journalists who recognized the deep cultural roots of the medium's forms of expression. Gilbert Seldes had dealt seriously with television in *The Public Arts* (1956), and in 1962 Robert Lewis Shayon, columnist for the *Saturday Review,* introduced *The Eighth Art,* a collection of essays, largely written by journalists. More significantly, Shayon again addressed a larger public with his 1971 book *Open to Criticism,* in which he reprinted a number of his columns and discussed them in a style of metacriticism. His book was a study of the critical process—that its subject was television made the analysis all the more remarkable.

Other cultural institutions were also "discovering" the significance of other discursive formations developing around the newer medium. As early as 1966, Patrick Hazard's *TV as Art: Some Essays in Criticism* had suggested a role for serious academic study of the medium. Published, significantly, for the National Council of Teachers of English, this collection went largely unnoticed. In the mid-1970s, the Aspen Institute for Humanistic Studies sponsored conferences that resulted in two influential anthologies, edited by Richard Adler and Douglass Cater, *Television as a Social Force* (1975) and *Television as a Cultural Force* (1976). These collections called for and provided examples of television analysis and criticism that resembled the best work in literary and film studies, as well as other essays that explored the reasons for a lack of serious cultural discussion of television.

Horace Newcomb's 1974 monograph *TV: The Most Popular Art* offered genre-by-genre analysis of American television's most popular program types, the first full-length study of this material from a perspective more directly grounded in the humanities than in the social sciences. In 1976, Newcomb's anthology of television criticism drawn from journalistic and academic writing, *Television: The Critical View,* became a widely used text-reader for the growing number of courses devoted to the study of television. (Four subsequent editions, each containing new essays, have traced the expansion of television studies.) From the mid-

1970s to the present, the field has grown rapidly and influences from the United Kingdom and from European critical theory have been central to this development.

Early U.S. approaches to television were focused largely on defining formal qualities of the medium, relating those forms to a heritage of generic influence from literature and film, and engaging in interpretive analyses of the relations of those forms to American culture. Although British and Continental approaches to mass culture generally, and television in particular, dealt with similar topics, they were also informed from the very beginning stages by concern for issues of politics, ideology, and all forms of social power. Clearly, much study of popular culture forms of all sorts was influenced by the work of Raymond Williams, long a television commentator for *The Listener.* But his *Television: Technology and Cultural Form* (1975) most clearly related study of this medium to economic and technological formations.

During this same period, significant work on television and other popular cultural formations was being conducted at the Centre for Contemporary Cultural Studies at the University of Birmingham, England. Working Papers in Cultural Studies, a mimeographed series describing ongoing studies and projects, was circulated with great influence in various academic circles. One of these papers, Stuart Hall's "Encoding/Decoding" (published in 1980 as "Encoding/Decoding in Television Discourse") was extremely significant in its articulation of relations among ideological formations, industrial structures, textual practices, and audience responses. In some ways, Hall's essay prefigured later, more fully developed studies exploring these fundamental elements of television.

An equally influential book, *Reading Television* by John Fiske and John Hartley (1978), was a powerful demonstration of the ways in which television required an approach that exceeded narrow formalism, methodologically driven social-scientific approaches, or subjective interpretation. Here again, ideology formations were central topics, but complex formal questions informed the ideological analysis. Recognizing the range of possible meanings within individual television programs and genres, Fiske and Hartley presented television content as a site of struggle for cultural and social meanings. Television was presented as a "bardic" voice, at once the presenter of the pressures within social formations and a centralizing force that tends to "claw back" alternative ideological notions to an acceptable manner of representation.

By this point in the development of television studies, several issues were constantly in play. Concern for the ideological power of television led to a strong influence from Continental sources. Significant among these was the recognition, following Louis Althusser, of television's role as an ideological state apparatus. Other forms of structuralism and psychoanalysis were central to film studies during this

period, and attempts to apply approaches from film theory had brought an increasing number of film scholars to the study of the related medium. "Screen Theory" (from the journal *Screen*) sought to relate television viewing to processes of "subject positioning" prominent in the study of film. Here again, the final concern was with the reinforcement of dominant ideology. But Screen Theory argued that the process not only occurred through narrative techniques, story, and plot, but was located as well within the very cinematic apparatus. Ways of filming, modes of exhibition, and the resulting forced forms of spectatorship led (almost) inevitably to certain ideological "effects" or "effectivities." The apparatus forced a replication of psychological states and stages of development, and these deeper structures, it was argued, reestablished unequal gender relations and other forms and expressions of power. When applied to television, the range of genres and modes of address led the argument toward the conclusion that these psychological functions were structured, especially in U.S. television, within an ideology of consumer capitalism. All desire was directed, in some cases toward products, but more generally toward the acceptance of consumerism as both "natural" and appropriate.

But various forms of structuralism, ideology studies, and audience analysis soon seemed to falter on the recognition of actual differences between film and television. In 1980, Hall and others published an edited collection, *Culture, Media, Language:Working Papers in Cultural Studies, 1972–79*. Here, Hall's "Encoding/Decoding" essay received much wider dissemination. Following Antonio Gramsci's use of the concept of hegemony as a noncoercive means of ideological persuasion and enforcement, Hall suggested that the producers of television (encoders) worked within unstated, professionally defined, dominant ideological boundaries. The resulting messages/meanings/representations were thus "structured in dominance." But his attention was also focused on the "decoding" process in which audiences variably interpreted and responded to these messages. Although there is relatively little detailed analysis in the essay, Hall points to possible differences in interpreting ideological central messages. Substantial portions of an audience would, he argued, "read" the content within the accepted, dominant framework. Others, however, because of particular social formations, would perform an "oppositional" reading. His example here is of trade unionists rejecting a news report explaining causes of and responses to a labor dispute. He also holds out the possibility of a middle ground, a "negotiated" reading, that would draw on a range of possible meanings. With this outline of the social processes surrounding television, Hall effectively established a taxonomy of foci for television studies. That arrangement of conceptual issues can be presented as follows:

- The encoding process, which is sometimes also termed "production studies." This work focuses on the modes of production, organization of labor, technological apparatus and influence, policy and regulatory contexts (including specific national variations), and fundamentally, the economic system in which television is produced, transmitted, and received (ever more frequently focusing on the roles of transnational corporations).

- The programs/texts of television. Work here includes studies of narrative structures, the analysis of particular genres and individual programs, the roles of individual performers, writers, producers, and directors. Additional attention is paid to the arrangement of television programs into a "schedule," a far more complex notion of "text." Much of this work is descriptive and interpretive in nature, often focusing on the representation of specific groups (racial, ethnic, class, gender-defined) and on ideological constructs. Examining and explaining the hegemonic processes that appear in the content of television are central goals of much textual analysis, and general issues of ideology are often at the forefront of this work.

- The television audience. Work related to understanding the behavior and interpretive processes of television audiences has become increasingly central to television studies since the mid-1980s. Often arguing against narrowly defined "effects studies," audience analysis has oscillated between two radical poles, one seeing the audience as effectively positioned by the apparatus of television (industry, text, modes of transmission and exhibition), the other positing an audience radically free to create individual or group judgments and interpretations. Actually, few studies would be found at either extreme. Most focus on specific cases and operate cautiously in some more moderate space.

In practice, many specific instances of television studies combine some aspects of all these categories, and placement of any particular project in one or the other suggests a central focus or tendency rather than purity of accomplishment.

In the earlier stages of television studies, relatively few works concentrated on production studies, and those that did often placed significant emphasis on the texts that emerged from the production process. One major approach in this body of work involves case studies or particular productions. Philip Elliot's *The Making of a Television Series* (1972), and Manuel Alvarado and Ed Buscombe's *Hazel: The Making of a Television Series* (1978), follow an entire production process in order to explain how a particular text emerges. These studies depend on participation or close observation, and both require intimate access to the production arena for primary sources. Another approach focuses on the role of individuals within this production process, often attempting to identify degrees of control and the use of this industrial medium as a means of personal expression (e.g., David Marc and Robert J. Thompson's *Prime Time, Prime Movers: From I Love Lucy to L.A. Law,* Boston, 1992). A related concern finds this logic of control and expression not in individuals, but in organizations such as production companies. *MTM: Quality Television* (Feuer et al., 1984) is the most thorough exploration of the "company signature" approach to understanding commonalities in a body of work for television. Todd Gitlin's *Inside Prime Time* (1983) provides case studies in an overview that combines several of these approaches; but his focus, again, is thrust toward understanding the large ideological significance of the medium as a whole. The study is the strongest recent example of the legacy of the Frankfurt School attitudes toward mass culture, and, in Gitlin's view, television is the fullest expression of "recombinant culture," a culture of exhaustion.

Gitlin draws his conclusion from his combined study of production (encoding) and interpretive (textual) practices. But specific textual studies of television are far more extensive and varied than studies of production, and offer a wider range of conclusions. They can be indicated here only by representative instances such as David Marc's highly personalized accounts of television programs, particularly television comedy (1989, 1996), or Robert Thompson's study of quality programming in the 1990s (1996). Numerous studies of individual genres exist, but perhaps the soap opera has been studied more thoroughly than any other. In some ways, this emphasis is exemplary of the rise of television studies, for in a suspect medium, soap opera is perhaps the most suspect instance. It is also one of the most complicated; for here, fundamental issues and problems of television's textuality come to prominence. The central questions may be put this way: What is it that one studies when one studies "television"? What is a television text? Do we study individual episodes of programs, the entire run of a program's episodes (impossible until the advent of videocassette recording devices), the genre in which the program exists, or the schedule in which the program, and the episode, are embedded?

In the United States, the soap opera, specifically designed for industrial purposes, not only raises all these questions, but also requires consideration of fundamental notions of textuality developed for literary, dramatic, and film study. Programmed daily and constructed around an intertwined set of never-ending narratives, the form explodes the Aristotelian dictum that stories have beginnings, middles, and ends. The American soap opera is designed as a perpetual middle, a perpetual second act. The very fact that the form is created for such continuous attendance and potential pleasure contributes, in some views, to its debased status. Much of this discrimination is related to the designation of soap opera as not merely a "women's genre," but as a genre for "woman domesticated."

Yet, feminist scholars have examined the form frequently, often recouping a substantial range of value and significance, and in so doing, claiming a power for both creators and viewers. Studies by Muriel Cantor and Suzanne Pingree (*The Soap Opera,* Beverly Hills, Calif., 1983), Suzanne Frentz (*Staying Tuned,* Bowling Green, Ohio, 1992), and Carol Traynor Williams (*"It's Time for My Story,"* Westport, Conn., 1992) explore a range of production practices, social experience, and textual strategies. Martha Nochimson (*No End to Her,* Berkeley, 1994) examines soaps in light of feminist social and psychological theory. Mary Ellen Brown (*Soap Opera and Women's Talk,* Thousand Oaks, Calif., 1994), Christine Geraghty (*Women and Soap Opera,* Cambridge, 1991), C. Lee Harrington and Denise D. Bielby (*Soap Fans,* Philadelphia, 1995), and Laura Stempel Mumford (*Love and Ideology in the Afternoon,* Bloomington, Ind., 1995) all study the form with a view of social relations, seeking to identify and analyze the particular pleasures and uses of soap opera by viewers. Like Robert C. Allen in *Speaking of Soap Operas* (1985), many of these studies also present crucial elements of the production and industrial processes underlying soap opera. This has particularly been the case as the influence of soap opera has spread to prime-time television. The massive international response to programs such as *Dallas* and *Dynasty,* as well as the generic experimentation in such crime programs as *Hill Street Blues,* are directly related to the adoption of serial narration in these programs; and because soap operas are increasingly international in their production, distribution, and popularity (as the Latin American *telenovela* and the Quebecois *téléroman* attest), they raise questions focused on international economics and policy as well as cultural influence.

If the soap opera is a concentrated version of the problem of television textuality and the locus of fundamental questions related to the place of television in both social and cultural formations, it is also the site on which textual studies blur into the study of television audiences. No area has received so much attention in the recent past as the study of the television audience. The central issue of this discussion has focused on possible degrees of audience freedom, the freedom to variously interpret and apply discourse presented in television constructed within dominant industrial, economic, regulatory, and expressive contexts. These issues were being presented and refined as early as the publication of Hall et al.'s *Culture, Media, Language.* There, Dave Morley, in the essay "Texts, Readers, Subjects," expanded on Hall's notion of variable decoding, and, in later work on the television program *Nationwide,* offered grounded analyses of how these variations might rise from the social contexts of viewers. His findings—that social class might not always be a defining predictor of interpretive strategies and that gender and domestic arrangements, as well as technology (the remote control device), are major factors in the decoding process—have been supported in a range of other studies with reference to other programs and genres. Ien Ang (1991, 1996) has provided the most thorough theoretical surveys of this issue, as well as close analysis of specific cases (1985). In almost every case, the issue of interpretation continues to be framed in terms of viewer relations to ideological formations. As such, these projects have continued an emphasis on the ideological role of the medium, and questions of form and history have been subordinated to that fundamental concern.

This brief survey of some core issues and texts in television studies (which has not cited a burgeoning periodical literature) suggests a progressive identification of issues, topics, themes, and approaches to the medium. These studies also reflect a continuing application of critical theory common to other expressive forms such as literature and film. Structuralism, semiotics, genre study, cultural studies, feminist theories and other approaches have been honed and focused in terms of their specific subjects, and television has often proved exceptionally difficult to "capture" with any single method. Among the most useful texts for television studies have been Robert C. Allen's *Channels of Discourse: Television and Contemporary Criticism* (1987) and *Channels of Discourse: Reassembled* (1992). These collections demonstrate specific connections between television and a wide range of theoretical perspectives. But they also illustrate the difficulty of explaining the medium with any single theory, any unified approach.

As suggested earlier, television demands, and television studies now acknowledges, the application of intersecting theoretical and methodological examinations. Early examples of this sort of work already cited include Gitlin (1983) and Feuer et al. (1984), both of which explored interactions of industrial practice and textual strategy, but offered less specific analysis of audiences. The most recent contributions to this field have maintained an interest in specific topics, but have more and more often sought to explore that topic as the locus of interacting forces. Jostein Gripsrud's study of the television series *Dynasty* (*The Dynasty Years: Hollywood Television and Critical Media Studies,* London and New York, 1995), for example, explores the international circulation of that program and others, the cultural responses in differing national contexts, and consequent problems for the entire field of "critical media studies." He demonstrates the necessity for framing much of television in terms of international cultural and policy issues, while pointing to the role of multinational flows of capital as another central means by which to understand television. At the same time, however, Herman Gray's (*Watching Race: Television and the Struggle for Blackness,* Minneapolis, 1995) examination of the representation of "blackness" on U.S. television focuses on specific *national* issues. He forges a context comprising economic conditions, Reaganism, the growing power of certain black performers, and changes in the television industry. The acknowledgment of both spe-

cific local sites of production and cultural significance, as well as the international implications of artifacts and their economic and cultural roles, is now a necessary part of television studies. The oscillation between local and global contexts—so common a theme in much culturally based work—is increasingly acknowledged and practiced in the study of this medium.

Still, for all its familiarity, all its massive cultural influence on a global scale, few of the details of the development of television are known. Fortunately, therefore, many of the more recent studies demonstrating complex webs of explanation have been cast as histories. As such, they acknowledge the fact that there are now sufficient supplementary studies of specific programs, genres, individuals, archival institutions, events, and policies to support such explorations, as well as minimal technical devices such as the videocassette recorder to make detailed study possible. Additionally, they demonstrate strong forays into relatively unsupported primary sources—the television industry is notorious for randomly disposing of its own product as well as for its close proprietary control of records and details, but new archival endeavors have uncovered important resources, and oral histories and case studies of events have added vastly to the store of knowledge regarding the medium.

William Boddy's *Fifties Television: The Industry and Its Critics* (1990) is a model for the analysis of complex interactivity that must be untangled in any definition of "television." Examining industrial strategies, critical response in both journalistic and public interest arenas, and governmental actions, he outlines television's shift from the context of "live" production in New York to the culture industry in Hollywood. By providing detailed industrial and policy contexts for the development of the medium at a crucial time, he presents a new perspective on the nation's adoption of this medium as a central aspect of social and cultural life. Moreover, he presents these events in the history of television as a struggle to control "television," and shows how the outcome of these contests related to and reinforced other interests and power relations. From a very different perspective, Lynn Spigel's *Make Room for TV: Television and the Family Ideal in Postwar America* (1992) provides a social history to detail the more personal, home-centered responses to television as a domestic device and a general entertainment medium. Relying on sources such as print advertisements for television sets, Spigel shows how the very spaces in which American families lived were transformed by this technology. But she also shows how the redefinitions generally reinforced existing gender relations, child-rearing practices, and personal interactions. On yet another front, Christopher Anderson's *Hollywood TV: The Studio System in the Fifties* (1994) offers a series of detailed case studies providing specific information about the transformation of the film industry and the invention of television's narrative structures. He also explains how television was deeply implicated in large-scale leisure industries, such as Disneyland, which were on the verge of transforming leisure and entertainment experiences.

These three studies all employ a variety of interpretive strategies, sources, and analytic approaches, and in so doing demonstrate the now-recognized necessity for examining television as an intersection of social and cultural forces. More important, however, they can be seen as interlocking pieces of the "map" of television as it developed from the late 1940s through the 1950s. Only by shifting from the national, policy, and industrial arenas limned by Boddy, to the specific studios and individuals making television as presented by Anderson, and finally to the domestic and personal experiences analyzed by Spigel can we capture anything approaching the more complete sense of what the coming of television meant in a particular place at a particular time. Television exists in the making of policy and the exchange of huge capital outlays, in the industrial processes that produce programs and schedules, and in the experience of families and individuals who live with it in quotidian experience. Perhaps no single study can capture the overlapping layers of influence and participation. But, as the new television histories provide more and more detail, the map is drawn more precisely.

One of the most recent additions to television studies comes close to providing such a detailed map for a particular period. John Thornton Caldwell's *Televisuality: Style, Crisis, and Authority in American Television* (1995) seeks to define closure for the "network era." His argument holds that by the 1980s "television" as it had been commonly produced, recognized, and received no longer existed. In its place was something quite familiar, but now defined by constant efforts for stylistic distinction that might draw attention, stop the ceaseless "channel surfing," and afford economic success. The situation he describes is dependent on a rigorously detailed delineation of changes in technology, government policy, and industrial composition. His explanations of how economic and technological shifts altered the fundamental structure of the television industry, and consequently, the fundamental structures of television programs, are powerful examples of such interactions; and his interpretations of specific texts, fully cognizant of their multiple meaning structures, provide extraordinarily subtle connections to the shifting ideological and cultural formations of this crucial period. Although he does not depend on specific ethnographic or observational studies of audiences, he makes clear the options open for varieties of interpretation. He also offers a thorough analysis of industry attempts to manufacture new audiences and interpretive communities, often defined demographically in the interests of sponsors and advertising agencies. Thus, Caldwell, as much as any scholar to date, has managed to present the complex interactions of the three broad categories of television studies: encoding/text/decoding.

Claims such as Caldwell's—attempts to define truly transitional moments of huge import—are always fragile in some respects, but there is little question that "television" as it has been known for a brief period of half a century is in a stage of momentous alteration. New technologies have outstripped existing policies. Fundamental terms such as *broadcasting* are now obsolete. Once a central and centralizing medium comparable in power to the church of the Middle Ages, "television" has become fragmented and personalized, and the linkage of "television" with the personal computer suggests even more individualization to come. In some ways, cultures and societies intimately familiar with television are moving from a relationship defined by that earlier ecclesiastical model to that of the newsstand or the massive lending library. The probability of hundreds of available channels is inevitably, perhaps ironically, linked to the probability of control by fewer and fewer massive media conglomerates. The relation of these institutions, these channels of distribution, to these audiences lacks clear focus and perspective. Barely two decades of television studies have only begun to offer an understanding of the period just ending, yet the field already faces an imperative to make sense of a fluid future.

BIBLIOGRAPHY

Adler, Richard, and Douglass Cater, eds. *Television as a Social Force.* New York, 1975.

Adler, Richard, and Douglass Cater, eds. *Television as a Cultural Force.* New York, 1976.

Allen, Robert C., ed. *Channels of Discourse: Television and Contemporary Criticism.* Chapel Hill, N.C., 1987. Second edition published as *Channels of Discourse: Reassembled: Television and Contemporary Criticism* (Chapel Hill, N.C., 1992).

Ang, Ien. *Watching Dallas: Soap Opera and the Melodramatic Imagination.* Translated by Della Couling. London and New York, 1985.

Ang, Ien. *Desperately Seeking the Audience.* London and New York, 1991.

Ang, Ien. *Living Room Wars: Rethinking Media Audiences for a Postmodern World.* London and New York, 1996.

Boddy, William. *Fifties Television: The Industry and Its Critics.* Urbana, Ill., 1990.

Brown, Mary Ellen. *Soap Opera and Women's Talk: The Pleasure of Resistance.* Thousand Oaks, Calif., 1994.

Caldwell, John Thornton. *Televisuality: Style, Crisis, and Authority in American Television.* New Brunswick, N.J., 1995.

Feuer, Jane. *Seeing through the Eighties: Television and Reaganism.* Durham, N.C., 1995.

Feuer, Jane, et al., eds. *MTM: Quality Television.* London, 1984.

Fiske, John. *Media Matters: Everyday Culture and Political Change.* Minneapolis, 1994.

Fiske, John, and John Hartley. *Reading Television.* London, 1978.

Gitlin, Todd. *Inside Prime Time.* New York, 1983.

Hall, Stuart, et al., eds. *Culture, Media, Language: Working Papers in Cultural Studies, 1972–1979.* London, 1980.

Hartley, John. *Tele-ology: Studies in Television.* London and New York, 1992.

Hilmes, Michelle. *Hollywood and Broadcasting: From Radio to Cable.* Urbana, Ill., 1990.

Marc, David. *Comic Visions: Television Comedy and American Culture.* Boston, 1989.

Marc, David. *Demographic Vistas: Television in American Culture*. Rev. ed. Philadelphia, 1996.

Morley, Dave. *The Nationwide Audience: Structure and Decoding*. London, 1980.

Morley, Dave. *Family Television: Cultural Power and Domestic Leisure*. London, 1986.

Newcomb, Horace. *TV: The Most Popular Art*. Garden City, N.Y., 1974.

Newcomb, Horace, ed. *Television: The Critical View*. 5th ed. New York and Oxford, 1994.

Newcomb, Horace, and Robert S. Alley. *The Producer's Medium: Conversations with Creators of American TV*. New York, 1983.

Pribram, E. Diedre, ed. *Female Spectactors* [*sic*]: *Looking at Film and Television*. London and New York, 1988.

Spigel, Lynn. *Make Room for TV: Television and the Family Ideal in Postwar America*. Chicago, 1992.

Thompson, Robert J. *Adventures on Prime Time: The Television Programs of Stephen J. Cannell*. New York, 1990.

Thompson, Robert J. *Television's Second Golden Age: From Hill Street Blues to ER*. New York, 1996.

Thompson, Robert J., and Gary Burns, eds. *Making Television: Authorship and the Production Process*. New York, 1990.

Williams, Raymond. *Television: Technology and Cultural Form*. New York, 1975.

HORACE NEWCOMB

Contemporary Thought

The technical possibilities of television, and with them the aesthetics of television, have been changing and will continue to change with great rapidity. For some time, however, a staple of television has been standard commercial broadcasting, and much of it remains in place despite recent alterations. It remains a good, difficult topic for the philosophy of art. This essay considers only those thirty-minute, sixty-minute, and occasionally longer programs that constitute what are called "series." These include so-called dramatic series, often involving police, detectives, hospitals, lawyers, and the like, and also comedy series. Other staples of television programming are certainly of interest, but it is with these that the philosophy of art might first begin to make its way.

Two main topics are the objects themselves and the audience for these objects. In both cases, theorists are confronted with virtually unprecedented phenomena, and it is of the first importance to describe these phenomena accurately. Television is often held in low esteem, especially by American academic intellectuals, and, whether or not that opinion is justified, it often seems to arise from a failure to apprehend the phenomena accurately.

The Objects. Just what is a television series, metaphysically, so to speak? An example likely to be chosen from the "narrative" arts—say, a movie, a short story, a novel, or a play—is a self-contained entity, however its temporal and spatial dimensions are to be described. So is a television program. But a television series is different. It is discontinuous: its elements are spread out in time, separated from one another, typically, by a week. Thus, it is a very peculiar object of aesthetic appreciation. In some cases—for instance,

those of some "situation comedies"—each episode is largely self-contained, with plots that are resolved entirely during one program, but even with them the sustaining characters appear week after week, and a sense of the characters—especially of those that develop throughout the series—requires attention to more than a single program. In other cases, in which plots are not begun, developed, and concluded in the same program in which they begin, there is a profound difference from other kinds of narrations. The tempo and rhythm of such a continuing series is manifest not in a single program, but in a succession of them, sometimes occupying many weeks or even more than a year. When such a series is done with appreciable skill, use is made of the temporal separation of programs; that is, the series is constructed to exploit the fact that anyone watching one of the programs has not seen the series for the last seven days. The simplest exploitation of this fact is the use of a presumption that a week has elapsed since the characters in the program were last seen: the viewer is made to feel that the characters he sees have been active during the week in which they have not been seen; that is, it is not as if one put aside a novel for a week and then resumed reading at the point at which one broke off, but it is as if one were periodically witnessing an hour's worth of the time in the lives of the program's characters, having missed all the time since seeing them for an hour a week ago.

A failure to credit television series with their ample dimensions, with the fact that the actual object of appreciation is spread out over a very long time, often leads to the idea that television is a rather simple medium, producing objects that, if they are artistic at all, are of very little complexity or subtlety. It is difficult to sustain this idea once one attempts to account for the structural features of a genuine series. Correlatively, the idea that television programs are "easy" to appreciate, perhaps too easy to be genuine works of art, may have to give way in the face of the fact that those members of the audience who do engage in easy viewing (often called "passive") are simply viewers not responding to all that is there. Standard commercial television series may just be examples of a kind of art familiar elsewhere, namely, that kind of art that somehow supports both sophisticated, intense audience responses and less arduous, easier, more superficial responses. Operas by Giuseppe Verdi, novels by Charles Dickens, poems by Robert Frost, much jazz music, and even some plays by William Shakespeare are all like that. It scarcely shows the inferiority or slightness of these works that they have long sustained audiences deriving simple pleasures and enjoyment, because they also support very complicated and intricate considerations from audiences with a taste for that. Neither should that fact about television, by itself, underwrite a low estimation of television programs, should it be possible—as it almost certainly is—to subject television series to complex aesthetic analyses.

The Audience. It is arguable that the appreciation of movies, certainly in the early history of movies and in some quarters even today, suffers from a persistent tendency to view movies as if one were seeing a play. Whatever we make of that misapprehension and how damaging it may be to an adequate appreciation of movies, it seems true that the appreciation of television often derives from a tendency to view television as if one were seeing a movie. Even if it does not increase one's estimate of at least some television to correct this misapprehension, it is useful to approach the description of television programs in terms of their difference from movies. To begin, one might note that for almost all the history of commercial television, television pictures have had less vivid and interesting colors than movie pictures, they have been less sharply and accurately focused than movie pictures, and because of their much smaller size they have not had the capacity for the same spatial dynamism available to movie pictures.

The development of a sensibility adequate to television, or to the movies, or perhaps to any art, is different for different people, especially when the people are of different ages and the art in question has developed during their lives. For a certain group of people, now among the oldest part of the population, in the development of movies they witnessed the addition of sound (to silent pictures), whereas in the development of television they witnessed the addition of pictures (to radio). Thus in "talking pictures" they heard the people they had been seeing, whereas in television they saw the people they had been hearing. In both cases, it took some time for the newly added element to seem more than a novel, contingent addition, that is, for the new element to begin to seem essential and to be "exploited" artistically. But for those born later, and especially those born, say, since 1950, both the movies and television were sight and sound from the beginning. These younger viewers are far less likely to have assimilated movies to theater, or television to movies. Indeed, for many of them, their earliest experience of movies was on television sets, and these people have had to separate movies from television, not television from movies, and there has been no background sense of theater in play at all.

No art has had an audience like the audience for television. Television's audience has a size and structure unique in the history of art. This is changing with alterations in television programming and especially with the increasingly wide use of recording devices, but for a time the situation of the television audience was this: At a certain time—say, 10 P.M. United States Eastern Standard Time—a certain program, say, an episode of *Hill Street Blues,* came on, and several million people spent the following hour watching. Movies have had audiences of millions, no doubt, and so have musical works and literary works, but these audience members are spread out in time. The television audience is spread out in space, but not in time. This means that when

one is watching that particular program, even though one might be watching alone in one's own room, one is part of an enormous audience, none of which is present to oneself. The members of this audience know that one another are watching, and a concomitant feature of the appreciation of television is the ongoing conversation supported by the communal experience. Thus, the mornings after *Hill Street Blues* was shown, millions of viewers engaged one another in conversation about the preceding night's episode. Some people, no doubt, experience art in isolation, and it is no part of their appreciation to share this experience, but for many people it is a vital dimension of their aesthetic experience that others participate in it. It is one thing, and a very important one, that a person be enraptured by a Wolfgang Amadeus Mozart divertimento. It is another thing, and a very common and vital one, that the person so enraptured be aware that his rapture is available to all those to whom the divertimento is accessible. Thus, one recommends the piece or a particular performance of it to another. But with the mass television audience, the experience is not only shared, but it is participated in cotemporally. So it is with the audience at a movie or a musical performance. But, paradoxically, the television audience is immensely larger while, at the same time, a much smaller part of it is present to any other part. Whether the experience of television is an "aesthetic experience" or not, it is still of interest that it is a common shared human experience in which the aspect of sharing is unique. If art does indeed have the power to create communities of those who respond to it, television does this in a particularly direct and dramatic way.

BIBLIOGRAPHY

Adler, Richard, and Douglass Cater, eds. *Television as a Cultural Force.* New York, 1976.

Cavell, Stanley. "The Fact of Television." *Daedalus* (Fall 1982).

Cohen, Ted. "Objects of Appreciation: Early Reflections on Television with Further Remarks on Baseball." In *Philosophy and Art,* Studies in Philosophy and the History of Philosophy, vol. 23, edited by Daniel O. Dahlstrom. Washington, D.C., 1991.

Nehamas, Alexander. "Plato and the Mass Media." *Monist* 71 (April 1988).

Newcomb, Horace, ed. *Television: The Critical View.* 5th ed. New York and Oxford, 1994.

TED COHEN

TEXT. Despite being one of the more frequently used terms in contemporary aesthetics, cultural studies, literary theory, and critical theory, *text* is one of the more difficult to define. It is used in a number of radically different and even conflicting senses for varying sets of purposes. The history of the concept of text is long and somewhat convoluted, and is complicated even more by the exponential growth of varying theories of the text during the twentieth century. Nevertheless, one might divide conceptions of text into two distinct groups: the classical concept of text and the contemporary concept of text. Making a fundamental distinction between two conceptions of text will help to avoid the unfortunate trend in aesthetics toward conflating these widely differing conceptions.

Textus. Variations of the concept of text have been in circulation since Greek antiquity, but whereas contemporary usage of the concept tends to make distinctions among related concepts such as work, artifact, and artistic production, the classical usage of the term does not. One frequently finds the term *text* used interchangeably with, say, *work,* to denote the concept of text. What is more, there is a long history of arguments by philosophers in support of the impossibility of even defining the concept of text, from Aristotle's *Physics* (192b20) through Ludwig Wittgenstein's *Philosophical Investigations* (sections 65–67).

The first use, though, of *textus,* the Latin root of *text,* is in Quintilian's major contribution to rhetoric and literary theory, the *Institutio oratoria* (IX, 4, 13). Here, *textus* is used by Quintilian as a metaphor that regards an instance of language use as a woven tissue or texture. This metaphor has been employed in many of the classical and contemporary codifications of the meaning of *text.* The idea of woven texture appears, for example, in the Romance language regard for the term as representing the connection of the different parts of a literary work. It also plays a central role in the contemporary notion of intertextuality—an idea developed by the semiotician Roland Barthes that involves the notion that all texts have other texts present within them to some degree. As such, most of the usage of the term *text* up to the twentieth century (that is to say, what we shall call the classical usage of the term) has treated the domain of *text* to be exclusively a linguistic or written domain. Even Barthes, in his entry on *text* for the *Encyclopaedia universalis,* limits the concept of text only to written entities, and not spoken ones. *Text* has thus become widely regarded as the linguistic texture of the written discourse that constitutes it. As we shall see, one of the hallmarks of the contemporary concept of text is that its domain is not limited to written entities.

Since the Middle Ages, the denotation of *text* has ranged from (1) an abstract, immaterial, verbal entity that may be instantiated in different concrete, material entities to (2) a specific, concrete verbal inscription existing as a particular material object or event. One important difference between the former entity and the latter is that the abstract, verbal text is repeatable, whereas the specific, concrete text is not. Contemporary aesthetics, following a distinction made by Charles Peirce, has called these transcribable texts "tokens," and the original or archetype of the transcription a "type." The type-token distinction compels us to see in every written realization a more or less veiled reflection of a text whose nature has been taken by many philosophers to be purely mental. To a great extent, the ways in which texts are produced and reproduced determine our position as to what a text is. It has also led to the widespread belief that the text is not part of the "furniture of the world," so to speak—that it is something toward which particular transcriptions or tokens approach but never replicate.

The Classical Concept of Text. Although there are many variations of the classical concept of text, each regards *text* as an autonomous, stable, and coherent object with a determinate identity. From the Stoics through the middle of the twentieth century, this classical concept of text maintained that a text is a written message involving two major components: a signifier and a signified. The former, the signifier, manifests itself in the materiality of the text, that is to say, its letters, words, sentences, and so on. The latter, the signified, is a univocal and definitive meaning—a meaning that is positively closed to multiple meanings. This notion of text, while firmly established by Geoffrey Chaucer's time, gained particular prominence through the work of the American literary critical movement known as the New Criticism.

During its heyday in the 1960s through the 1960s, the New Criticism had a monumental effect on the focus of literary studies. Although the members of this movement differed on many of the specifics of criticism, they were united in the view that literature should be treated objectively, and that works of literature are self-contained, autonomous, and exist for their own sake. Extrinsic factors such as authorial intention are not important for a determination of the identity and meaning as they serve only to divert the reader from the text. W. K. Wimsatt and Monroe Beardsley (1946) dubbed such diversions the "intentional fallacy." Oddly enough, with regard to authorship, there is some similarity of view between the New Critical and the seemingly antithetical poststructuralist position on authorship, which was presented most famously in Barthes's "The Death of the Author" (1968).

The New Critics sought to replace biographical and philological approaches to literary works with a text-centered approach. In this regard, they stood squarely in opposition to philological views of the text that not only emphasized the material boundaries of the text, but also insisted that understanding texts involved determining the intentions of the writer. The New Critics insisted that emphasis be placed on close reading of the text with an eye toward the complex interrelations of form and content—a distinction that would later be dismantled by the contemporary, semiological concept of text. By championing the beauty, complexity, and speciality of literary language, the New Criticism foregrounded the text as an object of aesthetic appreciation. Both the aesthetic qualities and the meaning of the literature come from its text and not its author, and form and content are inexorably linked. [*See* New Criticism.]

One of the major debates in twentieth-century aesthetics, especially in the United States and Britain, was over the source of the identity of the autonomous, stable, and coherent classical notion of text. For some, from Roman Ingarden in *The Literary Work of Art* (1931) to Wolfgang Iser in *The Implied Reader* (1974), the text is a set of schemata with indeterminacies awaiting concretization. For Stanley Fish (1980), a reception theorist like Ingarden and Iser, the identity of the artistic text is bestowed on it by its interpreter, and is not an inherent property of the object. Fish's position that textual identity is a social construction implies, for example, that authorial intention plays little role in the identity of the text. It also implies that different interpretations entail different texts. For Fish, there is no difference between explaining a text and changing it. His view might be said to conflate questions of interpretation with those of identity.

Other theorists of the classical text associate textual identity with inherent properties of the text. Nelson Goodman (1976), for example, argues that the identity of a text is defined by the identity of its syntax and its language—the former involves all of the characters and marks that constitute the text, and the latter implies that translation, for example, will yield a text with a different identity.

A number of attempts have been made in Anglo-American aesthetics to define a text that stands somewhere between the flexibility of Fish's classical concept of text and the rigidity of Goodman's. However disparate the definitions may seem, at the center remains a text with some type of an essence and identity—a notion of text that is squarely opposed to notions of the text developing on the Continent. Some theorists, such as Richard Rorty (1991), have tried to find a type of middle ground for texts between essentialist Anglo-American positions and antiessentialist Continental views. One particularly rich source in this area is the work on text by Umberto Eco (1976, 1979).

A text, for Eco, is a "lazy machinery" that asks someone to do part of its job, and is meant to be an experience of transformation for its reader. Aesthetic or open texts serve as the "structured model for an unstructured process of communicative interplay" (Eco, 1979). Labyrinthine structures can be located at the foundation of every aesthetic text, as well as every sign function. These mazelike structures of the aesthetic text stimulate reactions, rather than communicate contents. Open texts are organized such that their interpretation by a reader forms a significant part of the compositional and narrative strategy of the author. The completion of the open text is possible only through the participation of the reader, yet even so, the completion of a truly open work is only temporary and provisional. The opposite of the open text—the closed text—elicits almost a predetermined response from its reader. A good example of a closed text would be Ian Fleming's James Bond novels, and an exemplary open text would be James Joyce's *Finnegans Wake*. Open texts lack the specific, privileged point of view of closed texts from which the message may be interpreted. Nevertheless, for Eco, closed texts, like open texts, are always texts, and as such can elicit infinite readings. [*See* Eco.]

Classical conceptions of text, then, are closely associated with criticism's demand for a fixed textual meaning; and, if meaning necessarily involves some degree of identity, then classical notions of text must determine the amount and source of textual identity. Although each of the positions defended necessarily involves maintaining some degree of stability and determinate identity between signifier and signified, there is no consensus as to the source of that identity. It is located to varying degrees and combinations, in the text, the author and the critic.

The Contemporary Concept of Text. By the 1960s, the domain of text had extended from its traditionally delimited space of written discourse to that of any object whatsoever—written or spoken, aesthetic or otherwise. Some theorists, including Juri Lotman and Jacques Derrida, went so far as to view the world itself as text. Why did this shift take place? What compelled theorists to broaden the scope of text to such a degree?

The key to understanding this shift is to recognize that it involves nothing less than a rejection of the classical notion of text, and a reconceptualization of the linguistic and philosophical foundations of language. The contemporary concept of text departs from the classical concept by following through on some of the implications of the structural linguistics of Ferdinand de Saussure. He held that the material and nonmaterial differences among signs determine language, and that language is not representational. The sign system is a convention, and signs have neither an existential nor an analogical relation to what is represented. Saussure began nothing less than a revolution in the way in which we view the structure of the elements of language—a revolution that in turn compelled many to explore a new conception of text. [*See* Structuralism.]

Saussure and the structuralists proposed that it is only through functional structures that we are in any sense aware of reality, and maintained that language, including art, abstracts utterances or cultural products from their existential and historical context. Language, in effect, imposes form on nature and makes it manifest as the given of a certain structure. For some structuralists, such as Michel Foucault, codes are the sum total of a discourse, whereas for others, such as Barthes, the forms of the already given order themselves into the cultural codes of the language. For Barthes, then, codes are the forms imposed by language on reality that determine our perception of it, and the text of art amounts to nothing more than a set of codes that control its production. All told, the structuralist text can be said to be motivated by three elements: the sign; the codes that order the signs into the already said of a culture; and the discourses to which sets of codes belong.

In the twentieth century, the multifarious semiological movements and their successors became the major forces shaping the contemporary concept of text. From the philological tradition, the semiologists inherited a reverence for the materiality of the text. They also removed it, however, from an idealism which philologists contended stabilized and fixed textual meaning. One of the major figures in the semiological reshaping of the concept of text was Louis Hjelmslev. In the early 1960s, Hjelmslev proposed the innovative view of text as process. By replacing Saussure's opposition of *langue* to *parole* with an opposition of *system* to *process*—that is to say, *language itself* to the *text*—Hjelmslev was able to argue that language cannot be individuated and defined except by starting from processes. Texts come into existence *against* the background of systems that govern and determine their development. The tradition established by Hjelmslev regarded texts as related to linguistic systems, but not coextensive with them. [*See* Semiotics.]

Clearly, though, the most influential group of writers on the contemporary concept of text in the twentieth century was the *Tel Quel* group. Founded in 1960, the avant-garde journal *Tel Quel* included among its associates three seminal theorists of the text: Barthes, Julia Kristeva, and Jacques Derrida. The *Tel Quel* group's concept of text as *écriture* displaced the idea that the meaning of a text is singular and upheld the notion that textual meaning is polysemic. Derrida's (1976) view of *écriture* is based on the idea that the meaning of texts is not stable or fixed, but is rather a series of supplements, deferrals, and substitutions. Derrida contests long-standing philosophical tradition when he argues that speech is not to be privileged over writing. For Derrida, speech is *always already* writing, and both speech and writing lack presence and are indeterminate. [*See* Barthes; Kristeva; *and* Derrida.]

According to Barthes (1975), texts are structures of language in which authorial intention has no role in the meaning of the text. Meaning not only is produced independently of the author, but also resists closure. The reader interacts with the text to produce meaning that is many times a source of *jouissance*. Barthes makes a sharp distinction between this type of entity, which he calls a text, and something he calls a work. The latter is laden with authorial intent, finitely meaningful, and ultimately interpretable. Whereas a text is an unstable entity that is produced by the reader, a work is a stable entity consumed by the reader. The predominant view among Anglo-American aestheticians is that the objects of aesthetic inquiry are works, whereas among Continental theorists, the view is quite the opposite: the objects of aesthetics are more like Barthes's texts. Generally speaking, the differences between works and texts mirror the differences between classical and contemporary concepts of text.

It should be noted that even though Barthes restricts the domain of *text* to written entities only, and treats spoken entities as the domain of *discourse*, many of the poststructuralists who succeeded him do not follow this practice. Rather, they use the term *text* to refer to any entity—written, spoken, or otherwise—that produces meaning through the infinite play of signs. Others, such as Émile Benveniste, extend the range of *discourse* to include both spoken and written entities, thus using *text* synonomously with *discourse*.

Kristeva (1969) treats the text not as a communicative process of social exchange based on the sender-receiver model of communication, but rather as a generative activity that she calls "productivity." As productivity, texts—aesthetic and otherwise—have a redistributive relationship to the language in which they are situated, and because of this are regarded by her as translinguistic entities. For Kristeva, texts are regarded as revolutionary transformations of the language because of the dialectical relationship that she establishes between language and text. Of primary concern is the dynamics of the production of texts, rather than the actual product. One of the factors determining the polyphonous character of texts, intertextuality, is not simply a matter of literary influence. The text is an intersection, absorption, and transformation of other texts and codes, and comprises in some sense the entirety of contemporary and historical language. The analytic process, comprised of the *phenotext* and *genotext* stages, is one of dissolution that inevitably leads to the hidden meanings of the text. The phenotext is the textual surface structure that can be described empirically by the methods of structural linguistics. The genotext is the level of textual deep structure wherein the production of signification takes place. Characteristics of the genotext include exteriority to the subject, timelessness, and a lack of structure. The genotext contains the possibilities of all languages and signifying practices as its predisposition before it is masked or censured by the phenotext. Textual analysis, for Kristeva, shows that, whenever a text signifies, it participates in the transformation of reality by capturing it at the moment of its nonclosure.

The World as Text. As mentioned earlier, since the 1960s, there has been not only a reshaping, but also a broadening, of our sense of text. Although Hjelmslev, Barthes, and Kristeva capture some of the broadening, the domain of text for them is narrow when compared with the text theories of Mikhail Bakhtin, Juri Lotman, and Derrida. Perhaps the broadest sense that text can take is reference to entities of *any* code. It is this sense of text that many theorists employ when they regard all cultural phenomena—from film and dance to music and carnival—as text. According to this broad definition, all of the objects of aesthetics should be treated as texts.

As a proponent of this position, Bakhtin (1986) regarded the text, both written and oral, as the primary given of all of the disciplines making up the human sciences, including literary studies, aesthetics, and philosophy in general. For Bakhtin, the text is the unmediated reality of thought and experience, and the only reality from which the disciplines of the human sciences can emerge. Where there is no text, claims Bakhtin, there is no object of study, or even an object of thought. A text is any coherent complex of signs. The structure of the sign complex is such that in itself it reflects all texts with the bounds of a given area—texts are a type of monad. According to Bakhtin, the study of the arts is the study of texts whose structures are a mosaic. Through his close readings of writers such as Fyodor Dostoyevsky and François Rabelais, Bakhtin has shown how literary texts, in particular, have a *dialogic* or *polyphonous* structure because they are a layered mosaic of other texts. [*See* Bakhtin.]

Other theorists have worked to refine this broad sense by narrowing the notion of text to mean the basic unit of culture, and claim that texts are the product of cultural codes. Texts occur within a situational context that involves textual and extratextual elements. In *The Structure of the Artistic Text* (1977), Lotman differentiates the textual and extratextual by the criteria of expression and demarcation. Because the text *is* its expression, it is materially fixed in the signs of a system. According to Lotman, the textual is opposed to the extratextual structures of *langue*, which are not expressed within the text. By its demarcation, the text is opposed to all material signs of the context not contained in the text. In general, any kind of sign activity within a given sign system may be called a text. "From this point of view," Lotman explains, "we may speak of a ballet, of a play, of a military parade, and of all of the other sign systems for behavior of texts, in the same measure in which we apply this term to a text written in a natural language, to a poem or to a picture" (1977).

Lotman also observes that in widely different cultures a tendency arises to see the world as text, and, as a consequence, to treat our knowledge of the world as tantamount to a reading, understanding, and interpretation of this text. This view of the world as text is related to long-standing religious views of the text—a position that is nicely summarized in Francis Bacon's quip from *The Advancement of Learning* that there are two texts laid before us by God: Scripture and the creatures that express God's power (I. vi. 16). A similar position can be seen in the Russian Symbolists' view that the world presents itself as a hierarchy of texts dominated by one universal text.

The vision of the "world as text" outlined by Derrida argues that there is nothing outside of the text ("il n'y a pas de hors-texte"). Aesthetic texts, as well as all others, are, for Derrida, a place of the effaced trace—the play of presence and absence. The breadth of Derrida's notion of textuality is evident when one considers that not only is textuality the object of study, it is also the subject that studies. As such, the subject-object distinction does not hold for Derrida—he is said to have *deconstructed* it. Whereas structuralists such as Barthes contended that reconstruction of the object in a way that manifests the rules of its functioning is the goal of critical activity, Derrida challenged a position predicated on the ability to objectively describe objects in the world. His textualism asserts that we cannot provide answers to questions such as "What is X?"—whether X is art in general or

a particular painting or musical composition. Although Derrida's grammatological structure is discernible, it denies us the possibility of objective description in aesthetics.

The Limits of Expansion. One of the reasons for the expansion of *text* as a key term in philosophy in general, and aesthetics in particular, is the impact of the "linguistic turn" on twentieth-century philosophers. Interest in language among philosophers has achieved a status unprecedented in the history of philosophy. Philosophers from differing philosophical trends have together agreed that not only are philosophical questions closely related to questions of language, but also that truth is linked in some ultimate sense to language. Some philosophers have even gone so far as to say that outside of language there are no facts, and that reality is only available to us through language—that the dream of "seeing through" language or making it more precise is not the way to knowledge and truth. As such, the contemporary concept of text has appealed to many philosophers, as has viewing the world as text. One of the problems with this approach, though, is that it can easily give way to forms of relativism or linguistic idealism.

The main tension that has arisen in the expansion of text is not whether the concept should be central to philosophy, but whether it should be the classical or the contemporary concept of text that is fundamental. On the one hand, the classical concept of text allows us to conceive of text as an autonomous object capable of being evaluated in terms of its formal unity, and as integrating various historical, literary, and sociological influences and sources into a new unity. On the other hand, the contemporary concept of text pushes us to reveal the codes that integrate the text into a whole of signification, and suggests that we view text as a function of linguistic and ideological discourse. The latter concept of text is also theoretically more fruitful in a technological world that reinscribes texts into an economy of production and consumption, and does not value uniqueness. Despite attempts by some, such Rorty and Eco, to bridge the two conceptions, however, there has yet to be an entirely satisfactory compromise between the two conceptions. The differences between them seem almost insurmountable.

[*See also* Discourse; Ecphrasis; Hypertext; Imagery; *and* Ut Pictura Poesis.]

BIBLIOGRAPHY

Bakhtin, Mikhail M. "The Problem of the Text in Linguistics, Philology, and the Human Sciences: An Experiment in Philosophical Analysis." In *Speech Genres and Other Late Essays,* translated by Vern W. McGee, edited by Caryl Emerson and Michael Holquist, pp. 103–131. Austin, 1986. English translation of "Problema teksta v lingvistike, filologii i drugikh gumanitarnykh naukakh: Opyt filosofskogo analiza" (1959–1961).
Barthes, Roland. "The Death of the Author" (1968). In *The Rustle of Language,* translated by Richard Howard, pp. 49–55. New York, 1986.

Barthes, Roland. "From Work to Text" (1971). In *The Rustle of Language,* translated by Richard Howard, pp. 56–64. New York, 1986.

Barthes, Roland. "Texte (théorie du)" (1973). In *Encyclopaedia universalis,* vol. 7, pp. 996–1000. Paris, 1985.

Barthes, Roland. *The Pleasure of the Text.* Translated by Richard Miller. New York, 1975. English translation of *Le plaisir du text* (Paris, 1973).

Benveniste, Émile. "The Semiology of Language" (1969). In *Semiotics: An Introductory Anthology,* edited by Robert E. Innis, pp. 226–246. Bloomington, Ind., 1985.

Derrida, Jacques. *Of Grammatology.* Translated by Gayatri Chakravorty Spivak. Baltimore, 1976. English translation of *De la grammatologie* (Paris, 1967).

Ducrot, Oswald, and Tzvetan Todorov. *Encyclopedic Dictionary of the Sciences of Language.* Translated by Catherine Porter. Baltimore, 1979. English translation of *Dictionnaire encyclopédique des sciences du langage* (Paris, 1972).

Eagleton, Terry. *Criticism and Ideology: A Study in Marxist Literary Theory.* London, 1976.

Eagleton, Terry. *Literary Theory: An Introduction.* Minneapolis, 1983.

Eco, Umberto. *A Theory of Semiotics.* Bloomington, Ind., 1976.

Eco, Umberto. *The Role of the Reader: Explorations in the Semiotics of Texts.* Bloomington, Ind., 1979.

Fish, Stanley. *Is There a Text in This Class? The Authority of Interpretive Communities.* Cambridge, Mass., 1980.

Goodman, Nelson. *Languages of Art: An Approach to a Theory of Symbols.* 2d ed. Indianapolis, 1976.

Hjelmslev, Louis. *Prolegomena to a Theory of Language.* Rev. ed. Translated by Francis J. Whitfield. Madison, Wis., 1961.

Jameson, Frederic. "The Ideology of the Text." In *The Ideologies of Theory: Essays, 1971–1986,* vol. 1, pp. 17–71. Minneapolis, 1988.

Kristeva, Julia. *Séméiotiké: recherches pour une sémanalyse.* Paris, 1969.

Kristeva, Julia. *The Kristeva Reader.* Edited by Toril Moi. New York, 1986.

Lotman, Jurij. *The Structure of the Artistic Text.* Translated by Ronald Vroon and Gail Lenhoff. Ann Arbor, 1977. English translation of *Struktura khudozhestvennogo teksta* (Moscow, 1970).

Mowitt, John. *Text: The Genealogy of an Antidisciplinary Object.* Durham, N.C., 1992.

Ricoeur, Paul. "What Is a Text? Explanation and Understanding." In *Hermeneutics and the Human Sciences: Essays on Language, Action, and Interpretation,* edited and translated by John B. Thompson, pp. 145–164. Cambridge and New York, 1981.

Rorty, Richard. "Texts and Lumps." In *Objectivity, Relativism and Truth: Philosophical Papers,* vol. 1, pp. 78–92. Cambridge and New York, 1991.

Wimsatt, W. K., Jr., and Monroe Beardsley. "The Intentional Fallacy" (1946). In *The Verbal Icon: Studies in the Meaning of Poetry* by W. K. Wimsatt, Jr., pp. 3–20. Lexington, Ky., 1954.

JEFFREY R. DI LEO

THEATER. Until recently, there have been remarkably few sustained investigations into the nature of theater, by either philosophers, theater scholars, or practitioners. For a comprehensive overview of important theoretical positions, one must ferret through a disparate assortment of texts in disciplines that have had little discourse with one another. With a few notable exceptions—such as Georg Wilhelm Friedrich Hegel, for whom theater occupied the "highest phase" of all the arts—philosophers have examined theater only fleetingly in the context of aesthetic theories developed through detailed analyses of the visual arts or music. Theater scholars have produced mostly critical studies of particular dramatic texts or performances and historical studies of particular periods or movements, and theater practitioners typically advance manifestos declaring what theater *should* be. Such descriptive and prescriptive analyses inevitably rest on assumptions about the general features of theater, but rarely do they explicitly articulate, and even more rarely do they defend, these assumptions.

The most basic assumption concerns what sort of thing theater is. The issue is not how to *define* theater in the sense of identifying necessary and sufficient conditions (an issue considered later in this essay), but how to *categorize* it, situating theater among related phenomena. The perspective one assumes toward theater helps to determine both the way one answers many basic questions and the questions that one sees fit to ask in the first place, much as a scientific paradigm determines the terms of scientific research.

Paradigms. Various approaches have been taken to categorizing theater. This section examines several paradigms.

Theater as enacted literature. In the *Poetics,* Aristotle defines tragedy as a species of mimesis or imitation, and specifically as a genre of poetry. The four most important elements in his ranking of the six elements of tragedy—plot *(mythos),* character *(ethos),* thought *(dianoia),* and diction *(lexis)*—pertain exclusively to the dramatic text; only the last two elements—song *(melos)* and spectacle *(opsis)*—pertain to theatrical performance. Aristotle describes these two performance-related elements as "embellishments" and ascribes the power of tragedy chiefly to dramatic structure. Aristotle's *Poetics* dictated the terms of dramatic theory from the time that text was rediscovered in the Renaissance through the Enlightenment, with the primary goal of most theorists, from Julius Caesar Scaliger in the sixteenth century to Voltaire in the eighteenth century, being to establish rules for the proper construction of tragedies and, by extension, plays in other genres. Even after the authority of Aristotle's *Poetics* waned after the Enlightenment, many serious thinkers who concerned themselves with drama continued to follow Aristotle in devaluing performance. In the nineteenth century, the British critic Charles Lamb argued that William Shakespeare's plays exist fully only on the page, and that performances corrupt the texts' purity. For a generation of scholars following World War II, the dominant paradigm for analyzing plays was New Criticism, which treated plays as extended metaphors to be subjected to "close readings," minimizing the significance of even such quasi-theatrical features as the sequence of the dialogue and its attribution to specific characters.

Theater as sign system. In the twentieth century, the most extensive body of theory analyzing the general nature of theater employed an approach that combines, in varying proportions, the structuralist semiology of the Swiss linguist

Ferdinand de Saussure and the pragmatic semiotics of the American philosopher Charles Sanders Peirce. The underlying assumptions of semiotic theories of theater are that the primary function of theater is communicative and that theater constitutes a distinctive system of signs with its own syntax and semantics. Theater semiotics has come in two waves. The first occurred in Prague during the 1930s and 1940s, when members of the Prague Linguistic Circle emphasized the conventional and dynamic nature of theatrical signs: a single signifier, such as an actor or a prop, can convey virtually any type of meaning, including information about a character or place. This early semiotic program paid particular attention to those theatrical practices that highlighted the conventionality of the theater event, such as puppetry, and folk and experimental theater. It came to an abrupt halt when the Soviet authorities—who had declared Socialist Realism the only valid style for drama and theater—disbanded the Prague Linguistic Circle in 1948. The second wave of theater semiotics, beginning in the late 1960s, was international in scope. Theater semioticians such as Tadeusz Kowsan, Patrice Pavis, Marco De Marinis, Keir Elam, and Erika Fischer-Lichte worked to provide a systematic account of the theatrical sign system. This project involved, among other things, breaking theater down into component sign systems such as language, gesture, and costume, determining the way these component systems operate both separately and together, and, most problematically, trying to identify a minimal syntactical and semantic unit equivalent to words in verbal language. By the early 1990s, the semiotic paradigm seemed to have fallen out of favor, and many self-described theater semioticians had abandoned the effort to identify universal features of the supposed "language" of the stage, turning instead to issues concerning the ideology and historical contingency of theater practices. [*See* Prague School; *and* Semiotics.]

Theater as phenomenon. One objection to the semiotic paradigm is that it fails to account for the vitality of human presence on the stage. In response to this limitation, a number of theater theorists, such as Bert States and Stanton Garner, have adopted an approach they call "phenomenological," loosely inspired by the work of such Continental philosophers as Maurice Merleau-Ponty, Gaston Bachelard, and to a lesser extent Roman Ingarden and Mikel Dufrenne. From a semiotic perspective, a live actor is just another kind of signifier, and theater is little different than film; indeed, according to some semioticians, the former is a subset of the latter, which incorporates virtually all of the sign systems of theater and adds additional systems such as montage. From a phenomenological perspective, however, live performance and film are radically different. Phenomenology shifts the focus away from theater as a medium for communication and examines the way different dramatic and performance strategies manipulate spectators' perceptions of the performance event, and in partic-

ular their subjective experience of time and space, their sensitivity to the elements of risk and spontaneity implicit in live performance, and their awareness of the corporeality of the actor's body. This emphasis on the body dovetails with issues in feminist theory such as "gender construction" and "the gaze," and theorists including Judith Butler and Peggy Phelan have employed variations of the phenomenological approach to analyze the way performance manipulates people's perception of gender and sexuality. [*See* Phenomenology.]

Theater as art form. Philosophers of art such as Susanne Knauth Langer, Richard Wollheim, Nicholas Wolterstorff, and Kendall Walton have carved out a place for theater within their aesthetic theories, albeit usually as an afterthought. Analyzing theater as an art form tends to deemphasize the relationship between theater and literature that, until recently, has preoccupied most academic theater specialists, and highlights theater's kinship with other art forms. As a medium of representation, theater has much in common with both painting and sculpture; scenery often incorporates elements of both these media, and one might view an actor as a sculpture made of flesh. At the same time, many of theater's nonrepresentational features relate theater more closely to music: both music and theater involve a temporal dimension and the concept of "performing a work." Because theater shares key features with other art forms, philosophers often find it easy to apply to theater their solutions to problems presented by other forms. Theater, however, also presents some distinctive philosophical challenges of its own, and these have received less attention. By using flesh-and-blood human beings to represent human beings, and real actions to represent fictional actions, theater blurs the lines between reality and representation in a way that no other art form does. Actors function at once as artists and media, analogous to both the musician and the music, simultaneously giving voice to dramatic language and becoming aesthetic objects in their own right.

Theater as performance. Since the mid-1970s, an increasing number of theorists have situated theater within a larger field called performance studies, whose earliest champions were the experimental theater director Richard Schechner and the anthropologist Victor Turner. Performance studies encompasses not only Western and non-Western theater traditions, but also dance, performance art, circus, shamanistic rituals, sporting events, political rallies, parades, wedding ceremonies, and medieval tournaments. Performance studies inherits its populist, antiliterary impulses from 1960s avant-garde theater and performance art, and at the same time responds to the growing emphasis on multiculturalism in all disciplines in the arts and humanities. A number of writers have followed Schechner in defining performance as "restored behavior," that is, any behavior that can be rehearsed and repeated, but there is little emphasis on establishing a rigid definition; the focus is rather on identifying multiple points of similarity and variation within an open-ended range of phenomena. A precedent for the performance studies paradigm occurred early in the twentieth century when the "Cambridge school anthropologists" Gilbert Murray and F. M. Cornford argued that Greek tragedy and comedy, respectively, evolved from pagan rituals enacting the myth of the Year-Daemon. Although most classical scholars rejected this proposal, the underlying idea of analyzing theater from an anthropological perspective rather than a literary or aesthetic one has had enormous influence. Another key influence on performance studies was sociologist Erving Goffman's use of theater as a governing metaphor to analyze a wide range of social behavior, demonstrating the usefulness of an extended concept of "performance."

Theater as play. A number of theorists—among the most prominent being the cultural historian Johan Huizinga and the hermeneutic philosopher Hans-Georg Gadamer—have analyzed theater as a species of play, classing theater with children's games of make-believe and other games that involve an element of role playing. The performance studies approach sometimes subsumes this paradigm, for it includes any game performed for spectators within its province. [*See* Play.]

Theater as mode of cultural production. Starting in the 1980s, a great deal of theory set out to de-aestheticize theater, analyzing it as a mode of cultural production alongside such practices as advertising, news reporting, popular music, and television. This approach is grounded in Marxist theory, and in particular the work of twentieth-century cultural materialists such as Antonio Gramsci, Louis Althusser, and the Frankfurt School, as well as Michel Foucault's analyses of history and power. Its objective is to explore the way theater—both as an institution and through particular works—participates in the propagation or subversion of the "dominant ideology." Advocates of this approach emphasize the need to "historicize" theory, that is, to base it in an understanding of a particular cultural context, and so tend to be skeptical of "essentializing" claims about the nature of theater.

Problems. Regardless of which paradigm is adopted in the analysis of theater, certain problems arise. They will be discussed in this section.

Definition of theater. Most theorists, whatever their preferred paradigm, agree that theater as conventionally practiced within the Western tradition consists of one or more actors performing a play for an audience, which in turn entails conveying a narrative by means of role playing. Not all theorists would accept every element of this loose definition of theater as a necessary condition. In particular, some regard the existence of a "play" as optional, thereby allowing for improvised forms of theater—though certain definitions of "play" do accommodate certain kinds of improvisation. Others regard "narrative" as optional, thereby

allowing for Happenings and other types of avant-garde performance—though even many avant-garde performance artists consider some hint of narrative content, however fragmented or ambiguous, to be integral to theater. For example, Alan Kaprow, who coined the term *Happening* in the late 1950s, insists that Happenings *not* be regarded as theater. Some even question the necessity of "audience," thereby making room for fully participatory events that do not distinguish between performer and spectator. Most philosophical controversies concerning theater, however, arise from the way theorists characterize the constituent elements of this definition and, even more, the precise relationship between these elements. The most salient controversies have concerned the relationships between play and performance, performance and narrative, and actor and role.

Play and performance. Semiotic theories distinguish between the "dramatic text" that a reader encounters on the page and the "performance text" that an audience encounters in the theater. This "two-text" model is consistent with at least six ways of characterizing the relationship of performance text to dramatic text, each of which has had prominent proponents. Proponents of an *incorporation* theory (e.g., Jiří Veltruský) regard the dramatic text merely as the "verbal component" of the performance. The relationship between play and performance, on this view, is one of part to whole: a performance, in addition to containing other kinds of signs, contains the dialogue of the play. According to a *translation* theory (such as Pavis's view), dramatic text and performance are related by virtue of what they represent, with the performance attempting to say in the language of the stage what the text says in words. A *realization* theory (such as Jean Alter's) is similar to a translation theory, but instead of regarding the dramatic text as the representation of a fictional narrative, it regards it as the representation of an idealized performance. An *interpretation* theory (such as Fischer-Lichte's) responds to the fact that performances do not strive merely to replicate content already present in the text or that once existed in the mind of the playwright, as the translation and realization theories imply, but inevitably add a tremendous amount of information, including, but not limited to, the specific appearance of the props and scenery and the actors' inflections and movements. These creative contributions convey the director's, designer's, and actors' interpretation of the play. Advocates of *adaptation* theories (e.g., Benedetto Croce, Ingarden) are similarly impressed by the extent of a production's creative contribution, but draw the conclusion that the resulting production should therefore be regarded as a new work altogether, analogous to a film based on a novel. Finally, proponents of *execution* theories (e.g., John Searle, De Marinis, Anne Ubersfeld) regard the dramatic text as a series of instructions, commands, or suggestions to actors and designers, though they offer contrasting proposals regarding the specific illocutionary force of the stage directions and dialogue.

Many contemporary analytic philosophers conceive of plays as logical *types* whose *instances* are performances. This proposal, first advanced by Wollheim in *Art and Its Objects* (1968; 1992), implicitly rejects the two-text model, which conflates the concept of the "play" with that of the dramatic text. The relationship between a play and its performances, on this view, is less like that of a novel to its translations than a novel to its copies or a silk screen to the prints made from it. One strength of this view is that the concept of a "play" need not presuppose the existence of written dialogue, as long as it is capable of providing a set of principles that allow performers and audience members to determine what counts as a performance of the work. Among the areas of contention surrounding the type-token theory are when a performance ceases to be an instance of the play and becomes a new work, and whether the primary object of aesthetic interest for the audience is the type (the play) or the token (the performance). Wollheim, for example, regards the play as the aesthetic object and the performance as a means of access to it; Paul Thom, by contrast, concedes that theatrical performances are not artistic "works," as plays are, but maintains nonetheless that they are primary objects of aesthetic interest. The theory also raises many issues that have as yet received little attention, such as the status of the production. A play such as *Hamlet*, for example, receives a great many productions by different directors and casts of actors, and each of these productions usually has many performances. Hence, a theatrical performance is typically the token of two types: a play and a production, and productions themselves are simultaneously tokens with respect to plays and types with respect to performances.

Performance and narrative. Precisely how theatrical performances convey narrative information is one of the key issues in theater theory. [*See* Narrative.] A major concern has been the relative role of what Peirce called "symbols" (convention), "icons" (which can be characterized in terms of either resemblance or exemplification, concepts that some theories conflate), and "indexes" (physical cause or contiguity). Prague school semioticians emphasized the role of convention, as did the American playwright Thornton Wilder in his reflections on theater theory; many more recent semioticians, such as Umberto Eco, have emphasized iconicity, and some, such as Elam, have argued that indexical signs play an extensive role. Other theorists, such as Jean-Paul Sartre and Walton, have offered nonsemiotic theories of theatrical representation emphasizing the role of the spectators' imagination. According to Walton, for example, representational art functions in general by serving as "props" in the spectators' "games of make-believe" (1990). What distinguishes theater from other art forms is its extensive use of *reflexive* props: when spectators watch an actor playing Hamlet, they not only imagine that they are seeing Hamlet, as they would if confronted with a painting of Hamlet, but they imagine *of the actor* that *he* is Hamlet.

In addition to analyzing how theater works as a medium of representation, some theorists have questioned the possibility of a nonrepresentational theater. Some theorists, such as Michael Kirby, Josette Feral, and Jean-François Lyotard, argue that "de-semiotic" strategies of performance can arrest signification and produce a theatre of pure "surfaces" or "libidinal energy." Others, such as States, Marvin Carlson, and Herbert Blau, argue that all such strategies are doomed to failure, and nothing can ever simply be "itself" on the stage; the theatrical frame inevitably initiates a process of signification or illusion.

Actor and role. A hotly contested issue, especially since the posthumous publication of Denis Diderot's *Paradox of Acting* in 1830, has been the degree to which actors should identify with their roles. Diderot took the position that actors should remain psychologically detached from their characters and acutely aware of their audiences. At the same time, they should produce the illusion of identification with the character and immersion in the fictional scene, creating the impression that an invisible "fourth wall" separates the world of the stage from that of the audience. Diderot's advocacy of fourth-wall realism in the theater correlates with his illusionistic theory of painting, which Michael Fried aptly describes as "dramatic," and anticipates the realistic aesthetic that was to dominate the Western stage by the end of the nineteenth century. At the same time, Joseph Roach (1985) has traced an intimate connection between Diderot's theory of acting and the arguments about emotion, sensibility, and spontaneity set forth in his writings about physiology and biology.

During the first three decades of the twentieth century, the Russian director and actor Konstantin Stanislavsky (1948) developed a systematic approach to actor training known simply as the "System." Stanislavsky's objective was to help actors consistently achieve a state of inspired creativity and intense emotional involvement with their parts. His quasi-scientific attempt to uncover timeless laws of acting drew inspiration from the nascent science of psychology, and in particular the work of the French psychologist Théodule Ribot. Stanislavsky insists that the *illusion* of identification is not sufficient; actors must act "truthfully" and "become the character." According to Stanislavsky, a commitment to "inner truth" does not entail a realistic aesthetic; on the contrary, he began work on the System precisely as his interests as a director shifted from Naturalism to Symbolism. Consequently, Stanislavsky's position inverts Diderot's: whereas the former insists on the identification between actor and character but not the illusion of external realism, the latter insists on the illusion of reality but rejects actor-character identification. Nevertheless, the System has become closely associated with realism, and in particular American domestic realism, through its appropriation and modification by members of New York's Group Theatre in the 1930s. The various American incarnations of the System became known collectively as the "Method," and achieved worldwide fame through the spectacular film success of Method-trained actors such as Marlon Brando. Method performances have proved especially well suited to film, because they are not only capable of withstanding the close scrutiny of the camera, but they thrive on the camera's ability to convey subtleties of expression and subtext. In turn, film's emphasis on the visual elements of the performance has no doubt contributed to the diminution of language's role in much modern and postmodern theater.

Bertolt Brecht devised his widely influential theory of "epic acting" in the late 1920s when he embraced Marxism, and abandoned it toward the end of his career in favor of a more nuanced approach. This theory shares Diderot's position regarding the means, but disagrees with both Diderot and Stanislavsky about the desired ends. Actors should not even *appear* to identify with their characters or be immersed in the fictional scene. They should adopt a third person perspective on their characters, cultivating a "gestus of showing" to keep the audience conscious at all times that it is watching a play, and conveying a clear attitude toward the character for the audience to assess critically. Humanist approaches to acting that cultivate empathy between character, actor, and spectator, Brecht argues, universalize the play's meaning by encouraging the spectator to focus on individual psychology rather than the larger sociopolitical context.

Diderot, Stanislavsky, and Brecht differ in their empirical assumptions (for example, about what approach to acting most effectively elicits the audience's empathy) and artistic objectives (for example, whether audience empathy is to be encouraged or avoided), but not in the range of possibilities for which their theories allow. Brecht, for example, presupposes the possibility of identifying with one's character, just as Stanislavsky presupposes the possibility of adopting an objectified attitude toward one's character. Underlying all these theories, however, are unresolved philosophical issues concerning the concepts of both character and identification. What is a dramatic role? Is that concept the same as literary character? Is it the same in all forms of theater? Little philosophical work has been done to address these questions explicitly, though philosophers often, with little reflection, construe their general theories about fictional character to extend to the case of theater. Both Diderot and Brecht describe dramatic characters as social types; Stanislavsky, by contrast, advocates a humanist view of characters, explicitly warning actors to avoid playing general types and instructing them to invent details about the character's biography. This view of character links Stanislavsky to nineteenth-century literary critics such as A. C. Bradley, who scoured through Shakespeare's plays for hints about the characters' lives; but whereas Bradley analyzes literary characters as if they were autonomous human beings, Stanislavsky does not ultimately grant characters an autonomous existence. Stanislavsky maintains that, in the end, actors should play themselves, acting truthfully *as if they* were in the character's given circumstances.

The influential director and theorist Jerzy Grotowski (1968), inspired by Antonin Artaud's vision of a "Theater of Cruelty," similarly regards character on stage as a role that the actor must truthfully assume, but he "depsychologizes" the concept. Rather than defining the role in terms of a character's fictional situation, he defines it as a "score" of precise physical actions, and conceives of the actor's disciplined performance as a ritualistic process, an act of self-sacrifice with symbolic overtones. Although Grotowski's approach has been described as apolitical, Grotowski has retrospectively described his productions in the Soviet-controlled Poland of the 1960s as subversive rituals of freedom and self-expression within an oppressive society. Grotowski's work assumed a different significance in the United States during the 1960s, where its raw, uncompromising emotional expressiveness and physicality, coupled with its rejection of realistic conventions, constituted a rebellion against the values and restrictions of the bourgeois "establishment," and a utopian attempt to achieve a more authentic mode of being.

A second philosophical issue underlying the debates about whether the actor should identify with the character concerns the notion of "identification." Many writers have defined the idea of "becoming the character" in terms of emotional empathy. The philosophical problem then becomes explaining what an actor's emotional empathy with a character entails. Although philosophers have devoted little attention to this problem, the many conflicting theories about the nature of an audience's emotional involvement with music and fiction clearly have a bearing here.

In his later work, Stanislavsky de-emphasized the significance of emotional identification and argued that the key challenge for the actor is to truthfully perform a character's actions. This goal raises one of the few sharply defined philosophical controversies about acting's logical limitations. A number of philosophers have asserted that actors do not perform *real* actions on stage, but only *pretend* to perform actions. Although some philosophers have argued that *all* action on stage is pretense, the most influential position has been Searle's, which applies specifically to the status of speech acts. Searle argues that the fictional frame of a theatrical performance suspends the illocutionary force of any utterance made during a play. Theater semioticians regularly cite this argument with approval, because it supports the semiotic view that everything placed on stage becomes a sign. If this argument is correct, then Stanislavsky's insistence that actors "really" perform actions is quixotic, and boils down to an injunction for actors to create a particularly effective illusion of real action. The argument that the theatrical frame eliminates illocutionary force, however, fails to account for the function of speech acts in improvisations, where, for example, one actor's command that a partner sit down often does cause the partner to sit down. If speech acts performed during improvisations retain some degree of illocutionary force, so, at least under certain circumstances, might speech acts performed during scripted performances.

[*See also* Alembert; Brecht; Diderot; Dryden; Goethe; Performance; Performance Art; Rousseau; Sartre; Tragedy; *and* Wilde.]

BIBLIOGRAPHY

Artaud, Antonin. *The Theater and Its Double.* Translated by Mary Caroline Richards. New York, 1958.
Blau, Herbert. *To All Appearances: Ideology and Performance.* New York and London, 1992.
Brecht, Bertolt. *Brecht on Theatre: The Development of an Aesthetic.* Translated and edited by John Willett. New York, 1964.
Carlson, Marvin. *Theories of the Theatre: A Historical and Critical Survey, from the Greeks to the Present.* Exp. ed. Ithaca, N.Y., 1993.
Cole, Toby, and Helen Krich Chinoy, eds. *Actors on Acting.* New rev. ed. New York, 1970.
Dukore, Bernard F., ed. *Dramatic Theory and Criticism: Greeks to Grotowski.* New York, 1974.
Elam, Keir. *The Semiotics of Theatre and Drama.* London and New York, 1980.
Fischer-Lichte, Erika. *The Semiotics of Theater.* Translated by Jeremy Gaines and Doris L. Jones. Bloomington, Ind., 1992.
Grotowski, Jerzy. *Towards a Poor Theatre.* New York, 1968.
Pavis, Patrice. *Languages of the Stage: Essays in the Semiology of the Theatre.* New York, 1982.
Phelan, Peggy. *Unmarked: The Politics of Performance.* London and New York, 1993.
Reinelt, Janelle G., and Joseph R. Roach, eds. *Critical Theory and Performance.* Ann Arbor, 1992.
Roach, Joseph. *The Player's Passion: Studies in the Science of Acting.* Newark, Del., 1985.
Saltz, David Z. "How to Do Things on Stage." *Journal of Aesthetics and Art Criticism* 49.1 (Winter 1991): 32–45.
Schechner, Richard. *Performance Theory.* Rev. exp. ed. New York and London, 1988.
Searle, John R. "The Logical Status of Fictional Discourse." In *Expression and Meaning: Studies in the Theory of Speech Acts*, pp. 58–75. Cambridge and New York, 1979.
Stanislavsky, Konstantin. *An Actor Prepares.* Translated by Elizabeth Reynolds Hapgood. New York, 1948.
States, Bert O. *Great Reckonings in Little Rooms: On the Phenomenology of Theater.* Berkeley, 1985.
Thom, Paul. *For an Audience: A Philosophy of the Performing Arts.* Philadelphia, 1993.
Walton, Kendall L. *Mimesis as Make-Believe: On the Foundations of the Representational Arts.* Cambridge, Mass. 1990.
Zarrilli, Phillip B., ed. *Acting (Re)Considered: Theories and Practices.* London and New York, 1995.

DAVID Z. SALTZ

THEORIES OF ART. There is no limit to the number of theories that might be applied to art. Almost any account of social life or of human concerns might be extended to it.

There are also many possibilities for theories focusing specifically on art's various aspects, such as artistic creativity, performance, reception, criticism, and the histories and sociologies of these. Another area involves comparison of the arts of different cultures. One rather special theoretical enterprise, that of definition, attempts to outline what it is in virtue of which a thing is what it is. Definitions of art take different theoretical approaches—the functional, the procedural, and the historical. Moreover, individual philosophers (Plato, Plotinus, Thomas Aquinas, Francis Hutcheson, Alexander Baumgarten, Immanuel Kant, David Hume, Georg Wilhelm Friedrich Hegel, Arthur Schopenhauer, Friedrich von Schiller, Søren Kierkegaard, Friedrich Nietzsche, Martin Heidegger, John Dewey, and Roman Ingarden) developed philosophical systems in which the analysis of the aesthetic and of art was accorded an important place. Theories of art also have been developed by artists (such as Samuel Taylor Coleridge, John Ruskin, Oscar Wilde, T. S. Eliot, Wassily Kandinsky, Richard Wagner, and Igor Stravinsky) and by critics and historians (such as F. R. Leavis, Clement Greenberg, Susan Sontag, E. H. Gombrich, and Heinrich Wölfflin).

This essay begins by sketching some views that have been historically important in the aesthetics of Western art. These variously identify mimesis, expression, form, or historical process as central to art's distinctive character or purpose. Two broad trends in the approach to art—autonomism and contextualism—are then contrasted. The suppositions of autonomism have dominated the discussion of art over much of the past two hundred years; contextualism represents a recent reaction to autonomism. Next, the suppositions of modernism and their rejection by postmodernists are outlined. A final section considers Marxism, psychoanalysis, and feminism in their application to art. These accounts of psychological and social life have widely influenced the way in which art is discussed, analyzed, and made, just as they have affected the wider intellectual climate of the times.

Art as Mimesis. Plato (c.427–347 BCE) characterizes art as mimetic—a notion covering imitation, representation, and embodiment. Because he regards the appearance of reality as but a shadow of the world of the Forms, wherein truth and stability reside, and art merely as a copy of that shadow, he sees art as doubly removed from the eternal verities. Accordingly, his conclusions are negative: art is an unreliable source of truth and is faulty as a pedagogical tool. Moreover, its power to work on the emotions, thereby subverting reason, makes it liable to mislead. In arriving at this assessment, Plato seems to assume that art would be valuable only if it could convey reliable information about the world of the Forms. One could challenge this assumption in two ways: by rejecting the Platonic doctrine of the Forms while arguing that art reveals truths about reality; or by suggesting that art's value does not depend solely on its capacity to inform us about the way the world is. In developing this last idea, it could be suggested that many artworks represent or generate fictional worlds the exploration and comprehension of which are interesting and worthwhile independently of the extent to which these fictions correspond to the real world. The point was made by Aristotle (384–322 BCE), who argued that the mimetic arts present the idea of a *possible* world. [*See* Aristotle.]

Provided one includes narration within the scope of mimesis, the mimetic theory applies to many of the arts—to drama, song, dance, poetry, and literature, as well as to painted or sculpted depictions—but it does not cover all the forms of art and it does not capture all that is important about some of the arts to which it does pertain. Instrumental music and some paintings, sculptures, and dances appear to be abstract in nature. Meanwhile, the expressive power of many pieces, not their depictive character, is the more distinctive of them as art.

There are several ways by which one could try to save the mimetic theory by extending it to these alleged counterexamples. It might be argued that, as well as description and depiction, mimesis includes any form of symbolization or expression. Contra Plato, all art, including the abstract varieties, could be said to represent aspects of human experience that are not immediately apparent in appearances presented directly to the senses. If we cannot always describe what art represents, this might be because the aspects of human experience depicted in artworks are not readily describable. One might maintain, alternatively, that abstract works represent themselves, the materials from which they are constructed, or the techniques used in their construction.

None of these strategies is attractive, however. Given the differences between them, the assimilation of description, depiction, symbolization, and expression, rather than discovering an underlying commonality, imposes an artificial unity. Also, it is difficult to support the claim that art communicates the ineffable when there is so little agreement about the profundities allegedly conveyed by artworks, especially abstract ones. Moreover, there is no reason to think that abstract works refer to their properties or materials, as opposed merely to possessing or using these. To follow the suggestions mooted would drain the notion of mimesis of explanatory power and resilience.

It might be thought that no theory describing art as serving a referential function via mimesis can do justice to the fact that artworks interest us for themselves, not as instruments for conveying ideas lying beyond their boundaries. This objection is not so compelling as might first appear, though. Where it is fictional, or offered as such, a work's contents draw one in, rather than directing one elsewhere. It is a distinctive feature of art that the "message" is not easily to be separated from the "medium," that the significance of a work and the means by which this is imparted to it are re-

lated so intimately that a pursuit of the former usually leads to an awareness of the latter. If art serves a referential function in being mimetic, it does so in a fashion drawing attention to its own nature and to the techniques employed in it. It is opaque, not transparent, with respect to its import. Thus, an interest in representational artworks for themselves is consistent with a concern with their mimetic character. Even if it is not the prime purpose of artistic depictions to convey information about the world, it does not follow that an aesthetic interest in them could or should be indifferent to their depictive character or to the subjects they represent.

Art as Expression. Leo Tolstoy (1828–1910) maintains that the function of art is the communication of feeling from the artist to the audience. The relevant feelings should encompass or be consistent with the highest religious and moral perceptions. Art derives its value and purpose from its expressing those feelings (such as ones of human fellowship) that give meaning to life in general. Works whose sole aim is to be beautiful are dismissed as mere entertainment, whereas those that promote cultural elitism and social division are rejected for opposing art's true function.

Tolstoy's is a revisionist theory; on his view, works that do not conform to his analysis are not art. He explicitly rejects the art credentials of many works, including some of William Shakespeare's plays, that are generally recognized as artistic paradigms. But if we think of artworks as generating and exploring fictional worlds that remain distinct from, even if they take inspiration from, the actual world, and if we are inclined to value them not solely for the moral lessons they might teach but also for the pleasure we gain from contemplating them on their own terms, we might prefer to stand by the notion of art with which we are already familiar. It should be noted, moreover, that a theory such as Tolstoy's does not apply readily to abstract works, such as Johann Sebastian Bach's fugues. [*See* Tolstoy.]

A different version of the expression theory, one that highlights the expression of emotion as against expression of the more general feelings that concern Tolstoy, is propounded by Benedetto Croce (1866–1952) and R. G. Collingwood (1889–1943). They regard artistic creation as a process through which the artist's inchoate feelings and impulses are brought to a definite form. The emotion present in, and communicated by, the artwork is constituted through the act of expression, having no prior identity; that is, the unique character of the emotion expressed is a product of the manner of the emotion's artistic expression. Collingwood regards art as expression at the level of imagination, whereas Croce characterizes art as intuitive expression. Like Tolstoy, both tend to dismiss as not genuine artworks that do not accord with their theories.

These authors regard the work as existing in the artist's mind and as inseparable from the act of expression. A work can be created without being "externalized," but the creation of a public object in a physical medium is necessary if the artist wishes to communicate his work to others. This public object is not strictly the work, but is, rather, a vehicle by which awareness of the work is transmitted to the audience. The audience comes to know the work if contemplation of the public object leads it to recognize or share the mental condition that is the work's existence. Collingwood denies, however, that it is the function of art to arouse emotion. This is because an artist could aim to arouse a particular emotion only if he could identify in advance the emotion he intended to provoke, which he cannot do because the emotion expressed in his work cannot be identified prior to its successful expression. Collingwood holds that art is primarily concerned with the self-awareness accomplished by the artist through his act of expression. [*See* Collingwood; *and* Croce.]

This version of the expression theory invites some obvious objections: It overemphasizes the private, mental dimension of both artworks and emotions, and thereby relegates their public forms and embodiments to the role of dispensable concomitants. In consequence, it renders mysterious the process by which the audience becomes acquainted with, and confirms its knowledge of, the artwork. Moreover, it must treat the work's content as largely independent of the physical medium in which the artist works, whereas many artistic properties seem to rely on, or otherwise derive from, the manner in which the work's material is treated.

Another philosopher who regards art as primarily concerned with the expression of emotion is Susanne Knauth Langer (1895–1985). She argues that artworks are symbols of the emotions. Unlike discursive symbols, of which ordinary language is the main example, artworks are presentational symbols that represent feelings by echoing their forms. The various art forms differ in the manner in which they generate structures iconic with those of feelings. Neither the rules governing the projection of feeling into narrative, paint, sound, and the like, nor the individual character of the emotions thereby expressed, can be described in language. But the similarity between the forms of artworks and the forms of feeling, as well as reference from the former to the latter, is intuitively recognized by those who appreciate art.

There is a tension in Langer's theory produced by her attempt to account in language for that which she characterizes as ineffable and indescribable. Moreover, it is doubtful that the phenomenological forms of emotional experiences serve to distinguish adequately between their various types and instances, or between emotions and other kinds of dynamic processes, including nonmental ones. Finally, it might be thought that art expresses the content or feeling of emotions, not merely their structures. [*See* Langer.]

Art as Form. Aesthetic formalism often is associated with the theory of beauty offered by Kant (1724–1804),

who, in his *Critique of Judgment*, is concerned to characterize judgments of taste as objective, even though they do not provide knowledge. He regards judgments of aesthetic value (as distinct from moral and practical ones) as "disinterested." The objects of such judgments are viewed apart from their conceptual categorizations, functions, moral relevance, and existence, as well as the subjective interests, goals, desires, and appetites of the judger. Normally, the faculty of "imagination" collects and presents sensory "intuitions" that are synthesized and brought under concepts by the faculty of understanding. The knowledge that results, when harnessed to desire or duty, might then issue in action. In the case of aesthetic judgments, by contrast, the exercise of these faculties leads to their combination in a kind of contemplative "play" that is free in being both disinterested and nonconceptual. Where their interaction is harmonious, the free play of the imagination and understanding is pleasurable. We judge to be beautiful those objects of sensory intuition that produce delight when contemplated disinterestedly, and we regard beauty as autonomously valuable because its apprehension affords us a kind of pleasure unobtainable in other ways. Although aesthetic judgments are grounded only in feeling, and are not subsumable under rules, therefore, they have the character of universal, rather than subjective, judgments because they are made disinterestedly and, hence, ought to be arrived at by every person.

The formalism apparent in Kant's theory is a function of the nonconceptual, noncognitive character of aesthetic experience as he describes it. The raw data for aesthetic experience are delivered by the imagination and consist of that which is perceived without being brought under definite concepts by the understanding. In Kant's view, these data, as explored by the faculty of understanding, are the *form* of the object of intuition. The understanding seeks "purposiveness without purpose"; that is, it looks for, or considers the possibility of, design, while approaching its object as divorced from the ideas, concepts, or functions that would give moral or practical point to that design. The outcome, as previously noted, is "free play" of the imagination and the understanding, a pleasurable process coming to no natural conclusion or completion. [*See* Kant.]

In the early twentieth century, Clive Bell (1881–1964) argued that the feature distinctive of paintings is "significant form." Because all works have some kind of form, the qualifying adjective must carry the explanatory burden. Bell's account of significant form seems to render the notion both empty and circular. Works are said to possess significant form if they are artistically meritorious, and artistic merit then is analyzed as the possession of significant form. A more perspicuous account of formal significance, however, will likely lead one either to an unacceptably narrow formalism, one that treats representation and expression as artistically irrelevant, or to a notion of "form" that, in acknowledging the contribution of representational and expressive elements to the artistic whole, does not treat structural factors as the sole source of aesthetic interest and value. [*See* Bell.*]

For the reasons just indicated, formalism is at its most appealing when applied to art forms that are essentially abstract, with "pure" instrumental music being the prime candidate. The music critic Eduard Hanslick (1825–1904) developed such a view. He claimed that beauty in music resides solely in the attractiveness of "tonally moving forms." Music is not capable of expressing or embodying emotions, he holds, though it might be described metaphorically in terms of emotions or processes (such as the weather) that are analogous in their dynamic structure. Peter Kivy has advocated an "enhanced formalism" for instrumental music. He differs from Hanslick in holding that musical features can be intrinsically expressive of emotions and also in maintaining that limited representation is possible in instrumental music. If Kivy's is the more plausible account, it is so to the extent that it rejects narrow formalism by conceding that the appreciation of music frequently depends on an awareness of much more than purely sonic structures. [*See* Hanslick.]

Art as Historical Process. Hegel (1770–1831) regards art as a source of metaphysical knowledge; art has the aim of presenting truth, or insight into the divine, through a sensuous medium. When this goal is achieved, art is superseded by religion and then by philosophy, which offer progressively higher, conceptually based acquaintances with the nature of metaphysical and cultural truth. Human history is a progress toward self-consciousness and self-revelation. Art provides an essential step in this process, but progress in the history of art comes to an end when art's purpose is fulfilled. At that time, art no longer advances the dialectic of human history; doing so becomes the task of religion and philosophy.

According to Hegel, Greek art attained a harmony and consistency between its subject matter and its sensuous mode of expression. Accordingly, he maintains that art fulfilled its historical destiny some two thousand years ago; it had conveyed about the nature of spirit all of which it was capable. Subsequent historical developments left art behind, as it were. By the Christian era, art could only present truths already known through religion. There was no longer a perfectly balanced connection between form and content in art, between Beauty and Truth. From that time to the late eighteenth century, art increasingly concerned itself with its own techniques and forms; that is, with the mechanics of style.

The interpretation of Hegel's thesis is difficult and controversial. Some commentators have pointed out that Hegel draws attention to changes in the attitude to art, from a devotional to a critical one that evaluates art against other sources of knowledge and questions its authority. By contrast, other commentators have recommended the view that art returns to importance as the epochs of a civilization replace each other cyclically. The philosophical consciousness attained at the end of one epoch might give way to art that represents a higher level of self-awareness at the beginning of the next, and so the spiral continues. In that case, it is not obvious how Hegel would regard the art of the present day. Whatever interpretation is appropriate, it is plain that Hegel's theory of the end of art presupposes his more general philosophies of culture and history. The obscure metaphysics and teleological assumptions that underpin these might always be questioned. [*See* Hegel.]

Arthur C. Danto (b.1924) has taken inspiration from Hegel's views in offering a different theory that stresses the self-referential, inward-looking character of recent art: the purpose of art's historical progress has been the revelation of its own essence. The past tense is appropriate here because art completed its historical destiny in the twentieth century, according to Danto. Marcel Duchamp's ready-mades and Andy Warhol's appropriations of the images of popular culture raise within art the question of its own nature and intimate the answer to that question. The query could not have been posed within art at an earlier time because it was only with the twentieth century that it became acceptable to create as art items that, to the untutored eye, are perceptually indistinguishable from "mere real things." These revealed that what makes something art is not, as traditionally thought, its appearance, nor is it a matter of mimetic or expressive function. Something is art if it is surrounded by an "atmosphere" generated by the traditions, practices, and institutions of artists, performers, critics, and audiences. A piece so located cannot collapse the differences between itself and blank reality, or between itself and items with a different cultural or historical location. The history of art, as a progress toward that moment of self-discovery and awareness, then came to an end. Art continues to be made in its posthistorical phase, but it can have nothing new to say.

One wonders how readily Danto's apocalyptic vision can be generalized from the visual, plastic arts to others. There may be different ways of explaining the presently confused condition of art, and the alienation from it of the wider public, without committing oneself to a view according to which artistic change is irreversible and seemingly inevitable. Even if this were a plausible account of the development of artistic traditions, one might doubt that their development involves progress, as opposed merely to change, or that current artistic practice better reveals the nature of art than did historically prior ones. [*See* Danto.]

Accounts that focus on art's self-referential character might miss a crucial consideration that the theories characterized earlier aimed to capture. Art possesses interest and value only because it engages human concerns, aspirations, and sympathies. It might make this connection through narration, depiction, expression, or in other, less direct, ways.

Even outwardly abstract artworks are experienced as infused with the effort, intellect, and feeling that go into their creation and elaboration. Not every artwork establishes a direct link to the world of human experience, but we approach and appreciate art as such against a background that supposes the regularity and vitality of that bond. Without acknowledgment of this, it is difficult to explain the importance of art and the role it occupies in any culture's attempt to define itself.

Autonomism versus Contextualism. From the eighteenth to the early twentieth century, the philosophy of art was dominated by views such as the following: The fine arts are to be distinguished from crafts and decorative practices. Works are to be approached "for their own sakes"—for the enjoyment of their aesthetic properties, which are given directly to the senses. Beauty and sublimity are the primary aesthetic qualities and these are displayed more often in form than in content. The beautiful and the sublime are present in nature, just as they are in art. Access to a piece's aesthetic properties is provided by the faculty of taste, the exercise of which might require the adoption of a special perceptual mode or frame of mind, the aesthetic attitude. In adopting this attitude, the audience is to separate the work from its historical and social context and to divorce it from all practical concerns. This is deemed necessary for the perception and appreciation of its aesthetic character. Great artworks are produced by geniuses and artistic creation cannot be formulaic but must be unconstrained by rules. Works are valued for their individuality and originality.

Much of the philosophical aesthetics of the second half of the twentieth century might be seen as a reaction against the aesthetic autonomism just caricatured. This response was ignited by developments in the world of art, such as the revolutionary character of Duchamp's readymades and the rise of mass art, as well as by changes within the discipline of philosophy, which witnessed a move toward relativism, antirealism, and nihilism. The recent trend is toward a contextualized, historicized account of art's place and purpose.

Central planks of the autonomist platform have been challenged. For example, George Dickie (b.1926) argues against the idea that there is a distinctively aesthetic mode of perception or psychological attitude. Also, a wider range of aesthetic properties are considered relevant and attention is devoted more to artistic properties—nonsensuous features depending for their significance on semantic or referential relations—than to aesthetic qualities. [See Dickie.] As Danto has argued, if an artwork has properties different from "mere real things" from which it would be perceptually indistinguishable were it mistaken for another of their kind, then the artistic significance of artworks cannot reside in the appearances they present to the uninformed observer. The character of an artwork will be apparent only to the person who can locate it within or against an appropriate context, which is generated by the institutions, practices,

writings, and actions of artists, critics, and audiences. As Joseph Margolis (b.1924) puts it, artworks are culturally emergent artifacts. Art has a history of making and of appreciation; it takes place within a tradition. This means not only that artists are inspired or revolted by the art of others and by the writings of commentators and historians, with this reaction showing in their own works, but also that what it is possible for artists to achieve depends on their place within the tradition. What might be a plausible continuation of the "narrative" that is art's history will depend both on who offers it (on what that person has done and said so far) and on the tradition as it then stands (on its works, its prevailing ideas, and its values). As a result, no artist can achieve by the same means what some other artist has done, which explains, as the autonomist view cannot readily do, the differences between an original and a forgery. It follows, then, that we can appreciate and understand art only if we bring to it a knowledge of its provenance and background, of the practical problems posed by its medium, of its intended and likely function, and so forth. The work takes its identity and its character from its relation to the art world and, more generally, to its social and historical surroundings; so, contrary to autonomism, it cannot be appreciated "for itself" if these relations are disregarded.

Modernism versus Postmodernism. *Modernism* is an umbrella term for the assumptions, values, and methods derived from the autonomism of writers such as Kant and Schopenhauer (1788–1860) by their followers in the twentieth century, such as Bell and the Bauhaus. Modernists stress the autonomy, unity, integrity, and high purpose of the fine arts, regard art as distinct from the other products of culture, and see art as a providing knowledge of absolute, transcendental truths that could not be communicated by other means. They assign to art a central place in systematic, overarching, totalizing theories that dealt more generally with metaphysical reality, morality, and historical inevitability.

As used within philosophy, *postmodernism* is a term applying to a range of theories that find their roots in contextualism and are united in their rejection of modernist doctrines. Postmodernism is suspicious of "metanarratives," of grand theories and systems. It rejects claims to absolute value or truth, along with the possibility of total consensus, of authority, and of neutral, objective, exterior perspectives on the nature of culture or history. Such notions are replaced by a commitment to indeterminacy, instability, openness, and multiplicity. More particularly, principled distinctions between fine art and mass art, and between art and the other products of social life, are discarded. Postmodernism favors eclecticism, individuality, pastiche, incongruity, and difference in art, and celebrates the polyglot impurity of popular art, while treating all explicit pretension to aesthetic value with irony. All this is accompanied not with the angst that so often attends the rebellious overthrow of one set of ideals by another but, rather, with a deflationary "who cares?"

Some philosophers whose accounts are regarded as postmodern include Derrida, Foucault, Lyotard, and Baudrillard. Jacques Derrida (b.1930) considers texts not as repositories of given, fixed meanings determined by their authors, but as intrinsically dynamic, linguistic arrays to be treated creatively by the playful reader who, in exploring their multidimensional resonances, thereby contributes to their significance. Michel Foucault (1926–1984) stresses the extent to which social "realities" are fabricated as discourses; that is, are culturally and linguistically relative. Jean-François Lyotard (b.1925) argues that social groups and the roles of authority within them are constituted by self-legitimating narratives. The values invoked in such narratives are internal to them and different narratives appeal to incommensurable values, so none can justify its superiority to another. Jean Baudrillard (b.1929) suggests that the signs and social images of mass culture now function as "hyperreal" commodities. They have become reified simulcra, replacing, rather than referring to, reality. The works of these authors are not solely (nor even primarily) concerned with art, but nevertheless are frequently taken to entail the aestheticization of life and culture. Where meaning and culture are arbitrarily constructed and there is no fundamental difference between the actual and the fictional, life cannot be distinguished from art.

The Continental philosophers with whom postmodernist aesthetics is associated often seem to make these equations: the collapse of the ideals and values of modernism with the end of artistic value as such; the historicity of art with the inaccessibility of the past (so that past art must be entirely remade by its current audience in light of their own values and desires); multivalency, ambiguity, and multiple interpretability with radical insecurity of meaning; the recognition that fundamental perspectives are relative to changeable, socially grounded conventions and practices with the demise of most standards for truth and objectivity. By contrast, some Anglo-American philosophers draw a different moral and philosophical goal from the demise of modernism. Their project appears to be that of demonstrating that a naturalized, historicized, socialized contextualism is compatible with objectivity in the description, interpretation, and evaluation of both present and past art. To this end, they argue that the multiple interpretability of artworks does not entail the legitimacy of all interpretations of a given work; that a knowledge of the history and conventions of art can make it possible to understand and appreciate the art of the past for what it was created to be, as well as permit the benefits of hindsight; and, more generally, that appropriate relativizations are not inconsistent with widely applicable standards for meaning, acceptability, merit, or truth.

Psychological or Social Theories External to Art.
This section discusses the place of some general accounts of human psychology and social structure as these have been applied to the discussion of art: Marxism, psychoanalysis, and feminism (treated as if they were unitary theories).

Karl Marx (1818–1883), in his attempt to explain the material (economic) relations that determine social relations, and the implications of these for the unfolding of history, regarded art, and "culture" in general, as belonging to sets of ideas (the "superstructure") in a society that are determined by economic relations (the "infrastructure") and the patterns of power generated by these relations. [*See* Marxism.] Sigmund Freud (1856–1939) presented an account of human psychosexual development and of the mental structures and forces that govern transactions between the public and private aspects of the individual. Although he viewed artworks much as he did dreams and fantasies—as symptomatic of unconscious desires from which they are derived by a process of symbolization—he took inspiration from art and myth and named thematic patterns of human development after Oedipus (and Elektra). [*See* Freud.] Feminism, as a political and intellectual movement, has been concerned to uncover and alter the masculinist attitudes that have led to the suppression, deprivation, and exclusion of women with respect not only to their proper social, political, and economic place, but also to their spirit, moral ethos, and character. Art, as a prime manifestation of culture, has been viewed by feminists both as an instrument employed for women's oppression and as providing an opportunity for renewal and change. [*See* Feminism.]

These theories are relevant to art in three ways. First, they provide theoretical frameworks in terms of which to view artistic practice as a whole, either to illustrate the theories or to expose the forces shaping that practice. The theories can be applied in producing broad-based accounts of the creative process, of performance, of audience reception, of the social dynamics of the art world, and of themes persistently presented within artworks. For instance, the Marxist György Lukács (1885–1971) considers many literary works for their modernist (bourgeois) or realist (socialist) tendencies and John Berger (b.1926) notes how the contents of paintings serve to illustrate or imply the social status of the owner or commissioner, thereby revealing the role of art as an economic commodity. The Freudian Otto Rank (1884–1939) offers a detailed account of artistic creativity. Feminists such as Kate Millett (b. 1934) have exposed masculinist attitudes expressed toward women in literature in *Sexual Politics* (New York, 1970). Feminists also have drawn attention to the fact that skilled women's work, such as needlepoint, has been denied the status of art by being dismissed as a decorative, domestic craft. Germaine Greer (b.1939), among others, has—in *The Obstacle Race: The Fortunes of Women Painters and their Work* (New York, 1979) pointed—to the past exclusion of women from the leagues of creative artists and she documents the frequent dismissal and trivialization of the works of the comparatively few women artists who produced artworks under their own names.

When it comes to discussing the contents of artworks, such theories do not always confine themselves to the straightforwardly narrative or depictive types. Theodor W. Adorno (1903–1969), a Marxist and a progressivist, looks for social meaning in instrumental music. When the composer takes control of the material of music, as Arnold Schoenberg did with his method of composing with twelve tones, greater creative freedom results. Regressive artworks, such as Stravinsky's neoclassical pieces, do not look forward to social transformation, Adorno claims. The feminist Susan McClary suggests in *Feminine Endings: Music, Gender, and Sexuality,* (Minneapolis, 1991) that the confrontational and combative ethos of the sonata form—the structure most commonly used in classical music between about 1760 and 1910—is essentially phallocentric. She concludes that truly feminist music requires the evolution of different structural patterns. Freud himself made intriguing observations about a striking feature of the symphonies of Gustav Mahler—the prevalence at moments of high emotional intensity of banal themes, such as those played by brass bands—as a result of questioning the composer about his childhood.

Second, the theories can be applied to the interpretation of particular pieces, providing new insights into the artist or the work. Ernest Jones's (1879–1958) explanation of Hamlet's (alleged) procrastination and Freud's accounts of Leonardo da Vinci's painting of Saint Anne, Mary, and the Christ child, as well as of Michelangelo's *Moses*, are examples of the psychoanalytic approach. McClary's feminist analysis of Georges Bizet's *Carmen* points to an association between Carmen's sensuality and chromaticism in the music associated with her. Chromaticism, which is connected in music's history with instability and deviation, calls for resolution and a return to order. Carmen also is expected to conform (for the sake of the patriarchal social order) and is sacrificed for failing to do so.

Third, such theories may inspire or provoke artists in their creative efforts. Under Joseph Stalin, Marxism was interpreted as suggesting that art should serve the proletariat. It could do so by pursuing realism while idealizing the goals and values of socialism and condemning those of capitalism. This political agenda was forced upon artists, many of whom did not find it congenial. Alternatively, it is argued by Adorno and Bertolt Brecht (1898–1956) that Marxism is compatible with antirealist styles of art that audiences will find challenging and sophisticated. In his plays, Brecht sets out to reveal both the social forces lying behind the events considered and the mechanisms employed in bringing all this to the stage. Meanwhile, the painters of the Surrealist movement, among many others, self-consciously employed a mode of symbolism with a Freudian character; and the artworks of many contemporary women artists express a distinctive female consciousness and celebrate the place, lives, interests, and values of women.

Three kinds of objections, none of which is entirely convincing, are often raised against the analysis and interpretation of art in terms of theories such as these. The first objection is to the theories' generality: because they focus on broad patterns and trends, and in doing so must overlook the welter of detail, such theories are ill suited to characterizing that in which the interest and importance of art resides, which is the individuality of works. If people's choices in clothes, or cars, or friends can illustrate the themes of Marxism, or psychoanalysis, or feminism as readily as do their arts, then these theories fail to reveal what is distinctive to, and valuable in, art.

In response, one can note that, although art might be used (as the objection recognizes) with the purpose of illustrating the theory, this is by no means the only way the two can be brought into relation. These theories can provide revealing perspectives on the wider social settings within which art is created, presented, and received. That background is of interest in its own right, but it also connects intimately with the work's character, because artistically significant properties of the work can be affected by its relation to these contexts. Moreover, the individual work and its interpretation can become the focus of concern. Just as a general theory of gravity and force can be applied to the specific case, say, of explaining how a plane becomes airborne, so Marxist, psychoanalytic, or feminist theories can be applied to the detail of a particular artwork. The generality of these theories is a function of the range over which they might be applied, not of the manner of their operation on the particular.

The second complaint is raised against the anachronistic use of such theories in interpreting works created prior to their espousal. How could it be that Hamlet is paralyzed by an inner Oedipal conflict when Shakespeare could not have conceived of such a possibility? Is it not arrogant of us to judge art depicting the treatment of women in other times by standards grounded in, and shaped by, our own sociotemporal location?

A reply might take this form. The theories under discussion claim to be true—if not of all cultures at all times, then of patriarchal or capitalist/feudal ones, and of those in which children are raised by their parents against a background of sexual taboos. Thus, they deal with most societies, if not all. If they are true, for example, of the societies in which John Bunyan penned *The Pilgrim's Progress,* Sophocles scripted *Oedipus Rex,* and Samuel Richardson wrote *Clarissa,* and if these authors are astute observers of custom and human nature, then the theories can be employed to discuss their works. Artists of any time might see and record the effects of the psychological processes and social forces analyzed by Marxism, psychoanalysis, and feminism, because these processes and forces predated their systematic description and categorization.

This is not to say that artists always think about the psychological or social significance of their ideas as they work. They might remain unaware of the underlying causes of the outcomes they describe, depict, or convey. Indeed, psychoanalysis predicts that the processes it discusses are often cloaked from consciousness. It is likely that the social dynamics discussed by Marxists and feminists often operate like Adam Smith's famous "hidden hand"—as producing overall patterns that are not aimed at directly, but that occur as a consequence of many individual decisions, each of which is made with a view only to immediate, local goals.

The third objection takes up a point mentioned in the previous reply by questioning the truth or credibility of the theories under discussion. Marxism and psychoanalytic theory now are, if not entirely discredited, treated with reserve and skepticism, and feminism is not without its critics. If the appropriateness of using such theories in art criticism depends on their claim to truth, then there is room for doubting their applicability.

A first line of response remarks that the theories in question might contain many insightful parts even if the whole is flawed. (More than a hundred years' persistent attractiveness speaks for the likely truth of elements in Marxism and psychoanalysis, and the depth of recognition and engagement awakened in many women by feminist theory suggests that, at worst, it contains an important kernel of truth.) Because Marxist, psychoanalytic, and feminist theories usually are applied to art in piecemeal fashion, their use in analyzing the art of the past is sufficiently justified by the insights they encompass. The second response was foreshadowed above: contemporary artists constantly draw on these theories, false or not, so interpretation of the resulting pieces requires reference to them. To take some obvious examples, George Orwell's novels are overtly political; the protagonists of J. D. Salinger's *The Catcher in the Rye* and Philip Roth's *Portnoy's Complaint* address their stories to their psychoanalysts; Doris Lessing's *The Golden Notebook*, Marge Piercy's *Woman on the Edge of Time,* and Marilyn French's *The Women's Room* are all about women's personal liberation. The theories of Marxism, psychoanalysis, and feminism are embedded so pervasively and deeply in the intellectual life of our times that it is legitimate to extend their use even to works that seem not to invite this regard.

[*See also* Autonomy; Discourse; Expression Theory of Art; Formalism; Historicism; Mimesis; Modernism; Ontology of Art; Postmodernism; Semiotics; Sociology of Art; Text; *and* Theory.]

BIBLIOGRAPHY

Adorno, Theodor W. *The Philosophy of Modern Music.* Translated by Anne G. Mitchell and Wesley V. Blomster. London, 1973.
Adorno, Theodor W. *Aesthetic Theory.* Edited by Gretel Adorno and Rolf Tiedemann, translated by Robert Hullot-Kentor. Minneapolis, 1997.
Aristotle. *The Poetics of Aristotle: Translation and Commentary.* Translated by Stephen Halliwell. London, 1987.
Baudrillard, Jean. *Jean Baudrillard: Selected Writings.* Edited by Mark Poster. Stanford, Calif., 1988.
Bell, Clive. *Art.* Reprint, New York, 1958.
Berger, John. *Ways of Seeing.* London, 1972.
Brecht, Bertolt. *On Theatre: The Development of an Aesthetic.* Edited and translated by John Willett. London, 1964.
Collingwood, R. G. *Principles of Art.* Oxford, 1938.
Croce, Benedetto. *Aesthetic as Science of Expression and General Linguistics.* Translated by Douglas Ainslie. Reprint, London, 1953.
Danto, Arthur C. *The Transfiguration of the Commonplace: A Philosophy of Art.* Cambridge Mass., 1981.
Danto, Arthur C. *The Philosophical Disenfranchisement of Art.* New York, 1986.
Derrida, Jacques. *Writing and Difference.* Translated by Alan Bass. Chicago, 1978.
Dickie, George. *Art and the Aesthetic: An Institutional Analysis.* Ithaca, N.Y., 1974.
Eagleton, Terry. *The Ideology of the Aesthetic.* Oxford and Cambridge, Mass., 1990.
Freud, Sigmund. "The Moses of Michelangelo." In *Collected Papers,* vol. 4, translated by Joan Riviere, pp. 257–287. London, 1957.
Freud, Sigmund. *Leonardo da Vinci and a Memory of Childhood.* Translated by Alan Tyson. Harmondsworth, England, 1963.
Hanslick, Eduard. *On the Musically Beautiful: A Contribution Towards the Revision of the Aesthetics of Music* (8th edition of 1891). Translated and edited by Geoffrey Payzant. Indianapolis, 1986.
Hegel, Georg Wilhelm Friedrich. *Aesthetics: Lectures on Fine Art.* 2 vols. Translated by T. M. Knox. Oxford, 1975.
Kant, Immanuel. *The Critique of Judgement.* 2d rev. ed. Translated by J. H. Bernard. London, 1914.
Kivy, Peter. *Sound Sentiment: An Essay on the Musical Emotions.* Philadelphia, 1989.
Kristeller, Paul Oskar. "The Modern System of the Arts: A Study in the History of Aesthetics." *Journal of the History of Ideas* 12.4 (October 1951): 496–527; 13.1 (January 1952): 17–46.
Langer, Susanne Knauth. *Philosophy in a New Key.* Cambridge, Mass., 1942.
Langer, Susanne Knauth. *Feeling and Form.* New York, 1953.
Lukács, György. *The Meaning of Contemporary Realism.* Translated by John Mander and Necke Mander. London, 1962.
Lyotard, Jean-François. *The Postmodern Condition: A Report on Knowledge.* Translated by Geoffrey Bennington and Brian Massumi. Minneapolis, 1984.
Margolis, Joseph. *Art and Philosophy.* Atlantic Highlands, N.J., 1980.
Plato. *The Republic.* Translated by H. D. P. Lee. Harmondsworth, England, 1955.
Rank, Otto. *Art and Artist: Creative Urge and Personality Development.* Translated by Charles Francis Atkinson. New York, 1932.
Sparshott, Francis. *The Theory of the Arts.* Princeton, N.J., 1982.
Tolstoy, Leo. *What Is Art? and Essays on Art.* Translated by Aylmer Maude. Oxford, 1930.

STEPHEN DAVIES

THEORY, HISTORY OF. [*The role of theory has become an important, if controversial, topic in contemporary aesthetics, art history, literary studies, cultural studies, and many other disciplines related to art and culture. This entry provides the conceptual background for such debates by tracing the history and practice of the concept of theory in general (not just in connection* *with art) from the Greeks up to the end of the nineteenth century, when theory seems to get displaced (for reasons analyzed here), only to reemerge late in the twentieth century.]*

A theory is a consistent, coherent, complete, critical body of ideas believed to provide a clearer, more comprehensive, or more adequate understanding of some object or objects than less systematic, pretheoretical perspectives. In aesthetics, theory is a body of ideas about the aesthetic, including within its scope topics such as the phenomenology of processes through which natural or cultural objects come to be perceived or designated as aesthetic, the ontology of such objects, and the analysis of ways in which art is created, experienced, and/or critically understood and evaluated.

In ancient Greek philosophy, Aristotle established the philosophical contrast between theory and other forms of activity with a tripartite distinction between *theoria* (an activity whose end is knowledge of the universal and eternal), *poiēsis* (an activity whose end is things made rather than knowledge), and *praxis* (an activity that produces change in the agent; good or worthwhile action in the sense of *praxis* is its own end). This triple division was subsequently simplified to a distinction between theory and practice, and in its contemporary usage theory is usually contrasted with practice (or praxis) in a modern philosophical tradition extending from Immanuel Kant through Georg Wilhelm Friedrich Hegel to Karl Marx and beyond. Contemporary discussion of relationships between theory and practice also occurs in other areas of philosophy besides aesthetics, such as ethics and political philosophy, and in the social-scientific disciplines of cultural anthropology, sociology, clinical psychology, and political science. This expanding discussion across and within academic disciplines and fields has produced an impact on aesthetic discussions of the topic. Although current discussion of theory inside and outside of aesthetics differs in significant ways from the views expressed in ancient philosophical texts, it is necessary to grasp the understanding of theory present in Plato and Aristotle in order to appreciate contemporary discussion. The following summary of views about theory thus begins with ancient Greece, then turns to a brief survey of contributions to the topic by Kant, Hegel, and Marx, and concludes with suggestions about the relationship between contemporary understandings of theory and aesthetics.

Etymology. Greek understanding of theory as a topic in philosophy presupposes a complex etymology. The origins of the English word *theory* are found in three Greek words associated with vision—*theorein, theoros, theoria*—and word for the divine, *theos*. Together, these words imply root ideas that informed the work of Plato and Aristotle and that continue to play a role in modern and contemporary discussions. These ideas include the priority of sight over other senses, the truthfulness or reliability of a privileged way of seeing, and a possible link between this reliable way of see-

ing and transcendence of the merely visible. *Theorein* means to look at attentively, to behold, to contemplate, or to survey. The centrality of sight over other senses in Greek culture is captured by Hans Blumenberg: "The light in which the landscape and things that surround the life of Greeks stood gave to everything a clarity and (in terms of optics alone) unquestionable presence that left room for doubt regarding the accessibility of nature to man only late, and only as a result of thought" (1983). Hans Jonas, in his essay "The Nobility of Sight," notes several consequences of the Greek visual bias, including the atemporal quality of sight and a resulting Greek preoccupation with unchanging and eternal presence; the distance between subject and object established by sight accompanied by a predisposition to believe in the neutral observation of the latter by the former; and the great reach of sight as an influence on the idea of infinity.

A *theoros* was originally a spectator at festival theater performances, athletic contests, and other public events. In later usage, the term assumed a more restricted, technical sense of one who has a faculty for seeing farther, for discriminating, judging, comparing, criticizing, or savoring what he sees. According to Terence Ball, "A spectator in this sense is not one who seeks immediate sensual or perceptual gratification but rather one who seeks understanding and wisdom" (1979). Hans-Georg Gadamer emphasizes the sacral character attributed to the vision of a *theoros:*

> We can recall the concept of sacral communion that lies behind the original Greek concept of *theoria*. *Theoros* means someone who takes part in a delegation to a festival. Such a person has no other distinction or function than to be there. Thus the *theoros* is a spectator in the proper sense of the word since he participates in the solemn act through his presence at it. Thus sacred law accords him a distinction: for example, inviolability. (1989)

Finally, according to Hartmut Böhme (1984), this communion-oriented emphasis on vision was especially evident in pre-Socratic thought. Böhme implies cultural movement from an earlier, communion-oriented understanding of vision to a subsequent understanding of vision emphasizing separation between the viewer and the object of vision. This suggestion is further supported by F. M. Cornford's (1991) observation that the Orphic version of *theoria* included a sense of emotional involvement, whereas its later Pythagorean replacement did not.

The question as to whether theory represents a way of seeing separating the theoretician from the theorized, or rather indicates a unique form of insight leading to communion between theoretician and object, is further complicated by the change from Greek to Latin. As Martin Jay notes, "The Latin *speculatio*—along with *contemplatio,* the translation of *theoria*—contained within it the same root as *speculum* and *specular* which designate mirroring. Rather than implying the distance between subject and object, the specular tradition . . . tended to collapse them" (1993). The question of theory as communion or separation from its objects returns in Kant and Hegel.

Theory also has links to *theoria*. A *theoria* was an official delegation from one Greek polis to another. It served an important function in Greek civic life by attesting to the occurrence of an important event, first witnessing the event as it occurred, and later certifying that it had actually taken place. Wlad Godzich, in his "Forward: The Tiger on the Mat" (in Paul de Man, *The Resistance to Theory*), emphasizes the contrast between the collective, official work of the *theoria* and individual acts of perception or *aesthēsis.*

> Their [the *theorias'*] function was one of see-and-tell. . . . while other individuals in the city could see and tell . . . the city needed a more official and ascertainable form of knowledge if it was not to lose itself in endless claims and counterclaims. The *theoria* provided such a bedrock of certainty: what it certified as having seen could become the object of public discourse.
>
> (1986)

There are, finally, associations between *theorein, theoros, theoria,* and *theos* or god. The gods of Greece were believed to have been visibly manifest to humans, and were frequently depicted in sculpture, mosaics, and painting, suggesting links between the visualization associated with theory and the sacred. Plutarch and early Christian authors such as Gregory of Nyssa, Basil the Great, and Pseudo-Dionysius all note the link between *theorein* and *theos,* suggesting that true *theoria* involves more than mere seeing; it may involve observation of nature from a divine perspective. At the same time, the dangers of vision misdirected—to the one who sees or to the object of seeing—are the subject of Greek myths, notably those of Narcissus, Orpheus, and Medusa. The possibility implied by these myths—that sight/insight improperly used may lead to death—does not diminish the importance of vision, but serves rather as a balance to the otherwise positive understanding of vision in Greek iconography.

The etymology of *theory/theoria* demonstrates that prior to Plato's discussion of theory as a unique kind of seeing done by a philosopher, or Aristotle's praise of a life dedicated to theory over one given to practice, there was already a complex background in Greek culture and language that emphasized the precedence of vision over other senses in the search for truth, recognized the sight of some persons as privileged, and implied the possibility of such sight performing a positive or a negative revelatory role.

Plato and Aristotle. For Plato, theory is a superior form of seeing not wholly communicable in language. In the *Republic* (474B–478), Glaucon mentions a resemblance between the sightseers at festivals and philosophers. Socrates, while conceding a resemblance between the two forms of activity, emphasizes the philosopher's task as more than mere seeing. Philosophy is the pursuit and love of knowledge *(epistēmē),* defined by Plato as an understanding of an eternal, immutable, and unchanging *eidos* or idea, "which is like a visible form blanched of color" (Jay, 1993). Such knowledge is direct, unmediated, in some ways similar to a religious vision, as well as being incommunicable in speech according to the image of the dazed philosophical visionary returning to the cave from his encounter with the central *eidos*—the good—in the *Republic.* While there is no sharp separation in Plato between theory in the transformative sense of contemplation of the divine, and theory in the reductive sense of scientific analysis through dialectic, in later dialogues such as the *Statesman,* the *Laws,* and the *Sophist,* the theorist is cast as a "stranger" and given no name, thus emphasizing the strangeness of philosophy. At times, Plato even suggests that theorizing means taking leave of life, a kind of separation or type of death. Plato's final understanding of theory in effect replaces the collective citizen *theoria* with an individual philosopher, who is to perform that office by virtue of unique qualities of soul. Plato also assumes that a philosopher cannot fully achieve the final goal of *theoria*—knowledge of the good—until a polis is governed by philosophers.

In later, Neoplatonic thinking, this Platonic inheritance of the strangeness of philosophy and longing for an ideal city is developed in the light of a different ideal: union with the divine One. This otherworldly ideal leads to a further distinction between theory as science and theory as contemplation. "With Gregory of Nyssa Christian theology . . . takes over this distinction. In his homily on the Song of Songs Gregory distinguishes between two sorts of *theoria:* one which corresponds to the Platonic dialogues and thus to science . . . and another which is a 'seeing of God in darkness,' that is, contemplation" (Lobkowicz, 1977). For Aristotle, as noted earlier, theory is one of three distinctive ways or forms of life. *Theoria* is the highest or best way of life consisting of noninstrumental, continuous activity aiming at self-sufficiency *(autarkēs).* This activity is dedicated to a wisdom (nous) capable of grasping undemonstrable first principles, the permanent, unchanging characteristics of being as such (*Nicomachean Ethics,* 6.2, 1140b31–41a8). It is in such theoretical activity that human minds most closely approximate the pure, unmediated activity of God as pure thought, a form of life in which there is perfect coincidence between subject and object of knowledge. A life devoted to *theoria* is in marked contrast to the leisured life of desire pursued by the wealthy. This way of life is sharply criticized by Aristotle (in the *Rhetoric* 2.15–16. 1390b14–91a19) as "worthless" *(euteles)* or "foolish" *(aonoētos).* Finally, there is the life of an engaged citizen of a polis, dedicated to praxis. Praxis is a form of activity whose goal is the perfection of the doer, requiring practical wisdom *(phronēsis):* the ability to deliberate about "living well as a whole" (*Nicomachean Ethics,* 6, 1141a20–25). Such practical wisdom can only be acquired through repeated experience in the exercise of the various moral and intellectual excellences *(aretē)* of character, for it is in this way that an individual actor comes to recognize and embody a mean of excellence relative to himself. This form of practical rationality, about one's life and the lives of people one knows, enables one to resolve the problems of a city, while simultaneously developing one's character. All of these ways of life presume a degree of leisured independence, unlike the life of an artisan or daily wage earner focused on poeisis, the form of intentional activity through which various objects are made according to a plan.

Aristotle assumes, in his account of *theoria*, that human beings have a natural desire to know, ultimately to comprehend reality in the fullest sense possible, and further, that when the mind is fully engaged in such activity, it achieves a type of unity with its object in ways that echo the notion of communion between seer and seen present in the vision of a *theoros*. [*See* Plato; *and* Aristotle.]

Kant and Modernity. To understand Kant's contribution to the idea of theory, it is important to recall the ways in which the philosophical context of his work differs from the work of Plato and Aristotle. Medieval Christianity's understanding of the distinction between theory and practice had moved between the alternatives of Plato and Aristotle as these were developed by Augustine and Thomas Aquinas and their followers, with the obvious difference that, for Christians, the world, however understood, was to be seen as the good product of an all-powerful, benevolent Creator as only the penultimate locus of human life. Whether theory was understood in a Neoplatonic sense as a form of inner, mystical union with the One or in a neo-Aristotelian sense as the work of the active intellect in grasping the forms of sensible things, the common theological and ecclesial background of thought about theory precluded development of the idea of theory as critical in the modern sense.

In the period of scientific discovery and creativity in western European society that immediately preceded Kant, this commonly accepted theological and ecclesial background either disappeared altogether or was relegated to a minor place in the progress of scientific discovery. With both traditional practices and beliefs of Christianity under increasing attack within and outside churches, theory was no longer commonly understood as necessarily linked to a religious tradition or as serving religious purposes. To the contrary, true theory now came to be seen by many secular intellectuals as the result of independent, empirical, scientific investigation in explicit contrast to the received understandings and practices of religious tradition. Such scientific discoveries, though requiring no justification in practice, were nevertheless believed by many modern thinkers, such as Thomas Hobbes, to offer an independent, material basis for human conduct thanks to an accurate, empirical understanding of the fundamental characteristics of reality. At the same time, progress in mathematical discovery in thinkers

as diverse as René Descartes and Gottfried Wilhelm Leibniz suggested an alternative to this empirical tradition: that theory as an understanding of the fundamental structures of reality was closer to the deductive work of mathematicians than to the inductive work of scientific experimentation. The philosophical work of Descartes, Leibniz, and Baruch Spinoza follows this model of theory.

Kant rejects the claims of both "speculative metaphysics" (his term for the mathematically based form of theory) and empiricism to have achieved reliable, truthful knowledge about the nature of reality as it might exist independent of the human mind. For Kant, theory is to be understood in three different and somewhat contradictory ways. First, Kant sharply rejects and criticizes theory as useless and illusory the claims of "speculative metaphysics," the rationalists' attempt to achieve knowledge of reality independent of the empirical work of science. There is no knowledge of an independent reality "as it is," prior to experience. Second, Kant challenges the claims of modern scientific theory to have achieved the truth about reality in his logical criticism of the limits of scientific understanding (what he calls a "metaphysics of nature"). The task of theoretical reason as presented in the *Critique of Pure Reason* is largely negative: to demonstrate that the methods of science can achieve nothing more than an interpretation of sense-data. Theoretical reason in its strictest sense denies the knowableness of "things in themselves." Third, there is a positive understanding of theory in Kant such as can be found in his definition in a 1793 essay, "On the Proverb: That May Be True in Theory, but Is of No Practical Use." There theory is "a collection of rules, even of practical rules . . . envisaged as principles of a fairly general nature . . . which, nonetheless, necessarily influence their practical application" (Kant, 1983). In this essay, as well as in the *Critique of Practical Reason* and other writings on morality, Kant understands theory as providing an account of the rational basis for moral action, a basis that includes both the general rules governing moral action (the categorical imperative) and a grasp of necessary "postulates" (God, freedom, and immortality) that allow men to believe their pursuit of virtue to be in accord with reality. Theory in this final sense is the basis of normative judgment capable of shaping and directing an autonomous moral will.

Kant also introduces the idea of judgment as a middle term between theory and practice in this essay: "For to the concept of the understanding that contains the rule must be added an act of judgment by means of which the practitioner decides whether or not something is an instance of that rule" (1983). Further development of this "middle term" occurs in the later *Critique of Judgment,* whose import is especially evident for aesthetics in Kant's discussion of the "antinomy of taste." Kant proposes a "dialectical" tension between a thesis—that "A judgement of taste is not based on concepts; for otherwise one could dispute about it (decide by means of proof)" (ibid.)—and an antithesis: "A judgement of taste is based on concepts; for otherwise . . . one could not lay claim to other people's necessary assent to one's judgment" (ibid.). He resolves the antinomy by claiming that whereas judgments of taste are indeed based on a concept, the concept is "of a general basis of nature's subjective purposiveness for our power of judgement" (ibid.). Although this concept is indeterminate, telling us nothing about the perceived object that has inspired it, it is still the basis for a universal claim about the kind of being who makes the judgment—what Kant calls the "supersensible substrate of humanity."

Kant's often-quoted remark, in his preface to the second edition of the *Critique of Pure Reason,* that he had intended to "abolish [speculative] knowledge [in order] to make room for [moral] belief" suggests both the radical character of his work and his intent to maintain a determinative role for theory. Kant's work is radical to the extent that he denies the possibility, implied in the Greek notion of *theoros,* of a form of human activity that unites the theorist with the object of his knowledge, if by "object" one means anything other than the content of one's mind. Yet, for Kant, a properly chastened theory still has a (negative) role to play in guiding the work of science, and, in its normative applications, theory as a form of practical rationality can provide a positive, principled basis for understanding the universal character of moral and aesthetic judgments in marked contrast to the empirical, psychological basis for claiming that such judgments are subjective, as found in Scottish Enlightenment figures such as David Hume, Francis Hutcheson, and Adam Smith. Where the latter must appeal to "common sentiments" or cultural convention to secure a possible basis for shared normative judgments about particulars, Kant claimed to provide a link between the particular objects of sensation and universal ideas in his notion of judgment as an aspect of (practical) reason itself. Hegel and Marx attempt to provide a stronger theoretical basis for the link between theory and practice in their different understandings of reason as a historical process and a social product. [*See* Kant.]

Hegel and Marx. Although Hegel and Marx are often seen as polar opposites on questions of theory and practice, they share a strong appreciation for the cultural, social, and political power of theory. Hegel shares Aristotle's understanding of theory as the highest form of activity and Kant's appreciation for the limits of classical speculative metaphysics. Unlike Aristotle, who saw God as independent of the world, Hegel understands Spirit *(Geist)* to be immanent and evident in the processes of natural and historical change. These processes always involve a dialectical movement between three basic terms—thought, action, and object (thing)—each of which is able to play its distinctive role only in interplay with the other two; one of these three terms must always mediate between the others. Hegel's ac-

count of the evolution of human consciousness in *The Phenomenology of Spirit* equates the historical and social processes by which persons have become able to grant recognition to each other as fully autonomous beings with the gradual growth in God's recognition of God in that which is truly "Other"—natural and human conscious processes. Unlike Kant, for whom theory had a primarily limiting function, theoretical reason was expansive and radically inclusive for Hegel. Although powered by the "negative" (i.e., by consciousness's ability to reject a partial truth about an initial object of awareness and move dialectically to a higher perspective), reason is not separate from historical process; it always reflects the determinate stage of development reached by that process. Ultimately, all of the contradictions experienced in historical life, such as those between nature and culture, self and other, God and world, or being and nonbeing, are to be understood as overcome in a form of knowing that combines permanence and process in a cohesive vision of the whole. Partial truths, such as those implicit in art or religion as contrasts or contradictions, are finally understood as aspects of an overarching unity in philosophical discourse, the truest medium of Spirit. Hegel writes:

> The essential category is that of unity, the inner connection of all these diverse forms. We must firmly grasp this, that there is only *one* Spirit, *one* principle, which leaves its impress on the political situation as well as manifesting itself in religion, art, ethics, sociability, commerce and industry, so that these different forms are only branches of one trunk.   *(History of Philosophy)*

Marx decisively rejects Hegel's idealism in the name of dialectical materialism and insists on the supremacy of praxis over theory, claiming that all social life is practical and, in his famous eleventh thesis on Ludwig Feuerbach, that "The philosophers have only *interpreted* the world in various ways; the point is, to *change* it" *(Theses on Feuerbach).* Yet, Marx was no less confident than Hegel in the power of theory. Where, for Hegel, theory in the form of philosophical wisdom fully expresses the sense of a culture or age, making further development possible, for Marx, theory, in uncovering the material forces and processes that have produced cultural institutions, objects, and relations, is a critical tool, one that can enable revolutionary change led by those most profoundly alienated by modern culture, the urban workers whom he designated a "proletariat." The first task of such a critical theory in Marx's sense is to expose the oppressive ideology embedded in cultural institutions and the role played by that ideology in producing resistance to change when internalized by members of an oppressed class. Genuine change in the direction of an egalitarian community can only come about through a combination of theoretical understanding and action. The former prevents action's ineffectiveness or dissipation, while the latter, altering the material conditions under which men live, provides the necessary basis for a humane social order. Criticizing Hegel for collapsing theory and practice into one, Marx claimed that only a revolutionary yet genuinely self-critical practice could mediate between thought and things, that only such a practice was already thoughtful enough to be "objective" in a nonpositivistic sense. Objectivity, for Marx, means constant awareness of real, human individuals as the basic units of thought rather than of statistical patterns. Marx writes: "The chief defect of all hitherto existing materialism . . . is that the thing, reality, sensuousness is conceived only in the form of *object* or *contemplation*, but not as *human sensuous activity, practice*" (ibid.). Where Hegel defined the activity of a theorist as an attempt to render a phenomenon comprehensible, Marx saw theoretical activity as the attempt to master the phenomenon. Reason is an instrument or weapon of living, sensuous men who suffer, and true thinking is a form of practice, not contemplation at a distance. These extraordinary, albeit different, claims for the power of theory in Hegel and Marx failed to be realized in the twentieth century. Hegel's vision of theory achieving a comprehensive grasp of the "objective spirit" of an age manifest in a unified, common culture has been rendered problematic, in part by the development of a global, multicultural society, fragmented into distinctive cultural identities based on nation, language, race, religion, and ethnicity. In spite of this apparent fragmentation of culture into cultures, some cultural theorists continue to argue for a more expansive role for theory, as James Clifford does in his essay "On Collecting Art and Culture" (1988). For Clifford, it is possible for a theorist to gasp universal, dynamic processes at work in contemporary culture, such as the movement of cultural artifacts between points on a semiotic grid. These "points" are represented by terms such as "fine art objects," "representative artifacts of material culture," "examples of technology," and "curios or commodities," and it is claimed that artifacts are routinely displaced from point to point on the grid by a system of cultural institutions and meanings that classifies them and assigns them relative value. Although a Marxist or neo-Marxist version of critical theory is capable of seeing through the machinery such as Clifford's "art-culture system," belief in the power of critical practice to bring about any final, progressive, revolutionary change has also been rendered suspect by the betrayal of Marx's humanism in Soviet and Chinese state Communism, and by the collapse of self-identified "Marxist" or socialist regimes throughout eastern Europe. Yet, in spite of these theoretical and empirical difficulties, combinations of Hegel's and Marx's understanding of theory continue to provide a necessary starting point for the ideas of theory found in the work of such diverse contemporary French thinkers as Jean Baudrillard, Maurice Blanchot, Gilles Deleuze, Jacques Derrida, Michel Foucault, Jacques Lacan, Emmanuel Lévinas, and Jean-François Lyotard, taken in combination with the work of Friedrich Nietzsche,

Edmund Husserl, Martin Heidegger, and other existential phenomenologists, such as Jean-Paul Sartre, Maurice Merleau-Ponty, and Paul Ricoeur. Another, parallel discussion of theory in the Frankfurt School among authors such as Theodor W. Adorno, Walter Benjamin, Max Horkheimer, Herbert Marcuse, and Jürgen Habermas also presupposes the work of Hegel and Marx. The discussion of such work, however, belongs more properly to survey essays on postmodernism and on individual French and German authors than to this general survey of ideas about theory. [*See* Hegel; *and* Marx.]

Theory and Contemporary Aesthetics. This brief summary of perspectives on theory ends with the nineteenth century, well before the phenomena of modernism and postmodernism. Although it would be possible to expand discussion of work on theory into the twentieth century in a similar survey fashion, covering some or all the individual Continental authors just mentioned, apart from limitations of space, the greater problem is that much of what has been traditionally understood as "theory" has been displaced today into cultural locations other than philosophy. Part of this displacement is the result of the influence of a growing number of interdisciplinary or cross-disciplinary texts such as those of Foucault. It is increasingly difficult, in the work of contemporary academic authors on aesthetics influenced by such texts, to draw sharp lines separating the humanities and the social sciences or dividing discrete disciplines such as philosophy, literary criticism, religious studies, anthropology, or psychology. Combinations of elements of all of these and other disciplinary conversations, not always clearly designated or noted as such by authors, often shape texts "occasioned" by an artwork or a traditional aesthetic problem. When reading a contemporary work of theory dealing with a familiar topics in aesthetics such as Pierre Bourdieu's *Distinction: A Social Critique of the Judgement of Taste,* it may be possible to discern an educational background focused on the literatures of specific fields (cultural anthropology and modern works on aesthetics in Bourdieu's case), but the primary evidence for such a background is often to be found less in the substance or style of the argument than in the texts referenced in footnotes or the bibliography.

The displacement of theory also involves the blurring of lines between text and context, work and commentary, or artist and audience, typically associated with postmodernism. Where modernism in art and art writing often rejected self-conscious efforts to be "theoretical," it is a commonplace of contemporary writing about art and the aesthetic that the work of many postmodern artists embodies explicit theoretical beliefs or positions, and that such work is directed at an audience presumed to be theoretically informed, if not always theoretically sophisticated. Sherrie Levine's, Barbara Kruger's, and Cindy Sherman's photographs all involve a theoretical stance on the defining characteristics of photography, on "originals" versus "copies," and on the role of the artist in the artwork, without which the visual experience of their work remains opaque. It is often the case in such works, and in writing about them by art critics and aestheticians, that a form of "praxis" response by an intended audience (i.e., action of some kind in a political, social, or communal sense rather than appreciation or contemplation of a work) is part of the primary aim of individual or collective artists. Whether "theory" is understood by such artists or in such works as a form of ideology, or as a constantly expanding metadiscourse about paradigms or epistemes of ideologies and their instantiations, or as itself a form of practice, it is increasingly difficult to draw precise lines distinguishing artworks from theory. Given the proliferation of a wide diversity of theories of art claiming an explicit basis in practice and/or in sui generis forms of experience of varied groups identified by sex, gender, ethnicity, or race, it is also difficult to find a common point of reference by which diverse theories could be compared, if not critically evaluated. The evaluation of a theoretical discourse in such instances is often found in its ability to provoke action or to consolidate the unique experience of members of a group sharing a common identity.

Finally, in the case of some contemporary site-specific works such as Robert Smithson's environmental works, John Ahern's South Bronx bronzes, or projects of new genre public artists such as Suzanne Lacy or the Chicago "Culture in Action" group, it is often difficult to determine at what point artists and/or a critical/appreciative audience is/are experiencing, analyzing, or acting. Many of these works, like much of the theoretical writing about them, have deliberately indeterminate, anticlosural qualities that invite supplementation, and resist framing by any one, unitary discourse. In such a cultural context, it is impossible to offer any definitive concluding generalization about theory in relation to aesthetics other than to remark that parallel work by philosophers in ethics and political theory faces a similar set of cultural challenges.

It is possible, however, to note how postmodern cultural contexts problematize the central ideas implied in the Greek etymology of theory. To the extent that one accepts an image-laden cultural background characterized by constant vacillation between signified and signifier as the defining attribute to postmodern culture, it is possible to imagine that the work of a *theoria* or the words of a *theoros* can no longer be confined to designated individuals recognized for their special abilities. The postmodern world is not one in which difference has been simply absorbed into identity. It is, rather, a world in which determinate identities, of either cultural objects or cultural fields—once said to be established by theory—can no longer be produced because the cultural conditions for such production are absent. It is not yet evident what forms of thought or genres of expression

will come to be regarded as theory in the twenty-first century.

[*See also* Theories of Art.]

BIBLIOGRAPHY

Ball, Terence. "Plato and Aristotle: The Unity versus the Autonomy of Theory and Practice." In *Political Theory and Praxis: New Perspectives*, pp. 57–69. Minneapolis, 1977a.

Ball, Terence, ed. *Political Theory and Praxis: New Perspectives*. Minneapolis, 1977b.

Bernstein, Richard J. *Praxis and Action: Contemporary Philosophies of Human Activity*. Philadelphia, 1971.

Blumenberg, Hans. *The Legitimacy of the Modern Age*. Translated by Robert M. Wallace. Cambridge, Mass., 1983.

Böhme, Hartmut. "Sinne und Blick: Variationen zur mythopoetischen Geschichte des Subjekts." In *Konkursbuch*, 13 (1984).

Bourdieu, Pierre. *Outline of a Theory of Practice*. Translated by Richard Nice. Cambridge and New York, 1977.

Clifford, James. *The Predicament of Culture: Twentieth-Century Ethnography, Literature, and Art*. Cambridge, Mass., 1988.

Cornford, F. M. *From Religion to Philosophy: A Study in the Origins of Western Speculation*. New York, 1957; reprint, Princeton, N.J., 1991.

de Man, Paul. *The Resistance to Theory*. Minneapolis, 1986.

Foster, Hal, ed. *The Anti-Aesthetic: Essays on Postmodern Culture*. Port Townsend, Wash., 1983.

Gadamer, Hans-Georg. *Truth and Method*. 2d rev. ed. Translation revised by Joel Weinsheimer and Donald G. Marshall. New York, 1989.

Godzich, Wlad. "Foreword: The Tiger on the Paper Mat." In Paul de Man, *The Resistance to Theory*, pp. ix–xviii. Minneapolis, 1986.

Harrison, Charles and Paul Wood. *Art in Theory, 1900–1990: An Anthology of Changing Ideas*. Oxford and Cambridge, Mass., 1992.

Jay, Martin. *Downcast Eyes: The Denigration of Vision in Twentieth-Century French Thought*. Berkeley, 1993.

Lobkowicz, Nicholas. "On the History of Theory and Practice." In *Political Theory and Praxis: New Perspectives*, edited by Terence Ball, pp. 13–27. Minneapolis, 1977.

Kant, Immanuel. "On the Proverb: That May Be True in Theory, but Is of No Practical Use." In *Perpetual Peace and Other Essays*, translated by Ted Humphrey. Indianapolis, 1983.

Salkever, Stephen G. *Finding the Mean: Theory and Practice in Aristotelian Political Philosophy*. Princeton, N.J., 1990.

Stepelevich, Lawrence S., and David Lamb, eds. *Hegel's Philosophy of Action*. Atlantic Highlands, N.J., 1983.

Taylor, Charles. *Hegel*. Cambridge and New York, 1975.

Tessitore, Aristide. *Reading Aristotle's Ethics: Virtue, Rhetoric, and Political Philosophy*. Albany, N.Y., 1996.

Wallis, Brian, ed. *Art after Modernism: Rethinking Representation*. New York, 1984.

DAVID H. FISHER

TOLSTOY, LEO NIKOLAEVICH (1828–1910), Russian novelist and theorist. Tolstoy was born on his family's estate, Yasnaya Polyana, in central Russia. He attended the University of Kazan for three years, from 1844 to 1847, but did not take a degree. He lived the dissolute life of many young Russian aristocrats during this period. He saw military service in the Caucasus, and in the Crimean War, during the 1850s. During this period, he also found his vocation as a fiction writer. Most of the rest of Tolstoy's life was spent at Yasnaya Polyana.

Tolstoy's writing life divides quite sharply between two periods, which are separated by a time of spiritual and psychic crisis. In the earlier period, he wrote his greatest works of fiction. In the later, although he continued to write fiction, he concentrated on the ethical, political, and aesthetic implications of the religious views he had developed during that crisis (which he describes in *A Confession*).

Tolstoy has special relevance for aesthetics in three ways. First, he was, by common critical assessment, one of the supreme fiction writers who has ever lived. Moreover, he was a writer who attempted self-consciously to engage philosophical issues in his fiction. In *War and Peace*, he not only wrote a great historical novel about the conflict between Napoleonic France and Russia filled with memorable characters (and much of his own family's history), but he also reflected on the nature of human history. Second, Tolstoy was concerned with the nature of fiction and participated in some of the lively critical debates in nineteenth-century Russia about the possibilities of fiction. Third, late in his life, he wrote a book titled *What Is Art?* in which he presented a critique of previous theories of art, and in which he proposed his own definition and analysis of art. This work, though not the product of a trained philosopher, has been one of the most provocative in the history of aesthetic theory. Interestingly, Tolstoy denounces his own earlier writings (including *War and Peace* and *Anna Karenina*) in this book from the perspective of his late religious views. After a brief overview of Tolstoy's view of fiction and *What Is Art?* this essay will discuss Tolstoy's own definition of art and some of the more common objections to it.

Tolstoy's View of Fiction. Although Tolstoy was not a philosopher, he began his career as a writer of fiction at a time when philosophical issues permeated the atmosphere of Russia. He both attempted to deal with philosophical—even metaphysical—issues in his fiction and engaged in the lively critical debates about the nature of fiction that were so prominent among writers in the 1850s and 1860s. A terminology derived from Georg Wilhelm Friedrich Hegel helped frame these debates. Much of the tradition of critical discussion about Tolstoy stresses what is seen as his divided nature. For Isaiah Berlin, for example, in *The Hedgehog and the Fox*, Tolstoy was best understood as a fox (someone who knows many different things) who wanted to be a hedgehog (someone who knows one big thing—who has achieved a systematic understanding of reality). It was, however, a commonplace of the time to think of analysis as the detailed understanding of individual elements and events, and synthesis as the capacity to integrate these particulars in a single unifying vision. Moreover, the relationship of these two capacities was thought of as dialectical—a Hegelian term often used of Tolstoy by his contemporaries. To a writer such as Henry James, the novels of Tolstoy with their natu-

ralistic and metaphysical ambitions must appear to be "large loose baggy monsters," but, for Tolstoy, the naturalistic representation of life would be incomplete without a reflective attempt to understand the meaning of life.

Tolstoy was obsessed by basic philosophical issues throughout his life—such issues as the true nature of a human being, the relationship of the individual to history, the nature of goodness, the possibility of human happiness—and he sought to embody, and to investigate, these issues, first in his fiction, later in his essays and in his life. Perhaps the most important philosophical influence on him was Jean-Jacques Rousseau; even late in life he identified Rousseau and the Gospels as the principal influences on his thought and art. Tolstoy's understanding of Rousseau's view of human nature underlies much of his fiction in the earlier period of his writing career. By the time he came to write *What Is Art?* Tolstoy had repudiated what most people judge to be his greatest artistic achievements. This was not because his fundamental concerns had changed, however, but because he had reached new religious conclusions about those concerns. Well before his religious conversion, he regarded his fiction as philosophical and didactic. He never held the view of "art for art's sake," and although he was committed to a broadly naturalistic view of fiction, he always felt that it was his task to go beyond the representation of possible realities in order to attempt to achieve an integrated understanding of those fictional realities.

What Is Art? The context of the title's question already shows the direction of Tolstoy's thought. He asks this question by considering the money that is spent on art, the effort and expense of training performing artists such as opera singers and ballet dancers, and the effort involved in a rehearsal of an opera. (In the famous passage describing the opera rehearsal, he achieves an alienated distance from what he describes by pretending that he has no acquaintance with the cultural practice of opera.) The question of the justification for all this activity requires an answer to the more basic question of what art is: what does it do for human beings?

Tolstoy gives a brief history of aesthetic theorizing (derived mainly from Max Schasler's history of aesthetics) in order to show that this history consists of a chaos of conflicting opinions. He writes that "Art in all its forms is bounded on one side by the practically useful, and on the other by unsuccessful attempts at art. How is art to be marked off from each of these?" (1959). This is the task of definition, and he goes on to give his own definition of art, which he then uses to judge what has been offered as art in his own time. Of that, he writes that he has come to the "conviction that almost all that our society considers to be art, good art, and the whole of art, far from being real and good art, and the whole of art, is not even art at all but only a counterfeit of it" (ibid.). It is his sense of the endemic threat of fraudulence in art that motivates much of what

Tolstoy writes. He gives special attention to the refutation of aesthetic theories that depend on notions of beauty or pleasure, though he also attempts to explain the historical origin of such theories. Tolstoy also devotes considerable attention to the evaluation of art.

Tolstoy's Theory of Art. At the outset, a number of different questions asked about art by Tolstoy should be distinguished:

1. What is art as opposed to nonart?
2. How is art, as art, to be evaluated? (Tolstoy makes a not always successful effort to separate this from the first question.)
3. How is the content of art to be evaluated? (It is here that Tolstoy introduces his own religious views.)
4. Which works are examples of good art, bad art, and nonart? (Tolstoy's critical judgments, presented as answers to this question, have occasioned outrage among most readers of his book.)

Tolstoy claims that the first question can only be answered by considering the purpose that art may serve "in the life of man and humanity. . . . [Art is] one of the conditions of human life. Viewing it in this way we cannot fail to observe that art is one of the means of intercourse between man and man" (1959). Tolstoy then draws a fairly crude distinction between thought and feeling, and suggests that whereas speech is the medium for the communication of thought, the essence of the intercourse of art is the transmission of feeling. Of course, not all transmission of feeling from one human being to another is art, though art is based on the human capacity to share the feelings of fellow humans. Here is Tolstoy's definition of art from *What Is Art?*:

> To evoke in oneself a feeling one has once experienced and having evoked it in oneself then by means of movements, lines, colours, sounds, or forms expressed in words, so to transmit that feeling that others experience the same feeling—this is the activity of art.
>
> Art is a human activity consisting in this, that one man consciously by means of certain external signs, hands on to others feelings he has lived through, and that others are infected by these feelings and also experience them.   (Ibid.)

Several aspects of this definition require comment. First, Tolstoy emphasizes both the expression of feeling by the artist and the reception of feeling by the audience. Because his theory is often broadly categorized as an "expression" theory, it is worth noting that, for Tolstoy, expression, to be achieved, requires reception by an *other*. Moreover, he requires that the audience experience the *same* feeling as that experienced by the artist, rather than that they understand what the feeling was that the artist experienced. (Unfortunately, Tolstoy has no philosophical account of feeling or emotion to offer here, so the implications of this definition are difficult to assess.) It is immediately obvious from this

definition that sincerity of the artist is required for something to be art (a requirement that Tolstoy shortly makes explicit.)

Second, one should note that his definition does include a reference to the media of the various arts ("movements, lines, colours, sounds, or forms expressed in words") and that he requires a conscious manipulation of the medium by the artist. Tolstoy has been criticized for his lack of attention to the formal elements of the arts, and it is true that he pays very little specific attention to these elements throughout *What Is Art?* Nonetheless, there is a place for them in his theory. The artist must have a command of these elements adequate to fashion an object capable of evoking in an audience the feeling experienced by the artist. Art is not produced by the simple spontaneous expression of emotion.

Third, however, it should be noted that this definition covers more than had come to be classified as part of the "fine arts" by the time Tolstoy wrote. His own example of artistic activity is of a boy telling of his frightening encounter with a wolf, producing in his audience the feelings he has experienced. This feature of Tolstoy's theory was welcome to its author who, as we shall see, was opposed to almost everything considered to be a part of the "fine arts" not only of his own time but throughout history.

The second question—"How is art, as art, to be evaluated?"—is the point at which Tolstoy's view of the relationship between art and morality/religion should be discussed. Tolstoy has commonly been interpreted as holding a moral view of art, which he specifically opposes to the "art-for-art's-sake" aestheticism of the nineteenth century. This interpretation may ultimately be compelling, but his presentation of his view is complex. He holds that it is a necessary condition of a work of art that it produce an "infection" of its audience of its author's "condition of soul" or feeling. When he gives a criterion for what he calls the "quality of art (which depends on its form) considered apart from its subject-matter," he writes that "not only is infection a sure sign of art, but the degree of infectiousness is also the sole measure of excellence in art. . . . *The stronger the infection the better is the art*, as art" (ibid.). Here we seem to have a criterion of evaluation that is decidedly nonmoral. That Tolstoy intends this seems to be confirmed by his statement, "If a work is a good work of art, then the feeling expressed by the artist—be it moral or immoral—transmits itself to other people" (ibid.). This seems to imply that there can be a good work of art whose content is immoral, which would be precluded by any simple equation of the artistically good with the morally good. Of course, this would still leave open the possibility that works of art can be subject to moral judgment—it would just refuse the claim that nothing can be a good work of art unless it is morally good.

Matters become complicated, however, with Tolstoy's answer to the third question: "How is the content of art to be evaluated?" Tolstoy carefully distinguishes the quality of art considered apart from its subject matter from the quality of the feelings that form the subject matter of works of art, and deals with these issues in separate chapters. For judgments about the former, the degree of infectiousness is the criterion, and that degree is determined by the individuality of the feeling, the clarity of its transmission, and the sincerity of the artist (and Tolstoy claims that sincerity entails individuality and clarity). For judgments about the latter, one must employ moral/religious truth. Tolstoy claims that the value of the feelings transmitted by works of art must be judged in terms of the highest religious perception of the age, and that the religious perception of *his* age is

> the consciousness that our well-being, both material and spiritual, individual and collective, temporal and eternal, lies in the growth of brotherhood among men—in their loving harmony with one another. . . . And it is on the basis of this perception that we should appraise all the phenomena of our life and among the rest our art also. (Ibid.)

It might seem that we now have two standards of evaluation that might not be in agreement: one standard evaluates the quality of the work of art in terms of infectiousness; the other evaluates the quality of the content of the work in terms of religious truth. This picture is complicated by the fact that Tolstoy has a normative view of sincerity, however. He holds that the religious perception articulated above is true; therefore, feelings not in accord with it are what he calls "perverted." Because an artist who expresses such feelings is necessarily alienated from the truth of his or her nature, such expression can never be deeply "sincere." Hence, despite that fact that he attempts to separate the evaluation of art as art, and the evaluation of its content, Tolstoy may have a moral criterion for true art after all.

Finally, the fourth question: which works are examples of good art, bad art, and nonart? The most famous feature of *What Is Art?* is Tolstoy's almost complete rejection of the traditional "canon" of fine arts. Here is a list of some of the artists whose work Tolstoy condemns as pseudoart or bad art: Aeschylus, Sophocles, Euripides, Aristophanes, Dante Alighieri, Torquato Tasso, William Shakespeare, John Milton, Johann Wolfgang von Goethe, Charles Baudelaire, Stéphane Mallarmé, Maurice-Polydone-Marie-Bernard Maeterlinck, Henrik Ibsen, Gerhart Hauptmann, Michelangelo, Raphael, Édouard Manet, Claude Monet, Auguste Renoir, Camille Pissarro, Alfred Sisley, most of Johann Sebastian Bach, late Ludwig van Beethoven (especially the Ninth Symphony), Franz Liszt, Hector Berlioz, Richard Wagner, Johannes Brahms, Émile Zola, Rudyard Kipling, and almost all of the literary works of Tolstoy (including *War and Peace* and *Anna Karenina*). Tolstoy does give some examples of works that satisfy his criteria of arthood and value; these include primarily folk art and religious literature of great antiquity, but also a few modern literary works. Among the latter are *Les Misérables,* some works of Charles Dickens, the works of Fyodor Dostoyevsky, George Eliot's *Adam Bede,* and some stories by Aleksandr Sergeevich Pushkin, Nikolai Gogol, and Guy de Maupassant. One might note that Tolstoy's particular critical judgments result from his application of his theory, and that one might agree with the theory and still dispute those particular judgments. Some have attributed Tolstoy's late repudiation of the tradition of high art that he had loved to his deeply divided personal nature. He was also a deeply sensual man, who railed against human sensuality. Ultimately, for Tolstoy, his aesthetic theory was one more weapon to be used against the social institutions of his culture. Nonetheless, his insistence that art is one of the conditions of human life, and must be understood in relationship to human nature and human communication, has provided inspiration to later theorists.

[*See also* Expression Theory of Art; Literature, *article on* Literary Aesthetics; *and* Russian Aesthetics.]

BIBLIOGRAPHY

Work by Leo Tolstoy

What is Art? and Essays on Art. Translated by Aylmer Maude. Reprint, New York and Oxford, 1959.

Other Sources

Bayley, John. *Tolstoy and the Novel.* New York, 1967; reprint, Chicago 1988.
Matlaw, Ralph, ed. *Tolstoy: A Collection of Critical Essays.* Englewood Cliffs, N.J., 1967.
Orwin, Donna Tussing. *Tolstoy's Art and Thought, 1847–1880.* Princeton, N.J., 1993.
Silbajoris, Rimvydas. *Tolstoy's Aesthetics and His Art.* Columbus, Ohio, 1990.
Steiner, George. *Tolstoy or Dostoevsky.* New York, 1959; 2d ed., New Haven, 1996.
Wasiolek, Edward. *Tolstoy's Major Fiction.* Chicago, 1978.
Wilson, A. N. *Tolstoy.* New York, 1988.

STANLEY BATES

TRAGEDY. [*To examine several of the key stages in the history and genre of tragedy within the history of aesthetics, this entry comprises three essays:*

Greek Tragedy

Hume on Tragedy

Freud on Tragedy

The first essay explains the origins of tragedy in Greek drama and philosophy. The second essay explains David Hume's contribution to the aesthetics of tragedy. The last essay examines Sigmund Freud's ideas on tragedy and their place in his psychoanalytic aesthetics. For his central analysis of tragedy, see Nietzsche. *See also* Music; *and* Theater.]

Greek Tragedy

Greek tragedy developed in the late sixth century BCE, in a society whose dominant form of communal organization was the "citizen state" (polis). As the modern traveler knows, impressive remains of ancient theaters can still be visited at sites in many areas where Hellenic civilization flourished; even in the fifth century BCE, a hundred years before the huge expansion of Greek culture in the wake of the conquests of Alexander the Great, tragedies were put on in a range of locations, from Sicily to Macedonia. Yet, the source of the tragic phenomenon lies within just one polis: democratic Athens. An understanding of the Athenian context of tragedy is a prerequisite for the interpretation of the genre.

Context. Tragedies were performed at the City Dionysia, a spring festival in honor of the god Dionysus. Three playwrights each put on four plays. First came three tragedies, in which stories from the mythical past were retold through the actions, speech, and song of masked actors and chorus. Each set of three tragedies was followed by a "satyr play," a mythological burlesque that raucously disrupted the tone of what went before. A panel of citizens, chosen by lot, awarded the prize to whichever dramatist they adjudged the best.

Several points about the Dionysia need to be emphasized. First, it involved citizen participation on a large scale. In addition to tragedies, there were also competitions for comic drama and choral singing, so around fifteen hundred people must have been actively involved in mounting each festival, quite apart from the audience of perhaps fifteen thousand. Second, the festival represented the polis on display, not just before its own members but, in symbolic terms, before the rest of Greece: tribute from states belonging to the city's empire was ostentatiously brought into the theater, and distinguished visitors from outside Athens had privileged seats. Third, the competitive element enabled the community to keep artistic innovation within the bounds of what was felt appropriate to tradition. It is clear, then, that Athenian tragedy was the very opposite of a coterie art form appealing exclusively to the taste of an elite. Although it is unlikely that many slaves ever attended performances, and although the presence of women in the audience is a matter of heated debate—some scholars rule it out altogether—it nevertheless remains undeniable that tragedy was aimed at a mass public to which it was directly accountable, for the point of selecting judges at random was surely to ensure a representative verdict.

Were performances "religious"? Were they "rituals"? Like the festival, the theater belonged to Dionysus: his priest sat in the middle of the front row. But the relationship between the god and the tragedies staged within his precinct is intricate and indirect. Although most plots explore the relations between humans and gods, few concern Dionysus himself. Because Dionysus was a god of reversals and "ecstasy" ("standing outside oneself"), however, tragedy may be thought of as "Dionysiac," at least insofar as it constituted an arena for temporary, licensed role reversal, in which masked, male citizens stood outside their own identities to portray slaves, women, heroes, and gods.

As for "ritual," the situation is equally complex. With rare exceptions, each play put on was new—not an exact repetition of a sacred drama, but a fresh reinterpretation of the past in the light of present concerns. Like other aspects of Athenian life, rituals (marriage songs, hymns, funeral dirges) were reworked for theatrical purposes. In spite of repeated attempts by modern scholars to find the key to tragedy's structure in a ritual pattern, however, the genre's fluidity resists the imposition of such a restrictive framework.

Tragic Myths. Tragedies explore experience by means of exaggeration. The dramatized myths portray some of the most extreme types of transgression imaginable: incest between son and mother (*Oedipus the King*), matricide (Aeschylus's *Oresteia,* and the *Electra* plays of Sophocles and Euripides), infanticide (Euripides' *Medea* and *Heracles Mad*), fratricide (Aeschylus's *Seven against Thebes*), cannibalism (the story of Thyestes' unwitting consumption of his own children, again recounted in the *Oresteia*). Yet, such stories simply take to their ultimate, catastrophic conclusion tensions potentially felt by any person living within a family. Similarly, the dilemma experienced by Sophocles' Antigone—whether to leave one's traitor-brother unburied or to defy the city's ruler—shows in extreme form some of the conflicts generated in ordinary life by that other framework for social life, the polis. Borrowing a phrase from engineering, one might describe tragedy as "testing to destruction" the norms of the society within which it grew. The Athenian polis was in precisely the kind of historical situation to foster such a self-examination: a democracy coming to terms with the aristocratic world out of which it had developed.

Action and Character. Aristotle famously observed that tragedy was "an imitation, not of human beings, but of action and life." The profound truth highlighted by this observation, sometimes obscured by critics interested in peeping behind the mask of tragic characters to examine the supposed person beneath, is nowadays widely recognized. Greek tragedy depicts *the unfolding of an action*. Thus, *Antigone* represents the consequences of Creon's edict forbidding the burial of a traitor, who happens to be the brother of Antigone. The work begins by focusing on the "heroine," yet ends by virtually ignoring her and concentrating on the shattered ruler, who enters bearing his son's dead body in his arms. Similarly, in another Sophoclean play, *Women of Trachis,* which explores the doomed attempt of Deianira to recover the love of her husband Heracles, the two central figures never meet onstage: as the action develops, it is first the wife who takes center stage, and only later the monster-slayer. The corollary of this emphasis on the unfolding of an action as opposed to the in-depth exploration of character is that the minutiae of an individualized, idiosyncratic personality play no part in this genre. To come to Greek tragedy with expectations derived from George

Eliot or Henry James is to forget the crucial importance of the mask.

Space. From their seats in the half-bowl-shaped auditorium beneath the Acropolis, the Athenian audience looked down on a multifaceted space. Immediately below lay the *orchestra,* the circular "dancing place" where the chorus (twelve, later fifteen in number) danced and sang to provide a context for and link between the "episodes" involving actors. Beyond the orchestra was the *skene,* a low, flat-roofed stage building with at least one door, allowing entrances and exits. Beyond, again, was the territory of the city outside the theater. No hermetically sealed theatrical world, this: the other public spaces of the polis, notably its arena for political debate, were a short walk away.

Greek theater did not aim at illusionistic realism. Instead, "reality" was created through language. In the manner celebrated by the chorus at the start of William Shakespeare's *Henry V,* the audience's imagination was called on to breathe life into the prospect before them. The imaginary space of tragedy was, indeed, varied and elaborate. The scene of the *Oresteia* shifts from Argos to Delphi to Athens, with the city of Troy looming repeatedly as a significant offstage presence; Euripides' *Helen* is set in Egypt, *Prometheus Bound* (ascribed to Aeschylus) in the Caucasus; numerous other stage sets occur, within and outside Greece. Recently, scholars have drawn attention to the way in which "other" places are used to explore contrasts and comparisons with the home city of Athens. Ideologically speaking, tragedy was both "here" and "not here," as well as being both "now" (thanks to its exploration of contemporary moral and political issues) and "not now" (being set in the mythical past). This combination of proximity ("here"/"now") and distance ("not here"/"not now") offers an intriguing analogy with the famous Aristotelian identification of pity and fear as the combination of emotions aroused by tragedy, because, for Aristotle at least, pity was aroused by contemplating the suffering of others, fear by the sense that "it might happen to *me.*"

Speech and Song. Tragedy incorporates many types of poetic meter and linguistic register. Choruses sang, to the accompaniment of a double-pipe player, in a variety of "lyric" rhythms, and in language whose tinge of Doric dialect set it, for an Athenian audience, apart from the everyday. Closer to the conversational was the iambic verse in which most dialogue between the actors was spoken. But actor speeches had their own stylizations, such as the extended passages of alternate-line dialogue known as "stichomythia," and the narratives of news bringers ("messengers"), who typically use a form of the past tense that approximates it linguistically to the narratives of Homeric epic.

Due attention to tragic language enables us to dispel the trivial observation that "nothing happens in Greek tragedy." For example, the violence that many theatrical traditions exhibit on stage was, in Greece, enacted in words. Oedipus's self-blinding, Hippolytus's gruesome downfall, and Pentheus's rending by his mother lose nothing by owing their theatrical realization to an audience's imagination rather than its eyesight. Again, a recurring aspect of tragic "action" is persuasion. The psychic invasion of Pentheus by Dionysus in Euripides' *Bacchae* is as clear a case as there could be of "something happening"; the same goes for Clytemnestra's mastering of Agamemnon's will in the *Oresteia,* as a result of which he leaves the stage, trampling over fabric the color of darkened blood, on his way to meet death within the house.

Stagecraft. Greek tragedy may be, supremely, a drama of the spoken word, but it also derives much of its power from apparently simple gestures and stage movements. Toward the end of *Heracles Mad,* the returning hero lies onstage a shattered wreck, surrounded by the corpses of his family, whom he had just slaughtered in a fit of madness sent by the goddess Hera. Heracles has shrouded his head, through fear of bringing religious pollution upon those around him; but his friend Theseus uncovers him, so restoring him to the world of human intercourse. A comparably momentous act occurs in Sophocles' *Philoctetes,* when the exiled, naively trusting hero places his one, priceless possession—his magic bow—into the hands of Neoptolemus, the young man who, as the audience knows, is part of a conspiracy to steal the bow. Many significant exits and entrances in tragedy tell the same story, as a powerful emotional charge is concentrated into a simple movement—nowhere more impressively than in the case of the deathward exit of Agamemnon just mentioned.

The Uses of Convention. The commonest difficulty faced by anyone attempting to introduce Greek tragedy to a contemporary public is that the plays' conventions may be felt to constitute a barrier to appreciation. Two such conventions are the chorus and the *ekkuklema.* Brief consideration of these should demonstrate that the barrier need not exist.

The chorus's contribution to dramatic meaning is often underestimated by modern audiences/readers because the frequent cross-references to other stories from the corpus of mythology can seem obscure or tedious. Yet, in fact, choruses have a pivotal role within the overall dramatic structure. Typically, they occupy a position of "ritual centrality." They may sometimes be wrong; their lack of perception may set them at an ironical disadvantage compared with characters or audience; but their proverbial, communal voice remains a vital counterpoint to the transgressions and exaggerations implicit in the conduct of those who decide and act. "Why should I dance?" sings the chorus of old men in *Oedipus the King,* faced with the prospect that the direction in which the action is vertiginously heading may threaten everything—including ritual dancing—which they have hitherto regarded as securely rooted in experience and tradition.

The *ekkuklema* was, it seems, a platform that could be rolled out from the *skene,* bearing a tableau of characters from within. Like any sharply defined theatrical convention, it lent itself to parody—as Aristophanes gleefully showed. But, within its tragic context, it had a perfectly valid function. Thanks to this piece of machinery, a moment of past action could be frozen onstage, for the contemplation of the audience. In the first two plays of the *Oresteia,* the corpses of Agamemnon and Cassandra, and later those of Clytemnestra and Aegisthus, are brought from the house, their postures fixed as at the moment of death, to be gazed at and meditated upon by dramatic characters and audience alike. One central theme of the trilogy is the dragging of the dark past into the glare of the present; another is the revealing of the generations of horrors concealed within the household. The *ekkuklema* is not a *restrictive* convention, but one that allows a particular kind of dramatic statement to be made.

Evaluation. How, finally, do ancient and modern evaluations of Greek tragedy differ? Many modern critics relish the presence in the genre of paradox, ambiguity, and irony, and stress what they see as the questioning and even subversiveness to be found there. There is, however, no evidence that the *admiration* for tragic paradox/ambiguity/ subversion was so widely shared in antiquity. (Intriguingly, the tetralogy of which *Oedipus the King* formed part came no higher than second in the dramatic competition; this *might* imply that the qualities that modern critics find in that play were not so highly valued by the ancient jury.) Where the issue of evaluation is addressed, the angle of approach usually concerns either a play's effectiveness in "teaching" its audience, or its success in arousing emotion. Neither of these is unproblematic. The sense in which tragedy could be said to "teach" is far from certain—"by providing moral paradigms" is one answer implicit in our sources, but this obviously leaves out much of the genre's complexity. Again, privileging emotional arousal (as some modern critics would wish to do, following Aristotle and the Sophist Gorgias) risks belittling the undeniable presence of intellectual, speculative elements in these works.

Surely, the most sensible strategy is to accept that Greek tragedy can accommodate all of these approaches: the plays are unsettling *and* paradigmatic *and* moving. Such multivalence is one of the reasons why this remarkable art form—both popular and profound—has continued to fascinate for two and a half millennia.

[*See also* Aristotle, *survey article*; *and* Katharsis.]

BIBLIOGRAPHY

Goldhill, Simon. *Reading Greek Tragedy.* Cambridge and New York, 1986.
Heath, Malcolm. *The Poetics of Greek Tragedy.* London, 1987.
Jones, John. *On Aristotle and Greek Tragedy.* London, 1962; reprint, Stanford, Calif., 1980.
Pickard-Cambridge, Arthur. *The Dramatic Festivals of Athens.* 2d ed. Revised by John Gould and D. M. Lewis. Oxford, 1968.
Silk, Michael S., ed. *Tragedy and the Tragic: Greek Theatre and Beyond.* Oxford, 1996.
Taplin, Oliver. *Greek Tragedy in Action.* London, 1978.
Vernant, Jean-Pierre, and Pierre Vidal-Naquet. *Tragedy and Myth in Ancient Greece.* Translated by Janet Lloyd. Atlantic Highlands, N.J., 1981. Reprinted as *Myth and Tragedy in Ancient Greece* (New York, 1988).
Winkler, John J., and Froma I. Zeitlin, eds. *Nothing to Do with Dionysos? Athenian Drama in Its Social Context.* Princeton, N.J., 1990.

RICHARD BUXTON

Hume on Tragedy

Although "Of the Standard of Taste" is undoubtedly David Hume's most significant contribution to philosophical aesthetics, his essay "Of Tragedy" is of considerable interest, both as a contribution to the philosophical discussion of the "paradox of tragedy" and as an application of the theory of the passions worked out in book 2 of his *A Treatise of Human Nature.* The topic of the essay has been the subject of debate by philosophers and literary theorists at least since Aristotle's statement that "The tragic pleasure is that of pity and fear" (*Poetics,* chap. 14): how is it that we can take pleasure in tragedy, given that the sorts of response that it characteristically elicits from us (indeed, which on Aristotle's view are partly definitive of the genre) are on the face of it far from pleasant? What sort of pleasure is it, Hume asks, that stems "from the bosom of uneasiness" and "which still retains all the features and outward symptoms of distress and sorrow" (1987)?

Hume begins by considering two attempts to explain the appeal of tragedy, both of which he finds inadequate. The first claims that human beings naturally prefer emotional excitement, even if the emotions involved are negative, to the "languid, listless state of indolence, into which [the mind] falls upon the removal of all passion" (ibid.). Hume accepts that there is something in this, but argues that it fails to explain the pleasure that we take in tragedy: after all, "real-life" tragedies are hardly a source of pleasure, despite their invigorating powers. The second explanation suggests that we can take pleasure in literary or dramatic tragedy because we know that it is fictional; this knowledge, in Bernard Le Bovier de Fontenelle's words (quoted by Hume), "serves to diminish the pain which we suffer . . . and to reduce that affliction to such a pitch as converts it into a pleasure" (ibid.). Hume has more sympathy with this suggestion, but again finds it inadequate. He notes, first, that the distress we experience in response to fictional tragedy may be acute, and second, that in some cases we take pleasure in the tragic representation of events that we do not take to be fictional. How can this be?

Hume's suggestion is that the key to understanding the peculiarly ambiguous nature of our experience of tragedy lies in recognizing that the pleasure and the distress that we may experience in responding to tragic works have different causes and objects. The negative emotional responses that are aroused in us are directed at *what is depicted*—at the suffering of the characters, the horror of the events, and so on. In contrast, the pleasure that tragedy affords us is directed at *the manner of depiction*—at what he describes as "that very eloquence with which the melancholy scene is represented" (ibid.). This pleasure "predominates" over the feelings of distress that we also experience, and "converts" them into pleasurable feelings. As Hume says, "The uneasiness of the melancholy passions is not only overpowered and effaced by something stronger of an opposite kind; but the whole impulse of those passions is converted into pleasure, and swells the delight which the eloquence raises in us" (ibid.). Thus, for example, in responding to *King Lear,* we attend not only to the plight of Lear and Cordelia and Gloucester, but also to William Shakespeare's eloquence and to the art of the actors, director, stage designer, and so on; and the pleasure that we take in the latter "overpowers" and "effaces" and "transforms" the distress that we feel at the former.

Understanding Hume's account of tragic pleasure clearly depends on understanding this rather obscure talk of the "conversion" and "transformation" of passions. What does this process amount to? Hume cannot mean that, in our experience of tragedy, sorrow or terror (say) are somehow rendered pleasant, for, in book 2 of his *A Treatise of Human Nature,* the passions are identified with "simple and uniform" reflective impressions; a change in the feeling of a passion from pain to pleasure would on this account be impossible, because it would necessitate a change in the impression and hence a change in the passion itself. As he says in "Of Tragedy," "You may by degrees weaken a real sorrow, till it totally disappears; yet in none of its gradations will it ever give pleasure" (ibid.).

But if Hume is not suggesting that painful passions are themselves rendered pleasant in our experience of tragedy, it is far from clear precisely what he *is* suggesting. At some points in the essay, he talks explicitly of the transformation of one passion into another: for example, "the subordinate passion is here readily transformed into the predominant one" (ibid.). At other points, he writes as though the conversion he has in mind is not strictly of the passions themselves, but of the "impulse" or "vehemence" or "motions" that accompany or "arise from" the passions: for example, "The impulse or vehemence, arising from sorrow, compassion, indignation, receives a new direction from the sentiments of beauty" (ibid.).

These remarks are reminiscent of parts of his discussion of the passions in the *Treatise* where, for example, Hume speaks of the "principle, that every emotion, which precedes or attends a passion, is easily converted into it" (1978, book 2, part 3, section 5). Unfortunately, however, the discussion of this principle in the *Treatise* is hardly less opaque than it is in "Of Tragedy." In both works, the best

that Hume offers by way of illumination is a series of examples of the phenomenon with which he is concerned. For instance, "parents commonly love that child most, whose sickly infirm frame of body has occasioned them the greatest pains, trouble, and anxiety in rearing him. The agreeable sentiment here acquires force from the sentiments of uneasiness." Again, "jealousy is a painful passion; yet without some share of it, the agreeable affection of love has difficulty to subsist in its full force and violence." These and the other examples that Hume gives in both the *Treatise* and "Of Tragedy" constitute virtually the only support he offers for the principle that underlies his view of tragic pleasure, and commentators have differed over just how much support they do actually provide.

The central difficulty facing Hume's account of tragic pleasure, then, lies in the obscurity of his talk of the conversion and transformation of passion. Doubtless not least as a result of that obscurity, Hume's account has found few supporters in subsequent philosophical discussion of tragedy. Attenuated versions of his account, however, which abandon his notion of conversion but retain his suggestion that the pleasure and the distress involved in our experience of tragedy have different causes and objects, have not been uncommon. It is questionable whether this sort of position represents any advance on Hume's account, however. As Hume recognized, we value tragedy in large part because of, and not despite, the fact that it arouses in us the sort of "uneasy" or distressing emotional experience that it does. To construe the pleasure afforded us by tragedy as essentially separate from the distress that it also evokes, then, is to pull apart one of the crucial respects in which we value tragedy from the pleasure that it affords us. For Hume, who held a hedonic theory of value, that would be unacceptable; hence, his insistence that tragic pleasure has its source at least partly *in* the distress. In his words, the seemingly "unaccountable pleasure" is pleasure "which the spectators of a well-written tragedy *receive from* sorrow, terror, anxiety and other passions that are in themselves disagreeable and uneasy" (ibid.; emphasis added): not a pleasure that accompanies or runs alongside the "uneasiness" of "passions that are in themselves disagreeable," but—paradoxical though it seems—the pleasure *of* those passions. The tragic experience has a unitary character, albeit a difficult and ambiguous one; and it is just this that Hume's thesis about the conversion and transformation of passion in our experience of tragedy is meant to account for. Without that thesis, we are left with an account that misses a crucial aspect of the nature of the "singular phenomenon" with which he was concerned. With the thesis, however, we have an account that is at best highly obscure, based on associative principles that Hume himself never fully explains.

[*See also* Hume, *survey article.*]

BIBLIOGRAPHY

Works by Hume

A Treatise of Human Nature. 2d ed. Edited by P. H. Nidditch. Oxford, 1978.
"Of Tragedy." In *Essays Moral, Political and Literary,* rev. ed., edited by Eugene F. Miller. Indianapolis, 1987.

Other Sources

Budd, Malcolm. "Hume's Tragic Emotions." *Hume Studies* 17 (1991).
Eaton, Marcia. "A Strange Kind of Sadness." *Journal of Aesthetics and Art Criticism* 41 (1982): 51–63.
Feagin, Susan. "The Pleasures of Tragedy." *American Philosophical Quarterly* 20 (1983): 95–104.
Hill, Eric. "Hume and the Delightful Tragedy Problem." *Philosophy* 57 (1982): 319–326.
Hipple, Walter. "The Logic of Hume's Essay 'Of Tragedy'." *Philosophical Quarterly* 6 (1956): 43–52.
Neill, Alex. "Yanal and Others on Hume and Tragedy." *Journal of Aesthetics and Art Criticism* 50 (1992): 151–154.
Packer, Mark. "Dissolving the Paradox of Tragedy." *Journal of Aesthetics and Art Criticism* 47 (1989): 212–219.
Paton, Margaret. "Hume on Tragedy." *British Journal of Aesthetics* 13 (1973): 121–132.
Quinton, Anthony. "Tragedy." *Proceedings of the Aristotelian Society* Suppl. vol. 34 (1960): 245–264.
Schier, Flint. "Tragedy and the Community of Sentiment." In *Philosophy and Fiction,* edited by Peter Lamarque. Aberdeen, 1983.
Schier, Flint. "The Claims of Tragedy: An Essay in Moral Psychology and Aesthetic Theory." *Philosophical Papers* 18 (1989): 7–26.
Yanal, Robert J. "Hume and Others on the Paradox of Tragedy." *Journal of Aesthetics and Art Criticism* 49 (1991): 75–76.

ALEX NEILL

Freud on Tragedy

Sigmund Freud's contribution to the study and interpretation of tragedy begins with his letters to Wilhelm Fliess, for it is there that he announces that he has discovered a thematic continuity between the tragic drama *Oedipus the King* by Sophocles and William Shakespeare's *Hamlet.* That reading of the two plays established a lifelong involvement and fascination with Greek classical and Shakespearean tragedy. It also set the interpretive pattern for Freud's commitment to a biographical element in literary psychology, for he believed that the authors of tragedies gained their deep psychological insights through personal experience, though usually unconscious, of inner conflict. Two programs are initiated in the letter of 15 October 1897: the first, to examine great literary writings for psychoanalytic insights; the second, to connect those insights to the private life of the author.

> The Greek legend [of Oedipus] seizes upon a compulsion which everyone recognizes because he senses its existence within himself. Everyone in the audience was once a budding Oedipus in fantasy and each recoils in horror from the dream fulfillment here transplanted into reality. . . . the same thing might be at the bottom of *Hamlet* as well. I am not thinking of Shakespeare's conscious intention, but believe, rather, that a real event stimu-

lated the poet to his representation, in that his unconscious understood the unconscious of his hero.   (Freud, 1985)

Freud's wide reading in European literature, especially drama, led him to discoveries that he believed supported his own understanding of psychic development, and lent support to his theoretical observations. This support encouraged him to extend the literary interpretations even further in the light of the clinical, and thus psychoanalytic inquiry and the literary analysis of character came to reinforce one another. Psychoanalytic essays, in which long-debated literary problems are given psychological solutions, and neglected passages brought into the center of interpretation, and thus are seen in a new light, appear throughout Freud's writings.

In his many books and essays, Freud frequently returned to tragic drama because, of all the arts, it offered the most compelling and insightful representations of the kinds of family constellations and conflicts that psychoanalysis discovered in the consulting room. When *The Interpretation of Dreams* (1900) was published, Freud elaborated on the insight communicated to Fliess, making it clear that one may postulate a historical development in tragedy that shapes the tragic conflict in its various representations, though the psychological roots remain constant. The psychoanalytic theory of tragedy distinguishes two components, historical and psychological: "Shakespeare's *Hamlet* has roots in the same soil as [Sophocles'] *Oedipus Rex,*" Freud wrote.

> But the changed treatment of the same material reveals the whole difference of the mental life of these two widely separated epochs of civilization: the secular advance of repression in the emotional life of mankind. In the *Oedipus* the child's wishful phantasy that underlies it is brought into the open and realized as it would be in a dream. In *Hamlet* it remains repressed; and—just as in the case of neurosis—we only learn of its existence from its inhibiting consequences.   (1953, vol. 4, p. 264)

Modern audiences remain unknowing about Hamlet's psychological problem, that is, his inability to act, because of the psychological repression characteristic of our time. Freud argued that while literary critics advance a variety of interpretations to explain Hamlet as a person, they all miss the essential, unconscious conflict that immobilizes him:

> Hamlet is able to do anything—except take vengeance on the man who did away with his father and took that father's place with his mother, the man, who shows him the repressed wishes of his own childhood realized. . . . I have translated into conscious terms what was bound to remain unconscious in Hamlet's mind.   (Ibid., p. 265)

Beyond the historical and psychological forces that shape tragedy, Freud insisted, a biographical cause can be postulated in the case of Shakespeare because there is sufficient evidence to tie the plot of Hamlet to the playwright's life:

> It can only be the poet's own mind that confronts us in Hamlet. . . . *Hamlet* was written immediately after the death of

Shakespeare's father (1601), that is, under the immediate impact of his bereavement and, as we may well assume, while his child-hood feelings about his father had been freshly revived.   (Ibid.)

Freud, like his predecessor in the interpretation of tragedy, the philosopher Georg Wilhelm Friedrich Hegel, used the method he had evolved for solving problems outside the aesthetic to read and interpret a number of tragic dramas. Whereas in Hegel's case the method was his general philosophy, then relied on as an interpretive tool to analyze a variety of problems, in Freud's case it was his psychoanalytic theory and its method of interpretation that opened up a number of cultural problems, especially in the arts. The two thinkers are alike in that both postulate a manifest content and a latent content in tragedy, to be connected through the method of inquiry that each has worked out. For the psychoanalytic, that means a double connectedness: first from the manifest content of the drama, as in Hamlet's inability to act, with its unconscious underpinnings in infantile psychic conflict, Hamlet's "Oedipus complex," and then to search in the biography of the author for evidences of the conflict, expressed in conduct, letters, and contemporary historical facts. Freud's method thus led him to explore a wide variety of conditions, internal and external to the particular drama in question. He was able to observe, in a sensitive application of his theory, common themes that tied together plots from various sources. Freud discovered in both linguistic and material art a universal preoccupation with conflicts that necessarily emerged in the sexual development of men and women. Tragedy derives its emotional force in part from its establishment of the irresolvability of these conflicts. Tragic pessimism mirrors the psychoanalytic view of human nature.

In contrast, it might be pointed out, that Hegel's readings of tragedy, for all his recognition of tragic conflict, emphasized a progressive movement toward resolution and enlightenment in the historical process. Freud, although firmly committed to the power of his method in the clinic to better the human condition, saw no optimism in the tragic dramas he analyzed. Their clear-sighted representations of the ever-present political and sexual conflicts stood as evidence that human nature has not changed and does not change through the ages.

Two major essays develop the psychoanalytic interpretation of tragedy, and exemplify the broad scope of the theory: "The Theme of the Three Caskets" (1913) and "Some Character-Types Met with in Psychoanalytic Work" (1916). In the first, Freud analyzes scenes from *The Merchant of Venice* and *King Lear;* in the second, themes in *Richard III, Macbeth,* and Henrik Ibsen's *Rosmersholm.*

Tying together dramas that at first seem as disparate as the *Merchant of Venice* and *King Lear* is the subject, Freud observes, of a man making a choice of one among three women. The women, symbolized in the *Merchant of Venice* by the three caskets from which the suitors must choose, and directly represented in *King Lear* by the three daughters, are a manifest dramatic presence symbolizing a latent meaning. The essay "The Theme of the Three Caskets" searches for the hidden inner meaning of such a dramatic presentation. Freud suggests that underlying the choice in both cases of the most beautiful yet silent woman lies the human necessity to deny life's finitude, to turn that which is most repellent, death, into that which is most alluring, beautiful, and sexually desirable. Both dramas perpetuate a mythic theme, choosing one of three women, a theme that is seen in other stories: the choice by Paris of Aphrodite, who promises him the most beautiful woman in the world, Helen, and the choice in fairy tales of the most beautiful, though apparently least worthy, Cinderella. Another example of the choice is to be found in Apuleius's tale of Psyche.

In the *Merchant of Venice,* Bassanio chooses the lead casket, characterized as silent and unworthy, but within is hidden the painting of Portia, so beautiful it stuns the beholder. Silence and lead symbolize death, as does Cordelia's silence before Lear. Freud made this identification with the help of his own clinical work, for, he observed, in dreams reported by patients, dumbness symbolized death, and therefore he was led to ask if the same symbolization appeared outside of dreams. Setting as a hypothesis that the symbolization does indeed extend beyond dreams, he examined the way tragic drama intensifies the dream thoughts in dramatic scenes of great power. He also observed audience response, for these dramas make clear to the audience the high worth and sexual attractiveness of the woman. One may then postulate that the woman, so attractive and so desirable is at the same time a symbol of death and death's loss of dominion, a deep and universal wish of all human beings: let death be transformed into that which is most to be sought.

Freud goes on to argue that in every life there are three women, the woman who is mother, the woman who is lover, and finally the woman who, as in Nordic myth, carries away the dying person, death itself. Underlying all of these narrative representations in which there is affirmation of choice, yet recognition of finality, is the Greek trio of the Fates, women who preside over every life. The terror of death they inspire becomes transformed in dramas such as the *Merchant of Venice* and *King Lear* into the one beautiful woman, freely, joyfully chosen from among her two companions.

Latent and manifest content are woven into a denial and an affirmation that penetrate into the audience's unconscious, for, Freud argued, works of tragic art are able to show us that through an aesthetic structure we are enabled to look upon that which, outside of art, would simply force us to turn away. Freud concludes his remarks on *King Lear:* "Let us now recall the moving final scene, one of the culminating points of tragedy in modern drama. Lear carries Cordelia's dead body on to the stage. Cordelia is death" (1958 vol. 12, p. 301). With this bold *is* of psychoanalytic interpretation, Freud demonstrates the identification on which his whole theory rests: a manifest representation is translatable into a latent meaning. Once that is discovered, the force and power, the hidden inner meaning, of the dramatic scene is disclosed, and we gain an understanding of why and how tragedy moves us so deeply.

Discussing *Macbeth*, in the essay "Some Character-Types Met with in Psychoanalytic Work," Freud discovers a theme at once obvious, yet implying hidden meanings. Central to the tragedy is the childlessness of Macbeth and Lady Macbeth. Moving beyond the tragic plot, Freud saw its political implications, for tragedy always hides, even in its psychological shrewdness, a political reality with which all societies must cope. Psychoanalytic theory of tragedy is sensitive to the close affinity between tragic conflict and the real political conflicts in everyday life. In the case of *Macbeth*, the political reality is a covert mirroring of the childlessness of Queen Elizabeth: "The accession of James I," Freud points out, "was like a demonstration of the curse of unfruitfulness and the blessings of continuous generation. And the action of Shakespeare's *Macbeth* is based on this same contrast" (1957, vol. 14). Childlessness has many ramifications, and in following them out, Freud gives a psychoanalytic reading of the play that pulls together several seemingly disparate scenes.

Scenes that appear remote from one another gain consistency and coherence. The words of the Weird Sisters, the fate of Banquo, the advancing "trees" of the forest, the terrifying night noises, all contribute to a cosmic ruin politically expressed by Macbeth in his cruel violence, and psychologically by Lady Macbeth in her madness. The protagonists are driven to tear apart the public social fabric and to pervert the private psychic balance as a consequence of the despair induced by lack of descendants. Freud writes:

> I believe Lady Macbeth's illness, the transformation of her callousness into penitence, could be explained directly as a reaction to her childlessness, by which she is convinced of her impotence against the decrees of nature. . . . The dramatist can indeed, during the representation, overwhelm us by his art and paralyse our powers of reflection; but he cannot prevent us from attempting subsequently to grasp its effect by studying its psychological mechanism.   (Ibid. Vol. 14, pp. 321–323)

Freud's studies of tragedy led him to conclude that these "mechanisms" are represented in the same terms in literature as they are in clinical experience.

In order to apply the psychoanalytic method to its fullest extent, the interpreter of works of art ought to be conversant with psychoanalytic narratives produced as "case histories," for they themselves are stories with tragic elements embedded in them. A study of Freud's cases highlights two recurring elements that appear frequently in tragic drama. One is the riddle, the other a psychological process to which Freud applied the term *splitting*.

Riddles appear over and over again in tragic drama, the most obvious in *Oedipus the King*. They are central also in *Hamlet, King Lear, Macbeth,* and many of the Greek tragedies. The person setting forth into psychoanalytic treatment pursues the deepest riddle that all human beings confront, their own innermost nature. So too the tragic heroes are engaged in a like searching, and in the search come upon the contradictions human being sees in itself. Watching a tragic drama unfold is very like a quest into the self. This observation led Freud to propose tentatively a hypothesis about how audience response to tragedy can be at once frightening and pleasurable. Splitting is the psychoanalytic answer to Aristotle's inquiry into the pleasure appropriate to tragedy, even while the audience suffers the emotions of pity and fear. Splitting allows the audience to gain pleasure from witnessing even the terrifying scenes in tragedy. Freud describes the psychological process of splitting in his late essay "An Outline of Psychoanalysis": "Two psychical attitudes [coexist], one which takes account of reality, and another which under the influence of the drives detaches the ego from reality. The two exist alongside of each other." Even though they are "contrary and independent of each other" they can be maintained at the same time. This doubleness allows the audience to identify both with the action on the stage, its aesthetic wholeness as narrative representation, beautifully composed, and the reality of private conflict within the self, which though it may remain unconscious, is brought into congruity with the dramatic unfolding (1964, vol. 23, pp. 202–204, 275–277).

Although Freud created a method of interpretation that stands beside those of Aristotle, Hegel, and Friedrich Nietzsche, from all of whom the psychoanalytic draws some of its powers, the psychoanalytic emphasizes interpretations of tragedy that complement those sources by discovering the deep unconscious conflicts that all cultural traditions must confront, and that in the West were best represented and aesthetically tamed in tragic drama.

[*See also* Freud, *article on* Survey of Thought.]

BIBLIOGRAPHY

Euben, J. Peter. *The Tragedy of Political Theory.* Princeton, N.J., 1990.

Freud, Sigmund. *The Interpretation of Dreams* (1900). In *The Standard Edition of the Complete Psychological Works of Sigmund Freud,* vols. 4 and 5, edited by James Strachey. London, 1953.

Freud, Sigmund. "Some Character-Types Met with in Psychoanalytic Work." In *The Standard Edition of the Complete Psychological Works of Sigmund Freud,* vol. 14, edited by James Strachey, pp. 309–333, London, 1957.

Freud, Sigmund. "The Theme of the Three Caskets." In *The Standard Edition of the Complete Psychological Works of Sigmund Freud,* vol. 12, edited by James Strachey, pp. 289–301. London, 1958.

Freud, Sigmund. "An Outline of Psychoanalysis." In *The Standard Edition of the Complete Psychological Works of Sigmund Freud,* vol. 23, edited by James Strachey, pp. 141–207. London, 1964.

Freud, Sigmund. "Splitting of the Ego in the Process of Defense." In *The Standard Edition of the Complete Psychological Works of Sigmund*

Freud, vol. 23, edited by James Strachey, pp. 271–278. London, 1964.

Freud, Sigmund. *The Complete Letters of Sigmund Freud to Wilhelm Fliess, 1887–1904.* Edited and translated by Jeffrey Moussaieff Masson. Cambridge, Mass., 1985.

Garber, Marjorie. *Shakespeare's Ghost Writers: Literature as Uncanny Causality.* New York and London, 1987.

Girard, René. *Violence and the Sacred.* Translated by Patrick Gregory. Baltimore, 1977.

Green, André. *The Tragic Effect: The Oedipus Complex in Tragedy.* Translated by Alan Sheridan. Cambridge, 1979.

Jones, Ernest. *Hamlet and Oedipus.* New York, 1949.

Kuhns, Richard. *Tragedy: Contradiction and Repression.* Chicago, 1991.

Rorty, Amélie Oksenberg, ed. *Essays on Aristotle's Poetics.* Princeton, N.J., 1992.

Rudnytsky, Peter L., and Ellen Handler Spitz, eds. *Freud and Forbidden Knowledge.* New York, 1994.

Steiner, George. *Antigones.* New York and Oxford, 1984.

Vernant, Jean-Pierre, and Pierre Vidal-Naquet. *Tragedy and Myth in Ancient Greece.* Translated by Janet Lloyd. Atlantic Highlands, N.J., 1981. Reprinted as *Myth and Tragedy in Ancient Greece* (New York, 1988).

RICHARD KUHNS

TRIBAL ART. Also termed "ethnographic art" or, in an expression seldom used today, "primitive art," tribal art is the art of small-scale nonliterate societies. Some of the traditional artifacts to which the term refers may not be art in any obvious European sense, and many of the cultures where they occur may not, strictly speaking, be tribal in social structure. The rubric nevertheless persists because the arts produced by small-scale cultures share significant elements in common. The tribal arts that have gained the greatest attention in the West come from the Americas (such as the Inuit, Southwest and Plains Indians, and isolated areas of Central and South America), Oceania (including Melanesia and Australia, Polynesia and New Zealand), and sub-Saharan Africa. The characteristics that define a small-scale, traditional society are (1) isolation, politically and economically, from civilizations of Europe, North Africa, or Asia; (2) oral traditions in the absence of literacy; (3) small, independent population groupings, usually in villages of no more than a few hundred souls who live a life of face-to-face social interaction and informal social control; (4) a low level of labor/craft specialization; (5) subsistence by hunting, fishing, and gathering and/or small-scale agriculture; (6) little technology beyond hand tools, and that often of stone rather than metal; and (7) slow rates of cultural change prior to European contact. Of this list, small size, lack of written language, and isolation from large civilizations are the essential features of societies whose art is discussed here.

As the European interest in "primitive" art grew in the second half of the nineteenth century, attention was first captured by carvings and masks, as these were the easiest to transport back to the capitals of colonial empire. The arts of small-scale societies include, however, far more than transportable artifacts: musical and dance performance, oral literatures, textiles and jewelry, and relatively perishable or ephemeral arts, such as sandpainting and body painting. Cultures tend to specialize in some arts at the apparent expense of others; the Sepik peoples of northern New Guinea, for example, are renowned for their wood carving, whereas their countrymen in the interior highlands hardly carve at all, but focus extraordinary care and attention on stunning body decorations. The acute aesthetic sensibilities of peoples of small-scale societies extend beyond crafted arts. Nilotic cattle herders of east Africa, such as the Dinka, have a refined sense for the natural colors and forms of cattle markings, around which they have built a subtle aesthetic vocabulary for critical discourse.

Whether such activities and artifacts amount to art at all in the European meaning of the term is a question persistently raised in anthropological and aesthetic literature. Rudolf Arnheim has claimed that tribal art "is not made to produce pleasurable illusions," but is "a practical instrument for the important business of daily living" (1974). More recently, anthropologist Alfred Gell has argued that the importance of tribal art lies in its utility as a magical technology, rather than in its aesthetic appeal (1993). Thus, the colorful appearance of a canoe may dazzle a trading partner, the decorations on a spear may help it find its target, or a carving's importance may derive from the fact that it is occasionally inhabited by a god or by the ghost of an ancestor; it follows that the Europeans' valuing of such objects merely because of their beauty would be ethnocentric. Gell's emphasis on the remoteness of tribal arts from familiar European aesthetic interests can be bolstered by considering some of the remarkable practices in the local contexts of tribal arts: for instance, *malangan* figures of New Ireland are sometimes unceremoniously burned following the ritual for which they were a centerpiece.

Yet, it is arguable that too much stress has been placed on the differences between Western and tribal arts. For instance, there are folk traditions in European Christianity in which an icon of the Virgin may temporarily be inhabited by her spirit, and it develops that New Ireland artists may have very good reason for wanting to burn a laboriously produced *malangan,* if, in the course of a rite, the carving has acquired potent magical powers that could be put to malevolent use were it not destroyed. Generally, it is difficult to find a practice involving tribal art in its original magical, religious, political, or entertainment context for which there cannot be discovered a plausible analogue involving acknowledged "art" products and practices in the civilizations of Asia and Europe.

Moreover, even when Westerners are ignorant of the original context of use of tribal arts, the immediately perceptible visible organization of a putative work of tribal art—color, imaginative representation, order, and balance—seems often to mark its aesthetic status. In this respect, what Robert Goldwater (1938) has termed the "directly visual" impact of tribal arts is no more mysterious (and no less powerful) than the encounters, however decontextualized, with fragments of ancient artworks of the West. Furthermore, even the most culturally remote or naive audience will recognize a human face or human body in a work of art, and this can provide a point from which appreciation can begin (this fact may explain, incidentally, why the most desirable tribal carvings in the Western market for such art continue to be renderings of the human form).

The characteristics of the art of tribal societies have been cataloged by H. Gene Blocker (1994). According to Blocker, the tribal art object normally (1) is of aesthetic (sensual or imaginative) interest, (2) is made by a specialist producer of art, (3) is subject to critical appraisal, (4) is set apart from ordinary life, (5) represents the real or a mythological world or events either literally or symbolically, (6) is intended to be understood as a symbolic or as mimetic representation, (7) involves the possibility of novelty within a tradition, and (8) is made by a person often seen as "eccentric" or socially alienated within the indigenous context. Although one might dispute the applicability of any of these criteria to every small-scale society (e.g., carving is a special activity of an elite few in some Polynesian cultures, whereas in most of Melanesia virtually any man can try his hand at it), the list is nevertheless a useful reminder that tribal arts are very far from being crude or primitive in any aesthetic sense, but are the mature, fully developed arts of technologically less developed societies.

An imaginative challenge to the claim that the artistic status of tribal artifacts is necessarily perceptible in visible form has been mounted by Arthur C. Danto (1988), who suggests a thought experiment: imagine two tribes, the Pot People and the Basket Folk, both of whom produce what are, to European eyes, indistinguishable pots and baskets. In the minds of these tribal peoples, however, there is an enormous difference between Pot People pots and Basket Folk pots (and conversely with baskets), for the pots are works of art, embodying deep symbolism for the Pot People, whereas they are mere utilitarian artifacts for the Basket Folk. Because this is, for Danto, a conceivable situation, it follows that for these imagined tribes, and possibly generally as well, the status of an artifact as work of art results from the ideas a culture applies to it, rather than from its inherent physical or perceptible qualities. Cultural interpretation (an art theory of some kind) is therefore constitutive of an object's arthood.

If supportable, Danto's thought experiment would have important implications for the Western encounter with tribal arts, for it would follow from it that knowledge of the cultural context of, say, an Oceanic ancestor figure was not merely an enriching support to the immediate aesthetic impact of the object. Rather, its original culture would exhaustively determine whether the object was art at all; apprecia-

TRIBAL ART. *Canoe Prow* (nineteenth to twentieth century), Solomon Islands; private collection. (Photograph courtesy of Denis Dutton.)

tion of formal aesthetic qualities in the absence of considerable cultural knowledge therefore risks being completely delusive. Nevertheless, it is difficult to imagine circumstances where something like Danto's example could actually exist. Those works of tribal art that embody dense cultural meaning are in small-scale societies normally ones into which are invested the greatest care, craftsmanship, and critical discernment. In Danto's example, even though one can well imagine that Europeans might find it difficult or even impossible to distinguish between Basket Folk baskets (works of art) and Pot People baskets (utilitarian craft objects), it is hard to envision the situation where the basket weavers of the Basket Folk would not be able to tell the difference (one might mistake a Terborch for a Hals, but it is unlikely Terborch or Hals ever did so).

Nevertheless, Danto's approach to the problem of cross-cultural aesthetic understanding, even if overdrawn, is a useful reminder of the importance of cultural knowledge in grasping works of tribal art. As they are deeply embedded in their cultural contexts, tribal arts are governed by systems of rules as complex as those that govern Western art forms. Moreover, it seems probable that societies that lack writing as a means of recording information and tradition invest artworks with a greater density of meaning than do literate societies. It may also be the case that an isolated society that has no access to alternative visual representations outside of its own art develops highly sophisticated and aesthetically powerful stylizations. It is perhaps for this reason that many judges both from within and outside of small-scale societies have remarked on the degradation of tribal arts once they come in close contact with industrial societies.

Whether such a view is fair to indigenous artists or instead represents ethnocentric prejudice is a topic of fierce debate. Many knowledgeable collectors and curators of tribal arts wish mainly to acquire and display works made in a traditional style for a traditional religious or social use that are thus designated "authentic." The market in tribal art therefore places a premium on African masks that have been used in a dance, Philippine carvings encrusted with years of oil and blood offerings, or decorated New Guinean fighting shields peppered with arrowheads from combat. At the same time, contemporary tourist or "airport" art made explicitly for sale to foreigners is passed over as inferior, because it does not reflect the indigenous values of the society, but only the demands of an alien market. This Western valorization of authenticity has been sternly criticized by Larry Shiner, who argues that it "is not merely an ethnocentric reflection of the modern discourse of Fine Art; it is also a piece of ideology, an unintended justification of a continuing exploitative power relation" (1994). Westerners fantasize that old, authentic works were produced by tribal artists in the unspoiled, Edenic state of such societies prior to colonial contact. Yet, as Shiner points out, there was a healthy circulation of ideas with much artistic and cultural borrowing in tribal societies before European contact; the fact that tribal artists now borrow from the West itself is a continuation of an authentic tradition of cultural exchange. Such a value system works against contemporary indigenous artists, unless they become adept at producing the countless faked "old" masks and carvings that have flooded the tribal art market in recent years.

Yet, although it may be unjust that the airport art of developing societies should be disparaged by those more wealthy cultures that brought the airports in the first place, it is not unreasonable that historians and collectors should retain an abiding interest in the art of small-scale societies as they existed before the onslaught of the consumer economies of colonizing powers. The passionate, imaginative visions of tribal arts, expressing as they often do modes of life and thought that have been abandoned since contact

with Western culture, have significantly expanded the West's notion of how art can have meaning. For those in the West willing to open their eyes and minds, they offer a wondrous gift.

[*See also* African Aesthetics; *and* Folk Art.]

BIBLIOGRAPHY

Abusabib, Mohamed A. *African Art: An Aesthetic Inquiry.* Uppsala, 1995.

Arnheim, Rudolf. *Art and Visual Perception: A Psychology of the Creative Eye.* New rev. exp. ed. Berkeley, 1974.

Blocker, H. Gene. *The Aesthetics of Primitive Art.* Lanham, Md., 1994.

Coote, Jeremy, and Anthony Shelton, eds. *Anthropology, Art, and Aesthetics.* Oxford, 1992. Includes articles by Ruth Barnes, Ross Bowden, Raymond Firth, Alfred Gell, Susanne Küchler, Robert Layton, Howard Morphy, Jarich Oosten, Anthony Shelton, and Jeremy Coote.

Danto, Arthur C. "Artifact and Art." In *Art/Artifact: African Art in Anthropology Collections,* edited by Susan Vogel. New York, 1988.

Dissanayake, Ellen. *Homo Aestheticus: Where Art Comes from and Why.* Reprint, Seattle, 1996.

Dutton, Denis. "Tribal Art and Artifact." *Journal of Aesthetics and Art Criticism* 51.1 (Winter 1993): 13–21.

Dutton, Denis, "Mythologies of Tribal Art." *African Arts* 28.3 (Summer 1995): 32–43.

Gell, Alfred. *Wrapping in Images: Tatooing in Polynesia.* Oxford and New York, 1993.

Goldwater, Robert J. *Primitivism in Modern Painting* (1938). Enl. ed. Cambridge, Mass., 1986.

Shiner, Larry. "'Primitive Fakes,' 'Tourist Art,' and the Ideology of Authenticity." *Journal of Aesthetics and Art Criticism* 52.2 (Spring 1994): 225–234.

DENIS DUTTON

TRUTH. Underlying the ancient debate about truth and art—a debate at the very core of aesthetics—are profound philosophical issues concerning the acquisition of knowledge (epistemology), the ultimate nature of reality (metaphysics), and the sources of goodness (ethics). Beginning with some scattered observations in Homer about representation and the different functions of the poet and seer, the debate (in the Western philosophical tradition) has evolved considerably over two-and-a-half thousand years, reflecting not just changing views about art but radically different conceptions of truth, reality, and knowledge. In the broadest terms, the truth issue in aesthetics boils down to two fundamental questions: What features of art, in particular involving relations between works of art and reality, support the claim of art to truth? Is the conveying of truth to be counted among the primary functions and thus values of art?

It is a mark of the complexity of the topic that specialist terms have been developed to characterize the truth-bearing relations between art and reality: *mimesis,* representation, "mirror" (of nature), realism, verisimilitude, didacticism, and naturalism, among others. These conceptions are by no means interchangeable and confusion often results from running them together. Nor is their connection with truth by any means straightforward. The question, for example, whether art aims at lifelikeness or verisimilitude should be distinguished from the question whether art aims at truth in some more direct cognitive sense (in parallel to philosophy or science). Also, the imaginative truths that the Romantics (William Wordsworth, Samuel Taylor Coleridge, John Keats) claimed for lyric poetry are not the same—nor based on the same conception—as the truths that the eighteenth-century neoclassical theorists (Alexander Pope, John Dryden, Samuel Johnson) identified with poetry, nor indeed those sought by nineteenth-century Realist novelists (Honoré de Balzac, Émile Zola) or painters (Gustave Courbet, Edgar Degas), even though these views developed within a span of little more than one hundred years. Furthermore, not all arts lend themselves to the truth idiom, which is most commonly applied to the literary arts (drama, poetry, the novel) and the visual arts (painting, sculpture, film), but less to architecture, music, and dance, except where these are deemed to have representational content.

It is possible to discern different kinds of theories relating art and truth, which might be crudely sketched as follows:

1. *Mimetic theories.* The term *mimetic* covers a range of views, some of which will be discussed below, according to which works of art are seen as "imitating" or "mirroring" reality (be it a transcendent reality of Platonic Forms or a social reality or the mental reality of philosophical idealism or yet other kinds). The "imitating" might occur through verisimilitude (likeness), the transmission of universal truths, or the realization of an ideal type. [*See* Mimesis.]

2. *Didactic theories.* Characteristic of such theories is the notion that art is (can be, should be) a vehicle for instruction, be it religious doctrine, moral truth, or political ideology. The potential of art for teaching, imparting belief, even propaganda, has long been recognized, though as often deplored as applauded. [*See* Politics and Art; *and* Religion and Aesthetics, *article on* Religion and Art.]

3. *Moral theories.* Those theories that emphasize the moral nature and responsibilities of art, the idea that great art in some essential way is connected to moral truth, can often be viewed as a subclass of didactic theories; but they deserve a category of their own because they do not necessarily imply a teaching function for art and have at their core a criterion for art's fundamental value. [*See* Morality and Art.]

4. *Authenticity theories.* Sometimes the concept of truth in art is associated with truthfulness, sincerity, or authenticity. According to such theories, works of art are to be valued for their honesty, lack of sentimentality, clarity, or directness, whereby an artistic vision is presented without self-indulgence or distracting artifice; such works are praised for their "truth," though this need not be either moral truth or in any straightforward sense an "imitation" of nature.

The first three categories, in their varied manifestations, have found expression throughout the history of aesthetics. In contrast, authenticity theories, the fourth category, are essentially modern (post-eighteenth century), arising only when Romantic or expressive conceptions of art began to develop, although those who hold authenticity views often (however anachronistically) project them back onto earlier periods. Already the distinction between mimetic, didactic, moral, and personal or expressive truth shows just how diverse are the concerns in the debate about truth and art. Tracking the history of the debate is fraught with difficulty not only because of the profound changes in epistemological and metaphysical presuppositions, but also given the very elusiveness of the key terms *truth* and *art*. It would be deeply misleading to suppose that all the contributors to the debate shared any common, clearly defined set of premises or even any universal conception of the subject matter.

The Classical Foundations of the Historical Debate. In the classical debate, two fundamental positions on the question of how art might stake a claim to truth are defined by Plato (428–348 BCE) and Aristotle (384–322 BCE). Plato's views on knowledge and on the nature of reality played a determining role in his attitude to art. In the allegory of the Line (*Republic*, 1941, book 6), he divided cognition into four levels from the highest *(noesis)*, a form of reason giving access to the basic principles of reality, to the lowest *(eikasia)*, the perception of "shadows" and appearances. He assigns the products of art to the lowest level. The true reality of the world of ideas can only be grasped through a disciplined exercise of philosophical reasoning. Pictorial, sculptural, and literary art are all a form of mimesis or "imitation." But what the artist imitates is simply the imperfect and deceptive appearances found in this world. Plato illustrates the point in his famous example of the bed (ibid., book 10, pp. 597–599), according to which the craftsman (carpenter) imitates the Form of a bed while the painter merely imitates that imitation, thus locating his work at two removes from reality. In this same passage, Plato introduces the analogy of art and a mirror, a metaphor that was to become so influential among neoclassical theorists, by way of showing how easy it is to be a "maker" of (images of) all things on Earth (i.e., by holding up a mirror to them).

Of all Plato's strictures against art, none is stronger than his discrediting of art as a source of truth. For one thing, artists purport to a knowledge that they do not in fact possess and base their productions on unreliable opinion; a poet might successfully mimic the speech of a doctor without having any of the doctor's skills. Worse still, poets can beguile their readers, through the charm of their verse, into ascribing to them an authority that they have not earned. Plato recognized the seductive power of art and had much to say in its favor but on balance tended to stress its dangers over its benefits. In depicting the poets as irrational (even mildly insane), as lacking true knowledge of their subject matter, as mere "imitators" (in a largely negative sense), as pursuing pleasure before truth, as producers of potentially harmful effects, and therefore in need of censorship (ibid., book II; *Laws*, 801), he laid the foundations for a line of thought about art that has proved remarkably resilient. [*See* Plato.]

Aristotle's response to Plato comes in his *Poetics*, where he deals specifically with the genre of tragedy. He agrees with Plato that art must be defined as a type of mimesis, but he extends the possible objects of mimesis: the poet, like the painter, can imitate "one of three things, that is, what was or is, what is commonly said and thought to be the case, and what ought to be the case" (*Poetics*, 1972, 1460b). Aristotle emphasized the natural propensity of humans to take pleasure in imitations. In rejecting Plato's metaphysics of Forms and locating universals (the proper objects of knowledge) in particulars *(in re)* rather than in some ultimate reality of their own *(ante res)*, he was not committed to the idea of art as an "imitation of an imitation" and was able to accord to poetry an epistemically respectable place between philosophy and history: "poetry is at once more like philosophy and more worthwhile than history, since poetry tends to make general statements, while those of history are particular" (ibid., 1451b). Far from denigrating poetry as a source of truth, he even identified, at least in the case of tragedy, the nature of the truths it can impart: "the poet's function is to describe, not the thing that has happened, but a kind of thing that might happen" (ibid.). In tragedy, the principal object of imitation is human action (not character), and the way the plot is structured, with its own internal necessity, is of paramount importance in yielding both the cognitive and the emotional (cathartic) payoff that gives tragedy its unique artistic value.

In his response to Plato, then, Aristotle does not question the basic premise that it is a function of art to tell the truth or to "imitate" reality and that failure to do so makes art morally objectionable. But he meets Plato's worries about the poet's merely simulated knowledge by locating the dramatist's distinctive contribution not in the recounting of particulars but in the revelation of deeper universal principles. As for the poet's use of artifice, this is no longer seen as serving mere trickery or beguiling illusion but as part of the craft of constructing a convincing plot from which the universal truths can emerge. [*See* Aristotle.]

The notion, broadly conceived, of a mimetic function (and value) of art came to provide a basis for the discussion of truth in art for nearly two millennia, even though conceptions of the appropriate objects of imitation and the realities against which art was matched shifted radically. It is only with the Romantic period in Europe in the mid- and late eighteenth century that truth in the ordinary, cognitive sense came to be challenged as irrelevant to the nature and function of art.

Both Plato and Aristotle are concerned with the philosophical (or moral) rather than the historical (or factual) truth of art. It is indeed arguable that classical comments on art put a higher premium on verisimilitude or lifelikeness than on historical accuracy. In summarizing debates about the Arts in classical Greece, Plutarch (c.46–after 119 CE) says about Simonides (c.556–c.468? BCE) that he held that though painting and poetry (and in poetry he includes history) "differ in material and manner of imitation," they both have the same goal: the best historian "is he who brings his narrative to life like a picture with emotions and personalities"; and, continues Plutarch, the Greeks also held that "poetry owed its charm and honour to its power to express things in a lifelike way: as Homer says [*Odyssey*, 19.203], 'she spoke many lies, resembling truth'" (*Moralia*, 1972, 346^f ff.). The concern for verisimilitude also emerges in Aristotle's much-quoted dictum that "one ought to prefer likely impossibilities to unconvincing possibilities" (1972, 1460a). These remarks illustrate not only that the question of the verisimilitude of a work of art is different from that of its (literal) truth, but that it was commonly accepted through the classical period that historical truth and accuracy had lower priority than verisimilitude. The function of poetry, the art in which the question of truth has always arisen in its most acute form, was, in Horace's (65–8 BCE) words, held to be "to do good or to give pleasure—or, thirdly, to say things which are both pleasing and serviceable for life" (*Ars poetica*, 1972, pp. 333–334). Both poetry and history had the rhetorical function to edify or amuse, and it did not then matter whether the tale was literally true or not.

The Late-Classical and Medieval Period. Throughout the classical period, there was a continuous concern with verisimilitude in sculpture and painting. A great deal of virtuosity is displayed in rendering sculpturally the peculiar individuality and specific look of a subject, something commented on by Pliny (23–79 CE) in his *Natural History* (xxxv, 88). Pliny also gives an account of the development of the technique of painting from a simple beginning to something like full realism (ibid., xxxv, 56–62). There is, however, little sustained discussion of the issue of truth in aesthetics between the seminal writings of Plato and Aristotle and that of the Neoplatonist Plotinus (204–270 CE). In *Ars poetica*, Horace offered some fleeting contributions, but although his views are often quoted, out of context, they remain undeveloped. Sextus Empiricus (second century CE) used his general skepticism to question whether poetry contains truth *(Against the Grammarians)*.

What is notable about Plotinus is that although he adopted many of the metaphysical precepts of Plato, he more or less reversed the position that Plato assigns to art in the levels of cognition. Although the beauty of art (actual art objects) falls well short of the eternal Beauty (the essential Form, for Plotinus, identical with the Good), recognition of this worldly beauty is nevertheless a path to knowledge of the higher form. In a clear reference to, and repudiation of, Plato, he writes in *The Enneads:*

> Still the arts are not to be slighted on the ground that they create by imitation of natural objects; for, to begin with, these natural objects are themselves imitations; then we must recognize that they give no bare reproduction of the thing seen but go back to the Ideas from which Nature derives, and, furthermore, that much of their work is all their own; they are holders of beauty and add where nature is lacking. Thus Pheidias wrought the Zeus upon no model among things of sense but by apprehending what form Zeus must take if he chose to become manifest to sight. (1956, v.8.1, "On Intellectual Beauty")

Far from being restricted to imitating objects in the natural world, the artist, like the philosopher, can justly aspire to revealing truths at a higher plane.

In the early development of Christianity, the influence of Plato was strong, including his own ambivalence toward art and poetry. Classical literature was tolerated only to the extent that it could be useful in education, but drama was viewed—for example, by Saint Augustine (354–430 CE)—as morally suspect. Augustine observes that although poetry is often "full of lies," it nevertheless has "the aim . . . to delight rather than to deceive" (*Soliloquies,* II, ix, 16). By addressing the question of fiction and (in the case of stories and poems) replacing imitation with invention, he takes a significant step on from classical mimetic theories.

Perhaps a bigger step still comes in the theory of scriptural interpretation. Augustine (in *De doctrina christiana*) had discussed how to penetrate the obscure passages in Scripture to reveal their spiritual truth, but it was John Cassian (360–435) who postulated four levels of scriptural meaning—the literal, allegorical, tropological, and analogical—a distinction that was to become standard throughout the Middle Ages. The distinction allowed for the uncovering of otherwise unnoticed symbolic meanings (and thus truths) in the Bible, but it soon became connected to a wider metaphysical doctrine that the world itself was replete with symbolic meaning, natural objects doubling as things *(res)* and signs *(signa),* which could be "read" like a book. The development of allegorical literature, such as the *Divine Comedy, The Faerie Queen,* and *Pilgrim's Progress,* springs from the same intellectual sources. Truth was present in art, as in nature, but had to be elicited through interpretation. A parallel movement in pictorial representation led to increasingly arcane uses of Christian iconography to the point where the blending of Christian and pagan mythological figures in Baroque art makes the meanings virtually irrecoverable except to the cognoscenti. Nevertheless, medieval didactic art—morality plays, the frescoes of Giotto—whose function was to convey the revealed truths of Christian doctrine is often perfectly accessible.

The Renaissance. For all the flourishing of creative activity that occurred in the fifteenth and sixteenth centuries, especially in Italy, there is not a great deal of advance in the debate about art and truth. Leon Battista Alberti (1409–1472) conceived of a painting as a "window through which we look out into a section of the visible world" and insists, in a typically empiricist and nominalist manner, that "the painter has nothing to do with things that are not visible" (1956). The representational nature of painting and the need for verisimilitude are taken for granted. There is also an emphasis on painting as a species of natural philosophy, however, embodying general knowledge about the human form, the laws of nature, and mathematics. In his *Treatise on Painting,* Leonardo da Vinci (1452–1519) explicitly sought to incorporate painting into natural science, a view that led him to elevate painting above poetry, insisting that the former "represents the forms of nature's works with more truth than does the poet" (1956).

The spirit of Plato lived on in Puritan attacks on poetry and drama (e.g., Stephen Gosson's *School of Abuse,* 1571). The most notable, though by no means unique, "defense of poetry" is that of Sir Philip Sidney (1554–1586), whose *A Defence of Poetry* (1579/80) encapsulates the characteristic anti-Platonic (neo-Aristotelian) line in the Renaissance. The poet reveals the universal by combining the philosophical (teaching by precept) and the particular (teaching by example), but even where dealing with historical fact rather than "invention," the poet "nothing affirms, and therefore never lieth." Poetry in its productions "bodies forth" "in effect another nature," but the principles that govern this production are the same rational principles of probability and necessity that govern nature itself. Sidney thus retains the mimetic view of poetry, allied to the Horatian formula that its aim is to "teach and delight." The truths that poetry tells are not historical truths but truths about how things ideally should be: "[nature's] world is brazen, the poets only deliver a golden."

The Neoclassical Period. The seventeenth century saw a rapid growth in the prestige and spread of science as well as a new emphasis on reason as the source and guarantee of the validity of all human knowledge. Science was concerned with the exploration of nature, whereas reason guaranteed the validity of the mind's outlook on nature. Conceptions of art were developed that emphasized the importance of reason. "Love reason then," Nicolas Boileau (1636–1711) insists, "and let whate'er you Write / Borrow from her its Beauty, Force, and Light" (*Ars poetica* [1674], canto 1, lines 37–38). The goal of art was to imitate nature correctly, as Pope (1688–1744) wrote in *An Essay on Criticism* (1711):

> First follow NATURE, and your Judgement frame
> By her just Standard, which is still the same:
> *Unerring Nature,* still divinely bright,
> One *clear, unchang'd,* and *Universal* Light,

> Life, Force, and Beauty, must to all impart,
> At once the *Source,* and *End,* and *Test of Art.*
>> (1961, lines 68–73)

The view that nature, properly understood, is the standard against which art is measured is found equally in theories about painting. "Have recourse to nature herself," says Joshua Reynolds (1723–1792), "who is always at hand, and in comparison of whose true splendour, the best coloured pictures are but faint and feeble" (1852, vol. 1, p. 320). Art is not merely an imitation of nature as casually perceived, however, but of universal nature:

> There is an absolute necessity for the painter to generalize his notion; to paint particulars is not to paint nature, it is only to paint circumstances. When the artist has conceived in his imagination the image of perfect beauty, or the abstract idea of forms, he may be said to be admitted to the great council of Nature.
>> (Ibid., vol. 2, p. 257)

Similar remarks abound in the writings of the literary critics of the period, perhaps the most famous being Johnson's (1709–1784) remark in *Rasselas* (1759) that "The business of the poet is to examine, not the individual, but the species; to remark general properties and large appearances; he does not number the streaks of the tulip, or describe the different shades of verdure of the forest" (1990); or his remark in his "Preface to Shakespeare" (1765) that "Nothing can please many, and please long, but just representations of general nature" (1968). For the neoclassical theorist, then, the highest aim of art is to exhibit those eternally valid truths that the rational mind discloses, and to do so with the clarity, simplicity, and moral seriousness that was thought to be the mark of a classical golden age.

The development of science, however, also pointed in another direction, which in philosophy manifested itself in empiricism, in particular in Britain. In scientific reports, it was important to get the facts right and empiricist philosophy insisted on the importance of particular sense impressions as the building blocks of knowledge. In the arts, this empirical emphasis showed itself in an insistence on close observation and lifelike detail. In literature, it provided part of the background that made possible the development of the novel, with what Ian Watt (1957) has called its formal realism. In early novelists such as Henry Fielding (1707–1754) and Samuel Richardson (1689–1761), there is a marked concern with verisimilitude grounded in accuracy of observation and knowledge of the world. "First then," says Fielding in chapter 1, book 8 of *Tom Jones,* "I think it may be very reasonably required of every writer, that he keeps within the bounds of possibility. . . . Nor is possibility alone sufficient to justify us, we must keep likewise within the rules of probability." Richardson, too, in the "Preface" and "Postscript" to *Clarissa* (1747–1748), defends his portrayal of the character of Clarissa as well as his technique (the epistolary form and the amount of minute, circumstantial detail) in terms of the probable and the lifelike.

The Romantic Period. Until the last quarter of the eighteenth century, the notion of artistic truth was nearly always closely bound up with prevailing notions of philosophical or scientific truth. In the most general terms, artistic truth was taken to consist in some sort of "imitation" or reproduction of an external reality (however conceived), and the debate about truth in art was a debate about how far, if at all, art could successfully present important truths about such a reality. With the change in the intellectual climate toward the end of the century, however, which saw the breakdown of the Enlightenment confidence in reason and the increased emphasis on the irrational and passionate side of man's nature, views on the aspirations of art, and consequently on artistic truth itself, underwent a radical change. What became paramount was not, as for the neoclassicists, the studied delineation of a rationally ordered world but the artist's own sensibility, an inner world of intense, sometimes disorderly, feelings.

Art came to be seen as the expression of these feelings; as the poet Charles Baudelaire (1821–1867) remarked later, "Romanticism is precisely located neither in choice of subject nor in exact truth, but in a way of feeling." Art was both caused by emotion and affected its audience emotionally, and the value of art was seen as in a large part bound up with its emotive origins and impact. The emotions that were essentially linked to art, however, were also a source of knowledge. Poets and painters were thought to possess a special gift, a sort of emotional intuition, which enabled them to participate feelingly not only in the inner life of other human beings, but in the inner life of the world itself. As Wordsworth (1770–1850) says in the "Preface" to the 1802 edition of *Lyrical Ballads:*

> It will be the wish of the Poet to bring his feelings near to those of the persons whose feelings he describes, nay, for short spaces of time perhaps, to identify his own feelings with theirs; [the] object [of poetry] is truth, not individual and local, but general, and operative; not standing upon external testimony, but carried alive into the heart by passion; truth which is its own testimony.

Reason being discredited, the key faculty for the artist became imagination, which came to be seen as a mode of thought seizing directly on deep, mysterious truths involving man's sentience, which reason could not reach: artistic truth became imaginative truth.

This new role for the imagination required a new conception of imagination itself. Coleridge (1772–1834) distinguished between imagination and fancy, the *primary* imagination being "the living Power and Prime Agent of all human Perception," the *secondary* imagination being "an echo of the former" but a faculty that can be exercised at will in artistic creation: "It dissolves, diffuses, dissipates, in order to recreate; or where this process is rendered impossible, yet still at all events it struggles to idealize and to unify." The fancy, on the other hand, was what had heretofore been called imagination, having "no counters to play with, but fixities and definites," and being "no other than a mode of Memory emancipated from the order of time and space" (1983, chap. 13). Imagination affects, in the words of William Hazlitt (1778–1830), "the intuitive perception of the hidden analogies of things" and is "what stamps the character of genius on the productions of art more than any other circumstance: for it works unconsciously, like nature" ("On the English Novelists" [1819], in *Works*, 1967, vol. 6, p. 109). Similar views of the role of the imagination were developed on the Continent by theorists such as Joseph Joubert (1754–1824) ("Imagination is the faculty of making sensuous what is intellectual, of making corporeal what is spirit: in a word, of bringing to light, without depriving it of its nature, that which in itself is invisible" [*Les Carnets* (1938 ed.), vol. 2, p. 493]) and poets and artists such as Baudelaire: "Imagination is, as it were, a divine faculty, which perceives directly, without the use of philosophical methods, the secret and intimate relationships of things, their correspondences and analogies" (Introduction to his translation of Edgar Allan Poe, *Nouvelles histoires extraordinaires* [1857], *Œuvres complètes*, vol. 7 [1933], p. xv).

For all the grand claims made on its behalf, the Romantic conception of imaginative truth is deeply problematic. Because imaginative truth is essentially subjective—literally the product of one subject's felt response to the world—the line between truth and falsehood must itself rest on subjective criteria, for example, that which "rings true" or is "true to" another individual's own response. This means that only like-minded people will recognize each other's truths. Yet, if imaginative truth contrasts so strongly with more familiar notions of truth, in science and common sense, which at least aspire to objectivity (so important for Enlightenment thought), then it is not clear that "truth" is being used univocally; nor is it clear in what sense imaginative truth could be "deeper" or more important than scientific truth. These have been recurring problems for all attempts to shore up the otherwise attractive conception of imaginative truth that has been an enduring legacy of Romanticism. [*See* Romanticism.]

It is significant that the two towering figures of philosophical aesthetics in this period, Immanuel Kant (1724–1804) and Georg Wilhelm Friedrich Hegel (1770–1831), took quite different views on the truth debate. For Kant, who stressed the beauty of nature over art, who played down the cognitive elements in aesthetic appreciation, and was a key architect of Romantic conceptions of genius and the sublime, the question of truth in art held little interest. For Hegel, on the other hand, the truth issue was central, but his approach to it was eccentric. Art occupied a key role in Hegel's elaborate Idealist philosophy, being, along with religion and philosophy, one of the three modes of apprehension of the Absolute Idea. The basic aim or "vocation" of art is "to unveil the *truth* in the form of sensuous artistic configuration" (1975, vol. 1, p. 55). Hegel emphasized the historical development of art and the changing relations between the spiritual and the material: in Symbolic art, the spiritual Idea is overwhelmed by the material medium; in classical art, the two are perfectly in harmony; in Romantic art, the Idea dominates the sensuous. This in turn allows Hegel to propose a hierarchy of the arts: architecture is supreme in Symbolic art, sculpture in classical art, and poetry (ahead of painting and music) represents, in Romantic art, the final stage of freedom from the material. Nowhere is it plainer than in Hegel's philosophy how the truth debate in aesthetics hinges on a wider metaphysical context. [*See* Kant *and* Hegel.]

Later Nineteenth-Century Developments. Another leading conception in the nineteenth-century truth-in-art debate after the Romantic period was that of Realism, although the idea was developed more by artists themselves than by philosophers, who remained mostly under the spell of Idealism and Romanticism. The term *réalisme* first appeared in print in 1826 *(Le Mercure français du XIXᵉ siècle)* and was immediately associated with truth ("la littérature du vrai"). At a superficial level, the guiding notion once again was that of verisimilitude, but there were more interesting currents at a deeper level. One was the continuing influence of experimental science. For Zola (1840–1902), a leading exponent of the doctrine (though he preferred the term *naturalism*), "the novelist is equally an observer and an experimentalist . . . the naturalistic novel . . . [being] . . . a real experiment that a novelist makes on man by the help of observation" (1894). Gustave Flaubert had spoken of "the precision of the physical sciences" and the "pitiless method" of his novels (1857; *Correspondance IV*), and earlier still, Balzac identified the need to "study the causes or central cause of . . . social facts, and discover the meaning hidden in [them]" ("Preface" to *La comédie humaine*, 1846). In painting too the same language was being deployed; John Constable (1776–1837), in his fourth lecture to the Royal Institution (1836), described painting as "a branch of natural philosophy, of which pictures are but the experiments."

In contrast to the Romantic view, the pursuit of truth for the Realists was conceived in terms of scientific objectivity and fidelity to fact. The means adopted in this pursuit took various forms. There was a preference (not universally adhered to) for a subject matter representing lowlier aspects of life, the gritty struggles of ordinary people, rather than the idealized (and exotic) lives of romantic heroes. In novels, characters were drawn in highly particularized detail set in a real-life background; conventional plots were replaced by individualized stories displaying a finely meshed causal and temporal nexus; and the narrative language lacked undue ornament or embellishment. The overall (desired) effect—

in the service of truth—was to make the narrative more like reportage, concealing the art (or artifice) in the name of "scientific" neutrality. What is evident in the development of Realism as an aesthetic conception is the markedly different emphases given to these various aspects: Realism being associated sometimes with a strong scientific view of truth, sometimes with mere verisimilitude; as primarily a feature of subject matter or just as a mode of writing; as a mirror held up to society or as a tool for deeper explanation.

It is interesting to note that, as an aesthetic doctrine, Realism declined in France just as the new social sciences were being established. It is arguable that this decline was partly the result of the recognition that the social sciences performed much better at the task the Realists had set themselves. What is notable is that although the strong cognitive claim for Realism—that realistic art afforded a special neo-scientific access to (social) truth—was abandoned or modified, the Realist mode of writing (and, indeed, painting) survived into the twentieth century, even if for a time it was overshadowed by modernism. Realism did not need the strong claim to truth, nor, as we shall see, did the claim to truth need realism.

In the twentieth century, the debate about realism (and truth) took different forms. Within Marxist aesthetics, for example, the idea of "Socialist Realism" was used both as a theoretical weapon against modernism and as a renewed attempt to identify a truth role for art. György Lukács (1885–1971), a Marxist theoretician who helped refine the notion of realism, admired the literary form of the nineteenth-century Realist novel but rejected what he called the "pseudo-objectivity" of the "mechanical imitation of life" ("Art and Objective Truth," 1965), preferring the "partisanship of objectivity," which drew on, and revealed, deeper processes of historical change. Another Marxist, Bertolt Brecht (1898–1956), in "The Popular and the Realistic" (1958), sought a conception of realism "broad and political, free from aesthetic restrictions and independent of convention," but nevertheless one with a cognitive function, "laying bare society's causal network / showing up the dominant viewpoint as the viewpoint of the dominators" (1964). He rejected the constraint of verisimilitude (in effect disagreeing with Lukács) and famously advocated in the theater the "alienation effect" *(Verfremdung)*, thereby breaking down the illusion of reality and the tendency of audiences to empathize with the characters. Theodor W. Adorno (1903–1969) took a similar view, yet had no hesitation in speaking, in an unqualified way, of "truth" in art; he championed (e.g., in *Aesthetic Theory*) the most austere modernist art against all forms of popular culture on the grounds that the latter colluded with prevailing ideologies, whereas the former could give a truthful, if "negative," image of the fragmented and alienated condition of bourgeois society. For these latter theorists, the notions of realism, truth, and verisimilitude are pulled apart altogether. [*See* Realism.]

There are tendencies in this direction from other quarters as well. Nelson Goodman (b.1906) has argued (1976) that realism need not imply verisimilitude, claiming that realistic depiction is fundamentally a matter of convention; what seems realistic is a function only of how familiar is the system of representation used. Roland Barthes (1915–1980), who (unlike Goodman) denied any representational function in narrative ("Introduction to the Structural Analysis of Narrative," 1966), described realism as simply "a reality effect" ("The Reality Effect," 1967). It should be emphasized, though, that the relation between realism and verisimilitude, like that of representation and resemblance, is still a matter of contention among aestheticians, even if the strong claims of the early French theorists probably have few remaining supporters.

Another later nineteenth-century development was the art-for-art's-sake movement, which grew up alongside, although in opposition to, that of French Realism. Like Romanticism, it involved a sharp repudiation of the classical mimetic theory. The phrase *l'art pour l'art* was first popularized by Théophile Gautier (1811–1872) in the preface to *Mademoiselle de Maupin* (1834). Oscar Wilde's (1854–1900) often-quoted paradox that "Life imitates art far more than Art imitates Life" nicely pokes fun at centuries of orthodoxy about mimesis, as does his view that "the more we study Art, the less we care for Nature" (both in "The Decay of Lying," 1891). In fact, the ideas can be traced back to the Kantian aesthetics of disinterestedness and Friedrich von Schiller's conception of art as "play"; they also anticipate formalist developments in the twentieth century. The aestheticist movement emphasized the autonomy of art, conceived sometimes in terms of the social isolation of the artist, sometimes, more philosophically, in terms of the intrinsic value of aesthetic experience and the subjection of art to its own law-governed sphere. A. C. Bradley (1851–1935) wrote of poetry that it is "not a part, nor yet a copy, of the real world . . . but . . . a world by itself, independent, complete, autonomous," though he qualifies this by speaking of a "connection underground" between "life and poetry" ("Poetry for Poetry's Sake," 1909). Aestheticism broke not only with mimetic theories, but also with moralistic theories. Clive Bell's (1881–1964) assertion that "Once we have judged a thing a work of art, we have judged it ethically of the first importance and put it beyond the reach of the moralist" (1914) is not far removed from Wilde's aestheticist's epigram that "There is no such thing as a moral or an immoral book. Books are well written, or badly written. That is all" (*The Picture of Dorian Gray*, 1891). [*See* Aestheticism.]

Twentieth-Century Developments. Descendants of the Romantics, the art-for-art's-sake movement, and the cognitive Realists have manifested themselves in diverse strands of the twentieth-century truth-in-art debate. Formalists, autonomists, and structuralists, on the one hand, as well as those who adopt wider skeptical attitudes to truth itself, take a broadly "antitruth" stance, while realists, Marxists, and certain metaphysicians and moral philosophers, on the other, form the "pro-truth" camp.

The truth idiom is prominent, for example, in Martin Heidegger's (1889–1976) aesthetics in accord with his sense of truth as "unconcealment." Art can uncover the "hiddenness" of being. In Heidegger's famous discussion of Vincent van Gogh's painting of what Heidegger takes to be peasant shoes, he argues that the painting, through revealing facets of the peasant's work, "has shown us what shoes are in truth" (1964). Jean-Paul Sartre's (1905–1980) existentialist philosophy stressed the freedom of artistic creation and the use of imagination to disclose the world, but in a more political vein he encouraged the idea of "la littérature engagée" (*What Is Literature?* 1948) whereby writers could not shirk political commitment in the name of artistic autonomy. [*See* Heidegger *and* Sartre.]

The dominant and most vocal form of antitruth theories in the twentieth century have been structuralism and its descendants, poststructuralism and postmodernism. Four antecedents (at least) helped shape this complex of ideas. First, there is Friedrich Nietzsche's (1844–1900) view that there are "no facts only interpretations" a view he dubbed "Perspectivism" (*The Will to Power*, 1901); the rejection of absolute or universal truth is a central tenet of poststructuralism. Second, there is the general Marxist doctrine that the significance of art lies as much in what it conceals—its ideology, the conditions of its production—as in what it overtly displays. Third, there is the antihumanist attack on the autonomous self or subject, drawing on (but going far beyond) the work of Sigmund Freud (1856–1939). Fourth, there is the crucial influence of Ferdinand de Saussure (1857–1913), whose *Cours de linguistique générale* (1916) was interpreted as claiming that language (into which human beings are born) does not mirror reality but helps constitute reality.

For structuralists, all cultural phenomena, including works of art, are products of "systems of signification" whose signs acquire sense through their internal relationships rather than their relations with an external reality. Such phenomena are viewed essentially as "texts" constituted in much the same way as linguistic texts. The sentence analogy is imposed on all sign systems, including painting, architecture, sculpture, or film, whose general meaning properties are taken to be conventional and "arbitrary" on the pattern of the linguistic sign in Saussure's theory. This view is often thought to be encapsulated in the slogan, lifted from Jacques Derrida's (b.1930) *De la grammatologie* (1969), "Il n'y a pas de hors-texte" (p. 227) (deliberately ambiguous between "There is nothing outside the text" and "There is no outside text," that is, no ultimate urtext or master text that can be used as a point of reference for truth). On the issue of art and truth, this can only imply a strong "antitruth" stance. What is rejected are not only all forms of mimesis (there is nothing for art to imitate, and even verisimilitude is a mere "reality effect"), but also the Romantic notion of an expressive (authorial) self, which is seen as one more social construct. At best, works of art are deemed to be self-referential, tracking their own history of production and the sign systems in which they are embedded. Poststructuralism goes further, emphasizing the inherent instability of all sign systems, suggesting that determinate meaning (not to speak of truth) is permanently undermined in every text. The traditional ascendancy of philosophy over literature is reversed, as the latter, through foregrounding its rhetorical tropes and fictionality, is judged to be less "deluded" than the former, which still strives vainly for universal truth and rational argument. Poststructuralists also have little use for the concept of "art" itself; the concept embodies too many humanist assumptions that they reject, as well as a value system that they see as ungrounded. [*See* Structuralism *and* Poststructuralism.]

Postmodernism, both as a body of theory and as an art practice, owes much to certain strands of poststructuralism. Characteristically, postmodernist theory rejects, as based on spurious "metanarratives" (Lyotard, 1984), any intellectual enterprise—that of aesthetics par excellence—that aspires to universal application; the very concepts of truth, meaning, value, reality, and reason, which have been thought to provide foundations for theorizing, are radically relativized or dismissed as repressive and authoritarian. Postmodernist artists also self-consciously turn against the aesthetic; their principal mode is ironic self-reflection, delighting in the ephemeral and the fragmented, denouncing the false reverence of the art gallery or the museum, rejecting the distinction between "high art" and "popular art," and, above all, mocking the higher aspirations of art in terms of truth, self-expression, or morality. Curiously, one of the more outlandish postmodernists, Jean Baudrillard, has come to see reality itself as a kind of simulacrum or simulation ("the cinema and TV are America's reality" [Baudrillard, 1988, p. 104]), suggesting the ultimate collapse of the distinction between art and the world. [*See* Postmodernism.]

Within analytic aesthetics, the truth debate has largely been focused on the logical peculiarities of fiction, but opinions remain divided for and against artistic truth. Early in this strand of the debate, I. A. Richards (1893–1979) had proposed a sharp distinction between two "functions of language," the "referential" and the "emotive," identifying science broadly with the former and poetry with the latter (1923, chap. 7). In his *Principles of Literary Criticism* (1924), he insists that the "scientific sense" of "truth" is "little involved by any of the arts" and that within criticism "truth" is most commonly used to mean "acceptability" and "sincerity" (1926, pp. 212–213). He speaks of the "pseudostatements" of poetry. Although the notion of "emotive" meaning largely ran out of steam with the demise of logical positivism, the idea that the language of fiction fulfills a special, nonreferential, function has had wide support. The idea, as a logical thesis, probably originated with Gottlob Frege (1848–1925), who had written in his essay "On Sense and Reference" (1892) that, in the case of poetry (i.e., fiction), "the question of truth would cause us to abandon aesthetic delight for the attitude of scientific investigation. Hence it is a matter of no concern to us whether the name 'Odysseus', for instance, has reference, so long as we accept the poem as a work of art" (1980). Many logicians, and in turn logically minded aestheticians, came to think of poetic or fictional language as lacking truth-value (a view anticipated perhaps by Sidney, as quoted earlier); a stronger view still, though less influential, deriving from Bertrand Russell's theory of names, sees fictional sentences as simply false.

For many, though, it is far from clear that such logical theses imply the cognitive inertness of all fictional literature (and, by analogy, other representational arts). On this issue, a vigorous debate has been pursued. The proponents of truth have moved in two directions, either relocating the truths of fiction or seeking different conceptions of truth. On the former, it is pointed out that although works of fiction do contain sentences describing fictional states of affairs that cannot literally be true, they also contain, explicitly and implicitly, propositions that make a legitimate claim to truth: these are generalizations found in fictional texts (King Lear's "As flies to wanton boys, are we to th'Gods; / They kill us for their sport") or implied truth claims elicited by readers ("Even Kings are mere mortals," identified as a theme of Shakespeare's history plays). The crucial step in the pro-truth argument is not that these propositions are genuine truth-bearers, which can be readily conceded, but that their truth is relevant to the aesthetic value and interest of the works. The latter is hotly disputed: Morris Weitz (1955), John Hospers (1946, 1960–1961), Francis Sparshott (1967), R. K. Elliott (1966–1967), D. H. Mellor (1968), and Richard Miller (1979) have argued in favor, while Arnold Isenberg (1954–1955), Joseph Margolis (1965), Mary Sirridge (1974–1975), Peter Lamarque and Stein Haugom Olsen (1994) have argued against. The case against often rests on emphasizing the distinctive ("institutional" or aesthetic) nature of literary works (including the generalized propositions in or derived from them) and the dangers of assimilating them to other (truth-centered) modes of discourse.

A different strategy on the pro-truth side involves loosening the connection between truth and propositions. The notions of "truth to" (Hospers, 1946) or of truth as "authenticity" (Dorothy Walsh, 1969) or of "knowing how" (David Novitz, 1987) or "knowing what it is like" (Walsh, 1969) in contrast to "knowing that" are sometimes proposed. Iris Murdoch has sought to explain the "truth" of great works of art in terms of their "vision" as against the propositions they express (Murdoch, 1970, 1992, 1997). Other philoso-

phers (e.g., Martha Nussbaum, 1990) have tried to assimilate literary works into moral philosophy. The objection to such moves is that they either deploy a weakened and unexplained notion of truth or that they lose sight of the unique contribution of literature.

One thing is clear, namely, that merely investigating the logic of fictional sentences is not sufficient to resolve the deeper, more long-standing issues about literary truth. It should be noted that there is a conception of "truth in fiction" that is not to be confused with this wider issue: the idea of truth "within a fictional world," whereby a distinction is drawn between, say, the truth of "Sherlock Holmes is a detective" and the falsity of "Sherlock Holmes took up ballet dancing." This distinction between truth and falsity is drawn within the parameters of the fictional context. There is extensive debate as to how best to explicate this notion: in terms of "possible worlds" (David Lewis, 1978) or speech act theory (John Searle, 1979) or even to play down the significance altogether (Richard Rorty, 1982).

The deeper questions about literature and art in relation to truth are not amenable to any simple categorizations in logic. Among other things, they go to the heart of what counts as, and might be the benefits of, a liberal humanist education. As intellectual and philosophical fashions come and go, it is unlikely that this debate will find any determinate and uncontested resolution.

[*See also* Alienation, Aesthetic; Epistemology and Aesthetics; *and* Fiction.]

BIBLIOGRAPHY

Alberti, Leon Battista. *On Painting.* Translated by John R. Spencer. New Haven, 1956.

Aristotle. *Poetics.* Translated by M. E. Hubbard. In *Ancient Literary Criticism: The Principal Texts in New Translations,* edited by D. A. Russell and M. Winterbottom. Oxford, 1972.

Auerbach, Erich. *Mimesis: The Representation of Reality in Western Literature.* Translated by Willard R. Trask. Princeton, N.J., 1953.

Augustine. *De doctrina christiana.* Translated by Thérèse Sullivan. Washington, D.C., 1930.

Barthes, Roland. "From Work to Text." In *Textual Strategies: Perspectives in Post-Structural Criticism,* edited by Josué V. Harari. Ithaca, N.Y., 1979.

Barthes, Roland. "The Reality Effect" (1967). In *The Rustle of Language,* translated by Richard Howard New York. 1986.

Baudrillard, Jean. *America.* Translated by Chris Turner. London and New York, 1988.

Beardsley, Monroe C. *Aesthetics from Classical Greece to the Present: A Short History.* New York, 1966.

Beardsley, Monroe C. *Aesthetics: Problems in the Philosophy of Criticism.* 2d ed. Indianapolis, 1981.

Bell, Clive. *Art.* London, 1914.

Bradley, A. C. "Poetry for Poetry's Sake" (1909). In *Oxford Lectures on Poetry* (1909). Reprint, London, 1965.

Brecht, Bertolt. "The Popular and the Realistic" (1958). In *Brecht on Theatre: The Development of an Aesthetic,* edited and translated by John Willet. New York, 1964.

Coleridge, Samuel Taylor. *The Collected Works of Samuel Taylor Coleridge,* vol. 7. 1–2. *Biographia Literaria; or, Biographical Sketches of*

My Literary Life and Opinions, edited by James Engell and W. Jackson Bate. Princeton, N.J., 1983.

Culler, Jonathan. *Structuralist Poetics: Structuralism, Linguistics, and the Study of Literature.* Ithaca, N.Y., 1975.

Culler, Jonathan. *On Deconstruction: Theory and Criticism after Structuralism.* Ithaca, N.Y., 1982.

Derrida, Jacques. *Of Grammatology* (1969). Translated by Gayatri Chakravarty Spivak. Baltimore, 1976.

Elliott, R. K. "Poetry and Truth." *Analysis* 27 (1966–1967): 77–85.

Falck, Colin. *Myth, Truth, and Literature: Towards a True Post-Modernism.* Cambridge and New York, 1989.

Frege, Gottlob. "On Sense and Reference." In *Translations from the Philosophical Writings of Gottlob Frege,* 3d ed., edited by Peter Geach and Max Black. Oxford, 1978.

Goodman, Nelson. *The Languages of Art: An Approach to a Theory of Symbols.* 2d ed. Indianapolis, 1976.

Hart, H. L. A. "A Logician's Fairy Tale." *Philosophical Review* 60 (1951): 198–212.

Hegel, G. W. F. *Aesthetics: Lectures on Fine Art.* 2 vols. Translated by T. M. Knox. Oxford, 1975.

Heidegger, Martin. "The Origin of the Work of Art." In *Philosophies of Art and Beauty,* edited by Albert Hofstadter and Richard Kuhns. New York, 1964.

Horace. *Ars poetica.* Translated by D. A. Russell. In *Ancient Literary Criticism: The Principal Texts in New Translations,* edited by D. A. Russell and M. Winterbottom. Oxford, 1972.

Hospers, John. *Meaning and Truth in the Arts.* Chapel Hill, N.C., 1946.

Hospers, John. "Literature and Human Nature." *Journal of Aesthetics and Art Criticism* 17 (1958–1959): 45–57.

Hospers, John. "Implied Truths in Literature." *Journal of Aesthetics and Art Criticism* 19 (1960–1961): 37–46.

Isenberg, Arnold. "The Problem of Belief." *Journal of Aesthetics and Art Criticism* 13 (1954–1955): 395–407.

Johnson, Samuel. *The Yale Edition of the Works of Samuel Johnson,* vols. 7–8, *Johnson on Shakespeare,* edited by Arthur Sherbo. New Haven, 1968.

Johnson, Samuel. *The Yale Edition of the Works of Samuel Johnson,* vol. 16, *Rasselas and Other Tales,* edited by Gwin J. Kolb. New Haven, 1990.

Lamarque, Peter. *Fictional Points of View.* Ithaca, N.Y., 1996.

Lamarque, Peter, and Stein Haugom Olsen. *Truth, Fiction, and Literature: A Philosophical Perspective.* Oxford and New York, 1994.

Leonardo da Vinci. *Treatise on Painting.* 2 vols. Translated by A. Philip McMahon. Princeton, N.J., 1956.

Lerner, Laurence. *The Truest Poetry: An Essay on the Question: What Is Literature?* London, 1960.

Lewis, David. "Truth in Fiction." *American Philosophical Quarterly* 15 (1978): 37–46.

Lukács, György. "Art and Objective Truth" (1965). In *Writer and Critic and Other Essays,* edited and translated by Arthur D. Kahn. London, 1970.

Lyotard, Jean-François. *The Postmodern Condition: A Report on Knowledge.* Translated by Geoff Bennington and Brian Massumi. Minneapolis, 1984.

Martin, Graham Dunstan. *Language, Truth, and Poetry: Notes towards a Philosophy of Literature.* Edinburgh, 1975.

McCormick, Peter J. *Fictions, Philosophies, and the Problems of Poetics.* Ithaca, N.Y., 1988.

Mellor, D. H. "On Literary Truth." *Ratio* 10.1 (1968): 150–168.

Miller, Richard W. "Truth in Beauty." *American Philosophical Quarterly* 16 (1979): 317–326.

Murdoch, Iris. *The Sovereignty of Good.* London, 1970.

Murdoch, Iris. *Metaphysics as a Guide to Morals.* London, 1992.

Murdoch, Iris. *Existentialists and Mystics: Writings on Philosophy and Literature.* Edited by Peter Conradi. London, 1997.

Nelson, William. *Fact or Fiction: The Dilemma of the Renaissance Storyteller.* Cambridge, Mass., 1973.

Newsom, Robert. *A Likely Story: Probability and Play in Fiction.* New Brunswick, N.J., 1988.

Nietzsche, Friedrich. *The Will to Power* (1901). Translated by Walter Kaufmann and R. J. Hollingdale, edited by Walter Kaufmann. New York, 1967.

Nussbaum, Martha C. *The Fragility of Goodness: Luck and Ethics in Greek Tragedy and Philosophy.* Cambridge and New York, 1986.

Nussbaum, Martha C. *Love's Knowledge: Essays on Philosophy and Literature.* New York and Oxford, 1990.

Nuttall, A. D. *A New Mimesis: Shakespeare and the Representation of Reality.* London and New York, 1983.

Plato. *Republic.* Translated by Francis MacDonald Cornford. Oxford, 1941.

Pliny. *The Elder Pliny's Chapters on the History of Art.* Translated by K. Jex-Blake, commentary by E. Sellers. London, 1896; reprint, Chicago, 1968.

Plotinus. *The Enneads.* 2d ed. Translated by Stephen McKenna, revised by B. S. Page. New York, 1956.

Plutarch. *Moralia.* Translated by D. A. Russell. In *Ancient Literary Criticism: The Principal Texts in New Translations,* edited by D. A. Russell and M. Winterbottom. Oxford, 1972.

Pope, Alexander. *The Poems of Alexander Pope: The Twickenham Edition,* vol. 1; *Pastoral Poetry and An Essay on Criticism,* edited by E. Audra and A. Williams. New Haven, 1961.

Reynolds, Joshua. *The Literary Works of Sir Joshua Reynolds.* 2 vols. London, 1852.

Richards, I. A. *Principles of Literary Criticism* (1924). 2d ed. London, 1926.

Richards, I. A., and C. K. Ogden. *The Meaning of Meaning.* London, 1923.

Rorty, Richard. "Is There a Problem about Fictional Discourse?" In *Consequences of Pragmatism: Essays, 1972–1980.* Minneapolis, 1982.

Sartre, Jean-Paul. *What Is Literature?* Translated by Bernard Frechtman. New York, 1965.

Saussure, Ferdinand de. *Course in General Linguistics* (1916). Edited by Charles Bally, Albert Sechehaye, with Albert Riedlinger, translated by Roy Harris. London, 1983; reprint, La Salle, Ill., 1986.

Searle, John R. "The Logical Status of Fictional Discourse." In *Expression and Meaning: Studies in the Theory of Speech Acts.* Cambridge and New York, 1979.

Sirridge, Mary J. "Truth from Fiction?" *Philosophy and Phenomenological Research* 35 (1974–1975): 453–471.

Sparshott, Francis E. "Truth in Fiction." *Journal of Aesthetics and Art Criticism* 26 (1967): 3–7.

Stern, J. P. *On Realism.* London and Boston, 1973.

Walsh, Dorothy. "The Cognitive Content of Art." *Philosophical Review* 52 (1943): 433–451.

Walsh, Dorothy. *Literature and Knowledge.* Middletown, Conn., 1969.

Walton, Kendall L. *Mimesis as Make-Believe: On the Foundations of the Representational Arts.* Cambridge, Mass., 1990.

Watt, Ian. *The Rise of the Novel: Studies in Defoe, Richardson, and Fielding.* Berkeley, 1957.

Weitz, Morris. *Philosophy of the Arts.* Cambridge, Mass., 1950.

Weitz, Morris. "Truth in Literature." *Revue Internationale de Philosophie* 9 (1955): 116–129.

Wilde, Oscar. "The Decay of Lying" (1891). In *The Works of Oscar Wilde,* new coll. ed., edited by G. F. Maine. London, 1948.

Zola, Émile. "The Experimental Novel." In *The Experimental Novel and Other Essays,* translated by Belle M. Sherman. New York, 1894.

PETER LAMARQUE and STEIN HAUGOM OLSEN

U

UGLINESS. The common conception that ugliness is simply the antonym of beauty, its polar opposite on the spectrum of aesthetic value, can easily obscure the subject's inherent subtlety and complexity—features that have made it both fascinating and perplexing to aesthetic theorists throughout the ages. Although there is no doubt an opposition between beauty and ugliness, it is an opposition that can be understood in a good many ways; and although beauty marks an extreme of aesthetic positivity, ugliness sometimes present itself in manifestations whose effects are not altogether negative. Philosophical reflection on the nature of aesthetic ugliness has centered on three issues: (1) the conceptual problem of providing a correct analysis of ugliness, particularly in its relation to beauty; (2) the ontological problem of determining whether ugliness exists (i.e., whether there are any things that truly *are* ugly) and, if it does, how it becomes engaged in aesthetic judgment; and (3) the critical problem of accounting for ugliness's salubrious effects both within and without the world of art.

The Analysis of Ugliness. It seems apparent that ugliness cannot be abstractly identified with some set of characteristics common and peculiar to all ugly objects. For one thing, the kinds of ugly objects and the ways in which they can be ugly are remarkably diverse; for another, ugliness is often supposed to consist less in features of things than in a form of reaction they call up. It might be thought that this reaction, an expression of serious aesthetic disfavor or disapproval, could itself serve as a defining characteristic of ugliness, except that there are arguably many instances of ugly objects—grotesques appearing in certain artworks, for instance—that, far from evoking disfavor or disapproval, seem to evoke something approaching their opposite. It is hardly surprising, therefore, that the consensus view throughout the history of debate on the concept has been that attempts to analyze ugliness in terms of this or that feature in things or in our reactions to things are destined to miss the mark unless they frame the analysis as an expression of the complementarity of these features or reactions to those of beauty. This is because, as nearly everyone agrees, the chief point of the standard deployment of this concept is to mark a pronounced contrast or distance between objects we call ugly and those we call beautiful. In ascribing ugliness to this thing or that, we are at the very least declaring it to be unbeautiful, or at odds with beauty (or perhaps very

unbeautiful, very much at odds with it). But in what way is this opposition to be understood? Quite different accounts of ugliness follow from different accounts of its way of contrasting with beauty, and controversies over these differences have proved especially heated and long-lived.

Four main camps have emerged from the debate. The first takes the view that ugliness is related to beauty as its absence, or privation, much as cold is simply the absence of heat. This view is rooted in Plato's treatment of the ugly as this or that detraction from the power of beauty—as what is less than fitting, inappropriate, or limited in practical value. Plato's point is extrapolated and given a moral-theological cast by Plotinus:

> All shapelessness whose kind admits of pattern and of form, as long as it remains outside of Reason and Idea, has not been entirely mastered by Reason, the matter not yielding at all points and in all respects to Ideal Form, is ugly by that very isolation from the Divine Thought. . . . We may even say that Beauty *is* the Authentic-Existents and Ugliness is the Principle contrary to Existence: and the Ugly is also the primal evil; therefore its contrary is at once good and beautiful, or is Good and Beauty: and hence the one method will discover to us the Beauty-Good and the Ugliness-Evil.

Similarly, Saint Augustine speaks of ugliness as simply the inverse of beauty, a "privation of form," and most medieval philosophers down through Saint Thomas Aquinas follow his lead. As they saw it, one principle governs both beauty and ugliness, so that the presence or absence, increase or decrease, of the one is ipso facto the absence or presence, decrease or increase, of the other. A fundamental problem facing this view is that of accounting for callilogical neutrality. Not everything that fails to be beautiful is generally taken to be to that degree ugly. In fact, some things (the number seventeen, for example) seem to be altogether unbeautiful without thereby being in the least bit ugly.

A second view responds to this problem. It is the position that ugliness is not just the inverse of the scale of beauty; instead, it and beauty occupy polar extremes on a single scale of aesthetic value whose gradations descend from each pole toward a middle state of neutrality. On this account, beauty and ugliness are related more as pleasure to pain than as heat to cold. Just as some experiences are neither pleasurable nor painful, so some objects are neither beautiful nor ugly. Early modern philosophers seem generally to have gravitated to such a position. Thomas Hobbes, David Hume, and Edmund Burke apparently held such a view. More recent thinkers often complicate the position with moral or practical judgments flavoring the way in which both "beautiful" and "ugly" are to be understood. John Dewey, for example, attributed beauty to whatever serves the purpose for which an artifact was designed and ugliness to whatever thwarts that purpose. In *Art as Experience,* he illustrates the distinction with the example of a common chair:

> A chair may serve the purpose of affording a comfortable and hygienically efficient seat, without serving at the same time the needs of the eye. If, on the contrary, it blocks rather than promotes the role of vision in an experience, it will be ugly no matter how well adapted to use as a seat.

But it is clear that Dewey accepted the view that some artifacts are neither so successful in their design to be counted beautiful nor so unsuccessful as to be deemed ugly. In this second version of opposition, whatever is credited to the account of beauty is not thereby deducted from that of ugliness; still, anything that is found beautiful cannot be to any degree ugly, and vice versa, because ascriptions of each are made on opposite sides of neutrality. This view is, therefore, no more capable than its predecessor of making sense of the claim that things may be both ugly and beautiful at once.

The third view accepts the plausibility of this conflation by placing beauty and ugliness on the same scale and allowing either or both to permeate the neutral meridian. Here, ugliness is conceived of as related to beauty much as humility is to pride; while some actions may be purely proud or purely humble, some display what seems aptly described as humble pride or, conversely, proud humility. Two prominent versions of this view have emerged. In the first, ugliness is seen as a negative species of beauty distinguished from the more familiar, positive species by the challenge its negative aspects pose to appreciation. George Santayana, Bernard Bosanquet, and W. T. Stace, among others, subscribed to variations of this view; but it was Samuel Alexander who embraced it most explicitly as a pivotal point in his aesthetic theory: "Ugliness . . . is an ingredient in aesthetic beauty, as the discords in music or the horrors of the tragedy. When it becomes ugly as a kind of beauty it has been transmuted. Such ugliness is difficult beauty" (Alexander, 1968). Thus understood, ugliness contributes to the effect of (positive) beauty by challenging the attentive intellect to respond in unorthodox ways to phenomena in which appealing elements are combined with repelling ones. No doubt such a view owes some of its credibility to the emergence of modern psychology, a study that points up the constructive contribution made by elements of experience hitherto regarded as altogether untoward. (It is worth noting that some theorists—for example, Burke—retain the idea that beauty and ugliness are mutually exclusive opposites while allowing that ugliness partially overlaps with the sublime. Others (e.g., August Schlegel) propose that, while the two are opposites, certain forms of ugliness may contain elements of the beautiful). The second version derives from Hegelian idealism rather than empirical science; it characterizes the ugly as one stage in a dialectical process whereby the beautiful is more perfectly realized. In this view, most ambitiously expressed in the work of Benedetto Croce, ugliness abets beauty's role in the development of spirit's progress toward its ultimate destiny by serving as its aesthetic counterpoint. Just as the individual consciousness cannot discover what it is without considering what it is not, beauty requires an antithetical value to evolve through synthesis into something that goes beyond both on the path of intellectual liberation. Far from relegating ugliness to the role of beauty's foil or sparring partner, the dialectical accounts often speak quite admiringly of its constructive partnership with beauty, especially as the two are linked together in art. As Karl Rosenkranz puts it, "If art is not to represent the idea in a merely one-sided way it cannot dispense with the ugly. . . . If mind and nature are to be admitted to presentation in their full dramatic depth, then the ugly of nature, and the evil and diabolic, must not be omitted" (*The Aesthetic of Ugliness,* 1853).

The chief complaint against both versions of the third view is that they equivocate on the question of whether ugliness is really negative. In trying to establish the claim that aesthetic awareness of the ugly can be valuable, proponents of this view are driven to say that ugliness is both appealing and unappealing, both pleasant and unpleasant, both positive and negative. But it can be argued that this is not so much a concession to aesthetic complexity as it is to muddle a thing's ugly aspects with others coexisting in close proximity to them. Just as a bad man may do a good deed because he sometimes is motivated otherwise than by his badness, so an ugly thing may have its appealing, even beautiful aspects without thereby becoming "negatively beautiful," or beautifully ugly.

The fourth view avoids the conflation problem by denying that ugliness and beauty occupy the same scale of aesthetic value. The contrast between the two might be thought of as similar to that between the risible and the pathetic. While these characteristics occupy independent scales, so that any degree of risibility is consistent with any degree of pathos in a subject, an attenuated form of opposition between them persists in that, in civil society, the recognition of the truly pathetic rightly inhibits laughter, rendering it boorish and contemptible. Likewise, ugliness and beauty might be conceptually independent yet exercise a shaping or braking influence on each other as they operate in certain contexts. The seeds of such a view were planted by Schlegel and Bosanquet, who insisted that while ugliness and beauty both express positive value, they do so in altogether different ways. More recently, Stephen C. Pepper distinguished ugliness from the lack of beauty (in artworks) by turning the former, but not the latter, into an ascription of moral disapproval. Artworks might be ugly, he supposed, if they exhibit "aesthetic dishonesty" through actions by artists that sacrifice the integrity of their work by deliberately distorting or perverting the audience's attention. A particularly strident defense of the view has been mounted by Mark Cousins, who insists that because aesthetics cannot deal with ugliness save as a negation of beauty, its proper analysis must be left to other disciplines. His own deconstructive, psychoanalytic account presents ugliness as the experience of dislocation or mislocation; "The ugly object is an object which is experienced both as being there and as something that should not be there. That is, the ugly object is an object which is in the wrong place" (Cousins, 1996). Although on this account ugliness has admittedly little to do with beauty, an opposing relation between the two may still be detected at a certain level of experience. For, while the dislocating force of ugliness makes our relations to the experienced world seem "precarious," the countervailing force of beauty makes them seem less so.

The obvious charge to be leveled against theories that put beauty and ugliness on different scales is that in so doing they abandon the very notion of complementary opposition without which ugliness is freed from beauty only to be bound in confusion with a host of other values. If ugliness has nothing to do with beauty it becomes the expression of any aesthetic antipathy one pleases, dissipating its force in the vagaries of taste, intuition, and ideology. Efforts by proponents of the different-scales view to retain some portion of the polarity they reject, as in admitting the "natural" conflict between the lessons of beauty and ugliness in certain contexts, are bound to seem desperate expedients, or unwitting betrayals of an incapacity to abandon what has been disavowed.

The Ontology of Ugliness. A common indictment of theories equating ugliness with the privation of beauty is that they tend to deny reality to ugliness altogether. If all things are beautiful in varying degrees—say, in proportion to the excellence of their form—then ugliness is simply a hypothetical limit on quotients of beauty, an absence beyond its smallest presence. But this absence, like formlessness itself, simply does not exist, so nothing can truly be ugly. Such a conclusion is, of course, impossible to square with the general acknowledgment that many real things are ugly; and this consequence is widely regarded as a reductio ad absurdum of ugliness-as-privation theories.

Not everyone, however, regards the unreality of ugliness as an unwelcome, let alone absurd, belief. To Augustine, for example, it is simply a reflection of the recognition that God's handiwork in this world is permeated with aesthetic as well as moral goodness. If something should seem ugly, that fact is taken as symptomatic of a deficiency in perceptual capacities

or in responsiveness to the formal order and harmony pervading all things. One need not share Augustine's sanguine theological outlook to discount the reality of ugliness as a failure of appreciation. Bosanquet, for instance, regards apparent ugliness simply as a matter of incomplete expressiveness, a condition growing out of humanity's as-yet-unsuccessful attempt to relate freely and fully to the objects of our awareness. Since, in his view, every object of awareness is already to some extent expressive, and since what is expressive is beautiful, what at first seems ugly is properly understood as a stimulus to aesthetic effort on the part of the observer— an effort whose success consists in the conversion of initial ugliness to eventual beauty. Nor need one subscribe to idealist metaphysics to take such a view. Pepper rejects all negative aesthetic value on the ground that value runs through all of life. Francis J. Kovach argues along Deweyan lines that the ugly is simply a limitation on the beauty of beautiful things— a condition of impediment or shortcoming—and, while this condition may add piquancy or depth of meaning to experience as a whole, it is only a deficit in real things, and no real thing itself.

Philosophers are not the only ones to deny the reality of ugliness. It is a point of pride among some artists to insist that a special, heightened aesthetic awareness permits them to see beauty in all things, nullifying whatever ugliness others see. Thus, for example, John Constable is said to have boasted: "No, madam, there is nothing ugly; *I never saw an ugly thing in my life:* for let the form of an object be what it may, —light, shade, and perspective will always make it beautiful." Frequently, it is difficult to determine from what they say whether artists are claiming that nothing is ugly and they have a facility for seeing that this is so or that whatever things are ugly can be transformed and presented as beautiful under the spell of their talents. It is, in fact, apparent that among both theorists and practitioners rejecting the reality of ugliness rarely has the effect of denying its real consequences, and for this reason it is usually more instructive to take note in these expressions of what existences are affirmed than of what are denied. In general, the lines between affirming a thing's existence and commending it and between denying its existence and condemning it are extremely thin.

It would be natural to suppose that theorists who defend the reality of ugliness break into the two familiar camps of objectivism (locating the existence of ugliness in things and their qualities) and subjectivism (locating it in the reactions of consciousness to things perceived) along the Kantian divide, paralleling the historical development of corresponding positions in the theory of beauty. But this would be a mistake. After Immanuel Kant, ugliness theorists are overwhelmingly subjectivists, and before him most theorists denied independent existence to ugliness altogether. Consequently, there are virtually no objectivist ugliness theories. All the interesting debates among the reality affirmers have been between rival conceptions of the experiential process involved in making judgments about ugliness rather than between claims about its location.

One strand of theory takes judgments of ugliness to mark a distinctive species of painful experience—usually involving a kind of pain that rises above the merely unpleasant by virtue of its perceived contrast to the pleasures supplied by beauty. Stace is a prominent defender of such a view, strands of which he derives from Aristotle's earlier reflections on the value of aesthetic pain. Another strand emphasizes disapproval rather than displeasure. It identifies the ugly with the inappropriate, the ignoble, the unseemly, and so forth, even when the experience of these does not occasion a painful response. Theorists as various as Schlegel, Croce, and Cousins have defended such views. Sometimes the disapproval takes on a moral tone, and the judgment involved mingles with ethical judgments, as when in Hobbes, for instance, the ugly is associated with the base, or when in G. E. Moore, it is identified as whatever it is evil to contemplate admiringly. Yet another strand regards the experience of ugliness as consisting mainly of pleasure, albeit of a peculiar kind—a contorted form of allure, fascination, or amusement. Santayana sometimes seems inclined to such a view (on the ground that "everything is capable in some degree of interesting and charming our attention"), and several of his followers have embraced it explicitly. Of course, we have already mentioned the Hegelian position that ugliness is not a feature of any one human faculty, response, or taste verdict but rather a reiterated component in a complex, dialectical action incorporating many elements of evolving consciousness. There are other views as well—perhaps as many as there are aesthetic epistemologies. While the diversity of these views exposes the depth of historical controversy over the conceptual mechanism of aesthetic judgment, it also reveals the breadth of effort that has been expended on extracting value from ugliness in the exercise of that mechanism. For, in almost all instances, the theorists have built their theories with one eye fixed on the objective of showing how our experience of ugliness can be edifying, no matter how negative its inherent character.

The Value of Ugliness. If our contact with ugly things is usually or always distasteful or disagreeable, it would seem we should wish to avoid or minimize our exposure to them. The displeasure we feel is more than just a feeling of dislike or a bad taste; it involves a cognitive aversion to what is wrongly formed and therefore debilitating or debilitated. Yet, curiously enough, the experience we derive from that contact is frequently pleasant, engaging, and even ennobling. We may call this the "paradox of ugliness." It is easily recognized to be the generic parent of the better-known "paradox of tragedy." The latter concerns our special reactions to representations of ugly, untoward, and hideous objects and conduct on stage, whereas the former concerns the way we react to ugly objects and events wherever we find them. Explanatory accounts of our admiration of ugliness in art often founder on the issue of what object is being admired, diverting attention to the skill or ingenuity of the artist and away from the ugly thing portrayed. Questions about how an artist manages to convert what was once ugly into beauty and why we are pleasantly moved by the ugly so converted are neither as fundamental nor as challenging as the question of how ugliness can be so powerfully and positively affecting, whether or not it is touched by art. At least four kinds of answers have been given to this question.

Descending from Aristotle's treatment of the therapeutic effects of unpleasant elements in tragedy, the dominant early strand of answers took the negativity of ugliness seriously and conceived of its salubrious effects as strictly antidotal. Some exposure to ugly things and actions can, according to this account, defend and improve us by providing what amounts to inoculation against later, more dangerous uglinesses. The pleasure we experience in relation to ugly objects is taken to be a symptom of the rightful satisfaction we feel at being well warned and armed against hazards that might confront us from without or erupt from our own unwary souls.

A second pattern of answers began to appear in the heady turbulence of post-Renaissance individualism, when introspective curiosity demanded a full accounting of our mental powers and their interplay. Ugliness was deemed particularly instructive in acquainting us with internal tensions between these powers. A strong antipathetic reaction to something might awaken an awareness not only of the grounds of aversion but of the distinctive way we consider and manage such a response. Kant's analysis of sublimity set the tone for advocacy of this position in the modern period. In the experience of sublimity, horror of the overwhelming is a vital element in revealing the grounds of human dignity. Similarly, ugliness could be seen to show us hidden corners of our powers that are activated in facing and overcoming the untoward. Later, Hegelian strands of the self-awareness answer insisted that ugliness could not properly be understood except in its partnership relations with other elements (the comic, the sublime, the beautiful, etc.) in the wider scheme of intellectual and spiritual fulfillment.

A third kind of answer emerged from postindustrial realism, a strident reaction to what was seen as the excesses of theory in preceding ages. If philosophers held that ugliness was unreal, that it was an odd kind of beauty, or that it was only part of a grand process of human improvement, then, the realists responded, they had to be wrong. For the world, as people normally experience it, is gritty, messy, and indelibly ugly here and there. We should, they insisted, see it for what it is, not what it is imagined or hoped to be; and in doing so we will reap the benefits of honest vision, ontological tolerance, and respect for the natural order of things. Inspired by the ascendancy of anti-Panglossian scientism (especially in the field of psychology), they insisted that ugliness, like death, malevolence, and disease, should be faced up to and not denied.

In recent times the role of ugliness as a concept expressing aesthetic disapproval has fallen into disuse. The negative force it once had has largely been transferred to ethics. Beginning with the *fin de siècle* decadence movement, literature and the arts undertook to challenge old divisions between bad and good on the broadest front. They called on us to look again at ugly things with eyes prepared to find beauty. Or perhaps it would be more accurate to say that they asked us to look at things through neither concept so that we might see them beyond the distortion of both. What had been realist respect for ugliness as part of common experience now became avant-garde fascination with ugliness as an exciting frontier of unusual experience. That positive effects might be experienced in relation to objects commonly regarded as ugly is not hard to understand; they are simply the undiscovered aspects of things that could be revealed only after the old, dichotomous borders were broken down. Postmodernism has, of course, led this assault on old lines of theory, but it has not been alone. Analytic aestheticians like Guy Sircello have not hesitated to join in this response, urging that what we gain from experiencing ugliness is surprisingly similar to what we gain from experiencing beauty; it is an intensification of our awareness of the qualities in our world most deserving of attention.

Each of these approaches throws light on facets of the contribution that appreciative awareness of ugliness makes to aesthetic intelligence. No doubt any fully satisfactory rejoinder to the paradox of ugliness will need to take stock of all of them. That there is considerable value to be gained from contemplation of the ugly things in life is beyond dispute; the debate has shifted to consider what part of this contemplation should involve rejection of ugliness in defense of beauty and other positive aesthetic values and what part can be given over to enjoying its dark, exotic pleasures.

[*See also* Beauty; Ontology of Art; *and* Value.]

BIBLIOGRAPHY

Alexander, Samuel. *Beauty and Other Forms of Value.* Reprint, New York, 1968.

Beardsley, Monroe C. *Aesthetics from Classical Greece to the Present.* New York, 1966.

Bosanquet, Bernard. *Three Lectures on Aesthetic.* London, 1915.

Cousins, Mark. "The Ugly." *AA Files* 28 (1996): 61–64; 29 (1996): 3–6.

Garvin, Lucius. "The Problem of Ugliness in Art." *Philosophical Review* 17 (1948): 404–409.

Kovach, Francis J. *Philosophy of Beauty.* Norman, Okla., 1974.

Pepper, Stephen C. *The Basis of Criticism in the Arts.* Cambridge, Mass., 1945.

Stace, W. T. *The Meaning of Beauty.* London, 1929.

Stolnitz, Jerome. "On Ugliness in Art." *Philosophy and Phenomenological Research* 11 (September 1950): 1–24.

Stolnitz, Jerome. "Ugliness." In *Encyclopedia of Philosophy*, edited by Paul Edwards, vol. 8, pp. 174–177. New York, 1967.

RONALD MOORE

UNIVERSALS. What impresses any observer of art, and our human interactions with art, is how much these differ from place to place, even from person to person, and how much they change over time. Nonetheless there have been persistent attempts by theorists of the arts to identify, beneath all the diversity and change, certain universals. One can usefully distinguish four different dimensions of art and interactions with art in which theorists have claimed to spy universality—of one sort or another.

Begin with evaluations. It is here especially that the observer is struck by diversity and variation: what one person judges admirable, another judges despicable or boring. Relativism seems unavoidable. Now no one denies that judgments of quality in works of art are in fact extremely diverse and variable. But there is a powerful body of thought about art that invites the observer to look deeper.

From within this whole mass of evaluations, one must, first, single out those that are aesthetic evaluations. It has proved extremely difficult to state, with rigor and precision, which evaluations those are. The general idea that guides the attempt to do so is clear enough, however. Aesthetic evaluations are those based on what one finds good in the object itself when contemplating it—as opposed to those based on what one finds good in how the object fits into the fabric of human purposes and desires. Aesthetic evaluations are those made when one contemplates the object disinterestedly.

A question that inevitably comes to mind is this: When contemplating objects disinterestedly, which features of those objects are in fact found good? Which features of objects make such contemplation of them rewarding? Which features give satisfaction in such contemplation? Which features ground, account for, aesthetic delight? To this question it would, of course, be possible to answer, "It varies"— and let it go at that. But few of those who have struggled to isolate the aesthetic dimension have in fact been content with that answer. The strategy for answering the question that Monroe Beardsley adopts in his now-classic book *Aesthetics* is paradigmatic. Beardsley concedes that human beings find aesthetic delight in a wide variety of different features of objects. But he does not regard these features as an unstructured smattering. To the contrary: he argues that everything humans find aesthetically good in objects is a specific case of either unity, complexity (richness), or expressiveness. Beneath all the variety, there are these universals.

A modern aestheticist like Beardsley is continuing the line of thought found in the medieval reflections on beauty. The medievals thought of beauty as that which pleases upon contemplation. They did not explicitly add the qualifier *disinterested*. But that they implicitly assumed this qualifier is clear from the answers they offered to the question, What is it in objects that accounts for pleasure upon contemplation? In their terminology that question is the same as, What is it about objects that makes them beautiful? Among the answers standardly offered were *unity, due proportion, clarity, brightness,* and *perfection.* The relevant point is that these were understood as features of objects that always and everywhere make for beauty.

Immanuel Kant, in his *Critique of Judgment,* pressed the quest for universality, in grounds for evaluation, one decisive step further. Suppose that what gives one person delight in contemplating some object is its melancholy character, whereas that very same character makes another person dislike contemplating it. For Beardsley, the fact that the latter person differs from the former in this way does not imply that the former person's satisfaction is not aesthetic. Our tastes for particular species of expressiveness may differ, as may our tastes for particular species of unity and of complexity; but if it is the unity, the complexity, or the expressiveness of an object that grounds one's satisfaction in contemplation, it is certain that the satisfaction in question is aesthetic. The medievals would happily make the parallel point for beauty. Although the due proportion of an object makes it beautiful, it may well be that human beings differ from each other in their tastes for specific versions of due proportion. Kant, however, laid down as a condition of aesthetic satisfaction not only that it be disinterested, but that it be universal, in the sense that it be grounded in shared human nature rather than in any particularity of makeup or training. If the melancholy character of the work gives a person no delight in the contemplation thereof, that establishes that the delight experienced in its melancholy character is not aesthetic. Indeed, if it is so much as possible that someone have no taste for melancholy expressiveness, that is sufficient to establish that such expressiveness is irrelevant to judgments of beauty. It is not possible in this discussion to explain which features of objects Kant regarded as grounding judgments of beauty, given his double requirement of disinterestedness and universality.

From evaluation consider what might be called artistic impulse. Nobody would deny that what motivates the composition and creation of works of art is multiple and diverse. But on this point, too, a rather large number of theorists have contended that if one digs through the variety and diversity one comes to a universal—to the universal artistic impulse. Although in every specific case other impulses may be operative as well, one always finds this universal. For example, Johan Huizinga, in his well-known *Homo Ludens,* suggests that it is the play-impulse that generates art.

Most of these attempts to discover some universal artistic impulse come and go with considerable rapidity. Various attempts to define "art," or "work of art," presuppose some such universal, however; and some of these definitions have proved of more abiding interest. Two examples will suffice to make the point. In *What Is Art?* Leo Tolstoy argues that art comes about when someone evokes in others an emotion that he or she has had by composing or creating an ar-

tifact expressive of that emotion. Such an artifact, and only such an artifact, is a work of art, said Tolstoy. From this it can be inferred that Tolstoy was of the view that the impulse to communicate or transmit emotions in the way indicated is the universal artistic impulse. R. G. Collingwood's view, expounded in his *Principles of Art,* is similar to Tolstoy's in its emphasis on emotions, but is nonetheless significantly different. Human beings often try to form constructs of the imagination with expressive qualities that match (fit, correspond with) some emotion that is felt. Such a construct of the imagination, says Collingwood, is a work of art. The artist may try to "objectify" this construct of the imagination in some medium, with the intent of producing in other persons knowledge of the emotion of which that construct was expressive—perhaps even with the intent of evoking that emotion in others. But this is not essential to art, and whatever impulse there may be to produce such objectifications, that is not the artistic impulse. The universal artistic impulse is just that impulse to "express" one's emotions by forming imaginative constructs that are expressive of one's emotions.

This reference to expressiveness leads naturally into a third dimension of art and commerce therewith in which theorists have claimed to spy universality beneath diversity and variability. It was suggested above that human beings differ from each other with respect to the kinds of artistic expressiveness that they like and dislike: some like works of melancholy character, others do not. In that way they differ in their tastes. It is equally obvious that they disagree in their identification of the expressiveness of objects: where one person spies melancholy, nothing of the sort. More generally, people differ in how they respond to works of art. People differ in construals of what the works represent or symbolize, in interpretations of what is said, in emotional reactions—and, as mentioned, in apprehensions of their expressiveness. Yet here, too, in this vast realm of actuality of response, theorists have claimed to spy universals.

Among the most interesting and provocative of such claims are those that emerge from the experiments of the psychologist Charles E. Osgood and associates, in which universals in the apprehension of the expressiveness of objects were uncovered. Osgood freely admitted that if one took complex objects and simply asked people to state what they perceived them as expressive of, highly diverse answers would be forthcoming. Nonetheless, he uncovered two fascinating phenomena beneath the diversity. He invited people to judge the expressive character of objects by locating the object on a qualitative continuum, with the two ends of the continuum picked out by antonyms. Is the object more fast than slow or more slow than fast? Is it more joyful than sad or more sad than joyful? And so on. What Osgood discovered is that, for all subjects, if sufficient continua for evaluation are offered, and those offered are selected randomly, these continua fall into three groups, of the following sort: If I know how a subject would evaluate an object on one of the continua belonging to a certain group, I can predict, with considerable reliability, how that subject will evaluate that object on other continua belonging to that same group. If a subject, for example, evaluates the expressive character of a painting as more fast than slow, then it is likely that she will also evaluate it as more sharp than dull. Second, Osgood and his associates discovered that if the entities given for evaluation are qualities rather than highly complex objects, then there is often astonishing agreement across cultures on their expressive character. There is massive agreement across cultures, for example, that heavy is more thick than thin, and that sharp is more red than green. (The Osgood results are summarized and scrutinized in Nicholas Wolterstorff, 1980a pp. 96–110.)

The fourth dimension of art concerns the claim by a good many theorists that universals are discovered when considering the ontological status of works of art. One hears two musical performances. But fully to describe the situation, one is compelled to say something more; namely, that the two performances are of the same sonata. One scrutinizes two graphic-art impressions—two etchings. But fully to describe the situation one is compelled to say something more; namely, that they are both impressions of the same print. One reads a poem in two different books. But fully to describe the situation, one is compelled to say something more; namely, that it was the same poem read in two different books. And so forth. What then is the sonata, as distinct from performances thereof, the print, as distinct from impressions thereof, and the poem, as distinct from copies thereof? A considerable number of theorists (including the author of this article) have contended that there genuinely are these entities—sonatas, prints, poems, and that given that they are capable of multiple instantiation in performances, impressions, and copies, these entities are universals. As one would expect, this claim has been controversial. Some, while conceding that there are ontological universals in art, would contend that they are of a somewhat different nature than that suggested above. More radically, "conceptualists" have argued that in addition to such spatiotemporal particulars as performances, impressions, and copies, there are only such mental entities as images, memories, concepts, and so forth; and "nominalists" have argued that in addition to the spatiotemporal particulars, there's nothing at all. Talk about sonatas, prints, and poems is nothing but a dispensable—albeit useful—fashion of speech.

These, then, are four dimensions of art and of interactions therewith in which theorists have claimed to discover universals. Within each dimension, many more examples could be given. And in every case, the claims made have proved controversial. Indeed, some of the most fascinating and perennial debates concerning art are clustered around these claims of universality. On this occasion we have only been able to indicate the focus of these debates, not to enter them.

[*See also* Definition of Art; Essentialism; Evaluation; Ontology of Art; Qualities, Aesthetic; *and* Relativism.]

BIBLIOGRAPHY

Beardsley, Monroe. *Aesthetics: Problems in the Philosophy of Criticism.* New York, 1958.
Collingwood, R. G. *The Principles of Art.* Oxford, 1938.
Currie, George. *An Ontology of Art.* New York, 1989.
Kant, Immanuel *Critique of Judgment.* Translated by Werner S. Pluhar. Indianapolis, 1987.
Huizinga, Johan. *Homo Ludens: A Study of the Play-Element in Culture.* Translated by R. F. C. Hull. London, 1949.
Goodman, Nelson. *The Languages of Art: An Approach to a Theory of Symbols* (1968). 2d ed. Indianapolis, 1976.
Kivy, Peter. *The Corded Shell: Reflections on Musical Expression.* Princeton, N.J., 1980.
Tatarkiewicz, Wladyslaw. *A History of Six Ideas.* Translated by Christopher Kaspareh. The Hague, 1980.
Tolstoy, Leo. *What Is Art?* Translated by Almyer Maude. New York, 1930.
Wolterstorff, Nicholas. *Art in Action: Toward a Christian Aesthetic.* Grand Rapids, Mich. 1980a.
Wolterstorff, Nicholas. *Works and Worlds of Art.* Oxford, 1980b.

NICHOLAS WOLTERSTORFF

UT PICTURA POESIS. The phrase *ut pictura poesis* first appears in the *Ars poetica* of Horace. Translated literally it means "as a painting, so a poem," and it occurs in a passage urging greater flexibility in critical judgments of poetry when Horace implies that a poem, like a painting, can please both in its detail and in its overall conception. The passage, in Latin, reads:

> Ut pictura poesis: erit quae, si propius stes,
> te capiat magis, et quaedam, si longius abstes.
> haec amat obscurum, volet haec sub luce videri,
> iudicis argutum quae non formidat acumen;
> haec placuit semel, haec deciens repetita placebit.

Ben Jonson's translation is as follows:

> As Painting, so is Poësie: some man's hand
> Will take you more, the nearer that you stand;
> As some the farther off: this loves the dark.
> This, fearing not the subtlest Judge's mark
> Will in the light be viewed: this, once, the sight
> Doth please, this ten times over will delight.

Thus, in a casual, incidental way appears the simile that becomes one of the great commonplaces in the history of aesthetics, initiating the tradition of comparisons between the sister arts of painting and poetry. Its basic assumption, that painting and poetry shared a common objective—namely, the vivid representation of nature—was not argued but simply implied. Nonetheless, it provided the departure point for countless discussions of the similarity and differences between these two liberal arts, discussions that reached their greatest application and refinement between the fifteenth and eighteenth centuries. After the eighteenth century, as theories of poetic inspiration shifted to a Romantic doctrine of original genius, references to *ut pictura poesis* diminish, although it can be argued that many of its preoccupations are reformulated to reappear in other guises in modern aesthetic thought.

In antiquity, the phrase did not possess the full theoretical meaning it was later to accrue. It appears, for example, in Plutarch's *De gloria Atheniensium* in another phrasing that would reappear in more extended discussions. When quoting Simonides of Ceos, Plutarch refers to painting as "mute poetry" and to poetry as a "speaking picture," a version of the comparison that would shift the balance from visual to verbal art in later formulations. Plutarch also invokes the analogy between painting and poetry when, in his *Moralia* (17f–18a), he suggests that a young man studying poetry be given "a general description of the poetic art as an imitative art and faculty analogous to painting."

The assumption that poetry and painting are mimetic arts, unstated by Horace and unargued by Plutarch, is more directly addressed by Plato in book 10 of *The Republic*. As is well known, Plato found the efforts of both poets and painters to imitate ideal beauty to be defective. His conception of Beauty as an ideal form, both ontologically real and having a metaphysical status prior to the existence of material nature, inevitably relegated both verbal and visual art to a secondary role relative to the work of the philosopher, but his emphasis on the mimetic nature of the sister arts would become a fundamental aspect of subsequent discussions of *ut pictura poesis*. Moreover, in his discussion he gave to this developing aesthetic theory one of its most persistent metaphors relative to the concept of *ut pictura poesis*, the idea of the painting or poem functioning as a mirror held up to nature.

Aristotle, in his *Poetics* (2, 1), also emphasized the mimetic function of painting and poetry as the essential meeting place of these two sister arts, but he redirected that mirroring function toward the material world. In doing so, he added yet another element to the accrual of associations around the phrase *ut pictura poesis*, the notion that the proper object of imitation for both painters and poets was human nature in action. Moreover, Aristotle also stressed that, as mimetic arts, poetry and painting are nonetheless distinguished from each other: painting by imitating through color and form and poetry by imitating through language, rhythm, and harmony. Thus, he opened the discussion of the likeness between the sister arts to a consideration not only of their distinguishing features but also of their respective strengths and weaknesses. Painting, limited to form and color, could portray many but not all things. Poetry, conversely, would excel in depicting those topics whose sequential nature made them best presented through language. Aristotle thus introduced an important refinement to the aesthetic theories originating in *ut pictura poesis*: he made clear that when the arts were classified by the means of imitation, they would differ from each other; when classified by the objects of imitation, they would be more closely associated.

Finally, Aristotle introduced one more variable to the discussions premised on the assumptions of *ut pictura poesis*. In section 5 of the *Poetics*, he noted that the tragic dramatist should follow the example of the painter who produces a portrait that, without losing the likeness, yet idealizes the sitter. Thus, to his assertion that the proper object of imitation is human nature, Aristotle added the notion that the poet should seek not simply to imitate but to improve nature, and in this endeavor his best role model was the painter. [*See* Aristotle.]

One other figure from antiquity should also be mentioned in the history of the evolution of *ut pictura poesis*. Chrysostom (Dion of Prusa), in his *XII Olympic Speech*, anticipates some of the differences between painting and poetry that Gotthold Ephraim Lessing would detail at greater length in the eighteenth century, when he observes that a poem develops in time whereas a painting remains the same. Additionally, he asserts, a poem can "evoke images of anything that comes to mind," including things that cannot be visually depicted, like abstract thought. A painting, according to him, can only represent the human image. Finally, other classical writers (e.g., Cicero, in his *Tusculans*, 5) also made reference to analogies between painting and poetry, but these too, like the other mentions from antiquity, were only in passing and remained undeveloped.

In the Middle Ages, the formula *ut pictura poesis* was known and commented on, usually in periods of classical renaissance like the Carolingian and Ottonian revivals. Many *arts poétiques*, influenced by Horace, were produced (and have been collected and summarized by Edmond Faral). At the same time, most medieval discussions of the association of poetry with painting also emphasized the greater difficulty in understanding and processing poetry but identified this difficulty as both source and sign of the greater value of the written text. They concurred with Augustine (*In Ioannis Evangelium*, 24.2) that writing was capable of addressing spiritual matters and in stimulating spiritual responses in ways that painting could not. Thus, the Middle Ages gave to the *ut pictura poesis* discussion the argument that writing had the greater moral and religious value. It offered more lasting satisfaction than paintings could produce.

Whereas the classical world saw painting as the model for poetry insofar as its use of color and form made it superior in representing material nature, the early Christian world not only privileged the superior spiritual efficacy of words but, in its more iconoclastic moments actively distrusted painting. Isidore of Seville is typical in his definition of painting:

Pictura is a representation expressing the appearance of anything, which when it is beheld makes the mind remember. *Pic-*

tura is, moreover, pronounced almost *fictura*. For it is a feigned representation, not the truth. Hence it is also counterfeited, that is, it is smeared over with a fabricated color and possesses nothing of credibility or truth.   (*Etymologarium,* 19)

While the medieval world, deeply divided in its attitudes toward its classical past, thus added little to the aesthetic theories that were being shaped by the evolution of the phrase *ut pictura poesis,* Renaissance theorists welcomed, revived, and extended it. In fact, the period from the fifteenth century in Italy to the eighteenth century throughout Europe made the greatest identification of painting and poetry, sometimes collapsing altogether any distinction between them.

Fifteenth- and sixteenth-century Italian theorists, responding to both Horace and Aristotle, extended the growing complex of ideas surrounding *ut pictura poesis* in two directions. On the one hand, following Aristotle, they gave greatest attention to that aspect of "nature" that emphasized the nobility of human nature in action. On the other, they developed two, partially antithetical, extensions of the mimetic function of art, one toward greater naturalism, or the trompe l'oeil effect, the other toward greater idealism through a doctrine of imitation that argued for the imitation of human beings not as they are but, in Aristotle's phrasing, "as they ought to be." Over time the arguments shifted from an emphasis on the exact imitation of nature to an emphasis on an ideal imitation of nature, but the two could coexist, and the same theoretician who argued for art as imitating the ideal within the natural might also be found describing the painter's ability to be the "ape of nature" as his most important accomplishment.

Leon Battista Alberti, in his *De pictura* (c.1435), represents the first category of theorist, those who stressed that reality should be imitated closely and exactly. In his technical discussions of perspective and composition, he relies heavily on the sister-arts comparison, arguing that the painter should be like the poet in compiling the different levels of a painting. Just as the poet first joins letters into syllables, then syllables into words, and words into sentences, so the painter must compose a painting by first outlining surfaces, then joining surfaces, and finally combining these surfaces into forms. When Alberti moves his discussion from technical matters to choices of subject, he again touches on the poet/painter comparison, but here he moves more in the direction of suggesting that what poet and painter imitate is not simply human experience but an enhanced version of that experience. The "historia" that is the painter's subject will move the spectator more if it is inspiring, and, in a later section, Alberti recommends that the painter turn for inspiration to the poet. In reminding his readers that Phidias was said to have learned how best to depict Jupiter by reading Homer and that it is Lucian's verbal description of Apelles' lost painting of Calumnia that

"excites our imagination when we read it," Alberti inverts *ut pictura poesis* to serve the painter's needs. [*See* Alberti.]

As one scholar, Jean H. Hagstrum, has observed, "The chief, if not sole, reason for the importance of *ut pictura poesis* in Renaissance criticism was that it somehow served the purposes of artistic naturalism" (Hagstrum, 1958). The shift from the exact to the ideal imitation of nature suggests that the complex of theoretical approaches subsumed under *ut pictura poesis* also served a concept of both arts that saw them as mirroring not only human experience but also the hidden order of the universe. Boccaccio, for example, although he uses the reference "ape of nature," which is more frequently associated with exact imitation, seems to be gesturing toward something hidden in nature as equally the poet's objective:

> The epithet [ape of nature] might be less irritating [than ape of philosopher] since the poet tries with all his powers to set forth in noble verse the effects, either of Nature herself, or of her eternal and unalterable operation . . . the forms, habits, discourse, and actions of all animate things, the course of heaven and the stars, the shattering force of the winds, the roar and crackling of flames, the thunder of the waves, high mountains and shady groves, and rivers in their course . . . so vividly set forth that the very objects will seem actually present.
>
> (*Geneaologiae Deorum* 14.7)

Here the "forms, habits, discourse, and actions of all animate things" imply that the poet's objective is moving beyond literal representation.

Thus, although the concept of literal representation was, in Rensselaer W. Lee's words, "a realistic point of view and practice among those artists who were striving strenuously to capture the perfect illusion of visible nature," it can be seen that even for those who, like Alberti, were deeply engaged in the technical aspects of producing realistic effects, the sister arts' mirror could be held up to an idealized nature.

This latter point is most important for the author of the major humanist treatise on painting in the late Italian Renaissance, Lodovico Dolce (*Dialogo della pittura,* 1558). Dolce invokes the usual comparison of painters and poets, saying not only that "writers are painters" but also that "poetry is painting, history is painting, any composition by a learned man is painting," and he retells the familiar stories about Zeuxis and Parrhasius in which painted objects deceive the viewer. In his more precise discussion of imitation, however, Dolce demonstrates how that fundamental empiricism becomes qualified by the idealism that marked many Renaissance departures from strict mimeticism. Discussing the perennial question of whether the painter should imitate nature directly or rather be guided by imitating his classical predecessors (who had the advantage of living closer to nature in the golden age), Dolce makes it clear that imitation is not an end in itself but a means to an end, the representation not of empirical nature but of the ideal hidden within or behind it.

Exactly how the ideal was associated with the empirical remained an open question, not just for Dolce but for others as well. Theorists varied in their emphases (occasionally within the same discussion), sliding between Aristotle's theory of the selective imitation of nature and the Neoplatonic emphasis on ideal beauty, the image of which might be reflected in the artist's mind but whose source was in God rather than in nature.

Dolce is also important in respect to *ut pictura poesis,* moreover, for his discussion of the response of the spectator to painting. According to him—relying on the Renaissance understanding of faculty psychology whereby the imagination was seen as that capacity of the soul that created and refined images out of materials collected by the senses—a profoundly religious painting could stimulate and even improve the viewer's soul. Thus the painter, at least in a few instances, could generate as empathetic a response as could the poet, historian, or orator. Images, Dolce concluded, were thus not only books for the ignorant, they could also arouse devotion in those who had understanding by directing them toward the contemplation of what was being represented. Dolce thus offered a corrective to the medieval emphasis on the word as the more spiritually efficacious medium.

A more ardent and passionate champion of this point of view—although unfortunately without influence, since his observations remained hidden in his notebooks—was Leonardo da Vinci. Leonardo argued aggressively for the superiority of painting to poetry, contending that painting appealed to the eye, the highest of the senses, that painting engaged directly with nature, the creation of God, and that painting in its immediacy could effectively represent the harmonious nature of beauty, whereas poetry's successive depiction of it could only result in the tedium of boring description. In language, he asserted, the parts of beauty are divided in time and thus forgetfulness intervenes and the effects, which painting could present simultaneously, are separated from each other in language and lose their focus. Parodying Simonides, he observed sarcastically that "if you call painting mute poetry, poetry can itself be called blind painting" (1956, p. 18).

Leonardo's position was extreme, however, and most Renaissance critics engaging with *ut pictura poesis* held the dominant view of poetry that stressed its image-making capacity and superior ethical and spiritual value. English theorists were no exception here. As Sir Philip Sidney, the best known among them, observed in his *Defense of Poesy,*

> Only the poet, disdaining to be tied to any . . . subjection, lifted up with the vigor of his own invention, doth grow in effect another nature, in making things better than nature bringeth forth, or, quite anew, forms such as never were in nature . . . so as he

goeth hand in hand with nature, not enclosed with in the narrow warrant of her gifts, but freely ranging only within the zodiac of his own wit. Nature never set forth the earth in so rich tapestry as divers poets have done . . . Her world is brazen, the poets only deliver a golden.

Sidney's words thus sum up the dominant view of *ut pictura poesis* in the Renaissance: while the splendors of painting—especially naturalistic painting profiting from the technical developments achieved through the use of perspective and oil-based paints—were impressive, poetry was still privileged for its greater epistemological and spiritual efficacy. Nevertheless, Sidney's use of the vocabulary of painting to describe the effects of poetic inspiration and accomplishment demonstrates just how closely each of the sister arts had affected the other. [*See* Sidney.]

Although theorists of the Enlightenment still used the vocabulary and assumptions associated with *ut pictura poesis,* there are several indications that that influence was fading and had run its course. Late seventeenth- and eighteenth-century theorists, for example, accepted as axiomatic the sister-arts analogy so fundamental to *ut pictura poesis,* and, at least initially, they seem to differ little from their Renaissance predecessors. Charles Dufresnoy's Latin poem, *De arte graphica* (c. 1644–1653), translated into French by Roger de Piles (1668) and into English by John Dryden (1695), summarized the doctrine of *ut pictura poesis* and reinvested it with some of the vigor of its initial formulations. Nevertheless, opposition to the unity of the sister arts had begun to surface. That opposition was most clearly and fully expressed by Lessing in *Laocoön; or, The Limits of Painting and Poetry* (1776).

Lessing's argument was similar to Leonardo's, although presented in more unified and accessible fashion. Essentially, he argued that painting should concern itself with bodies in space and that the proper domain of poetry lay in action through time. Additionally, the signs that comprised language were largely arbitrary, their significance established by convention, while the signs composing a painting were natural. The highest genre, however, was that which came closest to converting arbitrary signs into natural, and that was drama. [*See* Lessing.]

Moreover, the image-making capacity of poetry also began to be questioned. Edmund Burke in *A Philosophical Enquiry into the Origin of Our Ideas on the Sublime* (1757) pointed out that words do not necessarily generate images and indeed that the visual imagery produced by poetic images can sometimes be absurd, even chaotic. Poetry, he concluded, affects by "sympathy" rather than by imitation. It is not truly an imitative art. [*See* Burke.]

The similarities that had linked the sister arts were thus increasingly downplayed or denied while their differences were accentuated. Most critically, the element that had originally united them, the assumption that they were each mimetic arts with the common goal of representing the natural world, came increasingly into question. Poetry came to be seen as less and less like a picture, and the phrase *ut pictura poesis* disappeared almost entirely from aesthetic discussions. In the Romantic era, interest in the topic was limited. In fact, poetry was more frequently compared to music than to painting, and when its image-making potential was discussed, it was in the context of a new phrase, the picturesque. By the end of the nineteenth century, although there was much discussion on the nature of poetic imagery and although in the twentieth considerable attention has been given (in the Symbolist movement, for example) to the image-making potential of language, little of this discussion has been in the context of *ut pictura poesis*, largely because painting itself had begun to turn toward abstraction and thus away from the mimetic function on which its analogy with poetry had been predicated. Moreover, it has been generally agreed that the mental images evoked by a literary text are selectively constructed, varying enormously among individual viewers and thus not fundamentally susceptible to visual analysis.

One might argue, however, that some of the attention to the representational aspects of painting and poetry that concerned the theorists of *ut pictura poesis* has returned in part through semiotic poetics. The work of C. S. Peirce, for example, can be seen to reformulate *ut pictura poesis* as the thesis that the iconicity of a literary work is attributable to systems of signs in which there exists a resemblance between the signifier and the signified. Since, however, certain elements of iconicity must also be in the form of symbols, which semioticians term conventional signs, they thereby lack any natural resemblance to their signified objects. More fundamentally, since the dominant thrust of such systems is to turn everything to text, the sister-arts analogy no longer works in both directions, and thus *ut pictura poesis* has really been erased rather than reinstated.

Thus, while the final word on *ut pictura poesis* has doubtless not yet been written, its epitaph has been prepared. In the words of John Ashbery from his poem "And *Ut Pictura Poesis* Is Her Name," "You can't say it that way any more."

[*See also* Discourse; Ecphrasis; Imagery; Literature, *article on* Literary Aesthetics; Poetics; Renaissance Italian Aesthetics; *and* Text.]

BIBLIOGRAPHY

Dundas, Judith. *Pencils Rhetorique: Renaissance Poets and the Art of Painting.* Newark, Del., 1993.

Faral, Edmond. *Les arts poétiques du XIIe et du XIIIe siècle.* Paris, 1924.

Farmer, Norman K., Jr. *Poets and the Visual Arts in Renaissance England.* Austin, Tex., 1984.

Gent, Lucy. *Picture and Poetry, 1560–1620.* Leamington Spa, England, 1981.

Hagstrum, Jean H. *The Sister Arts: The Tradition of Literary Pictorialism and English Poetry from Dryden to Gray.* Chicago, 1958.

Land, Norman E. *The Viewer as Poet: The Renaissance Response to Art.* University Park, Pa., 1994.

Lee, Rensselaer W. *Ut Pictura Poesis: The Humanistic Theory of Painting.* New York, 1967.

Leonardo da Vinci. *Treatise on Painting.* Translated by A. Philip McMahon. Princeton, N.J., 1956.

Markiewicz, Henryk. "Ut Pictura Poesis: A History of the Topos and the Problem." *New Literary History* 18 (1987): 535–559.

Mitchell, W. J. T. "*Ut Pictura Theoria:* Abstract Painting and Language." In *Picture Theory: Essays on Verbal and Visual Representation,* pp. 213–239. Chicago, 1994.

Park, Roy. "*Ut Pictura Poesis:* The Nineteenth Century Aftermath." *Journal of Aesthetics and Art Criticism* 28 (Winter 1969): 155–169.

Steiner, Wendy. *The Colors of Rhetoric: Problems in the Relation between Modern Literature and Painting.* Chicago, 1982.

"Ut Pictura Poesis: A Selective, Annotated Bibliography of Books and Articles, Published between 1900 and 1980, on the Interrelations of Literature and Painting from 1400 to 1800." *Yearbook of Comparative and General Literature* 32 (1983): 65–124.

Word and Image: A Journal of Verbal and Visual Inquiry 4.1 (1988).

ANN HURLEY

V

VALUE. Value is one of the weightiest, most indispensable, and perhaps most mystified concepts in aesthetics and, beyond that, in formal thought. Like a number of other terms, such as *meaning* and *reality,* that have strong currency in informal speech and long histories as the focus of theoretical analysis, the term seems to name an aspect of the world so fundamental to our thinking—so elementary and at the same time so general—as to be both irreducible and irreplaceable. Like any other term, however, *value* has a history of variable and complex usage.

From the time of its earliest recorded occurrences through to the present, the English word *value* (like *worth* and the corresponding French and German terms *valeur* and *Wert*) has maintained two parallel—related but distinct—senses. In the first sense, value is understood as the equivalence-in-exchange of a thing: its price in some cash market, its equivalent when compared to or traded for something else in some more general domain of reciprocal transactions. In the second broad sense, the value of a thing is a more abstract matter of its utility in relation to some purpose, its measure with respect to some dimension, or its position on some scale (e.g., courage in battle, temporal duration of a musical tone, or abstract numerosity of a variable in a mathematical equation). Value in this second sense, then, is something like relative plusness or amount or degree of positivity. Because both senses of the term involve two key ideas (namely, comparison and positivity) that relate to an extensive range of human practices, it is not surprising that the concept of value appears so important and, so to speak, invaluable.

As this last somewhat paradoxical possibility reminds us, however, the more or less pragmatic, quotidian senses of the term may be negated or reversed in the specification of one or another highly privileged (i.e., valued) type of value. Thus, it may be asserted that the essential, spiritual, moral, sentimental, symbolic, or aesthetic value of a thing has nothing to do with comparison, measure, utility, money, materiality, or exchange, but is, on the contrary, unique, noninstrumental, ineffable, immeasurable, and unexchangeable. It appears that when the experienced positive operations or effects of a thing are especially intense, extensive, or significant but also especially heterogeneous and subtle, those operations and effects are likely to be indicated and theorized by way of contradistinction from other rela-

tively more specific, palpable, or readily describable values. There also seems to be a strong general tendency to project the experienced effects of any complex set of conditions back into the most salient (i.e., visible, concrete, palpable) of those conditions—with the resulting idea of value as an autonomous and inherently objective property of objects themselves that is independent of the actual, possible, posited, or even imagined experience of those objects by particular situated subjects.

Although the general idea of essential or intrinsic value is more closely associated with the humanistic disciplines and ethics or aesthetics than with social theory, various social theorists—including anthropologists, sociologists, and economists—have entertained or been affected by the idea of an essentially inherent and fixed value that is distinct both from fluctuating market price and from subject-variable experienced or attributed value (Appadurai, 1986). The conception of value as embodied labor could be explored in this connection (Steedman et al., 1981), as could Karl Marx's somewhat ambiguous allusions to use-value as a historically, subjectively, and otherwise variable attribute of objects and as a product or shadowy twin of their physical, material, and presumably objective properties.

Complicating current conceptualizations of value are the classically perplexed relations between objects and subjects in the realm of human experience. It seems clear that experiences and judgments of the value of particular objects—in the sense of subjective registerings and overt verbal assessments of their adequacy in satisfying certain needs, serving certain purposes, or eliciting certain desired or desirable effects—are, like all other experiences and judgments, more or less subject variable and shaped by numerous other more or less variable conditions (contextual, cultural, historical). It could be said, then, that (the experience or judgment of) the value of any object is irreducibly contingent, meaning not arbitrary but, rather, dependent on conditions that are always to some extent variable and unpredictable. It may still be asked, of course, whether the value of an object (or at least some aspect of its value) could not be (or is not properly conceived of as) independent of the experiences and judgments of particular subjects, and thus as essentially intrinsic and objective. Given these classic perplexities, however, there seems no way to approach that question without also engaging a number of other chronic and currently significant philosophical issues—or, of course, presupposing particular but currently contested positions on them (essentialist or nominalist, realist or constructivist, phenomenological or naturalistic, and so forth).

An important consequence of the history of usage and conceptualization of value is the emergence, in the West, of a double discourse of value, that is, the stabilization of two strenuously antithetical discursive domains, both centered on articulations of value but defined largely through mutual contradistinction. In the first (profane, naturalistic) discourse, value is understood as instrumental, economic, material, often monetary, and essentially mutable and contingent: this is the domain of trade and industry, accumulation and profit, production and consumption, and individual self-interest. Value in the second (sacred, humanistic) domain is understood as nonutilitarian, noneconomic, immaterial, inherent, and essentially transcendent: this is the domain of ethics and religion, gifts and sacrifice, creation and appreciation, and, traditionally, art—at least high art. Differences among types and degrees of value are, of course, both individually and communally significant, but these polarized oppositions are evidently discursively constituted and only institutionally stabilized; that is, they are not otherwise given in the nature of things. Accordingly, the boundaries of the double domain of value require careful patrol and continuous (re)establishment, tasks characteristically undertaken by religious institutions and also, in relation especially to cultural productions, by the humanistic disciplines. Thus, the familiar implicit admonitions to discriminate between intrinsic value and mere utility, aesthetic value and mere hedonic enjoyment, artistic value and mere technical display, literary value and mere sociological interest, and so on. For the reasons already suggested, the differences thus set in polarized, hierarchized opposition can usually be recast as matters of relative or gradient difference in relation to some configuration of dimensions: for example, range of uses and effects, degree of subtlety, intensity, or heterogeneity, or extent of individual or contextual variability. It could also be argued, however, that there are important communal, long-range values served by the strenuous maintenance of at least some such absolute distinctions and hierarchies: notably, the protection of certain goods (in all senses) from commodification, debasement, and the risk of ultimate destruction.

Aesthetic value, often equated with the concept of beauty and associated with a particular type of pleasurable and otherwise (e.g., morally or politically) valuable sensory/perceptual experience, is widely understood as a distinctively noninstrumental positivity elicited by certain purely or at least primarily formal properties of certain natural or artifactual phenomena. So understood, it is also seen as especially characteristic or defining of (genuine) works of (fine) art, and as the product, expression, or manifestation of exceptional creative gifts on the part of artists and performers. The proper or full experience of aesthetic value, so understood, is sometimes seen as limited to persons with special training or appropriate innate sensibilities but is also—and sometimes simultaneously—posited as ideally or potentially universal.

These interrelated characterizations and understandings of aesthetic value have operated quite well over the past two centuries for purposes of critical discourse (description, classification, explanation, interpretation, assessment, and so forth), at least among those (artists, audiences, patrons, critics, curators, academic scholars, and so forth) educated in the classical high culture of Europe. Certain conceptual incoherences and otherwise problematic features of that set of ideas have become more evident, however, as relevant research and analysis in empirical fields such as anthropology, cultural history, psychology, and sociology have been disseminated more broadly (see, e.g., Becker, 1982; Bourdieu, 1984; Braudel, 1982; and Douglas, 1979) and also as more conceptually exacting formulations have been attempted in formal aesthetics and elsewhere in philosophy (Danto, 1981; Derrida, 1981, 1987; Goodman, 1976, and Mothersill, 1984). At the same time and to some extent relatedly, the cultural provincialism and sometimes narrowly self-privileging normative assumptions of much traditional critical theory have become more notable as alternative formulations—many of them with significant political and institutional implications—have been developed and promoted by the members of a now more culturally diverse and heterogeneous academic, artistic, and critical community. Accordingly, contemporary discussions of aesthetic value are likely to stress the subjectively individuated, historically and culturally variable, and contextually specific nature of the experience and effects of artworks (Stewart, 1991); the historically and institutionally variable constitution of categories such as works of (fine) art, works of literature, and aesthetic experiences (Williams, 1977); and the social and political operations of aesthetic theory itself (Bennett, 1979; Eagleton, 1990; and Connor, 1992). More or less sophisticated efforts to redeem the idea of an essential aesthetic value and, with it, of a potentially or ideally universal aesthetic experience, do, however, continue to be pursued (Eagleton, 1990; and Guillory, 1993).

Most current conceptions of aesthetic value derive more or less directly from Immanuel Kant's *Critique of Judgment,* in which such value, under the term *beauty,* is associated with certain configurations of pure form. Although the details of Kant's elaborations of this idea have been a rich resource for phenomenological aesthetics and critical theory more generally, some of his relevant assumptions concerning the operations of human perception and cognition now appear dubious—and with them the related idea of an objectively (or universally subjectively) valid aesthetic judgment. Most significantly, it appears that our perceptual experiences of even such ostensibly pure stimuli as single musical tones, basic geometric figures, and simple visual or auditory patterns will be shaped by our experiential history of similar and related forms and by the particular contextual conditions in which we encounter them—which is to say, the experience and judgment of beauty will inevitably be both impure (in Kant's terms) and, contrary to the idea of universal subjective validity, more or less personally individuated.

The term *aesthetic value* operates in many informal critical discourses with more or less specific and stable senses (though not the same ones in all those discourses), and the idea of aesthetic value as a distinctive, determinate attribute has been important and perhaps indispensable in the development of Romantic and modernist critical theory. One reason for the increasing questioning of such theory, however, is that, in spite of the many painstaking attempts to do so, there does not appear to be any way to define clearly, consistently, substantively, and without circularity a particular type of value that is characteristic of just those phenomena or features of phenomena that are generally spoken of as aesthetically valuable or just the set of objects generally referred to as art at any particular time. Rather, it appears that the phenomena indicated as aesthetically valuable are irreducibly heterogeneous and that those highly specific, intensely focused, uniquely exciting or pleasing, richly evocative, analysis-defying, category-dissolving effects that we (sometimes) experience in our engagements with (what some of us now call) artworks are more or less continuous with our experiences of numerous other putatively nonartistic, nonaesthetic artifacts, activities, and states, including mass-produced commodities, popular entertainment, sex, sports, work, dreaming, drunkenness, and madness.

[*See also* Evaluation; Historicism; Qualities, Aesthetic; Relativism; *and* Universals.]

BIBLIOGRAPHY

Appadurai, Arjun, ed. *The Social Life of Things: Commodities in Cultural Perspective.* Cambridge and New York, 1986.

Bataille, Georges. "The Notion of Expenditure" (1933). In *Visions of Excess: Selected Writings, 1927–1939,* edited and translated by Allan Stoekl. Minneapolis, 1985.

Becker, Howard S. *Art Worlds.* Berkeley, 1982.

Bennett, Tony. *Formalism and Marxism.* London, 1979.

Bourdieu, Pierre. *Distinction: A Social Critique of the Judgement of Taste.* Translated by Richard Nice. Cambridge, Mass., 1984.

Braudel, Fernand. *Civilization and Capitalism,* vol. 2, *The Wheels of Commerce* (1979). Translated by Sian Reynolds. New York, 1982.

Connor, Steven. *Theory and Cultural Value.* Oxford and Cambridge, Mass., 1992.

Danto, Arthur C. *The Transfiguration of the Commonplace: A Philosophy of Art.* Cambridge, Mass., 1981.

Derrida, Jacques. "Economimesis" (1975). Translated by Richard Klein. *Diacritics* 11 (1981) 2: 3–25.

Derrida, Jacques. "Parergon" (1978). In *The Truth in Painting,* translated by Geoff Bennington and Ian McLeod, pp. 15–148. Chicago, 1987.

Douglas, Mary, and Baron Isherwood. *The World of Goods.* New York, 1979.

Eagleton, Terry. *The Ideology of the Aesthetic.* Oxford and Cambridge, Mass., 1990.

Fekete, John, ed. *Life after Post-Modernism: Essays on Value and Culture.* New York, 1987.

Goodman, Nelson. *Languages of Art: An Approach to a Theory of Symbols.* 2d ed. Indianapolis, 1976.

Guillory, John. *Cultural Capital: The Problem of Literary Canon Formation.* Chicago, 1993.

Kant, Immanuel. *Critique of Judgment* (1790). Translated by J. H. Bernard. New York, 1951.

Mothersill, Mary. *Beauty Restored.* Oxford, 1984.

Mukarovsky, Jan. *Aesthetic Function, Norm and Value as Social Facts* (1936). Translated by Mark E. Suino. Ann Arbor, 1970.

Smith, Barbara Herrnstein. *Contingencies of Value: Alternative Perspectives for Critical Theory.* Cambridge, Mass., 1988.

Steedman, Ian, et al. *The Value Controversy.* London, 1981.

Stewart, Stewart. *Crimes of Writing: Problems in the Containment of Representation.* New York and Oxford, 1991.

Williams, Raymond. *Marxism and Literature.* Oxford, 1977.

BARBARA HERRNSTEIN SMITH

VASARI, GIORGIO

VASARI, GIORGIO (1511–1574), Italian painter, architect, and art historian. Giorgio Vasari was born in Arezzo to a family of artisans, and his education in the Medici household in Florence prepared him well to become a highly successful courtier-artist. After some initial setbacks linked to political turmoil, he enjoyed the favor of many of the leading patrons of his day; from 1555 he worked for Cosimo I, duke of Florence, whom he served as painter, architect, and designer of elaborate court spectacles. Although his painting is now generally held in low regard (his architecture, on the other hand, still commands admiration), his achievement in bringing a new degree of rationalization to the productive process, especially to the management of large, complex collaborative projects involving literary advisers, on the one hand, and teams of artist-assistants, on the other, deserves recognition. The Accadémia del Diségno, the first formally incorporated academy of art, which he helped to establish in Florence in 1563 with the aim of imposing a similar kind of rationalization on artistic education, also set an example imitated throughout early modern Europe.

Vasari's enduring fame, and his interest in this context, depend on his book, *The Lives of the Most Eminent Painters, Sculptors and Architects,* first published in 1550, then again, in a greatly expanded edition, in 1568. The *Lives* is the first sustained account of the history of the visual arts in modern times, and it is as important for the interpretive structure it imposes on that history as for the information it provides about individual artists and their works. Written for cultivated amateurs as well as artists, it helped to establish and disseminate a system of aesthetic standards and a critical vocabulary for the discussion of art, the fundamental elements of which continued to enjoy currency all over Europe until the nineteenth century. Written in a lively style, with colorful descriptions, anecdotes, and character sketches, it is also a classic of Italian literature.

The biographies that make up the *Lives* are grouped into three sections corresponding to three phases that Vasari discerned in the development of Italian art from the late-thirteenth to the mid-sixteenth century, the period we have come to call the Renaissance. Vasari understood this development as one of progress, and likened the phases to stages in the growth of an individual: the first, extending roughly to the end of the fourteenth century, is represented as the "infancy" of art; the second, which covers the fifteenth century, as its "youth." The third phase, from the last years of the fifteenth century to Vasari's own time, is the period when art reaches "maturity" and perfection. The notion of the progress of art was available from ancient sources such as Pliny; the metaphor of organic development is found among ancient historians, and three-phase patterns are commonplace, but Vasari's combination of these ingredients deserves to be recognized as an original achievement: it creates an intepretive structure that has survived even the many revisions modern scholarship has offered to the substance of his account.

The progress of art involves the gradual improvement of the ability to "imitate nature": in the case of painting, the perfection of the ability to suggest the illusion of three-dimensionality and, in figures, of living presence. The leading artist of the first period, Giotto, is able to suggest the volume of forms by virtue of accurate drawing, consistent modeling in light and shade, and attentiveness to spatial relationships; Masaccio, an innovator of the second phase, refines on his predecessors by using the technique of linear perspective to create an altogether more consistent and convincing illusion of space; by making a careful study of anatomy he is also able to improve on earlier representations of the figure. Leonardo da Vinci, the artist who inaugurates the third phase, develops a style distinctive for its extremely delicate modeling, capable of capturing the subtlest and most fleeting effects: he brings to the mastery of linear perspective a sensitivity to the way in which forms are perceived through atmosphere—so-called atmospheric perspective—and his comprehensive study of nature enables him to represent all things, not just human anatomy, with extraordinary depth of understanding.

Besides naturalism there are other aspects to the progress of art. One is storytelling: an early painter like Giotto gives plausibility to his narrative scenes by appropriate costumes and effective characterization. Two hundred years later, Raphael possesses such a comprehensive sense of decorum that his pictures seem like the perfect equivalents of the texts they illustrate; beyond that, they seem to reflect a systematic, "philosophical" understanding of human nature, so that they become occasions for the contemplation of larger and deeper truths. Another aspect of the progress of art is the capacity of pictures to convey abstract ideas through symbolism and allegory. Giotto pioneers allegorical representation in frescoes at Assisi; Vasari and his contemporaries are able, with the help of scholar-advisers, to concoct elaborate decorative schemes deploying all the resources of theology and humanist learning.

If art becomes more naturalistic, it also becomes more beautiful: at its best, it no longer imitates but surpasses nature. On the one hand, the path toward beauty is indicated by ancient art: the progress of sculpture, for instance, has as much to do with approaching the look of ancient statuary as with fidelity to nature, and Vasari believed that the study of ancient models had enabled the artists of his own time—Michelangelo above all—to surpass nature. On the other hand, the authority of ancient sculpture rests on the belief that the ancient masters selected only the best natural forms to imitate, often combining the most beautiful features of several specimens in order to produce an ideal form, a principle illustrated in the famous story of the painter Zeuxis and the maidens of Croton. The modern artist might also proceed in this manner, without having recourse to ancient models (some theorists, like Leonardo da Vinci, argued that the artist should only rely directly on nature), and thus even the standard of ancient art might be subject to critical revision, as it were, and surpassed. Vasari believed that, like nature, antiquity too had been surpassed in his own time, and again, by Michelangelo, whose figures must therefore be understood to possess a beauty unprecedented in the world.

Another feature of the progress of art, often neglected in accounts of the *Lives*, is the integration of the three arts of painting, sculpture, and architecture. The idea that painting and sculpture are kindred arts, dependent on the practice of drawing, and thus on the principle of design (the Italian word *diségno* can mean both an individual drawing and the concept of design in the abstract), was already a commonplace in the mid-fourteenth century; the notion that design *(lineaménta)* is an essential principle of architecture is found in Vitruvius. Ambitious art theorists—Leonardo among them—had suggested that design actually serves as the basis of many other disciplines as well: writing, mathematics, geometry, optics, astronomy, and mechanics. Vasari combined these ideas, and again made use of a biological metaphor, when he claimed that the three arts are daughters of the one father, *diségno*—thereby establishing the unity of the visual arts as well as the basis of their distinctness from other arts. This unity exists a priori, in principle, but the historical development that he traces brings it to realization or fulfillment: increasingly, artists are able to work in all three art forms and to integrate them into single works. This process, too, reaches its climax in Michelangelo, who brings each of the arts to perfection individually, but in so doing also demonstrates their unity in the principle of design.

Wishing to emphasize its importance, Vasari elaborated and clarified his treatment of design in the second edition of the *Lives:* he added discussions of individual artists' drawing styles to many of the biographies, and included at the beginning of the book, in an introductory section on the materials and techniques of art, a definition of design as a principle. This definition is the most explicitly philosophical passage in the *Lives:*

> Because design, the father of our three arts of architecture, sculpture and painting, proceeding from the intellect, derives from many things a universal judgment, like a form or idea of all things in nature—which [nature] is most consistent in its measures—it happens that not only in human bodies and those of animals, but in plants as well and buildings and sculptures and paintings, it [design] understands the proportion that the whole has to the parts and the parts to one another and to the whole. And because from this there arises a certain notion and judgment which forms in the mind that which, when expressed with the hands, is called design, one may conclude that this design is nothing other than a visible expression and declaration of that notion of the mind, or of that which others have conceived in their minds or given shape to in their imaginations.

The concept of "universal judgment" comes from the beginning of Aristotle's *Metaphysics;* the phrase "like a form or idea" invokes Platonic tradition. Vasari's point is simply that design is something that requires philosophical definition, a faculty of mind that qualifies the visual arts as modes of rational operation. Although scholars have criticized the rather superficial juxtaposition of the two philosophical vocabularies, Vasari's intention is obviously to suggest that no serious incompatibility exists between them as far as the definition of design is concerned.

The idea that design is the principle of the visual arts was given an institutional form in the Accadémia del Diségno. The first edition of the *Lives* ended with the biography of Michelangelo; the second edition carries the account forward in time to include discussion of the work of many of the young academicians and the projects in which they collaborated: the emphasis is less on the culmination of the history of art in Michelangelo and more on the perfection of the rules of art and their propagation through the teaching of the academy. In this way, too, the position of design as the fundamental rule or essence of art is confirmed by historical demonstration.

Another important dimension of Vasari's concept of artistic progress is the way in which it is linked to the progress of other disciplines during the same period and to the progress of art in antiquity:

> Having carefully considered these things, I conclude that it is a property and natural quality of these arts that they improve themselves little by little from a humble beginning, finally attaining the height of perfection; and I am further convinced, seeing that virtually the same thing happened in other disciplines, which, because there is a certain kinship among all the liberal arts, is no small argument in favor of its truth. Something so

similar must have occurred in ancient times that if the names were exchanged, the account would be exactly the same.

The correspondence between the progress of art and the simultaneous progress in other areas of learning serves to support Vasari's claim for the status of the visual arts as liberal disciplines; the correspondence between the progress of art in his own time and in antiquity suggests that even the pattern of its development in time is governed by rule, a formal consistency that further testifies to its rational nature. Both correspondences, synchronic and diachronic, serve to confirm for Vasari the real perfection of the art of his own time and the universal validity of the principles on which it is based; at the same time they confirm the correctness of his account of its history.

Belief in the relation between the liberal disciplines and their revival in modern times was central to the cultural ideology of humanism, and insisting on the kinship between, say, painting and poetry was a common way of allowing the visual arts a share in the prestige of the humanist project. This idea, often denoted by the phrase *ut pictura poesis,* would be rejected by modern aesthetics—along with the assumption that art is fundamentally rational—but Vasari's suggestion that a single pattern underlies the historical development of art in all times seems to have been the starting point for modern formalist notions of an internal necessity governing the evolution of style.

Although the progress of art might be defined as the discovery and application of the rules for making good art, Vasari also acknowledges that the highest perfection sometimes involves a willful disregard of rules. In contrast to the artists of Vasari's own time, those of the second phase are deficient because they lack "a certain license, which, while not of the rule, is yet governed by the rule." Neither did these artists possess "that correctness of judgment by means of which their figures, without having been measured, might have, in proper relation to their dimensions, a grace surpassing measure." The idea that perfection can involve something beyond rational calculation could have come from any one of a number of sources: the literature of manners, for instance, extolled the studied negligence of demeanor that produces the aura of effortless grace; essays on female beauty often praised the stray curl that enhances rather than detracts from the overall effect; ancient rhetorical theory always reserved a place for the bold and effective breaking of rules. The tension between freedom and rule need not pose much of a problem if one remembers what Vasari himself says: that successful departures from rule give the impression of pointing toward another, higher rule.

A similar sort of apparent tension is found in Vasari's sensitivity to the diversity of individual styles, on the one hand, and his sense, on the other, of there being a single all comprehending standard. Some contemporaries had claimed that Raphael was a better painter than Michelangelo: although admitting Michelangelo's preeminence in sculpture and architecture, they felt that his painting, concerned almost entirely with the ideal male nude, lacked the pleasant color harmonies, facile grace, and richness of narrative interest found in Raphael. Others argued that Titian possessed similar virtues in even greater measure. Vasari acknowledged the merits of these painters; still, he took care, in the second edition of the *Lives,* to insist that Michelangelo's mastery of the principle of design gives his paintings a profundity that compensates for their lack of incidental charm. Raphael's style, marvelous as it is, owes much of its strength to the example of Michelangelo; Titian's voluptuous color masks a deficiency in design.

Appreciative as he was of different styles, then, there were limits to Vasari's tolerance; indeed, his conception of the progress of art presupposes rather narrow and rigid standards. His exclusivity is sometimes shocking to the modern reader: because good architecture is classicizing in style, for instance, what we call Gothic is simply barbaric—not an alternative style but a nonstyle. His attitude toward older art in general is condescending: although Giotto deserves credit for having made brave efforts in a benighted age, his work merits only qualified admiration. Such confidence in current standards was characteristic of the time: cultivated people could believe that the art of Giotto and his contemporaries was simply outmoded—quaint at best, clumsy and downright ugly at worst; one writer even criticized Vasari for giving Giotto more attention than he deserved. Seen against this background, Vasari's commitment to a historical understanding of the way art had come to achieve perfection stands out as markedly enlightened; one might even say that his historical perspective points beyond the limitations of his art theory. An appreciation for medieval art, a sense of its representing an alternative as valid as that of classical antiquity, on the one hand, or the High Renaissance, on the other, did not begin to emerge until the mid-eighteenth century and was not generally accepted until the mid-nineteenth: it was only with John Ruskin that Vasari's account of history, grounded in a particular set of values, was effectively supplanted.

Vasari is often faulted for his regional loyalties and prejudices. His taste is that of an artist trained in Florence and Rome, and his view of history gives overwhelming preponderance to central Italian developments. In the second edition he tried to present more information about other centers, both in Italy and northern Europe, but he still treats them as provincial, and sometimes uses the occasion to insist on the superiority of Florentine and Roman practice. His reservations about Venetian painters such as Titian, for instance, are partly explicable in terms of regional preference.

In addition to the exclusivity, there is another feature of Vasari's conception of progress that surprises and disturbs modern readers:

> This art is nowadays reduced to such perfection, and is so easy for someone who possesses skill in design, in invention and in the handling of colors, that where it once took a master painter six years to make one picture, we can now make six pictures in one year; I can swear to this for I have seen it done and done it myself; and [what is more] our works are more finished and perfect than those of even the leading masters of the past.

Such a passage reveals not only Vasari's smug attitude toward earlier art, but also that, on a deeper level, his notion of progress is rooted in a narrow, pragmatic—and frankly prosaic—conception of art as technique. His delight in the new facility of productive method seems to us almost embarrassingly simpleminded: disillusioned as we are by industrialization and nourished on the assumption that any such approach is alien to art virtually by definition, we must make an effort to imagine how he could regard it as something to be proud of. He could do so because the susceptibility of the creative process to this kind of rationalization was for him yet another sign of the rationality, hence the intellectual dignity, of art.

Much of Vasari's aesthetics is derivative, and much does not stand up to close philosophical scrutiny; one often hears it said that he was not an original or rigorous thinker. In his own way, however, he was both original and rigorous: he used a historical approach to gather and integrate, to superimpose, as it were, the various sources of art's interest; in so doing, he made history a means of demonstrating its intellectual depth and richness. The humanist historiography that he adopted as a model was regarded as a mode of philosophical inquiry: its aim was not simply to describe events, but to extract from them the enduring principles of human conduct. The *Lives* works in the same way: preserving the sources of art's human interest—in biography, in the drama of gradual development over time, for instance—it also tries to show how the universally and eternally true are revealed in time, and even how that process conforms to a pattern that transcends history. One might say that Vasari's philosophical achievement was to insist that art has a history, and that its historicity is essential to its philosophical interest.

[*See also* Art History; Narrative; *and* Renaissance Italian Aesthetics.]

BIBLIOGRAPHY

Works by Vasari

Le opere di Giorgio Vasari. 8 vols. Edited by Gaetano Milanesi. Florence, 1878–1885.

Le vite de' più eccellènti pittóri, scultóri e architéttori, nélle redazióni del 1550 e 1568. Edited by Rosanna Bettarini and Paola Barocchi. Florence, 1966–.

The Lives of the Most Eminent Painters, Sculptors, and Architects. 3 vols. Translated by Gaston du C. de Vere (1910). New York, 1979.

Other Sources

Belting, Hans. "Vasari and His Legacy: The History of Art as a Process?" In *The End of the History of Art?*, translated by Christopher S. Wood, pp. 65–120. Chicago, 1987.

Cast, David. "Reading Vasari Again: History, Philosophy." *Word and Image* 9 (1993): 29–38.

Kliemann, Julian. "Giorgio Vasari." In *The Dictionary of Art,* edited by Jane Turner, vol. 32, pp. 10–25. London, 1996.

Rubin, Patricia Lee. *Giorgio Vasari: Art and History.* New Haven, 1995.

Schlosser-Magnino, Julius von. *La letteratura artistica* (1924). 3d ed. Edited by Otto Kurz, translated by F. Rossi. Florence, 1977. See pp. 289–346.

ROBERT WILLIAMS

VENTURI, ROBERT. *See* Architecture; *article on* Modernism to Postmodernism.

VICO, GIOVANNI BATTISTA (1668–1744), Italian philosopher. Giambattista Vico was born in Naples and lived the whole of his life there, except for nine years (1686–1695) spent at Vatolla in the region of the Cilento south of Naples, where he served as tutor to the Rocca family at their castle, occasionally visiting Naples. He was professor of Latin eloquence at the University of Naples from 1699 to 1741. In 1735, under the rule of Charles of Bourbon, he was appointed royal historiographer.

Vico's major work is *Principles of New Science concerning the Common Nature of Nations,* which he published in two versions, the first in 1725 and the second in 1730 (the second was printed in a new edition in the year of his death). Vico is commonly considered to be the founder of the modern philosophy of history, but his *New Science* is also important for the origins of the philosophy of mythology and the philosophy of culture. Among his other works are a series of university orations presented in the first decade of his teaching career (1699–1707); these develop a conception of human education advocating the early study of poetry, metaphor, and rhetoric. Another book, *On the Most Ancient Wisdom of the Italians* (1710) is a refutation of Cartesian metaphysics. Vico opposes to René Descartes's method of certainty through doubt the principle he derived from Latin, that "the true is the made" ("verum esse ipsum factum"). He published a three-volume work on jurisprudence in the 1720s, under the general title *Il diritto universale* (Universal Law), in which he grounds natural law in the development of culture. Important to the understanding of Vico's philosophy is his autobiography, published in 1728 and continued in 1731. It is a first example of an original thinker providing a genetic account of his own intellectual development and discoveries. Vico wrote a large number of poems reflecting his knowledge of classical forms of composition, but these are occasional or commissioned pieces and are not regarded as having intrinsic artistic merit.

Although his career falls within the eighteenth century, Vico is not a figure of the Enlightenment. He does not hold doctrines of *illuminismo* or of specific progress either in history or in the development of the arts and sciences. Some commentators regard Vico as an enemy of the Enlightenment; others present him as accepting but transforming certain themes of modern science, and others consider him to be the final, summary figure of the tradition of Italian Renaissance humanism.

For aesthetics, the most important part of Vico's philosophy is his conception of "poetic wisdom" *(la sapiènza poètica),* which is the subject of the longest book in the *New Science.* Poetic wisdom is the form of thought and social life common to all nations at their origin. Poetic wisdom is the primordial state in which humans comprehend the world in terms of myths and create a world of civil institutions through rituals, customs, and common feelings. Vico claims that the first humans were poets who thought in terms of "imaginative universals" *(universali fantastici).* Vico uses the term *poetic* for what more modern thinkers such as Ernst Cassirer or Claude Lévi-Strauss would designate as "mythic." Vico's "poetic wisdom" is closer to the ancient notion of the poet as mythmaker, closer to *poiein* ("to make" and "to compose poetry"), on which concept Plato plays in book 10 of *The Republic,* and closer to the Latin *poeta* (maker, poet) than it is to the modern conception of poetry as a specific art form distinct from other forms of thought and consciousness. Vico claims that the first science to be studied should be mythology or the interpretation of fables because it is through the power of myths and fables that humans first organized their world and developed social institutions.

Vico's conception of poetic wisdom is based on his conception of *fantasìa.* Although normally translated as "imagination," *fantasìa* is not precisely equivalent to "imagination." Vico's notion of *fantasìa* has none of the sense of "fantasy," that is, nothing of the experience of a mental image of the "unreal," an illusion or phantasm. *Imagination,* when used not as a synonym for fantasy but in its sense of a deeply creative faculty that can perceive basic resemblances between things, is close to what Vico means by *fantasìa.* In the first stages of culture, according to Vico, human beings are unable to form abstract universals *(universali intelligibili)* such as are found in Aristotelian class logic, in which a given property can be univocally predicated of a number of things that compose a class. Humans are originally capable only of forming "imaginative universals"; through their power of *fantasìa* they are able to turn a particular experience into an image that carries universal meaning. A particular image formed by *fantasìa* can be univocally "predicated" of a multiplicity of particular entities. Thus, a hero or a totem is not one individual or thing among others but contains the total reality of the group. They all share in and fully embody its identity.

Vico's conception of imaginative universals is tied to his conception of history. Vico claims that history is cyclic. The life of any nation occurs in terms of *córso* and *ricórso*. Any given *córso* or *ricórso* moves through three ages, which Vico calls "ideal eternal history" *(stòria ideale etèrna)*: an age of gods, of heroes, and of humans. In the age of gods, all natural phenomena, as well as all basic social institutions (religion, marriage, burial, etc.), are formed as gods. Thunder is formed by the imaginative universal of Jove; the thunderous sky, with lightning, is literally Jove. Juno is literally the institution of marriage. In the age of heroes, virtues that guide conduct and character cannot be formed as concepts but are formed in the poetic character of the hero. Thus, Vico says, valor is formed as Achilles, wisdom as Ulysses. In the age of humans, the primordial power of *fantasìa* fades, as a dominant force guiding human thought and society, giving way to written laws and conceptual structures. *Fantasìa* remains within the third age as the power that underlies poetry and art. Within the sphere of aesthetic experience the imaginative universal holds sway, but it is no longer what guides thought and the cultural world at large.

Vico's imaginative universal—that is, the basis of fables and myths in the ages of gods and heroes—remains a way to form "ideal truths" about the human world in popular consciousness. Because of this, Vico says there "springs this important consideration in poetic theory: the true war chief, for example, is the Godfrey that Torquato Tasso imagines; and all the chiefs who do not conform throughout to Godfrey are not true chiefs of war" (1984, axiom 47). Vico suggests that there is a poetry of everyday life in which "ideal truths" or characters that embody virtues or various features of the human condition are first imagined, and these continue to be basic to our organization and interpretation of the world. The imagination continuously supplies us with the *archai* from which to know and act in the world. There is an interplay between the poet, who often formulates master images such as Tasso's Godfrey, and the common or vulgar imagination through which we approach the world on an everyday basis.

Based on his conception of the three ages of ideal eternal history, Vico has a conception of the "true Homer" and the "true Dante" that is relevant to literary history. Vico considers Homer to be the summary poet of the first two ages of the *córso* of Western history, the age of gods and the age of heroes. The "true Homer" is the Greek people themselves. Homer represents the transition from poetic wisdom to the conceptual wisdom of the philosophers, who appear in the third age, the age of humans. With the fall of the ancient world, the *ricórso* of the West is marked both by a return to religion and by the later development of the heroes of medieval society. The summary poet of the *ricórso* is Dante,

whom Vico calls the "Tuscan Homer." Dante's *Divina commèdia* marks the transition from the poetic wisdom of the *ricórso* to the philosophical wisdom of the Renaissance philosophers. For Vico, any work of literature can be read within the context of its place in the order of the ideal eternal history. What a work of literature means, for Vico, must include an understanding of its relationship to human culture.

Vico says that "imagination is the same as memory" ("la memòria è la stessa che la fantasìa). Thus the poet, in the modern age of humans, performs an act of memory; the poet is always attempting to recover that primordial power of *fantasìa* in an age in which such power is nearly lost. Behind the poet is always the ancient power of the myth and the fact that all words are centers of memory. Each word carries its own "truth" in its history of meanings, its etymology. James Joyce, who consciously used Vico's *New Science* as a "trellis" on which to base *Finnegans Wake* (as he had used Homer's poem for his novel *Ulysses*), adopted Vico's equation of imagination and memory as an aesthetic maxim. Joyce, as well as Ezra Pound and also William Butler Yeats, would be excellent examples of the view of the modern poet that emerges from Vico's approach to literature.

In aesthetic theory, the two thinkers who are most associated with the name of Vico are Benedetto Croce and R. G. Collingwood. Croce, in *Aesthetic as Science of Expression and General Linguistic*, devoted a chapter to the views of Vico. Indeed, Croce is one of the great figures in Vico scholarship generally. His *Philosophy of Giambattista Vico* was translated into English by R. G. Collingwood in 1913. Croce saw Vico as a precursor of Hegelian idealism and thus as an important source of his own idealist conception of culture. Croce credits Vico with the discovery of the true nature of poetry, in his conception of poetic wisdom, and calls Vico the inventor of the "science of aesthetic." Croce claims that in Vico's view, poetry and language are substantially the same, meaning that in its original form language is poetic and the instrument of the imagination. [*See* Croce.] Collingwood mentions Vico only twice in his *Principles of Art*, but Collingwood's general interest in developing a theory of imagination for understanding the principles of art, and his claim that art is knowledge, knowledge of the individual, are Vichian in spirit. [*See* Collingwood.] A third thinker who has given attention to Vico as important for a conception of myth and art is Cassirer. In his chapter on art in *An Essay on Man*, Cassirer presents Vico as the creator of a "logic of imagination," and he recounts Vico's conception of three ages as a basis for his own claim, that the mythmaker and the poet seem to live in the same world, that the symbolic form of myth always underlies and in one way or another is recalled in the productive activity of the poet.

Vico's *New Science* has historically had its greatest impact on the views of art and aesthetic experience in the idealist tradition. Vico has not become a source for work in contemporary aesthetics, although in literary studies such a writer as Herbert Read has praised Vico and been influenced by him. Vico does not have an aesthetic doctrine that is separate from his philosophy of history and philosophy of culture. Besides what Vico says specifically about the nature of the imagination and of poetic wisdom, the point that Vico's work holds out, to contemporary aesthetic theory, is the importance of grounding questions about art and aesthetics in the larger context of a philosophy of human culture.

Much work in the history of aesthetics has gone into the search for a definition of the artwork and for the determination of the essence of the artwork—the expression of emotion, pleasure, feeling, and so forth. In contemporary aesthetics a great deal of attention has been given to the cognitive status of the artwork and to the language of art. Most of such work in aesthetic theory is conducted as though art could be understood as something purely in itself, apart from the grounding of what art is in terms of a general theory of knowledge, philosophy of culture, or conception of society. When attention is given to art in these respects, a reductionist theory of art is often advanced in which art is reduced to politics, for example, in materialist or Marxist or other ideological terms.

Vico's view is instructive in that it implies that any proper conception of art, the arts, or aesthetic experience must begin where culture itself begins: with an understanding of myth or poetic wisdom, in the primordial use of *fantasia*. Although Vico does not formulate a theory of aesthetics per se, his *New Science* suggests that any aesthetics must be developed from an understanding of the origin of aesthetic experience in the origin of culture itself and that it must be understood against the particular stage of culture in which art occurs. This is not simply to advocate a historicist conception of art, because in Vico's view all development follows an ideal eternal pattern; thus, ultimately for Vico, any aesthetic view would require a grounding in a metaphysics of the nature of the human or civil world, one Vico claims to have given in his *New Science*.

[*See also* Poetics; *and* Renaissance Italian Aesthetics.]

BIBLIOGRAPHY

Works by Vico

The Autobiography of Giambattista Vico. Corr. rev. ed. Translated by Max Harold Fisch and Thomas Goddard Bergin (1944). Ithaca, N.Y., 1975.
The New Science of Giambattista Vico. Unabr. rev. ed. Translated from the 1744 edition by Thomas Goddard Bergin and Max Harold Fisch (1948). Ithaca, N.Y., 1984. Includes Vico's "Practic of the New Science."
On Humanistic Education: Six Inaugural Orations, 1699–1707. Translated by Giorgio A. Pinton and Arthur W. Shippee. Ithaca, N.Y., 1993. From the definitive Latin text, introduction, and notes of Gian Galeazzo Visconti.
On the Most Ancient Wisdom of the Italians, Unearthed from the Origins of the Latin Language. Translated by Lucia M. Palmer. Ithaca, N.Y., 1988. Includes Vico's *Disputations with the Giornale de' Letterati d'Italia.*
On the Study Methods of Our Time. Translated by Elio Gianturco (1965). Ithaca, N.Y., 1990. Includes Vico's "The Academies and the Relation between Philosophy and Eloquence," translated by Donald Phillip Verene.
Opere di G. B. Vico. 8 vols. in 11. Edited by Fausto Nicolini. Bari, 1911–1941.

Other Sources

Berlin, Isaiah. *Vico and Herder: Two Studies in the History of Ideas.* New York, 1976.
Danesi, Marcel. *Vico, Metaphor, and the Origin of Language.* Bloomington, Ind., 1993.
Grassi, Ernesto. *Rhetoric as Philosophy: The Humanist Tradition.* University Park, Pa., 1980.
Mali, Joseph. *The Rehabilitation of Myth: Vico's New Science.* Cambridge and New York, 1992.
Schaeffer, John D. *Sensus communis: Vico, Rhetoric, and the Limits of Relativism.* Durham, N.C., 1990.
Verene, Donald Phillip. *Vico's Science of Imagination.* Ithaca, N.Y., 1981.
Verene, Donald Phillip. *The New Art of Autobiography: An Essay on the "Life of Giambattista Vico Written by Himself."* Oxford, 1991.

DONALD VERENE

VIDEO. Defining video as an aesthetic medium has historically been a perplexing project. Written primarily as the evolution of its technology, video's history has been one of rapid, and of late, accelerating change. Since the introduction of the Sony Portapak in 1965, technological transformations of the video apparatus, such as the addition of color, high-resolution monitors, and on-line digital editing, have been inextricably allied with transformations of aesthetic effects. At the same time, video's diversity of formats, flexibility as a means of recording, and multimedia configurations have increasingly escaped traditional and modernist ontological categories. This chameleon-like quality, video's ceaseless process of becoming, can in part be traced to the specificity of the historical moment of its advent and cultural diffusion. Developed to complement broadcast technologies, videotape and video recorders were designed initially as accessories to commercial network television, which inflected the formal and technical properties of the video medium itself. Thus, at its origin, video lacked a secure and distinctive identity. Moreover, as a medium coming of age in the postindustrial era of information, video increasingly served as the audiovisual interface for interactive computer technologies, resulting in hybrid rather than pure video forms. From this perspective, the evolution of a unique video aesthetic can be read as the dialectical story of video's simultaneous self-discovery and abnegation as a medium, which can be charted in three roughly chronological periods: video's struggle for independence from the specificities of television, video's establishment of autonomy as a medium with distinct inherent properties, and video's re-

VIDEO. Nam June Paik, *Magnet T.V.* (1969), Television set and magnet, Television: 11 × 17 × 11 in., Magnet: 5 1/4 × 1 3/4 × 1 3/4 inches. (Photograph courtesy of the artist and the Holly Solomon Gallery, New York; used by permission.)

turn to indeterminacy as an adjunct technology of multimedia.

Video as Antitelevision. As an accident of history, video contested the tenets of technological determinism, a prescriptive discourse concerned with the belief that technology dictates aesthetics. Coinciding with the determinist theories of television popularized by Marshall McLuhan, video's first practitioners appropriated the medium precisely in opposition to television; thus, video by default signified antideterminism and the negation of institutional mandates, advocating cultural resistance to and formal experimentation with a broadcast medium previously theorized as monolithic and inert. Shattering David Sarnoff's model of broadcast from a single point of active production (the professional studio) to a constellation of passive receivers (domestic television sets), the invention of the Portapak and video recorder released the medium of videotape from the industrial and aesthetic confines of commercial networks into the hands of individual artists, activists, and home consumers. These constituencies, concerned respectively with art, politics, and entertainment, began to distinguish the term *video* from *television* as an inverse relation. Whereas television became regarded as a conservative medium of transmission (of other media forms, of capitalist ideology, of conventional programming), video was championed as a revolutionary medium of transformation (of art institutions, of the establishment status quo, of the network schedule).

In general, video artists adopted two strategies of negation: the first, a minimalist aesthetic and an assertion of real time as an interrogation into and detoxification of passive television spectatorship; the second, the modification of the codes of commercial television through quotation, allusion, parody, and protest in order to cue recognition of and distantiation from the objectionable qualities believed to inhere in industrial forms. Perhaps the video installations of Nam June Paik are most representative of these strategies of deconstruction and demystification: his prepared televisions (*TV Chair,* 1968), minimalist video sculptures (*TV Garden,* 1974–1978), recontextualized monitors (*TV Bra,* 1969), and distortions of received broadcast signals (*Magnet TV,* 1965) stripped television from its institutional and domestic environments in order to restore video as an aesthetic object.

Social activists who were contemporaries of Paik's appropriated video in order to intervene in the politics of television by organizing alternative production practices (variously referred to as street video, community video, or grassroots video) as modes of communication, consciousness-raising, and social change. Groups such as Videofreex, People's Video Theater, Global Village, and Ant Farm produced, distributed, and exhibited innovative underground documentaries, posed audiovisual culture as a positive alternative to print, and attempted to sublate the art/life dichotomy reified by bourgeois capitalism by integrating video into everyday praxis. In 1971, Michael Shamberg, a leader of the Raindance cooperative, advocated the decentralization of television as an aesthetically bankrupt and commercially corrupt medium in a manifesto titled *Guerrilla Television*. The appellation has persisted as a generic term for alternative video practices sharing similar sociopolitical goals.

Like early video art, activist video developed its aesthetic in opposition to commercial television. Against the slick postproduction values of network journalism, street video promoted an aesthetic of immediacy, which in part was technologically based. The unobtrusive nature of lightweight video equipment, its synchronous recording of sound and image, and the instantaneous replay of information encouraged a naturalistic, "real time" approach, which was, in turn, translated in terms of style as "realism" and of epistemology as "truth." Also opposed to the commodification of news as a product to be sponsored by commercial advertisers, activist video celebrated a more autotelic process accented by intimacy (an informal relationship between producers and subjects constituted by mutual participation and feedback) and by democracy (video's portability as a means to greater access and engagement for typically disenfranchised constituencies).

As many of the practitioners and goals of guerrilla video were absorbed and neutralized by television in the 1980s, the advent of home video consumer technologies, while domesticated in design and function, have been defended in some quarters for their potential resistance to broadcast imperatives for passive consumption. A substantial body of scholarship has documented the methods by which the video home system (VHS) video recorder has reactivated television reception. Its capacity for "time shifting," a function that records and saves broadcast programming for viewing at the spectator's convenience, intervenes in television's imperious "flow" by upsetting the designs of the network schedule to suit the idiosyncratic temporal rhythms of the household. The VCR's interactive features, such as pause, slow motion, and fast-forward, not only foster a writerly response to television texts but also liberate the viewer from ubiquitous advertisements and objectionable content. Finally, the growing market of prerecorded videocassettes available for playback increases access to subject matter not procurable from broadcast or cable, as well as preserves a corpus of texts for archival retention.

If the video recorder has fostered interactive reception, the video camcorder has encouraged proactive production.

As opposed to the economic and material restrictions of Super-8 film stock, videotape's low cost, extended recording time, and instant playback, as well as its capacity to be recycled, dubbed, and edited cleanly and efficiently, have substantially increased the range and volume of home-mode production practices exploring the possibility of non-broadcast forms (e.g., electronic diary, amateur porn, video will). As improvements to consumer equipment narrow the gap in quality between amateur and professional images, broadcast institutions have reacted by both adopting and adapting conventions of home video to fit those of commercial television. For example, the stylistic idioms associated with home video (hand-held camera movement, zooming, low light levels) have been embraced by advertising as markers of authenticity. More significantly, the subgenre of reality programming that solicits and airs amateur videotapes has substantially altered both audience expectations and Federal Communications Commission regulations of what constitutes broadcast image standards. The journalistic variation, inspired by George Halliday's footage of the Rodney King beating (1991) and represented by series such as *I Witness Video*, employs home video documents of crime, accidents, and disasters as eyewitness evidence; the more successful domestic variation, most notably *America's Funniest Home Videos*, blends the privatized experience associated with ritual family photography with the public, mass-marketed conventions of prime-time television. Commissioning amateur imagery for professional exploitation, reality-based programming of this nature in effect resituates activist video's populist origins as a democratic practice within a commercial context where, paradoxically, home video's ideologies of self-determination and familialism conflict. If amateur video may contest institutional hegemony, its commercial broadcast resurrects television's historic domestic ideologies, which may neutralize home video's potential for resistance.

Video as Video. Once liberated from its dependence on television, in order to achieve autonomy as a medium on an equal footing with the traditional arts, video would have to be reintroduced on its own terms, develop its own practices, and argue for the validity of its own aesthetic value. Resituating video within the Greenbergian discourse of inherent properties, which defines a medium by its supposed essential, unique formal characteristics, video artists began to create individual works foregrounding the materiality of the video apparatus, experimenting with its technological capabilities and constraints, and exploring its relation to painting, sculpture, Happenings, and kinetic, conceptual, and performance art.

If video's aesthetic of negation rejects the institution of television, video's aesthetic of inherent properties challenges the institution of art, in particular, the museum's archival agenda, sites of delivery, and modes of reception. Impermanent, videotape's signal decay and incompatibility with ever-changing delivery formats represent a denial of art as a precious, eternal object. Reproducible, video deviates from any policy dedicated to the protection and display of unique artifacts. Whether linear or multichannel, video's temporality, usually requiring a period of extended or intense viewing, clashes with the self-guided time of the museum's more leisurely pace.

Video installations, for example, reinvigorate the pedantic atmosphere of the museum by synthesizing real and electronic spaces into a visual, aural, and kinesthetic environment in which spectators can freely interact, moving about and behind the apparatus, while often appearing framed within monitors as part of the installation's raw material. Seminal works such as *Wipe Cycle* (Schneider and Gillette, 1969), *Corridor* (Nauman, 1970), *Dachau* (Korot, 1974), and *Mem* (Campus, 1975) aspired to the aesthetic of sculpture, by bringing separate units of image production (monitor, camera, VCR) into complex recorded and live closed-circuit configurations, and by treating the video signal as a tactile source of light rather than as a conduit of story or information.

Single-channel videotapes, like installations, often display a similar lack of commitment to narrative temporality and causal relations. Artists dedicated to a technique of synaesthetic abstraction reject the conception of videotape as a neutral recording device or a medium of representation, and instead generate electronic landscapes enabled by color processing, video keying, superimpositions, and computer inserts. Many early experimental tapes of this type focus on and exhaust the possibilities of one particular aspect of video's specificity: for example, instant replay (*Noise*, Benglis, 1972), live feedback (*Locating #2*, Holt, 1972), and electronic dubbing (*Generations*, Bolling, 1972).

Another genre of single-channel videotapes adopts the avant-garde aesthetic of montage as a method of parodic appropriation. At times referred to as "scratch" or "pastiche" video, works such as *P. M. Magazine* (Birnbaum, 1982), *Perfect Leader* (Almy, 1983), *Scenes from the Microwar* (Millner, 1985), and *Joan Does Dynasty* (Braderman, 1986) refashion popular and commercial imagery through a variety of editing and image-processing strategies, including the repetition of sound bites to expose the nonsensical redundancy of anonymous, authoritarian voice-overs; and the paradigmatic stacking of audiovisual fragments to betray the predictability and ideology of conventional narrative. As video dé-collage, these works offer a Brechtian metacritical discourse about industrial media's overt and hidden agendas, while reinvesting the appropriated material with a new understanding from a novel perspective.

Perhaps the most influential genre of single-channel tapes, performance videos foreground the presence of the artist's body as raw material, emphasize the author as both subject and object of enunciation, and incorporate personal experience for public display. The medium of video first at-

tracted performance artists who had been staging live exhibitions as a way to control, edit, and preserve each piece in its final, perfected form; to repeat performances without having to be physically present; and to seek refuge from the unpredictable responses of a live audience in real time and space.

In particular, the economy of video production, as opposed to film, recommended the medium to feminists, who discovered through performance video a mode of electronic consciousness-raising and an audiovisual means to illustrate the popular liberationist slogan "The Personal Is Political." Works such as *Semiotics of the Kitchen* (Rosler, 1975), *Kaleidoscope* (Barry, 1977), *Binge* (Hershman, 1987), and *It Wasn't Love* (Benning, 1992) typify feminist concerns with revising female stereotypes, expanding the self through projective role-playing, and exercising the right of women to assert themselves as creative, speaking subjects. Generally produced in the artist's home or alone in a production facility and structured rhetorically by direct address to the camera, feminist performance videos in particular have inflected art video with an aesthetic of intimacy.

Other performance videos have achieved a variety of aesthetic effects by imagining the video apparatus as a distinctive metaphor of self-identity. For example, seminal works such as *Centers* (Acconci, 1971), *Now* (Benglis, 1973), and *Boomerang* (Serra, 1974), exploit video's technological capacity to record and transmit the image of the artist simultaneously as both the object and subject of the gaze, constructing a solipsistic model of the apparatus as an electronic mirror, thereby achieving an aesthetic of narcissism. Not all performance videos are, however, essentially narcissistic. *Anger* (Cohen, 1986) and *The Love Tapes* (Clarke, 1978–1994), for instance, use video as a mode of confession and as a channel for dialogue with the self and an undisclosed other. In these works, wherein subjects disclose private thoughts and feelings alone to a camera as a method of therapy, the apparatus is constructed as both mirror and screen, a vehicle for self-confrontation and for intimate face-to-face encounters made safe by the buffer of a private and anonymous electronic space.

This is not to say that all performance videos are purely autobiographical. In videotapes as varied as *Weather Diary I* (Kuchar, 1986), *I Do Not Know What It Is I Am Like* (Viola, 1986), *My Puberty* (Segalove, 1987), and *Everyday Echo Street* (Mogul, 1993), the artist's subjectivity is split between inscribing personal history and documenting the external world. These works construct the monitor and camera lens as mirror and window, a dialectical apparatus calibrating the gap between introjective musings about self-identity and projective representations of an environment in which the artist maintains a libidinal, social, or cultural investment. Conceiving of the video apparatus variously as mirror, screen, or window, performance videos illustrate that the medium lacks a basal ontology. Video's so-called inherent properties are, rather, revealed as enabling fictions that reconfigure the differential aesthetic, cognitive, and cultural effects of individual works into metaphorical models of the apparatus that can claim for video a specific essence as justification of the artist's preferred mode of practice.

Video as Multimedia. The modernist pursuit of video's specificity in the 1970s and 1980s often conflated received conventions, established art idioms, and available technologies as intrinsic aspects of the medium rather than as the cultural elaborations of its material capacities at a specific historical moment. In the 1990s, video's manifold affiliations with multimedia, its assimilation by cinema, and its protean transformations by computer machinations have even further undermined the search for video's inherent properties as a propitious enterprise. Once the idea of a necessarily fixed site for the production and reception of images has been attenuated by issues of interface, hybridity, and digitization, the very designation of a unique video aesthetic loses signifying force. Increasingly, video serves as a medium of interface networking previously disparate media: for example, the computer (video games, CD-ROM, on-line editing), photography (photo-CD, video printer), telephone (teleconferencing, electronic mail), and architecture (video walls, closed-circuit surveillance). Neither an autonomous medium free of all links to other forms of art and communication, nor entirely dependent on any one of them, video can only be described by the plurality of its multimedia relationships rather than as pure in and of itself.

For example, video's supplemental relationship to film has generated hybrid forms and practices transforming modes of cinematic production and reception. Complementing celluloid as a production tool, video has been employed to record rehearsals, animate storyboards, scout locations, and check for continuity. Film-to-tape transfers of exposed footage have increased the speed and flexibility of editing, allowed for the rapid execution of special effects, and shortened the time lag between production and distribution.

Films on video have also radically transformed cinema reception in the form of the videocassette. Not only are motion pictures more frequently viewed at home than in movie theaters, privatizing a previously public viewing environment, but in order to accommodate for the different aspect ratios of the cinema screen and the television monitor, video must write its own technology over the original film text, introducing peculiar effects such as panning, scanning, letterboxing, and image reduction.

The employment of video images within film also modifies the phenomenology of classical Hollywood narration. Appearing in works such as *sex, lies, and videotape* (Steven Soderbergh, 1989) and *Speaking Parts* (Atom Egoyan, 1989), video scan lines, pixels, SLR-framing, LED messages, and shuttle effects comprise a new set of hybrid codes. This "video in the text" reframed by the cinema screen becomes a factor in the spectator's viewing strategy by calling attention to the source of its images, often implicating the viewer as a voyeur of private moments.

If film has increasingly incorporated video, computer digitization threatens to subsume it altogether. Digitized video replaces traditional image-making tools (VCR, camcorder, videotape) with a set of algorithmic models that code and decode the analog image as a series of binary symbols not mediated by physical processes, but rather stored in abstract structures independent of the dispositions and aesthetic qualities of the original video substrate. While digital icons are not subject to distortion or degradation when processed or reproduced, they do undermine the authority of the video image and distance the artist from the actual process of image creation: whereas analog video's aesthetic has been perceived as immediate, literal, actual, and naturalistic, digitized video is construed as contrived, distanced, synthetic, and analytic.

The indeterminacies of multimedia derail the notion that video's essence will inevitably unfold as it evolves progressively toward its self-identity. Such media teleology myths have been countered by postmodern arguments claiming that, because of its radical heterogeneity (capacity for interface and hybridity) and radical homogeneity (capacity for digital simulation), video simultaneously explodes and implodes modernist boundaries. From these apparently paradoxical qualities, according to this logic, the medium's essence can be extrapolated: that is, the specificity of video is precisely that it lacks one.

While multimedia may suggest that video's ontology will remain amorphous, the question of its aesthetic continues to be reframed and newly posed in works that stress content as well as form. Exploring issues of history (*The Art of Memory*, Vasulka, 1987), postmodernism (*Leaving the Twentieth Century*, Almy, 1982), creativity (*J. S. Bach*, Downey, 1986), ethnicity (*Meta Mayan II*, Veldez, 1981), feminism (*A Spy in the House That Ruth Built*, Green 1981), postcolonialism (*History and Memory*, Tajiri, 1991), and homophobia (*Tongues Untied*, Riggs, 1989), contemporary videos experiment with the medium's formal properties not merely in and for themselves, but as innovative material signifiers by which to express a unique social, cultural, or political vision. In these experimental works, the indeterminacies of video reflect the precarious conditions of contemporary life.

[*See also* Film; *and* Television.]

BIBLIOGRAPHY

Armes, Roy. *On Video*. London and New York, 1988.

Battcock, Gregory, ed. *New Artists Video: A Critical Anthology*. New York, 1978.

Berko, Lili. "Video: In Search of a Discourse." *Quarterly Review of Film Studies* 10.4 (1989): 289–307.

Cubitt, Sean. *Timeshift: On Video Culture*. London and New York, 1991.

Cubitt, Sean. *Videography: Video Media as Art and Culture*. New York, 1993.

d'Agostino, Peter, ed. *Transmission: Theory and Practice for a New Television Aesthetic*. New York, 1985.

Garnham, Nicholas. "The Myths of Video: A Disciplinary Reminder." *Capitalism and Communication: Global Culture and the Economics of Information*, pp. 64–69. London, 1990.

Hall, Doug, and Sally Jo Fifer, eds. *Illuminating Video: An Essential Guide to Video Art*. New York, 1990.

Hanhardt, John G., ed. *Video Culture: A Critical Investigation*. Rochester, N.Y., 1986.

James, David E. "inTerVention: The Contexts of Negation for Video and Video Criticism." *Millennium Film Journal* 20/21 (Fall/Winter 1988–1989): 46–55.

Jameson, Fredric. "Video: Surrealism without the Unconscious." In *Postmodernism: or, The Cultural Logic of Late Capitalism*, pp. 67–96. Durham, N.C., 1991.

Kurtz, Bruce. "Video Is Being Invented." *Arts Magazine* 47 (December/January 1973): 37–44.

Marshall, Stuart. "Video: Technology and Practice." *Screen* 20.1 (Spring 1979): 109–119.

Marshall, Stuart. "Television/Video: Technology/Forms." *Afterimage* 8/9 (Spring 1981): 70–85.

Nmungwun, Aaron Foisi. *Video Recording Technology: Its Impact on Media and Home Entertainment*. Hillsdale, N.J., 1989.

Podesta, Patti, ed. *Resolution: A Critique of Video Art*. Los Angeles, 1986.

Renov, Michael, and Erika Suderburg, eds. *Resolutions: Contemporary Video Practices*. Minneapolis, 1996.

Shamberg, Michael, and Raindance Corporation. *Guerrilla Television*. New York, 1971.

JAMES M. MORAN

VIOLLET-LE-DUC, EUGÈNE-EMMANUEL. *See* Gothic Aesthetics.

VIRTUAL REALITY. Virtual Reality is a synthetic technology combining three-dimensional video, audio, and other sensory components to achieve a sense of immersion in an interactive, computer-generated environment. Virtual Reality also appears under the title Virtual Environments or Virtual Worlds. Popular culture now uses the terms *virtual* and *virtual reality* in a weak sense that refers loosely to any kind of computer-mediated experience or even to any kind of imaginative experience, but the stronger usage of the term implies the application of immersion techniques that remain under development and are not yet widely available in the mid-1990s. It is these immersion techniques that distinguish the aesthetic novelty introduced by Virtual Reality.

Whereas traditional sculpture and architecture involve the viewer in three-dimensional space, Virtual Reality insulates the human sensorium in a full-surround computerized sensory feedback loop. The technical configuration used to achieve immersion differs, ranging from head-mounted displays and datagloves to room-size projections for unencumbered full-body interaction with artificial entities and autonomous agents. High-speed computing allows Virtual Reality systems to track the user's sensory responses and to provide real-time feedback of appropriate images, sounds,

and tactile pressure to create the feeling of immersion or being in a world. Some see in Virtual Reality the evolution of human–computer symbiosis, progressing from multimedia to cyberspace to virtual reality. A designer must take into account the specific immersion techniques and the kind of presence needed for the specific virtual world. The Virtual Reality artist can draw on a wide range of realism, from photographic realism to the softer realism of archetypal imagination. Virtual Reality has numerous applications in education, science, and industrial prototyping, as well as in telepresence and robotics, where it is used in surgery and in the exploration of outer space. As a metamedium, Virtual Reality will unfold its full potential only as artists gradually release it from the constraints of commercial and entertainment applications.

Definition in Historical Context. Virtual Reality functions as an umbrella concept for related research and commercial developments. The term *virtual reality* first appeared in the late 1980s with Jaron Lanier and his Virtual Programming Languages Incorporated (VPL), which introduced the first commercial system for controlling computer simulations through a dataglove and a stereoscopic head-mounted display (HMD). An artist himself, Lanier introduced Virtual Reality as a medium for shared self-expression. The fiber-optic glove or "dataglove" measures hand and finger movements and the helmet tracks the user's point of view so that the computer can adjust the stereo images to fit the user's position and hand gestures. The basic research behind the HMD and dataglove had been going on for twenty years before VPL, stretching back to Ivan Sutherland at Harvard and to several NASA research projects. Over the past decades, two major streams of Virtual Reality emerged: the one stream based on the HMD and the other stream based on the room-size projection of graphics for unencumbered interaction.

The helmet-based stream of Virtual Reality emerged not from the art world but from military flight simulators. The "supercockpit" was begun in the 1970s by Thomas A. Furness at Wright-Patterson Air Force Base. Along similar lines was the groundbreaking work of Ivan Sutherland during the 1960s at Harvard and at the University of Utah. Sutherland's head-mounted displays could work with primitive graphic simulations, not just aircraft flight. Early computer art, stemming from Michael Noll's experiments at Bell Labs, provided the computer graphics. Sutherland influenced Frederick P. Brooks, who founded the virtual worlds laboratory at the University of North Carolina. Brooks began designing virtual worlds for solving problems in medicine, physics, and engineering. The HMD pilot trainer became a universal simulator.

The other stream of Virtual Reality development came from the art world. Some of the kinetic and electronic art of the 1960s used cameras to create a feedback loop between the art objects and the participants. Interactive art, such as

Myron Krueger's Videoplace, suggested an unencumbered way of participating in real-time, computer-generated, graphic worlds. Krueger's Videoplace put people in separate rooms who could then relate interactively by mutual body painting, free-fall gymnastics, and tickling. Krueger's Glowflow, a light-and-sound room, responds to people's movements by lighting phosphorescent tubes and issuing synthetic sounds. Another environment, Psychic Space, allows participants to explore an interactive maze where each footstep corresponds to a musical tone, all produced with live video images that can be moved, scaled, rotated, without regard to the usual laws of cause and effect.

Krueger's line of Virtual Reality inspired commercial products such as the Mandala System and scientific research such as the CAVE at the Electronic Visualization Lab (EVL) of the University of Illinois at Chicago. At EVL, the CAVE (CAVE Automatic Virtual Environment) uses surround-screen, projection-based techniques to create an entire room in which users can explore virtual worlds unencumbered by physical trackers. Applications in the CAVE have included virtual environments for astronomy and physics. Krueger's influence was also manifest in the 1993 ALIVE (Artificial Life Interactive Video Environment) at the Massachusetts Institute of Technology Media Lab where semi-intelligent artificial agents with animated graphic bodies join human users who can relate to them with natural gestures.

Both streams of HMD and projection Virtual Reality share the common goal of providing an immersive experience. The user feels surrounded or immersed in a world of artificial, computer-generated entities with which he or she can interact. The "virtual" in *virtual reality* comes from the experience of being immersed in a world of entities that feel present when in fact they are not actually present, "virtual" meaning "in effect but not in fact." It is this illusory quality of Virtual Reality that establishes its link with trompe l'oeil painting and the many variants of aesthetic realism.

Virtual Reality can shade into telepresence. Telepresent Virtual Reality is an interactive immersion in a simulation linked causally, usually through robotics, to real-world entities. Virtual Reality telepresence allows NASA operators in Houston to move a Moon Rover across the lunar landscape while feeling as if they were actually present in the vehicle on the Moon. When linked to robotic graphics, Virtual Reality becomes a technology for telepresence, which means presence at a remote location.

The complex notion of presence is tied to subtle shadings of human experience. Research in Virtual Reality continues to explore the issues of what constitutes presence and what gives humans the ontological confidence to declare something to be real.

A related meaning of virtual reality has arrived with the advances in computer graphics. As sound systems were once praised for their high fidelity, present-day imaging systems now deliver "virtual reality." The images have a shaded texture and light radiosity that pull the eye into the flat plane with the power of a detailed etching. Landscapes produced on the GE Aerospace "Visionics" equipment, for instance, are photorealistic real-time, texture-mapped worlds through which users can navigate. These graphic dataworlds spring from the context of mission rehearsal and training in military flight simulators. Researchers now seek to bring these techniques to medicine, entertainment, and education. The claim of Virtual Reality aestheticians often goes beyond the claims of photographic realism or representation as users may experience the virtual entities to have ontological properties indistinguishable from the ontological properties of actual entities. Aesthetics in the virtual realm then often involves questions of presence and of ontological identity.

Relation to Tradition. Early Western psychology distinguished five senses plus a sixth or common sense *(sensus communis)* that coordinates the five other senses. The sixth or common sense produces the feeling of being focused on a unified, substantial entity on the basis of which the perceptions of the other senses are synthesized. Later aestheticians conceived this common sense as "sensibility" (called "universal subjectivity" in Immanuel Kant's *Critique of Judgment*), which changes over time and differs according to cultural conditioning. Cultural historians trace the variations in this conventional sensibility as shifts in perceptions. A similar postulate underpins Virtual Reality research. The notion of presence is intimately connected with whatever the senses perceive as given. The right sensory input can activate the sixth sense or feeling of presence, and the user experiences being present (virtually) among real entities in a real world. In this way, Virtual Reality brings aesthetics closer to ontology. Much twentieth-century philosophy—especially existentialism—revolved around presence as the key to reality. Pragmatists like William James also stressed the power of the human senses to entrain belief: you see it, you believe it—unless you consciously choose not to believe it. Because Virtual Reality raises basic questions of ontology and epistemology, its vocabulary resonates with much of Western art and philosophy, from Plato to Maurice Merleau-Ponty and Martin Heidegger. The scholars who one day will detail these connections will very likely cause the maps we have of past philosophies to be redrawn. Art, philosophy, and religion have from time immemorial discussed ways of transcending the immediate world. Knowledge, art, and thinking have achieved a considerable self-reflection on how to transcend bodily life. To this tradition Virtual Reality adds the factor of technology. Involvement with Virtual Reality may bring art, philosophy, and religion closer to the world of information.

Special Problems. The reference in Virtual Reality to "reality" or realism suggests a fundamental problem running throughout art history. If we want to create realistic experience, what indeed is reality? Is it largely a function of psychology or of empirical sense impressions? The introduction of technology does not answer this question but only heightens it—unless, that is, virtual reality shrinks to entertainment trivia and commercial applications. To achieve its potential as an art form, Virtual Reality will necessarily explore degrees of realism and of verisimilitude. What complicates the issue is the broad spread of disciplines from which Virtual Reality draws its sustenance: Virtual Reality combines art with technology, psychology with computer science, and electrical engineering with metaphysics. Another related problem is how to bridge the gap between the great expectations raised by the Virtual Reality concept and the actual achievements of research. The most widely available Virtual Reality systems today serve the limited goals of arcade games and commercial applications.

As Virtual Reality becomes a metamedium—combining theater, film, sculpture, dance, and so forth—artists will break it loose from the constraints of entertainment and commercial applications. Only in this way will its full potential unfold and truly appropriate applications appear. The learning curve will be high as Virtual Reality deviates from the experiential norms of previous art. One current example of such experiments is the visual sculpture done at the Institute for Simulation and Training in Florida. An interactive painting and sculpture environment gives participants some fuzzy-ball primitives to work with in three-dimensional space. The balls float scattered either loosely or densely in space according to the speed at which the user's hand moves through the space. The tracker sensor determines x, y, and z coordinates of the ball placement, but the other three degrees of hand movement (pitch, yaw, and roll) give color mappings for the balls. Colors change with the pitch of the hand, yaw controls the color saturation, and the intensity is controlled by the roll of the hand. Such nonisomorphic mapping requires considerable practice before art can be created, but the experiment shows the rich potential of Virtual Reality as a metamedium.

Closely related to the question of realism is the notion of immersion or presence. Granted that immersion is part of Virtual Reality, the question remains: How are users best immersed in virtual environments? Should users feel totally immersed? That is, should they forget where they are (in a graphics environment) and see, hear, and touch the world much in the same way we experience the primary phenomenological world? (We cannot see our own heads in the phenomenological world.) Or should users be allowed to see themselves as a cyberbody? Should they be aware of their primary body as a separate entity outside the graphic environment? What makes full-body immersion? The two different answers to this question split the field into the two kinds of immersion: the one derived from Krueger's Videoplace and the other from the head-mounted displays of Virtual Programming Languages, NASA, and Brooks's lab at the University of North Carolina. The choice of different Virtual Reality platforms (HMD or projection) points to a deeper issue of Virtual Reality and concerns its relationship to primary reality. The aesthetic questions then impinge on ethical issues. Our bodies remain in primary reality, and our cyberbodies (whether first person headless, full graphic, or telepresent surrogate) add a secondary level of self-awareness. The unity of the human mind and its primary body becomes more tenuous than ever in virtual worlds. Pilots in the Persian Gulf War experienced an extraordinary detachment from their bombing raids after having trained themselves virtually on the same missions for weeks. The skills required to wield computer precision and power are producing what the Pentagon calls "Nintendo soldiers." Avant-garde doctors also speak of the Nintendo surgeon who operates through telemedicine and whose patients evaporate into bodiless bits and bytes. Similar to jet lag and flight-simulator sickness, the Virtual Reality gap between mind and body leads to alternate world syndrome (AWS) or alternate world disorder (AWD) where fragments of the psyche get stuck in one world while working in another. Researchers find Virtual Reality users pointing their fingers in the real world and expecting to fly as they do in virtual environments. The positive side of such maladies is the possibility that Virtual Reality artworks in "augmented reality" will be able to connect virtual and real images in ways that enhance and transform the human connection to primary reality.

[*See also* Artificial Intelligence and Aesthetics; Computer Art; Cyberspace; Digital Media; Hypertext; *and* Multimedia.]

BIBLIOGRAPHY

Aukstakalnis, Steve, and David Blatner. *Silicon Mirage: The Art and Science of Virtual Reality.* Berkeley, 1992.

Biocca, Frank. "Will Simulation Sickness Slow Down the Diffusion of VE Technology?" *Presence: Teleoperators and Virtual Environments* 1.3 (Summer 1992): 334–343.

Burdea, Grigore, and Philippe Coiffet. *Virtual Reality Technology.* New York, 1994.

Heim, Michael. *The Metaphysics of Virtual Reality.* New York and Oxford, 1994.

Heim, Michael. *Virtual Realism: The Art of Emerging Technology.* New York and Oxford, 1998.

Krueger, Myron W. *Artificial Reality II.* Reading, Mass., 1991.

Pimental, Ken, and Kevin Teixeira. *Virtual Reality: Through the New Looking Glass.* 2d ed. New York, 1995.

Rheingold, Howard. *Virtual Reality.* New York, 1991.

MICHAEL HEIM

VOLTAIRE, FRANÇOIS-MARIE AROUET DE.

See French Aesthetics, *article on* Eighteenth-Century French Aesthetics.

W–Z

WAGNER, RICHARD (1813–1883), German composer. From *Der Fliegende Holländer* (1841), his first fully characteristic work, through *Tannhäuser, Lohengrin,* the mighty *Ring* cycle *(Das Rheingold, Die Walküre, Siegfried,* and *Götterdämmerung),* through *Tristan und Isolde, Die Meistersinger von Nürnberg,* to his final work, *Parsifal* (1882), Wagner's musical and dramatic explorations opened up terrains of the imagination that were to haunt almost every significant composer since his time. As a strictly musical phenomenon, then, Wagner's place in history is as secure and as clear as that of any seismic event could be. But why does he matter for aesthetics?

The answer to this question is immensely complex. One might begin, somewhat artificially, by distinguishing four separate senses in which Wagner's relationship to aesthetics is significant. First, Wagner can be seen as the product, or at least the accomplice, of an aesthetic—Arthur Schopenhauer's. Second, he can be seen as the inspirer of an aesthetic—most notably Friedrich Nietzsche's. Third, he can be seen as the producer of an aesthetic—through his own copious writings. Fourth, and most diaphanous, he can be seen as a disrupter of aesthetics—his musical works, and the reception of them, disturb and continue to disturb any settled sense of what art can be and do.

The first two of these can be dealt with quite quickly. Wagner discovered Schopenhauer's *The World as Will and Representation* in 1854, and what he found there was exciting and congenial. The innermost nature of the world, according to Schopenhauer, is vile: a blind, endlessly, and meaninglessly striving Will whose refracted representations constitute the world of human experience. Music, and music alone, is capable of penetrating the veil of representation. Indeed, music enjoys a uniquely privileged mode of access: it is (or can be) a "copy" of the Will. The sheer grandeur of Schopenhauer's vision, if not perhaps the actual vileness of it, appealed to Wagner immensely, as it would to any musician of ambition. Finding in Schopenhauer a warrant for his own most extravagant estimation of music's capacities, for his conviction that music was *the* metaphysically significant activity, he became an ardent admirer—to the extent that his book about Beethoven, supposed to be ardently admiring of Beethoven, refers to Schopenhauer about ten times as often as to its ostensible subject. Then, in 1868, Wagner met Nietzsche, himself already an avid Schopenhauerian. Nietzsche was hungry for a hero and was swiftly convinced that in Wagner he had found one. The final ten sections of *The Birth of Tragedy,* Nietzsche's first book, hail Wagner as the modern incarnation of Aeschylus, as a doer of metaphysical deeds whose like had not been seen since antiquity. Specifically, Nietzsche hails Wagner as the first post-Socratic artist to have penetrated the ("Apollonian") veil of representation so as to touch ground again with the ("Dionysian") reality beneath—a reality so dreadful that it could be borne only in the kind of intoxicated state that Wagner's music was so capable of inducing. Nietzsche fell out with Wagner shortly afterward. He also repudiated Schopenhauer. But whereas the break with Schopenhauer marked the decisive move into Nietzsche's all-too-brief philosophical maturity, the break with Wagner was much less clean. Nietzsche's estimation of the significance of art, and of music in particular, was permanently conditioned by his experience of Wagner. He returned to him again and again, as if to a peculiarly seductive sore—picking, squeezing, probing, hating, fond—and remains Wagner's most intimate and devastating critic.

No artist has so directly fed off or into the major philosophers of art as has Wagner. But if he had merely done that he would have been a prodigy, not a phenomenon. To capture his phenomenal quality better, one must turn to the third and fourth of the considerations mentioned earlier. The third concerned Wagner's own writings. Verbose, grandiloquent, and often tiresomely obscure, Wagner's reflections on music and musical drama represent by far the most sustained attempt by a musician of genius to express his hopes for and understanding of his own art (only Arnold Schoenberg comes close to him in this regard). Two of his larger ideas should be enough to suggest the thrust, and indeed the thrustingness, of his thought. First, there is the conception of the *Gesamtkunstwerk* (the "total work of art"). Wagner longed for a synthesis of the arts in a single work—a work in which the various arts would come together to yield a power and a totality of vision unavailable to any of them individually; and he sought, with a degree of success that is still the subject of debate, to realize that ideal in his own music dramas (for which he wrote both texts and music and, when he could, designed the sets). The second large idea concerns the relation of thought to feeling: "Nothing should remain," he said, "for the synthesizing intellect to do in the face of a performance of a dramatic work of art. . . . In drama we must become *knowers* through *feeling.*" Here, in all likelihood, Wagner felt that a sufficiently openhearted response to his own works would be enough to bear him out. These two ideas are not unrelated. Historically, both kick against the most important trend in nineteenth-century musical aesthetics. Music, it was increasingly coming to be held, was autonomous: it bore no natural allegiance to the other arts, did not depend on them or anything else for its significance, and was, in that sense, *pure,* that is, meaningful in a purely musical way. The *Gesamtkunstwerk* ideal turns this on its head. Music, for Wagner, is to be seen as a mere ingredient, as just one force in a field of significance whose import exceeds, no doubt impurely, anything that music might achieve by itself. Add to this the claim that dramatic art operates on thought via feeling, so that music, in its dramatic capacity, is significant for reasons other than purely musical reasons, and the repudiation of musical autonomy is complete. At a historical level, then, Wagner's aesthetic is strikingly nonconformist.

It is at a level that one might describe as cultural that Wagner's aesthetic is most striking. Nietzsche was probably the first to put his finger on (and to be disturbed by) the wider character of Wagner's artistic ambitions. The aspiration to a totality of vision, to an all-encompassing interpretation whose authority was to be grounded on the primacy of feeling, seemed, on Nietzsche's diagnosis, to be symptomatic less of an artistic impulse than of a religious one. Founders and furtherers of religions, he insisted, set out to combat the dissatisfactions engendered by the immanent, contingent nature of human existence. They do this by inventing for existence *complete,* and therefore transcendental, interpretations—that is, interpretations that, because they offer to account for everything, to make sense of everything, remove that "illusion" of contingency that dissatisfaction is caused by and feeds off; and the founders of religions exploit the passions of the dissatisfied in order to force those interpretations on them or, at any rate, to render them irresistible. In this sense at least, Wagner's aesthetic turns out to be a kind of substitute theology, expressly designed to comfort the afflicted and to foreclose the possibility of living in that honest acknowledgment of immanence and contingency that Nietzsche calls "noble" and "tragic." Small wonder that, having made this diagnosis, Nietzsche withdrew his youthful identification of Wagner's art as the *rebirth* of tragedy. Of course, the situation is more complicated than this. For one thing, Wagner—under the influence of Schopenhauer—came to accord to music a far greater significance than was consistent with his original conception of the *Gesamtkunstwerk.* But this is offset by his acceptance of Schopenhauer's metaphysics, itself a totalizing interpretation of existence driven, if the later Nietzsche is right, by the acutest feelings of dissatisfaction (Schopenhauer's "Will" is an all-embracing explanatory principle

that, once grasped, is supposed to alleviate pain by fostering renunciation—renunciation being a response to which Wagner had always attached great significance). Thus, Wagner's aesthetic remains quasi-religious, in Nietzsche's sense, even if his conception of the precise character of the metaphysical task to be fulfilled by art, and by music in particular, changed. What is beyond doubt, though, is that in a century on which religion proper had started to lose its grip, art was increasingly seen as its natural successor (*something* must comfort the afflicted); and of this new cult (which counted Hector Berlioz and Franz Liszt among its early adepts), few, including Wagner, seriously doubted that Wagner was to be high priest. Where "religion becomes artificial," he wrote, "it is the duty of art to save religion's essential core"; and when he opened the Festspielhaus at Bayreuth in 1876, built by him and specifically designed for the performance of his own works, its character as a temple and a place of worship was widely appreciated.

Many have been tempted to see rather more in Wagner's efforts to "save religion's essential core." Specifically, many have been tempted to see in it a commitment to another major nineteenth-century trend—the trend toward romantic nationalism. Insofar as Wagner would have liked, in part and at times, to reinvent Germany in the images of Nordic mythology, it is said, so his aesthetic/religious ambitions must necessarily have had a political dimension. But this is surely questionable. Wagner was, after all, a Schopenhauerian—and Schopenhauer's separation of aesthetics from politics was uncompromising. Nor is the suggestion, regularly made, that Wagner instead drew encouragement for an aestheticized nationalism from Nietzsche at all compelling: the nearest to a political position of any kind to be found in Nietzsche is an extreme contempt for nationalism in general and for German nationalism in particular. If the link between Wagner's quasi-religious ambitions and a romantic politics is to be made good, then, the evidence for it will have to be drawn from his music dramas; and here it is doubtful that what is needed can be found. Even *Die Meistersinger,* which might at first sight appear to offer the richest pickings, turns out to wear its nationalism lightly; and, to the extent that its politics is an aestheticized politics, it implies nothing more romantic than the musical or dramatic equivalent of a republic of letters. It seems unlikely, then, that Wagner is best to be regarded as a political phenomenon, however much politics may have figured in the reception of him in some quarters. The political is not, in other words, integral to an understanding of Wagner's work in the way that the religious is.

No one who is at all serious about life can remain indifferent to religion. Its claims and demands are unconditional; it abolishes, by fiat, the possibility of remaining neutral. One must be for it or against it; and so, for closely analogous reasons, and to an extent unequaled by any other artist, with Wagner. No one who is at all serious about music can be (or has been) indifferent to him; for the astonishing thing—and this brings us to the fourth of the considerations mentioned at the outset—is that Wagner's art succeeds, to a remarkable degree, in realizing and giving form to the fundamental tenor of his aesthetic. The larger-than-life, mythic quality of the characters and actions of his dramas, the huge and yet somehow hermetically sealed worlds in which they unfold, offer, or appear to offer, totalizing interpretations as complete and unconditional as those of any religion. As for the music, when Wagner demanded that a dramatic work of art should leave "Nothing . . . for the synthesizing intellect to do"—that "we must become *knowers*" of his interpretations "through *feeling*"—he neither overestimated the expressive capacities of his own music nor underestimated the radical power that such capacities might have. For sheer extremism, his is the most expressive music ever written. In its effects—seductive and intoxicating to the admirer, cynical and manipulative to the detractor—its power to polarize is unprecedented. No other artist has inspired worshipful fervor as Wagner has, nor has any artist been so brutally vilified. *Tristan und Isolde* is Wagner at his most Wagnerian. It is, as Michael Tanner has shown, his one fully religious work—not in the sense of having overtly religious subject matter, in which case the religious work would have been *Parsifal* (in fact his least religious work), but in the sense that it pushes so uncompromisingly at the limits of immanence and contingency that the only possible resolution of its dramatic impetus is transcendental—a possibility, moreover, of whose reality Wagner's music more than half persuades one. "Every religion," as Tanner puts it, is "a doctrine of extremes"; and in *Tristan*, "so paralysingly absolute in its demands," that doctrine is "humanism pressed to its limits, then exploded into transcendent metaphysics"—a metaphysics set to and apparently embodied in "music which has a compelling beauty of a kind that none other possesses" (1996). It is this sort of thing that makes neutrality in the face of Wagner a nonoption. Either one is prepared to be seduced by him, to be converted, however briefly, into a (quasi-religious) "knower" through "feeling," or else, because one suspects that this is what Wagner can do, and one refuses him the authority to do it, one must recoil from him and denounce the means through which his effects are attempted.

Yet, neither of these options has proved easy to pursue with any grace. The first, as the young Nietzsche found, degenerates too readily into idolatry: Wagner becomes a shrine at which one offers up one's integrity. The second, on the other hand, tests one's integrity to the limit: it requires that one first acknowledge the power of Wagner's music to do *to oneself* what one refuses it the authority to do—which, as the mature Nietzsche repeatedly discovered, makes the moral high ground almost impossible to identify, let alone to occupy. This, in turn, explains why the rejection of Wagner's own extremism—a rejection that may be attempted in all se-

riousness and good faith—so often, in his less courageous critics, degenerates into those extreme and self-serving modes of denunciation with which we are all familiar, for instance, the perennially popular one of pretending to have discovered traces, or even swaths, of proto-Nazism in his music (something that, music being music, could not be there). It is no accident, in light of this, that Wagner's most penetrating critics—Nietzsche, Thomas Mann—have also been the most ambivalent, perpetually torn between gratitude and revulsion, never settling for long into either. Wagner, like Christianity, puts the critic—indeed, Western culture itself—on the spot, to an extent that no other artist even begins to equal; and it is in this huge and acute sense that he continues to matter for aesthetics. What, as Nietzsche asked, is the *meaning* of Wagner?

[*See also* Music, *historical overview article;* Nietzsche; Opera; *and* Schopenhauer.]

BIBLIOGRAPHY

Work by Wagner

Prose Works. 8 vols. Translated by William Ashton Ellis. London, 1892–1899.

Other Sources

Cooke, Deryck. *I Saw the World End: A Study of Wagner's Ring.* New York and Oxford, 1979.
Dahlhaus, Carl. *Richard Wagner's Music Dramas.* Translated by Mary Whittall. Cambridge and New York, 1979.
Deathridge, John, and Carl Dahlhaus. *The New Grove Wagner.* London, 1984.
Donington, Robert. *Wagner's "Ring" and Its Symbols: The Music and the Myth.* London, 1963.
Kerman, Joseph. "Opera as Symphonic Poem." *Opera as Drama,* new rev. ed., pp. 158–177. London, 1989.
Large, David C., and William Weber, eds. *Wagnerism in European Culture and Politics.* Ithaca, N.Y., 1984.
Mann, Thomas. *Pro and Contra Wagner.* Translated by Allan Blunden. London, 1985.
Muller, Ulrich, and Peter Wapnewski, eds. *Wagner Handbook.* Translation edited by John Deathridge. Cambridge, Mass., 1992.
Nietzsche, Friedrich. *Nietzsche contra Wagner.* In *The Portable Nietzsche,* edited and translated by Walter Kaufmann. New York, 1954.
Nietzsche, Friedrich. *The Case of Wagner.* In *The Birth of Tragedy and the Case of Wagner.* Translated by Walter Kaufmann. New York, 1967.
Schopenhauer, Arthur. *The World as Will and Representation.* 2 vols. Translated by E. F. J. Payne. Reprint, New York, 1966.
Tanner, Michael. "The Total Work of Art." In *The Wagner Companion,* edited by Peter Burbidge and Richard Sutton, pp. 140–224. London, 1979.
Tanner, Michael. *Wagner.* London, 1996.

AARON RIDLEY

WARHOL, ANDY. *See* Pop Art.

WILDE, OSCAR (1854–1900), Irish poet, playwright, and critic. Perhaps the most entertaining aesthetic theorist of all time, Wilde's contribution to the transition between Victorian and modern views of art in society has been consistently underrated—even, as Jorge Luis Borges once observed, by his most ardent defenders, who tend to celebrate his irreverence and wit over the lucidity and insight that bore them out. In the more than a century since his release from prison, Wilde has been championed as a martyr to Victorian morality, as a radical and boisterous minister of an otherwise rather effete aesthetic gospel, and, more recently, as a fountainhead of such postmodern phenomena as queer self-consciousness, identity politics, and commercial self-promotion. Although none of these views is false or useless, they all tend to de-emphasize the intellectual aspect of his achievement in favor of its social and political aspect, and thus do Wilde the same disservice—much as contemporary accounts of his outrageous affectation and brilliantly modulated conversation once tended to obscure his remarkable kindness and generosity. This essay considers Wilde's critical theory on its own terms—that is, those of the main currents of Victorian thinking about art's function in society—and, equally, in terms of his own personal development.

Life. Oscar Fingal O'Flahertie Wills Wilde was born in Dublin in 1854, second son of Sir William Wilde and Lady Jane Francesca. Reared in an atmosphere of high-minded, intellectual bohemianism, Wilde spent three years at Trinity College, Dublin, before going up to Magdalen College, Oxford, in 1874, where he studied with John Ruskin and Walter Pater and distinguished himself as a first-rate classical scholar and flamboyant personality. In 1878, he moved to London, where he published a volume of poems and a verse play, and acquired almost instant celebrity as a wit and apostle of art, often sharing weekly headlines with James McNeill Whistler. In 1882, his fame firmly linked to that of Reginald Bunthorne, the aesthetic caricature in W. S. Gilbert's *Patience* (1881), Wilde embarked on a yearlong lecture tour of the United States, delivering his largely Ruskinian gospel of beauty in everyday life. On his return to England, he married Constance Lloyd in 1884 and had two sons, Cyril and Vyvyan. In 1886, he gave up lecturing in order to pursue a career in letters, writing numerous reviews, occasional pieces, and the fairy tales collected in *The Happy Prince and Other Tales* (1888). Between 1887 and 1889, he edited *The Woman's World,* a popular ladies' magazine, which he revamped to include articles on politics and social issues as well as fashion. In the ensuing years, Wilde wrote his most important works of criticism: "The Portrait of Mr W. H. (1889), "The Soul of Man under Socialism" (1891), and the four essays later published as *Intentions* (1891): "The Decay of Lying," an attack on realism; "Pen, Pencil and Poison," which explores the affinities of art and crime; "The Critic as Artist," the most complete statement of Wilde's critical theory; and "The Truth of Masks," a meditation on Shakespearean stage costume. The year 1891 also

saw the publication of two volumes of Wilde's fiction: *A House of Pomegranates,* a collection of allegorical tales, and *The Picture of Dorian Gray,* the now classic fable of a beautiful young man whose portrait bears the marks of age and debauchery, while he himself retains the innocent beauty that it first depicted. Although its initial notoriety proceeded largely from its distinctly homosexual overtones, the novel is now most fruitfully viewed as a culmination of this critical phase.

It was in the wake of *Dorian Gray*'s controversial reception that Wilde met Lord Alfred Douglas, the love of his life, and the instrument of Wilde's spectacular fall from public grace. During the early 1890s, Wilde found a lucrative market as a popular dramatist. Although *Salomé* (1891), written in French, was banned from the English stage, his series of comedies, *Lady Windermere's Fan* (1891), *A Woman of No Importance* (1892), *An Ideal Husband* (1893), and his masterpiece, *The Importance of Being Earnest* (1894), were all critical and financial successes. The last two were running simultaneously in the West End when the marquess of Queensberry, Douglas's father, delivered the last of a string of public insults with which he had been harassing Wilde for some time. At Douglas's urging, Wilde sued for libel, lost, and was subsequently tried, convicted, and sentenced to two years at hard labor for homosexual practices. In prison he wrote the long, cathartic letter to Douglas published posthumously as *De Profundis* (1905). Shortly after his release, he wrote "The Ballad of Reading Gaol" (1898), his best poem and last completed work. A social and professional pariah, Wilde lived out the remaining years of his life on the Continent under the assumed name of Sebastian Melmoth. He died in Paris, from complications of an ear infection, in 1900.

The Aestheticism of Self. Ian Small (1993) and other critics have argued that Wilde's celebrity as a social figure and the tragic trajectory of his later life have obscured the nature of his work as a critic and theorist. But Wilde's theory of self-cultivation is far too closely bound up with his own career of self-promotion, spectacular rise, and fall to allow for any easy suppression of his biography. Wilde himself famously remarked to André Gide that he had put his genius into his life, and only his talent into his works, and taking this claim seriously does illuminate certain important elements of Wilde's very particular contribution to aesthetic theory. Wilde's genius in life was for producing extreme and quite often opposing effects while sustaining a remarkably unified and consistent persona. In society he combined self-serving dissimulation with a radically satirical honesty. Professionally he advocated an aristocracy of art while devoting his energies to popular and financial success. His intellectual tastes combined the exquisite languors of Charles Baudelaire with the energetic rigors of Ruskin; his morals were equally narcissistic and public-spirited; his ethics were as radically individualistic as Friedrich Nietzsche's or Ralph

Waldo Emerson's, yet more sensitive to the effective operation of conventional norms than either. In personal matters, he was known for his extraordinary kindness and generosity, yet his conduct toward his wife can only be called cruel.

Many original personalities can be said to contradict themselves this way, but Wilde was the only one to claim it as a mode, rather than merely a symptom, of creative genius. "To turn truth into a paradox is not difficult," he once wrote in praising a modern novelist, "but [he] makes all his paradoxes truths, and no Theseus can thread his labyrinth, no Oedipus solve his secret." It was crucial to Wilde's work that he had a secret of his own, which he was always both careful to preserve and eager to flaunt. Richard Ellmann has suggested that Wilde's critical period of productivity was linked to his seduction and initiation into homosexuality by Robert Ross in 1886, and that the illicit, duplicitous existence into which it propelled him provided not only the basis for his fiction but the grounding of his critical thought as well, although it can as easily be said that Wilde's preoccupations with duplicity influenced the conduct of his erotic life. Either way, the public revelation of Wilde's sexuality is clearly central to his importance as a figure of Victorian transition into modernity, not only socially, but intellectually as well. Wilde's eloquent defenses of male love as a cultural inheritance of classical Greece revealed the erotic aspect of a familiar mode of thought and discourse; his defeat and decline underscored the irreconcilability of human experience to simple classifications of moral value. Other figures of the period—Charles Stewart Parnell, for example—had challenged conventional morality, demanding that one aspect of a man's character guarantee forgiveness for another. But Wilde's homosexuality was far more acutely linked to his public persona than any public man's private adulteries could be: rather than demanding forgiveness, it was a revelation that gave everything he had said and done before a new meaning, producing precisely the kind of shift in consciousness that, according to Wilde, it is art's business to effect.

The course of Wilde's life is a remarkable illustration of just those tensions between self and society, conceptual and perceptual experience, that came to define modernist self-consciousness. Wilde was himself a great exponent of modern selfhood, which identifies the individual as existing in opposition to a communal standard, albeit not completely alienated from it. In "The Soul of Man under Socialism," Wilde propounds his view of the artist's perfect freedom to cultivate sensation and experiment with new forms as the ultimate type of personal autonomy. According to his libertarian socialism, the elimination of private property and industrial labor will free everyone, rich and poor, to realize themselves fully in this manner, resulting in an entirely uninhibited culture, in which it will be possible "to express everything," as the artist is able to do. Although Wilde's belief in socialism's commitment to the supreme rights of the individual was sincere, his utopia is more of a platform than a projection. The abolition of authority in a state of perfect socialism is a step toward the abolition of "public opinion," a philistine monstrosity that limits the exercise of artistic temperament. Yet, it is in setting the counterexample for this very public that the artistic temperament is meaningful and empowering, and it is in this essay that Wilde asserts the possibility of good art being able to affect and improve public taste, provided that the artist is free from the need to satisfy public expectation; and he praises a great theatrical producer for having "created in the public both taste and temperament." Art, then, is for Wilde the means by which individual efforts at self-realization can be shared without resorting to the universalizing effects that invariably proceed from the imposition of moral standards or social prejudices.

Art also provides a model for the synthetic, rather than organic, development of the self, which for Wilde was a crucial feature of modern existence. Dorian Gray's identity composes and decomposes itself around a picture and a book, each brought into his life by a different man; Willie Hughes, the notional boy actor on whom the central theory of "The Portrait of Mr. W. H." is based, is literally composed of lines from Shakespeare's sonnets and the frustrated passion of an actor turned critic; in *The Importance of Being Earnest,* Jack Worthing's false identity trades places with his real one when the latter turns out to be the result of a substitution of a person for a work of fiction. The point is not only that the self is grounded in artifice, but that it grows and changes as art does, in the consciousness of other people as well as one's self. Conflicting attitudes toward the public—indifference and confrontation, deception and disclosure—are at the heart of all the phases of Wilde's individualism. In the Preface to *Dorian Gray,* he says that the artist commits himself to "reveal art and conceal the artist," while the critic's work is always "a mode of autobiography"—a species of self-disclosure that emerges from serious engagement with nature of his aesthetic responses. Yet, this engagement is precisely what makes the critic *into* an artist. In *De Profundis,* the source of self-realization has mutated from aesthetic experience to suffering, and takes the despised, redemptive Christ as the figure for the Ultimate Artist. The idea still partakes of the same paradoxical relation between a perfectly universal individualism—toward which Wilde saw all good as tending—and the communal background of social and moral standards against which it must be exercised. That he insists on sustaining this contradictory attitude toward others, rather than attempting either to evade to resolve it, is finally what makes Wilde's individualism more of a personal and practical philosophy than a social or political one.

The Aestheticism of Form. In the figure of the artist/dandy/critic, Wilde found his own method of enacting critical ideas of self-development that might well be (and has been, by Philip Rieff [1970]) called therapeutic, especially considering that Wilde was almost an exact contemporary of Sigmund Freud. But whereas Freud's theory depends on working out a relationship to authority through transference, Wilde's model of self realization presupposes an indifference to any authority save beauty, that interplay between form and feeling by means of which Wilde saw art doing its therapeutic work: "mere expression is a mode of consolation," he says in "The Critic as Artist": "form, which is the birth of passion, is also the death of pain." The birth of passion is also the birth of external, not just internal, experience of self. For Wilde, as Leon Chai puts it, "form belongs to life rather than simply to our perception of it" (1990). The apprehension of form is a means of connecting interior experience to exterior reality.

Both in Wilde's theory and in the course of his own life, the development of the self begins in this attentiveness to form. During his Oxford years, Wilde traveled to Greece with a former Trinity tutor, and returned with a fully "Hellenized" view of civilization and a settled commitment to the creed of beauty that would later qualify him to be representative of the so-called Aesthetic movement. A school of self-presentation as much as of ideas, its doctrine of sensational experiment and artistic detachment—the French dictum "art for art's sake" was its catchphrase—was to be expounded in a languid demeanor and various affectations of "exquisiteness" (long hair, cigarettes, anachronistic dress) as well as in an artistic and critical disdain for realism and a commitment to technique and atmosphere, principles influenced by such French writers as Baudelaire, Théophile Gautier, and Stéphane Mallarmé as well as by the English Pre-Raphaelites, Ruskin, and Pater. As he matured, Wilde's commitment to beauty crystallized into a commitment to individualism, but it maintained its grounding in aesthetic effects. It is precisely this aesthetic conception of self—an identity derived from experience rather than from universal precepts—that Wilde rightly understood to be a crucial aspect of modernity.

One of paradoxical things about Wilde that has confused his critics is that his aesthetic judgments—especially of poetry—often seem to belie his ideology. Wilde had none of the taste for hard, intellectual unprettiness that came to be a hallmark of modernist aesthetics; nevertheless, he recognized the greatness of two of its most important poetic precursors, Walt Whitman and Robert Browning: even as he denigrated the sounds of their poetry, he correctly understood and valued the more general aspect of their respective enterprises as modern artists. Grasping this distinction between deeper and more superficial modes of aesthetic affinity is crucial to understanding Wilde's thinking. For Wilde, form meant style and treatment, rather than structure or genre. It also meant, very importantly, a sense of beauty as a substantial element of experience. A great advocate of what he called "vitality" in art (a word he retained from Ruskin), Wilde despised the naturalism that emphasized quotidian

verisimilitude over the kind of truth that only beauty could make compelling. But although Wilde's resistance to "the morbid and unhealthy faculty of truth-telling" affects a superficially Romantic posture, it derives from a relation between art and life that, quite contrary to the transcendent operation of the sublime, deliberately asserted the limits of both. In an aphoristic couplet from the Preface to *Dorian Gray,* he makes it clear that the relation between beauty and realism, though conflicted, is not a simple opposition:

> The nineteenth-century dislike of Realism is the rage of Caliban seeing his own face in a glass.
>   The nineteenth-century dislike of Romanticism is the rage of Caliban not seeing his own face in a glass.

It is Caliban Wilde rebukes here—that is, expectations of art that limit its function *either* to decoration or to description—not the tendencies of Realism or Romanticism, which in this case represent what he called conditions of art.

Much confusion about Wilde's aesthetic doctrine has derived from his association with decadence, that belated mutation of Romantic aestheticism. Although decadence certainly appealed to Wilde's tastes (which were in many respects rather conservative), and indeed he came to represent its precepts to many people, it had far less to do with his aesthetic theory than is generally supposed. According to decadent theory, the artist's detachment from sordid reality was essentially an escape—or at any rate a refuge—from society. For Wilde, the artist's relation to society was, on the contrary, exemplary and dynamic, and most important, vulnerable. All his myths of individuality—with perhaps the exception of his socialist utopia—entail risk: the artist's freedom had nothing to do with privacy, or insulation from the public, but rather freedom from restriction and censorship, which implies public exposure.

The aspect of Wilde's thought most significantly influenced by decadence was the affinity of art with crime that he explores in "Pen, Pencil and Poison" and that, in *Dorian Gray,* was predicated not just on the transgressive nature of artistic experiment but more specifically on the radical disjunction of moral valuation from aesthetic experience. But although Wilde saw the artistic judgment as legitimately deriving only from the latter, he by no means considered the artist himself as unavailable to the former. Wilde was far too steeped in Ruskin to adhere to the outright rejection of middle-class morality espoused by his French colleagues. Rather, he adopted the posture of rejection to serve what was for him the important truth: that there is more to a good society than good morals, that indeed a modern society cannot rely only on ethical or sentimental principles to sustain coherence and growth. He denounced Victorian didacticism not because it accorded works of art too much responsibility for moral behavior, but because it mistook and underestimated the power of aesthetic effectiveness, reducing art's enormous capacity for conveying and modifying individual experience to the schematic representation of social and moral codes. "An ethical sympathy," he wrote, "is an unpardonable mannerism of style."

Wilde's idea of the nature of aesthetic effectiveness is best outlined in "The Decay of Lying," which attacks not didacticism but realism, on the ground that art develops its own forms, which life can only imitate:

> The highest art rejects the burden of the human spirit, and gains more from new medium or a fresh material than she does from any enthusiasm for art, or from any lofty passion, or for any great awakening of the human consciousness. She develops purely on her own lines. She is not symbolic of any age. It is the ages that are her symbols.

When Wilde's argument extends from life to nature, it takes a more clearly phenomenological turn, and gives rise to one of his most famous critical paradoxes: that the brown fogs hovering over London were the invention of Impressionist painters. In glossing this very pointed turn on Ruskin's formulation in "The Nature of Gothic" (i.e., that the vaulted ceilings and archways of Gothic architecture had gradually assimilated the organic forms of trees, rather than the other way around), Wilde then pays homage to the creative susceptibility of Ruskin's eye. "Nature is no great mother who has borne us. She is our creation. It is in our brain that she quickens to life. Things are because we see them, and what we see, and how we see it, depends on the Arts that have influenced us."

The Critic as Artist. At this point, Wilde's agenda begins to emerge: he had shown that the priority of individual method and style over social convention was the expressive basis of modern art, and that the displacement of nature by artifice had become the material basis of modern life. It remained for him to demonstrate the superiority of interpretation over representation or instruction as the intellectual basis of aesthetic response, and so to deliver his version of the function of criticism. The influence of Matthew Arnold becomes important here, not so much in terms of critical method—Wilde was far more indebted in this sense to Ruskin and Pater—but as a benchmark in the critical tradition against which it was necessary for Wilde to define himself. It was Arnold, even more than Ruskin, who had established the scope of critical activity, and set the goal of a society informed and directed by the critic's aesthetic attunement to art.

Although Wilde rejected Arnold's utilitarian model of aesthetic cultivation, as also he outgrew his early Ruskinian socialism, his belief in art's beneficent effects on society remained quite as sincere and urgent as theirs. It is art's capacity to inform general perceptions *through* individual experience that engages Wilde's moral attention, and it is at the crux of his relationship to, and departure from, his precursors. Where Arnold and Ruskin adopted social rationales

for criticism, and Pater avoided its public or social implications, Wilde recognized that criticism was both an aesthetic enterprise that, like works of art, should not be held accountable to moral standards of value, and a communicative medium, whose purpose was to convey a comprehensive experience of beauty.

The concept of "The Critic as Artist" is inspired by Pater, but it is clear that Wilde did not use Pater's own procedure but rather the effects of it as an example of what criticism could be made to do. The difference is subtle but important, for Wilde's thinking was far more attentive to the interplay of personalities—in both art and criticism—than Pater would ever allow his to be. In conflating the activities of producing art and interpreting it, Wilde's critic as artist argues for a dynamic relation between perceptual and conceptual experience that recasts the old Romantic link between reality and imagination. In taking artifice and gesture rather than spirit and motive to be the touchstones of aesthetic experience, Pater had done something like this, but Pater stops short of acknowledging any relationship whatever between individual experience and the realities of common life, whether social or material. For Pater, to contemplate a work of art was to absorb its existence into one's own—and so to be relieved of the Ruskinian responsibility for considering how it has come to be made. Wilde, on the other hand, saw criticism as a kind of recapitulation of the creative process, transferred to another personality. He argued that the critic is the ultimate artist, not because the primacy of his own impressions is unencumbered by the material considerations of technique, but rather because his detachment from the exigencies of technique allows him to comprehend a wider range of material considerations than can the artist himself.

In setting a premium on the dissemination of aesthetic perception, Wilde's theory of the critic as artist owes more to Ruskin than either to Arnold, whose claims to objectivity he entirely inverted, or to Pater, whose impressionism Wilde criticized for being too passive, too disengaged from the production and the consequences of aesthetic effects. Wilde came to see, albeit in different terms from Ruskin, that the disposition to address the process by which aesthetic properties and values are communicated did not derive solely from the capacity to appreciate beauty in existing forms, but also from the impulse—Ruskin would call it duty—to participate actively in the world of persons and things and institutions, and to address them on new terms. Interpretation as Wilde understood it was itself a gesture of imaginative community, both with the artist and with the audience. He saw that the fundamental link between art and activism that Ruskin insisted on could only be effected in a criticism devoted to the mechanisms by which experience of objects informs a subject, and by which subjects in turn create objects of their own. The impressionism that was for Pater a retreat from—or a resistance to—the artist's representative function was for Wilde a means for engaging in and vindicating the same role.

This ability to cope with both the sources and the consequences of aesthetic effects, in which Wilde recognized the key to a truly modern artistry, extended beyond the scope of an individual work of art; it was, indeed, the means by which art could comprehend and leave behind its history. "The development of the critical spirit" will allow us

> to realize not merely our own lives, but the collective lives of the race, and so make us absolutely modern. . . . For he to whom the present is the only thing that is present, knows nothing of the age in which he lives. To realize the nineteenth century, one must realize every century that has preceded it and that has contributed to its making.

Here Wilde's radical individualism finds its balancing force: the critical intellect as an instrument of communication with the past. Wilde's critic thus prefigures T. S. Eliot's individual talent, which inevitably contributes to and alters the totality of the tradition that precedes him.

Critical Fictions. For all his hymns to fantasy in "The Decay of Lying," imagination was for Wilde an essentially interpretive faculty, a matter of selection and emphasis rather than invention or vision. Personality, the force of temperament, was the true essence of artistic activity. It is not surprising, then, that the critical art form for Wilde, the representative medium for his theory, turned out to be not poetry or fiction but drama. Wilde's own plays may appear to be rather conventional, but the role of the drama in his critical work afforded him a very potent model for artistic experience and practice. Where Ruskin found in architecture a totalizing, concrete medium through which nature's genius could be realized, and translated, as it were, into a society, Wilde recognized the ideal conditions for modern artistry in the actor, an individual who realizes—interprets, enacts, and communicates—a supreme fiction. This affinity of criticism and acting is a manifestation of a dramaturgical element in Wilde's thinking that is discernible in his earliest work, and that Edouard Roditi (1947) has recognized in the dialectical grace of Wilde's criticism. Nowhere, however, is it more potent than in his fiction.

The most important example of what might be called Wilde's critical dramaturgy is "The Portrait of Mr. W. H.," a work of criticism in the form of a fiction, in which Wilde sets up a dizzying sequence of personal and rhetorical relationships among his protagonists to frame the critical theory at its center, which is that the dedicatee of Shakespeare's sonnets was a boy actor named Will Hughes, who portrayed the great heroines and inspired the playwright to create his greatest female roles. This theory, derived from purely internal evidence of the sonnets by Cyril Graham, a young man whose genius for acting has been thwarted by Victorian mores and so has turned to literary criticism, is an authentic work of critical art, while the eponymous portrait,

which Graham finally produces to corroborate his theory, is exposed as a forgery. Unable to realize his genius legitimately either on stage or in the world of letters, Graham martyrs himself to his own idea to convince his doubting disciple, the older critic Erskine; the latter in turn forges his own suicidal martyrdom to convince the disillusioned narrator, who has the last equivocal word. In its multiple layers of narration, the story makes explicit the complexity of the link between criticism and acting discussed in "The Critic as Artist." That the critic's coup is the revelation of the unsuspected existence of an actor, and that that revealed actor should be in turn the impetus behind the greatest works of English literature, suggests at once the interdependence of creation and interpretation, and the inevitable pressure of ordinary life that this contingency brings to bear on the life of art.

The mimetic aspect of this pressure is pursued in *The Picture of Dorian Gray*. Here Wilde acknowledges his own mentors in Dorian Gray's relationship to Basil Hallward, the painter whose repressed love for Dorian initially manifests itself in the portrait, and Lord Henry Wotton, the aesthetic-minded critic who persuades Dorian that youth is itself an art and better than anything life can offer. Alone together in the opening sequence, they argue about whether or not the unfinished portrait should be shown, and the substance of their debate forms a subtle counterpoint to the clear echoes of Ruskin and Pater in their rhetoric: Lord Henry, the Paterian voice of self-engrossed aestheticism, unexpectedly argues that art's place in society must preserve a balance between aesthetic and human reality, while Basil, the more righteous and sentimental Ruskinite, turns out to be morbidly obsessed with keeping both his picture and his friend out of sight. In this equivocal fashion, the two men's influence on Dorian culminates finally in Dorian's peculiar, and entirely secret, relation to the portrait itself. The ensuing struggle for moral identity that occurs between the man and the work of art is enlarged by the figure of an actress, whose perfect artistry Dorian worships, but whom he rejects when, having found love, she loses her talent. Sybil Vane's art, the perfect realization of a personality not her own, is a morally purified version of Dorian's own development. Both pay—she with her life, he with his conscience—for their different confusions of art and life, which Wilde cannily arranges to undermine each other.

In light of his essays, it becomes clear that both these fictions were integral to Wilde's critical project. *The Picture of Dorian Gray* is not simply a prurient tale about the dangers of aestheticism, but rather a profound and complex meditation on the relation between the processes by which a self is formed, and those by which a work of art is made. Similarly, "The Portrait of Mr. W. H." is not simply a fanciful theory about Shakespeare prophylactically encased in a fiction, but a very economical presentation of two ideas: one is the difficult concept of persuasiveness in art, which raises questions not only about the conflict between aesthetic and ethical modes of integrity, but about the very possibility of belief; the other is the relation between interpretation and creation, which Wilde rightly understands is based on love. In the displacement of mentors by disciples, each story offers a different version of Wilde's central critical drama, whereby Romantic sincerity is supplanted by a critical self-consciousness, an acknowledgment of the inevitable artifice of every gesture.

But in the autobiographical flavor of his characters' sins, in the allegorical cast of his subjects, and in the tragic structure of his plots, Wilde's fiction also extends his criticism in a direction that his critical essays and dialogues could not go: it allows him to pursue to its fullest implications the fundamental trope of his critical thought: the identification of person with a work of art. Predicated in one way or another on a deception, both works of art in these stories survive their makers and even, in the case of Dorian's portrait—which returns to its original perfection once painter and subject are both dead—the corrupt contingencies of mimetic representation. Each figure—the enduring portrait, the ever-plausible theory—embodies a cluster of relationships between artifact and personality that are not only problematic and interconnected but continuous and unending, and thus perpetually open to fresh response. The life of culture in general is thus implicated in the processes of personal mythmaking engaged in by Dorian Gray and Cyril Graham, and crucially by Wilde himself. What we learn from their tragedies is that the connections between the moral life of the individual and the effectiveness of art cannot be reduced to the formulas either of vulgar sentimentalism or of aestheticized formalism; yet, it may not entirely escape them either, for the vitality of both art and artists depends on their openness to misinterpretation. If art is to express everything, it must risk everything as well.

[*See also* Aestheticism; Gay Aesthetics; Pater; Ruskin; *and* Theater.]

BIBLIOGRAPHY

Works by Wilde

The Artist as Critic: Critical Writings of Oscar Wilde. Edited by Richard Ellmann. New York, 1969; reprint, Chicago, 1982.
Letters of Oscar Wilde. Edited by Rupert Hart-Davis. London, 1962.
The Picture of Dorian Gray (1890, 1891). Edited by Donald Lawler. New York, 1988. Includes both versions.

Other Sources

Chai, Leon. *Aestheticism: The Religion of Art in Post-Romantic Literature.* New York, 1990. Chapter 5, "Art and Life," is on Wilde.
Cohen, Ed. *Talk on the Wilde Side: Toward a Genealogy of a Discourse on Male Sexualities.* New York and London, 1993.
Ellmann, Richard, ed. *Oscar Wilde: A Collection of Critical Essays.* Englewood Cliffs, N.J., 1969. Includes assessments by W. H. Auden, Jorge Luis Borges, Hart Crane, André Gide, James Joyce, Thomas Mann, Walter Pater, G. B. Shaw, and W. B. Yeats.
Ellmann, Richard. *Oscar Wilde.* New York, 1988.
Gagnier, Regenia A. *Idylls of the Marketplace: Oscar Wilde and the Victorian Public.* Stanford, Calif., 1986.
Knox, Melissa. *Oscar Wilde: A Long and Lovely Suicide.* New Haven, 1994.
Powell, Kerry. *Oscar Wilde and the Theatre of the 1890s.* Cambridge and New York, 1990.
Rieff, Philip. "The Impossible Culture: Oscar Wilde and the Charisma of the Artist." *Encounter* 35 (September 1970): 33–44.
Roditi, Edouard. *Oscar Wilde.* (1947) Rev. ed. New York, 1986.
Shewan, Rodney. *Oscar Wilde: Art and Egotism.* London, 1977.
Small, Ian. *Oscar Wilde Revalued.* Greensboro, N.C., 1993.
Woodcock, George. *Oscar Wilde: The Double Image.* Montreal and New York, 1989. Reissue of *The Paradox of Oscar Wilde* (1949).

ELIZABETH HOLLANDER

WILLIAMS, RAYMOND (1921–1988), literary and cultural critic who was one of the founders in the early 1960s of the intellectual movement known as "cultural studies." Williams was born in a Black Mountain village on the Welsh border in 1921, and followed a well-trod path from provincial isolation to upward mobility as a "scholarship boy" at Cambridge during the late 1930s and early 1940s. Between 1946 and 1960, Williams worked as an adult education tutor at Oxford University. The experience of teaching English literature to working-class students, combined with his own Welsh, working-class background, gave Williams an acute awareness of the contingency of ostensibly universal forms of cultural expression. His first book, *Culture and Society, 1780–1950,* was published in 1958 and, along with Richard Hoggart's *The Uses of Literacy* (1957) and Edward Palmer Thompson's *The Making of the English Working Class* (1963), is considered one of the founding texts of the cultural studies movement, and of the British New Left. Williams was professor of drama at the University of Cambridge until his retirement in 1983. His books include *The Long Revolution* (1961), *The Country and the City* (1973), *Keywords* (1976), *Marxism and Literature* (1977), *Politics and Letters* (1979), and *Problems in Materialism and Culture* (1980), among others, as well as several novels.

Williams's work as a cultural critic was influenced by two intellectual traditions. The first was the strain of "practical criticism" associated with the writings of Frank Raymond Leavis and the journal *Scrutiny* during the 1920s and 1930s. Leavis, along with Ivor Armstrong Richards, sought to bring greater rigor to the study of English literature through close attention to the specific aesthetic operations of a given text. This process of "close reading" required, however, that the text be isolated from its social and historical context. Williams embraced Leavis's concern with the material performance of the text, but rejected the social abstraction of practical criticism, developing instead a kind of "left-Leavisite" approach epitomized by his treatment of literary works in *Culture and Society* (Eagleton, 1976, p. 38).

Williams was concerned to relate the mechanisms by which cultural texts such as novels, plays, and films produce meaning for the viewer or reader to historically specific forms of social, economic, and cultural power. In *Culture and Society,* this linkage was based on a relatively organic concept of "culture" as the domain in which underlying social tensions could potentially be resolved. The second important influence in Williams's intellectual development was his gradual rapprochement with Marxist cultural theory, culminating in the publication of *Marxism and Literature* in 1977. Here, concepts such as "feeling," "creativity," "imagination," and the "aesthetic" were related to Williams's analysis of a "hegemonic" culture, based in part on the work of Antonio Gramsci and Louis Althusser.

As a writer, Williams was not, by and large, concerned with philosophical issues, although he did acknowledge the influence of theorists such as Lucien Goldmann and Görgy Lukács, along with Althusser and Gramsci, on his own intellectual development (Williams, 1980). There is little or no direct engagement with the traditions of aesthetic philosophy in his work; no critical exegesis of the writings of Immanuel Kant, Friedrich von Schiller, Francis Hutcheson, or Anthony Ashley Cooper, earl of Shaftesbury; no detailed investigation of the structures of taste or *sensus communis.* Moreover, at no point does Williams offer anything like a systematic philosophical account of his own definition of the aesthetic. Instead, the aesthetic is positioned within a loosely defined collection of terms—*culture, art, structures of feeling, creativity,* and *imagination*—that are at the center of his analysis of modernity. Williams defines the aesthetic pragmatically, through what he perceives to be its cultural effects. In *Keywords,* the aesthetic is described as an "element in the divided modern consciousness of art and society: reference beyond social use and social valuation which . . . is intended to express a human dimension which the dominant version of society appears to exclude" (1976, p. 32). The concept of a "divided" conscious links Williams's discussion of the aesthetic to a process of historical change and contestation that he defines elsewhere in terms of "dominant," "residual," and "emergent" cultural practices (1977, pp. 121–127). Thus, the aesthetic resides either in the past, at some point prior to the "division" of art and society, or in contemporary practices that have been suppressed or marginalized by the dominant social order. Alternately, the aesthetic might be understood here as a primarily symbolic form, the function of which is simply to "refer" to the possibility of a cultural practice that is "beyond social use."

The strength of Williams's approach to cultural analysis lies in his ability to chart the process by which apparently fixed concepts have shifted in meaning over time, through interaction with changes in the structure of social, political, and economic power. The aesthetic is understood not as having some absolute or a priori meaning, but rather, as having undergone a series of semantic transitions since its

original emergence in eighteenth-century German philosophy. This contextual specificity, however, is purchased at the expense of a certain conceptual clarity. At some points in Williams's work, the aesthetic is defined as the expression of an original creative, human impulse. In *Marxism and Literature,* he writes of the "aesthetic response" as "an affirmation . . . of certain human meanings and values which a dominant social system reduced and even tried to exclude" (1977, p. 151). Here, the aesthetic merges into Williams's definitions of "creativity" and "imagination" (it is "directly comparable with . . . creative imagination"). In other cases, Williams defines the aesthetic precisely as the process by which this creative impulse was abstracted from the totality of the human subject. It was the "controlling and categorizing specialization of the aesthetic," he writes, that functioned to reduce the "multiplicity" of writing into reified categories such as "fiction," "history," and biography" (ibid., p. 150). Williams associates this function of the aesthetic, and the consequent shift of focus in the philosophy of art from the intention of the producer to the experience of the viewer or reader, to the emergence in the nineteenth century of a "bourgeois economics" that privileged a model of subjectivity based on consumption (ibid.). The aesthetic is simultaneously a part of the system by which bourgeois culture contains and subdivides the "multiplicity" of writing and of the expressive human subject, and the germinal form of a common human desire to create and transform.

Williams is concerned to point to a transition that is particular to modernity in which an initially whole or integral subject underwent a process of fragmentation. This dynamic is clear in *The Long Revolution* when he writes of the "division" of human activity between "work" and "art," and between "Aesthetic Man" and "Economic Man" (1961, p. 38). As Williams points out, the term *art* first referred to a general skill or craft, but was gradually transformed during the nineteenth century to refer to a privileged form of production, elevated above culture in general. The aesthetic was initially defined in terms of sense perception, but gradually came to signify only those sensations produced by works of art (1977, p. 50). This passage from the general or common to the specific is accompanied by the attribution of a heightened moral value as well (art and the aesthetic are understood as superior and more civilized modes of production and of sense-based knowledge). The confusion in Williams's analysis between the isolation of a preexisting "aesthetic" experience and the "aestheticizing" operations of modernity is thus joined by a slippage among analytic terms such as *art, culture,* and the *aesthetic.* If these terms are not always fully differentiated in Williams's writing, it is in part because of the conceptual force generated by his underlying definition of modernity. This definition rests on a dynamic in which a whole or integral "way of life" is subject to a hierarchical division and segmentation, and on an implicit teleology leading to the eventual reintegration of the divided halves of human culture (Hunter, 1992). Williams is caught between the humanism of his Leavisite origins and the protostructuralism of his later work. As a result, it is not always easy to understand precisely how he might define the "subject" implied by his cultural analysis. Questions that have come to preoccupy cultural theorists concerning the construction of subjectivity or the specific relationship between discursive formations and individual experience or agency are left unresolved.

Despite this conceptual slippage, Williams nevertheless insists on the need to defend the "specificity of the aesthetic" (1977, p. 151). In *Marxism and Literature,* he offers what is perhaps his most nuanced and detailed account of this specificity. He compares the bourgeois commodification of art with the Marxist reduction of the aesthetic to mere epiphenomenal "ideology." Williams cites Lukács's work, specifically his situation of the aesthetic between the "practical" (instrumental) and the "magical" (ideal and unrealizable; the domain of "myth"), as an example of a more sophisticated Marxist cultural analysis. Williams is concerned, however, with the way in which Lukács's analytic system might be applied to the "multiple world of social and cultural processes," a world in which "actual making and reception" cannot simply be reduced to categorical forms (ibid., p. 152). He turns to the work of Jan Mukařovsky for a nonidealist definition of the aesthetic as a "function" or "practice." In *Aesthetic Function, Norm and Value as Social Facts* (1970), Mukařovsky argues that aesthetic value is not inherent in given objects (it is "not a real property of the object"), but rather is a condition that only manifests itself in objects "under certain conditions" (cited in Williams, 1977, p. 153). This contextual and pragmatic reading of the aesthetic clearly complements Williams's own analysis of the arbitrary division between fine art and mass culture. As he writes, art must "by ever more absolute abstraction" suppress and deny the social processes "within which it is contained" (ibid., p. 154). The virtue of Mukařovsky's approach, according to Williams, is that it effectively dismantles the framework of bourgeois aesthetics, thereby exposing the structural "function" of aesthetic value, and clearing the philosophical ground for a more fully developed Marxist aesthetic.

But what remains of a conceptually discrete aesthetic experience in the aftermath of Mukařovsky's demolition? On the one hand, Williams locates the specificity of the aesthetic in its status as the repository of a vaguely defined human essence ("known and pressing elements of human intention and response" that have been "excluded or undervalued" by "dominant elements of human practice") (ibid.). He argues that a "genuine" aesthetic practice can express a "humane response" and "human meanings and values" (ibid., p. 151) by registering a protest against the general instrumentalization and commodification of cul-

tural values in bourgeois society. The aesthetic, like the unconscious, is created by repression. At the same time, Williams wants to replace Mukařovsky's aesthetic "function" with the concept of an aesthetic "situation" that is even more clearly rooted in a specific temporal and spatial context. A given object does not generate a single, unvarying aesthetic meaning, but rather, a "range" of potential meanings that can be made available to specific viewers in specific social situations (ibid., p. 155). Williams's faith in "practice," "variability," "relativity," "materiality," and the ultimately uncategorizable "multiplicity" of "actual" social encounters emerges as the last redoubt of a resistant subjectivity against the rationalizing drive of bourgeois culture.

The semantic shift from "function" to "situation" does not necessarily resolve the problems of immanence or of specificity, however. Thus, Williams contends that "situations" still require "works which are . . . designed to occasion" an aesthetic response (ibid., p. 154). At the same time, he roots the specificity of the aesthetic in a bodily response: the "real experience" of the aesthetic, the "true effects" of writing, "are indeed quite physical," including "specific alterations of physical rhythms, physical organization: experiences of quickening and slowing, of expansion and of intensification" (ibid., p. 156). This mode of experience must be viewed in continuity with other, equally "aesthetic" experiences produced by a "deliberately dividing society," such as "dulling," "lulling," and "chiming" (ibid.). In this view, the aesthetic acts as a site within bourgeois culture at which the status of somatic knowledge can be staged and potentially contested. Williams's analysis thus presents two sets of aesthetic meanings, each of which expresses a particular form of conflict. The aesthetic as somatic experience (the "expansion and intensification" evoked by the work of art) is coupled with an anaesthetic "dulling" and "lulling" (Buck-Morss, 1992). The aesthetic as an expression of (noninstrumental) "human values" is coupled with the aesthetic as an expression of the "categorization and specialization" of bourgeois culture. The dynamic interaction between these two terms—the body and the specific social situation undetermined by a priori conceptual forms—gives Williams's account of the aesthetic a contemporary resonance. The fact that both of these models of aesthetic experience continue to inform current debates and criticism suggests the prescience of his scholarship.

[*See also* Cultural Studies; Gramsci; Lukács; *and* Marxism.]

BIBLIOGRAPHY

Works by Williams

Culture and Society, 1780–1950. London, 1958.
The Long Revolution. London, 1961.
Communications. Harmondsworth, England, 1962; 3d ed., Harmondsworth, England, and New York, 1976.
The Country and the City. London, 1973.

Keywords: A Vocabulary of Culture and Society. London, 1976; rev. exp. ed., London, 1983.

Marxism and Literature. Oxford and New York, 1977.

Problems in Materialism and Culture. London, 1980.

Writing in Society. London, 1983.

Resources of Hope: Culture, Democracy, Socialism. Edited by Robin Gable. London and New York, 1989.

Other Sources

Buck-Morss, Susan. "Aesthetics and Anaesthetics: Walter Benjamin's Artwork Essay Reconsidered." *October* 62 (Fall 1992): 3–41.

Dworkin, Dennis L., and Leslie G. Roman, eds. *Views beyond the Border Country: Raymond Williams and Cultural Politics.* London and New York, 1993.

Eagleton, Terry. *Criticism and Ideology.* London, 1976.

Eagleton, Terry, ed. *Raymond Williams: Critical Perspectives.* Boston, 1989.

Eldridge, John Eric Thomas, and Lizzie Eldridge. *Raymond Williams: Making Connections.* London and New York, 1994.

Frow, John. *Cultural Studies and Cultural Value.* Oxford, 1995.

Gorak, Jan. *The Alien Mind of Raymond Williams.* Columbia, Mo., 1988.

Hunter, Ian. "Aesthetics and Cultural Studies." In *Cultural Studies,* edited, by Lawrence Grossberg, Cary Nelson, and Paula A. Treichler, with Linda Baughman and John Macgregor Wise, pp. 347–367. London and New York, 1992.

Mukařovsky, Jan. *Aesthetic Function, Norm and Value as Social Facts.* Translated by Mark E. Suino. Ann Arbor, 1970.

O'Connor, Alan. *Raymond Williams: Writing, Culture, Politics.* Oxford and New York, 1989.

Pinkney, Tony. *Raymond Williams.* Bridgend, Wales, 1991.

Prendergast, Christopher, ed. *Cultural Materialism: On Raymond Williams.* Minneapolis, 1995.

GRANT KESTER

WINCKELMANN, JOHANN JOACHIM (1717–1768), German archaeologist and art historian. Winckelmann is best known for his *Reflections on the Imitation of Greek Works* (1755) and *History of Ancient Art* (published 1764, though written some years earlier and continually under revision). Celebrated in his own lifetime, he became still more so in cultural retrospect. His place in the development of aesthetics stems largely from that acquired cultural status, namely, as founder of neoclassicism and of systematic art history.

Johann Wolfgang von Goethe hailed Winckelmann as the Columbus of a forgotten land. His picture of an ideal antiquity transformed eighteenth-century taste in the visual arts; the clear outlines of "noble simplicity and quiet grandeur" (*edle Einfalt und stille Grösse*; Winckelmann, 1987, pp. 32–33) influenced John Flaxman in England, Jacques-Louis David in France, and many others. In Germany, Winckelmann had an even larger impact on the literary culture. His humanist norm of *Bildung*—self-cultivation, self-development—shaped an entire scholarly and pedagogical tradition effective well into the twentieth century.

Besides this general significance for cultural history, however, Winckelmann may be said more specifically to have founded art history as a scientific discipline. Although certain aspects of his archaeology were outmoded soon enough, the dominance of Winckelmann's formalist approach may be traced down through Heinrich Wölfflin and Erwin Panofsky. Winckelmann's originality lay not just in his analytic observations of individual works, but also in his shift away from biographical chronicle to conjectures on the system of stylistic forms. More broadly, he went beyond Enlightenment models of political, pragmatic, or "universal" histories to suggest a new, singular conception of history that foreshadowed *Historismus.*

Inspired by Montesquieu, Winckelmann sought to place the arts in geographic, climatic, and above all political perspective. Although later (for prudential reasons) he would play down any republican intent, Winckelmann held that Greek art stemmed from democratic freedom, an idea that found an ideological resonance at the time of the French Revolution. Yet, it is not merely a question of context: Winckelmann casts art in a still more central role, namely, in articulating a particular culture; he thus anticipates the model of "expressive" explanation found in Johann Gottfried von Herder. For Winckelmann, art gave an insight into the "essential" in human society, and supplied the "systematic" angle on history that he thought his special contribution. "I understand the word *history* [*Geschichte*] in the larger sense that it had in the Greek language," he writes, "and my aim is to make an attempt at a system [*eines Lehrgebäudes*]" (1968).

The expressive model displays also a changed attitude to the past: no longer an Enlightenment search for the origins of the present, it sees all cultures as subject to an intrinsic development of growth and decay. "The history of art should teach us its origin, growth, alteration, and fall, together with the various styles of people, periods, and artists, and demonstrate this as far as possible from the remaining works of antiquity" (ibid.). Winckelmann's aim was not to diagnose an overall progress or decline—universal history in Enlightenment fashion—but to show how art (preeminently Greek sculpture) develops of its own accord, passing from schematic rigidity through a "high" style still marked by the older abruptness of outline, then to a "beautiful" phase in which all is gracefully rounded off, before degenerating into imitation and pleasing effects. This fourfold pattern of stylistic development configured the history of art from then on. Ironically—and it is hardly the last of Winckelmann's ironies—the Greek Ideal itself is internally split into "high" (or sublime) and properly "beautiful" moments: a duality repeated in Friedrich von Schiller, Georg Wilhelm Friedrich Hegel, and many others.

Winckelmann was the first to historicize art in a thoroughgoing way. At the same time, that achievement remains ambiguous. As Herder noted, Winckelmann retains a normative primacy for the classical Ideal, for metaphysical Beauty in an almost Platonic sense at odds with any historicizing of art (which would judge each culture in its own terms, whether of context or internal development). Alex Potts suggests that to force such inconsistency on Winckelmann verges on anachronism, and that if he did indeed effect a "paradigm change," it was in the proper Kuhnian sense of shifting discussion to new terrain and a different agenda of problems to solve: how to square history with system, empirical observation with formal distinction, norms of taste (in which Winckelmann strongly believed) with variant circumstance (Potts, 1994, p. 24f.). Such aesthetic problems remain part of the "normal science" of history to this day; Winckelmann was merely their originator. It should be no surprise that divergent traditions such as Weimar classicism, Romantic historism, or Rankean positivism claimed Winckelmann as progenitor.

This procedural resort cannot decide a further ambivalence in Winckelmann, namely, the dialectical chiasmus between history and art; for if Winckelmann *historicized* art, in turn History becomes *aestheticized*—as if it were (in Herder's image) a collection of picture galleries illuminated by the flickering glance of the historian's consciousness. Not only does an aesthetic perspective unify the whole, but it also demands a certain originality in the historian's composing of his account. Hence, the famous set pieces evoking the effect of looking at Laocoön, the Belvedere Apollo, Niobe, and so on: memorably vivid ekphrases in their day as influential as the developmental account in which they were embedded. Further yet, Winckelmann could be regarded as a forerunner of the systematizing of art itself, whereby culture is made in the image of a newly conceptualized "Art": no longer the several "fine arts," but a self-defining normative field. Art no longer appeared under the aegis of the old classicist canon, nor was it merely the object of "cultivated taste." In that sense, Hegel was right to declare (in a passage cited by Walter Pater) that Winckelmann was one of those who had "opened up for the spirit a new organ . . . a new sense for considering art" (Hegel, 1975, p. 63). Hegel notes that this had less influence on the theory of art, though his own account of the "classical Ideal" imitates Winckelmann's *History* verbatim.

If Winckelmann set out to re-create the original, so to speak, a similar dialectic operates in the appeal to "imitation." He writes in the *Reflections:* "The only way for us to become great or, if this be possible, inimitable, is to imitate the ancients" (1987, p. 5). On the face of it, this is more than paradoxical. It figures the Ideal as necessarily absent, value as found only when lost. It is as if Christopher Columbus glimpses his new land of art only (to recall Winckelmann's image at the end of the *History*) in waving tearful farewell to his beloved Greece. Following Jacques Derrida, Michael Fried (1968) calls such doubling of origins "supplemental": it requires a third term—the Renaissance—to give it referential stability, for then retrospective invention is naturalized as cyclical process. That argument could be extended

to the very conception of the Ideal, of a divine yet human beauty: an impossible identity of Idea and corporeal shape that needs adjacent terms such as the high and the derivative style for its postulation. One can more readily speak about imperfection; the fusion of elements in the beautiful style can only be hinted at.

Even Winckelmann's method suggests ambivalence. Having published the *Reflections,* he went on to pen a biting critique under a pseudonym, then rushed to his own philosophical defense. It shows an ironic awareness of conditions of circulation and publicity framing high speculation. Equally, Winckelmann owns up to the conjectural nature of his activity, applying the metaphor of "scaffolding" *(Gerüst)* to his own building practices (1968). Truth and fiction go hand in hand. His appeal to a system linking art and history—akin to a Linnean *systema* (Dilly, 1979, p. 95)—is an empirical construction, testable against the natural world. (Nor, one might add, is this so far from Hegel's understanding of "philosophical" history, beyond pragmatic, particular, or critical modes, but merging epistemological self-awareness with narrative drive; neither thinker is served by charging their constructions with a priori dogmatism.)

A figure caught between eras, Winckelmann today appears more complex than his marmoreal image implies. He is of contemporary interest in at least two further respects, linked to current revision of eighteenth-century studies: gender, and the bourgeois public sphere *(bürgerliche Öffentlichkeit).* First, not only does Winckelmann split the classical Ideal into the sublime and the beautiful, but he genders them in surprising ways. Edmund Burke's association of sublime with male and beauty with female has provoked recent comment. One might compare Winckelmann's suggestion that the "high" Ideal resists and finally overwhelms sensuous embodiment: Potts sees here "an allegory of desire," as if the masculine Idea ravishes the helpless figure of woman. With the beautiful, by contrast—as in Laocoön's graceful disposition of limbs even in agony—Idea and human (now male) body melt into each other: in this centerpiece, Winckelmann's male gaze longs for a masculine form.

The second area of contemporary interest concerns Winckelmann's venture into the public sphere of civil society, with its journals, reviews, prize essays, and institutionalized conversation. Here, it is notable how he fought to escape not just his poor social origins, but also the usual resort to a functionary's life as secretary, librarian, or academic (he refused university offers) in a Prussia he detested. Opting instead to become a private scholar and intellectual, he concerned himself with the artistic composition and most effective circulation of his own work in a nascent public sphere. One might compare the situation of a predecessor, Anne Claude de Tubières, comte de Caylus, in 1740s France: an aristocrat who moved beyond patronage yet was unable finally to secure a public forum for discussion of values (Crow, 1985, pp. 116–17). Winckelmann was more successful, even if much of the "conversation" about his neoclassical Ideal was posthumous. Here, too, one should attend to his social ambitions to be part of and even help form a "cultivated" middle class. In this respect, his own homosexuality, hinted at in his charged descriptions of sculpture, reveals a tension between private and public never successfully resolved in Enlightenment, or indeed later, aesthetics.

[*See also* Art History; Classicism; Herder; *and* Historicism.]

BIBLIOGRAPHY

Works by Winckelmann

Gedanken über die Nachahmung der griechischen Werke in der Malerei und Bildhauerkunst. Dresden, 1755. Translated by Elfriede Heyer and Roger C. Norton as *Reflections on the Imitation of Greek Works in Painting and Sculpture* (La Salle, Ill., 1987).

Geschichte der Kunst des Alterthums. Dresden, 1764; Vienna, 1776. Translation of 1849–1873 edition, as *History of Ancient Art* in 4 vols. (New York, 1968).

Other Sources

Crow, Thomas E. *Painters and Public Life in Eighteenth-Century Paris.* New Haven, 1985.

Dilly, Heinrich. *Kunstgeschichte als Institution: Studien zur Geschichte einer Disziplin.* Frankfurt am Main, 1979.

Fried, Michael. "Antiquity Now: Reading Winckelmann on Imitation," *October* 37 (1986): 87–97.

Goethe, Johann Wolfgang von. "Winckelmann and His Age" (1805). In *Essays on Art and Literature,* edited by John Gearey, translated by Ellen von Nardroff and Ernest H. von Nardroff, pp. 99–121. Princeton, N.J., 1994.

Hegel, Georg Wilhelm Friedrich. *Aesthetics: Lectures on Fine Art.* 2 vols. Translated by T. M. Knox. Oxford, 1975.

Potts, Alex. *Flesh and the Ideal: Winckelmann and the Origins of Art History.* New Haven, 1994.

MARTIN DONOUGHO

WINNICOTT, DONALD WOODS (1896–1971), British pediatrician and psychoanalyst. Noted for his work with children, Winnicott's contribution to aesthetics centers on a developmental theory of culture and on his concept of the "transitional object." His theory of the work of art as cultural object rests on a triadic epistemology: external reality, inner psychic reality, and a "third area" of play and make-believe shared by child and adult (usually the mother). Within that area, the child is inducted into culture. Psychoanalytically considered, the third area is the space within which therapeutic inquiry with children is carried on. It is from observations made during therapy that Winnicott developed his wider theory of art and culture.

In the process of acculturation, the child meets the first "work of art" as a "transitional object"—a blanket, a doll, a teddy bear, or simply a bit of cloth that the child can carry into the space outside the third area. Winnicott observed children in their early forays away from the mother, carrying the transitional object, as if a bit of maternal protection that allows the child to explore beyond the third area and then return to it. Within the third area, aesthetic-artistic events have their initial creation, for there the child plays a role, engages in imitations, responds to maternal teaching as roles are assumed, exchanged, and analyzed, and narratives are made up. Play with objects is often accompanied by explanations and interpretations.

Winnicott develops his theory of the "potential space" or "third area" in several directions. First, he elaborates Jacques Lacan's description of the child's first mirror of self-recognition by moving back to the earliest experience of the child with the mother. What the baby sees when he or she looks at the mother's face ought not be construed as a mirror experience, but rather something like this: what the mother looks like is related to what the mother sees in the baby. The child's feeling that the child exists depends on how the mother sees the child. This interrelational exchange characterizes externalizations in the case of cultural objects. And thus painting, sculpture, and narrative all are "seen" as they themselves *see.*

Second, works of art express and project as they are perceived and interpreted. That which they come to mean is a function of an interchange in which the object sustains itself against the perceiver's unconscious acts of destruction ("The Mirror-Role of Mother and Family in Child Development," in Winnicott, 1989).

Third, learning to use an object—that is, play in the "third area"—thus exhibits a developmental trajectory that leads to adult creation and use of cultural objects. Stages in development are as follows: (1) subject (child) relates to object; (2) child discovers the object is an independent event, not placed by the subject in the world; (3) subject "destroys" the object (in fantasy); (4) object survives "destruction"; and (5) subject can now use object in a creative way, for example, endow it with character, place it in a narrative context, shape it as an expression of the self ("The Use of an Object and Relating through Identifications," in ibid.). This use of the object is the first use of a symbol, for the object becomes the child's "first not-me possession." This symbol "is at the place in space and time where and when the mother is in transition from being . . . merged with the infant and alternatively being experienced as an object to be perceived rather than conceived of" ("The Location of Cultural Experience," in ibid.). In so describing the idea of symbol, Winnicott suggests that there is a psychological precondition that enables human beings to become symbol-using beings. The child comes to realize, through an unconscious process of assimilation, that separation in space and time from the mother can be as well union with the mother, now on a level that needs no actual physicality. Winnicott implies that a psychological-cultural development of this kind leads from this realization to adult aesthetic experience in all its complexity. Winnicott has grounded symbolism on a stage in the process of play.

Fourth, Winnicott now relates the early stages of cultural development to the adult whose objects are works of art, religion, and philosophy:

> The task of reality-acceptance is never completed; no human being is free from the strain of relating inner and outer reality, and relief from this strain is provided by an intermediate area of experience [art, religion, philosophy], . . . which is in direct continuity with the play area of the small child who is "lost" in play.
> ("Transitional Objects and Transitional Phenomena," in ibid.)

Winnicott's developmental theory has wide application to both the content of works of art and the process of perceiving-interpreting works of art. Aesthetic theory calls for a psychology of cultural objects that explains how humans become cultural beings that use and respond to material, tonal, and linguistic objects endowed with historical powers. Artists themselves often represent this process to which Winnicott has given a psychoanalytic explanation. The work of art as "transitional object" relating perceiver to tradition is the subject of paintings by Nicolas Poussin, Dominique Ingres, and Gustave Courbet; literary works by Virgil, Dante, and Giovanni Boccaccio in classical and Renaissance tradition, and T. S. Eliot, Wallace Stevens, and W. H. Auden in modern poetry; and the music of Maurice Ravel, Gustav Mahler, George Crumb. For examples, see bibliography.

[*See also* Freud; *and* Psychology of Art.]

BIBLIOGRAPHY

Work by Winnicott

Playing and Reality. London, 1971; reprint, London and New York, 1989.

Other Sources

Carrier, David. *Poussin's Paintings: A Study in Art-Historical Methodology.* University Park, Pa., 1993.
Kuhns, Richard. *Psychoanalytic Theory of Art: A Philosophy of Art on Developmental Principles.* New York, 1983.
Spitz, Ellen Handler. *Image and Insight: Essays in Psychoanalysis and the Arts.* New York, 1991.
Wollheim, Richard. *Painting as an Art.* Princeton, N.J., 1987.

RICHARD KUHNS

WITTGENSTEIN, LUDWIG JOSEF JOHANN.

[*To explore the importance of Wittgenstein's thought for aesthetics, this entry comprises three essays:*

> Survey of Thought
> Reception of Wittgenstein
> Wittgenstein and Literary Theory

The first essay is a survey of Wittgenstein's thought as a background for his views on aesthetics. The second essay explains how he influenced aesthetic theory in the second half of the twentieth century. The third essay discusses recent literary theory that has been inspired by Wittgensteinian philosophy. For related discussion, see Cavell; Conceptual Art; *and* Essentialism.]

Survey of Thought

The Austrian philosopher Ludwig Wittgenstein (1889–1951) was born in Vienna, the youngest of eight children. His father was one of the wealthiest men in the Austro-Hungarian Empire, and his mother was highly cultured and made the house a center of musical culture—Joseph Joachim, Johannes Brahms, and Gustav Mahler were frequent visitors. His brother Paul was a well-known concert pianist, while Wittgenstein himself had considerable musical talent. Engineering studies brought him to Manchester in 1908 and led to an interest in mathematics and then, through reading Bertrand Russell's *The Principles of Mathematics,* to the philosophy of mathematics. In 1911, he went to Cambridge to study with Russell and there began work on what was to be the *Tractatus Logico-Philosophicus.*

Despite physical disabilities and family connections, he enlisted as a common soldier when World War I began. He eventually became an officer and sought the most dangerous assignments. He had the manuscript of the *Tractatus* in his knapsack when taken prisoner by the Italians in 1918.

The conclusion of the *Tractatus* was that everything that philosophy tried to say was senseless and could not be said. Wittgenstein's intellectual honesty led him to abandon philosophy and he became a schoolteacher in rural areas of Austria. This experience ended unfortunately and for a while he worked as a gardener in a monastery and even considered becoming a monk. During this period, he designed and supervised the construction of a house for his sister in Vienna. Conversations with friends and other philosophers, however, led him to realize that the *Tractatus* had not disposed of all philosophical problems and in 1929 he returned to Cambridge and took his doctoral degree, submitting the *Tractatus* as his dissertation. He then began to lecture at Cambridge and to develop the thought that would eventuate in the *Philosophical Investigations,* published posthumously in 1953. In 1939, he was appointed to the chair of philosophy that George Edward Moore had resigned, but during the war he took leave to do volunteer war work. Although he lectured again after the war, he resigned his chair in 1947. He died of cancer in 1951.

Wittgenstein never produced systematic or extended writings in aesthetics, but it is clear that, along with ethics, aesthetics was a lifelong concern. In 1949, he remarked that although he found scientific questions interesting, it was only conceptual and aesthetic questions that really gripped him; he said he could be indifferent to the solution of a scientific problem, but not the other sort. Wittgenstein regarded art, especially music, with passionate intensity and said that it was impossible for him to say how much music had meant to him throughout his life. This concern is part of the background against which his philosophical work must be understood.

The *Tractatus* makes a distinction between the world as the totality of facts, those things that can be said (i.e., described and talked about), and those things that cannot be said, but can only be shown. The latter include ethics, aesthetics, and religion as well as the relation between language and the world it describes. Wittgenstein called all this, perhaps misleadingly, "the mystical." Any attempt to talk about these topics results only in nonsense. The significance of this was misunderstood by the logical positivists, who were much taken with Wittgenstein's work in logic and language. If it is nonsense and "mystical," they thought, then it must be dismissed as of no importance. Wittgenstein's mysticism, however, is not the usual one, but signals a view of the world as a "limited whole" in which ethics and aesthetics are seen as standing outside the world of facts and marking the only things that are of vital human importance.

In the *Notebooks, 1914–1916*, from which much of the *Tractatus* material was drawn, he described art as a kind of expression and said that ethics is the world seen under the aspect of eternity, whereas a work of art is an object seen under the aspect of eternity. The only reference to aesthetics in the *Tractatus* is the statement that ethics and aesthetics are one. These remarks are enigmatic, but are probably best glossed as follows: value is not a fact in the world, but is the result of the way in which one sees the world. One's moral stance to the world is shown in the character seen in the world and that character may be one's own for, he says, the world of the happy man is different from that of the unhappy man. Aesthetics, on the other hand, presents us with a view of a particular object. In 1930, he said that a work of art forces us to see an object in the right perspective, that is, as the artist saw it.

Wittgenstein never abandoned the saying/showing distinction that was the central thesis of the *Tractatus*, although it underwent important changes. In the *Tractatus*, the distinction is puzzling and, for many, obfuscating, which is not surprising because that work is a thoroughgoing piece of metaphysics. The philosophical practice of his later work in the *Philosophical Investigations* is intended to clear away the confusions of metaphysics, with the result that one can find there the wherewithal to make clear sense of the distinction.

In 1936, Wittgenstein spoke of the odd resemblance between a philosophical investigation and an aesthetic one. One clue to understanding the resemblance is found in Moore's report of the 1930–1933 lectures, in which Wittgenstein said that what aesthetics does is to give reasons why, for example, this word rather than some other is used in the poem or this musical phrase in the composition. This is done by drawing attention to the work and placing works side by side. To understand a particular work of art, to understand what the artist is doing, the work must be seen alongside other of the artist's works, and even perhaps alongside that of other artists. In this way, attention is directed to the larger context of artistic endeavor with all its history, conventions, and practices that alone make the work intelligible. This is consistent with the remark in the *Lectures and Conversations on Aesthetics, Psychology and Religious Belief* that expressions of aesthetic judgments play a complicated role in the culture of a period, and to describe them the culture must be described. A description of the culture shows the role of these expressions.

A philosophical investigation also puts things side by side. Philosophical problems arise, Wittgenstein says, when language goes on holiday, that is, when words are taken out of any context in which they have a role to play. Wittgenstein's practice is to bring words back from their metaphysical to their everyday use by reminding us of their actual uses and by describing particular cases and situations in which words have a function and engage with life. These cases can then be put alongside the claims of philosophical theories so that we can see when work is being done and sense is being made and when it is not. Traditional philosophical arguments play little role in Wittgenstein's work; his procedure is to show language at work.

The aim of an aesthetic investigation is to realize the meaning and the value of a work of art for oneself and to change the way a painting is seen, a piece of music is heard, or a poem is read. Similarly, the aim of a philosophical investigation is to realize for oneself when language has gone on holiday and thus to bring us back to engagement with the world and with human affairs so that things are seen properly. In neither case is it of any avail simply to be told what is or what is not important, valuable, or intelligible. Both kinds of investigations aim at changing one's perspective.

In the *Lectures and Conversations*, Wittgenstein insists that the kind of reason and explanation that we seek in aesthetics is not causal and has nothing to do with psychology. He talks about aesthetic taste and appreciation with respect to such activities as selecting clothing, but says that we do not appreciate the tremendous things in art, that is, our reactions to great art are very different from our reactions to a well-cut suit.

In the *Philosophical Investigations*, Wittgenstein stressed the importance of language as an activity grounded in human life by constructing an analogy between language and games and spoke of the different uses of language as language games. He claimed that there was no essence of language, no factor common to all its multiple uses. To illustrate this, he pointed out that there is no essence of games, that is, no feature common to all games by virtue of which they are games. There are, however, characteristic and overlapping features that he described as family resemblances. He insisted that we "look and see" whether there are common features instead of assuming that there must be if the word *game* is to have a clear meaning. In the 1950s, philosophers such as Morris Weitz and William Kennick saw implications in this for attempts to construct theoretical definitions of "art" and argued that such attempts are fruitless because there is no factor common to all works of art and that, instead, "art" should be considered a "family-resemblance" concept.

Thus, it came to be thought that a Wittgensteinian aesthetics must be "antiessentialist." Although Wittgenstein did not discuss the notion of art in this way, his methods should suggest that there is no intelligible formulation of what could constitute the essence of art, of what could count as a common factor, and therefore he is neither an essentialist nor an antiessentialist. The question of whether there is an essence of art should be dismissed. The concentration on definition and theory makes it appear that the major concern is with identifying something as a work of art when the concern should be with the point of calling something art and with the way one engages with the work and reacts to it. The matter of engagement has important implications for our dealings with the avant-garde.

There are other issues relevant for aesthetics in the *Philosophical Investigations* of equal or greater importance than the matter of definition. Aesthetic appreciation and understanding are in large part a matter of how things are seen or heard. In part 2, section 11 of the *Philosophical Investigations*, there is an extended discussion of seeing that makes clear that there are a number of interrelated conceptions of perception and that many different kinds of things can count as objects of sight. Although much attention has been directed to the ambiguous duck-rabbit figure that can be seen either as a duck or as a rabbit, that curious creature serves only to introduce a whole series of different concepts of perception. The section begins with the notion of seeing likenesses and moves to seeing aspects and patterns of organization and investigates the relations between seeing, thinking, and interpreting and then modulates to the phenomenon of experiencing the meaning of a word. This, in turn, leads to the introduction of the idea of words having secondary senses.

This material has very important implications for understanding a number of issues that have puzzled philosophers—for example, the perception of design and composition in a work of art, the aesthetic character of language, and the use of expressions borrowed from other areas of human experience to describe works of art when those expressions do not appear to have any "literal" application to art (e.g., the ascription of emotional character to works of art).

Wittgenstein understands these questions to be conceptual or "grammatical" in nature. They are not psychological or in any way empirical. The problems arise because there is something about language that is misunderstood. The prob-

lem is to be dissolved by getting a better view of the actual workings of the relevant language. The implication for aesthetics is that these questions about aesthetic experience and aesthetic perception can be resolved without recourse to theories, whether of psychological processes or the ontology of "aesthetic objects."

Wittgenstein shared with twentieth-century analytic philosophy the view that philosophical problems are at bottom a matter of language, but he was not concerned, as analytic aesthetics has been, to construct theories of art or to map the logic of aesthetic concepts. His concern was always with the human importance of art and with those intellectual tendencies to misunderstand what is before our eyes that lead us to darken counsel by philosophical theory.

Although the *Philosophical Investigations* contains a number of insightful remarks and asides concerning aesthetics, aesthetics is not directly a major concern. The book's greatest importance is the view that it gives of the nature of philosophical problems and the techniques it teaches for resolving those problems. It is left to us to apply all that to aesthetics and the philosophy of art.

BIBLIOGRAPHY

Works by Wittgenstein

Tractatus Logico-Philosophicus. Translated by C. K. Ogden. London, 1922. Also translated by D. F. Pears and B. F. McGuinness (London, 1961).
Philosophical Investigations (1953). 3d ed. Translated by G. E. M. Anscombe. New York, 1968.
Notebooks, 1914–1916. Edited by G. H. von Wright and G. E. M. Anscombe. New York, 1961; 2d ed., Chicago, 1979.
Lectures and Conversations on Aesthetics, Psychology, and Religious Belief. Edited by Cyril Barrett. Berkeley, 1967. The material on aesthetics is from 1938.
Culture and Value. Edited by G. H. von Wright and translated by Peter Winch. Chicago, 1980. Material from 1914–1951.

Other Sources

Cavell, Stanley. *Must We Mean What We Say?* (1969). Cambridge and New York, 1976.
Elton, William, ed. *Aesthetics and Language.* Oxford, 1954.
Evans, Martyn. *Listening to Music.* Houndmills, 1990.
Haller, Rudolf, ed. *Aesthetics: Proceedings of the 8th International Wittgenstein Symposium.* Vienna, 1984.
Janik, Allan, and Stephen Toulmin. *Wittgenstein's Vienna.* New York, 1973.
Johannessen, Kjell S., and Tore Nordenstam, eds. *Wittgenstein: Ästhetik und transzendentale philosophie.* Vienna, 1981.
Kennick, William E. "Does Traditional Aesthetics Rest on a Mistake?" *Mind* 67.3 (July 1958): 317–334.
Mandelbaum, Maurice. "Family Resemblances and Generalization concerning the Arts." *American Philosophical Quarterly* (1965).
McGuinness, Brian. *Wittgenstein: A Life: Young Ludwig, 1889–1921.* Berkeley, 1988.
Monk, Ray. *Ludwig Wittgenstein: The Duty of Genius.* New York, 1990.
Moore, George Edward. "Wittgenstein's Lectures, 1930–1933." In *Philosophical Papers*, pp. 252–324. London, 1959.
Tilghman, B. R. *But Is It Art? The Value of Art and the Temptation of Theory.* Oxford and New York, 1984.

Tilghman, B. R. *Wittgenstein, Ethics and Aesthetics: The View from Eternity.* Houndmills, 1992.

Weitz, Morris. "The Role of Theory in Aesthetics." *Journal of Aesthetics and Art Criticism* 15.1 (September 1956): 27–35.

Wijdeveld, Paul. *Ludwig Wittgenstein, Architect.* Cambridge, Mass., 1994.

BENJAMIN R. TILGHMAN

Reception of Wittgenstein

It is remarkable that the writings of Ludwig Wittgenstein have exerted a great influence on aesthetics and the philosophy of art, because Wittgenstein actually wrote very little directly on the philosophical issues that arise in connection with the arts. But since the publication of the *Philosophical Investigations* in 1953, philosophers of art have found many of Wittgenstein's fundamental contributions to the philosophy of language and the philosophy of mind to hold significance for aesthetic questions, and like the impact his work made on the areas of language and mind, the aesthetic significance was regarded as revolutionary. Rather than accepting without question the problems that aestheticians traditionally faced and then proceeding to the development and elucidation of theories designed to answer those questions, Wittgenstein provided an avenue of escape from, or a new method for treating, those classic questions. Central among them were the essentialist questions of definition: "What essential properties must an object possess to qualify as a work of art?" and "What quality or property do all works of art have in common?" Wittgenstein's famous contribution to the problem of universals, the question asking why all members of a class are placed in that class (e.g., objects of knowledge, truth, beauty, justice, and art), was revolutionary in that it undercut rather than answered the question of universals. Wittgenstein's new proposal proceeded in terms of "family resemblance," but the great impact of this proposal led to the consensus that the significance that Wittgenstein's philosophical writings held for aesthetics could be summed up in antiessentialist terms. This is in fact untrue. Further topics include the often-hidden influences of language on our conceptions of artistic meaning; the complex interrelations among words, music, pictures, and gestures; the analogy between the arts and what Wittgenstein antireductively refers to as a "form of life"; the clarification of the ways in which art can embody thought; relations between philosophical conceptions of the self and conceptions of artworks; the role of the imagination in aesthetic perception; many complex interrelations between texts and contexts; nuances of self-revelation and autobiographical disclosure in literature; the relations between literary-interpretive and philosophical undertakings; the "logic" of criticism and the nature of critical reasoning and justification; and the separation of empirical and conceptual methods in aesthetics. There are also authors now reading Wittgenstein as a philosopher of culture, extracting from his writings new understanding of how a tradition is transmitted, how to evaluate and diagnose the ailments of a culture, how to better see the relation between Wittgenstein's work and his own time, and how to see in the *Philosophical Investigations* a subtle—and unsettling—depiction of our own times. There is much greater aesthetic and cultural illumination to be had from Wittgenstein's philosophy than the antiessentialist consensus would begin to suggest.

The writings discussed here divide into five broadly defined areas. The first concerns the relations between the arts and the philosophy of language; issues and strategies from Wittgenstein's multifaceted investigations into language are transplanted into aesthetic contexts. Under this heading, Rush Rhees (1969) has inquired into the very possibility of an artwork's *character;* this naturally led him into an investigation of the relations between judgments of persons and works of art. Following Wittgenstein's observation that "we learn logic as we learn to speak," he suggests that we learn the concept of art and—broadly speaking—art criticism as we learn to speak, and that such concepts are embedded in our linguistic practices. Rhees also opened the discussion of Wittgenstein's remarks on the meaning of ritual in his comments on James Frazer's *The Golden Bough,* a topic that resurfaces throughout the multifarious writings on Wittgenstein, aesthetics, and cultural understanding.

Beginning with Wittgenstein's replacement of problem-solution with problem-dissolution, Carolyn Korsmeyer moved beyond the definitional question in aesthetics to the ontological question, asking "What do aesthetic adjectives modify?"—particularly, how do critical descriptions such as "mysterious," "eerie," "corrosive," "pompous," "stately," and similar aesthetic predicates reside in (if they do) the physical objects we regard as artworks? Korsmeyer brings into play the concept of gesture as an illuminating way of understanding the relation between aesthetic predicates and physical objects. Yet, to speak of relations here is dangerously misleading because "a major part of understanding a poem or other work of art is 'seeing' the expression it embodies, although the expression is nothing different from the work itself, just as an expression of sadness is not a face plus sadness, but a sad face" (Korsmeyer, 1978). Aesthetic predicates are "verbal equivalences" to the "gesture" made by the expressive work, and thus artistic meaning is not—consistent with Wittgenstein's groundbreaking work within the philosophy of language—to be understood as a mental shadow or hidden intention only contingently attached to its outward expression.

Furthering the use of the concept of gesture in its connection with linguistic meaning, Karlheinz Lüdeking observed that whenever Wittgenstein "considers art, he shows a remarkable tendency to compare it to the gestures of the human body" (1990), and he uncovered the aesthetic significance of a claim that is central to Wittgenstein's mature thought, namely, that language is invariably viewed as having roots in concrete practices rather than as an abstract calculus. Indeed, gestures, like works of art, are understood only "when one is familiar with their role in a form of life," and it is by looking into some human gestures as depicted in painting that Lüdeking uncovers valuable connections between Wittgenstein's gestural conception of linguistic meaning and the perception of expressive properties in art.

Showing that references to musical experience appear throughout Wittgenstein's writings and that these are primarily used to explore logical and linguistic matters, P. B. Lewis (1977) examined the parallel that Wittgenstein draws between understanding a sentence and understanding music. But whereas Wittgenstein usually employs this parallel to cast light on linguistic understanding, Lewis reverses the direction and investigates how Wittgenstein conceives of the understanding of a musical theme. Not surprisingly, relations to understanding persons, and particularly to understanding facial expressions, enter into the discussion; these topics too have become major themes in Wittgensteinian aesthetics.

The phrase "a form of life" appears throughout Wittgensteinian aesthetics, referring to the "complex of habits, experiences, skills, with which language interlocks in that it could not be operated without them and, equally, they cannot be identified without reference to it," as Richard Wollheim captures the meaning of Wittgenstein's phrase (1980). Wollheim shows why it would be wrong to attempt—as many aesthetic theorists have done and continue to do—to locate the artistic impulse or intention apart from and prior to the institutions and practices of art. He offers a diagnostic analysis of the erroneous presumption that the expressive content of a work of art can always be propositionally expressed apart from the expressive artwork itself. Wollheim uncovers some of the subtleties, and the often-veiled power to direct subsequent thinking, of the larger or more general analogy between language and art. Answers to questions concerning art-language analogies, as Wollheim's writing shows, are anything but simple and unitary.

Yet, it may still be the case that the language we use in aesthetic or critical contexts can be characterized generally, and B. R. Tilghman has offered such a characterization in terms of the secondary senses of words, a conception of linguistic meaning found in the latter sections of the *Philosophical Investigations*. Tilghman finds much significance for aesthetics in some of Wittgenstein's remarks on experiencing the meaning of a word, on the "soul" of a word, and on "understanding a sentence in the sense in which it can be replaced by another which says the same, but also in the sense in which it cannot be replaced by any other." Tilghman also investigates the autonomy of language games, a topic discussed at length by others mentioned later in this essay.

The second broad area into which Wittgenstein's writings relevant to aesthetics can be divided concerns the relations between aesthetics and the philosophy of mind, and the work here undertaken has particularly cast light on the significance that Wittgenstein's work holds for our understanding of artistic creation and perception. Roger Shiner (1982) has shown the philosophically pernicious effects of holding a Cartesian or dualistic (i.e., mind and body) conception of the self for our understanding of meaning, and he too turns to the significance of gesture in sorting out the relations between expressive content in art and in human behavior. He also shows why, once dualism is seen to lead us into conceptual confusion when contemplating artistic expression, we should avoid reaching for the polemical alternative to dualism, a monistic or reductive behaviorism. To insist on the distinction between a person and that person's expressive behavior is to lay the groundwork for the analogous distinction between a tangible art object and its intangible expressive properties, and that is to remain locked inside the dualistic categories from which Wittgenstein's work, as Shiner shows, releases us.

Wittgenstein's philosophy of mind has much to say about the nature of the self. But it also has much to say about perception, and Malcolm Budd (1989) has focused on the central topic of aspect perception. We do on occasion see an object (or a much-discussed ambiguous line drawing that can be seen as a duck or as a rabbit) and, while seeing it, know that although it has not changed, the way we see it does change. In what does this change consist, and what does it tell (or show) us about the role the imagination plays in perception? As Budd says, Wittgenstein returned to this kind of perceptual-imaginative phenomenon (actually, phenomena—he shows that they are not all alike) time and again in his writings on the philosophy of psychology, and these writings have exerted considerable influence in philosophical aesthetics. Budd's work, extending into aspect shifts, aspects of organization, the relations between sensational and representational properties in visual experience, and—most fundamentally—the role of imagination in visual interpretation, is primarily about the philosophy of mind, but his close examination of Wittgenstein's remarks hold great significance for aesthetics.

Some, notably T. E. Wilkerson, have argued that "interpreting pictures is a special case of seeing aspects" (1991), and Wilkerson has identified five features of aspect perception: it is typically detached from belief; it is subject to the will; noticing a change of aspect is akin to the experience of a sudden dawning of understanding; in seeing a Y-aspect in S, we focus attention on a resemblance between X and Y (e.g., in seeing a landscape in cracked plaster we focus on the resemblance between the contour of the plaster lines and the contour of landscape depiction); and, most important, aspect seeing is an exercise of the imagination. One can see how these features are immediately relevant to fundamental aesthetic questions, and Wilkerson goes on to show how the explanation of pictorial representation in terms of aspect perception does not rely too heavily on resemblances between picture and object, yet it preserves a place for it.

R. K. Elliott (1973) has also explored imagination, but he has taken the discussion in a somewhat different direction. Noting the density of significance in Wittgenstein's remark that when a printed triangle is seen as a mountain "it is as if an image came into contact, and for a time remained in contact, with the visual impression," Elliott focuses his concern on "types of imaginal experience in which the image which seems to come into contact with what is perceived is an image of something which is *not* depicted or described in the work, but which nevertheless achieves a certain strength of presence" (1973), and conducts a Wittgensteinian investigation into the roles imagination plays in aesthetic perception. Just as Wilkerson secures a carefully described place for resemblance (through the use of Wittgenstein's analysis of aspect perception) in an account of pictorial representation, so Elliott secures a carefully nuanced place for imaginal experience in aesthetic perception, showing how a misbegotten aesthetic objectivism—a position holding that a true and verifiable perception of an artwork would derive only from a direct perception of its intrinsic properties—would severely mischaracterize and impoverish genuine aesthetic experience.

A third major area of research in Wittgensteinian aesthetics is devoted to the relations between philosophy and literature, but because the subject is addressed in the following essay, the reader is referred here to works listed in the bibliography.

G. E. Moore's record of Wittgenstein's lectures in 1930–1933 has proven a valuable resource for those working in a fourth area, the philosophy of criticism. Moore writes: "He introduced his whole discussion of aesthetics by dealing with one problem about the meaning of words" (1972), and then follows this with a discussion of Wittgenstein's remarks on the word *game* and its application to the word *beautiful*. Richard Shusterman opens an essay on the Wittgensteinian sense of critical reasoning by referring to these lectures, and identifies three central themes of Wittgensteinian aesthetics: (1) the "radical indeterminacy of aesthetic concepts" (illustrated by the concept "game") but applied to genre concepts (tragedy, comedy, epic, etc.), to period concepts (Gothic, Baroque, Cubist, etc.), to the very concept of art itself, and to specific critical concepts (vivid, delicate, unified, elegant, etc.); (2) "the logical plurality of critical discourse," involving both the logical variety of critical statements and the critical plurality of critical frameworks; and (3) the "cultural historicity of art and art appreciation" (1986). But by returning to those lectures, and by proceeding to an examination of the rhetorically persuasive rather than strictly inductive or deductive nature of critical argumentation, Shusterman cautions that a *theory* of criticism built on these foundations "seems inconsistent with the very doctrines that engendered

it" (ibid.), and that if we are insufficiently mindful of the plurality of critical "language games"—indeed, a *family* of critical games—we may well ironically fall victim to the very conceptual dangers of which Wittgenstein's philosophy is designed to warn us.

Theory construction, or building, is anything but Wittgenstein's motivation, and Kjell S. Johannessen (1990) opens his study with an epigraph from Wittgenstein: "I am not interested in constructing a building so much as in having a perspicuous view of the foundations of possible buildings." And he employs a particularly resonant passage from Wittgenstein, that there is a "queer resemblance between a philosophical investigation . . . and an aesthetic one." Johannessen turns our attention to various critical activities and to how we actually get rid of aesthetic puzzlement; these show the kinds of things Wittgenstein had in mind by "aesthetic investigation."

Beginning with a discussion of some of Wittgenstein's observations on inexpressibility in aesthetics and the analogy between aesthetics and ethics, Joachim Schulte (1989) considers nuances of the expressibility and inexpressibility of the content communicated by works of art, thus implicitly furthering the discussion of intransitivity and explicitly furthering the discussion of the nature of criticism. Like other authors, Schulte integrates remarks from Moore's record of Wittgenstein's lectures, and he further advances the investigation into the delicate role of subjective judgment and personal taste within Wittgensteinian aesthetics. A central theme of Wittgenstein's philosophy of language and his philosophy of mathematics enters in here, specifically that of rule following in connection with the perception of aesthetic correctness. But Schulte shows that, indeed, rule following in artistic contexts does not reduce to one single mental phenomenon, nor do the experiences of noticing unusual aspects or particular features of works where those experiences play roles in our critical language specifically as they pertain to aesthetic rightness. Frank Cioffi (1984) has pursued these topics in detail, asking particularly when and why empirical methods bypass questions of aesthetic meaning and significance. Cioffi reminds us that Wittgenstein criticized Frazer for having launched an investigation into the origins of ritual, and Sigmund Freud for having responded to dreams by searching for causal relations between dreams and other aspects of our experience. These doubts concerning empirical explanation, extending, as Cioffi observes, well beyond Wittgensteinian exegesis, give rise to this problem:

There are questions which present themselves as empirical, i.e. such that they require further information for their resolution, but with respect to which we are told, or come to feel obscurely for ourselves, that this is an illusion, that the consummation we are seeking is not to be found in more empirical knowledge, or via scientific explanation, but elsewhere and otherwise. What is the character of this "elsewhere and otherwise"? (Cioffi, 1984)

In answering, Cioffi identifies errors (e.g., the conceptual model of dualism, taking causal explanation for all explanation, the mimicking of science) that Wittgenstein was opposing in his remarks on aesthetics. In sorting out these errors and in elucidating their significance for aesthetics, Cioffi relies on a quotation from an author who exerted a profound influence on Wittgenstein's thought, Heinrich Herz in *Principles of Mechanics:* "When these painful contradictions are removed, the question as to the nature of the force will not have been answered; but our minds, no longer vexed, will cease to ask illegitimate questions." This brings to the fore the replacement of problem-solution by problem-dissolution in Wittgenstein's philosophy, an idea also central to Wittgensteinian aesthetics.

The dissipation of perplexity is thus a fundamental aim of Wittgenstein's philosophical methods, and Richard Eldridge (1987) has provided an overview of these methods as they have influenced aesthetics since the publication of the *Philosophical Investigations;* he particularly sets the rooting of aesthetic and artistic concepts in human practices against the misleading influences of Cartesian dualism and definitional essentialism, and considers the possibility of a Wittgensteinian phenomenology of art. For this, he refers to the ideas of Immanuel Kant, particularly concerning the capacity of the arts to exhibit the mind's freedom.

A fifth major area of work in Wittgensteinian aesthetics is the philosophy of culture. This naturally involves further investigation into aesthetic practices, as well as into central areas of Wittgenstein's philosophy of language, including private language and rule following. Anthony O'Hear (1991) has shown the significance that these linguistic themes hold for our understanding of the cohesion and style of a culture and the transmission of that culture generationally. O'Hear views Wittgenstein's work not only from the more familiar point of view of Gottlob Frege, Bertrand Russell, and British empiricism, but also from that of Austro-Hungarian conservative thought and the "philosophical anthropology" one can extrapolate from it. Indeed, the very idea of tradition is illuminated, as O'Hear shows, by Wittgenstein's analysis of rule following, of the ineradicably social nature of language, and more specifically of linguistic meaning, and of the nature of the relations between self and society. O'Hear asks where the grounds of our practices are and are not intelligibly called into question, and he shows that Wittgenstein had a good deal of immediate relevance to the understanding of cultural activity on this score. But Wittgenstein's emphasis on the rootedness of the concepts of our community and, more widely, our culture, does not imply that these practices are immune to criticism. Wittgenstein was hardly complacent or satisfied with the state of his own culture.

J. Bouveresse (1991) quotes a phrase from a passage in the Preface to the *Philosophical Investigations* written in 1945: "It is not impossible that it should fall to the lot of this work in its poverty and in the darkness of this time, to bring light into one brain or another—but, of course, it is not likely." Wittgenstein's perception of cultural darkness was such that he wrote in the remarks published as *Culture and Value*, "My own thinking about art and values is far more disillusioned than would have been *possible* for someone one hundred years ago." But Wittgenstein adds that, rather than showing that his view is more correct than someone's a century ago, this "only means that I have examples of degeneration in the forefront of my mind which were not in the *forefront* of men's minds then." Also looking into the Austro-Hungarian and European contexts for Wittgenstein's cultural thinking, Bouveresse reconsiders his cultural pessimism and in particular his sense of *decline* and the relations of his view to those of Oswald Spengler, Robert Musil, Friedrich Nietzsche, and others. Appropriate to a Wittgensteinian study, Bouveresse assembles a large picture of the cultural context within which Wittgenstein developed these views and the set of cultural practices in which these concepts were rooted, particularly emphasizing Wittgenstein's doubts concerning the concept of progress. Indeed, Wittgenstein's preference for clarity and perspicuity, "values in themselves," over progress and the building of ever more complicated theories or explanations, is given a fuller context here, as is his remark, "I am not interested in constructing a building so much as having a perspicuous view of the foundations of possible buildings" (ibid.).

Wittgenstein had personal doubts about his philosophical work being properly understood in his cultural context, and such doubts may have been common, as George H. von Wright has pointed out, to many great philosophers. Did not many believe that they "could not be properly understood until an entirely new climate of opinion had come to prevail?" (von Wright, 1981). Perhaps not, for von Wright writes: "I still think that Wittgenstein's attitude to his time makes him unique among the great philosophers" (ibid.). In a line that resonates with some work surveyed earlier in this essay, von Wright shows how in Wittgenstein's thoughts on these and related matters (e.g., the belief that in a future culture with different patterns, the questions that tormented him will not arise), the "philosophic conviction that the life of the human individual and therefore also all individual manifestations of culture are deeply entrenched in basic structures of a *social* nature" (ibid.) is absolutely central. These structures are, as discussed throughout the larger field of Wittgensteinian aesthetics, *Lebensformen,* or forms of life, and language games. Von Wright also shows how the emphasis on the social (in language and in the psychology of the individual) is intertwined with Wittgenstein's conception of the nature of philosophy itself. If problems of philosophy have their origins in the malfunctions or conflations of language games, similar problems can manifest as "unhealthy habits of thought, permeating the intellectual culture of a time" (ibid.). Wittgenstein's philosophical methods are designed to do battle with such problems and pernicious habits, but a profound change in our practices (following a thorough investigation of them), which of course are inseparable from our concepts, can prove therapeutic and problem-dissolving. Von Wright quotes Wittgenstein from the *Remarks on the Foundations of Mathematics:* "The sickness of a time is cured by an alteration in the mode of life of human beings . . ."; von Wright goes on to consider the deep connections between language and ways of life, and he too pursues the comparison between Spengler and Wittgenstein on these issues. Von Wright reveals that Wittgenstein's "conception of philosophy is intimately allied to a way of viewing contemporary civilization" (1981), a view constituted in large part by the artistic and aesthetic dimensions of his culture.

Von Wright's essay is Stanley Cavell's (1989) point of departure in pursuing further questions in Wittgensteinian philosophy of culture. Is Wittgenstein's attitude to his times essential not only to understanding his intellectual personality, but also to understanding his philosophy? Cavell reconsiders the similarities, but primarily the contrasts, between Wittgenstein's position on culture and Spenglerian pessimism, and this naturally leads to a reconsideration of the idea of a form of life and the question whether Wittgenstein found disorders in language itself. In casting light on Wittgenstein's conception of philosophy and of philosophical problems (not by any means a straightforward task, as Cavell shows), he observes that although "Wittgenstein speaks of pictures holding us captive, of unsatisfiable cravings, of disabling sublimizings," he does not "say very much about why we are the victims of these fortunes, as if his mission is not to explain why we sin but to show us that we do, and its places" (1989). For Cavell, the multifarious philosophical undertakings of the *Philosophical Investigations* constitute an interminable war with skepticism; and we can link to this perspective the related observation that within some contexts, some language games, the question of giving grounds cannot arise, as argued by O'Hear. But, more specifically, Cavell is claiming that "there is a perspective from which the *Philosophical Investigations* may be seen as presenting a philosophy of culture," and can be seen as it stands, "as a portrait, or say as a sequence of sketches (Wittgenstein calls his text an album) of our civilization, of the details of what Spengler phrases as our 'spiritual history,' the image of '*our own* inner life'" (ibid.). In reading the *Philosophical Investigations* as an artistic representation, Cavell uncovers a good deal concerning the conception of philosophy that Wittgenstein's book slowly articulates.

Further works demonstrate various aspects of the influence of Wittgenstein's philosophy on aesthetics. For example, Roger Scruton's groundbreaking *Art and Imagination,* (1974), while extending its account of aesthetic experience far beyond the bounds of Wittgensteinian exegesis or commentary, incorporates a Wittgensteinian account of the imagination; more recently, Martyn Evans's *Listening to Music* (1990) incorporates Wittgensteinian conceptions of expressivity, judgment, and gesture into its subject; Frank Palmer's *Literature and Moral Understanding* (1992) incorporates the concept of the language game in its account of literary experience; G. L. Hagberg's *Meaning and Interpretation* (1994) explores literary interpretation as Wittgensteinian investigation and his *Art as Language* (1995) examines analogies between language and art as these have shaped much aesthetic theory.

Exclusive focus on the question of artistic definition would greatly impoverish our understanding of the significance of Wittgenstein's philosophy for aesthetics: work in this field, although perhaps generally unified in its broadly antitheoretical stance, in fact ranges throughout, and in many cases crosses over, the five major areas of Wittgensteinian aesthetics mentioned here. It uncovers and elucidates complex interrelations among visual art, language, gesture, imagination, music, architecture, literature, criticism, self-understanding, culture, aesthetic theory, methodology, and philosophy itself.

BIBLIOGRAPHY

Work by Wittgenstein

Lectures and Conversations on Aesthetics, Psychology, and Religious Belief. Edited by Cyril Barrett. Berkeley, 1967.

Other Sources

Bouveresse, J. "'The Darkness of This Time': Wittgenstein and the Modern World." In *Wittgenstein Centenary Essays,* edited by A. Phillips Griffiths, Royal Institute of Philosophy Lecture Series 28, pp. 11–38. Cambridge and New York, 1991.
Budd, Malcolm. "Seeing Aspects." In *Wittgenstein's Philosophy of Psychology.* London and New York, 1989.
Cavell, Stanley. "The *Investigations* as a Depiction of Our Times." In *This New Yet Unapproachable America: Lectures after Emerson after Wittgenstein.* Albuquerque, N.Mex., 1989.
Cioffi, Frank. "When Do Empirical Methods Bypass 'The Problems Which Trouble Us'?" *Philosophy and Literature,* edited by A. Phillips Griffiths, Royal Institute of Philosophy Lecture Series 16 (1983), pp. 155–172. Cambridge and New York, 1984.
Eldridge, Richard. "Problems and Prospects of Wittgensteinian Aesthetics." *Journal of Aesthetics and Art Criticism* 45.3 (1987): 251–261.
Elliott, R. K. "Imagination in the Experience of Art." In *Philosophy and the Arts,* edited by Godfrey Vesey, Royal Institute of Philosophy Lectures 1971–1972, vol. 6, pp. 88–105. London, 1973.
Evans, Martyn. *Listening to Music.* Houndmills, 1990.
Hagberg, Garry L. *Meaning and Interpretation: Wittgenstein, Henry James, and Literary Knowledge.* Ithaca, N.Y., 1994.
Hagberg, Garry L. *Art as Language: Wittgenstein, Meaning, and Aesthetic Theory.* Ithaca, N.Y., 1995.
Johannessen, Kjell S. "Art, Philosophy, and Intransitive Understanding." In *Wittgenstein: Towards a Re-evaluation,* edited by Rudolf Haller and Johannes Brandl, Proceedings of the 14th International Wittgenstein Symposium, pp. 323–333. Vienna, 1990.
Korsmeyer, Carolyn. "Wittgenstein and the Ontological Problem of Art." *Personalist* 59.2 (April 1978): 152–161.
Lewis, P. B. "Wittgenstein on Words and Music." *British Journal of Aesthetics* 17.2 (Spring 1977): 111–121.

Lüdeking, Karlheinz. "Pictures and Gestures." *British Journal of Aesthetics* 30.3 (July 1990): 218–232.

Moore, George Edward. "Wittgenstein's Lectures, 1930–1933." In *Aesthetics,* edited by Harold Osborne, pp. 86–88. Oxford and New York, 1972.

O'Hear, Anthony. "Wittgenstein and the Transmission of Traditions." In *Wittgenstein Centenary Essays,* edited by A. Phillips Griffiths, Royal Institute of Philosophy Lecture Series 28. Cambridge and New York, 1991.

Palmer, Frank. *Literature and Moral Understanding.* Oxford, 1992.

Rhees, Rush. "Art and Philosophy." In *Without Answers,* edited by D. Z. Phillips. London, 1969.

Schulte, Joachim. "Aesthetic Correctness." *Revue Internationale de Philosophie* 43.169 (1989): 298–310.

Scruton, Roger. *Art and Imagination: A Study in the Philosophy of Mind.* London, 1974.

Shiner, Roger. "The Mental Life of a Work of Art." *Journal of Aesthetics and Art Criticism* 40.3 (Spring 1982): 253–268.

Shusterman, Richard. "Wittgenstein and Critical Reasoning." *Philosophy and Phenomenological Research* 47.1 (September 1986): 91–110.

Tilghman, B. R. *Wittgenstein, Ethics, and Aesthetics: The View from Eternity.* Houndmills, 1991.

von Wright, George H. "Wittgenstein in Relation to His Times." In *Wittgenstein and His Times,* edited by Brian McGuinness, pp. 108–120. Oxford, 1981.

Wilkerson, T. E. "Pictorial Representation: A Defense of the Aspect Theory." *Midwest Studies in Philosophy* 16 (1991): 152–166.

Wollheim, Richard. *Arts and Its Objects.* 2d ed. with six supplementary essays. Cambridge and New York, 1980. See especially pp. 104–132.

GARRY HAGBERG

Wittgenstein and Literary Theory

Ludwig Wittgenstein has had considerable impact on contemporary literary theory and criticism in spite of the fact that he wrote very little about literature and did not regard himself as producing a "theory" of language, literary or otherwise. Wittgenstein's thinking has nonetheless been important for contemporary literary theorists because it offers nuanced perspectives on the antifoundationalist assumptions that govern the most prominent work in criticism today. Moreover, the antifoundationalism of Wittgenstein's *Philosophical Investigations* may also offer a way beyond the impasses with which both deconstruction and neo-pragmatism have found themselves confronted. Wittgenstein's work can help move critics away from debates over what can or cannot be known with certainty about the (literary) text toward a deeper understanding of the responsibilities placed on readers when faced with the facts of the text's "undecidability."

Wittgenstein's importance for contemporary literary theory first became apparent in the context of the American appropriation of ordinary-language philosophy and speech act theory, especially in the work of Stanley Cavell, who drew extensively on Wittgenstein's later writings in the course of his engagement with the work of J. L. Austin. In the essays gathered in *Must We Mean What We Say?* and even more so in the chapters that comprise *The Claim of Reason,* Cavell's understanding of what is at stake in the claims of "ordinary language" centers on a drama in which philosophy encounters the limits of what it can reasonably claim to know in the form of skepticism's irrepressible doubts. In Cavell's reading of Wittgenstein, skepticism is not so much opposed to philosophy as it is the condition and limit of philosophical discourse: as long as philosophy is to attempt to validate its claims to knowledge, it must acknowledge the threat of skepticism. Skepticism represents something that philosophy cannot overcome, but only avoid.

In this reading of Wittgenstein, skepticism and epistemology represent twin distortions of our relationship to the world and to others. When faced with the fact of these distortions, the task of philosophy must be to overcome itself. This process of therapeutic overcoming yields a return to the world of the ordinary, or to the "everyday." Its intent is to bring words back "home," or to a region in which their sense is obvious. Although the hope expressed in the *Philosophical Investigations* is for a "complete clarity," in which philosophical problems would finally disappear, later readers of Wittgenstein such as Cavell stress the fact that any return to the ordinary must take place in full view of the fact that skepticism cannot be defeated. In contrast to the Wittgenstein of the *Philosophical Investigations,* for whom our response to doubt must be to return words to their "home," the world of the ordinary in many of the recent literary-theoretical uses of Wittgenstein is seen as a space of contingent relationships in which rational coherence is available only within the framework of some provisional "language game" and in which there is no justification for, or theory of, what constitutes a language game in general. The "language game" has been taken as Wittgenstein's way of formulating what other antifoundationalist philosophers, from Martin Heidegger to Michel Foucault, have described in terms of the background "practices" against which all forms of human action establish their meaning.

The many dimensions of our contingent relationship to the world become especially visible in a Wittgensteinian reading of the literary forms of tragedy, romance, and novel. In tragedy (Cavell deals principally with *King Lear* and *Othello,* but others, including Anthony J. Cascardi and Richard Eldridge, have dealt with the novel), we find revealed the limits of what we can claim to know with certainty about the world. In disclosing the limits of knowledge, tragedy discovers that the demand for responsible action with respect to other human beings is without end. It leads to a demand for acknowledgment rather than knowledge as the basis for our dealings with others. In romance (Cavell looks at William Shakespeare's romances, especially *The Winter's Tale,* and at a genre of Hollywood film called the "comedy of remarriage"), Wittgenstein's understanding of the provisionality of language games helps disclose the fact that we stand in a contingent relationship to the world. For example, "marriage" is not the description of an original or natural set of facts; in these plays and films, "marriage" involves acceptance and consent; moreover, every "marriage" seems also to be a form of remarriage. In the case of the novel, a Wittgensteinian approach reveals the ways in which the coherence and continuity of narrative are at best internally generated; similarly, the forms of life that novelistic narrative supports are the products of deeply rooted conventions. In all these instances, the antifoundationalism of Wittgenstein's *Philosophical Investigations* informs and supports a nonnaturalist vision of the social self.

Wittgenstein's insights into the nature of "language games" has helped provide many other theorists with a richer understanding of what is at stake in the development of a nonfoundationalist philosophy. This work overlaps with, and in some respects surpasses, the assumptions that contemporary literary theory has adopted from deconstruction and neopragmatism. For the philosopher Richard Rorty, who approaches Wittgenstein via the work of John Dewey rather than Austin, Wittgenstein's thought represents a valuable lesson in "overcoming" philosophy that is every bit as powerful as the lessons that Friedrich Nietzsche and Heidegger taught in this regard. For Rorty, the problem facing philosophy that a Wittgensteinian approach can help resolve is how to "circumvent" the tradition of metaphysics. Especially during the Enlightenment, when philosophy staked its identity on the ability to locate a truly impartial critical position, the practice of critique amounted to an attempt to "unmask" every prior critical stance, to show that each is marked by some form of blindness, of which it is unaware. But at the end of the Enlightenment tradition it has become apparent that none of these so-called critical stances was powerful enough to put an end to the motives of suspicion that drive the demand for further unmasking, and indeed that no stance could ever have such power. Wittgenstein's philosophical therapy is particularly instructive in showing what philosophy might look like if it could overcome the desire for a final unmasking and set aside its desire to pronounce the final word on any given subject.

In Wittgenstein's work, the problem with traditional philosophy (metaphysics) lies in that it has been held captive by ideals of systematic completion and closure that it has never been able to achieve. The task of philosophy as Wittgenstein sees it is rather "to shew [*sic*] the fly the way out of the fly-bottle" (1958, p. 309). This does not mean finding the right solutions to all the "problems," but rather working to bring words back home, so that the "problems" of philosophy disappear. Thus, Wittgenstein can insist that the clarity he is seeking in his work is "complete clarity" (ibid., p. 133). Rather than find a better answer to a Kantian question such as "How is synthetic a priori knowledge possible?" Wittgenstein might propose to diagnose and resolve the strangeness of the desires that motivate such a question in the first place. By focusing on the problems of philosophy and the linguistic distortions that produce them,

Wittgenstein's work is nonetheless congruent with the irony that Rorty identifies as characteristic of literary discourse as opposed to philosophy. In Rorty's work, however, a much greater emphasis falls on the contingency of our relationship to language (and, for that matter, to social practices). For Rorty, the "ironic" writer recognizes the fact that his or her pronouncements can never aspire to be the final words, the summation of a discourse. The "ironic" writer foregrounds the facts that permeate all literary discourse: contingency, provisionality, and openness to revision by redescription. Rather than aim to be an accurate representation of the world, Rorty has proposed that philosophy should strive to be an edifying form of discourse; and, rather than aim to be complete, philosophy should strive to approximate the irony of literature by revoking its claims to necessity and to closure, recognizing instead the contingency of its own ambitions and goals. Rorty's neopragmatist desire to circumvent the tradition of metaphysics thus shares central assumptions with Wittgensteinian "therapy" even while it diverges from Wittgenstein's desire for "complete clarity."

The neopragmatist use of Wittgenstein is complemented by the deconstructive interest in Wittgenstein. Stressing the affinities between the Heidegger of the "end of metaphysics" tradition, the work of Jacques Derrida, and Wittgenstein's later writings, numerous poststructuralist theorists and practitioners of deconstruction have drawn on Wittgenstein in order to press a series of assumptions about the indeterminacy of the text. (Some, such as Henry Staten, have also emphasized the irreconcilability of Wittgenstein and Derrida.) Deconstructive uses of Wittgenstein often begin from the commonplace position that Wittgenstein's notion of the "language game" can support claims about the indeterminacy of meaning (and, by implication, of all structures); in so doing, they may betray Wittgenstein's desire for "complete clarity." But deconstructive and other poststructuralist uses of Wittgenstein can also yield insightful treatments of the notion of the "language game" as the expression of the contingency of human relations. Jean-François Lyotard's appropriation of Wittgenstein in the discussion of justice in *The Differend* (1988) is a prominent example of the latter. For Lyotard, Wittgenstein's philosophy fits squarely within the domain of poststructuralism. He argues that this is so because the Wittgensteinian notion of "language game" makes sense only where we accept the fact that there can be no a priori hierarchy of language games, no transcendental position from which all such games can be surveyed, coordinated, or ranked. Lyotard's use of Wittgenstein is placed in the service of a stance that he describes as "pagan." This postmodern "paganism" describes a world founded on a belief in the irreducible heterogeneity of language games. Lyotard remains sensitive to the demands for justice that arise from claims that fall between the language games that rule a given world; and although his use of Wittgenstein's notion of language games allows us to hear the claims of those who have been denied a voice and thus victimized by the reigning language games, it comes at the price of a blindness to other, equally attractive, conceptions of justice. Specifically, Lyotard advances a notion of justice that does not acknowledge the validity of principles such as "fairness" or "desert." By stressing instead the affinity between justice and notions of taste and tact *(justesse)*, Lyotard uses Wittgenstein in order to revoke the notion of "principle" itself. Many would argue that although a revocation of the notion of principle suits Wittgenstein quite well, Lyotard's world simply does not aspire to the "complete clarity" of the *Philosophical Investigations*. [*See* Lyotard.]

Wittgenstein's affinities with aesthetic modernism can offer literary theory something that both neopragmatism and deconstruction are bound to miss insofar as they remain preoccupied with the incommensurability of language games and the indeterminacy of meaning. This lies in Wittgenstein's insights into the qualities of action or modes of relation of the subject, which tend to be omitted from critical practices that stress strategic rather than purposive modes of action. Rather than simply provide the ground for an ironic questioning of identities, and rather than provide us with instruction in the incommensurabilities of language games, Wittgenstein's work in the *Philosophical Investigations* can be seen as calling for further reflection on the qualities we display and the attitudes we adopt in relation to the language games we accept as contingent. This further reflection, which does not follow any strict methodological path, is represented by Wittgenstein's emphasis in the *Philosophical Investigations* on the particular modes in which a subject speaks or acts. It involves an emphasis on articulation that requires us to turn our attention to the "rough ground" of experience rather than to the transcendental or quasi-transcendental issues that philosophical advocates of discourse theory, such as Jürgen Habermas, have continued to pursue. Among contemporary literary scholars who have detected such possibilities in Wittgenstein's work, Charles Altieri (1976, 1981) has argued cogently that this attention to quality has affinities with modernist literary and artistic practice. First, modernist art stands in an ironic relationship to the aesthetic tradition, which it cannot conclusively surpass. Instead, modernism takes its problematic relationship to the past as the basis for foregrounding the particular qualities of action that the subject is empowered to put into play. Second, where modernist art approaches the ideal of a subjectless work, it relieves us of the desire to approach the work of art as an accurate representation of the world and asks us instead to focus on the modes of being or qualities of action that are displayed in and through it. Ideally, the modernist work of art is not "about" the world; it is itself a field in which the qualities of subjects can be demonstrated, put in play.

Wittgenstein thus enables literary theorists to confront a set of questions that remain to be addressed even after deconstruction and neopragmatism have succeeded in gaining universal agreement about the undecidability of the text and the contingency of discourse. These further questions are remarkably close to the ones Cavell was asking in the course of his interlacings of Wittgenstein, ordinary-language philosophy, tragedy, and romance. Rather than concentrate on what we can know, can Wittgenstein prompt us to ask how we should act in light of the contingency that surrounds anything we might claim to know? Wittgenstein's work thus opens a further avenue of research into the links between ethics and aesthetics for contemporary theorists working at the intersection of literature and philosophy. Wittgenstein's critique of the philosophical tradition and its modes of discourse provides convincing evidence that there remain viable models of subjective agency to be recovered from literary discourse even after we have accepted its ironic and contingent nature.

[*See also* Literature, *article on* Literary Aesthetics.]

BIBLIOGRAPHY

Work by Wittgenstein

Philosophical Investigations (1953). 3d ed. Translated by G. E. M. Anscombe. New York, 1968.

Other Sources

Altieri, Charles. "Wittgenstein on Consciousness and Language: A Challenge to Derridean Theory." *MLN* 91 (1976): 1397–1423.

Altieri, Charles. *Act and Quality: A Theory of Literary Meaning and Humanistic Understanding*. Amherst, Mass., 1981.

Cascardi, Anthony J. *The Bounds of Reason: Cervantes, Dostoevsky, Flaubert*. New York, 1986.

Cascardi, Anthony J. "The Grammar of Telling." *New Literary History* 19 (1988): 403–417.

Cavell, Stanley. *Must We Mean What We Say?* (1969). Cambridge and New York, 1976.

Cavell, Stanley. *The Claim of Reason: Wittgenstein, Skepticism, Morality and Tragedy*. New York and Oxford, 1979.

Cavell, Stanley. *Pursuits of Happiness: The Hollywood Comedy of Remarriage*. Cambridge, Mass., 1981.

Eldridge, Richard. *On Moral Personhood: Philosophy, Literature, Criticism, and Self-Understanding*. Chicago, 1989.

Fischer, Michael. "Stanley Cavell's Wittgenstein." In *Redrawing the Lines: Analytic Philosophy, Deconstruction, and Literary Theory*, edited by Reed Way Dasenbrock, pp. 49–60. Minneapolis, 1989.

Law, Jules David. "Reading with Wittgenstein and Derrida." In *Redrawing the Lines: Analytic Philosophy, Deconstruction, and Literary Theory*, edited by Reed Way Dasenbrock, pp. 169–188. Minneapolis, 1989.

Lyotard, Jean-François. *The Differend: Phrases in Dispute*. Translated by Georges Van Den Abbeele. Minneapolis, 1988.

Rorty, Richard. *Philosophy and the Mirror of Nature*. Princeton, N.J., 1979.

Rorty, Richard. *Contingency, Irony, and Solidarity*. Cambridge and New York, 1989.

Staten, Henry. *Wittgenstein and Derrida*. Lincoln, Nebr., 1984.

ANTHONY CASCARDI

WITTKOWER, RUDOLF (1901–1971), German-American art historian. Wittkower studied at Munich and Berlin and taught at Cologne, London (Warburg Institute and University College), and Columbia. He was long considered one of the principal theoretical art historians writing in English, thanks to his *Architectural Principles in the Age of Humanism* (1949; 3d ed. 1962) for decoding the metaphysical (Pythagorean-Neoplatonic) aspect of Italian Renaissance church architecture as a manifestation of a humanist spirituality, thus revising the nineteenth-century secularist understanding of the Renaissance. In its diversity, however, Wittkower's larger project has become more legendary than familiar.

Like his mentor Adolf Goldschmidt, Wittkower did not believe that art-historical scholarship existed to advance grand Hegelian theory: he was interested in theory, notably Renaissance and Baroque architectural theory and eighteenth-century British aesthetics, for the sake of culture-historical understanding. One of several general papers on art history, a 1959 address to the Winterthur (Delaware) Seminar on Museum Operation and Connoisseurship titled "Art History as a Discipline" (1961) not only relates to Erwin Panofsky's "The History of Art as a Humanistic Discipline" (1940) but stands against the extreme of connoisseurship declared in Roger Fry's "Art-History as an Academic Study" (in *Last Lectures*, 1939), where German scholarship is criticized for taking artworks "almost entirely from a chronological point of view, as coefficients of a time sequence, without reference to their aesthetic significance": not that sensibility is unworthy, but Wittkower could not have acknowledged as a historical discipline a subject aiming (symbolistically) to "compare the state of mind which results from contemplating one work of art with that which results from contemplating another."

In one theoretical matter of his generation, Wittkower took a firm position: he was ethnologically a *diffusionist*, a believer that similar forms imply historical contact and transmission. Of course, the opposite term to diffusionism is not always clear: "functionalism," "independent invention" (which, not unlike spontaneous generation as false start to germ theory, may hide diffusion), psychologizing universalism, uncritical nominalism. In "East and West: The Problem of Cultural Exchange" (1966, p. iii), Wittkower cites Adolf Bastian as posing the question in the late nineteenth century with an evolutionary view of parallel cultural manifestations at equivalent developmental stages, "independent convergence." In the more synoptic than syncretic lectures *The Impact of Non-European Civilizations on the Art of the West* (1989), Bastian leads "antidiffusionists" as Wittkower warns that both sides may "forget that for the high civilizations with literary traditions diffusionism has been developed into a universally accepted technique of research; in art-historical controversies the degree and character of diffusion may be disputed but not the principle of diffusion"—provided that lines of contact are verifiable and that "alert, critical judgment . . . be exercised at all times," for not all things that look similar are related.

Despite a strong skepticism toward the reification of period style, Wittkower participated in the modern (even modernist) establishment of Mannerism as a style occurring between "Renaissance" and "Baroque" and entailing a dialectic of classical and anticlassical tendencies. His joining the cause of Mannerism, however, not only shows Wittkower's implicit theoretical bent, but it also testifies to his opposition to Wölfflinian formal systematics even as he exercised subtly penetrating formal analysis. As for the Baroque itself, when he took up Gianlorenzo Bernini's case (first with H. Brauer, in *Die Zeichnungen des Gianlorenzo Bernini*, 1931), the emotive Counter-Reformation sculptor cannot have been any more respected in Berlin than in England, where he would still be distained by Wittkower's friend, that "Yorkshire Protestant" Herbert Read. As a writer, Wittkower can show stunning concision—famously in his Pelican handbook of Italian Baroque painting, sculpture, and architecture (1958). A few careful strokes, in his Bernini monograph (1955), and one knows exactly what is meant by saying (against much literary commentary confused by the concretization of metaphor) that *The Ecstasy of St. Theresa* (1645–1652) makes that mystic's text "real and visionary at the same time"; he also dilates eloquently, as on a certain drapery fold in *The Blessed Ludovica Albertoni* (1671–1674) as the "pang of death" (1955).

Wittkower was intellectually at home in the Enlightenment even with his passion for the Italian Baroque, Jesuits, and all (1972), the honor in which he (be)held the High Renaissance and its "Divine Michelangelo" (1964), his own humanist re-cognition of the earlier Renaissance, and even his fascination with the ancient East as point of origination: these were all features of a singular encyclopedic enthusiasm. If it were possible to build a system, like one building, to house such supposedly incompatible enthusiasms, its classical lintel might be inscribed "Burke," for his having rendered up to understanding the subjective aspect of art (also for being Roman-oratorical and writing handsome *prose*); first, however, at the entrance to the surrounding *jardin anglais*, one would have to pass the name of Anthony Ashley Cooper, earl of Shaftesbury, or the word *Design* from his title "Letter concerning Design" (1712)—the ideo-historical key not only to Wittkower's happy Anglo-Palladianism, but also to the ideal of his English king peacefully pronouncing directives of even a Labour government as hardly utopian. Like his hero Bernini, he did not bother much with France (leaving it to Anthony Blunt, with whom he collaborated on Nicolas Poussin's drawings in the 1930s under Walter Friedländer): when he said "Enlightenment," he might as likely have been thinking of Potsdam as of Paris. He always insisted that Lord Shaftesbury's influence on the French Enlightenment was underestimated.

Although in his early collaborations he might well be mistaken for a connoisseur, Wittkower became a prime member of the "iconological" avant-garde. When Aby Warburg introduced the concept of "iconology"—more culturally hermeneutical than simple iconography—in a lecture in Rome in 1912, Panofsky, present as a student, soon joined in Warburg's project. Wittkower (nine years younger) met Warburg in 1927 and was invited to work in the Warburg Library in 1928; he joined the staff after it left Hamburg to become the Warburg Institute in London in the 1930s. Recent theoreticians have tended to install Panofsky as unique heir to the Warburg iconological tradition at the expense of others now less read—Gertrud Bing, Fritz Saxl (Frances Yates is read, but more remotely from art), as well as Wittkower—who were long active in the inner orbit. Panofsky and Wittkower were friendly colleagues, and there are significant points of thematic convergence in their work (e.g., implications of the dichotomy "Gothic" versus "classic" [Wittkower, 1974]) as well as a shared anti-Wölfflinian pedagogical influence in America (on the latter, see C. Eisler, "Kunstgeschichte American Style: A Study in Migration," in D. Fleming and B. Bailyn, eds., *The Intellectual Migration: Europe and America 1930–1960* [1969]). But their work was different. To put the matter crudely, Panofsky mainly pursued a history of illustrated concepts (such as Francis Bacon's "notions"), mythic or rational, that have fortunately taken roost from time to time in written texts and datable objects; it is no wonder that his position seems close to the neo-Kantian thinking of Ernst Cassirer, who was at home in the Warburg Library early on. Wittkower was as fascinated by the way a motif could travel independently of meaning as by the ways meaning could take different forms. Where current "critical theory" tends to install Panofsky as the Warburgian hero of (synchronic) "contextualism" versus (diachronic) "formalism," whereas both scholars were more dialectical in praxis, there may be repressed idealism in an automatic preference for Panofsky as the more "theoretical."

Wittkower was ultra-Warburgian. Even his popular *Born under Saturn* (1963)—praised by Stefan Morawski for "a keen insight into the precapitalist situation of the artist" ("Major and Minor Functions of Art in a Context of Alienation," 1964)—is in the direct Warburgian line of Ernst Kris and Otto Kurtz's catalog of topoi, *Legend, Myth and Magic in the Image of the Artist: An Historical Experiment* (1929). As with Panofsky, the classical tradition was his C major key (the "classical tradition" being what the Warburg Institute is "for the study of"), though in Wittkower's Warburgianism it was the very basis of cosmopolitanism: compare the postwar London exhibition and catalog by him and Saxl, *British Art and the Mediterranean* (1948), with his Germano-British contemporary Sir Nikolaus Pevsner's *The Englishness of English Art* (Reith Lectures, 1955).

As a humanist, Panofsky tended to take art as a more or less crafty illustration of *literae humaniores;* in his different but equally humanist practice, Wittkower, who taught artists at the Slade School (University College London), was a proponent of painting, sculpture, and architecture as *artes liberales*. Panofsky might seem closer to having been a philosopher, not only as associated with Cassirer, but also in his philological bent; but it deserves to be asked if Wittkower's pragmatic directness toward all made things, including ideas, was not also philosophical. If expanded historical understanding expands the range of aesthetic awareness, for Wittkower that was itself a historical consequence of the framing in eighteenth-century British aesthetics of new categories, the picturesque and the sublime. Methodologically, this teacher conveyed a sense that the field of examples of any motif (formal or iconographic) potentially includes every instance ever, everywhere, as if in Random Access Memory: Warburg might have liked to cross-index the whole world, but Wittkowerian synthesis wanted selectivity and hierarchy (subject to change). The canonical work served as a nexus facilitating operational extension of typology and discourse into the unknown.

Unlike Panofsky's "The History of the Theory of Human Proportions as a Reflection of the History of Styles" (1921; in *Meaning in the Visual Arts,* 1955), concerned with representation of the human body from Egyptian antiquity to Albrecht Dürer, Wittkower's "The Changing Concept of Proportion" pertains to architecture and was first aimed at architects. Panofsky sets out from the Cassireresque idea that normative bodily proportions change as a function of artistic style; Wittkower begins, à la Edmund Husserl's "Origin of Geometry" (not cited), with Galileo Galilei's first treating proportion in the abstract, and the detachment of mathematics from priestly mystique in ancient Greece. Pythagoras (not mentioned by Panofsky) establishes "theoretical geometry," including "musical consonances," as canonized in the *Timaeus* (Plato is barely mentioned in Panofsky's longer essay); and the Pythagorean-Platonic understanding persists in medieval "geometric" proportion, with "irrational dimensions" and incommensurable ratios, followed by a Renaissance "arithmetic" proportion of commensurable ratios. Why, then, a Renaissance cult of the square? Its appeal was not only geometric but as a figure of "the ratio 1:1 (unison in music)." When, beginning in the seventeenth century, art had to escape "a universe of mechanical laws, of iron necessity," Edmund Burke's *Philosophical Enquiry into the Origin of Our Ideas of the Sublime and Beautiful* (1757) was crucial for its emphasis on the perceiver. From René Descartes down to Jay Hambidge in the twentieth century, the quasi-superstitious "golden section" has nothing serious to offer; but Le Corbusier's resort to modular elements cannily combines construction efficiency and Renaissance-classical arithmetic proportion in the abstract. Alfred North Whitehead testifies that physics has "vindicated" some Platonic sense of harmony in nature.

Wittkower could be as imaginative as he was rigorous. In "Interpretation of Visual Symbols" (1955, p. iii), contributed to A. J. Ayer et al., *Studies in Communication* (1955), he denotatively equates "A Child's Drawing" of a figure with a nude by Leonardo da Vinci. When the present writer once noticed a curious detail and asked Wittkower if he had drawn the figure, he smiled; years later, the image turned up in an early child psychology book, James Sully's *Children's Ways* (1897), given as a "reproduction" of a little girl's drawing (from an American source). Wittkower's illustration is a further redrawing, identical for purpose of argument but mimetically distinct in its halting line, details of feet, and, particularly, one hand. Now the source left hand is a zigzagged letter "W," the right, another "W" but haphazardly drawn; however, Wittkower's figure's right hand is like a good "R," so that the hands thus read from the viewer's left as the initials "R" and W": even in hypothesis, he did not tell a documentary lie.

The burgeoning of art history in postwar America and its unfortunate overspecialization diminished the potential influence of Wittkower's orthodox but creative art history in the modern field. In the opening "Non-European" lecture, he maintains that the art of the whole nomadic Eurasian North "was to a large extent . . . abstract and non-representational" (followed up in the present writer's notes by the sentence, lacking in the *Selected Lectures of Rudolf Wittkower*, "Only after contact with the Southern civilizations did they incorporate animals into their style"). The last page of "'Sacri Monti' in the Italian Alps" (1959, p. iv) better accounts for the modern split between "high" and "popular" art, as a consequence of "idealistic classical art theory," than most studies of that question. Wittkower himself was contemporary with the first Bauhaus *student* generation, and he published contemporary exhibition reviews in the mid-1920s and an article on the politics of museums in the Soviet Union in 1931; in later life, he was prepared to analogize the young Raphael's stylistic pluralism to the young Pablo Picasso's (ibid.), and he spoke of Henry Moore, his contemporary, as "our Bernini"; as for architects, Le Corbusier had obviously inherited the mantle. Wittkower must have had other latter-day influences that would be more difficult to track (to his diffusionist satisfaction) than that in which this writer, while still his student, had occasion to explain his dialectical theory of the "English garden" to the artist Robert Smithson. Wittkower was an actively generalist-humanist art historian who said never to forget that to most people the "history of art" per se seems like a very specialized subject.

[*See also* Architecture; Classicism; Iconography and Iconology; Panofsky; *and* Renaissance Italian Aesthetics.]

BIBLIOGRAPHY

Works by Wittkower

Architectural Principles in the Age of Humanism (1949). 3d rev. ed. London, 1962.

Gian Lorenzo Bernini: The Sculptor of the Roman Baroque (1955). 3d rev. ed. Ithaca, N.Y., 1981.

Art and Architecture in Italy, 1600–1750 (1958). 3d ed. New York, 1980.

Born under Saturn: The Character and Conduct of Artists: A Documented History from Antiquity to the French Revolution. Collaboration with Margot Wittkower. New York, 1963.

The Divine Michelangelo: The Florentine Academy's Homage on His Death in 1564. Edited and translated by Rudolf Wittkower and Margot Wittkower. London, 1964.

Baroque Art: The Jesuit Contribution. Edited by Rudolf Wittkower and Irma Jaffe. New York, 1972.

Gothic versus Classic: Architectural Projects in Seventeenth-Century Italy. New York, 1974.

Collected Essays of Rudolf Wittkower. Edited by Margot Wittkower. London, 1974–1978. Consists of vol. 1, *Palladio and Palladianism;* vol. 2, *Studies in the Italian Baroque;* vol. 3, *Allegory and the Migration of Symbols;* vol. 4, *Idea and Image: Studies in the Italian Renaissance.*

Selected Lectures of Rudolf Wittkower: The Impact of Non-European Civilizations on the Art of the West (1964). Edited by Donald Martin Reynolds. Cambridge and New York, 1989.

Other Sources

Reynolds, Donald Martin, ed. *The Writings of Rudolf Wittkower: A Bibliography.* Rome and New York, 1989. Contains a reprint of Howard Hibbard, "Rudolf Wittkower (1901–1971): An Obituary," originally published in *Burlington Magazine* 114 (1972): 173–177.

JOSEPH MASHECK

WÖLFFLIN, HEINRICH (1864–1945), Swiss art historian. Born in Winterthur, Switzerland, Wölfflin grew to maturity in the fin de siècle world. His new art history became an influential part of this revolutionary world.

Wölfflin's continued influence lies in the two methods he devised for studying the history of art: the formal analysis of works of art and the comparison of formal characteristics of art from different periods and nations to determine the prevailing style. The power of Wölfflin's approach has always been in the ability to replicate these two methods. Through empirical means, Wölfflin discovered that a small number of forms were consistently used in the Renaissance and Baroque periods, and from this morphology of forms he created a lawful concept of style for both periods. From the outset, Wölfflin's scholarly work challenged the status quo by posing a radical reordering of the components of art history and aesthetics.

His books were short and spare compared to those of his contemporaries. They signified a turn away from philosophizing about art and its development to psychologizing about it. Wölfflin's psychological hypotheses mediated between art and its creators, viewers, critics, and historians. Early on, in his dissertation of 1886, his preferred psychological mediation was a one-to-one empathetic correspondence between man and his objects. The psychological mediations changed from book to book: from an organic analogy between man and architecture in his dissertation, to mood in his first book *Renaissance and Baroque* (1888), to attitude and vision in *Classic Art* (1899), to just vision in *The Art of Albrecht Dürer* (1905) and *Principles of Art History* (1915), and back to mood and feeling in *The Sense of Form in Art* (1931).

His theory of art has been considered purist and modern, or Hegelian and teleological, and even positivist in the Anglo-American tradition. There is some truth to all these claims, but when Wölfflin's work is considered as a whole, the consistency, complexity, and independence of his construct from all these interpretations becomes clear.

The cumulative image of Wölfflin is of a scholar who, at an early stage in his career, knew what kind of contribution he wanted to make and what he wanted to avoid. He refused to write the already popular biographies and monographs concerning artists, and concentrated on the material record of the works of art. He was inclined toward systematic and inductive research, and rarely diverged from it into anecdotal material. He balanced theoretical concerns against empirical research; he did not often exceed the bounds of what could be demonstrated. He was a circumspect humanist.

He was educated in a remarkable, intellectual milieu and was trained by some of the great minds of his time, such as historian Jacob Burckhardt, philosopher Wilhelm Dilthey, psychologist Hermann Ebbinghaus, philosopher and educator Friedrich Paulsen, historian Wilhelm Riehl, philosopher Johannes Volkelt, and classical archaeologist Heinrich Brunn. They all left a significant imprint on Wölfflin's work, which is evident in his thesis for Munich University, *Prolegomena zu einer Psychologie der Architektur* (1886). This "prolegomena for a psychology of architecture" summarized his university education. Philosophers Volkelt and Dilthey were both attempting to find the basis of artistic production and other cultural endeavors in psychology, although each proposed a different psychology. To investigate the idea of an "organic analogy" between man and architecture, Wölfflin found various common features, a similar organization, and function in man and architecture.

In finding these correspondences, he set the stage for his life's work: to discover a psychology of art. The new discipline of psychology, however, offered two discrepant models: an abstract and universal one in the work of philosophers Rudolf Hermann Lotze, Friedrich Theodor Vischer, and Volkelt, and a psychology based on low-level sensory functioning in the work of experimental psychologists Hermann von Helmholtz, Wilhelm Max Wundt, Gustav Theodor Fechner, and Ebbinghaus. Wölfflin used both models in his thesis, which explains the absence of the artist or other actors in his theory—they were missing in late nineteenth-century psychology also. [*See* Psychology of Art.]

The thesis on architecture for his degree in philosophy at Munich University was interdisciplinary, joining ideas from philosophy, art history, psychology, and aesthetics. Wölfflin was still uncertain about which of these paths would form

his life's work until he lived in Rome in 1886. In Rome, his interest in architecture flourished. With his first book, *Renaissance and Baroque* (1888), Wölfflin introduced the comparative analysis of the two styles, Renaissance and Baroque, with opposite characteristics—the method that became the hallmark of his work. He now favored a different psychological mediation—the "mood" *(Stimmung)* of a period.

Wölfflin became Burckhardt's successor as professor of art history at Basel University in 1893. In the intervening years up to the publication of *Classic Art* in 1899, Wölfflin was deeply influenced by the sculptor Adolf von Hildebrand, the writer Conrad Fiedler, and the connoisseur Giovanni Morelli.

Hildebrand and Fiedler believed that perception was the single most important element in artistic creation. Hildebrand developed a theory of perception to reinforce the superiority of his favorite art form, the classical relief, against Impressionism. He devised a modern form of the *paragone*, or comparison of media to determine which is superior, using new scientific theories of perception. Hildebrand defended his view in *The Problem of Form in the Fine Arts* (1893), which was extremely influential, primarily because he used new ideas from perceptual psychology.

Wölfflin reconciled historical practice with a "history of vision" in *Classic Art* (1899), which relied on Hildebrand's account of the effect of perceptual functioning on art forms. In *Classic Art*, Wölfflin compared fifteenth- and sixteenth-century Italian art. Again he chose to resurrect an unpopular style, this time sixteenth-century Italian art—notably of Leonardo da Vinci, Raphael, and Michelangelo—to demonstrate its beauty. Quattrocento art was much more highly valued at the end of the nineteenth century, as the works of Bernard Berenson, Aby Warburg, and Morelli attest and Wölfflin noted. The first part of *Classic Art* resembled *Renaissance and Baroque* with a characterization of classic art in terms of its opposite, fifteenth-century art. Differences in art as markers for cultural change were of the greatest importance to Wölfflin.

The second part of the book presented three different ways of analyzing the classic style and explaining its development: he described the subject matter in terms of patronage, society, and the artist; then he derived the nature of the style from the then current attitude toward beauty; and, finally, he determined the formal composition of images from the artist's vision. By 1899, Wölfflin had determined that art was clearly the result of both internal artistic and external social influences, which were interrelated.

Perception became the leading new explanatory variable for change in style. The autonomy of art and vision, however, jeopardized the claim that other, external factors played a part in creation. It was not until his classic book *Principles of Art History* (1915) that Wölfflin clarified this issue.

In 1901, Wölfflin became professor of art history at Berlin University, the most prestigious university in central Europe. He was cast into a foreign milieu, from small republican Basel to large and imperial Berlin. Kaiser William II virulently and emphatically opposed modern art and placed Wölfflin in the position of having to defend his friends, as well as his Swiss nationality. It is in this context that Wölfflin's next book, *The Art of Albrecht Dürer* (1905), must be understood, for it is exceptional among his publications. Despite concentrating on a single artist, Wölfflin did not relinquish his comparative method, for Dürer sought to integrate classic elements into his style.

The underlying theme of this book was national differences in art. By focusing on the premier northern artist, he described what was characteristic in northern art and its opposite southern style. Wölfflin claimed that Dürer was unique among northern artists in that he sought to become a classic artist. Perception, broadly defined, was the force that altered Dürer's course: he gradually abandoned his northern vision for that of the south. The irony is that Dürer was cherished as the great German artist, with all the nationalistic connotations of that faith. Wölfflin abandoned this myth by accentuating Dürer's Italian ambitions.

At the time Wölfflin was working on the Dürer book, he was living a life that emulated Dürer's and that of all the other great northerners who had lived in Italy. He took sabbaticals in Italy to paint and to associate with artists. Wölfflin was so enthralled with Italy that he planned to write a novel about a modern German artist who seeks salvation in Italy. Instead, he wrote about Dürer.

Wölfflin integrated the artist's life into the historian's. He identified with Dürer's creative path, as he followed it work by work, re-creating his aesthetic world using historical methods. Dürer's eye was initially naive and northern, recording nature in a realistic style. But, as Dürer matured, Wölfflin felt he was able to move from realism to idealism. Dürer transcended his native vision and attained an individual vision that he used to create at will. In a sense, Wölfflin was intent on enacting a realist epistemology, while he continued to theorize, to idealize, to find patterns that explained the experience of both artist and historian. The northern artist began with a realist epistemology, while the southern artist simplified, idealized, and monumentalized. The antinomies of Wölfflin's intellectual activity were allegorized and symbolized in the art he studied.

For the next ten years, up to World War I, Wölfflin worked on a synthesis of the many ideas he had considered since the beginning of his academic career. (He moved home to Munich University in 1912, where his father had ended his career.) The result was his classic book *Principles of Art History* (1915), which summarized the results of his comparative approach as applied to the two leading European styles—the Renaissance and the Baroque. In it, he compared northern and southern examples of Renaissance and Baroque painting, sculpture, and architecture. He concluded that there are two primary ways of perceiving and transcribing the world into art, corresponding to the Renaissance and Baroque styles. These two visions recurred over time, in the same order, with a classical, linear style the precursor to a baroque and painterly style. Like his method in *Renaissance and Baroque,* Wölfflin distinguished five essential characteristics of each style or schema: linear, planar, closed, clear, and multiplicity of focii for the Renaissance style versus painterly, recessional, open, unclear, and unity of focus for the Baroque style. Each characteristic mode of representation derived from vision, again the single most important factor for changes in style. [*See* Style.]

In *Principles of Art History,* Wölfflin asserted that perception has a history, which was revealed and reified in art: "not everything is possible at all times"; only at certain times could some perceptions occur. He attempted to harmonize the real historical flow of art with a theoretical construct to interpret it. Crucial to his notion of perception was his statement: "Determining and determined, it always overlaps into different spiritual spheres" (1932). In other words, perception was always simultaneously an independent agent and yet determined by other agents of culture and life. The visual schemas of the two styles were the end product of an ongoing exploration of a large amount of visual material.

Wölfflin combined an empirical, scientific method of analyzing art with a circular hermeneutical interpretation of artistic development. [*See* Hermeneutics.] Perception, defined as rational and psychological, mediated between them, because it preceded and grounded both. [*See* Perception.]

There are affinities between Wölfflin's theory and the sociologist Max Weber's theory of ideal types. One could compare an internally logical ideal type or style with the actual art. In comparing the hypothetical and the concrete, one could speculate about the differences. In making the comparison, an interpretive strategy was begun that might add new objects of analysis, change the initial ideal type or schema, and end in the construction of laws. Empirical and interpretive acts were intertwined. Weber and Wölfflin intended such a union. Wölfflin continually demonstrated that each publication was a work in progress, modified and elaborated in succeeding works. Unlike most scientists at work, humanists can revise, reinterpret, reengage; conclusion is not necessary, although readers generally expect it. Early on, Wölfflin reached closure on his overall strategy of interpretation of art's history, but not on the causes for historical change.

Wölfflin described his task as speculative. Perception was determining, but was itself driven by external forces; it incorporated a number of cognitive states: imagination, interpretation, representation. Perception was malleable, but conformed to a rather rigid framework of the visual schemas of five pairs of concepts that recurred, periodically, in a regular sequence. But Wölfflin never fully explicated how the whole system operated, for he claimed that more empirical work was necessary before the whole theory could be perfected. The ideal schemas of style and real works of art remained in permanent tension in Wölfflin's theory.

The last thirty years of Wölfflin's life reveal both continuity and discontinuity in his theorizing. He wrote four rebuttals to the critics of *Principles of Art History* between 1920 and 1940, in which he defended his earlier work by restating the arguments while slightly shifting ground. At the same time, he revised his theory quite substantially in his only major publication after 1915, *The Sense of Form in Art* (1931), as it is known in English, or *Italien und das deutsche Formgefühl*.

In this last unified book, Wölfflin examined national differences, comparing art in Italy and the Germanic world between 1490 and 1530, the late Renaissance and early Mannerist periods. Contradicting his claim in *Principles of Art History* that Renaissance art possessed the same features in the north and the south, he now attempted to demonstrate that there were significant national variations in the Renaissance style. He refashioned the five pairs of concepts from *Principles*, concentrating on classic stylistic traits.

One fundamental change was the status of the "eye," which now retreated into the background of the theory and was replaced by "form-psychological hypotheses," meaning primarily feeling and sensation. The "organic analogy" reappeared, along with the "mood of a nation." Now Wölfflin proposed a sociological approach: he suggested that one could examine national food preferences and sleeping habits and still discover the same types of differences found in a nation's art. The core of his theory was no longer perception, but the patterns of imagination and thought that nations possess and that inform their art. The intellectual climate had moved away from the dominance of rational, scientific perceptual theories to *Lebensphilosophie*, the irrational, spiritual, antipositivist. Wölfflin adapted to and participated in new general philosophical trends.

Fascism was ascendant in 1931 when *The Sense of Form in Art* was published. In his book, however, Wölfflin favored the Italians over the Germans. Wölfflin had been repelled by what was happening in Germany during the 1920s and fled back to Zurich in 1924 to live out his days in the safety of his neutral, republican homeland. Nonetheless, one cannot ignore that he claimed that each nation possessed a "racially different bodily organization." This kind of notion relates to the then popular belief in eugenics that became integrated into Nazi medical and social practice. Determining factors in the creation of art became more confused and contradictory in Wölfflin's book. National traits seemed to negate psychological forces and yet he still argued that psychological causes were responsible for the supremacy of certain forms. He subverted his previous argument that the development of European art was uniform.

Wölfflin dismantled the entire framework of *Principles of Art History* in *The Sense of Form in Art,* and also the harmony of hermeneutical, inductive, and perceptual psychological approaches. He returned to his earlier psychological theories without uniting them into a coherent whole. It appears that, in this last systematic book, he was attempting to humanize his abstract and logical theory. The artist became the "seer" and "feeler" who expressed through forms. Wölfflin, however, seemed to be moving the old variables around like pieces on a chessboard and the outcome was a stalemate.

Wölfflin struggled to create a systematic history of art. He was most successful in *Principles of Art History*. The basic framework of interpretation, with an empirical, hermeneutical, and psychological union was impressive. Like Weber, he created a heuristic model of art-historical styles against which he could compare individual works of art. Wölfflin laid an impressive foundation for even more ambitious models—particularly that of Erwin Panofsky, who understood the need to proceed from a formal analysis to a larger interpretive framework and who also used a hermeneutic method of interpretation. Wölfflin concentrated on formal design, much as the artists of the Bauhaus and other modern artists did. Current interpretations in the history of art propose a greater emphasis on the language of art—a project that Wölfflin initiated. Art for him was a language of form, to which signs either conformed through contour, color, and shading and were Renaissance, or did not conform in those ways and were Baroque. The hegemonic constructs today are the ones Wölfflin engaged: empiricism, hermeneutics, psychology.

[*See also* Art History; Baroque Aesthetics; Iconography and Iconology; *and* Renaissance Italian Aesthetics.]

BIBLIOGRAPHY

Works by Wölfflin

Renaissance and Baroque (1888). Translated by Kathrin Simon. Ithaca, N.Y., 1966.
Classic Art: An Introduction to the Italian Renaissance (1899). London and New York, 1952.
The Art of Albrecht Dürer (1905). Translated by Alastair Grieve and Heide Grieve. London and New York, 1971.
Principles of Art History: The Problem of the Development of Style in Later Art (1915). Translated by M. D. Hottinger from the 7th ed. New York, 1932.
The Sense of Form in Art: A Comparative Psychological Study (1931). Translated by Alice Muehsam and Norma A. Shatan. New York, 1958.

Other Sources

Gantner, Joseph, ed. *Jacob Burckhardt und Heinrich Wölfflin: Briefwechsel und andere Dokumente ihrer Begegnung, 1882–1897.* Basel, 1948.
Gantner, Joseph, ed. *Heinrich Wölfflin, 1864–1945.* Basel, 1982.
Hart, Joan. "Reinterpreting Wölfflin: Neo-Kantianism and Hermeneutics." *Art Journal* 42 (1982): 292–300.

Hart, Joan, Roland Recht, and Martin Warnke. *Relire Wölfflin*. Paris, 1995.

Hauser, Arnold. *The Philosophy of Art History* (1958). Cleveland, Ohio, 1965.

Mallgrave, Harry Francis, and Eleftherios Ikonomou, eds. *Empathy, Form, and Space: Problems in German Aesthetics, 1873–1893*. Santa Monica, Calif., 1994.

Minor, Vernon Hyde. *Art History's History*. Englewood Cliffs, N.J., 1994.

Podro, Michael. *The Critical Historians of Art*. New Haven, 1982.

JOAN HART

WOLLHEIM, RICHARD (b.1923), a British philosopher who has both contributed to aesthetics and written in a serious systematic way about art history. Analytic philosophers, it has often been observed, typically have little to say about art. Perhaps this reflects insensitivity to the properly poetic qualities of language; maybe it demonstrates that traditional philosophical aesthetics cannot survive modern critical scrutiny. Wollheim's work is a valiant attempt to develop a systematic aesthetic employing the standards of reasoning and the style of argumentation found in analytic philosophy.

The starting point of his *Art and Its Objects* is the ontological question: what is art? Posing this ontological question is a good way of comparing the various arts. In painting, the artwork is identified with a unique physical object; in literature, there are many copies of the artwork; and in music, the artwork might be identified with the score, or its performances. Therefore, really one should ask: What is painting? What is a novel? What is a musical work? and so on. When one then asks how artworks represent, or are expressive, discussion must take account of these distinctions. With painting, for example, the question to ask is how a physical object has expressive qualities. Until one thus understands how to define the arts, it is not possible to understand the nature of representation or expression; how interpretation works; or the strengths and limitations of psychoanalytic theorizing, Marxism, and other interpretive approaches.

As befits an analytic philosopher, Wollheim is cautious about making generalizations. He tends less to assert his own viewpoint directly than to back into it by identifying problems with less subtle approaches. For example, the view that art is a language, although it identifies the way that art communicates emotion, breaks down when we observe that artworks are not grammatical in the way that sentences are. The most illuminating statement of Wollheim's general position is provided by a preface, later suppressed, in one 1968 edition of *Art and Its Objects:* "As the audience of art or as the makers of it, we seem to be engaged simultaneously with artefacts and with a concept. Art, and its objects, come indissolubly linked. . . . Aesthetics . . . may be thought of as the attempt to understand this envelope in which works of art invariably arrive." Wollheim provides a piecemeal reconstruction of this envelope. His inability to give sweeping generalizations is compensated for by his capacity to provide numerous details about the relationships between the various arts and their corresponding objects.

The starting point of *Painting as an Art,* as one would expect in a book on painting, is narrower. The theory of representation is discussed, first from the artist's viewpoint, then from the spectator's. A significant artist has an individual style, which is to say that there is an internal relationship between his works. What we spectators see has been described by aestheticians in terms of illusion, make-believe, "seeing as," information conveyed; and using semiotic theories. What is important for Wollheim is less the details of his disagreements with other theorists than his deployment of a very far-reaching account of projection. Often in everyday life, one finds a scene in the external world that matches an emotion. Then "expressed emotion and perception fuse" (Wollheim, 1987, p. 82). In art, projection is guided by the artist. What one sees depicted is what the artist intended to show. Seeing the picture properly, one observes the artist's attitude toward his pictorial content. In his account of Adrian Stokes, Wollheim notes how "it becomes for the reader the most natural thing in the world . . . to assimilate a shape to a feeling" (Wollheim, 1973, p. 334). That is what happens also for the reader of his writing.

Once this theory is presented, Wollheim is prepared to look at the procedures of individual artists: Édouard Manet's appeal to a spectator within the picture; Pablo Picasso's play with the power of the gaze; Titian's metaphoric association of the painting with the body; and so forth. What links this account to traditional psychoanalytic approaches to art is the concern with art as a form of personal expression. We best understand Manet, Picasso, and some (not all) other painters, Wollheim suggests, by knowing something of their lives. (Such approaches, it has been often argued, are essentially reductive; they reduce art to mere autobiography. This is correct, Wollheim implies, only if we hold an impoverished view of the psychic processes that generate art.) The interesting complications arise in fitting Wollheim's practice of art-historical interpretation into his broader vision of mental activity. In the Preface to *Painting as an Art,* he argues that connoisseurship is the "best hope for the objective study of painting" (1987, p. 10). Connoisseurship usually is understood as the skill needed to separate the genuine works of a master from the school pieces, copies, and forgeries; and then to identify the sequence in which those genuine works were made. Connoisseurship is thus characteristically opposed to iconography, whose concern is with the meaning of the visual image, with its sources and its possible symbolic sense.

Connoisseurs' preoccupation with identifying quality closely associates them with collectors, who need reliable attributions to guarantee the value of the art they purchase.

Wollheim does not accept this characterization of connoisseurship, nor this conservative view of its political implications. Wollheim calls himself a socialist, but he is not interested in the radical protest art so influential during the 1980s. (It really is not clear, from his published writings, how exactly he would understand the link between politics, philosophy of mind, and aesthetics.) Politically leftist, Wollheim is, within the context of the American art world, aesthetically conservative; his is the prose of an aesthete, but he has the morality of a socialist. (His novel *A Family Romance* gives a vivid sense of his ways of dealing with what, to an outsider, would seem the obvious conflicts here.) Wollheim is not especially concerned with attributions. What for him defines connoisseurship is close, attentive looking, which reveals what the artist intended to depict. The essential qualities of the artwork can be identified visually. Study of the historical context can support, but never supplant, this evidence of the eye.

How, then, can Wollheim's accounts of what close looking reveals be tested? Not by any abstract philosophical argument; nor by appeal to historical evidence. We must see—literally, *see*—if his accounts of Manet, Picasso, Titian, and Nicolas Poussin are consistent with our experience. What is to be done when, inevitably, disagreements arise? Wollheim implies that the only ultimate source of disagreements is the inability of some viewers to see the artwork as it really is. Here, he rejects decisively the claims of cultural historians. Wollheim's version of connoisseurship depends on a bold faith in the universality of human nature. He does not have any way to explain different responses, except to assert that they arise because some people do not see the artwork accurately.

Is this a weakness of his position? Perhaps not, because for Wollheim, as with more traditional connoisseurs, focusing on disagreements may be misleading. Some attributions remain controversial, but on the whole connoisseurs achieve remarkable agreement. The easiest way to explain that agreement is to suppose that most people interested in visual art learn to see it correctly. Analogously, in interpreting art, interpersonal agreement very often is achieved. *Painting as an Art* in effect asks that the readers test Wollheim's claims to see if they match their experience. What is merely personal in his analyses thus can be corrected.

Wollheim attributes highly complex internal structures to the mind, giving special emphasis to our capacity to fantasize; rejecting historicism, positivism, and relativism, he is very optimistic about our capacity to retrieve these inner feelings revealed in our experience of art. Psychoanalysis, he argues, in extending commonsense ways of thinking, builds on the classical tradition of philosophy of mind. Connecting his view of visual art with the view of persons and morality presented in his *The Thread of Life* is no easy task. Nor is it easy to directly relate the reading of psychoanalysis in his *Freud* to the kinds of fantasy play discussed in *Painting as an Art*. In *Art and Its Objects,* Wollheim appeals to Ludwig Wittgenstein's much-discussed phrase, "form of life": "Art is, in Wittgenstein's sense, a form of life" (1980, p. 104). The significance of this enigmatic claim takes us back, again, to the title of the book. To understand art, we cannot merely appeal to the psychic processes characteristic of the artist; nor, as social historians would suggest, to the institutions that constitute the art world. Such understanding requires, rather, that we grasp the finely entangled relationship between the traditions of art, and the modification (or dismantlement) of those traditions such as occur in the practice of any interestingly original artist. To speak of art *and* its objects is to note, tersely, this unity of history and ongoing practice. When a great deal of traditional philosophy—especially philosophy in the analytic tradition—marginalizes art, as if art making were merely a rather subsidiary human activity, what is really revealed, Wollheim is suggesting, is an impoverished view of the mind and its activities. A politically sensitive aesthete, he implies, would understand the relation between art and social life.

The easiest way to unpack the interconnections here within Wollheim's aesthetic is through a comparison with the work of his near contemporary, Arthur C. Danto. Both are analytic philosophers; and both, seeking to define art, are centrally concerned with visual art. But they disagree entirely about the philosophical significance of contemporary art. Danto claims that Marcel Duchamp's readymade *Fountain* (1917) and Andy Warhol's *Brillo Box* (1964) show that visual art cannot be defined by its visual properties. What defines an artwork, he says, is not its visual qualities, but what he calls "a certain theory of art" (Danto, 1964, p. 581); what distinguishes *Brillo Box* from a Brillo box in the grocery store is the availability of some such theory. But Wollheim resists this claim. He argues that Duchamp's work has exercised more influence over contemporary aesthetics than it deserves.

What is at stake here is something more, and something other than disagreements about taste. Wollheim grants that readymades are artworks. (His 1965 essay "Minimal Art" [Wollheim, 1973, chap. 5], which discusses Duchamp, was probably the source for the name of that art movement, "Minimalism.") Danto, in turn, allows that the painterly art that Wollheim loves is the kind of art he also cares about most. But what Danto claims, and Wollheim certainly denies, is that such work is very significant for the philosophy of art. Why, then, do they disagree? Here, it is necessary to return to the ontological discussion in *Art and Its Objects*. If the goal is to define art, and the readymades are artworks, then what follows? "As our attention spreads over the object, more and more of its properties may become incorporated into its aesthetic nature" (Wollheim, 1980, p. 123). It seems impossible to view such banal objects as *Fountain* and *Brillo Box* in this way.

In "Minimal Art," Wollheim made a further helpful suggestion: "In the visual arts . . . we are called upon to concentrate our attention upon individual bits of the world" (1973, p. 110). Now, in one obvious way, this claim seems to be either false or circular. If *Fountain* and *Brillo Box* are artworks, then do they not show that in the visual arts one is not always called on to take this kind of aesthetic attitude toward individual bits of the world? They must be counterexamples to his general characterization of art. If, however, Wollheim is only saying that in *traditional* visual art individuals concentrate their attention thus, then his analysis is just circular. He simply rules out in advance any counterexamples such as Danto's.

But there is more going on here than this characterization of his claims indicates. Allowing that the readymades are artworks, Wollheim implies that they are an impoverished kind of art. It is revealing that in speaking of how art calls our attention to individuals, he speaks also of loving a particular individual, and not merely someone with certain qualities. At this point there are deep connections between his account of persons, his passionate interest in psychoanalysis, his socialism, and his aesthetics. His "Babylon, Babylone" (1962) dealt with Impressionism in a way that makes these connections. This remarkable essay, not much discussed in the art-historical literature, thus anticipated the concerns of recent social historians of Impressionism. These political themes are not taken up explicitly in Wollheim's recent work, but perhaps a similar approach is needed to do justice to this debate about Minimalism and defining art. Wollheim's aesthetic reveals its full significance only when linked with the broader concerns of his social philosophy.

There has been a great deal of discussion of Wollheim's work within the aesthetics journals. Mostly what has been discussed are points of detail. What remains to be explored are these broader ways in which he links aesthetic theory to philosophy of mind and social philosophy.

[*See also* Danto; Formalism; *and* Minimalism.]

BIBLIOGRAPHY

Works by Wollheim

"Babylon, Babylone." *Encounter* 18.5 (May 1962): 25–36.
Art and Its Objects. New York, 1968; 2d ed. with six supplementary essays, Cambridge and New York, 1980.
A Family Romance. New York, 1969.
Freud. London, 1971; 2d ed. London, 1991.
On Art and the Mind: Essays and Lectures. London, 1973; reprint, Cambridge, Mass., 1974.
The Thread of Life. Cambridge, Mass., 1984.
Painting as an Art. Princeton, N.J., 1987.
"Danto's Gallery of Indiscernibles." In *Danto and His Critics,* edited by Mark Rollins, pp. 28–38. Oxford and Cambridge, Mass., 1993.

Other Sources

Danto, Arthur C. "The Artworld." *The Journal of Philosophy* 61.19 October 15, 1964): 581.

DAVID CARRIER

WORDSWORTH, WILLIAM (1770–1850), English Romantic poet. Wordsworth's significance for aesthetics rests on (1) his theory of poetry, particularly as set out in his Prefaces to *Lyrical Ballads;* (2) his passion for and reflective interest in natural beauty as expressed not only in his poems but above all in his *A Guide Through the District of the Lakes in the North of England,* a work that was highly popular in its day and that has something to contribute to contemporary interest in environmental aesthetics; (3) the preoccupations manifest in his best poetry with the nature and power of the imagination and with the sublime, a heightened interest in which are bequeathed to aesthetics by the Romantic movement in poetry; and (4) what might be called Wordsworth's apology for poetry, that is, his claims for the moral seriousness of poetry.

Theory of Poetry. Wordsworth's most familiar reflections on poetry are to be found in his Preface to the *Lyrical Ballads,* a collection of poems, some written by himself and the others by Samuel Taylor Coleridge, and first published in 1798. The Preface is his and has often been reprinted (for example, in Paul Zall's edition of the *Literary Criticism of William Wordsworth*). Wordsworth's best-known proposition is that

> Poetry is the spontaneous overflow of powerful feelings: it takes its origin from emotion recollected in tranquillity: the emotion is contemplated till by a species of reaction the tranquillity gradually disappears, and an emotion, similar ["Kindred" is substituted for "similar" in the version of the Preface attached to the 1802 edition of *Lyrical Ballads* (Wordsworth, 1996, pp. 57–58)] to that which was before the subject of contemplation, is gradually produced, and does itself actually exist in the mind.
>
> (Ibid., p. 27)

"Poetry," Wordsworth observes in the Advertisement to *Lyrical Ballads, with a Few Other Poems* (1798), is "a word of very disputed meaning" (ibid., p. 10): what philosophers in our time have variously characterized as a fit subject for persuasive definition (Charles Stevenson, 1944), or as an instance of an essentially contested concept (W. B. Gallie 1955–1956). The poems in *Lyrical Ballads,* Wordsworth says, "are to be considered as experiments. They were written chiefly with a view to ascertain how far the language of conversation in the middle and lower classes of society is adapted to the purposes of poetic pleasure" (Advertisement, in Wordsworth, 1966, p. 10). Wordsworth's aim was "to make the incidents of common life interesting by tracing in them . . . the primary laws of our nature." "Low and rustic life was generally chosen [as the subjects of the poems] because in that situation . . . our elementary feelings exist in a state of greater simplicity and consequently may be more accurately contemplated and more forcibly communicated" (Preface [1800], in ibid., p. 18).

Wordsworth rejected the language of poetry that he inherited from eighteenth-century writers such as Alexander

Pope and Samuel Johnson and proposed "to myself to imitate, and, as far as possible, to adopt the very language of men" (ibid., p. 22). In the Preface to the 1802 edition, he adds the phrase: "the real language of men in a state of vivid sensation" (ibid., p. 38). The poet "is a man speaking to men: a man, it is true, endued with more lively sensibility, more enthusiasm and tenderness, who has a greater knowledge of human nature, and a more comprehensive soul, than are supposed to be common among mankind" (ibid., p. 48). Although the poet "describes and imitates passions, his situation is altogether slavish and mechanical, compared with the freedom and power of real and substantial action and suffering. So that it will be the wish of the Poet to bring his feelings near to those of the persons whose feelings he describes" (ibid., p. 49). "The Poet writes under one restriction only, namely, that of the necessity of giving immediate pleasure to a human Being possessed of that information which may be expected from him, not as a lawyer, a physician, a mariner, an astronomer or a natural philosopher, but as a Man" (ibid., p. 50). The gender expressions here may give offense today but, allowing for that, the thought is not so different from that expressed in Friedrich von Schiller's *Letters on the Aesthetic Education of Man* (again, the title may be provocative today). The idea is that it is a crucial task for the arts to speak to the whole person, many of whose mental powers will have become atrophied in the specialization demanded by the division of labor in the modern world. It is not only Schiller who deplores this; Karl Marx in his early writings identifies and analyzes it as a fundamental historical fact in the development of modern capitalism.

Zall cautions that "Wordsworth later maintained that he 'never cared a straw about the theory, and the Preface was written at the request of Mr. Coleridge out of sheer good nature'" (ibid., p. 15). It is right that we should be informed of this disclaimer but also right not to take it too seriously. For one thing, certain of Wordsworth's observations bear obvious connections with claims made in other works that have not been ejected from the history of aesthetics. This has already been suggested in the case of Schiller but it also applies to works by Edmund Burke and Joshua Reynolds. For example, Burke's distinction between a clear expression and a strong expression may profitably be compared with Wordsworth's account of what the language of poetry should be. For Burke, a clear expression "regards the understanding" and "describes a thing as it is," whereas a strong expression "belongs to the passions" and describes a thing "as it is felt." Later, Burke writes: "Uncultivated people are but ordinary observers of things, and not critical in distinguishing them; but, for that reason, they admire more, and are more affected by what they see, and therefore express themselves in a warmer and more passionate manner" (1970).

Wordsworth makes specific use of Reynolds's ideas in both editions of his Preface: "an *accurate* taste in Poetry and in all the other arts, as Sir Joshua Reynolds has observed, is an *acquired* talent, which can only be produced by thought and a long continued intercourse with the best models of composition" ([1800] Wordsworth, 1966, p. 31; [1802] ibid., p. 61). If, however, Wordsworth's theoretical views are to be accorded the same seriousness as those of other theorists in aesthetics, that requires the admission that Wordsworth is inconsistent. He invokes Reynolds's support for the view that taste in poetry is to be trained and educated, that is, improved, but also ridicules eighteenth-century talk of a taste for poetry (ibid., p. 50).

Wordsworth says that several of his friends urged him to provide "a systematic defence of the theory, upon which the poems were written," but, with an evasiveness worthy of his friend and co-contributor Coleridge, he replies: "the Reader would look coldly upon my arguments, since I might be suspected of having been principally influenced by the selfish and foolish hope of *reasoning* him into an approbation of these particular Poems" (Preface [1800], ibid., p. 16). Although this has been quoted with approval by Margaret Macdonald in a paper on the nature of arguments used in literary criticism ("Certainly, it does seem queer to suppose that anyone could be *argued* into admiring *Persuasion* or condemning *The Stag at Eve*" [Macdonald, 1959, p. 114]), Wordsworth's excuse confuses the description of poetic aim with the grounds on which a poem may be admired, which may or may not coincide. Macdonald, in turn, confuses the adducing of grounds for admiring a poem with the rhetoric that would persuade readers to admire it.

Natural Beauty. Wordsworth is himself often meticulous in giving reasons for his aesthetic judgments. In his *A Guide Through the District of the Lakes in the North of England* (in this case, we are speaking not of poems, of course, but of scenery, but the point holds good for both), there is no question of Wordsworth's trying to defend a preference for, say, native vegetation rather than plantations of foreign larch (Wordsworth, 1970, pp. 82–83), but only an attempt to get us to see the local landscape as he does. In like manner, he explains how the comparatively small size of the English lakes is favorable to the beauty of the area (ibid., p. 33) and why white is the wrong color for a house in the mountains (ibid., p. 80). The invitation to accept these judgments is one people can freely accept or not depending on how they respond to the reasons he presents for their assent or dissent.

In the *Guide*, Wordsworth seeks to adduce what one might call principles of landscape criticism, which is why the work has a continuing value transcending the usually ephemeral nature of guidebooks: "It is to be hoped . . . that this Essay may become generally serviceable, by leading to habits of more exact and considerate observation than . . . have hitherto been applied to local scenery" (ibid., p. 22). For example: "The form of the lake is most perfect when, like Derwent-water, and some of the smaller lakes, it least resembles that of a river" (ibid., p. 32). Or, because of the "craving for prospect," "which is immoderate, particularly in new settlers," their habit of placing their new houses on the "summits of naked hills in staring contrast to the snugness and privacy of the ancient houses" (ibid., p. 74) is having a deleterious effect on the landscape.

The Imagination and the Sublime. The importance of the imagination is a leading tenet of Romanticism, but there is a severe tension between a tendency, on the one hand, to regard it as a unique faculty of mind through which only access and insight into otherworldly, supersensible, or transcendental reality is to be had, and a tendency, on the other hand, to suppose "imagination" names various faculties of mind (e.g., perception, understanding, emotion) in heightened and quickened states. Notwithstanding imagination, as Wordsworth puts it, "having been our theme" of his great poem, *The Prelude* (1805 edition, book 13, line 185), it would be folly to expect a philosophically worked-out account; but, with that caveat, it can be said that Wordsworth tends to the second view of imagination:

> Imagination, which, in truth,
> Is but another name for absolute strength
> And clearest insight, amplitude of mind,
> And Reason in her most exalted mood.
> (*The Prelude*, 1805; book 13, lines 167–170)

Certainly, "imagination" for Wordsworth does not have the common connotations of illusion or the fabrication of fiction; these, one suspects owing to the influence of his friend Coleridge, he is inclined to hive off under the secondary category of fancy.

The Prelude does not, of course, offer a *theory* of the sublime in the manner of Burke or Immanuel Kant, though in fact theory is by no means absent from the poem, far from it; rather, the poem expresses sublimity. The best-known passages, not surprisingly both to do with mountains, are Wordsworth's accounts of his descent from the Alps and his ascent of Snowdon. The passages are too long to quote in full but the following should give a flavor:

> The immeasurable height
> Of woods decaying, never to be decayed,
> The stationary blasts of waterfalls,
> And everywhere along the hollow rent
> Winds thwarting winds, bewildered and forlorn,
> The torrents shooting from the clear blue sky . . .
> (Ibid., book 6, lines 556–561)

> The moon stood naked in the heavens, at height
> Immense above my head, and on the shore
> I found myself of a huge sea of mist,
> Which, meek and silent, rested at my feet.
> A hundred hills their dusky backs upheaved
> All over this still ocean . . .
> (Ibid., book 13, lines 41–46)

Wordsworth does not discourage the reader who would go to his poetry for his philosophy, for his doctrines. He is himself impatient with the artifices and contrivances of art, as already seen in his remarks on the language of poetry. Fictionality, artifice, and artistic cunning are nevertheless present in Wordsworth's poetry and the metaphysical grand statements apparently setting out a doctrine of nature that, on a first reading, seem to comprise the poem "Lines Composed a Few Miles above Tintern Abbey," on a closer reading are seen to be much more tentative and elusive.

For all that, Wordsworth is attracted to the ideal of the poet as teacher: "Every great Poet is a Teacher; I wish either to be considered as a Teacher, or as nothing," he writes in a letter (1966, p. xv). This was recognized by his early followers who treated him as leader, moralist, and sage, not primarily, it should be noted, on the subjects of art, poetry, and the other specific concerns of aesthetics but on the subjects of nature and of man, so Wordsworth can be seen in a tradition of nature philosopher-poets more familiar perhaps in the works of Ralph Waldo Emerson, Walt Whitman, and Henry Thoreau in American literature than in English. Another way to put this point is to say that Wordsworth's work, whether poetry or prose, does not sit happily within the conventional academic boundaries maintained between religion, philosophy, and poetry.

Moral Importance of Literature. Wordsworth's passionate belief in the importance of literature is recognizably in the tradition that later critics such as Matthew Arnold and F. R. Leavis also embraced when they spoke of its moral seriousness. In *Lyrical Ballads*, Wordsworth aimed to produce poetry "well adapted to interest mankind permanently, and not unimportant in the multiplicity and in the quality of its moral relations" (Preface [1800], ibid., p. 16). This tradition accordingly sees an approach to literature through the categories of aesthetics, especially those of taste and beauty, as distorting and reductive. Indeed, Wordsworth himself could be dismissive of these categories, when, for example, given his passion for poetry, he is scornful of those who speak, as philosophers and critics of his own and immediately preceding time indeed did, of a taste for literature:

> Further, it is the language of men who speak of what they do not understand; who talk of Poetry as of a matter of amusement and idle pleasure; who will converse with us as gravely about a *taste* for Poetry, as they express it, as if it were a thing as indifferent as a taste for Rope-dancing, or Frontiniac or Sherry.
> (Preface [1802], ibid., p. 50)

In Wordsworth's view, we go to poetry for teaching and for truth. As if this is not enough, "Poetry," he says in his Essay Supplementary to the Preface to *Poems* 1815, "is most just to its own divine origin when it administers the comforts and breathes the spirit of religion" (ibid., p. 162). The conjunction of truth with religion is further found in what, to borrow Richard Rorty's term, might be called Wordsworth's edificatory account of truth:

> Aristotle, I have been told, hath said, that Poetry is the most philosophic of all writing: it is so: its object is truth, not individual and local, but general, and operative; not standing upon external testimony, but carried alive into the heart by passion; truth which is its own testimony, which gives strength and divinity to the tribunal to which it appeals, and receives them from the same tribunal. Poetry is the image of man and nature.
> (Preface [1802], ibid., p. 50)

Wordsworth's Prefaces broaden out from an account of poetry into a more general critique of his contemporary culture, and what Wordsworth objected to in his own time has been seen by literary critics such as Leavis to have become worse since then. Wordsworth objects to the craving for excitement, a "degrading thirst after outrageous stimulation," the blunting of the "discriminating powers of the mind" that has various causes, including the "encreasing accumulation of men in cities, where the uniformity of their occupations produces a craving for extraordinary incident, which the rapid communication of intelligence [news] hourly gratifies" (Preface [1800], ibid., p. 21; [1802] ibid., p. 44). Wordsworth professes a philosophy of nature and integral to that, a critique of the cultural condition of the England of his day, which was then undergoing unprecedentedly rapid modernization. Wordsworth, then, was a writer much exercised by the experience of modernity.

The headings under which Wordsworth's contributions to aesthetics have been considered here do not, of course, encompass—nor are they intended to—the range and scope of Wordsworth's poetry, nor do they explain the devotion it aroused and still does (or, for that matter, the intense dislike that it can also cause. For instance, a poem celebrating a beautiful scene, the poem about daffodils ["I wandered lonely as a cloud"], may be picked out for especial ridicule and obloquy by those who have to study poetry at school but who develop no love for it). All this is to say that the effect of Wordsworth's poetry on the reader, whether favorable or unfavorable, is often strong, so to offer an expository account of his aesthetic ideas as if they were those of a dedicated philosopher is plainly no substitute for experiencing (itself another important notion for Wordsworth) the poetry itself.

The nineteenth-century British philosopher John Stuart Mill well catches the strong positive effect that Wordsworth could have on readers, turning them into followers. That a poet might create a following is perhaps a new development in English literature; previously, a poet was admired for talent and skill but even the greatest poets, such as William Shakespeare, Geoffrey Chaucer, and Edmund Spenser, were hardly seen by their contemporaries as spiritual advisers.

Mill, in his *Autobiography*, was careful to distinguish the question of poetic merit from the effect Wordsworth had in transforming and redirecting his own personal experience: "The result was that I gradually, but completely, emerged from my habitual depression, and was never again subject to it. I long continued to value Wordsworth less according to his intrinsic merits, than by the measure of what he had done for me" (Mill, 1969, p. 90). The influence a poet might have as spiritual guide or counselor is distinguishable from the question of how good the poetry is as poetry. Not that we have any reason to be apologetic about the poetic value of Wordsworth's poetry. Some is very bad (e.g., certain lines in "When to the attraction of the busy world," "Peter Bell," and "Vaudrecour and Julia"), but the best poems (e.g., *The Prelude*, "Lines Composed a Few Miles above Tintern Abbey," "Michael," the sonnet "Upon Westminster Bridge," and the "Lucy" poems) hold their own as and with the finest poems in English.

Mill describes Wordsworth's restorative effect on him in chapter 5 of his *Autobiography* and pays tribute to Wordsworth's poems for their effect in resolving what he calls "a crisis in my mental history"; they offered him "a medicine for my state of mind." Mill found in Wordsworth gratification of his own "love of rural objects and natural scenery," but more deeply from the poems, "I seemed to learn what would be the perennial sources of happiness, when all the greater evils of life shall have been removed," for they "seemed to be the very culture of the feelings, which I was in quest of" (Mill, 1969, pp. 88–89.) It is an interesting thought about the nature of Wordsworth's poetry that this moving tribute to it is paid by a philosopher.

[*See also* Coleridge; Imagination; Literature, *article on* Literary Aesthetics; Poetics; Romanticism, *article on* Philosophy and Literature; *and* Sublime.]

BIBLIOGRAPHY

Works by Wordsworth

A Guide through the District of the Lakes in the North of England (5th ed., 1835). Edited by Ernest de Selincourt. London, 1970.

Literary Criticism of William Wordsworth. Edited by Paul M. Zall. Lincoln, Nebr., 1966.

The Prelude: A Parallel Text. Edited by J. C. Maxwell. Harmondsworth, England, 1971.

Other Sources

Bate, Jonathan. *Romantic Ecology: Wordsworth and the Environmental Tradition*. London and New York, 1991.

Bateson, Frederick Wilse. *Wordsworth: A Re-interpretation*. London and New York, 1956.

Burke, Edmund. *A Philosophical Enquiry into the Origin of Our Ideas of the Sublime and Beautiful*. 2d ed. London, 1759; reprint, Menston, England, 1970. See part 5, section 7, "How Words Influence the Passions."

Davies, Hunter. *William Wordsworth: A Biography*. London, 1980.

Gallie, W. B. "Essentially Contested Concepts." *Proceedings of the Aristotelian Society* 56 (1955–1956): 167–198.

Hartman, Geoffrey H. *Wordsworth's Poetry, 1787–1814*. New Haven, 1964.

Hartman, Geoffrey H. *The Unremarkable Wordsworth*. Minneapolis, 1987.

Jones, J. *The Egotistical Sublime: A History of Wordsworth's Imagination*. London, 1954.

Macdonald, Margaret. "Some Distinctive Features of Arguments Used in Criticism of the Arts." In *Aesthetics and Language,* edited by William Elton, pp. 114–130. Oxford, 1959.

Mill, John Stuart. *Autobiography*. Edited by Jack Stillinger. London, 1969.

Noyes, Russell. *Wordsworth and the Art of Landscape*. Bloomington, Ind., 1968.

Stallknecht, Newton P. *Strange Seas of Thought: Studies in William Wordsworth's Philosophy of Man and Nature*. 2d ed. Bloomington, Ind., 1958.

Stevenson, Charles L. *Ethics and Language*. New Haven, 1944. See chap. 9.

Weiskel, Thomas. *The Romantic Sublime: Studies in the Structure and Psychology of Transcendence*. Baltimore, 1976.

T. J. DIFFEY

WORK OF ART. *See* Art World; Definition of Art; Essentialism; *and* Ontology of Art.

WORRINGER, WILHELM (1881–1965), German art historian and theorist. Any assessment of Worringer's aesthetics has to begin with its reception. Although he was an academic art historian, Worringer had a greater impact in other areas than in his own field. His early works, mainly *Abstraction and Empathy* (1908) and, to a lesser extent, *Form Problems of the Gothic* (1911), exercised an uncommonly broad influence on discussions of aesthetics in the years before World War I, as well as on German Expressionist painters themselves, on writers of the period (mainly 1910–1920), on early film theory in the 1920s, on psychologists and social theorists, on later art critics such as Herbert Read, and even on American literary criticism after World War II in Joseph Frank's influential theory of "spatial form." Frank credits Worringer with a stature for aesthetics in the early twentieth century equal to Gotthold Ephraim Lessing (the author of *Laocoön* [1766]) in the eighteenth century, and Frank's use of Worringer gave another life to the latter's ideas in the second half of the twentieth century.

Nonetheless, the academic discipline of art history has been slow to consider Worringer's stature in modernism for several reasons. Worringer's scholarship departed from traditional humanism and its exaltation of Greco-Roman, Renaissance, and eighteenth-century classicism. By writing mainly about the art of so-called primitive cultures and of the Middle Ages, Worringer gave aesthetic priority to nonnaturalistic forms of representation. Also, although his studies appeared historical in topic and scope, his work addressed artistic and cultural issues of his own contemporaries—a very unconventional scholarly activism on behalf of contemporary art that at the time was not considered the domain of academic scholarship. Further, in his art-historical studies, Worringer was less a systematic, historical positivist than a cultural theorist, who subordinated empirical detail to a comprehensive, but also speculative and hypothetical, "method" that seemed almost visionary in its provocative originality and its uncertain validity. Most notably perhaps, Worringer employed a simple but forceful and dramatic rhetoric, unencumbered by footnotes, that won him an audience outside the academy but suspicion within it.

Worringer's first book, *Abstraction and Empathy* (1908), was a sensation and remains his most well known, and is still in print. In it, Worringer developed the very first aesthetics for abstract or nonrepresentational art, whether it be Egyptian or African, Gothic or Baroque (or modernist), which also coincided with the earliest experiments in modern abstraction (cf. Pablo Picasso's *Demoiselles d'Avignon* of 1907); his work provided a theoretical justification and a genealogy for that tendency (in French Cubism and German Expressionism), and was duly embraced. Yet, the volume was not a history; its subtitle identifies it as *A Contribution to the Psychology of Style*, whereby formal and stylistic particularities (in any genre or medium) reflect the psychological disposition of the artist and, in turn, of the historical epoch, its "world feeling" *(Weltgefühl).* That "world feeling" directs the artist's and epoch's "artistic volition" *(Kunstwollen),* a concept and term borrowed from Alois Riegl. Different styles in art do not reflect progress or its lack, but simply a different "world feeling" and "artistic volition." The art of each period is thus the fullest realization of those impulses, and not a chapter in the "progress" of technical ability to copy nature. Art does not represent the external world; art presents a metaphysical disposition. Thus, Worringer's views in 1908 refute the materialist and evolutionary views of art that dominated the nineteenth century, and anticipate Expressionism, whereby *Stil* (style) in art reveals profound emotions and metaphysical depths.

Worringer's dichotomy distinguishes sharply between naturalistic and expressive tendencies in art. Naturalistic art (from the ancient Greeks to the Renaissance to nineteenth-century Realism and Impressionism) reflects, in its attempts to attain mimetic fidelity, a metaphysical disposition of existential comfort in the world, based on science and humankind's ability to understand and control nature. Such naturalistic art reveals what Worringer called "empathy" (a term adopted from Theodor Lipps) or the tautological desire to identify with what is familiar. Aestheticians such as Jakob Burckhardt (and later E. H. Gombrich) had described the history of art as a narrative of progress in mimetic depiction and equated beauty to harmony, proportion and fidelity to external appearances. In stark contrast, nonnaturalistic or abstract forms reflect primordial psychic anguish, an existential alienation from the natural world, or what Worringer famously called "spiritual agoraphobia"

(*Platzangst*). Abstract art in any period expresses a desire to transcend reality by transfixing the contingency and relativity of existence in timeless, static forms: in visual terms, this meant eliminating three-dimensional depth perspectives. Thus, abstract art is not representational; it expresses as a secular icon both metaphysical anxiety (*Angst*) and the urge to spiritual transcendence, an instinct for an irrational permanence beyond visible phenomena.

Worringer's second book, a study of Lucas Cranach (also 1908), expands the social dimension to his "psychology of style." Worringer goes against prevailing "genius" theories of the artist to read the "mass psyche" of the Reformation in the production of Cranach's workshop for the art market of a new German burgher class. Worringer's discussion there of the "multiple production of images" for the market may well have influenced Walter Benjamin's famous essay "The Work of Art in the Age of Mechanical Reproduction" (1936). Worringer also announced there his desire to see German art in terms of native German-Gothic traditions instead of the Greco-Roman Renaissance. The introduction to *Form Problems of the Gothic* (1911) describes his hypothetical method of art history (and his antipathy to positivism) and the text applies his general aesthetics to a specific area of nonclassical art. As in his first work, Worringer's aesthetics is based on psychological types (that influenced Carl Gustav Jung), but here also on racialist lines: "primitive," "classical," "Oriental," and Germanic "Gothic" man(kind). Worringer locates in the forms of Gothic architecture the transcendental impulse of Gothic mankind's "sublime hysteria," a "madness with method" that translates matter into the formal, constructivist expression of spiritual longing. His study figured as a disguised manifesto for German Expressionism, for which he became a leading spokesman.

Worringer's thesis countered reactionary criticism against non-German (French) influences on modern art in Germany. Indeed, Wassily Kandinsky invited him to lead the rebuttal to Carl Vinnen's nationalistic *Protest of German Artists* (1911); Worringer declined the editorship but contributed an essay, "On the Historical Development of the Most Modern Art" (1911), to the volume. Later, in an elegiac essay of 1919, "Critical Thoughts on the New Art," Worringer reflected on the yearnings and shortcomings of Expressionism, its failed attempt to spiritualize expression, and in 1921, in his *Questions about Contemporary Art*, he publicly declared its end. In his famous essay "Greatness and Decline of Expressionism" (1934), György Lukács seized on Worringer's remarks to indict the spiritual pretentions of Expressionism as an escapist mystification designed to avoid politics and accommodate reigning bourgeois ideology. Yet, Lukács, whose own early work has affinities to Worringer's, ignores the sociological dimension of Worringer's argument and the historical context of art-historical debates. In fact, Worringer argued that the Expressionist spirit had only migrated out of art and into scholarly works of critical intellect (in line with the notion of "New Objectivity" [*Neue Sachlichkeit*] in Weimar society).

By the time of his *Egyptian Art* (1927), Worringer had reversed his famous early views on "primitive" abstraction. He still engaged his historical scholarship in contemporary issues, but the parallel he draws between ancient Egypt and modern America reveals the book as a diatribe against "Americanization" and a symptom of general anxieties about social instability and change in the Weimar period. All of Worringer's work stands in relation to the thesis he developed in *Abstraction and Empathy* (1908) and elaborated on in *Form Problems of the Gothic* (1911) and in his essays. But his later scholarship never matched the suggestiveness of his early, provocative ideas on the psychological genesis of abstract art. In fact, his own career through the 1920s and then after World War II appears as only one line (and not even the most important) of the influence that extended from his early work in so many different directions.

[*See also* Abstraction; *and* Expressionism.]

BIBLIOGRAPHY

Works by Worringer

Abstraktion und Einfühlung: Ein Beitrag zur Stilpsychologie. Munich, 1908. In English as *Abstraction and Empathy: A Contribution to the Psychology of Style,* translated by Michael Bullock (New York, 1953; 4th ed., New York, 1980).

Lukas Cranach. Munich, 1908.

"Entwicklungsgeschichtliches zur modernsten Kunst." In *Im Kampf um die Kunst: Die Antwort zum "Protest deutscher Künstler,"* pp. 92–99. Munich, 1911.

Formprobleme der Gotik. Munich, 1911. In English as *Form Problems of the Gothic,* translation unattributed (New York, 1920); *Form in Gothic,* edited by Herbert Read (London, 1927; rev. ed., New York, 1964).

Die altdeutsche Buchillustration. Munich, 1912.

"Kritische Gedanken zur neuen Kunst." *Genius* 1 (1919): 221–236. Included in *Fragen und Gegenfragen.*

Künstlerische Zeitfragen. Munich, 1921. Reprinted in *Fragen und Gegenfragen.*

Die Anfänge der Tafelmalerei. Leipzig, 1924.

Ägyptische Kunst: Probleme ihrer Wertung. Munich, 1927. In English as *Egyptian Art,* authorized translation, edited by Bernhard Rackham (London, 1928).

Griechentum und Gotik: Vom Weltreich des Hellenismus. Munich, 1928.

Fragen und Gegenfragen: Schriften zum Kunstproblem. Munich, 1956.

Other Sources

Bushart, Magdalena. *Der Geist der Gotik und die expressionistische Kunst: Kunstgeschichte und Kunsttheorie, 1911–1925.* Munich, 1990.

Donahue, Neil H. *Forms of Disruption: Abstraction in Modern German Prose.* Ann Arbor, 1993.

Donahue, Neil H., ed. *Invisible Cathedrals: The Expressionist Art History of Wilhelm Worringer.* University Park, Pa., 1995.

Nachtsheim, Stephan. *Kunstphilosophie und empirische Kunstforschung, 1870–1920.* Berlin, 1984.

Perkins, Geoffrey. *Contemporary Theory of Expressionism.* Frankfurt am Main, 1974.

NEIL H. DONAHUE

WRIGHT, FRANK LLOYD (1867–1959), modern American architect. Wright's designs are more popular today, more than a century after he began his practice in 1893 and decades after his death in 1959, than they were during his lifetime. Although it is no doubt increasingly difficult to understand how Wright's designs emerged at the moment of their conception and construction, the built works that Wright left are immediately accessible to those who inhabit their precisely articulated, experientially determined spaces for living.

Born in 1867, Wright was raised in a household where the study of nature, the Unitarian faith, the ideas of American Transcendental philosophy, and the Froebel system of kindergarten training were all powerfully present. These complex yet complementary systems of thought had in common the belief that the material and spiritual worlds could not be separated, but were in fact one; that every physical thing was the consequence of, and had consequences for, spiritual thought—"All form is an effect of character," as Ralph Waldo Emerson said—and therefore that all form had moral meaning.

Wright's development as an architect involved the evolution of this moral imperative through the search for a more principled relation to historical form, for a monumentality appropriate to the young American nation, and for a systematic yet personal process of architectural design for the American house through the engagement of the landscape, the materials of construction, and the experience of inhabitation. Wright was thirty-three years of age in 1900: to be fully understood, therefore, Wright's architecture should be seen as issuing not from twentieth-century society, but from the American culture of the nineteenth century.

Toward an American Architecture. Wright's mentor and architectural father figure, Louis Sullivan, while calling attention to the absence in his own time of an appropriate American architecture, also warned against efforts to speed its arrival by transplanting historical styles onto the American continent. Any truly organic American architecture would only develop on a regional basis, he felt, with variations dependent on local climate, landscape, building methods and materials. Sullivan, together with his young apprentice Wright, searched for alternatives to what they believed to be the exhausted Western classical tradition, analyzing the ornamental patterns from Islamic and Oriental sources presented by Owen Jones in *The Grammar of Ornament*.

In an attempt to develop an indigenous American architecture, the "Chicago school," with Sullivan at its center, was established by 1890. The efforts of this group were soon overwhelmed, however, by the classical architecture dictated for the World Columbian Exposition, which opened in Chicago in 1893: uniform, academically correct, explicitly noncontextual and intended to be the same around the world. That this academically defined "tradition" was so appealing to a young America eager to establish and display its recently attained position as a global power reveals a basic aspect of the American character that Wright was to struggle against throughout his life—the belief that historical form alone is sufficient to produce architecture of significance.

Although Wright's later attacks on his academically correct contemporaries are well known, few have noted the degree to which he directly engaged the formal order underlying the architecture of classical antiquity in his own early work of the Prairie Period (1895–1915). Yet, in the first comprehensive national publication of Wright's work in 1908 when he was forty years old, Wright challenged the academic classicists' exclusive control over the interpretation of architectural history, and indicated how his own early work, with its symmetry, axial planning, hierarchical ordering from earth to sky, and attention to the nature of materials, demonstrated a more principled manner of relating to architectural history. Despite what he termed the "radical" appearance of his forms, Wright's designs were the result of exhaustive analyses of the great architecture of the past.

A Modern Monumentality. At the time Wright left Sullivan's office in 1893, an appropriate monumental form had failed to emerge in American architecture. The legacy of the steel-framed office tower, which Wright had received from Sullivan and the Chicago school, had in fact proved totally incapable of dealing with the need for monumentality in giving form to the public realm. As a manifestation of the economic determination of scale and massing, the universal planning grid, and the production of uniform interiors to be "styled" later by tenants, the Chicago frame skyscraper was a projection of private commercial interests at a scale heretofore given only to public buildings, yet totally lacking the qualities inherent in a monument. Therefore, a primary motivation for Wright's reclaiming of the buildings of antiquity was their undeniable monumentality.

Wright understood that the systematic production of universal space resulting from the office building's column grid could not give form to monumental public buildings, and this was reflected in his work as early as 1894, only a year after leaving Sullivan's office, with his project for the Monolithic Concrete Bank. Wright achieved his fully developed vision of an appropriate monumentality for public buildings ten years later with his designs for the Larkin Building of 1904 and Unity Temple of 1905.

The plans of these buildings are simple rectangles, the spaces within ordered by the exposed structural rhythm, with mezzanines surrounding and overlooking a central multiheight space, lit by high clerestory windows and skylights, and allowing no views out at eye level. On the outside, these buildings are closed, solid, and possessed a severity unlike anything else of their time, seeming to relate more to the stark rectilinearity of ancient monuments. Like Wright's later public buildings, such as the superb Johnson

Wax Building of 1936, the singularity of their central spaces, and the manner in which these are born from a fusion of their form, structure, and material, are experienced as profoundly monumental.

For Wright, the monumentality appropriate to American public spaces would inevitably take the form of introverted compounds, seen from the outside as groupings of powerful independent elements bound together by mutual purpose; a primary and secondary (service) volume with entry occurring between, leading to the low, dark, horizontal, rotating entry sequence, which compresses and then releases us into the tall, light, hidden, vertical central space—the whole admirably demonstrating Wright's mastery in orchestrating the perceptions of those inhabiting his buildings through movement, space, and light. The entire spatial and ornamental program for Wright's public buildings, from plans and massing to furniture and carpet patterns, was ordered through formal manipulations of the square and cube, which Wright considered the most perfect of geometries. Wright intended that his public buildings be experienced as sacred spaces, whatever their function, their introspective interiors flooded with transcendent light to create a morally edifying effect for those inhabiting the public place.

The Natural House. Throughout his career, the design of the American single-family house was the primary task and mission that Wright gave himself as an architect. He considered each of his house designs as a variation of an evolving ideal theme, so that each design in-formed or gave form to the next in the sequence. Wright's house designs make place through his comprehensive understanding of inhabitation, wherein site, space, and material are woven together to become the setting for the repeated rituals of daily life—his houses are places of shelter and outlook, with the fireplace as center, the horizon as edge, and the inhabitant's experience as an unfolding of space. Wright believed that the quality and integrity of spaces positively affected those who lived in them, and that a life taking place in the beneficial influence of nature would be infinitely better for it.

For Wright, it was essential that daily life be lived in direct communion with nature, and that the American house be designed as a natural place. Wright believed—as did Ralph Waldo Emerson and Henry David Thoreau—that because man was a product of nature, he was capable of learning about his own essential nature from regular and intimate contact with the natural landscape. He gave all his houses a horizontal emphasis in their form and space, believing that this grounded the house, making it a suitable foundation for the domestic life within. He began by incorporating the formative power of the landscape as the primal place of occupation—the building began with the ground on which it stood.

Wright's Prairie Period houses, such as the Robie House and the Coonley House, both of 1908, are extroverted counterparts to his introverted public buildings. The house is anchored by the central solid fireplace mass, and the spaces open out in all directions at eye level, outriding walls and overhanging eaves layering the house into the earth, projecting its grid out into the landscape and simultaneously pulling the landscape into the house. In this way, Wright gave the entire suburban site a geometric order so that the house and site were inextricably bound to one another.

Wright believed that the house should not merely mimic or repeat or even merge with the form of the landscape, but rather that architecture clarifies and makes present the spatial and habitable qualities latent but hidden in the landform. Wright sought to construct buildings that acknowledged their influence on the site and the changes inevitably accompanying man's settlement of the landscape, with the intention that the site be a better place after construction of the house.

This is exemplified by Wright's domestic masterpiece for Edgar Kaufman, called "Fallingwater" and built outside Pittsburgh in 1935 along and over a waterfall in a heavily wooded landscape. The house draws all the profiles of the landforms to itself, resolving them within its order, so that Fallingwater appears to have grown out of the ground and into the light, making present the latent power of the boulders on which it sits above the waterfall—the same boulders that emerge from the rippling "water" of the slate living room floor to provide a place of refuge in front of the fireplace. The natural setting is so integrated into this house that in occupying it people are constantly reminded of where they are by the sound of the waterfall, the flow of space and movement inside and outside across the floors and terraces, and the views and sunlight framed by the steel windows—to inhabit Fallingwater is to engage in the most intimate communion with nature.

The year after he designed Fallingwater, Wright designed the Herbert Jacobs House of 1936, the first of his Usonian Houses, affordable homes for the emerging American middle class. Unlike the cruciform Prairie Houses, the Usonian Houses (1936–1959) were L-shaped in plan, folding inward to make a corner, anchoring their sites without completely enclosing them, so that the spatial weaving is applied to the enclosed landscape as well as interior space, and the center of the spatial composition is outside the house, in the garden. Protecting the garden as its "interior," the house presents a closed facade to the street, and the living room focuses sideways or laterally toward the garden. Wright was careful to assure that the spaces of his houses were oriented to receive sun at appropriate times during the day, insisting on a southern orientation for the living room elevation, which faced the garden; flooded with southern sun, these courts or gardens became the focus of the house and the life that went on within it.

Wright's designs emphasized the topographic, and included in that the natural landform and the history of hu-

WRIGHT. Frank Lloyd Wright, *Exterior, Fallingwater House,* Bear Run, Pennsylvania. (Copyright by the Frank Lloyd Wright Foundation; photograph courtesy of Art Resource, New York; used by permission.)

man occupation of the site. In his design for Broadacre City of 1935, intended to merge city and countryside in a seamless unity, benefiting from the attributes of both, as well as the individual houses conceived as being stitched into Broadacre City's fabric, Wright's work acknowledged and made experiential the close relationship between agriculture and architecture; agriculture (to care for and cultivate the land) and architecture (to build and edify) as related activities on the earth—tending and transforming the landscape.

The Nature of Materials. The ideal of integrating space and form with the structure and materials with which it is made was primary for Wright, and he engaged in a constant search for a comprehensive order that would encompass both composition and construction, an order similar to the fusion of structure, material, form, and space that he found in his studies of nature. Essential to Wright's archi-

tecture was his understanding that the way a space is made or constructed is directly related to the way it is experienced. Construction was not simply a means to some end— it was an essential part of the final experience of life that took place within the house, and thus was to be fully integrated in the process of design.

Wright felt that this integrated understanding of structure, construction, space, and experience was capable of giving habitable form to the concepts and ideals of the American Transcendental philosophers, and he indicated that his compositions with squares and cubes were intended to connect his houses with nature, as called for in the poetry of Walt Whitman, "chanting the square deific." The square grid that underlay all of Wright's house designs operated as an essential compositional and scaling device, a measure and organizational method for construction, and a means of achieving economy—all required in his view to accomplish the integral order that resulted in the making of beautiful spaces. In synthesizing and integrating spatial and constructive grammars, Wright brought space into presence by articulating both the physical and emotional qualities that may be experienced in materials, structure, and the act of construction.

In his search for order that would be reinforced and edified in the process of construction and material realization, Wright grappled throughout his life with the one material that proved perfectly "plastic," able to be formed into any formal or structural shape: reinforced concrete. Wright was often critical of concrete's inherent lack of internal order—the type of modular order evident in the brick and standardized wood studs and boards he had used so effectively to give rhythm to his house designs. In seeking a more direct revelation of concrete's construction module, Wright developed the custom-cast concrete block, used most convincingly in the superb Freeman House of 1923. The organizing square grid operates in both plan and section, constituting a veritable knitting together of the surfaces, resulting in a fully integrated building mass that, despite its cubic form and the weight of its concrete construction, imparts an impression of being fabricated from a lightweight textile.

Wright achieved his highest level of resolution of spatial, constructive, and experiential forms in his Usonian Houses, where the horizontal (plan) grid operates at an entirely different scale than the vertical (section) layering, recognizing the fact that in inhabiting space, human beings experience horizontal dimensions (distances on the ground) very differently from vertical dimensions (distances off the ground). These houses, although physically small, feel much larger because of their asymmetrical volumes, which do not allow the inhabitant to see the entire space as a result of its wrapping around a corner and being out of sight; their horizontally layered walls, where shelves, tables, desks, seats, and storage units appear to be either pulled out of or pushed into the wooden surfaces; and the three overlapping but differing plans at floor, door top, and ceiling. Each space is literally built into the next, so that even the heating is cast into the concrete floor slab—as a result these houses feel remarkably like large pieces of furniture, with subtle articulations within the constructed spatial fabric to accommodate even the most modest of domestic events.

Intimate Possession of Every Interior. In the end, the question of Wright's importance to architecture and modern culture centers not on issues of style or form but on the aspect of expanded experiential possibilities made evident in his works. As the primary method he used to order and construct spatial experiences, Wright stated early in his career that the floor plan was of preeminent importance in his conception of architecture; the building was conceived as being generated from the plan, which gave form and order to the space within to be lived in. For Wright, the only reason to shape space in plan was for the experience of man; architecture was first and foremost concerned with the presentation of man. Architecture gave order to man's experience, and thus made him present in the world—in space conceived and formed as being occupied; the act of inhabitation embodied.

Denying that architecture was directed toward the production of isolated sculptural objects, Wright defined buildings as the background or framework for human existence; architecture gave dignity to daily life. Wright's architecture appealed at a fundamental level to the occupant's sense of embodied presence, bodily movement, and the position of the eye. Wright's system of design was measured, scaled, and calibrated precisely by the human body and its experience, and although the geometric rigor of Wright's planning is well known, the esteem in which he held the concepts of use and comfort is not as widely understood. The intellectual and formal order of Wright's plans was balanced by the physical and spiritual engagement of the inhabitant; for Wright, concept and experience were one and the same.

Wright's designs condensed natural light in way that reflected light's complex and multivalent effect on the experience of architecture's inhabitants. Wright utilized roofs as shadow makers, and defined the place of inhabitation as the space made by shadows cast on the earth. Although Wright's house plans often projected the main rooms out so that light could enter from two or even three sides, what increased was not the interior light level but the ability to view out, to survey the landscape from within the shadowed interior. In his house designs, Wright developed a culture of light as it relates to the landscape, the creation of a sense of refuge—seeing without being seen.

Wright understood that humans inhabit architecture through movement, allowing space and material to be woven together in their experience. The dynamic spatial development of Wright's architecture originated in his understanding of inhabitation and experience as nonstatic, indivisible events, capable of being framed only by boundless space.

In his houses, Wright achieved what few if any others have in our time: the systematic production of unique places. Yet, Wright insisted that the principles on which his work was based were not invented by one man or one age, and that his work was founded on architecture understood as a discipline—a history of principled place making. Indeed, it could be argued that Wright's contribution is virtually unmatched in the twentieth century, which produced a rich assortment of new forms but few systematic conceptions that link spatial form and order to human occupation and experience. Wright's definition of architecture is exemplified in his works: each building is a celebration of man embodied in a world of his own making.

[*See also* Architecture; *and* Modernism, *article on* Modernity and Tradition in Architecture.]

BIBLIOGRAPHY

Works by Wright

Ausgeführte Bauten und Entwürfe von Frank Lloyd Wright. Berlin, 1910. Reprinted as *Drawings and Plans of Frank Lloyd Wright: The Early Period, 1893–1909* (New York, 1983) and as *Studies and Executed Buildings by Frank Lloyd Wright* (New York, 1986).

An Autobiography. New York, 1932; reprint, New York, 1977.

The Natural House. New York, 1954.

In the Cause of Architecture. Edited by Frederick Gutheim. New York, 1975. Reprint of *Architectural Record* essays, 1908–1952.

Frank Lloyd Wright: Collected Writings. 5 vols. Edited by Bruce Brooks Pfeiffer. New York, 1992–1995.

Other Sources

Alofsin, Anthony. *Frank Lloyd Wright: The Lost Years, 1910–1922.* Chicago, 1993.

Bolon, Carol R., Robert S. Nelson, and Linda Seidel, eds. *The Nature of Frank Lloyd Wright.* Chicago, 1988.

Brooks, H. Allen, ed. *Writings on Wright.* Cambridge, Mass., 1981.

Futagawa, Yokio, ed. *Frank Lloyd Wright.* 12 vols. Text by Bruce B. Pfeiffer. Tokyo, 1984–1988.

Hitchcock, Henry Russell. *In the Nature of Materials, 1887–1941: The Buildings of Frank Lloyd Wright.* New York, 1942.

Hoffmann, Donald. *Frank Lloyd Wright's Fallingwater: The House and Its History.* New York, 1978; 2d rev. ed., New York, 1993.

Levine, Neil. *The Architecture of Frank Lloyd Wright.* Princeton, N.J., 1996.

Lipman, Jonathan. *Frank Lloyd Wright and the Johnson Wax Buildings.* New York, 1986.

Manson, Grant Carpenter. *Frank Lloyd Wright to 1910: The First Golden Age.* New York, 1958.

McCarter, Robert, ed. *Frank Lloyd Wright: A Primer on Architectural Principles.* New York, 1991.

Nute, Kevin. *Frank Lloyd Wright and Japan.* New York, 1993.

Quinan, Jack. *Frank Lloyd Wright's Larkin Building: Myth and Fact.* Cambridge, Mass., 1987.

Riley, Terence, and Peter Reed, eds. *Frank Lloyd Wright: Architect.* New York, 1994.

Secrest, Meryle. *Frank Lloyd Wright.* New York, 1992.

Sergeant, John. *Frank Lloyd Wright's Usonian Houses: The Case for Organic Architecture.* New York, 1976.

Siry, Joseph M. *Unity Temple: Frank Lloyd Wright and Architecture for Liberal Religion.* Cambridge and New York, 1996.

Smith, Norris Kelly. *Frank Lloyd Wright: A Study in Architectural Content.* Englewood Cliffs, N.J., 1966.

Storrer, William Allin. *The Frank Lloyd Wright Companion.* Chicago, 1993.

Sweeney, Robert. *Frank Lloyd Wright: An Annotated Bibliography.* Los Angeles, 1978.

ROBERT MCCARTER

ZHUANGZI. *See* Daoist Aesthetics.

DIRECTORY OF CONTRIBUTORS

James S. Ackerman
Arthur Kingsley Porter Professor Emeritus of Fine Arts, Sackler Museum, Harvard University
Architecture, *article on* Italian Renaissance Aesthetics

Craig Adcock
Professor of Art History, University of Iowa
Marcel Duchamp, *article on* Survey of Art

Jan A. Aertsen
Professor of Philosophy and Director, Thomas-Institut, Universität zu Köln
Beauty, *article on* Medieval Concepts

Alexander Alberro
Assistant Professor of Art History, University of Florida, Gainesville
Conceptual Art, *historical and theoretical overview article*

Tamara Albertini
Assistant Professor of Philosophy, University of Hawaii at Manoa
Renaissance Italian Aesthetics

Daniel Albright
Richard L. Turner Professor in the Humanities, University of Rochester
Ineffability

Thomas Alexander
Associate Professor of Philosophy, Southern Illinois University
John Dewey, *article on* Theory of Expression

Philip A. Alperson
Professor of Philosophy, University of Louisville; Editor, Journal of Aesthetics and Art Criticism
Improvisation, *overview article;* Performance

Ernst van Alphen
Director of Education and Communication, Museum Boymans–Van Beuningen, Rotterdam
Morality and Aesthetics, *article on* Art, Morality, and the Holocaust

Charles Altieri
Professor of English, University of California, Berkeley
Postmodernism, *article on* Postmodern American Poetry

Douglas R. Anderson
Associate Professor of Philosophy, Pennsylvania State University
Robin George Collingwood

Richard L. Anderson
Professor of Liberal Arts, Kansas City Art Institute
Anthropology and Aesthetics

Simon Anderson
Associate Professor and Chair, Department of Art History, Theory, and Criticism, School of the Art Institute of Chicago
Anti-Art; Situationist Aesthetics

Dudley Andrew
Angelo Bertocci Professor of Critical Studies and Director, Institute for Cinema and Culture, University of Iowa
André Bazin

Keith Ansell-Pearson
Senior Lecturer in Philosophy, University of Warwick
Friedrich Wilhelm Nietzsche, *article on* Nietzsche on Art and Politics

Mark Antliff
Associate Professor of Art, Queen's University, Kingston, Canada
Henry-Louis Bergson; Politics and Aesthetics, *article on* Aestheticized Politics

David Armstrong
Professor of Classics, University of Texas, Austin
Longinus

Philip Armstrong
Visiting Lecturer, Ohio State University
Iconography and Iconology

Rudolf Arnheim
Professor Emeritus of Psychology of Art, Harvard University
Rudolf Arnheim, *article on* Dynamics of Art; Psychology of Art

Elizabeth Asmis
Professor of Classics, University of Chicago
Hellenistic Aesthetics, *article on* Philosophers and Literary Critics

George W. S. Bailey
Associate Professor of Philosophy, East Carolina University
George Dickie

George Baird
G. Ware Travelstead Professor of Architecture, Graduate School of Design, Harvard University
Semiotics, *article on* Semiotics and Architecture

Mieke Bal
Professor of the Theory of Literature and Director, Amsterdam School of Cultural Analysis, Universiteit van Amsterdam
Narrative, *article on* Narrative and the Visual and Literary Arts; Charles Sanders Peirce; Semiotics, *article on* Semiotics as a Theory of Art

Anna Balakian
Professor of Comparative Literature, New York University (deceased)
Symbolism

Michael Baldwin
Artist, Oxford, United Kingdom
Conceptual Art, *article on* History of the Unformed

Sally Banes
Marian Hannah Winter Professor of Theatre History and Dance Studies, University of Wisconsin, Madison
Postmodernism, *article on* Postmodern Dance

Stephen Bann
Professor of Modern Cultural Studies, School of Arts and Image Studies, Rutherford College, University of Kent
Victor Cousin; Walter Horatio Pater

Annette Barnes
Professor of Philosophy, University of Maryland, Baltimore County
Definition of Art; Interpretation, *article on* Analytic Interpretation

Stanley Bates
Walter Cerf Distinguished College Professor of Philosophy, Middlebury College
Leo Nikolaevich Tolstoy

Norton Batkin
Director, Graduate Program, Center for Curatorial Studies and Art in Contemporary Culture, and Associate Professor of Philosophy and Art History, Bard College
Formalism, *article on* Formalism in Analytic Aesthetics

Christine Battersby
Senior Lecturer in Philosophy, University of Warwick
Genius, *article on* Genius and Feminism

Bruce Baugh
Associate Professor of Philosophy, University College of the Cariboo, Kamloops, Canada
Rock Music

Michael Baxandall
Professor of Art History, University of California, Berkeley
Jean-Baptiste Du Bos

Gordon C. F. Bearn
Associate Professor and Chair, Department of Philosophy, Lehigh University
Kitsch

Howard S. Becker
Professor of Sociology and Music, University of Washington
Art World

Frederick Beiser
Associate Professor of Philosophy, Indiana University
Johann Georg Hamann; Johann Gottfried Herder; Johann Christoph Friedrich von Schiller; Karl Wilhelm Friedrich von Schlegel

Elizabeth Belfiore
Professor of Classical and Near Eastern Studies, University of Minnesota
Aristotle, *article on* Survey of Thought

Antonio Benítez-Rojo
Thomas B. Walton, Jr., Memorial Professor of Romance Languages, Amherst College
Caribbean Aesthetics

Maurice Berger
Senior Fellow, Vera List Center for Art and Politics, New School for Social Research
Politics and Aesthetics, *article on* Difference and Culture

Arnold Berleant
Professor Emeritus of Philosophy, Long Island University
Environmental Aesthetics

Robert Bernasconi
Moss Chair of Excellence in Philosophy, University of Memphis
Martin Heidegger, *article on* Heidegger's Displacement of the Concept of Art

J. M. Bernstein
W. Alton Jones Professor of Philosophy, Vanderbilt University
Alienation, Aesthetic

J. Duncan Berry
Independent scholar, Harwich Port, Massachusetts
Heinrich Hübsch

Monika Betzler
Assistant Professor of Philosophy, Georg-August-Universität Göttingen
Georg Simmel

Timothy Binkley
Chair, Graduate Computer Art Department, School of Visual Arts, New York
Computer Art; Digital Media, *overview article*

Inge Boer
Associate Professor of Literary Studies and Multiculturalism, Universiteit van Amsterdam
Orientalism

Ron Bontekoe
Associate Professor of Philosophy, University of Hawaii at Manoa
Paul Ricoeur; Friedrich Daniel Ernst Schleiermacher

David Bordwell
Jacques Ledoux Professor of Film Studies, University of Wisconsin, Madison
Film, *article on* Film Theory

Leon Botstein
President and Leon Levy Professor in the Arts and Humanities, Bard College; Editor, The Musical Quarterly; and Music Director, American Symphony Orchestra
Modernism, *article on* Modern Music

Curtis Bowman

Lecturer in Philosophy, University of Pennsylvania
Karl Philipp Moritz

Peggy Zeglin Brand

Assistant Professor of Philosophy and Women's Studies, Indiana University
Feminism, *article on* Feminism and Tradition; Parody; Pastiche

Richard Brilliant

A. S. Garbedian Professor in the Humanities, Art History, and Archaeology, Columbia University
Hellenistic Aesthetics, *article on* Visual Arts; Portraiture; Roman Aesthetics

Joyce Brodsky

Professor of Art, University of California, Santa Cruz
Feminism, *article on* Feminist Art History

Elisabeth Bronfen

Professor of English and American Literatures, Universität Zurich
Death and Aesthetics

Lee Brown

Associate Professor of Philosophy, Ohio State University
Jazz

Gerald L. Bruns

William P. and Hazel B. White Professor of English, University of Notre Dame
Hermeneutics

Norman Bryson

Professor of Art History, Harvard University
Semiotics, *article on* Semiotics as a Theory of Art

Peter Bürger

Professor of Linguistics and Cultural Studies, Universität Bremen
Autonomy, *article on* Critique of Autonomy; Avant Garde

Ronna Burger

Associate Professor of Philosophy, Tulane University
Aristotle, *article on* Aristole on Mimesis

Susan Bush

Associate in Research, Fairbank Center for East Asian Research, Harvard University
Chinese Aesthetics, *article on* Painting Theory and Criticism

Joseph Buttigieg

Professor of English and Fellow of the Nanovic Institute for European Studies, University of Notre Dame
Antonio Gramsci

Richard Buxton

Professor of Greek Languages and Literatures, University of Bristol
Tragedy, *article on* Greek Tragedy

Oleg V. Bychkov

Lecturer, Franciscan Institute, St. Bonaventure University
Russian Aesthetics, *article on* Religious Aesthetics

Victor V. Bychkov

Head, Department of Nonclassical Aesthetics, Institute of Philosophy, Moscow
Byzantine Aesthetics; Icon; Russian Aesthetics, *article on* Religious Aesthetics

David Cahan

Professor of History, University of Nebraska, Lincoln
Hermann von Helmholtz

Mary Ann Calo

Associate Professor of Art History, Colgate University
Bernard Berenson

Joseph Keim Campbell

Assistant Professor of Philosophy, Washington State University
Hugh Blair

Allen C. Carlson

Professor of Philosophy, University of Alberta
Landscape, *article on* Landscape Assessment; Nature, *article on* Contemporary Thought

Taylor Carman

Assistant Professor of Philosophy, Barnard College, Columbia University
Martin Heidegger, *article on* Survey of Thought

David Carrier

Professor of Philosophy, Carnegie Mellon University
Charles Baudelaire, *article on* Survey of Thought; Adrian Durham Stokes; Richard Wollheim

Joseph Carroll

Professor of English, University of Missouri, St. Louis
Matthew Arnold

Noël Carroll

Monroe C. Beardsley Professor of Philosophy, University of Wisconsin, Madison
Film, *article on* Motion Pictures; Morality and Aesthetics, *historical and conceptual overview article;* Politics and Aesthetics, *historical and conceptual overview article*

Curtis L. Carter

Professor of Aesthetics and Director, Haggerty Museum of Art, Marquette University, Milwaukee
Dadaism

Anthony Cascardi

Professor of Comparative Literature, University of California, Berkeley
Ludwig Joseph Johann Wittgenstein, *article on* Wittgenstein and Literary Theory

Allan Casebier

Professor of Communication, University of Miami, Coral Gables
Phenomenology

Terry Castle

Professor of English and Walter Haas Chair in the Humanities, Stanford University
Lesbian Aesthetics

Marcia Cavell
Occasional Associate Professor of Philosophy, University of California, Berkeley
Sigmund Freud, *article on* Freud and Literature

Mary Ann Caws
Professor of Comparative Literature, Graduate School and University Center, City University of New York
Surrealism, *article on* Surrealism and Literature

Howard Caygill
Professor of Cultural History, Goldsmiths College, University of London
Henry Home

Kermit Swiler Champa
Andrea V. Rosenthal Professor of the History of Art and Architecture, Brown University
Piet Mondrian

V. K. Chari
Adjunct Professor of English, Carleton University, Ottawa
Abhinavagupta; Indian Aesthetics, *article on* Indian Theories of Interpretation; Rasa

Michael Charlesworth
Assistant Professor of Art History, University of Texas, Austin
Uvedale Price

Mark A. Cheetham
Professor of Visual Arts, University of Western Ontario
Immanuel Kant, *article on* Kant and Art History

Thomas Christensen
Associate Professor of Music, University of Iowa
Johann Mattheson

Olivier Christin
Professor of History, Université de Lyon II
Religion and Aesthetics, *article on* Religion and Art

Margaret Cohen
Associate Professor of Comparative Literature, New York University
Walter Benjamin, *article on* Benjamin and Surrealism

Ted Cohen
Professor of Philosophy, University of Chicago
Jokes; Sports; Television, *article on* Contemporary Thought

David Cole
Professor of Law, Georgetown University Law Center
Law and Art, *article on* Government-Funded Art and the First Amendment

Frances Colpitt
Associate Professor of Art History and Criticism, University of Texas, San Antonio
Minimalism

Frances S. Connelly
Associate Professor of Art History, University of Missouri, Kansas City
Grotesque; Primitivism

David E. Cooper
Professor of Philosophy, University of Durham, United Kingdom
Romanticism, *article on* Visual Arts

Elizabeth Cornwell
Preceptor, Art History Department, Columbia University
Postcolonialism

Gregory Currie
Professor of Philosophy and Head, School of Arts, Flinders University of South Australia
Ontology of Art, *article on* Analytic Ontology

Daniel O. Dahlstrom
Professor of Philosophy, Boston University
Johann Christoph Gottsched; Edmund Gustav Albrecht Husserl; Johann Ulrich von König

Arthur C. Danto
Johnsonian Professor Emeritus of Philosophy, Columbia University
Pop Art, *article on* Aesthetics of Andy Warhol

Stephen Davies
Associate Professor of Philosophy, University of Auckland, New Zealand
Authenticity, *conceptual overview article;* Theories of Art

Whitney Davis
John Evans Professor of Art History, Northwestern University
Formalism, *article on* Formalism in Art History; Sexuality

Martine Debaisieux
Professor of French, University of Wisconsin, Madison
Nicolas Boileau-Despreaux; Charles Sorel

Mark DeBellis
Associate Professor of Music, Columbia University
Perception, *article on* Music Perception

Thierry de Duve
Elliot and Roslyn Jaffe Visiting Professor of History of Art, University of Pennsylvania
Immanuel Kant, *article on* Kant, Duchamp, and Judgment

Kelly Dennis
Assistant Professor of Art History, Theory, and Criticism, School of the Art Institute of Chicago
Performance Art, *historical overview article*

Eliot Deutsch
Professor and Chair, Department of Philosophy, University of Hawaii at Manoa
Comparative Aesthetics

Mary Devereaux
Associate Professor of Philosophy, University of California, San Diego
Autonomy, *article on* Autonomy and Its Feminist Critics

George Dickie
Professor Emeritus of Philosophy, University of Illinois, Chicago
Evaluation, *article on* Aesthetic Evaluation

T. J. Diffey
Reader in Philosophy, School of Cultural and Community Studies, University of Sussex
Essentialism, *conceptual overview article;* William Wordsworth

Jeffrey R. Di Leo
Editor in Chief, symplokē, *School of Literature, Communication, and Culture, Georgia Institute of Technology*
Text

Paul J. DiMaggio
Professor of Sociology, Princeton University
Museums, *article on* Sociological Perspectives on Museums

Edward Dimendberg
Film, Architecture, and German Departments, University of Michigan
Film, *article on* Film Noir

Randall Dipert
Professor of English and Philosophy, United States Military Academy, West Point
Artifact

Beth Ann Dobie
Assistant Professor, Division of Human Studies, Alfred University
Intention, *article on* Speech Act Theory and the Interpretation of Images

Mo Dodson
Principal Lecturer in Communications, London Guildhall University
Design

Neil H. Donahue
Associate Professor of German and Comparative Linguistics, Hofstra University
Wilhelm Worringer

Martin Donougho
Associate Professor of Philosophy, University of South Carolina
Georg Wilhelm Friedrich Hegel, *article on* Hegel on the Historicity of Art; Johann Joachim Winckelmann

Linda Dowling
Independent scholar, Princeton, New Jersey
Aestheticism

Johanna Drucker
Associate Professor of History of Art, Yale University
Modernism, *overview article*

Aruna D'Souza
Doctoral candidate, Institute of Fine Arts, New York University
Surrealism, *article on* Surrealism and the Visual Arts

Steven C. Dubin
Associate Professor of Sociology, State University of New York, Purchase
Politics and Aesthetics, *article on* Politicized Art

Daniel Dumouchel
Assistant Professor of Philosophy, Université de Montréal
Georg Friedrich Meier; Johann Georg Sulzer

Denis Dutton
Senior Lecturer in the Philosophy of Art, University of Canterbury, New Zealand
Forgery; Tribal Art

Wayne R. Dynes
Professor of Art History, Hunter College, City University of New York
Gothic Aesthetics

Marcia Muelder Eaton
Professor of Philosophy, University of Minnesota
Morality and Aesthetics, *article on* Contemporary Aesthetics and Ethics

Katherine Eggert
Assistant Professor of English, University of Colorado, Boulder
Historicism, *article on* New Historicism in Literary Theory

Richard Eldridge
Associate Professor of Philosophy, Swarthmore College
Romanticism, *article on* Philosophy and Literature

Catherine Z. Elgin
Visiting Professor of Philosophy, Princeton University
Science and Aesthetics, *article on* Contemporary Thought

Aaron H. Esman
Professor Emeritus of Clinical Psychiatry, Cornell University Medical College
Insane, Art of the

Ellen Esrock
Associate Professor of Literature, Rensselaer Polytechnic Institute
Imagery, *article on* Visual Imagery in Reading

Susan L. Feagin
Professor of Philosophy, University of Missouri, Kansas City
Drawing; Emotions, *article on* Emotions and Literature; Imagination, *article on* Contemporary Thought

Stuart Feder
Clinical Associate Professor of Psychiatry, Albert Einstein College of Medicine, New York
Sigmund Freud, *article on* Freud and Music

Rita Felski
Professor of English, University of Virginia
Feminism, *article on* Critique of Feminist Aesthetics

David Fenner
Assistant Professor of History, Philosophy, and Religious Studies, University of North Florida
Attitude, *article on* Aesthetic Attitude

Peter Fenves
Professor of German and Comparative Literature and Herman and Beulah Pearce-Miller Research Professor in Literature, Northwestern University
Johann Christian Friedrich Hölderlin

Frances Ferguson
Professor of English and the Humanities, Johns Hopkins University
Edmund Burke; Sublime, *article on* The Sublime from Burke to the
Present

David H. Fisher
*Professor of Philosophy and Chair, Department of Philosophy, North
Central College, Illinois*
Theory, History of

Christopher Fitter
Assistant Professor of English, Rutgers University
Landscape, *article on* Landscape from the Ancients to the
Seventeenth Century

Lisa Florman
Assistant Professor of History of Art, Ohio State University
Pablo Picasso

Thomas R. Flynn
Samuel Candler Dobbs Professor of Philosophy, Emory University
Jean-Paul Sartre

Cheryl Foster
Assistant Professor of Philosophy, University of Rhode Island
Nature, *article on* Nature and Artistic Creation

Kenneth Frampton
Ware Professor, School of Architecture, Columbia University
Futurism

Henry Frankel
Professor of Philosophy, University of Missouri, Kansas City
Glass, *article on* Aesthetics of Glass

Susanne K. Frantz
Curator of Twentieth-Century Glass, Corning Museum of Glass
Glass, *article on* Glass Art

Francis Frascina
John Raven Professor of Visual Arts, Keele University, United Kingdom
Collage, *conceptual and historical overview article*

Cynthia Freeland
*Associate Dean, College of Humanities, Fine Arts, and Communication,
University of Houston*
Film, *article on* Feminist Film Theory

Barbara Claire Freeman
*Associate Professor of English and American Literature and Language,
Harvard University*
Sublime, *article on* Feminine Sublime

Eli Friedlander
Assistant Professor of Philosophy, Tel Aviv University
Opera

Michal Grover Friedlander
Assistant Professor of Musicology, Tel Aviv University
Opera

Josef Früchtl
Department of Philosophy, Westfälische Wilhelms-Universität Münster
Theodor Wiesengrund Adorno, *article on* Adorno and Mimesis

Thomas Furniss
*Senior Lecturer, Department of English Studies, University of
Strathclyde, Glasgow*
Joseph Addison

John Gage
Reader in the History of Western Art, University of Cambridge
Synaesthesia

Claude Gandelman
Professor of French, University of Haifa, Israel (deceased)
Imagery, *article on* Reading Images

Gunter Gebauer
Professor, Institute of Philosophy, Freie Universität Berlin
Mimesis

Alexander Gelley
Professor of Comparative Literature, University of California, Irvine
Rhetoric, *article on* Exemplarity

Jeremy Gilbert-Rolfe
*Chair, Graduate Program in Fine Art, Art Center College of Design,
Pasadena*
Contemporary Art, *article on* Aesthetics of Contemporary Art

Jonathan Gilmore
*Visiting Assistant Professor of Philosophy, Barnard College, Columbia
University*
Arthur Coleman Danto, *article on* Danto's End of Art Thesis;
Narrative, *article on* Internal Narratives of Art History; Realism,
article on Pictorial Realism

David L. Gitomer
Associate Professor of Religious Studies, DePaul University
Indian Aesthetics, *historical and conceptual overview article*

Sima Godfrey
Associate Professor of French, University of British Columbia
Charles Baudelaire, *article on* Baudelaire and Art

David Goldblatt
Professor of Philosophy, Denison University, Granville, Ohio
Architecture, *article on* Modernism to Postmodernism

Leon Golden
Professor of Classics, Florida State University
Aristotle, *article on* Reception of Aristotle in Modernity

Alan Goldman
Professor and Chair, Department of Philosophy, University of Miami
Realism, *article on* Realism and Aesthetics; Representation,
conceptual and historical overview article

Jennifer González
Assistant Professor of Art History, University of California, Santa Cruz
Installation Art

John Goodman
Translator and art historian, Brooklyn, New York
Denis Diderot, *article on* Diderot and the Salon

Nelson Goodman
Professor Emeritus of Philosophy, Harvard University
Nelson Goodman, *article on* Art in Action

Carol Gould
Assistant Professor of Philosophy, Florida Atlantic University
Arthur Clive Howard Bell

Timothy Gould
Professor of Philosophy, Metropolitan State College of Denver
Stanley Cavell, *article on* Survey of Thought; Ralph Waldo
Emerson; Genius, *conceptual and historical overview article*

Oleg Grabar
*Professor, School of Historical Studies, Institute for Advanced Study,
Princeton, New Jersey*
Islamic Aesthetics, *historical and conceptual overview article*

Theodore A. Gracyk
*Professor and Chair, Department of Philosophy, Moorhead State
University, Minnesota*
Immanuel Kant, *article on* Kant on Nature and Art

Jean Grondin
Professor of Philosophy, Université de Montréal
Hans-Georg Gadamer, *article on* Gadamer and the Truth of Art

Ann Hutchinson Guest
Director, Language of Dance Centre, London
Notation, *article on* Dance Notation

Yair Guttmann
Assistant Professor of Philosophy, Stanford University
Conceptual Art, *article on* Conceptual Art and Philosophy

Paul Guyer
Professor of Philosophy, University of Pennsylvania
Alexander Gottlieb Baumgarten; George Berkeley; Marcus Herz;
Karl Heinrich Heydenreich; Immanuel Kant, *article on* Survey of
Thought; Rudolph Hermann Lotze; Moses Mendelssohn

Garry Hagberg
Associate Professor of Philosophy, Bard College
Improvisation, *article on* Jazz Improvisation; Ludwig Josef Johann
Wittgenstein, *article on* Reception of Wittgenstein

Margaret A. Hagen
Professor of Psychology, Boston University
Perception, *article on* Psychology of Perception

Barry Hallen
*Fellow, W. E. B. Du Bois Institute for Afro-American Research, Harvard
University*
African Aesthetics

Stephen Halliwell
Professor of Greek, University of Saint Andrews, Scotland
Aristotle, *article on* Aristotle on Form and Unity

James R. Hamilton
Associate Professor of Philosophy, Kansas State University
Bertolt Brecht

Michele Hannoosh
Professor of French, University College London
Caricature; Ferdinand-Victor-Eugène Delacroix

Forest Hansen
Professor Emeritus of Philosophy, Lake Forest College
Susanne Knauth Langer

Karen Hanson
Professor of Philosophy, Indiana University
Fashion, *article on* Fashion and Philosophy

C. L. Hardin
Professor Emeritus of Philosophy, Syracuse University
Color, *article on* Color Science

William E. Harkins
Professor Emeritus of Slavic Languages, Columbia University
Russian Aesthetics, *articles on* Russian Formalism *and* Socialist
Realism

Karsten Harries
Professor of Philosophy, Yale University
Architecture, *modern overview article;* Martin Heidegger, *article on*
Heidegger's Confrontation with Aesthetics

Andrew Harrison
Senior Lecturer in Philosophy, University of Bristol, United Kingdom
Medium

Bernard Harrison
E. E. Erickson Professor of Philosophy, University of Utah
Literature, *article on* Literature and Cognition

Charles Harrison
*Professor of the History and Theory of Art, The Open University,
Oxford*
Conceptual Art, *article on* History of the Unformed

Joan Hart
Independent scholar, Bloomington, Indiana
Heinrich Wölfflin

Casey Haskins
*Assistant Professor of Philosophy, State University of New York,
Purchase*
Autonomy, *historical overview article;* John Dewey, *article on* Survey
of Thought

Carl R. Hausman
Professor Emeritus of Philosophy, Pennsylvania State University
Creativity, *conceptual and historical overview article;* Metaphor,
article on Metaphor and Nonverbal Arts

Deborah J. Haynes
*Director, Women's Studies Program, and Associate Professor of Fine
Arts, Washington State University*
Mikhail Mikhailovich Bakhtin

K. Michael Hays
Professor of Architectural Theory, Graduate School of Design, Harvard University
Autonomy, *article on* Autonomy and Architecture; Ludwig Mies van der Rohe

Michael Heim
Researcher in Digital Media, Art Center College of Design, Pasadena
Cyberspace; Multimedia; Virtual Reality

Hilde Hein
Professor of Philosophy, College of the Holy Cross
Law and Art, *article on* Aesthetic Concepts in Law; Museums, *article on* Museums and Aesthetics

Marjorie Heins
Director and Staff Counsel, Arts Censorship Project, American Civil Liberties Union Foundation, New York
Law and Art, *article on* Censorship

Reinhold Heller
Professor of Art History and of Germanic Studies, University of Chicago
Expressionism

James D. Herbert
Associate Professor of Art History, University of California, Irvine
Impressionism

Göran Hermerén
Chair, Department of Medical Ethics, Lunds Universitet
Qualities, Aesthetic

María Herrera
Senior Research Associate and Professor of Philosophy, Institute for Philosophical Research, Universidad Nacional Autónoma de México
Latin American Aesthetics, *article on* Latin American Aesthetics and Modernity

Daniel Herwitz
Professor and Chair, Department of Philosophy, University of Natal, Durban, South Africa
John Cage; Constructivism; Arthur Coleman Danto, *article on* Survey of Thought; Pleasure; Postmodernism, *historical and conceptual overview article*

Patricia Herzog
Visiting Assistant Professor of Philosophy, Brandeis University
Criticism, *article on* Music Criticism

Kathleen Higgins
Professor of Philosophy, University of Texas, Austin
Emotions, *historical overview article;* Friedrich Wilhelm Nietzche, *article on* Nietzsche's Literary Style

Stephen Hinton
Associate Professor and Chair, Department of Music, Stanford University
Theodor Wiesengrund Adorno, *article on* Adorno's Philosophy of Music

Harvey Hix
Professor, Department of Liberal Arts, Kansas City Art Institute
Poetics

Anne Hollander
Writer, New York
Fashion, *articles on* Dress in the World *and* La Haute Couture

Elizabeth Hollander
Doctoral candidate in English, City University of New York
Artists' Models; Oscar Wilde

John Hollander
Sterling Professor of English, Yale University
Ecphrasis

Martha Hollander
Assistant Professor of Art History, New College, Hofstra University
Baroque Aesthetics

Michael Ann Holly
Professor of Art History, University of Rochester
Erwin Panofsky

Robert C. Holub
Professor of German, University of California, Berkeley
Reception Aesthetics

Gregg Horowitz
Assistant Professor of Philosophy, Vanderbilt University
Ernst Hans Josef Gombrich

Stephen Houlgate
Professor of Philosophy, University of Warwick, United Kingdom
Georg Wilhelm Friedrich Hegel, *article on* Survey of Thought

Tom Huhn
Visiting Assistant Professor of Philosophy, Wesleyan University
Theodor Wiesengrund Adorno, *article on* Adorno and Kant

John Dixon Hunt
Professor and Chairman, Department of Landscape Architecture and Regional Planning, University of Pennsylvania
Gardens, *historical overview article*

Ian Hunter
Associate Professor in Humanities and Queen Elizabeth II Fellow, School of Humanities, Griffith University, Nathan, Australia
Cultural Studies

Ann Hurley
Professor of English, Wagner College, Staten Island, New York
Ut Pictura Poesis

Eleftherios Ikonomou
Architect, London Architectural Association
August Schmarsow

Gary Iseminger
William H. Laird Professor of Philosophy and Liberal Arts, Cartleton College
Intention, *article on* Intentional Fallacy

Wolfgang Iser
Professor Emeritus of Literary Studies, Konstanz Universität; and Professor of English, University of California, Irvine
Fiction, *article on* Contemporary and Literary Account of the Fictive; Imagination, *article on* The Imaginary

Daniel Jacobson
Assistant Professor of Philosophy, College of Charleston
Philip Sidney

Dale Jacquette
Professor of Philosophy, Pennsylvania State University
Johann Wolfgang von Goethe

Christopher Janaway
Senior Lecturer in Philosophy, University of London
Plato, *article on* Survey of Thought

Richard Janko
Professor of Greek, University College London
Aristotle, *article on* Reception of Aristotle in Antiquity

I. C. Jarvie
Professor of Philosophy, University of York, Canada
Creativity, *article on* Explaining Creativity

Mark Jarzombek
Professor of Architecture, Massachusetts Institute of Technology
Leon Battista Alberti

Joan Jeffri
Director, Research Center for Arts and Culture, Columbia University; and Director, Program in Arts Administration, Teachers College, Columbia University
Artist, *article on* Sociology of the Artist

Galen A. Johnson
Professor and Chair, Department of Philosophy, University of Rhode Island
Maurice Merleau-Ponty

Jeannine Johnson
Visiting Instructor of English, Wake Forest University
New Criticism

Mark Johnson
Professor and Chair, Department of Philosophy, University of Oregon
Metaphor, *overview article*

Amelia Jones
Associate Professor of Art History, University of California, Riverside
Marcel Duchamp, *article on* En-Gendering of the Artistic Subject; Performance Art, *article on* Feminist Performance Art

Caroline A. Jones
Assistant Professor of Art History, Boston University
Abstract Expressionism

Peter Jones
Director, Institute for Advanced Studies in the Humanities, and Professor of Philosophy, University of Edinburgh
David Hume, *article on* Survey of Thought; Adam Smith

Guillemette Morel Journel
Editor, Les cahiers de la recherche architecturale, *Paris*
Le Corbusier

Deborah Jowitt
Dance Faculty, Tisch School of the Arts, New York University; Senior Dance Critic, The Village Voice
Modernism, *article on* Modern Dance

Peggy Kamuf
Professor of French and Comparative Literature, University of Southern California
Jacques Derrida, *article on* Derrida and Literature

Peter H. Karlen
Attorney, La Jolla, California
Moral Rights of Art, *article on* Moral Rights Legislation

Douglas Kellner
George F. Kneller Philosophy of Education Chair, University of California, Los Angeles
Jean Baudrillard; Fredric Jameson

Mary Kelly
Professor and Chair, Department of Art, School of the Arts and Architecture, University of California, Los Angeles
Contemporary Art, *article on* Images and Desire

Norman Kelvin
Professor of English, City College and Graduate Center, City University of New York
William Morris

Salim Kemal
Professor of Philosophy, University of Dundee, Scotland
Arab Aesthetics; Muḥammad al-Fārābī; Ibn Rushd; Ibn Sīnā; Immanuel Kant, *article on* Kant on Beauty

Grant Kester
Assistant Professor of Modern Art History and Theory, Washington State University
Raymond Williams

Peter Kivy
Professor of Philosophy, Rutgers University
Edmund Gurney

Jane Kneller
Assistant Professor of Philosophy, Colorado State University
Disinterestedness; Immanuel Kant, *article on* Feminism and Kantian Aesthetics

David Kolb
Charles A. Dana Professor of Philosophy, Bates College
Modernism, *article on* Modernity and Tradition in Architecture

Katherine Kolb
Lecturer, Department of French and Italian, University of Minnesota
Romanticism, *article on* Music

Nikolas Kompridis
Assistant Professor of Philosophy, Wilfrid Laurier University, Waterloo, Canada
Jürgen Habermas

Franz Koppe
Professor of Philosophy, Institute for Philosophy and Social Sciences, Hochschule der Künst, Berlin
Herbert Marcuse

Carolyn Korsmeyer
Associate Professor of Philosophy, State University of New York, Buffalo
Perception, *article on* Aesthetics of Perception; Taste, *article on* Modern and Recent History

Michael Krausz
Professor and Chair, Department of Philosophy, Bryn Mawr College
Interpretation, *article on* Interpretation in Art

Paul Oskar Kristeller
Woodbridge Professor Emeritus of Philosophy, Columbia University
Origins of Aesthetics, *historical and conceptual overview article*

Lucian Krukowski
Professor of Philosophy, Washington University, St. Louis
Abstraction; Formalism, *conceptual and historical overview article*

Michael Kubovy
Professor of Psychology, University of Virginia
Perspective, *article on* Psychology of Perspective

Margaret P. Kuhns
Adjunct Clinical Associate, Psychology Doctoral Program, Pace University
Sigmund Freud, *article on* Survey of Thought

Richard Kuhns
Professor Emeritus of Philosophy, Columbia University
Augustine; Sigmund Freud, *article on* Survey of Thought; Katharsis; Karl Mannheim; Tragedy, *article on* Freud on Tragedy; Donald Woods Winnicott

Peter Lamarque
Professor of Philosophy, University of Hull
Truth

George P. Landow
Professor of English and Art History, Brown University
Hypertext

Berel Lang
Professor of Philosophy, State University of New York, Albany
Marxism, *historical and conceptual overview article;* Style

Neil Larsen
Associate Professor of Spanish and Classics, University of California, Davis
Marxism, *article on* Marxism and Materialism

Thomas Leddy
Professor of Philosophy, San Jose State University
Essentialism, *article on* Anti-Essentialism

Richard Lehv
Attorney, New York
Law and Art, *article on* Trademarks and Art

Barbara Lekatsas
Professor of Comparative Literature, Hofstra University
André Breton

Jerrold Levinson
Professor of Philosophy, University of Maryland, College Park
Arthur Schopenhauer

Tamara Levitz
Associate Professor of Musicology, McGill University
Igor Fedorovich Stravinsky

Edward A. Lippman
Professor Emeritus of Music, Columbia University
Music, *historical overview article*

Rosemary Lloyd
Chair, Department of French and Italian, Indiana University, Bloomington
Stéphane Mallarmé

Patrizia Lombardo
Professor of French and Comparative Literature, Université de Genève
Hippolyte Adolphe Taine

Dominic M. McIver Lopes
Associate Professor of Philosophy, Indiana University, Kokomo
Representation, *article on* Depiction

Renée Lorraine
Professor of Music, University of Tennessee, Chattanooga
Music, *article on* Music and Feminism

Tommy Lott
Professor of Philosophy, San Jose State University
Alain Leroy Locke

Colin A. Lyas
Senior Lecturer in Philosophy, Lancaster University, United Kingdom
Benedetto Croce; Giovanni Gentile; Luigi Pareyson

Bernd Magnus
Professor of Philosophy and Humanities, University of California, Riverside
Friedrich Wilhelm Nietzsche, *article on* Survey of Thought

Rudolf Makkreel
Professor of Philosophy, Emory University
Wilhelm Dilthey; Immanuel Kant, *article on* Kant and Hermeneutics

Harry F. Mallgrave
Senior Research Fellow, Getty Research Institute for the History of Art and the Humanities
Gottfried Semper

Avishai Margalit
Professor of Philosophy, Center for Rationality and Interactive Decision Theory, Hebrew University of Jerusalem
Nelson Goodman, *article on* Survey of Thought

Joseph Margolis
Laura H. Carnell Professor of Philosophy, Temple University
Historicism, *article on* Historicism and Philosophy; Ontology of Art, *article on* Historical Ontology

Sally Markowitz
Professor of Philosophy, Willamette University
Edward Bullough

György Márkus
Professor of General Philosophy, University of Sydney
György Lukács

Richard Martin
Curator, Costume Institute, Metropolitan Museum of Art, New York
Fashion, *article on* Fashion as Art

Robert L. Martin
Professor of Philosophy and Music and Dean of Graduate Studies, Bard College
Ontology of Art, *article on* Ontology of Music

Colin Martindale
Professor of Psychology, University of Maine
Empirical Aesthetics

Joseph Masheck
Professor of Art History, Hofstra University
Rudolf Wittkower

Paul Mattick
Associate Professor of Philosophy, Adelphi University
Pierre Bourdieu, *article on* Survey of Thought; Ideology

Carol Mavor
Associate Professor of Art, University of North Carolina, Chapel Hill
Obscenity, *article on* Obscenity in Art

Gita May
Professor of French and Romance Philology, Columbia University
Jean Le Rond D'Alembert; Denis Diderot, *article on* Survey of Thought; French Aesthetics, *article on* Eighteenth-Century French Aesthetics

Patrick Maynard
Associate Professor of Philosophy, University of Western Ontario
Photography, *article on* Photography and Technology

Robert McCarter
Professor and Chair, Department of Architecture, University of Florida
Frank Lloyd Wright

Peter McCormick
Professor of Philosophy, University of Ottawa
Fiction, *historical and conceptual overview article*

Thomas McEvilley
Distinguished Lecturer in Art History, Rice University
Contemporary Art, *article on* Postmodern Transformation of Art

Indra Kagis McEwen
Faculty Lecturer, Department of Art History, McGill University
Architecture, *article on* Early Greek Aesthetics

Graham McFee
Lecturer, Chelsea School of Physical Education, Sports Science, Dance and Leisure, University of Brighton
Criticism, *article on* Dance Criticism; Dance, *article on* Contemporary Thought

Reginald McGinnis
Associate Professor of French and Italian, University of Arizona
Irony

Ralph McInerny
Professor of Philosophy, Jacques Maritain Center, University of Notre Dame
Jacques Maritain

Sheila McTighe
Assistant Professor of Art History, Barnard College, Columbia University
Nicolas Poussin

Françoise Meltzer
Chair and Professor of Comparative Literature and Professor of French and Divinity, University of Chicago
Originality, *article on* Originality in Literature

Stephen Melville
Professor of History of Art, Ohio State University
Jacques Derrida, *article on* Survey of Thought; Gaze; Clement Greenberg; Jacques Marie Lacan, *article on* Survey of Thought; Metonymy

Christoph Menke
Associate Professor of Philosophy, Graduate Faculty, New School for Social Research
Theodor Wiesengrund Adorno, *article on* Adorno's Dialectic of Appearance

Detlef Mertins
Assistant Professor of Architecture, School of Architecture and Landscape Architecture, University of Toronto
Bauhaus; Sigfried Giedion

Paul Messaris
Professor of Communications, Annenberg School of Communications, University of Pennsylvania
Film, *article on* Visual Literacy

Kerstin Mey
Lecturer in History and Theory of Art, Duncan of Jordanstone College of Art and Design, University of Dundee, Scotland
Sculpture

Christian Michel
Professor of History of Modern Art, Université de Paris X, Nanterre
Charles-Nicolas Cochin

Robin Middleton
Professor of Art History, Columbia University
Jean-Nicolas-Louis Durand

James Miller
Faculty Professor of Art, University of Western Ontario
Politics and Art, *article on* AIDS, Aesthetics, and Activism

Mara Miller
Research Fellow in Art History, Emory University
Gardens, *article on* Gardens as Art

William J. Mitchell
Professor of Architecture and Media Arts and Sciences and Dean, School of Architecture and Planning, Massachusetts Institute of Technology
Digital Media, *article on* The Postphotographic Image

Michael Mitias
Professor and Chair, Department of Philosophy, Millsaps College, Jackson, Mississippi
Mikel Dufrenne

Jeff Mitscherling
Associate Professor of Philosophy, University of Guelph, Canada
Roman Witold Ingarden

Ronald Moore
Associate Professor of Philosophy, University of Washington
Education, Aesthetic, *article on* History of Aesthetic Education; Moral Rights of Art, *historical and conceptual overview article;* Ugliness

James M. Moran
Doctoral Candidate in Critical Studies of Cinema and Television, University of Southern California
Video

Julius Moravcsik
Professor of Philosophy, Stanford University
Plato, *articles on* Plato on the Effects of Art *and* Plato and Modern Aesthetics

Robert P. Morgan
Professor of Music, Yale University
Arnold Franz Walter Schoenberg

John Morreall
Professor of Religious Studies, Univeristy of South Florida
Comics

Mary Mothersill
Professor Emerita of Philosophy, Barnard College, Columbia University
David Hume, *article on* "Of the Standard of Taste"

Keith Moxey
Professor of Art History, Barnard College, Columbia University
Canon, *article on* Politicizing the Canon in Art History

Myroslava M. Mudrak
Associate Professor in the History of Art, Ohio State University
Suprematism

Daniel Joseph Nadenicek
Director, Center for Studies in Landscape History, and Associate Professor of Landscape Architecture, Pennsylvania State University
Landscape, *article on* Landscape Architecture

Jean-Jacques Nattiez
Professor of Musicology, Université de Montréal
Semiotics, *article on* Semiology of Music

Josefine Nauckhoff
Assistant Professor of Philosophy, Wake Forest University
Archibald Alison; Thomas Reid

Alex Neill
Lecturer, Department of Moral Philosophy, University of Saint Andrews, Scotland
Tragedy, *article on* Hume on Tragedy

John Neubauer
Professor of Comparative Literature, Universiteit van Amsterdam
Novalis

Horace Newcomb
F. J. Heyne Centennial Professor in Communication, University of Texas, Austin
Television, *overview article*

H. B. Nisbet
Vice-Master, Department of Modern Languages, University of Cambridge
Gotthold Ephraim Lessing

Mignon Nixon
Lecturer in the History of American Art, Courtauld Institute of Art, University of London
Louise Bourgeois

David Novitz
Reader in Philosophy, University of Canterbury, New Zealand
Epistemology and Aesthetics

Ōhashi Ryōsuke
Professor of Philosophy and Aesthetics, Kyoto Institute of Technology
Japanese Aesthetics, *article on* Kire and Iki

Jeffrey K. Olick
Assistant Professor of Sociology, Columbia University
Popular Culture

Margaret Olin
Associate Professor of Art History, Theory and Criticism, School of the Art Institute of Chicago
Alois Riegl

Kelly Oliver
Associate Professor of Philosophy, University of Texas, Austin
Julia Kristeva

Stein Haugom Olsen
Chair Professor of Humanities and Director, School of General Education, Lingnan College, Hong Kong
Appreciation; Literature, *article on* Literary Aesthetics; Truth

Michael Orwicz
Professor of Art History, University of Connecticut, Storrs
Criticism, *article on* Art Criticism

Jerry Palmer
Professor of Communications, London Guildhall University
Design

Nickolas Pappas
Associate Professor of Philosophy, City College, City University of New York
Beauty, *article on* Classical Concepts

Esther Pasztory
Professor of Art History and Archaeology, Columbia University
Pre-Columbian Aesthetics

Thomas Pavel
Professor of Comparative Literature and Romance Languages and Literatures, Princeton University
Classicism

Geoffrey Payzant
Professor of Philosophy, University of Toronto
Eduard Hanslick

Joan Crystal Pearlman
Independent scholar, New York
Outsider Art

Max Pensky
Associate Professor of Philosophy, State University of New York, Binghamton
Walter Benjamin, *article on* Survey of Thought

Marjorie Perloff
Sadie Dernham Patek Professor of Humanities, Stanford University
Collage, *article on* Collage and Poetry; Gertrude Stein

Gloria Phares
Attorney, Paul, Hastings, Janofsky, & Walker, New York
Appropriation, *article on* Appropriation Art and Copyright Law

Carl Plantinga
Professor of Theatre Arts, Hollins College, Roanoke, Virginia
Film, *article on* Film and Documentary

Arkady Plotnitsky
Visiting Associate Professor of Literature, Duke University
Mathematics and Aesthetics; Science and Aesthetics, *conceptual and historical overview article*

Christine Poggi
Associate Professor of Art History, University of Pennsylvania
Collage, *article on* "The Pasted-Paper Revolution" Revisited

Larsen Powell
Instructor of German, Barnard College, Columbia University
Pierre Boulez

Donald Preziosi
Professor of Art History, University of California, Los Angeles
Museums, *article on* Museology

Stephen Prince
Associate Professor of Communication Studies, Virginia Polytechnic Institute and State University
Film, *article on* Film and Ideology

Jessica Prinz
Associate Professor of English, Ohio State University
Discourse

Thomas Puttfarken
Professor of History and Theory of Art, University of Essex, United Kingdom
Roger de Piles

Mel Ramsden
Artist, London
Conceptual Art, *article on* History of the Unformed

Herman Rapaport
Helen DeRoy Professor of English, Wayne State University
Jacques Marie Lacan, *article on* Visual and Literary Arts

Mary Rawlinson
Associate Professor of Philosophy, State University of New York, Stony Brook
Michel Foucault

Christopher Reed
Assistant Professor of Art History, Lake Forest College
Bloomsbury Group; Gay Aesthetics

Cedric D. Reverand II
Professor of English, University of Wyoming, Laramie
John Dryden

Michele H. Richman
Associate Professor of French, University of Pennsylvania
Georges Bataille

Aaron Ridley
Senior Lecturer in Philosophy, University of Southampton, United Kingdom
Emotions, *article on* Emotions and Music; Richard Wagner

Charles A. Riley II
Associate Professor of English, Baruch College, City University of New York; Editor in Chief, WE magazine
Color, *article on* Color in the Arts

Bruce Robbins
Professor of English and Comparative Literature, Rutgers University
Literature, *article on* What is Literature?

Hilary Robinson
Lecturer in the History and Theory of Art, University of Ulster at Belfast
Luce Irigaray

D. N. Rodowick
Professor of English and Visual/Cultural Studies, University of Rochester
Jacques Derrida, *article on* Derrida and Kant

Mark Rollins
Associate Professor of Philosophy, Washington University, Saint Louis
Attitude, *article on* Pictorial Attitude; Perception, *article on* Picture Perception

Holmes Rolston III
University Distinguished Professor, Colorado State University
Landscape, *article on* Landscape from the Eighteenth Century to the Present

Carlin Romano
Professor of Philosophy, Bennington College; literary critic, Philadelphia Inquirer
Umberto Eco

David Rosand
Meyer Schapiro Professor of Art History, Columbia University
Meyer Schapiro

Jason M. Rosenfeld
Adjunct Assistant Professor of Fine Arts, New York University
Joshua Reynolds

Mark Roskill
Professor of History of Modern Art, University of Massachusetts, Amherst
Cubism; Wassily Kandinsky

Stephanie Ross
Associate Professor of Philosophy, University of Missouri, Saint Louis
Picturesque

Stephen David Ross
Professor of Philosophy, State University of New York, Binghamton
Beauty, *conceptual and historical overview article*

Cynthia Rostankowski
Associate Professor of Philosophy, San Jose State University
Children's Art

Albert Rothenberg
Clinical Professor of Psychiatry, Harvard University
Creativity, *article on* Creativity and Psychology

William Rothman
Professor of Film, School of Communications, University of Miami
Stanley Cavell, *article on* Cavell and Film

Fred L. Rush, Jr.
Assistant Professor of Philosophy, University of Kansas
Georg Wilhelm Friedrich Hegel, *article on* Hegel's Conception of the End of Art; Richard Payne Knight; Jean Paul

John Paul Russo
Professor of English, University of Miami
Ivor Armstrong Richards

John Russon
Assistant Professor of Philosophy, Pennsylvania State University
Plotinus

Herman Saatkamp, Jr.
Professor, Department of Humanities in Medicine, Texas A&M University
George Santayana

Warren Sack
Research Assistant and doctoral candidate, Media Laboratory, Massachusetts Institute of Technology
Artificial Intelligence and Aesthetics

Baldine Saint Girons
Professor of Philosophy, Université de Paris X, Nanterre
Sublime, *article on* The Sublime from Longinus to Montesquieu

Yuriko Saito
Associate Professor of Liberal Arts, Rhode Island School of Design
Japanese Aesthetics, *historical overview article;* Nature, *article on* Japanese Aesthetic Appreciation of Nature

Gabriela Sakamoto
Doctoral candidate in Philosophy, University of Chicago
Representation, *article on* Resemblance

Lucia Saks
Associate Professor of Communications, Rand Afrikaans University, South Africa
Camp

David Z. Saltz
Assistant Professor of Drama, University of Georgia
Theater

Crispin Sartwell
Assistant Professor of Philosophy, University of Alabama, Tuscaloosa
Appropriation, *historical overview article;* Art for Art's Sake

David Saunders
Dean Faculty of Arts, Griffith University, Nathan, Australia
Obscenity, *article on* Aesthetics in Obscenity Law

Haun Saussy
Associate Professor of Asian Languages and Comparative Literature and Chair, Department of Asian Languages, Stanford University
Chinese Aesthetics, *historical overview article*

Barbara Savedoff
Associate Professor of Philosophy, Bernard Baruch College, City University of New York
Photography, *article on* Photography and Digital Technology

Ofelia Schutte
Professor of Philosophy, University of Florida, Gainesville
Latin American Aesthetics, *article on* Twentieth-Century Latin American Aesthetics

Mitchell Schwarzer
Associate Professor of Architectural History and Theory, California College of Arts and Crafts, San Francisco
Karl Gottlieb Wilhelm Botticher

Martin Seel
Professor of Philosophy, Justus-Liebig-Universität Giessen
Nature, *article on* Aesthetics of Nature and Ethics

Grace Seiberling
Associate Professor of Art History and Visual and Cultural Studies, University of Rochester
Art Market

David I. Seiple
Independent scholar, New York
John Dewey, *article on* Experience and the Organic Unity of Artworks

Azade Seyhan
Fairbank Professor in the Humanities, Professor of German and Comparative Literature, and Chair, Department of German, Bryn Mawr College
August Wilhelm von Schlegel

Elinor Shaffer
Visiting Fellow, All Souls College, University of Oxford
Samuel Taylor Coleridge

David Grahame Shane
Adjunct Professor of Architecture, Graduate School of Architecture, Planning, and Preservation, Columbia University
Louis Isadore Kahn

Daniel Shapiro
Attorney, New York
Law and Art, *overview article and article on* Cultural Property

Gary Shapiro
Professor of Philosophy and Tucker-Boatwright Professor in the Humanities, University of Richmond
French Aesthetics, *article on* Contemporary Painting Theory; Friedrich Wilhelm Nietzsche, *article on* Nietzsche and Visuality

Fadlou Shehadi
Professor Emeritus of Philosophy, Rutgers University
Islamic Aesthetics, *article on* Islamic Music

Bernard D. Sherman
Independent scholar, Fairfield, Iowa
Authenticity, *article on* Authenticity in Music

Richard Shiff
Professor of Art and Art History, University of Texas, Austin
Originality, *article on* Originality in the Visual Arts; Photography, *article on* Catachresis

Larry Shiner
Professor and Chair, Department of Philosophy, Sangamon State University, Springfield, Illinois
Craft; Folk Art

Roger A. Shiner
Professor Emeritus of Philosophy, University of Alberta
Law and Art, *article on* Law and Literature

Ellis Shookman
Associate Professor of German, Dartmouth College
Johann Caspar Lavater

Katy Siegel
Assistant Professor of Art, University of Memphis
Pop Art, *overview article*

Anita Silvers
Professor of Philosophy, San Francisco State University
Canon, *article on* The Canon in Aesthetics; Feminism, *overview article*

Stuart Sim
Professor of English Studies, University of Sunderland, United Kingdom
Structuralism

Barbara Herrnstein Smith
Braxton Craven Professor of Comparative Literature and English, Duke University
Evaluation, *article on* Cultural Evaluation; Value

Ralph Smith
Professor of Cultural and Educational Policy, University of Illinois, Urbana-Champaign; and Editor, Journal of Aesthetic Education
Education, Aesthetic, *article on* Contemporary Aesthetic Education

Roch C. Smith
Professor of French, University of North Carolina, Greensboro
Gaston Bachelard

John Smylie
Editorial Assistant, Journal of Philosophy, Columbia University
Comics

John Vignaux Smyth
Head, Department of English, Northeast Louisiana University
Irony

Joel Snyder
Professor and Chair, Department of Art History, University of Chicago
Photography, *overview article*

Robert Solomon
Professor of Philosophy, University of Texas, Austin
Emotions, *overview article*

Ruth Sonderegger
Lecturer in Philosophy, Freie Universität Berlin
Play

Priscilla Soucek
Professor of Fine Arts, Institute of Fine Arts, New York University
Islamic Aesthetics, *article on* Visual Experience in Islamic Culture

Catherine Soussloff
Associate Professor of Art History, University of California, Santa Cruz
Artist, *article on* History of the Concept of the Artist; Historicism, *article on* Historicism in Art History

John Spackman
Independent scholar, Middlebury, Vermont
Expression Theory of Art

Francis Sparshott
Professor Emeritus of Philosophy, University of Toronto
Dance, *historical and conceptual overview article*

Andreas Speer
Associate Professor of Philosophy, Thomas-Institut, Universität zu Köln
Thomas Aquinas

Ellen Handler Spitz
Lecturer on Aesthetics in Psychiatry, New York Hospital–Cornell Medical Center
Sigmund Freud, *article on* Pathography; Melanie Klein

Gayatri Chakravorty Spivak
Avalon Foundation Professor in Humanities, Columbia University
Jacques Derrida, *article on* Derrida and Deconstruction

Robert Stecker
Associate Professor of Philosophy, Central Michigan University
Relativism

Peter Steiner
Associate Professor of Slavic Literature, University of Pennsylvania
Prague School

Josef Stern
Associate Professor of Philosophy, University of Chicago
Metaphor, *article on* Metaphor and Philosophy of Language

Randall Stevenson
Reader in English Literature, University of Edinburgh
Modernism, *article on* Modern Literature

John Stopford
Visiting Lecturer in Philosophy, Universität Hannover
Politics and Aesthetics, *article on* Culture and Political Theory

Nancy S. Struever
Professor of History, Humanities Center, Johns Hopkins University
Rhetoric, *historical and conceptual overview article*

Marita Sturken
Assistant Professor of Communication, Annenberg School for Communication, University of Southern California
Monuments, *historical overview article*

David Summers
William R. Kenan, Jr., Professor of the History of Art, University of Virginia
Origins of Aesthetics, *article on* History of Aisthēsis; Metaphor, *article on* Metaphor and Art History

Kevin W. Sweeney
Associate Professor and Chair, Department of Philosophy, University of Tampa
Alexander Gerard

Jacques Taminiaux
Adelmann Professor of Philosophy, Boston College
Martin Heidegger, *article on* Philosophical Heritage in Heidegger's Concept of Art

Paul Taylor
Associate Professor of Philosophy, University of Cape Town
Intention, *overview article*

Elizabeth Telfer
Reader in Philosophy, University of Glasgow
Food

Benjamin R. Tilghman
Professor Emeritus of Philosophy, Kansas State University
Ludwig Josef Johann Wittgenstein, *article on* Survey of Thought

Marianna DeMarco Torgovnick
Professor and Chair, Department of English, Duke University
Criticism, *article on* Cultural Criticism

Dabney Townsend
Professor of Philosophy, University of Texas, Arlington
Anthony Ashley Cooper; Francis Hutcheson; Joseph Priestley; Taste, *article on* Early History

Alan Trachtenberg
Neil Grey, Jr., Professor of English and American Studies, Yale University
Photography, *article on* Daguerreotype

Zev Trachtenberg
Associate Professor of Philosophy, University of Oklahoma
Jean-Jacques Rousseau

Leo Treitler
Distinguished Professor of Music, Graduate School and University Center, City University of New York
Notation, *article on* Musical Notation

Richard Tristman
Independent scholar, New York
Canon, *historical and conceptual overview article*

Willis Truitt
Professor of Philosophy, University of South Florida
Max Raphael

Yuri Tsivian
Associate Professor of Film, University of Chicago
Sergei Mikhailovich Eisenstein

Makoto Ueda
Professor of Japanese, Stanford University
Haiku

Yayoi Uno
Assistant Professor of Music Theory, University of Colorado, Boulder
Aleatoric Processes

Julie Van Camp

Associate Professor of Philosophy, California State University, Long Beach
National Endowment of the Arts, *historical survey article and article on* Controversies; Ontology of Art, *article on* Ontology of Dance

Robert Jan van Pelt

Professor of Cultural History, University of Waterloo, Canada
Historicism, *article on* Historicism and Architecture

Michael G. Vater

Associate Professor of Philosophy, Marquette University
Friedrich Wilhelm Joseph von Schelling

Donald Verene

Charles Howard Candler Professor of Metaphysics and Moral Philosophy, Emory University
Ernst Cassirer; Giovanni Battista Vico

Ian Verstegen

Doctoral candidate in Art History, Temple University
Rudolf Arnheim, *article on* Survey of Thought

Anne Vila

Associate Professor of French, University of Wisconsin, Madison
Étienne Bonnot de Condillac; Sensibilité

Loïc Wacquant

Associate Professor of Sociology, University of California, Berkeley, and Research Associate, Center for European Sociology, Collège de France
Pierre Bourdieu, *article on* Artistic Field

Sylvia Walsh

Adjunct Professor of Philosophy, Stetson University
Søren Aabye Kierkegaard

Kenneth W. Warren

Associate Professor of English, University of Chicago
Harlem Renaissance

Samuel Weber

Professor of English and Comparative Literature, University of California, Los Angeles
Walter Benjamin, *article on* Benjamin's Writing Style

Joel Weinsheimer

Professor of English, University of Minnesota
Hans-Georg Gadamer, *article on* Gadamer and Aesthetics

Marjorie Welish

Adjunct Associate Professor of Graduate Fine Arts, Pratt Institute, New York
Donald Judd; Ad Reinhardt

Carroll William Westfall

Professor of Architectural History, University of Virginia
Historicism, *article on* Historicism and Architecture

Kenneth R. Westphal

Associate Professor of Philosophy, University of New Hampshire
Immanuel Kant, *article on* Kant on the Sublime

Samuel C. Wheeler III

Professor of Philosophy, University of Connecticut
Metaphor, *article on* Derrida and de Man on Metaphor

Cynthia White

Independent scholar, Washington, Maine
John Ruskin

Harrison Colyar White

Giddings Professor of Sociology, Columbia University
John Ruskin

James Williams

Lecturer in Philosophy, University of Dundee, Scotland
Gilles Deleuze; Jean-François Lyotard

Robert Williams

Associate Professor of History of Art and Architecture, University of California, Santa Barbara
Giorgio Vasari

Catherine Wilson

Professor of Philosophy, University of Alberta
Fiction, *article on* Epistemology of Fiction

Mary Wiseman

Professor of Philosophy, Brooklyn College, City University of New York
Roland Barthes; Poststructuralism

Nicholas Wolterstorff

Noah Porter Professor of Philosophical Theology, Yale University
Religion and Aesthetics, *overview article;* Universals

Christopher S. Wood

Associate Professor of History of Art, Yale University
Iconoclasm and Iconophobia; Perspective, *overview article*

Paul Woodruff

Professor of Philosophy, University of Texas, Austin
Plato, *articles on* Plato on Mimēsis *and* Plato's Use of Poetry

Michael J. Wreen

Associate Professor of Philosophy, Marquette University
Monroe C. Beardsley

Kathleen Wright

Professor of Philosophy, Haverford College
Hans-Georg Gadamer, *article on* Survey of Thought; Martin Heidegger, *article on* Heidegger and Hölderlin

Christoph Wulf

Professor, Institute for Sports Science, Freie Universität Berlin
Mimesis

Sylvia Wynter

Professor Emerita of Spanish and Portuguese and Afro-American Studies, Stanford University
Black Aesthetic

Robert J. Yanal

Professor of Philosophy, Wayne State University
Institutional Theory of Art

Wai-lim Yip
Professor of Chinese and Comparative Literature, University of California, San Diego
Daoist Aesthetics

James E. Young
Professor of English and Judaic Studies, University of Massachusetts, Amherst
Monuments, *article on* Twentieth-Century Countermonuments

Julian Young
Senior Lecturer in Philosophy, University of Auckland, New Zealand
Friedrich Wilhelm Nietzsche, *article on* Nietzsche, Schopenhauer, and Disinterestedness

Jan Ziolkowski
Professor of Comparative Literature and Medieval Latin and Chair, Department of Comparative Literature, Harvard University
Erick Auerbach

Vera Zolberg
Senior Lecturer in Sociology, Graduate Faculty, New School for Social Research
Sociology of Art

Günter Zöller
Professor and Chair, Department of Philosophy, University of Iowa
Joseph Beuys; Immanuel Kant, *article on* History of Kantian Aesthetics

Lambert Zuidervaart
Professor of Philosophy, Calvin College, Grand Rapids, Michigan
Theodor Wiesengrund Adorno, *article on* Survey of Thought

Marina van Zuylen
Associate Professor of French, Bard College
Difficulty, Aesthetics of

INDEX

Note: Volume numbers are printed in boldface type, followed by a colon and relevant page numbers. Page numbers printed in boldface indicate a major discussion; those in italics refer to illustrations.

ENCYCLOPEDIA OF AESTHETICS

ENCYCLOPEDIA OF

AESTHETICS

MICHAEL KELLY

Editor in Chief

Volume 3

OXFORD UNIVERSITY PRESS

New York   1998   Oxford

OXFORD UNIVERSITY PRESS

Oxford   New York
Athens   Auckland   Bangkok   Bogotá
Buenos Aires   Calcutta   Cape Town   Chennai
Dar es Salaam   Delhi   Florence   Hong Kong   Istanbul
Karachi   Kuala Lumpur   Madrid   Melbourne   Mexico City
Mumbai   Nairobi   Paris   São Paulo   Singapore
Taipei   Tokyo   Toronto   Warsaw

and associated companies in
Berlin   Ibadan

Copyright © 1998 by Oxford University Press, Inc.

Published by Oxford University Press, Inc.,
198 Madison Avenue, New York, New York 10016
http://www.oup-usa.org

Oxford is a registered trademark of Oxford University Press

Library of Congress Cataloging-in-Publication Data
Encyclopedia of aesthetics / editor in chief, Michael Kelly.
p.   cm
Includes bibliographical references and index.
1. Aesthetics—Encyclopedias.   I. Kelly, Michael, 1953–
BH56.E53   1998   111'.85'03—dc21   98-18741 CIP
ISBN 0-19-511307-1 (set)
ISBN 0-19-512647-5 (vol. 3)

Printing (last digit): 9 8 7 6 5 4 3 2 1

Printed in the United States of America
on acid-free paper

J

CONTINUED

JAZZ. By the end of the second decade of the twentieth century, a new musical art form arose in America. No flash in the pan, jazz remains a living, evolving music, garnering the attention of music lovers around the world. Groaning shelves continue to fill with books devoted to histories and criticism of all eras of jazz. For the standard European "fine" arts, there exists a distinguishable body of literature devoted to aesthetic theory. Jazz theory exists, to be sure, but it is often embedded in literature that is primarily biographical, educational, journalistic, historical, or critical in nature. Authors who command respect—in various quarters—include André Hodeir, Winthrop Sargeant, Martin Williams, Marshall Stearns, A. B. Spellman, Mark Gridley, Stanley Crouch, James Lincoln Collier, Frank Tirro, and Gary Giddens. Among works distinguished for their full-fledged analytic and historical scholarship are Gunther Schuller's two volumes, *Early Jazz: Its Roots and Musical Development* (New York, 1968) and *The Swing Era* (New York, 1989).

Afropurism. Two questions chronically arise in discussions of jazz, typically intertwined: *Can* white people play the music authentically? Do they have a legitimate *right* to play it? Curiously, it was white writers who, in the early years, first gave ammunition for a negative answer to the first question. Influential critics of the thirties and forties argued that the purest jazz is the kind that lies closest to its African roots. This claim they typically combined with a characteristic picture of the African "soul." The Afropurists saw the jazz improvisation, for instance, as a manifestation of untrammeled spontaneity, devoid of the benefits of training and skill, and undistorted by European musical culture. For such a view, see *Jazz from the Congo to the Metropolitan* (1944) by the French critic Robert Goffin who believed that the "real" jazz musician is able to "whip himself up" into a complete state of primitive "frenzy" as he plays.

It is likely—although not certain—that some features of jazz can be traced in a fairly linear way to African roots. For instance, the jazz "riff," as well as the practice of "trading fours"—where a pair of improvisers play four-bar segments in alternation—may have their antecedent in the call-and-response format of African sources of the music. Additionally, the master drummer's trick of trying to draw others off the beat in western African music may have affinities with similar practices in jazz. Finally, it is possible that African roots also can be detected in what Schuller calls the "democratization" of note values (Schuller, 1968, pp. 15–16). By boosting many weak beats up and making them nearly equivalent to, or even stronger than, strong beats, players partly satisfy, within the alien framework of the European metrical system, the impulse to generate self-propelled African polyrhythms. In many fundamentals, however—as just suggested—African music is quite different both from European music and from jazz.

In most European concert music, rhythm imposes order on sounds that form musical episodes and thereby assists, through metrical contrast, in the generation of large dramatic designs—as exemplified by the broad metrical changes in a classical symphony. By contrast, although African music may gradually change rhythmically over the course of a "performance," it does not make use of dramatic shifts from one rhythmic pattern to another as an organizational principle. Instead, rhythm is an engine for the liberation of musical values on a continuous basis. In European music, rhythmic deviations only make sense given measures divided with regularity into certain numbers of beats. Within this context, such music can, of course, be polyrhythmic—as when three beats are sounded against four. But African music begins with the idea of superimposed rhythmic patterns. This gives rise to hierarchies of such complex interaction that a time lapse between a beat in one line may regularly occur only a fraction of a second after the occurrence of a beat in a parallel line without the former becoming absorbed into the orbit of the latter.

André Hodeir made a strong case about the differences between African and European music and jazz in his *Hommes et problémes du jazz: Suivi de la religion du jazz* (1954), which was translated in 1956 by David Noakes as *Jazz: Its Evolution and Essence*. For Hodeir, Afropurists lay themselves open to rebuttal in the form of a *reductio:* to be consistent, Afropurists should legislate against every non-African element in jazz. In positive terms, Hodeir's central point is that with exceptions that lie at opposite ends of a spectrum, the sources of jazz music, whether European or African, are, in jazz, transfigured by their interaction with each other. Distinctive qualities of jazz are emergent results of the interplay of originally distinct practices.

A good example of the generality is "blue" tonality, that is, the tendency, in different degrees, to flatten notes at the third, seventh, and sometimes fifth intervals of the tempered scale, thereby generating the so-called blue notes. At least part of the explanation of this striking feature of jazz is probably the interaction of distinct scalar practices, one of which tends toward pentatonism. (See, e.g., Gridley, 1988, pp. 52–53; Stearns, 1956, p. 7; and Hodeir, 1956, p. 42.) The idea is that when African-Americans were taught songs in Western scales, the overprinting of the one tonality by the other resulted in the tendency to flatten the notes. From a purist's standpoint, blue notes are, as Hodeir puts it, "just as *impure* as the 'altered notes' of modern jazz seem to the present-day believer in 'original purity'" (p. 42).

Much the same could be argued for jazz improvisation. The sheer wonder at the spectacle of players making up music while playing it is central to our interest in jazz. The purist's appeal to an indefinable "primitive" capacity native to African musicians is probably unfounded, however. The exact steps by which jazz improvisation as we know it originated constitute a question still shrouded in mystery. Early sources of the modern practice may be discerned in a nineteenth-century article on African-American singing styles by Jeannette Robinson Murphy in *Popular Science Monthly* (1899). Murphy describes how people actually sang the material in the *Jubilee* and *Hampton Song Books*: The singer is supposed to "make his voice exceedingly nasal and undulating." Around "every prominent note he must place a variety of small notes, called 'trimmings.'" He "should carry over his breath from line to line and from verse to verse." He "must often drop from a high note to a very low one; he must be very careful to divide many of his monosyllabic words in two syllables, placing a forcible accent on the last one, so that 'dead' will be 'da-*ade*,' 'back' becomes 'ba-*ack*,' 'chain' becomes 'cha-*ain*.'" Furthermore, singing takes place, so to speak, between the notes, in both a rhythmic and a scalar sense. Words are often added between notes or phrases (e.g., "tell me 'bout it"), or are repeated over and over again, in a mantra-like way.

These practices are still identifiable in African-American church music, as well as in blues and jazz. The blues tradition restricted itself to altering the sound of a single sustained tone by varying the timing, timbre, volume, and pitch at various points during its sounding—or by toying with rhythms, for example, starting tones a bit earlier or later, repeating a tone several times instead of sounding it just once, or displacing a phrase rhythmically. Contrary to Afropurism, however, the full-fledged improvisatory practices that are distinctive in jazz cannot be clearly traced back to the earliest prototypes of the music. The Memphis clarinetist Buster Bailey said that although he was embellishing melodies in 1917–1918, he did not know then what was meant by "improvisation" (see Shapiro and Hentoff, 1955, pp. 77–78). Even when we turn to a slightly later period (e.g., the music of King Oliver's Creole Jazz Band), *free* is hardly the word we should use to describe the control exhibited by this band's playing. Although Oliver and his musicians did play brief "hot breaks," improvisation then was still restricted to rhythmically articulated paraphrases.

Although African music is Dionysian in its emphasis on music as a shared communal process, the jazz that comes from it is, in that same respect, much more Apollonian. In traditional African drum music, individualism is carefully hedged with dos and don'ts. Musical variation in traditional African music would be prized, not for its blatant individualism, but for its subtlety. Allowable changes in African drumming patterns were tolerated only within a complex and rigorous discipline (Hodeir, p. 42; Chernoff, 1979, is also a good antidote to common misconceptions about this matter). In jazz, however, risky and highly individualized additions and variations are not merely tolerated but encouraged. To such individualism, the Afropurist ought to object. Jazz improvisation as we know it did not exist in its prototypes.

This is made doubly convincing when we realize that jazz improvisation as it was known by 1930 depends on a harmonic organization of the musical material that is distinctively European. It is this organization that enables a jazz player to improvise on the harmonic changes that define a tune. On these harmonic matters, the Afropurist again faces a *reductio*. Purists who object to the more ambitious harmonic agendas of mid-century modern jazz have to face the fact that even King Oliver's early recordings—which supposedly do pass the purist's test—already contain "dangerous" diminished sevenths. Not even the music Murphy describes should be acceptable to the purist, since, by rights, the purist ought not to accept any chords at all in "real" jazz.

Similar comments apply to jazz melody. African melody does have distinctive features that partly find their way into jazz. For instance, jazz melody almost certainly reflects the peculiarly close relationship between speech and music in African practice. Many of the distortions that Hodeir classifies under *matière sonore* (sonority) undoubtedly reflect the African tie between speech and song. In jazz, horns are taught to speak—a fact that Duke Ellington made an essential part of his writing for "growling" brass instruments. (By a reverse twist, jazz singers learned to imitate growling horns.) Further, the center of gravity in European melody tends to fall at the end of the melodic phrase, typically leading to a climactic end point. In African music, the melodic burden tends to fall on the beginning, with a consequent tapering off, both in loudness and emotional intensity, toward the end of a phrase. Finally, unlike European melodies, African ones are typically "end-repeating." That is, when African melodies are varied, the part that changes is usually the beginning, whereas the endings remain comparatively similar to each other. Improvised choruses in jazz often reflect these latter two features. Nothing is clear-cut in this sphere, however. At one end of the spectrum—where lie the slow jazz ballads—the familiar beginning-middle-and-end structure of European melody looms larger. The generalization holds, however: without the interaction of African and European practices, the music of a paradigmatic jazz singer such as Billie Holiday could not be imagined.

One reason for the emergent character of jazz melody is that European melodic material is also skewed by other jazz qualities—which themselves represent the interaction of African and European qualities (e.g., jazz rhythm). The melodies characteristic of improvised jazz reflect the way players toy rhythmically with the musical line, for instance. Louis Armstrong could generate jazz interest in a melody, however paltry, by simply dancing around a single tone, or by ping-ponging a note back and forth within a single harmonic interval for several measures. If one listens to such a performance as either a straightforward European or African melody, one could hardly get the point of the effort.

Hodeir's argument against Afropurism, if sound, is equally telling against a view that seems, at first glance, to be the very opposite of Afropurism—namely, Europurism. It makes no more sense to say that in jazz we hear a genuinely African impulse breaking through the surface of a European interference than it does to say that we hear in it the European soul expressing itself in an alien African context. Hodeir's critique would apply, for instance, to Theodor Adorno's view that the genuine music in jazz is really European—albeit of a paltry sort. This comes out in Adorno's peculiar assumption that what we know as blue must simply be mistakes—presumably because they fall "within the cracks" of the keys on a tempered keyboard (Adorno, 1941, p. 26; for a clarifying recent study of some of the foregoing questions, see Rudinow, 1994).

Defining the Music. Most texts are agnostic about defining jazz, settling for a generous plurality of unrefined "views" on the matter. Partial exceptions to this are Joachim Ernst Berendt's *Das grosse Jazzbuch* (1981) and Schuller's *Early Jazz*. Jan Slawe's *Einführung in die Jazzmusic* (1948) is bolder. The definitions contained in these books, not surprisingly, have strong affinities with each other. Hodeir's account, however, stands out among the others for its severe essentialism. His theory reflects his critique of the Afropurist.

Hodeir's account of jazz is as striking for what it denies as for what it says. Jazz, he claims, is not defined by (1) a connection with "architecture," meaning, roughly, "form" (e.g., the sonata-allegro form, pp. 139–140), (2) its use of special metrical devices (pp. 140, 235), or (3) any special relationship to tonality (e.g., blues, pp. 140–143, 234). Finally, (4) it has, surprisingly, no essential connection with improvisation (pp. 80, 234–236). By the first point, Hodeir means that it is not part of jazz's telos to exploit musical form—as the European symphonic tradition has done. (The form most characteristic of the music—theme and variation—is a mere framework for other aims.) The second point, similarly, is

that, in jazz, the familiar family of meters in duple or march time used in jazz are put to specifically jazz uses. But what about Hodeir's third and fourth points?

For many, jazz seems unthinkable without its connection with blues tonality. Hodeir's defense of point (3) is simple: there are counterexamples to the supposed dependence of jazz on the blues—Coleman Hawkins's classic Victor recording of "Body and Soul," for instance (pp. 145, 235). As neat as Hodeir's argument is, it may not have put the issue to rest. He was not aware of Winthrop Sargeant's earlier study of the issue (Sargeant, 1975). Sargeant analyzed a set of recorded jazz pieces, many of which are not blues in the strict sense. He showed how even "in the most extended and florid solos" of these performances, "little melodic whirlpools will be found continuously centering about one or the other of . . . two tetrachordal groupings" (p. 168). It happens that when these tetrachords are put together, they make up the blues scale. Since Sargeant does not insist that this is so in every case, Hodeir's position may, technically, stand. Of course, Hodeir never denies that much of our jazz music is founded on blues tonality. Furthermore, it is not clear how to evaluate the putative counterexamples. A jazz performance devoid of blues tonality is not unrelated to the blues in the same sense that Mozart's *Il tesòro mio* is unrelated to the blues. If blue tonality is as endemic to the music as even Hodeir admits, then its *absence* in exceptional cases ought to have special significance. Some exceptions really may "prove" the rule, in short.

One way to disparage the role of improvisation in jazz music is to apply a criterion of "genuine" improvisation so strict that it can never be met in practice. (See Adorno, 1941, for an example of this kind of position.) In fact, of course, any reasonable theory about jazz improvisation has to acknowledge that improvisers do not simply take up instruments and improvise ex nihilo, but rather begin by mastering a repertoire of musical material, out of which they gradually learn to construct solos of their own. Jazz improvisers always, however, feel the call of a *secondary* regulative ideal to take serious risks. This secondary ideal is not jazz specific, by the way. It governs classical Iranian music, for example, where the "exceptional and unexpected is [most highly] valued" (Bruno Nettl, "'Musical Thinking' and 'Thinking about Music,'" *Journal of Aesthetics and Art Criticism* [winter 1994], p. 142).

Hodeir's argument that improvisation is not essential to jazz is, like his argument about the blues, simplicity itself: cases exist in which improvisation plays virtually no role, for example, the Ellington trumpet "concerto" for Charles "Cootie" Williams. If we construe *improvisation* narrowly, to include only extended *melodic* variations, such works may vindicate Hodeir's claim. Of course, if we count as improvisational all the impromptu inflections that give a performance such as Williams's much of its character, then perhaps the case is not a counterexample at all. The problem with this rebuttal, however, is that it construes improvisation so broadly that the concept could no longer be regarded as the relatively late phenomenon we have assumed it to be. Further, what if Williams plays these details the same way every time? Alternate recording "takes" tell us that as improvised as Jelly Roll Morton's band pieces sound, they were probably often worked out in advance. The matter is complex, in short—more so if we introduce one final consideration. Composed jazz has always sought to capture the characteristic "feel" of solo jazz performance. The pianist and composer George Russell has said that even if jazz is written out, it should sound "intuitive," that is, as though it is being improvised (quoted in Harrison, 1976, p. 61). Clearly, this is a concession to the centrality of improvisation in jazz. Finally, it should be noted that a possible explanation of Hodeir's position on the matter is that he is focused almost entirely on jazz recordings—a matter to which we shall return.

According to Hodeir, "jazz consists essentially of *an inseparable but extremely variable mixture of* . . . swing and the 'hot' manner of playing" (p. 240). The term *inseparable* here bears a bigger burden than might be gathered. For Hodeir, jazz cannot be defined simply by giving a list of necessary and sufficient conditions. A mere list, even if arguably complete, will leave us with a nagging question: what is it about the interaction of the factors that transforms them into jazz?

Along with a kind of forward momentum that Hodeir terms *drive,* hot playing includes certain aspects of the music's sonority. He provides no definition of sonority, except by ostention—for example, distorted timbres, unschooled portamenti, harmonics, and exaggerated dynamics—in short, features we recognize by their contrast with the "legitimate" sounds of European concert music. The famous growl brass effects of the Duke Ellington orchestra are paradigms.

The centerpiece of the definition is Hodeir's attempt to isolate the conditions of the first component, jazz rhythm. We earlier pointed out aspects of jazz rhythm that might be traceable in a linear way back to African music. What the purist does not acknowledge is that the European four-bar metric format—or some close analogue—is a necessary condition for the production of characteristically jazz rhythm. In other words, African and European rhythm practices dissolve into each other in jazz in a much more complete way than the linear tracings alone suggest. They make for what Hodeir calls swing. Hodeir explains swing with an infrastructure/superstructure model, according to which, in jazz, notes in the superstructure are eccentrically placed above a relatively steady rhythmic base in the infrastructure. The result of an effective placement of notes in the superstructure is that musical phrases are felt as moving independently of the underlying pulse and then as being recaptured by it, so that the strata catalyze each other. The relationship between tempo and swing can be modified by variations in rhythmic strategy—as when a soloist doubles his or her pace in relationship to an unchanging tempo in the rhythm section or maintains a slow tempo, but complicates his or her playing with quavers and semiquavers. Special interest can be aroused if the pulsation is not always beaten out explicitly, as in "stop-time breaks."

Hodeir's use of the term swing is a slightly technical one, obviously. An arranged jazz ensemble can have swing "feeling," if only because of its use of so-called swinging eighth notes. The common feature in both cases is displacement. (Because of this displacement, a typical representation of swinging eighths in scores—as dotted eighths plus sixteenths—is really a misrepresentation, as every jazz player knows.) Igor Stravinsky was speaking of swing in this broad sense in his *Poetics of Music,* where he describes the giddy sensation we register when jazz tries "persistently to stress irregular accents," but "cannot succeed in turning our ear away from the regular pulsation of the meter drummed out by the percussion" (1947, p. 30).

European music capitalizes on alternations between tension and relaxation—between movement and repose, between dissonance and consonance. In jazz, Hodeir suggests, tension and relaxation are perpetually bound together within a single structure (pp. 195–196). When bound together in this way, we might say that the music has a continuous tension-release function—or "T-R function." So what are the sources of T-R function in jazz? Hodeir's main position casts swing as the source of relaxation, and hot playing as the source of tension (p. 240). Matters are complicated, however, when he also suggests that swing itself involves a complex interaction of tension and relaxation, since it involves an internal relationship between an underlying pulsation and a rhythmic overlay that pulls against it, if only to reconfirm it (p. 196). The basic question the account needs to work out is the connection between hot playing and swing. Otherwise, the parts of the definiens collapse into a mere disjunction, which does not satisfy Hodeir's requirement that the components of jazz are essential to the extent that they contribute to a unified jazz effect.

Furthermore, a survey of jazz styles threatens to turn up counterexamples to the theory. For instance, there are clear rhythmic differences between high modernist and classic jazz. In the latter, phrases will often begin with an emphasis of strong beats and conclude with rhythmically disorienting placements. Bebop jazz likes to reverse the procedure by using a series of displaced accents to draw our interest toward a subsequent strong beat. Perhaps Hodeir's concept of swing can embrace both sorts of music. But consider Ornette Coleman's use of a very loose "spread" rhythm that was liberated from all metrical consistency. Alongside mainstream jazz, we may feel it does not swing. But we might say otherwise if we place Coleman's music alongside the boiling piano music of Cecil Taylor. The latter allows the hearer to relax only when the performance is over—hardly a recipe for swing. Or consider the fusion-funk movement that began in the 1960s. Like high-energy rock, such music often creates unrelenting tension quite different from Hodeir's picture of swing. The rhythm is not the itchy, flowing lilt of the so-called swing era. Nor is it the "cooking" flow of high modernist bop rhythm sections. As Mark Gridley puts it, fusion likes to "sit on each beat instead of pulling it along or leading it, as [traditional] jazz does" (1988, p. 317). Furthermore, as in the early 1970s work of the band Weather Report, it is not easy to distinguish rhythmic infrastructure and superstructure. Individual players surface briefly, only to return to the blended textures of the whole, to which every instrument is busy making its contribution. Further, there exists jazz whose T-R function does not seem to be a function of jazz rhythm at all. The rhapsodic, unaccompanied piano playing of Keith Jarrett, for instance, owes its rhythmic character more to Sergei Rachmaninoff or Maurice Ravel than to mainstream jazz. Tension and release in such music are not features of swing feeling but of other devices, for example, figures repeated over and over, ecstatic running passages, and romantic tonalities.

Perhaps the main difficulty with Hodeir's approach can be best identified by reference to his *reductio* of Afropurism. The problem is that Hodeir's trenchant critique is a double-edged sword. It tacitly delimits jazz to its most recently emergent features. By his own reckoning, Hodeir's account, framed basically in terms of the classic small band swing of the late thirties and forties, ought to be superseded—indeed, continuously—by revised accounts that essentialize the music's more recent versions. There is clearly something wrong with such an outcome.

The New "Critical Theory" of Jazz. Afropurism continues to surface in jazz discourse. A seminal book in this vein is *Blues People: Negro Music in White America* (1963), by Imamu Amiri Baraka (LeRoi Jones), in which it is argued, for example, that the phrase "white blues singer" is simply oxymoronic. Afropurist themes also have been given a boost more recently by what might be called the critical theory of jazz.

In effect, the movement that began in literary studies eventually found a new subject—jazz. Two volumes edited by Krin Gabbard—*Jazz among the Discourses* (1995a) and *Representing Jazz* (1995b)—present good surveys of representatives of the approach. The critical theory of jazz proposes a full-scale critique of traditional approaches. Authors who come under fire include Williams, Schuller, and Hodeir. The following points summarize some of the putative errors of the tradition, by the lights of the new theory.

1. "Exclusionary" (i.e., *essentialist*) views of jazz are out.
2. So is essentialism's supposed first cousin, elitism—the attempt to turn it into "America's classical music" (Gabbard, 1995a, p. 14).

3. The essentialist is also typically an internalist, that is, a theorist who mistakenly fixates on formal features of the music at the expense of externals. By contrast, the critical theory of jazz holds that we can only get at the heart of jazz by placing the music within its cultural context.
4. This entails that the study of jazz should treat the social problem of race as central to the study of the music.
5. Because of this, the critical theory of jazz emphasizes non-European forms of communication in the music. Jazz, it is said, exhibits pointedly *dis*unified voices, "strategically contrapuntal" forms of speech intended to "glance off and otherwise evade the dominant code" (ibid., p. 155).
6. For the critical theory of jazz, historical developmentalism sponsors the misguided idea of jazz history as traceable back to certain "heroicized" originary figures. A better approach is to look for *dis*continuity and *non*-development.
7. The critical theory of jazz rejects the legitimacy of a jazz canon. The charges are the ones familiar in literary studies: for example, canonizations are "determined by the last few generations of university professors" (p. 3).
8. The new approach tacitly opposes the theoretical focus on musical product at the expense of the process of making the music.
9. A corollary complaint is lodged against the assumption that the history of the music is simply the history of its sound recordings.
10. For the critical theory of jazz, evaluative commentary, whether positive or negative, has no place in serious jazz analysis.

It is to the general credit of the critical theory of jazz that it reminds us that part of the significance of jazz reflects its social circumstances and its tacit intentions in light of those circumstances. (True, the critical theory of jazz has precursors in this regard. *The Jazz Scene,* first published in 1959 by the social historian Eric Hobsbawm, detailed a multitude of jazz's social crosscurrents.) In particular, the critical theory of jazz addresses an aspect of popular music that aestheticians have barely begun to address, namely, its role as a reference point for social self-definition. For example, Howard McGhee, the trumpet player, explains that when his generation of African-American players came out of the army after the war, they felt that their music had been stolen in their absence by the white music system (Gitler, pp. 314–315). Their response was a species of rough justice: novice white players who tried to join in and play were often put to new musical tests it would prove difficult to pass.

A social dimension of jazz that one would expect the critical theory of jazz to pay more attention to eventually is the place of women in jazz. Jazz has been fertile ground for the cultivation of a "macho" culture that has not been open to women seeking jobs in jazz, let alone provide them with opportunities for self-definition within the field.

The critical theory of jazz also draws attention to dimensions of jazz that are likely to be neglected in overidealizing approaches. For example, Hodeir's ground rule that the elements of jazz that belong to its definition must work together to create a unified effect may be too strict—perhaps too strict for any kind of music, let alone the music of this imperfect art. The new approach insists that jazz often appropriates diverse—even discordant—materials. The critical theory of jazz's strategy for maintaining its nominalism against the likes of Hodeir may not convince every reader either, however. Sometimes, the antiessentialism is expressed simply by using *essentialist* as a pejorative term. Sometimes, the official position is tacitly compromised—whether knowingly or not, it is hard to say. Gendron, for instance, believes he knows that jazz is *not* folk music (Gabbard, 1995a, p. 39). William Kenny describes certain attempts to "dilute [real] jazz" into a more commercial product (ibid., p. 106). Further, the assumed connection between essentialism and elitism diagnosed by the new discourse will need to be made clearer. André Hodeir, a notorious essentialist in the eyes of the new theorists, took special note of the difference between jazz and European concert music.

Presumably as the critical theory of jazz develops its resources, it will further clarify these matters. It may also make a better case for its view that by approaching jazz externally, formalism can be avoided. There is no doubt that a sociological story lurks behind the rise of high modernist jazz. However, any representation of the matter that did not take differences between the forms of the old and the new music into consideration would have bound and gagged itself. The challenge posed by bop music is not a sheer sociological fact. The new jazz players challenged their opponents with new forms.

Jed Rasula urges that the exemplary is always "alienated from its subject by its speaker's purpose" (p. 154). It is not clear, however, how discourse about any sphere of art can do without a tacit list of exemplary cases. It is thus hard to see how solid musical analysis could be as value free as the critical theory of jazz would like it to be. True enough, discourse that merely gushes over its subject matter is uninformative. But an analytic approach that was utterly value free would not know where to begin, or how to go on, once begun. In fact, what differentiates the critical theory of jazz may really be its desire to rewrite the canonical list in terms of its own set of values. It is hard not to notice that the new discourse tends to advance the cause of artists the industry has chosen to marginalize, in varying degrees, for example, Anthony Braxton, Archie Shepp, Pharoah Sanders, Henry Threadgill, Evan Parker, and Albert Ayler. What these figures have in common is a family of traits: free improvisation, "fragmentation of subjectivity," and resistance to prior categorization. Music made by "unified musical subjects" is now out—not quite the real thing.

The critical theory of jazz is undoubtedly right that attempts to understand jazz from a purely synchronic point of view will be lacking. In European concert music, the original sources of the music—in dance forms, for instance—have been almost completely lost to the ear. Jazz, by contrast, trails its nonjazz sources behind. As a result, it is constantly reevaluating the authenticity and validity of its origins. Hodeir tried to unseat oldtime jazzmen such as Jelly Roll Morton and Johnny Dodds. (On this matter, Gabbard's remarks about Hodeir are either inaccurate or misleading; see 1995a, p. 14.) The revivalists of the 1940s then tried to recanonize what Hodeir had earlier decanonized. Any version of jazz history will marginalize somebody or other. Canonization and recanonization in jazz have been going on almost since the beginning. Under the label of "theory" the new discourse is simply joining in the old tug of war. These recent writings do not so much prove as illustrate certain facts of jazz life that have been illustrated again and again from the beginning in both jazz practice and its commentary.

The Jazz Culture Wars. The second half of the twentieth century is marked by a series of battle lines drawn not only in the arts, humanities, and education, but in the cultural generally. Jazz is no exception. In fact, the jazz wars form an oppositional triangle: in one corner, we find the mainstream, represented by the contentious Wynton Marsalis and his Lincoln Center repertory jazz band. In another corner, we find the nonelectric avant-garde. In the third, we have electrofusion. To illustrate the affinities and divisions, consider that the agendas of Marsalis and Lincoln Center, for instance, are not much appreciated by the experimentalists, such as Muhal Richard Abrams, associated with the Association for the Advancement of Creative Musicians (AACM) group in Chicago. Neither group, however, has much patience with jazz fusion, whether in its more formulaic later pop versions or in its early "harder" versions—as played by John McLaughlin, Herbie Hancock, or Weather Report.

By concentrating on traditional white jazz journalism, the new critical theory of jazz may not have found a worthy target. For instance, Marsalis ought to be far more problematic for the critical theory of jazz than would be indicated by the attention he receives in the Gabbard volumes cited earlier. The reason may be that for the critical theory of jazz, he is something of a hot potato. From one point of view, Marsalis is clearly on the wrong side of the line. He is a blatant elitist, declaring jazz to be America's *real* classical music. He is a blatant canonizer. But, given the new critical theorists' talk about the "erasure" of black voices by white appropriation, Marsalis ought to be on the right side of the line. Further, he has taken the "right" position about who "owns" the music, in both the financial and the spiritual sense. Jazz fusion gets even less play in Gabbard's collections. Even a cursory survey of the scene suggests that if we want to identify the forces that do have real power over jazz taste, we should look to the popular music industry, rather than to the academy. (On this matter, Adorno was certainly right.) As commercially viable music on radio, there is no doubt that jazz fusion currently leads the field. For the critical theory of jazz, however, late-century fusion seems to be so far beneath contempt that it is barely mentioned—a curious stance, given the new perspective's official anti-elitism.

The Apollonian and the Dionysian. Jazz does not fit nicely into typical European views of artistic reception. On this point, Hodeir's account of the music is probably lacking. With the possible exception of John Dewey's *Art as Experience* (1934), traditional European aesthetics since Immanuel Kant and Arthur Schopenhauer tends to emphasize the intellectualistic aspects of the aesthetic experience of art. Art, on this account, consists of a controlled display of abstract patterns pleasing to the mind. This way of looking at jazz would be, so to speak, Apollonian. Indeed, earlier reference was made to an Apollonian feature of jazz improvisation. Other aspects of the music, however—in particular, communal and somatic ones—mock the temptation to think of aesthetic experience in these terms alone. The Apollonian and the Dionysian come together in collective improvisation, when each player tries to anticipate, reinforce, but also challenge each other. Sargeant describes the situation this way:

> When even the players themselves are not quite sure what is going to happen next the music takes on the aspect of a tussle in which individual players . . . try to unhorse each other, as well as the audience, by means of conflicting rhythmic impacts, . . . the result is jazz in its purist form. (Sargeant, 1975, pp. 241–242)

The effect is augmented by the presence of an interactive audience aware of what is happening and appropriately energized. Sargeant emphasizes the music's powerful physical manifestations and effects—foot stamping, finger snapping, head bobbing—by which the audience tries to maintain its "sense of orientation" as it listens to a rhythmically charged jazz performance. The responses of both players and audience become positive feedback loops integral to the whole event. Naturally, jazz and dancing went hand in hand in the early days. The Apollonian and the Dionysian in jazz fall apart again, however, given that the music nowadays is presented in very different ways, in very different kinds of venues.

With African music, it would have been hard to speak of an audience, indeed of a performance, in the Western sense. These negative attributes color jazz itself, particularly in the early days. As Tom Bethell argues convincingly in his *George Lewis: A Jazzman from New Orleans*, the music in the early days was not its own raison d'être, but was secondary to the function at hand—functions integral to a wide array of quotidian activities of ordinary people—dances, picnic excursions, parades, funerals, and so on. Eventually, this "natural" relationship of the music to daily life was eroded, at least in certain contexts. Even before the first half-century of its life had passed, the motor responses of jazz audiences in many jazz venues had become discreet so as not to interfere with the more cerebral pleasures of the music's aficionados, who preferred to listen with studiously quiet concentration. Dancing, of course, would be utterly taboo. A new complexity in the music's modernist forms also contributed to its "arty" status. In some ways similar in function to the hard-core jazz club is the concert hall, home to the jazz repertory orchestra, of which Lincoln Center is only the best-known example.

But the elite jazz club and the jazz concert hall are not the only venues in which the music exists. If members of a jazz concert audience go across town, they might find the raucous atmosphere Bethell described in early New Orleans still alive—albeit modified by the dominance of electric instruments. Audience participation is de rigeur. Customers dance, clap their hands, or spontaneously get up on stage to perform. Here, the Dionysian looms large again. The contrast between the two kinds of venues, with their distinct messages—although embodied in sounds that are, historically and stylistically, family members—is palpable.

High Art and Low. So, when we think of this invidious "high art"/"low art" dichotomy, we need not confine ourselves to the writings of a strident elitist such as Adorno. Even Sargeant caps off his brilliant book with a rather shrill chapter explaining why jazz cannot provide values as important as those of "serious" art. He argues that jazz has created no polished masterpieces. One might reply with a limited concession: the degree of metrical regularity demanded by the rhythmic agendas of jazz—among other features of the music—may be inconsistent with the kind of large-scale formal development exploited in European "serious" music. Of course, if one insists on making invidious cross-categorial comparisons, one could just as reasonably argue that "serious" music is deficient because it fails to relate tension and release in the way jazz does.

Part of the high/low issue is the relationship of jazz to the music business. Adorno's picture of all popular music as mere commodity is, of course, oversimplified. The truth is that jazz is caught between conflicting pressures. While beholden to the music industry for their lifeblood, jazz musicians have also struggled against pressures to play "down" to a broad public and to record "hits." To some extent—but only some—the music has become a species of self-conscious art music. Adorno also insists that popular music is not oppositional enough to qualify as art. In fact, not even rock music bears out his claim. The unpredictable and uncontrollable crosscurrents peculiar to rock music's audiences both support and resist the commodity system, thereby contributing to the music's ferment. As for the oppositional features of jazz, consider the anger and frustration in the music of players like Eric Dolphy and John Coltrane.

Process/Product. Another way jazz challenges the European tradition of music aesthetics is its tendency to reverse the Eurocentric priority of musical product over process. (In this respect, the stance of the new critical theory of jazz is a salutary one.) The tradition typically makes two closely related assumptions, namely, that music comes packaged in musical works and that all musical works are subject to criteria of reidentification. Nelson Goodman's division of the sphere of art in his *Languages of Art* (1968) into two central categories—the autographic and the allographic—is a perspicuous example of the standard approach. (The two categories specify the two ways artworks can be reidentified.) Fitting jazz into such a format poses problems, however. A phenomenology of the experience of improvised music might be some evidence that improvisational performances are not at all subject to reidentification.

Such a phenomenology ought to profile what might be called presence. The sense that unscripted music is being generated as one listens gives an improvisatory performance its special sense of moment. One has to be there at the right time to hear a specific improvisation; yet, one cannot plan to hear that particular improvisation. Further, much of the focus of informed attention on such music is on the activity by which a performer makes use of his or her opportunity to create the music being played. Even if two improvisatory actions coincidentally had the same acoustic output, each would possess a kind of aesthetic indexicality, so to speak. Essential to the one is its being *this* spontaneous action; essential to the other is its being *that* one. A request that a pianist, who has just played Ludwig von Beethoven's *opus* 111, play *that* piece again is an intelligible one. By contrast, when Coleman Hawkins improvised a solo, a request that he improvise *that* solo again is not intelligible. So, there may simply be no entity with which an improvisation can be reidentified—nor any entity with which an improvisation might be mistakenly reidentified. The situation with a work of autographic art (e.g., Édouard Manet's *Olympia*) and a work of allographic art (e.g., Beethoven's *op.* 111) is that we can return to each work again and again. One cannot return, however, even once, to an improvisational performance.

Yet, with rare exceptions, improvised jazz is based on modest works—folk tunes, "parlor" songs, marches, rags, blues songs, and Broadway show tunes. Typical jazz performances seem to be work performances and improvisations at the same time. The explanation may be that the sense in which improvisers perform works is, with exceptions discussed earlier in this essay, much looser than the sense in which, for example, Rudolf Serkin played *opus* 111. A listener who said of Hawkins's performances, "That's just not 'Body and Soul,'" because it did not conform to a scored representation of it, would misunderstand the point of the performance. Consider, too, that for many jazz ears, what identifies a "work" is its pattern of harmonic motion. From one point of view, a player who has performed the bop tune "Koko" has not played "Cherokee"; from another, he has. Given the built-in lack of precision about what counts as playing "the work" in such contexts, it seems harmless to say that an improvisation on such a work does two things at once. Jazz practice lives with this lack of precision. Indeed, it thrives on it. Jazz players continually reshape jazz's fluid musical materials for new musical purposes.

Jazz and Phonography. Consider that in a world without recording technology, we might never apply the concept of work identity to improvised music. But the question arises whether, given the preservative features of recording technology, improvisations might become fodder for reidentifiable works anyway. Consider the fact that recording technology seems to have made possible a new type of musical work hitherto unknown, and deserving of its own ontological analysis. One might call these new entities works of phonography. Unlike standard musical works, they are not performable. Like them, however, they are subject to criteria of reidentification. Obvious examples are the grandiose studio productions of the later Beatles, for instance, or the manipulations of sound in *musique concrète,* works made for electronic tape, and computer-generated music. But now consider that as recorded an improvisatory performance can be visited, and revisited, as easily as one can return to a Beethoven's *op.* 111 or to Manet's *Olympia*—indeed, far more easily. In that context, do they not acquire the status of reidentifiable works after all? As evidence for an altered ontology, consider the fact that, once the music is recorded, the phenomenology seems to change. It takes only one punch of the "repeat" button to bring it home that even though I am listening to a jazz performance, no spontaneous action is taking place now—as I listen.

The result is ironic. Much of our understanding of improvised jazz—indeed, jazz's evolving understanding of itself—is based on its recorded history. The many masterpieces embedded in the grooves of phonograph records owe much of their beauty to the economy imposed by the roughly three-minute limit for a recorded performance in the 78 rpm recording era. The history of jazz and the history of recording technology are intertwined, in short. But once embedded in the grooves of phonograph records, or their equivalents, the music cannot but be affected in ways that have potentially transforming effects on the music. It is to the credit of the new critical theory of jazz that it has shown sensitivity to these issues.

An Imperfect Art. Two things are hard to avoid when addressing the topic of jazz music—mystificationist reverence and elitist condescension. Opposite sides of a coin, they both assume either that music must conform to familiar European practices or that it lies beyond the bound of rational musical understanding. The element of truth in the antinomy is that jazz is caught between partly incommensurate musical cultures—an imperfect art, as Ted Gioia calls it in his book of that title (1988). The situation is made more complicated by the fact that jazz is nowadays encroaching on the territory of fine art more than ever before. So, a consideration of jazz will partly confirm, partly blur, conceptual boundary lines routinely drawn when aestheticians address the arts. No mere conceptual jockeying by philosophers will make the untidiness disappear.

[*See also* Improvisation, *article on* Jazz Improvisation; *and* Music, *historical overview article.*]

BIBLIOGRAPHY

Adorno, Theodor. "Abschied vom Jazz." *Europäische Revue* 9 (1933): 313–316.

Adorno, Theodor (Pseud. Hektor Rottweiler). "Über Jazz." *Zeitschrift für Socialforschung* 5 (1936): 84–115.

Adorno, Theodor. "On Popular Music." *Studies in Philosophy and Social Science* 9.1 (1941): 17–48.

Adorno, Theodor. "Jazz." In *Encyclopedia of the Arts,* edited by Dagobert D. Runes and Harry G. Schrickel, pp. 511–513. New York, 1946.

Adorno, Theodor W. "Zeitlöse Mode: Zum Jazz." In *Gesammelte Schriften,* edited by Rolf Tiedemann, vol. 10.1, pp. 123–137. Frankfurt am Main, 1977. Translated by Samuel Weber and Shierry Weber as "Perennial Fashion—Jazz" in *Prisms* (London, 1967), pp. 119–132.

Alperson, Philip. "On Musical Improvisation." *Journal of Aesthetics and Art Criticism* 43.1 (Fall 1984): 17–29.

Baraka, Imamu Amiri (LeRoi Jones). *Blues People: Negro Music in White America.* New York, 1963.

Baraka, Imamu Amiri, and Amina Baraka. *The Music: Reflections on Jazz and Blues.* New York, 1987.

Berendt, Joachim Ernst. *Das grosse Jazzbuch.* Frankfurt am Main, 1981. Translated by H. Bredigkeit and B. Bredigkeit with Dan Morgenstern and Tim Nevill as *The Jazz Book: From Ragtime to Fusion and Beyond* (6th ed., Brooklyn, N.Y., 1992).

Bethell, Tom. *George Lewis: A Jazzman from New Orleans.* Berkeley, 1977.

Brown, Lee B. "The Theory of Jazz Music." *Journal of Aesthetics and Art Criticism* 49.2 (Spring 1991): 115–127.

Brown, Lee B. "Adorno's Critique of Popular Culture: The Case of Jazz Music." *Journal of Aesthetic Education* 26 (Spring 1992): 17–31.

Brown, Lee B. "Musical Works, Improvisation, and the Principle of Continuity." *Journal of Aesthetics and Art Criticism* 54.4 (Fall 1996): 353–369.

Brown, Lee B. "Phonography." In *Aesthetics: A Reader in Philosophy of the Arts,* edited by David Goldblatt and Lee B. Brown, pp. 252–257. Upper Saddle River, N.J., 1996.

Brown, Lee B. "Adorno's Case against Popular Music." In *Aesthetics: A Reader in Philosophy of the Arts,* edited by David Goldblatt and Lee B. Brown, pp. 426–432. Upper Saddle River, N.J., 1996.

Buckner, Reginald T., and Steven Weiland, eds. *Jazz in Mind: Essays on the History and Meanings of Jazz.* Detroit, 1991.

Chernoff, John Miller. *African Rhythm and African Sensibility: Aesthetics and Social Action in African Musical Idioms.* Chicago, 1979.

Collier, James Lincoln. *The Making of Jazz: A Comprehensive History.* Boston, 1978.

Crouch, Stanley. "Jazz Criticism and Its Effect on the Art Form." In *New Perspectives on Jazz,* edited by David N. Baker. Washington, D.C., 1990.

Gabbard, Krin, ed. *Jazz among the Discourses.* Durham, N.C., 1995a.

Gabbard, Krin, ed. *Representing Jazz.* Durham, N.C., 1995b.

Gioia, Ted. *The Imperfect Art: Reflections on Jazz and Modern Culture.* New York and Oxford, 1988.

Giddens, Gary. *Riding on a Blue Note: Jazz and American Pop.* New York and Oxford, 1981.

Gitler, Ira. *Swing to Bop: An Oral History of the Tradition of Jazz in the Forties.* New York, 1985.

Goffin, Robert. *Jazz from the Congo to the Metropolitan.* Garden City, N.Y., 1944.

Gridley, Mark C. *Jazz Styles: History and Analysis.* 3d ed. Englewood Cliffs, N.J., 1988.

Harrison, Max. *A Jazz Retrospect.* Boston, 1976.

Hobsbawm, Eric J. *The Jazz Scene.* Rev. ed. New York, 1993.

Hodeir, André. *Hommes et problèmes du jazz: Suivi de la religion du jazz.* Paris, 1954. Translated by David Noakes as *Jazz: Its Evolution and Essence* (New York, 1956).

Hodeir, André. *Toward Jazz.* Translated by Noel Burch. New York, 1962.

Jones, A. M. *Studies in African Music.* 2 vols. New York and Oxford, 1959.

Kernfeld, Barry, ed. *The New Grove Dictionary of Jazz.* 2 vols. New York, 1988.

Murphy, Jeannette Robinson. "The Survival of African Music in America." *Popular Science Monthly* (September 1899): 660–721.

Ogren, Kathy J. *The Jazz Revolution: Twenties America and the Meaning of Jazz.* New York and Oxford, 1989.

Rudinow, Joel. "Race, Ethnicity, Expressive Authenticity: Can White People Sing the Blues?" *Journal of Aesthetics and Art Criticism* 52.1 (Winter 1994): 127–137.

Sargeant, Winthrop. *Jazz: Hot and Hybrid.* 3d enl. ed. New York, 1975.

Sartre, J.-P. "Jazz in America." In *Frontiers of Jazz,* edited by Ralph de Toledano, pp. 66–68. London, 1966.

Shapiro, Nat, and Nat Hentoff, eds. *Hear Me Talkin' to Ya: The Story of Jazz as Told by the Men Who Made It.* New York, 1955.

Slawe, Jan. *Einführung in die Jazzmusic.* Bern, 1948.

Spellman, A. B. *Black Music: Four Lives.* New York, 1970.

Stearns, Marshall W. *The Story of Jazz.* New York and Oxford, 1956.

Tirro, Frank. *Jazz: A History.* 2d ed. New York, 1993.

Williams, Martin. *The Jazz Tradition.* 2d rev. ed. New York and Oxford, 1993.

LEE BROWN

JEANNERET, CHARLES-ÉDOUARD. *See* Le Corbusier.

JOKES.

Jokes are an astonishingly rich topic for philosophical reflection, carrying one into areas of moral philosophy, the philosophy of culture, the philosophy of language, and the philosophy of mind. This article, however, considers jokes only with regard to a few respects in which they are an obvious matter of interest in the philosophy of art.

Here jokes are taken to be certain kinds of fictional stories, usually relatively short, culminating in some final sentence or two, often called the punch line, which is meant to be amusing when it comes at the end of the story. Amusing stories, humorous stories, witty stories, practical jokes, and many other enterprises may well be similar to these jokes, and although it would be of considerable interest to discover how they are similar and how they are different, they are not addressed here.

The Structure of Some Jokes. It is a common feature of jokes that their success depends on the accuracy of certain assumptions concerning what the audience knows or believes or can be expected to recognize. Although not all jokes are like this, many are, and the dynamics of such jokes exploit two related features of joke telling and joke hearing. The first is the evident need for concision. The second is the implication of the hearer in the joke transaction.

It is possible to begin jokes with lines like these: "There was once a very clever man who was grasping and unscrupulous . . ."; "There was a man who would do anything in order to make money, including attempting to further unjust causes . . ."; "There was a man of considerable intellect and learning who was utterly incapable of applying his intelligence and knowledge to any genuinely practical matter . . ." But such beginnings are unlikely to lead to very successful joke telling. Instead, one begins "There was a Jew . . ."; "There was a lawyer . . ."; "There was a philosopher . . ." Why? Why does joke telling often require that one begin with an abbreviation, a kind of formulaic invocation? Before looking for an answer, it would be good to turn briefly to an initial and partial consideration of the "moral" implications of such jokes.

Jokes with this kind of abbreviated beginning are often castigated as being in bad taste, defamatory, and even downright immoral. They may be, but if so it is not because they explicitly trade on falsehoods, defamatory or not. To follow such a joke, one need no more believe that Jews are grasping, that lawyers are amoral, or that philosophers are practical incompetents than one needs to believe that owls are wise or pigs are dirty in order to understand metaphors like "Tom is an owl" and "Dick is a pig." What one needs to know is that these characteristics have a customary association with Jews, lawyers, philosophers, owls, and pigs. It is not truths about these things that are relied on, nor even beliefs about them, but only a shared awareness of their associations. (These are the things called associated commonplaces by Max Black in his discussion of metaphor.) It might be unfortunate, and even damaging that such associations have been established, and it may be appropriate to blame such jokes for keeping these associations current, but it is wrongheaded to blame the jokes for purveying falsehoods or negative prejudices in any simpleminded way.

But why is there a need for this kind of coded reference to the associations, a need that is not typically satisfied by spelling out the associations themselves? Part of the answer is in the second related feature of joke telling: at least in this kind of joking, the active complicity of the hearer is sought and is made a part of the dynamics of the enterprise. Thus, the hearer must know the associations that go with these references to Jews, lawyers, and philosophers. Thus, this is,

in the classical sense, a rhetorical exercise and not an exercise in simple exposition. The aim of the joke teller is to move the audience, and toward that end, he or she virtually forces the hearer to join in the enterprise from the start. The hearer must supply some background over and above merely understanding the words, rather as the recipient of a rhetorical demonstration must himself supply a missing premise.

Noting this common feature of much joke telling is the beginning of an explanation—although it is far from a complete explanation—of why it is so common to joke about topical matters, including those involving terrible matters. The joke teller needs to be able to presume the audience's acquaintance with some fact, say, something about the president of the United States or the pope or an airplane crash or an earthquake or a serial killer. The morbidity of some of these topics is striking, and it requires additional explanation to get at their special attraction (perhaps they are attractive because they offer a way of confronting things so disagreeable that it is difficult to deal with them straightforwardly), but in the first instance it is merely their publicity that makes them suitable topics. They will do to bring joke hearers into the enterprise virtually against their will, since they cannot help but bring what they have heard to mind as soon as they hear the reference.

In these cases the solicitation of a contribution from the audience is made quite generally. A corollary feature of some jokes is precisely that they do not do this, but instead ask for something that only a specialized audience can supply. Thus, there are jokes with words from foreign languages, jokes with special references, for instance, to arcane terms of law or mathematics or plumbing. For these jokes the only possible audience will be made up of those who can supply the associations that go with these references. This possibility yields "Jewish jokes," for instance, in the sense of jokes that can be understood only by those who are familiar with certain Jewish references, as contrasted with Jewish jokes in the sense of jokes about Jews, for which all the audience needs to know is certain commonplace associations with Jewish people.

These narrowly aimed jokes, the ones requiring the audience to possess relatively specialized knowledge, deliver an augmented delight. The competent hearer is not only amused by the joke but is also aware that the amusement is unavailable to those not sharing his or her qualifications. In this regard, one suspects, these jokes have a kinship with certain objects of advanced, "elitist" art. Their appreciators are relatively few, and those few rejoice in their special achievement in appreciating these special things.

Jokes and Art. Jokes share some other characteristics with art as it is generally conceived. Although it is often unclear just what this means, it is common for art to be spoken of in terms of problems and their solutions. For instance, various versions of perspectival drawing and painting are said to be solutions to the problem of the depiction of three-dimensional space on a two-dimensional surface; the flying buttresses common to Gothic cathedral architecture are said to solve the problem of supplying an immense interior space with adequate support not visible from within that space; the saxophone is said to be a solution to the problem of sounding a reed musical line loud enough to be heard from within a large orchestra; certain modernist paintings are said to address the problem of the framing edge; the use of a specified narrator like Marlow in some novels by Joseph Conrad is described as a solution to the problem of how to distance the author from some distinct authorial voice. Of course, these are not all the same kind of problem, they may not even all be problems in the same sense of "problem," and a corresponding variability attaches automatically to the idea that these devices and implements and techniques are "solutions." The very general idea of problems and solutions, however, is a persistent theme in writing about works of art, and the idea has an obvious application to the creation of jokes.

Those who create jokes are commonly in the position of people looking for solutions to problems. Riddles, puns, and plays on words very often look like loose equivalents to solutions to simultaneous equations in algebra. Thus, "find an x and a y such that x plus y is equal to 6, and x times y is equal to 8" is a little like finding a word that will connect clothing with battle, as in "The general keeps his armies in his sleeves."

Any eye-catching public event is an obvious occasion for creating a joke, and so are occasions on which one needs to create a joke that, say, makes fun of a particular person or thing. Just as art is sometimes defended against charges of immorality by reference to some assertion of a transcendental value in art that outweighs any possible negative considerations, considerable cruelty in jokes is commonly excused on the grounds that the jokes are, after all, funny, and that is taken to be a compelling warrant.

Jokes as problem solutions are best known, probably, in the case of certain kinds of generic jokes. So-called ethnic jokes take some person of recognizable ethnicity, to which has been attached the association of clumsiness or stupidity or ignorance, and ask how this person would (or did) perform some task. This kind of joke is to be found in many parts of the world. In the United States its most common form, probably, is the Polish joke, although in this country there are also Iowa legislator jokes, Aggie jokes, Maria jokes, redneck jokes, and a few others. In India there are Sikh jokes; in England, Irish jokes; in Poland, Russian jokes; in Russia, Ukrainian jokes; in Canada, Newfie jokes; and so on. It is of minor interest to compare these ethnic jokes—how would, say, a Sikh change a lightbulb, buy an airline ticket, drive an automobile—with their logical opposite number, of which the most common example, probably, is lightbulb-changing jokes. With these, one asks, how many

Sikhs, Poles, Jews, Christian Scientists, psychiatrists, graduate students, and so on, does it take to change a lightbulb? In the first case, the ethnicity is held constant while the task changes; in the second case, the task is set and the ethnicity changes. Although not everyone seems able to make up a joke, most people can, if given enough time and some healthy encouragement, make up one of these problem-solving jokes. Their efforts may not be altogether successful, but it seems clear that what they have made up is a joke. Is this like what happens when someone is given enough time, enough help studying, enough exposure to prior examples, and then, as an exercise, composes a musical fugue? Or is that just a joke?

As with art, there is a critical question about the particularity or selectivity of jokes. It is clear that many jokes appeal—and sometimes are designed to appeal—only to audiences who satisfy certain conditions. First is the matter of what the audience knows. When Hamlet says "Get thee to a nunnery," for instance, the force of his remark, and along with it a considerable part of one's sense of Hamlet's character, is lost on any audience that does not know that the word nunnery is a slang term for a brothel. Similarly, one who does not know the meaning of the Yiddish/German word *ungepotchke* will be unable to grasp a joke that, although otherwise told in plain English, uses this word in its punch line. One must know at least a little of the history of astronomy to appreciate John Donne's line including the phrase "trepidation of the spheres," and one must also know at least a little astronomy to get a joke in whose punch line a man intending to fly a rocket to the sun says the heat will not be a problem because he will make the flight at night.

The second kind of particularity appears when the work of art, or joke, essentially calls into play the audience's feelings or dispositions to feel. Not everyone is able to apprehend the feelings of Shylock in *The Merchant of Venice*, and among those who can, not all of them can appreciate the feelings of Antonio. So it is with jokes. Not everyone can be amused by a joke in which the character portrayed as stupid or foolish is very like oneself.

What is to be made of this particularity, in either of its forms? First is the minor but significant implication that it is not at all clear what it could mean to declare that the appeal of art or of jokes is "universal." Those who hold that the proper appreciation of a work of art must be confined to "the work itself," and must not require external considerations must explain just how this is to be understood. Perhaps it will be said that all these seemingly external matters, including knowledge of astronomy, information about the meanings of words in Elizabethan England, and the rest, are simply prerequisites for *understanding* the work, rather like having to know the language in which it is written. Perhaps that is so, but it becomes increasingly difficult to say that truly successful works of art must be accessible to everyone, at least "in principle." One might as well say that late twentieth-century particle physics is in principle comprehensible to everyone. In both cases, it may well turn out that an enormous number of people, whatever they might do "in principle," are incapable of the concentration, memory, and combinatorial ability required to comprehend quantum gravity or to appreciate James Joyce's *Ulysses* or Arnold Schoenberg's *Moses und Aron*.

The second implication is even more serious, for here we are speaking of a prospective audience's feelings. To grasp some of T. S. Eliot's poetry, for instance, or Conrad's *Heart of Darkness* or Mark Twain's *Huckleberry Finn* or William Shakespeare's *Merchant of Venice*, it is arguable that one must be able to appreciate certain feelings about Jews, African-Americans, and native Africans. What if one does not have these feelings oneself, and what if these are negative feelings that sometimes lead to disagreeable actions? How is one to feel what needs to be felt in any complete appreciation of such works? So it is with jokes. What is required to be amused by jokes in which specific people or groups of people are portrayed as inferior or immoral, and are therein offered as objects of derision?

The exclusivity of some works of art and of some jokes is not always an accidental matter. Although there are cases in which one is excluded from the audience of appreciation only contingently, because of something one fails to know, for instance, or perhaps, if David Hume is right, because of one's age, there are still cases in which the exclusion is deliberate. Prominent examples are to be found among musical works intended to appeal to the young. It is sometimes a mark of such music that its appeal is constituted in part by the fact that it does not—indeed, seemingly cannot—appeal to its audience's elders. When an older person, like the author of this essay, for instance, says of some current music popular among teenagers that she does not care for this music, that she cannot imagine how anyone *could* care for it, she should reflect on the possibility that the music is meant, precisely, to be something that she cannot attach herself to. That music thus helps those who are attached to it to identify themselves, to make it clear that they have an individuality distinct from that of their elders. This, too, happens with jokes. There are especially gruesome jokes whose narratives include unspeakable horrors (dismemberments, dead babies), and these jokes tend to be agreeable only to the very young. Their youthful delight in such jokes incorporates the sense that these jokes are essentially inaccessible to older people. These jokes, and this kind of art may be—in principle—universally accessible, but in fact they are deliberately offered as in fact inaccessible to many. This selective appeal is a part of the very dynamics of their effect.

Although the selection of a young audience is an especially clear example of the exclusivity of some jokes and some art, particularity in other respects is a feature of many kinds of jokes and much art. Some art, for instance, is designed to appeal to Christian or conservative or hedonistic sensibilities, and it does so to a point at which other possible audiences are virtually excluded. The same is true of many jokes: for instance, jokes meant to celebrate the cleverness of Jews, jokes meant to castigate the venality of Jews. In all these cases, we are faced, philosophically, with the question of whether they are essentially parochial, and if so whether this adds to or detracts from their value; or whether their limited appeal is merely contingent, resulting from failures of imagination on the part of those who cannot appreciate them.

It is useful to think of what is often called "taste" in matters of art in comparison with what is called "a sense of humor." To fail to laugh at a good joke is to be without a sense of humor, or at least not to be bringing it to this joke. To fail to appreciate a good work of art is to be without taste, or at least not to be able to exercise it in this case. Should we think of the capacity for aesthetic appreciation and the capacity to be amused by jokes as universal, so that those who do not appreciate and those who do not laugh are deficient in their responses? We can be justified in thinking this only if we can establish that certain works of art are valuable and that certain jokes are truly funny, and we must establish this independently of the reactions of the very audiences whose sensibilities we aim to impugn. Can this be done? That is a question for the topic of art criticism, and that topic is enriched if it is extended to include the criticism of jokes.

[*See also* Comedy.]

BIBLIOGRAPHY

Carroll, Noël. "On Jokes." *Midwest Studies in Philosophy* 16 (1991).

Cohen, Ted. "Jokes." In *Pleasure, Preference, and Value: Studies in Philosophical Aesthetics,* edited by Eva Schaper. Cambridge and New York, 1983.

De Sousa, Ronald. *The Rationality of Emotion.* Cambridge, Mass., 1987.

Freud, Sigmund. *Jokes and Their Relation to the Unconscious.* Translated and edited by James Strachey. New York, 1960.

Kant, Immanuel. *Critique of Judgment.* Translated by Werner S. Pluhar. Indianapolis, 1987. See section 54.

Morreall, John. *Taking Laughter Seriously.* Albany, N.Y., 1983.

Morreall, John, ed. *The Philosophy of Laughter and Humor.* Albany, N.Y., 1987.

TED COHEN

JUDD, DONALD

JUDD, DONALD (1928–1994), American artist and critic who brought Constructivist principles to the project of Minimalism and thereby gave definitive form to American sculptural materialism.

An autodidact, Donald Judd arrived at the practice of art through art history and art criticism. From 1949 to 1953, Judd studied at Columbia University, receiving his bachelor's degree in philosophy, cum laude, and from 1957 to 1962, continued his studies toward his master's degree in art history. From 1959 to 1965 he wrote art criticism, principally for *Arts Magazine*. Given his determinedly partisan aesthetic for the art of the 1960s, Judd's gallery reviews are tolerant of styles and inclusive of artists. (Wasilly Kandinsky is well considered even as Judd's aesthetic ideology attaches itself to Kasimir Malevich; both Stuart Davis and Jackson Pollock; Boberto Echauren Matta as well as Josef Albers. Robert Rauschenberg and Jasper Johns, but also John Chamberlain and Kenneth Noland, are favorites, and although these last are not surprising alliances, Judd's scope also includes Jacques Lipchitz, Kenzo Okada, and Roy Lichtenstein; Alfred Jensen, H. C. Westermann, and Oyvind Fahlstrom. "Unknowns" are frequent subjects of praise.) He is impatient with sensibility, the proficiency of "borrowed means," and parochialism.

With the sense of urgency to contribute to modern art by advancing the art-historical dialogue, Judd's own art soon fashioned itself as a synthetic response to the radical challenge proposed by the New York school. Judd saw the urgency of conceiving a form of artwork as advanced as the linear fields brought into being by Pollock and the color fields embedded by Barnett Newman, and as necessary as theirs to the history of modern art.

Judd gave the term *Specific Objects* to his project and fabricated monochromatic reliefs that, in confounding painting with sculpture, forced the issue of classification. From 1962 is a work that would be a painting were it not exploited for its sculptural physicality: a textured cadmium red masonite board into whose surface a lateral slit is wedged with a folded metal element to reveal the physical depth of the object. In other early works three-dimensional tactile aspects of reliefs and floor pieces dominate two-dimensional optical conditions. As though to co-opt the color fields of Newman, the tactile surfaces of Clyfford Still and Yves Klein, and the commonplace physical existence put forth in the constructed composites of painting and sculpture that Johns and Frank Stella had already effected in painting, Judd made a point of synthesizing painting and sculpture without, however, repeating these contemporary exempla of modern art.

By 1964 concrete demonstrations of the most barely necessary and sufficient conditions for sculpture had led Judd to concentrate on large boxes or deep frames suspended in series from the wall, or single or multiple modular boxes or serial frames placed on the floor. Metals vary from galvanized iron to stainless steel, while lacquer and Plexiglas supply physical vehicles for color that articulate the interior faces of boxes, to revivify a fixed morphology. After 1971, structural complexity comes about primarily through the tactical deployment of variably oriented internal divisions within such boxes. In Judd's own objects (as he had noted in

a 1963 review of Lee Bontecou's reliefs), "the entire shape, the structure and the image are coextensive."

Specific Object designates an artwork that, in Judd's own words, is "neither painting nor sculpture. Usually, it has been related, closely or distantly, to one or the other" (*Arts Yearbook* 8, 1965). This category amalgamates a variety of modes of assemblages and constructions. Assembled and constructed objects made by Rauschenberg and Johns qualify in Judd's scheme of things, as do industrial fluorescent fixtures by Dan Flavin, accretions of crushed automobile fenders by Chamberlain, as well as compulsive Surrealist aggregates by Lucas Samaras and Yayoi Kusama, and, pointedly, merely built structures by Robert Morris. With Judd, the relation—and antagonistic argument—has been decidedly with the notion of sculpture.

Taken as sculpture, Judd's objects are easiest to understand through a boundary definition: what sculpture is not. Sculptures are certainly not *statues*. At their most basic, they do not depict people, scenes, or anecdotes, nor do they commemorate history or render idealizations of history into mythological allegories. The subject matter traditionally portrayed through sculpture is disallowed in Judd's negation of the category of statuary. Not that he invented abstraction. But even allowing that sculpture is abstract, in Judd's aesthetic, subdividing wholes into parts traditionally jeopardizes abstraction by suggesting content extraneous to sculptural space. So, while adhering to the Humean notion of beauty as "an order and construction of parts," Judd has nonetheless stoutly insisted that that order remain aesthetically autonomous through what he termed a "non-relational" order of parts. Series, sequence, but not anthropological segmentation, will allow sculpture its own structural integrity.

In other words, the human anatomy from which the notion of order was derived is, in Judd's thinking, a biological metaphor retarding the development of consequential modern sculpture. Sculpture should have to found itself on another order, through a system of coordination without the hierarchy of part to whole characteristic of much sculptural convention.

Put positively, sculpture is essentially a three-dimensional entity: a volume in which space and solid accord and exist in structural and formal parity, a volume of real, not illusive or allusive, space. Following a precept of early modernism from Cubism on, Judd assumes the essential condition of sculpture to be volumetric rather than massive, and, although at times he allows closed forms, it is to explicate the volumetric concept that he does this. Indeed, density does not display the conditions of space as much as form does the interior that is available to sight.

If a volume defines sculpture, then, Judd assumes, whatever is done to the volume ought to clarify the essential reality of the volume. The "box," large, yet open to view, is the morphology on which Judd relies for this purpose. Then, too, if a volume defines that three-dimensional entity called sculpture, an ordering of parts should reiterate or explain the volume's essential nature. The so-called stacks, composed of deep galvanized aluminum or steel frames interleaved with equal measures of space and mounted in vertical series, would be an example of this sort of sculptural object. Work exemplifying real space are "boxes" placed on the floor, singly or arrayed in groups, to display the formal structure achieved by depressing the top face or displacing it diagonally within the volume of the box. Although the stacks exemplify coordinated structure, these boxes, which displace an inward surface, reveal Judd's later willingness to introduce a subordinated element, provided that the entity of the volume still dominates. Cognitively obdurate as are the "stacks," the "boxes" for the most part present themselves as transparent, that is, self-evident.

Despite the fact that Judd resisted the term *order* for its rational connotations, his primary strategy was to derive orders for sculptural objects that accorded them aesthetic autonomy. Like modern artists denying the biological metaphor before him, Judd's notion of ordering and construction of parts expresses itself in formal orders of logic and simplified mathematics. In a sense as apprentices together, American artists at work during the 1960s and early 1970s pursued a mathematical formal alternative to biological order governing traditional form. In the 1960s, this resulted in an inventive reconception of both painting and sculpture, of which Stella's deductive structures, Mel Bochner's measurements and additions, Dorothea Rockburne's folded drawings, and Jeremy Gilbert-Rolfe's and Bruce Boice's logical paintings are only a few examples.

Arithmetic series also informed Judd's work. Early on and intermittently throughout his career, Judd elected to compose wall elements in arithmetic progression, the length of metal elements diminishing as the intervals augmented. These elements, mounted horizontally under a continuous bar, showed their discontinuity purposefully. In other similarly conceived works, the edge of a single horizontal bar in relief created the focus of an arithmetically sequenced dentilation.

To Judd's way of thinking, varying the materials helped concretize the shape and structure that might otherwise remain cognitive abstractions. Introducing plywood into his material repertory in 1974 significantly contributed to the vernacular form, and content of that form. Plywood is not an overexposed material for sculpture, as even steel has become almost a cliché of modernist aesthetic. Then, too, plywood's coarse grain may be considered a fortuitously "found pattern" in nature, a *factura* that comes to be read as intrisically natural to the material. Rendering Judd's effects a function of democratic content, the grain of plywood also displays the strong-yet-flexible laminations of the structure, for plywood is a material structure expressly developed to suit the engineering needed in the pioneering aviation industry. The concrete references to Constructivist utility and immanence, yet also to the Russian avant-garde utilization of real materials in real space, cannot be missed.

Lecturing on art and architecture at the Yale School of Art and Architecture in September 1983, Judd did acknowledge limited early familiarity with Malevich, who, together with Piet Mondrian and Henri Matisse, were exemplary artists available on view since his youth at the Museum of Modern Art. "It's been 'the actual force of red' alongside 'a worker in a red apron.' Of those who began the tradition of the force of red, Malevich was the most clear in his painting and writing, as was Mondrian," noted Judd in his lecture. He also made clear that works by Naum Gabo and Antoine Pevsner were known to him. (Even before Camilla Gray's pioneering book *The Great Experiment: Russian Art, 1863–1922* finally introduced Russian art to an American public in 1962, her mentor, Alfred Barr, the first director of the Museum of Modern Art, had integrated the vision of a Russian avant-garde into the museum from the outset and had incorporated that vision into a permanent history of twentieth-century art when issuing the exhibition catalog *Cubism and Abstract Art* in 1936.)

Acknowledged or not, Minimalism's precedents are decidedly in Constructivism. Real, rather illusory, space is integral to Contructivist sculptural definition; indeed, space itself is treated as a material, palpable element. In the engineering aesthetic advanced by some Constructivists, industrial materials such as plastic and aluminum, along with common building materials, come into favor. Industrial methods are preferable to the organic techniques that attach to handicrafts. Preconceived and then executed, Judd's engineered fabrication is not a "realization," as Paul Cézanne would understand it—yet, it is a concretization of conception planned in advance. A practical approach to real materials in real space does not preclude planning, however, and in design Constructivism presumes an a priori structure to art, as it is decidedly biased toward rational form. (Although Vladimir Tatlin took an intuitive approach to rational form, an intuitive or expressive *content* would be as unwelcome as it would become in the name of materialist Minimalism.)

Eventually, by 1984, Judd will have produced fifteen designs for objects of furniture that exploit the formal union of sculpture and furniture, prompted in part by a commission, and in part (one suspects) by having to solve the many practical construction problems of renovating former artillery hangars and grounds of a disused military base to a studio compound when he moved in 1971 to Marfa, Texas. Yet, despite his late pursuit in furniture design and in integrating sculpture, applied arts, and architecture into the landscape, Judd remained decidedly aloof from collectivity, and shared with the engineer Gabo a commitment to solving the problem of sculptural autonomy. Indeed, from the 1970s onward, Judd made a point of dissecting his volumes in a way reminiscent of the stereometric analysis by Gabo. This may be seen not only in specific works (Bois, 1991), but also in a general preoccupation with the diagrammatic possibilities of rationalizing an interior space. The negative space of a box became a domain for Judd to exploit for a logic of operations peculiar to him. Meanwhile, as with his predecessor, applied and pure projects remained distinct aspects of, as Alan Colquhoun (1989) might say, the search for a vernacular classicism.

Assumed by Constructivists as by modernists at large is the autonomy of the artwork. Once the analytic revolution precipitated by the Cubist "destruction [and] the formal unity of the external world was suddenly laid down on their canvases, torn in pieces and dissected," then it became possible to create art. The Constructivist idea would come "to prepare a state of mind which will be able . . . to construct, co-ordinate and perfect," as Gabo wrote in a 1937 *Circle* editorial. With the Cubist sum of destructions turned constructive, "material values will reveal such a state." Meanwhile, insofar as real space is the subject of Judd's art, his objects are informed by the antecedent material values of Constructivism precedents coincident with the precepts of the de Stijl movement in the Netherlands. As voiced, for instance, in the manifesto of "concrete" art issued by Theo van Doesburg in 1930, there are the beliefs that art is universal; that it is "formed by the mind before its execution"; that its plastic form "means nothing but itself"; that the elements and their construction are "visually controllable"; that the execution is "mechanical, that is [,] exact"; and that clarity is the result. All these precepts, however they may have applied to painting, are also coincident with the stylistic register assumed by proponents of what will be called Minimalism in the 1960s.

The Minimalism of which Judd was arguably the indispensable protagonist does enter into aggravated sculptural dialogue with Constructivism. Judd challenges the notion of sculpture as a construction by asserting that before all else a sculpture is a thing. It is a thing in that it exists, and it exists in actuality. An extended review that Judd wrote in the March 1964 issue of *Arts Magazine* establishes this point. The occasion for the review, "Black, White and Gray," a group exhibition at the Wadsworth Atheneum in Hartford, Connecticut, provokes discussion, of Robert Morris's contribution especially. Of the several entries, the ones that seize Judd's interest are *Column* and *Slab*. They, like Rauschenberg's early four-paneled white painting,

> are next to nothing. You wonder why anyone would build something only barely present. . . . Morris' pieces exist after all, as meager as they are. Things that exist exist, and everything is on their side. . . . Things exist in the same way if that is all that is considered—which may be because we feel that or because that is what the word means or both. Everything is equal, just existing, and the values and interests they have are only adventitious.
>
> (Judd, 1975)

Intent on the semantic content of a thing, Judd will seek to advance that sense in which delimiting and defining its own fundamental being coincide with being an actuality. "Art means 'what is,'" observed sculptor John Chamberlain (quoted in Colpitt, 1993). Or, as Judd himself puts it in the *Arts Yearbook* for 1964, "The most unusual part of three-dimensional work is that which approaches 'being an object'" (ibid.). A Minimal object is an actuality to be taken literally (Fried, *Artforum*, June 1967). Before all else, Judd seems to insist, a sculpture is a thing that presents itself; it is a presentation, not a representation. Hence, its reality. Or, as Arthur Danto puts it, "Something is 'real' when it satisfies the representation of itself" (1981).

Gravitationally at rest, Judd's box is antithetical to Gabo's visualized topologies, with its Constructivist kineticism that in linear progression and volumetric evolution ingeniously calibrates a space of "continuous depth." Volumetrically static, Judd's objects extend themselves early on through repetition, unchanging and easily visualized, and later on through group permutation rather than development in the conventional sense. Compared with the compositionally complex forms of Gabo and Pevsner, simple unity of shape allows perception of the Minimal object as a single whole.

Beyond the matter-of-fact implementation of geometry, Minimalism differs from Constructivism in another way, as later work by Judd reveals. It is disconcerting that some of Judd's work that appears to be geometric evades those proportional harmonies of ratio traditionally said to induce beauty through mathematics. The intellectual power attained through his appeal to unprepossessing arithmetic sequences frustrates the expectations of even those viewers conversant with Constructivist reliance on mathematical models and the visualization of topologies created from the 1920s through the 1950s—from Gabo and Pevsner to Max Bill. Rather, Judd's understanding of the cultural situation inherited from the Constructivists is to present a sculpture that must retain the status of an object by virtue of its being a constructed entity in space yet must resist even certain geometric inventiveness, to reinstate and manifest the simple formal rigor. Instead of Gabo's sensuously unfolding topologies elaborating form is Judd's display of limited arithmetic operations: divide in half, then half again—left, then right of the median. In this way, then, the sets of boxes subdivided by partitioning to reveal successively their ratios of halves, then fourths, display the operation of division concretely—as though to demonstrate the algebraic content of the geometric volumes thereby produced. Judd's need to make algorithmic reckoning synonymous with formalism has early modern roots. Citing Oswald Spengler in his history of modern sculpture, Jack Burnham underlines Spengler's observation that in the early twentieth century mathematics had turned to the "general morphology of mathematical operation" (Burnham, 1968). Judd participates in this aesthetic of number without strain.

So in Judd's later practice especially, a thing is an object, so-called, by virtue of exercising the potentiality of a "scheme" (Agee, 1994). In maturity, it was increasingly true that Judd relied on the fixed morphology of a box. Once his morphology stabilized, then a fixity of exterior shape demonstrably dramatized the systematic variability articulating the interior. As discussed above, the louvers subdividing the whole into parts exploit the relationship left and right of the center median, to create a logical focus on the formalism. In other instances, the articulated relationship of the sculptural volume to the orientation and placement of the plane(s) within the volume enhances the coincidence of formal essentialism and structural analysis. Where color is introduced, it either articulates the recessive structural dimension of the box—its interior—or, as in early work, gives the surface emphasis: surface may be colored or patterned only insofar as articulating the surface does not interfere with the volume's dominance. (It has been suggested that the Constructivist formalist aesthetic anticipates Roland Barthes's own Structuralist approach to literature [Bann, 1990], and Judd's own semiotic display of formal visual language historically coincides with the general literary interest newly taken in these matters.)

"Minimalism," a designation resisted by Judd, is arguably advantageous in lending expedient classification to a praxis with which his work is identified. Literal abstract constructions and industrial materials, placed simply, constitute an art of aesthetic economy—just what is deemed necessary and sufficient in an art object.

Aside from the layperson's usage, in which Minimalism means anything apparently simple, Minimalism is a contested term. As John Graham employed the term in *System and Dialectics of Art* (1937), *minimalism* applies to the process of attaining form through patient carving that eventually yields its essential form, in such sculptors as Constantin Brancusi and Jean Arp. Historically, minimalism is a reduction arrived at intuitively and gradually. In contrast, Minimalism is preconceived and constructed of prefabricated, commonly available, industrial units.

Minimalism is at once a style, a method, and a value, as it is variously appropriated to designate the art of the early 1960s. The philosopher Richard Wollheim, for whom the aesthetic object is essentially a mental, not a physical, entity, has allowed that minimal art applies to artifacts ranging from those of Marcel Duchamp to Ad Reinhardt and beyond, artifacts of "very low content" yet of decision-driven consequence (Wollheim, 1968). For Judd, however, the content of the object is unavoidably determined through its relation to sculpture as a type and in history. Further, its content is expressible as the totality of its materials; indeed, palpable objects are intrinsic to the making of art, and material differences among materials carry discriminative content integral to the criticality that results in substantive and normative judgments. When considering the content of works that appear nearly identical, such discriminations of content reveal themselves. (In Judd's review of "Black, White and Gray," the sheer existence established through Morris's *Slab*, distinguishable from Tony Smith's modular constructions, was, in turn, not to be confused with Reinhardt's nearly black paintings "close to nothingness.") Statements of intelligible definition aside, for Judd, training in the rigors of art history does entail analytic expertise in ascertaining consequential aspects of style that will culturally elevate or indict an object. Yet, Wollheim and Judd do concur that the conceptual content of an artwork will significantly govern its cultural significance.

Applicable here is the convergence of Minimalism with a possibility of "form exhaustion," which posits an alternative to the furtherance of beautiful things, through an aesthetic of ideas or "informational systems" organized along non-aestheticized principles (Burnham, 1968, 1973). Minimalism does indeed put forth artifacts organized in ways to defeat conventional delectation. By borrowing patterns of recurrence and change from other disciplines, orders that make explicit the self-referential realism of structure in itself, Minimalism may be said to exhibit a profound aesthetic disinterestedness—but not indifference.

A normative definition of art that centers a form concentrated through the elimination of nonessentials likens the "realist" project of Judd's with that of avant-garde early modern art throughout Europe. In Minimalism, as Judd practices it, a materialism coincides with the analytic approach to form in art.

[*See also* Minimalism; *and* Sculpture.]

BIBLIOGRAPHY

Works by Judd

Complete Writings, 1959–1975. Halifax, 1975.
Complete Writings, 1975–1986. Eindhoven, 1987.

Other Sources

Agee, William. *Donald Judd.* New York, 1968.
Agee, William. "Donald Judd in Retrospect: An Appreciation." In *Donald Judd.* New York, 1994.
Arts Council of Great Britain. *Art in Revolution: Soviet Art and Design since 1917.* London, 1971.
Bann, Stephen, ed. *The Tradition of Constructivism.* New York, 1974; reprint, New York, 1990.
Battcock, Gregory, ed. *Minimal Art: A Critical Anthology.* New York, 1968.
Bois, Yve-Alain. *Donald Judd.* Paris, 1991.
Burnham, Jack. *Beyond Modern Sculpture.* New York, 1968.
Burnham, Jack. *The Structure of Art.* Rev. ed. New York, 1973.
Colpitt, Frances. *Minimalism.* Seattle, 1993.
Colquhoun, Alan. *Modernity and the Classical Tradition: Architectural Essays, 1980–1987.* Cambridge, Mass., 1989.
Crone, Rainer. *Donald Judd, 1987–1988.* Eindhoven, 1987.
Danto, Arthur C. *The Transfiguration of the Commonplace: A Philosophy of Art.* Cambridge, Mass., 1981.
Fried, Michael. "Art and Objecthood." In *Minimal Art: A Critical Anthology,* edited by Gregory Battcock, pp. 116–147. New York, 1968.

Gabo, Naum. "The Constructive Idea in Art." In *Circle: An International Survey of Constructive Art,* edited by J. L. Martin, Ben Nicholson, and N. Gabo, pp. 1–10. Reprint, New York, 1971.

Gabo, Naum. "Sculpture: Carving and Construction in Space." In *Circle: An International Survey of Constructive Art,* edited by J. L. Martin, Ben Nicholson, and N. Gabo, pp. 102–111. Reprint, New York, 1971.

Gray, Camilla. *The Great Experiment: Russian Art, 1863–1922.* London, 1962.

Krauss, Rosalind E. "Allusion and Illusion in Donald Judd." *Artforum* 4.9 (May 1966): 24–26.

Poetter, Jochen, and Rosemarie E. Pahlke. *Donald Judd.* Baden-Baden, 1989.

Smith, Brydon. *Donald Judd: Catalogue Raisonné of Painting, Objects and Wood blocks, 1960–1974.* Ottawa, 1975.

Wollheim, Richard. "Minimal Art." In *Minimal Art: A Critical Anthology,* edited by Gregory Battcock, pp. 387–399. New York, 1968.

MARJORIE WELISH

JUDGMENT. *See* Appreciation; Epistemology and Aesthetics; Evaluation; Interpretation; Kant, *article on* Kant, Duchamp, and Judgment; Perception; Realism; *and* Taste.

K

KAHN, LOUIS ISADORE (1901–1974), American architect. Louis Kahn's aesthetic formation encompassed two very different worldviews: one based on stasis, enclosure, and centering (the Beaux-Arts); another based on dynamics, transparency, and flow (modernism). Rationalism served as a universal, symbolic, and abstract bridge between these two worlds. Kahn switched from the Beaux-Arts of his training to the Moderne and then modernism of his early career. He then helped develop a third, imperial, proto-postmodernist style, which critics have identified with America's emergence on the world stage as a superpower after World War II. In his maturity, Kahn switched again to break with modernism on some key issues. He became more guarded, phenomenological, and mystical, anticipating postmodernism. Kahn based his late work on the ideal concept of the "Room," which distinguished him from his colleagues. Kahn's statements at the last conference of the Congress of International Architects (CIAM) at Oterloo in 1959 were crucial to the development of the postmodern aesthetic. After Oterloo, Kahn built the works that have enshrined him as one of the last great Modern Masters, while his aesthetic position remains one that all subsequent practitioners have had to acknowledge.

Kahn's Aesthetic Formation. Louis Kahn was born in Estonia. His parents immigrated to Philadelphia, and in his youth Kahn won several citywide drawing contests before he went to a special magnet high school, which took him across the city and out of his neighborhood. Kahn's first recorded childhood ink sketch shows a port clustered on the shore of a bay, with a tall steeple to guide sailors. Kahn entered the University of Pennsylvania as a scholarship student and studied with Paul Cret, when the school was perhaps the preeminent Beaux-Arts school in America. He later worked for Cret, who was involved with the committee to create the Benjamin Franklin Parkway. Cret was a rationalist trained in the French Beaux-Arts tradition, but one who, like Charles McKim, W. R. Mead, and Stanford White, accepted modern industry. As a student Kahn emulated the Pencil Points picturesque drawing style of the period and studied the great urban illustrators of New York, such as Hugh Ferris, whose stepped skyscrapers allowed light to penetrate down to the street. After a period of work in Philadelphia, Kahn traveled to Europe on an idiosyncratic Grand Tour, viewing romantic and picturesque British castles, the romantic classicism of the newly constructed Stockholm town hall, and his family home in Estonia, ending up in Italy sketching picturesque hill towns.

Like his entire generation, Kahn was deeply affected by the global failure of monopoly capitalism in 1929, the Great Depression, the rise of international fascism, and anti-Semitism. Kahn became an ardent supporter of Franklin Roosevelt, the New Deal, and the change to a state-managed capitalist system. At the onset of the depression he converted to a liberal, Moderne, Art Deco architectural aesthetic, which was still quite conservative and retained many elements of the Beaux-Arts (axiality, hierarchies, compositional values, entourage, etc.). In the depths of the depression Kahn became a more radical modernist and accepted the mechanist aesthetic of Le Corbusier, believing in standardized mass production as the solution for the ills of the city and country. Kahn developed a linear, scrawling, sketching style, which he employed to illustrate various utopian schemes for the redevelopment of downtown Philadelphia, equipping it for the arrival of the automobile as envisaged by Le Corbusier in his *Ville radieure*. Kahn was employed on several WPA-sponsored housing projects, while absorbing the more flexible, idealized, avant-garde American industrial philosophy of Buckminster Fuller. As a convinced modernist, Kahn worked for George Howe and William Lescaze on the Philadelphia Savings Fund Society skyscraper office tower in downtown Philadelphia. Kahn formed a lifelong friendship with the Harvard-trained Howe, whose partner on the PSFS was one of the designers of the Museum of Modern Art in New York.

After World War II, Howe's advocacy helped Kahn to teach at Yale and to study at the American Academy in Rome in 1951. At Yale, Kahn taught an urban history course with the city planner Christopher Tunnard (whose later *American Skyline* [1956], written with Henry Hope Reed, placed a great emphasis on typologies, industrial development, and the continuity of the monumental tradition). Kahn's design juries were attended by the architectural historian Vincent Scully, Jr. (author of *The Earth, the Temple, and the Gods: Greek Sacred Architecture,* as well as the first monograph on Kahn in 1962). During the late 1940s Kahn continued to work on utopian modern schemes for Philadelphia, planning to replace the existing railway viaduct with an auto-based business center, the Penn Center. He then extended this project, linking it to a renewed civic center with a new geodesic town hall tower designed with Anne Tyng in the early 1950s. Later, Kahn expanded this utopian plan to include a new commercial center at Market Street East. After the war Kahn's sketching style developed from his earlier picturesque realism to a radical, flat, abstract style influenced by the light-and-dark enclosures of Giorgio De Chirico's metaphysical cityscapes and Josef Albers's relational color field theories. Kahn's red-and-orange portrayal of the amphitheatral Piazza Del Campo at Siena gave enormous prominence to shadows across the bowl of the space. Kahn filled his notebooks on his second European tour and residency in Rome with such drawings from Greece and Egypt, as well as the ruins of the Roman Forum and Hadrian's Villa, with their collisive plane geometries and monumental scale. On his return, Kahn sketched a revision of his imaginary Penn Center Business Complex, creating a large, triangular, metaphysical plaza, stretching De Chirico down toward the river. The first publication of Henri Matisse's paper cutouts in the early 1950s influenced Kahn's later work deeply, with their lyrical freedom and use of line and color, as well as their dematerialization and emphasis on light.

Kahn's "Imperial" Aesthetics. After the war, when Kahn sought to move beyond the aesthetic horizons of functionalism, he was forced to invent spatial devices that broke the free-flowing universality of the rationalist grid (perhaps best represented in the transparent, open, grid plans of the pavilions of the Illinois Institute of Technology campus in Chicago by Ludwig Mies van der Rohe). Kahn and his colleagues at Yale, especially Philip Johnson (an associate of Mies's) and Eero Saarinen, developed a new muscular, abstract, monumental, structural module scaled to dwarf the individual (framing many standardized and repetitive bays and details). This representation of state or corporate power was applied in many situations, varying from Edward Durell Stone's embassy at New Delhi of 1957, to Saarinen's embassy in London completed in 1960 and Johnson's work at the Lincoln Center in New York completed in 1963. Kahn himself in 1959 designed an unrealized U.S. consulate in Angola using this giant bay system, setting cubic pavilions below its giant roof, carried on monumental structural columns. Manfredo Tafuri and Francesco Dal Co, in *Modern Architecture* describe these experiments at Yale as the origins of a new American "imperial" style in the cold-war years. Kenneth Frampton, in *Modern Architecture: A Critical History,* also notes the importance of Yale and its dean, Kahn's friend Howe, when this new monumental style emerged.

Kahn played a crucial role in the definition of this new modular "imperial" aesthetic, but his emphasis, as Frampton noted, was on the monumental wall or skin, a secondary nonstructural surface. At Yale, Kahn was especially suscep-

tible to his colleague Fuller, whose rotational geometries and three-dimensional geodesic domes and vaults so influenced Tyng, Kahn's associate and companion of his last thirty years. Kahn's first big public commission at Yale, for the University Art Gallery (1950–1954), contained a giant structural bay unit wrapped in walls of glass or brick. This bay concept was further developed in the Richards Medical Research Center at the University of Pennsylvania in 1955. Here the horizontal segregation of the cellular, "servant" and "served," spaces was given dramatic, picturesque vertical expression, reminiscent of Kahn's romantic English castle sketches and breaking the continuity of the modernist floor plate into discrete towers.

Kahn's geometric interest was further complicated by an encounter with Colin Rowe, the author of *The Mathematics of the Ideal Villa.* Rowe introduced him to Rudolf Wittkower's work on Andrea Palladio, mathematics, symbolism, and geometry in 1955, including his distinctive analysis patterns of bay sizes that set rhythms and alternative scales in the building structure and facade. These rhythms disrupted the standardized reticulations of the modernist grid, creating an uneven tartan of possibilities. Rowe identifies Kahn's key role in redefining this new cellular and monumental aesthetic in "Neo-Classicism and Modern Architecture II" (written 1956–1957). In the Trenton, New Jersey, Jewish Community Bath House of 1955, the "servant" corner pavilions first began to clearly define the central, pyramidal roofed space as a top-lit room (in the Wrightian tradition of the Unity Temple in Oak Park, Illinois, or the Larkin Building in Buffalo, New York). In the Sephardic synagogue projected for historic downtown Philadelphia (Mickeh Israel Synagogue, 1961–1972) Kahn would convert these corner pavilions into light towers around a central room. Rowe points out how in Trenton, Kahn set out the differentiated tartan grid and then centered each module using a vaulted roof structure and peripheral pavilions to define the cellular bays. These, Kahn rapidly realized, were the equivalent of traditional rooms.

Kahn's "Rooms": Urban, Institutional, and Domestic Aesthetics. Kahn gave the clearest exposition of his "Room" concept at the last meeting of the CIAM in Oterloo in 1959. This concept was profoundly at odds with the modernist's belief in the universality of space, expressed in the grid, representing the universal rationalism of modern science. Kahn adopted a Matisse-like drafting style, using soft pencils or charcoal, to make a series of iconic cartoons describing the "Room." Kahn showed an annotated vision of this "Room" space, as an ideal architectural type, which he called a fundamental, existential "Form." Its space was defined by four walls and opened to the light at window punctures. It was monumental in scale with large, blank wall surfaces which dwarfed elements scaled to human habitation, like a bay window, door or table. The sketch evoked his earlier drawings of Romanesque chapels, as well as memories of the great rooms of Philadelphia (the richy detailed and multiple-scaled reading room at Frank Furness's library at the University of Pennsylvania, the sublime height of the Great Hall in the Thirtieth Street station, or the Modern, smoothe, round-cornered, double-height banking hall at the PSFS Building). The monumental, cubic volume of the room sketch was given further definition by a vaulted ceiling, which centered the void, giving it increased stability. Kahn explicitly detailed the metaphysical qualities of his "Room": its light and silence, the immanent presence of its space. Within these fragmentary enclaves, Kahn was concerned with a slowing of time, with the long duration, a sense of timelessness, in contrast to the space-time acceleration of the technophilic, modern world. Phenomenological concepts like tradition, especially craft tradition shared in a community as an alternative source of knowledge, became important to him, as was a phenomenological sense of materials eroding as traces through time. Each piece of the building had its own identity and tradition. Kahn conceived of his "Rooms" as sacred entities: sculpted, plastic voids acting like solids, controlled by geometry (in the Beaux-Arts tradition of Choisy). While in Europe for Oterloo Kahn visited Le Corbusier's Ronchamps Chapel (1950–1954), which confirmed his intuitions about the "Room": light and mass, the dematerialization of architecture and the importance of the wall (as a screen, independent of structure). Kahn acknowledged the importance of Le Corbusier in his work. He often stayed in Le Corbusier's Villa Sarabhai at Ahmadabad (1955), with its barrel vaults and screen walls, when he was supervising his own work in India.

Kahn applied his "Room" concept on various scales, extending it to "Institutions" (groups of rooms clustered about a common idea or community) and to the city itself, where "Streets" functioned as urban rooms connecting communities and institutions. This implied the fragmentation of the modernist city into enormous, institutional units, a model influenced by his admiration for Giambattista Piranesi. At Oterloo Kahn showed his last project for Philadelphia, in which the core became a "Room" defined by a cluster of enormous, Piranesian, institutional fragments. These in turn were surrounded by a ring wall of highways with enormous, circular parking towers, which he called "harbors" and "gateways" (based on his visit to the defensive walls and towers of Carcassonne in 1959). The hybrid parking buildings (perhaps related to the circular hybrid parking/living towers of Wright's Pittsburgh Triangle project) were to be painted different colors to aid navigation on the highway (anticipating Kevin Lynch's theories about urban markers). Within these defenses Kahn proposed a mechanized raised pedestrian "Street" as an armature linking his earlier institutional enclave projects. This "Street" crossed an enormous urban room created by his towers and

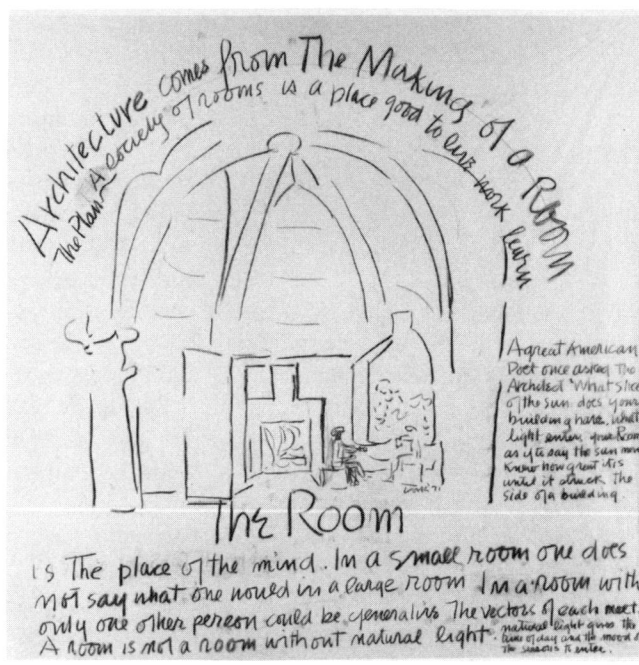

KAHN. Louis Kahn, *Drawings for City/2 Exhibition* (1971), charcoal on paper, 34 × 34 in.; Philadelphia Museum of Art (Given by Louis Kahn). (Copyright by the Philadelphia Museum of Art; used by permission.)

a new Forum entertainment complex, leading down to the historic Independence Mall area by the river.

Kahn built his first great "Room" in the Margaret Esheric house of 1959–1961. The beautifully scaled, double-height living room was both domestic and intimate, as well as monumental. This ambiguous double scale was achieved by virtue of precise details like human-scaled folding wooden shutters that modulated the light, and sliding library stairs against a wall of books. On one side of the room a visible, cramped, staircase-service zone and balcony contrasted with the monumental scale of the white exterior wall opposite, whose surface was incised with a window slot surrounding a fireplace. Here Kahn's characteristic "keyhole" windows appeared, indicating the double scale of human and monumental. It was also here that the attention to detail and to materials, wood and stone, zinc and brick, broke the modernist, standardized mold, returning to a craft tradition.

"Rooms" at various scales became a unifying aesthetic theme in Kahn's later work. In the late 1950s, he began his association with Jonas Salk, which would produce a "Great Room," this time open, facing the horizon and the Pacific Ocean at the Salk Institute in La Jolla, California (1956–1965). Kahn originally planned to landscape this space with an allée of cypress trees, but the Mexican landscape designer Luis Barragán (consulted on-site after his show at the Museum of Modern Art) advised Kahn, "Not one leaf, nothing green." While working on the Esheric House, Kahn developed for the Erdman Dormitories at Bryn Mawr College a series of three diagonally interlinked, top-lit "Great Rooms," surrounded by rotated rings of smaller, dormitory rooms. The Esheric House and the Bryn Mawr dormitories established the pattern of setting large rooms inside rings of smaller ones, wrapping the monumental within the domestic, which came to characterize Kahn's double-scaled work in postcolonial India: the Indian Institute of Management in Ahmadabad, Pakistan (1962–1974), and the National Assembly Hall and the Presidential Palace at Dhaka, Bangladesh (1962–1983). An alternative line of research concerned the interstitial spaces between "Rooms," developed in many unbuilt projects of the 1960s such as Saint Andrew's Priory in California (1966–1967) or the Dominican Motherhouse at Media, Pennsylvania (1965–1969). For these projects Kahn used a compositional technique explicitly based on Matisse's paper cutouts.

In the library at the Phillips Exeter Academy (1965–1972), Kahn imported the giant circle motif from India to define his first American institutional "Great Room." It is a gigantic cube awkwardly entered from below via a baroque double stair. The interior facades of this top-lit cube are faced with great concrete screen walls inscribed with circles. The sublime scale of this abstract incised geometry, combined with the light descending from the monumental, diagonal baffles overhead, make this a truly memorable space. Kahn arranged for the stacks to be visible though the circular punctures, scaling the human presence through these giant oculi, positioning the readers and research rooms on the exterior, with small wooden carrels close to natural light. The brick skin of the library registers the rhythm of these carrels to the exterior facade, while the building's red brick mass functions as the prominent hinge between two great, green, open-air rooms that make up the campus enclosure. In the Mellon Center for English Art at Yale (1969–1974), facing his earlier University Gallery, Kahn again organized the building around two top-lit, multistory interior "Rooms." One of these awkwardly drops down to street level to provide diagonal access from the corner (via a circular staircase tower). Picture galleries open off these two courts, with wooden folding shutters providing a flexible sense of enclosure, light control, and domestic intimacy (reminiscent of the Esheric House). In the Kimbell Art Museum in Fort Worth, Texas (1966–1972), Kahn achieves a successful entry to his building. He and landscape architect Harriet Pattison have drawn a small grove of trees, with gravel underfoot, into the grid of the building, while the space is filled with the gentle sound of water from a black marble slab fountain. The Kimbell combines the intimate scale of his "Room" concept at the same time suggesting a mysterious ambiguity, as the roof and natural lighting system span in long vaults toward infinity. It was here that Kahn speaks of light as his great theme. At the end of his life

Kahn again worked on an outdoor landscape "Room" without planting, this time as a memorial for FDR at the southern tip of Roosevelt Island in New York (1973–1974).

Kahn's Aesthetic Legacy: Postmodern Aesthetics. Kahn defined many of the basic questions for later architects in his moves to fracture the modernist grid, without giving up on the dream of universality and equal opportunity. The centrality of his position and depth of his aesthetic achievement may be realized by a brief survey of his legacy. Robert Venturi (whom he had met in Rome in 1951), Charles Moore (his student at Yale), and Paul Rudolf (Howe's successor), the next generation of young teachers at Yale, developed his preoccupation with monuments and fragmentation in their appreciation of Pop art, pop culture, and mass consumerism in the postwar suburban sprawl. Team Ten, especially Alison Smithson and Peter Smithson, combined this pop sensibility with an appreciation of Kahn's restructuring of the urban infrastructure as modern monument (also appreciated by Reyner Banham). Kahn's rationalism, monumental institutions, and phenomenological emphasis on silence, stillness, and light were appreciated by Aldo Rossi, leader of the Italian rationalists of the 1970s. In *Deconstructing the Kimbell: An Essay on Meaning and Architecture*, Michael Benedikt makes a convincing case that Kahn, in his questioning and inversions of the logic of modernism, anticipated the strategies of the literary critic Jacques Derrida and architects like Peter Eisenman.

Both the Beaux-Arts and modernism in their American formulations accepted the machine, but within very different aesthetics. In order to grow and develop, Kahn had to question the machine aesthetic and thus opened the door for the postmodern critique of the machine. He clung to his abstract and rational capacity even as he crossed this boundary so that he could translate between codes, maintain continuities, and negotiate differences. His personal world was deeply shaped by this ecumenical universalism, which encompassed both the technical world of the machine and the ethical world of art in the neo-Kantian or Hegelian interpretation. He had to master multiple codes and maintain a strong aesthetic identity in a rapidly shifting world. In this he was helped enormously by his powerful, interior, visual and spatial imagination, which grew over time not only to occupy the conventional professional visual codes, but also to explore the previously uncharted formal, spatial, and multisensual worlds beyond them.

[*See also* Architecture.]

BIBLIOGRAPHY

Works by Kahn

Light Is the Theme: Louis I. Kahn and the Kimbell Art Museum: Comments on Architecture by Louis Kahn. Edited by Nell E. Johnson. Fort Worth, Tex., 1975.
Louis I. Kahn: Writings, Lectures, Interviews. Edited by Alessandra La Tour. New York, 1991.

Other Sources

Benedikt, Michael. *Deconstructing the Kimbell: An Essay on Meaning and Architecture.* New York, 1991.

Brownlee, David B., and David G. De Long. *Louis I. Kahn: In the Realm of Architecture.* New York, 1991.

Frampton, Kenneth. *Modern Architecture: A Critical History.* New York, 1980.

Johnson, Eugene J., and Michael J. Lewis. *Drawn from the Source: The Travel Sketches of Louis I. Kahn.* Cambridge, Mass., 1996.

Plattus, Alan J. "Kahn and the Order of the City." *Design Book Review* 21 (1991): 17–21.

Rowe, Colin. "Neo-Classicism and Modern Architecture II." In *The Mathematics of the Ideal Villa and Other Essays.* Cambridge, Mass., 1976.

Scully, Vincent. *Louis I. Kahn.* New York, 1962.

Scully, Vincent. *The Earth, the Temple, and the Gods: Greek Sacred Architecture,* rev. ed. New York, 1969.

Smithson, Alison, ed. *The Team Ten Primer.* Cambridge, Mass., 1968.

Tafuri, Manfredo, and Francesco Dal Co. *Modern Architecture.* Translated by Robert Erich Wolf. New York, 1979.

Tunnard, Christopher, and Henry Hope Read. *The American Skyline: The Growth and Form of Our Cities and Towns.* Boston, 1955.

Tyng, Alexandra. *Beginnings: Louis I. Kahn's Philosophy of Architecture.* New York, 1984.

DAVID GRAHAME SHANE

KAMES, LORD. *See* Home.

KANDINSKY, WASSILY (1866–1944), Russian painter. Wassily Kandinsky described in his memoir *Reminiscences* (1913) how, shortly after his return to Munich in 1908, he had had a "revelation" of an unexpected and enchanting kind:

> I returned home [at dusk] having finished a study, still dreamy and absorbed in the work I had completed, and suddenly saw an indescribably beautiful picture, pervaded by an inner glow. At first, I stopped short and then quickly approached this mysterious picture, on which I could discern only forms and colors and whose content was incomprehensible. At once, I discovered the key to the puzzle: it was a picture I had painted, standing on its side against the wall. (Kandinsky, 1994)

The philosophical interest of this passage, which forms part of Kandinsky's account of how his search for "pure painting" developed, lies not only in the mystically charged nature of the incident, as later recounted, but also in the intellectual sources and exposures that motivated such a way of responding.

Kandinsky was born in Moscow. He did not begin to devote himself to painting until, at the age of thirty, he moved to Munich for this purpose, attending first the school of Anton Ažbe and then studying under Franz von Stuck at the Munich Academy. Prior to that he had spent a decade studying and teaching law; and in 1889, on an ethnographic expedition to the Vologda province, he had seen and sketched carved and painted examples of folk art in the re-

mote villages there. On entering one particular room so decorated, he had "felt surrounded on all sides by painting, into which I had thus penetrated." This experience repeated itself over time in churches and chapels that he visited. At some point also in 1890s (the exact date remains uncertain), Kandinsky attended an exhibition of the French Impressionists in Moscow and, confronted with one of Claude Monet's *Haystacks,* was surprised to discover that he failed to recognize in it the subject identified by the accompanying catalog. Clearly, he had already learned that it was more important initially to respond to the play of colors and shapes than to recognize what a painting, or an ensemble of images in the case of folk art, actually showed.

The analogy between painting and music—claimed from the Romantic period onward as the most "abstract" of the arts—was familiar to Kandinsky, who responded fervently to the "music dramas" of Richard Wagner and would bring musical analogies, as early as 1902, into the reviews of art exhibitions in Munich that he wrote that year for a Saint Petersburg periodical. Subsequently, during his years of association with the Blue Rider group (Der Blaue Reiter) in Munich, whose exhibitions of 1911 and 1912 he organized and whose almanac he compiled and edited jointly with Franz Marc, he wrote on Arnold Schoenberg's pictures. He published in the almanac music, analyses of it, and theoretical essays by Schoenberg, Anton Webern, Aleksandr Scriabin, and others. He also created his own stage compositions, such as the *Yellow Sound,* deploying sound, color, and light in expressive correlations with one another.

The power of Friedrich Nietzsche's example was important here, as it impacted on European thought from the 1880s onward, and on Munich as an intellectual environment. In an article of 1911 for the Russian press, "Whither the 'New Art'?" Kandinsky referred to the "transvaluation of values" that "consciously or unconsciously, the genius of Nietzsche began." In his major theoretical text composed prior to 1914, *On the Spiritual in Art,* which was drafted in a Russian version in 1911, he added to the text as first published in German that year a reference to Nietzsche's "mighty hand" in shaking the values of religion, science, and morality. [*See* Nietzsche.] He was attracted correspondingly to the Nietzschean concept of "contradiction," as it could be applied in a deep sense to the structure of paintings. Symbolist art and theory were equally important stimuli. Kandinsky referred in the same context to the dramas of Maurice Maeterlinck, which had gained considerable currency in Munich. He would also have known, as a student newly arrived there, the ringing statement by the *Jugendstil* painter and designer August Endell to the effect that "we stand on the threshold of an altogether new art, an art with forms that mean or represent nothing, yet which can stimulate our soul as deeply as the tones of music have been able to do."

But while Endell applied this claim to the imaginative creation of rugs, furnishings, and metal and stucco decorations, Kandinsky had grasped its application to painting further back in time, from his exposure to Russian Symbolist art and thought. In a tradition of religious philosophizing that claimed the insufficiency of rational thought alone, art had been conceived of in Russia, from the later nineteenth century onward, as, in Kandinsky's own words, renouncing the rendering of "states of mind" in favor of communicating with the spectator by means of a "language of the soul," with the uniquely held power to develop and refine it. Nietzsche was a much venerated figure in that tradition, as he was with Kandinsky's contact in Saint Petersburg, Nikolai Kulbin, who shared the idea introduced near the close of *On the Spiritual* of the "spiritual triangle" that moves slowly "onward and upward." There are references also made in that text to theosophical writings: to the Russian Helena Blavatsky's contribution in her *Key to Theosophy* of 1889 (German version, 1907), and to Rudolph Steiner, whose lectures Kandinsky attended in Berlin in 1908, and whose ideas promulgated there about harmony and flux, circles and colors were being actively discussed in Munich—in line with its liberalizing and strongly spiritual orientation as an intellectual environment—by 1908–1909. Kandinsky may also arguably have drawn, for his own imaginative purposes, on the plates illustrating "Thought-Forms" in Annie Besant's and C. W. Leadbetter's 1901 book of that title (German version, 1908); but those small-scale images, made by artists on the authors' instruction, could only have served to confirm, in an indirect and suggestive way, what Kandinsky already had in mind.

Kandinsky did not apply the term *abstract* to his production as a painter from 1910 or 1911 onward until 1919, and in revising his *On the Spiritual* in 1914, he expressed the sense he had then of the inadequacy of this term, by qualifying it with *purely*. In his *Reminiscences* of 1912–1913 he used the term "nonobjective painting" *(gegenstandslöse Malerei)* to designate a branch of development in art in general, explaining it as involving work that "springs mainly or exclusively from 'out of the artist,'" without coming down firmly in favor of the second of those alternatives. Prior to that he had used the phrase "pure painting" to describe what he had arrived at by 1911: expression achieved primarily by the treatment of color, form, plane, and line, with real objects serving only as "an allusion or aroma." "Veiling" or disguising the object by "dissolving" its originary identity acted in this context to intensify the "purely painterly composition."

As to what lay behind this in the development of Kandinsky's practice as a painter: his cosmopolitan personality, as well as taking him back and forth between central Europe and Russia, had led him to travel extensively throughout Europe and to spend a year in France in 1906. Based in Sèvres and exhibiting both in Paris and, as a member of the cooperative group Les Tendances Nouvelles, in Angers, he was exposed that year to the same Neo-Impressionist and Symbolist pictorial practices as the Fauvist painters had drawn on in 1905–1906. He also showed with the Bridge group (Die Brücke) in Dresden in the winter of 1906, and in 1910 he had, through the exhibition of Islamic art held in Munich that year, an exposure to Near Eastern carpets, ceramics, textiles, and miniatures that proved important for his interest in embroidery and ornamental design. During those same years the imagery of his paintings shifted from landscape and coastal scenes and fairy-tale subjects of old Russia to the mountain ranges and village streets of Murnau and its surroundings—where he began spending summers in 1908 and acquired a house a year later, decorated by him and his companion, the painter Gabriele Münter, who equally admired and collected examples of the folk art of that region. From those subjects he then moved to biblical scenes of creation, resurrection, and apocalypse, saints and knights, and evocations of battle and conflict in generalized landscape settings. These in turn became the basis of his first "abstract" works, which he called, in their evolved form, "Compositions" or alternatively—borrowing the terminology of music—"Impressions" or "Improvisations."

The role of Kandinsky's theorizing, answering from the beginning to a different strain in his personality than fueled the work itself, had as its principal aim, as he put it in his *Reminiscences,* to "awaken [the] capacity to experience the spiritual in material and in abstract phenomena"; and he concluded *On the Spiritual* with the affirmation that "an age of purposeful creation" already lay ahead, informed by a "spirit in painting" that stood "in a direct organic relationship to the creation of a new spiritual reality." But what he had to go through, in order to arrive at a fully committed version of "abstraction"—devoid of readily recognized objects or presences within what constitutes, in the most broadly evocative sense, a landscape setting—was the maturation of a conviction that an audience for such art really existed, or could exist.

The viability of such a conviction, as it lays itself open to debate in modern art more generally, beginning at this period, parallels the philosophical issue of whether there can be such a thing as a truly private language, and especially one that some creative individual might seek to devise, to express thoughts and ideas that lie beyond the bounds of commonly shared experience, and its interpretative understanding on the part of others. At the time that he put *On the Spiritual* into its final form, Kandinsky was still ambivalent as to how inner experience could derive from composing with "wholly emancipated forms and colors." For the time being the approach to a work of art should entail "conversation" about ideas and feelings that might convey what was expressed in the way of a "direct, abstract effect." Then, later, the possibility would arise of "speaking through purely artistic means," without it being necessary any longer "to borrow the forms for this inner speech from the external world." But by the time of his *Reminiscences* Kandinsky had come to regard as a "delusion" such positing of an open-mindedness on the viewer's part, together with the capacity to pick out in the picture "a language to which he can relate." Rare in principle, such viewers where they existed would be ones who, "without possessing a personal affinity with the language of the work," could nonetheless "give themselves to it and derive something from it." But in terms of "pure forms," seen now as the expressive vehicle of "emotion or emotions" in themselves, there could be, at best, only a small and specialized, educated elite that had the requisite capability and preparation to respond as was called for.

Kandinsky moved back to Moscow following the outbreak of World War I, and remained mainly there for the next seven years. In the wake of the Russian Revolution he found himself appointed in 1919 to the Publication section of the People's Commissariat of the Enlightenment. Through contact with Roman Jakobson, who was then secretary of the Visual Arts section, he was exposed both to Cubo-Futurist developments in Russian art—favoring an abstraction based on rhythmic and broadly geometric organization of planes and contours—and, more indirectly, to the second phase of Russian Formalism. As a method of critical analysis devised for works of literature, but applicable also to the visual arts, this entailed seeking to understand the workings of a given art form in terms of how specific effects were technically and structurally achieved. In "On Point" and "On Line," articles prepared in 1919 for an encyclopedia of fine arts—in parallel to a publication that Jakobson projected on the "science of painting," for which he invited Kandinsky to write on its "semantics"—Kandinsky brought in principles of perception answering to inner cognitive and associative needs. This continuing orientation on his part to the psychological effect of a work of art on its reader or viewer became a bone of contention in 1920–1921, when the All-Russian Union of Professional Artists and Painters of the New Art (NARKOMPROS), of which Kandinsky was a founding member, spawned the Institute of Artistic Culture (INKhuK), with Kandinsky placed in charge of devising a work program that would join artists, theorists, and critics in studying in depth the theoretical principles underlying innovation in the arts. Other members—notably Aleksandr Rodchenko and his wife, Stepanova—set up their own working group to study systematically the "underlying laws" of artistic expression, placing particular emphasis on the material quality of objects. But Kandinsky clung to his own viewpoint, which put him in the minority, and in September 1921 he chose to resign and leave. He had moved meanwhile as a painter to a more geometric and constructively organized treatment of forms in space. He took with him to Germany this visual

language, and along with it the plan for a companion volume to *On the Spiritual,* which in its eventually published form of 1926 would be titled *Point and Line to Plane,* on the model of the 1919 articles.

Appointed by Walter Gropius to teach at the newly founded Bauhaus in Weimar, Kandinsky developed further, in his teaching and curricular planning there and also in his paintings, the corresponding idea of a "science of painting." The spirit of Constructivism, as an interarts movement in Germany and other mid-European countries now, favored this with its emphasis on the relation of works of art, in such forms as wall paintings or reliefs, to a public space or gallery environment. Kandinsky moved with the Bauhaus to its second home, in Dessau, in June 1925, but found the emphasis placed on painting in the curriculum there progressively reduced in favor of a concern with the application of artistic and artisanal skills to commercially viable ends. At the instigation of National Socialism, the dissolution of the Bauhaus would be decreed in 1932, and its final closure as an institution came a year later. [*See* Bauhaus.]

Kandinsky then left for France and established himself in Neuilly, a suburb of Paris, where he remained until his death in 1944, continuing to paint ambitiously, but on a smaller scale after the outbreak of World War II limited his choices and access to materials. He defended "abstract painting" afresh in an article of 1936 for an Amsterdam periodical and in an interview of 1937–1938, in opposition particularly to the recognition now given to Cubism, as a seminal language within the development of art since 1900. He also adopted for his work at that time the label "Concrete art," which was used by a group of artists centered in Paris who were, after 1933, allied under the loose banner of Abstraction-Création. He began at this point to draw on biological and zoological imagery as a consistent source of inspiration, but employed organic motifs quite differently from the contemporary work of the Surrealists, led by Jean Arp.

Kandinsky's last works, on wood or board with a more totemic imagery, represent, in a now less exalted but very distinguished vein, the phenomenon of *Spätstil,* or "late style" in a long-lived artist. They bring to a close a career and contribution to aesthetics that would increasingly win art-historical and critical recognition after World War II. Through his participation in international exhibitions, through critical reviews drawing on his writings, and through the entry of his work into major museums, Kandinsky had attained recognition as a figure of major importance. Such recognition was aided also by the appearance of the first monographs on his work, by Will Grohmann, in 1924 and 1930, and by the keeping in print and translation of his major publications.

Kandinsky's claims for the role of the "spiritual" in art distinguish themselves from more narrowly mystical and sectarian claims on the part of artists (like the Rose-Croix group active in France at the end of the nineteenth century) insofar as his commitment was, like William Blake's, to the expansion of consciousness in general and the forging of a language that would direct and inform the viewer's participatory response, in the way that religious icons had traditionally done. The tradition of the spiritual, so understood, has many branches in the art of this century, and at the same time a larger continuity that reaches down to present times, as part of "New Age" consciousness. Kandinsky's conception of artistic creation and its goals forms a major link in this chain.

The practice of *abstraction* in art, understood as the use of color and shape to simplify and distill key qualities or aspects of appearance, and to essentialize or synthesize in the interests of an underlying "truth"—as opposed to seeking to transcribe individual sensations, in a fashion that is directed to their character as the eye, rather than the imagination, discerns this—has its own trajectory in European art, from the 1880s onward. This trajectory includes in its unfolding lines of development Henri Matisse's work of 1905–1915 and aspects of Cubism and Futurism. Contemporary with Kandinsky, Robert and Sonia Delaunay in Paris, and also František Kupka, who had come there from Prague via Vienna, were doing color compositions that could be thought of comparably as exemplifying "pure painting."

After World War I, more geometric forms of abstraction—those of the Constructivists, working in Russia, Hungary, and Germany, and those evolved by Piet Mondrian and his colleagues in the Dutch de Stijl movement—attained wider currency, as reflected in the curriculum of the Bauhaus, and the artists brought there to teach or lecture. The linkage of abstraction with avant-garde tendencies, and with modernism more generally, in all of the arts that gave a leading role to the visual (as with experimental theater production, in which Kandinsky notably participated, and equally in photography between the wars) became, against that background, a fixture of the twentieth-century scene with considerable staying power to it.

In addition, the material and technical components of the artist's visual language became, over the same time span, increasingly self-referential; that is, they pointed inward to the creative processes by means of which they were achieved, and called for interpretative understanding in those reflexive terms. Kandinsky became a preeminent participant in this ongoing development, as seen in the way in which the painters of the New York school who would be grouped together as Abstract Expressionists, notably Jackson Pollock and Arshile Gorky, drew on his example in the 1940s. Although he had no disciples or direct followers in the domain of aesthetic theory, the demonstration afforded by Kandinsky's work that the free operation of line, plane, and color and their interactive power can serve in themselves as

means of expressive communication proved its applicability across a wider front than simply his own kind of painting. It established itself as a more general principle of artistic practice that could be read back confirmingly into the art of other times and places.

[*See also* Abstraction; Color; *and* Modernism.]

BIBLIOGRAPHY

Work by Kandinsky

Kandinsky: Complete Writings on Art. Edited by Kenneth C. Lindsay and Peter Vergo. Boston, 1982; reprint, New York, 1994.

Other Sources

Hahl-Koch, Jelena. *Kandinsky.* New York, 1993.
Lassaigne, Jacques. *Kandinsky: Biographical and Critical Study.* Translated by H. S. B. Harrison. Geneva, 1970.
Long, Rose-Carol Washton. *Kandinsky: The Development of an Abstract Style.* New York and Oxford, 1980.
Overy, Paul. *Kandinsky: The Language of the Eye.* New York and London, 1969.
Ringbom, Sixten. *The Sounding Cosmos: A Study in the Spiritualism of Kandinsky and the Genesis of Abstract Painting.* Turku, Finland, 1970.
Roethel, Hans K., and Jean K. Benjamin. *Kandinsky: Catalogue Raisonné of the Oil-Painting, vol. 1, 1900–1915; vol. 2, 1916–1944.* Ithaca, N.Y., 1982, 1984.
Roskill, Mark. *Klee, Kandinsky, and the Thought of Their Time: A Critical Perspective.* Urbana, Ill., 1992.
Tuchman, Maurice, et al. *The Spiritual in Art: Abstract Painting, 1890–1985.* New York, 1986. Los Angeles County Museum of Art exhibition catalog.
Weiss, Peg. *Kandinsky in Munich: The Formative Jugendstil Years.* Princeton, N.J., 1979.

MARK ROSKILL

KANT, IMMANUEL. [*To treat the thought of one of the pivotal figures in the history of aesthetics, this entry comprises nine essays:*

The first essay is a survey of Kant's philosophy in general and the place of his aesthetics therein. The next three essays concern major issues in the Critique of Judgment, *his main text on aesthetics: beauty, the sublime, and nature. The fifth essay traces the history of Kantian aesthetics from his time to the present, while the sixth essay examines the appropriation of Kant by art history. The seventh and eighth essays reflect contemporary critiques of Kantian aesthetics in hermeneutics and in feminism. The final essay links Kant to contemporary discussions of mod-*

ernism and to the continued relevance of judgment in contemporary art.]

Survey of Thought

Immanuel Kant (1724–1804) is the central figure in the transition from early modern to modern philosophy, and his work still defines key issues and positions in epistemology, metaphysics, and moral and political philosophy. Kant published only two works in aesthetics, the early *Observations on Feeling of the Beautiful and the Sublime* of 1764 and the "Critique of Aesthetic Judgment," the first half of the last of his three great critiques, the *Critique of Judgment* of 1790. In fact, the *Observations* is concerned more with social and moral psychology than with art and beauty, so the *Critique of Judgment* alone contains Kant's crucial contribution to aesthetics. But the surviving evidence of his intellectual development and teaching, such as his own notes for and student transcriptions of his lectures in logic and anthropology, show that Kant's mature aesthetics was the product of several decades of thought; and the influence of the *Critique of Judgment* within aesthetics has been just as great as that of Kant's other works in their areas of philosophy.

Background. Kant was born in the East Prussian capital of Königsberg to a family of extremely modest means, but his education, first at a Pietist academy and then at the university in Königsberg, was facilitated by the leading Pietist pastor of the city. Kant studied both the rationalist philosophy of Gottfried Wilhelm Leibniz and Christian Wolff and the modern science of Isaac Newton under the tutelage of Martin Knutzen, a promising philosopher whose own career was cut short by early death. After finishing his studies in 1747, Kant spent the next eight years as a household tutor, returning to the university as a *Privatdozent* in 1755 and lecturing in that capacity for fifteen years before becoming professor of logic and metaphysics in 1770, the position he then held until his retirement in 1797. From the outset of his career, Kant tried to mediate the great intellectual debates of his day. In his earliest work, he attempted to resolve the debate between René Descartes and Leibniz on "living forces," and in subsequent writings of the 1750s and 1760s he attempted to reconcile Newtonian physics with Leibnizian metaphysics, as well as to mediate the more general debate between rationalism and empiricism. These efforts came to fruition in Kant's magnum opus, the *Critique of Pure Reason* of 1781 (substantially revised in 1787). Kant's moral philosophy, published in the *Groundwork of the Metaphysics of Morals* of 1785, the *Critique of Practical Reason* of 1788, and the *Metaphysics of Morals* of 1797, likewise attempts to preserve what was sound in both rationalism and empiricism, the perfectionist doctrine of duties of Wolff and Alexander Gottlieb Baumgarten, on the one hand, and a theory of respect related to the moral sense philosophy of Francis Hutcheson, David Hume, and Adam Smith, on the other, while placing both on a deeper foundation in pure practical reason and the intrinsic value of human freedom. In aesthetics, too, Kant pursued a syncretist path, preserving many of the insights of both empiricists like Hutcheson and his British successors as well as rationalists such as Baumgarten and Moses Mendelssohn, while seeking to place these insights within a radically new epistemological, metaphysical, and ultimately moral framework.

Unlike many other key figures in the history of aesthetics, Kant was not obviously inspired by a personal engagement with the arts. His knowledge of both classical and modern literature appears to have been limited in comparison with many of his contemporaries, and his acquaintance with music and the visual arts was even more restricted. Instead, Kant seems to have thought about issues in aesthetics initially because the German pioneers of the discipline, Baumgarten and his disciple Georg Friedrich Meier included some elements of their aesthetic theories in their handbooks of logic and metaphysics, which were the texts for Kant's lectures in these subjects; and even when his interest grew beyond these authors, Kant still seems to have reflected more on the writings of other philosophers and critics than on literary and artistic materials themselves. Nevertheless, Kant focused on aesthetics in the last few years of the 1780s, when he thought he saw how to reconstruct some of the key results of his century's extraordinary efforts in aesthetics within the terms of his own transcendental philosophy, and especially when he saw how to resolve the debate about the disinterestedness of the experience of beauty that had been started between Anthony Ashley Cooper, third earl of Shaftesbury, and Hutcheson, and that had continued through the century, by showing how the very autonomy of aesthetic experience from external constraint, including didactic constraint by morality, allows it to serve as a palpable experience of the freedom that is the essence of morality.

In Kant's own view (stated in a letter of December 1787 to his disciple Karl Leonhard Reinhold), he was able to give a satisfactory philosophical treatment of the judgment of taste, paradigmatically the judgment that a particular object is beautiful, only when he saw how to bring it under a general a priori principle of a newly recognized faculty of reflective judgment, which was also the source of teleological judgment, or the judgment that a particular organism, system of organisms, or nature as a whole is purposive. The subsumption of both aesthetic and teleological judgments under a single principle of reflective judgment is reflected in the structure of the *Critique of Judgment*, which is divided into a "Critique of Aesthetic Judgment" and a "Critique of Teleological Judgment." Judgments of taste are supposed to be reflective judgments on the form of particular objects, while teleological judgments are reflective judgments on the internal organizations of the parts of natural organisms and their external relations to other natural objects. In fact, there are important disanalogies between aesthetic and teleological judgment as well as analogies, and Kant's attempt to show that judgments of taste rest on a genuinely a priori principle analogous to the fundamental principles of natural science and morality is complex in ways that contemporary scholarship is only beginning to see. In spite of the new framework, much of what is most important in Kant's mature aesthetics is continuous with views that he held long before 1787. In the exposition of the *Critique of Judgment* that follows, more attention will be paid to the issues internal to the "Critique of Aesthetic Judgment" than to the theoretical innovations that may have facilitated its completion as part of a larger work on reflective judgment after 1787, even though this new framework may have been what made aesthetics important enough in Kant's own eyes for him finally to publish his views in this field of philosophy.

The Basic Theory. In some of his earlier reflections, Kant had defined the judgment of taste as a judgment claiming general agreement about pleasures in objects due neither to their immediate impact on our external senses nor to their moral significance, and then sought an explanation of such pleasures. He canvassed two different explanations: on one account, influenced by the Germans Baumgarten and Johann Georg Sulzer but perhaps also by the Scot Alexander Gerard, he placed the source of such pleasure in satisfaction of laws of sensibility in general, but in particular in conditions especially facilitating the sensible apprehension of objects; on another account, more reminiscent of Hume but also of his own disciple Marcus Herz, he placed the source of aesthetic pleasure in the possibility of mutual agreement itself (which obviously risked circularity). In the *Critique of Judgment*, this straightforward approach, first offering a logical analysis of what is claimed by the judgment of taste and then proposing an epistemological and/or psychological explanation of aesthetic response showing how it can satisfy the requirements of the logical analysis of the judgment of taste, is submerged in a structure borrowed from the *Critique of Pure Reason*, but in the end may remain the best way to understand Kant's ideas about taste and aesthetic experience.

In both the first part of the text of the "Critique of Aesthetic Judgment," its "Analytic of the Beautiful," and the first draft of the introduction to the whole *Critique*, which he wrote early during the composition of the work but replaced with another version shortly before publication, Kant began by analyzing the concept of an aesthetic judgment as a judgment that is both about and made on the basis of a necessarily subjective feeling—this is what he took to be connoted by the term *aesthetic*—which in turn could only be the feeling of pleasure (or, in the case of a negative judgment, of pain). It would have been natural for him then to have continued in an analytic mode, turning from the term *aesthetic* to *judgment,* and arguing that as a form of judgment an aesthetic judgment must claim general intersubjective validity in spite of the fact that it concerns merely pleasure,

after which he could then have sought to characterize and explain the kind of pleasure that permits of intersubjectively valid judgment. But, forcing his discussion into the theory of categories developed in the *Critique of Pure Reason,* Kant made his argument more complicated than that.

In the *Critique of Pure Reason,* Kant had argued that human thought consists of judgments requiring the application of concepts of objects formed in accordance with twelve general categories of understanding to data, or intuitions, presented in two forms of intuition, space and time. The twelve categories were organized under the four headings of quantity, quality, relation, and modality, which were in turn derived from a logical analysis of the structure of judgments. In the *Critique of Judgment,* Kant used these four headings, renamed "moments," to organize his discussion of the judgment of beauty and then the judgment of the sublime, although in both cases the connection between the logical structure of judgments and Kant's real subject matter is tenuous at best. In the "Analytic of the Beautiful," he began with the moment of "Quality." After his initial, analytic claim that the judgment of taste, as aesthetic, necessarily concerns pleasure (section 1), he then proceeded to assert that the judgment is "disinterested," which he defined as being concerned with the "appearance" rather than the "existence" of its object (section 2). He then argued that the judgment of the beautiful could be distinguished from mere sensory gratification, or the "agreeable," as well as from the "good," including judgments of both utility and moral goodness, because it neither presupposes nor gives rise to an interest in the existence of its object (sections 3–4). Next, under the heading of "Quantity," Kant argued that because the judgment of taste is disinterested, it is necessarily intersubjectively valid (sections 6, 8), a claim he illustrated by an appeal to ordinary language: we can defuse the claim to intersubjective agreement inherent in the use of the linguistic form of a judgment when we state that something is merely agreeable, as when we say, "This wine is agreeable *to me,*" but we do not relinquish this claim in the case of a judgment of beauty—we do not countenance a disclaimer like "This painting is beautiful *to me*" (section 7). In a passage with many misleading suggestions, the interpretation of which has been much contested, Kant then argued that the possibility of a judgment of taste depends on the existence of a "free play" or harmony between the cognitive faculties of imagination and understanding, a state in which in response to the perception of an object both of these faculties are "enlivened" without the use of any particular concept (section 9). Because this pleasurable state is achieved without the application of a concept to the object, it is subjective in the sense required by the term *aesthetic,* but because it involves general faculties of cognition that can be expected to operate in the same way in all people, it gives rise to an intersubjectively valid judgment. (Kant subsequently formalized this argument under the title of the "deduction of judgments of taste" in sections 21 and 38.) Third, under the heading of "Relation," Kant argued that because the judgment of taste must be made without a determinate concept, its object must possess *Zweckmässigkeit,* which has been variously translated as "finality," "purposiveness," or "suitability," without being seen as having a determinate purpose *(Zweck).* This claim has also been difficult to understand: Kant seems to say that a beautiful object has the appearance of having a purpose and of having been designed to have that purpose without actually having such a purpose (sections 10–11); but since there is no particular appearance that is characteristic of objects that have a purpose, it is better to understand Kant as arguing that a beautiful object satisfies our *subjective* purpose of cognition without being judged to have any actual objective purpose. In another obscure move, Kant also insists that purposiveness without purpose, or what can be called the "form of purposiveness," is equivalent to "purposiveness of form," thus that beauty arises only from formal features of perceptual objects (sections 13–14); this claim has been taken as an endorsement of formalist theories of the visual arts by later critics, such as Clement Greenberg, which Kant's own treatment of fine art later in the *Critique of Judgment* (sections 43–53) makes clear he never could have intended. Finally, under the heading of "Modality," Kant claims that a judgment of beauty possesses "exemplary necessity," or claims necessity of agreement in response to a particular object (exemplar), not in response to any determinate class of objects under any formulable rule (section 18). Here he also emphasizes that our judgments of beauty are always "conditional" rather than certain (section 19), even though we do suppose that they have a basis in shared cognitive faculties or a *sensus communis* (sections 20–21).

There are many obscurities and confusions in Kant's exposition: notably, the claim that judgments of taste are universally valid does not logically follow from the claim that they are disinterested, which in any case was a controversial point from which to begin; the claim that beauty lies only in perceptual form does not follow from the characterization of it as the form of purposiveness; and it is difficult to distinguish the idea of universal subjective validity from that of exemplary necessity. For these and other reasons, it seems preferable to understand Kant's underlying argument along lines suggested by his earlier reflections, as well as earlier and later portions of the text (such as section 7 of the published introduction and sections 31–38), where Kant suggests not a fourfold but a twofold division of his argument: first, an analytic phase, in which a judgment of beauty is described as a judgment about pleasure that claims universal agreement in spite of its subjectivity, and, second, an explanatory and justificatory phase, in which it is argued that only a pleasure produced by the free play of imagination and understanding can satisfy this analysis. In further steps, constraints on the objects of aesthetic judgment are drawn

from the general idea of a harmony of cognitive faculties, and it is also argued that this harmony necessarily occurs in all persons under the same conditions—although this is the a priori principle of taste that Kant never successfully proves.

The Enriched Theory. However precisely the logical structure of Kant's basis analysis of judgments of beauty should be understood, it is only the beginning of his aesthetic theory, which quickly undergoes a process of enrichment in the course of which many of Kant's most interesting ideas are first presented. This amplification takes place in four stages: first, within the "Analytic of the Beautiful" itself, the basic conception of the pure judgment of beauty is supplemented by the notions of the dependent judgment of beauty and the ideal of beauty; second, the analysis of beauty is supplemented by an analysis of the sublime; third, the original account, intended primarily as an account of natural beauty, is supplemented by a brief but profound account of art and genius; and finally, an account of the aesthetic that has been cast largely in aesthetic terms is given metaphysical and moral significance.

The "Analytic of the Beautiful" is cast primarily as a theory of judgments of natural beauty, conceived primarily as judgments about the beauty of particular objects in nature, whether inorganic, such as crystals, or organic, such as flowers and birds. In its third moment, however, two ideas are introduced that begin the extension of the theory to art and its connection to morality. First, Kant draws a distinction between pure and dependent judgments of beauty: the former require no concept of their objects at all, but the latter are constrained by concepts after all—what may appear beautiful in a summerhouse will not appear beautiful in an arsenal (section 16). Typical examples of free beauties are natural objects, such as flowers, appreciated without any reference to concepts of their function, but artworks without any content, such as wallpaper designs, may also be appreciated as free beauties; dependent beauties are typically works of human artifice, such as structures built for a purpose, but may include natural objects our response to which is constrained by our own purposes, such as racehorses, or even human beings themselves, where our aesthetic response is always constrained by moral considerations. This distinction presents an interpretative difficulty: if the judgment of dependent beauty is fully determined by the relevant concept of the object, then it is not clear why it should be a judgment of beauty at all; the answer would seem to be that in this case the concept of what the object is intended to be places certain constraints on its possible appearance, but still leaves considerable scope for the freedom of the imagination to be exercised in both the production of and response to the object. In fact, although the category of dependent beauty is not coextensive with the category of fine art, the theory of dependent beauty offers a model for Kant's subsequent theory of fine art, by showing how our response to an object may be constrained by concepts of an object's intended form and function but still leave room for the free play of the imagination going beyond the limits of such concepts, or even for free play of the imagination in responding to the relation between the form and intended function of the object. Second, Kant introduces the notion of an "ideal of beauty," supposing not just that there must be universal agreement about any beautiful object, but that there must be some one object that is agreed to be maximally beautiful, which, he maintains, will be the human form as the expression of the moral (section 17). Here the puzzle is that the requirement of a single maximally beautiful object does not seem to follow from the logical analysis of aesthetic judgment at all; rather, it seems to be a requirement of reason, specifically the need of practical reason to find sensible representation for the abstract ideas of morality.

Next, Kant adds an "Analytic of the Sublime." The sublime was a standard theme in eighteenth-century aesthetics, given particular prominence by Edmund Burke and in Germany by Felix Mendelssohn, although in some ways Kant's treatment is more closely related to the earlier account by Joseph Addison. Again, Kant's exposition is somewhat distorted by his use of the categorial framework of the *Critique of Pure Reason*, but its basic outline is clear enough. The experience of the sublime is not an undiluted experience of pleasure, but a mixed experience of displeasure superseded by pleasure (here the influence of Mendelssohn is obvious). This mixture is due to the fact that the attempt to comprehend the boundless in nature is initially perceived as a frustrating disharmony between imagination and understanding, but ultimately as a pleasing harmony between imagination and reason, which alone is capable of conceiving of the infinite. The sublime takes two forms: the "mathematical sublime," in which theoretical reason's capacity to conceive the infinite is revealed in the very attempt to apprehend things of vast size (sections 25–26), and the "dynamical sublime," in which what is ultimately revealed is the power of practical reason—namely, our power to preserve our moral personality by acting in accordance with pure reason even in the face of the physically most threatening forces of nature (sections 28–29), which might seem to be able to compel us to act in accordance with our inclinations. This interpretation of the dynamic sublime is Kant's fundamental addition to the view of Mendelssohn and Burke, and represents his radical revision of Addison's idea that the sublime is an "image of liberty."

Third, Kant expands his initial account of judgments of natural beauty with a theory of art and its source in genius. For Kant, a work of art is a product of intention, and must be judged to be beautiful in spite of the recognition of its intentionality (sections 43–45). Further, Kant also assumes that works of art are characteristically mimetic, and thus have a content that can be grasped through concepts (section 48). The only way these assumptions can be reconciled with the requirement that a beautiful object induce a free harmony of the cognitive faculties is through the idea that a beautiful work of art is a work of genius, with a richness of both form and content that goes beyond anything that can be derived from any determinate concept, thus (as in the earlier case of dependent beauty) leaving ample scope for the freedom of the imagination of both artist and audience (sections 46, 49). Specifically, artistic genius finds expression in aesthetic ideas, themes for works that, on the one hand, intimate a rational idea not directly perceivable in sense, typically a moral idea, and, on the other, induce an inexhaustible wealth of particular imagery (section 49). This conception of the aesthetic idea is Kant's reconstruction of Baumgarten's idea that beauty lies in clear but confused perception with extensive rather than intensive clarity. Kant also adds a classification of the different media of art in terms of their expressive potential (section 51) that stands in a long tradition leading from Baumgarten and Mendelssohn to Arthur Schopenhauer and Nelson Goodman.

Finally, Kant intimates deep connections between the aesthetic, on the one hand, and the metaphysical and the moral, on the other. The connection with metaphysics is drawn in the "Dialectic of Aesthetic Judgment" that concludes the "Critique of Aesthetic Judgment." Here Kant argues that the antinomy between the thesis that judgments of taste are not based on concepts, for then they would admit of proofs, and the antithesis that they must be based on concepts, for otherwise they could not claim necessary agreement (section 56), can only be solved by linking beauty with the indeterminate idea of the supersensible substratum lying at the basis of both object and judging subject (section 58), or the thing-in-itself. The ground for this argument is obscure, since in the idea of the free play of imagination and understanding Kant had already introduced an indeterminate concept adequate for solving the antinomy without invoking metaphysics. In its concluding section, however, the "Dialectic" takes a different tack, arguing that the beautiful can serve as a symbol of the morally good because of analogies between the freedom of the imagination inherent in the experience of beauty and the freedom of the will that is the essence of morality, but which can never be directly experienced (section 59). Thus, the aesthetic can serve as a symbol of the moral, which needs a symbol because it is not itself an object of experience, without losing its own autonomy, but rather precisely because of its own autonomy. This resolution of the problem of the relation between aesthetics and morality, which had run throughout eighteenth-century aesthetics, may have been Kant's deepest motivation for including aesthetics within his philosophical purview. It was deeply influential on a few successors, such as Friedrich von Schiller, although many later critics and aestheticians seem not to have gotten past the formalism of the "Analytic of the Beautiful" and have failed to see the moral significance of Kant's aesthetic theory.

BIBLIOGRAPHY

Works by Kant

Beobachtungen über das Gefühl des Schönen und Erhabenen. Königsberg, 1764.

Kritik der Urteilskraft. Berlin, 1790.

Kants gesammelte Schriften. Edited by the Royal Prussian (later German) Academy of Sciences. Berlin, 1900–. This is the standard modern edition of Kant's works. The *Beobachtungen* is contained in volume 2, the *Kritik der Urteilskraft* in volume 5, and the first draft of the introduction to the latter in volume 20. Fragments of Kant's early views can be found in the reflections on anthropology and logic reproduced in volumes 14 and 15 and in the lectures on logic transcribed in volume 24, especially the *Logik Blomberg* and *Logik Philippi* of 1770–1771.

Works by Kant in Translation

Critique of Judgment. Translated by J. H. Bernard. London, 1892; reprint, New York, 1951.

The Critique of Judgement. Translated by James Creed Meredith. Oxford, 1952. Originally published in two parts, with interpretative essays, in 1911 and 1928.

Observations on the Feeling of the Beautiful and Sublime. Translated by John T. Goldthwait. Berkeley, 1960.

First Introduction to the Critique of Judgment. Translated by James Haden. Indianapolis, 1965.

Critique of Judgment. Translated by Werner S. Pluhar. Indianapolis, 1987. Includes the First Introduction.

Lectures on Logic. Translated by J. Michael Young. Cambridge and New York, 1992.

Other Sources

Caygill, Howard. *Art of Judgement.* Oxford and Cambridge, Mass., 1989.

Cohen, Ted, and Paul Guyer, eds. *Essays in Kant's Aesthetics.* Chicago, 1982. Contains extensive bibliography through 1980.

Coleman, Francis X. J. *The Harmony of Reason: A Study in Kant's Aesthetics.* Pittsburgh, 1974.

Crawford, Donald W. *Kant's Aesthetic Theory.* Madison, Wis., 1974.

Crowther, Paul. *The Kantian Sublime: From Morality to Art.* Oxford, 1989.

Esser, Andrea, ed. *Autonomie der Kunst? Zur Aktualität von Kants Ästhetik.* Berlin, 1995.

Fricke, Christel. *Kants Theorie des reinen Geschmacksurteil.* Berlin and New York, 1990.

Gibbons, Sarah. *Kant's Theory of Imagination: Bridging Gaps in Judgment and Experience.* Oxford, 1994.

Ginsborg, Hanna. *The Role of Taste in Kant's Theory of Cognition.* New York, 1990.

Guyer, Paul. *Kant and the Claims of Taste* (1979). Enl. ed. Cambridge and New York, 1997.

Guyer, Paul. *Kant and the Experience of Freedom: Essays on Aesthetics and Morality.* Cambridge and New York, 1993.

Henrich, Dieter. *Aesthetic Judgment and the Moral Image of the World: Studies in Kant.* Stanford, Calif., 1992.

Kemal, Salim. *Kant and Fine Art: An Essay on Kant and the Philosophy of Fine Art and Culture.* Oxford and New York, 1986.

Kemal, Salim. *Kant's Aesthetic Theory: An Introduction.* New York, 1992.

Kulenkampff, Jens. *Kants Logik des ästhetischen Urteils.* Frankfurt am Main, 1978.

Lyotard, Jean-François. *Lessons on the Analytic of the Sublime.* Translated by Elizabeth Rottenberg. Stanford, Calif., 1994.

Makkreel, Rudolf A. *Imagination and Interpretation in Kant: The Hermeneutical Import of the Critique of Judgment.* Chicago, 1990.

Meerbote, Ralf, and Hud Hudson, eds. *Kant's Aesthetics.* North American Kant Society Studies in Philosophy, vol. 1. Atascadero, Calif., 1991. Includes extensive bibliography of the period 1980–1990.

Parret, Herman, ed. *Kants Ästhetik/Kant's Aesthetics/L'esthétique de Kant.* Berlin and New York, 1997.

Rogerson, Kenneth F. *Kant's Aesthetics: The Roles of Form and Expression.* Lanham, Md., 1986.

Savile, Anthony. *Aesthetic Reconstructions: The Seminal Writings of Lessing, Kant, and Schiller.* Aristotelian Society Series, vol. 8. Oxford and New York, 1987.

Savile, Anthony. *Kantian Aesthetics Pursued.* Edinburgh, 1993.

Schaper, Eva. *Studies in Kant's Aesthetics.* Edinburgh, 1979.

Uehling, Theodore E., Jr. *The Notion of Form in Kant's Critique of Aesthetic Judgment.* De Proprietatibus Litterarum, Series Minor 5. The Hague, 1971.

Zammito, John H. *The Genesis of Kant's Critique of Judgment.* Chicago, 1992.

PAUL GUYER

Kant on Beauty

Immanuel Kant characterizes beauty in some detail in "The Analytic of the Beautiful" of the *Critique of Judgment* before going on to consider its relation to morality.

Beauty: Disinterested, Subjective, and Universal. "The Analytic of the Beautiful" explains beauty through four moments or declarations of its character:

1. "Taste is the ability to judge an object, or a way of presenting it, by means of liking or disliking devoid of all interest. The object of such a liking is called beautiful" (section 5).
2. "*Beautiful* is what, without a concept, is liked universally" (section 9).
3. "Beauty is an object's form of purposiveness insofar as it is perceived in the object without the presentation of a purpose" (section 17).
4. *Beautiful* is what, without a concept, is cognized as the object of a necessary liking" (section 22).

The central feature of Kant's theory is that beauty consists in the subject's pleasurable experience of a judgment of taste that is subjective yet universal and necessary. The explanation of our ability to talk of beauty depends on our capacity to judge or assess objects in particular ways. Kant understands *interest* as the pleasure we feel in the existence of an object because it satisfies a desire or some moral purpose. When we have an interest, we assess how well objects can serve these purposes. By contrast, the assessment that an object is beautiful is not concerned with the existence of objects or representations for the use we can make of them, nor for their relation to other objects within the system of scientific knowledge. Our concern with objects is then not so much with the physical qualities of the oils, stone, or metal, of the canvas, paper, ink, and so on, that constitute them and that are necessary to satisfy desires and moral demands. Rather, a judgment of taste is disinterested in that it assesses the presentation of the object for itself: it considers the structure of elements, their order, complexity, and unity, their coherence, meaning, and expression, the balance between the elements of the presentation, and the features that make up these items.

Kant talks of the grasp of objects in terms of a relation between our rational capacities—the mental equipment we must have in order to have experience we can understand. A cognitive grasp or judgment of an object depends on a determinate relation between the cognitive faculties of imagination (which provide sensible intuitions) and understanding (which provides the concepts we apply to intuitions). The relation between cognitive faculties is determined by the particular perceptual qualities we intuit the object has and the cognitively determinate concepts we apply to it. Kant also allows for a cognitively indeterminate use of concepts in a judgment, which he sometimes talks of as "indeterminate" concepts, that depends on a commensurately less determinate relation between faculties. In these cases, an assessment of the object does not extend to considering the moral and sensuous purposes the object can satisfy since considerations of the latter must use determinate concepts to identify the object, its physical properties, and their causal relation with other objects, properties, and selves. In some cases, the indeterminate use of concepts in a judgment depends on a harmonious relation between faculties. Kant maintains that this harmony of faculties, the cognitively indeterminate use of concepts in our judgment of taste that it allows, occasions pleasure. In other words, the particular grasp of the object that is our assessment of beauty, this judgment of taste, occasions a feeling of pleasure resulting from a "harmony of faculties" (as contrasted with a determinate relation between faculties). In effect, a successful judgment of taste is the pleasurable disinterested grasp of the order and meaning of an object or representation.

In this case we must refer the object "only to the subject, namely, to his feeling of life, under the name of feeling of pleasure or displeasure" (section 1). A "feeling for life" is principally "the ability of a being to act" in conformity with its representations (Kant, 1993, and 1991, p. 211). When an object permits such a pleasurable grasp or such a liking, we say it is beautiful. And since the judgment of taste occasions a pleasurable relation between the subject's faculties in assessing the object, when we say an object is beautiful, our claim is really an appraisal of the subject and its pleasurable grasp. Another implication of this subject dependency is that the claim that an object is beautiful is autonomous in the following sense. The subjectivity or basis in pleasure of claims about the beauty of objects means that, first, no one else can feel the subjects' pleasure and make the concomitant aesthetic judgment for them; second, pleasure results from a use of mind that the subjects must make for themselves.

After arguing that beauty is this pleasurable grasp of objects that is disinterested (because it concerns the object for itself rather than any further purpose it may serve) and subjective (because it depends on experiences of pleasure), Kant goes on to propose that this pleasure is universally valid. Pleasure is generally subjective in the sense that it depends on the subject and its occasioning varies from subject to subject. The fact that swimming in cold water gives one person pleasure does not imply that anyone else will find the same activity pleasurable. Yet, despite the basis of judgments of taste in pleasure or a feeling for life, despite their subjectivity, Kant maintains that they have universal validity in the sense that we may expect and, further, can demand similar experiences of pleasure from other subjects like ourselves on the basis of which they will find beautiful the objects that we value. This is part of what it means for the beautiful to be liked universally and will be a basis for it being the object of a necessary liking.

The universality of this pleasure, our expectation that others can experience it, rests on the rational nature of the judgment of taste. In the "Deduction" of the *Critique of Judgment* Kant argues that our grasp of the object in judgments of taste depends on using our cognitive capacities (section 38). Since we can expect that all other subjects possess the same capacities, because these are necessary for us to have the ordinary experiences we all have, and since a grasp of the object by using these capacities is pleasurable, we can expect that all other subjects capable of having our ordinary experience will also be capable of having this pleasure—the pleasure is universalizable in that the judgment of taste is comprehensive over all subjects.

This deduction of the universal validity of the experience of pleasure that constitutes beauty has a restricted scope: it shows at best that our aesthetic valuations can be valid; it does not show which particular objects, if any, we will find beautiful. Nor does it tell us how to decide on the correctness of any particular claim that an object is beautiful, for the universality of our pleasure does not occur to us in our experience as one of its phenomenal properties. To understand the scope and validity of this conception of beauty, then, we need to examine how we deal with actual claims that an object is beautiful, how we might confirm them.

Beauty, Confirmation, and Community. Initially, Kant maintains that to confirm our actual assessments of beauty we reflect internally on our pleasurable response. This allows us to "separate out" whatever is merely agreeable or good because it satisfies some desires and therefore fails to be disinterested (section 8). He complains, however, that subjects' internal reflection is corrigible because it can confuse disinterested pleasure with pleasure in charm, emotion, sensation, moral connotations, or successful communication. Moreover, although they take it that aesthetic judgments have universal subjective validity, subjects cannot suppose that everyone will agree with their actual judgments. Therefore, to ensure that they can rely on their actual judgments, subjects need some criteria, apart from a fallible reflection, by which to confirm their own judgments. For Kant, it is not enough to know generally that aesthetic judgments are possible. We must also know how to confirm particular actual aesthetic judgments, for where aesthetic judgments are problematic, subjects do not simply make a wrong judgment, they fail to make aesthetic judgments at all: they then have only an experience of pleasure in charm, emotion, sensation, moral connotations, or successful communication. If we lack criteria for success for particular judgments, and cannot distinguish actual judgments from other instances of pleasure, then even if we know that it is possible generally to make aesthetic judgments, we will never know that we are making particular judgments.

Since the claim that an object is beautiful depends essentially on an experience of pleasure in the subject, these judgments are not subject to the usual way of generating assent (section 8). An objective claim is comprehensive over objects, contending that every object of a certain kind would have a given property. By contrast, aesthetic evaluations are universal in being comprehensive over subjects and their experiences of pleasure. That is, the judgment that an object is beautiful contends that every *subject* who is capable of experience will have the same pleasurable exercise of mind. Therefore, Kant proposes, the subject must seek confirmation for the putatively universally valid subjective judgment through agreement from other subjects when they, too, make the same pleasurable judgment.

This confirmation through agreement has to be of a particular kind. A common experience of pleasure by itself is not enough. Given the autonomy of judgments, other subjects will want to submit the object to [their] own eyes before they can confirm a subject's claim (section 8). Two subjects may independently think an object beautiful because it generates a pleasurable use of mind, yet their feelings may nonetheless differ because they find the object beautiful for different reasons. Such confirmation would surely be false, and to avoid its occurrence Kant insists that communication is crucial: we gain confirmation when subjects successfully communicate their feeling of pleasure or displeasure, enabling another subject to make the same judgment and, based on that communication, to agree about the beauty of the object.

This raises the further problems that since other subjects' judgments and internal reflections are also fallible, it is not clear that we can escape the fallibility of one subject's reflection by relying on several fallible reflections by other members of the community. Further, the importance of confirmation through communication also changes our focus: we are no longer concerned simply with the object that has aesthetic value; instead, the relation to an object becomes secondary to the relation between subjects in a community who supposedly confirm the actual individual pleasurable judgments. The object seems to lose its independent status.

That the object is secondary is not an objection to this theory, since that is what Kant claims: references to the beautiful, he argues, denote subjects whose experience of a universalizable pleasure constitutes the judgment that an object is beautiful. If confirmation from the community warrants that experience, then the relation between subjects will naturally gain prominence. The occurrence of pleasure by itself may not guarantee communication, but we can point to features of the object to explain why we gain a pleasurable yet rule-governed use of mind. The presence of these rules allows us to divine whether pleasure is a result of communication rather than a mere accident.

Kant can also find a positive use for the corrigibility of judgments. The objection that if the judgments are fallible, then no confirmation is possible, so we can never know if our judgments are correct, leads aesthetic judgments to sustain an exploration of the nature and form of a community of subjects, whom we need to understand to grasp the viability of claims about the beauty of objects. In other words, the aesthetic community militates in favor of a continuing and developing interrelation between subjects. The relation develops through deepening and enlarging the community of subjects. Its subjectivity prevents the experience from being imposed on others on the grounds of its objectivity, and is available to others only to the extent that they deploy their own subjectivity. Individuals must be treated as rational and feeling ends who must themselves give assent to a judgment by making one in confirmation. Their agreement cannot be legislated; instead, subjects in effect construct the community through their agreement based on capacities they share with other subjects. The source of social forms in individuals' participation allows them the power to confirm the social order, giving them the possibility of producing new and liberating ones, for the relation of individual to community is constantly in process; the individual's autonomous judgment is always in search of a warrant from the community, which is itself always developing through the assent of its members.

That judgments are fallible means that it is always possible that our confirmation might be mistaken. But it does not follow from this that every claim is useless because it must be mistaken in some part. If there is some error in the confirmation, a critic would have to analyze the agreement given in any instance to diagnose where the error lies. That requires a deepening understanding of the ways of rational and feeling creatures like ourselves, in their relation to each other.

In these ways claims about the beauty of objects are intersubjective and communal in structure even while they are autonomous. This has other implications for Kant's account of beauty.

Beauty and Necessity. Kant uses this formation of a community of subjects making disinterested judgments to argue that judgments of taste have a necessity in that they can, "like an objective principle, *demand* universal assent" (section 22; see also sections 18, 19, and 21). He maintains that we can have an interest in beauty that will not determine what, if anything, we will find beautiful, but will give value to the experiences of beauty we do have. In diverse ways, including his talk of culture and methodology in the *Critique of Judgment* at sections 60 and 83–86, and in other texts, including the methodology of the *Critique of Practical Reason,* Kant points out that aesthetic value is an important participant in the construction of culture. Briefly, an experience of beauty encultures us by facilitating the purchase on us of rational and moral incentives. It denotes our capacity for reasoning and treating other subjects as ends in themselves in a community of actors who are capable of being moved by reason rather than by nature. Insofar as beauty brings about this state, our experience of its pleasure transmits us from being merely receptive to objects and feeling sensual pleasure to engaging our rational faculties, experiencing their harmonious and disinterested interrelation in a manner that presages our engagement with moral maxims. In *The Metaphysics of Morals,* Kant proposes a duty to culture as part of the search for natural perfection; and if beauty promotes culture, then it will be subject to a commensurate moral requirement. By this duty we have an obligation to promote our humanity, possessed of both an animal and a rational character, by developing the capacity for reason and setting ends. Judgments of taste are significant only to humanity because they depend on a harmonious relation between rational faculties and feelings of pleasure. They develop every individual's capacity for reason: because such judgments have subjective universal validity and depend on a relation of rational faculties that are possessed by all those who are capable of empirical experience, all subjects can make these judgments. Accordingly, every successful judgment is an example of an accord between reason and nature that requires the relation of subjects to each other as ends in themselves, in the ways set out above, and consequently promotes human culture. Therefore, given the participation of beauty in culture, subjects making a judgment of taste are justified in demanding that every other rational individual should assent to their judgments about the beauty of an object.

Kant clarifies aspects of the nature of this necessity by considering beauty as a symbol of morality. He does not, however, argue that its symbolic relation to moral good justifies the necessity of beauty; rather, beauty is able to symbolize morality because it claims necessity, and the symbolic relation brings attention to particular features of beauty that generate an interest. We need to explain the connections to morality Kant proposes in order to understand some of the implications of the demands beauty can make.

Kant writes in the *Critique of Judgment* that "the beautiful is a symbol of the morally good; and only because we refer the beautiful to the morally good (we all do so naturally and require all others to do so, as a duty) does our liking for it include a claim to everyone else's assent" (section 59). Two features of the symbolic relation are important to this context. First, for Kant a symbol contains an "indirect . . . exhibition of [a] concept" (section 59). He cites the example of a handmill serving as a symbol of "a monarchy ruled by an individual absolute will," saying that "although there is no similarity between the despotic state and a handmill, there certainly is one between the rules by which we reflect upon the two and on how they operate" (section 59). The mill operates according to mechanisms fixed by its maker and its user's will; similarly, the parts of the despotic state operate in their assigned ways at the despot's will. The mill exhibits indirectly, because it replicates only inexactly and only insofar as it is necessary to bring attention to certain features, the operation of the despotic state. Second, while indirect, the relation nonetheless depends on certain analogies holding between the symbol and what it symbolizes.

One of these features, the analogies, show how an agent who appreciates beauty will be capable of acting well. The other, the indirectness, shows why a symbolic relation of beauty to morality will fail to justify aesthetic necessity. To begin with the first: a symbolic relation between beauty and morality depends on their possessing analogous "modes" or "forms" of reflection or similar rules by which we reflect on both. The analogy depends on four formal characteristics set out in section 59 of the *Critique of Judgment:* we like both directly and without any interest, both embody a harmony between law and the freedom of imagination or will, and both are universal in scope. To begin with the third comparison, which perhaps best exemplifies the analogy between beauty and moral good, both moral and aesthetic judgment denote freedom, a set of possibilities for action and imagination. Yet, the imagination and choice are free only when they claim a rational coherence. Without these rational standards, behavior and associations of images and ideas would be merely arbitrary rather than free; they would be incoherent rather than rule governed and neither purposeful nor ordered.

To be free here both moral and aesthetic judgments must be autonomous at least in the important sense that agents must make judgments for themselves, making the material their own. Neither an action that obeys someone else's rule nor a judgment that claims beauty for an object on the basis of someone else's authority can be successful as a moral or aesthetic judgment. To make an aesthetic judgment the subject must grasp the order of an object, without which no valid experience of pleasure is possible, and moral agents must adopt the relevant maxims, without which their own action is impossible.

Judgment is crucial for both morality and beauty in this exercise of autonomy. A morally good action is based on a maxim, or recommends a rule for action, embodying a judgment about the morally relevant features of a given situation that satisfies the Categorical Imperative. The maxim sets out a choice whose validity consists in satisfying the will *(Wille)*. Similarly, beauty is the experience of a judgment embodying a recommendation that a discerned order or structure of material generates a pleasure that can claim validity over all rational human beings because it satisfies the lawfulness of the understanding.

Both aesthetic and moral judgments are also universalizable. The moral judgment or maxim is valid for all human subjects insofar as they are rational, while the aesthetic judgment postulates that all other rational and feeling human subjects can achieve and appreciate its ordering of material. The suggestion is, then, that both kinds of judgments claim for themselves a reflection guided by standards that are comprehensive over all human beings. The freedom of imagination and choice that satisfies a standard, and thus gains validity, is a freedom that all human agents can possess, and so the standard is universal or appropriate for all human beings. Of course, aesthetic judgment remains bound to the experience of pleasure arising from the relation of faculties, from discerning the structure of material in an object, while the moral judgment articulates a particular intention that can be expected of all rational individuals in that morally relevant situation. But this difference does not cloud their analogy.

Both moral and aesthetic judgments are immediate in that they value their objects for themselves. The moral good is an end in itself, and the beautiful object generates pleasure for itself rather than for any other moral or sensuous purpose it may serve. Further, since moral maxims are universal, through the maxim other rational beings are treated as ends in themselves. Where the freedom of the will is thought as the harmony of the latter with itself according to universal laws of Reason, agents exercise their independence in another kind of autonomy. Their universalizable judgments are independent of arbitrary factors and of determination by personal idiosyncrasies, habits, and other "external" constraints, and thereby without interest. The result is that the judgments are capable of being made by other subjects, who exercise their own autonomy, making their own judgments based on reason and feeling, and in other ways behaving according to a *conception* of the law.

The restriction on judgments that treats other subjects as rational and feeling subjects is also able to embody their point of view, to the extent that the latter is not itself idiosyncratic. The interconnection between those judgments and viewpoints, moreover, is systematic because it sustains an order of judgments and judgers in which autonomous agents have their own place among the collection of universalizable and, therefore, mutually consistent proposals, projects, and persons.

In other words, by comparing moral good and beauty in terms of freedom, universality, immediacy, disinterestedness, and the interrelation between subjects, Kant affirms the three maxims he has identified for judgment: that individuals must be autonomous, must think from the viewpoint of everyone else, and must be consistent. Both aesthetic and moral judgments are universalizable by being autonomous yet rule governed. They treat other subjects as ends in themselves, neither as objects to be manipulated nor as subjects to be merely seduced into appreciation of an object, but as beings who are capable of reason and freedom and can reflect on events and objects in ways that ennoble the mind "above mere sensibility to pleasure from impressions of sense." An agent who appreciates beauty, where the latter bears such strong analogies with moral good, must construe objects and events in a manner crucial also to moral judgment.

This analogy that beauty bears to morality, which is crucial to its symbolic relation to moral good, rests in part on beauty being necessary in the way explained here. The discussion now proceeds to some difficulties with, among other things, supposing that its symbolic relation to moral good explains the necessity of beauty.

Beauty, Expression, and Morality. The account in the *Critique of Judgment* of the relation between beauty and morality based on "a certain analogy in our reflection upon both" (section 60) avoids some of the difficulties afflicting other possible readings of Kant's wording. One such reading is that, first, beauty symbolizes the basis of morality because of an analogy between them; second, whatever symbolizes the basis of morality demands our attention; and third, beauty therefore imposes an obligation on us, or is necessary. Such an argument would be unsuccessful, first of all, because the relation of analogy is wild and, unless particular similarities between beauty and morality are clearly most significant, any claim about necessity based on an analogy between beauty and morality will remain arbitrary. We need, therefore, already to have some account of the significant relation between beauty and morality. But now, second, the significant connection between them seems to be the necessity each possesses, for not much else will justify the reference to the basis of morality that is apparently crucial to their similarity. Therefore, beauty will already have to claim necessity before it can enter into this symbolic relation, and the latter cannot explain the necessity of beauty.

Arguably, there is an analogy between beauty and morality based on their respective necessities: one claims a subjective universal validity and the other an objective validity. But, to move to the third reason for this argument's lack of success, even if there were such necessities, or even if the symbolic relation between beauty and morality were independent of the necessity of beauty, its symbolic relation to morality does not clearly allow us to impute a "duty-like" necessity to beauty. This is because symbolic relations do not seem to be so powerful. If there is only a symbolic relation, then the necessity attaching to the moral good, which supposedly extends to beauty, would be at best a commensurately symbolic necessity. It is difficult to know, however, what sense we can make of this symbolic necessity or of how it fails to include everything analogous to morality.

At other times Kant's wording suggests that beauty expresses moral ideas, and that such expression partly explains the value of beauty. This suggests that moral ideas are the content of the works we find beautiful. But for Kant aesthetic pleasure cannot come from the content. He maintains that "the pleasure in the beautiful is . . . neither a pleasure of enjoyment nor of an activity according to the law, nor yet one of rationalizing contemplation according to ideas, but rather of mere reflection" (*Critique of Judgment* section 39). Accordingly, when he talks of connecting beautiful art with moral ideas, he must be referring to the analogy between modes of reflection in beauty and morality rather than to the moral ideas that might serve as the content of what is expressed. He can therefore say, as he does, that "the pleasure [we take in form] is . . . culture, and disposes the soul to ideas," and mean that the purposive form of aesthetic judgments on the beauty of objects makes them analogous to moral good, rather than imply that beauty's purchase on morality arises from ideas expressed as the content of judgments. The content of works of fine art need not itself be made up of moral ideas.

Nor is it clear how the expression of moral ideas in a work can make its beauty necessary. In one interpretation, the claim that beauty is necessary because it expresses moral ideas consists of four theses. The first is that aesthetic judgments are disinterested, and the second is that disinterested judgments may have an interest attached to them. Thus, being disinterested, capable of a subjective general validity or necessity, and expressive, third, they may express moral ideas as easily and fluently as they express other ideas. Indeed, since they are disinterested, they may only express moral or other ideas rather than, say, embody moral ideas as imperatives, and, fourth, only when they express moral ideas are they beautiful objects of interest. All other expressions of ideas yield at best superficial and dissipated pleasures.

One difficulty with this sort of argument is that it introduces a distinction between morally interesting and morally uninspiring content for beauty, and valorizes the former in a manner that seems restrictive of aesthetic and artistic practices. The distinction relies on an indeterminate relation to morality—on the expression of moral ideas, with all the rational uncertainties concomitant with such loosely structured and infinitely variable associations of ideas. Such infinite variety renders expression unwieldy, since it can make almost any association of ideas capable of being moral, and therefore militates against the distinction between interesting and uninteresting works.

Another problem is that the attempt to give beauty seriousness through its expression of moral ideas shares the problem faced by the symbolic relation between beauty and morality considered above. An expression of moral ideas will clearly carry the seriousness attendant on moral ideas only if there is some "expressive necessity" that extends from moral ideas to their expression in beautiful objects. Yet it is far from clear that the latter is any more plausible than a "symbolic necessity" was earlier.

On the other hand, if moral ideas were more determinate in expression, if beauty claimed serious worth because and insofar as moral ideas were made real in expression, then our aesthetic judgments would be interested rather than disinterested. We would find them important because of what they were about rather than because of their aesthetic nature.

Certainly, Kant does not obviously stake out any such grounds in his account of beauty. He gives examples of portraying Neptune as an expression of divine power without implying that beauty can express only this kind of idea. Instead, he apparently wants to validate and affirm the importance of all beauty, not just a morally expressive kind (see *Critique of Judgment,* sections 59 and 60). Since none of the possibilities proposed so far is very attractive or plausible in relation to other theses in Kant's theory, we must be circumspect in interpreting Kant's claim that

> Where fine arts are not, either proximately or remotely, brought into combination with moral ideas, which alone are attended with self-sufficing delight, [dullness of the soul] is the fate that ultimately awaits them. They then only serve for a diversion, of which one continually feels an increasing need in proportion as one has availed oneself of it as a means of dispelling the discontent of one's mind, with the result that one makes oneself ever more and more unprofitable and dissatisfied with oneself.
>
> (section 54)

Although this seems to affirm the need for moral ideas as content, the argument and context are more complicated. In this context Kant is arguing that we cannot consider only the matter of sensations when valuing works of fine art, because these do not sustain the validity of aesthetic judgments. Art must be meaningful, and although simple sensations, such as the experience of color, can claim intersubjective validity, their experience does not provide a proper occasion for reflective judgment. So he can say that the mere play of sensations, where "the aim is merely enjoyment, which leaves nothing behind as an idea . . . renders the soul dull, the object in the course of time distasteful, and the mind dissatisfied with itself and ill-humored, owing to a consciousness that in the judgment of reason its disposition is perverse" (ibid.). But this does not affirm the importance of moral ideas as expression over the analogy with moral good. Rather, the context of Kant's complaint is a concern with mere plays of sensation and therefore with the kind of formalism that ignores all content. In this passage he is criticizing any attempt to claim a ratiocinative universality for a merely meaningless play of sensation. His argument cannot justify the claim that beauty must express moral ideas (as content) in order to have serious weight.

This discussion set out Kant's conception of beauty by explaining that it is an experience of pleasure that is disinterested, subjective, universally valid, and necessary. In order to explain the last feature it was necessary to examine beauty's symbolic relation to morality and its expression of moral ideas. Kant also develops his theory of beauty by distinguishing natural beauty from fine art and between pure and dependent beauty—distinctions that are outside the province of this entry.

[*See also* Beauty; *and* Morality and Aesthetics.]

BIBLIOGRAPHY

Works by Kant

Foundations of the Metaphysics of Morals (1785). 2d rev. ed. Translated by Lewis White Beck. New York, 1990.

Critique of Practical Reason (1788). 3d ed. Edited and translated by Lewis White Beck. New York, 1993.

Critique of Judgment (1790). Translated by Werner S. Pluhar. Indianapolis, 1987.

The Metaphysics of Morals (1797). Translated by Mary Gregor. Cambridge and New York, 1991.

Anthropology from a Pragmatic Point of View (1798). Translated by Mary J. Gregor. The Hague, 1974.

Über die Fortschritte der Metaphysik seit Leibniz und Wolff (On the Progress of Metaphysics since Leibniz and Wolff, 1804). In *Kants gesammelte Schriften*, vol. 20, pp. 253–351. Berlin, 1900–.

Other Sources

Crawford, Donald W. *Kant's Aesthetic Theory.* Madison, Wis., 1974.

Guyer, Paul. *Kant and the Claims of Taste* (1979). Enl. ed. Cambridge and New York, 1997.

Kemal, Salim. *Kant and Fine Art: An Essay on Kant and the Philosophy of Fine Art and Culture.* Oxford and New York, 1986.

Kemal, Salim. *Kant's Aesthetic Theory: An Introduction.* New York, 1992.

Rogerson, Kenneth F. *Kant's Aesthetics: The Roles of Form and Expression.* Lanham, Md., 1986.

Savile, Anthony. *Aesthetic Reconstructions: The Seminal Writings of Lessing, Kant, and Schiller.* Aristotelian Society Series, vol. 8. Oxford and New York, 1987.

SALIM KEMAL

Kant on the Sublime

Immanuel Kant's account of the sublime is profound, provocative, and problematic; the focus here will be on his mature analysis of the sublime in the *Critique of Judgment* (1790), sections 23–30 and 39. Kant's critical philosophy explicates the fundamental, rightful role of reason in human affairs. His "transcendental" analyses set out the necessary a priori conditions of cognitive, moral, and aesthetic judgments. The peculiar logical feature of aesthetic judgments, in Kant's view, is that they concern single objects and command universal assent, even though they are not based on interests, on determinate concepts, or on sensory qualities.

Aesthetic judgments are universally valid because aesthetic experience is based on the universal features of our minds that make experience possible. Aesthetic judgments are much more than a logical curiosity because aesthetic experience symbolizes and facilitates our moral vocation to guide our behavior by rational precepts. Kant concludes his *Critique of Practical Reason* (1788) with a statement suggesting the moral tenor of his later analysis of the sublime: "two things always fill the mind with renewed and increasing wonder and awe . . . the starry heavens above me and the moral law within me" (Kant, 1993, p. 166). Our reason enables us to understand and to act on the requirements of the moral law; thus, we are able to judge and act independently of both authority and empirical givens. This is the key to human freedom and autonomy, to our independence from external circumstances and our empirically given desires and aversions. The experience of the natural sublime, according to Kant, makes us aware of the sublimity of our moral capacities and vocation.

Experience of the natural sublime emerged with the revival of interest in Longinus's *On the Sublime,* with John Milton's masterpiece *Paradise Lost,* and with the advent of travel, especially across the Alps, in the latter seventeenth century. Travelers (including Milton) were deeply moved by grand scenes of nature, despite their not fitting the traditional requirements of beauty, namely, order, harmony, and proportion. Kant did not travel, but he avidly read travelogues and was a prized conversationalist at dinners hosting visitors to Königsberg. His examples of the sublime are borrowed: the Egyptian pyramids, Saint Peter's Basilica in Rome, formless masses of mountains piled on one another, the stormy sea, thunderclouds billowing up into the vault of heaven, volcanoes, hurricanes, and mighty waterfalls. Kant concentrates on the natural sublime because the sublime in art must correspond to (i.e., represent) the natural sublime (section 23) and because only judgments of the natural sublime are pure, since they involve no concepts of the purpose of the objects judged (section 26). Kant's description of the experience of the natural sublime follows his British predecessors, although his analysis of it differs sharply from theirs. Unlike the contemplative pleasures of beauty, the pleasure of the sublime involves agitation and displeasure. Whereas beauty is found in the formal characteristics of objects, Kant finds the sublime in the formlessness, the unboundedness of natural objects, provided they are perceived as totalities (not aggregates) displaying size and might. The sublime is absolutely great; in comparison to it, all else is small (section 25). *Absolute* greatness cannot be found in any object of the senses; for any object perceived, a larger one can be given. Consequently, our ability simply to think of the sublime shows that our mind has the ability to exceed every standard based on the senses. British analyses of the sublime wavered about whether sublimity is properly ascribed to the object, to the subject's state of mind, or to both. Kant contends that sublimity is properly ascribed to our rational capacities and ideas, and is only ascribed to nature by a "subreption." Kant thus incorporates a classical observation: "within the scope of human enterprises there lie such powers of contemplation and thought that even the whole universe cannot satisfy them, but our ideas often pass beyond the limits that enring us" (Longinus, 1939, p. 125).

Kant's reference to size or might in natural totalities reflects his view that we are led to contemplate the sublime by two distinct kinds of causes. Kant analyzes these as the "mathematical" and the "dynamical" sublime. In the former, we refer the scene we apprehend to our rational powers of cognition; the mathematically sublime concerns quantitative features of our experience and our rational aim to comprehend an extensive (spatial and temporal) totality. Kant maintains that to have experience at all we must integrate our sensations into a temporal and spatial whole. The "productive imagination" integrates sensations in accord with our basic concepts, the twelve categories of cognitive judgment. Integrating our sensations into a whole requires a concept of a whole to guide that integration. That concept cannot be presented to us in sense experience, because that concept is presupposed by experience and because, for any totality presented to us in sense experience, we can imagine a greater totality (just as for any number we count to, we can count higher). Because the concept of infinity as totality cannot be exhibited in sensory experience, it is supersensible. Kant further maintains that units of measure are useful only through their (mathematically proportional) relation to some standard unit of sensed extension. The only fundamental natural unit of measure is nature as an absolute whole, "infinity comprehended," although no such genuine totality can be perceived by our senses. For these reasons, infinity as totality is a supersensuous, rational idea.

Kant's transcendental analysis of the mathematically sublime reconstructs Edmund Burke's quaint physiological claim that the idea of the sublime results from the eye strain involved in perceiving a vast object (Burke, 1968, part 4, section 9). Kant's analysis of the mathematically sublime holds that those natural phenomena that exceed our capacity to perceive their extent strain our faculty of sensory presentation, the (productive) imagination. According to Kant, the experience of the mathematically sublime involves discord between the perceptual estimation of a natural object and our rational idea of infinite totality. In this circumstance, our (productive) imagination is incapable, and is experienced to be incapable, of matching reason's idea of infinity. The strain and pain of this discord are "purposive" because they make us aware, first, that our pain results from imagination's attempt to comprehend a quantitative infinity, even if it cannot achieve it, and second, that we have an ultimate standard of comparison that is great beyond all comparison, namely, the rational idea of infinity as a given totality. Because this pain is purposive, it is ultimately plea-

surable. In this way, Kant reconciles the painful and the pleasurable aspects of the experience of the sublime, without recourse to a third affective category.

The "dynamical sublime" concerns might. We refer our apprehension of it to our own source of might, our will; it concerns active features of our experience and our rational aim to overcome the merely sensuous limitations of our volition. Kant's analysis turns on defining *might* as something superior to great obstacles and defining *dominance* as something superior to might. Kant claims that nature is dynamically sublime when it is considered aesthetically as might that has no dominion over us. He contends that might can be estimated perceptually only by how much the object judged resists us. Whatever we resist we regard as evil; if it can overpower us, it is fearsome. Hence, nature must be fearsome in order to be dynamically sublime (though fearsomeness does not suffice for sublimity). Kant grants that we cannot judge aesthetically when we are actually afraid of something; such judgments would not be disinterested. While in safety, however, we can recognize the potentially overwhelming might of nature. Recognizing the might of nature leads us to recognize both our own physical impotence and our capacity to judge and to determine our will morally, independently of nature and of our sensuous interests. Due to this rational autonomy from nature within and without us (from our psychological fears and from fearsome nature), "the humanity in our person remains undiminished, even though the human being would have to succumb to [the] dominance [of nature]" (section 28). Once again, sublimity is a feature not of nature but of ourselves: "nature is here called sublime merely because it arouses our imagination to exhibit those cases where the mind can feel the proper sublimity of its [rational] vocation over nature" (ibid.).

Kant does not detail the feeling of the dynamically sublime. A plausible conjecture is that the fear it involves concerns the threat of physical pain or mortality, while that fear can be overcome by recognizing our moral supremacy to nature by recognizing and respecting our free rational agency. According to Kant, the moral law is a law of reason that demands such supremacy, and we can take pleasure in our supersensuous rational or "noumenal" agency. This conjecture maintains a reasonable parallel between the feelings engaged in the two varieties of sublime. Kant claims that the satisfaction in the sublime is marked by a mixture of pain and a negative pleasure of respect and admiration. This pleasure is generated by the need to judge in accordance with ideas of reason. Kant defines respect as "the feeling of our incapacity to achieve an idea which is a law for us" (section 27). This definition of respect is broad enough to cover both kinds of sublime as well as Kant's account of respect for the moral law, which requires us to act on the basis of rationally determined duty, regardless of our psychological desires and aversions—an ideal we cannot humanly attain.

In both kinds of experience of the sublime, the feeling of the superiority of our rational capacities over our sensibility and over nature leads us to recognize the sublime—the sublimity of our vocation to triumph rationally over nature and ourselves qua natural beings. This "use" of the objects of nature to generate a conflict between our sensuous and rational capacities, and thus to be aware of the necessary ascendancy of reason over sensibility, is subjectively purposive in the sublime. The "sublime" in nature can be understood only as if it had the purpose of making us aware of our own purpose, although we cannot ascribe this purpose to nature. This purposiveness is itself a source of pleasure, for by arousing this feeling nature accords with the laws of our reason.

Kant holds that judgments of the sublime impute a necessary agreement among all potential judges. This is tenuous because a certain degree of education is required to be receptive to the sublime, and such receptivity requires the mind to be receptive to rational ideas (section 29). Kant maintains that culture is required only for developing an innate (nonconventional) moral tendency "to have feeling for (practical) ideas, *i.e.* for what is moral" (section 29). This moral basis grounds the necessity of universal agreement, and this imputation of necessary universal agreement shows that judgments of the sublime rest on an a priori principle. Judgments of the sublime thus transcend empirical psychology and belong to transcendental philosophy. This is Kant's main disagreement with British aesthetics, especially Burke's, namely, that British aesthetic theories were insensitive to the normative character of aesthetic judgments and to the theoretical implications of that normativity (cf. Burke, part 3, section 9).

Kant is not precise about our relation to natural danger in experiencing the dynamically sublime. He recognizes that we cannot be in actual danger to have this experience, but overcoming sensuously based fear is crucial to his analysis of this experience, and he does not say how merely regarding objects as fearful or feeling fear of such things by "aid of the imagination" can put us in the right state of mind. Kant's analysis also reduces natural objects to the mere occasions of sublime reflection on rational ideas. Furthermore, Kant's four arguments for ascribing sublimity to the mind rather than to nature are unconvincing. These arguments are important, for they provide Kant's reasons for denying that judgments of the sublime require a distinct "deduction"—justification—of their claim to universal agreement: they require no deduction because they are not about objects (section 30).

Kant's first reason for not ascribing sublimity to the objects that give rise to its experience is that consciousness of the sublime leads to no objective principles, hence to no principles concerning the object that occasions the sublime (section 23). It appears, however, that Kant's ultimate analysis of the significance of our experience of the sublime involves a regulative principle for our power of rational judgment. Kant holds that what is "absolutely great"— "great beyond all comparison" (section 25)—is ultimately our practical reason in its ability to transcend the limits of sensibility (section 26). If so, then the sublime does suggest a regulative principle regarding objects, parallel to the case of beauty (pace section 23). The principle of purposiveness (without a definite purpose) in the case of beauty concerns the suitability of (beautiful) objects, or indeed nature as a system, for our cognitive powers (sections 11, 12). The principle of purposiveness of the sublime concerns the suitability of nature to our moral vocation, expressed in the judgment, "That which I ought rationally to do, I have the rational power to do." Kant does not discuss this kind of principle in the first part of the *Critique of Judgment,* but it is crucial to his discussions of the moral postulates in the *Critique of Practical Reason,* and should not be ignored here. Kant's first argument is at best inconclusive.

Kant's second argument is based on his explication: "we call that *sublime* which is *absolutely [schlechthin] large*"; or (alternatively), *"That is sublime in comparison with which everything else is small."* The magnitude of any perceived object is only comparatively large, and can be small or large, depending on our standard of comparison or unit of measure. Thus, no perceived object is absolutely large; thus, no perceived object is sublime (section 25). Kant's conclusion follows from his explication *(Namenerklärung),* but his explication is highly stipulative, it presupposes Kant's pre-Cantorian notion of infinity as a specific (maximal) quantity, and it diverges significantly from the actual usage of most of the writers and theorists who reported or analyzed the sublime, who ascribe sublimity to the objects of their experience and do not call those objects "absolutely" large. Kant's explication does not provide an independently plausible premise to support his conclusion.

Kant argues, third, that our satisfaction in the sublime may be found in boundlessness. Hence, our satisfaction in the sublime is not based on properties of the object, and so our satisfaction is not a satisfaction in the object (section 25). Two problems arise here, both stemming from Kant's attempt, like Burke, to distinguish absolutely between beauty and sublimity. Kant's account of beauty can only specify the beautiful features of objects in terms of their forms being found purposive for our cognitive faculties. Accordingly, he distinguishes sublime objects from beautiful ones by denying that formal features of objects have anything to do with their sublimity; hence his emphasis on sublime "formlessness" (sections 23, 30). One problem with Kant's notion of formlessness is that it is strictly incompatible with the unity, specifically the *totality,* that must be presented by objects which give rise to the sublime (section 23). Thus, at least this one formal feature of objects must be relevant to their eliciting the sublime response: their manifest unity. Kant is mistaken that the experience of the sublime rests on *no* principles concerning the object (section 23), and therefore this premise cannot be used to show that sublimity is properly ascribed to us rather than to objects. (Kant could instead distinguish beauty and sublimity by their distinct kinds of purposiveness; the sublime is purposive for reason, beauty for understanding.) Second, Kant's own examples of objects of the sublime are not, in fact, infinite in extent and do not, in fact, exceed our capacity to perceive them as unitary objects; they are not literally formless in the way required by Kant's argument against ascribing sublimity to objects due to their formlessness. Kant needs to explain how large but actually finite and perceivable objects suggest to us our rational idea of an infinite totality; his claim that they overload the capacity of our productive imagination to synthesize the manifold of sensation is insufficient.

Kant contends, fourth, that the natural objects that give rise to the sublime violate the purpose of our cognitive powers, and no such violation can be satisfying, whereas our experience of the sublime plainly is (section 26). This reasoning, however, is inconsistent with his later, more detailed account of our experience of the sublime, in which Kant recognizes that the violence of nature is contrapurposive for our (productive) imagination, but this very contrapurposiveness is ultimately purposive for our entire mind (section 27). This is Kant's considered view, but on this view the objects that give rise to the sublime are purposive for our entire mind, and this can be their source of satisfaction.

Analyzing our experience of the sublime in terms of our rational capacities and ideas may ground the possibility of universal agreement in judgments of the sublime. Kant does not thereby, however, show the necessity of such universal agreement. The close analogy between judgments of the sublime and moral judgments does not bring these aesthetic judgments within the moral domain. Also, if the above objections are sound, judgments of the sublime are about objects and so, like judgments of beauty, require a deduction. Can there be a "deduction," that is, a justification, of the necessary universal validity of pure judgments of the sublime?

One way to fill this lacuna lies in a parallel between judgments of beauty, of mathematical sublimity, and of dynamical sublimity. In his analysis of judgments of beauty Kant suggests that we are justified in presuming a common sense—a common aesthetic sensibility or sensitivity to beauty—because we all have common cognitive capacities and because experiencing and judging beauty involves a noncognitive use of exactly those same capacities (sections 20, 21, 38). Our intellectual capacities are identical in kind and are defined functionally. Thus their nonpurposive activity should have the same results for each of us, just as does their purposeful activity. If this is true, then Kant could argue that the same points hold for judgments of the sublime, because such judgments involve the interaction of our imagination and ideas of reason (section 26).

A further way to fill this lacuna emerges in Kant's discussion of beauty as the symbol of morality (section 59). There he notes that, in judging the beautiful, judgment "gives the law to itself in respect of the faculty of desire" (section 59), just as reason does in morality. Judgments of the sublime involve the same kind of aesthetic self-legislation as judgments of the beautiful. By virtue of such isomorphism, the sublime, too, symbolizes the moral. The experience of the sublime symbolizes morality because it presents reason as ascendant over sensuous nature, just as morality requires. Moreover, morality requires a connection between the rational and the sensible (natural) realms. The experience of the sublime expresses one such connection. In these ways, Kant's "deduction" of judgments of taste (section 59) can be extended to judgments of the sublime as well.

Despite its difficulties, Kant's analysis of the sublime is very suggestive and had great influence on subsequent German aesthetics and on literature through Friedrich von Schiller, the brothers August Wilhelm and Friedrich von Schlegel, Samuel Taylor Coleridge, and the New England Transcendentalists. Despite his criticism of most of Kant's main doctrines, Arthur Schopenhauer modeled his account of the sublime closely on Kant's. Schiller filled Kant's contrast between beauty and sublimity with the blood of a highly creative artist, ultimately transmuting it into a contrast between naive and sentimental poetry. Schiller's essay "On Naive and Sentimental Poetry" (1795–1796) fed the apotheosis of Romanticism developed in Friedrich von Schlegel's contrast between classical and Romantic art.

G. W. F. Hegel rejected Kant's subjectivism, but nevertheless based his account of the sublime on the Kantian notion that rational ideas—which Hegel held were objective structures of the world—transcend and thus cannot be fully exhibited in the particulars that instantiate them. Hegel associated the art of the sublime especially with the ancient literature of India and Persia and the Muslim, Hebrew, and early Christian religions.

Interest in the sublime faded later in the nineteenth century, but has recently been revived by Theodor Adorno and by postmodernists who tend to treat Kant's analysis as a palimpsest for their own issues. The exception is Jean-François Lyotard, whose detailed *Lessons on the Analytic of the Sublime* aims to show that aesthetic judgment provides the model for philosophical reflection in general because it specifies our powers of judgment by a feeling for the integrity of its subject matter, and that the sublime reveals that our powers of judgment and experience transcend the limits of cognition set out in Kant's theory of knowledge.

[*See also* Sublime.]

BIBLIOGRAPHY

Works by Kant

Critique of Practical Reason (1788). 3d ed. Edited and translated by Lewis White Beck. New York, 1993.

Critique of Judgment (1790). Translated by Werner S. Pluhar. Indianapolis, 1987. See part 1, division 1, book 2, "Analytic of the Sublime," sections 23–30, 39.

Other Sources

Adorno, Theodor W. *Aesthetic Theory.* Edited by Gretel Adorno and Rolf Tiedemann, translated by Robert Hullot-Kentor. Minneapolis, 1997.

Burke, Edmund. *A Philosophical Enquiry into the Origin of Our Ideas of the Sublime and Beautiful* (1757). Edited by James T. Boulton. New York, 1958; 2d ed., Notre Dame, Ind., 1968.

Crawford, Donald W. "The Place of the Sublime in Kant's Aesthetic Theory." In *The Philosophy of Immanuel Kant*, edited by Richard Kennington, pp. 161–183. Washington, D.C., 1985.

Crowther, Paul. *The Kantian Sublime: From Morality to Art.* Oxford, 1989.

Guyer, Paul. *Kant and the Experience of Freedom: Essays on Aesthetics and Morality.* Cambridge, 1993. See chap. 6, "The Beautiful and the Sublime," and chap. 7, "Nature, Art, and Autonomy," pp. 187–274.

Hegel, G. W. F. *Aesthetics: Lectures on Fine Art* (1830). 2 vols. Translated by T. M. Knox, Oxford, 1975. See vol. 1, part 2, chap. 2, "Symbolism of the Sublime," pp. 362–377.

Hipple, Walter John, Jr. *The Beautiful, the Sublime, and the Picturesque in Eighteenth-Century British Aesthetic Theory.* Carbondale, Ill., 1957.

Lokke, Kari Elise. "The Role of Sublimity in the Development of Modern Aesthetics." *Journal of Aesthetics and Art Criticism* 40.4 (summer 1982): 421–429.

Longinus. *On the Sublime.* Translated by W. Hamilton Fyfe. Loeb Classical Library. Cambridge, Mass., 1939.

Lyotard, Jean-François. *Lessons on the Analytic of the Sublime* (1991). Translated by Elizabeth Rottenberg. Stanford, Calif., 1994.

Makkreel, Rudolf A. *Imagination and Interpretation in Kant: The Hermeneutical Import of the Critique of Judgment.* Chicago, 1990. See chap. 4, "The Regress of Imagination: The Sublime and the Form of the Subject," pp. 67–87.

Monk, Samuel H. *The Sublime: A Study of Critical Theories in Eighteenth-Century England.* New York, 1935; reprint, Ann Arbor, 1960.

Schiller, Friedrich. *Essays.* Edited by Walter Hinderer and Daniel O. Dahlstrom, translated by Daniel O. Dahlstrom. New York, 1993. See chap. 2, "On the Sublime (Toward the Further Development of Some Kantian Ideas)" (1793), chap. 4, "Concerning the Sublime" (1801), and chap. 6, "On Naive and Sentimental Poetry" (1795–1796), pp. 22–44, 70–85, and 179–260, respectively.

Schlegel, August Wilhelm von. *Vorlesungen über dramatische Kunst und Literatur* (1808). 2 vols. Edited by Edgar Lohner. Stuttgart, 1966–1967.

Schopenhauer, Arthur. *The World as Will and Representation* (1819). 2 vols. Translated by E. F. J. Payne. Reprint, New York, 1966. See vol. 1, sections 39–41.

Wellmer, Albrecht. "Adorno, die Moderne und das Erhabene." In *Ästhetik im Widerstreit: Interventionen zum Werk von Jean-François Lyotard,* edited by Wolfgang Welsch and Christine Pries, pp. 45–66. Weinheim, 1991.

KENNETH R. WESTPHAL

Kant on Nature and Art

Immanuel Kant's aesthetic theory invites conflicting readings concerning the relation of fine art to natural beauty. Kant's *Critique of Judgment* has been interpreted as making art secondary to nature, assigning less value to the beauty of fine art than to natural objects. Although natural beauty seems to take methodological priority in Kant's argument that formal purposiveness accounts for the pleasure of pure judgments of taste, it is not clear that his theory favors either art or nature as objects of aesthetic interest: "in the judgment of mere taste neither would vie for superiority over the other" (section 42). When Kant variously prioritizes one or the other, it is by reference to factors supplementing the pure judgment of taste. Examining passages that imply or specify a superiority of natural beauty over that of art, it becomes clear that none do so other than in a qualified way (i.e., the introductions and sections 16, 30, 42, and 52).

A passage that may seem to denigrate art appears in Kant's initial contrast between "the beautiful in nature" and "beautiful art":

> In a critique of Judgment, the part that deals with aesthetic judgment belongs in it essentially. For this power alone contains a principle that judgment lays completely a priori at the basis of its reflection in nature: the principle of a formal purposiveness of nature . . . without which principle the understanding could not find its way about in nature.   (section 8)

Kant proposes that the a priori principle of the formal purposiveness of nature accounts for all judgments of taste. Because it is a principle concerning nature *(Natur)*, however, Kant has been taken to mean that objects of nature rather than of art are primary for aesthetic judgment, thereby limiting genuine aesthetic response to objects of nature. As such, the principle of purposiveness cannot account for the beauty of fine art, undercutting Kant's proposal that all judgments of taste require an a priori principle about nature. It is tempting to conclude that Kant needs a separate principle of taste to account for art.

Such a reading emphasizes passages in which Kant treats the realms of art and nature as mutually exclusive, as in the remark that "art can be called fine art only if we are conscious that it is art while yet it looks to us like nature" (i.e., "free from all constraint of chosen rules"; section 45). Again, it seems that Kant confusedly treats nature, or objects with the appearance of nature, as aesthetically primary. But such a reading is unnecessarily harsh, for the purposiveness of nature does not concern the purposiveness of natural objects in a manner excluding artworks.

As Kant uses the term, *Natur* does not uniformly exclude fine art. It sometimes means the totality of objects experienced according to the categories, as in the *Prolegomena*'s equation of nature and possible experience. Under this usage, both the Mona Lisa and a rose are parts of nature. They are objects about which we discover empirical regularities, in contrast to God and the human soul, which are not. But there are many passages where *Natur* has a different meaning, indicating the organized complex of all laws (including empirical laws) through which we impose a systematic unity on objects of experience. In these cases, *Natur* means something like "the order of nature." Although these two different senses of *Natur* are found throughout Kant's mature writings, they predominate in the two introductions to the *Critique of Judgment*.

According to the unpublished first introduction, "nature as the sum of all objects of experience" is unproblematic. Yet, this version of the introduction goes on to emphasize that "it does not follow from this that nature is a system *comprehensible* by human cognition through *empirical* laws." Kant now recognizes that the schematized categories cannot ensure the order of nature. The schematized categories are necessary for cognition of phenomena as law-governed nature, but they cannot secure the coherence of "natural things as such" as a law-governed whole (section 5). The *Critique of Judgment* thus supplements the first by acknowledging that the categories only provide nature qua objects of experience, comprehended in an unsystematic aggregate of empirical judgments. For instance, the empirical judgment that unsupported objects fall may seem unrelated to Venus's changing location in the sky. Without a transcendental principle supplementing the categories, we would not suppose that there must be a general theory that will systematically unify these disparate empirical facts. Empirical science has the goal of unifying all phenomena under universal laws that hold with strict necessity. As such, it presupposes some additional a priori principle for the possibility of nature. Kant calls it "the *law of the specification of nature* in terms of its empirical laws" (section 5).

Kant therefore posits the principle of purposiveness as accounting for reflective judgments in which we move "from the particular in nature to the universal." This principle does not imply that objects subsumed under empirical concepts will be found to have any purpose, finality, or natural end. The purposiveness at issue is relative to human inquiry. Because human cognition is discursive rather than intuitive, we do not know in advance what system of laws will ultimately accomplish the goal of unification. We can only investigate nature on the a priori assumption that there is some "harmony of nature with our cognitive power" (ibid.).

Significantly, these senses of *Natur* can include artworks. Paintings and sculptures are objects of experience, subject to the categories and comprehensible under a system of empirical laws. As objects of experience, their rate and direction of fall are explained by the same laws of physics that account for the observed motions of Venus. The principle of the purposiveness of nature does not itself establish art and nature as mutually exclusive realms for cognition.

Complications arise when the *Critique of Judgment* introduces a third sense of *Natur*, singling out natural objects and excluding artworks. Kant uses this third sense alongside the other two: "our receptivity to a pleasure arising from our reflection on the forms of things (both of nature and of art) does not always indicate a purposiveness of objects in relation to the subject's reflective power of judgment, in accordance with the concept of nature" (section 7). This passage initially treats nature and art as mutually exclusive. It then claims that sometimes the pleasure "does not indicate a purposiveness . . . in accordance with the concept of *nature*." With both natural objects and art, judgments concerning sublimity presuppose a failure to regard the object as nature (in the sense of comprehending it within the order of nature). Taken in any other way, Kant would contradict himself by saying that we discover sublimity in nature only when we do not have a natural object. Kant subsequently argues that sublimity is paradigmatically found in natural objects when they initially seem "contrapurposive for our power of judgment," namely, when the objects do not seem comprehensible within a system of empirical laws (section 23).

The exclusive sense of *Natur* predominates in part 2 of the *Critique of Judgment*, where Kant's focus on the intelligibility of nonhuman purposes limits his consideration of artworks and other products of purposeful human agency. Human action has objective purposiveness, so the products of human agency reflect a plan according to a concept of such an object. Natural objects may seem to have purposes, yet for a thing to have a *natural* purpose it must be "both cause and effect of itself" (section 64). Kant thus raises the question of whether nature (qua natural objects) requires comprehension under a system of laws (the order of nature) involving final causes. In this context, Kant also uses *Natur* to mean the total system of natural objects, as when he asks whether "spruce forests are a purpose of nature" (section 63). However, neither the introductions nor Kant's earlier writings exhibit this exclusivity of focus on natural objects.

Thus, Kant introduces multiple senses of *Natur* and he does not uniformly intend the restricted sense of "natural object" that excludes works of art. Although the restricted usage predominates in the *Critique of Judgment*, the less restrictive usage underlies the doctrine of nature's purposiveness. Because the principle of the purposiveness does not systematically exclude art and other "nonnatural" objects, Kant does not denigrate nonnatural objects (e.g., fine art) when he claims that nature's purposiveness grounds pure judgments of taste. Kant's principle of purposiveness does not limit or even favor the application of his aesthetic theory to natural objects.

There are, however, further passages suggesting that Kant values natural beauty over art. Section 30 concludes that "the only deduction we will have to attempt is that of judgments of taste, i.e., judgments about beauty in natural things." Kant's qualification suggests that pure judgments of taste concern only natural beauty. A few pages later, he says that "the actuality of natural beauties" is a condition of the deduction's success (section 38).

Kant apparently focuses on natural beauty because it invites a direct interest in a way that artworks cannot. Natural beauty is discovered in contexts in which our cognitive activity is not determined by specific practical, cognitive, or moral objectives: "our judgment is not based on an interest and also gives rise to none" (section 42). Because artworks are artifacts, their existence presupposes an objective purpose and a corresponding interest, that is, "pleasure in the existence of the object" (section 41). Strictly speaking, a free response to an artwork is possible, provided one judges it without making a determinate judgment. Kant offers an example of a botanist admiring a flower, who "pays no attention to [its] natural purpose when he judges the flower by taste" (section 15). This admiration presupposes an ability to ignore its causal history and objective purpose. Presumably, the same is true of artworks.

However, as long as an object's form can be interpreted as resulting from some objective purpose (including designs "for our liking"), its purposiveness does not confirm the contingent harmony between the object's appearance and our cognitive faculties. Only natural beauty provides actual cases where the perceived purposiveness can only be interpreted as "ideal" and where it simply cannot be a response to intentional design. So only natural beauty offers independent confirmation of the contingent fact that appearances reveal forms harmonious with our cognitive powers (the idea governing the general principle of reflective judgment).

Kant does not presume that contexts devoid of objective purposes are unique to nature. Some artifacts are "free beauties." Furthermore, natural beauty can be discovered while one satisfies practical objectives such as gaining knowledge. If the judgment is free of determination under an empirical concept, natural beauty can be included in the category of free beauties with musical fantasias and wallpaper patterns. Some formalists recommend appreciating all art, even representational artworks, independent of any practical objective (e.g., obtaining knowledge of how something looks). Like a free beauty of nature, the Mona Lisa can be enjoyed in a pure judgment by a viewer who remains ignorant of or "abstract[s] from" its purpose (section 16). Kant's regard for fine art as a stimulus to thought suggests, however, that he would dismiss such responses to the painting. Yet, he does not regard natural objects as uniquely suited to the discovery of beauty in a pure judgment.

Some commentators hold that Kant emphasizes natural objects because such objects can appear purposive apart from any interest on our part, whereas fine art cannot. Again, it is not immediately clear how to reconcile Kant's comment (that only natural beauty belongs to the deduction of taste) with his doctrine that the beauty of fine art reflects the same principle. What is needed is a relevant difference between natural objects and artworks that is compatible with their both being *Natur* in the broad sense of being subject to the understanding's criteria for a system of empirical laws. Kant stipulates one such difference. In the unpublished introduction, he says that the principle of

purposiveness underlying pure beauty accounts for unintentional purposiveness and so belongs only to nature. Such purposiveness concerns subjective finality in the mere mode of representation.

Here, Kant offers an epistemological justification for nature's superiority. It is consistent with the subsequent claim that "idealism concerning purposiveness" accounts for pure judgments of taste directed at both art and nature (section 58). Because human artifacts reflect objective purpose, their appearance always reflects objective finality in "an actual (intentional) purpose . . . on the basis of an idea of [beauty] in the producing cause" (section 58). When an object's form invites a "realistic" interpretation, the viewing subject's aesthetic response "would not be free and based on autonomy" (section 58).

This rationale for restricting the deduction to natural beauty clarifies Kant's decision to place his only extended treatment of fine art as an addendum to the main argument. It also elucidates Kant's remark that when an artwork pleases in a pure judgment of taste, it must "have the *look* of nature" (section 45). This requirement is not a call for unmannered, realistic representation of natural forms. Kant means that a beautiful artwork must seem purposive—as if evidencing subjective purposiveness—when the viewer "pays no attention" to its status as an artifact. Fine art must also exhibit the originality of genius, animated by spirit. In practical terms, the work must express "ineffable" ideas that prompt the viewer's imagination "to spread over a multitude of kindred presentations" (section 49). The content of the work thus escapes any determinate judgment, and its expression is not constrained by artistic rules.

Kant offers another reason why natural beauty is superior to that of art:

> the superiority of natural beauty over that of art, namely, that . . . it is the only beauty that arouses a direct interest. . . . A man who has taste enough to judge the products of *fine art* with the greatest correctness and refinement may still be glad to leave a room in which he finds those beauties that minister to vanity and perhaps social joys, and to turn instead to beautiful nature.
>
> (section 42)

The relative superiority of nature rests on its power to "arouse" a direct interest. Because fine art is a "production through freedom" exhibiting spirit (section 43), it invites an indirect interest. In this context, Kant allows that the preference involves an "estimation of [the] two kinds of objects" (section 42). As with his other comparisons of fine art and nature, he ties nature's qualified superiority to an impure (determinate) judgment. The viewer is conscious of the object as art or as nature: "we must become conscious that it is art rather than nature" (section 45), and a further pleasure arises to supplement the pure judgment of taste. Consequently, this claim of nature's superiority to fine art is not a general endorsement of the superiority of natural beauty and it is consistent with Kant's position that in a pure judgment neither is superior. Pure judgments of taste treat all appearances as nature, not in opposition to art, but simply insofar as imagination is in harmony with the understanding's lawfulness.

If one is delighted with natural beauty and subsequently "meditates" on beautiful nature as natural, reason "must take an interest" in its harmonious accord with our a priori demands. An object's status as nature is a necessary but insufficient condition for a direct interest in natural beauty: "not only does [one] like nature's product for its form, but [one] also likes its existence" (section 42). Because the link between beauty and our common sense accounts for the existence of beautiful artifacts, only natural beauty can "show a trace" or "hint" that our moral ideas contingently fit the objective order of things (nature as the sum of objects of experience). Few people are gratified by the actual existence of such beauty, but those "rare" persons reveal a predisposition to morality. The soundness of the deduction of pure judgments of taste does not, however, depend on there being such persons. So Kant's approval of a direct, intellectual interest in nature does not privilege natural beauty.

Kant recognizes that some art is like natural beauty in yielding its rewards in a pure judgment of taste. Fine art is distinguished from "aesthetic," "agreeable art." The former is restricted to products of genius, whereas the latter includes entertainment and the decorative arts. Like birdsongs and flowers, "table music" can be beautiful apart from objective purpose. Yet the existence of such beauties does not further the deduction, for their existence does nothing to bridge the "immense gulf" between principles of nature and principles of freedom (section 2).

Kant offers multiple examples of persons who are disturbed to find that they have been admiring artificial flowers or faked bird calls. The flower is now classified as either a beautiful flower or an imitation of one; "this (which happens to be a rose) is beautiful" gives way to "this is a beautiful rose" or "this is an imitation of a beautiful rose." The object is judged in terms of its causal history, under determinate concepts. When it is recognized as an imitation, some people will be disgusted by the trick while others will take an empirical interest in it. But, neither response remains a pure judgment of taste.

Finally, Kant thinks that both nature and art express aesthetic ideas and can symbolize the morally good. But only art can express moral ideas and invite reflection on them and hence on the supersensible, and so fine art is superior to natural objects when judged as such. This situation holds only for fine art as the art of genius, and again the priority is not aesthetic. Although natural objects do not express moral ideas, the harmful effects of amoral art lead Kant to conclude that "it is generally the beauties of nature that are most beneficial" in attuning the spirit to ideas (section 52). (The decorative arts have no special superiority, inviting

neither a direct interest nor any reflection on ideas.) The lingering paradox, of course, is how Kant can hold both that artworks must be recognized as such and that a judgment of taste is impure if determined by a concept. Recognition of something as art demands a determination of the object—how it came to be and so of its "determinate intrinsic purpose"—and thus its beauty seems unrelated to its status as an artwork (section 16).

[*See also* Adorno; *and* Nature.]

BIBLIOGRAPHY

Work by Kant

Kritik der Urtheilskraft. In *Kants gesammelte Schriften,* edited by Wilhelm Windelband, vol. 5. Berlin, 1908. Translated by Werner S. Pluhar as *Critique of Judgment.* Indianapolis, 1987.

Other Sources

Buchdahl, Gerd. *Metaphysics and the Philosophy of Science: The Classical Origins: Descartes to Kant.* Cambridge, Mass., 1969.
Butts, Robert E. "The Methodological Structure of Kant's Metaphysics of Science." In *Kant's Philosophy of Physical Science,* edited by Robert E. Butts, pp. 163–199. Dordrecht and Boston, 1986.
Crawford, Donald. "Kant's Principles of Judgment and Taste." In *Proceedings of the Sixth International Kant Congress,* edited by Gerhard Funke and Thomas M. Seebohm, vol. 2.2, pp. 281–292. Washington, D.C., 1989.
Guyer, Paul. *Kant and the Claims of Taste* (1979). Enl. ed. Cambridge and New York, 1997.
Kemal, Salim. *Kant and Fine Art: An Essay on Kant and the Philosophy of Fine Art and Culture.* Oxford and New York, 1986.
McCloskey, Mary A. *Kant's Aesthetic.* Albany, N.Y., 1987.
Pluhar, Werner. "Translator's Preface." In Immanuel Kant, *Critique of Judgment,* translated by Werner S. Pluhar. Indianapolis, 1987.
Scruton, Roger. *Kant.* Oxford and New York, 1982.
Walker, Ralph C. S. *Kant.* London and Boston, 1978.

THEODORE A. GRACYK

History of Kantian Aesthetics

Immanuel Kant's aesthetic theory, as presented in the *Critique of Judgment,* stands at the juncture of two main periods in the history of aesthetics. With its focus on the faculty of taste, on nature as the primary site of beauty, on the role of genius in artistic creation, and on the moral dimension of art, it belongs squarely in the eighteenth century, as the creative synthesis and culmination of that period's multiform aesthetic culture. Yet, Kant's aesthetics is also the starting point of the many forms of aesthetic discourse that have followed it in the past two centuries—from the idealist aesthetics of the immediate post-Kantians to the various Kantianisms in aesthetics and the theory of art in the nineteenth and twentieth centuries. In particular, Kant's insistence on the autonomy of the aesthetic sphere, on the formal nature of aesthetic properties, on the distinct character of the aesthetic attitude, and on the expressive dimension of aesthetic ideas has been taken up by subsequent aesthetic theorizing.

For the most part, Kant's influence on the history of aesthetics has taken the form of a productive reception and transformation of one or more central aspects of his philosophy. The dissemination of Kant's aesthetics among different theories and even different disciplines is part of the general development of post-Kantian thinking away from comprehensive philosophical system building toward specialized work in emerging academic disciplines such as epistemology, psychology, and art history.

The particular fate of Kant's aesthetic theory in this overall development of professionalization and specialization is moreover due to the vaulting ambition of Kant's aesthetic project and the resultant sheer complexity of his theory. Kant's power in bringing together vastly divergent sets of problems and doctrines under the notion of a "critique of aesthetic judgment" remains a one-time achievement. Subsequent thinking on aesthetic matters has for the most part not even attempted to follow up on Kant's grandiose synthesis. For the most part, Kant's work in aesthetics has been selectively appropriated rather than systematically absorbed. Hence, from the viewpoint of current scholarship on Kant, the history of Kantian aesthetics may even appear as a sequence of misinterpretations. Yet, the appropriation of Kantian features into new aesthetic theories has often been highly productive and a genuine enrichment of the aesthetic discourse. It could be argued that Kant's aesthetics provided the inspiration, orientation, and authority for the main developments in the field for more than two centuries.

The presence of Kantian themes, insights, and arguments is especially prominent in the German-speaking countries. In fact, the emergence of aesthetics as an academic discipline took place almost entirely within the German university culture of the nineteenth century. Similarly, the development of a scientific theory of art *(Kunstwissenschaft)* in the late nineteenth and early twentieth century was almost entirely a German academic phenomenon. The following overview of Kantian traits in nineteenth- and twentieth-century aesthetics therefore focuses mainly on the German-speaking countries.

The earliest productive transformation of Kant's aesthetics is to be found in the theoretical writings of the playwright, poet, and historian Friedrich von Schiller. Schiller's main concern is with the role of the beautiful and the sublime in the cultivation of morality. In a series of essays on the sublime in life and art Schiller appropriates Kant's theory for the poetics of tragedy, arguing that the experience of physical limitations and even physical annihilation can incite in the tragic hero as well as the spectator an increased awareness of the mind's ultimate independence from nature in us and outside of us. While Schiller's aesthetics of the sublime emphasizes the contrast between human sensuous and supersensuous existence, his aesthetics of the beautiful aims at the integration of sense and reason in a humanity reconciled with nature. For Schiller the "aesthetic state" is the real-life anticipation as well as preparation of this social-political ideal. An influential contemporary alternative to Schiller's moral interpretation of the sublime can be found in the theories of irony and humor in the Romantic generation. The literary theorist and philosopher Friedrich Schlegel advocates extreme aesthetic playfulness ("irony") as a means of negatively approximating the infinite under conditions of human finitude. The novelist and literary theorist Jean Paul Richter defines humor as the "inverted sublime," arguing that the misproportion between the finite and the infinite in human existence is comical as much as it is tragical.

The most sweeping wave of Kantianism in nineteenth-century aesthetics originates with Johann Friedrich Herbart, a follower of Kant and opponent of G. W. F. Hegel. While the German idealists treat aesthetic objects in metaphysical terms, as manifestations of the absolute, Herbart takes up the Kantian epistemological project of elucidating the subjective conditions for aesthetic judgments. To be sure, Herbart replaces Kant's apriorism regarding judgments of taste with a thoroughly empiricist account of pleasure and pain, and eschews Kant's faculty psychology in favor of an associationist account of the mind as the arena of dynamically related presentations, including processes of mutual reinforcement in the case of pleasurable experiences. Yet, under the guise of psychologism, Herbart and his school preserve the Kantian insight that, on the part of the subject, there are necessary conditions for all our experience and that those conditions, moreover, determine the objects of all such experience. Accordingly, Herbart and his followers treat philosophical aesthetics as a branch of psychology. The most important of those philosopher-scientists, whose work often includes physiological research in aesthetics, are Hermann Helmholtz, Gustav Fechner, Hermann Lotze, and Wilhelm Wundt.

Herbart's influential project of a science of the human mind gives rise to a formalist orientation in nineteenth-century aesthetics. The scientific view of human mental life as law-governed interaction of mental events leads a number of philosophers to conceive of aesthetics as the scientific study of the regularities that elicit aesthetic responses. On the formalist view, the grounds of aesthetic liking are formal features of the object that trigger the mind's lawfully determined affective responses. Kant's point that pleasure in the beautiful as such is freely taken pleasure in some perceptual form has been transformed into the investigation of nomological correlations between perceptible relations and aesthetic reactions to them. The main representatives of formalism in nineteenth-century aesthetics are the philosopher Robert Zimmermann and the music critic Eduard Hanslick. Zimmermann extended the psychophysiological approach in aesthetics from the field of music, where it was first developed, into the visual arts. Hanslick was the author of an influential polemical tract on music as "forms in sound motion," in which he argued for the aesthetic superiority of absolute over programmatic music.

The purist extremes of aesthetic formalism were opposed by those philosophers who sought to preserve Kant's insight, as modernized by Herbart, that the aesthetic object is determined by subjective, mental processes. Drawing on the concept of the symbol as the unity of spiritual meaning and perceptible form, the antiformalists argued that the mind is forever animating natural and geometric forms with meaning and significance. The basic concepts of this eminently psychological aesthetics are "empathy" *(Einfühlung)* and "expression" *(Ausdruck):* the human being is seen as endowing objects with psychological content; those objects are then experienced as bringing out the inner psychic life. For many decades the aesthetics of empathy remained a popular and influential approach to understanding the production and reception of art. Its main proponents were Friedrich Theodor Vischer, his son Robert Vischer, Lotze, Johannes Volkelt, and Theodor Lipps.

In the last third of the nineteenth century, the formalist tendencies of the dominant philosophical aesthetics began to influence artistic theories set forth by historians and critics of art. A chief representative of this development is the collector, patron, and critic Conrad Fiedler, who applied formalist considerations to the aesthetics of architecture, treating the latter as the introduction of formal articulation into three-dimensional space. Fiedler modeled his theory on Kant's treatment of space in the "Transcendental Aesthetic" of the *Critique of Pure Reason* rather than on Kant's explicit pronouncements on beautiful form and fine art in the *Critique of Judgment.* The shift in aesthetic orientation toward Kant's cognitive theory reflected a more general reluctance to base aesthetic judgments on such notoriously elusive grounds as taste, and prepared the way for an autonomous understanding of nonrepresentational or abstract art as independent from traditional aesthetic values.

The coexistence of formalist and expressivist tendencies in aesthetic theory at the turn of the century, both of them Kantian in inspiration, is nicely illustrated in the work of the historian of art Heinrich Wölfflin. Early on, Wölfflin sought to provide a psychological foundation for the historical study of art, arguing that one's own bodily and emotional self-experience determines the experience of objects in general and of aesthetic objects in particular. He later came to supplement the belief in universal mental constants governing artistic expression and its recognition with formalist considerations regarding the specific aesthetic requirements and possibilities of different artistic media as well as different historical styles. The normative and supraindividual nature of style in Wölfflin can be seen as a historically enriched successor concept to Kant's notion of an aesthetic common sense. Wölfflin shared with the other aesthetic formalists the basic belief that art is an autonomous mode of knowledge that must be understood strictly on its own terms.

The only challenge to the prevailing psychological orientation of nineteenth-century aesthetics comes from the movement of neo-Kantianism in German academic philosophy. Yet, while the neo-Kantians dominated professional philosophy late in the nineteenth and early in the twentieth century, they exercised little influence on contemporary aesthetic debates and theories of art. The neo-Kantians agreed with psychological Kantianism on the foundational role of the subject in the constitution of the world and its objects. But on the neo-Kantian view, the subject in question is not some concrete, empirically existing entity that can be an object of psychological study, but a logical construct representing the a priori laws governing all instances of human consciousness. According to the neo-Kantians, aesthetics is not a branch of human psychology but the study of the methodological requirements of aesthetic culture. The aesthetic sphere and the feeling subject underlying it are seen in strict analogy to the world-constituting functions of the subject in knowing and willing. The most detailed system of neo-Kantian aesthetics is to be found in the work of one of the movement's founders, Hermann Cohen, but the movement became influential on wider developments in aesthetics and art history only through the work of Ernst Cassirer, a student of Cohen's, who sought to complete the post-Kantian project of linking the formal and expressive dimensions of aesthetic consciousness through a comprehensive philosophy of symbolic representation, in which the constitution of meaning in culture is seen in dynamic, developmental terms. Following Cassirer, the historian and theoretician of art Erwin Panofsky, viewed art under the Kantian cognitive ideal of achieving consistency both within the individual work of art and between it and the surrounding culture.

Compared to the pervasive presence of Kantian elements in nineteenth-century philosophy, twentieth-century work in aesthetics is considerably more diverse in method as well as subject matter. The relation to Kant is more subtle and often obscured by the presence of other historical reference points, most notably Hegel. On the Continent, the development of a philosophical hermeneutics or theory of understanding cultural artifacts of all kinds in the works of Wilhelm Dilthey, Martin Heidegger, and Hans-Georg Gadamer moved the notion of "aesthetic experience" *(ästhetische Erfahrung)* to the forefront of the aesthetic debate. The discussion of art in terms of its experience combines a Kantian insistence on the constitutive role of subjectivity with the recognition of the role of objective, historically specific factors that determine aesthetic phenomena. Kant's account of the beautiful in nature has received a prominent place in the aesthetic theorizing and social critique of Theodor W. Adorno.

Much of the debate in analytic aesthetics has been carried out in ahistorical terms. Yet, many of the issues, such as the nature of aesthetic concepts, have a distinctly Kantian ring to them—although most of the positions argued for resemble David Hume's rather than Kant's views on aesthetic judgments. To a growing extent, the aesthetic orientation of recent French thought has been informed by Kantian themes, as evidenced in the appropriations of Kant's analytic of the sublime through Jacques Derrida and Jean-François Lyotard and the reading of Kant through twentieth-century avant-gardism in Thierry de Duve. Finally, the significant growth of Anglo-American scholarship on the *Critique of Judgment* since the 1980s, with its emphasis on the systematic, historical, and cultural dimension of the work in authors such as Paul Guyer, Salim Kemal, and Rudolf Makkreel, is evidence for the continued influence of Kant on the development of aesthetic thought.

[*See also* Formalism.]

BIBLIOGRAPHY

Cohen, Hermann. *Ästhetik des reinen Gefühls.* 2d ed. 2 vols. Berlin, 1972.

Dessoir, Max. *Aesthetics and Theory of Art.* Translated by Stephen A. Emery. Detroit, 1970.

de Duve, Thierry. *Kant after Duchamp.* Cambridge, Mass., 1996.

Fechner, Gustav Theodor. *Zur experimenten Ästhetik.* Leipzig, 1871.

Ferretti, Silvia. *Cassirer, Panofsky, and Warburg: Symbol, Art, and History.* Translated by Richard Pierce. New Haven, 1989.

Fiedler, Konrad. *Schriften zur Kunst.* 2 vols. 2d ed. Edited by Gottfried Boehm. Munich, 1991.

Guyer, Paul. *Kant and the Experience of Freedom: Essays on Aesthetics and Morality.* Cambridge and New York, 1993.

Helmholtz, Hermann von. *Selected Writings.* Edited by Russell Kahl. Middletown, Conn., 1971.

Herbart, Johann Friedrich. *Psychologie als Wissenschaft.* 2 vols. Königsberg, 1824–1825.

Kemal, Salim. *Kant and Fine Art: An Essay on Kant and the Philosophy of Fine Art and Culture.* Oxford, 1986.

Lipps, Theodor. *Ästhetik: Psychologie des Schönen und der Kunst.* 2 vols. Leipzig, 1903–1906.

Lotze, Hermann. *Outlines of Aesthetics.* Translated and edited by George T. Ladd. Boston, 1885.

Lotze, Hermann. *Geschichte der Ästhetik in Deutschland.* Leipzig, 1913.

Mallgrave, Harry Francis, and Eleftherios Ikonomou, eds. *Empathy, Form and Space: Problems in German Aesthetics, 1873–1893.* Santa Monica, Calif., 1994.

Makkreel, Rudolf A. *Imagination and Interpretation in Kant: The Hermeneutical Import of the Critique of Judgment.* Chicago, 1990.

Nachtsheim, Stephan. *Kunstphilosophie und empirische Kunstforschung, 1870–1920.* Berlin, 1984.

Podro, Michael. *The Manifold in Perception: Theories of Art from Kant to Hildebrand.* Oxford, 1972.

Podro, Michael. *The Critical Historians of Art.* New Haven, 1982.

Richter, Jean Paul. *Horn of Oberon: Jean Paul Richter's School for Aesthetics.* Edited and translated by Margaret R. Hale. Detroit, 1973.

Vischer, Friedrich Theodor. *Ästhetik: oder, Wissenschaft des Schönen.* 3 vols. Leipzig, 1846–1857.

Vischer, Robert. *Über das optische Formgefühl: Ein Beitrag zur Ästhetik.* Leipzig, 1873.

Volkelt, Johannes Immanuel. *System der Ästhetik.* 2d ed. 3 vols. Munich, 1925–1927.

Wundt, Wilhelm. *Beiträge zur Theorie der Sinneswahrnehmung.* Leipzig, 1862.

Zimmermann, Robert. *Ästhetik.* 3 vols. Vienna, 1858–1865.

GÜNTER ZÖLLER

Kant and Art History

Students of the humanities know Immanuel Kant as an important figure in the European Enlightenment and its aftermath and as central to this day in philosophical aesthetics, a field he consolidated with the publication of the *Critique of Judgment* in 1790. In his own time, as today, his works were held to be difficult, technical, and best adapted to a strictly philosophical setting. In keeping with this view, John H. Zammito has claimed that "Kant was primarily and professionally enmeshed in the Aufklärung's epistemological project. He was not interested in fine art, in its system, in creativity or artistic taste" (Zammito, 1992, p. 21). Ted Cohen and Paul Guyer refer to "mere digressions on some specific issues raised by judgments about works of art" in the *Critique of Judgment* (Cohen and Guyer, 1982, p. 4). But how can these accounts explain the art topics—evidently important to Kant—examined in the 1764 *Observations on the Feeling of the Beautiful and Sublime,* not to mention large parts of the *Critique of Judgment?* Some recent commentators from within the discipline of philosophy have written extensively on Kant's ideas about art—especially Sarah L. Gibbons, Salim Kemal, and Rudolf Makkreel—and while Kant's writings have little to do explicitly with the historical or current arts (as he makes clear in the preface to the *Critique of Judgment,* where he apologizes—not without irony—for his book's "deficiency" in empirical matters, p. 7), he is of central importance for theorists who are concerned with intersections among philosophy, art history, and the visual arts, especially Jacques Derrida, Jean-François Lyotard, Jean-Luc Nancy, and Philippe Lacoue-Labarthe. Kant's theory of the sublime is the prime interest of these writers (see Courtine et al., 1993). Significantly, and to introduce yet another context for his reception, the sublime and its Kantian associations is also an active concern for many practicing visual artists (Cheetham, 1995, and Crowther 1985). Finally, in art history and indeed art practice, Kant's "patronage" is unusual in that his name is frequently "dropped," in both senses of the word. His influence in and around the arts, while pervasive, is less overt—and much less analyzed—than G. W. F. Hegel's, for example, and frequently stems from his writings in areas other than art and aesthetics. Certainly, Kant did not seek to have an influence in the arts, but as we can see by looking at the historical reception of his ideas, he was frequently understood to have an interest in and relevance to this field. By examining briefly the kinds of effects his thinking has had across so many disciplines—rather than separating these areas artificially to suit our own, not the historical, disposition of these fields—we may gain a fuller sense of Kant's importance to the arts in our own time and his.

What we witness in art history is a practice that might best be deemed an informal if widespread "Kantianism," rather than the systematic neo-Kantianism of the nineteenth century. Kant's name becomes a synecdoche for his doctrines (or those attributed to him), which in turn, through their reception in art history and the visual arts, come to stand for philosophy, the discipline of which he is a part and whose supremacy he explicitly asserts. As seen from the perspective of the visual arts, "Kantianism" invokes the "notion that consciousness constitutes its world" (Summers, 1989, p. 373). As defined by Christopher Norris, his doctrines characteristically raise "certain questions—of agency, autonomy, ethical conduct, reflective self-knowledge—which were also some of Kant's most important concerns throughout the three *Critiques*" (Norris, 1993, p. 71). Thomas McEvilley adds:

> The foundation of the Kantian doctrine is the notion of a [disinterested] sense of taste through which we respond to art. . . . this quality is noncognitive, nonconceptual; it is a *sensus communis,* innate and identical in everyone; it is a higher faculty, above worldly concerns; it is governed by its own inner necessity.
> (McEvilley, 1988, p. 125)

How do these summaries compare with what Kant wrote on the arts in the *Critique of Judgment,* especially in sections 14 and 43–53?

In section 14, Kant seeks to establish that "only pure aesthetic judgments (since they are formal) are properly judgments of taste." The judgment that a work of art or an object in nature is beautiful is, for Kant, not an empirical statement but rather a pure—and thus universalizable— recognition of the "form" of this judgment, which is "purposive" without a specific purpose or interest of any kind. Kant attempts to transfer this insight to the fine arts generally by stating that here "*design* is what is essential" (p. 71) and that color is merely supplemental. Kant ends this section with a passage on the essential versus ornamental in art, made famous by Jacques Derrida in the "Parergon" section of *The Truth in Painting,* where he describes as an impossible though potent dream Kant's attempt to delimit the essential in this way. In sections 43–53, we find a more sustained discussion of the principles of aesthetic judgment as they interact with the arts. Kant distinguishes art and craft and promotes the "fine" arts as universal. He discusses in some detail the notion of genius as that power that gives the rule to art and is productive of "aesthetic ideas." And he provides a thoroughly conventional "division" or hierarchy of the arts, with the literary forms foremost, the visual arts in a middle position, and music below. In all these instances, it is important to ask to what degree Kant's arguments and principles in fact derive from contemporary art-historical styles and debates and his own limited experience of the arts. His emphasis on line or contour, for example, is thoroughly neoclassical and not at all surprising in one who saw most works of art in graphic reproduction. His lengthy machinations about genius seem caught in the structures of emerging academies of art, which sought both to teach according to tradition and to cultivate the new—genius—in order to legitimize national schools of art.

Kant's most pervasive influences in the visual arts and art history are found in the work of the central founders of academic art history—that of Heinrich Wölfflin and Erwin Panofsky especially—and in the art criticism of Clement Greenberg. As Joan Hart has shown, Wölfflin was acquainted with Kantian views in part through his teachers Friedrich Paulson, a professor of philosophy and psychology in Berlin in the late nineteenth century and a biographer of Kant, and Wilhelm Dilthey. Wölfflin shared Kant's idea that perception was blind without the mind's concepts, and he sought from this basis to explain in a scientific way how stylistic change in art's history occurred. He reacted against the personal, unverifiable cultural analysis of Jacob Burckhardt and developed instead an ultimately Kantian system of formal categories with which the eye historically sees and organizes the world. Wölfflin's extraordinarily influential "categories of beholding" (linear/painterly, plane/depth, closed form/open form, multiple unity/fused unity, absolute clarity/relative clarity), which he articulated in *The Principles of Art History: The Problem of the Development of Style in Later Art* (1915), are not themselves Kantian, but their necessity in our "subjective" perception of the world and art follows a Kantian pattern. Although he disputed many of Wölfflin's ideas in his early essays, Panofsky too sought the stability of what he called an "Archimedean" point of view, beyond—or perhaps prior to—the exigencies of history. Both turned to Kant's epistemology for a secure understanding of art.

Panofsky's Kantianism—much of which he developed from the theories of Ernst Cassirer, himself a pupil of the famous Marburg neo-Kantian Hermann Cohen, and which is more explicit than Wölfflin's—can be seen at work in his famous 1924–1925 essay "Perspective as Symbolic Form." In this essay (though less so elsewhere, as Keith Moxey has shown [1995]), Panofsky views one-point, "Renaissance" perspective as a cultural convention that mediates in a Kantian sense between subject and object. "Perspective," Panofsky argues,

> subjects the artistic phenomenon to stable and even mathematically exact rules, but on the other hand, makes that phenomenon contingent upon human beings, indeed upon the individual: for these rules refer to the psychological and physical conditions of the visual impression, and the way they take effect is determined by the freely chosen position of a subjective "point of view."
> (p. 67)

Panofsky made his reliance on Kant even more evident in *Idea: A Concept in Art Theory,* published during the same period as the essay on perspective. Referring to section 38 of Kant's *Prolegomena,* he claimed that "artistic perception is no more faced with a 'thing in itself' than is the process of cognition" (Panofsky, 1968, p. 126). Artists' perspective, it seems, was for Panofsky analogous to Kant's a priori intuition of space itself. As it was for Kant, freedom is also crucial in Panofsky's account of artists' use of perspective (see Podro, 1982, p. 6). As we will see shortly, however, that freedom was not seen by artists as simply formal and epistemological, as in Panofsky's account, but also as "political."

The late American art critic Clement Greenberg, arguably this century's most influential and controversial art writer, rested a good deal of his reading of modernism on an interpretation of Kant, especially the philosopher's idea of critique as a method. Almost because Kant had what Greenberg deems "bad taste and relatively meagre experience of art," he wrote, "his capacity for abstraction enabled him . . . to establish in his *Critique of Aesthetic Judgment* what is the most satisfactory basis for aesthetics we yet have. Kant asked how art in general worked" (Greenberg, 1955, p. 151). More than Kant's celebrated "formalism," what Greenberg adopts to explain how art works—how it changes, and, in a very Hegelian way, evolves—is Kant's fundamental notion of critique as self-criticism. Greenberg wrote in "Modernist Painting": "I identify Modernism with the intensification, almost the exacerbation, of this self-critical tendency that began with the philosopher Kant. Because he was the first to criticize the means itself of criticism, I conceive of Kant as the first real Modernist" (Greenberg, 1982, p. 5). Notoriously, for Greenberg Kant's "immanent" criticism is an analogy for art's own autocriticism and reduction to the "purity" of its essence, whether in painting or sculpture. In a legislative gesture reminiscent of Kant's typical boundary work, Greenberg argues that each art can only remain autonomous by excluding those qualities that truly belong to other art forms. This Kantian attention to each art medium's area of "competence," as Greenberg put it, allows us to know that painting's essence is flatness, for example. "The essential norms or conventions of painting are also the limiting conditions with which a marked-up surface must comply in order to be experienced as a picture" (ibid., p. 8). Despite the attention to formal qualities that these remarks encourage, Greenberg uses Kant in the service of what is ultimately a historical argument. To keep painting and the other art forms viable historically, they must remain themselves. He sees this achievement as the definitive victory of modernism in the arts.

Discussions of Greenberg bring us closer to Kant's influences in the visual arts themselves. While some examples of his impact are so obvious that they tend to slip from our consciousness, here as in art history, Kant remains an outsider. Many of the earliest responses to Kant were to the *Critique of Judgment,* to its apparent claims that we do not have access to the noumenal and that our knowledge of the world rests on our own faculties. Kant's *Critique of Pure Reason* is also the source for the famous analytic/synthetic distinction used early in discussions of Cubism to distinguish both working methods and chronological development.

ments. In both cases, Kant's terminology entered nonphilosophical discourse, with artists, critics, and historians referring to the "thing-in-itself" or to "analytic" procedures in Cubist composition. The use of his terminology is neither innocent nor superficial. Thus, for Daniel-Henry Kahnweiler, the famous art dealer and critic, Cubism's

> new language has given painting an unprecedented freedom . . . coloured planes, through their direction and relative position, can bring together the formal scheme without uniting in closed forms. . . . Instead of an analytical description, the painter can . . . also create in this way a synthesis of the object, or in the words of Kant, "put together the various conceptions and comprehend their variety in our perception."
>
> (Kahnweiler, 1949, p. 12)

In Kahnweiler's view of Cubism, *analytic* refers to a painterly process of fragmenting—analyzing—the subject matter, whereas "synthetic" refers to the chronologically later habit that Pablo Picasso, Georges Braque, and others had of adding materials such as sand, newspaper, and even chair caning to their images. Although Kant would never have employed these terms to describe art or its making, we can see how Kahnweiler adapted the spirit of Kant's notion of the analytic, defined in the *Critique of Pure Reason* as adding "nothing through the predicate to the concept of the subject, but merely break[ing] it up into those constituent concepts that have all along been thought in it, though confusedly" (A7 / B11). We have here an excellent analogue for early Cubist paintings, which their creators and critics even saw as clarifying the visual world. *Synthetic* also accurately describes what Kant held as a going beyond the given and what Cubism practiced literally in its later phase. Kahnweiler read Kant and neo-Kantian texts by Wilhelm Wundt, Heinrich Rickert, and others in Bern during World War I. For him, the analytic/synthetic distinction, the notions of the thing-in-itself and disinterestedness, and the formal autonomy of the work of art provided nothing less than a way of conceptualizing and justifying Cubism.

Also largely forgotten today are examples of specific Kantian ideas that have been employed by contemporary artists as different but important as Joseph Kosuth and Barnett Newman in the United States and Anselm Kiefer in Germany, not to mention the fascinating use of Kant among artists and critics of his own time. In 1796, for example, the later eminent Danish sculptor Bertel Thorvaldsen was commissioned to bring with him on his way from northern Europe to Rome Kant's recently published essay "Perpetual Peace" ("Zum Ewigen Frieden"). His interest in Kant was made concrete by this text and gave him an entry into a vibrant German-speaking art community that based its sense of personal, artistic, and political autonomy largely on Kant's *political* views, precisely and not coincidentally at the time when Napoleon declared Rome a republic. For these artists, artistic freedom seemed to be guaranteed, however briefly, by political change. The leader of this artist colony in Rome around 1800, the Dane Asmus Jakob Carstens, was sufficiently earnest about Kantian ideas to produce a drawing titled *Raum und Zeit* (Space and Time, 1794). His rather literal yet allegorical rendition of the fundamental categories of space and time from the *Critique of Pure Reason* was the topic of a mirthful correspondence between Johann Wolfgang von Goethe and Friedrich von Schiller. But, Carstens employed the philosopher's political thinking to greater effect. He adopted Kant's distinction between public and private duty to justify his bold refusal to return from Rome to his position at the Prussian Academy in Berlin. "I belong to Humanity, not to the Academy of Berlin," he wrote in 1796, and "I am ready . . . to assert it in public, to justify myself to the world, as I feel justified in my own conscience" (quoted in Busch, 1982, p. 109). "By the public use of one's reason I understand the use which a person makes of it as a scholar before the reading public," Kant stated in "What Is Enlightenment?" ("Beantwortung der Frage: Was ist Aufklärung?" 1785–1787). Like Kant, Carstens asserts the "public" primacy of his conscience over the strictures of what Kant labeled any "private" "civil post or office."

The most profound and sustained interaction between Kant's philosophy and the Carstens circle was realized by the critic and historian Carl Ludwig Fernow, for whom Thorvaldsen's copy of Kant's new book was destined. Fernow knew Schiller (the main disseminator of Kantian ideas at this time) and had studied in Jena with the Kantian Karl Leonhard Reinhold from 1791 to 1793 before arriving in Rome in 1794. Fernow demonstrated that Kant's philosophy was important to more than specialists and that in its reception, his thinking bore directly on the contemporary visual arts. In the winter of 1795–1796, in Rome, he gave a series of lectures on Kant's aesthetics to an audience of thirty-six artists, intellectuals, and art lovers, two of whom were the artists Joseph Anton Koch and Carstens. Although more concrete than Kant, Fernow largely agreed with the philosopher on the need to ground our knowledge of beauty and reality itself in the subject. His letters also reveal his interest in other aspects of Kant's ideas. He notes favorably the formation of the contemporary Roman Republic while praising Kant's "Perpetual Peace" (Fernow, 1944, p. 231); indeed, Fernow and his compatriots styled their "Künstlerrepublik" on Kant's ideals and thus skillfully and effectively combined the political and aesthetic sides of his doctrines of freedom and autonomy. Through Fernow, Kant's ideas on politics, ethics, and aesthetics went a long way in structuring the self-image and artistic goals of these important artists.

Kant's preoccupation with drawing conceptual lines and promising epistemological certitude is perhaps partly responsible for his enduring appeal outside philosophy. In his 1764 *Observations on the Feeling of the Beautiful and Sublime,*

he tries to keep morality and aesthetics apart in ways that became crucial to his position in the *Critique of Judgment.* More generally, the architecture of the three Critiques was designed to maintain autonomy and thus proper relations among scientific inquiry, ethics, and aesthetics, respectively. But, of course, the *Critique of Judgment* was also Kant's self-consciously constructed bridge between what we can know of the world and how we ought to behave in it. As he makes clear in his late *Conflict of the Faculties* (1798), independence and proper relationships guarantee fruitful interactions among equals; autonomy guarantees the sorts of comparisons that Goethe found wonderful in the *Critique of Judgment,* those between science and the arts, nature and reason.

This habit and method of delineation is maintained on the most minute level in Kant's texts. In section 17 of the *Critique of Judgment,* for example, "On the Ideal of Beauty," Kant provides a typically complex discussion of how the mind arrives at the notion of the "average" or "common standard." He begins with an example of how we judge the average size of a man by looking at a thousand examples but moves immediately to a (not immediately helpful) "analogy from optics: in the space where most of the images are united, and within the *outline* where the area is illuminated by the colour applied most heavily, there the *average size* emerges . . . and that is the stature for a beautiful man" (section 17; first emphasis mine). In trying to explain how it is that we compare sizes by perceiving their overlapping extremities, Kant typically underscores outline *(Umriss)* rather than color. More than simply a neoclassical preference for linear simplicity, Kant's insistence on the supreme value of line is epistemological. In contour he can accurately *measure* the average or standard, the perfect line between too much and too little. Applying the result of this seeming digression in a comment that is reminiscent of Johann Winckelmann's interest in bodies' outlines, he then adds that it is in each case "this shape which underlines the standard idea of a beautiful man" (ibid.). He qualifies this statement in a manner that is reminiscent of Johann Lavater's interest in national and racial physiognomy (on which he cites Kant from another text): the "standard" operates "in the country where this comparison is made. That is why, given these empirical conditions, a Negro's standard idea of the beauty of the [human] figure necessarily differs from that of a white man, that of a Chinese from a European." "Rules for judging," Kant concludes, become possible not because of experience, but vice versa (ibid.). We discover the standard, the perfect contour that divides inside from outside, in ourselves, never in empirical experience. This is part of the reason for Kant's belief in a universally applicable faculty of judgment, a notion that has been widely accepted in art history and often applied in ways that underwrite the hegemony of a Western perspective on art (Moxey, 1994, pp. 37, 67). Kant has of course been criticized for his transcendentalist view of art. The sociologist Pierre Bourdieu argues persuasively that "Kant's analysis of the judgement of taste finds its real basis in a set of aesthetic principles which are the universalization of the dispositions associated with a particular social and economic position" (Bourdieu, 1984, p. 493). Kant's pure aesthetic disinterestedness is a learned attitude that follows class lines, according to Bourdieu's analysis of empirical data on taste. It is a way to maintain "distinction" in our hierarchical Western society. In a more recent study, Bourdieu builds on this research to admonish most philosophers for their "pure," ahistorical reading of Kant and other writers, their assumption that one can engage with arguments across history but ahistorically (Bourdieu, 1996, p. 306).

In art history, it is Kant's interest in form that encourages this ahistoricism. As David Summers claims, and as we have just seen, judgment works with form, and "form came to be regarded as the universal common denominator of human things. . . . It was largely under such auspices that the history of art came into existence and currency as an intellectual discipline" (Summers, 1989, p. 375). The "formal" precision allowed by measurement, by perceiving the contour here or the line of a forehead in physiognomy, is, perhaps, also related in a causal way to what Donald Preziosi has identified as art history's habit of "siting" works of art and their authors, what he specifies as the obsessive "assignment of an 'address' to the work within a nexus of synchronic and diachronic relationships" (Preziosi, 1995, p. 220).

In another "exotic" reference, Kant again invokes measurement in his discussion of the estimation of the overwhelming size of the pyramids as an example of the mathematically sublime (section 56). Again it is the line (literally in the sand), placed by the observer who is in the right place, neither too close to nor too far from the monuments, that allows the feeling of the sublime to occur. The sublime is in us; it is not a response to external art or nature. It is typical of Kant to invent a species of sublimity that relies on—instead of dismissing, as in Edmund Burke's 1757 model—the specificity and legibility of line and position within a "field." The sublime marks the outer limit of what we can know. In a disciplinary sense too, Kant is the master of emplacement. By placing art, philosophy, and the history of art in relation to one another, he established a pattern of disciplinary contouring that remains in effect today. It is the structuring, emplacing quality of Kant's thought that has allowed his name to travel so far in art history. As the epitome of reason's claims to autonomy through the establishment of domains, he is also now under suspicion in this field, as it tries to understand and revise its inclusions, exclusions, and relations with other domains. But Kant is not to be dismissed. Even for those who oppose his ideas today, he is necessary.

[*See also* Greenberg; Pantofsky; *and* Wölfflin.]

BIBLIOGRAPHY

Works by Kant

Foundations of the Metaphysics of Morals and What Is Enlightenment? (1785/1784). Translated by Lewis White Beck. Indianapolis, 1959.

Critique of Judgment (1790). Translated by Werner S. Pluhar. Indianapolis, 1987.

Perpetual Peace: A Philosophical Essay (1795). Translated by M. Campbell Smith. New York, 1972.

The Conflict of the Faculties (1798). Translated by Mary J. Gregor. Lincoln, Nebr., 1992.

Other Sources

Bois, Yve-Alain. "Kahnweiler's Lesson." In *Painting as Model*, pp. 65–97. Cambridge, Mass., 1990.

Bourdieu, Pierre. *Distinction: A Social Critique of the Judgement of Taste.* Translated by Richard Nice. Cambridge, Mass., 1984.

Bourdieu, Pierre. *The Rules of Art: Genesis and Structure of the Literary Field.* Translated by Susan Emanuel. Stanford, Calif., 1996.

Busch, Werner. "Kunsttheorie und Malerei." In *Kunsttheorie und Kunstgeschichte des 19. Jahrhunderts in Deutschland: Texte und Dokumente*, edited by W. Beyrodt, U. Bischoff, W. Busch, and H. Hammer-Schenk, vol. 1. Stuttgart, 1982.

Carstens, Jakob Asmus. Letter to Baron von Heinitz, 20 February 1796. In *Neoclassicism and Romanticism, 1750–1850: Sources and Documents*, edited by Lorenz Eitner, vol. 1, p. 109. Englewood Cliffs, N.J., 1970.

Cassirer, Ernst. *The Philosophy of the Enlightenment* (1932). Translated by Fritz C. A. Koelln and James P. Pettegrove. Princeton, N.J., 1951.

Cheetham, Mark A. "The Sublime Is Now (Again)." *C Magazine* (Toronto) 44 (Winter 1995): 27–39.

Cohen, Ted, and Paul Guyer, eds. *Essays in Kant's Aesthetics.* Chicago, 1982.

Courtine, Jean-François, et al. *Of the Sublime: Presence in Question.* Translated by Jeffrey S. Librett. Albany, N.Y., 1993.

Crowther, Paul. "Greenberg's Kant and the Problem of Modernist Painting." *British Journal of Aesthetics* 25.4 (Autumn 1985): 317–325.

Crowther, Paul. *The Kantian Sublime: From Morality to Art.* Oxford, 1989.

Curtin, Deane W. "Varieties of Aesthetic Formalism." *Journal of Aesthetics and Art Criticism* 40.3 (Spring 1982): 315–332.

Derrida, Jacques. *The Truth in Painting.* Translated by Geoff Bennington and Ian McLeod. Chicago, 1987.

Einem, Herbert von. *Carl Ludwig Fernow: Eine Studie zum Deutschen Klassizismus.* Berlin, 1935.

Fernow, Carl Ludwig. *Römische Briefe an Johann Pohrt, 1793–1798.* Edited by Herbert von Einem and Rudolf Pohrt. Berlin, 1944.

Gehlen, Arnold. "D.-H. Kahnweilers Kunstphilosophie." In *Pour Daniel-Henry Kahnweiler*, pp. 92–103. New York, 1965.

Gibbons, Sarah L. *Kant's Theory of Imagination: Bridging Gaps in Judgement and Experience.* Oxford, 1994.

Goetschel, Willi. *Constituting Critique: Kant's Writing as Critical Praxis.* Translated by Eric Schwab. Durham, N.C., 1994.

Green, Christopher. *Cubism and Its Enemies: Modern Movements and Reactions in French Art, 1916–1928.* New Haven, 1987.

Greenberg, Clement. "Greenberg on Berenson." *Perspectives USA* 11 (1955): 151–154.

Greenberg, Clement. "Modernist Painting" (1965). In *Modern Art and Modernism: A Critical Anthology*, edited by Francis Frascina and Charles Harrison, pp. 5–10. New York, 1982.

Guyer, Paul. *Kant and the Experience of Freedom: Essays on Aesthetics and Morality.* Cambridge and New York, 1993.

Hart, Joan. "Reinterpreting Wölfflin: Neo-Kantianism and Hermeneutics." *Art Journal* 42 (1982): 292–297.

Holly, Michael Ann. *Panofsky and the Foundations of Art History.* Ithaca, N.Y., 1984.

Kahnweiler, Daniel-Henry. *The Rise of Cubism* (1920). Translated by Henry Aronson. New York, 1949.

Kemal, Salim. *Kant and Fine Art: An Essay on Kant and the Philosophy of Fine Art and Culture.* Oxford, 1986.

Lyotard, Jean-François. *Lessons on the Analytic of the Sublime.* Translated by Elizabeth Rottenberg. Stanford, Calif., 1994.

Makkreel, Rudolf A. *Imagination and Interpretation in Kant: The Hermeneutical Import of the Critique of Judgment.* Chicago, 1990.

McEvilley, Thomas. "Empirical Thinking (and Why Kant Can't)." *Art Forum* 27. October 1988: 120–27.

Moxey, Keith. *The Practice of Theory: Poststructuralism, Cultural Politics, and Art History.* Ithaca, N.Y., 1994.

Moxey, Keith. "Perspective, Panofsky, and the Philosophy of History." *New Literary History* 26.4 (Autumn 1995): 775–786.

Norris, Christopher. *The Truth about Postmodernism.* Cambridge, Mass., 1993.

Panofsky, Erwin. *Idea: A Concept in Art Theory.* Translated by Joseph J. S. Peake. Reprint, New York, 1968.

Panofsky, Erwin. *Perspective as Symbolic Form.* Translated by Christopher S. Wood. New York, 1991.

Podro, Michael. *The Critical Historians of Art.* New Haven, 1982.

Preziosi, Donald. *Rethinking Art History: Meditations on a Coy Science.* New Haven, 1989.

Rodowick, D. N. "Impure Mimesis; or, The Ends of the Aesthetic." In *Deconstruction and the Visual Arts: Art, Media, Architecture,* edited by Peter Brunette and David Wills, pp. 96–117. Cambridge and New York, 1994.

Schoch, Rainer. "Rom 1797: Fluchpunkt der Freiheit." In *Künstlerleben in Rom: Bertel Thorwaldsen, 1770–1844: Der dänische Bildhauer und seine deutschen Freunde,* pp. 17–23. Nuremberg, 1992 Exhibition catalog, Germanischen Nationalmuseums.

Summers, David. "'Form,' Nineteenth-Century Metaphysics, and the Problem of Art Historical Description." *Critical Inquiry* 15 (Winter 1989): 372–406.

Summers, David. "Why Did Kant Call Taste a 'Common Sense'?" In *Eighteenth-Century Aesthetics and the Reconstruction of Art,* edited by Paul Mattick, Jr., pp. 120–151. Cambridge and New York, 1993.

Wölfflin, Heinrich. *Principles of Art History: The Problem of the Development of Style in Later Art.* Translated by M. D. Hottinger from the 7th ed. London 1932; reprint, New York, 1950.

Zammito, John H. *The Genesis of Kant's Critique of Judgment.* Chicago, 1992.

MARK A. CHEETHAM

Kant and Hermeneutics

Immanuel Kant's *Critique of Judgment* first inspired idealist successors such as Friedrich Schelling to project even more ambitious aesthetic-philosophical systems, but for subsequent hermeneutical philosophers such as Wilhelm Dilthey, Martin Heidegger, and Hans-Georg Gadamer it stands as a different kind of model. Dilthey found Kant's idea of immanent purposiveness useful for the understanding of more limited historical and cultural systems. Immanent purposiveness suggests the possibility of articulating order within specific contexts. Dilthey also concurred with Kant's decision to give feeling a central role in aesthetics. But whereas Kant isolated an a priori aesthetic feeling that is formal and disinterested, Dilthey explores a much broader range of feelings that can contribute to aesthetic appreciation. Artists express all kinds of human emotions and feelings, but their task is not so much to communicate their own state of mind as to transform it into a disinterested perspective that helps us more fully to understand the meaning of life in general.

Whereas Dilthey saw aesthetic feelings as important constituents of our overall cognitive response to the world, or what he calls a worldview, Heidegger and Gadamer regard an aesthetics based on feeling as too subjective. Rejecting Kant's celebration of aesthetic play as the felt harmony among the subject's faculties, Heidegger claims that art is above all a mode of work, an ontological mode of disclosure. Gadamer, in turn, reinterprets play on the model of a dramatic performance—not as a mere private imaginative process, but as the public process whereby meaning gets passed on through the dialogical interchange made possible by language. Because Kant distinguishes between aesthetic and logical judgments, Heidegger and Gadamer assume that only the latter produce knowledge and that aesthetic judgments lack cognitive import. To be sure, the aesthetic judgment declaring an object to be beautiful does not add to our empirical knowledge of that object. Yet, it can, according to Kant, contribute to the overall cognitive systematization of the world. [*See* Gadamer; *and* Heidegger.]

Kant's insistence on the limits of what can be understood directly by our finite intellect raises the question of what role the more indirect process of interpretation should assume. In some of his late writings Kant explicitly considers the problem of interpretation in relation to texts, and he sometimes speaks of interpreting the whole of nature as a text. Interpretations of nature derived solely from Kant's theoretical philosophy can be called systematic and architectonic. His aesthetics, however, suggests the possibility of a more open and flexible kind of interpretation based on reflective judgment. When Kant characterizes beauty as a symbol of morality and uses quasi-moral attributes such as majesty and innocence to describe aesthetic phenomena, he is employing what could be called "reflective interpretation." To develop this concept of reflective interpretation, Kant's views on reflective judgment in the *Critique of Judgment* must be linked to what he says elsewhere about how reflection in general makes it possible for the human subject to orient itself.

Among thinkers who have attempted to expand the role of reflective judgment beyond what Kant explicitly claims for it in the context of aesthetics and teleology, Hannah Arendt and Jean-François Lyotard readily come to mind. Arendt's main concern is to apply the reflective judgment of beauty to the specific domain of politics. In her *Lectures on Kant's Political Philosophy* she argues for the importance of the spectator stance in the evaluation of public discourse. Whereas beauty is exemplary for Arendt's ideal of social consensus, Lyotard focuses on the sublime in Kant to point to what transcends normal experience and cannot be readily assimilated. Reflective judgment in response to the sublime searches for a universal that remains out of the reach of present discourse, according to Lyotard. A new genre of discourse is demanded, and the feeling of pain that accompanies the awareness of its unavailability is the "differend." The gap felt here is like that between aesthetic ideas and ordinary concepts in Kant, but no *sensus communis* can be relied on to harmonize them, that is, to unify different genres of discourse. [*See* Lyotard.]

A hermeneutical understanding of reflective judgment extends beyond political-linguistic debates and juridical disputes in order to apply it to any domain where meaning is in question and interpretation appropriate. But more than that, it enables us to speak of the significance of aesthetic judgments in a way that integrates previously unrelated aspects of Kant's thought.

The basis for a theory of systematic interpretation is suggested in part by an image provided in the "Transcendental Dialectic" of the *Critique of Pure Reason*. Kant indicates there that whereas the understanding uses concepts "to spell out appearances" and "to read them as experience," reason expects its ideas to do more. Reason aims at a more encompassing systematization of all our experience. Since Kant speaks of the search for systematic order in the experience of nature as a kind of "interpretation *(Auslegung)*," it is possible to consider ideas of reason as being interpretive. Concepts of understanding can be construed as rules for reading the manifold of sense as objects of nature and ideas of reason as rules for interpreting these objects as a complete system of nature.

Whereas the rational ideas of the *Critique of Pure Reason* can be used to arrive at systematic interpretation, the aesthetic ideas introduced in the *Critique of Judgment* can be used to arrive at reflective interpretation. What is important here is the distinction between determinant and reflective judgment. Determinant judgments proceed from accepted universals to as yet unknown particulars. When the given universal is a concept of the understanding, then the determinant judgment relating it to a particular is the type of empirical judgment involved in our experiential reading of nature. It allows particular objects to be subordinated to the universal laws of nature. When the given universal is an idea of reason, the determinant judgment is merely regulative and extrapolates from the piecemeal or serial readings of experience to an integral or holistic interpretation of systematic order.

Reflective judgment reverses the deductive direction of determinant judgment. It proceeds from a given particular to an as yet unknown universal. When this definition of reflective judgment given in the *Critique of Judgment* is applied to the aesthetic judgment we see that it need not be an inductive judgment as it might seem at first. When one pronounces a rose beautiful one is not inquiring whether all roses should be called beautiful, but whether all other human beings can be expected to agree with one's judgment about this rose. In the *Logic* Kant argues that reflective judgments can generalize either inductively or by means of analogies. The aesthetic judgment involves the latter, for it intimates that others will take an analogous pleasure in this same object.

The aesthetic mode of reflective judgment can also be related to what Kant had claimed about transcendental reflection in the *Critique of Pure Reason*. There, transcendental reflection traces our judgments back to their mental sources (sense or intellect) and provides a kind of subjective "topology." When in the *Critique of Judgment* aesthetic reflective judgments are similarly considered in terms of their sources we discern a harmony among the cognitive faculties that suggests an analogous harmony among the parts of the beautiful object. At first the formal order apprehended in the object is said to "have no meaning, depend on no definite concepts," although it pleases. It is pleasurable because it is purposive in giving us a "trace" or a "hint" of a larger systematic order. The meaning that is here denied to the reflective judgment of taste is the objective meaning that determinant judgments make possible on the basis of the a priori concepts or categories of the understanding. In the *Critique of Pure Reason* Kant had appealed to the schematizing power of the imagination to bring out the implicit objective reference or intuitive meaning of these otherwise purely logical concepts. Imaginative schemata thus give the categories an intuitive presentation *(Darstellung)*.

In the *Critique of Judgment* Kant introduces a second, less direct, mode of intuitive presentation, which he calls "symbolical." Whereas the schematic presentation of concepts makes possible the objective intuitive "meaning" of the reading of experience, symbolical presentation allows us to give a comparable intuitive "significance" to ideas for a systematic interpretation of experience. Strictly speaking, rational ideas can have no intuitive reference, but now Kant adds aesthetic ideas as their intuitive counterparts. It is by creating analogies between rational ideas and aesthetic ideas that we can indirectly or symbolically present or exhibit systematic order. What was earlier characterized as a regulative and abstract interpretation of reality can now be specified into a reflective interpretation with intuitive content. Reflective interpretation can use the formal relations among parts and wholes found in aesthetically apprehended objects to symbolize abstract rational projections of systematic order. The analogies found between sense and reason can, of course, only be formal; they are not explicitly sensible but can be felt. The intuitive significance of reflective symbols draws on the implicit sense of wholeness that pervades aesthetic feelings and allows them to anticipate the totality projected by reason.

Aesthetic reflective judgments are based on a general comparison and coordination of the contents of consciousness in contrast to determinant judgments, which make universal connections on the basis of synthetic concepts. The latter can be said to impose an explanative order on the world, the former to draw out a descriptive order. In hermeneutical language, determinant judgments provide external explanations on the model of Kant's causal conditions, but reflective judgments generate internal understanding, meaning that they interpret the significance of things in light of their own specific context.

Lyotard assumes that because reflective judgments do not start with the clear and distinct rules of the understanding, they involve no rules at all. But, for Kant reflective judgment may be guided by the more abstract rules of reason. Moreover, by relating reflective judgment back to reflection in its original topographical sense we can obtain another kind of guidance for judgment, namely, that provided by a feeling of orientation. Kant's concern that judgment be able to "orient itself" requires us to recognize that orientation involves locating oneself in the world. In the *Critique of Pure Reason* the subject is either conceived as standing apart from the world, whether as a transcendental ego or as a noumenal ego, or it is conceived as an empirical ego that is a passive part of the world. But when the subject orients itself spatially it uses the a priori feeling that distinguishes between right and left to relate itself to the four quadrants of its visual horizon and to guide its movement in the world: the subject can become an agent in the world. Here again we find a feeling that is not pathological, as emotions and passions tend to be for Kant, but activating.

It is possible to conceive of two reflective counterparts to the feeling of spatial orientation: an aesthetic orientation based on our response to beauty and sublimity, and a teleological orientation based on a recognition of natural and cultural purposes. Kant defined the positive pleasure found in beauty as the simple feeling of the enhancement of our life. The aesthetically oriented subject is not merely a spectator (contra Arendt), but feels herself to be a participant in the world. The restfulness attributed to the contemplation of beauty is not a kind of passivity, but invokes an equilibrium in the play of mental powers. The sublime involves a negative pleasure that is described as a complex feeling of both a restriction and release of the vital powers. These aesthetically charged feelings of life can be said to orient us as we judge the things around us as either adding to or detracting from the value of our existence, thus allowing us to estimate the place of the self in the world. Hermeneutically, this constitutes the basis for contextual understanding. Just as the hermeneutical process is circular in moving back and forth between a context and its parts, so we can find in aesthetic orientation the basis for the claim that hermeneutical interpretation always returns to the problem of self-understanding.

To arrive at a teleological mode of reflective orientation, one can relate what Kant says about the *sensus communis* in section 40 of the *Critique of Judgment* to the teleological

question in section 83 on what it is in human beings that makes them the ultimate purpose of nature. Their ultimacy derives from the capacity to aim at public, cultural goals rather than just at the private goal of happiness. Moreover, in the process of furthering human culture, the *sensus communis* is indispensable, for it allows the judgment of the individual to be oriented to the larger perspective of the community. The *sensus communis* provides the felt basis for what Kant calls the enlarged modes of thought and interpretation necessary for an understanding of human culture. Kant defines the *sensus communis* as a communal sense:

> a sense *common to all*, i.e., a faculty of judgment which, in its reflection takes account *(a priori)* of the mode of representation of all other men in thought, in order, as it were, to compare its judgment with the collective reason of humanity, and thus to escape the illusion arising from the private conditions that could be so easily taken for objective.

The *sensus communis* orients reflective or interpretive judgments about the views and values of others in the community by means of a feeling that is universally communicable without the use of concepts. This reflective feeling of orientation can be said to estimate the relative positions of self and other in the public world.

By relating reflective judgment to common sense, the *Critique of Judgment* can be seen to stand at the intersection of two responses to the world—that of scientific experience and that of ordinary experience. On the one hand, the *Critique of Judgment* is the attempt to round out the doctrinal positions of the *Critique of Pure Reason* and *Critique of Practical Reason*. On the other hand, it addresses our common-sense views as part of a less abstract acquaintance with the world *(Weltkenntnis)*. Whereas critically grounded science is philosophical in a doctrinal sense, there are also generally useful sciences like pragmatic anthropology that are philosophical in a worldly sense: they allow us to participate in public life by helping us to anticipate human responses to situations. But such knowledge, rather than being predictive, is merely interpretive.

In several contexts Kant distinguishes between "doctrinal interpretations" that extend the theoretical approach of the natural sciences beyond its usual limits and "authentic interpretations" that are more modest in their claims and based on practical reason. The doctrinal interpretations of history found in traditional theodicies are rejected by Kant as "sophistical"—they are in effect pseudodeterminant judgments attempting to discern God's purposes in history. Kant opts for an authentic theodicy which initially seems nothing more than God's own self-interpretation. If we conceive God rationally as a moral being, however, it is "through our reason itself that God becomes the interpreter of his will as proclaimed in his creation." Thus, it is through the medium of human practical reason that the divine will is interpreted authentically. Similarly, in legal hermeneutics, an authentic interpretation allows the authority of a legislator to be passed on from generation to generation. In philological criticism, authenticity demands evidence for something really *being* an original source, but in Kant's philosophical critique authenticity involves *having* an appropriate relation to an original source. In the latter case, we can only have a reflective certainty based either on moral respect or on awe inspired by genius. As with aesthetic reflective judgments, Kant's conception of authentic interpretation points to the need to compare one's own subjective perspective with that of an ideal other.

Generally, a hermeneutical approach to reflective judgment allows for a better way of relating human feelings to our theoretical and practical concerns. It also reconceives aesthetic ideas as ways of integrating feeling and reason into the process of interpreting the world as orderly. Aesthetic ideas are said to complete our experience by arousing "an illimitable field of kindred representations" and to produce much thinking without, however, crystallizing into any definite thought or concept. A wealth of partial aesthetic attributes are suggested that give intuitive content to our thinking. Kant is well known for denying humans the possibility of an intellectual intuition. This means that we do not possess the intuitive concepts required for an absolute metaphysical comprehension of the world. What we can have instead is a broad interpretative vision based on thoughts that stir up intuitive counterparts. The quasi-intuitive thoughts involved in aesthetic ideas can give a completeness to experience that is ordinarily lacking, while falling short of the totality expected of intuitive concepts. Indirect but significant affinities can be suggested to feeling even where direct conceptual connections are unavailable to us.

[*See also* Hermeneutics.]

BIBLIOGRAPHY

Works by Kant

Critique of Pure Reason (1781). Translated by Norman Kemp Smith. New York, 1965.
Critique of Judgment (1790). Translated by J. H. Bernard. New York, 1951.
Metaphysical Principles of Virtue (1797). Translated by James Ellington. Indianapolis, 1964.
Anthropology from a Pragmatic Point of View (1798). Translated by Mary J. Gregor. The Hague, 1974.
"On the Failure of All Attempted Philosophical Theodicies." Translated by Michel Despland. In Despland, *Kant on History and Religion,* pp. 283–297. Montreal, 1973.
"What Is Orientation in Thinking?" In *Kant's Critique of Practical Reason and Other Writings on Moral Philosophy,* edited and translated by Lewis White Beck, pp. 293–305. Chicago, 1949.

Other Sources

Arendt, Hannah. *Lectures on Kant's Political Philosophy.* Edited by Ronald Beiner. Chicago, 1982.
Gadamer, Hans-Georg. *Truth and Method.* 2d rev. ed. Translation revised by Joel Weinsheimer and Donald G. Marshall. New York, 1989.
Heidegger, Martin. "The Origin of the Work of Art." Translated by Albert Hofstadter. In *Philosophies of Art and Beauty,* edited by Albert Hofstadter and Richard Kuhns. New York, 1964.
Lyotard, Jean-François. *The Differend: Phrases in Dispute.* Translated by Georges Van Den Abbeele. Minneapolis, 1988.
Makkreel, Rudolf A. *Imagination and Interpretation in Kant: The Hermeneutical Import of the Critique of Judgment.* Chicago, 1990.
Makkreel, Rudolf A. "The Confluence of Aesthetics and Hermeneutics in Baumgarten, Meier, and Kant." *Journal of Aesthetics and Art Criticism* 54.1 (Winter 1996): 65–75.
Makkreel, Rudolf A. "On Sublimity, Genius, and the Explication of Kant's Aesthetic Ideas." In *Kants Ästhetik/Kant's Aesthetics/L'esthétique de Kant,* edited by Herman Parret, pp. 615–629. Berlin, 1997.

RUDOLF MAKKREEL

Feminism and Kantian Aesthetics

Feminist aestheticians, like feminist philosophers generally, approach the work of historical figures in ways determined by their particular philosophical and political background and goals, so it is misleading to suggest that there might be a single reading of Immanuel Kant's aesthetics that can be labeled "the feminist reading." Still, as feminists have begun looking critically at aesthetic theory certain common themes have emerged, and it is possible to evaluate Kant's aesthetics in light of them. This discussion has as its focus two main difficulties that feminists are likely to have with Kant's aesthetics: (1) it imports his gender bias into aesthetic categories and the analysis of aesthetic judgements, and (2) he accounts for the universality of judgments of taste in terms of disinterest.

Explicit Treatment of Gender Themes: The Place of Women in Kant's Aesthetics. Some contemporary feminist critics have placed great weight on remarks made in Kant's 1764 essay "Observations on the Beautiful and the Sublime" in which he assumes that the standard aesthetic categories may be used to interpret gender and national character: beauty is a female characteristic, sublimity is male. To turn to this text as representative of Kant's aesthetic theory, however, is somewhat misleading. The essay, in the words of one biographer, is a "fashionable" piece of anthropology rather than a treatise in aesthetics, written prior to the Critical turn in his philosophy. Moreover, the view that aesthetic categories are themselves explicable by reference to gender does not square well with his subsequent project of finding a universal basis for aesthetic judgment in human subjectivity. In his mature work on natural and artistic beauty, Kant does not argue for a gendered aesthetic subject. It is thus better to look at Kant's *Critique of Judgment* and other work written after his critical turn in the 1770s for a definitive expression of his views on art and beauty and of the role of women with respect to these views.

Unfortunately, the fact that Kant's mature aesthetic theory is not explicitly gendered by no means implies that it is innocent of gender bias. Throughout the course of his teaching career, as evidenced by lecture notes from his course in anthropology, Kant professed a dim view of feminine subjectivity, both in the realm of knowledge (women with books are like people who wear watches that don't work) and of morality (women are more interested in outer appearance than inner moral worth; 1798, pp. 308–309). It is hardly surprising that traces of these popular stereotypes may still be detected in his aesthetic theory, where Kant extends the Critical philosophy into the empirical realm of feeling. In the "Critique of Aesthetic Judgment," Kant gives elaborate new analyses of both the beautiful and the sublime, finding in each elements that are present in human cognition a priori. At the same time his characterizations of the beautiful and the sublime tend to perpetuate the association of beauty with traditionally feminine and masculine attributes. Historically this characterization is nothing new. In a "general comment on the exposition of aesthetic reflective judgments" (section 29 of the *Critique of Judgment*), Kant cites Edmund Burke as the single best authority on the "empirical" approach, referring approvingly to his view that the sublime is based on the instinct of self-preservation and the feeling of fear, whereas beauty is based on the feeling of love. Because his task is critical, rather than empirical, Kant does not describe in detail the properties of objects that might give rise to the feeling of love without desire that is associated with beauty (although he does hold that the sublime is elicited in us by extremely large or powerful objects and scenes in nature). Certainly he does not go as far as Burke does in attributing beauty to the feelings aroused by the feminine: smallness, smoothness, curvaceousness, delicacy, and even weakness. Nevertheless, Kant does not object to these characterizations, and it is revealing that his paradigm instance of beauty is a flower. Although he is primarily concerned with the formal aspects of our experience that give rise to these feelings a priori, a surprising amount of masculine and feminine imagery is retained in his transcendental account. Thus, we find him arguing that the relationship of the faculties in reflecting on the beautiful is one of harmony between imagination and understanding, wherein the imagination is allowed to play freely, but only within the constraints set for it by the concepts of the understanding. The fact that this relationship bears considerable resemblance to Kant's account of the ideal marriage in his *Anthropology* (1798, pp. 309–310) is not entirely coincidental. In contrast to this rather domestic account of the relationship in judgments of beauty between imagination (the faculty most closely associated with sensibility in Kant's economy of the mind) and understanding, Kant characterizes the sublime as the experience of the dominance *(Gewalt)* of reason over sensibility, associating this dominance with military prowess and courage (section 28). If the reader does not find the military reference itself transparently masculine in nature, it should be read in light of his contrast in the *Anthropology* (1798, p. 257) between patience, which he labels a "feminine virtue," and courage, a principled virtue that is associated throughout this discussion *(Von der Furchtsamkeit und der Tapferkeit)* with soldierly behavior in battle. In short, there is little reason to interpret Kant's account of the beautiful and the sublime in the *Critique of Judgment* as in any way breaking with the eighteenth-century tradition that associates these aesthetic qualities with gender characteristics. On the contrary, in the context of the *Critique of Judgment,* where the beautiful and the sublime become systematically incorporated into the critical edifice, these associations become more than ever before deeply embedded in aesthetic theory.

Kant's account of the sublime involves a statement of its affinity to moral subjectivity. The sublime, although occasioned by displays of power and magnitude in nature, is really about the subject's experience of his own moral supremacy in the face of nature's physical threats. Thus, although Kant himself describes his section on the sublime as a "mere appendix to our aesthetic judging of the purposiveness of nature" (section 23), the sublime is clearly important for its close empirical link to the feeling of respect that is central to his moral theory. As long as the sublime is associated with masculine subjectivity, however, the implications for feminine subjectivity are unfortunate. If there is indeed an important link between the experience of the sublime and morality, then women, by nature timid rather than courageous according to Kant (1798, pp. 256–257), will find morality less accessible. Again, Kant does not explicitly state this in his aesthetic theory, but since he is elsewhere quite explicit that women tend to be morally shallow (ibid., pp. 307–308), his association of the sublime with masculinity rather than femininity is consistent.

Kant's emphasis on the triumphal nature of the sublime experience is worrisome to feminists, not only because it seems to incorporate a condescending attitude toward what Kant considers female subjectivity. It also may be taken as advocating the moral *superiority* of the experience of our inner selves over the experience of the world of nature, and hence as one more instance of modern philosophy denigrating the physical and natural in favor of reason. Beauty, as argued above, is characteristically more feminine. Kant cites with approval Burke's descriptions of the beautiful (in *A Philosophical Enquiry into the Origin of Our Ideas of the Sublime and Beautiful*) as based on love and "softening, dissolution, exhaustion, a fainting, a dying and melting away with delight" (General Comment after section 29). The sublime is associated with awe and respect for one's own inner fortitude in the face of overpowering external forces, but the beautiful directs the subject outward to nature. It is presumably the "outward" rather than "inward" direction of the contemplation of the beautiful that makes it, for Kant, more easily described as feminine in character.

Beauty, for Kant, is that aesthetic characteristic that finds expression in the judgment of taste. Kant's analysis of the judgment of taste is, like the rest of his systematic philosophy, gender neutral on the face of it. But, it is worth remembering that in the *Critique of Judgment* Kant intends to address lingering problems about the unity of the theoretical (a priori) and empirical aspects of human experience. It is thus no surprise to find his empirical or "anthropological" views on women's nature subtly but surely interwoven in his analysis of the pure judgment of taste. This becomes most evident when his depiction of the role of imagination in the judgment of taste is compared with his account of the role of women in society, and more specifically, of their role in marriage. Kant, like most of his contemporaries, believed that women were more ruled by inclination and sensibility, whereas men were more likely to be ruled by understanding and reason. Thus, in a marriage, he argued, the woman's tendency to "think only of amusement" must be governed by her husband so that she *feels* as if she is having her way even though he is in fact in control (1798, pp. 309–310). At the same time, Kant believed that women's morally shallow concerns for refinement and culture had a civilizing effect on men so that the latter "finds himself imperceptibly fettered by a child . . . and led by it, if not to morality itself, at least to its clothing" (ibid., p. 306).

This should be compared to Kant's characterization of the role of imagination in judgments of taste: in a way precisely analogous, the imagination in the judgment of taste is in need of the discipline and control of the understanding, even though it is also capable of promoting morality in men. The imagination in judgments of the beautiful, although engaging in "free play" with the form of the object, is not "lawful of itself." Rather, "the understanding alone gives the law" (General Comment after section 22). Still, "Ideal taste," Kant says, "has a tendency to promote morality in an external way. Making a man well-mannered as a social being falls short of forming a *morally good* man, but it still prepares him for it by the effort he makes, in society, to please others" (1798, p. 244).

Here again, Kant is espousing nothing new in associating imagination and taste with "feminine" characteristics. The imagination had long been linked with women and femininity in the theory and practice of Western philosophy. Kant's "contribution" is to metaphorically encode this stereotype in a sophisticated and systematic treatment of the faculty of imagination in the *Critique of Pure Reason* and in his analysis of disinterest in the *Critique of Judgment*. Feminists, depending on their own views about the nature of femininity, may respond to this by rejecting the account of imagination as tied to sensibility, arguing that that faculty is rather more closely associated with reason (Wheeler, 1989), or they may simply reject the "dualism" that makes this sharp distinction between imagination and sensibility, on the one hand, and understanding and reason, on the other (Schott, 1988).

Criticisms of the Disinterested Attitude. A second type of criticism of Kant's aesthetic theory has less to do with his views concerning the nature of the sexes and focuses rather on the very nature of his approach to beauty and art. Theoretical concerns about "objectivist" approaches to science and epistemology that have typified much of postmodern criticism have also been shared by feminists. The parallel concern among feminists working on aesthetic theory has been articulated as a critique of the notion of "disinterest." As Hilde Hein and Carolyn Korsmeyer write in their introduction to a 1993 collection of essays in feminist aesthetics,

> pure aesthetic attention is conceived to be incompatible with interest in other values, including moral and social values and cognitive concerns for truth and falsity . . . because awareness of gender necessarily directs one's attention not only to the act of perception but also to the perceiver and her or his position within a social and political context, one of the revisions that feminism implies is the abandonment of the doctrine that a disinterested state of contemplative attention characterizes aesthetic appreciation.

Since Kant's theory of taste is predicated on disinterest ("disinterested pleasure"), and was the first theory to incorporate this notion systematically into aesthetic theory, it is an obvious and important target for such critique. To see how such a critique might look, it is important to first sketch Kant's account of disinterested aesthetic reflection.

Disinterest, for Kant, is a mental state or attitude that must prevail in order to produce the sort of pleasure ("disinterested pleasure") that is the ground of a judgment of taste (a judgment about the beautiful). Kant gives a detailed analysis of this state in the first four "moments" of the "Critique of Aesthetic Judgment." Summarized briefly, it involves a special relation between imagination (the faculty of reproducing representations and schematizing concepts) and the understanding (the faculty of concepts). In ordinary cognition, these two faculties' interactions are "determining"; that is, the understanding provides the rules or concepts that the imagination then proceeds to apply to sense representations given in experience. For example, in the judgment "This is a rose," the imagination is said to determine the manifold representations given in an intuition of this particular thing by finding the concept "rose." In aesthetic reflective judgment, however, the relation of the two is "non-determining": the imagination, in Kant's words, is in "free play" with the concepts of the understanding, ranging over vast possibilities for conceptual application without ever determining that the given representation is an instance of a specific concept. Because it is not finally "objectified," that is, conceptualized, this free play of the imagination is experienced purely subjectively as a feeling of pleasure. This very specialized kind of pleasure Kant calls "disinterest" or disinterested pleasure, and it is expressed in a judgment about the beauty of the experience that Kant calls a judgment of taste. There is a moment of universality in such judgments, even though they are thoroughly subjective (i.e., felt), because even though the judgment of taste/beauty expresses a feeling rather than predicating a concept of an object, that feeling is universally communicable. Everyone could feel it were they to abstract, as the subject has done, from their cognitive, moral, and particular interests and concentrate on the formal properties only. [*See* Disinterestedness.]

This account might very well bother feminist critics because it gives rise to the general concern mentioned earlier that a disinterested aesthetic attitude requires complete abstraction from moral and social issues. Kant's analysis of aesthetic reflective judgment is typically cited as the locus classicus of the doctrine of "art for art's sake" or of formalism in aesthetics, and the "distanced" or disinterested aesthetic attitude is the cornerstone of the aesthetic psychology of these theories. Because the value of aesthetic appreciation on such accounts is purely recreational or cathartic, devoid of direct social and moral significance, it is viewed critically by philosophers, including feminists, who are profoundly concerned with social change.

Kant's aesthetic theory is far more comprehensive, however, than has often been generally recognized, at least until very recently. Early Anglo-American accounts focused primarily on his analysis and "deduction" of taste, and ignored or gave short shrift to other aspects of his theory that Kant himself clearly intended to be an integral part of his aesthetics. In fact, Kant intends his deduction of judgments of taste, which does rest on disinterestedness and a kind of formalism, to be part of a larger account. His discussion of the sublime in the *Critique of Judgment* is an excursus, a "mere appendix," to this larger story, a crucial aspect of which is the claim that the "mere universal communicability of our feeling [in judgments of taste] must carry with it an interest for us" (section 40). Kant argues for the interest produced by disinterest in sections 41 and 42 of the "Critique of Aesthetic Judgment," concluding that we have both an empirical and an a priori, or intellectual, interest in the beautiful that results from our disinterested appreciation of nature. The intellectual interest is especially important because it is in the end a moral interest. Due to this connection we can, Kant claims, require that others take a direct interest in beautiful nature. Thus, Kant's formalism and reliance on the disinterested attitude must be viewed in light of the larger purposes that he sees at work in our experience of aesthetic reflection.

For this reason, the fact that Kant associates the feminine with the disinterestedness of beauty and taste rather than with sublimity may be a saving grace. Although fraught with problems, the association of beauty with outwardness may provide insight into how this important work might be salvaged by feminists. When all is said and done, Kant attaches greater importance to taste than to sublimity because he believes that taste, although itself disinterested, can give rise to moral interest of a special sort. The sublime is also tied to moral experience, but it is a purely subjective and inward experience. The significance of aesthetic experience of beauty is that in it "we must seek a basis outside ourselves, but for the sublime [we seek] a basis merely within ourselves" (section 23). This is crucial to Kant's larger aims, since he wants the *Critique of Judgment* to help bridge the gap between the realm of freedom and the phenomenal world of nature. This last goal reaches far beyond a mere analysis of art for art's sake, and is of clear interest to contemporary debates about human subjectivity and its relation to nature and the physical world in general. Since feminists have typically been very critical of philosophies that separate humanity from the natural world, Kant's attempt to bridge this gap deserves attention.

His aesthetics may even require feminist aestheticians to reevaluate their global critique of the disinterested attitude and "aesthetic distance." For Kant, taste is outward looking, as mentioned, and as such is able to reveal a world that at least appears to be in harmony with our own subjectivity. That is, he holds that beauty discloses a system that at least appears to be purposive and hence compatible with our own highest ethical/social aspirations. Beauty feeds hope, and hope is the core of Kant's social ethic, of his insistence that morality requires of all individuals that they try to bring about a better world. Thus, if his account of disinterest is taken in the complete context of the *Critique of Judgment*, the second major objection to his theory may to a large extent be met. It cannot be said of Kant's account that the experience of beauty is completely abstracted from the social and moral concerns that are central to any feminist position. This may be true of later formalist positions that looked to one part of Kant's aesthetic theory for inspiration, but then these positions simply do not capture the whole of Kant's views.

Of the two objections, the first is harder to meet. That the theory imports gender bias into aesthetic categories is a fact, or, one hopes, a relic, of Enlightenment social categories. As these categories change, it is to be expected either that the aesthetic categories with which they are associated will be dramatically redefined or that, if the aesthetic categories are inseparably bound up with these old, discarded stereotypes, the former will simply wither away. Still, Kant's theory of beauty, with its demand that human subjectivity be connected to external nature and moral hope, is a potentially fruitful candidate for reconstruction. The sublime, with its heroic, even narcissistic, triumphalism, strikes this interpreter as less promising for feminist theory.

[*See also* Feminism.]

BIBLIOGRAPHY

Works by Kant

Beobachtungen über das Gefühl des Schönen und Erhabenen (Observations on the Beautiful and the Sublime, 1764). In *Kants Gesammelte Schriften,* vol. 2, pp. 205–256. Berlin, 1905.

Critique of Judgment. Translated by Werner S. Pluhar. Indianapolis, 1987.

Kritik der Urtheilskraft (Critique of Judgment, 1790). In *Kants gesammelte Schriften,* vol. 5, pp. 165–486. Berlin, 1908.

Anthropologie in pragmatischer Hinsicht (Anthropology from a Practical Point of View, 1798). In *Kants gesammelte Schriften,* vol. 7, pp. 117–334. Berlin, 1907.

Other Sources

Battersby, Christine. *Gender and Genius: Towards a Feminist Aesthetics.* Bloomington, Ind., 1989.

Burke, Edmund. *A Philosophical Enquiry into the Origin of Our Ideas of the Sublime and Beautiful.* Edited by James T. Boulton. New York, 1958.

Gould, Timothy. "Intensity and Its Audiences: Notes towards a Feminist Perspective on the Kantian Sublime." *Journal of Aesthetics and Art Criticism* 48.4 (Fall 1990): 305–315.

Hein, Hilde, and Carolyn Korsmeyer, eds. *Aesthetics in Feminist Perspective.* Bloomington, Ind., 1993.

Kneller, Jane. "Discipline and Silence: Women and Imagination in Kant's Theory of Taste." In *Aesthetics in Feminist Perspective,* edited by Hilde Hein and Carolyn Korsmeyer, pp. 179–192. Bloomington, Ind., 1993.

Kneller, Jane. "Kant's Immature Imagination." In *Modern Engendering: Critical Feminist Readings in Modern Western Philosophy,* edited by Bat-Ami Bar On, pp. 141–153. Albany, N.Y., 1994.

Kneller, Jane. "The Aesthetic Dimension of Kantian Autonomy." In *Rereading the Canon: Kant,* edited by Robin Schott. University Park, Pa., 1997.

Mattick, Paul. "Beautiful and Sublime: Gender Totemism in the Constitution of Art." *Journal of Aesthetics and Art Criticism* 48.4 (Fall 1990): 293–303.

Schott, Robin May. *Cognition and Eros: A Critique of the Kantian Paradigm.* Boston, 1988.

Wheeler, Kathleen M. "Kant and Romanticism." *Philosophy and Literature* 13 (1989): 42–56.

Wiseman, Mary Bittner. "Beautiful Exiles." In *Aesthetics in Feminist Perspective,* edited by Hilde Hein and Carolyn Korsmeyer, pp. 169–178. Bloomington, Ind., 1993.

JANE KNELLER

Kant, Duchamp, and Judgment

The pairing of Immanuel Kant, the thinker who achieved a Copernican revolution in the history of philosophy, with Marcel Duchamp, the enfant terrible of modern art who, in André Breton's estimation, accomplished "a total revolution in the object" is perhaps uncanny. Yet, the renewed aesthetic acquaintance with art in general and with contemporary art in particular suggests two things that relate these thinkers: (1) Kant's account of what humans do when they experience the world aesthetically and of what this means and implies for them is the best ever given; and (2) Duchamp is a great artist whose central place in twentieth-century art is deserved. To take both convictions seriously has at least two intriguing consequences: first, far from being dismissible as a Dadaist hoax, an oddity, or, at best, a borderline case, Duchamp's invention of the readymade should be granted a central and revelatory role in the theory of art required by

our time; and, second, whatever definition of art *after* Duchamp is arrived at, it must be valid for all art *before* Duchamp as well.

Clearly, the readymade has not simply challenged the traditional assumptions of aesthetics, it seems to have made aesthetics as such obsolete for the theory of art, in that it dispenses with the notions of taste and beauty—the sublime not being very helpful either. To say of a snow shovel, a bottle rack, or a urinal that they are beautiful (or ugly) does not turn them into art, and Duchamp's snow shovel, bottle rack, and urinal have claimed—and attained—the status of art, not something else. Quite paradoxically, the break in aesthetic theory lies in the fact that the same old name of art appears on both sides of the dividing line, making the line itself all the more conspicuous and yet incomprehensible. But, for that very reason, the new theory called for by Duchamp must have retroactive implications on the traditional approach of the art of the past. There are basically two opposed ways of accepting this. One might claim that "as far as art is concerned, [Vincent] van Gogh's paintings aren't worth any more than his palette is" (Kosuth, 1991, p. 19). Granted, anything perceptible can be an aesthetic phenomenon, but Duchamp's readymades have demonstrated that aesthetics does not matter as far as the phenomenon's art status is concerned. Art is a concept, and what van Gogh's paintings demonstrate that his palette does not is his own contribution to the definition of that concept. Or, one might claim that "what we agree to call art cannot be definitively or decisively separated from aesthetic experience at large" (Greenberg, 1973, p. 44). Granted, Duchamp's readymades demonstrated that anything that can be seen at all can be seen as art, but this demonstration merely puts the outrageous experiments of the avant-garde in continuity with the art of the past, thanks to the disappearance of all rules delimiting art's legitimate domain. Art is not a concept, then, and whether to grant or to refuse a readymade—or van Gogh's palette, for that matter—the status of art hinges on one's aesthetic judgment and whether one will find agreement for it.

Art is a concept versus art is not a concept is apparently the interpretive alternative commanded by the conviction that Duchamp's break with classical aesthetics ought to be taken seriously. Reading this alternative as an antinomy—an antinomy that needs to be resolved showing that both sides are right—stems from another conviction, namely, that Kant understood aesthetic experience better than anyone before or since, when he saw that at the core of every aesthetic judgment, there lies the same antinomy: concept versus nonconcept. Kant was talking not about art, however, but about taste:

Thesis: The judgment of taste is not based upon concepts; for, if it were, it would be open to dispute (decision by means of proofs).

Antithesis: The judgment of taste is based upon concepts; for otherwise, despite diversity of judgment, there could be no room even for contention in the matter (a claim to the necessary agreement of others with this judgment) (Meredith trans., p. 206).

Kant's definition of taste is that it is "the faculty of judging of the beautiful," and his main concern is with beauty in nature. A judgment of taste is private, subjective, not cognitive, and sentimental, that is, grounded in the feeling of pleasure (or pain). Yet, a judgment of taste claims universal assent. To solve the antinomy is to understand why and to show how this claim is justified even though reality denies it. The judgment of taste naturally expresses itself through a sentence such as "this is beautiful." Let's call it the classical aesthetic judgment. Works of art—all works of art, including a Duchamp readymade—can of course be appreciated with this sentence, but none is a work of art simply because it is beautiful, least of all a snow shovel, a bottle rack, or a urinal. What matters in the readymades' appreciation as art is the sentence "This is art," through which they were baptized as such, and whether one endorses it. The Kantian-after-Duchamp approach to aesthetic judgment rests on the hypothesis that the sentence "This is art," although not necessarily any longer a judgment of taste, is an aesthetic judgment. It even represents the paradigmatic formula for the modern aesthetic judgment. If this is so, then the theory of art required by our time takes on the Kantian shape of a "Critique of the Modern Aesthetic Judgment," the core of which is Kant's antinomy of taste rephrased as the antinomy of art:

Thesis: The sentence "This is art" is not based on concepts.
Antithesis: The sentence "This is art" is based on concepts.

Before asking what the Kantian-after-Duchamp approach leaves intact and what it changes of the strictly Kantian approach, let us see how Kant presents and develops both sides of the antinomy of taste. To choose two excerpts from among many, the first presenting the thesis:

Now the judgment of taste is applied to objects of sense, but not with a view of determining a *concept* of them for the understanding; for it is not a cognitive judgment. It is thus only a private judgment, in which a singular representation intuitively perceived is referred to the feeling of pleasure, and so far would be limited as regards its validity to the individual judging. The object is *for me* an object of satisfaction; by others it may be regarded quite differently—everyone has his own taste.
(Bernard trans., pp. 184–85)

The second excerpt presents the antithesis:

Nevertheless there is indoubtedly contained in the judgment of taste a wider reference of the representation of the object (as well as of the subject), whereon we base an extension of judgments of this kind as necessary for everyone. At the basis of this there must necessarily be a concept somewhere, though a concept which cannot be determined through intuition.
(ibid., p. 185)

How does Kant now present his solution? Again, two excerpts, in two different phrasings:

In the thesis we mean that the judgment of taste is not based upon *determinate* concepts, and in the antithesis that the judgment of taste is based upon a concept, but an *indeterminate* one (viz. of the supersensible substrate of phenomena). Between these two there is no contradiction.
(ibid., p. 186)

But all contradiction disappears if I say: the judgment of taste is based on a concept . . .; from which, however, nothing can be known and proved in respect of the object, because it is in itself undeterminable and useless for knowledge. Yet at the same time and on that very account the judgment has validity for everyone . . ., because its determining ground lies perhaps in the concept of that which may be regarded as the supersensible substrate of humanity.
(ibid., p. 185)

The solution to the antinomy lies in the supersensible, referred to in the above two phrasings of the solution as "the supersensible substrate of phenomena" on the side of the judged objects, and as "the supersensible substrate of humanity" on the side of the judging subjects. The supersensible, writes Kant, is "an unbounded but also inaccessible field" beyond the sensible, which "we must indeed occupy with ideas" (ibid., p. 11). Ideas that are beyond the sensible because nothing can be shown to the senses that could be subsumed under them; ideas, also, that are not demonstrable in the way the concepts of pure understanding are. The supersensible is therefore a transcendental idea, which means that it is known and recognized to be merely an idea, but a necessary, mandatory one. It is a requirement of reason, without which it is impossible to think that nature is intelligible *(Critique of Pure Reason)*, or that ethical freedom exists *(Critique of Practical Reason)*, or that the judgment of taste is entitled to claim universal validity, although it is the outcome of a merely subjective, personal, feeling. What the supersensible thus postulates, from the vantage point of the *Critique of Judgment,* is a subjective principle that, although subjective, is not merely personal but shared by all human beings.

If "faculty of taste" is the specifically aesthetic name Kant gave to this "subjective principle, which determines what pleases or displeases only by feeling and not by concepts, but yet with universal validity" ibid., p. 75), *sensus communis* is its general, anthropological name. Just like the supersensible, the *sensus communis*—common sense, or better, common sentiment—is a mere transcendental idea. Nothing proves that it exists. Witness the extraordinary skepticism accompanying Kant's reflexive movement of thought:

This indeterminate norm of a common sense is actually presupposed by us, as is shown by our claim to lay down judgments of taste. Whether there is in fact such a common sense, as a constitutive principle of the possibility of experience, or whether a higher principle of reason makes it only into a regulative principle for producing in us a common sense for higher purposes; whether, therefore, taste is an original and natural faculty or only the idea of an artificial one yet to be acquired, so that a judgment of taste with its assumption of a universal assent in fact is only a requirement of reason for producing such harmony of sentiment; whether the ought, i.e. the objective necessity of the confluence of the feeling of any one man with that of every other, only signifies the possibility of arriving at this accord, and the judgment of taste only affords an example of the application of this principle—these questions we have neither the wish nor the power to investigate as yet.   (ibid., p. 77)

When Kant finally takes up the task of investigating the postponed questions, his deduction of the judgment of taste is not of the same kind as the transcendental deduction of the categories in the *Critique of Pure Reason;* it is itself a reflexive and regulative usage of the faculty of judgment, which is why Kant, apparently to his own surprise, finds it easy:

> This deduction is thus easy, because it has no need to justify the objective reality of any concept, for beauty is not a concept of the object and the judgment of taste is not cognitive. It only maintains that we are justified in presupposing universally in every man those subjective conditions of the judgment which we find in ourselves.   (ibid., p. 133)

It is thus for Kant one and the same thing to call these subjective conditions the supersensible substrate of humanity, a *sensus communis,* or more simply the faculty of taste. Taste, not this or that taste, but the faculty of taste, which ought to be postulated as the endowment of every human being, is what justifies not the universality itself (one person's taste being no more universal than another's), but the claim to universality of every singular aesthetic judgment. Even after the deduction, the previously postponed questions receive a negative or, at best, an indeterminate answer. Kant does not think that the way we phrase judgments of taste demonstrates, but merely that it shows or indicates, the presence in every human being of a *sensus communis.* In the absence of proof, the common sense or sentiment is a regulative principle, not a constitutive one; not an actual faculty, but perhaps "the idea of an artificial one yet to be acquired," which Kant suggests we produce in ourselves "for higher purposes." These are the historical and political purposes attached to the cultivation of taste, in other words, to cultural progress—with not even a hint of utopianism, however: Kant does not believe in the universal communicability of feelings. He merely reads our unwarranted claim to lay down universally valid judgments of taste as a sign (not a proof) of the existence of a possibly shared faculty of taste, itself a mere sign of the existence in each of us of what could be termed a faculty of agreeing. Rather than an autonomous and separate faculty, taste, as the faculty of aesthetic, reflexive judgment, is the "go-between" capable of bridging the conflict among the faculties. By the same token it is also, if only symbolically or exemplarily, the very faculty of agreeing that the ethical and political prospect of perpetual peace transcendentally requires.

This is enough to show the strategic positioning of the faculty of taste in Kant's architectonic. Something that is poised on the pinhead of mere personal feeling is ultimately responsible for throwing a bridge over the gap between the jurisdiction of the *Critique of Pure Reason* and that of the *Critique of Practical Reason,* between the realm of the understanding—science, theory (where questions such as "What is art?" belong)—and the realm of practical reason—ethics, moral action (where questions such as "What is the function of art?" belong). The Kantian-after-Duchamp approach to aesthetic judgment is already in Kant: although the faculty of taste is no more than the faculty of judging the beautiful, beauty stands to freedom as the beaux-arts stand to art at large. Duchamp's readymades simply brought this equation into the open by being "art at large" and nothing else. A snow shovel, a bottle rack, or a urinal is neither painting nor music nor poetry, and they are sculpture only if you see them as art first. They are objects that have freed themselves of the rules and conventions of every one of the beaux-arts, the better to have their status as art rest on the freedom of any viewer's singular aesthetic judgment. To appreciate art means to judge, by dint of feeling, what is art and what is not. There is no limit to what can be called art and no infringement on a person's feeling that this or that should or should not be called art. Art is the proper name with which we baptize the things we feel to be art. It is not a concept, but it is an idea of reason. Indeed, if we read "art" wherever Kant wrote "the beautiful," and simply draw the consequences of this substitution, refraining from all interpretation, then the idea of a *sensus communis* shared by the whole of humankind becomes the idea of a faculty of judging art by dint of feeling common to all men and women. Whether this faculty actually exists or whether it is merely "the idea of an artificial one yet to be acquired" is as undecidable now as *sensus communis* was in Kant's time.

[*See also* Duchamp.]

BIBLIOGRAPHY

Works by Kant

Critique of Judgment. Translated by J. H. Bernard. Reprint, New York, 1951.
Critique of Judgment. Translated by James Creed Meredith. Reprint, Oxford, 1952.
Critique of Judgment. Translated by Werner S. Pluhar. Indianapolis, 1987.

Other Sources

de Duve, Thierry. *Kant after Duchamp.* Cambridge, Mass., 1996.
Greenberg, Clement. "Seminar One." *Arts Magazine* 48 (November 1973): 44–46.

Kosuth, Joseph. "Art after Philosophy." In *Art after Philosophy and After: Collected Writings, 1966–1990*, edited by Gabriele Guercio. Cambridge, Mass., 1991.

Thierry de Duve

KATHARSIS. The term *katharsis* or *catharsis* is derived from the Greek root word *katharos*, which means "clean, unsoiled." It has many metaphoric applications within classical Greek philosophy as applied to religious, ethical, physiological, viticultural, and ritualistic practices. From its earliest uses it was powerfully plurasignative but in nineteenth- and twentieth-century aesthetics the term appears most often in the context of audience response to an artistic event. Although its long career as a basic concept in analyzing aesthetic experience has been made possible by its metaphoric power, the exploitation of its many-sidedness we find in earliest uses diminishes in contemporary aesthetics. Now it is used to describe a much more limited psychological experience, which might be called the healing power of art.

When it was taken up by Aristotle in the *Poetics* and in the *Politics* as a word that could have its metaphoric powers further extended, it was given added dimensions of meaning, yet in only two places in the Aristotelian writings does the term *katharsis* appear, once in the *Poetics* at 1449b, and once in the *Politics* at 1341b–1342a. Since no detailed explication accompanies the use of the term, a great deal of scholarly effort has gone into fleshing out so skeletal a use of a clearly important concept.

Classical references to catharsis, brief as they are, set it in a communal context where a citizenry is engaged in watching a performance or are themselves performing, as in dance and gymnastics. The setting thus conjured up by philosophical description emphasizes deeply felt emotions and some change of state as a result. This could be then considered a psychological transformation, a feeling of being emotionally purged or intellectually enlightened, and even extended to a metamorphosis of the citizenry as a whole so that they become accepting of the absolute need to moderate destructive impulses within those who must reside together in harmony. Thus, the earliest uses of the term *catharsis* are introduced with a decidedly political emphasis even as the examples talked about have to do with tragic drama. There is no doubt that the term in its original aesthetic applications draws on its derivations from medicine and religion. Indeed, its medical connotations, especially relevant to the experience of music, dominated aesthetics in the long period from Hellenistic Greece to contemporary criticism. Cassiodorus (490–585), in his discussion of music, simply reiterates the Platonic interpretations of the musical modes and concludes that music is an agency of catharsis: it purifies the soul and quiets its disordered passions. Adelard of Bath (twelfth century, England) extended the concept of musical catharsis to the entire order of living things and to society as a whole. He had observed the power of music to influence the behavior of fish and the flight of birds, and assumed that a universal harmony not only was mirrored in music, but could be sustained through musical relationships.

In more recent times *catharsis* has found a place in philosophical and psychological aesthetics that look back to Aristotle's *Poetics* (only rediscovered in the thirteenth century) but become more and more psychological, almost totally ignoring its political connotations. In early psychoanalytic writing catharsis appears as a term denoting an aspect of cure, but also as having a place in the ways that art can be purging and therapeutic. Sigmund Freud compared the use of hypnosis and of analysis to the sorts of penetrating inquiries represented in dramatic works of art. His essay "On Psychotherapy" (1904) mentions both Leonardo da Vinci and William Shakespeare as sensitive to the processes of analytic interpretation, and although this is merely a comparison, it implies that works of art can, as does psychotherapy, function as agents of relief from neurotic symptoms. Freud then (1905) repeats Aristotle's theory, as understood in the nineteenth century, that pity and fear were "purged" in aesthetic experience, and that the domain of aesthetic experience as a whole has its roots in gratification of unconscious wishes so that for both artist and audience the creation and appreciation of art exhibits cathartic benefits (see Freud, 1908, 1911).

Several contemporary theories of aesthetic experience rest on concepts closely allied to catharsis. Of those who interpret painting, Richard Wollheim analyzes Willem de Kooning painting as representing "those sensations which give us our first access to the external world. . . . [he] crams his pictures with infantile experiences of sucking, touching, biting, excreting, retaining, smearing, sniffing, swallowing, gurgling, stroking, wetting." While these experiences are largely regressive, Wollheim's point is that they become objectified and contained, and although they are "heavily charged with excitation," they nevertheless allow us mastery of their threatening presence in unconscious experience (Wollheim, 1987, pp. 348–349).

Painters often built their images into forceful criticism of social and intimate private ills; it is usually assumed by the artist that no interpretation is needed to respond to the work of art as cathartic instrument. Powerful painters like Francisco José de Goya intended their works to be more than simply critiques; they were also curative, instruments to remove destructive emotions and induce in their place altruistic responsibility. Although they rarely used the language of catharsis their intentions were consistent with the medical-political tradition on which the concept rested.

Literary criticism of the kind often referred to as "expressionist" seeks to analyze linguistic art in terms of the feelings it arouses and the sequence of feelings reader/hearers are led through as they focus on the objects. The spirit of catharsis as an aesthetic principle informs the work of the critics I. A. Richards, F. R. Leavis, and Wolfgang Iser, and energizes the artistic achievements of many of our modern poets—D. H. Lawrence, Thomas Hardy, T. S. Eliot, W. H. Auden, and Wallace Stevens.

Works of art may induce feelings of great variety. It is generally believed today by many political leaders that art has the power to rend the social fabric and the power to mend it. It is correct to say that while the theory of catharsis has disappeared from aesthetics in an open explicit sense, it infects a great many beliefs we hold about the way art works on the human psyche.

[*See also* Aristotle, *survey article;* Emotions, *overview article; and* Tragedy.]

BIBLIOGRAPHY

Aristotle. *On Poetry and Style.* Translated by G. M. A. Grube. New York, 1958; reprint, Indianapolis, 1989.

Else, Gerald F. *Aristotle's Poetics: The Argument.* Cambridge, Mass., 1957. See pp. 224–232, 423–447.

Freud, Sigmund. "On Psychotherapy" (1904). In *The Standard Edition of the Complete Psychological Works of Sigmund Freud,* edited by James Strachey, vol. 7, pp. 257–268. London, 1953.

Freud, Sigmund. "Psychopathic Characters on the Stage" (1905). In *The Standard Edition of the Complete Psychological Works of Sigmund Freud,* edited by James Strachey, vol. 7, pp. 305–310. London, 1953.

Freud, Sigmund. "Creative Writers and Daydreaming" (1908). In *The Standard Edition of the Complete Psychological Works of Sigmund Freud,* edited by James Strachey, vol. 9, pp. 143–153. London, 1959.

Freud, Sigmund. "Creative Writers and Daydreaming" (1911). In *The Standard Edition of the Complete Psychological Works of Sigmund Freud,* edited by James Strachey, vol. 12, pp. 218–226. London, 1958.

Holland, Norman N. *The Dynamics of Literary Response.* New York, 1968; reprint, New York, 1989.

Iser, Wolfgang. *The Act of Reading: A Theory of Aesthetic Response.* Baltimore, 1978.

Jones, John. *On Aristotle and Greek Tragedy.* New York and Oxford, 1962.

Kuhns, Richard. *The House, the City, and the Judge: The Growth of Moral Awareness in the* Oresteia. Indianapolis, 1962. See chap. 5, "Dramatic and Moral Meaning of Catharsis."

Parker, Robert. *Miasma: Pollution and Purification in Early Greek Religion.* Oxford, 1983.

Plato. *Phaedrus.* Translated by R. Hackforth. Cambridge and New York, 1952.

Rorty, Amélie Oksenberg, ed. *Essays on Aristotle's Poetics.* Princeton, N.J., 1992.

Spector, Jack J. *The Aesthetics of Freud: A Study in Psychoanalysis and Art.* New York, 1972.

Vernant, Jean-Pierre, and Pierre Vidal-Naquet. *Tragedy and Myth in Ancient Greece.* Translated by Janet Lloyd. Atlantic Highlands, N.J., 1981; reprint, New York, 1988.

Winner, Ellen. *Invented Worlds: The Psychology of the Arts.* Cambridge, Mass., 1982.

Wollheim, Richard. *Painting as an Art.* Princeton, 1987.

RICHARD KUHNS

KIERKEGAARD, SØREN AABYE (1813–1855),

Danish philosopher. Unlike some philosophers of the modern period, Søren Kierkegaard did not produce a systematic aesthetics. His writings are nevertheless rich in aesthetic theory and the use of aesthetic categories, such as irony and humor, as well as literary techniques, in the form of pseudonyms and representative figures, that give his authorship a poetic, or artistic, character. Perhaps most renowned for his theoretical differentiations between, and literary characterizations of, three stages, or modes, of human life (the aesthetic, the ethical, and the religious) in his writings, winning him the philosophical distinction of being called "the father of existentialism," Kierkegaard seeks ultimately to show how these dimensions may be unified in human existence through a process of personal striving toward the realization of an artistic wholeness of being, or selfhood, that constitutes, in his view, the goal of human life and art.

Understanding the aesthetic fundamentally in terms of its etymological derivation from the Greek word *aisthēsis,* or sense perception, Kierkegaard associates the aesthetic stage with an immediate enjoyment of life through the senses, including sensuous enjoyment through poetic, or artistic, products of the creative imagination, and with the refinement of that lifestyle through aesthetic reflection. There is an integral connection in his thought, therefore, between the aesthetic as a stage of life, the creation of artworks as a means of obtaining sensuous enjoyment, and aesthetics as the theory of sensate or artistic representation.

At the level of aesthetic reflection, one may identify two types of aesthetics in Kierkegaard's writings. The first has to do with the interpretation of artistic representations through the various media of the fine arts, as in traditional aesthetics. The second focuses on the representation, or reduplication, of poetic possibilities, or idealities, in human life, in what may be termed an "existential aesthetics." Kierkegaard is highly critical, in both direct and indirect ways in his writings, of the prevailing objectivity, or disinterestedness, of Kantian aesthetics and Hegelian philosophy, and he is especially disdainful of what he regards as a tendency in early German Romantic poetry and aesthetics to privilege imagination and possibility in an ironic negation of personal striving and self-realization in the context of historical actuality. In Kierkegaard's view, the aesthetic stage or lifestyle—exemplified in the modern age by the reflective, self-centered romantic poet who seeks to reclaim and enjoy a lost immediacy through a momentary recollection of it in poetry and art—needs to be transcended in the choice of a higher form of life in the ethical and the religious, in which the individual is directed toward the realization of human selfhood through personal relations to others and to the divine. Although imagination and possibility are regarded by the philosopher as essential ingredients in the projection and existential realization of the ideal self, there are a number of problematic features of poetry, or the poetic (broadly conceived in his thought as incorporating all forms of the productive and reproductive imagination), that make it an unsatisfactory medium in and by itself for maintaining a proper relation to actuality. For example, as the medium of ideality and possibility, poetry tends to lead us away from, rather than toward, actuality, and has the effect of transfiguring, or distorting, actuality so as to give an untrue or inadequate representation of it.

This does not mean, however, that Kierkegaard has a negative attitude toward the poetic and aesthetic as such. On the contrary, in his early writings the aesthetic is seen as being preserved and ennobled in the ethical and as receiving its truest expression in the religious, understood as a new or second form of immediacy and self-enjoyment. In his later works (e.g., *The Sickness unto Death*), imagination is viewed as "the capacity *instar omnium*," or the capacity on which all other capacities, such as feeling, knowing, and willing, depend, and possibility is virtually identified with God, for whom and through whom all things are possible. Where the first type of aesthetic reflection is practiced in Kierkegaard's writings, therefore, it appears either in connection with a characterization of the modern aesthetic lifestyle he seeks to expose and transcend or as a positive attempt on his part to formulate an alternative understanding of what constitutes, in his view, the proper role of the aesthetic and poetic in the life of the creative artist and others.

An example of the type of aesthetic reflection associated with the modern aesthetic lifestyle may be seen in *Either/Or*, a literary masterpiece published pseudonymously by Kierkegaard with the use of representative figures so as to distance himself from the viewpoints expressed in the work. Composed in the form of a romantic arabesque novel, or mixture of literary genres (aphorisms, aesthetic essays, letters, a diary, and a sermon), and illustrative, in part 1, of a romantic-aesthetic lifestyle that seeks to "live poetically" as well as to create works of art, this work contains a great deal of aesthetic theory relating to traditional modes of artistic representation. For example, A, the anonymous aesthete who is presumably the author of most, if not all, of the aesthetic writings in part 1, sets forth a theory of music ("The Immediate Erotic Stages or The Musical-Erotic"), a theory of tragedy ("The Tragic in Ancient Drama Reflected in the Tragic in Modern Drama"), a theory of situation comedy ("The First Love"), a theory of artistic representation of the inner and the outer ("Silhouettes: Psychological Diversion"), a general theory of artistic enjoyment and living poetically on the basis of the principle of limitation ("Rotation of Crops") and the principle of the interesting ("The Seducer's Diary"), as well as a characterization of the fragmentary, contradictory, unhappy, restless, and despairing poet-existence of the modern romantic aesthete whom he exemplifies ("Diapsalmata" and "The Unhappiest One"). Although Kierkegaard may agree personally with some of the aesthetic theory set forth in this volume, such as the aesthete's association of music with the representation of the immediate sensuous-erotic in demonic form, in general the viewpoints expressed in part 1 of *Either/Or* should be understood as reflecting a romantic aesthetics rather than his own.

That Kierkegaard also envisions a legitimate role for the creative artist in the production of traditional forms of art is apparent from his earliest writings. In his very first book, *From the Papers of One Still Living*, a critical assessment of Hans Christian Andersen as a poetic writer of novels *(Romandigter)*, Kierkegaard identifies two aesthetic criteria for an authentic novelist: a life development and a life view. In adopting the first criterion he is influenced by the German neoclassical aesthetics of Friedrich von Schiller and Johann Wolfgang von Goethe, who viewed self-cultivation *(Bildung)* as the goal of human life and art. He is also influenced by the Hegelian aesthetics of the eminent nineteenth-century Danish aesthetician, J. L. Heiberg, who proposed a schema of genre development (contra G. W. F. Hegel in this instance) from the lyric (immediacy) to the epic (reflection) to a synthesis of these in drama. Anticipating the later distinction between the aesthetic and the ethical, which correspond respectively to the genres of the lyrical and the epical in this early work, Kierkegaard associates the life development of an authentic novelist with an epic development, or the forming of a positive relation to actuality through striving toward a single goal in life, as portrayed in classical epic literature. Such a development, he contends, is necessary for the novelist's work to be anything more than a lyrical projection of his or her own moods and unreflected life experiences. An authentic novelist also needs to form a positive, overarching life view by which to understand and transcend individual life experiences, so as not to identify with the fate of the hero or heroine in the novel or to make the perspective of a single age normative for all. Very early, then, Kierkegaard discerns an integral connection between aesthetic and existential categories and seeks to show how these are properly related in the life and artistic productions of the creative writer. In later works he continues to use these criteria in distinguishing between an essential, or true, author and a "premise author," or fake writer *(On Authority and Revelation: The Book on Adler)*, and in evaluating the work of other novelists *(Two Ages: The Age of Revolution and the Present Age)* and dramatic actresses *(The Crisis [and a Crisis] in the Life of an Actress)* of his time.

Although already prefigured in the association of aesthetic categories with stages of human development in *From the Papers of One Still Living*, the second form of aesthetics, or existential aesthetics, in Kierkegaard's thought receives its initial formulation in his doctoral dissertation, *The Concept of Irony, with Continual Reference to Socrates*. Here, Kierkegaard, writing under his own name, sketches an alternative to a romantic mode of living poetically in which, as he understands it, one seeks to create oneself as well as external works of art by imaginatively playing or experimenting with various poetic possibilities in life. Against this style of living poetically Kierkegaard poses a Christian mode of living poetically in which human life is understood as a process of self-development, rather than self-creation, through a cultivation of one's given potentialities carried out in cooperation with the divine. In this mode of living poetically, a "transubstantiation," or inward change, in the individual takes place so as to render the actuality of that person "inwardly infinite" by means of a relation to the infinite, eternal, or ideal as a possibility within, rather than outside or beyond, the self. In Kierkegaard's view, only an inward infinity is truly infinite and truly poetic, enabling one to become transparent or clear to oneself in one's absolute and eternal validity as a human being. An inward infinity thus constitutes the absolute condition for living poetically in an authentic manner.

This mode of living poetically receives further development in part 2 of *Either/Or,* where Judge William, the representative spokesman for an ethical mode of existence, defines the aesthetic not merely in terms of a sensuous immediacy, such as erotic love, but also as a historical ideal that is acquired and possessed through a process of inward striving, or reduplication, in human life rather than through the production of external works of art. In the judge's estimation, this form of the aesthetic—best exemplified in marriage, where the task is continually or repeatedly to realize the eternal in the form of inward qualities such as faithfulness, humility, patience, and long-suffering—is not susceptible to artistic portrayal in traditional forms of art because these concentrate on the moment and are incapable of representing that which has its reality in temporal succession. It is essential to conjugal love, for example, that one be an ideal spouse every day, not just once in one's married life. The judge concludes, therefore, that this form of the aesthetic ideal can be represented aesthetically only by living it, that is, by realizing it daily in the realm of actuality. In this way, human life itself becomes a mode of artistic representation, giving expression to inner qualities that other modes of artistic representation can only hint at or give a semblance of in time and actuality. In the judge's estimation, the highest in aesthetics is reached when one feels oneself a character in a divine drama in which one has lived oneself into one's part and assimilated the words of the prompter, or God, as one's own.

This emphasis on an existential realization of the aesthetic ideal continues in Kierkegaard's later authorship, particularly in *Concluding Unscientific Postscript to Philosophical Fragments,* where the subjective thinker is portrayed as an artist who is concerned first and foremost with fashioning his or her own life as a work of art. For this task, not only are imagination, thought, passion, and action required, but also a sense of the tragic and the comic as aesthetic expressions of the discrepancy, or contradiction, between the inner and the outer, the temporal and the eternal, the finite and the infinite in human life, together with an existential appropriation of the aesthetic elements of irony and humor as incognitos of ethical-religious inwardness in the external realm.

[*See also* Irony.]

BIBLIOGRAPHY

Works by Kierkegaard

Early Polemical Writings. Translated and edited by Julia Watkin. Princeton, N.J., 1990. Contains *From the Papers of One Still Living* (1838).
The Concept of Irony, with Continual Reference to Socrates (1841). Translated and edited by Howard V. Hong and Edna H. Hong. Princeton, N.J., 1989.
Either/Or (1843). 2 vols. Translated and edited by Howard V. Hong and Edna H. Hong. Princeton, N.J., 1987.
Stages on Life's Way (1845). Translated and edited by Howard V. Hong and Edna H. Hong. Princeton, N.J., 1988.
Concluding Unscientific Postscript to Philosophical Fragments (1846). 2 vols. Translated and edited by Howard V. Hong and Edna H. Hong. Princeton, N.J., 1992.
Two Ages: The Age of Revolution and the Present Age, A Literary Review (1846). Translated and edited by Howard V. Hong and Edna H. Hong. Princeton, N.J., 1978.
On Authority and Revelation: The Book on Adler: or, A Cycle of Ethico-Religious Essays (1846/1847, unpublished). Translated and edited by Walter Lowrie. Princeton, N.J., 1955.
The Crisis [and a Crisis] in the Life of an Actress (1848). Translated and edited by Stephen Crites. New York, 1967.
The Sickness unto Death (1849). Translated and edited by Howard V. Hong and Edna H. Hong. Princeton, N.J., 1980.

Other Sources

Connell, George. *To Be One Thing: Personal Unity in Kierkegaard's Thought.* Macon, Ga., 1985.
Ferreira, M. Jamie. *Transforming Vision: Imagination and Will in Kierkegaardian Faith.* Oxford, 1991.
Gouwens, David. *Kierkegaard's Dialectic of the Imagination.* New York, 1989.
Hall, Ronald. *Word and Spirit: A Kierkegaardian Critique of the Modern Age.* Bloomington, Ind., 1993.
Pattison, George. *Kierkegaard: The Aesthetic and the Religious.* New York, 1992.
Walsh, Sylvia. *Living Poetically: Kierkegaard's Existential Aesthetics.* University Park, Pa., 1994.

Sylvia Walsh

KITSCH. The German term *Kitsch* appears to have been invented around 1870 in the art circles of Munich, but its origins remain obscure. English dictionaries tell us the word derives from the orthographically identical German word, but German dictionaries tell us the word may actually come from English, from the word *sketch.* On this etymological hypothesis, the English, touring Bavaria and seeking souvenirs, would ask merchants and craftspeople to provide quick sketches of local scenery to take back home, and one can easily imagine that these Bavarian landscapes might have included saccharine, proto-Hummel inhabitants. According to another etymological hypothesis, *kitsch* derives from German's obscure, colloquial verb *kitschen,* which means to stroke, pet, smear, or lump together—a semantic space not too distant from *smarmy* and *unctuous,* which are among kitsch's tacky cousins. Thus, in spite of the widespread use of the term, "it is impossible to define what kitsch or artistic trash is" (Adorno, 1970 [1984], p. 53).

Kitsch presents a problem of what Immanuel Kant would have called reflective judgment: given a number of examples of kitsch, a critic will construct an account of what makes kitsch kitsch. But most discussions begin with putative examples of kitsch: Hummel figurines, paintings on black velvet of a tearful clown or a beatific Elvis Presley, Muzak, Eiffel tower pepper grinders, ice cubes shaped like breasts, peek-a-boo anything, paintings of mournful waifs with the outsized eyes made familiar by Margaret or Walter Keane, Walt Disney Tudoroid or Bavarioid architecture, heart-shaped grave stones, plates adorned with cute fluffy kittens; some critics provocatively include among examples of kitsch the paintings of Adolphe-William Bouguereau, Lawrence Alma-Tadema, Andrew Wyeth, Norman Rockwell, the poetry of Robinson Jeffers; some go so far as to proclaim Richard Wagner and Salvador Dalí "masters" of kitsch (Broch, 1950 [1968], p. 63). But the problem of kitsch is to decide what makes all these heterogeneous objects kitsch. The technical expertise of these examples is sufficient to silence the thought that the trashiness of kitsch is a function of technical incompetence. In fact, quite the reverse is true: a certain technical competence is necessary for the production of kitsch. But if not incompetent, what does the kitschiness of kitsch consist in?

Friedrich Nietzsche anticipated many later discussions of kitsch when he criticized Wagner for being decadent (Nietzsche, 1888a [1966]). He argued that Wagner was only concerned with effects, big effects, popular effects; thus, authenticity became a liability, and excessive size and theatricality became necessities. In brief, "Wagner's music is never true" (p. 173). In 1912, Roger Fry gave a detailed description of the interior of a railway refreshment-room replete with what would now be called kitsch but that, protecting high culture with quotation marks, Fry calls the "art"; produced by "artists" who have "not only learned to draw but . . . learned by sheer application to put forms together with a similitude of that coherence which creative impulse gives" (Fry, 1912 [1956], p. 69; see also Calinescu, 1977, p. 250).

Each of Nietzsche's and Fry's terms features in the explicit theoretical investigation of the phenomenon of kitsch that began in what has been called the "extraordinary theoretical moment of the later 1930's" (Crow, 1983, p. 16). At this time, the Nazi attack on modern art culminated in a pair of exhibitions that opened in 1937 in Munich: one of "Degenerate Art," including most of modernism, and the other of "Great German Art." It was during these same years that a number of theorists in Europe and North America undertook investigation of what they viewed as the sedimentation of two apparently separate and adversarial aesthetic traditions: on one side art or the avant-garde and on the other side mass art or kitsch (Broch, 1933 [1968], Benjamin, 1936 [1969], Schapiro, 1936 [1986], Adorno, 1938 [1982], Greenberg, 1939 [1986]). Of these theorists, Hermann Broch and Clement Greenberg were more concerned with the terms in which kitsch should be criticized, and the others were more concerned with the historical genesis of kitsch and of the relations between kitsch and art. But all of these theorists agreed that the difference between kitsch and art was the difference between nongenuine, inauthentic art and the real thing. If this approach is correct, it means that the investigation of kitsch, quite apart from other pleasures, promises an understanding not only of kitsch but, by implication, of the nature of art as well.

Kitsch: The Terms of Criticism. Although the claim will be challenged below, the discussion begins with the almost universal characterization of kitsch as being qualitatively different from art: kitsch is a simulacrum of genuine art. This familiar account of kitsch has been elaborated in a number of different terms, but it is possible to group the terms of these criticisms into three different classes. Kitsch is criticized for being too easy, for being too formulaic, and for being a lie.

Kitsch is too easy. Kitsch can be criticized for being too easy to enjoy, or as being merely enjoyable, as only appealing to the sensational senses and emotions, as being nothing but entertainment. In this class would be placed the charge that kitsch is too sentimental or too cute or too erotic or too didactic. Greenberg recalls Nietzsche's criticism of Wagner when he suggests that kitsch paints easy effects, not causes that would then have to work to achieve their effects (Greenberg, 1939 [1986], pp. 12, 16).

According to Broch there are two broad classes of easy emotional effect that kitsch indulges: "the kitsch novel depicts the world not 'as it really is' but 'as people want it to be' or 'as people fear it is'" (Broch, 1933 [1968], p. 71). Some years later, Broch helped to name these two kinds of kitsch when he observed of Adolf Hitler that "he lived the bloody and loved the saccharine kitsch," but it is now more usual to call these two types of kitsch sweet and sour (Broch, 1950 [1968], p. 65; see also Holthusen, 1954; Harries, 1968, p. 82; Higgins, 1992). Sweet kitsch offers the easy enjoyments of cute puppies and children, lovers in moonlight: the world as people want it to be. That many sweet things can become sticky may be part of the reason that, at least in North America, "kitsch" shares part of its force with "tacky"; in British English, "twee" almost says sweet kitsch. For its part, sour kitsch offers for our easy enjoyment the sanitized mourning of sympathy cards, the uplifting experiences provided by many war movies and war memorials, cheap thrills of horror movies: the world as we enjoy fearing it to be. Sour kitsch presents death, danger, and despair, but with the anguish removed, the pain anesthetized, the experiences become enjoyable.

The topic here so far has been what might be called the straight enjoyment of kitsch, but it is also possible to enjoy kitsch because it is kitsch. This is ordinarily spoken of as a camp sensibility: "it's good because it's awful" (Sontag, 1966, p. 292). The camp sensibility enjoys the kitschiness of kitsch, and camp objects are objects that—like *Attack of the Killer Tomatoes*—know they are kitsch. Camp is not, however, part of this discussion.

Kitsch is too formulaic, too mechanical. Part of the reason kitsch—sweet or sour—is so easy is that it follows familiar formulaic paths. There is nothing surprising about kitsch, except perhaps its own excesses, so kitsch is often neo-Tudor or Tudoroid. Greenberg insists that kitsch is so formulaic that it could not exist apart from "the availability close at hand of a fully matured cultural tradition, whose discoveries, acquisitions, and self-consciousness kitsch can take advantage of for its own ends" (Greenberg, 1939 [1986], p. 12). Broch describes kitsch's formulaic, mechanical dimension as kitsch's replacing the inaccessible, transcendental ideal of art—beauty—with an accessible, mundane, finite pseudoideal (Broch, 1950 [1968], p. 62; Harries, 1968, p. 151). He also suggests that this is what brings kitsch so close to all that is merely academic: "academic art . . . involves a continual search for rules of beauty, with which all works of art must comply, makes things finite in a similar manner [to that of kitsch]" (ibid.).

Being formulaic, kitsch images are frequently familiar, and this familiarity actually contributes to the enjoyment of kitsch. For part of the reassuring enjoyment of kitsch, sweet or sour, is knowing that one is not alone, that this pleasure is universal, or ought to be. Kitsch has a store-bought predictability, which like the predictability of McRestaurants, contributes to our enjoyment of kitsch. Milan Kundera refers to this as the kitsch's second tear:

> Kitsch causes two tears to flow in quick succession. The first tear says: How nice to see children running on the grass!
> The second tear says: How nice to be moved, together with all mankind, by children running in the grass!
> It is the second tear which makes kitsch kitsch.
> (Kundera, 1984, p. 251)

The second tear may already be on the cheek of anyone who says, "How nice to see children running on the grass," but wherever it appears, the second tear is stimulated by the recognition that there is nothing unusual about the sweet or sour scene—it is formulaic.

Kitsch is a lie and therefore evil. Included in this class are those who criticize kitsch because of its theatricality. The

life of the theater has traditionally been tinged with evil because theater, while not exactly lying, does not exactly tell the truth: it dissembles. Broch explicitly charged kitsch with being an enjoyable evil: "This satisfaction of impulses by finite and rational means, this never-ending sentimentalizing of the finite, this gazing at 'the beautiful,' imbues kitsch with a false element behind which one can sense ethical 'evil'" (Broch, 1933 [1968], p. 77). Kitsch's formulaic depictions of scenes sweet and sour are already part of its dissembling character. Kitsch's easy, sanitized representation of the world is, again in Kundera's terms, "the absolute denial of shit" (p. 248). The power of this characterization derives to some extent from the inflated extension of the word *shit*, which can refer to almost any unwanted aspect of anything. Kitsch denies that anything is difficult. Love, war, artistic invention—they are all easy. Evil can be glimpsed behind this denial because purveying pleasurable but lying, sanitized representations of the world is as potentially harmful as any efficient propaganda is, and here it is significant that these criticisms of kitsch were first published during the rise of fascism (Broch, 1933 [1968], p. 68; Higgins, 1992, p. 579).

Kitsch: The Genealogy of a Concept. I have said that the term *kitsch* was invented around 1870, but that while variously anticipated, for example, by Nietzsche and Fry, the explicit characterization of kitsch did not occur until the 1930s. But the characterization of kitsch just elaborated is strangely familiar from Kant's eighteenth-century characterization of fine art. Kant distinguished the fine arts both from the practical crafts and from the agreeable arts, whose only purpose was enjoyment; it is the later that are closest to kitsch (Kant, 1790 [1987], sections 43–44). Kant's examples of agreeable arts even include an eighteenth-century anticipation of Muzak: "table music—a strange thing which is meant to be only an agreeable noise serving to keep the minds in a cheerful mood, and which fosters the free flow of conversation between each person and his neighbor, without anyone's paying the slightest attention to the music's composition" (section 44; for a parallel characterization of the enjoyment of mass music, see Adorno, 1938 [1982], p. 288). Thus, it may be that Kant is not only the first modern theorist of the fine arts, but the first theorist, as well, of kitsch. Nor can this be thought of this as an accident. Kant's purification of the concept of fine art produced at the same time, and by the same movement, the concept of impure, pseudoart: kitsch, art's other.

Each of the three classes of criticism of kitsch singles out features that would make it impossible to be, in Kant's terms, fine art. Here is a sketch of some considerations that support this contention.

Fine art is not easy. Crafts can be work, and fine art is not work, but neither is it easy. Fine art stimulates the "play of the subject's cognitive powers" unlike the merely agreeable, which can charm us even when "the mind is passive" (Kant, section 12). One suspects it is the easy, passive enjoyment of what is merely charming that makes Kant refer to a taste for what charms as "barbaric" (section 13). Fear of barbarism, call it the fear of the body, may also explain Kant's insistence that although plastic art offers figures to both sight and touch, it "offers them to touch without regard to beauty" (section 51). The problem with the evident pleasures of touch is that like many pleasures of the body, they can be experienced while the mind is in a passive state, not unlike that of a "nonrational animal" (section 5).

The distinction between the easy enjoyment of sweet and sour kitsch can also, in a pinch, find itself anticipated by Kant. To do so we need to divide the agreeable arts into those that stimulate easy charms and those that stimulate easy emotions (section 13). Sweet kitsch may provide a barbaric simulation of the pure pleasures on offer to rational beings from the free beauties of fine art. Sweet kitsch might be ersatz beauty, the too easy enjoyment of life-affirming scenes: puppies and children. Sour kitsch might be ersatz sublime, the too easy enjoyment of the "negative pleasure" that follows the "momentary inhibition of vital forces": Rambo respect and hockey-mask terror (section 23).

Fine art is not formulaic. Quite the opposite, fine art is the product of genius, that is, "a *talent* for producing something for which no determinate rule can be given" (section 46). Hence, in an object of fine art, "the academic form must not show; there must be no hint that the rule was hovering before the artist's eyes and putting fetters on his mental powers" (section 45). Yet, kitsch is precisely characterized by its formulaic manner—the clown must be crying, the hurt puppy must not have an ugly wound, the ax murderer cannot kill the only surviving baby-sitter.

Fine art is not a lie, nor is it evil. Kant is fairly explicitly set against whatever appears artificial, mannered, or theatrical: "anything studied and painstaking must be avoided in art" (section 51). But Kant is not only opposed to dissembling in art; he thinks, positively, that fine art, if beautiful, is a symbol of the morally good (section 59). We like the beautiful, among other things, without interest, and we present our liking as universal. But in liking something because it is agreeable, we do so with a definite interest in the object that we find agreeable, and we present our liking as true, not universally, but for us alone (sections 3 and 8). A liking for kitsch is connected with an interest in the object, either the particular object or the depicted object: children, puppies, war heroes, valiant half-dressed baby-sitters. It must be conceded that kitsch's second tear is a universal tear, but its is a contingent universality, and so in Kant's scheme, it would be a diminished universality. Judgments that something gratifies (charms) us or pains us "make either no claim at all to universality, or a claim that is diminished to the extent that sensations of that kind are included among the bases determining the taste" (section 13). Thus,

kitsch judgments could at best symbolize a morality based on the universal desire to be happy, not on duty. This is perhaps why Kundera finds it easy to say that "kitsch is the aesthetic ideal of all politicians and all political parties and movements" (p. 251). Soviet kitsch, American kitsch, soft family-values kitsch, tough leftist kitsch—they all promise a dream world without shit.

If we now ask how old the concept and phenomenon of kitsch are, or if we ask how old the concept and phenomenon of pure autonomous art are, we get the same answer: no older than the eighteenth century. Apart from any concern with kitsch, Paul Kristeller is well known to have argued that the modern notion of the arts did not exist before the eighteenth century (Kristeller, 1990; see Benjamin, 1936 [1969], p. 226). Although most critics (Calinescu, 1987, p. 237) treat kitsch as though it also did not exist before the late eighteenth century, there are those (Broch, 1933 [1968], p. 77) who insist that kitsch will be a part of the decay of any culture. John Morreall and Jessica Loy (1989) observe that while there certainly are early examples of what might be kitsch (they mention Hellenic miniatures and medieval devotional pictures), it is nevertheless true that kitsch came more and more to dominate popular culture in the nineteenth and twentieth centuries. They point out that the rise of kitsch tracks the rise of the industrial ability to mass-produce kitsch objects, and the rise of a new market for these objects among the newly urbanized, factory-town populace out of touch with indigenous craft traditions.

Being nicely opposed concepts, and having the same age, it would be gratifying to find a single explanation for the birth of these archaeological twins: kitsch and art. Moreover, it is natural to seek this joint explanation in the rise of modern industrial culture, although any complete explanation in these terms would probably itself become an example of rather than an explanation of kitsch. A too formulaic account, itself cribbed from T. J. Clark and Thomas Crow, might proceed as follows. There was a time, before autonomous, modernist art, before the avant-garde, when art was produced for and answered to the needs of a politically empowered and economically secure cultured class. This situation may have persisted into the nineteenth century, but by mid-century, "[o]ut of the desolation of early nineteenth-century forms of collective life, which affected all classes of the city, adventurous members of the privileged classes led the way in colonizing the one remaining domain of relative freedom: the spaces of public leisure" (Crow, p. 16). Dreams of political community became realized as communal leisure activity, in Bavaria or Orlando, inciting the mass production of souvenir sketches and miniature mementos: kitsch. At the same time, there developed an autonomous artistic tradition, which in pursuit of aesthetic authenticity, maintained its distance from all that was merely kitsch. The appeal of this purified art to those who purchased it might have been that it preserved—in the realm of art—aristocratic ideals of honor, disdain for popularity, intransigence, and emotional intensity that were more and more impossible to find outside the frame of art (Clark, 1982, p. 211). Even in this sketch, it is possible to see how the social and political consequences of industrialization might account for the simultaneous birth of kitsch and art.

Some of those who would endorse a story such as this understand kitsch and art to be wholly separate and mutually despising traditions (Broch, Adorno, Greenberg). In this vein, Greenberg bleakly described the triumph of kitsch over art: kitsch was "crowding out and defacing native cultures in one colonial country after another . . . [kitsch] is now by way of becoming a universal culture, the first universal culture ever beheld" (Greenberg, 1939 [1986], p. 14). Benjamin was more optimistic about the consequences of the imperialism of kitsch, but he too thought that kitsch and art were pure opposites (Benjamin, 1936 [1969], p. 226).

Other theorists (Schapiro, 1936 [1986]; Crow, 1996) accept the general account of art and kitsch as twins born of industrial culture, but modify the picture of the relations between kitsch and art. These theorists suggest that kitsch is regularly brought within the tradition of genuine art to cure that tradition of creeping inauthenticity and the commodifying effects of kitsch academicism. Later, this revivified artistic tradition may discover itself, like Surrealism, sold back to the consumer culture as "chic and kitsch commodities" (Crow, p. 35). Writing not precisely of art and kitsch but of high and low, Crow summarizes his position:

> Advanced artists repeatedly make unsettling equations between high and low which dislocate the apparently fixed terms of that hierarchy into new and persuasive configurations, thus calling it into question from within. But the pattern of alternating provocation and retreat indicates that these equations are, in the end, as productive for affirmative culture as they are for the articulation of critical consciousness. (p. 33)

With a certain algebraic formality we can say that the rise of industrial culture gave birth to two opposed traditions—that of kitsch and that of autonomous art. Whether these traditions are fully insulated from each other or, as seems more plausible, interact in roughly the manner described by Schapiro and Crow, is a minor dispute in a field that shares one basic account of the genealogy of kitsch and art.

Art and Kitsch: Not Different in Kind. The fates of art and kitsch are linked because kitsch is simply what remains of the arts once we have removed from art all but its autonomous, formal delights. Sleight-of-hand philosophers might point out that this very account of the nature of art ruins the purity of the distinction between art and kitsch, for if kitsch is, in a certain sense, the shit that art excludes and if kitsch itself is the denial of shit, then art, too, by excluding kitsch becomes kitsch. But we do not need to decide if that argument is clever or just slippery, for the general point is that if, for whatever reasons, we have become suspicious of the category of autonomous art, we should at the same time, and for the same reasons, become suspicious of the category of kitsch.

It is not clear that anything has ever been either completely autonomous (the way art was meant to be) or completely heteronomous (the way kitsch was meant to be). So, one can think of the situation in terms of the following choice: either there is no such thing as kitsch and no such thing as art, or the difference between art and what is called kitsch must only be a matter of degree. The second option has greater appeal, but on that account the difference between kitsch and art could no longer be construed as that between impure, simulated art and the real thing. It perhaps makes greater sense to construe the difference between art and kitsch as a difference in degrees of intensity, but that suggestion will be pursued subjunctively.

Nietzsche's mature alternative to the self-absorbed conception of art as autonomous—as purposive, but without a purpose—is presented as a series of questions:

> A psychologist, on the other hand asks: what does all art do? does it not praise? glorify? choose? prefer? With all this it strengthens certain valuations. Is this merely a "moreover"? an accident? something in which the artist's instinct had no share? Or is it not the very presupposition of the artist's ability? Does his basic instinct aim at art, or rather at the sense of art, at life? at a desirability of life? Art as the great stimulus to life: how could one understand it as purposeless, as aimless, as *l'art pour l'art?*
> (Nietzsche, 1888b [1954], p. 529)

It might seem that if we adopted this account of art, then we would have to deny the possibility of enjoying the merely formal delights of a representation of a naked body. But this is not true: the fact that a nude is erotically stimulating does not mean that it is impossible to direct one's attention solely to the dynamism of forms in space. After all, one can direct one's attention solely to the aftertaste of a given wine, but there is more to the wine than its aftertaste, and the power of a good wine will depend on its many different strengths, not just its aftertaste. It may be the same with art: its intensity, power, strength depend not on its autonomy but on its multidimensionality.

One way to model intensity is to think of the tension on a wire: if the tension is to be increased, pressure must be put on the wire in opposite directions. A boat can be tied to a pier in a similar fashion, and although there are nautical reasons not to tie the boat too tightly, a boat can be tied down by tying a rope from the bow to the pier and by tying a second rope from the stern to a different part of the pier. Imagine a work of art as such a boat. A one-dimensional work of art will be tied in only one direction. A powerful work of art of great intensity will be tied tightly from its bow and from its stern in a multitude of different, possibly conflicting, directions, and in harbors, as in the arts, it is sometimes possible to stabilize a boat by tying it not to the pier at all but to another boat. On this account, merely sweet or merely sour works of art would be one-dimensional, and there would be no real tension on the work of art at all unless, perhaps, a second rope were, ironically, attached by the admirer of the work. A work of art of great intensity would be stretched in a number of different directions: autobiographical, political, theatrical, erotic, formal, sentimental, comical, aesthetic, historical, material, critical, majestical, philosophical, and so on.

There is no need to deny the real pleasures of what is called kitsch, but these pleasures are less intense than those of more complex objects. Even kitsch addicts rate multipurpose objects more than simple sweetness (Henry, 1979). The crying clown—as opposed to the merely cute kitten—is itself an instance of intensity at the level of what is called kitsch. Even more intense might be the wine bottle twelve inches high in the shape of a briar pipe, whose bowl is shaped like an ashtray and on whose sides is a picture of the Ponte Vecchio under a banner spelling "Florence." This bottle-pipe-ashtray-souvenir puts its intensity in the service of fun. The intensity of a work like Pablo Picasso's *Les Demoiselles d'Avignon* may be said to derive from the many directions that the work is pulled and pulls its viewers, not only toward new ways of representing space, but also toward a challenging unveiling of the frightening, dark truths normally masked in and by brothels.

If we think of kitsch and art not as different in kind but as differing only in degree of intensity, then we will be able to avoid the elitist sneer that is a feature of the very category of kitsch, a category known only to those who think themselves above it, either essentially or ironically. We will also be able to help ourselves to the historical genealogy of kitsch and art as a reaction to the colonization of the spaces of leisure, for art without much intensity will lend itself more easily to mass marketing, and museum art could itself be energized, intensified, by the insertion of references to popular culture. But the main reason, apart from its truth, for insisting that kitsch and art differ only in degree is that it makes it possible to add to the naked enjoyment of art, without either blushing or sneering.

[*See also* Camp.]

BIBLIOGRAPHY

Adorno, Theodor W. "On the Fetish-Character in Music and the Regression of Listening" (1938). In *The Essential Frankfurt School Reader*, edited by Andrew Arato and Eike Gebhardt, pp. 270–299. New York, 1982.

Adorno, Theodor W. *Aesthetic Theory* (1970). Edited by Gretel Adorno and Rolf Tiedemann, translated by C. Lenhardt. London and Boston, 1984.

Benjamin, Walter. "The Work of Art in the Age of Mechanical Reproduction" (1936). In *Illuminations*, edited by Hannah Arendt, translated by Harry Zohn, pp. 217–251. New York, 1969.

Broch, Hermann. "Kitsch" (1933). In *Kitsch: The World of Bad Taste*, edited by Gillo Dorfles, pp. 68–77. New York, 1968. Published as Part 5 of "Evil in the Value System of Art"; the complete text is in

Hermann Broch, *Schriften zur Literatur: Theorie* (Frankfurt am Main, 1975), pp. 119–157.

Broch, Hermann. "Notes on the Problem of Kitsch" (1950). In *Kitsch: The World of Bad Taste,* edited by Gillo Dorfles, pp. 49–67. New York, 1968.

Brown, Curtis F. *Star-Spangled Kitsch.* New York, 1975.

Calinescu, Matei. "Kitsch." In *Five Faces of Modernity: Modernism, Avant-Garde, Decadence, Kitsch, Postmodernism*, pp. 225–262. Durham, N.C., 1987.

Clark, T. J. "Clement Greenberg's Theory of Art." In *The Politics of Interpretation*, edited by W. J. T. Mitchell, pp. 203–220. Chicago, 1982.

Crick, Philip. "Kitsch." *British Journal of Aesthetics* 23.1 (Winter 1983): 48–52.

Crow, Thomas. "Modernism and Mass Culture in the Visual Arts." In *Modern Art in the Common Culture*, pp. 3–37. New Haven, 1996.

Dorfles, Gillo, ed. *Kitsch: The World of Bad Taste.* New York, 1968.

Fry, Roger. "Art and Socialism" (1912). In *Vision and Design,* pp. 55–78. Cleveland, 1956.

Greenberg, Clement. "Avant-Garde and Kitsch" (1939). In *Clement Greenberg: The Collected Essays and Criticism*, vol. 1, *Perceptions and Judgments, 1939–1944,* edited by John O'Brian, pp. 5–22. Chicago, 1986.

Greenberg, Clement. "Modernist Painting" (1960). In *Clement Greenberg: The Collected Essays and Criticism*, vol. 4, *Modernism with a Vengeance, 1957–1969,* edited by John O'Brian, pp. 85–94. Chicago, 1993.

Harries, Karsten. *The Meaning of Modern Art.* Evanston, Ill., 1968.

Henry, Lyell D., Jr. "Fetched by Beauty: Confessions of a Kitsch Addict." *Journal of Popular Culture* 13.2 (Fall 1979): 197–208.

Higgins, Kathleen. "Sweet Kitsch." In *The Philosophy of the Visual Arts,* edited by Philip Alperson, pp. 568–581. New York and Oxford, 1992.

Holthusen, Hans E. "Über den sauren Kitsch." In *Ja und Nein,* pp. 240–248. Munich, 1954.

Kant, Immanuel. *The Critique of Judgment* (1790). Translated by Werner S. Pluhar. Indianapolis, 1987.

Kristeller, Paul Oskar. "The Modern System of the Arts." In *Renaissance Thought and the Arts*, exp. ed., pp. 163–227. Princeton, N.J., 1990.

Kulka, Tomas. "Kitsch." *British Journal of Aesthetics* 28.1 (Winter 1988): 18–27.

Kulka, Tomas. *Kitsch and Art.* University Park, Pa., 1996.

Kundera, Milan. *The Unbearable Lightness of Being.* Translated by Michael Henry Heim. New York, 1984.

Morreall, John, and Jessica Loy. "Kitsch and Aesthetic Education." *Journal of Aesthetics and Art Criticism* 23.4 (Winter 1989): 63–73.

Nietzsche, Friedrich. *The Case of Wagner* (1888a). In *The Birth of Tragedy and The Case of Wagner.* Translated by Walter Kaufmann. New York, 1967.

Nietzsche, Friedrich. *Twilight of the Idols* (1888b). In *The Portable Nietzsche,* edited and translated by Walter Kaufmann, pp. 463–569. New York, 1954.

Schapiro, Meyer. "The Social Bases of Art" (1936). In *Artists against War and Fascism: Papers of the First American Artists Congress, 1936,* edited by Matthew Baigell and Julia Williams, pp. 103–113. New Brunswick, N.J., 1986.

Solomon, Robert C. "On Kitsch and Sentimentality." *Journal of Aesthetics and Art Criticism* 49.1 (Winter 1991): 1–14.

Sontag, Susan. "Notes on Camp." In *Against Interpretation,* pp. 275–292. New York, 1966.

Stern, Jane, and Michael Stern. *The Encyclopedia of Bad Taste.* New York, 1990.

GORDON C. F. BEARN

KLEIN, MELANIE (1882–1960), Viennese-born British psychoanalyst, a founder of object-relations theory. When aesthetics and psychoanalysis are brought together, it is Sigmund Freud's work that is generally taken as authoritative, but the work of Melanie Klein offers an additional mine of rich and largely untapped resources for aestheticians who wish to work psychologically with works of art, artistic creativity, and aesthetic experience. Owing to various prejudices against her (she was female, was never medically trained, held no advanced academic degrees, worked for many years mainly with children, and became the principal rival of Freud's daughter, Anna, who was likewise a major leader in the field of child analysis and also emigrated to England on the eve of the Nazi terror), Klein's corpus of work has met the Pyrrhic fate of being appropriated, imitated, and applied without receiving (in many instances) the acknowledgment and acclamation it deserves. Widely disseminated within the field of psychoanalysis, her ideas have influenced virtually all subsequent theorizing; yet, her work is still largely untapped for its potential relevance beyond the clinic in the general field of cultural studies. Only in England, where she made her home from 1927 until her death, are there established groups of followers who promulgate her views, practice and update her techniques, actively reissue her works, and publish those of her protégés.

With regard to aesthetics, Klein wrote two papers specifically devoted to the interpretation of works of art, the first published in 1929 and the second posthumously in 1963. These are, respectively, the Maurice Ravel-Colette opera, *L'enfant et les sortilèges* of 1925 (see below), and the *Oresteia* of Aeschylus. In both cases, Klein's enterprise can be seen as a kind of "specimen aesthetics," in which the work of art in question, like a ripe tree, is prodded with her unique instruments and its falling fruit then caught, collected, and examined. Such a method, while delimited in scope, yields a rich harvest of insightful and original interpretation.

Klein bases this interpretation on a theory of psychic life derived directly from Freud, but with three major shifts. First, whereas Freud emphasizes and tracks the ubiquitous role of libido (sexuality), Klein focuses on and tracks the role of aggression (the so-called death instinct). Second, whereas Freud is content to state that every drive has an aim and an object, Klein fleshes out this skeletal model by elaborating specifically on its final term, the object, and creating, in so doing, a complex picture of internal psychic life wherein objects (or part-objects) survive and interact. This picture of hers of an internal object world can be used as a powerful tool for understanding fantasy and behavior and has been subsequently refined by such thinkers as Edith Jacobson (1964) and Otto Kernberg (1980). Third, whereas the focus of Freud's patriarchal attention centers throughout his oeuvre on the figure of the father in the family and on the tripartite Oedipal constellation to which he gave pride of place, Klein, on the other hand, working closely with very young children, shifts her attention away from the father-dominated triad and turns to the earlier dyadic relation between mother and child. Her work in this area has interesting spin-offs for aesthetics where the relation between artwork and artist and between beholder and work are, likewise, dyadic in structure.

In relating psychoanalytic theory to aesthetics, moving from one frame of reference to another, it is most useful to treat the relevant ideas as metaphoric. Freud postulates that each component drive (initially, the oral) has an aim (sucking) and an object (the breast). Klein, in taking up this model and elaborating it, lays out two systems of structured interactions that occur sequentially with respect to it. This dual-stage sequence, the *paranoid-schizoid position* and the *depressive position,* occurs first in early infancy but recurs throughout the lifespan. Because of its recurrence, Klein prefers the term *position* to *stage,* which would imply developmental discreteness.

These two Kleinian positions presuppose radically different types of relationships, not only among internal objects (i.e., within the psyche), but between the self and external objects (animate and inanimate). In the more primitive paranoid-schizoid position, the relation to objects is based solely on need. The vulnerability of the infant dictates that no ambivalence can be tolerated; hence, splitting (dissociation) is the primary adaptive and defensive maneuver: good must be preserved within the self and bad projected outside. Klein's metaphoric paradigm of the paranoid-schizoid position is the hungry, helpless infant rooting for the breast. Attention and desire are directed exclusively toward that part of the mother's body. Her person, the whole object to which the needed part-object belongs, is irrelevant. She does not register as possessing an independent existence, subjectivity, or agency. She is reduced to what is desired by, and exists exclusively for the sake of, the dependent baby. Thus, the part-object is so in two senses: it is only a part of the whole mother, and it is experienced as good when it is gratifying and bad when it is not. Clearly, this part-object wields tremendous power: it can give or withhold, satisfy or frustrate. Since the infant's needs are labile, overwhelming, and, to him or her, unpredictable, life is experienced as unstable and potentially dangerous: a good object can reverse suddenly into a bad one.

Furthermore, since only extremes are possible in the paranoid-schizoid position (in-betweens and uncertainties being intolerable), the object, if it happens to be unavailable when needed, is experienced not as merely absent but as *bad.* This is so because the normal rage felt by the frustrated infant is intolerable; it must be disowned and is projected into the depriving mother, whose breast thus becomes "bad" while the child remains "good." Here, it is important to say that the terms *bad* and *good* carry no ethical valence but merely denote states of feeling. In this way, the mechanisms of projection and introjection are brought into play to protect the child from the dysphoria of facing his or her own destructive impulses. Such disavowal of aggression and the separation of good (inside) from intolerable bad (outside) constitute what is known as splitting.

The Kleinian story does not end here, however, for the mother, if she is bad, or, in the world of part-objects, if her breast is bad, cannot be allowed to remain so, for in that state, she is uncontrollable and threatening. Thus, another mechanism, that of projective identification, comes into play, wherein the bad breast, having been created as bad, is taken back, introjected, so as to be under control. This move in turn produces its own dangers, for the bad object, when it is reintroduced into the psyche, becomes an inner persecutory object, a threat yet again from within, and the cycle of projection must be repeated. Gratifying experiences, however, as well as frustrating ones, are also introjected, and Klein reasons that the ratio of good to bad objects (love versus hate) within the psyche of any individual determines his or her emotional equilibrium.

In aesthetics, these notions may be useful when we attempt to account for the instant positive or negative responses beholders often have to works of art and their inability or unwillingness to go beyond a first moment of asthetic experience when an object fails to satisfy pre-existent expectations, expectations not always within the realm of conscious awareness. The paranoid-schizoid position also provides a useful means of understanding the popularity of narrative plots and pictorial schemata that trade on splitting, that polarize good and evil (in literary characters, for example), thus evading the dysphoria of ambiguity. Manic triumph and contempt, defenses described by Klein and associated with this position, tend to be extreme and to cycle rapidly from one state to the other, a phenomenon not only depicted by works of art in many media but observable in the lives and behavior of many artists.

The depressive position, on the other hand, represents, for Klein, a psychological achievement, for in it, the object of love is no longer based exclusively on need. Experienced as a whole person by the child, the mother now becomes a more fully realized and autonomous other. In order to recognize her as such, however, the child must confront the possibility of actually losing her, a fate never faced in the paranoid-schizoid position where there is no mother to lose and where magical dissociative defenses are quickly mobilized. The depressive position brings with it the realization that one's love objects are necessarily both bad and good (frustrating as well as gratifying) and that this is correspondingly true of the self. To accept this more mature position, one must recognize one's own capability for harm as well as for reparation and thus shoulder the twin burdens of responsibility and guilt. Rather than the speedy solutions provided by the paranoid-schizoid position, the depressive position is associated with slower, more painful processes that Klein, after Freud, calls "working through."

In her paper on the Ravel-Colette opera, Klein provides a clear example of the way these ideas can be put to use in interpreting a work of art. Focusing her attention on the libretto and action onstage, she describes the opening moments wherein the protagonist, a little boy, is portrayed as irritable and bored. The child expresses his wish to hurt the family cat, destroy the furniture, and punish his mother. To the mother's initial affectionate overture, he grimaces. She then tells him that he will have only dry bread and no sugar for his tea. Flying into an immediate rage at this news, he attacks every object in sight, including a little squirrel. Magically, these attacked objects grow enormous and retaliate against him, forcing him to flee outdoors, where the mayhem continues. In the ensuing fray, a squirrel is wounded and at this point, the child feels pity and binds the creature's paw. With this, the objects return to their normal size, and as the boy whispers "Mama," the animals sing that he is a good and well-behaved child, and the opera ends. Klein interprets that the unhappy child, unable to contain his negative feelings, using projection, turns to the "omnipotent mother" as their source and aggresses orally against her so that she responds by withholding (orally) from him and he, introjecting what has now become her anger and reprojecting it, attacks every object around him as if it too were all bad. By means of projection, the whole world goes bad. Correspondingly, these objects and small animals, embued now with the child's anger, grow monstrous and threatening to him, puffed up as they are with his own disowned aggression. When, however, the child stops and experiences empathy toward the hurt animal, and then identifies with his mother by performing a spontaneous act of reparative kindness, the frightening world of split-off bad objects recedes, and normalcy is restored. The child, by indicating his capacity to accept suffering and acknowledge his responsibility toward it, for better or for worse, brings the opera to a healing and harmonious close.

Among the cultural critics who have used Klein's work to write about the arts in interesting ways are Adrian Stokes (1965), who has drawn on her theory in his discussions of Renaissance art, architecture, and sculpture, and C. Fred Alford (1989), who relates Klein's description of "working through" to Aristotle's notion of catharsis. Alford speaks of the creation of beauty in Kleinian terms as a means both of making reparation for hate and of adding goodness to the world, and he further inserts Klein into debates on art and morality by citing her confidence in the morality of the irrational; he defines tragedy in Kleinian terms as the terror of being utterly alone in the world when we fear that within ourselves there is insufficient love to combat our aggression and hatred. It remains for other scholars to carry this promising interdisciplinary dialogue into the future.

[*See also* Freud, *survey article.*]

BIBLIOGRAPHY

Work by Klein

The Collected Works of Melanie Klein. London, 1975. Consists of vol. 1, *Love, Guilt and Reparation, and Other Works;* vol. 2, *The Psychoanalysis of Children;* vol. 3, *Envy and Gratitude, and Other Works;* vol. 4, *Narrative of a Child Analysis.*

Other Sources

Alford, C. Fred. *Melanie Klein and Critical Social Theory: An Account of Politics, Art, and Reason Based on Her Psychoanalytic Theory.* New Haven, 1989.
Fuller, Peter. *Art and Psychoanalysis.* London, 1980.
Grosskurth, Phyllis. *Melanie Klein: Her World and Her Work.* New York, 1986.
Jacobson, Edith. *The Self and the Object World.* New York, 1964.
Kernberg, Otto. *Internal World and External Reality: Object Relations Theory Applied.* New York and London, 1980.
Segal, Hanna. "A Psycho-Analytical Approach to Aesthetics." In *New Directions in Psycho-Analysis: The Significance of Infant Conflict in the Pattern of Adult Behavior,* edited by Melanie Klein, Paula Heimann, and R. E. Money-Kyrle, pp. 384–405. London, 1955.
Segal, Hanna. *Introduction to the Work of Melanie Klein.* New enl. ed. New York, 1974.
Segal, Hanna. *Melanie Klein.* Harmondsworth, 1979.
Spillius, Elizabeth Bott, ed. *Melanie Klein Today: Developments in Theory and Practice.* London and New York, 1988.
Spitz, Ellen Handler. "Picturing the Child's Inner World of Fantasy: On the Dialectic between Image and World." *Psychoanalytic Study of the Child* 43 (1988): 433–447.
Stokes, Adrian. *The Invitation in Art.* New York, 1965.

ELLEN HANDLER SPITZ

KNIGHT, RICHARD PAYNE (1751–1824), British critic. One of the arbiters of taste of his day, Richard Payne Knight is important for his prominent role in several aesthetic debates of the time. His first significant foray was *An Account of the Remains of the Worship of Priapus* (1786), in which he claims that there is an extant cult of Priapus in Naples and, moreover, that much of Christianity could be traced to similar phallus cults (holding even the cross to be an oblique reference to the penis). He expands this account in the *Inquiry into the Symbolical Language of Ancient Art and Mythology* (1818) to include claims about non-European cultures and religions. Knight also embroiled himself (to limited effect) in the question of the historical Homer in *An Analytical Essay on the Greek Alphabet* (1790), arguing for a historical Homer as the author of *The Iliad,* but not of *The Odyssey.* Without a doubt the most famous, or infamous, of Knight's critical activities was his denunciation before Parliament of the authenticity of the Elgin marbles. The reasons for Knight's stand against the marbles are complex—motivated in equal part by artistic and political prejudice. In any case, the incident was an embarrassment, although Knight never recanted his negative assessment.

It was the didactic poem *The Landscape* (1793) that brought Knight to prominence as a critic. In it Knight attacks Capability Brown, advocating a more "natural" approach to landscape gardening, by which Knight means one that emphasizes "roughness" over "smoothness" and juxtaposition of elements over even transition and formality. Knight argues for the importance of the aesthetic category of the picturesque as an ideal for gardens. The defense of the autonomy and primacy of the picturesque in art (and particularly in landscape) is a project that occupies Knight for the remainder of his critical career and is surely his most lasting legacy.

The appropriate psychological and philosophical grounding of the picturesque forms the subject of Knight's most substantial work of aesthetics, *An Analytical Inquiry into the Principles of Taste* (1805)—although that work addresses more general aesthetic issues as well. Knight was prompted to write the work by what he took to be false views of Uvedale Price (also criticized in *The Landscape*) and Edmund Burke. [*See* Price; *and* Burke.] In his *Essays on the Picturesque,* Price attempts to apply Burke's philosophical psychology, developed in the context of an analysis of the beautiful and sublime, to the picturesque. Knight contested two central assumptions of Burke's theory, as received through Price:

1. that aesthetic ideas (here, the "ruggedness" definitive of the picturesque) arise immediately from the sensory effect of perceptual objects; and
2. that aesthetic ideas necessarily arise from joint exercise of the senses.

Following Thomas Reid, Knight pointed to the result of an operation performed by the surgeon William Cheselden that restored sight to a boy blind from birth as important to this question. What sort of visual perception such a person could be expected to have once his sight was restored was a much-debated question (known in the philosophical literature as "Molyeaux's problem") since John Locke first addressed it in the second edition of the *Essay* (1694). The findings of Cheselden seemed to vindicate Locke's contention that habit enters into what initially may be thought to be innate perceptual dispositions—the boy at first had perceptual awareness entirely lacking depth acuity, a "capacity" that had to be learned. Reid, and Knight after him, cite Cheselden's result as conclusive evidence that the only secondary perceptual qualities of objects that have a direct effect on sense organs are contrasts in light—that is, hues of color. With this in hand, Knight believes himself able to dismiss Price's contention that the ruggedness characteristic of the picturesque is directly apprehended—that is, is a feature of the object that we receive as such through the senses. Second, Knight thinks Cheselden's case refutes Burke's and Price's further assumption that the senses act in concert in any aesthetic experience. Although it is impossible here to reconstruct the reasons why some empiricists were led to hold the view that the senses *must* convey perceptual information to one another, it is easy to see why Knight might think the position refuted by the "resolution" of Molyneax's problem. If it is the case that a blind person, who can easily distinguish depth and three-dimensionality by means of touch or hearing, does not have at the restoration of sight a like visual capacity, it cannot be the case that perceptual capacities are distributed from sense to sense as Burke argued. Knight insists, therefore, that visual perception has a certain autonomy in aesthetic experience.

[*See also* Picturesque.]

BIBLIOGRAPHY

Works by Knight

An Account of the Remains of the Worship of Priapus, Lately Existing at Isernia, in the Kingdom of Naples. London, 1786.
An Analytical Essay on the Greek Alphabet. London, 1790.
The Landscape: A Didactic Poem in Three Books. London, 1793.
An Analytical Inquiry into the Principles of Taste. London, 1805.
Inquiry into the Symbolical Language of Ancient Art and Mythology. London, 1818.
Expedition into Sicily. Edited by Claudia Stumpf. London, 1986.

Other Sources

Burke, Edmund. *A Philosophical Enquiry into the Origin of Our Ideas of the Sublime and the Beautiful,* 2d ed. Edited by James T. Boulton. Notre Dame, Ind., 1968.
Cook, B. F. *The Elgin Marbles.* London, 1984.
Funnell, Peter. "Visible Appearances." In *The Arrogant Connoisseur: Richard Payne Knight, 1751–1824,* edited by Michael Clarke and Nicholas Penny, pp. 82–92. Manchester, 1982.
Hipple, Walter John. *The Beautiful, the Sublime, and the Picturesque in Eighteenth-Century British Aesthetic Theory.* Carbondale, Ill., 1957.
Monk, Samuel Holt. *The Sublime: A Study of Critical Theories in Eighteenth-Century England.* New York, 1935; reprint, Ann Arbor, 1960.
Price, Uvedale. *Essays on the Picturesque.* 3 vols. London, 1810.
Reid, Thomas. *An Inquiry into the Human Mind on the Principles of Common Sense.* Glasgow, 1817.
Robinson, Sidney K. *Inquiry into the Picturesque.* Chicago, 1991.

FRED L. RUSH, JR.

KÖNIG, JOHANN ULRICH VON

KÖNIG, JOHANN ULRICH VON (1688–1744), German playwright, librettist, and aesthetic theorist. The works of Johann König (for some of which Georg Philipp Telemann composed) include the very successful *Inverted World*, first staged in 1725 and performed as late as 1760. König's contribution to aesthetic theory is his 1727 *Investigation of Good Taste (Einer Untersuchung von dem guten Geschmack),* characterized by authorities on early German aesthetics as "the first German treatment of taste," "read by everyone at that time," and, together with some later correspondence between Johann Jakob Bodmer and Pietro di Calepio, "the best aesthetic work before [Alexander] Baumgarten" (Bäumler, 1967, pp. 22, 89, and Braitmaier, 1972, p. 56). König takes his bearings for his study of taste from the universality of the metaphor of good taste in art (synonyms in several European languages are noted). König emphasizes, in particular, the likeness of the meaning of taste in art with the literal meaning of taste in food. The emphasis on this likeness permits König to incorporate critically the more empiricist-minded approach to taste championed by Jean-Baptiste DuBos into the context of German thinking dominated by the rationalist psychology and epistemology of Christian Wolff. According to König, the likeness between the metaphorical and literal meanings of *taste* consists in (1) the immediacy of the feeling of attraction or repugnance in each case and yet (2) the fact that it is generally possible, in each case, to identify the source of these feelings in the object or the subject (thus, the opera or audience, the soup or person dining). In keeping with this understanding of the basis of the metaphor, König regards taste in the metaphorical sense as a definite and determinable complex of processes, continuous between subject and object, affected by the state of each. To the degree that the states of subject and object are respectively perfected, so is taste.

This characterization of taste as something determinable and relative to the degree of perfection of subject and object prefigures later rationalist accounts by Johann Christoph Gottsched and Alexander Gottlieb Baumgarten. Yet König also characterizes taste as the feeling of the degree of this perfection with or without the distinct conception of the arrangement—degree of perfection—that produces the feeling. König accordingly defines good taste as "the aptitude [*Fertigkeit*] of the intellect, produced by sound wit and keen powers of judgment, to feel correctly the true, good, and beautiful and to prefer the latter to the false, bad, and ugly" (p. 529). Thus, while taste is defined by König, not as a sixth sense (as DuBos defined it), but as an aptitude of the intellect or understanding *(Verstand),* it is, nonetheless, an aptitude of the intellect precisely to feel. As this definition also indicates, the domain of good taste is not confined by König to art, but instead extends from theology to scientific research, from moral deliberation to the arrangement of a household. The absoluteness of good taste sets a standard for peoples and things in all their possible relations. Indeed, in a self-proclaimed age of reason König unhesitatingly proclaims taste "the guide and steward of all the other noble powers of the soul" (p. 261).

BIBLIOGRAPHY

Work by König

Des Freyherrn von Canitz Gedichte: Mehrenteils aus seinen eigenhändigen Schrifften verbessert und vermehret, mit Kupfern und Anmerckungen, nebst dessen Leben und Einer Untersuchung von dem guten Geschmack in der Dicht-und Rede-Kunst. Leipzig, 1727.

Other Sources

Bäumler, Alfred. *Das Irrationalitätsproblem in der Ästhetik und Logik des 18. Jahrhunderts.* Reprint, Darmstadt, 1967.
Braitmaier, Friedrich. *Geschichte der poetischen Theorie und Kritik von den Diskursen der Maler bis auf Lessing.* Reprint, Hildesheim and New York, 1972.
Waniek, Gustav. *Gottsched und die deutsche Literatur seiner Zeit.* Leipzig, 1897.

DANIEL O. DAHLSTROM

KRISTEVA, JULIA, (b. 1941), French literary theorist and philosopher. Julia Kristeva was born in Bulgaria, where she was educated by French nuns. In 1966 she began a doctoral research fellowship in Paris, working with Lucien Goldmann. After the defense of her dissertation, Kristeva was appointed to the faculty of the Department of Science of Texts and Documents at the University of Paris VII, where she continues to teach in the Department of Literature and Humanities. She also holds a regular visiting appointment at Columbia University.

Aesthetic experience and the processes of artistic production have been a central focus in Kristeva's writings since she began publishing in the late 1960s. Her involvement with the journal *Tel Quel* in the 1970s was influential in the development of her particular combination of theory and avant-gardism. Although she has written on linguistics, philosophy, psychoanalysis, and contemporary culture, as well as art and music, Kristeva is best known for her work as a literary theorist and critic.

In order to understand Kristeva's contribution to aesthetics it is necessary to go back to her theory of the relation between signification and drives. Kristeva takes up Sigmund Freud's theory of drives as instinctual energies that operate between biology and culture. Drives have their source in organic tissue and aim at psychological satisfaction. Drives are heterogeneous; that is, there are several different drives that can conflict with each other. In *New Maladies of the Soul,* Kristeva describes the drives as "a pivot between 'soma' and 'psyche,' between biology and representation" (Kristeva, 1995, p. 30). Drives can be reduced neither to the biological nor to the social; they operate in between these two realms and bring one realm into the other. Drives are energies or forces that move between the body and representation.

For Kristeva all signification or representation—artistic and linguistic, from painting to logic—is composed of two elements, the semiotic and the symbolic. The semiotic element is the discharge of bodily drives through rhythms, tones, colors, and movement in signification. The semiotic element of signification is nonrepresentational, and yet it has meaning for the human psyche. It motivates signification even as it challenges the stability of signifying structures. The discharge of drives into signification is essential not only for the process of signification to succeed but also for the survival of the psyche. Semiotic drive force is the operator in any signification process.

In *Revolution in Poetic Language,* Kristeva maintains that rhythms and tones do not represent bodily drives; rather, bodily drives are discharged through rhythms and tones. In *New Maladies of the Soul,* she discusses different ways of representing that are not linguistic in a traditional sense. There, Kristeva says that the meaning of the semiotic element of language is "translinguistic" or "nonlinguistic" (pp. 32–33, 31); she explains this by describing these semiotic el-

ements as irreducible to language because they "turn toward language even though they are irreducible to its grammatical and logical structures" (p. 35). This is to say that they are irreducible to what she calls the *symbolic* element of language.

The symbolic element of signification provides the stability always threatened by its semiotic counterpart. Symbolic stability ensures that signification does not give way to delirium or psychotic babble. The symbolic is representational and provides signification with linguistic meaning. The structures of grammar and syntax are the symbolic support of the process of signification. Like the semiotic element, the symbolic element is essential for the process of signification to succeed as well as for the survival of the psyche.

Different forms of signification display different combinations of semiotic and symbolic elements. Logic and mathematics might be examples of signification in which the symbolic element is dominant, whereas music and dance might be examples in which the semiotic element is dominant. All signification is a constant negotiation between semiotic and symbolic elements. The tension between semiotic and symbolic is what produces signification. For this reason, signification is always a process in which stability is but a precarious moment.

Art and the Maternal Body. For Kristeva the semiotic aspect of signification is associated with the maternal body and the infant's first experiences in connection with it. Freudian psychoanalytic theory maintains that the process of becoming an individual subject requires the repression of those primary experiences in order that the subject leave the haven of the maternal body and enter the social. The semiotic rhythms, tones, and movements that make their way into signification are expressions of the return of that repressed primary bond. So, the semiotic elements in signification are expressions of tones, rhythms, and movements first experienced in this primary bodily relationship. In one way or another, then, artistic representation, through its emphasis on the semiotic element in signification, always takes us back to the maternal body.

Throughout her work, Kristeva's analyses of painting, music, and literature take us back to the maternal body. For example, in *Revolution in Poetic Language* she applauds the poetry of Stéphane Mallarmé and Isidore-Lucien Ducasse for its revolutionary movement, lifting inhibitions by breaking through prohibition to introduce liberating drives, drives that always bring us back to the primary relation with the maternal body. In *Desire in Language: A Semiotic Approach to Literature and Art,* she sees in Giotto di Bondone's use of color the sublimation of *jouissance* or ecstasy, which is always related to the forbidden mother and the pleasure that results from the discharge of drives into signification. There, too, she sees in the luminous colors of Giovanni Bellini's Madonna with Child paintings an expression of the luminosity of the maternal space. She suggests that even while displaying the split mother—both the object of desire and the object of fear—Bellini seeks reunion with the maternal body through painting.

In *Powers of Horror: An Essay on Abjection,* she diagnoses Louis-Ferdinand Céline's writings as a struggle with an abject maternal body that both fascinates and horrifies. In *Tales of Love,* figures from Wolfgang Amadeus Mozart, William Shakespeare, Christian mythology, tales of courtly love, Charles Baudelaire, Stendhal, and Georges Bataille are analyzed in terms of their relationship to the mother and her body; there Kristeva maintains that all love is ultimately love for the mother. In *Black Sun: Depression and Melancholy,* the paintings of Philip Holbein, the poetry of Gérard de Nerval, and the prose of Fyodor Dostoyevsky and Marguerite Duras are interpreted in terms of their ability or inability to mourn the lost maternal body. And, Kristeva begins her monumental study of Marcel Proust, *Time and Sense,* with a discussion of the *petite madeleine* as a remembrance of lost maternal time and space.

Artistic Production, Aesthetic Experience, and Revolution. The expression of the repressed connection to the maternal body is what makes art revolutionary. Art can present that which has been buried in the unconscious in a way that is both pleasurable and challenging. In *Revolution in Poetic Language,* Kristeva maintains that there is an analogy between poetic revolution and political revolution. The influx of drives into language challenges syntax and grammar and revolutionizes language. More than this, the semiotic element in poetic language—or language as art—displays something crucial in the process of signification itself.

For Kristeva, the revolutionary function of poetic language at the end of the nineteenth century was the result of the way that this language pointed to the semiotic element of signification even while discharging it. In this way, poetic language can show that the process of signification is always made up of both semiotic and symbolic elements; and that signification is a process that results from a constant tension between these two elements. Poetic language is revolutionary insofar as it displays the process of signification itself.

Kristeva also suggests that there can be no political revolution without a revolution in representation. In order to change the way that we act or think, we have to change the way that we represent ourselves. We have to change the relation between our drives, affects, and words or artistic representations. In addition, since subjectivity is always essentially linked to language, in order to change our conceptions of ourselves we need to change language; and any change in language is necessarily a change in the status of the subject. If language is a process, so is the subject. If language is ever changing, an open system, so is the subject. Like language, and all forms of representation, Kristeva's subject is always in process and on trial.

In *Revolution in Poetic Language,* Kristeva seems to propose a dialectical relationship between politics and artistic practice. While, on the one hand, political revolution requires a revolution in signifying practices, on the other, artists are always the products of their sociopolitical situations. Art is always a response to the return of repressed unconscious elements on both an individual and a social level. In this way art is often a response to psychic crises on both an individual and a social level. For this reason, art needs to be analyzed in relation to the social and individual history of the artist.

More than twenty years after the publication of *Revolution in Poetic Language,* in *Sens et non-sens de la révolte: Pouvoirs et limites de psychanalyse,* Kristeva proposes that all creativity is the result of revolt, psychic revolt, that takes us back to the most archaic psychic revolutions that initiate both individual and social identity. All artistic production and aesthetic experience require a revolt against, and an identification with, authority. Each artist makes the artistic medium and its logic his or her own by rejecting the rules of the medium as a transcendent authority that restricts his or her freedom and incorporating the authority of the rules into his or her own artistic vocabulary in order to say something new. Artistic creation and all creativity involve rejecting and reincorporating authority; they require revolt.

Creative revolt is necessary for the survival of psychic life. In this way, art responds to individual and cultural needs. Kristeva goes so far as to suggest that art and literature are other forms of religion. Just as religion provides us with a way to make our lives meaningful, so do art and literature. It is within the creative space opened up through revolt that meaning emerges. If our culture is plagued by feelings of meaninglessness and hopelessness this is because we are losing our creative space. Kristeva sees hope for revitalizing this creative space through art, literature, and psychoanalysis.

Even in seemingly anti-aesthetic art, or ugly art, Kristeva hears a response to the cultural need for meaning that comes through opening aesthetic space. For example, in *Sens et non-sens de la révolte,* Kristeva diagnoses installation pieces by Hans Hacke and Robert Wilson as meeting our need for foundations even as they attempt to shatter them. There, she says that these artists, without knowing it, are celebrating alternative foundations, broken ones. Instead of asking the viewer to relate to an object of art, these artists require the "viewer" to be a participant engaging the entire body and all of the senses. In the place of the object of art, these artists are creating a space in which the "viewer" contemplates not only the image but also his or her relation to being. In other words, these installation pieces ask the "viewer" to dwell in the psychic space required to contemplate the meaning of life and our relation to our environment. Kristeva suggests that in a time when psychic space is closing down these artists have asked us to contemplate this precarious space; they have touched what Kristeva calls our "new maladies of the soul."

Aesthetics and Meaning. As a practicing Freudian psychoanalyst, much of Kristeva's work explores the relationship between art and the unconscious. Kristeva maintains that art does not represent the unconscious but expresses it. Unconscious bodily drives are discharged through artistic practice. In this way, artistic production and aesthetic experience are essential to maintaining the psychic space required to make life meaningful for human beings.

Starting with *Tales of Love,* and continuing in *New Maladies of the Soul* and *Sens et non-sens de la révolte,* Kristeva has diagnosed a flattening or collapsing of psychic space in our culture. We experience this flattening as a crisis in meaning. Our words and experiences seem empty and life seems meaningless. In *New Maladies of the Soul,* Kristeva suggests that too often we turn to media images and drugs (especially antidepressants) to counter our feelings of emptiness. But these "remedies" only perpetuate the emptiness by projecting false and flat images of our lives. Filled with two-dimensional media images, our psyches or souls become as flat as those images themselves. We are losing the ability to imagine ourselves.

In contemporary culture, life takes place on the screen—movie screens, television screens, computer screens. Yet, these media images merely cover the surface of the emptiness that we feel facing the loss of meaning. Psychotropic drugs and antidepressants flatten the psyche. They relieve the feeling of crisis caused by a loss of meaning at the expense of a feeling of emptiness; they flatten or empty the patient's affects. Both drugs and media images provide only false or artificial selves that only temporarily smooth over the surface of an otherwise empty psyche. By substituting surface images for psychic depth, drugs and media images close psychic space.

Psychic space is the space between the human organism and its aims; it is the space between the biological and representation. It is the space of drives that move energy between these two interconnected spheres. It is within this psychic space that affects materialize between bodily organs and social customs. Our emotional lives depend on this space. Meaning is constituted in this space between the body and representation. Our words and our lives have meaning by virtue of their connection to affect. The meaning of words (the symbolic element of language) is charged with affective meaning (the semiotic element of language) through the movement of drive energy within psychic space.

As Kristeva says in *Tales of Love,* we are extraterrestrials wandering and lost without meaning as a result of this abolition of psychic space. We experience somatic symptoms cut off from their psychic or affective meaning. Psychoanalysis, literature, and art can give meaning to signification by reconnecting representation and affects. Artistic practice can open up psychic space and provide various interpretations with which to give meaning to representation and thus to life.

Psychoanalysis, literature, and art provide nourishment for a psyche that thrives on reinventing itself through imagination. It is through imagination that bodily drive force and affects are linked to signification. Without these creative links supplied through aesthetic experience, which is essential to psychic life, words and all forms of signification are cut off from affects; and this separation between signification and affect leaves us feeling dissatisfaction, if not despair. Aesthetic experience is not superfluous to human experience. Rather, in Kristeva's analysis, aesthetic experience is essential to human experience. Aesthetic experience is what makes it possible for human beings to find, and create, meaning in our lives and in our representations of ourselves.

Aesthetics and Ethics. Ultimately, for Kristeva it is aesthetic experience that makes ethics possible. Only through imagination can we enter into relations with others. Only through imagination can we embrace the return of the repressed within ourselves and within our culture. It is aesthetic experience that makes the embrace of difference possible. This is why we need to augment aesthetic experience in a culture that seems to be forgetting its importance.

In *New Maladies of the Soul,* Kristeva says that

> the role of aesthetic practices needs to be augmented, not only to counterbalance the mass-production and uniformity of the information age, but also to demystify the idea that the community of language is a universal, all-inclusive, and equalizing tool. Each artistic experience can also highlight the diversity of our identifications and the relativity of our symbolic and biological existence. Understood as such, aesthetics takes on the question of morality. (p. 223)

This new morality born out of aesthetic experience through imagination is not an ethics of law or reason per se. Rather, it is a pliable ethics that acknowledges its own sacrificial order. It is an ethics that reinvents the repressed by imagining it otherwise in order to embrace it, even while acknowledging the ultimate inaccessibility of the repressed unconscious other within each individual and the repressed other(s) within each culture.

[*See also* Feminism; Freud, *survey article;* Literature, *article on* Literary Aesthetics; Poetics; Semiotics; *and* Text.]

BIBLIOGRAPHY

Works by Kristeva

La révolution du langage poétique. Paris, 1974. Translated as *Revolution in Poetic Language* by Margaret Waller (New York, 1984).

Desire in Language: A Semiotic Approach to Literature and Art. Edited by Leon S. Roudiez, translated by Thomas Gora, Alice Jardine, and Leon S. Roudiez. New York, 1980.

Pouvoirs de l'horreur: Essai sur l'abjection. Paris, 1980. Translated as *Powers of Horror: An Essay on Abjection* by Leon S. Roudiez (New York, 1982).

Histoires d'amour. Paris, 1983. Translated as *Tales of Love* by Leon S. Roudiez (New York, 1987).

Soleil noir: Dépression et mélancolie. Paris, 1987. Translated as *Black Sun: Depression and Melancholy* by Leon S. Roudiez (New York, 1989).

Étrangers à nous-mêmes. Paris, 1988. Translated as *Strangers to Ourselves* by Leon S. Roudiez (New York, 1991).

Les nouvelles maladies de l'âme. Paris, 1993. Translated as *New Maladies of the Soul* by Ross Guberman (New York, 1995).

Le temps sensible: Proust et l'expérience littéraire. Paris, 1994. Translated as *Time and Sense: Proust and the Experience of Literature* by Ross Guberman (New York, 1996).

Sens et non-sens de la révolte: Pouvoirs et limites de la psychanalyse, vol. 1. Paris, 1996.

The Portable Kristeva. Edited by Kelly Oliver. New York, 1997.

Other Sources

Crownfield, David R., ed. *Body/Text in Julia Kristeva: Religion, Women, and Psychoanalysis.* Albany, N.Y., 1992.

Fletcher, John, and Andrew Benjamin, eds. *Abjection, Melancholia, and Love: The Work of Julia Kristeva.* London and New York, 1990.

Lechte, John. *Julia Kristeva.* London and New York, 1990.

Oliver, Kelly. *Reading Kristeva: Unraveling the Double-bind.* Bloomington, Ind., 1993.

Oliver, Kelly, ed. *Ethics, Politics and Difference in Julia Kristeva's Writing.* New York and London, 1993.

KELLY OLIVER

L

LACAN, JACQUES MARIE. [*To treat the psychoanalytic theory of the twentieth-century French philosopher Jacques-Marie Lacan and its influence on contemporary aesthetics, this entry comprises two essays:*

Survey of Thought

Visual and Literary Arts

The first essay clarifies the development of Lacan's thought and its general relevance to aesthetics. The second essay explores in greater detail Lacan's influence on film and other art theories, as well as on literary and cultural studies. For related discussion, see Feminism; Freud; Gaze; Lyotard; Metonymy; Sartre; *and* Sexuality.]

Survey of Thought

Jacques Marie Lacan (1901–1981) is the pivotal figure in a reception of psychoanalysis that has proved central to much postwar French thought. To a high degree, the work of such figures as Louis Althusser, Gilles Deleuze and Félix Guattari, Jacques Derrida, Jean-François Lyotard, and Michel Foucault remains incomprehensible apart from some grasp of their relation to Lacan's thought and writing. Lacan's influence beyond France—most strongly on literary theory—has been both direct and indirect.

Up until about 1940, Lacan would have appeared as a somewhat maverick psychoanalyst (his earliest psychoanalytic publications appeared in the Surrealist journal *Minotaure*) whose primary contribution to the field was the description of the dynamics of the infant's visual self-recognition in what Lacan called the "mirror stage." Beginning around 1950, with a significant impetus from the Claude Lévi-Strauss's magisterial mapping of Saussurean linguistics onto social structure in his *Elementary Structures of Kinship*, it becomes clear that Lacan has a vision of psychoanalysis in its entirety, a vision that first becomes fully public in his rebarbative collection of essays, *Écrits*. In the mid-1970s, the texts of his "seminars" (for most part lecture courses with occasional interventions by and questions from his ever-expanding audience) began to appear from Éditions du Seuil; to date nine volumes have been published, with English translations following in short order; in general, these are more accessible than the *Écrits*, although over time the difference between Lacan's spoken and written styles dissolves so that later seminars are often at least as

difficult as the *Écrits* themselves. Lacan's thought—much as he was prone to claim otherwise—is not without distinct periods and moments of development, although our view of that development remains constrained by the seminars to date. In a rough way, it seems useful to distinguish a first period ending in 1955 or 1956 with the crystallization of the central (and problematic) thesis of the "pure signifier" (this forms the object of sustained Derridean critique in "The Purveyor of Truth" [1975]); a second period lasting up to about 1970 or 1971, when the passage of Lacan's teachings beyond the explicit field of an audience of analysts-in-training begins to appear as an explicit problem for him; and a final period that sees him turning away from the terms that had seemed central to his teaching in favor of a new emphasis on the things he calls the Real and the Symptom (this last development appears to be accompanied by a renewed emphasis on explicit topological models and the quasi-formal notations that Lacan called "mathemes"). Slavoj Žižek has emerged as perhaps the leading interpreter of this period of Lacan's teaching.

While this entry will necessarily concentrate on the theoretical dimensions of Lacan's work, it is useful to know that he is also the center of a stormy institutional history beginning with his expulsion from the existing French psychoanalytic society (and so ultimately the International Psychoanalytic Association) in a dispute centered on both his practice of the "short session" and his training practices, and continuing through a repeated founding and fissioning of alternative psychoanalytic institutions, including his dissolution of his own École freudienne shortly before his death.

In *Being and Nothingness*, Jean-Paul Sartre argued forcefully against the notion of a psychoanalytic unconscious on the grounds that the continuing investment integral to the notion of repression assumed knowledge of what was to be repressed and maintained in that repression, and so was reducible in all cases to "bad faith"—an argument that Sartre backed up by an appeal to Wilhelm Stekel's clinical studies of frigidity in women. Lacan's position appears to respond to this by locating repression as a necessary consequence of linguistic articulation as such and prior to any claims to knowledge that language might advance or support. This is at the least a strong claim about the conditions under which something properly called an unconscious could come into existence, and in making it Lacan immediately specifies the claims of psychoanalysis as irreducible to any individual psychology. Lévi-Strauss's work then allows Lacan to move fluidly between the familiar psychoanalytic terms of family romance and the linguistic reference that will supplant Sigmund Freud's thermodynamics and offer a newly explicit connection between the terms of psychoanalytic theory and its crucially discursive practice.

Approached from this angle, the core of Lacan's thought appears contained in his distinction of three registers that he distinguishes as Real, Imaginary, and Symbolic through which he articulates a psychoanalytic field in which developmental or cross-sectional, intrapsychic or social accents may be variously distributed. The essential thought here is that when a "brute" reality—essentially full and continuous with itself—becomes remarkable, it divides from itself and creates a field of "logics" that are at once mutually dependent and not resolvable into one another's terms. If we begin from this Real, we will call its systematic remarking the Symbolic (we are looking at the passage from that real tree that is, to the extent that we can imagine it apart from us, wholly embedded in the continuous fabric of stuff to the "tree" that shows itself as distinct from a "ground" and "sky" and in contrast to such other things as "grass" or "shrubbery"), and we will call Imaginary the region of desires and identifications resulting from the tension between these two.

It is important that this is not the only way we can tell the story of the mutual imbrication of Lacan's registers. We can also—and this is indeed the more standard way of articulating the registers in the Lacan literature—begin from the moment at which the child, paradigmatically before a mirror, first gained access to its image both as other and as implicated in a relation to the other (equally paradigmatically its mother), thus finding itself first of all within the Imaginary's logic of identification and desire only to later run up against Symbolic facts of lineage and filiation, of naming and language, that have all along underlain and supported the possibility of what had once appeared as transparent self-recognition (and that now shows itself to have been, necessarily, misrecognition as well—if the developmental sequence appears to present a passage from Imaginary to Symbolic, the logical order is the reverse). The Real shows itself in this light as the tension we actually inhabit between the claims of the Imaginary and the limitations of the Symbolic. We can equally begin from the Imaginary logics of desire and identification insofar as they support themselves on a positing of the Real whose distance answers to the intervening insistence of a Symbolic order.

The three registers so described offer a revision of the Hegelian play of means and extremes within the "speculative proposition," just as the Borromean knots that come to fascinate Lacan late in his career refigure the self-enclosing harmonies of G. W. F. Hegel's circles within circles as so many instances of knotting and mutual interference, locking into place a singularity that cannot assume the structure of a simple point or center. This is a way of indicating the considerable support Lacan's thought takes from a sustained confrontation with the Hegelian account of consciousness, and so also a way of indicating the depth to which Lacan's psychoanalytic field presents itself as a field of determinate negations not susceptible to dialectical overcoming—a feature of his thinking abundantly in evidence in the many diagrams he produces that deploy his three registers across a grid of contradiction and opposition that can be variously described as founded in the Aristotelian logic of contraries and oppositions, the mathematician's Klein Group, and Greimas's "semiotic square," as well as in his distinctly unprincipled play with various forms of logical or mathematical notation.

The work of elaboration that follows from this fundamental scheme has been of interest to aesthetics and adjacent fields in at least four distinguishable ways.

The first of these lies in its apparent promise—just because Lacanian analysis takes text and unconscious to be made of essentially the same stuff—to let psychoanalysis address the specifically literary object in a way that sustains the established desire to secure an account of the role of a Freudian unconscious within the literary work while no longer seeming to leave the text for some other realm entirely. Notable work pursuing this track might include Shoshana Felman's extended study of the controversies attendant on Henry James's *The Turn of the Screw* and, in a significantly different vein, certain strands in Jacques Derrida's work, as, for example, his writings on Stéphane Mallarmé or Francis Ponge. Such studies typically do not raise the question, proper to a psychoanalytic aesthetics, of the sublimated character of the work of art.

The second, having its strongest impact in cinema studies and in art history, draws on Lacan's specific account of the workings of the visual. Within this general arena, it is useful to distinguish two distinct moments and tendencies. The historically earlier and so far most influential arises primarily from film studies, places a particular premium on the Imaginary logics of identification and desire, and tends to participate in what has been described as a distinctively antivisual discourse that passes easily from Lacan to certain moments in Foucault (particularly his analysis of the panopticon), as well as recalling strongly the earlier Sartrean stance toward the "regard" in *Being and Nothingness*. The genealogy of this position is complex, involving a passage from some of Lacan's Althusserian students to the British film journal *Screen* and thence into a more general circulation. Crucial to the success of this tendency has been its strong account of the construction of woman as object of the cinematic gaze, although questions arising from this account have also played a role in the emergence of the second tendency in this area.

Here it is a matter of turning away from the heavy emphasis on the mirror stage in favor of the extended dealings with vision by Lacan in perhaps the most accessible and widely read of his seminars, *The Four Fundamental Concepts of Psychoanalysis*. What we seem to get here is an account of the Symbolic underpinnings of the mirror stage worked out in close relation to Maurice Merleau-Ponty's posthumously published explorations of vision (in *The Visible and the Invisible*) and sharing with that material a distinct emphasis on questions of picture and painting. The burden of this account falls out in ways markedly different from the first, emphasizing facts not of identity but simultaneous social solidarity and heterogeneity as well as a certain priority of visibility, anchored in an essentially inhuman or Symbolic gaze, over the exercise of human vision—and with this a certain play of picturing and being pictured taken as integral to human being. It is an underappreciated feature of this account that it cannot go forward apart from a certain evidencing of taste (it is, for example, strongly anti-Expressionist). Although there is no necessary contradiction between these two tendencies in taking up Lacan on vision, there is a clear tension between them, and just accounts of their actual relation remain in short supply.

The third major moment of Lacan's interest for aesthetics is so far considerably the least developed, and it is his direct reflection on the aesthetic, an important relay in his effort, during 1959 and 1960, to explore the ethical implications of psychoanalysis. The central topic here is, as one would expect, sublimation in its difficult relation to both the pleasure principle and that which, within psychoanalysis, asserts the necessity of a movement beyond this principle. This is, for Lacan, to a considerable extent a question of what, both following and contesting Martin Heidegger, he calls the Thing and defines as what the real suffers from its submission to the signifier. What the real so suffers is, of course, nothing (it remains the real that it is), but it is also the quasi-Heideggerian "nothing" that is the difference between the tree and the ground in which it sits, and so it stands also as the thing the real implies, contains, and nonetheless cannot but withhold. Art, Lacan claims, is its tracing—as the jug, a figure he willingly borrows from Heidegger, is the containing of the nothing it renders (without thereby rendering it visible or palpable or . . .).

The fourth region in which Lacan's work has proved consequential for aesthetics and related areas is more oblique but nonetheless crucial. Indeed, Lacan's interest for feminist theory provided the occasion for his first sustained introduction in English—Juliet Mitchell's 1974 *Psychoanalysis and Feminism*. Psychoanalysis and feminism have always entertained an uneasy and contestatory relationship; Lacan can be said to have both renewed and exacerbated this situation. We have seen one instance of this already in Lacan's appropriation to film theory, but the larger promise of Lacan for feminism, where a promise has actually been perceived, has been in his general approach to gender as in some sense a linguistic fact or consequence, the dividedness of gender being for psychoanalysis roughly parallel in its fundamental logic to the dividedness of vision sketched earlier. The Lacanian analysis of gender, whether as something to be built on or argued against (in the best cases there is something of both), has been crucial for a generation or more of French feminists (including Luce Irigaray, Julia Kristeva, and others), has entered in complex ways into feminist art practice (one might instance in France the notion of an *écriture féminine* or in Anglo-American art the work of Mary Kelly and others), and has come to inform much of the most powerful recent work in feminist and related theory (as, for example, that of Judith Butler or Elizabeth Grosz).

[*See also* Irigary; *and* Kristeva.]

BIBLIOGRAPHY

Works by Lacan

Écrits. Paris, 1966. Partial translation as *Écrits: A Selection* by Alan Sheridan (New York, 1977).

Télévision. Paris, 1974. Translated, with additional materials, by Denis Hollier, Rosalind Krauss, and Annette Michelson. (New York, 1990).

Le séminaire. Edited by Jacques-Alain Miller. Paris, 1975–. Vols. to date:
  1. *Les écrits techniques de Freud* (1953–1954). Translated by John Forrester as *Freud's Papers on Technique* (New York, 1988).
  2. *Le moi dans la théorie de Freud et dans la technique de la psychanalyse* (1954–1955). Translated by Sylvana Tomaselli as *The Ego in Freud's Theory and in the Technique of Psychoanalysis* (New York, 1988).
  3. *Les psychoses* (1955–1956). Translated by Russell Grigg as *The Psychoses*. (New York, 1993).
  4. *La relation d'objet* (1956–1957).
  7. *L'éthique de la psychanalyse* (1959–1960). Translated by Dennis Porter as *The Ethics of Psychoanalysis*. (New York, 1992).
  8. *Le transfert* (1960–1961).
  11. *Les quatre concepts fondamentaux de la psychanalyse* (1964–1965). Translated by Alan Sheridan as *The Four Fundamental Concepts of Psychoanalysis* (New York, 1978).
  17. *L'envers de la psychanalyse* (1969–1970).
  20. *Encore* (1972–1972)
(and *l'école freudienne*). *Feminine Sexuality*. Edited by Juliet Mitchell and Jacqueline Rose, translated by Jacqueline Rose. New York, 1982.

Other Sources

Bowie, Malcolm. *Lacan*. Cambridge, Mass., 1991.

Butler, Judith. *Gender Trouble: Feminism and the Subversion of Identity*. New York and London, 1989.

Derrida, Jacques. "The Purveyor of Truth." Translated by Willis Domingo et al. *Yale French Studies* 52 (1975): 31–113.

Felman, Shoshana. "Turning the Screw of Interpretation." *Yale French Studies* 55–56 (1977): 94–207.

Felman, Shoshana. *Jacques Lacan and the Adventure of Insight: Psychoanalysis in Contemporary Culture*. Cambridge, Mass., 1987.

Gallop, Jane. *Reading Lacan*. Ithaca, N.Y., 1995.

Grosz, Elizabeth. *Jacques Lacan: A Feminist Introduction*. London and New York, 1990.

Irigaray, Luce. *This Sex Which Is Not One*. Translated by Catherine Porter with Carolyn Burke, Ithaca, N.Y., 1985.

Kelly, Mary. *Post-Partum Document*. London and Boston, 1983.

Kristeva, Julia. *Powers of Horror: An Essay on Abjection*. Translated by Leon S. Roudiez. New York, 1982.

Lévi-Strauss, Claude. *The Elementary Structures of Kinship*. Rev. ed. Translated by James Harle Bell et al. Boston, 1969.

Merleau-Ponty, Maurice. *The Visible and the Invisible*. Edited by Claude Lefort, translated by Alphonso Lingis. Evanston, Ill., 1968.

Mitchell, Juliet. *Psychoanalysis and Feminism*. London, 1974.

Roudinesco, Elizabeth. *Jacques Lacan: Esquisse d'une vie, histoire d'un système de pensée*. Paris, 1993.

Sartre, Jean-Paul. *Existential Psychoanalysis*. Translated by Hazel E. Barnes. New York, 1953.

Turkle, Sherry. *Psychoanalytic Politics: Freud's French Revolution*. New York, 1978.

Žižek, Slavoj. *Looking Awry: An Introduction to Jacques Lacan through Popular Culture*. Cambridge, Mass., 1991.

STEPHEN MELVILLE

Visual and Literary Arts

Just as Sigmund Freud has had an immense influence on literary and visual culture in the earlier part of the twentieth century, so the psychoanalytic writings of Jacques Lacan have had an impact on the way contemporary cultural critics have been conceptualizing the arts, in particular, those arts concerned with textual and visual media. Of these, Lacan is perhaps most relevant to cinema studies, which, to a large extent, was fateful in popularizing Lacan outside of France during the 1970s. Indeed, Lacanian psychoanalysis still remains central to the study of cinematic aesthetics, just as he remains influential in other domains.

Of immense interest to cinema critics was how Lacanian psychoanalysis could be used to talk about the intersection of the gaze with moving images that comprised a flow of signifiers (any represented entity to which one could ascribe a meaning). This flow was retroactively invested with significance as the image flow and sound track was punctuated by means of the subject's desire. Lacan's theory of retroaction enabled one to think of film not as a stream of moving pictures that are thoroughly decoded as they unfold, like one sentence after another or a series of still photographs, but as a libidinal flow in which the subject locates itself only in retrospect by way of latching on to a signifier that anchors the subject to its desire and, in so doing, makes the film legible from a certain libidinal perspective. Feminist film theorists were intrigued by the fact that Lacanian analysis determines the unfolding of meaning as essentially gendered or as sexually positioned. If a film interpellates the viewer into its flow by means of offering those signifiers whereby the subject latches on to its desire, it is not necessarily the case that this latching on to the signifier is uniform for all viewers. Males and females may not latch on to the same signifiers, or they may latch on differently to the same signifiers. Persons with different sexual orientations will not retroactively insert themselves into the libidinal flow of images identically, because desire is a determining factor. That

this retroactive positing of the desiring subject is an unconscious process of which one is not entirely aware—after all, we do not self-consciously decide what signifier will interpolate our desire at what moment—enabled film critics to more accurately account for the subliminal nature of how cinema is generally experienced. Indeed, it better accounts for *moving* images even as it approaches a theory in which the aesthetic necessarily bears on the libidinal. In *The Acoustic Mirror* (1988), Kaja Silverman makes a similar argument for sound, in particular, the cinematic female voice.

If Lacan's influence on film critics was motivated by the idea that cinema resembled the unconscious somewhat better than Lacan's own invocation of language, Lacan was also influential because he offered the hope of a cinematic analysis that could merge Freud, Karl Marx, and Ferdinand de Saussure. As a mechanical flow of signification, film was considered unconscious, an "automatic process" in the Freudian sense. In terms of Marx, however, film could be thought of as a mode of signifying production, whereas, in a Saussurean context it could be thought of as a "chain of signification" in which, to recall a formula by Lacan, a signifier represents a subject to another signifier. Lacan is key, because his emphasis on the priority of the signifier not only fits in well with the automatic process of turning a film that results in a streaming by of the signifier, but because it accounts for the interpellation of the subject as it emerges in the backwash or silt, as Lacan calls it, of signification. The subject is not indicative, therefore, of someone who exists independently of the work—recall the conception of the "consumer" implicit in television movie criticism—but rather is an effect or production of the work itself; that is to say, from a Lacanian point of view, the subject is residual—an aftereffect of the working of the work.

The aesthetic implication is that a film is not to be approached like an object that exists primarily for the purpose of being apprehended, known, or understood by a detached and disinterested viewer. Instead of thinking of the filmgoer as a fully realized and unattached subject to whom the film is subordinate and, hence, answerable, Lacanian film theory suggests that the viewer is constructed and positioned as an "interested" subject by means of an automatic enchaining of the signifier that follows from an industrialization of cultural production (lights, cameras, projectors, screens, etc.). That the subject is constituted by the work rather than constituting it in a Kantian or Husserlian sense is cardinal to a structuralist view in which emphasis falls on the idea that men and women are the signifying effects of language rather than the makers or authors of language.

In the visual art of figures such as Andy Warhol, Roy Lichtenstein, Cindy Sherman, Sigmar Polke, and David Salle, this retroactive construction of the subject by automatic signifiers of desire blatantly calls attention to itself as a trick or cliché that is essentially a conditioned response. All of these artists have focused on how modes of mechanical reproduction in the arts are capable, even at the crudest of levels, of interpellating subjects into desiring and desired positions, the result being that one can exploit a certain tension between the aesthetically tawdry quality of an image and its capacity to still produce a "good-enough" subject position for purposes of interpellation. Cindy Sherman's and David Salle's increasingly pornographic scenarios have been the logical extension of this line of thinking, because pornography is typical of an automatic and ready-made visual language that easily situates (or, as Lacan says, stitches) the viewer within positions of desire that are the result of cultural conditioning: the repetition of positions that the viewer has already taken up elsewhere in other contexts that are not specifically identifiable as pornographic. This is what Lacan meant by a signifier representing a subject to another signifier: the subject is an effect of the signifier insofar as one signifier occasions the subject position that another signifier will then repeat. Of course, this position is divided according to sex and sexual orientation, or may be available to some and not to others.

Another modality of subject positioning that is central to Lacan's influence on film and the visual arts generally is that of the mirror stage. Borrowed from the research of Henri Wallon, a psychologist at the Collège de France in the 1930s, Lacan posited the idea of a developmental encounter wherein a child first recognizes itself in a mirror *as itself*. This recognition is an illusion, Lacan argues, because the image seen by the child does not literally correspond to itself: mirror images are reversed. The moment of first recognition therefore is mediated by a misrecognition of which the child is entirely unaware. Indeed, this reversed image in the mirror could be considered the image of an other, of someone who is not me. Even if many older children and adults may not notice this consciously, their unconscious picks it up. Whereas in Jean-Paul Sartre's *Being and Nothingness* this kind of experience was thought of in terms of alienation, a moment that the subject could consciously and dialectically transcend, Lacan saw it as the veiled trait of an absolute difference or cut that no dialectic could heal. Hence, the mirror stage is post-Hegelian as well as a rejection of what came to be known as existential psychology, which often studied the subject in terms of alienation.

The mirror stage, however, also concerns Lacan's lectures on mirror apparatuses in which he argued that at the periphery of the mirror plane the subject always imagines an Other who is looking back. Should one incline the mirror plane just right, that Other will come into view even as the image one was looking at (oneself) turns into a blur. Initially, Lacan thought of that peripheral image as a parental one, the image of the subject whom the child imagines she is while looking at herself in the mirror. But, in the lectures on the mirror apparatuses, Lacan suggests that this peripheral other is the persecutionary Other of paranoia. His point is that somewhere in any given field of vision we imagine or

supply this peripheral Other, splitting off a part of our unconscious into the field of vision where we situate ourselves in relation to what we see. Anorexia would be typical of a case in which the person looking in the mirror sees with the eyes of an accusative peripheral Other who is split off, as it were, from the subject's unconscious. That the subject's image is distorted would be a logical consequence of looking awry in the mirror so as to see with an Other's eyes.

Probably the most penetrating use of Lacan's mirror stage concept in an aesthetic context occurs in Christian Metz's *Le signifiant imaginaire* (1977), in which we are told that the cinematic signifier differs from a painterly one in that in cinema the signifier is merely a shadow. In this the cinematic signifier has much in common with a mirror image, which is also in essence a shadow. Yet, unlike the mirror image, the cinematic shadow is not a direct reflection of the viewer; thus, with respect to the cinematic shadow, the viewer is entirely absent. Not to be overlooked, Metz says, is that although the child of six to eighteen months may be able to identify with itself in the mirror, she will not be able to follow a film. Only after the point when the mirror stage becomes foundational for apprehending things in the world in terms of self-identification does it become possible to map the cinematic experience onto this prior mirror stage of development. It is only because of the mirror stage, then, that cinema is decipherable, because cinema operates merely at a second remove. This notion of cinema as a secondary modeling system (the idea is borrowed from semiotics) has important implications for how the signifier turns into an anchorage point on which the subject discovers itself in the wake of its desire, because identification with the signifier is inherently established at the level of the mirror stage, which the film only reenacts at a second remove with the curious twist that the viewer is seeing everything in the field of vision but herself. In other words, the spectatorial me always already exists, because it is pre-given in the mirror-stage phase. The question, therefore, is where the spectatorial me is located psychologically during the running of the film. Clearly, as the spectator watches, the me is being substituted on-screen by images that take its place. Whereas it found itself in the mirror of the mirror stage, it now loses itself on the screen of the cinema. The screen, therefore, is the place of the "not me" where the "me" will be seduced into making an identification. Even this would be relatively simple, Metz argues, if cinema were not, in fact, an enchaining of mirror apparatuses that include storyboard, photo still, movie camera, film, projector, and screen. In other words, it would be problematic to set up a theory of cinema spectatorship wherein the relationship between spectator and screen is more typical of a painterly relationship between viewer and work than of a cinematic enchaining of mirror apparatuses that concerns a rather complex mode of visual production. Again, the consequences for an aesthetic understanding of cinema are evident in that an adaptation of Lacan's thinking can account for numerous perceptual stages and formations and not flatten perception into a simple geometry about whose gaze is looking at what or whom. From a Lacanian perspective, a film aesthetic differs markedly from a painterly one insofar as one has to be alert to the serial production of the image on something approximating an assembly line of apparatuses that automatically reproduce the image.

With respect to the Other in the visual field, Lacan gave a lecture titled "What Is a Picture?" in the famous seminar of 1964, *The Four Fundamental Concepts of Psychoanalysis.* (These concepts include the unconscious and repetition; the gaze; transference and the drive; and the field of the Other.) Lacan's starting point is that if man's desire is the desire of the Other, painting is the showing or exhibition of that desire. Lacan argues that when we look at a painting we notice an "appetite of the eye" that is not originally ours but that we come to identify with as we keep looking at the work, because only in that way can we truly see what is being represented. This Other eye, however, is malign. It is, in short, an "evil eye." Lacan justifies this perception by saying that the evil eye has the function of separating us out by casting a malicious glance in our direction, a glance reminiscent of envy or *invidia* (derived from the root *videre*). The glance of *invidia* is aimed at depriving one of a satisfactory experience of wholeness. It is, in essence, the glance whose purpose is to take something away for no other reason than that someone else is thought to be better off. The one who is separated is made desperate by this envious gaze, and that, Lacan says, is fundamental to the painted work of art whose social function is to veil and mitigate *invidia:* the competition of the gaze for the object of desire, which, in this case, is the painted scene itself. This speaks, then, to what Lacan calls the aggressivity of the eye as a precondition for art, whose function is to hide its malice. Concluding "What Is a Picture?" Lacan says that the eye "cannot be beneficient—it is maleficient."

The Four Fundamental Concepts of Psychoanalysis contains two other very well known theories that are relevant to the visual arts: aphanisis and anamorphosis. Aphanisis concerns the "fading" of the subject as it is carried from one signifier to the next. Even if one signifier represents the subject to another signifier, something is lost in this transference. Lacan calls this *Vorstellungsrepräsentanz*. In the context of cinema, this means that the subject is both an appearance and a disappearance, because our being made conscious of an appearance requires that something slip into the realm of the unconscious.

Anamorphosis corresponds to what one of Lacan's commentators has called "looking awry." In a famous painting by Hans Holbein, there is an elongated elliptical blur in the center of the painting that one does not ordinarily notice. But if one looks at it awry, one sees the deformed image of a skull. Of course, one then only sees that and not the rest of the image. Lacan equates this with the annihilation of the subject, because the Holbein painting is a ruse with which to entrap the gaze in that anamorphic spot where death is absolute. As in his discussion of the Other in painting, the point here is to consider how the gaze is being alienated from itself. Fundamental to an aesthetics of apprehension in Lacan would be the basic painterly strategies of such alienation.

At one point in *The Four Fundamental Concepts of Psychoanalysis,* Lacan makes reference to a concept known as the suture, which he defines as a pseudoidentification. As an aside, Lacan says that the suture refers to a gap between seeing and what he calls the terminal arrest of the gaze. In terms of painting, the obvious example that comes to mind would be Claude Monet's *Nymphéas* at the Musée de l'Orangerie. Well known is that these works encourage seeing and discourage the arrest of the gaze or what Lacan calls the "terminal time of the look" that objectifies and freezes the work as a static image for the sake of mastery. This arrest, according to Lacan, is a mortifying fascinatory effect because it suggests antimovement and antilife. "The moment of seeing can intervene here only as a suture, a conjunction of the imaginary and the symbolic, and it is taken up again in a dialectic, that sort of temporal progress that is called haste, thrust, forward movement, which is concluded in the fascinum" (1978).

A key essay in cinema studies that builds on Lacan's notion of the suture is Jean-Pierre Oudart's "La Suture" (1969). Oudart, who has the concept of aphanisis in mind, argues that whenever we see a film image we are at least subliminally aware of a missing fourth wall: the absence of a dimension. Because the image posits lack, we are immediately aware of its status as signifier that is part of an order of discourse. Suture refers to how the spectator fills in the absence by means of linking the images as if they were part of a complete discourse that explains or fills in the gaps. Crucial to Oudart's application of Lacan to cinema is the argument that signification depends on the absence or cut that the subject/spectator is trying to suture by means of situating the image in an imaginary field that presupposes a discourse that is sufficient or complete enough to stitch parts to a whole. Film critic Stephen Heath (1981) has literalized the concept of the suture by looking for strategic formal cinematic absences that the spectator is required to suture, say, the construction of a central absence (a character, a place) that refuses any singular suturing solution. It is in the failure of the suture that cinema enables us to become aware of how we "construct" the social reality in which we live by means of turning to a discourse that has the function of interpellating subjects into a ready-made narrative, what in the social world itself is called ideology.

In addition to cinema studies and, to a lesser degree, the visual arts, Lacan has been relevant to literary criticism, particularly because he developed a number of striking literary readings, among the most well known a stunning reading of Sophocles' *Antigone*, a crucial reinterpretation of William Shakespeare's *Hamlet*, and an enormously influential reading of Edgar Allan Poe's short story "The Purloined Letter." Like orthodox Freudians before him, Lacan allegorizes literature in such a way that it functions as an extended metaphor for psychoanalytic theory. "The Purloined Letter" is read largely as the repetition of a psychological structure that interpellates the characters into various Oedipal subject positions. As the letter in the story shifts its place from site to site, characters implicated by the letter are positioned and, later, repositioned. Lacan's argument is that the letter is equivalent to a fantasized object, the female phallus, and that the story is an economy wherein the identity of the subject is determined by how an imaginary object is being exchanged. Aesthetically, one notices that for Lacan the Poe story is to be thought of as a series of structural or logical permutations rather than as a poetic text on which we are encouraged to fantasize and free-associate.

Lacan's writings on *Hamlet*, only partially available in English, stress the idea that Hamlet's fantasies are the expression of the signifier of an Other before whom Hamlet undergoes aphanisis or fading. Drawing on the work of the analyst Ella Sharpe, Lacan stresses the feminine side of Hamlet, which is to say, his male hysteria. Subjected to the signifier of the Other, Hamlet is obsessed with a phallic object that he can never appropriate for himself, because it belongs either to the father, the mother, or Ophelia (Lacan argues that the name Ophelia stems from the ancient Greek term *O Phallos*). The women turn out to be variants of the father on whose demand Hamlet is dependent. Indeed, the women are anamorphic to the extent that they are distortions of the primal father who alienates Hamlet from his own desire. Aesthetically, this interpretation would lead to a very different kind of performance of Hamlet than we usually see, because it presupposes characters who are not figures in their own right but subject positions that are constructed in relation to the inaccessible and castrating desire of the father. One is reminded, perhaps, of the aesthetic of Heiner Müller's *Hamletmaschine*, where Ophelia emerges victorious as the persecutionary Other.

The examination of Sophocles' *Antigone* is unquestionably Lacan's most intriguing literary reading insofar as it is predicated on a careful reading of the ancient Greek text and yields a number of surprising interpretations. Situated in the context of a seminar on ethics in psychoanalysis, Lacan is taking issue with Hegel's reading of *Antigone* by arguing that Antigone is no ordinary citizen challenging the state. Given that much of the seminar on ethics in psychoanalysis bears on ethics as an essentially sadistic enterprise, it comes as no surprise in Lacan's final sessions on *Antigone* to learn that Antigone herself is someone who feels neither pity nor fear. For Lacan, the live entombment of Antigone is reminiscent of the Marquis de Sade, for whom such an or-

deal is "number seven or eight" on his list of torments. Lacan argues that because man mistakes evil for good, something beyond the limits of *Ate* (audaciousness, wickedness) has become Antigone's good. This is a good that is different from everyone else's and moves toward *Ate*. The ethics of Antigone rests precisely in this surpassing the limit of *Ate*, a surpassing that takes her beyond the limit of life and enables her to speak as if she were no longer speaking to the living. *Ate*, according to Lacan, concerns the field of the Other and is the place where Antigone is situated. Creon can know nothing of it. Lacan's thesis is essentially that Antigone can only live life from that place where life has already been lost and that she is already "on the other side" of life, a side where life can be lived in the form of something that is already lost. Not only that, but Lacan argues that the violent illumination of this position showers forth a "glow of beauty" that coincides with the moment of transgression and realization of Antigone's *Ate*. This beauty dazzles us, Lacan says, and in so doing separates us from its true function, which is to blind our critical faculties and not question Antigone's unreasonable demand, "I am dead and I desire death."

Although there is much in Lacan's work that touches directly or indirectly on aesthetic questions, there is no overarching aesthetic doctrine. Rather, one has to appreciate a diverse number of analytic approaches that have consequences for those interested in aesthetic problems. That Lacan offers diverse and suggestive analyses from which one can develop one's own thoughts about aesthetics is something that has made him attractive to a wide number of scholars interested in the arts.

[*See also* Film, *article on* Film Theory.]

BIBLIOGRAPHY

Works by Lacan

Le séminaire, vol. 1, *Les écrits techniques de Freud* (1953–1954). Paris, 1975.
Le séminaire, vol. 7, *L'éthique de la psychanalyse* (1959–1960). Paris, 1986.
Le séminaire, vol. 11, *Les quatre concepts fondamentaux de la psychanalyse* (1964–1965). Paris, 1973. Translated by Alan Sheridan as *The Four Fundamental Concepts of Psychoanalysis*. (New York, 1978).
Écrits. Paris, 1966.
"Desire and the Interpretation of Desire in Hamlet." *Yale French Studies* 55–56 (1977): 11–52.

Other Sources

Adams, Parveen. *The Emptiness of the Image: Psychoanalysis and Sexual Differences*. London and New York, 1996.
Copjec, Joan. *Read My Desire: Lacan against the Historicists*. Cambridge, Mass., 1994.
Heath, Stephen. *Questions of Cinema*. London, 1981.
Metz, Christian. *Le signifiant imaginaire: Psychanalyse et cinéma*. Paris, 1977.
Oudart, Jean-Pierre. "Cinema and Suture." *Screen* 18.4 (Winter 1977–1978): 46–89.
Rapaport, Herman. *Between the Sign and the Gaze*. Ithaca, N.Y., 1994.

Silverman, Kaja. *The Acoustic Mirror: The Female Voice in Psychoanalysis and Cinema.* Bloomington, Ind., 1988.

Žižek, Slavoj. *Looking Awry: An Introduction to Jacques Lacan through Popular Culture.* Cambridge, Mass., 1991.

HERMAN RAPAPORT

LANDSCAPE. [*To survey the extensive history of landscape art and aesthetics, this entry comprises four essays:*
Landscape from the Ancients to the Seventeenth Century
Landscape from the Eighteenth Century to the Present
Landscape Architecture
Landscape Assessment
The first essay explores the dual senses of landscape—as art and as natural setting—in the historical periods leading to modernity. The second essay picks up this same narrative and carries it into the twentieth century. The third essay explores the history and current status of landscape architecture. The final essay focuses on one of the central aesthetic issues in all the above discussions: how to assess or evaluate landscapes in their artistic and natural modes. For related discussion, see Environmental Aesthetics; Gardens; Nature; *and* Picturesque.]

Landscape from the Ancients to the Seventeenth Century

The word *landscape,* derived from the Dutch pictorial term *landschap,* was not introduced into English until the 1590s. As this fact suggests, the *concept* of landscape (i.e., the artistic representation of nature in terms of the physical "view"), far from proving a universal of literature and pictorial art, constitutes only one, comparatively recent, form of conceiving and representing the manifold reality of external nature. That the interpretation of nature as landscape is culturally subjective is partly concealed by the ambiguity of the term itself, because *landscape* has come to mean not only a genre of art but an objective expanse of terrain itself. The fact remains however that the emergence of landscape, relatively late in art history, entailed displacement of several earlier modes of representing the physical world. Within a preliterate, animistic worldview, for instance, the earth could not be expressed as a "landscape," because it was conceived as a volatile realm of supernatural immanence, dynamically interactive with human behavior, and thus incompletely representable. As a numinous and mythic field, spatial extension was irreducible to merely visual terms. (Something of the intractable inarticulability of this predescriptive condition can still be felt in the world's oldest poem, the *Epic of Gilgamesh,* whose treatment of space alternates between featureless blankness and the attempted generation of momentous effects from highly cryptic natural reference.) Other interpretations of nature, we shall see, produced formal languages of conceptual symbol, such as the pictographic conceits of pharaonic Egypt or the standardized emblems of Christian iconography. Concern for "landscape," in contrast, proceeds from a worldview recognizably more modern; for the term *landscape,* properly used, refers in art or literature not to one-word references to topography or to landmarks, but to something very distinctive: landscape is the definition of nature that organizes material features of the land into a composite whole set into defined spatial relations. Thus, Christopher Marlowe's poem "Come live with me and be my love / And we shall all the pleasures prove / That valleys, groves, hills and fields / Woods, or steepy mountain yield" gives us units of land, not landscape—unlike John Milton's *Paradise Lost,* which emulates the painter's feat of arranging topographic elements and optical impressions into a compressed unity. This kind of drive to a masterful, measuring, and sensuous recreation of nature within an imposed "frame" flows from the values of relatively secular cultures: confidently materialistic in their voyaging and map making, their scientific inquiry and technological command, culturally oriented toward sensuous pleasure in the particulars of organic life and the scenes of everyday experience. It is in the expansive, adventurist capitals of advanced commercial economies that landscape is born.

Much contemporary theorization of landscape response fails, in discussing the arts, to note this historical distinction between land and the Western concept of land*scape,* and further compounds confusion, in discussing environmental response, by expanding the word *landscape* to mean almost anything (topography, light effects, impressions of the city, landmarks, prospects, the external world, etc). Consequently, there is much disagreement over whether "landscape" response is innate or culturally relative, whether it observes or creates its perceptual field, indeed, whether it is necessarily an "aesthetic" experience at all. It has been suggested that human perception of terrain is unconsciously directed by at least four foundational drives of which the aesthetic is only one; and, although there is no space here to elaborate, because these innate drives are subject to cultural conditioning, they become attuned to and "discover" different elements and aspects of natural reality in various historical periods (see Fitter, 1995).

The elements of landscape focus are deeply culturally subjective, perceptual appraisal of every landscape being itself historically conditioned. Borrowing the terminology of the reader-response school of literary theory, one might say that a landscape is read, by mutable communities of perception, each with its own horizons of expectation. Cultural projection by a spectator will complete a landscape's necessarily partial self-formulation. No poet had ever described the sunset before the painters of Renaissance Venice "discovered" it; and autumn tints in verse are practically an invention of the eighteenth century. Consequently, to understand the emergence and evolution of landscape aesthetics within human perception of natural appearances, one must traverse the varied sceneries of historical development itself.

Prehistory and Early Civilizations. At the hunter-gatherer level, nature's significance had not been as "landscape," a determinate material order separated from a measuring observer, but as a surrounding, indivisible community, animal, vegetative, and divine, collectively centered on seasonal rhythms and the fortunes of fertility. Rather than standing "outside" this community, and conferring "perspective" upon it, human beings saw themselves as but one element of this teeming totality of organic life—christened a "topocosm" by the anthropologist T. H. Gaster. The irreducibility of such a vision to mere spatial extension is perhaps one reason why palaeolithic cave art was spaceless, jumbling acutely naturalistic animal forms at arbitrary angles upon a void. The advent of agriculture in the third millennium BCE, however, fostered a new mentality, distancing and schematic, for agriculture entailed the coercion and transformation of the natural world into a planned and regulated order. As agriculture produced a nature of systematic, standard design, so in art the natural world became correspondingly articulable through fixed schematic forms. As settled agrarian civilizations grew fiercely territorial, moreover, human figures came to require siting: Sumerian and Egyptian vases introduced the ruled groundline, and thus the defined image field: figures now are set in their "own," limited space. These developments—symbolism, groundline, and location—are all dramatically visible in the Akkadian Stele of Naramsin (c.2300 BCE), the world's first rudimentary landscape, which localizes a conquering king and his soldiers in distinctive, specified space: troops ascend on jagged rising lines through a formalized topographic imagery of cone-shaped hill and lozenge trees.

In literature, something of the rigorously functional and schematic representation of the natural world introduced by agrarian values remains evident as late as the eighth century BCE in Hesiod's *Works and Days*. This early Greek masterpiece, a didactic "wisdom" poem on mythological and farming themes, renders nature primarily as an expounded code of seasonal cues to calendar tasks. It is concerned relatively little for sensuous values, and never for an outspread view. Similar priorities were clear, too, in Egyptian tomb paintings, such as that of Ti at Saqqara (c.2450 BCE), which depicted slave-driven flocks and river-wading cattle in the austere mode of pictographs. Undramatic and nonnarrative, the images record the status and possessions of the deceased, rather than comprising self-validating delight in natural scenes. Egyptian royal reliefs furthered such antisensuous symbolization, elevating their hieratic figure beyond organic reality altogether into a timeless, placeless order of higher authority. Imaging eternity in the regal "static stride," pharaonic iconography, from the Palette of King Narmer (2950 BCE) onward, spurned the triviality of natural appearances. Dramatic exception arrived with the astonishing murals of the revolutionary pharaoh Akhenaten (c.1350 BCE), whose artists produced an Egyptian "picturesque": paintings of a new gaiety and lyricism feature birds and animals in papyrus thickets, hunting scenes, and Nilotics of fishing, fowling, and wild bulls leaping in the swamps. Even these, however, do not altogether break from conceptual stylization into sensuous representation. Rather, their limited movement toward naturalism (stylistic realism, aiming at physical verisimilitude) appears to be only the elevation of the ancestral "low style" normally consigned to slaves and animals, although their reverent concern for nature was politically instrumental: their function was to glorify the world of the Sun God (whose reigning son this pharaoh claimed to be) at the expense of underworld and Osirian deities, against whose priests Akhenaten was struggling.

The emergence of large-scale empires and of international commerce revolutionized relations with nature once more. Regular travel and geographic discovery fostered interest in natural variety, while the expansion and prosperity of city life recast rural hinterlands into the complementary recreative role of "countryside." Such a climate stimulated a fresh artistic engagement of nature, oriented toward spectacle and sensory pleasure. In Egypt, tomb paintings during the opulent metropolitan centuries of the New Kingdom now incorporated some sensuous relish of nature, as in their persistent and delicate wealth of tree and plant foliage, and revealed too a new concern for the empirical world, inserting contingent incidents into traditional canonic themes. There nonetheless remained sharp limits to Egyptian advances: despite a new expressiveness, Egyptian painting continued, in its groundlines and blocks of parallel registers, to cling to the wall surface rather than reach into depth. Restrained as it was by the profound traditionalism of pharaonic autocracy, it was rarely free to exhibit that celebration of the humble and transitory things of temporality on which landscape depends.

Assyrian autocracy developed a rather different artistic orientation. The commemorative reliefs in Assyrian royal palaces (ninth to seventh century BCE) unfolded continuous narratives that were secular and dramatic, portraying with a lively naturalism episodes of lion spearing, seige warfare, and the looting of great cities. Topographic indication, through a kind of empirical shorthand of simplified palmate tree forms or stands of uniform reeds, remained, however, entirely subsidiary to the compelling dynamic of savage clash between finely modeled warrior and animal forms. Despite some fascinating experiments in the rendering of large-scale scenic action, such as the "Battle in the Mountains" from the reign of Sennacherib, in which figures escape the usual confines of narrow parallel registers to become distributed instead across a single unified plane, and despite resultant moments of disorganized, almost accidental, rudimentary perspective, Assyrian reliefs developed little interest in spatial recession. They remained instead generally tied both to the groundline and to symbolic conventions such as bands of wavy lines for water or solid backgrounds of scaly pattern to suggest hilly terrain.

The extraordinarily free conditions of Minoan civilization, in contrast, stimulated remarkable advances. In a wealthy commercial society, where nonaristocrats exert cultural power, and the antitraditionalist spirit of the market enjoys comparatively free expression, an art may emerge that favors scenes of a literally "common" life, recreative and routine, over the mythical, esoteric, or propagandist concerns of theocratic and seigneurial tradition. Such a correlation between, in the words of Arnold Hauser, "naturalism and progressive politics, on the one hand, and between formal rigorism and conservatism on the other" (1962), is suggested on the prosperous and comparatively independent Minoan colony of Thera, where pictures of nature, apparently for its own sake, emerge for the first time in Western art about 1700 BCE. Frescoes on the walls of affluent homes depict in impressionistic naturalism riparian scenes of palm trees, monkeys, antelopes, and wild ducks. Mating swallows arc above sprays of blooming lilies atop undulating mountains. Here, finally, is an art of joy in the familiar world, delighting in both a free play of form and the observed detail and color of spontaneous exotic life.

Greco-Roman Landscape. Minoan painting never developed perspective, however, or thus, the composite view. It was Greece, and later Rome, that, innovating these, carried landscape representation to its fullest development in the ancient world. As early as Homer, Greek interest in landscape emerges as a function of a seafaring culture's comparativist orientation, a practical concern for sizing up variations of people and place. In the *Odyssey,* formulaic adjectives encode topographic difference ("deep-soiled Larissa," "rocky Calydon," "Ithome with its terraced hills," and so forth); digressive formulas feature descriptions of place such as the perfect natural harbor in Ithaca where Odysseus is dropped (13.96–105); and the verb *Theaomai* is frequently deployed for "gazing" on objects. The comparativist habit linked human identity to locale, producing "characterological" space: Circe, Eumaeus, Calypso, and Alcinous each have their "own" defined landscape. It may therefore be this ancient connection between demographic acumen and literary mise-en-scène that induced Agatharcus, in 456 BCE, to invent provision of "scenery" for plays. Background perspective scenes on scattered panels on the Gκηνή (or wooden stage), the innovation of scenery was developed by Sophocles. Although often no more, initially, than rudimentary cave-and-vine pictures, the concept was so to inspire Greco-Roman poets and painters that Virgil would term his sumptuously evoked Carthaginian harbor in

book 1 of the *Aeneid* a *scaena*. Vitruvius uses the word 'scaenographia' to indicate any perspective view.

Greco-Roman celebration of the "everyday" in art moved far beyond Minoan levels of specificity. Roman villas came to be adorned with illusionistic window views of citizens strolling by lakesides or of carriages passing before colonnaded facades. Theocritus's *Idylls* (or "Little Poems"), written to amuse at the sophisticated court of the Ptolemies, pioneered a new genre of wittily poeticized snatches of everyday life in diverse milieux; and those set in the countryside (founding the "pastoral" tradition) built a paradisal tone into mock-elegant narratives of poetical herdsmen, often set (as in *Idyll* 7) among careful accuracies of landscape and natural history. Thus, Simichidas and the shaggy, cheese-smelling goatherd Lycidas sing of country life and love en route to a harvest celebration, to sip wine on fragrant reed beds in a rustling grove of elm and aspen, as dove and goldfinch sing above, pears roll at their feet, and all nature smells of opulent, fruit-rich summer. Virgil's *Georgics,* as a nominal farming manual, renders nature as an essentially cyclic, practical reality; yet, as a patriotic anthem to the fertile Italian countryside, it transfigures the spare depiction of Hesiodic tradition into a poetry centered, for the first time in literary history, on sustained and consciously pictorializing landscape description.

With the poetry of Virgil, we move from the Homeric sense of land to the pictorial sense of landscape. Inheriting from Homer antiquity's repertoire of beauty spots, Virgil takes such features as the cradled natural harbor, the "pleasance" or *locus amoenus* of tree, rock, and water, and the "mixed grove" of varied stately trees, and coordinates them into rounded scenic fullness and specified depth. The influence of Hellenistic painting is again felt in Virgilian concern for chiaroscuro (the artful distribution of light and shadow) and subtle light effects, as sunshine flashes on a wall from a swaying bowl of water, or moonlight shimmers on rippling waves. From Virgil, too, came the tripartite division of landscape types still echoed in Renaissance: the leisurely grazing lands and beechen shade of the *Eclogues,* the busy agrarian landscapes of arable land and vineyards of the *Georgics,* and the wild, "epic" terrain of the *Aeneid,* with its rivers winding through primal forest, and its majestic crag citadels. Although natural description is indeed integral to Virgil's neo-Stoic philosophical vision, in most poets of Imperial Rome, landscape motifs are pursued as digressive decoration, a fashion censured by Horace (*Ars poetica* 17) as the sewing of trivial "purple patches" onto dignified work. The vogue notwithstanding, Greco-Roman landscape remains always background to human form and action.

Philosophical rationalism, with its demystifying, materialist forms of thought, helped stimulate landscape art to its zenith as Democritus, Anaxagoras, and others theorized problems of spatial representation in painting. Classical perspective never escaped internal inconsistency, however,

LANDSCAPE: Ancients to the Seventeenth Century. *The Boat of Odysseus Drawn to the Island of Circe,* fresco, Biblioteca Apostolica Vaticana, Vatican Museums, Vatican State. (Photograph courtesy of Alinari/Art Resource, New York.)

and Roman painting (very little Greek survives) swung permanently between naturalism and symbolic modes in which a mountain, for instance, might be personified as a nymph. Nonetheless, under the masterful humanism and ruthless technological dominion of imperial Rome, the archaic topocosmic instinct dwindled to sentimental "pathetic fallacy" in the nostalgic new genre of pastoral poetry, while antiquarian "sacro-idyllic" frescoes (rustic shrines, shepherds, and streamside offerings) decorated wealthy villas (visible today at Pompeii). In Lucretius, above all, rational materialism fostered nature-as-landscape: *De rerum natura* everywhere objectifies the invisible atomic energies of his Epicurean physics in the surging lines and forces of bravura landscape observation.

In late antiquity, as gnostic and Christian doctrines devalued the world of sense perception, and the western empire fragmented slowly into comparatively static economic local-ism, illusionistic space and Hellenistic pastoral were abandoned for an antiempirical art of stylized cryptic form and symbol. Skies were replaced by gold grounds, and individual features such as tree, flower, and creature were laid in spatial isolation across a flat picture surface to project allegoric meaning and transcendental truth in the unearthly dimensionlessness of the Byzantine manner. Classical poetry of place, affectionately sensuous, gave way to fixed schemata of seasonal depiction, consolingly expressive, as civilization foundered, of a providential design indestructible by even the barbarians.

Medieval and Renaissance Foundations. Notwithstanding its extramundane values, Christianity was not intrinsically hostile to sense perception and natural reality. A millennium later, in fifteenth-century Flanders and quattrocento Italy, when expansive, geographically minded cultures of international commerce rose again, an art of landscape more materially solid and detailed than any known to antiquity was to be reborn, within the sensibility of Christian humanism. Christian monotheism had labored to reject animistic beliefs, expelling indwelling presences from its vision of nature: gone were spirits from rocks and nymphs from trees. Rather than being the volatile playground of innumerable supernatural forces, all space, in theory at least, was thus filled and unified by the dependable omnipresence of a single benevolent deity. In consequence, far from reproducing the somewhat unsteady, disunified landscapes of classical antiquity (seen in the flickering thinness of impressionistic frescoes such as the harbor scenes from Stabiae, or in the mistiness and eerie latency of the Vatican *Odyssey* landscapes, where polytheism seems invoked in the very form), Christian art can rejoice in statements of a steady material world of unified extension. One major achievement of Renaissance art was precisely to establish and perfect this unitary spatial field, through the theory and practice of geometric perspective, whose mathematically coordinated, fixed-point recession homogenized space into a stable and systematic whole, in contrast to Greco-Roman "aggregate" perspective, which had always defined space discontinuously through the relations of a multiplicity of bodies.

Furthermore, Christian theology had from the beginning defined creation in terms of an "anagogic" materialism: landscapes, as the didactic pages of the Book of Nature, present material forms whose detailed particularity it is our duty to contemplate because they ingeniously embody symbols or anagoges of divine truth. Within this conception, landscapes sacred and secular are not easily dissociable: as the popularity of landscape grows, *Flights into Egypt* and *Jeromes in the Wilderness* turn flanking hinterlands into packed, even eclipsing, panoramas, which in turn yield spiritual allusion in dead tree and tempting fruit, erring sheep or busy vineyard.

But what saturated the tour de force depths of Renaissance landscape with a tender sense of the divine was light. As a traditional Christian symbol of the indwelling spiritual principle, and as an irresistible primal affection of humanity, the light that brightened and flowed across field and valley reconciled a potentially secular artistic technique to piety. A painting such as Giovanni Bellini's *St. Francis in Ecstasy* (1480–1485) expresses both humanist confidence in the luminous intelligibility of the world and the participation of that world in a higher reality figured in the creative visitation of light.

The growth of metropolitan cultures, distanced from rural toil, also encouraged landscape by idealizing the "restful" countryside. So popular became landscape by the early sixteenth century—when the term *paese* was already in use in Italy to denote landscape as an independent genre—that it was derided as vulgar. Giorgio Vasari sneered that not a cobbler's house was without a German landscape, and Michelangelo Buonarroti disdained the form as trivial.

Conversely, Italian neoclassical theorists praised it as a vogue of the ancients and as a field wherein moderns might surpass antiquity in technical virtuosity (as indeed proved the case with Filippo Brunelleschi and Leon Battista Alberti's pioneering of geometric perspective). Theorists such as Alberti and Paulo Lomazzo were less successful, however, in regimenting landscape (like poetry) into three thematic styles or degrees: the regal (magnificent architecture), comic (realistic scenes of townscape and topography), and satyric (caves, lonely and sinister sites). Artistic practice appears to have paid more heed to market forces, specializing in whatever paid, than to nicety of academic categorization.

As the painting of nature in the Middle Ages and the Renaissance wound a serpentine course from early taste for decorative botanical elements, through swelling landscape settings, to the final status of independent genre, it traversed a wide variety of media. Illuminated manuscripts, particularly prayer-book miniatures, produced the early masterpieces of Jan and Hubert van Eyck. Tapestries, the murals of palaces and villas, and altar panels all bore landscape, which came to flourish, in the period of fullest development and popularity, on great panoramic canvases and in massproduced prints.

Indeed, as naturalism developed in landscape painting from the High Middle Ages through the seventeenth century, so varied and discontinuous was its character that little may safely be generalized. Evolving without steady progression in a mosaic of regional traditions, naturalism emerged practically full-blown at a single miraculous leap in the meticulous miniature panoramas of the van Eyck brothers in the 1420s, and subsequently flourished, or retreated before more traditional symbolic modes, according to patron and region. The emblematic aspect of nature pictures diminished gradually; and increasingly secular priorities are likewise suggested by the form's gradual redirection of primary attention away from *time* (an uncontrollable, "religious" order, of mortality and teleology) toward *space* (the medium of mastery, field of human agency and acquisition). Thus, whereas landscape of the high-medieval period typically focused on divinely imposed seasonal rotation, often setting a zodiac arc of traveling planetary symbols above its busily responsive fields, by the late fifteenth century, landscape content was defined in terms of inventories of objects—rocks, cattle, rivers, groves—and windowscapes might present scenes of checkered urban bustle with no indication of season. Naturalism nonetheless retained marked formulaic tendencies, whether the fantastic medieval rock shapes that served for mountains, persisting even into Joachim Patinier and Pieter Breughel, or the winding rivervalley vistas of the quattrocento. Because this latter scenery of smoothly graduated landscape recession approximated handily to the simple mechanics of fixed-point perspective, and as these were often left to apprentices to paint while the master produced the human figures of the foreground, what often characterizes landscape in even the sixteenth century is a movement of art into landscape more than of landscape into art.

Medieval and Renaissance Landscape Traditions. The complex evolutions of the form during these centuries seem best suggested by a brief indication of nine distinct elements or traditions in landscape painting into which its history seems to be somewhat schematically divided. In monastic flower gardens of the Middle Ages, plants had been chosen for emblematic meaning as much as for visual pleasure; and early medieval paintings of nature, working more by focus on select objects such as flower, tree, and creature than through broad scenic impressions, produced a lasting tradition of symbolic depiction or reading of nature. Lilies and red roses (signifying purity and martyrdom, respectively) are particular favorites, but, influenced by meticulously drawn botanical studies in fourteenth-century Italian textbooks, European tapestries and paintings introduce *millefiori* or thickly flower-starred lawns into paradisal gardens, Annunciations, and Lady-and-Unicorn pictures for decorative richness. Dante Alighieri's Matilda is placed in such a flower-carpeted path (*Purgatorio* 28.40–43); and flower catalogs become a staple of verse natural description (as in Edmund Spenser, William Shakespeare, and Milton, following Virgil) before poetic evocation of "prospect" (deep landscape view) is developed. Emblem books assisting citizens in contemplating the Book of Nature prove vogue as late as seventeenth-century England, when John Denham, meditating the "moderation" of the Thames, gives *paysage moralisé* a political twist in *Cooper's Hill:* "O could I flow like thee and make thy stream/ My great example, as it is my theme:/ Though deep yet clear, though gentle yet not dull,/ Strong without rage, without o'erflowing full."

Seasonal landscape, like emblematic perception a standard descriptive mode of the church fathers, legitimates wide-scale pictorial engagement of the postlapsarian world through an edifying scenery of fallen hardship, mutability, and redemptive human labor. The "Labors of the Months" ran from the pollarding and soil turning of early spring through ploughing and sowing, hay making and reaping, autumnal vine harvest and swine fattening, to winter's swine slaughter and the cutting of firewood. Flourishing in a host of poetic forms, from folk rhymes to descriptive showpieces in narrative verse (as in *Sir Gawain and the Green Knight* or the Prologues to Gavin Douglas's translation of the *Aeneid*), calendar description in painting expanded empiricism to encompass large expanses of fresh natural and everyday observation from the early fifteenth century onward. Its incomparably rich legacy captivates landscape masters as late as Breughel. In two of the earliest masterpieces of empirical landscape painting, Ambrogio Lorenzetti's fresco *The Country of Good Government* (c.1340), and a Book of the Hours, the *Très Riches Heures du Duc de Berry,* illuminated by Herman, Paul, and Jean Limbourg

(1413–1416), calendar scenes combine, however, with a new and primary panegyric impulse to produce an early form of *estates painting.* Here, the city of Siena and the fairy-tale magnificence of the castles of Jean, Duc de Berry, loom above calendar action in what are detailed pictorial encomiums to swelling worldly power. Similarly eulogistic motives inhabit the almost superhuman photographic vistas of the van Eycks: chivalric splendor graces the castle across the lake in the Milan Hours's *Baptism of Jesus,* while the breathtaking minutiae of the *Rollin Madonna* windowscape commemorate architectural monuments achieved by Rollin's statesmanship. In verse, Eustache Deschamps's *Lay de Franchise* (late fourteenth century) waxes empirical in praising the château and parkland of Beauté-sur-Marne, just as in seventeenth-century England, poets pen Country House verse and the earliest topographic paintings focus on regal and baronial palaces.

A fourth landscape tradition is the provision of parerga, or flanking "accessory" scenery, in quattrocento portraits, history painting, and sacred narrative, whose tone and symbolic elements (serene skies or thunderclouds, fruitful orchard or frowning fortress) formed, at least theoretically, commentative *paysages moralisés.* Initially akin to the inclusion in contemporary Italian pastoral verse of subordinate, conventionally mellifluous, and mood-creating scenery, pictorial parerga could grow so lavish as to eclipse their nominal subjects. In this sense, Bellini's *Madonna of the Meadow* and *St. Francis in Ecstasy* are clearly emancipated parerga: expressive "backgrounds" to sacred figures have become, in fact, the substance and center of the composition, as towered cities, nuzzling cattle, and watchful herdsmen, caressed in the movement of a calm and infinitely subtle light from rich Venetian skies, prove spiritual statements in their own right of a harmony of heaven and earth.

The dominant form for the sixteenth century, however, is the vast "world landscape" or *weltlandschaften,* established by Patinier in Antwerp around 1520. Manifestly stimulated by travel and transoceanic discovery, painted by Brueghel, Albrecht Altdorfer, Jacopo Tintoretto, and others and later appropriated by Peter Paul Rubens, these canvases of high-view panorama, often stretching away to remote mountains and seacoast (also called Mannerist landscapes), may improbably weld Flemish villages, vast estuaries, and Alpine pinnacles together in a kind of pictorial equivalent to the large-scale maps in which Antwerp and Amsterdam were coming to specialize. Insofar as these paintings seek to be compilatory and comprehensive rather than topographic transcripts, they recall the Chinese tradition, which had similarly rendered a generalized universal nature, wrapping tiny human figures in philosophical statements of eternal mountain and misty infinity. Yet, the vaunted perspective and hungry encyclopedic detail of Western panorama are sharply distinctive; and seventeenth-century poets such as Milton and William Chamberlayne will seek to appropriate

LANDSCAPE: Ancients to the Seventeenth Century. Claude Gellee Lorraine, *Mill on the Tiber* (c.1650), oil on canvas, 20 × 27 in. (49.8 × 68.6 cm); Nelson-Atkins Museum of Art, Kansas City, Missouri (Purchase: Nelson Trust). (Photograph copyright by the Nelson Gallery Foundation; used by permission.)

for verse the charisma of their illusionistic sweep and teeming detail.

German painters such as Albrecht Dürer and Altdorfer produced around 1500 the first "pure" landscapes, unjustified by emblemata, figures, or narrative, and filled instead with almost expressionistic scenes of northern forest or woodland pond. A nature untamable and uncanny seems suggested in the writhing energies of Altdorfer's dense, dripping tree masses, in etchings and watercolors alike, whose nearest literary parallel lies perhaps in the trackless winter wilderness swallowing the hero of *Sir Gawain and the Green Knight* (late fourteenth century). The canvases of seventeenth-century Dutch landscape, though placid in tone and somber of color, share with German painting both the status of landscape as an independent subject and an antischematic orientation. In Salomon van Ruysdael, Meindert Hobbema, and Esaias van der Velde, an antiauthoritar-

ian preference for low viewpoint, asymmetry, parochial content, and vernacular topography of dune and plain replete with weighty skies embodies the self-consciously dissenting nationalism battling imperial Spain, as well as the love of a countryside won from the sea in massive drainage schemes. Homespun scenes restore patriotic calm in dun wartime chromatics. Finally, the same century produced both ideal and sublime landscape. Whether inspired by lyricism (as in Claude Lorraine, whose vast Arcadian distances in central perspective melt into golden light) or by an austere spirit of logic (as in Nicolas Poussin, whose sternly ordered vistas of balanced landmass and classical architecture recede within rhythmic horizontals and diagonals), the canvases of ideal landscape dream of a golden age of lost natural harmony. Sublime landscape, by contrast, dwells on "Precipices, mountains, torrents, wolves, rumblings—Salvator Rosa," in the words of Horace Walpole crossing the

Alps. The awesome grandeur and "pleasing horror" of sublime landscape sketch a reprise of northern taste with little equivalence in contemporary verse; although, less anarchically, Marc Antoine Girard de Saint-Amant in France and Andrew Marvell in England introduce a "romancey" poetry, whose indulgent, sensuous mood music establishes verse landscape description as a notation of subtle and passionate human feeling. Ideal or sublime, factual or symbolic, by the seventeenth century landscape, like the confident mercantilist humanism that nourished it, had come of age.

BIBLIOGRAPHY

Clark, Kenneth. *Landscape into Art* (1949). New ed. London, 1976.

Fitter, Chris. *Poetry, Space, Landscape: Toward a New Theory.* Cambridge and New York, 1995.

Gibson, Walter S. *Mirror of the Earth: The World Landscape in Sixteenth-Century Flemish Painting.* Princeton, N.J., 1989.

Gombrich, E. H. "The Renaissance Theory of Art and the Rise of Landscape." In *Norm and Form: Studies in the Art of the Renaissance,* vol. 1. London, 1966.

Groenewegen-Frankfort, H. A. *Arrest and Movement: Space and Time in the Representational Art of the Ancient Near East* (1951). Reprint, Cambridge, Mass., 1987.

Hauser, Arnold. *The Social History of Art* (1951). 4 vols. London, 1962.

Kemal, Salim, and Ivan Gaskell, eds. *Landscape, Natural Beauty, and the Arts.* Cambridge and New York, 1993.

Leach, Eleanor Winsor. *The Rhetoric of Space: Literary and Artistic Representations of Landscape in Republican and Augustan Rome.* Princeton, N.J., 1988.

Nicolson, Marjorie Hope. *Mountain Gloom and Mountain Glory: The Development of the Aesthetics of the Infinite.* Ithaca, N.Y. 1959; reprint, Seattle, 1997.

Panofsky, Erwin. *Perspective as Symbolic Form* (1927). Translated by Christopher S. Wood. New York, 1991.

Pearsall, Derek, and Elizabeth Salter. *Landscapes and Seasons of the Medieval World.* London, 1973.

Schama, Simon. *Landscape and Memory.* New York, 1995.

Stechow, Wolfgang. *Dutch Landscape Painting of the Seventeenth Century.* London, 1966.

Williams, Raymond. *The Country and the City.* New York, 1973.

Wood, Christopher S. *Albrecht Altdorfer and the Origins of Landscape.* Chicago, 1993.

CHRISTOPHER FITTER

Landscape from the Eighteenth Century to the Present

The term *landscape* has two main referents. The first is a territory that the eye can comprehend in a single view, such as those celebrated in the English Lake District. The second is a work of art that, usually, depicts a real-world landscape, such as the paintings of John Constable, or, with the coming of photography, the landscapes of Ansel Adams. At times, landscapes have been imaginary, or even fantastic; and they regularly blend an ideal with the real. Landscape is portrayed in literature, word pictures inviting response. Landscape figures in film, even in song, such as Katherine Lee Bates's "America the Beautiful." The landscapes of human geography are often rural scenes, with suggestions of indefinitely continuing nature, such as mountains, forests, rivers, or sky, in the background. There are also seascapes, remembered by Winslow Homer.

Landscape blends nature and human response. Hildegard Binder Johnson says:

> Landscape per se does not exist; it is amorphous—an indeterminate area of the earth's surface and a chaos of details incomprehensible to the perceptual system. A landscape requires selective viewing and a frame. The "line" of a mountain crest, woods, or prairie silhouetted against the sky is imaginary; it lies in the eye of the beholder. Landscapes need . . . the subjectivation of nature.
>
> (1979, p. 27)

The "land" exists, but the "scape" comes with human perspective.

Landscape in the Eighteenth and Nineteenth Centuries. Landscape art was much esteemed in the eighteenth century. Thomas Gainsborough, Richard Wilson, and Joseph Wright of Derby are English representatives. In the nineteenth century, interest remained strong, for example, in John Ruskin's *Modern Painters* (1843), praising especially the work of Joseph Mallord William Turner. Turner and Constable flourished at the turn of the centuries. In France, there was Jean-Baptiste-Camille Corot, followed by Impressionists such as Claude Monet and Pierre-Auguste Renoir. In Italy, Giuseppe De Nittis, Giuseppe Canella, and Giovanni Fattori flourished. Germany produced Caspar David Friedrich. The Romantic movement underlay much of this continuing interest.

In North America, Thomas Cole interpreted the Catskills. With the opening up of the West (especially prior to photography), Albert Bierstadt and Thomas Moran captured the imagination of a broad public. In America, interest was as often in wild as in rural landscapes. In the twentieth century, as artists became more interested in non-representational art, landscape art became less common. Since the rise of environmental concerns, however, from the 1960s onward, interest in landscape aesthetics has vigorously returned, although not especially in landscape painting.

In the eighteenth and nineteenth centuries, a recurrent question was whether art imitates or improves nature. How far is the artist a composer and how far is the artist to present, or re-present, nature? "In the vaunted works of Art, the master-stroke is Nature's part," insisted Ralph Waldo Emerson. Others demurred, thinking artists should be like flower arrangers, using nature but composing in their work. "We find the Works of Nature still more pleasant, the more they resemble those of Art," wrote Joseph Addison. Joshua Reynolds complained that Gainsborough had not looked at nature with enough of "a poet's eye." The eighteenth century typically favored a pleasing prospect, picturesque and

LANDSCAPE: Eighteenth Century to the Present. Paul Cézanne, *Mont Sainte-Victoire* (1902–1904), oil on canvas, 27 1/2 × 35 1/4 in.; Philadelphia Museum of Art: George W. Elkins Collection. (Copyright by the Philadelphia Museum of Art; used by permission.)

rural; the Victorian age became more interested in the sublime. Impressionists accentuated color, line, or form to present nature to the viewer, sensitizing the beholder to what was actually there, which beholders might otherwise miss.

The glory of nature is a characteristic theme; the countertheme is the appropriate presence of humans. The perennial in nature versus its ephemeral passing was an issue, as was the role of humans and their artifacts. Why include castle ruins? Tacitly to suggest the transient quality of human achievements? Or because the ruins gave a lingering sense of the pathetic? The balance between the glorious and the somber in nature was always of concern. How the artist used light, darkness, and shadow was important, accentuating and counterbalancing the "gloom and glory" (Nicolson, 1959) in nature.

Artists in these centuries emphasize the patterned shapes made by the various items of a landscape, the spatial relationships, near and far, the relative intensity of differing elements in the scene, the result perhaps of a stronger color or a more commanding shape. Paul Cézanne might oppose two forms—a roof ridge and a vertical tree—bringing the onlooker to focus there, only later to see colors and optical contrasts. Corot will invite the eye to wander along a flow and swing of shapes; the specific forms are more reticent—awareness of them sharpens later at the onlooker's option.

Turner may use a strong juxtaposition of color, almost to alarm the onlooker, for instance, in light and dark, or red clouds in the sky. Many artists use a strongly colored or strikingly formed tree as a starting point, creating an atmosphere of attention and yet tranquillity.

Such artists will characteristically have a plan, of which the viewer will not be unduly conscious, designed to lead deeper into the landscape reality. Vincent van Gogh might use a wooden fence line, or a dusty road, to invite looking further, or even a walk. There may be figures traveling, perhaps a cart drawn by horses. A river is a frequent device, suggesting a scene going on and on. Bridges over rivers, or boats create a similar atmosphere. Various features will give depth to the picture, something projecting or receding from the otherwise flat plane of the painting, inviting a kind of entrance, or catching up the onlooker into pursuing inquiry about what is going on, what is present in that place. George Lambert's *Woody Landscape with a Woman and Child Crossing a Bridge* (1757) is representative, as is Gainsborough's *The Harvest Wagon* (1767, and again, 1784–1785).

As travel became more affordable, there was recurrent discussion of its benefits in appreciating the actual landscapes, and the role of art. Country gentlemen in the eighteenth century carried small, amber-tinted lenses, "Claude glasses," with which to frame the countrysides through which they rode, making rural nature into art, and then returning to appreciate nature and the human place in it. Another interest was whether nature is a moral tutor. William Wordsworth claimed, "One impulse from a vernal wood, / May teach you more of man, / Of Moral evil and of God, / Than all the sages can." After Charles Darwin, critics held that nature might be glorious but was amoral and taught nothing in ethics. With the turn of the twentieth century, aestheticians were less sure even about the former, and turned their attention to human works of art.

Landscape and Art. In 1966, Ronald Hepburn complained that twentieth-century aesthetics had neglected natural beauty. Aesthetics had become synonymous with "philosophy of art." As a result, aesthetics had become impoverished, deprived of an entire dimension of experience appropriate to the discipline. A pivotal claim is that, despite the tradition of landscape painting, nature does not fit into the categories of art. An evident difference is that natural scenes have no frames or pedestals. Nothing has been composed with the design of being beheld. To the contrary, the processes generating the landscape—at least the dominantly geological, meteorological, evolutionary, and ecological processes—are indifferent to the beholder. The natural landscape is "just there," and the human aesthetic contribution more demanding and more evident. Where one is appreciating landscape architecture, or built landscapes, by contrast, the appropriate response differs radically.

Confronting the natural elements, the framing is up to the observer, who must make sense of the mixed order and disorder on an otherwise value-neutral landscape. Is the scenery interrupted or enhanced when mist drifts across the valley or when geese fly over unexpectedly? By shifting position, foreground and background are recomposed; or, if one waits, shadows will fall. Unlike landscape paintings, the beholder must do the arranging, and yet also is challenged to be, more or less, responsible, even "true" to what is beheld. What is one to make, for instance, of human contributions to the landscape—are they interruptions or complementary?

Landscapes, though a scenic whole, can be appreciated at multiple levels. One has binoculars on a bird that lighted nearby, then the eye falls on a patch of wildflowers, and afterward in sweeping gaze the beholder gathers all into one view. Again, with artworks, one can focus on detail, and then stand back, but there multileveled approaches are much more constrained.

Landscape and Participation. A frequent theme in art is that the observer needs to be detached from utilitarian needs. Appreciating nature, one needs similar distance, and yet there must be participation as well. The experiencer of landscapes is much less a spectator than the observer of landscape paintings. Genuinely experienced landscapes are those of one's resident environment, or at least of an environment in which the visitor is, for a time, immersed.

Arnold Berleant, in his *Aesthetics of Environment,* refuses to place a "the" before "environment" in the title precisely because he does not wish to suggest too much objective environment, but rather seeks the experience of the self in a vivid way, located in the world: "This is what environment *means:* a fusion of organic awareness, of meanings both conscious and unaware, of geographical location, of physical presence, personal time, pervasive movement. . . . There are no surroundings separate from my presence in that place" (1992, p. 34). Experience on landscapes is multisensory. Think of watching a gathering storm over the plains, hearing the thunder, feeling the rain, and smelling the wetted grass.

In the United States, the National Park Service builds roadside viewing sites at the best spots. But perhaps this makes a kind of found art object out of a landscape. Serious landscape appreciation eludes those who wish only to capture the scene in the camera viewfinder, producing something like a postcard, and then to drive off. The ecological processes are pervasively present on the landscape. They are on the landscapes left behind at home. The organic unity in a working landscape is not gained by treating it as scenery, though it might be found if one discovered its ecology, or made a living on the landscape. Such landscape experience spirals around two foci—the one that aesthetic experience must be participatory; the other that nature is objective to such beholders.

Landscape and Human Nature. Certain landscapes have an archetypal appeal, especially semiwooded savanna-type landscapes, where there is a blending of prospect, open vistas, and refuge, places of retreat and safety, a contrast of the horizontal and the vertical, with interest in both foreground and background. Some claim that these are innate preferences, going back to the environments in which early humans evolved. Statistical studies of eighteenth- and nineteenth-century landscape paintings find these features with high frequency. There is a growing body of research analyzing the psychological and health benefits of landscape amenities. There are even therapeutic benefits. Patients recover from surgery more quickly if their hospital rooms have pastoral views, or, failing that, landscape pictures on the walls.

Others are not so sure. David Lowenthal (1978) doubts that innate attractions are significant. If present, they are quite submerged in culturally acquired preferences. Welsh landscapes, he finds, have been variously out of favor, in favor, out of favor, and back in favor again from the 1700s to the present. Landscape appreciation may originate in the human evolutionary past, but that past does not govern all that can now be. Humans appreciate many landscapes that are not "homey," as when drawn to wilderness vistas, or to the taiga, or to tundra. Artists, such as Georgia O'Keeffe, have celebrated the desert Southwest. The Grand Tetons, to which millions are drawn, are not especially livable places.

Landscape Construction and Constitution. With rising doubts about realist epistemologies, many critics are claiming that nature is a social construction. When these ideas are pressed, landscape perceptions become almost entirely reflections of culture, and little appreciation of objective nature remains. The landscape becomes cultural symbol. John Rennie Short concludes a study of the "environmental myths" used in American westerns, English novels, and Australian landscape painting: "My aim is simple, to identify and decode the major sets of ideas about the wilderness, country and city in the belief that there is nothing so social as our ideas about the physical environment" (1991, p. xviii).

Social historians at work on the paintings of the eighteenth and nineteenth centuries now claim that landscape painters served to project a desired social order. They unearth "the dark side of the landscape" (Barrell, 1980). The poor are shaded or placed in the background, the wealthy in a well-lighted foreground. Landscape attitudes are used to justify the human occupation of some territory by legitimating the prevailing social and political powers, or to idealize some community, leaving out or shading this and celebrating that. Interestingly, by this account, the Romanticism often taken to be a protest against the ills of industrialization and urbanization is interpreted as protecting another form of domination.

Positive Landscape Aesthetics. A provocative claim is that natural landscapes in and of themselves are always beautiful. John Muir exclaimed, "None of Nature's landscapes are ugly so long as they are wild." After forty years of painting, Constable agreed: "I never saw an ugly thing in my life." The claim that natural environments are always aesthetically stimulating when appropriately encountered has been reaffirmed by Allen Carlson: "All virgin nature . . . is essentially aesthetically good" (1984, p. 5).

The claim is somewhat surprising because it may simultaneously be held that there is no beauty at all in nature, if humans are absent. *Aesthetic capacities* are found only in beholders although *aesthetic properties* may lie objectively in natural things. There is aesthetic stimulation in the sense of abyss overlooking a canyon, or with the fury of a storm. The experience is in the beholder, but the abyss and the fury (the aesthetic properties) are in nature. The world is beautiful in something like the way it is mathematical. Neither aesthetic nor mathematical experience exist prior to humans. But these inventions succeed because they map form, symmetry, harmony, distribution patterns, causal interrelationships, order, unity, and diversity, discovered to be actually there. Landscapes artists were catching some of this in their composing.

Rather like clouds, which are never ugly, only more or less beautiful, so too with mountains, forests, seashores, grasslands, cliffs, canyons, cascades, and rivers. As an area-level judgment, this claim does not deny that some items in nature are ugly viewed from certain perspectives, only that in a landscape perspective, in locale and ecosystemic perspective, there are only positive qualities—provided one has adequate categories of interpretation. It would seem implausible to say of human works of art that they are never badly done; yet, here the positive thesis claims that virgin landscapes are always (more or less) well formed aesthetically. All landscapes are not of equal aesthetic merit, but the scale runs from zero upward.

Landscape and Natural History. Considerable discussion turns on how far landscape appreciation needs natural science, a connection ignored or left implicit in the preceding centuries, when criteria were more formalist. So far as natural science entered, it was largely geology. The current debate features ecology. Yrjö Sepänmaa (1993) asks whether a scenic landscape is to be approached as one might a work of art, with formal criteria, or whether a landscape is to be viewed as a surrounding, living ecosystem; he prefers the second paradigm. Carlson (1984) argues that aesthetic appreciation of nature requires not so much the categories of formal art as relevant scientific knowledge. A drive through the country is not analogous to a walk through a gallery of landscape paintings.

When J. A. Walter (1983), from England, visited the Rocky Mountains, he was disappointed. The sun was too high in the sky, leaving a flattened effect; there were too many trees, all similar conifers, over great expanses, which was rather boring. There was not enough water. There were no cottages, cows, people, often no signs of humans; the scenery lacked balanced elements of form and color. The scale was overblown, the landscape not complex enough. The scenery was nowhere as stimulating as the English countryside. Walter's critics responded that he was wearing the wrong cultural filter. More appreciation of the American "great open spaces" mentality would help.

Even more, appreciation of the natural history might have educated Walter's eye. The dominant spruce in the montane zone are evergreen, with needles, and shaped so because they can photosynthesize year round and shed snow. Lodgepole pine replaces itself after a stand replacement fire, hence the many trees about the same age. A Rocky Mountain forest does not lack essences in balance; there life persists by a perpetual dialectic of environmental resistance and conductance, wind and water, hot and cold, life and death. It is a mistake to look for a prospect that pleases, using the English categories; here one seeks insight into wild processes that ignore humans completely. That is what is so aesthetically stimulating, positive, though not picturesque.

Neil Evernden (1983) argues that Americans themselves, unless reared on the prairies, have an insufficient capacity to appreciate prairie landscapes. Again, there is too much sun; now the land is too flat, and there is too much grass; homesteads may be infrequent, and there is too much open space, another boring landscape. There is little of evident form; again, no balance. Landscape artists seldom painted prairies. The prairie does not fit well into a camera frame, and tourists head toward the Rockies. Evernden responds that the void and the sky, the wind sweeping the grass, the clouds forming and re-forming, daybreak and dusk, the sense of time and space are just what is to be so positively experienced, if only the passerby will submit to the prairie's regimen. May Theilgaard Watts, *Reading the Landscape of America* (1975), exemplifies this blending of natural history with personal multisensory experiences.

Many people have loved landscapes that they inhabited but knew little about scientifically. At the same time, an animistic worldview ("an enchanted world") seems inadequate for appreciating landscapes, despite the multicultural approaches noted later in this essay. American Indians warned John Wesley Powell, the first European to travel the Colorado River through the Grand Canyon, that he would draw the god Tavwoats's awful wrath. But Powell saw the canyon geologically. He experienced awe at the erosional forces of time and the river flowing. Millions of visitors now experience the canyon appropriately only if they know some of its geology.

Landscape Art and Conservation. A related issue is the relevance of aesthetic appreciation of landscapes to their conservation, both in theory and in practice. Landscape and wildlife artists are, with increasing frequency, claiming that the obligation of an artist is not simply to invite aesthetic appreciation but to move the viewer to act to preserve nature, sustain landscapes, and create a society in harmony with nature. One can no longer afford elitist contemplation. In *Visions of America: Landscape as Metaphor in the Late Twentieth Century* (Friedman, 1994), the contributors find that, though the idyllic landscapes of nineteenth-century painting linger in the modern consciousness, the troubled state of America's landscapes assumes a particular urgency for many contemporary artists.

Landscape is, profoundly, a metaphoric means of eloquently expressing these artists' social, psychological, and technological concerns. Concern for landscape is caring for all life and its processes, as Leopold recognized a half century back. Conservationist journals, such as *Sierra* or *Wilderness,* steadily employ landscape photography in an appeal for saving nature.

Landscapes, Multiculturalism, and a Global View. Pluralism characterizes modern times, and postmodern times even more. Coupled with postcolonialism, the rise of Third World states, and the resurgence of Asian nations, there is a decreasing confidence that European and American value systems are as definitive as once claimed. That forces a reconsideration of how landscapes are appreciated in other cultures. The results have been positive, if mixed.

Yuriko Saito (1985), for example, analyzed how the Japanese appreciation of landscapes differs from that of the European and American West. The Japanese prefer a more manicured nature, often viewing the surrounding landscape from more immediately gardened or landscaped areas in which there is simplified nature, facilitating a focus on abstract expressive qualities, such as the transient character of nature (the petals of cherry blossoms falling, a butterfly flitting past in a scenic view). The Japanese love to dwell on the beauty and pathos in passing life. They are not so interested in either sublime or wild nature, but in a nature with which they can find a harmonious acceptance.

Other critics have found that Hispanic attitudes differ from those farther north, with more emphasis on land and family, responding to personal place and residential identity on a sparsely settled landscape, than on the scenic, the picturesque, the sublime, or the wild. Still others have been concerned to appreciate Native American and Australian aboriginal perspectives, reflected in their art, arguing that the religious nature of these perspectives, perhaps demythologized, can serve as a corrective to overly secular Western views.

Against the requirement that landscapes be seen in terms of their natural history, some critics protest that the scientific perspective is just the way Westerners currently "constitute" their world. There is no reason to think this the privileged view. Aesthetics is nothing that science can discover on landscapes objectively, independently of persons, as though it were some preexisting characteristic. Landscape is land taken into human scope, and nonscientific cultures can do that quite meaningfully by their own standards. Nature is a smorgasbord of opportunities. No one aesthetic response is more or less correct than any other; what counts is the imaginative play. What is remarkable is nature's richness in launching this play. Claims that humans panculturally have genetically innate dispositions to certain landscapes have to be accommodated to multicultural expressions.

The photographs with more aesthetic impact than any "landscapes" in the twentieth century have been the views of Earth from space: "a sparkling blue and white jewel, a light delicate sky-blue sphere laced with slowly swirling veils of white, rising gradually like a small pearl in a thick sea of black mystery" (Mitchell, 1996). More than two hundred men and women astronauts from twenty nations unanimously report being earthstruck. Their photographs have been seen by more than half the persons on Earth, who, almost without exception, have found these whole Earth pictures aesthetically stimulating.

Landscape, the Sublime, and the Sacred. The experience of the sublime was of much interest in the eighteenth century. Mountains, Wordsworth held, were Earth's supreme example of tranquil sublimity. The most famous analysis is that of Edmund Burke. By the twentieth century, the category was thought to have lapsed before a more secular outlook. That judgment has proved premature, or at least arguable. The sublime is perennial in encounter with nature because wherever persons step to the edge of the fa-

LANDSCAPE: Eighteenth Century to the Present. Robert Smithson, *Non-site (Palisades, Edgewater, New Jersey)* plus Map and Description (site) (1968), main work: painted aluminum, enamel, and stone, map: ink on paper; main work: 56 × 26 × 36 in. (142.2 × 66 × 91.4 cm.), map: 1 1/2 × 2 in. (3.8 × 5.1 cm.), description: 7 3/8 × 9 3/4 in. (18.7 × 24.8 cm.); Collection of Whitney Museum of American Art (Purchase, with funds from the Howard and Jean Lipman Foundation, Inc. [69.6a-b]), New York. (Photograph copyright 1997 by the Whitney Museum of American Art; used by permission.)

miliar, everyday world, they risk encounter with grander, more provocative forces that touch heights and depths beyond normal experience, forces that transcend humans both to attract and to threaten. Wild nature is never very modern or postmodern, or even classical or premodern. Aesthetic experience of nature, social construction though it sometimes is, explodes such categories and moves outside culture into fundamental nature.

Almost by definition, the sublime runs off scale. There is vertigo before vastness, antiquity, power, elemental forces austere and fierce, mysterious and enormously beyond human limits. At a forest vista, the trees point upward along the mountain slope, which rises to join the sky, and the scene soars off to heights unknown. One encounters what was aboriginally there in its present incarnation. Viewing the windswept bristlecone pines along a ridge in the Sierras, the aesthetic challenge is conflict and resolution presented on awesome scales. By contrast, fewer persons get goose bumps indoors, even in art museums. A challenge to landscape artists and photographers is to invite such experience, and landscape art with this capacity has proved enduring.

When beauty transforms into the sublime, the aesthetic can be elevated into the numinous. Natural landscapes invite transcending the human world and experiencing an archetypal realm, about as near to ultimacy as one can come in phenomenal experience, especially in an age doubtful of any ultimates. The wildness in, with, and under cultural landscapes, has an enduring capacity to elicit cosmic questions, differently from art and artifacts. An enthralling creativity characterizes this home planet. At landscape range, or, in those global Earth views, an appropriate aesthetics becomes spiritually demanding.

[*See also* Japanese Aesthetics.]

BIBLIOGRAPHY

Andrews, Malcolm. *The Search for the Picturesque: Landscape Aesthetics and Tourism in Britain, 1760–1800.* Stanford, Calif., 1989.
Appleton, Jay. *The Experience of Landscape.* Rev. ed. New York, 1996.
Barrell, John. *The Dark Side of the Landscape: The Rural Poor in English Painting, 1730–1840.* Cambridge and New York, 1980.
Berleant, Arnold. *The Aesthetics of Environment.* Philadelphia, 1992.
Bourassa, Steven C. *The Aesthetics of Landscape.* London and New York, 1991.
Carlson, Allen. "Nature, Aesthetic Judgment, and Objectivity." *Journal of Aesthetics and Art Criticism* 40.1 (Fall 1981): 15–27.
Carlson, Allen. "Nature and Positive Aesthetics." *Environmental Ethics* 6.1 (Spring 1984): 5–34.
Clark, Kenneth. *Landscape into Art* (1949). New York, 1976.
Evernden, Neil. "Beauty and Nothingness: Prairie as Failed Resource." *Landscape* 27.3 (1983): 1–8.
Friedman, Mildred, ed. *Visions of America: Landscape as Metaphor in the Late Twentieth Century.* Denver, 1994.
Hepburn, Ronald. "Contemporary Aesthetics and the Neglect of Natural Beauty." In *British Analytical Philosophy,* edited by Bernard Williams and Alan Montefiore, pp. 285–310. London, 1966.
Hipple, Walter John, Jr. *The Beautiful, the Sublime, and the Picturesque in Eighteenth-Century British Aesthetic Theory.* Carbondale, Ill., 1957.
Johnson, Hildegard Binder. "The Framed Landscape." *Landscape* 23.2 (1979): 26–32.
Kelley, Kevin W., ed. *The Home Planet.* Reading, Mass., 1988.
Kemal, Salim, and Ivan Gaskell, eds. *Landscape, Natural Beauty, and the Arts.* Cambridge and New York, 1993.
Lowenthal, David. "Finding Valued Landscapes." *Progress in Human Geography* 2.3 (1978): 373–417.
Mitchell, Edgar (with Dwight Williams). *The Way of the Explorer: An Apollo Astronaut's Journey through the Material and Mystical Worlds.* New York, 1996.
Nicolson, Marjorie Hope. *Mountain Gloom and Mountain Glory: The Development of the Aesthetics of the Infinite.* Ithaca, N.Y., 1959; reprint, Seattle, 1997.
Orians, Gordon H., and Judith H. Heerwagen. "Evolved Responses to Landscapes." In *The Adapted Mind: Evolutionary Psychology and the Generation of Culture,* edited by Jerome H. Barkow, Leda Cosmides, and John Tooby, pp. 555–580. New York and Oxford, 1992.
Penning-Rowsell, Edmund C., and David Lowenthal, eds. *Landscape Meanings and Values.* London and Boston, 1986.
Saito, Yuriko. "The Japanese Appreciation of Nature." *British Journal of Aesthetics* 25.3 (Summer 1985): 239–251.

Sepänmaa, Yrjö. *The Beauty of Environment: A General Model for Environmental Aesthetics.* Helsinki, 1986; 2d ed., Denton, Tex., 1993.

Short, John Rennie. *Imagined Country: Environment, Culture, and Society.* London and New York, 1991.

Tunnard, Christopher. *A World with a View: An Inquiry into the Nature of Scenic Values.* New Haven, 1978.

Walter, J. A. "You'll Love the Rockies." *Landscape* 17.3 (1983): 43–47.

Watts, May Theilgaard. *Reading the Landscape of America.* Rev. exp. ed. New York, 1975.

HOLMES ROLSTON III

Landscape Architecture

Landscape architecture is the art of arranging land to support human activity and ecological stability. The profession's development was inextricably tied to a number of important aesthetic theories. Although the organization of the American Society of Landscape Architects (ASLA) in 1899 marks the official establishment of the profession, its evolution began during the early nineteenth century in the United States and was greatly influenced by eighteenth-century English explorations in landscape art.

The general approach to landscape design in England shifted dramatically during the eighteenth century from axial and ordered estate designs influenced by the Renaissance and Baroque periods of Italy and France to a new approach often referred to as the English Landscape School style typified by curvilinear forms, asymmetrical balance, wide expanses of turf, and scattered groupings of trees. Employed by wealthy estate owners, landscape gardeners, such as Lancelot (Capability) Brown and Humphrey Repton, transformed a significant portion of the English countryside to resemble an Arcadian ideal. In 1794, Uvedale Price, in *An Essay on the Picturesque,* unfavorably compared the soft, undulating landscapes of Brown with rough irregular picturesque landscapes capable of affecting human emotion with a "tincture of the sublime."

Those ideas about landscape observation and design were brought to the United States during the early national period. Travelers used picturesque terminology to describe the richness and variety of wild and provocative American landscapes. Others such as Thomas Jefferson, in his design of Monticello, directly appropriated English Landscape School design principles.

By the first half of the nineteenth century in the United States, as eastern seaport towns and hinterland settlements grew into crowded and often unhealthy cities, and civilization slowly pushed its way west, writers and artists commented on the importance of nature to the moral, spiritual, and physical health of the people. The transcendentalists, Ralph Waldo Emerson and Henry David Thoreau, directly commented on the importance of nature as a conduit to spiritual understanding. The more rapidly the landscape changed, the more important it became as a subject of intellectual discourse.

An American landscape gardening tradition also developed during the first half of the nineteenth century in direct response to the rapidly changing landscape and the deplorable condition of densely packed urban environments. By the 1830s and 1840s, as thousands recreated in newly built rural cemeteries to escape the deplorable conditions of the city, a number of upper- and middle-class Americans emigrated from crowded urban centers to exurban environments. Those members of a new American gentry looked for guidance in developing their rural estates. Andrew Jackson Downing (1815–1852), in writing the *Treatise on the Theory and Practice of Landscape Gardening* (1841), provided a set of principles for them to follow. The approach to design that Downing promoted represented a simplified (if not simplistic) version of English design principles and picturesque theory. Downing advocated two approaches to what he called the modern style of design: the picturesque and the beautiful. In each case, he was interested in an appropriate fit between architecture and landscape form. Gothic architecture, for example, with an angular composition of multiple gables and dormers fit best with a picturesque landscape comprised of irregular compositions of wild understory, thickets, and craggy coniferous plantings, whereas classical structures were best suited to a beautiful landscape of managed turf, spreading deciduous trees, and soft luxuriant planting beds.

Downing's *Treatise,* which was republished in several editions, sold well throughout the nineteenth century. He also edited a journal, titled the *Horticulturist,* that included articles on agriculture, horticulture, and landscape aesthetics. That publication and other journals such as the *New England Farmer* were carefully read by a new breed of horticulture experts who searched the importance of the landscape to human life. Scientific farming, as the endeavor was called, was really a training ground for the new profession of landscape architecture. The principal pioneers of the profession, Horace William Shaler Cleveland (1814–1900), Robert Morris Copeland (1830–1874), and Frederick Law Olmsted (1822–1900), engaged in pomological experiments on their scientific farms, and wrote about the importance of the landscape to human existence.

The development of landscape architecture was also directly influenced by English picturesque theory and American literary explorations on the landscape and aesthetics. In his books *Social Life and Literature Fifty Years Ago* (1888) and *Landscape Architecture as Applied to the Wants of the West* (1873), Cleveland wrote of the importance of picturesque ideas and commented directly on the writing of Price. In letters to friends and other writing, he discussed the importance of Emerson's work to his aesthetic vision. Copeland and Olmsted were also influenced by Emerson's theories.

Emerson was an important early American aesthetic theorist who wrote about an "organic principle" in concert with the American sculptor Horatio Greenough. Emerson and Greenough discussed the inappropriateness of outmoded and decadent European ideas about aesthetics for America. A new aesthetic, they argued, should emerge from the new land. An essential component of the "organic principle" was "appropriateness" (also called naturalness or essential rightness). In the case of landscape art, the principle meant that design should always be true to place. Both Emerson and Greenough were particularly critical of artificial embellishment (superfluous decoration), claiming that extraneous showy details would be the ruin of any work of art.

Emerson was not simply a distant pundit wrapped in his own esoteric musings. He was convinced of the practical necessity of a new art to help plan for the movement of civilization across the American continent. In "Young American," he wrote that landscape art was "the fine art . . . left for us now that sculpture, painting, religious and civil architecture have become effete, and have passed into second childhood" (1903). In the same piece, he argued that because the landscape was "the appointed remedy for whatever is false and fantastic in our culture . . . the physic and food for our mind as well as our body" (ibid.), it needed to be carefully and artistically presented to the populace by leaders equipped for the task. Emerson's view of the Transcendental artist equipped to guide the masses influenced the early landscape architects, Cleveland, Copeland, and Olmsted. Emerson wrote that the artist was capable of higher perception than the average person, but with that gift came a responsibility to make greater understanding generally available to the mass of society through art.

In 1855, Copeland delivered an address at the Concord, Massachusetts, Lyceum titled the "Usefull and the Beautiful" illustrating a direct affinity to the aesthetic ideas of Emerson. In the same year, Copeland and Cleveland who had recently formed a landscape design partnership, were hired by the Concord Cemetery Committee—Emerson served on that committee—to design Sleepy Hollow Cemetery, which became Emerson's final resting place and the burial site for Thoreau, Amos Bronson Alcott, Louisa May Alcott, and Nathaniel Hawthorne. Sleepy Hollow was intended as a literary garden and a picturesque expression of a Transcendentalist ideal. Emerson's aesthetic principles were followed: the cemetery was designed true to its place; it was carefully set into a natural amphitheater; and native plants were used. Superfluous decoration was avoided, as Emerson had cautioned.

Olmsted left his farm on Staten Island in 1857 to become superintendent of New York's Central Park. He too was a literary man with a number of publications to his credit. In 1852, Olmsted published observations about English parks in *Walks and Talks of an American Farmer in England*. In 1858, he and Calvert Vaux (1824–1895) won the Central Park design competition with their "Greensward" plan. Olmsted not only studied Emerson, but was also influenced

by John Ruskin's writing on the arts. He adopted Ruskin's principles of repose, unity, and infinity and applied those principles in the design of Central Park. Given the deplorable urban conditions of the age, Olmsted artistically and abstractly presented what he believed to be the essential qualities of nature for the improvement of the people. The Central Park landscape, with its dark, wooded glades and vast sunlit meadows, was intended to provide the same healthful effects to visitors as a walk in the country. It was in 1863, when Olmsted and Vaux signed the words *landscape architects* in resigning their Central Park commission, that the fledgling profession was provided with a name.

In the years that followed the design of Central Park, landscape architects continued to think about how nature might be artistically provided for the benefit of the people. The work took place at all scales from residential landscapes to national parks. One of the most important developments was the connected parks system. Olmsted in Boston and Cleveland in Minneapolis devised a scheme whereby a system of parks connected by parkways would provide the armature on which cities would grow. Rather than providing an abstract version of nature in the center of a busy city, the Minneapolis system in particular left large portions of the existing landscape in place so that scenery resembling the original condition of the region might be left for the benefit of future generations.

In the 1890s, Charles Eliot (1859–1897), son of the renowned president of Harvard University of the same name, added the principles of modern science to the aesthetic ideas already in place. Prior to the establishment of university programs in landscape architecture, Eliot, in consultation with his father, crafted his own curriculum at Harvard's Bussey Institute. There, he studied the various sciences (botany, horticulture, geology) that he believed important to the practice of landscape architecture. During the 1890s, Eliot was the landscape architect of the Boston Metropolitan Park System. In 1893, after an intensive study of the landscape within a ten-mile radius of the Massachusetts State House, he campaigned to create a comprehensive system of parklands for the Boston area that included harbor islands and beaches, tidal estuaries, oceanfront beaches, woodland reservations, and urban parks. In promoting the system, Eliot advocated the melding of designed landscapes and existing natural landscapes.

By 1897, when Eliot died of spinal meningitis, a number of new practitioners were designing parks, park systems, suburban communities, cemeteries, and institutional landscapes in the tradition of design established by Cleveland, Copeland, and Olmsted (hereafter referred to as the Olmstedian approach). As the ranks of the profession grew, the direct connection to the in-depth aesthetic exploration of the past waned. Many directly copied styles and applied those styles to the landscape. Although a few practitioners—Warren Manning, Jens Jensen, and Osian Cole Simonds, for example—continued to be innovators after the formation of the ASLA in 1899, many practitioners adhered to a watered-down and frozen version of the Olmstedian approach. The trend toward the blind application of styles was also spurred by the movement toward historicism, particularly after the Chicago World's Columbian Exposition of 1893. During the 1890s, Charles Platt made a name for himself by replicating Italian villas for nouveau riches American clients, and many landscape architects followed his lead into the lucrative business.

Ironically, when the first landscape architecture program in the United States was initiated at Harvard in 1900, in memory of Charles Eliot, little of Eliot's multifaceted approach remained. After professional organization, landscape architects attempted to codify a set of principles that could be easily taught and applied in practice. At Harvard and in the landscape architecture programs that sprang up at a number of land-grant institutions throughout the nation, students were told that they must adhere to the two distinct styles: a simplified Olmstedian approach of soft curving lines and undulating landform, or ordered axial schemes, an American reflection of the Italian Renaissance.

The Olmstedian approach was distilled down even further for popular consumption as landscape architects working through land-grant college extension services traveled with lantern slides to present a residential design template to all Americans who cared. The well-maintained landscapes that resulted were considered outward reflections of the character of individual landowners. Landscape architects were highly successful in promoting an aesthetic ultimately accepted by a large portion of the American populace.

The formal approach to design, which continued during the same period, stifled innovation and undermined any social imperative associated with the profession because much of the work until the 1930s was for the wealthiest of clients. The work was thought to benefit the mass of society only through a trickle-down process whereby even common people would see the elegance of the designs and wish to obtain a simpler version of the grandeur for their own landscapes. Although that rationalization may have eased consciences, the elitist approach to design was ultimately ineffectual in making any significant change to the American landscape. During the Great Depression, much estate work dried up with the loss of private fortunes, and projects funded by the government pulled many landscape architects into the public arena. Although the client base changed, the formal style of design stubbornly remained.

Innovations in modern landscape design occurred in Europe earlier than in the United States. Practitioners such as Pierre-Émile Legrain designed dynamic and unconventional landscapes that resembled Cubist paintings. A few American designers attended conferences on garden art held in Europe and began to experiment with those ideas in the United States. One of the earliest to assay the new style of design was Fletcher Steele. By the 1930s, he flexed his mostly classical designs to include modernist moves. During that period, he also lectured at Harvard, informing students about the new approach.

When the modernist architect Walter Gropius came to Harvard to head the architecture program, landscape architecture students were given yet another example of modernist design to ponder. Despite all of that change, the landscape architecture faculty continued to teach the Renaissance design techniques. Beginning in the late 1930s, three students in the program, Garrett Eckbo, James Rose, and Dan Kiley, were influenced by the new thinking to the extent that they refused to work in the traditional mode, and introduced modernist solutions to the problems given. They published their ideas about modernist design in landscape architecture in the architectural journal *Pencil Points*. By the end of World War II, and throughout the 1950s and 1960s, the profession pushed headlong into modernism. Historicism and history itself in most cases were ceremoniously abandoned by modernist designers. Eckbo published *Landscape for Living* in 1950 and Thomas Church, a California practitioner, published *Gardens Are for People: How to Plan for Outdoor Living* a few years later, in 1955. Both books highlighted the new approach, which emphasized landscapes tailored for each individual client. On the surface, the design process was a rational inventory and analysis leading to an eventual synthesis unique to each site and client. The forms, however, were distinctly modernist. In the place of the axis were asymmetry, richness of color, the melding of spaces, and dynamic and changing forms. The modernist approach was reflected in built works at various scales from the private residence to urban plazas. In the private Donnell Garden in Sonoma, California, Church designed a kidney-shaped swimming pool (with a sinuous modernist sculpture by Adaline Kent) and other biomorphic forms cut into a rectilinear pattern of paving and decking. John O. Simonds designed Pittsburgh's Mellon Square, a public plaza and parking garage rooftop garden, comprised of asymmetrical plantings, an array of colors, and durable triangular terrazzo paving.

The rational strategy in design was taken even further by the late 1960s and early 1970s when modern science was brought back into the mix. Ian McHarg, in *Design With Nature* (1969), wrote that landscape architects must carefully study and better understand the systems of nature prior to any intervention in the landscape. McHarg's ideas greatly influenced the way landscape architecture was practiced in the succeeding years. The profession more frequently engaged in sophisticated analyses of huge parcels of land, and promoted techniques more typical of planning than design.

In 1966, Robert Venturi wrote *Complexity and Contradiction in Architecture*, which marks the movement toward postmodernism in that profession because the work questioned the underlying premises of modernism. By the late 1970s and 1980s, many wondered out loud about the negative effects of modernism in landscape architecture. In throwing out history, they argued, landscape architects had also discarded timeless principles of design that make places humane. The abandonment of those principles and the loss of spatial definition, it seemed, had yielded stark landscapes devoid of richness and comfort. During the same period, others openly challenged the emphasis on rational thinking and the scientific approach promoted by McHarg and his protégés. In response to those developments, Steven Krog wrote an article in 1981 for *Landscape Architecture* posing the question "Is It Art?" The challenge led to wholesale experimentation, which continues until the present time. History was resurrected, but in new and unusual ways.

Additionally, environmental artists argued that bold artistic statements about the human relationship to nature could potentially do more good in educating society about the importance of nature than McHarg's systematic scientific approach. New practitioners—Maya Lin, Martha Schwartz, George Hargreaves, and Michael van Valkenburg—moved to the forefront with provocative designs. Maya Lin's design for the Vietnam Veterans' Memorial stretched the bounds of the time-honored conception of memorial.

Despite the many innovations promoted by an avantgarde in landscape architecture in the 1990s, the watered-down and popularized Olmstedian aesthetic once promoted by the profession remains a commonly held representation of nature and a symbol of good citizenship. Softly undulating landforms covered by verdant lawns and plantings kept in consummate neatness today cover much of the American suburban landscape. Although that abstraction of nature is perceived to be natural by much of society, it is in fact a design cliché and a consumptive environment. Today, a number of landscape architects are focusing on the environmental consequences of the firmly fixed popular aesthetic. Firms such as Andropogon Associates are providing environmentally sensitive designs as an example for others to follow. Other landscape architects seek through their writing to educate the mass of society of the ecological and economic costs of maintaining the ubiquitous landscape. Change will not come easily, however. The popularity of the approach is deeply entrenched in the values of the American people, with roots that run deep in history.

[*See also* Architecture; Emerson; *and* Ruskin.]

BIBLIOGRAPHY

Church, Thomas Dolliver. *Gardens Are for People: How to Plan for Outdoor Living.* New York, 1955.

Cleveland, H. W. S. *Landscape Architecture as Applied to the Wants of the West with an Essay on Forest Planting on the Great Plains.* Chicago, 1873.

Cleveland, Horace William Shaler. *Social Life and Literature Fifty Years Ago.* Boston, 1888.

Downing, Andrew Jackson. *Treatise on the Theory and Practice of Landscape Gardening.* New York, 1841.

Eckbo, Garrett. *Landscape for Living.* New York, 1950.

Emerson, Ralph Waldo. "Young American." In *The Complete Works of Ralph Waldo Emerson,* vol. 1, *Nature, Addresses and Lectures,* edited by Edward W. Emerson, pp. 358–397. Boston, 1903.

Fisher, Irving D. *Frederick Law Olmsted and the City Planning Movement in the United States.* Ann Arbor, 1986.

Krog, Steven R. "Is It Art?" *Landscape Architecture* 71.3 (May 1981): 373–376.

McHarg, Ian L. *Design with Nature.* Garden City, N.Y., 1969.

Nadenicek, Daniel Joseph. "Nature in the City: Horace Cleveland's Aesthetic." *Landscape and Urban Planning* 26.1 (1993): 5–15.

Nadenicek, Daniel Joseph. "Civilization by Design: Emerson and Landscape Architecture." *Nineteenth Century Studies* 10.1 (1996): 33–48.

Nassauer, Joan Iverson. "Messy Ecosystems, Orderly Frames." *Landscape Journal* 14.2 (Fall 1995): 161–170.

Newton, Norman T. *Design on the Land: The Development of Landscape Architecture.* Cambridge, Mass., 1971.

Olmsted, Frederick Law. *Walks and Talks of an American Farmer in England.* New York, 1852.

Pregill, Philip, and Nancy Volkman. *Landscapes in History: Design and Planning in the Western Tradition.* New York, 1993.

Price, Uvedale. *An Essay on the Picturesque.* London, 1794.

Roper, Laura Wood. *FLO: A Biography of Frederick Law Olmsted.* Baltimore, 1973.

Rose, James C. "Freedom in the Garden." *Pencil Points* 19.10 (October 1938): 639–645.

Treib, Marc, ed. *Modern Landscape Architecture: A Critical Review.* Cambridge, Mass., 1993.

Venturi, Robert. *Complexity and Contradiction in Architecture.* Garden City, N.Y., 1966.

DANIEL JOSEPH NADENICEK

Landscape Assessment

In the last few decades, landscape assessment has been conceived of primarily as a practical, empirical endeavor. This emphasis comes into prominence in the 1960s in the following way: A general concern for enhanced "quality of life" brings attention to "environmental intangibles." These intangibles are environmental features traditionally considered immeasurable, including aesthetic qualities as well as others, such as the historical and educational dimensions of landscapes. Moreover, a specific interest in "beautification" and attendant legislation, together with the recognition of the recreational and tourist potential of aesthetic features, helps put a special focus on what one researcher describes as the "visual harvesting of scenic resources." It is assumed, however, that the newly recognized scenic resources must compete with other more conventional environmental resources such as timber, fuel, and food, and, because the former are considered intangibles, a means must be found to make comparisons possible. The challenge is to assess landscape quality by methods involving classification and measurement and thereby make the aesthetic quality of landscapes competitive with other environmental resources.

Responses to this challenge are diverse. One kind of approach grows out of the environmental design and planning disciplines such as landscape architecture. In these approaches, landscape assessment is typically in terms of design features traditionally recognized and valued by these disciplines, such as form, line, color, contrast, and texture, while classification and measurement involves grouping and enumeration of such features in light of established standards and categories. Such assessments are typically site-specific, involving the description, classification, and inventory of the valued landscape features of a particular area. Opponents of this kind of assessment find a number of difficulties. Critics claim that the whole point of classification and measurement is to achieve the kind of objectivity required for comparison with other resources. It is thought, however, that such objectivity is undercut by the site-specific nature of these assessments. More significantly, in design-based assessments the classification and measurement seem to involve little more than grouping and counting, which gives no more objectivity than that which is presupposed by the traditional standards and categories of the design disciplines. Moreover, these standards and categories are claimed to be both overly formalistic in that they involve primarily formal, design-based features and essentially elitist in that they reflect only the aesthetic preferences of landscape professionals in the planning and design disciplines.

The desire for a more rigorous objectivity fuels a second kind of empirical approach to landscape assessment. These approaches are more closely aligned with resource and recreational management fields. The goal is to "quantify" the aesthetic quality of landscapes in order to produce a "measurement of scenic beauty" that will be both site-independent and completely objective. One classic example of this kind of assessment involves what is called a "landscape preference model," which is claimed to predict the "aesthetic preferability" of a given landscape by measuring certain dimensions of a photograph and feeding the measurements into an equation that yields a value for the landscape as a whole. The relevant equation is developed by using techniques such as factor and multiple-regression analysis on the measurements of selected areas and features of sample sets of landscape photographs and the preference rankings of those same sample sets by randomly selected respondents. Such landscape preference models frequently provide impressive predictions of the order in which spectators will rank landscape photographs.

Such attempts to "quantify" the aesthetic quality of landscapes are, however, the focus of a number of objections. For example, it seems that if anything is quantified and thus subjected to objective measurement by these approaches, it is not the actual aesthetic quality of landscapes, but only the overall preference rankings of landscape photographs by randomly selected individuals. The issues concerning the relationships between the two are numerous and difficult. Aside from philosophical problems about the connections between values and preferences, there are problems concerning the correlations between, on the one hand, our multidimensional experiences of real, full-bodied landscapes and, on the other, our looking at two-dimensional, frequently black-and-white photographs. Moreover, these approaches, like those based on the design disciplines, are also open to—although not so obviously so—the charge of being overly formalistic, for the dimensions that are measured in the photographs in question are typically identified only in terms of formal features. Finally, although these approaches escape the criticism that they reflect only the preferences of landscape professionals and are thus elitist, they face the roughly opposite criticism that, in analyzing the aesthetic quality of landscapes in terms of the preferences of randomly selected individuals, they reduce landscape quality to the lowest common denominator.

The number and seriousness of the problems seemingly facing the different kinds of approaches to empirical landscape assessment lead some individuals to the conclusion that the whole area of endeavor is deeply flawed. These researchers claim that the overriding problem is that the field lacks adequate theoretical underpinnings in terms of which research methodologies and techniques can be properly conceived and justified. The field is said by these critics to have a "theoretical vacuum." It is suggested that a general "landscape assessment theory" is required and that such a theory should have at least three features: first, it should be underlying and foundational, involving principles more basic than other landscape research and on which such research can be built; second, it should be organizational and orientational, involving a framework that gives structure and direction to all landscape research; third, it should be explanatory, involving an account of why certain conditions obtain, such as specific landscape preferences and values.

Attempts to address the theoretical vacuum problem have produced further landscape assessment approaches, although typically of a more general and abstract nature than those emphasizing design features or quantification techniques. One set of approaches draws its paradigm from the sciences and focuses on the need to give an explanatory account of specific landscape preferences. For example, one particular version called "prospect-refuge theory" takes somewhat of a sociobiological tack, attempting to explain landscape preferences in terms of the survival needs of early humans for landscapes that provide both a prospect and a refuge. On this theory, landscapes with vistas offering a wide view from a secure position are perceived as aesthetically valuable. Other accounts of this general type rely more heavily on the social sciences, in particular fields such as environmental and developmental psychology. Various studies attempt to find correlations between landscape preferences and factors such as age, sex, race, nationality, upbringing, education, and profession and offer an assortment of features such as, on the one hand, familiarity and habitability and, on the other, mysteriousness and naturalness as the keys to the aesthetic quality of landscapes. The diversity and the sometimes seemingly conflicting nature of the results given by these approaches lead some observers to a degree of skepticism about the ultimate value of this kind of research.

A second kind of response to the theoretical vacuum problem stresses the need for a foundational framework giving structure and direction to the whole body of landscape assessment research. For example, one study distinguishes a number of different approaches and organizes them under four of what it calls "paradigms" in the hope of providing an "overriding system" for the identification of neglected research areas. Three of these paradigms—the expert, the psychophysical, and the cognitive—include, respectively, the above-mentioned research involving design professionals, quantification techniques, and explanatory accounts of landscape preferences. The fourth is called the experiential and includes the research of the landscape critics mentioned below. In a somewhat similar fashion, another study attempts to order the existing research by means of a tripartite structure of human development that involves three different "modes of aesthetic experience" involving, respectively, general biological laws, particular cultural rules, and individual personal strategies. The resultant organizational system is proposed as a "comprehensive theoretical framework for research in landscape aesthetics" that both classifies and orders the work in the field as well as indicating directions not only for promising lines of research, but also for future planning and design decisions. In general, this kind of work is permeated by a vague hope to the effect that once an impressive enough amount of research is brought together in a comprehensive system, then the system itself will perform some kind of overall theoretical function. In spite of this hope, however, these approaches seemingly do little more than organize preexisting work and therefore do not make much progress toward filling the theoretical vacuum.

One problem with both the explanatory accounts of landscape preferences and the organizational frameworks for landscape assessment research, as well as with approaches emphasizing design features or quantification techniques, is that they do not provide a means for justifying specific aesthetic assessments of landscapes. Although they are rich in orientational, organizational, and explanatory power, they are poor in justificatory power. For example, an explanatory account such as prospect-refuge theory may tell us why a certain landscape feature is preferred, but it does not demonstrate that such a feature is preferable, just as an explanation of why, for example, tobacco is desired does not demonstrate that it is desirable. But presumably, demonstrating that a specific landscape feature is preferable, rather than simply explaining why it is preferred, is what is required to justify a landscape assessment of that feature. Moreover, the way in which such explanatory accounts operate misleadingly suggests that they do indeed fulfill a justificatory role. This is because the causes that may explain, for example, why an individual prefers a certain landscape feature frequently involve the same phenomena as those referred to in the reasons that may justify that individual's assessment that the feature is preferable. It is easy, therefore, to mistake explanation for justification, concluding that the former does the job of the latter. In part for this reason, justificatory theory seems to be somewhat overlooked in the otherwise comprehensive work on landscape assessment. Perhaps what is needed to fill the theoretical vacuum is a theory of justification.

Landscape assessment is a relatively new field of inquiry, however, and within any field justificatory theory takes time to develop. Such theory is typically not successfully imposed from without, but rather grows naturally within a field as it matures into a proper discipline of its own. In landscape assessment, it is seemingly developed mainly by individuals who have devoted a whole lifetime to the experience and the appreciation of the landscape and to deep, reflective thought about the nature, meaning, and value of such experience and appreciation. Such researchers may be characterized as environmental or landscape critics; their contribution to the field is more aligned with the humanities than with the sciences. It frequently involves sensitive and detailed studies of particular landscapes, dwelling on features such as uniqueness of setting, expressiveness of site, and "sense of place." There is a growing body of such careful qualitative studies of landscapes, and they, perhaps more than other kinds of research in the field, demonstrate a means by which to justify specific assessments of particular landscapes. Thus, they complement the other work in landscape assessment and take one step toward filling the theoretical vacuum.

Unlike approaches to landscape assessment that emphasize design features or quantification techniques or explanations of preferences, however, the research of landscape critics does not constitute empirical landscape assessment in the conventional sense. Thus, whether and to what extent these studies provide a satisfactory means by which the aesthetic quality of the landscape may be directly compared with other environmental resources remains an open question. Moreover, this research must also confront the charges that it is site-specific and elitist. Nonetheless, insofar as these qualitative studies of the value of landscapes contribute to a theory of justification and provide a means by which to justify specific aesthetic assessments of landscapes, they thereby also provide a means by which to objectively assess the landscape. Objectivity resides not exclusively in quantified measurement, but also in properly justified judgments of quality.

[*See also* Evaluation.]

BIBLIOGRAPHY

Altman, Irwin, and Joachim F. Wohlwill, eds. *Behavior and the National Environment.* New York, 1984.

Arthur, Louise, Terry C. Daniel, and Ronald S. Boster. "Scenic Assessment: An Overview." *Landscape Planning* 4 (1977): 109–129.

Appleton, Jay. *The Experience of Landscape.* London, 1975.

Bourassa, Steven C. *The Aesthetics of Landscape.* London, 1991.

Carlson, Allen. "On the Possibility of Quantifying Scenic Beauty." *Landscape Planning* 4 (1977): 131–172.

Carlson, Allen. "On the Theoretical Vacuum in Landscape Assessment." *Landscape Journal* 12 (1993): 51–56.

Cats-Baril, William L., and Linda Gibson. "Evaluating Aesthetics: The Major Issues and a Bibliography." *Landscape Journal* 5 (1986): 93–102.

Elsner, Gary H., and Richard C. Smardon, eds. *The Proceedings of Our National Landscape: A Conference on Applied Techniques for Analysis and Management of the Visual Resource.* Berkeley, 1979.

Gold, John R., and Jacquelin Burgess, eds. *Valued Environments.* London and Boston, 1982.

Groth, Paul, ed. *Vision, Culture, and Landscape: The Berkeley Symposium on Cultural Landscape Interpretation.* Berkeley, 1990.

Jackson, John Brinckerhoff. *The Necessity for Ruins and Other Topics.* Amherst, Mass., 1980.

Jakle, John A. *The Visual Elements of Landscape.* Amherst, Mass., 1987.

Kaplan, Rachel, and Stephen Kaplan. *The Experience of Nature: A Psychological Perspective.* Cambridge and New York, 1989.

Meinig, Donald W., ed. *The Interpretation of Ordinary Landscapes: Geographical Essays.* New York and Oxford, 1979.

Nasar, Jack L., ed. *Environmental Aesthetics: Theory, Research, and Applications.* Cambridge and New York, 1988.

Penning-Rowsell, Edmund C., and David Lowenthal, eds. *Landscape Meanings and Values.* London and Boston, 1986.

Saarinen, Thomas F., David Seamon, and James L. Sell, eds. *Environmental Perception and Behavior: An Inventory and Prospect.* Chicago, 1984.

Sadler, Barry, and Allen Carlson, eds. *Environmental Aesthetics: Essays in Interpretation.* Victoria, British Columbia, 1982.

Sell, James L., Jonathan G. Taylor, and Ervin H. Zube. "Toward a Theoretical Framework for Landscape Perception." In *Environmental Perception and Behavior: An Inventory and Prospect,* edited by Thomas F. Saarinen et al., pp. 61–83. Chicago, 1984.

Zube, Ervin H., Robert O. Brush, and Julian G. Fabos. *Landscape Assessment: Values, Perceptions and Resources.* Stroudsburg, Pa., 1975.

ALLEN C. CARLSON

LANGER, SUSANNE KNAUTH (1895–1985),

American philosopher. In the middle of the twentieth century Susanne Langer was perhaps the most influential aesthetician in American academia and the one most read by the general public. Langer's *Philosophy in a New Key,* published in 1942, became required reading in many humanities courses in American colleges and universities. This was followed in 1953 by *Feeling and Form,* also widely read, which applied her theory to a variety of art forms. Essays and talks elaborating her theory were collected in *Problems of Art* (1957) and *Philosophical Sketches* (1962). In her final work, *Mind: An Essay on Human Feeling* (1967–1982), she used her aesthetic theory as a touchstone for understanding a range of fields, including linguistics, history, and biology. But from the start, Langer (who had earlier written *The Practice of Philosophy* and *Introduction to Symbolic Logic*) had a broad range of philosophical interests. *Philosophy in a New Key* was subtitled *A Study in the Symbolism of Reason, Rite, and Art.* Thus, aesthetics was never for her an isolated field. It was linked with studies of myth, magic, religion, biology, anthropology, psychology, logic, and linguistics. The breadth of her concerns, her eloquent writing style, and her thoughtful aesthetic theory all contributed to the popularity of *Philosophy in a New Key,* which is still in print and has been translated into a dozen languages.

Langer did not claim originality for her "new key," which was to give art equal status with science as symbolisms providing meanings for human understanding. She acknowledged Ernst Cassirer and his *Philosophy of Symbolic Forms* as a major influence. Because it linked art theory explicitly with contemporary philosophical concern with signs and symbols, her aesthetics is sometimes called "semiotic."

While acknowledging important differences among various intellectual symbolizations (mythology, religion, language, science, art), Langer claimed that they shared a common purpose in attempting to represent and/or elucidate features of the world. In the case of art, according to Langer, the features are human feelings and emotions; and this is why art is in some ways more fundamental and more important than other symbolizations. In addition, art's symbolization is primarily presentational or nondiscursive, as opposed to the discursiveness that is the normal characteristic of languages—with their more or less conventional and cumulatively established lexicons, grammars, and syntaxes—and the forms of knowledge expressed in language. The ultimate model of discursive language is science, where words and formulas attempt to provide objective, emotionally neutral descriptions of the world and its contents. Language can be used nondiscursively, but then it becomes metaphor and, ultimately, poetry (or a part of some other art form such as drama, opera, or literary fiction).

Because music was, for Langer, the paradigm case of artistic symbolization, it makes sense to elucidate her theory mostly by reference to that art form. (Langer's theory has been widely accepted among music educators as their main aesthetic position, as articulated by Bennett Reimer in *A Philosophy of Music Education.*)

Langer thought past and current aesthetics of music inadequate to explain the great value of music for people of all cultures. Formalists restricted themselves to analyses of musical structure, as if music presents nothing more than arrangements of tones, chords, and silences. Expressionists, on other hand, promoted fanciful associative daydreaming, romantic notions about composers' lives, or implausible and misguided causal psychological theses. Surely there must be a better explanation for what makes music vital in the lives of so many people. Langer concluded that the explanation lay in music's capability of being a form of knowledge. Although critical of their interpretations of the term, Langer lauded the central labeling of art by Clive Bell and Roger Fry as "significant form."

In terms of music, the essence of Langer's theory might be summed up in a sentence: musical passages are meaningful insofar as they articulate feeling or present feeling-semblances, and they do this by means of formal properties (tonal tensions and rhythms) that resemble the formal properties (tensions and rhythms) of feelings. She put it this way in *Feeling and Form*:

> The tonal structures we call "music" bear a close logical similarity to the forms of human feeling—forms of growth and of attenuation, flowing and stowing, conflict and resolution, speed, arrest, terrific excitement, calm, or subtle activation and dreamy lapses. . . . Such is the pattern, or logical form, of sentience; and the pattern of music is that same form worked out in pure, measured sound and silence. Music is a tonal analogue of emotive life.
>
> (1953, p. 27)

Langer was early on taken to task by other philosophers who objected to her use of the term *symbol*, tied by them to concepts such as denotation, signification, formal assignment, and reference. But she had announced in *Philosophy in a New Key* that she was talking not about referential symbols but about "presentational" ones, and she reiterated her differentiation in subsequent essays. (A lecture on this topic published in *Philosophical Sketches* is titled "On a New Definition of 'Symbol.'") As a gesture of compromise with her critics, she often tried to substitute other terms for *symbol*: *vital import, form, semblance, articulation*. But *symbol* kept creeping back into her writing, and appears in *Mind*, her final opus.

What are presentational symbols, and how do they differ from referential or discursive ones? The latter stand for, point to, name, or are about something else. When discursive symbols are linguistic, then in ordinary and (especially) scientific usage they are claimed to apply to facts—and they are barely attended to while we concentrate on those facts. Typically, such symbols are composed of more elementary symbolic parts (sentences, clauses, words) corresponding to the parts of the facts. By contrast, presentational symbols, according to Langer, give us their meaning directly in their very phenomenal form; when apprehending them aesthetically, we concentrate on them and do not move on to consideration of a meaning separate from that which is immediately given. In the case of artworks, each is "a single, indivisible symbol, although a highly articulated one; it is not . . . composite, analyzable into more elementary symbols" (1953, p. 369).

Although, in *Feeling and Form*, Langer tended to substitute terms such as *image, illusion, virtual object*, and *semblance* for *presentational symbol*, she had already used that terminology in *Philosophy in a New Key;* and perhaps those terms serve her theory better. Although one might not immediately know what to make of the claim that a presentational symbol has meaning because of its form, it is plausible (perhaps even obvious) that an image does. In explaining how we distinguish between a cat image and a rabbit image, for example, Langer had said that we do so on the basis of the differences between a cat form and a rabbit form—quite apart from the issue of whether either image represents a biologically real animal. Such an image is distinct from the physical materials that, along with a perceiver, provide its ground. "A picture is neither a person nor a vase of flowers. It is an image, created for the first time out of things that are not imaginal, but quite realistic—canvas or paper, and paints or carbon or ink" (1953, p. 46). In attending to a good representational painting, we become engrossed in the visual depiction—which may be a totally fictitious scene.

But there is something more: the painting simultaneously presents us with a feeling-depiction. This operates in all art forms. Music makes it most apparent, because so little music is representational in the customary sense. Langer held that, like rabbits and cats, feelings have forms whereby we identify them as feelings, even as certain kinds of feelings. Just as sometimes we can put a depicted thing in a family (calling it, e.g., "a Siamese cat"), we might classify a feeling-semblance as, for example, happy or sad. A depicted cat without much detail, however, may not warrant any classification other than being a cat, while a polka-dotted depicted cat may defy being put in any recognizable cat family box. Feeling-semblances may likewise be unclassifiable. But, in either case, that does not prevent us from seeing one as a cat depiction, the other as a feeling-semblance. Indeed, Langer at least implied, such specificity or ambiguity is of relatively little concern in our involvements with art paintings or art music.

Our experienced world is much populated by images: in family photo albums, advertisements, seasonal songs. But, according to Langer, only some images (or presentational symbols) are works of art—namely, those that present a feeling-form. Music most notably does this: presenting us with images of sadness, joy, poignancy, despair, sprightliness, and the like. These feeling-semblances belong to no one, but rather inhere in the music. The composer (or performer) may or may not have experienced something similar, and listeners may or may not have similar feelings while listening or in their past; all of that is irrelevant to aesthetic experience. What is relevant is the recognition of a musical feeling-semblance, usually a highly complex one and one for which verbal descriptive labels are always inadequate.

What is true of (good) music is true of all art forms, though their modes of expression may differ in important respects. The central feature of a work of art is its import, a depicted feeling or emotion that is attended to in the very act of attending to the work. In aesthetic appreciation, they cannot be distinguished. When we attend to the feeling-semblance of an artwork, we are engrossed in the work (the image, the virtual object), not diverted from it, and vice versa.

One stated implication of this thesis set Langer apart from many previous aestheticians and art theorists (though it harmonized with the position of the New Critics of literary theory): that creative causes and responding effects are largely or wholly irrelevant in aesthetic theory. This is at odds as well with much present-day aesthetic (and especially literary) theory. But Langer makes an eloquent and persuasive case, and contemporary thinkers might well profit from reading or rereading it.

We can and do consider many discursive statements ("The cat is on the mat," "D-Day took place on 6 June 1944," "2 + 3 = 5," "E = mc²") quite apart from the speaker's intention or our response, except for the customary one of relating the statement to a fact. Proper art appreciation, according to Langer, similarly ignores the artist and the response (and, further, relating the image to a fact). Although a work of art *might* be "an utterance, giving vent to its author's feelings," or it *might* be "a stimulus, producing sentiment in the spectator," or it might be both, for serious art criticism and philosophical esthetics these hypotheses are "silly" (1953, p. 18). The hypotheses psychologize the problems of aesthetics with hypotheses that are "empty . . . because there is no elementary success that indicates the direction in which neurological aesthetics could develop" (ibid., p. 38). As Langer had said about music in *Philosophy in a New Key*: "Its 'meaning' is evidently not that of a stimulus to evoke emotions, nor that of a signal to announce them; if it has an emotional content, it 'has' it in the same sense that language 'has' its conceptual content—symbolically" (1957, p. 218). She believed that good critics tend to discount the feelings or emotions of the creator and perceiver and "treat the emotive aspect of a work of art as something integral to it, something as objective as [its] physical form, color, sound pattern" (1953, p. 18).

Partly in response to her own critics and perhaps more as an outcome of rethinking her earlier statements, Langer seemed to move toward a position that put even greater distance between her and traditional expressionists. For one thing, her definition of "feeling" was enlarged, in the opening essay of *Philosophical Sketches*,

to designate *anything that may be felt*. In this sense it includes both sensation and emotion—the felt responses of our sense organs to the environment, of our proprioceptive mechanisms to

internal changes, and of the organism as a whole to its situation as a whole, the so-called "emotive feelings." We feel warmth, pinprick, ache, effort, and relaxation; vision is the way the optic apparatus feels the impingement of light, and hearing is the way the auditory structures feel sound waves; we feel bodily weakness or high tonus, and we feel expectation, frustration, yearning, fear, satisfaction. All these ways of feeling have characteristic forms.   (1962, p. 8)

These forms can be given artistic expression. For another thing, the notion of a depicted feeling was sometimes replaced by something more akin to simply a dynamic organic process, what Langer often called "living form." In *Feeling and Form,* for example, she wrote: "Feeling, life, motion and emotion constitute [the] import [of music]"; "'Living form' [in art] expresses life—feeling, growth, movement, emotion, and everything that characterizes vital existence"; The experiences relevant to the articulation of art "are the rhythms of life, organic, emotional and mental. . . . Altogether they compose the dynamic pattern of feeling" (1953, pp. 32, 82, 240–241). "Living form" was raised to the status of a chapter title in *Problems of Art* and the first volume of *Mind*. The latter work is replete with such usage: "The art image has an irresistible appearance of livingness and feeling . . ."; "If a piece of art is to express the pulse of life that underlies and pervades every passage of feeling, some semblance of that vital pulse has to be created by artistic means"; "The artist's symbolic projection provides a principle of analysis applicable to the actual living form his work reflects" (1967, vol. 1, pp. 96, 99, 272).

With these moves Langer seemed at times to depart radically from her earlier theorizing. The "forms of feelings" became *primarily* aspects of the "forms of vital processes" such as growth, motion, development, and decline. Music provides not so much images of feeling as illusions of organic vitality. Perhaps that is an even larger claim, though a more defensible one.

Among challenging issues that even sympathetic readers of Langer find difficult to resolve are clarification of the notion of forms of feelings; why the dynamic patterns of artworks should be claimed to manifest forms of feelings rather than other, nonfeeling dynamic processes; whether the alleged images of feeling or "living form" are anything more than simply dynamic properties of artworks; and how Langer's theory can be used to explain or inform judgments of aesthetic merit.

Although aestheticians have moved off in some different directions, questions about the nature of artistic expressiveness remain. Langer's proposals, ignored by some, have not been refuted. Even in the burgeoning subfield of philosophy of music, it is not apparent that proponents of versions of expressionism have surpassed her; many fall far short of the clarity, thoroughness, and beauty of her theorizing.

[*See also* Cassirer; Emotions; *and* Music.]

BIBLIOGRAPHY

Works by Langer

Philosophy in a New Key: A Study in the Symbolism of Reason, Rite, and Art (1942). 3d ed, Cambridge, Mass., 1957.
Feeling and Form: A Theory of Art Developed from Philosophy in a New Key. New York, 1953.
Problems of Art: Ten Philosophical Lectures. New York, 1957.
Philosophical Sketches. Baltimore, 1962.
Mind: An Essay on Human Feeling. 3 vols. Baltimore, 1967–1982.

Other Sources

Budd, Malcolm. "Music as Unconsummated Symbol." In *Music and the Emotions: The Philosophical Theories,* chap. 6. London and Boston, 1985.
Davies, Stephen. "Music and Symbols." In *Musical Meaning and Expression,* chap. 3. Ithaca, N.Y., 1994.
Hansen, Forest. "Philosophy of Music Education in a Slightly New Key." *Philosophy of Music Education Review* 1.1 (Spring 1993): 61–74.
Howes, Frank. *Music and Its Meanings.* London, 1958.
Nagel, Ernest. "Review of *Philosophy in a New Key.*" *Journal of Philosophy* 40.12 (10 June 1943): 323–329.
Price, Kingsley Blake. "Is a Work of Art a Symbol?" *Journal of Philosophy* 50.16 (30 July 1953): 485–503.
Price, Kingsley. "Philosophy in a New Key: An Interpretation." *Philosophy of Music Education Review* 1.1 (Spring 1993): 34–43.
Reimer, Bennett. *A Philosophy of Music Education.* 2d ed. Englewood Cliffs, N.J., 1989.

FOREST HANSEN

LAOZI. *See* Chinese Aesthetics, *overview article; and* Daoist Aesthetics.

LATIN AMERICAN AESTHETICS. [*To explore the field of Latin American aesthetics, this entry comprises two essays:*

Latin American Aesthetics and Modernity
Twentieth-Century Latin American Aesthetics

The first essay examines the very question of a Latin American aesthetic by discussing its place in the tradition of modern Western aesthetics. The second essay is an overview of some of the key theorists in twentieth-century Latin American aesthetics.]

Latin American Aesthetics and Modernity

The question of a Latin American aesthetics is, in the first place, a problem of its insertion in the larger domain of a general theory of aesthetics. Whether it is at all possible to qualify such a theory from a territorial or culturally specific perspective would depend on the way in which that theory is characterized. For this reason, one may begin by taking some distance from the strong universalistic claims of an abstract theory and rather see aesthetic theory as a historically changing field of conceptual problems—in a way consistent with the early critical theory program as expressed by Max Horkheimer: "there is no abstract theory of aesthetics, but rather the theory always corresponds to the history of an specific period" (Wiggershaus, 1994, p. 195).

Characterizations of its domain and scope have never achieved complete agreement among philosophers, even if the inquiry is restricted to modern times. From classical concerns with the problem of "beauty" to the eighteenth-century preoccupation with questions of "taste" and aesthetic judgment, to the Romantic demands of an inner connection of art with life and the importance of subjective experience, to the often contradictory indictment of "representation" and meaning of formalist aesthetics, thinking about art or "aesthetic questions" has, nevertheless, retained a core of themes and concerns that set some flexible limits to its conceptual field. Thus, one could think of this "conceptual arena" along the lines of a "family resemblances" model, assuming no fixed or metaphysical "essences," but rather shifting arrangements of interrelated problem domains. One might see "aesthetics" as a philosophical reflection on a historically specific practice or set of practices from which certain normative orientations (rules of production and appreciation of certain cultural artifacts—objects and events) are established. In this manner, not only is the practice of artistic production and reception historically specific, but also, to some extent, the categories to conceptualize it are cultural constructs with a history of their own.

There are other ambiguities in the use of the term *aesthetics* in addition to the shifts and turns of its historical meaning. On the one hand, it is employed as a descriptive term, as the distinctive mark for the artistic production of a style or of a given period, as in the "aesthetics of Cubism" or the "aesthetics of Mexican mural painting." On the other hand, it is assigned to the general theory of art and the philosophical study of aesthetic problems (perception, appreciation, the conceptual status of fictional works, and so on). In the first case, we are dealing mainly with questions of classification and evaluation of artistic works, with "rules" and prescriptions of the work of a group of artists, or with questions of influences or originality that usually belong to the territory of art criticism. In the second case, thinking on aesthetic matters understands itself as a theory that postulates general validity. These two uses of the term *aesthetics* are interrelated, but it is important to maintain an analytic distinction between the two insofar as one wants to preserve a general theory—as a historically changing field of conceptual issues—and, on the other hand, to account for the historically specific nature of some concrete aesthetic "prescriptions" and criteria of evaluation of artworks, although the question of a culturally specific "aesthetics" could be asked, in turn, about these two domains; that is, it could be a problem of the conceptions and aesthetic propositions of an artistic movement, or it could be something of a more general nature.

In this manner, if one accepts the historicity of aesthetic thinking, one would have to conclude not only its temporally restricted validity as an epochal phenomenon, but also its inextricable dependency on European history in a more general sense. Neither "art" nor "aesthetics" is a "neutral" concept that could immediately or unproblematically claim universal validity. Thus, the question of whether one can talk about "aesthetics" outside of the assumptions of its internal history has to be placed within the more general framework of the relations of European history with that of the rest of the world, that is, with "non-Western" cultures, or with those that as former colonies have an ambiguous status as ethnically and culturally mixed peoples, somehow "marginal" to mainstream Western civilization. In other words, one has to take into consideration the internal relations between aesthetic theory and the concept of modernity.

The very idea of "history" as an evolutionary concept, as "progress," or as the story of the civilizing process has been assigned restrictively—from G. W. F. Hegel to Karl Marx to contemporary theorists of modernization—to Europe and North America (the United States and Canada), the only former colonies that achieved "first world" status. This problem is particularly acute when attention is turned to the question of modernization, for this establishes in an explicit way both criteria of inclusion and of exclusion. From the perspective of modernization (and of cultural modernity), Latin American countries are only partially or insufficiently "modern." Their subordination to European development is simply regarded as a fact, as an uncritical assumption that permeates most accounts of economic and political history—as, for example, in the entry on the topic "modernization" in the *Encyclopedia of the Social Sciences* (1968, vol. 10, p. 387). Thus, it is rather unclear what one is talking about when one speaks of a Latin American aesthetics (both as art and as theory). Are its original contributions those that come close to the achievements of the leading Western avant-garde movements, or rather those that are "different," the premodern "other" of modernity?

As is well known, both characterizations are common in the history of Latin American art. In the first case, it is a chronicle of the process of becoming "truly modern"—for example, of the introduction of abstract painting as a reaction to the Socialist Realism of postrevolutionary muralist painting. In the second, it is a way to describe distinctive cultural motifs from an externalist perspective: as the "exotic," the "primitive," or "folklorism," assuming the point of view of the foreign observer, even by some local art historians. In both cases, these interpretations imply serious distortions as accounts of actual events, because Latin American artists belong to the same general development of artistic modernity and have learned from avant-garde movements, but, at the same time, they have made original contributions that influenced European and North Ameri-

LATIN AMERICAN AESTHETICS: Latin American Aesthetics and Modernity. Rufino Tamayo, *Woman in Grey (Mujer en gris;* 1959), oil on canvas, 76 3/4 × 51 in. (195 × 129.5 cm); Solomon R. Guggenheim Museum, New York (FN 59.1563). (Photograph by David Heald; copyright by the Solomon R. Guggenheim Foundation, New York; used by permission.)

can artists as well. An often overlooked fact is the influence of Mexican painters (Diego Rivera, José Clemente Orozco, David Alfaro Siqueiros) on North American artists in the 1930s. For example, Jackson Pollock, Philip Guston, Isamu Noguchi, and Louise Nevelson, among others, were not only influenced by them but actually worked in collaboration with Rivera and Siqueiros (Paz, 1993, p. 323). Thus, the interconnections between the different strands of aesthetic modernity are more complex and intertwined than what some simplistic Eurocentric versions of this history might lead one to believe, as is perhaps the case in most accounts of postcolonial history, as suggested by Edward Said in the *Oxford Amnesty Lectures* of 1992 (in Johnson, 1993, pp. 175–205). We must, then, start with a profound revision of received "interpretations" of cultural history in order to be able to answer the question of the originality of art and aesthetic ideas.

An alternative understanding of the connections of Latin American art with aesthetic modernity is found, however, in the actual work of artists, specially among some Mexican and other Latin American painters and writers of the first decades of the twentieth century who set for themselves the task of finding ways of defining in their own terms the access to "modernity"—even if the search for a postcolonial cultural identity began earlier, with the wars of independence in the early nineteenth century. This quest had to follow its own political agenda as well. With the end of colonial rule and the constitution of a modern nation-state came the demands for a symbolic representation of a multiethnic society that was perceived as more progressive politically than the previous system of racially based privileges (for the Spanish and those born in Spain), and with the Mexican Revolution of 1910 came the need to incorporate the Indians—at least programatically and symbolically—as full citizens of the new postrevolutionary republic. Thus, the demands for cultural legitimation of the new regime not only offered new "themes" to the artists (from pre-Hispanic civilization and contemporary Indian popular culture) but implied a new understanding of the past, more inclusive and heterogeneous in its sources than the European counterpart. Instead of a radical departure from tradition (of European modernity), the new regime attempted a reconstruction of a sense of continuity with the pre-Hispanic past, a recovery of non-Western sources of identity not as "antimodern" but rather as part of the same historical process of becoming a new, modern, nation.

As Octavio Paz, among others, has observed, the recovery of the past (pre-Columbian architecture and popular arts as well as other aesthetic motifs and attitudes from Mexican Indian culture) by Mexican painters came in part from having learned the lesson of "Western aesthetic curiosity," that is, from the adoption of the relativizing gaze of European cosmopolitanism (Paz, 1993, p. 184), and as such, it was "modern" in its own way. For many Latin American artists of the beginning of the century, living in Europe (Paris) opened up new ways of looking at their own cultural differences, while the experience of the Mexican revolutionary movement granted a new legitimacy to "Indian" and popular themes that became part of their aesthetic explorations ever since.

Consequently, the idea of the modern project implied for these artists more than just economic modernization (or, in the artistic domain, more than the adoption of new techniques). It was an entry into a universal process; it would mean "to insert the nation in the modern world," but at the same time, in the words of Paz, it would have to mean "a reconciliation with our own tradition" in order to become "truly modern." This reconciliation with a conflicting identity differs, in turn, from the image of the (utopian)

"reconciliation with nature" of European aesthetic discourse in that its object is not a remote "abstract" nature but rather concrete "nature" as it appears in the artists' actual, culturally heterogeneous past: as an encounter with a rediscovered sensibility, and as a problematic recovery of myth.

This recovery was not a "natural" form of continuity with tradition either, for tradition was brutally interrupted by European colonization (thus, it was not simply a premodern or "traditional" attitude toward tradition); it was instead a conscious, reflexive (and modern) attempt to reconstruct a fractured identity, one that had to take into account the colonial past as well, but from the new critical perspective acquired in the Mexican Revolution. One must also keep in mind the fact that not all the artists or the leading artistic movements shared a unified political outlook or agreed on issues of cultural identity. The richness and heterogeneous character of these cultural resources (pre-Hispanic and colonial, premodern and modern) gave rise to a variety of cultural interpretations and aesthetic proposals. As might be expected, these attempts, which can be observed in the visual arts and literature of the beginning of the twentieth century, are riddled with internal contradictions and incompatible claims and expectations. These are unavoidable in a cultural project that both attempts to find its way into the modern world and at the same time needs to define its cultural identity by way of recovering its "difference," its cultural specificity rooted in a non-European past.

These problems result, however, not only from a conceptually unclear appropriation of the concept of European modernity but from some tensions internal to this concept as well. The question of the entry into modernity puts forward an interesting philosophical problem: the concept of modernity presents itself as context-transcending, as a radical departure from the traditional understanding of local cultures, but at the same time, in the cultural domain—specifically in art and aesthetics—sets a list of prescriptions and prohibitions (a departure from "representational" not just "figurative" art, and so on) that arose from the particular history of art movements in Europe, and, for that reason, their status as "candidates" for generalizable validity stands in need of further justification. In other words, a distinction must be made between artistic modernity as a historical event and those general attributes of the process of (cultural) modernization that may claim universal validity.

A full revision of the self-conception of European modernity cannot be offered here, however. We can only suggest that a revised interpretation of the history of aesthetic modernity can be attempted not only from the perspective of "postmodernity" (or "antimodernity") but from the horizon of these "other" modernities as well. From this, one may conclude that the history of European art and aesthetic thought is not a unified development; nor can it be reduced to a simplistic opposition between "modern" and "anti-modern" tendencies. Rather, from the new perspective gained, one can see it as contingent process in which a general will toward "rationalization" and secularization in the arts (and an increased "autonomy" of an art concerned with itself and its own formal means—away from older forms of representation) runs a parallel course to the expression of the demands of a sensibility that feels dissatisfied with the development of modern life and the reduction of experience to the pursuit of practical ends. One can find strong affinities between the development of some of these "impure" strands of modernity both in Europe and in the United States and Latin America, especially among the last two, because they share at least a consciousness of being part of the "New World," and at some point in their history—in the 1930s—they also shared an interest in searching for their non-Western cultural origins. Paz has suggested that the program of American Abstract Expressionism demarcated itself from European abstraction in that it not only aimed at archetypes and geometry but looked for "concrete sensations" and "emotions"; if North American abstractionism came from Europe, "their Expressionism came from Mexico" (Paz, 1993, p. 227).

Some may find this suggestion disquieting, not because of the implied idea of a mixed, "impure," and contingent historical development—"postmodern" thought has already made that acceptable—but because it links the "modern" with the "premodern" in unorthodox ways. Perhaps, however, it is time to conclude the cycle of the idea of cultural history as "progress," assigning to the latter a univocal character. Thus, one could understand, on the one hand, that the ideals of freedom (in the public as well as in the private domains of experience) as authentically universal ideals may be realized at any corner of the "globalized" culture, and, on the other, that the connection between "the end of representation" and "modern" art is not a necessary one, but rather, one that belongs to the repertoire of "prescriptions" of the "aesthetics of modernism" as a concrete historical development.

Then, one can see as a progressive sign the artistic will to preserve in the sphere of art those experiences neglected or suppressed by modern life—even if the final determination of its moral or political significance requires contextual specification. One may regard the selective (and reflexive, critical) appropriation of attitudes and practices of other cultures (not only of their decontextualized and thus "sanitized" cultural objects, as formalist aesthetics would have it) as legitimate ways of learning, as forms of cultural "resistance" that belong as well to the actual history of avant-garde artistic movements—for example, in their demands for a form of "disclosure" of truth in authentic artworks (something entirely consistent with the aesthetic program of a great deal of Latin American artists, even if in a variety of ways—from the political agenda of Mexican muralist

painters to the exploration of Indian myths and motifs of Rufino Tamayo, Carlos Mérida, or Toledo, and so on); or in the acknowledgment that the acceptance of art as an "illusion" does not necessarily dictate an ascetic renunciation of "meaning" but rather a search of new ways of continuing aesthetic "play" (as the strong influence of Surrealism in Latin American painters testifies, from Wolfgang Paalen and Gunther Gerzso, to Leonora Carrington, Remedios Varo, and Frida Kahlo, or Roberto Matta, among others) (Rodríguez Prampolini, 1969); or, in architecture, the respectful and attentive way of looking at other cultures of a Louis Kahn, who wanted to join together aspects of "sedimented" traditional ways of building (that came from hundreds of years of experience in the use of materials and light, in the proportions and relations of inner and outer space, etc.) with the technical and formal means of modern architecture, in ways that resemble the work of Luis Barragán, the Mexican architect, as observed by Peter Frampton (Saito, 1992); finally, as a contribution to debates on aesthetic theory in support of a nonreductionist philosophical aesthetics, as in the arguments against formalist reductionism of Joseph Margolis (1980), and of a pragmatic conception of the universality of art—as an ability for resignification and openness to reception and appreciation beyond its horizon of production—and a plural conception of ways of entry into the historical process of a modernity that has not yet exhausted its possibilities.

[*See also* Comparative Aesthetics.]

BIBLIOGRAPHY

Adorno, Theodor W. *Ästhetische Theorie.* In *Gesammelte Schriften,* vol. 7, edited by Gretel Adorno and Rolf Tiedemann. Frankfurt am Main, 1970. Translated by Robert Hullot-Kentor as *Aesthetic Theory.* Minneapolis, 1997.

Charlot, Jean. *The Mexican Mural Renaissance, 1920–1925.* New Haven, 1963.

Johnson, Barbara, ed. *Freedom and Interpretation: The Oxford Amnesty Lectures of 1992.* New York, 1993. See "Freedom and Interpretation," by Edward Said, pp. 175–205.

Margolis, Joseph, *Art and Philosophy.* Atlantic Highlands, N.J., 1980.

"Modernization." In *International Encyclopedia of the Social Sciences,* vol. 10, pp. 386–409. New York, 1968.

Orozco, José Clemente. *An Autobiography.* Translated by Robert C. Stephenson. Austin, 1962.

Orozco, José Clemente. *El Artista en Nueva York.* Edited by Luis Cardoza y Aragón and Jean Charlot. Mexico City, 1971.

Paz, Octavio. *Los Privilegios de la Vista,* vol. 2, *Arte de México.* In *Obras Completas,* vol. 7. Mexico City, 1993. See chaps. 4–6.

Rivera, Diego. *Textos de Arte.* Edited by Xavier Moyssen. Mexico City, 1986.

Rodríguez Prampolini, Ida. *El surrealismo y el arte fantástico de México.* Mexico City, 1969.

Saito, Yutaka, ed. *Luis Barragán.* Tokyo, 1992. See "Luis Barragán, the Mexican Other," by Peter Frampton.

Wiggershaus, Rolf. *The Frankfurt School: Its History, Theories, and Political Significance.* Translated by Michael Robertson. Cambridge, Mass., 1994.

MARÍA HERRERA

Twentieth-Century Latin American Aesthetics

Twentieth-century Latin American aesthetics has been largely shaped by the relationship between traditionally ahistorical aesthetic principles or issues—such as beauty, creativity, artistic production, and aesthetic judgment—and ongoing social-historical debates about culture, education, and national identity. Among the principal theorists in this aesthetic tradition are the philosophers and social theorists José Vasconcelos, Antonio Caso, Alejandro Octavio Deústua, José Carlos Mariátegui, and Samuel Ramos.

The work of the Mexican philosopher Vasconcelos (1882–1959), a member of a generation for whom the Mexican Revolution (1910) was particularly significant as both a historical and a cultural event, typifies the practice of linking up aesthetic, metaphysical, anthropological, and cultural considerations. In a number of metaphysically oriented works, including *El monismo estético* (Aesthetic Monism, 1918) and *Todología* (1952), Vasconcelos develops an aesthetically arranged cosmology based on the notion of the design and ultimate harmony of different metaphysical elements (Vasconcelos, 1986). In *La raza cósmica* (The Cosmic Race, 1925), he prophesies an ultimate and superior fusion of races to emerge from the Hispanic American mixed races of South America. The mission of Latin Americans, he argues, will be to bring the world to a higher civilization based on universal principles of love, in contrast to the ethnic and nationalist egoisms that have prevailed in the European and Anglo-Saxon civilizations. Given its positive appraisal of Latin American culture, this view achieved widespread popularity throughout the region.

Linking aesthetic activity to the principle of disinterested action, the Mexican philosopher Caso (1883–1946), also influenced by the revolution, offered a carefully crafted perspective on aesthetic activity as central to civilization. In "La existencia como economía, como desinterés, y como caridad" ("Existence as Economy, Disinterest, and Charity," 1916; 3d ed., 1943), Caso argues that "life is always bound to interest" (Caso, 1986, p. 49), which may be calculated in utilitarian terms. At a superior level of human activity, however, aesthetic contemplation and disinterested acts of love are able to transcend the Darwinian struggle of all living beings for existence. Caso's views on aesthetics are linked to an anthropocentric personalist metaphysics ultimately based on Christian ideals. This position demonstrates the universalizing and important roles that art and aesthetics can play in the lives of Mexicans, or any other group of people, insofar as aesthetic awareness is deemed an important capability and element of the human condition.

A more conservative view of aesthetics was developed by the Peruvian philosopher Deústua (1849–1945). Appealing to an idealist metaphysics, Deústua argued in *Estética general* (General Aesthetics, 1923) that aesthetic judgment was wholly disinterested, a characteristic that linked aesthetics to the highest ideals of freedom (Deústua, 1986). Insofar as this view could be interpreted to mean that both aesthetics and freedom involved the release of the subject from all interested activity, including work, Deústua's position came under attack by one of Latin America's foremost Marxist thinkers, the Peruvian Mariátegui (1894–1930). Arguing that work, if only liberated from conditions of alienation under capitalism, was one of humanity's most creative activities, Mariátegui denounced Deústua's presumed philosophical idealism in terms of its political effects, which he suggested were to legitimate a "feudal" and "aristocratic" order in Peruvian national politics and higher education at a time when the forces of modernity were introducing more liberal or even revolutionary perspectives (Mariátegui, 1971, pp. 115–121). Mariátegui, in turn, offered a pro-indigenous unorthodox socialist position on art and myth, arguing that, without a will to believe and to create, there could be no genuine social revolution. His ideas on art and social change were put into practice with the publication of the influential journal *Amauta* (1926–1930).

The preoccupation with the disinterested quality of the aesthetic experience, found especially in Caso and Deústua, and criticized from a socialist position by Mariátegui, is indicative of whether aesthetics is read from an Enlightenment (universalist) or post-Enlightenment (historicist) theoretical position. Trying to mediate between these two tendencies is the work of the Mexican philosopher Ramos (1897–1959), a member of the second postpositivist generation in Mexico and author of works on Mexican culture and humanism. In *Filosofía de la vida artística* (Philosophy of the Artistic Life), Ramos argues that, despite the multiple forms that art can and does take both within a culture and across different cultures, human beings have an artistic sensibility that allows them to unify the differences under the general category of art (Ramos, 1950, pp. 15–17). In *Estudios de estética* (Aesthetics Studies), incorporating an earlier piece on Rivera's work (Ramos, 1935), the case for including Mexican art into the Western canon is made by appealing to universal qualities of the work of art present in Rivera's painting. Ramos distinguishes Rivera's ideological message from his artistic accomplishments, arguing that aesthetic merit resides only in the latter (Ramos, 1963, p. 254). Nevertheless, he also favors the notion that there is such a thing as a national aesthetic sensitivity, or a sensitivity expressing a certain aesthetics of national identity, as can be found in modern Mexican painting and in Rivera's work. The reason that some of the Mexican bourgeoisie found Rivera's art disturbing, he notes, is that it conveyed an image of Mexico that they wished to deny (ibid., pp. 220–221, 232–233). Ramos's measured acceptance of elements of Mexican nationalist, popular, and indigenous cultures under the category of universal aesthetics shows the creative adjustments that some Latin American intellectuals have made when negotiating the relationship of their own national or cultural heritage (in this case, pre-Columbian and Mexican history and artistic production) to the rest of the Western canon.

A transgression of the bourgeois cultural and academic orders reaching continental proportions took place beginning in the 1960s as a result of the Cuban Revolution of 1959. The Cuban cultural institute, Casa de las Américas (House of the Americas), was established in 1960. It has served as a catalyst for publications, competitions, and prizes for original work in Latin American and Caribbean literature. International conferences of writers and critics have been hosted periodically through this and other cultural centers in Cuba, drawing the participation of intellectuals from other parts of the hemisphere. With a progressive political climate later opening up in Chile until the death of the Chilean Socialist president Salvador Allende in 1973, conditions were ripe for the development of Marxist aesthetics in conjunction with Latin American intellectual and cultural protest movements.

In *Las ideas estéticas de Marx* (Marx's Aesthetic Ideas) (1965), the Spanish-born philosopher Adolfo Sánchez Vázquez, professor of aesthetics at the National Autonomous University of Mexico in Mexico City, argues on behalf of an undogmatic Marxist aesthetics, criticizing György Lukács's concern for realism as too narrow a reading of Karl Marx's ideas on art (Sánchez Vázquez, 1965, pp. 40–41). In an interesting critique of the alienation of art and the artist under the system of capitalist production and consumption, Sánchez Vázquez also argues that aesthetic enjoyment is characteristically unpossessive and therefore defies the capitalist laws of private property (ibid., pp. 228–234). The Marxist idea that art should not be exhibited, performed, or sold just for the benefit of the bourgeoisie's education and enjoyment was put into practice by the policies of the Cuban Revolution. Education and art in Cuba were subsidized so that their benefits could reach the widest number of people in both urban and rural areas. The distinction between high and low art was undercut when, as a norm, the popular sectors of society were able to attend performances and exhibitions previously reserved for the middle and upper classes, one of whose social benefits was to be associated with the patronage of the arts. The notion that the popular sectors were also capable of artistic creativity led to the increased valorization of forms of popular art and culture, including the African-Latin and African-Caribbean traditions of dance, music, poetry, and art. Although some prominent intellectuals such as the Mexican Octavio Paz favored dialogue with the West on relatively traditional grounds, a radical critical consciousness of Latin America's economic and cultural dependence on, and protest against, Western dominance gained visibility in the 1960s and 1970s (Fernández Retamar, 1986, 1989). One of

LATIN AMERICAN AESTHETICS: Twentieth-Century Latin American Aesthetics. Frida Kahlo, *Suicide of Dorothy Hale* (1939), oil on masonite panel with painted frame, 20 × 16 in.; Phoenix Art Museum (Gift of an Anonymous Donor). (Photograph courtesy of Phoenix Art Museum.)

the artistic genres that emerged in the 1960s out of the specific historical conditions of the Latin American region came to be known as the "New Latin American Cinema."

In a manifesto titled "The Aesthetics of Hunger," first published in 1965, the Brazilian film director Glauber Rocha claims that hunger is not only a symptom of the economically disadvantaged Latin American societies but the actual "essence" of these economically dependent (colonized) societies. An aesthetics of hunger is an aesthetics of violence against all forms of colonialism, both past and present. In film, this means the filmmaker's resistance against commercialism, exploitation, and the "tyranny of technique," as well as the engagement in raising consciousness about the misery endured by Latin Americans and how to fight such misery (in Chanan, 1983, p. 13). In "For an Imperfect Cinema" (1970), the Cuban film critic Julio García Espinosa argues against perfectionism in technique and style, noting that once such mastery is achieved, the filmmaker risks becoming part of an established elite who no longer relates to the audience as a subject, but as an object. "What can be done," he asks, "so that the audience stops being an object and transforms itself into the subject?" (in ibid., p. 29). García Espinosa takes the universality of art to mean not that "everyone must share the taste of a few, but that all can be creators of that culture" (ibid., p. 30). The Argentine director Fernando Birri's maxim, "Filming realistically, filming critically, filming underdevelopment with the optic of the people" (ibid., p. 12), set the tone for the general objectives of this critical genre, whose scope encompassed gender and race issues and extended to some Latino filmmakers in the United States, as is demonstrated by the classic documentary "La Operación" (The Operation) by director Ana María García (1982), on the subject of campaigns for the sterilization of black and Hispanic women in Puerto Rico and New York.

A different attempt to call into question Eurocentrism and to situate aesthetic and cultural theory on Latin American ground has resulted from the practice of a decentered postmodern criticism. Latin American postmodernism has its roots in the specific conditions of Latin American societies. Struggling against the established canons officially installed in countries such as Chile and Argentina during military dictatorships in the 1970s and early 1980s, extra-academic research focused on the possibility of studying new social and cultural movements that would challenge these dictatorships from the margins of the established institutions and from resistant sectors of the popular culture. The concept of the "hybridization" of cultures (after Néstor García Canclini's *Culturas híbridas,* 1990) defies the distinctions among high, popular, and mass cultures, as well as the view that culture should be the province of an elite. "Hybrid cultures" has come to refer to the combined results of the interaction of popular, mass, and high cultures, based on phenomena such as the simultaneous presence of the traditional and the modern, the central and the peripheral, the foreign and the domestic, in Latin American cultural consumption and production (García Canclini, 1990, pp. 338–343; Herlinghaus and Walter, 1994, pp. 32–33). The issue of economic dependence on the West has been reconsidered in the light of the heterogeneous cultural phenomena produced thereby, in contrast to the more essentialistic and totalized notion of a "culture of dependence" typical of earlier decades. Taking distance from the notion of authenticity, previously used by the right, the center, and the left to theorize their positions on art and culture, postmodern critics point to the replacement of the original by the copy, to the displacement of people from their places of origin, and to the accelerated construction of social identities by the mass media operating through multinational media conglomerates. For the French-born Chilean critic Nelly Richard (1994), a posture of suspicion and a disbelief in all final utopias are primary characteristics of the postmodern, postdictatorial Latin American cultural critique, though the South American critic Hugo Achugar (1994) still holds a place for utopian considerations even within the framework of the postmodern.

What is certain, however, is that Western conceptual paradigms (recently poststructuralism, as was the case earlier with pragmatism, phenomenology, and Marxism) continue to be a part of the Latin American intellectual scene. The extent to which this appeal is negotiated with a regard for local, regional, or continental concerns of special historical significance to Latin Americans, and is also able to include the importance of non-European, indigenous, or African-related cultural production in the region, is a process that changes definition as cultural contexts, intellectual movements, and historical conditions change. In the light of these observations, it is reasonable to hold that to remove issues regarding popular culture, cultural crossings and differences, and cultural politics from the province of Latin American aesthetics would be to deprive it of some of its most distinctive, as well as collectively significant, sources of meaning.

[*See also* Caribbean Aesthetics.]

BIBLIOGRAPHY

History of Aesthetics

Caso, Antonio. "Existence as Economy, Disinterest, and Charity" (1916; 3d ed., 1943). In *Latin American Philosophy in the Twentieth Century: Man, Values, and the Search for Philosophical Identity,* edited by Jorge J. E. Gracia, pp. 48–52. Buffalo, 1986.

Caso, Antonio. *Principios de estética* (1925). Mexico City, 1944.

Deústua, Alejandro Octavio. *Estética general.* Lima, 1923. Selection translated as "General Aesthetics" in *Latin American Philosophy in the Twentieth Century,* edited by Jorge J. E. Gracia, pp. 175–184. Buffalo, 1986.

Ramos, Samuel. *Diego Rivera.* Mexico City, 1935.

Ramos, Samuel. *Filosofía de la vida artística.* Mexico City, 1950.

Ramos, Samuel. *Estudios de estética.* Edited by Juan Hernández Luna. Mexico City, 1963.

Vasconcelos, José. *El monismo estético: Ensayos.* Mexico City, 1918.

Vasconcelos, José. *La raza cósmica* (1925). Mexico City, 1985.

Vasconcelos, José. "Todología" (1952). In *Latin American Philosophy in the Twentieth Century,* edited by Jorge J. E. Gracia, pp. 55–62. Buffalo, 1986.

Marxist Aesthetics

Fernández Retamar, Roberto. "Our America and the West." *Social Text* 15 (Fall 1986): 1–25.

Fernández Retamar, Roberto. *Caliban and Other Essays.* Translated by Edward Baker. Minneapolis, 1989.

Mariátegui, José Carlos, and Ricardo Martínez de la Torre, eds. *Amauta: Revista mensual de doctrina, literatura, arte, polémica* (1926–1930). Facs. ed. 6 vols. Lima, 1976.

Mariátegui, José Carlos. *Seven Interpretive Essays on Peruvian Reality* (1928). Translated by Marjory Urquidi. Austin, Tex., 1971.

Sánchez Vázquez, Adolfo. *Las ideas estéticas de Marx.* Mexico City, 1965.

New Latin American Cinema

Burton, Julianne. *Film Artisans and Film Industries in Latin America, 1956–1980.* Wilson Center Working Papers, No. 102. Washington, D.C., 1981.

Chanan, Michael, ed. *Twenty-Five Years of the New Latin American Cinema.* London, 1983.

Postdictatorial and Postmodern Criticism

Achugar, Hugo. "Fin de siglo. Reflexiones desde la periferia." *Posmodernidad en la periferia,* edited by Hermann Herlinghaus and Monika Walter, pp. 233–255. Berlin, 1994.

García Canclini, Néstor. *Culturas híbridas: Estrategias para entrar y salir de la modernidad.* Mexico City, 1990. Translated by Christopher L. Chiappari and Silvia L. López as *Hybrid Cultures: Strategies for Entering and Leaving Modernity* (Minneapolis: 1995).

García Canclini, Néstor. "Memory and Innovation in the Theory of Art." *South Atlantic Quarterly* 93.3 (Summer 1993): 423–443.

Herlinghaus, Hermann, and Monika Walter, eds. *Posmodernidad en la periferia: Enfoques latinoamericanos de la nueva teoría cultural.* Berlin, 1994.

Richard, Nelly. "The Latin American Problematic of Theoretical-Cultural Transference: Postmodern Appropriations and Counterappropriations." *South Atlantic Quarterly* 93.3 (Summer 1993): 453–459.

Richard, Nelly. "Latinoamérica y la posmodernidad." In *Posmodernidad en la periferia,* edited by Hermann Herlinghaus and Monika Walter, pp. 210–222. Berlin, 1994.

OFELIA SCHUTTE

LAVATER, JOHANN CASPAR (1741–1801), prominent Swiss pastor, theologian, author of books on metaphysics, and citizen of Zurich, remembered most for reviving physiognomy, the pseudoscience of finding people's moral character revealed in their physical—especially facial—features. Both he and his lavishly illustrated *Physiognomische Fragmente* (1775–1778) enjoyed tremendous success and suffered terrible ridicule. Lavater regarded man as made in God's image and "read" the human body, like Christ, as God's word made flesh. He distinguished *physiognomy,* the study of fixed facial features, from *pathognomy,* the study of features that change along with one's emotions. (Physiognomy should not be confused with phrenology, the interpretation of bumps on the skull.) In theory, his own correlations of good and bad with beauty and ugliness seem well meant; in practice, however, such judging by mere appearances often betrays or reinforces prejudices based on nationality, race, class, religion, and gender. While typifying many common eighteenth-century attitudes toward virtue and vice, *kalokagathia,* and beautiful souls, Lavater's intellectual legacy has thus always seemed dubious.

Besides speculating about natural beauty—the human body—Lavater often remarked on the visual arts. He frequently cited such art to prove physiognomy true, yet he also lamented that portraits were often caricatures instead of accurate copies of nature. He explained that every painter's style and subject matter were simply the "physiognomy of his age and of himself," and he ranked artists according to their "physiognomic insight." He criticized some artists for projecting their own facial features into their likenesses of others, and though portraits seemed more useful to him than nature itself, because one cannot stare at people as intently as one regards paintings, silhouettes drawn with

mechanical instruments struck him as more reliable evidence. He considered Greek statues mere reproductions of beautiful human beings and assumed that such ancient art naively mirrored nature, betraying his simplistic concepts of mimesis and imagination. His analyses of portraits of Christ illustrate his blend of theology, physiognomy, and aesthetics especially well. Lavater stressed visual impressions because he distrusted verbal language, but writers as well as artists have refined his focus on facial detail.

In its purview and problems, Lavater's "science" is much like aesthetics. Benedetto Croce argues that aesthetics, the science of human beings' spiritual expression, is not a semiotics, physiognomic or otherwise. Links between bodily and higher forms of beauty, however, have been posited since Plato's *Symposium,* Plotinus's analogies between sensual and spiritual beauty and ugliness, and the symbolic connections between visible and invisible worlds forged during the Middle Ages. Establishing ideal human proportions and the intersubjective validity of aesthetic judgments is as central to Lavater's work as it is to Albrecht Dürer's or Immanuel Kant's, though Lavater did not seriously address the subjectivity of beauty and taste that concerned eighteenth-century aestheticians such as David Hume. Instead, he instinctively embraced moral-sense philosophy. His physiognomic conclusions show him seeking truth through beauty and trying to articulate his experience of the latter in a systematic theory meant to justify value judgments given along with visual descriptions. In addition to its social, literary, and artistic import, then, and to its applications in anthropology, criminology, psychology, and medicine, physiognomy demonstrates how singularly Lavater related the traditional aesthetic concerns of truth, beauty, and goodness.

BIBLIOGRAPHY

Work by Lavater

Physiognomische Fragmente zur Beförderung der Menschenkenntnis und Menschenliebe. 4 vols. Leipzig, 1775–1778; reprint, Zurich, 1968–1969.

Other Sources

Cowling, Mary. *The Artist as Anthropologist: The Representation of Type and Character in Victorian Art.* Cambridge and New York, 1989.

Graham, John. *Lavater's Essays on Physiognomy: A Study in the History of Ideas.* Bern, 1979.

Jaton, Anne-Marie. *Jean Gaspard Lavater.* Lucerne, 1988.

Pestalozzi, Karl, and Horst Weigelt, eds. *Das Antlitz Gottes im Antlitz des Menschen: Zugänge zu Johann Kaspar Lavater.* Göttingen, 1994.

Rivers, Christopher. *Face Value: Physiognomical Thought and the Legible Body in Marivaux, Lavater, Balzac, Gautier, and Zola.* Madison, Wis., 1994.

Shookman, Ellis, ed. *The Faces of Physiognomy: Interdisciplinary Approaches to Johann Caspar Lavater.* Columbia, S.C., 1993.

Stafford, Barbara Maria. *Body Criticism: Imaging the Unseen in Enlightenment Art and Medicine.* Cambridge, Mass., 1991.

Tytler, Graeme. *Physiognomy in the European Novel: Faces and Fortunes.* Princeton, N.J., 1982.

Wechsler, Judith. *A Human Comedy: Physiognomy and Caricature in Nineteenth-Century Paris.* Chicago, 1982.

Weigelt, Horst. *Johann Kaspar Lavater: Leben, Werk und Wirkung.* Göttingen, 1991.

ELLIS SHOOKMAN

LAW AND ART. [*To treat legal issues as they relate to art and aesthetics, this entry comprises seven essays:*

> Conceptual Overview
> Aesthetic Concepts in Law
> Cultural Property
> Government-Funded Art and the First Amendment
> Censorship
> Trademarks and Art
> Law and Literature

The first is an overview essay that explains which legal issues are important in art and aesthetics and how they are related to one another. The second essay is about how aesthetics has historically and conceptually treated legal issues related to art. The third essay explains the meaning and history of cultural property as a legal concept, though one that has broad cultural significance. The next three essays are discussions of basic issues in contemporary aesthetic-legal controversies: First Amendment issues, censorship, and trademark. The final essay explores in more depth the relationship between law and aesthetics, using literature as the particular art that relates to law in various ways, especially through comparisons between legal and literary modes of interpretation. For other essays on art law, see Appropriation; Moral Rights of Art; *and* Obscenity.]

Conceptual Overview

Art law is the growing body of formal rules and regulations that society has developed to deal with artistic creations. It concerns matters such as the relations between government and art, artists' rights in their work, the public interest in art, and, on a more mundane level, art as a commodity: something owned, bought, and sold, and so subject to the more general laws of property and commerce.

Although furthest from the aesthetic, enriching, and elevating aspect of art, it is the economic interests in art that most drives the law; and so it is that the area of art that now has the most monetary value, the visual arts, leads to the lawsuits and legislation that gives rise to art law. Nevertheless, it is the uneasy relationship between art as something economic and the higher aesthetic and cultural purposes that art is thought to further that give art law its particular interest and complexity. Behind almost every conflict and case there is a tension between what a work of art is materially in society and the fact that we look to art as something that transforms and lifts us above the everyday world of business and law.

Perhaps the earliest manifestation of the crosscurrents of art as a part of, yet as transcending, society is arts censorship. At least since Plato, some have felt the need to censor the creative urge for the presumed good of society. The arts, without control, can provoke and push beyond the bounds thought needed for a stable society. Censorship or control of the arts by religious, political, and other authorities has left an indelible mark on permissible subjects and representation in the arts. Today, modern societies promote openness and limit censorship. In the United States, the First Amendment of the Constitution protects freedom of speech, which has been interpreted to include artistic expression. Nevertheless, the battle between what is and is not permissible remains and now rages over issues of sexuality and antisocial conduct in cases and constitutional review of legislation. Art is still hostage to society.

Governments not only censor art, they also promote it. Traditionally, state or religious institutions were art's patrons. Painting, architecture, music, drama, dance, and literature were all promoted in order to further established interests. In today's democratic societies, direct government support of the arts raises issues of how a central authority can justify spending taxpayers' money on art that only benefits some, while the actual choice of art that government subsidizes raises questions of how such support can be given without the specter of government self-aggrandizement or censorship of what is not supported.

With respect to justifying government subsidies, there are substantial difficulties with a benefit analysis or claim that the arts have intrinsic value, and democratic states are always faced with the justification of spending on high culture when some portion of the population is of necessity excluded from it because of lack of wealth, inadequate education, or other inability to appreciate it.

Assuming that government will invest in art, the question becomes how to decide what art can properly be promoted without either unreasonable indoctrination or censoring what is not supported. In the United States, this was satisfactorily resolved by having the National Endowment for the Arts (NEA), the government agency that directly subsidizes the arts, make its determinations of what to support on the content-neutral grounds of aesthetic merit and excellence. Since the 1980s, with the arts having become highly politicized, Congress has sought to impose limitations on grants that it found distasteful, usually because of overtly sexual content. This has led to lawsuits in which the courts have so far rejected encroachment on a purely aesthetic funding criteria. The underlying tension, however, between justification of government support of the arts and concern about the results will no doubt lead to implicit censorship, further lawsuits, and an uncertain future for the NEA. [*See* National Endowment for the Arts.]

Perhaps the most developed legal relationship of art in society is that between artist and artwork. Since the rise of artists as something more than craftsmen, their creative role has been recognized by laws reflecting their special relationship to their work. This manifests itself in copyright, trademark, and moral rights law.

Copyright recognizes artists' rights to economic rewards when others copy and use their creative expression. With the ever-increasing importance of created images and other icons of popular culture, a problem has arisen of artists' rights to use others' images to create their art. Whereas the noncopyrightable sea and sky were once the subjects that artists drew on to create their work, now it is copyrighted and trademarked Brillo boxes, Coke bottles, and other images of our media and consumer world that are the subject of artworks. Similarly, in a world ever more aware that creativity is context-bound, the very notion of the difference between copying and creating, imitating and originating, simulacrum and reality is being called in question by artists. This has led to the question of whether the law of copyright is too constraining, preventing a new breed of artists from appropriating others' images to comment on a copyrighted world. [*See* Appropriation.]

Trademarks are recognizable names or images that identify something as coming from a particular source. With respect to the arts, they can protect the right of artists to be associated with their works, and prevent public confusion about a work's source because of the use of an artist's name, signature, or even unique style. Here too appropriation art creates problems. For example, trademark protection may prevent an artist's use of known logos or other marks arguably needed to comment visually on the commodification of culture.

Moral rights are the most interesting legal relationship between artists and their art. Originally developed in French law, moral rights include the right to have a work attributed to its author, the right to prevent mutilation or destruction of one's work, and the right to disclose or withhold a work from publication. Theoretically, these rights derive from the idea that a work of art is an expression of the person who creates it. As such, there is a continuing connection between the artist's personality and his work, one that can, for instance, affect the artist's reputation, and this connection justifies crediting the artist as the author of a work and not permitting false attributions, as well as prohibiting the destruction of a work or the display of one that has been altered or distorted. Some of the protections provided by moral rights law may also be provided by copyright, trademark, and other legal protections. The most interesting aspect of moral rights, however, is the continuing, noneconomic, almost metaphysical connection between art and artist, which may give the artwork a right to a life of its own, preventing its destruction or mutilation even after the death of the artist.

This recognition of art as having a potential life of its own has led some philosophers to consider whether artworks themselves can be said to be legal entities that have rights. Thus, for example, if artworks cannot be destroyed and in certain circumstances must be protected, should this be analyzed in terms of the rights of artworks? Although the philosophical discussion of this question goes well beyond present legal concepts, it provides grounds for approaching aesthetic interests in terms of the public's or a culture's rights rather than as a matter of individual artist's rights. [*See* Moral Rights of Art.]

Public art, from the bronzed public figures of the past to Christos and interactive media, is a developing concept. As groundbreaking art requiring a public audience, it often raises strong aesthetic responses and a complex of social and legal issues. Not surprisingly, resolution of these issues leads to lawsuits. The government's decision to remove Richard Serra's unpopular site-specific *Tilted Arc* was a seminal case involving the artist's assertion of First Amendment, copyright, trademark, and moral rights claims to prevent the removal. The court's answer—that, essentially, the government could do what it wanted with art that it owned—indicates that the complexity of issues raised by public art (questions of free speech, government funding, artists' rights, and the public interest in art) are in the earliest stages of development.

Cultural property is also a developing legal concept. It involves a community's, a country's, or a culture's right to art. Certain art and other cultural manifestations are thought to be so integral to a people's identity, or so aesthetically, politically, or historically important, that legal restrictions are placed on their treatment or removal. This can lead to conflicting claims depending on who is regarded as the appropriate custodian: the heirs of the local people who created the work, the nation in which it resides, or all mankind when the work is taken as an expression of human creativity. The result is a thorny web of legal and political issues of whether artworks should remain with or be returned to the heirs of their original creators, whether they should be allowed out of or returned to their country of origin, or whether they should freely travel the world, residing in different museums and collections. As a legal matter, whose laws and claims should be enforced? Behind these questions are deeper philosophical ones that are rarely raised: How does art manifest culture? How is it related to that culture's identity, its past, and its future? How are competing claims to it to be decided?

Law is also linked to the arts through literature. Both use words. Some of the greatest jurists of the past, such as John Marshall, Oliver Wendell Holmes, and Benjamin Cardozo, were great writers whose decisions were convincing either as narratives, by evoking scenes that justified their conclusions, or through metaphors, which created models that formed new law. Law's present relation to literature is typically through critical theory. Lawsuits and decisions are treated like other narratives, to be analyzed and unpacked to see how society works, or criticized as metaphors that mythologize roles and structures now thought overly confining or wrong. Law, like literature, is now also seen as text to be interpreted, and statutes are viewed as open structures whose intentions are not givens, set for all time, but to be used or discarded, and necessarily open to interpretation in order to be applied.

Even more broadly, law as literature, or otherwise, can be interpreted as itself embodying aesthetic as well as moral elements. For example, censorship of the arts as obscene can itself be seen to be built on aesthetic judgments of the beautiful or the profane. Indeed, law as a whole can be interpreted as expressing aesthetic concepts, such as order and harmony. [See Obscenity.]

Although law can rise to these aesthetic and philosophical heights, it is mostly concerned with more mundane matters: art as commerce and commodity, the residue of aesthetic creation that is bought and sold, dealt in and collected, valued and invested in, insured, loaned to, and exhibited in museums, damaged in transit, poorly restored or conserved, wrongly disparaged, faked, and stolen. It is the business of art, the life of art as a commodity, that is the usual concern of art law; and it is the fact that art is an unusual commodity, unlike cars and can openers, unique, not of the everyday, aesthetic and cultured, that makes art law different.

The problems that arise in art law show the confluence of art as a material thing with an ethereal, aesthetic side. Art, like other things bought and sold, is the subject of contracts. But unlike cars and houses, what is being bargained for is not just a practical matter, even though what is being purchased is often more expensive than a car or even a house. Thus, unlike cars and houses, there is no registration procedure that clearly determines ownership. Moreover, the sale of art is often wrapped in the mystique of the art market, where knowledge about a piece and its owner is usually not known or given, and inquiry is often frowned on. The reasons for this are many. Dealers do not want to reveal their sources; owners, concerned with security, want to shield their identity; and collectors, in search of the aesthetic, pursue art not as a business matter but as a cultural act, where the cautious behavior of the market may be thought inappropriate. [See Art Market.]

This leads to legal problems. For one, it is often hard to determine provenance, the history of ownership, and so definitively to know the chain of ownership and whether a piece was stolen. In addition, given cultural attitudes toward art, would-be buyers may be reluctant to inquire, and not be diligent in searching out sources, instead relying on the good faith of others. This has led to special problems that courts and legislatures have in dealing with stolen art. Should owners seeking the return of their art be precluded from obtaining it if they did not do what they could to notify a would-be innocent buyer that their work was stolen, and should a buyer be deemed an innocent, good-faith purchaser, with certain protections at law, if little or no inquiry was made at the time of purchase? Similarly, concerned that the unusual practices of the art market may dupe some, and the ways of dealers or auction houses may mystify others, legislatures have passed laws requiring various kinds of disclosure to protect a naive public and so affect the otherwise established art market.

Similar concerns arise with respect to issues of authenticity, whether the art is what it is said to be. Here both neophyte and sophisticate may be at a loss. When authenticity is unclear, as when provenance is murky or the art is old, there are usually no definitive tests or procedures to resolve the matter. Once scientific tests of age or the appropriateness of the materials have been passed, the ultimate determination is based on technique and subject as viewed by an experienced, good eye. Further, scholars whose opinions are sought on these matters are often reticent to speak for fear that they will be sued by owner or buyer, unhappy with the result, for negligence or wrongly disparaging their work. Here too courts and legislatures have often stepped forward and created laws requiring certain disclosures, standardizing language, and imposing warranties on supposedly knowledgeable sellers, such as dealers and auction houses, in order to protect the public. At the same time, successful fakers of art tend to be lauded in the press as masters of deceit, their success used to deflate a highfalutin art world, where the distortion of the historical record or an artist's reputation is of little concern. [See Forgery.]

This is but the tip of what art law is about. These matters, together with how art is taxed, how museums are treated, censorship, government funding, artists' rights, copyright, trademark, and moral rights, are the stuff of art law. Aside from the practical issues they raise and the disputes they are asked to decide, who owns a work and who is to suffer if it is not authentic, art law raises larger, more philosophical, issues. After all, the artists and the works they create arise in the context of an art world more and more formed by legal decisions and constraints. There is no reason to think that, if artists cannot rely on dealers for subsidies, dealers on handshakes, collectors on the good faith of the market, but all must better know and be enmeshed with the law, then both the attitude toward art and the approach to it will change. The formal rules and regulations that society places on artistic creation through law are not a world apart from art's creation, but are intrinsic to it. In the end, art law should not just be paid attention to in doing the business of art, but also, and perhaps more important, be seen as reflecting the society that ultimately nurtures art and its creation and so is formative of what art is and will be.

BIBLIOGRAPHY

DuBoff, Leonard D., and Sally Holt Caplan. *The Desk Book of Art Law.* 2d ed. 2 vols. Dobbs Ferry, N.Y., 1993.

Darraby, Jessica L. *Art, Artifact, and Architecture Law.* New York, 1995.

Feldman, Franklin, and Stephen E. Weil. *Art Law: Rights and Liabilities of Creators and Collectors.* 2 vols. Boston, 1986.

Lerner, Ralph E. and Judith Bressler. *Art Law: The Guide for Collectors, Investors, Dealers, and Artists*, 2nd ed. New York, 1998.

Merryman, John Henry, and Albert E. Elsen. *Law, Ethics, and the Visual Arts.* 3d ed. Dordrecht, 1997.

DANIEL SHAPIRO

Aesthetic Concepts in Law

Theorists of the law often exalt its elegant structure and majestic grandeur. Law's likeness to architecture is celebrated by idealists, who admire its logic, as much as by Realists, who applaud its functionalism. The use of aesthetic language in praise of the law seems uncontroversial, but the philosopher of law Ronald Dworkin goes so far as to acknowledge a sense that "politics, art, and law are united somehow, in philosophy" (1983). In a more dynamic vein, Oliver Wendell Holmes, Jr., observes that "The life of the law has not been in logic: it has been experience", a sentiment applied also to the arts by his fellow pragmatist John Dewey. Because both art and law address the deepest and most pervasive issues of infinitely mutating human experience, their linkage comes as no surprise. Yet, although legal and aesthetic concepts and the theories that construct them seem inextricably bound, few people assert the priority of aesthetic theory over law. The high seriousness of decisive actions and their inevitable consequence seemingly prevails over the luxury of contemplation.

From another perspective, the very notions of order, harmony, and tradition among humans may derive from aesthetic judgment. Two other concepts essential to law—interpretation and authorship/authority—have roots in aesthetics. Their position in the domains of aesthetics and law has shifted in conformity with material circumstance and philosophical fashion, but throughout deep social and theoretical upheavals they have perdured.

Interpretation. Interpreting the law was once the work of royal emissaries, charged with executing the will of the king, who periodically resolved accumulated conflicts in far-flung circuit courts. Their deliberate judgments could be received as the application of rules and principles to specific circumstances or, alternatively, as giving voice either to inspired insight or to common wisdom. Interpretation is involved in every phase of the law's being, beginning with its expression for general promulgation, then with its adaptive application to instances, and finally historically, with its cultural dissemination and influence on subsequent legal process.

Although not exclusively confined to verbal expression, legal interpretation today is understood to be a form of "doing things with words"—finding, affirming, declaring, or judging. Interpretative performance takes a variety of shapes, not infrequently aesthetic in character. Whatever its practical function and transformative consequence, modern law is communicated through language that is necessarily opaque, never specific enough, and always open-textured. Proponents of the contemporary "Law and Literature" movement have therefore drawn an analogy between the interpretation of literary and legal texts, and have suggested that the criteria for evaluating the former may be of use in assessing the latter. Notwithstanding differences in potential outcome, some of the instruments of literary analysis—point of view, emphasis, framing, elliptical reference, allusion by omission, and a family of tropes—reflect strategies of thought that are also present in legal texts. Moreover, their presence is not limited to the word of the law—to statute or written opinion—but can be traced in the dramatic environment of the courtroom, the conduct of arrest and arraignment, of deposition and witness testimony, of law school classroom procedure, and of lawyer-client etiquette. All of these are interpretative frameworks wherein more is transmitted than meets the eye or ear. What is recognized by looking to literature is that meaning is multiplex and that words and their written histories—not to mention gestures, looks, movements, and postures—"do things" in many simultaneous and mutually interactive ways.

Ronald Dworkin (1983), an advocate of the "Aesthetic Hypothesis," recommends selecting that interpretation of a text which reveals it as the best possible work of art that it can be. This proposal obviously entails a commitment on the critic's part to a normative theory of what art is. Seeking a parallel prescription for law, Dworkin appeals to the institution of legal precedent, itself justifiable in terms of the aesthetic categories of identity (unity), coherence, and integrity (wholeness). In addition, he believes that law has the practical merit of social amalgamation, a feature that is arguably not shared by art. In effect, Dworkin holds that laws are to be interpreted so as to preserve and perpetuate the most *beautiful* social system, namely, one that balances adherence to past doctrine against sensitive appreciation of novel circumstances. Whatever ideological reservations one may harbor with regard to Dworkin's view of social justice, his aesthetic agenda is not in doubt. Order, regularity, predictability with variation are aesthetic desiderata. They are formal rather than substantive descriptors. Their final appeal may be attributable to their conduciveness to survival, but that conjecture transcends the concerns of the present essay.

Grounding the law in the aesthetic evades the charge of arbitrary or idiosyncratic judgment, the claim that personal taste is socially isolated and without rational foundation. It avoids the equally arbitrary position known as strict constructionism, which ascribes absolute authority to a single, historically fixed source. The "intention of the founding fathers," equivalent in legal theory to the literary conceit of "author's intention," is, after all, no less subjective than any other. Assuming its accessibility, one must, in the end, assess the author's intention according to its own merits, just as one would measure the worth of the text itself. Little is therefore accomplished by declaring a personified "founder" apart from the introduction of a conventional authority whose legitimacy remains to be vindicated.

Authorship/Authority. The integrity of works of art is commonly believed to reflect the creative genius of their maker, who, in turn, retains spiritual authority over their disposition. Likewise in law, the legislator holds titular dominion over the law, although in reality no such control is possible. More plausibly, in literature as in law, the creator has a conventional function, serving as a conceptual originary site of the work's coherence, unity, and meaning.

The critic Roland Barthes rejects the psychologism implied by designating a historically personified Author and proclaims the "death" of the Author—as autonomous subject. In place of the Author, Barthes engendered the notion of the Text that does not owe its existence to authorial paternity. Neither does it permit genealogical descent. Without filiation, the text is a social collaboration that "allows no enunciative subject to hold the position of judge, teacher, analyst, confessor, or decoder" (Barthes, 1979). Subsequently, the philosopher Michel Foucault reinstated the author, but as a "subjecting" function or fiction that transforms discourse into a set of legal and cultural relations. Conventionally, the author sustains a body of discourses and practices—entitlements, liberties, rights, duties, obligations, constraints, prohibitions, and punishments—produces and reproduces them, and maintains jurisdiction over them. Cultural and civic discontinuities are heroically marked by "fundamental" authors, who, like imperfections in crystal structures, initiate new social and cultural practice.

As a model of the law, the subjectless creativity described by Barthes and Foucault can help explain the separation of product from producer, law from lawgiver, at the same time preserving continuity from past to present. We do not read the text that William Shakespeare wrote, however faithfully the work is transcribed. Neither is the Constitution today the same as that propagated by a group of gentleman lawyers assembled in Philadelphia in the late eighteenth century. Moreover, there would be no good reason to follow their prescription, given these people's individual fallibilities and contamination by the material and economic conditions of their time. Nonetheless, we revere their "authorial" identity, symbolized by such linguistic devices as "William Shakespeare" and the "Founding Fathers." They delineate a domain temporally and spatially continuous with our own, and the continuity thereby achieved ensures substantive legitimacy.

This legitimacy relies heavily on the faith of successive audiences. Author and audience are correlative intensional concepts. It is often said that an author is her own first audience; but audiences, whether taken collectively or as distinct individuals, are also components of authorship. The history of the reception of works of art affects subsequent experiences of those works at least as much as any intention reconstructively ascribed to a creator. Likewise in law, judicial interpretation and local applications concretize the meaning of laws. As Justice Holmes remarked, if you want to know what the law is, you must look at it from the point of view of the "bad man" who calculates its consequences to enliven its vacuous abstractness.

No subject-author, legislator, or judge has the absolute creative freedom attributed to divinity. Human art and human law are transcendent not by virtue of their imitation of God's voluntarism but in consequence of their own laborious historicity. The respect for precedent in law, which corresponds to reverence for canonicity in art, is prone to abuse. It is not above political diversion, and its own history is riddled with the prejudices of race, sex, and class. Nevertheless, it pretends to integrity and there is conviction in that pretense. The aspiration to produce art is intrinsically referential to the tradition that is art, just as the presumption to make, refine, or denounce law implicitly endorses the legal system and prolongs it.

Our willingness to abide by law or, more broadly, to experience culture canonically links us to a world that is not of our creation. It expresses our own sense of continuity—our self-transcendence—while holding to a claim for personal freedom and subjectivity. It is, after all, our own experience that counts—however overlaid by authority and indoctrination. We navigate between fallacies. On the one hand, we have faith in pure objectivity, believing that the world is simply there, given by decree and described by Scripture. On the other, we cling to the fallacy of pure subjectivity, a belief in our own (rather trivial) authority, expressed at every moment in our freedom to construct the world according to our choice.

The traditions of art and law, aesthetics and legal theory, are protection against both fallacies. Conventions with a history and discernible form invite further specification and ward against falsification. They open themselves to modification and advance, but serve notice that innovation must be justified and validated against a standard. Without history there is no basis for criticism, but with history comes the recognition of error, falsehood, and the temptation of fraudulence. There can be no wrong in immediate experience, but only in its misalliance with past and future. We require a certain restraint or even fixity in order to make evaluative judgments, and these acquire authority by virtue of the aesthetic fixity we fabricate to satisfy that need.

In law, as in art, canonic atrocities can be carried forward from generation to generation. Aesthetic theory has little to say about the concept of progress, mildly acknowledging both that influence is real and that technological innovation permits the exploration of unforeseen possibilities. The same conditions of fluidity pertain to law. We represent to ourselves a growth in the law's enlightenment and humanity, but this is easily challenged. Change alone does not represent advance and is anyway restricted by the imperative to follow precedent. The standards that we protest are the same standards we protect and by which our achievements are measured. The accomplishments of law reflect the state of human civilization in which creative freedom is balanced against the weight of convention and of formal order lightened by the play of subjectivity. In 1795, Friedrich von Schiller proposed a wedding of the sensuous aesthetic and the rational order as an ideal to be approached. This marriage, consummated long ago, has been a fruitful union, but, like most marriages, has had its desperate moments, and its foundations are never self-justifying.

BIBLIOGRAPHY

Barthes, Roland. "The Death of the Author." In *Image, Music, Text,* edited and translated by Stephen Heath, pp. 142–148. New York, 1977.

Barthes, Roland. "From Work to Text." In *Textual Strategies: Perspectives in Post-Structuralist Criticism,* edited by Josué V. Harari, pp. 73–82. Ithaca, N.Y., 1979.

Dworkin, Ronald. "Law as Interpretation." In *The Politics of Interpretation,* edited by W. J. T. Mitchell, pp. 249–271. Chicago, 1983.

Fish, Stanley E. *Doing What Comes Naturally: Change, Rhetoric, and the Practice of Theory in Literary and Legal Studies.* Durham, N.C., 1989.

Foucault, Michel. "What Is an Author?" In *Language, Counter-Memory, Practice: Selected Essays and Interviews,* edited by Donald F. Bouchard, translated by Donald F. Bouchard and Sherry Simon, pp. 113–138. Ithaca, N.Y., 1977.

Frank, Jerome. "Words and Music: Some Remarks on Statutory Interpretation." *Columbia Law Review* 47 (1947): 1259–1278.

Holmes, Oliver Wendell, Jr. *The Common Law.* Boston, 1881.

Holmes, Oliver Wendell, Jr. "The Path of the Law." *Harvard Law Review* 10 (1897): 457–478.

Levinson, Sanford, and Steven Mailloux, eds. *Interpreting Law and Literature: A Hermeneutic Reader.* Evanston, Ill., 1988.

Llewellyn, Karl N. "On the Good, the True, the Beautiful in Law." *University of Chicago Law Review* 9 (1942): 224–248.

Schiller, Friedrich. *Letters on the Aesthetic Education of Man.* Translated by Elizabeth M. Wilkinson and L. A. Willoughby. In *Friedrich von Schiller: Essays,* edited by Walter Hinderer and Daniel O. Dahlstrom. New York, 1993.

West, Robin. *Narrative, Authority and Law.* Ann Arbor, 1993.

White, James Boyd. *The Legal Imagination: Studies in the Nature of Legal Thought and Expression.* Boston, 1973.

White, James Boyd. *Heracles' Bow: Essays on the Rhetoric and Poetics of Law.* Madison, Wis., 1985.

White, James Boyd. *Justice as Translation: An Essay in Cultural and Legal Criticism.* Chicago, 1990.

HILDE HEIN

Cultural Property

Cultural property is what a country, community, or people claims as its own unique form of expression. It is art and architecture, ancient relics and ritual objects, aesthetic and scientific artifacts, myth, music, and customs, even natural wonders and distinctive wildlife, when seen as manifesting and belonging to a particular culture or nation. At the heart of cultural property concerns is determining what aesthetic and other forms of expression belong to a particular country or people and the legal, ethical, and other ramifications of this determination.

The Parthenon's sculptures taken by Lord Elgin and now in the British Museum are the best-known example of disputed cultural property. Without question, they belong to and are part of Greece's identity and inalienable heritage, and are universally recognized as such, including in their display at the British Museum. But for some, Greek and non-Greek alike, the recognition that the Parthenon's sculptures are Greek is not enough. Their return to Greece is sought, even though they can no longer be affixed to the Parthenon and, as in London, should be housed in a museum. Yet, for those who seek their return, their absence is a loss that is believed to diminish Greece and prevent the sculptures from being fully appreciated or understood. For others, what Elgin did, if otherwise questionable, at least saved the sculptures from destruction by the Turks, Greek lime kilns, and other disasters, and preserved them as part of all humanity's heritage, resulting in increased appreciation and understanding of ancient Greece.

Claims to cultural property arise everywhere, and apply to an endless variety of cultural manifestations in a nearly unlimited number of circumstances. Some of the strongest claims are for artifacts identified with a unique culture that were intended to be an immovable part of a site or structure. The return of such cultural property may be warranted as its removal can affect aesthetic integrity and coherence and cause a loss of knowledge and understanding. Examples are claims for the return of wantonly removed and dismembered statuary and wall reliefs in Egypt's Karnak, Cambodia's Angkor Wat, Indonesia's Borobudur, China's Dunhuang and Luoyang caves, and Central America's Mayan stele.

Perhaps even more compelling are cases where conduct affecting cultural property can radically change and even lead to the demise of a living culture, as in the desecration of burial sites or religious ceremonies, despoliation of ritual objects, and the wrongful appropriation of folklore, music, and dance. This can happen through military campaigns, as in the past with the Spanish conquest of the Americas, or the British, French, Dutch, and Portuguese sorties into Africa and Asia; or, less drastically, with adventurers, art dealers, anthropologists, ethnologists, and archaeologists, who, however well-meaning, can alter and transform traditional ways of life with their inquiries and even innocent acquisition of objects and other forms of expression. Canadian, Australian, and American aborigines thus believe that the recording of their oral traditions, music, dance, and other ceremonies, and the preservation and display of ritual objects in museums, can irremediably appropriate and taint them, affecting their purpose and the culture to which they belong.

More common are Iceland's successful claim for important runic manuscripts taken to Denmark and Germany's so far unsuccessful attempts to recover art taken by Russia's trophy brigades at the end of World War II. The least compelling claims are those where a state seeks to retain or obtain the return of important art having little to do with it other than its having been within the claiming country's borders. Such claims, such as France's refusal to permit export of the Swiss artist Philippe Leotard's painting of a Turkish scene, and Italy's request for the return of an undistinguished Matisse, have been repeatedly made by countries that have enormous quantities of more clearly connected cultural property remaining within their borders.

These cases, whether they involve immovable monuments, movable objects, or immaterial myths, customs, and practices, whether from the past or the present, involving cultures living and dead, are all part of the field of cultural property, an inchoate but fast-developing area of law that affects art and aesthetics. The importance of the issues involved is immense. The issues include such critical matters as whether museums should return much of their contents to their source, whether a country or people should retain or have returned to it whatever it considers part of its heritage, or whether cultural property is above tribe and nation, to be shared by all humanity. The question is who has the right to control, protect, and preserve a particular form of cultural expression. The answer, which involves political issues and intractable legal and ethical disputes, is being sought in cultural property debates.

Cultural Property in the Ancient World. What is now hotly debated was in the past less controversial. In the ancient world, aesthetic achievements, works of art, jewelry, and other artistic and decorative accomplishments were valued for their extrinsic worth, their rare materials (precious metals, expensive stones), or their magnificent craft. Cultural property was valued objects of exchange, symbols of prestige and power. Ancient Egyptian wall reliefs portray valuable, tangible possessions; Assyrian panels depict tribute and war booty. Although often obtained through economic or military dominance, cultural property acquired from others in triumph, tribute, or trade was accepted as the norm. It was the expected reward for military prowess: the recognized way to show wealth, success, and power.

The taking of cultural property was not vilified or thought evil. A major law case involving organized theft from pharaonic tombs during the reign of Rameses IX (1142–1123 BCE) was not viewed as cultural desecration but as a way to obtain wealth. Rome's decimation of Carthage a thousand years later in the Third Punic War (149–146 BCE) was a way finally to end the economic threat of a resilient and possibly resurgent competitor, not a means of destroying an enemy's culture. Although Rome's acts were ruinous to Carthage, Punic culture itself was untouched by Rome elsewhere, and was retained and even honored in Roman temples, where the display of piety to others' gods was thought to benefit Rome by possibly incurring divine favor. Vanquished ancient peoples mourned the loss of their aesthetic and religious artifacts, but there seems to have been little thought then of cultural disputes, or of a people or country's rights as a culture's originator. The Romans were not made to regret that their art came from Greece, and Rome in turn assumed that Greek art came from Egypt. There was little covetousness about culture. Other people's art and ways of life were openly accepted, often shared; cultural exclusivity, priority, and pride were not what they are today. What counted was what one had, not where it came from or how it was obtained.

This attitude gradually changed with time. The earliest criticism of it seems to be the view of Polybius (205–115? BCE) that Marcellus (271–208 BCE) was wrong in his unrestrained taking of war booty from Sicily, noting that it included superfluous luxury goods, which, unlike gold and silver, did not help pay for war, and could have a softening effect on traditional Roman virtues such as austerity. Polybius also seemed concerned that plundering religious goods could anger the gods without any compensating advantage to Rome. Plutarch (46–120 CE) expressed similar concerns about Marcellus's conduct and also criticized Sulla (138–78 BCE) for excesses in his conquest of Greece, including indiscriminate looting of religious sites. Cicero's prosecution of Gaius Verres, recounted in his *Verrine Orations* (70 BCE), focused on Verres's sharp practices and abuse of power in plundering cultural property when he was governor of Sicily. These criticisms appear to be based on excesses that could ultimately prove harmful to Rome, rather than on respect for another culture's right to its property, for which there does not seem to be any particular concern, moral, religious, legal, or otherwise.

The first clear expression of concern for a culture's property came much later with a twelfth-century Roman Senate's edict that Trajan's column be preserved and not despoiled. This was followed by sixteenth-century papal bulls that sought to preserve ancient monuments. Notwithstanding the papal decrees, huge amounts of ancient marble were turned to lime to help build a new Rome. In this the papal see was one of the worst offenders. Ancient Saint Peter's was destroyed to build the new Saint Peter's, with much of the mortar for it and other new buildings coming from the burning of classical monuments—from which the papacy earned money through a substantial tax on such operations. Although popes and others were concerned that removal of newly discovered and valued classical remains could impoverish Rome and the prestige of the papal state, much of the finest statuary nevertheless found its way into private collections, ultimately to be removed from Rome.

Growing Importance of Cultural Property. Even so, there was a growing awareness of the importance of cultural property. During the War of 1812, a judge in Halifax, Nova

Scotia, refused to award a British ship Italian art captured from an American merchant vessel and destined for the Pennsylvania Academy of Fine Arts and ordered that it be returned because the arts and sciences "are considered not as the peculium of this or that nation, but as the property of mankind at large, and as belonging to the common interests of the whole species." Even the British Parliament condemned its navy's destruction of Washington by bombardment in the War of 1812.

This recognition of limits to conduct affecting cultural property followed Napoleon's systematic pillage of the art of Europe in the wake of his military conquests, with the spoils displayed in triumph at the Musée Napoléon, now the Louvre, in Paris. Napoleon and France's justification for such conduct was that cultural property, like culture itself, had its natural home in France, should be redistributed from the aristocracy to the people, and would be better cared for, appreciated, and understood in Paris. It was also argued that the seizures of cultural property were legal because the conquered later agreed to them in treaties. France's conduct and attitude were considered outrageous by the rest of Europe and had the effect of strengthening other nations' awareness of the importance of their cultural property. After Napoleon's defeat, much of the pillaged art was returned to the nations of origin on the ground that it was part of their artistic heritage and could not legitimately be removed through coercion.

Cultural Property in Time of War. In addition to effecting increased importance in cultural property, Napoleon's conquests also led to an awareness that cultural property should be protected from the vicissitudes of war. The first legal approach to cultural property was thus to create provisions for its protection in time of conflict. The earliest effort, the Lieber Code, was drafted by a professor for the United States Army during the Civil War. International codification followed through conferences in The Hague in 1899 and 1907.

After the Nazis' unprecedented destruction and pillage of cultural property, the 1954 Hague Convention was adopted to protect movable and immovable cultural property, such as works of art and historic monuments, and also the museums and other centers that contain them, regardless of origin or ownership. The justification for this international legal approach was that damage to cultural property belonging to any people whatsoever means damage to the cultural heritage of all mankind, since each people makes its contribution to the culture of the world. Nearly ninety parties have signed the convention, but some critical nations, such as the United States and the United Kingdom, are still not signatories. Moreover, in conflicts since 1954, such as the Persian Gulf war and the demise of Yugoslavia, the combatants did not protect cultural property and even made it an intended target.

Cultural Property in Time of Peace. Approaches to cultural property in time of peace have not fared any better.

Generally, they involve states' laws concerning their own cultural property. This legislation reflects the awareness that art, architecture, and other remains from the past are important in forming a national consciousness and identity. But the impetus for them is generally that, without such laws, others will acquire that nation's cultural property—not a concern that the cultural property should be conserved and protected. For example, Greeks purportedly made little effort to protect their classical antiquities and only acted to retain what remained of it after obtaining independence from the Ottoman Empire. Similarly, Egyptians showed little concern with French and then English appropriations, only later promulgating legislation to retain their heritage because of Egyptologists' promptings. The laws of South and Central American countries enacted at the end of the nineteenth century likewise sought to control export of pre-Columbian artifacts rather than protect and conserve them. By the beginning of the twentieth century, European countries also began enacting laws restricting export of cultural property because the United States and other wealthy countries were collecting it. Countries in Asia, Africa, and other colonially dominated parts of the world similarly focused their laws on retaining, not conserving, their cultural property once they became independent.

Almost all of these laws were reactive. The stimulus for them was concern that interest by others would deplete the heritage that remained. Less important was preservation and study of what remained. Thus, with very few exceptions, almost all countries have adopted restrictive legislation aimed at keeping cultural property within their borders, with much less emphasis on uncovering and understanding its importance and place in the nation's history and identity. One of the few exceptions is the United States, which has done little to retain its heritage, enacting legislation only for Indian remains on federal land. Unlike most other countries, the United States does not claim ownership or restrict export of cultural property—but this apparently is the result of its government's lack of interest in culture generally, and perhaps because it is assumed that the United States' wealth will keep its cultural treasures at home.

National Cultural Property Laws. For countries that have enacted cultural property laws, there are three types of approach. The most restrictive is where a country claims ownership and inalienability of cultural property—often very broadly defined—to be found within its borders, prohibiting any commerce in it and suing for its return as stolen property. Such ownership claims can apply to undiscovered artifacts still in the ground, known objects in private collections, as well as those in national museums and at recognized sites. This completely retentive approach is most often followed by art-rich countries that have been plundered in the past, such as Greece, Egypt, Mexico, and Peru. But it has also been taken by nations such as Turkey that were not systematically plundered and whose cultural property may have originally come from other cultures. The effect of such retentive policies is overflowing museum storerooms in Mexico City, Lima, Athens, and Ankara, where artifacts are unattended, unstudied, and unavailable.

A second, more moderate approach, is to classify and list a limited amount of important cultural property and restrict its export. Such an approach can only apply to known objects whose importance has been determined. It thus requires a comprehensive understanding and inventory of a nation's cultural property, and cannot apply to unknown, unreported, or clandestinely discovered objects, or where fairly complete and comprehensive knowledge of a culture is lacking. Germany, Japan, to some extent France and Italy, and other developed countries have followed this approach.

A third approach requires licenses for export of cultural property. This approach has the advantage of not requiring extensive preexisting knowledge of a country's cultural property, and can apply to previously unknown or unreported objects. It does, however, require criteria for determining what cannot be exported, with sufficient resources and incentives allocated to a licensing procedure and an often substantial enforcement effort to ensure compliance. The United Kingdom, Canada, Italy, France, and numerous other countries have taken this approach with various effects. To ensure retention of important cultural property, sometimes the listing and licensing approaches are used together, and either can be linked with a state's preemption by purchase or otherwise precluding export, but this also requires sufficient monetary and other resources to be effective.

Creating national legislation to retain cultural property by declaring ownership of it or by requiring government approval for its export is relatively easy. The difficulty is making it work. The most retentive schemes can have the least effect because of the problems inherent in their implementation. Limiting the availability of art and artifacts where there is demand for them is likely to drive up prices, creating incentives to get around even the most stringent methods of enforcement. Moreover, the most restrictive approaches are often taken by the poorest countries, those least able to police their borders, most prone to corruption from underpaid officials, and whose populace is more likely interested in the income that can come from trafficking in cultural property than in attempts to retain it. The consequence can be a powerful black market that multiplies the difficulty of safeguarding cultural property.

International Approaches to Cultural Property. A nation's cultural property law, in particular a very restrictive one, may be of limited effect without the cooperation of other nations. Under principles of international law, however, one country does not usually enforce another country's laws unless there is a specific agreement to do so. Consequently, international agreements or treaties are needed for extraterritorial enforcement of national cultural property laws.

The ease or difficulty in obtaining international agreements illustrates what is involved. At one extreme is a nation's attempt to recover cultural property stolen from a museum collection. Because such property is generally well documented, its identification is relatively easy and the claim of ownership clear. Moreover, because all countries have laws protecting ownership, a nation can usually seek the return of stolen documented cultural property under the existing stolen property law of the country where the property is found. Consequently, in the case of documented stolen cultural property, existing national laws make international agreements less important but presumably easy to obtain.

It is when the sought-for cultural property is not well documented or a state's claim to it can be questioned that international cooperation is needed and more difficult to obtain. The examples on this extreme are claims to clandestinely excavated cultural property that cannot be definitively described and where the sought-for cultural property is not especially unique or critical to the country claiming it. In these circumstances, an importing country may be reluctant to enforce national ownership or export restrictions where they are based solely on the fact that the sought-for cultural property had been located within the claiming country's borders. For one thing, ownership or restricting export of objects never actually possessed or not even previously known to exist may go beyond the limits of what another country is willing to recognize as "owned," "stolen," or even properly subject to another country's export controls. For another, many countries want their own collections to be representative of the world's cultures and may be unwilling to give up access to examples of other cultures for study and display absent a more compelling rationale than that they came from the country seeking their return. Further, enforcing claims for the return of cultural property can require substantial effort and resources. Most countries are unwilling to commit their often limited enforcement capabilities to other than domestic purposes. When those capabilities are to be expended on enforcing other countries' cultural property claims, which may be especially difficult because there are no exact means of identification, and may be contrary to the importing country's own interest in creating worldwide collections, there may be insurmountable obstacles to obtaining international cooperation.

The UNESCO Convention. The 1970 UNESCO Convention on the Means of Prohibiting and Preventing the Illicit Import, Export, and Transfer of Ownership of Cultural Property was one of the earliest and most important international attempts to deal with these issues. The convention broadly defines cultural property as designated objects of importance for archaeology, prehistory, history, literature, art, or science, including ethnological and paleontological objects, manuscripts, coins, stamps, even specimens of flora and fauna. In early drafts, authored by recently independent, poor but art-rich countries, UNESCO championed their position seeking to prohibit import of their cultural property by other countries without export certificates. This approach was rejected by the United States and other importing countries as too broad and restrictive, in effect giving the exporting countries a blank check in limiting access to their cultural property. It was also considered problematic as it potentially obligated importing countries to expend enormous resources to enforce another country's export laws—even though that country might itself be doing little or nothing to restrict exports.

The revised compromise treaty now adopted by more than eighty countries has only precatory language regarding export certificates, and prohibits import of documented cultural property stolen from state institutions and the acquisition by state institutions of illegally exported cultural property. With respect to archaeological and ethnological materials that are in jeopardy of pillage, the adopting parties agree to undertake concerted international efforts to prevent irremediable injury. In practice, UNESCO has accomplished little. The prohibition on importing documented stolen property adds little to existing law, and the provisions against collecting illegally exported materials by state institutions or undertaking concerted action in extreme cases means little as very few art-importing countries have adopted the UNESCO Convention.

The UNIDROIT Convention. As a result, UNESCO sponsored the use of national laws, such as stolen property laws, to enforce claims for the return of cultural property in the courts of the countries where found. The 1995 UNIDROIT Convention on Stolen or Illegally Exported Cultural Objects differs from the UNESCO Convention by providing for the return of undocumented, unlawfully excavated objects as stolen. UNIDROIT also, unlike UNESCO, provides for the return of objects exported contrary to law.

Not surprisingly, the problems involved in getting international acceptance of these provisions remain. With respect to UNIDROIT's application to illegally exported objects, the question is whether its restriction to objects whose removal significantly impairs their integrity, understanding, context, or ritual use, or the overall limitation to what has "significant cultural importance," is realistic and not overbroad. The reasonableness of providing for the return of anything with "significant cultural importance" has been criticized as permitting the return of all cultural property because a country's determination to bring a lawsuit for an object's return may in itself be considered sufficient to establish the significance of the cultural property for the country seeking its return. In the case of excavated objects, UNIDROIT has been criticized for defining excavated objects as "stolen" merely because they are "owned" as the result of a national decree, without any consideration of whether they have any cultural significance or relationship (other than location) to the country claiming ownership. On the other side, countries of origin are dissatisfied with UNIDROIT because it requires them to compensate innocent purchasers of stolen or illegally exported cultural property, thus making them pay for what they already owned or what others illegally obtained. In short, the UNIDROIT Convention may not be any better accepted or any more effective than the UNESCO Convention it was intended to supplant.

Difficulties with Present Approaches. The problems in developing a workable international approach reflect serious differences in underlying concerns. Poor and developing countries, especially those whose cultural heritage was depleted through colonialism, enact restrictive laws for political reasons that they cannot enforce and that few other countries will help them to effect. Countries that do not have restrictive laws that prohibit export of all cultural property are nevertheless often troubled by the loss of cultural property that is either not subject to legal restrictions or that slips through them. On the other side, the United States and other art-importing countries, including those that reasonably try to restrict export, would like representative collections of other peoples' cultural property and may be concerned about the difficulty and cost in policing imports to help effect other countries' claims, especially when those countries may do little to "protect" their cultural property other than trying to retain it. In sum, there are important differences and conflicts in national interests with few, if any, countries satisfied with matters as they now stand.

In addition, different countries can lay claim to the same cultural property. England refuses to return the Parthenon marbles taken by Elgin because they are considered part of its heritage, not simply because they are now part of all humanity's birthright, but because of the tremendous effect the sculptures have had on English art and culture since they were displayed in London in the early nineteenth century. Further, it is even difficult to maintain incontestable claims to cultural property when its location has not changed. Most nations are of recent origin and cultural remains found in one can often be claimed by another. In areas such as Africa, where boundaries are newly created, the originating cultural group may be on both sides of a border and have little to do with whatever nation now claims their cultural property. Further, much cultural property, such as coins, pottery, and statuary, was made for commerce and export, so that present-day claims that it should remain within the borders where found are not very convincing. This is especially true where the country claiming the property as part of its cultural heritage did not share a common culture or was even antagonistic to that culture, as in the case of Turkey's claims to Greek and Byzantine treasures. On the other hand, where there is a shared heritage, as in the Mediterranean states, northern Europe, Asia, and the Americas, there is often a common background and underlying context to support the claims of numerous countries to the same cultural property. The absence of natural exclusivity helps explain why there are so many dissatisfied countries with competing claims and why international agreement is so difficult to obtain.

Dissatisfied Constituents. Interested constituents that are affected by national cultural property laws are also dissatisfied. In addition to conflicting claims between countries, groups within countries may contest ownership. For example, when the tribally important Afo-A-Kom statue was returned to Cameroon, the national government was reluctant to return it to the Kom people. The government of Cameroon wanted to build national loyalty, and in order to do so thought it necessary to weaken tribal identities, such as those of the Kom people, which tribal artifacts reinforce. Similar conflicts can and do occur whenever a central authority seeks to dominate or repress a minority culture. Thus, in numerous places throughout the world, including China's treatment of Tibet or Brazil's and Indonesia's treatment of their indigenous peoples, the cultural identity and property of minority groups may be at risk to dominant national interests.

A host of interest groups that cut across national and intranational lines are also dissatisfied with the present state of cultural property claims. Archaeologists, who usually express sympathy for national claims, may be hostage to a source country's ideological and political needs in order to do their work, and so remain silent but critical of the nations that do little to protect their cultural property from the nonscientific excavation that results in the loss of knowledge. Anthropologists, ethnologists, art historians, and others may similarly be critical of above ground cultural property that is not properly maintained and protected. Art historians, who can glean much from art even without knowledge of provenance and context, may be critical of archaeologists and ethnologists who refuse to preserve or publish information about nonprovenanced pieces. Additionally, anthropologists and ethnologists may deplore the lack of concern for and pressures on indigenous peoples and cultures that are ignored or made subservient to national priorities and be critical of the archaeologists who further national priorities at the expense of minority cultures.

Market forces, reflecting dealer, collector, and museum interests, also affect cultural property. There are dealers, collectors, and even museum professionals whose conduct may evince no concern other than their own pleasure and profit. But many dealers are also scholars, whose concerns, like those of museum curators, are to preserve and share art and artifacts from diverse places and cultures. Collectors with similar concerns have been the holders and protectors of cultural property, with their collections often eventually ending up in museums, and without whom whole areas of human achievement might have been lost. While deploring the loss of knowledge from clandestine digs, chary of breaking export restrictions, and concerned to honor others' ownership claims, these participants in the market for cultural property reasonably deny the incontrovertibility of a nation's claim to all cultural property within its borders. Their refusal to abstain from acquiring unprovenanced pieces on the practical ground that it is unrealistic to think that this would end clandestine excavation is not unreasonable or unprincipled. Although not ideal, more good may come from their collecting than from abandoning the field to unscrupulous or neophyte collectors, who are less likely to preserve the cultural property involved.

Inadequacies in Present Approaches. In the end, all interested parties are dissatisfied with the present situation. Most nations do not consider that their right to cultural property is sufficiently respected. Indigenous peoples complain that their cultural interests are not recognized. The scientific community—archaeologists, anthropologists, ethnologists, and other scholars—is concerned that access to and protection of cultural property as a source of knowledge is inadequate. Art historians, dealers, collectors, museums, and others for whom aesthetic concerns may be paramount believe that there is a lack of appreciation and interest in the artifacts themselves.

All may deplore the present situation, but little improvement is likely. This is because each group, convinced that it is right, has been unwilling to work with others to fashion an effective solution. The inadequacy of the present approaches is illustrated by unscientific excavations. All except the completely unprincipled lose when cultural property is unearthed in nonprofessional, clandestine digs. Nation, tribe, scientist, dealer, collector, and museum are all the poorer for information lost and potentially irreplaceable. No one truly interested would prefer an object lacking its history to the same object with its history. Yet, unless all parties are willing to compromise, recognize the interests of others, and work together with them, there will be no solution. Thus, most source countries' claims to cultural property tend to ignore local populations whose heritage may be in issue, the independent claims of science, and the effect of market forces. In turn, these parties may ignore conflicting overly broad national claims.

The ineffectiveness of one-sided approaches is also evident on the international level. First UNESCO and now UNIDROIT, both with special provisions for dealing with excavated objects, have or can be expected to have limited success because of their proponents' inability to recognize other constituents' concerns. UNIDROIT is most telling. Rather than limit the convention's provisions to cover a list of specific noncontroversial abuses, its sponsors added language to declare that unauthorized excavated objects were "stolen," creating problems for the importing countries needed to ratify it—without creating any real benefit. Thus, rather than limit themselves to what was practicable, the convention's sponsors pushed a principled position unlikely to obtain the consensus needed to improve the existing, unsatisfactory situation. Other interest groups are equally likely to push one-sided positions, precluding compromise that could benefit all. Obvious but limited solutions, such as joint sponsorship by all interested groups in scientific excavations, which could save knowledge of cultural property that might otherwise be lost, are ignored.

The Difficulty in Making Things Better. Given all this, the central question in cultural property discussions should be why the various participants, whose common interests outweigh their differences, are so unable to work together to improve the situation. Rather than "Who should own a culture's property?" the question should be "Why so much dissension?"

A review of cultural property's history sheds some light. Although the ancient world was harsh and unforgiving, with whole populations subject to devastation and their property destroyed or taken as spoils in war, there seems to have been an easier acceptance then than now of the interrelations between peoples and cultures. Ancient peoples freely took from one another. They did not seek to be self-inventing; they did not seek priority or purity for their own culture; and they did not seem concerned that they would lose their own identity and uniqueness if they took from or gave to others. A large part of the intransigence and intractable nature of the current cultural property debate is a false arrogance, the self-aggrandizing view that aesthetic and scientific achievements reflect only the culture or people who took the last step in their creation. The reality is that there is little totally unique cultural property. Humans are more the product of a common past and heritage than of self-created differences. This is why they understand, appreciate, and want to share in the cultural achievements of others.

A second, related, misconception helps fuel the cultural property debate. It is that we are diminished by sharing what is supposedly uniquely ours. Greece is not less great because the Parthenon's frieze is in London. France is not less French because there are more Impressionist paintings outside that country than within its borders. Nor is nineteenth-century English art less English because England's artists were deeply influenced by Greece's classical sculpture, nor is American Impressionism less American because of French influence. Generally, we better understand what is special to one culture when other cultures want to share it. Herodotus, Marco Polo, and Ibn Baṭṭūṭah, like tourists today, were better able to understand what was unique about themselves by being exposed to cultural differences on their travels. Locking Mexican, Peruvian, Greek, and Turkish duplicative artifacts in museum storage vaults does not help protect some innate national identity—it diminishes it. The concern that seems to drive a good deal of the

retentive, nationalistic approach to cultural property—that a culture's distinctiveness will be lost or distorted if shared—is usually mistaken.

Moreover, the cultural property that a nation, community, or people consciously identifies with functions symbolically. The definitive icons of a culture are not what is yet to be excavated or what exists in another country's museum—unless indoctrination makes it so. What is critical to a nation or a people's sense of identity is the long-established myths, images, and customs that are part of the fabric of a culture. It is what is collectively taught and imagined as the core of a community or people, something that is more created than found. Invariably, little is actually changed when cultural property moves across borders. The exception is when removal is nearly complete, when few or no examples remain. Cultural genocide requires a determined effort to decimate and eradicate. Whatever the law, it is unlikely that it alone can ever stem such catastrophes.

Although these aspects of cultural property would appear to make a more satisfactory general approach possible, the opposite is more likely the case. The fact is that the source of the debate is basically psychological and political. Ultimately, what drives a country, community, or people's claim that certain property belongs to them is a need to define themselves as separate and distinct. To claim something as a culture's property is, at least in part, to declare that it is distinctive and exclusive. However unrealistic, imagined, and ideological, and ultimately unlikely to create the recognition and self-regard sought, cultural property serves as a symbolic bond that helps makes a nation, community, or people who they are—and necessarily unlike others. It is like family portraits and heirlooms: something special to those who claim it as their own. Cultural property both manifests and creates a sense of belonging and shared heritage. Like family portraits and heirlooms, it does not matter how inappropriate, posed, and touched-up the picture, or how recent and artificial the heirloom, cultural property gives a needed personal perspective and identity, however inaccurate.

Not only is cultural property ultimately highly personal and political, it also is related to needs that are becoming more strident. The need for a nation and people to assert their own identity that was provoked by Napoleon now seems innate and universal. The threat to a separate cultural identity that France represented with Napoleon's military conquests now seems to arise from global commerce's new internationalism, which offers standardized ubiquitous products. With the exception of those for whom such products reflect their culture, the reaction to the dominance and homogeneity of a commercial world culture seems to be the increased need to assert differences, for which claims to cultural property play an important part. Modern technology, communication, and commerce's tendency to assimilate cultural differences have provoked an increased need to assert those differences.

In effect, there seems to be an inherent conflict between cultural property as a source of a nation's or a people's individuality and identity and humanity's claim to cultural property as its shared heritage, to be discovered through science, displayed in the world's museums, and otherwise universally manifested. If this is so, there can be no satisfactory, comprehensive, overarching approach to cultural property. A better understanding of this may lead to more effective piecemeal solutions.

[*See also* Cultural Studies; *and* Museums.]

BIBLIOGRAPHY

Bator, Paul M. *The International Trade in Art.* Chicago, 1983.
International Journal of Cultural Property 1– (1992–). Web site http://www.oup.co.uk/intjcp
Merryman, John Henry. "Thinking about the Elgin Marbles." *Michigan Law Review* 83 (1985).
Merryman, John Henry. "Two Ways of Thinking about Cultural Property." *American Journal of International Law* 80 (1986): 831–853.
Merryman, John Henry. "The Retention of Cultural Property." *Davis Law Review* 21 (1988).
Merryman, John Henry. "The Public Interest in Cultural Property." *California Law Review* 77 (1989): 339–364.
Merryman, John Henry. "The UNIDROIT Convention: Three Significant Departures from the *Urtext.*" *International Journal of Cultural Property* 5 (1996): 11–18.
Prott, Lyndel V., and P. J. O'Keefe. *Law and the Cultural Heritage,* vol. 1, *Discovery and Evacuation.* Oxford, 1984.
Prott, Lyndel V., and P. J. O'Keefe. *Law and the Cultural Heritage,* vol. 3, *Movement.* London, 1989.

DANIEL SHAPIRO

Government-Funded Art and the First Amendment

Art has long been considered an important aspect of freedom of expression. Although art does not always communicate in rational ways, and may take many nonliteral forms, it remains a basic form of human expression: it is created by humans for each other, as a way of communicating. Accordingly, the United States Supreme Court has long protected artistic expression from government suppression. For example, under the Court's "obscenity" doctrine, if sexually explicit expression has artistic value, it cannot be censored, even if it is otherwise offensive. Moreover, the Court has protected as "symbolic speech" such acts as wearing a flag patch on one's pants, burning a flag, and wearing an armband. In such cases, the Court has acknowledged that communication can take many forms, and that as long as the government's interest in regulating particular conduct (such as flag burning) is motivated by what the conduct communicates, it should be treated as a restriction on speech. Thus, artistic expression is generally protected by the First Amendment from direct suppression.

Less well established, however, is the extent to which the freedom of expression protects the rights of artists who re-

ceive some sort of government subsidy or support. Public support of the arts is an institution in most Western democracies, and has become an area of great controversy in the United States. How should the freedom of expression apply where government is not directly censoring an artist, but is merely declining to subsidize her work? United States legislators intent on barring the National Endowment for the Arts (NEA) from funding controversial art argue that artists may have a constitutional right to make art, but not on the government's dime. Thus, Senator Jesse Helms, the leading congressional proponent of content restrictions, has written: "The [NEA] legislation in no way 'censors' artists; it does not prevent artists from producing, creating, or displaying blasphemous or obscene 'art' at their own expense in the private sector" (1990). Such arguments were fueled by the Supreme Court's 1991 decision in *Rust v. Sullivan,* which upheld restrictions on what federally funded family planning counselors could tell their clients about abortion.

At first reading, *Rust* appears to support the sweeping proposition that government is free to restrict speech whenever it is footing the bill. If the government can bar federally funded family planning counselors from mentioning abortion in pregnancy counseling, why should it not be permitted to require artists who receive federal grants to refrain from creating indecent art? But the Court in *Rust* asserted that its reasoning does *not* mean that "funding by the Government . . . is invariably sufficient to justify government control over the content of expression." It noted, for example, that in public forums and public universities, First Amendment dictates restrict the government's ability to control expression even where it is subsidizing speech. Nor did the Court overrule prior decisions mandating strict content neutrality in government subsidies to the press.

More recently, in the 1995 case of *Rosenberger v. Rectors and Visitors of the University of Virginia,* the Supreme Court ruled that the principle applied to uphold speech restrictions in *Rust* does not apply where the government is funding a forum designed to encourage a diverse expression of views from private speakers, but applies *only* where the government itself "is the speaker or when it enlists private entities to convey its own message."

What makes this area of the law so difficult is that government control over the content of the speech it funds is both necessary to and potentially subversive of a vital democracy. The citizenry has a First Amendment interest in knowing the government's point of view; self-government requires nonneutral government speech, so that citizens know whether their representatives' ideas reflect their own. If the government were required to remain neutral in all of the speech it funds, the president could not express his own ideas without providing equal time to all opposing points of view.

At the same time, government funding of speech may subvert the democratic process by skewing public debate toward ideas that the government favors. The public's interest in a robust public debate would be undermined if the government remained free to control the content of speech in all funded settings. A public university directed to teach only ideas supportive of government policies would raise First Amendment concerns even (or indeed, especially) if it were staffed entirely by committed ideologues happy to teach within the government's directive, and free to engage in unrestricted speech off campus. Such a university would provide an impoverished speech forum for its students, and would be unable to play an independent role in the broader public dialogue.

Where the government seeks to prohibit speech directly, the First Amendment demands that it maintain neutrality toward the content and viewpoint of the speech. This rule is designed to curb government action that threatens to skew the marketplace of ideas or to indoctrinate the citizenry. Government funding of speech raises similar concerns, but one cannot require across-the-board government neutrality in funding without placing a stranglehold on the business of government.

Citizens are caught in a bind. They want the government to provide them with information but not to overwhelm them with propaganda. They want public education but not indoctrination. They want publicly funded art, but not government art. The rub is that these lines are extremely difficult, and often impossible, to draw in a specific case.

Without explicitly saying so, the Supreme Court has sought to balance these competing concerns through a structural accommodation of the competing values and dangers of government-funded speech. It recognizes the legitimacy of nonneutral government support of speech, but at the same time insists on protecting certain spheres of independence and neutrality as institutional checks against the dangers of government propaganda and indoctrination. In these protected spheres, government must afford a degree of independence to institutions and speakers notwithstanding the presence of government funding, toward the end of ensuring a vigorous public debate. In other funded settings, such as when it undertakes an advertising and educational campaign to discourage smoking or drinking, the government remains free to support specific viewpoints and dictate content.

A spheres-of-neutrality approach to First Amendment doctrine explains what the *Rust* Court acknowledged but left unexplained: that in spheres such as public forums, public universities, and the press, government cannot avoid First Amendment scrutiny by arguing that it is merely declining to subsidize the exercise of a constitutional right. First Amendment strictures of neutrality and independence apply to government funding in these settings because each of these institutions plays a central role in shaping and contributing to public debate, and because the internal functioning of each institution demands insulation from government content control.

For its first twenty-four years of existence, the National Endowment for the Arts operated consistently within these principles and was in effect treated as a "sphere of neutrality." Its statutory criteria focused on aesthetic excellence, without imposing substantive restrictions on the content of funded art. In 1989, however, Congress prohibited funding of art that "may be considered obscene, including but not limited to, depictions of sadomasochism, homoeroticism, the sexual exploitation of children, or individuals engaged in sex acts and which, when taken as a whole, do not have serious literary, artistic, political, or scientific value." This language was hopelessly vague—on one view, it effected no change in NEA funding, because anything the NEA funded would virtually by definition have "serious literary [or] artistic . . . value." It did send a chilling effect through the arts community, however, which it was no doubt intended to do. Several NEA recipients challenged the standard on First Amendment grounds, and in *Bella Lewitzky Dance Foundation v. Frohnmayer,* one court struck it down as unconstitutionally vague.

In 1990, Congress superseded the obscenity language by requiring the NEA to award grants on the basis of "excellence and artistic merit . . . taking into consideration general standards of decency and respect for the diverse beliefs and values of the American public." This provision similarly had a broad chilling effect, because artists seeking grants could not possibly know whether their projects would be deemed consistent with "general standards of decency."

Four performance artists whose grants had previously been vetoed because of their controversial content and the National Association of Artists' Organizations challenged the constitutionality of the "decency" provision, and in 1992, a federal district court declared the provision unconstitutional. The court in *Finley v. National Endowment for the Arts* found that the decency standard, like the obscenity standard that preceded it, was unconstitutionally vague. More important, however, the court held that the standard violated the First Amendment mandate of neutrality that governs publicly funded art programs. In 1996, the *Finley* decision was affirmed by the U.S. Court of Appeals for the Ninth Circuit.

The district court reasoned that the arts, like public forums, universities, and the press, are central to public debate and dialogue. Artistic expression, no less than academic speech, journalism, or a soapbox address, is at the core of a democratic society's cultural and political vitality. Congress recognized as much in creating the NEA. The Senate report that accompanied the NEA legislation stated that the arts "are at the center of our lives and are of prime importance to the Nation and to ourselves."

Moreover, as in the public university or public forum, a requirement of neutrality in NEA funding is fully consistent with the institution's purposes. When President Lyndon Baines Johnson proposed the creation of a national program to fund the arts, he insisted that in doing so government should not "seek to restrict the freedom of the artist to pursue his calling in his own way. Freedom is an essential condition for the artist, and in proportion as freedom is diminished so is the prospect of artistic achievement." Congress agreed, and the NEA statute provides that the Endowment was designed "to help create and sustain . . . a climate encouraging freedom of thought, imagination, and inquiry." This freedom can be maintained only if the NEA awards grants based on aesthetic merit. A standard of "aesthetic excellence," of course, is not content-neutral. The NEA will fund works whose content has aesthetic merit, and will not fund works whose content lacks aesthetic merit. Some have argued that an "aesthetic merit" standard is at least as vague as "decency," and therefore if the government can impose a standard of "aesthetic excellence," it should also be permitted to impose a standard of decency.

There are three responses to this argument. First, aesthetic merit, like academic merit in the university context, is a qualitative standard that, as long as it is not abused, poses less danger of censorship and indoctrination than a substantive standard such as "decency." This is because its content, while not easily defined, is enforced and given meaning by a community of professionals, distinct from government. By contrast, a substantive standard such as "decency" is imposed by government itself. Second, standards such as aesthetic and academic merit do have a shared meaning in the culture as a whole, largely as a result of the work of the community of arts and academic professionals. They are the criteria by which awards, grants, employment, and tenure are regularly judged by that community. "Decency," by contrast, has no such shared meaning, and its enforcement will be left to wholly subjective decisions of government officials. Third, unlike "artistic merit," "decency" is a code word for avoiding controversy, and thus will have a far broader chilling effect on artists interested in obtaining arts funding.

In the end, government funding of the arts will best serve its purpose of encouraging artistic freedom and innovation if it is implemented in a way that respects freedom of expression. Just as academic freedom in the public university is required by the First Amendment, so artistic freedom is required in public funding of the arts. That freedom can be maintained only if aesthetic rather than political standards guide the allocation of government largesse.

[*See also* National Endowment for the Arts; *and* Politics and Aesthetics.]

BIBLIOGRAPHY

Cases

Bella Lewitzky Dance Foundation v. Frohnmayer, 754 F. Supp. 774 (C.D. Cal. 1991).
Finley v. National Endowment for the Arts, 795 F. Supp. 1457 (C.D. Cal. 1992).

Rosenberger v. Rectors and Visitors of the University of Virginia, 115 S. Ct. 2510 (1995).
Rust v. Sullivan, 111 S. Ct. 1759 (1991).

Other Sources

Cole, David. "Beyond Unconstitutional Conditions: Charting Spheres of Neutrality in Government-Funded Speech." *New York University Law Review* 67 (1992).
Helms, Jesse. "Tax-Paid Obscenity." *Nova Law Review* 14 (1990).

DAVID COLE

Censorship

Censorship is the suppression of information, images, or ideas because they are considered dangerous or objectionable. It is one of the oldest and most familiar practices of human societies. Those who hold political power in any society almost always seek to suppress information and ideas that they find critical or embarrassing, or that otherwise threaten their hegemony. Artists (including not only visual artists but writers, performers, and musicians) have never been immune from censorship, and in fact have been among its most frequent targets.

This essay focuses on censorship of the arts—that is, creative expression—in the United States. The United States is unique in having in the First Amendment to its Constitution a prohibition on government action "abridging the freedom of speech," and a judicial tradition, at least in the twentieth century, of protecting that First Amendment right in the courts. "Freedom of speech" certainly includes artistic expression, as the U.S. Supreme Court noted in 1995 when it mentioned "the painting of Jackson Pollock, music of Arnold Schoenberg, or Jabberwocky verse of Lewis Carroll" as examples of expression that is "unquestionably" protected by the Constitution *(Hurley v. Irish-American Gay, Lesbian and Bisexual Group)*. Nevertheless, censorship of the arts and entertainment does exist in the United States in many forms.

The most direct and obvious form of arts censorship is found in criminal or civil laws that ban certain types of expression outright. Among the most common subjects or ideas that have been suppressed in this way are sexuality, subversive political beliefs, and "blasphemy," broadly defined to include ideas or images that question, contradict, or reflect disrespect toward particular religious beliefs. At least since the 1960s, however, the U.S. Supreme Court has interpreted the First Amendment to limit, if not completely invalidate, laws suppressing subversive or blasphemous ideas. This has left sexuality as the one area where direct, official censorship of artistic expression is still widely practiced in the United States.

The reasons for affording speech on sexual subjects less constitutional protection than other forms of expression are complex, both sociologically and historically. Certainly there is nothing in the First Amendment itself that relegates sexual speech to second-class status. In 1957, however, the Supreme Court ruled that "obscenity" is not protected by the First Amendment because it is "no essential part of any exposition of ideas" and is a type of expression "utterly without redeeming social importance" *(Roth v. United States)*.

In 1973, the Court reaffirmed this conclusion, and made "obscenity" easier for government prosecutors to prove by establishing a three-part test: (1) the material must depict or describe sexual conduct in a manner that is "patently offensive" according to "contemporary community standards"; (2) the material, taken as a whole, must appeal to the "prurient interest"; and (3) the material, taken as a whole, must lack any "serious literary, artistic, political, or scientific value" *(Miller v. California)*. All three parts of this obscenity definition are extremely vague and subjective: what is "patently offensive," appeals to the "prurient interest," or lacks "serious value" will obviously differ depending on the attitudes and tastes of the person making the judgment.

Although the third part of the *Miller v. California* obscenity test would appear to protect serious art or literature, in reality government officials do rely on obscenity laws to threaten, and sometimes pursue, prosecutions of creative works, much as they used these laws earlier in the century to exclude James Joyce's *Ulysses* from being imported into the United States, and to suppress works by major authors ranging from Aristophanes, Chaucer, and Boccaccio to Theodore Dreiser, Ernest Hemingway, William Faulkner, Edmund Wilson, D. H. Lawrence, Ralph Ellison, Walt Whitman, and many others. Art prosecuted for obscenity as recently as the 1990s has included a museum retrospective of works by the acclaimed photographer Robert Mapplethorpe, rap music by the popular band 2 Live Crew, safe-sex posters at an Oklahoma health clinic, provocative alternative journalism on the subject of rape, and the avant-garde antifascist film *Salò*, directed by one of the leading Italian postwar intellectuals and cinema artists, Pier Paolo Pasolini.

Judgments about whether a creative work has "serious" literary, artistic, or other value are so inherently subjective that, at least outside the obscenity context, the Supreme Court has recognized that "it is largely because government officials cannot make principled distinctions in this area that the Constitution leaves matters of taste and style so largely to the individual" *(Cohen v. California, 1971)*. Paradoxically, however, when it comes to art or entertainment dealing with sex, government agencies in the United States—police, prosecutors, and courts—are empowered to make precisely these value judgments under state and federal obscenity laws.

In addition to obscenity laws, other direct censorship of sexual subject matter is accomplished through prohibitions on the dissemination of "child pornography," "indecency," and material that is "harmful to minors." Each of these laws raises its own set of constitutional and political issues.

"Harmful to minors" laws ban the distribution to children or teenagers of material that is constitutionally protected for adults and that meets a modified version of the three-part *Miller v. California* obscenity test: whether a local community thinks the material lacks "serious value" for, is "patently offensive" to, and appeals to the "prurient interest" of those under age eighteen. Because minors vary greatly in their level of maturity, and because the attitudes of adults regarding what art, entertainment, or information is suitable for minors also varies, "harmful to minors" laws suffer even more severe problems of vagueness and subjectivity than do "adult" obscenity bans.

Prohibitions on "indecency" have also been justified in the interests of protecting the young. "Indecency," unlike obscenity, is constitutionally protected speech, and until the early 1990s its regulation was therefore confined primarily to radio and television broadcasting, where the U.S. government's Federal Communications Commission (FCC) already has broad supervisory powers. The FCC defines indecency as "language or material that, in context, depicts or describes, in terms patently offensive as measured by contemporary community standards for the broadcast medium, sexual or excretory activities or organs." In 1978, the Supreme Court ruled that the government may "channel" such indecent communications to late-night broadcast hours, but may not ban them outright *(FCC v. Pacifica Foundation)*. The program at issue in *Pacifica* was a comic monologue that satirized social taboos against the use of "dirty words." As a result of the *Pacifica* decision, the FCC operates as a freewheeling censorship agency for radio and television in the United States. In the early 1990s, it imposed heavy fines on broadcasters who carried the Howard Stern radio talk show because of Stern's style of humorous, and, to some listeners, offensive, sexual innuendo.

Congress has applied the "indecency" standard to other media, with uneven results. A ban on "indecent" telephone messages was struck down by the Supreme Court in 1989 *(Sable Communications v. FCC)*, but a later law requiring that telephone service providers take steps to ensure that minors do not have access to "indecency" was upheld by two federal courts. In 1992, the U.S. Congress authorized censorship of "indecency" on some cable television channels, but the Supreme Court struck down portions of this law in June 1996. Meanwhile, in February 1996 Congress passed the "Communications Decency Act," whose effect was to criminalize all "indecent" messages on the Internet or other parts of the expanding computer communications system. Because the Internet is a global medium, the task of determining what computer messages are "patently offensive" according to "contemporary community standards" would be formidable. In June 1996, a three-judge federal district court in Philadelphia ruled that the "indecency" provisions of the law were unconstitutional.

Images that are deemed to constitute "child pornography" are, like obscenity, an exception to the First Amendment, and are justified in the interests of protecting children from sexual abuse (*New York v. Ferber,* 1982). Criminalizing child pornography, however, is at best an indirect means of deterring actual abuse, and zealous prosecutors have used these laws repeatedly to pursue artists who work with child subjects but who have not in fact abused or exploited their models.

In 1990, for example, federal agents began a sixteen-month investigation of a well-respected art photographer, Jock Sturges, after raiding his home and studio and seizing many thousands of negatives and prints, some of which pictured child nudes. Art galleries that handled Sturges's work were questioned and asked for their customer lists. Ultimately, a grand jury refused to indict the artist.

Similarly, in 1992 the U.S. Customs Service seized photographic proofs for a book by the British artist Graham Ovenden, and would not return them until the editor to whom they were addressed filed a motion in federal court. The nudes showed no sexual conduct. In 1993, the state of New Jersey indicted an art photography student, Ejlat Feuer, for images of his daughter, made as part of a class assignment; again, no sexual activity was involved. The case was finally dismissed, but only after nearly two years of court proceedings and a temporary order by the state social-service department expelling Feuer from his home for several weeks pending investigation of child abuse charges. (He was eventually exonerated.)

The criminal and civil prohibitions on "obscene" or "indecent" speech, and on "child pornography," have a dramatic effect on artistic expression in the United States. Visual artists, including photographers and filmmakers, are increasingly forced to avoid any depiction of child nudes, a time-honored artistic subject. Any artist who hopes to have her work presented on radio or television must avoid explicit depiction or description of sexuality, or even of certain forbidden words. To this day, condoms are not advertised on broadcast television, and despite its importance for public health, explicit education about safe-sex techniques is also inhibited by obscenity and "indecency" laws.

Obscenity, indecency, and child pornography laws are direct forms of censorship and, as noted, focus mostly on sexual subject matter. A far broader range of material is censored *indirectly* in the United States, through restrictions on government funding, other benefits, and use of public property, and through control of public schools and colleges. Not only sexuality and nudity, but subjects such as violence, drugs, racism, homosexuality, flag desecration, other imagery or ideas that are deemed unpatriotic, and art or literature considered offensive to religious beliefs are among the frequent targets.

The government owns a great deal of property, for example, on which citizens congregate, often specifically for free-speech activities. Public parks and sidewalks are in this category, as are many civic buildings. Often, local officials invite members of the community to exhibit artwork in public areas of government buildings, or musicians entertain the public on city streets. Books, magazines, posters, and other artwork may also be displayed or sold on public property. Frequently, however, officials will remove a particular work of art from display because they, or some of their constituents, consider it "offensive" or "pornographic" (for example, a nude), or because its symbolism offends majoritarian religious or political sentiments.

This is a less direct form of censorship than criminal prosecution because, as the government will maintain, no absolute suppression of ideas is involved; the artist can always exhibit her work in a private museum or gallery. The government, so the argument goes, is merely declining to assist or "sponsor" the exhibition. Similar justifications are offered for denying government arts grants on the basis of "indecency" or "disrespect for the diverse beliefs and values of the American public" (the language of a 1990 statute restricting the National Endowment for the Arts). But because so much property is owned by the government, and so many programs rely on government support—including libraries, scientific and academic research, public universities, and public broadcasting—censorship is often accomplished indirectly through the denial of funding, other benefits, or access to public space.

In fact, indirect censorship of artistic expression through the manipulation of government funding or benefit programs probably has greater potential to force artists and arts institutions to self-censor than does the existence of direct legal prohibitions against obscenity or indecency. In the wake of controversies surrounding the National Endowment for the Arts in the early 1990s, museums and theater companies that depended on government or corporate grants became more cautious about presenting controversial material, and in some instances canceled or censored programs. In 1991, for example, an Idaho theater director was forced to eliminate a brief nude scene from the play *Bent,* about Nazi treatment of homosexuals, which was scheduled to be presented at the Idaho Shakespeare Festival. The festival had canceled an earlier play entirely because of "community standards." In 1990, the Corcoran Gallery in Washington, D.C., canceled a Robert Mapplethorpe show for fear of antagonizing government funders. By the mid-1990s, public and school librarians were increasingly removing books that were offensive to their government funders.

Censorship in public schools also increased dramatically in the 1990s. Student publications, dramatic productions, library books, and curriculum were among the frequent targets. The books most commonly attacked have included

Mark Twain's *Huckleberry Finn* (because of its portrayal of racism and use of the word *nigger*), Maya Angelou's *I Know Why the Caged Bird Sings* (because of sexual content and a description of a childhood rape), and almost anything by the celebrated children's author Judy Blume (because of realistic discussions of subjects interesting to teenagers, including menstruation and masturbation).

State and local governments in the United States control primary and secondary public education, and fund many public universities as well. These are important and traditional settings for the free exchange of ideas, yet the Supreme Court has ruled that local authorities have broad discretion to decide what materials shall be in the curriculum and in school libraries, and to reject or eliminate works that are "vulgar" or otherwise "educationally unsuitable."

There are constitutional limits, however. In *Board of Education, Island Trees School District v. Pico* (1982), the Supreme Court said that the "transcendent imperatives" of the First Amendment require some restriction on local officials' power to censor art and literature. School boards may not exercise their discretion "in a narrowly partisan or political manner," said the Court, because "our Constitution does not permit the official suppression of ideas."

It is on the basis of this principle that students, parents, teachers, and librarians have sometimes challenged school authorities' censorship decisions in the courts. In the early 1990s, the American Civil Liberties Union brought several such cases. In one, students and parents in Kansas claimed that the removal of a gay-themed novel, *Annie on My Mind*, from local high-school libraries violated the First Amendment because the school board's reasons for removing the book were based on its members' ideological and religious objections to any affirmative depiction of homosexuality. After a lengthy trial in 1995, a judge ruled that the school board had violated the First Amendment rights of the students, and ordered the book returned to the shelves. Another case, in Montana, challenged the firing of a library aide who had lent junior-high students two books about women's history to assist them with a research project on witchcraft. Parents and school board members objected to what they perceived as satanism, feminism, and sexual explicitness in the books. The case was settled after the aide won an administrative ruling that her firing was arbitrary and unjustified.

In both of these cases, the local school board decisions were driven by hostility to particular ideas, precisely the motives condemned by the Supreme Court in its *Pico* decision. Yet, many would maintain that removing books from libraries, or punishing librarians for lending them, is not censorship because the books are not being directly suppressed: they may still be available at bookstores or by mail; and the government simply has no obligation to sponsor or pay for books or other forms of expression that the majority of citizens find objectionable.

Thus, the debate over censorship continues. Despite the "transcendent imperatives" of the First Amendment, censorship remains a superficially attractive, if ultimately false, solution to social problems.

[*See also* Morality and Aesthetics; *and* Obscenity.]

BIBLIOGRAPHY

Beahm, George, ed. *War of Words: The Censorship Debate.* Kansas City, Mo., 1993.

Bolton, Richard, ed. *Culture Wars: Documents from the Recent Controversies in the Arts.* New York, 1992.

Carmilly-Weinberger, Moshe. *Fear of Art: Censorship and Freedom of Expression in Art.* New York, 1986.

Clapp, Jane. *Art Censorship: A Chronology of Proscribed and Prescribed Art.* Metuchen, N.J., 1972.

de Grazia, Edward. *Girls Lean Back Everywhere: The Law of Obscenity and the Assault on Genius.* New York, 1992.

DelFattore, Joan. *What Johnny Shouldn't Read: Textbook Censorship in America.* New Haven, 1992.

Dubin, Stephen C. *Arresting Images: Impolitic Art and Uncivil Actions.* London and New York, 1992.

Heins, Marjorie. *Sex, Sin, and Blasphemy: A Guide to America's Censorship Wars.* New York, 1993.

Kendrick, Walter. *The Secret Museum: Pornography in Modern Culture.* New York, 1987.

People for the American Way. *Attacks on the Freedom to Learn.* Washington, 1983. Yearly report on library censorship.

Pally, Marcia. *Sense and Censorship: The Vanity of Bonfires.* New York, 1991.

Wallace, Jonathan, and Mark Mangin. *Sex, Laws, and Cyberspace.* New York, 1996.

Marjorie Heins

Trademarks and Art

Copyright protects works of literary and artistic expression; trademarks protect names and symbols that identify the source of goods, including works of art. Thus, copyright law deals with the contents of a novel or a painting, while trademark law deals with the title of the work and the author's or painter's right of attribution. One case has even held that trademark law can protect a painter's "style." Sometimes copyright and trademark overlap: for example, cartoon characters may be protected by copyright law, and, because they are often used to market goods and services, they serve as indicators of origin and may therefore be protected as trademarks as well.

Copyright infringement generally consists of unauthorized use or copying of the protected work. This can be shown by proving that the infringer had access to the work and that the infringing work is "substantially similar" to the protected work. Trademark infringement generally depends on whether the use of the infringing mark creates a "likelihood of confusion" among an appreciable number of consumers. The type of confusion that generally gives rise to liability is confusion as to the source of the infringing goods, but other types of confusion can also arise; for example, as a result of the defendant's acts, the public may be confused into thinking that the plaintiff approved the defendant's goods, or licensed the use of the trademark on the defendant's goods.

In perhaps the first legal decision involving trademarks and art, the Council of Nuremberg in 1512 issued a decree stating:

> Whereas, a certain foreigner, who sells engravings under the Council Chamber has, among others, certain ones bearing the signature of Albrecht Dürer,
>
> Now, therefore, it is ordered that he shall obliterate all such signatures, and keep no more such engravings in future, and if he shall neglect so to do, he shall be brought before the Council for fraud.

The "signature" referred to in the decree is probably Dürer's famous monogram:

The wording of the decision shows that the law of trademarks is an outgrowth of the law of fraud; what the "foreigner" had done was use Dürer's signature (his trademark) to "pass off" the foreigner's engravings as Dürer's.

Would Dürer (or his modern-day counterpart) be able to use the trademark laws today to protect his art or his reputation? Clearly, the laws of fraud would today, as in Dürer's day, prohibit the use of an artist's signature on a fake. But more complex issues arise today: appropriation art, the commercial exploitation of art on calendars and other commercial products, and even claims that an artist's "style" has been infringed on all raise trademark issues. To understand how trademark law might apply to these issues, the following background might be helpful.

The Lanham Act. Federal trademark law is embodied in the Trademark Act of 1946, also known as the Lanham Act. The Lanham Act defines trademarks as words, names, or symbols used to identify and distinguish the goods and services of one person from those of another. In addition to protecting trademarks, the Lanham Act proscribes unfair competition, including false advertising and the use of "false designations of origin."

The act provides for injunctions against acts of unfair competition and trademark infringement, as well as monetary relief. It also provides for the destruction of reproductions, plates, molds, and similar materials in the possession of the defendant.

The unfair competition provisions of the Lanham Act have been held to guarantee an artist proper credit or attribution in appropriate cases. In one case, for example, an actor contracted to star in a film and to receive "star billing."

He sued under the Lanham Act (and prevailed) when the film studio substituted the name of another actor for his own in the credits and in advertising. The court held that use of the substitute name was a misrepresentation, technically known as "reverse passing off." ("Passing Off" is the sale of one's goods as those of a competitor; "reverse passing off" is the sale of a competitor's goods as one's own.)

The Lanham Act also grant artists a kind of moral right to prevent distortions of their works. For example, the famous Monty Python troupe was able to enjoin an American television network from broadcasting edited versions of programs the troupe had originally done in England for the British Broadcasting Corporation (BBC). The court held that the editing by the American network "impairs the integrity of the original work." It found that the "truncated version at times omitted the climax of the skits to which [Monty Python's] rare brand of humor was leading and at other times deleted essential elements of the schematic development of the story line." It was the use of the Monty Python name, however, rather than the editing itself, that violated the Lanham Act. The use of that name, the court said, created "a false impression of the product's origin."

Dilution. In 1996, a provision was added to the Lanham Act protecting famous trademarks from the somewhat nebulous act of "dilution." Dilution has been held to encompass two separate wrongs: (1) "blurring" the distinctiveness of a mark, and (2) tarnishing a mark, or injuring the business reputation symbolized by the mark, through use of a mark on inferior goods or in an unwholesome context. An example of blurring the distinctiveness of a mark would be use of a famous mark on an unrelated product: for example, Kodak pianos. Many parodies of famous marks involve tarnishment: for example, the sale of a poster with the words "Enjoy Cocaine" printed in the famous Coca-Cola script was held to tarnish the Coca-Cola mark.

State Law. The common law of unfair competition provides remedies against the kinds of activities prohibited under the Lanham Act. In addition, many states have their own trademark statutes. About half the states, including New York and California, have adopted "dilution" statutes.

Reproduction and Appropriation. To return to the modern-day counterpart of Dürer, let us assume someone has obtained a genuine engraving by a famous artist, and has made exact copies of the work. The unfortunate artist whose name is used on a reproduction probably has no remedy under the Lanham Act or state law (although copyright law probably would provide a remedy). Assuming the work has not been mutilated in some way, the use of the artist's name is simply a truthful statement of the origin of the work.

If the artist's name is removed, does the artist have a right to compel attribution? The courts have not held that artists have such a right. Although the Lanham Act prohibits affirmative misrepresentations, it is difficult to find any court decisions in which the act was held to extend to omissions, and Congress probably intended that it not extend to omissions.

In appropriation art, the artist makes an exact reproduction of a work (often a famous work) and presents it as his or her own, in an effort to question fundamental concepts of originality. In such cases, the artist whose work has been appropriated would seem to have a good claim of "reverse passing off," based on the false attribution. Moreover, the act of copying may result in alterations to the work, which could give rise to liability, as in the Monty Python case.

Protection of Style. Not just the name or signature of an artist may be a trademark; so may an image, because the Lanham Act does not limit trademarks to words or names, but also includes "symbols" or "devices."

Can an artist whose work has been copied claim that the work itself is a trademark? Further, can the artist claim that his or her "style" is a trademark, and that, although no single work has been reproduced, the artist's style has been copied? These issues have arisen in three cases. In one, the estate of Andy Warhol brought suit against a publisher who planned to bring out a calendar featuring Warhol's works. No copyright issues were raised in the suit, and the publisher had been granted permission from the collectors who owned the works to publish them in a calendar. The estate argued that the images themselves, because of the unique style of Andy Warhol, were trademarks of Warhol and the estate. The court held that an image could, in appropriate circumstances, serve as a trademark. The estate failed in its suit, however, because it could not meet the other critical part of the definition of a trademark: it could not show that the Warhol images were used "to identify and distinguish" goods, namely, calendars. As the court put it, the plaintiffs were required to show "not that these images have come to signify Andy Warhol as the artist" but that the images identify the plaintiffs as the source of the calendars. Because neither Warhol nor the estate had ever used the images to identify the source of any goods, including calendars, the plaintiffs could not meet their burden.

In a similar case, a publisher of etchings by Salvador Dalí sued defendants for selling unauthorized reproductions of Dalí's works. The plaintiff claimed that the images themselves were trademarks, because Dalí's unique style and interpretation of a subject set his works apart from those of other artists and allowed the public to identify his works. The court rejected this claim, on the ground that it was merely an attempt to enforce a copyright claim through trademark law. The subject matter of copyright law is "original works of authorship," and Dalí's "unique style and interpretation," the court said, constituted his "authorship." Therefore, the claim should have been brought under copyright law, not trademark law. The courts in both the Warhol and Dalí cases rejected claims under the New York dilution law.

In the third case, a court held that limited-edition prints and posters of artist Itzchak Tarkay were entitled to trademark protection under the Lanham Act against similar, but not identical, limited editions by another artist. The court did not discuss the Warhol or Dalí decisions or address the issues raised by those decisions. The *Tarkay* decision has been criticized by the author of the leading treatise on trademark law as "a unique result that seriously impinges on the policy of copyright law that artistic style is no one's exclusive property" (McCarthy, 1992–1993).

Use of Commercial Trademarks in Art. Artists often include labels of consumer products in collages, and Warhol was famous for copying Brillo boxes and Campbell's soup cans. The test for infringement in such cases would be whether there is a likelihood of confusion (which generally is not the case) or whether the famous mark has been tarnished. Where an artist uses a trademark to comment on, or poke fun at, the product, the courts will also consider the artist's First Amendment rights.

BIBLIOGRAPHY

Cases

Coca-Cola Co. v. Gemini Rising, Inc., 346 F. Supp. 1183 (E.D.N.Y. 1972).
Galerie Furstenberg v. Coffaro, 697 F. Supp. 1282 (S.D.N.Y. 1988).
Gilliam v. American Broadcasting Companies, Inc., 538 F.2d 14 (2d Cir. 1976).
Hughes v. Design Look, Inc., 693 F. Supp. 1500 (S.D.N.Y. 1988).
Romm Art Creations Ltd. v. Simcha International, Inc., 786 F. Supp. 1126 (E.D.N.Y. 1992).
Smith v. Montoro, 648 F.2d 602 (9th Cir. 1981).

Other Sources

Carlin, John. "Culture Vultures: Artistic Appropriation and Intellectual Property Law." *Columbia-VLA Journal of Law and the Arts* 13 (1988).
McCarthy, J. Thomas. *McCarthy on Trademarks and Unfair Competition.* 3d ed. 5 vols. and supp. Deerfield, Ill., 1992–1993.

Statutes

Copyright Act, 17 U.S.C. § 101 *et seq.*
Lanham Act, 15 U.S.C. § 1051 *et seq.* 1946.

RICHARD LEHV

Law and Literature

Systematic interest among lawyers and legal theorists in literature increased significantly in the first half of the 1980s. An informal movement appeared, the so-called law and literature movement. The movement seems to have been a response to a conjunction of different events in late twentieth-century cultural history. First, philosophy and theory in general in the second half of the century became very self-conscious about interpretation as a mode of inquiry. The three paradigm areas where interpretation is significant are religion, art, and the law. In a secular world, it is natural that art, and especially literature, and the law be linked as both dependent on interpretation. Not only that, postmodern theorists became preoccupied with the status of a literary work as a text, and the notion of text is central also to law. Second, humanist legal scholars seemed to feel the need for their own enterprise to conduct alongside, and even in opposition to, the links between law and the social sciences, especially the law and economics movement and sociolegal studies.

Within law and literature, two seemingly quite different projects may be distinguished. The first project is theoretical and jurisprudential—the comparison of law and literature as intellectual endeavors, with the aim of shedding light on conceptual questions in (primarily) the law. Legal theorists have found it more helpful to them to compare law with literature than literary theorists have found it helpful to compare literature with the law. The second project is pedagogical and educational—the attempt to introduce into the law-school curriculum works of literature, to break up the monopoly of the doctrinal casebook and the legal treatise on usage as textbooks. How far these two projects are themselves linked is a question addressed at the end of this essay.

Jurisprudence. There are two main ways in which theory has thought it to be profitable to compare law and literature. First, there is the issue already mentioned of interpretation and textuality. Within the law, there are three different and canonical sources of positive (settled, or black-letter) law—the constitution or charter of countries that have one; legislation or statute law; and the common law, or judge-made law, the accumulation of judicial decisions and precedents. These are arranged hierarchically, in the order just given. Both the constitution and a legislative bill are formal documents, sets of determinate words in a language, deploying the syntax and the semantics of that language. Even the best legal draftsmanship in the world cannot compensate for what the legal philosopher H. L. A. Hart called our relative ignorance of fact and our relative indeterminacy of aim. A statute is passed today. But today's legislators have no idea what the world will be like in ten or twenty years' time, nor do they know everything about today's world. The actual wording they use, however clear now, may well not seem clear tomorrow. Nor can today's legislators formulate clearly every specific aim that might fall within the purposive content of the statute. The passing of a statute is inevitably the giving of a hostage to fortune. Constitutions and statutes thus will require *interpretation*. Statutes referring to vehicles were passed before off-road all-terrain vehicles (ATVs) were invented; is an off-road ATV a "vehicle"? The First Amendment to the U.S. Constitution affirming freedom of speech was passed long before the Internet was invented. Does the amendment apply unconditionally to the Internet?

Analogously, literary texts do not always wear their meaning on their faces; they need interpretation. Not only that,

different theories of interpretation look very similar in law and in literature. In law, the theory of interpretation that restricts the interpreter to the "four corners of the document" and the plain meaning of the words looks very like the approach of the New Critics to the interpretation of a poem or a novel. The theory that calls for courts to interpret by determining the intentions of the original framers of the constitution, or of the enacting legislature, looks very much like the literary theory that makes authorial intention determine meaning.

It seems, therefore, that very profitable comparisons of interpretation in law with interpretation in literature could be made. All the same, caution is needed. The legal theorist Joseph Raz has argued that the dependence of the law on interpretation is linked to the role in the law of authority and continuity (Raz, 1979). The moral position of the citizen governed by law puts normative constraints on the law. Citizens are judged by whether they conform to the law, and so they must have a fair chance to conform. That means that at the least there must be continuity in the law. The law makes authoritative claims on people's obedience, so there is a special need to know what the law is demanding. Put those factors together, and one has a necessarily stable body of written norms whose meaning one needs to know. Hence, the prominence of interpretation. Literature is quite different. Despite the limited control exercised by genres and traditions, originality and creativity are valued in literature in a way that is offensive in the practice of adjudication. Interpretation in the law needs to be a source of determinacy and certainty. Interpretation in literature arguably can accept indeterminacy, or plurality of meanings. Literary texts do not claim authority over our lives, or demand allegiance from us. The fact that the reasons for interpreting have to be very different in literature from how they must be in law (religion is perhaps more like law than it is like literature) does not, of course, in itself mean that interpreting in law is structurally different from interpreting in literature. But care in drawing comparisons is required.

The legal theorist Ronald Dworkin has drawn interpretation in law and in literature into his ongoing opposition to legal positivism as a theory of law. Legal positivism is the theory that defines the existence and content of law by a value-free or content-independent test such as the commands of a sovereign, or the enactments of a legislature and the actual decisions of courts. As the nineteenth-century English positivist John Austin put it, "The existence of law is one thing; its merit or demerit another." As Dworkin (1985, 1986) has noted, such a view has the implication that there may be candidate propositions of law whose truth-value is not determined—because the law speaks with an unclear voice, or with many voices, or (more controversially) because the law is silent. Dworkin draws the analogy with a novel, for example. The novelist's literary fiction leaves many candidate propositions about, say, characters in the novel without a truth-value in the sense of correspondence with fact. Dworkin's favorite examples are David Copperfield's blood group and whether David had a homosexual affair with Steerforth. If David were a real person, there would be a truth to the matter, in either case; but because he is a fictional character, there is not. The literary interpreter, however, can use conventions of coherence, rather than correspondence, to argue that the proposition that David had such an affair, for example, makes for a more coherent novel than the proposition that he did not, and therefore that it is to be regarded as true by coherence.

Dworkin argues that legal positivism is problematic, because it can make no room for analogous considerations of coherence in legal interpretation. His thought is that legal positivism claims that a proposition of law is true just in case (for example) the legislature enacted it, and that is that. This argument is weak. In the first place, it is compatible with legal positivism that propositions that cohere with the propositional content of positive law are to be regarded as true. Courts often appeal to coherence considerations of exactly this sort. Of course, such a claim does not meet Dworkin's other challenge to positivism, that law should cohere with moral principle—but that claim raises entirely different issues from those of interpretation and coherence. Moreover, the whole world of the law itself can be plausibly regarded as a fiction, just like the whole world of a novel. Things are required or forbidden by law not in themselves but because the law says as much. If that is true, then Dworkin and legal positivism are differing only over what the approved conventions for interpreting the law are. They are not differing over whether propositions of law are true by correspondence with fact or are warranted by the conventions of legal interpretation.

The second, quite different, jurisprudential comparison between law and literature starts out from the fact that a legal system is an institutionalized normative system. A norm is a norm of the legal system only because an institution says that it is. Clearly, there is a very tempting comparison to be made with the institutional theory of art, as proposed in different forms by Arthur C. Danto and George Dickie. But again, the comparison must be handled with care. The institutional theory of art is a radical and skeptical theory of art. Its purpose is to deny to artworks any objective status as such, and to norms of interpretation and evaluation any objective validity. An institutional theory of law, on the other hand, is at a minimum a truism about law. Exactly how law differs from, for example, morality or etiquette is that its norms have status as legal norms via the activities of legal institutions. The features about the nature of art that are brought out by the institutional theory are puzzling ones having to do with the role of the appreciator and the artist in defining art. The features about the nature of law brought out by legal positivism and institutional theories of law are those commonplace features that precede, and do not conclude, philosophical wonderment. Thus, again, any jurisprudential comparison between law and literature needs to be carried out with great care.

Pedagogy. Initially, the law and literature movement constituted simply a call for expansion of the traditional law-school curriculum to include discussions of the law and legal matters in works of literature, as well as in legal decisions, casebooks, and doctrinal treatises. Often, the call was inspired by ethical and political ideals. Writers such as Charles Dickens and Franz Kafka presented compelling pictures of the law in action, as it actually affected people's lives, instead of the dry abstractions of P the plaintiff, D the defendant, and V the victim. The movement also (more cynically) afforded a chance for legal academics to display their humanistic learning by publishing their "readings" of literary texts.

The social value of using alternatives to the traditional repositories of legal doctrine is and has been real. Although the institutional nature of the law means that it would be irresponsible to turn entirely away from the casebook and treatise, there is no doubt that a humanist leavening of the curriculum might well produce a more humane profession. But there is a deeper point behind this one. Suppose one believes, as many do, that the fundamental categories through which we see the world, especially the normative world, are those given to us by our society and our culture. Traditional legal pedagogy attempts to reveal a legal world stripped of these cultural constructions. Thus, it presents the law in false guise. In the typical narrative of a novel, the law is presented with its attendant social constructions intact. The novelist presents us in the process of constructing legal and social reality, and thus we can see and come to a deeper theoretical appreciation of the process itself, and of the fact of the socially constructed nature of lives. This is a compelling theoretical reason for the technique of using novels, plays, films, and so forth in the legal classroom.

Perhaps in the end there is a link between the jurisprudential project of trying to understand the nature of positive law (Is it an institution? Is it a text? What is legal interpretation?) and the pedagogical project of using literature in legal classrooms (see how the institution constructs reality; see how the legal text defines its own meaning; see how interpretation creates meaning). But perhaps there is not—both law and literature are what they are and not another thing, and especially, law is not literature, nor literature law.

[See also Institutional Theory of Art; Interpretation; and Literature, article on Literary Aesthetics.]

BIBLIOGRAPHY

Dworkin, Ronald. *A Matter of Principle.* Cambridge, Mass., 1985.
Dworkin, Ronald. *Law's Empire.* Cambridge, Mass., 1986.
Fish, Stanley. *Doing What Comes Naturally: Change, Rhetoric, and the Practice of Theory in Literary and Legal Studies.* Durham, N.C., 1989.

Goodrich, Peter. "Rhetoric as Jurisprudence: An Introduction to the Politics of Legal Language." *Oxford Journal of Legal Studies* 4 (1984): 88–122.

Levinson, Sanford. "Law As Literature." *Texas Law Review* 60 (1982): 373–403.

Levinson, Sanford, and Steven Mailloux, eds. *Interpreting Law and Literature: A Hermeneutic Reader.* Evanston, Ill., 1988.

Marmor, Andrei, ed. *Law and Interpretation.* Oxford, 1995.

Minow, Martha. "Identities." *Yale Journal of Law and the Humanities* 3 (1991): 97–130.

Nerhot, Patrick. *Law, Writing, Meaning: An Essay in Legal Hermeneutics.* Edinburgh, 1992.

Patterson, Dennis. "The Poverty of Interpretive Universalism: Toward the Reconstruction of Legal Theory." *Texas Law Review* 72 (1993): 1–77.

Raz, Joseph. *The Authority of Law: Essays on Law and Morality.* New York, 1979.

Symposium Issue: Interpretation. Southern California Law Review 58.2 (January 1985): 1–725.

van Roermund, Bert C. "Narrative Coherence and the Guises of Legalism." In *Law, Interpretation and Reality: Essays in Epistemology, Hermeneutics and Jurisprudence,* edited by Patrick Nerhot, pp. 310–345. Law and Philosophy Library, vol. 11. Dordrecht and Boston, 1990.

Weisberg, Richard H. *The Failure of the Word: The Protagonist as Lawyer in Modern Fiction.* New Haven, 1984.

Weisberg, Robert. "The Law-Literature Enterprise." *Yale Journal of Law and the Humanities* 1 (1988): 1–67.

West, Robin. "Authority, Autonomy and Choice: The Role of Consent in the Moral and Political Visions of Franz Kafka and Richard Posner." *Harvard Law Review* 99 (1985): 384–428.

West, Robin. "Jurisprudence as Narrative: An Aesthetic Analysis of Modern Legal Theory." *New York University Law Review* 60 (1985): 145–211.

White, James Boyd. *When Words Lose Their Meaning: Constitutions and Reconstitutions of Language, Character, and Community.* Chicago, 1984.

ROGER A. SHINER

LE CORBUSIER (1887–1965), French modern architect. Le Corbusier, whose real name was Charles-Édouard Jeanneret, was born in La Chaux de Fonds, Switzerland. After learning the craft of watch engraving, he turned to architecture and worked as a draftsman in Paris (in 1908–1909) for Auguste Perret, a master builder in reenforced concrete, and in Berlin (in 1911) for Peter Behrens, the architect.

Le Corbusier settled in Paris permanently (in 1917) after building regionalist-style villas in his hometown. With the painter Amédée Ozenfant and the Dadaist poet Paul Dermée, he founded the avant-garde journal *L'esprit nouveau,* of which twenty-eight issues appeared from 1920 to 1925. While he pursued his work as an architect and urbanist— seventy buildings were constructed in Europe, the United States, and India, and many unbuilt projects were drawn— he was a painter (as well as a sculptor after 1947) and a polemicist, writing hundreds of articles and publishing more than sixty books. Le Corbusier never taught, but his buildings as well as his theoretical works received consider-

able attention from both his contemporaries and students, in part because of his active participation in the International Congress of Modern Architecture (CIAM, ten meetings held between 1928 and 1956). As a result, his work exerted a strong impact on twentieth-century architecture and urbanism, as one can see by examining architectural magazines from 1930 onward.

All of Le Corbusier's work can be stylistically divided between his prewar and postwar buildings, paintings, and writings. Detailed research does show underlying recurring themes, such as a fascination for the order of nature or for an atemporal Platonism. Le Corbusier's lyrical forms and materials anticipated his future work: for example, his "objets à réaction poétique," which appeared at the end of the 1920s in his paintings, prefigure a formal explosion and lyricism in his buildings, as in the "Ronchamp Chapel" (1951–1955); and the "Weekend House," which he built in 1935 in La Celle-Saint-Cloud with concrete catalonian vaults, millstone walls, and glass pavements to convey a worn, defaced, unpolished ruggedness and serene contextualization, prefigures the Sarabhai (in Ahmedabad, India, 1954–1956) and the Jaoul (in Neuilly-sur-Seine, 1951–1955) houses. Nevertheless, there is an irreducible discontinuity in all this work that resists analysis, a kind of mystery that magnifies the work of Le Corbusier. Thus, some secrecy and a lack of unified interpretation seem unavoidable because, as Kenneth Frampton observes (1997, p. 6), it is difficult to escape the evocation of the "quality of genius."

Can an unexperienced eye attribute the same hand to the "Stein House" and the "Unité d'Habitation" in Marseille, the "Plan Voisin" ("Paris Plan") and the Venice Hospital project? Aside from the personal evolution of every creator, it is as though the entire work of Le Corbusier was marked by a dramatic tension between a classic, atemporal, Platonic, quasi-disembodied aspiration, on the one hand, and a strong expressionist, artistic will of unbridled lyricism and passion for the sensuality of materials, on the other. As a result, it is difficult to forgo a chronological approach in any interpretation of his work. Without lingering on his formative years and initial buildings—or on his transitional phase around World War II—the focus here will be on the purist period (the 1920s), the period of the Radiant City (the 1930s), and the postwar period (the 1950s–1960s).

Purist Period. A year after moving permanently to Paris, in the Autumn of 1918, Ozenfant and Jeanneret signed a short treatise called *After Cubism.* In conjunction with the exhibition of their paintings in Paris at the Galerie Thomas, this text initiated a new pictorial movement known as "Purism." It was an appeal to the rediscovery of the simple beauty of everyday reality beyond Cubism's formal, esoteric search of the fourth dimension: "The purist ideology opens the way for a true rationalist cosmology. Nature is no longer an enchanting and fantastic world, nor is it a miraculous secret; instead, it is an exact machine in which perfection and beauty constitute an identity" (Moos, 1979, p. 42).

This first manifesto, in which Ozenfant undoubtedly still played the upper hand, combined two dimensions: first, a quasi-reactionary dimension that seemed like a return to a French tradition of order; and, second, a more contemporary dimension that displayed a fascination for objects of that time. Jeanneret, who later on adopted the signature of "Le Corbusier" in his articles for *L'esprit nouveau* (which are admirably analyzed by Reyner Banham, 1960), referred to these themes later on. They revealed a true understanding of *la formule:* for example, "architecture is the masterly, correct and magnificent play of volumes brought together in light" and "the house is a machine-for-living-in" ["machine à habiter"] (1927, pp. 16, 73); "a town is a working tool" (1925, p. i); "The human-limb objects are type-objects responding to type-needs," and "Law of Ripolin, coat of whitewash: elimination of the equivocal" (1930, pp. 76, 192, 193).

Le Corbusier left behind abundant material for his commentators and followers. Besides the archives preserved at the Fondation Le Corbusier in Paris, there are the eight volumes of his *Complete Works*—an accessible and precious research tool—collected and written by himself or under his very strict supervision. They represent a veritable auto-analysis and theoretical reconstruction of his work. The first volume, dedicated to the years 1910–1929, defines in a very concentrated manner the various founding theoretical principles of a modern vocabulary that are reflected in his buildings. It is mainly about the "Five Points of a New Architecture" and the notion of "architectural promenade."

The architectural promenade allows for a shifting viewpoint, a perspective in motion that brings about a fourth dimension of time and movement. (Sigfried Giedion, the historian and promoter of the "modern movement," gave great importance to this dimension in his classic book, *Space, Time and Architecture*, 1940.) The use of the ramp, which is developed by the neomodernists in a quasi-icon way in the 1980s, is fundamental here. It is not systematic, however, as the Villa Stein at Garches (1926–1928) reveals, because it provides an elaborate example of a promenade without a ramp. One sees this form evolve from an earlier, quite simple version—a single flight along a curved exterior wall of the La Roche House (Paris, 1923–1925)—into more elaborate versions in later projects, such as the Meyer (never realized, 1925–1926) and Savoye houses (Poissy, 1928–1931). This promenade reappeared and was magnified in subsequent public buildings: for example, in the project for the Palace of Soviets competition (1931); in the Millowners' Building (Ahmedabad, India, 1951–1957); in the three major buildings for the capitol of Chandigarh (the High Court, the Palace of Assembly, and the secretariat building, 1951–1958), and in the Carpenter Center (Cambridge, Massachusetts, 1959–1965).

The "five points," which later became the "ukases" of the modernist vocabulary, were defined for the first time in 1927, when Le Corbusier participated in the Weissenhof Siedlung Exhibition in Stuttgart. They were reformulated and commented on several times later on, but their titles—constituting a veritable system of architectural composition—changed very little:

1. *The pilotis.* Freestanding thin concrete posts rise from the ground to the first floor in such a way as to conserve the visual transparency of the building.

2. *The roof garden (Le toit-jardin).* The ground level surface reappears at the top of the building. The reinforced concrete allows for level, accessible terraces instead of slanted roofs. The building stands out neatly against the sky forming a horizontal pure line, without cornices.

3. *The free plan (Le plan libre).* In opposition to the traditional construction of the "plan paralysé" (paralyzed plan), where the partitions are bearing walls and must be superimposed on one another from floor to floor, the free plan leads to the disassociation of structural and dividing functions. The concrete floorboarding meets the poles placed at a great distance from one another, whereas the partitions are placed according to the desired architectural design.

4. *The free facade (La façade libre).* The envelope of the building is also independent from the structure. The posts can be recessed from the facades in the interior of the building. The composition of the facade—the positioning of the openings—is theoretically only dictated by the light and views of the interior.

5. *The ribbon or elongated windows (La fenêtre en longueur).* Again, the reinforced concrete has "liberated" the plan and the facade. The openings of the construction can run from one side to the other free of interruption. The elongated window "bandeau," which lends itself to panoramic views, to this day remains the stamp of modern architecture.

The fundamental point is the third, of course, because it makes the other four possible; this fantasy of freeing the "rigid plan" or "paralyzed plan" of traditional stone architecture could be compared to *Raumplan*, developed a few years earlier by Adolf Loos. The Savoye Villa—an immaculate parallelepiped split by only one horizontal opening and placed on thin pilotis in the middle of a field—may be interpreted as a built manifesto encompassing the five points. Tim Benton described it as "the last attempt to reconcile the absolute platonic ideals, nature and man, . . . the almost automatic manifestation of the synthesis of ten years of research, . . . just at the moment when a unified language of purist architecture was about to be abandoned" (1987, pp. 191–193).

Period of the Radiant City. When Le Corbusier built this last "villa blanche" in 1931—an icon of international style and a paragon of the machine-for-living-in—he had already distanced himself from the machine aesthetic and its strict functionalist orthodoxy. In this sense, the "International Style" exhibition at the Museum of Modern Art (1932)—which was curated by Henry-Russell Hitchcock and Philip Johnson and in which Le Corbusier was a major player among the "masters of the second generation"—was historically misleading because of its primary focus on formal vocabulary. In the journal *L'architecture vivante* (published by Jean Badovici in the Albert Morance Edition series) that came out in the fall of 1927, Le Corbusier answered the question that became the title of his contribution—"Where is architecture?": "It is beyond the machine." Two years later, within the polemical framework of his opposition to the Czech critic Karel Teige—who accused Le Corbusier's project for the Mundaneum of formalism and metaphysical monumentalism, which were both reactionary defects—Le Corbusier wrote a significant article, again with an eminently programmatic title: "Défense de l'architecture." He indicated his evolution:

> Today among the avant-garde of the "neue Sachlichkeit" (new objectivity), two meanings have been killed: Baukunst (architecture) and Kunst (art). They have been replaced by Bauen (construction) and Lieben (life). In 1921, in *L'esprit nouveau*, we returned to zero in order to try and see clearly. But if we have gone back to zero, it is not to remain there but to gain ground. (1933)

These comments reflect a direction that he turned into a definitive formula: "The useful is not the beautiful." Here we are far away from the purist machine-for-living-in, but also from two despised themes of the 1970s when the anti-Corbusier discourse flourished: the "tabula rasa" and city "zoning," which are based on four functions—"to dwell, to work, to re-create, to circulate"—that extol the "Radiant City" and *The Athenes Charter* (1943).

Here again, we find an ambivalence in Le Corbusier's work. Even in these years when his urban discourse theory became more dogmatic, he planned sensuous curves in the Obus plan for Algiers (1931–1933)—and, surely, they were more contextual than "rational." He exposed unmanufactured stone in the only three houses he built during that decade (in Le Pradet, Les Mathes, and in La Celle-Saint-Cloud), and in his studio at 24, rue Nungesser-et-Coli (1931–1934), where in 1935 he organized the strange exhibition, "The Primitive Arts in the Homes of Today."

The "primitive" works were exhibited next to paintings by his friend Fernand Léger, and the statuettes of the Cyclades; in 1937, for the International Exhibition in Paris, he built a pavilion of cloth like a tent. Le Corbusier's competition entries for two important international competitions with similar programs—the League of Nations Palace in Geneva, designed in 1926–1927, and the Palace of Soviets in Moscow, submitted in December 1931—evoked the same evolution: from a certain classical stiffness in the composition of the masses in the first, to a spatial fluidity and quasi euphoria about structural expression in the second.

Postwar Period. The enigmatic turn to Brutalism after World War II may be illustrated in the work Le Corbusier made for the Salvation Army site (Paris, 1929–1933), one of his most important buildings of the 1930s. In 1948, he was asked to renovate the building, which had originally been poorly constructed—Le Corbusier had a passion for new technologies, but not for their practical application—and which had suffered from the war and the way its inhabitants used it. He did not hesitate to replace the vast glass wall at the southern facade—a prototype for the "neutralizing wall" or "exact respiration"—with a series of painted concrete sunbreakers. The refinement, uniqueness, and transparency were replaced by massiveness and modular articulation. The control of interior environment (of light and air) was no longer based on the virtues of the machine—which were visually absent—but fastened by a fixed, extremely present mason device. The sunbreaker—which was a recurrent shape in the Corbusian postwar facades, as in the "Unités d'Habitation," in the Indian buildings, in the Convent of La Tourette, and in the Carpenter Center—"became an element of style and expression rather than of efficient environmental management." It had "a visual function comparable to that of the windows, pillars, balustrades, cornices, and loggias in earlier architecture; they were a means of making a building's dimensions recognizable even at a distance." An inappreciable tool of "contour and profile [*modénature*]"—which, as early as in *Vers une architecture*, Le Corbusier called "the touchstone of the architect"—the sunbreaker, like his earlier principles of design (free plan and free facade) "transcended its utilitarian roots and became an instrument of sculptural dramatization" (Moos, 1979, p. 95). It also embodied a new way to work with light: no longer concerned with transparency and spatial fluidity, but rather with sharp and dramatic contrasts between shadow and light.

The two great religious buildings by Le Corbusier—the Ronchamp Chapel (1951–1955) and the Convent of La Tourette (in Eveux-sur-Arbresle, 1953–1960)—also utilize devices that are connected to light and that reveal the interior dramatization of space. In the first building, the projection of the conch shell roof creates a dynamic luminous split wing. The splayed cutting and the diverse orientation of the thick south wall vibrate against the colored glass embedded in the wall. Soft gleams of sunlight pour periscopically from the lateral chapels, inspired by a 1910 sketch by Jeanneret of "serapeum" from the Adriana house. In La Tourette, the public spaces, particularly the central atrium, are stimulated by the rhythmic play of the lines of the "musical walls" or "pans de verre ondulatoire," whereas the static concrete box of the adjacent church has vertical perforations that reach up behind the altar. The lateral chapels are animated with machine guns of light (*mitraillettes à lumière*) painted in vibrant colors in the crypt and the sacristy.

In 1960, speaking of this convent, Le Corbusier evoked a theme that he had been working on since the 1940s:

> When a work reaches its maximum level of intensity, proportion, quality of execution, and perfection, a phenomenon of ineffable space occurs: the places radiate, physically they radiate. They become what I call "ineffable space," that is to say, an impact based not on dimensions but on perfection. This is about the ineffable domain. (1960)

This ineffable perfection, which arose after a long, "patient investigation" of the "box of miracles" and the "synthesis of art" (three of Le Corbusier's leitmotifs that are invaluable and difficult to communicate to anyone), also went through a more operative process of reflection about an eminently traditional architectural theme: proportion. *L'esprit nouveau* was already displaying an interest in "regulating lines" (*tracés régulateurs*) and "golden section" (*nombre d'or*). From 1943 onward, Le Corbusier focused on a universal system of measurement based on the human scale and simple mathematic series called the "Modulor," that which dominated his later practice and was subsequently used by a number of other architects. In a conference in 1951, the art historian Rudolf Wittkower said: "The Modulor demonstrated the coherence of our cultural heritage. Just like proportional geometry used in the Middle Ages, or like musical arithmetic proportions in the time of the Renaissance, the dual system of irrational measures of Le Corbusier was based on the Pythagorean-Platonic tradition of the West" (Wittkower, 1962).

In all his buildings and writings, the work of Le Corbusier oscillated between "modernity and archaism" (Curtis, 1986) and between "machine and memory" (Tafuri, 1983). That is what makes Le Corbusier both an emblematic and a paradoxical figure in architectural modernity.

[*See also* Architecture; *and* Modernism, *article on* Modernity and Tradition in Architecture.]

BIBLIOGRAPHY

Works by Le Corbusier

Vers une architecture. Paris, 1923; 3d (and final) ed., Paris, 1928. English translation by Frederick Etchells published as *Towards a New Architecture* (London, 1927).
Œuvre complète. 8 vols. Zurich, 1929–1970.
Précisions sur un état présent de l'architecture et de l'urbanisme. Paris, 1930.
"Défense de l'architecture." In special issue, "Le Corbusier et Pierre Jeanneret." *L'architecture d'aujourd'hui* (1933).
La ville radieuse. Boulogne, 1935.
La charte d'Athènes. Paris, 1943.
Le modulor: essai sur une mesure harmonique à l'échelle humaine applicable universellement à l'architecture et à la mécanique. Boulogne, 1950.
"Entretien avec la communauté religieuse de la Tourette." *L'art sacré* (March–April 1960).
Le voyage d'Orient. Paris, 1966. First publication of notes taken by Jeanneret during his trip in 1911.

Other Sources

Banham, Reyner. *Theory and Design in the First Machine Age.* London, 1960; 2d ed., reprint, Cambridge, Mass., 1980.
Benton, Tim. *Les villas de Le Corbusier et Pierre Jeanneret, 1920–1930.* Paris, 1984. Published in English as *The Villas of Le Corbusier, 1920–1930* (New Haven, 1987).
Cohen, Jean-Louis. *Le Corbusier et la mystique de l'URSS: Théories et projets pour Moscow, 1928–1936.* Brussels, 1987. Translated as *Le Corbusier and the Mystique of the USSR: Theories and Projects for Moscow 1928–1936* by Kenneth Hylton (Princeton, N.J., 1992).
Curtis, William. J.R. *Le Corbusier: Ideas and Forms.* Oxford, 1986.
Frampton, Kenneth. *Le Corbusier.* Paris, 1997.
Lucan, Jacques, ed. *Le Corbusier: Une Encyclopédie.* Paris, 1987. Catalog, Georges Pompidou Center, Paris.
Moos, Stanislaus von. *Le Corbusier: Elemente einer Synthese.* Frauenfeld, 1968. Translated as *Le Corbusier: Elements of a Synthesis* (Cambridge, Mass., 1979).
Raeburn, Michael, and Victoria Wilson, eds. *Le Corbusier: Architect of the Century.* London, 1987. Catalog, Hayward Gallery, London.
Tafuri, Manfredo. "Ville: Machine et mémoire." Published initially in English as "Machine et mémoire": The City in the Work of Le Corbusier," in *The Le Corbusier Archive,* vol. 10, p. xxxi–xivi. New York and London, 1983.
Taylor, Brian Brace. *La Cité de Refuge di Le Corbusier, 1929–1933.* Rome, 1979. In English as *Le Corbusier: The City of Refuge, Paris, 1929–1933* (Chicago, 1987).
Wittkower, Rudolf. *Architectural Principles in the Age of Humanism.* London, 1949: 3d rev. ed., London, 1962.

GUILLEMETTE MOREL JOURNEL
Translated by Annabel Manning

LENIN, VLADIMIR ILICH. *See* Marxism; Russian Aesthetics, *article on* Socialist Realism.

LESBIAN AESTHETICS. Historically speaking, the term *lesbian aesthetics* might be taken for a tautology. Whatever the result of contemporary debates among lesbian critics on the subject—does such a thing exist? ought such a thing to exist?—the history of aesthetics since the Enlightenment offers up its own would-be primordial truths. The extraordinary proliferation of lesbian imagery in nineteenth-century "art for art's sake" discourse—a phenomenon first noted by Mario Praz in *The Romantic Agony* in the 1930s—suggests that the lesbian topos is in some sense necessary to Romantic conceptualizations of the beautiful, and is indeed one of the means by which post-Kantian aesthetics symbolizes to itself one of its fundamental concepts. What else to make of the countless sapphic lovers who haunt the writings of Théophile Gautier, Charles Baudelaire, Paul Verlaine, Josephin Péladan, Algernon Charles Swinburne, Arthur William Symons, Jules Barbey d'Aurevilly, Pierre Louÿs, Marcel Proust, and other French and English proponents of *l'art pour l'art?* Like the voyeur, the male aesthete needs his lesbians in order to know himself, and, in the "double caress" of woman and woman—his rationalized fantasy of female homosexual love—finds a fetishistic emblem of Beauty itself.

If, in a sense, the doctrine of art for art's sake is a "lesbian" aesthetics, it may be because of Gautier, author of both the first and most important nineteenth-century aestheticist manifesto, the celebrated Preface to *Mademoiselle de Maupin* (1835) and the first and most important nineteenth-century lesbian novel, *Mademoiselle de Maupin* itself. Gautier was the first modern writer to link the beautiful with the vicissitudes of a sapphic desire. In the Preface, a coruscating satire on the utilitarian notion of art put forward by Louis de Rouvroy, duc de Saint-Simon, Charles Fourier, and their followers, he gave a brilliant inaugural expression to what would become the standard maxims of the nineteenth-century cult of Beauty:

> Nothing is really beautiful unless it is useless; everything useful is ugly, for it expresses a need, and the needs of man are ignoble and disgusting, like his poor weak nature. The most useful place in a house is a latrine.
>
> . . . I am among those to whom the superfluous is necessary—and I prefer things and people in the inverse ratio to the services that they perform for me. I prefer to a certain useful pot a Chinese pot which is sprinkled with mandarins and dragons.
> (Gautier, 1984, p. 39)

In the titillating fable that followed—detailing the curious amorous exploits of Madelaine de Maupin, a beautiful young woman who disguises herself, Queen Christina-like, as a handsome cavalier in order to see the world, and thus attired, inspires ambiguous passions in men and women alike—he sought to give these axioms a living and breathing form.

This is not to suggest that historians of aestheticism have been prepared to acknowledge the link between preface and text. The preface has often been printed apart from its companion-fiction, as if to rescue it from any contamination by Gautier's lascivious transvestite fantasy. (With a primness that later critics would imitate, Henry James [1984] spoke of the latter as Gautier's one "disagreeable performance.") Even when the two texts are conjoined, commentators frequently attempt to maintain a kind of rhetorical cordon sanitaire between them. Gautier's English translator, Joanna Richardson, writes: "The Preface bears little relation to the novel itself, and is probably included on its own brilliant merits as a polemic" (in Gautier, 1984). As for the perverse tale that follows—Mademoiselle de Maupin ends up sleeping first with a young poet, D'Albert, then with his elegant courtesan-mistress—Richardson argues that "the story is the least important part of the book. . . . It is only important in so far as the equivocal position of the heroine enables Gautier to suggest that beauty may be loved independently of sex, for itself alone" (ibid.).

Yet such hygienic (often homophobic) gestures cannot disguise the fact that the introductory polemic and the les-

bian romance of *Mademoiselle de Maupin* are bound up together in what one might call an emblematic way. In the classic emblem books of the late Renaissance, abstract philosophical concepts—say, of Art, Virtue, Wisdom, or Taste—found allegorical representation in conventionalized visual images. In Cesare Ripa's 1593 *Iconologia*—a work that Gautier would have known in its many eighteenth- and nineteenth-century redactions—Art, for example, was described as taking the form, iconographically, "of a seated woman robed in green, with a flame rising out of her head, who with one hand holds a scroll with a drawing on it, a brush, and a chisel, and with the other points to a statue of a woman, who in turn points to her own naked breast." Ripa's many illustrators over several hundred years obliged with an array of allegorical images drawn to these specifications.

In a similar fashion, the numerous lesbian tableaux of *Mademoiselle de Maupin* might be considered emblematic figurations of the antiutilitarian concept of beauty posited in Gautier's preface. For Gautier, as for virtually every Western writer who has philosophized on the subject, Beauty is associated at the most primitive symbolic level with the female form. Within the novel, the hapless narrator D'Albert, who will lose both his heart and his mistress to the dashing Mademoiselle de Maupin, asserts this primary association with compulsive—indeed, tedious—regularity. When others are taken in by the pseudomasculinity of "Théodore de Sérannes" (the disguised Mademoiselle de Maupin), D'Albert alone recognizes that "he" must be a woman because, as he puts it, in a postlapsarian modern world, no male body could express such ideal beauty. "Adonis and Hermaphroditus are dead," he explains in a love letter to the mock-cavalier:

> and this degree of beauty may no longer be attained by a man; for, since the heroes and the gods have gone, you alone preserve in your statuesque bodies, as in a Greek temple, the precious gift of form which was declared accursed by Christ, and you alone show that the earth has nothing to envy heaven; you represent, with dignity, the first divinity in the world, the purest symbol of the eternal essence—beauty.
> (Ibid., 297)

But D'Albert's unitary conception of the beautiful will be shown to be insufficient. The problem with the simplistic equation Woman = Beauty is that it does not in the end express the central innovation in Gautier's avidly post-Kantian theory of the aesthetic: that the beautiful must be estranged from use-value. As long as the male aesthete desires the beautiful in the form of a single longed-for woman, his desire must remain suspect; for it cannot be distinguished from instinct, the primordial force requiring Man to "use" Woman for the production of offspring and the creation of human society. Heterosexually structured aesthetic emotion is inevitably compromised by its involvement in a preordained and necessary reproductive economy, and no amount of sublimation—as D'Albert himself will painfully discover—can ultimately obviate that fact.

Gautier's repeated foregrounding, within the fiction, of the "double caress"—the image of two women locked in an erotic embrace—is, from one angle, an attempt to elaborate a more expressive emblem of the beautiful. The term *double caress* here—the title of an 1879 Edgar Degas image of two women making love—highlights Gautier's intense predisposition, even as he ostensibly tells a story, toward a kind of visual allegory. Although *Mademoiselle de Maupin* has a "plot" of sorts—having to do with the various rivalrous stratagems used by D'Albert and Rosette (the mistress) to attract the love of the elusive "Théodore"—the narrative is perhaps more appropriately described as a succession of painterly vignettes, a series of moments of "stoppage" during which the reader's attention is focused on a particularly charismatic human configuration. The effect might be compared to a freeze-frame in cinematic narrative: Gautier repeatedly suspends his fictional characters in time and space for emblematic ends.

The configuration he turns to again and again—hence *Mademoiselle de Maupin*'s status as a lesbian classic—is the image of two female bodies combining in an ecstatic, timeless, and wholly "useless" love. A few examples, selected out of many, will have to do here to symbolize the textual phenomenon. Gautier obsessively stages—then freezes—scenes of kissing and sexual arousal between female characters. When the infatuated Rosette attempts to seduce Madelaine/Théodore, for example, the bodies of the two women come to a standstill, like exquisite living statues, precisely at the moment of the kiss. "She came to me"—Mademoiselle de Maupin tells her female confidant Graciosa—

> sat down on my lap quicker than lightning, clasped her hands behind my head, and her mouth clung to mine in a wild embrace; I felt her breasts, half-naked and aroused, buoyant against my breasts, and her interlaced fingers tighten in my hair. A quiver ran through all my body, and my nipples stood out.

"Rosette didn't leave my mouth," she continues, "her lips enveloped mine, her teeth struck against my teeth, our breaths merged with each other. I recoiled for a moment, and two or three times I turned my head away to avoid this kiss; but an invincible attraction made me turn back again, and I returned it almost as ardently as she had given it" (ibid., pp. 283–284).

A few pages later, when Rosette comes to "Théodore"'s bedroom and they kiss again, there is a similar fixing of the lesbian image:

> From the outer edge of her cheek, which I brushed with an almost imperceptible kiss, I came to her half-open mouth; we stayed like that for some time. But I don't know if it was two minutes, or a quarter of an hour, or an hour; for I had completely lost count of time, and I didn't know if I was in heaven or on earth, here or elsewhere, dead or living.   (Ibid., p. 306)

Elsewhere, like a painter posing his models, Gautier arranges the lovers in strange Siamese twin-like postures, then invites his reader to dwell on the captivating image created:

> Her body, supple and fluent [writes Mademoiselle de Maupin], modelled itself like wax on my own, and followed its whole external line as closely as possible; water wouldn't have flowed more precisely into its every curve. Fixed to my side like this, she looked like the double line which painters add to their drawing on the shadow side, to make it thicker and stronger. Only a woman in love could undulate and entwine herself like that. Ivy and willows are nothing in comparison.   (Ibid., p. 282)

Even at the end of the novel, although D'Albert will realize his own erotic dream by spending an evening of love with Mademoiselle de Maupin before she leaves in search of new adventures, his triumph is undercut by the "frozen" sapphic image on which the fiction suspends—of the "rumpled and disturbed" bed, bearing the faint "imprint of two bodies," which D'Albert finds when he enters Rosette's chamber the next morning. The aesthete's humiliation: Mademoiselle de Maupin, now departed forever, went straight from his bed to Rosette's. Thus, even as heterosexual passion appears to achieve its goal, it is superseded—here in a metonymic or spectral fashion—by the charismatic image of two women entwined.

At such moments, Gautier in effect rewrites the aesthetic equation: not Woman = Beauty, but Woman + Woman = Beauty; and in so doing, he injects a new and distinctly modern pathos into the history of the beautiful. The emblematic embrace of woman and woman—Beauty in Love with Itself, Beauty Redoubled, Supersaturated Beauty—at once realizes perfectly the central aestheticist notion of superfluity (this lesbian loving is "work" that results in nothing) and renders the aesthete himself superfluous: he remains an impotent onlooker, caught up in longing, yet excluded eternally, masochistically, from the scene before him. In a terminally romantic age, such an image of the beautiful might be construed as making a perverse kind of emotional as well as intellectual sense. "If Don Juan had once found his ideal," writes Gautier, "he would have been the most faithful of lovers; but his greatness lay in not meeting it, for he sought absolute beauty, and absolute beauty is God"—or, less metaphysically, Beauty is a couple of women who care nothing for Don Juan.

The pathos injected here circulates permanently in the bloodstream of nineteenth-century art and literature. In *Les fleurs du mal* (1857), a work he dedicated to Gautier, Baudelaire figures the beautiful in the exquisite, time-stopping kisses ("légers commes ces éphémères / Qui caressent le soir les grands lacs transparents") that the lesbian Delphine implants—forever—on the lips of Hippolyte in "Femmes damnées." In "Sur le balcon" in *Scènes d'amour sapphique* (1867), Verlaine takes from Gautier the image of the empty bed vacated by two women lovers ("défait" and "emphatique comme un trône de mélodrames") and makes of it his own allegory for poetic inspiration. Similar emblematic appropriations can be found in Swinburne's *Poems and Ballads* (1866), Catulle Mendès's *Méphistophéla* (1890), Louÿs's *Chansons de Bilitis* (1894), and Proust's *À la recherche du temps perdu* (1913–1927). Not surprisingly, the "double caress" becomes a cherished topos in late nineteenth- and early twentieth-century visual art: in the paintings and sketches of Gustave Courbet, Gustave Doré, Degas, Honoré Daumier, Félicien Rops, Auguste Rodin, Henri de Toulouse-Lautrec, Aubrey Beardsley, Egon Schiele, Aristide Maillol, Willy Jaeckel, and countless others.

One might ask, parenthetically, whether the spectacle of two *men* embracing—male homosexuality also being a culturally "useless" phenomenon—can function in a similarly emblematic manner. For Gautier, as for most of his nineteenth-century followers, the answer would seem to be no: male bodies—pace D'Albert's comment on Adonis and Hermaphroditus—are no longer beautiful enough in the corrupt modern age to stand *for* the beautiful. Only a few nineteenth-century writers and artists made a self-conscious attempt to aestheticize the male-male sexual caress: the poet Walt Whitman was one; the German homosexual photographer of the 1880s, Baron von Gloeden, another.

There is a paradox in the Beauty = Woman + Woman equation, of course—and indeed, in the insistent Romantic reification of the aesthetic as the beautiful and nothing else. In the fantasy life of modernity, the aesthetic has become increasingly indistinguishable from the pornographic. Always a central topos in the underground world of pornography from the Renaissance onward, female homosexuality makes its way, via Gautier, into the mainstream of Western philosophical reflection and artistic production. Yet, what is this validation of the sapphic, after all, but a kind of "polite," second-order rationalization of the masturbatory pleasures of pornography? Even as they seek to overlay it with the most exquisite and diaphanous philosophical finery, what Gautier and the other glamorizers of the "double caress" cannot obfuscate is the crude power of the image to gratify precisely those "ignoble and disgusting" needs of "man" elsewhere satirized in aestheticist discourse. The emblem of uselessness turns out to be as guiltily "useful" as any other—a kind of Saint-Simonian wet dream.

It is beyond the scope of this essay to say why the image of the "double caress" should exert such a provocative affective force or what prompted its historic rationalization and mainstreaming in the nineteenth century. Psychoanalysis hints at possible answers: if the archaic human association of beauty with the female form seems a displacement of infantile fantasies of the mother, then the aestheticist celebration of double-bodied, tribadistic beauty may represent this fantasy redoubled, so to speak, and transformed into a mode of psychic defense. (The doubling of images in dreams, wrote Sigmund Freud in "The 'Uncanny,'" is a kind of magical "insurance" by which the unconscious attempts to defuse its fear of castration and the destruction of the ego.) Rather, it must do for now—like the uncanny Mademoiselle de Maupin herself—merely to suggest aestheticism's guilty secret: in the autotelism of the beautiful, the autoeroticism of its lovers.

[*See also* Aestheticism; Art for Art's Sake; Feminism; Gay Aesthetics; *and* Sexuality.]

BIBLIOGRAPHY

Castle, Terry. *The Apparitional Lesbian: Female Homosexuality and Modern Culture.* New York, 1993.

Dijkstra, Bram. *Idols of Perversity: Fantasies of Feminine Evil in Fin-de-Siècle Culture.* New York and Oxford, 1986.

Federman, Lillian. *Surpassing the Love of Men: Romantic Friendship and Love between Women from the Renaissance to the Present.* New York, 1981.

Foster, Jeannette. *Sex Variant Women in Literature.* New York, 1956; reprint, Tallahassee, Fla., 1985.

Freud, Sigmund. "The Uncanny." In *The Standard Edition of the Complete Psychological Works of Sigmund Freud,* edited by James Strachey, vol. 17, pp. 217–252. London, 1955.

Gautier, Théophile. *Mademoiselle de Maupin.* Translated by Joanna Richardson. Harmondsworth, England, 1984.

James, Henry. "Théophile Gautier." In *Literary Criticism,* vol. 2, *French Writers, Other European Writers, the Prefaces to the New York Edition,* edited by Leon Edel, pp. 353–389. New York, 1984.

Maser, Edward A., ed. *Baroque and Rococo Pictorial Imagery: The 1758–1760 Hertel Edition of Ripa's Iconologia with 200 Engraved Illustrations.* New York, 1971.

Néret, Gilles. *Erotica Universalis.* Cologne, 1994.

Praz, Mario. *The Romantic Agony.* 2d ed. Translated by Angus Davidson. Oxford and New York, 1951.

Sadoff, Janet. *Ambivalence, Ambiguity, and Androgyny in Théophile Gautier's "Mademoiselle de Maupin."* Ann Arbor, 1988. Microfiche.

TERRY CASTLE

LESSING, GOTTHOLD EPHRAIM (1729–1781), German philosopher, dramatist, and critic. Lessing's chief contribution to aesthetics is his treatise *Laocoön: An Essay on the Limits of Painting and Poetry* (1766). This brilliant, if tendentious, treatise is of characteristically polemical inspiration. It takes its title from the famous Hellenistic sculpture, now in the Vatican, depicting the death throes of the Trojan priest Laocoön and his two sons in the coils of two enormous serpents, and its point of departure is a disagreement with the art historian Johann Joachim Winckelmann over the interpretation of this statue. Lessing's disagreement with Winckelmann is, on the face of it, a minor one, for he accepts Winckelmann's neoclassical premise that the supreme law that governed the visual arts in antiquity was the law of beauty. What he objects to is the *moral* component in Winckelmann's theory of beauty. He does not deny that the Greeks were morally admirable; he denies merely that their visual art, as distinct from their literature and way of life, was determined by moral considerations. Thus, Laocoön's half-closed mouth is not a sign of his stoical fortitude, that is, of his moral excellence, for, Lessing points out, Laocoön *does* scream aloud in Virgil's version of the story in the *Aeneid*, and other Greek heroes did not consider it unmanly to do likewise in similar predicaments. The statue shows him at the moment just before he screams, because to show him actually screaming, with his mouth gaping open, would offend the rule of beauty. It was therefore solely in the interests of beauty that the sculptors avoided showing him screaming, whereas in literature (for example, the *Aeneid*), the law of beauty does not apply as it does in the visual arts, so that the poet is perfectly free to describe Laocoön's screams. In other words, Lessing insists on a narrowly aesthetic definition of classical beauty. Winckelmann's supporting, ethical arguments, though not incompatible with the aesthetic thesis, have the effect of blurring a distinction that Lessing wishes above all to establish.

Lessing uses this apparently minor disagreement with Winckelmann to demonstrate something fundamental to aesthetics: that poetry and visual art are subject to quite different laws. His aesthetic principles, like those of his age as a whole, are normative: each art form has rules of its own, and the arts must not be assimilated to one another, as the Horatian dictum "ut pictura poesis" had suggested. The central arguments in Lessing's *Laocoön* are not by any means original: most of them can be found in the work of earlier theorists such as Jean-Baptiste Du Bos, James Harris, Moses Mendelssohn, and Denis Diderot. But they had never before been stated so fully and so lucidly. The treatise *Laocoön* shows Lessing at his analytic best: he is a master of logical distinctions. Although he attempted, in the final version of his work, to give it as formal and relaxed an appearance as possible (before Winckelmann and Lessing, German aesthetics, having grown out of academic philosophy, had been all too addicted to abstract systems, such as that of Alexander Gottlieb Baumgarten), the early drafts show that it began, in the manner of Wolffian rationalism, as a rigorous piece of deduction from the concepts of space and time, along the lines of chapter 16 in the final version. Like the aesthetic theories of most of his immediate predecessors, Lessing's is a mimetic, representational one: it is the business of art to render imaginary objects present, to create an illusion of reality. It follows from this that there must be a natural relationship between sign and signified. Poetry uses words, which follow each other in time; hence, it must deal with objects that follow each other in time, that is, actions. The visual arts use shapes and surfaces, which coexist in space; hence, they must depict objects that coexist in space, that is, bodies. It is one of the strengths of Lessing's treatise that it supplements, and indeed builds up to, these a priori arguments with empirical ones (chiefly derived from the practice of the Greeks): Homer, as a poet, depicted primarily actions, and the Greek sculptors depicted primarily

bodies. Lessing thus arrives at identical conclusions by two distinct routes: by the analytic methods of Baumgarten, Mendelssohn, and other thinkers of the Leibniz-Wolffian school, and by the empirical methods favored by the art historian Winckelmann and by British theorists such as David Hume and Edmund Burke.

Lessing's treatise extends to literature the service that Winckelmann had performed for the visual arts. Just as Winckelmann had drawn his conclusions directly from the art of antiquity, so Lessing formulates the laws of poetry by direct reference to Homer, Sophocles, and (in his essays on drama, the *Hamburg Dramaturgy* of 1767–1769) the poetics of Aristotle. French literary classicism is either ignored or (again in the *Hamburg Dramaturgy*) attacked as weakly derivative and inauthentic. Greece supersedes France as a model for German culture, and the foundations of that Hellenism that became almost an obsession for German writers from Johann Wolfgang von Goethe to Friedrich Nietzsche were laid.

It is a great misfortune that the *Laocoön* is unfinished. Its continuation was to have dealt with, among other things, music, dance, and mime, and with drama as an art form that combines visual art and poetry. As a dramatist himself, Lessing would have been well qualified to tackle this issue. The *Hamburg Dramaturgy* is no real substitute, for it consists of unsystematic reflections, chiefly designed to undermine the authority of French tragedy as practiced by Pierre Corneille and François-Mane Arouet de Voltaire, and to supply a theoretical justification for psychological and domestic drama in a more realistic idiom such as Lessing himself, Diderot, and a few other contemporaries were then developing. The continuation of the *Laocoön* would have approached drama more systematically, working from first principles. Lessing gave an indication of how he would have proceeded, however, in his letter of 26 May 1769 to Friedrich Nicolai.

The conceptual framework of the *Laocoön* is supplemented by Lessing's semiotic theory of "natural" and "arbitrary" signs (which is itself foreshadowed in the work of earlier Enlightenment thinkers). A "natural" sign resembles the object it signifies, as do the shapes and colors of figurative sculpture and painting. An "arbitrary" sign (and all language, with rare exceptions such as onomatopoetic words, consists of "arbitrary" signs) has no necessary connection with its object: the connection is a purely conventional one. Because the aim of all art, according to Lessing's mimetic theory, is to present the imitated object to the intuitive cognition of the recipient in as direct a manner as possible, it follows that poetry must endeavor by all possible means to transform its "arbitrary" (that is, conventional) linguistic signs into "natural" ones. In depicting only actions and eschewing description of bodies—for the visual arts are more suited to the latter task—poetry takes a major step in this direction. Its use of images and metaphors (rather than abstractions) also enhances its concreteness and immediacy. But the genre of poetry best equipped to convert symbolic or linguistic cognition into intuitive or perceptual cognition—that is, to convert "arbitrary" signs into "natural" signs—is drama, as Lessing explains in the letter to Nicolai. Drama is not an *imitation* of speech, as the third-person narrative often is: the sign (the dramatic dialogue) coincides completely with the signified (the speech of the characters); and the linguistic signs are reinforced by the purely "natural" signs of the actors' gestures and expression.

It is clear that, at this point, Lessing has reached the limits of the mimetic theory of art, and of the conceptual framework of his original treatise. The letter to Nicolai points the way to a new, nonreferential theory of art and poetry. Lessing did not develop such a theory himself. But his insistence that art should be judged only by aesthetic (as distinct from ethical, religious, political, or any other) standards consolidated Baumgarten's defense of aesthetic autonomy, and prepared the way for the aesthetics of Immanuel Kant; and his close attention to the artistic medium laid the basis for Johann Gottfried von Herder's attempts to relate the different arts to different senses, including touch.

One other of Lessing's aesthetic achievements deserves mention. In his short treatise of 1769, *How the Ancients Portrayed Death,* he further reinforced German Hellenism and the neoclassical movement in the visual arts. Death, he argues, was never depicted in classical (as distinct from Christian) art as an ugly skeleton, but as a beautiful youth, the brother of sleep; even on tombstones and sarcophagi, the law of beauty prevailed. This elegant little essay furnishes a theoretical justification for the neoclassical funerary sculpture of Antonio Canova, John Flaxman, and their followers, and is a landmark in the post-Christian iconography of death.

It cannot be denied, however, that Lessing's interest is above all in poetry, and that, in the *Laocoön,* the visual arts come off poorly by comparison. Winckelmann's conception of classical beauty had itself been narrow and restrictive. Lessing has the same limitations, in that he is just as indifferent as his predecessor toward landscape, genre painting, still life, and other nonclassical art forms. But he adds further restrictions on top of these. Although he endorses Winckelmann's contention that the visual arts should depict beautiful and idealized human figures, he goes on to maintain that this is their exclusive task. Not only does he outlaw the ethical content of Winckelmann's conception of beauty; he also condemns allegorical and historical painting—forms held in high esteem by Winckelmann—as unwarranted intrusions by the visual arts upon the province of poetry. His censures of descriptive poetry (descriptive in the sense of indulging in enumeration of physical detail) diminish the province of poetry far less drastically than his corresponding strictures on whole areas of sculpture and painting diminish that of the visual arts; and whereas he deals separately with the different genres of poetry—and would have distinguished between them further had he completed his treatise—he simply lumps together painting and sculpture as if they were a single art form. (It was left to Herder, in his essay *Plastic Art [Plastik]* of 1778, to supplement Lessing's work with a separate aesthetics of sculpture as a three-dimensional form, relating less to vision than to the sense of touch.) The effect of all this was to confine the visual arts to depicting only a restrained and, in the last resort, empty variety of human beauty. Poetry, meanwhile, remains undisputed sovereign of the realm that interested the dramatist Lessing most: the boundless sphere of human activity, which affects us far more immediately than the lofty, but ultimately frigid, beauty of Greek art. It is probable, as E. H. Gombrich (1957) has suggested, that Lessing's attack on Winckelmann's interpretation of Laocoön as a paragon of fortitude is part of his campaign against French classicism, against the idealized stoical heroes of Cornelian tragedy. By banishing heroic images to the visual arts, and at the same time emptying them of all but aesthetic content, Lessing hopes to clear the way for literature—especially the dramatic and narrative forms—to get on with more important things, and to enjoy a monopoly of realism.

The limitations of the *Laocoön* are thus conspicuous, particularly in its treatment of the visual arts. As regards poetry, its limitations are not so much those of Lessing himself as of the representational aesthetics and neoclassical principles of his time. The mimetic theory is less than adequate to the more subjective varieties of poetry, especially the lyric. The role of unconscious factors in expression, the role of mood and atmosphere, and of the associative qualities of languages, are almost completely neglected. And although Lessing tries valiantly, in his *Hamburg Dramaturgy,* to harmonize Aristotle's *Poetics* with modern forms of drama, his attempts are strained. Despite his frequent praise of William Shakespeare, he nowhere seriously attempts to reconcile Shakespeare's plays with his own neoclassical principles. Based as the latter were on the art forms of antiquity, their inadequacy in relation to newer, post-Renaissance forms was becoming ever more obvious. What was now required was an aesthetics capable of doing justice to the psychological, social, and cultural origins of works of art—of art as expression rather than as imitation. Herder's expressive theory of poetry (further developed by the Romantics) and his historical relativism (further developed by Georg Wilhelm Friedrich Hegel) were among the first attempts to meet this need.

[*See also* Winckelmann.]

BIBLIOGRAPHY

Works by Lessing

Laocoön: An Essay on the Limits of Painting and Poetry. Translated by Edward Allen McCormick. Indianapolis, 1962; reprint, Baltimore, 1984.

Laokoon. In *Werke und Briefe,* edited by Wilfried Barner et al., vol. 5.2, pp. 11–321. Frankfurt am Main, 1990. A modern critical edition with a full commentary.

Laokoon: Lessing, Herder, Goethe: Selections. Edited by William Guild Howard. New York, 1910.

Lessings Laokoon. Edited by Hugo Blümner. 2d ed. Berlin, 1880. Includes all drafts and manuscript variants.

Wie die Alten den Tod gebildet (How the Ancients Portrayed Death). In *Werke und Briefe,* edited by Wilfried Barner et al., vol. 6, pp. 715–778. Frankfurt am Main, 1985.

Other Sources

Bieber, Margarete. *Laocoön: The Influence of the Group since Its Rediscovery.* 2d ed. Detroit, 1967.

Gebauer, Gunter, ed. *Das Laokoon-Projekt: Pläne einer semiotischen Ästhetik.* Stuttgart, 1984.

Gombrich, E. H. "Lessing." *Proceedings of the British Academy* 43 (1957): 133–156.

Gustafson, Susan E. "Beautiful Statues, Beautiful Men: The Abjection of Feminine Imagination in Lessing's *Laokoon.*" *Publications of the Modern Language Association of America* 108 (1993): 1083–1095.

Hatfield, Henry Caraway. *Winckelmann and His German Critics, 1755–1781: A Prelude to the Classical Age.* New York, 1943.

Howard, William Guild. "Ut pictura poesis." *Publications of the Modern Language Association of America* 24 (1909): 40–123.

Nisbet, Hugh Barr. "Laocoön in Germany: The Reception of the Group since Winckelmann." *Oxford German Studies* 10 (1979): 22–63.

Nolte, Fred O. *Lessing's "Laokoon."* Lancaster, Pa., 1940.

Richter, Simon. *Laocoön's Body and the Aesthetics of Pain.* Detroit, 1992.

Rudowski, Victor Anthony. *Lessing's "Aesthetica in nuce": An Analysis of the May 26, 1769, Letter to Nicolai.* Chapel Hill, N.C., 1971.

Szarota, Elida Maria. *Lessings "Laokoon": Eine Kampfschrift für eine realistische Kunst und Poesie.* Weimar, 1959.

Wellbery, David E. *Lessing's "Laokoon": Semiotics and Aesthetics in the Age of Reason.* Cambridge and New York, 1984.

Wessell, Leonard P. "Lessing as an Aesthetic Thinker." *Lessing Yearbook* 15 (1983): 177–211.

H. B. NISBET

LITERATURE. [*To treat the subject of literature and related topics, this entry comprises three essays:*

> Literary Aesthetics
> What Is Literature?
> Literature and Cognition

The first essay traces the history of literature and literary aesthetics, including criticism and theory, from Plato to the present. The second essay offers a brief overview of the history of the concept of literature, which in turn sets the background for contemporary debates about the nature and role(s) of literature in culture. The third essay treats cognitive issues in literary aesthetics, that is, whether claims to knowledge can be made in or on behalf of literature; this has been a primary concern of philosophers from Plato until the present. For theories of literature, see Arnold; Blanchot; Coleridge; Derrida; Dryden; Hellenistic Aesthetics; Kristeva; New Criticism; Plato, *article on* Philosophy and Literature; Sartre; Sidney; Tolstoy; Wittgenstein; *and* Wordsworth. *For related discussion, see* Emotions, *article on* Emotions and Literature; Epistemology and Aesthetics; Law and Art, *article on* Law and Literature; Poetics; *and* Ut Pictura Poesis.]

Literary Aesthetics

From its very beginning literature has elicited responses of a kind that one today would recognize as criticism. Already in the oral bards of Archaic Greece there is self-reference and reference to the poetry of others. From the fifth century onward, there is quite a lot of what one today might call practical criticism: comments with reference to specific works and authors on the necessary connection between content and style, as well as comments on diction, meter, and construction. General reflection by philosophers on the nature and function of literature, that is, literary aesthetics, comes into being with the birth of Greek philosophy and its conceptualization of ideas of nature and man.

Classical Period. Early Greek criticism as one finds it in the early fragments, in the authors of the Old Comedy and in Plato (428–348 BCE), is mainly concerned with literature from the point of view of ultimate moral values: works and authors are criticized insofar as they are taken to contribute to the political and moral decline of Athens. Plato, in the *Republic,* has the famous reference to the "old quarrel between poetry and philosophy" (book 10, 607). He wants to banish the poets from his ideal state. "the only poetry admissible in our city," he says, "is hymns to the gods and encomia to good men" (ibid.). Although Plato's perspective on literature was external and his interest in it motivated by ethical and educational considerations rather than by a passion for literature itself, his work brought into focus two problems that were to be central in all later writings on literature: the problem of *mimesis* and the problem concerning the relationship between the literary work and the emotional aspect of human nature.

Very roughly, there are two reasons why Plato wants to banish poetry from the ideal society. Poetry, like the pictorial and sculptural arts, is a form of *mimēsis* or imitation. But what the poet imitates is not the ultimate reality, which, according to Plato, can only be found in the world of ideas, but simply the imperfect and deceptive appearances found in this world. Poetry leads the mind away from, while philosophy tries to show the mind the way to grasp, the true reality of the world of ideas. The consequence of indulging regularly in literature is therefore "ruination to the listeners' mind, unless they are protected by the knowledge of what really is" (ibid., 595). The second reason that Plato wants to ban poetry, is that "poetical imitation" "waters . . . and nourishes" "all the desires and pleasures and pains of the mind" when "they ought to be dried up" and "under control" (ibid., 606), so that our ability to live in accordance with the idea of what is just is not undermined.

Reacting to Plato's views of literature, Aristotle (384–322 BCE), in his *Poetics*, approaches literature as a distinctive art, and therefore a distinctive area of inquiry, attempting to define its essential characteristics, to distinguish it from other types of discourse as well as to identify the species or genres of literature. While agreeing with Plato that all art offers images of possible reality, Aristotle argues that such images cannot be tested against any fixed conception of reality; for the poet can have as the object of his *mimēsis* "one of three things, that is, what was or is, what is commonly said and thought to be the case, and what ought to be the case" (*Poetics*, 1460b). Aristotle had a view of the relationship between particulars and universals that permitted him to accord to literature an epistemically respectable place between philosophy and history: "poetry is at once more like philosophy and more worthwhile than history, since poetry tends to make general statements, while those of history are particular" (ibid., 1451b).

On the issue of literature and emotion Aristotle makes only a few comments, but it is clear that these meet Plato's objection. According to Aristotle, there are two kinds of emotions involved in the apprehension of a literary work. One is the pleasure felt when one understands what the imitation is an imitation of: "All men enjoy getting to understand something" (ibid., 1448b). But *mimēsis* also induces ordinary emotions appropriate to the situation that is the object of the *mimēsis*. Thus, for tragedy, which is Aristotle's concern in the *Poetics*, pity and fear are the emotions appropriate to the represented action. But tragedy does not encourage habits of excessive emotive reaction. On the contrary, by arousing pity and fear, it effects the *katharsis* of those feelings (ibid., 1449b), thus contributing to emotional balance.

In the *Poetics*, Aristotle also deals with the intrinsic qualities of the genre of tragedy. He introduces the idea that good tragedy should have unity of action, and he also briefly mentions that the action should take place within one revolution of the sun, and that the location of the action should be restricted. In addition, he makes comments about the kind of action suitable for tragedy, the kind of ideas tragedy should deal with, and in what kind of language it should be written.

In the centuries after Aristotle there developed a rich critical culture in the Greek-speaking world, a culture that also developed scholarly methods of textual criticism as well as methods of interpretation. Already from the time of Aristophanes (c.450–380 BCE) there had been a historical awareness of literary change, and Aristotle had a theory of the origins of tragedy and comedy. This historical consciousness grows throughout the Hellenic period, and in Latin criticism there is also an awareness that criticism has a history: Horace (65–8 BCE) looks back to Democritus (c.460–360 BCE) as well as to Aristophanes and Aristotle. The historical consciousness in Latin criticism almost grows into a feeling of belatedness: that the great authors of classical Greece had established patterns and standards for literature that one could not really compete with, but at best copy. Thus, in Latin criticism the concept of *imitatio*, which was the Latin translation of *mimēsis*, took on an additional meaning. "My advice to the skilled imitator," says Horace, "will be to keep his eye on the model of life and manners, and draw his speech living from there" (*Ars poetica*). But it is equally important to "Study Greek models night and day" (ibid.). Imitation thus became imitation of classical models as well as of nature.

In addition to Aristotle's *Poetics*, Horace's *Ars poetica* and Longinus's *Peri hypsous (On the Sublime)* were the outstandingly influential works from antiquity. The former was written toward the end of Horace's life, probably some time between 12 and 8 BCE. *On the Sublime* is more difficult to date as one does not know who Longinus was, nor when he lived. *Ars poetica* is a verse epistle written by a poet to advise the sons of a nobleman by the name of Piso how to write a literary work. It is not a philosophical treatise but represents a genre that was to become very common in criticism: general reflections on literature by artists and critics who did not necessarily have any philosophical background or interest. Thus, it does not, like Aristotle's *Poetics*, belong in literary aesthetics and the general principles it propounds are not argued. It is full of humor and allusion and the main themes are bewilderingly interlaced. These themes are, however, easy to identify: consistency, unity, propriety or decorum, the debt to Greece, the importance of technique, and the need for moral seriousness. Horace declares the aim of the poet to be "to do good or to give pleasure—or, thirdly, to say things which are both pleasing and serviceable for life" (*Ars poetica*), and, he says, "The man who combines pleasure with usefulness wins every suffrage, delighting the reader and also giving his advice" (ibid.).

Longinus's *On the Sublime*, probably written in the first century CE rather than by the third-century rhetorician Cassius Longinus, who is traditionally held to be the author, is not concerned specifically with poetry, nor with any poem in its entirety, but only with the quality of "the sublime." Longinus takes this to be the "source of the distinction of the very greatest poets and prose writers and the means by which they have given eternal life to their own fame" (1.3–1.4). Sublimity is not simply pleasing or useful, but "produces ecstasy rather than persuasion in the hearer" and "tears everything up like a whirlwind" (1.4). There are, according to Longinus, five sources of the sublime. The first two ("the power to conceive great thoughts" and "strong and inspired emotion") are "for the most part natural," while the last three (figurative language, noble diction, and dignified and elevated word arrangement) "involve art" (8.1). It is the first two sources that play the most important part in the creation of a great work, and the grand, if flawed, products of natural genius must be preferred to the mediocre but artistically faultless. Because of the emphasis he puts on the "power to conceive great thoughts" and "strong and inspired emotion," Longinus shows a tendency to move from the quality of the work to the mind of the author: "Sublimity is the echo of a noble mind" (9.2). Again, *On the Sublime* is not a philosophical treatise but the work of what we would call an enthusiastic critic.

Together with Plato's strictures on poetry, these three works define the problems and concerns that have dominated reflections on literature up to the present day: the nature of the literary work itself and the relative role of style, structure, and ideas or thought within the work; the nature of the relationship between the work and the world, between the work and its creator, and between the work and the reader's emotions; and the instrumental value (positive or negative) of literature. But these works can also be seen to represent a development in the way in which criticism was written and becomes established as a special kind of discourse different from, for example, philosophy. Neither Horace nor Longinus writes as a philosopher but rather as an adviser to poets or as a connoisseur of the art. They propound general principles, but they do not do so systematically, nor do they support these principles by argument. Criticism was never to enter the realm of philosophy again.

Medieval Period. In the Middle Ages, the study of literature as an activity with principles of its own disappeared altogether, as the concept of literature itself became blurred. When literature was made the object of reflection, it was from within two of the three disciplines of the trivium, grammar and rhetoric. There had been affinities between rhetoric and poetics in classical antiquity, but now literature was seen simply as another way of using ornate language for public speech; and rhetoric itself moved away from reflection on the way in which language worked, toward a merely classificatory concern with linguistic and rhetorical devices of a steadily more ornate character. In grammar, the "art of speaking correctly," metrics and style as well as the use and misuse of words, were discussed. The most important legacy of the Middle Ages for criticism, however, was a strengthening of the notion that allegorical and etymological meanings were present in poetic texts and deserved explication. This idea was not new, but as a result of the church applying it in the interpretation of sacred texts when these texts were introduced to a hostile society, it became established by analogy as a general principle that allegory formed part of all literary creation. The notion that the meaning is hidden in the text, and that this is even what distinguishes a literary work from other texts, plays a central role in criticism even today.

Neither Aristotle's *Poetics* nor Longinus's *On the Sublime* was known in the Middle Ages. Of the *Poetics* there existed in the later Middle Ages an almost unknown translation from the abridged Arabic version of Ibn Rushd (Averroës). It was with the westward movement of Byzantine manuscripts in the decades before and after the fall of Constantinople in 1453 that Europe rediscovered both these books. The many newly discovered Greek texts were translated into Latin to make them available to the literate public of the day. And the discovery of both classical Greek and Roman texts gave impetus to a new kind of criticism: textual criticism. Critical editions of the newly discovered texts started to appear in Italy in the first half of the sixteenth century. The vast stores of new literature that were acquired in Europe at this time reconstituted literature as an object of independent interest. The discovery of the magnificence and scope of ancient literature created an enthusiasm for literature itself. Enlightened scholarship in Italy discerned in literature a vitality that one did not experience in other kinds of text. Consequently, attempts were now also made to explain in more specific terms the nature and function of literature.

These attempts did not, however, constitute a coherent discipline, nor even a coherent and continuous type of discourse. The important documents of criticism from the Renaissance to the middle of the nineteenth century were sometimes systematic "scientific" treatises modeled on Aristotle's *Poetics*, but often they were prefaces, dialogues, and so on, written to defend a certain practice (John Dryden, Henry Fielding, William Wordsworth), advice to poets and critics based on the model of Horace's *Ars poetica* (Nicholas Boileau, Alexander Pope), or defenses against moralists or other enemies of poetry (Philip Sidney, Percy Bysshe Shelley). Criticism was defined through the set of concerns on which Plato, Aristotle, Horace, and Longinus had focused, but the way in which these concerns were addressed and discussed depended on the what ideas were current in other areas of intellectual life and on what was the purpose of the discussion.

The Renaissance. Although respect for classical Greek and Roman models dominated thinking about literature in the Renaissance, the period was one of rebellion against ancient authority, in religion, in science, in the view of man and his place in the world. Among the areas in which this tension manifested itself in criticism was the conflict between classical models and vernacular literature, which either extended or did not obey classical rules. This raised the question about the extent to which the ancients were to be imitated, and how far to respect their authority. The latter question was given a special twist because one came to read Aristotle's brief comments on the necessary restrictions on place and time, together with his emphasis on the unity of action, as *rules*. The French critic Jules-César Scaliger (1484–1558) turned them into the three *unités scaligeriennes,* the unities of time, place, and action, which came to dictate the form of French classical drama in the seventeenth century and to justify the dismissal for two centuries of William Shakespeare in France as a major dramatist. Related to this was the problem concerning the relative importance in the creation of poetry of natural genius and acquired skills. There was also the question of how literature was to imitate nature: was it to imitate ideal nature, typical nature, or nature in its particulars? "Nature," says Sidney (1554–1586), whose *The Apology for Poetry* (1579/80 [1595]) is in many ways a summary of Renaissance poetic doctrine, "never sets forth the earth in so rich a tapestry as divers poets have done; neither with so pleasant rivers, fruitful trees, sweet-smelling flowers, nor whatsoever else may make the too much loved earth more lovely. Her world is brazen, the poets only deliver a golden." For Sidney, then, poetry presents the ideal and not only ideal *nature*, but also the *ideal man* and what is *morally ideal*. The question of what literature was to imitate was connected with the question of what was the function of literature. Here the Horatian formula "to teach and delight" was taken over, and Sidney combines it with the notion of mimesis in his definition of poetry as "an art of imitation . . . with this end, to teach and delight." This again is linked to the question of the moral status of literature, a question that Sidney's *Apology* answers by making the moral content of poetry a part of its essential requirement.

As the Renaissance period came to an end, the main seat of literary criticism moved from Italy to France. One main difference between French classicism and the earlier Italian classicism was the former's greater emphasis on ancient authority. French criticism was dominated by a much more rigid conception of how classical rules and models should be applied and it imposed this view on the creative writers of the time. The period thus earned the name of neoclassicism. Under the influence from France, this stricter observance of rules and models also defined English neoclassicism and distinguished it from the classicism of the English Renaissance. The sources of Sidney's *Apology* had been classical, but the spirit was wholly different from the much stricter neoclassical spirit that arose later.

Neoclassicism. The spirit of neoclassicism can be defined by reference not only to the attitude to classical rules and models, but also to the attitude to imitation, and to reason and genius. Whereas a typical representative of Renaissance poetics such as Sidney insisted that the poet imitates ideal nature, that poets create a golden world where nature only delivers one of brass, neoclassical critics tended to insist more on literature as imitating commonplace reality or, more frequently, as imitating what is typical, general nature, that is, the principles and order of nature. This view of imitation is epitomized in Samuel Johnson's (1709–1784) remark that "Nothing can please many, and please long, but just representations of general nature" (Preface to his edition of Shakespeare, 1765). Also, in neoclassical criticism, imitation of nature was narrowly linked to imitation of the best works from classical antiquity. "To copy Nature is to copy Them," says Pope (1688–1744) in *An Essay on Criticism* (1711; l.140), which, like another central neoclassical

work, Boileau's (1636–1711) *L'art poétique* (1674), was an imitation of Horace's *Ars poetica*.

The interpretation of mimesis as meaning that literature should imitate only typical or general nature led to the doctrine of decorum or propriety. The poet must not, says La Mesnadière, describe the "meanness of avarice, the infamy of indulgence, the blackness of perfidy, the horror of cruelty, the smell of poverty" (*La poétique*, 1639). Violent events on the stage were banned. Medea must kill her children off stage, Agamemnon must be murdered behind the scenes. The characters in literary works must be typical and preserve their typical and proper behavior throughout. A king must always speak like a king and behave as one. A soldier likewise. Thus, one finds that in the neoclassical period, Shakespeare stands condemned for introducing an ungrateful, scheming soldier in Iago (for soldiers are typically honest and straightforward). Propriety or decorum was extended to style as well. The Metaphysical Poets used conceits: the yoking together in metaphor of two disparate elements that had to be connected through logical reasoning rather than seeming intuitively connected. They stand condemned by neoclassical criticism, which instead demanded an urbane and polished style.

Neoclassical criticism was the criticism of the Age of Reason. It rested on an assumption that all men shared a common human nature that was the same whatever the external conditions were. "Mankind," says Dryden (1631–1700), "is ever the same and nothing lost out of nature, though everything is altered" (Preface to *Fables, Ancient and Modern*, 1700). What distinguished man from the beasts and made him human was his reason. All men were rational creatures, governed by the light of reason. This idea influenced criticism in two ways. First, if there is a common human nature, then what appeals to one generation will appeal to all. This was the basis for assuming that worthy models would guarantee worthiness in the imitation. Second, if man is governed by reason in general, so is his creation of a literary work. Natural talent and natural gifts are fully recognized by neoclassical criticism, but such gifts can only be used to full effect when they are controlled by reason. In neoclassical theory, the emphasis is on precedent and tradition, on the skill and handiwork of writing rather than on genius and natural talent.

Neoclassical poetic doctrine carried with it the seeds of its own destruction. The notion that literature is subject to rules that can be recognized by reason as being the right rules, and the notion that literature is best produced in imitation of models, are ultimately restrictive notions. Neoclassical rules, in particular those concerning the three unities of time, place, and action, and those concerning propriety, fairly quickly came into conflict with the literary reality they were supposed to regulate. In particular, they came into conflict with Shakespearean plays and Shakespearean style: Shakespeare, by the neoclassical rules, stands condemned.

In England, he had to be defended by all the great critics against such strictures as the neoclassical rules gave rise to. In France, where the rules meant much more than they did in England, Shakespeare was simply ignored. In such a conflict, however, Shakespeare was bound to win and the rules to lose, for Shakespeare's plays are paradigms of great literature. If there are to be rules for literature at all, they must permit one to explain the greatness of Shakespeare and they must not exclude him. The neoclassical rules were also too restrictive in another area. The eighteenth century saw the development of the novel as a major literary genre, and this new literary genre posed an even greater challenge to the neoclassical rules than did Shakespeare. It was not that the novel appeared to pose a problem for these rules seen from inside the neoclassical framework; from such an inside point of view, the novel simply could not be conceived as a major literary genre or a serious form of literature. The whole development of the novel, however, was toward becoming a new manifestation of an age-old main genre: the epic mode. Furthermore, the novel appealed to a wider audience than the poetry and drama of the time—to the new and expanding middle classes. This audience was growing in economic and political importance year by year. Therefore, the novel could not be dismissed. What is more, once the neoclassical rules were given up, the novel could easily be seen as a new development of the epic and as having essential similarities with other literary genres such as drama and poetry. All in all, the neoclassical rules broke under this strain.

Romanticism. The change from neoclassicism to Romanticism in literature was part of a deep change in the intellectual outlook and mood of Europe. Various developments in the course of the eighteenth century undermined the basic assumptions on which the Age of Enlightenment views rested: that man's distinguishing feature was reason and that the universe and man would in the end yield to an analysis by reason. The empiricism of John Locke (1632–1704) and David Hume (1711–1776) led in the end to a new emphasis on the irrational side of man's nature in the acquisition of knowledge, as well as in the moral sphere. The Kantian answer to this Humean challenge led to an emphasis on the mind as actively creating the world about which man could have knowledge. In literary criticism, this shift toward a view of man as an irrational and a passionate being, together with the view of the mind as creative rather than passive, led to momentous changes. The imitation theory that was so important in the neoclassical period now became almost impossible to hold. A creative artistic mind does not repeat the process of creation that it has already accomplished when it participates actively in forming the real, external world, but, in making a work of art, it engages in a new and *different* process of creation. It does not imitate something that has already been brought into existence, but it creates instead a fresh, new, and independent reality. The poet thus becomes a creator rather than an imitator and the key faculty becomes the imagination rather than reason. If original creation is the only genuine form of artistic activity, then the imitation of models and the adherence to rules is alien to and even inimical to the artistic process. What is more, if man is an irrational and passionate being rather than a rational one, then the interesting reality is not the external world but the internal world. Moving the passions closer to the center of attention, as did the British empiricists, leads in Romantic doctrine to an emphasis on the need for man to express, and understand in expression, these passions. Literature, as opposed to science and philosophy, which use the language of reason, comes to be seen not only as particularly suitable for the expression of emotion, but as the language of the emotions itself. The metaphor of literature as a mirror of life that gives either an idealized, a typical, or a realistic reflection of an external reality is now exchanged for that of a lamp that, by its colored light, also colors reality as the single subjective consciousness sees it.

The metaphor of the lamp was supplemented by a series of other metaphors that suggested that the activity of the mind, in creating of a work of art, is not a willed activity, an activity controlled by the poet's deliberate choices. The mind is active, but its activity is natural and beyond the control of the individual. "Poetry," says Wordsworth (1770–1850), "is the spontaneous overflow of powerful feeling" (Preface to the 1802 edition of *Lyrical Ballads*). The analogy here is between the mind and a container. When the container is full, it overflows, and what results is poetry. Another metaphor is that of the aeolian harp, a harp whose strings vibrate with the wind and in this way produce wonderful music. Impressions, provided by the primary imagination that creates the real world, touch off in the poetic soul a vibration that the poet then transforms into poetry. From this there follows an interesting change in the status of the lyric poem, which, until the Romantic period, had been a minor genre. The favored genres in the neoclassical period had been the objective genres—the drama, the epistle, and so on—where there was no room for the poet to declare his own feelings. In the Romantic period, the lyric poem becomes a major genre, because it is eminently suited to the expression of moods and emotions.

Nineteenth Century. Although periodization in historical accounts is always dangerous and periods must never be conceived as explanatory principles, in surveying the development of modern critical thought it makes some sense to identify a Renaissance, a neoclassical, and a Romantic period where a poetic theory existed that emerged out of the general climate of ideas of the time and that influenced literary practice. In the sixteenth, seventeenth, and eighteenth centuries, and even at the beginning of the nineteenth, authors and critics were often the same people, or they were people in some way closely involved with literature, and there was no differentiation between theoretical speculation and critical comments on specific works.

In the nineteenth century, it is not possible to identify a poetic theory that had, on the one hand, a connection with the general climate of ideas and, on the other hand, with poetic practice. At the same time, the way in which literary critical thought was organized changed. A differentiation of function developed: general literary criticism (evaluative and interpretative comments on single works, groups of work or oeuvres), literary history, and, ultimately, literary theory became separate intellectual activities, practiced by different people. Toward the end of the century, these activities also became academic disciplines as they migrated into the universities.

The development of literary history took place in the wake of the development of modern political history as a discipline rather than an art, and as such came to suffer from the same positivistic bias. This was reinforced by Hippolyte Taine's (1828–1893) widely adopted formula *race, milieu, moment* from his *Histoire de la littérature anglaise* (1864–1869), which led to an emphasis on genetic factors, the study of sources, the detailed accumulation of facts, and all the facts. The reaction against positivism in literary history was given a theoretical foundation in Wilhelm Dilthey's (1833–1911) *Einleitung in die Geisteswissenschaften* (1883), in which it was argued that the disciplines that deal with man's spirit, the social sciences and the humanities, have a goal and method of their own that is completely different from that of the natural sciences. Dilthey inspired a special discipline, *Geistesgeschichte,* which tended to invoke notions such as weltanschauung (worldview) and zeitgeist (spirit of the age) to explain an author and his work. Neither positivist literary history nor *Geistesgeschichte* had much to say about the literary work of art itself, however, and therefore led to a reaction in the twentieth century against biographical and historical criticism.

It is also in Dilthey's *Einleitung in die Geisteswissenschaften* that the roots of literary theory can be found. The notion that there is a distinct discipline for the human sciences, with its own methods and goals, raises the question of what these methods and goals are as well as what the object of study is. Dilthey's own view was that there was a discipline of hermeneutics that would provide an answer to these questions, but as developments in the twentieth century have demonstrated, there can be many approaches to these theoretical problems.

Germany and France provided the impetus for the development of literary history and theory, but it was above all in England that criticism was given a new direction. Starting with his first series of *Essays in Criticism* (1865) and continuing in *Culture and Anarchy* (1869), Matthew Arnold (1822–1888) developed an extended concept of criticism. By the term *criticism,* Arnold intends something much broader than literary scholarship. Criticism embraces all branches of knowledge and its object is to make what Arnold calls "the best" in the world of ideas prevail. The critic, drawing on all the resources of cosmopolitan culture, seeks to supply what is lacking in the English character and thus to remedy the defects of English society. With Arnold, criticism becomes an essential humanist discipline, an area of intellectual activity that claims to be taken as seriously as philosophy, and indeed, as seriously as literature itself. This criticism was not merely literary, but also cultural, criticism.

Although a number of Victorian critics could be said to practice cultural rather than narrowly literary criticism, it was within the discipline of literary studies that humanist criticism of the Arnoldian kind was to be influential. With the rise of the social sciences and history as academic disciplines, cultural criticism as practiced by Thomas Carlyle (1795–1781), Arnold, John Stuart Mill (1806–1873), William Morris (1834–1896), John Ruskin (1819–1900), and other distinguished Victorians lost its authority and its role as it had no basis in the kind of systematic knowledge about culture and society that the universities now began to produce and of which they became the custodians. When criticism finally found a home within the university, it was as a part of literary studies, and only after a long struggle. It was not clear that criticism could be developed as a *discipline,* for it was not clear in what sense criticism was a specialty that needed professional practitioners. The notion of a critic, however, incorporated in its conceptual basis the idea of someone who, by virtue of his superior knowledge and taste, is a guide and mentor, and the academic critic became a guardian of the literary tradition and of standards of literary judgment.

Twentieth Century. In the twentieth century, criticism in the sense of interpretative and evaluative arguments about particular literary works, about groups of works and oeuvres, became a main type of critical activity. It was flanked on the one side by literary history, which, however, was logically secondary to interpretative criticism because it necessarily rested on interpretation. On the other side, it was flanked by literary theory, but literary theory was not a part of criticism, and, at least in the English-speaking world, criticism was atheoretical and sometimes, as in the case of F. R. Leavis (1895–1978), antitheoretical: it was what Leavis called practical criticism. Similar to the practical criticism of Leavis was the New Criticism that developed from the reflections on criticism by T. S. Eliot (1888–1965), the theoretical work of I. A. Richards, and the verbal analyses of William Empson (b. 1906), and that had Yvor Winters, Cleanth Brooks, and William K. Wimsatt as some of its most distinguished practitioners. The New Criticism focused on the literary work of art in isolation from its historical context and its origin with an author. It was thus ahistorical as well as atheoretical. Both practical criticism of the kind practiced by Leavis and his followers and the New Criticism could be seen as a reaction against the historical and biographical criticism that had its roots in literary history of the positivist and *Geistesgeschichtliches* kind.

Although the New Criticism was atheoretical, it was not antitheoretical, and parallel to interpretative analyses of single works and groups of work there developed a literary theory rationalizing the New Criticism. This theory was not developed by critics but by philosophers such as Monroe C. Beardsley (in *Aesthetics: Problems in the Philosophy of Criticism* [New York, 1957]) who also made important contributions to general aesthetics. Other kinds of theoretical approaches to literature, such as the Wittgensteinian approach (e.g., Morris Weitz's *Hamlet and the Philosophy of Literary Criticism* [London, 1965]), were also developed by philosophers. The differentiation of function that took place toward the end of the nineteenth century was thus still in force in the 1960s. Literary theory was literary aesthetics and sometimes, more narrowly, philosophy of criticism.

The view that literary theory and literary criticism were logically different activities was summed up in an article by René Wellek in 1962 in which he declared that theory was "concerned with principles, categories, devices, etc.," and criticism with "a discussion of concrete works of literature" (Wellek, 1963, p. 36). Literature is an art, literary criticism a discipline of thought, and literary theory a branch of philosophy. On this view, the concept of criticism is a pretheoretical concept that might be the object of analysis and description as it is in the "philosophy of criticism," but is not itself a critical or theoretical instrument defined *within a theory* that gives the concept both meaning and legitimacy. Criticism is atheoretical in the sense that the validity of its arguments and methods is not guaranteed by a set of theoretical premises, and it does not employ a set of theoretical concepts to formulate its arguments or conclusions. This does not mean that a piece of atheoretical criticism is without a logic or a set of presuppositions that governs the argument, but the logic and presuppositions will not be defined or motivated *within* a theory of literature. Because criticism can be of many kinds, different types of criticism will be based on different sets of presuppositions. Insofar as criticism is *literary* criticism, however, there must be presuppositions that define its status as literary criticism and therefore underlie critical practice. These are presuppositions fundamental to the existence of literary criticism as such. Criticism that dispenses with these presuppositions will not be literary criticism. These presuppositions can be made explicit, and when they are, they can be used to discriminate between what is literary criticism and other types of critical discourse, but they cannot be used to discriminate against a *type* of literary criticism, that is, criticism based on these presuppositions that is also governed by further presuppositions.

One fundamental presupposition defining this conception of literary criticism is that the object of criticism is an object of appreciation, an object that might be expected, given the right sort of attention, to yield an experience of value, and that it is part of the value of this experience that it offers the reader a shaped and concentrated presentation of situations raising questions that are important for human life. This does not mean that all literary criticism is interpretative criticism aimed at revealing the object of appreciation. Literary criticism can be concerned with any aspect of literature at any level of generality—with a literary work, a literary oeuvre, a literary period, a literary technique, a literary genre. The presupposition that the particular literary work is an object of appreciation is what provides atheoretical criticism with its motivation and purpose. Presuppositions such as this one, do not, however, make critical practice an application of *theoretical* concepts and conventions. Literary criticism is as little governed by theory as are one's financial transactions, all kinds of which can be undertaken without an economic theory.

Literary theory, on this view, is conceived of as independent of, and posterior to, the practice of producing, reading, and discussing literary works. It is assumed that literary theory can only have a purpose if there exists such a literary practice: without the existence of such a practice, there would be no questions for theory to answer. As a branch of philosophy, literary theory is seen as having the task of addressing the ontological, epistemological, and evaluative questions that arise in connection with literature and literary criticism. These are questions such as the following: What is the nature of the literary work? How can one identify/define a literary work? What is the mode of apprehension through which the literary work is grasped? What are the criteria for validity in interpretation? What is the nature of the value judgments passed on literary works and what are the criteria for valid value judgements? Moreover, as a branch of philosophy, literary theory would have at its disposal the insights reached and the arguments developed in other areas of philosophy—in metaphysics, epistemology, the philosophy of language, and ethics. The standards of argument in literary theory would be governed by the standards of argument in these philosophical subdisciplines.

The conception of literary criticism as independent of theory is still the dominant one of the relationship between criticism and theory. The majority of critics still go about their work without finding it necessary or illuminating to base their work in some kind of theory. Since the beginning of the 1960s, however, literary theory has developed as a subdiscipline *within* literary studies itself. The discipline has been labeled just "theory," or "critical theory," or "theoretical criticism." It has acquired its own institutional framework with journals, chairs, and other university posts dealing with "theory." Publishers have their separate lists with titles in "literary theory," just as they have lists in "Renaissance studies," "Victorian studies," and so on. Critical theory is not confined to literary studies, however, but has appeared in other areas of the humanities as well, such as art history, music, and even history. Indeed, critical theory often manifests aspirations to become global theory, a theory that takes as its province the whole field of the humanities—to become, that is, a general theory of culture. Critical theory thus claims to produce knowledge by establishing general propositions about cultural phenomena such as literature, art, music, architecture, and history. Moreover, this knowledge is the kind of knowledge that is the product of a research effort. Representatives of critical theory refer to what has been "shown" or "demonstrated" by an academic authority (though this authority is always personalized) and the knowledge produced is taken to be progressive. There is a clear ambition in critical theory to adopt from the hard sciences a *strong* concept of theory. Some theorists invoke an analogy between the advent of critical theory and what they call the Copernican revolution in science, while others adopt the concept of "paradigm" and "paradigm shift" from Thomas Kuhn's *The Structure of Scientific Revolutions* (1962; 2d ed., 1970), to characterize the development that critical theory represents.

Critical theory challenges the assumption that literary criticism is independent of, and logically prior to, the practice of producing, reading, and discussing literary works. As a general theory of literature and culture, critical theory provides the concepts for describing literature and other cultural phenomena and the criteria for what constitute valid descriptions. Critical theory thus lays down the rules for how individual literary works can be interpreted and evaluated. Although the concept of criticism that developed as a consequence of the differentiation of functions at the end of the nineteenth century is atheoretical, this new concept of criticism is theoretical. Criticism becomes an extension or an application of theory. This application has taken two forms. Some theorists have sought to ground the reading of literary texts in methods designed to guarantee the objectivity and validity of interpretations. Others, impressed by the inability of such procedures to produce agreement among interpreters, have translated that failure into an alternative mode of theory that denies the possibility of distinguishing between correct and incorrect interpretation. Critical theory in its various forms thus represents an attempt to guide practice from a position above or outside it, and, where existing practice does not conform with the recommendations of the theory, to revolutionize existing practice. The development of critical theory has therefore had as a consequence that its proponents try to initiate "new readings" of well-known literary works.

Opponents of critical theory have argued that these new readings are not simply readings but constitute "a new dogmatics of reading" (Parrinder, 1987, p. 18), and that the introduction of the theoretical concept of criticism amounts to a recommendation to stop doing criticism in the recognized sense of that word and start doing something else.

The fundamental reason for contesting the idea that theoretical criticism is "literary criticism" would be that it does not rest on the same humanist basis as the interpretative and evaluative activity that became recognized as the discipline of literary criticism in the last century. Criticism in the humanist sense is a many-faceted activity based on many different principles, dealing with many types of subject and using many types of methodology. The underlying rationale of this activity, however, is that it contributes in some way to the appreciation within the community of the single literary work and thus to the reproduction of cultural value. The recommendation implicit in the theoretical concept of criticism is that this many-faceted activity be reduced to one consistent practice grounded not in a conception of humanist value, but in a theory of literature or culture. Thus, there would be no link between theoretical and humanist atheoretical criticism.

Proponents of the various kinds of critical theory would not necessarily object to such a description. These types of theory have the ambition to be general theories of texts rather than just theories of literature. Consequently, criticism can have as its object other types of work than literary works. The objects of theoretical criticism are not works at all but discourses or texts, and criticism should deal with any questions concerning the use of language and rhetoric in texts in general. If criticism is conceived in this way, then the link between criticism and appreciation is simply inappropriate. The texts with which criticism deals are not singled out because they have any particular aesthetic values that criticism either reveals, comments on, or presupposes. Thus, the very notion of literature as an aesthetic category is questioned or denied by critical theory, and one is in a situation not unlike the one that existed in the Middle Ages when the concept of literature itself became blurred and literary criticism had no object on which to focus.

Because the various types of critical theory can be construed as being aimed not at explaining present critical practice but at changing it, the real issue that this conception of theory and criticism raises is not theoretical but political and, some would argue, moral. The choice between atheoretical, humanist criticism and theoretical criticism is a choice between different kinds of value. This choice cannot be grounded within literary theory itself or within critical theory, because it is a choice concerning the evaluative basis that constitutes the rationale for such theories.

BIBLIOGRAPHY

Abrams, M. H. *The Mirror and the Lamp: Romantic Theory and the Critical Tradition.* New York and Oxford, 1953.

Atkins, J. W. H. *Literary Criticism in Antiquity: A Sketch of Its Development,* vol. 1, *Greek.* London, 1934.

Atkins, J. W. H. *Literary Criticism in Antiquity: A Sketch of Its Development,* vol. 2, *Graeco-Roman.* London, 1934.

Atkins, J. W. H. *English Literary Criticism: The Medieval Phase.* London, 1943.

Atkins, J. W. H. *English Literary Criticism: The Renascence.* London, 1947.

Atkins, J. W. H. *English Literary Criticism: 17th and 18th Centuries.* London, 1951.

Culler, Jonathan. "Literary Criticism and the American University." In *Framing the Sign: Criticism and Its Institutions,* pp. 3–40. Oxford and New York, 1988.

Eagleton, Terry. *The Function of Criticism: From* The Spectator *to Post-Structuralism.* London, 1984.

Easthope, Anthony. "Paradigm Lost and Paradigm Regained." In *The State of Theory,* edited by Richard Bradford, pp. 90–104. London and New York, 1993.

Eliot, T. S. "The Function of Criticism." In *Selected Essays,* 3d ed., pp. 23–34. London, 1951.

Kennedy, George A., ed. *The Cambridge History of Literary Criticism,* vol. 1, *Classical Criticism.* Cambridge and New York, 1989.

Leavis, F. R. "Literary Criticism and Philosophy." In *The Common Pursuit,* pp. 211–222. London, 1952.

Leavis, F. R. *The Living Principle: 'English' as a Discipline of Thought.* London, 1975.

Mitchell, W. J. T., ed. *Against Theory: Literary Studies and the New Pragmatism.* Chicago, 1985.

Olsen, Stein Haugom. "Literary Theory and Literary Aesthetics." In *The End of Literary Theory,* pp. 196–211. Cambridge and New York, 1987.

Olsen, Stein Haugom. "Critical Theory and Atheoretical Criticism." In *Understanding the Arts: Contemporary Scandinavian Aesthetics,* edited by Jeanette Emt and Gøran Hermerén, pp. 81–94. Lund, 1992.

Olsen, Stein Haugom. "The Role of Theory in Literary Studies." In *Aesthetic Matters: Essays Presented to Göran Sörbom on his 60th Birthday,* edited by Lars-Olof Åhlberg and Tommie Zaine, pp. 101–113. Uppsala, 1994.

Parrinder, Patrick. *The Failure of Theory: Essays on Criticism and Contemporary Fiction.* Brighton, 1987.

Righter, William. *The Myth of Theory.* Cambridge and New York, 1994.

Selden, Raman, ed. *The Cambridge History of Literary Criticism,* vol. 8, *From Formalism to Poststructuralism.* Cambridge and New York, 1995.

Small, Ian. *Conditions for Criticism: Authority, Knowledge, and Literature in the Late Nineteenth Century.* Oxford, 1991.

Sidney, Philip. *The Apology for Poetry.* (1579–1580 [1595]). Edited by Mary R. Mahl. Northridge, Calif., 1969.

Vickers, Brian. *Appropriating Shakespeare.* New Haven, 1993.

Wellek, René. "Literary Criticism and Philosophy." *Scrutiny* 5 (1937): 375–383. Reprinted in *The Importance of Scrutiny,* edited by Eric Bentley (New York, 1948), pp. 23–30.

Wellek, René. *A History of Modern Criticism, 1750–1950.* 8 vols. New Haven, 1955–1992.

Wellek, René. "The Term and Concept of Literary Criticism." In *Concepts of Criticism,* edited by Stephen G. Nichols, Jr., pp. 21–36. New Haven, 1963. Originally in *Proceedings of the Third Congress of the International Association of Comparative Literature* (The Hague, 1962), pp. 35–47.

Wimsatt, William K., Jr., and Cleanth Brooks. *Literary Criticism: A Short History.* New York, 1957; reprint, Chicago, 1978.

Stein Haugom Olsen

What Is Literature?

The term *literature* has existed in its current sense for about two hundred years. From classical Rome through the Renaissance (with a large gap for the medieval period, when the word disappeared), the two primary senses of literature were (1) literacy, the simple ability to read and write, and (2) possession of that further degree of general knowledge that would cause one to be considered well-read, erudite, or "cultured." In the latter sense, it figures on lists of good qualities; Julius Caesar is said to have *litteratura* along with "good sense, memory, reflection, and diligence."

The term does not become firmly attached to the now familiar third sense of a valued body of secular writings until the early eighteenth century, and it is only around the time of Immanuel Kant and the Romantics that it acquires the still more specialized fourth sense of creative or imaginative writing, as distinguished from the moral, the true, and the useful. For most of the eighteenth century, René Wellek writes in "The Attack on Literature" (1972),

> literature is used very inclusively. It refers to all kinds of writing, including those of erudite nature, history, theology, philosophy, and even natural science. Only very slowly was the term narrowed down to what we today call "imaginative" literature: the poem, the tale, the play in particular. This is a process intimately connected with the rise of aesthetics.   (Wellek, 1982, p. 15)

To say that literature is a recent and historically shifting concept is of course not to imply that the concept must be abandoned. Many, like Wellek, remain committed to some version of post-Romantic "established usage" (ibid., p. 19) without bothering over literature's earlier, unspecialized senses. But what Wellek calls the "attack on literature" should perhaps be seen less as an attack than as a complex return of and to those earlier senses, a reinvigoration—alongside and in combination with the full set of aesthetic meanings—of usages established before the rise of aesthetics.

In its meanings of literacy and general reading knowledge, literature was of course a strong marker of class identity. This was not lost on earlier observers. When Pierre Bourdieu (1993) argues that literary taste, like other sorts of aesthetic preference, serves as cultural capital for purposes of social reproduction and social climbing, he extends Voltaire's already pronounced contempt for literature in the sense of an intellectually insubstantial "smattering" of knowledge serving as a badge of membership in the circles of upper-class fashion.

A similar point can be made concerning contemporary debates about literature and ideology. What is really at stake in such debates is often not literature's autonomy but its value. The separability of value from autonomy, a point registered by recent critics, is an eighteenth-century lesson. For post-Romantics, literature's value seems to depend on its autonomy, which seems in turn to depend on imagination. (As Wellek himself acknowledges, imagination or fictionality is in fact no guarantee of value; "subliterary" genres of questionable value are equally fictional. The only sufficient guarantee, for Wellek, is reflexivity.) But the eighteenth-century understanding of literature as writings that rise above a certain threshold of quality, whether or not they are especially creative or reflexive, suggested grounds of inclusion based on literature's functions in the public sphere, and thus called attention to the process by which quality was determined in and by society. The question of whether "the quality" (a social elite) is defining quality in its own image is thus a pre- as well as a post-aesthetic question. When Tony Bennett calls for "a non-literary theory of literature which will theorize its object as a set of social rather than formal realities and processes" (1990, p. 139), the replacement of *form* by *society* does not reduce formal ambiguity to a single exhaustive social meaning, nor a meaning determined by *contemporary* society. Rather, it returns us to the ambiguities of society itself, which include those that the pre-Romantic definition of literature already offered for examination in phrases such as "polite learning" (which is by no means to say that form is irrelevant to such an examination).

According to Terry Eagleton, "Literature, in the sense of a set of works of assured and unalterable value, distinguished by certain shared inherent properties, does not exist" (1983, p. 11). This conclusion, which exposes a rift between the third and fourth senses of literature mentioned at the beginning of this essay, would seem to be the most glaring and unavoidable effect of literature's semantic history; that is, literature cannot claim without anachronism to be both imaginative/creative and a canon extending back to classical antiquity. We have no reason, for example, to believe that Sophocles, Dante, William Shakespeare, or even Voltaire was self-consciously trying to produce literature in the modern imaginative/creative sense, or that such a goal existed for anyone to strive for. To the extent that the so-called canon is indeed literary—many of the authors included, such as Michel de Montaigne and Jules Michelet, Thomas Babington Macaulay and John Stuart Mill, suggest that it is not—it is the product of a retroactive imposition of the modern sense upon works that recognized no such criterion.

According to Wellek, the first book that calls itself a "history of *English* literature" dates from as late as 1836. Clearly, a given body of writings often commands respect and reverence for reasons that have nothing to do with imagination in any of its numerous, mutually contradictory senses. Estrangement and empathy, organic form and the subversion of organic form, the exciting of intense emotion and the withdrawing from any moral or instrumental purposes, the self-consciousness of an author or period and the display of the workings of the unconscious—none of these explains how the literary canon comes to be entangled with reverence for the past, for a local or universal heritage and its monuments, for nations and nationalism.

Of course, one can see imagination as a positive value without seeing it as embodied either in a canon or in knowledge of any sort. And one can value literature as a sort of knowledge, whether or not it is uniquely imaginative and whether or not it is embodied in a canon. Indeed, literariness of the sort championed by Roland Barthes largely defines itself *against* the canon. "Et tout le reste est littérature": Paul Verlaine's famous outburst of condescension anticipates Barthes's distinction between literature that has gone dead (the merely readable, deserving of nothing better than scholarly analysis) and that which remains so alive as to be worthy of (re)writing today. A perpetually renewed contempt for the canon may be the protest of an avant-garde, or simply a means by which active writers make room for new and diverse forms of writing. It is in the latter terms that Raymond Williams, whose history of the term in *Keywords* does not disagree with Wellek's, expresses his resistance to the "specialization" that leads from "all works within the orbit of polite learning" to "well-written books of an *imaginative or creative* kind" (1983, p. 152). Williams is enthusiastic about recent challenges to literature "by concepts of *writing* and *communication* which seek to recover the most active and general senses which the extreme specialization seemed to exclude" (ibid., p. 154).

According to Williams's *Culture and Society* (1958), the birth of the concept of literature belongs to a new and higher valuation of the past that also arose in the era of the industrial revolution and the French Revolution. In this period, as Jonathan Kramnick has shown, literary history emerges as a reversal of the earlier progressivism that saw "*modern* literature improving on the works of the past" (1997). Instead of figuring as an obstacle to be overcome in one's reading of an older author, a stigma of barbarism yielding slowly to refinement, pastness became an unquestioned marker of the older author's presumed higher merit. Hence, the category of literature participates in "an aesthetics of well-nigh unapproachable oldness" (ibid.).

On the one hand, the concept of literature derives a critical, subversive value from its association with a disappearing preindustrial way of life, and this association explains the oblique but forceful politicizing that the concept of literature has so strangely provoked. On the other hand, this critical, political impulse tends to be drawn helplessly into a vague, amorphous confrontation between past and present and thus finds itself blunted and distracted. Critique of the past is severely limited by a presumptive admiration of everything not modern; critique of the present too easily becomes peremptory and absolute. For all the many appeals to politics that ground recent literary studies, this logic has not lost its power. So-called constructive critique, critique that aims at matters of policy and assumes both urgency and moral messiness, still tends to be abandoned to the social sciences.

If literature thus becomes identified with the past, the past also becomes identified with literature. When literary critics complain about the rise of cultural studies, often the real object of complaint is not disrespect for literature or literariness as such. (Cultural studies, like literary theory, could as easily be seen not as doing away with literariness but on the contrary insisting on its presence in a much vaster field of texts. Indeed, one could well call this situation, in David Simpson's phrase, "the rule of literature" [1995].) The real source of complaint would seem to be the arrogance of a perceived presentism; for cultural studies in and of the past, however extensively it may seem to favor social-scientific perspectives at the expense of a pure aesthetic, does not seem to excite the same ire. If not always conventionally respectful to literature, it is certainly respectful to the past. In many situations, pastness is equivalent to honorary literariness.

The past is another country. Respect for communities distant both in time and in space is another value that has remained largely implicit in the literature concept, perhaps because it bridges the divide between pre- and post-Romantic understandings. The aesthetic understanding of literature offers a protected enclave in which respect for the expression of cultural uniqueness or otherness can be taken for granted. The pre-aesthetic understanding values literature's instrumental role in furthering sociability, civility, open and rational debate. Both give literature a function in articulating, preserving, and translating collective experience—though, of course, not without collisions: At what point, for example, does respect for cultural particularity serve to close down rational debate? Can collective experience survive the subversive force of an aesthetic of indeterminacy? Thus, literature has meant much to recent projects of feminist and minority community building; and the same function can, of course, be read backwards into the works of the canon.

Much of the debate over the concept of literature can be resolved into a debate over which community—for example, writers or academics—should be allowed to impose its definition. John Gross argues that literature cannot serve as the object of an academic discipline. "Isn't there a certain basic antagonism between the very nature of the university and the very spirit of literature?" Literature "can be a hundred things—but a discipline is not one of them" (Gross, 1969). Pleading for an amateur criticism, Gross concludes:

> Criticism remains the most miscellaneous, the most ill-defined of occupations. At any given moment it is liable to start turning into something else: history or politics, psychology or ethics, autobiography or ethics, autobiography or gossip. In a world which favours experts and specialists, this means that the critic is increasingly liable to be dismissed as a dilettante or resented as a trespasser. But if his uncertain status puts him at a disadvantage, it also makes possible, ideally, the breadth and independence which are his ultimate justification. (Ibid.)

Here the "ill-defined" nature of literature, which keeps literary criticism from being a true discipline, is offered as criticism's strongest competitive advantage, and it has been greeted as such by the discipline itself, which embraces it as a sustaining mythology.

There are also ironies on the other side of this disagreement. In "The Order of Discourse," Michel Foucault suggested that primary texts are credited with "multiple or hidden meaning," with an "essential reticence and richness," in order to become "the basis for an open possibility of speaking" (1981). This demonstration of how objects of knowledge such as literature served the purposes of disciplines like criticism was only possible, however, because (as Foucault confessed in an interview) he had learned how to adopt a viewpoint outside disciplines, and especially outside philosophy, from literature itself.

Stanley Fish explains "how, in the absence of formal criteria, literary texts come to be identified." He argues that literature

> is a conventional category. What will, at any time, be recognized as literature is a function of a communal decision as to what will count as literature. All texts have the potential of so counting, in that it is possible to regard any stretch of language in such a way that it will display those properties presently understood to be literary. (1980, p. 10)

In other words, "it is the reader who 'makes' literature" (ibid., p. 11). Here the irony is that the authority of the community that makes this "collective decision" is itself undermined by the generalizing of the category of literature. Nothing could be more characteristic of "the rule of literature" than the demonstration of what a given community neglects, elides, or excludes, hence of the limits to its authority.

Yet, this does not mean that literature possesses some uniquely subversive capacity denied to (other) disciplinary objects. Writers since William Wordsworth have always claimed, according to Derek Attridge, that literature

> can engage with the language and thoughts of everyone who speaks the same tongue, and that it attains thereby the power to intervene in the ethical and political life of a community or a nation. To push this claim too far, however, is to endanger the existence of literature itself as a distinct entity, for if literature does *not* employ a special language, from what does it derive its appeal and its strength? (1988, p. 3)

Hence, there are "two mutually inconsistent demands—that the language of literature be recognizably different from the language we encounter in other contexts, and that it be recognizably the same" (ibid.). Attridge's solution to this problem is to define literature as this very impossibility of definition. But it is a happy impossibility, for this seems to be a paradox that literature can be proud to call its own. The problem is that this paradox is *not* its own, but rather a general characteristic of disciplinary objects as such. As Attridge himself notes, in its ability to "destabiliz[e] the discourses and institutions within which it has its being," "the word *literature*" is "a term like *writing* or *law*" (ibid., p. 17).

The analysis of literature as a disciplinary object emerged from the Althusserian argument, developed by Étienne Balibar and Pierre Macherey, that "the old idealist question 'What is literature?'" should be rejected and replaced by a view of literature as part of "the ideology of bourgeois education" (1981). This argument should be distinguished from the apparently similar position, expressed by Tony Bennett and Terry Eagleton, that literature is an ideological formation, hence an enemy to be combated. In the Althusserian position, the concept of "ideology" is itself weakened, diluted, rendered more complex and more "literary." Above all, it is no longer identified with simple false consciousness. Hence, to say that literature is produced by and functions in the apparatus of education is no longer to identify it as an ideological *antagonist*. As in the eighteenth century, literature is here seen as less autonomous but not necessarily as less valuable.

In this and related arguments, what is proposed is something like a compromise between pre-Romantic and post-Romantic definitions of literature. Once again, according to this view, literature becomes a particular mode of valued knowledge that need not be attached to any restricted body of texts. It is asserted that almost anything can be looked at in an aesthetic way; that to do so is to produce or discover value, but is not invariably the most valuable thing to do with a given text; that the modes of literary knowledge include both versions of imagination and creativity, on the one hand, and the sorts of rational discourse to which these were initially opposed, on the other; and finally, that these modes are themselves subject to significant historical change. No pronouncement is made as to whether literature should or should not be defended against challenges from more comprehensive, less value-laden terms such as writing, rhetoric, communication, and culture.

[*See also* Ideology; *and* Williams.]

BIBLIOGRAPHY

Attridge, Derek. *Peculiar Language: Literature as Difference from the Renaissance to James Joyce.* London, 1988.

Balibar, Étienne, and Pierre Macherey. "On Literature as an Ideological Form." In *Untying the Text: A Post-Structuralist Reader,* edited by Robert Young, pp. 79–99. London and Boston, 1981.

Bennett, Tony. *Outside Literature.* London and New York, 1990.

Bourdieu, Pierre. *The Field of Cultural Production: Essays on Art and Literature.* Edited by Randal Johnson. New York, 1993.

Derrida, Jacques. *Acts of Literature.* Edited by Derek Attridge. New York and London, 1992.

During, Simon. *Foucault and Literature: Towards a Genealogy of Writing.* London and New York, 1992.

Eagleton, Terry. *Literary Theory: An Introduction.* Minneapolis, 1983.

Eagleton, Terry. *The Ideology of the Aesthetic.* Oxford and, Cambridge, Mass., 1990.

Fish, Stanley. *Is There a Text in This Class? The Authority of Interpretive Communities.* Cambridge, Mass., 1980.

Foucault, Michel. "The Order of Discourse." In *Untying the Text: A Post-Structuralist Reader,* edited by Robert Young, pp. 48–78. London and Boston, 1981.

Gross, John. *The Rise and Fall of the Man of Letters.* New York, 1969.

Kramnick, Jonathan. "The Emergence of English Literary History." *PMLA* (October 1997).

Levine, George, ed. *Aesthetics and Ideology.* New Brunswick, N.J., 1994.

Macherey, Pierre. *The Object of Literature.* Translated by David Macey. Cambridge and New York, 1995.

Simpson, David. *The Academic Postmodern and the Rule of Literature: A Report on Half-Knowledge.* Chicago, 1995.

Wellek, René. *The Attack on Literature and Other Essays.* Chapel Hill, N.C., 1982.

Williams, Raymond. *Culture and Society, 1780–1950.* New York, 1958.

Williams, Raymond. *Keywords.* Rev. ed. New York and Oxford, 1983.

BRUCE ROBBINS

Literature and Cognition

Literature manifestly offers readers pleasure and amusement. But does it offer cognitive gains? Despite the current prevalence of the entrenched collection of views widely defended under the label "critical theory," the issues are probably still best introduced historically, in terms of the evolution of theories of criticism in association with parallel developments in general philosophy.

Plato famously argues (*Republic*, 595–601) that it is possible to make a representation of something without possessing anything seriously worth calling knowledge of that thing. The poet's craft, like that of other sorts of artist, lies in the production of persuasive simulacra, not in knowledge of the things he thus represents. Although a poet may represent virtue, knowledge of the nature of virtue lies rather with the philosopher. The function of literature is thus not to improve our knowledge but to move our passions, for the most part, Plato thinks (605–608), in a way corrupting to character.

The authority of these arguments remains overwhelming up to (and in some quarters beyond) the Renaissance. However, in Philip Sidney's (1554–1586) *Apology for Poetry* (1579–1580 [1595]), we encounter a critical transformation of them capable of standing on its own feet. Sidney grants that "the poet nothing affirmeth": literature offers the reader no true statements concerning what David Hume was later to call "matter of fact and existence." But that is because poetry transcends the mundane world. The poet is a second Creator, who either ennobles nature or envisages things entirely new. Poetry, as Plato thought, works on the emotions, but it does so not to corrupt but to improve us by making us enamored of ideal rather than existing forms of virtue. The most important departure from Plato in Sidney's typically Renaissance outlook, at least from the present point of view, is the uncoupling of literature from the job of producing simulacra of what already exists. That move gives Sidney the conception of literature as a central mechanism in the constitution of a human world that is doubtless founded on the natural world, but is to a great extent independent of it. From that it is only a short step to the idea that literature does offer cognitive gains after all, at least in the sense that it offers readers acquaintance with certain of the forms and possibilities of that world.

That is an idea taken further in a variety of ways by Romantic literary theory. Between Sidney's Neoplatonism and the Romantics, however, lies the very different Neoplatonism of the scientific revolution and its philosophical supporters. One expression of the new spirit is an interest in the question of what kind of writing is most appropriate for the expression of scientific truth, a topic given impetus in England by the foundation of the Royal Society. The demands yielded by that seventeenth-century discussion are familiar enough: scientific language should be stripped of all rhetoric, avoiding especially metaphor and trope, and should consist of plain declarative sentences couched in explicitly defined general terms. The spirit of the age, aided by the immense prestige of John Locke's *Essay Concerning Human Understanding* (1690), rapidly spreads the idea that these are not merely desiderata for scientific language, but for any language aiming at the expression of truth.

The trouble is not that such a conception of truth-directed discourse makes literature impossible. After all, the Augustan style exemplified by Alexander Pope or Samuel Johnson offers a remarkable testimony to the extent to which it is possible to create a serious and even imposing literature within the restraints of a roughly Lockean conception of how language can best serve truth. The type of nineteenth-century Realism that claims to offer fictions that acquaint the reader with real *general* features of social or political reality, even though all the *particulars* of the story may be invented, offers another. The real problem is that such a view restricts literature, pace the proto-Romantic Sidney, to the representation of general features of nature or manners as they actually exist or are taken to exist.

It is resistance to this latter drawback of the grand Augustan manner that motivates most of the main Romantic attempts to reconceive the relationship between literature and truth. Within this large enterprise one can roughly distinguish at least three major strands of thought. First there is the line of theorizing opened up by the denial that there is any one point of view from which the "truth of things" can be wholly, or finally, apprehended. Friedrich Nietzsche's "perspectivism" is one expression of this, as is William Blake's rejection of "single vision and Newton's sleep" in favor of the kind of "Vision" invoked by such lines as "The Vision of Christ that thou dost see / Is my Vision's Greatest Enemy" (*The Everlasting Gospel*, 1818).

A second line of Romantic theorizing questions the Augustan conviction that literature, like science, should concern itself with general features of nature: that the "business of a poet" as Imlac assures us in Johnson's *Rasselas* (1759), "is to examine, not the individual but the species." Blake, as usual, takes a short way with this: "To Generalise is to be an Idiot. To Particularise is the alone Distinction of Merit"

(Annotations to Joshua Reynolds's *Discourses on Art*, 1808). Laurence Sterne, another proto-Romantic, does better. In *Tristram Shandy* (1761–1767), he presents characters whose whole interest and charm lie in their utter particularity, not to say idiosyncracy. Sterne's novel, moreover, is packed with sly digs at Locke; its general tendency is to articulate a serious point against Locke's account of the relationship between language and truth: that the "objective" language fitted for natural science, founded as it is on the discounting of idiosyncracies of observational viewpoint and on the pursuit of general laws, is ill fitted to describe the human world, constituted as the latter is out of irreducible particularities and differences of viewpoint and outlook. To the speaker of a Lockean language founded on "judgment," indeed, the whole human world simply vanishes from view: it is only the writer who disposes of the resources of Sterne's "wit" who can bring it back into focus.

A third line of (this time full-blown) Romantic thinking about literature and truth, discernible everywhere in the period from G. W. F. Hegel to William Wordsworth and Samuel Taylor Coleridge (Abrams, 1971), exploits the notion of transcendence, in association with that of growth. Natural science can describe growth and development in the natural world. But, proceeding—as, for the most part, pace Thomas Kuhn, it does—from a single, stable point of view, it cannot describe the growth of the mind, because that involves transcendence of outlook, vision, and even conceptual vocabulary (this is the thrust of Coleridge's celebrated if opaque distinction between *fancy* and *imagination*) by the mind experiencing it. Wordsworth's *Prelude* and Marcel Proust's great novel are no doubt the high points of the literary Romanticism that takes this thought as its raison d'être.

Versions of these Romantic defenses of the cognitive claims of literature were dominant in English-speaking literary theory until the 1960s. Since then they have come under threat from a number of directions. One influential line of attack common to structuralists (Barthes, 1974), poststructuralists (Derrida, 1978; de Man, 1984), and others (Fish, 1980; Kermode, 1979) has dwelt on the hermetic aspects of writing, and perhaps of language itself, in the attempt to show that the construction and interpretation of literary works are exclusively responsive not to features of the world, natural or human, but to considerations internal to literary traditions, interpretative communities, or language itself. These arguments have fueled in turn a revival of "historicist" criticism that, tracing its stance and methods ultimately to the Marxist critique of ideology, treats literature primarily as a mystified expression of "underlying" economic or social relations, whose "real" significance can only be uncovered by critics capable of wielding the tools of some special theory or tradition of social criticism.

The effect of all these arguments is to deny cognitive significance to literature itself by, in effect, draining it out of literature into current literary criticism, or "theory," which retains whatever cognitive significance attaches to it in virtue of its own theoretical commitments, together with its exposure of the delusive cognitive claims of its subject matter. It is tempting to see in this bid for cognitive autonomy on the part of academic theorists a new skirmish in Plato's long-running "war between the poets and the philosophers": a new way of assigning to "theory" the pursuit of truth and to literature the fabrication of illusion.

Indeed, at the heart of recent critical "theory" lies a deeply Platonic discontent with literature: that literature, most notably in forms, such as the nineteenth-century novel, held to have Realist ambitions, fails to represent Reality as it is, offering instead only persuasive simulacra constructed according to canons internal to literature itself. But a reading of Sidney should already have taught us a reply to this: literary writing does not mimic life: it is alive. What its life secretes—a moral that, for that matter, might equally be drawn from a reading of Derrida—are not simulacra of already existing things, but new things existing in their own right. This suggests (Harrison, 1991) a different account of the relationship between literature and theory: one with roots both in Romantic notions of transcendence and in Derridean ones of margins and transgression. Theory provides us with construals of Reality each of which presents itself as a putative representation of the truth of things, and thus as exhaustive and final. The function of literature is not to compete in this pursuit, but rather, in presenting us, as Aristotle claimed it did, not with "what happens" but with "what would happen," to offer elaborations of possibility that continually transgress and exceed the limits of theory. On such a view, the cognitive gains characteristically offered by literature are of the negative kind that come from seeing how things that the limitations of a former outlook had led us to fancy impossible might, after all, be envisaged. To take a familiar example, *Sense and Sensibility* is not an attempt at a description of manners or of social conditions; it is an exploration of a possible outlook on life, an outlook that, although it has its roots in many sources, from Stoicism to the novels of Henry Fielding, is ultimately Jane Austen's own creation. The novel exposes the reader to the same surprise to which the plot exposes Marianne Dashwood: that of discovering that such an outlook is not necessarily cold, or overformal, or lacking in humanity. Those who find such an outlook very unsympathetic will, of course, be inclined to say of the novel, as Ludwig Wittgenstein said of William Shakespeare, that it is not "true": that the book is a confidence trick, the work of a mere "wordsmith," and so on. Such complaints merely thrash the air, leaving Austen and Shakespeare to survive uninjured in the estimation of other readers, because they miss the point: literature does not record truths; it articulates, of course with differing degrees of adequacy and persuasiveness, ways of responding to life, ways, thus, of being human. It is for that reason that literature quite legitimately engages us as readers in a relationship of trust that accepts the risk of being surprised, and possibly changed and enlarged, by what we read; and for that reason, too, that the stance of "hermeneutic suspicion" (Paul Ricoeur) so widely recommended by recent critical theory is ultimately unsustainable, as well as antiliterary.

Such a view is, of course, opposed by various versions of philosophical skepticism (primarily skepticism concerning the possibility of control by the text over the meanings readers attach to it), and by metaphysics, in the sense of any philosophical theory that claims finality for its vision of things. These further issues raise questions more extensive than can be entered into here.

BIBLIOGRAPHY

Abrams, M. H. *Natural Supernaturalism: Tradition and Revolution in Romantic Literature*. New York, 1971.

Barthes, Roland. *S/Z*. Translated by Richard Miller. New York, 1974.

de Man, Paul. *The Rhetoric of Romanticism*. New York, 1984.

Derrida, Jacques. *Writing and Difference*. Translated by Alan Bass. Chicago, 1978.

Fish, Stanley. *Is There a Text in This Class? The Authority of Interpretive Communities*. Cambridge, Mass., 1980.

Harrison, Bernard. *Inconvenient Fictions: Literature and the Limits of Theory*. New Haven, 1991.

Kermode, Frank. *The Genesis of Secrecy: On the Interpretation of Narrative*. Cambridge, Mass., 1979.

Sidney, Philip. *The Apology for Poetry* (1579–1580 [1595]). Edited by Mary R. Mahl. Northridge, Calif., 1969.

BERNARD HARRISON

LOCKE, ALAIN LEROY (1886–1954), American philosopher. Locke elected to forego the formal study of philosophy and instead devoted himself to the development of a group-conscious school of African-American art and literature. He was a mentor of several well-known writers and artists, including Aaron Douglas, Langston Hughes, and Zora Neale Hurston. His thesis, "The Problem of Classification in the Theory of Value," was completed under the direction of Ralph Barton Perry at Harvard in 1918. This early work in value theory provided the philosophical ground on which he developed his view of aesthetics. Value relativism, the centerpiece of his cultural pluralism, framed his account of art as instrumental in the social elevation of African Americans. Even though he believed that African Americans had already contributed many native elements to the national culture in the areas of music, dance, and folklore, he did not think that full recognition would be granted until they also contributed to the more sophisticated art forms, such as the novel and drama in the literary field, or painting and sculpture in the fine arts. Along with his effort to organize support for African-American writers, he became directly involved in the promotion of African-American art by arranging exhibitions, including some of

African art. In 1925, he edited a special Harlem issue of *Survey Graphic* that highlighted African-American art and literature. It was expanded the same year into the celebrated anthology *The New Negro.* These two works are hallmarks of the Negro Renaissance.

Locke was a prolific writer throughout his forty-year teaching career at Howard University. In addition to his published and unpublished articles on history, education, and anthropology, several anthologies on African-American art, poetry, and drama, and numerous critical essays on these subjects, he completed two volumes that presented a comprehensive historical survey of African-American art and music. He died before completing most of the manuscript for his magnum opus, *The Negro in American Culture,* which would have provided a single authoritative source for his aesthetic theory. The best source remains Locke's earlier work in *Negro Art: Past and Present* (1936) and *The Negro and His Music* (1936), which he completed for the *Bronze Booklet* series. In these two scholarly treatments, Locke presented a sociohistorical account of African-American cultural progress, tracing the development of various forms of folk expression from their early manifestation in antebellum plantation life to their twentieth-century transformation. Certain basic rudiments of his aesthetic theory can be gleaned from his sociohistorical analysis of music and art.

African Retentions and Folk Culture. The historical schema that Locke employed to represent the various stages of cultural development indicated progress in each phase by reference to whether folk forms have entered a process of transformation into high art. The uneven development of music and art is explained in terms of African retentions. Noting that advancement had occurred in those areas of cultural expression where there had been an early start in well-developed folk art forms, Locke concluded that faster progress had been made where African retentions were strongest. In the *Bronze Booklets,* he remarked that there was some memory of beauty in song, graceful movement and poetic speech, a list he expanded to include retentions in pantomime and folklore. By contrast with these forms, he believed that no such retentions existed in sculpture or the decorative arts. He appealed to environmental influences to explain both what was retained and what was lost of the African cultural heritage.

This view of retentions was a basis for Locke's advocacy of a Negro racial idiom in art that aimed to restore a lost African tradition in sculpture and the decorative arts that had been literally erased by the toils of slavery. The crudeness of slave labor caused physical damage to the hands of the slave; consequently, there was an eventual loss of the manual dexterity required for sculpturing, carving, and similar physical skills. By comparison with music, dance, and poetry, slavery reduced African Americans to a "cultural zero" in visual art. The uneven development of various art forms was used by Locke to support his claim that, with

regard to artistic temperament, there is no kinship between African and African-American cultures. The ordeal of slavery had caused African Americans to emphasize the "emotional" forms of cultural expression. This lopsided development and neglect of the plastic and pictorial forms has resulted in a reversal of the African artistic temperament. Beneath the African American's acquired artistic temperament, however, "slumbers" an original, more basic, one waiting to be reawakened. According to Locke, because the African spirit is at its best in abstract decorative forms, it is this "slumbering gift" that needs "reachievement and reexpression" (*The New Negro,* 1925).

Locke's appeal to a Negro artistic temperament to account for the unique element in Negro art and music sometimes has been interpreted to imply that the kinship between African and African-American cultures is rooted in genetics (Washington, 1986). None of his remarks need be construed in this fashion, given that he only assumed an emotional bond between peoples of African origin. For example, his remark that "we must believe that there still slumbers in the blood something which once stirred will react with peculiar emotional intensity toward African art" has been taken to mean that, because of a blood tie, the emotional bond between African-American and African artists is genetically determined. Here, as in several other places, Locke's use of the term *blood* is misleading because he only meant this bond to be understood in terms of a reconstructed social memory peculiar to those whose cultural roots trace back to Africa. The rapid progress of African-American self-expression in art following the Negro Renaissance emboldened Locke to predict in 1933 that sculpture would be the African-American artists' forte. He seems to deny any role for retentions in this case: "It is rather the feeling that there is some connection between plastic sense and the naive emotional approach to life" (Locke, 1936). He instead drew a parallel with African-American artistic achievement in music: "The instinctive spontaneous harmony of the Negro in music ought to be expected to have some counterpart in the other arts, and here, I think, it is" (Locke, 1936). When specifically discussing the work of African-American artists, Locke shifted his paradigm of the underlying African aesthetic endowment to music, whereas in his article on Negro art in the *Encyclopaedia Britannica* (1951) he maintained that the reason the African-American artistic temperament found expression in music was that it was unable to express itself in the characteristic African forms of sculpture, smithing, and weaving. Taken altogether, these remarks suggest that the underlying African-American aesthetic endowment has not been a static African retention; rather, it too has undergone transformation along with the African-American artistic temperament.

The invention of a tradition that cultivates a racial idiom required a collective effort by both the African-American community and African-American artists. In a voice directed toward the community, Locke expressed his concern about the lack of support for the work of African-American art, lamenting that the African-American community had not assumed responsibility for the establishment of a permanent collection. In the *Bronze Booklets,* Locke acknowledged that the African-American artist had not yet completely "recaptured his ancestral gifts or recovered his ancient skills." He believed that this recovery of a lost African tradition in the plastic arts would occur "not as a carry-over of instinct," but instead as "a formal revival of historical memory" based on "the proud inspiration of the reconstructed past." It was important that African-American artists gain inspiration from exposure to their lost African heritage—both to creatively express racial themes in their art and to acquire the advanced skill and technique of their ancestors. The rediscovery of an African tradition in art by African-American artists would be at second remove, through the work of European masters such as Pablo Picasso, Ernst Barlach, Jacques Lipchitz, and Amedeo Modigliani. Consequently, the race tradition instituted by African-American artists would draw on both European and African masters to produce a uniquely African-American art.

When Locke referred to a Negro temperament transplanted to the soil of the New World, he meant this to be consistent with his claim that, although the strength of African retentions might vary in the three Americas, there remains a common cultural denominator. He held that, even when the interpenetration of European and African cultures has rendered the African element difficult to specify, this element is not difficult to recognize, for it dominates "like rum in the punch." He appealed to the retention of an African aesthetic endowment to explain the diverse ways that European music and art have been reconfigured by African descendants throughout the New World. He proposed to understand the lack of affinity, as well as the close affinity, of African and New World cultures in terms of a relationship between environmental influences and the retention of a basic aesthetic endowment responsible for the African artistic temperament "creeping back" into the "overtones" of creative expression.

Cultural Self-Expression. Locke considered the self-conscious racialism and self-expression represented by the work of the Negro Renaissance artists to be a necessary phase of African-American cultural development. In the mature stages of development, Negro elements combine with various modes of European classical music, or modern art, to produce hybrid forms that are both racial and national. This objective of fusing of the musical and artistic self-expression of black people with European music and art was a guiding principle for his conception of the aesthetic outcome of the Negro Renaissance and dictated the criteria by which he evaluated its success. He argued that the race consciousness of the Negro Renaissance was an

important step toward the integration of the Negro subject into American art. Once Negro art, and the Negro subject in art, has gained acceptance as representative American art, there will be a true cultural democracy in America. Art, therefore, can be a means of social change, given that cultural pluralism in art will pave the way for greater social equality. This pragmatic orientation of African-American art toward social change is perhaps the most prominent feature of Locke's aesthetic theory.

The key to understanding Locke's concept of cultural democracy lies in his characterization of African-American art as both racial and national. Given the social outcome he envisioned, one might think that his commitment to this objective would reduce African-American art to group propaganda. In "The Negro's Contribution to American Art and Literature," he touted the Negro Renaissance as "a minority promotion move—an attempt to capitalize and bring one's own stock to par, and to have a quotable market rating and a recognized market standing" (1928b). He often spoke of African-American culture as a kind of capital that provides leverage for social change. He insisted, however, that recognition and respect for the African-American contribution to the national culture would be achieved only on the basis of the aesthetic value of African-American art. For this reason, he insisted on authentic forms of cultural expression, which he defined as self-expression representative of the group. He rejected well-intentioned positive portrayals that lacked aesthetic merit along with other nonrepresentative "Nordicized" and minstrel images. He argued that the capitalization of the race's endowments and particular inheritances of temperamental experience must eschew propaganda in favor of beauty. Art that meets the highest standards is the best group propaganda.

Although his theory did not constrain African-American artists to work exclusively in a racial idiom, Locke was frequently criticized for promoting racialism. His detractors invariably overlooked the fact that he distinguished between the traditionalist and modernist Eurocentric schools and the Africanist school. Although only the latter represent a race tradition, all African-American artists benefit from their success. Moreover, race-conscious African-American artists are not precluded from creating nonracial art. A major tenet of Locke's theory was that folk elements drawn from black peasant culture would come to be viewed by both black and white artists as native material for a national high art. This process of cultural reciprocity between black and white artists is the primary social outcome of the cultural democracy he championed in the *Bronze Booklets* and heralded in his later essays.

What is the difference between the cultural democracy made possible by Negro Renaissance artists, in which black and white artists reciprocally employ both African-American and European idioms, and the situation of African-American artists such as Robert Duncanson and

Henry Tanner prior to the Negro Renaissance? Locke cites Duncanson's successful career painting portraits and murals for patrician families as an illustration of the fact that, even in the South, a talented black artist was given recognition. In a similar vein, he claimed that Tanner's success was a result of his talent. Nonetheless, he was critical of African-American artists whose work evaded the black subject, maintaining that it was possible for an artist to be race-conscious and expressive without hindrance to his cosmopolitan scope. His remark that the work of Tanner "showed no racial path or social significance" indicates the connection between his theory of African-American art and his conception of the Negro Renaissance as an important cultural component of the New Negro movement. He argued that a racially conscious art, produced by a group of African-American artists, would be less apologetic and stultifyingly imitative and would stimulate a more "vigorous creativity" by introducing a decidedly black aesthetic into the work of African-American artists.

In addition to criticism for his openness to white artists, Locke was criticized for promoting racialism in African-American art (Porter, 1943). What lent credence to the charge of racialism was his commitment to the idea that to be a representative Negro is to have a certain set of character traits, both physical and psychological. When he proposed that African-American artists develop a race tradition, he envisioned the development of a Negro art that expresses what he considered to be genuine Negro racial characteristics. He wanted African-American art to become racially representative, but recognized that to break with the limited genre treatment of current tradition, a new idiom, a fresh technique, and a revised social perspective were needed. He argued that the Negro physiognomy must be objectively conceived in order to seriously interpret it on its own patterns. With regard to negative stereotypes, "Art must discover and reveal the beauty which prejudice and caricature have obscured and overlaid." He likewise denounced the use of "Nordicized transcription" and "Caucasian type-ideals" that aim to present a positive image, remarking that "No great art will impose alien canons of beauty upon its subject matter" ("Internationalism—Friend or Foe?"). Instead, Locke insisted on "good type portraiture," which he defined as "free from cant and compassion, self-pity and pose" (Locke "Negro Portraiture" 1928).

Race and Nationality. The Negro Renaissance had succeeded in creating a group of African-American artists who had a common bond of race consciousness in their work. Locke's insistence on the racial idiom as vital to African-American art seems to follow W. E. B. Du Bois's proclamation that African Americans will make a unique cultural contribution. Artists such as Aaron Douglas, Edouard Scott, Laura Wheeler Waring, Hale Woodruff, Archibald Motley, and James Lesesne Wells ran the gamut of modern techniques and schools. Each nonetheless had a distinguishable note or accent that could as easily have a racial explanation as a national one. For Locke, the difference between the racial and national aspects of African-American art is only a matter of degree. White and black artists can have almost the same "depth of attitude," except that, perhaps, in most cases the white artist will display "more technical and emotional detachment." What accounts for this difference is the history of slavery and racial oppression. The African-American experience of racial discrimination has emotionally and intellectually intensified group feelings, reactions, and traditions that have become an important part of African-American culture. This experience is the basis of what is of "distinctive worth and originality" in African-American self-expression. According to Locke, "The materials were all American, but the design and the pattern were different" (*The New Negro*, 1925).

In a letter sent to Locke in May 1924, the African art collector Albert Barnes tells Locke that he intends to roast a curator at the University of Pennsylvania for his remark that "the Negro has not progressed since the savage era in Africa" (Helbling, 1982). The underlying assumption of the curator's remark, as well as Barnes's disagreement with it, was that art provides an index of a group's cultural development. Some of Locke's claims regarding the use of art and crafts to interpret African culture levels and characteristic culture traits indicate that he shared a similar assumption. He maintained that history could be rewritten from art, given that art is always a mirror of social ideals. If there were no other sources, one could discover through art the history of a cultural group. For Locke, the history of the Negro subject in American art is also a history of the Negro in America.

Although Locke was generally dissatisfied with anthropology, this should not be taken to mean that he considered all anthropological studies of African culture worthless. He understood his own account of African-American art and music in the *Bronze Booklets* to be a scientifically grounded cultural history, and he urged a similar method to analyze African art. With the understanding that the cultural significance of African art is important for assessing its aesthetic value, Locke's analysis considered the function of masks, cups, and swords in religious and ceremonial practices and sometimes classified them into historical periods that included a classical era. In his zeal to establish the aesthetic worth of African art, Locke may very well have attributed to such functional art an abstract significance that it rarely possessed for those who created it. He quoted the noted art critic Roger Fry to support his claim that African sculpture is an advanced art form, placing a special emphasis on Fry's assertion that African artists had mastered with absolute virtuosity some of the technical problems of spatial representation that preoccupied European modern art. This technical accomplishment, according to Locke, explained the influence of African sculpture on modern art.

Despite his own use of the term *primitive* on occasion, Locke maintained that "things primitive have had far from a primitive influence and effect in modern art; most African art is by no means primitive, especially those phases of it which have so profoundly influenced European art. He wanted to shift the discussion of the abstract significance of African art away from the anthropological paradigm of the primitive; for he thought that European art was largely responsible for transmitting this African heritage to the younger generation of African-American artists, who, by being modernistic, were indirectly being African. According to Locke, the influence of African art on European art is evidence of an aesthetic endowment of the highest order.

Greater Democracy in Art and through Art. Because Locke was primarily concerned with the inclusion of a Negro subject in art, one might wonder why it mattered whether the transformation of African-American folk expression be achieved by black or by white artists. In a pivotal essay he wrote in 1931, "The American Negro as Artist," Locke referred to the five annual Harmon exhibitions devoted to the work of African-American artists as indicating a trend toward racialism with an increasing emphasis on racial themes and types. He proclaimed that this marked the passing of the childhood period of African-American art, the advent of a representative school of African-American self-expression, and the contribution of something new to American art. The purpose of this racial school of African-American art would be to carry out the twofold function of interpreting the African American to the nation at large and interpreting the African American to himself.

In response to critics who failed to see the relevance of African art to the African-American cultural tradition, Locke pointed out that for truly great art there is no essential conflict between racial or national traits and universal human values. It is worth noting that Locke's earlier dichotomy between race and nationality is replaced with another conflation. He used several cases to illustrate his point about the universal aspects of African-American art. With regard to a distinctively African-American aesthetic in music, he claims that, "as in the art of Miss Anderson, the more deeply representative it is racially, the broader and more universal it is in appeal and scope" (ibid., 1936). Locke is commenting on Marian Anderson's renditions of the spirituals as representative of the race. He characterized the spirituals in terms of the transformation of a strong African retention into a distinctly African-American hybrid that is both racial and national. In visual art, he cites the work of Richmond Barthes. He claimed that Barthes had dealt with subjects, such as lynching, that are racial to the core. According to Locke, Barthes's famous sculpture of a mother cradling the broken-necked body of her lynched son displays several components of African-American art. It is striking enough to be more potent antilynching propaganda than an armful of pamphlets—a decidedly racial theme. It would move with pity a spectator who was unfamiliar with lynching—a universal response. It would be of interest to an art critic who merely has an appreciation of the problems of sculptural form and tradition—a technical achievement.

In addition to the high standard of technical skill, the most important lesson that Locke wanted African-American artists to derive from African art had more to do with the essence of that tradition, namely, its vigorous simplicity and vitality. He worried that African-American artists would follow European art into the indirect inoculation of African abstraction and simplification, which will only lead to slavish imitation and sterile sophistication. He wanted the African influence on African-American art to be largely inspirational and technical. As in the case of Anderson and Barthes, the racial aspect of African-American art would not necessarily invoke the memory of an anterior culture. Locke believed that, by dealing with the African-American experience, the younger generation of artists such as Ernest Crichlow, Jacob Lawrence, Elizabeth Catlett, Norman Lewis, Charles White, and John Wiley had displayed their ability to blend a social message with the abstractly aesthetic into a balanced, mutually reinforcing synthesis. This hybrid form of expression is a defining characteristic of African-American art. More than any of the artists Locke promoted, the work of Jacob Lawrence most embodied his view. Lawrence's work was technically accomplished and deeply committed to social issues. He employed African principles of design and focused on African-American history as his subject matter. With regard to the universal elements in works such as the Toussaint L'Ouverture and Migration series, Locke asked: "Which cause owed the greater debt to him? Haitian national history, Negro historical pride, or expressionism as idiom for interpreting tropics, peasant action and emotion" (Locke, 1936).

Locke sometimes spoke of the universal qualities of art in terms of the common denominators of world art. He considered African art to be closer to the style, idioms, and forms of most non-European cultures, with the exception of perhaps the primitive or archaic periods such as early Greek or early Gothic. From the standpoint of global art, painting and sculpture are the special art forms of traditional Europe. This somewhat critical stance toward Europe must be viewed in the light of Locke's cultural pluralism, which provided a broader context for his account of art and aesthetics. In his writings on race and cultural contacts, Locke relied on a notion of value relativism to address the political problems generated by value absolutism. He considered value absolutism to be a basis for authoritarian political dogmatisms and maintained that value relativism could play a harmonizing role in dealing with competing social ideals and the problem of cultural antagonism. The assertion of absolutist notions of values only leads to illiberalism, bigotry, and cultural conceit. For Locke, relativism provides a means of escaping the ethnocentric predicament of hypostasizing one's own values, traditions, and loyalties. He proposed cultural reciprocity as a way to avoid cultural antagonism in a pluralistic society and argued that value relativism combined with reciprocity allows greater toleration of cultural differences by bridging cultural divergence. Value relativism was employed by Locke to show that antagonism caused by contact between diverse cultures can be overcome through a recognition of their universal elements. With the global context of intercultural contacts in mind, he presented a general theory of Negro art, along with its application to African-American culture, that was consistent with his account of value relativism. Aside from his dissertation and several articles, he wrote very little about values that was slated for a strictly philosophical audience. Nonetheless, he wrote a great deal about the history of African-American culture that was philosophically interesting.

[*See also* African Aesthetics; Black Aesthetic; *and* Harlem Renaissance.]

BIBLIOGRAPHY

Works by Locke

"The Problem of Classification in the Theory of Value." Ph.D. diss., Harvard University, 1918.

"Art of the Ancestors." *Survey Graphic* 6.6 (March 1925): 673.

"The Art of Auguste Mambour." *Opportunity* 3 (August 1925): 240–241, 252.

"Internationalism—Friend or Foe of Art?" *The World Tomorrow* 8 (March 1925): 75–76.

"The Legacy of the Ancestral Arts." In *The New Negro,* edited by Alain L. Locke, pp. 3–16. 1925; New York, 1992.

"More of the Negro in Art." *Opportunity* 3 (December 1925): 363–365.

The New Negro: Voices of the Harlem Renaissance (1925). Edited by Alain L. Locke. New York, 1992.

"To Certain of Our Philistines." *Opportunity* 3 (May 1925): 155–156.

"Negro Portraiture." *Nation* 126 (11 April 1928): 414. Review of *Portraits in Color,* by Mary White Ovington.

"The Negro's Contribution to American Art and Literature." *Annals of the American Academy of Political and Social Science* 140 (1928): 234–247.

Preface to *A Decade of Negro Self Expression,* Occasional Paper, no. 26, edited by Alain L. Locke, pp. 5–8. Charlottesville, Va., 1928.

"The American Negro as Artist." *American Magazine of Art* 23 (September 1931): 210–220.

"Values and Imperatives" (1935). In *The Philosophy of Alain Locke,* edited by Leonard Harris, pp. 34–50. Philadelphia, 1989.

The Negro and His Music (1936). Salem, N.H., 1991.

Negro Art: Past and Present (1936). Salem, N.H., 1991.

The Negro in Art: A Pictorial Record of the Negro Artist and of the Negro Theme in Art. Washington, D.C., 1940.

"Up Till Now." Introduction to *The Negro Artist Comes of Age: A National Survey of Contemporary American Artists,* pp. iii–vi. Albany, N.Y., 1945.

"Negro Art." *Encyclopaedia Britannica,* vol. 16, pp. 198–199. New York, 1951.

Other Sources

Helbling, Mark. "African Art: Albert C. Barnes and Alain Locke." *Phylon* 43.1 (1982): 57–67.

Porter, James A. *Modern Negro Art* (1943). Washington, D.C., 1992.

Washington, Johnny. *Alain Locke and Philosophy: A Quest for Cultural Pluralism.* Westport, Conn., 1986.

TOMMY LOTT

LONGINUS, or Pseudo-Longinus (fl. first century CE), the name commonly given to the Greek author of *Peri Hypsous, On the Sublime.* About two thirds of this work of ancient Greek literary criticism survives. Scholars from its first editor Francesco Robertello (1564) until well into the nineteenth century misunderstood the attribution of the treatise to "Dionysius Longinus" as identifying its author with Cassius Longinus, rhetorician and courtier of the third century CE rebel against the Roman Empire, Zenobia, queen of Palmyra, who was killed by the Emperor Aurelian for advising her to revolt. Thus, the author was long taken to be a sublime person himself, a hero in the great ancient tradition. In fact, the attribution is to "Dionysius *or* Longinus," meaning that the scribes had no idea whether it was written by Longinus or by the Augustan critic Dionysius of Halicarnassus, neither of whose surviving work it at all resembles. The treatise ascribes the lack of sublimity in literature contemporary with itself to the spirit of submission to imperial rule and to the profound peace reigning in the empire (chap. 44). This cannot have been said much later than the early years of Marcus Aurelius (161–180 CE), after which the long Augustan peace began to unravel. Most modern critics agree in placing the treatise sometime in the first century CE. Because Longinus couches his treatise as polemic against a *Peri hypsous* by the Augustan critic Caecilius of Calacte, which he considers tame, dry, and rule-bound, it may well be itself a product of Augustus's reign, as William K. Wimsatt and others have believed. An alternative theory is that he was more nearly contemporary with Tacitus, who, in his *Dialogus* (c.100 CE), ascribes the decline of Roman oratory to similar causes.

The treatise is an extraordinary and highly individual work, which left only a few traces of its influence in antiquity and the Middle Ages, but is central to the understanding of Renaissance and especially eighteenth-century and early Romantic literary and aesthetic theory. Longinus's canon of favorite authors is a conventional one: Homer, Pindar, Sophocles and Euripides (not Aeschylus), Plato, and Demosthenes. His references to other fourth-century BCE and Hellenistic prose writers and poets are nearly all intended to show their inferiority to these great classics. He also preserves for us the great ode of Sappho, *phainetai moi* (chap. 10) and compares the art with which she unifies her picture of the physical effects of passion favorably with

Homer's own. But his way of praising and criticizing their great passages in what he considers the "sublime" (*hypselon*) style is unique in the surviving literature of antiquity.

"Sublimity," Longinus claims at the beginning, "is a certain height and majesty in words" with which the greatest poets and prose writers have "attained pre-eminence and decorated eternity itself with their own glories; for things of this superior nature do not persuade their hearers but put them in transport (*ekplexis*)" and "by their power and irresistible might reign supreme over everyone who hears." This sublimity, which "scatters everything before it like a thunderbolt, when it comes at the exact right time (*kairios*)," is superior even to the power of laboriously uniting every element of a large composition so that its unity "appears little by little from the whole web of the words" (chap. 1). The sublime essentially comes only from inborn genius, but art can help it, for it may need "the curb as well as the spur" (chap. 2). Longinus begins with warning examples of passages where it has been aimed at, but the result has been bombast; or frigidity; or mere adolescent trifling; or an inappropriate display of passion at the wrong moment, for which he quotes from another contemporary, Theodorus of Gadara, the term *parenthyrson*, "picking up the wand of Bacchus out of season" (chap. 3). Longinus's Greek style, which has more in common with *koiné* in usage and syntax than the formal, artificially Atticized prose the empire mostly patronized, is densely packed with similes, metaphors, and coined words such as that just quoted, thus not easy to do justice in translation.

The real sublime, he continues, has nothing to do with such faults, which come from striving after temporary novelty. Its source is what pleases always and everywhere, not what makes a temporary effect here and now, and it bears repeated examination, because its effect and its deeper meanings are not exhausted after many hearings. To try for the sublime and fail of it, he says later, is *aschemonein pros ton aiona*, to make a fool of oneself before eternity; for great writing aims at no less an audience.

The greater part of the treatise is then divided formally (chap. 8) into four sections treating what Longinus considers the principal causes of sublimity: the power of forming elevated thoughts and conceptions, otherwise "great-spiritedness" (*to megalophues*) (9–15); the use of figures of thought and speech (16–29); nobility of diction, which has three parts, choice of the right words, metaphoric speech, and elaboration of language (30–38); and composition (i.e., word order, rhythm, and euphony; 39–42). The treatise as we have it breaks off with melancholy reflections on the unfavorable conditions for producing great literature in the contemporary world (44). Actually, chapter 8 gives as a fifth cause of the sublime emotion, *pathos*, emotion, but in the surviving parts of the treatise there is no separate section devoted to it. At the end, Longinus promises to write a

separate treatise on the emotions. But *pathos* figures prominently in the first two sections as a source of sublimity, and the second section concludes (29) with the comment that figures of speech used rightly rouse strong emotion, "something as essential to the sublime as character-drawing is to entertainment."

This scheme is Longinus's own and original, no stereotype drawn after the standard treatises on rhetoric and composition, and each part of this exposition has striking and original features. The section on the subject "grandeur of thought" is notable for its brilliant tributes to Homer—especially the famous ninth chapter, with its comparison of Homer's grander passages about his deities to the "Let there be light" of the opening of Genesis, a famous exception to the general ignorance among the pagans of any literary values to be found in the Jewish Scriptures; its characterization of the poet as himself the "wind from heaven breathing into his own battles" and the Ares or war god of his own poem; and its deprecation of the *Odyssey* in comparison with the *Iliad* as an evening sun compared with the noonday, a decline into the mere old man's love of narrative from the depiction of vital action and conflict. Also, it is notable that Longinus appreciates as keenly as any modern critic the essential intertextuality of the later poem with the earlier ("it is the *Iliad*'s epilogue"). Here the examples are mainly from Longinus's favorites among favorites—Homer, Sappho, and especially a long tribute to Plato as, ironically (because he is such a critic of the morality of the Homeric poems), the most Homeric of prose writers. The section on the topic "figures of speech," though it takes examples also from tragedy, is basically an anthology of great passages from the orators, especially Demosthenes, with comments that are well suited to show a modern reader why the art of oratory roused such passionate admiration in antiquity. This section also expands the notion of the sublime writer as possessed by, and creating in the reader, the emotion—and indeed, the very experience—that his words convey. Longinus quotes Euripides' speech of the Sun giving the chariot to Phaethon, and asks, "Would you not say the soul of the writer climbs into the chariot with him and takes wings and shares the peril with the horses? That soul could never have fantasized these things if it had not been carried along in flight through just this journey in heaven." "Nobility of diction" is the power of "breathing a soul and a voice into mere dead things" (30). Taking risks in diction is preferable to mere "correctness," or Lysias would be a greater writer than Plato, Apollonius and Theocritus than Homer, Bacchylides than Pindar (33). Going directly against the canon of the great Hellenistic poet Callimachus that the pure but slender spring is preferable to the voluminous but muddy river, Longinus defiantly holds that it is not small streams that we admire but "the Nile, the Danube, the Rhine, and still more the Ocean," the terrors of Etna, not our household fire on the hearth. This is because nature herself intends by these spectacles to raise us to the heights of our own human nature, or even further, and take us out of and beyond ourselves, to thoughts that exceed our mortal span (35). What is truly sublime in literature is produced by writers exalted in the same way, and exalts us in the same way by its influence.

Longinus is a memorable practical critic. From dozens of striking examples one could choose his remark in the section on "composition" that overrhythmic writing "conveys to the hearers not the feeling of the words, just the feeling of the rhythm" (41), or the elaborate analysis of the most famous paragraph of Demosthenes' *On the Crown* (16). But it is this general doctrine of "sublimity" as related, not to religion, but to the grandeur of nature, and to the release of suppressed emotion and the realization of hidden potentialities in human nature by the transports produced by the sublime both in nature and in art, that is responsible for Longinus's influence in the history of artistic and literary criticism. Although Longinus was admired from the time of his first republication in the sixteenth century, it was at the end of the seventeenth century, when disillusion with Christianity was becoming general, and in the Age of Reason and among the early Romantics that he had his greatest influence. *On the Sublime* seemed then to offer a ready refuge for those who still believed in the greatness of human nature and the sublimity of artistic experience from the threats of atheism and scientism. It also seemed to offer classical authority against the mere elegance and "correctness" that many thought the disease of eighteenth-century art and literature. The first enthusiasts among European writers and artists for such examples of the natural sublime as the Alps and the Scottish Highlands are contemporary, or nearly, with Nicolas Boileau's immensely influential translation and commentary (1674). By 1728, Longinus was so well known in literary England that Alexander Pope could parody him in the *Peri Bathous* or "On the Art of Sinking in Poetry" appended to his *Dunciad*. His influence lasted through the eighteenth century—evident in (among many others) Sir Joshua Reynolds, Gotthold Ephraim Lessing, Edmund Burke, and even Samuel Johnson and Edward Gibbon—and longer. George Saintsbury's pointed tribute to him, that he was the greatest critic of the whole fifteen hundred years before Samuel Taylor Coleridge, has much point, and his deep feeling for the sublimity of nature and humanity is part of the foundation of William Wordsworth's and Coleridge's attitudes and does not, for example, disappear from French artistic theories before Eugène Delacroix.

In the modern world Longinus's treatise is admired and somewhat out of use (but cf. Neil Hertz, 1985), a long elaborate reference to a power of the arts and perhaps of nature that one may recognize, but finds difficulty in bringing into ordinary critical practice and teaching. His ideal of elevation, *enthusiasmos* and *ekstasis*, which (granted) does not exclude wholly rational and canny accounts of the means by which they are produced, is a little discordant with systems of criticism that analyze literature as discourse and treat its social values from outside as suspect. It is no accident that the most understanding and readable account of him in "modern" literature is in Saintsbury's old-fashioned and (even for its time) antitheoretical *History of Criticism* (1900), or that the most "Longinian" critics of literature anyone reads nowadays are Coleridge and Matthew Arnold. The task of keeping up with Longinus's secondary literature, even in classical studies, is not great and seems to lessen with the decades, as a look through recent volumes of the *Année Classique* will easily show. But the treatise will always remain an unparalleled monument to its own old-fashioned, enthusiastic point of view about art and literature as enlargers and expanders of the human soul.

[*See also* Sublime, *article on* The Sublime from Longinus to Montesquieu.]

BIBLIOGRAPHY

Works by Longinus

'*Longinus' on the Sublime*. Edited by D. A. Russell. Oxford, 1964.
On Great Writing (On the Sublime). Translated by G. M. A. Grube. New York, 1957; reprint, Indianapolis, 1991.

Other Sources

Hertz, Neil. "A Reading of Longinus." In *The End of the Line: Essays on Psychoanalysis and the Sublime*, pp. 1–20. New York, 1985.
Logan, John L. "Longinus." In *Ancient Writers: Greece and Rome*, edited by T. James Luce, vol. 2, pp. 1063–1080. New York, 1982.
Saintsbury, George. *A History of Criticism and Literary Taste in Europe from the Earliest Texts to the Present Day*. 3 vols. London, 1900. See vol. 1, pp. 152–174.
Wimsatt, William K., Jr., and Cleanth Brooks. *Literary Criticism: A Short History*. New York, 1957. See pp. 97–111.

DAVID ARMSTRONG

LOTZE, RUDOLF HERMANN (1817–1881), a German philosopher trained in philosophy and medicine. Lotze spent most of his career as professor of philosophy at Göttingen. His combination of scientific and philosophical studies left him vigorously opposed to reductionism in either of the forms prevalent in nineteenth-century Germany, the idealist reduction of all reality to a few simple abstractions of thought, and the mechanistic reduction of all reality to what can be explained by a few simple laws of motion. Instead, he portrayed the empirical knowledge obtained by means of natural science as only a part, though an indispensable part, of the access that humans have to the cosmos of which they are a part; both practical reason and feeling, the latter expressed in many forms including both religion and art, are also means of access to the many forms of order in the cosmos. Lotze expressed this vision in numerous works, both technical works such as his *Metaphysics* and more popular works such as his *Microcosmus*, a vast study of mankind and its place in nature and history. The scope of this work sometimes leads to the characterization of Lotze as a Hegelian, but his philosophical vision seems more closely related to the views of Gottfried Wilhelm Leibniz and Immanuel Kant, especially the Kant of the Third Critique, because on his account natural science, religion, and art are never superseded by any form of absolute knowing, but always remain necessary and compatible means of access to the world.

Lotze's main contributions to aesthetics were a massive history of aesthetics in Germany from Alexander Gottlieb Baumgarten's day to his own (*Geschichte der Ästhetik in Deutschland,* 1868), and a slender work, derived from his lectures, on the fundamentals of aesthetics (*Grundzüge der Ästhetik,* 1884). The *Geschichte* deals with the views of the main figures in German philosophical aesthetics, the main concepts of aesthetics, and theories of the specific arts. In its first part, Lotze gives special prominence to Friedrich von Schiller, who must be considered, along with Kant, as one of the important influences on his own views. In the *Grundzüge,* Lotze focuses on the concept of beauty and its exemplification in the various arts. Against Kant, he argues that beauty cannot be defined simply as universal and disinterested pleasure, but rather that what is special about the pleasure in our experience of beauty is that it is the product of our attempt to grasp both the particularity and the wholeness of the world through the active use of all of our mental capacities. Different media and genres of art are characterized by differences in how they do this, beginning with their use of our various senses as irreplaceable modes of experience of the world. Music, for example, exhibits the "entire happy structure of the world" through rhythm, melody, and harmony, "and is not merely *capable* of but *determined* to arouse the intensive *nameless* feelings that attach to this structure"; genre painting "makes intuitive how external circumstances such as profession, wealth or poverty, and surroundings leave indestructible traces on the [human] form, but how, nevertheless, the power of spiritual nature is so durable" that it shows through all such circumstances; and literature, in the various forms of poetry and fiction, "can undertake to exhibit the sense and spirit of the whole [world] in a little fragment [of it]." Lotze's characterizations of the various arts are based on a deep familiarity with them, and remain thoughtful and suggestive.

Lotze's works were widely circulated in German as well as in English translations. He was influential on British philosophers such as Bernard Bosanquet (who translated his *Logic* and *Metaphysics*) and later Alfred North Whitehead, and on American philosophers such as Borden Parker Bowne, William James, Josiah Royce, George Santayana (who wrote his dissertation on Lotze under Royce's supervision), and John Dewey.

BIBLIOGRAPHY

Works by Lotze

Metaphysik: Drei Bücher der Ontologie, Kosmologie und Psychologie (1841). Leipzig, 1879. In English as *Metaphysic in Three Books: Ontology, Cosmology, and Psychology,* translation edited by Bernard Bosanquet (Oxford, 1884).

Logik: Drei Bücher vom Denken, vom Untersuchen und vom Erkennen (1843). Leipzig, 1874. In English as *Logic, in Three Books, of Thought, of Investigation, and of Knowledge,* translation edited by Bernard Bosanquet (Oxford, 1884).

Über den Begriff der Schönheit. Göttingen, 1845.

Mikrokosmus: Ideen zur Naturgeschichte und Geschichte der Menschheit. 3 vols. Leipzig, 1856–1864. In English as *Microcosmus: An Essay Concerning Man and His Relation to the World,* in 2 vols., translated by Elizabeth Hamilton and E. E. Constance Jones (Edinburgh, 1885).

Geschichte der Ästhetik in Deutschland. Munich, 1868.

Grundzüge der Ästhetik: Diktate aus den Vorlesungen. Leipzig, 1884. Modern edition edited by Hein Stünke, in *Schriften zur Kunsttheorie* (Berlin, 1990). In English as *Outlines of Aesthetics: Dictated Portions of the Lectures of Hermann Lotze,* translated by George T. Ladd (Boston, 1886).

Other Sources

Jones, Henry. *A Critical Account of the Philosophy of Lotze: The Doctrine of Thought.* Glasgow and New York, 1895.

Santayana, George. *Lotze's System of Philosophy.* Edited by Paul Grimley Kuntz. Bloomington, Ind., 1971. Contains Lotze bibliography.

PAUL GUYER

LUKÁCS, GYÖRGY

LUKÁCS, GYÖRGY (1885–1971), Hungarian writer and philosopher, one of the creators of Marxist aesthetics. Born in Budapest, Lukács joined the Communist Party of Hungary in 1918. During the months of the Hungarian Soviet Republic of 1919, he was effectively responsible for the cultural policy of the regime. After its collapse, he lived as an émigré in Vienna, Berlin, and Moscow. The condemnation of his views as right-wing opportunism by the Comintern in 1928 resulted in his withdrawal from direct participation in politics. He returned to Hungary in 1945. A new wave of official attacks in 1949 again led to his retreat from political activity. During the Hungarian revolution of 1956, he was minister of culture in the short-lived government of Imre Nagy. After internment in Romania, he worked in a virtual internal emigration in Hungary until 1967, when he was allowed to return to public cultural life.

His Marxist turn divides Lukács's aesthetic activity into two periods, though there is a significant degree of continuity between them. His pre-Marxist oeuvre centers on the problem of the crisis of culture in modern society: the impossibility under its conditions to form a common communal understanding of the world and to give a unified meaning to the life of the individual. Questions concerning the arts are raised by Lukács within this context, to be approached in two distinct ways: as problems related to the history of modern art and as metaphysical-existential questions.

The historical works of this period—*History of Development of the Modern Drama* (1911) and *The Theory of Novel* (1916)—share a fundamental methodological premise: the historicity of works of art is ultimately determined not at the level of their content, but by their form; not by what they directly mean, but by the way they create meaning. The largely sociologically oriented *Drama* book follows up the growing dissolution of the dramatic form under the dual impact of the unsuitability of the material of contemporary life for dramatic presentation, on the one hand, and the transformations in the social characteristics and cultural expectations of the theater audience, on the other. *The Theory of Novel*—a major influence on the later work of Walter Benjamin, Theodor Adorno, and Lucien Goldmann—offers, within the framework of a philosophy of history, a historical typology of the form of the novel as the representative literary genre of modernity. In opposition to the premodern epic, which grew out of the soil of a meaningful social totality—and represented it—the novel is paradigmatic for an epoch in which the individual can no longer find meaning in the world, but can only strive to create such a meaning. This is reflected in its very form, in the paradoxical and problematic fusion of heterogeneous components into a never-completed unity, kept together only by the self-reflection of the narrator. The development of the novel leads toward its growing psychologization, to an ever more pronounced disillusioned, ironic self-reflexivity, and finally (with Dostoyevsky), to the transgression of its own formative principles harboring a utopian hope.

At the same time, in his volume of essays *Soul and Form* (1910), Lukács already posed the problem of art in the context of the ultimate existential question: is it possible at all to give a "form," that is, unified meaning, to everyday life itself? This constitutes the problem of departure for his two (unfinished) attempts at a systematic aesthetics: the *Heidelberg Philosophy of Art* (1912–1914) and the *Heidelberg Aesthetics* (1916–1918), both published posthumously. The Heidelberg manuscripts in some respects anticipate later developments both in the phenomenology of artistic creativity and in the hermeneutic theory of aesthetic meaning and receptivity. Art emerges out of the fundamental human dissatisfaction with the ambiguity, context-dependence, and pragmatic limitedness of everyday processes of communication, always prone to be misunderstood. It is an attempt at the creation of a cosmos of transparent meanings, understandable and eternally valid for everyone. This is the accomplishment of aesthetic forms originating in the homogenization, intensive stylization, and autonomization of the everyday schemes of communication. But precisely because of this forming, the perfect work of art—an objectivization in which all the opposition between the meaning-creating form and the experienceable content, between the subjective and the objective, disappears—constitutes a self-enclosed totality that in itself is elevated above, and insulated from, the actual, always heterogeneous, and contingent experiences both of the author and of the recipient. Lukács's early aesthetics, one of the most extreme formulations of the idea of the autonomy of art, conceives the artwork as the pure scheme of experienceable satisfaction, the universal validity of which is based solely on the fact that every potential recipient can introject into it his or her uncomparably unique experiences. As the actual identity of the subject and the object, the work of art represents a utopian reality, but one that in no way can be reconnected with everyday life. It overcomes the empirical misunderstandings characterizing everyday communication only by making misunderstanding constitutive and eternalized. In this sense, art is diabolical: it offers full, but momentary, satisfaction without the redemption of life.

In the decade following his Marxist turn of 1918, Lukács dealt with the problems of art only marginally. In 1923, he published the volume of essays *History and Class Consciousness*, the founding text of "Western" Marxism, offering a radically new understanding of the philosophical sense and significance of Karl Marx's thought. Although the theory of reification elaborated by him here had a lasting impact on later Marxist and post-Marxist theories of art, in this period Lukács himself paid rather scant attention to such potential consequences.

It was only after his withdrawal from direct participation in politics that Lukács again returned to the field of aesthetics. From the early 1930s until the end of the 1950s, he was primarily active (and became known so also in the West) as the leading Marxist literary critic and theorist of literature. He partly continued, though on a new, historical-materialist foundation, his earlier preoccupation with the social history of literary forms (*The Historical Novel*, 1937). But his influence was primarily the result of his theory of realism, and its critical-negative obverse, the theory of decadence of artistic modernism.

"Realism," in Lukács's understanding, does not designate a particular literary style or epoch; it certainly has nothing to do with the narrowly conceived verisimilitude of content. For him it means the fundamental accomplishment of all authentic works of art (though its concept was actually explicated by him almost exclusively in relation to the novel and the drama) through which they fulfill their basic function of the disclosure of truth. Realism is the ability of the artwork to illuminate through the representation of concrete individual phenomena the essential conflicts and dynamic tendencies of a whole epoch of social development. The realist work of art organically connects, through aesthetic typification, the individual with the general, the appearance with the historical essence.

Lukács's conception of realism reconciled a cognitivist theory of literature with the epistemological framework of a

Leninist theory of "reflection" that became the unquestionable dogma of Soviet philosophy. At the same time, under conditions of a rampant Stalinism, his critique of "tendentious literature" (*Tendenzliteratur*), his insistence on the necessity to distinguish the author's own worldview and intentions from the actual meaning of his or her work, represented the defense of the autonomy of art against the predominant tendencies of its crude politicization; and his struggle for the recognition of the abiding significance of the great artistic tradition of the past ("classical realism") affirmed the values of Enlightenment and democratic humanism.

In theoretical respects, however, Lukács's conception of realism, as presented in the writings of this period, was deeply ambiguous. Not infrequently, especially in his criticism of "decadent" modernism, it amounted to a rather simplistic sociologizing, normative content aesthetics. The understanding of literary personae as social types allowed the reduction of the meaning of the work to some general sociological statements, the "truth" of which then could be measured by comparison with the relevant theses of a Marxist social theory. Similarly, the characterization of realism as a "creative method" made possible the wholesale rejection of some artistic techniques or stylistic solutions (e.g., montage or allegory) as irreconcilable with the requirements of the dialectical method.

At the same time, however, especially in his great interpretative essays about the paradigmatic works of eighteenth- and nineteenth-century literature, a substantively different concept of realism was present. It was understood primarily as the accomplishment of the successful literary form. The great realist novel makes manifest the way in which the fate and the character of the represented figures are formed by their own actions under the depicted circumstances. It allows the reader to see through the reified surface of life, the seemingly sheer accidentalness of events, and to directly apprehend their sense: the connection between the objective situations and the actions of the characters. Its personae illuminate in an irreducibly individual form the essential variety of human possibilities under the evoked conditions, while their ethical hierarchy and the connection of this latter with their destinies are made transparent by the very narrative. In this sense, it constitutes an intensive totality: a world made meaningful. In these contexts, the critique of modernism as decadence also acquired a changed emphasis. It accentuated not so much the inadequacy of particular artistic techniques, but formulated a morally informed criticism of artworks that merely express a fetishistic consciousness, evoke—even if with the subjective attitude of despair—a world of inescapable alienation that excludes the very possibility of free and rational human agency.

This latter concept of realism received its generalization and philosophical justification in Lukács's late work *The Specificity of the Aesthetic* (1963). It represents a unique attempt to elaborate a systematic aesthetic theory on the basis of Marxist philosophy. The work is undoubtedly of Hegelian inspiration: a cognitivist and normative aesthetics focusing on the analysis of the authentic work of art as a special type of ideal-cultural objectivization characterized by the organic unity of its form and content allowing a truth of universal significance to appear in a directly apprehensible, sensuous-concrete embodiment. At the same time, this late aesthetics reintroduces in a new interpretation a number of ideas that Lukács first elaborated in his pre-Marxist, Heidelberg writings.

The central organizing concept of *The Specificity of the Aesthetic* is that of the mimesis understood as the active-selective mental appropriation of reality through its modeling, the principles and norms of which, however, differ in the various spheres of social life activity. Lukács undertakes the explication of the genesis of the principles of aesthetic mimesis, of the general categorial structure of the work of art, out of the characteristics of the thinking of everyday life, the undifferentiated and ultimate ground of all higher objectifying activities, including the sciences and the arts. The sciences, in their historical evolution, realize a tendency toward disanthropomorphization, toward the ever-stricter demarcation of the objective from the subjective and the ever-greater approximation of their ideal objectivizations—that is, theories—to the lawful characteristics of their object alone. They operate with universal concepts and theoretical constructs transcending the limits of the directly experienceable. Aesthetic mimesis, on the other hand, is always anthropomorphizing; it relates back, whatever be the object of artistic presentation, to the human subject as a social species-being. From this most basic feature of aesthetic mimesis, Lukács then derives the fundamental constitutive categories of its sphere: particularity, that is, the coincidence of the concrete individual presentation with universal meaning, as the fundamental principle of artistic forming; the immediately experienceable and evocative character of works of art ensuring the sensuous-emotive nature of aesthetic meaning; their immanent closure, the principle of aesthetic totality, making them incomparable individualities with the character of "worldliness"; their self-reflexivity, as a result of which they do not appear in their immediate materiality but as representations of a reality. The explication of the genesis of these categorial characteristics out of the everyday (and magical) forms of mimesis also explains the essential pluralism of the aesthetic sphere, the existence of art as a system of arts, each with its characteristic "homogeneous medium" of representation and with a corresponding modality of possible meanings.

These characteristics of the authentic artwork determine its possible receptive effect and the social function of art in general. The objective meaning structure of the work leads the experience and understanding of the recipient. First of all, in its closure, it demands the suspension of the pragmatic orientation of everyday life. Just for this reason, aesthetic experience cannot be directly transformed into practical action; it provides no immediate instruction for social activity. But the reorientation demanded by, and effected in, aesthetic experience means something positive: a transformation of the experiencing subjectivity. In the reception of the work of art, the individual casts off the self-centered particularism of everyday life with its unreflexively accepted schemata of reality perception, and learns to apprehend the world from the historically achieved level and standpoint of the human species. This change in the structure of personality ("catharsis") can open up for imagination and understanding new general possibilities of an active relation to the human world. In this consists the great educative and emancipatory function of art; for, in its unity of the subjective and the objective with the sensuous, this-worldly immanence of its meaning, the artwork not only allows us to apprehend reality from the universal perspective of species development, but also offers a defetishized understanding of it in a form that is in principle available for everyone. At the same time, the great artistic legacy of the past makes reexperienceable the historical path of the development of human self- and world-understanding, laying bare our own historicity. Art is the living memory and the actual self-consciousness of humankind.

[*See also* Marxism; *and* Realism.]

BIBLIOGRAPHY

Works by Lukács

Soul and Form (1910). Translated by Anna Bostock. Cambridge, Mass., 1974.
A Modern Drama fejlödésének története (History of the Development of Modern Drama). 2 vols. Budapest, 1911.
The Theory of the Novel: A Historico-Philosophical Essay on the Forms of Great Epic Literature (1916). Translated by Anna Bostock. Cambridge, Mass., 1971.
History and Class Consciousness: Studies in Marxist Dialectics (1923). Translated by Rodney Livingstone. Cambridge, Mass., 1971.
The Historical Novel (1937). Translated by Hannah Mitchell and Stanley Mitchell. London, 1962; reprint, Lincoln, Nebr., 1983.
Studies in European Realism. Translated by Edith Bone. London, 1950.
The Meaning of Contemporary Realism (1958). Translated by John Mander and Necke Mander. London, 1963.
Die Eigenart des Ästhetischen (The Specificity of the Aesthetic). 2 vols. Neuwied, 1963.
Heidelberger Ästhetik, 1916–1918 (Heidelberg Aesthetics). Edited by György Márkus and Frank Benseler. Darmstadt, 1974.
Heidelberger Philosophie der Kunst, 1912–1914 (Heidelberg Philosophy of Art). Edited by György Márkus and Frank Benseler. Darmstadt, 1974.

Other Sources

Bernstein, J. M. *The Philosophy of the Novel: Lukács, Marxism, and the Dialectics of Form.* Minneapolis, 1984.
Corredor, Eva L. *György Lukács and the Literary Pretext.* New York, 1987.
Heller, Agnes, ed. *Lukács Revalued.* Oxford, 1983.
Jung, Werner. *Georg Lukács.* Stuttgart, 1989.
Kadarkay, Arpad. *Georg Lukács: Life, Thought, and Politics.* Oxford and Cambridge, Mass., 1991.
Parkinson, G. H. R. *Georg Lukács.* London and Boston, 1977.
Pasternack, Gerhard. *Georg Lukács: Späte Ästhetik und Literaturtheorie.* Frankfurt am Main, 1986.
Tertulian, Nicolae. *Georges Lukács: Étapes de sa pensée esthétique.* Paris, 1980.

GYÖRGY MÁRKUS

LYOTARD, JEAN-FRANÇOIS (b. 1925), French philosopher. Professor emeritus at the University of Paris and professor at the University of California at Irvine, Lyotard's early career was spent teaching in Algeria, followed by the University of Nanterre in France. He was politically active in left-wing groups, writing mainly on Algeria. Toward the end of the 1970s, he developed an influential analysis of the postmodern condition. His work covers a great range of philosophical topics and styles including aesthetics, philosophy of language, political philosophy, the history of philosophy, and philosophy and literature. He has entered into debates with a significant number of his philosophical contemporaries, notably Jacques Derrida, Jean-Luc Nancy, Gilles Deleuze, Philippe Lacoue-Labarthe, Jürgen Habermas, and Richard Rorty. His influence and collaborations extend to art and artists, in particular in his work at the Centre Georges Pompidou in Paris.

The most important aesthetic intuition running through Lyotard's philosophy is that events cannot be fully represented in discourse. In the two main periods of his philosophy, this intuition is grounded and made clear in distinctive aesthetics developed in key philosophical works: *Discours, figure* (1971) and *Économie libidinale* (1974), for the first period, and *Le différend* (1983) for the second. The intuition that events are beyond representation is also the mainstay of his philosophy and criticism of art. The artwork enjoys a privileged relation to the event because, in art, that which stands over and above representation can be communicated through feelings and desires. This gives art an all-important political and ethical role associated with the disclosure of the limits of discourse in general, as well as the limits between particular forms of discourse. For Lyotard, aesthetics must take on a central philosophical role because the most important truths are a matter of sensibility rather than understanding. Artworks allow for the communication of otherness independently of cognition; therefore, they participate in an ethics and politics free of the hegemony of reason and of the demand for knowledge prior to the respect for difference.

Lyotard's best-known work, his influential *La condition postmoderne* (1979) on postmodern knowledge and culture, is given a philosophical rather than a sociological or historical basis through his work on these intrinsic limits of discourse. In *La condition postmoderne*, Lyotard analyzes the different types of narrative that are used in society to legitimate social practices such as science. He draws a distinction between grand narratives, accounts that bring together all forms of legitimation into a single unified account, and local language games. Lyotard claims, first, that all-encompassing grand narratives, designed to legitimize claims to truth in different arenas, fail to take full account of the event: "In contemporary society and culture—postindustrial society, postmodern culture—the question of the legitimation of knowledge is formulated in different terms. The grand narrative has lost its credibility, regardless of what mode of unification it uses, regardless of whether it is a speculative narrative or a narrative of emancipation" (1984, p. 37). Second, Lyotard claims that legitimation takes place within specific rule-driven linguistic practices, defined as language games. Any social practice can be interpreted according to a language game, that is, according to the rules on proper and improper statements governing correct moves within the practice (the rules of chess, for instance). He argues that language games are incommensurable, because there can be no shared system of rules for the resolution of conflicts. Therefore, there can be no universal basis for legitimation, because such a basis would have to act as a bridge between incommensurable language games. These claims are consistent with Lyotard's poststructuralist anti-Hegelianism, that is, with his opposition to the possibility of totalization and to the resolution of difference through dialectics. They are also consistent with his concern for a politics and ethics based on otherness. There is no common discourse that can legitimate all true statements. There are true statements in one language game that cannot be translated into others.

Once modern art, philosophy, and politics are defined in terms of grand narratives, the link between Lyotard's work on narrative and the modern–postmodern debate in aesthetics becomes clear. Some artworks depend on and serve to further the dominance of grand narratives, whereas others testify to the illusory quality of that dominance and to the limits between language games. This allows an understanding of Lyotard's deep commitment to the avant-garde. The aesthetic avant-garde creates works that escape from the formation of aesthetic and political consensus by creating new artworks that call for forms of judgment counter to established rules and values. The avant-garde work is a break with tradition; it challenges viewers and readers to reevaluate their systems of values and beliefs. Indeed, the ineffable shock generated by the break with the consensus on the meaningful and the beautiful is itself a testimony to the independence of events from discourse.

A dangerous confusion concerning the modern–postmodern debate can be avoided at this point; although Lyotard is defined as a postmodern thinker, this does not mean that he defends what is commonly understood as postmodern art and literature. On the contrary, his definition of the avant-garde often coincides with modern avant-

garde works of art—Abstract Expressionism in painting or modernism in literature, for example—and with the radical claim that avant-garde works always have the ability to shock and to generate new ways of thinking and feeling. This position must be dissociated from the postmodern epoch and standard definitions of postmodern art as antimodern and counterrevolutionary; the historical period of a work is not a factor in Lyotard's definition of avant-garde. When Lyotard seeks to answer the question "What is the postmodern?" his response draws a distinction between avant-garde works in their time, that is, works that forced a rethink of established values and norms and works that upheld the tradition. What is important in this distinction is Lyotard's belief that avant-garde works do not lose their ability to shock and make us think anew. Thus, the avant-garde is as timeless as the modern–postmodern distinction. This explains why Lyotard appeals to definitions of feelings, desires, and events that are not historically conditioned. This does not mean that works cannot become less and more influential or shocking. Instead, it implies that even when the influence of the avant-garde is on the wane, its ability to shock is still latent.

In order to understand why the artwork is a special kind of event, it is necessary to analyze the two main definitions of the event that coincide with the main periods of Lyotard's work. This will also allow an understanding of why the aesthetic event is of the highest philosophical, social, and political importance. After Lyotard's early critical book on phenomenology and his political essays on Algeria, for the Socialisme ou Barbarie group, Lyotard published his doctoral thesis as *Discours, figure*. The book puts forward an anti-Hegelian, antiphenomenological, and, ultimately, antistructuralist study of discourse in terms of a study of the difference between figure and discourse. Figure is the basic aesthetic form that must occur prior to meaning and representation; there can be no meaning without figure, but the occurrence of figure is registered prior to meaning and representation. Starting from a critique of structuralist linguistics and from a study of Paul Valéry's prose poems, Lyotard uses Sigmund Freud to distinguish the conscious cognitive element of communication (discourse) from the unconscious libidinal element (figure). Any occurrence involves both, but any account of the event purely in terms of discourse and meaning must necessarily miss the impact of figure. This impact involves feelings and desires as opposed to cognitions. It is at work in any event as the sign not only of the limit of what can be said, but also of the effect of the libidinal in what is said: "We have to pose the identity of wanting to know and to desire. . . . The will to know is implicated within discourse: turning *around* its object, in deep space, the object always concealing one of its faces" (1971, p. 128). There can be no discourse without figures, but any commentary on those figures within discourse fails to capture the intensity of feelings and desires associated with figures: "Which means that when we speak we are not what we speak of, and that our speech awaits its respondent (its reference), on the other side, as does our desire" (ibid., pp. 128–129).

In this libidinal period, Lyotard uses many studies of artworks to illustrate and test his aesthetics. Among the most important artists studied by Lyotard are Paul Cézanne, Marcel Duchamp, and the artists of the quattrocento, where his Freudian analysis contrasts with phenomenological studies, notably by Maurice Merleau-Ponty (*Discours, figure, Des dispositifs pulsionnels,* 1973). Lyotard argues that with Cézanne the dominance of representation in painting, established in the quattrocento, is overturned in favor of figures associated with intense feelings and desires. He is therefore interested in the mechanics of how desire is channeled and released in paintings when there is a revolt against representation: "There is a polymorphism of modern painting that attests to an analogical dissolution of the objects, states, places, configurations, and modalities that up to now bound that institution called painting" (1973, p. 233). Lyotard charts the pure forms that allow for a release from systems of representation (perspective, for example) into more energetic systems (the flow of colors through a painting by Robert Delaunay). The positive force of painting is, then, to release desire, rather than to communicate the meaning of something to which it stands in a position of lack: "the force of what is painted lies not in its power of returning, or of seduction, or in its 'difference,' in its status of signifier (or signified), that is, in its lack; it lies instead in its . . . communicable libido" (ibid., p. 266). Later, in *Économie libidinale,* the terminology from *Discours, figure* is altered in order to convey better the idea of these economic flows of energy. Pure intensity appears in tensors, that is, intense contents such as color, that can take on many different functions within different formal systems called dispositions. An economy consists of heterogeneous dispositions channeling energy from tensors. This completes Lyotard's move away from an aesthetics based on meaning to an aesthetics of form and intensity. *Économie libidinale* is, however, in many ways a difficult and forbidding book, because it puts forward its main terms with an explicit hostility to argument and a frustrating metaphysical loftiness. This explains the unsympathetic reception to its publication. Yet, in later years the book has been reconsidered by commentators (David Carroll [1987] and Geoffrey Bennington [1988]) and, despite its avowed antitheoretical stance, the book can be seen as consistent not only with Lyotard's early work, but also with his later, more Kantian, philosophy.

Lyotard's libidinal philosophy is one of the prime examples of post-1968 iconoclastic and liberating French philosophy. Its energy and revolutionary violence leave little space, however, for precise values and judgments. This need for judgment influences a marked turn in his philosophy at the end of the 1970s; the turn shows up first in *Au juste* [1979] and *La condition postmoderne.* After the turn, the questions "What are the limits of judgment?" and, more important, "What are the political and ethical consequences of these limits?" take on great importance. Although Lyotard does not abandon his interest in the event and aesthetics, the philosophical frame of reference moves toward Immanuel Kant's aesthetics and Ludwig Wittgenstein's philosophy of language. In *Le différend,* Lyotard attempts to show the limits of different types of statements (of knowledge, judgment, ethics) in terms of events. When something occurs, that occurrence can be interpreted as a linguistic entity called a phrase. He argues that there is no one correct way of following on from any given phrase and that different ways of following the phrase cannot be judged as appropriate according to a single frame of reference. The basis for this argument is aesthetic in two ways: first, the phrase itself is felt, prior to being understood (Lyotard first illustrates this point in his work on the painter Henri Maccheroni); second, the events that indicate the limits of types of statements are sublime. For example, the limits of knowledge statements are indicated by events accompanied by the feeling of the sublime: something occurs that exceeds our understanding. How do we "know" this? We fall prey to contradictory feelings of terror and delight or pleasure and pain that indicate an insufficiency on the part of our cognitive faculties.

Again, Lyotard's philosophy of art and art criticism has a strong influence on the second period of his work. This is made most clear in his work on the sublime in Abstract Expressionism, and in his study of the works of Barnett Newman in particular. The analysis of Newman's work in terms of the sublime is not original in itself. Lyotard combines it with his philosophy of the event and with a sustained reflection on the ethical and political consequences of the feeling of the sublime. He thereby departs from the theological interpretation of the sublime, though he has always retained an interest in Judaism and ethics; this is reflected in his work on Newman, but more strongly in his constant study of the philosophy of Emmanuel Lévinas. Newman's paintings are sublime events because, though viewers are aware of something of importance happening with them, they do not know what: "What is sublime is the feeling that something will happen, despite everything, within this threatened void, that something will take 'place' and will announce that everything is not over. That place is mere 'here,' the most minimal occurrence" (1991, p. 84). Thus, the feeling of the sublime subverts presence in favor of an ever-deferred future event. Although one may know what is occurring in the present, one is also called to witness by an unknown and unknowable future. The sublime event limits claims to knowledge in the present in favor of an awareness of difference; something is occurring that exceeds our understanding but that we are called to testify to. This difference forms the basis for the main concept of Lyotard's later philosophy, the differend: "The differend is the unstable state of language wherein something that must be able to be put into language cannot yet be. . . . This state is signaled by what one ordinarily calls a feeling" (1988, p. 13). With the differend, Lyotard makes clear the ethical and political stakes concomitant with his aesthetics, because a differend is a radical difference that shows the limits of present ways of resolving conflicts: "The differend is reborn from the very resolution of supposed litigations" (ibid., p. 181).

Lyotard's critique of presence on the basis of the sublime belongs to the set of critical attacks on the role of the subject in art and philosophy. In his work on Kant, he uses the feeling of the sublime to turn Kant's critique against itself. Where the Kantian sublime is a matter of greatness in size or number, for Lyotard the contradictory feelings of pleasure and pain caused by the deregulation of the understanding can be caused by any event that indicates a presence, but also something unknown and unknowable. Thus, by applying the deregulatory effect of the sublime in the *Critique of Judgment* to the aesthetics of time and space of the *Critique of Pure Reason,* Lyotard destroys the certainties of the understanding and extends deregulation to the transcendental subject (see *L'enthousiasme: La critique kantienne de l'histoire,* 1986). This move against the transcendental subject situates Lyotard at the heart of a series of such "deconstructions" on the basis of the *Critique of Judgment,* most notably by Derrida, Nancy, and Lacoue-Labarthe (see *Du sublime,* 1988). Lyotard's critique of the subject and of the organization of time and space in terms of the subjective present is distinctive, however, because of its dependence on his philosophy of art and literature. His books on contemporary artists (Georges Guiffrey, Albert Ayme, Gianfranco Baruchello, Jacques Monory, Valerio Adami, Shusaku Arakawa, Daniel Buren) chart the way in which experience in art cannot be explained in terms of the subject; on the contrary, modern art and literature depend on a disorientation of the subject and a dismantling of human time and space. In line with this idea, Lyotard was the curator for a large exhibition at the Centre Georges Pompidou on the dematerialization of the world, *Les immatériaux* (1985), which brought together exhibits on the effect of the media and art on the experience of space and matter. In his latest works, Lyotard takes this dehumanization to the limit in a philosophy that begins to resemble science fiction. The point of these works, however, is always to readdress question of politics and ethics in a universe stripped of human values.

Because of its influence on the definition of the postmodern, the latter period of Lyotard's work has been criticized much more extensively than the former. More specifically, his theorizing of the postmodern has come under strong attack by the thinkers influenced by the Frankfurt School, Habermas in particular. Two critical arguments stand out.

First, it is claimed that Lyotard's postmodernism and his insistence on incommensurability form part of an attack on the project of the Enlightenment. This attack endangers the political benefits of modernity and negates the positive social and political function of art. This implies that Habermas's label of neoconservative, coined as a response to the influence of poststructuralist thinkers through the concept of the postmodern, is applicable to Lyotard's work. Because Lyotard denies the progressive aspect of the Enlightenment and the critical function of art, he is seen as leaving the field free for reactionary political and economic forces. He has responded to this point by emphasizing the positive ethical and political function of art and philosophy as witnesses to difference and as forms of resistance to totalization (see *Le postmoderne expliqué aux enfants,* 1986). Indeed, it is possible to view his work as a search for a valid basis for a reaction to the power of capital after the failure of Marxism. Second, it is claimed that Lyotard's work falls prey to a performative contradiction because it depends on a recognition of difference while also claiming that a differend is a case of radical difference that does not allow for knowledge of why there is a difference. The response in this case depends on Lyotard's aesthetic of the sublime and on whether one is convinced that the feeling of the sublime is an indication of a radical difference. Notwithstanding these criticisms, Lyotard's philosophy of the event has contributed to the central debate on difference that runs through the poststructuralist and deconstructive strands of postwar French philosophy. No philosophical study of the postmodern can bypass his work.

[*See also* Narrative; Postmodernism, *historical and conceptual overview article;* Poststructuralism; *and* Sublime, *article on* The Sublime from Burke to the Present.]

BIBLIOGRAPHY

Works by Lyotard

La phénoménologie. Paris, 1954. Translated by Brian Beakley as *Phenomenology* (Albany, N.Y., 1991).

Discours, figure. Paris, 1971.

Dérive à partir de Marx et Freud. Paris, 1973.

Des dispositifs pulsionnels. Paris, 1973.

Économie libidinale. Paris, 1974. Translated by Iain Hamilton Grant as *Libidinal Economy* (Bloomington, Ind., 1993).

Les transformateurs Duchamp. Paris, 1977. Translated by Ian McLeod as *Duchamp's Transformers* (Venice, Calif., 1990).

La condition postmoderne: Rapport sur le savoir. Paris, 1979. Translated by Geoff Bennington and Brian Massumi as *The Postmodern Condition: A Report on Knowledge* (Minneapolis, 1984).

Le différend. Paris, 1983. Translated by Georges Van Den Abbeele as *The Differend: Phrases in Dispute* (Minneapolis, 1988).

L'enthousiasme: la critique kantienne de l'histoire. Paris, 1986.

Le postmoderne expliqué aux enfants: Correspondence, 1982–1985. Paris, 1986. Translated by Don Barry et al. as *The Postmodern Explained: Correspondence, 1982–1985,* translation edited by Julian Pefanis and Morgan Thomas (Minneapolis, 1992).

Que peindre? Adami, Arakawa, Buren. 2 vols. Paris, 1987.

L'inhumain: causeries sur le temps. Paris, 1988. Translated by Geoffrey Bennington and Rachel Bowlby as *The Inhuman: Reflection on Time* (Stanford, Calif., 1991). See "Newman: The Instant," pp. 78–88.

Collaborative Works

Lyotard, Jean-François, and Jean-Loup Thébaud. *Au juste: Conversations*. Paris, 1979. Translated by Wlad Godzich as *Just Gaming* (Minneapolis, 1985).

Lyotard, Jean-François, and Thierry Chaput, eds. *Les immatériaux*. Paris, 1985.

Lyotard, Jean-François, et al. *Du sublime*. Paris, 1988. Translated by Jeffrey S. Librett as *Of the Sublime: Presence in Question* (Albany, N.Y., 1993).

Other Sources

Benjamin, Andrew, ed. *Judging Lyotard*. London and New York, 1992.

Bennington, Geoffrey. *Lyotard: Writing the Event*. New York, 1988.

Carroll, David. *Paraesthetics: Foucault, Lyotard, Derrida*, London and New York, 1987.

Readings, Bill. *Introducing Lyotard: Art and Politics*. London and New York, 1991.

JAMES WILLIAMS

M

MALEVICH, KAZIMIR SEVERINOVICH. *See* Suprematism.

MALLARMÉ, STÉPHANE (1842–1898), French Symbolist poet. Few poets can have reflected on art and culture with greater constancy, clarity, and intelligence than Stéphane Mallarmé. A prolific letter writer and a frequent contributor to the review sections of newspapers and periodicals, he devoted to music and the theater, to art, ballet, and literature many passages that are as intense as they are enigmatic. Rejecting comfortable bourgeois positions on art as decoration and entertainment, Mallarmé consistently presents it as an intellectual and existential challenge with broad political and metaphysical implications. Because of the way he sets them out on the page, in paragraphs isolated from each other by large white spaces, as well as because of their hauntingly unusual formulations, his statements tend to reverberate in the mind, provoking, enticing, and challenging their readers to respond. They are also robustly resistant to translation, not merely into another language, but also into more standard French, since the experimental nature of their syntax constitutes part of Mallarmé's constant rejection of the hackneyed in his aesthetic thinking.

That unexpected, demanding use of language is central to Mallarmé's critical vision. All great art, in his view, yields its full delight, and therefore its deepest significance, only as a result of an intense cerebral effort on the part of its audience. What, after all, is the use of transposing into language any response to the natural world, he pertinently asks, if we do not do so in such a way as to release the essence of that phenomenon, set free from whatever may originally have caused it? The task of art, moreover, is not to mimic what already exists, but to create. The writer represents all artists in that, even when describing the scintillation of the stars, he or she has to transform that light, reproduce it not as radiance on a black background but through black ink on a white page. In that pregnant metaphor, exemplified most powerfully in *Un coup de dés,* is distilled much of Mallarmé's thinking on aesthetics: while the beauty of the external world has to be reduced and transformed by the individual poet into a dark lace of universal thoughts and responses, that black drop of ink nevertheless contains infinity and is therefore capable of releasing the dazzling intensity of the stars. Impersonality is essential to such art since the universe speaks through the great creative artist, who sets aside individual preoccupations for this greater purpose.

> Pure poetry implies that the poet refrain from speaking and yield the initiative to words, mobilized by the clash of their inequalities. They set each other aglow with reciprocal reflections, like a potential tongue of fire over stones, replacing both the perceptible respiration that occurs in the old lyric and the personal thrust that drives the sentence. (Mallarmé, 1945, p. 277)

At issue in this seminal quotation are two images, that of pure, depersonalized art, and that of the creative power of the medium itself. Language may be imperfect (Mallarmé gives as illustration the conflict between the intellectual and the emotional impact of *nuit* [night] with its bright clear sounds and *jour* [day] with its heavy dark sounds), but such imperfections can be overcome by allowing free play to the phonetic and intertextual values of words in combination with each other. After all, as he also reminds us, if language were transparent, there would be no need for poetry.

Aware from an early stage of the importance of Impressionism, Mallarmé suggests that painting operates in similar ways to poetry: "As no artist has on his palette a transparent and neutral color corresponding to open air, the desired effect can only be obtained by lightness or heaviness of touch, or by the regulation of tone," he argued in his review of Édouard Manet for the *London Art Monthly* of 30 September 1877, for which we possess only the English text. Mallarmé had close ties not only to the Impressionists, whose exploration of light has much in common with his own, but also with such fresco painters as Pierre-Cécile Puvis de Chavannes, whose flat surfaces and elliptical suggestions of time passing demand of their viewers the same energetically interpretative response that Mallarmé sought from his readers.

Music undoubtedly posed Mallarmé greater problems than did painting. While several musicians and music critics were part of the charmed circle that regularly met at his home on Tuesday evenings, his response to the aesthetic possibilities and demands of music seems to remain more that of an amateur, however enlightened and enthusiastic. What attracts him is something equivalent to the suggestive power of language and Impressionist art, where the notes themselves are less evocative than the silences between them: "Silence, the only luxury after rhymes, an orchestra creating with its gold, with its strokes of thought and evening, nothing but the outline of meaning, like a silent ode that the poet is thus challenged to translate!" (1945, p. 310). Richard Wagner's concept of the *Gesamtkunstwerk,* his determination to exercise complete control over his viewer's response through everything from lighting and stage sets to music and text, implied a relationship that Mallarmé found unconducive. There can be no doubt that he admired Wagner's immense intellectual energy and aesthetic ambition, but both the highly condensed sonnet he wrote in homage to the composer, and the longer, more intricately expressed prose "Rêverie" convey, with a suggestive mixture of courtesy, firmness, and regret, the conviction that Wagner has not reached the mountain peak, that poetry will always remain the most demanding, but also the most rewarding, of all the arts.

Best known, no doubt, among Mallarmé's essays are those written in response partly to this upsurge in popularity of Wagner's concept of art, and partly to the fashion for free verse. Initially given as lectures in Oxford and Cambridge, "La musique et les lettres" (Music and Letters, 1894), together with its companion pieces, "Crise de vers" (Crisis of Poetry, 1886–1896) and "Quant au livre" (As for the Book, 1895), have come to be regarded as primary texts in the development of aesthetic thinking. To some extent they exemplify his conviction that the world is made to culminate in a book, an ideal book that would be the distillation of humanity's aesthetic convictions and discoveries. Among the most challenging of his prose pieces, these meditations on the function of art contain some of Mallarmé's finest, if most elliptical, formulations on the function of the symbol, the role of personal experience, and the play of language.

Richest of all his meditations on the performing arts are those on mime and ballet, less for their perceptions of specific works than for their meditation on general aesthetic questions, and their inventive and untiring attempt to draw general precepts from individual examples. (Theater, for Mallarmé, is not a performing art, sensu stricto, since, as he amusingly remarks: "At a pinch, an entire play can be evoked by paper alone: with the help of our multiple personalities, all of us can perform it in imagination, something which cannot be said for pirouettes" [1945, p. 315].) In ballet and mime, performers use their bodies as instruments, allowing an unmediated expression of the work. Thus, the manipulation of time, where the present is always a symbol of past or future, the correspondence between gesture and thought, the silence of the medium, which recalls what Mallarmé terms the condition and delight of reading (p. 310)—all these elements invite the reader's aesthetic response without interposing the barrier of an interpreter, as is the case in music. Loïe Fuller, whose innovative manipulation of veils, fabrics, and movement transformed her body into a constantly changing work of art, thus becomes in Mallarmé's memorable phrase an "endless fountain of herself" (p. 311). Equally, classical theater strives to reproduce archetypal situations and to incarnate universal emotions. Thus, like mime and ballet, true theater enables within its audience that internal and individual festival that allows the imagination to reveal both perennial and intensely private truths. Here lies the key to much of Mallarmé's meditation on aesthetic questions, for the impersonality of poet or performer is precisely what is required to allow the reader or watcher to enter most deeply into contact with his or her personal mythology, a discovery of self that results from intellectual effort but that brings with it powerful, frequently erotic, pleasure.

If Mallarmé occasionally donned, as he put it, the crimson robe of the critic, his aesthetic response to the work of others was always at its most acute in regard to literature and especially to poetry. When he spoke to audiences in Oxford and Cambridge in 1894, the message he wanted to bring them, one that he claimed was infinitely more significant than the fall of monarchies and governments, was that French poetry had freed itself from the demands of traditional metrics, forging in its place a pattern of rhythm that responded not to any preexisting formula, but to the demands both of the individual poet, and the poem itself. Mallarmé's response to vers libre is typical of him. Profoundly interested in current experiments and deeply sympathetic to the attempts of younger poets, he himself continued to value the alexandrine, not as standard and inevitable coinage, but as a jewel to be drawn out only when the thought or emotion demanded the perfection of that finely wrought form. In countless letters to other poets he reflects on thematics and techniques with a lucidity that balances keen awareness of what his correspondent has attempted with an unshakable conviction in the value of what he himself is driven to attempt. Writing to Henri de Régnier in 1886, for example, he crisply affirms the value of retaining traditional metrical forms within a broader experimentation: "Today you possess the most subtle fingering, retaining the art of the old, unchangeable poetry while mingling with it the delightful discoveries of the present, with the result that your reverie is at once precise and vague, having found a perfect vehicle" (1959–1985, 3.70). Then to Paul Valéry in 1891, he sums up in lapidary fashion the interrelationship of poetry and music:

> Yes, dear poet, if poetry is to be conceived and if it is to have a meaning, we must attain that "lofty symphony" that, perhaps, no one will achieve; but such a symphony has haunted even the least conscious of minds, and its main features, whether commonplace or subtle, mark every written work. It's music, strictly speaking, which we must pillage, which we must plagiarize if our own music, because it is silent, is insufficient, it's music that suggests just such a poem.   (4.233)

Mallarmé's impact on aesthetics, both in fin de siècle France, and far more broadly in the latter half of the twentieth century, has been considerable. His reflections on the interplay of the erotic and the aesthetic in "L'après-midi d'un faune," to give just one example, inspired the music of Claude Debussy, the ballet of Sergei Diaghilev and Vaslav Nijinsky, and the poetry of Rubén Darío and Chris Brennan. Those reflections continue to haunt and challenge readers through the suggestive power of rhythms and metaphors, through the evocative force of the poem's rhymes and its intermingled time sequences, and through the allusions provided by such visual clues as its white spaces and its typology. His poetry and his critical writing, as well as his conversation, reverberated worldwide through Symbolist poets in Belgium and Germany, Australia and South America. Readings of his poems inform central aesthetic debates in such widely differing novels as Marcel Proust's *À la recherche du temps perdu* and Iris Murdoch's *The Philosopher's Pupil*. Yet, there can be little doubt that his greatest impact has made itself felt more recently, as his writing, particularly his aesthetic theory, has acted as a catalyst on the thinking of major French philosophers and literary critics. Thus, Jean-Paul Sartre uses Mallarmé to construct a psychoanalytic argument concerning the interrelationships of gender and aesthetics. Julia Kristeva's semiotic reading explores what she sees as a poetic revolution that took place under the explosive impetus of Isidore-Lucien Ducasse and Mallarmé. Jacques Derrida offers an intertextual reading of Plato's famous passage on mimesis and Mallarmé's "Mimique," exploring the poet's economical demonstration of the ultimate impossibility of the mimetic art and his affirmation of the endless displacement of meaning. The last few years have seen a broadening of the focus, a turning away from the somewhat stultifying desire to transform Mallarmé from poet to philosopher, to a closer exploration of his political convictions and, in particular, his assertion that creative writing constitutes a far more powerful vehicle for social change than does an anarchist's bomb. With the approach of the centenary of his death, Mallarmé's aesthetics, as expressed both in his criticism and in his creative writing, are certain to attract even closer attention and to occupy an even more important position in the evolution of contemporary thought.

[*See also* Art for Art's Sake; Poetics; *and* Symbolism.]

BIBLIOGRAPHY

Works by Mallarmé

Œuvres complètes. Edited by Henri Mondor and G. Jean-Aubry. Paris, 1945.
Œuvres complètes, vol. 1 *Poésies.* Edited by Carl Barbier and Charles Gordon Millan. Paris, 1983.
Œuvres. Edited by Yves-Alain Favre. Paris, 1985.
Poésies. Edited by Lloyd James Austin. Paris, 1989.
Collected Poems. Translated by Henry Weinfield. Berkeley, 1994.

Correspondence of Mallarmé

Correspondance. 11 vols. Edited by Lloyd James Austin. Paris, 1959–1985.
Correspondance complète, 1862–1871: Suivi de lettres sur la poésie, 1872–1898. Edited by Bertrand Marchal. Paris, 1995.
Selected Letters of Stéphane Mallarmé. Edited and translated by Rosemary Lloyd. Chicago, 1988.

Other Works

Austin, Lloyd James. *Poetic Principles and Practice.* Cambridge and New York, 1986.
Austin, Lloyd James. *Essais sur Mallarmé.* Edited by Malcolm Bowie. Manchester, 1995.
Bellet, Roger. *Mallarmé: L'encre et le ciel.* Seyssel, 1987.
Bersani, Léo. *The Death of Stéphane Mallarmé.* Cambridge and New York, 1982.
Bowie, Malcolm. *Mallarmé and the Art of Being Difficult.* Cambridge and New York, 1978.
Cohn, Robert Greer. *Toward the Poems of Mallarmé* (1965). Exp. ed. Berkeley, 1980.
Davies, Gardner. *Mallarmé et la "couche suffisante d'intelligibilité."* Paris, 1988.
Delfel, Guy. *L'esthétique de Stéphane Mallarmé.* Paris, 1951.
Derrida, Jacques. *La dissemination.* Paris, 1972.
Florence, Penny. *Mallarmé, Manet and Redon: Visual and Aural Signs and the Generation of Meaning.* Cambridge and New York, 1986.
Grauby, Françoise. *La création mythique à l'époque du symbolisme.* Paris, 1994.
Kearns, James. *Symbolist Landscapes: The Place of Painting in the Poetry and Criticism of Mallarmé and His Circle.* London, 1989.
Kristeva, Julia. *La révolution du langage poétique.* Paris, 1974.
Lawler, James R. *The Language of French Symbolism.* Princeton, N.J., 1969.
Lloyd, Rosemary. *Mallarmé: Poésies.* London, 1984.
Marchal, Bertrand. *La religion de Mallarmé.* Paris, 1988.
Marvick, Louis Wirth. *Mallarmé and the Sublime.* Albany, N.Y., 1986.
Michaud, Guy. *Mallarmé.* Novv. ed. Paris, 1971.
Michaud, Guy, et al. *Le symbolisme tel qu'en lui-même.* Paris, 1995.
Millan, Gordon. *Mallarmé: A Throw of the Dice: The Life of Stéphane Mallarmé.* London, 1994.
Noulet, Emilie. *Vingt poèmes de Stéphane Mallarmé.* Geneva, 1967.
Paxton, Norman. *The Development of Mallarmé's Prose Style.* Geneva, 1968.
Pistone, Daniele. *Symbolisme et musique, 1870–1914.* Paris, 1995.
Richard, Jean-Pierre. *L'univers imaginaire de Mallarmé.* Paris, 1961.
Sartre, Jean-Paul. *Mallarmé: La lucidité et sa face d'ombre.* Edited by Arlette Elkaim-Sartre. Paris, 1986.
Vial, André. *Mallarmé: Tétralogie d'un enfant mort.* Paris, 1976.

ROSEMARY LLOYD

MANNHEIM, KARL (1893–1947), German sociologist. Born in Budapest, Mannheim's formative intellectual development was in Germany, and in 1933 he emigrated to Great Britain, where he taught at the University of London until his death. Mannheim contributed to and shaped the sociology of knowledge, a body of inquiry into history, culture, and art that drew on Hegelian idealism, Marxist theory of society, Diltheyan historicism, and Entstehen theory. His thinking followed closely the art-historical work of Alois Riegl and Max Dvorák. One task Mannheim assumed as sociologist of culture was to analyze the methods of art history and philosophy of art that relied on the structure G. W. F. Hegel had given in his lectures on aesthetics (1823–1828).

Mannheim's most important essay that undertakes to introduce clarity into a confused mélange of approaches to cultural objects is "On the Interpretation of 'Weltanschauung,'" (1923).

The problem Mannheim posed is as follows: how are we to deal with the way past moments of culture saw themselves and their own past when any theory we articulate as a mode of interpretation will use cognitive categories meaningful to us but inapplicable to the past? The past, insofar as it expresses a world outlook or point of view, expresses that weltanschauung through thoughts and objects that are not cognitive, and we, in our cultural actions, do the same. It would seem therefore that we cannot understand the past, nor be fully self–conscious of our present. We must develop an atheoretical (i.e., interpretative) method that is not irrational. Mannheim sought, in the manner of Edmund Husserl, a phenomenology of intentional cultural acts that could be applied to the past. In this way, cultural history could be written, but with admitted and accepted unconscious elements as part of it. Those elements would necessarily await future interpretative acts to become conscious.

Mannheim proposes that we view past cultural events, for example, works of art, as exhibiting three aspects of meaning: objective, expressive, documentary. Objective meaning can be grasped in our present without knowledge of intentional acts of the artist. This includes "pure visibility"—that which all can see immediately. (Obvious problems with this present themselves: we know that we often fail to "see" that which becomes evident upon further inquiry into a cultural past.) Expressive meaning connotes what an event meant to the artist as it appeared to past consciousness, known in the present through affective properties of the object, most clearly represented in the formal artistic structures. (Again, where we look into past values, interpretative verification is difficult.) Documentary meaning refers to the unconscious "ethos" of the object, not knowable by the creator or the period in which the work was created. Documentary meaning becomes part of cultural consciousness only through later interpretations. Every dimension of a cultural object, even the seemingly most trivial, suggests a world outlook, a point of view, a set of unconscious values and presuppositions. Subsequent documentary interpretations (e.g., those we today propose) themselves hide unconscious documentary meanings that will become available only in the future. Endless interpretative acts are imposed on us by the very nature of cultural life. The history of documentary meanings of past ages is thus also a history of the interpreting subjects themselves. Mannheim pushes to its logical interpretative conclusion the central theme of Hegel's grand survey of past cultures.

This analysis leads Mannheim to distinguish interpretations (the necessary method for determining a weltanschauung) from explanations, the goal of scientific inquiry. An interpretation would ask, What does X mean? An explanation would ask, Why does X express A? What led X to have the content it does? How is X related to the artist? Explanations may be possible when we turn to the past, and may be part of our understanding of ourselves. But explanations cannot articulate the weltanschauung of the past. That is achieved through a kind of feeling into the past in the manner pursued by Wilhelm Dilthey. As for ourselves, we are almost wholly excluded from that which a future interpretation will call our weltanschauung.

[See also Croce; Dilthey; Panofsky; and Sociology of Art.]

BIBLIOGRAPHY

Works by Mannheim

Essays on the Sociology of Knowledge. Edited by Paul Kecskemeti. London, 1952. See "On the Interpretation of 'Weltanschauung,'" pp. 33–83.

Other Sources

Dvorák, Max. *Kunstgeschichte als Geistesgeschichte.* Munich, 1924.
Hauser, Arnold. *The Philosophy of Art History.* New York, 1959.
Mandelbaum, Maurice. *The Problem of Historical Knowledge: An Answer to Relativism.* New York, 1938.
Panofsky, Erwin. *Meaning in the Visual Arts.* Garden City, N.Y., 1955; reprint, Chicago, 1982.
Podro, Michael. *The Critical Historians of Art.* New Haven, 1982.
Riegl, Alois. *Stilfragen: Grundlegungen zu einer Geschichte der Ornamentik.* Berlin, 1893.

RICHARD KUHNS

MARCUSE, HERBERT (1898–1979), German philosopher who emigrated to the United States. Aesthetic reflection runs like a red thread through Herbert Marcuse's lifework, from his first book (*Der deutsche Künstlerroman*, 1922) through his last (*The Aesthetic Dimension: Toward a Critique of Marxist Aesthetics*, 1977). After his immigration in 1934, it also plays an essential role in connection with the New Left movement at the end of the 1960s, which catapulted Marcuse, the movement's favorite mentor, to the heights of his publicity. At the same time, however, a certain opposition between a liberating trust in the future and a diagnosis of the gradual stabilization of repressive forms of rule was overlooked. This inner tension in Marcuse's work characterizes the elaboration of his conception of social theory. This is also true of Marcuse's art criticism. More detailed presentations of Herbert Marcuse's life and of the lines of development of his critical writings on art and society will be presented in this article. The discussion will be restricted to a reconstruction of Marcuse's relevant range of ideas, thereby distilling a concept of the theory of art that can be a valid, durable, and fruitful starting point for a philosophy of art, especially one that extends to semiotics.

An Outline of a Social Theory. Marcuse is concerned with the perspective of "secular redemption" (Marcuse, 1972, p. 89) in art: art as "reconciliation between man and man, man and nature" (p. 90)—in short, he is concerned with utopia. In contrast to other social forces, art shows itself to be the promoter of utopia in that art permits utopia to take on material forms. Herein lies art's ability to transcend the repressive reality of life in a class-based society. Despite art's concrete material nature, its "transcendence" is not, however, the reality of utopia, but rather illusion *(Schein)*. It is, to be sure, a beautiful illusion because of its material nature. By all means, art is, as such, conscious illusion, and if "art wills itself as illusion" it acquires "another dimension" of reality, "that of possible liberation" (p. 87). Art does not thereby efface its own class character, but rather realizes what it at the same time surpasses. In this doubled perspective, the living reality becomes "transparent as the condition and as the dream of humanity" (p. 90). The "subversive power" of art is to be found in this dialectic.

Therein lies a profound conflict. If art is, on the one hand, always a revolutionary negation of the given by virtue of its "alienation from the alienated society" through the transcendence of the beautiful, art is at the same time, on the other hand, always a compensatory affirmation of the established order as well. Art can go as far as to be the decorative appeasement of the established order: it can "beautify and justify" it (p. 92). This conflict is, however, not merely unavoidable: it is constitutive of what makes art art. For the affirmative moment of the beautiful is "also the power which denies this affirmation" (p. 97). Where art cannot endure this tension, "art has lost its truth, has lost itself (p. 93).

What, however, would become of art, if it were to reach its goal of a concrete utopia? It would cease to be art in conflict. That would mean that art would cease to be art at all—not because it would have lost its potential, but rather because it would have fulfilled itself as social reality. Art would be, in G. W. F. Hegel's sense, neutralized and elevated to the next level *(aufgehoben)*. The fulfillment of art's mission is at the same time the end of art (Marcuse, 1964).

This perspectival vanishing point in Marcuse's philosophy of art experienced a traceable displacement and radicalization in the New Left movement of the 1960s. The "end" of "utopia" is no longer present in art as a moving sensual nearness. The new avant-garde aspired much more to truncate this process in that it anticipated and tried immediately to hasten this end of art in the form of "living art." That is the movement of revolutionary happenings, guerrilla theater, and art as agitation.

Despite the closeness to the New Leftists that he inspired (Marcuse, 1969), the first impetus for Marcuse's own revi-

sion of his philosophy of art came in the 1970s (Marcuse, 1972). The structure of his theory remains the same, however. But one thing has changed: the conclusion and telos of the whole. This is accomplished through insight into the perspective permanence of utopia and, thereby, into the "permanence of art." It is the insight that "no matter in what form, art can never eliminate the tension between art and reality" (p. 108). Whoever supposes this would deny "the insurmountable limit to the mutability of human nature: a biological, not theological limit" (ibid.). For, writes Marcuse,

> the institutions of a socialist society, even in their most democratic form, could never resolve all the conflicts between the universal and the particular, between human beings and nature, between individual and individual. Socialism does not and cannot liberate Eros from Thanatos.   (1978, pp. 71–72)

Marcuse had already used the title of this last small work, *The Aesthetic Dimension,* once before, as the title of a chapter in his larger work *Eros and Civilization: A Philosophical Inquiry into Freud* (1955). Marcuse had referred in that work to Friedrich von Schiller's *Letters on the Aesthetic Education of Man.* Like Schiller, Marcuse saw in artistic beauty the synthesis of individual sensual experience and universal rational knowledge, and in this synthesis, true human freedom, to which aesthetic education should lead as its real goal. [*See* Schiller.] In *The Aesthetic Dimension* of 1978, this creed of Schiller's is no longer shared. For Marcuse, who confronts already the horizon of his own death, the chasm between individual happiness and the common good is no longer fully or really to be closed, not even in a utopian perspective. In Marcuse's understanding, this means the move from the protofactual anticipation to the contrafactual permanence of art (as in the German title of this last text: *Die Permanenz der Kunst,* 1977). That is, seen from the point of view of his biography, the final version of Marcuse's reflections on art.

An Analysis of Methodology. Marcuse did not limit himself to saying *what* art brings about; he also tried to grasp *how* art brings it about. As we will see, Marcuse's ultimate version of the "what" is confirmed from the point of view of the "how." According to Marcuse, it is as language that art is unique—as language sui generis that can hear and see what language is otherwise incapable of expressing (Marcuse, 1978, p. 98). The transcendence of art is thus the transcendence of language: "[images, sound, and rhythm . . . reveal and communicate] facts and possibilities of the human existence; they 'see' this existence in a very different form from that in which reality appears in ordinary (and scientific) language and communication" (p. 88).

But, can the language of art accomplish this? How can the language of art be differentiated from everyday language and the language of the sciences? Where is the transcendent power in this difference? The answer is unequivocal. The element that distinguishes art is the "aesthetic form"—in short, "style." Marcuse describes this as follows: "in the aesthetic form are . . . the critical, negating, transcending qualities" of art (p. 93). Herein lies "the achievement of style, which is the poem, the novel, the painting, the composition" (pp. 98–99). Thus, for Marcuse, style determines aesthetic difference. Style is art's transcendent language. To summarize: style, the aesthetic form, is art. As a stylized image, art explodes the limited horizon of its social origin into its anthropological context: "the aesthetic transformation reveals the human condition . . . over and above any specific condition" in history (p. 87). Through the "miracle of the aesthetic form, . . . another dimension . . . appears in the particular content" (p. 90). In this new dimension, the socially and historically determined figures in art "incarnate the species man: the human being" (ibid.).

Marcuse thus positions himself, on the one hand, against a false avant-garde that, in the name of cultural revolution and the overcoming of art, appears as the enemy of aesthetic form (p. 91). Accordingly, guerrilla theater is termed a *contradictio in adiecto* (p. 113). The attempt to create "living art" that erases the difference between art and reality is doomed to failure, as is the attempt to annul the gap between reality and language (pp. 85, 101). This is true, as well, of art as its own kind of language: "To the degree to which it makes itself part of real life, it loses the transcendence which opposes art to the established order—it remains immanent in this order, one dimensional" (p. 101).

Art can express its "radical potential only as art," which means as aesthetic form, as style (p. 103). In this sense, art has the permanence, the stability of language. As an example, Marcuse, following André Breton, refers to Arthur Rimbaud, who, as a supporter of the 1871 Paris Commune, wrote poems no different than he did before, because it was his intention from the beginning "to translate the world into a new language" (p. 106). Marcuse also refers to Gustave Courbet, who, although he belonged in the forefront of the Commune, kept painting still lifes. Marcuse writes that "some of these apples . . . are more powerful and more 'protestaire' than any political painting" (p. 106).

On the other hand, Marcuse contradicts György Lukács, who demands that art reveal basic socioeconomic principles: "But precisely this requirement offends the very nature of art. The basic structure and dynamic of society can never find sensuous, aesthetic expression" (p. 125). Both critical tendencies are simultaneously critiques of language. If Lukács does not recognize art as style, the pseudo-avant-garde misses art's linguistic character along with art's stylistic elements. At the same time, both fail to grasp the transcendental moment of art as language: as the language of the aesthetic form, as the language of style. Recalling Francisco José de Goya's etchings, Marcuse sees art's transforming potential confirmed by the fact that in art, "even the ugly, [the] cruel, [the] sick" becomes a part of the aesthetic

structure (p. 99). "The style," writes Marcuse, "embodiment of the aesthetic form, in subjecting to another order, subjects it to the 'laws of beauty'" (p. 99).

What is this "aesthetic form"? What is "style"? Marcuse gives us an answer: "'Aesthetic form' means the total of qualities (harmony, rhythm, contrast) which make an oeuvre a self-contained whole, with a structure and order of its own (the style)" (p. 81). In the German edition, the quality of "meaning" *(Bedeutung)* is added to the list *(Konterrevolution und Revolt,* Frankfurt am Main, 1973, p. 98). Thus, style constitutes itself out of the respective work elements: whether these are directly physical (as is rhythm) or semantic (as is meaning) or both (as is contrast). All these qualities, taken on their own, are merely material, at the same time merely linguistic elements, which only in connection with one another comprise the language of aesthetic form, of style. To be sure, Marcuse introduces elements of order and closure. This appears to be an orientation on classicist models, or, at the minimum, on art's traditional work character. There is, however, also art as "open form," as fragment: even the fragmentary and the chaotic are elements of style. This does not alter the idea that it is the structural connection that constitutes style. As art, the fragment remains a structural whole, and as art, chaos is an aesthetic form: thus, they are languages of style.

Open Questions. Not only does Marcuse theorize what art accomplishes, he theorizes how it accomplishes it. Previously, this linkage of the semantic and functional aspects of art to the elements of the artistic process was rarely so clearly developed and articulated as a practical-semiotic unity. This raises questions as well, however, especially the following two interrelated problems. First, how can art, as an image of style, and especially when it is without understandable words or recognizable images, realize situations of living reality, if necessary, exclusively through colors, forms, rhythms, sounds, or contrasts? Second, how can art at the same time transcend the present situation in the sense of a Janus-faced realization of the "situation and dream" of humanity, so that the two can authentically unite? Marcuse never developed this double question of the unique semiotic character of art. An attempt at a solution that could correspond to Marcuse's line of thought appears to rest in the comprehension of the entirety of the elements (with or without understandable words or recognizable images) that comprise an artistic image, as the synonymless embodiment of a reference to the world in which we live.

[*See also* Adorno; *and* Marxism.]

BIBLIOGRAPHY

Works by Marcuse

An Essay on Liberation. Boston, 1969.
Counterrevolution and Revolt. Boston, 1972.
Die Permanenz der Kunst: Wider eine bestimmte marxistische Ästhetick: Ein Essay. Munich, 1977.

Eros and Civilisation: A Philosophical Inquiry into Freud. Boston, 1955.

One-Dimensional Man: Studies in the Ideology of Advanced Industrial Society. Boston, 1964.

Schriften. 9 vols. Frankfurt am Main, 1978–1989.

The Aesthetic Dimension: Toward a Critique of Marxist Aesthetics. Boston, 1978.

"Über den affirmativen Charakter der Kultur." *Zeitschrift für Sozialforschung* 6 (1937): 54–94.

Other Sources

Görtzen, R. "Kommentierte Bibliographie der Schriften über Herbert Marcuse." In *Kritik und Utopie im Werk von Herbert Marcuse*, edited by Institut für Sozialforschung. Frankfurt am Main, 1992. Contains 413 titles.

Kellner, Douglas. *Herbert Marcuse and the Crisis of Marxism.* Berkeley, 1984.

FRANZ KOPPE

MARINETTI, FILLIPPO TOMMASO. *See* Futurism.

MARITAIN, JACQUES (1882–1973), French philosopher. The aesthetics of Jacques Maritain must be understood within his commitment to the philosophy of Thomas Aquinas. "Woe is me," Maritain wrote, in a variation on Saint Paul, "if I do not teach Thomism." Because it is not the case that Aquinas developed anything that could be called an aesthetics, however, Maritain's aesthetics, while it stems from features of Aquinas's philosophy, must be seen as an original extension of it.

Readers of James Joyce will have encountered Stephen Dedalus's reflections on Aquinas's definition of the beautiful as "that which when seen pleases." Aquinas numbers beauty among the transcendental attributes of being, adding it to the more traditional One and Good. An attribute of being is transcendental when we can say, for example, "Whatever is, is one," and "Whatever is, is good." Aquinas holds that we can also say, "Whatever is, is beautiful." This somewhat puzzling claim will not seem promising for those who are seeking a criterion enabling them to distinguish the beautiful from the nonbeautiful.

Maritain wrote two major works in aesthetics, *Art and Scholasticism* (1920) and *Creative Intuition in Art and Poetry,* the Mellon Lectures in the Fine Arts that were delivered at the National Gallery in Washington, D.C., in 1952. To these may be added *The Frontiers of Poetry* (1935) and *Situation de la poésie* (1938), written with his wife, Raissa. (It would be difficult to overestimate the influence of Raissa on Maritain's aesthetics. She was a poet, he makes overt mention of her help and dedicates two of his aesthetic works to Raissa, applying to her the Horatian phrase, *dimidium animae meae:* half my soul.)

At first glance, *Art and Scholasticism* is deceptive. Written when Maritain was still a neophyte Thomist, it brings together in a somewhat pedestrian way a series of discussions, each of them familiar to the student of Aquinas, but linked by Maritain in such a way that they take on a new significance. After an initial indication that Aquinas and the other Scholastics did not develop an aesthetics or theory of the fine arts, he draws attention to the discussions of the liberal and the mechanical arts to be found in the texts of Aquinas and, most notably, the divine art of creation. All human art is considered with reference to the divine art and is interpreted as a sharing in or participation in it. This is the profound significance of speaking of the work of the artist as creation. Maritain also develops for his reader the familiar distinction between the theoretical or speculative use of the mind and the practical use of it. Instances of the latter are the knowledge embedded in moral action and the activity of the artist.

As in Aristotle, the "artist" is primarily exemplified by someone who reshapes a natural material, for example, the hide of an animal, first tanning it, then making a pair of shoes. The coming into being of natural things is taken to be the acquisition by matter of a form it did not previously have. The making of art is modeled on this: the "shape" or form of the shoe is imposed on a natural matter, hide. In this humble instance of it, art is seen as supplying what nature does not supply and *homo faber,* the human maker, emerges as unique among cosmic creatures. Birds, animals, insects make things—nests, hives, and the like—but they do so in a way that, however remarkable, is repetitive. Human art as a manifestation of reason involves a free choice of ends and an endless variation in ways of achieving the end.

The route from such mechanical art to fine art passes through the liberal arts. Liberal arts are sciences that essentially involve a making: grammar, rhetoric, logic,—the trivium—shape speech and thought, making sentences, assertions, arguments. The arts of the quadrivium—arithmetic, geometry, music, and astronomy—bear on quantity as such or impose a quantitative shape on sound and the movement of the planets.

The *Poetics* of Aristotle was not translated into Latin in Aquinas's lifetime, so his knowledge of it was at best oblique (he did not read Greek, and his dozen commentaries on Aristotelian works are based on Latin translations of them). It is interesting to speculate on what Aquinas would have had to say of the *Poetics.* Some intimation can be found in his commentary on the *Metaphysics* when he deals with texts in which Aristotle likens the poet and the philosopher. The latter is a lover of wisdom (*philosophos*), the former a lover of myth (*philomythos*). Moreover, they are akin in taking their rise from wonder and awe.

Maritain's aesthetics, particularly in this first work, can be seen as an effort to take cues from Thomas and develop them into the account of fine art that Aquinas did not give. First he takes what Thomas said of the beautiful and fashions an account of the fine arts. Moreover, he insists on the view that Aquinas learned from Aristotle that art is a virtue of the practical intellect bearing on things to be made, just as prudence is a virtue of the practical intellect dealing with things to be done. Nowadays, we are likely to restrict our use of *virtue* to moral virtue, but in the Aristotelian scheme sciences are virtues since, thanks to them, we are able consistently to make true judgments in a given subject matter. If calling such determinations of speculative intelligence virtues seems remote from our usage, calling prudence a virtue will not, since it is the cognitive side of those appetitive dispositions—courage, temperance, justice—that are virtues in the primary sense, for us as well as for Aquinas. It is the difference between art and prudence that receives Maritain's particular attention.

What is the relationship between art and morality? Obviously, one can be a good shoemaker and morally reprehensible—dishonest, intemperate, cowardly. By the same token, the fine artist seems to possess skill in indifference to his or her moral character. The Romantic impulse was to suggest that artists are more or less exempt from the moral law, beyond good and evil, since they must master them both in their creations. This was Oscar Wilde's view in *Intentions*. Maritain does not want to make artistic creation dependent on the moral virtue of the artist, but he suggests that just as prudence must be acquired along with the moral virtues (and vice versa), so art is dependent on nonmoral appetitive dispositions that function like the moral virtues vis-à-vis prudence. He does not develop this suggestion to the point where an appraisal of it can easily be made. But it is rather in the use of the artifact that Maritain concentrates his discussion of art and morality early on and to the social context into which the artifact is introduced.

Turning to a discussion of Christian art, Maritain explores the possibility that religious art bears a tighter relation to the moral condition of the artist than does secular art. All in all, his positions in this first work are more inchoative than definitive. A good deal of the interest of the book resides in the appendixes and notes Maritain added to subsequent editions. In one of these, he makes the provocative remark that in order to write Marcel Proust's *Remembrance of Things Past* as it ought to be written, one would need the sanctity of a Saint Augustine. A remarkable suggestion, that profound moral virtue is a prerequisite for writing well of moral decadence. Among these addenda one will find discussions of Immanuel Kant, of transcendental beauty, the relation between the beautiful and the good, Charles Baudelaire, on contemporary art, the novel, and art as imitation of nature.

There is a superficial resemblance between *Creative Intuition in Art and Poetry* and *Art and Scholasticism*. Some of the same themes are taken up: art as a virtue of the practical intellect, poetry, and beauty. But the Mellon Lectures represent a very different aesthetics, one that Maritain had slowly developed over the intervening years. The first chapter treats of the advent of the self as crucial in the development of art, and chapter 3 speaks of the preconscious life of the intellect: Maritain sees poetry as an attempt to escape from reason. The poetic knowledge that interests him is not that which goes into the conscious making of the poem, but rather that which precedes creation and indeed need never be manifested in an artifact. Poetic knowledge thus is something even nonpoets can have. What is this poetic knowledge?

In what is perhaps his most daring development of a Thomistic theme, certainly in the realm of aesthetics, Maritain takes Aquinas's discussion of the knowledge that is at work in the moral act and distinguishes a version of it that is the soul of poetic knowledge. The distinction as found in Aquinas is this. If we ask a moral philosopher about a given virtue, for example, what chastity might demand of an agent in certain circumstances, the reply will remain at the level of knowledge. That is, what we are being given is a bit of knowledge that could be known by someone even if he himself does not practice the virtue being discussed. On the other hand, we might ask advice of someone who is not a moral philosopher but who possesses the virtue in question. You ask your venerable aunt for advice in resolving a moral problem. Her response would likely be in the mode of, "Well, what I would do . . ." Such a response is essentially colored by the woman's virtuous character, her disposition or inclination to the good of that virtue. Thomas says such knowledge involves a judgment through inclination toward or connaturality with what is being discussed.

It will be seen that this distinction is a contribution to the recurrent question of what the relationship is between knowledge and conduct. The kind of knowledge that makes up ethics could be acquired by morally immature persons and on the basis of it they could give advice. But the knowledge that is at the heart of action—actions are singular—involves a judgment that is shaped by our appetitive condition, our disposition or inclination to the good. We can know truths about the good, but the good as such is an object of appetite and our judgments about it will be the better insofar as they are guided by a state of character involving a steady appetitive relation to the good. "Incline our hearts, O God," in the words of the familiar prayer.

Maritain suggests that poetic knowledge, too, is a judgment by disposition or connaturality. It is like the judgment of prudence, but unlike it as well, since it is not concerned with moral decisions. It is the artist's peculiar grasp of reality that is at the heart of Maritain's aesthetics, creative intuition. The poet possesses a peculiar connaturality with the world. The Mellon Lectures move through a wider range of the fine arts than did the first work, this expansion being visible in the lesser aesthetic works that intervened between *Art and Scholasticism* and *Creative Intuition in Art and Poetry*. Maritain's profound sympathy with the direction of modern painting, fueled by his close friendships with a number of artists, is of particular note. One might have thought that nonrepresentational art would be frowned on by one whose aesthetics has its roots in Aquinas, but this is not so. Music is the subject of a most interesting meditation. Here, too, the Maritains' lifelong friendship with musicians has its effect.

It is not rare for working scientists to find a philosophy of science curiously remote and irrelevant to what they do. The same fate perhaps awaits many aesthetic theories. It is worth noting, accordingly, that working artists found inspiration and encouragement in Maritain, particularly (and surprisingly) in *Art and Scholasticism*. Poets like Thomas Merton, Allen Tate, and Robert Lowell, and writers like Flannery O'Connor are examples of this. O'Connor was particularly struck by the view that the aim of art is the perfection of the thing made, not the self-revelation of the artist. Many, first attracted by Maritain's aesthetic works, go on to the other writings that provide the ultimate support for his views. His masterpiece, *The Degrees of Knowledge*, requires the supplement of his theory of poetic knowledge in order to be complete.

BIBLIOGRAPHY

Works by Maritain

Art and Scholasticism and The Frontiers of Poetry. Translated by Joseph W. Evans. New York, 1962; reprint, Notre Dame, Ind., 1974.
Creative Intuition in Art and Poetry. New York, 1953; reprint, Princeton, N.J., 1978.
Œuvres complètes, 15 vols. Edited by René Mougel et al. Fribourg, 1986–1995. Edition includes work of Raissa Maritain.
Works. 20 vols. Edited by Ralph McInerny, Bernard Doering, and Frederick Crosson. Notre Dame, Ind. 1995–.

Other Sources

Aloysius, M. "The Epistemological Value of Sense Intuition." *Philosophical Studies* 5 (December 1955): 71–88.
Barre, Jean-Luc. *Jacques et Raissa Maritain: Les mendiants du ciel.* Paris, 1995.
Belgion, Montgomery. "Art and Mr. Maritain." *Dublin Review* 187 (October 1930): 201–215.
Clancy, William P. "The Intuition of Jacques Maritain." *Commonweal* 59 (25 December 1953): 309–310.
Cocteau, Jean. "Rencontres." *La revue de Paris* 60 (September 1953): 31–35.
Doering, Bernard E. *Jacques Maritain and the French Catholic Intellectuals.* Notre Dame, Ind., 1983.
Evans, Joseph W. "Jacques Maritain's Personalism." *Review of Politics* 14 (April 1952): 166–177.
Fitzgerald, Robert. "The Power of a Mind." *New Republic* 128 (6 April 1953): 22–23.
Frank, Joseph. "Maritain's View on Modern Art." *New Republic* (30 May 1955): 17–18.
Hamm, Victor M. "Creative Intuition and Scholasticism." *America* 90 (31 October 1953).
Hook, Sidney. "The Integral Humanism of Jacques Maritain." *Partisan Review* 7 (1940): 204–229.
McInerny, Ralph. *Art and Prudence.* Notre Dame, Ind., 1988.
O'Connor, Flannery. "The Catholic Novelist in the Protestant South." In *Collected Works,* pp. 853–864. New York, 1988.
Philippe, M. D. "L'esthétique de Jacques Maritain." *Revue des science philosophiques et théologiques* 41 (1957): 245–248.

RALPH McINERNY

MARX, KARL HEINRICH. *See* Marxism.

MARXISM. [*To explore the traditions of Marxist aesthetics, this entry comprises two essays:*
Historical and Conceptual Overview
Marxism and Materialism
The first essay discusses the historical and theoretical roots of Marxism and its aesthetics. The second essay focuses on Marxism's commitment to materialism, especially in connection with contemporary aesthetics. For related discussion, see Cultural Studies; Gramsci; Hegel; Historicism, *article on* Historicism and Philosophy; Ideology; Jameson; Merleau-Ponty; Raphael; Russian Aesthetics, *article on* Socialist Realism; Sartre; Schapiro; *and* Williams.]

Historical and Conceptual Overview

Reiterating Marxism's general concern with the relation between theory and practice, Marxist aesthetics has emphasized issues in art criticism and history (and recently, in cultural studies), as well as the systematic questions of aesthetic theory. These efforts have sometimes originated or ensued in explicit political programs; they have also led to disagreements about which positions count as "authentically" Marxist as well as skepticism among other philosophers and critics who question the status of Marxist theory in general. But for a tradition that claims figures as important for twentieth-century thought as György Lukács, Walter Benjamin, Raymond Williams, Jean-Paul Sartre, Theodor W. Adorno, and Mikhail Bakhtin, such issues and even the differences among its most notable "members" are less significant for assessing the impact of Marxist aesthetics than is their common focus on art as a distinctive and powerful representation of class relations, historical tendencies, and social formations. Art, like all other human activities, originates and takes its varied forms in relation to the historical situation and material needs of those who make it and their audience; this same basis would then be reflected in the method and direction of Marxist inquiry in aesthetics.

That Karl Marx himself wrote little explicitly about aesthetics is misleading as a measure of its importance for him. Aside from his own literary interests (including his unrealized plan for a book on Honoré de Balzac after completing *Capital*), his systematic thinking discloses significant aesthetic influences at its source. Having proposed to turn G. W. F. Hegel "right side up" with the displacement of idealism by materialism, Marx nonetheless retains the formal—and unifying—aesthetic configuration of the Hegelian dialectic in characterizing the movement of history; moreover, the "true beginning" of history that he predicted for the end of class conflict anticipates in that image of the future an intensification of sense experience that recalls the original emphasis of the term *aesthetics* in its use at the beginning of the modern tradition by Alexander C. Baumgarten. ("The forming of the five senses," Marx writes, "is a labor of the entire history of the world down to the present.") In these and other references to the patterns of historical development, the influence is evident of Marx's close reading of Hegel's own *Philosophy of Fine Art* (1835) and of the *Aesthetics* (1846) by Hegel's follower, F. T. Vischer.

In substantive terms, the analysis of history for Marx and then Marxism centers on the relation between the material "base" of economic existence and a "superstructure" of cultural institutions, including that of art. The exact terms of this relation remain a disputed question for Marxism; it is also one on which the central concept of representation in art bears directly. Marx himself anticipates and rejects the "vulgar" Marxist view according to which the material conditions of a society mechanically imprint themselves on and thus determine the character of its cultural superstructure. The inadequacy of that account is evident for Marx in respect to Greek art and William Shakespeare's writings, both of which in his judgment transcended the ideological context in which they appeared. Indeed, art may not only reflect more than its own context, it also has the capacity to *act* on (or even against) that source; the relationship is thus more complex than would be an apologia or even only a literally accurate description of the prevailing social hierarchy. Thus, too, the specific representation in the individual work of art need not—ought not—be tendentious; so Friedrich Engels emphasizes, "The more fully concealed the author's views, the better for the work of art."

The Marxist concept of representation in art as at once rooted in history and aesthetically self-conscious also anticipates the Marxist position on other traditional aesthetic issues. In respect to art's cognitive status, Marxism consistently rejects the varieties of formalism, distancing itself from the many variations on a Kantian abstract or "free" (and noncognitive) beauty, and rather emphasizing (in Lukács's version) a representation of the "typical" in human experience, that is, of what, in a particular context, would be necessary and universal. What art communicates, then, is knowledge mediated by history—thus, historically expressive—and heightened in its sensible affect: at once

abstract and concrete. (This combination resembles, although still with differences, the "universal" character of art claimed in Aristotle's *Poetics*.)

On related grounds, the distinction between form and content in the ontology of art and thus in the individual artwork becomes problematic. Hegel's reaction against that distinction's own formalist bias—as in his claim that "every definite content determines a form suitable to it"—is extended in its Marxist revision also against the opposite position in which form is no more than an epiphenomenon of content (so Lukács, for example, insists that form itself *has* a content). Thus, too, Marxist stylistics rejects the often subjectivist practice of connoisseurship in fine art and the antihistorical disposition of the Russian Formalists or the American New Criticism in literary criticism and theory. Objections to historicist interpretation, like that of the "intentional fallacy," succeed only in making a fetish of the work of art; they must themselves fail because, analyzed apart from their social and human origins, the "formal" features of art are vacuous, of no interest either within or outside aesthetics.

The problem raised first by Plato of the relation between ethical and aesthetic judgment evokes in Marxist aesthetics a response that, like Plato's, stresses the connection between the two. Contrary to the "art for art's sake" doctrine, the social origins and consequences of the artwork are intrinsically related to it *as* art, with the aesthetic experience thus also involving a moral point of view: no "benefit of clergy" (in George Orwell's phrase) insulates either the creative or the critical process. Such links between artistic and other objects lead Marxist aesthetics to oppose positions that emphasize the disembodiment of aesthetic experience—as claimed, for example, in the Kantian view of aesthetic disengagement from all utilitarian interests that has dominated modern aesthetics. The Marxist objection to the Kantian view suggests a conception of art as materially "interested" rather than "disinterested," thus also linking up with the possibility they insist on more generally that aspects of the social superstructure can act on elements of the material "base" as well as the other way around. To this extent, it seems that despite the Marxists' own (occasional) disclaimers, art would be actively, even if subtly tendentious; that art as it thus acted might be claimed to have history on its side would not alter the fact of this role. Even in this anti-"aestheticist" reaction, however, Marxist aesthetics attempts to avoid both the extremes of reductionism, on one side, and appeals to transcendent or ahistorical values, on the other, by combining a cognitive (and historically grounded) version of artistic representation with the intensification through art of the concrete affect. The "aesthetic" would then reflect a conjunction of thought and feeling that—so the claim goes—is objective or "realistic" without being emotively or morally neutral.

The composite view thus summarized leaves open such central issues as the relation between art and ideology (specifically, of how art can be at once inside and outside ideology). But then, no summary could provide a comprehensive (or perhaps even a consistent) statement of the sort that Marx and Engels themselves never ventured. Their emphasis on historical, social, and economic issues rather than on others like those of aesthetics anticipates also the order of priority in most of their successors. Even the most politically engaged of twentieth-century Marxists, however, attach importance to art and at times to aesthetics, as is evident, for example, in writings by Leon Trotsky and Georgy Plekhanov. Analyses by V. I. Lenin and Mao Zedong found art significant, at least instrumentally, as a means of communication and persuasion. The emergence in the Soviet Union and then elsewhere of Socialist Realism—officially "adopted" as an artistic standard at the 1934 Congress of Soviet Writers—remains more notable for the political and moral extremes to which it contributed than for the art it fostered or for its bearing on problems of aesthetics.

On the other hand, initiatives suggested by Marx and Engels in their social theory continue to influence thinkers who find in that framework a basis for addressing issues of aesthetics in relation to specific arts as well as to art as such. (Like most aesthetic theories, Marxist aesthetics has closer affinities to one art—in its case, literature—than to others; that emphasis is undoubtedly due to the cognitive emphasis in the Marxist view of representation.) Among the important early or mid-twentieth-century writers on Marxist aesthetics, one group in particular—the "Frankfurt School," which included Adorno, Max Horkheimer, Leo Loewenthal, and Herbert Marcuse (peripherally, also Walter Benjamin, and in his early work, Jürgen Habermas)—has had a continuing impact on aesthetics and social theory more generally. Influenced by them but in the end independently, a later generation of writers on aesthetics also associate their work with Marxism, although again without being bound by any but the most general orthodoxy. These include Terry Eagleton and John Berger in England; Louis Althusser, Pierre Macherey, and Pierre Bourdieu in France; Robert Weimann in Germany; and Fredric Jameson and Richard Ohmann in the United States.

The range of issues and methods considered by the latter authors is, if anything, broader than that of their predecessors; because of changes in the international political landscape, both the external and the internal pressures that constrained earlier Marxist thinkers have diminished. Despite this change, however, neither analytic aesthetics (influenced by recent Anglo-American linguistic philosophy) nor structuralist and poststructuralist aesthetics, which together have dominated recent aesthetic theory, has been responsive to the Marxist criticism of their common antihistorical and antifoundationalist claims. (If anything, the influence has moved in the other direction, with certain ostensibly Marxist writers scaling back the traditional centrality for Marxism of both historical explanation and the essentialist definition of human nature.)

On the other hand, Marxist themes figure in a number of contemporary aesthetic theories and theories of criticism that do not represent themselves as primarily Marxist. (Whether these would gain from being more explicitly or consistently Marxist is a matter of dispute within the accounts themselves.) Thus, "reader-response" or "reception" theory and the more general versions of hermeneutics, both of which cite the process of reading and the reader's historical situation as determinants of literary meaning, have evident precedents in Marxist analysis (this, without any more basic commitment to materialism and sometimes in direct opposition to it). A complement to this appears in the "New Historicism," which again typically brackets the issue of materialism at the level of ontology, focusing rather on the contextual implications of the origins and consequences of art and criticizing the indifference to such historical factors in poststructuralism. The attentiveness by certain art historians to aspects of the production of fine art—like the development of technology and the roles of patrons or sponsors—carries further the analyses of social structure anticipated in earlier Marxist writers on the visual arts like Arnold Hauser and Max Raphael. (This work links up with other recent writing on "intellectual property" as related to aesthetic issues such as the ownership—and then the identity—of art.) Feminist aesthetics, examining the social causality of art's origins and the relation between the historical status of women artists and the supposed "nature" of art, has also looked (sometimes overtly, sometimes tacitly) to Marxist grounds. Various writers have drawn on "speech act" theory as a key to aesthetic issues of meaning—and again, the conception of art as an individual or institutional means of action has been an important and basic (and, if anything, more fully developed) theme of Marxist analysis. (By contrast, the influential "institutional" and related "artworld" theories of George Dickie and Arthur Danto, respectively, have relatively little to say about the status of institutions as such.)

Whatever strains occur in proposals to link these apparently diverse theories of art or criticism with Marxism, narrower definitions of Marxism are still more likely to misrepresent the status and transmission of the central aesthetic concepts in that tradition. Aesthetic theories that emphasize the roles of intuition, form, and the absence or indeterminacy of meaning—and the sharp distinction between aesthetic and other experience—do not constitute a single position in the history of aesthetics. But those theories are in any event distinguishable as a group from a second one for which the significance of art is social, cognitive, and connected through the transformations of art to the causal grounds of a historical and materialist setting. Marxist aesthetics is not unique in stressing the latter elements, but its emphasis on the social context as integral to the creation and understanding of art—through the role of the material medium, the lived worlds of creators and audiences, the relationship between history outside and inside art—offers valuable points of entry for both analyzing and experiencing art and the aesthetic. For aesthetic theories that acknowledge the importance of such considerations, the Marxist position would be obviously relevant; even for theories that dispute that importance, Marxist aesthetics provides a useful framework for addressing the disagreement itself.

BIBLIOGRAPHY

Alpers, Svetlana. *Rembrandt's Enterprise: The Studio and the Market.* Chicago, 1988.

Althusser, Louis. *For Marx.* Translated by Ben Brewster. New York, 1969.

Arvon, Henri. *Marxist Esthetics.* Translated by Helen R. Lane. Ithaca, N.Y., 1973.

Baxandall, Lee. *Marxism and Aesthetics: A Selected Annotated Bibliography.* New York, 1968.

Baxandall, Lee, and Stefan Morawski, eds. *Marx and Engels on Literature and Art.* Saint Louis, 1973.

Baxandall, Michael. *Patterns of Intention: On the Historical Explanation of Pictures.* New Haven, 1985.

Berger, John. *About Looking.* New York, 1980.

Bourdieu, Pierre. *Distinction: A Social Critique of the Judgement of Taste.* Translated by Richard Nice. Cambridge, Mass., 1984.

Dickie, George. *Art and the Aesthetic: An Institutional Analysis.* Ithaca, N.Y., 1974.

Eagleton, Terry. *Criticism and Ideology.* London, 1976.

Eagleton, Terry. *The Ideology of the Aesthetic.* Oxford and Cambridge, Mass., 1990.

Frow, John. *Marxism and Literary History.* Cambridge, Mass., 1986.

Gadamer, Hans-Georg. *Truth and Method.* 2d rev. ed. Translation revised by Joel Weinsheimer and Donald G. Marshall. New York, 1989.

Hauser, Arnold. *The Philosophy of Art History.* New York, 1959.

Iser, Wolfgang. *The Act of Reading: A Theory of Aesthetic Response.* Baltimore, 1978.

Jameson, Fredric. *Marxism and Form: Twentieth-Century Dialectical Theories of Literature.* Princeton, N.J., 1971.

Lang, Berel, and Forrest Williams, eds. *Marxism and Art: Writings in Aesthetics and Criticism.* New York, 1972.

Lenin, V. I. "Party Organization and Party Literature." In *Collected Works*, vol. 10. New York, 1975.

Lukács, Georg (György). *Studies in European Realism.* Translated by Edith Bone. New York, 1964.

Macherey, Pierre. *A Theory of Literary Production.* Translated by Geoffrey Wall. London and Boston, 1978.

Mao Tse-tung. *Five Documents on Literature and Art.* Peking, 1967.

Marx, Karl. *Economic and Philosophic Manuscripts.* Edited by Dirk J. Struik, translated by Martin Milligan. New York, 1964.

Nelson, Cary, and Lawrence Grossberg, eds. *Marxism and the Interpretation of Culture.* Urbana, Ill., 1988.

Nochlin, Linda. *Women, Art, and Power and Other Essays.* New York, 1988.

Plekhanov, Georgy. *Art and Social Life.* Edited by Andrew Rothstein London, 1953.

Raphael, Max. *The Demands of Art.* Translated by Norbert Guterman. Princeton, N.J., 1968.

Solomon, Maynard, ed. *Marxism and Art: Essays Classic and Contemporary.* New York, 1973.

Spivak, Gayatri Chakravorty. *In Other Worlds: Essays in Cultural Politics.* New York and London, 1987.

Trotsky, Leon. *Literature and Revolution.* Translated by Rose Strunsky. Reprint, Ann Arbor, 1960.

Veeser, H. Aram, ed. *The New Historicism.* New York and London, 1989.

Weimann, Robert. *Structure and Society in Literary History.* Charlottesville, Va., 1976.

BEREL LANG

Marxism and Materialism

The question of a "materialist aesthetics," as evidenced in the words themselves, implies some foregrounding state of tension or variance with an "idealist aesthetics." This in turn points to a prior embeddedness of the aesthetic question itself within the larger, governing framework of a theory of knowledge. Thus an idealist aesthetics conceives art, like knowledge, to be autonomous in relation to a (putative) world of material realities, whereas a materialist aesthetics holds art to be inseparable from this world. At this level of generality, one might trace a materialist aesthetics as far back as Aristotle's *Poetics* and its implicit break from Platonic idealism. Scanning down the checklist of canonical Western philosophy, the aesthetic theories of Enlightenment thinkers such as Denis Diderot or David Hume might also be considered to take up something like a materialist position, although here any distinction between the material and the empirical effectively disappears.

In contemporary practice and parlance, however, the question of a materialist aesthetics is rarely raised, except in reference to historical and dialectical materialism, that is, to Marxism. It is to materialist aesthetics in this currently accepted sense that the following remarks are directed.

The question of the aesthetic for Karl Marx and Friedrich Engels was superordinately a question of its specific form of truth. Was the truth of art something strictly internal to the aesthetic sphere, or did it, on the contrary, reside in its relationship to an independent, material reality? Reacting, in particular, against the aesthetic doctrines of Friedrich von Schiller, Marx and Engels took the latter position. But in what, then, did this relation to material (i.e., social and historical) reality consist? Clearly, in its imitation, or conscious representation, as Aristotle had long before stipulated.

> A spider conducts operations that resemble those of a weaver, and a bee puts to shame many an architect in the construction of her cells. But what distinguishes the worst architect from the best of bees is this, that the architect raises his structure in imagination before he erects it in reality. (Marx and Engels, 1973)

Insofar, however, as this material object of artistic representation had come to coincide with the alienated and debased relations of bourgeois society, the materialist demand for aesthetic truth implied the demand for aesthetic negativity as well, the demand for a "glimpse" of what lay beyond, or trapped within, the fallen world of the present. Here the Aristotelian aesthetic fell short, in ways that the German idealist tradition—"standing on its head"—had been the first to seek systematically to redress.

Given the background of the truth question, an important current within materialist aesthetics concerns itself primarily with the practice of art as part of the material world of labor and production. If human labor itself has become alienated from the human laborer, how, materialistically speaking, can the art of such an alienated existence be anything but a pale shadow of the truly and fully human creative process it once was (under conditions of primitive communal being), and may yet again become (in a future classless society)? So conceived, art or aesthetic practice counts as a process whereby a human being, unlike an animal that "forms things in accordance with the standard and the need of the species to which it belongs," "produce[s] in accordance with the standard of every species and knows how to apply everywhere the inherent standard to the object." In its full self-realization, such a "species being" thus "forms things in accordance with the laws of beauty," according to Marx in his *Economic and Philosophic Manuscripts* (Marx and Engels, 1973).

Perhaps the most brilliant, if highly idiosyncratic, development of a materialist aesthetics in this sense we owe to the British Marxist Christopher Caudwell, who, in *Studies and Further Studies in a Dying Culture,* conceived beauty as arising from "the social ordering of affective elements in social things." This "social ordering" was itself inseparable from the labor process, which Caudwell characterized as not only a community of action and perception but a "community of desire." Caudwell's aesthetics appear even more remarkable when one considers that—like William Morris, in some ways his precursor—he wrote with no knowledge at all of the *Economic and Philosophic Manuscripts.* Caudwell had perhaps read Georgy Plekhanov, who, in works such as *The Role of the Individual in History* and *Art and Social Life,* had attempted a "materialist" and rigidly determinist explanation for such "aesthetic" phenomena as talent and "art for art's sake." But where Plekhanov's "materialism" went no further than a "Marxist" sociology of art, Caudwell's (in ways analogous to the otherwise utterly distinct approach of the early aesthetic writings of Herbert Marcuse) not only examined and denounced the crippling effects of class division and alienation on the aesthetic faculty, but traced both this faculty and its "social conditions" to a common source in the most elemental human and social processes.

At bottom, the radical, materialist humanism of Marx's *Economic and Philosophic Manuscripts* as well as of work such as Caudwell's treats the question of artistic truth as inseparable from the question of its roots in "species being." But the former question nevertheless lies at the center of what has been a far more developed and polemical tradition in materialist aesthetics, if only because it bears much more immediately on the social and political criticism of artistic works themselves. The truth of art in relation to its material conditions may itself be of fundamental, material importance to concrete, emancipatory practice. So it is that such a materialist aesthetic, as applied to literature, becomes a demand for realism—"socialist" insofar as "by conscientiously describing the real mutual relations . . . [it] instills doubt as to the eternal character of the existing order" (Marx and Engels, 1973). V. I. Lenin, in his fragmentary, but brilliantly insightful, writings on Leo Tolstoy, outlined what such a realism meant in the context of the Russian revolutionary experience—a lesson effectively ignored, if apotheosized, in subsequent Soviet doctrines of Socialist Realism. But it is in the aesthetic theory of the Marxist philosopher György Lukács that this strand within orthodox Marxism receives its great and systematic elaboration, leading to a theory of the aesthetic as a special mode of cognition within the total process of reflection, in consciousness, of a preconscious, material realm of being. "The effect of art," according to Lukács, "results from the fact that the work [of art] by its very nature offers a truer, more complete, more vivid and more dynamic reflection of reality than the receptant otherwise possesses" (Lukács, 1971). Such a materialist aesthetics became linked, in Lukács's thinking, to a defense of the "classics" of literary realism—above all, nineteenth-century European realists on the order of Honoré de Balzac and Tolstoy and twentieth-century Social Realists on the order of Maxim Gorky.

Under the influence of modernist and avant-garde artistic practice, however, this epistemological approach is displaced by an aesthetic that declares itself "materialist," not because it claims for art and literature the status of a particular form of reflectively true, or "concrete" consciousness, but rather by virtue of the supposed power of art to intervene directly on the level of the practical and behavioral. Art's claim to the "material" thus implicitly postulates an aesthetic act pure and simple, as distinct from an aesthetic act of consciousness. A truly revolutionary work of art would not simply enter the field of general consciousness as a special instance of knowledge, but would work more directly, and perhaps unconsciously, to challenge, to subvert, or to alter conscious existence itself on the level of praxis. The governing conceptual framework or "problematic" within which a materialist aesthetics is posited and debated thus shifts, in effect, from that of the theory of knowledge to something more akin to a theory of agency in an ethico-political sense. In this spirit, aesthetics as otherwise divergent as Surrealism ("an unconscious, immediate action of the internal on the external"; Breton, 1989) and Brechtian epic theater (a theater that, instead of "provid[ing]" the spectator with "sensations . . . forces him to take decisions"; Brecht, 1964) center on the artistic process of producing an "effect" on the artistic public—a "shock" or an "estrangement"—that will somehow mobilize the receptant into action for social or cultural change. As elaborated by Walter Benjamin, this ethically framed materialist aesthetic requires of the artist that her "work will never be merely work on products but always, at the same time, on the means of production" (Benjamin, 1978). Technique as such, or the "organizing function" of a work of art, will principally determine whether the materialist demands of this aesthetic can be met. "The best political tendency is wrong if it does not demonstrate the attitude with which it is to be followed" (Benjamin). In the wake of the "linguistic turn" introduced by structuralist linguistics and semiotics, this materialism of "effects" and "attitudes" even manages to lodge itself entirely within the scope of language and signification. Witness, for example, Julia Kristeva's characterization of "signifying practice" (a.k.a. "poetic language") as radically "materialist" by virtue of its capacity to marshal the transgressive power of the "heterogeneous" (i.e., the noncodifiable) against established linguistic codes or sign systems (Kristeva, 1975). In its feminist and psychoanalytic inflection, what was at first a strictly semiotic conception of heterogeneity is then linked to theories of a radical, antipatriarchal agency. In Kristeva's case, the "matter" of signs outside or previous to the "symbolic" order of the sign system is identified with the pre-Oedipal female body as such. The material, aesthetically speaking, merges with the maternal.

Theodor W. Adorno's aesthetic philosophy represents what is probably the most systematic and self-conscious expression of this trend—but is also the announcement of its decline. It is the work of art alone, unbound to either artist or receptant, that embodies what is now perhaps no more than the possibility of an emancipatory agency. Here, however, the cognitive frame reappears, if only in the ironic sense that Adorno views the very process of rational cognition with suspicion, reason itself having been, as he and Max Horkheimer were to claim, "instrumentalized" by totalitarian late capitalism. With Adorno, the radically pre- or even transcognitive attribute of the work of art becomes a site for a paradoxical kind of "knowledge" that is neither consciously rational nor an irrational act of pure intuition. "Total unfreedom" can be recognized, but not represented. But this is still, at least by its own account of itself, a materialist aesthetic, if only because the realm of the "ideal" has fallen. If all ideals have become false, the work of art, by refusing such ideals, becomes itself a novel instance of the material, but one in which the true ideal can "hibernate." "Art draws its power of resistance from the fact that the realization of materialism would also be the abolition of mate-

rialism, that is, of the domination of material interests. Weak as it may be, art anticipates a spirit that would step forth at that point" (Adorno, 1987).

More recently, the trend within materialist approaches to art and literature has been to devolve a species of "materialism" that is, at best, agnostic concerning the pertinence of aesthetics as such to the aims of radical theory and practice. This trend corresponds roughly to what we now often consent to call postmodernism in the arts and literature, as well as to the philosophical ascendancy of poststructuralism. Within "Western" Marxist discourse, its roots undoubtedly lie in Louis Althusser, who, in a kind of unintended parody of classical Marxist aesthetics, argued that art was not directly reducible to ideology insofar as it really did make it possible to "'see' . . . something which alludes to reality" (Althusser, 1971). But this "something" turns out not to be the truth of this reality, but only that of its ideology per se, an ideology "identical with the 'lived' experience of human existence itself." Works of art "make us 'perceive' (but not know) in some sense from the inside, by an internal distance, the very ideology in which they are held"). The ultimate effect of Althusser's theoretical intervention, however, has been to pave the way for the elimination of the aesthetic altogether as a materialist category, since, given the purportedly ideological saturation of "lived" experience as such, the theory of the aesthetic as a miraculously transparent wrinkle within ideology is reduced to an effectively theological principle that even Althusser's former disciples have found it difficult to credit.

The least one can say is that—post-Althusser—contemporary Western Marxists seem to take less and less interest in aesthetics, unless it is, following Terry Eagleton in *The Ideology of the Aesthetic*, to reduce the aesthetic question itself to one of bourgeois hegemonic and ideological provenance: "The aesthetic is . . . no more than a name for the political unconscious: it is simply the way social harmony registers itself on our senses, imprints itself on our sensibilities" (Eagleton, 1990). On the whole, the categories of judgment and critique that once served—qua "materialism"—to distinguish art from what was simply "culture" are set aside. The outwardly dominant ethicopolitical framework of aesthetic vanguardism remains in place, but aesthetic categories have seemingly been rendered irrelevant within it. "Cultural studies" takes the stage. So, for example, in the thinking of John Fiske, "high culture" maintains a "distance between the art object and reader/spectator," one that "devalues socially and historically specific reading practices in favor of a transcendent appreciation or aesthetic sensibility with claims to universality" (Fiske, p. 154). "Distance" here implies a strict separation of the "aesthetic" and the "socially and historically specific"—of art and the "material." The "culture of the people," however, "denies categorical boundaries [distances] between art and life: popular art is part of the every day, not distanced from it." This sounds unobjectionable enough, until it becomes apparent that every trace of negativity and alienated existence has been summarily erased from this "every day." With an inadvertent irony, one of the most basic tenets of Marxian, materialist aesthetics is reaffirmed even as it is blithely set aside: welcomed merely for what it *is* in the everyday popular experience of capitalism, the material abjures all need for the aesthetic.

As a final observation: it is noteworthy how, in the overall tendency within materialist aesthetics to disregard questions of artistic truth in preference for the question of art as direct, material agent, the emphasis placed on dialectics within the process of aesthetic theorization has steadily waned. Thus, for example, the relationship of art to the social totality—central to Lukácsian aesthetics—seems to be all but forgotten by contemporary materialists. (Fredric Jameson, in his guise as a latter-day Adornian, may be one of the few significant exceptions here.) This leads one to speculate whether, for all its cautionary virtues in combating the escapist proclivities of a purely contemplative, aestheticist ideal, the "materialism" of a left-oriented aesthetic avant-garde has not itself progressively succumbed to the reifying and fragmenting pull of late capitalist society and culture.

[*See also* Adorno; Benjamin; Brecht; Ideology; Kristeva; Lukács; *and* Marcuse.]

BIBLIOGRAPHY

Adorno, Theodor W. *Aesthetic Theory.* Edited by Gretel Adorno and Rolf Tiedemann, translated by Robert Hullot-Kentor. Minneapolis, 1997.
Althusser, Louis. "Letter on Art in Reply to André Daspre." In *Lenin and Philosophy and Other Essays,* translated by Ben Brewster, pp. 221–227. New York, 1971.
Benjamin, Walter. "The Author as Producer." In *Reflections: Essays, Aphorisms, Autobiographical Writings,* edited by Peter Demetz, translated by Edmund Jephcott, pp. 220–238. New York, 1978.
Brecht, Bertolt. *Brecht on Theatre: The Development of an Aesthetic.* Edited and translated by John Willett. New York, 1964.
Breton, André. "The Poet's Function." From *Les vases communicants.* In Maurice Nadeau, *The History of Surrealism,* pp. 304–305. New York, 1965; reprint, Cambridge, Mass., 1989.
Caudwell, Christopher. "Beauty: A Study in Bourgeois Aesthetics." In *Studies and Further Studies in a Dying Culture,* 2 vols. in 1, pp. 77–115. New York, 1971.
Eagleton, Terry. *The Ideology of the Aesthetic.* Oxford and Cambridge, Mass., 1990.
Fiske, John. "Cultural Studies and the Culture of Everyday Life." In *Cultural Studies,* edited by Lawrence Grossberg et al. New York, 1992.
Jameson, Fredric. *Marxism and Form: Twentieth-Century Dialectical Theories of Literature.* Princeton, N.J., 1971.
Kristeva, Julia. "The System and the Speaking Subject." In *The Tell-Tale Sign: A Survey of Semiotics,* edited by Thomas A. Sebeok, pp. 47–55. Lisse, Netherlands, 1975.
Larsen, Neil. *Modernism and Hegemony: A Materialist Critique of Aesthetic Agencies.* Minneapolis, 1990.
Lukács, Georg (György). "Art and Objective Truth." In *Writer and Critic and Other Essays,* translated by Arthur D. Kahn, pp. 25–60. New York, 1971.
Lukács, Georg (György). *Ästhetik I: Der Eigenart des Ästhetischen.* Neuwied, 1963.
Marx, Karl, and Friedrich Engels. *Marx and Engels on Literature and Art.* Edited by Lee Baxandall and Stefan Morawski. New York, 1973.
Solomon, Maynard, ed., *Marxism and Art: Essays Classic and Contemporary.* New York, 1973; reprint, Detroit, 1979. See for extensive bibliography.

NEIL LARSEN

MATHEMATICS AND AESTHETICS. The history of mathematics and science is indissociable from the history of their aesthetics. In this history, mathematics and its aesthetics have the primary role, for several reasons. First, along with astronomy, mathematics appears to be the oldest form of what we now understand as scientific inquiry (keeping in mind historical changes, evolutions and revolutions, in the nature of what we now designate as scientific inquiry). Second, mathematics has been indispensable to other sciences and, as such, inevitably affected their aesthetics. Third, most attempts to theorize aesthetic experience and practice, such as art, in philosophy and elsewhere, and (a more complex claim) aesthetic experience and practice themselves are deeply, if sometimes indirectly, connected to mathematics and its aesthetics. As a result, both mathematics and the aesthetics of mathematics also had a major importance in the history of the discipline of aesthetics, whether one traces this history, in more rigorous historical terms, to Immanuel Kant and his predecessors (with whom the term *aesthetics* originates) or, in more general conceptual terms, to Plato and his predecessors. Beyond its role in mathematics itself, then, the aesthetics of mathematics (of its objects, logical structures, and so forth) may be seen as a primary aesthetic model in science, philosophy, and the arts. The mathematically beautiful has been a primary model of the beautiful, just as mathematical rigor has been a primary model of analytic rigor in science, philosophy, and other disciplines. Or, since both beauty and rigor do have their nonmathematical genealogies and models, it would be more precise to say that aesthetic concepts have often been conceived in terms of mathematical models, which may themselves conform to or derive from models originating elsewhere. Indeed, the most fundamental feature of aesthetics in and of mathematics (or science) may well be the reciprocity of these connections, and of the connections between the aesthetics in mathematics, which may come from elsewhere, and the aesthetics of mathematics, which extends elsewhere and gives the latter its significance in Western aesthetics and culture. By virtue of this reciprocity, the aesthetics in and of mathematics and science acquires a complex constitution, which requires and has received a critical analysis—conceptual, historical, and political—as rigorous and profound as philosophy or other disciplines are able to offer.

For the pre-Socratics—in particular, Thales (who is sometimes seen as the first geometer), and Pythagoras and the Pythagoreans—and then for Plato and the Platonist tradition, mathematical objects and ideas were primary examples and often fundamental archetypes of the beautiful. From Pythagoras and before, to Johannes Kepler and beyond, the music of the spheres was literally a conjunction or even a harmony of its own of music and the sphere. It was also a conjunction (sometimes a harmony, sometimes a conflict) of arithmetic and geometric harmonies, a conjunction crucial for the Greek and the subsequent European mathematics, which eventually supplemented it by algebra and analysis. The principle itself of harmony—in particular, that between the parts and the whole, and among the parts within a whole, and sometimes without a single ambient whole—may well be the single most significant aesthetic principle in the history of mathematics and science. This principle is sometimes accompanied by a closely related, but not identical, principle of proportion. Harmony and proportion can also be conceived without (the ambient) wholeness, unity, or oneness. Although related, and sometimes used interchangeably, the concepts of wholeness, unity, and oneness are different, and each has a complex constitution of its own. Accordingly, they can serve and have served to define different aesthetic configurations in mathematics, or elsewhere.

A graphic example of the principle of harmony between the parts and the whole is offered by a mathematical argument that establishes the connections between the properties of integer numbers and the geometric problem of dividing a circle into equal parts, with which Werner Heisenberg opens, by way of Leopold Kronecker, his reflections on "the meaning of the beauty in exact sciences" in *Across the Frontiers*. (One of Heisenberg's books is titled, revealingly, *The Part and the Whole* [*Der Teil und das Ganze*].) It is not necessary to consider this argument itself in order to make the main aesthetic point, namely, that the principle of harmony between the parts and the whole operates here on two levels, in turn mutually reflecting each other. The first level is that of the geometric object under consideration, the circle, and its partitioning. Fittingly (and perhaps not altogether coincidentally), the circle is also the symbol of the highest perfection or/as of eternity—"a great *Ring* of pure and endless light," in Henry Vaughan's famous description. The second level is that of the structure of interconnections, defined by the axioms of arithmetics and geometry as the whole and the mathematical properties of numbers and geometric constructions as the parts. In the process, an aesthetic configuration also becomes, and emerges from, a powerful analytic tool. This joint functioning of aesthetics and reason is often traced to Thales, who (it is claimed) makes harmony between the parts and the whole a grounding principle of his mathematics and philosophy. The principle of harmony of the parts and the whole, on the one

hand, and the conjunction of aesthetics and reason, on the other, have shaped the history of mathematical inquiry at various levels of its operation or (beginning at least with Euclid) systematization. Of course, throughout this history these elements of mathematical inquiry and their own conjunctions have functioned in a variety of ways and in a variety of interactions between and among them. One finds this various and varied functioning even in specific cases, for example and in particular, in Euclid's *Elements*.

From very early on, then, mathematics involves two defining types of aesthetic configurations and the interactions between them. The first is the beauty of particular mathematical objects. The second is the beauty of theorems and, then, of the mathematical system(s) involved, extending all the way to mathematics itself as a whole and connecting its various areas or fields, such as geometry and arithmetic. The example considered above offers a reflective configuration of precisely that type: the structure of a given object, here the circle, becomes an embodiment or reflection of the structure of the system, the plane geometry, to which that object belongs. This example also connects geometry and arithmetic (and in fact, certainly in Kronecker's analysis, algebra as well). The overall configuration itself thus defined has a very long history, and it appears to accompany and even define all known origins or genealogies of mathematical inquiry. At least in this sense, mathematics appears always to have been an aesthetic project, or conceivably to have emerged from a protomathematical project that was in part aesthetic, as both (although differently) Kant's introduction to the *Critique of Judgment* and Edmund Husserl's "The Origin of Geometry" may suggest.

From early on, too, mathematical aesthetic principles showed their influence and impact elsewhere, although, once again, such connections and influences have always been reciprocal. Most obviously, Plato's conception of the beautiful (and even of the good) was greatly indebted to these principles and to their functioning in both objects and methods of Greek mathematics. In modern times, Kepler's astronomy and (differently) Galileo Galilei's astronomy and physics replayed the configuration delineated above in all of its aspects. By doing so they offered the first modern examples of connecting the rigor of science to mathematics (indeed, of making science mathematical) and grounding the aesthetics of science in the aesthetics of mathematics. This combined configuration has served as a central, if not *the* central, theoretical and aesthetic paradigm for modern mathematics and science ever since, especially in the wake of Sir Isaac Newton's work and his version of scientific project. In actuality, this configuration is still richer, since it also includes the beauty (elegance, compactness, richness of potential implications, and so forth) of an argument or a proof—for example, the proof that would proceed by way of or would itself establish connections between geometric and arithmetic or algebraic objects, logical structures, or different areas of inquiry. In the process, aesthetics and rigor often emerge as linked, and both can be shown to be further connected to the epistemological and ontological questions concerning mathematical objects, such as numbers or geometric forms, or of course physical objects and concepts, and (or in) their mathematical idealization.

Aristotle is rarely seen as a particularly mathematical philosopher, not altogether justly, since there is much mathematics and much on mathematics in his works. Instead, he is often seen, justly, as one of the founders of nonmathematical science. The *Poetics,* however, arguably the first systematic aesthetic treatise or what we would so call now, opens with a discussion of musical, and hence also numerical, harmony. Later on in the book, he defines the beautiful *(to kalon)* in terms of both harmony between the whole and the parts, and proportion. Finally, Aristotle considers (or "constructs") tragedy itself on the model of harmony between the whole and the parts, making this and other mathematical or quasi-mathematical aesthetic principles the basis for a rigorous philosophical analytics. The credit here may well belong to the tragedians themselves, who might be seen as having enacted these types of interactions in their works. Friedrich Nietzsche, well aware of Aristotle's strategy, offered a very different—Dionysian, he called it—aesthetics of the Greek tragedy, and by implication a different aesthetics in general, which can be and has been applied to mathematics as well, since at least the *practice* of mathematics has Dionysian dimensions. Mathematics can be and has been modeled on tragedy no less than tragedy on mathematics. This mutual modeling can proceed either on the principle of mathematical (or logical) harmony, as in (more) Aristotelian interpretations, or on irrationality and chaos, as in (more) Nietzschean interpretations, and on the beauty and the *mathematical* beauty of both.

The concept of mathematical irrationality was, of course, familiar to Greek mathematics. One of its great discoveries (often attributed to Theaetetus, Socrates' younger contemporary and pupil) was that the diagonal of the square is incommensurable with the side and is thus not a rational number. The diagonal was a vestige or trace of chaos in the order and harmony of mathematics. *Chaos* is used here more in the sense of something that cannot be expressed, the ineffable, an *areton*, rather than that of a disordered, chaotic multiplicity. The topic is invoked on several important occasions by both Plato and Aristotle. In *Greater Hippias,* Socrates brings up arithmetics and specifically irrational numbers in his discussion of the category of the beautiful as possibly mixed in this sense—that is, as a mixture of the rational and the irrational. The harmonies of mathematics were, at all levels, a complex mixture of order and chaos (now in both senses), harmony and dissonance, rationality and irrationality, from the outset of its history. Such was certainly the case in both Plato and Plotinus, whose "forms" entail the traces of chaos or, more radically,

of that which is neither order nor chaos. As such, they also suggest that we may not in truth be able to conceive of either, as twentieth-century mathematics and science, especially quantum physics, have revealed so poignantly. Deriving in part from Parmenides and Plato, Plotinus's concept of the beautiful as the translucence of the eternal splendor of the One through the material world has been one of the great defining principles of classical aesthetics. It may not be possible, however, to conceive of such a unity without it carrying within itself not only the indelible traces of division (Plotinus does not refer to the parts), disharmony, and chaos (or that which is neither order nor chaos), but also of the material contamination, and even material constitution, of the ideal. Although it is often seen as and claimed to be the most ordered and the most ideal and in part for that reason also (this is not quite the same as being ideal) the most dematerialized of sciences, mathematics, too, carries within itself the ghost—and the aesthetics—of chaos and materiality. Both mathematics and art, such as music or/as tragedy, are capable of offering the ideas of order and chaos and an aesthetics based on both, or on the complex interplay of and "proportion" of both, with, in Francis Bacon's words, some strangeness in it. Following and intermixing both Plotinus's and Nietzsche's philosophy and/as aesthetics, James Joyce calls this mixture of strangeness and proportion, of chaos and cosmos, "chaosmos."

Aristotelian science is usually seen as nonmathematical because it is based on classification rather than measurement and its mathematization, a point stressed by Alfred North Whitehead in *Science and the Modern World.* The mathematical project of science in the modern sense emerges, in its various, including aesthetic, aspects, with Kepler, Galileo, and Newton, and the mathematical science developed in the wake of their work. Classification, however, may be seen as an embodiment of the principle of harmony between the parts and the whole, or multileveled harmonies between the classes of the parts and different partitions of the whole—or of genus and species, another defining principle of Aristotle's philosophy. Throughout their history and indeed what may called their prehistory (for example, in Babylonian and Chinese mathematics and astronomy), mathematical or mathematized sciences are based both on the mathematization of experimental data and the classification of these data. Tycho Brahe's data, for example, provided the basis for Kepler's laws and his "harmony of the world," and certainly Babylonian and Chinese astronomy must be seen as both classificatory and mathematical. It would, in fact, be difficult to claim that Aristotle was not aware of various, including aesthetic, connections between classification and mathematics. Classification has, of course, played a crucial role in mathematics itself, since collecting various numerical data has been and continues to be an important part of mathematics. The main point here is that classificatory science and its aesthetics are in part based on and embody an aesthetic and (at the very least in this sense) mathematically aesthetic principle, that of the relationship between the parts and the whole.

The role of both mathematics itself (as a model) and its aesthetics has been just as significant in modern as in ancient philosophy, beginning with major figures of precritical (i.e., pre-Kantian) philosophy—René Descartes, Blaise Pascal, Gottfried Wilhelm Leibniz, and Baruch Spinoza. The first three were, of course, also mathematicians, and their mathematics and mathematical writings would require a separate consideration in this context. Spinoza's *Ethics* famously models itself on mathematical (specifically Euclidean) discourse, and this strategy can be shown to have and to connect both logical and aesthetic dimensions.

Arguably the most significant for the subsequent intellectual history, however, was Kant's aesthetics, as developed in the *Critique of Judgment*. This aesthetics is defined in terms of feelings of pleasure *(Lust)* and displeasure *(Unlust)* independent of concepts, and this definition is, among other things, designed to account for the conditions of possibility of beautiful objects. Such objects please universally and as such may, in all rigor, not be seen as mathematical. It may be argued, however, that in effect, following a long tradition (perhaps especially Plotinus), Kant approaches the beautiful in part through a certain model of geometric or quasi-geometric play *(Spiel)*, insofar as it is "form" and "delineation" that are most fundamental to his definition of the beautiful and his concept of taste (as opposed to, for example, colors, equally lacking in both purity and universality). It is the purity and universality of this quasi-geometric play (and of the objects that it produces) that make the experience of the beautiful universal and universally pleasing. It can be further shown that Kant's conception becomes a complex rendition of the principle of harmony, but also extends it and anticipates subsequent ideas in psychology and cognitive science, and their own connections to mathematics and its aesthetics. It is a complex question whether and to what degree "beautiful" mathematical objects as such (that is, objects that would be considered beautiful in mathematics itself) would satisfy Kant's requirements for the beautiful, since our pleasure in experiencing such objects may not be independent of (here mathematical) concepts— an independence that defines *aesthetic* pleasure in Kant. The aesthetics in and of mathematics is closer to Kant's economy of the beautiful arts, which involves conceptual along with aesthetic play. Mathematical objects are sometimes seen as beautiful (or sublime) in a more strictly Kantian sense; that is, while emerging within mathematics, they are experienced aesthetically, outside their mathematical significance. Conversely, along the lines of Kant's general thinking concerning the beautiful in the *Critique*, the beautiful may be seen as mathematical without being mathematics. To paraphrase John Keats, however, "truth is mathematical

beauty, beauty mathematical truth," has been a far more common principle of mathematical aesthetics. [*See* Kant.]

Kant's analytics of the sublime, too, involves mathematical concepts and introduces the concept of the mathematically sublime emerging in the experience of mathematical infinitude. The concept of infinity has played an especially, perhaps uniquely, complex role both in the epistemology and the aesthetics of mathematics. This complexity is reflected in Kant's considerations of the mathematical sublime and its aesthetics (in Kant's sense). In contrast to the experience of the beautiful, the experience of the mathematical sublime has no object (no sublime does in Kant). Kant's second example of the sublime, the dynamically sublime of nature, may in turn be seen as based on quasi-geometric concepts, closer to those of modern-day mathematics, for example, chaos theory. Even more significantly, certain mathematical or quasi-mathematical objects and theories underlie Kant's general conceptuality of the sublime. Conversely or, again, reciprocally, the aesthetics of the sublime, either proceeding closer to Kant or others (for example, Friedrich von Schiller and G. W. F. Hegel), has its place in mathematics and is applied both to certain types of mathematical objects and mathematics itself, now seen (along more Nietzschean lines considered earlier), as unstructured or chaotic, or inaccessible, including infinite. The aesthetics of sublime is also key for understanding the complex relationships (both proximities and differences) between the aesthetics of mathematics or mathematics itself and Hegel's *Aesthetics,* in part in comparison with the role of mathematics and its aesthetics in the *Critique of Judgment* or elsewhere in Kant. In addition, the sublime is a crucial juncture in the history of the relationships between mathematical aesthetics and theology. This history, too, extends from Kepler (or, again, the pre-Socratics, especially the Pythagoreans) to our own time, and includes both Kant and Hegel, or Pascal and Leibniz, whose thought is especially significant in this context, as well as many others figures mentioned here. [*See* Sublime.]

The concept of harmony of the parts and the whole was one of the earliest junctures of mathematics and aesthetics. Many other concepts defining aesthetic considerations in mathematics and science, such as innovation or economy, acquire their aesthetic determination and definition when they are related to this principle of harmony. An innovation is often seen as beautiful when it either demonstrates or establishes connections, or more harmonious connections, within a certain (perhaps implicit) whole, or when it extends a whole or creates a new whole and a new harmony of connections. The latter may be attempted either by creating a new mathematical object, or by extending a given theory or field, or by connecting several theories or fields within a whole, or in a more modern (or postmodern) fashion without assuming an ambient whole or (which is, again, not the same) unity or oneness. The aesthetic applications of various parsimony principles (such as Occam's razor), too, usually function so as to maintain an economy of harmonization either for a given argument or for a given field.

Many concepts or principles associated with the beautiful in mathematics (including harmony and proportion) can also be related to the general concept of symmetry, understood in its most general sense as invariance under transformations. The overall relationships between symmetry and beauty are complex and sometimes ambiguous even in mathematics, let alone in general. Considerations of symmetry are, however, fundamental to both aesthetics and mathematics (or physics and other sciences), and to the interconnections between them. In mathematics, the idea of symmetry finds its most powerful manifestations or indeed definitions in group theory, introduced by Evariste Galois in the early nineteenth century, and, then, in representation theory (the objects of both are transformations and their structures). In addition, group theory profoundly connects algebra (in considering the relation between transformations) and geometry (for example, that of the geometric figures manifesting such symmetries, remaining the same under transformations), and their respective aesthetics. Here, too, then, one of the most aesthetic concepts of mathematics, symmetry becomes one of its most powerful analytic tools, and a mathematical principle—the principle of symmetry—and the objects embodying it define an aesthetic (or epistemological) model. The principle of symmetry has also been crucial to most figures whose work defines modern physics, which is profoundly linked to group theory. Mathematically and philosophically, quantum physics is often seen as and functions as a symmetry theory, and its aesthetics is defined accordingly, and many other theories of modern physics, including relativity, can be formulated in these terms as well. This approach can be seen as an example of the implementation of earlier ideas of Felix Klein and others, which had already found powerful applications in mathematics itself, as in the work of Klein himself, or such figures as Henri Poincaré, David Hilbert, Hermann Weyl, and Emmy Noether, especially in her famous theorem linking physical conservation laws to the principles of symmetry. More recently, in part inspired by these earlier developments, Robert Langlands's program in representation theory (the latter term, again, refers to a mathematical theory) is arguably the most general and the deepest application of the principle of symmetry in modern mathematics. It connects many areas of mathematics within a complex network by means of several concepts or methods derived from and extending the symmetry principle.

At the same time, however, Langlands's program and other developments just mentioned (in particular, quantum physics) are also among the areas where the classical aesthetics and epistemology of mathematics and science encounter their limit and, while retaining their significance, open the space to a different form of epistemology and aesthetics. The main reason for this change is that such theories make mathematical (or perhaps all) descriptions irreducibly oblique, irreducibly metaphorical, rather than characterizing mathematical objects at issue themselves, which appears no longer possible. By so doing, these theories also suggest a very complex, multileveled aesthetics, to be considered in more detail below. The history of the aesthetics in mathematics (or science) has, however, always been the history of its complexity and the complexity of the economy in which this aesthetics functions. Certainly, the aesthetics in mathematics (or science), cannot be restricted to the aesthetics of mathematics (or science). First of all, both have also depended on aesthetic practices and theories elsewhere. One can, for example, argue, as Gilles Deleuze does, for the interdependence of Leibniz's philosophy and mathematics, and their aesthetics, and the aesthetics of the Baroque, or for the interdependence of preceding, more classical, art and architecture and the classical mathematical aesthetics. Multiple examples of that type can be found throughout history, from the interconnections between musical and mathematical harmonies in the pre-Socratics, as discussed earlier, to the impact of Cubism or Joyce on the epistemology and aesthetics of quantum physics.

One must also consider such more or less nonmathematical aesthetic dimensions of mathematics as rhetorical presentation of argument, even writing style, or usage of diagrams and other visual dimensions of presentation. These subjects have become explicit (and pointed) subjects of scholarly and philosophical analysis only relatively recently, especially during the last two decades. The questions themselves, however, of the relationships between mathematical and philosophical rhetoric, argumentation, and so forth, and the aesthetic aspects of these questions, have been a major concern throughout the history of philosophy. In modern times, one can think in particular of Descartes's and then Pascal's commentaries on these issues and of their discursive practices from this perspective, or, again, of Spinoza's *Ethics* and its mathematical discursive models, from Euclid onward. In the nineteenth century, extraordinarily profound reflections on these issues were offered by Galois, whom we have already encountered as the discoverer of group theory and who is considered one of the greatest mathematical geniuses who ever lived (even though and perhaps because he was killed in a duel at the age of twenty-one).

One can also attempt to formalize in one degree or another mathematical (or, indeed, philosophical) argument itself, write it out in term of mathematical symbols, for example. Extending from Leibniz (and his predecessors) into the present, this project was responsible for the emergence of mathematical logic and, finally, led to Kurt Gödel's famous incompleteness theorems. The first theorem proves that most mathematical systems (at least those containing arithmetic) contain, as they are called, undecidable propositions, that is, propositions that cannot be proven as either true or false within the system in which they arise. The second theorem proves further that the proposition (it can be formalized) concerning the mathematical consistency of any such system is itself an undecidable proposition. Hence the full consistency of such systems cannot be proved (provided that such systems are free of contradiction). Gödel's theorems also suggest that a (mathematical) formalization of mathematics may never be possible in full measure. One of the epistemological and aesthetic implications of this impossibility is that the richness of mathematics exceeds (mathematical) formalization, just as the richness of physics may exceed mathematization, or the richness of nature (or mind) any representation. This irreducible excess of nature and mind over any formalization or even representation of any kind is one of the key epistemological and aesthetic implications of modern mathematics and science.

Gödel's theorems do suggest that the *logical* harmony, as it were, of the whole (even if it existed) is unattainable, even by approximation. As a result, the aesthetics of such a harmony, too, requires a radical rethinking. These theorems have by no means undermined traditional aesthetic (or philosophical) convictions of leading mathematicians, scientists, and philosophers, Gödel himself included. Some of them did realize that Gödel's findings and other radical mathematical and scientific discoveries of the twentieth century signal great epistemological and aesthetic complexities in and of mathematics, science, and philosophy. They were not, however, willing to surrender the key classical epistemological and aesthetic principles here considered. Kepler's discoveries of his laws and the new more complex harmonies that they helped establish (replacing the old harmonies) have continued to serve as a great example and inspiration in this hope that mathematical harmonies can always be reintroduced at new levels, rather than lost altogether.

Until recently, the aesthetics in and of mathematics and science functioned primarily along the lines of classical aesthetics, as just considered. As the preceding discussion suggests, however, just as does classical philosophy, this classical aesthetics entails considerable and sometimes radical complexities, to the point of bringing it to and crossing the threshold of what may be seen as the nonclassical aesthetics. Still, for most of this history practical aesthetic considerations were connected to very old mathematical objects and principles, while most attempts to theorize the aesthetics of mathematics and science followed the development of aesthetic theories in philosophy. Several major developments in mathematics and science themselves, however, have had a powerful impact on modern philosophy and aesthetics and, more recently, on the aesthetics of mathematics itself.

In a more subterranean fashion, new, very radical forms of aesthetics were operative in mathematics and science for about a century (leaving aside still earlier intimations), with the emergence of topology in the works of Henri Poincaré, Georg Cantor's work on set theory, or the introduction of statistical physics. The introduction of non-Euclidean geometries has questioned, if not changed, key aspects of classical aesthetics, along with the underlying epistemology and ontology, both in mathematics itself and elsewhere. These aesthetic and philosophical complications have still earlier roots, beginning with the irrationality of the diagonal of the square or the atomic theories of Democritus. As we have seen, more generally, key concepts of classical aesthetics have always had great complexity, and such counteraesthetic forces as disorder, disfiguration, and irrationality have been part of classical aesthetics beginning with its Greek origins.

With these qualifications in mind, however, arguably the most significant transformation in the aesthetics of both mathematics and science begins around 1900, in the wake of, on the one hand, certain key developments in mathematics and science and, on the other, parallel trends in philosophy (especially in and the wake of Nietzsche), literature, and the arts, where one can mention such icons as James Joyce and Franz Kafka in literature, Arnold Schoenberg and other serialists in music, and Pablo Picasso and Cubism, or Marcel Duchamp in the visual arts. On the scientific side, the key areas include quantum physics and its extensions, and modern biology and genetics. In mathematics, arguably the most prominent have been investigations into the foundational questions and mathematical logic leading to Gödel's incompleteness theorems. Other developments extend and join new areas of topology, algebra, and analysis, initiated in the works of such earlier figures as Galois, Bernhard Riemann, and Poincaré. Among major developments in our own time, one can note the infinite-dimensional group representations and Langlands's program, modern differential and algebraic topology, André Weil's (more classical) program and then Alexandre Grothendieck's (more nonclassical) program in algebraic geometry, which has extraordinary links to many other areas of mathematics and even (by means of the so-called topos theory) to mathematical logic, as well as such even more recent developments as catastrophe theory, fractals, and chaos and complexities theories. Equally important are connections among such programs and fields, and their connections to other sciences, such as quantum physics. Many of these programs themselves and their interactions embody both classical and nonclassical aesthetic (or epistemological and ontological) principles, for example, by introducing radically new concepts of wholeness and partitioning (or fragmentation), centering and decentering, connectedness and disconnectedness, at the level of both mathematical objects and theories themselves.

On the classical side, the networks emerging as a result may have an appearance of a certain grand unity or whole, however complex the parts and the interactions among them within such networks. The appeal to wholeness and unity and, indeed, especially to complex (and even partly chaotic or chaosmic) types of both has certainly been and remains a central aesthetic and epistemological-ontological aspect of modern mathematics and science. These networks may, however, not represent or even allow any classical or indeed any unity, however complex, and may lead to a very different aesthetics and epistemology. As both Nietzsche and Jacques Derrida argue in more general terms, we may be forever hampered by the absence of any fundamental, absolute center—*the* center—and, hence, by the absence of the One, however conceived. What transpires or is translucent here is the irreducible multiplicity of the Heraclitean Many, rather than Parmenides' or Plotinus's One. The resulting aesthetics and epistemology may be seen as the aesthetics and epistemology of networks that are both radically decentered and radically oblique. Although it has crucial aesthetic dimensions, the last characterization is fundamentally of an epistemological nature in the sense that such networks have at best highly indirect connections to the object they are supposed to represent and, by the same token, complicate the status or indeed the very possibility of existence of such objects themselves. These networks emerge at the level both of the mathematical objects themselves and of such new fields and their interactions, or even mathematics or physics as a whole.

The transformation at issue arises in part from what may be called the crisis of representation (a concept crucial to all classical aesthetics) in modern and then in postmodern culture, including mathematics and science. The situation is perhaps most dramatic in quantum physics, where both mathematical and physical concepts have at best an oblique relation to reality in the sense just indicated. More radically, it may no longer be possible to speak, even metaphorically, of reality in any sense that is (or perhaps will ever be) available to us. Still more radically, quantum physics involves a mathematics, such as that of infinite-dimensional spaces, that is itself subject to an analogous economy. One is dealing not only with representing ultimately unrepresentable or otherwise inaccessible objects, which have always been part of aesthetics and philosophy, but one must also (obliquely) relate to this unrepresentable by means of models that are, in all rigor, themselves ultimately inaccessible. That is, although we might be able to describe certain key properties of such objects and models that represent them or even classify them up to isomorphism, we can at best conceive of these "objects" and "models" as such only on the basis of irreducibly oblique, remote, metaphorical approximations. The very concept of the existence of both such "objects" and such "models" (for example, as objects or models) requires major rethinking. In semiotic terms,

one must deal both with the radical and irreducible inaccessibility of both the signifieds and the signifiers involved. This obliqueness-inaccessibility cannot be reduced by any degree of mathematical rigor and precision, and in fact is enhanced or indeed produced by rigor and precision. Thus, in quantum physics one can obliquely approach what may be called the radical—that is, radically inaccessible—reality or, which is perhaps more precise, "alterity" of matter only by means of mathematical objects, such as infinite-dimensional spaces, that themselves allow only for similar (i.e., at best oblique) metaphorical descriptions, a point crucial to Langlands's program and other radical mathematical theories mentioned above. As a result, the aesthetic properties of both objects and models describing them within these theories, and aesthetic claims about these objects or models, too, can only be based on tentative and imperfect metaphors.

In one degree or another, however, one finds the nonclassical features just indicated in classical mathematics (or of course philosophy, or art), beginning with Descartes or indeed Euclid, certainly in much of nineteenth-century mathematics. One could even argue that, at least to some degree, the epistemology and aesthetics of numbers and geometrical figures have always been oblique in this sense. They have always been the epistemology and aesthetics of the oblique and the unknowable. Hence, in some measure—in some proportion—they have always been nonclassical, or at least are rigorously reconstructible as such.

Nietzsche was arguably the first to grasp this situation in its most general terms, both epistemological-ontological and aesthetic, and in the full measure of its radical implications, and to understand the role modern science played in bringing it about. He argued that all our aesthetics is irreducibly, uncircumventably oblique in the sense just considered, and he made this understanding a crucial part of his Dionysian aesthetics. He traced the latter to Greek tragedy, whose aesthetics, as we have seen, may be indissociable from (the aesthetics of) Greek mathematics, as the aesthetics and mathematics of both the rational and irrational, order and chaos—the aesthetics of chaosmos. Our aesthetic or, again, epistemological ideas and ideals may have nothing to do either with the world or even with the ideas (if they are ideas) that make beautiful ideas and images possible, and the structure of the latter, too, may already be ultimately inaccessible. Gods, if they were not dead or if they existed, could have very different ideas of beauty—mathematical, artistic, or other. Against the hope of all great believers in the mathematical harmony of the world, from Plato to Kepler to Albert Einstein, we might never—in all our sciences and arts, in any form of knowledge we can ever have—reach anything in common with the mind of God, or with the harmony of nature, if it is harmony and if it is indeed nature.

As a result, the radical aesthetics of mathematics and science that may emerge, and that has already emerged, may no longer be fully mathematical either; that is, mathematics or science will no longer be able to offer its own objects or structures as direct or even indirect models in this respect. The aesthetics of mathematics and science exceeds both of them, in part because they both exceed themselves. (The latter point is fundamental to Ludwig Wittgenstein's investigations into the foundations of mathematics.) These irreducibly excessive workings of mathematics, science, and aesthetics do, however, offer something new to us, namely, a new relation to the unmathematizable, the unrepresentable, the inaccessible, the unknowable, and new concepts designated by these terms and interactively, by their counterparts—mathematization, representation, accessibility, knowledge. Classical aesthetics and classical epistemology need not be and should not be—and, in truth, cannot be—abandoned, even though the retheorizing or even reformulation of many old principles becomes exceedingly complex and in part for that very reason, since new nonclassical aesthetic or epistemological configurations also emerge and indeed require this process of reworking the classical. Radical mathematical and scientific theories invoked above offer an extraordinarily rich and, one might say, beautiful or sublime, conjunction or proportion (again, with some strangeness in it) of classical aesthetic principles and nonclassical—irreducibly chaotic and irreducibly oblique—epistemology and aesthetics. The new aesthetics is the aesthetics of multiple interconnections, and the same may indeed be said about aesthetics in mathematics and science throughout its history. One deals here with the extraordinary richness of the aesthetics in and of mathematics and science at all levels and throughout its history, from Thales and Pythagoras, to Plato and Plotinus, to Kepler and Newton, to Kant and Hegel, to Galois and Riemann, to Poincaré and Einstein, to Niels Bohr and Gödel, to Weil, Grothendieck, and Langlands. This history has continuously opened new, sometimes immense, spaces of both the known and the unknown, the knowable and the unknowable, even though—and because—the very concepts of knowledge or of the unknowable are continuously reconceived in the process. This conjunction of the known and the unknown, the knowable and the unknowable, may well be the best, the most sublime, feature of mathematics and science. It is their greatest aesthetic principle and a crucial driving force that connects fantastically tangled trajectories of their history and holds them and this history together.

[See also Science and Aesthetics.]

BIBLIOGRAPHY

Cartier, Pierre. "Kepler et la music du monde." *La recherche* 278.26 (1995).

Curtin, Deane W., ed. *The Aesthetic Dimension of Science.* New York, 1982.

Davis, Philip J., and Reuben Hirsh. *The Mathematical Experience.* Boston, 1982.

Fomenko, Anatoly T. *Mathematical Impressions.* Providence, R.I., 1990.

Heisenberg, Werner. "The Meaning of the Beauty in Exact Sciences." In *Across the Frontiers,* translated by Peter Heath. Woodbridge, Conn., 1990.

Hildebrandt, Stefan, and Anthony Tromba. *Mathematics and Optimal Form.* New York, 1985.

James, Jamie. *The Music of the Spheres: Music, Science, and the Natural Order of the Universe.* New York, 1993.

Kant, Immanuel. *Critique of Judgment.* Translated by J. H. Bernard. New York, 1951.

Langlands, Robert P. "Representation Theory: Its Rise and Its Role in Number Theory." In *Proceedings of the Gibbs Symposium,* edited by D. G. Caldi and G. D. Mostow. Providence, R.I., 1990.

Lyotard, Jean-François. *The Postmodern Condition: A Report on Knowledge.* Translated by Geoff Bennington and Brian Massumi. Minneapolis, 1984.

Poincaré, Henri. *Science and Method.* Translated by Francis Maitland. Reprint, New York, 1960.

Reed, David. *Figures of Thought: Mathematics and Mathematical Texts.* London and New York, 1995.

Weyl, Hermann. *Symmetry.* Princeton, N.J., 1952.

Wigner, Eugene. *Symmetries and Reflections.* Bloomington, Ind., 1967.

ARKADY PLOTNITSKY

MATTHESON, JOHANN (1681–1764), German music theorist and critic. In a period during which questions of changing musical style and taste constituted a central topic of public debate, there was no one who weighed in with a louder or more influential voice than Johann Mattheson. Trained as both a composer and performer, astoundingly well read in both classical and contemporaneous literature, and uncommonly loquacious and opinionated even by the standards of the eighteenth century, Mattheson expressed his views on virtually every subject of music theory and aesthetics during his prolific publishing career spanning some sixty years and seventy-seven-odd works.

Mattheson's training in music was both wide-ranging and thorough. As a youth, he gained valuable experience at the Hamburg opera, working variously as a singer, harpsichordist, and composer. His involvement at the opera kindled in Mattheson a love of theatrical music and did much to shape his progressive views on musical style and expression. But he was also passionately devoted to church music, and he defended it vigorously in his later years from the attacks of the Pietists.

In 1706, Mattheson secured employment as secretary to the British ambassador in Hamburg, Sir John Wich. This was to prove a fortunate change for Mattheson, as his new position allowed him to exercise his considerable literary ambitions. With ready access to the most up-to-date literature and philosophy published in Britain—much of which he would translate into German—Mattheson launched a successful and stormy career as music critic and theorist. The writings of the moral philosophers were of particular influence on Mattheson, as were those of the empiricists (particularly John Locke).

But Mattheson's literary interests were by no means restricted to English sources. He proved to be extraordinarily erudite as a scholar. Fluent in a half dozen languages, he was able to cite large numbers of classical and foreign authors in his own writings (if, as it sometimes seemed, only for the sake of impressing and intimidating his opponents). In 1713, Mattheson published his first comprehensive treatise on music, *Das neu-eröffnete Orchestre*. Setting a tone that would be emulated in most of his subsequent publications, Mattheson offered an encyclopedic inventory and critique of received music theories, as well as contemporary compositional styles. Yet, despite his vast learning—or perhaps because of it—Mattheson was never able to organize his own views in any systematic or coherent fashion. His musical philosophy, such as it was, tended to be eclectic and often poorly worked out.

Still, a few key ideas remain constant throughout his writings, and these ideas give focus to his importance as a critic during the period of Western music in which "Baroque" ebullience was giving way to the more refined sensibility of classical style. Above all, Mattheson attempted to promote the "good taste" characteristic of an enlightened *galant homme*. This meant, first of all, exposing the tastelessness and bombasity of music that relied on excessive contrapuntal artifice, harmonic complexity, or melodic embellishment. It also prompted Mattheson to condemn those Cartesian writers who indulged in over abstract music speculation (such as the French theorist Jean-Philippe Rameau) or who defended obsolete practices such as the ancient modal system (Johann Buttstett and Johann Fux). Instead, Mattheson advised all composers to seek clarity of melodic line, a simplification of harmonic accompaniment, clear and expressive declamation of texts, and a general lightening of musical texture. Mattheson was by no means the first theorist to identify melody as the chief defining parameter of the new *galant* style, but he was the first to offer detailed criteria for its composition and evaluation. He held a "noble and simple melody" as the fount of all musical expressiveness. In *Der vollkommene Capellmeister* of 1739—his most important and comprehensive treatise of music—Mattheson included a large section devoted to the composition and evaluation of melody in which he recognized the importance of phrase symmetry, tonal balance, and cadential articulation in the shaping of the nascent classical style. Above all, melodic lines must be conceived vocally, even if written as instrumental music, and they should possess qualities of "accessibility, clarity, fluidity and loveliness" (*Der vollkommene Capellmeister*, 1981, pp. 140–141). Harmony and counterpoint must always be subordinate to melody, he argued (anticipating Jean-Jacques Rousseau), neither being capable of conveying the expressiveness and sheer sensory potency of a vocally conceived melody.

Mattheson sought justification for his empirical aesthetics in the sensationalist psychology of John Locke, whose writings Mattheson read eagerly in his youth. Articulating what was probably the most uncompromising empirical theory of music to be presented in the eighteenth century, Mattheson argued that all musical judgments must be based on the sensory evidence of the ear. Music theorists who rely on arguments of Pythagorean numerology, Scholastic logic, Cartesian a priori principles, or simple authority, thus commit a grave epistemological error by ignoring the sensible judgment afforded by hearing.

An emblematic test for this empirical philosophy was found by Mattheson in the interval of the perfect fourth. As articulated in *Das forschende Orchestre* of 1721—his longest and most explicitly Lockean treatise—any musical evaluation of the consonance value of the perfect fourth must be made by the ear in musical context, not on some a priori evaluation based on the simplicity of the interval's ratio. (Traditional Pythagorean theory had taught that the fourth—expressed as an epitritic ratio 4:3—lay within the sacred *Tetraktys* and therefore must always be classified as a consonance.) In practice, however, the fourth could be a dissonance depending on its contrapuntal context. Mathematics should never dictate to the ear, Mattheson would continually remind his readers:

> [N]umbers in music do not govern but merely instruct; hearing is the only channel by which the force [of music] is communicated to the inner soul of the attentive listener. . . . Hence, if the testimony of the ear is followed it will be discovered that in its relation to the surrounding sounds and harmony, the fourth will be either consonant or dissonant.
>
> (Mattheson, 1713, pp. 126–127)

For all the progressiveness of Mattheson's musical philosophy, there were a number of quite traditional elements to his aesthetic views that betray a more conservative, ambivalent personality. Whereas for a later generation of music theorists, a rigidly applied empirical epistemology led to a loosening of classical mimetic strictures, for Mattheson no such slackening was possible. Tenaciously, he identified with the traditional neoclassical view that music was fundamentally an imitative art, and that the goal of all music—or more specifically, perhaps, of all melody—was the "enjoyment of the ear through the arousal of affections in the soul" (*Der vollkommene Cappelmeister*, 1981, p. 207). (Although whether in fact music aroused such affections or merely portrayed them was an issue on which Mattheson seemed to waver.)

To elucidate his *Affektenlehre* (Theory of Affects), Mattheson invoked the venerable analogy with rhetoric. Like a moving speech, a good composition must depict and sustain some emotion in the audience, although the composer could obviously not do this with the precision of the orator. Still, Mattheson was one of the first music theorists to link in any detail affections with musical techniques. (For example, "since joy is an expansion of our soul, it is reasonable and natural that I could best express this affect by large and expanded intervals"; ibid., p. 16.) As would any music theorist who has tried to map varieties of emotion to specific compositional elements, Mattheson had to concede that this quality of musical expressiveness—as with the construction of any good melody—eluded systematic codification. In many of his later writings, in which surprising evidence of latent Pietist sympathies becomes manifest, Mattheson seemed to falter further in his goal to articulate a comprehensive *Affektenlehre* by reifying a moral soul within each individual that resonates in sympathy to the acoustic stimulus of music, thus endowing sound with unique ethical and cathartic power.

[*See also* Music, *overview article.*]

BIBLIOGRAPHY

Works by Mattheson

Das neu-eröffnete Orchestre. Hamburg, 1713.
Das forschende Orchestre. Hamburg, 1721.
Der vollkommene Capellmeister. Hamburg, 1739. Translated by Ernest Harriss as *Johann Mattheson's Der vollkommene Capellmeister: A Revised Translation with Critical Commentary* (Ann Arbor, 1981).

Other Sources

Berg, Darrell. "Johann Mattheson and John Locke: Sensus Vindiciae." *Musica Antiqua (Acta Musicologica Bydgoszca)* 8 (1988): 81–99.
Buelow, George J., and Hans Joachim Marx, eds. *New Mattheson Studies.* Cambridge and New York, 1983.
Cannon, Beekman C. *Johann Mattheson: Spectator in Music.* New Haven, 1947.
Christensen, Thomas. "*Sensus, Ratio,* and *Phthongos:* Mattheson's Theory of Musical Perception." In *Musical Transformation and Musical Intuition: Eleven Essays in Honor of David Lewin,* edited by Raphael Atlas and Michael Cherlin, pp. 1–16. Roxbury, Mass., 1994.
Kivy, Peter. "Mattheson as Philosopher of Art." *Musical Quarterly* 70.2 (1984): 248–265.
Lester, Joel. *Compositional Theory in the Eighteenth Century.* Cambridge, Mass., 1992.
Lippman, Edward. *A History of Western Musical Aesthetics.* Lincoln, Nebr., 1992.

THOMAS CHRISTENSEN

MEDIEVAL AESTHETICS. *See* Aquinas; Arab Aesthetics; Augustine; Beauty; Icon; Islamic Aesthetics; Origins of Aesthetics; Plotinus; Religion and Aesthetics; Rhetoric; *and* Russian Aesthetics, *article on* Religious Aesthetics.

MEDIUM. A medium, literally something that stands between two other things and, thus, something that may transmit from one thing to another, has long come to be thought of as the most general category for a means of communication. This sense of the word seems not to predate the seventeenth century, though the issues it raises are inevitably far older and more complex; an early use of the word *medium*

in this sense is found in Francis Bacon's *The Advancement of Learning:* "But it is not of necessity that Cogitations be expressed by the Medium of Wordes." The issues here are inevitably much older and range far wider than this specific use of the word: for example, Aristotle's central thought in the *Ethics* may be read as supposing that the process of rational, practical thought may be as much expressed in rightness of action as in words, and central to Renaissance thought was the idea, typified by Leon Battista Alberti's *De pictura* and in Leonardo da Vinci's *Treatise on Painting,* of what we might call the "medium" of painting's claim to be a universal "language." What Bacon says presupposes what comes very close to the necessary truth that—the doubtful possibility of direct telepathy aside—communication requires a means, something that by standing between the originator of a thought and an audience or beholder, conveys the message. In this sense any language is a medium. But what of the converse? Bacon here raises the quite different bone of contention whether in any proper sense of *cogitation,* or thought, there might either be thought apart from language or thought that could be formed and communicated in a medium for which there was not some linguistic equivalent. Could there be, for example, musical or pictorial thought that would not be capable of being spoken or written? A dominant tradition in twentieth-century analytic philosophy has been to provide a clear no to this unclear question. For example, the famous final line of Ludwig Wittgenstein's *Tractatus*—"of what we cannot speak we must remain silent"—invoked the very nearly as famous riposte from Frank Ramsey, "And you can't whistle it otherwise." A serious commitment to the idea of communication in the arts might suggest, however, that there may well be communication via other media than the linguistic.

Recently, and most popularly, *the media* has come to be a single collective noun for the various devices of mass communication—the "mass media" of film, television, newsprint, even theater, music, and dance. This term, which invites the thought that there is a clear concept behind the idea of there being a discipline of "media studies" or a single social or political phenomenon of mass communication, is perhaps the least interesting of all concepts of media and would be much better replaced by a discussion of performance, film, television, newsprint, and the like in their own right. The danger, otherwise, can be of falling into quite unilluminating talk of such things as the "language of" such "media." It is certainly best approached against the background of some reflection about different mediums on smaller, more modest scales. For that reason this currently most common idea of media will not be pursued here.

In the visual arts the idea of a medium as a means for expressing pictorial thought retains some vigor right down to the smallest scale, where we may refer to the medium of painting or drawing in terms of the material means of mark making. Here the word's use elides the two concepts of the liquid "vehicle" that carries a pigment such as oil paint, watercolor, or tempera with the wider one of the general material conditions of pictorial expression. It is here that we may most easily focus on the quite general philosophical issues associated with the very idea of a medium, the twin problems of what we might call *medium indifference* and *medium specificity*. In a fairly focused way these issues are easy to outline. They center on the difficult problem of the "identity" of what may be communicated by different means, an issue very closely connected to that of the concept of style, as discussed, for example, by Nelson Goodman. It might well seem that if a medium is a means of communication, it should be correspondingly possible to distinguish between what is communicated and how, or by what means, it is communicated. Then, could *it,* whatever this pronoun may refer to, have been communicated by some other perhaps very different means or medium? In this way we might attempt to distinguish between a drawing of a certain sort, of a specific subject, and the medium of pencil, watercolor, oils, and so on, in which it is made, as if it might have been made in a different medium, while still in a significant manner being the same general work. But can we really talk of the same picture—say, a study of a child's head—being expressed, on the one hand, in the medium of pencil and, on the other hand, in silver point or charcoal, or of the same picture being produced in the spontaneous medium of a free-flowing pen as part of the process of etching as opposed to the careful medium of engraving? The practice, for example, of making studies in color for a work to be finalized as an engraving was deeply established as fine book printing developed: J. M. W. Turner's studies in gouache on blue paper of French river scenery (c.1830) can be read as providing color clues for specific monochrome engraved effects. It is tempting to suppose that because of the radical change in medium we should be reluctant to identify what it is that survives the alteration. Yet, despite the fact that the engraver needed subtly to change the composition in order to comply with the visual spirit of the originals, and that the visual appearances are manifestly altered by the translation from one medium to the other, there still seems to be good reason to suppose that the engravings are indeed versions of the same works. How may we do this?

A precedent for the idea that we must be able to do this might seem to be naturally provided by the "medium" of language. A set of assertions in English might be communicated in handwriting, print, or by voice while remaining the same assertions; they express the same proposition. The problem is then that in nonlinguistic contexts we seem to lack any systematic replacement for this abstract identifier of content. "Same work" or "same picture" clearly begs the question. Even in linguistic contexts the possibility of peeling what is said away from the means of transmission is obviously far more difficult to do where we may wish to identify not merely the propositional content but what is "expressed" in the saying. Even if the words are the same, a handwritten letter to a bereaved friend may perform a quite different act of condolence and express quite different attitudes from the same words written on a word processor. What is said face-to-face may express something quite different from the "same" message (the same words) transmitted by fax or E-mail. We might think of standard philosophical ideas of propositional content, or of "the sense" of the words as deriving from the pursuit of medium indifference in communication. We may seem to have no such concepts outside language. The pursuit of medium indifference clearly must have its limitations, and equally clearly, these could not in principle be total. For any theory of a medium of communication must imply some account of relative medium indifference. Marshall McLuhan's once-fashionable slogan, "The medium is the message," is self-defeating, since taken seriously it would rob the idea of a medium of communication of all content. The dilemma seems to be that, while it is not easy to see what a general theory of medium indifference might be, it seems just as clear that for there to be a concept of a medium of communication at all we should be able to find such a theory.

To escape from this impasse small-scale examples can help. A central debate in the theory of visual depiction has been how one should relate the fact that a beholder may attend to what is depicted to the fact that the beholder may attend to the handling of the materials of depiction as they may be manifest in the marked surface, to brushwork, the handling of a drawn line, and so on. E. H. Gombrich has been fairly consistently attacked by Richard Wollheim and many others for supposing that such forms of attention are both quite distinct and indeed may exclude one another at any one time. This would certainly, if true, provide a starting point for a theory of medium indifference in pictorial contexts. It seems, however, to be rather obviously false. What must strike one most forcibly about any sensitive response to painting or drawing is that we attend to what is depicted in terms of how we attend to the marked surface as a medium of depiction. All responses to the expressivity of such work seem manifestly to depend on what Wollheim has called the "twofoldness" of a beholder's response in such cases. For example, we respond to how Hans Holbein invites us to attend to the subjects of his portraits in terms of the precision and unerasability of his silverpoint. By the same token our response to much of the drawing of Dominique Ingres may depend on our attending to his use of graphite (that most erasable of mediums) as if to give the appearance of the older medium. The "twofoldness" enables us to incorporate our grasp of a work's "facture" (that is, the manifest evidence of the process of its making) within our response to what the work depicts. This thought might then invite the further thought that any distinction between medium and content is vacuous. In fact, the reverse follows. For just as no concept of the object-as-depicted-by-means-of-the-marked surface can make sense divorced from some concept of twofold attention, so similarly there can be no concept of facture as such that can have force for us in our understanding of the work except in terms of what we take the work to be—whether a portrait, still life, landscape, or even abstract. In other words, the unity of our informed response itself implies the very conceptual distinctions we are seeking. Similarly, the fact that in the expressive language of poetry our unified response to the subject matter of a poem must be in terms of the expressive use of the linguistic medium, of meter, rhyme, and stress, such a unified response can only be possible if such facets of the work are indeed different from one another and different again from whatever (to express the matter loosely) the poem is "about." The idea that there can be no concept of medium indifference is to confuse the phenomenology of our response to a work with the cognitive content of our understanding, which alone may explain it.

If we widen the scope of the concept of a medium so that it may contrast "the pictorial," "the musical," "the choreographic," perhaps, with "the linguistic" the problem will center not so much on the concept of medium indifference as on the converse idea of medium specificity, where there may be "cogitations" expressible in one such medium but not in any or all others, or conversely whether the only proper medium of thought is language. This is a thought that, for example, runs through Gotthold Ephraim Lessing's discussion in Laocoön of the visual arts in contrast to literature. It makes no contribution to this debate to extend the notion of language to uncritically include these other mediums. Either way this can pose a dilemma for the language of art criticism. As raised by Michael Baxandall in *Patterns of Intention* and elsewhere, the question becomes to what does good art criticism refer? On the first assumption, illustrative writing and speech can at best only approximate to the "thought" of the work; on the second, as far as it may be regarded as work in a particular medium, it literally expresses no thought. Thus, either way we could not be able to ascribe specific painterly, musical, or choreographic thoughts to the work's makers. This seems unsatisfactory. Imagine, however, a picture of three horses, drawn to show how they group, how the rhythms of their planes and volumes interplay within the pattern of the group: it would seem that no elaboration of the drawing as such could extend the picture so that it could express the linguistic thought that these might be the only horses left on earth if such and such were to happen, while on the other hand no extension of language that was not aided by an invitation to attend to the picture itself could in principle capture how the retreat of the surface planes of their volumes might in the drawing modify into rhythmic horizons. Similarly, one might challenge a "pure" linguistic description to replace the musical experience of the resolution of a tune. For one who supposed that there was sense to the idea

of a form of thought that was medium specific, requiring for its understanding an education in the grasp of its particular medium, it might be convenient to distinguish between two uses of critical language, one that served to draw a beholder's attention to the relevant aspects of the work, and was a more or less elaborate form of ostension to the work in its own medium right, and one that explained and expanded the specifically linguistic thought to which the work related, such as the intentions of its maker and the beliefs or stories it sought to illustrate. Here again, negotiating the distinction between the unity of our phenomenological response and the complex variety of our interpretative explanation of, and justification for, such a response would not be easy. It would not in principle be impossible. The lesson of the concept of a medium—thus, of various mediums of art— is then, to be learned in the difficult but not quite impossible task of intelligent art criticism. The continuing philosophical issue then becomes the complex epistemology of that task.

[*See also* Digital Media; *and* Multimedia.]

BIBLIOGRAPHY

Aristotle. *Nicomachean Ethics.* Translated by J. A. K. Thomson. Harmondsworth, England, 1953.

Aristotle. *Poetics.* Translated by Gerald F. Else. Ann Arbor, 1967.

Alberti, Leon Battista. *On Painting.* Translated by Cecil Grayson. London, 1991.

Baxandall, Michael. *Patterns of Intention: On the Historical Explanation of Pictures.* New Haven, 1985. See chap. 2.

Baxandall, Michael. "The Language of Art Criticism." In *The Language of Art History,* edited by Salim Kemal and Ivan Gaskell, pp. 67–75. Cambridge and New York, 1991.

Gombrich, E. H. *Art and Illusion* (1960). 2d rev. ed. New York, 1961; reprint, Princeton, N.J., 1969.

Goodman, Nelson. *Languages of Art: An Approach to a Theory of Symbols.* 2d ed. Indianapolis, 1976.

Goodman, Nelson. *Ways of Worldmaking.* Indianapolis, 1978.

Goodman, Nelson, and Catherine Z. Elgin. *Reconceptions in Philosophy.* Indianapolis, 1988.

Harrison, Andrew. *Making and Thinking.* Indianapolis, 1978.

Harrison, Andrew. "Dimensions of Meaning." In *Philosophy and the Visual Arts: Seeing and Abstracting,* edited by Andrew Harrison, pp. 51–76. Dordrecht and Boston, 1987.

Harrison, Andrew. "Style." In *A Companion to Aesthetics,* edited by David Cooper, pp. 403–407. Oxford and Cambridge, Mass., 1992.

Harrison, Andrew. "A Minimal Syntax for the Pictorial." In *The Language of Art History,* edited by Salim Kemal and Ivan Gaskell, pp. 213–239. Cambridge and New York, 1991.

Leonardo da Vinci. *Leonardo on Painting: An Anthology of Writings.* Edited by Martin Kemp, translated by Martin Kemp and Margaret Walker. New Haven, 1989.

Lessing, G. E. *Laocoön.* Translated by Robert Phillimore (1874). Boston, 1978.

McLuhan, Marshall. *Understanding Media: The Extensions of Man.* New York, 1964; reprint, Cambridge, Mass., 1994.

Podro, Michael. "Depiction and the Golden Calf." In *Philosophy and the Visual Arts: Seeing and Abstracting,* edited by Andrew Harrison, pp. 3–22. Dordrecht and Boston, 1987.

Wollheim, Richard. *Art and Its Objects.* 2d ed. with six supplementary essays. Cambridge and New York, 1980.

Wollheim, Richard. *Painting as an Art.* Princeton, N.J., 1987.

Ziff, Paul. "On Being an Abstract Artist." In *Philosophy and the Visual Arts: Seeing and Abstracting,* edited by Andrew Harrison, pp. 155–166. Dordrecht and Boston, 1987.

ANDREW HARRISON

MEIER, GEORG FRIEDRICH (1718–1777), German philosopher and aesthetician. Georg Friedrich Meier studied Protestant theology and philosophy at the University of Halle, where he succeeded his master, A. G. Baumgarten, often considered to be the founder of aesthetics. Like Baumgarten, Meier attempted to extend, complete, and popularize Christian Wolff's rationalism. While closely related to Baumgarten's thought, Meier's works (written in German) are reminiscent of the "popular philosophers" of the German Enlightenment. He wrote on all the major philosophical fields of his time, but his original contributions were chiefly in the so-called instrumental philosophical sciences, such as aesthetics and logic (the latter being understood in the broad sense given to the term at the time, which included the theory of knowledge and scientific methodology). Thus, Meier broadened the theoretical scope of Wolffian philosophy, both by emphasizing the limits of human knowledge (*Metaphysik; Schranken der menschlichen Erkenntnis* [The Limits of Human Knowledge]) and by recognizing that the nature of our understanding determines what we can think. Mindful of empirical psychology (Metaphysik; Anfangsgründe aller schönen Künste und Wissenschaften [Principles of All the Fine Arts and Letters]; Vernunftlehre [Logic]), Meier emphasized the inadequacy of intellectual knowledge and gave theoretical importance to sensual or "sensible" knowledge (the *sinnliche Erkenntnis,* which stems from what Wolff called the *pars inferior* of the soul) in the generative process of rational knowledge. Meier, more so than Baumgarten, was attentive to the pedagogical role of logic (in the broad sense of the term) and, more particularly, of aesthetics, in the overall context of the improvement and refinement of the perceptual and intellectual faculties.

In section 2 of his *Anfangsgründe aller schönen Künste und Wissenschaften,* Meier develops his project of "aesthetics," understood as the "science that deals with sensual *(sinnlich)* knowledge" (following the post-Leibnizian classification, a knowledge that is clear but not distinct). Aesthetics is an instrumental science of the faculty of inferior knowledge (i.e., of *Sinnlichkeit*) that serves as a complement to logic; its role is to produce the systematic organization of the rules all knowledge must follow in order to be "beautiful." Meier's work, like Baumgarten's unfinished *Aesthetica,* is divided into three sections that correspond, respectively, to three points of view regarding "beautiful knowledge":

the beauty of the thoughts themselves (aesthetic heuristics);

the beautiful order of thoughts (aesthetic methodology); and

the expression of thoughts (aesthetic semiotics).

Of the three sections, the first, which coincides with the classical theory of poetic invention, is both the most important and the richest. It includes two essential parts: the first is a study of what constitutes the beauty of sensual knowledge in general and the analysis of its particular "perfections" (richness, greatness, aesthetic verisimilitude, clarity, certainty, aesthetic life); the second is a study of the sensual or "inferior" faculty of knowing that is founded on "empirical psychology" (attention, sense, imagination, wit, perspicacity, memory, poetic faculty, taste). Like Baumgarten, Meier was criticized, in large measure rightly, for having tried to base his universal aesthetic rules on the rules of eloquence and poetry.

Although Meier's work remains relatively faithful to the terminology and spirit of his master's project, it has none of the theoretical boldness of Baumgarten's *Aesthetica.* Meier's aesthetics remains closer to Wolffian orthodoxy in its conception of the nature of beauty and of the task of aesthetics. Sections 23–24 of the *Anfangsgründe* develop a Wolffian conception of beauty as a "confused perception of perfection," whereas the *Aesthetica* (section 14), where beauty is thought of as the "perfection of sensual knowledge," had already opened the path to the relative independence of the field of aesthetics, a question that later occupied Moses Mendelssohn, Johann Georg Sulzer, and Immanuel Kant (although Kant, who used Meier's logic as the basis for his teaching in logic, seems to have encountered rational aesthetics through Meier rather than through Baumgarten's *Aesthetica*). Meier is less aware than his master had been of the importance of reflecting on an autonomous aesthetic domain. He does not distinguish between aesthetics and a "psychology of effect" oriented toward a moral end; instead, he aims at integrating aesthetics within a more global strategy of developing sensual sources of human knowledge.

[*See also* Baumgarten; *and* Kant.]

BIBLIOGRAPHY

Works by Meier

Anfangsgründe aller schönen Künste und Wissenschaften. Halle, 1748–1750. Reprinted in the 1754 edition published as *Anfangsgründe aller schönen Wissenschaften,* 3 vols. (Hildesheim and New York, 1976).

Vernunftlehre. Halle, 1752.

Philosophische Sittenlehre. Halle, 1753–1761.

Metaphysik. Halle, 1755–1759.
Versuch einer allgemeinen Auslegekunst. Halle, 1756.
Betrachtungen über die Schranken der menschlichen Erkenntnis. Halle, 1775.

Other Sources

Bergmann, Ernst. *Die Begründung der deutschen Ästhetik durch A. G. Baumgarten und G. F. Meier*. Leipzig, 1911.

Böhm, H. "Das Schönheitsproblem bei G. F. Meier." *Archiv für die gesamte Psychologie* 56 (1926).

Nivelle, Armand. *Les théories esthétiques en Allemagne de Baumgarten à Kant*. Paris, 1955. German translation published as *Kunst- und Dichtungstheorien zwischen Aufklärung und Klassik*, 2d ed. (Berlin, 1971).

Schaffrath, J. "Die Philosophie des G. F. Meier." Thesis, Freiburg, 1940.

Schenk, Günter. *Leben und Werk des Halleschen Aufklärers Georg Friedrich Meier*. Halle, 1994.

Sommer, Robert. *Grundzüge einer Geschichte der deutschen Psychologie und Aesthetik von Wolff-Baumgarten bis Kant-Schiller*. Würzburg, 1892.

DANIEL DUMOUCHEL

MENDELSSOHN, MOSES (1729–1786), German philosopher. A leading figure in Enlightenment philosophy in Germany as well as in both the intellectual reform of Judaism and the argument for the civil acceptance of the Jews, Moses Mendelssohn also made significant contributions to the development of aesthetics. Educated in traditional Jewish studies in his hometown of Dessau, he followed his rabbi to Berlin at the age of sixteen and rapidly acquired profound knowledge of classical and modern languages and their literature. At twenty-one, he entered the service of a wealthy Jewish merchant as a tutor, subsequently becoming a bookkeeper and then a partner in the business. Denied membership in the Prussian academy of sciences by Frederick the Great, Mendelssohn produced his vast body of writing in his hours of leisure from business. Plagued by weak health in later years, he died at the height of a notorious dispute with Friedrich Jacobi over whether his lifelong friend Gotthold Ephraim Lessing had been a pantheist and Spinozist.

Mendelssohn's works include three elegant and by no means unoriginal essays in rationalist metaphysics: the *Treatise on Evidence* (1764), *Phaedo; or, The Immortality of the Soul* (1767), and *Morning-Hours; or, Lectures on the Existence of God* (1785); many works of Jewish scholarship, including a commentary on Maimonides and the first translation of the Pentateuch into German for a Jewish audience; and his great plea for religious freedom, *Jerusalem* (1783). His works in aesthetics, produced early in his career, include the *Letters on the Sensations* (1755), "On the Chief Principles of the Fine Arts and Sciences" (1757), "On the Sublime and the Naive" (1758), and the "Rhapsody or Supplements to the Letters on the Sensations," included in the first collection of his philosophical writings in 1761.

Writing within a framework provided by Gottfried Wilhelm Leibniz, Christian Wolff, and Alexander Baumgarten, but enriched by the writings of the earl of Shaftesbury, Jean-Baptiste Dubos, Johann Georg Sulzer, Edmund Burke, and many others, Mendelssohn was notable for his insistence on the irreducible complexity of aesthetic experience. In his earliest work, he essentially combined the standpoints of Wolff and Baumgarten to argue that our pleasure in beauty is a response to the recognition of both the objective perfections of external objects and the perfection of our own capacity for sensory representation, which he interpreted to comprise in turn the perfection of both our intellectual and our bodily condition. In ensuing essays, he complicated this picture further, emphasizing that we take pleasure not only in the perfection of external objects and our own condition but in the medium of artistic signs or representations as well, and also adding our admiration of artistry, both the divine artistry that produces external objects and the human artistry that produces their representation, as yet another source of pleasure.

Mendelssohn summarized this complexity of the sources of aesthetic response by calling it a "mixed sensation" *(vermischte Empfindung)*. Finally, in his last metaphysical work, the *Morning-Hours*, Mendelssohn clearly distinguished aesthetic pleasure from the pleasures of both knowledge and desire, and assigned it to a third "faculty of approval" *(Billigungsvermögen)*. This may well have influenced Immanuel Kant's decision to assign the judgment of taste to the newly distinguished faculty of reflective judgment in his *Critique of Judgment* (1790), published five years after Mendelssohn's work.

Mendelssohn applied his doctrine of the complexity of aesthetic response to a number of the major debates in eighteenth-century aesthetics. He offered a solution to the problem of tragedy, arguing that we enjoy the perfections of artistic representation and the activity of our own faculties even when the represented object is unpleasant or evil. He provided a trenchant criticism of Charles de Batteux's thesis that all art is the imitation of nature, arguing that our pleasure in the beauty of represented objects is only one part of our pleasure in art. He drew a distinction between natural and artificial signs, and between simultaneous and successive representation in the visual and verbal arts, respectively, which provided the conceptual framework for Lessing's *Laocoön*. Influential in their own time, much of the substance of Mendelssohn's views was reconstructed in Kant's different metaphysical and epistemological framework, and Mendelssohn's recognition of the complexity of aesthetic experience should endure as an admonition against reductionist theories of art and aesthetic experience.

[*See also* Baumgarten; Kant; *and* Lessing.]

BIBLIOGRAPHY

Works by Mendelssohn

Ästhetische Schriften in Auswahl. Edited by Otto F. Best. Darmstadt, 1974.

Gesammelte Schriften, Jubiläumsausgabe. Edited by I. Elbogen, J. Guttmann, and E. Mittwoch. Berlin, 1929–.

Moses Mendelssohns philosophische Schriften. 2 vols. Corr. ed. Berlin, 1771.

Other Sources

Altmann, Alexander. *Moses Mendelssohns Frühschriften zur Metaphysik.* Tübingen, 1969.

Beck, Lewis White. *Early German Philosophy: Kant and His Predecessors.* Cambridge, Mass., 1969. See pp. 324–339.

Guyer, Paul. "The Perfections of Art: Mendelssohn, Moritz, and Kant." In *Kant and the Experience of Freedom: Essays on Aesthetics and Morality,* chap. 4. Cambridge and New York, 1993.

Nivelle, Armand. *Kunst- und Dichtungstheorien zwischen Aufklärung und Klassik.* Berlin, 1960.

PAUL GUYER

MERLEAU-PONTY, MAURICE (1908–1961), French philosopher. Maurice Merleau-Ponty's contributions to aesthetics are focused on the arts of painting and literature. His insights into painting are particularly unique for their emphasis on modern painting, and his belief that the paintings of Paul Cézanne and the post-Cézanne painters, rather than classical painting, have clarified the task of the artist and instituted the outlines of a new ontology of the visible and the invisible. Merleau-Ponty's aesthetic is grounded within the phenomenological philosophy of Edmund Husserl, which he explored and tested to discover a phenomenology of painting and literature, but a tradition that he also exceeded toward a new ontology of the work of art.

Merleau-Ponty's philosophy of painting is found in three essays: "Cézanne's Doubt," "Indirect Language and the Voices of Silence," and "Eye and Mind." These are supported by selected texts from Merleau-Ponty's major works, *Phenomenology of Perception* and *The Visible and the Invisible.* The philosophy of literature is found principally in *The Prose of the World,* but also the early and last parts of "Indirect Language and the Voices of Silence."

"Cézanne's Doubt" offers an antiformalist, phenomenological interpretation of the meaning of Cézanne's art. Although the critical studies of Cézanne had already appeared that viewed his work as proto-Cubism and focused on Cézanne's design, geometric forms, and use of planes on the two-dimensional surface, Merleau-Ponty was interested in Cézanne for his attempts to paint the "lived" prescientific experience of the world. In Cézanne, Merleau-Ponty believed he had found the artistic analogue to phenomenological "seeing." Husserl's phenomenological *epoché* was meant to provide access to the phenomena and forms of our experience of the world as they are given to us and not as the world is supposed to appear according to Galilean science and Cartesian philosophy. Cézanne was undertaking something similar, a faithful, observant, and ordered interlacing of himself with the world in which the visible world was reconstructed on canvas in its process of appearing to perception as colored, solid, weighty, and monumental. According to Cézanne's own account, he was "attempting a piece of nature," which did not mean an empirical "imitation" of nature or an intellectual projection outward of the artist's imaginative response to nature. This was remarkably parallel to Merleau-Ponty's lifelong philosophical project of articulating a philosophy in between empiricism-naturalism and rationalism-idealism. "The landscape thinks itself in me," Cézanne had said, "and I am its consciousness." Merleau-Ponty had qualified his endorsement of Husserl's *epoché* in his *Phenomenology,* but he was nevertheless moved by Cézanne's belief in a peculiar kind of reversibility or overlapping in which the artist is literally present "at the world" (*l'être au monde*).

As a phenomenologist, Merleau-Ponty was especially interested in Cézanne as a colorist, for color is one of the sensible "secondary" qualities, secondary to the "primary" mathematical qualities such as point, line, plane, and ratio. The secondary qualities provide our original contact with the world and institute the voluminosity and solidity of things. Mathematical properties are second-order and more abstract. Merleau-Ponty prized Cézanne for his insistence on the objectivity of the dense local colors of things, and his departure from the atmospheric colors featured in the works of the Impressionists. Later, in "Eye and Mind," Merleau-Ponty wrote that although there is "no one master key to the visible," the return to color gets us nearer to "the heart of things."

With Cézanne as exemplar, Merleau-Ponty's phenomenology of painting highlighted a number of touchstone themes: the bracketing of the natural attitude, an emphasis on prescientific lived perception, the solidity and constancy of secondary qualities like colors, and the interpenetrating, reversible relationship between the painter and the world. As for painting itself, Merleau-Ponty was persuaded by his studies of Cézanne to believe that the task of painting is expressing what exists, rendering visible a world that is taken for granted, hurried by, and seldom noticed. Painting is an intentional, noetic-noematic act, and therefore referential, but a painting is not about itself as formal elements and relations on a canvas, nor is it about the history of painting, but about the visible world that is all too often invisible. We live with someone we love all our lives but never "see" her or him. In privileging Cézanne to develop this aesthetic, Merleau-Ponty did not mean to speak for one moment in the history of painting or art in order to exclude others such as classical perspectivism or Cubism or Abstract Expressionism, as has sometimes been claimed (Jean-François Lyotard, *Discours, Figure;* Michel Haar, in Fóti, ed., 1996). He argued that Cézanne, in spite all his own self-doubts, in spite of the withering attacks of the critics and "official art" establishment, had rendered the task of all painting from Lascaux to our times more manifest.

Merleau-Ponty brought the structures of history and institutions to bear on his phenomenology of painting in his second essay, "Indirect Language and the Voices of Silence," through a critique of André Malraux's three-volume history and psychology of art collected as *The Voices of Silence.* Written for the journal *Les temps modernes,* which Merleau-Ponty coedited for a time with Jean-Paul Sartre, "Indirect Language" also took Sartre's existentialism with its ahistorical thesis of radical subjectivity and freedom as the implicit subtext demanding a response. Merleau-Ponty was a political philosopher and philosopher of history who was engaged with his own assessment of Marx's historical materialism, and his account of "experience" pushed downward Husserl's intellectualist phenomenology of immanent consciousness toward a new phenomenology of the body. Although not materialist in a strong Marxist sense, Merleau-Ponty took seriously the historical structures of economics, politics, and language as they form and preform our bodies. Whereas Husserl had focused phenomenological description on isolated, individual, and conscious perceptions of a scene or sound, Merleau-Ponty elaborated the "primacy of perception," that is, our kinesthetic, lived-bodily presence to the world. This set of operative intentionalities by which each of us "has it out with the world" is grounded in an anonymous tradition of gesture and speech inherited as an acquisition.

Therefore, the artist's expression does not arise from nowhere as an ungrounded, arbitrary act, but neither is it a wholly determined production. Merleau-Ponty's solution to this philosophical impasse centered on a rethinking of the notion of style focused on the artist's work (*peindre,* "to paint") or the process of painting, rather than on the works (*les peintures*) that appear in the museums and galleries. Merleau-Ponty criticized modern-day museums, institutions of power and money that have only existed for about two hundred years and only in Western countries, that render artists' living works as gallery rivals. Institutions should be understood in Husserl's sense as fecund foundations (*Stiftung*) that open a field for investigation. Thus, style is a historical and intersubjective phenomenon, the special way in which our living body trains, practices, and thereby takes up a tradition of gesture and meaning both to perpetuate it and to challenge it in a "coherent deformation." All embodiment stylizes or accents the variants the world offers, and the artist is the one who is capable of condensing and expressing his or her bodily encounter with the perceived world onto paper, canvas, stone, or clay. Whereas Malraux's account in subjective terms of "genius" and an "inner gaze"

or objective terms of a "Spirit of painting" rendered the artist as "mysterious as octopuses or lobsters," Merleau-Ponty's account drew the painter's production close to everyday work, where it is mixed with bodies and life, schools, mistresses, creditors, the police and revolutions, as the everyday bread his or her painting crystallizes and consecrates. One's life and situation do not impose any particular work, but provide categories and a call that is given expression in all the works. A painting expresses this encounter with the world tacitly and allusively, and its meaning is not singular and determinate but overdetermined.

In addition to painting, Merleau-Ponty was concerned with a general theory of expression, language, and signs, and "Indirect Language" appeared originally as the third chapter of Merleau-Ponty's work that he left unpublished and that was titled *The Prose of the World.* Merleau-Ponty also taught a course on modern poetry in 1947 at the University of Lyons, gave lecture courses at the Sorbonne on the child's acquisition of language, and published an essay on the novel in *Sense and Non-Sense.* All expression is indirect, Merleau-Ponty argued, just as history advances obliquely and ambiguously rather than straight toward ends or concepts. Therefore, Sartre was wrong to privilege literature over painting, as he did in *What Is Literature?* when he wrote that the painter, in contrast with the writer, "is mute." The living body "is essentially an expressive space," and the meanings of the gestures of a painter at work are intermingled with the structures of the world they outline, just as words, vowels, and phonemes are so many ways of gesturing with teeth and tongue to "sing the world's praises." Everything, Merleau-Ponty says, is both manufactured and natural in human life, in which actions and language deviate from their preordained direction and institute new forms "through a sort of *leakage* and through a genius for ambiguity which might serve to define man." There are different layers of significance, from the gestural to the visual to the conceptual, and a novel, like a painting, must also express the most important things allusively or tacitly. In Stendhal's *The Red and the Black,* for example, Julien Sorel's desire to kill Madame de Rênal for her betrayal is nowhere said, but is between the words and lines, marked out by the hollows of space and time in Julien's dreamlike journey toward Verières, like an invisible lining of the visible.

In these views on language and literature, Merleau-Ponty was developing a number of theses that mark the outlines of a theory of signs: first, a gestural theory of language; second, a theory of signs as more than conventional but "natural" emergents from the relations of body and lived world; third, an account of meaning as allusive, metaphorical and multivocal. In "Indirect Language," he brought these theses into relation to Ferdinand de Saussure's semiotics, and introduced important supplements within the gestural theory of signs.

In "Eye and Mind," the circle of Merleau-Ponty's aesthetic concerns widened once again, from a general theory of expression to a theory of Being. "Eye and Mind" announced the themes of the ontology on which Merleau-Ponty was working from 1959 until his death in 1961, and which appeared posthumously as *The Visible and the Invisible*. Merleau-Ponty contended that painting has a "metaphysical significance," and every theory of painting enters into metaphysical claims regarding space, time and the "there is" (*il y a*). It is clear that greater meditation on painting would have changed René Descartes's "flat" metaphysics without depth. Why is it that painters have so often said, as did Cézanne and Paul Klee, that the forest was speaking in them, or the trees were looking at them? It must be that there is a system of exchanges between body and world such that eye and hand become the obverse side of things, the inside of an outside in which both are enveloped. This envelopment, generality, and anonymity Merleau-Ponty named Flesh (*la chair*), a term he compared to the Greek idea of an element, which is not Substance nor Mind nor Matter. We are held by a Speech and a Thought that have us. The world and the painter are the inverse and obverse of one sole Power that breaks open in an unending generosity of creation and expression. This ontology of Flesh and reversibility, learned from the painter, may be approximated as a new neutral monism, but a loosely knit monism that preserves the gaps (*écarts*), strife, and differences among colors and things and between self and world. The incarnate principle of Flesh imbues the world with a longing for unity that is deferred, but a deferral that keeps open the genesis and metamorphosis of expression.

The gains for Merleau-Ponty's aesthetic theory offered by "Eye and Mind" are multiple, for the essay is condensed and complex, including discussions of color, iconography, etchings, sculpture, mirrors, motion, depth, voluminosity, line, and abstraction. Merleau-Ponty's discussion of line emphasizes the free line such as found in the self-portraits of Leonardo da Vinci or the drawings of Henri Matisse and Alberto Giacometti, and cites Henri Michaux's phrase "to go line" (*aller ligne*). A single line can crystallize the entire meaning of a face or hand, and thereby convey the visible world's lining of transcendence and invisibility. Klee's lectures and notebooks are the new inspiration for many of the ideas of "Eye and Mind," and the original essay published by *Art de France* (1960) included an abstract work by Klee entitled "Park near Lucerne," as well as an abstraction consisting of several juxtaposed planes by a little-known French artist named Alain de la Bourdonnaye titled simply "Composition. 1960." The reflections on line and abstraction emphasize that the "metaphysical significance" and the aesthetics of expression that Merleau-Ponty found in modern painting are not limited to a few painters or works at the turn of the century, but as Merleau-Ponty himself concluded, every creation, from the paintings of the caves at Lascaux to Matisse, from the sculptures of Auguste Rodin to Ligier Richier, clarifies, deepens, confirms, and exalts the mystery and wonder of Being.

The influence of Merleau-Ponty's aesthetics has been profound, and is not easily summarized in a few sentences. In France, his aesthetic ideas have been carried forward by Hubert Damisch, who was the editor of the edition of the *Bulletin de psychologie* (November 1964) containing the summaries of Merleau-Ponty's University of Paris-Sorbonne psychology lectures, as well as by Claude Lefort, Mikel Dufrenne, Lyotard, Françoise Dastur, and Oliver Mongin. There are traces of Merleau-Ponty's themes of visibility and invisibility in much of the work of Michel Foucault, and Jacques Derrida has taken up the theme of blindness and invisibility from Merleau-Ponty explicitly in the catalog for his Louvre exhibition titled *Memoires d'aveugle: L'autoportrait et autres ruines* (1990). In Germany, the main line of influence has been through the work of Bernard Waldenfels at the Ruhr-University of Bochum. The work of the Belgian philosophers should also be mentioned, especially Rudolf Bernet, Marc Richir, and Jan Van der Veken. It is perhaps in the United States that Merleau-Ponty's influence has been felt most widely. Chief among his interpreters in the philosophy of art and literature are Hugh Silverman, Véronique Fóti, Samuel Mallin, Glen Mazis, Michael Smith, Anthony Steinbock, and Dorothea Olkowski, and in art criticism, the effects of Merleau-Ponty's ideas are seen in the works of Annette Michelson on cinema studies, Rosalind Krauss on the optical unconscious as well as modern sculpture, and Michael Fried on painting.

[*See also* French Aesthetics, *article on* Contemporary Painting Theory; Marxism; Perception, *article on* Aesthetics of Perception; *and* Phenomenology.]

BIBLIOGRAPHY

Works by Merleau-Ponty

Phenomenology of Perception (1945). Translated by Colin Smith. London, 1962. Reprinted with translation revisions by Forrest Williams and David Guerrière, 1989, 1992.

"Cézanne's Doubt" (1945), "Metaphysics and the Novel" (1945), and "The Film and the New Psychology" (1946). In *Sense and Non-Sense* (1948), translated by Hubert L. Dreyfus and Patricia Allen Dreyfus. Evanston, Ill., 1964. Retranslated by Michael B. Smith in *The Merleau-Ponty Aesthetics Reader: Philosophy and Painting*, edited by Galen A. Johnson (Evanston, Ill., 1993).

Adventures of the Dialectic (1955). Translated by Joseph Bien. Evanston, Ill., 1973.

"Indirect Language and the Voices of Silence" (1952). In *Signs* (1960), translated by Richard C. McCleary. Evanston, Ill., 1964. Retranslated by Michael B. Smith in *The Merleau-Ponty Aesthetics Reader: Philosophy and Painting*, edited by Galen A. Johnson (Evanston, Ill., 1993).

"Eye and Mind" (1961). Translated by C. Dallery. In *The Primacy of Perception*, edited by James E. Edie. Evanston, Ill., 1964. Retranslated by Michael B. Smith in *The Merleau-Ponty Aesthetics Reader: Philosophy and Painting*, edited by Galen A. Johnson (Evanston, Ill., 1993).

The Primacy of Perception and Other Essays. Edited by James E. Edie. Evanston, Ill., 1964.

The Visible and the Invisible (1964). Translated by Alphonso Lingis, edited by Claude Lefort. Evanston, Ill., 1968.

Consciousness and the Acquisition of Language (1964). Translated by Hugh J. Silverman. Evanston, Ill., 1973. Lecture course for 1949–1950 at the University of Paris, Sorbonne.

The Prose of the World (1969). Translated by John O'Neill, edited by Claude Lefort. Evanston, Ill., 1973.

Texts and Dialogues. Edited by Hugh J. Silverman and James Barry, Jr., translated by Michael B. Smith et al. Atlantic Highlands, N.J., 1991.

Other Sources

Behnke, Elizabeth A. "At the Service of the Sonata: Music Lessons with Merleau-Ponty." *Somatics,* 4, 2 (1983): 32–34. Reprinted in *Merleau-Ponty: Critical Essays,* edited by Henry Pietersma. (Lanham, Md., 1989), pp. 23–29.

Fóti, Véronique M., ed. *Merleau-Ponty: Difference, Materiality, Painting.* Atlantic Highlands, N.J., 1996.

Johnson, Galen A., ed. *The Merleau-Ponty Aesthetics Reader: Philosophy and Painting.* Evanston, Ill., 1994. Contains essays by Forrest Williams, Alphonse de Waelhens, Michael Smith, Marjorie Grene, Linda Singer, Olivier Mongin, Mikel Dufrenne, Hugh Silverman, Jacques Taminiaux, Véronique Fóti, Jean-François Lyotard, René Magritte, Wayne Froman, and Robert Burch.

Jones, Edwin. *Reading the Book of Nature: A Phenomenological Study of Creative Expression in Science and Painting.* Athens, Ohio, 1989.

Madison, Gary Brent. *The Phenomenology of Merleau-Ponty: A Search for the Limits of Consciousness.* Athens, Ohio, 1981.

Mallin, Samuel. "Chiasm, Line and Art." In *Merleau-Ponty: Critical Essays,* edited by Henry Pietersma, pp. 219–250. Lanham, Md., 1989.

Mazis, Glen A. "*La chair et l'imaginaire:* The Developing Role of Imagination in Merleau-Ponty's Philosophy." *Philosophy Today* 32.4 (Spring 1988): 30–42.

Sartre, Jean-Paul. "Merleau-Ponty." Translated by William S. Hamrick. *Journal of the British Society for Phenomenology,* 15.2 (May 1984). This is the original version of Sartre's homage to Merleau-Ponty, translated from Sartre's posthumous manuscripts. The second, or public, version was published earlier in *Situations,* translated by Benita Eisler (New York, 1965), pp. 156–226.

Watson, Stephen. "Merleau-Ponty and Foucault: De-Aestheticization of the Work of Art." *Philosophy Today* 28 (Summer 1984): 148–167.

GALEN A. JOHNSON

METAPHOR. [*To explore the role of metaphor in aesthetic theory and art, this entry comprises five essays:*

> An Overview
> Metaphor and Philosophy of Language
> Metaphor and Nonverbal Arts
> Metaphor and Art History
> Derrida and de Man on Metaphor

The first essay is an overview of different philosophical approaches to the topic of metaphor. The next four essays represent in more depth at least five of these approaches. The differences are due both to disciplinary concerns—philosophy of language (second essay) as compared to art history (fourth essay)—and to differences between linguistic and nonlinguistic senses of metaphor (third essay). The fourth essay specifically explores the notion of "real" metaphor, that is, a metaphor in which real displacement takes place between two things in art, particularly in sculpture. The last essay discusses Jacques Derrida's and Paul de Man's theories of metaphor as examples of the Continental theories distinct from the analytic ones discussed in the previous essays. For related discussion, see Metonymy; *and* Rhetoric.]

An Overview

Metaphor theory is one of those rare areas in which we can actually identify a monolithic conception that has dominated philosophy and literary theory for almost two thousand years. Within this framework, metaphor was regarded as an optional rhetorical and stylistic device, and it was thus relegated to the status of a secondary problem in aesthetics. Since about 1975, however, this received view has been subject to devastating critiques that have led to a complete reappraisal of the topic. We now recognize metaphor to be a fundamental principle of human understanding that operates in all forms of our symbolic activity. Consequently, a person's view of metaphor has become a divining rod with which to discover his most basic philosophical commitments about the mind, knowledge, and language.

The received view that has dominated the Western tradition is both objectivist and literalist in character. It is made up of related views about the nature of the world, how the mind works, and how language can be about the world. The core set of defining beliefs includes the following:

1. The world consists of mind-independent objects that have properties and stand in various determinate relationships.

2. Meaning is an abstract relation between symbolic representations (either words or mental representations) and objective reality.

3. Meaning is sentential; that is, it consists of propositions that are capable of being true or false.

4. Meaning is fundamentally literal. By definition, literal concepts are those that directly represent, or map, the objects, properties, and relations that make up our world.

5. Metaphoric expressions cannot be cognitively basic or fundamental, since metaphors are cross-domain projections, whereas the world consists of fixed domains defined in their own terms.

6. A metaphor, therefore, is a derivative, cognitively dispensable phenomenon, since its meaning should be reducible to a set of literal propositions.

This traditional view thus involves an ontology and an epistemology that marginalize the imaginative dimensions of human cognition. It underwrites a comparison theory, which reduces metaphor to a cross-domain comparison of preexisting similarities that are specifiable in literal terms. Such a view grants rhetorical force and ornamental value to metaphor, but denies its crucial role in conceptualization and reasoning, dismissing it as nothing more than a set of literal similarity statements (such as "X is similar to Y in respects $R, S, T, \ldots$").

It is a much-debated question whether Aristotle, who gave us our first extended treatment of the subject, actually held this traditional comparison theory. His classic definition is that "metaphor consists in giving the thing a name that belongs to something else; the transference being either from genus to species, or from species to genus, or from species to species, or on grounds of analogy" (*Poetics*, 1457b). He does seem to hold some of the literalist tenets, since he regards metaphor as a matter of words, treats concepts as literal, and defines metaphor as a deviation from the proper sense of a term. On the other hand, Aristotle's remarks on the power of good metaphors (*Rhetoric*, 1405a, 1410b) and on metaphor as a product of genius (*Poetics*, 1459a) suggest that he regarded it as an indispensable cognitive device. [*See* Aristotle.]

Whether or not Aristotle was a thoroughgoing objectivist and literalist, he was interpreted in this way by succeeding generations of philosophers who codified the traditional comparison theory of metaphor. In this sense, it is not wrong to read the next twenty-two hundred years of metaphor theory as variations on Aristotelian (if not Aristotle's) themes. Classical rhetoric focused on Aristotle's view that metaphor is powerful because it presents "similarity in dissimilars" (*Poetics*, 1459a). Cicero is representative of the rhetorical concern with what makes a metaphor fitting and forceful: "A metaphor is a brief similitude contracted into a single word; which word being put in the place of another, as if it were in its own place, conveys, if the resemblance be acknowledged, delight; if there is no resemblance, it is condemned" (*De oratore*, 3.38.156–39.157).

Medieval rhetoric and theology reveal an ambivalence toward metaphor. On the one hand, it was acknowledged that both Scripture and theology are shot through with metaphor. Thomas Aquinas recognizes the central role of metaphoric understanding in our knowledge of God. We try to grasp the Being of God in the only way we can, by means of metaphors based on our finite human experience (*Summa Theologiae*, 1, 1, 9ad.1). On the other hand, we must always remember that there can be no direct predication of attributes of God, so we must never mistake our metaphoric understanding for knowledge. Throughout medieval theology we therefore find strong and sustained warnings against the charms of metaphor, which can be used to mask untruths and to lead us astray. [*See* Aquinas.]

This suspicion of metaphor as a powerful and deceptive device of imagination reached its peak in the writings of Thomas Hobbes, John Locke, and other early empiricists. Hobbes, the archobjectivist, argues that "metaphors, and senseless and ambiguous words, are like *ignes fatui;* and reasoning upon them is wandering amongst innumerable absurdities; and their end, contention, and sedition, or contempt" (*Leviathan*, part 1, chap. 5). Locke regards metaphors and other figurative devices as being "for nothing else but to insinuate wrong ideas, move the passions, and thereby mislead the judgment; and so indeed are perfect cheats" (*Essay concerning Human Understanding*, book 3, chap. 10). Even G. W. F. Hegel carries forward this prejudice toward the figurative, defining metaphor as an "abridged comparison" and arguing that "metaphor cannot pretend to the value of an independent representation, but only to that of an accessory one. Even in its highest degree it can appear only as a simple ornament for a work of art" (*The Philosophy of Fine Art*, pp. 40–41).

The most flamboyant exception to this general Enlightenment derogation of metaphor is Friedrich Nietzsche, who, as in most things, turns the entire subject on its head by claiming that metaphor is the basic principle of all meaning and thought. He sees perception, conception, and reasoning as irreducibly metaphoric processes, and he argues that all our knowledge is based on metaphor. The stable truths of any culture are metaphors whose metaphoric nature has been forgotten and suppressed: "What therefore is truth? A mobile army of metaphors, metonymies, anthropomorphisms: in short a sum of human relations which become poetically and rhetorically intensified, metamorphosed, adorned, and after long usage seem to a nation fixed, canonic and binding" (*On Truth and Falsity in Their Ultramoral Sense*, p. 180). [*See* Nietzsche.]

It would take another century for this view of the metaphoric nature of thought to be taken seriously and to be supported by empirical research on cognition. In the interim, philosophy ignored Nietzsche's exaltation of metaphor and drifted back into the most stringent forms of reductive empiricism. Metaphor was seen as, at best, a temporary placeholder useful in developing theories, but something to be eliminated within a mature science, which would supposedly consist only of clearly defined literal propositions. At worst, it was treated as having only "emotive" meaning, and as lacking any cognitive content whatever (C. K. Ogden and I. A. Richards, *The Meaning of Meaning*, 1923).

Against this logical empiricist dismissal of metaphor, Max Black (1954–1955) sparked a revolution within Anglo-American philosophy by arguing that metaphor cannot be reduced to literal meaning and is, therefore, indispensable for the practice of science and all other forms of knowing. Black drew heavily on I. A. Richards's earlier argument, in *The Philosophy of Rhetoric* (1936), that metaphor is an omnipresent principle of thought and that our linguistic metaphors are manifestations of these underlying metaphoric concepts. Moreover, Richards saw metaphor as an ontological principle that structures our very understanding of our world: "the processes of metaphor in language, the exchanges between the meanings of words which we study in explicit verbal metaphors, are superimposed upon a perceived world which is itself a product of earlier or unwitting metaphor" (pp. 108–109).

Black's theory became the focus of discussion within analytic philosophy because of his claims that metaphor is a semantic phenomenon, that some metaphors are not reducible to cognitively equivalent literal propositions, and that metaphors may even "create" similarities, rather than merely presenting preexisting ones. Black's account of metaphoric creativity starts by showing that a certain class of metaphors does not work by picking out features common to two different domains. Instead, a metaphor is a cross-domain interaction between the "systems of associated commonplaces" that define each of the two domains. The key to Black's theory is that it is the entire *systems* of implications that interact to reorganize each of the systems themselves, generating new meaning from some of the elements within each system and inducing a novel cognitive perspective on the domain that is metaphorically redescribed.

Black's provocative claims influenced a number of philosophers, psychologists, and linguists to take a much more serious look at metaphor, and this has given rise, since the mid-1970s, to a proliferation of theories about the cognitive status and workings of metaphor. There are at least four major orientations that have dominated recent debates. The first set of theories is a more or less direct exploration of themes in Black's general theory of the irreducibility of metaphor. Earl R. MacCormac (1985) accepts the very traditional view that literal language gives us a foundational tie to the objective world, and he sees metaphor as a device for conceptual change that transforms the literal conceptual base. Metaphors are creative when hitherto unassociated features of two conceptual domains are brought together in a novel way. MacCormac rejects any simplistic true/false dichotomy for metaphor, emphasizes its crucial role in the evolution of knowledge, and defends a fallibilist position regarding the creative operation of metaphor as a force for linguistic, conceptual, and cultural change. Another "cognitivist" approach is that of Eva Feder Kittay (1986), who follows Black in treating metaphor as a semantic phenomenon, and who uses semantic field theory to explore the cognitive force of creative metaphor. She argues that the two "semantic fields" (one for each term in the metaphor) interact to produce a transference of meaning from one domain to the other.

In this same antireductionist spirit, Paul Ricoeur (1977) offers a far more ontologically ambitious analysis of metaphor as a suspension of the ordinary reference of an expression that opens up the possibility of semantic innovation, thereby restructuring our experience of the world. Like Richards, Ricoeur regards metaphor as a deep ontological principle involving a unified process of understanding that is at once cognitive, imaginative, and emotive. He also tries to rethink the notion of reference in a way that could make sense of a metaphor as reorganizing our world, and not just our thoughts about it. [*See* Ricoeur.]

The second major approach that has sparked considerable controversy in recent years is Donald Davidson's (1978) wholesale rejection of the traditional view of metaphor as a semantic phenomenon. Davidson claims that all meaning is literal (i.e., there is no such thing as "metaphorical meaning") and that metaphors are merely pragmatic devices by which we use the literal meaning of the expression to "suggest" or "intimate" something that was previously unnoticed. Both David Cooper (1986) and Richard Rorty (1989) accept Davidson's denial of meaning to metaphor and his claim that the only truth conditions of a metaphor are those of the literal expression used metaphorically. For Rorty, metaphors are not structures for motivated semantic change but rather merely irrational leaps from one "language game" or "vocabulary" to another: "Nietzschean history of culture, and Davidsonian philosophy of language, see language as we now see evolution, as new forms of life constantly killing off old forms—not to accomplish a higher purpose, but blindly" (Rorty, 1989, p. 19). On this view, powerful metaphors are the result of the genius of "strong poets" who succeed in instituting new metaphors that redefine our vocabularies, not because the metaphors are better or truer, but simply because they just happen to catch on.

Rorty's irrationalist view of metaphor, with its emphasis on the ungrounded, unconstrained nature of metaphor, has affinities with versions of the third major contemporary orientation, which is deconstructivist in character. Taking inspiration from Nietzsche's view of the omnipresence of metaphor, and appropriating a view of language as an ungrounded system of differentiations, Jacques Derrida (1974) has used metaphor as a tool of deconstruction. For example, he analyzes classical metaphysical positions as being based on a set of shifting metaphors whose openendedness undercuts the foundationalist and absolutist claims of the metaphysical systems themselves. On this view, to discover the underlying metaphors that constitute our most fundamental concepts is to reject any possibility of grounded meaning and truth claims for those concepts. This would apply equally to our understanding of metaphor itself, or to any of our knowledge claims. From this perspective, metaphor is thought to epitomize the constant shifting and deferment of meaning that allegedly characterize all language.

Against Davidsonian deflation and Derridean deconstruction of metaphor, a fourth major orientation claims to marshal empirical evidence from linguistics, psychology, and anthropology to show that metaphoric concepts are grounded in our bodily experience and thereby constrain our understanding and reasoning. George Lakoff and Mark Johnson (1980) argue that all of our most basic abstract concepts are defined by clusters of often inconsistent metaphors, most of which operate unconsciously and automatically in our understanding. What we think of as "literal" language is actually based on underlying conceptual metaphors that define its conceptual structure and the inferences we draw from that structure. Conceptual metaphors are mappings of structure from one domain of experience (the source) onto another domain of a different kind (the target). Source domains are typically grounded in our bodily experience and are used to structure our more abstract concepts. For example, we have a vast metaphor system in which aspects of vision are used metaphorically to structure our understanding of mental operations and reasoning (as in "I *see* what you mean"; "Could you *shed some light* on that hypothesis?"; and, "His argument was utterly *opaque*"). We then use our knowledge of the source domain to draw inferences about the target domain. Citing empirical linguistic and psychological studies of meaning, conceptualization, and inference, Lakoff and Johnson argue, contra Davidson, that metaphors are semantic and that they are capable of being true or false. Against deconstructivist views, they cite the experiential grounding of metaphor source domains as constraining meaning and thought.

METAPHOR: Overview. Robert Morris, *Blind Time IV (Drawing with Davidson)* (1991), graphite on paper, 38 × 50 in.; text by Donald Davidson (Copyright 1998 by Robert Morris/Artists Rights Society, New York/Donald Davidson; photograph courtesy of Leo Castelli Gallery, New York; used by permission.)

First two crosses are laid out on the page in the upper section. Then working blindfolded and estimating the lapsed time, the hands attempt to enlarge the cross on the left. The same thing is tried again on the right. Time estimation error: +20"

Let the large cross on the left stand for the Stuka that crashed in a snowstorm somewhere in the wastes of the Russian steppe in 1942, and from which the pilot, Joseph Beuys, was pulled by Tartar tribesmen who wrapped the unconscious airman in felt and butter, preserving his warmth for the 12 coma-like days he lay near death in a frozen yurt. Let the large cross on the right stand for the Stuka listed in the Luftwaffe archives which notes a crash in 1944 a few miles from an airfield at the Russian front and records that corporal Joseph Beuys, tail gunner and radio operator was brought to hospital by Russian workers a half hour after the accident.

"What makes the difference between a lie and a metaphor is not a difference in the words used or what they mean (in any strict sense of meaning) but in how the words are used. Using a sentence to tell a lie and using it to make a metaphor are, of course, totally different uses, so different that they do not interfere with one another, as say, acting and lying do. In lying, one must make an assertion so as to represent oneself as believing what one does not; in acting, assertion is excluded. Metaphor is careless of the difference."—Donald Davidson

Lakoff and Mark Turner (1989) then extend this analysis to poetic metaphor, which they see as based on, and using the same cognitive principles as, conventional conceptual metaphor.

These four approaches represent the most prominent philosophical projects now under discussion. There is also, however, a massive and rapidly expanding psychological literature that cannot be described here (see Gibbs, 1994, for a survey). The focal problems around which various research programs have organized themselves include the following: How do we recognize an expression as metaphorical? Does processing a metaphor take more time than literal comprehension? Are metaphors conceptual (and, if so, how do they constrain reasoning)? What are the underlying cognitive mechanisms for metaphor comprehension? Do people at different stages of development (e.g., children versus adults) understand metaphors differently? How do congenitally blind people process metaphor?

In all of these discussions, one thing seems clear—metaphor has come of age, and it can never again be dismissed as ornament or rhetorical flourish. The traditional objectivist view that has defined so much of our thinking about concepts and meaning has been demolished by attacks from every side. Even the most deflationary views recognize the pervasiveness of metaphor, and they see that there are persistent imaginative phenomena that require explanation. Metaphor must be taken seriously as lying at the heart of human understanding, not just in language, but in all forms of symbolic activity. Human beings are metaphoric animals whose experience, thought, and symbolic communication are the product of deep metaphoric processes. What we now need, but do not yet have, are adequate treatments of the nature and role of metaphor, not just as a linguistic phenomenon, but also in our visual, tactile, and auditory experience.

BIBLIOGRAPHY

Black, Max. "Metaphor." *Proceedings of the Aristotelian Society.* New Series 55 (1954-1955): 273-294.

Cooper, David E. *Metaphor.* Oxford and New York, 1986.

Davidson, Donald. "What Metaphors Mean." *Critical Inquiry* 5.1 (Autumn 1978): 31-47.

Derrida, Jacques. "The White Mythology: Metaphor in the Text of Philosophy." *New Literary History* 6.1 (Autumn 1974): 5-74.

Gibbs, Raymond W., Jr. *The Poetics of Mind: Figurative Thought, Language, and Understanding.* Cambridge and New York, 1994.

Kittay, Eva Feder. *Metaphor: Its Cognitive Force and Structure.* Oxford, 1986.

Lakoff, George, and Mark Johnson. *Metaphors We Live By.* Chicago, 1980.

Lakoff, George, and Mark Turner. *More than Cool Reason: A Field Guide to Poetic Metaphor.* Chicago, 1989.

MacCormac, Earl R. *A Cognitive Theory of Metaphor.* Cambridge, Mass., 1985.

Richards, I. A. *The Philosophy of Rhetoric.* New York and Oxford, 1936.

Ricoeur, Paul. *The Rule of Metaphor.* Translated by Robert Czerny with Kathleen McLaughlin and John Costello. Toronto, 1977.

Rorty, Richard. "The Contingency of Language." In *Contingency, Irony, and Solidarity,* pp. 3-27. Cambridge and New York, 1989.

MARK JOHNSON

Metaphor and Philosophy of Language

No topic in aesthetics has been more deeply transformed during the twentieth century by the philosophy of language than metaphor. Three landmarks stand out in this story. The first was Max Black's essay "Metaphor." Influenced by the English literary theorist, I. A. Richards, Black put the problem of metaphor on the agenda of Anglo-American philosophy by presenting it, in the Oxford vocabulary of his day, as a question about its "logical grammar." After criticizing the received substitution, similarity, and elliptical simile theories for making metaphor a merely decorative rhetorical device, Black argued for its distinctive cognitive value, claiming that metaphors "create" rather than "formulate" similarities and that they resist literal paraphrase. To explain the unique "insight" of a metaphor, Black proposed his own "interaction" theory according to which the novel meaning of the metaphor emerges out of the selective projection of systematically related presuppositions—"associated commonplaces"—related to the metaphorically used predicate onto the subject of the sentence. It remains unclear how Black's interaction theory differs from a more complicated, bidirectional version of a similarity, or analogical, theory, but his essay proved seminal for proposing that metaphors can be cognitively significant in ways that differ from the literal.

The second important moment was the central place Nelson Goodman assigned to metaphor in his *Languages of Art,* a work that gave aesthetics in general a newfound prominence in mainstream philosophy. As part of his greater program to show that there are common modes of symbolization that cross the various media in the arts and sciences, Goodman uses metaphor to exemplify a generic symbolic competence that applies equally to language and art. Recasting it in the mold of his extensionalist semantics and nominalist, irrealist metaphysics—the themes that underlie much of his analysis of art—Goodman also employs metaphor to show off their explanatory power. For example, he argues that what is wrong with the comparison theory of metaphor is just a special case of what is wrong with the explanatorily vacuous idea of similarity *tout court.* He nominalistically reformulates the classic Aristotelian account of metaphor as "transfer" as the transfer of labels, sans properties, from one realm of extensions to another. He also explicates the novelty of metaphor in terms of its role in creating new categories and classifications, reflecting his vision that the basic cognitive activity is symbolization. [*See* Goodman.]

The third important development in the recent history of metaphor has been the explosion of interdisciplinary work since the early 1970s in which philosophers and literary theorists have been joined by linguists, psychologists, anthropologists, and cognitive scientists. As the study of natural language has moved on to what previously were peripheral topics, these inquirers have brought well-developed, formally rigorous semantic, psychological, and linguistic theories to the analysis of metaphor. Furthermore, the kind of interest metaphor holds for these theorists differs from the intrinsic interest it held for many earlier philosophers. Like "exotic" phenomena in the physical sciences whose primary significance lies in the ways they indirectly confirm or disconfirm remote abstract laws or theories, metaphor has now come to serve as a test case for general theories of language, its interest consisting primarily in its implications for the specific theoretical frameworks within which it is investigated.

These contemporary accounts of metaphor focus on three main questions:

1. How do we identify or recognize an utterance as (containing at least one expression used or interpreted as) a metaphor? Is there a syntactic or semantic feature that marks an utterance as a metaphor or is a metaphor identified only pragmatically?

2. How do we metaphorically interpret an utterance? What kind of knowledge or ability or competence—semantic or extralinguistic—do we employ that enables us to assign a metaphorical interpretation to an utterance? Is this knowledge rule-governed, a nonpropositional skill, or a special kind of genius that transcends rules and constraints?

3. What is the semantic status of the content of a metaphoric interpretation of language? Is the metaphoric mode of expression of the utterance merely stylistic, with no additional content beyond that expressed by its literally meant words? Or, does it express propositional content specific to its metaphoric interpretation though of the same type as the kind of content expressed by literal language? Or, is the "cognitive content" of the metaphor cognitively significant in some unique way completely unlike the information conveyed by literal language? Closely related to these are the questions whether metaphors are truth-valued and, as a litmus test, whether they are literally translatable or paraphrasable.

One approach whose strongest influence was in the 1970s promised to answer all these questions about metaphorical recognition and interpretation in one fell swoop. Theories in this vein (proposed, e.g., by Monroe Beardsley, Robert J. Matthews, Samuel Levin, L. Jonathan Cohen, and Avishai Margalit) explicated the "tension" often identified with metaphor using the thesis that metaphors are literally false, absurd, or grammatically deviant. This syntactic or semantic feature of the sentence itself excludes its literal interpretation—from which these authors conclude that it is ipso facto identified as a metaphor—and the same violation among features of the literal meaning serves as the

mechanism for generation of its metaphoric interpretation. For some authors, the new metaphoric sense emerges from secondary connotations to which the interpreter shifts when the literal meanings fail; for others, it is the result of cancellation-, weighting-, and transference-operations performed on the lexical entries of the words. On either view, however, metaphoric meaning is a reinterpretation of language that cannot be understood in its primary, privileged literal sense.

The doctrine underlying all these accounts—that all or typical metaphors, were they interpreted literally, would be false, grammatically deviant, or semantically anomalous—was one of the most widely held dogmas about metaphor of its day. In the mid-1970s, however, it was decisively challenged. As Ted Cohen has aptly put it, there are many "twice-true metaphors"—for example, "No man is an island"—that would be perfectly fine and equally true in the very same context whether they were interpreted literally or metaphorically. More generally, the import of the critique was that there need be nothing deviant or irregular—syntactically, semantically, or pragmatically—about the literal meaning of a sentence that is used or interpreted metaphorically. Hence, neither its metaphoric recognition nor its interpretation should be explained by way of its literal impossibility.

How, then, is an utterance identified as a metaphor? We are unlikely to have a good general answer to this question until we have a better theoretical understanding of how arbitrary (literal) types are assigned to utterances or tokens. The most promising recent attempts in this direction appeal to Paul Grice's maxims of conversational implicature, emphasizing the role of contextual cues rather than necessary and sufficient conditions involving syntactic or semantic properties of the sentence uttered. Even those who still defend the grammatical deviance thesis hold it, explicitly or implicitly, as a pragmatic thesis: that were the metaphor interpreted literally, it would be unacceptable or inappropriate in its context because it contravenes one or another of Grice's maxims. Nonetheless, even these pragmatic versions still take the narrow-sighted view that utterances are identified as metaphors only when they cannot be taken literally, ignoring the broader possibility that a metaphoric interpretation may sometimes be the best rather than the only interpretation of the utterance. Instead of being a reinterpretation that is serially processed after the literal interpretation of the utterance is rejected, the metaphoric interpretation may be identified and processed in parallel with literal interpretations, just as alternative literal interpretations themselves seem to be processed in parallel. The moral, as psychologists now emphasize, is that the same processes that appear to be used to type and interpret literal language are employed to type and interpret metaphors.

Once it was acknowledged that metaphoric recognition is largely a function of context, it was only natural to take metaphoric interpretation also to be pragmatic rather than semantic, to be explained as a use of language rather than as a type of meaning. Within this approach two kinds of accounts should be distinguished. The first holds that just as there are semantic theories, so there are pragmatic theories—and metaphor is no exception. Hence, this approach includes theories that treat metaphor as a kind of speaker's meaning like that expressed by an indirect speech act (John Searle) or as a kind of figurative speech act (Cohen, Ina Loewenberg) or as a type of Gricean interpretation of speech that depends on mutual recognition of intentions (Robert J. Fogelin). The second approach takes metaphor to be a matter of use in the sense that its interpretation seems to follow no lawlike regularities and, in particular, those that are encoded in context-independent meanings assigned to word types. The best-known proponent of this approach, Donald Davidson, denies both the possibility of a theory of metaphor (i.e., a finitistic account of its content) and that a metaphor should be awarded any kind of meaning—even speaker's meaning—beyond the literal meaning of its words. What a metaphor "conveys" is just an unpredictable causal effect of its utterance event, largely nonpropositional, the product of a non-rule-governed "creative" skill.

All of these use theories of metaphor, including Davidson's "no-theory" theory, begin from the correct observation that metaphoric interpretation is highly context dependent. That is to say two things. First, metaphoric interpretations of utterances of the same expression may vary widely from one occasion to another, depending on a not easily systematizable variety of factors. Second, the interpretation of a metaphor is a function, not simply of the speaker's linguistic or semantic competence, his or her knowledge of meaning in a strict sense, but of all sorts of contextual, or extralinguistic, presuppositions and of skills or abilities (like the perception of similarity) that are not language specific. Both these ways in which metaphor is context dependent demonstrate, however, only that metaphor cannot be an object solely of a speaker's semantic competence; they do not show, as the use theorists conclude, that metaphor lies entirely outside semantics. There is, moreover, evidence of constraints on what a speaker can use a given expression to metaphorically express like the linguistic constraints that determine which of a speaker's intentions can be (literally) communicated by which expressions. Use theories cannot account for these constraints. Searle, for example, cites eight principles that catalog the heterogeneous range of "grounds" that can serve as sources of metaphoric interpretations. But he cannot explain how or why one rather than another is determined as the interpretation of a given expression. Because it is the (literal) meaning of a word that in general constrains possible contents, this in turn raises the question whether some notion of metaphoric meaning might nonetheless be necessary and

what it would be—since such meaning must be more abstract than the content it constrains.

One reaction by recent authors (e.g., Merrie Bergmann, Josef Stern) has consequently been to construct semantic theories that articulate the constraints on metaphorical interpretation that are due to linguistic structure. These accounts emphasize the context-dependent character of metaphoric interpretation (e.g., its dependence on contextual presuppositions) but distinguish, on the model of other kinds of context-dependent expressions like indexicals, between their content, or truth conditions, in a context, and their meaning, rules that determine but do not belong to their interpretation.

A second reaction, whose best-known proponents are George Lakoff and Mark Johnson, argues that metaphors are less context dependent and more systematic than the use theories allow and, furthermore, that metaphors govern not merely speech but the very ways in which we "think about" domains. As evidence for this view, these authors appeal to a rich, detailed body of structured networks of "conventional" metaphors—nonpoetic metaphors that pervade ordinary language in organized systems (e.g., that love is a journey, argument is a war, time is money). The original credit for this idea that the schema rather than the individual expression is the basic unit of metaphoric interpretation really belongs to Goodman, but Lakoff and Johnson's corpus of conventional metaphors demonstrates to a degree no one anticipated both the ubiquity and the subtlety with which metaphors structure the ways in which we express our beliefs and concepts. Their work has had a significant impact on psychologists and cognitive scientists, but less on philosophers, in part because they have used it to mount wholesale refutations of grandiose philosophical positions (e.g., "Objectivism in Semantics, Epistemology, and Linguistics") that have convinced very few.

Lakoff and Johnson's descriptive work nonetheless raises a number of important methodological questions. Should evidence consist primarily in one rather than another kind of metaphor—poetic or ordinary? Is metaphor, as Lakoff and Johnson claim, a mapping of one domain onto another or should metaphors be primarily understood as predicative, or class-inclusion, statements? Connected to this second question is the role of similarity or resemblance as a "ground" for metaphoric interpretation. Since Black's and Goodman's critiques, the notion of similarity has undergone a rehabilitation, initiated by Amos Tversky. At the same time, its application to metaphor has been challenged, by Sam Glucksberg and Boaz Keysar, on the grounds that metaphors are not relational or comparative in form but are instead devices for expressing novel, ad hoc categories. This work, which has been conducted mainly by psychologists, is only now being assimilated by philosophers. It promises, however, to throw new light on issues relevant to the third of the questions mentioned earlier, the semantic and cognitive status of the content conveyed by metaphors.

Until now progress on this last question has been hindered by an almost exclusive focus on the literal paraphrasability test with its inherently unclear criteria for success. In recent years, however, philosophers have turned the issue in new, more promising directions. Richard Boyd has investigated the constitutive roles of metaphors in scientific theories, and William Alston and Richard Swinburne in religious language. Martin Davies and Richard Moran (replying to Davidson) have discussed how a metaphor can make us see something as something else in a way that cannot be captured by, although it interacts with, the attitude of belief. Stern has explored how the metaphoric mode of expression of the contents of certain beliefs must be taken into account in order to show how they explain actions. Recent work on the noncognitive significance of metaphors (e.g., by Cohen, on creating a sense of intimacy), and their relation to jokes and riddles, also promises to illuminate other cognitive aspects of metaphor, for example, their sense of surprise. Although we are still far from possessing good answers to these many questions, the questions themselves exemplify how the study of metaphor, enriched and deepened by the philosophy of language, is philosophically more exciting now than it has probably ever been before in its history.

BIBLIOGRAPHY

Beardsley, Monroe. "Metaphorical Senses." *Noûs* 12.1 (March 1978): 3–16.

Bergmann, Merrie. "Metaphorical Assertions." *Philosophical Review* 91.2 (April 1982): 229–242.

Black, Max. "Metaphor." In *Models and Metaphors: Studies in Language and Philosophy*, pp. 25–47. Ithaca, N.Y., 1962. Reprinted in *Philosophical Perspectives on Metaphor*, edited by Mark Johnson (Minneapolis, 1981), pp. 63–82.

Boyd, Richard. "Metaphor and Theory Change: What Is 'Metaphor' a Metaphor For?" In *Metaphor and Thought*, 2d ed., edited by Andrew Ortony, pp. 481–533. Cambridge and New York, 1993.

Cohen, L. Jonathan, and Avishai Margalit. "The Role of Inductive Reasoning in the Interpretation of Metaphor." In *Semantics of Natural Language*, edited by Donald Davidson and Gilbert Harman, pp. 722–740. Dordrecht, 1972.

Cohen, Ted. "Notes on Metaphor." *Journal of Aesthetics and Art Criticism* 34.3 (Spring 1976): 249–259.

Cohen, Ted. "Figurative Language and Figurative Arts." *Journal of Philosophy* 72.19 (6 November 1975): 669–690. Reprinted in *Philosophical Perspectives on Metaphor*, edited by Mark Johnson (Minneapolis, 1981), pp. 182–199.

Davidson, Donald. "What Metaphors Mean." *Critical Inquiry* 5.1 (Autumn 1978): 31–47. Reprinted in *Inquiries into Truth and Interpretation* (Oxford, 1984); and in *Philosophical Perspectives on Metaphor*, edited by Mark Johnson (Minneapolis, 1981), pp. 200–220.

Davies, Martin. "Idiom and Metaphor." *Proceedings of the Aristotelian Society* 83 (1982–1983): 67–85.

Fogelin, Robert J. *Figuratively Speaking*. New Haven, 1988.

Glucksberg, Sam, and Boaz Keysar. "Understanding Metaphorical Comparisons: Beyond Similarity." *Psychological Review* 97.1 (1990): 3–18.

Goodman, Nelson. *Languages of Art: An Approach to a Theory of Symbols*. 2d ed. Indianapolis, 1976.

Johnson, Mark, ed. *Philosophical Perspectives on Metaphor*. Minneapolis, 1981.

Kittay, Eva Feder. *Metaphor: Its Cognitive Force and Linguistic Structure*. Oxford, 1987.

Lakoff, George, and Mark Johnson. *Metaphors We Live By*. Chicago, 1980.

Levin, Samuel R. *The Semantics of Metaphor*. Baltimore, 1977.

Loewenberg, Ina. "Identifying Metaphors." *Foundations of Language* 12 (1975): 315–338. Reprinted in *Philosophical Perspectives on Metaphor*, edited by Mark Johnson (Minneapolis, 1981), pp. 154–181.

Matthews, Robert J. "Concerning a 'Linguistic Theory' of Metaphor." *Foundations of Language* 7 (1971): 413–425.

Moran, Richard. "Seeing and Believing: Metaphor, Image, and Force." *Critical Inquiry* 16.1 (Autumn 1989): 87–112.

Ortony, Andrew, ed. *Metaphor and Thought*. 2d ed. Cambridge and New York, 1993.

Sacks, Sheldon, ed. *On Metaphor*. Chicago, 1979.

Searle, John. "Metaphor." In *Metaphor and Thought*, 2d ed., edited by Andrew Ortony, pp. 92–123. Cambridge and New York, 1993.

Stern, Josef. "Metaphor as Demonstrative." *Journal of Philosophy* 82.12 (December 1985): 677–710.

Stern, Josef. "What Metaphors Do Not Mean." In *Philosophy and the Arts*, edited by Peter A. French, Theodore E. Uehling, Jr., and Howard K. Wettstein, pp. 13–52. Midwest Studies in Philosophy, vol. 16. Notre Dame, Ind., 1991.

Tirrell, Lynne. "Extending: The Structure of Metaphor." *Noûs* 23.1 (March 1989): 17–34.

Tversky, Amos. "Features of Similarity." *Psychological Review* 84.3 (July 1977): 322–352.

JOSEF STERN

Metaphor and Nonverbal Arts

Studies of metaphor have appropriately centered on verbal expression, for it is in words, phrases, sentences, and larger verbal units that examples of metaphors seem most obvious. However, insofar as interest is directed toward poetic expressions, metaphor theory is obviously relevant at least to that aspect of aesthetics that is concerned with the literary arts (Hester, 1967). Not only are verbal metaphors crucial, even central, in poetry and works of prose, but whole poems have been viewed as metaphors. Moreover, some accounts of metaphor—in philosophy, notably that of Paul Henle (1958)—have regarded iconic significance as the basis for verbal metaphors, thus suggesting that verbal metaphors are rooted in more fundamental meanings. Just as important, nonverbal expressions have been thought to offer insights within their own media. Inquiries, especially in psychology, have also explored the ways mental processes that are associated with these verbal examples have common ground with the processing of nonverbal expressions. Theories of metaphor that have been directed toward verbal examples, then, seem to be applicable to nonverbal contexts, and metaphor studies have implications for aesthetics in general—for the visual arts and music as well as for the literary arts.

Antecedents for this broader view of metaphor are found in Immanuel Kant's (1790 [1987]) account of the power of genius in fine art in terms of what he named "aesthetical ideas," which, although not explicitly called metaphors by Kant, seem to have been conceived as metaphoric in function and achievement. Aesthetic ideas give "soul" to works of artistic genius. They serve as prompters for presenting meaning that is not determinable through conceptualization. They may restructure experience, following principles "higher" than analogical laws. They thus serve as the sources of artworks' insights, and they succeed in doing this by combining formerly unrelated images and conceptually dissonant, but meaningful, concepts.

Kant's examples include nonverbal presentations, for instance, *Jupiter's eagle with its lightning in its claws,* which presents attributes of aesthetic ideas expressive of divine power. Kant's account of the insight-generating components of works of art, then, offers a perspective that expands views about metaphor from an interest in poetic utterances to considerations of nonverbal expressions in general.

It seems reasonable to assume that pre-Kantian interest in metaphor also would have been directed toward some nonverbal expressions such as painting and music, at least insofar as metaphoric expressions were regarded as symbolic. Anything that refers to something beyond itself and has connotative meaning (rather than indexicality alone) may be thought of as a symbol. Nonverbal works of art have also been thought of, however, as symbols in the sense of exhibiting meanings that refer to experience (external to the immediate appreciation of the symbol for its own character) such as moral and religious themes and ideals. If works of art are metaphors in this sense of being symbols, then they may be understood as expressing insights. More recently, works of art have been considered as symbols in a more special sense, as referring to events or objects that are most appropriately, even exclusively, referred to through those works. This view is found in Susanne K. Langer (1953) and Philip Wheelwright (1962), and it is anticipated in Carl Jung (1923).

To regard works of art as metaphoric because they are symbolic in this way points to one of the most basic issues that brings together metaphor theory and aesthetic theories in general. Insofar as it is the expression of significance or the insight-giving function of works of art that leads to the idea that artworks may be seen as metaphors, the issue at hand concerns how works of art or metaphors work so that they have cognitive import. It should be noted that even theories of metaphor that deny cognitive significance to metaphors—such as emotive theories and Davidsonian treatments of metaphors (1978)—are relevant to this issue of cognitive meaning. Although such theories reject the idea that metaphors are cognitively meaningful in themselves, they do acknowledge that metaphors may be prompters of insights. Thus, the question of the way they can condition

the provocations of insights still arises. If we assume that at least some works of art have been designed so that their content is expressive of (or provokes) insights, then the question of how the insights of art can be new and a function of the way the work is organized arises as one of the fundamental issues in aesthetics. Correlating theories of metaphor that bear on verbal examples with views about the ways works of art may produce insights will be our main concern.

Of the views that metaphors are cognitively significant, and with respect to the idea that they are relevant to the central aesthetic problem of meaning, two general perspectives on metaphor can be distinguished: the comparison and the interaction views. In philosophical writings, what was the most commonly adopted view of metaphor, at least until recently, is reductive; it interprets metaphors as nonliteral uses of language that are translatable or paraphrasable into literally understandable statements. Metaphors are based on transferences of meaning to conceptually or conventionally incompatible contexts. The incompatibility, however, is overcome, because the metaphoric expressions are said to be traceable to analogies or similes made explicit in the translations and recognized in mental processing for both utterer and interpreter. "The human being is a wolf" is translatable into "The human being is ferocious and predatory." This way of accounting for how metaphors can be meaningful generally is associated with what has been called the comparison view, which treats metaphors as utterances that are based on comparing one thing with another with which the first is not literally or conventionally associated but which is seen to be related to it by some similarity. Presumably, in "The human being is a wolf," *Human being* and *wolf* are understood as referring to the quality of ferocity and being predatory, thought by the comparisonist to be common to humans and wolves.

The other main perspective dominant in metaphor theories during the second half of the twentieth century, the interaction view, interprets metaphors as nonliteral utterances that express or at least prompt cognitive insights that could not otherwise be articulated. They connect literally or conventionally incompatible systems ("The world is an unweeded garden"), or they utter meanings seemingly incongruous with their contexts ("Bob is cold," when Bob is obviously physically warm, or "New York is no island" when geographic considerations are absent). The interactions of incompatible meanings or of utterances and their meanings and contexts force interpreters to recognize new meanings. Metaphors (presumably the best ones) can be creations—the outcomes of creative acts—for the insights such metaphors offer are new and not simply discoveries of formerly unnoticed similarities or different formulations of what was already known. Thus, the significance of at least some metaphors is untranslatable and not paraphrasable without loss of meaning. Metaphors work by bringing otherwise incompatible meanings together such that the clusters of meanings associated with the main terms of the metaphor interact—"interanimate" one another—so that a new insight is generated.

The interaction view was initiated by I. A. Richards (1936) and developed by Max Black (1954–1955, 1977). Although he does not identify himself explicitly with interactionism, Monroe C. Beardsley (1958, 1962) gives an account that he believes supports the idea of the creativeness of metaphors—in a uniqueness of the "senses" that their interrelated meanings bring about.

The idea that metaphors are analogies and the idea that they are interactions between meanings expressing new meanings have distinct implications for one's conception of the way works of art are significant and how they function for the creator's and appreciator's experiences. One of the most explicit efforts to make such an application in the visual arts was made by Virgil Aldrich (1968, 1971). His thesis that there are visual metaphors seems at first sight to be based in part on a version of the comparison view: metaphors invite interpreters to see one thing as another thing with which the first is not ordinarily associated. Paintings can be metaphorical in the sense that they exhibit a way of seeing one kind of image as another kind of image. In Oskar Kokoschka's *Courmayeur et les dents des géants* (1927), mountains are seen as "domesticated" by the images of houses that appear almost embedded in them, and, at the same time, the houses are "aggrandized" by virtue of their integration with the mountains.

If works of art are, then, metaphors, and, in accordance with the comparison view, metaphors are thought to be based on similarities, then works of art might be thought to be at bottom representational, in the sense of imitating things in the world outside the work, with respect to the insights or force they have in getting appreciators to see (or hear) these things in the world in unprecedented ways. For, on this view, works of art as metaphors represent their objects or referents by virtue of underlying similarities. Houses are mountainous when "seen as" houses, and vice versa—for example, in terms of their structural integrity.

In Aldrich's view, however, there are suggestions that metaphors are more than instances of unusual ways of seeing something as something else on the basis of recognizing some common underlying quality. According to Aldrich's account, there is an intimate relation of images from different category-schemes: however different they are with respect to the categories in which they may be classified, the houses and mountains are painted in such a way that they are interdependent with respect to textures, lines, colors, or, generally, the visual qualities articulated on the surface of the painting. The visual metaphor introduces a constituting interrelation unique to the medium and in turn unique to the interacting images. Aldrich's view, then, leans toward the interaction view.

From a much different perspective, Nelson Goodman (1976) offers a thesis about metaphor in the context of a general account of aesthetic significance based on interrelations of symbol systems, and his conclusions bear on all the arts. These, too, are relevant to the interactionist, nonreductive approach. Within the field of psychology, Albert Rothenberg (1979) offers a view that draws on philosophical literature (Aldrich in particular) as well as his own empirical research, which is explained with the interaction view in mind.

It seems clear that the first, comparison theory, implies that works of art are metaphoric forms that refer to something antecedent—to formerly unnoticed resemblances. A portrait that is not simply photographic in the sense of being a snapshot, but is one that exhibits features that are normally ignored, and thus apparently "remote" from normally noticed features, shows characteristics pointing to an attentive appreciator's different way of seeing the subject of the portrait. For the comparativist, Leonardo da Vinci's Mona Lisa, then, may refer to a mysterious warmth in women, and this insight is the outcome of discovering overlooked qualities common to the image in the painting and live females.

On the other hand, for the interactionist, the insight emerges from recognition of unique (internal) relations among visual qualities—imbalance of horizon and haziness (vagueness) in the context of the main figure, subtlety in the suggestion of a smile—all related so that the "similarity" connecting mystery and womanhood is new (created) and the object of a visual insight. If the insight concerning mysterious warmth is dependent on the uniqueness of the way Leonardo exhibited interrelated qualities, then the mysterious warmth would be unique as a referent of the painting and for the interactionist (including Black) would be a created quality.

Given this interpretation, it may seem that works of art are being viewed as metaphoric in the sense of the special-symbol thesis, that is, in the sense that works of art are symbols that are not translatable into terms other than those of the symbol. This sense of symbol is surely comparable to, although not identical with, the sense of metaphor adopted by interactionists, for symbols in this special sense—Jung (1923), Langer (1953), and Wheelright (1962)—are symbolic in offering the only way to refer to their objects. Ludwig van Beethoven's Ninth Symphony expresses a celebration of the victoriousness of human striving in a way that no other complex of ordered qualities—verbally or visually as well as sonically (aurally) articulated—can duplicate.

There is a difference, however, between these special conceptions of symbol and interactionists' metaphors: although the symbols in question articulate new ways of referring, it is not clear that the special symbol views understand what is symbolized as being new. For instance, Jung proposed that what is symbolized consists of fundamental archetypes—ideas common to the collective (general) human unconscious; and Langer suggested that what is symbolized is founded on certain dynamic structures of human emotion. An insight recognized by interactionists refers to something that is created. What the insights are about is new in the world.

It is the uniqueness and thus fundamental newness of their way of presenting their significance that suggests a special relevance of the interactionist to the application of metaphor to art in general. Unless the significance of the symbol or metaphor shows something that was not there to be identified through closer scrutiny or through reordering established meanings, the work would not in a strong sense be creative—both created as the outcome of a creative act and as generative of future insight. As created, it is an outcome that is unprecedented, unpredictable, and in some respect valuable. As Kant put it, it makes its own rules and is thus exemplary rather than informative concerning rules for other artists to use. As creative, again as Kant said, a work of genius ought to inspire more genius, which is not to produce mannerism or to prompt imitators to ape the genius. And as Black put it, the metaphoric expression has resonance. On his interaction view, interacting meanings bring about a new significant quality, which Black calls a new similarity and which, he explains, is a new perspective.

One reason for this application of the comparison and interaction views to art in general is to suggest that construing artworks as metaphors may throw some light on the object of critical analysis and interpretation. This suggestion is supported by the point that insofar as metaphoric expressions are used in critical theories and interpretations of works of art, it is reasonable to consider the ways in which the objects of these critical accounts are organized so that the accounts are applicable to them.

The comparison theory is suggestive for closer analysis of how symbols work—that is, the ways in which analogical relations and comparisons are constitutive of the work's significance. Interactionism may throw light on ways of analyzing the interactions of nonverbal meanings—visual and aural qualities and relations—for example, using Black's proposal that systems of meaning function by emphasizing, suppressing, and producing resonance. Such processes point to ways visual and aural qualities interact in systems of internal relations, yielding visual and musical significance. Recently, Robert S. Hatten (1994) has discussed the relevance of metaphoric expression to music, in some respects, assuming an interaction approach. Carl R. Hausman (1989) has applied an interactionist view to the visual arts and music, proposing that the metaphoric structure of works of art includes levels of integrations among the ways elements function internally for interpretation and externally in relation to extra-aesthetic conditions.

The motive for applying metaphor theory to the arts, as was suggested earlier, is the question of how metaphors yield insights. Thus far, the kinds of answers mentioned have centered primarily on the forms or kinds of orderings among qualities that may be examined. The question of insight, however, also implies assumptions about the kinds of referents that metaphoric or metaphorically inspired expressions might have. This is a second reason for viewing artworks as metaphors. This dimension of the question points to the differences between issues concerning the relation of form and content and what aspects of the world (what objects) aesthetic insights are about. On formalist and emotivist views, there should be no external reference directly linked to the work. On a realist view, there should be some referent to which insights refer. The same questions are mobilized in metaphor theory. The prevailing view of the interactionists seems to confine metaphoric reference to what is found uniquely in the metaphor, thus apparently paralleling formalist views in aesthetics and, incidentally, going hand in hand with developments in the "linguistic turn" in philosophy—the so-called neopragmatist movements and deconstructionism. The comparison views seem to support a realist conception of aesthetic meaning, for they assume that there is in some sense an external object—an extralinguistic condition for the artistic insight. They provide a way of accounting for truth-value in metaphors or works of art in general, and the idea that truth somehow is relevant where insight is claimed needs to be faced.

On the one hand, then, interactionists give us accounts that preserve the newness and creativity of aesthetic meaning but leave open the question of the relevance of aesthetic insight to anything but themselves, since their objects are products of creative insights. Most interactionists realize this and refer to insights as perspectives or "ways of seeing"—or as "about the world"—but do not pursue the issue of just what the perspectives are about as anything considered to be independent, determinate referents that make up "the world." Bipin Indurkhya (1992) and Hausman (1989) have tried to come to grips with this issue, the former primarily in terms of verbal metaphors and the latter through an application to nonverbal examples. Goodman (1968) also has proposed extensionalist theories, but as a nominalist, he rejects the ontological dimensions of the issue. This is to say that the ontological or metaphysical status of things in the world, which are referred to and thus are extralinguistic or extraschematic and extraformal, is left open. This is not because his view of metaphor requires it, but because of his general theory of language.

At the root of the consideration of the question of metaphoric or aesthetic meaning is the underlying, fundamental issue, which should be emphasized, although it cannot be pursued further. The issue concerns the relation itself between the linguistic (verbal and nonverbal) utterances that are understood metaphorically and their objects, or referents: is the relation analogical or metaphoric? In either case, the answer bears on the meaningfulness of saying that metaphoric-aesthetic insights are creative, and at the same time, about something.

BIBLIOGRAPHY

Aldrich, Virgil. "Visual Metaphor." *Journal of Aesthetic Education* 2 (1968): 73–78.

Aldrich, Virgil. "Form in the Visual Arts." *British Journal of Aesthetics* 11 (1971): 215–226.

Beardsley, Monroe C. *Aesthetics: Problems in the Philosophy of Criticism.* New York, 1958; 2d ed., Indianapolis, 1981.

Beardsley, Monroe C. "The Metaphorical Twist." *Philosophy and Phenomenological Research* 22 (1962): 293–307.

Black, Max. "Metaphor." *Proceedings of the Aristotelian Society* n.s. 55 (1954–1955): 273–294.

Black, Max. "More about Metaphor." *Dialectica* 31.3–4 (1977): 431–457. Reprinted in a slightly modified version in *Metaphor and Thought,* edited by Andrew Ortony (Cambridge and New York, 1979), pp. 19–43.

Davidson, Donald. "What Metaphors Mean." *Critical Inquiry* 5.1 (Autumn 1978): 31–47.

Goodman, Nelson. *Languages of Art: An Approach to a Theory of Symbols.* 2d ed. Indianapolis, 1976.

Hatten, Robert S. *Musical Meaning in Beethoven: Markedness, Correlation, and Interpretation.* Bloomington, Ind., 1994.

Hausman, Carl R. *Metaphor and Art: Interactionism and Reference in the Verbal and Nonverbal Arts.* Cambridge and New York, 1989.

Henle, Paul, ed. *Language, Thought, and Culture.* Ann Arbor, 1958. *See* pp. 173–195.

Hesse, Mary, and Michael A. Arbib. *The Construction of Reality.* Cambridge and New York, 1986.

Hester, Marcus B. *The Meaning of Poetic Metaphor.* The Hague, 1967.

Indurkhya, Bipin, *Metaphor and Cognition: An Interactionist Approach.* Dordrecht and Boston, 1992.

Johnson, Mark, ed. *Philosophical Perspectives on Metaphor.* Minneapolis, 1981.

Jung, Carl. *Psychological Types.* Translated by H. Godwin Baynes. London, 1923. *See* pp. 601–610.

Kant, Immanuel. *Critique of Judgment* (1790). Translated by Werner S. Pluhar. Indianapolis, 1987. *See* section 49.

Langer, Susanne K. *Feeling and Form.* New York, 1953.

Richards, I. A. *Philosophy of Rhetoric.* New York and Oxford, 1936.

Ricoeur, Paul. *The Rule of Metaphor: Multidisciplinary Studies of the Creation of Meaning in Language.* Translated by Robert Czerny with Kathleen McLaughlin and John Costello. Toronto, 1977.

Rothenberg, Albert. *The Emerging Goddess: The Creative Process in Art, Science, and Other Fields.* Chicago, 1979.

Wheelwright, Philip. *Metaphor and Reality.* Bloomington, Ind., 1962.

CARL R. HAUSMAN

Metaphor and Art History

The word *metaphor* is from the Greek *metapherein,* "to carry over or across." In the Latin rhetorical writers, *metaphor* became *translatio* or *transferentia,* both closely preserving the same idea of movement and carrying. Taken together, these terms provide a schema according to which something (and not just a word) is moved from one place to another. In what will be called here *real* metaphor, this displacement actually occurs. More specifically, a real metaphor is the consequence of putting something available in place of something else, something else that is absent or not present, or not actually present—that is, not present in a way that allows it to be treated or addressed. Real metaphor thus makes the absent present and accessible through the transfer of what is already at hand. A stone, for example, might "take the place" or be "put in the place" of a dead chieftain in order for his power to continue to be addressed. Such substitution is a fundamental mode of image making, issuing directly from the most basic conditions of human spatiality, namely, actual presence and absence. Real metaphor is thus an irreducible basis for the construction of meaning within the prelinguistic spatial relations and possibilities acknowledged and indicated by language itself.

Like a metaphor in language, the significance or value of a real metaphor depends on context. The context in question, however, is real *spatial.* A real metaphor is not a "sign" in the way that a mark or set of marks might be; and it is a "representation," not in the sense of being a symbol, but rather in the sense of making present again, or, more specifically, of making the already present present again, but in another circumstance as something else. Finally, a real metaphor is not simply a substitute, although the *standing* buried in the etymology of the word *substitute* is essential for a real metaphor's definition of and by real spatial context.

As suggested above, a real metaphor is not only a displacement, it is also a removal to a place in which it may be treated as if it were what it is able to be treated as if being. But however the matter is phrased, place is fundamental, and the stone/chieftain is not simply designated as such, but is rather made to be such by being set in a place of use, a precinct with more or less definite boundaries. Boundaries in themselves define and determine the stone, making it central, for example, and circumambulatable. The spaces correlative to real metaphors are intrinsically social, providing the basis for both inclusion and exclusion. Only certain persons, for example, might know the significance of a real metaphor, or be allowed to enter its precinct, or the precinct might be entered only on certain occasions. Real metaphor always entails a decorum and is integral with culturally specific behavior, of which ritual in some sense of the word is a part. Those who know such decorum, that is, who know what to do in the space in which the real metaphor has its value and meanings, are not so much "observers" of works of art as they are "observant" of rite and custom.

In West Africa there are stories of stones at crossroads ministered to as the messenger god Eshu; homage was said to have been paid to Eshu by means of these stones before there were anthropomorphic wooden images. A stone, in other words, was the effective presence of Eshu at a crossroads, in relation not only to a certain space, but in relation to a certain social space, and to a more or less specific social behavior. In India, the effective presence of Śiva may be stated by a stone or mound at the center of an oriented precinct. In both cases, the deity may also be shown in highly developed anthropomorphic form, but the minimal presentation of a real metaphor may still be perfectly adequate. The point of these examples is not that the real metaphor is "early" and the anthropomorphic images "more advanced"; rather, the later images should be explained as amplifications and elaborations of what might be called a real metaphoric core. What is constant through such a range of representations of the same thing is the correlative real spatial decorum all the images involve.

Regarded simply as a sign, the identity of a real metaphor as what it makes present would be lost without its correlative social space and practice. Any real metaphor, however, is not a mere cipher, and the conditions of its existence are themselves positive and may make it significant by analogy in many ways. In language, a metaphor tellingly replaces another word by virtue of some similarity. To say that Alexander is a lion is to say, for example, that he shares characteristics with the king of beasts, and a stone might have been chosen because of its supposed qualities or powers, which are at least implicitly associated with or attributed to what the stone represents. To the degree that it is distinguished in some way, a real metaphor may be more or less separable from its context, even though it must quickly be said that these meanings are also culturally specific. Green or blue stones, for example, have high value in some cultures but not in others. Real metaphors may also be enhanced by facture, by the addition of pigment, by shaping, rounding, or smoothing, or by ornamentation. They may also be both distinguished and empowered by resemblant elements—eyes, mouth and hands—that allow what has been made present to see, speak, and act. Such elements may be very schematic, or resemblant only because of location. Eyes may be no more than depressions or knobs set side by side in the upper part of a stone, and have more to do with increasing or articulating the power of a presence than with the duplication of appearances. The meanings to be inferred from such specification, it should be noted, can only be general and provisional. If a stone has schematic but recognizable "eyes," we may see that it is anthropomorphic, and this recognition is relatively independent of context of use. We can say little more specific about it, however, not least because its use may change, and its specific "meaning" might be circumstantial in important respects, thus to be explained in many ways by those who use it.

Analogy raises other issues. At the level addressed here, the implicit "this is that" of a real metaphor means "this may be treated as if it were that." What makes this treatment possible is, in the simplest case, mere presence, which allows facing and address. But as I have said, actual presence has its own conditions and coordinates; a stone occupies space, "stands" in some way in relation to us, is permanent and of a certain size. A stone given eyes has also been made more explicitly to face, and this facing may be magnified by orientation in a precinct and fit to ritual.

Presences of the kind being associated here with real metaphor are evidently desirable to those who make them, but for that very reason they may have a range of uses and meanings. The forces made addressable may be positive, negative, or ambivalent. The great stone figures of Easter Island are called "the living faces of our ancestors." If that is something like what they were called from the beginning, this does not mean that they are likenesses of ancestors; rather, it means that the figures make those (or the "greatest" of those) who have come before able to be appropriately addressed in the present. If this presence becomes undesirable for some reason, or ineffective, the humiliation or disempowering of the images—toppling, breaking, gouging out of eyes—is a reversal of their original placement and empowerment, significant in terms of the same conditional categories, but negatively significant.

In order to be a real metaphor, an object must be manageable, which is real spatially continuous with its being treatable, or "observable." In these terms, a large stone might also be significant for having required concerted collective effort to move (like the statues of Easter Island or the colossal heads of the Olmecs); or, at the other end of the scale, images may be primarily significant because of their manipulability, portability, and possessability (from which the general principle might be drawn that the size of all images is determined by human purpose). There are countless examples of manipulable images, some of them close at hand, such as snapshots of friends and family members. Paleolithic "Venuses" were fashioned in shapes close to those of tools, as if by figuration to make an implement with special powers, and at the same time to make those powers manipulable, thus changing the value of both tool and image. Examples could be extended, from the vast numbers of clay figurines made in agricultural societies in many parts of the world, to the dolls and toys by which social behavior is taught and learned through modeling and imitation.

Real metaphor provides a base of substitutive value relative to which all images may be considered. To take a familiar historical example, the perennial disputes and conflicts of Western iconoclasm turn on the question of whether or not images are adequate presentations of what they represent.

The paradigm for real metaphor is sculpture. Words such as *statue* and *monument* preserve these meanings in fairly pure form, although sculpture (like European sculpture, especially since the Renaissance) may also be predominantly "pictorial." For their part, images on surfaces, for which painting may be taken as the paradigm, are not simply integral with real space, but rather possess a double distance. That is, the surface itself—always a specific format—is in a real space of some specific social significance at some distance; in addition, any image on the surface also entails a virtual space and distance. Whatever is represented on a surface, precisely because of its being on a surface, entails the more or less explicit assertion of an apparent place (of space or time) "in" the surface. Virtual space may be articulated in any number of ways, and the possible structures of virtuality are in their turn reducible neither to the structures of language nor to those of real space, at the same time that formats, as real spatial, involve decorum and "observance" as well as the "viewing" of virtual spaces. In the case of images on surfaces, materials are brought and applied in order to make it seem as if forms had been placed in a virtual space. From the standpoint afforded by this framework, Western optical naturalism is a construction of virtual space as primarily metric, physical, and egocentric, that is, a construction of virtual forms in virtual light in relation to a single viewer. For the most part, Western art history and criticism have been preoccupied with the construction of virtual spaces, their problems and implications, and much less concerned with their correlative real spaces, which is not to mention the neglect of real metaphor and its values. Western art history continues to be written as a development from rudimentary to fully realized optical naturalism. According to the options sketched here, however, changes in emphasis from real to virtual space are exchanges of one kind of positive meaning for another. The general principle urged by real metaphor is that all images, both real and virtual spatial, are primarily significant in terms of their conditions of presentation.

BIBLIOGRAPHY

Gombrich, E. H. *Meditations on a Hobby Horse and Other Essays on the Theory of Art* (1963). 3d ed. London, 1978.

Summers, David. "Real Metaphor: Toward a Redefinition of the Conceptual Image." In *Visual Theory: Painting and Interpretation*, edited by Norman Bryson, Michael Ann Holly, and Keith Moxey, pp. 231–259. New York, 1991.

Summers, David. "Conditions and Conventions: On the Disanalogy of Art and Language." In *The Language of Art History*, edited by Salim Kemal and Ivan Gaskell, pp. 181–212. Cambridge and New York, 1991.

DAVID SUMMERS

Derrida and de Man on Metaphor

Jacques Derrida's and Paul de Man's remarks on metaphor are complementary developments from the same general perspective. The two thinkers share a thesis about language that shapes much of their thought: Derrida and de Man hold that linguistic meaning does not rest on non-language-like meaning bearers. The absence of "meanings," in the sense of magic tokens of thought that, by their very nature, pick out their extensions, means that an account of metaphor must be constructed entirely within language and its use. Terms are applied to objects not because the objects naturally fit an interior concept that is somehow nonarbitrarily apt for the object. The denial of such natural fit is also the denial of a "given." The relationship even between thought and object is like the relationship between "f-r-o-g" and a frog. Thus, many familiar ways of thinking of metaphors cannot be part of their account.

For example, neither Derrida nor de Man can appeal to "metaphorical meanings" for metaphors to mean, given that any account of the meaning of a term will be in words that can be interpreted "metaphorically" or not. For the same reason, de Man analyzes metaphor in terms of the rhetorical force with which something is said. Given that there are no intended meanings to distinguish the literal from the metaphoric, different force is the only equipment for the distinction between literal and figural, a distinction that de Man retains, at least verbally.

De Man and Derrida both reject accounts of metaphor that "marginalize" it, that is, treat it as a mere supplement to a theory of the workings of language. De Man's rejection amounts to making metaphor the fundamental mechanism of predication. Derrida's rejection questions the very categories in which the concept "literal" language is thought.

Derrida. Jacques Derrida's most direct and extended treatment of metaphor occurs in "White Mythology" (see also "The Supplement of Copula"). This essay starts with Anatole France's critique of philosophical concepts as metaphors that have had their genuine sensory meaning eroded so that philosophy deals in ideas that have lost the richness of ordinary words. Derrida evolves a very nuanced position in relation to France's critique: on the one hand, he agrees that philosophy is based on metaphors and that philosophical concepts are suspect as a consequence; on the other hand, he rejects France's critique as presupposing the very philosophical conceptions it is trying to attack (one aspect of "deconstruction"). The France piece is the point of departure for an examination of metaphor and its relation to philosophy. This examination is not so much a theory of metaphor as a "deconstruction," a demonstration that metaphor, although conceived as an addition to the central workings of language, is in fact not only a construction of philosophy, but also the founding device of philosophical accounts of language and meaning.

If extensions of terms are not "dictated by nature" in general, then the concept of metaphor does not pick out a phenomenon that is there independently of the theory in which it is articulated. The "theory" with which the concept of metaphor is particularly laden is the philosophical theory of meaning. "Meanings" allow us to think that something can be "transported" from the "proper" domain of a predicate to something else.

So, "metaphor" presupposes philosophy by presupposing the theory of meanings as logoi, the theory of the contrast between the sensory and the intellectual, and the persistent analogy in philosophy between thinking and seeing. Given that there are no "meanings" in the sense of magic thought tokens that, by their nature, determine extensions, thoughts are as remote from or close to what is represented as written inscriptions are. Extending a term to a new case is always underdetermined by previous applications—"the same kind of thing" is undetermined either by internal dispositions of speakers or by natural necessities. So, "metaphor," although it can be applied in cases, cannot be separated from the philosophical accounts that inform it.

In this respect, Derrida's account of "metaphor" resembles Willard Van Orman Quine's account of analyticity. Quine and Derrida allow that the predicates can be applied in cases, but deny that the theories that "metaphor" and "analyticity" contain are appropriate. Like Quine on analyticity also, Derrida does not try to refute every possible account of metaphor. Rather, his project is to bring the reader to think of what has been called metaphor in a different way.

Derrida claims that philosophy and philosophical theories of metaphor have always rested on some "tutelary tropes," the most important of which is the contrast/analogy between the sensory and the intellectual, which produces the idea of intellectual "clarity," the light of reason, and meanings themselves as entities that are grasped by reason and carried by words. Plato's analogy of the sun in *The Republic* is taken as the paradigm of such a conception.

The philosophical account of meanings as something "present to the mind" that magically pick out their referents has another role in many accounts of metaphor. How do we tell when a use is metaphoric? If metaphoricity were determined by interior intentions or consciousness, there would have to be a level of thought representation where no figural interpretation was possible. Such a level could only be the "magic language" of present-to-the-mind logoi.

Derrida "shows" that these tropes have always characterized philosophy by discussing Plato, G. W. F. Hegel, Aristotle, and other philosophers and theorists of metaphor. As the framework for the whole essay, his discussion of Anatole France argues that France's critique of philosophy as worn-out metaphor uses in its theorizing precisely the tropes that constitute and organize philosophical accounts. Thus, France's denunciation of philosophy presupposes the legitimacy and accuracy of philosophical accounts.

Another aspect of the philosophical application of the concept of metaphor emerges from the notion of "wearing away" or "usure." Usure also can be understood as usury, excessive return on capital. When a term is used as a philosophical concept, it is supposed to become clarified and purified and therefore appropriate for "technical" philosophical use. Hegel's theory of *Aufhebung* is a paradigm of this process. But the idea that philosophy has concepts purified by being removed from the sensory to a "higher" realm is a widespread notion of how philosophical concepts can transcend the inadequacies of "ordinary" discourse.

What would an account of the phenomena we call metaphor be like, apart from its philosophical roots? Derrida suggests that an alternative would see breaks rather than continuity—sudden departures into a different way of thinking about a subject matter. So, the philosophical tropes would be regarded as contingent breaks, rather than naturally forced developments of thought.

Besides resting on a theory of meanings and a contrast between the sensory and the intellectual, "metaphor" is a metonym for the relation of language to the world. Words are not naturally proper to their referents. A metaphor, likewise, is not properly or literally applied to what it is a metaphor for. But, for a metaphor to work, there has to be something "appropriate" about the application of the term to the case. Metaphors therefore need to be both fitting and not.

Derrida has thus argued several theses on metaphor. First, "metaphor" itself is a metaphor. Something called "meaning" is "carried across" from its proper home to something to which it is appropriate but not proper. Second, philosophy is founded on a family of metaphors connecting vision, light, intellect, and intelligibility. Most important, "meanings" are a product of this metaphor. Third, nothing in nature dictates that knowing is like seeing. Fourth, philosophical concepts produce the illusion of precision and superiority to ordinary language by using metaphoric processes.

These theses support Derrida's conclusion that there can be no philosophical account of metaphor, for such an account of metaphor would have to include itself. On philosophical, logical priority grounds, there is a self-referential paradox in the idea of a subject matter, philosophy, explaining itself. So, strictly speaking, philosophy, as founded on metaphor, cannot give an account of metaphor. Thus, Derrida's critique is a deconstruction of, rather than an alternative theory of, metaphor. Note that this argument is not an argument that there is something about self-reference that really makes metaphor incompletely explainable. Rather, on the Husserlian model that Derrida takes to be the paradigm, philosophy insists on generating concepts with conceptual equipment that does not presuppose the very concepts being generated. Given that conception of philosophy, philosophy indeed cannot give an account of metaphor, since its concepts are themselves metaphorical.

The idea of an intelligible account of the world, in which the order of thought corresponds to the order of the world (i.e., in which logical priority corresponds to ontological priority), is an insistence on a founding metaphor.

de Man. Paul de Man discusses many of the philosophical questions about metaphor in the chapter of *Allegories of Reading* on Jean-Jacques Rousseau, entitled "Metaphor (Second Discourse)" and in his article "The Epistemology of Metaphor." According to de Man, Rousseau says two apparently incompatible things about the relation between naming and conceptualization. In the *Discourse on the Origin of Inequality (Second Discourse),* Rousseau takes naming to be the primitive linguistic act, while predicating is an articulation, a division into categories, of the named objects.

Since predication is an exchange or substitution of properties on the basis of resemblance, predication is metaphor. So, this account seems to make nomination literal and predication figurative and thus to divide language into the literal and the figurative.

In the *Essay on the Origin of Languages,* on the other hand, Rousseau supposes language to start with an expression of passion, specifically through the use of a general term. De Man makes these two doctrines constitute parts of a single view.

In the *Essay,* Rousseau takes the first general term to be an expression of fear, when a person applies a term more or less translated "giant" to a fellow human being. In *Allegories of Reading,* de Man calls this application metaphoric and metalinguistic (pp. 152–153)

As a first approximation, this utterance of "giant" is metaphoric because an outer item, the human being, is called by a term proper to an inner item, the fear, thus meeting the conditions for carrying across meaning. For de Man, figuration is essentially a matter of rhetorical force. He even speaks of the fear felt at the approach of another human as a "figural state" because that fear is a hypothesis of future harm rather than a known fact.

De Man says, "The metaphor 'giant,' used to connote man, has indeed a proper meaning (fear), but this meaning is not really proper" (p. 151).

De Man thinks of propositional attitudes, or "passions," as different rhetorical forces with which propositional contents can be entertained or uttered. De Man calls such deviations of force "figural." His notion is that there is a turning from a direct ascription of a description to reality. Something other is meant by the representation. De Man identifies the rhetorical explicitly with the figural. Meaning is a feature of speech acts, primarily, for de Man, so a turning of meaning is a turning of a speech act. Troping is the use of a representation for something other than direct reporting of what is the case. So, "giant" is a metaphor, even in this narrative in which such a word is being uttered for the first time in a stimulus situation.

De Man's account of language, however, seems to require an emotional given and an empirical given relative to which human language can be described as figured and disfigured. De Man's argument appeals to a distinction between the given facts, the "empirically verifiable" and the emotional reactions that somehow are the meanings of utterances. One wonders whether this distinction can be made without presupposing distinctions that should not be available, given that de Man is discussing the origins of language.

For de Man, then, rhetoric begins at home, in the interiority of the person who has attitudes toward the contents of sentences. A person in relation to her own representations is in a rhetorical situation. Since, on de Man's view, the representations themselves have a dubious rhetorical standing,

the special status of a person in relation to his own utterances begins to be erased. That is, the representations themselves already have rhetorical histories due to their use of general terms. These "emotionally contaminated" histories raise the same questions about their relation to some originating intention that the utterance has to its originating intention.

There are other important features of this case. This metaphor *disfigures,* which is de Man's paradoxical term for the change that takes place when a figural state is put into words. The figural state, when put into words, can be taken literally, so the metaphoric expression, qua expression, falsifies something. A "literal" reading is the prima facie force of whatever is put in a declarative sentence. As an utterance, "giant" cannot carry a "rhetorical force marker," a sign that would say how it was intended. Force cannot be put into words, because words, by being words, are detached from any necessary connection with an intention. As soon as intention is expressed, it must be expressed in something that need not carry that intention. There are no intentions apart from language and no language without ulterior rhetorical force, that is, undirected by intention.

The "falsification" in the metaphoric use of a term, then, is twofold. First, the inner state, a passion, is ascribed to the external world—the object is characterized by something representing the passion. Second, by being put into words, the representation loses its privileged tie to a particular rhetorical force, namely, hypothesis, and is turned into what can legitimately be read as an assertion of what is the case.

De Man calls metaphor "metalinguistic" because he thinks of the rhetorical force with which something is thought as something like the intention with which a sentence is said. So, saying something sarcastically or ironically presupposes a consciousness of and a representation of the sentence said. So, the rhetorical use of language requires that the user have a metalanguage in which sentences of the object language can be represented.

De Man treats disfigurement as universal in Rousseau even when, on the surface, Rousseau takes acts of denomination to be primitive linguistic operations, rather than the expression of passions through general terms. Rousseau's picture on the surface is that objects are first named, and then, on the basis of resemblances among named objects, a general term is applied that labels distinct things the same. Distinct objects are all called by the same name—say, "tree"—so that a transfer of meaning from one case to the next takes place. Thus, for Rousseau the use of predicates, what de Man calls "conceptualization," is essentially metaphoric.

De Man resists the usual interpretation of this passage as contrasting the literal, denominative stage of language with the conceptual, figural stage. Rousseau says that denomination depends on noticing difference, so that individuals are given distinct names only when they are noticed to be distinct. But "different" is a concept that would have to have been applied to new pairs on the basis of the metaphoric extension described above and explicated in detail below. So, Rousseau actually takes denomination to presuppose conceptualization.

De Man thus accepts Rousseau's narrative of conceptualization, but does not suppose that "natural resemblance" fixes the language into a system. For de Man, there are multiple "natural" bases in "resemblance," and therefore the metaphors that constitute the predicate "system" will not be a system.

Figural displacement is fundamental to language in two ways, according to de Man. First, language is figural in the sense that it involves disfiguration, the misrepresentation of the force of a propositional content. The gap between an intended force at a particular level and the liberation from any necessary connection with that force when the utterance is produced makes every level of representation subject to misrepresentation.

Second, de Man holds that all predication is calling one thing by a term that is not by nature appropriate to it. Here is the crucial point at which the assimilation of all metaphor to rhetoric needs to be made: this characterization, which is used to label predication as metaphoric, sounds like the typical definition of metaphor as calling one thing by another's name, as de Man notes. So he seems to have two notions of figure—the figural as intending a different rhetorical force, and the figural as using a name for an object to which it does not properly apply. The first is his general conception of figure, whereas the second is used to describe metaphor, a special case of figure. De Man needs some account of how the second notion is really a special case of the first, in order to maintain the identification of the rhetorical with the figural.

How is meaning some other referent than is said a matter of rhetorical force? How does de Man assimilate the account of conceptual extension as metaphoric to the rhetorical analysis of saying something other than is meant?

Conceptualization is calling one thing by another's name. When Charles is discovered and is about to be said to be a frog, while Albert and Bertha are familiar frogs, the term *frog* at that point has the set (Albert, Bertha) as its extension. So, when Charles is said to be a member of that set, to be a "frog," the remark is not strictly true, and is not strictly "meant." The speaker or thinker does not seriously believe that Charles is identical to Bertha or to Albert. De Man, that is, assuming at this point that the application of predicates in new cases is not fixed by nature, can assimilate the application of a predicate to a new case as metaphor based on, but not determined by, objective resemblance.

The rhetorical force involved in the predication is then exactly like the force that Donald Davidson ascribes to metaphor: the sentence is not asserted as true but rather in order to point up something. It is recognized as not literally true, but said for some other point. In this case, the point is to bring out a felt resemblance or to illuminate Charles by calling him a element of the set (Bertha, Albert).

When one *says* "Charles is a frog," however, the utterance loses special attachment to the complex metaphoric intention. This "disfiguring" amounts to literalization, so that Charles is said to *be* a frog. Then the "extension" is in effect the set (Albert, Bertha, Charles), and the feeling that there is something about Doris that makes it appropriate to call her a frog sets the narrative on another cycle.

In short, Rousseau's narrative as transcribed by de Man pictures ordinary predication as involving exactly the kind of rhetorical force, the intention that the utterance not be understood as strictly a description of how the object really is.

De Man continues to use the figural/literal distinction as a way of emphasizing the centrality of the figural in the apparently literal. It is not clear, however, that de Man's use of this distinction can be merely rhetorical. De Man's metalanguage seems to require genuine applications of *literal* and *empirical*. Whereas Derrida's account manages to disengage from the distinctions being questioned, by not proposing another account of metaphor, de Man uses the "literal" and the "figurative" in their traditional sense when explaining how the literal is really figurative.

[*See also* Derrida.]

BIBLIOGRAPHY

Davidson, Donald. "What Metaphors Mean." In *Inquiries into Truth and Interpretation,* pp. 245–264. Oxford, 1984.
de Man, Paul. "The Epistemology of Metaphor." *Critical Inquiry* 5.1 (Autumn 1978): 13–30.
de Man, Paul. *Allegories of Reading: Figural Language in Rousseau, Nietzsche, Rilke, and Proust.* New Haven, 1979.
Derrida, Jacques. *Speech and Phenomena and Other Essays on Husserl's Theory of Signs.* Translated by David Allison. Evanston, Ill., 1973.
Derrida, Jacques. "The Supplement of Copula: Philosophy before Linguistics." In *Margins of Philosophy,* translated by Alan Bass, pp. 175–205. Chicago, 1982.
Derrida, Jacques. "White Mythology." In *Margins of Philosophy,* translated by Alan Bass, pp. 209–271. Chicago, 1982.
Quine, Willard Van Orman. "Two Dogmas of Empiricism." In *From a Logical Point of View,* 2d rev. ed. pp. 20–46. Cambridge, Mass., 1961.

SAMUEL C. WHEELER III

METAPHYSICS OF ART. *See* Ontology of Art.

METONYMY. *Merriam-Webster's Collegiate Dictionary,* tenth edition, defines *metonymy* as "a figure of speech consisting of the use of the name of one thing for that of another of which it is an attribute or with which it is associated" and gives "crown" in "lands belonging to the crown" as its example. More expansive, the *Oxford English Dictionary* offers for *metonym* "a word used in a transferred sense," instancing "testimony" for "witness" in the 1837 edition, and for *metonymy* "a figure of speech which consists in substituting for the name of a thing the name of an attribute of it or of something closely related." The examples and citations display a considerable range: bread for the body of Christ (1547); a 1562 definition as "when the name of the thynge is given unto the signe"; a staff or truncheon signifying authority (1625); effect being put for cause (1657); and "times" standing for "things done in those times" (1676).

The uneasiness reflected in these various instances and definitions continues to the present, where influential examples of metonymy (a notable instance would be Jacques Lacan's citation of "thirty sails" for "thirty boats") often turn out to be better put in other terms (as, in this case, synecdoche, the use of a less comprehensive term for one more comprehensive, or vice versa—one can feel the pressure of this slide in a number of the examples and definitions cited above). But this uneasiness may seem fundamentally a specialist matter and resolvable only within, and thus relative to, a particular elaboration of the system of tropes; it casts little light on the role metonymy has come to play within a certain range of contemporary thought and hardly explains why it seem appropriate as an entry in an encyclopedia of aesthetics.

For that, one might appeal to, for example, Friedrich Nietzsche's lately famous assertion of truth as a mobile army of metaphors and metonymies. Nietzsche's use of the term is certainly informed by a firm grasp of rhetorical theory, and we have come to see it as profoundly connected with other strong Nietzschean motifs—as, for example, what he argues to be an endemic human reversal of cause and effect, taking the bee for the cause of the sting rather than, as Nietzsche evidently would have it, the sting as the cause of (our noticing of) the bee. But Nietzsche's use, however considered, would have remained largely unremarked were it not for a particular sequence of developments in linguistics that have had a signal effect on the shape assumed by certain textual theories and practices in the second half of the twentieth century.

Ferdinand de Saussure's seminal *Course in General Linguistics* offered a number of distinctions crucial to the creation of language as an object of systematic study. Prominent among them is the distinction between syntagmatic (or associative) and paradigmatic (or substitutive) dimensions of language. The core thought here is that any language consists both of elements that can be substituted for one another and of rules governing their permissible sequences, so that if we begin from "the cat sat on the mat" we can create a number of other utterances by paradigmatic substitution in a variety of registers ("the feline sat on the mat"; "the hat sat on the mat;" and so on) but must order those substitutions always within a framework outside of which we make only nonsense ("the cat mat sat on"). Saussure noted that with respect to any given utterance the alternative members of a paradigmatic set are absent, whereas syntagmatic relations exist wholly *in presentia* as the order of that utterance. Studies of linguistic aphasia led the Russian-born linguist Roman Jakobson to rename this distinction in rhetorical terms, replacing paradigm with metaphor and syntagm with metonymy, thus setting what traditional rhetoric had taken to be a particular form of substitution (of an adjunct for the thing it adjoins) in opposition to substitution as such (along the way he suggested one see poetry as the projection of the metaphoric axis onto the metonymic, thus locating the doggerel effect of the classic mat-sitting cat).

Jakobson appears to take the substitutability of his rhetorical terms for Saussure's as more or less self-evident and so does not dwell on his motives in doing so; it seems fair to say that a number of factors combine to push him in this direction, including an interest in integrating C. S. Peirce's notion of intepretant into the Saussurean picture, a strong general interest on Jakobson's part in semantics and symbolic processes, especially literature, and the clinical facts of aphasia, a disorder that produces, in either of its forms, modes of speech characterized by an apparent breakdown in the literal grasp of things and so an efflorescence of "rhetorical" utterances. Whatever Jakobson's explicit motives, the effect of his shift in terminology is to render language in its entirety rhetorical, sense becoming wholly the effect of signs in their various relations with one another, one effect arising from their substitutability and the other arising from their enchainment to one another. This can appear entirely in keeping with Saussure's initial impulse, including his suspension of questions of reference; at the same time, however, it opens an obscure possibility of imagining language as wholly a turning from itself, away from the meanings we presume it to depend on and which Saussure's theory intends to describe.

Metonymy's problematic definition as substitution by contiguity or adjacency now settles into the nonsubstitutive consequences of adjacency: an instance might be the way in which *rose* added to *water* engenders *rosewater*. This is a model for the generation of literal sense out of rhetorical movement, as opposed to the traditional tendency to define (and limit) rhetorical movement by its grounding in prior literal sense (it is worth noting that the word *literal* is used here in ways that can and will be contested by the model being used to lay it out). The traditional tendency finds its classic formulation in the Aristotelian theory of metaphor as rational proportion; Jakobson's formulation in effect offers a systematic way of recovering and placing what Surrealism had opposed to it, albeit still as a presumed doctrine of metaphor whose actual metonymic weight is nonetheless clear in the privileged examples of Lautréamont's umbrella and sewing machine meeting on a dissecting table or in Max Ernst's canoe and vacuum cleaner making love in the forest. That the Surrealists got their own theory wrong this way is instructively unsurprising: given their insistence on the imagination, they took their object to lie in moving beyond language in its literal usage and so more or less naturally took their interest to lie in a doctrine of metaphor as a paradigm of language's escape from mere signifying; but in accepting that description of their interest, they continued to seek a literal name for that which could then stand for the rhetoricity of the rhetorical (*metaphor* has a long history of filling this role; in recent literary history *irony* has been another such name). Jakobson makes it clear that there is another possibility here—naming the literal as itself a modification of the rhetorical.

It is possible to distinguish three sometimes converging and sometimes diverging lines that will ultimately determine the emergence of metonymy as a key term in structuralist and poststructuralist thought. The first one carries, at least initially, an aspiration toward a generalization of Saussure's claim to scientific understanding and is first carried on from Jakobson by the anthropologist Claude Lévi-Strauss and then taken up by such figures as Roland Barthes and Jacques Lacan. On its own, this line will have no more than a technical use for the term *metonymy* that will simply cover the same ground as Saussure's *syntagm*. The second has one root in the history of Surrealism and its undivorceable dissidents, most notably Georges Bataille, and another root in Martin Heidegger's writings on language; it finds a certain intellectual continuation in the writings of both Lacan and the philosopher Jacques Derrida. The third arises from literary study's recurrent modern interest in the specific literariness of its object. While these are issues that are of central importance to Derrida, they are especially important to the American reception of much French theory; in this reception, the notions of metaphor and metonymy are immediately entered into a field in which such terms as *irony* (for American New Criticism) and *allegory* (in Northrop Frye) are already doing substantial work that will be variously extended and transformed by, for example, Paul de Man. The various patterns of overlap, interference, and avoidance among these three lines, including the frequent failure to distinguish them at all, continue to render contemporary appeals to metonymy difficult and often obscure, so that metonymy sometimes appears as a piece of linguistic terminology, sometimes as the name of a trope among other tropes, sometimes as a switch point between the literal and the rhetorical, and sometimes as a switch point between the discursive and the visible. Partly because of this confusion and partly for the more substantial reasons this essay explores, metonymy has rarely risen to the status of an explicit theoretical topic and has tended to make its presence felt most often as a certain awkwardness to be negotiated.

Nonetheless, it seems possible to sketch a sort of history of this trope or antitrope as it enters into, and ultimately disappears from, poststructuralist writing. The history being proposed here passes through three specific points: the psychoanalysis of Lacan, the literary criticism of de Man, and the philosophical work of Philippe Lacoue-Labarthe.

Lacan makes both metaphor and metonymy central to his vision of psychoanalysis, first, by using their ability to replace the Freudian notions of condensation and displacement as a part of his general claim that the unconscious is structured as a language, and then by extending them to take in the fundamental dimensions of human being as psychoanalysis proposes them—identity and its support in repression, which Lacan argues to be fundamentally metaphoric (the submission of one signifier to another, forcing the first into the unconscious), and desire, the movement of which Lacan takes to be fundamentally metonymic, enchaining one object to another, with the subject always finding itself only as sliding beneath that movement. That human beings should be torn between these two, Lacan takes to follow from its more general submission to "the signifier," understood to be abstractable from the unity of the sign, pursuing its own logic and generating a necessarily mobile web of sense as one of its effects. The relative stability of that web is assured by its buttoning back on itself through the privileged signifier he calls the phallus and defines as "the signifier intended to designate as whole the effects of the signified, in that the signifier conditions them by its presence as a signifier," which is to say that Lacan takes the phallus as a "pure signifier," one capable of rendering explicit the truth of signification in general. Lacan's doctrine of the priority of the signifier and so of the order he calls symbolic can be seen as a particular way of taking up and transforming Jakobson's rhetoricization of language.

At the same time, Lacan integrates into his account elements that can be seen to arise from his early involvement with Surrealism and Bataille's dissidence within it. In particular, Lacan sets up the symbolic on the basis of and in opposition to a real characterized by the fact that in it everything is always in its place. In becoming remarkable, in being exposed to language, the real both stays in place and passes over wholly into an order in which things can be only either in one another's place or in continuity with one another. On this view, metaphor looks to name language insofar as it supplants the real, while metonymy registers within language the real's radical continuity with itself, a continuity that demands registration just because language itself cannot be simply outside the real. [*See* Lacan.]

In a long essay from 1975 entitled "Le facteur de la vérité" (The Purveyor of Truth, or, The Truth Factor), Derrida mounted a forceful critique of Lacan's psychoanalysis through a close reading of the latter's key essay, "The Seminar on 'The Purloined Letter.'" While the essay does not directly raise issues of metaphor and metonymy, it argues that the effect of Lacanian theory is to seal itself wholly within itself and away from a world whose actual existence it could no longer acknowledge. It is thus interesting that the work of de Man, often seen as Derrida's most significant American literary critical disciple and himself at times an explicitly and forcefully antipsychoanalytic theorist, can nonetheless seem to renew and extend the fundamental logic of Lacan's position and to render particularly explicit its skeptical underpinnings.

While de Man's version of deconstruction is fixed in its essential lineaments quite early in his career (well in advance of his encounter with Derrida's work—their eventual encounter is to a degree determined by their relatively independent encounters with the work of Heidegger and Maurice Blanchot), its preferred sites, registers, and vocabularies display considerable fluidity. It is in his 1979 book *Allegories of Reading* that metaphor and metonymy take their turn at organizing de Man's readings (even as they also operate a turn toward the questions of linguistic performance that will supplant them). The introductory essay, "Semiology and Rhetoric," summarizes the stakes, developed in a reading of Marcel Proust, through two moments:

> By passing from a paradigmatic structure based on substitution, such as metaphor, to a syntagmatic structure based on contingent association such as metonymy, the mechanical, repetitive aspect of grammatical forms is shown to be operative in a passage that seemed at first sight to celebrate the self-willed and autonomous inventiveness of a subject. . . . The deconstruction of metaphor and of all rhetorical patterns . . . that use resemblance as a way to disguise differences, takes us back to the impersonal precision of grammar and of a semiology derived from grammatical patterns.

> It cannot pause there however. Individual metaphors are shown to be subordinate figures in a general clause whose syntax is metonymic; from this point of view, it seems that the rhetoric is superseded by the grammar that deconstructs it. But this metonymic clause has as its subject a voice whose relationship to this clause is again metaphorical. The narrator who tells us about the impossibility of metaphor is himself, or itself, a metaphor, the metaphor of a grammatical syntagm whose meaning is the denial of metaphor stated, by antiphrasis, as its priority.

> (de Man, 1979, pp. 16, 18)

The conclusion is then that "literature as well as criticism—the difference between them being delusive—is condemned (or privileged) to be forever the most rigorous and, consequently, the most unreliable language in terms of which man names and transforms himself" (p. 19). Although the structuring terms shift considerably over the course of de Man's career—from, for example, an early opposition of *symbol* to *allegory* to a late opposition of *the aesthetic* and *the material*, the fundamental form of the argument remains the same: the essential rhetoricity of language obliges it to name a literal order of sense it cannot reach, ei-

ther beyond itself (as something like the world) or within itself (as a proper name for its own rhetoricity) and so we find ourselves sealed within a system that runs by itself. Lacan's symbolic gains, through the privileged signifier of the phallus, a kind of closure that is available to de Man only through a momentary figure like metonymy that is itself a moment of sliding and displacement, so that if Derrida is right to say of Lacan's psychoanalysis that it ever finds only itself, it will be equally right to say of de Man's deconstruction that it only ever finds the displacement of its self as that from which it is a pure flight.

Both Lacan and de Man can be well described as distinctly anti-Heideggerian thinkers (de Man's repeated early negotiations with Heidegger's readings of Friedrich Hölderlin are particularly explicit about the stakes here). The fate of metonymy along a line more markedly sympathetic to—but also distinctly critical of—Heidegger is notably different. Here things start from the Heideggerian assertion, offered wholly apart from the Saussurean-Jakobsonian opposition of metaphor and metonymy, that the language is both absolutely continuous with the world (thus effectively taking Saussure's suspension of reference in a radically different direction) and, in its essence and origin, wholly metaphoric. Derrida takes this thought as a repeated object of his deconstructive reading, most directly in the 1978 essay "The *Retrait* of Metaphor," but the Heideggerian view of language also serves as an important early ground for his critique of Saussurean binarism, as in *Of Grammatology*. Jean-François Lyotard, closer to Maurice Merleau-Ponty than to Heidegger, pursues a parallel critique of Saussure in *Discours, Figure* that is perhaps particularly notable in its explicit engagement of the nexus of Jakobson, Lacan, and Surrealism. Gilles Deleuze and Félix Guattari can be said to address the same complex of issues by abandoning both Saussure and Heidegger in favor of an expressive problematic enabled by Louis Hjelmslev's linguistics backed by an appeal to Baruch Spinoza's systematic philosophy. In this range of writing *metonymy* retains its visibility as a pivotal term and topic only for Lyotard, and its presence there can be taken as a marker of his somewhat wavering stance toward the underlying issues.

These issues find perhaps their fullest expression in Lacoue-Labarthe's long and difficult essay "Typography." Reading its way back and forth between Plato and Heidegger around the topic of mimesis, "Typography" resists argumentative summary with unusual success, and the focus here is on but one particular moment within it. It is at this point a question of reading both a particular Platonic/ Socratic ruse and of seeing the internal relationship of that ruse to the emergence of what Lacoue-Labarthe calls "mimetologism." The ruse is the displacement of the question "who is the tragic poet?" into the question "what is mimesis?" One might imagine this displacement as amounting to taking a mirror that is held up in the world as a part of and continuation of it as if were outside that world reflecting (on) it.

> One can then speak of what is seen and of what is not seen, of what appears and of what does not appear (or not so clearly), of what shows itself, of what gives itself to be seen as this or that, just as it is or not, etc. In short, we can be installed within the visible realm: we do *theory*.   (Lacoue-Labarthe, 1989, p. 91)

With this trick turned, the radical and continuous lability of the world, including the subject who participates in it, freezes, as it were, into visibility, opening a field of presence and absence for a subject who now finds itself structured by that field. This is, Lacoue-Labarthe goes on to argue, an inevitable consequence of just that continuity and lability but it is one that renders its own cause and condition inaccessible: "That is to say, the ruse or trope in which the very will to capture the mimetic evasion simultaneously marks and betrays itself, is caught in its own device and recovers itself. This operation *already* has a mirror, a theoretical trap . . . in it" (p. 134).

Metonymy has, in effect, vanished into the actual stuff of the world (as it does more deeply still for Deleuze and Guattari), where it is registerable only as the fact of the world's passage over into language that will thenceforth be caught between the literal and the rhetorical and will be able to think that division only on the basis of the mirror (something we will now call a metaphor and that will be privileged insofar as it would be its own ground, thus giving rise to the image of a mirror fastened wholly to itself as the shape of a knowledge that would be both absolute and speculative). Lacoue-Labarthe reads, between Plato and Heidegger, the story of metonymy's appearance at the border of the literal and the rhetorical as the story equally of its disappearance, its becoming illegible (the story is thus close to the one Nietzsche tells about Apollo and Dionysus). This would be the strange fate of a trope both marginal and central to much contemporary theory.

[*See also* Metaphor; *and* Rhetoric.]

BIBLIOGRAPHY

Deleuze, Gilles, and Félix Guattari. *A Thousand Plateaus.* Translated by Brian Massumi. Minneapolis, 1987.

de Man, Paul. *Allegories of Reading: Figural Language in Rousseau, Nietzsche, Rilke, and Proust.* New Haven, 1979.

Derrida, Jacques. "The Purveyor of Truth." Translated by Willis Domingo, Moshe Ron, James Hurlbert, and Marie-Rose Logan. *Yale French Studies* 52 (1975): 31–113.

Derrida, Jacques. *Of Grammatology.* Translated by Gayatri Chakravorty Spivak. Baltimore, 1976.

Derrida, Jacques. "The *Retrait* of Metaphor." *Enclitic* 2 (1978): 5–33.

Jakobson, Roman. *Language in Literature.* Edited Krystyna Pomorska and Stephen Rudy. Cambridge, Mass., 1987.

Lacan, Jacques. *Ecrits: A Selection.* Translated by Alan Sheridan. New York, 1977.

Lacoue-Labarthe, Philippe. *Typography: Mimesis, Politics, Philosophy.* Edited by Christopher Fynsk. Cambridge, Mass., 1989.

Lyotard, Jean-François. *Discours, Figure.* Paris, 1971.

Saussure, Ferdinand de. *Course in General Linguistics.* Edited by Charles Bally and Albert Reidlinger, translated by Wade Baskin. New York, 1959.

STEPHEN MELVILLE

MIES VAN DER ROHE, LUDWIG (1886–1969), German-born American architect. Ludwig Mies van der Rohe is among the most influential architects of the twentieth century; his buildings help form the very basis for the definition of modern architecture for both supporters and detractors alike. He was the third director of the Bauhaus, director of the School of Architecture at the Illinois Institute of Technology (IIT) from 1938 to 1958, and a recipient of the Presidential Medal of Freedom from John F. Kennedy in 1963.

After a few houses in the tradition of Karl Friedrich Schinkel, Mies made his debut on the avant-garde scene with a series of studies for a glass skyscraper (1921–1922) that combined advanced building techniques with a Dadaist taste for the aleatory conditions of the metropolis. His projects for the Concrete House (1923) and the Brick Country House (1924) synthesize various formal lessons from the early buildings of Frank Lloyd Wright and the pictorial work of Theo van Doesburg and El Lissitzky to produce asymmetrical groupings of prismatic, interlocking masses and open "free plans" with independent walls that direct movement but do not create traditional rooms. All of these reappear in the German Pavilion for the Barcelona International Exposition of 1929, where Mies was first able to realize in built form the earlier formal experiments.

After World War II, having immigrated to the United States, Mies emerged as the architect whose work would shape the contours of American architecture for the next two decades. The campus of IIT (1939–1941), the house for Edith Fransworth in Plano, Illinois (1947–1951), the 860–880 Lakeshore Drive apartments in Chicago (1948–1951), and the zenith of his career, the Seagram Building, New York (1954–1958)—which won the American Institute of Architects' "25-Year Award" in 1984—were the paradigms other architects emulated, revised, and copied over and over again.

The received view of Mies's work—from commentators as different as Sigfried Giedion (1941), Philip C. Johnson (1947), Ludwig Hilberseimer (1956), and Arthur Drexler (1960)—has canonized it in a set of idealist terms that include technical perfection, timeless geometry, and aloof formal abstraction, all manifest in the universal space of the clear-span pavilion and the transcendent structure of the prismatic tower. Indeed, Mies did translate the heritage of romantic classicism into the modern steel frame, often with shifting planes suspended in a diaphanous space that seemed to flow uninterrupted through his buildings out into a universe commonly described as "Platonic." More recent readings of his work, however, have seen Mies's insistence on the unchanging truths of architecture as belying a complex struggle with the gritty contingencies of mass culture that modulates the meaning of his modernist abstraction.

Consider the 1922 skyscraper project. On the one hand, the skyscraper's newly achieved optics of mechanical reproduction is a thorough encoding of post–World War I society's technical advances. The vivid coordination of the reflective and refractive glass surface, the repetitive steel structural elements and floor plates, the contingent plan and aleatory volume, and the technical form of the high-rise building itself attest to architecture's social power of representation. The glass curtain wall—alternately transparent, reflective, or refractive, depending on light conditions and viewing positions—absorbs, mirrors, or distorts the immediate, constantly changing images of city life. The very body of the building contorts to assume the form demanded by the contingent configuration of the site and to register the circumstantial images of the context; and the reiterative steel structure mimics the anonymous repetition of the assembly line.

On the other side of the mimetic submission to its context, however, the skyscraper demonstrates architecture's power of resistance through its autonomy and independent material existence. For the other aspect of the project—most apparent in the thick, black, silent elevational drawing—strives toward an immediate materiality of the surface, attempting to oppose and negate the contextual status quo and assert itself as a radically intrusive, nonidentical object within an unsatisfactory social and physical fabric, an opaque refusal of the situation that was its sponsor. Mies seems eager here to escape the kinds of interiority bequeathed to aesthetic practice by the traditional bourgeois cultural values from which his early work had emerged. But he also wants to escape the degradation that modernity can bring. His later work would emphasize again and again its ambition to salvage the purity of high art from the encroachment of mass production, technological modernization, urbanization—in short, of modern mass culture and everyday life. But already in the skyscraper project—or at least in this one of its aspects, the elevational drawing seeming incompatible with the socially "reflective" model—Mies has reserved a dimension of antisociality and refusal.

The two aspects of Mies's project are, then, the result of the encounter between these contradictory impulses: representation and resistance, submission and refusal, mimesis and expression. A similarly contradictory structure is operative in his early masterwork, the 1929 German Pavilion in Barcelona. The building begins with a horizontally extended space produced by the low plinth and terraces, the uninterrupted roof slab, the freestanding columns and walls, and the corresponding constancy of section. Space is, quite literally, continuous between the pavilion and its site. Inside, however, the viewer is presented with an assemblage of different parts of disparate materials—the travertine pavement and walls surrounding the large pool, the marble walls facing the court, the tinted glass diaphragms, onyx slab and light wall, the chromium columns and glazing bars—the particular quality of each material registered as a kind of absolute. The relationships among these parts are in constant flux as one moves through the building; space itself becomes a function of the specificities of material and the time in which one experiences them.

The normal system of expectations about materials, however, is quickly shattered as materials begin to contradict their own nature. Supporting columns dissolve in an invasion of light on their surfaces; the highly polished green marble reflects the highlights of the chromium glazing bars and seems to become transparent, as does the onyx slab; the green-tinted glass, in turn, becomes an insuperable mirrored screen; the pool in the small court—shielded from the wind and lined in black glass—is a perfect mirror. The fragmentation and distortion of the space are total. Any transcendent order of space and time that would confer an unchanging unity on this assemblage is systematically and utterly dispersed. Mies's clearspan pavilion has become a labyrinth that denies us access to the ideal moment of organization lying beyond the actual experience of this montage of contradictory perceptual facts. A participant in the world yet disjunctive with it, it does not simply represent a preexisting reality. The built artifact is nothing less than the production of an alternative reality. The architectural reality takes its place alongside the real world, sharing temporal and spatial conditions of that world, but resisting their absolute authority with an alternative of material, technical, and conceptual precision.

In his study of Mies's writings, Fritz Neumeyer has alerted us to the persistence of a dialectical structure in Mies's thought, a "double way to order." Rehearsing a manuscript of Mies's from 1927, Neumeyer notes "a regular two-step of opposites: life and form, inside and outside, unformed and overformed, nothing or appearances, what had been or what had been thought, how and what, classical and Gothic, constructivist or functionalist" (Neumeyer, 1991, p. 197). Neumeyer continues, interpreting Mies through his underlinings of Romano Guardini's 1925 *Der Gegensatz*: "This conflict of opposites was not resolvable by a redeeming formula. Life could not be thought as a 'synthesis of disparities' nor even as a whole the two sides of which are complementary 'parts.' It exists rather as an elemental form, a 'bound duality'" (p. 200). This problematic subtends the trajectory of Mies's architectural program begun in 1922 to

MIES VAN DER ROHE. *Seagram Building* (1991). (Photograph by Ezra Stoller; copyright by Esto, Mamaroneck, New York; used by permission.)

intersect with another skyscraper, the Seagram Building, in the altogether different time and place of Park Avenue, New York City, 1954–1958.

The focus of Mies's attention in this project seems, at first, to be the plaza itself, with the building surface understood as a kind of frame or support for that primary clearing in the deadening thickness of the Manhattan grid. We can think of the plaza as Mies's attempt to pass beyond the contradictions of representation and resistance manifest in the two aspects of the 1922 skyscraper project toward some third term or "bound duality." The plaza is a cut out in the city, a literal nothing endowed nevertheless with a positive presence through its material and dimensional precision. Like the space-time montage of the Barcelona pavilion, it is a simultaneous production of difference and integration with the social city.

What would become the most significant feature of the Seagram Building, its curtain wall of glass and steel, like the curtain wall of 1922, has a mimetic dimension. Here the Seagram's famous I-section steel mullion is crucial; it is the nexus of meaning of the entire building surface: functional, factural, symbolic; utterly commonplace yet raised to representational status in the matrix that is the Seagram's sur-

face. What is more, the I-section mullion can be construed as the final stage in a set of transformations from a purely technical, instrumental fragment to a new form that organizes the visual exchange between the work and its reader; that is to say, from the I-section's use as a load-bearing component in some hypothetical steel-frame building to its tectonic role in the trabeated frame and brick infill at IIT (where the I-section still functions as a structural support behind the glass line or embedded in the wall), to the Seagram Building where the I-section, for one thing, stands as a synecdoche for the steel construction now pushed behind, but, by dissolving its factural identity into a mode of address, becomes strikingly more thing-like and present than ever.

But as we move back to view the curtain wall at a distance, the facture of the primal elements is taken over by their visual effect, which is to say by a logic of surface perception. The series of bronzed steel mullions now casts shadows on the bronze glass, erasing themselves as figures and the glass curtain wall as ground into a continuous spread of surface. The modulations of the surface—the reticulated grid of welded mullions and panels—as tectonically thick as they are, cannot be read "deeply" like the agonized surface of the 1922 building, which still projects subjective disturbances and contextual dissonances onto the full body of the building. Rather, they can only be scanned for textural information: they are metal-marked calibrations of a vision that has excluded everything from its domain except the idea of surface itself. Although they trace a manufacture and a certain skill, these marks signal precisely the renunciation of expression and of a controlling agency in favor of an immanent evenness of surface persisting from start to finish as if unencumbered by subjective intent. This is Mies's abstraction: the effort to turn subjective experience into objectivized form and images but that now flow back into the space of experience thus left open.

It is helpful to consider the built wall of the Seagram Building together with Mies's sketches for the sculptures of the plaza, the wall seemingly having come into existence fully conceptualized, with little intermediate development, the sculptures churned out in variation after variation, then finally discarded. The sketches have a kind of hit-or-miss quality: they can be taken as a search or as a catharsis, as if they were never meant to go into production, as if they had flowed from Mies's ruminations over the famous cigar and vodka back in his Chicago apartment. There is this implacable optical field of the building and the unsure plastic figure of the sculpture, the object found already and the object not-being-found. The two make sense only as negations of one another. By 1958, it seems, if there is to be an appearance at all, it will not be built up out of the human body (as the sculptures are, as all of Mies's chosen sculptures were) but rather out of architectural materials already reified, which have sucked in all corporeality. The abstract field will displace the figurative object, put it in the back pages of the notebook, or submerge it in the pools that finally appeared in the plaza in its stead, and then itself take on just enough of the aesthetic substance necessary to remain in experience at all.

One is reminded of Piet Mondrian, who, while dancing to his favorite Broadway boogie-woogie, suddenly turned to his partner and said, "Let's sit down, I hear a melody." Now, perhaps Mies's abstraction harbors just this negativity of modernist refusal; perhaps Mies is just like all the others of the avant-garde, only more so. It is true that Mies's famous desire to build "almost nothing" is at one with his abstraction. But abstraction as negation only is not adequate to explain the Seagram Building, where abstraction is more the presence of a new sort of experience, rather than the mere absence of experiences previously had. If abstraction could finally dispose of any conciliatory melody, but in such a way that one could still "dance" to it, then architecture might discover some other means of signifying experience; it might put itself in a different sort of relation to the world, create an experience that culture had not yet invented or not yet banalized. "Almost nothing," indeed, because there is not much left to work on.

Abstraction is late modern architecture's way of working through the social fact. Manfredo Tafuri, in perhaps the most provocative and most elliptical of recent interpretations of Mies's building in North America, sees the abstraction of its surface as a poignant endgame played out with the alienating forces of modernity—the last, desperate nonsolution to the historical guilt of modern architecture:

> The "almost nothing" has become a "big glass" . . . reflecting images of the urban chaos that surrounds the timeless Miesian purity . . . in the neutral mirror that breaks the city web. In this, architecture arrives at the ultimate limits of its own possibilities. Like the last notes sounded by the Doctor Faustus of Thomas Mann, alienation, having become absolute, testifies uniquely to its own presence, separating itself from the world to declare the world's incurable malady.   (Tafuri and Dal Co, p. 342)

For Tafuri, abstraction is a sign of formal closure and withdrawal in the face of overwhelming historical forces. Architectural abstraction is legitimate precisely because it reproduces the abstraction of the social system of exchange itself, putting the best face on the society's rationalization and planification of the subject that ultimately dispenses altogether with that inconvenience and reduces subjective choice to market desire. At the same time, Tafuri sees in Mies's work a wish to neutralize the social, which is not to say that it succeeded in doing so, or even that such a project makes any sense, for the social will still be found, but, for Tafuri, *outside* the work.

It is important, however, to find the social still inherent in the work, and we must therefore attempt to historicize Mies's effort at Seagram and factor in the anthropological shock of the self-constructed European mandarin (Mies famously changed his name in 1921 from Ludwig Mies to the aristocratic-sounding Mies van der Rohe) in contact with the new American democracy, and in particular with social practices that assured the destruction of the last remnants of surviving aristocratic forms, but came into being independently of the class struggle with an *ancien régime,* as had been the case in the Old World. For American popular culture in the 1950s had, on its own so to speak, become as technologically advanced as anything modernism could have hoped for—or better, there was a simultaneous leap forward both technologically and culturally and in which these two developments were consciously linked, resulting in the emergence of what we now call media culture. In the United States in the 1950s, unlike in modernism's earlier stages, it was the image of mass production and consumption, and the logic of mass advertising and image reception, that were foregrounded over the mechanical production techniques of the modern "masters." The logic of image reception began to displace that of object production.

The emergence just later of so-called pop architecture is enough verification of this, and the work of Archigram, Alison Smithson and Peter Smithson, and the Independent Group in Great Britain, and even more so the semiotic surfaces of Robert Venturi and Denise Scott-Brown in the United States are only the most obvious examples of architecture's close involvement with consumer culture and mass advertising and the consequent challenge to the cherished modernist ideals of profundity and autonomy. During the years of the Seagram Building and just after, more intensely than any other time in modern history, architecture itself began to be seen as part of commodity cultural generally. Not only does this mean that the aesthetic tastes of the new mass-cultural subject will be different in kind from those of the controlled and more comfortable identities of either the older aristocratic or bourgeois publics; it means ultimately the end of any doctrine of aesthetic universals or invariables, the tendency going even so far as to break up the very concept of the aesthetic unity and organicity of the work. It means that aesthetic self-referentiality begins to recede as a possible defense against mass culture.

The reemerging consumer culture of the 1950s, with its newly devised strategies of advertising—the technique of large-scale color printing on outdoor billboards and the use of electric lighting for advertisement, both on a scale and pervasiveness not previously imaginable—changed the very nature of the experience of urban public space. For now, visual reception challenged tactility and the perception of architectural surfaces began to overtake the experience of urban space in the traditional sense. The extensive development of buildings on the outskirts of the city and the new distribution of services to suburban commercial zones made the control of the quality of urban space through traditional compositional, tectonic, and constructional means more and more difficult. Thus is abstraction—very much including its most sophisticated philosophical and architectural equivalents, and especially that of surface—revealed at another level to be at one with the logic of equivalence and exchange, that is to say, with the logic of the commodity. Consequently, a split was felt to open between the world of high-quality building, in the European tradition of *Bauen* or *Baukunst,* and the everyday world of the American popular environment; and this would later (with Venturi and others) become a fundamental split in architectural theory.

It is precisely the isolation, self-referentiality, and conceptual opacity of modernist abstraction that have been fixed on by historians and critics as the definitive characteristics of the resistant abstraction of modernism. But when read through a logic of the surface—a perceptual logic that must now understand as having been given to us by consumer culture itself—self-referential or autonomous is too passive an adjective for Mies's abstraction. Abstraction in its fullest sense as a historically specific mode of organizing both subject and object comes into our perception in forms that are themselves produced by society, not by architecture alone. The experience of abstraction therefore belies architecture's autonomy, pinning that "inside" and that "appearance" to its "outside" (Mies) and the nothingness of reification.

The result is something that maintains the aspirations of modernism toward a visual logic derived from the qualities of materials and the nature of construction processes, but, at the same time, is not impervious to the gritty world of commercial culture that modernism, in its most famous moments, tried to refuse. The particular experience of this something, which is at once autonomous and porous, opaque and transparent, which reproduces social development in aesthetic terms without directly representing it, is rather more complex and dialectical than the abstraction that has been fixed on by historians and critics as the definitive characteristic of the resistant abstraction of modernism. One who would experience this manifestation is encouraged to adopt the perspective of just what is vilified (commodity culture) in order to see its "other."

The crucial move of Mies is to pose abstraction as at one and the same time the ultimate achievement of reification—the separation and neutralization of the full range of experience being the precondition of abstract thought—and a historically new experience, the only possible experience adequate to everything we have lost in reification. What results in the Seagram Building is, then, not so much an aesthetic representation of, or a resistance to, the social, but rather a series of transductions whereby abstraction changes its nature as it passes from the social to the aesthetic and back again. The plaza at the Seagram Building is perhaps the first pulling back from the alienating life of the metropolis, and the assertion of the architectural surface as the support for that space is commensurate with that with-

drawal. At this point, however, reification is borrowed back from the social in the form of the volumetric ready-made of the high-rise building and, even more, in the perception of the abstract surface. Then, in a final moment of transfer, reification appears as the experience of abstraction. By producing the abstract, architecture acquires a means to escape that same status, to refuse to become a mere thing among things.

[*See also* Architecture; *and* Modernism, *article on* Modernity and Tradition in Architecture.]

BIBLIOGRAPHY

Work by Mies van der Rohe

The Mies van der Rohe Archive. 20 vols. Edited by Arthur Drexler. New York, 1986–1992.

Other Sources

Blake, Peter. *Mies van der Rohe: Architecture and Structure.* Harmondsworth, England, 1963.

Blaser, Werner. *Mies van der Rohe: The Art of Structure.* New York, 1965.

Carter, Peter James. *Mies van der Rohe at Work.* New York, 1974.

Drexler, Arthur. *Ludwig Mies van der Rohe.* New York, 1960.

Evans, Robin. "Mies van der Rohe's Paradoxical Symmetries." *AA Files* 19 (Spring 1990): 56–68.

Giedion, Sigfried. *Space, Time, and Architecture: The Growth of a New Tradition.* 5th rev. enl. ed. Cambridge, Mass., 1967.

Hays, K. Michael. "Critical Architecture: Between Culture and Form." *Perspecta* 21 (1984): 14–29.

Hilberseimer, Ludwig. *Mies van der Rohe.* Chicago, 1956.

Johnson, Philip C. *Mies van der Rohe.* 3d rev. ed. New York, 1978.

Mertins, Detlef, ed. *The Presence of Mies.* New York, 1994.

Neumeyer, Fritz. *The Artless Word: Mies van der Rohe on the Building Art.* Translated by Mark Jarzombek. Cambridge, Mass., 1991.

Quetglas, José. "Fear of Glass: The Barcelona Pavilion." In *Architecture-production,* edited by Beatriz Colomina, pp. 122–151. New York, 1988.

Schulze, Franz. *Mies van der Rohe: A Critical Biography.* Chicago, 1985.

Smithson, Allison, and Peter Smithson. *Without Rhetoric: An Architectural Aesthetic, 1955–1972.* London, 1973.

Spaeth, David A. *Ludwig Mies van der Rohe: An Annotated Bibliography and Chronology.* New York, 1979.

Tafuri, Manfredo, and Francesco Dal Co, *Modern Architecture.* Translated by Robert Erich Wolf. New York, 1979.

Tegethoff, Wolf. *Mies van der Rohe: The Villas and Country Houses.* Translated by Russell M. Stockman, edited by William Dyckes. New York, 1985.

K. MICHAEL HAYS

MIMESIS. If we examine the history of the word *mimesis,* often rendered as imitation, we discover that the ease with which it is used cloaks a myriad of meanings that can be and have been attached to the term. Indeed, this indeterminacy is perhaps the most constant feature of mimesis. Mimesis moves with history and takes on forms appropriate to each historical period. Today the concept is experiencing a renaissance all the more astounding in light of the criticism on it received during the artistic upheavals at the turn of the century. Erich Auerbach's book returned mimesis as a kind of leitmotif for representing social reality in Western literature. Describing mimesis as an ongoing attempt to approximate social reality, Auerbach wrote a purely intellectual history, without considering semiotics, the material conditions of written communication, and the anthropological dimension of literature. Exactly these aspects form the crux of twentieth-century efforts to take up the concept of mimesis. Picking up on Walter Benjamin, Theodor W. Adorno elaborates mimesis as the core of his aesthetic theory. In the work of Jacques Derrida, mimesis is used to see processes of signification from a new perspective, one that is to overcome the boundaries of semiotics.

Mimesis and Its Shifting History. *Mimesis* is a broad term with a wide range of possibilities for how a self-sufficient world created by people (as in Nelson Goodman's understanding of "worldmaking") can relate to any given real world, or even a postulated or imagined one (see Gebauer and Wulf, 1995). Each historical epoch tailors its own mimesis concept. We can distinguish among various historical stages and thus underscore those aspects of mimesis that dominate at a particular time. In the early use of *mimesis,* even before Plato, there is an emphasis on its representational aspect. Hermann Koller, Gerald F. Else, and Göran Sörbom show that *mimos* is the root word. *Mimēisthai* and *mimēsis, mimēma, mimētēs,* and *mimētikos* all derive from this stem. *Mimēisthai* denotes imitation, representation, or portrayal. *Mimos* and *mimētēs* designate the persons who imitate or represent, whereby *mimos* also refers to the context of the dramatic action. *Mimēma* is the result of mimetic behavior, *mimēsis* the action itself. Mimētikos refers to something that can be imitated or is subject to imitation. The cultural historical background of the word family *mimēsis* is disputed. Refuting Koller's assertion that the origin of mimesis lies in music and dance, Else derives three central definitions of the concept from his own work:

1. the direct imitation of animal and human utterances;
2. one person's imitation of another person, without direct physical mimicry; and
3. the imitation of persons and things in an inanimate medium.

The origin of the *mimēisthai* group lies in the word *mimos* (mime). It designates either a recitation composed of several parts and delivered by one person, or a dramatic performance by two or more persons. Koller, Else, and Sörbom scholars agree that the concept was applied to more and more areas; mimesis came to mean the representation of "something animate and concrete with characteristics that are similar to the characteristics of other phenomena."

Mimesis has numerous heterogeneous meanings in Plato's work: in addition to imitation, representation, and expression, he attaches particular weight to the production of appearances (and illusion). No less important than Plato's strategic use of the concept is his alertness to how mimesis affects the attitudes and behavior of people. Mimesis is attributed with the ability to spread in subliminal, almost epidemic waves; in response, Plato places mimesis, with its moment of danger, in theoretical quarantine.

In Aristotle's understanding, mimesis embraces not only the re-creation of existing objects, but also the changes introduced in this process. Mimesis thus includes the possibility to beautify, improve, and generalize individual qualities. In literature, for example, mimesis invokes the possible and the universal. Mimesis can be understood as the capacity for literary representation, expressed in the verbal and imaginary design for human actions.

Later epochs turn from representation to other aspects of mimesis. For the authors of the Renaissance, mimesis becomes a matter of intertextuality, the direct reference of texts to each other. They see themselves with their literary productions in a mimetic relationship, successors to the ancient authors, under whose authority and protection they struggle to create their own forms of personal expression. In this sense, the Renaissance historicizes mimesis by interrogating the relative merits of each period's cultural achievements and accentuates the social relation enclosing the mimetic. During the Middle Ages, the concept of *imitatio* likewise underscored the social embeddedness of mimesis; here, however, the model remained of divine origin and was not a figure from science or literature. Nor could the Middle Ages see in the individual a source of creative power. This was reserved for God, the supreme object of imitation.

With a return to representation, mimesis is appropriated in the seventeenth century by high politics—as representation of power, mimesis becomes a constitutive element for expressing the symbolism of the state. Mimesis elevates and enacts the state as manifestation of supreme power; mimesis then cloaks this representation in the illusion of a higher reality. Even the king, who in fact bears state power, must bow to this illusion.

The bourgeois age finally brings the breakthrough in realism so pivotal to Auerbach's book. Literature continues to produce an elevated social reality, but this is no longer a world of ideal politics but instead a world of model bourgeois life and emotion. "Imitation of nature" supplies the motto; what is imitated is nothing other than that produced according to the laws of reason—that is, according to human rules. In the nineteenth century, the bourgeois person and his or her social practices, sensuous and driven, becomes the object of literary representation. The bourgeois subject is represented as someone who makes his or her world in reference to others, with the same desires and striving for the same goals, oriented along the same lines—in short, imitating and, in the end, disoriented. Bourgeois society itself is described as mimetic.

At the turn of the century, the upheavals in modern art turned mimesis, in the sense of imitation, into an obsolete concept. New approaches to mimesis must search for a different understanding, one outside the tradition cast by Plato and Aristotle. The concept of mimesis has entered anthropological theories; here mimesis designates something other than the purely rational modus of making, a production of artifacts with particular emphasis on the body, the senses, the emotions, the temporal. With the help of mimetic insights, authors such as Benjamin, Adorno, René Girard, and Derrida have taken up the search for another way of viewing human action, one that focuses both on social practice and interpersonal relations. The following discussion will examine the profoundly historic character of mimesis as it moves among certain positions.

Plato and Aristotle. *Mimēsis* has a range of meanings in Plato's work. Along with imitation, representation, and expression, as well as emulation, transformation, and creation of similarity, *mimēsis* designates the production of appearances and illusion. In *The Republic,* Plato emphasizes the preeminent meaning of mimesis in education. In their attempts to emulate models, young people strive to achieve similarity. Poor examples pose the risk of spoiling youth. Plato therefore insists on the strict supervision of poetry and its models. Imitation for Plato falls short in that it is not the capacity for producing the things themselves, but only their images. Definitive of these images is that they bear a relation of similarity to objects, one that combines the real and the imaginary. If similarity determines images, they belong to the world of appearances and make something visible that they themselves are not. In terms of recognition, the illusion produced by mimesis is deceptive, defective, and thus inferior. Illusion finds its place in a special domain that is not subordinate to the ends of knowledge; Plato furnishes illusion with a new space, in aesthetics. Plato's work intimates the later import of mimesis for art, literature, and music, but sees aesthetics very critically.

According to Eric Havelock (1963), Plato's critique of mimesis is bound up in the larger social transition from the old, oral tradition of philosophy, embodied by his teacher, Socrates, to written teachings. The shift from orality to literacy made possible in turn some of the characteristic features of Plato's position. Plato's assessment of mimesis is closely tied to his efforts to replace the image-based discourse of orality, and its strongly performative character, with a conceptual discourse. During Plato's period, an elaborated and widespread literality gave rise to a new language of facts and theory. In this context, mimesis becomes a concept characteristic of both poetic speech and the unique power of the poet to represent the world. Over against the absolute certainties of the *epistēmē*, mimesis can claim to produce only relative or conditional statements.

Plato confronts the legacy of knowledge based on mimesis under the new conditions of literate culture. In oral culture, mimesis had taken shape within the complex relationships among poet and audience, physically emotional processes, and recited material. Plato draws on the myriad applications of the word *mimēsis* to construct a philosophical concept able to comprehend a second-class procedure in epistemological terms: mimesis is opinion *(doxa)*. It comprises a form of knowledge coupled to practical experiences; disassembled into discrete units, these are pluralistic and resist integration into systems of cause and effect. For Plato, *doxa* involves the becoming instead of the being, the many instead of the single, and the visible instead of the invisible and conceivable. In Havelock's interpretation, Plato stands as the first representative of a new, text-oriented culture at the end of the period of orality. He uses mimesis within a strategy to break the oral tradition, stripping it of its ways of knowing and recognition. The relegation of mimesis to its own sphere, aesthetics, opens the way for mimesis-based theories of art and music, which Aristotle would soon elaborate in a systematic way.

In the *Poetics,* Aristotle develops two aspects of the mimesis concept. Picking up on Plato, Aristotle emphasizes the significance of mimesis in the production of images. He then develops a unique conception of literary mimesis. For Aristotle, mimesis embraces not only the re-creation of existing objects but also the possibility to change them and thus to beautify, improve, and universalize individual qualities. In literature, the possible and the general are products of mimesis. Mimesis, says the *Poetics,* leads to the construction of the "fable" or the "plot," an embodiment of myth. In tragedy, mimesis aims to dramatize and embody the speaking and acting person. Mimesis can be understood as the capacity for literary representation, expressed in the verbal and imaginary design of actions. Mimesis creates fictional worlds in which there is no nonmediated reference to reality. The artistic organization gains prominence over the individual elements of action in producing the cathartic effects of tragedy. In contrast to Plato, who feared the repercussions of negative models, Aristotle identifies the possibility of lessening their effects precisely in their mimetic recapitulation.

Aristotle turns mimesis into a theoretical concept bound into a series of systematic relationships. In his work, mimesis also comes to designate the imitation and the manner in which, in art as in nature, creation takes place *(natura naturans)*. The creative force emerges as something that nature and humans have in common; it characterizes a fundamental feature of the human being, a source of pleasure and a capacity to learn. At the same time, Aristotle's mimesis refuses to become a philosophical concept to be used like others; its resistance to theory building expresses itself in the indeterminacy of how the concept is applied, in the absence of an exact definition, and in its embeddedness deep in the realm of what is assumed (and not to be discussed) to constitute a human being. Given this anthropological turn, any attempt to give a semiotic structure to the Aristotelian concept of mimesis is destined to fail.

Mimesis in the Seventeenth and Eighteenth Centuries. During the period of French absolutism, mimesis is used to organize a colossal machine for representing and interpreting political power. At the court of Louis XIV, diverse individuals—historians, dramatists, painters, palace and garden architects—are authorized to design and build political representation and political power. This realm of signs and imagination is understood as a source of royal authority. The absolutist state engages the artist, maker of mimetic worlds, to produce the "portrait of the king," his symbolic being, a representation of his essence. This image is more important than how the king might himself look; indeed, the empirical king, the occupier of power, is subordinate to his image.

Louis Marin uses the example of the historian, chronicler of symbolic power, to reveal the force of mimesis under Louis XIV. The chronicler takes things and events, even as they occur, to forge a succession of significant state actions. He understands how to read the world of events, to apprehend the appropriate symbols, to construct their narrative contexts. In these writings we see an image of the king as the world's most powerful man take shape; the historian's representation transforms the king's actions into wonders. A vast fictionalization of history, including its main actor, more real than the world of events, flows from the historian's portrayal of the king.

The reader of these histories, in turn, is seated in a kind of theater for world history. On the stage, Louis XIV pulls the strings of historical actors as marionettes in his production. In reality, however, this scenario is produced by the narrator, who simulates the images for the reader-audience. To this end, the historian Paul Pellisson, appointed the official chronicler of the king, develops a performative writing style, designed to render his readers into an admiring audience. In its own way, on the field of narrative, the account of war must follow strategies and tactics. Events in space and time appear as a constant, universal attribute of the king's substance. Repetition inscribes this into history. All differentiations among event, speech, image, and text must be transcended: for the reader, what is written must spring to life as speech; the text invokes images; the tableau captures the substance of history; the written text makes it possible for this substance to assume form. The reader must be able to see the portrait of the king as the incarnation of absolute power. Legibility creates visibility, and the visible is readable.

Throughout seventeenth- and eighteenth-century aesthetics, the concept of mimesis is restricted to the imitation of nature. Indeed, contemporary debates on the object and rules of art preclude other possibilities. In the long term, however, this aesthetic dictate helps free literature from the conventions of rhetoric. At the end of this process, the author no longer is required to select ways of speaking and representing from the prevailing rhetorical canon. The author gains the freedom to orient his or her writings on the characteristics of the objects to be described, even while adhering to an exacting set of artistic rules. In both the seventeenth and eighteenth centuries, the concept of nature embraces not the empirically given but rather an idealized nature.

This aesthetic debate finds its point of departure in the controversies (the *querelles,* "quarrels") of the French court, in particular in the "Querelle des Anciens et des Modernes." Artists, critics, and aestheticians all have their say in this dispute on the relationship of the present to the past. The "Anciens," among them Jean Racine, Jean de La Bruyère, and Jean de La Fontaine, see themselves as normatively bound to the classical heritage, observing a strict understanding of Aristotelian thought. They claim to practice a direct imitation of antiquity. The "Modernes," on the other hand, understand mimesis as a historical category; mimesis implies change appropriate to modern times. At the same time, they do not advocate a break with antiquity. On the contrary, they see themselves as continuing and perfecting the classical tradition, but fully aware of the legitimacy exerted in their own aesthetic practices. For their part, the ancients reject the idea that later ages could surpass antiquity.

In the eighteenth century, writers and thinkers gradually abandon what had become a rigidified school of neo-Aristotelian thought. Of course, the centuries-long debate on the correct form of the imitation of nature was requisite to this move. In particular, English philosophy (the earl of Shaftesbury) and aesthetic practice (for example, Joseph Addison and dramatists such as George Lillo) provided new impulses. Aesthetic theory began to open itself to new ways of looking at the world. Inner images, subjective impressions, and wonders find their way into drama. At the beginning of the eighteenth century, the discussion surrounding the imitative approximation of nature—the task of literature, drama, and painting—is very vague and invokes Aristotle, although such claims still lack a philological foundation. This situation changes profoundly over the course of the century. Aesthetic thinkers such as Jean-Baptiste Du Bos, Charles Batteux, Denis Diderot, and Gotthold Ephraim Lessing, rigorously trained in philosophy, give new momentum to the discussion about the rules of mimesis and its relationship to the artistic medium itself. Rational thought plays an increasingly important role. Aristotle continues to serve as the point of reference; moreover, eighteenth-century thinkers have a much more precise reception of his work. It is not always clear whether, as such authors insist, they are interested in understanding Aristotle's writings, or whether their avowal of Aristotle is meant to provide the basis for their forays into the unknown.

For all its professions to Aristotle, a new kind of drama arises in this aesthetic discussion and theater, one with emphasis on subjectivity and emotion. The rise of bourgeois sensibility recasts mimesis. Theatrical imitation helps stage models of bourgeois life, legitimating the representation of inner human nature by enacting it as a mirror of outer nature. The inner is expressed in imitating outer nature. On the bourgeois stage, mimesis mediates between the public sphere and the world of feeling. Through the representation of acting bourgeois models, mimesis provides the audience with models of the inner world. Mimesis helps shape the ways that emotions are felt and expressed.

The bourgeoisie's claim to social leadership manifests itself in a culture of taste and emotion. Mimesis becomes central to the articulation of fine taste and lofty emotion. The bourgeois drama proves a fitting stage for the representation of emotions as universal (not class-specific) human characteristics, even though only the bourgeoisie is accorded the privilege of realizing them in their ideal sense. By staging moral guidance, the theater offers its audience interpretations of behavior and models of self-representation. In the eighteenth-century discussion of the imitation of nature, the role of mimesis in artistic creation, new concerns emerge: to unleash the individual's own creative power, and the autonomy of the artwork.

With the assertion of human creativity, the individual capacity to comprehend nature, nature loses its role as preceptor. The search for rules and ideal models moves to the inner realm of the creative person. The aesthetic theory of genius, Lessing's *Laocoön*, and Jean-Jacques Rousseau's work—all announce the turn away from the Aristotelian concept of nature. Mimesis is freed from the imitation of nature. Karl Philipp Moritz and Immanuel Kant put an end to the automatic reference of artistic works to the model of a given world, renouncing the productive relationship of the mimetic world to another. As a principle of art, mimesis (usually narrowed to imitation) seems to have run its course for aesthetics.

Mimesis as an Anthropological Category. The twentieth century has rediscovered mimesis as a fundamental human property. Walter Benjamin postulates a "mimetic faculty" in people to discern a special kind of similarity, not always obvious, the "nonsensuous similarities." The human body has always been used to produce and express similarities in such things as dance, gesture, language, and imagination. In this process, representation and expression appeared as two indivisible, entwined aspects of the mimetic faculty. The gradual repression of the mimetic relation to the world, to others, and to the self led to a loss of sensuous similarity. Benjamin notes that parts of the mimetic relation to the world have been made over into writing and language as an "archive of nonsensuous similarities." Individuals can use the mimetic powers available to them to decode and revitalize these mimetic aspects in reading and writing. Such processes, including the child's mimetic encounters with its surroundings (in Benjamin's *Berliner Kindheit*), capture flashes of nonsensuous correspondence among objects, their meanings, and their past.

Like few other writers of this century, Benjamin appreciates the fundamental anthropological significance of mimesis. Theodor W. Adorno too sees in mimetic processes a kind of anthropological basis for the use of signs, although he takes a direction different from that suggested by Benjamin. Starting with *Dialectic of Enlightenment,* Adorno and Max Horkheimer use the mimesis concept to describe an irreconcilable ambivalence manifest in the relation of the human being to outer and inner nature—what is also the glimmering of a chance for people to liberate themselves from domination. By feigning death in the face of a hostile nature, early humans assumed a kind of mask to stave off terror. Adorno sees the engraving of human features in the mask as the first form of technology. This later becomes freely available as an instrument of the subject's domination over nature itself, as well as other subjects. The spread of rationality later turns into the suppression of nature within humans. Only artistic works have preserved the old remnants of mimesis, capable of saving the individual; art is, in Adorno's words, a "refuge for mimetic behavior," yet shares in the rationality of its time. In their ambivalent constitution, both as bridge to the stage of archaic mimesis and as artifacts rationally and technologically fabricated, artworks can provide modernity with a possibility to revise or neutralize the domination of nature.

Adorno uses the image of an individual clinging to social reality to characterize the peculiarity of the mimetic in art. Aesthetic mimesis creates a kind of stamp that delineates social relations with all their ruptures. In the artwork, the assimilation of social reality takes place without the involvement of forces which subordinate nature: the subject disappears in the work of art. The mimetic of art "is rationality, which criticizes art without evading it." So seen, the artwork cannot be less cruel and violent than social reality itself—not in reality, but in a gestural sign. As autonomous, self-referential artifact, the artwork recovers access to levels that in the civilizing process have been cut off or repressed. In aesthetics, we find the potential to produce images that permit us to hope for a reconciliation with nature.

Jacques Derrida focuses his treatment of mimesis on the concept of text. Texts are nondisposable; they stand in relation to what has preceded them. They are never the origin, never inner, never outer, but always doubled. Every text begins as double. There is no beginning without that which has gone before it. The mimesis of the text lacks an original model. Its intertextuality demands to be deconstructed. As with hieroglyphics, we must decipher that which cannot be said within them. Texts are traces of the people who write them; each is a beginning and a repetition. The mimetic approach to texts precedes the ability to comprehend them in theory. It plays with unveiling, concealment, masking, and oscillates between extremes. This interplay becomes clear in Derrida's "Economimésis" (1975). Derrida demands the study of mimesis itself, as revealed in "theoretical and practical formations." Mimetic processes play with unveiling; they conceal and mask. "Mimose" oscillates between plant and animal, an image for a mimesis that transgresses the boundaries between science, literature, art, and society. *Différence* is the principle of mimesis, a productive freedom, not the elimination of ambiguity; mimesis contributes to the profusion of images, words, thoughts, theories, and action, without itself becoming tangible.

In Derrida's work, mimesis has a doubled or "between" character; it remains ambivalent. No cognition is possible without mimesis; mimesis actualizes itself in play, in the simulacrum of apocryphal textuality. Mimesis is not drawn to a notion of truth; at the same time, there is no truth without and outside of mimetic movement. An expression of human freedom, mimesis articulates itself in how it deals with texts and signs, in the play of presence and absence.

Derrida's access to texts is itself mimetic. In deconstruction, he takes elements and positions of the text, sets them in motion, scatters (disseminates) them, makes them fruitful in new (and uncontrollable) ways. Their elements combine with others in new texts. Each is a game of coincidence and necessity, related to other texts. Texts proliferate in mimetic play. The meanings of all texts are, in principle, indeterminate and elude closure.

Despite his interpretative twist, Derrida's mimesis sets forth certain traditions that have repeatedly marked the history of mimesis. Mimetic actions can often be described as processes of how signs are used, interpreted, and assigned meaning. In this sense, we can, for example, identify basic features of mimesis in Aristotle, in French absolutism, and in the rise of the bourgeoisie in the eighteenth century. Perhaps the other side of mimesis is even more compelling: the performative, the physical and the sensuous, the spread of mimetic processes, the use of magical signs, the pictorial, the indeterminable, the effects on social life and people. All these hone our appreciation of the social genesis of mimesis. We recognize social situations of performance even in the first moments of the concept, before Plato.

The original rhythmic act, the performance with a strong emphasis on the body, receives different accents over the passage of time: as painting or writing, as making with one's own hands, as producing sounds in speaking or in playing a musical instrument. But a physical remnant always remains in mimetic actions. Here, in the body's participation in mimesis, and in the relationship to other people of the person acting, we find the essential difference of mimesis to purely cognitive knowing. Mimesis aims at influence, appropriation, change, repetition, or the new interpretation of existing worlds.

Mimesis resists the construction of theory. We violate mimesis if we try to specify it in conceptual and logical terms: mimetic actions, open and indeterminate, elude unequivocal, fixed, and logical interpretations. Not only would we impose such things, themselves alien to mimesis, on the concept, we would rob mimesis of precisely its essential indeterminacy. Mimesis is stamped, as we recall from its long history, by its openness to interpretation, its ties to each epoch, and its inner relationships, themselves given in mimetic practice. The power of mimesis lies in the images that it creates. Mimesis makes a world of appearances, illusion, aesthetics. Images have, of course, a material existence, but what they represent is not an integrative part of empirical reality; it belongs to another way of knowing. Images forge a connection between the person and empirical reality, but they retain their aspect of illusion, fiction, and deception. We recognize an inclination toward autonomy in images, a hint of sensuous experience beyond reference to reality.

[*See also* Adorno, *article on* Adorno and Mimesis; Aristotle, *article on* Aristotle on Mimesis; Auerbach; Derrida; Perception; Photography, *article on* Catechresis; Plato; Realism; Representation; *and* Theories of Art.]

BIBLIOGRAPHY

Adorno, Theodor W. *Aesthetic Theory*. Edited by Gretel Adorno and Rolf Tiedemann, translated by Robert Hullot-Kentor. Minneapolis, 1997.

Adorno, Theodor W., and Max Horkheimer. *Dialectic of Enlightenment*. Translated by John Cumming. New York, 1972.

Aristotle. *Poetics*. Translated by Stephen Halliwell. Chapel Hill, N.C., 1987.

Auerbach, Erich. *Mimesis: The Representation of Reality in Western Literature*. Translated by Willard R. Trask. Princeton, N.J., 1953.

Benjamin, Walter. "Lehre vom Ähnlichen." In *Walter Benjamin: Gesammelte Schriften*, vol. 2. 1, edited by R. Tiedemann and H. Schweppenhäuser, pp. 204–210. Frankfurt am Main, 1977.

Benjamin, Walter. *Berliner Kindheit um Neunzehnhundert*. Frankfurt am Main, 1950.

Benjamin, Walter. "On the Mimetic Faculty." In *Reflections: Essays, Aphorisms, Autobiographical Writings*. Edited by Peter Demetz, translated by Edmund Jephcott. New York, 1978.

Derrida, Jacques. "Economimésis." In *Mimésis des articulations*, edited by Sylviane Agacinski et al., pp. 55–93. Paris, 1975.

Derrida, Jacques. *Dissemination*. Translated by Barbara Johnson. Chicago, 1981.

Else, Gerald F. *Aristotle's Poetics: The Argument*. Cambridge, Mass., 1957.

Gebauer, Gunter, and Christoph Wulf. *Mimesis: Culture-Art-Society*. Translated by Don Reneau. Berkeley, 1995.

Goodman, Nelson. *Ways of Worldmaking*. Indianapolis, 1978.

Havelock, Eric. *Preface to Plato*. Cambridge, Mass., 1963.

Hermann, H. P. *Naturnachahmung und Einbildungskraft: Zur Entwicklung der deutschen Poetik von 1670 bis 1740*. Bad Homburg. 1970.

Jauss, Hans Robert. "Ästhetische Normen und geschichtliche Reflexion in der 'Querelle des Anciens et des Modernes'." In *Parallèle des Anciens et des Modernes*, edited by Charles Perrault, pp. 8–64. Munich, 1964.

Kant, Immanuel. *Critique of Judgment*. Translated by J. H. Bernard. New York, 1951.

Koller, Hermann. *Die Mimesis in der Antike: Nachahmung, Darstellung, Ausdruck*. Bern, 1954.

Lessing, Gotthold Ephraim. *Laocoön: An Essay on the Limits of Painting and Poetry*. Translated by Edward Allen McCormick. Indianapolis, 1962; reprint, Baltimore, 1984.

Marin, Louis. *Portrait of the King.* Translated by Martha M. Houle. Minneapolis, 1988.

Plato. *The Collected Dialogues of Plato.* Edited by Edith Hamilton and Huntington Cairns. New York, 1961; reprint, Princeton, N.J., 1969.

Sörbom, Göran. *Mimesis and Art: Studies in the Origin and Early Development of an Aesthetic Vocabulary.* Stockholm, 1966.

Weimann, Robert. *Shakespeare und die Macht der Mimesis: Autorität und Repräsentation im Elisabethanischen Theater.* Berlin, 1988.

Zimbardo, Rose A. *A Mirror to Nature: Transformations in Drama and Aesthetics, 1660–1732.* Lexington, Ky., 1986.

GUNTER GEBAUER and CHRISTOPH WULF

MINIMALISM. As a style and a philosophically based movement, Minimal art developed to its fullest extent in the 1960s, although its repercussions continue to affect contemporary art into the 1990s. Like Pop art, which appeared in galleries in New York and Los Angeles only a year before Minimalism, it is characterized by hard-edged planes, anonymous facture, and an industrial sensibility developed in reaction to the painterly, emotion-driven forms of Abstract Expressionism. Unlike the Abstract Expressionists, many of the artists associated with Minimal art produced three-dimensional works. Although most had been trained as painters, the desire to suppress the illusionism inherent in painting and to explore the possibilities of real space led many of them to wallbound reliefs and finally to sculpture. The distinctions between painting and sculpture had begun to blur in the 1950s, and by 1965 Donald Judd was able to assert that much contemporary three-dimensional work might resemble sculpture but that it was nearer to painting, from which it retained its predominantly rectangular format and the use of color. While sculptors explored the effects of polychromy, painters associated with Minimalism tended to work monochromatically, in neutral, industrial colors. Resolutely abstract, Minimal art avoided figure-ground relationships in painting and any anthropomorphic reference that might associate it with sculptural statuary.

Minimal art was an American phenomenon, limited primarily to New York City, where most artists lived and exhibited. Donald Judd, Robert Morris, Dan Flavin, Carl Andre, and Sol LeWitt, along with Tony Smith and Anne Truitt, who had more direct ties to Abstract Expressionism, comprised the central group on the East Coast. A related movement in Los Angeles, whose practitioners often participated in Minimal exhibits, was known as Finish Feush. Inspired by the bright light, popular techniques of automobile modification associated with the car culture, and the burgeoning plastics industry in southern California, John McCracken and Larry Bell, in particular, made significant contributions to the Minimalist aesthetic. The most influential painter was Frank Stella, whose nonillusionistic, slablike paintings of 1959–1960 inspired both sculptors and painters. Brice Marden, Robert Mangold, David Novros, Robert Ryman, and Jo Baer began exhibiting Minimal paintings in the mid-1960s. Their older colleagues were Ellsworth Kelly and Agnes Martin. Outside of a few English artists such as Anthony Caro and Richard Smith, and later several of Caro's students at St. Martin's School of Art in London, Minimalism had no original adherents in Europe or Asia, although it was more widely collected in Europe than in the United States.

The major developments of Minimal art took place between 1963 and 1968. Following Truitt's exhibition of the first recognizably Minimal work at the André Emmerich Gallery in New York in early 1963, Judd and Morris exhibited individually at the Green Gallery, under the direction of Richard Bellamy. Although many of the artists later showed at the Leo Castelli Gallery, Bellamy remained an ardent supporter of Minimalism. The first major group exhibition, *Primary Structures,* was presented in 1966 at the Jewish Museum in New York, followed by *Systemic Painting* at the Solomon R. Guggenheim Museum in 1967. Summarized in 1968 by the *Minimal Art* exhibition at the Gemeentemuseum in The Hague and the publication of Gregory Battcock's edited collection, *Minimal Art: A Critical Anthology,* Minimal art reflects a particular system of beliefs pertaining to the function of artworks and their relationship to space and the viewer. As a style term, however, it is often used to refer to abstract art of the 1960s and 1970s (or even later). Younger artists such as Robert Smithson, Eva Hesse, Bruce Nauman, and Richard Serra, who were originally classified as postminimalists, are sometimes included in the larger category of "minimal art."

One of the definitive characteristics of Minimalism is the condition of objecthood. Eschewing representation, illusion, and expressive form, Minimal objects aspired to the ontological status of furniture or other real things, but without practicality or function. Marcel Duchamp's readymade objects of the 1910s constitute a precedence for Minimal artworks as does the Surrealists' use of the term *object* to characterize their three-dimensional works. Minimal objecthood was indebted to the work of Jasper Johns, who referred to his paintings of flags and targets of the 1950s as "objects" to convey the notion that they were self-sufficient things-in-themselves. Johns's choice of a flat image for reproduction on a flat canvas avoided any kind of pictorial depth and resulted in his paintings appearing to be objects, rather than pictures or windows, with real material presence. The term object gained currency with the publication of Donald Judd's article "Specific Objects" in 1965, in which the artist-critic defined art objects as singular, or single things, distinct from assemblages and environments, and as neither painting nor sculpture, at least as they had existed up to that point. The debate over Minimal objecthood generated much controversy in art publications, which had become overwhelmingly theoretical by the late 1960s and early 1970s. British artist William Tucker maintained that objecthood is the distinguishing feature of Minimal sculpture,

MINIMALISM. Donald Judd *Untitled* (1966) and *Untitled* (1966); Robert Morris, *Untitled (2 L beams);* and Robert Grosvenor, *Transoxiana* (1965); installations from Primary Structures, 27 April–12 June 1966; Jewish Museum, New York. (Copyright by Donald Judd Estate/VAGA, New York; Robert Morris/ARS, New York; Robert Grosvenor/Paula Cooper Gallery, New York. Photograph courtesy of the Jewish Museum/Art Resource, New York; used by permission.)

while Garth Evans held that sculpture gives up its claim to objecthood by the very fact of its being art, and thus being treated differently than plain objects. Still the most influential essay on Minimalism, despite its negative assessment of the movement, is Michael Fried's "Art and Objecthood" in which objecthood is equated with nonart, thus denying to Minimal objects the status of art. Philosophers also contributed to the dialogue, with Richard Wollheim's contention that in modernist theory a work of art is significantly held to be a physical object, and Arthur C. Danto's investigation of the relationship between "artworks and real things." Modernism can, in fact, be characterized by a driving "search for the real," as Hans Hofmann titled his book in 1948, from nineteenth-century French Realist Gustave Courbet's refusal to paint an angel because he had never seen one to the Museum of Modern Art's exhibition, *Art of the Real: USA, 1948–1968.* The reality principle arrived at its purest manifestation in the concept of objecthood embraced by Minimal artists.

"Real materials in real space," the motto of Russian Constructivist Vladimir Tatlin, was equally applicable to sculptors of the 1960s. Art critics cited parallels between the two movements, although much less was known at the time about the Russian avant-garde than after increased scholarly investigation in the 1980s. At the time of his 1960 proposals for the *Element* series of uncarved, stacked wooden beams, for example, Andre was unaware of Aleksandr Rodchenko's similar constructions of 1920, although they were soon brought to his attention. In his "Notes on Sculpture [Part 1]," Morris acknowledged Rodchenko and Tatlin as influences, and Flavin dedicated a series of fluorescent light works to Tatlin. While the Minimalists' use of common industrial materials was less overtly political than the Constructivists', the image of the artist as a worker rather than an aesthete, often relying on factory production of his art, prevailed. Formally, however, the inertia of Minimal objects was in stark contrast to the dynamic and essentially Cubist compositions of most Russian painting and sculpture. More closely related to Minimalism was the work of Constantin Brancusi, with its emphasis on simplicity of shape or repetitive structure. Brancusi was the topic of Morris's 1966 master's thesis at Hunter College and the inspiration for Flavin's and Andre's earliest Minimal works.

Motivated by an overwhelming desire for formal unity, the Minimalists adopted the allover balance of Abstract Expressionist painting, which had replaced the standard part-to-part, relational composition of Cubism. Stella was the first Minimalist to extend the possibilities of allover composition by substituting geometry for gesture and adhering to a rigid symmetry. Morris also advocated nonrelational composition through the use of "unitary forms," characterized by strong gestalts. The unitary form is perceived as a single, whole shape, which does not subdivide into a composition of multiple elements. For this reason, Morris preferred boxes, slabs, and right-angular or triangular forms whose shapes were immediately comprehensible to the spectator.

While Judd's basic modules were not unlike Morris's, he often repeated a shape in a linear arrangement, a compositional technique he described as "one thing after another." Repetition avoided traditional methods of balance as well as symmetry, which was too obvious a solution to nonrelational composition. In 1964, Judd began to use arithmetic and geometric progressions to determine the sizes and arrangement of boxes or cylindrical projections in his wall-bound work. Many other artists used simple mathematics, primarily arithmetic progressions in which the size of an element or the spaces between elements are increased by the addition of a constant unit of measure. Permutations, in which a limited set of variables are arranged in every possible combination, provided another neutral method of composition by not privileging any one arrangement of elements over any other. With this method, LeWitt produced elaborate serial structures of closed and open cubes, and, during the course of an exhibition in 1967, Morris periodically altered the arrangement of eight fiberglass modules. Repetition, progressions, and permutations were considered anonymous methods of arrangement that avoided the expression of a subjective sensibility. Serial systems established the logical parameters of a composition from which the artist could not deviate once the terms of the system had been established. This approach was preferable to what Judd considered the "discredited rationalism" associated with relational composition and characteristic of European art. In compositions determined by a rational decision-making process, the placement of each element in a work depends on a prior compositional decision. At any point along the way, the artist has multiple options. Logical systems are essentially irrational, according to LeWitt, and must be followed in the manner of a syllogism. Once the first terms are established, the conclusion is inevitable.

The rejection of compositional relationships resulted in works with fewer parts or works in which formal balance of the parts was negligible. In "Notes on Sculpture, Part 2," Morris observed that "the better new work takes relationships out of the work and makes them a function of space, light, and the viewer's field of vision. . . . One is more aware than ever before that he himself is establishing relationships as he apprehends the object" (Morris, 1993). The external constitution of meaning initiated by Minimalism is one of its most radical contributions, as critics Rosalind E. Krauss and Kenneth Baker have acknowledged. Against the private space of the mind proposed by Cartesian philosophy, Krauss and Baker argue for meanings that occur in a public space. Based on a similar thesis and coincident with the ascendancy of Minimal art, Roland Barthes's seminal essay, "The Death of the Author," also attributes the responsibility for determining the meaning of a work of art to the reader/viewer rather than the author/artist. Phenomenology, especially as it was articulated by Maurice Merleau-Ponty in his widely read *Phenomenolgy of Perception*, proposed another influential alternative to traditional aesthetics by identifying the perceiver's body as the site of perception. Acknowledgments of the role of the body appear in critical writings by and about Morris, as well as subsequent art-historical texts by Krauss and Hal Foster, who posit Minimal art as a significant break with formalism's appeal to the eye alone.

The body is implicated not only through the haptic recognition of shape, but through the phenomenon of scale. Suppressing incident and texture, Minimal paintings and sculptures are characterized by a large scale that relates to the size of the human body or—in the case of Andre's plate pieces placed directly on the floor for the viewer to walk on—requires physical interaction to be fully appreciated. To ensure that their artworks were understood to occupy the same space as the viewer's body, Minimal artists dispensed with frames and pedestals, which have the effect of distancing and isolating their objects. Presented directly on the floor, or in some cases on the wall or suspended from the ceiling, the works' scale and physical presence are immediate and direct in their impact.

Rather than carving or modeling forms in traditional materials, Minimal artists used industrial materials to create precisely defined, primarily right-angular shapes. Painted plywood, inexpensive and relatively easy to use, was the material of choice in the early 1960s. As artists' economic situations and access to technology improved, metal and plastic were used more frequently. Although some Minimal painters continued to work on canvas, others turned to masonite, fiberglass, and other rigid supports that, like the materials used by sculptors, were solicited for their anti-illusionistic nature. Because of their traditional uses, marble and bronze had come to appear inherently figurative by standing for the flesh of the sculpted body, while the canvas rectangle is almost inescapably read as a window. Variations on Duchamp's concept of the readymade can be seen in Flavin's employment of fluorescent lamps involving no manipulation of form other than their placement, and Andre's reliance on brickyards or metal suppliers for his preformed modules.

Minimal artworks exhibit little or no evidence of facture. Often, this is the result of turning to industrial fabrication. While Pop artists such as Andy Warhol and Roy Lichtenstein wanted their work to look industrial and thus initiated studio practices simulating the commercial, Minimal artists achieved an industrial appearance as a result of relying on fabricators to provide them with efficient and practical means of production. Metal and wood shops, and eventually Lippincott, Inc., a Connecticut factory devoted solely to the fabrication of sculpture, were equipped and staffed to facilitate artists' conceptions. Despite the tradition of the foundry devoted to bronze casting, many critics in the 1960s found the prevalence of industrial fabrication troubling. The Canadian sculptor Robert Murray, in 1959 the first to commission a large welded steel work from a fabricator, was almost unanimously criticized for not making the sculpture himself. In the early 1960s, Truitt and Tony Smith had their works fabricated at a lumberyard and a welding company, respectively. Judd began to employ Bernstein Brothers Shop in Long Island City, New York, to produce his metal pieces in 1964. By the end of the decade, factory-produced sculpture was a widespread phenomenon.

Anonymous and manufactured, lacking the expressive moment conveyed through the artist's hand, Minimal art appears to many critics to reflect or even celebrate the dehumanization of industrial society symbolized by the assembly line. As such, it is often condemned as a collusion with capital, a critique reinforced by its popularity with corporate art collectors and decorators. Equally problematic is the potential for refabrication of industrially generated works of art in cases of damage or loss. Refabrication, with or without the artist's approval, is not uncommon and has refueled the controversy over industrial production. Now, questions of authenticity, originality, and ownership have superseded critical despair at the lack of personal touch in Minimal art.

One summary interpretation of modern art holds that its development is reductive. Ludwig Mies van der Rohe's "less is more" is symptomatic, as is Clement Greenberg's influential assertion that the conventions not essential to the viability of a medium be discarded as soon as they are rec-

ognized. To many viewers, Minimal art appeared to be concrete evidence that modern art had reached ground zero. Minimal artists, on the other hand, were mostly opposed to the reductivist reading of their work. Judd argued that the "new work is just as complex and developed as old work. Its color and structure and its quality aren't more simple than before. . . . Prior work could be called reductive too; it would have less color, less scale and less clear form (1975). Like all art before it, he maintained, Minimalism was only comparatively reductive. In order to reinforce the positive, progressive concerns of the artists, critic Lucy Lippard substituted the term *rejective* for reductive. Other descriptors proposed for the movement included Structurist, Literalist, ABC Art, and Cool Art. The style term Minimalism, although it had been used earlier in the century by Russian artists David Burliuk and John Graham, derives from a 1965 essay by Wollheim. Also linking the term to the phenomenon of reduction by identifying a lack of constructive work or manifest effort, Wollheim focused on Duchamp and Ad Reinhardt rather than the artists who would come to be known as Minimalists in the 1960s. The designation was immediately adopted, however, by critics to describe the new work, and was widely accepted by 1967. Of the major Minimalists, only two artists expressed approval of the term and its implications of reductive intentions. McCracken's leaning fiberglass planks were developed with the explicit goal of producing the most reduced or simplest form possible. Determined that a work should make use of only what is necessary, Andre followed his own "rules of parsimony and sufficiency." The same idea is expressed in Occam's razor—"Entities are not to be multiplied without necessity"—which Flavin referenced in the title of a 1963 work *(The Nominal Three: To William of Occam)*, although he was opposed to the label of Minimalist.

As a highly theoretical movement, Minimalism was the subject of a great deal of critical writing, with the artists themselves authoring many of the most influential texts. Never before in history had artists played such a prominent role in intelligently articulating the ideas behind their art, a responsibility usually left to critics. This shift in authority is partially due to the fact that the Minimalists' generation was the first to be educated not in art schools or academies but universities, where studies in art history and philosophy complemented studio training. Educated to think and write, the artists conceived of their contributions in historical and philosophical terms. The Minimalists' tendency to explain their own art influenced the following movement of Conceptual art, which used language itself as a medium.

Among the most supportive critics associated with Minimal art were Lippard and Barbara Rose. A few years after its inception, Krauss and Annette Michelson provided insightful theoretical commentary on Minimalism. Greenberg, the most influential critic of the previous generation,

was not predisposed toward Minimal art, which he classified as "novelty art" along with Pop. Once a follower of
Greenberg, Fried launched the most controversial attack on
what he called "literalist art" by defining it as theatrical,
based on its dependence on the spectator for its meaning.
Although he quoted Judd and Tony Smith, Fried was responding primarily to Morris's ideas expressed in the first
two installments of his "Notes on Sculpture." As a dancer,
Morris had in fact performed with some of the objects he
would later exhibit as Minimal artworks. Fried's acknowledgment of the performative aspect of Minimal art led
postmodern critic Douglas Crimp to posit a connection between Minimalism and what he called "the pictures generation," a group of young artists in the late 1970s exploring
the theatrical effects of reproductive media.

Although Fried's indictment was a wholesale dismissal of
Minimalism as nonart, other critics recognized the seriousness of the movement, but found the work essentially boring. Rose went so far as to suggest that the boredom it
evoked was a test of the viewer's commitment. The spectator who was bored was the one who approached the work
with expectations informed by previous art, from the spatial
complexities of Cubist compositions to the emotional intricacies of Abstract Expressionism. Minimalists, however,
considered interest rather than boredom to be the chief
value of their works. LeWitt's objective was to make his
work "mentally interesting for the spectator." According to
Judd, "A work needs only to be interesting," and what
makes it interesting is "its quality as a whole" (1975). Resistant to formal analysis or expressive readings, Minimal art
inspired a form of criticism that was more phenomenologically based. Through its emphasis on indivisible structures
and its appeal to the body, it offered an integrated and objective reality.

Many subsequent interpretations of Minimal art have rejected its claim to objectivity. Seeking to connect it to the
world that spawned it, critics have identified it with the conditions of late capitalism, whether through its "serial mode
of production," which according to Hal Foster is indicative
of the socioeconomic order of our time, or its "logical systems that reiterated the cold, hard geometry of our oppression," according to Maurice Berger. The strongest opposition to Minimalism's assumed political neutrality was
presented by Anna C. Chave, who condemned its authoritarian ideology as a form of cultural terrorism.

After a period of inattention in the late 1970s and early
1980s, Minimal art resurfaced as an influence on work identified as Neo-Geo. New meanings were given to Minimalism's disinterested use of geometry and serial structures in
the paintings of Peter Halley, which reflect the "geometric
orderings of industrial society." Jeff Koons's pristine Plexiglas boxes illuminated by fluorescent fixtures and containing
mass-produced consumer items such as vacuum cleaners
collapse the forms and materials of Judd and Flavin into an
institutional critique of the commodity system. Symptomatic of the socially engaged art and criticism of postmodernism, these interpretations acknowledge the pivotal position of Minimalism at the end of the modern period.

[*See also* Sculpture.]

BIBLIOGRAPHY

Baker, Kenneth. *Minimalism: Art of Circumstance.* New York, 1988.
Battcock, Gregory, ed. *Minimal Art: A Critical Anthology.* 2d ed. Berke-
ley, 1995.
Berger, Maurice. *Labyrinths: Robert Morris, Minimalism, and the 1960s.*
New York, 1989.
Bourdon, David. *Carl Andre: Sculpture, 1959–1977.* New York, 1978.
Chave, Anna C. "Minimalism and the Rhetoric of Power." *Arts Maga-
zine* 64.5 (January 1990): 44–63.
Colpitt, Frances. *Minimal Art: The Critical Perspective.* 2d ed. Seattle,
1993.
Coplans, John. *Don Judd.* Pasadena, Calif., 1971.
Crimp, Douglas. "Pictures." *October* 8 (Spring 1979): 75–88.
Danto, Arthur C. "The Last Work of Art: Artworks and Real Things."
Theoria 39 (1973): 1–17. Reprinted in *Aesthetics: A Critical Anthol-
ogy,* edited by George Dickie and Richard J. Sclafani (New York,
1977), pp. 551–562.
Evans, Garth. "Sculpture and Reality." *Studio International* 177.908
(February 1969): 61–62.
Foster, Hal. "The Crux of Minimalism." In *Individuals: A Selected His-
tory of Contemporary Art, 1945–1986,* edited by Howard Singerman
pp. 162–183. Los Angeles, 1986.
Fried, Michael. "Art and Objecthood." *Artforum* 5.10 (June 1967):
12–23. Revised version in *Minimal Art,* edited by Gregory Battcock
(Berkeley, 1995), pp. 116–147.
Glaser, Bruce. "Questions to Stella and Judd." Edited by Lucy R. Lip-
pard. *Art News* 65.5 (September 1966): 55–61. Reprinted in *Minimal Art,* edited by Gregory Battcock (Berkeley, 1995), pp. 148–164.
Greenberg, Clement. "Recentness of Sculpture." In *American Sculpture
of the Sixties,* edited by Maurice Tuchman, pp. 24–26. Los Angeles,
1967.
Haskell, Barbara. *BLAM! The Explosion of Pop, Minimalism, and Perfor-
mance, 1958–1964.* New York, 1984.
Judd, Donald. *Complete Writings, 1959–1975.* Halifax, Nova Scotia,
1975.
Krauss, Rosalind E. *Passages in Modern Sculpture.* New York, 1977;
reprint, Cambridge, Mass., 1981.
LeWitt, Sol. "Paragraphs on Conceptual Art." *Artforum* 5.10 (June
1967): 79–83. Reprinted in *Sol LeWitt,* edited by Alicia Legg (New
York, 1978), pp. 166–167.
Lippard, Lucy R. *Changing: Essays in Art Criticism.* New York, 1971.
Merleau-Ponty, Maurice. *Phenomenology of Perception.* Translated by
Colin Smith. London, 1962.
Michelson, Annette. *Robert Morris.* Washington, D.C., 1969.
Morris, Robert. "Notes on Sculpture [Part 1]." *Artforum* 4.6 (February
1966): 42–44. Reprinted in *Minimal Art,* edited by Gregory Battcock
(Berkeley, 1995), pp. 222–228; and Robert Morris, *Continuous Pro-
ject Altered Daily: The Writings of Robert Morris* (Cambridge, Mass.,
1993), pp. 1–8.
Morris, Robert. "Notes on Sculpture, Part 2." *Artforum* 5.2 (October
1966): 21–23. Reprinted in *Minimal Art,* edited by Gregory Battcock
(Berkeley, 1995), pp. 228–235; and Robert Morris, *Continuous Project Altered Daily: The Writings of Robert Morris* (Cambridge, Mass),
pp. 11–21.
Rose, Barbara. "ABC Art." *Art in America* 53.5 (October–November
1965): 57–69. Revised version in *Minimal Art,* edited by Gregory
Battcock (Berkeley, 1995), pp. 274–297.

Smith, Brydon. *Donald Judd.* Ottawa, 1975.

Tuchman, Phyllis. "Minimalism and Critical Response." *Artforum* 15.9 (May 1977): 26–31.

Tucker, William. "An Essay on Sculpture." *Studio International* 177.907 (January 1969): 12–13.

Wollheim, Richard. "Minimal Art." *Arts Magazine* 39.4 (January 1965): 26–32. Reprinted in *Minimal Art,* edited by Gregory Battcock (Berkeley, 1995), pp. 387–399.

Wollheim, Richard. "The Work of Art as Object." *Studio International* 180.928 (December 1970): 231–235.

FRANCES COLPITT

MODELS, ARTISTS'. Since few people who have not drawn in a life class have any idea what artists' models actually do, it would be useful to begin with a description. In the plastic arts of the West, a human model has two basic functions: to convey visual information about the body, and to create an effect with the body that will stimulate work in an artist. These roles may be fulfilled simultaneously or separately. A sculptor may position a model's body (or part of it) in a very particular way to study a particular visual phenomenon: light falling on a joint or insertion of a muscle, a set of proportional relationships among various parts of the body in space. At the other extreme, an abstract painter might work with a model to develop ideas for images derived from figures. Here, the model would move autonomously, working through a sequence of poses derived from the artist's responsiveness to particular shapes or gestures or distributions of light. Models can also be called on to function as actors, animating roles or ideas already imagined to one extent or another by an artist. This work ranges from something approaching that of a movie stand-in, who replicates an existing image (which in the model's case might be mental, pictorial, or actual) and sustains it for the purposes of observation—to an improvisatory invention of the model's own that generates a concrete image for the mood or idea or situation that the artist wants to convey or present. In general, models make their own poses, especially in drawing classes or sessions in which the aim is to study the figure. Even in carefully conceived compositions it is unusual for an artist to pose a model down to every detail.

Of personal relations between artists and models, very little can be said in a general way that does not partake either of stereotype or fatuity. Like all working intimacies, relations between artists and models are so heavily charged with the personalities involved that they defy speculation by outsiders, even as they irresistibly invite it. The erotic element that is inevitably part of any intense personal relationship is hopelessly overplayed when it comes to artists and models: while it is undeniably of enormous importance to certain artists, it is only one possible aspect of the partnership; furthermore, it is one that may (as in many perfectly successful partnerships, even marriages) be entirely beside the point. What is never beside the point is the discipline of productive work and the demands of the eye, to which both personalities must be accountable, even if the artist is in charge.

The choice of a model is thus a key element of the artist's way of working, and may indicate very deep commitments or fears or fantasies about what it means to make art out of people. An artist may interact with a model as with any other sort of person, but will usually choose to impute a very specific sort of status to the model's presence in the studio: the hired model may thus function as servant, witness, inanimate object, professional collaborator, or simply an economic incentive to work on a regular schedule. Because many artists use models only for study and never paint or sculpt directly from the figure, the model's role in the studio may take on the qualities of a pupil or an assistant—and so indeed the model often turns out to be. Other artists resist both the tutelary and the collaborative aspects of the relationship, preferring instead to think of the model as alien or neutral to the specific processes of looking or making. Some will not use professional models at all, on the ground that they are too mannered or jaded or egotistical or "academic" (an attitude held over from the Realist and Impressionist agendas of the nineteenth century), and set a premium on an idea of authenticity that can be satisfied by using only members of the family, or nonartist acquaintances, as models.

Such differences in attitude toward the model's presence in the studio are essentially differences of artistic method and rationale; they reveal as much about what artists think they are doing as about what they do, and they allow an artist a means of correlating personal ideas and impulses and habits with prevailing theories or expectations about figurative practice. Although the technical aspects of using models have until this century been more circumscribed, individual artists have always been able to impute any number of psychological or imaginative functions to the model, and the results of this are so wide ranging as to preclude discussion here: indeed, a good deal of the history of figurative art in the West has consisted of exploring the effects of artists' imputations to their subject matter in particular works or bodies of work. What is less commonly considered are the interesting ways in which the model's flexibility of function extends both to popular and theoretical ideas about the role of models in the plastic arts, which have been no less influential in Western aesthetics. What follows is an attempt to indicate some of the most important currents in the history of the idea of the model, based not on the evidence of individual practice but on the history of the idea of modeling itself.

Origins. Although the word itself probably did not come to designate the person from whom an image is drawn until the seventeenth century, the term *model,* with its connotations both of abstract paradigm and concrete example, conveys very well the combination of stylization and observation to which the human figure has been subject as long as it has been represented at all. Traditionally, use of the live model in the West is held to have emerged, with the science of perspective, as an innovation of the Italian Renaissance. Just as skeptical analysis and empirical science displaced medieval dogma, these technical advances in mimetic realism—one empirical, the other systematic—undermined the scheme of Gothic image making, which relied chiefly on the iteration of paradigms for the rendering of the human figure. But the reliance on ideals or types always entails continually consulting sources—in nature as well as in art—from which formulas may be distilled, and through which they are consequently always being revised. Historically, the use of pattern books, casts of antique sculpture, or other stylizations tended to supplement, rather than compete with, direct observation as a technical basis for the representation of the human figure. In rationalizing their techniques, different eras have emphasized different aspects of the work of representation, and it is here that the function of the model emerges as a kind of fulcrum, a point of reference that may serve to embody a number of different principles.

A good example of how the model figures in the elusive engagement between ideal and concrete values in representation can be found in the classical story of the Greek painter Zeuxis, whose mimetic gifts, like those of Apelles, were legendary. Commissioned to paint a Helen by the people of Crotona, he was given his choice of their most beautiful virgins to serve as his model. According to legend, the painter chose five different maidens, each with her own perfect feature, to arrive at his image of flawless beauty. It should be noted that although mimetic persuasiveness was a value in antique art, few classical allusions to the successful imitation of nature, Greek or Roman, make any reference to direct observation, and any mention of an artist's use of a living model invokes the erotic power or divine authority of beauty, rather than nature's challenge to realistic representation. Naturalism of effect, although valued differently in different eras, was never discussed in terms of successful copying, but of successful illusion, and continued to be associated not with the transmutation of a real thing into another medium, but with the intelligent manipulation of formulas within that medium. Quintilian, for example, recommended making use of a wider variety of types—paradigmatic postures and expressions set down in pattern books—in the composition of the figures, to achieve not a more beautiful but a more naturalistic effect. To ancient readers, then, Zeuxis's composite Helen expressed the principle that good art, whether its aim is to be beautiful or natural, involves the ability to incorporate disparate elements into a unified effect. Renaissance neoclassicism added an interesting twist to the story. When Leon Battista Alberti retold the Zeuxis story in his 1435 handbook, he used it as an example, not of the need for multiple sources in composing

an image, but of the importance of close observation of nature. Neither the story nor the reverent spirit in which it was told changed, but in paying homage to the master the emphasis shifted from the artist's capacity for synthesis to a subtlety of perception, and humility of discipline. What is fundamentally different is the empirical attitude, whereby each model is an object of attention, rather than the constituent of a process.

Just how far back the modern practice of drawing from the live model actually goes is difficult to know. In the late thirteenth century, Cennino Cennini's handbook for artists makes no mention of live models, but it does give instructions on the making of body casts, which were presumably studied in drawing, and for whom living human bodies of some kind were needed. The extraordinary subtlety of Gothic sculpture in particular suggests that sculptors were looking hard at human bodies far earlier than painters were, but no drawings exist to document it. What began with the Renaissance was not so much the practice of observing the human form for the purpose of representing it as a way of thinking about representation, especially in two dimensions, that rationalized and necessitated that practice. Whatever the degree to which the living model may have been employed earlier, certain innovations of the late fifteenth and early sixteenth centuries did in fact bring life drawing into standard practice. The development of a systematic study of anatomy placed new emphasis on the understanding of human proportion and musculature, which for many artists entailed a far more thorough examination of the body's capacity for movement than either cadavers or casts could provide. Most important, the increasing rationalization of the fine arts brought about the establishment of arts academies, and with them the institution of life class. Although the earliest academies were formed for the purposes of establishing and debating theoretical precepts, they soon became sites of organized practical study. The Carracci started their academy in 1582 expressly to promote the study of live models, as did many of the smaller organizations of artists throughout Europe in the sixteenth and seventeenth centuries. The study of the live model did not, however, supplant the study of antique casts or the formulation of standard rules and practices, which remained the unquestioned basis of all art training until well into the twentieth century. An ongoing debate between precepts of naturalistic realism and formal idealism came to be symbolized by the juxtaposition of antique casts and live models in the images of the classrooms and workshops that became common in the seventeenth and eighteenth centuries.

In addition to the academies, the other major legacy of the Renaissance was the enhanced prestige of artists, and the slow but steady elevation of the fine arts, especially painting, to the status of philosophy and poetry. The higher the status that painters enjoyed, the more pronounced the presence of individual persons in their work became, and with a more personal subject matter came a more personal image of the model. Between 1600 and 1800, moreover, portraiture, both of patrons and of models in various mythical or allegorical guises, became a more important vehicle for painterly achievement than it had been. Thus, great painters of this epoch who seem to embody this shift from artisan to humanist—Rembrandt van Rijn, Peter Paul Rubens, Diego Velázquez, and, later, Francisco José de Goya—all had celebrated relationships with their models, whereas the masters of earlier generations did not. For the first time since the legends of antiquity, an artist's fame was being expressed in terms of this relationship, and the model—whether a great patron like King Philip or a common Dutchwoman like Hendrijke Stoeffels—had an individual status that might either contribute to or be defined by the prestige of the artist.

The Modeling Profession. It was not until the beginning of the nineteenth century that the figure we would now recognize as a professional artists' model came into being. Models had been posing in individual artists' studios and workshops for some time, probably according to a rule of thumb that still holds today: a servant, an acquaintance of a lower class, a performer, or a prostitute would be compensated in some way, while a student or spouse or family member would pose gratis. In the academies, on the other hand, a standard of payment had to be established, and it is in the academic context that modeling eventually evolved into a proper trade. Several factors contributed to the consolidation of the trade into a recognized profession. One was the enormous general increase of the number of people engaged in the formal study of art, both in the academies and later in the teaching ateliers that grew in prestige, size, and number as the century progressed. Another was Romanticism's revision of neoclassical canons of form, which, together with its modern deference to nature, combined to emphasize the importance of working from the live model both in and outside the classroom. It was during the Romantic movement that principles of artistic technique were linked for the first time to social and political principles, and a new kind of distinction emerged between institutional and individual ideals for artists. Among the models who served on both sides, this new mode of artistic polarization was reflected, interestingly, in terms of gender.

In the great long-standing art centers of Italy and Germany, the profession was relatively ungendered: Italy, in particular, was famous for whole families of models, many of whom immigrated in the 1860s to France and especially to the United States, where a growing number of art schools likewise provided a market for models of both sexes. But in the great state-run academies of England and France the use of female models was prohibited, and male models were the norm until 1850. This meant that although female models were certainly paid to pose in private studios and teaching ateliers—as they had been for more than a century—

their professional status was still determined by factors other than the private and ad hoc relationship of posing for artists. Male models, on the other hand, because of their fixed place in the academies, developed a professional standing that partook of the prestige of the artists and institutions that employed them, especially in France. The model Charles Alix DuBosc, the son of a laundress employed by a whole circuit of artists in the early part of the nineteenth century, built an entire career and professional persona on the basis of having posed for Jacques-Louis David at the age of eight. Dubosc became such a fixture of the École des Beaux-Arts that he actually endowed a trust to provide an annual stipend for the winners of the Prix de Rome. Although few models claimed Dubosc's eminence, many were well known outside their immediate circles for their expertise, experience, and physical perfection. Female models, by contrast, operated in a much greater degree of obscurity, working irregularly and temporarily, associating with a far more limited number of artists.

The second half of the nineteenth century saw a complete reversal of the relative status of male and female models, a shift in public perceptions that lingers today in the unthinking assumption that all artists' models are women who pose without clothes for male painters who abuse, exalt, or mystify them. Among the complex economic and cultural shifts of balance that brought this about—attitudes toward gender were, for example, further complicated by strong national prejudices stimulated by the great influx of Italian models to Paris in the middle of the century—perhaps the most important was a new sense of authority and responsibility in the visual artist, the increased use of the female nude in painting to represent their artistic commitments. Although history and genre painting, and fancy portraiture (which used clothed models of both sexes), continued to be the dominant forms well into the 1880s, representing prevailing issues of social and moral value, it was the female nude, an emblem of truth since the Renaissance, now stripped of allegorical trappings, that became the authoritative vehicle for those who wanted to proclaim the verities of art, especially in the last quarter of the century. Whatever spirit her image might convey—Eugène Delacroix's Romantic heroism or Jean-Auguste-Dominique Ingres's peculiar ideal, Gustave Courbet's raunchy realism or Édouard Manet's canny artifice, Edgar Degas's intense absorption or Adolphe-William Bouguereau's slick perfection, Thomas Eakins's passionate discipline or August Renoir's bourgeois sensuality—the female nude became its quintessential expression.

Meanwhile, the putative model from whom these images were made was understood to have an independent existence of her own, which became correspondingly emblematic of an artistic culture increasingly aware of its own power, both as a psychological and as a social phenomenon. It was at this point that artists and models became the subject of contemporary fiction, rather than just traditional lore. The second half of the nineteenth century produced an unprecedented amount of printed material—novels, stories, verses, cartoons, periodical pieces ranging from serious arts journalism to near pornography—dealing with artists and models: Honoré de Balzac's *Le chef-d'œuvre inconnu* (1845), Émile Zola's *L'œuvre* (1886), Oscar Wilde's *The Picture of Dorian Gray* (1891), Henry James's "The Real Thing" (1892), and George Du Maurier's *Trilby* (1894) are among the most distinguished literary examples. The ascendancy of the female model coincided with the increasingly professionalistic character of the artist whose accessory—and, often, foil—she became. By the end of the century their shared, equal prominence in glossy high society and chic bohemian counterculture had become an important emblem of the artistic privilege and autonomy so essential to modernism. The male model, meanwhile, remained a fixture of the arts establishment, donning or doffing classical, biblical, or historical costume according to demand. In popular consciousness, he partook of the notoriety, but not the glamour of the female models; in England, especially, he came to represent the verities not of art but of class, an increasingly alienated worker in the great industry of art production.

Twentieth-Century Models. Throughout the first half of this century, drawing from the figure remained the staple exercise of serious artists that it had been for three hundred years. But although models were still very much in use, they ceased to be on view: the visible impact of the model on finished pictures was considerably diminished. Where earlier generations of artists had relied on the model not only to instruct their eyes but to inform their images, twentieth-century artists tended to deal more idiosyncratically with the figure, emphasizing and experimenting with different, often isolated, aspects of the figural presence in their images, eventually abandoning any suggestion that the coherence of a figure on a canvas derived from any physical body other than their own. With Henri Matisse and Pablo Picasso the topos of the female nude as an expression of the fundamental drives of a male artist developed into something more abstract than it had been before; in each case, the artist employs not just the figure but the model herself as a sort of theoretical muse, an entirely private resource that in the end becomes so wholly identified with the artist that the model as a personality—even of the most idealized or degraded kind—disappears entirely.

Over the course of the twentieth century, artist's models of both sexes have gradually retreated into the rather obscure existence that female models had at the beginning of the nineteenth. This decline in professional art modeling is usually attributed to the advent of modernism, which responded to the literalness of the camera by displacing the representation of figures from the center of its technical attention. But what did the most to change the practice of modeling in the twentieth century was the rise of photography, not as a fine art but as the primary medium of commercial illustration. The art school boom of the 1870s, which had launched life models into public prominence, occurred largely in response to a newly expanded market for graphic advertising, which remained an important commercial medium until well into the 1930s. Even today, more than half the figure drawing classes that employ models train more commercial illustrators than fine artists or dilettantes. But the overwhelming majority of commercial picture making came to be done by photographers in the middle of this century, and the effects on the practice of modeling professionally, both in life classes and in the studios of individual artists, was profound.

Where models became invisible in the process of making paintings or sculpture, the reverse occurred in the making of a commercial photograph, where only the model is visible, and the work of staging, lighting, processing, and cropping is carefully hidden. Thus, the personal glamour that had adhered to painters' models in the late nineteenth century became the province of fashion models and movie stars, who seemed to address—often to command—the camera without having to capitulate to the dominant presence of an artist's intervening hand. But while fashion models—and the imagery derived from them—are now the locus of the same concerns about gender, self-presentation, body consciousness, and erotic power that surrounded artists' models in the late nineteenth century, their complete identification with the images made from them removes all issues of mimetic persuasiveness and technique from those concerns. Implicit in the older iconography of artists' models is the active dialectic between originals and copies, conceptual and perceptual ideals, universally comprehended or individually apprehended forms. In drawing, the artist's physical effort to make flat images carry the freight of things and bodies engages directly with the model's capacity to generate an image with the body, so that seeing and being seen operate as modes of physical understanding, not just aspects of desire.

This deep continuity between somatic work and optical experience, although it is of importance to some photographers, seldom figures in the impact of photographic images themselves, especially those of commercial photography and film that have pervaded all aspects of twentieth-century vision. On the contrary, the success of photography as a medium of fantasy is predicated precisely on the ease with which it can be made to suppress the distinctions between image and body, and thus any skeptical or exploratory interest in the mimetic relationship between them. This is why the most compelling issues of visual art in previous centuries—whether a form is "ideal" or "natural," whether a phenomenon is experienced or conceptualized, whether the authority of a subject has been recorded or created, have become of more social and ideological than visual interest. E. H. Gombrich's formulation of the priority of making to matching, having become a commonplace of plastic art, still raises lively questions for photography, where the technical problem of matching is nonexistent, and the impression of it absolute.

We all intuitively accept, even if we do not understand, that the photographic image, especially of a much-photographed person, is a unique kind of entity—a trace of that person, an emanation far more direct, however contrived, than any plastic representation, and yet at the same time far more abstract. Paintings or drawings of human figures always in some sense record or interpret or analyze the experience of seeing a body, and so draw the viewer into that experience by virtue of that work, that process of expression. In a photograph, what impels us to experience is not what we see the artist has done but what we feel the subject is: the fact of the photograph's being a made, flat, thing—so untextured and untouched as to be an antithing—is the desire-enhancing obstacle to direct experience, not the means of access to it.

Yet, these very exigencies have in recent decades led to developments in the photographic treatment of figures that seem to advance the old questions in a new direction. Where once we had Picasso projecting an endless sequence of visual and erotic obsessions with representation into the image of artist and model, now we have Cindy Sherman using her own body as the primary material for an exploration of the huge range of figurative imagery in contemporary culture. Whether we want to call William Wegman's use of his dogs the result of perverse vulgarity or of profoundly disinterested, uncannily respectful rapport, the question clearly belongs in the same discussion as similar debates over Degas's attitudes toward the female figures in his pastels.

What photography *has* caused to disappear is the old idea of the model's capacity for embodying both the work and the play of representation in a single figure. Instead, the concept of the model has acquired a double valence: one associated with the phantasms of commercial photography, fashion, and film, and the other with the most sordid and unglamorous travails of the fine arts. The latter, collapsing nineteenth-century distinctions, includes both the academic model, unsung hero or heroine of arts education, and the vague, but still potent, image of the bohemian muse, who has been variously mythologized: an old image of bohemia has dedicated male artists alternately tormented and inspired by their model/mistresses; a more recent one has dedicated female artists (Gwen John, Camille Claudel, Tina Modotti) alternately inspired and abused by the successful male mentor/lovers for whom they posed. However entrenched in melodrama, this composite conception understands living models as something both emotionally (and perhaps politically) more real and intellectually less interesting than the images made from them. Worshipers and debunkers of the cult of artistic genius alike have rendered the

model's personality as always the enemy or victim of representation, the exploited or appropriated or suppressed underside of the image whose outer face stands for creativity.

Thus alienated from the images made from them, artists' models have occupied a very different sphere from that of fashion models or media stars, whose reality seems entirely subsumed by the demands of commerce and fantasy that define their image. But, although it is no closer to concreteness than it ever was, the image of the model-as-icon has undergone its own species of progressive revision: the relentless activity of the unformed, beleaguered ego that once destroyed Marilyn Monroe is now understood to have fueled and empowered Madonna, and the independence of mind that cut short the career of Louise Brooks has extended and amplified that of Lauren Hutton.

Current Prospects. Abstract art, particularly in its mid-century Expressionist aspects, was supposed to be the death of the model, but although the market for artists' models declined considerably after World War II, since the 1970s it has stabilized. The demoralization of the profession of artists' models in recent years turns out to have had far more to do with declining technical standards in all forms of education and an economy increasingly hostile to short-term freelance contractual service than with the artistic revolution that during the 1950s threatened to obliterate it: the demand persists. Most art schools still rely on models to demonstrate the principles of proportion and anatomy, the complexity of articulating form and communicating movement. The private market for artists' models is likewise a small but steady trickle of painters, sculptors, photographers, even architects who, for one reason or another, believe that paying careful attention to the human body is of value to their work. At no time have artists' personal rationales for using the model been more diverse and less codified.

Despite the large shadow cast by their cousins in the fashion industry, artists' models continue to enjoy an obscure glamour of their own. Even to the artists who employ them, models carry the suggestion of a bygone world that seems at once grittier and gentler than today's gleaming treadmill of grant application politics, space shortages, and distended markets. Bohemian nostalgia aside, the aura of detachment conferred on the figure of the studio model has served to complement, even to relieve, the intense engagement with prevailing cultural norms demanded of modern artists since the Romantic movement. Nineteenth-century artists' models occupied a role deliberately set apart from, and inaccessible to, the traditional standards or values of the bourgeois classes with which their artist clients were constantly expected to address. Similarly, twentieth-century models have remained entirely irrelevant to the otherwise universal pressure on artists to be avant-garde, thus providing both a scapegoat for and relief from the relentlessly competitive, progressive demands of twentieth-century artistic culture.

Indeed, it seems that, having stood at one or another pole in all manner of technical conflicts inherent in healthy artistic practice, models have come to stand in some way for the value of technique itself, not just the ability to render, but the very discipline of seeing. Yet, this too is changing. We have already seen how both bohemian muses and commercial models have been reimagined according to ideas of gender politics developed since the 1960s. Moreover, since the 1970s both aesthetic and ethical questions have been raised regarding the rights and status of persons used as subject matter in works of theatrical and literary, as well as visual, art. New technologies, an increasingly porous boundary between fact and fiction, and the permanent disruption of modernist assumptions about claims of authorship promise still further modulations in the idea of serving as a model for artists; but, although they may shock, they cannot surprise, for in the end the only fixed function of artists' models is to be available for revision.

BIBLIOGRAPHY

Borel, France. *The Seduction of Venus: Artists and Models.* Translated by Jean-Marie Clarke. New York, 1990.

Borzello, Frances. *The Artists' Model.* London, 1982.

Crisp, Quentin. *The Naked Civil Servant* (1968). New York, 1977.

Delectorskaya, Lydia. *With Apparent Ease: Henri Matisse.* Translated by Olga Tourkoff. Paris, 1988.

DuBosc, Charles Alix. *DuBosc modèle: Soixante ans dans les ateliers des artistes.* Reprint, Paris, 1986.

Fink, Lois Marie, and Joshua Charles Taylor. *Academy: The Academic Tradition in the Fine Arts.* Chicago, 1978.

Flam, Jack D., ed. *Matisse on Art.* New York, 1973; rev. ed., Berkeley, 1995.

Goldwater, Robert, and Marco Treves, eds. *Artists on Art: From the XIV to the XX Century* (1945). New York, 1972.

Gombrich, E. H. *The Heritage of Apelles: Studies in the Art of the Renaissance.* Ithaca, N.Y., 1976.

Hollander, Elizabeth. "On the Pedestal: Notes on Being an Artists' Model." *Raritan* 6.1 (Summer 1986): 26–37.

Hollander, Elizabeth. "Subject Matter: Models for Different Media." *Representations* 36 (Fall 1991): 133–146.

Hollander, Elizabeth. "Artists' Models in 19th Century America: A Study of Professional Identity." *Annals of Scholarship* 10.3/4 (1993): 281–304.

Kiki. *Kiki's Memoirs.* Translated by Samuel Putnam (1930). Hopewell, N.J., 1996.

Kleinfelder, Karen L. *The Artist, His Model, Her Image, His Gaze: Picasso's Pursuit of the Model.* Chicago, 1993.

Klüver, Billy, and Julie Martin. *Kiki's Paris: Artists and Lovers, 1900–1930.* New York, 1989.

Lathers, Marie. "The Social Construction and Deconstruction of the Model in 19th Century France." *Mosaic* 29.2 (June 1996): 23–52.

Nochlin, Linda. *Realism.* New York, 1971.

Panofsky, Erwin. *Renaissance and Renascences in Western Art.* Stockholm, 1960; reprint, New York, 1969.

Pevsner, Nikolaus. *Academies of Art, Past and Present.* Cambridge, 1940; reprint, New York, 1973.

Taylor, Pegi. "In the Classroom." *Art and Academe* 7.2 (Spring 1995): 52–70.

Taylor, Pegi. "Quartet." *Denver Quarterly* 2.31 (Fall 1996): 103–111.

ELIZABETH HOLLANDER

MODERNISM. [*To explore the complex meanings and legacy of modernism as a distinct historical and aesthetic topic, this entry comprises five essays:*

> An Overview
> Modernity and Tradition in Architecture
> Modern Music
> Modern Dance
> Modern Literature

The first essay is an overview of the historical parameters and aesthetic import of modernism in the various arts. The next four essays focus on the arts—architecture, music, dance, and literature—not fully covered in the overview. The architecture essay also explores the role of tradition in modernism, an art period that typically defines itself as breaking from all tradition. For related discussion, see Abstraction; Avant-Garde; Collage; Constructivism; Cubism; Dadaism; Formalism; Futurism; Originality; Postmodernism; Primitivism; Suprematism; *and* Surrealism.]

An Overview

Modernism cannot be defined as an aesthetic position but must be understood as an extended historical moment in which various aesthetic issues develop in counterpoint with the emergence of modern culture (characterized by the formation of the nation-state, of the concept of the individual, and of industrial and consumer capitalism). These aesthetic issues are explored by modern visual and literary artists as an ongoing tension between a search for legitimacy according to scientific, universal, ahistorical, or transcendent terms and a self-conscious sense of the historical specificity and cultural effect of artistic forms. Latent in this tension is another opposition between the critical concepts of autonomy and contingency. An autonomous work is one whose formal means are presumed to be sufficient in themselves: the work is presumed significant without recourse to considerations (such as causality, intention, historical events, political and cultural circumstances, or other referents) beyond its formal properties. By contrast, the concept of contingency insists on the embeddedness of artistic forms within cultural, ideological, or political contexts in which their significance is generated. The concept of autonomy in particular served as a distinctive element of the rhetoric on which modern art functioned as a cultural formation (especially in the later nineteenth and twentieth centuries) and has implications for the formal development of modern visual and literary art, the aesthetic claims on which it operated, and ultimately for the terms (such as claims to neutrality) in which it has been critiqued.

The aesthetic positions that provided the springboard for modernism can be traced to late Renaissance discussions concerning "the ancients and the moderns." These reopened debates about the relative virtues of painting and poetry as mimetic forms that had their origins in the work of Plato and Aristotle. After the seventeenth century, in the search for a solution to the problematic perception of painting as an inadequate mode of imitation (as a mere sign of a sign, or image of an image), mimesis was gradually jettisoned as a philosophical basis for beauty and also as the conceptual foundation of visual artistic practice. With the appearance of aesthetics proper in the eighteenth century, the focus shifted to an investigation of the specificity of each individual medium or mode of art. Gotthold Ephraim Lessing's 1766 *Laocoön: An Essay on the Limits of Painting and Poetry* put in place a founding tenet of modern art: that each medium can best fulfill itself through maximizing its own formal properties. Immanuel Kant, in his *Critique of Judgment* (1790), formulated a notion of aesthetic judgment as disinterested (without motivation in desire or need) and intersubjectively universal (independent of individual preference or idiosyncratic taste), while his concept of beauty resided in purposive form. In Kant's work there was no prescription for linking beauty or aesthetic judgment to art through engagement with the integrity of a work, but the tenets of self-sufficient perfection and self-reflexive attention to a medium were taken up as features of twentieth-century modernism, often with reference to Kant as their source. G. W. F. Hegel's *Philosophy of Fine Art* (published posthumously in 1835) provided a philosophical justification for fine art as a revelation of truth, an aspect of the process of self-knowledge of the Absolute in the approach of Mind and Spirit. Hegel's emphasis on the self-reflexive aspect of the definition of beauty permitted an easy, if dubious, slippage into an artistic practice of self-referentiality (self-conscious attention to the process of art making as a subject for art and also a privileging of formal means as an end in themselves). Although German Idealism provided an important foundation for modern aesthetics, it would be a mistake to equate modernism with its aesthetics, since the visual and literary arts were continually modified through their relation to broader cultural and historical concerns.

In the early nineteenth century, another tension—between the subjective expression of Romanticism and the empirical tenets of Realism—contributed to the erosion of belief in idealist perfection and increased attention to the location of artistic practice within social and psychological frameworks. August Wilhelm von Schlegel established the premises for a Romantic aesthetics in which a work of art was born of passionate imagination and brought into being as an expressive form with no precedent or prior referent. Romantic expression preserved the idea that art and beauty were valuable because they revealed truth, although they did this through feeling, rather than logic or judgment, and emphasized form and effect over structure and order.

In literary and artistic terms, modernism is commonly associated with the mid- to late nineteenth century. In art-historical terms, the crucial moment at which stylistic and institutional breaks with the academic (and classical) tradi-

tion occurs is in the 1860s, particularly in France. Artistic autonomy stressed the increasing independence of visual art from literary sources, its perceived capacity to serve as a site of critical social commentary, and its ability to pose a self-conscious investigation of the cultural and aesthetic terms of art making through thematic and formal interrogations of the premises of art production. Édouard Manet's visible brushwork, controversial subject matter, and attention to the picture plane and Gustave Courbet's workmanlike surfaces and attention to nontraditional themes (such as labor) served as paradigmatic examples of these positions. The movement of autonomy from a philosophical frame (Hegel's concept of Idea recognizing itself) into a cultural one (art as an independent site with its own rules, agendas, and identity) was fundamental to modernism's use of an aesthetic rhetoric that claimed that formal means were instrumental for achieving cultural ends. The tension between autonomy and contingency was thus evident in a contrast between the artwork as a product or object among others (autonomous, freely circulating, and yet distinct in its identity) and the work of art as an integral element in and quintessential expression of modern life. This tension is evident in Charles Baudelaire's 1863 essay, "The Painter of Modern Life," which initiated a critical call for an aesthetic appropriate to modernity, defined as modern life, but differentiated from modernism as the cultural expression of the modern period. The role of art was to provide an accurate image of modernity but also to be independent of it to a sufficient degree to offer a critique of or escape from its conditions. Stressing the ephemerality of modern life, the transient, the fleeting aspects of lived experience, Baudelaire articulated the fundamental duality of modernism in which one aspect is the "contingent . . . whose other half is the eternal and immutable" (Baudelaire, 1964). Baudelaire's poetry, with its emphatic rejection of the classical verse forms, and its combination of vernacular imagery and mythic eroticism, embodies this dualism as the opposition of *spleen* and *idéal*. [*See* Baudelaire.]

Late nineteenth-century artists continued to explore the potential of visual representation to exist and function independently of a reference: the Post-Impressionist attention to the surface arrangement of pigment into form and the Symbolist investment in color as a replete medium helped secure features of twentieth-century visual modernism's claims to autonomy. Nonetheless, the spiritual uneasiness expressed in the work of such Symbolist artists as Edvard Munch or Odilon Redon bespeaks a profound spiritual and psychological anxiety about the condition of contemporary culture and the problems of sexuality, gender, and the unconscious fostered by social changes brought on by urbanization, secularization, and industrialization. Likewise, the work of Georges Seurat, with its precise optical manipulation, its repetitive, rational ordering of the application of pigment, and its thematic engagement with the fragmenta-

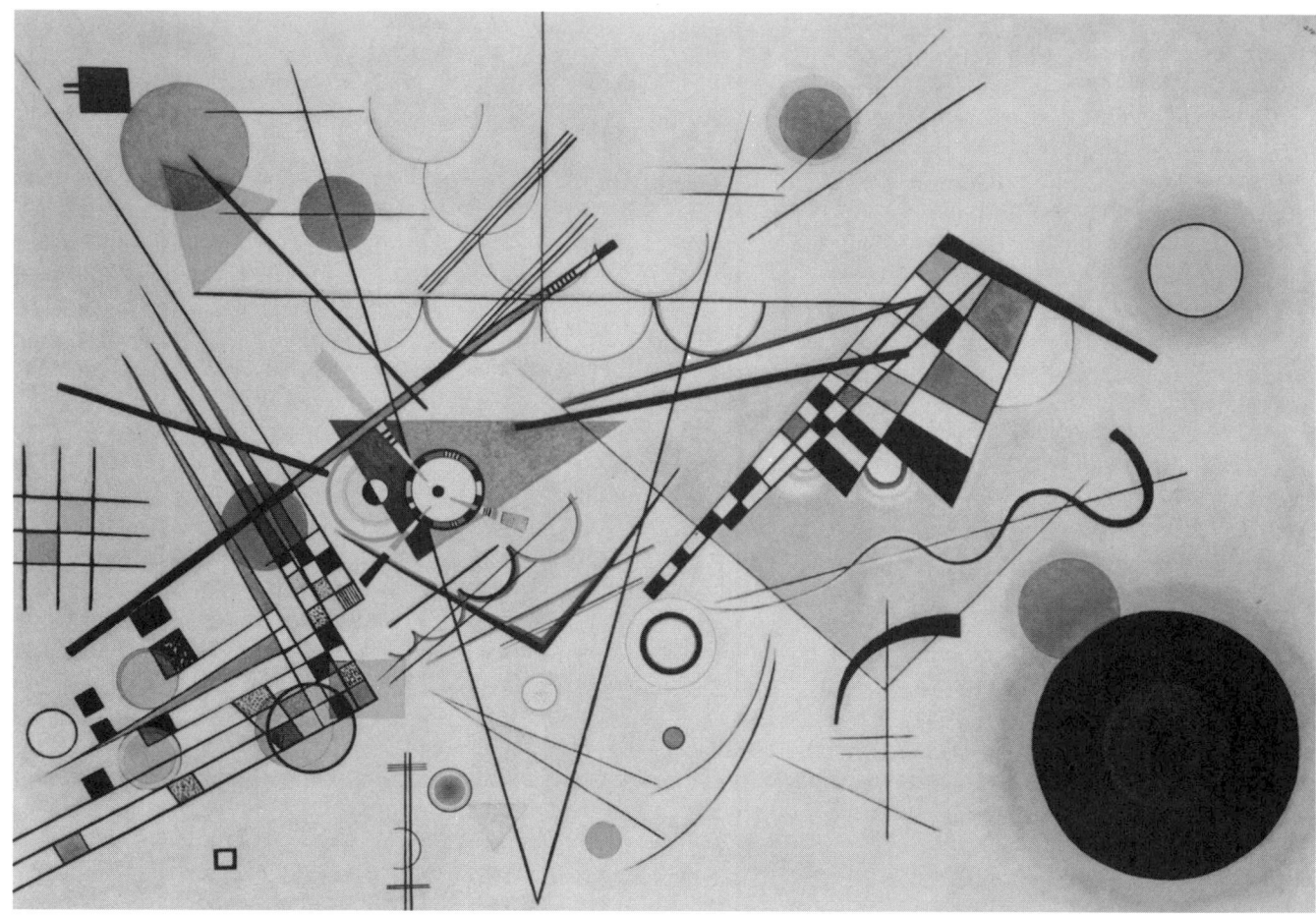

MODERNISM: Overview. Wassily Kandinsky, *Composition 8* (1923), oil on canvas, 55 1/8 × 29 5/8 in.; Solomon R. Guggenheim Museum, New York. (Photograph by Robert E. Mates; copyright by the Solomon R. Guggenheim Foundation; used by permission.)

tion of modern life, demonstrates the extent to which modern art reflected and critiqued the contemporary condition. In the same decades of the late nineteenth century, the compelling conviction that art could be a potent social force for transforming modern life or resisting some of its more perfidious effects provided the impetus behind the Arts and Crafts movements, especially that of William Morris in England, which struggled to make artistic practice a model for individual labor that was not subsumed under industrial production.

Conrad Fiedler, writing in the late nineteenth century, attempted to establish a philosophical basis for works of visual art that signified entirely through formal relations, a position taken up and expanded in the early twentieth-century aesthetics of Clive Bell and Roger Fry. Two metaphors—that of music and that of language—provided the basis for two distinct formalist tendencies at the turn of the century. Both depended on a concept of autonomy to sustain their convictions of visual meaning as independent of reference: in the musical analogy, form is presentational (its expressive means are its meaning), and in the linguistic model, form is discursive (its rule-bound systemic character allows it to produce meaning differentially). The Russian artist Wassily Kandinsky attempted to distill a systematic language of visual form in his work, and identify the essential properties of elements of color, composition, shape, and relations within the canvas in a search for universal, stable meaning according to a quasi-scientific investigation of visual effects. Such work continued the long-standing quest to find legitimacy for visual representation as a natural, essential mode of representation rather than as a merely conventional one, extending earlier debates about visual representation and mimesis. Such investigations supported the assertion that visual art could function as a form of presentation and not merely as a mode of representation. For Cubists, Futurists, and a range of modern abstract painters and writers, therefore, an autonomous work claims to be a thing in its own right—a creation—in the same sense as a work of nature. Few works of modern art took this premise to the limit (as visual art engaged solely with color, composition, material, texture, mass, line, or literary compositions foregrounding sound, rhythm, or word patterns). Nonetheless, this premise provided a basis on which much modern art was assumed to emphasize self-conscious attention to art making and process.

In the twentieth century modernism (visual and literary art) and modernity (modern life) came to be increasingly antagonistic, and artistic practice began to be perceived as a site of resistance to the negative effects of technological advances, social transformations, and the development of mass culture. Artistic modernism split into a formalist investigation (of the purity of the medium, often staged as universal and transcendent—as in the work of Ezra Pound or Piet Mondrian) and an avant-garde (dedicated to using art to produce a resistant counterdiscourse, as in the work of Dadaists and Surrealists, or to help bring about a revolutionary new society in which the role of artist and aesthetics can be functional, integral, and productive, as in the work of Bertolt Brecht and Aleksandr Rodchenko). In the avant-garde, autonomy served to define two different aspects of artistic practice: the capacity of visual art to circumscribe an arena of privileged activity within the culture (and thus serve as a site for symbolic disruption and strategic political intervention) and, second, the emphatic insistence on the utterly discrete identity of this work of art as against, opposed to, and distinct from other culture productions. In this definition, visual, literary, musical, or any other art as an autonomous form assumed a political dimension—its very identity as autonomous distinguished it from industrial production (at first at the level of manufacture through preservation of the handmade touch, mark, or other sign of uniqueness and later at the level of cultural production through the self-reflexive attention to conceptual premises as well as an increased insistence on unconsumability within artistic work). The emphasis on the laying bare of devices articulated by Russian formalist Viktor Shklovsky, of the usefulness of negation or aesthetic difficulty asserted by Frankfurt School critic Theodor W. Adorno, found its artistic parallel in the work of early twentieth-century artists such as Gertrude Stein, James Joyce, and Marcel Duchamp, or in later decades, the work of John Cage and Samuel Beckett. But as a force in shifting the terms of artistic identity from the formal plane of production to the conceptual plane, Duchamp was inarguably the strongest influence in the visual arts, especially after about 1950.

By the middle of the twentieth-century modernism had become highly codified in philosophical, artistic, critical, and cultural terms. In the visual arts, the concept of autonomy was associated with the idea of the "purity" of the medium, that is, a self-conscious attention to the formal properties of production, and with the accompanying belief that work produced through this principle had an immediately apprehensible presence and meaning. New Criticism in literature (especially the work of Cleanth Brooks and

W. K. Wimsatt) and high modernism in the visual arts shared the critical premise that intention, biography, and history were secondary considerations—much less important in assessing a work of art than the formal properties of the poem, painting, or sculpture itself. [*See* New Criticism.] In the visual arts this critical formulation is associated with the work of Clement Greenberg, who asserted a teleological basis for the material purity of a medium, particularly painting. While attributing the idea of an aesthetics of self-critical awareness to Kant, Greenberg recast the notions of disinterest and purposive form that were Kant's aesthetic principles into an active property of artistic process. Greenberg's attention to the purity of the medium was in fact more properly an extension of the earlier eighteenth-century aesthetic position of Lessing and later formalists such as Fry and Bell. By its very autonomous and discrete identity, Greenberg felt that art could serve as a site for the preservation of cultural values. But the mere admission that cultural values are at stake and available to preservation within the formal means of fine art demonstrates the extent to which the concept of autonomy is compromised by a web of contingencies—all of which continually reinscribe the work of art within its historical and cultural moment. [*See* Greenberg.]

In the 1960s both Pop and Minimalist artists sought new solutions to the problem of the identity of the fine-art image in relation to that of mass culture. To maintain the distinction between the forms, images, and production of visual art and those of the culture industry, consumer capitalism, and mass-market media, many artists emphasized a shift from formal qualities to conceptual ones as the basis of an artwork's identity, thus moving away from Greenberg's focus on the medium as the distinguishing characteristic of a work of art. Conceptual artists of the 1960s emphasized the idea that art depended on the conventions according to which a work could be recognized as art in nonessentialist terms. Thus, the central issue for art in the latter half of the twentieth century came to be the idea of art as an idea: concept replaced form as the essence of a work's identity in the later modern aesthetic.

Critiques of modernism have focused on the concept of autonomy, noting that modernism effectively concealed or participated in practices of oppression with regard to class, gender, ethnicity, and colonial politics. The ideological structure of artistic autonomy, it turned out, in its very claim to transcend historical circumstances in favor of universal investigations of form, aligned readily with hegemonic cultural agendas intent on effacing their self-interested programs in the name of values of humanity, civilization, or an advanced social order. On examination, the idea of aesthetics as a disinterested arena engaged with such values turned out to legitimate, conceal, and otherwise serve the interests of a first-world culture. By focusing on the historicization of concepts of abstraction, self-sufficiency of formal means, and nonreferentiality, critics of modernism demonstrated that these very claims were symptomatic of and linked to specific agendas. Writers committed to an analysis of art through the lens of historical materialism made specific analysis of the relations between visual form and the dynamics of social life in terms of class structure (e.g., Fredric Jameson, Timothy Clark, and Griselda Pollock). Increasing awareness of the heterogeneity of modern art stressed the necessity of understanding the ways in which the concept of autonomy had served to repress practices that deviated from the formalist or avant-garde lines—such as figurative work or work in a more traditional or conventional mode, often produced in communities of women or by people of color. Recent critiques of the biases central to modernism's claims to autonomy have come from the areas of feminism, cultural studies, and postcolonial theory (e.g., Gayatri Spivak and Homi Bhabha) for which the term *representation* always invokes the cultural networks within which the artistic strategies function and the agendas of power in which they participate. The concept of autonomy as an aesthetic premise is thus attacked and dismantled through an assertion of the cultural context as a condition for conceiving of autonomy as an aesthetic strategy in the first place.

The notion of a society of the spectacle (in the work of Guy Debord) or of the simulacrum (Jean Baudrillard) that developed in the late twentieth century signaled the demise of modernism as a cultural, critical, and aesthetic paradigm, and the founding myths of formal visual modernism and the avant-garde have now been severely qualified. Modern autonomy has been replaced with postmodern contingency (historical and cultural specificity, the social embeddedness of form and interpretation, a highly qualified notion of artistic identity and originality, and a self-consciousness about the hegemonic agenda of discursive practices) as the dominant formulation of the basis of artistic activity.

BIBLIOGRAPHY

Adorno, Theodor W. *Aesthetic Theory.* Edited by Gretel Adorno and Rolf Tiedemann, translated by Robert Hullot-Kentor. Minneapolis, 1997.
Baudelaire, Charles. *The Painter of Modern Life and Other Essays.* Translated and edited by Jonathan Mayne. London, 1964.
Bloch, Ernst, et al. *Aesthetics and Politics.* Translation edited by Ronald Taylor. London and New York, 1977.
Drucker, Johanna. *Theorizing Modernism: Visual Art and the Critical Tradition.* New York, 1994.
Frascina, Francis, ed. *Pollock and After: The Critical Debate.* New York, 1985.
Greenberg, Clement. *Art and Culture.* Boston, 1961.
Hegel, Georg Wilhelm Friedrich. *Aesthetics: Lectures on Fine Art.* 2 vols. Translated by T. M. Knox. Oxford, 1975.
Kant, Immanuel. *Critique of Judgment.* Translated by J. H. Bernard. New York, 1951.
Krauss, Rosalind E. *The Originality of the Avant-Garde and Other Modernist Myths.* Cambridge, Mass., 1985.
Lessing, Gotthold Ephraim. *Laocoön: An Essay on the Limits of Painting and Poetry.* Translated by Edward Allen McCormick. Indianapolis, 1962; reprint, Baltimore, 1984.
Nochlin, Linda. *The Politics of Vision: Essays on Nineteenth-Century Art and Society.* New York, 1989.
Roberts, John, ed. *Art Has No History! The Making and Unmaking of Modern Art.* New York and London, 1994.
Williams, Raymond. *The Politics of Modernism.* London and New York, 1989.

JOHANNA DRUCKER

Modernity and Tradition in Architecture

The defining events for architectural discourse in the twentieth century have been the rise and decline of orthodox modernism—*orthodox,* because it came to dominate many architectural schools, and *modernism* typified by the pronouncements of the Congrès Internationaux d'Architecture Moderne (CIAM) and the writings of Le Corbusier and Walter Gropius that inculcated a design strategy based on rationality and functional analysis of the program, the ideal of the building as a single aesthetic object, the proscription of applied ornament, and the refusal of overt historical references. Modernism was never so monolithic as its apologists claimed, nor as restrictive as its opponents averred, nor was it ever the only current of architectural design. Nevertheless, modernism remained either the dominant set of ideas to be espoused or the fraternal antagonist to be opposed in architectural discourse for a large part of the twentieth century, even as modern rationalized construction and planning techniques swept almost all before them.

The weakening of modernism's hold on architectural discourse began during the very period that modern design appeared almost everywhere in the rebuilding following World War II. Gradually, movements against strict abstraction and rationalism urged the incorporation, if not the reproduction, of historical references and multiple architectural traditions. Even more radical movements in literature and the visual arts began to find their way into architectural discourse and some practice.

While the term *postmodern* could be and originally was applied to any movement that relaxed high modernism's purity and prohibitions, gradually the term has narrowed to indicate a particular mode of historicist quotation and irony, often simplified into a standard vocabulary of semi-classicized columns, arches, fenestration, and rooflines. Despite a great deal of discussion about the needs of local communities for increased meaning and self-expression, the social concerns that characterized high modernist theory seem to have weakened in postmodern design practice.

As the "postmodern" became the name of a particular style, other stylistic options were generated, "high tech," "deconstructive," "late modern," and "neomodern" styles being prominent in discourse, with others no doubt soon to follow. Some of these new styles proclaimed themselves not to be styles all but rather to be based on some understanding of building and design that reached beneath the eclecticism that was perceived as threatening on all sides. This was also the very claim made by the modernist pioneers about their own designs during their period of reaction against nineteenth-century eclecticism. Indeed, architectural discourse seems more fractured in the late twentieth than it was in the late nineteenth century.

The deeper question raised by this story of a succession from modern to postmodern styles is the appropriateness of any such narrative of stylistic periods. In fact, discerning unified periods and traditions in architecture is not as straightforward a task as it might seem, because architecture as a cooperative and constructional art involves many processes and groups with their own sometimes parallel and sometimes divergent histories and modes of transmission.

Buildings receive influence from many directions, for instance, where the designers and builders came from, their training, what methods they take for granted, or what is featured in the current publications and media that have great power for spreading and crossbreeding styles. Kinds of decoration, ways of massing, what functions are taken as primary, the ways of organizing architectural firms and developing designs and communicating with the clients and builders, methods of financing, community decision or approval processes: all of these have their own histories. Methods of construction and engineering develop at their own pace of innovation that does not correlate directly with styles of design. The efficiencies of steel frame and concrete construction techniques have fostered both modernist functionalism and postmodernist applied historical decoration. All these influences do not necessarily change as a whole or in step with one another. Among these many processes and factors, "style" is only one variable. No single process of design or production is so dominant within one time or one locale that we can speak of it as carrying "the tradition." Nonetheless, architectural theory has until recently been dominated by the notion of unified periods and styles.

Critical practice inherited from the nineteenth century relied on such periodization. Unified styles and matched sets of philosophical and artistic options were seen as dominating successive periods and fitting into an underlying narrative of development in society and civilization as a whole, as influenced by Johann Gottfried von Herder and G. W. F. Hegel, and the development of art history as a separate discipline. More recently, such narratives have come under attack, even if the assault often continues to tell similar narratives with an expanded cast of characters.

The idea that architecture has been dominated by one sequence of styles has been contested, as has the ideal that design should continue to be dominated by some unique style that will provide a proper expression for the current age. Under the pressure of multiple cultures and better historical knowledge, the underlying narrative of society or civilization as advancing through defined stages seems less certain, and it is not so obvious that there is a unified "spirit of the age" that is to be maintained and expressed in architecture and other cultural productions. The more we learn about marginal and deviant practices, about background connections among supposedly separate areas of culture or building, as well as about the variety of interpretations and interactions that happen with supposedly similar buildings, the more questionable becomes the unity of the presumed periods. Even the unity of modernism seems less evident when we compare the simplified and commercialized versions of the International Style to the more flexible and regionally inflected variants of modernism that neither accepted the full CIAM doctrine nor simply continued local vernaculars.

As modernism's hold was relaxed, we might have expected that one or more historical styles of building would become dominant, but this has not happened. Aside from the fact that contemporary construction techniques make it more expensive to construct buildings in older ways, there is no simple opposition of modernism versus tradition. Nor has modernism gone away, since postmodern reactions against it remain modernist at heart.

The word *tradition* in the sixteenth century referred to the act of handing something over to another or passing something down through time, as well as to the items or practices so handed along. There were many separated zones of such passing down: family and community rituals, schools of painting, craft lineages, religious organizations, and so on. In the nineteenth century, however, as *culture* came to signify the unity of a people's outlook, values, and practices, *tradition* became the historical transmission and development of cultural totalities. Present cultural identity could be located in a historical stream that brought it both content and legitimacy.

Modernism in architecture developed as an unstable mix, accepting the notion of a cultural totality but seeking content and legitimacy within itself rather than from any historical stream. Contemporaries were to concretize the spirit of the times. In architecture this meant a rejection of historical styles and a search for new technological solutions, universal functions, and self-referential buildings that showed only their functions and their mode of construction.

There is no simple opposition of modernism with tradition. Modernism itself became a tradition in the sense of a visually and spatially recognizable mode of building, with a traceable history and a style that can be handed down, quoted, parodied, mixed with others. It became an identity with its own values and past heroes to be lived up to. Inevitably, then, modernism came to be felt as a constraint on freedom. The modernist gesture applies to itself, leaving the modernist style and narrative behind. This involves denying modernism's totalizing narrative and its separation from history, but without the supposed narrowness of past traditions. An avant-garde postmodern architecture picks and chooses from among historical and modernist references, refusing unified identities either across history or in the present time.

This approach is still modernist at heart. Modernism claimed to offer wider possibilities through new building technology and new analyses of function, and through the freedom of a design process that was no longer restricted to a standard vocabulary of historical forms. In postmodern polemics modernism was in turn accused of imposing restricted possibilities because the modernist rational maximizing of function led to a narrow formal vocabulary of its own. The breadth of modernist building somewhat refutes that accusation, but what is important is that the whole dispute is carried out with both sides agreeing with the modern presupposition that opening an ever wider sphere of self-conscious possibilities is the only proper move toward progress in design. Thus, the reactions against modernism agree with the modern esteem for ever increased self-consciousness in design and what is presumed to be a liberating distance from history, even when citing past styles or monuments. In this sense, all of the reactions to modernism remain firmly modernist.

Disputing such modern presuppositions about self-consciousness and progress is much more difficult than attacking the rigors of the International Style, especially since such a dispute seems too easily connected with attempts to enforce a reactionary fixed identity or retrograde vocabulary. Many fields of cultural production and analysis today are haunted by the question whether it is possible to deviate from the great Enlightenment and modernist presuppositions, reducing modern self-consciousness and subjectivity to one mode of self-relation among others.

What, at the close of the twentieth century, is the relation of modernism and tradition? If modernism means universal rational functionalism, architecture can no longer appeal to those universals. But modern individual or social subjects still attempt to give themselves content and legitimacy. In architecture, the search for more self-conscious design and wider possibilities continues, but amid a less unified field of possibilities that cannot be neatly periodized or furnish a single guiding narrative. Tradition continues in something like the premodern sense: plural, uncoordinated zones where practices and meanings are handed along, but now with less unified subjects doing the receiving and reworking possibilities and meanings, which, in turn, questions the modern project of self-foundation.

This leaves architects unsure of their vocation. Architecture has concerned itself with who and where we are, but today the unity of the *we* is both affirmed and denied in complex ways that perplex the architect. Can a city be composed of multiple fragments? Should there be a relaxation of the architectural imperative to represent ourselves? Can architecture have a civic expressive function if there is no unified spirit to express? What are buildings to do or be beyond or alongside their functional and representational roles?

Thus, the declines of modernist theory and the International Style pose questions more far reaching than "what style shall we build now?" The issues touch our identity and our conception of history in an age that is self-consciously pluralistic. None of these issues are being resolved in architectural theory any more than they are in society at large. They are, however, being addressed in theoretical writings (e.g., by Christian Norberg-Schulz, Christopher Alexander, Karsten Harries, Anthony Vidler, and Mark Wigley), and they underlie practical disputes such as those over the choice of modernism or classicism in England, neotraditional planning in the United States, and the importation of Western designs into the expanding cities of Asia.

[*See also* Architecture, *modern overview article;* Bauhaus; Le Corbusier; *and* Mies van der Rohe.]

BIBLIOGRAPHY

Alexander, Christopher. *The Timeless Way of Building.* New York and Oxford, 1979.

Blumenberg, Hans. *The Legitimacy of the Modern Age.* Translated by Robert M. Wallace. Cambridge, Mass., 1983.

Gropius, Walter. *The New Architecture and the Bauhaus.* Translated by P. Morton Schand. Reprint, Cambridge, Mass., 1965.

Harries, Karsten. *The Ethical Function of Architecture.* Cambridge, Mass., 1997.

Hegel, G. W. F. *Aesthetics: Lectures on Fine Art.* 2 vols. Translated by T. M. Knox. Oxford, 1974–1975.

Jencks, Charles. *The Language of Postmodern Architecture.* 6th ed. New York, 1991.

Klotz, Heinrich. *The History of Postmodern Architecture.* Translated by Radka Donnell. Cambridge, Mass., 1988.

Le Corbusier. *The Athens Charter.* Translated by Anthony Eardley. New York, 1973.

Le Corbusier. *Towards a New Architecture.* Translated with and introduction by Frederick Etchells. Reprint, London, 1970.

Norberg-Schulz, Christian. *The Concept of Dwelling: On the Way to Figurative Architecture.* New York, 1985.

Rykwert, Joseph. *The First Moderns: The Architects of the Eighteenth Century.* Cambridge, Mass., 1980.

Tafuri, Manfredo, and Francesco Dal Co. *Modern Architecture.* Translated by Robert Erich Wolf. New York, 1979.

Vidler, Anthony. *The Architectural Uncanny: Essays in the Modern Unhomely.* Cambridge, Mass., 1992.

Wigley, Mark. *The Architecture of Deconstruction: Derrida's Haunt.* Cambridge, Mass., 1993.

David Kolb

Modern Music

Modernism in music refers to a distinct aesthetic outlook and set of compositional practices prevalent within a pivotal cadre of twentieth-century composers. Among nonmusicians, modernism, when used in connection with music, has been linked to the rejection of the expectations and standards of musical beauty associated with the dominant practices of eighteenth- and nineteenth-century music. The qualities that musical modernism is understood to have dispensed with are the adherence to tonality (and therefore a particular ideal of consonance), the maintenance of recognizable rhythmic patterns and structures, and the employment of integrated and pleasing sounds and timbres. The traditions that modernism upset placed a premium on continuities of form and structure in the organization of sound (e.g., the evident presence of melodic or thematic coherence) that were readily apparent to the turn-of-the-century educated audience of music lovers who considered themselves well schooled. Consequently, musical modernism has been identified with dissonance, discontinuity, fragmentation, atonality, and sound experiments. Insofar as this is true, a key characteristic of one subgroup within musical modernism is properly revealed: the conscious abandonment of the common technical and aesthetic ground between popular and high-art music, and therefore also of the audience historically shared by both.

Modernism came into being at the turn of the century and assumed a distinct shape during the 1920s. For the most part, its protagonists continued to write music within a late nineteenth-century framework of opera and instrumental concert music. The historical transition from late romantic musical practice to modernism can be located in the music of Gustav Mahler, Claude Debussy, Max Reger, Ferruccio Busoni, and Aleksandr Scriabin. Musical modernism flourished primarily within the German and Austrian traditions (i.e., with the second Viennese school of Arnold Schoenberg, Alban Berg, and Anton von Webern and their aesthetic progeny, which included Ernst Krenek, Egon Wellesz, Stefan Wolpe, Nikos Skalkottas, and Karl Amadeus Hartmann). Modernism possessed a Russian and French aesthetic axis, which centered on Igor Stravinsky. In the United States, musical modernism had its first great independent exponent in Charles Ives. A host of innovators followed in his footsteps, including Henry Cowell and John Cage. This American trajectory resulted in the experimental aspect of modernism, including the embracing of non-Western musics, conceptual composition, minimalism, indeterminacy, and new technology. This direction in modernism, contrary to the second Viennese school, embraced aspects of popular music and ambient sound in an effort to expand the idea of music and its audience beyond what was regarded as the limiting and limited terms of nineteenth- and eighteenth-century European aesthetic discourse regarding music as an "art."

Modernism also aptly covers the work of Edgard Varèse in the United States and Olivier Messaien in France, as well as part of the Hungarian Béla Bartók's mature oeuvre. Before 1939, there were European and American experiments in microtonality and, after 1945, the use of electronically generated sound. The threads of early twentieth-century modernism merged somewhat after World War II, particularly in France and America. The result was the high point of musical modernism as represented in part by American students of Nadia Boulanger (Stravinsky's advocate) and Schoenberg, who taught in America during the late 1930s and 1940s. Leading exponents of postwar modernism include Pierre Boulez, Karlheinz Stockhausen, Elliott Carter, György Ligeti, Roger Sessions, and Milton Babbitt.

Within the history of musical aesthetics, modernism is best understood as a phenomenon of reaction. Its direction was defined by the conception held by both its protagonists and antagonists regarding the history of music. The premises of modernism were historicist. Each epoch was said to possess a unique zeitgeist that demanded of its artists an appropriate, imaginative mirror in expression. Modernism conceived of the critique of late nineteenth-century bourgeois tradition and taste as a historical imperative. Innovation became an essential hallmark. Insofar as an appeal to historical precedent within the history of music was invoked by modernists, that appeal redefined the traditional compositional patterns of imitation and emulation as requiring radical transformation and the disfigurement of the surface of stylistic continuity.

The explicit dialogue with the history of music focused on the dominant musical practices of late romanticism, including the use of large orchestral sonorities, extended forms, evident repetition, and the reliance in instrumental music on "extramusical" programs, as in Richard Strauss's tone poems. The historical realities and philosophical questions of the twentieth century seemed to demand a new music. Modernism sought to create a musical equivalent to Sigmund Freud, post-Newtonian physics, modern warfare and technology, and the critique of positivism and language.

On closer examination, musical modernism does not represent a coherent aesthetic category, even though it has been and remains a useful way of identifying the leading directions in concert music during the initial two-thirds of the twentieth century. Modernism's utility as an analytic and historical category has always been underscored by the reaction against it, which accompanied it from its first appearance. Since the 1970s, composers once identified with post–World War II modernist techniques, including George Rochberg, David del Tredici, Krzysztof Penderecki, and Philip Glass, each explicitly abandoned modernism. This ushered in an era in which modernism lost its dominant position in contemporary concert music. Minimalism, postmodernism, and neo-Romanticism came to the fore. Once again, a desire to break free from what had come to be widely regarded as a dominant aesthetic outlook took hold. Ironically, that dominant outlook was modernism, which after 1945 sought to retain its aura as a symbol of authentic aesthetic rebellion and the avant-garde.

The centrality of modernism in music at mid-century was such that other parallel directions in twentieth-century music have been overshadowed in terms of the way music history is written and the rhetoric and philosophical justification of twentieth-century musical aesthetics. The most influential polemical arguments on behalf of the priority of musical modernism at mid-century came from the writings of Theodor W. Adorno and René Leibowitz. Since the post-1970 success of an eclectic reaction against modernism, the history of music in the twentieth century has undergone a revision, stripping modernism of its status as uniquely emblematic of the music of the century.

Therefore, what lends musical modernism its character and conceptual importance are the shared historical circumstances and impulses surrounding its initial appearance. The idea of the modern as a self-conscious desideratum of music first appeared in a decisive manner in the writings of Richard Wagner. Wagner sought to justify his compositional innovations in terms of historical imperatives explicit in the present and future. To the generation of composers that came of age during the last quarter of the nineteenth century—particularly Mahler, Strauss, Schoenberg (before the early 1920s) in the German-Austrian context, Debussy in the French, and Ives in the American—Wagner's music and aesthetic theories were at one and the same time primary influences and the target of rebellion.

Wagner placed himself within a historical teleology. The forms of music, the harmonic practices—particularly the conception of the structural function of tonality—and the dynamics between listener and music were understood as requiring a necessary progressive process of adaptation to modernity. Music had to assume a revolutionary spirit adequate to the historical moment and anticipatory of the future. The composer was challenged to offer an overt attack on a perceived complacency and corruption in taste. Music, in Wagner's view (and in the view of the young Friedrich Nietzsche), needed to play both a philosophical and a political role in expressing the latent spiritual and political possibilities of a new age in explicit opposition to the inherited aesthetic modes of cultural consumption and the academic pieties of the mid-nineteenth century.

Wagner declared himself the true successor to Ludwig von Beethoven, who, by the mid-nineteenth century, had become the model of pathbreaking, transformative originality and innovation. As Beethoven demonstrated, true historical succession in music history took the character of an altered sound world. In Wagner's case, that meant replacing the symphony with the music drama. Wagner sought to transcend a sharp mid-nineteenth-century differentiation between the extramusical and the purely musical.

Although Wagner proclaimed himself the founder of a new aesthetic, the modernist generation of the turn of the century asserted its own voice by finding a way to integrate key Wagnerian experiments with compositional principles located in the work of Wagner's supposed archrival and polar opposite, Johannes Brahms. In articulating the principles of musical modernism in his writings in the 1930s, Schoen-

berg found in Brahms's music the progressive formal procedures considered crucial to a unique musical art in the twentieth century.

While musical modernism owed much to Wagner, in part because of the spectacular success and popularity that Wagner enjoyed, the turn-of-the-century generation of modernists sought to cut its own distinct path out of Wagner's shadow by returning to preromantic, eighteenth-century principles of musical composition and realizing those principles with new sounds and strategies in the use of pitch relations, timbres, and time. A constructed ideal of late eighteenth-century classicism led to neoclassicism, the return to an ideal of "absolute" music, and the rejection of music as narrative and illustration became the foundation of a distinct twentieth-century modernist aesthetic. At the same time, as in Ives, Berg, and ultimately Cage, the return to a formalist pre-Wagnerian definition of music as abstract and self-referential, in both modernist composition and criticism, was never complete.

While nineteenth-century music, inclusive of Wagner, does not permit a facile comparison with forms of visual or literary realism as practiced during the nineteenth century, a sufficiently powerful canonic tradition in aesthetic expectations in music had developed by 1900 that provided the equivalent of realist expectations. In the mid-eighteenth century, as the Baroque era ended, a new, simpler, homophonic tonal style at odds with Baroque polyphony and with an emphasis on linear expressiveness became widespread in Europe. Its emergence ran parallel with a growing audience for instrumental music and the beginning of a sustained acceleration in the rates at which musical literacy expanded. These processes coincided with the flourishing of philosophical speculation on the nature and character of music, which lasted throughout the nineteenth century.

The initial period of reaction to the Baroque was followed by the great age of Viennese classicism. Wolfgang Amadeus Mozart and Franz Joseph Haydn (particularly the latter) reintroduced a contrapuntal complexity into classical style, augmented the range and variety of operatic convention, and spawned large-scale models for purely instrumental music, particularly in the quartet, sonata, and symphony, in which an extended, "purely musical" logic could be discerned. That logic included notions of thematic development, formal symmetry, and organic integration in multiple-movement works of music. The Viennese school of classicism (as it later became known) created the benchmark for all future aesthetic debates and movements in European music, particularly if one includes in the Viennese classical canon the work of Beethoven. Beethoven was regarded by all subsequent generations as a nascent Romantic individualist who brought the immanent possibilities of expression audible in Mozart and Haydn to completion in a manner adequate to both Romanticism and classicism.

The first generation of nineteenth-century composers—Felix Mendelssohn, Robert Schumann, and Hector Berlioz, for example—struggled with the overpowering example of Beethoven. At the core of the Romantic engagement with Beethoven were fundamental aesthetic questions regarding the nature of music: Was music a vehicle for emotional expression? Was it abstract in the sense that its aesthetics were contingent on a self-referential logic? Was it an art form that inhabited a realm otherwise unreachable, beyond the grasp of the pictorial and the literary? Furthermore, in what sense could music be representational, narrative, or illustrative and yet realize the inherent unique possibilities of musical discourse, form, and conversation? Beethoven's work lent itself to being used by mid-nineteenth-century proponents of radically differing answers to these questions.

In 1854, Eduard Hanslick published his famous tract *On the Musically Beautiful*. He was understood as arguing for a formalist approach to the importance and beauty of music based in a belief in its autonomy. His polemic set the terms of the divide between absolute and program music in the nineteenth century. The programmatic direction was heralded by the so-called new German school, which included Franz Liszt and Wagner. A contradiction that was not apparent to Beethoven or Schumann and Mendelssohn, or even Mozart and Haydn, was constructed between what was termed pure music and music subordinated to so-called extramusical logics.

A key factor in this mid-nineteenth-century philosophical and aesthetic debate was the social and economic context, particularly the rapid explosion of a public for music. The sale of sheet music, the demand for pianos, the expansion of an international concert life, and the popularity of music instruction and writings about music created a suspicion that an elite art form associated with a highly cultivated aristocratic tradition of amateurism and connoisseurship was being debased by rendering it contingent on visual and literary criteria of meaning. Indeed, Wagner's success in using music to illustrate the visual and the dramatic was derided as a corruption of the true nature of music and a concession to a new and lamentably philistine public. For every young enthusiast who embraced Wagner as a rebel against bourgeois convention, there was a so-called conservative who saw in Wagner the failure to realize the inherent and exclusive power of music evident in the traditions of Viennese classicism.

Musical modernism was inspired in part by a reaction against the late-Romantic rage for "program" music and the explicit manipulation of musical sounds to illustrate ordinary narratives and stimulate emotions that reached its apogee around 1900, particularly in the music of Strauss and the operatic work of the Italian verismo composers, including Giacomo Puccini. Schoenberg, for example, saw modernism as the emancipation of music from a dependency on nonmusical programs derived from poetry,

drama, and images. When worlds and music were combined, as in Schoenberg's *Pierrot Lunaire* (1912) or later *Moses und Aron* (1932), the music was not composed to "illustrate" or represent the meaning of the words. The tone poems of Strauss and the orchestral music of the late nineteenth-century Russian composers, particularly Pyotr Ilich Tchaikovsky, were characterized as trapped in a dead end created by the extramusical illustrative expectations of the audience.

Modernism required that longer musical forms (the musical equivalents of the nineteenth-century novel)—the extended, multimovement symphony, the music drama, and the tone poem—be recast or abandoned in favor of more succinct genres and transparent timbres. The lush sound of late-Romantic music was set aside, and so too was the dependency on thematic repetition. Schoenberg called for a return to a technique by which miniature musical ideas—musical cells of pitch and rhythm—were transformed, developed, and varied, and through that process, given meaning and form over the elapsed time of a single composition. Ironically, many critics of modernism in composition, such as the great theorist Heinrich Schenker, shared in this rejection of late nineteenth-century, post-Wagnerian habits. Modernism was part of the early twentieth century's effort to reclaim music's autonomy and reassert it as an abstract and inherently formalist language of expression.

If one were to identify a moral equivalent to realist techniques in music, one might turn to the uses of harmony and the nature of melody. Schenker, for example, argued that tonality was normative and possessed a transhistorical aesthetic and psychological validity. Composers who followed in the wake of late Wagner (Debussy, for example) saw themselves as stretching the boundaries of tonal practice. From the standpoint of the 1920s, one could describe an evolutionary development in harmonic practice leading up to the abandonment of tonality. It began with extended tonality, the transformation and emancipation of the idea of dissonance, and the embracing of atonality, as well as alternatives to the harmonic system of whole and semitones. The hallmark of early twentieth-century musical modernism from the vantage point of both composer and listener was ultimately the abandonment of conventions with respect to pitch relations. The most important innovation was twelve-tone composition or serialism, which dates from the 1920s. Serialism, too, was inspired in part by frustration at the extent to which in the post-Wagnerian age tonal practice had successfully made instrumental music into the purveyor of nonmusical clichés and images.

By the mid-1920s, the main features of musical modernism had become clear. Tonality was either abandoned or radically redefined. A distinct neoclassical tendency toward formal genres independent of any so-called extramusical program became discernible. The combinations of instruments and voices were generally smaller in scale. The overarching aesthetic was anti-Romantic, resembling the revival of Biedermeier design on the part of early twentieth-century modernist architects and designers. This led, in turn, to an economy of means and experimentation with the uses of silence.

Among the classic polemical writings on behalf of the varieties of musical modernism are Schoenberg's *Theory of Harmony* (1911), Busoni's *New Aesthetics of Music* (1920), Ives's *Essays before a Sonata* (1920), Stravinsky's *Poetics of Music* (1947), and the shorter writings of Schoenberg, Bartók, and Sessions. The most significant historical events associated with musical modernism are the public scandals that attended performances of Schoenberg's music between 1907 and 1913 in Vienna and Berlin, the famous melee that erupted in 1913 at the first performance of Stravinsky's *Rite of Spring*. The history of modernism also includes Strauss's own foray into innovative practice, particularly in the operas *Salome* and *Elektra*. Although his music was discovered only in the 1920s, Ives's radical innovations and formal procedures, particularly the layering of disparate elements and the uses of fragments of found music that result in a dissonant and discontinuous surface, also date from the first two decades of the twentieth century.

Musical modernism's status as a rebellion against the all-too-comfortable tastes of the late nineteenth-century, middle-class audience for music turned out to be more successful perhaps than was bargained for. The lure of modernism captured the imagination of composers throughout Europe, from England to eastern Europe, during the 1920s and early 1930s. From the 1920s onward, as modernism gained in prestige among composers and performers, it struggled in vain to keep the allegiance of the audience of the era, which showed its recalcitrant preference for eighteenth- and nineteenth-century music.

Modernism's promising emergence in music after World War I was profoundly influenced by the politics of the 1930s. Musical modernism became the object of attack by fascism in Italy, Nazism in Germany, and Stalinism in the Soviet Union. Declared "degenerate" by the Nazis, musical modernism became a rallying point for modern philosophical aesthetics and critical theory. Yet, many socialist critics and musicians, particularly Hanns Eisler and Kurt Weill (both of whom had a modernist phase and then a rejectionist period), recognized in musical modernism a nostalgia for an aristocratic public and even a distaste for the mass of humanity at odds with its progressive ideology. Indeed, despite the use of the term *modern,* a basically reactionary attitude to mass society and modern technology lay behind the harsh and dissonant surface of new music. Modernism's radical break with past practice seemed necessary, however, to the critique of bourgeois culture and capitalism. In part, this view was shared even by Ives, who, despite his business career, was a radical democrat and populist. This defense of modernism was best articulated by Adorno. Schoenberg be-

came at one and the same time a progressive radical as a political symbol and a radical conservative in compositional procedures.

The effect of the Nazi critique and the Zhdanov decrees of 1948 against modernism promulgated in the late 1940s by Joseph Stalin was to lend musical modernism an unimpeachable ethical prestige among the generation of composers who emerged after 1945 in the West. In the United States, the innovations of Ives and the arrival of modernist composers with the emigration of the 1930s fueled the development of a distinct American tradition that involved the exploration of non-European musics and traditions. Henry Cowell was its most distinguished practitioner. It led, in turn, to the work of Lou Harrison, Cage, Steve Reich, LaMonte Young, and Terry Riley. In postwar Europe—particularly in France and Germany—schools of composition arose that continued the work of the second Viennese school, particularly the refined, elegant, and austere music of Webern, who experimented not only with pitch and rhythm, but with silence. Centers of the new European postwar modernism were Darmstadt and Donauschingen, and, later in the century, Paris through the work of Boulez at the Institut pour la Recherche et Coordination Acoustique-Musique.

In the United States, the music of Carter, Sessions, Babbitt, and a host of younger academic composers dominated the teaching of composition in the decades following 1945. Many of these composers, along with Stockhausen in Germany, began to experiment with mixing acoustic and electronic sources of sound. In all of these trends, the emphasis on a formalist and autonomously musical conception of sound and time predominated. Likewise, there was a rigid avoidance of what would have been viewed as a regressive reliance on tonality and tonal procedures. In turn, the modernist music of the post–World War II era, although critically acclaimed and ideologically privileged, struggled in vain to achieve a stable place in the repertory of the concert hall, the opera house, the radio, and especially the phonograph in the home.

In the late 1960s, when the political linkage between modernism and the politics of resistance against pre-1945 political oppression faded, the dominance of modernism began to weaken as well. George Crumb's music of the late 1960s signaled a more eclectic and sensual approach. Fin de siècle and nineteenth-century sources became audible in contemporary music. Despite the visibility and prestige of modernism throughout the twentieth century, a tradition of composition seemingly more conservative and overtly skeptical of modernism had always existed. During the 1930s, many composers who had once embraced modernism in the 1920s (e.g., Aaron Copland) modified their stance precisely because of its lack of wide appeal. The politics of socialism and progressive democracy cast suspicion on the assertion that musical modernism was the historically true aesthetic medium of spiritual and political liberation. In other circumstances, the direct patronage of fascism and communism sustained an antimodernist compositional tradition. In the 1940s, Bartók made fun of Dmitri Shostakovich precisely because of his lack of modernism. By the 1970s, Shostakovich had emerged as a highly influential figure of twentieth-century music alongside his relatively conservative British contemporary Benjamin Britten. Curiously, they, like the modernists, identified Mahler as a key source of inspiration.

By the 1980s, the drift away from modernism revealed a revived interest in the relation between music and narrative, music and illustration, and music and emotions. The claims on behalf of an exclusive, self-referential logic in music, dependent exclusively on the composer's ability to manipulate procedures of musical transformation, were rejected, despite the uncomfortable comparisons made between this postmodern movement and the worlds of popular music, commercial music, and Hollywood film music. The antimodernist musical legacy within the twentieth century was rehabilitated.

What is perhaps most distinctive about European musical modernism is its striking philosophical conservatism. It picked up implicitly the cultural critique inherent in Hanslick's 1854 attack on "program" music. It seemed in search of an audience that could think in a purely musical manner, as defined by tenets of formalist aesthetics. It sought to realize in sound alone the philosophical privilege accorded music by Romantic aesthetics, even though it rejected the traditions of tone painting and expressiveness of the eighteenth century and of program music and music drama of the late nineteenth century.

The failure of modernism in music vis-à-vis the public is perhaps unique with respect to twentieth-century modernism in general. Unlike modernism in architecture, painting, and literature, musical modernism did not experience any form of generalization or imitation in mass culture owing to its failure to win the wide allegiance of any of the traditional audiences for high culture. Modernism effectively isolated the tradition of concert music from the mainstream of twentieth-century art. It helped to lend undue prestige to a standard repertory of the eighteenth and nineteenth centuries in the concert hall. Modernism stimulated the revival of Renaissance and Baroque music (and the concomitant embracing of period performance practices) in the post–World War II era. Last, it implicitly encouraged, as a result of its arcane surface, renewed enthusiasm for popular and commercial music among late twentieth-century intellectuals and artists as worthy of high status and critical attention.

The leading writers and painters of this century in the main kept on listening to music written before 1914, with few exceptions. Those exceptions included the alliance between musical minimalism and abstract and geometric min-

imalism (e.g., in the music of Morton Feldman), and, to a limited extent, the link between modernist choreography and the music of Stravinsky and Copland.

Nevertheless, in the late twentieth century, new music by composers who have absorbed and sustained many of the key aesthetic strategies of musical modernism, particularly the search for a distinctly twentieth-century use of pitch and rhythm, continues to appear. This has helped lend the surface of much of late twentieth-century music a contemporaneity based in early twentieth-century modernism. Modernism, as understood as a strategy of music writing that emerged from the innovations of Schoenberg, Varèse, and Ives, and the modernist aspects of Bartók, Messaien, and Stravinsky, continues as a force in musical composition.

[*See also* Adorno; Boulez; Cage; Music, *historical overview article;* Schoenberg; *and* Stravinsky.]

BIBLIOGRAPHY

Adorno, Theodor W. *The Philosophy of Modern Music.* Translated by Anne G. Mitchell and Wesley V. Blomster. New York, 1973.

Born, Georgina. *Rationalizing Culture: IRCAM, Boulez, and the Institutionalization of the Musical Avant-Garde.* Berkeley, 1995.

Goehr, Lydia. *The Imaginary Museum of Musical Works: An Essay in the Philosophy of Music.* Oxford, 1992.

Griffiths, Paul. *Modern Music and After: Directions since 1945.* Oxford and New York, 1995.

Ives, Charles. *Essays before a Sonata and Other Writings.* New York, 1961.

Leibowitz, René. *Schoenberg and His School: The Contemporary Stage of the Language of Music.* Translated by Dika Newlin. Reprint, New York, 1970.

Morgan, Robert P. *Twentieth-Century Music: A History of Musical Style in Modern Europe and America.* New York, 1991.

Rochberg, George. *The Aesthetics of Survival: A Composer's View of Twentieth Century Music.* Edited by William Bolcan. Ann Arbor, 1984.

Schoenberg, Arnold. *Style and Idea: Selected Writings of Arnold Schoenberg.* Edited by Leonard Stein, translations by Leo Black. Reprint, Berkeley, 1985.

LEON BOTSTEIN

Modern Dance

Modern dance (also known at various times and in various countries as contemporary dance, new dance, free dance, and *Ausdrucktanz*) has resisted classification since its beginnings in twentieth-century Germany and America. The term was first applied sometime in the early 1930s to its pioneering American practitioners (Martha Graham, Doris Humphrey, and Charles Weidman, among others), in part because they strongly believed that their work should reflect contemporary life in its themes, forms, and movement styles. The first modern dancers would all have supported a statement José Limón (1908–1972) made in an essay for Selma Jeanne Cohen's *Modern Dance:* "The artist's function is perpetually to be the voice and conscience of his time"

(Cohen, 1966). By the 1990s, however, when the postmodern movement born in the 1960s was in full swing, "modern dance" had come to suggest established styles rather than innovation.

Modern has other implications. Especially during the late 1920s and early 1930s, the tenets of modern dance could be linked to those of modernism in art, architecture, and design. The choreographers focused on what they deemed to be the essence of dance, on what set it apart from the other arts. Movement and form, not literary content or visual spectacle, were to dominate. In a 1935 statement quoted in Merle Armitage's *Martha Graham: The Early Years*, Graham (1893–1991) sounded a clarion call: "This is a time of action, not re-action. The dance is action, not an attitude, not an interpretation" (Armitage, 1978). (It should be noted that her style of the 1940s and afterward modified this position.)

Also, like artists associated with modernism in other fields, choreographers sought to discover the intrinsic nature of their material, in this case, the human body—not just the physical mechanism, but the mental and emotional states it projected. Finally, their interest in stripping away ornament and paring an idea to its essence echoed the ideas of prominent modernist designers.

Certain of these principles can also be found as early as 1900 in the work of Isadora Duncan (1877–1927), claimed variously as a forerunner or founding mother or inspirational force for modern dance—mainly in her emphasis on simple, natural movements. The idea that movement is dance's great subject continues to be held and practiced in highly uncompromised ways by Merce Cunningham (b. 1919) and others.

It could be said that modern dance developed in part as a reaction against ballet. Ballet evolved from the elaborate entertainments and social dances of the sixteenth-century French court; the first modern dancers deplored what they felt to be an outmoded illusion of aristocracy and built systems rooted in movements common to all humans: breathing, falling, walking, running. Ballet prized the image of lightness; modern dance acknowledged the pull of gravity. Ballet dancers emphasized the straight spine, with action in the limbs dominant; modern dancers brought the torso into play, frequently making its movements impel those of the legs. Ballet drew its subject matter—and still draws it to some extent—from fairy tales, often putting story in thrall to spectacle. Humphrey (1895–1958) wrote disparagingly in *The Art of Making Dances* that "the drama [in ballet] was interrupted by display pieces of technique, thought to be much more important than the story. All had to be airy, charming, with sadness the mere shadow of a butterfly's wing" (Humphrey, 1959). Modern dance asserted its right to tackle dark, thought-provoking subjects. Said Graham in 1928, "Ugliness may actually be beautiful if it cries out with the voice of power."

These dancer-choreographers tended to be articulate. They wrote manifestos and essays, and gave interviews. In their printed work, one often finds the idea that dance had once been a profound part of religious life. Exposure to the ceremonies of Sufi monks (Whirling Dervishes) impressed on Rudolf Laban (1879–1958), the Hungarian theoretician and choreographer, the nature of dance as spiritual communication. The early solos of his pupil Mary Wigman (1886–1973) also revealed a vision of dance as rituals of sacrifice, offering, and possession. Ted Shawn (1891–1972), the cofounder (with Ruth St. Denis) of the Denishawn school and company, pointed out in *Gods Who Dance* the serious status accorded dance in Asian cultures. Duncan's mission was to elevate dance to the stature and power she imagined it to have had in ancient Greece. Most appeared to believe that dance could and should reveal powerful human drives and universal forces, taming these through form. In other words, the choreographers intended this "serious" art they were practicing to illuminate, stir, and inspire spectators, not simply to entertain them.

It is difficult to make generalizations, and misleading to suggest that choreographers associated with modern dance over a period of close to one hundred years have shared an identical vision—especially since another essential property distinguishing modern dance from ballet is its shunning of a single lexicon of steps or training excercises. This very heterogeneity, considered a sign of weakness by traditionalists, lies at the core of its aesthetic. Beginning with Duncan, the choreographer was not conceived of as a ballet master manipulating a common vocabulary, but as a choreographer-dancer creating and performing an individual body of work. Although Laban based his work on analyses of observed elements of space, rhythm, and dynamics in human movement, most choreographers aimed to discover a distinctive lexicon of movement, rooted inevitably in his or her own body and psyche, and responsive to era and country. (As Helen Tamiris wrote in a 1928 "Manifest" printed in a program for her second New York concert, "Art is international, but the artist is the product of a nationality, and his principal duty to himself is to express the spirit of his race.")

Despite the diversity of styles and the changes resulting over time, it is possible to isolate some common values. These are particularly marked during the first part of the twentieth century, when radical dance artists laid out their aesthetic credos. Although the German choreographers preceded the Americans in allying their art with the principles of modernism and expressionism in the visual arts, only a few direct influences can be proved; yet the dances of Wigman and Graham from the 1920s and 1930s, for example, seem in retrospect to have more in common than was allowed at the time.

Duncan, like Paul Taylor and Mark Morris (two and three generations later, respectively), found inspiration in music. She imagined the works of the great composers she idolized as animating forces, as if she were a dynamo to receive music and transform it into dancing. Other choreographers, however, have approached music in more unusual ways: dancing in silence, creating a dance in silence and having a composer then create a score for it, collaborating with a composer as the dance is evolving. The dancing may follow the music's structure and quality closely or work against it at times. The music may function more to provide atmosphere than a rhythmic beat. The most radical approach, exemplified by Cunningham, is to consider the musical score as a separate and independent entity running concurrently with the dance, but not heeded by the dancers.

When music does not dictate a dance's form, other structuring principles come to the fore. Another statement of Graham's collected by Armitage dates from 1927: "Out of emotion comes form." (Her words correspond closely to those of Expressionist painter Wassily Kandinsky.) Her great rival Humphrey issued similar statements. The choreographers also made it clear, however, that, despite the emphasis on feelings and individual discovery as sources, attention to structure elevated the work over sheer self-expression. Duncan, Wigman, Graham, and Humphrey are known to have found inspiration in Friedrich Nietzsche, especially in his *Birth of Tragedy from the Spirit of Music,* and were mindful of the power that objectivity should exert over subjectivity. By using various forms of abstraction, they could suggest universal conditions that transcended personal histories. In Humphrey's autobiography (completed by Selma Jeanne Cohen as *Doris Humphrey: An Artist First*), is found this statement, dating from 1931: "I believe that the more impersonal and abstract art is, the greater it will be. The farther from the individual, the farther from personality, the closer to perfection" (Humphrey, 1972).

For these choreographers, abstraction became condensation, the modernist stripping of an idea to its essence, as exemplified by Graham's 1929 *Heretic.* The inspiration is believed to be Joan of Arc. Graham reduced it to a single performer in white (herself) confronting, over and over, a stern, unresponsive group of identically dressed women. To each of her brief "statements," they responded by assembling themselves, instantly and obdurately, into frozen images of walls, jeering mobs, advancing phalanxes. By the end, she was prone, powerless to resist. The result was not the story of a particular heroine, but a dramatic essay on the individual spirit battling a conformist society (the individual in relation to the group was a popular theme in both America and Germany of the 1920s and early 1930s).

Modern dancers have tended to perform as themselves—understanding always that this self is a created entity. In dances involving narrative and character, such as the major works Graham created between 1944 and 1958, the issue seems less one of impersonation than of allying this "self" with a character. Even Ruth St. Denis (1879–1968), who cast herself as numerous and glamorous Asian goddesses, nevertheless made her principal subject the transformation of flesh into spirit, the revealing of the soul under accumulated layers of "maya. She, her husband, Shawn, and dancers they trained (among them Graham, Humphrey, and Weidman) performed on the vaudeville circuit as well as the concert stage, but apparently felt no discrepancy between entertaining the public with their exotic genre pieces and tackling themes of redemption and transcendence. The effect she gave in her more reverent solos was of an individual transfigured by revelation.

Many of the created movement styles were based on gesture rather than on "steps." By *gesture* is not meant pantomime, but the gesture that suffuses the whole body: the reach, the contraction, the swoon, the gathering in. Some theories, and the training systems they engendered, involved the expression of natural duality within the individual, as basic as inhaling and exhaling. The notion of duality also related to Nietzsche's concepts of the Dionysian and the Apollonian. For Wigman, this duality took form as tension and relaxation, for Humphrey as fall and recovery, for Graham as contraction and release. The concepts had a strongly idealistic component: for instance, Dionysian turbulence—whether interior or from an outside force—might knock the individual off balance, with the dance born in the struggle to regain equilibrium. The emphasis was on the rise, not on the fall, even though one of the features common to most early modern dance styles was an extensive vocabulary of falls.

Some choreographers have articulated the intuitive beginnings of creation in highly mystical ways, as if dance were a force speaking through them. In *The Language of Dance,* Wigman wrote of the genesis of her solo *Ceremonial Figure,*

> I shut myself in my golden room, leaned my head against the softly singing Siamese gong, and listened to myself deep within. I did so until a pose emerged out of this musing and resolved itself into the stylistically corresponding gesture and, with it, into the first careful step which released the now awakened body and surrendered it to space.　　　　　　　　(Wigman, 1966)

Decades later, Cunningham wrote in an essay, "The Impermanent Art," that the dancer's tranquil concentration on doing the movement allowed him "to present freely and liberally. Making of himself such a kind of nature puppet that he is as if dancing on a string which is like an umbellical [*sic*] cord:—mother-nature and father-spirit moving his limbs without thought" (Cunningham, 1955).

A belief in the inherent expressiveness of forms and human movement may influence choreographic choices: a circle to convey unity and shared belief, a fugue to convey similar impulses gradually coming together. Among the generation of choreographers approaching artistic maturity in the 1940s were some who rejected narrative and suggested that dancing is its own subject—notably Erick Hawkins (1909–1994), Alwin Nikolais (1912–1993), and Cunningham. But they did not mean that dancing was therefore just an amalgam of steps. Hawkins wrote eloquently in his essay for *The Modern Dance* of discovering "the wondrous, immediate knowledge of existence that you get in the pure fact of movement," provided you find what he calls its "inner quality" (Hawkins, 1992). Cunningham, who has asserted that his dances are not "about" anything, or rather are about movement and however we wish to construe it, told Jacqueline Lesschaeve in interviews published as *The Dancer and the Dance*, "I always feel that movement itself is expressive, regardless of intentions of expressivity, beyond intention" (Cunningham, 1985).

Cunningham's aesthetic may seem diametrically opposed to that of choreographers working from an inner source, yet, like them, he believes in the expressive nature of movements; he simply will not inflict a prior interpretation on them or choose them for their particular emotional suggestiveness. Cunningham began in 1951 to employ chance procedures to thwart his own movement preferences. Yet, his deep belief in the profundity of dancing links him with earlier modern dance practitioners, and "chance" has only enriched a personal movement style essentially serene and Apollonian, but full of unexpected coordinations, speeds, and direction changes.

Choreographers have often spoken of bringing their art in tune with nature, although, since the understanding of nature's processes is constantly reshaped by scientific thinking, the resultant styles differ. For instance, Duncan, through an idyllic vision of wave motion, connected herself with a harmonious universe. In a circa 1905 essay collected in *The Art of the Dance*, she wrote,

> This great wave movement runs through all Nature, for when we look over the waters to the long line of hills on the shore, they seem also to have the great undulating movement of the sea; and all movements in Nature seem to me to have as their ground-plan the law of wave movement.   (Duncan, 1977)

Cunningham's view of nature, on the other hand, was more influenced by particle physics. Random selection, chance, indeterminacy, and acausality found their way into his processes and the look of the finished work. For Nikolais, acknowledging nature meant deemphasizing the role of the dancer as a representative of dominant humankind and making him or her one spatial element in a patterned universe of color and light.

Connected with an interest in nature is the concept of "natural" movement, what is peculiar and essential to humans. Only in postmodern dance of the 1960s, however, was *natural* construed as everyday. Modern dance choreographers, in varying ways, idealized or stylized basic movements and functions. Cunningham applied a direct and natural performing style to difficult and virtuosic dancing.

The idea that gestures evolve organically, crucial to Wigman's thinking and to Duncan's, can also be related to "naturalness." So can the interest in gravity that has informed much modern dance. Acknowledging the pull of gravity—whether fighting it as the early moderns did, or playfully cooperating with it, as Hawkins advocated—is another way of affirming nature.

Possibly because many modern dance choreographers wished to sense a connection between their work and primal rituals, they tended to conceive of space as an active animating force, not simply the patterned ground they associated with ballet. Elizabeth Selden wrote in *The Dancer's Quest* that what she called "The New Dance" envisioned the body as a three-dimensional object, like sculpture, to be viewed from all sides. The movement of the dance makes the "lines 'roll' around his body," turning the dancer into "an instrument for projecting space" (Selden, 1935). In her solos, Duncan animated the space around her, peopled it with imagined friends and enemies, perhaps coloring one place onstage as dangerous, another as alluring. The connection between gesture and points in space was central to Laban's theory of Space Harmony. In his work and that of Wigman and her pupils (Hanya Holm, for example), the dancer often collaborated with space—attracted toward depth, torn between opposite poles. The great dance dramas that Graham began to make in the 1940s, many with the crucial collaboration of designer Isamu Noguchi, were set in an arena in which space and time were flexible concepts: Troy and Mycenae, past and present, events and dreams might coexist simultaneously on the stage. Cunningham conceived of space as an "open field," with no point more important than any other, thus undermining the traditional proscenium stage as a picture box in which events are arranged in hierarchical layers according to their importance.

An important difference in philosophy distinguished ballet from modern dance during the latter's formative years. Ballet training, by and large, has focused on the would-be professional dancer, whereas the teaching of modern dance, particularly in Germany and England (to which Laban immigrated in 1938) extended to the amateur as well. Dancing was everyone's birthright. Laban wrote in *The Mastery of Movement* that "Man's desire to orientate himself in the maze of his drives results in definite effort rhythms," and that a tribe or community's characteristic "effort configurations" play a role in the creation of dances that teach and reinforce moral values (Laban, 1971). Through performances of movement choirs, therefore, he sought to create artificial and liberating communities in which large numbers of mostly untrained dancers moved together in harmonious unison or counterpoint, roused to an awareness of their individuality in relation to a greater whole. His ideas, like those of Duncan, St. Denis, and Shawn, show the influence of French theorist and singing teacher François Delsarte

(1811–1871), whose ideas (systematically linking the mental, the spiritual, and the physical) encompassed the belief that movement had the power to ennoble character.

Certainly not all choreographers deemed part of modern dance have articulated their ideas with the fervor of some of those quoted above, yet they share many of those beliefs or have been influenced by them. Beginning in the 1950s, modern dance, spreading throughout the world, developed a generic side, with choreographers blending styles or merging them with ballet, making it more difficult to isolate what categorizes a work as "modern dance." Confusingly, the early stages of postmodernism were in some ways modernist by nature; the vanguard choreographers of the 1960s sought to strip away accretions, to scrutinize natural human movement, and to discover what was basic and particular to dance. That their works looked so radically different from anything that preceded them only confirms that they inherited much from modern dance: sensitivity to the times in which they lived, esteem for change, and the need to pursue an individual vision.

[*See also* Dance.]

BIBLIOGRAPHY

Armitage, Merle, ed. *Martha Graham: The Early Years* (1937). New York, 1978.

Cohen, Selma Jeanne, ed. *The Modern Dance: Seven Statements of Belief.* Middletown, Conn., 1966.

Cunningham, Merce. "The Impermanent Art." In *7 Arts,* no. 3, edited by Fernando Puma, pp. 69–77. Indian Hills, Colo., 1955.

Cunningham, Merce. *The Dancer and the Dance.* In conversation with Jacqueline Lesschaeve. New York, 1985.

Duncan, Isadora. *The Art of the Dance.* Edited by Sheldon Cheney (1928). New York, 1977.

Fancher, Gordon, and Gerald Myers, eds. *Philosophical Essays on Dance, with Responses by Choreographers, Critics, and Dancers.* Brooklyn, N.Y., 1981. Based on a conference at the American Dance Festival.

Hawkins, Erick. *The Body Is a Clear Place and Other Statements on Dance.* Pennington, N.J., 1992.

Humphrey, Doris. *The Art of Making Dances.* Edited by Barbara Pollack. New York, 1959.

Humphrey, Doris. *Doris Humphrey: An Artist First.* Edited and completed by Selma Jeanne Cohen. Middletown, Conn., 1972.

Jowitt, Deborah. *Time and the Dancing Image.* New York, 1988.

Laban, Rudolf. *The Mastery of Movement.* 3d ed. Revised and enlarged by Lisa Ullmann. Boston, 1971.

Langer, Susanne K. *Feeling and Form.* New York, 1953.

Nietzsche, Friedrich. *Ecce Homo and The Birth of Tragedy.* Translated by Clifton P. Fadiman. New York, 1927.

Partsch-Bergsohn, Isa. *Modern Dance in Germany and the United States: Crosscurrents and Influences.* Chur, Switzerland, 1994.

Selden, Elizabeth. *The Dancer's Quest: Essays on the Aesthetic of the Contemporary Dance.* Berkeley, 1935.

Shawn, Ted. *Gods Who Dance.* New York, 1929.

Siegel, Marcia B., ed. "Nik: A Documentary." *Dance Perspectives* 48 (Winter 1971).

Wigman, Mary. *The Language of Dance.* Translated by Walter Sorell. Middletown, Conn., 1966.

DEBORAH JOWITT

Modern Literature

Modernist literature is usually thought to belong to a period between 1890 and the 1930s, and to have been at its height in the 1920s. Like some other forms of modernism, or indeed the Romanticism of which it sometimes seems a late heir, modernist literature is often considered to be distinguished by its reactions to the challenging pressures of modernity, although it can nevertheless be seen to practice a kind of modernization of its own. This commitment to change and innovation within literature is often summed up by reference to Ezra Pound's perennial demand that his contemporaries "make it new" within "a new civilisation"; or to Virginia Woolf's view, in her celebrated essay "Modern Fiction" (1919), that the proper material of the novel is "other than custom would have us believe it."

Literary modernism's departures from custom and convention are most significant in terms of form, rather than subject or theme. Throughout the period, many writers took as their subject the new experience of the twentieth century, yet continued to present it through styles and structures carried on from the end of the nineteenth. Modernist writing, on the other hand, is distinguished by its attempt to make literature itself a new experience. The fractured complexity of modern city life, for example, not only figures as a subject in James Joyce's *Ulysses* (1922) and T. S. Eliot's *The Waste Land* (1922), but is installed within the form of texts that alternate abruptly between different perspectives and voices and fracture their style into diverse linguistic registers. Likewise, the concern with sex that appears in the fiction of Joyce and D. H. Lawrence seemed new and explicit enough to lead each author into difficulties with censorship. Yet, what really sets their work apart is not the subject of sex but the new intensity and subjective inwardness with which this and other aspects of private experience are presented. Following Woolf's advice to "look within" and "examine the mind," this move toward inner consciousness and away from conventional realism is characteristic of modernism and of its fiction in particular: like the subject of sex, it also parallels the age's new interest in psychology, following the work of Sigmund Freud.

Shifts from the surface of experience toward recording the inner workings of the mind required developments in the styles and strategies of fiction that appear in several phases in the early twentieth century. Henry James focuses the point of view of novels such as *The Ambassadors* (1903) largely through the personal perspective of a single observer, while in *Lord Jim* (1900) and *Heart of Darkness* (1902) Joseph Conrad refracts experience through the subjective vision and voice of a narrator, as does Ford Madox Ford in *The Good Soldier* (1915). Especially in *The Rainbow* (1915) and its sequel, *Women in Love* (1921), Lawrence extensively transcribes the inner voice of characters, often by means of free indirect style. A further, decisive step in presenting inner mental life appears in the stream-of-consciousness style developed for English-language fiction by Dorothy Richardson in the early volumes of *Pilgrimage* (1915–1967), a style extended or alternated with other forms of interior monologue in the work of Woolf and Joyce. The range and subtlety of the latter's representations of inner consciousness help make *Ulysses* the principal achievement of modernist fiction, although the stream-of-consciousness form is later put to particular and challenging use—sometimes in representing disturbed minds—in William Faulkner's *The Sound and the Fury* (1929). The complex, nonchronological form of Faulkner's novel is also typical of consequences of movement within the mind for the overall structure of modernist fiction, which often departs from the historical sweep of nineteenth-century novels in favor of narratives contained in one or a few days of consciousness, with the fickle, associative memories of characters or narrators used to stitch in significant past episodes alongside present ones.

Such strategies can be seen as forms of resistance to the stresses of the modern age, and attempts to find imaginative alternatives. World War I added conviction to the view in *Ulysses* of history as "nightmare." Long before the end of the nineteenth century, Karl Marx had highlighted the commodification of time and the reification of the individual within capitalist industry, processes accelerated after the turn of the century under the influence of Frederick W. Taylor and Henry Ford. War, work, and many aspects of everyday existence in the early twentieth century shaped modernist fiction's departures from the compromised dimensions of time and history, and its preference for deeper visions of the self—less rational spaces of the mind—as refuges from some of the negative, rationalizing forces of modernity.

Modernist poetry was equally ready to fracture or abandon conventional forms—in favor of new or unruly rhythms and rhymes, complex tones, apparently casual rather than causal connections—and in ways comparable to the intentions of modernist fiction. Symbolism projects on—or discovers within—an inhospitable external world, often urban or industrialized, some continuing resonance of personal or emotional significance. A sense of collapse rather than coherence in the life in time offers modernist poetry not only a problem but the possibility of juxtaposing cultural or historical markers for purposes of its own. In *The Waste Land*, Eliot echoes or alludes to a wide range of past culture—Dante Alighieri and William Shakespeare most frequently—as a means of contextualizing yet also criticizing a confused, dispirited postwar existence by contrast with its supposedly splendid past.

Pound did much to edit *The Waste Land* into its published form, although his own career had begun with some different priorities, shaped by a leading role in the Imagist movement. A number of early twentieth-century poets shared Imagism's determination to substitute clarity and exactness in place of the rhetoric, abstraction, and sentiment of nineteenth-century verse, and to concretize personal states through reference to a firmly described world of objects, and the movement's influence was extended into later years by the work of William Carlos Williams. By "Hugh Selwyn Mauberley" (1920), however, Pound himself had moved closer to Eliot's wider vision of a "botched civilisation," and to his tactics for describing it, and he extends into his major work, the *Cantos* (published in various sections from 1925 onward), a determination to set modern life within the "arena" of all world culture, presented through a bewildering range of tones, styles, and personal references.

Recurrent mythic themes help provide the *Cantos* with some coherence. In an age of rapidly declining religious faith, influenced by skeptical or antirational philosophers such as Friedrich Nietzsche and Henri Bergson, modernist writing often relies on myth as a last potential source of order and coherence for contemporary life—Eliot using the Grail legends in *The Waste Land*, and Joyce sustaining parallels with Homer's *Odyssey* throughout *Ulysses*. William Butler Yeats also came to rely on a personal, esoteric, mythic/magical system, set out in *A Vision* (1925), although he differs from the modernists in some other respects: his early poetry is romantic and escapist; his middle period was directly concerned with contemporary Irish politics; and much of his work is relatively regular in rhythm and rhyme. Later poems such as "Sailing to Byzantium" or "Byzantium," however, are typical of a characteristic modernist interest in art. In these poems, and much of Eliot's and Pound's work, art functions rather like myth—as a means of escaping the vicissitudes and mutability of contemporary life, or of finding some visionary coherence beneath or beyond its fractured surface.

Sometimes simultaneously, modernist texts' reflections on art draw attention to their own practices and proceedings. Much of Wallace Stevens's poetry broods over the nature of relations between creative imagination and reality, an issue further highlighted by the richly imaginative landscapes, mental and physical, of the poems themselves. Comparable self-consciousness appears in the semiautobiographical artist figures who turn up in modernist fiction, sometimes helping elucidate the complicated textual strategies of the works in which they appear. Figures such as Lily Briscoe in Virginia Woolf's *To the Lighthouse* (1927), Stephen Dedalus in Joyce's *Portrait of the Artist as a Young Man* (1916), or the eponymous hero of Wyndham Lewis's *Tarr* (1918) all highlight or discuss in this way aesthetic issues of interest to their authors—although in Lewis's case such aesthetics is as often antithetical to modernism as consistent with it, part of a position as "The Enemy" of his age that he develops further in wide-ranging, revealing analyses of contemporary culture such as *Time and Western Man* (1927).

While literary self-examination can be figuratively presented through painters such as Lily or Tarr, it ultimately comes to rest on issues of language and its capacities to represent reality. These are issues of interest to the age as a whole: to thinkers such as Nietzsche, Bergson, and the linguist Ferdinand de Saussure; to most of the poets, Eliot perhaps most explicitly in the reflective self-examination of *Four Quartets* (1936–1943); and to many novelists—to experimenters with language and style such as Gertrude Stein and Ernest Hemingway, and to Joyce, above all. Stephen's fascination with words in *A Portrait of the Artist as a Young Man* extends into Joyce's constant parody and verbal play in *Ulysses,* and the punning, invented, half-nonsensical language of the "Work in Progress" that followed, eventually published as *Finnegans Wake* in 1939. As contemporary commentators such as Samuel Beckett pointed out, Joyce's language in this late phase largely ceases to represent any recognizable reality and reflects principally on its own nature and movements.

Almost a stream of *un*consciousness, the language of *Finnegans Wake* is an extreme example of the difficulty and complexity for which modernist literature has often been criticized—whether in the dense allusions of Pound and Eliot, the esoteric system of Yeats, or the more generalized challenge to readers of new, unfamiliar forms, unreliable narrators and fractured perspectives. Such challenges have been seen as elitist; parts of a deliberate or perhaps unconscious attempt to preserve high art for the privileged, leisured, educated few at a time when—in the form of cinema, radio, journalism, or cheaper books—culture seemed to be more and more a possession of the masses. Such elitism can be seen as consistent with the antidemocratic politics of a number of modernist authors—Pound and Lewis, in particular, embraced the fascism that emerged as the major political threat of the 1930s. Modernist difficulty can, of course, be defended as only an unfortunate side effect of complex strategies necessary to confront or resist the difficulties and challenges of modern life. Yet, literary modernism is sometimes so successful in distancing or effacing these challenges, imaginatively or formally, that it has also remained open to the charge that it evades them altogether.

This charge of irresponsibility to contemporary life and history receives its strongest summary in György Lukács's essay "The Ideology of Modernism," published in 1957. Such criticisms were already prevalent in the 1930s, however, when immediate economic and political crises, the rise of fascism particularly, encouraged authors to move away from modernism toward more direct political and social commentary, often presented through more conventional styles. There was nevertheless some 1930s fiction—John Dos Passos's *U.S.A.,* or Lewis Grassic Gibbon's *A Scots Quair*—as well as the poetry of W. H. Auden, which found ways of combining contemporary left-wing commitments with modernist innovations in style and form. By the end of

the decade, a new generation of innovative writers, Beckett among them, had emerged to help carry forward some of the characteristics of modernism—its self-reflexive, self-scrutinizing concerns with art and writing perhaps primarily—toward the later twentieth-century literature often defined as "postmodernist." Critical debate continues about how far, and in what ways, this literature can be seen to descend from modernism, and how far it shares in a wider postmodern outlook also traceable in architecture, music, philosophy and the culture of the later twentieth century as a whole.

Modernist innovations in style and form are much less apparent in drama than in fiction and poetry, in the anglophone context at any rate. In continental Europe, on the other hand, the early twentieth century saw a number of reactions against, or developments beyond, modes of Realism and Naturalism dominant at the end of the nineteenth. Alfred Jarry's plays challenged almost all established conventions of drama, an attack later extended by the influential theories of Antonin Artaud, favoring a return to primal, ritualistic aspects of theater. The work of August Strindberg and German authors who followed him developed an Expressionist drama whose interest in staging inner or dreamlike states bears comparison with contemporary fiction's streams of consciousness. Initially close to Expressionism, Bertolt Brecht eventually established new anti-illusionistic strategies (partly shared with the director Erwin Piscator) specifically appropriate to a Marxist theater of instruction as well as entertainment. In Italy, Luigi Pirandello provided a kind of dramatized commentary on relations between realism, reality, and illusion, while Italian Futurism and Russian Constructivism's settings, representative of an industrialized machine age, added to the range of antinaturalistic staging strategies. None of these movements, however, had a very strong or immediate impact in the English-speaking world. Expressionist influence can be traced in some of the 1930s drama of Auden and Christopher Isherwood, and in the early work of Eugene O'Neill (such as *The Emperor Jones,* 1920), but it is probably clearest in fiction—in the "Nighttown" chapter of *Ulysses,* or in Wyndham Lewis's *The Enemy of the Stars,* included in his radical Vorticist journal, *Blast* (1914), and not much more than nominally a play. Although Brecht eventually became a commanding figure for the twentieth-century stage generally, his influence was not much felt internationally until around the middle of the century.

While English-language drama in the modernist idiom is therefore overshadowed by developments in continental Europe, more equable comparisons can be made in relation to fiction and poetry. Marcel Proust's *À la recherche du temps perdu* (In Search of Lost Time, 1913–1927) offers an early, influential example of modernist concentration on time and art, and the latter area is further, self-reflexively examined in André Gide's *The Counterfeiters* (1925). Modernist interests in time and history also figure strongly in Thomas

Mann's *The Magic Mountain* (1924), and a concern with individual consciousnesses, isolated by alienating societies, shapes much of the writing of Franz Kafka and Robert Musil. The Symbolist poetry of Stéphane Mallarmé appealed to both Yeats and Stevens, while successors such as Paul Verlaine, Arthur Rimbaud, and Paul Valéry all share in the formal innovations of modernism. Influences from Symbolist poetry and from Jules Laforgue also figure in the work of Eliot, whose early cityscapes may owe something to Charles Baudelaire's somber, dreamy visions of Paris. Comparisons and connections of this kind figure significantly throughout modernist writing, often the work of authors—such as Eliot, Joyce, Pound, Conrad, and James—living in countries not originally their own, and therefore especially attuned to cultural contrasts and the increasing internationalism of outlook in the modern age generally.

Acknowledgment of European parallels and influences is one part of a necessary broadening of the context in which modernist writing should be considered. Unlike related developments such as Imagism, Futurism, or Vorticism, modernism was not a movement deliberately organized by a group of authors sharing an agreed agenda of ideas and priorities. Modernism is a critical construct: an agreement among later commentators that certain writers who may differ in other ways nevertheless share significant, dominant interests—in innovation and formal experiment particularly. This critical conclusion, however, leaves the boundaries of modernism inexactly defined. Much debate has resulted about where they should be drawn, especially as modernism has been increasingly assessed as the most exciting phase of twentieth-century writing, and its contributions to "the international store of literary technique," as Pound calls it, seen as important influences on the literature that has followed. Culminating in Bonnie Kime Scott's anthology *The Gender of Modernism* (1990), much of this recent debate has emphasized the significance of women authors excluded from full attention during the period and since—writers of poetry, such as H. D. (Hilda Doolittle), Mina Loy, or Amy Lowell, for example, or of fiction, such as May Sinclair, Rebecca West, Jean Rhys, or Katherine Mansfield. Recent commentary has also reemphasized the kind of gender issues stressed at the time in Woolf's essay *A Room of One's Own* (1929)—needs for a new language and literary strategy to reflect the consciousness of women—as among contemporary factors underlying the development of modernism generally, as well as specific features such as stream of consciousness.

As historical distance from modernism increases, commentators have also grown more inclined toward the position outlined in Peter Nicholls's *Modernisms* (1995), which sees literary modernism not as a single coherent phenomenon but an amalgam of many cognate ones—a broad phase of experiment including Imagism, Vorticism, Expressionism, Futurism, Symbolism, and much besides. Critics have also recently emphasized analogies between literary developments and those in other contemporary arts such as painting and music—the work of Pablo Picasso, Arnold Schoenberg, and many others bearing obvious comparison with modernist literature's fracturing of conventional artistic forms and modes of construction. Lengthening perspectives, however, help clarify not only the great range of modernism's manifestations but also the historical particularity of the period that underlies them. Stevens's "ghostlier demarcations, keener sounds," Woolf's determination to "look within" the mind, Proust's search for lost time—all contribute to the achievement of this outstanding period of twentieth-century literature. All are also ways of seeking subtler structures and languages, deeper senses of self, to resist the chaotic history and diverse threats to the individual experienced in the modern machine age.

[*See also* Baudelaire; New Criticism; *and* Stein.]

BIBLIOGRAPHY

Bradbury, Malcolm, and James McFarlane, eds. *Modernism, 1890–1930*. Harmondsworth, England, 1976.

Chefdor, Monique, Ricardo Quinones, and Albert Wachtel, eds. *Modernism: Challenges and Perspectives*. Urbana, 1986.

Eysteinsson, Astradur. *The Concept of Modernism*. Ithaca, N.Y., 1990.

Kenner, Hugh. *The Pound Era*. London, 1972.

Lewis, Wyndham. *Time and Western Man* (1927). Edited by Paul Edwards. Santa Rosa, Calif., 1993.

Lukács, Georg. "The Ideology of Modernism." In *Marxist Literary Theory: A Reader,* edited by Terry Eagleton and Drew Milne, pp. 141–162. Oxford and Cambridge, Mass., 1996.

Nicholls, Peter. *Modernisms: A Literary Guide*. London, 1995.

Quinones, Ricardo J. *Mapping Literary Modernism: Time and Development*. Princeton, N.J., 1985.

Schwartz, Sanford. *The Matrix of Modernism: Pound, Eliot, and Early Twentieth-Century Thought*. Princeton, 1985.

Scott, Bonnie Kime, ed. *The Gender of Modernism: An Anthology*. Bloomington, Ind., 1990.

Stead, C. K. *Pound, Yeats, Eliot, and the Modernist Movement*. London, 1986.

Stevenson, Randall. *Modernist Fiction: An Introduction*. New York and London, 1992.

Woolf, Virginia. "Modern Fiction." In *Collected Essays*, vol. 2, pp. 103–110. London, 1966.

Woolf, Virginia. *A Room of One's Own* (1929). Harmondsworth, England, 1975.

RANDALL STEVENSON

MONDRIAN, PIET (1872–1944), Dutch artist. When he died in New York City on 1 February 1944, Piet Mondrian was broadly hailed as Holland's greatest modern painter. This was perhaps small tribute to an artist who had, along with Wassily Kandinsky, provided first theoretically and then through sustained practice the foundational demonstrations of what seemed to them the aesthetically inevitable, namely, abstract art. For both artists, modern conditions of being, combined with the recognized momentum of modern painting, were seen to demand the abandonment of natural representation in favor of imaging structures derived from personal confrontation with what was variously conceived as a higher reality. This higher reality as a notion derived in the instance of both artists from loose—in fact, wholly hybrid—conceptualizations of reality based on Platonic, Neoplatonic, and theosophical premises. Neither artist was formally trained in philosophy, but together (and separately) they produced the nearest thing to tightly argued philosophical analyses for the enabling conditions of modernist pictorial practice as such were seen to exist in the second decade of the twentieth century.

The role of artist-theorist (or ideologue) was firmly established by the time Mondrian and Kandinsky entered the arena of modern painting in a serious fashion. Eugène Delacroix's journal had been published (fragmentarily at first) beginning in the late 1870s. Paul Gauguin's *Noa Noa* and other writings appeared through the 1890s hard on the heels of James Whistler's *Ten O'clock Lecture* as translated into French by Stéphane Mallarmé. After the turn of the century, Vincent van Gogh's letters (to his brother and to other artists and family members) began to appear in print, as did various forms of quasi-theoretical statements squeezed out of Paul Cézanne by young admirers. From the 1890s onward, artists like Maurice Denis and Paul Signac increasingly used critical and theoretical writing in tandem with painting to convey their various aesthetic positionings. Finally, in 1907, and coordinating with the opening of his private art school, the established leader of advanced modern painting in France, Henri Matisse, published his highly influential and self-promoting *Notes of a Painter*. To enter modern painting successfully after the publication of Matisse's long essay virtually mandated writing and painting at once—or, if not writing, as with Pablo Picasso, having plenty of others writing for one, thereby producing at least an aura of theory to support spectator-challenging practice and to control interpretation of that practice.

Theoretical expectations for modern painters were certainly driven as well by a substantial thickening of art-historical discourse in the years after 1900. Following on his groundbreaking study *Renaissance and Baroque* of 1888, the Swiss art historian Heinrich Wölfflin produced *Classic Art* in 1899 and in 1915 *Principles of Art History*. Together these books applied a quasi-Hegelian model of a historically driven dialectic to account for the progressive behavior of art considered as pure form—a notion derived from the "pure visibility" aesthetic discourse of Conrad Fiedler and Adolf von Hildebrand as it had emerged in the 1880s and 1890s. Like other totalizing formalist behavioral constructions of the period, Sigmund Freud's or Georg Simmel's for example, Wölfflin stressed inevitable conditions but, more important, he stressed implicit historical determinants. Applied to newly defined "modern art," Wölfflin's analysis produced remarkable results, particularly in Julius Meier-Graefe's massively influential *Development of Modern Art* of 1904 (written in German and translated into several other languages before 1910). Meier-Graefe's complex historical and critical portrayal of the trajectory of modern art as he defined it merged powerfully with the evolving historical and critical formulations of the Englishman Roger Fry to produce a tightly theorized discourse working from recent history toward an impending future. What the so-called critical historians of art provided to the enterprise of artist-theorist was the presumedly historically based impulse to project both artistically and theoretically ahead, with the projection guided by an established understanding of the progressive behavior of artistic form.

It would be a gross oversimplification to attribute the entirety of Mondrian's (or Kandinsky's) artistic project to discursive conditions—whether aesthetic, historical, or both—circa 1910. By the same token, it would be intellectually limiting to view their behavior practically and theoretically in a discursive void. In fact, it is at least arguable that the very intensity of aesthetic discourse circa 1910 largely constituted the incendiary conditions necessary for so revolutionary an aesthetic maneuver as abstraction. Compared to the conceptual noise level and general impatience of contemporary Italian Futurist or, in Russia, Suprematist and Constructivist theoretical rhetoric, Mondrian's (and Kandinsky's) projects appear highly reasonable and procedurally confident. But this comparison simply highlights what can be viewed as profoundly similar gestures toward that which appeared historically inevitable.

Born into a politically and religiously conservative family in Amersfoort, Holland, Pieter Cornelius Mondriaan was interested in drawing from a very early age. By 1892, he had managed sufficient training to obtain a secondary-school teaching diploma. Thereafter and until 1896, he attended various classes at the Dutch national art school (the Rijksacademie), and he qualified for the Dutch Prix de Rome competition in 1898, but his candidacy was rejected because his figure drawing was seen to be insufficiently accomplished. Over the next decade he was an active participant in most of the exhibitions of contemporary Dutch art mounted under various auspices in and around Amsterdam. He gained a respectable level of recognition as a landscape painter. After 1907 and several summers on the Dutch coast working with the most ambitious of his Dutch contemporaries, he began to be viewed as an artist routinely seeking to establish himself as someone both interested in and increasingly conversant with international artistic trends—particularly those visible in Paris. Yet, Mondrian seemed at first reluctant to travel in order to confront international trends firsthand and in depth, relying instead for his understanding on the descriptions of his more cosmopolitan associates, on international art magazines, and on the comparatively few examples of French modern work that were exhibited in Holland before 1910.

By 1909, Mondrian's reputation as a potentially significant international painter brought him into exhibitions, first in Belgium and then in France. By the time he moved to Paris on a more or less permanent basis in 1912, he was sufficiently well connected there to begin exhibitions regularly at the Salon des Indépendants, and after 1913 in important German venues as well. During these years his clientele remained predominantly Dutch, even though his work departed increasingly from the norms of contemporary art as practiced in Holland. During World War I Mondrian took comfortable refuge in his native country, rapidly becoming a moving force both artistically and theoretically in the de Stijl group and in its house journal, also called *De Stijl*. Along with his friend and associate, Theo van Doesburg, he managed to bring de Stijl into the forefront of modernist practice and discourse in the immediate postwar period.

Returning to France after the war Mondrian was increasingly visible as primary exponent of the most radically simplified version of abstract painting, as well as that version's most articulate apologist. Although he never established a reliable commercial relationship with a private gallery, the artist managed, largely through participation in group exhibitions, to develop a more or less dependable international market consisting of museums (particularly in Germany), collections of advanced contemporary art, artists and architects. His work passed into American collections facilitated in one way or another by Marcel Duchamp in the late 1920s. In England he was revered (if not widely collected) by various artists related to the English Modern movement in the 1930s.

Mondrian remained a highly visible fixture in the Parisian art scene of the 1920s and 1930s, but his celebrity blossomed increasingly among American and British artists in the years before World War II. Geometric abstraction was a prominent force in the contemporary art of the two principal parts of the English-speaking world. Mondrian as artist (and as persona) seems uniquely to have served to represent the aesthetic cutting edge of modernity, even more so outside Paris than within. As extreme as his paintings were his ideas regarding the appropriate modern habitat. His stark white studio-apartments in Paris, decorated only by his paintings and assorted rectangles of pure colors, were pilgrimage stops for artists and collectors from many lands. His insatiable taste for American jazz and for ballroom dancing completed the thoroughly modern image his paintings had begun.

Mondrian's connections with London and New York served him well when he chose to exile himself from events in Europe. Moving to the former in 1938 and the latter in 1940, with the financial support of artists from both countries, he managed a surprisingly productive late career in the United States. When he arrived he found himself preinstalled in major museum collections, most notably at the Museum of Modern Art. His New York years surpassed all prior ones in terms of one-man exhibitions, sales, and prestige. Mondrian's presence in New York during the war years, like that of several other important artists immigrating from Europe, served significantly to cosmopolitanize artists' tastes and practices in America both during the war and after. Additionally, the artist seems to have found himself secure and confident to a degree never experienced before, surrounded as he was by many friends and admirers. Without achieving much wealth he was nevertheless relatively comfortable, and without becoming conventionally social he enjoyed his expanded range of personal contacts.

There is not much in the basic biographical scan of Mondrian's life that casts more than circumstantial light on his artistic project. As twentieth-century artists' biographies go, his is uninteresting, and he may well have intended it to be so in order that he not get in the way of what he considered most important, namely, his aesthetic performance. As already suggested, this performance consisted of two tightly interconnected efforts, one pictorial and one theoretical. At different points in his life one or the other effort appears dominant, even though the artist himself firmly believed that the painting came first and then the theory.

Historically speaking, Mondrian had painted for a long time before he undertook to theorize what he was doing and why. Only after joining the Dutch Theosophical Society in 1909, and only after receiving extensive critical coverage of his exhibited work around the same time, did Mondrian begin seriously to consider writing as a complement to painting. His earlier work had featured landscape images very typical of postrealist practice in Holland, Belgium, and northwestern Germany. Heavily impastoed, densely colored, and often developed with prominent decorative features, his paintings showed a recurrent fascination with direct reflections of trees and real buildings positioned close to rivers and canals. This fascination produced and supported a severe flattening of spatial representation and encouraged various degrees of frontality in the presentation of motifs.

With these characteristics in place, Mondrian gradually accepted a sequence of more "modern" influences, largely secondhand from France. Neo-Impressionist, Cézannian, and Fauvist procedures appear in somewhat hybrid fashion starting in 1908. In order to accommodate them, Mondrian simplified his landscape motifs even further, concentrating on stretches of coast, on individual sand dunes, and on isolated towers and windmills. His color is simplified and often emphatically bright. His paint structure is the result of continuously dotted and dashed brushstrokes carrying considerable material weight. His drawing alternates between an emphasis on intricate webs and on severe simplifications of contour. The general aspect of the 1908–1910 work is experimental. Some new motifs appear—some half-length figures and some single flowers.

Theosophical subtexts are more or less overt in certain paintings in which such states as contemplation, devotion,

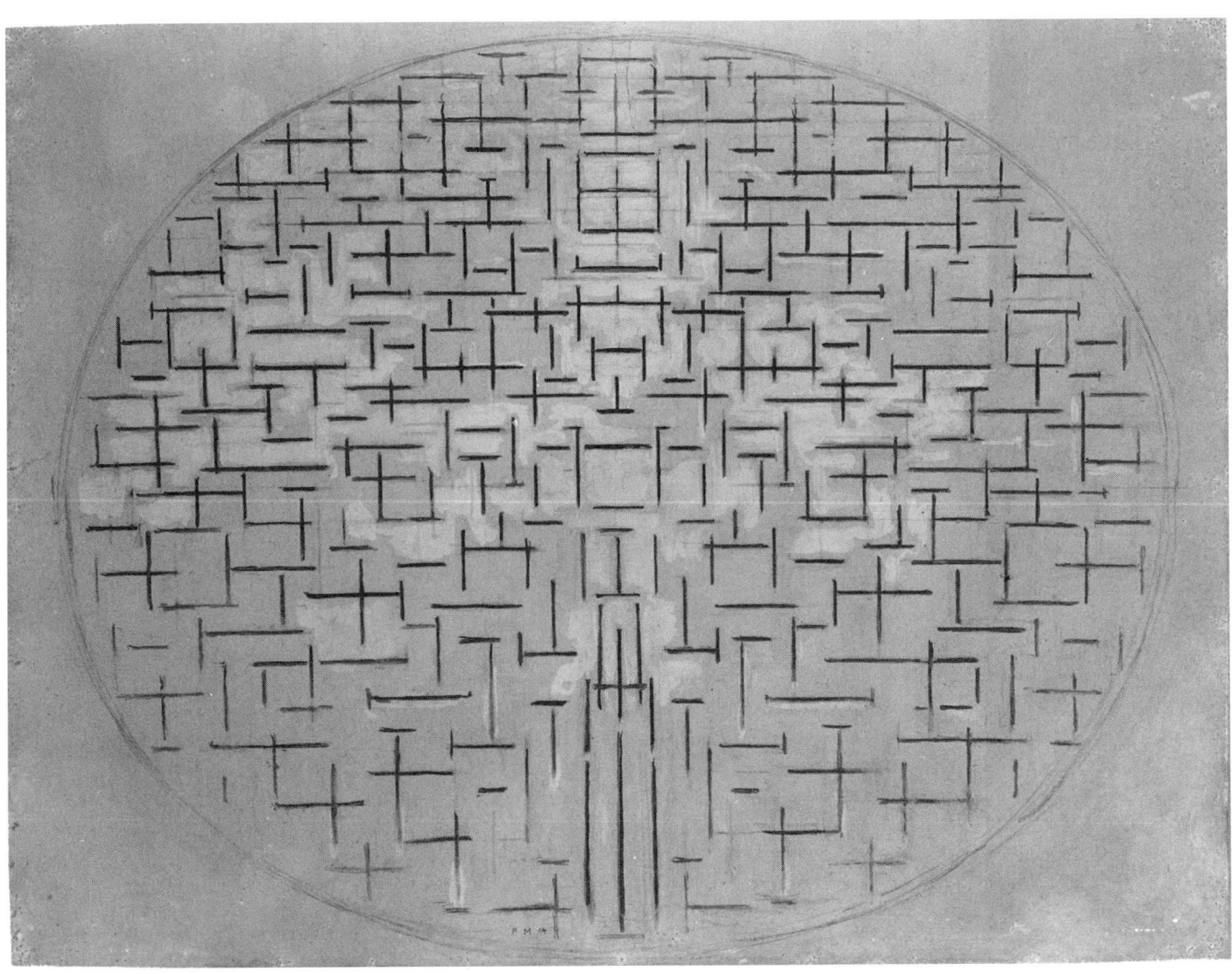

MONDRIAN. Piet Mondrian, *Pier and Ocean* (1914), charcoal and white watercolor on buff paper, 34 5/8 × 44 in. (87.9 × 111.2 cm), oval composition 33 × 40 in. (83.8 × 101.6 cm); Museum of Modern Art, New York (Mrs. Simon Guggenheim Fund). (Photograph copyright 1998 by Museum of Modern Art; used by permission.)

and unfolding are loosely thematized, but not until a large-scale work of 1910–1911, the *Evolution Tryptich*, is it possible to define an elaborated theosophical program. In that work, which was not well received when first exhibited, Mondrian presented three torso-length female nudes, geometrically simplified with faces positioned to alternate among expressed conditions of upwardness, outwardness, and inwardness. Ascending degrees of consciousness are named, so to speak, by theosophical emblems worked around the figures' upper bodies. Producing a painting obviously intended to be both seen and read, the artist was clearly signaling a shift in his aesthetic strategy—a shift away from the material in any form and toward the spiritually ideological in some form. *Evolution* did not suffice in itself to direct Mondrian in any clear fashion, but it did establish the conditions for a much more self-conscious and

conceptually intricate project. This project would feature prominently the clearest demonstration possible of a continuing search for the least materially impeded offerings painting might manage. Painting is here conceived as a unique locus of knowledge and of feeling—one that could be configured to aim outward at the spectator with the purpose of confronting her with the platonically "real" in its most intense modern form.

In theoretical writing published after 1917 Mondrian would mark out as precisely as he could how universal and antisubjective his project was. In this sense, he would distance himself absolutely from the more conventionally mystical and musical subjectivity operative in Kandinsky's privileging of "inner necessity" as a creative point of origin. Over a period of years between 1912, the year of his move to Paris, and 1917, when he undertook to theorize his art comprehensively, Mondrian gradually deduced the pictorial terms of his project through an ongoing process of acceptance, rejection, and synthetic conclusion. It cannot be determined with any certainty how systematically he worked in this period. The paintings that remain demonstrate a certainty of development that probably masks a good deal of trial and error. In any event, Mondrian had by 1917 established a secure position from which to paint abstractly and to undertake discourse on that painting.

Mondrian's decision to locate himself in Paris rather than Holland can be viewed as an attempt to mark clearly an intended radical reconfiguration of his artistic strategy. With *Evolution* completed and standing as a monument of mixed messages, both symbolic and pictorial, the artist seems to have sensed in the mature Cubism of Georges Braque and Picasso (of which he had only recently become aware) the potential means for measuring a new self—one wholly unencumbered by overfamiliar habits of seeing and feeling. Cubism revealed a way to oppose and ultimately to destroy all forms of the pictorially conventional and to deposit certain still-theosophical beliefs in a much more precise way than had been managed in *Evolution*. Helena Blavatsky's *Isis Unveiled*, theosophy's foundational text, was crucial (whether in itself or in more accessible reductions) in installing Mondrian's belief in the so-called secret codes of geometry and mathematics that Blavatsky had sensed in the systems of Euclid and Pythagoras. Similarly, the balanced opposition of male and female forces reducible to straight vertical and horizontal line oppositions figured strongly in the written images of Blavatsky and her followers.

Geometry as a stylistic device had appeared in *Evolution* but not as a pictorial generator. Cubism, on the other hand, demonstrated geometry as a primary, virtually exclusive generative force for developing form in two dimensions. The attraction of the Cubist demonstration for Mondrian seems in retrospect predestined to have been immensely powerful. But, by the same token, Mondrian's ways of seeing and responding to Cubism were predestined to be heavily programmed from the start. More than any other contemporary artist, Mondrian seems to have seen Cubism primarily as featuring webs and grids of powerfully equivocal sorts, successively and simultaneously sculptural and two-dimensional in their expression, yet seemingly poised in some unexpected condition of perceptible balance.

From 1912 onward, Mondrian's painting explores what he found to be the mandatory implications of Cubism. Working with still life and tree motifs, he applied first rough, then increasingly severe, networks of geometrical drawing that marked profiled edges of represented shapes and also of the areas between shapes, drawing positive and negative spaces together into a single pictorial field. Elements of apparent figure and apparent ground (as background) conversed equivocally within and across the web/grids. As these became more complex and more regular geometrically, architectural motifs began to be favored as points of image origin. Their preexistent geometry served more "naturally" to initiate the particular energies Mondrian sought to elaborate. Color in the most Cubist of his paintings serves as a distinguishing element, connecting or separating one area from another. But it operates as well to unify by being restricted within individual paintings to closely coupled hues and intensities.

By the middle of the decade Mondrian has progressively regularized his paint surface. His touch is very even, responding, it seems, to the dominance of right-angle geometry evident in drawing and in shaping. Working in Holland from mid-1914 to mid-1919, Mondrian pressed ahead relentlessly to determine and then define the operative essentials of his immanently abstract version of Cubism. Reduction of representational means and the foregrounding of all-encompassing geometric relationships—this is the ongoing project and the one the artist undertook to defend theoretically as necessary to the existential condition of being modern.

Three ambitious theoretical exercises, all produced for the magazine *De Stijl*, announce Mondrian as a formal theorist. They include an essay, "The New Plastic in Painting," and the dialogues "Natural Reality and Abstract Reality" and "Dialogue on the New Plastic." The writings feature a highly evangelical tone couched in persistent dialectical form using essential binary oppositions—nature versus reality, objective (free, reasonable, and modern) versus subjective (tragic, personal, and stuck in the past), and male versus female. Aesthetic and social missions are addressed simultaneously as Mondrian undertakes to demonstrate what the "modern" necessarily includes or excludes and why. To begin with, Mondrian takes pains, particularly in "The New Plastic in Painting," to establish his reason for writing publicly at all, since prior to 1917 he had been content simply with notes to himself in his sketchbooks. He starts with an apology: "Although the new plastic in painting reveals itself only through the actual work—needs no explanation in words—nevertheless much concerning the new plastic can be expressed directly in words and clarified by reasoning." This statement presents in capsule form the basis for an ongoing question regarding the priority of practice over theory, or vice versa, that, unanswered in any definitive way, hangs over Mondrian's art after 1917. When defining art and then the artist, Mondrian actually amplifies the significance of the question without intending to:

> Only that art is truly alive which gives expression to the contemporary—the future consciousness. . . . the artist, then, is only the more or less appropriate instrument through which the culture of a people (i.e., the degree of universality in the consciousness of the time) is expressed aesthetically. Aesthetically because *all* people—insofar as they have matured in this

respect—are part of the spirit of our age, and in one way or an-other, all represent it. Thus, modern art, where is appears *completely in the manner of art* is finally nothing other than the exact plastic expression of a more inward culture.

As regards what painting addresses specifically Mondrian uses the term *reality* in a very loaded way. It is his concep-tual device for excluding nature in any form as an appropri-ate frame of reference for pictorial imaging. He accepts the Platonic contention that mimesis involves an illusion of an illusion and is therefore twice removed from truth. Beyond this he sees "nature" in its self-sufficient grandness as disre-spected and reduced in stature through representation. Fi-nally, he sees nature and what he interprets as natural feel-ing as imbued with what he terms the tragic, hence, unmodern. It is basic to his theory that he situates painting next to nature as an alternative source of sublime sensation and a unique source for modern sensation that is antinat-ural. To accomplish this he has to reject nature (in the Rousseauian sense) as the de facto positive ambience of modern existence. He substitutes the metropolis for the for-est, the well-serving machine for the benevolent tree, and so on. The metropolis is the new cultural reality of the twenti-eth century as he perceives it, and his correspondent belief is that for modern painting to act as a conduit for modern reality, it must derive all its feelings and all its values from the metropolis in order to secure its modernity. Painting, however, must imitate only feelings, not images, or the old trap of mimesis (already rejected) is reset.

In his early theoretical writing, Mondrian argued for a range of axiomatic positions that, if granted, managed two things. First, it situated his art as the true and original mod-ern, and, second, it insisted that it be understood in a very specific way. With the theory in place, what remained for Mondrian was to paint from within it, proving by ongoing pictorial examples that he had discovered a true breadth of expressive terrain rather than a desert.

An art of intensely pure relationships built efficiently from fixed pictorial members—black lines always intersect-ing at right angles and bounding rectangles of white (some gray early on), red, yellow, and blue—this Mondrian de-vises and develops over the years from 1921 until his death in 1944. With his theory in place and available for occa-sional updating or modified emphasis, Mondrian chal-lenged himself to practice the freedom he preached. In painting after painting, his highly reduced pictorial lan-guage was made to yield a seemingly endless range of ex-pressive possibilities. At first, his structures were almost ar-chitecturally responsive to the framing edge of his regular rectangular formats. In the early 1920s he favors keeping open an inside square or near square of white, teasing it with color planes and line intersections positioned in the area between this square and the painting's outer limits.

Later in the 1920s, and after some experimentation with the canvas (stretched as a square) positioned at forty-five degrees to normal and with its bottom being a corner, more diagonal kinds of organization become favored, but despite much apparent asymmetry the paintings always read as balanced (or at rest) whether read two- or three-dimensionally.

In the early 1930s, the elements set into balance become somewhat thinner as the white field of the images is allowed to expand as a pictorial dominant with often fragile line and color plane interruptions serving to inflect this spread with-out in any way seeming to control it absolutely. Often only one or two of the primary colors will appear in a given painting. When this occurs the visual importance of the in-tersection of black lines is amplified substantially. Reacting to this, Mondrian first doubles and then multiplies the units of intersecting lines, sometimes thickening them or thinning them as well. When the doubling and then multiplying oc-curs, an optically active phenomenon develops as the view-ing eye reacts to the crossing points as flickering or light generating. The more of these points and the wider their distribution across a painting, the more the paintings lose their statically resolved architectural character and become visually animated and dynamic. The term *dynamic equilib-rium* begins to appear in late versions of Mondrian's theo-retical writing, responding, it seems, to the dominance of the new pictorial voice of optical vibrancy.

The paintings made in New York over the last four years of Mondrian's life seem literally to celebrate this new voice by translating it into color. The means for accomplishing this appear fortuitously in the commercial availability of half-inch colored tape. Working with the tape the artist was able to lay out and to adjust his images with much physical ease. At the same time, complicated grid studies with the color and drawing combined into a single line/plane unit could be developed and evaluated without massive invest-ments of time. Much was made spontaneously available by means of the tape, and Mondrian thrived in the new techni-cal condition, letting the spontaneity breed a kind of ner-vousness into his late pictures that likely seemed appropri-ate to the high visual stimulation environment of New York, both in normal and in wartime conditions. Blackouts alter-nated with daylight images laced with streams of yellow taxis and spectacular city lights at night, just as feelings of safety and vulnerability alternated relentlessly. In his group of *New York City* paintings from 1941–1942, in his *Broad-way Boogie Woogie* of 1943, and his unfinished *Victory Boogie Woogie*, Mondrian managed, working from theoretical premises left largely unformed by the time of his death, to project his final views of modernity in what were (as he had hoped) always his strongest and most original terms—namely, his paintings.

[*See also* Modernism.]

BIBLIOGRAPHY

Work by Mondrian

The New Art—The New Life: The Collected Writings of Piet Mondrian. Edited and translated by Harry Holtzman and Martin James. Boston, 1986.

Other Sources

Blok, Cor. *Piet Mondriaan: Een Catalogus van zijn werk in Nederlands openhaar bezit.* Amsterdam, 1974.

Blotkamp, Carel. *Mondrian: The Art of Destruction.* London, 1994.

Bois, Yve-Alain, Joop Joosten, Angelica Zander Rudenstein, and Hans Janssen. *Piet Mondrian, 1872–1944.* New York, 1994. Exhibition catalog, National Gallery of Art, Washington, D.C., and the Museum of Modern Art.

Carmean, E. A., Jr., *Mondrian: The Diamond Compositions.* Washington, D.C., 1979. Exhibition catalog, National Gallery of Art.

Celant, Germano, Michael Govan, et al. *Mondrian e De Stijl: L'ideale moderno.* Milan, 1990.

Champa, Kermit Swiler. *Mondrian Studies.* Chicago, 1985.

Henkels, Herbert, Harry Holtzman, et al. *Mondrian: Drawings, Watercolours, New York Paintings* Baltimore, 1981. Exhibition catalog, Staatsgalerie Stuttgart, Haags Gemeentemuseum, Baltimore Museum of Art.

Jaffé, Hans L. C. *Piet Mondrian.* New York, 1970.

Joosten, Joop M., "Mondrian between Cubism and Abstraction." In *Piet Mondrian Centennial Exhibition,* pp. 53–66. New York, 1971. Exhibition catalog, Solomon R. Guggenheim Museum.

Milner, John. *Mondrian.* New York, 1992.

Ottolenghi, Maria Grazia. *L'opera completa di Mondrian.* Milan, 1974.

Seuphor, Michel. *Piet Mondrian: Life and Work.* New York, 1956.

Troy, Nancy J. *Mondrian and Neo-plasticism in America.* New Haven, 1979. Exhibition catalog, Beinecke Rare Book and Manuscript Library.

Welsh, Robert P. "Mondrian and Theosophy." In *Piet Mondrian: Centennial Exhibition,* pp. 35–51. New York, 1971. Exhibition catalog, Solomon R. Guggenheim Museum.

KERMIT SWILER CHAMPA

MONTAGE. *See* Collage; Film, *article on* Motion Pictures; *and* Pastiche.

MONTESQUIEU, BARON DE LA BRÈDE ET DE (Charles-Louis de Secondat). *See* French Aesthetics, *article on* Eighteenth-Century Aesthetic Theory; *and* Sublime.

MONUMENTS [*To appreciate the relevance of monuments as subjects of aesthetic inquiry, this entry comprises two essays:*

Historical Overview

Twentieth-Century Countermonuments

The first essay discusses the history of the aesthetics of monuments in the West. The second essay explores how monuments have been understood and constructed in the twentieth century all over the world and explains the prevalence of countermonuments in this same period. For related discussion, see Sculpture.]

Historical Overview

Monuments have existed throughout history as means to speak to posterity about a specific event, action, or person. Monuments establish events as both deserving of glorification and worth remembering. They are built to demand that events and persons be perpetually, if not eternally, remembered, and they have been constructed throughout history to signify a sense of permanence. Hence, the concept of monumentality indicates a structure that will survive all potential tests of time—weather, war, political regimes, and changed values. The monument is supposed to pass down through history the essence of a past event and, in its immobility, to hold it stable in time—indeed, to render it timeless. That monuments have often been erected on a massive scale can thus be attributed as much to the desire that they are lasting as to the particular importance they attempt to apply to a given past.

Monuments are a form of pedagogy; they instruct on historical values, persons, and events, designating those that should be passed on, returned to, and learned from. Some monuments speak the language of celebration, while others indicate codes of nobility, valor, sacrifice, and heroism. Monuments can serve a variety of purposes—as tombs for the dead, signs of triumph, honor, or hatred, and as memorials. They can be demonstrations of authority, power, or ownership. Until the rise of modernism and the subsequent twentieth-century reevaluation of the aesthetic codes of depicting the past, monuments were built primarily to signify particular abstract values that were perceived to be universal and timeless. The modernist turn away from the massive and the monumental can thus also be seen as a recognition that such truths are not universally understood.

Origins of Monumental Aesthetics. Many of the originary codes of the monument were established by the monuments of antiquity, specifically through styles of Egyptian, Greek, and Roman architectures, and in Asia through the styles of ancient Chinese and Mongolian edifices. Certain central styles of the monument emerged from these legacies—the monument as tomb, the pyramid, the obelisk, the monumental figure, the war memorial, the victory monument, and the triumphal arch. Pyramids were constructed throughout the Americas, where they served both for military defense and as temples for worship. Yet, because of their immense size and durability, the Egyptian pyramids have often been regarded as icons for the ancient monument. The durability, immensity, and elaborate decoration of the monuments of ancient Egypt have allowed them to serve as icons of the colossal.

The function of the monument as both a site for religious practice and as a tribute to the dead is evidenced in the pyramids throughout the world. The early tombs as mounds of dirt evolved into increasingly elaborate forms that culminated in the Egyptian pyramids, built before 2000 BCE.

These were highly decorated houses for the dead—huge, elaborate edifices that established their importance and indicated a desire to speak their legacy to the future. At the same time, the pyramids of the Americas functioned both as tombs and as sites of worship, their monumental structures thus indicating a desire to speak and make sacrifice to the gods.

While traditions of freestanding figures had been established in Assyrian and Sumerian monuments, the legacy of the Greeks can be seen in the enduring aesthetic of the realist figure as a form of monumental tribute. The monumental Greek figure depicted great men, athletes, gods, and public citizens in life-size or larger-than-life works that signified dignity and physical prowess. The rendering of human likeness in stone was thus perceived to establish significance and historical weight, codes of realism to convey the individuality of the human figure, and massive size to imply an enduring, godlike, superhuman aura. Through the Greeks' glorification of the athletic aesthetic that characterized the Olympic Games, the figurative was monumentalized.

The victory monument derives its primary aesthetic elements from ancient artistic traditions. Historians have noted that the codes of triumph in the Greek victory monument departed radically from the victory monuments of previous ancient civilizations. Whereas the Egyptians and Assyrians constructed enormous limestone reliefs of leaders tormenting their opponents, and later the Romans built monuments with superhuman victors riding chariots over the spoils of their defeated enemies, the Greek victory monument subscribed to an ethic of no hubris, and a central theme of sorrow over the dead of both the victorious and the defeated.

The Romans created the triumphal arch as a monumental structure. Ironically, however, the Roman arch was designated as an edifice that straddled a road or bridge and was intended to hold triumphal sculpture. While many Roman arches were originally plain and seen merely as a form of pedestal, they gradually became adorned with decorative relief. The fact, however, that many arches survived through time without their original sculptures has allowed for the arch itself, rather than the statue that once stood on top of it, to acquire the meaning of triumph.

Throughout the Middle Ages and into the Renaissance era of European architecture, Christian styles of marking history and what should be remembered were manifested primarily in elaborate churches, private chapels, and narratives of transcendence and redemption. The relic (which by its very nature is antimonumental) took on the role of creating a cult of the past, and codes of monumentality were subsumed into religious narratives. The Baroque period, however, returned to the aesthetics of elaboration, decoration, and theatricality, and this was followed by a neoclassical revival that succeeded in installing classical codes for monuments up through modernism. This neoclassical return to the traditional forms continues to this day. Hence, Greek and Roman styles of antiquity are seen as evoking the entire tradition of the Western monument.

Because of their declarative and often baldly self-aggrandizing statements, monuments have also served as particularly symbolic spoils of war. Many leaders have stolen monuments of the territories they conquered in order to mark their imperialist triumphs. A monument as a spoil of war is thus both a trophy to be removed from its original context and displayed as a sign of victory, and a means to erase and potentially defile the triumphant history of the defeated regime. Obelisks in particular were transported from Egypt to Rome and then Europe, perhaps most famously by Napoleon, and eventually the meaning of an imperialist trophy became incorporated into their connotations. These moves to appropriate the monumental pasts of other places succeeded in disseminating architectural styles as well.

Throughout time, the concept of the monument as a temple to the body of the dead has endured. In the seventeenth century, Saint Peter's Basilica in Rome, while it functions primarily as a site of worship, was built over the grave of the first pope, and the Taj Mahal in Agra, India, was built for a Mughal queen. Monumental mausoleums to Napoleon, in the Hôtel des Invalides in Paris, to Ulysses S. Grant in New York, and to V. I. Lenin in Red Square in Moscow continue to operate as sites of tribute. These enormous structures, which are often also sites of worship, serve as a means to celebrate past leaders triumphantly and to compensate architecturally for the inadequacy of the corpse itself to evoke the impact of a life.

Since the establishment of the codes of monumentality of classical forms, the history of monuments and memorials has often been one of marking history by referencing the architectural and artistic styles of the past. Thus, the Egyptian obelisk and the Roman triumphant arch are found in Paris and evoked in Third Reich architecture, and the monuments of Washington, D.C., borrow styles from the Greek Parthenon. To create a monument in classical style is to refer to the history of monuments, to espouse codes of durability through time, and to chart a lineage from the past in order to speak to the future. The traditional Western monument thus glorifies not only its subject but the history of architecture as well.

The Monument as Memorial. The traditional function of the monument was to establish codes of heroism, triumph, nobility, glorification, and affirmation of a particular regime, state, or leader, to instruct pedagogically on what should be remembered and to what purpose, and to speak with some permanence to the future as a means of guiding the values of the present. Insofar as all monuments do speak to the question of remembering, they can be seen as memorials. Yet, the relationship of the memorial—in particular, war memorials—and the monument is complex. Like the cautionary Greek trophy monument, which eschewed boasting over the dead, the war memorial often privileges signs of sacrifice and martyrdom over triumph and glorification. Traditional war memorials, although often through the architectural codes of monuments, call to mind loss, either as the valorization of a cause or as legitimation for the sacrifice of individual lives. There has been some debate over the usefulness of separating the category of memorials from that of monuments, because throughout history many monuments have functioned as both. Yet, there are often important cultural and aesthetic reasons to distinguish them. Monuments are a means to honor the past, whereas memorials focus specifically on paying tribute to the dead. Memorials can take many forms (including specific days), but monuments are always concerned with the process of remembering.

Yet, while monuments always can be said to engage with issues of memory, the term *monument* may seem inappropriate to contemporary concepts of the memorial that work against the codes of monumentality. Although many monuments to victorious wars act as both monuments and memorials, the memorial to a defeat does not necessarily reflect the codes of the monument. Its primary narrative is of loss and sacrifice rather than triumph and conquest. In addition, memorials tend to isolate and mark individuals through either direct or implied naming. For example, a World War I memorial designed by Sir Edwin Landseer Lutyens, in Thiepval, France, contains the names of 73,000 men who died in the battle of the Somme. Its monumental style, however—a massive arch on which many of the names are inaccessible to the viewer—indicates the ways in which the functions of memorials and monuments can often work in tension. Monuments have a tendency to rely on abstract visual codes to convey their messages, whereas memorials usually are more inscription and text driven—the narrative of loss seeming to need more explanation than the simple narrative of triumph.

Monuments and the Passage of Time. The fact that monuments age over time, and often fall into ruin, has changed the aesthetics of their portrayal of durability. The pyramids, statues, and obelisks of Egypt have been regarded as evoking the poignancy and majestic qualities of aging works of stone. Because the tradition of monument building has returned in the past few centuries to the aesthetic of classical styles, contemporary neoclassical styles always refer at some level to the aging ruins of ancient monuments. Hence, they incorporate within their styles the sense of time passing, stone aging, and a recognition of the monument's ultimate ephemerality. The monument, under threat not only from natural causes but also the onslaught of tourism, consistently raises issues of preservation: When is a ruin appropriate? When should it be restored? The aging monument thus comes to symbolize testimony to time's relentless

movement forward, and has inspired reflections in literature and the other arts on the monument's evocation of time. For instance, the dramatic quality of the ruined monument, evoking both the tragic loss of the past as well as the hubris in believing one could survive through time, intrigued the Romantic poets, who wrote movingly of the remnants of ancient Egypt. In Percy Bysshe Shelley's famous poem *Ozymandias,* all that remains of the monument are "two vast and trunkless legs of stone" that form a "colossal wreck" taken over by sand. For Shelley, this ruin displayed the capacity of the sculptor to "mock" the desire of the king (supposedly Ramses II) to lay claim to the future.

Alois Riegl philosophized this aging quality at the turn of the century by defining monuments within specific categories: the "intentional monument," the "historical monument," and the "age-value" of monuments. These designations respond in part to nineteenth-century concerns about preservation and historical value. For Riegl, the traditional, intentional monument could be distinguished from the historical monument, which acquired its monumental status specifically through the passage of time. He saw the "intentional monument" as acquiring its commemorative value from its maker, whereas the viewers define the values of unintentional monuments. Riegl's work was an early attempt to understand the ways in which monuments change meaning over time, lose their original meaning, yet remain monumental. This Riegl termed "age-value," the power of a monument to mark, without specific references, the passage of time. The age-value of a monument allows it to convey monumental values even when its original signification is lost, and, for instance, when it is transported to new locales or survives political and national regimes.

The Modern Monument. Through its function to commemorate, display victory, glorify accomplishments, and attribute significance and grandeur to specific events and persons, the monument has played a role throughout history in the affirmation of nationalism. In modern history, monuments have become synonymous with national monuments, and they most often speak in the voice of the state. As such, with the exception of public figures who stand in for the nation, they have tended to subsume the individual into broader definitions of a people. The monumentality of immense size, abstract symbols, and larger-than-life figures thus incorporates the individual into discourses of sacrifice, citizenship, and the priorities of the collective.

With the rise of modernism, the aesthetics of monumentality became both exaggerated and increasingly self-conscious. Many monuments of the nineteenth and twentieth centuries have been referred to as "monstrous" monuments, in which an aesthetic of size has become overwhelming at the expense of form. The massive monuments of fascist architecture, most obviously realized in the enormous structures and monuments of Nazi Germany and fascist Italy during the 1930s and 1940s, borrowed classical forms, trimmed them of decorative excess, and exaggerated their scale. The excessive size of Third Reich monuments and buildings was a deliberate attempt to create "ruin value" that would speak to many future generations. Rudy Koshar writes: "The 'theory' of ruin value encapsulates much about Nazism's violent fear of time. The regime's architecture would be built so that it would resemble Roman models after centuries had passed" (Koshar, 1994). The exaggerated monumentality of Nazi and fascist architecture in general irrevocably changed the meaning of classical forms in the Western monument. In the postwar era, the classical forms that had become appropriated into fascist architecture could no longer be seen within conventions of democracy.

At the same time, Socialist Realist art borrowed and appropriated many of these same forms, often with an emphasis on the figure of the worker. While this was not the realist figure of the tradition of the Greek athletic aesthetic, in its depiction of the modern, angled body of the worker in poses of glorification or the ubiquitous statues of a larger-than-life Lenin, Socialist Realist art emphasized physicality and monumentality. In addition, both Lenin in the Soviet Union and Mao Zedong in China used the poster as a form of monument that was intended to speak directly to the populace and to allow for an endless recycling and variation of the same message.

This indicates another important stage in the concept of the monument, specifically in terms of the emerging technologies of memory in the nineteenth and twentieth centuries. Photography, cinema, television, and the mass production of public images emerged as new forms of remembrance and acquired many of the codes of historical posterity previously ascribed to the monument. Roland Barthes has written:

> Earlier societies managed so that memory, the substitute for life, was eternal and that at least the thing which spoke Death should itself be immortal: this was the Monument. But by making the (mortal) Photograph in the general and somehow natural witness of "what has been," modern society has renounced the Monument. (Barthes, 1981)

The image thus calls into question the durability of the monument as well as its central capacity to speak in the form of architecture and stone to the narratives of history. Indeed, it can be said that the historic events of the late nineteenth and twentieth centuries have been remembered more through photographs than through the monuments and memorials they have generated. Ironically, this has meant that some famous photographs have been monumentalized. An emblem of modern realism, the Marine Corps War Memorial in Arlington, Virginia, is based on a famous photograph of men raising the flag at Iwo Jima.

Contemporary Monument Building. In the twentieth century, changing aesthetics of monuments and memo-

rials have produced an active culture of antimonuments and countermonuments, which are aesthetically oppositional to the codes of monumentality. Underlying these works, which have proliferated throughout Europe and the United States in the late twentieth century, is the idea that monuments are in themselves inherently forgetful, that the values they intend to perpetrate need to be questioned, and that the monument itself is an ancient and ideological form. Hence, the monument's capacity to obliterate cultural memory in the process of preserving specific versions of history has been increasingly part of its contemporary reputation. Many of these new monuments and memorials have sparked intense debate, precisely because of the ways in which they defy the traditional codes of commemoration. Thus, the Vietnam Veterans Memorial was built in Washington, D.C., in 1982 amidst a volatile debate about what its dark granite walls, which are engraved with names, could connote about sacrifice and nationalism, a controversy that has resulted in two additional figurative statues being added to the site. The countermonuments of Germany, which have attempted to reckon with the remembrance of the Holocaust, have not simply broken the codes of monuments, but actively opposed them by refusing to rise above the ground, speak to heroism, or, indeed, to espouse a sense of history.

The culture of monuments in the late twentieth century throughout the world is, in fact, tremendously complex. In the United States, the traditional codes of monumentality are enacted through the kitsch forms of commercial architecture in cities like Las Vegas, yet a surge of memorial building has gripped the capital. In the late 1980s and 1990s, the post–cold war dismantling of monuments throughout the Soviet Union and in Eastern Europe has been regarded as a kind of death of the monument. Images of these larger-than-life monuments pulled down by crowds, warehoused, and obsolete, have had profound symbolic value in signaling the end of Soviet power and the aesthetic codes of Socialist Realism. At the same time, monuments of political power continue to be erected. In Iraq, a bombastic arch of swords pays tribute to the power of Saddam Hussein. In China, the conflicting codes of remembrance have been vividly in evidence in Tiananmen Square in Beijing, where monuments have been erected for five hundred years. When protesting students erected a new statue, the "Goddess of Democracy," in the likeness of the Statue of Liberty, amidst the Chinese obelisks, monumental gates, Mao's mausoleum, and massive buildings of the square, it intervened in both the political and aesthetic codes of this symbolic place and was quickly destroyed. Wu Hung writes, "The statue of the Goddess of Democracy was a monument that was *intended* to be destroyed, because its monumentality would derive from such self-sacrifice" (Wu, 1991).

Postmodern aesthetics thus seems to encompass this reconfiguration of the concept of monumentality—one that can derive from impermanence as well as endurance—in addition to the monument as kitsch and the countermonument. While the antimonuments and innovative memorials of the late twentieth century would seem to question the core attributes of the monument, they are also deeply engaged with the question of how to commemorate the past and to speak to the future. As such, they are evidence of the monument's durability and social function, one that will continue to survive dramatic changes in aesthetic codes.

BIBLIOGRAPHY

Barthes, Roland. *Camera Lucida: Reflections on Photography.* Translated by Richard Howard. New York, 1981.

Curl, James Stephen. *A Celebration of Death.* New York, 1980.

Danto, Arthur. "The Vietnam Veterans Memorial." *Nation* (31 August 1985): 152–155.

Fehl, Philipp. *The Classical Monument: Reflections on the Connection between Morality and Art in Greek and Roman Sculpture.* New York, 1972.

Forster, Kurt W. "Monument/Memory and the Mortality of Architecture." *Oppositions* 25 (Fall 1982): 2–19.

Gillis, John R., ed. *Commemorations: The Politics of National Identity.* Princeton, N.J., 1994.

Heiferman, Marvin. "One Nation, Chiseled in Pictures: The Monumental Nature of American Photography." *Archive* 25 (1989): 6–14.

Khalil, Samir al-. *The Monument: Art, Vulgarity, and Responsibility in Iraq.* Berkeley, 1991.

Koshar, Rudy. "Building Pasts: Historic Preservation and Identity in Twentieth-Century Germany." In *Commemorations: The Politics of National Identity,* edited by John R. Gillis, pp. 215–238. Princeton, N.J., 1994.

Kostof, Spiro. *A History of Architecture: Settings and Rituals.* New York and Oxford, 1985.

Ragon, Michel. *The Space of Death: A Study of Funerary Architecture, Decoration, and Urbanism.* Translated by Alan Sheridan. Charlottesville, Va., 1983.

Riegl, Alois. "The Modern Cult of Monuments: Its Character and Its Origin." Translated by Kurt W. Forster and Diane Ghirardo. *Oppositions* 25 (Fall 1982): 21–51.

Sturken, Marita. *Tangled Memories: The Vietnam War, the AIDS Epidemic, and the Politics of Remembering.* Berkeley, 1997.

Wu, Hung. "Tiananmen Square: A Political History of Monuments." *Representations* 35 (Summer 1991): 84–117.

Young, James E. *The Texture of Memory: Holocaust Memorials and Meaning.* New Haven, 1993.

MARITA STURKEN

Twentieth-Century Countermonuments

Like other cultural and aesthetic forms in Europe and North America, the monument—in both idea and practice—has undergone a radical transformation over the course of the twentieth century. As intersection between public art and political memory, the monument has necessarily reflected the aesthetic and political revolutions, as well as the wider crises of representation, following all of this century's major upheavals—including both world wars, the Vietnam War, and the rise and fall of Communist regimes in the former Soviet Union and its eastern European satellites.

In every case, the monument reflects both its sociohistorical and aesthetic context: artists working in eras of Cubism, Expressionism, Socialist Realism, earthworks, or conceptual art remain answerable to both the needs of art and official history. The result has been a metamorphosis of the monument from the heroic, self-aggrandizing figurative icons of the late nineteenth century celebrating national ideals and triumphs to the antiheroic, often ironic and self-effacing conceptual installations marking the national ambivalence and uncertainty of late twentieth-century postmodernism.

In fact, the monument as both institution and concept had already come under withering attack well before the beginning of the twentieth century. "Away with the monuments!" Friedrich Nietzsche declared in his blistering attack on a nineteenth-century German historicism that oppressed the living with stultified versions of the past—what Nietzsche called "monumental history" (Nietzsche, 1985, pp. 14-17). To this sentiment, a chorus of artists and cultural historians have since added their voices. "The notion of a modern monument is veritably a contradiction in terms," Lewis Mumford wrote in the 1930s (Mumford, 1938, p. 438). "If it is a monument it is not modern, and if it is modern, it cannot be a monument (ibid)." Believing that modern architecture invites the perpetuation of life itself, encourages renewal and change, and scorns the illusion of permanence, Mumford wrote, "Stone gives a false sense of continuity, a deceptive assurance of life (ibid)." Indeed, Mumford went on to suggest that traditionally it seems to have been the least effectual of regimes that chose to compensate their paucity of achievement in self-aggrandizing stone and mortar.

More recently, the late German historian Martin Broszat and Saul Friedlander have suggested that in their references to history, monuments may not remember events so much as bury them altogether beneath layers of national myths and explanations (Broszat and Friedlander, 1990, p. 129). As cultural reifications, in this view, monuments reduce or, in Broszat's words, "coarsen" historical understanding as much as they generate it. In another vein, art historian Rosalind E. Krauss finds that the modernist period produces monuments unable to refer to anything beyond themselves as pure marker or base (Krauss, 1988, p. 280). After Krauss, critics have asked whether an abstract, self-referential monument can ever commemorate events outside of itself, or whether it only motions endlessly to its own gesture to the past, a commemoration of its essence as dislocated sign.

Still others have argued that rather than preserving public memory, the monument displaces it altogether, supplanting a community's memory work with its own material form. "The less memory is experienced from the inside," Pierre Nora warns, "the more it exists through its exterior scaffolding and outward signs." In fact, Andreas Huyssen has even suggested that in a contemporary age of mass memory production and consumption, there seems to be an inverse proportion between the memorialization of the past and its contemplation and study. It is as if once we assign monumental form to memory, we have to some degree divested ourselves of the obligation to remember.

In the eyes of modern critics and artists, the traditional monument's essential stiffness and gradiose pretensions to permanence thus doom it to an archaic, premodern status. Even worse, by insisting that its meaning is as fixed as its place in the landscape, the monument seems oblivious to the essential mutability in all cultural artifacts, the ways the significance in all art evolves over time. In this way, monuments have long sought to provide a naturalizing locus for memory, in which a state's triumphs and martyrs, its ideals and founding myths are cast as naturally true as the landscape in which they stand. These are the monument's sustaining illusions, the principles of its seeming longevity and power. But, in fact, as several generations of artists—modern and postmodern alike—have made scathingly clear, neither the monument nor its meaning is really everlasting. Both a monument and its significance are constructed in particular times and places, contingent on the political, historical, and aesthetic realities of the moment.

The early modernist ambivalence toward the monument hardened into outright hostility in the wake of World War I. Both artists and some governments shared a general distaste for the ways the monument seemed formally to recapitulate the archaic values of a past world now discredited by the slaughter of the war. A new generation of Cubists and Expressionists, in particular, rejected traditional mimetic and heroic evocations of events, contending that any such remembrance would elevate and mythologize events. In their view, yet another classically proportioned Prometheus would have falsely glorified and thereby redeemed the horrible suffering they were called on to mourn. The traditional aim of war monuments had been to valorize the suffering in such a way as to justify, and even redeem, it historically. But for these artists, such monuments would have been tantamount to betraying not only their experience of the Great War, but also their new reasons for art's existence after the war: to challenge the world's realities, not affirm them.

As Albert E. Elsen has noted, modern and avant-garde sculptors between the wars in Europe were thus rarely invited to commemorate either the victories or losses, battles or war dead of World War I. If figurative statuary were demanded of them, then only antiheroic figures would do, as exemplified in the pathetic heroes of Wilhelm Lehmbruck's *Fallen Man* and *Seated Youth* (1917). As true to the artists' interwar vision as such work may have been, however, neither public nor state seemed ready to abide memorial edifices built on foundations of doubt instead of valor. The pathetic hero was thus condemned by emerging totalitarian regimes in Germany and Russia as defeatist for seeming to embody all that was worth forgetting—not remembering—in the war. Moreover, between the Nazi abhorrence of abstract art—or what it called *entartete Kunst* (decadent art)—and the officially mandated Socialist Realism of the Soviet Union, the traditional figurative monument even enjoyed something of a rebirth in totalitarian societies. Indeed, only the figurative statuary of officially sanctioned artists, like Germany's Arno Breker, or styles like the Soviet Union's Socialist Realism, could be trusted to embody the Nazi ideals of "Aryan race" or the Communist Party's vision of a heroic proletariat. In its consort with two of this century's most egregiously totalitarian regimes, the monument's credibility as public art was thus eroded further still.

Even so, it is also true that before his eventual embrace of Socialist Realism, V. I. Lenin had recognized the essentially antipopulist character of the everlasting monument. In an early gesture intended to win the support of the masses, he proposed a humanly proportioned environment of ever-perishable monuments. His "Plan for Monumental Propaganda" was founded in the revolutionary notion of a monument's essential impermanence. Instead of bronze, marble, and granite, Lenin turned to posters, public slogans, and temporary plaster casts. Although the mutability of the state's monuments was to have reflected the people's own changing lives and needs, it was not long before the people discovered that only the forms were changing: the monumental message, on the other hand, was always the same and so grew increasingly ossified over time. The more entrenched the party became, the more traditionally proportioned and materially static its monuments grew in their glorification of the October Revolution, the workers, and party leaders. By the time the Communist regime fell in 1991, the only violent uprising on the part of the masses came not against the party leadership but against the countless Socialist Realist monuments dotting the landscape of the former Soviet Union.

Meanwhile, the question that abstraction posed for the monument continued to divide artists from their publics and sponsors. The reluctance on the part of governments to commission abstract memorials, in particular, seems to have stemmed from two parallel impulses in the public and state. On the one hand, in their sense of mimetic witness to great figures and events, figurative images seemed to naturalize best the state's memorial messages. In contrast, by seeming to ameliorate a work's sense of witness, abstraction seemed to confound the monument's capacity as locus for shared self-image and commonly held ideals—one of the state's best reasons for monuments. Furthermore, in its hermetic and personal vision, abstraction encouraged private responses in viewers, which seemed to defeat the communal and collective aims of public monuments.

With the defeat of Nazi Germany during World War II and the dissolution of the Soviet Union in 1991, however, along with a new willingness in governments to commemorate their defeats and crimes as well as their triumphs and ideals, abstract and conceptual monuments have found more receptive audiences. For in referring to the general condition of the world, an inner state of mind, broken trust in humankind, or even art's inability to represent the real, abstract and conceptual forms have expanded the monument's capacity to simultaneously fix and destabilize its referent in the public mind. Maya Lin's succinctly abstract Vietnam War Memorial, for example, challenges every one of Washington's white, phallic, neoclassical conventions to commemorate America's ambivalence toward the Vietnam War and its dead in ways altogether unavailable in figuration.

Nearly fifty years after the defeat of the Nazi regime, contemporary artists in Germany still have difficulty separating the monument there from its fascist past. In their eyes, the didactic logic of monuments—their demagogic rigidity and certainty of history—continues to recall too closely traits associated with fascism itself. How else would totalitarian regimes commemorate themselves except through totalitarian art like the monument? Conversely, how better to celebrate the fall of totalitarian regimes than by celebrating the fall of their monuments? A monument against fascism, therefore, would have to be a monument against itself: against the traditionally didactic function of monuments, against their tendency to displace the past they would have us contemplate—and finally, against the authoritarian propensity in monumental spaces that reduces viewers to passive spectators.

For artists like Hans Haacke, Jochen Gerz, Norbert Radermacher, Renata Stih, and Frieder Schnock, the possibility that memory of the Holocaust, in particular, might be reduced to exhibitions of public artisanship or cheap pathos is intolerable. These artists have rejected the traditional forms and reasons for public memorial art, those spaces that either console viewers or redeem such tragic events, or indulge in a facile kind of *Wiedergutmachung*. Instead of searing memory into public consciousness, they fear, conventional memorials seal memory off from awareness altogether. For these artists and architects like Lin, Daniel Libeskind, and James Ingo Freed, the most important "space of memory" has not been that in the ground or above it, but that between the monument and viewer, between viewers and their own memory. To this end, they have proposed a generation of countermonuments, non-monuments, negative-form monuments, and deconstructivist museums designed to estrange memory and highlight the visitor's role in it. In the cases of vanishing or invisible monuments (by Gerz), or those built into the ground (by Horst Hoheisel and Micha Ullman), or conceived of as performative installations (by Haacke), visitors thus "become the monument."

The status of monuments in the twentieth century remains double-edged and is fraught with an essential tension: outside of those nations with totalitarian pasts, the public and governmental hunger for traditional, self-aggrandizing monuments is matched only by contemporary artists' skepticism toward the monument. As a result, even as monuments continue to be commissioned and designed by governments and public agencies eager to assign singular meaning to complicated events and people, artists increasingly plant in them the seeds of self-doubt and impermanence. The state's need for monuments is acknowledged, even as the traditional forms and functions of monuments are increasingly challenged. Monuments at the end of the twentieth century are thus born resisting the very premises of their birth. As a result, the monument has increasingly become the site of contested and competing meanings, more likely the site of cultural conflict than of shared national values and ideals.

BIBLIOGRAPHY

Broszat, Martin, and Saul Friedlander. "A Controversy about the Historicization of National Socialism. In Peter Baldwin, ed. *Reworking the Past: Hitler, the Holocaust, and the Historians' Controversy.* Boston, 1990.

Diers, Michael, ed. *Mo(nu)mente: Formen und Funktionen ephemerer Denkmaler.* Berlin, 1993.

Doezema, Marianne, and June Hargrove. *The Public Monument and Its Audience.* Cleveland, Ohio, 1977.

Elsen, Albert E. *Rodin's "Thinker" and the Dilemmas of Modern Public Sculpture.* New Haven, 1985.

Koselleck, Reinhart, and Michael Jeismann, eds. *Der politische Totenkult: Kriegerdenkmaler in der Moderne.* Munich, 1994.

Krauss, Rosalind, *The Originality of the Avant-Garde and Other Modernist Myths.* Cambridge, Mass. and London, 1988.

Mai, Ekkehard, and Gisela Schmirber, eds. *Denkmal—Zeichen—Monument: Skulptur und öffentlicher Raum Heute.* Munich, 1989.

Mitchell, W. J. T., ed. *Art in the Public Sphere.* Chicago, 1992.

Mumford, Lewis. *The Culture of Cities.* New York, Jovanovich, 1938.

Nietzsche, Friedrich, *The Use and Abuse of History.* Translated by Adrian Collins. New York, 1985.

Nora, Pierre. *Les lieux de memoire.* 4 vols. Paris, 1984–1993.

Wu, Hung. "Tiananmen Square: A Political History of Monuments." *Representations* 35 (Summer 1991): 84–117.

Young, James E. *The Texture of Memory: Holocaust Memorials and Meaning.* New Haven, 1993.

Young, James E., ed. *The Art of Memory: Holocaust Memorials in History.* Munich and New York, 1994.

JAMES E. YOUNG

MORALITY AND AESTHETICS. [*To explore the relationships between art and morality or between aesthetics and ethics, this entry comprises three essays:*

Historical and Conceptual Overview
Contemporary Aesthetics and Ethics
Art, Morality, and the Holocaust

The overview essay critically surveys many different approaches to the understanding of these relationships in the history of Western aesthetics. Against the background of this same history, the second essay explains the various attempts in contemporary aesthetics to overcome the conventional separation between aesthetics and ethics. The final essay discusses the difficulties art has had responding to a specific moral problem, the Holocaust. For related discussion, see Law and Art; Moral Rights of Art; Obscenity; *and* Politics and Aesthetics.]

Historical and Conceptual Overview

Throughout history, art and morality have been linked in various ways. Much early art served the purpose of religion, commanding not only reverence for gods but also illustrating moral precepts. Even in our own day, a great deal of art engages in social criticism, a fact acknowledged by most philosophers, from Plato through David Hume. In the eighteenth century, however, a new view of art began to emerge, one that, by the early twentieth century, argued that the realm of art and the realm of morality were categorically distinct. Whereas previous philosophers, like Plato, presumed that it was appropriate to evaluate art from a moral perspective—a position that we might call moralism—an opposing view, espoused by figures like Clive Bell, maintained that art was its own domain of value with its own canons of evaluation (canons of evaluation, moreover, that precluded moral assessment as a legitimate enterprise with respect to art). This view—call it autonomism—has exerted a profound influence on the course of art theory in the twentieth century. If it has not been the dominant position, it is still at least the position that anyone wishing to advance the moral claims of art must address in order to sound plausible.

The earliest systematic theory of art in the West was propounded by Plato. In his *Republic,* Plato analyzed poetry and painting, concluding, for a variety of reasons, that they addressed the irrational parts of the soul and therefore constituted a threat to justice. This led Plato to recommend that poets be banished from the good city. Thus, the earliest art theorizing in the Western tradition was a species of moralism. Moralism comes in several varieties, however, and it is useful to draw some distinctions among them.

Plato's moralism is what may be called extreme moralism. Extreme moralism is the view that art always possesses a moral dimension and can be assessed in terms of its contribution to morality. Extreme moralism, in turn, comes in three basic types: Platonism, utopianism, and comprehensive variable moralism. Each category of extreme moralism maintains that all art is susceptible to moral evaluation. It is extreme simply because its claims are universal. But each category possesses a different view of the way in which that assessment is to go. Platonism maintains that all art can be evaluated as morally pernicious; utopianism regards all art as morally good; and comprehensive variable moralism contends that moral evaluation is relevant to all art but that those evaluations are morally variable—that is, that morally art can be either good or bad.

Platonism, perhaps unfairly, takes its name from Plato. He argued that by its very nature mimetic poetry was morally discreditable. This view is philosophical insofar as it is based on a conception of the nature of the art in question. Poetry, according to Plato, unavoidably elicited identification with morally unsavory role models and, in consequence, induced morally disreputable emotions from audiences. Versions of Platonism continue into our own day, as media critics voice similar worries in their denunciations of television, the movies, and rap music for encouraging identification with aggressive behaviors.

Whereas Platonism tends to regard all art as morally suspect, utopianism regards all art as morally uplifting. Perhaps utopianism emerges as a reaction or antidote to Platonism. Both are examples of extreme moralism, inasmuch as both render moral evaluations of art *tout court.* Their overall assessments of art go in different, indeed opposite, directions, however.

An example of the utopianian tradition may be found in the aesthetics of Herbert Marcuse. For Marcuse, art is always on the side of the angels, because of its ontology. That is, core features of art—such as fiction and representation—have the capacity to show that the world can be otherwise, thus encouraging the conviction that it is at least possible to change the way things are (an obvious precondition for moral practice and ethical rejuvenation). That artworks are distinct from mere real things counts as an affirmation of the possibility of the kingdom of ends and, therefore, makes of art a de facto acknowledgment of moral freedom.

Utopianism, however, need not, and most frequently does not, come with such heady metaphysical trappings. It is evident in much of the unreflective, sanctimonious platitudinizing of reformers and educators who defend the expansion of museums and arts education on the grounds that art, as such, is morally ennobling.

Because they are such extreme positions, Platonism and utopianism are easily criticized. Despite their optimistic attitude, utopianists must confront the embarrassing fact there are many examples of morally disreputable art, such as the Nazi film spectacle *Triumph of the Will.* Even if an intelligible case could be made for the claim that its formal properties projected the possibility of an alternative moral state of affairs, the state of affairs in question would turn out to be one of irredeemable evil. Similarly, even if Platonists could show that all art trafficked in identification and role modeling—an unlikely prospect, since much art, like much pure orchestral music, does not afford the possibility of role modeling—the Platonist would have to show that all of the role modeling in question is necessarily morally pernicious. Plato might have thought that he could do this by maintaining that all art is addressed to the emotions. But even if that were so, not all of the emotions are morally suspect. Consequently, if spectators do model their emotional responses on those affective reactions elicited by artworks, there is no reason to suspect that this is, in all cases, morally problematic.

Due to the obvious shortcomings of Platonism and utopianism, a more likely form of extreme moralism is comprehensive variable moralism. On this view, which is exemplified by someone like Leo Tolstoy, all artworks are the appropriate target for moral evaluation. The evaluation in question is variable, however. Art as such is neither all good nor all bad. Rather, some artworks are morally good and some are morally bad. This approach is certainly more reasonable than either Platonism or utopianism. Any position on the relation of art to morality should make room for variable moral assessment of art. But comprehensive variable moralism, nevertheless, is still an example of extreme moralism, since, for any artwork, it maintains that it must be either good or bad, although this will have to be determined on a case-by-case basis.

The comprehensive variable moralist may assess the moral merits and demerits of artworks on the basis of the presumed consequences of the works in question. Call this consequentialism. An example of such a judgment is that such and such a television show is bad because it causes violent behavior or that such and such a novel is good because it promotes tolerance. Artworks may also be criticized morally in terms of the moral beliefs that they engender in audiences. A racist, sexist, or homophobic film is bad because it encourages the audience to accept certain immoral propositions, whereas a drama that proposes that all people are equal is, ceteris paribus, morally good. Call this propositionalism.

Propositionalism and consequentialism, of course, can be combined by contending that artworks bring about the behavioral consequences they do just because they engender the relevant moral (or immoral) beliefs in their audiences. Undoubtedly, there are even more models than these two for assessing the moral dimension of artworks. But what remains the mark of the comprehensive variable moralist is the presupposition that every artwork can be evaluated in terms of its moral merits or demerits by some such method.

It is at this point in the dialectic that the autonomist steps into the fray. The autonomist might also be regarded as proposing an antidote to Platonism. The autonomist argues that all forms of extreme moralism must be wrong, since it is not conceptually intelligible to regard all artworks as appropriate objects of moral evaluation. Many artworks, such as many pure visual designs and much orchestral music, have no moral dimension, and it is just conceptually confused to attempt to assess them morally.

Moreover, in response to consequentialism, the autonomist may point out that we really have little or no knowledge of the behavioral consequences of consuming artworks. Why are rates of violence lower in Japan than in the United States, despite the fact that Japanese programming is much more graphic in its depiction of gore and mayhem than American programming? No one really knows. Thus, insofar as the knowledge presupposed by consequentialism is not there to be had, consequentialism can be dismissed as so much arm waving.

Further, with respect to propositionalism, the autonomist can point out that it is unlikely that artworks really engender beliefs, moral or otherwise, in audiences, since when one looks at the beliefs on offer in artworks, they are more often than not of the nature of truisms and commonplaces that audiences already embrace. If D. W. Griffith's *Birth of a Nation* trumpeted the morally pernicious proposition that "black people are morally inferior to white people," it was not really instilling that view in white audiences, but exploiting a view that most of the white spectators probably already held. Art does not create moral opinions in audiences but rather plays off preexisting ones. Thus, if one is concerned to uproot those opinions, the place to look, the autonomist says, is not at art, but at whatever social factors caused audiences to have those beliefs before they entered the theater.

Undoubtedly, the autonomist has some good arguments against extreme moralism. However, autonomism becomes extreme autonomism when it argues that art can never be evaluated morally. This conjecture is advanced on several grounds. The first may be called the common denominator argument. This argument begins by pointing out that morality cannot be taken as a general canon of artistic evaluation because not all artworks have a moral dimension. As we have seen, it makes no sense to judge many abstract designs morally where they are proposed simply for the pleasure of the eye. But, the extreme autonomist argues, if moral quality is not always a canon of artistic evaluation, then it is not a general canon of assessment that can be brought to all artworks. Thus, in assessing whether any artwork qua artwork is good, we should refrain from asking whether it is morally good. Moral goodness is simply not a general evaluative category for art.

The extreme autonomist can bolster this argument with an appeal to essentialism. Art, the extreme autonomist claims, is its own domain of practice and value. It is ontologically separate or autonomous from other domains such as religion, politics, cognitive inquiry, and morality. The essence of art (formal play) and its aim (affording disinterested pleasure) are not reducible to those of other human practices. It has its own domain of methods, effects, and values. Art on the autonomist view is intrinsically valuable; it should not be subservient to ulterior purposes such as producing moral consequences or inducing moral education. For the autonomist, anything devoted to such ulterior purposes could not be art, properly so called.

There are, of course, a number of problems with this approach. The extreme autonomist maintains that the moral evaluation of art is somehow at variance with the essence of art. Unfortunately, to date, no autonomist has been able to provide an adequate account of what might comprise that essence. Some say that a work of art is an artifact designed to support the play of disinterested attention in audiences. After two centuries of discussion, however, no one has been able to offer a compelling characterization of disinterestedness. Thus, autonomist arguments that rely on claims about the purity of the essence of art seem to rest on little more than a vastly overrated presumption.

Furthermore, on the other hand, there is much reason to believe that art is impure—that it mixes freely and naturally with other realms of human practice. As already noted, much art, including Western art, was religious for long periods, while art has also characteristically served political and social purposes cross-culturally for as long as anyone can remember. Moreover, a great many artworks, notably narrative fictions, also rely on audiences filling in the presuppositions of the relevant artworks by using what they know of the world in terms of schemata of ordinary human behavior, moral judgment, and practical deliberation.

Much art, that is, would be unintelligible if audiences could not bring their knowledge of other realms of human practice to their commerce with artworks. Narrative address typically engages the knowledge, moral and otherwise, of audiences. Activating such knowledge is a condition of possibility for most art of this sort. Thus, it strains credulity to suppose that art in general is independent of other realms of practice. That is, one cannot preclude the ethical evaluation of art on the grounds that art is utterly independent of morality. For much art is not, in any straightforward way.

There is also a ready reply to the autonomist's common denominator argument. The autonomist has shown that moral evaluation is not always an appropriate standard to bring to bear on artworks. Perhaps it would be a category error to evaluate an abstraction by Josef Albers morally. But it does not follow from this that it is never appropriate to assess an artwork morally. One may evaluate a tractor and a sports car in terms of their capacity to locomote. But then one may go on to evaluate the tractor in terms of its pulling power and the sports car in terms of its capacity to execute hairpin turns. Tractors and sports cars are both vehicles, but this does not preclude their evaluation in virtue of different standards, standards appropriate to the different subcategories to which they belong.

This point has relevance for the evaluation of art. Morality may not be a universal standard of assessment for all artworks. But some artworks may be members of subcategories of art for which moral assessment is appropriate. Novels like *The Grapes of Wrath* and films like *Potemkin* address their audiences morally. They are the kinds of things that are, in fact, designed to address their audiences morally. Thus, prima facie, it seems obvious that it is appropriate to evaluate them in terms of their moral address, since they belong to categories of art for which moral assessment is apposite. It is no argument against morally assessing works of art like this to point out that some abstractions by Albers should not be evaluated morally.

Moreover, an observation like this may breathe new life into moralism. Whereas extreme moralism is clearly wrong insofar as not all art is genuinely susceptible to moral evaluation, we have just seen that some art may be. That is, some art,

because of the kind of thing it is—because of the category of art it belongs to—may be an appropriate object of moral evaluation. Let us call this position moderate moralism.

Where the extreme moralist claims that all art is ethically assessable, the moderate moralist only maintains that some art is—where that is a function of the category or kind that the artwork inhabits. The extreme autonomist has failed to show that art is necessarily independent from other realms of human practice and concern. The moderate moralist conjoins a recognition of this failure with the reasonable conjecture—based on the history of art—that that leaves open the very likely possibility that some art does connect with the moral realm and that, with respect to such art, moral evaluation may be appropriate.

Given these arguments, it is open to the autonomist to change his line of defense. The autonomist may concede that with certain artworks—given their category or kind—it does make sense to evaluate them morally. Nevertheless, the autonomist is inclined to qualify this concession immediately by proposing that with such works of art we need to distinguish between various levels of address.

A given artwork may legitimately deal in aesthetic, moral, cognitive, or political value. But these levels, it will be said, are independent or autonomous. An artwork may be aesthetically valuable and morally defective, or vice versa. But these different strata of value do not mix. An aesthetically defective artwork is not bad because it is morally defective, and that provides a large part of the story about why a work can be aesthetically valuable, but evil. Let us call this view moderate autonomism because, although it allows that the moral discussion and evaluation of artworks, or at least some artworks, are coherent and appropriate, moderate autonomism remains committed to the view that the aesthetic dimension of the artwork is autonomous from other dimensions, notably from the moral dimension.

The moderate moralist says that it is appropriate to evaluate some artworks morally. The moderate autonomist concedes this much, but hastens to add that such evaluation is never aesthetic evaluation. Moral evaluation of artworks is irrelevant to the aesthetic evaluation of artworks. A negative moral evaluation of an artwork never, the moderate autonomist claims, counts toward a negative aesthetic evaluation of the same artwork. Moderate moralism, as here construed, maintains on the other hand that sometimes a moral defect in an artwork can figure in a negative aesthetic evaluation of that artwork. Which position is more compelling? Let us conclude with a test case.

In the *Poetics,* Aristotle proposes that for tragedy to take hold, the major character must be of a certain moral sort, if we are to pity him. He cannot be evil, because then we will regard his destruction as well deserved. The historical Adolf Hitler could not be a tragic character; his ignominious death would not prompt us to pity him. Indeed, we might applaud it. Likewise, Aristotle points out that tragic characters cannot be flawless. For then when disaster befalls them we will be moved to outrage, not pity. Mother Teresa could not be a figure of tragedy, because she had no known fatal flaw. The right kind of character, Aristotle hypothesizes, is morally mixed, elevated, but in other respects more like the average viewer.

Here Aristotle is pointing out that for tragedy to succeed on its own terms (qua tragedy), it must elicit certain moral judgments from the audience. But to elicit the moral emotion of pity, certain conditions have to be met by the play. Characters and situations have to be depicted in a certain way. Specifically, they must be depicted in such a way that they meet the morally appropriate conditions for pity. This requires that the playwright choose morally appropriate characters and situations and show them in a morally appropriate way. In short, the playwright must bring a morally appropriate understanding of characters and situations to the composition of a drama. Where the playwright's understanding is defective, and where those defects are manifest in the composition of the drama, the drama will not elicit a morally appropriate response. The play will not secure tragic uptake qua tragedy. This should count as an aesthetic defect, if anything does. But it is also a moral defect.

The Nazi propagandist who portrays Hitler as an object of pity fails to elicit pity from morally sensitive and reflective audiences. This is certainly an aesthetic failure. But it is an aesthetic failure because it manifests a defective moral understanding on the part of the author of the protagonist of the tragedy. The play cannot move morally sensitive and reflective audiences in the aesthetically appropriate way, because the moral perspective it promotes is evil. The drama is aesthetically defective—dramatically inert—because it is morally defective. Its aesthetic defect and its moral defect are two sides of the same coin. As well, cases like these are easy to multiply. Thus, the moderate moralist argues that moderate autonomism is too strong a view. There are some cases where a moral defect in a work amounts to an aesthetic defect. In those cases, a negative moral evaluation of a work will count toward an negative aesthetic evaluation of the same work. The moral structure of an artwork may in certain cases be coeval with the aesthetic structure of the work. In those cases, morally evaluating a work is not a matter of bringing ulterior considerations to the artwork. It may be responding to the express design of the work, given the kind of thing the artwork in question is.

BIBLIOGRAPHY

Aristotle. *Poetics*. In *The Complete Works of Aristotle*, edited by Jonathan Barnes, vol. 2. Princeton, N.J., 1984.
Beardsmore, R. W. *Art and Morality*. London, 1971.
Bell, Clive. *Art*. Reprint, New York, 1958.
Carroll, Noël. "Beauty and the Genealogy of Art Theory." *Philosophical Forum* 22.4 (1991).
Carroll, Noël. "Moderate Moralism." *British Journal of Aesthetics* 36.3 (July 1996): 223–238.
Carroll, Noël. "Art, Narrative and Morality." In *Aesthetics and Ethics*, edited by Jerrold Levinson. Cambridge and New York, 1997.
Currie, Gregory. "The Moral Psychology of Fiction." *Australasian Journal of Philosophy* 73.2 (1995).
Gaut, Berys. "The Ethical Criticism of Art." In *Aesthetics and Ethics*, edited by Jerrold Levinson. Cambridge and New York, 1997.
Marcuse, Herbert. *The Aesthetic Dimension: Toward a Critique of Marxist Aesthetics*. Boston, 1978.
Nussbaum, Martha C. *Poetic Justice: The Literary Imagination and Public Life*. Boston, 1995.
Plato. *Republic*. In *The Collected Dialogues of Plato*, edited by Edith Hamilton and Huntington Cairns. Corr. ed Reprint, Princeton, N.J. 1969.
Tolstoy, Leo. *What Is Art?* Translated by A. Maude. Indianapolis, 1960.
Walton, Kendall. "Morals in Fictions and Fictional Morality." *Proceedings of the Aristotelian Society* suppl. vol. 67 (1993).

NOËL CARROLL

Contemporary Aesthetics and Ethics

Philosophers since Plato and Aristotle have debated the relation between ethical and aesthetic value. Plato argued that artists' interest in stimulating emotions and imitating the physical world (a realm that itself already merely imitates reality) inevitably leads them and their audiences to contribute to a society's moral decline. Aristotle, believing that imitation is at the core of learning and that the emotional outlet provided by art is therapeutic, had a much higher opinion of art. Indeed, he believed that aesthetic excellence and moral excellence are connected. For example, the best tragedies, according to him, must be structured in such a way that what is presented (what happens when good people make mistakes) is consistent with correct moral principles. Moral flaws will be aesthetic flaws, and vice versa.

In the two millennia since, a wide range of positions have been taken as philosophers have aligned themselves in the debate. Many have argued that aesthetic and moral value are mutually exclusive, some taking the extreme position that they are so essentially different that moral and aesthetic experiences can never be simultaneous. Immanuel Kant is the most influential of those philosophers who argue for a complete separation of the moral and the aesthetic. The aesthetic for him was a matter of subjective feelings of pleasure or pain that accompany certain experiences—looking at or smelling a rose, for example. Since morality and science go far beyond purely individual responses, they are in different realms. Among contemporary writers, Monroe Beardsley has clearly articulated a position that insists on a separation of aesthetic and moral values.

Others have argued that the pinnacle of aesthetic value requires connections to morality, even going so far as to claim that great art actually improves moral character. Leo Tolstoy believed that the value of art lies in its ability to create spiritually united communities; when artists successfully express their emotions, the emotions are actually transmitted to the audience, thus connecting all involved. People who have similar feelings will treat one another fairly and with respect.

Others have argued that the aesthetic and the moral are different, but not always, nor necessarily, separate. Thus, Thomas Aquinas viewed the beautiful and the good as two aspects of the same thing. Beauty has to do with making, goodness with acting. Even Kant, in a move that indicates how strong the pull both toward and away from connecting ethics and aesthetics can be, asserted that the beautiful is a symbol of the morally good.

In the twentieth century a separatist attitude emphasizing the role of formal properties, and positing a unique experience detached from everyday concerns and pursuits, has often characterized aesthetic theories. Recently, however, the number of theorists who are less inclined to distinguish sharply between the aesthetic and the ethical has increased. A contextual turn in value theory has resulted from greater interest in the ways in which values generally are socially constructed. Considerations deemed irrelevant by strict formalists (author biography, historical consequences, the political power of the artist, viewer, and presenter, etc.) are more often seen to impinge on and shape aesthetic experience and judgment. Confronted by a host of practical problems, nonphilosophers as well as philosophers have been forced to look at the connections between a variety of value sources. The insistence that one must or even can take an aesthetic point of view that entails putting moral considerations aside becomes less comprehensible as it becomes more and more difficult for individuals to do this.

There are several examples that show why, even if one can differentiate ethical and aesthetic value sometimes, one cannot, often does not, and often should not separate them. One problem is what could be called "the purple loosestrife problem." This plant, which boasts a brilliant purple spiky flower, thrives in wetlands and, indeed, is so hardy that it tends to take over vast areas, wiping out other plant species and hence upsetting regional biological balances. Admittedly, the result is colorful, but is it "beautiful"? Knowledgeable ecologists often say that they find this plant positively ugly, but not everyone agrees with them. There are many more examples of objects and events that evoke conflicting responses—even in the same individual. Consumers are often both attracted to and repelled by fur coats, for instance. Pornography, of course, provides another test case. Can there really be beautiful photographs of children being sexually abused? In all of these cases, moral considerations seem to override or at least seriously to influence aesthetic response. The formalist admonition to concentrate solely on the properties that matter aesthetically is at best simplistic here.

A different sort of example is provided by quilts. Once dismissed as "mere craft" or "women's work," these artifacts are increasingly found in museums of fine art—a development applauded by many. But others object that quilts do not belong in museums, not because they are not real (and "fine") art, but because full or genuine aesthetic experience of them demands that they be viewed in the appropriate context: on beds keeping warm the bodies of loved ones who know the history of the materials used. The latter group insists that only a wrongheaded aesthetic/moral/political view would sell out to the dominant power group that historically dictated that value is defined by such practices as displaying artifacts in museums.

A wide range of other problems reflects the possibility or necessity of integrating moral and aesthetic concerns. Is the high-low-art distinction based on genuine aesthetic differences between objects, or is it simply a sign of political or economic oppression? Who should make decisions about which works of art are to be displayed in public spaces often paid for from public coffers? Who decides, and on what grounds, whether and how restoration projects should be carried out? All of these issues are complex; it would be amazing if they could satisfactorily be dealt with by attending exclusively to formal properties. A narrow aesthetic formalism that denies considerations of moral (and political or religious or ecological or economic, etc.) factors misses the very importance of art. Artistic and aesthetic value are not given their due when they are separated from other areas of deep human interest.

Yet, one feels the pull both in the direction of separating aesthetic and moral value as well as connecting them. Thus, when one reads Oscar Wilde's quip, "The fact of a man being a poisoner is nothing against his prose," something correct seems to be expressed. Supporters of the arts insist that great works of art make societies and individuals better, that they actually contribute to the public welfare. The arts are credited with binding communities, stimulating and developing imaginative and reflective powers, reinforcing the moral order, and creating morally sensitive people. But, if there is empirical evidence that this sometimes happens, there is also ample evidence that art often fails to have such consequences. Tales of Nazi Gestapo officers who loved music and surrounded themselves with masterpieces of painting and sculpture counter claims of a causal connection between aesthetic sensitivity and moral uprightness, and vice versa. It may be that the honorable ending of *Casablanca* makes it an aesthetically better film than one with a less morally admirable conclusion. But, there also are good films with evil protagonists.

Indeed, when one asks how the moral and the aesthetic might be connected, there are several possible answers, and it is not always clear which connection (or lack thereof) a theorist has in mind. The empirical connection referred to above seems at most contingent. Connecting ethics and aesthetics logically or conceptually, where the beautiful and the good are, for example, considered two aspects of the same thing, only helps if one is clear about what is meant or entailed by "aspect" or "the same thing." Gestalt shifts between the good and the beautiful may occur sometimes, but they do not always occur. This view presupposes a metaphysics not shared by everyone.

At the very least, the terms *ethical* or *moral* and *aesthetic* play different roles in language games; that is, they fulfill different functions in human discourse. Moral considerations typically involve references to principles, consequences, or sustainability of human relationships. One knows when asked to make an ethical judgment that what is relevant is human action and interaction. Asked to make an aesthetic judgment, one recognizes that attention to an object or event on something like its own terms is called for.

In many ways, my own definition of *aesthetic* is formalistic, for it relies heavily on intrinsic properties:

A is an aesthetic property of *x* in a culture, *C*,
if and only if *A* is an intrinsic property of *x*
and *A* is considered worthy of attention in *C*;
that is, in *C* it is widely believed that attending
to *A* (perceiving and/or reflecting on *A*) will
be rewarding.

Unlike strict formalists, however, one need not insist that attention must be restricted to intrinsic properties. Anything can be aesthetically relevant in the sense of drawing attention to the valued intrinsic properties. Memories of one's parents may lead one to attend more closely to shapes in a painting; thinking about tyranny may result in one's focusing on a trumpet trill. This is one of the reasons that art has so profound an effect on individuals' and communities' lives, and vice versa. Human experience is not segregated into the moral, the aesthetic, the religious, the political, and so on. Aesthetic experience is special, but that does not imply that it is separate from the rest of one's life. Moral considerations do not necessarily distract one's attention from the aesthetic; quite the contrary—they may draw one's attention to precisely those intrinsic features of objects or events that a culture values.

One way in which one comes to realize that the aesthetic is sometimes connected to the moral involves recognizing what is required for an aesthetic experience to occur at all. If aesthetic response is response to certain intrinsic properties, then an individual must have access to those properties. Access can be "morally blocked" in at least two ways.

First, a person's moral view may make it impossible for that person to perceive or concentrate on the aesthetic properties. David Hume, like other British empiricists, grounded aesthetic response in human nature; by nature, he thought, all people respond positively to such things as order, proportion, utility. But, he pointed out, even if a work is beautifully proportioned and ordered, if it expresses moral sentiments that one abhors, there will be no positive aesthetic judgment. One can indeed find many examples of this. The animal lover is so distressed by the knowledge that a rare animal was slaughtered just so that a wealthy con-

sumer could indulge vanity that he or she simply fails to notice or disregards the way the pelts have been combined to achieve certain color patterns or linearity. A pedestrian is so enraged that funding a pile of rusting metal blocks was given priority over funding a homeless shelter that he or she is blind to the clever arrangement of forms and shapes. An individual's outrage at a picture taken of a nude child makes it impossible for him or her to attend to focus or lighting effects. In all of these examples one's morality "anaesthetizes" one to the relevant aesthetic features.

Second, a person may be able to perceive the relevant properties but lack awareness of the moral implication of those properties and in turn will overlook aesthetic relationships. The clearest example of this comes from an analysis of sentimentality. The charge of being sentimental does both moral and aesthetic jobs in contemporary English. It is used (most often negatively) both with respect to people and works of art. People who shallowly display emotions too easily or inappropriately (e.g., cry at the death of a snail) are sentimental. Poems or plays that jerk tears through the use of trite images (e.g., the death of an incredibly sweet, innocent child) are also sentimental. But we do not have one term with two meanings. Rather, full perception of sentimentality requires due attention both to behavior (ethics) and to intrinsic properties (aesthetics). One must perceive both what is done and how it is done before one has access to the relationships that lead to the ethical/aesthetic judgment, "That is sentimental."

There are other examples of ways in which attention to the moral is required for aesthetic response. It is hard to imagine one responding aesthetically to the ending of *Casablanca* or *Don Giovanni* in the absence of an appreciation (perhaps even a sharing) of the moral codes that are therein instantiated. The very existence of certain aesthetic experiences is thus dependent on moral access to relevant features.

Thus far we have seen various ways of connecting ethics and aesthetics that concentrate on refusal to interpret "the aesthetic" formalistically. Another approach has been taken by several contemporary theorists, for example, Cora Diamond, R. W. Hepburn, and Iris Murdoch. These writers have urged that "the ethical" be construed rather differently than it has been typically interpreted. Instead of thinking of morality in terms of decisions about what one should do in particular circumstances in order to assure conformity to a particular code, one should think of morality as ways of envisioning the overall patterns of lives. Diamond says that ethics is a matter of reflecting on one's "texture of being"— a holistic picture of the sort of person one is or hopes to be. And art plays a very significant role in helping one to develop such a vision. In attempting to shape one's life, one needs to pay attention not just to the content of specific actions, but to things that are normally categorized as "aesthetic": one's choice of vocabulary, one's choice of style, what one finds boring or amusing. Thus, the aesthetic and the ethical become essentially intertwined.

Both a view of the aesthetic that goes beyond narrow formalism, and a view of the ethical that goes beyond following deontological or consequentialist principles, exemplify the contextualist turn referred to at the beginning of this article. Either way of integrating the aesthetic and the ethical offers much insight into the complexity of human experience.

BIBLIOGRAPHY

Aristotle. *Poetics*. Translated by Malcolm Heath. London and New York, 1996.

Beardsley, Monroe C. *The Aesthetic Point of View: Selected Essays*. Edited by Michael J. Wreen and Donald M. Callen. Ithaca, N.Y., 1982.

Carroll, Noël. "Moderate Moralism." *British Journal of Aesthetics* 36.3 (July 1996): 223–238.

Diamond, Cora. "Having a Rough Story about What Moral Philosophy Is." In *The Realistic Spirit: Wittgenstein, Philosophy, and the Mind*. Cambridge, Mass., 1991.

Eaton, Marcia Muelder. "Where's the Spear: The Nature of Aesthetic Relevance." *British Journal of Aesthetics* (January 1992).

Eaton, Marcia Muelder. "Integrating Moral and Aesthetic Value." *Philosophical Studies* 67 (1992).

Hampshire, Stuart. "The Logic of Appreciation." In *Aesthetics and Language,* edited by William Elton. Oxford, 1954.

Hepburn, R. W. "Vision and Choice in Morality." *Proceedings of the Aristotelian Society* suppl. vol. 30 (1956). Part 1 of a symposium with Iris Murdoch.

Hume, David. "Of the Standard of Taste" (1757). In *Essays: Moral, Political, and Literary,* rev. ed., edited by Eugene F. Miller, pp. 226–249. Indianapolis, 1987.

Kant, Immanuel. *Critique of Judgment* (1790). Translated by Werner S. Pluhar. Indianapolis, 1987.

Murdoch, Iris. Reply to Hepburn. *Proceedings of the Aristotelian Society* suppl. vol. 30 (1956). Part 2 of a symposium with R. W. Hepburn.

Plato. *Republic*. Translated by G. M. A. Grube, revised by C. D. C. Reeve. Indianapolis, 1992.

Tolstoy, Leo. *What Is Art?* (1896). In *What Is Art? and Essays on Art,* translated by Almyer Maude. Oxford, 1930.

MARCIA MUELDER EATON

Art, Morality, and the Holocaust

Representations of the Holocaust are faced with two types of problems. First, such representations lead to ethical problems that do not arise with representations of other historical events. Second, the representation of the Holocaust confronts the writer or artist with semiotic problems, which is to say that the discourse of the writer or artist does not provide means by which the uniqueness and extremity of the Holocaust can be represented. This semiotic problem is the background of the widespread conviction that the Holocaust is unrepresentable.

The ethical problem can be illustrated best through Theodor W. Adorno's famous statement that "after Auschwitz it is barbaric to continue writing poetry." This statement appears to condemn poetry, or artistic representations in general, as barbaric. By this statement Adorno has set the tone for the suspicious approach of literary or artistic representations of the Holocaust. Whereas up to World War II the creation of art and literature had a serious, almost religious aura, after Auschwitz it suddenly appeared to be a shockingly frivolous occupation. This explains why for many years literary representations of the Holocaust were especially valued if they made people think of literature as little as possible. The mode of writing had to be bare and realistic. Fictionalizing was taboo, and ego documents (personal testimonies modeled on journalistic or documentary accounts) were supposed to be the most adequate and proper genre for representations of the Holocaust.

Yet, when Adorno's statement recurred in many contexts as bearing on the Holocaust, and not on the inappropriateness of literature, Adorno referred back to it. In an essay of 1962 on commitment and literature, he specifies that a particular kind of literature is inappropriate after Auschwitz:

> I do not want to soften my statement that it is barbaric to continue to write poetry after Auschwitz; it expresses, negatively, the impulse that animates committed literature. . . . It is the situation of literature itself and not simply one's relation to it that is paradoxical. The abundance of real suffering permits no forgetting. . . . But that suffering—what Hegel called the awareness of affliction—also demands the continued existence of the very art it forbids.   (Adorno, 1992, pp. 87–88)

The Holocaust has entailed a paradoxical problem. From one perspective the necessity of remembering and representing has never been as acute as it is today. In order to avoid another systematic attempt to exterminate an entire people, the commemoration of this apocalyptic event in Western history is more than a moral obligation to its victims. At the same time, however, many Holocaust representations entail forgetting instead of maintaining contact with it. How is this possible? How can representation be the cause of forgetting?

Adorno's judgment turns out to condemn the aesthetic, stylistic principle that underlies the production of images or poetry out of experiences:

> When [the Holocaust] is turned into an image, however, for all its harshness and discordance it is as though the embarrassment one feels before the victims were being violated. The victims are turned into works of art, tossed out to be gobbled up by the world that did them in. The so-called artistic rendering of the naked physical pain of those who were beaten down with butts contains, however distantly, the possibility that pleasure can be squeezed from it. The morality that forbids art to forget this for a second slides off into the abyss of its opposite. The aesthetic stylistic principle, and even the chorus's solemn prayer, make the unthinkable appear to have had some meaning; it becomes transfigured, something of its horror removed.   (p. 88)

In short, Adorno objects to transfiguration. The transposition of events and experiences like those of the Holocaust ought not to be transformed into images or artworks so as to be read with aesthetic pleasure. At the same time, art is utterly indispensable: according to Adorno we need an art form that keeps Holocaust experiences from being forgotten.

Objections against literary imaginings of the Holocaust based on Adorno's early statement are in fact contingent on a rather limited conception of literature, limiting that form of representation to sheer aesthetics in the sense of enjoyment. The most important function that Walter Scott assigned to the historical novel, the transmission of historical knowledge through fictional means, has completely disappeared. When Adorno sharpens his statement later, this function returns: we must keep the world informed of the suffering of the victims, and literature must provide that knowledge. Aesthetic experience cannot be reduced to "pleasure" in the sense of (distracting) amusement. It is striking that in many discussions about the (un)representability of the Holocaust, aesthetic experience and the transmission of (historical) knowledge are conceptualized as polar opposites instead of as mutually supportive processes.

But the ethical problem is not limited to the impropriety of "aesthetic pleasure." A second problem is caused by the so-called redemptive function of art. According to the generally accepted conception, art and literature redeem from the singular and mortal. That is how this function provides religious dimensions to the human production of artworks. The artist or poet is able to transform passing experiences into eternal objects. The human being is an artist like God, because she or he creates immortal artifacts. From this perspective, the artist is a redeemer, as Christ was.

The American literary scholar Leo Bersani has recently argued, however, that this exalted conception of art and literature is based on a highly problematic conception of life and history. On the one hand, art redeems us from experiences of reality and history, which are apparently unbearable. But on the other hand, this insufferability of life is extremely frivolous. The horrors of individual, human experiences function as material or medium for eternal artifacts. Thus, these horrors are ultimately subordinated to that which is of real importance: art.

This lofty conception of art and literature suddenly becomes controversial when art redeems us not from average historical experiences but from the Holocaust. It could imply, for instance, that the Holocaust has been meaningful because it has given rise to monumental works of art such as Charlotte Salomon's *Leben oder Theater?* or the poems of Paul Celan. The Holocaust is over, but its monuments have eternal value. The Holocaust has not only been apocalyptic, it has also yielded fruits, namely, works of art. The Holocaust experiences have ennobled life. The so-called redemptive function of art is improper in the case of the Holocaust, precisely because it leads us away from the historical reality that has to be imprinted on the memory.

Critique of the redemptive function of art manifests itself more concretely in a suspicion of realist narrative plots with their redemptive closure. For instance, Claude Lanzmann, maker of the Holocaust documentary *Shoah*, criticizes Steven Spielberg's *Schindler's List* because its end would suggest that the Holocaust was meaningful: it led to the birth of Israel. The film's closure, in color, while the rest of the film is in black and white, looks, according to Lanzmann, like a reconciliation with the Holocaust. To avoid this idea of reconciliation, Lanzmann ended *Shoah* with images of a moving train, in order to signify his conviction that the Holocaust never ends. Redemption is impossible.

The second problem concerning imagining the Holocaust is not ethical but semiotic. Language allegedly falls short in its mimetic capacities; the historical reality to be represented exceeds language's grasp, because it exceeds human understanding. This conception of the intrinsic limitations of language and representation in the face of the exceptionality, the uniqueness, of this part of history, can be compared with the Jewish tradition according to which Yahweh is too magnificent and comprehensive to be represented by a visual or verbal expression.

The semiotic problem of language is felt not only in literature but also in history writing, although differently. The historian Saul Friedlander recognizes two problems in history writing. The first is so-called revisionism, which means that historical facts are simply disregarded, for instance, by denying that the Holocaust ever happened. The second problem is caused by traditional, positivistic historiography, which has as its only goal tracking the facts of the Holocaust. According to Friedlander, this kind of historiography paradoxically leads also to a forgetting of the Holocaust. At first sight it is rather amazing that revisionism and systematic, objective historiography are claimed to have the same negative effect. In the case of the historical representation of the Holocaust they both lead away from the Holocaust. Traditional historiography creates a distance from the Holocaust. That distance lies in the reading attitude the reader is encouraged to adopt—the attitude of the expert charged with verifying the facts and the connections between them:

> That neutralizes the whole discussion and suddenly places each one of us, before we have had time to take hold of ourselves, in a situation not unrelated to the detached position of an administrator of extermination: Interest is fixed on an administrative process, an activity of building and transportation, words used for record keeping. And that's all.   (Friedlander, 1992, p. 91)

Friedlander indicates that the historian has no way out. The historian cannot work in any other way, and historical studies have to be pursued along accepted lines. The events described are what is unusual, not the historian's work. Historiography has reached the limit of its means of expression.

The following question then arises: could literature rather than history have the means to represent the unusual, unique, incomparable aspect of history? In the volume Friedlander edited, *Probing the Limits of Interpretation: Nazism and the "Final Solution"* (1992), historians such as Dominick LaCapra and Hayden White declare that for the Holocaust we need "a new rhetorical mode." They look at literature and the other arts to find such a rhetorical mode. Friedlander even indicates that much contemporary literature on the Holocaust—he mentions the novels of Aharon Appelfeld and David Grossman—consists of a mixture of allegory and realism. Realistic elements are necessary in order to avoid too much allegorical distance, to preclude the possibility of total disjunction. Hence, the function of realistic elements within such allegorical representations of the Holocaust is fundamentally different from their function in other literature:

> A common denominator appears: the exclusion of straight, documentary realism, but the use of some sort of *allusive or distanced realism*. Reality is there, in its starkness, but perceived through a filter: that of memory (distance in time), that of spatial displacement, that of some sort of narrative margin which leaves the unsayable unsaid. (p. 17)

While for a long time, straightforward realism was supposed to be the most adequate and proper mode for representing the Holocaust, postmodern literature of the 1980s and 1990s has pointed to the limitations and consequences of a mimetic, realistic representation of the Holocaust. Such a representation is not only impossible but also undesirable: it threatens to make this history familiar. As one of the characters of Walter Abish's novel *How German Is It?* (1980) puts it, "When something becomes terribly familiar we stop seeing it."

But this caution does not imply that the Holocaust cannot or should not be represented. Instead, there is a need to explore and develop modes and means of representation that guard the contact with this extreme history—means that keep transmitting the knowledge of it, that simultaneously prevent forgetting and making familiar.

The Holocaust is a frequent theme in postmodern art and literature. On the one hand, this is because the historical situation of crisis is imagined as apocalyptic: the ideals of Enlightenment and modernity have not been able to prevent the barbaric excesses of World War II, and are even read by some as continuous with these, so that this "bankruptcy of modernity" necessitates postmodernism. But there is also a connection between postmodernism and the Holocaust of an entirely different kind. Postmodernism involves, among many other issues, a rethinking of the relationship between representation and reality, and an attempt at proposing new possibilities for that relationship. Such an alternative is acutely necessary for representation of this specific historical happening. Many postmodernist writers and artists establish such a relation emphatically rather than mimetically. Their attempts to develop alternative strategies of representation seem to be particularly appropriate in the case of trauma.

Whereas realist, mimetic Holocaust literature is structured on the model of memory, many postmodernist works are best understood through the model of trauma. This distinction assumes that memory is structurally different from trauma. Memories are representations of a past. According to research in cognitive psychology, memories have a narrative structure and contribute to the formation of identity, individually and collectively. Memories, including painful ones, thus have a constructive effect. Traumas are different, both structurally and in effect. A traumatic event cannot be fully experienced at the moment it happens; as a consequence, it cannot be remembered. Only in repetition, after the fact, can a trauma retrospectively become an experienced event. Whereas a memory is clearly distinct from the event—it is the memory *of* something—the reality and the representation of trauma are inseparable, so as to make the distinction void. The representation *is* the event.

In recent literature on the representation of the Holocaust, the notion of trauma and its difference from memory is the central issue (see Felman and Laub, 1992). When we think through the problems of trauma, notions like witness and testimony also change, notions that are used in their general sense in discussions of literature and history. Psychoanalyst Dori Laub has argued that the Holocaust is therefore also the collapse of the notion of bearing testimony: "History was taking place with no witness . . . it was also the very circumstance of *being inside the event* that made unthinkable the very notion that a witness could exist. . . . The historical imperative to bear witness could essentially not be met during the actual occurrence" (Felman and Laub). When we attempt to understand the consequences of Laub's statement concerning the impossibility of bearing testimony, the reflection on the representation of the Holocaust has to trade a mimetic conception of literature and art for a rhetorical one. The main function of representing the Holocaust becomes performative. The traumatic event that could not be experienced because there was no language available for it must be experienced for the first time in its representation. This implies that representation seen as a repetition of the event is no longer a mediated repetition as representation, but a real repetition in the form of representation.

[*See also* Adorno; Ineffability; *and* Semiotics.]

BIBLIOGRAPHY

Adorno, Theodor W. "Engagement." In *Notes to Literature*, edited by Rolf Tiedemann, translated by Shierry Weber Nicholsen, vol. 2, pp. 76–94. New York, 1992.

Bersani, Leo. *The Culture of Redemption*. Cambridge, Mass., 1990.

Felman, Shoshana, and Dori Laub. *Testimony: Crises of Witnessing in Literature, Psychoanalysis, and History*. New York and London, 1992.

Friedlander, Saul, ed. *Probing the Limits of Interpretation: Nazism and the "Final Solution."* Cambridge, Mass., 1992.

Longer, Lawrence L. *Holocaust Testimonies: The Ruins of Memory.* New Haven, 1991.

ERNST VAN ALPHEN

MORAL RIGHTS OF ART. [*To define and examine the rights morally and legally afforded artists and artworks, this entry comprises two essays:*

Historical and Conceptual Overview
Moral Rights Legislation

The first essay clarifies the philosophical history of the moral rights tradition. The second essay explains the concrete legislation that has been introduced to protect these rights. For further discussion, see Law and Art; *and* Morality and Aesthetics.]

Historical and Conceptual Overview

Do artworks have rights? The deceptively simple form in which the question is usually put masks its daunting internal complexity. For one thing, the rights in question may aim at protecting works against a host of harms, among them deliberate alteration, mutilation, destruction, misattribution, and inappropriate display. For another, they may aim at enacting these protections in a variety of ways; they may be thought of as being located in different entities, enjoying different deontic modalities, carrying different quotients of normative force, and being aimed at achieving different effect. To determine the validity of any given rights claim made on behalf of an artwork, it will be necessary first to sift through these differences and identify which combination of traits is appropriate to the work in its particular normative context, then to make the argument that the traits identified add up to a right. This is no easy matter, for the differences in question rest on thorny conceptual issues, and the philosophical debate over these issues renders any argument in support of rights of artworks problematic.

Conceptual Issues. First, there is the issue of the locus of putative rights: If artworks have rights, where do they reside? In the artists who created them (or their legatees), in the audience that may appreciate them, in the wider community that provides them a cultural home, or in the artworks themselves? The last alternative is the simplest, but possibly the most difficult to maintain, because it would entail the survival of aesthetic rights beyond the extinction of all claims by any persons having stakes in them. It may seem conceptually jarring to speak of, say, the destruction of Frank Lloyd Wright's Imperial Hotel as violating the building's rights rather than those of Wright, Tokyo, or the art-world public. But if this result seems counterintuitive, each of the other alternatives can be shown to suffer no less serious shortcomings. Artists, who may seem to have an obvious interest in the well-being of their works, are sometimes the very persons against whom the works need to be protected. Under the influence of Girolamo Savanarola, many great Renaissance painters (including Sandro Botticelli) threw their masterpieces on the bonfire, and over the centuries many more have made deathbed declarations ordering destruction of their works. So it would seem hazardous to suppose that if artworks have rights they are exhausted by the property interests of the artists. Precisely because artworks are frequently unpopular and critically disdained during the early years of their display (the Eiffel Tower, *Ulysses,* and *Sacre du printemps* were all initially reviled and despised), it will seem equally hazardous to suppose that the rights of artworks are exhausted by the claims of their audiences.

The celebrated controversy over the posthumous treatment of David Smith's sculptures illustrates the difficulties of settling questions of the locus of rights in a practical context. The distinguished art critic Clement Greenberg, acting as Smith's executor, authorized the removal of white paint from certain of these outdoor works so that they could be transformed by the patinizing effect of the weather. In doing so, he might have argued that he was protecting the rights of legatees in Smith's estate by improving the pieces' monetary value (as the stripping may well have done). It might also be argued that the right of the art-world public to enjoy the work is respected by whatever treatment maximizes its aesthetic quality. But it might equally be argued that Smith has a right surviving his death that his works not be treated in unauthorized ways (in fact, he had published vociferous complaints when one of his sculptures was stripped by its owner), or the work itself has a right to its integrity, requiring that it be left in the state the artist regarded as finished. If the artist's reputation (as distinguished from his or her wishes) has a right to protection, it could be argued either that certain changes promise to enhance Smith's artistic legacy, and hence should be tolerated, or that a reputation is always best served by preserving or restoring works to the state best known to reflect the artist's intent. Clearly, there is no way to weigh these conflicting putative rights claims apart from a determination of their legitimating force.

This takes us to the second issue, that of deontic modality: do the rights in question create moral or legal duties, or should aesthetic obligations instead be understood to be *sui generis*? Moral duties may seem either too weak or too controversial a basis to provide the protections sought by proponents of rights in artworks. They are too weak if the ruination of an artwork is taken to be as inconsequential as the average broken promise. They are too strong if any change to a work is deemed a moral outrage and its motivation conflated automatically with wickedness. It may, moreover, be argued that it is unwise to dilute the general utility of these concepts in guiding human conduct by extending them into areas where their application is controversial. While it is unquestionably a moral offense to deny an artist agreed-on payment for a work, whatever offense might arise from, say, hanging it in a bathroom is less clearly moral. But while conceiving rights of artworks as enforcing moral duties may seem to go too far, limiting them to the enforcement of legal duties may seem not to go far enough. Legal duties may seem insufficiently extensive to account for many of the rights claimed for artworks. A New York judge hearing a complaint brought against Greenberg's alteration of Smith's sculptures would, under the law in effect at the time, have been forced to conclude that even if a moral right had been violated, no legal right had. Of course, evidence of the former violation might be offered in promotion (through legislation or judicial interpretation) of a legal right not yet in existence. (In fact, later New York courts probably would have recognized the alleged legal right.) But at no time and nowhere in America have legal rights been granted to artworks independently of the rights artists or owners exercise in them. Smith's rights in his sculptures died with him (although, of course, his estate enjoyed certain survival rights in the works). If, however, rights of artworks are interpreted as sui generis, reducible neither to moral rights nor to legal rights, it is difficult to determine what protections they should be understood to afford. When Alexander Calder complained of the repainting of his mobile *Pittsburgh* (in the official Allegheny colors, green and gold) for its display in the Greater Pittsburgh International Airport, he could not claim the owners were violating any legal rights, nor could he argue that the act violated any clearly legible moral duty. But his insistence that rights in some sense—aesthetic rights—were being breached proved unpersuasive, and the work was not restored during his lifetime.

Third, there are the issues of normative force and its source. Rights are, by their nature, privileged in competition with interests; so, for example, the claim that an owner has a right to destroy artworks in her possession is a claim that she may do so no matter how many people would oppose her action and no matter how strong the interests they assert. But, this privilege may not be absolute. Similarly, if artworks are conceded to have rights, that fact alone will not immunize them from competition with all other values in all circumstances. An owner's property right to do as she pleases with a work may be superseded by an artist's property right through protective legislation. Conversely, an artist's right to display his work as he pleases may be superseded by contravening claims, for example, by a public right to safety where the nature of the work imperils audiences. (When, in 1996, Jason Sprinkle parked his artwork, a truck containing a large metal broken heart and covered with various graffiti including the word *bomb*, in a downtown mall, a large part of Seattle's commercial core was evacuated and the artist was arrested and charged with violation of antiterrorist ordinances.) If artworks are conceded to have rights,

should these rights be considered to have a high or low threshold of preemption, and, if so, how high or how low? It may be supposed that a public artwork's right to preservation is exhausted when conditions have rendered it more a nuisance than a benefit, while it could be argued that no urban renewal projects, no matter how noble and well conceived, could justify destruction of a distinguished architectural landmark. If rights in artworks are held to be natural rights (i.e., rights inhering in them independently of any political right-granting authority), they will likely be thought to enjoy special stringency, comparative prescriptive weight, or scope. If, instead, they are held to be positive rights (i.e., rights deriving from specific enactments), they will be understood to draw their force from the legitimacy and effectiveness of the positing authority.

Finally, whatever their locus, modality, source, and force, there remains the fundamental question of what effects rights in artworks are supposed to achieve. While assertions of rights in artworks are most frequently aimed at strengthening their resistance to damage and destruction, they are also invoked to ensure the alteration, or even demolition, of artworks. Sacred Tibetan sand paintings, for instance, are ritually demolished on their completion, and some Native Americans insist that their totem poles be mounted outdoors so that they can be subjected to the same weathering and eventual disintegration as are their makers. Aesthetic rights are often asserted as mandates of respect, requiring that artworks be treated, presented, displayed, or performed in ways recognized to be appropriate; but such rights might also be invoked to ensure that works be treated or presented in other, unconventional ways, out of respect for the aesthetic value of innovation. Rights are sometimes invoked to preserve older works in their integrity, even when they are dilapidated, yet they are also invoked in the contrary-seeming causes of restoration and reconstruction. Beyond all the respects in which rights are ascribed to existing artworks and artistic enterprises, rights are also sometimes asserted on behalf of future claims on appreciation and creation, and in particular on the public's interest in future benefits deriving from continuing artistic traditions.

The Philosophical Debate. Controversy over this welter of issues has burgeoned since the 1970s. This development has paralleled, and has no doubt been inspired by, a recent marked inflation in the inventory of entities that have been popularly held to have (legal as well as moral) rights. If neighborhoods, fetuses, corporations, historic edifices, household pets, spotted owls, and possibly even groves of trees have rights, it may well be asked why it should not be appropriate to recognize rights in artworks, too. It is already well established, of course, that artists, architects, authors, curators, composers, performers, publishers, impresarios, critics, and others engaged in artistic activities enjoy a variety of property rights in relation to their work; but most of these rights, created by contract or specific legislation, are in no substantial way different from other long-standing legal rights held by makers, displayers, and purveyors of all manner of nonartistic artifacts. Most proponents of rights in artworks argue that certain features peculiar to them (including aspects of appreciation and criticism, as well as production) should be recognized as imbuing them with additional, more stringent, rights. Opponents commonly complain that the invocation of aesthetic rights as a strategy of arts protection is a mistaken means to an otherwise admirable end. Without denying that artworks (or at least some of them) are owed substantial respect and that we are morally obliged to treat things we respect in specially protective ways, they insist that the extension of the ascription of rights to inanimate, impersonal entities is a spurious, or at best metaphoric, usage that plays havoc with normative categories and undercuts the effectiveness of rights claims in their standard moral and legal contexts.

The roots of modern discussion of aesthetic rights lie in the venerable French doctrine of *droit moral,* a sweeping legal protection of artworks deriving from postrevolutionary moral imperatives. Until recently, the disparity between rights afforded artworks under this doctrine and rights available in American courts has been sufficiently glaring to inspire complaints that the conversion of moral to legal rights has been inexplicably retarded on this side of the Atlantic. But this conversion requires a consensus on the locus and normative force of aesthetic rights that has not been achieved. *Droit moral* has been interpreted to adhere to artworks themselves or to the public at large as aesthetic stakeholders, and to draw its stringency from popular acceptance of the importance of national treasures. In the United States, agreement about cultural values is less pronounced and traditional protections of property interests a greater impediment to public interest legislation. From the beginning, theoretical argument favoring the recognition of rights of artworks has usually stressed the adverse social consequences of tolerating injury to artworks more than the positive consequences of sustaining a cultural legacy by protecting art. Typically, they have aimed to demonstrate a close relation between the offense we take at harms to artworks and our offense at the harms suffered by sentient beings.

Alan Tormey's early article, "Aesthetic Rights" (1973), exemplifies this approach. Tormey defends the thesis that because artworks may be subjects of "aesthetic pain" and may therefore be treated in objectionable ways that amount to victimization, they may legitimately claim interests that generate obligations on us that amount to rights. He boldly locates these rights in works themselves, arguing that our duties to them are equivalent to our duties to other parties who have a right not to be injured by us, and that such duties are not discharged by satisfying any particular persons, artists or performers, say, who may after all be unavailable to benefit. He argues that our way of speaking and acting with respect to artworks betrays the fact that we already accept the entitlements he describes. Nowhere in the article does Tormey address the distinction between moral and legal rights, but it seems implied by what he does say that his argument is meant to establish artworks that already enjoy moral rights that might, if deemed sufficiently stringent, be given legal force. The normative force they enjoy is a product of regarding artworks as quasi persons, and the Kantian injunctions that apply to the latter are taken to apply with equal force to the former.

To Tormey's critics, this position seems to trade illegitimately on its metaphors: artworks do not really feel pain; they are not really persons; and therefore they are not entitled to the rights reserved to social beings. As David Goldblatt points out (1976), if it is essential to the concept of rights that their possessors be capable of claiming them and choosing to deploy or waive them, it perverts the concept to apply it to entities that can do none of these things. Moreover, in the absence of support for the claim that rights attached to artworks are justified (and not just de facto entitlements), their normative force is unmeasurable and hence vulnerable to any fluctuations in moral convictions. Goldblatt's chief argument against Tormey's account of the locus of aesthetic rights is a reductio ad absurdum: if rights inhere in artworks because they can be injured, they will inhere in stereo speakers, rocking chairs, lamps, and so forth as well; but that is ridiculous. Goldblatt rejects altogether the claim that artworks have rights. His rejection is based on a conviction that the (Wittgensteinian) form of life we—presumably present-day Americans—have adopted restricts the domain of application of the ingredient concepts (entitlements, obligations, etc.) to social beings. But, of course, a form of life is a de facto practice, no less unjustified than the entitlements Tormey describes. So it remains open, even accepting Goldblatt's criticisms, to imbue artworks with rights by changing our ascriptive practices.

Hilde Hein argues (1978) that changes of this kind are very much in order. She interprets Tormey's idea that injury to artworks is in a way "painful" as a fruitful, if fanciful, way of indicating the precariousness of depending on standard societal protections to defend objects of great value. She points out that in a world in which persons holding traditional rights (usually white men) have held hegemonic sway over those who do not, it is sometimes useful to indulge what amounts to a normative fiction, speaking of artworks as having rights as a way of expressing the demand of community protectiveness toward objects whose worth transcends the conventional bounds of privilege. Like familiar legal fictions (common-law marriage, corporate personality, etc.), such fictions serve as "interim measures," pending a more satisfactory revision of social relations. Locating the right in artworks rather than their creators or possessors can help do for the disenfranchised putative right bearers what they cannot do for themselves; and presenting them as potentially legal, and not just moral, rights acknowledges future generations as parties whose interests are protected by them.

Arguments opposing the recognition rights in artworks reached a crescendo in 1983 with the publication of Francis Sparshott's essay "Why Artworks Have No Right to Have Rights." Sparshott argues that we must resist the "fool's gold" temptation to ascribe rights to artworks on the ground that doing so would enable us to consolidate the various categories of obligation under which we are normally disposed to respect them. Such a consolidation, he insisted, would obscure the fact that the several ingredient duties are owed by different parties, have different strengths, rationales, sources, and so on, and are frequently asserted in protection of the artwork against the property rights of owners and artists, rather than the marauding public. If the strand that holds all these duties is simply the interest we have in protecting things we cherish, Sparshott argues, it is not the artwork that should be understood to be the locus of the corresponding right, but the community of present and future cherishers, a community whose membership is controversial, whose opinions are hard to measure, and that has done nothing to deserve the right in question. It should not be overlooked, Sparshott points out, that any ascription of rights (to artworks, artists, or the art world) that entails that they are not to be destroyed faces the unhappy consequence of unthinking accumulation of works. If old things cannot die, it is harder and harder for new things to live.

Both Hein and Sparshott observe that the value of a work of art is in part contingent on its being recognized as a work of art. This determination is a notoriously fragile base on which to rest weighty normative protections, as the celebrated controversy over Constantin Brancusi's *Bird in Flight* dramatically illustrates. Brancusi's sculpture was intercepted by customs agents on its arrival in the United States and held for payment of duty as a "manufacture of metal." The Customs Court subsequently determined that it was instead a work of art and hence not subject to duty (*Brancusi v United States*, TD 43062, 54 Treas. Dec. 428 [1929]). But, as philosophical reflection on the institutional character of art recognition proceeds, it is likely that the effects sought by invoking the language of rights will be attached to artworks through various less controversial status claims linking conduct in the art world with conduct in wider social institutions. It may, in the end, not matter much if the status of a work of art is held to vest it with rights or with substantial value—say, presumptive cherishability (in Sparshott's terms)—that establishes expectations of respectful treatment.

Legal Rights of Artworks. Remarkably, in the midst of this philosophical controversy, and cognizant of the political turmoil surrounding controversial artworks, the American electorate has recently been disposed to secure protection for cherished artworks through newly created legal rights.

This tendency, manifested in a wide array of landmark preservation, copyright extension, artists' rights bills, and other similar instruments, is a marked departure from the established principle of Anglo-American jurisprudence, affirmed in *Crimi v Rutgers Presbyterian Church*, 89 NYS 2d 813 (1949), that, in the absence of reservations in contract, works of art are the property of their owners and subject to alteration or destruction without remedy. That the plaintiff in *Crimi* was unsuccessful in urging judicial recognition of a "moral right" securing the artist's interest beyond the point of sale is hardly surprising since the United States was not among the seventy signatory nations joining in the Berne Convention for the Protection of Literary and Artistic Works (1886; revised 1971) and had not followed European nations in reducing the moral right to statute. What is surprising is the rapidity with which states reversed direction and adopted the essence of the European rights position, beginning in 1979.

The French *droit moral,* codified in 1957, extends protection for artists against damage to their names, authorship, and works as a right of personality, that is, of artists' repute and personal integrity, rather than a right of property defending a pecuniary interest in artistic possessions or creations (much like copyright). It provides that the right enjoyed is "perpetual, inalienable, and imprescribable," and that it may be passed on to heirs or legatees. The statute specifically forbids the distortion, dismemberment, or misrepresentation of works of art, creates a "right of paternity" that protects artists' prerogative of demanding that their works be associated with their names (and equally that works of others *not* be associated with their names), and a "right of divulgation" that reserves to artists all decisions about when, and whether, to show their work to the public. Italian law suggests an additional public right, in that it may be pressed by a public official as well as by the artist or the artist's heirs. The California Art Preservation Act of 1979 created very similar protections (specifically declaring rights of paternity in artists and of integrity in "distinguished" artworks); and while it is less sweeping in one sense, in that the rights it creates are all explicitly alienable, it is more extensive in another, in that it proscribes the destruction, and not just the mutilation, of artworks. New York followed in 1983 with an Authorship Rights Act more closely adhering to the European model in attaching rights to artists' personality interests (i.e., artistic reputation) rather than to any public interest in the integrity of the artworks themselves. Two years later, Massachusetts passed a near copy of the California act; and a number of other states (at least ten, to date) have followed suit.

State-by-state rejection of the *Crimi* rule culminated in 1990 with congressional passage of the Visual Artists' Rights Act, a law providing nationwide protection of rights of attribution and integrity for works of visual art. Under it, artists are guaranteed the right to claim authorship of their works, to prevent use of their names as authors of works they did not create, and to prevent any intentional distortion, mutilation, or other modification of the work that would be prejudicial to their honor or reputation. The act is narrower than most of its state-adopted forebears in that its provisions are limited to the length of the artist's life, applicable only to original visual artworks (and signed limited editions) not "made for hire," and inapplicable to films (against colorization, for example), crafts, books, models, and so forth. It does, however, protect works (such as frescoes) incorporated into buildings against uncompensated destruction (which was the precise issue litigated in *Crimi*). It is too early to forecast the full effects of the Visual Artists' Rights Act, including the normative stringency it will be taken to imply; but early litigation under it has made clear that its provisions (including such undefined terms as *honor, reputation,* and *stature*) are not on their face unconstitutionally vague, and that federal courts are willing to enforce those provisions against substantial property interests to prevent damage to the integrity of artworks of recognized stature. The cumulative effect of the state and federal statutes has been to give the notion of aesthetic rights a firm foothold in the law of the land.

Whatever bearing these recent legal developments may eventually have in securing rights for artists (and owners et al.), they undeniably stop short of establishing rights in artworks themselves. Thus, the question of the locus of legal rights in artworks remains juridically unresolved. One tantalizing intimation of possible future legal argument in support of inherent rights in artworks was presented in Justice William O. Douglas's dissent in *Sierra Club v Morton*, 405 US 727 (1972). Enthusiastically endorsing an argument Christopher D. Stone had made in "Should Trees Have Standing? Toward Legal Rights for Natural Objects" (1972), Douglas urged the Court to permit redwood trees to sue the government for their own protection through appointed guardians. Although Douglas's position did not garner majority support, it provided considerable impetus to those who would extend trustee protections through guardianship to an indefinite class of culturally prized objects, both animate and inanimate. If artworks should be counted in this class, it would hardly matter whether the rights at issue were ascribed to the works themselves or to the community that endorses them, because the point of the protection would be directed beyond both of these to the perpetuation of aesthetic values for succeeding generations; and this is a value to which all parties to the philosophical and political disputes declare allegiance.

BIBLIOGRAPHY

Dworkin, Ronald. *A Matter of Principle.* Cambridge, Mass., 1985. See pp. 221–233, 335–372.
Feldman, Franklin, and Stephen E. Weil. *Art Law: Rights and Liabilities of Creators and Collectors.* Boston, 1986.
Goldblatt, David A. "Do Works of Art Have Rights?" *Journal of Aesthetics and Art Criticism* 35.1 (Fall 1976): 69–77.
Goodwin, Matthew. "The Visual Rights Act of 1990: Further Defining the Rights and Duties of Artists and Real Property Owners." *Golden State University Law Review* 22 (1992).
Hein, Hilde. "Aesthetic Rights: Vindication and Vilification." *Journal of Aesthetics and Art Criticism* 37.2 (Winter 1978): 169–176.
Karlen, Peter. "The 'Moral Right' Comes to California." In *Beauty and the Beasts: On Museums, Art, the Law, and the Market,* edited by Stephen E. Weil, pp. 226–239. Washington, D.C., 1983.
Karlen, Peter. "Worldmaking: Property Rights in Aesthetic Creations." *Journal of Aesthetics and Art Criticism* 45.2 (Winter 1986): 183–192.
Merryman, John Henry, and Albert E. Elsen. *Law, Ethics, and the Visual Arts.* 2d ed. Philadelphia, 1987.
Sparshott, Francis. "Why Artworks Have No Right to Have Rights." *Journal of Aesthetics and Art Criticism* 42.1 (Fall 1983): 5–15.
Stone, Christopher D. *Should Trees Have Standing? Toward Legal Rights for Natural Objects.* Los Altos, Calif., 1974.
Tormey, Alan. "Aesthetic Rights." *Journal of Aesthetics and Art Criticism* 32.2 (Winter 1973): 163–170.
VerSteeg, Russ. "Federal Moral Rights for Visual Artists: Contract Theory and Analysis." *Washington Law Review* 867 (1992).

RONALD MOORE

Moral Rights Legislation

The term *moral rights* is derived from the French *droit moral*. Perhaps the concept is best expressed by the German term *Urheberpersönlichkeitsrecht*, which refers to the "right of the author's personality."

The doctrine encompasses various kinds of authors' rights that have been categorized in a number of ways. Moral rights may be classified into three basic categories:

1. disclosure rights, including the rights to create or not to create and to control disclosure and publication of creative works, even to the extent of withholding or withdrawing them from publication
2. the rights of authorship, often called "paternity" rights, including the right to be acknowledged as the author of a work under one's own name or pseudonym, the rights to limited protection of anonymity and protection against false attribution, and the right to object to excessive criticism and attacks on the author's professional reputation
3. the rights of integrity, including the rights to object to the destruction of one's work and to prevent its mutilation, distortion, or alteration.

The salient aspect of moral rights is enforcement by authors and their heirs against the legal owners of physical objects in which the creative work is embodied, and sometimes even against copyright owners of the work. For example, the sculptor enjoying moral rights can prevent the mutilation of his sculpture by its owner, or the writer entitled to withdraw the work can do so even against the wishes of an authorized book publisher.

These authors' rights extend to a broad range of creative persons and works. Although frequently associated with visual artists and their works, moral rights also apply to the literary realm, cinematography, music, and other established creative fields.

The moral rights doctrine serves a number of purposes. The most important is protection of the author's reputation. Moral rights also protect the author's economic interests. For example, the author able to claim credit for a valuable work, which would otherwise be published with no credit or credit for someone else, achieves recognition that may lead toward commissioning of new works by the named author. Moral rights also help preserve a nation's cultural heritage. For instance, enforcement of integrity rights is often the only means of preserving the existence or completeness of an artistic work that would otherwise be lost forever because of those who would destroy or mutilate it. Moreover, from an art-historical perspective, moral rights are valuable for preserving the integrity of any author's oeuvre. As an example, the very identity of an artist's work is preserved over time by enforcement of paternity rights, especially by preventing falsely attributed forgeries and fakes from entering the marketplace.

Moral rights are personal rights, not property rights. As such, moral rights are generally inalienable and cannot be bought or sold, although in many jurisdictions they can be waived. During the author's lifetime, they adhere to the author; after the author's death, they are generally enforced by the author's heirs-at-law. In some jurisdictions, the rights are perpetual, but in the majority of jurisdictions where moral rights are recognized, they extend for a limited period after the author's death, for example, the term of copyright protection, which is often the author's life plus a fixed number of years (e.g., fifty or seventy). In a few jurisdictions, even the state can enforce these rights whenever the author or the heirs refuse to act and in rare cases even against the wishes of the heirs. For instance, the state may bring a legal action to preserve a famous work of art against those who would otherwise destroy it.

As explained below, rights equivalent to moral rights were previously enforced by applying diverse legal theories. Not until the early part of the twentieth century, however, did jurists recognize or fully develop the comprehensive concept of the *droit moral*.

The *droit moral* had its origins primarily in two sweeping changes that became evident in the nineteenth century. One of these changes was economic. The creative person, particularly the visual artist, could no longer rely on aristocratic patronage or church commissions but instead became subject to the whims of middle-class tastes. No longer was the commissioned work the primary source of income for artists and other creative persons. Instead, works were thrust on the open market just like other commodities and subjected to the vicissitudes of the free-market economy in aesthetic creations. As entrepreneurs, authors became dependent on their public reputations in order to develop clienteles. An artist's reputation was easily damaged if she were deprived of credit or associated with a work that was not hers, or if her works were altered so that they did not represent her artistic personality. After all, authors were never again to be the creatures of salons and court chambers but rather were business people who had to guard name and reputation in the same way that merchants must prevent the tarnishment, dilution, or infringement of their trademark.

The other change giving rise to the *droit moral* was a matter of aesthetics. With the flowering of Romanticism in the nineteenth century the author's right to "follow the call of feelings and individual disposition" was emphasized as never before. The work of authorship, particularly the work of visual art, was no longer severely restricted by patrons in terms of subject matter, form, or content. Rather, it became the personal expression of the author, revealing individual perceptions and sensibilities. Thus, false attribution of the work and interference with the integrity of the work by mutilation, alteration, distortion, or presentation out of context were increasingly seen as personal attacks on the author. The public, also imbued with romantic notions about art, was sympathetic regarding moral rights, and vociferous authors and their allies were able to persuade the courts to recognize new residual rights in creative works that went beyond copyright protection.

If moral rights had a birthplace it would be France. Shortly following the establishment of authors' property rights in their works by legislation dating back to the French Revolution, the French courts in the early nineteenth century, relying primarily on criminal plagiarism statutes, began to recognize authors' rights to prevent deformation of their works.

By the middle of the nineteenth century, the opinions begin to reflect the courts' willingness to recognize the special needs of authors to protect their works. In *Clesinger et Laneuville c. Gauvain*, [1850] D.P. III. 14 (Trib. Corr. de Lyon), reversed, [1852] D.P. II. 159 (Cour de Paris), a criminal action for defacing a work of art was not allowed, but the appellate court hinted that a civil action might be permitted: "independent of the economic interest there exists for the artist a more valuable interest, that of his reputation."

As early as 1837 the Paris Court of Appeal upheld paternity rights in saying that "the collaborator whose name has been omitted from the titling of the work without his knowledge may obtain recognition of his authorship and his rights through the courts" (De Repertoire de Jurisprudence V. Prop. Lit. et Art. no. 194).

In the latter part of the nineteenth century almost the full panoply of moral rights was recognized by the French courts. Finally, in *Cinquin c. Lecocq* [1902] D.P. 1903. I.5, the highest court, the Cour de Cassation, officially recognized the *droit moral*.

French jurisprudence surrounding the *droit moral* was so well developed and well received that the *droit moral* was incorporated, in part, in the 1928 Rome text of the Berne Convention for the Protection of Literary and Artistic Works (2 Copyright Laws of the World, Item E-1), discussed below.

But the crowning achievement of French moral rights law was the Law of II March 1957 (Law no. 57-298 on Literary and Artistic Property), perhaps the most comprehensive and wide-ranging statutory recognition of the *droit moral* in the world. This legislation, as amended, covers a wide range of creative works such as works of the visual arts, choreography, music, and literary and dramatic arts. Under this statutory scheme the rights are perpetual, inalienable, and imprescriptible, and on an author's death pass to his heirs.

The first international recognition of the *droit moral* came with the 1928 draft of the Berne Convention. Article 6bis read:

> (1) Independently of the patrimonial rights of the author, and even after the assignment of the said rights, the author retains the right to claim the paternity of the work, as well as the right to object to every deformation, mutilation or other modification of the said work, which may be prejudicial to his honor or to his reputation.
>
> (2) It is left to the national legislation of each of the countries of the Union to establish the conditions for the exercise of these rights. The means for safeguarding them shall be regulated by the legislation of the country where protection is claimed.

Because the Berne Convention in its latest version still embodies article 6bis, moral rights now enjoy protection throughout the world among Berne Convention countries, which at the time of this writing number more than eighty. The Berne Convention requires its member nations to enact legislation implementing the moral rights recognized under article 6bis, although the scope of statutory protection varies from country to country. For instance, in the United States, national moral rights legislation in the form of the Visual Artists Rights Act of 1990 (largely embodied in 17 U.S.C. Sections 101, 106A, 113(d), and 301(f)) only extends to a limited number of "works of visual art." Moreover, many countries, particularly common-law countries such as the United States and the United Kingdom, took quite some time to enact moral rights legislation.

Even though moral rights are now widely recognized throughout the world, the full complement of rights recognized in France is usually not found elsewhere. As an example, the right to withdraw one's work from publication is not a universally recognized right since it sharply conflicts with publishers' contract rights.

Before and even after the recognition of moral rights, authors have been able to enforce these rights using other legal doctrines. For instance, an author deprived of credit or wrongfully credited may have an action for unfair competition based on false attribution. An author whose name is wrongfully used in connection with a mutilated work may have a claim for defamation. Moreover, copyright law can be used to effectuate moral rights. For example, publication of an altered work will sometimes violate the author's exclusive right under copyright law to adapt the work. Also, publishing an author's work without his or her permission may be a copyright violation. Wrongfully associating an author with a work that is not his or hers may invade the author's right of privacy wherever recognized. Failure to give an author credit may violate the author's contractual right to credit, and attributing a work to someone other than the author may be an actionable slander of title.

The following are some noteworthy cases involving moral rights or their attempted enforcement using other legal doctrines. James McNeill Whistler filed suit for defamation in *Whistler v. Ruskin* (reported in the London *Times*, 26–27 November 1878, and discussed in Hollander, 1959). The critic John Ruskin had described one of Whistler's *Nocturnes* thus: "I have seen and heard much of Cockney impudence before now; but I never expected to hear a coxcomb ask two hundred guineas [the painting's price] for flinging a pot of paint in the public's face." Whistler's suit was questionably successful. Following a dispute about payment for a commissioned portrait of Lady Eden, Whistler painted out the already completed head on the portrait and refused to complete the work, which prompted a lawsuit by Lord Eden to compel Whistler to complete the portrait (*Eden c. Whistler*), [1898] Recueil Periodique et Critique II.4.65 (Civ. Trib. Seine), [1900] S.II.201 (Cour d'Appel, Paris), [1900] Recueil Periodique Sirey 1.490 (Cass. Civ.). The French court held that an artist cannot be forced to complete a work but also sustained Lord Eden's right to damages). *Carco c. Camoin* [1931] D.P.II.88 (Cour d'Appel, Paris) (note by Nast) was a successful suit by an artist who had cut his paintings to pieces and thrown them away against an entrepreneur who had filched the pieces from the garbage, reassembled them, and sold them at auction. In a reverse action, *Buffet c. Fersig* [1962] Recueil Dalloz (D. Jur.) 570 (Cour d'Appel, Paris) (note by Desbois), *aff'd*, [1965] Gaz.Pal II.126, discussed in Merryman, "The Refrigerator of Bernard Buffet," 27 Hastings L.J. 1023 (1976), the artist Bernard Buffet, who had painted work on a refrigerator, brought successful suit against an entrepreneur who had separated the refrigerator into panels with the aim of selling them as individual works. In *Shostakovich v. 20th Century-Fox Film Corp.* 196 Misc. 67, 80 N.Y.S.2d 575 (Sup. Ct. 1948), *aff'd*, 275 App. Div. 692, 87 N.Y.S. 2d 430 (1st Dept. 1949) the Russian composer brought unsuccessful suit in New York on the claim that his music had been wrongfully used in an anticommunist film. The opposite result obtained in France in *Soc. Le Chant du Monde c. Soc. Fox Europe et Fox Americaine Twentieth Century* [1954] D. Jur. 16, 80 (Cour d' Appel, Paris) in which the composer was successful in making similar claims regarding use of his music in an anticommunist film. In *Huston c. La Cinq*, discussed in Boyer, "The Asphalt Jungle"—in France—Entitlement to Moral Rights," 2 Ent. Law Rev. E-55 (1991) the film director John Huston commenced suit for unauthorized colorization of his film *The Asphalt Jungle*. In *Anatole France c. Lemerre* [1911] Pataille 1912.1.98, the author's right to withhold his work from publication was upheld when the work no longer represented his views. In *Clemens v. Press Publishing Co.*, 67 Misc. 183, 122 N.Y.S. 206 (Sup. Ct. 1910), in New York jurisdiction not then recognizing moral rights, and without a written contract providing for credits, Mark Twain was not able to obtain authorship credit for a book he had written.

BIBLIOGRAPHY

Diamond, Sidney A. "Legal Protection for the 'Moral Rights' of Authors and Other Creators." *Trademark Reporter* 68 (1978).

Giocanti, Dominique. "Moral Rights: Authors' Protection and Business Needs." *Journal of International Law and Economics* 10 (1975).

Hollander, Barnett. *The International Law of Art: For Lawyers, Collectors, and Artists.* London, 1959.

Karlen, Peter H. "What's Wrong with VARA: A Critique of Federal Moral Rights." *Hastings COMM/ENT Law Journal* 15 (1993).

Ladas, Stephen P. *The International Protection of Literary and Artistic Property.* New York, 1938.

Marvin, Charles A. "The Author's Status in the United Kingdom and France: Common Law and the Moral Right Doctrine." *International and Comparative Law Quarterly* 20 (1971).

Merryman, John H. "The Refrigerator of Bernard Buffet." *Hastings Law Journal* 27 (1976).

Michaélidès-Nouaros, George. *Le droit moral de l'auteur.* Paris, 1935.

Roeder, Martin A. "The Doctrine of Moral Right: A Study in the Law of Artists, Authors and Creators." *Harvard Law Review* 53 (1940).

Sarraute, Raymond. "Current Theory on the Moral Right of Authors and Artists under French Law." *American Journal of Comparative Law* 16 (1968).

Strauss, William. "The Moral Right of the Author." *American Journal of Comparative Law* 4 (1955).

Stromholm, Stig. *Le droit moral de l'auteur en droit Allemand, Français et Scandinave avec un aperçu de l'évolution internationale.* Stockholm, 1966.

PETER H. KARLEN

MORITZ, KARL PHILIPP (1756–1793), German author. A literary jack-of-all-trades whose prodigious output included novels, poetry, travelogues, studies in pedagogy and classical mythology, and works on the German, English, and Italian languages, Karl Philipp Moritz is best known for his autobiographical novel *Anton Reiser* (1785–1790) and two contributions to aesthetics, "Attempt at a Unification of All the Fine Arts and Sciences under the Concept of That Which Is Perfect in Itself" (1785) and "On the Creative Imitation of Beauty" (1788).

During his school years at the Hannover gymnasium from 1771 to 1776 he became obsessed with art because it gave him a refuge from the misery caused by his poverty and unhappy childhood. In later years, he continued his studies in Erfurt and Wittenberg; and moved to Berlin, where he met Moses Mendelssohn and Marcus Herz. Moritz traveled to England in 1782, and stayed in Italy from 1786 to 1788, where he befriended Johann Wolfgang von Goethe. In 1789, he returned to Berlin as professor of the theory of the fine arts and died four years later of tuberculosis.

In "On the Concept of That Which Is Perfect in Itself" (as the essay from 1785 is commonly known), Moritz distinguishes the useful from the beautiful and discusses the pleasure that they produce in us. An object that is merely useful (e.g., a knife) offers us pleasure by serving as a means to our ends. Since it is we who endow it with a purpose that it is to fulfill, it is imperfect and thus not a completed whole of rationally organized parts; it becomes one only by our endowing it with a purpose. The useful object, imperfect in itself, is perfected in us. A beautiful object, however, is perfected in itself. It does not need us to perfect it by endowing it with an extrinsic purpose. Instead, it possesses an intrinsic purpose whose fulfillment produces in the viewer a sympathetic pleasurable response. Thus, beautiful objects are treated as if they were agents with their own purposes. For example, Moritz says that we feel displeasure at a performance in an empty theater: the frustration of the play's intrinsic purpose—presumably, the intention of being enjoyed by an appreciative audience—evokes our pity. Furthermore, because we are absorbed in the object itself and thus are not concerned with any purposes of our own that it might fulfill, it commands our attention for its own sake and draws us away from the merely useful world around us. Our everyday desires are momentarily stilled, and we experience a loss of ourselves, which causes in us the highest pleasure. Thus, pleasure in the beautiful is akin to unselfish love, for in both states the object, treated as an end in itself untouched by our purposes, removes us from our ordinary concerns.

In "On the Creative Imitation of Beauty," Moritz claims that creative geniuses produce beautiful objects that are microcosms of the rationally organized whole of nature. The mind can dimly grasp this whole in thought but cannot represent it sensibly. The artistic genius creatively imitates nature by producing a beautiful object with an organization analogous to that of nature itself: such an object can be represented by the mind. What we cannot think in its particularity can be analogically imitated in what we can sense. This sensible representation of the structure of nature affords us pleasure that we cannot obtain otherwise.

Moritz's aesthetics is ably illustrated in *Anton Reiser*. Anton writes poetry and pursues a theatrical career, not from a desire to imitate nature creatively, but rather from a desire to escape his emotional and material wretchedness and win the approval of others. Thus, he treats works of arts as means to his ends. True artists, however, create in accordance with the demands of the work itself—that is, its internal requirements for being a perfected whole—and thus not to satisfy their audience's desires or any desire of their own except that of creating a perfected whole. Anton's inability to create in the proper spirit, says Moritz, is the source of his failure as an artist. With this judgment Moritz harshly condemns his own youthful artistic efforts in light of his mature aesthetic theory.

Moritz's influence was diverse. Immanuel Kant, it seems, formulated his notion of the subjective purposiveness of works of art in tacit opposition to Moritz's rather implausible claim that they possess intrinsic purposiveness. Also, Moritz anticipated Arthur Schopenhauer's claim that aesthetic experience momentarily extinguishes the impertinent demands of the will. Finally, his proposal that creative imitation affords us some sort of metaphysical insight into nature is an early expression of a doctrine that later aestheticians, especially those among the Romantics, developed in greater detail.

BIBLIOGRAPHY

Works by Moritz

Anton Reiser: Ein psychologisher Roman. Berlin, 1785–1790.
Versuch einer Vereinigung aller schönen Künste und Wissenschaften unter dem Begriff des in sich selbst Vollendeten. An Herrn Moses Mendelssohn. Berlin, 1785.
Über die bildende Nachahmung des Schönen. Braunschweig, 1788.
Selections. In *Beiträge zur Ästhetik,* edited by Hans Joachim Schrimpf and Hans Adler. Mainz, 1989.
Excerpts from "On the Creative Imitation of Beauty." In Johann Wolfgang von Goethe, *Italian Journey,* translated by Robert R. Heitner, edited by Thomas P. Saine and Jeffrey L. Sammons, pp. 431–436. New York, 1989.
"On the Concept of That Which Is Perfect in Itself." In *Eighteenth Century German Criticism,* translated and edited by Timothy L. Chamberlain, pp. 245–251. New York, 1992.
Werke. 3 vols. 2d ed. Edited by Horst Günther. Frankfurt am Main, 1993.
Anton Reiser: A Psychological Novel. Translated by John R. Russell. Columbia, S.C., 1996.

Other Sources

Boulby, Mark. *Karl Philipp Moritz: At the Fringe of Genius.* Toronto, 1979.
Guyer, Paul. *Kant and the Experience of Freedom: Essays on Aesthetics and Morality.* Cambridge and New York, 1993. See chap. 4, "The Perfections of Art: Mendelssohn, Moritz, and Kant."
Schrimpf, Hans Joachim. *Karl Philipp Moritz.* Stuttgart, 1980.
Waniek, Erdmann. "Karl Philipp Moritz's Concept of the Whole in His 'Versuch einer Vereinigung . . .' 1785." *Studies in Eighteenth-Century Culture* 12 (1983): 213–222.
Woodmansee, Martha. "The Interests in Disinterestedness: Karl Philipp Moritz and the Emergence of the Theory of Aesthetic Autonomy in Eighteenth-Century Germany." *Modern Language Quarterly* 45 (1984): 22–47.

CURTIS BOWMAN

MORRIS, WILLIAM (1834–1896), English artist and poet. Since William Morris's had no interest in formal analytic philosophy, his aesthetic theory must be pieced together by noting what he said in practical situations and in lectures; by looking closely at his work, both visual and verbal; and by acknowledging his indebtedness to John Ruskins's ideas, while at the same time observing the limits of that indebtedness. The last consideration is particularly relevant, first, because Morris, unlike his master, was a practicing artist—a maker of both visual patterns and verbal lyrics and narratives both prose and poetic—and, second, because Ruskin, although he supported and encouraged the decorative arts, was equally enthusiastic about easel painting. Morris, although ready at times to acknowledge the beauty and importance of certain paintings on canvas, had a preoccupation with the decorative arts whenever he set out to lecture about art as a presumably general idea.

Nevertheless, present in the sources named here are key concepts that act as lines of perspective and converge on a very substantive aesthetic theory in Morris's work, though—let it be added—his practice as an artist only partially reinforces what his verbal utterances say.

Another matter, essential to note in any discussion of Morris's aesthetic theory, is his commitment to socialism, beginning in 1883. This is not the place to detail the history of Morris's involvement with the nineteenth-century British socialist movement, an interest and activity lasting until his death in 1896, but it should be emphasized that socialist lecturing and writing were important parts of his life and career. As for his aesthetic theory, however, the significance of his socialism is more problematic. He had already, before 1883, expressed his strong preference for the decorative arts, calling them in an 1879 lecture "the art of the people," and, in an 1880 talk, "the beauty of life," contrasting the traditional decorative arts with the ugly luxury goods produced for the wealthy. What Morris's commitment to socialism did was enable him to confirm and articulate his strong belief by relating it to a broad historical view of the transformation of early European society into modern capitalist society, marked by its own class system. Already deploring the death of "the art of the people," the crafts, he now tied their disappearance to the absorption of farm laborers and artisans into the urban factory centers and the manufacture for their consumption of cheap and shoddy goods.

Already disliking the art of the late Renaissance, the eighteenth century, and most of the nineteenth century, Morris now argued that all this bad art had been made to suit the degenerate taste of the wealthy, entrepreneurial middle classes, who produced nothing themselves but demanded that ugly luxury items be provided for their gratification, corrupting the artists thus employed. Socialism gave Morris a historical explanation of why the arts had declined and reinforced his commitment to the decorative arts, particularly as they were pursued in the precapitalist Middle Ages. The principles of the art of the Middle Ages, by definition decorative, expressive of the stonecutter, the illuminator, the weaver, became for Morris the principles on which to base a future art of a future socialist society.

Morris's preoccupation with the decorative arts led to a number of reiterated admonitions delivered in lectures to art students and to general audiences. A central one—an aesthetic commandment—is "Have nothing in your house that you do not know to be useful and think to be beautiful," and it defines one class of objects capable of expressing beauty. Although he does not spell out the implications, the grounding in functionalism sets limits on the material forms that can be regarded as beautiful. Pottery, for example, is included, but ornamental objets d'art presumably are not. As for painting, the admonition avoids the question of how to regard a picture on canvas. Morris's ambivalence toward easel painting in theory comes down on the positive side when he could regard a painted canvas as a wall decoration, as living architecture, which for Morris was the mother of all the other arts. Nevertheless, he strongly preferred walls to be decorated with wallpaper or simply whitewashed, and the potential decorative function of an easel painting in a nineteenth-century home remains in his discourse just that—a potential, and an ignored one. It should be added, however, that Morris had strong opinions, both positive and negative, about paintings in museums; he strongly supported art museums—indeed, museums in general—as repositories of the past, and he was also very much in favor of museums as sites for education. Nevertheless, the fact that most of the particular references to painting in his lectures and letters have to do with Pre-Raphaelite works is at once an expression of true admiration, of loyalty to friends who were Pre-Raphaelite painters (and who had also been praised by Ruskin), and a measure of how limited Morris's interest in oil painting was.

Another rule for Morris is that all forms be conceived in the mind of the artist before being committed to paper or other material, and that outline—his synonym for form—be definite; as an implicit corollary, outline should be regarded as prior to color, however important color may be in larger historical terms. Morris affirms the linear and rejects the painterly mode of creating images in color; and *image* in a discussion of Morris must be regarded as including such terms as *design* and *pattern*. There is also a clear antecedent in Morris's sinuous wallpaper designs based on stylized natural forms—flowers, vines, and leaves—to the approach to drawing of the aesthetic movement at the end of the century, particularly Aubrey Beardsley's sinuous lines creating "unnatural" human forms. Line, moreover, is for Morris the basis of mimesis, and mimesis is much involved for him in what art should do. There is a continuous admonition in his lectures to students, and indeed in letters to artists employed as illustrators of Kelmscott Press editions of Morris's own work, to "get it right"; and *right* invariably means depicting correct proportion in the human figure, rendering in accurate detail a building facade, and observing Ruskinian "truth to nature" in the depiction of leaves, flowers, and other vegetation. Yet, there was also in Morris's aesthetic, as in Ruskin's, a keen sense of pattern as abstraction from the natural—though still with heavy emphasis on outline—usually demonstrated in his practice as designer of wallpaper and chintz patterns.

All of the above is important for assembling Morris's aesthetic, but the most challenging and profound of his aesthetic ideas is drawn from—or leads to—his social and political egalitarianism, confirmed and reinforced by his commitment to socialism in 1883. All work done with pleasure is art, he asserts. This is a striking challenge to one of his other positions, and a contradiction of another. Pleasurable work that produced objects intended for the home, but useless there, would presumably not qualify, although Morris gets around this by asserting in his essays that it is impossible to get real pleasure from producing useless objects. As for outright contradiction, Morris advised several petitioners for his encouragement that it takes a special "gift" to draw patterns or the human figure, although he added—again, strikingly—that the pleasure of enjoying art was equal on any scale of human values to the pleasure of making art. Be it also said that nowhere is he on record as discouraging anyone from embroidery or textile weaving—if the fingers are nimble enough.

Carefully outlined forms; a commitment to functionalism, with emphasis on the decorative arts in the home; an implicit grounding of aesthetic experience in the material; mimesis in modern painting and in illustration; a faith that creativity is universal—that pleasure in work inspires the creative imagination in everyone: all of these inform Morris's aesthetic. These are constants, but as noted, the contradiction, variation, and extension are also there. The belief that the production of art depends on a "gift" contradicts the belief that creativity is universal, but Morris's compensatory assertion that one person's pleasure in enjoying a work of art is equal to another's pleasure in making a work, opens up an aesthetic of receptivity. In this respect, Morris's position is congenial, it should be added, with Walter Pater's viewer-centered aesthetic, but shifts away from Ruskin's stress on the "truth" inherent in a work of art and accessible only to a cultivated sensibility. Of course, when Ruskin generalizes about art he has high art in mind, and so for that matter does Pater, whereas Morris, when he generalizes, is thinking of the decorative arts (and at times of poetry). Nevertheless, the force of Morris's position is to democratize Pater's onlooker philosophy of art rather than to search, as Ruskin does, for essence.

As a poet, Morris wrote lyrics, brief dramatic verse, and long narrative poems. The models for his lyrics were John

Keats and Percy Bysshe Shelley; for his brief dramatic poems, Robert Browning (to some extent); and for the long narratives, Geoffrey Chaucer's work and the Icelandic poetic Eddas. For poetry, more than any other art, Morris denied that there was for him anything that could be called an aesthetic theory. Early in his career, while he was still an undergraduate at Oxford, occurred the famous incident in which he read his first poem to a group of friends, was praised by them, and answered, "Well, if this is poetry, it is very easy to write." His utterance epitomizes a lifelong attitude toward the writing of verse. Nevertheless, the assertion that he resisted naming an aesthetic of poetry should be qualified by observing that he strongly preferred rhymed to unrhymed verse and that as a writer he preferred composing long narrative poems to short, lyric ones. Although he hardly had praise for any poet other than Chaucer, his enthusiasm for *The Canterbury Tales* equaled what he felt for his other true love in verbal art, the novels of Walter Scott, Charles Dickens, and Alexandre Dumas the elder.

What Morris does enjoy in poetry is "incident," a term that instantly links together his ideas about verse, prose narrative, and illustrations for books—for the illuminated medieval manuscripts and early printed books he loved, and for those he produced and had illustrated at his Kelmscott Press. Significantly, his "truth to nature" in art is restricted, like Ruskin's, to the representation of vegetable nature. "Naturalism," as a literary phenomenon, he disliked (as did Ruskin). The great irony is that while he followed Ruskin and the Pre-Raphaelite painters in denouncing Sir Joshua Reynolds's assertion that painting should idealize the human face and form, Morris created only idealized protagonists for his romances (including *News from Nowhere*, his socialist romance). "Truth to nature" meant only truth to the forms and details of leaves, flowers, and the exterior world in general.

Arguably, however, and indeed as Jerome McGann has demonstrated, Morris's concern with the typography and page layout of his poems and romances, his revolutionizing the printing arts at the end of the nineteenth century through his own Kelmscott Press, demonstrate the profoundest kind of "naturalism" in literature of all. It demonstrates—indeed, constitutes—a recognition that books are material objects, and that pleasurably experiencing their visual and tactile materiality is an essential aspect of the aesthetic experience of reading, not an adjunct to it.

Nevertheless, there remains in Morris's practice and in his lectures on art some division along the visual/verbal line: partially different approaches to realism for each. The difficulty persists in attempting to find a perspective from which we might perceive a unified aesthetic theory in his lectures and his practice as an artist. Standing in the way is the difference between his insistence on the useful in the decorative arts ("have nothing in your home you do not know to be useful . . .") and the "useless" in poetry, epitomized by

Morris's self-description in the prologue to *The Earthly Paradise* (a long narrative poem written early in his career) as "the idle singer of an empty day" (although he later wrote socialist poems, too). Along the same dividing line, form comes before color in the making of patterns and images in general, but a setting for his prose romances that is vague, *seemingly* medieval, but only seemingly. Only as a reader, as author of *The Defence of Guenevere* (his early lyric and dramatic poems), and as translator and adapter of Icelandic sagas did Morris experience in verbal art a pleasure in characteristics akin to those he required for the decorative arts and book illustrations: sharply defined incidents against clearly rendered backgrounds; a minimum of sentiment; and, in the saga translations and adaptations, depictions of survival in a world in which humans and nature are treacherous—that is, a depiction of "truth" to both external and human nature: a kingly version of naturalism in characterization set against a sharply defined background.

Putting aside these achievements, which, given the many attributes of his narrative writing and the extent of it, represent in total only a few aspects of his verbal art, it can be said that Morris strove for directness and vigor in all his art but achieved these largely in his decorative designs for wallpapers, chintzes, and borders for pages and illustrations for the Kelmscott Press volumes. For the most part, the verbal arts in reality were for him a letting go rather than a screwing himself up to pitch: writing poetry and prose romances was for Morris an escape from the rigor of "form." Of course, his verbal compositions have their own forms. There is in them an air of ease and a feeling of verbal plenitude. These are determining characteristics, as valid of assessment as aesthetic characteristics as any other. But the forcefulness that one feels when looking at his visual patterns is not there.

There is, too, Morris's view of himself as a writer. If it is at variance with his practice, it is nevertheless essential to add this view to the information from which we derive his aesthetic theory. Perhaps because Pater in the late nineteenth century had introduced into aesthetic discourse the term "euphuism" in a laudatory way, Morris was at pains to assert his freedom from "euphuism," expressing pleasure to Theodore Watts-Dunton for declaring him guiltless of it (as well as of "didacticism" and "the curse of rhetoric"), in a review of one of Morris's prose romances, *The Wood beyond the World*.

This romance is lush and eloquent and moves at an easy pace, and indeed is characterized by what some might regard as archaic and therefore artificial language. Morris, however, would deny this, and the denial would be plausible. A mimetic absorption into his own work of the language of medieval romance was natural for him. All told, Morris regarded himself as writing "naturally," as doing analogously in prose what he and Ruskin believed painters should do—remain "true to nature"—and what he believed pattern designers (like himself) should begin by doing, however flattened and thus abstracted the forms in the pattern derived from nature ultimately were.

There is finally, despite difficulty, a large, embracing view enabling a perspective that discloses a coherent aesthetic theory. Morris was the epitome of his own seemingly divided aesthetic made whole. Whereas for him people to an extent were divided for aesthetic purposes into the categories of those capable of making art and those capable only of enjoying it as onlookers or users, he reunited the roles in his own actions as both designer and writer of romances. The pleasure he took in designing and in writing shared an etiology. They were both preceded by the pleasure Morris took in seeing the medieval patterns and reading the medieval tales he often used as a basis for his own art. Observer and maker, he testified that pleasure for him meant any relationship at all to art, and that both visual design and verbal incident in his work resulted from the pleasure of recalling design and incident in the art of the past and the pleasure of then transforming them—and thus making art that was new. "Pleasure" in making is Morris's substitute for "inspired vision," "genius," and even for imagination, when this last is, in use, too closely allied with genius, a term Morris never employed to express his admiration for any artist's ability and achievement. The modesty of pleasure's claim lays the ground of an egalitarian aesthetic in the verbal and the visual arts and in a way that reaches for a simultaneous embrace of both.

Yet, still impeaching Morris's democratic aesthetic is the distinct feature that characterizes his own art: the vigor of his designs and of some passages at least in his narrative poems, long and short. It creates the tension, the presence of compressed energy, so characteristic of his designs and of his best poetry—and not only energy but aggressive energy, a fact about himself and his art that he did not see. It is the aggressive energy within his work that pulls together his verbal art, in which undercurrents of violence or longing underlie seemingly languorous episodes, and his decorative work, in which the vigor of his lines makes immanent a will that to an extent bends nature—the lines of natural objects—to itself and that thus substitutes creative vision for truth to nature. Finally, this powerful stylizing impulse, profound in its implications, and among other things replacing "truth to nature" with a calm violence toward it, puts Morris's aesthetic practice into the Aesthetic movement, which he ignored or reproved, but helped to found, and in which he continued as a presence recognized by fellow members of the movement. That Morris was both a socialist and an inspiration to the aesthetic movement, particularly to its younger members in the 1890s, is not a contradiction. It is an invitation to see the prophetic quality of his vision: his understanding that aesthetic sensibility is part of the definition of the human and that a political reconstituting of society to realize more fully human life must mean, whatever else it means, reconstituting opportunities for expression and gratification of that sensibility.

[*See also* Design.]

BIBLIOGRAPHY

Works by Morris

The Collected Works. 24 vols. London, 1910–1915; reprint, New York, 1966. See vol. 22, "The Art of the People," pp. 28–50; "The Beauty of Life," pp. 51–80.

"The Ideal Book." In *The Ideal Book,* edited by William S. Peterson, pp. 67–73. Berkeley, 1982.

The Collected Letters of William Morris. Edited by Norman Kelvin. 4 vols. Princeton, N.J., 1984–1996.

Other Sources

Auerbach, Eric. *Mimesis: The Representation of Reality in Western Literature.* Translated by Willard R. Trask. Princeton, 1953.

Christ, Carol T. *Victorian and Modern Poetics.* Chicago, 1984.

Eagleton, Terry. *The Ideology of the Aesthetic.* Oxford and Cambridge, Mass., 1990.

Jackson, Holbrook. *The Eighteen Nineties.* London, 1913; reprint, London, 1988.

MacCarthy, Fiona. *William Morris: A Life for Our Time.* London, 1994.

Martin, Wallace. *Recent Theories of Narrative.* Ithaca, N.Y., 1986.

McGann, Jerome. "Thing to Mind: The Materialist Aesthetic of William Morris." In *Black Riders: The Visible Language of Modernism,* pp. 45–75. Princeton, N.J., 1993.

Nochlin, Linda. *Realism.* Harmondsworth, England, 1971.

Pater, Walter. "The Earthly Paradise" (unsigned review). *Westminster Review* (October 1868): 300–312. Final section reprinted as the "Conclusion" to *The Renaissance* (1873); reprinted in *William Morris: The Critical Heritage,* edited by Peter Faulkner (London and Boston, 1973), pp. 79–92.

Pater, Walter. "Preface." In *The Renaissance* (1873). London, 1910.

Ruskin, John. *The Works of John Ruskin.* 39 vols. Edited by E. T. Cook and Alexander Wedderburn. London and New York, 1903–1912. See "The Nature of Gothic" in vol. 10.2, *The Stones of Venice,* chap. 6, pp. 180–269, and "Pre-Raphaelitism" in vol. 12, pp. 339–393.

Tillyard, S. K. *The Impact of Modernism, 1900–1920: Early Modernism and the Arts and Crafts Movement in Edwardian England.* London and New York, 1988.

Trilling, Lionel. "Aggression and Utopia: A Note on William Morris's 'News from Nowhere.'" In *The Last Decade: Essays and Reviews, 1965–1975,* edited by Diana Trilling, pp. 148–159. New York, 1979.

Wölfflin, Heinrich. *Principles of Art History: The Problem of the Development of Style in Later Art.* Translated by M. D. Hottinger. New York, 1932.

Yeats, W. B. "The Happiest of the Poets." In *Essays and Introductions,* pp. 53–64. New York, 1961.

NORMAN KELVIN

MOVIES. *See* Film.

MULTIMEDIA. Multimedia combines sound, graphics, video, text, and animation to present interactive stories, games, and educational materials. Electronic storage—whether on CD-ROM discs or on the Internet—allows symphonies, films, and even whole museums to exist online with instant access to background, history, and relevant commentary. Hypertext (nonlinear linkage) encourages browsing through encyclopedic knowledge bases. The interactive nature of multimedia requires a high degree of user participation, making it a powerful tool for training and education, as well as for new forms of communication. Designing multimedia requires collaborative work among artists and software developers. Because of its interactivity and nonclosure, multimedia challenges the aesthetics of telic, author-centered artworks. At the same time, the digital basis of multimedia raises concerns about its applications in legal proceedings, and its psychological power raises concerns about its impact on young people who play interactive games or browse the World Wide Web on the Internet. The shift of sensibility from contemplative to interactive modes suggests a cultural change that reaches far beyond the usual domain of the fine arts.

Definition in Historical Context. Interactivity is a key feature of digital multimedia. But long before multimedia, artwork in the twentieth century showed an interactive side. As early as the 1950s, some television programs experimented with interactive media. One CBS show in the 1950s, *Winky Dink and You,* instructed children to cover the TV screen with a thin sheet of plastic so they could draw with color crayons on televised images. In the 1960s, the term *multimedia,* along with cognates like intermedia or mixed media, characterized the work of art groups like USCO in Garnersville, New York, who combined films, tapes, and slides in their audiovisual performances. The mixed media of the 1960s flooded the senses with electronic multiscreen audiovisual "worlds" and strobe-light environments. Mixed-media artists drew upon what they took to be Marshall McLuhan's ideas about the sophisticated tribalism created by electronic worlds. In the 1970s, artists introduced "happenings" or elements of spontaneous audience participation, much as John Cage had done in music performance, and much like the action painters of the 1950s who emphasized dynamic process. Some of these media happenings later fed into the artificial realities explored by pioneers of virtual reality like Myron Krueger.

By the 1980s, the personal computer enabled artists to combine several media on the same digital platform. Instead of patching single films, slides, or recordings, the artist could integrate vast amounts of audio and video stored on computers, including whole movies, libraries of text, and historical video clips, as well as recordings that span music history. In the 1980s, researchers at Apple Computer began using the term *media integration* to describe the use of digital sound, graphics, and text on a single desktop. Eventually, *multimedia* became an umbrella term for applying computer power to integrate a wide range of material for interactive use. By the 1990s, multimedia had spread to game arcades, compact-disc educational programs, museum tours,

real estate guides. The multimedia approach of the World Wide Web browsing software made the Internet computer network a commercial gold rush in the mid-1990s. The David Sarnoff Research Laboratory, among others, has been developing interactive television that combines interactive multimedia with traditional television.

The essential tool for navigating multimedia is hypertext. Hypertext represents an important concept for designing information, but the aesthetic implementations of hypertext vary considerably. Originally conceived by Vannevar Bush in 1945, then detailed by Theodor Nelson in the 1960s, hypertext makes it possible to choose among alternate pathways in a data landscape. The user can choose whatever seems at the moment to be the relevant pathway. The term *hypertext* (coined by Nelson) originally referred to an information aesthetics for written literature, but soon it came to characterize a broader navigation tool for multimedia, sometimes called hypermedia. The same cognitive aesthetics for data-linked literature could be applied to any digitized sensory material. Hypermedia provides the user with software links that cross-reference a body of digitized data. The user can then choose to explore layers of meaning at any particular juncture. A backtracking or history function enables the user to review or revisit a previous series of choices. While the artist provides the initial set of links, the user has the option of activating the links in any order at will. In this way, the sequential structure of linear media— traditional books, films, music—becomes a subset of hypermedia. Hypermedia offers aesthetic freedom in controlling the art experience and calls for a new relationship between the artist, the artwork, and the art audience.

Relation to Tradition. Multimedia undercuts the traditional relationship between the art object and the art audience. Traditionally, the audience receives the artwork as an object to contemplate or as information to consume passively. Interactive multimedia undermines this unilateral notion of media. The user's own choices become an intrinsic part of the multimedia experience. Likewise, with the artist's autonomy. While the artist must still shape the material or software for contemplation, the multimedia designer must at every step take into account the user's involvement. The unilateral artistic decision changes into an ongoing consultation with users. Instead of buyers or viewers, the art audience becomes participants. Because of its interactive nature, multimedia falls under the ecological, holistic paradigm, undercutting both the isolated software designer and the unilateral communications media. In this way, technology combines with art to achieve a synthesis similar to the ancient Greek techē: not a one-way technology for manipulating attention but an art shaped by usage. What also distinguishes hypermedia with its mixture of sound, graphics, video, and animation is the user's access to nonlinear background material. A score, for example, can include a video clip of a film while at the same time it can offer additional materials not included in the author's print of the film. Extra material, such as outtakes and documentation, can illuminate the initial conception. Related artworks can exist in juxtaposition to reveal the substructure on which the work stands. The hypertextual selection of relevant content makes it possible to navigate documentary material that would otherwise be daunting in its bulk. A listener might want, for example, to hear to the fifteen hours of Richard Wagner's Ring opera, isolate individual leitmotivs linked to their musical occurrences, look at the vocal score, read commentaries synchronized to the music, and see full-color images from historical performances—all of which is possible today on a single CD-ROM. With hypermedia, the user can choose to explore different sensory modes at the click of a button in a convenient format that offers instant searches. The multimedia artist can create linked materials that make it possible to know an artwork from many angles. What, therefore, distinguishes multimedia is not the combination of sensory materials but rather the underlying digital structure and the high-speed hypertextual access.

Special Problems. Like real-time experience, multimedia authoring permits the serendipity of choices and the branches of multiple associations—something excluded by the closed form of traditional art objects. Since the ancient Greeks, Western art sought to satisfy the viewer by presenting a well-made object, something finished and complete. Art promised polished structures, whether through symmetrical patterns or through reversal and recapitulation. Drama, according to Aristotle, imitates a completed action, and Thomas Aquinas saw in *integritas* the hallmark of beauty. Only later, with Immanuel Kant and the Romantics, did open-ended infinity—under the guise of the "sublime"— enter into the art experience. Multimedia brings out the indeterminacy of meaning and what John Cage promoted as the tychic, oleatory aspects of experience. Chance and change can translate into the cognitive disorder and information overload. So, to achieve aesthetic unity, multimedia may draw on atmospherics (opera's *tinta*), on Wagner's leitmotifs, or on menu-like overviews that provide a bridge between the interpreter and the indefinite, multifaceted art object. Future multimedia may evolve its own special integrity, when the artwork appears in the stored collaboration that has evolved from both the participants' response to the art object and the author's postulates. As in chaos theory, the artist's starting point functions less like a final cause and more like an initial starting condition. The artist's design "causes" the evolving product in an important but not in a final or deterministic sense.

A shift to interactive multimedia throughout a society implies a broader shift in how human intelligence functions. The shift brings with it changes in education and in how knowledge gets shaped. Since Plato, the model of human intellect has revolved around contemplative wholeness, the ability to sustain a fixed mental vision. The epistemic function was largely identified with the ability to integrate experience into a single, differentiated whole (Plato's idea or *eidos*). Multimedia manifests the movement of modern and postmodern culture away from the contemplative spectator who can grasp wholes. Knowledge in the interactive mode works as a collage of images, sounds, photos, and bits of information. The fragmentation faced by multimedia has precedents in early and late modern art. One example comes from music composition.

Music composers, at least since Richard Wagner, confront the question of wholeness and closure. For centuries, the harmonic scale supported the melodic line of Western music so that a melodic series conveys an internal feeling of completion as its last note sounds, usually a tonic note of the established key or a note harmonically close to the tonic. Classical stylists like Wolfgang Amadeus Mozart or Ludwig van Beethoven play with the ear's anticipation of harmonic closure, injecting wit, elegance, and varying moods that exploit the listener's harmonic expectations. Wagner's operas pushed this musical legacy to the edge. Instead of closed pieces connected by spoken recitative passages, Wagner presented hours of a seamless, uninterrupted unity, an "endless melody." The *unendliche Melodie* preserves buoyancy and flow by continuously raising and shifting the ear's expectations so that the harmonic line seems to hover without settling or closing. Wagner used harmonic tonality against itself to the point at which the ear detects forward momentum but, just before arriving at the final tonic, the tonal line subtly slides into another harmonic scale. The effect is one of continuously ambiguous tonality in an endless musical process. Wagner's Ring cycle weaves together fifteen hours of music with recurrent motifs and dramatic sound textures. Inheritors of Wagner's style, such as Richard Strauss, turned symphonic music into tone poems held loosely together by floating harmonies, instrumental color, and recurrent figures.

Twentieth-century music continued Wagner's quest for greater melodic freedom and nonclosure. Arnold Schoenberg and the second Viennese school abandoned tonal closure in principle. Schoenberg advanced the flow of free sequences, of the unending series. The hostile public reaction to the Schoenberg school can serve as a warning to multimedia authors who face analogous problems of compositional unity. The pleasure of recognizing an entire pattern may belong intrinsically to the contemplative, compositional act of mind. If multimedia manifests a deeper shift of cultural energies away from the contemplative habit, then perhaps the artist need not face the opposition that greeted modern atonal music. Nevertheless, multimedia fosters a scanning/sampling cognitive mode that is sure to cause discomfort for traditional epistemic temperaments.

When viewed online, multimedia often functions under metaphors of place, space, and architecture rather than under the more liquid metaphors of music. Multimedia then shades into cyberspace. The issue of contemplative attention appears as the search for habitable places and for Internet "home pages." Artists and critics vacillate between the dynamic power of moving images and more stable depth rendered by immersive images and alphabetic text.

One further issue for multimedia artists is how to preserve the credibility and authenticity of content. Already, lawyers and judges use multimedia to present evidence in court. Previously, photographs and videotape served to establish evidence in courts of law. Now, with the application of multimedia to organize legal materials, special standards of authentication seem necessary. Digital information is inherently manipulable. Digital photos, video, text, and music do not inherently preserve real-world references; they can easily be altered. Digital signals consist of numbers on a computer, and any number can be altered without a trace of its having been so. Film studios currently digitize analog films and in seconds can convert night scenes to day scenes, and vice versa. The security and authenticity of data remain troubling issues.

[*See also* Artificial Intelligence and Aesthetics; Computer Art; Cyberspace; Digital Media; Hypertext; Medium; *and* Virtual Reality.]

BIBLIOGRAPHY

Barrett, Edward, ed. *Sociomedia: Multimedia, Hypermedia, and the Social Construction of Knowledge.* Cambridge, Mass., 1992.

Davis, Douglas. *Art and the Future: A History-Prophecy of the Collaboration between Science, Technology, and Art.* New York, 1973.

Heim, Michael. *Virtual Realism: The Art of Emerging Technology.* New York and Oxford, 1998.

Landow, George P. *Hypertext: The Convergence of Contemporary Critical Theory and Technology.* Baltimore, 1992.

Laurel, Brenda, ed. *The Art of Human-Computer Interface Design.* Reading, Mass., 1990.

Mitchell, William J. *City of Bits: Space, Place, and the Infobahn.* Cambridge, Mass., 1995.

MICHAEL HEIM

MUSEUMS. [*To explore the history, development, and current status of art museums and their role in the history of art and aesthetics, this entry comprises three essays:*

Museums and Aesthetics

Museology

Sociological Perspectives on Museums

Art museums were first introduced around the same time as aesthetics emerged, so their histories are intertwined, as the first essay demonstrates by tracing both from the eighteenth century up to the present. The second and third essays explain how museums have been understood in the disciplines of art history and sociology. See also Art Market; Art World; Artist; Cultural Studies; *and* Law and Art, *article on* Cultural Property.]

Museums and Aesthetics

The word *museum* originally designated a place consecrated to the nine Muses or the arts over which they presided. The most famous one was founded in fourth-century (BCE) Alexandria by the Macedonian ruler, Ptolemy Soter, and maintained for centuries by succeeding generations of Ptolemies and Caesars. This structure, like some contemporary multiplex arts and humanities institutions, included a library, a scholarly research center, and a collection of antiquities. Between that time and the present, however, museums have undergone profound conceptual changes, and they are currently in a state of rapid transition. Defined in 1983 under the United States Museum Services Act, which created the Institute of Museum Services, a museum is defined as "a public or private nonprofit agency or institution organized on a permanent basis for essentially educational or esthetic purposes which, utilizing a professional staff, owns or utilizes tangible objects, cares for them, and exhibits them to the public on a regular basis." Art museums are a special subcategory, more recent in origin than collections of other artifacts and natural specimens, and somewhat more narrowly defined as "permanent, nonprofit institution(s) essentially educational and aesthetic in purpose, with professional staff, which acquires or owns works of art, cares for them, interprets them, and exhibits them to the public on some regular schedule."

Following the vagaries of historic fashion, museums have concentrated with greater or less intensity on one or another of their defining elements. At the present time, education is a primary focus, and, while the enculturation of a segment of the public has always been a component of the museum's mission, pedagogy today has a more democratic scope than at earlier times. Like many public institutions, museums have become less assertive of their own authority and more responsive to claims of subjective diversity and independent knowledge systems. These adjustments are still in process and are affecting both the procedures by which museums acquire and dispose of objects, and their approach to human resources of the past and present. As cultural institutions, museums are not exempt from the pressures of politics and technological change, and their function of social mediation has become a topic of public examination as well as considerable self-scrutiny.

The modern European concept of the museum emerged after the Crusades, elaborating an apparently universal human inclination to accumulate and hoard things that satisfy interest and provide pleasure. Private collection is the foundation of the modern museum, but its institutionalization is marked by a shift from sheer gratification and glorification of the individual collector to the commemoration of what are perceived as collective social values. Most important, museums, through their collections, function to create and propagate social knowledge and to ground its validity in a system of meanings.

Renaissance princes, prelates, and commercial traders throughout Italy, northern Europe, and England sought enthusiastically to know and learn everything about a world whose resources were newly opened to them. They collected rarities of art and nature, experimented and made discoveries, and assembled those materials in which they were interested in designated spaces for study and display. These spaces, variously called "cabinets of curiosities," "Wunderkammern," "Kunstkammern," "galleria," or "musaea," depending on their location and content, were the forerunners of today's museums. Art collections were somewhat specialized aesthetically, but included the accoutrements of religious observation and military expedition as well as pictures, books, and statuary. They were not meant so much as celebrations of artistic genius, but rather as testimony to the power, wisdom, splendor, and taste for antiquity of the collector. Collections of Greek and Roman antiquities were especially prized as testimony to the universality of human nature and to the splendor of its earthly achievements. Cabinets of curiosities might also contain aesthetic artifacts, but were wider in scope, including all sorts of organic and inorganic substances, both common instances and "freaks of nature." These, as the word *musaeum* also entailed, represented the categorizing cast of mind by which the assembled collection was organized. The museum was to reflect not only the order of human achievement but also divinely ordained relationships such that a microcosmic model of universal nature could be privately possessed.

In the seventeenth century, these collections became widely renowned scholarly resources for what would become modern science. The philosopher Gottfried Wilhelm Leibniz conceived "An Odd Thought concerning a New Sort of Exhibition" (1675), which was a combination scientific academy and world's fair that would feature a succession of scientific exhibitions, inventions, and models, in addition to the conventional assortment of games, military exercises, animal programs, theater, concerts, athletic performances, pictures, craft displays, and entertainment. Devised to "open people's eyes, stimulate inventions, present beautiful sights, instruct people with an endless number of useful or ingenious novelties . . . [it] would become a museum of everything that could be imagined." No less important, the museum would come to represent all that could be known, physically displaying the intelligible order of reality encased in the clarifying miniature of the museum shelves and architecture. Gradually, princely collections were augmented and rationalized. The encyclopedic idea of the world in microcosm gave way to a new typology as scholarly disciplines split and discriminated between the natural sciences, history, and the human production of art and artifact. The collections contributed to the growth of knowledge and also grew as a result of it. No longer sustainable as private, many were turned into public institutions by royal decree or through affiliation with institutions of higher learning.

By the end of the eighteenth century, museums had assumed a role of national unification. Napoleon created a monumental museum system, freely accessible to all, and with the mission to inculcate within the individual soul a sense of national identity and patriotic pride that would powerfully proclaim the illustriousness of the French Republic. The Louvre, previously a palace of kings, became the Museum of the Republic, dedicated to transforming collected material goods into a collective spirit of citizenship that culturally reified the new nation. The celebration of great works of art created by newly revered great artists also spawned the new professions of art historian and museum curator. Their civic responsibility was to instill a sense of community among citizens and between them and their historic ancestors whose visible endeavor had paved the way to present greatness.

Most of the major American museums were founded in the mid-nineteenth century with a similar spiritual intent. Whereas natural history museums were to edify, art museums were to uplift, since art was proclaimed to have intrinsically redemptive power. This quasi-religious character of art was modulated in the 1880s into a more secular therapeutic function that continued to mark the American museum. Wealthy Americans aspired to possess the "avenues of transcendental escape" from all parts of the earth, but also bestowed them munificently on a deserving public. American philanthropists further promoted the values represented by the objects they cherished by funding the educational and cultural means of their transmission to the general public. Serving as trustees of the institutions they funded, they could maintain authority over cultural expression and were able, without apparently compromising democracy, to define the limits of taste that museums encompassed.

Modernism, with its formalist aesthetic doctrine, only gave the socially embedded philosophy of the museum a new twist; for while it advanced the doctrine of art's autonomy, it continued also to hold that art is morally beneficial. The ideologues of the twentieth-century museum still consider art spiritually regenerative, but repudiate propagandistic didacticism or the representation of familiar moral content. The certifiable presence of an object as art in the museum suffices to cancel out whatever (mundane or sublime) message it might carry, and to replace it with pristine and supervenient "aesthetic value." The educational benefit thereby conveyed is thus neither historically instructive nor conventionally moral. It is presumed to be of a higher order, possessing universal aesthetic quality that purportedly makes a better person of whoever experiences it. Such aestheticism is repudiated by postmodernists and others who doubt art's universality and deny the museum's ability to decontextualize it. The modernist ideal, however, still in-

MUSEUMS: Museums and Aesthetics. *Musée du Louvre, Paris; panoramic view.* (Photograph courtesy of Alinari/Art Resource, New York.)

fuses the view that the art museum's chief goal and obligation are to inculcate visual—not cultural—literacy.

A seemingly opposite objective, that of entertainment, has also been ascribed to museums and has coexisted with their educational mission almost from the beginning. The first American museum, intended by its founder, Charles Wilson Peale, to be a "school of useful knowledge" as well as "rational amusement," was purchased after his death by Moses Kimball and P. T. Barnum, of circus fame. Perhaps the uneasy alliance of spectacle and scholarship that followed is an inevitable consequence of financial dependence. Museums are condemned to beggary. Although charged with the oversight of enormous wealth and capital investment, American museums are quasi-legally confined to nonprofit status. Government support attracts the charge of political pressure or, more insidiously, the risk of self-censorship within the art world. The pressure to please and not to offend has caused museums to vacillate precariously

between a style of presentation designed for commercial success and scholarly research. Moreover, as the opportunities for collection building have grown scarcer and more competitive, attention to exhibition and audience development has increased. This, too, reflects an epistemic shift as museums assume a more theatrical stance, replacing didactic presentation with selective narration.

Curation, traditionally the central museum profession that combines sleuthing for objects with research and day-to-day care, has become both more custodial and more dramatically interpretive. Charged with identifying, gathering, and preserving culturally significant materials, curators face compounded practical and philosophical restrictions. Art museums are constrained by conflicting aesthetic and art-historical paradigms. The taxonomic legislation that construes "fine art" as distinguished from other artifacts is arbitrary, and the content of art museums is dictated as much by the history of donors' tastes as by discriminating research. Art history, which is premised on the supposition of a prior recognition of art, is itself an artifact of the museum, produced by and in the museum by successive generations of curators, exhibitors, and viewers. At the close of the twentieth century, the ideology of historical progress has given way to relativism and contextualism, and concurrently there are vast disagreements over what belongs in the art museum.

Curatorial judgment is neither pure aesthetic sensibility nor sheer historical expertise, although these are both necessary ingredients of professional ability. Curation does require technical skills of authentication, however these must be refined to match revised ideas on the nature of authorship. As long as "works of art" referred to discrete items of human-made reality in accordance with the objectivist views of the Enlightenment, they might be thought "collectibles"; but artworks are now more likely to be apprehended as unstable components in a metanarrative that bespeaks a multiplicity of interpretive intentions. Museum exhibitions are metalevel expressive performances in which the displayed objects collectively activate meaning potentials.

Audiences also bring agendas with them to the museum, and these may not coincide with that proposed by the curator(s), whose authority has shrunk to that of a single culturally inflected consciousness. One consequence of the plurality of interpretive schemata is that they cannot be assessed according to one normative evidentiary standard. Not truth but the intensity of engendered experience becomes the test of their reality. Museums, as a result, are competing with other providers of spectacle and "virtual reality" for the attention of the public. Presented with objects in dramatic context, visitors are creatively challenged to complete the structure of their meaning. In doing so, they are guided in part by history, by aesthetic conventions, and by class and cultural traditions, but also by a host of personal and local factors that disrupt the solidity of these cohesive social forces. This dialectical confrontation enculturates visitors, helping them forge a sense of their own identity while it furthers the consecration of the museum objects. As legitimating institutions, museums stabilize the identity of their holdings, not by precepts, but by manipulating a "semantic repertoire" found in things and their uses.

Estimates of the worldwide number of museums as of 1992 ran as high as twenty-five thousand—eight thousand of them located in the United States alone. But, notwithstanding their worldwide proliferation and growing popularity, museums are under stress. They are struggling to promote vivid experiences competitive with those purveyed by theme parks and other forms of entertainment. Postmodernists and neo-Marxists implicate museums within the capitalist property system that commodifies even knowledge and values. Museums do project and fabricate reified meaning; that is what constitutes the objects they collect. Yet, while these objects are not transparently real—or perhaps for that very reason—their historic and context-based understanding, negotiated through discourse, can help human societies communicate and establish bonds with one another. Ordinarily, the spoken and written word is privileged in the transmission of meaning. Museums have a powerful role to play in this regard; for they alone privilege objects—responsibly approached, preserved with care and affection, and studied respectfully from multiple points of reference.

BIBLIOGRAPHY

Alexander, Edward P. *Museums in Motion: An Introduction to the History and Functions of Museums.* Nashville, Tenn., 1979.

Bloom, Joel N., Earl A. Powell III, Ellen Cochran Hicks, and Mary Ellen Munley. *Museums for a New Century: A Report of the Commission on Museums for a New Century.* Washington, D.C., 1984.

Burt, Nathaniel. *Palaces for the People: A Social History of the American Art Museum.* Boston, 1977.

Hughes, Robert. *Culture of Complaint: The Fraying of America.* New York and Oxford, 1993.

Impey, Oliver, and Arthur MacGregor, eds. *The Origins of Museums: The Cabinet of Curiosities in Sixteenth- and Seventeenth-Century Europe.* Oxford, 1985.

Karp, Ivan, and Steven D. Lavine, eds. *Exhibiting Cultures: The Poetics and Politics of Museum Display.* Washington, D.C., 1991.

Lee, Sherman E. *Past, Present, East and West.* New York, 1983.

Malaro, Marie C. *A Legal Primer on Managing Museum Collections.* Washington, D.C., 1985.

Pearce, Susan M. *Museums, Objects, and Collections: A Cultural Study.* Washington, D.C., 1993.

Taylor, Francis Henry. *The Taste of Angels: A History of Art Collecting from Rameses to Napoleon.* Boston, 1948.

HILDE HEIN

Museology

Since antiquity the term *museum* has had encyclopedic associations and has not been connected exclusively either to words or things. At times referring to places set aside for study and contemplation, the word has equally denoted a collection of objects suitable for study, as well as a method—often closely associated with the medieval arts of memory—of formatting objects and information in space.

The most familiar modern usage of the word—indicating a particular kind of institution or building devoted primarily to the ordered storage and display of artifactual or natural objects—dates largely from the European Enlightenment. The same eighteenth century that saw the rise of aesthetic philosophy in Europe also saw the invention of civic institutions (to which the term *museum* came to be universally applied over time) that sought to balance the scholarly needs of specialists with the more broadly based instruction, enlightenment, and social indoctrination of a general (and in most cases a newly enfranchised) populace or citizenry.

This form of mass pedagogy that came to be known as the "museum movement" in the nineteenth century gained powerful momentum in Europe and America, under both state and private patronage, in concert with the growth of the modern nation-state and its supportive ideologies of ethnic homogeneity and uniqueness. By the beginning of the twentieth century hundreds of museum institutions were in operation or were being established, not only in Europe, but in virtually every country touched by European colonization and expansion.

In the most general and fundamental sense, a museum is an epistemological technology: an instrument for producing, ordering, and legitimizing historical knowledge. Sharing certain methods with other modern institutions and disciplines, museums have been closely associated with and indispensable to many professional fields, from art history to ethnography to zoology, over the past two centuries.

Museology and the museum's ancillary discursive practices and professions—such as art history and criticism; art theory and aesthetic philosophy; connoisseurship and art marketing; and the heritage or infotainment industry—are interdependent facets of the distinctively modernist ideology of representational adequacy. Within such a framework, specimens distinguished and naturalized by the formatting of information are presumed to make present or *re*present in a determinate manner historical circumstances taken to preexist their portrayal in exhibitionary space.

Museums are most commonly understood today as repositories of objects of historical significance whose spatial deployment simulates the historical ambience or genealogical development of a form, theme, style, or artistic technique native to and expressive of a person or people. In some cases, museums are constru(ct)ed as portraying the developmental evolution or historical progress of an artist, people, nation, race, or ethnic group through objects taken as uniquely characteristic.

More generally, the association of objects in a museum constitutes a system of representation with dramaturgical implications. The historical or evolutionary import of a specimen is a function of its syntactic connections and contrasts in museological space: its position in a series or its place in a synoptic tableau. Museums stage historical narratives through the associative juxtapositions of objects: structural contiguities explicitly or implicitly simulating linked series of historical events over time. The series of objects is legible insofar as it is palpably genealogical in some sense: if it may be read as a set of causal relationships in one or more dimensions. These may be thematic, stylistic, functional; or they may simulate, reflect, or symbolize steps or grades in the evolution, progress, or descent of a person, people or species, or of a scientific or technical problem.

At the same time, museum specimens may be staged so as to imply certain kinds of causal relationships to their makers or sources, appearing to reconstitute a semblance of past or absent circumstances. As such, they may be legible as relics uniquely evocative of their sources—which can be

anything from an individual maker to a society, age, or milieu. In short, a museum (of any kind) is an instrument for the articulation of continuity in variation and variation in continuity: for the management of change and the control of difference. It is most clearly understood, historically, in its fuller sense as both a distinct institution for the spatial deployment and association of objects (of all kinds) and a practice or discipline for the formatting of causal and associative information, applicable to a wide variety of modern institutions and professions.

The nature and status of museum specimens themselves may vary with the type of item and museum, as well as the circumstances of its stagecraft. Various facets may be dominant or subordinate in a given situation, and the same item may play different epistemic and semiotic roles in different settings. In what follows, attention will be given primarily to art museum objects.

Perhaps the most powerful agency by which the enterprise of museology has been successful in its virtually universal colonization of the world's cultures has been its naturalization of a totalizing notion of "art" as a pan-human phenomenon. As one of the most remarkable and powerful of modern European inventions, art—the art of art history—has been one of the most effective instruments for the retroactive rewriting of the history of human societies.

The idea of art as a universal phenomenon provided nineteenth-century racial and ethnic theorists, historians of culture, and proponents of nationalism and folk identity with a standard of measurement applicable to questions of individual or group mentality, cognitive capacity, or relative progress in ethics, technology, philosophy, or civilization. Art came to be the paradigm of all production from the beginnings of the Industrial Revolution onward—its ideal horizon, and a standard against which to measure all forms of manufacture—as well as a paradigmatic instrument for the articulation and maintenance of individual and social identities.

Within the specular order of the museum, the work of art is an object that is simultaneously an instrument: both what is museologically staged and discursively cited, and the framework of study itself. As with the term *history* (denoting equally a disciplinary practice of writing—historiography—and the referential field or object of that scriptural practice), "art" is most clearly understood in its fuller modern sense as both the instrumentality or metalanguage of the museum's historiographical and psychic confabulations, and the framed domain of objects itself. Since the Enlightenment delineation of an aesthetic dimension of sensory phenomena as an object of attention in its own right, comprising the obverse of the phenomenon of "fetishism" postulated for certain non-European societies, art came to constitute a powerful method of organizing whole fields of activity so as to render legible and natural certain notions of the social subject and its agency.

Since the eighteenth century, museums have been heterotopic sites within social space that provide subjects with some

MUSEUM: Museology. *Guggenheim Museum, Bilbao, Spain.* (Photograph by David Heald; copyright 1997 by the Solomon R. Guggenheim Foundation, New York; used by permission.)

of the means to simulate mastery of their lives while compensating for life's contradictions and confusions. What this has entailed since then has been nothing less than the disciplining of whole populations through a desire-driven interaction with objects that were "object lessons" in at least two principal ways.

They were, first, documentary indexes of a history of the world and its people, construed as teleological dramaturgy (evolution or social progress), as having a direction and point and leading up to the spectator in the present, at the apex of this development; second, they were metaphoric simulacra of a variety of subject positions that might be admired, desired, emulated, or rejected. Just as the museum object came to serve as a synthesizing paradigm or perspective on the complex evolution of attitudes, values, styles, or peoples, so also did the new modern social subject itself come to be constituted as an anamorphic perspective on the bits and pieces of its own life and experience. The art museum object became a screen for a dramaturgy of the desiring self.

The semiotic character of this art museum object has had a distinctly hybrid status, staged (as it has been since the late eighteenth century without substantial change) in a spatiotemporal framework of oscillating determinacy and causality.

On the one hand, the object's significance exists within a network of associations defined by formal or thematic relationships: it is similar to or distinct from other comparable objects. Staged as a specimen of a class of like objects that may or may not be physically present in the same space, and each of which seems to provide evidence for the progressive solution to similar problems of construction or representation, the object's meaning is a function of its position in a universal art-historical evolution. On the other hand, it is foregrounded as unique and irreplaceable, its significance rooted in expressive properties metaphorically related to its maker or source. The form of the work is commonly construed as the figure of its "truth"—a truth expressive of the vision, intentions, mentality, or character of the maker or source.

In art-historical exegesis and museological dramaturgy, the museum object is thus simultaneously referential and differential in character. This simultaneity, however, is akin to that of an optical illusion, wherein there is an oscillating determinacy such that either one or the other facet is foregrounded at any one time, only to be subject to a perpetual slippage or alternation with its other.

In the art museum, referentiality is paradoxically both the foreground and background to differentiality, and vice versa, in an oscillation that can never finally be fixed in place, and that itself mirrors the paradoxical and ambivalent status of the viewing subject. Historically, it has been the very slippage or incompleteness of any one mode of art-historical explanation that has literally kept disciplinary discourse in play for so long, by the perennial oscillation between formalist and contextualist paradigms.

All this is complementary, at a different scale, to the object/instrument character of art itself. The distinctly ambivalent semiotic character of the art museum object is such that, in effect, the specimen is both "there" and "not there" in two ways.

First, while the object is physically present in the historiographic theater of the museum it is at the same time unnaturally abstracted there from some "original" historical situation: its present site is in one sense fraudulent (this museum is not "its" place, even where the object's authenticity value might support its exhibition value). Second, the object's significance is both present and absent, in the manner described above: its semiotic status is both referential and differential, being directly and indirectly meaningful.

Formalism and contextualism are thus prefabricated and coconstructed positions in the same museological system of representation; coordinated facets not only of art history, but also of the sociopolitical enterprise of modernity more generally. Inexplicable without each other, both museology and art history are also continuous with other epistemological technologies for the fabrication and maintenance of the modern nation-state and for the naturalization and validation of the kind of subjects it requires to function effectively, and the marginalization or occlusion of (what thereby become) deviant types.

As a device for distributing the spaces of social memory within a totalizing schema of coordination and commensurability, the museum provided both the stage and the instruments for envisioning all times, places, and peoples within a common, universal, and seemingly neutral laboratory frame. For every nation, race, and people no less than for every individual, there could be imagined legitimate and proper "art histories," each articulating a distinctive aesthetic paradigm with its own unique spirit; its own archaisms and classicisms; its own stylistic problem-solving adventures; its own fitness and decorum; and its own potentials for growth or decline.

In the contemporary world, virtually anything can be deployed as a specimen in a museum, and virtually anything can be staged or designated as a museum. This phenomenon—given force, weight, and direction with the historical institution of the modern museum—renders problematic any understanding of the latter in isolation from its epistemic milieu.

BIBLIOGRAPHY

Alsop, Joseph W. *The Rare Art Traditions: The History of Art Collecting and Its Linked Phenomena Wherever These Have Appeared.* New York, 1982.

Apter, Emily, and William Pietz, eds. *Fetishism as Cultural Discourse.* Ithaca, N.Y., 1993.

Bann, Stephen. *The Clothing of Clio: A Study of the Representation of History in Nineteenth-Century Britain and France.* Cambridge and New York, 1984.

Carruthers, Mary J. *The Book of Memory: A Study of Memory in Medieval Culture.* Cambridge and New York, 1990.

Déotte, Jean-Louis. *Le musée: L'origine de l'esthétique.* Paris, 1993.

Duncan, Carol. *Civilizing Rituals: Inside Public Art Museums.* London and New York, 1995.

Hooper-Greenhill, Eilean. *Museums and the Shaping of Knowledge.* London and New York, 1992.

Impey, Oliver, and Arthur MacGregor, eds. *The Origins of Museums: The Cabinet of Curiosities in Sixteenth- and Seventeenth-Century Europe.* Oxford, 1985.

Lugli, Adalgisa. *Naturalia et mirabilia: Il collezionismo enciclopedico nelle Wunderkammern d'Europa.* Milan, 1983.

McClellan, Andrew. *Inventing the Louvre: Art, Politics, and the Origins of the Modern Museum in Eighteenth-Century Paris.* Cambridge and New York, 1994.

Mitchell, Timothy. "Orientalism and the Exhibitionary Order." In *Colonialism and Culture,* edited by Nicholas B. Dirks, pp. 289–317. Ann Arbor, 1992.

Pearce, Susan M. *Museums, Objects, and Collections: A Cultural Study.* Washington, D.C., 1993.

Preziosi, Donald. *Rethinking Art History: Meditations on a Coy Science.* New Haven, 1989.

Preziosi, Donald, ed. *The Art of Art History.* Oxford, forthcoming.

DONALD PREZIOSI

Sociological Perspectives on Museums

Social scientists have studied art museums (and the behavior of people in them) at the individual, organizational, and societal levels of analysis. The perspective here is sociological, but the enterprise is multidisciplinary, and, although most of the works discussed are by sociologists, the list includes studies by scholars from the fields of economics, psychology, art history, literature, cultural studies, communications, and marketing.

Research on individuals has focused on the composition of the museum's public and the behavior of art museum visitors. Motivation for such research has varied from abstract and theoretical (e.g., understanding the role of aesthetic taste in reinforcing or attenuating social hierarchies) to the concrete and pragmatic (e.g., advising policymakers in developing grant programs, or assisting museum managers).

Research on museums as organizations has articulated with the major thrust of the sociological approach to the arts: to explore the influence of social arrangements on the life chances of artworks and artistic movements. Standing between artist and public, aesthetic institutions (patronage systems, markets, career structures, and the formal organizations and informal networks that constitute these) shape the opportunities for artists to reach publics, find critical favor, and develop reputations. Because art museums are central institutions of the artworld, social scientists concerned with the visual and plastic arts have studied and written about them.

Finally, researchers have addressed the subject of museums as part of broader examinations of cultural change. Art museums have played central roles in the emergence of cultural hierarchy, the rise of postmodernity, and the construction of collective memory, and studies of each of these topics have taken them into account.

Individuals and Museums. The classic work on the museum's public is by Pierre Bourdieu and Alain Darbel (1990; see also Bourdieu, 1984). Synthesizing classical ideas on status cultures (Max Weber), ritual (Émile Durkheim), and status competition (Thorstein Veblen), the authors reported two key findings: first, the overrepresentation among art museum visitors of high-status and, especially, highly educated persons; and, second, the tendency within the "dominant class" for greater attendance among the less wealthy "class fractions." Bourdieu argued that aesthetic perception and confidence are inculcated in well-educated families, rendering high-status persons more interested in and capable of enjoying the visual and plastic arts. Participation in high-status arts activities like visiting museums was especially attractive to teachers, professors, and members of the social and cultural semiprofessions, who, lacking substantial economic resources, depend on accumulating and transmitting "cultural capital" in order to ensure the success of their offspring in a system of formal education that defines as gifted students who have acquired such cultural capital at home.

Studies from a dozen countries and four continents replicate Bourdieu's basic findings on the composition of the art museum's public. Other studies have found that highly educated parents provide more aesthetic socialization to their children than do less-educated parents (Bergonzi and Smith, 1996). Still others have documented positive effects of young people's cultural capital on their success in the educational system (DiMaggio and Mohr, 1985).

The relationship between family background and arts participation is looser than one might infer from Bourdieu's theory, however. For one thing, many factors other than class, especially gender, influence frequency of art museum visiting. Many people in the categories most likely to attend do not do so, suggesting that "cultural capital" is an optional part of the high-status lifestyle for individuals. Rather than exacerbating inequality, as Bourdieu's argument suggests, elementary and secondary school arts education, in the United States at least, appears to reduce inequality in adult participation (Kracman, 1997). Moreover, research in the United States demonstrates that taste is not so much class stratified as it is pyramidal, with more-educated people more likely than others to consume almost every kind of culture, not just high art (a generalization that John Robinson [1993] calls the "more-more" principle). Richard Peterson (1992) argues that the highly educated are no longer snobs (if they ever were), but rather are omnivores, a conclusion supported by research indicating that museum visitors have unusually democratic attitudes toward aesthetic value and judgment (DiMaggio, 1997).

Although Bourdieu's paradigm has grown in influence, much research on museum visitors has been pragmatic in intent. Since the 1920s, psychologists and others have studied visitor behavior, writing about such topics as "museum fatigue," the effectiveness of different types of documentation, the ways in which visitors organize their movement through the museum, and the preferences of different kinds of visitors. Such museums as New York's Metropolitan Museum of Art, the Smithsonian Institution in Washington, D.C., the Royal Ontario Museum, and Saint Petersburg's Russian State Museum have maintained active research programs, some results of which are of broad interest. For example, Ludmila E. Gaav and Marina V. Potapova (1997) studied audiences for the Russian State Museum during *glasnost,* documenting change in the composition and reactions of Russia's art public during the first public exhibits of modernist art in more than fifty years. Jeffrey K. Smith and Lisa F. Wolff (1997) found visitors to the Metropolitan who knew about art were more likely to report planning their visit in detail ahead of time, spent more time with fewer artworks, and were oriented more toward learning and less toward "fun."

Other studies have been sponsored by public arts agencies concerned with documenting or expanding the reach of the institutions they support. Surveys of national samples suggest that the same kinds of people visit art museums throughout Europe and North America, and that educational attainment is by far the most important predictor of participation (Schuster and Davidson, 1991). Research based on the Survey of Public Participation in the Arts, a U.S. study unusual because it has asked the same questions of comparable samples of the public over a ten-year span, has revealed that, compared to performing arts organizations, which have lost audience among the young with the rise of new media technologies during the 1970s and 1980s, art museums have become increasingly popular, attracting larger publics even among young people (Peterson and Sherkat, 1996). Such results suggest a divergence in the social role of the visual arts from that of the high-culture performing arts, with which they have been associated.

Museums as Organizations. In contemporary Western societies, the art museum shares with university art-history departments the role of guarantor of aesthetic value. Consequently, scholars interested in the creation of value—the market value of artworks and the reputations of works and their creators—are keenly interested in how art museums decide what works to acquire and exhibit.

Distinctive features of art museums as organizations. Vera Zolberg (1980) has explored the differences between art museums and performing arts organizations that follow from their distinctive technologies. Museums place stationary exhibits throughout a large space through which visitors may move at their own pace, and invest heavily in physical plant and the preservation of objects. Performing arts companies, by contrast, organize productions that concentrate artists and audience in time and space. It follows from this that most art museums have higher ratios of fixed to variable costs; require larger endowments; are better equipped to accommodate diversity in both artworks and audience than performing arts institutions; face less risk in exhibiting new works than orchestras, for example, do in performing them; and have more formal departmental structures.

Students of formal organizations often focus on the way institutions are influenced by those on whom they depend for vital resources, a perspective that casts much light on art museums. Paul DiMaggio (1992) describes U.S. art museums as confederations of at least three administrative/staff structures, each with a distinctive mission, external environment, and understanding of its public. One, which keeps alive the museum's commitment to "culture" in Matthew Arnold's sense, consists of curators and allies, and is oriented to patrons and connoisseurs. A second, whose principals possess business and financial training, conceives of the museum's public as a middle mass, to be reached with the language and techniques of marketing. A third, consisting of education and outreach staff, focuses on needs of "underserved" audiences, and is oriented to public and private grant makers (see also Zolberg, 1986).

This complexity reflects change in the support base of art museums from private patrons (and, in some cases, municipal subsidies) in the United States, and from the state in Europe, to a more complex mix of revenues from several kinds of commercial, philanthropic, and government sources. DiMaggio (1987) argues that these changes account for a transformation in the backgrounds of museum directors between the early 1960s and the early 1980s, during which period the social credentials of art museum directors declined while their educational credentials gained luster; and curatorship, once the key stepping-stone to directorships, became just one of many routes to the top.

Simpler environments yield simpler structures with smaller administrative components. Before the 1960s, the major divisions within U.S. museums were between departments organized around types of art (and the collectors, patrons, and trustees with whom each was allied); and the director's function was to act as peacemaker among these interests and to provide a modicum of planning and administration. In Europe, the major relationship the art museum had to manage was with the ministry that provided its budget, and the director's primary role was to protect the autonomy of professional staff (Frey and Pommerehne, 1989). By contrast, contemporary museum administration requires the full gamut of business skills, changing the criteria for director selection and expanding greatly the size of administrative staff.

Institutional change in art museums has elicited much research attention. Diana Crane (1987) examines the role of U.S. art museums in the consecration and diffusion of new art movements in the 1970s and 1980s, during which time the hegemony of Abstract Expressionism gave way to a multiplicity of contending schools and styles. Her account illuminates several distinctive dynamics.

Importance of numbers. Cultural institutions change when the pressure of numbers exceeds the capacity of existing forms to accommodate them. Harrison C. White and Cynthia A. White's classic study of the emergence of Impressionism (1994) illustrates the breakdown of the academic system under the weight of aspiring artists who flooded Paris during the mid-nineteenth century. Change in the U.S. art world responded to increased demand rather than supply: the creation of hundreds of new art museums, and the expansion of exhibition space in hundreds of others, created exhibition niches into which new art movements could move (Blau, 1995; Crane, 1987).

Interaction of museums and markets. The art market expanded during the 1970s and 1980s to include collectors of new kinds of artwork, who importuned the growing number of art museums to consecrate this work by hanging it in their galleries (Lang and Lang, 1990). The strategies of artists, some types of whom depend more on museum exposure than others, also influence the chances that museums will accept a new style (Greenfield, 1989). Since the 1920s, art museums have made room for many new forms, such as architecture, photography, folk art, and crafts, enhancing the market for the forms they exhibited.

Influence of institutional patronage. New visual arts movements require sponsorship in order to receive recognition. Collectors and critics can play this role, of course, but increasingly institutional patrons are primary sponsors. The postwar rise of corporate collections raised to prominence several styles that eventually found their way into museum collections, and some that did not (Martorella, 1990; Crane, 1987). So did patterns of public patronage, especially in the United States, where state arts agencies encouraged the definition of regional aesthetics (Crane, 1987).

Based on rigorous study of more than four thousand exhibitions at fifteen major U.S. art museums over a quarter century, Victoria D. Alexander (1996) reported that government and corporate grant makers disproportionately supported blockbuster exhibits and thematic shows. As institutional patronage increased in scale, the sorts of exhibitions that grant makers favored became more numerous, and the kinds they did not (exhibits of particular patrons' collections, work by local artists, and subjects of community interest) declined in prominence. Alexander also found that the proliferation of external funders increased conflict between staff whose priorities matched those of institutional patrons and those whose priorities did not.

Influence of political movements. Other research has demonstrated the influence of broad political movements on art museums' aesthetic choices (Zolberg, 1994). Censorship, often due to agitation by movements outside the state, is an obvious source of pressure (Dubin, 1992), although we know little about why comparably provocative artworks elicit such different reactions in different exhibition sites. Perhaps more subtly, exhibition policies are shaped by political movements that alter norms of international conduct (such as calls for repatriation of art objects) or promote the salience of ethnic, racial, or other social identities (Karp et al., 1992).

Museums and Societal Change. Art museums not only mediate the influence of markets and organizations on aesthetic norms, they also participate in broader cultural change. Art museums are repositories of collective memory and physical embodiments of cultural authority and symbolic power (Duncan, 1995, chap. 3). They define and patrol aesthetic boundaries between art and nonart, and between great art and the merely mundane.

Museums originated in the democratization of Western polities, as royal collections were opened to the masses, and in the rise of colonialism, as military power rendered objects of antiquity accessible to Western collectors (Harris, 1962). Yet museums, and the view of art that museums convey, have articulated closely with structures of inequality and elite mobilization in both Europe and the United States (Fox, 1963; McCarthy, 1992; Beisel, 1993). In the latter, the rise of great museums coincided with the emergence of urban upper classes, and served to define a high culture that sanctified elite taste, distinguished from fashion or sentiment, as a badge of distinction (Abrams, 1985). Whereas early U.S. and British museums focused on mass education and the improvement of manufactures and design, after 1900 many became preoccupied with collection and connoisseurship, and their commitment to mass education diminished (DiMaggio, 1982; Levine, 1988).

In the United States, where art museums received little state support, the boundaries of canonical art have been almost continually challenged. During the 1920s, progressives turned on art museums, invoking Veblen's work on conspicuous consumption to denounce wealthy patrons as selfish and short-sighted. (Ironically, Veblen [1934] saw museum founding as a sign that even the most barbarous plutocrats retained some small social conscience.) Progressives challenged art museums' goals, calling on museum workers to build an autonomous profession that would pursue a mission of social enlightenment, and their content, urging increased exhibition of crafts and manufactured objects of good design. Although the progressives influenced the New Deal's arts programs, art museums were professionalized by art historians, not educators, and the reform wave passed with the Depression (DiMaggio, 1991).

Art museums remain at the boundary between art and nonart, which like all boundaries is most visible when challenged. Museums have been awkward in incorporating the art of socially disprivileged groups (Lachmann, 1988; Gross, 1995; and Metcalf, 1985), finding it difficult to separate aesthetic hierarchies from social hierarchies in which they have been embedded. As Russell W. Belk puts it, " 'Museum quality' more often than not also means museum inequality" (Belk, 1995, p. 155).

Many recent changes in art museums appear consistent with arguments of postmodern theorists, who contend that cultural hierarchy is eroding and cultural order is being replaced by bricolage. Museums have participated in the creation of multifaceted urban cultural centers, replacing defunct manufacturing economies with symbolic economies that reinterpret a community's history to itself (Zukin, 1995). Symbolic hierarchies among genres within art museums have weakened, perhaps reflecting the museum's immediate resource environment more than a general zeitgeist. As Zolberg (1988) has argued, the art museum was in a sense born postmodern, committed from the start by its very structure and mission to yanking objects from their contexts and displaying them in awkward juxtaposition. This affinity between the art museum's technology and broader trends in contemporary culture may in part explain the extraordinary popularity of the art museum in the late twentieth century.

Sociology, by its nature, focuses on the way that social factors influence art—not because it denies the autonomy of the creative act (although it would insist that this autonomy is partial and relative), but because it seeks purchase on the patterned aspects of cultural life. Nonetheless, most sociologists would agree with Judith R. Blau (1995, p. 88) that aesthetic ideas, as much as formal organizations and flows of revenues, are consequential parts of the museum's environment, shaping the way in which patrons, curators, and directors interpret the opportunities and challenges that they face. Social scientists are a bit like the fabled religion student who, coming to a fork in the road with one path marked "To Heaven" and the other marked "To a Discussion Group about What Heaven Would Be Like," chose the latter. Most would rather study the conditions under which different aesthetic doctrines capture philosophical and lay imaginations than take part in the philosophical debates themselves. If forced, however, they would doubtless admit to a distaste for Kantian idealism (Bourdieu, 1984) and an affinity for institutionalism (Becker, 1982). It is the precisely the centrality of the art museum among the institutions of art that has made it such an appealing object for social-scientific attention.

[*See also* Sociology of Art.]

BIBLIOGRAPHY

Abrams, M. A. "Art-as-Such: The Sociology of Modern Aesthetics." *Bulletin of the American Academy of Arts and Sciences* 38 (1985): 8–33.

Alexander, Victoria D. "Pictures at an Exhibition: Conflicting Pressures in Museums and the Display of Art." *American Journal of Sociology* 101 (1996): 797–839.

Becker, Howard S. *Art Worlds.* Berkeley, 1982.

Beisel, Nicola. "Censorship, the Politics of Interpretation, and the Victorian Nude." *American Sociological Review* 58 (1993): 145–162.

Belk, Russell W. *Collecting in a Consumer Society.* London and New York, 1995.

Bergonzi, Louis, and Julia Smith. *Effects of Arts Education on Participation in the Arts.* National Endowment for the Arts Research Division Report No. 36. Santa Ana, Calif., 1996.

Blau, Judith R. "Art Museums." In *Organizations in Industry: Strategy, Structure, and Selection,* edited by Glenn R. Carroll and Michael T. Hannan, pp. 87–114. New York and Oxford, 1995.

Bourdieu, Pierre. *Distinction: A Social Critique of the Judgement of Taste.* Translated by Richard Nice. Cambridge, Mass., 1984.

Bourdieu, Pierre, and Alain Darbel, with Dominique Shnapper. *The Love of Art: European Art Museums and Their Public.* Translated by Caroline Beattie and Nick Merriman. Stanford, Calif., 1990.

Crane, Diana. *The Transformation of the Avant-Garde: The New York Art World, 1940–1985.* Chicago, 1987.

DiMaggio, Paul. "Cultural Entrepreneurship in Nineteenth-Century Boston." *Media, Culture and Society* (U.K.) 4 (1982): 33–50 and 4 (1982): 303–321.

DiMaggio, Paul. *Managers of the Arts: Careers and Opinions of Senior Administrators of U.S. Art Museums, Symphony Orchestras, Resident Theatres, and Local Arts Agencies.* Washington, D.C., 1987.

DiMaggio, Paul. "Constructing an Organizational Field as a Professional Project: U.S. Art Museums, 1920–1940." In *The New Institutionalism in Organizational Analysis,* edited by Walter W. Powell and Paul DiMaggio, pp. 267–292. Chicago, 1991.

DiMaggio, Paul. "Notes on the Relationship between Art Museums and Their Publics." In *The Economics of Art Museums,* edited by Martin Feldstein, pp. 39–49. Chicago, 1992.

DiMaggio, Paul. "Are Art-Museum Visitors Different from Other People? The Relationship between Attendance and Social and Political Attitudes in the United States." *Poetics: Journal of Empirical Research on Literature, the Media, and the Arts* 24 (1997): 161–180.

DiMaggio, Paul, and John Mohr. "Cultural Capital, Educational Attainment, and Marital Selection." *American Journal of Sociology* 90 (1985): 1231–1262.

Dubin, Steven C. *Arresting Images: Impolitic Art and Uncivil Actions.* London and New York, 1992.

Duncan, Carol. *Civilizing Rituals: Inside Public Art Museums.* London and New York, 1995.

Fox, Daniel M. *Engines of Culture: Philanthropy and Art Museums.* Madison, Wis., 1963; 2d ed., New Brunswick, N.J., 1995.

Frey, Bruno S., and Werner W. Pommerehne. *Muses and Markets: Explorations in the Economics of the Arts.* Oxford and Cambridge, Mass., 1989.

Gaav, Ludmila E., and Marina V. Potapova. "New Audiences for New Art: The Public for the Avant-Garde Exhibitions at the Russian State Museum." *Poetics: Journal of Empirical Research on Literature, the Media, and the Arts* 24 (1997): 131–160.

Greenfield, Liah. *Different Worlds: A Sociological Study of Taste, Choice, and Success in Art.* Cambridge and New York, 1989.

Gross, Larry, ed. *On the Margins of Art Worlds.* Boulder, Colo., 1995.

Harris, Neil. "The Gilded Age Revisited: Boston and the Museum Movement." *American Quarterly* 14 (1962): 545–566.

Karp, Ivan, Christine Mullen Kreamer, and Steven D. Lavine, eds. *Museums and Communities: The Politics of Public Culture.* Washington, D.C., 1992.

Kracman, Kimberly. "The Effect of School-Based Arts Instruction on Attendance at Museums and the Performing Arts." *Poetics: Journal of Empirical Research on Literature, the Media, and the Arts* 24 (1997): 203–218.

Lachmann, Richard. "Graffiti as Career and Ideology." *American Journal of Sociology* 94 (1988): 229–250.

Lang, Gladys Engel, and Kurt Lang. *Etched in Memory: The Building and Survival of Artistic Reputation.* Chapel Hill, N.C., 1990.

Levine, Lawrence W. *Highbrow/Lowbrow: The Emergence of Cultural Hierarchy in America.* Cambridge, Mass., 1988.

Martorella, Rosanne. *Corporate Art.* New Brunswick, N.J., 1990.

McCarthy, Kathleen D. *Women's Culture: American Philanthropy and Art, 1830–1930.* Chicago, 1991.

Metcalf, Eugene. "Black Folk Art and the Politics of Art." In *Art, Ideology, and Politics,* edited by Judith H. Balfe and Margaret Jane Wyszomirski, pp. 169–194. New York, 1985.

Peterson, Richard A. "Understanding Audience Segmentation: From Elite and Mass to Omnivore and Univore." *Poetics: Journal of Empirical Research on Literature, the Media, and the Arts* 21 (1992): 243–258.

Peterson, Richard A., and Darren Sherkat. "Effects of Age on Arts Participation." In *Age and Arts Participation, with a Focus on the Baby Boom Cohort,* edited by Erin V. Lehman, pp. 13–67. National Endowment for the Arts Research Division Report No. 34. Santa Ana, Calif., 1996.

Robinson, John. *Arts Participation in America, 1982–1992.* National Endowment for the Arts Research Division Report No. 27. Washington, D.C., 1993.

Schuster, J., and Mark Davidson. *The Audience for American Art Museums.* National Endowment for the Arts Research Division Report No. 23. Washington, D.C., 1991.

Smith, Jeffrey K., and Lisa F. Wolff. "Museum Visitor Preferences and Intentions in Constructing Artistic Experiences." *Poetics: Journal of Empirical Research on Literature, the Media, and the Arts* 24 (1997): 219–238.

Veblen, Thorstein. *The Theory of the Leisure Class* (1899). New York, 1934.

White, Harrison C., and Cynthia A. White. *Canvases and Careers: Institutional Change in the French Painting World.* New York, 1965; 2d ed., Chicago, 1994.

Zolberg, Vera L. "Displayed Art and Performed Music: Selective Innovation and the Structure of Artistic Media." *Sociological Quarterly* 21 (1980): 219–231.

Zolberg, Vera L. "Tensions of Mission in American Art Museums." In *Nonprofit Enterprise in the Arts: Studies in Mission and Constraint,* edited by Paul DiMaggio, pp. 184–198. New York and Oxford, 1986.

Zolberg, Vera L. "Postmodernism Previewed: Aesthetic Eclecticism in the 19th Century Art Museum." Paper presented at Annual Conference on Social Theory, Politics, and the Arts. Washington, D.C., 28–30 October 1988.

Zolberg, Vera L. "Art Museums and Cultural Policies: Challenges of Privatization, New Publics and New Arts." *Journal of Arts Management and Law* 23 (1994): 277–290.

Zukin, Sharon. *The Cultures of Cities.* Oxford and Cambridge, Mass., 1995.

PAUL J. DiMAGGIO

MUSIC. [*To analyze the rich history of music aesthetics, this entry comprises two essays:*

> Historical Overview
>
> Music and Feminism

The first essay is an extensive overview of the history of music aesthetics both in relation to aesthetic theory in general and as a distinct field. The essay on feminism explains how feminists have recently entered the debates on the aesthetics and politics of music. See also Aleatoric Processes; Authenticity; Emotions; Expression Theory of Art; Islamic Aesthetics, *article on* Islamic Music; Modernism, *article on* Modern Music; Notation, *article on* Musical Notation; Opera; Rock Music; Romanticism, *article on* Music; *and* Semiotics, *article on* Semiology of Music.]

Historical Overview

Aesthetic properties have always been part of musical experience—properties such as the sensuous beauty of sound and tone and of combinations of tone or the sensuous beauty of rhythmic successions of sound or tone. But these aesthetic properties do not belong to musical aesthetics unless they provoke verbal comment that is committed to written form. In addition, such comment or reflection will characteristically be organized and systematic in some way, and even—for the history of aesthetics in particular—be part of a more or less continuous tradition of thought. These conditions are fully complied with in the West only during the eighteenth century, when additional components of musical aesthetics also become prominent. The first of these is the "musical work"—a conceptual entity that had appeared and been characterized in the sixteenth century. The "work" was fixed and recorded in notation, and was consequently regarded as the finished product of the composer's constructive activity (known in Greek philosophy as *poiēsis*). It stood in the sharpest possible contrast to the ongoing improvisation of unrecorded music making. Thus, alongside action, or praxis (performance), and theoretical contemplation (philosophy and theory), a third sphere of music came into existence: poetics. (Or, in the customary musical terminology of the present day—performance, theory, and composition.)

The second of these additional components, which had emerged during the seventeenth and eighteenth centuries, is the integration of music into a "system of the arts"—a family of various fine arts that have been regarded as fundamentally related to one another. Thus, the "liberal arts," a distinguished group of studies that can be traced to antiquity, finally found a counterpart in the new and very different group of "fine arts." The system of the arts had its remote ancestry in the Muses of antiquity and its immediate antecedents in the comparisons of the arts *(paragone)* that were common in the sixteenth, seventeenth, and eighteenth centuries but continued into the nineteenth and twentieth as well. These also had variously distant predecessors: for architecture and music, Vitruvius (first century BCE) and Leon Battista Alberti (fifteenth century); for painting and poetry, Horace (first century BCE, *ut pictura poiesis*).

The formal systems of the arts follow many different principles of organization, from the logical and historical progressive order of G. W. F. Hegel's *Aesthetics* to the articulation of the arts into contrasted subgroups. Sometimes a single art will occupy a special position, as music does in Arthur Schopenhauer's aesthetics. Often, the arts of time will be set against those of space, or the representational arts against the nonrepresentational. Subsequently, the properties of an art may be deduced from its place in a given system, although these properties are often the reason it was given that place to begin with.

The very existence of aesthetics, finally, is made possible by an attitude of contemplation in the approach to works of art. This is not a purely passive attitude, but one of openness and receptivity to the properties of the work and to its quality as a whole. The work must engage our interest and attention for its own sake, yet also as a reflection and expression of its time and place of origin and of the creative personality of its producer. All of this can properly be regarded as a "disinterested" view, for ownership and economic value are excluded. What the work of art calls for ideally, then, is the historical knowledge and trained sensitivity of a connoisseur. The appropriate appreciative attitude will depend on a certain degree of leisure in society such as exists for an aristocracy or, more generally, for a wealthy middle class. A certain detachment is intrinsic to an aesthetic view, rather than the more active intercourse of a painter or a composer with the materials and constructive techniques of his or her art.

In the isolated discussions of music that have come down to us from antiquity the specifically aesthetic properties of music are never examined in their own right, but are characteristically mentioned in passing in connection with other philosophical concerns of a metaphysical or ethical nature. Indeed, the most widespread and tenacious ideas of music in Greco-Roman antiquity were traditional views of the nature of harmony and of the ethical or moral influence of music. Ideas of this kind seem to have prevailed not just in Greece and Rome, but in the ancient world in general. Even beyond this, they have persisted to some extent throughout the centuries of Western thought and up to the present. The idea of harmony often has no apparent point of contact with music, but encompasses an astonishing variety of manifestations in which patterns of certain mathematical ratios and proportions have been shown to prevail or are believed to prevail.

At least a partial identity, therefore, can exist (or can be thought to exist) between the structure of the musical system or the structure of scales and the structures of numerous manifestations that are otherwise unrelated to music. Accounts of such mathematical harmony are often completely abstract; any connection with music remains implicit and is simply suggested by the fact that the ratios and proportions given are known to be characteristic of tonal structures in particular. Even when sounding music is discussed, it is really an attendant circumstance, not the central concern.

By way of contrast, the ethical or moral influence of music, like its influence on physical health, almost always depends on music that is actually heard. The Dialogues of Plato are the most important ancient source for ideas of this kind, which range from the effect of music on the character and temper of the individual to its effect on the social and political order. The regulation of music, especially in its educational role, becomes a matter of the greatest urgency, and it is considered carefully in a number of the Dialogues, most notably in the *Republic* and in the *Laws*. But the values of music in this context are again not aesthetic values, but rather those of education and government.

The history of musical aesthetics can be said to have its inception in the Renaissance. During the course of this period the sensuous properties of music increased in prominence until they came into balance with the mathematical properties of musical structure that had prevailed previously. A simple flowing style of accompanied melody had already been conspicuous in the Italian secular song of the fourteenth century, which can be regarded as a kind of proto-Renaissance. But an increased sonority due to the use of lower tones and of three or even four simultaneous parts instead of two became evident in the fifteenth century, while in the sixteenth century there was a crucial change in the mathematical basis of simultaneous intervals, the ratios of which were derived from the senaria (the first six integers) instead of the quaternary, or tetractys (the first four integers). As a result, the angular and relatively hard quality of medieval sonority and medieval melody, which had already given way to some extent in the fifteenth century to the use of melodic and harmonic thirds, was replaced by the euphony of triadic construction.

In the early sixteenth century, in the motets and masses of Josquin Desprez, for example, the balance of mathematical structure and harmonious auditory quality was brought to a remarkable state of perfection with the further enhancement of sonority due to the tendency to exclude instruments, and the choral rather than solo performance of each vocal line. The uniformly vocal sonority and the blending due to the predominance of thirds and triads produced the greatest possible blending of the different voices and the greatest sensuousness of tone. In addition, not only the same melody but a single text as well was used for all the voices instead of the various texts and even the different languages sung simultaneously in the medieval motet. Each section of the text with the corresponding section of the melody that accompanied it was taken up in turn by the four or five groups of singers taking part in the performance to constitute a motet in imitative polyphony—the principal style of church music in the sixteenth century. Dissonance was regulated; it was limited to specific unobtrusive types.

In the course of the century, however, a growing interest in expression, which was motivated chiefly by an increasing concern with the text, upset the balance of this *ars perfecta*. Aesthetics appears in the writings of the leading musical theorists around the middle of the century—Glearanus, Nicola Vicentino, and Gioseffo Zarlino. Established rules are relaxed in favor of the expression (or "imitation") of the concepts and affects represented by the words, and authority for the innovations is found in ancient Greek writings, notably those of Plato and Aristotle. The object of the musical imitation has to be clear, and this is possible only if the text is clearly audible and only if it controls the other aspects of the musical expressiveness. The new and old polyphonic practices came into open conflict in a notorious dispute between Claudio Monteverdi and the theorist Giovanni Maria Artusi, who defended the traditional style.

More fateful than this conflict of two opposed practices in polyphony is the dispute between polyphony and monody. What is at stake here is a duplication of the effects of ancient Greek tragedy, as these had been described by Plato and Aristotle. Girolamo Mei, a respected classical scholar, wrote in 1572 that both the solo songs and the choruses of the ancients had been monophonic, and that this had given ancient music unlimited power. Some years later the cause of monody attracted considerable attention when it was advocated by Vincenzo Galilei in his famous *Dialogo* of 1581, which contained an unqualified rejection of polyphony. Later discussions of the new expressive style appear in prefaces and dedications of operatic scores. From the very beginning of opera in the early seventeenth century, however, the problem of boredom is evident. Even though the new song-speech was emotionally intensified, it also had to be varied by the introduction of other styles—by the insertion occasionally of solo or choral songs or of dance songs, or even of interludes of purely instrumental music. In the operatic treatise of Giovanni Battista Doni (1633–1635), there is a systematic discussion of all the aspects of opera. Doni emphasizes the need for variety. He distinguishes three types of monody, devoted respectively to narration, recitation, and expression.

During the last half of the seventeenth century, opera in Venice was no longer restricted to the private performances presented by aristocrats, as it had been in Florence, but was given in public theaters starting in 1637. Venetian opera, however, was characterized by complexity, confusion, and even incoherence of plot, together with numerous and highly varied roles. The aria became longer and more prominent, sacrificing dramatic quality to purely musical values and to vocal display. These developments stood in striking contrast to the dramatic simplicity and poetic quality of early librettos, and they were accompanied by a new aesthetic that made its appearance in the prefaces of Venetian librettos. Instead of the serious emotional and moral effects sought for originally, the later aesthetic stressed the values of delight and astonishment; it aimed at entertainment rather than edification and emotional impact. From a social point of view, the change was a consequence of a public rather than an aristocratic genre.

In France, Charles de Saint-Évremond and Nicolas Boileau expressed sharply critical views of opera, the one disapproving of the deus ex machina and the negative effect of opera on spoken tragedy, and the other of the use of love as a central theme. In place of the French concern with the corruption of morals by opera, the German criticism of opera was part of a religious condemnation of theatrical entertainment in general. Apart from this, however, opera tended to be regarded as the highest form of theater because of its synthesis of the different arts.

Eighteenth-century musical aesthetics is dominated by the ideal of expressive vocal melody that has a direct and wide appeal. This ideal—which extends to instrumental as well as vocal music—is shaped largely by German writers, but it is also influenced by French and English ideas and by Italian music. Johann Mattheson is its first and most important spokesman. The *galant* (as the style was called) is illuminated continually by its antithesis, the traditional learned polyphony of the German church musicians. To a great extent, this conflict of new and old is grounded in a contrast of secular and religious, of an urbane, basically international style and a specifically German, more provincial, contrapuntal complexity. The ideal Mattheson espouses is really derived from opera, the genre, itself international, that was favored both by Mattheson and by Hamburg in general. But aesthetics seems to thrive on controversy, even to demand it: on the conflict, typically, of new and old and of simplicity and complexity. Thus, Germany, with its powerful tradition of church polyphony on which there impinged the attractive newer style of secular melody, was fertile ground for aesthetics. Contrapuntal technique and complexity continually called forth critical attacks that served as the foil for newer ideals. Mathematics was pitted against rhetoric, craft against taste, and learning against the *galant*. Behind the aesthetic conflict there was often a contest of social ideals—

of the church with the aristocracy, of the town cantor with the court kapellmeister. And much as in the later sixteenth century and the earlier seventeenth, the foundation of the new musical style could not be provided by training and rules. Instead, the traditional contrapuntal curriculum had its competitor in auditory experience, taste, and judgment, and the composer turned for guidance to principles of rhetoric and aesthetics.

Imitation and expression represent major eighteenth-century conceptions of the nature of music, the one giving way to the other starting around 1750. The prominence of imitation has its explanation in the prevailing reliance on reason and objectivity, with a corollary mistrust of feeling. The highest values were found in clarity and distinctness, which could best be exemplified in music by fidelity to a clearly defined model that was being represented. Music was thus connected at once with the charted realm of objectivity and knowledge. For René Descartes, clarity was a criterion of scientific truth, but Boileau made it a criterion of beauty also, as a consequence of his principle "Nothing is beautiful but the true." The chief object of musical imitation was impassioned speech.

As early as the 1740s, however, it became evident that the concept of imitation is inadequate as a basic principle for the aesthetics of music, however well it might serve in that capacity for the other arts. Even Charles Batteux's important *Les beaux-arts réduits a un même principe* of 1746, which undertakes expressly to demonstrate that imitation is the basis of all the fine arts, does not appeal consistently to the imitative principle, but quite often instead to the principle of expression. Later French writers, with the surprising exception of some of the Encyclopedists, increasingly call imitation into question, until with François-Jean de Chastellux, and Michel Paul Gui de Chabanon, it is conclusively demonstrated that some principle other than imitation would have to provide the basis for musical aesthetics as well as for unifying the family of fine arts.

Other countries followed the leadership of France in eighteenth-century aesthetics; from Francis Hutcheson and James Harris to Adam Smith in England, and from Mattheson and Johann Elias Schlegel to Immanuel Kant, Friedrich von Schiller, and Christian Gottfried Körner in Germany, a surprising number of illustrious writers testified to the evolution of musical aesthetics from imitation and its shortcomings to expression. Beyond this, the appearance of many translations, some with commentaries, ensures a considerable community of ideas between France, England, and Germany. Important for the future, finally, was the replacement of imitation, which is hostile to an aesthetic of instrumental music, by expression, which is receptive to such an aesthetic.

Just as in the seventeenth century, operatic aesthetics in the eighteenth century continued to be discussed largely by literary figures and librettists rather than composers. Their attention was devoted primarily to questions of reform, since the major development in opera itself was the appearance in Venice during the second half of the seventeenth century of several features that were subject to criticism, especially when viewed in the light of traditional dramatic theory. Italian opera had come to be dominated by arias and vocal display at the expense of dramatic coherence and dramatic values. There was a mixture of serious and comic scenes, a profusion of characters, and a flagrant disregard of the dramatic unities of time, place, and action. Italian disapproval had its chief source in the Arcadian Academies, the first of which was founded in Rome in 1690.

The literary historian Lodovico Muratori was perhaps the severest of the Arcadian critics. Italian operatic criticism seems to be strongly influenced by France, and it is very much in the vein of Saint-Évremond that Muratori blames opera for the poor state of the Italian theater. He asserts that the theatrical music of his time is effeminate and more calculated to corrupt the minds of the audience than to purge and improve them as ancient music did. His criticism is really moral indignation, and he laments the fact that poetry obeys music rather than commanding it. Muratori finds fault with every feature of opera, from arias—which are extraneous to the drama—to word repetition. The drama must imitate real behavior, he maintains, and angry or grieving people, or those engaged in serious discussion, do not sing. Opera violates the principle of imitation, and it is morally corrupting as well.

The main mode of criticism in Italy, however, was satire, and the most notorious example of this was *Il teatro all mòda* (1720) by the composer Benedetto Marcello, who pokes fun at every aspect and feature of opera. Marcello presents a lively picture of operatic practice in Venice during his time, although there is doubtless a certain amount of exaggeration and just plain silliness in his account.

A more positive attitude toward opera was characteristic of the second half of the eighteenth century in spite of ceaseless fault-finding with respect to particular features. The benefits of such a positive approach can be seen at once in the judicious and highly influential *Sàggio sopra l'òpera in mùsica* of Francesco Algarotti. Algarotti was a cultivated and cosmopolitan connoisseur, and his underlying principle was the cooperation of all the components of opera toward a single dramatic purpose. The poet, consequently, is regarded as the most important participant in the operatic enterprise.

At the very beginning of the eighteenth century in France, operatic aesthetics becomes a prominent public issue as part of an ongoing controversy over the relative merits of French and Italian music. Not only do the essays of François Raguenet and Jean Laurent Le Cerf de la Viéville signal a new intensity in this quarrel of the two national

styles, but they also establish the outlook that remains dominant for most of the century. Discussions of opera, even when they are directed to French opera alone, cannot seem to pursue their argument without reference to Italy, either as a standard or as the target of criticism, for the controversy belonged to a general habit of thought, with manifestations in other types of music, in poetry and drama, and, indeed, in every aspect of culture.

The production of Jean-Philippe Rameau's *Hippolyte et Aricie* in 1733 precipitated a second operatic controversy in France that to a certain extent revived the views of Raguenet and Le Cerf concerning French and Italian opera. One camp supported the opera of Jean-Baptiste Lully, with the "ancient" simplicity and naturalness, and the other the "modern" opera of Rameau, the character of which, according to some of its opponents, derived from Italy. Nevertheless, the two competing styles were both French, and the contest of national styles was not literally present. At stake were qualities more abstractly defined: simplicity versus complexity, melody versus harmony, moderation and unity versus imagination and variety.

The Parisian performance of Giovanni Battista Pergolesi's *La serva pardona* in 1752 set off a third controversy, once again over the relative merits of French and Italian opera—the war of the buffoons. The almost numberless pamphlets and articles, most of them published anonymously, that document this quarrel are less concerned with operatic aesthetics than they are with quibbling and displays of wit. Many essays simply rehearse the known characteristics of French and Italian opera. But there are a few that exerted considerable influence, that possessed literary merit, and that dealt with matters of substance. The most renowned document of the buffoon war was Jean-Jacques Rousseau's *Lettre sur la musique française*. Rousseau did not hesitate to assert that Italian opera met his criteria of possessing a flexible language, bold modulation, exact rhythm and tempo, and melodic unity, the last requirement ruling out both counterpoint and complex harmony in the interest of a single effect. Rousseau also undertakes a general demonstration that French opera, and indeed French music of any kind, is essentially impossible since the language itself is intrinsically unsuitable for music. The reliance on harmony to conceal the deficiencies of melody does not help matters; it only creates a learned music in which harmony and melody obstruct one another. In Denis Diderot's very different view, musical imitation must be based on the natural expression of passion in vocal cries and declamation, and it is created by the composer and singer when they are in the grip of very real emotion, which is thought of as duplicating the nature and intensity of the "original" expression.

The last of the great wars of words in French operatic aesthetics was occasioned by the introduction to Paris of

Christoph Willibald Gluck and his epochal French operas of the 1770s. In the new battle of French and Italian styles, France and Italy were represented by Gluck and Niccolò Piccini, respectively. To some extent, the conflict was one between the older *galant* aesthetic and the new intensity of a *Sturm und Drang*.

In Hamburg, the city in which a continuous tradition of German opera reached an efflorescence in the early eighteenth century, operatic aesthetics was importantly shaped by the reaction to a tide of neoclassicism that had its source in seventeenth-century France. Chief among the early Hamburg proponents of opera was the librettist Barthold Feind, who insisted that the nature of drama was relative to time and place and who suggested William Shakespeare as a model for the Germans rather than French neoclassical writers. Feind maintained that opera was not bound by traditional dramatic rules and that it was devoted to the pleasure of the audience. Yet, he emphasized, as a librettist, that the drama was primary and that opera was a genre of significance. He also effectively combated the requirement of verisimilitude, as it was expressed by Saint-Évremond, and repeatedly emphasized the fictional character of opera and the necessity of its dramatic conventions.

Johann Mattheson was connected with the Hamburg opera as a singer and composer. He was its lifelong champion, continually examining its aesthetics and supporting it. In *Der musikalische Patriot*, Mattheson criticized Saint-Évremond and the criterion of verisimilitude, maintaining that "the opera in itself is a little art world" constructed from a variety of materials. He thus introduces an alternative to verisimilitude, and in fact to artistic imitation in general, that was probably the most powerful conceptual image of the century. In the theater, Mattheson points out elsewhere, daytime actions are depicted in the evening with artificial illumination. Opera is intrinsically different from the real world, like any other play, because it is art, and as such presents "a new kind of pleasing order." It is also characteristic of Mattheson, and of German operatic aesthetics in general, to take a positive view of the numerous and varied components of opera, sometimes as the basis of the values of pleasure and entertainment, sometimes as the foundation of moral and educative value and of the highest status among the arts.

Gotthold Ephraim Lessing's *Laocoön* (1766), which studied the distinctive differences between poetry and the plastic arts, was intended as the first part of a comprehensive three-part work devoted to the individual limitations and distinguishing properties of all the arts. This would not only help the creative artist formulate appropriate goals and projects and avoid unsuitable ones but also point the way to successful syntheses of the arts, an achievement entailed in every form of theater. Lessing found music and poetry fundamentally akin, for they both appealed to hearing and they both progressed in time. Lessing's speculations on artistic combinations were continued in his *Hamburgische Dramaturgie* (1767–1769). The use of instrumental music in drama is one of his recurrent themes. Among other things, we find a consideration of melodrama and also an idea usually connected with Richard Wagner, that the orchestra can play a role in drama comparable to that of the ancient Greek chorus.

The poet and novelist Christoph Martin Wieland was also active in the cause of native opera, particularly from the time of his arrival in Weimar in 1772, where he spent the remainder of his life. He proposed a new and distinctly German form of opera to be called *Singspiel*. This would affect the emotions through simplicity of plot, poignancy of action, and poetic quality of text. Instead of using the subjects of ancient tragedy, which would be senseless because society and culture had become so different, the *Singspiel* was to emphasize the lyrical rather than the dramatic, for music seems to contain certain intrinsic limitations. *Singspiele* should be devoted to mood and sentiment; their plots should permit music to reveal psychological states and inner action and to intensify the effects of these on the feelings of the audience.

After the advent of Gluck's so-called reform operas, starting with *Orfeo ed Euridice* and *Alceste* in Vienna, German operatic aesthetics was concerned mostly with the properties of these works and with the issues that were made concrete by the contrast between Gluck's innovations and the more traditional feature of Italian opera, especially of the operas of Johann Adolf Hasse and Pietro Metastasio. Thus, a traditional Italian art of sensuous melody and soft sentiment stood in sharp contrast to an apparently unprecedented art of powerful emotions that was compounded of Italian, French, and German ingredients. It is this contrast that underlies the aesthetic discussions that are scattered throughout Wilhelm Heinse's large novel *Hildegard von Hohenthal* (1795–1796). Gluck is discussed repeatedly and in considerable detail. In his expression of the violent, the powerful, and the sorrowful, Heinse claims, he belongs with the finest masters of tragedy. "Gluck created a unique genre," Heinse also asserts, "between tragedy and opera."

Heinse is particularly concerned with the newly prominent achievement of characterization in opera. Melody characterizes powerful passions, compliant persons, coarse ones, those who are calm, and so forth. Castrati represent an impoverishment of vocal music, for they can produce no contrast between a man and a woman, or between people of different ages. Also important in its novel strength is the unified effect made by one of Gluck's operas as a whole. In "the deep impression of the whole," Gluck ranks with the greatest of dramatists.

German Romantic aesthetics, especially musical aesthetics, is often embedded in a literary work, and the context provides a kind of justification for the poetic style in which ideas about art are expressed. For Romantic aesthetics is generally infused with emotion: with enthusiasm and even ecstasy. Thought and rationality alone seem inadequate to serve as its vehicle. It is further characteristic of this aesthetics that the unique status and quality of music with respect to the other arts is always apparent. Music is the highest, or ideal, art. The musician Joseph Berglinger, a character created by Wilhelm Wackenroder, invokes music as follows:

> But why do I, foolish one, try to melt words into tones? It is never as I feel it. Come, Thou musical strains, draw near and rescue me from this painful earthly striving for words, envelop me in Thy shining clouds with Thy thousandfold beams, and raise me up into the old embrace of all-loving heaven.

In the primary matter of presenting feeling, at any rate, the other arts, and especially literature, must give way to music.

Instrumental music in particular takes on a new value in evoking the magical realm of musical feeling, and this in turn suggests the idea of music as a separate world of its own. Social considerations, finally, are absent from Romantic aesthetics: the musical experience is that of an individual who is alone or withdrawn, related only to music and the world it reveals.

The philosophical aesthetics that developed in Germany during the early years of the nineteenth century seems to provide a metaphysical account of the imaginative and poetic descriptions of music found in German literature and criticism during the same period. Friedrich Wilhelm von Schelling, Schopenhauer, and Hegel thus constitute a systematic counterpart of Ludwig Tieck, Johann Gottfried von Herder, and E. T. W. Hoffmann, and taken together, both groups become the basis of the aesthetics of the second half of the century, which is less a time of originality than of reworking and elaboration. Alongside this continuation of Romantic ideas, however, other conceptions of music gained currency.

After the efflorescence of musical Romanticism in the 1820s and 1830s a new and more vivid kind of music became prominent in the decades from 1840 to 1860. The veiled and suggestive feelings of Romanticism, nostalgic and unfulfilled, gave way before specific and clearly defined feelings along with the representation of external scenes and events. The ideal was vocal music rather than instrumental, and in particular, opera, in which the greatest realism and force could be achieved and the feelings in fact made coincident and apparently identical with those of experience outside music. Environmentally and psychologically realistic program music was also responsive to demands of this kind. The central subject matter was sensuous and erotic feeling, which found direct and forceful expression.

In addition to this, where Romantic aesthetics had entailed a metaphysical outlook, realistic aesthetics entailed a social one. Quite clearly in the treatises of Wagner around mid-century, art is conceived as a manifestation of society—a perspective inevitable for a man of political mentality, shortly before engaged as an active revolutionary. Greek art was conservative, Wagner maintained, because it was a worthy expression of the public conscience. "With us, true art is revolutionary because its very existence is opposed to the ruling spirit of the community." The new work of art Wagner envisages is intimately tied to revolution: it can be made possible only through revolution, and it will at the same time help this revolution to succeed. Furthermore, the human being as artist can be fully satisfied only in the highest collective work of art, which includes all the individual types of art, each in its ultimate completeness. In these elaborate aesthetic treatises of the middle of the century, Wagner focuses more and more narrowly on the details of both theory and construction for the "work of art of the future."

During the second half of the century the realistic conception of musical feeling assumed a more specifically biological character. A number of prominent writers were active in this more or less scientific kind of aesthetics: Herbert Spencer, Charles Darwin, Edmund Gurney, Carl Stumpf, Ernest Newman, and Friedrich von Hausegger.

Nineteenth-century formalism in aesthetics doubtless has its chief source in Kant's *Critique of Judgment* (1790). Kant considers art in the light of cognition, for it is cognition that he takes to be the province of philosophy in general. But it is form that we know, not the material that is formed; aesthetics deals with judgment and with the pleasure that is attached to the apprehension of form. This pleasure expresses the formal purposiveness of an object in its appearance as perceived. But there is a type of beauty that Kant calls "free beauty," which he regards as independent of any concept of what the object ought to be. This is found in instrumental music, as it is in decorative visual designs. At least some instrumental music, then, is not considered "fine" art (which involves judgment and cognition), but "pleasant" art (which involves merely sensations and enjoyment).

In the formalism of Johann Herbart, the concept of a work of art is based on the unity of effect. Since the beautiful is objective, he argues, it must be separated from emotion and from general attributes such as "lovely." Musical beauty has to do specifically with the relations of tones. What the listener contributes—which Herbart calls the apperception of the aesthetic object—produces a great variety of judgments; but it is difficult, he concedes, to escape the demand that the work of art represent, depict, or mean something, or the belief that music expresses feelings.

For Hans Georg Nägeli, the essence of music is play. Music possesses only forms, regulated tones and series of tones combined into a whole. Its ceaseless play of forms dispels every particular affection, every mixture of affections. Eduard Hanslick, whose important treatise on music is largely a sustained polemic against the aesthetic role of feeling, draws on both Nägeli and Herbart. Music is confined to the dynamics of feeling, to patterns of motion. Feelings are at most the causes or effects of music; they cannot be either represented or expressed, for they are necessarily defined by ideas, and these cannot be conveyed by music. Most of the musical formalists after Hanslick are strongly influenced by him. They include Moritz Lazarus, who employed a psychological and social approach to aesthetics; the versatile scientist Hermann Helmholtz, whose scientific aesthetics is largely restricted to tonal sensations; the philosopher Robert Zimmermann, whose totally abstract aesthetics deals with forms that are apprehended only by thought, not by sense perception; Gustav Fechner, for whom the essential (as opposed to associative) effects of music include musical moods, so that music is really autonomous rather than formalist; Ottokar Hostinsky, who sought to reconcile the views of Hanslick with those of Wagner; and Gurney, who finds support for his theory of a special musical faculty in the writings of Darwin.

The course of idealism after Hegel is characterized chiefly by a secularization in which the Absolute recedes in importance or plays no easily discernible role. At the same time, the other major foundation of idealist views that is represented by Kant's conception of the aesthetic idea increases in importance. There is also a tendency during the course of the nineteenth century to eclecticism and syncretism in musical aesthetics, which stands in contrast to an earlier phase of the century in which ideas were presented in more definite or more striking form.

Kant's conception of the aesthetic idea has a persuasive exponent in the Danish scientist Hans Christian Oersted. Musical pleasure depends on reason, Oersted maintains, as well as on the senses. But we are not conscious of the rational basis of this pleasure, for the rationality contained in tones and their relations is a hidden one, which unconsciously penetrates our soul. The figure of the circle furnishes an example of the idea in aesthetics. The circle as a contemplated whole will contain properties intrinsic to its nature that are not included in its concept. The contemplation is of a multiplicity that is fused into a unity, and the beauty we perceive in this way is not dependent on our recognition of the properties. The circle is beautiful as the representation of an idea that is one with its nature; it is beautiful as a consequence of its nature or its idea.

Oersted finds convincing evidence for his theory in the famous acoustic demonstration of Ernst Chladni, who produced a tone by bowing a metal disc that was covered with powder. The vibration creates a striking symmetrical pattern of hills and nodes, which leaves no doubt, Chladni feels, of the operation of a hidden reason even in what we perceive as a single tone. But this secret reason is clearly operative also in the octave, the fifth, and the triad, and it is operative as well—without being known to the listener or even to the composer—in a musical work of art.

In his comprehensive *Aesthetics*, which was strongly influenced by Hegel, Friedrich Vischer regards music as an art of subjectivity and feeling. He considers feeling to be the center of mental life, and he undertakes to characterize it by reference to consciousness, on the one hand, and self-consciousness, on the other. The most important aspect of the ambiguous character of music is found in the relations between vocal music and instrumental music. In the connection of music and word, the word says more than the music in that it points to a definite object, but it says less than the music in respect of feeling. The absolute inwardness of feeling, however, dissolves the object. Purely instrumental music, which gives us feeling in all its purity, in its unconsciousness, suffers from the deficiency of feeling with respect to clarity and determinate content. In his search for a solution to the problem of vocal and instrumental music, Vischer comes close to the ideas of Wagner.

Many of the writers on musical aesthetics after Hanslick (1854) are concerned with endorsing or refuting his ideas. Of the negative critics, all of whom are understandably idealists of one kind or another, Friedrich Stade (1870) is the most thorough and the most penetrating. For example, in dealing with Hanslick's proposition that the sole content of music is tonal forms in motion, Stade argues that the content in music is inseparably bound to the tonal forms. Hanslick is therefore misled by the immediate immanence of the content in the tonal forms into believing that the content *is* the tonal forms.

In another instance, Hanslick evicts the feelings of the composer or the listener are evicted from aesthetics, but Stade believes that they are closely related to musical content. This positive view of feeling is made possible by the conception of apparency. The feeling involved in composing and in listening is a feeling through the medium of the fantasy, or a contemplation of feeling in the fantasy. Because there is in reality no actual cause that arouses a commensurate feeling, the feeling that is provoked by music alone is (somewhat illogically) called "apparent." Stade also believes that the course of music is reflected in detail in the course of the apparent feeling of the listener.

Not only is Stade's tract a thorough and persuasive revision of Hanslick, it is also a valuable contribution to the field in its own right, exceeding Hanslick's contribution in its anticipation of future conceptions, although not approaching it, of course, in fame and direct influence. Other important representatives of aesthetic idealism in music are the historian Wilhelm Ambros, the critic Adolf Kullak, the scholar Karl Köstlin, the critic Gustav Engel, and the philosopher Eduard von Hartmann. The various types of idealism that can be surveyed at the end of the century are described in Hartmann's history, *Die deutsche Ästhetik seit Kant* (1886). Hartmann himself represents "concrete idealism," which concerns ideas that are specific to music and is entirely free of metaphysics.

In the present century, a concern with meaning in music has doubtless become the chief object of musical speculation. Meaning has replaced the traditional interest in emotional content and has been the common concern of four different fields of study: hermeneutics, which was elaborated by Wilhelm Dilthey, symbolism, which was investigated by Arnold Schering and by Susanne Langer, semiotics, which was examined by C. S. Peirce, Ferdinand de Saussure, Claude Lévi-Strauss, Umberto Eco, and Nicolas Ruwet, and understanding, which has been investigated by Hans Eggebrecht and by Roger Scruton.

Another characteristic concern of musical thought in this century has been the property of objectivity, which is connected with neoclassicism. The ideal of objectivity appeared in the 1920s in the stylistic term *Neue Sachlichkeit,* and eventually, New Objectivity came to be attached particularly to Paul Hindemith and his disciples, and neoclassicism particularly to Igor Stravinsky. Even when the concept of objectivity gives way to the ideals of order and organization, it remains present as the fundamental presupposition of musical discussion. The explicit concern with musical order and musical organization always rests on the inexpressivity of tonal materials and tonal formulations. Thus, the antiexpressive cast of musical thought remains characteristic of the century throughout, even when music itself becomes highly expressive, as it often does toward the end of the century. The value of order and organization in music is therefore a recurrent theme of Karlheinz Stockhaussen, who in respect of objectivity is the logical successor of Stravinsky, even though in respect of structure his point of departure is Viennese serialism.

The phenomenology of music is still another important area of thought in twentieth-century aesthetics. Edmund Husserl's work on the inner consciousness of time was faithfully continued and directed more specifically to music by Alfred Schutz. The ontological nature of the musical work was studied by Roman Ingarden, while phenomenology not specifically Husserlian can be found in various forms in a number of different writers, among them Gisèle Brelet, Jeanne Vial, Thomas Clifton, and David Greene.

The last of the major streams of thought in the musical aesthetics of this century is the sociology of music. The specific concern of this field as defined by Theodor W. Adorno is the identification of structural properties of music that are the counterpart of the characteristics of society. In this rather speculative enterprise, Adorno's fundamental work has secured a considerable following. While Adorno is the outstanding representative of Western Marxism, with its concentration on the penetrating criticism of the negative ramifications of capitalism, Zofia Lissa and György Lukács are the most important representatives of the communist sphere of influence. Lissa's work is based on the writings of Joseph Stalin, and she insists on the class-bound character of

musical works. Beyond this, however, her treatment of music is remarkably flexible. It is not strictly confined to a Marxist perspective, but does full justice to the details of change and influence in a variety of styles and genres. For Lukács the central problem of musical aesthetics is the reflection of reality in music. According to his theory of "double imitation," the complete unfolding of human feelings occurred not as an inner reaction to the events of life, but rather as a mimetic representation of this reaction. The range of complexity and subtlety of human feelings is thus twice removed from the practical world, but still a reflection of it.

During the final two decades of the twentieth century a number of important new trends have appeared. Central among these has been the attempt to supersede the well-grounded and historically confirmed duality of music and art and to replace it with the full equivalence of the two spheres—a radical project that would seem at the very least to be ill conceived. What has been revealed from this vantage point in the way of previously unexamined issues has had little philosophical value for the understanding of music, and has simply reinforced the growing misgivings that had been evident for sometime concerning the shortcomings of semantic analysis as a productive method for aesthetics in general. This problem is confronted directly by a valuable work by Lydia Goehr, *The Imaginary Museum of Musical Works,* (1992) which is devoted to the concept of the "musical work." Examining this concept first by the application of semantic analysis and then through recourse to the obviously antithetical approach of historical understanding, Goehr provides nothing less than a convincing demonstration of the superiority of history to linguistic analysis in questions of aesthetics.

Other trends in these decades are not really new but rather developments that had been predicted somewhat earlier: the integration of ethnomusicology and "historical musicology" to form a single inclusive musicology, the consideration of the social nature of music not as an added dimension of study but as an intrinsic part of music itself, and the treatment of jazz, reproduced music, entertainment music, and the musics of all the various strata and segments of society as manifestations that are all equally worthy of musicological examination.

[*See also* Adorno, *article on* Adorno's Philosophy of Music; Boulez; Cage; Gurney; Hanslick; Improvisation; Jazz; Perception, *article on* Music Perception; Performance; Rasa; Schoenberg; Stravinsky; *and* Wagner.]

BIBLIOGRAPHY

Adorno, Theodor W. *Philosophy of Modern Music.* Translated by Anne G. Mitchell and Wesley V. Blomster. New York, 1973.
Adorno, Theodor W. "On the Fetish-Character of Music and the Regression of Listening." In *The Essential Frankfurt School Reader,* edited by Andrew Arato and Eike Gebhardt. New York, 1978.

Adorno, Theodor W. *Aesthetic Theory.* Edited by Gretel Adorno and Rolf Tiedemann, translated by Robert Hullot-Kentor. Minneapolis, 1997.

Besseler, Heinrich. "Grundfragen des musikalischen Hörens." *Jahrbuch der Musikbibliothek Peters für 1926* 33 (1926).

Bücken, Ernst. *Geist und Form im musikalischen Kunstwerk.* Potsdam, 1929.

Bujic, Bojan. *Music in European Thought, 1851–1912.* Cambridge and New York, 1988.

Dahlhaus, Carl. "Eduard Hanslick und der musikalische Formbegriff." *Musikforschung* 20 (1967).

Dahlhaus, Carl. *Esthetics of Music.* Translated by William W. Austin. Cambridge and New York, 1982.

Dahlhaus, Carl. *Klassische und romantische Musikästhetik.* Laaber, 1988.

Gatz, Felix. *Musik-Ästhetik in ihren Hauptrichtungen.* Stuttgart, 1929.

Goehr, Lydia. *The Imaginary Museum of Musical Works.* Oxford, 1992.

Handschin, Jacques. "Zur Musikästhetik des 19. Jahrhunderts." *Deutsche Vierteljahresschrift für Literaturwissenschaft und Geistesgeschichte* 10 (1932).

International Review of the Aesthetics and Sociology of Music. 1– (1970–).

Le Huray, Peter, and James Day, eds. *Music and Aesthetics in the Eighteenth and Early Nineteenth Centuries.* Cambridge and New York, 1981.

Lippman, Edward. "The Tonal Ideal of Romanticism." In *Festschrift für Walter Wiora,* edited by Ludwig Finscher and Christoph-Hellmuth Mahling. Kassel, 1967.

Lippman, Edward. "The Dilemma of Musical Meaning." *International Review of the Aesthetics and Sociology of Music* 12 (1981).

Lippman, Edward A., ed. *Musical Aesthetics: A Historical Reader.* 3 vols. Stuyvesant, N.Y., 1986–1990.

Lippman, Edward. *A History of Western Musical Aesthetics.* Lincoln, Nebr., 1992. Contains extensive bibliography.

Moos, Paul. *Die Philosophie der Musik von Kant bis Eduard von Hartmann.* 2d ed. Stuttgart, 1922.

Pfrogner, Hermann. *Musik: Geschichte ihrer Deutung.* Freiburg, 1954.

Salmen, Walter, ed. *Beiträge zur Geschichte der Musikanschauung im 19. Jahrhundert.* Regensburg, 1965.

Schäfke, Rudolf. *Geschichte der Musikästhetik in Umrissen.* 2d ed. Tutzing, 1964.

Schering, Arnold. "Symbol in der Musik." *Zeitschrift für Ästhetik* 21 (1927).

Schering, Arnold. "Das Entstehen der instrumentalen Symbolwelt." *Jahrbuch der Musikbibliothek Peters für 1935* 42 (1935).

Serauky, Walter. *Die musikalische Nachahmungsästhetik im Zeitraum vom 1700 bis 1850.* Münster, 1929.

Zoltai, Denes. *Ethos und Affekt: Geschichte der philosophischen Musikästhetik.* Translated by B. Weingarten. Budapest, 1970.

EDWARD A. LIPPMAN

Music and Feminism

There is much work in feminist musicology and music theory that is relevant to or might qualify as aesthetics, although there is at present relatively little scholarship that is identified as "feminist musical aesthetics." Much of this work has dealt with historical and cultural constructions of the masculine and feminine in music. Ancient writers such as Plato, Aristotle, Atheneus, Clement, Basil, and Boethius associated music they regarded as masculine or manly with rationality, order, and control; music they connected with women they associated with effeminacy, sensuality, excitement, passion, or madness. These early writings have had an impact on conceptions of music throughout history. Leo Treitler has identified both ancient and more recent descriptions of Old Roman and Gregorian chants that have gendered implications. The older Old Roman chant tends to be recursive, highly melismatic, and highly decorated, and is described as soft, charming, elegant, graceful, round, and voluptuous. The simpler and relatively stable nature of the more favored Gregorian chant is reported to display strength, vigor, power, and reason. Linda Phyllis Austern has shown that in the English Renaissance music was often associated with women or the womanly. The "eternal attraction between men and music" was likened either to the sacred bond of marriage, or as something dangerously sensual. Suzanne G. Cusick and Susan McClary have demonstrated that in the early Baroque, music associated with female characters or the feminine is likely to be more ornamented, exciting, and unstable than the more straightforward and controlled music associated with male characters or masculinity.

In the eighteenth, nineteenth, and early twentieth centuries, the tonal system and sonata structure were often used to defeat musical processes associated with the unacceptable feminine. In operas such as *The Magic Flute, Tannhäuser, Carmen,* and *Samson and Delilah,* the female antagonist, who is usually independent, powerful, and often sexual, usually has relatively chromatic, dissonant, syncopated, minor, open-ended, or generally unstable music. The protagonists, whether males or acceptable females, are likely to have clear, diatonic music in a major key that eventually provides resolution or closure. While the music of the antagonist is often exciting and beautiful, it is also disturbing, unsettling; on some level we are likely to want her music to resolve—and her music does resolve, usually precisely at the moment that she is killed or destroyed. The fact that we want the independent and powerful female character's music to resolve may be conditioning, or at least contributing toward, a desire for her death.

Some women composers, intentionally or not, have opposed these musical processes by presenting positive associations of feminine open-endedness. In her *Feminine Endings,* musicologist McClary has shown how the conclusion of avant-garde artist Laurie Anderson's *Langue d'amour* consists of a prolonged section in which a woman's pleasure or *jouissance* is expressed with chromatic inflections, irregular rhythms, lack of closure, and vocal sounds such as: *"Oooo là là là là. Voici. Voila. Oooo là là là là"* (McClary, 1991). McClary also suggests that composer Janika Vandervelde, in her *Genesis II,* may present a culturally conditioned feminine concept of temporality in contrasting cyclic and "timeless" music with more "masculine" teleological or climactic processes.

In an attempt to avoid viewing female operatic characters as victims, other authors have shown how female characters who are eventually defeated can usurp a good deal of power and authority in spite of, or by means of, their unstable music. Gretchen A. Wheelock has demonstrated that while theorists and critics from the eighteenth century have generally described the minor mode as representing melancholy, weeping, laments, hesitation, indecision, and (thus) the feminine, Wolfgang Amadeus Mozart often uses the minor mode to destablize the masculine/feminine dichotomy and the tonal order that contains them. Of Mozart's twenty-three minor arias, seventeen are sung by women and two by castrati. But the modes are not used simply to communicate feminine weakness or indecision but also death and the supernatural, or fury and rage (as in minor arias of Zaide, Electra, and the Queen of the Night). These characters' voices, then, can undermine conventional gendered expression, and can represent that which is "out of control" or beyond rational control. The minor mode so often associated with these characters is unstable yet powerful in its association to the inner world of passion, fear, and desire.

An example of a secret victory in an operatic work is suggested by Cusick's interpretation of Francesca Caccini's opera *La liberazione di Ruggerio dall'isola d'Alcina* (1625). In this work the knight Ruggerio is rescued by the sorceress Melissa from the love spell of the sorceress Alcina. Melissa appears to Ruggerio as a man, Atlante, and her/his music is characteristic of music regarded as "masculine" in the seventeenth century: diatonic, firmly tonal, and with careful text declamation. Melissa's success in liberating Ruggerio becomes a warning to those who seek power that they must speak in the language of patriarchy and repress what is regarded as feminine. Caccini's opera, Cusick suggests, thus affirms the political agenda of its patroness, Archduchess Maria Maddalena. In contrast to the music of Melissa/Atlante, the music of Alcina, with its "feminine" chromaticism, extraordinary tonal range, and expressivity, is relatively unstable. Yet, even though Alcina is defeated, her captivating song lingers seductively, Cusick suggests, in the ear and imagination, and subtly exposes the deceit and oppression of the political and gender systems Melissa's triumph seemed to affirm. So Caccini, Cusick thinks, has succeeded where Alcina has failed. The beauty of the more unstable music continues to enchant, and seventeenth-century notions of the "feminine" are affirmed in the process. Cusick's important thesis might also be applied to powerful but doomed operatic characters created by men—the Queen of the Night, Venus, Carmen, Delilah. Although some of the composers may have felt ambivalent at best toward their characters, they empowered or "envoiced" the characters, perhaps in spite of themselves, by treating the characters with such memorable music.

Such a point is made in Carolyn Abbate's recent interpretation of Richard Strauss's *Salome* in "Opera; or, The Envoicing of Women" (a wordplay on Catherine Clément's *Opera: or, The Undoing of Women*). Here Abbate suggests that even though she is eventually killed and literally hidden from sight by soldiers' shields, Salome manages, through her gender mobility, to usurp the authorial voice in the opera. Rather than being a passive object, she renders the audience passive through the sheer volume and forceful nature of her sound. It might be added that Salome's voice is also privileged in that her final music, although accompanied by a repugnant act, is diatonic, ethereal, and beautiful, whereas the music accompanying her death is unstable and dissonant. From a purely musical point of view, then, the death of Salome is not a triumph but a tragedy, lending weight to the power of her voice. Now, it could be argued here that the authority of certain powerful operatic women is Clément's very point: the louder the powerful female characters sing, the harder they fall. But focusing on just how much authority these characters can usurp, especially in an era when women are often regarded as largely voiceless, is an important insight.

Attempts by women to subvert the appropriation of the musical feminine to the masculine have also been applied, in a few cases, to instrumental music. In the nineteenth century, the first theme in a sonata or symphony was considered to be masculine, the second theme, feminine. Musicologist Marcia J. Citron suggests that Cécile Chaminade, in the first movement of her sonata for piano (1853), seems to avoid the objectification of the feminine through avoiding tonal Otherness. The "feminine" second theme in a sonata is supposed to appear in another key and drive the narrative toward final closure through allowing itself to be reined back to the tonic, the key of the masculine, in the recapitulation. But Chaminade's movement does not establish an Other key. It hints at other keys, but denies their strong definition. Although the feminine is a major presence in the movement, it is too slippery, dynamic, or shifting to be defined and appropriated or conquered.

Feminist musicologists have also pointed out processes in instrumental music that could be regarded as misogynistic. McClary hears the forceful mastery of "feminine" elements in Ludwig von Beethoven's Ninth Symphony in terms of sexual violence, a hearing that has given rise to considerable controversy. She also suggests that in Johannes Brahms's Third Symphony the second, more feminine theme is trivialized and incidental to the central Oedipal struggle in the work between the "Law of the Father" (conventional tonality) and Brahms the rebellious son (who seeks to defy conventional norms).

Judith Tick and others have considered Charles Ives's notorious comments on what he regarded as the feminine and the effeminate in music. (For Ives, Sergei Rachmaninoff became "Rachnotmanenough," Franz Joseph Haydn, Mozart, early Beethoven, and Brahms were "too much of the sugar plum for soft ears," various European masters were "pussies" or "cherries.") Tick stresses that Ives's comments, while extreme, were not atypical of the times; Ives inherited a "social grammar of prejudice" and an ideology of gender differences in music. Tick's primary point is that Ives used his prejudicial statements, which coincided with his radical, modernist experiments in music, to retaliate against traditional critics and to effect a break from a European heritage he found overbearing. Specifically, Ives sought to "weaken his adversaries by inverting gender discourse, rendering [European] patrimony—the heritage of male achievement—suspect on its own terms" (Tick, 1993). By denying the masculinity of the masters he sought to reorder power relationships and artistic entitlements. Along these lines, Catharine Parsons Smith has suggested that musical modernism was a response to the first wave of feminism, and that the misogyny of modernism suppressed female and enabled male composers of art music.

There have been a few attempts to define "women's musics" based, for example, on the cultural experience of (at least some) women. Most scholars avoid this area of interest, fearing the possibility of essentialism. Yet, Citron quotes a number of composers who are women as suggesting, variously, that the music of women tends to emphasize communication more than abstraction, substance more than innovation, holism or organicism, extensive development of a limited amount of material, compositional flexibility, a fascination with process as opposed to an adherence to set structures or techniques, and a lyricism characterized by long lines and connectedness. Anthropologist/ethnomusicologist Alan Lomax has theorized that in cultures such as gatherer-hunter bands in which the "feminine aesthetic is dominant," music (and dance) tends toward "varied synchrony": everyone has an equal voice or expression but all expressions come together in a dissonant harmony. This aesthetic might be considered "feminine" due to a culturally conditioned feminine tendency to connect with others (a result of the female child's prolonged identification with the mother) and a culturally conditioned feminine tendency toward subject-to-subject rather than subject-to-object or hierarchical relationships. It has also been suggested that the music of some women might be analogous to *l'écriture féminine* of certain French women writers, a style that involves "writing the body." Fluidity, multiplicity, and open-endedness also figure prominently here. While it might be argued that this would be perpetuating musical stereotypes that have been damaging to women, a *musique féminine* might also invite us to learn to cherish traditional femininities.

A growing field within musicology and theory is gay and lesbian studies. Lesbian studies in music often concentrate on body and voice, important topics in feminist aesthetics as well as feminist theory in general. Elizabeth Wood relates what she has termed "Sapphonics" to the female voice, identifying the term as "a mode of articulation, a way of describing a space of lesbian possibility, for a range of erotic and emotional relationships among women who sing and women who listen" (Wood, 1994). A Sapphonic voice is also a particular voice that Wood finds thrilling or exciting. Cusick likens falling in love with a woman to falling in love with a piece of music.

BIBLIOGRAPHY

Abbate, Caroline. "Opera; or, The Envoicing of Women." In *Musicology and Difference: Gender and Sexuality in Music Scholarship*, edited by Ruth A. Solie, pp. 225–258. Berkeley, 1993.

Austern, Linda Phyllis. "Music and the English Renaissance Controversy over Women." In *Cecilia Reclaimed: Feminist Perspectives on Gender and Music*, edited by Susan C. Cook and Judy S. Tsou, pp. 52–69. Urbana, Ill., 1994.

Brett, Philip, Elizabeth Wood, and Gary C. Thomas, eds. *Queering the Pitch: The New Gay and Lesbian Musicology*. New York and London, 1994.

Citron, Marcia J. *Gender and the Musical Canon*. Cambridge and New York, 1993.

Clément, Catherine. *Opera: or, The Undoing of Women*. Translated by Betsy Wing. Minneapolis, 1988.

Cook, Susan C., and Judy S. Tsou, eds. *Cecilia Reclaimed: Feminist Perspectives on Gender and Music*. Urbana, Ill., 1994.

Cox, Renée. "A Gynecentric Aesthetic." *Hypatia* 5.2 (1990): 43–62.

Cox, Renée. "Recovering *Jouissance*: Feminist Aesthetics and Music." In *Women and Music: A History*, edited by Karin Pendle, Bloomington, Ind., 1991.

Cusick, Suzanne G. "Gendering Modern Music: Thoughts on the Monteverdi-Artusi Controversy." *Journal of the American Musicological Society* 46.1 (1993): 1–25.

Cusick, Suzanne G. "Of Women, Music, and Power: A Model from Seicènto Florence." In *Musicology and Difference: Gender and Sexuality in Music Scholarship*, edited by Ruth A. Solie, pp. 281–304. Berkeley, 1993.

Cusick, Suzanne G. "On a Lesbian Relation with Music: A Serious Effort Not to Think Straight." In *Queering the Pitch: The New Gay and Lesbian Musicology*, edited by Philip Brett, Elizabeth Wood, and Gary C. Thomas, pp. 67–84. New York and London, 1994.

Lomax, Alan, and Norman Berkowitz. "The Evolutionary Taxonomy of Culture." *Science* 177 (1972): 230–238.

Lorraine, Renée Cox. "A History of Music." In *Feminism and Tradition in Aesthetics*, edited by Peggy Zeglin Brand and Carolyn Korsmeyer, pp. 160–185. University Park, Pa., 1995.

McClary, Susan. *Feminine Endings: Music, Gender, and Sexuality*. Minneapolis, 1991.

McClary, Susan. "Narrative Agendas in 'Absolute' Music: Identity and Difference in Brahms's Third Symphony." In *Musicology and Difference: Gender and Sexuality in Music Scholarship*, edited by Ruth A. Solie, pp. 326–344. Berkeley, 1993.

Smith, Catharine Parsons. "A 'Distinguishing Virility': Feminism and Modernism in American Music." In *Cecilia Reclaimed: Feminist Perspectives on Gender and Music*, edited by Susan C. Cook and Judy S. Tsou, pp. 90–106. Urbana, Ill., 1994.

Solie, Ruth A., ed. *Musicology and Difference: Gender and Sexuality in Music Scholarship*. Berkeley, 1993.

Tick, Judith. "Charles Ives and Gender Ideology." In *Musicology and Difference: Gender and Sexuality in Music Scholarship,* edited by Ruth A. Solie, pp. 83–106. Berkeley, 1993.

Treitler, Leo. "Gender and Other Dualities of Music History." In *Musicology and Difference: Gender and Sexuality in Music Scholarship,* edited by Ruth A. Solie, pp. 23–45. Berkeley, 1993.

Wheelock, Gretchen A. "*Schwarze Gredel* and the Engendered Minor Mode in Mozart's Operas." In *Musicology and Difference: Gender and Sexuality in Music Scholarship,* edited by Ruth A. Solie, pp. 201–224. Berkeley, 1993.

Wood, Elizabeth. "Sapphonics." In *Queering the Pitch: The New Gay and Lesbian Musicology,* edited by Philip Brett, Elizabeth Wood, and Gary C. Thomas, pp. 27–66. New York and London, 1994.

Zaimont, Judith Lang, ed. *The Musical Woman: An International Perspective.* 3 vols. to date. Westport, Conn., 1983–.

RENÉE LORRAINE

N

NARRATIVE. [*To explore the role of the concept of narrative in aesthetics, art, and art history, this entry comprises two essays:*
    Internal Narratives of Art History
    Narrative and the Visual and Literary Arts
The first essay explains the philosophical issues of narrative (covering both art and art history, with some reference to literary theory) and how they are related to art history from Vasari to the twentieth century. The second essay examines how narratives are understood and constructed in art and literature. For related discussion, see Lyotard; *and* Vasari.]

Internal Narratives of Art History

Saying that he undertook to provide more than a "mere list of the artists," the Renaissance humanist and artist Giorgio Vasari is perhaps the first to speak of art as having its own history. For him, it was "inherent in the very nature of these arts to progress step by step from modest beginnings, and finally to reach the summit of perfection" (1987). For Vasari, this progressive development begins with the "imperfect" art of Giotto and Masaccio, which attempts to represent nature faithfully, and ends with the supreme achievements of Michelangelo, who triumphs, Vasari writes, not only over nature but over the arts of antiquity. It is in relation to the arts of antiquity that Vasari sees the arts of his time as undergoing a renaissance, and it is a particular account of the arts of antiquity on which Vasari's narrative is modeled: Pliny the Elder's *Natural History*. In this work, Pliny describes, in the narrative structure that Vasari later employs, how Zeuxis completes the task in painting begun by Appollodorus and "Polykleitos is considered to have perfected the art of sculpture," whose potential Phidias had revealed. Although these and the other artistic achievements Pliny describes would fit naturally in any history of ancient art, they are presented in Pliny's account as part of his inventory of what was known in the natural sciences. This is because for Pliny the history of art was an *external* development, in the sense that he explained changes in the history of art not by reference to anything intrinsic to the art itself, but by the progress of the general human enterprise of trying to understand and manipulate the various elements—bronze, gold, stone, gems, and so on—of the natural world.

The history of art that Vasari narrated was, by contrast, *internal*, in that the form the development of art took was,

for Vasari, explained by the nature of the art whose history it was. In this sense, Vasari found an appropriate analogy in the life history or natural development of an organism, the contours of which development are explained by the nature of the organism itself, even if certain external conditions must be in place for the development to occur at all. Thus, in Vasari's narrative, art has a kind of natural life, like the life of a human being, with periods of birth, growth, maturity, and decline. Vasari, and later writers (such as Karl van Mander, Giovanni Bellori, and Johann Joachim Winckelmann) who adopted his organic analogy, also saw the history of art as progressive, where later stages were compared to earlier stages as greater realizations of some defining goal. Only with the institutionalization of academic art history do these two ways of speaking about art's development—as organic and progressive—become disengaged. Stressing the conceptual independence of these two kinds of development, Heinrich Wölfflin, a founder of academic art history, writes, "It is an arbitrary judgement to say that the rose-bush lives its supreme moment in the formation of the flower, the apple-tree in that of the fruit" (1932).

Wölfflin changed his views over time, but central to his final account of how to explain changes in art history was what he called the "two roots of artistic style," which he identified as the culture or society of the artist and the visual tradition that the artist belonged to. Rather than seeing the explanatory roles played by these two factors as identifiable on only a case by case basis, as Jacob Burckhardt, Wölfflin's teacher, proposed, Wölfflin asserted that it was the visual tradition the artist belonged to that uniquely explains the way in which the artist's work developed from his or her predecessors. So in Wölfflin's account, art develops autonomously, in a sense, as a "form working itself out inwardly," where the artist's social context does not enter into the explanation of the form of the work, except as the initial conditions that allow or frustrate the visual tradition's development along its own trajectory.

Other early art historians such as Alois Riegl, Paul Frankl, and Henri Focillon similarly described art developing not in response to external demands or functions, but from immanent or internal drives, such as the desire to make manifest the potential variations of a form, or the need to attain greater order in design.

A fundamental difficulty in these accounts of art's development is that although they speak of causes or explanatory factors "internal" and "external" to an allegedly autonomous visual tradition, they do not provide any systematic distinction through which the internal and the external can be isolated. Such a distinction is required, however, if sense is to be made of the assertion that it is in reference to exclusively intrinsic features of the tradition that the development of art must be explained.

To be sure, some such intrinsic features were assumed in the analogy made between art and organic forms; that is, as it was assumed that some natural or biological law referring to the intrinsic features of an organism could describe the shape of its life history from beginning to end, so some historical law referring to the intrinsic features of art, or the tradition of art, could explain the putative life cycle of artistic styles or the history of art as a whole. The problem here was not just that no credible examples of such a "law of form" (as Focillon called it) could be discovered to explain the beginning, development, and end of artistic styles, but that there was no obvious reason why the analogy between the development of artistic styles and development of organic forms that promised the notion of a law of form was a valid analogy at all. Why, one might ask, should the explanatory structures that explain the internal development of organic forms function in the development of artistic styles? Of course, artistic forms may appear to have the developmental history, described in these narratives, of growth, maturity, and decline. But the relevant question is whether those descriptions of the development from beginning to end are underwritten by whatever genuinely explains the development from beginning to end. If the identification of a development's beginning and ending is not constrained by what explains the development, such an identification seems to be without objectivity, or, as in the view of many contemporary art historians, merely a product of the narrative form used to represent the so-called development.

Earlier narrative historians of art held what can be called a *realist* view of historical narratives, a view that narratives are in some respects structurally homologous with developments in the past, where a narrative's beginning and ending really match a historical development's beginning and ending. Contemporary historians, however, tend to hold a constructivist view of narrative histories, in which the identification by a narrative of a development's beginning and ending is held to be only part of the rhetoric of history writing, serving ends auxiliary to, but not identical with, factual exposition (see Hayden White, 1987). Whether a development appears to unfold internally, with its own beginning and ending, is, from the constructivist position, only a matter of how the development is represented in the form of a narrative.

What is misleading in the preceding treatment of historical narratives as a matter of a debate between realists and constructivists is that it suggests a satisfactory analysis is available of just what it is the debate would cede to either historical fact or historical representation. But at present there is no unequivocal theory of what constitutes a genuinely narrative structure and what is contained in the concepts of beginnings and endings. An even cursory survey of the work of literary theorists (e.g., Frank Kermode, Edward Said, Robert Scholes and Robert Kellogg, and Meir Sternberg) reveals that theories of plot and closure exist in a great variety of often contrary forms. Even if there were unanimity among theorists of fictional narratives about what is entailed in the claim that an event in a fiction is a beginning or an ending, this would still leave unanswered the question of how fictional closure is related to beginnings and endings in the history or historical representation of actual events. Thus, historical realists and constructivists argue over whether there are so-called real beginnings and endings in history, without a clear sense emerging of just what each side is denying or affirming the existence of.

Given that narratives can explain historical changes, rather than just represent historical events the way a chronicle does, one way to approach the concepts of beginnings and endings in art history is through considering the role they play in historical explanations. Perhaps the identification of beginnings and endings can be shown to bear explanatory commitments, where, that is, their identification is constrained by whatever is the correct explanation of the historical development they are the beginning and ending of. What is required here is a sense in which a beginning and an ending do not just individuate or identify some historical development, where they are just the first and last events within that development. Rather, what is needed is a sense in which a development's beginning can explain its ending, where the ending follows in some sense necessarily from the beginning, even if, as the early internal narrative histories of art allowed, contingent external conditions are required for the development to occur at all.

One such an explanatory connection between a beginning and an ending is suggested by the way the style of an artistic movement seems, once formed, to reach in its development a kind of natural limit. Here the ending to a movement can be said to be explained by its beginning, as the limit to a style is explained by the style's formation. Some examples may make this more perspicuous.

Although the problem of how to negotiate between the surface qualities of an object represented in a painting and the surface of the painting itself occupied both the Impressionists and the Cubists, this problem was treated by the two movements in different ways. The Impressionists construed the problem as a matter of how to negotiate between the thick dabbed-on paint on the canvas surface and the "sense impressions" of the objects represented. But the same problem was treated by Pablo Picasso, Georges Braque, and Juan Gris as a matter of adapting the form of

NARRATIVE: Internal Narratives of Art History. Giovanni Domenico Tiepolo, *Title Page to the Punchinello Series* (c.1800), brown ink and wash over black chalk on paper, 11 1/2 × 16 in. (29.2 × 40.6 cm); Nelson-Atkins Museum of Art, Kansas City, Missouri (Purchase: Nelson Trust). (Photograph copyright by the Nelson Gallery Foundation; used by permission.)

the represented objects to the surface of the canvas construed as a grid or set of interlocking planes. That the problem was formulated this way for the Cubists may, in fact, be explained by what they thought of the previous movement's success or failure in its treatment of the problem. Cubism's stylistic development in these terms was carried to a stage when its paintings threatened to appear abstract. Here, the surface qualities and form of the represented objects were almost completely subsumed in the allover effect of the painting's surface. Even if Abstract Expressionist painting would later carry this development toward an allover effect without a represented figure, the allover effect of the Cubist paintings seemed to constitute a limit for the movement because its style was essentially conceived, in its formation, in terms of a figurative or representational art; that is to say, whatever were the goals or problems pursued by the Cubists, these were articulated in terms that took for granted the notion that an image always represents a motif. Al-

though the intrinsically representational character of Cubism may not have been realized as such by those who formed the style, such a feature prevented the style from reaching a point in its development where it could function in making abstract art. Piet Mondrian developed out of Cubism a type of lattice-like composition similar to Cubism's, but, because he was not subject to Cubism's stylistic parameters, he could employ this lattice-like composition in paintings *without* a represented object.

One built-in limit that did not belong to the style of Cubism was that it should address pictorial problems in terms only of paint. The Fauves explored ways of disassociating the surface color of a painting from the local color of its represented objects. But, because of the nature of the Fauvist style, this investigation was limited to manipulating the color of paint on the surface of the canvas. Cubism as a style possessed no such intrinsic limit and thus as a movement was able to address this problem further and differently in the colored and printed paper imported into collage. But although Picasso and Braque made use of the most diverse media in their collages, it was a still a limit to Cubism's development, because a feature of its style, that it remained, with few exceptions, an art of the tableau, a flat surface with objects represented on it.

Finally, although Cubism invented a different form of pictorial space than that of linear perspective, its development was nonetheless carried out in terms of representing an object, as still life, portrait, or landscape, in some form of pictorial space. Extruding all represented space from their images, or representing space without an object to define it, was outside the limits of—because inconsistent with—the style in which Cubism was conceived, and thus the terms in which its development was carried out.

Thus, Cubism's development exhibits an internal structure in that it reaches an ending explained by limits built into its style. Of course, not all movements reach their limits, leaving, perhaps, opportunities or potentials unexplored. Such movements may be said to merely stop rather than end. Speaking this way allows one to distinguish between the final point of a movement that really does feel like an ending, because no further development could be conceived in the same direction, and the final point of a movement whose stopping is externally required, while it seems that the movement could have gone on further than it did if the external ending had not been imposed. It is a consequence of such an internal form of development that when a movement does reach an ending, that ending, signifying the limits to the movement's style, may reveal the nature of the movement as a whole; that is, sometimes seeing the ending that a development reaches lets one better understand the identity of that which developed. For example, many of the Cubist paintings of Picasso and Braque look so superficially similar as to have been painted by the same man. But the respective developments of Picasso's and Braque's individual styles turn out to have such different limits that those superficially similar paintings can be seen, retrospectively, to embody different principles, to be emerging from different conceptions of the proper means and ends of art. The identities of the paintings—what kinds of processes they emerge from—are revealed by the limits to the individual stylistic developments in which, respectively, they figure.

In the preceding examples, style serves as the central subject or continuant in narratives that explain the development of artistic movements. The point is not lack of interest in factors other than style that are part of artistic developments; many other forms and levels of description are appropriate to representing developments within art history. But it is through adverting to the artistic style that, once formed, exists throughout a development that one can see how the development's beginning explains its ending. The ending is explained by the beginning as a limit to the style,

even if it takes the development of the movement over time for that limit to be revealed.

[*See also* Constructivism; Cubism; *and* Realism.]

BIBLIOGRAPHY

Belting, Hans. *The End of the History of Art?* Translated by Christopher S. Wood. Chicago, 1987.

Carr, David. *Time, Narrative, and History.* Bloomington, Ind., 1986.

Carrier, David. *Artwriting.* Amherst, Mass., 1987.

Danto, Arthur C. *Narration and Knowledge.* New York, 1985.

Danto, Arthur C. "Narrative and Style." In *Beyond the Brillo Box,* pp. 233–248. New York, 1992.

Holly, Michael Ann. *Panofsky and the Foundations of Art History.* Ithaca, N.Y., 1984.

Kermode, Frank. *The Sense of an Ending.* New York and Oxford, 1967.

Podro, Michael. *The Critical Historians of Art.* New Haven, 1982.

Said, Edward W. *Beginnings: Intention and Method.* New York, 1975; reprint, New York, 1985.

Scholes, Robert, and Robert Kellogg. *The Nature of Narrative.* New York and Oxford, 1967.

Sternberg, Meir. *Expositional Modes and Temporal Ordering in Fiction.* Baltimore, 1978.

Vasari, Giorgio. *The Lives of the Artists* (2d ed. of 1568). Translated by George Bull. London and New York, 1987.

White, Hayden. *The Content of the Form: Narrative Discourse and Historical Representation.* Baltimore, 1987.

Wölfflin, Heinrich. *Principles of Art History: The Problem of the Development of Style in Later Art* (1915). New York, 1932.

Wollheim, Richard. *Art and Its Objects.* 2d ed. with six supplementary essays. Cambridge and New York, 1980.

JONATHAN GILMORE

Narrative and the Visual and Literary Arts

Narratology is the theory of narrative, mainly consisting of a definition and a set of derived concepts. These concepts can be used for the analysis of actual narratives, be they literary or visual, or mixed media, be they fictional or "true" reports on events. Narrative is one of the most pervasive modes of meaning production. By means of narrative, members of a given culture represent and convey happenings, ideas, arguments, experiences, imagined states of the world, and mythical theories of origin. According to a simple definition, a narrative is a semiotic construction in which a "speaker," the narrator, conveys his or her view of a series of events to a listener, viewer, or reader. From this definition the key concepts of narratology are derived. Although this definition holds for narratives in a variety of media, narratological analysis tends to be derived from literary practice.

Although narratology has developed mainly within the field of literary studies, it has been brought to bear, or "applied" (with the obvious emendations), to film, anthropology, scientific discourse, and visual art. The examples below are derived from the latter field. Accounts of narrative in visual art, for example, tend to focus on the question of how images are able to narrate stories. The underlying presupposition seems to be that images are a priori handicapped in this competition; narrating is primarily a matter of discourse, not of visuality. Hence, attempts to overcome the limits of the visual, brave as they are, will have to be considered with indulgence. But narratological analysis of images is possible without presupposing that narrative is somehow a foreign mode in visual art. A well-known example is the one implied in Barthes's book *S/Z*. Barthes develops an interpretation of Balzac's short story "Sarrasine" through an analysis of five codes that the reader allegedly activates when reading this story. The essay is attractive because it is reader-oriented, while placing the act of reading within cultural constraints.

The *proraïretic* code is a "series of models of action that help readers place details in plot sequences: because we have stereotyped models of 'falling in love,' or 'kidnapping,' or 'undertaking a perilous mission,' we can tentatively place and organize the details we encounter as we read" (Barthes, 1974). In a way, this is a narrative version of an iconographic code. In *Travels in Hyperreality*, Umberto Eco analyzes *Casablanca* as a "cult film" because of the predominance and intertextual play of the stories projected by what Barthes calls the proraitic code. The *hermeneutic* code presupposes an enigma and induces us into seeking out details that can contribute to its solution. The *semic* code inserts cultural stereotypes, "background information," which one brings in to make sense of figures in the text or image in terms of class, gender, ethnicity, age, and the like. With the help of the *symbolic* code, one brings in symbolic interpretation to read certain details, for example, "love," "hostility," "loneliness," or, for that matter, "theatricality," "vanitas," or "self-referentiality." Finally, the *referential* code brings in cultural knowledge, such as the history of the character "Napoleon" in Tolstoy's *War and Peace*, or the identity of the sitter for a portrait, the program of an artistic movement, or the social status of the figures represented. Together, these (and other) codes produce a "narrative," as a satisfying interpretation of the image in which every detail receives a place. This narrative is emphatically produced by the reader to deal with the image; it produces the story through the processing of a strange image into a familiar mind-set.

The intertwining of codes produced by prior discourses of a culture makes Barthes's approach congenial with Mikhail Bakhtin's theory of narrative. Barthes starts from the receiver, the reader (or viewer) of the work. Bakhtin's concept of polyphony, the intertwining of different voices in the novel, resulting in heteroglossia or the cacophony of incongruous strands of cultural discourses, takes the same issue up from the other side, the side of the sender or writer, or the maker of the image. The major gain this view yields is the awareness that the text or image is not unified. Indeed, classical criticism has tended to seek the interpretation that

accounts for each and every detail of the work within the same framework. Thus, details that do not fit are ignored or set aside as unimportant or as "mistakes," evidence of a foreign hand, of studio practice, ultimately discounting the work as nonautographic rather than contributing to a heteroglossic view of the work. Bakhtin helps us to accept that even when the image or text is made by one artist, the inherent heterodiscursive nature of the culture of which this artist is a product necessarily brings in elements of alterity, if only to be repressed to the margins. Thus, an image that overtly represents the intervention of women in a fight between men such as David's *Sabine Women* (Paris, Louvre) cannot help inserting indexes of homosexual interest. Diego Velázquez's *Las Meninas* has been argued to present a visual heteroglossia in that it is at the same time narrative and descriptive, displaying the act of painting within the description of courtly life as still life. This mix of modes is fundamentally different from the famous self-referentiality (famously, in Michel Foucault's first chapter of *The Order of Things*, on *Las Meninas*), paradox (in John Searle's [1980] response to that analysis), or unity (Joel Snyder and Ted Cohen's [1980] response to both) proclaimed by other critics. All these critics ultimately gave the painting a unity it so stubbornly refuses to yield; they interpreted the painting on the basis of the placement of the mirror in relation to geometrical perspective. Paradoxically, Svetlana Alpers's (1983) refusal to appropriate the entire painting for the narrative mode enabled the critic to do more justice to the painting as narrative than the other, simple narrative readings.

In spite of the importance of Barthes's and Bakhtin's insights into the various factors that collaborate or compete to produce narrative, the one factor that keeps slipping away is the traffic of meaning from source to destination and back. In traditional narrative theory, the concept of the narrator as the source of information or the utterer of the speech act of narrating has favored a model of a unified voice: one narrator determines what the reader is going to get. Replacing the author by the narrator, or the artist by an implied orchestrator of the image, does not really help in understanding the various signs at work in a text.

Attempts to atomize the informational sources of narrative in view of a semiotic conception of texts may be more useful. One such attempt distinguishes between three narrative agents: the *narrator* or speaker, source of the utterance; the *focalizer* or source of the vision presented in the utterance; and the *actor* or agent acting out the fabula (the sequence of events presented). This model allows for integration of two important views: the idea that signs are organized, and the possibility of the "difference within." Precisely because the narrators of a text hold discursive power, they are also able to embed the vision of somebody else, as in the phrase "She saw that he noticed that the lipstick on his collar had not escaped her." Here one narrator conveys three views, embedded like Russian dolls, and each based on signs positioned on different levels: in the fabula, two actors are confronted, one of whom, the woman, constructs on the basis of a sign of facial expression that the other, the man, has in turn constructed on the basis of the sign of her own facial expression, a third construction, the sign of lipstick on his collar, which he may until then have been unaware of himself.

In this structure of embedding, one voice conveys in a single discourse a visual dialogue that seems typical of language. In fact, something like free indirect discourse might seem impossible in visual images. In free indirect discourse, not just the vision but even aspects of the voice of another figure are embedded within the narrator's monological voice. In visual representation, this hierarchical ordering is replaced with the presence of all elements of the configuration of subjects on the one surface. Yet, this is a deceptive unification of the status of the various elements. Imagine the story of Susanna surprised by the Elders, a literary story conveyed through the biblical Book of Daniel. In a traditional painting of *Susanna and the Elders* by, say, Peter Paul Rubens, the figure of the naked woman is presented to the viewer, exposed for sight and delight (Munich, Alte Pinakothek). The elders, the represented focalizers, provide a position from which the viewer can interpret the woman's body; in other words, they offer a point of identification. The woman, either looking away or looking at the viewer in compliance, does not counter the voyeuristic position offered. This is, then, a simple, one-strand narrative. In contrast, Artemisia Gentileschi's *Susanna* (Pommersfelden, Schloss Weissenstein) is claimed by Mary Garrard (1989) to suggest discomfort at the situation of voyeurism, implying a critique of it.

What are the narrative signs of this critique? To give one example, Garrard mentions the uncomfortable stone bench that Susanna is sitting on. As opposed to the lush foliage that, alluding to the garden of earthly delight, traditionally represents the cheerful focalization of the Elders, this stone bench foregrounds the experience of the threatened woman. The structure of focalization in this painting is more complex than in the Rubens: the men exchange glances, "telling" each other visually their scheme; Susanna looks away, refusing to interact with her assailants; and the hard and unpleasant features of the Elders counter any tendency to identify with their viewing position—spying on Susanna. Instead, Susanna's distressed look, although not directed at the viewer so as to preclude the idea of compliance, and not directed at the men either with a similar effect, suggests that the unpleasant men we see are as she sees them: Susanna, here, focalizes her assailants, and the result of that focalization is signified to the viewer, before the latter reaches their focalization, which in its mutuality excludes the viewer. Thus, within the single "discourse" of

voyeurism, so prevailing in the Western tradition, instead of a narrative of voyeurism we have a counternarrative of anguish and vulnerability.

Between Rubens's and Gentileschi's Susannas we can read Rembrandt van Rijn's *Susanna* in Berlin, where one Elder is sitting on a throne while the other is busying himself with Susanna differently. On the one hand, the female nude, vulnerable, young, and iconographically recalling the Venus pudica (hence, evoking eroticism), looks at the viewer, who can read her as helpless and calling for sympathy, or as an object of sadistic lust. But the Elder who, with one hand, is undressing her is, with the other hand, signifying the direction of his look, which literally overlooks Susanna's body. With the help of another iconographic reference, to Albrecht Dürer's *Melencolia I,* one can construct a narrative that complicates and critiques voyeurism. This effect is produced not so much with reference to the woman's focalization, but rather to the man's failed focalization. Once a viewer identifies with this man, he or she is struck by the failure of looking and the resulting paralyzing melancholy. Again, the image presents three figures looking in different directions and different modes, breaking up the unity that would cast this work in the too-encompassing category of "the nude."

What this view of narrative suggests, then, is that the act of looking at a narrative painting is as much a dynamic process as reading a text is. The viewer moves about the surface to anchor his or her look at a variety of positions. These positions are not just alternatives, as a pluralistic view would have it, but they are interrelated and embedded. Bakhtin's radical view of heteroglossia, as well as Derrida's account of polysemy in the concept of dissemination, are often followed up as liberal pluralism. This is a mistaken interpretation of both theorists' positions. Both theories allow, even encourage, awareness of the power relations *among* the elements of the plurality. Whichever position one chooses to endorse in the Rembrandt, the other two cast their shadow over it. If one looks with the man in the upper right, comfortably sitting and watching the scene, one's eye travels with him to his colleague, and once that embedded position is occupied, the failure to see happens. If one responds to Susanna's look, her experience of already being attacked then leads to the awareness that the man undressing her is also emphatically not looking at her. In Bakhtin's terms, the discourse of melancholy and the discourse of rape are in dialogue with each other and with the discourse of voyeurism. But that view does not account for the embedding of the former two into the overall concept of the latter. Therefore, it appears better to state that both melancholy and rape, as well as the opposition between these two, are embedded within the discourse of voyeurism, embodied by the man at the upper right.

The semiotic nature of this model emphasizes the sign-status of the elements involved in this reading. As abandons the illusion of unity, the focused eye of the active Elder, engaged in an act of looking unrelated to the nude body, stands out as a sign of a whole range of meanings that include the ideas about melancholy as an index of artistry; and these meanings are close to losing any connection with the Susanna theme. In competition with this cluster of meanings stands the allusion to the Venus pudica in Susanna's left hand. But this sign is in turn overruled by the slight shift backwards, turning the sign of statuesque display into that of a narrative agency pushing back the threatening presence.

This example also demonstrates that the atomization of narrative within a discursive order—the integration of pluralization with embeddedness—allows for an account of ideology that breaks away from monolithic readings without falling back into an "innocent" relativism. Thus, those paintings by Anselm Kiefer that have disturbed some viewers because of their allusions to Nazism, while being hailed by others as a critique of fascism, can be seen as a debate with Nazism. This dialogic approach refuses to silence, ignore, repress, and thereby conserve fascism today. By integrating another partner in this debate, the tradition of linear perspective, that emblem of realism and objectivity, Kiefer's works also signify the complicity of art with politics. The suggestion is that perspective and the scientific pursuit it stands for, collaborate with the fascist tendencies that an obliteration of the Nazi past facilitates. The resulting narrative presents a highly complex account of both fascism and painting, within which the various possible focalizers take their share in the production of meaning. The narrative of the paintings is constituted by the tensions between these focalizers.

Narratology does not merely identify subjects within the image and their relations of embedding; it also allows one to specify the nature, place, and effectivity of each subject's agency. It provides a possibility for reading texts and images against the grain of the alleged opposition between discourse and image by interpreting elements as signs of negation, as in the Elder's not-seeing; as signs of syntactical connection, as in the bench in the Gentileschi shifting focalization from the Elders to the victim; as signs of causality, as in the anguished look of Susanna in the Rembrandt caused by the physical attack on her person by the man. Most important, narrative semiotics provides insight into visual narrative, as distinct from visual allusions to verbal narratives.

It is crucial to keep in mind that narrative is not a one-sided structure. Address, the ways in which a viewer is invited to participate in the representation, is perhaps the most relevant aspect of a semiotics of subjectivity. According to the linguist Émile Benveniste (1971), language inscribes the subject of discourse as the implicit "I" who speaks. Certain linguistic categories (such as, precisely, *I* and its correlate, *you,* but also other elements such as pronouns and adverbs such as *here* or *yesterday*) have no referential value but only have meaning in terms of the discourse itself. Thus, the subject of discourse is defined by these deictic words, whether or not she or he is the same person as the speaker who conveys the speech, say, the narrator. The noncoincidence between the speaker and the subject of the discourse is precisely the condition of possibility of narrative. The equivalent of "I" in a painting is often the figure whose act of looking is represented, thereby suggesting participation in a story: "I" takes the shape of an "eye." But that story involves the onlooker as well. If Édouard Manet's *Olympia* scandalized its contemporary viewers, we now say it was because, precisely, the woman participated too fully in her own display; rather than contenting herself with being the "third person" whose body was objectified in an impersonal narration for the sake of the onlooker, this woman looks actively at the viewer, so much so that her objectification is nullified, and the viewer, who is now no longer the "I" who can take possession of the woman, is offered the position of the "you" hailed by the woman and held accountable for his act of looking; for any "I" implies a "you" whom it addresses. The French philosopher Louis Althusser claimed that this address, this "hailing," constitutes the subject in ideology: it forms the subject as what the "ideological state apparatuses" wish the subject to identify with. However much autonomy a particular reader may have (or assume to have) in front of a narrative, according to this theory subjectivity is always produced at least by the interaction between the "I" of the work and the "you" this "I" addresses.

[*See also* Bakhtin; Barthes; *and* Derrida.]

BIBLIOGRAPHY

Alpers, Svetlana. "Interpretation without Representation." *Representations* 1.1 (February 1983): 31–42.

Bakhtin, Mikhail M. *The Dialogic Imagination.* Edited by Michael Holquist, translated by Caryl Emerson and Michael Holquist. Austin, Tex., 1981.

Bal, Mieke. *Narratology: Introduction to the Theory of Narrative.* Translated by Christine van Boheemen. Toronto, 1985.

Bal, Mieke. "The Point of Narratology." *Poetics Today* 11.4 (Winter 1990): 727–753.

Barthes, Roland. *S/Z.* Translated by Richard Miller. New York, 1974.

Benveniste, Émile. *Problems in General Linguistics.* Translated by Mary Elizabeth Meek. Coral Gables, Fla., 1971.

Booth, Wayne C. *The Rhetoric of Fiction* (1961). 2d ed. Chicago, 1983.

Foucault, Michel. "Las Meninas." In *The Order of Things,* pp. 3–16. New York, 1970.

Garrard, Mary D. *Artemisia Gentileschi: The Image of the Female Hero in Italian Baroque Art.* Princeton, N. J. 1989.

Searle, John R. "*Las Meninas* and the Paradoxes of Pictorial Representation." *Critical Inquiry* 6.3 (Spring 1980): 477–488.

Snyder, Joel, and Ted Cohen. "Reflections on *Las Meninas:* Paradox Lost." *Critical Inquiry* 7.2 (Winter 1980): 429–447.

MIEKE BAL

NATIONAL ENDOWMENT FOR THE ARTS. [*To treat issues relating to government funding for the arts, this entry comprises two essays:*

Historical Survey
Controversies

The first essay explains the history of when, how, and for what purposes the National Endowment for the Arts (NEA) was formed in the United States, as compared with government funding for the arts in other countries around the world. The second essay analyzes debates about the NEA that will determine whether it has a future and what kind of future that might be. Although there are other models for government funding for the arts, both the formation and current debates about the NEA make it a compact and telling case study for further reflection on the issue of public support for the arts by modern national governments. For related discussion, see Law and Art; *and* Politics and Aesthetics.]

Historical Survey

The National Endowment for the Arts (NEA), founded in 1965, is the best-known source of government funding for the arts in the United States, although free-market capitalism has favored a dominant role for private funding from corporations, foundations, and individual consumers. Yet, federal support is almost as old as the nation itself, and the complex American model of public and private financing is not unusual among industrialized nations.

France is the leading example of support for the arts through a governmental "ministry of culture," which provides not only funding, but also a dominant artistic and cultural vision for the nation. Even so, private support from individuals and now corporations has played an important, sometimes overlooked, role in funding the arts in France. In contrast, the United States, Canada, Australia, and other nations have combined funding from various private sources and hands-off government funding, with artistic decisions made by citizen-peer reviewers.

In the United States, indirect support consistent with individualism and capitalism began with the U.S. Constitution, which authorized the establishment of a copyright system (article 1, section 8). Allowing creators to reap the financial benefit of a monopoly on their intellectual property is believed to encourage creativity, which is in the national interest, and copyright is enjoyed by artists in most nations.

In the twentieth century, the United States has provided significant financial encouragement for artistic activities by permitting tax deductions for charitable contributions to nonprofit educational and artistic institutions, such as museums, symphony orchestras, and dance companies. This indirect government subsidy supports the arts through the tax code, an approach that enjoys support from the entire political spectrum in the United States and, increasingly, in other countries.

The United States also has a history of direct support for the arts that is often overlooked. The establishment of the Marine Band in 1790 was the first government support of a musical ensemble. The first support for the visual arts came in 1817, when Congress commissioned painter John Trumball to paint Revolutionary War scenes for the Capitol Rotunda. Books on art and music were included in the Library of Congress, established in 1800. The National Conservatory of Music was established by Congress in 1891, with Antonín Dvořák as its first artistic director.

Consistent with American capitalism, Congress established several arts institutions with funds donated by wealthy private individuals. The Smithsonian Institution, which includes several major art museums, was established in 1846 with funds from James Smithson. The Freer Gallery was founded under the Smithsonian umbrella in 1906, with Oriental art and funds for a building donated by Charles Lang Freer. The National Gallery of Art opened in 1941 on the Mall in Washington, D.C., after art and construction funds were donated by Andrew W. Mellon.

Several American presidents have considered ways to provide support for artists. A National Arts Commission was appointed by President James Buchanan in 1859 to promote the arts, but it was disbanded during the American Civil War for lack of funding. Theodore Roosevelt appointed a Council of Fine Arts in 1909, although it too was disbanded for lack of funding. But a Commission on Fine Arts, established one year later by Congress "to advise generally upon questions of art," continues even today, dealing primarily with the architecture of the nation's capital.

The four-term presidency of Franklin D. Roosevelt included significant developments in government support. In 1934, during the Great Depression, Roosevelt established a Section on Painting and Sculpture in the Treasury Department, to assign artists to decorate federal buildings. One year later, the government established the Works Progress Administration (WPA), which provided over 40,000 artists with direct employment in programs for writing, theater, art, and music.

After World War II, the United States Information Agency supported artists by sending them abroad for goodwill tours. In the 1970s and early 1980s, support for unemployed artists was provided through the federal Comprehensive Employment and Training Act (CETA).

Efforts to establish a federal agency to provide direct support for the arts date back to the nineteenth century, with legislation proposed in Congress in 1879 by a New York congressman. In the late 1930s, bills to establish a Bureau of Fine Arts were repeatedly introduced, although never reported out of committee.

The efforts to establish a national arts agency grew in vigor and intensity after World War II. New York Senator Jacob K. Javits, a leader in the bipartisan efforts that led to the establishment of the NEA, introduced a resolution in 1949 calling for a national theater, opera, and ballet. President Harry S. Truman asked the Commission on Fine Arts to recommend ways that the federal government could support the arts.

In 1955, President Dwight D. Eisenhower urged the establishment of a Federal Advisory Commission on the Arts and legislation was introduced with his encouragement, although no formal action was taken. In 1958, while Eisenhower was president, Congress did approve establishment of a National Cultural Center, which opened years later as the John F. Kennedy Center for the Performing Arts.

Some considered the establishment of the NEA in 1965 a tribute to the memory of Kennedy, who, with his wife Jacqueline, had ushered in an era of grace and culture. Kennedy himself nurtured the process that led to the founding of the NEA, including appointment of a special consultant to provide recommendations for how best to support the arts. Months before his assassination in 1963, Kennedy received the report recommending establishment of a National Arts Foundation. He signed an executive order to establish a President's Advisory Council on the Arts, and a bipartisan coalition introduced legislation to establish the foundation.

In the months after the assassination, Congress passed legislation to establish a National Council on the Arts, signed into law by President Lyndon Baines Johnson on September 3, 1964. The purpose of the new council was to "recommend ways to maintain and increase the cultural resources of the Nation and to encourage and develop greater appreciation and enjoyment of the arts by its citizens." Over the next year, hearings were held in both the House of Representatives and the Senate and an influential report was issued by the Rockefeller Brothers Fund titled "The Performing Arts: Problems and Prospects."

After years of effort, the NEA was established in September 1965, when President Johnson signed the National Foundation on the Arts and the Humanities Act (20 U.S.C. section 921 et seq.). The act established the NEA jointly with its sister agency, the National Endowment for the Humanities, under the umbrella of the National Foundation on the Arts and the Humanities. The act also established the Federal Council on the Arts and the Humanities, an interagency advisory group of various federal officials.

From the beginning, the NEA was organized to avoid being a "ministry of culture," as European funding decisions were perceived in the United States. Rather than allowing government bureaucrats to determine precisely what would be funded, an elaborate system of panel review brought in experts from around the country to review proposals and make recommendations for funding.

As the panelists were selected by the agency's professional staff, Congress mandated diversity requirements, including geographic, ethnic, cultural, and artistic points of view. NEA critics have charged that panelists have been mainly professional artists looking out for each other, leading to stagnation in true creativity. Congress added a requirement that all panels include laypersons knowledgeable about the arts but not themselves professionals in the arts, yet the influence of such a lone individual on a large panel is questionable.

All applications for funding are reviewed by the panels "solely on the basis of artistic excellence and artistic merit," as required in the NEA authorizing legislation, but critics wonder if such determinations can be made objectively. Difficulties in applying the funding criteria are compounded by the congressional directive that the agency not favor any particular aesthetic standard or school.

Recommendations of panelists go to the National Council on the Arts, an advisory group of twenty-six citizens appointed by the president and confirmed by the Senate, another safeguard against an ingrown professional staff dictating cultural policy to the nation. The recommendations from the National Council then go to the head of the agency, the chairperson, who makes the final funding decisions.

These safeguards are a double-edged sword. The extensive involvement of the "public" (members of the National Council and proposal review panels) can be seen as protection of the freedom of artists against federal bureaucrats who might impose their personal cultural agendas on the artists. But the public involvement also can be seen as suppressing artistic freedom, by restricting funded grants to the safe and the mainstream, whereas NEA staff members might otherwise fund riskier, experimental art.

The concern to avoid a ministry of culture is echoed in other nations, such as Australia. Arts groups advocate that the government should continue to provide direct financial support to encourage artistic development and give greater access to the arts to all citizens, but without dictating a national cultural policy or artistic identity. The government's Australia Council uses a system of peer review and arm's-length funding decisions strikingly similar to that of the NEA. Tax policy supports donations to arts organizations, as in the United States, although activists believe that it should be more generous to encourage greater corporate support.

As in Australia and the United States, an important principle in Canada has been peer review with arm's-length involvement of the government in actual cultural policy. Direct and continuing government support for the arts began in Canada in 1957 with establishment of the Canada Council.

The NEA budget, beginning with only $2.5 million in 1965, grew rapidly through the 1970s, reaching almost $159 million by 1981. That year, President Ronald Reagan's administration proposed cutting the NEA budget by 50 percent. In the face of a firestorm of opposition, much of it from mainstream Republicans who sat on boards of directors of museums and symphonies around the country, the actual cut was only 10 percent. The budget increased gradually during the 1980s, reaching almost $176 million in 1992, the largest budget in the history of the agency. After several years of controversy over the funding of art by Robert Mapplethorpe, Andres Serrano, and others, the budget for 1996 was cut 40 percent to $100 million.

While the NEA struggles with this drastic budget cut, other nations have recently provided dramatic increases in their support for the arts. The budget for the government Arts Council in Ireland has increased by almost 40 percent since 1994. The South African Department of Arts, Culture, Science and Technology, established in 1994, has distributed funds to all the provinces to further its goal of enabling artistic expression to revitalize its diverse national identity.

Mexico also has enhanced government support of the arts, with the 1989 creation of the National Fund for Culture and the Arts. Some prominent artists and arts organizations claim that they find cooperation with government funding sources stultifying and restrictive, while others enjoy the freedom to work on their art without crippling economic difficulties. (In most of Latin America, however, government support is limited and unreliable, with principal support for the arts coming from private patrons and foundations associated with local corporations and wealthy families.)

Even at its peak, the per capita funding of the NEA was small, less than seventy cents per citizen, compared with the equivalent of thirty-three dollars in the Netherlands and twelve dollars in Great Britain. Although exact numbers are difficult to establish, a Presidential Task Force on the Arts and Humanities reported to President Reagan in 1981 that only about 10 percent of funding for the arts in the nation came directly from the NEA. Other sources included state and local governments, as well as foundations and other private sources. But NEA supporters point to the strong impetus of NEA dollars in leveraging those additional funds.

Supporters of government funding in the United States note the social benefit of the arts and the symbolic importance of lending the stature of government support to the endeavor, even though the dollar value is miniscule compared to funds from other sources. Supporters also cite studies that appeal to American capitalism, showing that the arts stimulate economic growth, jobs, and tourism.

Opponents of government funding argue that art is dangerous to the nation's morals and that it is inappropriate to use tax funds for anything other than the most narrowly defined functions of government. Some argue that attempts to draw guidelines on acceptable programming unavoidably infringe on freedom of expression and that the arts thus should be left to the private sector. Others regard the NEA as a luxury that the nation can no longer afford.

Although artists often argue for the importance of government funds to provide economic necessities for working artists and art institutions, others wonder if overdependence on government subsidies stifles the creative work that such subsidies supposedly encourage. The former Soviet Union is cited by some as a system in which extensive financial dependence on the state led artists to toe the party line as effectively as overt censorship by the regime. The explosion of artistic creativity during the European Renaissance was made possible, critics note, by the market forces of the emerging middle class, newly rich merchants, and patrons from the nobility, not by government subsidies.

American artists sometimes look longingly to what they believe is a European model of art heavily subsidized by the state. But in Europe, the combination of private and state support, both direct and indirect, is increasingly the norm, even though the proportions and public attitudes might contrast with those in the United States.

In Britain, the House of Commons established a select committee to improve British art education in 1835. Members of Parliament expressed concern that Britain lagged behind the French at encouraging both producers and consumers of fine art. Yet the National Theatre in Britain was established by the government Arts Council only in 1963, three decades after the Federal Theater Project in America. The British Government Art Collection was established in 1898 to acquire art for government buildings, but reluctance to provide significant funds persists through the present day, with excuses ranging from national economic problems to the dangers of direct patronage.

Sharper contrast with American practices can be found in France. The Royal Academy for Painting and Sculpture, established by Louis XIV in 1667, a century before the American Revolution, provided the primary support for national cultivation of art. But by the nineteenth century, art supported by the academy seemed to many to be stagnant. Impressionists, excluded from the official exhibitions, found their principal support from the free economic market and the middle class.

France has moved to incorporate the increased freedom possible from diverse sources of private support, yet it remains a nation where the concept of a "ministry of culture" is praised, not shunned, as in the United States, Australia, and Canada. Novelist André Malraux became minister for cultural affairs in 1959, consolidating a variety of state funding programs and promoting a strong vision of making culture available to all citizens. In the 1980s, when the Reagan administration was attempting to drastically reduce NEA funding, the budget for the French Ministry of Culture was doubled, with a new emphasis on decentralization to improve broad access to the arts throughout France. In the 1990s, this national priority has continued, with additional support from private French corporations, a recent, more "American" development.

Modern Japan provides another contrast to the American model of mixed private and public support. In the United

States, mainstream art is supported by corporate sponsors fearful of controversy and commercial backers catering to popular taste, whereas experimental work that is not "commercially viable" has found support at the NEA. In Japan, private funds also favor traditional works in museums (60 percent of which are owned by business interests) and wealthy art buyers concentrate on stockpiling Western masters. But government funding sources (the Japan Art and Culture Foundation, the Agency of Cultural Affairs, and the Japan Foundation) also favor traditional work. Private galleries and a few private museums backed by wealthy businessmen provide the principal support for new art.

Nor does Japan provide the support for art in its tax code that is enjoyed by American art institutions. Not only are donations to the arts rarely tax-deductible, but some are actually taxed, although museums have lobbied heavily for tax deductions modeled on the American approach to nonprofit art institutions.

In another contrast, the city-state of Singapore has adopted a pragmatic approach in pursuing a role as a mecca for art in Asia. Hoping to benefit from uncertainty about future export policies in Hong Kong, Singapore has encouraged museums, galleries, and collections of Asian art. Although direct government funding is limited, generous tax benefits have developed extensive support from corporations, foundations, and wealthy patrons. Ironically, despite notorious state censorship of writers, other artists claim to enjoy considerable freedom of expression. A similar mix of economic prosperity and political ambition seems to be driving extensive investment in the arts by the government of Taiwan.

Spain, along with Japan, had been another holdout on tax incentives to support art, but tax reforms now allow deductions for donations of art to museums. This infusion of private support is expected to shift the balance of artistic control away from government support, which some believe stifles artistic creativity.

How to measure the effectiveness of government funding is a contentious issue worldwide. Does government support help or hinder creativity? Is the quantity of art produced relevant? Does improved nationwide access come at the cost of quality? Does artistic activity enhance national stature? Does it improve the economy?

The NEA cites impressive statistics to demonstrate its success in stimulating artistic output, as well as access. In the three decades since its establishment, more than one hundred thousand grants have been awarded to artists and arts organizations in all fifty states. With financial encouragement from the NEA, the number of state arts agencies has grown from five to fifty-six (including the fifty states, American Samoa, the District of Columbia, Guam, the Northern Marianas, Puerto Rico, and the U.S. Virgin Islands).

The NEA also cites impressive expansion of arts organizations around the country since its founding. Nonprofit

theaters have grown from forty-six to more than 425. Large orchestras have doubled in number. Opera companies have increased sixfold. Dance companies have increased tenfold. Yet, critics wonder whether this same growth would have occurred with state and local government support, along with private underwriting. Even some arts supporters wonder whether the quality of these new organizations justifies the continued infusion of federal funds. The long debate over "populist" access versus "elitist" quality has tilted heavily toward access in the NEA's fight for survival.

The symbolic importance of the arts in the United States was underscored in 1985 with the establishment of the National Medal of Arts, awarded annually at the White House. Perhaps only in the United States would the recipients of the nation's highest honor in the arts include such corporate patrons as the Dayton Hudson Corporation, Exxon Corporation, Hallmark Cards, Lila Wallace-Reader's Digest Fund, and Texaco Inc., along with outstanding artists and arts organizations.

Yet, the American mix of private support from individuals, corporations, and foundations, along with direct support from government subsidies and indirect support from the tax code, is increasingly the international norm, not the exception.

BIBLIOGRAPHY

Chapman, Christine. "Power and Patronage." *ARTnews* 89.3 (March 1990): 138–141. Contains information on Japan.

Dubin, Steven C. *Bureaucratizing the Muse: Public Funds and the Cultural Worker.* Chicago, 1987.

Enriquez, Mary Schneider. "Myths, Magic, Grunge, and Glamour." *ARTnews* 93.4 (April 1994): 134–138. Contains information on Mexico.

Howlett, D. Roger. "Donald DeLue and the Federal Government as Patron of the Arts." *American Art Review* 5.1 (Summer 1992): 114–119, 146–152.

Jones, Robert. "Art, the Great Persuader: A History of the Government Art Collections." *Apollo* 130.333 (November 1989): 297–303. Contains information on Great Britain.

Mattick, Paul, Jr. "Arts and the State." *Nation* 251 (October 1, 1990): 348–358.

National Endowment for the Arts. *National Endowment for the Arts, 1965–1995: A Brief Chronology of Federal Involvement in the Arts.* Washington, D.C., 1996.

Sproll, Paul A. C. "Matters of Taste and Matters of Commerce: British Government Intervention in Art Education in 1835." *Studies in Art Education* 35.2 (1994): 105–113.

Stolz, George. "Spain: Taking the Art Out of Politics." *ARTnews* 94.2 (February 1995): 108–111.

Veith, Gene Edward. "The National Endowment for the Arts: Liberator or Warden?" *Current* 377 (November 1995): 15–20.

JULIE VAN CAMP

Controversies

The United States Congress stressed the importance of freedom of expression at the National Endowment for the

Arts (NEA) when the agency was established in the National Foundation on the Arts and Humanities Act of 1965 (20 U.S.C. section 951 et seq.). In the Declaration of Purpose, Congress said that "it is necessary and appropriate for the Federal Government to help create and sustain . . . a climate encouraging freedom of thought, imagination, and inquiry."

Congress was concerned that the NEA not become a cultural "czar." The U.S. Senate urged that "there be given the fullest attention to freedom of artistic . . . expression. One of the artist's . . . great values to society is the mirror of self-examination which they raise so that society can become aware of its shortcomings as well as its strengths. . . . The standard should be artistic . . . excellence."

The minority report by the House of Representatives expressed concern that direct federal support of the arts "could lead to attempts at political control of culture." The report quoted Thornton Wilder that "Government should not subsidize a national theater because the voters would then become critics with the power of censorship at the polls."

Administrative safeguards, including the extensive involvement of persons outside government, provided important protection against an entrenched federal bureaucracy dictating cultural policy for the nation. Congress required the establishment of a National Council on the Arts to review proposals and make recommendations to the chairperson before grants could be made. The council consists of twenty-six members appointed by the president and confirmed by the Senate. They are private citizens, not government employees, with "broad knowledge of, or expertise in, or for their profound interest in, the arts and . . . established records of distinguished service, or achieved eminence, in the arts."

Another protection against a "ministry of culture" is the use of peer-review panels to evaluate all proposals. Panelists must reflect "a wide geographic, ethnic, and minority representation as well as . . . diverse artistic and cultural points of view." Panels must include "lay individuals who are knowledgeable about the arts but who are not engaged in the arts as a profession and are not members of either artists' organizations or arts organizations." All applications are reviewed "solely on the basis of artistic excellence and artistic merit."

The First Amendment to the United States Constitution ("Congress shall make no law . . . abridging the freedom of speech") protects speech that many find highly offensive. But this freedom seems less sacrosanct when the expression is financed by the taxpayer.

The use of grant money from the NEA to create what some consider pornographic or blasphemous art became the subject of enormous controversy in the late 1980s. Congress passed controversial prohibitions on the funding of such art and President George Bush fired the NEA chairman, John Frohnmayer. Some believe that the NEA should be shut down, as it cannot be trusted with the taxpayers' money. Others believe that the NEA is a luxury that the nation can no longer afford.

The NEA controversy has centered on obscenity, which is a recognized exception to First Amendment protection. In *Miller v. California*, 413 U.S. 15 (1973), the U.S. Supreme Court established a three-pronged test for obscenity prohibitions that would not violate the First Amendment: "*(a)* whether the average person, applying contemporary community standards, would find that the work, taken as a whole, appeals to the prurient interest; *(b)* whether the work depicts or describes, in a patently offensive way, sexual conduct specifically defined by the applicable state law; and *(c)* whether the work, taken as a whole, lacks serious literary, artistic, political or scientific value."

Congress used this language in 1989 in an amendment to the annual NEA appropriations act:

> None of the funds . . . may be used to promote, disseminate, or produce materials which . . . may be considered obscene, including but not limited to, depictions of sadomasochism, homoeroticism, the sexual exploitation of children, or individuals engaged in sex acts and which, when taken as a whole, do not have serious literary artistic, political, or scientific value.

NEA required grant recipients to certify that they would not use grant funds "to promote, disseminate, or produce [obscene] materials."

Many artists and arts organizations refused to accept NEA grants in order to protest the prohibitions on the content of their art. Some filed lawsuits challenging these restrictions on their exercise of free speech. Federal courts sided with the artists, striking down as unconstitutional the certification required by the NEA. In *Bella Lewitsky Dance Foundation v. Frohnmayer,* 754 F. Supp. 774 (C.D. Cal. 1991), the court held that the requirement was unconstitutionally vague and that it violated the First Amendment protection of free speech.

"Vagueness" violates the Fifth Amendment due process clause. People may not be subject to statutes that are so vague that ordinary people do not understand what they mean and thus could not avoid the conduct prohibited. As NEA applicants would not know how to meet this standard in the future, the clause is unconstitutional. The court concluded that the NEA's promise to apply the *Miller* standard of obscenity did not cure the unconstitutional vagueness. The court also held that the NEA certification requirement violated the First Amendment protection of free speech, because it had an unconstitutional "chilling effect" on grant applicants.

Congress tried a different approach in the 1990 reauthorization of the NEA, requiring that the NEA take "into consideration general standards of decency and respect for the diverse beliefs and values of the American public." This provision was struck down as an unconstitutional violation of the Fifth and First Amendments in *Finley v. National Endowment for the Arts*, 795 F.Supp. 1457 (C.D. Cal. 1992). The court held that discretionary NEA grants are subject to First Amendment standards, using the analogy of academic freedom in American colleges and universities.

The U.S. Department of Justice filed an appeal to this decision. The NEA reached a $250,000 settlement with the four performance artists (Karen Finley, John Fleck, Holly Hughes, and Tim Miller), in exchange for an agreement by the artists to drop their claims involving procedural irregularities during the review of their proposals.

The U.S. Court of Appeals for the Ninth Circuit agreed with the lower court that the so-called decency clause in the NEA authorizing legislation "violated the Fifth and First Amendments because it was impermissibly vague and imposed content-based restrictions on protected speech" (*Finley v. National Endowment for the Arts*, No. 92-56028 [9th Cir. filed 5 November 1996]).

Freedom of expression has never been exactly the same in the context of federally funded activities as it is in the private sector. Over the years, the courts have established several principles, although not without continued debate and controversy.

No one has a constitutional right to a grant from the NEA. NEA grants are "discretionary" grants, not "entitlements." The pool of funds available each year is limited. Meeting the eligibility criteria does not entitle an applicant to funds, but only to the right to compete for funds. A denial for fiscal reasons, in and of itself, does not constitute a denial of the right of freedom of expression.

A right under the U.S. Constitution does not necessarily include a right to a subsidy to exercise that right. Even though an artist has a right of artistic expression as a citizen, the artist does not thereby have a right to receive a grant from the NEA to finance the exercise of that right of artistic expression.

In *Advocates for Arts v. Thomson*, 532 F.2d 792 (1st Cir., 1976), *affirming* 397 F.Supp. 1048 (D.N.H. 1975), a literary journal was denied funding by the New Hampshire Commission on the Arts on artistic grounds. (The commission was spending federal funds awarded to state arts councils by the NEA, under authority of the NEA enabling legislation, which governed the state grants.) The court made clear that denial of the grant did not constitute "suppression" of the work. "A disappointed grant applicant cannot complain that his work has been suppressed, but only that another's has been promoted in its stead."

The government may impose some restrictions on government-subsidized activities. The right to exercise free speech in the context of a government-subsidized activity is not absolute.

In accepting funds from the government, the recipient does not thereby forfeit all constitutional rights. State university professors paid with government funds retain rights of freedom of expression, for example.

In determining whether someone should get a grant from the NEA, the government cannot penalize the applicant for the exercise of the constitutional right of free speech prior to the grant. The NEA has argued that artists are free to exercise their First Amendment rights independently of the NEA funding and that the nonobscenity certification requirement did not place any obstacles to such exercise. But the *Lewitsky* court noted the NEA's "extensive role in the financing of the arts" and the frequency with which private funding decisions were made based on the NEA's decision to fund an applicant. The *Finley* court noted that, by law, the NEA could fund no more than 50 percent of a project activity. A restriction on NEA funds thus would penalize the activity supported with nonfederal funds.

The review process used by the NEA in deciding future grants also resulted in an unconstitutional penalty for an applicant's exercise of free speech prior to the grant. The applications of the four performance artists in *Finley* were rejected because of their previous work as artists, work that the chairperson and the National Council found objectionable on "decency" grounds, even though their overall work had been rated high on artistic standards.

Although rejected by American courts, some theorists argue that speech that is merely offensive to others should be another exception to the First Amendment. In a court challenge of an NEA-funded exhibit, "David Wojnarowicz: Tongues of Flame," David Fordyce and Yvonne Knickerbocker claimed that the exhibit caused them to suffer "a spiritual injury and that the exhibition caused offense to their religious sensibilities" (*Fordyce v. Frohnmayer*, 763 F.Supp. 654, 656 [D.D.C. 1991]). The court rejected the claim, especially as "plaintiffs do not even allege that they have either seen the exhibition or studied the catalogue . . . [and thus] have failed to show that they have endured any special burdens that justify their standing to sue as citizens." But the court left open the possibility that the plaintiffs might have a claim if "they had to confront the exhibition daily, . . . the exhibition was visible in the course of their normal routine, or . . . their usual driving or walking routes took them through or past the exhibition."

Some speech is restricted because it constitutes the establishment of religion, which is itself prohibited by the First Amendment to the U.S. Constitution. ("Congress shall make no law respecting an establishment of religion.") Prayer led by a principal in a public school would violate the establishment clause; a school policy prohibiting the principal from leading such prayers would not violate the right of free speech.

In challenging the Wojnarowicz exhibit, plaintiffs argued that the exhibit was critical of their Christian beliefs and thus violated the establishment clause. The plaintiffs "view the public display of the exhibition as an affront to their liberty to practice religion free from governmental entanglement and politically divisive governmental intrusion into the affairs of religion." But the court said that "merely asserting spiritual injury under the establishment clause is insufficient to support standing to sue as a citizen."

A future plaintiff might be able to show sufficient and direct suffering, but another consideration rules out such challenges to NEA grants. To violate the establishment clause, "Congress . . . [must have decided] how the . . . funds were to be spent, and the executive branch, in administering the statute, was merely carrying out Congress' scheme." At the NEA, Congress does not "[participate] in the decision to grant or deny applications for federal funding, . . . [nor does] NEA merely [administer] a congressional directive." This also means that the NEA could not deny a grant based on possible violation of the establishment clause without risking violation of the free-speech clause of the First Amendment.

Projects that seem to benefit from these decisions include those that are anti-Semitic, racist, or sexist. If the NEA supports controversial projects for artists who are admired, then the public must be prepared for the possibility that NEA funds could go to groups that many find unacceptable. This is the true test of the commitment to freedom of expression. If the freedom of artists is genuinely supported, then those rights apply to artists who are condemned as well as to those who are applauded.

BIBLIOGRAPHY

Arian, Edward. *The Unfulfilled Promise: Public Subsidy of the Arts in America.* Philadelphia, 1989.

Balfe, Judith Huggins, ed. *Paying the Piper: Causes and Consequences of Art Patronage.* Urbana, Ill., 1993.

Betsalel, Kenneth Aaron. "The First Amendment and Public Support for the Arts: A Symposium." *Journal of Arts Management and Law* 21 (Winter 1992): 329–354.

Bolton, Richard, ed. *Culture Wars: Documents from the Recent Controversies in the Arts.* New York, 1992.

Buchwalter, Andrew, ed. *Culture and Democracy: Social and Ethical Issues in Public Support for the Arts and Humanities.* Boulder, Colo., 1992.

Feinberg, Joel. "Not with My Tax Money: The Problem of Justifying Government Subsidies for the Arts." *Public Affairs Quarterly* 8 (April 1994): 101–123.

Frohnmayer, John. *Leaving Town Alive: Confessions of an Arts Warrior.* Boston, 1993.

Helms, Jesse. "Art, the First Amendment, and the NEA Controversy." *Nova Law Review* 14 (1990): 317–322.

Marquis, Alice Goldfarb. *Art Lessons: Learning from the Rise and Fall of Public Arts Funding.* New York, 1995.

Mulcahy, Kevin V., and C. Richard Swaim, eds. *Public Policy and the Arts.* Boulder, Colo., 1982.

Mulcahy, Kevin V., and Margaret Jane Wyszomirski, eds. *America's Commitment to Culture: Government and the Arts.* Boulder, Colo., 1995.

Netzer, Dick. *The Subsidized Muse: Public Support for the Arts in the United States.* Cambridge and New York, 1978.

Pankratz, David B., and Valerie B. Morris, eds. *The Future of the Arts: Public Policy and Arts Research.* New York, 1990.

Sabrin, Amy. "Thinking about Content: Can It Play an Appropriate Role in Government Funding of the Arts?" *Yale Law Journal* 102 (1993): 1209–1233.

Serra, Richard. "Art and Censorship." *Nova Law Review* 14 (1990): 323–332.

Smith, Ralph A., and Ronald Berman, eds. *Public Policy and the Aesthetic Interest: Critical Essays on Defining Cultural and Educational Relations.* Urbana, Ill., 1992.

Sullivan, Kathleen M. "Are Content Restrictions Constitutional?" *Journal of Arts Management and Law* 21 (Winter 1992): 323–327.

Van Camp, Julie. "Freedom of Expression at the National Endowment for the Arts: An Opportunity for Interdisciplinary Education." *Journal of Aesthetic Education* 30 (Fall 1996): 43–65.

Wyszomirski, Margaret Jane, ed. *Congress and the Arts: A Precarious Alliance?* New York, 1987.

JULIE VAN CAMP

NATURE. [*To treat the concept of nature in aesthetics, this entry comprises four essays:*

> Nature and Artistic Creation
> Aesthetics of Nature and Ethics
> Japanese Aesthetic Appreciation of Nature
> Contemporary Thought

The first essay is an overview of the aesthetics of nature in the history of philosophy. The second essay explores the links between the aesthetics of nature and ethics, linking the concepts of beauty and the sublime with freedom. The third essay demonstrates how nature is understood in the Japanese tradition of aesthetics wherein nature has meanings distinct from those characteristic of the Western tradition. The final essay is a survey of how the experience and concept of nature are understood in contemporary aesthetics.]

Nature and Artistic Creation

"Nature" in the Western aesthetic tradition has long served as an inspiration for, subject of, or allegory to artistic depiction. Yet, the importance of nature for artistic understanding and production oscillates between its significance as a total *realm of being* outside or beyond human intentions and its status as a series of *perceived environments* outside ourselves, where particular entities evolve within explicit nonhuman contexts. At times in Western tradition, philosophers have conceived of nature as an inferior dimension of being or a raw first phase of dialectical progression or a supine, neutral tool for the refraction of human emotion. At other points, however, they have configured it more positively as a patchwork of pleasing forms or the catalyst for artistic vision or the ecosystemic habitat of creatures great and small. Can one comprehend precisely what philosophers and theorists mean when they refer to art as "imitating" nature, or revealing its "expressiveness," or emerging in the "overflow of intellect" that marks the possession of genius?

If one looks back to ancient thinking on the subject and conceives of art as imitating or representing reality, one first must discern the unusual depreciation of reality implied in the Platonic idea of nature. Plato's metaphysics equates reality wholly and unequivocally with the immaterial Forms, which are abstract, idealized concepts accessible primarily through the soul's power of reason. Earthly pseudorealities such as trees, towns, and persons constitute, for Plato, a second-order universe, one that inherits what little reality it possesses from partial participation in the more lucid, first-order Forms. If earthly nature itself aspires at best to mere imitation of first-order reality, then nature cannot be synonymous with that reality. Taking this reasoning one step further, attempts to reveal truth through artistic depiction of a second-order reality, nature, are metaphysically misguided, being no more than copies of inferior versions of reality. At their most powerful, artworks do provide a haven for the emotions, but even in this capacity their relation to untimbred truth will determine their lowly place within any Platonic approach to art's value.

If Plato's truth emerges from the soul's contemplation of abstract ideas rather than the body's encounter with the tangible world, Plotinus modifies Plato's sense of truth to make it more amenable to or continuous with material embodiment, and hence, most forms of art. For both Plato and Plotinus, the soul as the seat of reason is indivisible, but in Plotinus that power which makes the soul indivisible touches things of nature too, suffusing all with beauty as light dispels the dark. Plotinus's aesthetic light, while incorporeal, nevertheless remains on kindred terms with things of the world: an inner Idea of harmonized parts in a whole pervades *any* object, act, or person endowed with beauty. Bringing familiar single essence to alien diversity, Plotinus envisions beauty as an intelligible Idea that masters matter by bringing it into communion with mind. Works of art, even when imitating the beauty of nature, foster spiritual progress. One makes such progress through acquaintance with beautiful things to beautiful acts and, then, to beauty itself as it shines through the pure primal soul. No longer does nature mimic Plato's unsensed reality. In the thinking of Plotinus, nature, our artistic glimpses of it, and our acts within its sphere serve as tiny but treasured first steps on the human ascent to self-love. Love unveils beauty, making it apparent and signaling our passion. Responding to a vision of pervasive intellection, emotion in the face of nature's beauty, or art's depiction of that beauty, leads to final love of one's own soul.

Plotinus, like Plato, locates beauty in what is ultimately immaterial. Aristotle refrains from examining earthly nature aesthetically and instead uses his theory on tragedy as a vehicle for the portrayal of *human* nature in action. In this way, he sidesteps the ontological ambiguity of what constitutes the nonhuman, natural environment and, in claiming that art imitates nature, focuses instead on the capriciousness of nature or life force as it plays itself out in the drama of human decision and character.

Human character and action continue to figure prominently in Leo Tolstoy's view of nature as that which disrupts human complacency. Powerful and resolute, nature's par-

ticular beauty may inspire the artist to express his or her feelings about nature to others. The artist in turn creates an artifact that thrives on mere contagion, provoking in others the symptom of aesthetic desire. Art functions as an emotional infection that seizes admirers of the artwork and leaves behind a community united by feverish raptures and praise; their unity serves as the index of genuine art. Religious in impulse, Tolstoy's theory praises painting and sculpture of animals and landscapes as most efficacious in spreading proper, acceptable human emotions, which for Tolstoy come to fruition through exposure to unfettered depiction of nature's gentler vistas and creatures.

Yet, as John Ruskin or George Santayana might protest, nature as an empirical entity has no emotional or expressive qualities inherent in it. For them, only a misguided human-centeredness would lead one to suppose that nature, considered aesthetically, does anything other than reflect human associations and accept the impress of human projections. Expression of emotion begins with the human artist and ends with the human spectator, filtering itself through the organic topography of natural environments but never accountable to them as kith to their kin. Ruskin and Santayana deny the possibility of nature having any inherent aesthetic value of its own.

Other philosophers disagree, seeing the artist moved to expression by the beauty of nature as the plaything of nature itself, the small and unwitting depository of far too resilient a mind. For these thinkers, possession of genius hoists one's efforts exponentially. The purveyor of new artistic rules and standards, the genius bears the untimely burden of productive sense. For Tolstoy, the artistic impulse of genius satisfies a demand of nature, the desire to communicate the passions of a soul. Arthur Schopenhauer's view of genius, by contrast, involves possession of intellect in excess of that needed to survive. The genius uses this excess power to elicit from the perception of nature the static, timeless patterns beneath nature's ever-swift motions. Still another variation, Immanuel Kant's artistic genius, as if captivated and at once held captive by nature, creates pleasing forms as ideas for reflection. Engendered by beauty and sired by skill, works of fine art bespeak much that mere craft cannot fathom. For Tolstoy, Schopenhauer, and Kant, genius pays tribute to natural forms full of meaning, and art in its hands cannot help but evolve to point back.

Such a pointing back to nature through symbolic or discursive meaning, however, cannot be Georg Wilhelm Friedrich Hegel's concern. Nature, for Hegel, gives rise to its own source of redemption in human spirit. Once superseded by spirit, mute nature cannot reminisce. Aesthetic theory breaks abruptly with nature when Hegel has his way, for nature cannot be untouched by human interpretation when encountered and, as interpreted, nature progresses through art to its dialectical end. The image of progress captures Hegel's intent: nature in raw form remains deficiently mute and requires the intervention of human articulation to be worthy of hearing. For Theodor Adorno, however, nature's muteness need not be construed as a deficiency, despite Hegel's devaluation of it as such. On the contrary, nature's inability to squeeze into human conventions signifies its indomitability, its powerful presence resisting the lair of words. Even William Wordsworth, whose work celebrates open service to nature, confesses that for persons most sensitive to natural beauty, "Words are but under-agents in their souls / When grasping with their greatest strength / They do not breathe among them" (*Prelude* [1805], book 12, lines 272–274). In this way, nature's muteness, far from requiring salvation through human symbolic forms, inspires devoted imitation in the silence of its human subjects.

Devotion, nonetheless, need not always be contemplative, for according to Friedrich Wilhelm von Schelling, the artist forges the keystone of the arch that is philosophy and his efforts make nature conscious of itself. Nature stays to the unconsciously objective side of a distinction that polarizes real and ideal, while art collects worldly and disparate objects from nature and offers them to consciousness through subjective, productive intuition. Yet, for Schelling, not unlike Plotinus, the very same power works through nature and the artist. In nature, the formation of parts into wholes stays unconscious until art reveals that formation as the freely conscious act of creative intelligence. As revelation, art secures the identity of intelligence itself, pointing without ambivalence to an absolute power at work in all things of the world. Thus, in Schelling, the infinite progress of nature finds expression in the finite product of the artist, spawning symbolic representations of itself through the agency of the natural human creature. The identity of the absolute undergoes self-revelation in humanity's artistic representation of the natural world.

Still, not all issues of aesthetic identity between nature and art require linear progression *from* nature to art as proposed by Schelling, Hegel, or even Plotinus. In a powerful concession to the analogical imagination, Kant asserts that "Nature proved beautiful when it wore the appearance of art; and art can only be beautiful, where we are conscious of its being art, while yet it has the appearance of nature" (Kant, 1987, section 45). For Kant, art and nature, while not reciprocal in their allusions, nevertheless derive their greatest powers in reference to each other. Nature appears beautiful, without the intervention of human arrangement, when it displays itself in forms that suggest such intentional arrangement. Art conjures the recognition of beauty, not when it literally mimics the unfree products of nature, but rather when it strikes us as free from too labored an effect, too obvious an effort. For Kant, nature can be a beautiful thing and art a beautiful representation of a thing, but, at their most powerful, each calls for aid from the other. Nature offers forms of artistic appearance, while art manifests rule-governed forms with seemingly natural ease.

Kant's idea of seeing art as natural, and nature as artistic, has been developed consistently in current thinking about aesthetics. By achieving their identities through analogical interpenetration, art and nature enter into a philosophical marriage, one in which separate but conjoined entities sustain and renew their bonds. The artist, as an instrument of nature endowed with conscious freedom, serves as high priest at the aesthetic altar by calling on the community to validate the union taking place. Whether art be the imitation of an abstract realm of being or an homage to the concrete local environment, it often draws attention to its ancestry in natural forms or processes—often, that is, but not always, for a particular type of art allows the artist to disrobe and nullify his or her role.

If, in the Kantian spirit, the identity of art and nature come together analogically in natural or traditionally artistic products, they blend quite literally in the genre of environmental art. Natural materials cleverly arranged deconstruct their own arrangement, abandoning their maker by rejecting all convention. Of course, some works cling securely to "art," being composed of natural materials but presenting themselves as just what they are—human works. Such entities, however unusual the members or methods of their assemblage, fall easily into artistic traditions, announcing themselves as conscious products of intentional agency. These cases pose no problem for the ontology of nature reflected in art. More difficult to fathom are those entities that, once mustered by imagination and executed in the world, leave no trace of ancestry, thus questioning the relevance of genesis. Both Kant and John Dewey address the epistemological discomfort inherent in aesthetic ambiguity: we wrestle with genesis in order to place an object in its proper category. When errors are made—the finely wrought object turns out to be driftwood, the song of the nightingale reveals itself as roguish youth—mental adjustments take place and aesthetic judgment reorients itself to its proper object.

But, when authorship, artistry, and intention disappear entirely, the identity of art and nature melts into sensuous obscurity, forbidding us to indulge our obsession with makers and their marks while coercing attention to surrounding surfaces. Questions of beginnings are tolerated but ultimately deflected and, like a gender-blending androgyne, environmental art makes no marriage at all but appears as one being resisting dichotomous distinction. The apogee of artistic yearning for communion with the earth, environmental art offers consummation at a price: abandon the desire for curious rank and behold the plane of nature as continuous with our own.

BIBLIOGRAPHY

Adorno, Theodor W. *Aesthetic Theory.* Edited by Gretel Adorno and Rolf Tiedemann, translated by Robert Hullot-Kentor. Minneapolis, 1997.

Aristotle. *The Basic Works of Aristotle*. Edited by Richard McKeon. New York, 1941.

Dewey, John. *Art as Experience*. Reprint, New York, 1980.

Gadamer, Hans-Georg. *The Relevance of the Beautiful and Other Essays*. Translated by Nicholas Walker, edited by Robert Bernasconi. Cambridge and New York, 1986.

Hegel, Georg Wilhelm Friedrich. *Hegel's Introduction to Aesthetics: Being the Introduction to the Berlin Aesthetics Lectures of the 1820s*. Translated by T. M. Knox. Oxford, 1979.

Heidegger, Martin. *Poetry, Language, Thought*. Translated by Albert Hofstadter. New York, 1971.

Kant, Immanuel. *The Critique of Judgment*. Translated by Werner S. Pluhar. Indianapolis, 1987.

Plato. *The Dialogues of Plato*. 3d rev. corr. ed. 5 vols. Translated by Benjamin Jowett. New York, 1892.

Plotinus. *The Essential Plotinus*. Translated and edited by Elmer O'Brien. Reprint, Indianapolis, 1975.

Ross, Stephanie. "Comparing Natural and Artistic Beauty." In *Landscape, Natural Beauty, and the Arts*, edited by Salim Kemal and Ivan Gaskell, pp. 183–198. Cambridge and New York, 1993.

Ruskin, John. *Modern Painters*. Edited by David Barrie. London, 1987.

Santayana, George. *The Sense of Beauty: Being the Outlines of Aesthetic Theory*. Reprint, New York, 1955.

Schelling, Friedrich Wilhelm Joseph. *The Philosophy of Art*. Edited and translated by Douglas W. Stott. Minneapolis, 1989.

Schopenhauer, Arthur. *The World as Will and Representation*. 2 vols. Translated by E. F. J. Payne. Reprint, New York, 1966.

Tolstoy, Leo. *What Is Art?* Translated by Aylmer Maude. Oxford, 1930.

Tuan, Yi-Fu. "Gardens, Earthworks and Environmental Art." In *Landscape, Natural Beauty and the Arts*, edited by Salim Kemal and Ivan Gaskell, pp. 158–182. Cambridge and New York, 1993.

Wordsworth, William. *The Prelude: 1799, 1805, 1850*. Edited by Jonathan Wordsworth, M. H. Abrams, and Stephen Gill. New York, 1979.

CHERYL FOSTER

Aesthetics of Nature and Ethics

The topic of aesthetics is forms and possibilities of process-oriented perception. Aesthetics is concerned with modes of perception whose exercise is worthwhile for its own sake. This is, of course, a minimal notion of aesthetics and aesthetic perception; it isolates a specific element of awareness that is constitutive of every kind of aesthetic practice, however much this practice may transcend the "disinterestedness" that Immanuel Kant attributed to all genuinely aesthetic perception in his *Critique of Judgment* (1987). Whatever function and constitution have been ascribed to aesthetic perception in the theories succeeding Kant—sensible knowledge of the absolute in Georg Wilhelm Friedrich Hegel (1975), the contemplation of Platonic "ideas" in Arthur Schopenhauer (1969), the subversion of cultural conventions in Friedrich Nietzsche (1967), or the encounter with a higher "truth" in Martin Heidegger (1971)—it has always been determined by a tarrying with or losing oneself in its objects. This tarrying is a state whose presence is affirmed without hesitation, however much it can be linked to additional ends.

In a pretheoretical use of the word, the objects of this activity are called "beautiful." Everything that is pleasing for its own sake is considered beautiful—a beautiful work of art, a beautiful tree, beautiful weather, a beautiful piece of jewelry, a beautiful couch, even a beautiful argument. That something "is pleasing for its own sake" also means that perceiving the matter involved or abiding in the situation concerned is worthwhile in itself. Thus, *beautiful* is a term for everything with which we have dealings in such a manner that we are concerned with these dealings themselves.

Aesthetics, however, does not have to do with all kinds of self-fulfilling pursuits in this minimal sense; it is concerned with forms of a *perceiving* activity as an end in itself. To be more precise, that ought to read: aesthetics concerns itself with forms of sense-guided perception that are concerned—to various degrees—with the sensible, affective, and imaginative exercise of this perception; and it deals with the preferred *objects* of such perception. The preferred objects of aesthetic perception are called "beautiful" (or designated with any other aesthetically favored term) because they are excellent opportunities for aesthetic perception. The use of the term *beautiful* (or other predicates) in the narrower aesthetic sense refers to objects or situations that are worth encountering under conditions of sensible-imaginative attention. In contrast to the beautiful or sublime *moment*, however, beautiful (sublime, etc.) objects or domains are *enduring* opportunities for process-oriented, sense-guided perception. To understand the meaning of these opportunities, it is necessary to understand for what they are opportunities—for a form of perception that turns to them for their own sake.

When aesthetics refers to the beauty or sublimity of nature, it relates to nature as an excellent opportunity for human perception. It refers to its beauty (or sublimity, etc.) *for us*. Beauty does not exist "in itself," as contemporary writers such as Gernot Böhme (1989) and Hartmut Böhme (1988), alluding to the pre-Kantian tradition, would like to have it. Aesthetics could perhaps refer to nature's aesthetic attraction for other living beings; but even then it would refer to its beauty for someone who has certain possibilities for a sense-guided perception that is an end in itself. In any case, the perception of natural beauty, like the perception of everything aesthetically attractive, is closely connected to the sensible intelligence of the particular subject of this perception. The sensibility of intelligent living beings—that is to say, both their natural and culturally formed sensibility—decides what phenomena they are able to consider as candidates for the beautiful. Only those phenomena that they can appreciate in their sensibly filled particularity are potential objects of aesthetic recognition.

This means that an aesthetics of nature (inasmuch as it has the human being's aesthetic sense in view) has to refer to that which is perceivable for human beings in a bodily sensible manner as nature. It has to take the sensual appearance of natural things and environments as its starting point. Its subject matter is the sense-catching [*sinnenfällig*] forms of what is addressed, in the life-world, as nature and natural processes in contrast to human works and human action. The particularity of these forms constitutes its topic. An aesthetics of nature has to be able to make clear what the beauty of nature is all about in contrast to all other kinds of beauty (or sublimity, etc.).

A Location of Freedom. Which nature is an aesthetics of nature concerned with? That nature from which everything originates, which is interwoven with everything, and into which everything passes is not an aesthetic object in contrast to other kinds of aesthetic objects. A perspective that is concerned with the particularity of natural, as distinct from artificial, forms does not have reason to make this concept of nature its basic concept. Rather, the location of aesthetic perception—and the topic of the aesthetics of nature—is that relation to nature in which we encounter a nature that, first, we can *individuate* as animal, vegetable, mineral, or landscape and, second, we can grasp as more or less *free* nature, as distinct from human artifacts. Although they may be supported, arranged, and shaped in manifold ways by human intervention, aesthetically attractive natural objects are distinct from human artifacts in that they appear in their own gestalt. They are not products of style. A total arrangement of natural things and scenes would destroy the very possibility of an ecstatic distance to the intentional design of the human world. That nature that an aesthetics of nature is concerned with is an endangered domain within human reality.

The fact that the contrast between nature and culture, or between natural and artificial environments, is an entirely gradual distinction in today's world does not modify this at all. Quite a few distinctions make good sense and are precise even though they are gradual—just think of the difference between children and youths, between turquoise and blue, between spitting with rain and drizzling, or between analytic and synthetic sentences. Correspondingly, knowing that what we address as outer nature is in many cases artificially formed does not prevent us from distinguishing between the objects of this nature and mere artifacts, between the events of this nature and teleological action. Our aesthetic sense of nature's beauty is based on this distinction—as is our sense of awareness for the destruction of aesthetically attractive nature.

This distinction's perspective can best be presented as follows: What we are looking for, with aesthetic intention, in nature is figures and realms of a contingent life of form. In other words, nature is aesthetically interesting because of a processuality not brought about by humans, because of the independence and changeability of its formations, because of the unguided fullness of the appearances it presents to our senses. Under these aspects, nature appears different from everything that can be accomplished by the human

being. Because of this otherness, it is an independent source of aesthetic attraction.

We can react in very different ways to this phenomenal turbulence of nature. As the theorists of natural beauty from Kant to Theodor W. Adorno (1997) have repeatedly emphasized, it is precisely this inevitable difference in our aesthetic responsiveness that transfigures the space of a free nature into a unique possibility for aesthetic experience. We encounter aesthetically attractive nature not in a single but in a threefold manner (Seel, 1991). Beautiful or sublime nature presents itself to us simultaneously as an asemantic [*sinnfremd*] interplay of appearances; as a formative—and thus thoroughly meaningful—location of life; and, finally, as a pictorial place of art. In doing so, aesthetically viewed nature puts its observers in a position different from the life-worldly context of meaning in which it appears to them. In the contemplative relation, this context dissolves; in the corresponsive relation, it appears; in the imaginative disposition, it is transgressed in the projection of artistic works onto nature's appearances. In each of these attractions granted by nature, one can say, a different form of freedom is unlocked: first, freedom from all posited meanings; second, a freedom to perceive one's particular situation sensibly; third, a freedom to vary creatively artistic interpretations of life. What constitutes the particularity of natural beauty is its being a reality that simultaneously opens these three possibilities for freedom.

This complex relation in the aesthetic perception of nature suggests two conclusions. First, the aesthetic sense of nature is a product of the human life-form, but a quite paradoxical one. The pleasure generated by natural beauty is a pleasure that we get from the fact that not everything is the work of humans, not everything is of human design, and not everything has a posited meaning. The experience of natural beauty is an experience of positive contingency. The aesthetic interest in nature includes the interest in maintaining a distance to the humanly made and humanly interpreted world. Second, the fact that the presence of natural beauty generates a manifold freedom vis-à-vis cultural projects and perspectives is evidence that nature is a genuine possibility for the life of human beings. Natural beauty is a location of fulfilled time. That is to say that beautiful nature is not a means to happiness, it is a form of happiness. It is not in the service of those who seek it, it is an end for them—and, indeed, one that they themselves cannot bring about.

Ethical-Political Consequences. If this is the case, then the aesthetics of nature is simultaneously part of an ethics of the individual conduct of life. It enlightens us on a genuine possibility for the good life. That should not be very surprising, for aesthetics, being concerned with specific forms of and opportunities for process-oriented activity, is generally part of an ethics of the good life. This, of course, applies to an aesthetics of nature in particular; for it is directly concerned with conduct to an essential reality of human life, to life in and with outer nature. Beautiful or sublime nature, aesthetics can show us, is an irreplaceable location of noninstrumentalized and noninstrumentalizing existence. Ethics can take up this insight and, for its part, make clear that the experience of freedom in the domain of natural beauty has exemplary value for the human conduct of life as a whole. Hence, it follows that it is far better not only for our relation to outer nature, but also for our general mode of life to live in and with a polymorphous world that is not entirely dominated by us.

From this individual ethics of natural beauty there follows, almost directly, a social and political ethics. If it is the case that beautiful nature is a central place for a successful individual life, then the protection of free nature, in which this beauty is possible, is an imperative based on social and political respect for the possibility of each individual's development. If free nature is a general condition for happiness in human existence, then maintaining this condition is part of the respect that we have for the human person. Hence, the conservation (and, wherever possible, expansion) of free nature constitutes a norm of universal morality. Thus, the ethics of nature does not need to adopt a metaphysically grounded "right of nature" vis-à-vis human beings in order to justify a strong obligation to protect the environment. It can claim much more modestly that the *human being* has a right to free nature—vis-à-vis other human beings.

The meaning of this right (and its corresponding duties) becomes clearer when we observe the effects of its violation. Here, the moral scandal is to be found not so much—or not solely—in the destruction of the necessary conditions of a life beneficial to all, as in the destruction of a universal *form* of beneficial life itself. The devastation or preclusion of natural beauty constitutes a decimation of noninstrumental relations to life-worldly nature. It is thus a destruction of positive contingency, realized freedom, and fulfilled time. It is the destruction of a crucial and irreplaceable sphere of the human world. Just as there is no life without nature as a regenerating sustenance for human beings and no tolerable life without nature as an intact sphere of life, there is for human beings only a less-flourishing life without zones of free nature.

An Augustine Maxim. At the end of the fourth century CE, Augustine (1961, p. 216) wrote in book 10 of his *Confessions,* "Yet men go out and gaze in astonishment at high mountains, the huge waves of the sea, the broad reaches of rivers, the ocean that encircles the world, or the stars in their courses. But they pay no attention to themselves." People, Augustine claims, gape at the contingency of the outer world instead of attending to the inner world of their souls—with a view to the Almighty. Here, disdain for exter-

nal, nonanimated, nonspiritual reality becomes apparent, a disdain that persisted up to Hegel's (1975) devaluation of natural beauty in contrast to artistic beauty—and, indeed, continued long thereafter. It is rooted in the assumption that human beings can feel at home, be at one with themselves, be free only where they have cast off the contingency of their own situation in life. As a consequence, this of course means that their existence can succeed only when they manage to establish cultural freedom at the expense of the freedom of nature. The experience of the modern domination of nature has shown, however, that this program is aimed, in the short or long run, at the curtailment and destruction of human life itself. The modern experience of natural beauty gives reason in this situation to see in the failure to overcome contingency a condition for succeeding in individual and social practice; for it makes clear that there cannot be a free culture at the expense of free nature—that a free culture can come about only by abandoning exhaustive world appropriation. This insight can hardly be more beautifully expressed than by Augustine's words, though slightly altered: "Yet men go out and gaze in astonishment at high mountains, the huge waves of the sea, the broad reaches of rivers, the ocean that encircles the world, or the stars in their courses. And they thereby pay attention to themselves."

[*See also* Environmental Aesthetics.]

BIBLIOGRAPHY

Adorno, Theodor W. *Aesthetic Theory.* Edited by Gretel Adorno and Rolf Tiedemann, translated by Robert Hullot-Kentor. Minneapolis, 1997.

Augustine. *Confessions.* Translated by R. S. Pine-Coffin. Harmondsworth, England, 1961.

Böhme, Gernot. *Für eine ökologische Naturästhetik.* Frankfurt am Main, 1989.

Böhme, Harmut. *Natur und Subjekt.* Frankfurt am Main, 1988.

Hegel, Georg Wilhelm Friedrich. *Aesthetics: Lectures on Fine Art.* 2 vols. Translated by T. M. Knox. Oxford, 1975.

Heidegger, Martin. "The Origin of the Work of Art." In *Poetry, Language, Thought,* translated by Albert Hofstadter, pp. 15–87. New York, 1971.

Kant, Immanuel. *Critique of Judgement.* Translated by Werner S. Pluhar. Indianapolis, 1987.

Nietzsche, Friedrich. *The Birth of Tragedy* (with *The Case of Wagner*). Translated by Walter Kaufmann. New York, 1967.

Schopenhauer, Arthur. *The World as Will and Representation.* 2 vols. Translated by E. F. J. Payne. Reprint, New York, 1966.

Seel, Martin. *Eine Ästhetik der Natur.* Frankfurt am Main, 1991.

MARTIN SEEL
Translated from German by John Farrell

Japanese Aesthetic Appreciation of Nature

Nature has always constituted the most prominent aesthetic object in Japanese culture. The subject matter of Japanese fine arts, such as poetry and painting, has been predominantly nature, ranging from landscape and weather to flowers and birds. Furthermore, the aesthetic appreciation of nature is thoroughly integrated into the Japanese people's daily lives through their architecture, interior decoration, gardens, food, clothing, and festivals.

In the Western tradition, though relatively neglected by aesthetic theorists, nature has been appreciated in a number of different ways. Perhaps the most prevalent today is purely pictorial appreciation, evident in the penchant for postcards and landscape photographs, a trend rooted in the eighteenth-century notion of the picturesque. At the same time, the legacy of Romanticism continues in appreciating a series of associations, whether historical, literary, social, or mythological, triggered by a natural object or a phenomenon. Yet other times, nature is celebrated for embodying moral or religious symbols, as most notably advocated by Ralph Waldo Emerson, the founder of American Transcendentalism. On the other hand, recently hailed by ecologically minded thinkers is the appreciation of nature informed by scientific knowledge. This was advocated by Aldo Leopold, who proposed a new land aesthetic as well as a land ethic. Finally, the experience of the sublime, according to a philosopher such as Immanuel Kant, is possible only with certain natural objects and phenomena.

The Japanese aesthetic appreciation of nature has also consisted of pictorial, associational, and symbolic approaches. The long-held tradition of the Japanese aesthetic appreciation of nature, however, exhibits some distinct characteristics as well. First, the aspects of nature frequently praised for their aesthetic appeal are relatively small, intimate, tame, and friendly. Little appreciation is given to the gigantic, overpowering, frightening, or aloof. Second, nature is considered fundamentally identical to humans, and the sensuous expression of this identity becomes the object of aesthetic appreciation. Finally, nature is respected for its inherent characteristics, and this attitude underlies the Japanese design principle of making use of and enhancing nature's quintessential qualities.

One characteristic of the Japanese aesthetic appreciation of nature is the fact that it lacks the experience of the sublime, which, according to the Western theories of the eighteenth century, is typically invoked by overpowering, gigantic, or dangerous aspects of nature. This absence is not the result of a lack of natural objects exhibiting these features in Japan. Typhoons and earthquakes with destructive power, for example, occur frequently in Japan. It is noteworthy, however, that in the two best-known references to typhoons in the Japanese classical literature, *The Tale of Genji* (1008–1020) and *The Pillow Book* (c.1002), the storm itself is mentioned very little. Instead, both authors offer detailed depictions of the aesthetic effects of the aftermath of the storm. Or, take the description of nature by a Japanese

Henry David Thoreau: Kamo no Chōmei (1153–1216), a retired Buddhist monk who retreated into Mount Hino away from the capital city of Kyoto at the age of sixty. In *An Account of My Hut* (1212), which records his experience of living alone in a small hut surrounded by mountain wilderness, he describes nature as being always friendly and approachable rather than threatening and aloof.

There is a historical reason for this Japanese taste for experiencing nature as being affable. It was during the Heian period (794–1185) that the subsequent Japanese aesthetic traditions became established by the ruling aristocrats. Their daily lives were dominated by aesthetic pursuits, including nature appreciation. Although nature permeated their aesthetic lives, however, it was nature experienced primarily within the safety of their urban setting rather than in the wilderness. Their protected and comfortable space afforded the spectators a view of nature as friendly rather than menacing and overpowering. As a result, the typical objects of their nature appreciation consisted of things such as crickets caught in the field, a snow-clad garden, the scent of plum blossoms carried to the veranda by a spring breeze, and a distant landscape shrouded in mist.

There is also a conceptual reason for the absence of the sublime in the Japanese appreciation of nature. The Western experience of the sublime generally presupposes a perceived contrast between humans and nature. According to Kant, for example, a desert or a stormy ocean at first appears to overpower us through its size or power, but ultimately becomes surpassed by us through our intellectual capacity. Here the relationship between the two is based on contrast and dominance. One of the Japanese cultural assumptions, however, is that humans and nature are fundamentally alike, their relationship one of harmony or identity rather than contrast or dominion.

This human identification with nature embedded in the Japanese aesthetic appreciation can be either emotive or metaphysical. The content of emotive identification with nature was first put into a theory by an Edo-period philologist and literary critic Motoori Norinaga (1730–1801), in his discussion of *mono no aware*. Variously translated as "pathos of things" or "sensitivity of things," and sometimes compared to the Latin notion of *lacrimae rerum* (tears of things), *mono no aware* refers to the sympathetic identification with natural objects or situations.

The emotive identification with natural objects or situations occurs in two ways, according to Norinaga's theory of *mono no aware*. Sometimes when we are possessed with a strong emotion, we appreciate the way in which natural objects and events reverberate with our emotion. Initially suggested by the poet Ki no Tsurayuki (868?–946) in the preface to *Kokinshū* (The Anthology of Ancient and Modern Poems, 905), this emotive identification with nature finds its most notable expression in Japanese literature, which typically expresses human emotions and experiences *in terms of nature*. This experience of *mono no aware* may be regarded as what the Western tradition considers pathetic fallacy or affective fallacy. The experience of *mono no aware* remains object-centered, however; it is an aesthetic appreciation of the way in which human emotion is embodied or manifested in the sensuous qualities of the natural object.

Mono no aware is also experienced when we intuit the *kokoro* (essence, spirit) of the object or situation and sympathize with it. In this case, purity and openness of mind are necessary for one to experience *mono no aware*. To recognize and become deeply moved by the beauty of cherry blossoms or autumn landscapes at dusk is to know *mono no aware*. Sympathetic identification with these objects is facilitated not simply by their delicate outlines and colors, however. It is ultimately derived from our intuitive grasp of and sympathy with the fragility of their existence.

The recognition that existence is transient—the most important Buddhist teaching—has given impetus to various aesthetic pursuits in Japanese culture, including the aesthetic appreciation of nature. Transience of human life is generally regarded as one major source of misery and suffering. Different sects of Buddhism throughout history have suggested ways of delivering humans from this universal predicament, ranging from the belief in the otherworld to the absolute affirmation of this life. Japanese culture provides yet another means of salvation through the aesthetic appreciation of nature. Selecting not only the friendly parts of nature but also emphasizing their transient aspects, such as short-lived insects, passing showers, melting snow, and falling cherry blossoms, the Japanese aesthetic tradition aestheticizes the evanescence of natural phenomena. The impermanence of natural phenomena is appreciated as providing an analogy to human transience, and this affinity gives solace to the otherwise pessimistic outlook on life. A sense of camaraderie with nature is felt through this identity, which leads to the realization that nothing can escape the transience of existence, ultimately rendering our own mortality easier to accept. Furthermore, by aesthetically appreciating the poignancy and pathos expressed by the fleeting beauty of nature, the Japanese also succeed in aestheticizing human transience.

Nowhere is this preoccupation with transience more evident than in the Japanese celebration of seasonal change. Seasons in Japan, though cyclical, are always a passing phenomenon, each accompanied by its distinct qualities. To capture and express the unique characteristics of each season becomes a canon for many Japanese aesthetic activities. For example, a haiku must include a *kigo* (the season word) within its short five-seven-five syllable verse to indicate the appropriate season befitting the content. Similarly, the flower arrangement must express the season through its design, and the tea ceremony must incorporate the sensitivity to the season in its choice of various vessels and utensils, as well as its interior decorations. Finally, Japanese cooking must reflect the season not only in its ingredients but also in its cooking method, containers, and presentation.

This preoccupation with seasonableness and the resultant attempt to express it in various aesthetic activities indicates another characteristic of the Japanese appreciation of nature: respect for nature's inherent and quintessential features. This attitude is rooted in Shintō, a religion indigenous to Japan, which attributes spiritual qualities to natural objects, and subsequently developed by Zen Buddhism with its recognition of Buddha nature in everything for simply being what it is. Among the various elements constituting the sensuous surface of natural objects and phenomena, the Japanese particularly appreciate what is perceived as their essential, defining characteristics. For example, the strangely twisted, gnarled branches of a pine tree are appreciated not merely for their interesting appearance, but, more important, for their definition of what makes this particular tree quintessentially pine. This appreciation encourages careful attention to what nature has to offer, as well as submission to and grateful acceptance of each natural object with its individual characteristics.

This respectful attitude underlying the appreciation of nature is reflected in the depiction and utilization of nature in Japanese arts and crafts. For example, nature as a subject matter must be carefully listened to in composing a haiku, instructs the seventeenth-century master Matsuo Bashō (1644–1694). Similarly, visual depictions of nature must capture the defining characteristics of the subject matter, by distilling the essential features of the object through eliminating adventitious, nonessential elements. This forceful articulation of the object's defining characteristics also constitutes the design principle used in flower arrangements, bonsai, and pruning trees in gardens.

The use of natural materials in crafts, utensils, architecture, and cooking is another reflection of this respect for and appreciation of nature's characteristics. For example, the versatile qualities of bamboo, including both strength and flexibility resulting from its strong fiber, its potential to be split into thin pieces, and its tubular shape with regularly spaced partitions, are fully utilized and respected in making objects ranging from fences and verandas to vases, scoops, baskets, containers, and musical instruments. It is also noteworthy that the Japanese use of natural materials involves minimum human alteration and manipulation. In traditional Japanese architecture, for example, wood is never painted, thereby encouraging the appreciation of its grains, which become pronounced with age. Furthermore, a pillar in a tea hut sometimes consists of a crooked tree that has not been straightened. It is also well known that Japanese cooking highlights the fresh and natural state of each ingredient.

The Japanese aesthetic appreciation of nature is thus distinguished by its underlying cultural assumptions concerning the identity between humans and nature through shared emotive qualities and transience. It also reflects the important Japanese attitude of respecting nature's characteristics through grateful acceptance and submission. What is noteworthy about this Japanese respectful attitude toward nature is that it is facilitated primarily through appreciating its aesthetic values.

[*See also* Japanese Aesthetics; Landscape; Picturesque; *and* Sublime.]

BIBLIOGRAPHY

Berque, Augustin. *Le sauvage et l'artifice: Les Japonais devant la nature.* Paris, 1986.
Callicott, J. Baird. *Earth's Insights: A Survey of Ecological Ethics from the Mediterranean Basin to the Australian Outback.* Berkeley, 1994.
Greenbie, Barrie B. *Space and Spirit in Modern Japan.* New Haven, 1988.
Higuchi, Tadahiko. *The Visual and Spatial Structure of Landscapes* (1981). Translated by Charles S. Terry. Cambridge, Mass., 1983.
Ikagawa, Toshi. "White Sand and Blue Pines: A Nostalgic Landscape of Japan." *Landscape* 32.1 (1993): 1–7.
Kamo no Chōmei. *An Account of My Hut* (1212). Translated by Donald Keene. In *Anthology of Japanese Literature from the Earliest Era to the mid-Nineteenth Century,* edited by Donald Keene. New York, 1955.
Karaki, Junzō. *Zen to Shizen* (Zen and Nature). Kyoto, 1981.
McLuhan, T. C. *The Way of the Earth: Encounters with Nature in Ancient and Contemporary Thought.* New York, 1994.
Saito, Yuriko. "The Japanese Appreciation of Nature." *British Journal of Aesthetics* 25.3 (Summer 1985): 239–251.
Saito, Yuriko. "The Japanese Love of Nature: A Paradox." *Landscape* 31 (1992): 42–47.
Sandrisser, Barbara. "Valuing the Ordinary: The Poetics of Wood in Traditional Japan." *Journal of Value Inquiry* 28 (1994): 281–295.
Shiga, Shigetaka. *Nihon Fūkei Ron* (Theory of Japanese Landscape) (1895). Tokyo, 1976.
Shimomura, Toratarō. "A Systematic Consideration of the Concept of 'Nature': With Especial Reference to Landscape Painting." In *Philosophical Studies of Japan,* vol. 10. Tokyo, 1970.
Slawson, David A. *Secret Teachings in the Art of Japanese Gardens: Design Principles, Aesthetic Values.* Tokyo, 1987.
Stewart-Smith, Jo. *In the Shadow of Fujisan: Japan and Its Wildlife.* Harmondsworth, England, 1987.
Watsuji, Tetsurō. *Climate: A Philosophical Study* (1935). Translated by Geoffrey Bownas. Tokyo, 1961.

YURIKO SAITO

Contemporary Thought

Most of the issues in contemporary research on the aesthetics of nature are foreshadowed in Ronald W. Hepburn's seminal article "Contemporary Aesthetics and the Neglect of Natural Beauty" (1966). After noting that by essentially reducing aesthetics to the philosophy of art, analytic aesthetics virtually ignores the natural world, Hepburn sets the agenda for the contemporary discussion of the aesthetics of nature. He argues that aesthetic appreciation of art frequently provides misleading guidelines for appreciation of nature, yet he observes that there is in the aesthetic appreciation of nature, as in appreciation of art, a distinction between appreciation that is only trivial and superficial and that which is serious and deep. He suggests furthermore that, in the case of nature, such serious appreciation may require different approaches that can accommodate not only nature's indeterminate and varying character, but also both our multisensory experience and our diverse understanding of it.

The contemporary discussion of the aesthetics of nature thus focuses on different approaches to or models for the appreciation of nature: models intended to realize serious, appropriate aesthetic appreciation of nature. Certain more traditional models derived from the aesthetic appreciation of the arts are seemingly inadequate. Two such models are the object model and the landscape model. The former assimilates nature to sculpture and the latter assimilates it to landscape painting. On the object model, we appreciate natural objects as we might appreciate pieces of abstract sculpture, mentally or physically extracting them from their contexts and focusing on their formal properties. On the landscape model, we appreciate nature as we might a landscape painting, seeing it as a two-dimensional scene and again focusing largely on formal properties. Neither of these models realizes a serious, appropriate appreciation of nature: each distorts the true character of nature in that the former rips natural objects from their larger environments while the latter frames them and flattens them into scenery, and, in focusing mainly on formal properties, both models neglect much of our normal experience and understanding of nature.

Although the aesthetic appreciation of the arts does not directly provide adequate models for the appreciation of nature, it does suggest some of what is required in a more adequate model. In serious, appropriate aesthetic appreciation of works of art, it is essential that we appreciate works as what they in fact are and in light of full knowledge of their real natures. Thus, for instance, serious, appropriate aesthetic appreciation of Pablo Picasso's *Guernica* requires that we appreciate it as a painting, as a Cubist painting, and so on, and that we appreciate it in light of our knowledge of paintings, of Cubist paintings, and so forth. This suggests a third model for the aesthetic appreciation of nature, the natural environmental model. This model recommends that, as in our appreciation of works of art, we should appreciate nature as what it in fact is (that is, as natural and as an environment), and that we should, moreover, appreciate it in light of our knowledge of what it is (that is, in light of knowledge provided by the natural sciences, and especially the environmental sciences such as geology, biology, and ecology). The natural environmental model thus accommodates both the true character of nature and our normal experience and understanding of it.

Nonetheless, the natural environmental model may not fully capture our appropriate aesthetic appreciation of nature. Although it does not, as do the object and the landscape models, distort nature itself, it may yet be thought to distort our appreciation of nature. Its emphasis on scientific knowledge gives such appreciation a highly cognitive, and perhaps overly intellectual, quality. In contrast to the cognitive emphasis of the natural environmental model, the engagement model stresses the contextual dimensions of nature and our multisensory experience of it. Viewing the environment as a seamless unity of organisms, perceptions, and places, the engagement model beckons us to immerse ourselves in our natural environment in an attempt to obliterate traditional dichotomies such as subject and object and ultimately to reduce to as small a degree as possible the distance between ourselves and nature. It may be thought, however, that in calling for the total absorption of the appreciator into the natural environment, the engagement model goes too far. First, in attempting to eliminate any distance between ourselves and nature, it may lose that in terms of which the resultant experience is aesthetic, for within the Western tradition the very notion of the aesthetic is conceptually tied to the idea of distance between the appreciator and the appreciated. Second, in attempting to obliterate dichotomies such as that between subject and object, it may also lose the possibility of distinguishing between trivial, superficial appreciation and that which is serious and appropriate, for the latter revolves around the object and its true nature, whereas the former frequently involves only whatever the subject happens to bring to the experience. Without the subject-object distinction, aesthetic appreciation of nature is in danger of degenerating into little more than a subjective flight of fancy.

A second view that also seems to diverge from the natural environmental model is the arousal model. This model challenges the central place in aesthetic appreciation of nature that the natural environmental model grants to scientific knowledge, holding that we may appreciate nature simply by opening ourselves to it and thus being emotionally aroused by it. The view holds that this less intellectual, more visceral experience of nature is a way of legitimately appreciating nature without involving knowledge gained from science. Unlike the engagement model, however, this model does not call for a total immersion in nature, but only for an emotional relationship with it based on common, everyday knowledge and experience of it. Consequently, in contrast to the engagement model, the arousal model does not seem to risk the right to call its experience of nature aesthetic. Nor does it undercut the distinction between trivial and serious appreciation of nature, even though the appreciation it stresses may be more the former than the latter. The contrast between the arousal model and the natural environmental model, however, is less clear. If we recognize our scientific knowledge of the natural world as only a finer-grained and theoretically richer version of our common, everyday knowledge of it, and not as something es-

sentially different in kind, then the difference between the arousal model and the natural environmental model is mainly one of emphasis. Both models track the same kind of appreciation of nature, although the arousal model focuses on the more common, less cognitively rich end of the continuum.

A more fundamental challenge to the natural environmental model comes from what might be called the mystery model of nature appreciation. This view holds that the natural environmental model, in requiring that we must have knowledge of what we appreciate, has no place for the way in which nature is alien, aloof, distant, and unknowable. It contends that the only appropriate experience of nature is a sense of mystery involving a state of appreciative incomprehension, a sense of not belonging to and of being separate from nature. The mystery model, however, faces major difficulties. With only mystery and aloofness, there seems to be no grounding for appreciation of any kind, let alone aesthetic appreciation. The mystery and aloofness of nature are a gulf, an emptiness, between us and nature; they are that by which we are separate from nature. Thus, they cannot constitute a means by which we can attain any appreciation of nature whatsoever. In short, insofar as nature is unknowable, it is also beyond aesthetic appreciation. Even though mystery and aloofness cannot support appreciation, however, they can support worship. Thus, perhaps the mystery model should be characterized not as an aesthetic of nature, but rather as a religious approach to nature. If this is the case, then rather than revealing a dimension of our appropriate aesthetic appreciation of nature, the mystery model leaves the realm of the aesthetic altogether.

If the mystery model of nature appreciation moves such appreciation outside the realm of the aesthetic, it does so unintentionally. This possibility, however, the possibility that our appreciation of nature is not aesthetic, is embraced as the central tenet of the nonaesthetic model of nature appreciation. This view constitutes a radical alternative to all other models in explicitly claiming that nature appreciation is not a species of aesthetic appreciation. It holds that aesthetic appreciation is paradigmatically appreciation of works of art and is minimally appreciation of artifacts, of that which is human-made. Thus, on this view the appreciation of nature itself cannot be aesthetic appreciation of any kind whatsoever. Such a view is deeply problematic, however. Although the view finds some support in the tendency in analytic aesthetics to reduce all of aesthetics to philosophy of art, it remains essentially counterintuitive. Many of our fundamental paradigms of aesthetic appreciation are instances of appreciation of nature, such as our appreciation of the radiance of a glowing sunset, the grace of a bird in flight, or the simple beauty of a flower. Moreover, the Western tradition in aesthetics—not to mention other traditions, such as the Japanese—is committed to a doctrine that explicitly excludes the nonaesthetic model of nature appreciation: the doctrine that, as one writer puts it, anything that can be viewed can be viewed aesthetically.

There is nonetheless a grain of truth in the nonaesthetic model of nature appreciation that is worth preserving. This model makes a virtue of what the mystery model encounters unintentionally: the fact that the more removed, the more separate, something is from humankind and its artifactualization, the more problematic is its aesthetic appreciation. The limiting case is marked by the impossibility of aesthetically appreciating the completely unknowable. The insight of the nonaesthetic model is thus that some degree of artifactualization is necessary for aesthetic appreciation, but what this model fails to recognize is that human conceptualization and understanding of nature is itself a minimal form of artifactualization—and, although minimal, it is nevertheless adequate to underwrite aesthetic appreciation. To aesthetically appreciate the natural world, we do not need to actually make it, as we make works of art; nor do we need to conceptualize it in artistic categories, as is done by the object and landscape models. When we cast the conceptual net of common sense and scientific understanding over nature, we do enough to it to make possible its aesthetic appreciation. This fact sheds some light on the other models, suggesting that granting a place in nature appreciation to at least our common sense and scientific knowledge may be a necessary condition for providing an adequate account of serious, appropriate aesthetic appreciation of nature.

The realization that human conceptualization and understanding are a form of artifactualization adequate for underwriting aesthetic appreciation of nature opens the door to further possibilities. The conceptual net of common sense and scientific understanding is not the only one we cast over nature. There are also the numerous other nets woven by human culture in its many forms—not only by art, but also by literature, folklore, and myth. This realization gives rise to what might be called the postmodern model of nature appreciation. This view compares nature to a text, contending that, in reading a text, we appropriately appreciate not just the meaning its author intended, but any of various meanings that it may have acquired or that we may find in it. Moreover, none of these possible meanings has priority; no reading of a text is privileged. Thus, on the postmodern model of nature appreciation, whatever cultural significance nature may have acquired and that we may find in it, the rich and varied deposits from our art, literature, folklore, and myth are all accepted as proper dimensions of our aesthetic appreciation of nature; and of such dimensions, none is given priority, no particular appreciation is privileged as more serious or more appropriate than any other.

The postmodern model focuses attention on the many layers of human deposit that overlie pure nature. These layers range from the thin film of common sense, through the rich stratum of science, to the abundant accumulations of culture. In our encounters with nature, we confront this diversity and the postmodern model eagerly welcomes it all. In sharp contrast, some other models, such as the engagement model and the mystery model, strive toward attempting to appreciate pure, unadulterated nature, to look on nature bare, as Euclid looked on beauty. But the nonaesthetic model demonstrates that to go too far in this direction is to go beyond the realm of the aesthetic, making any aesthetic appreciation of nature impossible. Nonetheless, contained in the purist's inclination is the antidote for the potential excesses of the postmodern view. We must keep in mind that, as in appreciation of art, serious appreciation of nature means appreciating it as what it in fact is; and yet at the same time, we must recognize that this also means appreciating nature as what it is *for us*. This idea limits, yet enriches, what is involved in appropriate aesthetic appreciation. Contra the postmodern model, it is not the case that just any fanciful reverie we happen to bring to nature will do as well as anything else; but contra the purist, nature is what it is for us, is what we have made of it, and to miss or deny this is to miss or deny much of the richness that serious, appropriate aesthetic appreciation of nature has to offer.

The idea that nature is what it is for us, is what we have made of it, widens the scope of appropriate aesthetic appreciation, but it also constrains the postmodern model. In part, this is because neither nature nor we are one unitary thing, and thus not all of humankind's cultural deposits are aesthetically significant either to all parts of nature or for all of humankind. For any particular part of nature and for any particular appreciator, some cultural overlay is relevant and some is not—is indeed only the fanciful daydreams of a particular appreciator. In light of this, perhaps the pluralist model of nature appreciation should supplant the postmodern model. The pluralist model accepts the diversity and the richness of the cultural overlay in which the postmodern model delights, but also recognizes that, for any particular part of nature, only a small part of that cultural overlay is really relevant to its serious, appropriate appreciation, and that for any particular appreciator, only a small part of the overlay can truly be claimed as his or her own. The pluralist model endorses diversity, yet holds that in appropriate aesthetic appreciation not all nature either can or should be all things to all humans.

Although the pluralist model thus restricts the role of our cultural overlay in appropriate aesthetic appreciation of nature, this restriction does not apply equally to all layers of the human deposit. Perhaps the more basic layers, those of common sense and science, are dimensions of the appropriate appreciation of all of nature by any of its appreciators. Thus, even in light of the pluralist model, models such as the arousal model and the natural environmental model maintain a special place as general guides to appropriate aesthetic appreciation of nature. This is because these models concentrate on the most fundamental layers of the human overlay, those at the very foundations of our relationship with and our understanding of nature. There may be other layers relevant to our appreciation that are equally universal, however, although they may constitute the spires rather than the foundations of the human deposit. Such layers are the focus of the metaphysical imagination model of nature appreciation. According to this view, our metaphysical imagination interprets nature as revealing things about the whole of experience, about the meaning of life, about the human condition, about humankind's place in the cosmos. Thus, this model includes in appropriate aesthetic appreciation of nature those abstract meditations and speculations about the true nature of reality that our encounters with nature frequently engender in us.

The metaphysical imagination model invites us to entertain, in our aesthetic appreciation of nature, deep meditations and possibly wild speculations, but again the question of what is and what is not relevant arises. Which of such meditations and speculations are only trivial and fanciful and which are serious and sustainable? In essence, the question is again that of what does and what does not actually focus on and reveal nature as it in fact is. But in the context of the metaphysical imagination model, this question arises as a general metaphysical question about the real nature of the natural world. Thus, the metaphysical imagination model indicates a new agenda for the aesthetics of nature, for it suggests that in order to ultimately adjudicate among the different models of aesthetic appreciation of nature, we must first resolve more fundamental metaphysical issues about the true character of nature and about our proper place in it. Because Hepburn's initial work set the agenda for the contemporary discussion of the aesthetics of nature, it is appropriate that the metaphysical imagination model should set an agenda for future discussion, for this model is his most recent contribution to the field.

BIBLIOGRAPHY

Berleant, Arnold. *The Aesthetics of Environment.* Philadelphia, 1992.

Berleant, Arnold, and Allen Carlson, eds. Special Issue on Environmental Aesthetics. *Journal of Aesthetics and Art Criticism* 56 (1998).

Carlson, Allen. "Appreciation and the Natural Environment." *Journal of Aesthetics and Art Criticism* 37.3 (Spring 1979): 267–276.

Carlson, Allen. "Nature, Aesthetic Judgment, and Objectivity." *Journal of Aesthetics and Art Criticism* 40.1 (Fall 1981): 15–27.

Carlson, Allen. "Nature and Positive Aesthetics." *Environmental Ethics* 6.1 (Spring 1984): 5–34.

Carlson, Allen. "Nature, Aesthetic Appreciation, and Knowledge." *Journal of Aesthetics and Art Criticism* 53.4 (Fall 1995): 393–400.

Carroll, Noel. "On Being Moved by Nature: Between Religion and Natural History." In *Landscape, Natural Beauty, and the Arts,* edited by Salim Kemal and Ivan Gaskell, pp. 244–266. Cambridge and New York, 1993.

Crawford, Donald. "Nature and Art: Some Dialectical Relationships." *Journal of Aesthetics and Art Criticism* 42.1 (Fall 1983): 49–58.

Godlovitch, Stan. "Icebreakers: Environmentalism and Natural Aesthetics." *Journal of Applied Philosophy* 11 (1994): 15–30.

Hepburn, Ronald W. "Contemporary Aesthetics and the Neglect of Natural Beauty." In *British Analytical Philosophy,* edited by Bernard Williams and Alan Montefiore, pp. 285–310. London, 1966.

Hepburn, Ronald W. "Trivial and Serious in Aesthetic Appreciation of Nature." In *Landscape, Natural Beauty, and the Arts,* edited by Salim Kemal and Ivan Gaskell, pp. 65–80. Cambridge and New York, 1993.

Hepburn, Ronald W. "Landscape and the Metaphysical Imagination." *Environmental Values* 5 (1996): 191–204.

Kemal, Salim, and Ivan Gaskell, eds. *Landscape, Natural Beauty, and the Arts.* Cambridge and New York, 1993.

Mannison, Don. "A Prolegomenon to a Human Chauvinistic Aesthetic." In *Environmental Philosophy,* edited by Don Mannison, Michael McRobbie, and Richard Routley, pp. 212–216. Canberra, 1980.

Saito, Yuriko. "The Japanese Appreciation of Nature," *British Journal of Aesthetics* 25.3 (Summer 1985): 239–251.

Sepänmaa, Yrjö. *The Beauty of Environment: A General Model for Environmental Aesthetics* (1986). 2d ed. Denton, Tex., 1993.

Ziff, Paul. "Anything Viewed." In *Antiaesthetics: An Appreciation of the Cow with the Subtile Nose,* pp. 129–139. Dordrecht and Boston, 1984.

ALLEN C. CARLSON

NEW CRITICISM. The New Criticism is an applied literary theory that presumes that a text is, in itself, sufficient material for sound critical analysis: as Allen Tate testified, "We must return to, we must never leave, the poem itself" (1968). Although there has never been a self-identified New Critical school, the figures usually associated with its practices are Tate, I. A. Richards, William Empson, T. S. Eliot, Yvor Winters, John Crowe Ransom, R. P. Blackmur, Robert Penn Warren, Cleanth Brooks, William K. Wimsatt, and Monroe C. Beardsley. The work of this diverse group of scholars, many of whom were also poets, dominated Anglo-American literary studies in the 1940s and early 1950s. The New Critics granted priority to the poem itself, rather than to the conditions of its production or the effects of its reception. Thus, New Critical analysis often emphasized textual explication, investigating relationships between prosody and subject, rhetoric and tropes, and other formal features of the poem. Even more than its signature practice of "close reading," what distinguished the New Criticism from other critical positions was a belief that poetry constitutes a special kind of knowledge. On the basis of this supposition that poetry not only conveys knowledge or meaning but instantiates it, New Critics invalidated a traditional separation of form and content, and declared for poetry an autonomous epistemological and semantic context.

The term "New Criticism" became current after the publication of Ransom's *The New Criticism* (1941). The book's title seemed to point to a cohesive movement, but the book was an assessment, not an anthology, of the theories of Richards, Empson, Eliot, and Winters, and it demonstrated the variations and contradictions within this loose confederation of critics. In the end, Ransom's study collected figures (with the possible exception of Winters) who stand as the immediate precursors, rather than practitioners, of what is today known as the New Criticism. Ransom praised these critics for pursuing a "criticism of the structural properties of poetry," but he expressed disappointment with the psychological bias of Richards and Empson, with Eliot's emphasis on cultural and literary traditions, and with Winters's insistent rationalism. He found lacking in these "New Critics" an aesthetic affirming that poetry produces the terms by which it should be investigated and evaluated. Such an aesthetic position was fundamental to Brooks, Tate, and others, who subscribed to the idea that poetry constitutes an organic unity, as well as to Ransom himself, who called for critics to attend first and foremost to a poem's "ontology."

Ransom identified in poetry the presence of a distinct and self-generative quality of literariness. But, unlike some other New Criticisms, his ontological criticism, as he termed it, was finally more concerned with a poem's being, or structure of meaning, than with its meaning per se. One might include Richards and Empson, with their systematizing tendencies, in this protostructuralist strain of New Criticism, as well as Philip Wheelwright, who is sometimes associated with the New Critics despite his archetypal readings of literature. In a separate camp, one might place Brooks, Tate, and Warren, whose more localized approaches implied that nothing outside a literary text determines its meaning. In denying that an external source or structure governs literature, these critics anticipated poststructuralist semantic theory. Yet, their organicist concept of poetry—which trained their focus on the material presence of the poem—has more in common with Ransom's ontology than with poststructuralism and its destruction of the "metaphysics of presence."

This New Critical concern for poetry's materiality derived in part from Richards. Although he is often named as the New Criticism's originator, he might more accurately be characterized as its herald. Richards was among the first to apply semantics to literary study in English, laying the groundwork for Empson and others to elucidate poetry's unique capacity to create and contain multiple meanings. His modernized distinction between poetry and the language of science was championed most vigorously by Brooks, and found expression in a general antipositivism evinced by almost all of the New Critics. In addition, New Criticism's interest in the unified tensional structures (ironic, dramatic, paradoxical) of poetry proceeded from Richards's idea that poetry possesses a completeness that the critic must seek not to solve so much as to preserve. As Wimsatt and Beardsley pointed out, however, Richards's emphasis on the affective operation of literature conflicted with a central New Critical tenet that always privileged the material of the text over the reader's experience or the intentions of the author. Furthermore, Richards was primarily a theorist, and one of the defining features of the New

Criticism was its commitment to apply its precepts to literature, and especially to poetry.

The practical application of New Criticism was in abundant evidence in Brooks's and Warren's landmark textbook, *Understanding Poetry* (1938). Brooks says that it was the publisher who conferred on the book its rather immodest title and that the authors had originally titled it *Reading Poetry*. Certainly, the latter title more accurately reflected the fact that the authors valued a continuous and mutable process of discovery over a goal of acquiring final "understanding" of a given text. Brooks and Warren introduced this book, which would revolutionize American pedagogy, with a "Letter to the Teacher." In it they articulated their belief that poetry should be taught as poetry, and disparaged the custom of inculcating students with inadequate "substitutes" for a poem: "The substitutes are various, but the most common ones are: 1. Paraphrase of logical and narrative content; 2. Study of biographical and historical materials; 3. Inspirational and didactic interpretation" (Brooks and Warren, 1950). By contrast, Brooks and Warren minimized (which is not to say that they altogether dismissed) the importance of subjective reactions and historical contexts. They advocated "intensive" before "extensive" reading, urging students to linger over a poem, to recognize its semantic contradictions, and to account for its structural properties' contribution to poetic meaning.

The principles that Brooks and Warren outlined in their "Letter" were directed as much to scholars and professional students as to undergraduates, and provide a neat, if somewhat simplified, summary of New Critical thought. They bespeak an organic philosophy of poetry in which tropes and elements of prosody (verse form, rhythm, meter, sound, syntax) engender, rather than merely enhance, meaning. Warren, for instance, did not define poetry by the statement it makes, but located the poetic in the relationships—in tensions and resistances—between what a poem says and what it does. In a good or strong poem, these tensions never fully resolve, and there always remains a semantic excess or structural "impurity" that the critic must not attempt to eliminate in order to provide a coherent reading of the text. (Informing this idea that poetry incarnates unity through paradox are a Kantian precept of unified consciousness and Samuel Taylor Coleridge's description of poetry as fusion of opposing forces.) Although more rigid in his measure of what makes a good poem, Blackmur too celebrated inconsistencies and certified that a poem could contain a moment "when words fail though meaning persists" (1952). These critics would agree that a reader can only do injury to a poem by equating it with its paraphrasable content.

Brooks further exposed the limitations of prose restatements of poetry in "The Heresy of Paraphrase," one of his exemplary New Critical essays collected in *The Well Wrought Urn* (1947). In the essay, he took Winters, the sometime New Critic, to task for failing to recognize that a poem's "rational statement" should never be measured according to more common standards of logic (i.e., "scientific language" or prose in general) because those standards cannot take into account the poetic context in which the statement was made. Brooks's well-known phrase reflected his conviction—shared by many of the New Critics—that any inquiry that does not allow poetry to establish the terms by which it is to be evaluated violates the critic's fundamental duty to privilege poetic language. Ronald S. Crane who, as a member of the Chicago school, was a contemporaneous academic opponent of the New Criticism, contested the idea of poetry as in competition with—or as differentiated by—other discursive modes. Crane's Aristotelian approach to poetic structure inclined him to emphasize generic traditions, and he faulted the New Critics for neglecting the history of poetic genres and for failing to measure a poem's success by comparing it to its formal predecessors.

But historical contexts and traditions were a secondary concern for the New Critics, though they were not, as some have charged, willfully ignorant of these dimensions in poetry. Brooks and Warren responded to such a charge in their revised edition of *Understanding Poetry* (1950): "we are perfectly well aware that no intelligent teacher has ever presented poetry in a vacuum—that, on the contrary, he brings every resource he possesses to bear upon the poem." Even so, Brooks elsewhere insisted that professional critics must rigorously avoid and denounce an analytic method that "reduces literature to cultural history." Wimsatt and Beardsley (1954) argued that it is in poems themselves that one may find the best evidence of the attitudes, values, and customs of the past, and not in any attempt to reconstruct the cultural conditions that reigned when the poem is written.

Not surprisingly, the New Criticism has been and continues to be most forcefully attacked by those whose readings of literature are heavily invested in sociohistorical critiques. The New Critics garnered the antipathy of modernist cultural critics, such as Malcolm Cowley and Van Wyck Brooks, who disdained their "atomistic" approaches to literature. Such formalist readings were, in their view, grievously irrelevant to society as a whole. But Tate, for one, argued that poetry (and, presumably, the study of poetry) should be free from all political obligations. He said of those who use poetry as a platform for any kind of explicit political purpose: "whatever other desirable things they may believe in, they do not believe in poetry" (1968).

Tate's extreme position nevertheless admits what was underlying all New Critical inquiry, namely, a powerful humanist impulse and a confidence in the possibilities for individual and collective improvement through the training of the linguistic faculty. Still, given that they were skeptical of efforts to delineate literature's moral or psychological effects on the reader, the New Critics were for the most part content with literary study's indirect, if profound, effect on human events. (An exception to this was Kenneth Burke,

affiliated with the New Critics in his analytic methods, but set apart from them by his interest in the sociological consequences of literature.)

The New Critics also located themselves at a certain remove from literary modernism. Implicitly, New Criticism approved a modernist distinction between high and low culture. It also retained high modernism's insistence that literature possesses a nonutilitarian value, and its belief that literature creates its own reality, separate from that of quotidian life. On the other hand, the New Critical commitment to the integrity of a single text sometimes blinded it to modernism's linguistic dislocations, and by focusing almost exclusively on the lyric, New Criticism largely neglected modernist experiments with narrative form. Yet, in some ways, the New Criticism was more aware of its literary-historical moment than previous generations because, though many of them favored neoclassical authors, all contributed to a relatively new phenomenon of analyzing contemporary literature.

Although the New Critics generally subordinated to their rhetorical studies these broader contexts of culture and history, the extraliterary resource they found most objectionable and least relevant in critical interpretation was an author's biography. Their formalist approach to literature was in part a reaction to the preponderance of biographical-historical criticism in the late nineteenth and early twentieth centuries (well represented by the intense pursuit of the "Homeric question" and debates over the identity of Shakespeare's W. H.). In "The Intentional Fallacy," an essay more often ridiculed than read, Wimsatt and Beardsley denied that questions put to an author about his intentions or ken could expediently illuminate a work: "Critical inquiries, unlike bets, are not settled in this way. Critical inquiries are not settled by consulting the oracle" (1954). For these two exemplars of the New Critical position, the poem represented the only authority for determining the validity of a given reading.

How, precisely, a poem adjudicates stronger and weaker readings is never made clear by any of the New Critics, and certainly they did not grant equal merit to all readings. Brooks in particular inveighed against what he perceived to be a climate of increasing tolerance for critical relativism and a widespread reluctance on the part of critics to fulfill their responsibility to make value judgments about literature. Despite the implication that the New Criticism was an elitist enterprise (one observer characterized it as a "blatant mockery of certain works dear to the popular imagination"), it did invite the possibility of a critical plurality, and its vehement antipositivism always guarded against any claim to a demonstrably definitive reading of a text. Ransom characterized poetry itself as a kind of "democratic state," by which he meant that it accommodates a multiple and varied semantic constituency that is never subordinated to a single, "totalitarian" meaning or purpose. Warren, too, believed that an approach based on close reading would not reduce the possibilities for critical examination but increase them. To his mind, variegated poetic elements provide more—and potentially more contradictory—interpretations than textual explications based on external materials, thereby mitigating the authority of any single reading.

Yet, indeed, the New Criticism's advocacy and refinement of the practice of close reading has proved both its strength and its limitation. Contemporary critics such as Gerald Graff and Jonathan Culler have espoused an anti-hermeneutic stance, in opposition to a rather reductive conception of the New Critical position. Culler, for instance, rejects the New Criticism by defining its formal explication of literary texts as uncomplicated "interpretation." He endorses a context-based (rather than a text-based) literary criticism, and calls for scholars to exert themselves "beyond interpretation," which is to say beyond their common critical heritage. Culler fears that this is a difficult task because "Whatever critical affiliations we may proclaim, we are all New Critics, in that it requires a strenuous effort to escape notions of the autonomy of the literary work, the importance of demonstrating its unity, and the requirement of 'close reading'" (1981).

Some New Critical strategies have been absorbed into so many different critical practices as to have become invisible (or insidious, in Culler's view). A continuing commitment to close reading and to the study of individual works of literature—maintained by critics as dissimilar as Louis L. Martz, Helen Vendler, J. Hillis Miller, and Harold Bloom—owes a great debt to the New Critics. At another remove, the New Criticism's attentiveness to the subtle interdependencies of structure and content has facilitated certain forms of feminist and queer theory, particularly those that excavate from literary texts latent gendered readings and levels of meaning informed by issues of sexuality.

Deconstruction, too, recalls the New Criticism as it takes pleasure in verbal allusions and in language's general elasticity, and deconstruction's negation of logocentrism may be an extreme form of the New Criticism's antipositivism. New Critical ideas of ironic tension in poetry also echo in deconstructionist theories of the infinite "play" of linguistic meaning: Jacques Derrida's *différance*, like Warren's dramatic irony, is an enabling dynamic of literature. Of course, for the New Critics, irony simply never allows a poem to resolve itself: it reflects a motion toward stasis, as Warren suggests. Conversely, for the deconstructionists, play ultimately dissolves a poem (or, more properly, a poem dissolves itself through the operation of play): it is a movement toward more movement. Although deconstruction privileges literary texts, its dissolution of linguistic boundaries points up a fundamental condition of intertextuality that the New Critics never endorsed.

One of the most astute arbiters of the New Criticism's legacy has been Murray Krieger. In *The New Apologists for Poetry* (1956), Krieger identified a New Critic by his endeavor to defend poetry and to articulate poetry's unique function, especially as distinguished from the function of science. By associating the New Criticism and apologetics, Krieger underscored their determination to place criticism at the service of literature and not vice versa. In his more recent work, Krieger has negotiated a truce between the New Criticism and poststructuralism, observing that these two ostensibly antagonistic positions actually share a general concept of language as ultimately devolving into an unstable complex of absent signifieds and empty signifiers. In contrast to poststructuralism, however, New Criticism exempted poetic language from this fate of deterioration, privileging it as a self-generative and self-contained system of positive reference. Whatever limitations inhered in this impulse to defend poetry from both internal and external adversaries, it issued from an abiding belief in the special value of literature. Although it belonged to a particular historical moment, the New Criticism will continue to influence contemporary scholarship as it attempts to absorb the lessons of the recent historicism and establish a new textual study that affirms the central role of literary value.

[*See also* Intention; Modernism; Poetics; *and* Text.]

BIBLIOGRAPHY

Blackmur, R. P. *Language as Gesture: Essays in Poetry.* New York, 1952.

Brooks, Cleanth. *The Well Wrought Urn: Studies in the Structure of Poetry.* New York, 1947.

Brooks, Cleanth. "In Search of the New Criticism." *American Scholar* 53 (Winter 1983–1984): 41–53.

Brooks, Cleanth, and Robert Penn Warren. *Understanding Poetry* (1938). Rev. ed. New York, 1950.

Culler, Jonathan. "Beyond Interpretation." In *The Pursuit of Signs: Semiotics, Literature, Deconstruction,* pp. 3–17. New York, 1981.

Empson, William. *Seven Types of Ambiguity.* New York, 1930.

The Explicator. Washington, D.C., 1942–present. A literary journal devoted to close reading.

Handy, W. J. *Kant and the Southern New Critics.* Austin, Tex., 1963.

Kenyon Review. Gambier, Ohio, 1939–1970. A literary journal in which many of the early essays and debates of New Criticism were published.

Krieger, Murray. *The New Apologists for Poetry.* Minneapolis, 1956.

Krieger, Murray. "An Apology for Poetics." In *Words about Words about Words: Theory, Criticism, and the Literary Text,* pp. 107–119. Baltimore, 1988.

Lentricchia, Frank. *After the New Criticism.* Chicago, 1980.

Ransom, John Crowe. "Criticism as Pure Speculation." In *The Intent of the Critic,* edited by Donald A. Stauffer, pp. 91–124. Princeton, N.J., 1941.

Ransom, John Crowe. *The New Criticism.* New York, 1941.

Richards, I. A. *Principles of Literary Criticism* (1924). London, 1976.

Spingarn, Joel. *The New Criticism.* New York, 1911.

Spurlin, William J., and Michael Fischer, eds. *The New Criticism and Contemporary Literary Theory: Connections and Continuities.* New York, 1995.

Tate, Allen. *Essays of Four Decades.* Chicago, 1968.

Warren, Robert Penn. "Pure and Impure Poetry." In *Critiques and Essays in Criticism, 1920–1948,* edited by Robert W. Stallman, pp. 85–104. New York, 1949.

Wellek, René. *A History of Modern Criticism,* vol. 6, *American Criticism 1900–1950.* New Haven, 1986.

Wimsatt, W. K., ed. *Explication as Criticism.* New York, 1963.

Wimsatt, William K., and Monroe C. Beardsley. "The Intentional Fallacy" and "The Affective Fallacy." In *The Verbal Icon: Studies in the Meaning of Poetry,* by W. K. Wimsatt, pp. 3–18 and 21–39. Lexington, Ky., 1954.

JEANNINE JOHNSON

NIETZSCHE, FRIEDRICH WILHELM. [*To treat the thought of the German philosopher Friedrich Nietzsche, this entry comprises five essays:*

Survey of Thought

Nietzsche, Schopenhauer, and Disinterestedness

Nietzsche's Literary Style

Nietzsche and Visuality

Nietzsche on Art and Politics

The first essay is an overview of Nietzsche's thought in general as the background for his aesthetic theory; the author discusses many of the ways Nietzsche has been interpreted and how they affect our understanding of his aesthetics. The second essay is on Nietzsche's relationship to a philosopher who was pivotal in the development of his thinking about art: Schopenhauer; it also explains Nietzsche's critique of aesthetic disinterestedness. The third essay concerns the apparent unity between Nietzsche's ideas about style and his aesthetics, whether in relation to literature, music, or any of the arts. The fourth essay examines Nietzsche's aesthetics in connection with the visual arts, while the final essay discusses the relationship between art and politics in Nietzsche's aesthetics. For further discussion, see Postmodernism; Tragedy; *and* Wagner.]

Survey of Thought

It is doubtful that there is a single Friedrich Nietzsche (1844–1900). There are only "Nietzsches." Very few philosophers, perhaps none before him, have had their works function so seemingly deliberately as the equivalent of Rorschach tests. His name and phrases—taken out of context—have been used to support virtually every ideological persuasion. In Germany and in Italy, for example, he has been read not only as a proto-Nazi and fascist, but as an enemy of nationalism and power politics of any sort as well ("Culture and the state—one should not deceive oneself about this—are antagonists. . . . One lives off the other, one thrives at the expense of the other" ["What the Germans Lack," in *Twilight of the Idols: Or How One Philosophizes with a Hammer* (1888) p. 4]). He has been read as an anti-Semite and as an ardent foe of anti-Semitism, as a misogynist and as a protofeminist. The English-speaking world has been equally divided about Nietzsche, whereas in France his "politics" have always been of less interest than his "philosophy." In Israel, he is the third most widely read philosopher, exceeded in popularity only by Moses Maimonides and Baruch Spinoza; and the currently standard Giorgio Colli and Mazzino Montinari critical edition of Nietzsche's works was translated long ago into Hebrew—by an ultra-orthodox rabbi—but only now is work going on to produce a critical edition in English. Not so long ago, Nietzsche's *Thus Spoke Zarathustra: A Book for All and None* was one of a small handful of Western philosophy readings on Japan's long list of "Classics of World Literature," required reading for those who hoped to continue their education at the university level. Finally, what could be more perplexing than the spectacle of "Der Rote Nietzsche" (The Red Nietzsche) celebrated at a meeting of Italy's Communist Party in the early 1980s?

Given this partial "political" kaleidoscope, how could one pretend to provide an "overview," a God's-eye view, as it were, of a subject as controversial as Nietzsche as a philosopher, because "Nietzsche" appears to be a construct among and within conflicting interpretative communities at different times and places?

Life and Work. For the sake of convenience, Nietzsche's adult life and work can be divided into two decades: the Basel years (1869–1879), followed by his decade as a rootless, struggling pensioner (1879–1889). This latter period ended with the total loss of his mental faculties, placing him, first, in his mother's care and subsequently—from approximately 1896 until his death in 1900—in the sole care of his sister, Elisabeth Förster-Nietzsche.

After having excelled at Germany's leading Protestant boarding school, Schulpforta, Nietzsche attended the University of Bonn in 1864 to study theology and classical philology. He soon became a pawn in an acrimonious debate between his two leading classics professors, Otto Jahn and Friedrich Wilhelm Ritschl, and he followed Ritschl to the University of Leipzig in 1865. There, he became the only student ever to publish in Ritschl's prestigious classics journal, *Rheinisches Museum,* and he did so quite frequently. He entered military service in October 1867, sustained a serious chest injury, and returned to resume his studies at Leipzig precisely one year later while on extended sick leave. When a professorship in classical philology fell vacant in 1869 in Basel, Switzerland, Ritschl recommended Nietzsche with lavish and unparalleled praise, despite the fact that he had completed neither his doctoral thesis nor the additional dissertation required for a German degree. Ritschl assured the University of Basel that Nietzsche could do absolutely anything, that he had never seen anyone like him in forty years of teaching. In 1869, the University of Leipzig hurriedly conferred the doctorate on Nietzsche, solely on the strength of his previous publications, so that he could assume the title of extraordinary professor of classical philology at the University of Basel (the equivalent of an American associate professorship). The following year, Nietzsche was promoted to ordinary professor (the equivalent of an American full professorship) and became a Swiss citizen.

During the Basel years, Nietzsche's ambivalent relationship to Richard Wagner—whom he had met during the Leipzig years—ripened. Nietzsche seized every opportunity to visit Wagner and his wife Cosima. It was under the spell of Arthur Schopenhauer and the charismatic persona of Wagner that Nietzsche wrote his much-anticipated first book in 1872, *Die Geburt der Tragödie aus dem Geiste der Musik* (The Birth of Tragedy out of the Spirit of Music). This first book also represented an emphatic break with the trappings of classical philology—the book had no footnotes, for example—and represented a speculative rather than a conventional exegetical work. It argued that Greek tragedy arose out of the fusion of what Nietzsche termed Apollonian and Dionysian elements. The Apollonian, roughly, was the principle of order, stasis, static beauty, and clearly demarcated boundaries. The Dionysian, in contrast, was the principle of frenzy, excess, and a corresponding collapse of clearly demarcated boundaries. One could almost say that the Apollonian represented the nascent principle of the aesthetics of presence, while the Dionysian represented nascent ambiguity, hidden depths, complexity—that which escapes full disclosure to a detached gaze; but not quite, for although Nietzsche argued that Greek tragedy emerged out of these two elements, he also argued that a third principle, Socratic rationalism and its attendant optimism, spelled the death of Greek tragedy. It is in the demand to be "absurdly rational" that Socratism spells the death knell of Greek tragedy by making an aesthetics of presence fully manifest and seemingly mandatory. The final ten sections of this text are a rhapsody about the rebirth of tragedy from the spirit of Wagner's music.

Greeted by stony silence at first, *The Birth of Tragedy* became an object of heated controversy among those who mistook it as a conventional work of classical philological scholarship. Germany's leading classicists, among them Wilhelm Willamowitz-Möllendorf, wrote screeds denouncing the work. Erwin Rhode, Nietzsche's lifelong friend, responded measure for measure. The debate, in retrospect, demeaned all participants, for *The Birth of Tragedy* was "a work of profound imaginative insight, which left the scholarship of a generation toiling in the rear," as the British classicist Francis M. Cornford wrote (1912). That it remains a classic (and controversial) text in the history of aesthetics to this day is clearly demonstrated by the attention it receives in the essays that follow this survey of Nietzsche's thought.

1873–1876 marked the appearance of a series of books under the heading *Unzeitgemässige Betrachtungen* (Unfashionable Observations, R. Gray, trans. in the in-progress *Complete Works of Friedrich Nietzsche* [in 20 vols.], vol. 2, E. Behler ed; all translated titles derive from this in-progress edition). The first *Unfashionable Observation*, an attack on the theologian David Strauss, was written at the urging of

Wagner. It appeared in 1873 bearing the subtitle "David Strauss the Confessor and the Writer." It was a book unworthy of Nietzsche's talents. The second *Unfashionable Observation*, "On the Advantages and Liabilities of History for Life" (1874), attacked the then-fashionable notion that historical knowledge is intrinsically valuable; and it introduced distinctions between "monumental," "antiquarian," and "critical" history. The same year brought the appearance of the third *Unfashionable Observation*, "Schopenhauer as Educator." As R. J. Hollingdale has remarked, this is wholly about Schopenhauer as "an exemplary type of man" and tells us rather more about Nietzsche than about its alleged subject. The fourth and last *Unfashionable Observation*, published in 1876, "Richard Wagner in Bayreuth," was delayed repeatedly, in part because Nietzsche was beginning to have serious reservations about Wagner, his music, his anti-Semitism, his chauvinism, and his increasing promotion of a vulgar form of Christian mythology. Nevertheless, he suppressed earlier, more critical versions and published a flattering psychology of Wagner—one that Wagner, in turn, sent to King Ludwig of Bavaria. The fierce break with Wagner lay just beyond the horizon, however.

Because Nietzsche's health deteriorated steadily, he resigned his professorial chair at the University of Basel on 14 June 1879 and was granted a pension of three thousand Swiss francs for a period of six years, which he supplemented with a small inheritance from a relative in England whom he had never met. Financial stringency—scarcely visible in any works authorized for publication—plagued Nietzsche for the remainder of his (lucid) years.

From 1878 to 1880, Nietzsche's *Menschliches, Allzumenschliches: Ein Buch für freie Geister* (Human, All Too Human: A Book for Free Spirits) appeared in two separate volumes. These substantial volumes are often thought to mark a second, new phase in Nietzsche's development, one that is carried through in *Morgenröthe: Gedanken über die moralischen Vorurtheile* (Daybreak: Thoughts concerning Moral Prejudices, 1881) and *Die fröhliche Wissenschaft*, (The Gay Science, 1882). The works of this period reflect Nietzsche's emancipation from his earlier Romanticism, as well as from Schopenhauer and Wagner. These volumes reflect, more than any others, the influence of the French aphorists; they extol the sciences and the virtues of the Enlightenment. They also begin Nietzsche's profound explorations of the relationship between reason and power, specifically the subterranean striving after power that dominates, self-deceptively, the ascetic and the martyr, themes that would be broadened and come to dominate much of his later writings.

Nietzsche's professed literary and philosophical masterpiece, *Also Sprach Zarathustra: Ein Buch für Alle und Keinen* (Thus Spoke Zarathustra: A Book for All and None), was published in four parts between 1883 and 1885, the last part a private printing at his own expense, whose copies he later attempted to retrieve. He referred to *Zarathustra* with predictable hyperbole in *Götzen-Dämmerung: oder wie man mit dem Hammer philosophiert* (Twilight of the Idols: Or How One Philosophizes with a Hammer, 1888) as "the most profound book [humankind] possesses" ["Skirmishes of an Unfashionable Man," p. 4]). *Zarathustra* remained for many decades the least admired and least referred to of Nietzsche's books in the English-speaking philosophical world, not least because of its narrative structure, its biblical posture, its apparent prophetic yet parodic tone, and its exploitation of biblical and Platonic allusions. Indeed, the culminating book 4 was seldom remarked upon, in part because its carnivalesque "chapters" seemed to parody the first three parts of *Zarathustra*: (an issue discussed later in this essay).

As with most of his works, *Zarathustra* received almost no attention. Its sales were slight and virtually no critical notice was taken of it. Nietzsche attempted a more direct approach to set forth his "philosophy" in two subsequent books, *Jenseits von Gut und Böse: Vorspiel einer Philosophie der Zukunft*, (Beyond Good and Evil: Overture to a Philosophy of the Future, 1886), and *Zur Genealogie der Moral: Eine Streitschrift* (Toward the Genealogy of Morality: A Polemic, 1887). Neither attempt fared much better than *Zarathustra*, although philosophers, especially in the "analytic" tradition, have made more consistent use of *Toward the Genealogy of Morality*—totally ignoring its subtitle—often treating it as an excessively shrill exercise in "moral philosophy."

Nietzsche's final lucid year, 1888, was a period of supreme productivity. He wrote and published *Der Fall Wagner: Ein Musikanten-Problem* (Wagner's Case: A Musician's Problem); he attempted to set out his views in outline, in characteristic Nietzschean fashion in *Twilight of the Idols*, a book whose title obliquely *refers to*, but never *mentions*, Wagner, *Götzen-Dämmerung: oder wie man mit dem Hammer philosophiert* being a pun on Wagner's opera *Götterdämmerung: Twilight of the Idols; Twilight of the Gods*. Nietzsche's subtitle ("Or How One Philosophizes with a Hammer") doubles the irony by indicating in the book's preface that "this little essay is a great declaration of war; and regarding the sounding out of idols, this time they are not just idols of the age, but eternal idols, which are here touched with a hammer as with a tuning fork." Wagner is referred to only by allusion and is dismissed, because it is "eternal idols" that become Nietzsche's principal target here, just as a "hammer" becomes a *Stimmgabel*, a tuning fork. In 1888, Nietzsche also composed *Der Antichrist: Fluch auf das Christenthum* (The Antichrist: A Curse upon Christendom), whose first twenty-five numbered sections were originally to be included in *Twilight of the Idols; Ecce Homo: Wie man wird, was man ist* (Ecce Homo: How One Becomes What One Is); *Dionysos-Dithyramben; Nietzsche contra Wagner: Aktenstücke eines Psychologen* (Nietzsche contra Wagner: File Copies of a Psychologist. *The Antichrist* and *Nietzsche contra Wagner* were not published until 1895, five years after Nietzsche's mental collapse, the former mistakenly as book 1 of *Der Wille zur Macht* (The Will to Power); and *Ecce Homo* was withheld from publication by Elisabeth until 1908, twenty years after its composition.

Several cautionary points are worth mentioning at this point. First, Nietzsche's many published books, as well as those authorized for publication, have typically been referred to as consisting of "aphorisms." In fact, however, Nietzsche experimented with a profusion of styles and genres, only a very small percentage of which could properly be characterized as aphorisms. *Twilight of the Idols*, for example, begins (following its preface) with forty-two entries that may properly be called "aphorisms," and Nietzsche titles this collection *Sprüche und Pfeile* (Epigrams and Arrows), as in the oft-repeated eighth epigram: "*Out of life's school of war*: Whatever does not destroy me makes me stronger." Nietzsche understood very well that poignant aphorisms pierce the receptive mind more surely than any complex philosophical argument can ever do; and he wrote on more than one occasion that great writers want to be learned by heart, to be memorized. A certain sort of memorization is not merely memorialization but is, in fact, *Bildung* ("education" or "edification") in the strictest literal German sense of building or erecting a person.

Second, *Ecce Homo* is still too often referred to as Nietzsche's "autobiography." As in the first case—"aphorisms"—linguistic resources are simply too impoverished to adequately capture the genre of which *Ecce Homo* consists. After all, who would write an "autobiography" whose hyperbolic chapters bear the titles "Why I Am So Wise," "Why I Am So Clever," "Why I Write Such Good Books," and "Why I Am a Destiny"?; and who, if not Nietzsche, could have ended such a book with the sentence, "Have I been understood?—*Dionysus versus the Crucified!*"

Third, and of perhaps greater importance to the history of the reception of Nietzsche's work, is the condition of his literary estate in Weimar, the so-called *Nachlass* problem. It has become clear that in the end Nietzsche never intended to write a book called *The Will to Power*. Moreover, the compilation of notes published under that title by his sister, twice—once in 1895 in a shorter version as an appendix to her book about her brother, and a second time as 1,067 literary fragments appended to a later edition of her book—is a fraud, despite the fact that philosophers seem addicted to its illusion of "clarity." The fact is that, after the collapse of the Berlin Wall in 1989, the proper job of conserving and restoring Nietzsche's literary estate was begun for the very first time. As it turns out, there is much more material still unpublished, and even the canonical Colli and Montinari editions are full of errors. Not only did Montinari's by far superior edition omit anything he regarded as "personal" (and what was *not* "personal" for Nietzsche?), but his editions of the collected works contain the penultimate version of *Ecce Homo,* not its final form. As a result of the intervention of an American donor, Nietzsche's manuscripts and letters have now been restored for posterity. They add up to about 120 volumes; and a second archival collection is to be housed in the New York Public Library as a gesture of gratitude. As a result, it is difficult to know what the "Nietzsche" of the next century will look like, save that the nonbook *The Will to Power* will recede into richly deserved obscurity, along with the many interpretations of his work based on that nonbook.

The Ascetic Ideal. With all of the previous disclaimers in mind, can a coherent philosophical position be derived from Nietzsche's works? One would think so, no matter how provisional such an alembic may be. As Nietzsche put it in "What Is the Meaning of Ascetic Ideals":

> For the longest time philosophy would not have *been possible at all* on earth without ascetic wraps and cloak, without an ascetic self-misunderstanding. To put it vividly: the *ascetic priest* provided until the most modern times the repulsive and gloomy caterpillar form in which alone the philosopher could live and creep about. (*Toward the Genealogy of Morality* p. 10)

In his mature writings, Nietzsche was preoccupied by the origins and function of values in human life. If, as he maintained in *Twilight of the Idols,* the value of life cannot be estimated, that existence neither possesses nor lacks intrinsic value and yet is always being evaluated, then such evaluations can usefully be read self-referentially, as symptoms of the condition of the evaluators. This led Nietzsche to some radical motivating assumptions, including the belief that (1) traditional philosophy, morality, and religion are more important than any other institutional forces in making Europeans and Americans who they are—not race, gender, ethnicity, nationality, sexual orientation, social or economic class; (2) that philosophy, morality, and religion—each one taken separately—share a common feature that is more important than the multiplicity that seems to separate each one; (3) that philosophy, morality, and religion—taken collectively—share a common feature more important than their obvious differences. This common feature Nietzsche called the "ascetic ideal," which finds expression and hides its function in philosophy, morality, and religion.

The ascetic ideal, put simply, just *is* the need to provide surcease from suffering, to provide expiation, atonement, justification, and even explanation for existence. Suffering existence must be atoned for, repented, surmounted, justified, or explained. Although it is certainly the case that animals suffer pain and deprivations of all sorts, it is the human animal alone that seeks a meaning for its suffering—often simply to continue to live. Nietzsche's subtlety is evident here, for if one marks a distinction between suffering in its extensional and its intensional sense, then the human animal alone experiences both sorts of suffering. An explanation for suffering provided at one time to combat suicide can itself become a source of suffering at a later time when the extensional cause no longer obtains, as in the case of religiously inspired guilt, especially sexual guilt and traditional body shame. A longish quote from Nietzsche puts these points in sharpest relief:

> Without taking account of the ascetic ideal, human beings—the *animal,* human being—had no meaning before. Its existence on earth had no goal. "Why human being at all?"—was a question without an answer. . . . Precisely this was the meaning of the ascetic ideal: that something was lacking, that a tremendous *gap* surrounded humanity: it did not know how to justify, explain, or affirm itself, it *suffered* from the problem of its meaning. . . . yet, suffering as such was not its problem, but that the answer was lacking to the cry of the question "Why suffer?" . . . The meaninglessness of suffering, not suffering itself, was the curse which hitherto lay spread out over humankind—and *the ascetic ideal offered humankind meaning.* So far it has been the only meaning; any meaning at all is better than no meaning at all. . . . Through this, suffering was *interpreted.* . . . The interpretation undoubtedly involved new suffering, even more profound, more inward, more poisonous, that gnawed at life more. . . . Yet, in spite of that—humankind was saved: it had a *meaning.* . . . it could now want something—and to begin with, it mattered not what, whereto, or how it wanted: *the will itself was saved.* In the end, one can hardly conceal what it was that this will really expressed when it received its direction from the ascetic ideal: that hatred against everything human, even more, against everything animal, everything material, this disgust with the senses, with reason itself, this fear of happiness and beauty, this desire to get away from all semblance, change, becoming, death, wish, desire itself—the meaning of all this, should we dare to comprehend it, is a *will to nothingness,* a will running counter to life, a revolt against the most fundamental presuppositions of life; yet, it is and remains a *will!* And, to repeat at the end what I said in the beginning: rather than want nothing, humankind even wants *nothingness.* (Ibid., p. 28)

Accordingly, it is not at all accidental that the Judeo-Christian tradition made suffering tolerable, for example, by interpreting it as God's intention and an occasion for atonement. Moreover, Nietzsche argued that Christianity owed its hegemony to the flattering doctrine of personal immortality, that is, to the "conceit" that each individual's life and death have cosmic significance. It is no accident, therefore, that binary oppositions should come to characterize humankind's self-interpretations.

In philosophy, "The fundamental faith of the metaphysician is the *faith in opposite values*" (*Beyond Good and Evil,* part 1, 2). Being versus becoming, reality versus appearance, necessity versus contingency, eternity versus temporality, duty versus desire, mind versus senses, soul versus body, good versus evil, logic versus rhetoric, reason versus emotion, knowledge versus opinion, and, arguably, male versus female became philosophy's stock in trade. Analogous binary oppositions dominate traditional religions: heaven versus earth, God versus creation, righteousness versus sin, salvation versus damnation, soul versus body, good versus evil, immortality versus death, faith versus reason, humility versus pride, asceticism versus hedonism, abstinence versus fornication, male versus female.

Nietzsche's critique of traditional morality centered on the typology of "master" and "slave" morality. By examining the German words *gut* (good), *schlecht* (bad), and *böse* (evil), Nietzsche maintained that the distinction between good and bad was originally a nonmoral reference to those who were privileged, the masters, as opposed to those who were base, the slaves. The good/evil contrast arose when slaves avenged themselves symbolically by converting attributes of mastery into vices. If the favored, the "good," were powerful, it was said that the meek would inherit the earth. If the "good" were active, noble, proud, beautiful, it was soon said that the reactive ("turn the other cheek"), the base, the humble, the ugly would enter the kingdom of heaven. Pride became sin. Charity, humility, chastity, and obedience became tickets out of this vale of tears. As the ideology of slave morality, it became crucial to Christianity that it be the only true religion and corresponding morality. As Nietzsche was later to write, Christianity is Platonism for the masses *(für's Volk)*. This insistence on absoluteness, this dogmatism, is as essential to philosophical as it is to religious ethics.

Nietzsche often thought of his writings as struggles with nihilism. But is the struggle itself not an instance of what it seeks to overcome? Insofar as the will to truth would ultimately undermine Christianity and philosophical dogmatism, is not the will to truth also an ascetic impulse, a problem disguising itself as a solution? This point can be put in another, general way: if the human animal is a meaning mongerer, the ascetic ideal incarnate whose search for meaning is a problem as much as it is a solution, is not all striving for explanations—including this "survey"—an instance of the ascetic ideal? Although Nietzsche mentions the "comedians" of the ascetic ideal as the only prophylactic, how are they to be understood? Put differently, is there any way to decide if Nietzsche is playing the same (ascetic) game with a different set of rules or is playing an altogether different game?

These questions gain urgency because many have thought of Nietzsche as offering a penetrating critique of the history of philosophy, morality, and religion, a critique that is parasitic on a "positive" set of doctrines, for example, the "will to power," "perspectivism," "eternal recurrence," and the *Übermensch* ("superman," "overman"). Viewed in this way, perspectivism is a concept that holds that there are no immaculate perceptions, that the idea of knowledge from no point of view is as incoherent a notion as is seeing from no particular vantage point. Perspectivism also denies the

possibility of an all-inclusive perspective that could contain all others, and, hence, make reality available as it is in itself, a God's-eye view. The notion of such an all-inclusive perspective is as incoherent as the concept of seeing an object from every possible vantage point simultaneously.

Viewed as a "positive" doctrine, perspectivism raises the question of how one is to understand Nietzsche's own theses, for example, that the dominant values of our common heritage have been underwritten by the ascetic ideal. Is this thesis true unconditionally or only from a certain perspective? It might also be asked whether perspectivism can be asserted consistently without self-contradiction, because it must presumably be true in an unmitigated sense.

Another favorite candidate for Nietzsche's "positive" doctrine is the "will to power." He often identified life itself with "will to power," that is, with an instinct for growth and durability. Construed in this way, it provides another way of interpreting the ascetic ideal, because Nietzsche contends that "all the supreme values of humankind *lack* this will— that values that are symptomatic of decline, *nihilistic* values, are lording it under the holiest names" (*The Antichrist*, p. 6). Thus, traditional philosophy, religion, and morality have been so many masks that a deficient will to power wears. Many commentators have attempted to extend the notion of the will to power to the organic and inorganic realms as well, ascribing an ontology of will to power to Nietzsche. But again, one asks, how does this square with his perspectivism—not to mention the published texts?

Nietzsche's "doctrine" of eternal recurrence is unarguably the subject of two of Zarathustra's speeches—"On the Vision and the Riddle" and "The Convalescent"—and it is fully rehearsed in *The Gay Science* under the heading "Das Grösste Schwergewicht." That entry (341) concludes by asking its interlocutors two questions framed as one:

> If this thought were to gain possession of you, it would transform you, as you are, or perhaps crush you. The question in each and every thing, "Do you want this once more and innumerable times more?" would weigh upon your actions as the greatest stress. Or how well disposed would you have to become to life and to yourself *to crave nothing more fervently [um nach nichts mehr zu verlangen]* than this ultimate eternal confirmation and seal?

Nietzsche refers to this very aphorism in *Ecce Homo* ("Why I Write Such Good Books") when he writes: "my *Gaya Scienza* . . . contains hundreds of signs of something incomparable; in the end it even offers the beginning of *Zarathustra*, and in the penultimate section of the fourth book the basic idea of *Zarathustra*" (*Ecce Homo*). Thus, the aphorism just cited is the "basic idea of *Zarathustra*." It asks "How well disposed would a person have to become to himself or herself to crave nothing more fervently than the infinite repetition, without alteration, of each and every moment?" Presumably, most people would or should find such a thought shattering because they should always find it possible to prefer the eternal recurrence of their lives in an edited version rather than to crave nothing more fervently than the eternal repetition of each of its horrors. The person who could embrace the teaching of eternal recurrence without self-deception, pathology, or evasion would be an *Übermensch*, whose distance from humans is greater than the distance between beasts and human beings, Nietzsche says in *Zarathustra*. Milan Kundera grasped this abysmal yet central thought well when he wrote, in *The Unbearable Lightness of Being*:

> If every second of our lives recurs an infinite number of times, we are nailed to eternity as Jesus Christ was nailed to the cross. It is a terrifying prospect. In the world of eternal return the weight of unbearable responsibility lies heavy on every move we make. That is why Nietzsche called the idea of eternal return the heaviest of burdens.

A useful way of understanding Nietzsche commentators, especially among anglophone philosophers, is in terms of a fundamental split: Is one paying Nietzsche a compliment by assimilating him to a tradition in which criticisms of his predecessors are parasitic on his "positive doctrines," or is one denigrating his more broadly therapeutic achievement by construing him in such a way? Is Nietzsche a Sublime Ann Landers, or does he more closely resemble, say, a Michel Foucault, for whom the critiques just *are* the positive achievement? Read in the latter way, the positive doctrines are little more than Nietzsche's bait and hook with which to snare a reader in the grip of the ascetic ideal.

The best example of this latter reading may very well be *Zarathustra* itself, Nietzsche's masterpiece, read not as a philosopher's cookbook leading to the creation of an *Übermensch*, but read strategically. Nietzsche believed that Zarathustra (a.k.a. Zoroaster) (1) had the honor of being the first cosmic dualist, seeing reality itself as the struggle between good and evil; (2) subscribed to the notion of an *eschaton*, an end of time; (3) subscribed to a doctrine of reward and punishment; and (4) subscribed to the notion of linear time leading to the *eschaton*. To affect a genuine transvaluation of values would require the self-consumption of all four elements. Reality is neither intrinsically good nor evil. It has no epiphany at the end of time. One's life itself, this life, is one's reward or one's punishment; and time is not linear but an eternal wheel of the recurrence of all things.

Read in this way, *Zarathustra* is indeed a *Bildungsroman* in which the attentive reader—initially seduced by the promise of authentic "doctrines"—discovers in part 4 that the ascetic ideal cannot be escaped, it can only be parodied and transmuted into art: "It is only as an *aesthetic phenomenon* that existence and the world are eternally *justified*" (*The Birth of Tragedy*, p. 5)—if any "justification" is required at all. *Incipit Zarathustra: Incipit Tragödia: Incipit Comedia.*

BIBLIOGRAPHY

Work by Nietzsche

All translations are my own. They are based on the *Kritische Gesamtausgabe: Werke*, edited by Giorgio Colli and Mazzino Montinari (Berlin, 1967–). Previous translations were consulted as the need arose.

Other Sources: General

Clark, Maudemarie. *Nietzsche on Truth and Philosophy*. Cambridge and New York, 1990.
Cornford, Francis M. *From Religion to Philosophy: A Study in the Origins of Western Speculation*. London, 1912.
Danto, Arthur C. *Nietzsche as Philosopher*. New York, 1965.
Heidegger, Martin. *Nietzsche*. 2 vols. Pfullingen, 1961.
Janz, Curt Paul. *Friedrich Nietzsche Biographie*. 3 vols. Munich, 1978–1979.
Kaufmann, Walter. *Nietzsche: Philosopher, Psychologist, Antichrist*. 4th rev. enl. ed. Princeton, N.J., 1974.
Magnus, Bernd. *Nietzsche's Existential Imperative*. Bloomington, Ind., 1978.
Nehamas, Alexander. *Nietzsche: Life as Literature*. Cambridge, Mass., 1985.
Parkes, Graham. *Composing the Soul: Reaches of Nietzsche's Psychology*. Chicago, 1994.
Schacht, Richard. *Nietzsche*. London and Boston, 1983.

Anthologies

Gillespie, Michael Allen, and Tracy B. Strong, eds. *Nietzsche's New Seas: Explorations in Philosophy, Aesthetics, and Politics*. Chicago, 1988.
Kemal, Salim, Ivan Gaskell, and Daniel W. Conway, eds. *Nietzsche: Philosophy and Art*. Cambridge and New York, 1997.
Magnus, Bernd, and Kathleen M. Higgins, eds. *The Cambridge Companion to Nietzsche*. Cambridge and New York, 1996.
Pasley, Malcolm, ed. *Nietzsche: Imagery and Thought*. Berkeley, 1978.
Schacht, Richard, ed. *Nietzsche, Genealogy, Morality*. Berkeley, 1994.
Solomon, Robert C., and Kathleen M. Higgins, eds. *Reading Nietzsche*. New York and Oxford, 1988.

Aesthetics and Related Topics

Blondel, Eric. *Nietzsche, the Body and Culture: Philosophy as a Philological Genealogy*. Translated by Sean Hand. Stanford, Calif., 1991.
Derrida, Jacques. *Spurs: Nietzsche's Styles*. Translated by Barbara Harlow. Chicago, 1979.
Foucault, Michel. "Nietzsche, Genealogy, History." In *Language, Counter-Memory, Practice: Selected Essays and Interviews*. Translated by Donald F. Bouchard and Sherry Simon, pp. 139–164. Ithaca, N.Y., 1977.
Foucault, Michel. "Ecce Homo, or the Written Body." Translated by Judith Still. *Oxford Literary Review* 7.1–2 (1985): 3–24.
Higgins, Kathleen Marie. *Nietzsche's Zarathustra*. Philadelphia, 1987.
Kofman, Sarah. *Nietzsche and Metaphor*. Translated by Duncan Large. Stanford, Calif., 1993.
Lampert, Laurence. *Nietzsche's Teaching: An Interpretation of "Thus Spoke Zarathustra."* New Haven, 1986.
Magnus, Bernd, Jean-Pierre Mileur, and Stanley Stewart. *Nietzsche's Case: Philosophy as/and Literature*. New York and London, 1993.
Shapiro, Gary. *Nietzschean Narratives*. Bloomington, Ind., 1989.

Silk, M. S., and J. P. Stern. *Nietzsche on Tragedy*. Cambridge and New York, 1981.
Staten, Henry. *Nietzsche's Voice*. Ithaca, N.Y., 1990.
Strong, Tracy B. *Friedrich Nietzsche and the Politics of Transfiguration*. Berkeley, 1975.
Young, Julian. *Nietzsche's Philosophy of Art*. Cambridge and New York, 1992.

BERND MAGNUS

Nietzsche, Schopenhauer, and Disinterestedness

As is becoming increasingly recognized, a great deal of Friedrich Nietzsche's mature philosophy is a struggle against Arthur Schopenhauer, the hero of his youth. This is true, in particular, of his discussions of disinterestedness in the field of art.

Adapting Immanuel Kant's terminology to his own ends, Schopenhauer's main work, *The World as Will and Representation*, contrasts two fundamental stances to the world: the "interested" stance of one who wills, and the disinterested stance of art, of the aesthetic perceiver. Why does Schopenhauer see will-lessness, disinterest, as essential to the aesthetic state? Because interest, the will, molds, he says, "not merely the judgement, but even the original perception of things" (1966). Schopenhauer's point here is more familiar as a Heideggerian one: in ordinary consciousness, we experience objects as, in Martin Heidegger's language, "equipment." We regard, he says, "houses, ships, machines and the like with the idea of their purpose and their suitability therefor; human beings with the idea of their relation to us, if they have any, . . . their position and vocation . . . and so on" (ibid.).

Why should this mode of perceiving be incompatible with the aesthetic state? Sometimes Schopenhauer says that, in perceiving things under instrumental descriptions, we have access only to their "relative" not their "absolute essence." But although plausible with respect to people or to nature, this cannot be a general truth, for where houses, ships, and the like are concerned, their essence really is given by their instrumental description. Schopenhauer's real point is rather that, in ordinary consciousness of things as equipment, we are oblivious to everything in an object save those few features that are required for it all to fall under the instrumental concept that it does:

> a traveller . . . in a hurry, will see the Rhine and its banks only as a dash or stroke, and the bridge over it as a line intersecting that stroke. In the head of a man filled with his own aims, the world appears just as a beautiful landscape does on the plan of a battlefield. (Ibid.)

Why should this, as it were, diminution of the fullness of being of an object be unaesthetic? After all, *any* human interpretation must select, must fail to capture most of the infinite richness that is out there in the world. The point that Schopenhauer wishes to make, however, is not that the aesthetic perceiver apprehends the world in the fullness of its being but that such fullness becomes *available* to her. The routines of ordinary consciousness are just that: "thin," impoverished perceptual routines. Clichés, in fact. No wonder that Schopenhauer picks "boredom" as the characteristic mood of humanity save in those circumstances where it finds itself in tangible danger or need. The clichés of quotidian instrumentalism are useful but oppressive: in ordinary consciousness, we are closed off from all but immediately instrumental aspects of objects.

The artist through the "silence" of his will escapes this tyranny of the ordinary. The full richness of the object becomes available to him so that he becomes open to novel disclosure. He becomes able to perceive something sparkling, new—in a word, beautiful—in the world. The artist "perceives a world different from [ordinary] perceivers, though only by looking more deeply into the world that lies before them also" (ibid.).

Nietzsche devoted much energy to a critique of Schopenhauer's claim that the aesthetic state is disinterested. (Wrongly supposing Schopenhauer to be merely repeating Kant's account of the aesthetic state, he took himself to be attacking, at the same time, Kant.) Why should he have taken exception to the claim? Because, having identified will-lessness as essential to the aesthetic state, Schopenhauer goes on to use this feature to draw art into his general philosophy, in particular, into his pessimism. According to this latter, to live is to will and to will is to suffer. But, in entering the aesthetic state, one enters a state of will-lessness. Hence, one experiences the pleasure of a brief escape from pain, from the "penal servitude" of willing, a pleasure that offers a fleeting intimation of "how blessed must be the life of a man in whom the will is silenced not for a few moments, as in enjoyment of the beautiful, but for ever."

For Nietzsche, needless to say, this is a fundamental error. Art, the *On the Genealogy of Morals* holds, far from serving such an "ascetic ideal," is its most profound antagonist. Schopenhauerian aesthetics is a "maliciously ingenious" attempt to stand the truth on its head, to "adduce in favour of a nihilistic, total depreciation of life" precisely the great "counter-instance," the great self-affirmation of the "will to live," life's form of "exuberance" (1967). Hence, Nietzsche sets out to squash that—as *Twilight of the Idols* calls it—"fat worm of error" that accounts for the aesthetic state in terms of disinterestedness.

For Nietzsche, as for Schopenhauer, the aesthetic state is common to both spectator and to creator: "The effect of works of art is to excite *the state that creates art*," Nietzsche says in *The Will to Power* (1968). It follows that, correctly described, the aesthetic state must be revealed as a *creative* state. This forms the basis of what appears to be a rather simple objection against Schopenhauer: "Immaculate [disinterested] Perception," he says in *Thus Spoke Zarathustra*, can never "give birth." Art essentially involves the will, demands that I "will with all my will that an image may not remain a mere image" (1954a).

To this part of Nietzsche's criticism Schopenhauer has a ready response. Of course, he admits in *Parerga and Paralipomena*, art involves the will—in the production of the artwork. Yet, where at least *good* art is concerned, distinct from this executive phase or aspect is a contemplative phase. It is this and this alone that is claimed to be disinterested.

There is, however, more to Nietzsche's emphasis on the dominant role of the will in art than meets the eye. This can be approached by considering what is, in fact, a point of agreement with Schopenhauer. Nietzsche holds that the essence of art, of "aesthetic doing and seeing," is what he variously calls "transfiguration," "idealizing," "transform[ing] into perfection." He thus agrees with Schopenhauer's basic assumption that there is a special state, "aesthetic seeing," in which the object appears in a radically different way from the way it appears in quotidian seeing.

How, for Nietzsche, does this transfigured seeing come to pass? It comes to pass through *Rausch* (frenzy), the one condition that is "indispensable" to the "psychology of the artist." Out of this condition, one "enriches" things: one "lends to things, one *forces* them to accept from us, one violates them—this process is called *idealizing*" (1954b.).

Nietzsche allows that many kinds of *Rausch* can produce aesthetic seeing. His emphasis and focus, however, are on sexual *Rausch*. The reason is the well-established link between sexual passion and transfiguration to which he is able to appeal to explicate the general idea that *Rausch* transfigures:

> *On the genesis of art.*—That making perfect, seeing as perfect which characterizes the cerebral system bursting with sexual energy (evening with the beloved, the smallest chance occurrences transfigured . . .) . . . as man sees woman and, as it were, makes her a present of everything excellent, so the sensuality of the artist puts into one object everything else that he honours and esteems—in this way he *perfects* an object ("idealizes" it).
>
> (1968)

Here, then, is the nub of Nietzsche's argument against Schopenhauer: not will-lessness, but precisely the opposite. The powerfully *aroused*, frenzied will is the motive power of aesthetic perception. There is, of course, a certain sense in which art is disinterested in its attitude to life: the artist *sublimates* his lust for life in the artwork—"Making music is another way of making children; chastity is merely the economy of the artist"—rather than allowing it its natural expression. But so far as "aesthetic *seeing*" goes, Nietzsche seems committed to the view that the lover who does not engage in "aesthetic doing" nonetheless inhabits that state.

Nietzsche's essential claim is that the interested stance to the world is, in the aesthetic state, heightened rather than abandoned. Desire, condemned by the "Immaculate Perceivers" as "looking at life . . . like a dog, with [one's] tongue hanging out" is precisely the stance of the artist *(Zarathustra)*.

Does Nietzsche's argument, however, really establish the interestedness of the aesthetic stance in any sense that conflicts with Schopenhauer's aesthetic theory? Let us remind ourselves of the heart of Schopenhauer's position, the claim that *perception* must be disinterested, that aesthetic seeing can only occur where the clichéd routines of instrumental, manipulative, will-molded perception have been dislodged. Does Nietzsche's explication of transfiguration really contradict this claim? Surely not. To focus on his paradigm of transfiguration, the transfiguration provided by sexual passion, there is, surely, nothing instrumental, nothing manipulative, about the romantic lover's perception of the beloved. On the contrary, his "perfecting" of her, his investing her with every conceivable excellence, imposes on him a kind of awed reverence (the kind celebrated in the literature of courtly love) that is incompatible with any kind of instrumental "using" of the beloved. For the latter to occur, not the heated perception of passion, but rather the categories of coolly calculational reason, must come into play.

In conclusion, it has to be said that Nietzsche succeeds in putting a dent into Schopenhauer's philosophy of art. Although he exaggerates its force—Schopenhauer is surely right that to enter a state of disinterested contemplation is *a* way of dislocating the clichés of ordinary perception—Nietzsche does show that a heightening of the will, of "interest," is also *a* way of achieving this end. Hence, he succeeds in disrupting the necessary association of the pleasure of will-lessness with the aesthetic state, and hence, too, Schopenhauer's characterization of the aesthetic as an intimation of the ascetic. On the other hand, the heart of Schopenhauer's theory of art—as distinct from his attempt to fit that theory into his general philosophy—is untouched by Nietzsche's criticism. Art must displace the routines of instrumental consciousness. There is, therefore, a good sense in which it is true that aesthetic perception is disinterested. Nietzsche should have seen this, should have seen that there is much, in fact, in Schopenhauer's philosophy of art with which he could agree.

[*See also* Disinterestedness; *and* Schopenhauer.]

BIBLIOGRAPHY

Works by Nietzsche

On the Genealogy of Morals (with *Ecce Homo*). Translated by Walter Kaufmann and R. J. Hollingdale. New York, 1967.
Thus Spoke Zarathustra. In *The Portable Nietzsche*, translated and edited by Walter Kaufmann. New York, 1954a.
Twilight of the Idols. In *The Portable Nietzsche*, translated and edited by Walter Kaufmann. New York, 1954b.

The Will to Power. Edited by Walter Kaufmann, translated by Kaufmann and R. J. Hollingdale. New York, 1968.

Works by Schopenhauer

Parerga and Paralipomena: Short Philosophical Essays. 2 vols. Translated by E. F. J. Payne. Oxford, 1974. See vol. 2.
The World as Will and Representation. 2 vols. Translated by E. F. J. Payne. Reprint, New York, 1966.

Other Sources

Young, Julian. *Willing and Unwilling: A Study in the Philosophy of Arthur Schopenhauer.* Dordrecht, 1987. See especially chap. 7.
Young, Julian. *Nietzsche's Philosophy of Art.* Cambridge and New York, 1992. See especially chaps. 1 and 5.
Young, Julian. "Immaculate Perception: Nietzsche contra Schopenhauer." *Schopenhauer Jahrbuch* 74 (1993).

JULIAN YOUNG

Nietzsche's Literary Style

In *Twilight of the Idols,* one of his final works, Friedrich Nietzsche describes his aim in his writing: to say in ten sentences "what others say in a book—what others do *not* say in a book" (1954b). Considering the headstrong challenges that Nietzsche makes to the fondest beliefs of his tradition, his goal seems to have been fulfilled with respect to content. Yet, his remark applies just as well to the manner in which he chose to write. Nietzsche was committed to experimentalism in literary style, so much so that the question of how to weigh his stylistics in interpreting his work remains a subject of continuing controversy.

Underlying Nietzsche's diverse literary experiments is an aesthetic vision that is already evident in his first book, *The Birth of Tragedy.* The work opens by urging the reader to compare the Apollonian and Dionysian principles, of orderly beauty and dynamic frenzy, respectively, with the experiences of dreaming and intoxication. Implicit in this comparison is an association between aesthetic aspirations and modes of self-consciousness. The Apollonian principle, which Nietzsche associates with sculpture, corresponds to the mental condition of feeling oneself to be distinct from one's environment. The Dionysian principle, by contrast, is evident in music and corresponds to the mental state in which one feels conjoined with the rest of reality. The opening suggestion is also an assault on the reader's complacency. Nietzsche insists, right away, that the reader become engaged, even to the extent of drawing possibly embarrassing experiences into the range of the discussion.

Ancient Athenian tragedy, according to Nietzsche, conjoined the two principles. The Apollonian presentation of the drama was an epiphenomenon, based on a more fundamental musical transmission of a Dionysian state to its audience. Music caused the spectator to identify, in a pleasurable way, with the whole of reality. Supported by this joyous condition, the spectator was able to face the content of the tragic drama: always the destruction of the individual, a content that would be intolerable from an individualistic Apollonian point of view. By experiencing joy at being part of a larger whole, the spectator came to feel, according to Nietzsche, that the bliss of being a participant in the tumultuous flux of reality is worth all the suffering that life brings with it.

Nietzsche's analysis of tragedy indicates the centrality of aesthetic phenomena to the meaning of life, as he understands it. Rejecting all views that seek to justify this life by reference to another, Nietzsche sees art as the means by which we make peace with our temporal existence. Art moves us to psychological states that awaken and reinforce our sense that life is intrinsically worthwhile. Aesthetic experiences are crucial to our sense that life is meaningful despite the pains involved. In aesthetic experience, we embody the conviction that life is joyous and wonderful. The question of life's meaning, though reasonable enough from the everyday point of view, becomes irrelevant through such experience. In it, we ourselves instantiate meaning and experience ourselves and our world as fundamentally valuable.

Nietzsche's remarks on writing reflect this idea that questions of the meaning of life are resolved by experiences that alter our ordinary perspective. He associates artistic media with mental states, for example, in his remarks on style in his autobiography, *Ecce Homo.* There Nietzsche claims that the meaning and value of style are the communication of an inward state by means of signs, and he explicitly includes the "tempo of these signs" as essential to this communication. Nietzsche's writings aim not only, or even primarily, to convey propositional information. Instead, they aim to transform his readers' self-consciousness, broadly understood, and to do this through stylistic maneuvers.

This transformation resembles that which Nietzsche saw as the goal of Greek tragedy. The profound religious question of what life means in a world in which every individual faces a death sentence was the problem Athenian tragedy posed and answered. Similarly, Nietzsche's writings dwell on the problem of life's meaning, a problem made particularly poignant by Western culture's growing suspicion that the earthly life of the individual may be his or her only life.

The Birth of Tragedy's account of the principles at work in Athenian tragedy helps to explain Nietzsche's description of his literary style as "musical." He suggests in *Ecce Homo,* for example, that his entire work *Thus Spoke Zarathustra* might appropriately be considered music. Music, the fundamental means by which the tragic audience was induced to confront irrational suffering, is analogous to the means by which Nietzsche compels his audience to confront his often disturbing suggestions.

In describing his writing as music, Nietzsche draws attention to the nonsemantic characteristics of well-constructed writing—the rhythms and pacing and momentum that move the reader physiologically as well as intellectually. Much as the Apollonian drama is epiphenomenal on the Dionysian musical mood in *The Birth of Tragedy*, Nietzsche sees thinking—and writing that expresses or motivates it—as epiphenomenal on physiological activity. He insists in *Twilight of the Idols* that thinking is a kind of dancing, which must be learned as dancing. To write philosophy is to rework the physiological, according to Nietzsche. He describes philosophy as the transfiguration of various states of health into spiritual form in the Preface to the second edition of *The Gay Science*. His character Zarathustra, similarly, claims to love only writing that has been written with one's blood.

How, precisely, does Nietzsche engage the physiological dimension in his own writing? Although the details vary from work to work, he uses a number of characteristic strategies, among them (1) juxtaposition, (2) allusion, (3) parody, and (4) wild humor.

Nietzsche's strategy of juxtaposition might be described as a literal by-product of his own physiological condition. Afflicted by blinding migraines at many points during his life, Nietzsche's adoption of a format of aphorisms and short sections was at times scarcely a matter of choice—he could not count on long periods during which he could concentrate. Nevertheless, Nietzsche discovered artistic and provocative possibilities for arranging these short sections. In *Daybreak*, for instance, he alternates noncontroversial historical reports about customs and outmoded scientific beliefs with calculatedly similar descriptions about morality. The reader, seeking some connection between serial sections, is led to recognize Nietzsche's insinuation: contemporary morality is like any other custom, subject to change, and like outmoded science, downright misleading, at best a short-lived cultural oddity.

In *The Gay Science*, another work built of short passages, Nietzsche inserts a series of sections on women into book 2, which mainly discusses art. Book 2's initial sections criticize Realism, both in art and beyond it. Nietzsche taunts the Realist by suggesting that the phantasm involved in one's experience simply cannot be subtracted. Moreover, he suggests, whatever appears *becomes* the essence as far as we are concerned. The sections that follow, on women, initially seem out of place. On closer inspection, however, the first two sections on women prove to be about phantasms—specifically the fantasies that men construct about women, and how deceptive these turn out to be.

Further sections sketch brief vignettes of women who appear different than they are. For example, Nietzsche describes a woman who appears to be of easy virtue as a "noble" woman who has given a man her honor as her most cherished possession and discovered that it was not received as the treasure she took it to be. Nietzsche, presupposing a predominantly male audience, is posing a challenge with these juxtapositions. Even the (male) reader who

concurs with Nietzsche's initial judgment that we cannot dispense with all phantasms is likely to be faced with a disturbing discrepancy in his own perspective. His phantasms regarding women, most likely, do not accord with the quite plausible pictures that Nietzsche sketches of how women might look "realistically"—or even, perhaps, to themselves.

Allusion abounds in Nietzsche. His fine education and his religious background are regularly evident in his free references to Scripture, classical sources, folk maxims, and popular slogans of his day. Even his titles are sometimes sarcastic allusions. *Twilight of the Idols (Götzen-Dämmerung)* alludes to (and makes a gesture of debunking) Richard Wagner's *Twilight of the Gods (Götterdämmerung)*, while also comparing his own targets to Francis Bacon's "Idols of the Marketplace." *Ecce Homo* (Behold the Man), the title to Nietzsche's autobiography, is a sacrilegious reference to Pontius Pilate's presentation of the beaten Christ to the crowd that was screaming for his death.

The condensations Nietzsche achieves with such allusions are sometimes remarkable and philosophically pregnant. The opening of *Zarathustra*, which alludes both to Plato's Myth of the Cave and to the beginning of Christ's mission, draws attention to the mythic similarities between the story of Socrates and that of Christ. At the same time, it challenges both by appealing to their Persian predecessor Zarathustra, who is presented as a more appropriate prophet for modern times than either of the West's great heroes.

In this project, Nietzsche employs sustained parody, the third of his characteristic literary strategies. By making Zarathustra a parodic counterpart of Christ and Socrates, Nietzsche endorses some of these figures' spiritual concerns while rejecting the orientations they represent. Like Christ and Socrates, Zarathustra spends more time talking than anything else, although his gospel diametrically opposes theirs in many respects. Unlike Christ and Socrates, we see Zarathustra's development as incomplete, even after he has begun his mission. *Zarathustra* is a *Bildungsroman*, a novel of education. Zarathustra learns as he proceeds, frequently finding it necessary to reformulate his teachings, at times making a fool of himself in the process.

A lively example of Zarathustra succumbing to folly occurs in the fourth and final part of the book. In a parody of both the Last Supper and Plato's Symposium, Zarathustra has invited a motley array of characters, all eager but somewhat benighted disciples, to dinner in his home. He steps out at one point for some fresh air and returns to discover his disciples worshiping the ass that had accompanied the two kings to the party. Like Moses accosting the Israelites who had worshiped a golden calf in his absence, Zarathustra bursts into a fury, admonishing his guests for their lapse into theism. They, however, make excuses for themselves that ought to impress Zarathustra. One, called the Ugliest Man, questions whether either of them knows for sure whether God lives, has returned to life, or is completely dead. He also points out Zarathustra's own doctrine that one kills most thoroughly through laughter. Foolishly, Zarathustra has lost his sense of humor. He has slipped into the dogmatism he criticizes in theists, insisting that his guests should be good atheists. Lest there be any doubt, another of his guests (the Conscientious Man) retorts that his wisdom and overabundance could turn Zarathustra himself into an ass.

The allusion to Zarathustra as an ass recalls Apuleius's *The Golden Ass,* an ancient Roman novel. The main character, eager to gain insight and power through magic, uses the wrong potion and turns himself into an ass. The bulk of the novel recounts the ass's misadventures and observations over the long span of time that it takes him to get the chance to eat roses, the antidote for his potion. Most of his experiences are grim: he is frequently stolen, beaten, and sold. Precisely because he is never taken seriously, he is often privy to human foibles, and many of the stories he recounts are ribald and absurd. After receiving directions from the goddess Isis, who appears in a dream, the ass finally does reach roses and restore himself to human form. Although it largely describes foibles and bawdy behavior, *The Golden Ass* is the story of a soul, in which the main character has gained spiritual maturity by means of an unlikely and ungainly route.

Nietzsche's use of *The Golden Ass* as a model in part 4 of *Zarathustra* is an instance of the fourth authorial strategy that he uses to engage his readers, wild humor. Despite the high biblical prose style of *Zarathustra* and the dignified, nineteenth-century phrasing of other writing, Nietzsche uses humor outlandishly. One of Zarathustra's first encounters with humanity after ten years as a hermit occurs when he steps into a circus crowd and starts a speech on the *Übermensch* (overman or superman)—only to be mistaken for the circus barker. The guests worshiping the ass recite a litany that sounds unnervingly plausible—some of the lines are virtually lifted from Scripture, but to rather unusual effect. The ass is one who carries humanity's burdens, walks on crooked paths, opts for different routes than human beings would choose. In the words of one of Zarathustra's guests, Nietzsche attacks his targets here by provoking laughter. Whether by allusion, parody, juxtaposition, or peculiar coinages, Nietzsche frequently seeks laughter, an unquestionably physiological response, when he writes.

At some point in his career as a writer, Nietzsche came to doubt that the readers he aimed to move actually existed. He murmurs somewhat despondently in *Ecce Homo* that, ultimately, one cannot get more from books than one already knows. Yet, even in that book, one of his last, he reiterates his commitment to an incautious strategy of provocation. His ideal reader, he reaffirms, is an adventurer who refuses the safety of following Ariadne's thread, instead choosing risk and vulnerability to the lure of the Sirens. Nietzsche, ac-

cordingly, does not offer methodical sequences of reasoning for his readers to follow. In keeping with the aesthetics of his first work, and the values that aesthetics embodies, he encourages his readers to hear him more than read him, and he resists whatever desire he may have to constrain or control their responses.

Nietzsche's literary experiments are premised on his rejection of certain platitudes of aesthetic theory, particularly those enunciated by Immanuel Kant. Rejecting Kant's theory that aesthetic experience is a function of the play of the cognitive faculties, Nietzsche aims to move his readers emotionally and physiologically. In opposition to Kant's view that art should be contemplated from a disinterested standpoint, Nietzsche defends and produces an art that is designed to engage the reader (even to the extent of inducing altered inner states). In defiance of Kant's insistence that art should aim at universal intelligibility, Nietzsche challenges his readers to make their own individual responses. Whereas Kant ranks poetry as the highest art and music the lowest, Nietzsche tries to conjoin the two in his writing, taking the musical characteristics of writing as his highest aspiration.

Nietzsche is not alone in his opposition to Kantian aesthetics. Many of his Romantic contemporaries similarly emphasized the transporting power and emotional impact of art on the individual and the unique stature of music among the arts. Nietzsche was also one of many nineteenth-century thinkers to be influenced by Arthur Schopenhauer, whose impact on Romantic art and aesthetics, enhanced by Wagner's endorsement of his theory, was significant. Nietzsche's Apollonian and Dionysian principles recall Schopenhauer's duality of representation and will. Nietzsche also follows Schopenhauer in rejecting the eighteenth-century doctrine of the unity of the arts and analyzing music's purpose as different from that of the visual arts.

From our historical vantage, however, Nietzsche's similarities to his contemporaries are at least noteworthy, if not decisive, in our characterizing his aesthetics, although he would probably not be pleased by such comparisons. After his early works, he had an apostasy from Schopenhauer, whom he strenuously attacked in his later writings for endorsing Kantian disinterestedness and describing the goal of art as the observer's experience of will-lessness. Nietzsche also took pains to differentiate himself from his Romantic contemporaries. In his late writings, he endorses the classical ideal of organic unity in explicit opposition to the Romantics' "chaos of the atoms."

Ultimately, however, Nietzsche's approach to writing reflects the rather Romantic view, evident throughout his works, that aesthetics is centrally important to our sense that life is valuable. Consistently urging that we take art, with the joy it engenders, as a model for living, Nietzsche writes in a style that reflects the musicality of our experience, particularly our experience as thinkers. The dynamics and pacing of Nietzsche's presentation display what he sees as the temporal movement of thought, its propulsions and reversals, its character as "a kind of dancing." Nietzsche's style, in this respect, reflects his conviction that temporality is fundamental to the structure of our experience and important for our ability to shape our experience in a meaningful fashion.

Nietzsche also constructs his writings artistically, integrating elements that themselves maintain independent importance. He is a pioneer of literary forms that reflect the perspectival character of our experience and our temporal traversal of perspectives. Like other nineteenth-century thinkers (most notably G. W. F. Hegel), Nietzsche was interested in the confrontation and mutual influence of opposing ideas. Unlike his Hegelian contemporaries, however, Nietzsche did not aim to find a culminating resolution to all tensions. Instead, he sought to reinterpret dynamic tension, not as a problem to be solved, but as the substance of life itself. Nietzsche's "musical" aesthetics of literary style is ultimately a reflection of (and propaganda for) the transvaluation of life's tensions and a recognition of their role in occasioning delight.

[*See also* Difficulty; *and* Style.]

BIBLIOGRAPHY

Works by Nietzsche

The Birth of Tragedy (with *The Case of Wagner*). Translated by Walter Kaufmann. New York, 1967a.
Daybreak: Thoughts on the Prejudices of Morality. Translated by R. J. Hollingdale. Cambridge and New York, 1982.
Ecce Homo (with *On the Genealogy of Morals*). Translated by Walter Kaufmann. New York, 1967b.
The Gay Science. Translated by Walter Kaufmann. New York, 1974.
Kritische Gesamtausgabe: Werke. Edited by Giorgio Colli and Mazzino Montinari. Berlin, 1967–.
Thus Spoke Zarathustra. Translated by Walter Kaufmann. In *The Portable Nietzsche*, edited by Walter Kaufmann. New York, 1954a.
Twilight of the Idols. Translated by Walter Kaufmann. In *The Portable Nietzsche*, edited by Walter Kaufmann. New York, 1954b.

Other Sources

Allison, David B., ed. *The New Nietzsche: Contemporary Styles of Interpretation*. New York, 1977.
Blondel, Eric. *Nietzsche, the Body and Culture: Philosophy as a Philological Genealogy*. Translated by Sean Hand. Stanford, Calif., 1991.
Conway, Daniel W. "Nietzsche's Art of This-Worldly Comfort: Self-Reference and Strategic Self-Parody." *History of Philosophy Quarterly* 9.3 (July 1992): 343–357.
Derrida, Jacques. *Spurs: Nietzsche's Styles*. Translated by Barbara Harlow. Chicago, 1979.
Gillespie, Michael Allen, and Tracy B. Strong, eds. *Nietzsche's New Seas: Explorations in Philosophy, Aesthetics, and Politics*. Chicago, 1988.
Gilman, Sander L. *Nietzschean Parody*. Bonn, 1976.
Heller, Erich. *The Importance of Nietzsche*. Chicago, 1988.
Higgins, Kathleen Marie. *Nietzsche's Zarathustra*. Philadelphia, 1987.
Koelb, Clayton, ed. *Nietzsche as Postmodernist: Essays Pro and Contra*. Albany, N.Y., 1990.
Kofman, Sarah. *Nietzsche and Metaphor*. Translated by Duncan Large. Stanford, Calif., 1993.
Magnus, Bernd, Jean-Pierre Mileur, and Stanley Stewart. *Nietzsche's Case: Philosophy as/and Literature*. New York and London, 1993.
Miller, J. Hillis. "Ariadne's Thread: Repetition and the Narrative Line." *Critical Inquiry* 3.1 (Autumn 1976): 57–77.
Nehamas, Alexander. *Nietzsche: Life as Literature*. Cambridge, Mass., 1985.
Shapiro, Gary. *Nietzschean Narratives*. Bloomington, Ind., 1989.
Staten, Henry. *Nietzsche's Voice*. Ithaca, N.Y., 1990.
Taylor, Mark C. *Deconstruction in Context: Literature and Philosophy*. Chicago, 1986.
Williams, Robert J. "Literary Fiction as Philosophy: The Case of Nietzsche's *Zarathustra*." *Journal of Philosophy* 83.11 (November 1986): 667–675.
Young, Julian. *Nietzsche's Philosophy of Art*. Cambridge and New York, 1992.

KATHLEEN HIGGINS

Nietzsche and Visuality

Those who take Friedrich Nietzsche's thoughts about the arts and related matters seriously have usually stressed his significance as a critic and theorist of literature, rhetoric, or music. From a biographical point of view, Nietzsche's notoriously poor eyesight would seem to make him a bad candidate to play a similar role with regard to the visual. His optical disability can also be turned into an asset by those who have been critical of the alleged ocularcentrism of Western thought. From that perspective, the philosophical tradition has been dominated by the model of what Plato called "the noblest of the senses," a model that, in the critics' view, is misleading insofar as it suggests that the world is completely open to and masterable by our gaze. The model is said to promote the notion that the seeing subject is independent of the object seen; analogously, the subject of knowledge would maintain a distance from the object that would allow for a purely theoretical (i.e., spectatorial) cognition. Vision is said to support the metaphysics of presence, understood as the notion that what is genuinely real and knowable must be capable of being made totally manifest. The metaphysics of presence, as understood by Martin Heidegger, begins with the Platonic conception of the Forms as that which can really be known, and proceeds to produce other candidates for that which is clearly and intrinsically present: God, the Cartesian cogito, the data of sense as conceived by empiricism, the will in German philosophy. It is such associations that have led thinkers such as Heidegger and John Dewey to question the traditional role of vision in philosophy. From the metaphysics of presence, it is a relatively easy transition to an aesthetics of presence that would comprehend and evaluate aesthetic and artistic experience in terms of their approximation to the ideal of full manifestation. This model of vision is also sometimes said to be complicit with a specifically male or sexist bias (phallocentrism), according to which it is the male gaze that objectifies the world and, paradigmatically, the bodies of women.

One can distinguish two different ways of challenging this traditional notion of the primacy of vision. One, which finds ample support in Nietzsche, emphasizes the importance of the other senses, especially touch, taste, and smell, stressing the way in which they require intimate involvement with their domains and do not produce the illusion of totalizing comprehension (a stimulating reading of Nietzsche on these senses is to be found in Eric Blondel (1991). Another route, which also runs through Nietzsche's texts, involves rethinking the nature and aesthetics of vision in such a way as to challenge the Platonic model of that sense. The "over-turning of Platonism" of which Nietzsche spoke can then be accomplished on the aesthetic plane by two complementary moves: dethroning vision from its position of primacy, while suggesting that vision itself has been misconstrued. Once one realizes that Nietzsche is making both of these moves, one should be able to read what he has to say about the role of vision in the arts in a more sympathetic way.

Vision and the analysis of a visual scene appear at a crucial point in *Thus Spoke Zarathustra*, the work that Nietzsche regarded as his most important. The chapter titled "On the Vision and the Riddle" introduces the crucial thought of the eternal recurrence of all things. But, as the title indicates, the chapter is concerned not only with the riddle of recurrence but with the riddle of vision itself. The visual setting of the episode is highly specific. Zarathustra trudges up a difficult mountain path in twilight, weighed down by a dwarf who represents the spirit of gravity. When they reach the top, they engage in a dialogue about the meaning of the visual scene before them, whose centerpiece is a gateway inscribed *Augenblick*. This term, conventionally translated as "moment," is the name for that which recurs in the recurrence. In German, *Augenblick* is highly visual, meaning a moment of vision or a twinkling of the eye. In reading this dialogue on the *Augenblick*, much depends on whether one construes the term within the metaphysics and aesthetics of presence, according to which it would name a discrete, bounded, and distanced experience. The alternative that Zarathustra suggests is that the *Augenblick* be seen as infinitely deep, as having the complexity and indeterminacy of the abyss. When Zarathustra challenges the dwarf to explain the meaning of the two paths that confront one another at the gateway, he receives this response: "All that is straight lies," the dwarf murmured contemptuously. "All truth is crooked; time itself is a circle." This is a reductive vision, one that fails to apprehend the gateway or the *Augenblick* as such. Zarathustra suggests the alternative with his question: "Is seeing itself not—seeing abysses?" The abyss in German is the *Abgrund,* that which lacks a ground or foundation; there is no getting to the bottom of it, and so there is no totalizing vision, no God's-eye view that would reveal the visible in its entirety. To see abysses is to become aware of the failure of the ground, of the giving way of all boundaries, and the impossibility of any presence that would fully manifest itself; it is to realize that there are only perspectives giving way to other perspectives. The abyssal structure is marked in the episode with the dwarf by the *mise-en-abîme* structure in which the moment is inscribed with its own name, a name that the dwarf fails to read. This inscription doubles the meaning of the moment of vision. Although Zarathustra recognizes that abysses tend to produce vertigo, he calls for a courageous vision that confronts the bottomlessness of the visual. If one recalls Nietzsche's project of overturning Platonism here, one can juxtapose the infinitely deep, abyssal *Augenblick* with the vision of the Forms or the Good that is evoked in Plato's dialogues. In each case, a figure of visual aesthetics is employed, but to the different ends of establishing an ascending hierarchy founded on complete presence for Plato, or of acknowledging the endless complexity of the moment of vision.

With this perspective in mind, we may turn to Nietzsche's best-known text in aesthetics, *The Birth of Tragedy*. The familiar distinction between the Apollonian and the Dionysian is often thought to be resolved in favor of the Dionysian, where the two gods are typically identified with light, vision, and the dream (Apollo) or with music and intoxication (Dionysus). Nietzsche devotes much attention in this work, however, to the theme of the visual, especially in explaining the role of the audience and its relation to the chorus. He offers a synchronic (perhaps a structuralist) account of the relations of audience, chorus, actors, within a space divided into *theatron* (the space for the spectators), *orchestra* (the circle within which the chorus sings and dances), and *skene* (the rather small and narrow space from which the individual actors emerge and within whose precincts they remain). Here the architecture of the Greek theater (using the latter word now in the broad, contemporary sense, which would include the *theatron*) is itself neither Apollonian nor Dionysian. The theatrical matrix is described in a specifically visual way, and much of what it makes possible is itself visionary. The chorus itself in "its primitive form" (but it is implied that the identification persists) is said to be the self-reflection or self-mirroring *(Selbstspiegelung)* of Dionysian man. Nietzsche sees the event in the theater as a nested set of visions: the actor "sees the role he is supposed to play quite palpably before his eyes" (1967). The chorus, in turn, is a vision of the "Dionysian mass, just as the world of the stage, in turn, is a vision of this satyr chorus" (ibid.). The framing *(Umrahmung)* or setup of the theater blinds the eye to everything else. Nietzsche implies that all visions are framed in some way and that it is essential for aesthetics to articulate the structure of the effective frame. The verb *umrahmen,* which generates the noun *Umrahmung* (frame), may mean either "to frame" or "to reframe." When Nietzsche writes of a transfiguring framing or reframing, he emphasizes the variability of the frame. In section 8 of *The Birth of Tragedy,* he develops a specific account of how the framing/reframing of the tragic theater works in order to produce a double vision, one that is intrinsically perspectival and so avoids the monocular illusions of the imaginary all-seeing eye. The spectators can look down at the scene, the tragic vision, from their place in the *theatron,* identifying with Bacchants on a mountainside, while, insofar as they identify with the theatrical chorus, they can be virtually looking up, from *orchestra* to *skene.* In tragedy, the frame is transfiguring; setting off the actors in their costumes and masks from the surrounding space, it makes the "eye insensitive and blind to the impression of 'reality'" (ibid.).

In thinking of the framing effect of tragedy and the work of the poet, one must understand the audience or spectators as also being constituted by the frame. What is transfigured is the viewing subject *(Zuschauer),* as well as the visions that are presented. Nietzsche speaks of the spectators as enabled to see beyond *(übersehen)* the world of culture around them, imagining themselves as chorists. *Übersehen* is a complex verb, which can mean "to overlook," in the sense either of scanning and surveying, or of neglecting, failing to see, and forgetting. Given Nietzsche's penchant for emphasizing the active and transformative sense given by *über-* in words such as *überwinden* and *Übermensch,* his *übersehen* may actually combine several of these meanings. The spectators, in their specially arranged and framed space, look beyond the ordinary world of their culture to imagine themselves one with the chorus, whose spectacle they see, and to have the visions had by the chorus as if they were their own. This would not be a mere neglect or failure to see the surroundings; it would rather be akin to the "active forgetfulness" that Nietzsche celebrates in *On the Genealogy of Morals.* Seeing beyond may entail not only having a vision, but also being able to behold a vision within a vision; and this, one might say, is to see abysses. In the tragic theater, on Nietzsche's analysis, vision is not overwhelmed by music but has its own complex structure or framing/reframing that enables a seeing beyond; the birth of tragedy is the condition of a continual rebirth of the visionary.

It is significant, in *The Birth of a Tragedy,* that Nietzsche contrasts the visual sensibility of tragedy with the "one great Cyclops eye of Socrates" that "was denied the pleasure of gazing into the Dionysian abysses." The Cyclops eye of Socrates is not capable of the complex vision required by the tragic frame, a vision that involves *übersehen* and that identifies with the chorus so as to behold its visions through them. Just as he cannot gaze into the abyss, so he cannot dwell with the shining figures that are projected out of it. He is blind to everything but the tragic plot, which he finds confused. Socrates' maxims—that virtue is knowledge, that no one does wrong knowingly, that the virtuous man is the happy man—all establish the frame of a new setup, which could be called the theater of dialectic and virtue. This is

precisely what Socrates plays out in his own life, turning himself into a theatrical figure in the Athenian agora; he constitutes a "new Socratic-optimistic stage world." The aesthetic consequence of Socratism, as Nietzsche sees it, is an intolerance of ambiguity, hidden depths, and complexity; it is the aesthetics of presence.

BIBLIOGRAPHY

Work by Nietzsche

The Birth of Tragedy (with *The Case of Wagner*). Translated by Walter Kaufmann. New York, 1967.

Other Sources

Blondel, Eric. *Nietzsche, the Body and Culture: Philosophy as a Philological Genealogy.* Translated by Sean Hand. Stanford, Calif., 1991.

Shapiro, Gary. "In the Shadows of Philosophy: Nietzsche and the Question of Vision." In *Modernity and the Hegemony of Vision,* edited by David Michel Levin, pp. 124–142. Berkeley, 1993.

Shapiro, Gary. "*Übersehen:* Nietzsche and Tragic Vision." *Research in Phenomenology* 25 (1995): 27–44.

GARY SHAPIRO

Nietzsche on Art and Politics

As a modern philosopher, Friedrich Nietzsche stands out for his espousal of an aesthetic interpretation of existence. For many commentators, the elevation of art to be found in his work is coupled with a corresponding denigration of politics, although for others, Nietzsche's political thought has become the object of serious attention. This "return" to a "political" Nietzsche has challenged the portrait of him as a purely existentialist or aestheticist philosopher that prevailed in the decades after World War II. In his autobiography, *Ecce Homo* (1888), Nietzsche described himself as a disciple of Dionysus and famously as the "last antipolitical German." Such a statement gives clear expression to Nietzsche's distaste for the national statism and militarism that characterized the aspirations of Germany under Otto von Bismarck, but it also conceals the fact that a notion of politics does inform Nietzsche's mature thinking on the need for social change and historical transformation in order to bring about a new culture and the production of new types of human being.

Nietzsche's early writings, it is true, contain a dismissive attitude toward politics. In his first published work, *The Birth of Tragedy* (1872), he criticizes attempts to locate a political meaning to Greek tragedy, insisting that its origins are solely religious. In his *Untimely Meditations* (1873–1876), he speaks of those who naively think that the ills of existence can be met with a political solution. It is only as an "aesthetic phenomenon" for the early Nietzsche that life can find any justification and ultimate meaning and significance. As Martin Heidegger noted, the position that Nietzsche embraces in his mature period (1883–1888), in which art is celebrated as the proper task of life, as its true metaphysical activity (*The Will to Power*, 853), represents a return to the position of *The Birth of Tragedy*. The writings of the mature period, however, are also characterized by a distinctive political philosophy in which Nietzsche extends his aesthetic appreciation of life to questions of human evolution in the sociohistorical domain.

In its broadest and most creative sense, the artistic impulse characterizes the "activity" of life, where life is conceived as "will to power" *(Wille zur Macht)*. In this compound formulation, the "will" is not to be understood as denoting a simple desire "for" power, in which the will strives to possess what it lacks, because "power" denotes not an object separate from, and independent of, a subject (such as the "will"), but simply the essence of the activity of willing, which is always an overpowering, an expansive becoming and an aggressive growing that are endogenously generated. In part, Nietzsche's formulation of life as will to power is presented as a rival to Darwinian conceptions in which the emphasis is placed on the adaptation of forms of life to external circumstances. Nietzsche argues that this is to neglect the priority of the spontaneous and expansive "form-shaping forces" that work from within and that provide life with new directions and interpretations (*On the Genealogy of Morals*, II, 12).

This emphasis on life as composed of internally generated "form-shaping forces" is crucial to grasping Nietzsche's articulation of an "artist's metaphysics." For example, the will to truth, which he believes has guided metaphysics since Plato onward, a will that expresses a desire for a "true" world not subject to semblance, illusion, or error, but consisting of a world of pure and immutable forms, has in turn to be understood as the expression of a deeper will to power. Through forms of knowledge, humankind has arrived not at "truth" but at a world it can master and control by imposing on it categories of reason and logic that make it appear as something calculable, uniform, and regular. This will to truth, however, suffers from an anthropic illusion, namely, that in the construction of a transcendent reality it is possible to discover "truth" and so attain the standpoint of eternity. Nietzsche's point is that the desire for a changeless world and for eternal truths is little more than the expression of a human—all too human—phobia of death, destruction, and decay. "Truths," for Nietzsche, are not discovered but created and made, and are an expression of the activity of the will to power.

The elevation of art in Nietzsche stems in large part from his reception of Immanuel Kant and his critique of metaphysics. Nietzsche believed that Kant's Copernican revolution had shown metaphysics to be impossible and, in the process, had opened the door to relativism and nihilism (*Philosophy and Truth*, 1979 pp. 11–12). This new modern philosophy, which showed the impossibility of transcending our limited anthropocentric standpoint, would lead to a cul-

ture of self-resignation and nihilistic despair. It is in this context of cultural decay and fragmentation that Nietzsche assigns to art the function of a cultural redeemer. He appeals to philosophers of "tragic knowledge" who will master the uncontrolled drive for knowledge, but not by means of any new metaphysics. These new philosophers consider it "tragic" that the ground of metaphysics has been withdrawn and will not rest content with the motley whirling game of the natural sciences. Instead, they "return to art its rights." Knowledge is now to be placed in the service of the "best life," and what makes this knowledge tragic is recognition that even illusion must be willed. For the tragic philosopher, therefore, the recognition of metaphysical activity as merely anthropomorphic simply "completes the picture of existence." He does not become a skeptic as a result and nihilism exists only as an experience to be overcome. A tragic culture is one that does not seek to flee the world of becoming, of change, of decay, and so on, but, through the primacy accorded to art, entices human beings to transcend a narrow egoism, to leave behind the *principium individuationis*, and to participate through tragic awareness in the eternally creative and eternally destructive forces of life, and to do so without being overcome by despair or resignation. Art enjoys the "good will to appearance"; it penetrates the abyss and looks into it, but also contains powers of form capable of producing a sense of play and enjoyment in the elusive mysteries of life (*The Gay Science*, 107). Art is thus more valuable than "truth" (the truth of Platonic-Christian metaphysics) and it is cultivated in order so that we may not perish of the "truth" (the truth of an "artist's metaphysics").

A sustained notion of politics appears late in the unfolding of Nietzsche's thinking. The conception he advances of a "great politics" refers to the artistic task he believes now faces those philosophical legislators who, in an age of nihilism, an age in which the will to truth has culminated in a paralyzing will to nothingness, must come up with new visions and riddles of what the human being is and of what may still become of it. They are to do this through new practices of discipline and new experiments in breeding (*Beyond Good and Evil*, 208). These are the philosophers of the future, the "artist-tyrants" who will impose on man the discipline of great suffering, which is the discipline, Nietzsche contends, that has created all enhancements of man so far (ibid., 225). Here art and artifice are conjoined so that willing and thinking the future become a matter of artistry and cultivation and in which politics comes to be based on methods of artificial selection. This, for example, is how Nietzsche designed his thought experiment of the eternal return of the same, writing of it as the "great cultivating thought" that will serve to enhance the strength of the strong and to enervate further the powers of the world-weary and the impotent (*The Will to Power*, 1053 and 1058).

Nietzsche appeals to artists "of" the future, but the "of" spoken about has a double meaning because it refers to artist-philosophers who belong to the future (whose time is not yet), but also to those artist-philosophers who are responsible for its invention as a measure of their gravity. The invention of the future is to be a matter for architects, designers, experimenters, and innovators, who will all teach man that the future is now dependent on his will and his will alone. In this way, an end will be put, Nietzsche holds, to the gruesome accident and nonsense that so far have been called "history" (*Beyond Good and Evil*, 203). Nietzsche has a particular conception of the future that is now to be created and willed into existence. The philosopher-legislators, who practice a craft that is an amalgamation of philosophical laboring, natural science, and artistic creativity, are to construct a vision of the human being that will show that its possibilities for advancement have yet to be exhausted. In this way, their constructions will combat the modern political tendency that favors a degeneration and diminution of the human being into a "perfect herd animal," or what Nietzsche calls the "animalization of man into the dwarf animal of equal rights and claims" (ibid.).

It should be noted that Nietzsche's vision of the future of evolution is not at all racialist. The breed of new philosophers that he sees as appearing on the horizon are depicted by him as modern human beings without a home who are too manifold and racially mixed in their descent to be tempted to participate in the "mendacious racial self-admiration and racial indecency that parades in Germany today" (*The Gay Science*, 377). Moreover, he argues that, beneath the rise of European democracy, an equally important "physiological" process is taking place in which the Europeans are evolving more and more similar to one another as they become "more and more detached from the conditions under which races originate" (ibid.). As a result, the future will be characterized, Nietzsche believes and hopes, by a "supra-national and nomadic type of man" who shall possess a "maximum of the art and power of adaptation as its typical distinction" (*Beyond Good and Evil*, 242). He also holds that the modern movement of democratization will produce at the same an involuntary arrangement for the cultivation of "tyrants." He adds that this word is to be heard in its most "spiritual" sense (ibid.).

Significant problems attach themselves to Nietzsche's thinking on art and politics, rendering his philosophical project incoherent and showing it to be entirely caught up in the antinomies and aporias of modern European thought. For example, it is not at all clear that with the central notion of his artistic understanding of life and reality—the will to power understood as a creative, form-building, inner force—Nietzsche has not fallen back on the kind of aesthetic anthropomorphism of existence that at one point in his writing he incisively shows to be illegitimate (*The Gay Science*, 109). If it is the case that to posit "self-preservation" as the cardinal drive of life is to impose an aesthetic and moral judgment on it, as Nietzsche argues, in what respects

does the theory of will to power, which holds that life displays a desire for perpetual self-overcoming, differ in this regard? The determination of life as will to power has a pernicious influence on Nietzsche's political thinking. The basic problem is that it ontologizes the historical reality of enslavement and violence, pronouncing exploitation to be the essence of what lives as a "basic organic function" and as the "primordial fact of all history" (*Beyond Good and Evil*, 259). It is this biologically informed ontology that Nietzsche dubiously deploys to legitimize his prejudices in favor of an aristocratic society rigidly constructed along hiearchical lines (ibid., 257). Nietzsche's philosophy of the future also shares in the dangerous myth peculiar to modernity of achieving emancipation or advancement through controlling the forces of history and evolution. This desire for control proved disastrous in the first half of the twentieth century, and unfortunately, humanity still shows no signs of shaking off its hubris and letting go of its anthropocentric conceits as it approaches the twenty-first century.

Perhaps the most disconcerting criticism to be made of Nietzsche's philosophy, however, is that its celebrated Dionysian affirmation of reality—that all is war and becoming, that the highest affirmation of life is attained once we are able to say yes to reality as it is without subtraction, addition, or selection—rests, ironically, on a static conception of historical evolution that is simply unable to allow for genuine becoming or progress. Nietzsche's positing of Dionysian truths is absolutist and a prioristic, and seems out of sync with the emphasis on perspectives and experimental conceptions of reality that characterizes other aspects of his philosophy. His Dionysian conception of reality is undialectically posited and susceptible to Marxist criticisms that would accuse it of reifying particular aspects of modern existence and offering false promises of happiness in its championing of an aesthetic solution in the form of a philosophy of life based on a tragic pessimism and a regressive cult of Dionysus. Thus, although it it is possible to divorce Nietzsche's aesthetics of life from its fateful association with the racialist ideology of National Socialism, it is by no means clear that one can redeem it from a series of contradictions, problems, and weaknesses, which seriously impair one's reception of it.

[*See also* Politics and Aesthetics.]

BIBLIOGRAPHY

Works by Nietzsche

Beyond Good and Evil: Prelude to a Philosophy of the Future. Translated by Walter Kaufmann. New York, 1966.
Ecce Homo (with *On the Genealogy of Morals*. Translated by Walter Kaufmann. New York, 1967.
The Gay Science. Translated by Walter Kaufmann. New York, 1974.
The Will to Power. Edited by Walter Kaufmann, translated by Kaufmann and R. J. Hollingdale. New York, 1968.

Other Sources

Ansell-Pearson, Keith. *An Introduction to Nietzsche as Political Thinker: The Perfect Nihilist.* Cambridge and New York, 1994.

Bataille, Georges. *On Nietzsche.* Translated by Bruce Boone. New York, 1992.

Deleuze, Gilles. *Nietzsche and Philosophy.* Translated by Hugh Tomlinson, New York, 1983.

Habermas, Jürgen. *The Philosophical Discourse of Modernity.* Translated by Frederick G. Lawrence. Cambridge, Mass., 1987.

Heidegger, Martin. *Nietzsche,* vol. I, *The Will to Power as Art.* Translated by David Farrell Krell. New York, 1979.

KEITH ANSELL-PEARSON

NOTATION. [*To analyze the meaning of notation, this entry comprises two essays:*

Musical Notation
Dance Notation

These essays explain the meaning of notation in the two art forms in which it has had important compositional and aesthetic roles: music and dance. For further discussion, see Dance; *and* Music, *historical overview article.*]

Musical Notation

Vitally relevant to all thought about the main concerns of the aesthetics of Western art music since the ninth century is its notation and the relations of its notation to the music that is its reference field, whether that is construed as performance acts, sound patterns, works, or in ultramusical meanings.

The first step that is recommended to anyone interested in this subject from the vantage point of aesthetics is to adopt an attitude of independence from a number of interlinked ways of thinking that are widely manifested—explicitly or tacitly—and that tend to obscure the breadth of notation's meaningfulness. They are the following:

1. that attention to notation should be focused mainly on its function as a practical aid for the production of music by composers and performers;

2. that its role in that capacity depends, as a norm, on a direct, unambiguous, and stable one-to-one correlation between notational units and the scores into which they are assembled, on one side, and the musical units and works that they denote, on the other;

3. that the notatability (or nonnotatability) of music is among its immanent properties;

4. that the significance of all notations should be judged by the standards and expectations of present-day Western art-music practice;

5. that a unitary account of notation based on any standard at all can be given, which explains the whole working of notation in terms of a single theoretical model;

6. that an account of the history of notation can be given in terms of a gradual transformation leading to the perfection of notation in accordance with any such model.

The widespread currency of the first of these assumptions should perhaps be attributed to the experience, usually from an early age, of learning one's music lessons with the aid of the scores of the pieces that were assigned by one's teacher. To learn musical notation was to gain access to the music that was hidden behind the score, however difficult the process of translating the notational signs into bodily acts that produced sounds, and however mysterious the process through which those sounds came gradually to cohere and make enough sense to constitute feedback information that would reinforce the whole sequence and encourage it to advance. As it did so, the patterns formed could be reconstituted from memory. The music would remain in that case, having achieved some autonomy, and the score would become dispensable. But it was not and is not necessary to carry the process that far. Orchestra musicians, string quartets, choruses, church organists, church congregations singing hymns, participants in the annual *Messiah* Sing, accompanists of solo singers—all perform from scores. For them, the score is identified with the music, in the looser sense in which one might say that someone is identified with a cause or a style, and in the stricter sense in which identity means isomorphism, dependency, inseparability.

Goodman (1976) has formalized this aspect, asserting that

> a score, whether or not ever used as a guide for a performance, has as a primary [and logically prior, he says elsewhere] function the authoritative identification of a work from performance to performance. . . . From this derive all the requisite theoretic properties of scores and of the notational systems in which they are written.   (p. 128)

The practical history of notation, the way it has been used—which in the stance taken in this essay must test such philosophical analysis—confirms this assertion, but only in part.

The oldest European musical notation—ancestor of our own—was invented in the early ninth century. The oldest surviving music books—written around 1000 CE—were not used as choir books; the performance of their contents was done from memory. They were likely learned indirectly from those books, by rote from teachers who used the books as references. In that sense, the scores served for the authoritative identification of the chants they denoted (they are not "works" in the sense of the "work aesthetic" that is described further on). But this was a highly practical, not a theoretical, function, and it was motivated by cultural, political, and religious considerations, not by aesthetic ones. Although the details of the causal connections are necessarily obscure, the invention of musical notation and its introduction into musical practice certainly took place in a historical context in which the identification of an authoritative tradition with its origin in Rome was of cardinal importance.

That served the aim of a uniform liturgical—and with it, musical—practice, as did the more or less contemporaneous invention of an author for that musical tradition, Pope Gregory the Great, who had reigned two centuries earlier (hence, "Gregorian chant"). The project of a uniform liturgical-musical practice was promoted less by ecclesiastical than by temporal authorities, who saw it in the light of their ideal of a politically and culturally unified and revivified church-state (Hucke, 1980; Treitler, 1974).

Rote learning with the aid of noted books for performance in oral tradition was common for centuries afterward and it remains common in many circumstances today. In all such circumstances, the score serves as a touchstone, a symbol, for the identification of the music to which it refers. This can be so with the most explicit and detailed notations, as well as with notations that show no concern for details of pitch and duration, and especially when the exact rendition of a score would have produced chaos and cacophony if it had been rendered literally, because it was made carelessly or incompetently. Pirrotta (1984) has put the matter most felicitously regarding such scores of the fourteenth century:

> writing down was, in the type of sources I am trying to describe, a sort of gratuitous gesture in most cases, dictated by a *religio* for the written book, and by an almost ritual habit of assembling around a lectern for singing. . . . Once a piece had been accepted in the repertory of a chapter choir . . . it was rapidly memorized, so that the written version was soon reduced to the status of a symbol [for the piece as a whole thing] or a vague mnemonic aid, and an oral tradition took over. (p. 124)

Such mixture or alternation of oral and written processes could function as late as the mid-nineteenth century in the transmission of instrumental music (Treitler, 1981).

The phrase *oral tradition* provides a hint of what must be put into this picture in order to make sense of it. To the extent that musical notations are tools for the production of music, it is not only through the process of translating notational signs into bodily acts that produce sounds, it is also through the reference of notations to performance traditions and to the numerous organizing principles on which musical production is based—which might be called aural paradigms. This can be illustrated with a rather ingenious and unusual example. On the menu of a French restaurant one Bastille Day, the following notation appeared:

la laa la laa laa laa laa laaa la laa la laa la laa laaa laa la laaa

It is a notation for the first line of the French national anthem, but certainly not one that would allow a reader to work out the tune from the individual signs. It is, rather, a cue to the melody that will work only for those who already know it, mainly via its rhythm. Indeed, it is only once we have realized the melody in our minds that we recognize the syllables as a notation at all. To put it in more generally ap-

plicable terms, it is only when we have recognized what has been represented that we know we are looking at a representation. This has been said about pictorial representation (Goodman, 1976; Gombrich, 1969).

Thus, to the account of our childhood learning of musical performance must be added the assimilation of such archetypal patterns of musical style as triads, scalar passages and arpeggios, appoggiaturas, bass patterns, and durational patterns such as measures, phrases, and paired phrases, all of which become established as mental images and frameworks and which we learn to recognize as the references of the patterns of notational figures on the page. Notation is to such images "as is geography in relation to the countryside in which we have learnt beforehand what a forest, a prairie or a river is" (Merleau-Ponty, 1962). What is denoted by notation, then, is not isolated sounds—correlated one-to-one with individual signs—but the musical material in its contextual setting.

Goodman's formulation is based on the assumption that performance follows denotation: "Whatever is denoted by a symbol complies with it" (1976, p. 144); earlier, he had written: "What is required is that all and only performances that comply with the scores be performances of the work" (ibid., p. 128). The implication is of a kind of airtight connection between score and compliant performance. This conception is an applied case of the early Ludwig Wittgenstein's "picture theory" in which "sign-languages [Wittgenstein explicitly includes musical notation] prove to be pictures, even in the ordinary sense, of what they represent" (1961). But actual practice in the real historical world reveals that there are no such airtight connections, except perhaps in the case of a score for certain electronic compositions.

It is the roles of notation for symbolic representation of music and as cues to performance traditions and aural paradigms that complicate the view of a direct correlation between notations and their fields of reference (this essay will adopt Goodman's [1976] useful concept of "compliance," which is meant not in the sense of "obedience," but in the sense in which, for example, certain planar horizontal objects comply with the word *table*). It is the second of these factors, especially, that makes it far from self-evident that the properties of notations follow from the role of scores for the identification of works from one performance to another. According to this idea, work preservation is paramount, and is dependent on score preservation. But what of musical traditions in which score preservation appears not to be highly valued?

From the first several centuries following the introduction of notation into the practice of Gregorian chant have survived hundreds of noted chant books. Students of the practice have remarked on the striking uniformity of the notational representations of the same chants in different books (Hughes, 1987). From the same period, there also exist large numbers of noted books containing songs of other genres: secular, religious but not liturgical, and various complements to the liturgical chants (tropes and sequences are the most familiar). With these, score identity between representations of the same songs in different books is not the rule. The difference is to be explained with reference not to fastidiousness or lack of it in either performance or notational practice, nor to different attitudes about work preservation as an aesthetic value, but to that same geo-cultural-political concern for uniformity that applied to the liturgical chant but did not reach the other genres (Treitler, 1982). This teaches us not only to exercise caution in making assumptions based on a universal ideal of work preservation and the attendant requirements on musical notation, but that the nature and function of musical notation can vary even within the same cultural-historical circumstances according to the nature and function of the music denoted, the social or institutional roles and competencies of the performers, and the nature of the audience. A medieval book, to take a simple example, can use a staff notation for new polyphonic chants and a nonstaff notation for old monophonic hymns.

But perhaps something can be learned nevertheless about the correlation between work preservation as a value and the rule of compliance from this negative evidence. Work preservation is more than an abstract philosophical principle. It is the premise of a work aesthetic that became the center of a new musical economy in Europe at the end of the eighteenth century. This has been very well documented by Goehr (1992), as the idea that the institution of music involved the "creation, performance, and reception not just of music *per se,* but of works of such," which were closed and organically unified (Solie, 1980) and made such by the creative activity of a composer, whose personal stamp the work bears. It is this conception that demands work preservation, that is, the essential identity of the work between performances and between score copies, and a musical notation that could establish an explicit, unambiguous, and stable correlation between score and performance. After all, in traditions such as the medieval ones that do not display score preservation for the same musical items, one cannot even be sure that performances based on any one score would necessarily have complied with that score to the letter, so to speak.

There is confirmation of that sort of suspicion in a much later tradition: the written transmission of waltzes and mazurkas by Frédéric Chopin and performances of them by pianists of the early twentieth century that have been preserved on phonograph recordings. Only one example can be described here, the Waltz in G-flat Major op. 70, no. 1, with recordings by Sergei Rachmaninoff and Alfred Cortot. This is one of five waltzes published posthumously by Chopin's friend Julian Fontana. For all but one, autograph scores have turned up after the publication of Fontana's

edition, which is never in full agreement with any of the autographs. For Opus 70, no. 1, there are two autograph scores: one in the Yale University library, dated 1832 (Y), and one in a private collection in the Château de Thoiry, France (T), possibly presented to the chatelaine in 1833, and published by Byron Janis in 1978 (Janis, 1978). In the same year, Ewald Zimmerman, unaware of the existence of T, published the Fontana version (F) and Y in his *Urtext* edition of the waltzes (Zimmerman, 1978). The two versions differ in two respects: first, in the rhythmic profile of the opening melody (see example 1); and second, in the form or sequence of the sections in which the piece is composed:

Example 1

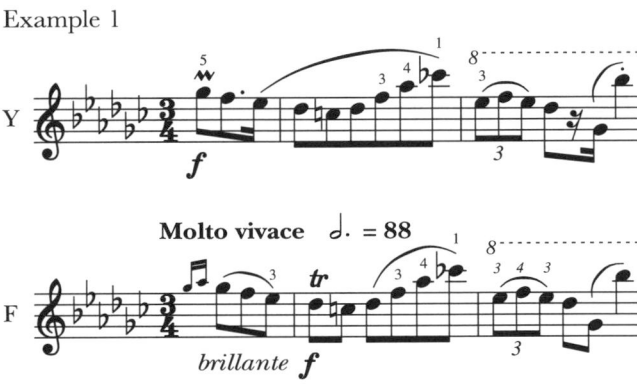

Y: AA BB CC DC AA
F: AA BB CC DC DC AA

T is identical to F with respect to the form, but to Y with respect to the rhythm of the principal melody; that is, Chopin recorded two different ideas about the form in his autograph scores, but just one about the rhythm.

When Rachmaninoff recorded the piece in 1921, he played it in the sequence of Y, but the performance follows the rhythmic details of F, which is the only version that was in circulation at the time. Either he arrived at this form on his own or he knew it through an unwritten performance tradition. In any case, the score constituted for him a point of departure, but it was not binding on his performance in so gross a matter as the form.

Cortot's 1934 recording follows the rhythmic profile of F, confirming again that his performance proceeded from the only published version in circulation, and its formal sequence is AA BB CC DC AA B A. This is the sequence of Y, with one additional playing each of B and A. The conclusion must be the same as that for the performance of Rachmaninoff.

This situation is typical on the sides of both composer and performer. Writing about the state of the aggregate of autograph and printed sources of his music published during Chopin's lifetime, Kallberg (1990) comments:

"Sketches, autographs, manuscript copies, 'simultaneous' first editions, . . . annotated editions—when we examine any of these sources we are almost certain to encounter alternate readings. Variants are pervasive in Chopin's music; indeed it is tempting to assert that they are essential to its aesthetic mode of existence."

Alternate readings, which can involve formal arrangements, as in this instance, and also the musical substance in matters of harmony, melody, rhythm, counterpoint, and so on, are a condition of the music's ontological status. They cannot be sufficiently explained as continuing efforts to improve the work, to find the best solution to particular musical problems, as in the case of the sketchbooks of Ludwig van Beethoven, for example (these have had their own special significance for aesthetic ideology, discussed later in this essay). In Chopin's case the completion of a manuscript, its submission to a publisher, and even his return of corrected proofs cannot be guaranteed to constitute the presentation of a closed work to the public.

On the performer's side, the sorts of rearrangements described in the case of Opus 70, no. 1, can be heard in recordings of other Chopin works by the same pianists and by others of equal stature; and alternate versions in details of musical substance are very common in recordings of that period. The performers at least behaved as though they had been left "considerable autonomy in the way they chose to play the work," as though, in some instances, they were called upon "to impose their judgment on the form of the piece" in "an act of improvised creation," as though the works "are quite literally 'unfinished' [and] the author seems to hand them on to the performer more or less like the components of a construction kit. . . . In other words the author offers the interpreter, the performer, the addressee a *work to be completed.*" The performers behaved as though a score was understood as an exemplification rather than a prescription in all its detail. Reports of Chopin's own playing and teaching are not inconsistent with such practice.

The cited passages seem to apply very well to the textual situation and performance tradition of the Chopin waltzes, but in fact they are taken from the first chapter—"The Poetics of the Open Work"—of *The Open Work* by Umberto Eco (1989), where their objects are "recent pieces of instrumental music" such as *Klavierstück XI* by Karlheinz Stockhausen, Henri Pousseur's *Scambi,* and Pierre Boulez's Third Sonata for Piano, all of which expressly call on the performer to determine the ordering of the musical material. Eco writes of

the macroscopic divergence between these forms of musical communication and the time-honored tradition of the classics [in which] a classical composition . . . posits an assemblage of sound units which the composer arranged in a closed, well-defined manner before presenting it to the listener. He converted his idea into the conventional symbols which more or less

oblige the eventual performer to reproduce the format devised by the composer himself [Goodman's "compliance"], whereas the new musical works referred to above reject the definitive, concluded message and multiply the formal possibilities of the distribution of their elements. . . . [T]hey offer themselves not as finite works . . . but as "open" works, which are brought to their conclusion by the performer at the same time as he experiences them on an aesthetic plane.
(Ibid.)

It is tempting to see in the composing and earlier performing tradition of such works by Chopin an aesthetic of the open work, in which notation did not have fully obligatory force. But again, the matter is not quite so one-dimensional. The historical record seems paradoxical. Vladimir de Pachmann, a pianist with a reputation for taking great liberties with musical texts, spoke of playing "like it is written down." If his word is suspect, there is the word of Josef Hofman, whose reputation as a modernist is sustained by this dictum: "The true interpretation of a piece of music results from a correct understanding of it, and this, in turn, depends solely upon scrupulously exact reading. The player should always feel convinced that he plays only what is written" (Schoneberg, 1987). It is a preachment that Hofman did not himself practice, at least in the most literal sense. At the extreme, he recorded Chopin's "Minute Waltz" in thirds, and he was in general free with many notated details. But perhaps there can be more than one understanding of the expression "playing what is written," with different senses in force under different circumstances and at different times.

The pianists who gladly rearranged the waltzes and mazurkas of Chopin did not rearrange the ballades, études, or preludes. For them, genre was a determinant of the relationship of score to performance. They did not rearrange any music of Wolfgang Amadeus Mozart or Beethoven. This is perhaps the perpetuation of a distinction that had its earliest formulation in a review of Chopin's first Paris concert on 26 February 1832 published in the *Revue Musicale.* The author, François-Joseph Fétis, wrote:

Here we have a young man who . . . has effected . . . a plethora of original ideas of a sort nowhere else to be found. This is not to say that M. Chopin is gifted with the powerful spirit . . . the majestic force . . . of a Beethoven. . . . Beethoven wrote music *for piano,* but here I am speaking of music *for pianists.* . . . Too many colorful modulations, so much confusion in linking phrases that it sometimes seems as though one is hearing an improvisation rather than a written composition—these are the imperfections that are found intermingled with the virtues I have just mentioned.
(Strunk, 1997)

One cannot miss the alignment of the duality of the godlike Beethoven and the brilliant composer-virtuoso with that of written and quasi-improvised music. (Ironically, Chopin later told his friend Eugène Delacroix that Beethoven's music is obscure because "he turns his back on eternal principles" [Delacroix, 1948].) Nor can one miss the identification of excess and confusion as signs of improvisation. In 1788, Johann Nickolaus Forkel—in his *Allgemeinen Geschichte der Musik*—associated the coherence of music with its susceptibility of notation. He actually put it the other way around, reporting that travelers in distant places populated by "wild and uncultivated" people were unable to write down the music of those people, and offering the explanation that it was because that music was too incoherent to be written down (Strunk, 1997). There is an implication of a link between notation and order that has continued to influence musical studies. Like other modes of representing music, notation is among the controls on the chaos into which music always threatens to erupt.

Eco writes "The *possibilities* which [a] work's openness makes available always work within a given *field of relations*. . . . The author is the one who proposed a number of possibilities which had already been rationally organized" (1989). Alternate readings of the score of a waltz by Chopin could be understood as the "actualization of a series of consequences whose premises are firmly rooted in the original data provided by the author" (ibid.). Under such a conception, the claim of "playing what is written down" about performances that are not strictly compliant with the score is not so paradoxical. The appearance of paradox is owing to the application of a notation that is highly specific and determining to music that is not determined to that degree, whereas there is always a tendency to assume that the levels of determinacy of a music and its notation are evenly matched. That assumption is a premise of the work aesthetic. But one can appreciate Eco's interpretation while recognizing that the historical evidence does not support his somewhat teleological construction of the historical evolution of the modern aesthetic sensibility.

In the remarks of Fétis and Forkel, as in the theory of Goodman, notation appears as an emblem of the work aesthetic. There is an interesting negative confirmation of that relationship in the behavior of musicians in the period of the ascendancy of the work aesthetic to notations in the music of the Baroque period. It is in the regularization of apparent inconsistencies of notation by editors and performers. Examples of such inconsistencies are shown in example 2. Criticisms of the regularizing practice attest to it. For example:

Example 2

One thing is certain: it is that in general the fussy quest for uniformity in the meanings of signs, which consists in settling on a single and even primitively expressed sign ideas of always the same type, removes from these ideas the charm of novelty which the author has here and there bestowed on them.

(E. M. E. Deldevez, 1873, quoted by Pont, 1979, p. 28)

It was a conflict between the work paradigm, which demands unity, and the notational paradigm, which demands that things be performed "as written." Deldevez's criticism seems to reflect an effort to bring them into alignment.

There are hints in this conflict, as there have been hints throughout this essay, that it can be a struggle to fit a musical idea to the grid of a notation, to impose the order of a notation on the different kind of order of a musical thought. Such a struggle is evident already in the original adaptation of the oral tradition of medieval chant to the notational matrix that had reference to a diatonic modal system (see Atkinson, 1990). The ideal of a straight correlation embodied in the compliance concept and the picture theory sometimes does not, as already noted, correspond to ordinary use. That does not call for the abandonment of the ideal, but for an accommodation of the discrepancies in our view of the nature and function of notation.

Our minds form and hold patterns, thoughts, ideas, and images. We sometimes bring them out to engage the world through gestures of body and voice, and through that engagement they change. Even when we externalize them through gestures of body and voice, they are ephemeral. It is a special and, in a way, unnatural and gargantuan ambition to aim to capture what is changing and fleeting in palpable and visible lasting signs. It also has its consequences.

Ferrucio Busoni wrote in defense of his many transcriptions:

Notation is itself the transcription of an abstract idea. The moment that the pen takes possession of it the thought loses its original form. The intention of writing down an idea necessitates already a choice of time and key. The composer is obliged to decide on the form and the key and they determine more and more clearly the course to be taken and the limitations. Even if much of the idea is original and indestructible and continues to exist this will be pressed down from the moment of decision, into the type belonging to a class. The idea becomes a sonata or a concerto; this is already an arrangement of the original. . . . The performance of a work is also a transcription, and this, too—however free the performance may be—can never do away with the original. For the musical work of art exists whole and intact before it has sounded and after the sound is finished. It is, at the same time, in and outside of time. (1974)

There is a parallel expression about literary texts and their contents that is very close to the sense of Busoni's argument. It is in Italo Calvino's book *If on a Winter's Night a Traveler:*

At times I think of the subject matter of the book to be written as of something that already exists: thoughts already thought, dialogue already spoken, stories already happened, places and settings seen; the book should be simply the equivalent of the unwritten world translated into writing. At other times, on the contrary, I seem to understand that between the book to be written and things that already exist there can be only a kind of complementary relationship: the book should be the written counterpart of the unwritten world; its subject should be what does not exist and cannot exist except when written, but whose absence is obscurely felt by that which exists, in its own incompleteness.

(Calvino, 1981)

The musician sketching a melody and the poet sketching a verse are something like the artist catching an image in a sketch. The sign is a trace of what the mind produced, and it can be the point of departure for its reconstruction. Artists and critics have valued sketches because they are as close to that boundary between mental image and visible sign as one can come.

Music historians and critics have been especially interested in the sketches of Beethoven, not only for their biographical value and for their potential contribution to the interpretation of the music, but as emblems of such a struggle—now made titanic and described in Romantic language. Gustave Nottebohm, well known for his early engagement with Beethoven's sketches, wrote that they

illustrate . . . a manner of composing that seems somewhat enigmatic to us. The enigma lies first and last in Beethoven's struggle with his demon, the wrestling with his own genius. The demon has dwelt in these sketchbooks. But the demon has vanished; the spirit that dictated a work does not appear in the sketches. The sketches do not reveal the law by which Beethoven was governed while creating. They can provide no conception of the idea that emerges only in the work of art itself. . . . What we term the organic development of a work of art is far removed from the sketches.

(Nottebohm, 1887)

The contrast is drawn between the final score, which shows the organic work, and the sketch, which displays both the intractable raw material and, through its chaotic condition, the struggle to bring it into order. This was interpreted in the later nineteenth century as a heroic struggle with ethical and moral dimensions, and it reflected on the character of Beethoven himself. In the earliest monuments of music writing from the tenth century, one cannot distinguish sketch from final score. But the circumstances alluded to earlier make a comparison with this interpretation of the Beethoven sketches not altogether far-fetched, and there is a clear note of triumph in announcements of the achievement of a written musical text and a method for learning to perform from it, as in this boast by the famous Guido of Arezzo: "We do not need to have constant recourse to the voice of a singer or to the sound of some instrument to become acquainted with an unknown melody" (quoted in Strunk, 1997).

Musical texts may be given a hermeneutic reading that is wholly independent of the music as sounding art form, even of the notes that the notation denotes. Notation has many ways of meaning.

There is a detail in this brief passage from the second movement of the Sonata for Clarinet and Piano in E-flat Major, op. 120, no. 2. (measures 187–188), that suggests an interpretation that is purely musical but conceptual and has nothing to do with the performance detail that the notational sign itself would seem to denote (see example 3).

Example 3

The instruction of the decrescendo sign in mm. 187–188 of the piano cannot be executed by the pianist, who could not, however, prevent the piano itself from carrying it out—the sound decays by the nature of the instrument. But this chord concludes the last statement of the movement's main theme, and what follows it is an ending of the movement through the gradual elimination and mulling over of the thematic material. It is music in a different narrative register from the more straightforward presentational mode of the preceding, and the decrescendo hairpin is a sign that the music before it must now fade away.

In his *Fantasiestücke* for clarinet and piano Opus 73, Robert Schumann made something thematic of a notational ambiguity, a Romantic gesture of ambivalence over what is denoted. At the very beginning of the piece, the clarinet plays a melody in quarters and duple eighth notes, accompanied by triplets in the piano right hand (see example 4).

Example 4

In measures 10–12, the clarinet and piano right hand upper voice play a quarter-note phrase in octaves, accompanied by triplets in the piano right hand lower voice. In measure 12, this phrase is played in eighth notes, and that forces the pianist to choose between playing the melody together with the clarinet or strictly in triplets (see example 5). That

Example 5

is the beginning of the notational ambiguity, which becomes more explicit in measures such as the one shown in example 6a. The piano left hand, the upper piano right hand, and the clarinet are in unison—or are they? Not if the upper piano right hand plays strictly in triplets. But if that were the intention, why would Schumann not have notated it as done in example 6b?

Example 6

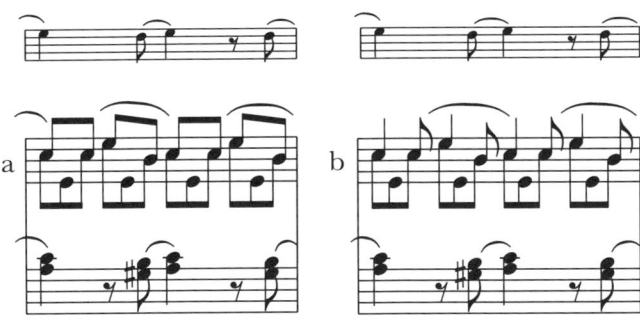

There is a German expression, *Augenmusik*, music for the eyes. The temptation to use it for such notations should be resisted, however, because of its judgmental connotations. It is simply a historical fact that notation has at times been a medium of communications from the composer to the performer or anyone else looking at the score, without going through the medium of sound. In this respect, Schumann's notation here is like Brahms's tempo indication for the first movement of the first of the Opus 120 clarinet sonatas, *Allegro amabile*. Both will influence the performance, but it is difficult, if not altogether impossible, to say just exactly how. It bespeaks a turning inward with respect to both the work and the beholder, and as such it is a property of Romantic formalism.

The implied notion here of a score as a content-laden text aside from its status as a character in a sign system denoting a performance has been spelled out sharply by Benjamin Boretz (1972), in a critique of Goodman. He writes: "When we apprehend something as art, it is structure we attend to" (p. 33). Hence, "Sounds are not part of music, [as] paint is not part of paintings" (ibid., p. 34), and "notes require prior music-structural interpretation to be regarded as music-determinately symbolic of sounds" (ibid., p. 35). This conception is a heritage of early nineteenth-century formalism. For example, Johann Friedrich Herbart, whom Eduard Hanslick identifies as the "first person to have attacked the feeling-theory in musical aesthetics," wrote in 1831 about the "old artists who developed the potential forms of the fugue" that "their thought went not outward but inward to the essence of art." He also wrote that "In strict composition music does not even depend on *forte* and *piano*. The tones need simply to be heard, indeed only to be read" (Herbart, 1831). Again, it is the turning inward of Romantic formalism.

But in the era of modernism, too, musical scores, under appropriate analysis, can be revealed to hold meanings that are not presented through sound, as an example, drawn from Alban Berg's opera *Wozzeck*, illustrates.

There are two moments in the first act that are, from a dramatic point of view, obviously the most portentous moments in the opera. The first is the moment (scene 2) when Wozzeck begins to have apocalyptic visions while cutting kindling in the field, visions that will shape his perception of events around him and lead him ultimately to be the executioner of his mistress. The second is the moment (scene 5) when an army drum major appears in front of the house of Wozzeck's mistress to put on a display of masculine swagger, initiating the act of infidelity that feeds into Wozzeck's paranoid vision and triggers the final events. At those crucial moments, the orchestra plays motivic material that is related through common properties in a way that must be explained. In each case, it involves a chord or an array of five notes (see example 7).

Example 7

What they have in common is what is called their pitch-class interval contents. A pitch-class is a class of all pitches having the same name, regardless of register—for example, all A-flats. A pitch-class interval is an interval between two pitch classes, for example, A-flats and E-flats, which would include both fourths and fifths having those two pitches as their constituents. In this type of analysis, one reckons all the intervals that can be made between any two pitches in the group and counts the number of intervals of each size that the group thus contains. The size is given in terms of the distance in half steps between the two notes of each interval—for example, a major third counts as four, a fourth counts as five, a tritone counts as six. It is in the number of intervals of each size contained in the two motives—that is, their intervallic contents—that they are identical. This certainly does limit the musical material of the two passages in similar ways. Hyde (1981) suggests that the sharing of this property is a musical counterpart of the linkage between the two dramatic elements as initiators of the catastrophic course of the opera. When one considers yet another constraint on the relationship between these two motives, it will seem unlikely that awareness of this correspondence can come through sound, at least not without the guidance of such laborious analysis of the score. It is that the two motives are not related through either inversion or transposition, relations that are the most readily recognizable. The suspicion is reinforced by the fact that in performance the two passages are separated by something like half an hour of very dense music.

If the reader senses a criticism in this, that is not at all the intention. The pivotal question for the evaluation of such claims is not the irresolvable one of whether the relationships are likely to be heard. What they amount to are claims of allegorical meaning in the score; that is the interpretation that should be pondered. That musical notation is capable of holding allegorical meanings is not something that can be rejected out of hand on the grounds of any aesthetic ideology; as with any language, the possibility deserves to be recognized on the grounds that its users—composers—have invested notation with such meanings, among others. Berg did it a great deal, as did Johann Sebastian Bach (see Chafe, 1981 and 1984) and numerous composers of the Renaissance and the Middle Ages. The question is, does it move you?

BIBLIOGRAPHY

Atkinson, Charles. "From 'Vitium' to 'Tonus acquisitus': On the Evolution of the Notational Matrix of Medieval Chant." In *Cantus Planus: Studia Musicologica Academiae Scientiarum Hungaricae,* edited by Laszlo Dobsay. Budapest, 1990.

Boretz, Benjamin. "Nelson Goodman's *Languages of Art* from a Musical Point of View." In *Perspectives on Contemporary Music Theory,* edited by Benjamin Boretz and Edward T. Cone, pp. 31–44. New York, 1972.

Busoni, Ferruccio. *Entwurf einer neuen Ästhetik der Tonkunst.* Facs. ed. Frankfurt am Main, 1974.

Calvino, Italo. *If on a Winter's Night a Traveler.* Translated by William Weaver. New York, 1981.

Chafe, Eric. "Key, Structure and 'Tonal Allegory' in Passions of J. S. Bach: An Introduction." *Current Musicology* 31 (1981): 39–54.

Chafe, Eric. "Allegorical Music: The Symbolism of Tonal Language in the Bach Canons." *Journal of Musicology* 3 (1984): 340–362.

Deldevez, E. M. E. *Curiosités musicales.* Paris, 1873.

Delacroix, Eugène. *The Journal of Eugène Delacroix.* Translated by Walter Pach. Reprint, New York, 1948.

Eco, Umberto. *The Open Work.* Translated by Anna Cancogni. Cambridge, Mass., 1989.

Goehr, Lydia. *The Imaginary Museum of Musical Works: An Essay in the Philosophy of Music.* Oxford, 1992.

Gombrich, E. H. *Art and Illusion: A Study in the Psychology of Pictorial Representation.* 2d rev. ed. Reprint, Princeton, N.J., 1969.

Goodman, Nelson. *Languages of Art: An Approach to a Theory of Symbols.* 2d ed. Indianapolis, 1976.

Herbart, Johann Friedrich. *Kurze Encyklopädie der Philosophie.* Halle, 1831.

Hucke, Helmut. "Toward a New Historical View of Gregorian Chant." *Journal of the American Musicological Society* 33 (1980): 437–467.

Hughes, David G. "Evidence for the Traditional View of the Transmission of Gregorian Chant." *Journal of the American Musicological Society* 40 (1987): 377–404.

Hyde, Martha MacLean. Review of *The Operas of Alban Berg. I: Wozzeck,* by George Perle. *Journal of the American Musicological Society* 34 (1981): 573–587.

Janis, Byron. *The Most Dramatic Musical Discovery of the Age.* n.p., 1978.

Kallberg, Jeffrey. "Are Variants a Problem? 'Composer's Intentions' in Editing Chopin." In *Chopin Studies* 3, pp. 257–276. Cambridge, 1990.

Merleau-Ponty, Maurice. *Phenomenology of Perception.* Translated by Colin Smith. London, 1962.

Nottebohm, Gustave. *Zweite Beethoveniana.* Leipzig, 1887.

Pirrotta, Nino. "Church Polyphony apropos of a New Fragment at Foligno." In *Music and Culture in Italy from the Middle Ages to the Baroque: A Collection of Essays.* Cambridge, Mass., 1984.

Pont, Graham. "A Revolution in the Science and Practice of Music." *Musicology* 5 (1979): 1–66.

Schönberg, Harold C. *The Great Pianists.* Rev. upd. ed. New York, 1987.

Solie, Ruth. "The Living Work: Organicism and Musical Analysis." *19th Century Music* 4 (1980): 147–156.

Strunk, Oliver. *Source Readings in Music History.* Rev. ed. New York, 1997.

Treitler, Leo. "Homer and Gregory: The Transmission of Epic Poetry and Plainchant." *Musical Quarterly* 60 (1974): 333–372.

Treitler, Leo. "Oral, Written, and Literate Process in the Transmission of Medieval Music." *Speculum* 56 (1981): 471–491.

Treitler, Leo. "Observations on the Transmission of Some Aquitanian Tropes." *Forum musicologicum* 3 (1982): 11–60.

Wittgenstein, Ludwig. *Tractatus Logico-Philosophicus.* Translated by D. F. Pears and B. F. McGuinness. London, 1961.

Zimmerman, Ewald. *Chopin Walzer: Urtext.* Munich, 1978.

LEO TREITLER

Dance Notation

The creation of a movement notation system requires both practical and philosophical decisions. What is the aim? Who will benefit and how? Over the centuries—harking back to the mid-1400s—there have been a wide range of choices in the method of conveying movement facts to paper, that is, the way of looking at movement and the drawings, the signs used. At one end of the scale is a brief memory aid for known movement patterns, at the other end a very precise movement analysis. Between these are many gradations.

The focus of such activity has long been the art of dance. You know the step? It has a name? Then an identifying letter will do—"R" for reverence, "s" for simple, "d" for double, and so on, the device much used in the *Dance Book of Margaret of Austria* and other manuscripts of the fifteenth century. Dances of that period were composed of a handful of simple steps; complications came later. In the mid-twentieth century, people began to be concerned with how the instrument, the body, can best be trained, and, with the recording in detail of how to achieve complex, demanding dance techniques such as that of classical ballet, or of Martha Graham technique. For example, the simple *grand plié* (deep knee bend) was analyzed in depth. What takes place? The knees bend to a considerable degree. What! Only the knees? Why no, flexion in the hip and ankle joints is also necessary for such an activity, but these are often not mentioned. To what degree does the knee/hip/ankle flexion occur? Within a slight tolerance, the appropriate degree is carefully prescribed. We analyze the anatomical changes, but dancing and gaining technique are not just about physical changes; other concerns can more readily produce the desired result. Is focus on the center of weight (center of gravity) lowering toward the floor on a straight line, like a bead sliding down a vertical string, the leg action accommodating this lowering? This lowering need not affect the rest of the body—the torso, head, and arms. The torso energy may actually be "pulling" upward, maintaining an energy link with the sky. Such upward energy can greatly help balance. But are we only concerned with mastering technique, with achieving the perfect physical rendition of a *grand plié*? Or might some content, some meaning, some expression, some other aim required? Is it a body shape to be produced, a diamond shape with the legs? Is the expression one of approaching the ground, the earth, our friend, our final resting place? Or are we retreating from the upward direction, away from the sky, from heaven? There are choices, and each serves a particular purpose. We must decide why are we writing this movement down. Is it for a particular need? If so, the differences described above can be conveyed in the choice of description, the choice of symbols in committing the movement to paper when a highly developed, flexible notation system is used. Dancers of long ago, striving to perfect their reverences, simples, doubles, and so on, would scarcely comprehend such an investigation into the meaning of and reason for a simple *grand plié*. It is also unfamiliar to most dance people of today. Here is the potential for a greater understanding of dance in all its aspects through its careful "spelling out" on paper. But the dance world is too

busy with the demands of actual dancing, with looking at video, an activity that requires no deep thinking or awareness of how a movement can be viewed, but rather of copying the superficial image. What do you see? Do you see what I see? Dancers must be trained to observe movement, to understand what is taking place, and to transfer the information to their bodies. A certain degree of intelligent thinking and awareness has to take place.

Between these two extremes, that of the simple use of letters to identify known steps, and a recording stemming from a deep inner awareness of the required performance of simple (or, indeed, complex) movements, lies a range of other levels of description, other points of view, and other reasons for recording dance, as well as other means used.

Most systems of dance notation were devised specifically to record the familiar dance steps and movements of the time, that is, to record the finished result, the structured form, the choreography. The need to remember, to preserve, and to pass on dance knowledge to the next generation was the driving force. Experimentation with movement, investigating the physical possibilities, and exploring the raw material of dance came only in recent decades.

It should be made clear that word notes to describe movement are not being considered here. Over the centuries, these have been found to be too vague and open to different interpretations. Any system of notation must, within its chosen range, provide a clear statement. Manner of performance will vary from person to person and era to era; that is expected. The signs, the indications used must, be clear in what they encompass. Such a system—that published in 1700, known now as the Beauchamps-Feuillet system—was well suited to the dance style of the period. This consisted mainly of footwork and pathways across the floor accompanied by a few simple arm gestures, danced by elegant ladies and gentlemen, impressing all with their social skills. Greater complexities in movement entered theatrical dancing and the system fell into disuse. A century later, in 1831, an English dancing master named E. A. Théleur (his first names are not known) presented a movement analysis approach indicated by abstract signs through which he notated gavottes and other social dances of the time. Later, a focus on music notes to show timing and an anatomical analysis of movement (the degree of flexion, extension, rotation, abduction, etc., of which the parts of the body are capable) formed the basis of the system devised by Vladimir Stepanov, published in 1892. Despite Stepanov's early death, this promising development was used in Russia at the turn of the century to record the classical ballets of Marius Petipa. This recording came to a halt when Michel Fokine's use of a wider range of flowing movement (harder to write than the "classroom" steps previously used on stage) discouraged the notators, who were untrained to cope with a deeper level of analysis. Notation had not yet become a profession and training was probably minimal. It took another mind, one that, until recently, never received acknowledgment for its scope, to develop a Stepanov-based system for a totally different style of movement. This was Vaslav Nijinsky, who, fascinated by notation, and having studied the Stepanov method as a student, used his own modification of it to record the whole of his first ballet, *L'Après-midi d'un Faune*. For this, the anatomical description proved practical, and, though he never left a key to his system, research by Ann Hutchinson Guest and Dr. Claudia Jeschke in 1987–1989 resulted in his score being revived for performance by professional companies—a marvelous example of a priceless work being preserved for the dance heritage.

Because dance is seen as a visual art, it was inevitable that down through the ages stick figures of different kinds would be used to capture dance on paper. Such visual representations faced the challenge of how to indicate on two-dimensional paper a four-dimensional activity (time being the fourth dimension). Of these, the most successful has been the Benesh system, created by Rudolf and Joan Benesh with an emphasis on serving classical ballet. Such visual representation devices did not incorporate movement analysis; their initial aim was to be a memory aid for established movement patterns, that is, choreography. Visual systems serve a need because some individuals find it easier to relate to such pictorial representations, whereas abstractions, the use of symbols to represent movement facts or concepts are difficult for them to grasp. But, in the twentieth century, more inquiring minds, willing to go to greater depths, have entered the picture.

In the 1950s, Noa Eshkol focused on the idea of composing movement sequences in a manner comparable to music notation, that is, in terms of intervals of progression—for her, spatial progressions. A simple formula could be repeated several times, producing displacements in space, a different effect being produced with each repetition. For this purpose, Eshkol analyzed movement anatomically and mathematically, movement being described as horizontal arcs or progressions rising or sinking on different coordinates (comparable to Earth's latitudes and longitudes). The movement description could be in terms of motion (departure from a previous point) or destination, the position to be reached. Eshkol was not interested in human expression; movement dynamics came from the spatial and temporal combinations. She used the performer as an "auto-mobile," one who physically produces the movement but is not expressing any human involvement. The results were intentionally emotionally blank; she was concerned with the shapes, the designs in space performed by torso and limbs and not with human interactions. Composing in this way, she evolved many very interesting and unusual movement sequences, producing actions that would not have emanated from movements into which the body falls naturally or sequences based on known dance techniques. The 1958

book *Movement Notation,* written by Eshkol with architect Abraham Wachmann, is clear, logical, and mathematically correct. The very use of numbers and analysis in terms of degrees of the few basic movement possibilities of which the body is capable makes the system less attractive to the average dancer and those who are concerned with the human condition, the subjective approach to dance movement. But for individuals exploring the "outer reaches" of movement, Eshkol's approach to movement and the results she achieves are of special interest.

Quite in contrast, although in many aspects very similar, was Léonide Massine's choreographic exploration. Whereas Eshkol was primarily trained in European modern dance, Massine was a product of the Imperial Ballet School in Moscow. Choreographer of many famous ballets, of both the storytelling and abstract genres, he became convinced that choreography was hamstrung by the heritage of the balletic vocabulary. In breaking away from this, he turned to the already mentioned Stepanov notation system. Trained in music, Massine believed that music and dance were sister arts, and therefore music notes were the most appropriate signs with which to record dance. Despite his belief in this system, Massine did not find time to become proficient in its use, and he did not produce scores of his ballets. But he made detailed use of it in his 1974 book *Massine on Choreography: Theory and Exercises in Composition* to record movements of the individual body segments, in isolation or in chordic unison, to illustrate his movement theories. For these, Massine drew from music practice in defining ideas such as "perfect" and "imperfect" intervals, and "chromatic" movement. Massine liked to point out where in his earlier choreographies he had featured a particular movement harmony, intimating that already at that time he had these theories in mind. This is very open to question. What Massine lacked was knowledge, or even curiosity, about the work of others. He might have been thrilled to learn of Rudolf von Laban's Space Harmony. He would have been fascinated in exchanging ideas with Eshkol; they had much in common. Despite his belief that music notes were the only way to show timing for dance, he never explored variations in the timing of movements; in his book on choreography, all his examples use only quarter notes (crotchets).

Laban's kicking-off point in developing a notation system was to record the various scales and sequences in his Space Harmony developments and subsequently to record his choreography. The system he originated, later called Labanotation (or Kinetography Laban) had, in fact, much in common with the Eshkol/Wachmann analysis of movement, but using a more compact staff and visually distinctive movement symbols. The Laban system really took off when practitioners developed the system further to record dances of many different styles and cultures. Focus was initially on capturing structured movement on paper, movements in which the part of the body used, the direction, degree of rotation, flexion, timing, and use of energy were all clearly established. A freer use of the symbols to pinpoint the main focus or intention of a movement developed later, particularly as an enrichment in dance education. For this, the focus is on how the raw material of dance, the basic "building blocks," can be used. The same basic symbols became a tool for exploration, experimentation, and creativity.

This survey has swiftly spanned six centuries. We have come from initial letters being used to indicate known steps, the dances being recorded through the appropriate sequence of these letters, to a deep investigation into the nature of movement and how movement can be conceived and perceived in the process of creativity, on the one hand, and into a very detailed description of subtleties of movement and how a particular technical feat is achieved, when such information, is needed, on the other. We have touched on different types of signs used, different analyses of movement, or absence of any in the visual representation systems (stick figures or abstractions from stick figures). Not mentioned are the many systems that focus on one type of dance, thereby evolving shorthand devices for that style.

To conclude, notation of human movement can be at many levels. Although no system is concerned with the action of particular muscles (it is the movement produced that is recorded), the need has arisen to state the use of inner tensions, the sensation of inner lengthening, expanding, or compressing, which have an effect on particular movements. These can be notated in the highly developed Laban system, as can the different types of breathing, when needed. Emotions as such are not described, but the physical results of these—yearning, being alarmed, loving, hating, mourning, and so on—can be recorded. Where words are more appropriate, they are used. Why notate the action of removing a belt unless the movements are stylized and specifically timed? Not all movement is worth recording in fine detail; if a brief description suffices, then use it.

BIBLIOGRAPHY

The Dance Book of Margaret of Austria (manuscript, c.1450). Royal Library, Brussels.

Eshkol, Noa, and Abraham Wachmann. *Movement Notation.* London, 1958.

Feuillet, Raoul-Auger. *Chorégraphie ou l'art de décrire la danse.* Paris, 1700.

Hutchinson Guest, Ann. *Labanotation.* 3d ed. New York, 1977.

Hutchinson Guest, Ann. *Your Move.* New York, 1983.

Hutchinson Guest, Ann. *Dance Notation.* London, 1984.

Hutchinson Guest, Ann. *Choreographics.* London, 1989.

Hutchinson Guest, Ann, and Claudia Jeschke. *Nijinsky's Faune Restored.* London, 1991.

Laban, Rudolf. *Choreographie.* Jena, 1926.

Laban, Rudolf. *Choreutics.* Edited by Lisa Ullmann. London, 1966.

Massine, Léonide. *Massine on Choreography: Theory and Exercises in Composition.* London, 1976.

Stepanov, Vladimir I. *L'alphabet des mouvements du corps humain.* Paris, 1892.

Théleur, E. A. *Letters on Dancing.* 2d ed. London, 1832.

ANN HUTCHINSON GUEST

NŌ THEATER. *See* Japanese Aesthetics, *historical overview article.*

NOVALIS (Friedrich Freiherr von Hardenberg; 1772–1801), German Romantic poet. Novalis was a member of the Jena Romantic group, which also included Friedrich and August Wilhelm von Schlegel, Friedrich's partner Dorothea Veit and August Wilhelm's wife Caroline Böhmer, Ludwig Tieck, Friedrich Schleiermacher, Friedrich Wilhelm von Schelling, and their philosophical mentor, Johann Gottlieb Fichte. Jena is where Fichte and Schelling taught and August Wilhelm lived for a while. A joint visit to the Dresden gallery in July 1798 and a meeting in Jena on 11–15 November 1799 were the central events; the group fell apart once Fichte left Jena and Novalis died.

The French Revolution, Fichte's *Wissenschaftslehre,* and Johann Wolfgang von Goethe's novel *Wilhelm Meisters Lehrjahre,* which Friedrich Schlegel in the Athenäum-fragment no. 216 defined as the momentous events of the age, were major forces in shaping Novalis's philosophical and artistic projects, most of which remained unfinished. Only the fragment collections *Blütenstaub* (Pollen; Novalis, vol. 2, pp. 412–470) and *Glauben und Liebe* (Faith and Love; ibid., pp. 483–498) and the poem cycle *Hymnen an die Nacht* (Hymns to the Night; Novalis, vol. 1, pp. 130–157) appeared during his lifetime. The rest, including *Das allgemeine Brouillon* (Novalis, vol. 2, pp. 242–478), a grandiose encyclopedia that Novalis started while studying at the mining academy of Freiberg, voluminous notes on philosophical, scientific, and professional matters, the essay *Christenheit oder Europa* (1799), and the unfinished novels, *Die Lehrlinge zu Saïs* (The Disciples at Saïs; 1798–1799) and *Heinrich von Ofterdingen* (1799–1801), was published posthumously, much of it only in recent editions.

Early death and an excessively ambitious project are the two main reasons for the fragmentariness of Novalis's oeuvre. His interest in the fragment as a form was vastly exaggerated by Tieck, who as editor of Novalis's works with Friedrich Schlegel, "manufactured" fragments by tearing his notes apart. The enigmatic quality of the resultant text was largely responsible for the legend of a mystic thinker, which joined that of the consumptive poet. Recent editorial work has revealed a much more coherent creative mind that dialogically reacted to the ideas of others.

Experience of nature was not the subject of Novalis's literary works, and organicism was not the basis of his aesthetics. Aesthetic concepts such as "beauty" and "harmony" seldom occur in his texts; among art theorists, only Frans Hemsterhuis interested him (Novalis, vol. 2, pp. 360–378). His central aesthetic concept, *Poesie* (e.g., ibid., pp. 533–536), covers all genres and all arts. His general project is to poeticize the world *(Poetisierung),* including mathematics (Novalis, vol. 3, p. 50), nature (ibid., p. 351), the sciences (Novalis, vol. 4, p. 252), and life itself (Novalis, vol. 3, p. 260). Novalis's famous romanticizing has the same meaning:

> The world must be romanticized. In that way one can find the original meaning again. To romanticize is nothing but a qualitative raising to a higher power. In this operation the lower self will be identified with a better self. Just as we ourselves are such a qualitative exponential series. This operation is as yet quite unknown. By endowing the commonplace with a higher meaning, the ordinary with a mysterious respect, the known with the dignity of the unknown, the finite with the semblance of the infinite, I romanticize it—the operation for the higher, unknown, mystic, infinite is the reverse—in this connection its logarithm will taken—it receives a familiar expression. (Novalis, vol. 2, p. 545)

This familiarization and alienation strikingly resembles the poetic operations that William Wordsworth and Samuel Taylor Coleridge divided among themselves in writing the *Lyrical Ballads* and clearly anticipates notions of the Russian Formalists, Bertolt Brecht, and others. Equally striking is how Novalis amalgamates here mathematical metaphors with concepts of higher and lower selves taken from Fichte's philosophy. His aesthetics responds not to traditional thinking about the arts but to other fields, including the philosophy of science, mathematics, and ethics. Indeed, poeticizing the world is no mere beautification for him, but "the great art of constructing transcendental health. The poet is thus the transcendental physician. *Poesie* . . . mixes everything together for the sake of its great purpose of all purposes—*mankind's elevation above itself"* (ibid., p. 535). More concretely, poeticizing becomes for Novalis the utopian project of gradually universalizing *poïēsis.*

To what extent Novalis welded together the Fichtean, mathematical, medical, and other metaphors into a coherent aesthetics is a matter of continuing scholarly debate. This essay discusses his aesthetic ideas primarily in relationship to Fichte's philosophy, Immanuel Kant's constructivist theory of mathematics, Gottfried Wilhelm Leibniz's combinatorics, and Goethe's *Wilhelm Meisters Lehrjahre,* for in this way the originality of Novalis's "adaptations" and the impulses radiating from them are best appreciable.

By consensus, Novalis began to develop his aesthetics in response to Fichte's *Wissenschaftslehre,* which starts with the originary act of "intellectual intuition," the simultaneous positing of subject and object. The world is the (unconscious) product of an absolute self; the task of the empirical self is to overcome the seeming objectivity of the "not-self" and recapture it by means of reflection as a form of self.

Diverse writers, including Walter Benjamin and H. A. Korff, hold that the Romantics, among them Novalis and Schelling, radicalized and poeticized Fichte's idealism by claiming that artistic creativity reenacts the intellectual intuition in the form of an aesthetic intuition. The full publication of Novalis's first Fichte-studies from 1795 to 1796 (Novalis, vol. 2, pp. 104–299) allowed a reassessment of this view (e.g., Géza von Molnár, 1970; Manfred Frank and Gerhard Kurz, 1977). Frank and Kurz argue that self-reflection is preceded in Novalis philosophy by a nonactive feeling of the self *(Selbstgefühl),* which can be represented as *Schein* but cannot be reached by means of philosophical reflection (Novalis, vol. 2, p. 114). Other studies direct attention to the sign theory that Novalis started to develop in connection with this notion of representation, and they emphasize that Novalis came to oppose Fichte's notion of a forceful subjugation of nature, with the formula "instead of not-self—thou" (Novalis, vol. 3, p. 430).

Novalis's notion of poeticization crosses the barriers that Kant erected between science, ethics, and aesthetics. Believing that "we know only inasmuch as we make" (Novalis, vol. 2, p. 378), he is closer to Giambattista Vico than to Kant. It is therefore both surprising and fitting that his aesthetics found inspiration not in Kant's *Critique of Judgment* but in the definition of mathematical knowledge as a construction of nonempirical intuitions for concepts that Kant gave in the *Critique of Pure Reason* (2d ed., section 742).

Novalis responded to this notion of mathematical construction with a longer commentary on Friedrich Murhard's Kantian *System der allgemeinen Grössenlehre* (1798), in which he suggests (going beyond Kant) that the method is not unique to mathematics. One should be able to construct intuitions for all kinds of concepts, to introduce the mathematical *Plastisirungsmethode* into all the sciences—and inversely to construct concepts for intuitions (Novalis, vol. 3, p. 123).

The construction of intuitions is a performative aesthetic act, no reproduction: just as Kant's mathematical construction of concepts emancipated mathematics (and only mathematics) from empirical experience, so too Novalis's aesthetic construction aimed at nonmimetic art forms. This does not conform to the generally held view that Romantic aesthetics shifts from imitative to expressive art. Novalis's aesthetic construction involves the projection of concepts rather than emotions and it anticipates therefore formalist, Symbolist, and conceptual rather than affective art.

The combinatorial tradition, Leibniz's refashioning of it into a universal calculus, and Carl Friedrich Hindenburg's theory of combinatorial mathematical progressions were another unlikely source of Novalis's aesthetics (Neubauer, 1978). He first applied combinatorial ideas in the *Brouillon,* which he planned as an encyclopedia that interlinked all fields of knowledge and forms discourse. The combinatorial principle found its decisive application, however, when Novalis transposed it into a poetics by conceiving of poetry and narrative fiction as combinatorial forms in which syntax assumed the primary role in semanticizing the signs:

> Combinatorial analysis leads to number fantasies—and teaches the compositorial art of numbers—the mathematical figured bass. (Pythagoras. Leibniz.) Language is a musical instrument of ideas. The poet, the rhetorician, and the philosopher play and compose grammatically. A fugue is thoroughly logical or scientific—it can also be treated poetically. (Novalis, vol. 3, p. 360)

This combinatorial aesthetics anticipates the symbolism of a Paul Valéry and nonrepresentational art in general. Instead of striving to become a representation of the absolute or an imitation of "reality," combinatorial art is an endlessly transformable experimental structure, a matrix of possible worlds. Its paradigmatic form is the fragment that is suggestive and open rather than aphoristically pointed (Uerlings, 1991, pp. 215–227). As the passage just quoted indicates, it reverses the hierarchy of arts by turning the musical calculus of sounds into a paradigm of all arts. Musicians, writes Novalis, cannot be suspected of even the slightest imitation (Novalis, vol. 2, p. 574).

By embarking on *Heinrich von Ofterdingen* and formulating for it an aesthetics of combinatorial progressions, Novalis turned to the novel in the last years of his life. Agreeing with Friedrich Schlegel that Romantic *Poesie* was a "progressive universal poetry" that incorporates all genres and knowledge (Schlegel, vol. 2, p. 182; Athenäum-fragment no. 116), Novalis now conceived of *Poesie* as an encyclopedic novel. In analogy to the *Wissenschaftslehre,* which was the science of science, science raised to a higher power, the novel was to become a genre of all genres, in which the sequence of reflection was to constitute progression, and the ceaselessly alternating forms would ironically relativize each others (Novalis, vol. 3, p. 689). The unity of this novel was not to be thematic but structural, based on the principles of progression, regression, inversion, variation, and transformation. In Goethe's *Wilhelm Meisters Lehrjahre,* Novalis noted, the characters fall into categories, and within each category they can be arranged into rising sequences (Novalis, vol. 2, pp. 312, 647). Novalis was first impressed by Goethe's structural principle, but he became critical of its direction, the point toward which the progression converged: *Wilhelm Meister* became for him a *Candide* against *Poesie,* a pilgrimage toward a "diploma of nobility" and a life without ideals (Novalis, vol. 3, p. 646).

Heinrich von Ofterdingen was to incorporate the structural, serial, and transformational principles found in *Wilhelm Meister* but shift the convergence point to infinity, where only desire could reach it (ibid., p. 308). In this sense,

it is a narrative critique of Goethe's novel, a matrix that reuses Goethe's formal parameters by inverting them. *Ofterdingen* had little to offer to nineteenth-century Realism and Naturalism, but as recent critical interest shows, it anticipated key modernist and postmodernist novelistic features, among them the shift from description of physical detail to dialogues and representation of minds, consistent focalization through the protagonist, *mise-en-abîme* through embedded stories, and the thematization of sexuality.

The paradoxical relationship between Novalis's formalist bent, his transcendental project, and his often allegorical representations is brilliantly portrayed in a brief *Monolog* (Novalis, vol. 2, p. 672f.), which asserts that language, like mathematics, is self-referential but immediately notes that in this case assertion is no longer possible. Indeed, if the formalist and autonomous art that Novalis advocated (and partially, but only partially, practiced) was to serve his utopian ethical and social project, it had to rely on exemplification and performance rather than assertions and rhetorical persuasion. The envisioned formalism, conceptual ambiguity, and openness of the artwork were to mobilize readers to active participation and to the development of their own constructive capabilities, diffusing thereby the exemplary artistic constructivity into the broader society. The fragment collection *Pollen* starts with the motto, "Friends, the soil is poor, we must spread plenty of seeds to reap even modest harvests" (ibid., p. 413), but ends with a call for new readers: "The true reader must be the extended author. He is the higher court that receives the case already prepared by the lower court" (ibid., p. 470).

Novalis responded to the collapse of normative aesthetics by hoping for new foundations in a humankind of the future that was to be paradoxically shaped by imaginative creativity. Whereas the earlier *disjecta membra* editions conveyed the image of a holistic mystic who nostalgically searched for lost foundations in the past, the more complete and coherent corpus of his texts shows him to be a utopian writer, whose evocations of the past (e.g., in *Christenheit oder Europa* and *Heinrich von Ofterdingen*) are not historical reconstructions but imaginative projections in service of constructing a new self and, via that self, a new world. To what extent Novalis believed in the necessary failure of the transcendental aesthetic project, to what extent he abandoned substantialist metaphysics, to what extent his aesthetics is consistent—these issues still divide scholarship today.

[*See also* Play; Poetics; *and* Romanticism.]

BIBLIOGRAPHY

Work by Novalis

Novalis. *Schriften: Historisch-kritische Ausgabe.* 5 vols. Edited by Richard Samuel in cooperation with Hans-Joachim Mähl and Gerhard Schulz. Stuttgart, 1960–1988.

Other Sources

Benjamin, Walter. *Der Begriff der Kunstkritik in der deutschen Romantik* (1920). Frankfurt am Main, 1973.

Frank, Manfred, and Gerhard Kurz. "Ordo inversus. Zu einer Reflexionsfigur bei Novalis, Hölderlin, Kleist und Kafka." In *Geist und Zeichen: Festschrift für Arthur Henkel,* edited by Herbert Anton, Bernhard Gajek, and Peter Pfaff, pp. 75–97. Heidelberg, 1977.

Kuzniar, Alice A. *Delayed Endings: Nonclosure in Novalis and Hölderlin.* Athens, Ga., 1987.

Link, Hannelore. *Abstraktion und Poesie im Werk des Novalis.* Stuttgart, 1971.

Mähl, Hans-Joachim. *Die Idee des goldenen Zeitalters im Werk des Novalis.* Heidelberg, 1965.

Molnár, Géza von. *Novalis' "Fichte Studies": The Foundation of His Aesthetics.* The Hague, 1970.

Molnár, Géza von. *Romantic Vision, Ethical Context: Novalis and Artistic Autonomy.* Minneapolis, 1987.

Neubauer, John. *Symbolismus und symbolische Logik: Die Idee der ars combinatoria in der Entwicklung der modernen Dichtung.* Munich, 1978.

Neubauer, John. *Novalis.* Boston, 1980.

Uerlings, Herbert. *Friedrich von Hardenberg, genannt Novalis: Werk und Forschung.* Stuttgart, 1991.

JOHN NEUBAUER

O

OBSCENITY. [*To examine legal definitions of obscenity and how they are applied to artistic and cultural practices, this entry comprises two essays:*

Aesthetics in Obscenity Law

Obscenity in Art

The first essay explains the role of aesthetics in the development and current status of obscenity law (in the United States and England), while the second essay explains key examples in the history of art that have provoked the legal disputes and precedents. For further discussion, see Law and Art; Morality and Aesthetics; *and* Politics and Aesthetics.]

Aesthetics in Obscenity Law

Aesthetic regulation will be a contradiction in terms for those who draw a fundamental line between aesthetic freedom and censorship, private moral judgment and public legal regulation. But what if aesthetics, deployed as a normative criterion, has played a central role in the legal regulation of pornography? If this were the case, would we so easily fall back into that immense moral knowingness that assumes aesthetics and obscenity law to be permanent adversaries, locked in a timeless struggle between the ideal of full and free self-expression and the dark forces of repression and censorship? In fact, this knowingness is ignorant of how twentieth-century Anglo-American obscenity law has taken up an aesthetic norm of conduct as the measure of what to count as moral maturity in dealing with erotic materials.

This norm represents a specialized derivation from the form of life whose recipe Friedrich von Schiller had already codified by the late eighteenth century: "the development of our sensual and spiritual powers in the greatest possible harmony" (Schiller, 1967, p. 143). Aesthetic "wholeness," achieved by balancing sensual experience against moral reflection so as to engage with both while becoming locked into neither, would characterize the persona fashioned by the "aesthetic education of man." This education—precisely a regimen of self-fashioning and not a school curriculum—was designed to support an elite conduct of life whereby enlightened German men of letters might distinguish themselves from an emerging mass culture and resist an instrumental state. Surprisingly perhaps, this persona has furnished the norm of personal maturity taken up by Anglo-American obscenity law. Operating as a legal norm inside the law, the aesthetic persona provides the means by which to distinguish mature persons who can safely be left to their own devices from those other kinds of persons unable to conduct themselves in a balanced (i.e., non-auto-erotic) manner with pornography. These latter remain the targets of legal regulation.

It was not inevitable that the law should accommodate aesthetics in this way. But there is no doubt that it has done so. By the early 1960s, reforming law professors William B. Lockhart and Robert C. McClure imported D. H. Lawrence into the legal sphere in order to endorse the American Law Institute's draft of a new obscenity statute for the Model Penal Code. They drew on Eberhard Kronhausen and Phyllis Kronhausen's (1959) influential *Pornography and the Law: The Psychology of Erotic Realism and Pornography.* Human maturation, the psychologists argued, rests on a balancing of primary sexual drives and social or moral standards that aims at an equilibrium of desire and norm. With what now seems an extraordinary faith in the transformative powers of literary culture and dialectical exercise, they accorded the literature of sexuality the task of "satisfying the natural and desirable interest in sex, without turning it into morbid channels, confusing and linking it with violence, or keeping it antiseptically detached from the physical sensations which should accompany it, and by connecting the sexual impulse with those love feelings which are its highest perfection" (p. 260).

A new psychoaesthetic threshold for measuring moral maturity was being assembled. On one side was "art"— "erotic realism"—that met the aesthetic criterion of balancing the sensuous and the moral; on the other side was a "hard core" pornography that failed this aesthetic test. Only the former was able to "depict life as it is, including man's basic biological needs" (ibid., p. 28), while keeping fully in touch with the necessity of moral judgment. The Kronhausens identify this moral ballast with the "philosophy" in Lawrence's novels, but also with literary features such as full characterization and developed settings that, they say, pornography lacks.

The law took note. The professors began to cite the new psychoaesthetic threshold: "Pornography is daydream material, divorced from reality, whose main or sole purpose is to nourish erotic fantasies or, as the psychologists say, psychic auto-eroticism" (Lockhart and McClure, 1960, p. 65).

For this kind of person, susceptible to a "psychic auto-eroticism" unmediated by the "realism" of moral norms or "philosophy," there was still a need for regulatory protective action: "hard core pornography appeals to the sexually immature because it feeds their craving for fantasy." By contrast, erotic art mediates sexual fantasy. On this basis, citing the line said to divide erotic art from pornography, "sexually mature" audiences were deemed immune from legal intervention.

This distinction between art and "failed art" was, in fact, a distinction between two different kinds of persons, only one of which had the specialized and—in literary and artistic circles—prestigious skill of balancing between sex and morality. But there was a problem for the new threshold. The aesthetic judgment on the work was dependent on the response the work received: "If it is true that the common man knows little and cares less about literary values, what is to be done with material of substantial aesthetic value that the common man peruses for his own private titillation, oblivious of its artistry?" (ibid., p. 72). The variability of audience response set limits to the deregulatory program that would have shifted the handling of obscene publication from coercive criminal law to private moral judgment.

In looking to the aesthetic norm, however, the law professors were not completely out of touch with a recent mutation in cultural reality. At least within the milieu of belles-lettres, the virtuoso persona defined by Schiller as the only "whole" form of life had established itself as the exemplary model of conduct to be emulated. But it was only later, at the start of the twentieth century, that this aesthetic persona was, so to speak, sexualized: sex now became the founding theme of serious literary writing and the key to fashioning a literary and artistic personality. As Michel Foucault notes in closing the first volume of his *History of Sexuality,* Lawrence's is the exemplary formulation of the change: "Now our business is to realise sex. Today, the full conscious realisation of sex is even more important than the act itself" (Foucault, 1979, p. 157). The same commitment to confront sex—which for literary intellectuals meant fashioning themselves by confronting their own response to pornography—was made by James Joyce "experimenting with the grossly masturbatory prose of 'dirty' books" (Charney, 1981, p. 5). By 1920, E. M. Forster had convinced himself and some of his readers that "nothing is more obdurate to artistic treatment than the carnal, but it has to be got in, I'm sure: everything has to be got in" (Forster, 1971, p. 9). Prior to this unforeseen cultural mutation, serious literature and mass pornography belonged to quite separate circuits. But by the time Lockhart and McClure were proposing reform of the law, this sexualization of aesthetics—which was also an aestheticization of sex—had seen the writing, publication, and circulation of works that were both of literary merit and pornographic. This unforeseen convergence brought serious literature and law into confrontation.

Not every reader or viewer had the benefit of training in the art of aesthetic balance in dealing with pornography. But with the rise and dissemination of a sophisticated literary schooling that involved a definite form of personality formation, many more students had had to learn and be examined on how to face up to direct literary expressions of sexual feeling without being utterly ruled by them. Having been focused on sex by avant-garde figures such as Lawrence, the capacity to balance "our sensual and spiritual powers in the greatest harmony" was thus subsequently distributed to an ever wider population by a literary pedagogy organized by the aesthetic norm.

Against this cultural backdrop, the courts took up this norm in two ways: first, in determining the nature of works; second, in determining the nature of audiences. We can follow the process in the U.S. Supreme Court judgments in *Roth v. United States,* 354 US 476; I L Ed 2d 1498 (1957), and in *Miller v. California,* 413 US 15; 37 Ed 419 (1973). In *Roth* the Court established the test of obscenity to be where "the dominant theme of the material taken as a whole appeals to prurient interest." The test builds an aesthetic criterion into legal judgment in dual fashion. First, it envisages individuals having the aesthetic capacity to impose on themselves an appreciation of the work as a whole in order to mediate their response to the erotic passages taken in isolation. Second, the reference to "prurient interest" shows the law admitting the aesthetic norm of optimal psychosexual development. The kind of person who can mediate fantasy and real experience, the primary drives and moral responsibilities, becomes the standard against which to define the other kind of person whose incomplete development has left them dominated by mere "prurient interest."

Yet, the problem remains: not all persons or populations conduct themselves in tune with this aesthetic norm. Hence, Chief Justice Earl Warren's observation in *Roth* (at 495): "It is manifest that the same object may have a different impact, varying according to the part of the community it reached. . . . A wholly different result might be reached in a different setting." In *Miller,* the Court follows the same line of reasoning, referring the test of obscenity to the local and contemporary "community standard." In this way, the judgment institutes a boundary or threshold that "floats," varying according to the level of aesthetic competence of different audiences or kinds of person. Where such a competence is taken to be present, the threshold can be set such that the responsibility for regulating the consumption of erotic materials passes from the legal system to the pedagogical apparatus.

British obscenity law has a different mode of operation, working through statutes and literary "show trials" rather than Supreme Court judgments of the constitutionality of decisions that might curtail First Amendment rights of speech and press. Yet, this has not meant a significance difference in the uptake of the aesthetic norm. The Obscene

Publications Act (1959) and the test case of *Regina v. Penguin Books* (1960) thus confirm what has been said concerning an aestheticization of the law. In the United Kingdom, as in the United States, by the late 1950s a social expansion of literary schooling was taking up the task of equipping students with the capacity to be "balanced" in their consumption of erotic literature. In both territories, then, a governmental program of aesthetic schooling allowed reforming jurists to call for freedom and a relaxation of direct legal intervention.

The historical interest of the 1959 Act and the 1960 trial of Penguin Books lies in their intermediate location between two different norms or standards that have organized legal judgments concerning obscenity. An earlier medical norm was retained from the 1868 *Hicklin* test of obscenity as a social toxin that had a "tendency to deprave and corrupt those into whose hands it is likely to fall." The newer norm was aesthetic, and provided the dual test of pornography as failed art and of the consumer of pornography as the aesthetically immature person. English law thus continued to guard an older medical boundary drawn to protect against a moral poison but also began to implement the new aesthetic criterion. From the latter came the requirement that the work be judged with the erotic passages balanced against its effect "as a whole," in other words, the sensual against the spiritual or moral. The 1959 Act also admitted literary critics to the legal status of expert witnesses, granting them standing to testify to the work's aesthetic—and thus social—value. Instability is built into the Act by virtue of its transitional situation, visible, for instance, in the fact that it allows for a work to be found to be obscene and therefore harmful, yet also to be found of aesthetic value and therefore publishable in the public good.

The trial of Penguin Books was a poor test case for the Act, since the court simply found Lawrence's novel not to be an obscene publication. To read the expert evidence given in the 1960 trial is to observe some vivid demonstrations of how to be a full-blown aesthetic personality, however. Witness after witness showed how to mediate one's response to sexual descriptions by turning them to morality, religious piety, or utopian politics. Lady Rebecca West showed the court how to read a series of thirteen detailed descriptions of sex as moments in "a return of the soul to the more intense life" (in Rolph, 1961, p. 67). But none of the literary experts demonstrated how to read the episode of anal intercourse in *Lady Chatterley's Lover* as a triumph of ethical self-completion achieved by a final confrontation with the dark secret of sexuality. Even so, the aesthetic skills demonstrated in the courtroom were daunting.

But these skills are anything but evenly distributed across the general population for whom the jury was supposed to speak. The prosecution asked how the boys at the factory gate would read the book. If the aesthetic norm is in fact a specialist practice of self-fashioning, adopted by a particular cultural faction, it cannot be a universal measure of the capacity of all humans. Writing before the time of mass aesthetic education, Lawrence himself assumed that only a "little band" of advanced literary intellectuals would be able to read *Lady Chatterley's Lover* in a nonpornographic manner. Aesthetic balancing in the face of pornography remains an extraordinary technique of self, an ethical discipline for bearing a distinctive persona that rests on a dialectical skill of being at once involved with and detached from the material. But, as such, aesthetic balance is too rare and technical to be treated as a universal test for human moral maturity in general.

If this aesthetic persona has now achieved sufficient social gravity to be taken up as a norm within the law, this is less a breakthrough to human freedom than a technical adjustment of the law to the circumstance in which this persona has been generalized by distribution through mass literary schooling. In its turn, this schooling was historically contingent on the cultural mutation whereby explicit sex became a central theme of serious literature, used as a primary vehicle for a form of self-development that had acquired prestige in a certain intellectual milieu. Obscenity law has responded to this cultural shift, displacing the earlier medical norm in favor of the aesthetic norm of personal development. The latter has become the key mechanism for determining when the regulation of erotic materials can—depending on the competence of the audience—be transferred from law to school.

Far from being marginal, the aesthetic norm has thus been adopted as a regulatory standard. The habit of opposing aesthetics to legal regulation no doubt sustains anticensorship postures and principles. It also sustains a story told about an epochal shift from public legal regulation to private moral—and aesthetic—judgment. No such fundamental divide between morality and law, private and public, can be sustained on the historical evidence, however. Rather, we observe a shift from one normative system to another. We thus do better to speak of a legal deregulation and an aesthetic reregulation of the pornographic field.

No doubt this proposition sits uneasily with feminist and gay critiques of obscenity law that claim to see beyond both the existing regulatory system and the norm of the "aesthetically mature person." Locked into the posture of transgression, critical advocates of affirmative but nonheterosexual uses of pornography easily align this latter norm with obscenity law and censorship as the instrument of a dominant power structure. But in fact these critics remain profoundly faithful to the aesthetic model of personal development. Two centuries ago Schiller articulated an art of living whereby the aesthetic person learns to reconcile and thus transcend two fundamental opposing drives: feeling and form. This dialectic found a sexualized expression when twentieth-century literary intellectuals began to acquire a stylized capacity to play with the unshaped force of pornography (feeling) while thinking of some shaping higher moral or "political" norm (form). Nothing has changed. The turn to the gay body or to female desire is a new variant—but still a variant—on the classic schema of aesthetic modeling. To call ordered society (or norm) into question one turns to the transgressive "body" (or desire). The pendulum swings against the established norm to the other end of its arc. But there one confronts unmediated bodily action such as spontaneous rape or mindless heterosexuality. The pendulum swings back toward the moral or social norm. Norm is called into question by body so that body can be called into question by norm. This oscillation provides the endless spiral of ascent by means of the dialectical discipline of aesthetic (self-)critique.

These mind and body games are tools of contemporary aesthetic cultivation and critique. For those pursuing a gay or feminist campaign objective, they have the transformative capacity to generate extraordinary dedication to a specialized belief: that a refunctioning of heterosexual pornography will progressively liberate and, at last, realize true self-determining subjectivity. For all their power, however, this liberation and realization remain within the aesthetic field. As such, they have no priority over law.

From within the aesthetic field it is all too easy—for the believers—to overestimate the transparency of the adjacent legal field to extralegal norms. To discuss the whole framework of relations between law and culture lies beyond the limits of this essay. Yet the main point can be made: the history of Anglo-American obscenity law provides an example of overlap and exchange between the legal and aesthetic fields. But the law is not absorbed into (sexual) culture. It is not governed by sexualized aesthetics. Obscenity law has given rise to its own ordering of conduct, bearing on those limited aspects of sexual relations that happen to have acquired the status of independent legal realities. In fashioning legally determined criteria to make a legal assessment of the susceptibility of some and the civil rights or criminal liabilities of others, obscenity law has looked first to a given medical norm and subsequently to the given aesthetic norm of the mature person—once this was sufficiently widely implanted. The law's objective remains: to draw and redraw a differential legal line between what have been deemed sexually self-governing populations and those populations in need of legal protection from harm by variously distributed pornography.

BIBLIOGRAPHY

Caputi, Mary. *Voluptuous Yearnings: A Feminist Theory of the Obscene.* Lanham, Md., 1994.

Charney, Maurice. *Sexual Fiction.* London and New York, 1981.

Forster, E. M. *Maurice.* London, 1971.

Foucault, Michel. *The History of Sexuality,* vol. 1., *An Introduction.* Translated by Robert Hurley. New York, 1978.

Hunter, Ian, David Saunders, and Dugald Williamson. *On Pornography: Literature, Sexuality, and Obscenity Law.* New York, 1993.

Kronhausen, Eberhard, and Phyllis Kronhausen. *Pornography and the Law: The Psychology of Erotic Realism and Pornography.* New York, 1959.

Lockhart, William B., and Robert C. McClure. "Censorship of Obscenity: The Developing Constitutional Standards." *Minnesota Law Review* 45 (1960): 5–121.

Rolph, C. H., ed. *The Trial of Lady Chatterley: Regina v. Penguin Books Limited: The Transcript of the Trial.* Harmondsworth, 1961.

Schiller, Friedrich. *On the Aesthetic Education of Man in a Series of Letters.* Translated by Elizabeth M. Wilkinson and L. A. Willoughby. Oxford, 1967.

DAVID SAUNDERS

Obscenity in Art

The words *obscenity, pornography,* and *indecency* occur interchangeably in everyday speech. Obscenity is most commonly linked to the sexual, but is also used as a strong term for describing the unacceptable horrors of everyday life: the obscenity of war, poverty, wealth, racism, murder. Whether the material at hand is itself a shocking, sexual representation or an allusion to what shocks us in everyday life, *obscenity* most often connotes excess, violence, and transgression.

In law, the distinction between the three terms (obscenity, pornography, and indecency) is a matter of ongoing debate. According to American legal precedent, obscenity is against the law; indecency is constitutionally protected speech; and pornography is legal if it does not depict a child under the age of sixteen engaged in explicit sexual activity. But when put into practice, such categories become vague at best and provoke, rather than settle, further debates on the definition of obscenity.

The first important legal definition of obscenity was provided in Britain in 1868 by the Lord Chief Justice, Sir Alexander Cockburn: "I think the test of obscenity is this, whether the tendency of the matter charged as obscenity is to deprave and corrupt those whose minds are open to such immoral influences, and into whose hands a publication of this sort may fall" *(Regina v. Cockburn).* Although hardly precise, Cockburn's definition was adapted by American courts and became known as the Hicklin Test. The Hicklin Test remained in service until it was finally rejected by the Supreme Court in 1957. In the United States today, obscenity is determined by the Miller Test (*Miller v. California,* 1973), which defines obscenity as violative of contemporary community standards, as risking the stimulation of prurient interests—to be mitigated only if the material (taken as a whole) has "serious literary, artistic, political, or scientific value."

It is artistic merit that turns the "obscene" into art, into legal obscenity. The defense lawyer H. Louis Sirkin successfully defended Dennis Barrie, the director of Cincinnati's Contemporary Arts Center (Barrie was accused of breaking the law for including sexually explicit photographs in the now infamous 1990 Robert Mapplethorpe exhibition *The*

Perfect Moment), by comparing the three-level test for obscenity to making an apple pie. "One or two ingredients may be present," he stressed, "but that does not make an apple pie" (Cembalest, 1990, p. 139). Although jurors on the trial have since admitted to finding the work troubling, offensive, immoral, gross, and lewd, the defense lawyers were able to convince all eight jurors that Mapplethorpe's pictures (even when they depict the genitals of a child or a man urinating into the mouth of another man) were art and not "apple pie." With the Cincinnati exhibition, artistic merit fed the disjunction between law and avant-garde practice, stretching it to previously unforeseen limits.

It is imperative to recognize that the late twentieth-century understanding of "obscenity" stems clearly from the mid-nineteenth century: not only through *Cockburn*—or even the legislation of Lord Campbell's Obscene Publications Act in Britain of 1857 (an act that would remain in force for a hundred years)—but also by way of the period's coinage of the word *sexuality*. The word *sexuality* was born at the dawn of the nineteenth century (in 1800) and originally referred only to reproductive biology; it was crystallized into its current meaning in 1889, when J. Matthews Duncan used the term to mean (as defined in the *Oxford English Dictionary*) a "possession of sexual powers, or capability of sexual feelings." An understanding of obscenity is dependent on the nineteenth century's fixing of the term *sexuality*.

Although current and past obscenity laws affect and have affected aesthetic practice, this essay is centered on aspects of obscenity within accepted (though disputed) aesthetic practices from the mid-nineteenth century to the late twentieth century. The following examples emphasize obscenity's integral relationship to sexuality, excess, violence, and transgression. The first example develops photography historically and emphasizes the urgency of this modern medium in relationship to obscenity, in that it was and still is able to convince the public that they are seeing the obscene. The second example investigates Georges Bataille's surrealistic novel, *Story of the Eye*, as a text that best fulfills notions of the obscene within academic discourses (anthropological, theoretical, feminist, literary, art historical). The third example offers a text from gay studies as a challenge to our modern, conventional notions of the obscene, especially in relationship to homosexuality.

Photography and Obscenity. It is significant that the invention and growth of photography occurred alongside the modern development of sexuality. Photography, too, was born in the beginning of the nineteenth century, with quicker and cheaper means of reproduction cascading forth from the mid-nineteenth century on. The result was that obscene representation in a new lurid (photographic) form became a booming industry. The *London Times* of 20 April 1874 "reports a police raid on a London shop in which 130,248 obscene photographs were seized, plus 5,000

stereoscopic slides" (Heath, 1982, 110). Likewise, urbanization fostered a full-blown economy of sex, with women selling their bodies in the streets of cities for a range of obscene practices: "the medical journal *The Lancet* estimated in 1857 that there were some 80,000 prostitutes in London for a total population of the capital of 2,362,000" (ibid., p. 12). Sexuality and photography were born and bred in the nineteenth century: obscene photographs were their offspring.

Due to its peculiar attachment to the "real," photography explicitly feeds the desire to see the illicit in ways that were impossible before its invention. As the famed philosopher of modern French life, Charles Baudelaire, remarked in 1859 (in regard to the period's love of obscene stereophotographs):

> It was not long before thousands of pairs of greedy eyes were glued to the peepholes of the stereoscope, as though they were the skylight of the infinite. The love of obscenity, which is as vigorous a growth in the heart of natural man as self-love, could not let slip such a glorious satisfaction.   (Baudelaire, 1980, p. 87)

Only with photography (as opposed to painting or sculpture) is one, relatively, assured of the fact that what was once before the camera—the photograph's referent, whether it be a nude child photographed by Lewis Carroll or a naked prostitute taken by an anonymous photographer—was there.

Yet, one cannot ignore the fact that photographs are also touched up, subject to new technologies, framed in illusory ways, in order to make a fiction register as truth. Certainly, photography's cousins, film and video, which can appear even more real than the photograph, make extensive use of illusory editing. Yet, even in such cases, the photographic presents us with an image that looks to be real. As the painter Eugène Delacroix astutely remarked in 1850, in regards to the daguerreotype, one of photography's earlier forms:

> One should not lose sight of the fact that the daguerreotype must be considered only a translator whose purpose is to further initiate us to the secrets of nature; for despite its astonishing reality in certain parts, it is only a reflection, a copy of the real that is false, in a way, because is is so exact.   (Delacroix, 1923, p. 17)

Such "exactness" in photographs of women, men, and children in compromising positions and settings is much more disturbing, shocking, troubling, than a painted body or a sculpted body (which may or may not be taken from the real). Photographs are traces of a once-present person and so, rightly or wrongly, may be seen to document practices that might be judged obscene.

The photograph's relationship to the "real" is dependent on two of obscenity's integral parts: violence and excess. From its very beginnings, photography has been associated with violently stealing the "real"—from Honoré de Balzac's fear of losing thin ghosts of himself with every photograph taken to Susan Sontag's musings on what it means "to shoot" a photograph. No doubt, the highly publicized controversies that have surrounded the work of such late twentieth-century artists as Mapplethorpe, Jock Sturges, and Sally Mann are as dependent on the medium's inherent violence and excess as they are on the subject matter depicted. Excessively real and violently taken (if only metaphorically), it is no wonder that photography's ventures into the sexual are often deemed obscene.

Georges Bataille and *Story of the Eye*. Sexuality, violence, excess, photography—all are central to Surrealism. Tellingly, Surrealism was the first movement in the history of art to take photography seriously as a medium. Although the Surrealists took on a range of mediums—including collage, sculpture, writing, painting—photography's special status as a "kind of deposit of the real," real but not real, like the dreams that were at the center of surrealist practice, had a special appeal (Krauss, 1985, p. 31). Corrupting modern culture's privileging of the original work of art and the authority of the artist, the Surrealist also exploited photography's inherent process of endless reduplication, repetition, twinning. Images like Man Ray's photograph of a cropped buttocks framed by a cross in his *Monument à D.A.F. de Sade* (1933) or Hans Bellmer's photographs (1930s) of violated, twisted dolls rest securely with the obscene surreality of Bataille's *Story of the Eye*. (Bellmer even took a series of illicit untitled photographs, in 1946, depicting scenes from Bataille's infamous text.)

Story of the Eye (which was first published in 1928 but never appeared under the author's name until after his death in 1962) is written in the space of excess that so characterizes the obscene (and much of Surrealism). Filled with violence, repetition, sexual encounters, *Story of the Eye* is one of the most revered works under the aesthetic rubric of the obscene. As the philosopher and cultural theorist Roland Barthes has remarked, Bataille defiles vision by associating the story's main character (who is not one of the book's named characters, but an object), the Eye, with a list of other orbs, from his father's blind eyes, to eggs, to the matador's eye ripped out by a bull's horn, to (severed) bull's testicles, to a saucer of milk, to a woman's breast, to the sun: the Eye migrates toward other objects and consequently "other functions than that of seeing" (Barthes, 1972, pp. 239–240). The historian Martin Jay has interpreted Bataille's defilement of the Eye to be a full-blown denigration of vision itself: in *Story of the Eye,* the eye is no longer privileged as "seeing the truth"—to see no longer means to know, to understand; the eye is nothing more nor less than other parts (flesh or excretion) of the body. Shockingly, these serial orbs, often severed from the body, are then placed in the orifices of other bodies: a man's eye in a vagina, a bull's testicle in a woman's mouth. Further denigrating these orbs is the mixing of "liquids associated with them (tears, egg yolks, sperm) and other liquids like urine, blood and milk" (Jay, 1994, p. 223). These liquids mark the story as especially obscene in their insistence on traversing margins, on exceeding the body, on becoming excess: the result is a defilement, a soiling, of both categories and bodies (including the category of Art itself).

The text and its bodies become filth. Yet, filth, as the philosopher Julia Kristeva, drawing on the anthropologist Mary Douglas, has pointed out, "is not a quality in itself, but it applies only to what relates to a *boundary* and, more particularly, represents the object jettisoned out of that boundary, its other side, a margin" (Kristeva, 1982, p. 69). Obscenity is frequently associated with this jettisoning of boundaries: whether it be children acting as adults, men "acting as women," the confusion of anuses, vaginas, and mouths in sexual activity, or the slipping of one body into another through matter issuing from bodily orifices. Douglas sees the transgression of the rules of the body as dangerous, yet suggestive of ways in which cultural experience can be effectively altered: "Spittle, blood, milk, urine, feces or tears . . . [traverse] the boundary of the body. . . . The mistake is to treat bodily margins in isolation from all other margins" (Douglas, 1966, p. 121).

Central to Bataille's obscene story is not only a denigration of vision and the defiling of the integrity of the body, but also the denigration of intimacy, which is no longer reserved for individuals loved or even known. *Story of the Eye* perversely celebrates intimacy with strangers, intimacy with inanimate objects, intimacy with animals, and (the ultimate horror of) intimacy with a body-in-pieces. Bataille's eye sees no differences between anything, especially between categories that structure our moral fabric: including, God and human being, human being and animal, parent and child, sex and defecation, death and life. Bataille insists on a body without hierarchy (especially without the privileged eye), without boundaries, prone to excess and obsessed with a twisted notion of intimacy: the end result is "the most ignoble eye imaginable" (Jay, p. 223). To see with Bataille's eye is to face the obscene as it lies waiting at the margins of socially constructed categories.

Bataille like other Surrealists—including not only Bellmer and Man Ray but also the painter Salvador Dalí and the filmmaker Luis Buñuel—sought artistic power by transgressing the boundaries of the body (emphasizing orifices and dreams) and the limits of aesthetic practice in order to challenge and call into question the meaning of life, especially sexual life. For some art, literary and cultural critics (such as Sontag, Rosalind Krauss, Susan Rubin Suleiman, Barthes, Jay), *Story of the Eye* is "a resource . . . for breaking through the limits of consciousness" (Sontag, 1969, p. 58). Likewise, Elinor Fuchs connects women performance artists (who since the 1970s have made use of their own bodies—often obscenely, as in the case of the controversial Karen Finley) as a progressive realization of Bataille's effort at erotic transgression. For others (such as the feminist writer-activist Andrea Dworkin), *Story of the Eye* is objectionably obscene—nothing more than "high-class pornography" for perpetuating violence and discrimination against women (Dworkin, 1981, p. 175).

Bataille's *Story of the Eye* transgresses a myriad of cultural beliefs by defiling them with sexuality: from religion to art to family to cleanliness, through a range of objects that are metaphorically dependent (eye, saucer of milk, boiled egg, bull's testicle)—until we can no longer see any use in the hierarchical structures that our culture has worked so hard to cultivate. As Barthes has noted, "Bataille transforms every experience into a warped [obscene] language" (pp. 246–247).

Gay Studies and the Challenge to Conventional Notions of the Obscene. Just as Bataille, although with different intentions, warps every experience with his perverse sexuality, our culture shadows every aspect of gay life with fantasies of the (homo)sexual. Homophobia has rendered the gay body as entirely obscene inside and out, in both everyday and sexual activities. (Even the most academic work on homosexuality has not escaped. For example, in 1993 *The Gay and Lesbian Studies Reader* was seized as obscene under Canadian law.) The result of this monological discourse (all gays are obscene) has torn the gay community between a need for privacy and protection "inside the closet" and the need for a political freedom that requires giving over all privacy, in order to be vocal, visible, "out of the closet."

The gay activist and critic Cindy Patton has usurped the term *obscene* as a political tool. Turning it back on its etymology, which suggests that the "ob-scene means something like *before staged* or indicates something before the moment of spatial visibility in official space," Patton uses obscenity to combat the obscenity of homophobia (Patton, 1996, p. 141). Patton's project envisions a gay transgression that is neither "safe but claustrophobic" like the closet, nor "proud, easier to target, agoraphobic" (p. 140). Patton proposes the breaking down of such rigid categories as in and out, homosexual and heterosexual, in order effectively to merge gay politics with the politics of race, class, and gender. Her utopian vision (her manifesto) does not erase gay subjects, nor does it seek a prior or "real" essence of homosexuality. Rather, she seeks an infrastructure in which gay bodies are "an insurrectional posture prior to staging, *being here before*" (p. 141). Although more of a vision than a viable practice, what Patton advocates defiles oppressive cultural categories, not unlike others who have made strategic uses of the obscene (i.e., the Surrealists, the anthropologist Mary Douglas, contemporary feminist body artists), through her insistence on returning to obscenity's etymology.

Despite laws and actions rendered to prevent it, "obscenity" as it manifests itself in photography, literature, art, and so forth transgresses not only cultural categories but presentation itself. Like its etymological meanings—which suggest "before staged," offstage, beyond visibility in official space—obscenity derives its meddling power from being there, but not at center stage. Obscenity's effective performance rests in its ability to provoke, while remaining as obscure and as impossible to define as that which so often celebrates it: art itself.

BIBLIOGRAPHY

Barthes, Roland. *Critical Essays.* Translated by Richard Howard. Evanston, Ill., 1972.

Bataille, Georges. *Story of the Eye.* Translated by Joachim Neugroschel. Reprint, San Francisco, 1987.

Baudelaire, Charles. "The Modern Public and Photography." In *Classic Essays on Photography,* edited by Alan Trachtenberg. New Haven, 1980.

Cembalest, Robin. "The Obscenity Trial: How They Voted to Acquit." *Art News* 89.1 (December 1990): 138–141.

Delacroix, Eugène. *Œuvres littéraires.* 2 vols. Paris, 1923.

Douglas, Mary. *Purity and Danger: An Analysis of Concepts of Pollution and Taboo.* London, 1966.

Dworkin, Andrea. *Pornography: Men Possessing Women.* New York, 1981.

Fuchs, Elinor. "Staging the Obscene Body." *Drama Review* 33.1 (Spring 1989): 33–58.

Heath, Stephen. *The Sexual Fix.* London, 1982.

Jay, Martin. *Downcast Eyes: The Denigration of Vision in Twentieth-Century French Thought.* Berkeley, 1994.

Krauss, Rosalind. "Photography in the Service of Surrealism." In *L'amour fou: Photography and Surrealism,* by Rosalind Krauss and Jane Livingston, pp. 13–54. New York, 1985.

Kristeva, Julia. *Powers of Horror: An Essay on Abjection.* Translated by Leon S. Roudiez. New York, 1982.

Mavor, Carol. *Pleasures Taken: Performances of Sexuality and Loss in Victorian Photographs.* Durham, N.C., 1995.

Nead, Lynda. *The Female Nude: Art, Obscenity and Sexuality.* London and New York, 1992.

Patton, Cindy. *Fatal Advice: How Safe-Sex Education Went Wrong.* Durham, N.C., 1996.

Roberts, M. J. D. "Morals, Art and the Law: The Passing of the Obscene Publications Act, 1857." *Victorian Studies* 28 (Summer 1985): 609–629.

Robertson, Geoffrey. *Obscenity: An Account of Censorship Laws and Their Enforcement in England and Wales.* London, 1979.

Solomon-Godeau, Abigail. *Photography at the Dock: Essays on Photographic History, Institutions, and Practices.* Minneapolis, 1991.

Sontag, Susan. *Styles of Radical Will.* New York, 1969.

Suleiman, Susan Rubin. *Subversive Intent: Gender, Politics, and the Avant-Garde.* Cambridge, Mass., 1990.

Weeks, Jeffrey. *Sex, Politics, and Society: The Regulation of Sexuality since 1800.* London and New York, 1981.

CAROL MAVOR

ONTOLOGY OF ART. [*To explore the ontology of art, that is, the nature of artworks, given that they exist in the empirical world as well as in the cultural-historical world, this entry comprises four essays:*

Historical Ontology
Analytic Ontology
Ontology of Music
Ontology of Dance

There have been at least two major ways of approaching these issues in Western aesthetics: analytically and historically. The first essay explains these two approaches, while emphasizing the latter. The second essay is an example of analytic ontology in contemporary aesthetics. The third essay explains how the two approaches have been applied to the field of music; this essay helps make the abstract discussion of the ontology of art more concrete by showing what it means in connection with one particular art form. The final essay continues the focus on a single art by examining the "identity" of dance that is one of its principal ontological concerns. For related discussion, see Definition of Art; Essentialism; Historicism; Realism; Theories of Art; *and* Universals.]

Historical Ontology

The puzzles of the ontology of artworks are no different from the puzzles of ontology in general, namely, those regarding the individuation, numerical identity, and nature of things. (The term *artwork* derives from Arthur Danto's coinage [1964] and has the advantage of disengaging the analysis of art from presumptions of intrinsic value and the tendentious history of the discussion of "works of art" and "the fine arts" [Kristeller, 1951, 1952].) Difficulties arise, however, as soon as we attempt to reconcile solutions regarding artworks with a general account of the ontology of nature or, in particular, the ontology of physical things. In general, Anglo-American philosophy, for reasons largely colored by the apparent success or promise—certainly, the considerable influence—of Positivism, the unity of science program, logical atomism, physicalism, and extensionalism, has sought to answer standard ontological questions about artworks (if it has allowed ontological questions at all) in ways that are intended to accord as much as possible with the approximate adequacy of our accounts of physical nature.

The most noticeable economy favored by such accounts (quite apart from whether they would be characterized as ontologies by their authors) concerns the treatment of a very large family of apparent properties of artworks that may be collected as *Intentional*—meaning by that term of art (Margolis, 1995) culturally significant attributes: linguistic, semiotic, significative, meaningful, symbolic, expressive, representational, rhetorical, informational, institutional, traditional, rulelike, hermeneutic, purposive, stylistic, genre bound, and the like. Here, the decisive issue bears on whether artworks, or cultural phenomena in general, may be treated as real, that is, as real as physical and biological phenomena; hence, such as to possess Intentional attributes in the same realist sense in which physical and biological attributes are ascribed.

The answer to that question collects the principal theories of art within the tradition of analytic aesthetics. The chief (by no means the only) options in accord with the constraints just mentioned are the following.

1. Artworks are (or are for the most part) physical objects to which Intentional attributes (for instance, representational and expressive properties) may be intrinsically ascribed (Wollheim, 1980).

2. Artworks are admitted to critical discourse when physical or natural entities (or, at any rate, extensionally manageable referents) are ascribed suitably selected Intentional "functions" (for instance, expressive and representational attributes), semiotic functions of the original referents rather than intrinsic attributes of antecedently admitted artworks (Goodman, 1976).

3. Artworks are not actually real as such, but admitting them to discourse signifies the "transfigurative" (or rhetorical) status assigned to "mere real things" (physical things, even artifacts like diagrams or snow shovels) rather than the "transformed" (or altered ontological) emergence or cultural constitution *of* actual artworks (Danto, 1981).

4. Real things (more or less in accord with extensionalist assumptions) are construed as artworks essentially by way of "make-believe" or by entertaining a fiction applied to the first (Walton, 1990).

Maneuvers of these reductive sorts suffer from a number of profound difficulties that implicate the linkage between the ontology of art and the ontology of persons or selves as well as the whole world of human culture. In analytic philosophy, these difficulties have been thought to come to little more than what is known as the mind/body problem. That, however, is implausible, for the resolution of the mind/body problem along physicalist and extensionalist lines tends to favor an initially solipsistic reading of the mental or psychological or "intentional" (Brentano, 1973); fails to address Intentional or cultural phenomena that are not mental (artworks, notably); treats discourse about the physical as never affected by intentional or Intentional complications; and regards the societal, collective, and historical aspects of human life (for instance, the linguistic) as entirely explicable in terms of, or as generated from, the processes of biological or solipsistic life (never vice versa). But the deepest puzzle posed by the ontology of art concerns the relation between nature and culture, not merely the mind/body problem; in fact, the mind/body problem is usually a special version of the other, and animal mentality is usually anthropomorphically modeled (however restrictedly) on linguistically qualified mental life. These caveats suggest quite promising analogies in the art world.

In any case, apart from the obvious fact that there is, at present, no satisfactorily detailed or convincing argument that shows how to resolve the mind/body problem in favor of the physicalist and extensionalist themes remarked, cognate ontologies of art are notably defective. In particular, none of the best-known views (those just tallied, for instance) offers an explicit analysis of persons or selves—the paradigms of cultural (or culturally emergent) entities—with which the intended treatment of artworks may be suitably reconciled. For if a reductive account of persons (or their Intentional nature) were not forthcoming, there would be no reason to anticipate a physicalist account of artworks.

If the distinctive properties of artworks are what have already been labeled here as Intentional—linguistic or semiotic properties, for instance—then there is every reason to believe that the distinguishing properties of persons or selves (their linguistic skills and whatever those skills make possible: notably, here, artworks that exhibit Intentional properties as a result of linguistically and similarly informed productive abilities) cannot be disjunctively analyzed in ontological terms. Encultured persons (or selves) and culturally formed artworks will present the same conceptual difficulties for any would-be reductive ontologies of the sorts mentioned. Arguably, a realist reading of speaking selves will extend to a realist reading of sentences and speech acts; similarly, a realist reading of culturally productive selves, whether in a poetic or technical sense (in Aristotle's idiom), will extend to a realist reading of artworks and tools and instruments. A strong reductionism will fail in the first instance, and the natural linkage between the two will question the advantage or plausibility—once the argument regarding the first is lost—of insisting on a strong reductionism in the second. The case is strengthened by conceding that the very existence and nature of art implicate the productive powers of human selves.

One way of featuring what is at stake is to ask, where in the world are Intentional attributes to be found? The best answer seems to be: in the collective space of human culture, not, or not merely, in any mind or minds, although (on the argument) the mental states of artists, critics, and ordinary people capable of linguistic behavior may be taken to have already internalized the collective practices of historical societies (natural languages and artistic practices, say). This much is the common theme of Ludwig Wittgenstein's *Lebenformen*, Hans-Georg Gadamer's "traditions," Michel Foucault's epistemes, variants of what Edmund Husserl calls the *Lebenswelt* and what Pierre Bourdieu calls the *habitus*. It is extraordinary that, with the exception of Thomas S. Kuhn's "paradigms," there is almost no Anglo-American philosopher, not otherwise drawn to the tradition of the British Hegelians or the early American pragmatists, who has favored a theme like the Intentional. The result has been an obvious lacuna at the level of ontology.

The importance of this single adjustment makes itself felt in elementary ways. For, of course, it is hard to suppose that artists do not compose or create or make or constitute something that rightly invites interpretation and appreciation along Intentional lines, robust enough (in realist terms) to support truth claims and presumptions of objectivity in some measure comparable with the objectivity of claims in the natural sciences. All the authors mentioned tend to favor the objectivity of critical discourse addressed to some range of Intentional ascriptions among artworks; nevertheless,

none has ever explained the conceptual basis for such a confidence. One may well wonder how the purchase of a $40 million painting by Vincent van Gogh could then be explained (that is, the purchase of a "mere real thing" to which, for merely transient or rhetorical reasons, we impute the expressive and representational properties we say we prize, but refuse to admit that artworks actually exist as such, and actually possess, as real properties, the expressive and representational properties imputed to them). The very idea of a market in art makes no sense if the Intentional properties ascribed to particular works can claim no objective standing or if they are subject to the vagaries of critical and appreciative practices antecedently committed to the notion that Intentional properties are not real—or are somehow real in persons but not in speech or art.

There is a great irony here. Among Continental theorists—Gadamer (1989), Roland Barthes (1979), Foucault (1970), for instance—informal concessions favoring the reality of the cultural world regularly obtain; nevertheless, there is noticeably little interest in contemporary European philosophy in addressing the specific puzzles of individuation, identity, and nature, although there is sympathy for the Intentional and for its pervasiveness in the whole of the intelligible world. On the other hand, Anglo-American analytic philosophers (who address art as well as nature) are pointedly interested in the technical issues; but they regularly impoverish the conceptual resources by which they may be effectively answered.

By and large, there have been only two distinctive ontological strategies within English-language philosophy that have sought to reverse the reductive tendencies mentioned. One, most fully and systematically developed by Nicholas Wolterstorff (1980), construes artworks as abstract entities, as universals in fact; the other, most systematically developed by Joseph Margolis (1980), construes artworks as culturally emergent particulars. Both are designed to ensure the Intentional features of artworks. The first faces the difficulty of vindicating a realism of universals; the second, the difficulty of vindicating a sufficiently robust form of cultural realism. Wolterstorff's account treats artworks as "kinds" (or "types" or "universals"), but also as "nonpredicable universals" (or "substance universals"), meaning that artworks may have plural instances, although not in the way of being predicable of anything else (for instance, in the form of multiple performances of Béla Bartók's First Quartet). Margolis's account offers the counterpart device of construing all and only cultural entities as "tokens-of-types": there may indeed be multiple instances of "the same work" but that there are no separable "types" and that "types" are introduced heuristically only to link particulars (for instance, performances of Bartók's quartet) for counting purposes—for attribution—as "tokens-of-the-same-type" ("Bartók's quartet"). (Regarding further difficulties involving tokens-of-types, of which there are many, see Margolis, 1980, chap. 4.)

Clearly, the issue rests with the plausibility and force with which universals may be assigned a cognitive function and reconciled with the perceived need to admit that universals exist; although (as Wolterstorff adds) kinds or universals need not occur (that is, may not have occurrent instances). There is evidence in Wolterstorff's account, furthermore, that kinds or universals are said to exist only on the strength of what is first admitted to be linguistically predicable of particular "works" or particular "occurrences" (among artworks: for instance, as between different printings of the same etching or different performances of the same quartet). (You will find the best evidence of this in Wolterstorff's account of "The Grizzly" as distinct from actual grizzly bears: 1970, chap. 10). There, Wolterstorff subscribes to something very close to the medieval realist reading of universals; whereas Margolis argues that there is no assignable cognitive role for universals anywhere: that none is needed and that the use of general predicables ("designated" by predicates, analogically invoked in the idiom of tokens-of-types) can only be explained in terms of something like Wittgensteinian *Lebensformen,* Gadamerian "traditions," or Foucauldian "epistemes" (see Margolis, 1995). Wolterstorff employs his notion of kinds to include the "projected worlds" (the represented "content" or "story") of artworks, which, in effect, corresponds to the Intentional predicables Margolis ascribes to his (sui generis) culturally emergent entities (particular artworks).

In this way, both lines of argument offset the reductive tendencies favored by the specimen views mentioned earlier: Wolterstorff, by way of a realism regarding universals; Margolis, by way of distinguishing between nature and culture, while denying Wolterstorff's sort of realism. The account of predicables, on Margolis's view, is neither realist nor nominalist, but depends on the "symbiosis" of "cognized world" and "worlded cognition"—that is, on the impossibility of a principled disjunction between "subjects" and "objects." (The thesis is anti-Kantian.) On the argument, Wolterstorff must fall back on the resources of something like those admitted in Margolis's account.

The principal focus of these two sorts of quarrels is afforded by attempts to "adequate" (or match conceptually) the ontology of artworks and the characteristic work of descriptive, interpretive, and evaluative criticism in the arts, particularly where objective claims are thought possible. In general, to attribute intrinsic expressive or representational properties presupposes that artworks have a suitable "nature" and may be individuated and reidentified congruently with such ascriptions. This confirms once again the importance of a realist reading of Intentionality.

There are at least three distinct puzzles that must be resolved and integrated with what has already been said:

1. concerning the conceptual relationship between natural and cultural entities and between natural and cultural attributes;

2. concerning the sense in which the linguistic resources of reference and predication can service the individuation and reidentification of artworks in ways congenial to interpretative truth claims; and

3. concerning the meaning of objectivity in the context of Intentional attributes.

These are strenuous matters. For the most part, they are ignored or not adequately analyzed in the analytic literature, and they are not cast in analytically congenial terms in the Continental. In both Gadamer's (1989) and Barthes's (1979) accounts, determining textual meanings proceeds extremely informally: readings are said to be constrained by the effective "horizons" or "codes" of an apt culture, but the practice is treated in a freewheeling way; similarly, imputed meanings are said to be affected by, and to affect, ongoing interpretation, but methodological questions are usually (deliberately) scanted. (Barthes is freer in this regard than Gadamer: Barthes, opposing francophone structuralism; Gadamer, Romantic hermeneutics). On the analytic side, one finds careful analyses of the "logic" of expressive properties (Tormey, 1971; Sircello, 1972) but little in the way of adequating objective criticism and the ontology of art. On the Continental side, one finds an appreciation of the complex nature of texts and artworks but little in the way of methodology.

On the first of the three puzzles mentioned, the trick is to avoid ontological dualism as well as reductionism, eliminationism, and "supervenience." (On supervenience, see Davidson, 1980.) Once we avoid dualism and physicalism, there seems to be only one possible line of analysis, namely, to treat entities that have Intentional "natures" as emergent sui generis with respect to the physical and biological world, as embodied in the entities of that world, and as possessing properties incarnate in the properties of that world. On Margolis's account, all and only cultural entities—artworks as well as persons or selves—are said to be:

1. tokens-of-types,
2. embodied,
3. possessing Intentional properties incarnate in physical properties,
4. intrinsically interpretable for these reasons,
5. accessible to standard referential and predicative resources,
6. capable of supporting objective claims, and
7. alterable in their Intentional properties as a result of ongoing interpretation within the *lebensformlich* practices of a historical society (see Margolis, 1995).

That is, if we treat Intentional properties in a realist way, if we oppose the usual forms of physicalism and extensionalism, if we refuse a realism regarding universals, if we mean to adequate ontology and criticism, then something like conditions 1–6 must obtain. Condition 7 is admittedly quarrelsome; it is also the nerve of the principal disputes affecting the objectivity of interpretive criticism.

Briefly, then, the proposal of conditions 2 and 3 is this: Intentional attributes are inseparable (indissolubly complex because they are inseparable) from the physical attributes ascribed to artworks (or persons). A thought or feeling, for instance, is an Intentional (mental) predicable inseparable from the neurophysiological attributes in which it is embedded; it is discernible, Intentionally, only in the cultural space of an apt community of human agents. Thus, the representational properties of Michelangelo's *Pietà* are Intentionally embedded in the marble of the sculpture and discernible only in the cultural world of producing and appreciating art. Our ontology should accommodate the conditions of objective truth claims, but what should count as true or false, with respect to particular interpretations, is an entirely separate matter. On the Romantic hermeneutic view (Hirsch, 1967), the objectivity with which "authorial intent" can be discerned justifies our supposing that there is a uniquely correct interpretation of that text; on Gadamer's post-Heideggerian hermeneutics, authorial intent is itself an artifact of the historically evolving horizontal perspective generated from the vantage from which our own interpretation arises. Hence, Gadamer, but not E. D. Hirsch, Jr., subscribes to condition 7.

The decisive metaphysical issue concerns the sense in which the cultural world emerges from physical nature in a sui generis way and in which, within the space of a particular culture, pertinent entities (artworks, persons) are posited, formed, discerned, interpreted. ("Embodiment" regarding entities is meant to be matched, of course, with the "incarnation" of their properties. In one stroke, we thereby avoid both dualism and reductionism.)

Beyond this, the most productive philosophical puzzle concerns the adequacy of our referential and identificatory resources—in speaking of artworks. The matter is adumbrated in the question posed earlier: "Where in the world are Intentional properties to be found?" The answer is quite straightforward. If artworks are discernible only within a cultural space that admits Intentionality, then clearly the individuation and reidentifiability of artworks also depend on the same resources. And if, on the argument sketched (against Wolterstorff), the objectivity of predication is inseparable from the historicized conditions of *lebensformlich* practices, then there can be no a priori objection against construing the effectiveness of individuation and reidentifiability as falling within the same *lebensformlich* world.

The result is that to admit the sui generis nature of Intentional attributes, the radical difference between such attributes and mere physical properties, the important fact that they can be objectively fixed only in some consensual way (within our collective practices), and the equally important fact that our practices change Intentionally with historical use, *is* to admit that what counts as objective in the consensual way proper to the world of human culture may not preclude divergent, even incompatible, interpretations as valid. What this signifies is that the ontology of art must make provision for the possible need for a relativistic logic, a logic in accord with which interpretative values that, on a bivalent scheme of truth claims (true/false) but not now, would be incompatible or contradictory, may be jointly confirmed without contradiction. Such a thesis would require a many-valued logic, an asymmetrical account of truth and falsity, the retirement of the term *true* in relevant contexts, and the introduction of many-valued truth-values such as *plausible* or *reasonable* (Margolis, 1991). The resultant claims might then be said to be "incongruent," not contradictory, although not in a way to disallow breaches of consistency. Such a proposal is both heterodox and quarrelsome. But, for one thing, it fits, in a natural way, certain strong intuitions about interpreting complex artworks; and, for another, if the general argument about the ontology of art is plausible, then the fixities of canonical logic are as open to reinterpretation as the realist nature of the entire world of human culture.

At the level of ontology, we must prepare for the admissibility of such complex epistemic claims. Ontically, entities (or referents) that are Intentionally qualified cannot fail to have somewhat indeterminate but determinable "natures," if their natures are alterable as a consequence of ongoing interpretation. The notion is neither referentially nor predicatively paradoxical; but it confirms the inseparability of alethic, epistemic, and ontic considerations.

BIBLIOGRAPHY

Barthes, Roland. "From Work to Text." Translated by Josué V. Harari. In *Textual Strategies: Perspectives in Post-structuralist Criticism*, edited by Josué V. Harari. Ithaca, N.Y., 1979.

Brentano, Franz. *Psychology from an Empirical Standpoint*. Edited by Oskar Kraus; English edition edited by Linda L. McAlister, translated by Antos C. Ranevrello et al. London, 1973.

Danto, Arthur C. "The Artworld." *Journal of Philosophy* 61.19 (15 October 1964): 571–584.

Danto, Arthur C. *The Transfiguration of the Commonplace: A Philosophy of Art*. Cambridge, Mass., 1981.

Davidson, Donald. "Mental Events." In *Essays on Actions and Events*. Oxford, 1980.

Foucault, Michel. *The Order of Things: An Archaeology of the Human Sciences*. New York, 1970.

Gadamer, Hans-Georg. *Truth and Method*. 2d rev. ed. Translation revised by Joel Weinsheimer and Donald G. Marshall. New York, 1989.

Goodman, Nelson. *Languages of Art: An Approach to a Theory of Symbols*. 2d ed. Indianapolis, 1976.

Hirsch, E. D., Jr. *Validity in Interpretation*. New Haven, 1967.

Kristeller, Oskar. "The Modern System of the Arts." *Journal of the History of Ideas* 12.4 (October 1951): 469–527; and 13.1 (January 1952): 17–46.

Margolis, Joseph. *Art and Philosophy*. Atlantic Highlands, N.J., 1980.

Margolis, Joseph. *The Truth about Relativism*. Oxford and Cambridge, Mass., 1991.

Margolis, Joseph. *Interpretation Radical but Not Unruly: The New Puzzle of the Arts and History*. Berkeley, 1995.

Sircello, Guy. *Mind and Art: An Essay on the Varieties of Expression*. Princeton, N.J., 1972.

Tormey, Alan. *The Concept of Expression: A Study in Philosophical Psychology and Aesthetics.* Princeton, N.J., 1971.

Walton, Kendall L. *Mimesis as Make-Believe: On the Foundations of the Representational Arts.* Cambridge, Mass., 1990.

Wollheim, Richard. *Art and Its Objects.* 2d ed. with six supplementary essays. Cambridge and New York, 1980.

Wolterstorff, Nicholas. *On Universals: An Essay in Ontology.* Chicago, 1970.

Wolterstorff, Nicholas. *Works and Worlds of Art.* Oxford, 1980.

JOSEPH MARGOLIS

Analytic Ontology

Ontology is concerned with the nature of things: the kinds of things that exist and the conditions for their existence. It raises such questions as: Are there universals, or is everything that exists a particular? Is everything that exists a material thing? Narrowing our focus so as to concentrate on one kind of thing—works of art—our questions become more specific: Is there one kind of things that artworks are, or does the category *art* cross the boundaries drawn by nature? Are all, or any, artworks material things? Ontology is to be contrasted with epistemology, which tells us how and what we know about the existence and natures of things. But how far ontology can be done in isolation from epistemology is a controversial issue. Yet, it is impossible to make progress in thinking about what art objects are without giving the closest consideration to questions about our knowledge of, and responses to, those objects.

In constructing a theory about the nature of art objects, we can be guided by two principles. First, as in all philosophy, we should aim for simplicity and generality. Second, our ontology should respect important aesthetic and artistic distinctions. These two principles are to some extent in conflict; we are sometimes able to mark aesthetic and artistic boundaries only at the cost of some complexity and by treating works of one kind differently from those of another. Perhaps there is no neutral perspective from which to determine how trade-offs should be made between these two principles. In that case, there may be more than one epistemically most desirable theory about the nature of art, and choosing one of them will then be a matter of preference. It may even be that there are no facts of the matter about precisely what art objects are, because our concept of art is consistent with a number of mutually incompatible ontologies. Each of these mutually incompatible theories could then be thought of as corresponding to an extension or refinement of our current conception of art works.

An admirably simple beginning in this deliberation has it that artworks are just physical objects. Leonardo da Vinci's *Madonna of the Rocks* is a canvas on a gallery wall, Donatello's *Saint George* is a certain shaped piece of stone. This theory, however, is not even remotely plausible for literary and musical works. In these arts the work cannot be the original manuscript or score (what we can call generally the autograph), since the work can exist when the autograph is destroyed. But there is no other physical object with which the work in these cases can plausibly be identified. Even for those works for which this proposal is plausible—painting and sculpture—the proposal is not correct. So, to take a most favorable case, if the statue *David, (D),* is identical with a certain block of stone, *B,* then *D* and *B* must have the same properties. But substantial deformation might destroy *D* without destroying *B.*

The argument just given is a familiar one from general metaphysics that applies to kinds of things other than artworks (e.g., functional kinds). We can add to it a specifically aesthetic consideration. The claim that paintings and sculptures are physical objects depends on the idea that in these cases the authentic object from the hand of the artist is of supreme aesthetic importance; a proper appreciation of the work requires that the viewer sees *that* object rather than any copy of it, however good. With novels, plays, and poems, on the other hand, the autograph has no special significance for the work itself; so far as access to the work itself is concerned, any word-for-word copy will do. Literature and music seem to allow for the unrestricted reproducibility of instances of the work, whereas painting and sculpture—and also printmaking and casting, where reproducibility seems restricted by the artist's say-so—do not. Now, one may argue that this contrast is simply the product of a technological limitation that makes it relatively easy to produce aesthetically adequate copies of literary works, and rather difficult to produce aesthetically adequate copies of paintings and statues; word-for-word sameness does not require strict identity of appearance. But, if the resources once devoted to space exploration were put into the manufacture of superb, mass-produced copies of paintings, prints, sculptures, and casts, would not the status of originals in these arts decline to that of autographs in literature and music? Original paintings and sculptures would continue to have a special interest for us, much as autographs of novels and poems do, but it would not be plausible to think of those originals as identical with the works themselves.

This argument—against which there is a host of objections not possible to consider here—suggests that we might be able to formulate a quite general ontology of art, at least for all the major, traditionally recognized forms. For literature and music, for example, where reproducibility has always been acknowledged as consistent with the integrity of the work, we might take the view that works are abstract structures or types, of which copies of their text or score are tokens. On this view, literary works are sequences of word types, or texts, and musical works are sequences of note types, or scores. Since texts and scores as here defined are abstract structures, we may call an approach of the kind just described a version of structuralism.

Since types are abstract objects, this proposal has the consequence that works are created rather than discovered.

This is not a significant drawback to the structuralist position. The structuralist need not deny that hard work and talent are required for the composition of significant works, or that without that talent and effort these works would not be available to us. We admire those who prove difficult and important mathematical theorems, and our admiration does not dissipate with the thought that these theorems are not created by the mathematicians. The creationist cannot appeal here to some evident fact about artistic creativity with which structuralism is in conflict. Rather, the structuralist and the creationist differ metaphysically, and whether artistic work is creation or discovery might reasonably be counted as spoils to the victor.

It is also objected against the version of structuralism just outlined that it makes no provision for the obvious difference between performance and nonperformance works, since it treats plays, symphonies, and novels alike as having tokens that are particular inscriptions of text. We can rectify this by saying musical works are sequences of sound types rather than note types. Whereas note types have as their tokens particular inscriptions, sound types have as their tokens particular sounds. A sound type might be specified in terms of a pitch, a duration, and a degree of loudness (all of which would have to be vague). Thus defined, an instance of the work would consist in the actual production of tokens of the sound types constitutive of the work; it would be a performance of the work. (A comparable stipulation can be made for plays and other nonmusical performance works.)

For the case of music, this proposal is open to objection. Musical works are typically intended to be performed on certain instruments, and the specification of the work in terms of sound types alone fails to accommodate this, as a sound type can be produced in ways that would be inappropriate for many works (see Levinson, 1991). We could meet the performance-means objection by specifying that the work is a sequence of sound types as performed on certain instruments. But we must go further. A person who produces the appropriate sequence of sounds on the appropriate instruments by accident, or while improvising, is not, strictly speaking, performing the work. We need to say that the work is a sequence of sound types as performed on certain instruments as a result of intentionally following a certain score.

What if our performer, Jones, were conforming to the score of an existing work—Ludwig van Beethoven's *Hammerklavier Sonata,* for instance—but was doing so as a result of having hit on that score himself by an act of composition undertaken in ignorance of Beethoven's previous efforts? Would Jones be performing the *Hammerklavier Sonata?* Structuralists say yes, assuming Jones was playing the instrument specified by Beethoven. Some writers have argued that the correct answer is that he is not playing Beethoven's work, and that consequently the theory so far elaborated is wrong; instead, he is playing a distinct work composed by

Jones himself (see Levinson, 1991; Currie, 1989; Danto, 1981). The argument for this is another version of the "distinct properties" argument presented earlier. Much of what, for the well-informed listener, is interesting and valuable in a musical work derives from the work's art-historical features. Works are variously describable as stunningly original, fresh, deliberately anachronistic, shamelessly plundered from better composers. We notice and enjoy or deplore their quotation from and commentary on other works. If such features are features of the works themselves, we cannot say that Beethoven's and Jones's works are identical just because they are correctly performed on the same instruments in accordance with the same score. Jones's twentieth-century work may reflect the influence of Johannes Brahms, express outrage at the practice of atonality, and consciously submit itself to the discipline of an earlier age—Beethoven's does none of these things. So these works have distinct properties and cannot be the same work. Parallel arguments show that literary works with the same structure—the same text—need not be identical (see Currie, 1991). Structuralism's identity conditions are ahistorical, so they falsely identify distinct works.

This antistructuralist argument is hard to answer. If it is accepted, we will have to specify the identity conditions of works in such a way that works will not automatically be identical when they have the same structure; we need, in addition, to specify a relation between the structure and an act of composition or authorship. Exactly how this is to be done is a matter of dispute between antistructuralists, and it is not clear that these disputes all admit of a fact. resolution. What does seem to be telling is the conclusion that the structuralist's identity conditions are insufficient to accommodate our deep sense of the historical nature of art.

Suppose we have two bundles of pages, alike with respect to the words printed on them. We cannot now automatically conclude that they are both instances of the same work, because we have allowed that two literary works can have the same structure, that is, the same text. The conditions for identity within the work, as we can call the conditions that must hold in order for a work instance to be an instance of this particular work, need a historical aspect, in the same way that identity of the work does. We might say that this bundle, B, is an instance of the novel *Emma* rather than of the textually identical novel *Schemme* because B derives causally from Jane Austen's act of authorship rather from that of her lesser-known rival, Schmausten. That is, B is a copy of something, which is a copy of something, which is . . . a copy of Austen's autograph. Similarly, this performance is a performance of Smith's First Symphony rather than of the identically structured Jones's Second Symphony because the players' knowledge of the score derives causally from Smith's act of composition rather than from Jones's.

Within the general framework so far outlined, we can accommodate the pictorial and plastic arts by saying that their identity conditions are also partly structural and partly historical. The structural component in these cases is specified in terms of what Nelson Goodman calls "pictorial properties." Two pictures have the same pictorial properties when they have the same colors at the same places on their faces (see Goodman, 1976, p. 42). For statuary, the structural condition would include a specification of three-dimensional shape as well as color. (Strictly speaking, shape would have to be specified for paintings also, since these works have, to varying degrees, a significant three-dimensionality.) Exactly how we are to specify the historical component in a work's identity is controversial: Should it include a reference to the identity of the artist? To the time and place of the artist's activity? Antistructuralists are, and probably will remain, divided on these issues. They are united only by their insistence that in some way or other, the identity conditions for works must be historical. So far as identity within the work goes, the matter is a little easier. Antistructuralists might agree on this: that an instance of the *Madonna of the Rocks,* or of the print *Tobit Blind,* must have a certain visible appearance, specifiable in terms of the location of colors on a surface, but it must also be a copy of something that is a copy of something, which . . . is a copy of the artist's original canvas, or is the result of an authorized pull from the original plate.

While focusing on some of the major areas of current theoretical discussion, it has been difficult here to specify the kind of theory we should aim for in devising an ontology of art. But something along the lines indicated here seems to have the best chance of achieving simplicity and generality while respecting those of our intuitions about the nature of art that are robust under philosophical reflection.

BIBLIOGRAPHY

Currie, Gregory. *An Ontology of Art.* New York, 1989.
Currie, Gregory. "Work and Text." *Mind* 100 (1991): 325–340.
Danto, Arthur C. *The Transfiguration of the Commonplace: A Philosophy of Art.* Cambridge, Mass., 1981.
Goodman, Nelson. *Languages of Art: An Approach to a Theory of Symbols.* 2d ed. Indianapolis, 1976.
Goodman, Nelson. "Remarks on Wollheim's Paper." *Ratio* 20 (1978): 49–51.
Goodman, Nelson, and Catherine Z. Elgin. "Interpretations and Identity: Can the Work Survive the World?" In *Reconceptions in Philosophy and Other Arts and Sciences.* London, 1988.
Kivy, Peter. "Platonism in Music: A Kind of Defence." *Grazer philosophische Studien* 19 (1983): 109–129.
Levinson, Jerrold. "What a Musical Work Is." In *Music, Art and Metaphysics: Essays in Philosophical Aesthetics.* Ithaca, N.Y., 1990.
Levinson, Jerrold. "Art as Action." In *The Pleasures of Aesthetics: Philosophical Essays.* Ithaca, N.Y., 1996.
Walton, Kendall. "Categories of Art." *Philosophical Review* 79 (1970): 334–367.
Wiggins, David. "Reply to Richard Wollheim." *Ratio* 20 (1978): 52–68.
Wollheim, Richard. "Are the Criteria of Identity That Hold for a Work of Art in the Different Arts Aesthetically Relevant?" *Ratio* 20 (1978): 29–48.
Wollheim, Richard. *Art and Its Objects.* 2d ed. with six supplementary essays. Cambridge and New York, 1980.
Wolterstorff, Nicholas. *Works and Worlds of Art.* Oxford, 1980.

GREGORY CURRIE

Ontology of Music

Philosophical questions about the ontology of music are generally concerned, not with acoustic events, but rather with the notion of "work" or "piece"; the core intuition is that a musical work can have repeated performances but is not identical with (though perhaps is experienced through) these performances. Paradigm cases of musical works are found among composed pieces of art music of the eighteenth century through the present day, such as J. S. Bach's C Major Cello Suite, Ludwig van Beethoven's opus 109 Piano Sonata, and Arnold Schoenberg's Second String Quartet. What sort of thing is a musical work? Even if this ontological question can be answered, there will remain the question whether the answer has application to music of other times, and music of other kinds. Only the first of these questions has been the subject of much sustained discussion among philosophers, and only that question will be considered here. But it is important to remember that much music making has little or nothing to do with the composition and performance of musical works.

There are, broadly speaking, two answers to our question: nominalist and realist. The nominalist view is that musical works, as distinct from performances and scores (or instructions) simply do not exist (exist in name only). The foremost nominalist of our century, Nelson Goodman, developed this view is detail in his 1968 *Languages of Art.* His position has not been widely accepted, but the influence of his work, novel in approaching the arts by means of epistemology rather than value theory and unprecedented in its rigor, has been enormous.

The challenge for the nominalist is to provide an alternative account for our intuition that works seem to exist and are revealed through performances; Goodman does this by explaining how performances (said to be *of the same work*) are linked together, absent works. Goodman places this burden on the score, requiring that it serve for authoritative identification of a particular set of performances. A musical work is characterized reductively as the set of performances determined by a score. (The notion of set is eliminable for Goodman, as explained in Goodman, 1966.) Goodman's version of this approach demands first that the score uniquely determine the set of performances belonging to the work, and second that the score be uniquely determined, given a performance and the notational system.

The second requirement seems implausible, and unnecessary even for a nominalist. What is to rule out the possibility that distinct scores could yield identical performances? Surely the technical possibility is no concern of the composer. Consider two brief scores, A and B:

A. Play any three notes of this chord; hold until sound disappears

B. Hold until sound disappears

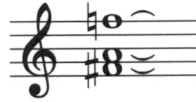

A single sound event can comply with both A and B, yet the works are distinct, since not every performance that complies with A also complies with B.

Goodman requires absolute compliance: he argues that a single wrong note disqualifies a sound event from being an instance of the work. His argument, a version of the sorites paradox, is powerfully general (it has been insufficiently noted that it is independent of his nominalist principles): from repeated applications of the premise that if a complex musical work sustains a single alteration (or addition or deletion) it remains the same work, and the transitivity of identity, one can apparently show that a performance of "Three Blind Mice" also counts as a performance of Beethoven's Fifth Symphony (Goodman, 1976, p. 187). This is essentially the same as the argument to show that a twenty-ton pile of sand weighs very little, given first, that a three-grain pile of sand weighs very little, and second, that if one grain of sand is added to a pile that weighs very little, the resulting pile still weighs very little. The problem is really a general one about vague predicates, of which both "weighs very little" and "is a performance of Beethoven's Fifth Symphony" are examples. A reasonable and paradox-free account of vagueness is needed. On the account of vagueness of Fine (1975), for example, the argument illustrated twice above fails.

A different nominalist treatment of musical works is possible. Suppose we hold that composers create instructions for performers, on the basis of which performers create performances that vary depending on their interpretation of the instructions. Suppose we hold that nothing else exists, beyond the instructions and the performances, to be called the "work"—that musical works are fictions that allow us to speak more conveniently about performances. On this view, all statements purportedly about musical works are really about past, present, or future performances, and the composer's instructions that give rise to performances. For example, "I am familiar with the work" goes into: "I have heard or imagined some performance." "I admire the work

but not any performance I have ever heard of it" goes into either: "On the basis of past performances I have heard but not admired, I can imagine an admirable one"; or, perhaps: "On the basis of my study of the instructions, I can imagine an admirable performance." "That work was never, and will never be, performed" goes into: "The relevant instructions never were, and never will be, carried out." "That work has taken on new and enriched meaning over the years" goes into something like: "Performances (following the given instructions) have changed over the years."

Goodman would object, I think, that this nominalist answer provides no account of the linking of performances—what on his account is provided by the strict requirements on the idea of a notation and compliance. It can be suggested in response that there is, in fact, no decision procedure for determining whether a given performance is sufficiently in accord with the instructions to count as one of the performances to be linked together. This second nominalist treatment is described briefly, though not embraced, in Martin (1993).

In the decade after Goodman's work, a number of realist accounts of musical works were proposed; one of the most fully developed was that of Nicholas Wolterstorff (Wolterstorff, 1980).

Just as a musical work and its performances share some predicates—for example, "is in C sharp minor" is true of Beethoven's opus 131 string quartet, and also true of its performances—so, Wolterstorff points out, do natural kinds and their instances share predicates: "has four feet" is true of the tiger, and also true of individual tigers. Wolterstorff proposes that natural kinds and artworks are "ontological allies"—two species of kinds. He notes that many kinds are such that it is possible for them to have properly formed examples and improperly formed examples; he calls such kinds norm kinds. For example, the kind Tiger is a norm kind, whereas the kinds Red Thing and Properly Formed Orchid are not norm kinds. Wolterstorff's suggestion is that musical works are norm kinds whose examples are performances. A property is normative within a kind if the kind is a norm kind, and it is impossible for something to lack the property and be a properly formed example of the kind. The property expressed by "has a C sharp in the first measure" is normative within the work (kind), Béla Bartók's Fifth Quartet.

Wolterstorff fills out his account of the ontological status of musical works with discussions of composing and performing. To compose a musical work is, for him, to select a set of properties that sound sequence occurrences can exemplify—such as being a violin sound of middle C pitch, being a quarter note long in 4/4 time at andante tempo, being forte in volume—for the purpose of their serving as criteria for judging correctness of occurrence. Wolterstorff includes instrumental properties (for example, produced by a violin), as well as acoustic properties, and allows that it will sometimes not be clear whether the composer has selected simply acoustic or also instrumental properties:

> In selecting a set of properties required for correctness, the composer composes a work—that one, namely, which has exactly those properties (plus any others presupposed by them) as normative within it. Any particular sound-sequence-occurrence which is correct by reference to that particular set of requirements for correctness will be a correct occurrence *of the work* composed. (p. 63)

It follows that one cannot uniquely extract a work from a performance. Even if one could discern all the properties of a sound sequence occurrence it would not be clear which are selected as required for correctness.

Not every sound sequence occurrence with the right properties is, for Wolterstorff, a performance: the right sounds accidentally produced do not constitute a performance. To perform a work is to bring about a sound sequence occurrence that "comes fairly close" (p. 79) to exemplifying the acoustic and instrumental properties normative within that work, and to do so by having beliefs largely correct as to what are the properties normative within the work; by aiming to produce a sound sequence occurrence that largely exemplifies most of the properties about which one has those beliefs; and by largely succeeding in achieving this aim. Kendall Walton argues, interestingly, that to perform is not only to bring about a sequence of sounds of the right pattern (as he puts it) but to present and portray that pattern in some particular way (Walton, 1988).

Musical works, because they are kinds, do not come into or go out of existence, according to Wolterstorff. In selecting a set of properties required for correctness, a composer brings it about that a preexistent kind becomes a work, but does not bring the work into existence. Similarly, musical works cannot change—what we might be inclined to describe as a single work changing is actually a series of slightly different works.

Jerrold Levinson (1980) can be seen as attempting to develop a plausible realist treatment of musical works compatible with intuitions that had been seen by earlier realist writers, including Wolterstorff, as unacceptable. Levinson argues first in support of these putative intuitions, then for a realist account of musical works congenial to them. His work, and the discussion prompted by it (see, for example, references in Levinson, 1990), is an interesting case study in the interaction between theory and intuitive desiderata. There is striking lack of agreement on the latter, and the theory that Levinson proposes to accommodate those intuitions seems not to have had a great deal of persuasive force by itself.

Levinson argues first that musical works are created by composers, even though they are abstract objects. He proposes an adjustment of the underlying metaphysics, introducing a distinction between implicit types and initiated types. The former are so called because their existence is implicitly granted, according to Levinson, when a general framework of possibilities is given: examples are all possible combinations of allowed moves of chess, sound structures simpliciter, performance-means structures (all possible sequences of ways of making sounds) simpliciter, and every compound of a sound structure and a performance-means structure. Initiated types are types that begin to exist only when they are initiated by an intentional human act; examples are the Ford Thunderbird and a compound sound structure/performing-means structure as indicated by Beethoven in 1797.

Levinson's view would be strengthened by evidence of independent plausibility of the distinction between implicit and initiated types. One could hold that the Ford Thunderbird is a type of the classic (implicit) variety and that it was directions for producing cars called Thunderbirds that was created in 1957 by the Ford designers.

Levinson argues, second, that the historical context in which a work is created informs its identity. This is surely the case, empirically. But Levinson takes it to imply the following. Suppose that in 1900 a score identical to that of Felix Mendelssohn's *Midsummer Night's Dream* (1826) was produced, in the same notational system and with the same conventions of interpretation in effect as in 1826; then, although in 1900 the same sound structure is determined as that determined in 1826 by Mendelssohn's score, the musical works composed are distinct (because of historical difference). Several points should be made.

1. The importance of historical context to the identity of a work might consist in it being extremely unlikely that two composers would compose (or discover) the same work.

2. Our intuitions about such cases are very weak because there are no such cases.

3. Levinson's strongest evidence is that musical works have properties (such as originality, or being a parody of a Shostakovitch-symphony, etc.) that they might not have were their historical context different. Mendelssohn's *Midsummer Night's Dream* is highly original; the 1900 hypothetical work, with the same sound structure, would be highly derivative and therefore, apparently, a distinct work. Hence, the work is not the sound structure. One could say, on the contrary, that the same work was composed, once in 1826, once in 1900, in the sense that they are indistinguishable in performance; it is Mendelssohn's originality in connection with this work that we admire, and generally no confusion can arise from attributing this originality to the work.

Levinson's idea to treat musical works as initiated types already provides accommodation for the role of historical context. Mendelssohn's work is the initiated type: sound structure as indicated by Mendelssohn in 1826; the derivative work is a distinct initiated type.

Levinson argues, third, for the importance of the performance means, not simply sound structure, to the identity of a musical work. He proposes to accommodate this through the notion of a combination of two abstract structures—one a sound structure, the other a performance means structure. To hold that every musical work includes such a combined structure seems to accomplish more than what is intuitively wanted. What is wanted is that performance means may be part of the identity of a musical work, not that every musical work comes with a specification of performance means.

Although she does not offer a direct answer to the question "What sort of thing is a musical work?" Lydia Goehr (1992) has enriched the literature on the question of the ontology of musical works and needs to be considered here, at least briefly. Goehr argues, first, that the proposals of a number of writers, including those considered above, are flawed, and suggests that all possible analytic proposals are inadequate: "there is something hidden in the method that forecloses the possibility of accounting satisfactorily for musical works" (p. 69).

Goehr proposes, second, a description of the historical process by which the concept of a work emerged in classical music practice and an account of how the concept has functioned in that practice. Goehr argues that the work concept emerged as central and regulative in European musical practice only around 1800, serving to define the norms, expectations, and behavior that we now associate with classical music. Within musical practice since 1800, musical works are posited as existants: they are seen as things produced by composers, independent of performances and scores; indeed, most aspects of current musical practice enshrine this "projection" or "hypostatization" of musical works. To press the question of the real existence of musical works is finally fruitless, according to Goehr; it assumes that "a practice has a "real," underlying structure existing independently of a theory of it" (p. 107).

It is not surprising, given this historical approach, that there is no direct treatment of the question "What sort of thing is a musical work?" This is an account of the history of the concept musical work; to ask about the nature of the things, the works themselves, falling under that concept, is apparently to miss the point that the view that there are such things (the "hypostatization") is itself a moment in the history of the concept.

The methodological underpinnings of Goehr's work differ too drastically from those of the present writer to be engaged fruitfully here. If one does not accept this methodology, there would appear to be no convincing basis for Goehr's claim that analytic philosophy is in principle incapable of giving a satisfactory answer to the question of the ontology of musical works.

BIBLIOGRAPHY

Fine, Kit. "Language, Truth and Vagueness." *Synthese* 30 (1975): 265–300.

Goehr, Lydia. *The Imaginary Museum of Musical Works: An Essay in the Philosophy of Music.* Oxford, 1992.

Goodman, Nelson. *The Structure of Appearance.* 2d ed. Indianapolis, 1966.

Goodman, Nelson. *Languages of Art: An Approach to a Theory of Symbols* (1968). 2d ed. Indianapolis, 1976.

Levinson, Jerrold. "What a Musical Work Is." *Journal of Philosophy* 77.1 (January 1980): 5–28. Reprinted in *Music, Art and Metaphysics: Essays in Philosophical Aesthetics,* Ithaca, N.Y., 1990, pp. 63–88.

Levinson, Jerrold. "What a Musical Work Is, Again." In *Music, Art and Metaphysics: Essays in Philosophical Aesthetics,* pp. 215–263. Ithaca, N.Y., 1990.

Martin, Robert L. "Musical Works in the Worlds of Performers and Listeners." In *The Interpretation of Music: Philosophical Essays,* edited by Michael Krausz, pp. 119–127. Oxford, 1993.

Walton, Kendall. "The Presentation and Portrayal of Sound Patterns." In *Human Agency: Language, Duty, and Value: Philosophical Essays in Honor of J. O. Urmson,* edited by Jonathan Dancy et al., pp. 237–257. Stanford, Calif., 1988.

Wolterstorff, Nicholas. *Works and Worlds of Art.* Oxford, 1980.

ROBERT L. MARTIN

Ontology of Dance

The ontology of dance encompasses questions of the nature of existence of individual dances and of dance as a cultural phenomenon and a type of art. Inquiry into the ontological status of dance considers what dance consists of. Proposals have included the physical bodies of the dancers, moving in time and space, at a particular performance; the sum total of all bodies that have ever performed the dance; the choreographer's mental concept of the choreographic design; the written notation; the archival videotape; or the perceptions and thoughts of the audience, at a particular performance of the work or at all performances ever given of the work.

Ontological inquiry also addresses the identity of a work of art in dance. The identity of works is whatever it is that makes two performances the same work. The various accounts of ontological status do not dictate a particular theory of the identity of a work. A theory of identity could be consistent with several ontological proposals, and a given ontological proposal could be consistent with several theories for establishing identity.

Identity in dance is difficult for several reasons. The development of standardized notations has been recent and controversial; no one form of notation has been universally accepted. The use of the entire human body as the principal instrument of the art form results in wider variation in performance than in other performing arts. The history and practice of dance accept astonishing variation among performances of works without loss of identity. The art form has complex standards for identity that vary among different subgenres, such as nineteenth-century classical ballets and twentieth-century modern works. Dance also has shifted in this century from an art of performers to an art of choreographers, with an evolving sense of repertory.

Philosophers have explained the identity of choreographic works by appealing to notational systems, production histories, and cultural context. None of these approaches has been accepted as adequately accounting for the ways in which identity is actually determined by performers, choreographers, audiences, historians, and critics. Nor do these accounts explain the increasing reliance on notation to establish identity, the ways in which compliance with notation is determined, and the ways in which people in dance actually understand the identity of choreographic works.

Prominent among philosophers addressing the identity of choreographic works is Joseph Margolis, who explicitly considered the issue in 1959. He first proposed that identity in dance be understood on the type/token model developed for other art forms. He later stressed the inadequacy of notational systems to account for identity, claiming only that "dance scores are primarily heuristic devices for recovering a minimal sense of the principal positions and movements of a given dance" (Margolis, 1981).

Margolis denied that dance is allographic, as proposed by Nelson Goodman, because of the discrepancy between "the emphasis on visual recognition *tout court* in the notation and the requirements of actually generating dance movements in terms of the dynamics of motor activity controlled proprioceptively" (ibid.). Critics charged that Margolis confused the establishment of the identity of a work with the separate activity of learning how to produce the movements of a certain work or produce them in a particular way. Musical notation explains nothing about how to blow or strike a musical instrument, but that does not render musical notation "a mere heuristic device" (ibid.).

Critics also charged that Margolis confused identity with evaluation, as when he said: "There simply is no reliable correspondence between a dancer's performing a set of movements in accord with a mere notation and an audience's seizing the expressive qualities somehow conveyed by those movements." The former (performance in accord with a notation) could be all that is needed for identity of the work, while the latter could be a separate matter of good performance of the work. Margolis also denied the allographic character of dance because of the central role of uniquely expressive human bodies as instruments, which "cannot be satisfactorily represented by any extensional notation" (ibid). This seems to confuse identity of a work with the evaluation of an individual dancer's interpretation of a work. Margolis may be correct in insisting that "the dance cannot be appreciated without some sense of how movements are actually generated" (ibid.), but it does not necessarily follow that this knowledge is necessary to establish identity of a work.

For Goodman, the identity of dance works is determined solely by compliance with a notational system. Dance is not an autographic art form, in which "even the most exact duplication of it does not thereby count as genuine." In allographic arts, such as music and dance, there is no distinction between original and forgery. In his landmark *Languages of Art*, he said that "the function of a score is to specify the essential properties a performance must have to belong to the work. . . . All other variations are permitted; and the differences among performances of the same work, even in music, are enormous" (Goodman, 1976).

Goodman's critics charged that this does not explain how audiences actually make comparisons for the purpose of establishing identity either before the emergence of notation or now that standardized notations are available. This is a serious flaw, as performances rarely if ever conform in every notated detail to the score. Goodman's initial account seemed to say that one wrong note or step would mean loss of identity for the work, which seems preposterous in practice. As Goodman notes in discussing the prerequisites to a notational system, consistent judgments regarding identity of dance performances are already made independently of a notational system. Although he later denied that he was describing actual practice in either music or dance, he never indicated how such identifications are made independently of the history of production.

Useful accounts of how identity is established in practice by audiences, choreographers, and dancers have been developed by Adina Armelagos and Mary Sirridge. They insist that performances must be characterized in terms of the history of production to establish identity. But these characterizations might be nothing but convenient descriptions that could be restated in terms of perceivable differences in performances and that could be notated or fixed in a tangible medium. They do not acknowledge the importance of new ways of establishing identity with notation to supplement long-established habits of transmitting dances from dancer to dancer.

Armelagos and Sirridge claim that Goodman's proposals show the inadequacy of notational systems to provide the necessary and sufficient determinants for the identity of dance performances. They argue that Goodman's view is "too weak, as it fails to include alleged 'incidentals,'" such as music, costuming, and lighting. These "incidentals" do not, however, show the inadequacy of all notation, but only that multiple notation or other methods for the different media of dance might be needed.

Armelagos and Sirridge also argue that the history of production is often essential in determining identity, as the use of dancers trained in a certain movement style might be essential for the work to meet identity requirements. Even though the training history of dancers is admittedly a convenient shorthand for characterizing performances, it is not essential for establishing identity. Different training results in perceivable differences in performance that can be described in other ways, including notation. It might be easier to describe those differences by reference to training, but that does not prove that notation is inherently inadequate to establish identity. The claim that scores are not adequate for producing a work "if the style, its vocabulary, and its characteristic kinesthetic motivator and ideals are not antecedently known" is irrelevant, as the adequacy of a score depends on its usefulness for identification, not on how useful it is for producing a work.

Graham McFee explains identity by using the type/token distinction promoted by Richard Wollheim for art generally and proposed many years earlier by Margolis. McFee accepts an important role for notation, citing with approval the work of Goodman and insisting that a work must instantiate the notation in order to be that work. But McFee also speaks approvingly of the work of Armelagos and Sirridge, which rejects the possibility of establishing identity through notation.

Sympathetic to the important role notation has taken in dance, Selma Jeanne Cohen believes the concerns raised by Armelagos, Sirridge, and Margolis can be addressed with supplementary information from effort/shape analysis. This analytic technique was developed by Rudolf Laban, who also developed Labanotation, one of the most widely accepted forms of dance notation. Suzanne Youngerman also extols the capacity of Labanotation to capture not only notation of steps but also style and expressiveness.

The philosophical identity of dance presents several questions. What notation or fixation, if any, is necessary to establish identity, in view of the unusual characteristics and evolving circumstances of dance? How much and what sort of compliance with those notations, fixations, or other standards is needed to constitute identity of a work in practice? Who makes those determinations and how? Identity theory must include both a standard for identity, through notation (or other fixation), and a test or method for application of that standard.

To understand how identity is established in practice, it is useful to consider the infringement of copyrighted choreographic works, an increasingly important application of identity theory since 1978, when choreography first became explicitly eligible for protection under federal copyright law in the United States. In considering actual practices in the dance world, philosophers look at the actual talk and actions of critics, historians, observers, and experts of various sorts. Considerations of copyright infringement look at the actual talk and actions of litigants, choreographers, lawyers, and judges.

Copyright of choreography also has received heightened attention in Europe, especially in an age of rapid dissemination of dance through television, film, video, and the travel of dance companies. Copyright laws vary in accepted methods for documenting the identity of protected works, but share the challenge of understanding how to determine when infringement has occurred. The complexity of the identity of dance knows no national boundaries.

Copyright infringement under U.S. law relies on a notation or other fixation (such as videotape) to fix an absolute standard of identity during registration. The notation is in service to the jury's lay observer test of "substantial similarity" to measure degrees of compliance with that notation. The test of substantial similarity is whether an ordinary observer, perceiving two works, considers them to be substantially similar. If so, and if the other requirements for copyright are met, one work is an infringement of the other, protected, work. The jury of lay observers functions in the same way as the community of the art world, which, through its talk and its actions, ultimately arbitrates identity.

In copyright infringement, the analysis of similarity by experts, using notational analysis or any other methodology, is relevant and admissible, but it is not conclusive on the jury of lay observers. The notation and expert testimony about production history inform the decision of the jury, but never dictate it.

Similarly, the identity of choreographic works can be understood pragmatically as ways of talking and acting by the communities of the dance world. These ways of talking and acting are informed by notational systems, as well as production histories and cultural histories. The community determines what counts as sufficient compliance with the notation. The pragmatic approach explains how communities actually function in determining the identity of artworks. These communities include overlapping communities of audiences, performers, choreographers, critics, historians, theater managers, and funding agencies.

The dance-legal community determining copyright infringement is yet another specialized dance community. The community reaching agreement about identity in this legal context is the jury of lay observers. Notation informs the decision of the jury, but identity (substantial similarity) is ultimately a matter of decision or agreement of the jury, just as it is for any community. The jury functions as the "art-world community" for that particular controversy.

Ways of talking and acting include the myriad activities that go on every day in these overlapping art worlds. Ways of talking include discussions by audience members during intermission and after the performance; conversations among dancers and their coaches about how to perform a work; deliberations by review panels at grant-making agencies about funding proposals; and conference discussions of critics and historians about various works. Ways of acting include the buying of tickets to certain performances; the distribution of funds by a grant-making agency to fund certain programs; the act of researching and writing by historians, critics, and other writers about various works; and the hiring of certain coaches by a company director to stage a work.

This pragmatic approach recognizes the increasing availability and acceptability of notation in the choreographic community. It also provides a way to determine compliance with that notation, short of the strict compliance demanded in some philosophical work. This proposal is a recognition of the important role of the communities of the art world, who are the final arbiters of compliance with the notation.

[*See also* Dance.]

BIBLIOGRAPHY

Alter, Judith B. *Dance-Based Dance Theory.* New York, 1991.

Anderson, Jack. "Idealists, Materialists, and the Thirty Two Fouettes." *Ballet Review* 5.1 (1975): 13–21.

Armelagos, Adina, and Mary Sirridge. "The In's and Out's of Dance: Expression as an Aspect of Style." *Journal of Aesthetics and Art Criticism* 36.1 (Fall 1977): 15–24.

Armelagos, Adina, and Mary Sirridge. "The Identity Crisis in Dance." *Journal of Aesthetics and Art Criticism* 37.2 (Winter 1978): 129–139.

Armelagos, Adina, and Mary Sirridge. "The Role of 'Natural Expressiveness' in Explaining Dance." *Journal of Aesthetics and Art Criticism* 41.3 (Spring 1983): 301–307.

Cohen, Selma Jeanne. *Next Week, Swan Lake: Reflections on Dance and Dances.* Middletown, Conn., 1982.

Goodman, Nelson. *Languages of Art: An Approach to a Theory of Symbols.* 2d ed. Indianapolis, 1976.

Margolis, Joseph. "The Identity of a Work of Art." *Mind* 68 (1959): 34–50.

Margolis, Joseph. "The Autographic Nature of the Dance." *Journal of Aesthetics and Art Criticism* 39.4 (Summer 1981): 419–427.

McFee, Graham. *Understanding Dance.* New York and London, 1992.

Scobie, W. D. L. "Margolis on 'The Identity of a Work of Art'." *Mind* 69 (1960): 256–258.

Sheets-Johnstone, Maxine, ed. *Illuminating Dance: Philosophical Explorations.* Lewisburg, Pa., 1984.

Sparshott, Francis. *Off the Ground: First Steps to a Philosophical Consideration of the Dance.* Princeton, N.J., 1988.

Van Camp, Julie. "Copyright of Choreographic Works." In *Entertainment, Publishing and the Arts Handbook, 1994–95 Edition,* edited by John David Viera and Robert Thorne, pp. 59–92. New York, 1994.

JULIE VAN CAMP

OPERA. The status of opera as an artistic medium is problematic. The difficulty derives primarily from the combination of various elements—music, text, drama, dance, stage design—to form the experience of opera. Opera is often viewed as a musical genre, but it has also been thought of, mostly through Richard Wagner's conception of the total artwork *(Gesamtkunstwerk),* as the form of art par excellence, the synthesis of all artistic media.

It is commonly held that opera originated in an act of invention by a circle of theoreticians, the Florentine Camerata, in the late sixteenth century. The aesthetic rationale was to develop a musical form that would revive the power that music originally had in Greek tragedy, or that would best serve the dramatic purposes. The reference to the authority of the original Greek model, which was at any rate nonexistent, marked the new form with a peculiar sense of expectation about the power of such music as well as with a certain nostalgic dimension that opera has retained ever since.

Whether or not opera did owe its original impetus to this self-conscious invention or developed continuously out of other practices, such as musical *intermedi* between acts of drama, the art form that developed very soon went beyond its original conditions of existence. In particular, such questions as opera's relation to Greek tragedy, the priority of words over music, the locus of the drama, the nature of the operatic voice, and the relation to other arts recurred through periodic crises and reforms, showing both a sense of the uniqueness of this art form and the difficulty of coming to terms with it.

Conceiving of opera as an independent medium or form of art demands tracing questions and issues that opera returns to and reworks. The medium is determined by a problematic of inheritance of concerns that are specific to it. The inner law of development of the medium is not limited to formal or stylistic issues but is also shown in the way opera provides us with a conception of human subjectivity and existence. Opera embodies an autonomous inner dialectic that reflects and interacts in its own way with culture at large.

The Myth of Opera. The myth of Orpheus is the founding myth of opera. Through its elaboration opera returns to its origin and refashions its self-understanding. Claudio Monteverdi's *La Favola d'Orfeo* and Christoph Gluck's *Orfeo ed Euridice* are the most famous instances of the setting of the myth.

The myth tells of Orpheus's loss at Euridice's death, and how his grief transforms itself into enchanting music that tries to overcome death. Orpheus's lament gains him access to the other world, and his entreaty to revive Euridice is granted. The Orphic myth provides an understanding of the power of operatic song. It arises out of the knowledge of suffering that has to do with human separateness, finitude, and mortality. Song manifests itself as the capacity to revive, or to infuse a world of death with life. But the myth is as much about the success of song as about the inability to sustain this success. Orpheus is permitted to bring back Euridice into this world on the condition that he does not turn back and look at her. Ultimately, Orpheus fails, as he turns around and by doing so loses Euridice again. Orphic knowledge does not permanently win back Euridice; she is resurrected for a fleeting moment, showing the inability to sustain the ecstatic power of song. Singing is essentially ephemeral; it reveals a world colored by transience. The temptation to slip back into conventional ways of experiencing the world is figured in the myth by a need for the gaze. This establishes one of the central tensions of opera as that between the auditory and the visual.

Words and Music. The relationship between text and music is often thought of as determining the development of opera as an oscillation, or pendulum movement, between the two poles of the primacy of words and the primacy of music: "prima la parola, prima la musica." This can also be thought of as the contrast between music and the dramatic element, where drama would include text and the whole visual world of the stage. Such delimitations are fluid and subject to reinterpretation as when music is considered the true locus of drama.

Opera originally defines itself in contrast to Renaissance principles of music composition, and the text-music relationship. There, what seemed to hinder the stirring of emotion was the unintelligibility of the meaning of the words, due to the several texts heard simultaneously, contrapuntally covering each other. The attempt to make the text intelligible led to the development of monody, the initial expression of opera. It is a form of intensified speech or of declamatory song that can be thought of equally as a new musical vehicle as well as a new rhetorical device. Later on, a division was established between recitative, whose function was essentially to advance the plot, and aria, in which the more reflective or emotional text called for intensified musical expression.

Jean-Jacques Rousseau's thinking on opera establishes a new model for the relationship of text and music insofar as it is embedded in a broader philosophical reevaluation of the conditions of language as such. Language itself is seen to be originally passionate utterance akin to singing. The various forms opera took were seen either as attempts to recover this original unity, or as further degeneration of language. This contrast was often conceived by Rousseau in terms of the difference between Italian opera, whose essence was melodic, and French opera, whose essence was harmonic. The decline of language shows itself in that opera cannot treat any more of ordinary human life, but must turn to the supernatural and the marvelous in order to create an effect of amazement. Rousseau, the only philosopher to have composed an opera, places his *Le Devin du Village* in a domestic setting and makes a point of problematizing the need for spectacles as well as the power of artifice and the supposed supernatural powers of the soothsayer.

Friedrich Nietzsche's *Birth of Tragedy Out of the Spirit of Music,* which he dedicated to Richard Wagner, expresses an ambivalence about the phenomenon of opera. Opera indeed originates in the privileging of text over music, and in its invention reflects perfectly what Nietzsche calls Socratic culture, but it comes into its own in the works of Wagner as an art form that is made possible by the opening of a new tragic era, which means essentially the resurgence of the priority of the musical, associated by Nietzsche with the Dionysian.

According to Nietzsche, Wagner has recognized a state of distress in modern culture that manifests itself as a sickness of language. Humankind is perceived as suffering from convention. Language becomes a power in its own right, whose exchange does not reflect the existence of a common culture. In *Der Ring des Nibelungen* Wagner provides music

with the role of reminding us of the original, all but forgotten condition of culture. Wagner's idea of the total artwork not only relates the various arts but also finds their inner relations to reflect the state of culture or the human spirit at that crossroad of history. Nietzsche found himself later on, in *The Case of Wagner,* to have overcome Wagner, in whose work he saw the most concentrated symptom of the modern mind. What he perceived as the overtheatrical nature of Wagner's operas—the striving for effect and the mise-en-scène, on the one hand, and the intoxication brought by the music, on the other—did not seem to Nietzsche anymore to embody the precarious alliance of the Dionysian and the Apollonian. Nietzsche's perception of the essentially redemptive form of Wagnerian opera further contributed to his estrangement from Wagner. Georges Bizet's "Mediterranization" of music in *Carmen* offered Nietzsche a different form of cheerfulness in the face of fate.

The very possibility of opera became an explicit topic for twentieth-century opera. It often reflects on the problematic of text and music, as well as on the future or possibility of development after the Wagnerian closure of opera. A prominent example is Arnold Schoenberg's *Moses und Aron.* The very characters and their form of expression, Moses' stuttering and Aaron's eloquence, express the fundamental tension of words and music. The form of a sacred work as well as the fragmentary nature of the work further reflect the problematic condition of the possibility of opera in a modern world. New options and problems concerning the relation of text, music, and drama are raised by the productions of traditional operas in contemporary settings, such as Peter Sellars's production of Wolfgang Amadeus Mozart's and Lorenzo Da Ponte's operas and Jonathan Miller's production of Giuseppe Verdi's *Rigoletto.*

Singing-Speaking. Opera seems unrealistic, or unnatural. It does not promote the illusion of mimetic realism. The singing in opera is on the face of it different from the speaking that takes place in real life. But, what is the nature of the operatic utterance? Operatic singing can be understood as a substitute for speech, or, alternatively, the character can be said to know it is singing, to mean to be singing.

Edward T. Cone argues that one cannot sustain the distinction between realistic singing (where the character really means to sing) and operatic singing (where singing takes place because of the condition of opera as such). Cone proposes to think of the character as the creator of its song, as one who composes its own music and thus as an Orphic figure. According to him, the character usually can also be said to hear its accompaniment. This is the case, for instance, in Salome's dance of the seven veils in Richard Strauss's *Salome.* Nevertheless, sometimes the accompaniment provides a commentary that goes beyond the character's conscious understanding as, for example, is the case with Wagnerian orchestration.

Peter Kivy aims at reducing the gap that Cone opens between the operatic and our ordinary ways of relating to the world. He argues that all instances of ordinary discourse are to some degree creative responses to novel situations. There is a continuum between speakers, improvisatory poets, improvisatory singers, composers, and the strange world of opera. The orchestral accompaniment then expresses the characters' gestures and bodily movements.

Stanley Cavell denies that singing in opera is a convention of the medium and should be viewed as standing in for speech. It is rather a condition of the medium as such, meaning that the fact of singing marks features of the operatic world and the human subject as it appears in opera. He recognizes the force of the idea that the character's singing is expressive of its essential being, but he does not want to interpret that through Cone's active idea of composition. Rather, song is the sign that opera is concerned with the vicissitudes of the human voice, with the possibility of gaining a voice for oneself as well as losing it, or being silenced by others. The voice raised in song shows the self's capacity for transformation, or, shows opera to partake in what Cavell calls the moral perfectionist conversation in Western culture.

Cavell finds it significant that opera originates together with the new understanding of the subject in the philosophy of René Descartes. Specifically, opera responds to the rise of modern skepticism. Operas are saturated with such issues as the suffocation of speech, and the stifling of voice and their relation to the withdrawal of the world and the division of the self, which are the preoccupation of philosophy in the advent of skepticism.

Voice. The attraction of the voice created one of the understandings of the essence of the operatic as such: the bel canto (Italian for "beautiful singing"). What was celebrated by composers such as Johann Hasse and Vincenzo Bellini in bel canto opera was the infinite flexibility, capacity for improvisation and virtuosity, nuance, and variety of the human voice. Bel canto signified the evocation of a sense of wonder through unusual quality of timbre, vocal display, and lyricism. The privileging of the voice implied the rejection of realism and naturalism in the plots and characters, and the creation of a mythical or fantastic world apart from human reality, whose inhabitants can show themselves through their rare and stylized voices. This accounts also for the suitability of bel canto to mad scenes, where the voice is further freed from the constraints of intelligibility and allowed the excess of coloratura and virtuosity.

The understanding of bel canto cannot be separated from the historical phenomenon of castrati in opera (boys who were castrated so as to retain a soprano register, which was especially effective in combination with the force and volume of a mature male body). It was in no way a substitute for a female voice but was unique in itself. What made the voice of the castrato attractive was its strangeness and ambiguity. The castrato's singing called attention to the voice as such, showing it to be akin to a musical instrument, thus creating a sense of the peculiar artificiality of human constitution and gendering. The cult of the prima donna came to replace castrati, and with it came a shift in plots that provided the female soprano with the central role. Nevertheless, the possibility of gender transcendence that was opened by the castrati roles remained part of the experience of bel canto opera. Recently, it has brought opera into the center of contemporary gay and lesbian criticism, two prominent examples being Wayne Koestenbaum's *The Queen's Throat* and Hélène Cixous's reading of Gioacchino Rossini's *Tancredi*.

Operatic reforms often followed the sense that opera turned into vocal display. Singers took over and used the performance primarily to display their virtuosity and the beauty of their voice. This has been viewed negatively for the most part and prompted reforms such as Gluck's that returned the total musicodramatic context to the forefront. The introduction of realism into nineteenth-century Italian opera meant the disappearance of bel canto. Such opera distanced itself from the plots and themes characteristic of bel canto, as well as from the allegorical and stylized portrayal of emotion. There was a striving for veracity that manifested itself in the intense and direct expression of the emotional undercurrents that are most of the time hidden from our perception of reality. Verdi's operas can be thought of as paradigmatic of this intensification of expression. As opposed to the smoothness *(legato)* and apparent lack of effort that characterized bel canto singing, the later Verdi uses the capacity of the voice to be stretched to the extreme, widening the range and intensity of vocal expression. In an opera such as Verdi's *Otello,* the voice is always on the verge of outburst.

Michel Poizat sees in opera the exclusive vicissitudes of voice. Plot or character delineation functions to highlight the supreme value of voice. The understanding of voice in Poizat draws on Jacques Lacan's elaboration of the condition of human articulation of desire in language as governed by the drive to recover an always already lost object (Mother, Woman, *jouissance*). Poizat's underlying supposition is that opera is the endless and painful quest for the original Object. The pleasure in opera is the result of an illusory structure that brings one into the proximity of the original *jouissance* as the voice turns into a cry without signification. It is an ecstatic pleasure in forgetting the fundamental attachments of desire to language.

Operatic Plots. The most famous philosophical reflection on an opera is no doubt Søren Kierkegaard's interpretation of Mozart's *Don Giovanni* in *Either/Or.* Kierkegaard chooses that opera to exemplify his understanding of the extreme form of the aesthetic life. In *Don Giovanni* we find a perfect match between character and the conditions of the operatic medium. Don Giovanni's power is identified with the power of music and its seductiveness. He is particularly suited for this identification insofar as he is not portrayed as a psychological character but rather as the embodiment of sheer desire. He is a life force partaking of the demonic rather than a specific human being. Don Giovanni is a musical character: he seduces not with the power of language but rather through the force and immediacy of his sensuous desire. This separation of Don Giovanni from the realm of language and articulation, represented through his inability to give his word, is what separates him from the ethical dimension.

Ivan Nagel views opera as the reflection of the engendering of the modern political subject. He views all expression in opera seria as arising from two fundamental gestures, both explicit in the myth of Orpheus: entreaty and mercy. These reflect the condition of existence of the subject under absolute sovereign authority. Opera buffa provides a model for a conversation of equality and for the appearance of the autonomous subject. Thus opera seria always involves hierarchy and its ending always involves mercy, whereas opera buffa's most fundamental ending is the condition of equality of marriage. It is in Mozart's operas that the complexities of that transformation and its various tensions and paradoxes are most strongly portrayed. *Idomeneo* and *La Clemenza di Tito* are his central examples of opera seria, and *Le Nozze di Figaro* of opera buffa.

Slavoj Žižek, following Nagel's line of thought, views Wagner's opera as a further stage in the enfolding of the medium's reflection on the subject. In particular, Wagner's *Parsifal* exemplifies the transition from a Kantian autonomous view of the subject to a Lacanian subject characterized by its nonessentiality, by a gap that is covered up by the same movement that opens it.

Catherine Clément argues that the pleasure in canonic operatic plot derives from the perpetual undoing of its heroines. Bizet's *Carmen*, Giacomo Puccini's *Madame Butterfly*, and Claude Debussy's *Pelléas et Mélisande* are but a few of the examples of such plots of undoing. The genre demands the heroine's death to bring the narrative to its end. Not hearing and not understanding the words, as is commonplace in the experience of opera, is precisely what sustains the pleasure in the victimization of women. The fact that the death is accompanied by the most beautiful music in the opera makes one further forget the plot that prepares for and executes this death.

Carolyn Abbate develops an understanding of voice in opera that stands in contrast to obvious character delineation and narrative plots. Voice for Abbate means a gesture in music that may be perceived as modes of subjects' enunciations. These gestures in the music have the power to subvert the plot. Voice, and the musical gestures that enfold the voice, is a realm beyond narrative plot.

From early on, opera has been the target of attacks. These have included charges that it is unnatural, boring, exotic, ridiculous, overstylized, and too conventional. The extravagance of emotion, the sense of excess of the drama that is associated with operatic narratives often led to a dismissal, or to various parodies and pastiches. The Marx brothers' involvement in a production of *Il Trovatore* in *A Night at the Opera* is probably the most famous instance of this parodying.

Theodor Adorno viewed opera as a bourgeois form of art. The disguises, costumes, and artifice are essential to the social function of opera. According to Adorno, opera is Orphic, but for him this means that it creates an illusion of enchantment or endeavors to preserve a magical dimension, an essentially auratic character, in the midst of a disenchanted world. The fixed repertoire of opera houses since the early twentieth century shows, according to Adorno, that opera can no longer cover up the tensions that formed it; it exists more as a sociological phenomenon than as a living art form. Adorno, thinking primarily of Alban Berg's achievement, in such works as *Wozzeck* and *Lulu*, nevertheless leaves open the possibility of a future for opera that would give prominence to reconciliation rather than a mythologization that hides society's alienation from nature.

[*See also* Cavell; Music, *historical overview article; and* Wagner.]

BIBLIOGRAPHY

Abbate, Carolyn. *Unsung Voices: Opera and Musical Narrative in the Nineteenth Century.* Princeton, N.J., 1991.

Adorno, Theodor. "Bourgeois Opera." In *Opera through Other Eyes*, edited by David Levin, pp. 25–44. Stanford, Calif., 1994.

Cavell, Stanley. "Opera and the Lease of Voice." In *A Pitch of Philosophy: Autobiographical Exercises*, pp. 129–170. Cambridge, Mass., 1994.

Cixous, Hélène. "Tancredi Continues." In *En Travesti: Women, Gender Subversion, Opera*, edited by Corinne Blackmer and Patricia Juliana Smith, pp. 152–168. New York, 1995.

Clément, Catherine. *Opera: or, The Undoing of Women* (1979). Translated by Betsy Wing. Minneapolis, 1988.

Cone, Edward T. "The World of Opera and Its Inhabitants." In *Music: A View from Delft*, edited by Robert Morgan, pp. 125–138. Chicago, 1989.

Dahlhaus, Carl. *Esthetics of Music.* Translated by William W. Austin. Cambridge and New York, 1983.

Kerman, Joseph. *Opera as Drama* (1956). New rev. ed. Berkeley, 1988.

Kierkegaard, Søren. *Either/Or.* 2 vols. Translated by David F. Swenson and Lillian Marvin Swenson. Princeton, N.J., 1944.

Kivy, Peter. "Opera Talk: A Philosophical 'Phantasie.'" In *The Fine Art of Repetition: Essays in the Philosophy of Music*, pp. 137–159. Cambridge and New York, 1993.

Koestenbaum, Wayne. *The Queen's Throat: Opera, Homosexuality, and the Mystery of Desire.* New York, 1993.

Nagel, Ivan. *Autonomy and Mercy: Reflections on Mozart's Operas.* Translated by Marion Faber and Ivan Nagel. Cambridge, Mass., 1991.

Nietzsche, Friedrich. *The Birth of Tragedy and The Case of Wagner.* Translated by Walter Kaufmann. New York, 1967.

Poizat, Michel. *The Angel's Cry: Beyond the Pleasure Principle in Opera.* Translated by Arthur Denner. Ithaca, N.Y., 1992.

Rousseau, Jean-Jacques. "Essay on the Origin of Languages." In Jean-Jacques Rousseau and Johann Gottfried Herder, *Two Essays on the Origin of Language,* translated by John H. Moran and Alexander Gode (1966). Chicago, 1986.

Wagner, Richard. *Wagner on Music and Drama: A Compendium of Richard Wagner's Prose Works.* Selected and arranged by Albert Goldman and Evert Sprinchorn, translated by H. Ashton Ellis. New York, 1964.

Žižek, Slavoj. "'The Wound Is Healed Only by the Spear That Smote You': The Operatic Subject and Its Vicissitudes." In *Opera through Other Eyes,* edited by David Levin, pp. 177–214. Stanford, Calif., 1994.

MICHAL GROVER FRIEDLANDER and
ELI FRIEDLANDER

ORIENTALISM. In encyclopedias of art, one searches in vain for the term *Orientalism,* although the "Oriental component" in Western taste or the "Orientalizing style" are common references. Descriptions of Orientalizing style center specifically on Eastern influences in Antiquity on objects and architectural styles in Mediterranean countries (which will not be considered here); those tracing the Oriental component in Western taste mostly do so in terms of periodization, region of origin, and particular themes or imagery. Both can be considered as part of a history of cross-cultural representations in texts and imagery produced in the West using Oriental(izing) elements.

This is a one-sided history, however. It is a history that traces, for example, Rembrandt van Rijn's interest in Mughal miniatures or the ways in which Antoine Galland's compilation and translation into French of the *Arabian Nights* (1704) exerted an extraordinary influence on novels, plays, and painting from the day of its publication. Numerous are the paintings depicting visits of embassies from Siam or the Ottoman Empire that displayed a marked interest in the costumes of the foreign dignitaries. Novels such as Baron de Montesquieu's *Persian Letters* (1721) described two Persian men struggling to understand life in Paris in the early eighteenth century, simultaneously attempting to maintain a hold on insubordinate women in their harem in Persia. Specific themes related to the Orient were very popular in Western representations, such as that of the despot, harem women, and eunuchs serving to guard the latter. Wolfgang Amadeus Mozart's opera *Die Entführung aus dem Serail (Abduction from the Seraglio,* 1782) is a good example of how these themes, in a comical sense, find their way into a repertory of representation.

Tracing a history of the Oriental components in Western taste, one finds a continuing fascination with non-European others, foregrounding their exoticism. Exoticism and representations of the Oriental other had both phantasmic overtones and aims to reflect a reality. In comparison to the eighteenth century, more men and women traveled to the Orient in the nineteenth and twentieth centuries. The list of authors and painters visiting Constantinople, Palestine, Egypt, or Algeria is long, and their names are well known. Yet, Gustave Flaubert, Richard F. Burton, John Frederick Lewis, Gérard de Nerval, Eugène Delacroix, or Henri Matisse can hardly be credited with representing the truth of the Orient. Travelogues, in offering accounts of life in the Orient, claimed a truth-value for their depictions, while simultaneously stimulating the appetite for fantasy about the Oriental other. The double strand of fantasy and epistemological enterprise continued to mark visual and textual representations of the Orient into the nineteenth and twentieth centuries.

Generally speaking, the Oriental component in Western taste was popular, yet this popularity did not necessarily accord with established literary or art-historical hierarchies in aesthetic appreciation. Whereas in the eyes of contemporary art critics, for instance, history paintings would elevate and educate the public, the popular Orientalist genre paintings lacked this quality.

Commonly, in histories of Oriental components in Western taste, a rift divides the nineteenth century from the eighteenth and earlier centuries. The latter are characterized by their love for Oriental elements, exotic, eclectically chosen and decorative in function. The playful and ornamental qualities, proliferating in the eighteenth century in particular, precluded exactitude in representing the Orient. According to these approaches, the nineteenth century, in contrast, showed a desire to describe and depict the Orient truthfully. Such a neat division between exoticism and claims for a "truth" about the Orient tells us more about the desire to label and categorize periods in Western history than it does about the dynamics of a continuous Western will to dominate the Orient.

Edward W. Said's *Orientalism* (1978) revealed the powerful ideological fabric of Orientalism underlying a seemingly apolitical structure of relations between the West and the Orient. *Orientalism* has subsequently had a major impact on the study of the Orient—extending beyond its geographically and historically specific meanings—in directing the focus on issues of power, knowledge, ideology, and culture. His work on Orientalism has led to fruitful analyses in the fields of cultural studies and aesthetics, combining the politics of culture and cross-cultural politics.

Said uses the term Orientalism in three interrelated and interdependent meanings. The first meaning is an academic one, designating "anyone who teaches, writes about, or researches the Orient" as doing Orientalism. In a more general sense, the second meaning pertains to "a style of thought based upon an ontological and epistemological distinction made between 'the Orient' and (most of the time) 'the Occident'." The third meaning is framed more historically, taking the late eighteenth century as point of departure, in which Orientalism is defined "as a Western style for dominating, restructuring, and having authority over the

Orient" (pp. 2–3). Said argues that Orientalism is a discourse in the Foucauldian sense, best understood as a system of possibility for knowledge. Crucial in Said's understanding is the assertion that the Occident possessed the power to represent the Orient. This structure of power did not permit the Orient a reciprocal capacity to represent the Occident. The production of knowledge about the Orient functioned as a concomitant factor in the representational power of Orientalism. Classificatory mechanisms, systematizing languages, religions, peoples, and so on were employed to continue and reinforce the indelible otherness of the Orient, an otherness that was characterized in terms of gender, sexuality, and ethnicity. In *Culture and Imperialism* (1993), Said stresses the role of cultural products such as novels, music, and imagery in Europe's overseas expansion, creating structures of feeling that support, elaborate, and consolidate the practice of empire.

In this discourse of Orientalism, the power/knowledge nexus works to reinforce inequalities frequently expressed in essentialist terms, in which the West most "naturally" assumes a dominant position over an Orient that it thinks is unable to know or represent itself, let alone rule itself. Western imaginings of the Orient and their acquisition of knowledge about it focused on the reality of inherent character traits connected to the Orient. In Said's interpretation, Orientalism thus operates on various levels, pertaining to the political, social, economic, and cultural domains.

Said's study of Orientalism provided a framework for the analysis of cross-cultural representations, explicitly pointing to the political, ideological, and historical contexts in which they functioned. Aesthetics was not denied its place, but was connected to the colonizing impulse of the West. Western literary and academic knowledge could not maintain its seemingly impartial status, and was shown to be complicit with the history of European colonialism. As a result of Said's work, textual and visual representations came to be studied not in terms of whether they represented the reality of the Orient, but rather in terms of how representational practices assigned specific characteristics to the Orient.

Although Said pays scant attention in *Orientalism* to visual materials, the work served as a source of inspiration for art historians and cultural critics to reconsider Orientalist painting, early colonial photography, postcards, and illustrated travelogues. Genre, then, is no longer a means to value one textual or visual tradition over another. High- or low-art forms were both implicated in the dominant regime of Orientalist representation. New questions concerning the particular representational practices of Orientalism developed, addressing who or what is present in paintings or photographs and what or who is absent. More often than not, Westerners were absent, although it was through their perspective that Orientalist visual representations came into being. The Orient itself was depicted as a timeless space, without history, unaffected by industrialization and moder-

nity. In Orientalist texts as well as imagery, stereotyped figures such as the despot, the odalisque, and the eunuch, as part of the Orient as a highly eroticized space, could now be analyzed in relation to a Western nineteenth-century history, in which anxiety about sexuality and gender relations was at play. Displacing those anxieties onto the Orient, the West produced a mirror image of its own desires and fantasies.

Another issue, only obliquely addressed in *Orientalism*, yet related to the depiction of the Orient as an eroticized space, is that of gender. Women were prominent in Orientalist representations, as in Dominique Ingres's *Turkish Bath*, for example, and numerous travelogues would routinely include a description of the harem and the position of women under Islam. Stereotyped twice over, as inhabitants of the Orient and as female, women were the focus for the Western desire to penetrate their inaccessibility. Moreover, gendered notions of the Orient as a feminine space were preeminent in Orientalist representations and served as justification for Western domination. Thus, gender and power are mutually implicated in the cross-cultural representations of the West and the Orient. The vital connections between culture, politics, and gender have become foregrounded through the study of Orientalism as a discourse.

Said's *Orientalism* stimulated a host of publications that paid specific attention to culture and politics, expanding to regions beyond those covered in his work. It will be clear that aesthetics, previously perceived as a relatively separate area of study dealing, for instance, with questions of value, beauty, and appreciation, has become part of a complex set of questions in which its ideological investments are explicitly linked to a politics of culture. If the history of tracing the Oriental components in Western taste was one-sided, it was because it ignored these important insights. In the emerging field of cultural studies, analyses of colonial discourse and the postcolonial condition took a leading role in debates concerning issues of power and how to theorize the relation between colonizer and colonized.

The attraction and problem of *Orientalism* are its seeming all-inclusiveness, leading some cultural critics to equate Orientalism with colonialism. Others have pointed to the specific histories of colonization in different parts of the world that cannot all be gathered under the heading of Orientalism. *Orientalism* has met with various critiques, one of which is the argument that Said has maintained a pervasive dualism in this work: a dualism between the West and the Orient, between colonizer and colonized, between those representing and those being represented. Possible solutions for overcoming or modifying these oppositions suggest different directions in which research on Orientalism might develop. On the one hand, developments have taken the direction of questioning the emphasis on differences and on the hostility inherent in the cross-cultural encounter. Therefore, in these approaches, one insists on the existence of sympathizing gestures from the West, on its true interest in the Orient, and on representations, textual and otherwise, which are neither essentialist nor pejorative. On the other hand, there is a development toward critiquing the two sides of the dualism invoked by Said. The West itself is too much of a homogeneous category that is thus in need of specification. Moreover, Orientalism then becomes a blanket term, whereas, in fact, it is a heterogeneous phenomenon. The other side of the dualism—the Orient—is approached fruitfully by various cultural critics by addressing the question of agency. In Said's analysis of Orientalism, the colonized are silenced and do not have or develop forms of counterdiscourse to that of the colonizers. With the theorization and critical elaboration of notions such as mimicry, ambivalence, hybridity, and the subaltern, the power of the colonizer is shown not to be complete. Some of these notions, such as hybridity and the subaltern, imply and enact active forms of resistance on the part of the colonized; others, such as mimicry and ambivalence, do so more through the effects they produce in both stabilizing and destabilizing the colonizer.

In conclusion, Said has outlined a set of issues showing the vital links between textual and visual representational practices, cross-cultural politics, and the politics of culture that had previously escaped scrutiny. We can state that *Orientalism,* and the debates surrounding it, has effectively challenged and changed the study of the Orient, colonial discourse, and postcolonial studies in general.

[*See also* Politics and Aesthetics; *and* Postcolonialism.]

BIBLIOGRAPHY

Alloula, Malek. *The Colonial Harem.* Translated by Myrna Godzich and Wlad Godzich. Minneapolis, 1986. Originally published as *Le harem colonial: Images d'un sous-érotisme* (Genèva, 1981).

Bhabha, Homi. *The Location of Culture.* London and New York, 1994.

Boer, Inge E. *Rereadings and Revisions: Gender in French Representations of the Orient.* Stanford, Calif., 1998.

Boppe, Auguste. *Les peintres du Bosphore au XVIIIe siècle* (1913). 2d rev. enl. ed. Courbevoie, 1989.

Dufrenoy, Marie-Louise. *L'Orient romanesque en France, 1704–1789.* Montreal, 1946–1975.

Graham-Brown, Sarah. *Images of Women: The Portrayal of Women in Photography of the Middle East, 1860–1950.* New York, 1988.

Kabbani, Rana. *Europe's Myths of Orient.* Bloomington, Ind., 1986.

Lewis, Reina. *Gendering Orientalism: Race, Femininity, and Representation.* London and New York, 1996.

MacKenzie, John M. *Orientalism: History, Theory and the Arts.* Manchester and New York, 1995.

Nochlin, Linda. "The Imaginary Orient." In *The Politics of Vision: Essays on Nineteenth-Century Art and Society,* pp. 33–60. New York, 1989.

Said, Edward W. *Orientalism.* New York, 1978.

Said, Edward W. *Culture and Imperialism.* New York, 1993.

Schwab, Raymond. *The Oriental Renaissance: Europe's Discovery of India and the East, 1680–1880.* Translated by Gene Patterson-Black and Victor Reinking. New York, 1984. Originally published as *La Renaissance orientale* (Paris, 1950).

Sharafuddin, Mohammed. *Islam and Romantic Orientalism: Literary Encounters with the Orient.* London and New York, 1994.

Spivak, Gayatri Chakravorty. *In Other Worlds: Essays in Cultural Politics.* New York and London, 1988.

Thornton, Lynne. *La femme dans la peinture orientaliste.* Courbevoie, 1985.

Young, Robert. *White Mythologies: Writing History and the West.* London and New York, 1990.

Inge Boer

ORIGINALITY. [*To analyze the concept of the originality of either the work of art or the artist, this entry comprises two essays:*

Originality in the Visual Arts
Originality in Literature

These essays explain how originality has been understood in both different and similar ways in the particular fields of literature and the visual arts; they also address contemporary critiques of originality. For related discussion, see Appropriation; Artist; Creativity; Genius; Intention; Law and Art; Postmodernism; *and* Romanticism.]

Originality in the Visual Arts

Original artists are "sons of no one," declared art critic Théophile Thoré in 1846; they proceed from their own "innateness." Thoré, a champion of modern democratic values, believed that universal self-regulation was the ultimate political good. Individuals might manifest such autonomy by interacting freely and asserting their idiosyncrasies in socially responsible ways; for artists, it was enough to be "original." Given a democratic, individualist orientation, what could be more natural? To be original would amount to being oneself and expressing one's innermost identity. Yet, because social beings communicate through inherited, shared languages (whether verbal or pictorial), representation of the unique identity each person presumably possesses is not to be achieved readily. The available means of expression threaten to mask the individual's originality, not only from others but from that very person.

How, then, is the origin of autonomous selfhood to be found? Perhaps operative principles of self-regulation and identification can be derived only from the collective language, never the individual person; this becomes but one of a number of realizations under which the principle of autonomy presents a social paradox. Such thoughts nagged at Thoré and other nineteenth-century modernists, whereas twentieth-century postmodernists accept them as truisms. The difference neither constitutes intellectual progress nor proves the triumph of nihilism, but is an overdetermined instance of a cultural shift. In exploring the issue of originality, it is important to note this shift along with certain others.

For Thoré and those engaged with social changes linked to conditions of early modernity, originality connoted genetic uniqueness (individuality at the end of an evolutionary process of progressive organic and social differentiation). Yet, this concept retained an older—original?—connotation of chronological uniqueness (the singular point of origin, the beginning of that same evolution). To be sure, originality has always suggested a coming first or doing first, some absolute priority; and in this sense it relates to issues of historical sequence as well as ontological essence. As if to answer ultimate questions of origin, originality, and precedence, Plato imagined a creator or prime mover who gave form to matter, instituting motion, time, and history itself. Saint Augustine provided a more economical account, with an immaterial Judeo-Christian God creating everything from nothing.

Jump forward. The modern world adds its complex social order to these pagan and early Christian considerations of history and ontology. The social and political forces of modernity create the now familiar distinction between classicism and Romanticism, with each perspective maintaining its particular sense of originality. The differences appear in contested issues of class, social priority, and lineage: just as one can inaugurate, inherit, or be introduced into a social rank and order of property, one can also be identified with an artistic style and tradition as another kind of privileged possession. If artists must rely on a language or medium, something shaped by predecessors who have already established the patterns of its use, then perhaps originality becomes analogous to membership in the highest social class, the status of which is both passively transmitted (by inheritance) and actively transferred (by authorization). Like a patrician, the artist becomes inheritor and bearer of original first principles, a set of primordial truths. He or she—the gender can vary just as the actual medium can—plays the role of creator, preserving the values of the first Creation in the form of preferred themes and authorized styles and practices. This is the essence of the classical position. There is, of course, another possibility: perhaps originality is manifested only when one alters existing directions or forces. In this instance, an artist becomes not the bearer of tradition but its countercultural deviator, that is, a social deviant or revolutionary. This Romantic scheme of deviance (innovation) opposes the classical scheme of transmission and transference (preservation).

It seems that the question of originality has answers, but they vary and conflict according to the social or political position with which they are identified. Originality is subject to the same irony that characterizes other formidable cultural constructs: because different social and political systems prevail in different eras, any particular cultural value, such as originality, appears to lack its own essence or fixed center, having instead an irregular history. As history moves on, what once might have seemed necessity appears to have been belief or fashion—a custom associated with a particular era, location, or social body, rather than an innate, eternal tendency. So, as well as asking what might be the moment of origin (divine or human) for a particular practice

or tradition, we can ask what might be the originating conditions or motivation for any given sense of originality. Just as there is no single correct solution to the political problems associated with inheritance and property, so there is no single answer to the theoretical problem of originality. Investigating it, we distinguish a "modern" or Romantic attitude from its "classical" counterpart, and perhaps also a "postmodern" variant. Such categories have historical foundation in a series of shifts from aristocratic or court culture with its relatively small units of authority and organization, to bourgeois culture with its industrial, urban economy, to mass culture with its postindustrial economy and global consumerism. Despite the apparent logic of this set of changes (from greater to lesser articulation or differentiation of social units), they do not correspond to a natural evolution with a definitive chronological sequence. The modern need not follow from the classical, nor, when it does, is the classical forever superseded; expressions of the classical position can be found in the modern and postmodern present.

The question of originality becomes a matter of what people at a given time believe, why they believe it, and how they express their belief. If it is apparent that Western culture shifted during the early nineteenth century from a predominantly classical attitude to a predominantly modern one, perhaps this is only because European Romantics proclaimed such a momentous event; they arrogated originality as their own and conceived themselves as the sole true moderns, forever beginning anew with their varied experiences. Given their stress on change, growth, and diversity, Romantics regarded classicism as a thing of the past because of its normalizing values and collective identity. As the bearer of order and hierarchy, classicism regularized and restrained, interfering with two forces that contributed to modernity and its particular form of originality: the private citizen's free movement and personal growth, open to the vicissitudes of individual experience; and the expansive social evolution fostered by an emerging industrial economy. Seen from a different angle, classicism promoted a sense of community and the spiritual harmony so difficult to maintain in the wake of modernity's social upheaval. In this respect, the loss of classicism was mourned as much as it was celebrated during the nineteenth century. It may be that this ambivalence, more than any inherent conservatism or inertia, is responsible for the somewhat paradoxical preservation of classical values within a definitively modern social order.

As a product of early modernism, Thoré's critical evaluation of the history of Western art (to return to this telling example) was appropriately complicated. He regarded classical Renaissance culture as an artificial *rebirth* (a seconding) of the ancient artists' faded originality, to be contrasted with the inspired natural *birth* (a first) of medieval culture; the medieval artist "imitated no one, and created everything spontaneously." Yet, many Renaissance masters "dared to paint what they saw," returning "naively to nature," a primordial and enduring origin ever available to the individual observer. Views of nature could be as liberating as the visions of a medieval artist's imagination. The final effect of the full range of Renaissance eclecticism—the use of models from both ancient art and newer masters, from both pagan and Judeo-Christian sources, and from nature as well—was to restore human culture to its original "universality." Given Thoré's reasoning, social harmony and individual well-being could derive, by somewhat different channels, from both medieval birth and Renaissance rebirth.

Nevertheless, because the practices of Renaissance or classical revival were codified and rigidified during the post-Renaissance era, Thoré joined other champions of modernity in regarding his latecoming classicist contemporaries as "academic." The term suggested an artistic order founded on rote learning and stereotype rather than expressive idiosyncrasy and diversity; it also alluded to the professional recognition (prizes, commissions) offered by institutions such as state academies of fine arts, which, consciously or not, promoted standardization, ranking, and a kind of subservience. So, when certain nineteenth-century critics advised painters to leave the studio and find their model in the natural landscape (or even in an urban environment), a political argument was implicit: artists, as well as anyone else, would prosper in the absence of those regulative authorities—in social terms, the aristocratic hierarchy—who served as traditional models in matters of culture and all aspects of public life. Confronting their surroundings and relying on their own experience, artists would find all they needed. The "natural" order of nature, observed and immediately represented, would free them from the otherwise formative influence of things artificial, namely, the existing culture and its accepted modes of representation. Yet, there remained a long-standing alternative to this modernist claim on the natural. It was often argued (Denis Diderot is an instance) that when classicists turned to Greek art for inspiration, this too was to work from nature, because the ancients, as the first artists, had themselves no classical model to follow; they used nature directly, capturing its truth for the first time. Nature's originality could be adequately transmitted to the moderns through these ancient sources, whose style of representation had no precedent and therefore nothing from which to deviate. The purest of classical art could remain as valid a source as nature.

Obviously, classical and modern variants of originality might share certain principles and nevertheless be at odds. A number of antiessentialist perspectives (associated with postmodernism) now cast suspicion on both of these views; particularly influential in recent years have been Jacques Derrida's critique of conventional theories of the "origin" of language and Jacques Lacan's account of the construction of the self in language. In each instance, linguistic or graphic representation not only preexists and limits the expressive actions of individuals, but also resists and exceeds efforts at authorial appropriation. Because language generates more meaning than any given user intends or perceives, it might be said that it encompasses and possesses the individual, rather than the other way around. The self, conceived as an origin or source of originality, loses its singularity and centrality as a result of the independent force of the primordial, generative medium (language or graphism in general).

Indeed, it has become common to argue that originality—whether associated with the individual self, nature, or God—has improperly entailed isolating a central origin. This is to privilege one term above all others from within what must instead be a continuously reconfigured matrix of representation lacking any fixed center. When the center is not evident, both classicists and modernists are likely to differ from postmodernists in their response: they assume the center exists, but is hidden or has been "lost"; it consequently becomes an object of artistic search. For classicists, the center, origin, or privileged representational term might be God, nature, community, or truth; for modernists, it might be true feeling, unmediated experience, individuality, or the essential self. Such "origins" are worthy ends, but may be no more than chimerical, the productions of mythologies and ideologies.

Even champions of traditional values recognize that history must involve change, so that values too may change, or perhaps appear to change because they reappear under different aspects. If there is a communal element to originality, how does it circulate even as it maintains itself? And how does it happen that origins and originality are themselves transformed or reconceived in transit? Before nineteenth-century Romantics complicated the matter, classically minded art theorists had no difficulty distinguishing two familiar modes of transformation: "imitation" and "copying." Imitation entailed a certain originality of its own because it was an interpretative act that generated a degree of difference between the model (the "original" in this instance) and its representation. In contradistinction, copying was an attempt at mechanistic replication. Both procedures amount to the creation of a form analogous, but not identical, to that of the original model. In the case of copying, the principle of transformation can be described in terms of a geometric or mathematical algorithm. An artist might "copy" either a natural scene or an existing painting by applying a grid and reducing all measurements to one-half or one-quarter the original, allowing no exceptions. Or an artist might systematically convert all hues to a limited number of grays. Photography does something of the sort, usually applying a reduction of both size and color according to the specifications of the lens and film—hence, the early modernist charge that this medium would inhibit spontaneously transformative originality. In the case of "imitation," however, the principle of transformation is free and irregular; it is as if new, potentially radical, interpretive decisions were being made at every moment in the process. The source of such idiosyncrasy is an artist who follows no codified rule but responds at every moment to changes in his or her environmental and psychological situation. If the artist's imitative practice follows a law, it is internalized and invisible: spontaneous rule by person rather than predictable rule by system. With such imitation, the individual artist becomes as much of an orienting center as the external model, perhaps seeking something hidden or lost within his or her own soul.

Does this mean that the originality to be associated with "imitation" must be the province of modernists? Not necessarily, as two related commentaries on the Renaissance master Raphael indicate. The authors in question are Sir Joshua Reynolds and A.-C. Quatremère de Quincy, both of whom presided over early modern academies for which they composed "classical" theory. According to Reynolds (1774), Raphael took "so many models, that he became himself a model for all succeeding painters, always imitating, and always original" (Reynolds, 1975). Reynolds's "imitation" verges on a composite "copying." His logic may seem obscure to those immersed in late modernist forms of creation: how can such imitation end in a fundamental originality? Reynolds appears to condone eclecticism and repetition at the expense of authenticity and innovation. An element of Quatremère's praise of Raphael resolves part of this apparent contradiction: "Once a beautiful thought has been struck with the mark of genius, there is also genius in refraining from giving it a new imprint" (Quatremère, 1837). So, an artist can exercise creativity by acknowledging what ought to be reiterated, that is, by repeating and even copying.

Where does this leave originality? Given Quatremère's position, Raphael's choice of features worthy of the effort of his imitation makes him original in two senses. First, he creates particularly effective combinations, actually enriching the standard imagery with new, albeit hybrid, forms derived from his multiple sources; classicists called this creative compositional technique "invention." The essence of pictorial invention lies in the arrangement of representational elements, not the style associated with the artist's hand. As if in recognition of the power of invention, the nineteenth-century landscapist Camille Corot sometimes acted like the master of a classical studio, perhaps like Raphael himself in a decorative project such as the Vatican Logge: Corot would add a few final touches and thereby authenticate compositions copied from his originals but executed by other artists; he was even willing to put his signature on paintings that would otherwise have been regarded as forgeries. Apparently, Corot believed that his worthy originality was adequately transferable through any compositional scheme or motif he had at one time initiated.

The second sense of originality that can be derived from the example of Raphael's "imitation" pertains to the maintenance of collective value. Raphael, it was argued, imitated only the very best of all discernible qualities. If we presume that Raphael's antecedents did the same—both Reynolds and Quatremère invoke the precedent of Masaccio, and before him the precedent of the ancients—then we understand that at least some element of the earliest artistic form necessarily passes into Raphael's art through a timeless process of genius recognizing, emulating, and recreating genius. What results is an expression of Western culture as a set of collaborative, anonymous values. There is a further implication: the principle of classical anonymity entails that predecessors resemble followers as much as followers resemble predecessors; thus, classical originality has little to do with one's position in a sequence of "geniuses" but depends instead on whether one participates in transmitting the essence of a culture's primordial character. Priority is not innovation but becomes a matter of rediscovering and disseminating first principles. The originality of classical artists renders them equally of the same "first" class or rank.

That, at least, is the classical position in the eyes of "modernist" artists, who tend to discredit the status of rank. They upset the given order, assuming the role of revolutionaries by introducing change, by returning to values long lost from the classical hierarchy (primitivism, unconventional forms of revival), and by representing truths in expressive, personalized, and perhaps deviant or marginalized form. It is sometimes justifiably argued that in Italian Renaissance art pictorial form had already become identified with its individual creator and was therefore "modern"; but this historical retrospect could not be shared by nineteenth-century Romantics, who adopted the fully developed modern position as their exclusive province. Often claiming that they lacked true precedent, such Romantic-modernists conceived of *themselves* (as opposed to their principles) as original and pursued originality by realizing their inner feelings, thoughts, and character. Édouard Manet once represented his aesthetic by stating that he "sought simply to be himself, and not another." Accordingly, Romantics and modernists associate artistic authenticity with an expressive manner so autonomous that it must also appear innovative, in contrast to the value a classicist might locate in selective repetition. Eugène Delacroix (Corot's exact contemporary) claimed that as a result of his having achieved mastery, others would seek to copy his original vision; but he himself would feel no need to reciprocate. Henceforth, he would follow only his own lead.

Because a borrowed or preexisting form has already served as another's expression, priority for the modern artist has little to do with existing principles. Instead, it becomes a matter of establishing a new principle in a new form, that is to say, an idiosyncratic manner of working. Originality amounts to becoming the first of oneself: "I am the primitive of my own way," Paul Cézanne was reported to say, albeit by a rather unreliable witness. This is tantamount to calling oneself the "son of no one" (Thoré's phrase), yet Cézanne was actually quite concerned to acknowledge precedessors within the European tradition, including both classical Italian masters and the romantic Delacroix. Because Cézanne's statement conveys such strongly modernist sentiment, it has been quoted endlessly by art historians and critics despite the questionableness of its fact. Cézanne's presumably modernist originality is marked by difference or divergence at the source ("my own way"). In this case, the source is the self, and mastery becomes self-mastery.

From Raphael to Delacroix to Cézanne the discourse of originality shifts. Raphael could be regarded as the ever-developing culmination of European originality, one who combined the best of everything while reconfiguring it in a personal manner that seemed, paradoxically, immediately accessible to all others—his style preserved original values and yet could be recognized as individually innovative (Raphael "kept his unique personality intact," Thoré wrote). Delacroix became the idiosyncratic master of tradition, an individual who led tradition forward by means of change, not Raphaelesque synthesis. With Cézanne, the "primitive" of his "own way," culture received an even greater jolt. His art displayed an original manner so crude and naive as to be incomprehensible to most initial viewers; responding to his radical difference, his supporters could acknowledge his sincerity long before they could articulate the nature of his formal excellence and power to communicate, which remained mysterious. To an unusual degree, Cézanne's form resisted academic appropriation. Unlike the situation of Raphael or perhaps even Delacroix, the appreciation of Cézanne's originality did not depend on a comprehensive understanding of his technical procedure, nor on a determination of the thematic message he wished to convey. While many critics reveled in the provocations of his modernism, others nevertheless credited him with reviving the character of classical universality, perhaps because they longed for the wholeness once believed to emanate from Raphael.

Originality is a foundational yet unstable, notion. There is still another shift, this one occurring simultaneously with all the others—it need only be recognized, as it often has been, by those who have reason to do so. Art, as a language or system of representation, always risks losing any exclusive hold on its referent. A work of art might be intended as a path to a divine origin, or to nature or the individual self; yet, it proves to be no more than an ever reversible trace, recording nothing beyond or deeper than other instances of itself, appearing to have multiple origins in the play of its medium. Art can be imitation without any identifiable source, what Jean Baudrillard has called "simulation."

As an explanation, consider once again certain parallels within the social realm. To seek originality by stressing one's deviation from others (as both Delacroix and Cézanne did in their different ways) encourages personal competition, which in turn has economic implications. Artists sell their unique difference, but not always directly. Modernists saw the irony of struggling for market recognition in a world ruled more by fashion than by absolute value and necessity. Fashion itself follows a principle of uniqueness of a peculiarly disarming kind: it is novelty produced in multiple and multiauthored editions. "Nobody wants my work because it is different from that of others," wrote Paul Gauguin to his dealer in 1900; "strange, illogical public which demands the greatest possible originality from a painter and yet will not accept him unless he resembles all the others—[but] I do resemble those who resemble me, that is, those who imitate me." Thus, Gauguin as modernist understood not only the conflict between significant innovation and passing fashion, but also one of the classical truths of originality—its commutability, the fact that the first in line might seem indistinguishable from the last, given successful acts of mediational imitation. Such imitation need not "copy" (that is, reproduce every detail) but need only preserve, and perhaps exaggerate, elements of particular interest and value to the society. "Original" artists themselves become commodities, subject to reproduction with respect to each one's transferable originality factor, the point of interest. Sometimes that factor can be marketed more effectively by followers who borrow it than by innovators who create it. As in the classical scheme, chronological sequence is not the final arbiter.

Gauguin knew that although artists might strive to express an inborn originality, they were attributed originality only if others saw the signs of it in their person, their works, or their following. This is something of a postmodern realization, parallel to a feature of classicism: originality appears as an attribute that might pass or be passed, like a sign or signifier, from one artist to another. Attributes or signs are communal entities, not private property; they can be appropriated by anyone with access to and authority to use the artistic language. Just as nineteenth-century artists and critics focused on the cultural value of expressing individualistic originality, so they doubted the entire enterprise because the general signs of originality and authenticity, like the more specific signs of individual identity and authorship, could be faked: "For those who aspire to truth . . . what temptation to imitate instead of creating, and to fall into the intentional and regulated naïveté that can only be a mannerism like the academic formulas" (Ludovic Vitet, 1841). Artists were fully capable of indulging themselves in a self-conscious "affectation of naïveté" (Étienne-Jean Delécluze, 1825), an academicized irregularity.

Such commentary indicates a general nineteenth-century awareness that representation forever threatens to displace, or even to rule over and determine, original and authentic truth. But such fear was not enough to prevent artists from acting on their desire for originality and self-expression as they created one romantic or modernist innovation after another—at least what passed for innovation. It remained for critics to accept or question the sincerity and effectiveness of each artistic manner, a process that left Cézanne standing as an exemplary modernist original. During the past two or three decades, a period characterized by postmodern perspectives, artists have internalized the critic's anxiety more than ever before to the detriment of their own claims to originality. If, among many contemporary artists, originality and other modernist values now seem discredited, it is because artists have radicalized old suspicions, adopting poststructuralist theory (Derrida, Lacan, Baudrillard) to make their case.

We need not end with an example from recent art, for Gauguin already experienced the postmodern in relation to those who appropriated his manner and its market. In one respect, he had little right to complain, for he himself appropriated Cézanne. There is an ironic possibility that Gauguin was pressured not only by his followers' postmodernist simulation but also by a kind of modernist backlash coming from his unilaterally chosen model. He admitted to "stealing" the thing most closely identified with Cézanne, a technique of painting with short parallel strokes of brilliantly contrasting color. Despite the fact that Cézanne had little concern to market his art, the situation irritated rather than flattered him; he believed that his character and originality had been violated. Yet, by modernist principles, Cézanne had no cause to worry: supposedly, his technique developed in himself alone and therefore should not have been subject to analysis into elements derived from predecessors; as such, it could neither be imitated in part nor with individualistic variation. If it were indeed to be used effectively by others, it would have to be appropriated whole. This is why critics claimed that Cézanne, like other modernist masters, was inimitable—one would have to appropriate an entire way of seeing, even a way of being. So, if Gauguin were to succeed in assuming Cézanne's technique, he would have to assume Cézanne's identity—all of it. That would convert Gauguin into Cézanne, the follower being absorbed into the predecessor.

Such is the danger of encountering the force of originality outside a classically structured environment, one designed to accommodate originality's play while maintaining its state of equilibrium. When classical values have been abandoned, the relations between the parties to an exchange of originality must become either passively or actively agonistic: they follow either the rule of fashion (Gauguin versus his imitators—a passive postmodernism) or the survival of the greatest ego (Gauguin versus Cézanne—an active modernism). It may seem that the originality of certain modernist artists actually does redirect the course of pictorial history—if not Gauguin's originality, then Cézanne's. But would such forcefulness constitute an unqualified triumph of the self, the ego? Not likely. The ego,

like originality, can be no greater than what the language of representation, operating in concert with the formative conditions of a particular society, allows. Even for the most individualistic of artists, originality remains a thoroughly social construct.

BIBLIOGRAPHY

Baudrillard, Jean. *Simulations*. Translated by Paul Foss, Paul Patton, and Philip Beitchman. New York, 1983.

Bloom, Harold. *The Anxiety of Influence: A Theory of Poetry*. New York and Oxford, 1973.

Derrida, Jacques. *Of Grammatology*. Translated by Gayatri Chakravorty Spivak. Baltimore, 1976.

Godfrey, Sima, ed. *The Anxiety of Anticipation*. Yale French Studies, vol. 66. New Haven, 1984.

Greene, Thomas M. *The Light in Troy: Imitation and Discovery in Renaissance Poetry*. New Haven, 1982.

Krauss, Rosalind E. *The Originality of the Avant-Garde and Other Modernist Myths*. Cambridge, Mass., 1985.

Lacan, Jacques. *Ecrits: A Selection*. Translated by Alan Sheridan. New York, 1977.

Lacoue-Labarthe, Philippe. *The Subject of Philosophy*. Edited by Thomas Trezise, translated by Gary M. Cole et al. Minneapolis, 1993.

Millon, Henry A., ed. *Retaining the Original: Multiple Originals, Copies, and Reproductions*. Studies in the History of Art, vol. 20. Washington, D.C., 1989.

Quatremère de Quincy, Antoine-Chrysostome. *Essai sur l'idéal*. Paris, 1837.

Reynolds, Joshua. *Discourses on Art*. Edited by Robert R. Wark. Reprint, New Haven, 1975.

Shiff, Richard. *Cézanne and the End of Impressionism: A Study of the Theory, Technique, and Critical Evaluation of Modern Art*. Chicago, 1984.

Thoré, Théophile. *Les salons*. 3 vols. Brussels, 1893.

RICHARD SHIFF

Originality in Literature

One of the best-known moments in literary mythology is the one in which a thirty-seven-year-old Jean-Jacques Rousseau has an epiphany and becomes a writer. Walking down the road to Vincennes, Rousseau has the *Mercure de France* with him. Glancing through it, he sees the question for the Dijon Academy Prize: "Has the progress of the sciences and arts done more to corrupt morals or to improve them?" The revelation is instantaneous: "The moment I read this I beheld another universe and became another man." Rousseau immediately writes the first part "in pencil under an oak tree." This act in turn creates a "fermentation" and intensity that were to last for "more than four or five years." The composition of this first essay leads Rousseau to dictation as a means of writing. He meditates at night on his writing and has decided that "the break caused by my getting up and dressing [makes] me lose everything." Writing here reflects the contents of a sacred, spontaneous moment that, if interrupted by daily life, is lost forever (Rousseau, 1953 pp. 327–329). (One is reminded here of Samuel Taylor Coleridge, who claimed that his poem "Kubla Kahn" was interrupted by a salesman ringing the front bell and thus annihilating the poem forever in the poet's mind.)

This moment of epiphany in Rousseau corresponds perfectly to the Western notion of literary originality. Rousseau is visited by some kind of flash intuition—something from the outside that then "ferments" on the inside to produce, in a dazzling but extremely vague fashion, a work of genius and indeed a genius. Moreover, what emerges is new, unthought of before, unique. The act of writing itself is a skill available to anyone. But talent, Rousseau tells us, is inherent and cannot be learned; one is or is not born with talent. Talent is in constant danger of being interrupted by the demands of daily life; writing itself, on the other hand, partakes of the quotidian. It is original thought—that most obscure and mysterious of all experiences, and yet the sine qua non of any genuine "author"—that remains outside the confines of the "real world." We have here a notion of a division of labor. One kind of labor ("talent") sees itself as resonant with the conversion experiences of a Saint Paul or a Saint Augustine, as happening "all at once." The other ("the act of writing") belongs to a Madame Levasseur, the secretary Rousseau hires to take dictation, and can be learned with time. The first is a sacred vocation; the second a learned skill. What matters is the epiphany, which the writing can only try to recapture. There are, then, two kinds of writing: writing as the moment of revelation (Blaise Pascal's "In Memoriam," for example), coming as close as possible to the notion of grace (the comments penciled under the oak tree), and writing as scribing, as industry. Originality, then, as Rousseau will come to describe it, has to do with a sudden inspiration rapidly recorded through dictation, the writing of which is merely the necessary intervention, or manual craft. This concept of inspiration will become the modern notion of what is original, in that the idea, the revolutionary or at least "new" thought, is believed to spring from within, or inside, the writer.

It should be remembered that the terms *inside* and *outside* have a complex history in the West with respect to inspiration (the two metaphors for the ancients were the spider and the bee). In the West, inspiration comes mainly from the "outside" (visits from gods, demons, prophetic dreams, and, of course, genies) until the organicist myths that spawned early Romanticism. The organicists (such as the earl of Shaftesbury, Edward Young, and, later, Friedrich Wilhelm von Schelling) argue that genius is like a seed, encapsulating its own substance; all the material is already there, inside, and needs only the proper watering to unfold. This move from the outside to the inside is mirrored at the linguistic level: in the latter part of the eighteenth century, in German, French, and English, for example, one begins to *be* a genius rather than to *have* genius.

Although it is tempting to imagine that the cult of originality springs from Romanticism, it should be remembered that writers have always worried that their ideas would be stolen and claimed by others. The cult of the individual, and its concomitant insistence on uniqueness, are at work long before the inexorable rise of the bourgeoisie and are implicit in any originary economy. René Descartes, for example, was constantly worried that his ideas would be stolen (see Scharfstein, 1969). Although some scholars have argued that until the seventeenth century originality as a notion carried no weight, and that theft was both expected and overlooked, even these same scholars will admit several instances in literature (and more in science) that demonstrate that authors have always been concerned about their intellectual property rights. Or, as Jacques Derrida would note, originality is an inevitable offshoot of logocentrism, and begins with the very notion of a beginning.

It is certainly true that classical literature makes imitation one of the cornerstones of education (McKeon, 1936; Greene, 1976), a tradition continued in the Renaissance (Pigman, 1980; White, 1965). It also seems to be the case, as Thomas Mallon (1989) has noted, that "something happened" in the seventeenth century that made copying (or imitation), until then an integral part of scholarship, reprehensible. This change may have begun as early as the Renaissance, and been brought to bear most heavily with the weighty influence of Young, with his emphasis on original rather than imitative genius (Young, 1750). The early European Romantics (Friedrich Schlegel, Novalis, Wilhelm Wackenroder, and Ludwig Tieck in Germany; Coleridge and William Wordsworth in England) developed the notion of "original genius," which, as several scholars have noted, complicated things immensely if only because the great literati were required to demonstrate both originality and genius in spontaneous and utterly convincing ways, recognizable only to literary criticism (Abrams, 1971). Moreover, literary criticism reserves the right to judge what is and what is not "original" and, by those lights, to alter the canon if necessary. Literary criticism, then, has a vested interest in maintaining what may be no more than a myth: that an original thought, entirely unique, can and must occur in what is judged to be great literature.

Two infamous examples of demotion from the constellation of literary greats will serve as examples: James Macpherson and Coleridge himself. Macpherson is of particular interest since his *Ossian* (1762) was a forgery, not a theft, and had been firmly pronounced "original" by the literary establishment. The influence of *Ossian* on literature is undeniable (Johann Wolfgang von Goethe's Werther, for example, reads from *Ossian* shortly before killing himself), as it is on translation theory. Yet, when it was discovered that Macpherson had largely invented a Scottish national epic, rather than having edited existing manuscripts and songs of such an epic, he and his warrior-bard were instantly thrown out of the pantheon (Stafford, 1988). Why? He had feigned a discovery, so that his writing became synonymous with inauthenticity—and authenticity is the hallmark of "spontaneous" originality. Paradoxically, then, Macpherson's very originality became the source of his undoing, since "genuine" originality is a stranger to any form of fakery.

Conversely, Norman Fruman and others have spent a great deal of time and effort demonstrating beyond doubt that Coleridge was a literary thief. The amount of resistance generated by such studies is finally more interesting than whether or not, and to what extent, Coleridge really did plagiarize. So, too, Stendhal, another canonized author of the nineteenth century, plagiarized "his" first three works, a fact that criticism similarly rushes to explain, excuse, or hotly deny.

As any study of Western notions on originality will uncover, the fear of plagiarism (a frequently well-founded anxiety and symptom of originality) does not suddenly appear in the eighteenth century. The Greeks, the Romans, the writers of the Renaissance, seventeenth-century Europeans (as we have noted)—all worried about having their ideas stolen. When Rousseau in his *Confessions* collapses into the prose of paranoia, accusing everyone of stealing from him (his ideas, his fame, his good reputation, his texts), he is not reflecting a new sensibility born of the preromantics; rather, he is echoing an anxiety that has always, to some degree, been in place. This anxiety is grounded in the idea of creating a sovereign textual subject, one that purports to double mimetically the authoritative and self-contained subjectivity of the author.

The modern idea of originality is also gendered, in the sense that what is original is a "first cause," an economy that is both masculinist and patriarchal. Woman is always secondary in such an economy (Eve, after all, is secondarily born of man); she has no place in the genealogy of ideas. Hence the constant suspicion concerning a woman writer's talent. The French writer Sidonie-Gabrielle Colette, for example, wrote her first novels under her husband's name. When she sued to retain the property rights for these works, much was written about the extent to which the books were hers, were original (Meltzer, 1994). The notion of originality does rest, it must be remembered, on the principle of private property and ownership. Even though one cannot (according to U.S. copyright law) "own" an idea, the curious resistance to a female original genius is in large part linked to the fact that women have, until recently, been in no position to own anything, including their private possessions (Hall, 1985). The mythology of originality relies on a principle of creation as first cause, as has already been noted. First cause in the West is male gendered: God, father; genius-woman is not inscribed in these categories.

Although it is no surprise that a culture of late capitalism should be so obsessed with the limits and boundaries of private property, we seem to be increasingly haunted by an odd anxiety every time the idea of originality is at issue. Derrida, in particular, has shown the extent to which we are wedded, in our Western metaphysical tradition, to the im-

portance of beginnings, of originary status, of first over second, of breath over text (Derrida, 1976). These are more than what Harold Bloom's psychoanalytic study calls "the anxiety of influence." These anxieties stem from the insistence on the new, the creative, the true. Underlying these convictions is another series of beliefs: in the individual and *his* sovereignty; in a patriarchal hegemony as dominating culture and metaphysics; in a concomitant feminine economy as eternally secondary, unable by definition to partake of an originary model; in private property and the exclusionary systems that ensue; in manual work as valid labor and product, to which writing remains a destabilized and ambiguous correlative. Is writing work? Is it "really" manual work, and if so, can its product, the text, be owned by the laborer?

Finally, at stake in every assertion of originality is the notion of ownership, which in turn entails that of the person. It was John Locke's *Two Treatises of Government* (1690) that gave the paradigm of the European idea that an individual's work and the fruit of his labor are his own property (Locke, 1960, pp. 305–306). This assertion was based on the declaration, surprising at the time, that every man owns his body and is therefore his own person. This remarkable statement not only marks a tenet central to modern European thought, but also leads to the assumption that literature is a form of labor and, as such, personal property as much as the product of any field or territory. It is such thinking that allows for the notion of author: the word *author* derives from the Latin *augere*, meaning "to increase, to augment" (terms of cultivating the land). There is no author without first a concept of personal property and hence of person. On the other hand, Michel de Certeau has pointed out that the present notion of *auctoritas* has shifted from author to expert, like the literary criticism that decides, from its expertise, what is and what is not original; and what "belongs" to any given author.

At least since the eighteenth century, it has been the literary critic's self-appointed, if at times unacknowledged, task to cull the "real" new from the false, to identify the point of origin and thus to recognize genuine originality. In our present era (despite protestations to the contrary), not much has changed since the pronouncements of Northrop Frye, who declared that the critic is "the pioneer of education and the shaper of cultural tradition" (Frye, 1957, p. 4). Originality remains a major requirement for criticism, first for the literary texts it professes to judge, but also (although this remains mostly unacknowledged) for itself, a move that allows for the dismissal, for example, of other kinds of criticism or theory. Critical texts, much like philosophical ones, leapfrog over each other, redefining the previous terms in what is purported to be a new way. Hence, criticism itself partakes both in judgment and in its very nature, in the myth of originality. The anxiety of being influenced (the Oedipal problem and so on) is but one symptom within the larger systemic disorder that one might call a metaphysics of origin.

BIBLIOGRAPHY

Abrams, M. H. *Natural Supernaturalism: Tradition and Revolution in Romantic Literature.* New York, 1971.

Blackall, Eric A. *The Emergence of German as a Literary Language, 1700–1775.* 2d ed. Ithaca, N.Y., 1978.

Bloom, Harold. *The Anxiety of Influence: A Theory of Poetry.* New York and Oxford, 1973.

de Certeau, Michel. *Heterologies: Discourse on the Other.* Translated by Brian Massumi. Minneapolis, 1986.

Derrida, Jacques. *Of Grammatology.* Translated by Gayatri Chakravorty Spivak. Baltimore, 1976.

Dutton, Denis, ed. *The Forger's Art: Forgery and the Philosophy of Art.* Berkeley, 1983.

Frye, Northrop. *Anatomy of Criticism: Four Essays.* Princeton, N.J., 1957.

Hall, Catherine. "Private Persons versus Public Someones: Class, Gender and Politics in England, 1780–1850." In *Language, Gender and Childhood,* edited by Carolyn Steedman, Cathy Urwin, and Valerie Walderdine. London and Boston, 1985.

Fruman, Norman. *Coleridge: The Damaged Archangel.* New York, 1971.

Grafton, Anthony. *Forgers and Critics: Creativity and Duplicity in Western Scholarship.* Princeton, N.J., 1990.

Greene, Thomas M. "Petrarch and the Humanist Hermeneutic." In *Italian Literature: Roots and Branches,* edited by Giose Rimanelli and Kenneth John Atchity. New Haven, 1976.

Kaplan, Benjamin. *An Unhurried View of Copyright.* New York, 1967.

Locke, John. *Two Treatises of Government.* Edited by Peter Laslett. Cambridge, 1960.

Macpherson, James. *The Poems of Ossian.* Edinburgh, 1926.

Mallon, Thomas. *Stolen Words: Forays into the Origins and Ravages of Plagiarism.* New York, 1989.

McKeon, Richard. "Literary Criticism and the Conception of Imitation in Antiquity." *Modern Philology* 34 (1936): 1–35.

Meltzer, Françoise. *Hot Property: The Stakes and Claims of Literary Originality.* Chicago, 1994.

Pigman, G. W., III. "Versions of Imitation in the Renaissance." *Renaissance Quarterly* 33 (1980).

Rose, Mark. "The Author as Proprietor: *Donaldson vs. Beckett* and the Genealogy of Modern Authorship." *Representations* 23 (Summer 1988): 51–85.

Rousseau, Jean-Jacques. *The Confessions.* Translated by J. M. Cohen. Harmondsworth, England, 1953.

Scharfstein, Ben-Ami. "Descartes' Dream." *Philosophical Forum* 1 (Spring 1969): 293–317.

Schelling, Friedrich Wilhelm Joseph von. *The Philosophy of Art.* Edited and translated by Douglas W. Stott. Minneapolis, 1989.

Stafford, Fiona. *The Sublime Savage: A Study of James MacPherson and the Poems of Ossian.* Edinburgh, 1988.

White, Harold Ogden. *Plagiarism and Imitation during the English Renaissance: A Study in Critical Distinctions* (1935). New York, 1965.

Young, Edward. *The Complaint; or, Night Thoughts on Life, Death and Immortality.* London, 1750.

FRANÇOISE MELTZER

ORIGINS OF AESTHETICS. [*The emergence of aesthetics in the eighteenth century was a unique event in Western culture not duplicated in any other culture in the world, before or since. To analyze the historical and conceptual factors that help to explain this development, this entry comprises two essays:*

> Historical and Conceptual Overview
> History of Aisthēsis

The first essay traces the emergence of aesthetics in relation to the development of the "System of the Arts" (painting, sculpture, architecture, music, and poetry) that developed in Europe between the Renaissance and the Enlightenment. Although this "system" has, of course, changed significantly, its cultural emergence is still an important measure of the origins of aesthetics because of the emphasis on system or generality that non-Western artistic or cultural traditions have largely chosen not to follow. The second essay examines the history of the concept of aisthēsis (or sensation) and how it shaped the etymological and conceptual roots of aesthetics. For related discussion, see Baumgarten; *and* Renaissance Italian Aesthetics.]

Historical and Conceptual Overview

The fundamental importance of the eighteenth century in the history of aesthetics and of art criticism is generally recognized. It is known that the very term *aesthetics* was coined at that time, and, at least in the opinion of some historians, the subject matter itself, the "philosophy of art," was invented in that comparatively recent period and can be applied to earlier phases of Western thought only with reservation. It is also generally agreed that such dominating concepts of modern aesthetics as taste, sentiment, genius, originality, and creative imagination did not assume their definite modern meaning before the eighteenth century. Some scholars have rightly noticed that only the eighteenth century produced a type of literature in which the various arts were compared with each other and discussed on the basis of common principles, whereas up to that period treatises on poetics and rhetoric, on painting and architecture, and on music had represented quite distinct branches of writing and were primarily concerned with technical precepts rather than with general ideas. Finally, at least a few scholars have noticed that the term *Art,* with a capital *A* and in its modern sense, and the related term *fine arts* (Beaux-Arts) originated in all probability in the eighteenth century.

If we take all these facts for granted, we can concentrate instead on a much simpler, and in a sense more fundamental, point that is closely related to the problems so far mentioned: the term *Art* in the eighteenth century comprises above all the five major arts of painting, sculpture, architecture, music, and poetry. These constitute the irreducible nucleus of the modern system of the arts, on which all modern writers and thinkers of aesthetics seem to agree. On the other hand, certain additional arts are sometimes added to the scheme, but with less regularity, depending on the different views and interests of the authors concerned: gardening, engraving and the decorative arts, the dance, and the theater, sometimes the opera, and finally eloquence and prose literature. This system of the five major arts, which underlies all modern aesthetics and is so familiar to us all, is of comparatively recent origin and did not assume definite shape before the eighteenth century, although it has many ingredients that go back to classical, medieval, and Renaissance thought. Because the classical and medieval periods did not have the modern notions of art or aesthetics, the present discussion of the modern system will focus on its emergence in the period between the Renaissance and the Enlightenment.

The Renaissance. The period of the Renaissance brought about many important changes in the social and cultural position of the various arts and thus prepared the ground for the later development of aesthetic theory. But the Renaissance did not formulate a system of the fine arts or a comprehensive theory of aesthetics.

Early Italian humanism, which in many respects continued the grammatical and rhetorical traditions of the Middle Ages, not merely provided the old trivium (grammar, rhetoric, dialectic) with a new and more ambitious name (*Studia humanitatis*) but also increased its actual scope, content, and significance in the curriculum of the schools and universities and in its own extensive literary production. The *Studia humanitatis* excluded logic, but they added to the traditional grammar and rhetoric not only history, Greek, and moral philosophy, but also made poetry, once a sequel of grammar and rhetoric, the most important member of the whole group. It is true that in the fourteenth and fifteenth centuries poetry was understood as the ability to write Latin verse and to interpret the ancient poets, and that the poetry the humanists defended against some of their theological contemporaries or for which they were crowned by popes and emperors was a quite different thing from what we understand by that name. Yet, the name poetry, meaning at first Latin poetry, received much honor and glamor through the early humanists, and by the sixteenth century vernacular poetry and prose began to share in the prestige of Latin literature. It was the various branches of Latin and vernacular poetry and literature that constituted the main pursuit of the numerous "academies" founded in Italy during that period and imitated later by the other European countries. The revival of Platonism also helped to spread the notion of the divine madness of the poet, a notion that by the second half of the sixteenth century began to be extended to the visual arts and became one of the ingredients of the modern concept of genius.

With the second third of the sixteenth century, Aristotle's *Poetics,* along with his *Rhetoric,* began to exercise increasing influence, not only through translations and commentaries, but also through a rising number of treatises on poetics in which the notions of Aristotle constituted one of the dominant features. Poetic imitation is regularly discussed along Aristotelian lines, and some authors also notice and stress the analogies between poetry, painting, sculpture, and music as forms of imitation. Most of them know, however, that for Aristotle music was a part of poetry, and that he knew other forms of imitation outside of the "fine arts," and hardly anyone among them is trying to establish the "imitative arts" as a separate class.

During the Renaissance, musical theory retained its status as one of the liberal arts, and the author of an early treatise on the dance tries to dignify his subject by the claim that his art, being a part of music, must be considered as a liberal art. It seems that the practice of the *Improvvisatori,* as well as the reading of classical sources, suggested to some humanists a closer link between music and poetry than had been customary in the preceding period. This tendency received a new impetus by the end of the sixteenth century, when the program of the Camerata and the creation of the opera brought about a reunion of the two arts. It would even seem that some of the features of *Marinismo* and Baroque poetry that were so repulsive to classicist critics were due to the fact that this poetry was written with the intention of being set to music and sung.

Still more characteristic of the Renaissance is the steady rise of painting and of the other visual arts that began in Italy with Giovanni Cimabue and Giotto di Bondone and reached its climax in the sixteenth century. An early expression of the increasing prestige of the visual arts is found on the Campanile of Florence, where painting, sculpture, and architecture appear as a separate group between the liberal and the mechanical arts. What characterizes the period is not only the quality of the works of art but also the close links that were established between the visual arts, the sciences, and literature. The appearance of a distinguished artist who also was a humanist and writer of merit, such as Leon Battista Alberti, was no coincidence in a period in which literary and classical learning, as well as religion, began to provide the subject matter for painters and sculptors. When a knowledge of perspective, anatomy, and geometric proportions was considered necessary for the painter and sculptor, it was no wonder that several artists should have made important contributions to the various sciences. On the other hand, ever since Filippo Villani, the humanists and their journalist successors in the sixteenth century looked with favor on the work of contemporary artists and would lend their pen to its praise. From the end of the fourteenth century through the sixteenth, the writings of the artists and of authors sympathetic to the visual arts repeat the claim that painting should be considered as one of the liberal, not of the mechanical, arts. It has been rightly noted that the classical testimonies in favor of painting, mainly from Pliny, Galen, and Philostratus, were not as authoritative and strong as the Renaissance authors who quoted them in support of their claim believed or pretended to believe. Yet, the claim of Renaissance writers on painting to have their art recognized as liberal, however weakly supported by classical authority, was significant as an attempt to enhance the social and cultural position of painting and of the other visual arts, and to obtain for them the same prestige that music, rhetoric, and poetry had long enjoyed. Since it was still apparent that the liberal arts were primarily sciences or teachable knowledge, we may well understand why Leonardo da Vinci tried to define painting as a science and to emphasize its close relationship with mathematics.

The rising social and cultural claims of the visual arts led in the sixteenth century in Italy to an important new development that occurred in the other European countries somewhat later: the three visual arts—painting, sculpture, and architecture—were for the first time clearly separated from the crafts with which they had been associated in the preceding period. The term *Arti del diségno*, on which Beaux-Arts was probably based, was coined by Giorgio Vasari, who used it as the guiding concept for his famous collection of biographies. This change in theory found its institutional expression in 1563 when in Florence, again under the personal influence of Vasari, the painters, sculptors, and architects cut their previous connections with the craftsmen's guilds and formed an academy of art (Accadèmia del Diségno), the first of its kind that served as a model for later similar institutions in Italy and other countries. The art academies followed the pattern of the literary academies that had been in existence for some time, and they replaced the older workshop tradition with a regular kind of instruction that included such scientific subjects as geometry and anatomy.

The ambition of painting to share in the traditional prestige of literature also accounts for the popularity of a notion that appears prominently for the first time in the treatises on painting of the sixteenth century and was to retain its appeal down to the eighteenth century: the parallel between painting and poetry. Its basis was the *Ut pictura poesis* of Horace, as well as the saying of Simonides reported by Plutarch, along with some other passages in Plato, Aristotle, and Horace. The history of this notion from the sixteenth to the eighteenth century has been carefully studied, and it has been justly pointed out that the use then made of the comparison exceeded anything done or intended by the ancients. Actually, the meaning of the comparison was reversed, since the ancients had compared poetry with painting when they were writing about poetry, whereas the modern authors more often compared painting with poetry while writing about painting. How seriously the comparison was taken we can see from the fact that Horace's *Ars poetica* was taken as a literary model for some treatises on painting and that many poetical theories and concepts were applied to painting by these authors in a more or less artificial manner. The persistent comparison between poetry and painting went a long way, as did the emancipation of the three visual arts from the crafts, to prepare the ground for the later system of the five fine arts, but it obviously does not yet presuppose or constitute such a system. Even the few treatises written in the late sixteenth and early seventeenth century that dealt with both poetry and painting do not seem to have gone beyond more or less external comparisons into an analysis of common principles.

The sixteenth century formulated still other ideas that pointed in the direction of later developments in the field of aesthetics. Just as the period attached great importance to questions of "precedence" at courts and in public ceremonies, so the academies and educated circles inherited from the medieval schools and universities the fancy for arguing the relative merits and superiority of the various sciences, arts, or other human activities. This type of debate was by no means limited to the arts, as appears from the old rivalry between medicine and jurisprudence, or from the new contest between "arms and letters." Yet, this kind of discussion was also applied to the arts and thus helped to strengthen the sense of their affinity. The parallel between painting and poetry, insofar as it often leads to a plea for the superiority of painting to poetry, shows the same general pattern. No less popular was the contest between painting and sculpture, on which Benedetto Varchi in 1546 held a regular inquiry among contemporary artists, whose answers are extant and constitute interesting documents for the artistic theories of the time. The question was still of interest to Galileo Galilei. The most important text of this type is Leonardo's *Paragone*, which argues for the superiority of painting to poetry, music, and sculpture. In a sense, this tract contains the most complete system of the fine arts that has come down to us from the Renaissance period. The text was not composed by Leonardo in its present form, however, but rather put together from his scattered notes by one of his pupils, and again rearranged by most of the modern editors. In any case, architecture is omitted, the separation between poetry and music is not consistently maintained, and the comparison seems to be extended to the mathematical disciplines with which painting, as a science, is closely linked for Leonardo.

Another line of thinking that might be called the amateur tradition appears in several writers of the sixteenth and seventeenth centuries, probably first in Baldassare Castiglione's *Courtier*. The exercise is grouped with the appreciation of poetry, music, and painting as pursuits appropriate for the courtier, the gentleman, or the prince. Again, the occupation with these "fine arts" is not clearly marked off from fencing, riding, classical learning, the collecting of coins and medals and of natural curiosities, or other equally worthy activities. But there seems to be a sense of the affinity between the various arts in their effect on the amateur, and by the first half of the seventeenth century, the taste and pleasure produced by painting, music, and poetry are felt by several authors to be of a similar nature. It does not seem that Plotinus's view that beauty resides in the objects of sight, hearing, and thought exercised any particular influence at that time.

The most explicit comparison between poetry, painting, and music in Renaissance literature is the appendix which the Bohemian Jesuit, Jacobus Pontanus, added to the third edition of his treatise on poetics. In stressing the affinity between the three arts as forms of imitation aiming at pleasure, the author goes beyond his classical sources. He argues for the status of painting as a liberal art, as many others had done before, but also places musical composition (not musical theory) as a separate art on the same plane with poetry and painting. The passage is quite remarkable and influential, since the work was often reprinted, in France also, where much of the later discussion on these topics took place.

Renaissance speculation on beauty was still unrelated to the arts and apparently influenced by ancient models. Agostino Nifo's treatise *De pulchro,* still quoted in the eighteenth century, dealt exclusively with personal beauty. Francesco da Diacceto's main philosophical work, which carries the same title, continues the metaphysical speculations of Plotinus and of his teacher Marsilio Ficino and does not seem to have exercised any lasting influence.

In spite of these notable changes, the Renaissance was still far from establishing the modern system of the fine arts. These schemes of that period continued in part the traditions of the Middle Ages, as is clear in the case of such Thomists as S. Antonino or Girolamo Savonarola. On the whole, however, there is a greater variety of ideas than in the preceding period, and some of the thinkers concerned were neither backward nor unrepresentative. Juan Luis Vives, Petrus Ramus, and Conrad Gesner largely follow the old scheme of the liberal arts and the university curriculum of their time. Neither Heinrich Cornelius Agrippa nor Julius Caesar Scaliger, nor in the seventeenth century Johann Heinrich Alsted or Gerardus Johannes Vossius, shows any attempt to separate the fine arts from the sciences; they list them scattered among all kinds of sciences and professions, and the same is still true of the eighteenth-century *Cyclopaedia* of Ephraim Chambers. Francis Bacon connects poetry with the faculty of imagination, but does not mention the other arts, and the same is true of Giambattista Vico, whom Benedetto Croce considers the founder of modern aesthetics. Giovanni Bonifacio stresses the link between poetry and painting, but otherwise does not separate the fine arts from the sciences, and the same is true of Alessandro Tassoni. Even Lodovico Antonio Muratori, who again stresses imagination in poetry and at times compares poetry and painting, when he speaks of the *arti* connected with poetry means eloquence and history, in other words, the *Studia humanitatis.* The modern system of the fine arts does not appear in Italy before the second half of the eighteenth century, when such writers as Saverio Bettinelli began to follow the lead of contemporary French, English, and German authors.

The Seventeenth Century. During the seventeenth century the cultural leadership of Europe passed from Italy to France, and many characteristic ideas and tendencies of the Italian Renaissance were continued and transformed by French classicism and the French Enlightenment before they became a part of later European thought and culture. Literary criticism and poetic theory, so prominent in the French classical period, seem to have taken little notice of the other fine arts. Only Jules de La Mesnardière in his *Poetics* has an introductory remark on the similarity between poetry, painting, and music, a point he calls a commonplace in Latin and Italian treatises on poetics, which is but vaguely reminiscent of such writers as Madius, Minturno, and Ludovico Zuccolo, but for which we can indicate no specific source unless we assume the author's familiarity with the appendix of Jacobus Pontanus.

Yet the *siècle de Louis XIV* was not limited in its achievements to poetry and literature. Painting and the other visual arts began to flourish, and with Nicolas Poussin France produced a painter of European fame. Later in the century, Jean-Baptiste Lully, although of Italian birth, developed a distinctive French style in music, and his great success with the Parisian public went a long way to win for his art the same popularity in France it had long possessed in Italy.

This rise of the various arts was accompanied by an institutional development that followed in many respects the earlier Italian model, but was guided by a conscious governmental policy and hence more centralized and consistent than had been the case in Italy. The Académie Française was organized in 1635 by Armand-Jean du Plessis Cardinal Richelieu for the cultivation of the French language, poetry, and literature after the model of the Accadèmia della Crusca. Several years later, in 1648, the Académie Royale de Peinture et de Sculpture was founded under Jules Mazarin after the model of the Accadèmia di Santo Luca in Rome, and tended to detach French artists from the artisans' guilds to which they had previously belonged. Many more academies were founded by Jean-Baptiste Colbert between 1660 and 1680. They included provincial academies of painting and sculpture, the French Academy in Rome, dedicated to the three visual arts, as well as academies of architecture, of music, and of the dance. The system of the arts that would seem to underlie these foundations is more apparent than real, however. The academies were founded at different times, and even if we limit ourselves to the period of Colbert, we should note that there were also the Académie des Sciences and the Académie des Inscriptions et Médailles, which have no relation to the fine arts; that there was at least a project for an Académie de Spectacles to be devoted to circus performances and other public shows; and that the Académie de Musique and the Académie de

Danse, like the projected Académie de Spectacles, were not organizations of distinguished professional artists or scientists, like the other academies, but merely licensed establishments for the regular preparation of public performances. Moreover, an extant paper from the time of Colbert that proposed to consolidate all academies in a single institution makes no clear distinction between the arts and the sciences and lends additional, though indirect, support to the view that Colbert's academies reflect a comprehensive system of cultural disciplines and professions, but not a clear conception of the fine arts in particular.

Along with the founding of the academies, and partly in close connection with their activities, there developed an important and extensive theoretical and critical literature on the visual arts. The conferences held at the Académie de Peinture et Sculpture are full of interesting critical views, and separate treatises were composed by Charles Dufresnoy, Roger de Piles, Fréart de Chambray, and André Sieur des Avaux et de Javercy Félibien. Dufresnoy's Latin poem *De arte graphica,* which was translated into French and English and made the subject of notes and commentaries, was in its form a conscious imitation of Horace's *Ars poetica,* and it begins characteristically by quoting Horace's *Ut pictora poesis* and then reversing the comparison. The parallel between painting and poetry, as well as the contest between the two arts, was important to these authors, as to their predecessors in Renaissance Italy, because they were anxious to acquire for painting a standing equal to that of poetry and literature. This notion, which has been fully studied, remained alive until the early eighteenth century, and it is significant that the honor painting derives from its similarity to poetry is sometimes extended, as occasionally in the Italian Renaissance, to sculpture, architecture, and even engraving as related arts. Even the term *Beaux-Arts,* which seems to have been intended at first for the visual arts alone, corresponding to *Arti del diségno,* seems sometimes for these authors to include also music or poetry. The comparison between painting and music is also made a few times, and Poussin himself, who lived in Italy, tried to transfer the theory of the Greek musical modes to poetry and especially to painting.

One of the great changes that occurred during the seventeenth century was the rise and emancipation of the natural sciences. By the second half of the century, after the work of Galileo and René Descartes had been completed and the Académie des Sciences and the Royal Society had begun their activities, this development could not fail to impress the literati and the general public. It has been rightly observed that the famous *Querelle des anciens et modernes,* which stirred many scholars in France and also in England during the last quarter of the century, was due largely to the recent discoveries in the natural sciences. The moderns, conscious of these achievements, definitely shook off the authority of classical antiquity that had weighed on the Re-

naissance no less than on the Middle Ages, and went a long way toward formulating the concept of human progress. Yet this is only one side of the *Querelle.*

The *Querelle* as it went on had two important consequences that have not been sufficiently appreciated. First, the moderns broadened the literary controversy into a systematic comparison between the achievements of antiquity and of modern times in the various fields of human endeavor, thus developing a classification of knowledge and culture that was in many respects novel, or more specific than previous systems. Second, a point-by-point examination of the claims of the ancients and moderns in the various fields led to the insight that in certain fields, where everything depends on mathematical calculation and the accumulation of knowledge, the progress of the moderns over the ancients can be clearly demonstrated, whereas in certain other fields, which depend on individual talent and on the taste of the critic, the relative merits of the ancients and moderns cannot be so clearly established but may be subject to controversy.

Thus, the ground is prepared for the first time for a clear distinction between the arts and the sciences, a distinction absent from ancient, medieval, or Renaissance discussions of such subjects even though the same terms were used. In other words, the separation between the arts and the sciences in the modern sense presupposes not only the actual progress of the sciences in the seventeenth century but also the reflection on the reasons why some other human intellectual activities that we now call the fine arts did not or could not participate in the same kind of progress. To be sure, the writings of the *Querelle* do not yet attain a complete clarity on these points, and this fact in itself definitely confirms our contention that the separation between the arts and the sciences and the modern system of the fine arts were just in the making at that time. Bernard Le Bovier de Fontenelle, as some scholars have noticed, indicates in an occasional statement of his *Digression* that he was aware of the distinction between the arts and the sciences.

Much more important and explicit is the work of Charles Perrault. His famous *Parallèle des anciens et des modernes* discusses the various fields in separate sections that reflect a system: the second dialogue is dedicated to the three visual arts, the third to eloquence, the fourth to poetry, and the fifth to the sciences. The separation of the fine arts from the sciences is almost complete, though not yet entirely, since music is treated in the last book among the sciences, whereas in his poem, *Le Siècle de Louis le Grand,* which gave rise to the whole controversy, Perrault seems to connect music with the other arts. Moreover, in his prefaces Perrault states explicitly that at least in the case of poetry and eloquence, where everything depends on talent and taste, progress cannot be asserted with the same confidence as in the case of the sciences, which depend on measurement. Equally interesting, although unrelated to the *Querelle,* is another writing of Perrault, *Le cabinet des beaux-arts* (1690). This is a description and explanation of eight allegorical paintings found in the studio of a French gentleman to whom the work is dedicated. In the preface, Perrault opposes the concept Beaux-Arts to the traditional *Arts libéraux,* which he rejects, and then lists and describes the eight "fine arts" that the gentleman had represented to suit his taste and interests: eloquence, poetry, music, architecture, painting, sculpture, optics, and mechanics. Thus, on the threshold of the eighteenth century we are very close to the modern system of the fine arts, but we have not yet quite reached it, as the inclusion of optics and mechanics clearly shows. The fluctuations of the scheme show how slowly emerged the notion that to us seems so thoroughly obvious.

The Eighteenth Century. During the first half of the eighteenth century the interest of amateurs, writers, and philosophers in the visual arts and in music increased. The age produced not only critical writings on these arts composed by and for laypersons, but also treatises in which the arts were compared with each other and with poetry, and thus finally arrived at the fixation of the modern system of the fine arts. Since this system seems to emerge gradually and after many fluctuations in the writings of authors who were in part of but secondary importance, although influential, it would appear that the notion and system of the fine arts may have grown and crystallized in the conversations and discussions of cultured circles in Paris and in London, and that the formal writings and treatises merely reflect a climate of opinion resulting from such conversations. A further study of letters, diaries, and articles in elegant journals may indeed supplement our brief survey, which we must limit to the better-known sources.

The *Treatise on Beauty* by Jean Pierre de Crousaz, which first appeared in 1714 and exercised a good deal of influence, is usually considered as the earliest French treatise on aesthetics. It has indeed something to say on the visual arts and on poetry, and devotes a whole section to music. Moreover, it is an important attempt to give a philosophical analysis of beauty as distinct from goodness, thus restating and developing the notions of ancient and Renaissance Platonists. Yet, the author has no system of the arts, and applies his notion of beauty without any marked distinction to the mathematical sciences and to the moral virtues and actions as well as to the arts; and the fluidity of his "aesthetic" thought is shown by the fact that in his second edition he substituted a chapter on the beauty of religion for the one dealing with music.

During the following years, the problem of the arts seems to have dominated the discussions of the Académie des Inscriptions, and several of its lectures that were printed somewhat later and exercised a good deal of influence stress the affinity between poetry, the visual arts, and music. These discussions no doubt influenced the important work of the Abbé Jean-Baptiste Du Bos that appeared first in 1719 and was reprinted many times in the original and in translations far into the second half of the century. Du Bos's merits in the history of aesthetic or artistic thought are generally recognized. It is apparent that he discusses not only the analogies between poetry and painting but also their differences, and that he is not interested in the superiority of one art to the others, as so many previous authors had been. His work is also significant as an early, although not the first, treatment of painting by an amateur writer, and his claim that the educated public rather than the professional artist is the best judge in matters of painting as well as of poetry is quite characteristic. He did not invent the term *Beaux-Arts,* nor was he the first to apply it to other than the visual arts, but he certainly popularized the notion that poetry was one of the Beaux-Arts. He also has a fairly clear notion of the difference between the arts that depend on "genius" or talent and the sciences based on accumulated knowledge, and it has been rightly observed that in this he continues the work of the "moderns" in the *Querelle des anciens et des modernes,* especially of Perrault.

Significant also is Du Bos's acquaintance with English authors such as Sir Henry Wotton and Joseph Addison. Finally, although the title of his work refers only to poetry and painting, he repeatedly has occasion to speak also of the other visual arts as linked with painting, especially of sculpture and engraving, and he discusses music so frequently that his English translator chose to mention this art in the very title of the book. Du Bos is as unsystematic in his presentation and arrangement as he is interesting for the variety of his ideas, however, and he fails to give anywhere a precise list of the arts other than poetry and painting or to separate them consistently from other fields of professions.

François-Marie Arouet de Voltaire in his *Temple du goût* (1733) seems also to link together several of the fine arts, but in an informal and rather elusive fashion that shows he was unable or unwilling to present a clear scheme. More important for the history of our problem is the *Essay on Beauty* of Père Yves-Marie André (1741), which exercised a good deal of influence. His Cartesian background is worth noticing, although it is not enough to ascribe an aesthetics to Descartes. The major sections of the work discuss visible beauty, which includes nature and the visual arts, the beauty of morals, the beauty of the works of the spirit, by which he means poetry and eloquence, and finally the beauty of music. André thus moves much closer to the system of the arts than either Crousaz or Du Bos had done, but in his treatise the arts are still combined with morality, and subordinated to the problem of beauty in a broader sense.

The decisive step toward a system of the fine arts was taken by the Abbé Charles Batteux in his famous and influential treatise, *Les beaux arts réduits à un même principe* (1746). It is true that many elements of his system were derived from previous authors, but at the same time it should not be overlooked that he was the first to set forth a clear-

ORIGINS OF AESTHETICS: Overview. Saul Steinberg, *Detail from Poster Celebrating 50th Anniversary of American Society of Aesthetics* (1991), lithograph, 19 × 13½ inches. (Copyright by Saul Steinberg; photograph by Anthony L. Stankiewicz; used by permission.)

cut system of the fine arts in a treatise devoted exclusively to this subject. This alone may account for his claim to originality as well as for the enormous influence he exercised both in France and abroad, especially in Germany. Batteux codified the modern system of the fine arts almost in its final form, whereas all previous authors had merely prepared it. He started from the poetic theories of Aristotle and Horace, as he states in his preface, and tried to extend their principles from poetry and painting to the other arts. In his first chapter, Batteux gives a clear division of the arts. He separates the fine arts, which have pleasure as their end, from the mechanical arts, and lists the fine arts as follows: music, poetry, painting, sculpture, and the dance. He adds a third group that combines pleasure and usefulness and puts eloquence and architecture in this category. In the central part of his treatise, Batteux tries to show that the "imitation of beautiful nature" is the principle common to all the arts, and he concludes with a discussion of the theater as a combination of all the other arts. The German critics of the later

eighteenth century, and their recent historians, criticized Batteux for his theory of imitation and often failed to recognize that he formulated the system of the arts that they took for granted and for which they were merely trying to find different principles. They also overlooked the fact that the much maligned principle of imitation was the only one a classicist critic such as Batteux could use when he wanted to group the fine arts together with even an appearance of ancient authority. For the "imitative" arts were the only authentic ancient precedent for the "fine arts," and the principle of imitation could be replaced only after the system of the latter had been so firmly established as no longer to need the ancient principle of imitation to link them together. Denis Diderot's criticism of Batteux has been overemphasized, for it concerned only the manner in which Batteux defined and applied his principle, but neither the principle itself nor the system of the arts for which it had been designed.

As a matter of fact, Diderot and the other authors of the *Encyclopédie* not only followed Batteux's system of the fine arts, they also furnished the final touch and thus helped to give it a general currency not only in France but also in the other European countries. Baron de Montesquieu in his essay on taste written for the *Encyclopédie* takes the fine arts for granted. Diderot, whose interests included music and the visual arts and who was also acquainted with such English authors as the earl of Shaftesbury, Joseph Addison, and Francis Hutcheson, criticizes Batteux in his *Lettre sur les sourds et muets* (1751), in which he demands a better and more detailed comparison between poetry, painting, and music that would take into account the different modes of expression of those arts as they would affect their treatment of even the same subject matter. In the article on the arts for the *Encyclopédie*, Diderot does not discuss the fine arts, but uses the old distinction between the liberal and mechanical arts and stresses the importance of the latter. Yet, in his article on beauty, he does discuss the fine arts, mentions Crousaz and Hutcheson, and gives qualified approval to both André and Batteux, calling each of these two good works the best in its category and criticizing Batteux merely for his failure to define his concept of "beautiful nature" more clearly and explicitly.

Still more interesting is Jean Le Rond D'Alembert's famous *Discours préliminaire*. In his division of knowledge, purportedly based on Francis Bacon, d'Alembert makes a clear distinction between philosophy, which comprises both the natural sciences and such fields as grammar, eloquence, and history, and "those cognitions which consist of imitation," listing among the latter painting, sculpture, architecture, poetry, and music. He criticizes the old distinction between the liberal and mechanical arts, and then subdivides the liberal arts into the fine arts, which have pleasure as their end, and the more necessary or useful liberal arts, such as grammar, logic, and morals. He concludes with a main division of knowledge into philosophy, history, and the fine arts. This treatment shows still a few signs of fluctuation and of older notions, but it sets forth the modern system of the fine arts in its final form, and at the same time reflects its genesis. The threefold division of knowledge follows Bacon, but significantly d'Alembert speaks of the five fine arts, whereas Bacon had mentioned only poetry. D'Alembert is aware that the new concept of the fine arts is taking the place of the older concept of the liberal arts, which he criticizes, and he tries to compromise by treating the fine arts as a subdivision of the liberal arts, thus leaving a last trace of the liberal arts that was soon to disappear. Finally, he reveals his dependence on Batteux in certain phrases and in the principle of imitation, but against Batteux and the classical tradition he now includes architecture among the imitative arts, thus removing the last irregularity that had separated Batteux's system from the modern scheme of the fine arts. Thus, we may conclude that the *Encyclopédie,* and especially its famous introduction, codified the system of the fine arts after and beyond Batteux and through its prestige and authority gave it the widest possible currency all over Europe.

After the middle of the century and after the publication of the *Encyclopédie,* speculation on the fine arts in France does not seem to have undergone any basic changes for some time. The notion was popularized and stabilized through such works as Jacques Lacombe's portable dictionary of the fine arts, which covered architecture, sculpture, painting, engraving, poetry, and music, and through other similar works. The term *Beaux-Arts,* and "Art," in the new sense, found its way into the dictionaries of the French language that had ignored it before. The Revolution also gave the novel term a new institutional expression when it merged several of the older academies into the Académie des Beaux-Arts. Gradually, the further developments of aesthetics in Germany began to affect French philosophy and literature. The second edition of the *Encyclopédie,* published in Switzerland in 1781, has additions by Johann Georg Sulzer, including an article on aesthetics and a section on fine arts appended to the article on art that had not appeared in the first edition. Early in the nineteenth century, the philosopher Victor Cousin, following Immanuel Kant and the Scottish thinkers of the eighteenth century, as well as what he believed he found in Plato, Proclus, and other classical sources, centered his philosophical system on the three concepts of the Good, the True, and the Beautiful, understanding by the latter the realm of art and aesthetics. Cousin's wide influence in the later nineteenth century served greatly to establish this triad in modern value theory and to fortify the place of aesthetics in the system of philosophical disciplines. It also induced many thinkers and historians to interpret in terms of this scheme a number of ancient and medieval notions that resembled it superficially but that in reality had a very different meaning and context. Meanwhile, as Cousin's doctrine was spreading among

philosophers and historians, French literature and criticism had long been feeling the impact of Romanticism. They were beginning to develop modern problems and theories concerning the arts and their interpretation, no longer related to the discussions of the eighteenth century, and were laying the ground for other, more recent tendencies.

English and Scottish Contributions. The English writers were strongly influenced by the French down to the end of the seventeenth century and later, but during the eighteenth century they made important contributions of their own and in turn influenced Continental thought, especially in France and Germany. Interest in the arts other than poetry began to rise slowly in the English literature of the seventeenth century. Works of an encyclopedic nature show little awareness of the separate function of the fine arts, whereas an author such as Henry Peacham, who continued the amateur tradition of the Renaissance, would not only write a treatise on drawing but also recommend the cultivation of painting, music, and poetry, of classical studies, and the collecting of coins and other antiquities and of natural curiosities, for the education of a perfect gentleman. John Evelyn, who was the model of a virtuoso, included artistic and scientific interests, but the work of the virtuosi of the Royal Society soon led to a separation between the arts and the sciences. The *Querelle,* which was at least partly caused by the emancipation of the natural sciences in the seventeenth century, spread from France to England. The most important treatise in England representing the views of the moderns, that of Henry Wotton, tried to cover systematically all the human arts and activities, just as Perrault had done, and, like Perrault, emphasized the fundamental difference between the sciences that had made progress since antiquity and the arts that had not. A translation of one of the French works related to the *Querelle,* François de Callières's *History of the War of the Ancients and Moderns,* was published as late as 1705, and reveals in its very title the growing sense of the affinity of the fine arts. Even before the end of the seventeenth century, John Dryden had translated Dufresnoy's poem on painting with de Piles's commentary and had added his famous introduction on "The Parallel of Painting and Poetry," which popularized the notion in England. This translation was still of interest to Joshua Reynolds, who wrote some notes on it. Early in the eighteenth century, Jonathan Richardson was praising painting as a liberal art, and John Dennis, in some of his critical treatises on poetics, stressed the affinity between poetry, painting, and music.

Of greater importance were the writings of Anthony Ashley Cooper, earl of Shaftesbury, one of the most influential thinkers of the eighteenth century, not only in England but also on the Continent. His interest in and taste for literature and the arts are well known, and his writings are full of references to the various arts and to the beauty of their works. The ideal of the virtuoso that he embodied and advocated no longer included the sciences, as in the seventeenth century, but had its center in the arts and in the moral life. Because Shaftesbury was the first major philosopher in modern Europe in whose writings the discussion of the arts occupied a prominent place, there is some reason for considering him as the founder of modern aesthetics. Yet, Shaftesbury was influenced primarily by Plato and Plotinus, as well as by Cicero, and he consequently did not make a clear distinction between artistic and moral beauty. His moral sense continues to includes both ethical and aesthetic objects. Moreover, although references to the particular arts are frequent in his writings, and some of his works are even entirely devoted to the subjects of painting or of poetry, the passages in which he mentions poetry, the visual arts, and music together are infrequent, and do not contain any more specific notions than may be found in earlier authors. Poetry, especially, appears in the company not only of eloquence but also of history, thus reflecting the Renaissance tradition of the *Studia humanitatis*. Almost equally influential in England as well as on the Continent, at least in literary circles, was Addison. His famous essays on imagination, which appeared in the *Spectator* in 1712, are remarkable not merely for their early emphasis on that faculty, but also for the manner in which Addison attributes the pleasures of the imagination to the various arts as well as to natural sights. Without ever giving a definite system, he constantly refers to gardening and architecture, painting and sculpture, poetry and music, and makes it clear that the pleasures of the imagination are to be found in their works and products.

The philosophical implications of Shaftesbury's doctrine were further developed by a group of Scottish thinkers. Hutcheson, who considered himself Shaftesbury's pupil, modified his doctrine by distinguishing between the moral sense and the sense of beauty. This distinction, which was adopted by David Hume and quoted by Diderot, played a strong part in preparing the separation of ethics and aesthetics, although Hutcheson still assigned the taste of poetry to the moral sense. A later philosopher of the Scottish school, Thomas Reid, introduced common sense as a direct criterion of truth, and although he was no doubt influenced by Aristotle's notion of common sense and the Stoic and modern views on "common notions," it has been suggested that his common sense was conceived as a counterpart to Hutcheson's two senses. Thus, the psychology of the Scottish school led the way for the doctrine of the three faculties of the soul, which found its final development in Kant and its application in Cousin.

Other English authors motivated by critical rather than philosophical interests and probably influenced by French authors, popularized the notion of the affinity between poetry, painting, and music (e.g., Charles Lamotte and Hildebrand Jacobs). More philosophical are the essays of James Harris, who continued Shaftesbury and had some influence on German writers. In the first of his three essays, which are written in an elegant dialogue form but heavily annotated with references to classical authors, Harris expounds the concept of art on the basis of Aristotle and with its older comprehensive meaning. In the second essay, he distinguishes between the necessary arts and the arts of elegance, putting under the latter category especially music, painting, and poetry, and comparing these three arts with each other according to their relative merits. The third essay deals with happiness as the art of human conduct. About the same time, the poet Mark Akenside continued the work of Addison; and before the middle of the century the important French works of Du Bos and Batteux were presented to English readers, the former in a translation, the latter in an anonymous version or summary, titled *The Polite Arts*.

During the second half of the eighteenth century, English writers continued to discuss the various arts. But they were not so much interested in expounding and developing a system of the fine arts, which they largely took for granted, as in discussing general concepts and principles concerning the arts (e.g., Henry Home, Edmund Burke, and Alexander Gerard); or else the relations between the particular arts (e.g., Daniel Webb or John Brown). All these English and Scottish writers show a strong preoccupation with psychology, as might be expected from the general trend of English thought in that century. They exercised considerable influence on the Continent, especially in Germany, where many of their works appeared in translations. It has been noted that the emphasis of writers and literary critics on the affinity between poetry and painting was followed after the middle of the century by an increasing insistence on the links between poetry and music. One reason for this may have been the public attention music received in London after the appearance of George Frideric Handel, just as had been the case in Paris after the success of Lully. On the other hand, if poetry really tended to exchange the company of painting for that of music, this merely reflects a change in style and taste from descriptive to emotional poetry that corresponds to the transition from classicism to Romanticism. A new epoch in English critical and artistic theory begins toward the very end of the century with Samuel Taylor Coleridge, who imported from Germany some of the aesthetic notions of Kant and of the early Romantics.

German Contributions. Discussion of the arts does not seem to have occupied many German-language writers in the seventeenth century, which was on the whole a period of cultural decline. The poet Martin Opitz showed familiarity with the parallel of poetry and painting, but otherwise the Germans did not take part in the development we are trying to describe before the eighteenth century. During the first part of that century interest in literature and literary criticism began to rise, but did not yet lead to a detailed or comparative treatment of the other arts. Some of the French and English writers we have mentioned were widely read, however, and were also translated into German during the course of the century, such as Du Bos and Batteux, Cooper and Harris. The critical writings of the Swiss authors Johann Georg Bodmer and Johann Jakob Breitinger focus from the beginning on the parallel between painting and poetry, and reflect the influence of Addison and perhaps of Dubos. Even their classicist opponent, Johann Christoph Gottsched, occasionally mentions the affinity between poetry, painting, music, and the other arts, as does Johann Elias Schlegel, who is said to have been influenced by the lectures of Claude-François Fraguier and other authors published in the *Memoirs of the Académie des Inscriptions*. His brother Johann Adolf Schlegel, who was one of the translators of Batteux, added to his version several original essays in which he criticizes the theory of imitation and also presents a modified system of the fine arts. Yet, all these writers were primarily interested in poetics and literary criticism and drew on the other arts only for occasional analogies.

These critical discussions among poets and literati constitute the general background for the important work of the philosopher Alexander Gottlieb Baumgarten and of his pupil Georg Friedrich Meier. Baumgarten is famous for having coined the term *aesthetics,* but opinions differ as to whether he must be considered the founder of that discipline or what place he occupies in its history and development. The original meaning of the term aesthetics as coined by Baumgarten, which has been all but forgotten by now, is the theory of sensuous knowledge, as a counterpart to logic as a theory of intellectual knowledge. The definitions Baumgarten gives of aesthetics show that he is concerned with the arts and with beauty as one of their main attributes, but he still uses the old term *liberal arts,* and he considers them as forms of knowledge. The question whether Baumgarten really propounded a theory of all the fine arts, or merely a poetics and rhetoric with a new name, has been debated but can be answered easily. In his earlier work, in which he first coined the term aesthetics, Baumgarten was exclusively concerned with poetics and rhetoric. In his later, unfinished work, to which he gave the title *Aesthetica,* Baumgarten states in his introduction that he intends to put forth a theory of all the arts, and actually makes occasional references to the visual arts and to music. This impression is confirmed by the text of Baumgarten's lectures published only recently, and by the writings of his pupil Meier. On the other hand, it is quite obvious, and was noted by contemporary critics, that Baumgarten and Meier develop their actual theories only in terms of poetry and eloquence and take nearly all their examples from literature. Baumgarten is the founder of aesthetics insofar as he first conceived a general theory of the arts as a separate philosophical discipline with a distinctive and well-defined place in the system of philosophy. He failed to develop his doctrine with reference to the arts other than poetry and eloquence, or even to propose a systematic list and division of these other arts. In this latter respect, he was preceded and surpassed by the French writ-

ers, especially by Batteux and the Encyclopedists, whereas the latter failed to develop a theory of the arts as part of a philosophical system. It was the result of German thought and criticism during the second half of the eighteenth century that the more concrete French conception of the fine arts was utilized in a philosophical theory of aesthetics for which Baumgarten had formulated the general scope and program.

When Meier tried to answer Baumgarten's critics, he stated that both Baumgarten and he had spoken only about literature, since they did not know enough about the other arts. The broadening scope of German aesthetics after Baumgarten, which we must now try to trace, was due not only to the influence of Batteux, of the Encyclopedists, and of other French and English writers, but also to the increasing interest taken by writers, philosophers, and the lay public in the visual arts and in music. Johann Joachim Winckelmann's studies of classical art are important for the history of our problem for the enthusiasm he stimulated among his German readers for ancient sculpture and architecture, but not for any opinion he may have expressed on the relation between the visual arts and literature. Gotthold Ephraim Lessing's *Laocoön* (1766) also has a notable importance, not only for its particular theories on matters of poetry and of the visual arts, but also for the very attention given to the latter by one of the most brilliant and most respected German writers of the time. Yet, the place of the *Laocoön* in the history of our problem has been misjudged. To say that the *Laocoön* put an end to the age-old tradition of the parallel between painting and poetry that had its ultimate roots in classical antiquity and found its greatest development in the writers of the sixteenth, seventeenth, and early eighteenth century, and thus freed poetry from the emphasis on description, is to give only one side of the picture. It is to forget that the parallel between painting and poetry was one of the most important elements that preceded the formation of the modern system of the fine arts, although it had lost this function as a link between two different arts by the time of Lessing, when the more comprehensive system of the fine arts had been firmly established. Insofar as Lessing paid no attention to the broader system of the fine arts, especially to music, his *Laocoön* constituted a detour or a dead end in terms of the development leading to a comprehensive system of the fine arts. It is significant that the *Laocoön* was criticized for this very reason by two prominent contemporary critics, and that in the posthumous notes for the second part of the work Lessing gave some consideration to this criticism, although we have no evidence that he actually planned to extend his analysis to music and to a coherent system of the arts.

The greatest contributions to the history of our problem in the interval between Baumgarten and Kant came from Moses Mendelssohn, Sulzer, and Johann Gottfried Herder. Mendelssohn, who was well acquainted with French and

English writings on the subject, demanded in a famous article that the fine arts (painting, sculpture, music, the dance, and architecture) and belles-lettres (poetry and eloquence) should be reduced to some common principle better than imitation, and thus was the first among the Germans to formulate a system of the fine arts. Shortly afterward, in a book review, he criticized Baumgarten and Meier for not having carried out the program of their new science, aesthetics. They wrote as if they had been thinking exclusively in terms of poetry and literature, whereas aesthetic principles should be formulated in such a way as to apply to the visual arts and to music as well. In his annotations to Lessing's *Laocoön*, published long after his death, Mendelssohn persistently criticizes Lessing for not giving any consideration to music and to the system of the arts as a whole; we have seen how Lessing, in the fragmentary notes for a continuation of the *Laocoön*, tried to meet this criticism. Mendelssohn also formulated a doctrine of the three faculties of the soul corresponding to the three basic realms of goodness, truth, and beauty, thus continuing the work of the Scottish philosophers. He did not work out an explicit theory of aesthetics, but under the impact of French and English authors he indicated the direction in which German aesthetics was to develop from Baumgarten to Kant.

What Mendelssohn had merely set forth in a general outline and program, the Swiss thinker Sulzer, who was well versed in French literature but spent the greater part of his life in northern Germany, was able to develop in a more systematic and elaborate fashion. Sulzer began his literary activity with a few short philosophical articles in which his interest for aesthetics was already apparent, and in which he also leaned toward the conception of an aesthetic faculty of the soul separate from the intellectual and moral faculties, a conception in whose development Mendelssohn and the philosopher Johannes Nikolaus Tetens also took their part. Some years later, he was prompted by the example of Jacques Lacombe's little dictionary of the fine arts to compile a similar dictionary in German on a much larger scale. This *General Theory of the Fine Arts,* which appeared in several editions, has been disparaged because of its pedantic arrangement, but it is clear, comprehensive, and learned, and had a considerable importance in its time. The work covers all the fine arts, not only poetry and eloquence, but also music and the visual arts, and thus represents the first attempt to carry out on a large scale the program formulated by Baumgarten and Mendelssohn. Thanks to its wide diffusion, Sulzer's work helped acquaint the German public with the idea that all the fine arts are connected with each other. Sulzer's influence extended also to France, for when the great *Encyclopédie* was published in Switzerland in a second edition, many additions were based on his *General Theory,* including the article on aesthetics and the section on the fine arts.

In the decades after 1760, the interest in the new field of aesthetics spread rapidly in Germany. Courses on aesthetics were offered at a number of universities after the example set by Baumgarten and Meier, and new tracts and textbooks, partly based on these courses, appeared almost every year. These authors have been listed, but their individual contributions remain to be investigated. The influence of the *Encyclopédie* is attested to by a curious engraving printed in Weimar in 1769 and attached to a famous copy of the *Encyclopédie*. It represents the tree of the arts and sciences as given in the text of d'Alembert's *Discours*, putting the visual arts, poetry, and music with their subdivisions under the general branch of imagination. Among the minor aesthetic writers of this period, Friedrich Riedel has attracted some scholarly attention, probably because he was the target of Herder's criticism. In his treatise on aesthetics, based on university lectures, Riedel gives a full discussion of all the fine arts, and also sets out with a general division of philosophical subjects into the True, the Good, and the Beautiful.

It is interesting to note the reaction to this aesthetic literature of the leaders of the younger generation, especially of Johann Wolfgang von Goethe and of Herder. Goethe in his early years published a review of Sulzer that was quite unfavorable. Noticing the French background of Sulzer's conception, Goethe ridicules the grouping together of all the arts that are so different from each other in their aims and means of expression, a system that reminds him of the old-fashioned system of the seven liberal arts, and adds that this system may be useful to the amateur but certainly not to the artist. This reaction shows that the system of the fine arts was novel and not yet firmly established, and that Goethe, just like Lessing, did not take an active part in developing the notion that was to become generally accepted. Toward the very end of his life, in the *Wanderjahre*, Goethe shows that he had by then accepted the system of the fine arts, for he assigns a place to each of them in his pedagogical province. Yet his awareness of the older meaning of art is apparent when in a group of aphorisms originally appended to the same work he defines art as knowledge and concludes that poetry, being based on genius, should not be called an art.

Herder, on the other hand, took an active part in the development of the system of the fine arts and used the weight of his literary authority to have it generally accepted. In an early but important critical work (*Kritische Wälder*, 1769), he dedicates the entire first section to a critique of Lessing's *Laocoön*. Lessing shows merely, Herder argues, what poetry is not, by comparing it with painting. In order to see what its essence is, we should compare it with all its sister arts, such as music, the dance, and eloquence. Quoting Aristotle and Harris, Herder stresses the comparison between poetry and music, and concludes that this problem would require another Lessing. In the fourth section, he quotes Mendelssohn as well as the more important English and French authors, and presents his own system of the fine arts, which includes all the essential elements, although it differs from previous authors in some detail. Herder's later contributions to aesthetics are beyond the scope of this article.

It is only fitting to conclude this survey with Kant, since he was the first major philosopher who included aesthetics and the philosophical theory of the arts as an integral part of his system. Kant's interest in aesthetic problems appears already in his early writing on the beautiful and sublime, which was influenced in its general conception by Burke. He also had occasion to discuss aesthetic problems in several of his courses. Notes based on these courses extant in manuscript form have not been published, but have been used by a student of Kant's aesthetics. It appears that Kant cited in these lectures many authors he does not mention in his published works, and that he was thoroughly familiar with most of the French, English, and German writers on aesthetics. At the time when he published the *Critique of Pure Reason,* he still used the term *aesthetics* in a sense different from the common one, and explains in an interesting footnote that he does not follow Baumgarten's terminology because he does not believe in the possibility of a philosophical theory of the arts. In the following years, however, he changed his view, and in his *Critique of Judgment,* which constitutes the third and concluding part of his philosophical system, the larger of its two major divisions is dedicated to aesthetics, whereas the other section deals with teleology. The system of the three Critiques as presented in this last volume is based on a threefold division of the faculties of the mind, which adds the faculty of judgment, aesthetic and teleological, to pure and practical reason. Aesthetics, as the philosophical theory of beauty and the arts, acquires equal standing with the theory of truth (metaphysics or epistemology) and the theory of goodness (ethics).

In the tradition of systematic philosophy this was an important innovation, for neither Descartes nor Baruch Spinoza nor Gottfried Wilhelm Leibniz nor any of their ancient or medieval predecessors had found a separate or independent place in their system for the theory of the arts and of beauty, although they had expressed occasional opinions on these subjects. If Kant took this decisive step after some hesitation, he was obviously influenced by the example of Baumgarten and by the rich French, English, and German literature on the arts his century had produced, with which he was well acquainted. In his critique of aesthetic judgment, Kant discusses also the concepts of the sublime and of natural beauty, but his major emphasis is on beauty in the arts, and he discusses many concepts and principles common to all the arts. In section 51 he also gives a division of the fine arts: speaking arts (poetry, eloquence); plastic arts (sculpture, architecture, painting, and gardening); arts of the beautiful play of sentiments (music and the art of color). This scheme contains a few ephemeral details that were not retained by Kant's successors. Since Kant, however, aesthetics has occupied a permanent place among the major philosophical disciplines, and the core of the system of the fine arts fixed in the eighteenth century has been generally accepted as a matter of course by most later writers on the subject, except for variations of detail or of explanation.

BIBLIOGRAPHY

Addison, Joseph. *Works.* Edited by Thomas Tickell. London, 1721.

Alembert, Jean Le Rond d'. *Œuvres.* Paris, 1853.

André (Père). *Essai sur le beau* (1741). Amsterdam, 1759.

Batteux (Abbé). *Les beaux arts réduits à un même principe* (1746). Paris, 1747.

Baumgarten, Alexander. *Aesthetica* (1750–1758). Edited by Benedetto Croce. Bari, 1936.

Callières, François de. *Characters and Criticisms, upon the Ancient and Modern Orators, Poets, Painters, Musicians, Statuaries, and other Arts and Sciences.* London, 1705. Anonymous translation of *Histoire poëtique de la querre nouvellement déclarée entre les anciens et les modernes* (Paris, 1687).

Castiglione, Baldassare. *The Book of the Courtier* (1528). Translated by George Bull. New York, 1967.

Chambers, Ephraim. *Cyclopaedia.* 5th ed. London, 1741–1743.

Cooper, Anthony Ashley, Earl of Shaftesbury. *Characteristics of Men, Manners, Opinions, Times* (1711). Edited by John M. Robertson. Indianapolis, 1964.

Cousin, Victor. *Du Vrai, du beau et du bien* (1836). 29th ed. Paris, 1904.

Crousaz, J. P. de. *Traité du beau* (1714). New ed. 2 vols. Amsterdam, 1724.

Diderot, Denis. *Œuvres complètes de Diderot.* Edited by J. Assézat. 20 vols. Paris, 1875–1877.

Du Bos, Jean-Baptiste (Abbé). *Critical Reflections on Poetry, Painting, and Music* (1719). 3 vols. Translated by Thomas Nugent. London, 1748.

Duffresnoy, Charles Alphonse. *De arte graphica: The Art of Painting.* Translated by John Dryden. London, 1695.

Fontenelle, Bernard. *Digression sur les anciens et les modernes* (1688). In *Œuvres,* vol. 4. Amsterdam, 1764.

Goethe, Johann Wolfgang von. Review of Sulzer's *Die schönen Künste in ihrem Ursprung* (1772). In *Goethes Werke* (*Sophien-Ausgabe*), vol. 37. Weimar, 1896.

Goethe, Johann Wolfgang von. *Wilhelm Meister's Years of Travel* (1895). Translated by H. M. Waidson. London, 1980–1982.

Harris, James. *Three Treatises, the first concerning art, the second concerning music, painting, and poetry, and the third concerning happiness.* London, 1744.

Herder, Johann Gottfried. *Kritische Wälder* (1769). In *Herders sämmtliche Werke,* edited by B. Suphan, vol. 3. Berlin, 1878.

Horace. *Ars poetica.* Edited by Augustus S. Wilkins. London, 1939.

Hutcheson, Francis. *An Inquiry into the Original of Our Ideas of Beauty and Virtue* (1725). Glasgow, 1772.

Jacobi Pontani de Societate Jesu (Jacobus Pontanus). *Poeticarum institutionum libri III.* Ingolstadt, 1600.

Kant, Immanuel. *Critique of Pure Reason* (1781/1787). Translated by Werner S. Pluhar. Indianapolis, 1996.

Kant, Immanuel. *Critique of Judgment* (1790). Translated by Werner S. Pluhar. Indianapolis, 1987.

Lacombe, Jacques. *Dictionnaire portatif des Beaux Arts; ou, Abrégé de ce qui concerne l'architecture, la sculpture, la peinture, la gravure, la poésie et la musique, avec la définition de ces arts, l'explication des termes et des choses qui leur appartiennent.* New ed. Paris, 1753.

Leonardo da Vinci. *The Literary Works of Leonardo da Vinci.* Edited by Jean Paul Richter and Irma A. Richter. 2d enl. rev. ed. 2 vols. London, 1939.

Lessing, Georg Ephraim. *Laocoön: An Essay on the Limits of Painting and Poetry* (1766). Translated by Edwin Allen McCormick. Baltimore, 1984.

Meier, Georg Friedrich. *Abbildung eines Kunstrichters.* Halle, 1745.

Meier, Georg Friedrich. *Anfangsgründe aller schönen Wissenschaften* (1748–1750). 2d ed. Halle, 1754–1759.

Mendelssohn, Moses. "Betrachtungen über die Quellen und die Verbindungen der schönen Künste und Wissenschaften" (1757). In *Gesammelte Schriften (Jubiläumsausgabe)*, vol. 1. Berlin, 1929.

Mesnardière, Jules de la. *La Poétique.* Paris, 1639.

Montesquieu, Charles de Secondat. *Essai sur le goût.* In *Œuvres complètes de Montesquieu*, edited by E. Laboulaye, vol. 7. Paris, 1879.

Niphus, Augustinus (Nifo). *De pulchro, de amore.* Lyons, 1549.

Perrault, Charles. *Parallele des anciens et des modernes.* 4 vols. Paris, 1688–1696.

Reid, Thomas. *Works.* 4th ed. Edinburgh, 1854.

Sulzer, Johann Georg. *Allgemeine Theorie der schönen Künste* (1771–1774). New ed. 4 vols. Leipzig, 1792–1799.

Voltaire, François-Marie Arouet de. *Le temple du goût* (1733). Edited by E. Carcasonne. Paris, 1938.

PAUL OSKAR KRISTELLER

History of Aisthēsis

Aisthēsis descends from a word meaning "to breathe," an archaic metaphor for perception as pneumatic, but certain aspects of the notion of *aisthēsis* led to its being adapted to the purpose of naming Alexander Baumgarten's new field of aesthetics in the middle of the eighteenth century. Things, as it were, breathe themselves out, we, as it were, breathe them in, and on this etymological view *aisthēsis* is of a piece with life itself. In the philosophies of Plato and Aristotle, *aisthēsis* became the agent of a higher principle, the soul, conceived as distinct from sense and essentially rational, specifically in being homologous with the reasons and causes of the larger world. At this point, *aisthēsis* assumed other meanings. Most *aisthēsis* was still perception, the basis for experience; but some *aisthēsis* provided reflective access to the nature of the soul itself, and the congruence between soul and sense, experienced as a kind of pleasure, constituted a judgment. Perhaps the formative example is the variously told story of the discovery of the laws of harmony by Pythagoras. Those sounds that pleased the ear could be shown to possess a *harmonia*, that is, to be well made and fitted to one another in ratios of whole integers. It is crucially important that *aisthēsis*, and therefore the human soul itself, resonated with this harmony, like apprehending like.

A related argument is advanced by Plato in the *Philebus* (51B). Pleasures are not necessarily the absence of pain (although some are, he says, like scratching an itch); true pleasures are those that fill no want, such as the sight of beautiful colors or figures, or certain smells ("less divine") and sounds, by which in this case he means pure tones. Beautiful "figures" (*schemata*) are not those of animals or those to be found in painting, but rather "the straight line; and the circle and the plane and solid figures formed from these by turning lathes and rulers and patterns of angles." These are absolutely, not relatively, beautiful in themselves. He adds the beauty of learning (*mathemata*) to this list. Later (67C), he reviews and slightly revises this argument; those pleasures that are painless are "pure pleasures of the soul (*psyche*) itself," which accompany knowledge (*epistēmē*) and, sometimes, perception (*aisthēsis*).

This statement comes as the fifth and last stage in a descending order of pure pleasures at the top of which are those to be taken in "measure, moderation and fitness." These pleasures, which descend through those of the virtues and sciences, are interrelated, and have in common the soul's delight in finding (or for Plato and Platonists, remembering) what is "pure" in being like the soul itself. The *schemata* of ruler, compass, and lathe are like the *kosmos* constructed by the *demiurgos* of the *Timaeus* (28A); like the *kosmos*, they teach the soul its own movements, the curative "harmonies and revolutions" that bring the rational soul at once to self-awareness and to true knowledge of the world. This consonance between *aisthēsis* and mind is beauty, or the highest beauty, a principle that would become basic to the long Platonic tradition. Plotinus, for example (*Ennead*, I.6.2), states as a principle that "things in the world are beautiful by participating in form," meaning that the soul itself delights in experience recalling it to its own origins in a realm of intelligible forms. By the same token, light is beautiful because it is like the soul in being an immaterial unity. Saint Augustine would argue that bilateral symmetry is immediately pleasing, and departures from it displeasing, because its unity adumbrates the unity of the soul and God.

If, according to Plato, *aisthēsis* might reveal the nature of that which senses, it also had other much less positive meanings that were crucial for the tradition to follow. As normal perception, *aisthēsis* provides the adequate basis for most experience, which it does both infallibly and with error; that is, sight does not tell us that a finger is not a finger (*Republic* 523B ff.), but it always presents the given for which the finger is exemplary as possessing variable qualities describable in terms of polarities, such as near and far, dark and light. These, Plato argued, are "productive of thought." The changing coexistences of these qualities make us wonder what they might be in themselves. By this reflective wondering about *aisthēsis* we transcend it, thus to find ourselves thinking about forms, qualities, and relations in themselves. Plato used such examples to make what proved to be a millennial distinction (*Republic* 524B–C) between the intelligible and the visible (or sensible): the intelligible is clear and distinct; the sensible is confused and confounded in the sense that what might be analyzed has not been analyzed. This distinction had many echoes in the tradition down to Baumgarten. Taken altogether, *aisthēsis* had thus become "sense" with the pejorative meaning the idea has had in Platonic philosophies and their many tributaries and adaptations. At the same time, it is important to stress that the intelligible was there in sense to be analyzed. Plotinus argued (*Ennead* 4.6.3) that the human soul is the farthest (lowest) extension of reason in the world and that sense is the farthest extension of the human soul. There is reason in *aisthēsis*, but potentially.

Plato's extremely general division between *aisthēsis* and *noesis* has shaped some of the foundations of Western culture. In the *Philebus* (56D), for example, he argued that there are two arithmetics, one of the many and one of the philosophers; the first is empirical and deals with the approximate; the second is abstract and deals with the exact. The cultural force of this distinction may be seen in Plutarch's account of Archimedes (*Marcellus* 14, 4–6). The inventors of mechanics argued not by word and diagram but with "sensible and tool-like models," and Plato condemned them for abandoning the noetic for the aesthetic. He added to this the condemnation of the manual labor necessary for such demonstrations, which, because they involved handiwork, could not be liberal, that is, not worthy of free men, and certainly not worthy of philosophers. Fearing such rebuke, Archimedes would not write of his machines, tainted as they were with the mathematics of the many. This social distinction survived to modern times in classifications of the liberal and mechanical arts, and still haunts modern attitudes toward theory and practice.

Plato's distinction also had the effect of opposing all kinds of human circumstantial judgment to reason. Aristotle, as we shall see, gave much more weight to such judgment. In Latin rhetoric, the *iudicium aurium*, the judgment of the ear, was a final arbiter, as it would later be argued to be by some theorists of Renaissance music. Vitruvius (*De architectura* 6, 2, 2) argued that the architect displays the greatest judgment in adjusting the proportions of buildings to their actual circumstances.

Aristotle defined *aisthēsis* in general as the apprehension of a magnitude through a magnitude, imagining the senses as lyres, instruments mute when not struck, broken when struck too hard. The five "special" senses are infallible in telling us that we are sensing what is fitted to them (light to vision, sound to hearing), and they also express judgments in pleasure and displeasure, always preferring the mean. If it is dark, we cannot see, and if we look at the sun, we experience irritation, pain, or damage. If light is moderate, sight is pleased. Such homologies, again evident to reflection on the pleasure of sense, point to the nature of the soul itself. Aristotle cites with approval the opinion of "wise men," who ar-

gue that the soul itself is a *harmonia* (*Politics* 1340 bff.), by nature seeking a mean.

Aristotle elaborated the idea of a common sense (*koinē aisthēsis*) from Plato's idea of the five senses as organs of the *psyche* (*Theatetus* 184ff.). The common sense is the central, unitary principle of perception, subsuming the particular senses, but also integral with reflection, imagination, and memory. It perceives what is common to the other senses, the so-called common sensibles, which, in their fullest list (*De anima* 425a15) were movement, rest, shape, magnitude, number, and unity. Again, the common sensibles (called "mathematicals" by some medieval writers) were judged imprecisely, and these judgments were necessarily subject to error. Important as it obviously was to his psychology, Aristotle never fully developed the idea of *koinē aisthēsis*. There are, however, indications that he also understood the common sense to "judge" according to a mean, or that he thought the mean with regard to common sensibles to be most pleasing. He states that the common sense judges the goodness and badness of things (*De anima* 426b, perhaps varying the argument just cited in Plato's *Theatetus*). In order for any whole made up of parts to be beautiful, Aristotle wrote, it must be neither imperceptibly small nor incomprehensibly large; it must be able to be taken in by the eye, just as the plot of a drama must not be too long to remember (*Poetics* 1450b34ff.; *Rhetoric* 1409a35). Comparing judgments about art to ethical judgments (*Nichomachean Ethics* 1109b), Aristotle notes that finding the mean by reasoning is difficult because the judgment must be made with respect to the particular. The judgment rests with perception (*aisthēsis*):

> Every art does its work well by looking to the intermediate and judging its works by this standard (so that we often say of good works of art that it is not possible either to take away or add anything, implying that excess and defect destroy the goodness of works of art, while the mean preserves it.

Aristotle (*Nicomachean Ethics* 1142a15ff.) gave great importance to *koinē aisthēsis* in the exercise of the central virtue of prudence (*phronēsis*). Prudence depends on experience and on the right judgment of the particular matter at hand, a judgment expressly opposed to general, mathematical judgments. Principles applied without respect to the particular case will be imprudent and unjust, and we have the capacity—*koinē aisthēsis*—to make judgments about particular cases. Following such clues, later Arabic and then Western writers consolidated a system of what they called the "internal senses," clustering around one or another account of the common sense (of which Aristotle sometimes spoke as a kind of *hegemonikon*), and combining what Aristotle had said about human sense with what he had written about lower reasons (productive and practical) and capacities for judgment (e.g., prudence). On the whole, it must be stressed that the internal senses were faculties of the rational soul, although they were not faculties of speculative reason. The system of the internal senses, which has now entirely slid into oblivion, was part of philosophical discourse at least until Immanuel Kant and Friedrich von Schiller. When Kant argued in the *Critique of Judgment* that taste is a *sensus communis* he was still making use of this system. Schiller lamented in the first of his letters in *On the Aesthetic Education of Man* that "intellect must first destroy the object of Inner Sense if it would make it its own."

The internal senses were opposed to the five external senses, with which they were often said to be symmetrical, at least in being the same in number. The complete list of internal senses—which combined and overlapped in various ways—consisted of *sensus communis, phantasia* or *imaginativa, estimativa, cogitativa,* and *memoria.* The internal senses were regarded as more spiritual than their external counterparts, but they were senses in that they too were concerned with particulars, and thus were opposed to pure or speculative intellect, which, in a pattern without deviation from Plato onward, was concerned with the general. Their particularity meant specifically that they were primarily concerned with images, so that imagination was always central to their discussion. The most complete and elegant version of the internal senses was given by Ibn Rushd (Averroës), who arranged them in a Neoplatonic hierarchy stretching between external sense and reason. The highest internal sense was what Ibn Rushd called the *vis cogitativa,* sometimes the *distinctiva.* For him, the *cogitativa,* summarizing the faculties below it, was the particular intellect, which was concerned with the negotiation of particular things and circumstances, but was also the soul of one mortal individual, concentric with, but separate from, the eternal intellect above it, concentric in its turn with the reasons of the structure of the world.

Ibn Rushd's notion of the particular intellect was widely associated in the West with the completely unacceptable idea of the mortality of the individual soul. In refuting him, Saint Thomas Aquinas did not reject the idea of the *cogitativa;* rather he incorporated it into his definition of the individual soul, but argued that it was immortal. By this means, the eternal principle in the human soul was distinguished from the eternal principles of God and nature and linked to human understanding and experience.

Aquinas's arguments represent only one important part of the vast reclamation, consolidation, and criticism of the philosophy of Aristotle in the late Western Middle Ages. Aquinas sometimes argued that the experience of the beautiful makes us aware of the nature of the soul itself, as I have described above; and he also argued, as I have quoted Plotinus to say, that sense participates in reason. He repeated the Aristotelian argument that only human beings are delighted in the very beauty of the sensible itself. But more important than such arguments is the acceptance of the Aristotelian principle that all human knowledge proceeds from mental images arising from sensation and that art is rational when it is fitted to the capacities of human sense and judgment. The beautiful is an "assimilation" to the higher faculties of the rational soul, but it is also the consequence of the proportion between what is to be perceived and the physical mean of human perception. It follows from the latter principle that people should be addressed according to the ways in which they know, and such arguments, full of implications for education, provided a powerful justification for the development of arts appealing to sense and imagination—and to the pleasures of sense and imagination—in the later Middle Ages.

The great *Optics* of Ibn al-Haytham (965–1039), called Alhazen in the West, provided the basis of the modern theory of light and vision and added a major new element to the mostly psychological (or protopsychological) arguments considered so far here. Al-Haytham's *Optics* had been translated into Latin by the early thirteenth century, and by the end of that century it had been joined by the closely variant optics of Witelo, the derivative optics of John Peckam, and the speculations of Roger Bacon. (In the fifteenth century, the Florentine sculptor Lorenzo Ghiberti used an Italian translation of al-Haytham.) Al-Haytham's optics was based on Stoic psychology, but it was quickly adapted to the mostly Aristotelian psychology we have been following. Al-Haytham distinguished between visual judgments made by the eye alone and those made by a higher faculty that he called the *virtus distinctiva.* We know light and color by sense alone, for example, but the comparison of colors requires the second faculty. The *virtus distinctiva* also judges a great many other "visible intentions," the most complex of which is *pulchritudo,* which is always a unique proportion (or relation) of the other intentions.

As it became a fixture in late medieval psychology and brain physiology, the *sensus communis* was often defined as the "center of all the senses" and characterized as *iudex,* judge. The judgments of al-Haytham's *virtus distinctiva* were added to the capacities of common sense by fourteenth-century commentators on Aristotle's *De anima,* and it was against such a background that Leon Battista Alberti was able to make the neo-Ciceronian argument that architecture should appeal to the human sense of *concinnitas,* and that Leonardo da Vinci could write of the *senso comune* as the faculty of what we would call aesthetic judgment. Significantly, Leonardo also identified this principle of judgment with the individual soul of the painter, thus, as was often done, conflating the *sensus communis* and the *cogitativa,* or particular intellect. The categories of internal sense thus gave substance to the emerging modern notion of subjectivity, becoming part of Leonardo's explanation of the Florentine proverb that "every painter paints himself," and serving to establish physical and spiritual individuality, much as related one-point perspective established "point of view."

In his sixth *Meditation,* René Descartes makes the extraordinary argument that the real world must be supposed to exist because his imagination otherwise unaccountably interferes with the ability of his mind to think purely in terms of the laws of mathematics. He might, he says, understand and think the laws that govern any possible polygon—his example is a chiliagon—but he is unable to *imagine* any possible polygon; the power of imagination, then, is alien to his reason and must therefore be fitted to another reality altogether. That reality is the actual world. Descartes is appealing to the distinction between confused and clear thought, the first of which is represented by the faculty of imagination. His distinction has the force not only of the ancient Platonic division, but also of the Galilean (and neo-Democritean) distinction between secondary and primary qualities (often compared to Aristotle's special and common sensibles), that is, between subjective experience and the objective world, the latter the mathematical Book of Nature, and the world of emerging modern science and technology. Gottfried Wilhelm Leibniz, who often makes the same fundamental distinction, added a new, quasi-optical refinement. Ideas may be confused and clear (or obscure.) He uses Descartes's example of the chiliagon (*New Essays on Human Understanding,* 2, 13). Even if one could recognize (or imagine) a chiliagon, the idea would only be clear, not distinct. A laborer (again, a social difference) may have more clarity of perception in such matters than a great geometrician, but this clarity arises from sensation and experience, not from an understanding of causes and general rules. The stage is set for Baumgarten.

The "subjective" experience of secondary qualities is the paradigm for Leibniz's notion of confused ideas, which are particular and can only be elucidated by example. They are a *je ne sais quoi.* This is a version of the traditional phrase for the possession of spiritual grace rather than more material beauty, defined by proportion and color, but it also clearly means that the confused is unanalyzed. We literally do not know what it is; we may name confused things, but we cannot define or classify them. To do so is to cross a divide.

So far the "confused" is simply the particular; Baumgarten made it into the "aesthetic" in its modern sense by discriminating some "representations" of the "lower part of the cognitive faculty" from others in order to achieve an *ars pulchre cogitandi,* which might be best translated as an art of thinking beautifully in images, taking *cogitatio* as the highest of the internal senses. This parallels the classical definition of rhetoric as the *ars bene dicendi,* and in fact Baumgarten discusses many of the traditional "colors," the figures and tropes, of rhetoric and poetry, as means of achieving desirable clarity (not distinctness). Figural language had been banished early on from the prose of natural science, the purpose of which was not to persuade by eloquence, but to convince by fact, analysis, and logic, to demonstrate the replicable, not reproduce the unique; figural language became, in short, part of the "fine arts," now distinct from the "mechanical arts," what in the nineteenth century would begin to be called the "technology" dependent on natural science. The "aesthetic" was defined in terms of the pleasure afforded by expressly particular or unique objects—works of art—fitted to the faculty of imagination itself, which was necessarily individual.

Baumgarten's aesthetics was thus based on the ancient definition of the beautiful in terms of conformity to the structure of perception and consciousness. Sublimity in its modern form, however, is a crucial variant of, and departure from, the ideas I have traced. Burke retained the idea of the proportion between physical sense and stimulus in his definition of the beautiful, but the sublime was based on a *disproportion* in the same terms, and the aesthetic ideal of sublimity, embracing both the fine arts and the feats of technology, has been crucial for modernity. The ancient assumption of the conformity of perception or consciousness to structure in the larger world is lost, although Kant might be seen to have reintegrated the sublime with the traditional scheme by pointing out the mind's capacity to think and thus transcend the sublime, if not to imagine it; and by replacing the classical idea of the soul as rational with the Christian idea of the soul as radically free, defining art as the expression and symbol of that freedom. In general, the old scheme of the particular intellect, of imagination and memory, so intimately related to the emergence of the aesthetic, might be seen as an armature for the development of modern subjectivity in all its forms, a development to which aesthetics has also been central.

BIBLIOGRAPHY

Burke, Edmund. *A Philosophical Enquiry into the Origin of Our Ideas on the Sublime and the Beautiful.* Edited by James T. Boulton. New York, 1958.

Gadamer, Hans-Georg. *Truth and Method.* 2d rev. ed. Translation revised by Joel Weinsheimer and Donald G. Marshall. New York, 1989.

Harvey, E. Ruth. *The Inward Wits: Psychological Theory in the Middle Ages and the Renaissance.* London, 1975.

Lindberg, David C. *Theories of Vision from al-Kindi to Kepler.* Chicago, 1976.

Onians, Richard Broxton. *The Origins of European Thought about the Body, the Mind, the Soul, the World, Time, and Fate.* Cambridge, 1951.

Panofsky, Erwin. "The History of the Theory of Human Proportions as a Reflection of the History of Styles." In *Meaning in the Visual Arts: Papers in and on Art History,* pp. 55–107. Garden City, N.Y., 1955; reprint, Chicago, 1982.

Schiller, Friedrich. *On the Aesthetic Education of Man in a Series of Letters.* Edited and translated by Elizabeth M. Wilkinson and L. A. Willoughby. Oxford, 1967.

Summers, David. *Michelangelo and the Language of Art.* Princeton, N.J., 1981.

Summers, David. *The Judgment of Sense: Renaissance Naturalism and the Rise of Aesthetics.* Cambridge and New York, 1987.

Summers, David. "Why Did Kant Call Taste a 'Common Sense'?" In *Eighteenth-Century Aesthetics and the Reconstruction of Art,* edited by Paul Mattick, Jr., pp. 120–151. Cambridge and New York, 1993.

Wolfson, Harry Austryn. *Studies in the History of Philosophy and Religion.* 2 vols. Edited by Isadore Twersky and George H. Williams. Cambridge, Mass., 1973–1977.

DAVID SUMMERS

ORNAMENT. *See* Islamic Aesthetics, *historical and conceptual overview article; and* Postmodernism, *historical and conceptual overview article.*

OUTSIDER ART. The term *Outsider Art* was introduced into the fine-art lexicon in 1972 by the British art historian Roger Cardinal. It was originally meant to be the English equivalent of the term *Art Brut,* coined by Jean Dubuffet in 1945 to describe the works that were created by individuals outside established society such as inmates in mental institutions and prisoners. More important, these artists had not had exposure to academic art training, art theory, or the infrastructure of the art establishment, and many, who simply responded to a creative drive, may not have even felt they were producing art. Art Brut indicates that the art was "raw" or "unadulterated," and described an authentic dynamism that sprang directly from a person with an overwhelming need to create who was not only uninfluenced but also unfettered by art-world trends and training. The term *Art Brut* was also adopted by the Collection de l'Art Brut in Lausanne (opened in 1976) to house Dubuffet's personal collection of Art Brut works and other related works. In a catalog for a 1967 exhibition, Dubuffet elaborates: "The aim of our enterprise is to seek out works that as far as possible escape cultural conditioning and proceed from truly original mental attitudes" (quoted in Cardinal, 1972, p. 26).

The anglicized term and concept of *Outsider* has been contested for many reasons, one being that it is no longer true to the spirit and the purity of meaning of Art Brut. In the United States especially, it is frequently used to refer to almost any untrained artist who lives in marginal circumstances, not just those who have been essentially isolated from society and the art world. A composite, more inclusive (albeit tentative) definition offered in the exhibition catalog for *Parallel Visions* (1992–1993) reflects the way the term has evolved in America: "These outsiders have usually been self-taught individuals, sometimes mentally disturbed who have created their work while isolated generally from mainstream culture and particularly from the complex infrastructure of the art world, that is, from galleries, museums, and universities with which mainstream artists are regularly associated" (Tuchman, 1992, p. 10).

In an article in 1993 in *Raw Vision: International Journal of Intuitive and Visionary Art,* John Maizels proposed to establish an agreed upon vocabulary of compiled definitions that would keep *Outsider Art* synonymous with Art Brut and

clarify meanings and distinctions among related subcategories that spring from the theme of "self-taught." Because these subcategories intersect, precise definitions and boundaries are subject to debate. The following—a summary of Maizel's terms—demonstrates how these related concepts are intended to diverge from the concept of *Outsider Art:*

Neuve Invention (New Invention): Dubuffet's term for the category of artists of comparable impact who have had greater contact with society, and have a greater awareness of their creations as art works; some try to earn a living from their art. To acknowledge them he formed the "Annex Collection," and in 1982 this became the "Neuve Invention" part of the Collection de l'Art Brut.

Contemporary Folk Art: It has a crossover with Outsider Art, but with its own traditions and without the psychic state associated with Outsider artists.

Naïve Art: Done by untrained artists, often sophisticated amateurs, who depict realistic scenes in detail, sometimes using fantasy images.

Marginal Art/Art Singulier: Similar to Dubuffet's Neuve Invention, this art is close to Outsider both in appearance and expression. Usually self-taught, the artists are in the margins between Outsider and mainstream art.

Visionary and *Intuitive Art:* Used together, these deliberate umbrella terms can encompass the categories described above, and almost everything in the field including much tribal and urban folk art of the third world.

Visionary Environments (or Grassroots Art): Buildings, and sculpture parks built by intuitive artists such as Simon Rodia (Watts Towers), Ferdinand Cheval (Le Palais Idèal), and Nek Chand (The Rock Garden at Chandigarh).

(Maizels, 1993, pp. 18–19)

It is not yet clear whether Maizel's distinctions will have an impact on what has become the broader, more common usage of the term *Outsider Art,* extended by gallery owners, curators, writers, and *Outsider* art fair organizers in the United States to include or encroach on the related terms. Critics of the term *Outsider Art* have faulted it for reasons other than not remaining true to the early spirit and meaning of Art Brut. While it was disparaged on the one hand for being too inclusive, a catchall term for all manner of autodidact artists, the connotations of the word were also seen as promoting separation of its practitioners who are "outside" from the mainstream of high art by the very act of labeling them as such. This criticism of the process of categorization concerns the sociopolitical implications in assuming there are those who have the right and authority to designate who is "outside" and who is "inside," especially when the designation is based on mental states of the artists, or on class differences, and race. If, for instance, a primary contributing factor for inclusion in the category is the mental state of the artist, it could be argued that the category be limited to the art of the psychotic. If not, how far should it extend?

Should we include the neurotic vainly trying to cope with the pressure of civilizing trends? If the *Outsider* category were to cover all "mad" artists, then it is close to becoming another category, the art of the insane, which reflects profoundly unusual internal experiences and involves altered states of consciousness (MacGregor, 1989). Some claim that the advent of chemotherapy and art therapy as a means of adaptation marked the end of Art Brut or *Outsider Art* in psychiatric hospitals (MacGregor and Thévoz in Carr, 1990, pp. 13, 19–20). Although some of his collection came from patients in mental institutions, Dubuffet himself maintained that there was no art of the insane any more than an art of the dyspeptic or of people with knee complaints. In choosing the term Art Brut Dubuffet sought to avoid a term associated with mental disability.

When designation is based on the artist's social status (or lack of it) then, at the very least, an artist must be of marginal status—outside the "mainstream"—to be considered an *Outsider* in the broader definition. This marginal status has been construed to include those with mental disorders, certain African Americans (usually poor, old, or isolated), religious visionaries, mediums, angst-filled misfits, prisoners, and reclusives. Many began creating their artworks when they were older, often without jobs or in subservient roles and had physical problems. If the marginal societal position of these artists is made to be a condition, it can be argued that many, perhaps most, artists are living on the margins of society, either because of financial circumstances or by choice. Of course, whether someone is living marginally, and where that line is drawn, is not clear.

Race has been used to justify the inclusion of a number of African Americans—probably, the largest portion of *Outsider* artists in the United States—on the grounds that racism has excluded them from the dominant culture, thus denying power, opportunities, and resources. This marginalization has also been seen as a "mixed blessing" that allowed for the continuation and development of ideas and images that would have otherwise "been swept away in the mainstream" (Lippard, 1990, p. 58). No matter what causes these artists to be identified as being outside mainstream society, the bond they share is of being self-taught and outside the art establishment.

An issue in the discussion of *Outsider Art* has been whether it can be identified and defined by aesthetic similarities. Some recognizable similarities often cited include obsessive-compulsive detail and ornamentation (the "horror vacuii"), use of bold coloration, a visionary tone with spiritual, religious, or futuristic overtones, use of repeated patterns, written messages, and childlike rendering (e.g., Adolf Wölfli, Madge Gill, William Hawkins, Bessie Harvey, Oscar Tschirtner, Sister Gertrude Morgan, Mary T. Smith). Use of unsophisticated materials such as discarded plywood, house paint, and corrugated tin is also common because these are materials to which artists have access, and

may, to the uninitiated eye, cause some works to look similar. Although these characteristics appear with frequency, there are also many counterexamples of simple, spare images, abstract graphic power, subtle coloration, enigmatic calligraphy, and strong, sure rendering (e.g., Mose Tolliver, Bill Traylor, Joseph Yoakum, J. B. Murry, Martin Ramirez). They may share certain elements, but each artist has a self-consistent vocabulary that individualizes his or her unique vision. The works may be more distinguished as a group by the way they differ from most traditional museum art than in how much they have in common. Aesthetic similarities may not be strong enough to define *Outsider Art,* but if the term has an accrued meaning through usage and remains viable, aesthetic similarities will probably be used to provide a characterization for the art. As an art category, however, *Outsider Art* differs from others in that it is not coextensive with a period in the development of art history where artists communicate with and influence each other or respond to public acclaim, critical theorizing, or benefactors' tastes resulting in a cohesive style.

Many strongly believe that *Outsider Art* should not constitute a separate category at all, but should be included in the broader category of "art." In fact, this process may have already begun. Some of the problems with this position concern the danger in being judged by current criteria of tastemakers who might be prone to ignore or denigrate an art that does not fit accepted conventions or theories. Absorption could also result in a loss of the information concerning the authenticity of untutored creative talent provided by the categorizing and assimilation into an institutionalized art world. This could contradict the basic criterion of Art Brut as independent of instituted visual communication.

These controversies revolving around the term and concept of *Outsider Art* reveal the issues of hierarchies, inclusion/exclusion, and the political implications of identification according to status of the artist. Although one can question the accuracy and appropriateness of the term, it may, by now, have a life and connotation of its own comparable to the use of the term *Gothic art,* which we no longer associate with its root Germanic tribal meaning. It could also be defended on the grounds that this term tells the story of this art in a more meaningful way than others. Alternative terms such as *self-taught, visionary,* and *contemporary folk art,* which are becoming increasingly popular replacements, can also be faulted for being broad, narrow, or unfocused.

Whether *Outsider Art* is a subset of folk art is another issue. *The Museum of American Folk Art Encyclopedia of Twentieth-Century American Folk Art and Artists* included most of those American artists now considered *Outsiders* side by side with such folk artists as the mountain-fiddling, wood sculptor S. L. Jones, and the memory painter Grandma Moses. One of the strongest arguments for including

Outsider Art under the folk art umbrella is that the artists share the characteristics of being self-taught and nonacademic. Also, courses on *Outsider Art* are taught in the only graduate program in folk art studies and in the Folk Art Institute in New York. Although *Outsider* artists have been classified as part of contemporary folk art, their differing intentions support the argument for keeping them separate. Traditional folk artists intend that their artwork be able to decorate or to be displayed. The tradition of decorating utilitarian objects is more closely associated with the ethnosyncratic European model based on the art of the peasant classes and the collective expression within a common culture that handed design traditions down through the generations. In the United States, which initially did not have a peasant class or many skilled artisans, folk art style of original character sprang up to reflect American needs, experience, and ingenuity, and went beyond tradition-based form. *Outsider Art* springs from an obsessive need to create, unrelated to the art-world trends, and does not require peer admiration. Although no artwork can help but relate to the artist's cultural background in some way, *Outsider Art* in the Art Brut sense is not part of a collective cultural tradition, is generally idiosyncratic, and is made without intent to produce an object for the art market.

As in most aesthetic categorizations, boundaries and language usage are disputed as scholars continue to refine their thinking and debate their conclusions. Whether or not *Outsider Art* remains a category, how this art will be defined depends on whether the concept remains close to the idea of *art brut* or expands to include all self-taught contemporary folk art. No doubt, there will be a continuum with many hybrid creations in this field that is neither a school, a style, nor a movement. In the meantime, the art continues to present itself with visual eloquence as more and more of the art world and general public respond to its power.

Besides the strong aesthetic qualities, the images in *Outsider Art* evoke a deep psychic response in viewers. There may even be a concordance between creativity and emotional instability resulting in more freedom for those artists who are not bound by societal conditioning, restrictions, and rewards, and do not renounce their deepest impulses in order to mimic or conform to artistic fashions. As writer and gallery owner Randall Morris says:

This art is about magic. It is about the unexplainable powers a human being feels no matter where in the world he or she comes from that cause him/her to make art from deep within the soul. It is about a power that has no regard for art school. or cultural background. or age. or religion. . . . When it is right (like any art), when accomplished in execution, authentic in intent, and unique in point of view it packs a force that instantly reminds us that art began as magic, and still has the power to be important magic.   (Morris, Lynch, and Kerrigan, 1993, p. 4)

This moves us from arguments about definitions and conceptual boundaries, and puts the emphasis back on the art, on its impact and scope, and on its contribution to the field of aesthetics.

[*See also* Folk Art; *and* Insane, Art of the.]

BIBLIOGRAPHY

Cardinal, Roger. *Outsider Art.* New York, 1972.

Cardinal, Roger. "Toward an Outsider Aesthetic." In *The Artist Outsider: Creativity and the Boundaries of Culture,* edited by Michael D. Hall and Eugene W. Metcalf, Jr., pp. 20–43. Washington, D.C., 1994.

Carr, Simon, et al., eds. *Portraits from the Outside: Figurative Expression in Outsider Art.* New York, 1990.

Carter, Curtis L. *Contemporary American Folk Art: The Balsey Collection.* Milwaukee, 1992. Exhibition catalogue, Patrick and Beatrice Haggerty Museum of Art.

Lippard, Lucy R. *Mixed Blessings: New Art in a Multicultural America.* New York, 1990.

Livingston, Jane, and John Beardsley. *Black Folk Art in America, 1930–1980.* Jackson, Miss., 1982.

MacGregor, John M. *The Discovery of the Art of the Insane.* Princeton, N.J., 1989.

Maizels, John. *Raw Creation: Outsider Art and Beyond.* London, 1996.

Maizels, John. "Raw Visions Definitions." *Raw Vision: International Journal of Intuitive and Visionary Art* 7 (Summer 1993): 18–19.

Morris, Randall, Colin Lynch, and Caroline Kerrigan. "Outsider Art." In *Outsider Art Fair,* pp. 4–7. New York, 1993.

Rosenak, Chuck, and Jan Rosenak. *Contemporary American Folk Art: A Collector's Guide.* New York, 1996.

Rosenak, Chuck, and Jan Rosenak. *The Museum of American Folk Art Encyclopedia of Twentieth-Century American Folk Art and Artists.* New York, 1990.

Thévoz, Michel. *Art Brut.* New York, 1976.

Tuchman, Maurice, and Carol S. Eliel, eds. *Parallel Visions: Modern Artists and Outsider Art.* Princeton, N.J., 1992. Exhibition catalog, Los Angeles County Museum of Art.

Yelen, Alice Rae. *Passionate Visions of the American South: Self-Taught Artists from 1940 to the Present.* Jackson, Miss., 1993. Exhibition catalog, New Orleans Museum of Art.

JOAN CRYSTAL PEARLMAN

P

PAINTING. *For discussion of different theories of art that focus on painting, see* Alberti; Baudelaire; Bell; Berenson; Danto; Derrida; Diderot; Gombrich; Greenberg; Lacan; Lyotard; Merleau-Ponty; Panofsky; Perspective; de Piles; *and* Wollheim. *For discussion of historical movements in painting, see* Abstract Expressionism; Abstraction; Classicism; Contemporary Art; Expressionism; Formalism; Impressionism; Landscape; Pop Art; Portraiture; Renaissance Italian Aesthetics; Romanticism, *article on* Visual Arts; Russian Aesthetics; Suprematism; *and* Surrealism. *For discussion of individual painters, see* Delacroix; Kandinsky; Mondrian; Picasso; Poussin; Reinhardt; *and* Reynolds. *For related discussion, see* Artist; Chinese Aesthetics, *article on* Painting Theory and Criticism; Collage; Color; Criticism, *article on* Art Criticism; Ecphrasis; French Aesthetics, *article on* Contemporary Painting Theory; Icon; Iconography and Iconology; Imagery; Models, Artists'; Originality; Perception; Photography; *and* Ut Pictura Poesis.

PANOFSKY, ERWIN (1892–1968), German-born American art historian and philosopher of art. Erwin Panofsky has often been called the most influential historian of art of the twentieth century. In numerous essays and books written over the course of a fifty-year scholarly career, his inquiries into the ways in which medieval and Renaissance images function as artistic embodiments of larger cultural and intellectual ideals have shaped many subsequent social and cultural histories of art. In his focus on content, Panofsky not only challenged the dominant fin de siècle aesthetic preoccupation with issues of form and the metahistorical principles underlying stylistic change, he also initiated a methodological approach for reading visual representations from a range of geographic places and historical periods (all Western). His "iconological" perspective is still very much in the foreground of debates in critical theory from a variety of disciplines at the end of this century. To understand the history of the concept of iconology, a brief review of the intellectual biography of its most famous advocate seems in order.

Born in Hannover, Germany, on 30 March 1892, Panofsky began his formal education at the Joachimsthalsches Gymnasium in Berlin and went on to attend the universities of Freiburg, Berlin, and Munich before receiving his doctorate from the University of Freiburg in 1914 under the tutelage of Wilhelm Vöge and Adolf Goldschmidt. Appointed *Privatdozent* at the newly founded University of Hamburg in 1921, he became a professor there in 1926, and held the post of *Ordinarius* throughout the years of the Weimar Republic. His intellectual home soon became the private Warburg library of cultural studies (Kulturwissenschaftliche Bibliothek Warburg) in the cosmopolitan port of Hamburg, and his associations with its resident scholars, including Aby Warburg, Edgar Wind, Gertrud Bing, Fritz Saxl, Rudolf Wittkower, and Ernst Cassirer, were epistemologically crucial for his professional evolution. By 1933, when he was dismissed by the Nazi regime from his university post for being Jewish, Panofsky had already achieved scholarly acclamation for a number of theoretical and historical studies of medieval and Renaissance imagery, such as "Die Entwicklung der Proportionslehre als Abbild der Stilentwicklung" (1921), "Dürers Stellung zur Antike" (1922), "Dürers 'Melancolia I'" (with Fritz Saxl, 1923), *Die Deutsche Plastik des 11. bis 13. Jahrhunderts* (1924), *Idee* (1924), "Die Perspektive als 'symbolische Form'" (1924–1925), "Über das Verhältnis der Kunstegeschichte zur Kunsttheorie" (1925), "'Imago Pietatis'" (1927), "Hercules am Scheidewege" (1931), and "Zum Problem der Beschreibung und Inhaltsdeutung von Werken der bildenden Kunst" (1932).

Compelled to emigrate with his family from Germany (the site of many of his historical studies), Panofsky, with the aid of American colleagues, assumed a position of visiting professor of fine arts at New York University in 1934, where, for the previous three years, he had been invited to give periodic lectures in the basement of the Metropolitan Museum of Art under the auspices of what soon became the Institute of Fine Arts. In 1934 he also assumed the rank of visiting lecturer at Princeton University, and became a member of its Institute for Advanced Study in 1935. This latter association would prove to be as intellectually stimulating an environment as the Warburg Institute (whose scholars and books were similarly exiled to Bloomsbury in London during these years) had been for the first part of his career. With colleagues such as Albert Einstein, Jacques Maritain, Thomas Mann, and J. Robert Oppenheimer, Panofsky claimed that he suffered an "expulsion into paradise," at a place "where members do their research openly and their teaching surreptitiously." After occupying the Charles Eliot Norton lectureship at Harvard University in

1947–1948, Panofsky returned to Princeton and taught and wrote there (in English) until his death twenty years later. Among his magisterial studies produced in these American decades are *Studies in Iconology* (1939), *The Codex Huygens and Leonardo's Art Theory* (1940), "The History of Art as a Humanistic Discipline" (1940), "Style and Medium in the Motion Picture" (1947), *Albrecht Dürer* (1943; titled *The Life and Art of Albrecht Dürer* after the fourth edition in 1955), *Gothic Architecture and Scholasticism* (1951), *Early Netherlandish Painting* (1953), "Three Decades of Art History in the United States: Impressions of a Transplanted European" (1954), *Galileo as a Critic of the Arts* (1954), *Meaning in the Visual Arts: Papers In and On Art History* (1957), *Renaissance and Renascences in Western Art* (1960), *Tomb Sculpture* (1964), and *Problems in Titian, Mostly Iconographic* (1969). His wife, Dora, with whom he punningly composed *Pandora's Box: The Changing Aspects of a Medieval Symbol* (1956), died in 1965. He subsequently married Gerda Sörgel, also an art historian. During his thirty-five years in the United States, Panofsky received many academic honors and awards, both on this continent and abroad. He died in Princeton on 14 March 1968.

Besides his publications, Panofsky's great legacy was his students. Over the years, he trained many scholars whose collected work would come to rival his own. Among his early disciples in the "Hamburg school" of art history were Hugo Buchtal, Adolf Katzenellenbogen, Walter Horn, Lise Lotte Möller, Lotte Brand Philip, P. H. van Blanckenhagen, William Heckscher, Charles de Tolnay, H. W. Janson, Hanns Swarzenski, and Ludwig Heinrich Heydenreich. His American students, both too well known and too numerous to list here, initiated the study of the history of art as a serious humanistic pursuit, and a sort of third-generation "Panofskyianism" might even be said to be alive and flourishing in the academy today. In point of fact, many departments of art history across the United States, directly or indirectly, owe their present existence and disciplinary outlook to Panofsky's original scholarship and persuasive pedagogy.

His impact on twentieth-century intellectuals, however, far exceeds the boundaries of a single discipline. Literary critics, cultural and intellectual historians, anthropologists, and philosophers of science, among others, have turned both to Panofsky's empirical studies of early modern European imagery and to his theoretical inquiries into the connectedness between works of art and the cultural universe that encircles them. The deviser of a method or approach to analyzing visual representation that depends on a well-thought-out theory of the relation of mind to world, Panofsky is more appropriately remembered as a philosopher of art rather than simply an art historian.

Several historiographers, in echoing the split between his early theoretical German essays and later historical research collated in books written during his American career, have spoken of "two Panofskys." Ironically, the "first" Panofsky—the one, until recently, less familiar to his English-speaking audience—is the thinker whose ideas and scholarly protocol would be more congenial to the impulse toward critical revisionism taking place in the humanities today. Although sometimes mired in the abstruse philosophical prose of 1920s academic writing, his early essays are full of self-reflexive speculation, interdisciplinary insights, and the bold desire to make new meanings rather than perpetuate received knowledge. Trained in neo-Kantian epistemology and much influenced by Ernst Cassirer's *Philosophy of Symbolic Forms,* as well as by Aby Warburg's aggressive institutional trespassing of disciplinary boundaries, the young scholar abhorred the simpleminded aesthetic "appreciationism" of his disciplinary peers, an approach to visual imagery that he asserted "deprives naivete of its charms without correcting its errors," with about the same frequency that he snubbed the labors of simpleminded antiquarians. When he first began writing, he openly challenged the formal analyses and connoisseurship of his predecessors, and even took on the theoretical giants of the field, Heinrich Wölfflin and Alois Riegl. Panofsky admired the formalist criticism of both authors, especially because of their efforts to reveal the laws of development underlying stylistic metamorphosis. Riegl's propensity, however, to locate a *Kunstwollen* to explain why visual material looks different in different times was more attractive to his own tendency to ask the grand questions. What Panofsky attempted to do—although his latent Hegelianism passes largely unremarked—was comprehend visual forms as part of a larger phenomenology of culture, in which works of art could almost always be deciphered as embodiments of philosophical ideals situated in a specific time and place. His 1924–1925 essay, "Perspective as a Symbolic Form," is a case in point.

In this project he is clearly indebted to Cassirer's notion of symbolic forms, through which the neo-Kantian philosopher argued that all cultural manifestations, from mathematics to music, function as a kind of symbolic language through which human beings disclose meanings to each other at the same time as they try to impose order on the chaos of experience. In his own essay, Panofsky argues that the system of linear perspective, codified by Leon Battista Alberti during the Italian Renaissance, rapidly gained momentum as a persuasive spatial convention, one whose geometric mandates served to convince most of its contemporary and historical practitioners that this is how human beings actually perceive the world. In order to underscore linear perspective's conventionality—what we might today call its "constructedness" or "fictionality"—the young Panofsky guides the committed reader through elaborate, and very often suggestively contradictory, diachronic and synchronic analyses to explain its hegemony in different sections of his essay. His vexed indecisiveness (i.e., his willingness to open up meaning rather than close it down) about which question to ask—how accurate is linear perspective, or is verisimilitude not relevant?—leads to all sorts of brilliant meditations on how the faculty of sight relates (or does not relate) to other imaginative constructs of the age. The creative associative thinking through which he links the various branches of Renaissance learning is fluid testimony to the range and depth of his learning and imagination. For Panofsky, perspective is an ambiguous organon located precisely at the midpoint on the representational spectrum between a device of representation and the object represented, and yet functioning as both at once. The formal system of perspective interrelates with other issues in the Renaissance (scientific, social, philosophical, and so forth), but at the same time it exhibits—because it is transparently a system of relationships—the formal principles underlying all Renaissance structures, including itself.

What makes this ambitious, imaginative, and often provocatively inconsistent essay emblematic of several of Panofsky's early essays is its desire to go beyond historical recitation into rigorous theoretical speculation. He performs the same sort of maneuver in his "The History of the Theory of Human Proportions as a Reflection of the History of Styles" essay, for example, where he suggests that canons of proportion are dependent on cultural constructs, which in turn can be read as philosophical issues. His commitment to humanist values—the idea that "man" is maker and center of the historical universe—is never forsaken. One could say, in fact, that his early studies of Dürer effectively situate the northern Renaissance "genius" in the tradition of Italian humanism, thus legitimating the artist as not only an authentic representative of the Renaissance, but also a revered predecessor of German Enlightenment thinking, a tradition to which Panofsky himself is a worthy heir. In this light, it is obvious why Panofsky found the mechanics of perspective such a suggestive topic. Perspective deifies the viewer, places his or her lone eye at the center of the seen world, and makes everything assume position around this special viewpoint. In these early theoretical essays (translated only recently), he yearned for an "Archimedian viewpoint" from which he could objectively survey the vast panorama of visual culture. The notion of distancing, so crucial to the Renaissance system of perspective, could also effectively serve as a working metaphor for historical insight in the investigative work to come.

Although Panofsky was a long way from abandoning an interest in theoretical issues, on his arrival in America his writing took a decidedly "practical" turn. Numerous well-known essays—on Dürer's Italianate humanism (again), on Michelangelo's Neoplatonism, on the Scholasticism of Gothic architects, on the hidden symbolism of northern Renaissance painting, and so on—dazzlingly demonstrate how reigning philosophical issues eventually become embodied in material works of art. The orderliness of cause and effect (a strategy not always paramount in the earlier, more theoretical essays) offers an epistemologically secure footing, as long as the historian is erudite enough to know what to read and where to look. Here Panofsky's sleuthing became legendary: a fancier of the deductive logic of the master detective Sherlock Holmes, he once declared that "if all that which is impossible has been eliminated, the improbable that remains must be true."

The empirical thrust of the American Panofsky's research, however, might legitimately be regarded as a partial renunciation of his early speculative commitments. If his later works abandon a concentration on the ways in which the formal systems of an age are interlinked synchronically in a social, ideological, and psychological matrix, and turn instead to a plotting of how philosophical or theological doctrine impinges on artistic production, then two linked interpretive principles of the early Panofsky have been put aside. First, if texts are always assigned a generative role in the making of visual representations, it is difficult to see how he could continue to claim that both words and images work together simultaneously to constitute a particular historical "worldview." Second, the restriction of analysis to the identification of literary themes significantly reduced his attention to the theoretically complex structure of visual signification.

This is not to claim, however, that Panofsky neglected methodological meditations per se, for his 1939 introduction to *Studies in Iconology* convincingly proves that he did not (even if this essay is a partial reworking of his 1932 "Zum Problem der Beschreibung und Inhaltsdeutung von Werken der bildenden Kunst"). Perhaps his most famous work, this essay posits three levels or layers of reading an image in order to decipher both latent and manifest content: the preiconographic, the iconographic, and the iconological. Because their articulation has become a functional part of the interpretive subconscious of the history of art, his stages (akin to Sigmund Freud's stratigraphy of the unconscious) merit a brief summary.

A "preiconographic description" on the basis of "practical experience" interprets "primary or natural subject matter." This stage is concerned with "factual" meaning, with the recognition of the work in its most elementary sense. Applied to a work of art—Panofsky's example is Leonardo's *Last Supper*—this primary reading would record only that thirteen men are seated at a table laden with food. The preiconographic level calls attention to the preverbal, almost preliterate, perception of the image.

An "iconographic analysis" is interested in the "secondary or conventional" meanings that can be discovered or detected by a familiarity with literary precedents. Here, the *Last Supper* is read as having its conscious source in the Christian ethos as it is expressed in the well-known Gospel story. On this level, the subject of the painting is identified: its moment and place of enactment, the names of its actors, its historical precedents, and so forth.

Iconology proper is the subject of the third level of analysis (in the original 1939 edition, Panofsky had called this stage "iconography in a deeper sense," but by the 1955 revision of *Meaning in the Visual Arts,* he had become clearly uncomfortable with the pragmatic connotations and epistemological limitations suggested by the term "iconography"). Iconology (a term appropriated from Aby Warburg) concerns itself with "intrinsic meaning or content." To reveal the meaning of a work on this level, the art historian must familiarize himself or herself with the "essential tendencies of the human mind" as they are conditioned by personal psychology and cultural predispositions. The iconological stage hinges on a reading of the work as a possible "unconscious" bearer of meaning beyond what the artist might have intended; in other words, this level involves an analysis of the meaning in terms of underlying cultural principles. The *Last Supper* might be read not only as a "document" of Leonardo's personality but also as an expression of the worldview of the Italian High Renaissance.

In practice, of course, it is much easier to pin down meaning by deciphering iconographic content (i.e., subject matter) than it is to open it up to a proliferation of cultural meanings. Worrying that there is some danger that "iconology will behave, not like ethnology as opposed to ethnography, but like astrology as opposed to astrography," Panofsky, the hermeneuticist, builds into his method an elaborate system of historical checks and balances as a reasonable guarantor of objectivity. But the thoughtful interpreter is also keenly aware that the subjectivity, interests, and intuitive predispositions of the historian also play a part in any meaningful historical analysis.

In "The History of Art as a Humanistic Discipline," written slightly later than the overtly methodological *Studies in Iconology,* Panofsky engages in a metahistorical reflection on the differences between the humanities and the sciences, and concludes that the role of the humanistic interpreter is paramount:

> The humanist, dealing as he does with human actions and creations, has to engage in a mental process of a synthetic and subjective character; he has mentally to re-enact the actions and to re-create the creations. It is in fact by this process that the real objects of the humanities come into being. (1982)

As evocative of the principles of German Enlightenment thinking as these words may sound, for this exiled scholar, the ideological rationale for championing humanist convictions on the other side of the Atlantic during the dark days of 1940 was undoubtedly a profoundly political one.

It is his very confidence in "humanist" values that has come under attack in recent poststructuralist critiques of the legacy of Panofsky. For several decades of its scholarly life, the method had promised transparency and accessibility. If enough sources could be collated, if enough research was accomplished, the historian could indeed hope to see through the works of art into the high-culture world from which they came. Panofsky's appeal to tradition, reason, and objectivity, however, has itself been characterized by some as an ideological agenda masking numerous exclusionary practices: the lack of acknowledgment, for example, of class and gender differences (representations of Virgins on pedestals or peasants tilling fields, for example), or the privileging of certain periods and cultures and certain kinds of works at the expense of others (Italian High Renaissance paintings as the standard against which to judge the visual productions of other geographic times and places). Coupled with the epistemological security that comes from recognizing how context acts on text, the ultimate knowability of Panofsky's symbols, that is to say, his faith in the historian's skills in their decipherment, has sometimes been perceived as robbing the works of a continuously active agency of their own. Meaning, in many iconographic case studies, seems to have been closed down rather than opened up.

How fair is this kind of poststructuralist indictment, with which certainly not all practicing art historians (such as traditional iconographers) today would agree? A sound historiographic review would appear to be able to uncover many cases over the years where this way of investigating works of art has degenerated into the sterility of decoding: of finding a text that "explains" an image, of locating a context that fits a text, of finding origins that presage endings, and so on. Yet, even if some of Panofsky's disciplinary heirs rigidified the original impulses behind iconology, and in doing so, neglected to recall and rework the theoretical bases on which he developed his working "method," the originator himself need not necessarily be blamed for similar blindness. Reviewing the body of his scholarship would reveal to any attentive reader that his thought was much more sophisticated and nuanced than that. To put it simply, Panofsky posed two very compelling interpretive principles: (1) he drew attention to the links between words and images; and (2) he re-emplotted works of visual art into their historical and ideological contexts.

Yet it is also the case that neither commitment stood on a solid foundation. The tremors that have shaken the artifice so confidently blueprinted by Panofsky more than half a century ago have originated from a number of different sources. The most tenable can be only summarized in relation to these two tenets. If poststructuralism has taught late twentieth-century art theorists anything, it is that both word and image cannot do anything other than function as symbolic mediations, and that every sign derives its power from a system of differences that circulates through and around social practices and ideological constructs. The loosening of interpretive fixity, moreover, is just the beginning of the contemporary art historian's predicament. Not only is the written text no longer securely serving as the context for the visual image (as traditional iconographic protocol would have it: thirteen men seated at a dinner table represents the *Last Supper*), but the very notion of context (social or metahistorical), the bedrock of all cultural histories since G. W. F. Hegel, has been excavated and exposed as textual fabrication.

But then again, the concept of iconology (and not necessarily its practice), as it originated once upon a time, is rich and supple enough to accommodate a wide range of theoretical alternatives now available, even if contemporary theoreticians of art are compelled to abandon some of its most revered commitments: to "Art," universal aesthetic value, hermeneutic understanding, cultural unity, intentionality, historical verifiability, and univocal meaning. Contemporary art history is no longer exclusively the empirical pursuit it once was. The shape of art history as a discipline has been irrevocably altered by deconstructionist debates in all of the humanities that have enticed scholars to cross disciplinary boundaries. It might not be too outrageous to call this changing art-historical field the "new iconology." But to do so would require an expansion of the always "something else" of iconological readings (which Panofsky himself tended to confine to literary, philosophical, theological, and autobiographical contexts) to issues of politics, social behavior, economic realities, gender construction, and sexual orientation that have come to characterize the recent study of something going by the name of "visual culture." The practice of late twentieth-century art iconology as a "method" requires the recognition that the art historian brings as much to interpretation as he or she finds in the historical record. If "new iconologists" study cultural systems now, they almost inevitably study them in conflict, stressing their instabilities and unpredictability, highlighting processes of subjectivity and identity formation.

This evolution might well be construed as the expression of the healthy afterlife of iconology, of what Panofsky once called "iconography turned interpretive." The name for such interdisciplinary pursuits has now changed to "word and image critiques" or "visual and cultural studies" rather than iconology, but that semantic metamorphosis is not very significant since Panofsky himself appropriated the term *iconology* out of the desire to give "something more" to the term *iconography*. Like any vigorous intellectual construct, as Panofsky showed us by way of the topic of the perspective, ideas change. Whereas he regarded art-historical knowledge as guaranteed by a Kantian correspondence between mind and world, many contemporary "new" art historians refuse to countenance such epistemological claims. Just as late twentieth-century theorists have become committed to the conviction that there are no autonomous objects of art that exist in splendid transcendental isolation, so too they have come to think that there can be no master narratives about their history and meaning.

Keeping the past alive and meaningful—that is, open to new interpretations—in the present is what is important.

Rather than pretending that conflict over what they are doing does not exist, many contemporary art historians tend, in general, to labor to protect and promote the intellectual unsettlement of the field. It is a matter of insight rather than knowledge, something that Panofsky, in many, but certainly not all of his essays, seems to have understood very well. While the goal of the sciences, he once said, may be "something like mastery, that of the humanities [is] something like wisdom."

[*See also* Iconography and Iconology; Perspective; *and* Renaissance Italian Aesthetics.]

BIBLIOGRAPHY

Works by Panofsky

"Das Problem des Stils in der bildenden Kunst." *Zeitschrift für Ästhetik und allgemeine Kunstwissenschaft* 10 (1915): 460–467.

"Des Begriff des Kunstwollens." *Zeitschrift für Ästhetik und allgemeine Kunstwissenschaft* 14 (1920): 321–339. Translated as "The Concept of Artistic Volition" by Kenneth J. Northcott and Joel Snyder in *Critical Inquiry* 8 (Autumn 1981): 17–23.

"Die Entwicklung der Proportionslehre als Abbild der Stilentwicklung." *Monatshefte für Kunstwissenschaft* 14 (1921): 188–219. In English as "The History of the Theory of Human Proportions as a Reflection of the History of Styles," in *Meaning in the Visual Arts* (Garden City, N.Y., 1955; reprint, Chicago, 1982).

Dürers "Melencolia I": Eine quellen- und typengeschichtliche Untersuchung. Studien der Bibliothek Warburg 2. Leipzig, 1923.

"Idee": Ein Beitrag zur Begriffsgeschichte der älteren Kunsttheorie. Studien der Bibliothek Warburg 5. Leipzig, 1924. In English as *Idea: A Concept in Art Theory,* edited by Joseph J. S. Peake (Columbia, S.C., 1968).

"Über das Verhältnis der Kunstgeschichte zur Kunsttheorie: Ein Beitrag zu der Erörterung über die Möglichkeit 'kunstwissenschaftlicher Grundbegriffe.'" *Zeitschrift für Ästhetik und allgemeine Kunstwissenschaft* 18 (1924–1925): 129–161.

"Die Perspektive als 'symbolische Form.'" In *Vorträge der Bibliothek Warburg, 1924–1925,* pp. 258–330. Leipzig, 1927. Translated as *Perspective as Symbolic Form* by Christopher S. Wood (New York, 1991).

Hercules am Scheidewege und andere antike Bildstoffe in der neueren Kunst. Studien der Bibliothek Warburg 18. Leipzig, 1930.

Studies in Iconology: Humanistic Themes in the Art of the Renaissance (1939). Mary Flexner Lectures in the Humanities, 1939. Reprint, New York, 1962.

"The History of Art as a Humanistic Discipline." In *The Meaning of the Humanities,* edited by T. M. Greene, pp. 89–118. Princeton, N.J., 1940. Reprinted in *Meaning in the Visual Arts* (Garden City, N.Y., 1955; reprint, Chicago, 1982).

The Life and Art of Albrecht Dürer (1943). 4th ed. Princeton, N.J., 1955.

Gothic Architecture and Scholasticism: An Inquiry into the Analogy of the Arts, Philosophy, and Religion in the Middle Ages (1951). Reprint, New York, 1957.

Early Netherlandish Painting: Its Origins and Character (1953). 2 vols. Charles Eliot Norton Lectures, 1947–1948. Reprint, New York, 1971.

Renaissance and Renascences in Western Art (1960). 2 vols. Reprint, New York, 1969.

Other Sources

Białostocki, Jan. "Erwin Panofsky, 1892–1968: Thinker, Historian, Human Being." *Simiolus kunsthistorisch tijdschrift* 4 (1970): 68–89.

Bonnet, Jacques, ed. *Erwin Panofsky*. Cahiers pour un temps. Paris, 1983.

Didi-Huberman, Georges. *Devant l'image: Question posée aux fins de l'histoire de l'art*. Paris, 1990.

Ferretti, Silvia. *Cassirer, Panofsky, and Warburg: Symbol, Art, Theory*. Translated by Richard Pierce. New Haven, 1989.

Hasenmueller, Christine. "Panofsky, Iconography, and Semiotics." *Journal of Aesthetics and Art Criticism* 36.3 (Spring 1978): 289–301.

Heckscher, William S. *Erwin Panofsky: A Curriculum Vitae*. Princeton, N.J., 1969.

Holly, Michael Ann. *Panofsky and the Foundations of Art History*. Ithaca, N.Y., 1984.

Kaemmerling, Ekkehard, ed. *Ikonographie und Ikonologie: Theorien, Entwicklung, Probleme*. Cologne, 1979.

Landauer, Carl. "Erwin Panofsky and the Renascence of the Renaissance." *Renaissance Quarterly* 47 (1994): 255–281.

Lavin, Irving, ed. *Meaning in the Visual Arts: Views from the Outside: A Centennial Commemoration of Erwin Panofsky, 1892–1968*. Princeton, N.J., 1995.

Mitchell, W. J. T. *Picture Theory: Essays on Verbal and Visual Representation*. Chicago, 1994.

Moxey, Keith. "Panofsky's Melancholia." In *The Practice of Theory: Poststructuralism, Cultural Politics, and Art History*. Ithaca, N.Y., 1994.

Oberer, Hariolf, and Egon Verheyen, eds. *Erwin Panofsky: Aufsätze zu Grundfragen der Kunstwissenschaft*. Berlin, 1964. Contains a complete bibliographic listing of Panofsky's works.

Podro, Michael. *The Critical Historians of Art*. New Haven, 1982.

MICHAEL ANN HOLLY

PAREYSON, LUIGI (1918–1991), Italian philosopher. Italian philosophy, particularly in the twentieth century, derives much of its fascination and importance from the way in which philosophical theories, such as, to mention but a few, idealism (Benedetto Croce and Giovanni Gentile), positivism (Roberto Ardigò, Galvano della Volpe, Ludovico Geymonat), Marxism (Antonio Labriola and Antonio Gramsci), and, of course, various forms of philosophical theology, are appropriated into Italian intellectual culture and given an often deeply original twist by their appropriators. That importance is enhanced by the fact that these philosophies are always thought to bear directly on how political and moral life should be conducted.

Originally influenced by Augusto Guzzo, Luigi Pareyson's work (like that of Stefanani and Abbagnano) is part of the Italian intellectual involvement with existentialism, and, in the case of Pareyson, in particular, with its German versions, as found in Karl Jaspers and Martin Heidegger. As with Croce, Gentile, and indeed any great systematic philosopher, such as Immanuel Kant or G. W. F. Hegel, aesthetics is not treated by Pareyson as a separate discipline but is integrated into an overall account of human beings and their constructions of reality. In those accounts, and in this Pareyson is at one with Croce and Gentile, the aesthetic often assumes a central role. It is arguable that the failure in Anglo-Saxon analytic traditions similarly to embed aesthetics in some comprehensive picture of the mind and its intellectual and spiritual powers is what often leads to the marginalization of aesthetics as a philosophical discipline. The task now is to explain briefly Pareyson's intellectual position and the place of aesthetics in it.

That overall position takes its departure from existentialism. Central to the appeal of that philosophy for Pareyson is its stress on liberty. Pareyson writes that "existentialism presents itself straight off as a philosophy of liberty." That, he thinks, is amply demonstrated not only by the terminology used in existentialism, but also from the fact that it was born of a revolt against Hegelianism, conceived, rightly or wrongly, as a rationalist metaphysics at odds with the possibility of freedom. In 1948, however, in *Attaulità dell'esistezialismo*, Pareyson asserted that although much was worthwhile in the polemical stance of existentialism, it was necessary to transcend it, the only two possibilities for such a transcendence being a frank espousal of a materialistic humanism (or a reformed spiritualism), or a modernized and reformed idealism. He preferred the latter alternative.

Pareyson's mature existentialism-transcending philosophizing elaborates what he calls "the ontology of liberty." This has its foundation in a thought, deriving from Friedrich Wilhelm von Schelling (for whom, too, in his earlier philosophy, art was central to the life of humanity), of an "ontology of the inexhaustible." Schelling had viewed the progress of thought as the endless activity of the practical and theoretical self as it transforms unconscious reason into feeling, perception, and thought, and as it transforms unconscious reality into individual morality, political life, and history.

For Pareyson this process of thought reaches its peak in what is called the *pensiero tragico*, tragic thinking, in which the problem of evil is the thinker's protagonist. Evil and suffering cannot be transcended or avoided. (Indeed, even God must face their reality.) For Pareyson, evil, in the form of "suffering," is liberty's reference point, that with which we must freely engage. Pareyson was in this regard deeply affected by Fyodor Dostoyevsky's work, which he thought of as a significant expression of our present condition in both religion and art. In aesthetics, about which he wrote copiously, and which he made central to this thought, he postulates the notion of the aesthetic as that which is given form. For this reason he may be thought to be an appropriator, for his own purposes, and with his own distinctive manner of thinking, of a central feature of Croce's theory, namely, the account of the aesthetic as an account of that part of the human spirit that expresses by giving form to our thought and feeling.

Pareyson's thinking about aesthetics is, then, deeply integrated with his overall thinking about ontology. Thus, for example, in his talk to the 1948 International Aesthetics Congress in Venice he began by remarking that the problem of the interpretation of works of art, in which the spiritual and the physical appear as one, was worth pursuing because that investigation would "reveal fundamental characteristics of the human spirit." For example, the work of art is inexhaustibly interpretable, and exists to be interpreted (a view not much remote from certain postmodernist views of art).

Like much that is interesting in Italian philosophy, Pareyson's views have been little disseminated. I know of no work that has been translated into English, and English reference works seem entirely to ignore him and his recent confreres. To redress that a translation follows of a short passage from the conclusion of his Venice paper that gives some of the flavor of his thinking:

> Everything finds its explanation in the fact that the work of art is form. As form gathers together an infinity of things, which it contains but does not exhaust, so a person is an infinity, and each one of the points of view which we can adopt contains us entirely although not exhausting our possibilities. Understanding only obtains when there occurs a correspondence, a consonance, a sympathy, between an aspect of a work of art and the point of view of a person. A work of art entirely reveals itself in one of its aspects, and the interpreter penetrates into it entirely from his or her point of view. The work does not change even if the aspect under which it is considered or the perspective of the viewer changes. Rather it is accessible only through ever diverse interpretations. These do not compromise its identity but, rather, acknowledge its infinity. These, far from subordinating the work, are something it desires, sustains and solicits. So the study of the interpretation of art casts light on the indivisible bond that exists between the philosophy of forms and any philosophy of persons.

[*See also* Italian Aesthetics.]

BIBLIOGRAPHY

Works by Pareyson

Estetica: Teoria della formatività. 2d ed. Bologna, 1960.
L'etica di Kierkegaard. Turin, 1965.
Teoria dell'arte. Milan, 1965.
Conversazioni di estetica. Milan, 1966.
Esistenza e persona. 3d ed. Turin, 1966.
I problemi d'estetica. 2d ed. Milan, 1966.
L'estetica di Kant. Milan, 1968.
Estetica e etica Etica ed estetica in Schiller. Milan, 1968.
Essere e libertà. Turin, 1970.
Studi sull'esistenzialismo. 2d rev. ed. Florence, 1971.
Verità e interpretazione. Milan, 1971.

COLIN A. LYAS

PARODY. The term *parody* derives from the ancient Greek word *parodia* and has come to accumulate a variety of meanings connected with correlative terms such as *pastiche, quotation, satire,* and *allusion.* Currently enjoying a postmodern revival and attendant appreciation, the history of parody can be traced from its ancient origins through its modern, late modern, and postmodern changes, noting the accumulation of negative associations along the way. At the present time, there are more than a few commentators eager to discuss contemporary parody as an art form particularly relevant to the twentieth century. Most approaches share a basic foundation that treats parody as a complex multilayered type of imitation (sometimes referred to as intertextuality). They differ, however, in that only some theorists include a comic element in the defining character of parody.

Based on evidence from writers of *parodia* in Athenaeus's *Deipnosophists,* parody has been defined as a narrative poem in moderate length, in epic meter, using epic vocabulary, and treating a light, satirical, or mock-heroic subject. An earlier use of the term, *parados* (from *para,* "beside, alongside, from the side of," plus *ode,* "ode" or "song") designating "an imitating singer," gave rise to *parode* ("beside song": in German, *Beigesang,* and in French, *contre-chant*). In ancient Greece, rhapsodes created the first parodies at the same time that they produced the first great epics of Western literature. A surviving example is Hegemon's *Batrachomyomachia* (Battle of the Frogs and Mice), a composition once thought to be the work of Homer himself, which reproduces the epic style of the *Iliad* but substitutes frogs and mice for Achaians and Trojans. This incentive to provide "imitations" as counterpoints to the originals continued into the later Greek playwrights who created satyr plays in addition to serious dramas.

As Margaret A. Rose sees it, the admission of a slight change of subject matter is significant for the subsequent development of the term, as it shows that imitation of form was only part of what was essential to a parody from the beginning. In looking at the *Battle of the Frogs and Mice* as well as other accounts or fragments of works like it, she concludes that Greek *parodia* not only imitated the form of heroic epics but also created humor by "rewriting the plot or characters so that there was some comic contrast with the more 'serious' epic form of the work, and/or . . . by mixing references to the more serious aspects and characters of the epic with comically lowly and inappropriate figures from the everyday or animal world" (Rose, 1979).

Consider this example from Hipponax's *Hexameters,* which parodies the opening lines of the *Odyssey.* The original lines of the *Odyssey* read: "Tell me, O Muse, of the man of many devices, who wandered full many ways after he had sacked the sacred citadel of Troy." Hipponax's parody reads: "Tell me, Muse, of that maelstrom wide as the sea, that belly-knife, son of Eurymedon who eats indecently, how that he, miserable one, shall in miserable doom perish by stoning at the people's decree by the shore of the unharvested sea." Unlike the original's praise of Odysseus expressed in the epithet "the man of many devices," the parody injects the comic element of the lowly and everyday world, of creative language to characterize "that belly-knife, son . . . who eats indecently . . . miserable one, [who] shall in miserable doom perish by stoning."

There is another sort of ancient writing that does not depend on the epic form as its model but rather parodies the conventions of Greek tragedy (the *paratragoedia* or "paratragedy"). Aristotle used the term *parody* to refer to the first works of the type written by Hegemon of Thasos, a contemporary of Aristophanes (c.450–c.388 BCE), who wrote *The Frogs*. Like the *Dilead* by Nicochares and other comedies, parodies showed men in a bad light (i.e., worse than they are), in contrast to tragedy, which showed them better than they are. For Aristotle, tragedy always surpassed comedy in its role of education and socialization. Further extension of the term (in usage by the Aristophanic scholiasts) broadened the meaning to "any device for comic quotation," thus setting the historic precedent for defining parody in terms of a comic element. Even the visual apparatus of the mask used in ancient comedy, with its upturned mouth and smile, seemed conclusively to confirm mirth and laughter as an identifying feature.

According to one theorist, the *Battle of the Frogs and Mice* is an example of a relatively pure or absolute parody in that it does not impute "fundamental imperfections" in the conception or the execution of the *Iliad* and hence is created for the sake of its nonmenacing humor. The parodies of Aristophanes *(The Frogs)* and those following him, however, were not so pure; such authors used parody to launch a "bitterly moral critique" of individual authors, their works, generalized modes of belief, and philosophical systems of the times. This satiric trend continued into seventeenth-century France, where parodies such as those by Louis Fuzelier (in the Theatre Italien) were justified by the claim that parody will strike only at what is degrading and false, so it is not so much a piece of buffoonery as a critical exposition far from degrading the truth. Negative associations arose in the sixteenth century, however, when Julius Caesar Scaliger introduced the Latin word *ridiculus* to describe the comic aspects of parody. In his widely distributed work of 1711, the *Spectator*, Joseph Addison furthered this trend by treating Miguel de Cervantes's *Don Quixote* as a burlesque and not as a parody. In the eighteenth century, parody was relegated to a subcategory of the burlesque (originating in the Italian, *burla*, "a joke or a trick"). By the nineteenth century, the *parodoi* were sometimes defined as "buffoons" that followed the Homeric rhapsodists from town to town, but in other accounts, parody settled down to become a rather "gentlemanly art" in such publications as *Punch*, eventually considered a form of harmless homage to the original.

According to Rose, parody's association with a modern notion of the burlesque as ridicule left it condemned to a status of triviality in the twentieth century; late modern commentators have "denied the importance of its comic effect or structure altogether in order both to save parody from such denigration and to stretch its meaning and function to cover other fashionable meta-fictional and 'intertextual' forms." In defense of parody, Rose defines it as an intertextual form: a work of fiction that comments or reflects on another text by re-presenting the words, passages, or messages of the model text. This notion of intertextuality comes from Julia Kristeva, who coined the term to capture a reader's experience of a text: the decoding of the author's encoded meaning based on the three elements of author, reader, and other exterior texts (in the case of parody, the original text). A similar notion is that of dual coding or double hybridization, a form of textual dialogism, as advanced by Mikhail Bakhtin, who also wrote accounts of the origins of comedy within the carnivalesque and Mardi Gras.

In Rose's account, the comic plays a crucial role. Parody can be "ambivalent" toward its target (original model) and can involve—in its creative re-presenting of the original—a mixture of criticism and sympathy for the parodied text. It is defined, however, as "the comic refunctioning of preformed linguistic or artistic material," where the comic element involves the creation of incongruity between the original and the parody traceable to the way the parodist "foregrounds" the original in the parodied work: by highlighting it, complicating it, or confusing it. Such incongruity stems from the effect on the reader of shock or surprise arising from a conflict (or clash) between one's expectations about the text parodied and what one actually encounters. Unlike forms of satire or burlesque that do not make their target a significant part of themselves, parody allows for comedy that laughs "both at and with its target." Rose believes this definition is consistent with the history and origin of the term. Her choice of paradigms of *Don Quixote*, James Joyce's *Ulysses*, Malcolm Bradbury's *Who Do You Think You Are?*, and David Lodge's works *(The British Museum Is Falling Down, Changing Places, and Small World)* bears this out.

In contrast to the mode of theorizing advanced by Rose that stipulates humor as necessary to the genre, Linda Hutcheon defines parody as "repetition with critical [ironic] distance, which marks difference rather than similarity" (Hutcheon, 1985). Following Gilles Deleuze, where parody is defined as "repetition that includes difference," she severs its connection to the comic, reserving the comic or ridiculous element for only burlesque and travesty. Thus, she denies the association of humor with the classical meaning of the term, and her definition comes to depend entirely on an explanation of the crucial phrase "critical ironic distance."

Hutcheon agrees with Rose that, in contrast to pastiche, which is a simple borrowing or imitating of material allowing for very little variation, parody seeks to do something more than just imitate the original. There is a connection between the original and the parody (imitation) that is deeper than surface repetition. Rose called it "intertextuality"; Hutcheon calls it imitation plus "ironic inversion":

> When we speak of parody, we do not just mean two texts that interrelate in a certain way. We also imply an intention to parody another work (or set of conventions) and both a recognition of

that intent and an ability to find and interpret the backgrounded text in its relation to the parody.

The inversion takes place when there is a change or alteration in the imitation as compared with its original, for instance, when Max Ernst parodies Michelangelo's *Pietà* by replacing the living mother and her dead son, Christ, with a petrified father holding a living son in his arms. Another example is Euripides' play, *Medea*, which inverts the convention followed in plays by Aeschylus and Sophocles of a male protagonist who is a member of a Greek family of renown who is saved by the gods. In *Medea*, the protagonist is female, an outsider to the established Greek families of renown, and the male hero turns out to be hypocritical and shallow. The difference in critical ironic distance appears to result from the process of "revising, replaying, inverting, and 'transcontextualizing' previous works of art."

Another example is Larry Rivers's painting of Napoleon Bonaparte, based on a work by Jacques-Louis David, ironically titled *The Greatest Homosexual*. In addition to Rivers parodying David's compositional elements (the stance of Napoleon, the right hand hidden in his vest, even the artist's obvious signature), his title playfully judges the content of the image as it critically inverts or transcontextualizes the revered statesman by focusing on his sexual orientation.

Such irony is "playful" and can range from scornful ridicule to reverential homage. It constitutes the central paradox of parody, that "its transgression is always authorized"; that in spite of its critical difference—its tendency to critique the original—"parody reinforces." (Recall the historical moment of the nineteenth century in which parody was theorized as paying homage to the original.) In other words, "irony judges," but it need not be humorous or comic. Other theorists concur. J. D. Kiremidjian, for instance, defines parody as "a work which retains the form but alters the contents of the work or tradition of works it imitates." Humor is not even mentioned.

Allowing for broader definitions, there are many well-known examples of works of art considered parodies. Wolfgang Amadeus Mozart's "A Musical Joke" (also known as the "Village Musician's Sextet") parodied certain musical conventions: the unnecessary repetition of banalities, incorrect modulation, disjointed melodic ideas—in other words, incompetent playing. The second movement of Charles Ives's Fourth Symphony suggests a parody of Mozart's and others' music, also in imitation of the playing of incompetent performers. Franz Liszt's *Reminiscences de Don Juan* developed certain themes of Mozart's *Don Giovanni*. In the third part of his String Quartet No. 3, George Rochberg combined new atonality with parodied nineteenth-century melodic-harmonic language of the styles of Ludwig von Beethoven and Gustav Mahler. Similarly, Luciano Berio's *Sinfonia* "transcontextualizes" fragmented quotations of J. S. Bach, Arnold Schoenberg, Claude Debussy, Maurice Ravel, Richard Strauss, Johannes Brahms, Hector Berlioz, and others within the context of the third movement of Mahler's Second Symphony. Eighteenth- and nineteenth-century parodies of the most popular operas often appeared on stage contemporaneously with the originals. It is even reported that parodies of Richard Wagner's *Tannhäuser* and *Tristan und Isolde* were performed before the original operas were staged. Jimi Hendrix's rock version of "The Star-Spangled Banner" shows that parody need not be restricted to the classical tradition.

In addition, Jane Austen parodied the popular romance fiction of her day in *Love and Friendship* and *Pride and Prejudice*. According to Hutcheon, Austen ended *Northanger Abbey* "parodying gothic conventions while still relying on them for her novel's shape." Mary Shelley, Emily and Charlotte Brontë, and others used parody as an element of social satire, prefiguring numerous women writers of today. Contemporary women have used parody within the visual arts as well. Sylvia Sleigh has represented the most noted art critics of the 1970s art world in a work parodying Eugène Delacroix's nineteenth-century harem scenes. Mary Beth Edelson has revised Leonardo da Vinci's *Last Supper* by replacing the central figure of Christ with Georgia O'Keeffe in *Some American Living Women Artists,* and Judy Chicago has gone so far as to portray thirty-nine women not invited to the Last Supper in her infamous work *The Dinner Party*. More recently, Cindy Sherman has photographed herself as the woman or man depicted in Renaissance portraiture, and the Australian artist Sally Swain has mounted the most thorough and humorous challenge to the entire tradition of the "great masterpieces" of Western art in her series of great housewives of famous artists.

Even filmmakers have used parody to comment on the predominance of men in the field and to communicate uniquely female outlooks on the world; consider director Rachel Talay's recent parody of Mad Max films, *Tank Girl*, as well as works of the New German Cinema: Wim Wenders's *The State of Things,* which parodies John Ford's classic Western *The Searchers;* Rainer Werner Fassbinder's *The Desire of Veronika Voss,* seen as a "parodic inscription" of Billy Wilder's *Sunset Boulevard;* and feminist filmmakers like Helma Sanders-Brahms, Helke Sanders, and Margerethe von Trotta. According to film theorist Marsha Kinder, von Trotta's films—for example, *Germany Pale Mother, Trouble with Love,* and *Sheer Madness*—are multifaceted, parodying "an even wider selection of patriarchal forms, including fairy tales, poems, classical films and genres, and even progressive works by male auteurs in the New German Cinema" (Kinder, 1990).

Whether comic or not, the continued exploration within the parameters of the genre and the abundance of the forms of parody testify to its continuing popularity and importance as an artistic manner of expression.

[*See also* Comedy; *and* Irony.]

BIBLIOGRAPHY

Bakhtin, Mikhail M. *The Dialogic Imagination: Four Essays.* Edited by Michael Holquist, translated by Caryl Emerson and Michael Holquist. Austin, 1981.

Deleuze, Gilles. *Différence et répétition.* Paris, 1968.

Hutcheon, Linda. *A Theory of Parody: The Teachings of Twentieth-Century Art Forms.* New York and London, 1985.

Kinder, Marsha. "Ideological Parody in the New German Cinema: Reading *The State of Things, The Desire of Veronika Voss,* and *Germany Pale Mother* as Postmodernist Rewritings of *The Searchers, Sunset Boulevard,* and *Blonde Venus." Quarterly Review of Film and Video* 12. 1–2 (1990): 73–103. Special issue edited by Ronald Gottesman.

Kiremidjian, J. D. "The Aesthetics of Parody." *Journal of Aesthetics and Art Criticism* 28 (1969): 231–242.

Rose, Margaret A. *Parody//Meta-Fiction: An Analysis of Parody as a Critical Mirror to the Writing and Reception of Fiction.* London, 1979.

Rose, Margaret A. *Parody: Ancient, Modern, and Post-Modern.* Cambridge and New York, 1993.

Swain, Sally. *Great Housewives of Art.* New York, 1989.

Swain, Sally. *Great Housewives of Art Revisited.* New York, 1992.

PEGGY ZEGLIN BRAND

PASTICHE. The term *pastiche* comes from the French *pastiche* or the Italian *pasticcio,* which originally meant a "pasty" or "pie" dish containing several different ingredients. It has come to be used synonymously with a variety of terms whose meanings are rarely fixed with clarity: *parody, montage, quotation, allusion, irony, burlesque, travesty,* and *plagiarism.* Most of them share, to some degree or other, what is essential to the notion of pastiche, namely, the imitation of one form of artistic medium (text, representation, music) by another. More often than not, *pastiche* is defined in comparison to the notion of parody. Although some definitions of pastiche strive to remain neutral, others have taken on a pejorative sense. Still others are more positive, especially within the architectural realm.

At the most basic level, pastiche is considered to be a simple imitation—at the level of stylistic elements and identifiable structure—in comparison to the more complex type of imitation particular to parody. A strict formal textual imitation, it is a borrowing of words, phrases, visual, or musical motifs from the original that are reproduced in an imitation. According to Leif Ludwig Albertsen, pastiche involves the reproduction of both the form and the content of a work that constitutes a revival of things from the past. In *A Dictionary of Architecture and Building,* Russell Sturgis defines "pastiche" as:

A. A work of art produced in deliberate imitation of another or several others, as of the works of a master taken together, and
B. Especially, in decorative art, the modification for transference to another medium, of any design.   (Sturgis, 1902)

Other neutral definitions are offered by Linda Hutcheon and Margaret A. Rose in their analyses of the corresponding notion of parody. For both, pastiche is more like quotation: a reproducing of the substance of a thought or image without alteration or afterthought. Like allusion, it adds a layer of reference to the past or to other contemporaneous works without construing it into something more than it is: simple reference. For example, Chippendale furniture reproduced the facades and decorations of classical stone and marble architecture in reduced wooden form; likewise, Philip Johnson's postmodern AT&T building in Manhattan imitates and refers back to Chippendale furniture.

Hutcheon comments on the fact that in pastiche there is little or no room for creativity—"Pastiche usually has to remain within the same genre as its model, whereas parody allows for adaptation" (Hutcheon, 1985)—and that pastiche may be an imitation not of a single text but rather of an indefinite number of texts. Whereas pastiche merely imitates or corresponds to the original, parody has been labeled a dual- or double-coded (double-voiced) hybridization. Parody seeks to do something more than just imitate, to differentiate itself from the original. It is repetition that includes some difference: "imitation with critical ironic distance." There is a connection between the original and parody that is deeper than surface repetition. Thus, the parody is doubled or multilayered in meaning, more adaptive to playful commentary on the original. According to Hutcheon, neither ridicule nor humor is essential to parody or pastiche; they are, however, essential to both burlesque and travesty.

Rose also sees parody as double-coded, but includes a comic or humorous element to its essential characteristics. For her, pastiche is not "blind" or "blank" parody, as Fredric Jameson suggests, since on her definition of parody, humor is essential. Pastiche is not lacking humor; it was never originally constituted in terms of humor. Rose notes the confusion of the term with *parody,* especially in French literature, clarifying that "pastiche, however, is not only a much more recent term than parody, but differs from the latter in describing a more neutral practice of compilation which is neither necessarily critical of its sources, nor necessarily comic" (Rose). Pastiche is further distinguished from fakes or forgeries (plagiarism) in terms of intention; for example, in architecture, pastiche is a compilation of different styles or motifs used deliberately and without the concealment which is characteristic of both the forgery and the more serious hoax. Unlike montage, it involves some added element of integration among the elements; far from slavish imitation, it can be used in a variety of "imaginative rather than derivative ways."

Pastiche has had its detractors, even in its short history. Edward Lucie-Smith's *Thames and Hudson Dictionary of Art Terms* begins with neutral terms ("a work of art using a borrowed style and usually made up of borrowed elements, but not necessarily a direct copy") but then adds that pastiche "often verges on conscious or unconscious caricature, through its exaggeration of what seems most typical in the original model" (Lucie-Smith, 1984). In Peter Murray and Linda Murray's analysis in *A Dictionary of Art and Artists,* the meaning of *pastiche* borders on plagiarism: "an imitation or forgery which consists of a number of motives taken from several genuine works by any one artist recombined in such a way as to give the impression of being an independent original creation by that artist" (Murray and Murray, 1959).

Some theorists have gone so far as to condemn its use, especially in the borrowing of past classical elements in the compilation of postmodern architecture. Jean-François Lyotard considered it "a feckless or meaningless compilation of styles," and Jameson—taking his cue from Jean Beaudrillard—reduced it to a "blind" or "blank" form of parody, something negative as well as "something humorless." On this view, pastiche is an acknowledged, intentional imitation that still falls short of the layered meaning essential to parody.

But pastiche has its champions as well. Filmmaker Jean-Luc Godard was known for having referred back to the genre of film noir and also for paying tribute to François Truffaut in his 1966 film, *Masculine-Feminine,* where a female character sings a song from Truffaut's *Jules et Jim.* One theorist, Hal Foster, has gone so far as to consider pastiche the distinguishing mark of postmodern art: "Yet nearly every postmodern artist and architect has resorted, in the name of style and history, to pastiche; indeed it is fair to say that pastiche is the official style of this postmodernist camp" (Foster, 1985).

Charles Jencks sees pastiche (like parody) as a method for positive, playful, and meaningful double-coding in postmodern art and architecture. He cites the example of Carlo Maria Mariani's *The Constellation of Leo,* also called *The School of Rome,* of 1980–1981, as an example of the role pastiche (combined with satire) can play in referring back to both modern neoclassical and modernist art, including (among others) *The School of Athens* by Raphael and *The Red Model* by René Magritte. The coupling of these borrowed elements with Mariani's fresher vision (the placing of Magritte's disembodied feet at the base of a classical statue) results in a double-coding of meaning within the elements of the work of art itself as well as at the level of historical style referring back in time: "modernism is also 'double-coded' with other periods via the use of pastiche, and the art of the 'modern' or of 'now' itself made a part of history" (Jencks).

Far from being a simple imitation, pastiche assumes the complexity of meaning previously reserved for parody. It still remains pastiche, however. It is an imitation *without* critical commentary on the original (thus it fails as parody for Rose); it repeats *without* difference (it fails as parody for Hutcheon). Such "failures" do not, however, hinder its role as a unique creative force within the art world.

[*See also* Collage; *and* Parody.]

BIBLIOGRAPHY

Albertson, Leif Ludwig. "Der Begriff des Pastiche." *Orbis Litterarum* 26.1 (1971): 1–8.

Foster, Hal. *Recodings: Art, Spectacle, Cultural Politics.* Port Townsend, Wash., 1985.

Hutcheon, Linda. *A Theory of Parody: The Teachings of Twentieth-Century Art Forms.* New York and London, 1985.

Jameson, Fredric. "Postmodernism and Consumer Society." In *Postmodern Culture,* edited by Hal Foster. London, 1985.

Jameson, Fredric. "Postmodernism; or, The Cultural Logic of Late Capitalism." *New Left Review* 146 (July–August 1984): 53–92.

Jencks, Charles A. *The Language of Post-Modern Architecture* (1977). 6th ed. New York, 1997.

Jencks, Charles A. *Late-Modern Architecture and Other Essays.* New York, 1980.

Lucie-Smith, Edward. *The Thames and Hudson Dictionary of Art Terms.* London and New York, 1984.

Murray, Peter, and Linda Murray. *A Dictionary of Art and Artists.* Harmondsworth, England, 1959.

Rose, Margaret A. "Post-Modern Pastiche," *British Journal of Aesthetics* 31 (January 1991): 26–38.

Rose, Margaret A. *Parody: Ancient, Modern and Post-Modern.* Cambridge and New York, 1993.

Sturgis, Russell. *A Dictionary of Architecture and Building.* 3 vols. London and New York, 1902.

PEGGY ZEGLIN BRAND

PATER, WALTER HORATIO

PATER, WALTER HORATIO (1839–1894), English essayist and critic. When Walter Pater died, Henry James commented on his achievement in a typically double-edged manner. In one of his most celebrated pieces of writing, the conclusion to the volume of essays known as *The Renaissance* (1873), Pater had equated "success in life" with the ability to "burn always with this hard, gemlike flame." James doubted whether he had lived up to the ideal: "he shines in the uneasy gloom—vaguely, a phosphorescence, not a flame." Nevertheless, he was willing to concede to his correspondent that "he is not of the little day—but of the longer time." Now that more than a century has elapsed since Pater's death, we can see the justice of the last remark. Pater has indeed proved capable of surviving, and of renewing his message for the end of the twentieth century.

To explain why this has been so requires at least some attempt to distentangle the different threads in Pater's production as a writer, and to trace his reception in the intervening period. Pater's writings were not voluminous, set beside the life's work of Victorian sages like John Ruskin and Thomas Carlyle. His preferred form was the individual essay, published in a contemporary journal like the *Fortnightly Review* or *Macmillan's Magazine;* this might take the form of a book review, like his first published essay, "Coleridge's Writings," or, at a later stage, of the more ambitious genre of the "imaginary portrait," in which he opened a viewpoint on a particular age and culture through the eyes of a usually fictive protagonist.

Pater's essays have never been gathered together in a complete edition, which would maintain the chronological order in which they were written and thus permit an overview of the development of his thought. They remain accessible for the most part in the groupings to which they were allocated in Pater's lifetime, and shortly afterward. *The Renaissance* (originally published as *Studies in the History of the Renaissance* and retitled *Studies in Art and Poetry* to accommodate a reviewer's complaint about the lack of historical content) went through four editions before his death. Two other collections of essays, *Imaginary Portraits* (1887) and *Appreciations* (1889), followed in due course, and were complemented in 1895 by a further pair industriously and rapidly compiled by Pater's executor Charles Shadwell: *Greek Studies* and *Miscellaneous Studies*. It is indicative of the general difficulty of following the development of Pater's thought that the last published essay in the second posthumous collection should in fact be the very first of his writings to be preserved: a piece originally read to a student society at Oxford and dated July 1864, which bears the title "Diaphaneitè."

To these collections of essays should be added two other categories of related writings that make up the Pater canon. His concept of the imaginary portrait, which has been acknowledged as a wholly original mode of cultural reconstruction, also engendered more lengthy fictional texts that approach the condition of novels. *Marius the Epicurean: His Sensations and Ideas* (1885) is the only complete example of this type of writing that, as the subtitle suggests, was concerned with exploring and interpreting the life of the mind through a chosen historical persona, rather than with the narrative procedures characteristic of the nineteenth-century historical novel. *Gaston de Latour,* however, an incomplete text of the same kind first published in 1896, is important insofar as it establishes a close connection between Pater's view of the Renaissance in France and his prognosis of the features of "Modernity" in his own time. Beside these, the most ambitious of Pater's writings, must be set those that were the product of his teaching responsibilities at Oxford University, and which he reportedly expected to endure longer than his other works: the "series of lectures" published in 1893 under the title *Plato and Platonism.*

This very brief summary of Pater's output helps to pinpoint the difficulty of isolating the special feature that gives him a special claim to the attention of posterity. Is it as a philosopher that he deserves to be known? Despite his expectations, *Plato and Platonism* is almost certainly the least widely read of his books, and likely to remain so. Plausible claims could be made for his astute analysis of the implications of relativism in nineteenth-century thought, and Lothar Hönnighausen has compared his concept of "point of view" with that of Friedrich Nietzsche. But we can find no systematic discussion of aesthetics in his essays. Is it then as a novelist that he establishes his real originality? There is no doubt that his historical explorations, based on the genre of the imaginary portrait, run parallel to certain of the innovations of James, or indeed Marcel Proust, whose characterization of the writer Bergotte in *À la recherche du temps perdu* invokes many of the features associated with his style. But Pater is too negligent of the devices of fiction, even mod-

ernist fiction, to pass muster in this company. *Gaston de Latour,* despite the device of a fictional character who provides its title, reads to a great extent like a second collection of essays devoted, with a northern European emphasis on this occasion, to the theme of the Renaissance.

It seems as though the only category for assessing Pater's achievement is therefore the rather dubious one (at least in modern letters) of the essay. Or alternatively, we should attempt to build on the category that he himself, more than any other writer in the English language, established and provided with its own protocols: that of aesthetic criticism. But here the evaluation of Pater's work runs across a particular problem, which could be expressed in the following way. Since Pater's time, the predominant tradition of academic study with regard to the visual arts has been a historical one, which attaches great importance to connoisseurship and its role in establishing provenance. Yet, Pater made it quite clear in his essay "The School of Giorgione" that this consideration hardly entered into his concerns. At the same time, the predominant discipline advancing the cause of criticism has been, especially in the English-speaking world, that of literary criticism. To those who set up the canon of English literature, and provided tools for evaluating it, in the second quarter of the twentieth century, Pater was an inconvenient figure who could easily be dismissed. He was, indeed, an exemplar of the "decadent" movement that could safely be excluded from the company of the "Great Tradition."

Much more could be said about the downgrading of Pater in the half-century that followed his death. T. S. Eliot, for example, contests even his right to be regarded as a devotee of "art for art's sake," despite the fact that he included this phrase in the early formulation of the conclusion to *The Renaissance.* Eliot wants to relegate him to the company of more solidly Victorian sages like Carlyle, Ruskin, and Matthew Arnold. The connections are certainly there. As Denis Donoghue has pointed out, Pater borrows Carlyle's vivid characterization of Charlotte Corday when he formulates the example of the "clear, crystal nature" in "Diaphaneitè." But the divergences that Pater exhibits from this Victorian tradition are even more striking. Pater implicitly rejects Arnold's approach when he chooses as the epigraph to *The Renaissance* the injunction from the Psalms: "Yet shall ye be as the wings of the dove." It is an appropriate rejoinder to Arnold's stern injunction at the outset of *Culture and Anarchy:* "Be ye therefore perfect." Pater amplifies the disagreement when, in his preface, he caps Arnold's critical objective "to see the object as in itself it really is" with the reminder: "in aesthetic criticism the first step towards seeing one's object as it really is, is to know one's own impression as it really is, to realise it distinctly."

Pater's equally pronounced divergence from Ruskin has been well summed up in the writings of Harold Bloom, who epitomizes the resurgence of interest in Pater over the past twenty-five years. For Bloom, the achievement of Pater is precisely to purify the aesthetic vision represented so intensely by Ruskin of its inconvenient moral bias, while at the same time nurturing a "consciousness of belatedness" that was to be integral to the modernists' reworking of tradition. Pater, the self-appointed "Caliban" of modern letters who did not venture into the seductive realms of poetry, becomes nonetheless the indispensable link in the chain that binds a modernist poet like Wallace Stevens or John Ashbery to his Romantic forebears. Whereas Bloom puts forward the most formidable claim for Pater's centrality to the Anglo-American tradition, it is also noteworthy that a German critic, Wolfgang Iser, should have put forward the thesis as early as 1960 that Pater's importance can only be grasped against the background of the Western philosophical tradition. Iser, like Bloom, sees the essence of Pater's achievement as his ability to serve as intermediary between late Romanticism and early modernism. It is against the background of thinkers like Plato, G. W. F. Hegel, and Samuel Taylor Coleridge, in particular, that Pater develops his own skeptical attitude to all forms of systematization, and his concept of aesthetic experience as a way of countering human finiteness.

Maximal and minimal claims for the continuing importance of Pater will certainly continue to be made. It may be possible to question the extent of his role in the aesthetic movement, and to show (as Nicholas Shimpton has finely expressed it) that he forms no more than the "still centre" of the "aesthetical sect." But it is difficult to disagree with Elinor S. Shaffer's estimate that Pater incarnates the problem of decadence in its relation to modernism, and so anticipates many of the issues that are still being raised in our own fin de siècle. As she further points out, Pater's insistence on the variety of points of view has become a source and a reference point for contemporary gender politics. Revisionist histories of the Victorian period based on a gay political agenda cannot easily avoid taking Pater into account.

Commentators like Denis Donoghue, while freely conceding the presence of a "homosexual code" in Pater's writings, are concerned to locate his particular contribution to present-day cultural criticism in a more global way. Donoghue is ready to concede that Pater is not a close reader; he is concerned not with the formal analysis of texts and works of art, but with "the types of feeling they embodied" (Donoghue, 1995). But this apparently anachronistic and unscholarly preoccupation is the price Pater has to pay for rejecting the instrumentalist view of knowledge that was predominant in his own day. It enables him to develop an approach that has not lost its persuasiveness: "consciousness not as a mode of knowledge but as an alternative to knowledge." Richard Wollheim in part corroborates this estimate when he argues that, for Pater, "culture, or art, is essentially expressive, and theory is essentially pragmatic"

(Wollheim, 1983). In other words, there is no inconsistency, with regard to Pater's writings, between the fundamental contention that art expresses human life and the proposition that the work of art is also intrinsically worthy of study. For Wollheim, Pater's criticism is thus characteristically "Janus-faced": "it looks towards both [theory and art] and strives to do each justice."

It will be apparent from this brief account that Pater has recovered an actuality that he appeared to have lost in the early years of the century, when he was too hastily relegated among the "Eminent Victorians." Donoghue is not too sanguine when obliged to admit that "the modern literature I most love has come from Baudelaire, Pater and Mallarmé rather than from Newman, Arnold and Ruskin." Wollheim is uncomfortable with a critical theory that, in his interpretation of Pater, "will derive its appeal from considerations not of truth but of utility." Iser, however, is ready to see in *Plato and Platonism* "an awareness of how the very modality of discourse predetermines the way in which subject matter is captured" (Iser, 1987). According to this viewpoint, Pater's "diversity of differently operating discourses" acquires a self-reflexive dimension in directing us to compare the different modes, and their aptitude for interpretation. "To have made interpretation itself into an object of scrutiny and to have retooled the mechanics of discourse gives Pater an unprecedented presence one hundred years after his death" (Iser).

[*See also* Aestheticism.]

BIBLIOGRAPHY

Work by Pater

Selected Writings of Walter Pater. Edited by Harold Bloom. New York, 1974.

Other Sources

Dellamora, Richard. *Masculine Desire: The Sexual Politics of Victorian Aestheticism.* Chapel Hill, N.C., 1990.

Donoghue, Denis. *Walter Pater: Lover of Strange Souls.* New York, 1995.

Hönnighausen, Lothar. "'Point of View' and Its Background in Intellectual History." *Comparative Criticism: A Yearbook* 2 (1980): 151–166.

Inman, Billie Andrew. *Walter Pater's Reading: A Bibliography of His Library Borrowings and Literary References, 1858–1873.* New York, 1981.

Iser, Wolfgang. *Walter Pater: The Aesthetic Moment.* Translated by David Henry Wilson. Cambridge and New York, 1987.

Levey, Michael. *The Case of Walter Pater.* London, 1978.

Monsman, Gerald. *Pater's Portraits: Mythic Pattern in the Fiction of Walter Pater.* Baltimore, 1967.

Shaffer, E. S., ed. *Walter Pater and the Culture of the Fin-de-Siècle.* Special issue of *Comparative Criticism: A Yearbook* 17 (1995).

Wollheim, Richard. "Walter Pater as Critic of the Arts." In *On Art and the Mind: Essays and Lectures,* pp. 155–176. London, 1973; reprint, Cambridge, Mass., 1974.

STEPHEN BANN

PAUL, JEAN (Friedrich Richter, 1763–1825), German writer. Jean Paul is typically classed as a Romantic, but is only problematically considered to be of that school. While it is true that he is concerned with repudiating much of what he takes to be overformalistic tendencies of the Weimar aesthetic, Jean Paul is also wary of the ironism of August Wilhelm von Schlegel and Friedrich Schlegel on similar grounds. Although suffering neglect for much of this century, Jean Paul's writings, and particularly his novels, were very popular in his day. Outside of the intellectual circle of Berlin, he was primarily influential in England: Thomas Carlyle, Thomas De Quincey, and Samuel Taylor Coleridge were among his ardent admirers.

Jean Paul's lampoon of Johann Gottlieb Fichte in the *Clavis fichtiana* (1803) (published as one of a series of appendixes to the novel *Titan*) shows real philosophical wit, but his sole substantial work of criticism is the *School of Aesthetics* (*Vorschule der Ästhetik;* 1804). Its structure (or lack of it) is informed by Jean Paul's deeply rooted and idiosyncratic novelistic tendencies and is, accordingly, far less a work of systematic aesthetics than a compendium of critical observations and polemical remarks. In those sections of the work that do take a more systematic approach—those that treat issues of the relation of the various cognitive faculties in the activity of artistic creation—Jean Paul does little more than rework Kantian ideas as transmitted through Friedrich Schiller. Like Immanuel Kant and Schiller (and against the tendency of the age), Jean Paul adopts a "moderate" model of genius positioned between the radical Romantic "English" view, in which unbridled originality is the mark of the work of genius, and the competing neoclassical "French" model, which conceives of genius as ingenuity in employing rules of taste. The Romantic element of Jean Paul's conception of genius shows itself in his belief that a work of art contains an original view of life peculiar to its creator. Jean Paul is very interested in the idea of art as an extrusion of personality (and of personality itself as an artifact).

Were Jean Paul's importance to rest on these ideas, he would not reward much study. Much more interesting, however, are his discussions of the nature of Romantic poetry and of humor. Jean Paul's discussion of the Christian underpinnings of Romantic art is prescient, bearing striking similarities with G. W. F. Hegel's discussion of the issue. Jean Paul argues that the essence of Romantic art is the negation or death of the earthly and a valorizing of its opposite, introspective love. This introspection has as its essence a longing for a reconciliation with the material element. Jean Paul's account of humor can be seen as a precursor to Friedrich Nietzsche. Humor is the "inverse sublime." The sublime (and here, Jean Paul means the Kantian sublime) renders the finite subject's existence insignificant or endangered, thereby elevating the infinite nature of the subject as a free moral agent. Conversely, humor simultaneously deflates the great and raises the small to a point at which they are in equilibrium, thereby abolishing the distinction between them. Jean Paul calls this generic leveling of the distinction of the great and the small humor's "totalizing" effect. But humor also "annihilates" (here Jean Paul's debt to his friend Friedrich Heinrich Jacobi is clear). It views the infinite through the lens of the finite—and thus perfection through that of imperfection—and contains an irreducible element of sadness, even of tragedy. Humor is thus the recognition of the ultimate impossibility, chaos, incomprehensibility, or absurdity of life.

[*See also* Romanticism, *article on* Philosophy and Literature.]

BIBLIOGRAPHY

Works by Paul

Horn of Oberon: Jean Paul Richter's School of Aesthetics. Edited and translated by Margaret R. Hale. Detroit, 1973.
Jean Paul: A Reader. Edited by Timothy J. Casey, translated by Erika Casey. Baltimore, 1992.
Sämtliche Werke: Historisch-kritische Ausgabe, Königlich Preussischen Akademie der Wissenschaft edition. Berlin, 1927.
Werke in zwölf Bänden. Edited by Norbert Miller. Munich, 1975.

Other Sources

de Bruyn, Günter. *Das Leben des Jean Paul Friedrich Richter.* 2d ed. Frankfurt am Main, 1978.
Harich, Wolfgang. *Jean Pauls Revolutionsdichtung: Versuch einer neuen Deutung seiner heroischen Romane.* Reinbek, 1974.
Schweikert, Uwe. *Jean Paul.* Stuttgart, 1970.
Staël, Germaine de. *De l'Allemagne,* vol. 2. Paris, 1968.
Szondi, Peter. *Poetik und Geschichtsphilosophie,* vol. 1. Frankfurt am Main, 1974.
Wheeler, Kathleen, ed. *German Aesthetic and Literary Criticism: The Romantic Ironists and Goethe.* Cambridge and New York, 1984.

FRED L. RUSH, JR.

PEIRCE, CHARLES SANDERS (1839–1914), American physicist, mathematician, and logician. The semiotic philosophy of Charles Sanders Peirce is a complex logical system, much of which is relevant only to specialists. A few of his concepts, however, have had an important bearing on developments in semiotic criticism. Peirce's theory has a trichotomistic structure that accounts for the ways signs function. Peirce's view is primarily dynamic; it describes the process of signification, which is called semiosis. This process involves the production and the interpretation of signs. Hence, this theory provides a logical basis for a reader- or reception-oriented theory of art.

The process of semiosis works through three positions: a perceptible or virtually perceptible item—the sign or representamen—that stands in for something else; the mental image, called the interpretant, that the recipient forms of the sign; and the thing for which the sign stands—the object or referent. When one sees a painting, say a still life of a fruit bowl, the image is, among other things, a sign or representamen of something else. The viewer shapes in her or his mind an image of that something with which she or he associates this image. That mental image, not the person shaping it, is the interpretant. This interpretant points to an object. The object is different for each viewer: it can be real fruit for one, other still-life paintings for another, a huge amount of money for a third, "seventeenth-century Dutch" for a fourth, and so on. The object for which the painting stands is therefore fundamentally subjective and reception-determined.

Peirce's famous definition of the sign is as follows:

> A sign, or *representamen,* is something which stands to somebody for something in some respect or capacity. It addresses somebody, that is, creates in the mind of that person an equivalent sign, or perhaps a more developed sign. That sign which it creates I call the *interpretant* of the first sign. The sign stands for something, its *object.* It stands for that object, not in all respects, but in reference to a sort of idea, which I have sometimes called the *ground* of the representamen.   (Quoted in Innis, 1985)

The structure of address of the sign has been taken up by speech act theory; the "more developed sign" points at the complex acts of interpretation, for example, in scholarly work; the "ground" can be seen as the basis on which the interpretation takes place, and comes closest to the more common concept of code.

As for the process, the interpretant is constantly shifting. As soon as the mental image takes shape, it becomes a new sign, which will yield a new interpretant, and we are in the middle of the process of infinite semiosis. None of the aspects of this process can be isolated from the others, which is why this theory is incompatible with any dichotomistic theory of the sign, such as Ferdinand de Saussure's pair signifier/signified. Peirce insists that the thing that becomes a sign only does so when it begins to evoke its interpretant: "A *Sign* is a Representamen with a mental interpretant." This view is consistent with standard aesthetic theories, for example, the German phenomenological school of *Rezeptions-Ästhetik,* which stated that a work of art becomes a work of art only in its concretization by a recipient. The Prague school of semiotics adopted Jan Mukařovský's distinction between artifact, the mere object, and aesthetic object, the work when processed as a work of art by readers or viewers, which is another aesthetic account similar to Peirce's more general account of semiosis. In spite of the different epistemological backgrounds, there is a strong similarity in this respect between Peirce's and Jacques Lacan's concepts of the sign. Both concepts entail the notion that the fixation of the meaning of a sign is endlessly deferred, as is also held by Jacques Derrida. The major difference seems to be that Lacan insists on the social formation of the practice of interpretation (his concept of the symbolic order). But Peirce's interpretant, although presented as a mental image and therefore carrying the burden of

mentalism, can be redefined as radically social in origin. For the Peircean ground without which no interpretant can occur, is, precisely, a common ground.

The interpretant is a crucial concept in Peircean semiotics. A good example of the representation of an interpretant is Jan Vermeer's *The Artist in His Studio.* Because Vermeer cannot have seen this scene while painting it, we must conclude that he imagined it, as an outsider would see it, for example. "The scene was nowhere but in his head." Hence, the scene of the painting artist presented from the back is in the first place and emphatically a sign or rather, a sign of its own sign-ness.

Peirce elaborates this basic trichotomy of the semiotic process in at times exasperating detail. A primary division of the field of semiotic inquiry is based on the relations between the elements of semiosis. The relation between the sign and the ground leads to grammar, whose most commonly studied aspect is syntax. The relation between sign and object leads to questions of meaning or semantics. The relation between sign and interpretant can be linked to questions of rhetoric as part of pragmatics by virtue of the idea that one thought brings forth another. This division into three fields of inquiry is more common in linguistics than in art criticism. Pragmatics would be the dimension where the affective efficacy of a work is examined; semantics includes any hypothesis about the meaning of a work; syntactics studies the relations between elements of the work to codes or ways of meaning-production.

Although many of Peirce's elaborate typologies of signs derived from this basic theory have not been commonly taken up by art critics, the most famous of these, icon, index, symbol, is popular. Peirce's own definitions matter, because this typology is frequently misunderstood.

> An *icon* is a sign which would possess the character which renders it significant, even though its object had no existence; such as a lead-pencil streak as representing a geometric line. An *index* is a sign which would, at once, lose the character which makes it a sign if its object were removed, but would not lose that character if there were no interpretant. Such, for example, is a piece of mould with a bullet-hole in it as a sign of a shot; for without the shot there would have been no hole; but there is a hole there, whether anybody has the sense to attribute it to a shot or not. A *symbol* is a sign which would lose the character which renders it a sign if there were no interpretant. Such is any utterance of speech which signifies what it does only by virtue of its being understood to have that signification.   (Peirce, 1966, pp. 9–10)

First of all, any identification of icon and the entire domain of the visual is wrong. As Peirce clearly states, the iconic is a quality of the sign in relation to its object; it is best seen as a sign capable of evoking nonexistent objects because it proposes to imagine an object similar to the sign itself. Iconicity is in the first place a mode of reading, based on a hypothetical similarity between sign and object. Thus, when we see a portrait by Frans Hals, we imagine a person looking like the image and do not doubt the existence, in the time of Hals, of such a person; we do not demand substantiation of that existence by other sources, because we adopt the iconic way of reading when looking at portraits.

But the example of portraits might wrongly suggest that the icon is predicated on the degree of "realism" of the image. An abstract element like a triangular composition can become an iconic sign whenever we take it as a ground to interpret the image in relation to it, dividing the represented space into three interrelated areas (Leo Steinberg, for example, makes this division in his essay on *Las Meninas*). Instead of visuality in general, or realism for that matter, the decision to suppose that the image refers to something on the basis of likeness is the iconic act, and a sense of specularity is its result. A romantic sound of violins accompanying a romantic love scene in a film is as iconic as the graphic representation of Guillaume Apollinaire's poem about rain in the shape of rain.

The concept of index is implicated in analyses of subjectivity. Peirce's description of the index emphasizes its symmetrical opposition to the icon: although the icon does not need the object to exist, the index functions precisely on the ground of that existence. His example suggests that real, existential contiguity between indexical sign and object (or meaning) is indispensable. But that existence need not be confined to "reality"; the indexical sign and its meaning can entertain such a contiguous relationship within the image itself. The many recent publications on the gaze and the look that take the represented look of the figures in the painting as their starting point, for example, implicitly state that there is an indexical relationship between the look and what is looked at. The represented voyeur looking at the nude body of a woman is an effective figure precisely because he stands for a real, objectifying contiguity between look and object defined by looking as a real act. The index functions here in conjunction with the icon: the figure directing his eyes somewhere is taken to stand for a similar figure, a man looking at a woman. In the same way, the open mouths, iconically suggesting screams, of the popes in Francis Bacon's early portraits after Diego Velázquez, function iconically because they also function indexically; the contiguity between screaming and the pain that induces it enhances the effectivity of the works.

The most obvious use of the concept of index is the pointer. Pointing elements in an image are the most convincing case against the notion that the image is still and can be "read" in a momentary, punctual act. Pointers make us aware of the way our eyes move about the surface in different directions, some of which are suggested by indexical signs. When a figure points a finger in a certain direction, our look will follow the figure's directions. In language, elements of deixis that have no meaning outside the discourse are indexical (I and you, here and there, yesterday, tomorrow, etc.).

One category of indexical signs gives the illusion of expressivity. Those are all the signs that refer to the maker of the image, ranging from the recognizable "hand" of the artist, the will to be expressive as in Expressionist painting, to the signature. The signature of the artist, for example, is an index of the person of the maker, even if it is a false signature; that is precisely why it is a sign, a stand-in for an absent other. From the perspective of the sender, a false signature is an icon (of the real signature) parading as an index. This possibility of falsification of the most materially grounded of the three signs is fundamental. As Umberto Eco has written, the sign can be defined as everything that can be used in order to lie (Eco, 1976, p. 10).

The signature is the most typical case of the Derridean trace, the indexical sign that refers by contiguity, not simply to the past (the maker of the image) but to the future, the reading of it. The act of writing, which for Derrida is much more than graphic writing alone, is precisely the production of traces, and painting, drawing, and most emphatically, etching are also acts of writing in this sense. The notion of the index suggests that we do not only account for works in terms of their provenance and making, but also of their functioning in relation to the viewer: their structure of address.

Finally, the symbolic sign in Peirce's theory must not be confused with the many different and often vague colloquial meanings of the word *symbol*. As the definition in the quoted passage makes clear, it is dependent even more strongly than the two other terms on the act of interpretation that brings it to life, because without that interpretation it simply does not exist—as a sign, that is. What is not specified in this passage is the ground on which interpretation of a symbol comes about, which is the conventional rule of correlation between sign and object or meaning. The interpretant formed by the reader is possible because the latter knows what things usually mean in the culture in which the sign functions. The idiom of a particular language is conventional in the same sense as the idiom of iconographic traditions. "Translation" from one language into another, from an image into words that explain it, from one image into another image, all work by virtue of the knowledge of such codes. These conventional signs are always also involved when we read iconically and indexically. We only come up with an iconic interpretation of a portrait because we know the convention of portrayal.

Symbolic interpretation, which always underlies other kinds of interpretations, is the most convincing evidence of the cultural specificity of literary or pictorial traditions and styles. Even when we think the image is "realistic," we are in fact imbued in the convention that suggests that certain kinds of pictorial signs stand for "reality" more clearly than others. With the help of iconicity, which suggests that the image must have an object in the real world, and indexicality, which makes us aware of the real contiguities between elements of the image, and between those elements and ourselves, symbolicity by virtue of its very arbitariness is the most deceptive code.

Peirce's semiotic theory is relevant for the study of art because it helps us think about aspects of the process of art in society, in history, in a way that is not bound up with the artist's intention. It can contribute to the explanation of why certain elements of an image are particularly seductive or deceptive, suggesting depiction of something real while specularity, a return to the self away from the real, is in fact the basis of the seductiveness. The mix of iconicity, indexicality, and symbolicity that every text or image presents emphasizes the other side of the illusory unity that the image is so easily assumed to be: its fracturedness, the "difference within" that allows for a view of image seeing that is dynamic and positioned in time.

[*See also* Dewey; Eco; *and* Semiotics]

BIBLIOGRAPHY

Works by Peirce

Charles S. Peirce: Selected Writings. Edited by Philip P. Wiener. New York, 1966.
Philosophical Writings of Peirce. Edited by Justus Buchler. New York, 1955.
Writings of Charles S. Peirce: A Chronological Edition. Edited by Max H. Fisch. Bloomington, Ind., 1982–.

Other Sources

Bal, Mieke, and Norman Bryson. "Semiotics and Art History." *Art Bulletin* 73.2 (1991): 174–208.
Comprehensive Bibliography of the Published Works of Charles Sanders Peirce. 2d rev. ed. Edited by Kenneth Laine Ketner et al. Bowling Green, Ohio, 1986.
Eco, Umberto. *A Theory of Semiotics.* Bloomington, Ind., 1976.
Innis, Robert E., ed. *Semiotics: An Introductory Anthology.* Bloomington, Ind., 1985.
Kloesel, Christian J. W. "Bibliography of Charles Sanders Peirce, 1976 through 1980." *Monist* 65.2 (April 1982): 246–276.
Sebeok, Thomas A., ed. *A Perfusion of Signs.* Bloomington, Ind., 1977.

MIEKE BAL

PERCEPTION. [*To explore the concept of perception and its relevance to aesthetics, this entry comprises four essays:*

Aesthetics of Perception
Psychology of Perception
Picture Perception
Music Perception

The first explains how perception has been understood in philosophy, specifically in relation to issues of beauty, interpretation, and emotions. The second essay addresses how perception has been analyzed in the psychology of art. The third essay is an indepth analysis of two distinct approaches to the theory of picture perception in perceptual psychology: constructivism and direct realism. The final essay explores the debates about perception in contemporary music theory. For related discussion, see Im- agery; Imagination; Mimesis; Realism; Representation; *and* Synaesthesia.]

Aesthetics of Perception

The subject of perception arises in aesthetics when one considers beauty, the interpretation of art, the appreciation of the aesthetic, and the nature of aesthetic objects. It is related to issues in epistemology and philosophy of mind, and to questions concerning sensation, expression, emotions, and intentionality. All of these subjects are mutually connected, and an analysis of perception in aesthetics cannot be entirely abstracted from consideration of the objects of perception and of the assumptions about which objects occasion the clearest instances of aesthetic appreciation.

Understanding the nature of aesthetic perception begins with certain questions also addressed in epistemology, including, by what means is the object of attention delivered to consciousness? The immediacy and particularity of aesthetic experience are often contrasted with the inference drawn by means of general principles of reason, and this has led many theorists to ally aesthetic perception with sense experience. (When Alexander Baumgarten introduced the term into modern parlance, he used *aesthetics* to refer to things perceived, in contrast to noetics, or things known.) Whether the object of attention is art or nature, the senses provide the basis for the experience of such aesthetic values as beauty or sublimity. Sensory experience is also necessarily the foundation for the perception of regional aesthetic qualities such as grace, vigor, and harmony.

Not all of the senses can apprehend aesthetic objects, however. The senses believed to be most rooted in bodily sensation, namely, smell, taste, and touch, have since classical antiquity been ruled out as sources for experiences of beauty because the pleasures they deliver are considered merely sensuous. In later periods of philosophy this observation achieves central theoretical significance, for sight and hearing become designated aesthetic senses, and smell, taste, and touch, nonaesthetic. There are two grounds for this observation. First, the pleasures of the bodily senses direct attention to one's subjective state and therefore do not have the requisite distance that draws attention away from the body to an external aesthetic object. Second, partly because of this, the objects of the bodily senses are not considered appropriate media for the creation of one of the fine arts. Food, perfume, and so on may be refined into a practical or decorative art, but their purpose is sensuous pleasure; they remain rooted in desire. Only the objects of the eye and the ear become the bases for fine arts. G. W. F. Hegel dramatizes this view in his assertion that "the sensuous aspect of art is related only to the two theoretical senses of sight and hearing, while smell, taste, and touch remain excluded from the enjoyment of art. . . . What is agreeable for these senses is not the beauty of art" (Hegel, *Aesthetics: Lectures on*

Fine Art, vol. 1 [1835], trans. T. M. Knox, Oxford, 1975, pp. 38–39). Thus, when one speaks of perception in aesthetic theory of the Western tradition, the notion of perception is usually closely tied to two of the senses, hearing and sight. For the most part, as is the case in epistemology, sight has been the sensory model for analysis of aesthetic perception.

Aesthetic perception, however, is not fully accounted for by reference to the eyes and ears. By themselves these organs still furnish only sensations, which provide neither the cognitive complexity nor the appreciative delight involved in the experience of beauty. Some theorists have treated this problem as one that distinguishes natural objects from artistic representation, recognizing that the perception of representation requires comparison of an artwork with an original subject. Appreciation of natural objects often, however, also requires understanding of the function and character of an object—of the emergence of a moth from its chrysalis, for example. Nonetheless, the case for the distinction between sensation and perception may be clearest with artworks, for in this domain an account of perception must also recognize variations among the arts. Neither poetry nor prose, for example, particularly delivers its chief effects to a sense. Once this point is granted, it becomes clear that the perception that occasions aesthetic appreciation always goes beyond both the data and the pleasures gained from the senses and that perception is a concept referring to a complex mental activity that must include contributions from the imagination and the understanding.

Philosophers have attempted to distinguish aesthetic perception from perception in general by examining either distinctive objects of perception or modes of perception. Theorists of classical antiquity often focused on the perception of mimesis, analyzing the differences and commonalities between perceiving what is actual and what is imitative or fictional. This inquiry considers the relationship between experience of the arts and the development of knowledge and moral character. The two giants of this discussion are Plato, who suspected that routine exposure to imitation would feed ignorance and moral profligacy, and Aristotle, who regarded love of imitation as an extension of natural human pleasure in learning and defended tragic poetry as a source of moral understanding. Although Plato was cautious about the dangers of perceiving mimesis, he treated beauty more positively. In the *Symposium,* Socrates argues that the perception of beautiful objects can be a stage in the journey of the mind toward the intellectual apprehension of the Form of Beauty itself. Centuries later Neoplatonic art theorists such as John Dryden, Charles Dufresnoy, and Giovanni Bellori followed classical traditions in maintaining that perception of beautiful imitation in art leads the mind to a grasp of the essential qualities of depicted subjects, thereby informing while pleasing.

Theories of the premodern era in Europe generally treated perception of beauty in nature and in art by reflecting on the objects of perception. Many held a Platonic position: beauty is a quality possessed by the objects that appear to us as harmonious, well balanced, eloquent. (It was difficult to pin down the nature of this quality, which led many to employ the French phrase "je ne sais quoi" or "I know not what," to allude to the objective cause of the perception of beauty.) The growth of popularity of empiricism, however, brought about a shift in the basic analysis of value qualities such as beauty. From the later seventeenth century onward, beauty was increasingly denied objective status and analyzed as a type of pleasure. This gave rise to a host of new theories of aesthetic perception, chiefly because the pleasure that beauty was identified with required careful qualification to distinguish it from dubious nonaesthetic pleasures such as the satisfaction of sensuous desire. As the eighteenth century wore on, philosophies were developed that became the foundation for modern theories of aesthetic perception.

Modern theories of aesthetic perception and their twentieth-century legatees constitute the major views to be considered in examining perception in aesthetics. Virtually all approaches to this subject describe aesthetic perception by means of its contrast with other modes of perception. The contrast between sensation and perception, or more exactly between sensuous pleasure and aesthetic pleasure, again is invoked, for aesthetic pleasure needs to be distinguished from any kind of bodily gratification. Even more important, perceiving the aesthetic qualities of an object requires detaching it from the satisfaction of desire, setting its practical uses aside, and attending to its perceptual properties alone. Immanuel Kant's *Critique of Judgment* provides an extreme statement of these contrasts, for Kant asserts that the experience of pure beauty requires the perception of the form of an object only, absent all desire, practical interest, or even cognition of the objective category to which the perceived representation belongs. One of the terms that comes into wide use as a result of this line of thinking is *disinterested attention,* signifying a mode of perception that attends only to the perceptual qualities presented to the mind by an object of nature or art. The term *disinterest* sums up the absence of desire or of instrumental considerations, freeing the mind to perceive and appreciate an object's intrinsic beauty. [*See* Disinterestedness.]

Kantian influence shored up several trends in subsequent European theory, including formalism and aesthetic attitude theory. The former view distinguishes aesthetic perception by stipulating its proper objects; the latter examines the mode of perception that selects objects for aesthetic perception. Formalism as a theory of perception reached its peak of influence in the nineteenth and early twentieth centuries. A particularly clear statement of this view can be found in Clive Bell's *Art* (1914), where it is maintained that aesthetic emotion is triggered by the perception of what Bell termed "significant form"—a supervenient quality emerging from composition, relations, harmonies, and color. (Kant had emptied pure beauty even of color in his efforts to abstract aesthetic pleasure from sensuous pleasure.) Bell devotes his book explicitly to visual art, especially painting (though he speculates that his principles extend to music); it is an illustration of the centrality that vision holds as the model for theories of aesthetic perception.

Concentrating on the object of perception yields views of aesthetic perception that emphasize the properties that come into focus when extraneous considerations are ignored. Other theories approach this subject by focusing on the state of consciousness of the perceiver that permits aesthetic attention. The purity of aesthetic perception is advanced by Arthur Schopenhauer, who argues that only in aesthetic pleasure is the will suspended from its ceaseless striving for survival. Desire is expunged from the aesthetic, and the mind is freed to notice the beauty of art and of nature. Schopenhauer's theory of aesthetic perception has a metaphysical dimension, for the aesthetic object is the Idea of the object rather than the precise, singular object before one; reciprocally, the individual identity of the perceiver recedes from attention in aesthetic experience:

> Therefore if, for example, I contemplate a tree aesthetically, i.e., with artistic eyes, and thus recognize not it but its Idea, it is immediately of no importance whether it is this tree or its ancestor that flourished a thousand years ago, and whether the contemplator is this individual, or any other living anywhere and at any time. (*The World as Will and Representation,* vol. 1, trans. E. F. J. Payne, New York, 1969, p. 209)

Several popular theories of aesthetic perception can be summed up with the term *aesthetic attitude theory,* of which Schopenhauer's theory may be considered an early version. There are several varieties of this view, which prevails in the twentieth century particularly in the Anglo-American and the phenomenological traditions. Aesthetic attitude theorists approach the nature of the aesthetic by considering the mode of perception and the objects of attention that different modes select. A widely read essay on this subject by Edward Bullough contrasts practical attention with aesthetic concerns and recommends "psychical distance," a state of attention that permits apprehension of aesthetic qualities. Whether the object is nature or art, Bullough maintains, practical interests get in the way of noticing aesthetic qualities. Thus, aesthetic perception requires that one put practical interests "out of gear." While it is the case that certain objects do not invite aesthetic approaches (disgusting, obscene, or terrifying objects rarely can be approached with the requisite psychical distance), the chief responsibility for perceiving aesthetic values lies with the perceiver, whose mental set can be cleansed of extraneous interests in order that aesthetic qualities may be perceived. Jerome Stolnitz sees all perception as selective and argues that an aesthetic attitude is "disinterested and sympathetic attention to

and contemplation of any object of awareness whatever, for its own sake alone" (Stolnitz, 1960, p. 35).

The phenomenologist Roman Ingarden also distinguishes a type of aesthetic perception that relies on the percipient purging his or her perceptual field of interfering interests. But, whereas for writers such as Stolnitz the purpose of this exercise is to reveal the qualities present in the work of art, Ingarden argues that this attitude is required in order that the percipient complete the work of art as an aesthetic object. This approach takes aesthetic perception to involve active participation of the mind in discerning the sensuous vehicle of the work of art and recreating with sensitivity and imagination the full product of the artist's mind. Since the activity of different perceivers may employ different interpretations or emphases for the artwork, there may be more than one aesthetic object of art. This angle on perception raises issues about the contribution of the perceiver to the genesis of the aesthetic object. Aesthetic attitude theorists who stress the suspension of practical interest and desire in order to disclose an object's perceptual qualities often tend to analyze aesthetic perception as a state of directed receptivity. But other philosophers, including Ingarden, stress the activity of the mind that contributes to the production of aesthetic qualities. Similarly, expression theorists such as Robin Collingwood link the (re)creation of the aesthetic object with a combination of perception and imagination, especially that required to grasp the expression of the artist. Gestalt theories such as that of Rudolf Arnheim argue that the mind is an active compositor of forms into patterns, activities that must be considered if one is to understand the nature of aesthetic perception.

Consideration of the nature of perception goes hand in hand with language that refers to "aesthetic objects," in other words, the objects of which aesthetic qualities are predicated. The type of object aesthetic predicates modify needs to be distinguished from physical objects. For example, the Mona Lisa as a physical object is small, rectangular, flat; as an aesthetic object is possesses qualities such as "enigmatic" and "serene." Since not every viewer would agree with these descriptions, such aesthetic qualities evidently require some sort of special discernment, raising questions regarding the need to posit the existence of a special perceptual facility. Frank Sibley has provoked much discussion with his claim that aesthetic qualities exceed the abilities of "ordinary" perception to discern, and that therefore their presence requires something like "taste" to notice. An aesthetic quality such as "delicate" may be partially dependent on a nonaesthetic quality such as "thin," but one may correctly perceive thinness and fail to notice delicate because of an absence of aesthetic sensitivity or taste. This argument distinguishes a specific type of perception for aesthetic qualities that cannot be accounted for by reference to the functioning of the senses or by reflective analysis of sense experience.

Despite the complications of imagination, understanding, and expression, the accounts of aesthetic perception recounted thus far still rely on a concept of the aesthetic object as a perceptual object and aesthetic qualities as perceptual qualities. Much of the art produced in the twentieth century has proved problematic for this notion, however, if it is intended to be central to a philosophy of art. "Anti-art" movements that deliberately defy aesthetic standards do not present perceptual qualities for appreciation; similarly, conceptual art and arts whose point is to comment on the world of art history and criticism require for their appreciation not perceptual discrimination but knowledge of the state of the arts that produced them. (Famous cases that have been frequent reference points for philosophers include Marcel Duchamp's *Fountain* of 1917, a urinal perceptually indistinguishable from a bathroom fixture, and Robert Rauschenberg's *Erased De Kooning,* which consists of a drawing by Willem De Kooning that Rauschenberg erased, and which thereby became Rauschenberg's piece.) It is evident that appreciation of the wit and originality of such pieces requires far more than perception, and this observation has displaced the concept of aesthetic perception from the central position in philosophy of art that it once enjoyed.

Arthur C. Danto argues that for an object to be a work of art it must be interpretable, and interpretation requires familiarity with art theory. The old focus on perception misled theorists to believe that the essential properties of artworks were perceptually discernible; however, the concept of art is not accurately explored by analyses of the perceptual qualities of artworks. Criticisms of the notion of aesthetic perception, particularly the aesthetic attitude variants, have also been advanced by such philosophers as George Dickie. Dickie argues that there is no such thing as a special aesthetic attitude from which aesthetic qualities can be perceived; rather, familiarity with artistic conventions directs attention to the aesthetically salient aspects of art works.

Another approach to the concept of aesthetic perception as a requirement for the interpretation, understanding, and appreciation of artworks has arisen from scholars mindful of the social and political influences over what is perceived and valued. These writers criticize the old notion of pure aesthetic perception, or distanced or disinterested perception, and argue that it disguises the operation of cultural hegemonies. The disinterested attitude does not cleanse the mind of competing interests so that a work of art may be appreciated for its own qualities alone, according to these critics. Rather, the pose of disinterestedness cloaks the interests of the ideal appreciators of art, who are usually males with a certain cultural privilege. Arguably, few people are actually in a position to assume the disinterested pose of the aesthete, for such an attitude presumes a degree of leisure, not to mention an education of a certain sort to enjoy canonical works of art. Moreover, many works of art actually praised for their aesthetic virtues can be seen to perpetuate established patterns of social privilege and power. Feminist critics and postcolonial theorists have argued that works of the artistic canon very often position the perceiver to select a masculine point of view valorized by the dominant culture. Psychosexual and social influences over perception are emphasized by these analyses. If what is perceived is ineluctably tied to the subject position (partly defined by gender, class, nationality, and historical situation) of the viewer, then the experience of art and all the perception that contributes to this will vary indeterminately according to who is looking. These trends further the displacement of aesthetic perception from the center of philosophy of art, supplanting it with interests in the social and historical formation of subjectivity and point of view. These approaches, like expression theory before them, also assume the viewer of art to be an active participant in the formation of intentional objects, though the emphasis is less on the relation between the individual and the artist and more on the individual as a member of a historically determinant group appreciating an object valorized by tradition. In short, these scholarly movements attend to factors involved in the social construction of both the act and the objects of aesthetic perception.

[*See also* Attitude; *and* Epistemology and Aesthetics.]

BIBLIOGRAPHY

Arnheim, Rudolf. *Toward a Psychology of Art: Collected Essays.* Berkeley, 1966.

Bell, Clive. *Art.* London, 1914.

Binkley, Timothy. "Piece: Contra Aesthetics." *Journal of Aesthetics and Art Criticism* 35.3 (Spring 1977): 265–277.

Bullough, Edward. "Psychical Distance as a Factor in Art and an Aesthetic Experience." In *Art and Its Significance: An Anthology of Aesthetic Theory,* 3d ed., edited by Stephen David Ross. Albany, N.Y., 1994.

Cohen, Ted. "Aesthetic/Non-aesthetic and the Concept of Taste." *Theoria* 39.1–3 (1973): 113–152.

Danto, Arthur C. *The Transfiguration of the Commonplace: A Philosophy of Art.* Cambridge, Mass., 1981.

Devereaux, Mary. "Oppressive Texts, Resisting Readers, and the Gendered Spectator." In *Feminism and Tradition in Aesthetics,* edited by Peggy Zeglin Brand and Carolyn Korsmeyer, pp. 121–141. University Park, Pa., 1995.

Dickie, George. "The Myth of the Aesthetic Attitude." *American Philosophical Quarterly* 1.1 (January 1964): 56–65.

Jay, Martin. *Downcast Eyes: The Denigration of Vision in Twentieth-Century French Thought.* Berkeley, 1993.

Ingarden, Roman. "Artistic and Aesthetic Values." *British Journal of Aesthetics* 4 (1964): 198–213.

Sibley, Frank. "Aesthetic Concepts." *Philosophical Review* 68.4 (October 1959): 421–450.

Stolnitz, Jerome. *Aesthetics and Philosophy of Art Criticism.* Boston, 1960.

Summers, David. *The Judgment of Sense: Renaissance Naturalism and the Rise of Aesthetics.* Cambridge and New York, 1987.

CAROLYN KORSMEYER

Psychology of Perception

Theorizing about perception in the modern Western world derives from George Berkeley's assertion of the inadequacy of vision as a source of information about the spatial layout of the world.

The principal tenets of Berkeley's theoretical position concerning the acquisition of knowledge about the world through the senses were these: that the primary qualities accessed through the senses are essentially atomistic and meaningless sensations; that aggregates of sensations are created through repeated experience and the process of association among sensations co-occurring in time and space; and last, that the still meaningless sensory aggregates are in turn given meaning—become percepts—through the various channels of touch and movement, including the movement of the eyes and the focusing of the lenses as well as the actions of the hands and the movements of the whole body in space. Berkeley's analysis of the visual process explicitly rejected the utility of geometric, optical, or perspectival analyses of the visual stimulus deriving either from Euclid or from Renaissance theorists and painters.

Following Johannes Kepler's demonstration of the existence of a visual image projected onto the back of the mammalian eyeball, perceptionists subsequent to Berkeley usually took as their empirical starting position the retinal image itself rather than the hypothetically original sensations that preceded the retinal aggregate, although it was always assumed that theoretically the isolate sensations preceded developmentally both the intermediary retinal image aggregates and the subsequent perceptions informed by touch through past experience.

Helmholtzian Theory of Optics and Perception. Hermann von Helmholtz, the noted German scientist and mathematician, in his *Treatise on Physiological Optics* developed the most explicit and comprehensive application of Berkeley's principles to the understanding and study of visual perception. Helmholtz's analysis served as the foundation of reasoning about perception, and about perception-based theories of art and aesthetics, for nearly a century.

Helmholtz began with the assumption that retinal images—the effective starting point for the visual process leading to a more or less veridical perception of the world—are a pair of two-dimensional, geometric projections infinitely ambiguous as to their sources in the world. Thus, Helmholtz's research program addressed the problems of adding the third dimension of spatial perception to the flat images, of resolving projective ambiguities of the images, and of establishing the constancy of perceptions of objects' sizes and shapes across various distances and when viewed from varying angles. Proposed processes for effecting these ends were various touch and movement mechanisms and a process of what Helmholtz called unconscious inference based not on geometric optics but on knowledge gained from past experience with various visual stimuli. Helmholtz, like Berkeley, rejected the utility of perspectival or geometric analyses either of the retinal images or of the perceptual processes involved in apprehending them. The assumption of an essentially ambiguous visual stimulus as the starting point of the theoretical visual perceptual process led as well to an enduring interest among Helmholtzian theorists in the numerous visual illusions.

Following Helmholtz, most like-minded researchers devoted their attention to an analysis of the development and functioning of the various monocular and binocular "cues" for the layout and appearance of objects in three-dimensional space. [*See* Helmholtz.]

Helmholtzian Theory of Representation. Since in pragmatic if not in theoretical terms, the retinal image was usually the starting point for research for every perceptual scientist from Helmholtz to the present, it was natural that the perceptual processes involved in adding meaning to meaningless retinal images could likewise be invoked to explain both the process of the perception of pictures and the process of their creation.

Ernst Gombrich (1969, 1972) is the most distinguished and best known of all the modern Helmholtzian art historians. Gombrich based his analysis of the history and development of art on a sophisticated version of the traditional perceptual distinction between seeing and knowing. In Gombrich's theory, "seeing" is equivalent to the awareness of either naive sensations or uninterpretable retinal images, whereas "knowing" refers to the experience-based perceptual end product.

Gombrich's account of the history and development of art is an account of painters' discoveries of visual schemata for representing perceptual knowledge about objects and spatial layout, not just sensations. According to Gombrich, pictorial schemata were first discovered by early humankind as they appeared in various patterns of nature, and were then adopted and then modified when the images they produced no longer met evolving criteria for successful art. Gombrich argues that at least for Western art, the continuing modification and creation of pictorial schemata took place within the larger cultural context wherein the evolution of the purpose of representation moved from the depiction of knowledge (perceptions) to the depiction of pure seeing (sensations) to the abandonment of representation itself as an artistic goal.

In popular accounts, this theory is usually expressed in the form: "Children and primitives draw what they know while sophisticated people draw what they see." From Gombrich's point of view, the Impressionists' attempts to depict pure sensation represented the apex of artistic evolution and were doomed to failure because they denied or attempted to circumvent the purported visual truth that all adult vision is determined by past experience and is thus laden with knowledge—inferences and associations taken from experience. Pure sensation, then, is impossible for adults to experience either in ordinary perception or in the creation and perception of representational art. Thus, according to Gombrich, it was inevitable that following the collapse of Impressionism, representational depiction as a goal of artists was simply abandoned by the majority. [*See* Gombrich.*]

Nearly all theories of the development of art in children that derive from the Helmholtzian approach analyze children's works in terms of their putative developing proximity to photographic realism through the increasing use of linear perspective. No such developmental progression in childhood has ever been demonstrated, nor has it ever been shown that the majority of adults in any culture employ perspective in their depictions without instruction. The best evidence shows that most untutored adults draw what they "know" about objects and spatial layout (e.g., depicting a right-angled object with right angles), while the artists of various cultures employ a number of techniques for depicting what they "see" at single moments or single points of view (e.g., the momentary visual overlap of one object by another or the decrease in projected visual size with increasing distance).

Thus, there is little evidence supporting the Helmholtz-Gombrich position on the development of techniques for artistic renditions across history or across childhood.

Gestalt Theory of Perception: Anti-Helmholtzian Theory. A highly critical deviation from the Helmholtzian analysis was the theoretical position crafted in direct opposition to it, the Gestalt theory of the 1920s and 1930s, begun and developed in Germany and then spread to the wider Western world with the advent of World War II.

The Gestalt theory of perception was based on the direct rejection of one of the central tenets of traditional perceptual theory, namely, that the perceptual aggregates are built out of essentially unaltered but associated sensations, with the experience of sensation necessarily preceding in time the perception of the holistic aggregates. The Gestaltists argued that the whole is different from the sum of its parts and could never be reduced to them. They argued that the perception of form was primary, that the fundamental perception is the differentiation of figure from ground, and that the brain rather than the image provides the impetus and direction for the perception of various forms through the laws or principles of organization: symmetry, similarity, proximity, good continuation, and common fate, among others.

It was argued that these organizing principles would not only pull order or form out of two-dimensional stimuli but would effect the same organization on the perception of three-dimensional space. The role of the visual stimulus itself was almost entirely disregarded, as was the attendant issue of the relationship between what is to be perceived and the resultant perception. Moreover, the utility of the analysis of the geometric properties of the visual aggregates—the retinal images or projections—and of the geometry/trigonometry-like perceptual processes was also explicitly rejected by the Gestaltists.

Since the bulk of Gestaltist research dealt with the demonstration of the operation of the laws of organization on two-dimensional patterns, the extension of the analysis to depictions on flat surfaces should have been a simple matter. Nevertheless, the creation and perception of pictorial works received very little attention with the exception of the lifetime work of the psychologist and art historian Rudolf Arnheim. In his several works, Arnheim explicitly described himself and his theoretical position as Gestaltist, but in truth his exposition of the creation and perception of art represents not a simple application of Gestalt psychology to the field but indeed his own unique and significant departure.

In his exposition of the relations between psychology and art, Arnheim developed the construct of the visual concept. The idea was first presented in *Art and Visual Perception* (1954, 1974) and then further developed in *Visual Thinking* (1969) within the context of the traditional issue of perceptual constancy: how do we perceive the constant sizes and shapes of objects despite their varying appearances under projective transformations across the retinas? Arnheim argued that the mind perceives the momentary aspect or appearance of an object as an integral part of a larger integrated sequence of views. "When such a view is embedded with a sequence of other views, it will acquire the character of a deformation by the context and by its relations to its neighbors in the sequence" (Arnheim, 1969, p. 50). Abstraction of the visual concept is accomplished by seeing certain aspects of the particulars as deformations of an underlying structure that is visible within them, not through integrating the elements across the sequence.

Arnheim's visual concept has three important properties: "It conceives of the object as being three-dimensional, of constant shape, and not limited to any particular projective aspect" (1954, p. 90; again, these assumptions are very similar to those made by Gibson, 1966). Arnheim believed that visual concepts are not differentiated beyond necessity, and for everyday perception all that is needed is everyday object identity—constancy—with no awareness of momentary perspective appearances. The most sophisticated visual concept, the aesthetic attitude, embraces the multiplicity of its appearances, the foreshortenings, the slants, the symmetries and asymmetries, the partial concealments and the deployments, the head-on flatness, and the pronounced volumes. The reductive attitude apprehends a given object as changing its character when the context changes; thus, context is seen as an attribute of the object itself, and the object identity is reduced to object appearance. [*See* Arnheim.]

Gestalt Theory of Representation. According to Arnheim, the type of visual attitude adopted by a painter of his or her culture will determine the form of the representation produced. The problem of representation per se, however, is always the same: how to make a translation of the three-dimensional visual concept onto a two-dimensional picture plane, how to present the structural essentials of the object concept by using the laws of structure. Arnheim claimed that primitive art and the art of children are concerned primarily with depiction of the everyday level of perceptual abstraction, simple object identity, without attention to momentary appearances, and without any differentiation of flatness from depth. The depiction is considered to be a pictorial equivalent of the depicted object, not a snapshot of it. To accomplish this equivalence successfully, objects must be depicted in their "most characteristic aspects." The most characteristic aspects of objects were said by Arnheim to contain *renvois,* that is, references that point beyond the given view to adjacent, subsequent ones. Aspects with *renvois* also make reference to the simplest three-dimensional solid that could have generated them, just as the structural skeletons of projections with *renvois* are directly related to the structure of the object depicted. It is primarily the development of the aesthetic or reductive attitude toward visual concepts, along with development of media technology, that moves art away from these primitive renditions. Thus, just as Impressionism represents the reductive attitude at its extreme, so does Western post-Renaissance art up to the time of the Impressionists reflect the adoption of the aesthetic attitude.

Perspectivist Theory of Optics and Perception. From the modern perspective, the most significant departure from the traditional approach to the study of perception—and the analysis of representational art—began in 1950 with the publication of James J. Gibson's *The Perception of the Visual World.* Until that time, following Berkeley and Helmholtz, the assumption of researchers and theoreticians had been that the proximal stimulus for vision, the retinal image, was so devoid of information about the world that gave rise to it, that the principal task of the perceiver was to add the necessary information or decision criteria for perception to the ambiguous and relatively meaningless retinal image.

Gibson's contribution was to alter radically the view of the visual stimulus, reanalyzing the retinal image in terms of sources of information that are relatively deterministic about their sources in the environment. Gibson reintroduced the geometric optics of Euclid and capitalized on the work of Renaissance perspectivists, both their written analyses of visual information in pictures and their painted works. In this perceptual approach, the theory of art was driving the theory of perception, not the other way around.

The Gibsonian perspectivist analyses of visual perception and information rested on a number of assumptions:

there exists a world cluttered with objects with the sky overhead;

the ground plane is the basic reference surface, and most other surfaces rest either on it or on other surfaces resting on it;

the ground surface and most other surfaces are more or less regularly textured in that they have a more or less homogeneous substance or composition;

every difference in surface texture causes a border in or change of quality of the light reflected from it;

every change in surface slant will also cause a change in the light reflected from a surface; and

such structures in the light are specific to their sources and, as such, are directly informative about those sources.

Under these assumptions, Gibson and his colleagues demonstrated through empirical studies that the informative structure in the retinal image was sufficient to specify for perceivers the size, shape, slant, and relative distance of objects distributed in three-dimensional space.

Thus, the primary difference between early Gibsonian theory in the 1950s and early 1960s and traditional theory was in the amount of information for perception assumed to be contained in the stimulus, with the Gibsonians demonstrating conclusively that the earlier view of an uninformative visual stimulus was not empirically supported.

Perspectivist Theory of Representation. Since this Gibsonian view attributed so much meaningful, reliable information to the visual image—what was called the "optic array" in the theory—it was inevitable that the model of depiction deriving from this theory would evaluate the success or failure of a representation in terms of its degree of resemblance to a retinal image, a monocular geometric projection of a three-dimensional scene onto a two-dimensional surface: "A picture is a surface so treated that a delimited optic array is made available to a point of observation that contains the same kind of information as that found in the ordinary environment" (Gibson, 1979).

It soon became clear that this original formulation of the stimulus for vision was inadequate because it failed to account for the ordinary case of perception in which a moving observer with constantly varying retinal images (eyes themselves exhibit constant tremor and are moved purposively in their sockets) nevertheless accurately perceives the relative sizes, shapes, slants, and distances, as well as changes in all of those parameters, of objects in the environment.

The early information analysis also failed to account for the success in depiction of images such as line drawings, cartoons, and caricatures that although lacking in the strictly accurate portrayal of perspective geometry that characterizes a "realistic" depiction, nevertheless serve even for the untutored as effective carriers of information about their subject matter. [*See* Perspective.]

Theory of Ecological Optics and Perception: Invariant Information. Gibson's later theory of visual information held that information for perception is not just the optical structure available to a single static projection but is rather structure that is invariant across visual—retinal—projections as the observer moves through the environment, as the illumination in the environment changes, as various "local changes in the scene viewed change, and as the perceiver scans the environment by moving the head and the eyes" (1966, 1979).

This later formulation demonstrated the effectiveness of various classes of visual structure—invariants—persisting across various types of changes as sources of information for perception. It also included the rejection of a role for retinal images as a stimulus for vision because the eye constantly trembles, the aperture of the pupil is nearly always wide open, and the "plane of projection" at the retina is really several layers of cells deep in the eye. Thus, there are no images as such in the eye. Moreover, Gibson claimed, information carried by images cannot be sufficient to support the perception of a moving observer.

Theory of Representation of Invariant Information. With retinal images removed from the theoretical analysis of requisite information for visual perception, the analysis of representational depictions could no longer be restricted to a simple extension from a retinal projective surface to a canvas or paper one. Thus, the later Gibsonian analysis of the perception of pictures involved an analysis of what "invariant" information a picture, a single stationary image, could be said to contain, and, in a complete reversal from traditional thinking, attempted to resolve the problem of how invariant information for the layout of objects in space ordinarily derived from motion and picked up over time and across spatial transformations could be applied to the perception of a static pictorial scene. (Gibson's development of the concept of invariance is an echo of Arnheim's identification of persistent underlying optical structure from around the same time.)

Generative Theory of Representation: Varieties of Realism Theory. Gibson's analysis of representational art, like Arnheim's approach, although forward-looking in their references to some geometric concepts, actually made little use of the rich formulations of the concepts of invariants and informative structures afforded by modern geometric characterizations of projective geometry.

A more recent reconsideration of the relationship between geometry and art undertakes an evaluation of the perceptual information contained in all known styles of representational art, across cultures and through history. This approach was proposed by Margaret A. Hagen, an American perceptual psychologist, in *The Perception of Pictures* (1980, 1981) and more fully in *Varieties of Realism: Geometries of Representational Art* (1986). The approach classifies all representational styles according to the subbranch of the families of projective geometry identified by mathematicians with attention to the type of perceptual information available to each style of projection. It represents a formal,

mathematical extension both of Arnheim's concept of *renvois* and of Gibson's construct of informative invariants.

Today, the thrust of analysis seems to be more focused on the elaboration of hypothetical perceptual mechanisms than on the analysis of the stimulus for vision, but the field remains diverse in its approaches to both perception and to art.

[*See also* Psychology of Art.]

BIBLIOGRAPHY

Arnheim, Rudolf. *Art and Visual Perception: A Psychology of the Creative Eye* 1954. New exp. rev. ed. Berkeley, 1974.
Arnheim, Rudolf. *Toward a Psychology of Art: Collected Essays.* Berkeley, 1966.
Arnheim, Rudolf. *Visual Thinking.* Berkeley, 1969.
Gibson, James J. *The Perception of the Visual World.* Boston, 1950.
Gibson, James J. *The Senses Considered as Perceptual Systems.* Boston, 1966.
Gibson, James J. *The Ecological Approach to Visual Perception.* Boston, 1979.
Gombrich, E. H. *Art and Illusion: A Study in the Psychology of Pictorial Representation* (1960). 2d rev. ed. Reprint. Princeton, N.J., 1969.
Gombrich, E. H. *The Story of Art* (1950). 12th enl. ed. London, 1972.
Hagen, Margaret A. *Varieties of Realism: Geometries of Representational Art.* Cambridge and New York, 1986.
Hagen, Margaret A., ed. *The Perception of Pictures,* vol. 1, *Alberti's Window: The Projective Model of Pictures.* New York, 1980.
Hagen, Margaret A., ed. *The Perception of Pictures,* vol. 2, *Dürer's Devices: Beyond the Projective Model of Pictures.* New York, 1981.
Helmholtz, Hermann von. *Helmholtz's Treatise on Physiological Optics.* Edited by James P. C. Southall. New York, 1962.

MARGARET A. HAGEN

Picture Perception

Two types of perceptual psychology have figured centrally in theories of picture perception. One approach, Constructivism, holds that perception is indirect; it requires unconscious inference, resulting in a mental representation of the perceived object or scene. Perception is a matter of interpretation, hypothesis testing, or problem solving, based on the perceiver's background knowledge and experience. Because of the dependence on background knowledge, there are no neutral observations. Thus, perceptual constructions are theory laden. Hermann von Helmholtz is the classic source of this view.

In contrast, direct realism claims that perception consists in the direct "pickup" of invariant properties that provide information about objects in a scene. These properties are said to be found in the perceptual layout, embodied in features of the light surrounding the perceiver. The central examples of invariant properties are gradients of texture over distance and texture flow, the latter being produced by motion. This view was developed by James J. Gibson. According to him, direct detection of properties is possible because every distinct type of higher-order perceptual property provides a unique stimulus. Although perception will depend on internal processes and brain functions, those will merely be aspects of a complex response that corresponds exactly to the relevant type of stimulus. They will not be inductive inferences or interpretations. It is in that sense that perception is unmediated.

A third school, Gestalt psychology, has also made important contributions to the understanding of picture perception. But it can be treated as a second, noninductivist version of Constructivism. To be sure, Gestalt psychology shares certain features with Gibson's theory of direct perception. Both reject the need for any special perceptual learning and deny that perception requires an interpretation of sensory input. Both also emphasize higher-order relations among features as the irreducible objects of perception. But Gestalt psychology is more appropriately linked with Constructivism because of its emphasis on the idea that perceptual content or meaning is supplied by the perceiver. The difference is that Constructivism in Helmholtz's empiricist sense takes its stimuli to be basic elements that are unaffected by their combination in complex wholes, whereas Gestalt theory makes whole configurations or forms the relevant stimulus units. These forms have emergent properties that cannot be reduced to the properties of their parts. Further, as developed by Helmholtz, Constructivism treats unconscious inference as inductive; perceptual judgments are probabilistic. But on the Gestalt account, bringing the stimulus under organizational principles or "visual concepts" effectively determines important aspects of perceptual content, especially figure-ground relations. Perceptual experience is thus not probabilistic. Finally, Gestalt psychology holds that whole forms or *Gestalten* occur in the nervous system as states or physiological configurations that are isomorphic to the perceptual experiences they produce. The unconscious inference posited by Helmholtz and his followers does not, however, depend on isomorphism.

These three psychological theories can be compared more specifically in terms of the accounts of picture perception they provide, especially where the pictures are works of visual art.

Gombrich's Account. Constructivism in the Helmholtzian tradition figures centrally in the work of Ernst Gombrich and Richard L. Gregory on aesthetic perception and art history. According to Gombrich, perception always requires background knowledge. There is no "innocent eye" that could provide a standard for representing what is seen, as opposed to what is known. Indeed, picture production always depends on "schemata" or pictorial techniques that are used to express the artist's beliefs about the ways that objects appear. Picture perception, in turn, requires that the perceiver have some facility with the relevant schemata.

On this view, perceptual knowledge is acquired and schemata are discovered through a process of hypothesis testing, operating under a Popperian criterion of falsifiability. As with scientific hypotheses, the most acceptable visual hypotheses are those that, on the one hand, have the most empirical content and are thus susceptible to being shown false but which, on the other hand, resist falsification. This suggests a natural question, however: in what does pictorial "falsity" consist? Of course, visual forms may fail to properly express the artist's knowledge or beliefs. But the more basic problem is to explain how those beliefs are supported or rejected in the first place: what would, in principle, warrant the relevant beliefs? And how exactly are visual hypotheses and pictorial schemata put to the test? The most straightforward answer would seem to be that visual hypotheses are corroborated when the properties they depict correspond to the properties of the object and are falsified when they do not. But the problem is that more than one visual hypothesis will always be consistent with what is observed. So if the criterion of falsifiability is to be used to single out a preferred representation, it must consist in something more complex than mere noncorrespondence.

For Gombrich, there seem to be three possible solutions to this problem. First, he sometimes invokes simplicity as a nonevidential criterion for selecting visual hypotheses. But that is a historically troubled notion at best. In addition, simplicity is often said to be an aesthetic concept, which would make its application to artistic hypotheses circular.

Second, constructivism has often been associated with conventionalism, the view that pictures are composed of arbitrary symbols constituting a code. Conventionalism is typically opposed to resemblance theory, which takes pictures to represent objects by virtue of natural similarities they possess. Gombrich claims that any attempt to replicate the pure appearances of objects must fail; what is represented is really knowledge. More precisely, pictures express perceptual knowledge, while denoting the (usually public) objects that the knowledge is about. In that case, the pictorial content of a painting is very much like the propositional content of a written sentence. Pictorial styles are thus like languages: They depend on a choice of symbols that can differ in different contexts. Therefore, the degree of acceptability of a visual hypothesis might be determined by how well entrenched or common its terms are in a culture (to use Nelson Goodman's term). In that case, what is false (to perceptual experience) will be what does not fit current representational practices. This need not preclude change; but it does imply that any change in the acceptability of a representation or representational style will always depend on exposure to new types of experience, which available forms of representation cannot fully accommodate.

There are two problems with this appeal to convention. One is that the need for standards of acceptability for modes of representation and the beliefs they express can arise even within a single context and a set of conventions. In that case, competing hypotheses may use different, but equally entrenched, terms or forms. Thus, comportment with convention provides no criterion for deciding between them. The other problem is that conventionalism tends to be an overconservative account. It cannot explain the fact of radical change. Although new perceptual categories will have to be added, or old ones modified, whenever new things are seen, it is likely that continuity with preexisting categories will be taken as a condition on acceptance. The aim will be to revise categories while preserving as much of the background perceptual framework or "theory" as possible, rather than to replace the framework as a whole. Change should thus be gradual and build on visual hypotheses already in place. But it is not clear that this account fits very well with the actual history of art.

The third response to the problem of falsifiability for pictorial hypotheses is suggested by Gombrich's claim that pictures can create the illusion that represented objects look as they would in their ordinary state. Perhaps unacceptable representations are those that fail in that respect. According to Gombrich's principle of adapted stereotype, there is no way to simply represent things as they really are; pictorial representation always begins with available stereotypes or schemata, and familiarity with the schema is what makes a picture look realistic. But, Gombrich argues, that is compatible with paintings in different styles being equally accurate, despite their use of different schemata. That fact need not be explained by simply relativizing accuracy to local convention. Instead, an alternate explanation is provided by information theory. On this account, a picture is accurate if perceivers who understand the relevant notational schemes will derive no false information from it. But pictures painted in different styles may simply convey information in different ways, thus promoting various "illusions" of the real appearances of objects. Diverse visual hypotheses are warranted as long as they succeed in representing information.

This account, however, merely pushes the problem of falsifiability back onto the ambiguous notion of information. Moreover, it sidesteps the problem of how to evaluate two competing visual hypotheses that are both informative and address the perceiver's concerns. Of course, it could be argued that some pictorial schemata or styles simply convey more information than others. For instance, one might claim that linear perspective was discovered to produce the "illusion" of seeing objects in space especially well by providing most of the same relevant visual information that the objects provide. In that case, the properties exploited by perspectivist techniques (e.g., linear convergence or size/distance relations) could provide a standard against which competing visual hypotheses might be tested. Good perspectivist paintings might thus be treated as special exemplars of realism. They embody perceptual information better than other styles. But the precise sense in which perspectival paintings might contain the same information that is contained in the scenes they depict is unclear. And invok-

ing perspectivist paintings as the highest degree of realism is a controversial idea. Why this is so will emerge in the discussion of picture perception in terms of the other two psychological theories. [*See* Gombrich.]

Arnheim's Account. According to Rudolf Arnheim, Cubist paintings are as realistic as perspectivist ones. The reason is, in part, that picture perception depends not on sheer informational content but on structural patterns or forms that are present in Cubist as well as perspectivist work. On Arnheim's account, realism is also relative to various attitudes about how much emphasis the forms should be given. Because these attitudes are reflected in various devices and styles of representation, convention plays a role. (Gombrich has a similar, but not identical, idea.) But under any attitude, while Gestalt forms do not work by symbolizing information, they also do not ground realism on resemblance. Rather, the isomorphism or shared form between percepts and pictures is defined in terms of second-order figural properties, like relative symmetry and good continuation. Instead of representing objects faithfully, pictures aim to convey the expressive features of those forms—organizational forces that make them "good," as well as any feelings with which they might be associated. However, the claim that Gestalt forms are psychobiologically real—that Gestalt principles of organization actually correspond both to features of the brain and to features of experience—is now generally rejected. Further, some attempts have been made (e.g., by Julian Hochberg) to explain Gestalt phenomena in constructivist terms. [*See* Arnheim.]

Gibson's Account. The rejection of mental representation in general is central to Gibson's direct realism. Initially, Gibson made use of the notion of perspective invariance, in a sense that bears comparison to projective theories of picturing. Those theories treat the picture as a window on which light rays are projected according to geometric principles. This projection produces various perspectival features. The result is a representation that is faithful to ordinary experience. Going beyond the projective theory, Gibson argued that the picture conveys the same information that is contained in light that is reflected from the objects it represents. This is because static perspectival features depend on invariant textural properties. For example, texture compression is a function of distance, regardless of the position of the perceiver. (When Gombrich appeals to information theory, he acknowledges his debt to Gibson. But there is an important difference: Gombrich uses information theory to explain the content of mental constructions that mediate picture perception. Gibson uses it to show that such mental constructions are unnecessary.)

The problem, however, is that Gibson's early theory of perception cannot explain how we disambiguate projections coming from objects of different sizes and at different distances, for those can produce equivalent textural properties if they have the right surface slants. Moreover, as a theory of picture perception, it is inadequate to account for our recognition of objects in line drawings, which lack significant texture.

In his later work, therefore, Gibson emphasized the importance of movement by the perceiver through a scene, which provides additional information through gradients of texture flow. The general problem here, however, is to identify exactly the invariant properties, that is, the nature of the information specified by texture gradients and flow. This is a problem that some philosophers have argued cannot be solved in Gibson's terms, without invoking inference. Moreover, Gibson's later version of "ecological optics" is difficult to apply to pictures, because they provide a static point of view that is unaffected by the viewer's changes in position. It might be argued that pictures somehow "freeze" the invariant properties that are present in a scene. But that seems inconsistent with the claim that invariant properties are precisely those that remain constant when viewpoints change. Such information cannot have always been available in a static view. Or, putting it another way, if the information were available in the static scene, motion should be unnecessary in general. Therefore, there is an apparent dilemma: either invariant properties can be directly picked up from pictures, and motion is inessential; or the "frozen array" leaves something out, and picture perception cannot be explained in terms of direct perception. (Margaret A. Hagen offers a similar argument.)

One way out of the dilemma is to appeal to attention. Even in the absence of bodily movement through space, eye movements can provide for exploratory activity by the perceiver. When attention is shifted by redirecting the gaze, there will be many changes in the image on the retina. Thus, Gibson sometimes suggests that invariant properties can be detected in the relations among momentary aspects provided by eye movements. This explains how information could be extracted from a picture. What is not clear, however, is why the properties so detected should be seen as belonging to the object that is represented rather than to the display itself. In particular, it is not obvious how even careful attention can give a determinate content to displays that are ambiguous with respect to the spatial properties of objects. Such ambiguity is possible because the point of view that is represented remains fixed, even when the perceiver attends to different aspects of the picture.

A different solution is to modify Gibson's theory in light of research in cognitive science. For example, David Marr's computational theory of vision combines elements of direct realism with the basic constructivist commitment to mental representation and inference in perception. It does this by imposing constraints on the process of mental construction that ensure that information of certain sorts will be picked up. Thus, Marr rejects the idea that perception is theory laden, that is, always colored by the biases and background knowledge of the perceiver. (Hochberg has suggested a similar view.) Specifically, Marr claims that perceptual systems are modular—that visual inference depends only on knowledge from a very limited domain, and that the activation of this knowledge is mandatory whenever the perceiver is presented with the right sort of stimulus. Moreover, the principles and structures on which perception depends are common to all perceivers. These points apply to picture perception, and the result is that, to some extent at least, pictorial content should be the same for all perceivers. The problem is that this assumes that the modularity thesis is true and that mental representations are, in fact, constructed in stages from universally available elements in the way that Marr suggests. Both of those assumptions are currently in doubt on empirical grounds.

There is, however, another line of research in cognitive science that has been linked by some of its advocates to direct realism, and it does not posit modules or innately constrained symbolic processes. According to connectionist computational models, perception does not require inference, explicit rules, or mental representations in the form of descriptive interpretations. Instead, with proper training, brainlike networks of highly interconnected units (e.g., neurons) come to produce prototypical patterns of activity that allow them to categorize sensory inputs as objects. It might be argued, then, that directly detected invariant properties are just the ones that connectionist machines in fact can learn to pick up. Picture perception will thus be direct, insofar as such devices can successfully identify depicted objects. But in that case, perception will still be mediated by nonsymbolic representations in the form of prototypical activation patterns. Moreover, direct realism will take on constructivist dimensions, for connectionism is sometimes said (e.g., by Paul M. Churchland) to support the theory ladenness of perception. Finally, it remains to be seen whether the features to which connectionist models spontaneously respond are anything like the properties that Gibson himself took to be invariant.

BIBLIOGRAPHY

Arnheim, Rudolf. *Art and Visual Perception* (1954). Exp. rev. ed. Berkeley, 1974.

Churchland, Paul M. *A Neurocomputational Perspective: The Nature of Mind and the Structure of Science*. Cambridge, Mass., 1989.

Gibson, James J. *The Senses Considered as Perceptual Systems*. Boston, 1966.

Gibson, James J. *The Ecological Approach to Visual Perception*. Boston, 1979.

Gombrich, E. H. *Art and Illusion: A Study in the Psychology of Pictorial Representation* (1960). 2d rev. ed. New York, 1961; reprint, Princeton, N.J., 1969.

Goodman, Nelson. *Languages of Art: An Approach to a Theory of Symbols* (1968). 2d ed. Indianapolis, 1976.

Gregory, Richard L. *The Intelligent Eye*. New York, 1970.

Hagen, Margaret A., ed. *The Perception of Pictures*. 2 vols. New York, 1980, 1981.

Hochberg, Julian. "Pictorial Functions and Perceptual Structures." In *The Perception of Pictures,* edited by Margaret A. Hagen, vol. 2, pp. 47–93. New York, 1981.

Marr, David. *Vision: A Computational Investigation into the Human Representation and Processing of Visual Information.* San Francisco, 1982.

MARK ROLLINS

Music Perception

The perception of music lies at the intersection of aesthetics, the philosophy of mind, and the philosophy of language. Theories of musical understanding enrich and widen our conceptions of mind and mental representation. Conversely, the aesthetics of music is incomplete without an understanding of issues of mind and psychology: an adequate characterization of the logical and epistemic relations between musical hearing and theoretical understanding is a prerequisite to a full account of the nature of musical appreciation and informed enjoyment.

This is intended not as a general survey of philosophical problems related to music perception but rather as an indication of some issues of contemporary concern. The main points will be the following.

1. Certain musical hearing consists in nonconceptual mental representation. This nonconceptual kind of hearing is characteristic of listeners untrained in music theory, in contrast with the conceptual, theory-laden hearing enjoyed by trained listeners.

2. Theory-laden musical hearing is a counterexample to recent arguments, invoking modularity theory, for a distinction between perception and cognition.

3. The distinctive aesthetic value of theory-laden musical hearing derives, in part, from the fact that it contains its own explanation: it presents aesthetic properties, such as unity, in a way not phenomenally distinct from the presentation of the specifically musical features that explain them.

Musical understanding admits of different levels, ranging from a basic ability to recognize genres and tunes, detect mistakes, and so on, to the sort of theoretical understanding entailed by music analysis (Tanner, 1985). Theories of musical understanding have been proposed to capture what it is that a listener at one or another of these levels perceives and understands. Fred Lerdahl and Ray Jackendoff (1983), Carol L. Krumhansl (1990), and Eugene Narmour (1990) all deal with the basic sort of understanding of a musical idiom (Lerdahl and Jackendoff draw an explicit analogy to language). At more sophisticated levels, music analysts describe what they hear using a rich theoretical vocabulary derived from a wide range of theoretical systems—perhaps the best known of which is Schenkerian theory—as well as more ad hoc formulations (for surveys of music analysis and theoretical systems, see Bent, 1987, Cook, 1987, and Dunsby and Whittall, 1988).

For any account of musical understanding, or ascription of musical perception, we will want to know, for the concept of hearing thereby invoked, "its place among the concepts of experience" (Wittgenstein, 1958, IIxi). We will want to know, too, what differences there may be among mentalistic notions imported by different accounts of hearing, how such notions are related, and how those differences may help to characterize different levels of musical understanding.

Malcolm Budd has suggested that, at one level of musical understanding (characteristic of an ordinary listener untrained in music theory), it is possible that certain music-theoretical concepts should apply to a listener's hearing of a passage without his or her possessing (or at any rate exercising) those concepts (Budd, 1985; cf. Kivy, 1990). This is one meaning that might be attached to the claim that (this kind of) musical hearing is nonconceptual. That Budd's suggestion is correct is shown by Fregean considerations of cognitive significance: a listener who, according to the relevant theory, attributes a certain property to a passage may well find informative the statement that it has that property (DeBellis, 1995). This shows that the relevant sort of musical hearing is conceptually distinct from thinking about music in theoretical terms.

One question that arises here is whether musical hearing should be thought of as representational at all. It is part of a representational conception of musical hearing that the latter have truth conditions: that it represent the world, or in this case a musical passage, as being a certain way, such that it is satisfied by the passage just in case the passage *is* that way. On this conception, "hears . . . as *F*" (where *F* is some music-theoretical property, structure, or relationship) is semantically and conceptually dependent on "is *F*"; that is, music theory is prior to psychological attribution. An example of an alternative to the representational view would be one that treats musical hearing along the lines of a secondary quality, whereby "hears . . . as *F*" is thought of as prior to "is *F*" in much the way "is red" might be analyzed dispositionally in terms of "looks red." Such an alternative conception is consistent with an analysis of hearing in terms of sensational (vs. representational) properties of experience (see Peacocke, 1983). There is some intuitive appeal to a nonrepresentational view, and it has its defenders (Jackendoff, 1987, in different terminology), but the main problem faced by a nonrepresentational view is whether an account of the identity conditions for the relevant psychological states can be given in a way that does not lend even greater support to a representational conception. It is doubtful that it can; at any rate, the following discussion assumes the representational conception.

On the basis of the foregoing we must conclude that an ordinary listener's musical hearing is an instance of nonconceptual mental representation, in the sense that the listener need not have (or exercise) the concepts contained in a psychological attribution in order to satisfy the latter. But this leaves open the possibility that a listener has to have *some* concept (say, a perceptual one) of the property designated by a music-theoretical concept if he or she is to satisfy an attribution that employs it, even if it is not the same concept. We may ask, then, whether musical hearing is ever nonconceptual in the sense that a certain music-theoretical concept applies to the listener's hearing without the listener having *any* concept of the relevant property (cf. Peacocke, 1986). That musical hearing is sometimes nonconceptual in this stronger sense is demonstrated by the fact that listeners often cannot discriminate instances of properties they perceive (according to the relevant theories) from noninstances; such discrimination typically requires aural training. But having a perceptual concept entails a capacity for perceptual discrimination (Armstrong, 1993). It follows that the kind of perception attributed by theories of the ordinary listener's musical understanding is nonconceptual.

The distinction between conceptual and nonconceptual may be brought to bear on the distinction between an ordinary listener's musical perception and that of the music analyst. The arguments for nonconceptual representation do not go through for trained listeners of this kind. Their hearing is theory-laden: their perceptual concepts are integrated with theories of music and analytic frameworks. The musical training this sort of listener has undergone may be characterized, then, as one that makes conceptual what was formerly nonconceptual—it brings about conceptual representations of properties that the listener had heretofore represented, if at all, nonconceptually.

Theory-laden musical perception has import for wider debates about the relation between perception and cognition and the tenability of a distinction between the two. Jerry Fodor has defended a view of mental organization on which the mind is composed of informationally encapsulated modules (Fodor, 1983). The question relevant to musical training is whether perceptual systems are encapsulated "diachronically" in a way immune to influence by theoretical belief; if not, then Fodor's strategy for drawing a distinction between perception and cognition fails.

The main problem in stating the thesis that perception is diachronically encapsulated is to delimit the notion of the perceptual in a non–question begging way. Fodor's constraints are these: perception enters into conscious decision making and inference; its terms are ones we naturally use to describe what we see and hear—it has "phenomenological salience"; and it underlies judgments of phenomenal similarity. But by these criteria elementary aural training does constitute a counterexample to the diachronic encapsulation thesis (Churchland, 1988; see also Fodor, 1988, and DeBellis, 1995). Listeners with this sort of training hear music in a way laden with music-theoretical concepts. Moreover, hearing of this sort is as "perceptual" as anything else: it enters into perceptual reports, inference, decision

making, and so on, and has as much phenomenological salience as the ordinary perception of colors and shapes.

The aesthetic issue of greatest urgency in connection with theory-laden musical perception is that of identifying its characteristic and distinctive aesthetic benefits: how does hearing music in theoretical terms contribute to understanding and enjoyment? To insist on a strong separation between the explanatory and appreciation-guiding roles of music theory (Kivy, 1990) is to overstate the case. A theoretically informed appreciation of music typically involves the perception of features explanatorily relevant to aesthetic properties (Davies, 1983). Moreover, what is distinctive about such perception is that, often, explanans and explanandum are not only metaphysically but also phenomenally unitary: the relation in such cases is not that of cause and effect, but property identity, and moreover identity so perceived.

A (perhaps underappreciated) puzzle about music analysis then arises. It appears that one important goal of analysis is to point to the specifically musical features that explain aesthetic properties such as unity (Reti, 1978, Epstein, 1979). It appears, moreover, that claims about such explanatory connections are subject to empirical test. One would think, then, that the enterprise of music analysis would go hand in hand with the enterprise of confirming or disconfirming such claims. But in fact the latter does not seem either to be part of, or a necessary adjunct to, music analysis (cf. Cook, 1990). We are left, then, with the uneasy result that music analysts are, for the most part, content to state hypotheses about such explanatory connections without seriously undertaking to determine whether they are true. Moreover, if a hypothesis of this sort is false, someone who hears music in a way conditioned by that hypothesis is enjoying a false pleasure. It would seem a not fully coherent aesthetic position to approach music in this way: if one's hearing is theory-laden, one will want to be justified in believing the relevant theoretical premises.

One attempt to avoid this impasse would be to claim that once the alleged sources of unity are pointed out, it is self-evident that they are responsible for unity; but it is hard to see what would justify such a claim. Another response would be to give up entirely the idea that such features are explanatorily relevant in the way suggested. But such an extreme response is unnecessary. The prevailing absence of a concern with confirmation might be ascribed, instead, to the fact that the interest attached to music-theoretical properties is overdetermined: they would be interesting even if they did not explain what they are said to explain. This diminishes, though does not erase, the demand for empirical confirmation.

[*See also* Music, *historical overview article.*]

BIBLIOGRAPHY

Armstrong, D. M. *A Materialist Theory of the Mind* (1968). 2d ed. London and New York, 1993.

Bent, Ian. *Analysis.* New York, 1987.

Budd, Malcolm. "Understanding Music." *Proceedings of the Aristotelian Society, Supplementary Volume* 59 (1985): 233–248.

Churchland, Paul M. "Perceptual Plasticity and Theoretical Neutrality: A Reply to Jerry Fodor." *Philosophy of Science* 55 (June 1988): 167–187.

Cook, Nicholas. *A Guide to Musical Analysis.* New York, 1987.

Cook, Nicholas. *Music, Imagination, and Culture.* Oxford, 1990.

Davies, Stephen. "Attributing Significance to Unobvious Musical Relationships." *Journal of Music Theory* 27 (1983): 203–213.

DeBellis, Mark. *Music and Conceptualization.* Cambridge and New York, 1995.

Dunsby, Jonathan, and Arnold Whittall. *Music Analysis in Theory and Practice.* New Haven, 1988.

Epstein, David. *Beyond Orpheus: Studies in Musical Structure.* Cambridge, Mass., 1979.

Fodor, Jerry A. *The Modularity of Mind: An Essay on Faculty Psychology.* Cambridge, Mass., 1983.

Fodor, Jerry A. "A Reply to Churchland's 'Perceptual Plasticity and Theoretical Neutrality.'" *Philosophy of Science* 55 (1988): 188–198. Reprinted in *A Theory of Content and Other Essays* (Cambridge, Mass., 1990), pp. 253–263.

Jackendoff, Ray. *Consciousness and the Computational Mind.* Cambridge, Mass., 1987.

Kivy, Peter. *Music Alone: Philosophical Reflections on the Purely Musical Experience.* Ithaca, N.Y., 1990.

Krumhansl, Carol L. *Cognitive Foundations of Musical Pitch.* Oxford, 1990.

Lerdahl, Fred, and Ray Jackendoff. *A Generative Theory of Tonal Music.* Cambridge, Mass., 1983.

Narmour, Eugene. *The Analysis and Cognition of Basic Melodic Structures: The Implication-Realization Model.* Chicago, 1990.

Peacocke, Christopher. *Sense and Content: Experience, Thought, and Their Relations.* Oxford, 1983.

Peacocke, Christopher. "Analogue Content." *Proceedings of the Aristotelian Society,* suppl. vol. 60 (1986): 1–17.

Reti, Rudolph. *The Thematic Process in Music.* New York, 1951; reprint, Westport, Conn., 1978.

Tanner, Michael. "Understanding Music." *Proceedings of the Aristotelian Society* suppl. vol. 59 (1985): 215–232.

Wittgenstein, Ludwig. *Philosophical Investigations* (1953). 3d ed. Translated and edited by G. E. M. Anscombe. New York, 1958.

MARK DEBELLIS

PERFORMANCE. The notion of performance is a central one in aesthetics, pertaining to virtually every aspect of art, from its production and presentation, to the appreciation, understanding, and evaluation of particular works of art, and, ultimately, to our understanding of what a work of art is.

Generally speaking, the concept of performance can refer to the execution of a range of human actions that can be understood and appreciated as such. As Francis Sparshott has pointed out, our common ways of understanding specifically artistic performance have their roots in a classical line of thinking about art as "a corpus of knowledge and skills organized for the production of changes of a specific kind in matter of a specific kind," and in modern times we have come to think of performances as pertaining to a very broad compass of artistic making and doing. We frequently find ourselves isolating, contemplating, and discussing various aspects of artistic activities such as drawing, sculpting, or painting, music making, dancing, acting, writing, and so on, whether in situ or recorded in some form or other. This is where the complexity of the notion begins to arise. We may have bought tickets for a performance by Pinchas Zukerman of Ludwig von Beethoven's Violin Concerto, but whose performance exactly are we appreciating? Is the performance we admire in a Laurence Olivier production of *Hamlet* Olivier's, William Shakespeare's, Hamlet's, or someone else's?

In certain arts, such as music, we typically distinguish between two stages of productive activity: composing, which is usually taken to refer to the creative act of conceiving of and organizing the parts or elements that make up the pattern, design, or overall structure and content of an artistic whole, and performing, the executory activity by means of which an artistic composition is then rendered into a tangible, public object or event. In a suitably generous sense of the term *performance,* both of these activities are performances and may be valued as such. We may attend to a musical performance (say) as instantiating or providing a record of the compositional achievement of Beethoven, just as we may appreciate the executory activity of Zukerman—performance in the narrower sense. We may make a similar distinction even in the contingency that a composer performs his or her own previously created composition. Most often, however, our appreciation of a musical performance involves an admixture of both poles, as it does in the case of an improvisation, which, it might be argued, can be thought to blur the distinction between composition and performance in the narrower sense.

Of course, if one takes the proper aesthetic object to be the work as conceived by the original artist, and if one assumes the possibility of direct access to that work, the goal of performance might seem to be that of accurate reproduction, and the activity of interpretive performance might be looked on with perplexity, if not downright suspicion. Eduard Hanslick, for example, arguing that "philosophically speaking, the composed piece, regardless of whether it is performed or not, is the completed artwork," acknowledges the ability of performers to reveal the "spirit" of the composer but regards performance rather contemptuously as a site for the fabrication of distracting emotional displays.

This seems to be the minority view, however. Most people regard the performer as in some sense collaborating with the original artist to bring the work into full existence for a public. That is to say, we normally think of performances in the narrower sense as something more than mere reproductions or presentations of previously existing works. This is true even of philosophers such as Benedetto Croce and R. G. Collingwood who hold the ontological status of the work to reside in an act of intuition of the originating artist. In the case of an art such as music in which extensive notation is available, much is left to the discretion of the performer, even with respect to comparatively low-level technical matters such as phrasing, inflection, intonation, and dynamics. Susanne K. Langer argues that final decisions of what tones actually sound like necessarily rest with the performer. Theater people know that even in the case of dramatic warhorses, substantial rewriting often occurs on the rehearsal stage, as do decisions about gesture, staging, lighting, and so forth, all of which can affect the aesthetic quality of the final production. In dance, whose notational devices and systems seem less well developed those of music or drama, there is, arguably, even more room to maneuver. Certainly most performers see themselves as makers in their own right, not as slavish imitators. Despite occasional critical talk of "definitive" performances, the public and critics alike are generally quite comfortable with the view that different but equally rewarding performances of the "same" work are possible, and so we speak of both "Leonard Bernstein's Mahler" and "Herbert von Karajan's Mahler."

Whether there are critical standards of excellence in performance, and if there are, what they might be, are matters of much tangled debate, however. Lip service is often paid in critical commentary to the ideals of being "true to the work" and of being "creative" or "original" in one's performances, but in such discussions everything hangs on what is to count as the "artwork" and on what constraints are put on creativity and originality. It is common to hold that performers have an obligation to ensure a measure of authenticity with respect to the work being performed and that authenticity is a matter of recapturing the intentions of the originating artist insofar as these may be suggested by notational means such as scores, scripts, and videotapes. Given that even the most complete scores, scripts, and tapes do not determine all decisions to be made about performances, however, some aestheticians choose rather to speak about a reference class of performances defined by some set of broad features about the work in question as providing normative guidelines for performances. Even here one must take a position on the range of aesthetically relevant qualities that fall legitimately under the ambit of authentic performance. Furthermore, one cannot assume that judgments about the correctness of performance are sufficient to determine what is meant by excellence in performance. It is also an important question whether evaluations of performances must be relativized, not only to the works being performed, but also to performers, audiences, to considerations of style and genre, and so on. One can see why debates about authenticity, obligation, and excellence in performance loom large in aesthetic discourse and have done so since the time of Plato's *Ion*.

It must be granted, however, that we typically think of compositional and performative skills as substantially different in kind, as we do in the case of choreography and dancing, for example. When we concentrate on performance activity in the narrower sense, we are likely to focus on the executory and the interpretive aspects of the performer's action. The interpretation and presentation of a previously conceived work may involve a considerable degree of technical skill, and with that comes the temptation toward virtuosic technical displays. But excellence in performance is generally thought to go beyond mere technique to include the entire range of formal and expressive qualities. Indeed, as classical discussions made clear, to perform is to engage in the world by effecting changes in it, to manifest and exhibit one's intentions through action. It is small wonder that we find the performances of others so fascinating in themselves. There is also something captivating about the effort to interpret and present the intentional product of another human being, bringing one's own understandings to bear on it, and to do this for the appreciation of a public.

Some arts seem especially well suited to the aesthetic contemplation of performance in the narrower sense. We call these arts the "performing arts" and usually number among them music, drama, opera, and dance, but not, say, painting, sculpture, pottery, or architecture. This grouping is consistent with the fact that in the case of much music, drama, and dance, we can without much difficulty identify particular performers who execute or comply with a set of instructions more or less completely provided at a previous stage of artistic activity often (though not always) by a separate individual (the composer, the playwright, the choreographer) to bring a work of art into full existence for a public. In such cases one can attend to the manner or mode of presentation of the executing performer or even, through attention to relevant "performance practice" standards regarding notation and other factors, appreciate the likely manner of presentation of a work in a style characteristic of an earlier period. Since such arts normally involve the provision of a notation to facilitate the instructions from the first stage to the second stage of artistic production, there is a relation between a performing art of this sort and what Nelson Goodman has called the "allographic" arts, that is, arts for which a notation is present and in which the distinction between original and forgery does not rest on establishing that the object in question is the product of the artist's hand. But clearly our traditional understanding of the performing arts involves other expectations as well. The performing arts typically involve highly organized events or sequences of events, as in the case of large-scale balletic, dramatic, and musical works, where a performer's ability to render often subtle and complex actions and events is highly valued.

That is not to say that the distinction between performing and nonperforming arts is always an easy one to make. Literature, for example, has obvious affinities with music and drama, especially in virtue of its potential for sequential complexity and the provision of instructions for the presentation of a work by means of a text, much in the manner of musical scores and playscripts. There is also a sense in which, in reading a text, one interprets a work and realizes a world, much as the musical performer and the thespian help to bring into existence musical and dramatic worlds. Public readings of literary texts are not at all uncommon, and yet literature is not—at least nowadays—counted among the performing arts. Perhaps this has to do with spread of literacy in modern times and the fact that literate people can wring literary worlds at some level of convincingness from the texts they read in privacy and silence. In that sense they have no need for third-party presenters. There may also prevail the supposition that the public recitation of a literary work does not generally place the same demand on human capacities as does the singing of a song, the playing of a musical work on a musical instrument, or even the acting out of a scripted role on the stage, and so the performative activity involved seems a less apt object of aesthetic contemplation and valuation. Contemporary "performance art," which frequently combines live or recorded dramatic performances with static aesthetic objects such as paintings and graffiti, also strains to fit under the rubric of performing art, at least when considered alongside the paradigm cases. Technological innovations can also influence our sense of what counts as a performing art even among the paradigmatic cases, as in the examples of Glenn Gould's extensively tape-spliced "performances," the "performances" of the Yamaha Disklavier, and karaoke "performances." In fact, recording technologies such as film, video, computer storage systems, records, tapes, and compact discs raise an interesting question: if is true that a large part of the interest we take in performance is in the excitement that comes from the knowledge that decisions and actions we witness are the product of the moment, to what extent or in what sense are recordings of performances performances?

There is also an important sense in which viewing, hearing, reading, judging, scanning, surveying, discussing, criticizing, and all the other activities involved in attending to, understanding, and evaluating works of art are themselves performances, not only in the sense that they are performed actions, but also insofar as they contribute to bringing a work to completion or at least to a fuller realization in some sense. Recent developments in participatory and interactive art make much of this possibility, but performers know that the participation of audiences has always played an important role in the so-called performing arts. Actors, for example, are well aware of the reciprocal relationship between feelings expressed on the stage and resonances evoked in the audience. At a more general level, audiences typically appreciate performances in a synthetic and contextualizing way. Adherents of deconstruction, reception aesthetics, and reader-response theory have in their own ways emphasized the role of the reader in establishing the meaning of literary

works in particular. Indeed, recent work by Kendall Walton and others on the role of make-believe in the perception, appreciation, and understanding of representational and abstract art generally has shown that the actions of audiences may be the sorts of performances that are central to our understanding, not only of the so-called performing arts, but of all art.

[*See also* Authenticity; Dance; Music, *historical overview article;* Performance Art; *and* Theater.]

BIBLIOGRAPHY

Alperson, Philip. "On Musical Improvisation." *Journal of Aesthetics and Art Criticism* 43.1 (Fall 1984): 17–29.

Collingwood, R. G. *The Principles of Art.* Oxford, 1938.

Croce, Benedetto. *Guide to Aesthetics* (1913). Translated by Patrick Romanell. Indianapolis, 1965.

Davies, Stephen. "Authenticity in Musical Performance." *British Journal of Aesthetics* 27 (1987): 39–50.

Goodman, Nelson. *Languages of Art: An Approach to a Theory of Symbols.* 2d ed. Indianapolis, 1976.

Grossman, Morris. "Performance and Obligation." In *What Is Music? An Introduction to the Philosophy of Music,* edited by Philip Alperson. New York, 1987; reprint, University Park, Pa., 1994.

Hanslick, Eduard. *On the Musically Beautiful: A Contribution towards the Revision of the Aesthetics of Music.* Translated and edited by Geoffrey Payzant. Indianapolis, 1986.

Hein, Hilde. "Performance as an Aesthetic Category." *Journal of Aesthetics and Art Criticism* 28.3 (Spring 1970): 381–386.

Hughes, R. I. G. "Tolstoy, Stanislavski, and the Art of Acting." *The Journal of Aesthetics and Art Criticism* 51.1 (Winter 1993): 39–48.

Kivy, Peter. *Authenticities: Philosophical Reflections on Musical Performance.* Ithaca, N.Y., 1995.

Langer, Susanne K. *Feeling and Form.* New York, 1953.

Levinson, Jerrold. *Music, Art, and Metaphysics: Essays in Philosophical Aesthetics.* Ithaca, N.Y., 1990.

Payzant, Geoffrey. "Performance and the Existence of Art." *Dalhousie Review* 44.1 (Summer 1964): 83–95.

Price, Kingsley. "The Performing and the Non-Performing Arts." *Journal of Aesthetics and Art Criticism* 29.1 (Fall 1970): 53–62.

Sparshott, Francis. *The Theory of the Arts.* Princeton, N.J., 1982.

Thom, Paul. *For an Audience: A Philosophy of the Performing Arts.* Philadelphia, 1994.

Urmson, J. O. "The Performing Arts." In *Contemporary British Philosophy,* 4th series, edited by H. D. Lewis. London, 1976.

Walton, Kendall L. *Mimesis as Make-Believe: On the Foundations of the Representational Arts.* Cambridge, Mass., 1990.

Webster, William E. "Music Is Not a 'Notational System'." *Journal of Aesthetics and Art Criticism* 29.4 (Summer 1971): 489–497.

PHILIP A. ALPERSON

PERFORMANCE ART. [*To analyze this distinct development in art, this entry comprises two essays:*

Historical Overview

Feminist Performance Art

The first essay is an overview, both of performance art since it first emerged in the 1960s and of its impact on contemporary art in general. The second essay clarifies the important role that feminists have played in performance art and the significance of performance art for feminism, given that performance art is one of the few art forms ever that has included and recognized women in major creative roles from its inception. For related discussion, see Contemporary Art; Dance; Performance; *and* Theater.]

Historical Overview

Known variously as "live art," "body art," "event art," and "post-object art," performance art initially referred to artistic events wherein the body of the artist functioned as a medium in addition to, or in lieu of, paint, canvas, or sculptural raw material. Additionally, performance art describes a diverse array of contexts and events that emphasize the process or event of art and art making rather than the resulting object, thereby raising questions as to the nature and function of art and the accompanying institutions of the market, gallery, and museum. The term *performance art* has been applied retroactively to describe cabaret, theater, and "live art" in the context of early twentieth-century avant-garde movements such as Dada, Surrealism, Futurism, and the Bauhaus, suggesting a historical and political lineage for the art of performance. Further, the notion of the "performative" has become a strategic description of contemporary social and cultural processes of signification, including the performance of gender and sexuality, in order to denote the arbitrary and constructed nature of identity and its ability to disrupt ideological boundaries.

Performance art might best be described as "breaking frame" in four distinct but related ways:

1. By substituting the artist's body as the medium or object, the performance work breaks with the traditional, material frame of the canvas or art object.
2. Performance art breaks frame in the theatrical sense by eradicating and/or acknowledging the so-called fourth wall between stage and audience, artist and viewer.
3. Performance art breaks or disrupts the frame or boundary of the body itself as the presumed site for the integrity of the individual and his or her subjective identity.
4. The centrality of the body in performance work breaks down the boundary between public and private, invoking the relation between the individual and state laws or national ideology.

Performance art "breaks frame" by taking the traditional, framed notions of the art object and art making as its literalized parameters, and translates formal issues across a broad, ideological spectrum.

While Jackson Pollock's Abstract Expressionist "drip paintings" of the postwar era are held to be the origins of contemporary art in the United States, the discourse surrounding his work provides a formal context for early performance art. The breakthroughs for which Pollock is granted the mantle of modern art are numerous, as are the

means by which performance artists responded. By taking his canvas off the easel and placing it on the floor, Pollock is credited with definitively transforming painting from its three-dimensional, illusory status as a "window on the world." Further, the coincidence of the pictorial plane with the space of the artist, held to be a "breakthrough" in postwar painting, was taken to be a literal breakthrough in the 1950s by the Japanese artists' collective, Gutai (Japanese for "concreteness"): Saburo Murakami took a running leap in order to break through a series of frames hung with paper "canvas" (1955).

This emphasis on process, or painting as event rather than resulting object, is exemplified not only by critic Harold Rosenberg's term "Action Painting" for Abstract Expressionism, but by numerous early performance artists, such as George Mathieu's *Battle of the Bovines* (1955), in which the artist threw paint onto a canvas on the wall, and Gutai's *Action Painting* (1962), in which a fire extinguisher was the means by which paint was sprayed onto canvas, floor, walls, artist, and model, literalizing the distinction between the physical and conceptual frame of painting. Yves Klein moved from painting his signature blue canvases with a brush and began in 1958 to use the bodies of his nude female models to apply paint in an unmediated way to canvas, presenting his inherently theatrical *Anthropometries of the Blue Period* to live audiences in Paris in 1960.

That Pollock's process was as important to postwar art as the paintings themselves is further witnessed by Hans Namuth's obsessive photographic and filmic documentation of Pollock painting for *Life* magazine in 1950. Pollock's drip style of painting was filmed by Namuth from beneath a transparent glass "canvas," while black-and-white photographs of Pollock's blurred hands and crouched form further fetishized the physicality and the ephemerality of the event of painting and foreshadowed performance art's reliance on the photographic document. The Gutai Art Association, whose members had seen Namuth's photographs of Pollock, continued to concretize ideas of frame, gesture, and immediacy in art: Kazuo Shiraga dispensed with the paintbrush and applied paint directly with his feet to a canvas on the floor (1956). The latter gave new meaning to the immediacy attributed to Pollock's expressionist, gestural style, as well as lent a certain irony to critics' fetishization of appearances of Pollock's own painted shoe print on the canvas as indexes of the artist's presence in the work.

Postwar Performance. While critics throughout the 1960s debated the nature of Abstract Expressionism's legacy and the potential "theatricality" of Minimalist sculpture's existence in narrative time and space (most notably with the 1967 publication of Michael Fried's "Art and Objecthood" in *Artforum*), early performance artists were confronting modernism on their own grounds, often taking its formal boundaries as the literal parameters for performance.

Marina Abramovic and Ulay's *Relation Work* series explored mind/body limits through performances that translated the formal parameters of art into physical and psychological boundaries. In *Relation in Time* (1977) the artists were seated back to back, their twin-length dark hair tightly bound together: the duration of the performance was the length of time it took for their hair to naturally come unbound. Similarly, *Relation in Space* (1976) commenced with the two nude artists in opposite corners of the room: they proceeded to walk back and forth across the room, drawing nearer the center and one another with each pass, speeding up almost imperceptibly, until they began to brush, then bump, and finally to collide with one another, the parameters of the performance defined when the two exhausted artists could no longer continue their respective paths with the other as an obstacle. Thus, the issue of latent violence was raised early on by performance art, an issue that could be said to be inevitable in foregrounding the body and in the confrontation between artist and audience previously mediated by the art object.

Other performance-based artists, such as Tehching Hsieh and Linda Montano, use lengthy, definitive temporal frames, such as the span of a year, to establish the parameters of their performances and simultaneously to eradicate the boundaries between art and everyday experience. Further, their Art-Life works test personal endurance as a means to explore social boundaries and mores. Hsieh spent one year living inside a cage (1978–1979) and another living out-of-doors in the city as if homeless (1981–1982). Over the course of seven years Montano dresses entirely in one color annually, corresponding to each of the seven chakras. The two collaborated in 1983–1984 in a year living tied together around the waist with only a six-foot rope delimiting both the distance between and the proximity to each other. As in other performances, they shaved their heads at the beginning of the year in order for new growth to mark the passage of time. The performance, which was not for the benefit of an audience, highlighted the negotiation and compromise of time, space, and one another that we perform on a day-to-day basis.

Significantly, Montano and Hsieh each interpret the piece from opposite sides of the Art-Life boundary. In an interview toward the end of their year-long performance, Hsieh claimed that the performance was "subsumed by Art" and that the piece was not about the two of them but "all people," while Montano asserted her interest in the personal issues of claustrophobia, ego, and power being as important as Art. Montano further remarked on the gendered nature of their respective interpretations, contending that while women traditionally refer to their personal feelings, men evade personal issues by claiming their universality or status as "everyman" (Carr, 1993). Performance art became a primary arena for women artists to explore divisions between personal and political and actively reclaim their

bodies as creative subjects rather than objects of male creative expression. Artists such as Carolee Schneemann used the formal parameters of gesture, frame, and immediacy as physical ones in *Up to and Including Her Limits* (1976), providing a corrective to Yves Klein's directorial mediation of his models' bodies by authoring her own body-made images.

The blurring of the physical as well as the temporal and spatial boundaries of art was conducive to interest in the 1950s and 1960s in questioning the hierarchical status of art, which performance art, like Pop and conceptual art, explored by challenging the boundary between art and the objects and events of everyday life. Black Mountain College in the 1950s was a communal experiment in "living" art on a daily basis and provided an arena for early collaborations between Robert Rauschenberg, Merce Cunningham, and John Cage, the latter renowned for his musical performances with pianos whose strings had been "altered" by attaching ordinary objects such as wooden spoons, and for his infamous "framed" silences (*4′ 33″*, 1952).

The loosely defined group of Fluxus artists founded by George Maciunas, which included George Brecht, Nam June Paik, Wolf Vostell, and Yoko Ono, were conceptually based performers who undermined traditional notions of authorship and ownership attached to the art object, and along with Cage, were influenced by the 1951 publication of *The Dada Painters and Poets,* edited by painter Robert Motherwell. Consequently, Fluxus shared both the anti-institutional and absurdist aspects of Dada. Fluxus "Event Scores" were cards with simple directions and no dramaturgy. George Brecht's score for *Drip Music* (1959–1962) consisted solely of enumerated instructions to pour water from one container into another: it was left to the performer to determine other parameters, such as type of vessel, water speed, duration, and context. Likewise, Flux Kits were portable art kits containing scores and random objects intended to diminish the uniqueness of art production. Fluxus events and objects were deliberately left unauthorized, so as to critique the role of the artist's name in the christening of the art object. In a related fashion, Milanese artist Piero Manzoni's *Artist's Breath* (1961–1962) and *Artist's Shit* (1961) are descendants of Marcel Duchamp's *Fountain* and other Dada readymades in their recognition of the constructed nature of the "aura" of art and its dependence on the artist's patrimony. Ironically, the passage of time and the inevitability of the market have recently invested Fluxus objects with market value, and individual artist's names are being reattributed to the works in order to establish their collectibility and authenticity.

The collective environment of Fluxus provided a home for the German artist Joseph Beuys to invent a shamanistic, mythic individual to make up for the authentic individual sacrificed to National Socialism. Reclaiming prewar Expressionism, Beuys represents a pivotal, even cathartic figure for postwar Germany, marking its reentry into an avant-garde project disrupted by Adolf Hitler. Beuys utilized an eccentric combination of personal and heroic myth to create an archaeology of symbols—wool felt, fat, honey, a dead hare—for bodily transitions from cold to warm in his performances and installations: the tendency of these materials to deteriorate naturally cheated the museum's conservatory impulses in true Fluxus fashion. Claiming that everyone is an artist, Beuys expressed an antipathy for traditional art-historical means of granting meaning and legitimacy to art as well as for the "coldness" of the formal project of modernism, embodied for him by figures like Duchamp (*The Silence of Marcel Duchamp Is Overestimated*, live television broadcast, Germany, 1964). Dubbed "social sculpture," performances such as *How to Explain Pictures to a Dead Hare* (1965) satirized the art-historical interpretive quest for meaning as well as an audience indifferent to the artist; at the same time, Beuys cradled the hare tenderly, perhaps proffering a victim for whom the postwar German psyche might develop a redemptive empathy. Similarly, Beuys's three-day habitation with a coyote in *I Like America and America Likes Me* (Rene Block Gallery, New York, 1974) attempted to renegotiate the doomed relation between nature and society. The power of the work resides in the fact that Beuys points no easy moral fingers at American society, yet resonance with German history is unmistakable.

Describing his elaborately scripted Happenings, Allan Kaprow asserted that it was time to "increase the responsibility of the observer," which he did by making the audience active participants in his events but also by leaving interpretation of the works' meaning open to the audience as well. By rendering meaning external to the work of art rather than its hermeneutic result, performance artists raised ethical questions regarding the viewing and consumption of art, frequently placing themselves at considerable physical risk in order to highlight the presumed passivity of spectatorship and its social and ideological consequences.

Performances involving extremes in personal endurance for the artist tested the artifice of the conceptual space or frame between artist and audience and the ethical implications in the audience's complicity as witnesses. In *Doomed* (1975), Chris Burden lay motionless on a gallery floor beneath a pane of glass: the parameters of the piece, unbeknownst to the audience or gallery officials, were temporally contingent on the activity of someone besides Burden to alter the work. Burden remained motionless for more than forty-five hours in front of his perplexed audience before a sympathetic guard placed a cup of water near his head, whereupon Burden leaped up and smashed the clock to mark the end of the piece. If the power to terminate the performance was dormant within the audience in *Doomed*, the latent violence of the artist-viewer relation was more explicit in *Prelude to 110/220,* where Burden lay on the floor restrained by copper bands in close proximity to two pails of water into which live voltage wires had been placed. Here the viewers' passivity was recast as an active choice *not* to overturn the pails and electrocute Burden, leaving the audience with the uneasy knowledge that they could indeed be responsible for such an action.

The passivity of viewing and the reassuring artifice of the presumed gap between art and life were of particular concern to many artists during and after the American war in Vietnam. The presence of the "television war" in America's living rooms each night was responsible both for turning popular sentiment against the war and also for numbing viewers to violence and accountability through its repetition and familiarity. Many performance artists began to incorporate newly available video technology into their performances in order induce tension between live and remote events, presence and absence, and the distance of television's proximity. In *Velvet Water* (1974), Burden "breathed" water by submerging his face in a sink full of water until he choked. The audience witnessed Burden's near drowning via a series of monitors on stage; Burden himself, however, was only a short distance from the audience, concealed by a row of lockers. The audience could hear Burden choke and gasp nearby while witnessing the event on the monitor, and were thus denied the illusory comfort of the fully mediated distance television appears to offer. The use of video monitors in Gina Pane's *Money, Meat, Fire* (1971) and in the context of other self-abusive, "live" performances similarly functioned to defamiliarize television spectatorship and raise awareness of audience complicity in U.S. foreign policy by their complicity in self-destructive performance.

Despite criticism of such overt parallels at the time, the self-mutilation of the artist's body in Burden's *Shoot* (1971) and *Trans-fixed* (1974) was an apt metaphor, not only for the fragmented body of the American G.I. displaced by the abstracted, State Department rhetoric of "body counts," but also for the fragmenting of the Western ideological gestalt invested in the body, particularly the male body and its sexual potency, the latter targeted by Vietcong guerrilla tactics such as the "Bouncing Betty" land mine, which bounced in the air prior to detonating in the victim's genital area. In the context of Vietnam, the physical and psychic wounds of the G.I. embodied a particularly Western castration anxiety invested as much in the "whole" or "normal" body as in sexual function. The ostracizing of Vietnam veterans and the subsequent crisis in American masculinity in the wake of the war in Vietnam is the context for quadriplegic performer Frank Moore's staged orgies in the 1970–1980s, Vietnam veteran Kim Jones's performances as *Mudman,* and for the Asian body as racial signifier in Simon Leung's *Squatting Project* (Berlin, 1994) and *Warren Piece, in the '70s* (New York, 1993).

In her work on self-mutilating performance by Pane, Burden, Vito Acconci, and Ulay and Abramovic, Kathy O'Dell identifies the skin itself as a boundary or frame that does not merely circumscribe the body's internal organs but functions as an ego site, one invested with individuating the autonomous subject of history. The very permeability of the skin to cutting, pricking, bleeding, and biting in performance indicates not only the fragility of the body in modernity to war, technology, medicine, and more recently AIDS, but also the fragility of the modern, bourgeois myth of subjective unity as it is invested in the individual corpus. The fragility of the body and the cherished myth of subjective unity as the site for gender identity is powerfully examined in Simon Leung's complex video/performance, *Transcrypts: Some Notes between Pricks* (1991–1992). Leung's meditation on the "glory hole," which transforms the public men's restroom into a "tea room," the site of private, gay sexual encounters, is a nuanced analysis of the permeability of the body's real and symbolic borders, exacerbated in light of the AIDS epidemic. Thus, the architectural site for digestive elimination and sexual emissions becomes a metaphor for HIV transmission, itself a real and allegorical site for cultural anxiety about the body, sexual identity, and their presumed stability.

A recent performance by Ron Athey in Minneapolis, *Four Scenes from a Harsh Life* (1994), which involved consensual, ritual scarring by Athey on a black male colleague, provoked public ire neither for its sado-masochism, nor for its incendiary racial imagery, but rather for the blood shed during the course of the performance. As Athey, who is HIV-positive, cut the skin of his accomplice, he blotted the

PERFORMANCE ART: Overview. Adrian Piper, *Catalysis III* (1970), Street Performance, New York. (Photograph by Rosemary Mayer. Courtesy of the artist; used by permission.)

fine incisions with paper towels, which were then suspended on clotheslines over the audience. Inaccurate and hysterical accounts of the event were taken up and further exaggerated by the media, who reported that HIV-infected blood dripped onto audience member's heads, providing a threat to public health and playing into homophobic rhetoric of "innocent victims" of AIDS. In the late twentieth century, the AIDS epidemic has become a focal point for cultural, political, and personal anxiety regarding long-standing beliefs about bodily integrity and individual identity, particularly as expressed through gender and sexual relations.

The raced body produces a related anxiety about social and cultural borders. A visible sign of "difference," race, and cultural stereotypy are addressed by Guillermo Gomez-Peña and Coco Fusco in their caged performance "Two Undiscovered Aboriginals Visit Madrid" and "promotional" brochures (both part of *Year of the White Bear*, 1992) during the 500-year anniversary of Columbus's "discovery" of America. In particular, Gomez-Peña foregrounds the dual origins of Chicano identity as vanquished Mexico and conquering Spain, marking the anniversary celebration as self-annihilating in a quentecentennial souvenir T-shirt, "Me cago en el quentecentennial (El Untranslatable Vato)." Similarly, Adrian Piper calls attention to her ability to "pass" as a light-skinned black woman, using her "Calling Cards" as a corrective to the casual racism among whites when they assume those around them are also white. More potently, Piper uses her known mixed-raced history to point out that the majority of Americans are likely to have African-American blood in their ancestry due to the antebellum rape of black female slaves by their white owners, calling attention to the precarious investment of racial borders in bloodline and skin color. In *Sally's Rape*, black performer Robbie McCauley stands nude on the auction block while Caucasian Jeannie Hutchins conducts the audience "bidding"; the latter's presence on stage with McCauley renders a liberal, sympathetic identification with McCauley by her white audience impossible, leaving them instead with the irrefutable evidence of their privileged racial status.

Background. With the rise to political and social power of the middle classes in the nineteenth century, accompanied by the disconcerting visibility of women in the public sphere, the concurrent rise of capitalism, and the influx of refugees from colonialism, the body became the primary site for bourgeois notions of individuality as well as for myriad concerns regarding containment of the body's potential excesses that symbolized comparable social transgressions. Hygiene as well as sexual morality became litmus tests for distinctions between the middle and working classes, and between desirable and undesirable social elements, seeming to necessitate those personal restraints increasingly imposed by the state by means of social norms defining the family, sexual morality, and physical and psychological health. Throughout the nineteenth and twentieth centuries the body was increasingly coded as a site of unpleasant digestive functions, odors, fluids, wastes, and secretions in need of concealment, deodorizing, sanitizing, and application of the infinite number of hygiene products by which the capitalist marketplace simultaneously created and alleviated anxiety surrounding the body.

Thus, it was no small offense in 1896 that the first word uttered on a Paris stage in Alfred Jarry's *Ubu roi* was "merde": even rendered in Old French, the scatological epithet led bourgeois audience members to riots and hysteria, and positioned the body as a crucial if controversial site for political opposition and commentary as an avant-garde gesture.

Indeed, the avant-garde objective, *épater le bourgeois,* provided the earliest body-oriented performative works during World War I, and event-structured art played a crucial role in the formation and definition of the modernist avant-garde as a confrontational instrument of social change. Live art in the context of avant-garde movements such as Dada, Futurism, Surrealism, and the Bauhaus constituted early counters to already conventionalized institutional frameworks of art production, including style, middle-class patronage, and exhibition standards. Cabaret Voltaire, where the term *Dada* originated, is significant inasmuch as the alterity of the cabaret as a live art site mirrors its national setting, Zurich, as a refuge from the Great War.

Cabaret Voltaire founder, Hugo Ball, recited his sound-poem *Karawane* wearing an ostentatious, if physically restrictive, costume: his limbs, head, and physique wrapped in cardboard cylinders, Ball had to be carried onto the stage. The transformation of Ball's body by the costume rendered his movements a simultaneously regal and mad illustration of the nonsense poem chanted in a solemn and liturgical manner. The juxtaposition of anarchic verbiage and physical constraint provides a metaphor for the psychological liberation sought by Dada in the face of catastrophic world events. Having determined that the war confirmed the corruption of bourgeois society, the Dadaists set out to raze bourgeois culture. The cabaret (1916–1919) provided a venue for an ad hoc and international group of artists, poets, musicians, and dancers to stage live art that proposed to be as irrational as the events that caused them all to seek refuge in Switzerland. Embracing chaos and irrationality, the Dadaists operated under an anti-aesthetic, refusing to produce objects or performances that could be consumed or easily understood by the bourgeoisie, whom they held responsible for the war of technology, progress, and rationalization gone awry. Through his correspondence and distribution of Dada periodicals Tristan Tzara disseminated the name "Dada," where it was adopted and applied by similar avant-garde groups to activities in Paris (1920–1922) and New York (1916–1920).

Dada events in Berlin (1917–1920) were considerably more political than other European and New York counterparts, due in part to Germany's defeat in the war as well as increased class conflict resulting in the brutal suppression of the Spartacist uprising and Workers' Councils. Less concerned with psychological liberation than with genuine political emancipation, Dada events in Germany took place in the street rather than in cafés and cabarets, and its members participated in street fights, demonstrations, riots, and generating propaganda rather than making art. Their hostility toward the ruling middle class was aimed at its political and military edifices rather than its aesthetic conventions as in George Grosz's masquerade as Death on the streets of Berlin and John Heartfield's insulting parade, rumpled and unshaven, in German military dress. The body in this context was condemned as half-man, half-automaton: mindless and robotic in its participation in the war from which it returned crippled and mechanized by artificial limbs. In the highly nationalistic context of postwar Berlin, Dada events were both more potent and more volatile: the effigy of a German soldier with a pig's snout hung from the ceiling of the first Dada fair in 1920 resulted in the prosecution of both Heartfield and Grosz.

The Dada horror of the mechanized body stands in stark contrast to Italian Futurism and its contempt for the body in the face of technological progress. Aligned with fascism, the Italian Futurists glorified and aestheticized war as a form of ethnic cleansing (Filippo Tommaso Marinetti, *War, the Only Hygiene,* 1911–1915). Similar to Dada, however, the complacent, bourgeois audience was the target of its deliberately obfuscating and offensive performances, which the Futurists felt were successful only when met with thrown vegetables or booing. Futurist ballet employed movement and costumes that suggested dynamism and the perfectibility of the human body via machinery. Futurism in Russia similarly glorified the mechanized body through costume, set, movement, and lighting. Likewise, Futurists in Russia promoted a break with traditional art; however, it was in the name of a technology as yet available and marked a desire to progress more fully into the electricity-fortified twentieth century proposed by Vladimir Lenin.

The term *sur-realist* was first used by Guillaume Apollinaire as a subtitle for his play *The Breasts of Tiresias,* which featured bodies that morphed and disintegrated in the midst of declarations of love. On the stage, the breasts of the bearded Tiresias were two balloons that were burst with a cigarette lighter. The group of artists who later took the name Surrealist followed Apollinaire's lead in their early acknowledgment of the transgressive nature of gender ambiguity and bodies that erupted or whose sexuality was socially disruptive.

Many in the Surrealist group, such as André Breton, had participated in earlier Dada events. In the wake of World War I, however, the apparently aimless anarchy of Dada produced no alternatives to the bourgeois order it despised. Among the first to read the writings of Sigmund Freud in

France, the Surrealists sought to mine the unconscious as a source for poetry and art as well as a source for political action. Having served in a neuropsychiatric unit treating shell-shocked soldiers, Breton became fascinated with madness and the ability of the unconscious to produce an alternative reality. Taking their cue from Freud, the Surrealists experimented with automatic writing and drawing, the latter producing the collectively drawn *Exquisite Corpse* in an attempt to access the unconscious.

The Surrealists looked to psychoanalysis, particularly its theories of sexuality, to counter bourgeois order and institutions, such as church- and state-sanctioned marriage and reproduction. Flirting with the objects of everyday life that Freud identified as genital symbols in his dream analyses, early Surrealist events concentrated on the excess of desire and the inability of the state, law, or clergy to contain and control it: the Surrealists sought psychological emancipation from bourgeois mores by liberating sexual desire. Unlike Dada, which operated at the level of pure chaos and nonmeaning, Surrealist performance, such as *S'il vous plaît*, coauthored by Breton and Philippe Soupault, was more insidious, providing audience members with recognizable characters, such as lovers, and identifiable plot elements, only to disrupt them with abrupt, discontinuous transitions in narrative, absurd dialogue, or anticlimactic and deliberately antiromantic conclusions or violent death. The correspondence between Surrealist performance and Surrealist film, such as *Un chien Andalou* and *L'âge d'or,* are obvious: romantic love is depicted as ugly or ridiculous while the continued frustration of sexual desire by a repressive society inevitably ends in murder.

The ballet provided yet another performance form subverted by the Surrealists, as *Mercure* (1924) was more mime than dance. Most notable was Pablo Picasso's elaborate costume, marionette, and set design, with which the male dancers merged, collage-like, into the scenery only to erupt symptomatically from the tableau with outsized breasts. Gender ambiguity remained a powerful resource for the Surrealists, and they continued to flaunt *entre-guerre* concerns with masculinity. Masquerading in hat, dress, and furs as the delicate Rrose Sélavy ("eros is life"), Marcel Duchamp extended his self-portrayal in drag beyond Man Ray's photographic documentation, even signing "Rrose Sélavy" to many of his readymades. The intermission at the Surrealist ballet, *Relâche* (Performance Canceled), featured René Picabia's film performance in a tutu in René Clair's *Entr'acte* (1924). While the parallel between the filmic shot beneath glass of the bearded Francis Picabia twirling and Namuth's of Pollock painting is irresistible, Surrealism's influence on Abstract Expressionism remained within the confines of automatism and the unconscious as sources for mystical and artistic expression, since Pollock, among others, inherited a particularly American macho horror of the "effeminacy" of European art.

Institutional Issues. Performance art's focus on the body in a society where the body is cause for so much anxiety has, in our contemporary era, raised numerous questions from conservative quarters as to the legitimacy of the artistic status of performance art. As such, contemporary public outrage over performance art bears witness to its avant-garde status. Performances throughout the 1980s by Kim Jones, the Kipper Kids, and Karen Finley, which involved gross displays of the body smeared with mud, food, and chocolate, have been dismissed as childish tantrums. Such performative displays of the body covered with food substances that all too clearly suggested excrescence were profoundly disturbing and easily dismissed by those who did not care to hear the message, and established that a century after Jarry's *Ubu roi* is not such a long time after all.

Finley's work in particular received considerable attention from conservative members of Congress and religious groups who scoffed at its appellation as "art" in order to justify its patriarchal and even legal censure. The ambiguously gendered "personas" that materialized during her trancelike performances held forth on rape, violence, and incest from the perspectives of both male perpetrator and female victim, the former all the more shocking in a woman's voice. Further, Finley symbolized culturally sanctioned gender abuse by stuffing canned yams up her ass or smearing her body with chocolate, the latter an angry commentary on the internalization of abuse by women in the form of eating disorders, including overdosing on laxatives. Thus, as Finley notes, such abuse victims symbolically equate themselves and their world with shit and exteriorize the otherwise culturally concealed female body.

Finley, along with John Fleck, Holly Hughes, and Tim Miller, is one of the "NEA Four" artists who sued the National Endowment for the Arts in 1990 for rescinding grant funds as a result of political pressure from conservatives and religious groups. Three of the four defunded artists were openly gay, whereas Finley subverted patriarchally sanctioned and acceptable images of women. In the case of each defunded artist, boundaries were clearly at stake—between "normal" and "marginal" sexuality and gender identity, between acceptable and unacceptable bodily functions, and between public and private. That blurring these gender and identity boundaries presents a legitimate threat to the established social and political order is witnessed by the fury unleashed by attempts to maintain those boundaries. In the wake of further NEA budget cuts and restructuring of grant allocation criteria, hardest hit are local theater, symphony, and dance companies in cities and towns too small to have the kind of subscription patronage of New York or Los Angeles, and who received the bulk of NEA funds, whose prestige in turn attracted corporate funds. For better or worse, individual artists, not to say controversial ones, are but a minute percentage of NEA budget recipients. The imminent demise of the NEA attests all too well to national and patriarchal stakes in maintaining those boundaries questioned by performance art.

Performance art often has been trivialized by mainstream culture (witness the recitation of Hugo Ball's *Karawane* by Marie Osmond on the television program *Ripley's Believe It or Not*) and by traditional art history, which superficially characterized it as yet another example of public nudity sanctioned during the flower-strewn, hippie free-love era of the 1960s. Performance art remains a vital medium at the end of the millennium, however, extending to arts activism, virtual reality, and sites on the World Wide Web. The overlap of performance art with issues explored by artists in related media such as dance (Yvonne Rainer), music (John Cage, Diamanda Galàs), film (Valie Export, Laurie Anderson), theater (Robert Wilson, the Wooster Group), and comedy and cabaret (Ann Magnussen, Reno), helps both to legitimate and confound performance art's exclusion from the museum and the art-historical canon.

By its very nature, performance art subverts the function of the museum and art history to legitimate aesthetic boundaries. In its refusal to produce either an art object for the market or museum, or the kinds of scripted texts and repeated narratives of theater, contemporary performance shares with early live art the embracing of a contingent existence in the margins of culture, which is to say, beyond institutional and aesthetic frames. Blurring the boundaries between media, art, and life, public and private, artist and audience, performance art problematizes the institutional structures of the museum, the art market, and art-historical practice whose function is to reinforce those very boundaries in order to justify their continued existence as realms separate from culture, politics, and class interests.

Similar to early twentieth-century cabaret, performance at the end of the century has flourished in nightclubs and in alternative spaces. Performance in the 1980s was indissociable from the club scene in New York, San Francisco, and Los Angeles, where performance art resided between musical acts, video, and comedians in front of beer-drinking crowds who alternated between jeering and indifference. Alternative spaces such as the Kitchen and PS 122 in New York, Real Art Ways in Hartford, and LACE and Highways in Los Angeles sprang up to accommodate the growing body of alternative work unwilling and unable to find a home in museums, while galleries, traditionally the site of pure art commerce, mutated into performance spaces. In the absence of an art object facilitating the exchange of capital for rent, these alternative spaces were dependent on the NEA for support, and it is these very spaces that feel the demise of the NEA most keenly.

In the absence of an object of performance, photographic documentation has come to bear the precarious burden of objecthood. Yves Klein's document-as-event, *The Leap into the Void* (1960), a photograph in which it appears as though the artist has swan-dived out of a second-story window, has since become a symbol of the circular logic inherent in the performance documentation on which the museum and art history have come to rely in their scramble to keep up. The duration of performance art through time and space renders it difficult to assimilate within the formal, comparative method of art-historical analysis and teaching. Further, photographic reproductions represent only isolated moments in the performance art event, and their posthumous existence relies heavily on nonvisual oral and textual narratives that are often second-, third-, even fourth- and fifth-hand accounts, some apocryphal and mythic in their construction, which in no way detracts from the "truth-value" of such accounts to the continued impact of performance art; photographic documentation of performances in slide reproductions resides uneasily under extant archival classifications such as "sculpture," "three-dimensional media," or "photography," recent catchall designations such as "New Art Activity," or, more often, "miscellaneous." Ironically, it was Klein's pseudodocument that graced the cover of the exhibition catalog *Action/Performance and the Photograph* (Los Angeles, 1993), which featured the photographic documents of performances themselves as unique, aestheticized, and commodifiable "art objects." The ephemerality of performance is equal only to the ephemerality of its ability to subvert these institutions, the latter of which continue to expand the parameters of art in order to maintain them.

Yet, performance continues to expand the boundaries of art events beyond the purview of institutional constraints and remains largely unaccounted for within the art-historical canon. Even a cursory glance at the bibliographic sources on performance art reveals little in the way of canonically inscribed scholarship. RoseLee Goldberg (1979/1988) remains the sole author of a "survey" text of Performance Art, granting legitimation to the term by applying it retroactively to early avant-garde live art and cabaret. A recent curatorial effort, *Outside the Frame* (1994), includes a self-consciously problematized curatorial directive and diverse "timeline," while Lucy Lippard's *Six Years* (1973) remains a landmark effort to describe the conceptually oriented field from which performance art emerged. Nascent acceptability has resulted in some monographic work in the context of performance art, yet even this conventional format bears the less conventional mark of its subject matter by the monographs' interdisciplinary approach or overtly political agenda.

Rather than becoming the object of traditional scholarship, the capacity of performance art to break frame and blur boundaries has instead carried over into recent privileging of "the performative" as an interdisciplinary category rather than a specific artistic subculture or history. In *The Object of Performance* (1989), Henry Sayre extends performance beyond a discrete body or type of work to describe a characteristic of the present-day avant-garde which he applies not only to his discussion of performances by Laurie Anderson, Carolee Schneemann, and Eleanor Antin, but to the photo-conceptual work of Cindy Sherman and Joel Peter Witkin. Peggy Phelan (1993), on the other hand, uses "performance" to describe a politics and strategy of representation, addressing not only performance work by Adrian Piper and Yvonne Rainer, but the self-imposed limits of the "visibility" of identity politics and the farcical performance of antiabortion demonstrations.

The earliest art-history courses on the history of performance art were taught in 1978 by RoseLee Goldberg at the School of Visual Arts in New York and in 1979 by Kristine Stiles at the University of California, Berkeley, almost a decade after Allan Kaprow established performance as a separate discipline at the California Institute of the Arts in 1970. Although others have followed suit, incorporating performance as part of the postwar survey course in art schools across the country, in academic art-history programs, performance art is still rarely part of the curriculum, although perhaps no less so than contemporary art until the last decade of the millennium. However, the impact of cultural and interdisciplinary studies on art history, the exigencies of the global AIDS epidemic, and the relative mainstreaming of sexual alterity, drag, and gender ambiguity in popular culture by music and movie industries, coupled with increasing attention to discourse on "the body," create a context in which the absence of performance art or performance studies from the museum or from art-history curricula creates a serious credibility issue. It is nonetheless clear that the incorporation of performance art within the museum or art-historical narrative can only be accomplished by reconsidering the very topography of the institutional discourse on art.

[*See also* Conceptual Art; Contemporary Art; *and* Installation Art.]

BIBLIOGRAPHY

Works by Performance Artists

Bronson, A. A., and Peggy Gale, eds. *Performance by Artists.* Toronto, 1979.
From Action Painting to Actionism: Vienna, 1960–1965. Kassel, 1988. Exhibition catalog.
Loeffler, Carl E., and Darlene Tong, eds. *Performance Anthology: Source Book for a Decade of California Performance Art.* San Francisco, 1980.
Nitsch, Hermann. *Orgien Mysterien Theater/Orgies Mysteries Theatre.* Darmstadt, 1969.
Performance: Another Dimension. Berlin, 1983. Exhibition catalog.
Russell, Mark, ed. *Out of Character: Rants, Raves, and Monologues from Today's Top Performance Artists.* New York, 1997.
Ugwu, Catherine, ed. *Let's Get It On: The Politics of Black Performance.* Seattle, 1995.

Other Sources

Battcock, Gregory, and Robert Nickas, eds. *The Art of Performance: A Critical Anthology.* New York, 1984.
Béhar, Henri. *Étude sur le théâtre dada et surréaliste.* Paris, 1967.
Carr, C. *On Edge: Performance Art at the End of the Twentieth Century.* Hanover, N.H., 1993.
Corvin, Michel. *Le théâtre de recherche entre les deux guerres: Le laboratoire Art et Action.* Paris, 1973.
Foster, Stephen C., ed. *"Event" Arts and Art Events.* Ann Arbor, 1988.
Goldberg, RoseLee. *Performance: Live Art, 1909 to the Present.* New York, 1979. Revised and enlarged as *Performance Art: From Futurism to the Present* (New York, 1988).
In the Spirit of Fluxus. Minneapolis, 1993. Exhibition organized by Elizabeth Armstrong and Joan Rothfuss.
Lippard, Lucy, ed. *Six Years: The Dematerialization of the Art Object from 1966 to 1972.* New York, 1973.
Melzer, Annabelle. *Latest Rage the Big Drum: Dada and Surrealist Performance.* Ann Arbor, 1980.
O'Dell, Kathy. *Contract with the Skin: Masochism, Performance Art, and the 1970s.* Minneapolis, 1998.
Outside the Frame: Performance and the Object: A Survey History of Performance Art in the USA since 1950. Cleveland, Ohio, 1994. Exhibition catalog.
Performance Art into the 90s. Special issue of *Art & Design* (Australia-New Zealand) 9/10 (September-October 1994).
Phelan, Peggy. *Unmarked: The Politics of Performance.* London and New York, 1993.
Pluchart, François. *L'art corporel.* Paris, 1975.
Sayre, Henry. *The Object of Performance: The American Avant-Garde since 1970.* Chicago, 1989.
Segel, Harold B. *Turn-of-the-Century Cabaret: Paris, Barcelona, Berlin, Munich, Vienna, Cracow, Moscow, St. Petersburg, Zurich.* New York, 1987.
Vergine, Lea. *Il còrpo come linguàggio: La "Body-art" e storie sìmili.* Translated by Henry Martin. Milan, 1974.

KELLY DENNIS

Feminist Performance Art

In 1964 for an event called *Meat Joy* Carolee Schneemann choreographed an orgiastic, ecstatic celebration of free love, with male and female bodies rolling around together in raw meat and fish, wet paint, and paper. A decade later in *Interior Scroll* (1975) Schneemann unfurled a long, sinuous scroll from her vagina and read from it a text about her exclusion from aesthetic discourse.

In between *Meat Joy* and *Interior Scroll* the women's art movement had been officially inaugurated through a series of activist events, art works, and organizations centralized primarily in Los Angeles (where the movement was extensive and institutionalized) and in New York. Hence, within the trajectory of feminist art history, Schneemann can be seen as having moved from a Fluxus exploration of human experience to a feminist interrogation of the ways in which the human is inscribed within sexual difference. Like Shigeko Kubota's Fluxus *Vagina Painting* ([1965], where the artist painted on the floor with a brush attached to her crotch), *Interior Scroll* subverts mythical, modernist conceptions of creation as inexorably linked to male artistic authority.

Performance has been among the most important strategies in the formulation of a feminist art practice. A visceral response to women's conventional objectification in "high" as well as "low" culture and to women's abuse, harassment, and oppression in the arenas of family and work, performance has also resonated as a means of attaining cultural authority through the active enactment of the woman artist's creative role. Through performance, in the terms of Simone de Beauvoir, women attempted to break away from their consignment to corporeal "immanence" and align themselves with the "transcendence" afforded male subjects in Western culture (*The Second Sex*, 1949). Phenomenologically, the female-body-in-performance articulated the female self as active participant in, rather than passive object of, culture; it insistently displayed the interdependence for both women and men of body and mind, self and other, subject and object.

Performance in its early forms (often called "body art" and involving only the artist and perhaps several other performers in simple, iconic scenarios), frequently carried with it a set of beliefs that, in retrospect, seems idealistic. Caught up in the excitement of coalition building and of discovering their nascent abilities as artistic subjects, many feminist body artists worked from the assumption that performance delivered the female body/self in an unmediated way to the audience and thus countered the "false" constructions of femininity in Western culture that had ostensibly been imposed on women. Body art was seen as a way for the artist to express her positively valued "female experience" directly to the audience—as in the spiritually inflected goddess performances of Mary Beth Edelson and Rachel Rosenthal or in Ana Mendieta's ritualistic *silueta* series, in which she imprinted her body on the landscape to revalue the association of women and nature.

But, while feminist performance in the 1970s was often ecstatically exploratory of women's bodies and sexual experiences, it was hardly only celebratory. Feminist body artists strategically examined a number of interrelated areas of women's oppression in incisively critical ways. Performances exploring women's victimization as objects of violence and abuse are the most striking in this regard: Gina Pane's *Sentimental Action* (1973), in which she lacerated her own arms to form rosettes or vulval pools of blood that read as externalized signs of her interior pain; Hannah Wilke's *S.O.S. (Starification Object Series)* (1974–1975), in which the artist molded wads of gum chewed by her audience into tiny cock-cuntlike "wounds" placed on her naked flesh; and *Ablutions* (1972) by Judy Chicago, Suzanne Lacy, Sandra Orgel, and Aviva Rahmani, in which a woman was bathed in raw eggs, earth, and blood to the sound of women's voices describing their experiences as rape victims.

In the more oblique *Waiting* (1971–1972), Faith Wilding rocked back and forth intoning a long list of events in women's lives ("waiting for someone to feed me . . . for menopause . . . for the pain to go away"), emphasizing the passivity that women often assume to survive in male-dominated culture. Works by Joan Jonas (*Mirror Check*, 1970), Barbara Smith (*Feed Me*, 1975), Martha Wilson (*I Make Up the Image of My Perfection/I Make Up the Image of My Deformity*, 1974), Ulrike Rosenbach (*Reflections on the Birth of Venus*, 1976), and Martha Rosler (*Vital Statistics of a Citizen Simply Obtained*, 1977) explored the negative effects of culturally and commercially inscribed ideals of beauty on women's sense of self. Mierle Ukeles's "maintenance" pieces from the 1970s, like the real-time domestic labor performances at *Womanhouse* (a feminist installation in Los Angeles in 1972), made explicit the unacknowledged drudgery that traditionally defines the lives of maids and housewives. All of these performances enacted so as to subvert the processes by which women are interpellated into positions of objectivity, passivity, and unacknowledged labor in Western culture.

In the 1970s, "female experience" was often strategically universalized in the attempt to form a coalition of women to fight patriarchy; this universalization had the unfortunate side effect of erasing differences among women (and inevitably of privileging the "femininity" of those who dominated feminist discourse: heterosexual, white, upper-middle-class women). Issues of sexuality—rape and sexual abuse, women's objectification and lack of sexual freedom—occupied white women artists, some of whom worked with men to interrogate the ways in which femininity is conventionally defined in relation to masculinity (Marina Abramovic with Ulay, Linda Montano, and Tehching Hsieh). But, aside from Kubota and Yoko Ono (whose *Cut Piece*, 1964, literalized the violation women experience as the objects of spectatorial desire), feminist artists of color largely avoided exploring issues of sexuality in public.

As Lorraine O'Grady has pointed out, the stakes involved in exploring the body/self for a woman of color living in Euro-U.S. culture (who may well have descended from women slaves forced to bare themselves publicly) are clearly different from those of white women, who have a more privileged, sometimes idealized, relationship to female nudity. Other avenues of exploration were mined by feminists of color. Adrian Piper's probing *Catalysis* series from the early 1970s, in which she moved throughout New York City performing herself in disgusting or offensive ways (with, for example, bubble-gum covering her face), addressed the ways in which race and gender position people as objects of loathing and desire. O'Grady crashed an artworld event through a pointed attack on the whiteness of the art world (in *Mlle. Bourgeois Noire Goes to the New Museum*, 1981), and Piper, Faith Ringgold, and Howardena Pindell donned whiteface in various performances, public events, and videos to examine the privileging of white women in culture at large and in feminism in particular. While a few white women—Nancy Buchanan and Eleanor Antin—became "black" through costuming and skin coloring to comment from the position of privilege on this same issue, by and large Ringgold and other women of color were accurate in assessing dominant feminist art discourse as resistant to acknowledging the ways in which race and class inflect gender relations.

Lesbian feminists have been open about exploring their desires and pleasures within contexts that they control (such as lesbian journals), but less interested in exposing themselves to mixed audiences (their expressions of female-to-female desire are perhaps too easily absorbed into heterosexual male pleasures). Unusual in its extended focus on lesbian experiences presented in a mainstream feminist context (the Woman's Building in Los Angeles in 1979), Terry Wolverton's *Oral History of Lesbianism,* a series of collaborative, consciousness-raising performances, explored lesbian relationships through personal narratives.

In the late 1970s and 1980s, a hegemonic shift occurred in feminist discourse toward a more rigorously, if narrowly, theorized notion of criticality drawn from Brechtian theories of distantiation and Laura Mulvey's formulative 1975 theory of the "male gaze." Loosely speaking, feminist writing and practice linked up with Marxian, psychoanalytic models of "critique" that demanded that feminist artists avoid representing or presenting the female body at all and, instead, concentrate on dislocating spectatorial pleasure (especially the objectifying male gaze). Feminist art, wrote "Mulveyan" art theorists such as Griselda Pollock and Mary Kelly, must at all costs avoid any reference to the female body or female experience, emphases that would align it with an "essentialist" conception of identity as biologically rather than socially determined.

Nonetheless, while the feminist body was thus largely suppressed in 1980s discourse and practice, artists such as Laurie Anderson, Cheri Gaulke, Karen Finley, and Holly Hughes continued to perform (the latter two were targets of governmental attacks on sexually explicit performance art in the early 1990s). The emphasis in their work, however, was no longer on the actual body of the artist; rather, these artists explored broader issues of feminist politics through mainly monologic narratives that were staged like traditional theater events. Anderson became a rock star as she merged an examination of how sexual difference is articulated through technology and language into the appealing and highly popular format of rock performance (as in *United States,* 1979–1983).

Cindy Sherman, one of the artists lauded in 1980s feminist discourse as a "feminist postmodernist" for her effective critique of the psychic structures through which the objectification of women takes place in patriarchal culture, is also one of the few artists visible in the 1980s whose work sustained a strong link to the body-art practices of the 1970s. In her performative "film still" series she posed provocatively in corny Hollywood scenarios, subverting the cinematic mechanism of the male gaze by positing herself ironically as "victim" within scenes constructed through a Hitchcockian, predatory camera eye.

In the 1990s, with the rise of interest in "performance theory" and the simultaneous transformation of feminism—its loss of authority on the broader cultural scene and its intensification into poststructuralist theoretical models in academic discourse—feminism's relationship to performance has shifted once again. Identity politics themselves—those perhaps "essentializing" but also empowering strategies of naming common to 1960s and 1970s rights movements—have begun to implode with the wide-scale questioning of policies such as affirmative action and feminism's self-interrogation of what it means to try to establish a notion of "women's" oppression or "female" experience. Judith Butler's poststructuralist ruminations on the "performativity" of gender, and Peggy Phelan's critique of the trope of visibility so foundational to identity politics theorize these profound shifts.

In the 1990s, as signaled by Butler's and Phelan's work, art has returned to the body. But the body now is not performed as a predictable material "fact" securing the artist's explorations of self. Thus, in the early 1990s *Post Porn Modernist* performances, professional sex worker Annie Sprinkle uses her body as an always already alienated (commodified) physical instantiation of herself; she enacts her body as a visible, material, but also ever elusive and unfixable aspect of her self—one that is never to be fully "known" (either by herself or by her clients/audience).

Through her assertive self-display, Sprinkle turns "objectivity" inside out, suggesting that feminist artists doing performance today seem to want neither to guarantee the full "presence" of the female body nor to erase it in a refusal of male pleasure; they seek, rather, to exaggerate the indeterminacy of the body as a guarantor of identity so as to open out its paradoxical role as physical or visible "proof" of lack or absence. Thus, performers Anna Devere Smith, Rhodessa Jones, and Marga Gomez exacerbate the gaps between and within their bodies/selves by multiplying themselves across numerous identities (male, female, Latino/a, black, Asian, Jewish, Anglo, rich, poor). They confirm what earlier artists such as Piper and Antin had suggested—that identity as such does not lodge within the body, but hovers at its margins, emerging in moments of intersubjective negotiation.

Feminists also have returned to video, a medium Lynda Benglis, Joan Jonas, and Valie Export explored to interesting ends in the early 1970s. Maureen Connor, Dorit Cypis, and Cheryl Donegan have exploited video's capacity to distance the body from both the artist (its "self") and the viewer in order to remark on the subject's alienation in cyberculture; in addition, this work examines the corollary fragmentation of codes of gender difference, pointing to the ways in which this alienation subverts idealistic conceptions of femininity as immanent.

The work of French feminist artist Orlan refuses immanence with a vengeance. In *Omnipresence* (1993), a videotaped performance event, Orlan has a plastic surgeon reconfigure her features according to facial components drawn from art-historical examples of "ideal" women. The viewer must watch Orlan's skin be separated from the fat, muscle, and bone that constitute her body. The question of where identity resides is disturbingly laid bare by this horrific disconnection of flesh (that layer of Orlan's self that reads as her face) and body. The self, like the other, becomes a projection, congealed only through ideology; femininity's "lack" propels itself onto the masculine.

In the 1990s the Nietzschean conception of femininity as artifice implodes through its very exaggeration. As feminist performance works such as Orlan's suggest (extending de Beauvoir's now fifty-year-old insight), a "woman" is something we become through cultural inscription, a constant exercise in sustaining (or performing) the fiction of "femininity." This fiction can be articulated so as to stabilize the conventional structures of gender difference or, as in the work of Pane, Wolverton, Piper, Gomez, or Sprinkle, to glory in their perversion.

[*See also* Feminism.]

BIBLIOGRAPHY

Adams, Parveen. "Operation Orlan." In *The Emptiness of the Image: Psychoanalysis and Sexual Differences.* London and New York, 1996.

Apple, Jacki. "Performance Art Is Dead: Long Live Performance Art!" *High Performance* 17.2 (Summer 1994): 54–59.

Butler, Judith. *Bodies That Matter: On the Discursive Limits of "Sex."* New York and London, 1993.

Carr, C. *On Edge: Performance at the End of the Twentieth Century.* Hanover, N.H., 1993.

Case, Sue-Ellen, ed. *Performing Feminisms: Feminist Critical Theory and Theatre.* Baltimore, 1990.

Chicago, Judy. *Through the Flower: My Struggle as a Woman Artist.* Garden City, N.Y., 1975.

Dolan, Jill. "The Dynamics of Desire: Sexuality and Gender in Pornography and Performance." *Theatre Journal* 39.2 (May 1987).

Elwes, Catherine. "Floating Femininity: A Look at Performance Art by Women." In *Women's Images of Men,* edited by Sarah Kent and Jacqueline Moreau, pp. 164–193. London, 1980.

Fuchs, Elinor. "Staging the Obscene Body." *Drama Review* 33.1 (Spring 1989).

Hart, Lynda, and Peggy Phelan, eds. *Acting Out: Feminist Performances.* Ann Arbor, 1993.

Jones, Amelia. "Interpreting Feminist Bodies: The Unframeability of Desire." In *The Rhetoric of the Frame: Essays on the Boundaries of the Artwork,* edited by Paul Duro. Cambridge, and New York, 1996.

Lippard, Lucy R. *From the Center: Feminist Essays on Women's Art.* New York, 1976.

Mulvey, Laura. "Visual Pleasure and Narrative Cinema" (1975). In *Visual and Other Pleasures,* pp. 14–26. Bloomington, Ind., 1989.

O'Dell, Kathy. "Fluxus Feminis." Unpublished manuscript of paper given at the Walker Art Center, Minneapolis, Minn. (February 13, 1993).

O'Grady, Lorraine. "Olympia's Maid: Reclaiming Black Female Subjectivity." In *New Feminist Criticism: Art/Identity/Action,* edited by Joanna Frueh, Cassandra Langer, and Arlene Raven. New York, 1994.

Phelan, Peggy. *Unmarked: The Politics of Performance.* London and New York, 1993.

Pollock, Griselda. *Vision and Difference: Femininity, Feminism, and Histories of Art.* London and New York, 1988.

Rosler, Martha. "The Private and the Public: Feminist Art in California." *Artforum* 16.1 (September 1977).

Schneemann, Carolee. *More Than Meat Joy: Complete Performance Works and Selected Writings.* Edited by Bruce McPherson. New Paltz, N.Y., 1979.

Stiles, Kristin. "Between Water and Stone/Fluxus Performance: A Metaphysics of Acts." In *In the Spirit of Fluxus,* edited by Janet Jenkins. Minneapolis, 1993.

Withers, Josephine. "Feminist Performance Art: Performing, Discovering, Transforming Ourselves." In *The Power of Feminist Art: The American Movement of the 1970s, History and Impact,* edited by Norma Broude and Mary D. Garrard, pp. 158–173. New York, 1994.

Wolverton, Terry. "Oral Herstory of Lesbianism." *High Performance* 2.4 (Winter 1979–1980).

AMELIA JONES

PERSPECTIVE. [*To explore the history, development, and current status of the notion of perspective, this entry comprises two essays:*

An Overview
Psychology of Perspective

The first essay is a historical and conceptual overview of (linear) perspective within art history, which is also the notion of perspective that has been most prominent in aesthetics. The second essay discusses contemporary theories of perspective and pictorial representation in cognitive science and shows their relevance to art history and aesthetics.]

An Overview

Perspective refers generally to the devices used by painters to represent space on plane surfaces. Perspectival devices include the use of gradients of hue, brightness, or texture to simulate the optical distortions involved in the perception of objects from a distance; such devices are known as "atmospheric" perspective. But more interesting to philosophers, traditionally, are the geometric procedures used by painters to project lines, planes, and solid bodies onto plane surfaces. One system in particular, known as "linear," "central," or "one-point" perspective, has proved highly effective and indeed has dominated Western painting since the Renaissance. Linear perspective measures the regular diminishment in apparent size of objects as their distance from a stationary beholder increases. The method was first propounded and applied by fifteenth-century Italian artists. The mathematics of perspectival projection was established in the seventeenth century by Gérard Desargues and other French geometers.

The ordinary linear perspective used by painters is nearly correct within certain limits, for instance, for representations of a sufficiently narrow field of vision (smaller than about thirty-seven degrees across). More thorough transformations require the more complete theorems of projective geometry. But even correct perspective does not reproduce the results of actual perception. Perspective fails to take into account the effects of binocularity, the anatomically governed distortions and unclarity at the margins of the visual field, and the movement of the eyes and head. Only under very special conditions will the beholder of a perspectival projection actually be deceived. And since the main purpose of Western oil painting has been to represent fictional spaces rather than to create actual illusions of space, the strict correctness of the perspectival projection has not always been a major concern, even for Renaissance and post-Renaissance Western painters. Only at isolated moments has perspectival correctness been considered indispensable to the effectiveness or value of a painting. In fact, inaccurate or incomplete methods of projection are often used deliberately to produce desired pictorial effects or to display spatial information more clearly: for example, when architectural drawings use so-called isometric or non-convergent perspective, whereby straight lines in a given dimension are all drawn to the same scale and orthogonals are set a fixed angle.

The earliest written account of perspectival projection is found in the treatise *De pictura* (1435) of Leon Battista Alberti, a Florentine humanist and architect. Alberti defined a painting as "the intersection of a visual pyramid at a given distance, with a fixed center and certain position of lights, represented by art with lines and colors on a given surface." This conception of the painting as the transcription of an imaginary "picture plane" suspended between the beholder and the viewed scene was revolutionary. It linked the art of painting to the sciences, in particular to medieval optics and to Euclidean geometry. Alberti then explained how to draw a tiled floor on a plane surface so that it would appear to recede into the distance at a fixed rate. The floor would serve as a measured grid on which bodies, including human figures, could be placed in their proper scale and spatial relation to one another. Italian painters had been placing figures on squared floors for more than a century, often with considerable accuracy. But they seem to have used trial and error and workshop tricks rather than a theoretically grounded procedure. Alberti first explains the "picture plane" by comparing it to a window intersecting the bundle of light rays emanating from the world and converging on the eye of a stationary viewer (the "viewing point"). Then he explains how to construct the grid of the tiled floor as it appears foreshortened on the picture plane. The grid is plotted along both axes, first by connecting the points along the front of the original grid with the viewing point, and then by connecting the points along the side of the grid, seen in elevation, with the viewing point. This became known as the "plan and elevation" method or *costruzione legittima*. In the resulting projection, any lines perpendicular to the picture plane (the "orthogonals") will converge on a single point (the "centric point," later known as the "vanishing point"). The horizontal running through the vanishing point came to be called the "horizon."

Much of the rest of Alberti's treatise on painting explained how to construct pictorial narratives in virtual spaces, often on small panels and without illusionistic intent. Accurate diminishment of forms within these virtual spaces would contribute to the clarity of the pictorial narrative, which was especially crucial if mythological or historical subject matter was to compete with the familiar Christian narratives. Italian painting had been intensely occupied with the representation of boxlike interiors ever since Giotto, and this interest contributed to the development of Alberti's method.

An interest in surveying techniques and in representations of exterior views of buildings or cityscapes, meanwhile, may have led to the mysterious perspectival experiment conducted by the Florentine sculptor and architect Filippo Brunelleschi around 1415–1420. According to his biographer, Brunelleschi prepared two panels representing public buildings in Florence in correct perspective and meant to be held up in the field of vision while standing on the appropriate spots in the city. If used properly, the panels were supposed to replace reality with convincing illusions. The account does not reveal how Brunelleschi constructed his images, but he may well have been using the very method later explained by his friend Alberti.

One of the uses for linear perspective in Renaissance and post-Renaissance painting was the representation, usually directly on walls, of plausible continuations of architectural space. The *Trinity* (c.1426) by the Florentine painter Masaccio, for example, shows a hypothetical vaulted chapel extending beyond the wall it is painted on, in real dimensions. Later examples include the ceiling of the Camera degli Sposi in Mantua by Andrea Mantegna (1465–1474), with an oculus opening onto the sky and ringed by peering figures; the walls of the Sala delle Prospettive in the Palazzo Farnesina by Baldassare Peruzzi (1516–1517), which open onto painted views of Rome; or the many Baroque ceilings painted *dal di sottu in sù*, most famously the dome and nave of Sant' Ignazio in Rome by Andrea dal Pozzo (1688–1694). Such entertaining visual tricks often depend on the beholder occupying a fixed standpoint. It should be noted that those frescoes, panels, or canvases painted in perspective that do not strive for trompe l'oeil effects, that is to say, the great majority of perspectival pictures, do not require the beholder to stand in a particular spot in order for the perspective to look correct.

The other main perspectival construction devised in the Renaissance was the so-called distance point or third point method. This simpler procedure relies on the fact that the two vanishing points of lines making forty-five-degree angles with the picture plane stand at a distance from the center of the horizon equal to the distance from the viewing point to the center of the horizon. The painter chooses a point on the horizon line at the desired distance, and then determines the diagonals of the squares on the checkerboard by drawing lines that converge on that point. Like the plan and elevation method, this procedure provides the measurements of the squares in the floor grid and permits the painter to place objects and figures on the floor in true scale. The distance point method was first expounded in print by the French amateur Jean Pélerin (known as Viator) in his treatise *De artificiali perspectiva* (1505). A similar procedure had been demonstrated by the Paduan humanist Pomponius Gauricus in his *De sculptura* (1504). Distance point methods clearly derived from workshop traditions dating back to the time of Giotto. Their exponents generally did not share Alberti's interest in optics or in such abstract notions as the picture plane.

The next important theorist of perspective after Alberti was the painter Piero della Francesca. Piero, a student of mathematics, refined and improved on Alberti's method in his treatise *De prospectiva pingendi* (c.1474), and addressed in detail the problem of the proportional diminution of forms as they receded in space. The German artist Albrecht Dürer seems to have been especially affected by Piero's ideas. In the pages on perspective in his mathematical treatise *Underwyssung der Messung* (1525), Dürer demonstrated the full plan and elevation method. He also offered a more practical shortcut ("the shorter way") that combined *costruzione legittima* with the distance point method.

Leonardo da Vinci left hundreds of remarks on perspective in his notebooks. Leonardo notably worried about perspective's failure to account for the perceived curvature of straight lines at the margins of the visual field. He argued that differences in apparent size of objects ought to be governed by the angles subtended by the objects at the viewing point, and not by the lengths of their intersections of the picture plane, as in standard linear perspective. Certainly, the discrepancy between the two ways of calculating the ratios increases as the viewing angle increases, that is, at the edges of the picture. In general, Leonardo was interested in the limits of perspective's power and in all the other factors besides perspective that contribute to depth perception. Apparently to compensate for the flaws in the standard system, Leonardo made a number of adjustments to the perspective of his *Last Supper* fresco, resulting in an unintelligible fictive space.

The problem of wide-angle vision did become a major theme in the critique of linear perspective throughout its history. Some perspectivists offered systems for mapping curved lines onto the picture plane. There are two main reasons why curvilinear perspective did not supplant linear perspective as the standard method. First, it is not clear that we ever do perceive straight lines as curved. Second, if we do, then the extreme edges of pictures done in ordinary linear perspective will themselves appear distorted and therefore correct.

It has been argued that the discovery of perspective by Brunelleschi and Alberti, together with the writings of Piero, Leonardo, and Dürer, represented a singular moment when the fine arts made an actual contribution to the history of science. In the sixteenth and seventeenth centuries many more artists and amateurs wrote treatises on perspective. Some of the most important were Jean Cousin's *Livre de perspective* (1560), Daniele Barbaro's *La pratica della perspettiva* (1569), and Giacomo da Vignola's *Le due regole* (1583). But the theorems of projective geometry established in the seventeenth century did not directly derive from the earlier researches and writings of the painters. Before 1600, in fact, there was no theory or proof of the vanishing point at all. Nor did the extravagant perspectival illusions of the Baroque ceiling painters draw on the recent findings of the mathematical perspectivists.

Perspective became a basic feature of the academic training of painters. The pioneering Florentine and Roman academies of painting, founded in 1563 and 1593, offered instruction in mathematics. Representational painters ever since have acquired the basic principles of linear perspective with more or less enthusiasm. Few modern artists have devoted much attention to the deeper puzzles of perspective. The British painter J. M. W. Turner did teach perspective at the Royal Academy, but somewhat unsystematically. The American Thomas Eakins was perhaps the last major painter to make a serious study of perspective.

Western painting, it is fair to say, has only intermittently insisted on correct linear perspective. Even a perspective maven like Dürer rarely bothered to apply the method consistently in his paintings and prints. Painters routinely adjusted the correct perspective in order to avoid undesired visual effects. And the painters who did construct precise perspectives were often pursuing a personal inclination or an aesthetic ideal rather than a pedagogical or epistemological imperative. Giorgio Vasari, the first historian of Italian art, observed disapprovingly that the painter Paolo Uccello took an excessive delight in the method of linear perspective. Uccello ornamented his narrative pictures, for example, with dead bodies and broken lances lying neatly along orthogonal lines, producing highly implausible pictorial fictions. Perspective for some, in other words, became an end in itself.

Perspective made it possible to construct virtuoso illusions with bits of inlaid wood (a technique known as marquetry or intarsia); to depict complex polygonal objects from any point of view; to construct fantastic but vividly detailed architectures and cityscapes; to show human bodies sharply foreshortened from unfamiliar angles. Part of the appeal of perspective in the Renaissance, evidently, was the sheer delight taken in the formal tension between the objective pattern on the two-dimensional plane and the virtual space generated by reading the pattern as a projection. Perspective also made possible the ingenious device of anamorphosis, whereby an object is depicted from an unnaturally oblique point of view. When the picture itself is then observed from an angle, the two foreshortenings cancel each other out and the object looks normal.

Perspective proved a powerful rhetorical device in the hands of major painters. A vanishing point met by a bundle of unobstructed orthogonals can serve as an emblem of infinity. An eccentric vanishing point, as in some compositions by Tintoretto, can give an effect of drama and violent movement. The precisely constructed paintings of the theorist Piero della Francesca, by contrast, exude rationality, mastery, and cool detachment; this inevitably affects the response to the subject matter, whatever it might be. Some seventeenth-century Dutch painters (e.g., Pieter Saenredam) became famous for perspectival views of luminous church interiors; it is arguable that these complex and precise constructions themselves constituted the true subject matters of the pictures.

Early twentieth-century painters decisively repudiated the supposed ambition of earlier Western painting to reproduce optical experience. Ever since, linear perspective has been the principal emblem of that abandoned ambition. In twentieth-century thought, painterly perspective, with its hypothesis of a fixed and stationary beholder, its respect for the evidence of the senses, and its endowment of a subjective point of view with objective validity, has in turn been repeatedly enlisted as an emblem for Western empiricism, rationalism, individualism, anthropocentrism, or relativism. A central contention—found in Martin Heidegger's "Age of the World Picture," for example—is that the picture constructed according to a fixed point of view is the historical correlative and complement of subjectivity itself. For Heidegger, "what belongs properly to the essence of the picture is standing-together, system" (Heidegger, 1977, p. 141); and the constitution of the world as a picture "is one and the same event with the event of man's becoming *subiectum* in the midst of that which is" (p. 132). Perspective has long been used by modern philosophers as a metaphor for the conditions of knowledge, for example, by Gottfried Wilhelm Leibniz and Friedrich Nietzsche. The overall persuasiveness of such metaphors, however, does not seem to depend on more specific observations about the invention of linear perspective or its application in painting.

The first detailed challenge to the unique epistemological legitimacy of Western perspective was the art historian Erwin Panofsky's "Perspective as 'Symbolic Form'" (1927). Panofsky believed that curvilinear perspective produced a more accurate representation of our optical impressions. He therefore reasoned that the overwhelming success of the less accurate method, Alberti's linear perspective, must reflect the peculiar demands and conditions of Renaissance and post-Renaissance European culture. Panofsky saw each perspectival system as an expression or "symbolic form" (a concept borrowed from the philosopher Ernst Cassirer) of the culture that devised it. According to Panofsky, linear perspective's achievement was to have efficiently negotiated between the objecthood of the viewed scene and the subjecthood of the beholder. But the model for this epistemo-logical reconciliation was the Kantian "category," the cognitive framework that makes possible the mind's very apprehension of the world. Panofsky did not dismiss Immanuel Kant's epistemology as a mere "symbolic form" of European culture, but rather accepted it as a fundamental philosophical truth. Therefore, Panofsky's assessment of perspective is contradictory and his relativism limited.

Panofsky's thesis that perspective is a mere convention of the post-Renaissance West, however, was adopted and radicalized by later writers. Rudolf Arnheim in *Art and Visual Perception* (1954) argued that the "funnel" produced by the convergence of the orthogonals on the vanishing point in many Renaissance paintings is "a violent imposition" and a distortion "not caused by forces inherent in the represented world itself" (Arnheim, 1974, p. 294). Such paintings are thus "manifestations" of Renaissance individualism and of a "hierarchical conception of human existence." The classic philosophical statement of the relativist position is found in Nelson Goodman's *Languages of Art* (1976). Goodman argued that "the behavior of light sanctions neither our usual nor any other way of rendering space" (p. 19). He pointed out that in linear perspective lines parallel to the picture plane—for example, the vertical edges of a tall building—remain parallel, although in reality such lines will appear to converge. In general, he maintained that "no degree of resemblance is sufficient" to establish a relationship of reference between picture and an object (p. 5). For Goodman, then, linear perspective is a conventional procedure that needs to be learned to be understood. The phenomenologist Maurice Merleau-Ponty also repudiated perspective as a mode of seeing overlaid on top of perception by culture. Merleau-Ponty said that "Renaissance perspective is a cultural fact, that perception itself is polymorphous, and that if perception has become Euclidean, it is because it has let itself be oriented by the system." The idea of the conventionality of perspective has become a commonplace in much recent Continental and Anglo-American thought and has played a major role in the critical assault on painting as an art form, in the field of film theory, in ideology-critique, and in feminist and psychoanalytic theories of the image and the gaze.

Many other writers on perspective have tried to refute or modulate this extreme conventionalism. Ernst Gombrich in *Art and Illusion,* for example, used the findings of perceptual psychologists to show that linear perspective produces effective illusions of the appearance of the world. This basic confidence in the uniquely successful and indeed objective nature of perspectival projection is shared by Decio Gioseffi, Samuel Edgerton, Jr., and Michael Kubovy, among others. Western pictorial perspective is presented by these writers as a limited but legitimate application of geometric principles that enjoy universal validity.

A major intervention in the debate on perspective is Hubert Damisch's recent *Origin of Perspective*. For Damisch, linear perspective is the fundamental scene of Western painting's philosophical ambitions, namely, to participate, alongside other sign systems, in the constitution of subjectivity. Perspectival painting, by positing a grammatical subject, a second person, and even a third person (in the "distance point"), reproduces the basic conditions of intersubjectivity. Following Jacques Lacan, Damisch argues that perspective stages the originary "capture" of the subject in the gaze. Thus, perspective for Damisch is neither a mere simulation of our optical impressions of the world, nor a mere cultural imposition, but a model or machine that reveals the structure of the mind to itself, independent of the particular historical circumstances of its discovery or use.

[*See also* Alberti; Gombrich; Goodman; Panofsky; *and* Renaissance Italian Aesthetics.]

BIBLIOGRAPHY

Arnheim, Rudolf. *Art and Visual Perception: A Psychology of the Creative Eye.* Exp. rev. ed. Berkeley, 1974.

Damisch, Hubert. *The Origin of Perspective.* Translated by John Goodman. Cambridge, Mass., 1994.

Edgerton, Samuel Y. Jr. *The Renaissance Rediscovery of Linear Perspective.* New York, 1975.

Elkins, James. *The Poetics of Perspective.* Ithaca, N.Y., 1994.

Gioseffi, Decio. *Perspectiva artificialis.* Trieste, 1957.

Gombrich, E. H. *Art and Illusion: A Study in the Psychology of Pictorial Representation* (1960). 2d rev. ed. Reprint, Princeton, N.J., 1969.

Goodman, Nelson. *Languages of Art: An Approach to a Theory of Symbols.* 2d ed. Indianapolis, 1976.

Heidegger, Martin. "The Age of the World Picture." In *The Question concerning Technology,* translated by William Lovitt, pp. 115–154. New York, 1977.

Kemp, Martin. *The Science of Art: Optical Themes in Western Art from Brunelleschi to Seurat.* New Haven, 1990.

Klein, Robert. "Pomponius Gauricus on Perspective" and "Studies in Renaissance Perspective." In *Form and Meaning,* pp. 102–128, 129–140. New York, 1979.

Kubovy, Michael. *The Psychology of Perspective and Renaissance Art.* Cambridge and New York, 1986.

Merleau-Ponty, Maurice. *The Visible and the Invisible.* Edited by Claude Lefort, translated by Alphonso Lingis. Evanston, Ill., 1968.

Panofsky, Erwin. *Perspective as Symbolic Form.* Translated by Christopher S. Wood. New York, 1991.

White, John. *The Birth and Rebirth of Pictorial Space.* 3d ed. Cambridge, Mass., 1987.

CHRISTOPHER S. WOOD

Psychology of Perspective

A painter who wishes to represent a scene must convey at least two of its aspects: (1) its layout, including information about the viewer's implied station point, and (2) the solid shape of the objects in the scene. The artist may also choose to represent four additional aspects of the scene: (3) the illumination of the scene, including information about the number of sources, their location, their intensity, and their color; (4) the medium's tendency to absorb and diffuse light; (5) object color; and (6) surface texture (e.g., is it fur,

or is it skin?), including information about temporary features such as wetness.

These types of information are not independent. Consider the following three examples:

Since the atmosphere absorbs red light more than blue light (aspect 4), the artist may paint distant objects bluer than close ones, and thus provide the viewer with layout information (aspect 1).

If the scene is illuminated by the sun (aspect 3)—a strong light source at infinity—the artist may use shadows to provide the viewer with information about layout (aspect 1).

If the scene is illuminated by a weak source, such as a candle (aspect 3), the artist may use chiaroscuro to convey the solid shapes of the illuminated objects (aspect 2).

It may appear that there is a single procedure that suffices to convey the layout of a scene (aspect 1): construct the picture in accordance with the laws of perspective. For the historian, the existence of a single solution to the depiction of layout is plausible because perspective was invented at a known time (c. 1411), at a known place (Florence), by a known person (Filippo Brunelleschi). For the mathematician, it is also plausible, inasmuch as perspective consists of a coherent collection of rules implied by the axioms of projective geometry.

Cognitive scientists, on the other hand, do not treat perspective as a single device that conveys the layout of a scene. They think of pictorial representation as a collection of tricks, each of which triggers the response of one or more specialized modules in the visual system. As a result, perspective is neither a necessary nor a sufficient condition for felicitous representation.

First, we will see that the use of perspective is not a sufficient condition for the adequacy of a depiction. For instance, whenever three lines in a picture intersect to form an arrow juncture or a fork juncture (Figure 1) we tend to see them as a rectangular trihedron, that is, three orthogonal planes meeting at a point, like the corner of a cube. We see them this way, however, only insofar as they satisfy D. N. Perkins's laws (Perkins, 1968, 1972), summarized in Figure 1: the measure of each of the three angles of a fork juncture may not be less than ninety degrees; the measure of each of the two angles of an arrow juncture may not exceed ninety degrees; their sum must exceed ninety degrees. These are not laws of perspective, and can be violated by drawings in perspective.

When a picture violates Perkins's laws, the objects in the scene seem distorted. Consider an engraving by Jan Vredeman de Vries (1604–1605; see Perkins, 1968), illustrating his 1599 treatise on perspective (Figure 2). Even though this picture adheres to the rules of central projection, it looks distorted. We have no reason to think that Figure 2 is a rep-

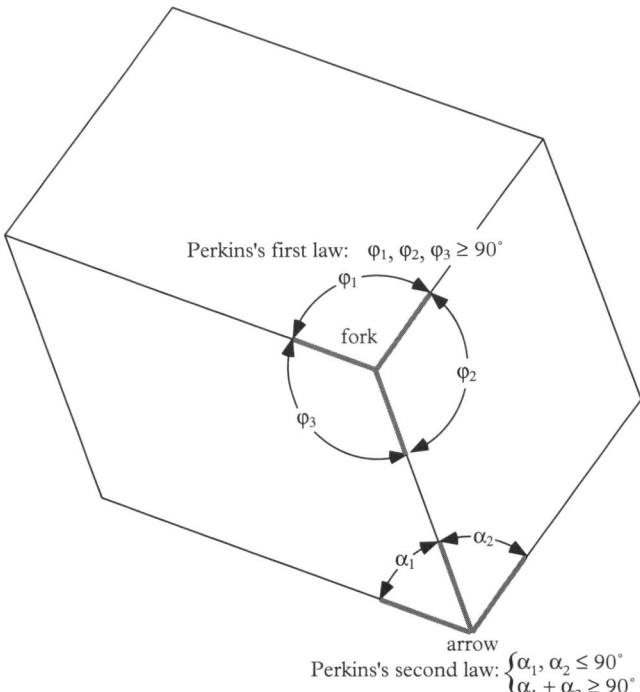

Perkins's first law: $\varphi_1, \varphi_2, \varphi_3 \geq 90°$

φ_1

fork

φ_2

φ_3

α_2

α_1

arrow

Perkins's second law: $\begin{cases} \alpha_1, \alpha_2 \leq 90° \\ \alpha_1 + \alpha_2 \geq 90° \end{cases}$

FIGURE 1. *Arrow and fork junctures, and Perkins's laws under which these junctures are seen as cubic corners.*

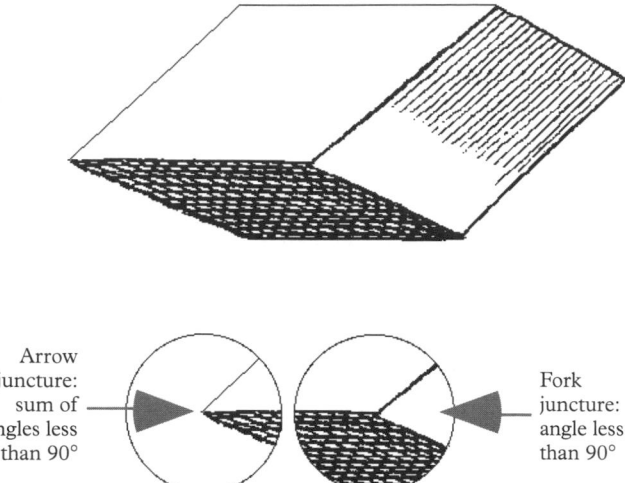

Arrow juncture: sum of angles less than 90°

Fork juncture: angle less than 90°

FIGURE 3. *Completed block at the base of the leftmost column in Figure 2.* The block does not look like a right parallelepiped because its depiction violates Perkins's laws.

resentation of a strange structure whose columns diverge from one floor to the next. So something must have gone wrong with the depiction. We assume that the base of each column is a right parallelepiped (a solid with six faces, each a rectangle and each being parallel to the opposite face). Let us examine the base of the leftmost column in Figure 2 more closely. Figure 3 shows this base completed and reveals that its arrow and fork junctures violate Perkins's laws.

Now we will see that the use of perspective is not a necessary condition for a depiction to be adequate. Figure 4 appears to be the depiction of a triangular frame. Upon scrutiny this frame reveals itself to be inconsistent. What we see—a closed triangular frame—could never be constructed as a closed triangular frame. Therefore, Figure 4 is a perspective representation of an object that could not exist. We

FIGURE 2. *Plate 22 from de Vries's* Perspective, *Part II.* The area marked by a circle is analyzed in Figure 3. The picture is a correct application of the rules of perspective, but it looks distorted.

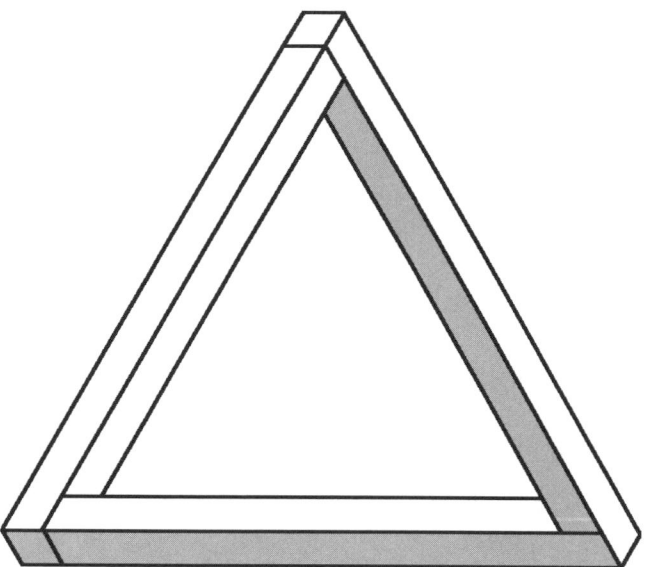

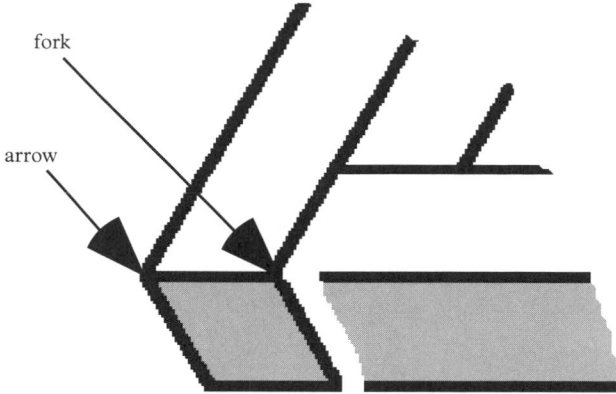

FIGURE 5. *Detail of the lower left-hand corner of the impossible object.*

FIGURE 4. *An impossible object.* The object shown seems to have a definite solid shape, and its angles all appear to be right angles, because its depiction conforms to Perkins's laws.

see it as a representation of an object because it conforms to Perkins's laws (see Figure 5).

If the use of perspective is neither necessary nor sufficient for the adequacy of a depiction, we have reason to view skeptically the two positions that have made perspective a focal point of debates in aesthetics: the thesis that perspective is the standard of adequate representation, held by E. H. Gombrich (1972) and James J. Gibson (1960, 1966,

pp. 231–234), on the one hand; and its antithesis that perspective is conventional, held by Erwin Panofsky (1991) and Nelson Goodman (1976), on the other.

The reader should not conclude, however, that it is equally wrong to argue the affirmative and the negative in this debate. Cognitive scientists have amassed considerable evidence against the conventionalist position. For instance, the preponderance of the empirical evidence argues against the relevance of Panofsky's concern that we see straight lines as curves, whereas in perspective straight lines project as straight lines (for a recent introduction to this topic, see J. E. Cutting and P. M. Vishton, 1995). Furthermore, we can readily disprove (Kubovy, 1986, pp. 122–125) Goodman's pivotal claim that it is no easier to learn to see the layout of

FIGURE 6. *Plate 1 from de Vries's* Perspective, *Part II.*

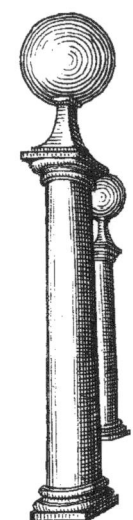

FIGURE 7. *Occlusion (detail of Figure 6).* The closer column occludes the farther one.

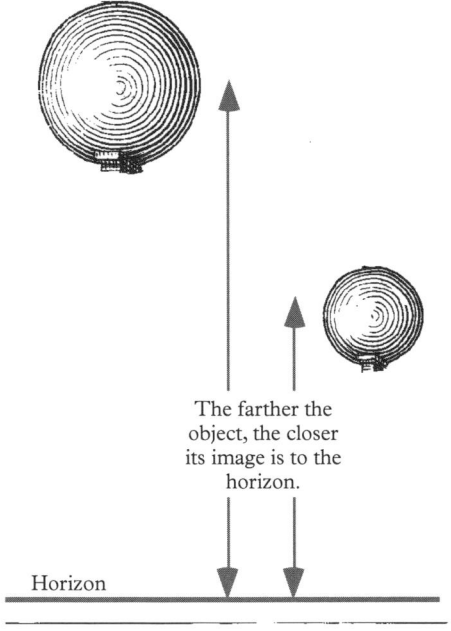

FIGURE 8. *Proximity to the horizon (detail of Figure 6).*

scenes represented in perspective than to learn how "to read pictures drawn in reversed or otherwise transformed perspective" (Goodman, 1976, p. 15).

In contrast, the Gombrich-Gibson position errs on the side of overgeneralization. As we saw earlier, pictorial representation draws on a repertoire of tricks, called pictorial layout cues (PLCs, or sometimes, less felicitously, pictorial depth cues) that trigger specialized perceptual modules. All these tricks are consistent with projective geometry.

We will now describe four PLCs, using Figure 6, another engraving by de Vries: occlusion (Figure 7), which provides depth-order information—one column is closer than the

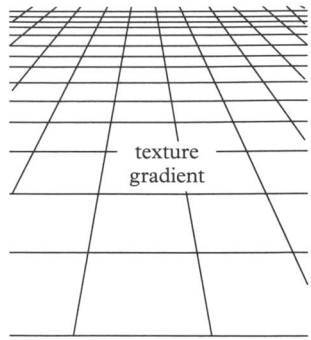

FIGURE 9. *Texture gradient (detail of Figure 6).*

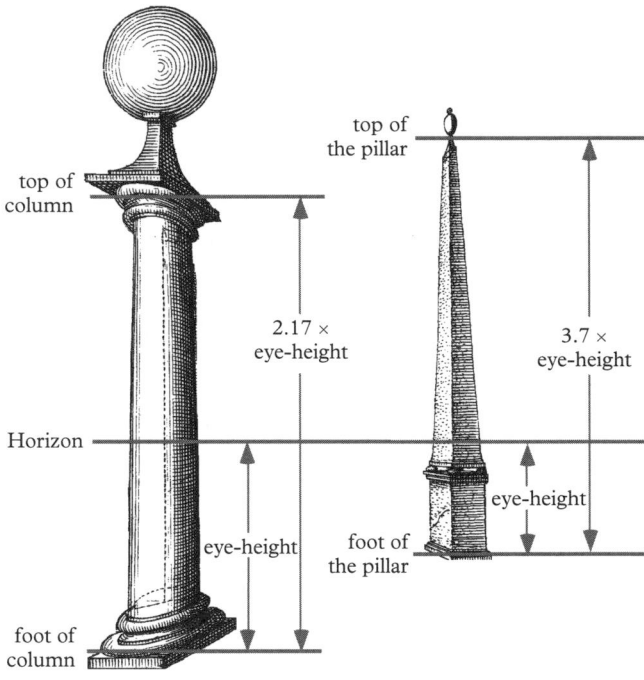

FIGURE 10. *Horizon-ratio relation.*

other—but does not convey a quantitative impression of distance; proximity to the horizon (Figure 8): the farther an object, the closer its image is to the horizon; texture density gradient (Figure 9): the pictorial size of texture elements of uniform texture decreases with distance; horizon-ratio (Figure 10): without evidence to the contrary, the viewer assumes that the horizon represents the eye level of a person standing on the ground level. The viewer automatically infers the height of objects in the scene, in units of eye height. Empirical evidence shows that these PLCs operate more or less independently of each other.

[*See also* Psychology of Art.]

BIBLIOGRAPHY

Cutting, J. E., and P. M. Vishton. "Perceiving Layout and Knowing Distances: The Integration, Relative Potency, and Contextual Use of Different Information about Depth." In *Perception of Space and Mo-*

tion edited by William Epstein and Sheena Rogers, pp. 69–117. Handbook of Perception and Cognition, vol. 5. San Diego, Calif., 1995.

Gibson, James J. "Pictures, Perspective, and Perception." *Daedalus* 89 (1960): 216–227.

Gibson, James J. *The Senses Considered as Perceptual Systems.* Boston, 1966.

Gombrich, E. H. *Art and Illusion: A Study in the Psychology of Pictorial Representation* (1960). 2d rev. ed. New York, 1961; reprint, Princeton, 1969.

Goodman, Nelson. *Languages of Art: A Theory of Symbols.* 2d ed. Indianapolis, 1976.

Kubovy, Michael. *The Psychology of Perspective and Renaissance Art.* Cambridge and New York, 1986.

Panofsky, Erwin. *Perspective as Symbolic Form* (1924–1925). Translated by Christopher S. Wood. New York, 1991.

Perkins, D. N. "Cubic Corners." *MIT Research Laboratory of Electronics Quarterly Research Report* 89 (1968): 207–214.

Perkins, D. N. "Visual Discrimination between Rectangular and Nonrectangular Parallelipipeds." *Perception and Psychophysics* 12 (1972): 396–400.

Vries, Jan Vredeman de. *Perspective* (1604–1605). New York, 1968.

The author wishes to acknowledge the support of NIMH (R01 MH47317).

Michael Kubovy

PHENOMENOLOGY. Phenomenology has and may continue to be a rich source for creative work in the fields of the philosophy of the arts (development of concepts for criticism of the various arts) and aesthetic theory (conceptualizing the epistemological, ontological, and axiological foundations of judgments about the arts). Whether or not one agrees with the programmatic of the phenomenological method as enunciated by Edmund Husserl and developed by his followers, the various theoretical formulations to be found in the writings of Husserl, Martin Heidegger, Edith Stein, Roman Ingarden, Maurice Merleau-Ponty, Jean-Paul Sartre, and the others who worked within this mode of analysis constitute a fertile field for reflections about central issues in the fields: representation, the meaning of aesthetic terms, the nature of aesthetic experience, the epistemological status of aesthetic verdicts, and the ontological grounding of aesthetic judgments.

The term *phenomenology* may be traced throughout the modern period in philosophy, with widely differing conceptions of its nature marking its successive appearances within the philosophical literature. There are two central meanings of *phenomenology*. In one sense, the term stands for a purely descriptive investigation of any object. Sources for this meaning may be found in the writing of William Hamilton in the mid-nineteenth century and in Charles Sanders Peirce in the earliest years of the twentieth century. Such descriptive activity is not restricted to real objects but applies as well to any content of consciousness. In another sense, *phenomenology* names a way of philosophizing. This latter meaning will be the focus here.

The intuitive core of the meaning of the term as naming a systematic method in philosophy is that phenomenology is the science of phenomena. For Johann Lambert of the mid-eighteenth century, phenomenology is a theory of illusion where the term *phenomena* stands for illusory features of experience. For G. W. F. Hegel in *Phenomenology of Spirit* (1807), phenomenology became a method for apprehending something real, that is, coming to know mind as it is in itself via phenomena, where phenomena are the ways in which mind appears to consciousness. In by far the most influential formulation of the meaning of *phenomenology,* Husserl argued for a view that this science of phenomena is the most fruitful way to pursue any philosophical investigation.

For Husserl, phenomenology is a presuppositionless descriptive study of phenomena (in a special sense of the term). Nonempirical in its approach, the objects it describes are essences that are apprehended by intuition. Phenomenology is nonempirical in that although it is a descriptive activity, a phenomenologist does not seek to describe empirically observable matters of fact. Such empirical facts are known only with a certain degree of probability, whereas the phenomena that phenomenology investigates are known with certainty. Phenomenological statements are arrived at, not by inductive generalizations or derivation from unexamined assumptions, but by apprehending phenomena via intuition in immediate experience. Phenomena are, however, not sense data or uninterpreted sensory objects. For phenomenology, any object is a phenomenon if apprehended in a particular way, namely, in conjunction with a process called reduction.

The presuppositionless aspect of phenomenology is supposed to be provided by the method of reduction. When one undertakes a reduction (bracketing or utilizing the *epoché*, different but related actions), there obtains a suspension of a belief in the existence of the objects to be described. As Eugene F. Kaelin puts it, "The subject must 'bracket the world' i.e., suspend belief in the reality of the real, physical world and hold in check the propensity to appeal to facts or laws of the sciences describing the real world." (Kaelin, 1970). Reduction is thus not to be conflated with Cartesian doubt (a method promulgated by the French philosopher René Descartes). Suspending a belief in the existence of an object that is bracketing the thesis of the natural standpoint, is not doubting the existence of the object. With the object bracketed, it becomes a phenomenon that may be described by the phenomenologist. Husserl would have phenomenologists utilize not only the reduction but also a process called free imaginative variation in order to describe phenomena. The objects described by those who would use the phenomenological method are essences in that what is described under a suspension of the thesis of the natural standpoint and in light of free imaginative variation are necessary and invariant features of a given kind of object.

Another feature of the phenomenological program is that statements about phenomena, that is, descriptions arrived at under the condition of the reduction, are statements about intentional acts. Consciousness is characterized in phenomenology as intentional in that it is always consciousness of something whether or not that something exists or not. The phenomenological program for Husserl thus consists in describing what is given to us in experience without the intervention of preconceptions or hypothetical speculations. We are, in a celebrated motto, asked to return to the things themselves. For Husserl, the only way out of the impasse into which philosophy had been led at the end of the nineteenth century, under the influence of a certain type of realism that insisted on the independent existence of the object and the influence of the idealists who made the subject the locus of the properties of the object, was a turn to a purely descriptive activity of what is given to consciousness, while affirming the thesis of intentionality—namely, that consciousness is always consciousness of something.

In the second volume of his *Ideas,* drafted in 1912 but not published until 1952 and not translated into English until 1990, Husserl presented a complex picture of the human self that when applied to problematics in aesthetics would provide a conceptual map of the relationship of self to art. It has often been thought that Heidegger and Merleau-Ponty, in different ways, overcame the Cartesian dualism in Husserl's theory of the self, but there was really no such dualism in Husserlian phenomenology. Later phenomenological accounts of the self proceed from Husserl's original conception: Heidegger's conception of being-with *(Mitsein)* in *Being and Time* (1927), Sartre's look of the other in *Being and Nothingness* (1943), and Merleau-Ponty's concept of the lived body in *The Phenomenology of Perception* (1945). *Ideas II* was a work known to all of these later phenomenologists.

In theorizing about the nature of the self, Husserl develops a monism of the self substance, the I, and a pluralism of aspects of that one substance. This complex aspect theory of the self stands in contrast to that of René Descartes wherein mind and body are distinct substances. In this phenomenological aspect theory, the mental and physical sides of experience are two aspects of a single event. Insofar as they are acts of consciousness, these events are understandable by means of intentionality, their directedness toward an object whether or not that object exists. This aspect theory of the self stands not only in opposition to Cartesian dualism, but also departs from a view of the self such as that of Immanuel Kant, who theorized the self as having its locus in a transcendental unity of apperception beyond the reach of any kind of apprehension except "thinking" it to be there.

Husserl's monism of substance and pluralism of aspects involves a complex and rich array of distinctions. The bodily aspect of the one individual human being is further divided into *Korper,* the physical body, and *Leib,* the living body. The mental aspect is further divided into *Seele,* the soul, *Geist,* the spirit, and the pure I, which is also called "the transcendental Ego," the locus of intentionality. My physical body, the material I, is my body qua physical. By contrast, my living body, the animate organism I, is this body insofar as it is living: my body is articulated by intentional attributes of volition and kinesthesis. The soul, the psychological aspect of myself, is that aspect of my living body that animates it; soul and physical body form a psychophysical animal unity. My spirit is I insofar as I am a human being, an embodied, personal, social, and cultural being who belongs to the life-world, the surrounding world defined not by science but by the possibilities and constraints of everyday life. The empirical I is the I as it appears to ourselves when we adopt what Husserl called "the natural attitude," that attitude toward things shaped by frameworks of common sense and natural science. Finally, the pure I is I qua subject of intentional experiences or acts of consciousness.

These distinctions among aspects of the one substrate reflect phenomenological distinctions among different ways we know, experience, and conceive of our minds and bodies. Psychology is viewed by Husserl as a natural science. It studies experiences so as to account for their role in nature. By contrast, phenomenology studies experiences from a first-person perspective through intuition of one's own experiences and their contents. The distinctions among aspects of the one substrate provide a basis for drawing distinctions between the natural sciences such as psychology, the human sciences, which study spirit, and phenomenology, which studies consciousness. In this ontology of the self, the soul depends on the physical body in that the soul is the psychic I that moves the physical body. The spirit is an ensouled and embodied I; the human I acts in the life-world. In this life-world, I find values and practicalities. I find works of art beautiful, and I find hammers useful. These distinctions are to be found in Heideggerian distinctions between mere things and tools. Cultural objects such as those with beauty as dealt with in aesthetics belong to the cultural world.

Empathy plays an important part in the Husserlian theory of the self. Husserl's concept of empathy has influenced, directly or indirectly, some of the most important phenomenological work. Edith Stein extended Husserl's account of empathy into a wide-ranging theory in *The Problem of Empathy* (1917). There, empathy consists in reproducing imaginatively the form of the other's experience. Empathy is the means by which we understand the motivations of others, both emotional and rational. Empathy is an attitude adopted insofar as the I is a spirit, that aspect of ourselves involving our membership in the life-world. In appreciating a drama, we adopt the spiritual attitude using empathy to apprehend the inner life of the characters. Husserl speaks of the role that the object plays in the experience in the following passages from *Ideas II:* "I experience the stimulus of the beautiful and I am motivated to turn to it, to pay attention to it, to take pleasure in it" (Husserl, 1991). With respect to our side of the experience, Husserl says:

> I am, in empathy, directed to the other Ego and Ego life and not to psychophysical reality, which is a double reality with physical reality as the found level. The other's body is for me a passageway . . . toward the understanding of the Ego there, the he. . . . The human being appears but I am focused on the human subject . . . in its nexuses of motivation.

Finally, of the spiritual aspect of ourselves, which is the locus of our empathetic relation to characters in an artwork, Husserl says: in the spiritual attitude I have as my exclusive theme purely and simply the subjects and their surrounding worlds . . . for the Chinese a symphony of Beethoven does not exist and is therefore not determining for them.

In subsequent developments of phenomenology and in the application to aesthetic theory and the philosophy of the arts, each thinker took a certain aspect of Husserlian phenomenology and either developed it or took a criticism of it as a departure for the formulation of their own theories.

For Heidegger, phenomenology remained a descriptive activity in which philosophical investigation starts with description devoid of obscuring preconceptions, of the nature of human existence. For Heidegger, however, the phenomena described in this purely descriptive activity reveal themselves in their relation to Being; they will reveal themselves if we do not coerce them into conceptual frameworks that reflect an estrangement from Being. For Heidegger, the descriptive activity must not proceed in a fashion as it did with Husserl in a context of an epistemological subject-object distinction. The art object is neither a represented object nor an expression of something within the subject, a feeling, an idea, and so on. Heidegger's *Dasein* is always already in the world; it does not seek an external form for something already within. The relation of inner and outer becomes transfigured into a relation with Being. The origin of the work of art is not in some inner vision within the artist or within the spectator but in the truth of Being that is already out there. Heidegger's aesthetic theory is a departure from the aesthetic tradition since Kant. He believed that modern aesthetics had lost connection with the central problem of Being by making beauty a merely optical phenomenon as well as imbedding its analysis in an unjustifiable subject-object distinction.

With Ingarden, there is a more direct application of Husserlian phenomenology to the theorization of the work of art. Ingarden analyzes the work of art as an intentional object. Fictional objects are classified as a kind of purely intentional objects, specifically consciousness-dependent entities obtaining in a different mode of being than ordinary spatiotemporal objects. In one notable analysis *(Controversy concerning the Existence of the World)* that Ingarden takes as his departure point, the Husserlian analysis of part/whole relationships (which Husserl develops in his *Logical Investigations*), Ingarden accepts Husserl's notion of moments but

expands on it with a series of distinctions among "existential moments": inseparateness/separateness, derivation/originality, contingency/self-dependence, heteronomy/autonomy. With these concepts of existential moments in hand, one may analyze the ontological differences between fictional objects and ordinary spatiotemporal objects.

Merleau-Ponty wanted to use the phenomenological method inherited from Husserl but alter it so as to acknowledge our lived bodily presence to the world. In Merleau-Ponty's view, Husserlian phenomenology dwelt in the realm of consciousness to the neglect of bodily incarnation. In developing a conception of the lived body, Merleau-Ponty aimed to orient phenomenological attention away from the Husserlian emphasis on single perceptions, logic, geometry and science, and toward intentionalities of body, desire, gesture, speech, and the entire range of human symbolic activities. In order to bring about this reorientation of phenomenology, Merleau-Ponty focuses on the phenomenological structures of perception. For instance, he invites an emphasis on the surface of a work of art. This surface is registered in the body as it intends an object in a sensuous field. This embodied dimension must be a central aspect of any analysis of the aesthetic experience. For Merleau-Ponty, perception is a fullness of real, embodied, ongoing relationship with the world; it is not outside that world but fully in it. In accordance with this vision, he regards painting as paradigmatic of the character of our condition of being in the world. Marjorie Grene states his view as follows: "Painting . . . as the art of and through vision, it displays as no other activity can the single equivocal unity of a person, a unity which Merleau Ponty expresses in the phrase le corps vécu, the lived body" (quoted in Merleau Ponty, 1993, p. 224).

Whereas Merleau-Ponty demonstrates a contunuity between perception and imagination, Sartre sets them in opposition. The notion of the intentionality of consciousness becomes a basis for Sartre to argue for the transcendence of the ego and against a supposed illusion of immanence. Sartre accepts the Husserlian method of reduction but only on a limited basis. He will follow him with the first two reductions but not the third. The reduction for Husserl takes three forms: phenomenological, transcendental, and eidetic. In the phenomenological, the aim is to focus attention on consciousness and its experiences while correspondingly turning attention away from external objects. In transcendentally reducing, an elimination of empirical or naturalistic assumptions about the stream of consciousness occurs. In the eidetic reduction (eidetic derives from *eidos*, meaning "essence"), there occurs a generalizing of the results attained through a transcendental study of consciousness. Reduction is thus a way of narrowing the scope of inquiry. The conclusion that Husserl had arrived at with the third reduction is that consciousness is never actually pure consciousness, for it is always existent as a locus for intentionality. As Sartre sees it, the ego is being granted a permanence that transcends the purity of consciousness as such. The reduction was supposed to suspend belief in existence, yet the third reduction confirms the existence of the transcendental ego. Sartre's aim is to show that the transcendental field of consciousness, purified of the existence of the ego, is really nothing: "since all physical, psychophysical, and psychic objects, all truths, all values are outside it; since my me has itself ceased to be any part of it. But this nothing is all since it is consciousness of all these objects" (Sartre, 1936).

From this view about the nature of the ego and consciousness, Sartre draws conclusions about the distinction between perception and imagination. In the case of perception, the object perceived is given against a background of the totality of reality. In contrast to this mode of givenness is the mode for the imagined object. Instead of being given against the totality of the real, the imagined object is given precisely as absent; that is, it is given as something that is nothing in relation to the background of real things. For Sartre, for the imagination to posit an image over against reality, it is necessary that consciousness not be "engulfed in the real." Consciousness must disentangle itself from reality in order to posit the image, for the image could only be one further real item unless it is a nothing in relation to the real. As he puts it: "For a consciousness to be able to imagine it ꞯust be able to escape from the world by its very nature, it ᴧust be able by its own efforts to withdraw from the world. In a word it must be free" (Sartre, 1962).

The artistic imagination, for Sartre, accordingly becomes essentially unfulfilled. Artists project what they lack onto their work; when they give their work the illusory quality of concreteness, this quality is due to perception. Like pure consciousness, the imagination is essentially spontaneous and active, but it can be diminished into what Sartre calls a "fascinated imagination."

In utilizing phenomenological concepts in analyzing aesthetic theoretical issues or developing metacritical concepts for appreciation and evaluation of the arts, it will be necessary to determine the viability of the phenomenological method as well as the centrality of the method to the epistemological and ontological grounds for the concepts. Even if one does not subscribe to the phenomenological program, the rich array of concepts that have issued from the movement may find other grounding and prove illuminating for the conceptual tasks in the field of aesthetics.

[See also Dufrenne; Heidegger; Husserl; Ingarden; Merleau-Ponty; and Sartre.]

BIBLIOGRAPHY

Primary Sources

Descartes, René. *Meditations de prima philosophia*. Paris, 1641. Translated as *Meditations on First Philosophy* by Elizabeth Haldane and George Robert Thomson Ross, edited by Stanley Tweyman (London and New York, 1993).

Hamilton, William, S. *The Metaphysics of Sir William Hamilton*. Edited by Francis Bowen. Boston, 1861.

Heidegger, Martin. *Sein und Zeit*. Tübingen, 1927. Translated as *Being and Time* by John Macquarrie and Edward Robinson (New York, 1962).

Hegel, Georg Wilhelm Friedrich. *Phänomenologie des Geistes*. Hamburg, 1830. Translated as *Phenomenology of Spirit: Selection*, by Howard P. Kainz (University Park, Pa., 1994).

Husserl, Edmund. *Logische Untersuchungen* (1900). 2d ed. Halle, 1913–1921. Translated as *Logical Investigations* by John Neimeyer Findlay in 2 vols. (New York, 1970).

Husserl, Edmund. *Ideen zu einer reinen Phänomenologie und phänomenologischen Philosophie*. Halle, 1913. Translated as *Ideas: General Introduction to Pure Phenomenology*, by W. R. Boyce Gibson (New York, 1962). *Ideen zu einer reinen Phänomenologie und phänomenologischen Philosophie, zweites Buch*. Drafted in 1912, revised in 1915 and in 1928, first published in German in 1952. Translated as *Ideas Book II* by Richard Rojcewicz and André Schuwer (Dordrecht and Boston, 1991).

Ingarden, Roman. *Der Streit um die Existenz der Welt*. Tübingen, 1964. A translation of *The Controversy concerning the Existence of the World*, vol. 1, by Helen R. Machejda is included in a volume under the title *Time and Modes of Being* (Springfield, Ill., 1964).

Kaelin, Eugene F. *Art and Existence: A Phenomenological Aesthetics*. Lewisburg, Pa., 1970.

Kant, Immanuel: *Kritik der reinen Vernunft*. Riga, 1781. Translated as *Critique of Pure Reason* by Norman Kemp Smith (Reprint, New York, 1965).

Lambert, Johann Heinrich. *Opera mathematica*. Turici, 1846.

Merleau-Ponty, Maurice. *Phénomenologie de la perception*. Paris, 1945. Translated as *Phenomenology of Perception* by Colin Smith (New York, 1962).

Merleau-Ponty, Maurice. *The Merleau-Ponty Asthetics Reader: Philosophy and Painting*. Edited by Galen A. Johnson, translation edited by Michael B. Smith. Evanston, Ill., 1993.

Peirce, Charles Sanders. *Collected Papers*. 6 vols. Edited by Charles Hartshorne and Paul Weiss. Cambridge, Mass., 1960.

Sartre, Jean-Paul. *La transcendance de l'ego. Recherches philosophiques 6* (1936–1937). Translated as *The Transcendence of the Ego* by Forrest Williams and Robert Kirkpatrick (New York, 1957).

Sartre, Jean-Paul. *L'imaginaire*. Paris, 1940. Translated as *Imagination: A Psychological Critique* by Forest Williams (Ann Arbor, 1962).

Stein, Edith. *Zum Problem der Einfühlung*. The Hague, 1917. Translated as *On the Problem of Empathy* by Waltraut Stein (The Hague, 1952).

Other Sources

Carr, David. *Interpreting Husserl: Critical and Comparative Studies*. Dordrecht and Boston, 1987.

Casebier, Allan. *Film and Phenomenology: Toward a Realist Theory of Cinematic Representation*. Cambridge and New York, 1991.

Dufrenne, Mikel. *Phénomenologie de l'expérience esthétique*. Paris, 1953. Translated as *Phenomenology of Aesthetic Experience* by Edward S. Casey (Evanston, Ill., 1973).

Follesdal, Dagfinn. "Husserl's Notion of Noema." *Journal of Philosophy* 66.20 (16 October 1969): 680–687.

Smith, Barry, and David Woodruff Smith, eds. *The Cambridge Companion to Husserl*. Cambridge and New York, 1995.

Sobchack, Vivian: *The Address of the Eye: A Phenomenology of Film Experience*. Princeton, N.J., 1992.

Spiegelberg, Herbert. *The Context of the Phenomenological Movement*. The Hague, 1981.

ALLAN CASEBIER

PHOTOGRAPHY. [*To analyze the history, technology, and aesthetics of photography, this entry comprises five essays:*

> An Overview
> Daguerreotype
> Photography and Technology
> Photography and Digital Technology
> Catachresis

The first essay is an overview of the history and current status of photography aesthetics. The second explains the daguerreotype and its role in the development of photography. The third essay concerns the technology of photography or, rather, photography as technology. The fourth essay explains the relationship between the aesthetics of photography and that of digital media, as this relationship is now central in shaping the aesthetics of photography, both in theory and practice. The final essay examines in depth the problem of catechresis (false metaphor) in photography, that is, the misuse of the term objectivity *in discussions of photography. For related discussion, see* Barthes; Bourdieu; Digital Media; Film; Mimesis; Realism; *and* Representation.]

An Overview

The term *photography* designates a number of distinct processes, most of which were designed to produce pictures on suitably treated supports by means of changes initiated by light or other forms of electromagnetic radiation. The earliest attempts at making what came to be called photographs began at the end of the eighteenth century, while the first successful, though primitive process for making pictures by means of light-sensitive coatings date to the early 1820s. The first practical processes—Louis-Jacques-Mandé Daguerre's daguerreotype, and William Henry Fox Talbot's photogenic drawing, the barely useful forerunner of modern negative/positive systems of photography—were invented in the 1830s and made public in 1839.

Understanding the motivations of the inventors of these processes does not reveal much about the character of the pictures they were able to produce, but it is nonetheless suggestive of the problems involved in gaining an appreciation of the conceptual, aesthetic, and historical issues involved in coming to terms with photography. Daguerre and Talbot saw their pictures as continuous with the tradition of picture making preceding them; each viewed his new process as a replacement for drawing pictures by hand, and each wrote of having invented means of fixing the image of the camera obscura, the forerunner of modern cameras. This inspiration for the invention of the processes—fixing camera imagery—might best be thought of as an enabling confusion. The leading idea of the inventors was not merely to make pictures by means of the action of light on a suitably prepared light-sensitive surface, but to secure "the" image of the camera ("a delicate, fairy picture," as Talbot called it) by somehow rendering it permanent. There are, however, strong reasons working against figuring photographic pictures resulting from camera exposures as stabilized images—quite apart from the obvious fact that they typically fail to look at all like the images on a ground glass (e.g., the products of in-camera exposure, after chemical treatment, are most typically negatives). Perhaps the primary reason for not identifying a photograph as the fixation of the image formed in a camera is that in most instances, there is no image that could usefully be thought of as a candidate for fixation. Take, for example, an early picture made in 1838, looking down at a vacant Parisian street from a window in Daguerre's studio. The exposure of the plate took about fifteen minutes, during which time people and horse-drawn carriages moved freely on the street and along the sidewalks. The daguerreotype, however, fails to show any figures, carriages, or anything else that moved during the exposure. The idea that photographs are simple records of preexisting camera images is tantalizing and was certainly productive for the inventors, but on examination, it turns out to be fantastic. Likewise, Talbot's notion that the negatives produced by exposing sensitized paper in his primitive cameras were pictures made by the objects they represented is similarly tempting, and equally fantastic.

One aspect of the reception of photography that is often overlooked is that despite the acclaim with which its products were greeted, and notwithstanding the often claimed "marvelous" and "prodigious" character of the pictures and the "inhuman detail" they provided, very few people saw any practical advantage to adopting photography over the older graphic media. The novelty of producing drawings by photographic means was insufficient by itself to create a market for them. Within two years of the publication of the inventions, however, each of the chemical processes had been sufficiently changed to permit relatively brief exposures (ranging about ten seconds in diffuse sunlight), and this encouraged the establishment of a commerce in the production of photographic portraits—primarily daguerreotypes. About a decade later, the invention of collodion wet plate photography brought an end to the production of daguerreotypes and prints from Talbot's improved paper negative system. Uniformity of print production via collodion negatives was established by the mid-1850s, and this brought with it large-scale photographic publication and the near-complete commercialization of the field.

Although the history of photography, understood as a history of technological change, is reasonably easy to follow, its social history is rather complicated. The first audience for the inventions of Daguerre and Talbot were the French Chambers of Deputies and Peers, the Academies of Science and Beaux-Arts, and the Royal Society in London. The initial reviewers of the processes were educated and prominent, and the discussions of the inventions were carried on in a relatively exalted environment. However, as photography was commercialized and the vocation of photographer was established by the mid-1850s as an occupation for low-level entrepreneurs and shopkeepers, critical attention to photography nearly disappeared and was replaced by an attitude of inattention. This stance reflected a more general snobbishness about the threatened disappearance of handicraft and its replacement by the products of industrial mass production. In the early years of photographic practice, prints were made on matte papers in various hues, and some purchasers confused them with engravings—which they were made to resemble. Beginning in the mid-1850s, however, photographic prints underwent a transformation: they took on a gloss—at first just a slight luster and then a very highly glazed, apparently machined surface—while the hues of the prints were uniformly restricted to the sepia-red, or purple-black range. Photographs came increasingly to look machined and mass produced, although they were made by hand. Photography itself came to be figured as a technical craft, one that required certain material skills, but that dispensed with the kind of talent then supposed to typify the production of works of art. It was quietly assimilated into the culture, becoming part of the assumed background of industrialized societies.

The idea that there is something mechanical about photography dates back to the period of invention as does the vague, though often advanced, notion that photographs are made automatically. These ideas are at the heart of continuing debates about its character and its legitimate use for the production of works of art. Although countless authors, most notably Walter Benjamin, have dismissed or recast the question of the possibility of making photographs that are works of art, the issue continues to haunt discussions about photography. One problem with addressing the question is that its most basic terms have been left unanalyzed.

What precisely does it mean to say that photographs are produced mechanically, or that they are made automatically? Part of the problem here centers on the characterization of photographs in terms of drawing, or copying by hand. What seems to be missing from any reasonably correct description of how a photograph is made is some account of how it is drawn. It seems right to think of photography as a kind of mechanical or automatic drawing, but there is no drawing in photography. The curious thing about making a photograph is that none of the actions a photographer takes in setting up a picture and making the exposure has any immediate pictorial result, in the way that making a painting constantly involves drawing marks onto a canvas, erasing and redrawing them, applying paint, scumbling, and so on. In making a photograph, the photographer loads film into the camera, arranges the items to be photographed, moves lights around, and then after setting the lens and shutter, makes the exposure. At this point there is absolutely nothing pictorial to show for all the effort. The next step, most usually done in complete darkness, is to develop the film, and it is here, finally, that something pictorial

takes shape, though it is in most cases, a negative and somewhat disappointing as a picture. The negative is then exposed very briefly to a sheet of white paper (which shows no sign of the exposure), and is inserted into a developer, whereupon—both predictably and magically—it appears and is completed in a matter of seconds. Writers advancing the notion of photography's inherent automatism want us to attend to the moment of exposure, the point at which all human agency ceases in the production of the picture. It is at this point, the moment at which agency seems to cease, that the automatic character of photography is said to take over.

It is difficult to know how to respond to this kind of argument. It is useful, though perhaps not terribly so, to insist on some account of "automatic" that would allow us to see just what it is that photography is said to do by itself. Most automatic devices substitute for work done by hand, or foot, or in times past, by animals. An automatic transmission replaces the hand- and footwork needed to engage and change gears, and similarly, an automatic rifle takes over the handwork of sliding the bolt forward, firing the round, sliding the bolt backward, advancing the next round, and so on. Similarly, in modern cameras, *auto focus, auto advance,* and *auto exposure* designate specific functions previously done by hand (and in the case of auto exposure, the judgment of the photographer is replaced as well). In other words, automatic devices like these perform activities in stages, by means of specifiable units—gears, cranks, pneumatic tubes, motors—which accomplish the desired action. In the case of *auto* as it appears in *automobile,* the Greek term functions to mark something about the source of the power—the vehicle can move itself, it does not need a horse to serve as a means of propulsion. There is a machine—the jacquard loom—that makes designs and pictures by itself, but for reasons that are not entirely clear, it has never been called an "automatic picture-making machine." The problem with thinking of photography as automatic is that it does not fit our generally accepted notions of what an automatic mechanism is or what it does. Photography is not an automatic way of drawing pictures, although photographs may substitute for handmade pictures and may even outperform them in various settings.

What is it, then, that is supposed to be mechanical about photography? The answer here is that in some reasonably straightforward sense, photographs are not handmade. This is perfectly true, but does not, by itself, separate photography from many other kinds of production. Lightbulbs and golf balls, infants and flowers, spider webs, volcanoes, commercial peanut butter, and mass-produced bread, among many other things, are not handmade. The claim that photographs are not handmade fails, by itself, to specify how they are made. What it does suggest, however, is that photography is best not conceived of as a form of mechanical or automated drawing.

The search for a general definition of photography has been complicated by the impulse of many authors to satisfy what they take to be the commonsense notion of what photographs are. The assumption here is that we have a single, generalized, albeit vague, notion about photographs that merely stands in need of precise formulation, but the supposition is incorrect. We have many different intuitions about what photography is and are quite facile in bringing one or another of them to bear on any particular picture. Unfortunately, each of these hunches is not always happy in the company of the others. One common intuition is that photographs stand in a special relation to the objects they represent. It is an easy step from this belief to the general proposition that photographs have a unique object relatedness, that a photograph can only show things in the world. We might suppose, for example, when looking at advertising photographs of food, that the pictures are traces or indexes of the things portrayed, and that a photograph of a cooked ham stands in the relation of effect to the cause provided by the photographed ham. Generalizing this notion, we might suppose that all photographs are indexes of objects in the world. This general proposition might seem to work for certain kinds of photographs—still lifes—but will not work at all for pictures made, for example, by photographing moving objects at slow shutter speeds. Imagine a car moving parallel to a camera during a one-second exposure. The resulting photograph shows an amorphous, unidentifiable blur in the middle of an otherwise well-delineated street. The blur is not an index of the car, at least not in any useful sense of the term. For the blur to function as an index (if we adhere, as we should, to C. S. Peirce's notion of indexicality), it would have to signify the car—would have to stand in relation to the car as effect to known cause—but it does not, because it cannot do this. To anyone accustomed to looking at photographs, the blur suggests that something moved past the camera during exposure, but knowing that it was caused by some moving thing provides no clue to the identity of the thing. If the blur is a trace, it is the trace of something unknowable. The impulse, at this point, to counter by arguing that the blur was indeed caused by something and that that thing was the action of light on the film only makes matters worse, since it is always light and never objects in the world that produces changes in photographic emulsions. To insist that all photographs are veritable indexes of the action of light is merely to repeat the obvious; *photograph* is a conjunction of Greek words and means "mark produced by light." It is a form of marching in place.

The idea that photographs stand in some special relation to what we see, or to the "visible facts of the moment," has been in circulation for nearly the entire history of photography. Charles Baudelaire, in his famous essay "The Salon of 1859" claims that photography is an industrial, technical skill and opposes it to the ideality that he supposes is at the core of painting considered as an art. For Baudelaire and for many of his contemporaries, photography is necessarily superficial, chained to the visible world. The oddness of photography for Baudelaire and for Edgar Allan Poe before him, is that it shows us what is in front of our eyes, if only we had the patience to look carefully at everything before our open eyes. This capacity is, for both authors, a function of the inhumanity of photography. Photographs are, in Poe's terms, "infinitely" more precise than any human hand, and no skills of manual dexterity can compete with them. On this view, photographs replicate the visible by mechanical means and leave no room for ideas, which are the product of imagination.

The advent of high-speed photography in the late 1870s, however, made it plain that the grounds for restricting the photographic to the visible were indefensible because instantaneous exposures often result in pictures that represent the movements of things in ways that never could be seen, but which are nonetheless (and often with good cause) taken to be accurate, although their accuracy can only be verified by other photographs—or by the use of mechanical detectors, transmitters, and inscribers.

The presumed mechanical character of photography and its alleged superficiality led to its classification in the mid to late nineteenth century as an industrial, and not a fine, art. Many writers on the art of the period concentrated on what they took to be the crucial distinctions between photography and painting, elaborating the differences in terms of oppositions between materiality and ideality, between the technical skills of photographic manipulation and the artist's practiced skills of hand (as if the photographer's skills were not skills of hand), between the mindless machine and the mind of the painter. Critics repeatedly emphasized the supposed lack of intentionality in photographic production and the complete intentionality of painting: the camera was supposed to represent whatever was in its optical field, while the painter exercised choice in respect to everything appearing in a painting. Photography helped these writers define what painting is by serving as the primary example of what it is not.

Despite the classification of photography as an industrial art, attempts at casting specific kinds of photographs as works of art began in the late 1880s in England, France, Germany, and the United States. Peter Henry Emerson, a British physician and photographer, initiated a fine-art photography movement in 1889 that he labeled "naturalistic" photography. Emerson's original position, which was adopted by others who followed his lead, maintained that a photograph could be a work of art, irrespective of its genetics, if it occasioned "aesthetic pleasure" in the viewer (although to qualify as art, the work had to be approved by an expert in the production and evaluation of visual art). Fine-art photography, in the hands of Emerson and his followers (most notably Alfred Stieglitz), was essentially an adapta-

PHOTOGRAPHY: Overview. Edward Weston, *Dunes, Oceano* (1936), gelatin silver print, 19.0 × 24.1 cm; Museum of Modern Art, New York. (Photograph copyright 1981 by the Center for Creative Photography, University of Arizona Board of Regents; used by permission.)

tion of Impressionist and Post-Impressionist painters' practices to the province of photography—practices regarding subject matter, ambiance, and manner of presentation. The utility of this position is that it grounds the determination of the artistic value of some photographs in the prints themselves and in the habits and expectations of viewers—not in the way the photographs come into being.

A more restrictive view of what constitutes an artful photograph began to emerge in the second decade of the twentieth century. Propounded by the photographers Paul Strand, Stieglitz, and, later, Edward Weston, the position is one of the many forms of photographic modernism and proposes to find the aesthetic principles peculiar to photography in the correct use of the medium and in the special relation photographs are said to establish with the objects they represent. On Weston's view, the peculiar, defining characteristics of

photography include its remarkable capacity to render fine detail by means of a microscopic mosaic of silver grains that cannot be reproduced by skills of hand. For Weston, the key to producing aesthetically notable photographs rests on the photographer's ability to look at a scene and to construct a "previsualized" image by imagining how the scene might be translated into a photograph. Weston places special emphasis on the difference between ordinary seeing and "seeing photographically," that is, constructing an image of the objects arrayed in front of the camera in terms of the choice of lens, film, exposure, film development, and printing technique. Weston's position assumes that photographs, when made by "purely photographic" means, are different in kind from other sorts of pictures and that good photographs declare their independence from all other graphic media. For Weston, the difference between photography and, say, painting is that when properly used, cameras introduce us to a domain that is unavailable to a painter, and it is the exploration of this domain that constitutes the art of photography. While premodernist photographers like Emerson and his followers saw the possibility that photography could become an art by aligning itself with the then current values of painting and graphic media, Weston deplored the imitation of the practices of artists in other depictive media and saw it as the major obstacle to the production of aesthetically valuable photographs.

Like all purist positions on photography, Weston's arguments are conditioned on suppositions that are impossible to warrant. For example, he believed that so-called soft-focus lenses (lenses that cannot resolve sharp images) must be avoided because they do not resolve detail in a way that he claimed is peculiar to photography, but of course such lenses are "purely optical" and pictures made with them are no less pure than his favored creations. Viewed positively, however, Weston's major achievement as a critic of photography can be found in his insistence on the difference between the objects placed in front of a camera and the subject of a photograph. For him, the subject of a photograph depends on the way in which the picture is formulated. If the formula is insipid and well known, it may well seem that there is an equivalence between an object photographed and the subject of the picture, but if the fashioning departs from the most usual or ordinary response, the subject of the picture may be a revelation of some aspect of the object photographed (or, for that matter, the subject might be a relationship between items depicted in the photograph). Of course, the notion of revelation in art is anything but revolutionary, but the thought that photographs might probe beyond the obvious, superficial aspects of what could be seen in front of a camera was new and served as a fundamental element of modernist photography.

These lines of conceptual and historical inquiry suggest that responses to the question of whether or not photographs can be works of art are heavily dependent on assumptions about what photographs are (to say nothing about what art is), and these suppositions are quite often false, fantastic, or simply trivial. Photographs are not restricted to showing what is available for all to see, or to showing what nobody could possibly see. Photographs are not peculiarly tied to "the facts of the moment" or to "visible reality." The supposed strict limitations on what a photographer can depict are more often than not constraints on the critic who writes out of ignorance of the extraordinary plasticity of the medium. The impulse to settle the question of the potential artfulness of photographs by resorting to a theory of "the photograph" or of "the index" is generally fed by a predisposition to argue for or against an art of photography, irrespective of the adequacy of the theory.

The issue of whether or not some photographs are works of art cannot be settled in advance of looking at them and cannot be answered outside of a variety of institutional contexts. The question, finally, is social and not conceptual in character.

BIBLIOGRAPHY

Arnheim, Rudolf. "On the Nature of Photography." *Critical Inquiry* 1.1 (Autumn 1974): 149–162.

Braun, Marta. "A History of the History of Photography." *Photo Communique* (Winter 1980–1981): 21–23.

Benjamin, Walter. "A Short History of Photography" (1936). In *Classic Essays on Photography,* edited by Alan Trachtenberg, pp. 199–216. New Haven, 1980.

Benjamin, Walter. "The Work of Art in the Age of Mechanical Reproduction." In *Illuminations,* edited by Hannah Arendt, translated by Harry Zohn, pp. 217–251. New York, 1969.

Bourdieu, Pierre. *Photography: A Middle-Brow Art.* Translated by Shaun Whiteside. Stanford, Calif., 1990.

Crary, Jonathan. *Techniques of the Observer: On Vision and Modernity in the Nineteenth Century.* Cambridge, Mass., 1990.

Galassi, Peter. *Before Photography: Painting and the Invention of Photography.* New York, 1981.

Krauss, Rosalind E. "Notes on the Index: Parts I and II." In *The Originality of the Avant Garde and Other Modernist Myths.* Cambridge, Mass., 1985.

Krauss, Rosalind E. "Photography's Discursive Spaces." In *The Originality of the Avant Garde and Other Modernist Myths.* Cambridge, Mass., 1985.

Newhall, Beaumont. *The History of Photography: From 1839 to the Present.* Rev. enl. ed. New York, 1982.

Phillips, David. "The Subject of Photography." *Oxford Art Journal* 12.2 (1989): 115–121.

Snyder, Joel. "Photography and Idolatry." In *The Pursuits of Reason: Essays in Honor of Stanley Cavell,* edited by Ted Cohen, Paul Guyer, and Hilary Putnam. Lubbock, Tex., 1992.

Snyder, Joel, and Neil Walsh Allen. "Photography, Vision and Representation." *Critical Inquiry* 2.1 (Fall 1975).

Tagg, John. *The Burden of Representation: Essays on Photographies and Histories.* Reprint, Minneapolis, 1993.

JOEL SNYDER

Daguerreotype

Named for its putative inventor, Louis-Jacques-Mandé Daguerre (1787–1851), the daguerreotype appeared in 1839 and was the most common form of the photograph until replaced by the glass-plate negative and paper print in the mid to late 1850s. Its special character, both as an object and as a picture, lay in its physicality. Typically small enough to rest in the palm of the hand, the daguerreotype was a cased image, similar to the miniature portrait. The image lay under glass on a highly polished copper plate. In its most popular form a gold-plated mat helped secure the glass and plate within a small wooden, leather, or thermoplastic case, while vignetting the image, usually a portrait. Unlike the paper print, which often appeared affixed to a stiffened sheet of paper, the daguerreotype had palpable weight, solidity, and heft.

Following from its artifactual character, the daguerrean image provided a unique viewing experience. Often, the image behaved in a manner that struck its viewers as uncanny, if not ghostlike. Partly this response arose from the extraordinary clarity of definition of a well-made daguerreotype. Especially in portraits, images seemed to have a lifelike character. Moreover, because of its peculiar image construction, built up, as one recent expert explains, through accumulated surface granules rather than suspended in an emulsion, what is required for the image to seem legible or to "come to life" is a specific triangulation of viewer, image, and light. The image seemed often to flicker, as if it indeed possessed animate life. It seemed, too, at times to pass away; when viewed at a certain angle, the image resolved into a negative shadow of itself. Then, too, the mirror-like polish of the plate cast back the viewer's own reflection, which could seem to mingle with that of the photograph's subject. These physical peculiarities of the daguerreotype gave rise to a popular and critical rhetoric that placed its strange representational behavior among things Gothic, romantic, and magical. The image seemed to possess a life of its own, a life fashioned of light and darkness, of shadow and substance. Was it a living portrait, or a magic mirror?

With the daguerreotype photography was born into a swarm of questions and speculations about the character of the photographic image. Was it no more than a "picture," a mundane concept, made by new means? The term *portrait*, applied quite early to daguerrean images of people posed as if for a face painting, seemed to affirm this familiarity. Or was it something different, something closer to the sort of reflection produced by mirrors, an identity rather than a likeness? Due largely to the daguerreotype, uncertainty about the character of the photographic image appeared at the birth of the medium and has persisted in critical discourse. But with the rise of the paper print in the middle 1850s and the demise of the daguerreotype, the question seemed to be settled on behalf of a new version of an old thing. The negative-positive process issued into a weightless image on paper, thus seeming to surpass or overcome the material-based limitations of the daguerreotype: its one-of-a-kind status, its instability of representation, its cumbersome solidity. While an important residue of the language of magic, alchemy, and the preternatural remained attached to popular discourses of photography, the sense of acute disruption, not without its frisson of acute pleasure, diminished in favor of a language of aesthetic value and cultivated taste. On the whole, the paper print was found to be more assimilable to discourses of high art and rational craft. Paper prints seemed to normalize the photograph by making it possible to speak of it as a picture in the usual sense of the word, a likeness, a representation. To be sure, some of the aura of mystery and speculation was transferred to the stereographic experience, the three-dimensional effect achieved by viewing paired images in a special viewing device. But the "coming to life" of an image with illusory substance and shadow remained peculiar to the daguerreotype.

Accustomed to viewing photographic images impressed on inked paper either as half-tone or, more recently, as dig-

ital reproductions or, in their classic form, as continuous-tone images in silver-based emulsions, modern viewers often find themselves at once disconcerted and charmed by the daguerreotype. Some viewers grow rapturous, others nostalgic for an original moment of the photographic craft. The modern rediscovery of the daguerreotype, including the revival of the process, has also revived the older language of enthrallment and mystique. Intellectually speaking, new attention to the old process offers an opportunity for criticism and theory. Especially at a time when digital images are rapidly challenging the hegemony of camera-made photography and its science-based claims to accuracy of representation, the reappearance of the daguerreotype offers a chance to reexamine fundamental assumptions about the aesthetic character of the medium as a whole.

Such an examination should begin with the sensuous and kinetic experience itself of viewing a daguerreotype. That experience always occurs within a setting of personal, social, and cultural life and history. Propositions about photography derived from the daguerreotype are inevitably time-bound and culture-specific. To ask what happens when the daguerrean image flickers into view and becomes legible is to ask what was thought to happen, how the daguerrean happening was understood, how the tension between likeness and identity was negotiated in specific discursive contexts.

Torn between thinking of the image as a likeness (a portrait) or an identity (a mirror), early viewers enacted in their quandary an implicit nineteenth-century debate about the character of photography and, beyond that, of representation as such. The daguerreotype seemed a simulacrum of the real, too real to be understood as just another kind of copy of the world, too immediately compelling to seem only a likeness. Its effect derived, too, from the image's capacity to negate itself when viewed in another light at another angle, to cancel itself into shadow, and rematerialize, as it were, from within itself. When the eyes go black and the eye cavity appears a blank socket, how startling it is to find in your hands the visage of a skull—as if the image contains its own death's head. Flipping from negative to positive and back, which accounts for the flickering effect, makes the daguerrean image seem not only alive but simultaneously dead and alive. Whereas some likened Daguerre's images to etchings and aquatints, and the American portrait painter and inventor of the telegraph, Samuel F. B. Morse, coined the phrase destined for fame, "Rembrandt perfected," this familiarizing and idealizing vocabulary competed with a more potent set of affective terms from Protestant theology, literary romanticism, and popular Gothicism, a syncretic allusive diction of breathing images, spiritual presence, living mirrors, haunted shadows, talismanic likenesses, spellbound viewers, and momenti mori.

Aesthetic theories of the daguerreotype proceed from the peculiarities of the viewing experience. Only those who know firsthand the sensation of succumbing to the charm of these objects can begin to understand what they might have meant to their makers and possessors in the past, and how their illusion of a living presence might make the photographic medium as a whole seem, as many of its twentieth-century theorists have claimed, something unique among the plastic arts: a uniquely immediate access to the "real." In the culture of the daguerreotype the photograph seemed a new, specifically modern opportunity to know reality by capturing its fleeting appearances with utmost clarity and brilliance of detail.

At the same time, another feature of the experience, when reflected on, tends to undercut the assumption of an entirely unmediated picture. The way the image presents itself on the mirrored metallic surface, legible only at a certain angle of view in a certain light, requires that the viewer play a decisive part in forming the image in his or her own eyes. How often the recorded experience of looking at a daguerreotype began with a testimony of amazement that there seemed to be nothing there, except the reflection of one's own face! The effort simply to see the image implicates the viewer in the making, the construction of the image. The daguerrean image allows for an engagement between viewer and subject unique in photography; literally, to see the image is to become an active agent in the picture's "coming to life." To see a paper print requires a less strenuous act: such images come to us as if objective facts, already constructed meanings.

It is possible to speak of the daguerreotype not only as a distinct photographic artifact, but also of daguerrean viewing as a distinct way of seeing and knowing the image: seeing it as a contingent act, and knowing it as a construction in which the viewer participates as an agent of meaning. Moreover, because of its continuing capacity to charm viewers, the daguerreotype provides a model occasion for a historicist methodology. To be sure, critical understanding might well find itself thwarted at the site of empathy, arrested in and by a discourse of mystique and nostalgia. Because daguerreotypes seen today are likely to be more than a hundred years old, frequently unidentified either by subject or maker, their power to excite sensations of beauty is more likely to arouse viewers than their discursive aspects, their capacity to mean something through and beyond their sensuous appearance. To the dubieties of the viewing experience must be added the uncertainties and frequent bafflements of efforts to interpret what is seen. Early commentators referred to a "language of its own" by which the daguerreotype "touched the common chords of life." That language was and is verbal as much as visual, a texture of words by which the daguerreotype was known and understood. Interpretation requires that current viewers become speakers of that language in order to converse with the image on its own terms.

It is not surprising that the early aesthetic discourse surrounding the daguerreotype shows an appropriation of key terms from formal art criticism: *likeness, chiaroscuro, compo-sition,* and so on. The fact is, and with its rigors of craft, the daguerreotype makes this especially apparent, the camera image can be made to resemble a resemblance, to give an effect of likeness, of intentional design, but only under controls (focus, framing, lighting) derived from formulas of likeness. Logically speaking, in Charles Sanders Peirce's terminology, what the camera produces in the first instance is a trace or index rather than an icon or symbol, something like a footprint or shadow, a literal impression of light delineating form and detail from a palpable surface. From any given camera position, variables of focus and light resolutely determine the extent of resemblance or nonresemblance produced by the image. Photographic images might function within semiotic systems as symbols (referring, in a loose construction of Peirce, to general ideas associated with the depicted referent) or icons (referring to an object by arbitrary convention), but their primary logical status remains that of a direct effect of a physical cause it replicates. Photographs contain within their representational range a depiction of their own causal agency: light struck from this or that surface. Not all photographs qualify as pictures in the sense of copy or likeness. The camera might be used to produce illusions of imitation, as in the staging of scenes, but the process itself does not imitate; it reproduces.

In this regard daguerreotypes are no different from photographs proper; their physical peculiarities only heighten the photographic experience, render it in a mode that served as an extraordinary initiation for modern culture into one of its fundamentally new conditions: the instant convertibility of experience into image, the potentiality of endless and continuous doubling of all tangible surfaces, and the reification of the eye as the leading instrument of everyday knowledge. As aesthetic experience the daguerreotype retains its uniqueness as long as viewers resist resolving its uncertainties into the fixity of paper prints. In this light it might help restore to discussions of camera-made images a sense of disbelief that once made photography an occasion for radical questioning of representation as such.

BIBLIOGRAPHY

Barger, M. Susan, and William B. White. *The Daguerreotype: Nineteenth-Century Technology and Modern Science.* Washington, D.C., 1991.

Buerger, Janet E. *French Daguerreotypes.* Chicago, 1989.

Gernsheim, Helmut, and Alison Gernsheim. *L. J. M. Daguerre: The History of the Diorama and the Daguerreotype.* London, 1956.

Newhall, Beaumont. *The Daguerreotype in America.* 3d rev. ed. New York, 1976.

Peirce, Charles Sanders. "Logic as Semiotic: The Theory of Signs." In *Philosophical Writings of Peirce,* edited by Justus Buchler. New York, 1955.

Pfister, Harold Francis. *Facing the Light: Historic American Portrait Daguerreotypes.* Washington, D.C., 1978.

Rinhart, Floyd, and Marion Rinhart. *The American Daguerreotype.* Athens, Ga., 1981.

Rudisill, Richard. *Mirror Image: The Influence of the Daguerreotype on American Society.* Albuquerque, N. Mex., 1971.

Taft, Robert. *Photography and the American Scene: A Social History, 1839–1889.* New York, 1938.

Trachtenberg, Alan. *Reading American Photographs: Images as History, Mathew Brady to Walker Evans.* New York, 1989.

Trachtenberg, Alan. "The Daguerreotype: American Icon." In *American Daguerreotypes from the Matthew R. Isenberg Collection.* New Haven, 1989.

Trachtenberg, Alan. "Mirror in the Marketplace: American Responses to the Daguerreotype, 1839–1851." In *The Daguerreotype: A Sequicentennial Celebration,* edited by John Wood. Iowa City, 1989.

Trachtenburg, Alan. "Photography: The Emergence of a Keyword." In *Photography in Nineteenth-Century America,* edited by Martha A. Sandweiss. New York, 1991.

Wood, John, ed. *The Daguerreotype: A Sequicentennial Celebration.* Iowa City, 1989.

Wood, John, ed. *America and the Daguerreotype.* Iowa City, 1991.

ALAN TRACHTENBERG

Photography and Technology

Photography names a diverse, burgeoning family of light-using technologies introduced in 1839 and increasingly pervasive since then throughout most of the world, where they are so entangled with other technologies and so deeply embedded in the social and economic fabrics of modern societies as almost to rival for importance the technologies of printing by movable type introduced four centuries earlier—technologies that photography combines. An important similarity between the spread of the photo and print families is their sheer bulk of production, causing massive changes in use. Photographic technologies now begin a similar entanglement with electronic information technologies. This article begins with a brief account of technology, which it then applies to photo technology, before turning to the meaning of this approach for matters of art and aesthetics. Our emphasis throughout will be on photography rather than on "the photograph": on actual, historical processes, rather than on an idealized "thing" or essence. Photography is so obviously a creature of developing technologies that accounts of it that do not include a general grasp of technology are in danger of obsolescence.

Technologies. A serious shortcoming of most accounts of photo-aesthetics is that they neglect to say what photography is. Photography is a modern technology, and technologies may be simply and generally characterized as amplifiers of our powers to do things. Powers thus amplified or enhanced may be part of our biological equipment or may be the results of earlier technologies. These include social organizations and teachable skills, as well as physical contrivances. Steam power, a slightly older technology that developed in tandem with photography in their early histories, provides, like printing, a revealing analogy for exploring photography in what follows. Whereas photography includes a set of cognitive technologies whose outputs feed into our perceptual systems, steam engines (and their internal combustion offshoots) are notable amplifiers of the motive powers of our own bodies, as well as of our previous motive technologies. The first inventors of photography saw that its technologies, like those of steam, "make the powers of nature work for you" (William Henry Fox Talbot), by channeling an abundant, renewable natural resource—light—toward the extension of existing human powers and the development of new ones. The following section will consider these photographically extended powers.

The origins of photo technologies, like those of steam or the later nineteenth-century technologies of concrete, iron, or steel construction, lay in engineering discoveries. Such innovations typically begin in an engineering concern with the properties of materials, then include invention of structures to exploit these. As the initial materials for steam power were water (with its capacity to expand when heated), fossil fuel, and iron, those for photography were solar light, in relationship with the chemistry of silver halide receptors. The delicacy and sensitivity of these chemical materials to light still abide as the basis of all photographic technologies.

Two very general facts about technologies help to fix a necessary perspective for understanding long-running debates about photography. First, if technologies are amplifiers of our powers, amplifiers are typically also *filters*—even suppressors—of other powers, in two ways. Our powers to do things are typically coordinated. When one power in a given domain is amplified while another is not, their previous relationships are disturbed. For example, amplification of motive power, as with steam and other power tools and engines, is inherently dangerous, as it tends to disable or to outrun our sensory and cognitive controls—unless these, in turn, are enhanced by parallel technologies. Suppression of some of our powers may indeed be required by amplification of others. Thus, speed over road surfaces is unbearable without springs and other shock absorbers, which suppress sensitivity to changes in those surfaces. Second, it is in the nature of successful technologies—much like our biological equipment—that they become taken for granted as inconspicuous background to a multitude of activities. As technologies such as photography evolve, it should be expected that their users will lose perspective on the increasingly complex amplifications, suppressions, and also side effects that they entail.

To apply our general technological perspective and to understand photo art better, we must next consider the most general uses of the photo technology family.

Photographic Technologies. People typically do one thing to accomplish another. Thus, besides being coordinated, human abilities and their technological extensions are usually sequenced. For example, increased motive lifting power by means of steam engines amplifies our power to build structures, which in turn extends powers of transport, storage, and shelter, each of which exfoliates into other interacting amplifications of powers—with their associated suppressions, inadvertent or not. By analogy, the photographic sequence of enhancements of our powers begins with what Lady Eastlake in 1857 called a method of producing "a stain designedly traced" on a prepared surface. As the second part of its name *(-graphy)* implies, photography arose, and persists, as an amplifier of a large and significant sector of human behavior: controlled surface marking. Humans are great intentional markers of surfaces—including their own—usually with the "display" intention that the marked surfaces be noticed to be so marked, for further purposes. As the human eye-brain channel is the most complex, sensitive information-processing system known, physically delicate deposits of visual information stored on prepared surfaces through minute quantities of energy exchange may carry potential for immense wealth of cognitive meaning. Mere mention of the two words *writing* and *drawing* should establish this point.

Surface markings hold much intrinsic interest, notably aesthetic and artistic. They have innumerable diverse and important further uses, for a multitude of cognitive activities, serving still other uses. Despite their social impact, interesting uses and promises, nineteenth-century photographic surface-marking technologies did not match or subsume the functions of older relief, intaglio, and planographic marking technologies until photography's successful combination with relief ink processes, sometimes termed its "second invention," in the first decades of the twentieth century. This allowed its confluence with, and propagation through, the older, still expanding, letterpress technologies of production and distribution. With the coincident invention of motion pictures, and later invention of television, a major branch of photography turned away from permanent surface "staining," in the direction of transient light modification of screens. This is achieved today, increasingly, by electronic rather than chemical agencies, interacting with light through optical technologies. Television shows the many advantages of electro-optic imaging technologies. These include greater sensitivity than chemical methods, easier storage, and faster mass distribution to remote reception sites. The further dramatic combination of electro-optic imaging with computer digital storage, transformation, and combination with other digitally stored imagery holds much promise. Yet, such methods fall far short of the fineness and permanence of the "classic" chemical ones, which show no obsolescence, and on which their own microcircuitry still relies.

Whether chemical or electronic, still or moving, photographic surface-marking technologies have thereby amplified four main areas of ancient cognitive technologies. These may be listed as depiction representation, reproduction, detection, and registration recording. We will consider these functions in order, both singly and in combination.

To depict is to incite to imagine. Humans are capable of imagining without such incitement. Depictions and like representations are made to stimulate, extend, and channel our imagining powers—particularly those of visualization. Therefore, to represent or depict is already to employ technology: imagining technology. Photodepictive technologies comprise a recent addition to a wide, vigorous, and very ancient family of these technologies, with which they are well integrated. Although making pictorial representations is the main imaginative use of photo technologies, their important contributions to modern mass reproduction of images of many sorts have been much discussed. Still, it needs to be emphasized that photographic technologies are well embedded in print productions, many of which are for purposes of imagining, and these include literary fiction and written music, as well as pictures.

For all its enormous amplification (and filtering) of our powers to imagine, through still and moving pictures, and its vital assistance to other industries of imagination, photography is especially notable for its amplifications of our detective powers and powers to record. Photography has unique and important uses for the detection of states and events, often remote from the viewer in time or space. Tracks, prints, and other natural kinds of surface markings are important means of detection for humans, as they are for other creatures. Photography provides a powerful set of technologies for extending such trace detection and recording powers, by means of the action of light on prepared surfaces. (These registrations need no more result in pictures than do footprints in the sand.) As mentioned above, chemical and electro-optic receptors have distinct advantages for these functions.

Much confusion and dispute about photography has been due to two simple facts about photographic use, which we are now in a position to indicate. First, by amplifying our detective powers, photography also filters or suppresses other powers—a general situation made graphic by the fact that photo technologies depend essentially on systems of physical filters, optical and other. Second, as the everyday term *photograph of* implies, we employ combinations of photography's depictive and detective uses. It is normal for technological uses to combine. It is also normal for imagining to serve detecting activities, as well as for detection to serve imagination. Imagining, like remembering, is an aid to detection in much of our visual perception. The reciprocal cases are also familiar: perceiving actual things is often an important incitement, guide, or vivifying factor in imagining about them or about other things. The photographic combination that has proved most mischievous to theory and popular thought is of the former kind: imagining in service of detecting. Photographic depiction provides a familiar "user-friendly" means to photographic detection. It enables us indirectly to detect situations and events, while pictorially imagining that we are directly seeing them. What is photographed need not be what is photographically depicted. Notorious problems arise out of ambiguities in the match between what we imagine seeing in such pictures and what we are actual able to detect from them.

Photography and the Arts. To address issues of photography and the arts from our technological perspective, it is first necessary to state generally what the *arts* are, in relation to technology. The resilient, modern idea of the fine arts, installed just a century before photography's first inventions, was itself technological: essentially that of the skilled production of representations, in the sense explained above, but as appealing to an alleged "faculty of Imagination." What was to be imagined was originally beautiful nature, and "genius" was supposed to crown productive skill—a requirement greatly elaborated in the nineteenth century, in terms of the free expression of the producer, whether understood as a person, a culture, or an epoch. These four elements of artisanal skill, self-expression, imaginative amplification, and aesthetic admiration have been highly valued in all societies throughout history. Their value did not wait on the invention of the idea of "fine arts." Their

PHOTOGRAPHY: Photography and Technology. Edward Steichen, *Rodin 'The Thinker'* (1902), photograph (platinum and pigment print), 17 × 12 5/16″ (43.2 × 31.3 cm), Museum of Modern Art, New York (Gift of the photographer). (Photograph copyright 1998 by the Museum of Modern Art; used by permission.)

fateful gathering in eighteenth-century Europe was distinctive in several ways, however: for the rather arbitrary listing of five "fine arts" that attended the event, for the secular context in which it cast those arts (each of which was rooted in religious traditions), and in orientation to the point of view of a new kind of audience, increasingly wide, secular, and amateur.

The four elements of the fine arts fall on two sides of a technological situation: that of production (productive skill, self-expression) and that of audience use (imagining, aesthetic admiration). Although notoriously in frequent conflict, these two general aspects, as well as their four components, turn out to be inseparable—in fact, internal to one another. Productive factors cannot be well specified independently of what they produce. Conversely, the "use" category, although more nearly separable, is not easily or lastingly separated from production. Audiences typically admire the productive skills such works exhibit—including skills in forming representations—and also admire the individual qualities of mind expressed in doing so. Again, artistic incitements to imagining typically display aspects of their own productive processes.

As simple illustration of the artistic inseparability of process and product, we may compare a most familiar surface-marking implement: production *of* pencils and production *with* them. The materials and processes for manufacture of pencils in varying grades of hardness (since 1795) do not, and need not, show up particularly well in their products. That it is unclear to many people how the "lead" is gotten through the wood casing has no effect on their use. By contrast, pencil actions in marking surfaces do show up clearly in their products and are typically noted there—almost as much as sounds are automatically understood in terms of the voices or instruments that produce them. Use of pencil markings for enhanced imagining typically calls on some understanding of them in terms of their mental and physical productive processes. The continued viability of such traditional hand surface-marking techniques as drawing and painting, in the face of suppressions of photographic mechanization, attests to their efficient use of such productive means.

Photography has affected the arts not only by producing important new varieties such as cinema but also through its interactions with each of the four interdependent constituents. We have already considered photography as an amplifier of our imagining powers, through its depictive, recording, and reproductive extensions, in the production and distribution of aids to elaborate imaginative projects. Especially as technology for figurative visual imagining, photography's repositioning of the human and the mechanical contributions to the productive process has obviously affected practices, conceptions, and also valuings of the two productive components of "art," craft and self-expression, incurring reactions to photography, as well as to art itself.

Photography has had more subtle, important impacts through the interdependence of art's four constituents. For example, aesthetic appreciation of form or of expression is usually affected by radical shifts in formative procedures, such as those instituted by photography. Photographic processes have histories of aesthetic comparison with other art forms, as well as of development of autonomous photo-aesthetics.

Reflexivity, or thematizing their own media, processes of production, and uses, is an oft-noted feature of all the modern arts. Photography, besides being a technological family of modern origin, is strikingly innovative, influential, and controversial with regard to physical production and social use, including the states and actions of subject, light, photographer, film, camera, reproductive process, and so on. Photographic technologies therefore provide a wealth of opportunities for reflexive, critical investigation, and may continue to do so as they become increasingly linked with expanding electronic technologies of visualization.

BIBLIOGRAPHY

Eder, Josef Maria. *The History of Photography.* 4th ed. Translated by Edward Epstean. Reprint, New York, 1978.
Newhall, Beaumont. *The History of Photography: From 1839 to the Present.* Comp. rev. enl. ed. New York, 1982.
Newhall, Beaumont, ed. *Photography: Essays and Images: Illustrated Readings in the History of Photography.* New York, 1980.
Sturge, John, Vivian Walworth, and Allan Shepp, eds. *Imaging Processes and Materials: Neblette's Eighth Edition.* New York, 1989.
Tausk, Petr. *A Short History of Press Photography.* Prague, 1988.

PATRICK MAYNARD

Photography and Digital Technology

A digital image is an image made up of a grid of discrete units known as pixels; the finer the grid, the higher the resolution of the image. With numbers used to specify the color or intensity of each pixel, the image can be stored in computer memory, copied, transmitted electronically, displayed, and printed. It can also be altered in innumerable ways.

This technology has implications for photography, because an ordinary photograph can be scanned and converted to digital format; or more directly, a digital camera can be used to record an image on disk, bypassing the photochemical process.

Are these images rightly considered a species of photograph? William J. Mitchell denies that they are, saying that digital imagery is as different from photography as photography is from painting. Whereas the photograph is an analog image formed by the action of light on a treated surface, the digital image, though it may be derived from a photograph, is formed by an array of integers describing a grid.

Mitchell points out that there are a multitude of differences between photographs and digital images—photographs can be enlarged to give increased information, whereas an enlarged digital image will just have decreased resolution as it begins to reveal the grid of which it is made. Furthermore, unlike a photograph, a digital image can be reproduced with no deterioration of the image. The photograph of a photograph will never have the precision of the original, but a digital copy can be indistinguishable from the original digital image. Finally, a digital image is more susceptible to alteration than a photograph. Once a photograph is digitized, its components can be rearranged, extended, deleted, and in other ways modified before it is printed, processes made all the easier by software designed expressly for these purposes.

Although these important differences do exist, they do not settle the matter of the digital image's exclusion from the category of photography, for a diversity of properties can be found even within the category of traditional photography. For instance, the problem raised by the alterability of the image is one of degree—we do not normally decline to call a retouched photograph, or a double exposure, a photograph. The extent to which the image can be reproduced or multiplied also varies—daguerreotypes are considered photographs, though they do not involve negatives and do not allow of multiple prints. Furthermore, images referred to as photographs exhibit a diversity of behaviors when enlarged—the halftone prints in books are often called photographs, although they are not analog images and although the resolution of such images deteriorates when enlarged. Finally, the term *digital photograph* does handily serve to distinguish those digital images that are either scanned from photographs or taken by digital "cameras." Mitchell may be right to describe the term *digital photograph* as misleading; however, his arguments against the use of the term are not wholly conclusive.

The Destruction of the Credibility of Photographs. Even if we follow Mitchell in refusing to use the term *digital photograph,* and even if we emphasize the distinct character of the digital medium, the way in which digital technology can be applied to photographs raises some important issues for photography.

Fred Ritchin gives some examples of this interaction in his book on digital technology's impact on photojournalism, *In Our Own Image.* He describes how the elements of a photograph can be repositioned, as in *National Geographic*'s 1982 cover image in which the pyramids of Giza were digitally pushed closer together so that they would fit the magazine's vertical format. He describes how the elements of a photograph can be deleted, as in *Rolling Stone*'s 1985 cover shot of Don Johnson, in which Johnson's shoulder holster and pistol were digitally removed for a less violent image. He also explains how different images can be combined or blended. For instance, Nancy Burson's *Warhead I* combines the features of Ronald Reagan, Leonid Brezhnev, Deng Xiaoping, François Mitterrand, and Margaret Thatcher, to form a composite portrait of the leaders, circa 1982, of the world's nuclear nations. With digital technology, the "photographer" has gained complete control over the image and has acquired the freedom of the painter to depict whatever he or she desires.

This new technology differs from older methods of alteration in several ways. Digital alterations can be effected with ease and rapidity—alteration no longer requires delicate, tedious, and time-consuming work; the range of things that can be done is expanded—faces can be aged or the features of several faces can be mixed; and the alteration itself can be made difficult, if not impossible, to detect. (This undetectability, however, is often greatly overestimated. Without careful matching of tone, lighting, scale, and perspective, a digital alteration will *not* be undetectable.)

The relative ease, freedom, and undetectability of digital manipulation make it hard to resist—and commonly employed. Whereas alteration is the exception for traditional photography, it can be seen as a defining characteristic of digital imagery. According to Mitchell, "Computational tools for transforming, combining, altering, and analyzing images are as essential to the digital artist as brushes and pigments are to a painter, and an understanding of them is the foundation of the craft of digital imaging" (Mitchell, 1992).

As Ritchin points out, the enhanced manipulability of photographs that results from applications of digital technology must ultimately change the way photographs are used—whether in journalism, law, or other areas. As it becomes more common to digitize photographs and to use digital cameras, and as it becomes easier to alter these digital images to reflect whatever scenarios we might dream up, the documentary usefulness of photographs is severely diminished.

With the ease of digital manipulation, alteration is becoming more widespread; with the relative seamlessness of digital manipulation, it becomes harder to detect (as compared with the previously available "cut and paste" methods); and with the use of digital and still video cameras, there is no negative against which an image can be checked for tampering. There is not necessarily anything about the digitally altered image to alert us to the fact that there has been manipulation, and in a world where manipulation is on the rise, all images, even photographs, become suspect. To the extent that we can see photographs as potentially indistinguishable from their digitally altered counterparts, photographs become suspect as carriers of even the most basic information, suspect as bearers of any evidence.

Since photographs can be digitized, since they can in that form be readily altered, and since the resulting images are potentially indistinguishable from straight (i.e., unaltered) photographs, the evidential authority of any putative straight photograph is threatened. This authority is what some (Rudolf Arnheim, Roland Barthes, André Bazin, Susan Sontag, and Kendall Walton, to name a few) consider to be a distinguishing characteristic of photography, and it is an authority that derives from how photographs are typically made. Because of the mechanical nature of its production, the photograph seems to have a special connection with reality and an independence of the photographer's intentions. For example, if there is a tree in a photograph, we assume that there must have been a tree in front of the camera, since the tree cannot just be a product of the photographer's imagination. This is not to say that a photograph can never distort or mislead—the photographer's choice of camera angle, lighting, and framing all influence the way in which the tree will be seen. But as Walton and others note, the credibility of the photograph does not rest on the exact duplication of appearances; rather, it rests on our knowledge of the way in which the photograph is produced. A photograph is thought to verify the existence of a tree in a way a painting never could—the photograph requires the presence of a tree for its production, while the painting could depend wholly on the artist's imagination.

This close connection between what the photograph shows and what exists in the world is what Bazin refers to when he speaks of the "realism" of the photograph, what Walton refers to when he speaks of the "transparency" of the photograph, and what Arnheim has in mind when he says that the objects in a photograph print their own images "by means of the optical and chemical action of light." Digital technology disrupts this connection between photography and reality, because it raises the possibility that the tree in what appears to be a straight photograph is actually a digital addition or simulation. The transparency, realism, and credibility of photographs are thus threatened.

Of course, there will always be some images whose altered or tampered status will be obvious, either because of technical clumsiness or because the scene shown is known to be utterly impossible. But when we look at a seemingly straight photograph, it will become more and more difficult to be confident that no manipulation has taken place.

Our implicit faith in the veracity of the photographic image is deeply ingrained, so it would take much more than a few digital "forgeries" to reshape our habits of seeing. After all, old-fashioned photographic forgeries have always been plentiful, for example, in the composites of supermarket tabloids and in retouched high-school yearbook photographs. But alongside manipulated images, there have always been a much greater number of straight photographs, some taken by journalists and other professionals, but many more taken by ordinary folks who send their exposed film to commercial developing labs. Digital scanners and cameras, however, put manipulation techniques at the fingertips of anyone with the appropriate software and a relatively modest amount of hardware—equipment that becomes more and more within the reach of the average person. Just as computers have made it much easier to revise papers—there is no laborious retyping of a whole manuscript to go through and no messy traces of cutting and pasting—computers will make it easier to "revise" a photograph. When something is easier to do, people do it with more frequency and less thought. One can easily imagine the vain routinely doctoring their photographs to take a few inches off their waists, and add a few hairs to their heads.

If we reach a point where photographs are as commonly digitized and altered as not, our faith in the veracity of photographs is likely to weaken, and one of the major differences in our conceptions of paintings and photographs may all but disappear. In this way, digital alteration may change the way in which we see *all* photographs.

Implications for the Aesthetics of Photography. Digital technology not only affects our ability to use photographs as evidence, it also has far-reaching implications for the aesthetics of photography. Most discussions of the computer's effects on art photography have emphasized the new opportunities afforded. The freedom of painting is wedded to the realism of photography—the digital artist can modify an image to fulfill his or her creative vision. But this freedom may be bought at the cost of photography's power, at least of one source of its power—that which derives from the photograph's credibility, from its perceived special connection with the world. With the loss of this perceived connection, photography's special surreal fascination may be lost.

Consider, for example, Henri Cartier-Bresson's *Behind the Gare St. Lazare*. The photograph shows a man jumping over a puddle; captured in mid-leap, his image is matched by the leaping figures on the circus posters in the background. Both the man and the figures on the posters are reflected in the puddle, creating a fortuitous repetition of images.

Behind the Gare St. Lazare has the potential to mislead as a putative documentary image (i.e., does it really show the area behind the Gare St. Lazare?); nevertheless, on the basis of this photograph, few of us would hesitate to say that leaping man, puddle, and posters existed, if only for an instant, in proximity to each other. Although it is perhaps possible to imagine that the photograph was created as a combination print, in the absence of any provocation to do so, we do not feel compelled to entertain this possibility. In an age where digital technology is widely used to create and alter images, we may come to view such a work differently, however. If we introduced the possibility of digital manipulation, we would not be so ready to assume that the posters bordered the puddle, or that the man attempted to leap it. We would not be so ready to dismiss the possibility that posters and man, along with their respective reflections, were electronically added to the image from other photographs—or from the artist's imagination, insofar as these elements of the image could be digitally simulated. Instead of the photograph being a happy confluence of reflected leaping figures caught at the "decisive moment" by the photographer, the possibility of digital manipulation would make the work seem much more contrived, and I believe it would give us less delight, or at least a delight of a different kind.

Or consider André Kertész's *Buy*, which is a cityscape taken from a position in front of but higher than a billboard. As a result of this vantage point, the billboard, which shows a smiling woman exhorting us to buy beer, fills the lower portion of the photograph. Beyond the billboard, we see the street, the sidewalk, and two people casting long shadows. The sidewalk scene fills the top of the photograph. The juxtaposition of the flat space of the billboard with the spare landscape of the sidewalk, the lack of a horizon, and the reversal of normal point of view (we usually see billboards *above* sidewalks) all add to a disjunction or confusion of space. Part of what fascinates us about this photograph is the way the vantage point and the framing can lead to such a surprising, defamiliarizing image. If, however, we entertain the possibility of digital montage, if we no longer assume that the composition shows a unified space, it becomes considerably less intriguing.

Our changing expectations for photographs could affect even the way we view the photographs of the past, those made long before the advent of digital technology—or could at least affect the way future generations look at such photographs. Those of us who started looking at photographs before the digital revolution will probably still retain, at least in part, our habitual ways of looking at works by Cartier-Bresson and Kertész. But those who grow up in an age where the photographic image is seen as fluid and manipulable may have trouble appreciating the aura of evidential authority surrounding traditional photographs.

Will future generations come to see the transformations of traditional photography—the apparent disjunctions of space or the fortuitously captured moments—as constructions of the photographer, rather than as revealing something uncanny about our world? It is impossible to know for certain, but changes in the way photographs are typically generated could very well lead to such changes in the way future viewers see all photographs, and in the kind of pleasure they are able to get from them.

BIBLIOGRAPHY

Arnheim, Rudolf. "On the Nature of Photography." *Critical Inquiry* 1 (September 1974): 149–161.

Arnheim, Rudolf. "The Two Authenticities of the Photographic Media." *Journal of Aesthetics and Art Criticism* 51.4 (Fall 1993): 537–540.

Bazin, André. "The Ontology of the Photographic Image." In *What Is Cinema?*, translated and edited by Hugh Gray, pp. 9–16. Berkeley, 1967.

Maynard, Patrick. "The Secular Icon: Photography and the Functions of Images." *Journal of Aesthetics and Art Criticism* 42.1 (Winter 1983): 155–169.

Mitchell, William J. *The Reconfigured Eye: Visual Truth in the Post-Photographic Era.* Cambridge, Mass., 1992.

Ritchin, Fred. *In Our Own Image: The Coming Revolution in Photography.* New York, 1990.

Savedoff, Barbara E. "Escaping Reality: Digital Imagery and the Resources of Photography." *Journal of Aesthetics and Art Criticism* 55.2 (Spring 1997): 201–214. Special issue titled "Perspectives on the Arts and Technology."

Walton, Kendall. "Transparent Pictures: On the Nature of Photographic Realism." *Critical Inquiry* 11.2 (December 1984): 246–277.

BARBARA SAVEDOFF

Catachresis

The capacity of photography to represent a vision true to every person and situation—its objectifying universality—has never gone unquestioned, despite popular trust in photographic images. Photography's apparent objectivity has merely been assessed in relation to that of its antecedent rivals, especially painting and drawing; and its success has been measured against those points at which the competition failed. Among its many advantages, photography has seemed to eliminate the variable of manual facility, which would bring difference to the products of any two painters attempting to render the same subject from the same viewpoint. Yet, in many respects, photography has been regarded as comparable to the various means of visual representation that preceded it; and even those who have denigrated rather than rejoiced in its "mechanical" evenhandedness (such as the nineteenth-century academician Charles Blanc) have noted that any photograph discloses the arbitrary human preferences of its maker through choice of view, lighting, and focus. Even its earliest critics believed that the "truth" of photography was a mix of subjective and objective factors; although, for better or worse, blind objectivity seemed to fare better in this optical medium than it ever had with painting.

The following argument concerning the perceived nature of photography and its place in modern culture emphasizes the historical circumstances surrounding its development and application, especially the fact that the critical discourse has always tended to compare it, explicitly or implicitly, with the more traditional mediums of painting, drawing, and associated methods of printmaking. Three propositions are at issue in this account.

1. At any moment in history the value of any given representation depends on the existence of some other representation that can be regarded (if only for that moment) as transparent, realistic, or natural. In other words, although the truth quotient of a given image may eventually be recognized as differential and therefore unstable, at the moment of the production of the image it will appear to be measurable against some fixed norm.

2. During the modern era photography provided a constructed or fabricated image that could successfully masquerade as a natural one (because it seemed the most natural one available).

3. As such, within a discourse of visual imagery, photography assumed by default the status of a proper term, a kind of norm, especially when opposed to modernist painting, which appeared as a heavily figured term.

This is to say that photography became catachresis in relation to the metaphor of painting. Modern viewers have accepted the photograph as natural by comparison with other kinds of images, yet they have also been able to recognize how deeply implicated in a system of arbitrary differential signs any product of photography remains. The photograph, that is, has been both natural and "natural."

Given recent developments in computer-assisted digitization of images, the photographic tradition of the past 150 years may have ended. During its history, photography was the dominant bearer of visual truth, at least for those living in modern, industrialized societies, who understood and tended to trust the medium's technology. As has been suggested, such trust was never entirely naive. Few, if any, doubted that individual photographs might reflect the partisan views of their makers and interpreters, that they might be manipulated, and that their messages might intentionally be skewed; but it was also generally believed that the photograph could approach objectivity more readily than other images having similarly dense construction (paintings or drawings, as opposed to more schematic diagrams or maps). The photograph needed only to compete successfully with other accepted mediums in order to represent the "truth." In its favor, the practice of photography involved a standardized technology, with lens, exposure, development, and other such factors being specifiable; this meant that its image would be consistently related to its model throughout. The causes of its results would be traceable, so long as one knew the specifications. Photography also entailed a good measure of mechanical automatism, lending a hands-off or tamperproof quality to the process. These features ensured that something approaching a common standard of judgment could be applied when interpreting the photographic product. Computer-assisted digitization changes the situation because it introduces remarkably nuanced ways of fabricating photographic images, in effect reintroducing the play of the human hand (as sequences of applied computer algorithms). The "hand" may always have been present in more conventional forms of photography, but digitization makes it especially difficult to entertain the fiction that such an intervening "hand" is lacking or that a fixed mechanism guides the medium's operation.

At the very moment that photography (as daguerreotype) entered public history, the announcement in London of its invention (*Literary Gazette*, 12 January 1839) inadvertently demonstrated its problematic status. The issue to raise here turns on the word *figured,* chosen by a translator from among any number of terms that might render the French word *reproduite* ("reproduced") as it appeared in the initial Parisian announcement of several days earlier. The English version of the statement, which aims to explain the novelty and significance of daguerreotypy, reads as follows: "Let our readers fancy the fidelity of the image of nature figured by the camera obscura, and add to it an action of the solar rays which fixes this image." Since the camera obscura was already a familiar device, it was not the image itself but the ability to stabilize and fix it that constituted photography's innovation.

Today, we can imagine the significance of things a bit differently. Consider the integral, hands-off character of the view seen within a camera obscura, and oppose it to the constructed or manipulated quality of composite, digitized imagery, which is also photographic. The practice of digitization in the 1990s (the capacity to alter or combine photographic elements without violating their "natural" system of color gradients) adds a level of irony to the use of the word *figured* in 1839. By referring to a process of figuration, the translator, whether consciously or not, introduced a metaphor, prefiguring our present situation. *Figure* can at times suggest nothing more than the most straightforward drawing or tracing, by hand or otherwise; indeed, according to William Henry Fox Talbot's famous reckoning, itself a metaphor, photography converted natural sunlight into nature's "pencil." But *figure* also implies a transformation of some kind, more of a change than to be expected from *reproduction,* perhaps a *quality* of change comparable to what we now recognize in digitized imagery.

The concept of figuration, so much debated by poststructuralist rhetorics from the 1960s through the 1980s, was hardly innocent even in 1839. In a treatise of 1823, the French art theorist Antoine Chrysostome Quatremère de Quincy denied that there could be any easy recourse to unfigured images, in this case literary ones: "Ordinary language is already itself almost entirely composed of figures: one cannot express oneself without using them; and, moreover, the word 'figure' [by alluding to a form or shape] is itself a 'figured' or metaphoric expression." So representations of all kinds were figured, even the most common ones. To be figured was to be metaphoric, not literal—that is to say, altered, distanced, ironic.

If even "ordinary" language is "almost entirely composed of figures," where do we find the "literal"? Perhaps only in practice, by consensus. Accordingly, the term *proper* better identifies what we usually refer to with the term *literal.* For *proper* connotes conventionality. A proper use of language, language seemingly free of figuration or at least of unusual degrees of figuration, does not guarantee truth; but being sanctioned by convention, it appears more acceptable, less problematic. According to Quatremère de Quincy and many other witnesses to the introduction of photography,

the most acceptable visual standard of the time was classic painting, exemplified by Raphael and carried on in conventional academic practice, as well as in Dominique Ingres, however idiosyncratically; and it was decidedly not what we would today regard as the "modern" art of 1839—Eugène Delacroix's romantic painting, with its expressive brushwork and dramatic extremes of color, now perceived as a foundation for modernist styles that sought to represent the artist's individuality and subjectivity more than any external object.

It would be wrong for the retrospective historian to judge either the classical or the romantic style as the more normative in any definitive way. Yet it is clear that for nineteenth-century viewers the two modes connoted varying (but not necessarily oppositional) social and political values and tended to be set into hierarchical frameworks. These two forms of representation were in competition just at the time of photography's appearance.

With its virtually immediate and immense success, photography became the third of three familiar modes of visual representation seeming to demand comparative evaluation from the nineteenth-century audience: first, the classical style of painting, which gradually lost its privileged cultural status as an aristocratic medium, because overt signs of privilege themselves lost favor in a political climate of republicanism; second, the modern (eventually, modernist) style of painting, which gained acceptance as an adequate representative of individual expression and liberty; and third, photography. Classical and modernist painting could be opposed in many respects, including their "originality"—a difference of kind rather than degree, for both could claim to be deeply original. Genius in classical art included the ability not only to capture the beauty or truth in nature, but also to emulate works created to that end by the imaginative geniuses of the past. Art in the classical tradition entailed reiteration, with its expressed "truth" becoming ever more ingrained for each passing generation. Originality in classical art was therefore a matter not of innovation but of a continual return to "original"—that is, first—principles, to knowledge of nature itself. Classical theorists of the early nineteenth century could therefore argue that Greek art was at once both real (natural) and ideal (principled, truthful), and the best modern classicism would equal the ancients' achievement. In contrast, the originality of modernist painting was expressed through difference and deviation, rather than a reassuring repetition; the modernist stressed individual authorship by inventing a recognizably personal manner of applying paint or composing forms. Classicism was collective; modernism was individualized. As a collective enterprise, classical painting readily assumed its status as conventional or proper; and with respect to it, the modernist manner became metaphorical or deviant. In contrast to both classical and modernist modes, photography concentrated on external appearances, as if without the vagaries of a personally motivated vision, nor need of guidance from collective genius.

If photography pictures its external world without manipulation of any kind, is it not necessarily more proper than even classical painting? Does it not set a higher standard for the representation of the real? It can be argued that the format and many of the visual features of the photograph were calculated to imitate the look of traditional paintings and graphic works, minimizing the pictorial difference. But the medium's mechanism, its automatism, is another matter. Walter Benjamin stated that "photography freed the hand." It might be said instead that photography freed representation *from* the hand. This is the foundation of an unrewarding debate—which Benjamin himself did not enter—about whether photography remains a matter of art (aesthetic choice and rhetorical construction) or becomes an unprecedented form of pure documentation (disengaged recording of visual data). The debate runs the entire course of photography's history, with photographers as well as their critics appearing on both sides of the issue. Why the debate has occurred may be far more significant than how it has been conducted. The majority of those who ponder the problem eventually conclude—perhaps too facilely—that photographic practice normally performs both as active art and as passive documentation. Benjamin's contemporary Hans Tietze, an art historian, wrote in 1936: "Even a mechanical photographic reproduction [of a work of art] is a kind of interpretation of its model" (Tietze, 1934–1936).

Ultimately, this response fails to illuminate any distinct character of photography as a medium; instead, it speaks to a cultural or psychological need to introduce or reintroduce into modern technological practices the signs of humanity such practices might seem to have lost or never developed. This is the problem Tietze's remark was addressing, if only indirectly. When photography threatened to convert the personalized recreation of collective images (that is, the practice of classical painting) into a depersonalized mass industry—with the immediate threat coming from the reproduction of classical artworks—the mark of the individual maker, the sign of the artist's hand, gained special value. Before the advent of photography, it was often argued that any self-conscious display of manual skills might indicate ignoble materialistic interests. But once photography liberated the hand and removed it from sight, there was little urgency to argue about how much it should show. The issue became all or nothing; and with the hand invisible, art also seemed to disappear. Sensitivity to the issue led the art historian Henri Delaborde to offer moral support to engravers in 1856; because the reproductive process of engraving involves direct use of the hand, Delaborde reasoned, it "copies and comments on painting simultaneously," whereas photography "begins and ends" with material facts, never extending beyond "blind fidelity."

To protect representation from inhumanity, hand and mind needed to be expressed in the practice of the dominant mediums. Painting of the modernist sort, with its exaggerated physical signs of individual authorship, offered an obvious solution to the cultural problem. It should come as no surprise that despite its mechanism and orientation toward the external, photography too could be rehabilitated as an individualized art of documentation. This is the argument that emerges from Lincoln Kirstein's commentary written to accompany Walker Evans's *American Photographs* of 1938. Kirstein distinguished photography's mechanism from painting's handicraft, but then proceeded to distinguish one manner of photographic documentation from another: Evans had astutely abandoned the familiar "candid-camera" style of angle shots and was taking his pictures "head on with the unsparing frankness of a Russian ikon or a Flemish portrait" (Kirstein, 1938). Kirstein gave Evans personal artistic credit for developing a depersonalized style of documentation that seemed to escape aesthetic convention.

But does it? After all, it resembles other manners familiar within the history of art (Russian icons, Flemish portraits). The ironies of Evans's canonical documentation easily become apparent: we realize that the documentary must itself be a recognizable genre, and that styles of documentation change. Whereas Evans cropped his images, sometimes radically, to enhance their effect, Diane Arbus's photographic prints display ragged edges, imperfections normally avoided by a neatly registered and slightly cropped printing. Her style, even more than Evans's, indicates that her approach is hands off, pure documentation, no cropping after the "fact" of exposure. Just as Arbus chooses to retain Evans's frontality, but gives her prints a different formal look, so the particular type of photograph that most obviously connotes the "real" changes from time to time. Yet, at all times within the modern period, the strongest claim to the real has been held by photography (with the serious challenges coming from related mediums perceived as equally indexical, such as holography or video). Then why have so many thinkers, somewhat paradoxically, followed Roland Barthes (1977) in arguing that photography is an art as rhetorical as any other—and therefore, despite its naturalness, also artificial? Because photography's particular manner of figuration subverts all proper representation and lends itself to this very paradox. For the photograph is neither proper nor figured, neither properly documentary nor properly art. The photograph is a catachresis.

What is catachresis? Many rhetorics list it as false metaphor or misuse of metaphor. In a book composed during the 1820s, just before photography's advent, Pierre Fontanier offered a more detailed explanation: catachresis appears when "a sign, already attached to a first idea [or image], is attached also to a new idea, which itself had no sign or has none that is proper within the language" (Fontanier, 1968). A catachretic term borrows from another field of discourse as if without recognizing the distance, seeming to convert a metaphor into the proper name for something; yet a hint of metaphor remains. A traditional example, given by Fontanier and others, is "arm" of a chair. This usage cannot be metaphor (in that figure's own proper sense) because there is no other, unfigured way of referring to the relevant part of the chair. Analogy to the human body is not sufficient to give "arm of a chair" genuine metaphorical force. If "arm" is here a metaphor, it is a "dead" one, a commonplace understanding or even a cliché, simply the usual and expected word or reference to apply to the thing in question, despite the fact that it does not strike one as "literal."

There is an obvious connection to be made between catachresis as dead metaphor (commonplace expression, conventional wisdom, accepted truth) and classical images of any kind. Such images go unchallenged because they are so proper, so expected, so satisfying, just like dead metaphors. Yet, to members of a classical tradition, such images live and are the foundation of the culture's very survival. If I have associated catachresis with the disruptive force of photography because it is a new figure that seems proper, might catachresis also be associated with any number of classic modes of visual representation, because their residual figuration is overlooked?

Among theorists educated at a time when the study of classical rhetoric was fundamental and its elaborate distinctions seemed suited to a desired hierarchical social structure, the standard rhetorical figures could be applied quite naturally to complex theories of the visual arts. Fontanier's contemporary Quatremère de Quincy, who had a very liberal sense of figuration, linked linguistic metaphor with a desirable visual transformation and idealization: "Every composition in which an artist proposes to express something other than a servile imitation or a copy of things is more or less a metaphoric composition." Thus, the accomplished academic artist's conventions, no matter how standardized, effected a metaphorical transformation from the "real" to what Quatremère de Quincy called the "figured." One can imagine that the most canonical modes of metaphoric transformation would generate images so familiar that—despite being figured—they would pass for "reality." Classical art claimed such a propriety, a literal reality that was also an ideality, also a particular, but right, way of seeing the world through ideal, nondeviant figuration. Thus, during the early years of both modernism and photography, Ingres and other supporters of classical doctrine spoke not of dead metaphors but of living classics and of the classical tradition as endlessly able to absorb and reflect new personalities—a classicism ever adequate to modern demands.

If classical art sought to represent reality with an all-powerful, proper form of figuration (a metaphor that, like catachresis, passed for the literal), then photography undermined classical art's claim to this kind of right representation. It did so, not because it was itself unfigured, but because it made all other representations look *more* figured.

To perceive the photograph as a representation of the "real" depends on an understanding of the camera's mechanism and in most cases on an association of the real with seamless detail. Classical painting traditionally offered the viewer all that one expected to see in terms of a proper degree of detail that would define or identify an object (at its outer limits were the special cases of anatomical and botanical illustration). Photography breaks with this past history of representation. The viewer of the photograph is shocked by its effortless extension of the standards of proper detail and is faced with representation more real than what the real has ever been. From the time of the announcement of the daguerreotype, both proponents and detractors of photography noted that anyone at all—whether aristocrat or commoner, educated or not—could master the operation of this medium. The photographic image entered its society full blown, without its public presuming a collective tradition of genius or a past record of distinguished achievement as with classical painting. Nor did photography necessarily reflect strong individual authorship, as in the case of modernist painting. Photography was neither classical nor modern, neither the accepted proper term, nor the idiosyncratic, metaphoric one. Like a catachresis, as soon as it appeared, it became the only available image of the real. It appropriated, instantaneously and forcefully, all claims to the real.

Photography provoked defensive reactions. Supporters of the idealizing force of classical art, Delaborde among them, argued that the new medium could not respond to imaginative experience; and this failure was linked not only to an absence of spiritual input but to photography's lack of handicraft. Not only classicists, but modernists too, who valued the subjectively expressive hand, argued that if photography triumphed over painting, its conquest involved only the realm of material reality—it could document but could not create. Yet, everyone knew, or at least suspected, that the photograph was a "figure."

That figure was catachresis. The advantage to considering photography as catachresis, once one grasps the concept, is that one understands why the various forms of the art/documentation debate lead nowhere. The historical circumstances in which photography arose established its products as catachretic representations. They were not improved pictures that merely replaced old ones but a different kind of picture that displaced the order of the old—a new term where there was none, yet a picture that resembled pictures generated by the older means.

One never quite recognizes catachresis for what it is. Thus, commentators struggle to push photography one way or the other. Most art historians (naturally enough) have regarded the medium as artistic and have created for it a narrative of its own tradition, articulated by masters, masterpieces, and acts of imitative emulation. To study photography in this manner is not only to transform documentary features into aesthetic ones, but also to convert a catachresis into a metaphor, into a proper and manageable figure. In art-historical accounts, the shocking originality peculiar to the photograph must be shaped to resemble either the repetitive originality of classicism (eternal return to classical or primitive origins) or the self-expressive originality of modernism (innovative with every artist). By this interpretive maneuver the effect of photography's third, catachretic term is annulled, and a traditional binary opposition of classic to modern (often now reconceived as modern to postmodern) can be retained. Yet, the commonplace photograph, with its potential to convince, continually threatens to overpower preexisting hierarchy, and to become itself the only proper figure, the figure of the real.

In recent years, commentators have been speaking especially insistently of a rhetoric of the photograph, thereby raising (or reducing) its status to that of an "art," a discipline of figuration like all others. The investigation of this photographic rhetoric has followed divergent paths. On the one hand, the photographic image is aestheticized, set into a formal history of visual art, and withdrawn from the world of commonplace documentary representation. On the other hand, any rarefied artistic status is denied, and photography is set into a world of institutions, disciplines, and practices motivated by a social struggle for power. From the latter perspective, the archives of a police department or a colonial administration may hold more interest than a distinguished private collection. The example of photography has led the study of paintings and other forms of visual representation to a similar division: witness museum collections being investigated as manifestations of both aesthetic principle and political hegemony. To recognize the complementarity of the two interpretive gestures—to see that a history of the document suits the photograph neither more nor less than a history of art—is to engage the catachretic force of this persistently problematic medium.

BIBLIOGRAPHY

Barthes, Roland. "The Photographic Message." In *Image, Music, Text*, edited and translated by Stephen Heath, pp. 15–31. New York, 1977.

Benjamin, Walter. "The Work of Art in the Age of Mechanical Reproduction" (1936). In *Illuminations*, edited by Hannah Arendt, translated by Harry Zohn, pp. 217–251. New York, 1969.

Blanc, Charles. "L'oeuvre de Marc-Antoine." *Gazette des beaux-arts* 15 (1 September 1863): 268–275.

Delaborde, Henri. "La photographie et la gravure" (1856). In *Mélanges sur l'art contemporain*, pp. 359–388. Paris, 1866.

de Man, Paul. "Pascal's Allegory of Persuasion." In *Allegory and Representation*, edited by Stephen J. Greenblatt, pp. 1–25. Baltimore, 1981.

Derrida, Jacques. "White Mythology." In *Margins of Philosophy*, translated by Alan Bass, pp. 207–271. Chicago, 1982.

Dubois, Philippe. *L'acte photographique*. Brussels, 1983.

Fontanier, Pierre. *Les figures du discours* (1821–1830). Paris, 1968.

Kirstein, Lincoln. "Photographs of America: Walker Evans." In Walker Evans, *American Photographs*, pp. 183–192. New York, 1938.

Mentienne, Adrien. *La découverte de la photographie en 1839*. Paris, 1892.

Newhall, Beaumont. *The History of Photography: From 1839 to the Present Day*. Rev. enl. ed. New York, 1964.

Quatremère de Quincy, Antoine Chrysostome. *Essai sur la nature, le but et les moyens de l'imitation dans les beaux-arts*. Paris, 1823.

Quintilian. *Institutio oratoria*. 4 vols. Translated by H. E. Butler. Loeb Classical Library. Cambridge, Mass., 1976–1980.

Talbot, William Henry Fox. *The Pencil of Nature* (1844–1846). New York, 1969.

Tietze, Hans. "The Psychology and Aesthetics of Forgery in Art." *Metropolitan Museum Studies* 5 (1934–1936): 1–19.

Todorov, Tzvetan. *Theories of the Symbol*. Translated by Catherine Porter. Ithaca, N.Y., 1982.

Walton, Kendall L. "Transparent Pictures: On the Nature of Photographic Realism." *Critical Inquiry* 11 (December 1984): 246–277.

RICHARD SHIFF

PICASSO, PABLO (1881–1973), Spanish painter and sculptor. No body of work figures more prominently in histories of modern art than that of Pablo Picasso. And yet, no body of work is more difficult to pin down. Its staggering heterogeneity is matched only by the diversity of the interpretations to which it has been subject. Anyone attempting to uncover some commonality running through all the paintings (to say nothing of the drawings, prints, sculptures, ceramics, collages, and papiers collés) faces an impossible task; there simply is no evident unifying thread. Too often, as a result, recourse has been sought in a biographical approach, and specifically one based on a conception of the individual as essentially that: individual, monadic, self-possessed. Thus, implicitly, the figure of the artist is held to provide the coherence and continuity lacking in his art. In the case of Picasso, this turn to biography receives its apparent sanction from the artist's own assertion that his work was like a diary in which he recorded his thoughts from day to day. Art historians and critics have unfortunately tended to envision in response a journal filled, not like Eugène Delacroix's, with ideas and observations regarding the practice of painting, but rather with details of Picasso's personal life, his marriages and many affairs.

To dismiss such biographical approaches as trivializing is not to say that Picasso's relationship to women—or at least that the myth of virility he cultivated—should be considered entirely irrelevant to his art. Indeed, Leo Steinberg has eloquently argued that that myth provides the guiding metaphor for much of Picasso's work: the canvas is a woman, the artist (and, later, the viewer) her ardent lover. Whereas other painters constrained themselves, like a camera, to a solitary and often distant vantage point, Picasso sought instead the visual equivalent of an embrace; hence the multisidedness of so many of his figures, especially the female nudes. (One thinks here principally of those women whose erogenous zones all somehow manage to congregate on the picture plane, and who therefore seem to provide us with simultaneous apprehension of their every aspect.) "Drawing or painting *as if to possess*" is how Steinberg describes the phenomenon. The experience these nudes offer as its consequence is in a sense less strictly visual than it is somatic, or even carnal.

Of course, not all of Picasso's works conform to this rule. In fact, those for which he is most widely known—the Cubist paintings and papiers collés—are glaring exceptions to it. Although the early champions of Cubism often claimed for those images a simultaneous presentation of multiple aspects, the overriding impression the works offer is one of dispossession, of the depicted figures' and objects' intangibility and elusiveness. To observe the development of Cubism over the course of its so-called Analytic phase is, in effect, to watch volume and depth, and therefore physicality, drain from the image. The illusionistically rendered, faceted forms of the early paintings gradually flatten and fracture to become complicated but nonetheless primarily two-dimensional intersections of lines. Chiaroscuro modeling, as intense as in any Renaissance painting, remains, yet it is so inconsistently applied as to prevent resolution into solid, volumetric form. It is as if the machinery of illusionism were malfunctioning, chugging on without purpose, its devices laid bare.

At the start of this process—that is, in the paintings of 1908 and 1909—there was a pronounced sense of three-dimensionality; that, after all, was much of what motivated the assignation of the "Cubist" epithet. Yet, simultaneously, and then with increasing frequency, flatness began to assert itself—as in those places where, for example, the facade of a house bleeds into the ground on which it sits, or where the neck of a guitar merges seamlessly with the wall behind. This marked tension between two- and three-dimensionality has its precedent, of course, in the art of Paul Cézanne. Not coincidentally, it also has a certain affinity with late nineteenth-century debates on the nature of perception. Associationist psychologists at that time asserted that, contrary to one's common sense of things, vision does not actually have access to depth. The images formed on the retina of the eye are, they claimed, utterly flat; it is only with the superaddition of remembered tactile or kinesthetic cues that that two-dimensional image is filled out into the spatial plenum of the world as we experience it. In Cézanne's still lifes and landscapes there appears to be a constant probing of these perceptual possibilities. In certain areas, and primarily through a careful modeling of hues, a strong sense of the palpable emerges; yet elsewhere within the same canvas there will be a *passage* or telescoping of planes through which the near and distant are made to abut like the interlocking pieces of a jigsaw puzzle. With Picasso's Cubist paintings, in turn, one senses an even greater conflict between the (retinally) flat and the (corporeally) three-dimensional. Again, in the early works the two are held in relatively equal tension. By 1910, however, with such paintings as *Girl with a Mandolin*, flatness has already gained the upper hand. In the maddening evasiveness of that nude figure and its partial submersion into the background, we can perhaps experience, as Rosalind E. Krauss has suggested, something of the poignant loss Picasso himself must have

felt "as he watched the outcome of his own visual convictions, as, that is, he watched depth and touch—what we could call the carnal dimensions—disappear, quite literally, from sight" (Krauss, 1985).

During the winter of 1911/12 the last vestiges of the figure were eradicated, assimilated beyond recognition to the gridded-off plane of the picture. Significantly, it was at precisely this moment that Picasso introduced language—actual letters and words—into the space of the painting. His *Ma Jolie,* the title of which is prominently written along the bottom edge of the canvas, underlines the significance of the move. That title, evoking as it does the beautiful woman who specifically is not there, serves to register the poignancy of her absence even as it reinscribes her in the face of it. Language is suited to this task in a way that iconic images are not, since, as the linguist Ferdinand de Saussure was insisting at almost exactly this same time, words not only function in the absence of their referents, they themselves belong to a system founded on absences and spacings, on the interstices between words.

Henceforth, linguistic signs would serve as a crucial model for Picasso's thinking about the nature of images. In the works of 1912, especially the constructed sculptures and papiers collés, Picasso began employing a number of elements that operate in a manner roughly analogous to the signs of language. One of the fundamental tenets of language emphasized by Saussure is its essentially arbitrary nature, the unmotivated connection between signifier and signified. In contrast to the iconic images of Western art, which point to their referents by virtue of a mimetic resemblance to them, words bear no likeness to the ideas or objects they denote. Rather, their significance derives from the position they occupy within the overall linguistic system (their differences from other words), and from the context in which they are used. The situation is similar with the pictorial signs of Picasso's papiers collés. An upended trapezoid, for example, can stand perfectly well for the neck of a wine bottle, even though—and here is where its difference from iconic representation is most evident—were it isolated from the rest of the image, its meaning would be impossible to discern. In fact, so much do these Cubist works emphasize the fundamentally arbitrary relationship between signifier and signified, and their dependence on context, that often an identical element is used to signify two entirely different things. In one collage, a rectangle with a semicircular indentation along its edge serves to represent, in abbreviated fashion, the sound hole and outer surface of a guitar; in another, the very same shape designates instead the notched silhouette of a violin. The pieces function, that is, like homonyms. But there are more scandalous cases as well. Krauss has pointed out that in certain instances—her example is the 1912 papier collé *Violin*—indistinguishable signifiers (here, two pieces of newspaper once belonging to a single sheet) have even been made to signify antithetical terms: the front face of the instrument and the space behind it, planar surface and atmospheric depth.

Of the many insights to be gleaned from Picasso's papiers collés, none would prove more important than this—that the meaning and value of any element is inherently unstable and derives only from its position within a larger field of signification. Time and again in the works to follow that point would be reiterated. Yet, it was a point frequently missed by Picasso's contemporaries, even in regard to Cubism itself. The semiological turn of the later Cubist paintings and papiers collés marked a radical departure from the tradition of iconic representation that had ruled painting since the Renaissance. Those works introduced into the history of Western art a mode of pictorial representation not tied to mimetic likeness. With but a few exceptions, however, artists and critics of the period overlooked the semiological import of the images, and misunderstood their abandonment of mimesis. The elements of Cubist composition were taken for signs of an altogether different sort—directional markers on the road to abstraction, to nonrepresentational art.

When histories of modernism first came to be written, Cubism was thus co-opted into a grand narrative of painting's inexorable drive toward nonobjectivity. Picasso himself wanted nothing to do with such histories. He shunned abstraction, and equally resisted the prescriptiveness of teleological views. "To me," he said, "there is no past or future in art. If a work cannot live always in the present it must not be considered." Indeed, his Cubist works were immediately followed by a group of images done in an extremely classicizing style, alluding above all to the sculpture of Greco-Roman antiquity. That is, as progressive or historicist accounts of painting became ever more frequent—principally among artists who traced its development through Cubism to their own most recent, abstract compositions—Picasso ever more fully engaged a style at the furthest remove from modernism, at the distant end, so to speak, of the teleological arrow. Borrowing once more the terminology of Saussure, we might say that, whereas explanations of abstract art tended to cling to a traditional, diachronic conception of style (one style following another in succession), Picasso's classical paintings asserted, by contrast, a synchronic view of things—any one style being but a selection from a range of simultaneously available alternatives.

Those same classical paintings also helped to reveal that that field of alternatives is structured, much like language, around oppositions, although oppositions that are intrinsically unstable and therefore subject to change. In the 1910s and early 1920s, when works such as *Three Women at a Fountain* and *The Pipes of Pan* appeared, there was one overarching opposition on the verge of dominating the field: that between modern art and art of the past, abstraction serving as the shibboleth distinguishing the two. Picasso's paintings, however, did much to upset that opposition and thereby restructure the field. What they brought into the open and used to their advantage was the prevalence within critical dis-

course at the time of the rhetoric of "purity." According to the logic undergirding this rhetoric, one of the aims of modern painting was the purification of the medium, the discovery and isolation of its absolute essence. Certainly, abstraction had its place here; illusionistic representation could easily be identified as an "impurity," extraneous to the medium of painting proper, and therefore quite dispensable. But illusionism was, in many ways, peripheral to the crux of the "purist" argument. It was an incidental target of censure, implicated only by being in the service of what was felt to be the true threat, namely, "anecdote" or narrative. Visible just beneath the surface of this argument are, of course, the contours of Gotthold Ephraim Lessing's *Laocoön*, with its emphatic insistence on the necessary separation of the visual and literary arts. According to Lessing, the different kinds of elements employed by painting and poetry give each art a distinctive quality and determine the sorts of things that each is able to represent effectively. The distinctive quality of painting—the unchanging essence of the medium—was seen by Lessing to be its own unchangingness, that is, the simultaneity of its parts as contrasted with the temporal successiveness of words. Following this same logic, many critics of the 1910s and 1920s advocated an emphasis on "pure form" over "literary content." It was by trading on precisely this antithesis that Picasso's classical paintings found their way into the modernist canon; with their stolidly impassive figures, they appeared as uncompromisingly nonnarrative as any of the artist's earlier Cubist works. In fact, it would be only a slight exaggeration to say that it was at this moment of their assimilation, and partially through the agency of the classical paintings themselves, that modernism found its preferred rallying cry in "purity" rather than "abstraction."

Yet Picasso's subsequent works adhered no more to this "purist" version of modernism than his earlier ones had to the dogma of abstraction. When "purity" was posited as its own teleological end, Picasso declined to follow. It seems clear that his classical paintings were intended less to set a new course for modern art than to destabilize the opposition that had been guiding the old. Such, in any case, was their effect. Following the intervention of Picasso's paintings, modernism was reconceived, this time with classicism as its ally. The opposing side was likewise redrawn, its ranks comprised of what were perceived to be the pair's common foes: the narrative, the nonunified (and therefore noninstantaneous), the otherwise "impure."

Of course, this general opposition in turn became dominant—and very much complicated by the fact that, during the interwar years, classicism was enlisted into the service of conservative and right-wing propaganda. (Classical *images* were doubly susceptible because, apart from any overt political content, both their style and the medium itself now carried connotations of timelessness and immutability.) Rather than ceding the field, however, Picasso reentered it—this time with several series of prints, all plainly classical on the face of things, but in which many of the features that had been opposed to or excluded by classicism also reentered. In their subversive aspect, Picasso's classicizing prints resemble what Roland Barthes referred to as a "third language." The function of the latter Barthes explained by means of a recollection from his childhood of playing the game prisoner's base: "What I liked best was not provoking the other team and boldly exposing myself to their right to take me prisoner; what I liked best was to free the prisoners—the effect of which was to put both teams back into circulation: the game started over again at zero." Like a third language, like the child playing prisoner's base, Picasso's prints were meant to scatter the terms and restart the game—in this case, by overturning the oppositions on which classicism's very identity was based.

The 1930 illustrations for the *Metamorphoses* of Ovid offer a prime example: not only were they made to accompany a literary work (and one, moreover, whose continuous narrative virtually thematizes temporality and change), they themselves establish separate pictorial narratives, largely independent of any reference to the text. For instance, within many of these illustrations—all of which are rendered with a spare, elegant line reminiscent of ancient Greek vase painting—the outermost contours of the principal figure are drawn so as to locate that body in two different positions, as if it were glimpsed from two different angles. As the viewer scans the image, traversing the blank space between these divergent contours, the figure actually appears to move, pivoting or falling in concert with each shift of gaze. The temptation is to say that, despite their insistent narrativity, the *Metamorphoses* illustrations are still at least stylistically classical. Yet it is difficult to point to any feature that is unequivocally so. Even the classicism of the images' line dissolves under scrutiny, subject as that line is to all the vagaries of perception and interpretation that had traditionally subordinated color to line and denied the former any classical status.

Equally subversive is the *Vollard Suite,* a series of 100 extremely diverse (if still mostly classicizing) prints. Here, clearly, is a "work" whose elements cannot be viewed (or even conceived) simultaneously, a "work" whose sheer bulk forcefully asserts the temporal dimension of both its making and its viewing. Perhaps more striking than either the number or the diversity of the plates, however, is their complex interrelatedness. The dense "cross-referencing" of the imagery encourages the viewer to continually shuffle through the prints, tracking down associations and discovering new connections. Ironically, many of the prints depict a classical artist contemplating, dispassionately and from a distance, his already completed work; a substantial fraction of these also include within the studio setting a sculpted head whose features resemble those of the artist-onlooker himself. Even as the imagery, then, seems fully to support both the classical ideal of aesthetic disinterest and the disembodied gaze theorized in modernism's appeal to the "purely visual," the "viewer" demanded by the *Vollard Suite* at large is, of necessity, physically involved with the work, and driven by an impulse that mimics the restlessness of unfulfilled desire.

The 1935 etching known as *The Minotauromachy* serves in many respects as the culmination of these classicizing series. Its imagery not only draws heavily on that of the *Vollard Suite,* it contains numerous references to ancient myths recounted in the *Metamorphoses.* In fact, there is a sense in which the mythological character of the etching makes it emblematic of Picasso's oeuvre as a whole—or would make it so, were it not in the nature of that oeuvre specifically to resist emblematic encapsulation. Myth is yet another field of signification in which the value of any element (say, a particular mythological character) is determined differentially, in relation to the network of oppositions structuring the entire field. Moreover, those oppositions are notoriously unstable. As mythologists in the early part of the century were realizing and beginning to emphasize, when studied in the context of the full mythological system, certain binary pairs (for instance, a god and his principle antagonist) appear to vacillate or reverse positions, with the result that there is a curious identification between the supposed adversaries. A similar phenomenon can be seen among the characters of the *Minotauromachy.* Much of their significance derives from the hierarchical opposition, set up both in the etching itself and in certain images of the *Vollard Suite,* between the antagonists of the bullfight: human versus beast, or more specifically, matador versus bull. Yet, the two sides of this antagonism are brought together in the prominent, hybrid figure of the Minotaur. His subversion of the antithesis is all the more complete in that his lowly, brutish features appear at the pinnacle of his human form, the site that should be the locus of the most elevated aspects of his being. What is more, the Minotaur carries slung over his shoulder a matador's cape. (In the two colored proofs that were made of the etching, the identification is unmistakable: the bright red cape stands out dramatically from the darker earth tones of the rest of the composition.) The Minotaur, then, is a figure of irreducible duality, a figure fundamentally divided against himself.

The classicist Jean-Pierre Vernant has written of myth (in language that might just as easily be applied to Picasso's *Minotauromachy*) that

> it brings into play shifts, slides, tensions and oscillations between the very terms that are distinguished and opposed in its categorical framework; it is as if, while being mutually exclusive, these terms at the same time imply one another. Thus myth brings into operation a form of logic which we may describe, in contrast to the logic of non-contradiction of the philosophers, as a logic of the ambiguous, the equivocal, . . . not the binary logic of yes or no but a logic different from that of the *logos.*
>
> (Vernant, 1988)

As we have seen, this same "logic" is brought into play by much of Picasso's work. It governs not only the figure of the

PICASSO. Pablo Picasso, *Minotauromachy* (23 March 1935), etching and engraving on copper plate, printed in black, plate: 19 1/2 × 27 3/8 in. (49.6 × 69.6 cm); Museum of Modern Art, New York (Abby Aldrich Rockefeller Fund). (Copyright 1998 by the Estate of Pablo Picasso/Artists Rights Society, New York; photograph copyright by the Museum of Modern Art; used by permission.)

Minotaur but the classicizing images more generally, as their primary function was to confound, and thereby unravel, the neat distinction between classicism and whatever else was currently serving as its defining antithesis. It is equally evident in the papiers collés—in the 1912 *Violin*, for example, where a single sheet of newspaper is made to signify a pair of opposing terms. Yet this logic decidedly does not enter (at least not directly) into those many works first discussed—those, produced throughout the length of Picasso's career, in which the presence and possessability of the figure are uncategorically asserted. The existence of those works seems contradictory, in opposition to the rest of Picasso's oeuvre. It is largely on their account that we are forced to concede that that oeuvre has no unifying principle at its origin. Instead, there is a fundamental, irreconcilable opposition, an antithetical set of artistic visions and practices. On the one hand are images (again, principally of female nudes) whose subjects are given to us in their seeming entirety, and who as a result appear palpably, unquestionably present; on the other are ambiguous, equivocal works,

each prone to "tensions and oscillations" between the very oppositions structuring its meaning. In light of this opposition, between two mutually exclusive—albeit mutually implicated—alternatives, it becomes possible to see that Picasso's oeuvre as a whole is much like the figure of the Minotaur—or better, that the Minotaur is an apt figure for the oeuvre as a whole. The half-bull, half-man hybrid has traditionally been regarded as a self-portrait of Picasso, and this essay is meant to suggest nothing different—provided, that is, we recognize that the reference is less importantly to Picasso the man than it is to the body of work, irremediably double, that is made to cohere under the name "Picasso."

[*See also* Collage; Cubism; *and* Primitivism.]

BIBLIOGRAPHY

Bois, Yve-Alain. "Kahnweiler's Lesson." In *Painting as Model*, pp. 65–97. Cambridge, Mass., 1990.

Bois, Yve-Alain. "The Semiotics of Cubism." In *Picasso and Braque: A Symposium*, edited by Lynn Zelevansky, pp. 169–208. New York, 1992.

Golding, John. *Cubism: A History and Analysis* (1959). 3d ed. Cambridge, Mass., 1988.

Hollier, Denis. "Portrait de l'artiste en son absence (Le peintre sans son modèle)." *Cahiers du Musée National d'Art Moderne* 30 (Winter 1989): 5–22.

Krauss, Rosalind E. "Re-Presenting Picasso." *Art in America* 68.10 (December 1980): 90–96.

Krauss, Rosalind E. "In the Name of Picasso." In *The Originality of the Avant-Garde and Other Modernist Myths,* pp. 23–40. Cambridge, Mass., 1985.

Krauss, Rosalind E. "The Motivation of the Sign." In *Picasso and Braque: A Symposium,* edited by Lynn Zelevansky, pp. 261–286. New York, 1992.

Leighten, Patricia. *Re-Ordering the Universe: Picasso and Anarchism, 1897–1914.* Princeton, N.J., 1989.

Penrose, Roland, and John Golding, eds. *Picasso in Retrospect.* New York, 1973.

Poggi, Christine. *In Defiance of Painting: Cubism, Futurism, and the Invention of Collage.* New Haven, 1992.

Richardson, John. *A Life of Picasso,* vol. 1, *1881–1906;* vol. 2, *1907–1917,* New York, 1991–1996.

Rubin, William, ed. *Pablo Picasso: A Retrospective.* New York, 1980.

Steinberg, Leo. "The Algerian Women and Picasso at Large." In *Other Criteria,* pp. 125–234. New York and Oxford, 1972.

Steinberg, Leo. "The Philosophical Brothel." *October* 44 (Spring 1988): 7–74.

Steinberg, Leo. "Le fin de partie de Picasso." *Les Cahiers du Musée National d'Art Moderne* 27 (Spring 1989): 11–38.

Vernant, Jean-Pierre. *Myth and Society in Ancient Greece.* Translated by Janet Lloyd. New York, 1988.

LISA FLORMAN

PICTURESQUE.

The picturesque is an aesthetic category that came into prominence in the last third of the eighteenth century. The word *picturesque* comes from the French *pittoresque* and the Italian *pittorésco,* meaning "in the style of a painter." The English term was in use early in the eighteenth century. For example, Alexander Pope wrote in notes to his translation of the *Iliad* (1717) that one of Homer's descriptive passages marked "circumstances the most Picturesque imaginable." Presumably, Pope meant that the passage created an engaging visual image in readers' minds. The term *picturesque* was used similarly by William S. Gilpin in his *Essay on Prints* (1768). Gilpin defined the picturesque as "expressive of that peculiar kind of beauty which is agreeable in a picture." Of course, pictures in many different styles and with many different subjects have pleased viewers over time, so Gilpin's comment does not yet fix a clear meaning for the term *picturesque.* It does, however, refer to whatever sorts of scenes most pleased audiences in mid-eighteenth-century England, and increasingly the pictures that pleased were landscape scenes in the style of the French and Italian masters.

Gilpin went on to use the term *picturesque* in the title of a series of travel books beginning in 1782. These books, each of whose subtitles referred to observations "Relative Chiefly to Picturesque Beauty," were intended to alert travelers to the aesthetic pleasures available through the contemplation of landscape scenes. Gilpin illustrated these volumes with aquatint sketches of the views he recommended. Thus by mid-century, the term *picturesque* had a dual application. It referred both to paintings and to natural scenes.

Because of volumes like Gilpin's, the picturesque became associated with travel. In *The Search for the Picturesque,* Malcolm Andrews speaks of picturesque tourists—travelers in search of quintessentially picturesque scenes. As Andrews characterizes this enterprise, "the object was not so much to find something new to describe . . . as to find scenery which resembled familiar paintings or poetic descriptions" (Andrews, 1989, p. 76). Andrews calls attention to one other aspect of picturesque travel: not only did tourists flock into the countryside seeking out the recommended scenes; they were also encouraged to create their own sketches and paintings of those scenes. Explicit directions were often included in the guidebooks, telling the tourists which "station points" to assume, how to frame their sketches, which features to include, and so on. Picturesque travel within Britain became a domestic equivalent to the grand tour that had flourished on the Continent a century earlier, and the instructions to amateur painters helped develop a formulaic notion of a picturesque scene.

A more precise and theoretical approach to the picturesque was offered by two "dueling" theorists in the 1790s, Uvedale Price and Richard Payne Knight. Their concerns differed from Gilpin's in important ways. First and foremost, their landscape preferences were fueled not by travel to wild locales in remote parts of England and Wales, but by views about estate improvement and a shared antipathy to the gardening style of Lancelot "Capability" Brown. (Brown, a professional gardener who redesigned between 120 and 140 estates in the course of his career, would move earth, dam streams, and destroy the formal gardens of his predecessors in order to create his signature landscapes. Typically, Brown's designs featured serpentine streams and limpid lakes, vast expanses of rolling lawn dotted with clumps of trees, and an assortment of classical and Gothic temples, cascades and grottoes, rustic cottages, and Palladian bridges.)

Two publications in 1794 marked the beginning of this phase of the picturesque. Subtitled "a Didactic Poem in Three Books . . . Addressed to Uvedale Price, Esq.," Knight's *The Landscape* covered a variety of topics. Knight not only outlined principles of taste—just congruity of parts was the primary one—and rules of gardening, but also celebrated older formal gardens and offered savage criticisms of the landscapes of Brown and his followers, who "shave the goddess [Nature] whom they come to dress." The poem's third and final book is devoted to trees.

The opening question of Price's 1794 publication, *An Essay on the Picturesque,* shows a concern for landscape design. He asked whether "the present system of improving is founded on any just principles of taste." His answer was no. Price hoped to inaugurate a new system of improving, one grounded in the theory of the picturesque. His theory of the picturesque was modeled on Edmund Burke's account of the beautiful and the sublime. In his treatise *A Philosophical Inquiry into the Origins of our Ideas of the Sublime and Beautiful* (1757), Burke had argued that the sublime and the beautiful were distinct aesthetic categories, associated with characteristic qualities and giving rise to characteristic passions and ideas. Thus, sublime objects and situations aroused terror in their viewers and were typically immense, powerful, and obscure; beautiful objects, by contrast, aroused love and were typically smooth, small, and delicate. Price in effect added a middle aesthetic category—the picturesque—between the two poles singled out by Burke. Price defined the picturesque in terms of objective qualities—its hallmarks were roughness, sudden variation, and irregularity. He believed that intricacy and variety were sources of pleasure and that they aroused in viewers the passion of curiosity.

One doctrinal difference between Price's and Gilpin's versions of the picturesque is apparent from the titles of their books. Gilpin understood the picturesque to be a species or variety of beauty; recall the subtitle appended to each of his tourbooks. Price, on the other hand, took the picturesque and the beautiful to be distinct aesthetic categories. He applied the category "picturesque" to all manner of items in the *Essay*, discussing the picturesqueness of such diverse objects as water, trees, buildings, ruins, dogs, sheep, horses, birds of prey, women, music, and painting. But Price was interested above all in the creation of picturesque landscapes. His estate, Foxley, in Herefordshire, had wild wooded paths with narrow bridges crossing turbulent streams. Presumably, he deemed such picturesque scenes the most aesthetically satisfying.

In addition to characterizing picturesque landscape scenes, Price also defended a view about their creation. He believed that landscape gardening should take its principles from the art of painting. That is, he claimed that aspiring designers should apply the principles of painting (general composition, grouping of parts, harmony of tints, unity of character, breadth and effect of light and shade, and connection) to natural scenes. Price did not see a need for landscape professionals. On his view, young aristocrats, who had honed their taste by viewing landscape scenes on the grand tour, viewing and collecting landscape paintings, and attempting their own landscape sketches, would internalize the principles of good landscape painting and then apply those principles in improving their own estates.

Whether the principles of painting were applicable to the area of landscape design became the subject of an extended debate between Price and the garden designer Humphrey Repton. Repton, who set himself up as a landscape professional and was considered by many to be the heir to Capability Brown, initially agreed with Price's dictum regarding the rules of painting. The two gentlemen took a tour together

along the Wye Valley. But reminiscing about it later, Repton averred that "during the pleasant hours we passed together amidst the romantic scenery of the Wye, I do remember my acknowledging that an enthusiasm for the picturesque had originally led me to fancy greater affinity between *Painting* and *Gardening* than I found to exist after more mature consideration and greater experience" (Repton, 1794, p. 70n.). Repton worked out his doubts about this issue in a "Letter to Sir Uvedale Price, Esq." Price soon fired back a book-length response, "Letter to H. Repton, Esq., on the Application of the Practice as well as the Principles of Landscape-Painting to Landscape-Gardening, Intended as a Supplement to the Essay on the Picturesque." While both theorists are identified as proponents of a "picturesque" style of gardening, they disagreed about a theoretical matter—the importability of principles of painting—and a practical one—how close to the house picturesque elements should be carried.

The actual debate between Price and Repton foundered on some silly issues—for instance, whether certain views like that down a steep prospect could be painted, and whether the visual elements that made a desirable foreground in a painting would serve equally well as the "foreground" to a house, that is, whether houses should be surrounded by a picturesque tangle of rocks, brambles, and rotting logs. Nevertheless, the two disputants may well have agreed in their judgments of particular paintings, gardens, and natural landscapes.

Knight defended a distinctly different theory of the picturesque. His poem *The Landscape* was a critique of contemporary styles in landscape gardening and estate improvement. In 1805, however, he produced a much more theoretical and wide-ranging work, *An Analytical Inquiry into the Principles of Taste*. Intended to provide an entire theory of taste on a par with works by Alexander Gerard, Archibald Alison, and, ultimately, Immanuel Kant, Knight's volume engaged the intellectual work of philosophers past and present. The *Inquiry* was structured according to the three faculties of sense, association of ideas (including imagination and judgment), and the passions. The picturesque is defined in book 2 on the association of ideas, although Knight's discussion of the senses provided many examples of aesthetic judgment and preference.

The crucial difference between Knight's and Price's take on the picturesque is summed up in Knight's accusation that Price's "great, fundamental error [was] seeking for distinctions in external objects which only exist in the modes and habits of viewing and considering them" (Knight, 1805, p. 196). For Knight, the picturesque was a principle of association, not an objective property marked by a set of perceptible traits:

This very relation to painting expressed by the word picturesque, is that which affords the whole pleasure derived from association; which can, therefore, only be felt by persons who

PICTURESQUE. Thomas Hearne, *Wooded Glen at Downton, Herefordshire* (c. 1790), oil on canvas; Victoria & Albert Museum, London. (Photography copyright by the Board of Trustees of the Victoria & Albert Museum, London; courtesy of Victoria & Albert Museum, London/Art Resource, New York; used by permission.)

have correspondent ideas to associate; that is, by persons in a certain degree conversant in that art. Such persons being in the habit of viewing, and receiving pleasure from fine pictures, will naturally feel pleasure in viewing those objects in nature, which have called forth those powers of imitation and embellishment.

(pp. 154–155)

From this passage it is clear that art played a central role in the picturesque as Knight understood it. In minds suitably primed by experience of art, certain scenes call up memories of sketches and paintings. This is what makes those scenes picturesque.

Can associative links of this sort constitute the picturesque? Some might object that Knight's formulation makes the picturesque ubiquitous. Anything can be picturesque if it summons up appropriate associations in appropriate viewers. It is possible that the theory can be shored up by specifying in more detail what counts as "appropriate" in each sense here. Gentlemen of Knight's era, who had received similar educations, viewed many of the same paintings, and savored many of the same scenes on the grand tour

and while traveling within the United Kingdom, would tend to have similar associations. They might admire many of the same landscape paintings and agree on such practical matters as eschewing brambles and rotting logs in the area immediately surrounding a house. Thus, within Knight's social and cultural circle, the picturesque might indeed have a fixed sense, yet his definition leaves it open in principle that the process of association could be utterly promiscuous.

A second and competing characterization of the picturesque emerges in some portions of Knight's treatise. Discussing the senses in book 1, Knight insisted again and again that smooth and unchanging sights and sounds soon bore their viewers and hearers. Our senses crave novelty and irritation. Not to such a degree as would yield pain or defeat generalization. Yet, Knight declared that "all change, not so violent as to produce a degree of irritation in the organs absolutely painful, is pleasing; and preferable to any uniform and unvaried gratification" (quoted in Hipple, 1957, p. 275). Thus, Knight suggested we have preferences at the physiological level—for dappled hues, varying lines, mixed tones, and so on—that accord with the properties Price pointed out as the defining traits of the picturesque. This rapprochement between Price and Knight fails in the end, however, because Knight believed that taste was determined not by sensory factors but by the association of ideas.

The physiologically based argument just offered for Knight conflicts with the more stringent definition of the picturesque he offers in book 2 of his treatise, which conflicts in turn with the definition offered by Price in his *Essay*. Of course, none of these views creates any clear connection between the picturesque and the art of painting. In fact, the definitions of the term *picturesque* were so varied and wideranging even in the time Knight was writing that the term can seem without critical weight. Thus, John Dixon Hunt and Peter Willis report that

> by 1801 a supplement to Johnson's *Dictionary* allowed a range of meanings which include what is pleasing to the eye, what strikes the viewer as singular or appeals to him with the force of a painting or would either afford a good subject for a painted landscape or help in conceiving one. (Hunt and Willis, 1988, p. 337)

Stephen Copley and Peter Garside write that "widespread adoption of Picturesque terminology in conversational use in the late eighteenth century, in relation to a broad range of cultural practices, confirms the problematic nature of the aesthetic: even in this period, it can seem so ill-defined as to be virtually meaningless" (Copley and Garside, 1994, p. 1).

The picturesque has been resurrected in recent times as an interesting aesthetic, cultural, and critical category. The first person to play a role in its rehabilitation was Christopher Hussey, whose book *The Picturesque* appeared in 1927. Hussey had direct connections to the nineteenth-century manifestations of the picturesque, for he inherited Scotney Castle, with picturesque grounds designed by Willam Sawry Gilpin (nephew of the clergyman responsible for the many volumes of picturesque tours), from his father's elder brother. Hussey placed the picturesque as a necessary bridge between the classic and the romantic in the history of art and appreciation. He defined the picturesque as a moment when "the relation of all the arts to one another, through the pictorial appreciation of nature, was so close that poetry, painting, gardening, architecture, and the art of travel may be said to have been fused into the single 'art of landscape'" (Hussey, 1927, p. 4). He claimed that "the picturesque interregnum between classic and romantic art was necessary in order to enable the imagination to form the habit of feeling through the eyes" (ibid.).

Hussey did much to revitalize this fascinating aesthetic category, but many today criticize his interpretation, arguing that it diminishes the importance of the picturesque. Walter Hipple, in *The Beautiful, the Sublime, and the Picturesque in Eighteenth-Century British Aesthetic Theory,* gives a more evenhanded and judicious account of the picturesque, offering detailed accounts of the views of Gilpin, Price, and Knight. He does not, however, adjudicate the conflicts among these authors, aiming instead for a "closely literal survey of the arguments . . . without the superimposition of a more comprehensive theory" (p. 188).

Martin Price, in his essay "The Picturesque Moment," characterizes the picturesque as inherently unstable. He notes that

> "the picturesque in general recomends the rough or rugged, the crumbling form, the complex or difficult harmony. It seeks a tension between the disorderly or irrelevant and the perfected form. Its favorite scenes are those in which the form emerges only with study or is at the point of dissolution.
> (Price, 1964, p. 277)

Elsewhere Price maintains that "once the picturesque is given moral or religious grounds, the picturesque moves toward the sublime" (p. 262).

A more common complaint is that the picturesque evacuates or is antithetical to any moral outlook. For example, Malcolm Andrews claims that "the picturesque enterprise in its later stages, with its almost exclusive emphasis on visual appreciation, entailed a suppression of the spectator's moral response to those very subjects which it could least hope to divest of moral significance—the ruin, the hovel, and rural poverty" (Andrews, 1989, p. 59). Ann Bermingham, in *Landscape and Ideology,* states that "the aesthetic effect of the picturesque seems to be calculated precisely on poverty and misery" (Bermingham, 1986, p. 69). Overall, Bermingham links the rise of the picturesque with nostalgia for a bygone way of life and relation to the land lost irrevocably to the process of enclosure. Noting that "the aesthetically pleasing landscape was not the economically productive one" (p. 66), she explores a number of factors that irrevocably altered the relation between landowners, laborers, and the land, and asserts that a "new sentimentalizing of the rustic landscape was codified in an aesthetic of the 'picturesque'" (p. 54).

Bermingham concluded that a "profound pessimism lay at the root of picturesque theory" (p. 70). On her view, the picturesque combined a nostalgic look back at the old order with an acknowledgment of the "precariously temporal nature of the new order that replaced it" (ibid.). Other authors concur in finding a dark side to the picturesque. Andrews suggests that the low viewpoint characteristic of picturesque compositions indicates a failure of confidence, a repudiation of the panoramic prospect favored by earlier painters and poets. Nor does Andrews find the picturesque fascination with humble life and unelevated views at all egalitarian. Rather, he argues that Uvedale Price, in calling for variety, hoped "to restore the old hierarchy with its clear social distinctions" (p. 65).

Kim Ian Michasaw, in "Nine Revisionist Theses on the Picturesque," emphasizes additional class distinctions within the picturesque itself. In particular, he points to differences between the audiences for which Gilpin, on the one hand, and Price and Knight, on the other, were writing.

Gilpin's readers were tourists moving through the country-side in search of sights to admire. They had no power to alter the landscape through which they traveled. By contrast, the landowners addressed by Price and Knight were amateur improvers who could change their estates at will. The landscape was thus subject to them. Michasaw concludes, first, that the picturesque is not a homogeneous notion, and second, that William Gilpin is not rightly viewed as an inept theorist but rather as an important thinker whose rules make the landscape inviolable, thereby elevating Nature and the actual, and diminishing art (Michasaw, 1992, p. 94).

Recent theorists have played inventively with the themes and arguments of the eighteenth-century authors surveyed above. In some cases this has taken the form of moral critique. Many take the picturesque to task as a mode or conveyor of cultural imperialism. Several authors in W. J. T. Mitchell's anthology *Landscape and Power* (1994) suggest that English attitudes and conventions regarding the natural landscape were imported to the far reaches of the empire and imposed inappropriately on the native scenes and traditions. Other authors offer quite distinctive reinterpretations of the picturesque. For instance, Sidney K. Robinson, in *Inquiry into the Picturesque,* characterizes the picturesque not in terms of Price's three qualities but in terms of mixture. On Robinson's view, the picturesque requires ingredients that remain distinct and do not easily blend into the wholes of which they are parts. Robinson suggests that this happens only when creators do not use all their resources in perfecting their compositions (Robinson, 1991, p. 22). Robinson thus positions the picturesque in opposition to regularity, system, and homogeneity. He draws further political consequences from this account, aligning system with tyranny and singularity (p. 49), finding parallels between the picturesque championing of mixture and Whig politics in England in the 1790s, especially the career of Charles James Fox.

The political analogies that Robinson draws from the picturesque conflict with the analyses of Bermingham and Michasaw. Robinson's initial account in terms of mixture may in fact have little connection with the concerns and intents of the original picturesque theorists: Gilpin, Price, and Knight. Yet, this in itself is testimony to the fact that the picturesque remains an intriguing and vital aesthetic category, one that will continue to be reappropriated and reinterpreted as new generations of scholars build aesthetic theory that is increasingly sensitive to the social, the cultural, the economic, and the ideological.

[*See also* Beauty; Environmental Aesthetics; Gardens; Knight; Landscape; Nature; *and* Price.]

BIBLIOGRAPHY

Andrews, Malcolm. *The Search for the Picturesque: Landscape Aesthetics and Tourism in Britain, 1760–1800.* Stanford, Calif., 1989.
Bermingham, Ann. *Landscape and Ideology: The English Rustic Tradition, 1740–1860.* Berkeley, 1986.
Copley, Stephen and Peter Garside, eds. *The Politics of the Picturesque: Literature, Landscape, and Aesthetics since 1770.* Cambridge and New York, 1994.
Gilpin, William. *An Essay on Prints.* London, 1768.
Gilpin, William. *Observations on the River Wye, and Several Parts of South Wales, etc. Relative Chiefly to Picturesque Beauty; Made in the Summer of the Year 1770.* London, 1782.
Gilpin, William. *Observations, Relative Chiefly to Picturesque Beauty, Made in the Year 1772, on Several Parts of England; Particularly the Mountains, and Lakes of Cumberland, and Westmoreland.* London, 1786.
Gilpin, William. *Observations, Relative Chiefly to Picturesque Beauty, Made in the Year 1776, on Several Parts of Great Britain; Particularly the High-Lands of Scotland.* London, 1789.
Gilpin, William. *Observations on Several Parts of the Counties of Cambridge, Norfolk, Suffolk, and Essex. Also on Several Parts of North Wales, Relative Chiefly to Picturesque Beauty, in two Tours . . .* London, 1809.
Hipple, Walter John, Jr. *The Beautiful, the Sublime, and the Picturesque in Eighteenth-Century British Aesthetic Theory.* Carbondale, Ill., 1957.
Hunt, John Dixon and Peter Willis, eds. *The Genius of the Place: The English Landscape Garden, 1620–1820.* Cambridge, Mass., 1988.
Hussey, Christopher. *The Picturesque: Studies in a Point of View.* London, 1927.
Knight, Richard Payne. *The Landscape, a Didactic Poem in Three Books. Addressed to Uvedale Price, Esq.* London, 1794.
Knight, Richard Payne. *An Analytical Inquiry into the Principles of Taste.* London, 1805.
Michasaw, Kim Ian. "Nine Revisionist Theses on the Picturesque." *Representations* 38 (1992): 76–100.
Mitchell, W. J. T., ed. *Landscape and Power.* Chicago, 1994.
Price, Martin. "The Picturesque Moment." In *From Sensibility to Romanticism: Essays Presented to Frederick A. Pottle,* edited by Frederick W. Hilles and Harold Bloom. New York and Oxford, 1965.
Price, Uvedale. *An Essay on the Picturesque.* London, 1794.
Price, Uvedale. *Letter to H. Repton, Esq., on the Application of the Practice as well as the Principles of Landscape-Painting to Landscape-Gardening, Intended as a Supplement to the Essay on the Picturesque.* London, 1795.
Repton, Humphrey. *Letter to Sir Uvedale Price, Esq.* London, 1794.
Robinson, Sidney K. *Inquiry into the Picturesque.* Chicago, 1991.

STEPHANIE ROSS

PILES, ROGER DE (1635–1709), French aesthetician. Roger de Piles studied philosophy and theology at the Collège du Plessis and at the Sorbonne in Paris. A position as tutor and, later, as secretary to the French ambassador Michel Amelot provided lifelong financial security and opportunities to travel extensively in Italy, Portugal, Switzerland, Germany, and Spain. In 1668, when he published his translation of and commentary on Charles-Alphonse Dufresnoy's *De arte graphica,* he established himself as the theoretical leader of the *rubénistes* in their quarrel with the *poussinistes,* who, headed by Charles Lebrun, dominated the recently established Royal Academy of Painting and Sculpture. From 1692 to 1697 he was imprisoned in Holland on charges of espionage. He finally joined the academy in 1699 as *conseiller honoraire amateur* and was its chief theorist. His academic lectures, the sum total of his theory, were published in 1708 under the title *Cours de peinture par principes.*

For de Piles, the quarrel between the *rubénistes* and the *poussinistes* encompasses something more important than the relative achievements of Peter Paul Rubens or Nicolas Poussin, or the respective merits of drawing or coloring. It concerns the question of how properly to define the art of painting. Like Gotthold Ephraim Lessing a hundred years later, de Piles dismisses the equation ut pictura poesis as inappropriate in view of the different nature of the two arts; they speak differently to their respective audiences. In an important way de Piles is more radical than Lessing: while the German is determined to define the arts solely according to their means and what these means could achieve, he also insists on defining the end and aim of both the arts of sculpture and painting as the depiction of bodily beauty. It follows for Lessing that even in painting, drawing, being concerned with form, is more important than coloring, which is concerned only with the accidence of appearance of objects.

De Piles defines painting as the imitation of all the visible objects of nature on a flat surface. The nature and value of the respective object, whether a historical event or a still life, are extrinsic to this definition. Whether a painting is good or not does not depend on whether it is poetically moving or historically instructive, but whether it has the power to create a convincing illusion. This is not advocating crass naturalism: "A painter who only paints what he sees will never arrive at a perfect imitation." Moreover, "an able painter must never be the slave of nature; he must be her arbiter and discerning imitator . . . and as long as a painting makes its effect and impresses itself agreeably on our eyes, that is all one can expect in this respect."

De Piles is concerned neither with ideal bodily beauty nor with naturalism but with the specific visual nature of pictorial imitation—with the visual effect of pictures. His demand that a picture "make its effects" is based on two grounds. First, if any visible object is a potential *sujet* for a painting—no matter whether it is a flower or a heroic action—then painting cannot derive any intrinsic importance from the nature of its subject matter. It is not, by its own definition, an instructive or didactic art. It would therefore be wrong to assume that people would feel obliged to look at pictures. If an artist wants a work to be noticed, he or she must make sure that the work itself, by the force of its visual effect, catches spectators' attention and draws them near.

Second, the means of painting from which it derives its definition (i.e., lines and colors on a flat surface) will not by their own nature allow a convincing "naturalistic" imitation of the world (a point taken up later by Denis Diderot). Despite de Piles's own rhetorical use of some examples of complete visual deception, and despite his advocacy of the abbé Zumbo's colored wax sculptures, it is true to say that illusion or *tromperie* does not, for de Piles, refer to a state of mind in which we mistake the objects of the picture for objects of nature. It does mean that we abandon ourselves to a pictorial fiction that by its own force excludes our awareness of the real world (and, in particular, of the flat surface and the material presence of the picture).

The condition under which such a pictorial fiction can work, and work forcefully, is that of unity, of a unified total visual effect. Three closely related parts of painting are essential for this unity of effect: *l'oeconomie du tout ensemble, le coloris,* and *le clair-obscur.* In the *Cours de peinture* de Piles deals with them in three separate chapters, yet that separation is artificial: as light and shade are painted with colors, they are also part of coloring, the overall color composition, and this is virtually identical with the *tout ensemble.* As early as 1668 de Piles defines the rule of the unity of the whole, its overall composition, as the most important precept of painting:

> It belongs properly to the painter only, while all the others have been borrowed, from the *belles lettres,* from medicine, from mathematics, or from other arts: for it is sufficient to have *esprit* and *des lettres* in order to come up with a beautiful invention: in order to draw one needs to know anatomy: a mathematician will be well able to put buildings and other things into perspective . . . But as far as the *oeconomie du tout ensemble* is concerned, there is only the painter who understands it; because the end of the painter is to deceive the eyes in a pleasant way: he will never achieve that if he lacks this part. (de Piles, 1668)

The modernity of de Piles's notion of overall pictorial composition lies in the fact that he does not try to define its rules according to the nature of a particular kind of subject matter (e.g., history painting), but rather according to the nature of our visual perception, our faculty of sight. His is the first theory of formal pictorial composition. According to the difference between focal and peripheral vision, the picture—which according to de Piles must make its successful impact *au premier coup d'oeil* if it is to be noticed at all—must have a clearly defined and forceful center and become less defined and less forceful toward the margins. As a centralized composition, it also has to have space and depth, and in order to preserve the unity of the whole, de Piles recommends either convex or concave arrangements. These rules must be applied with discretion: they would defeat their own purpose if they were to become visually obvious.

For de Piles, the unified first effect of a painting is more than a merely initial introductory experience; it is a truly aesthetic effect in that our faculty of vision, presented with an object composed according to the very structure of this faculty, would gain a deep and lasting satisfaction in the full exercise of its powers. The dispersed objects of nature could never offer us the same satisfaction and pleasure. The formal unity of the *tout ensemble* can lead to, or can include, another profound visual effect: it allows painting to aspire to a universally approved and desired quality, that of harmony: "Harmony, wherever it is found, comes from arrangement and good order. There is harmony in morals as in physics; in the conduct of the lives of men, as in the bodies of men themselves." The *tout harmonieux* of painting is primarily that of *coloris,* and its overall *effet merveilleux,* brought about by the careful orchestration of the sympathies and antipathies of colors, is the visual equivalent to the moving aural effects of the accords and harmonies of music.

By insisting on the importance of both visual unity of effect and, as part of it, visual harmony of color composition, de Piles succeeds in undermining the orthodox division of artistic work into the highly regarded intellectual or mental activity of invention, and the lowly rated manual craft of execution. He is no longer worried about the position of painting within the traditional, and by now old-fashioned, system of the liberal and the mechanical arts. There is, according to de Piles, a specific science and intelligence of painting that embraces both the planning and the execution of the *tout hamonieux.* This science must comprise a thorough knowledge of artists' materials (like colors and their interaction), a full understanding of the ways in which these materials, applied to and partaking in the whole and its composition, will affect the vision of the viewer, and an ability both to plan and to execute a picture as a *tout harmonieux* and with *unité d'effet.* This is, strictly speaking, the painter's science and all that artists require in order to succeed in their art. For particular kinds of subject matter, a knowledge of poetry, history, or Scripture may be desirable, but that does not constitute an essential part of the business of being a painter.

If, in addition to having acquired and developed this *science de la peinture,* the artist is endowed by nature with *génie* and has cultivated his *fureur pittoresque,* he will instill in his work a force surpassing even the harmonious unity of the *tout ensemble.* To describe this ability, de Piles introduces the term *enthousiasme,* borrowed from Nicolas Boileau's translation of Longinus. For an artist to work in a state of enthusiasm does not mean that he or she may disregard the rules of his science; it is through the unity and harmony of the whole that artists transmit their enthusiasm to viewers, elevating them to a similarly lofty state of mind:

> Enthusiasm carries us away without our noticing it and transports us, so to speak, as from one country to another without our being aware of it except through the pleasure that it causes us. It is to that surprising, yet just and reasonable, elevation that the painter as much as the poet should carry his work, if both want to arrive at that extraordinary *vrai-semblable* that touches the heart and is the greatest merit of painting and of poetry.

Here, at last, de Piles enters again into the traditional *paragone* with poetry. In its supreme form of enthusiasm, wholly engaging us in an elevating, absorbing, and enthralling visual fiction, painting—different though it is in its means, its procedures, and its science—is the equal of the best works of poetry. Like its sister art, painting has the power to lift us out of our ordinary life and to transport us to a higher experience of an altogether different order.

De Piles's effects of unity, harmony, and enthusiasm are autonomous effects of painting, not continuous with our sense of the normal world. They provide us with an experience *sui generis* of painting. For the modern viewer, the art of Antoine Watteau or Jean-Baptiste-Siméon Chardin, of François Boucher or Jean-Honoré Fragonard provides this experience more easily, but perhaps also less forcefully, less "enthusiastically," than that of Rubens, which inspired de Piles in the first instance. Eugène Delacroix's notion of the dreamlike quality of art insists on a similar discontinuity between the two worlds; and while modern abstract art has taken the idea of autonomous visual effects to its logical conclusion, it may in the process have lost that essential part from which the whole of de Piles's theory developed, the experience of visual fiction.

In the context of eighteenth- and nineteenth-century thinking about the arts de Piles's theory appears as an important prephilosophical attempt to separate what came to be known as aesthetic effects from moral issues and a concern with knowledge. His development of a theory of painting that impresses itself on its viewers must be seen as part of an attempt to widen the public for art by positing the judgment of taste as largely independent from the knowledge of rules. De Piles's new public is no longer that of experts, of learned artists and erudite connoisseurs, represented and promulgated by the academy:

> It would be a very strange thing if pictures were made only for painters, and concerts for musicians. It is quite certain that *un homme d'esprit* who has not learned the rules of art, is well able to judge a picture, even if he cannot always give the reasons for his feeling . . . he will judge as *homme de bon sens.*

The *homme d'esprit, de bon sens,* or, elsewhere, the *honneste homme,* deserve, according to de Piles, the right to judge; the knowledge of the rules and the history of art required for that purpose is limited and is provided by de Piles himself in his dialogues and his *Abrégé de la vie des peintres.* This, by his own admission, contains little that is new, yet it contains all that is needed: to know more would be pedantic and boring, to know less would be scandalous. His playful *Balance des peintres,* appended to the *Cours de peinture,* in which he notoriously awards marks out of twenty for composition, drawing, coloring, and expression to all major European painters of the past, is often misunderstood as a pedantic application of rules. It was meant to be the opposite, an encouragement for a wider public to make up its own mind, and in this respect its popularity in eighteenth-century France is testimony to de Piles's success.

BIBLIOGRAPHY

Works by de Piles

L'art de peinture de Charles-Alphonse du Fresnoy, traduit en françois, avec des remarques nécessaires et tres-ample. Paris, 1668.
Dialogue sur le coloris. Paris, 1673.

Conversations sur la connoissance de la peinture, et sur le jugement qu'on doit faire des tableaux. Paris, 1677.

Dissertation sur les ouvrages des plus fameux peintres, dédiée à Monseigneur le duc de Richelieu. Paris, 1681.

Abrégé de la vie des peintres, avec des réflexions sur leurs ouvrages, et un traité du peintre parfait, de la connoissance des desseins, et de l'utilité des estampes. Paris, 1699.

Cours de peinture par principes. Paris, 1708.

Other Sources

Alpers, Svetlana. "Roger de Piles and the History of Art." In *Kunst und Kunsttheorie, 1400–1900,* edited by Peter Ganz, pp. 175–188. Wolffenbütteler Forschungen, vol. 48. Wiesbaden, 1991.

Démoris, René. "Le discour des tableaux ou le vin de Brie, d'après Roger de Piles." *Écrit-voir* 4 (1984): 75–85.

Lichtenstein, Jacqueline. *La couleur éloquente: Rhétorique et peinture à l'âge classique.* Paris, 1989.

Mirot, Léon. *Roger de Piles, peintre, amateur, critique, membre de l'Académie de Peinture, 1635–1709.* Paris, 1924.

Puttfarken, Thomas. *Roger de Piles' Theory of Art.* New Haven, 1985.

Puttfarken, Thomas. "Composition, Perspective and Presence: Observations on Early Academic Theory in France." In *Sight and Insight: Essays on Art and Culture in Honour of E. H. Gombrich at 85,* edited by John Onians, pp. 287–304. London, 1994.

Puttfarken, Thomas. "Roger de Piles, une littérature artistique destinée à un nouveau public." In *Les "Vies" d'artistes: Actes du colloque international organisé par le Service culturel du musée du Louvre les 1er et 2 octobre 1993,* edited by Matthias Waschek, pp. 81–102. Paris, 1996.

Teyssèdre, Bernard. *Roger de Piles et les débats sur le coloris au siècle de Louis XIV.* Paris, 1957.

Teyssèdre, Bernard. "Une collection française de Rubens au XVIIe siècle, le cabinet du duc de Richelieu décrit par Roger de Piles, 1676–1681." *Gazette des Beaux-Arts* 2 (1963).

Teyssèdre, Bernard. *L'histoire de l'art vue du grand siècle: Recherche sur l'abrégé de la vie des peintres par Roger de Piles et ses sources.* Paris, 1964.

THOMAS PUTTFARKEN

PLATO [*To explore Plato's philosophy of art, the first of its kind in the history of Western philosophy, this entry comprises five essays:*

> Survey of Thought
> Plato on Mimēsis
> Plato's Use of Poetry
> Plato on the Effects of Art
> Plato and Modern Aesthetics

The first essay is an overview of Plato's thought in general. The next three essays focus on issues that were central to his thinking about art (a term Plato, of course, did not use the way we now do, anymore than he ever used the word aesthetics*): "mimēsis," "the use of poetry," and "the effects of art." The final essay reflects the differences between Plato's philosophy of art and modern aesthetics. For related discussion, see* Aristotle; Beauty; Mimesis; Poetics; *and* Theories of Art.]

Survey of Thought

Plato (428–347 BCE) is one of the principal figures not only in ancient Greek thought but in the history of philosophy as a whole. His works have played a vital shaping role in many fields of the subject, and his discussions of art and beauty can be regarded as the first great monuments of philosophical aesthetics. Different aspects of his work have influenced artists and philosophers of art in many ages, including Aristotle (in the *Poetics*), medieval and Renaissance philosophy of art, and Romanticism. He is still regarded as an important contributor to debates about the nature and value of art.

The most prominent feature of Plato's philosophy of art is his hostility to artists, especially poets. This has tended to be regarded in two different ways. The first is to dismiss his position as a product of philistinism or political zeal. The second is to assume that so great and subtle a thinker cannot really have been hostile to poetry, and to seek clues that he has a more positive view of "genuine art." Both reactions rest on an apparent assurance that art has a supreme value that philosophers should not impugn. A third, more sympathetic approach sees Plato as highly sensitive to the appeal of poetry, yet fundamentally challenging art's value and its relationship to philosophy. This best reflects Plato's view in the *Republic*, book 10, where he rejects some forms of poetry as antithetical to the pursuit of truth and the good, but confesses that freeing oneself from their attractions is akin to keeping away from a person one loves.

Plato lacks the modern conception of art as a domain of life with a high and unquestionable value. No single Platonic term translates directly as *art*. On the other hand, it is appropriate to speak of his philosophy of art since he frequently treats poetry, drama, music, painting, and sculpture as kindred activities. His thinking about beauty inaugurated a long tradition in aesthetics, although Plato's own concern with the value of beauty is not purely aesthetic in the modern sense, and he makes no privileged link between beauty and the arts.

The chief Platonic texts bearing on art and beauty are the *Republic* (especially books 2, 3, and 10), *Ion, Hippias Major, Symposium, Phaedrus,* and *Laws* (especially books 2 and 7). Similar concerns permeate his philosophy in all its phases, however, and his discussions of art and beauty are best appreciated in the context of his ethics, metaphysics, and epistemology. The dominant questions are always whether the arts increase our knowledge or promote what is ethically valuable.

Republic, 2–3. Plato's best-known treatment of the arts occurs in the *Republic*, the central work of his mature "middle period." In books 2–3 of his description of the ideal human community he discusses *mousikē*, which includes music and dance, but also poetry and dramatic enactment. The concern is to produce the right moral character in the selected class of citizens Plato calls "guardians." He assumes that a training in the arts from infancy will achieve this, along with gymnastics. But it is not only the practices of the young that are to be controlled—he also wishes to set standards for the arts throughout the community.

Plato examines the content of mythical stories and poems, and proposes to remove portrayals of figures such as gods and heroes unless they present true paradigms of human behavior and give to rise to desirable moral attitudes. The staples of Greek education such as Homer and Hesiod are to be censored by the state in accordance with this rule. Plato has a rudimentary notion of fiction, but insists that a fiction should not be approved unless it gives a good likeness. For example, no divine being is capable of change, deception, or evil, so no fiction will be permitted in which gods are thus portrayed.

Plato makes a division between two forms of poetic diction: pure narration in the poet's own voice, and narration by means of *mimēsis*—dramatic enactment or representation. The two forms may occur separately or combined: tragedy and comedy use *mimēsis* alone, dithyrambic poetry uses pure narration without *mimēsis,* and Homeric epic is a combination of the two, in which dramatic speeches by characters in the story punctuate the poet's pure narration. Plato argues that the person of good character must not pursue dramatic *mimēsis* as an end in itself, despite the pleasure this can bring, but should always emulate people of appropriate character, whether inside or outside a fictional context. One may thus enact the part of a noble, restrained character, but indiscriminate pursuit of *mimēsis* will make one a double or multiple person. The idea is that one becomes similar to what one enacts, and that the guardians must have only a single character to fit them for their single role in the state. A parallel argument supports prescriptions as to which musical modes, rhythms, and instruments may be used, since these will also assimilate the performer to specific traits of character.

In this discussion Plato assigns the arts the high and honorable role of training the growing soul and impressing gracefulness on it, preparing it for the rational pursuit of the good. Yet, he sees no value in artistic products that give pleasure as such. He emphasizes that the most pleasure-giving and the "most poetic" artists will find no place in his community.

Republic, Book 10. In book 10 of the *Republic* Plato gives a new account of *mimēsis* and excludes "all mimetic poetry" from the ideal state. Painting is used as an example to explain the nature of *mimēsis* in a more general sense, which is the making of representational images or appearances. The painter paints the image of a bed. This is no real thing, but is derivative from real beds made by a carpenter, which are in turn "less real" than the Form of Bed. Plato is using the apparatus of his epistemology and metaphysics in order to analyze artistic activity. Knowledge, for him, requires contact with the eternal, unchanging Forms, such as Justice itself or Beauty itself, which alone have true being. His strategy is to show that a painter does not produce something with true being, but only the appearance of a thing of a certain kind. This is *mimēsis.*

The real focus of this argument is poetry. If poetry is mimetic (as Homer and the tragedians in particular are), then it too produces only appearances of things and people.

Supporters of Homer claim that a poet requires comprehensive knowledge of human life in order to make such appearances. But Plato argues that this is a false assumption. Poets who practice *mimēsis* are far from knowing the truth about human excellence and deficiency, and should not be regarded as "the educators of Greece" on the strength of their poems. Poets produce only images of virtue and everything else they write about.

Plato then examines the psychology of poetic *mimēsis,* asking what part of the psyche it appeals to. Again he uses an analogy with visual appearances. The mind has a split reaction to visual illusions—an "inferior" part of us continues to be deceived by them even when the rational part has attained the correct belief. Analogously, poetic *mimēsis* has the power to arouse a childish, emotional part of the psyche, which reacts independently of our rational beliefs. The "greatest charge" against mimetic poetry is that even disciplined Platonic individuals, whose soul is governed by reason and the search for the good, may be ruined by the pleasures of such poetry: sympathetically following its fictional images of emotional turmoil and excess, they allow the "inferior" part of the soul free rein, a habit that may spill over into their reactions to things in real life.

On the grounds, then, that it is a kind of appearance making masquerading falsely as knowledge, and that it has deleterious effects on the psyche, poetic *mimēsis* is to be banished from Plato's ideal community. Plato retains performances whose aim is moral edification rather than pleasure, considering these to be a kind of poetry. His criticisms are most sharply directed at Homer and tragedy, although he objects to every poetic form whose portrayal of scenes or characters aims at pleasure. Such poetry is to be banished, not only from the model community, but from the individual's soul, which throughout the *Republic* is held to be analogous to the city.

Inspiration. Elsewhere Plato suggests that good poets are divinely inspired. This has sometimes been thought to mitigate the criticisms of the *Republic,* but does so equivocally at best. For Plato opposes inspiration to genuine knowledge, which has the higher value.

The *Ion,* one of Plato's earliest dialogues, portrays Socrates in conversation with Ion, who is a rhapsode, a professional reciter of poetry and would-be literary critic. Socrates argues that the rhapsode's abilities stem not from genuine expertise *(technē)* but from inspiration. A typical *technē* is medicine, which embraces a clear subject matter, is teachable, and has general principles of which a rational account can be given. The rhapsode's ability to discourse effectively on Homer's merits is not of this kind, according to Socrates.

Instead, successful performance and discourse about poetry should be explained in the same way as fine poetry itself, as stemming from a state of possession in which one becomes temporarily "out of one's mind." Fine poetry speaks through the poet as a mouthpiece. The poet can write finely about any subject when in such a state, but can give no account of the poetry's source. We should admire poets as "divine" because of their beautiful, pleasure-giving works, but must not think that they or their interpreters have the kind of responsibility for their achievements that is characteristic of consciously applied expertise.

Similar views of poetic inspiration are repeated in other dialogues, including Plato's last work, the *Laws.* A more positive view appears to be present in the *Phaedrus,* written some time after the *Republic.* Here, Socrates praises the benefits of various kinds of "madness," including poetic inspiration or "the madness of the Muses." A good poet cannot rely on technical expertise alone, but must be "mad" or possessed in a particular way. This view, however, is compatible with the condemnation of poets as lacking knowledge or expertise. For while Plato recognizes that good poetry requires a special explanation, he does not necessarily think that it stands very high in the whole scheme of human values. Later in the *Phaedrus,* poets are ranked sixth out of nine in a list of lives entered by reincarnated souls, while the philosophical lover occupies first place. Although the philosopher is supposed to be "cultured" and enamored of beauty, there is nothing here corresponding to the honorific title of "artist" as used by modern theorists.

Technē (expertise or craft) does not stand in for the modern term *art.* Artistic pursuits such as poetry, painting, and music are deficient when compared with clear paradigms of *technē* such as medicine, building, or arithmetic. The beginnings of a philosophy of the "artistic" lie rather in the idea of inspiration, which is diametrically opposed to *technē.* Given his central belief that the healthy soul should be governed by the disciplined, rational search for knowledge of the good, Plato is suspicious of an activity that he thinks is outside the full control of the rational mind.

Beauty. The term for *beautiful* in Plato's Greek is *kalon.* It is a wide term of approbation, sometimes translated as "fine." Plato often praises poets as producing fine or beautiful works. How close does he come to an aesthetic notion of beauty?

The most notable treatments of beauty are in the *Symposium* and *Phaedrus.* It can scarcely be an accident that Plato's writing in these works reaches heights of brilliance that the modern reader must regard as supremely artistic. Nevertheless, the theme in both cases is love and its relation to philosophical aspiration. Beauty is not tied specifically to works of art, which are comparatively neglected. Plato thinks, first, of the physical beauty of a human individual regarded as the object of desire by a pederastic lover.

In the *Symposium* the objects to which this lover is attached are progressively elevated: attachment is first to bodily beauty, then to the beauty of souls, then to beauty in abstract objects of learning, and finally to a Platonic Form. The Beautiful itself, the eternal Form that is beautiful in a strict and unchanging way, is what the philosopher will as-

pire to love, despising as "mortal trash" the particular sensible objects that are beautiful, including all artifacts and human individuals.

In the *Phaedrus* the philosopher-lover enters a continuing association with the beautiful beloved, who serves as a visible reminder of Beauty itself. Beauty is the one Form that has an easily recognizable sensible aspect. These doctrines are enunciated by Socrates in a fine mythical speech that Plato marks as poetic and even inspired. But there is playfulness here, prompting the reader to question where Plato is being serious, and where the boundary lies between philosophical discourse and the poetic invocation of beauty and love.

Plato's conception of beauty is not straightforwardly aesthetic. The dialogue *Hippias Major* (whose authenticity has sometimes been disputed) gives some insights here. When a definition of beauty or fineness *(to kalon)* is sought, relevant notions are "the appropriate," "the beneficial," and "the useful"—taking us into areas of approbation that are not aesthetic. On the other hand, Plato finds it natural to associate something's being fine with its having a fine appearance, and one species of the fine is "that which pleases through sight or hearing." This category prominently includes the visual arts, music, and poetry. Plato thus recognizes the arts as an area in which objects are praised for being pleasing to the senses, and sees this as one of the areas covered by his term *kalon.*

Pleasure and the Good. A persistent theme in Plato's writings is the opposition between what is pleasing and what is good. In the *Gorgias,* he laments that dramatists and musical performers resemble practitioners of rhetoric, who try to win over the audience with whatever gratifies them, rather than seeking to make them better by imparting to them genuine knowledge of what is good. The most desirable use of the arts would be the opposite of this, as Plato explains in his last dialogue, the *Laws.* In this work he develops a blueprint for a city on more realistic lines than those followed in the *Republic* and makes detailed provision for the arts within it.

One of the questions raised by the *Laws* is what the standard of evaluation for the arts should be. Many people maintain, says Plato, that "the power of music to give pleasure is the sole standard by which it should be judged." But this leads to an unacceptable relativism, in which good music is simply music that a particular audience likes. Plato proposes to institute superior judges, who are familiar with the art form in question, but, more important, have a proper knowledge of what is ethically good. They would use this as the true criterion of music, and similarly with all the arts. Pleasure is not allowed to be a criterion of artistic success in an indiscriminate way. In this way innovations in style are to be curbed.

Nevertheless, Plato is not opposed to pleasure; rather, he demands it for his citizens in the *Laws,* much of whose life will be spent in play *(paidia)*. They must take part in choric dances and music at all stages of their life, which will provide them with "harmless pleasure," at the same time cementing the community and transmitting the correct values. In Plato's view there are correct values, which it is not the business of artists to decide, so play is not allowed to be free. It must be ensured that no new styles develop without the city's approval. The arts are declared not to be personal to anyone, but to belong to the state. Plato gives the arts a weightier role than they enjoy in many modern communities, yet at the same time scorns any notion of self-expression or artistic freedom.

In the *Philebus*, another late dialogue, Plato examines pleasure at length. Pleasure in the beauty of colors, shapes, and sounds is classified as "pure" pleasure, which does not depend on desires or an admixture of distress. Such pleasures are truer than others, and receive approval because they "go with health and self-control" in the psyche. This suggests a positive aesthetic, albeit of an austere kind. But the pleasures of tragedy, which for Plato rely on emotional involvement with images of the morally ambiguous or false, will not be included in the pure pleasures of beauty.

Poetry and Philosophy. Book 10 of the *Republic* refers to an "ancient quarrel between poetry and philosophy." Plato is one of the chief contributors to this quarrel, yet both sides of it play themselves out in his dialogues. His writing is often akin to poetry in its supremely skillful use of metaphor, myth, and rhetoric. The traditional story that Plato was a writer of tragedies in his youth, however reliable, is not belied by the nature of his philosophical writing. It may also be asked why it is dialogues that Plato writes: he is critical of *mimēsis*, yet uses it himself, giving us words that present the mere appearance of what the character Socrates says and does.

A plausible interpretation is that Plato's writings are a deliberate attempt to oust mimetic poetry from its central role in the culture of his day. The ultimate aim of Plato's dramatic portrayals and his poetic use of language is, however, not to bring pleasure or to engage the mind in emotional experiences. Rather, it is to prompt independent inquiry into the truth by means of rational argument. Plato aims to supplant poetry in order to establish philosophy as a discipline. In so doing, he raises profound questions about the relationship between philosophy and art that touch on the very nature of philosophy itself.

BIBLIOGRAPHY

Works by Plato

The Collected Dialogues of Plato. Edited by Edith Hamilton and Huntington Cairns, translated by Lane Cooper et al. Corr. ed. Princeton, N.J., 1963.

Plato: Republic 10, with translation and commentary. Translated by S. Halliwell. Warminster, 1988.

Other Sources

Ferrari, G. R. F. "Plato and Poetry." In *The Cambridge History of Literary Criticism*, vol. 1, *Classical Criticism*, edited by George A. Kennedy, pp. 92–148. Cambridge and New York, 1989.

Havelock, Eric Alfred. *Preface to Plato.* Cambridge, Mass., 1963.

Janaway, Christopher. *Images of Excellence: Plato's Critique of the Arts.* Oxford, 1995.

Nehamas, Alexander. "Plato and the Mass Media." *Monist* 71.2 (April 1988): 214–233.

Moravcsik, Julius, and Philip Temko, eds. *Plato on Beauty, Wisdom, and the Arts.* Totowa, N.J., 1982.

Murdoch, Iris. *The Fire and the Sun: Why Plato Banished the Artists.* Oxford, 1977.

CHRISTOPHER JANAWAY

Plato on Mimēsis

"Poets tell many lies," says Plutarch, citing a proverb (*Moralia* 16A), and elsewhere reports that Gorgias said that a poet who deceives is wiser than one who does not (348c). Philostratus may record an even earlier view when he claims that it is pleasant and harmless to be affected by things that do not exist as if they did (*Proemium* 391k.4). Plato is the first to raise alarm about deception in poetry, appealing in two different ways to the concept of *mimēsis*.

In Plato's criticism of poetry, *mimēsis* picks out, first, a certain sort of poetry that is to be condemned as deceptive and, second, a broad range of artistic production, including poetry, all of which may be deceptive. The two uses are not consistent, but *mimēsis* carries certain dangers in both of them, and its products are always inferior to their originals. The broader use is probably closer to standard ancient usage, for Aristotle, in the *Poetics*, classifies poetry, theater, music, dance, and the visual arts all under *mimēsis*. To understand the background concept, then, we must first see how poetry, music, and sculpture could all be considered mimetic.

Frequently translated as "imitation," *mimēsis* does not correspond perfectly to any English term and is best left untranslated. As such, it has become a term of art in twentieth-century discussions. Generally speaking, *mimēsis* is the process by which a poet, artist, or other imitator adapts selected features of an original to a product *(mimēma)* in such a way that the product has an effect through its maker's art that the original would have by its nature. A mimetic statue may have the look of a real nude, whereas mimetic poetry or drama may have some of the emotional impact of the action it represents. Even medicine is mimetic when it reproduces, through treatment, the healing of nature. Although not inherently deceptive, *mimēsis* deceives if it deliberately passes off a product in place of its original. So much for the background of the Greek concept.

Plato narrows the focus of *mimēsis*. In his first use of the term in the *Republic*, as a classification within poetry, *mimēsis* is primarily limited to impersonation. In his second and wider critique of poetry, he uses it for the reproduction of mere images, *image making*, not limited to the visual. Elsewhere, in a third, more neutral, approach to the topic, Plato treats *mimēsis* as *reproduction*.

Impersonation. In book 3 of the *Republic*, Plato defines *mimēsis* as: "likening oneself to another either in voice or in appearance" (*Republic* 393c5; cf. *Sophist* 267a). This is the art of an actor or performer; its product is performance, and its original is speech or other action in real life. Since poetry was made in ancient Greece to be presented orally, all poetry that contains direct discourse is mimetic in that it is written to be performed (392d5). Indirect discourse is not performable in the same way, and is therefore not mimetic (394a). Plato thus has three modes of poetry (394c, 392d):

1. pure *mimēsis*, which produces the direct discourse of tragedy and comedy,
2. pure narrative, such as is found in many dithyrambs; and
3. a mixture of the two, as is found in epic.

Because he holds that poetry can be purely narrative and thus made without *mimēsis*, Plato can bar mimetic poetry from education without barring poetry altogether (398a).

Plato illustrates *mimēsis* with the speech of Chrysis (*Iliad* I.17ff.): the poet "tries his best to make us think that the speaker is not Homer, but a priest, and he an old man" (393b1–2). Here, Plato is clear that it is the author who impersonates the speaker in direct discourse; later in the same passage, he will treat the performer as the impersonator. Both cases satisfy the general definition of *mimēsis*: in the first, the poet borrows words from the original; in the second, the performer borrows expressive features of the original's speech—or, more accurately for a Homeric scene, both poet and performer borrow features from what they imagine the original to have been. Whether the artists are working from an actual or imagined original scene, listeners will have an experience close to that of hearing an old man wailing for the loss of his daughter. Thus, *mimēsis* can be carried out for fiction as well as for fact, and by those who know their original as well as by those who do not. The Aristotelian distinction between history and poetry is not relevant to Plato's criticism of *mimēsis*: a performance is no less deceptive if what it brings to life is history.

The main danger Plato treats in book 3 is that citizens may be beguiled by such poetry; but no audience really believes that the speaker in Homer is Chrysis. Everyone knows Homer wrote the poem. What, then, is Plato's objection to *mimēsis* as impersonation?

1. The first objection to impersonation is that it aims at deception concerning the identity of the speaker, and it entices us to do the same: the poet "tries his best to make us think" what is not the case, and so must the performer. Here is the kernel of Plato's concern. It is not that we are really likely to be taken in by a deception, but that we may be beguiled into becoming performers, and therefore into taking

deception as our aim; and this is morally an unhealthy aim to take.

2. A second objection concerns the bad moral qualities of the people who are to be impersonated in ancient epic and tragedy. Ancient Greek education depended on the recitation (i.e., the performance) of poetry by upper-class youngsters, and Plato was afraid that students would tend to become like the characters they impersonated. Certainly, ancient poetry teems with characters no peer of Plato would want his children to emulate.

3. A third objection is more Platonic: on Plato's account of the ideal state, each student must learn to play only the role proper to his station in life and to avoid all others, in order that justice may be preserved in the city. A course of mimetic performances, however, would require a student to take many parts, and this would be bad practice for the pure life of a guardian.

4. In case the poet does not know the original, a second act of *mimēsis* takes place along with the first, for the poet is then playing the part of one who knows, borrowing the trappings of knowledge to win the confidence of listeners—trying to have, by art, the effect on his listeners that a truly wise person should have by his wisdom (*Republic* 10, esp. 598c). Impersonation of a wise person is the most dangerous of all deceptions, in Plato's view, and he has shown Socrates making a career of bringing such deceptions to light.

Image Making. Plato treats *mimēsis* differently in book 10 of the *Republic*, where he uses the example of the production of images in a mirror (596d) to illuminate the production of images by painters, and, in turn, the production of poems by Homer and the tragedians. Here, he drops his earlier distinction between narrative and nonnarrative forms to build a line of criticism aimed at poetry in any form. His two objections are that *mimēsis* carries a false pretension to knowledge and that it depicts, appeals to, and strengthens the worst element in the human soul.

He compares poets to painters to illustrate his view that poetic *mimēsis* deceives its audience if it makes them accept its expert authority on the subject of the poem (598c). No one would believe that a painter is expert on bridle making merely because he can present us a convincing visual image of a bridle. Poets, on the other hand, offer themselves as moral teachers to the Greeks on the strength of their powerful presentations of heroic action in verse. A poet who paints a convincing word picture of a general beguiles his audience at the same time into thinking they are learning from his poetry what it is to be a good general. Indeed, Plato implies, much of Greece has been fooled into thinking that poets have the authority of experts on moral education.

The analogy to painters is meant to show how foolish this is; and such deception, concerning ethics, is especially dangerous in Plato's view. Unlike statesmen, who may do well without expert knowledge if they have true opinions, poets work only from images, and so are void even of true opinion.

In this too, poets are like painters—third down from those who know. A bed maker works from a unique original Form of bed (made by a god); a painter representing a bed looks only to the manufactured bed, and not even to the bed as it is in its three dimensions, but as it appears from one angle or another. The painter thus ranks third behind god and bed maker, and, because the painter's product is mediated by a mere appearance, it is too remote from the truth to be useful in education. So it is with poets, who occupy an analogous third-ranking position. The "colors" they use are meter, rhythm, and harmony, and the appearances they make convincing by these means are merely vulgar opinions as to what is good or noble (602ab). We have nothing whatever to learn from the reproduction of such opinions in poetry.

The case against poetry is more serious than this; it is bound up with Plato's case against emotion as arising from an inferior part of the soul—the same part of the soul that is unable to distinguish appearance from reality. In a decent person, the rational element in the soul reins in emotion; but poetry is most effectively mimetic when it overrides the better judgment of an audience in order to induce an emotional response. Poetry is most effective in engaging emotions when it represents characters who themselves give way to emotion, and these are bad models. Decent people who are not given to emotion in their private lives may yet find their self-control disarmed in the theater, their intelligence disabled, and their moral character damaged in consequence.

Reproduction. *Mimēsis* is not always based on mere appearances, however, and does not always play to our weaknesses. In the *Laws*, *mimēsis* is a kind of reproduction that can be accurate (668b); in the *Timaeus*, it is the ideal relation between sound thought or speech and the divine reality of the Forms (47bc); and in the *Statesman*, the laws are *mimēmata* of the truth that is known by experts. The rule of such laws is second best to direct rule by the experts themselves, but, in the absence of experts, it is the best we can have (300c; cf. *Laws* 817b). All of these positive uses of *mimēsis* depend on the idea that a product of *mimēsis* should have at least some of the good qualities of the original object. Sound thought as described in the *Laws* is a proper *mimēma* of reality because it has some of the stability of the intelligible world. Thus a *mimēma* can serve a useful purpose so long as its limitations are known.

Every *mimēma* has some features that belong also to its original, but the taking of features from an original is not always a case of *mimēsis*: a child has many of its mother's physical features but is not her *mimēma* by virtue of them, because the child was not produced to take her place by having an effect that is properly hers. By contrast, the laws were produced to take the place of experts in maintaining—albeit weakly—the stability that is the proper result of rule by experts. A *mimēma* takes on just those features of its object that it needs to take over the effect at which it aims. *Mimēsis* does not aim at the same sort of effect in every case; but it does in every case aim at an effect, and that effect explains the selection of features that are reproduced in *mimēsis*.

Mimēsis in Plato, then, is the reproduction of at least some of the qualities of an original, through impersonation, image making or reproduction. In itself, it is neither a good nor a bad thing to do. When it flows from ignorance, as in the case of poets, it has the aim of deceiving its audience; when it aims to reproduce the emotion-engaging properties of action, as in the theater, it is morally corrupting. But when it provides us with the next best thing to a lost and divine original, then *mimēsis* is our best hope.

BIBLIOGRAPHY

Work by Plato

Plato: Republic 10, with translation and commentary. Translated by S. Halliwell. Warminster, 1988.

Other Sources

Halliwell, Stephen. *Aristotle's Poetics.* London, 1986.
Havelock, Eric Alfred. *Preface to Plato.* Cambridge, Mass., 1963.
Keuls, Eva C. *Plato and Greek Painting.* Leiden, 1978.
Koller, Hermann. *Die Mimesis in der Antike.* Bern, 1954.
Moravcsik, Julius, and Philip Temko, eds. *Plato on Beauty, Wisdom, and the Arts.* Totowa, N.J., 1982.
Murdoch, Iris. *The Fire and the Sun: Why Plato Banished the Artists.* Oxford, 1977.
Nehamas, Alexander. "Plato on Imitation and Poetry in *Republic* 10." In *Plato on Beauty, Wisdom, and the Arts,* edited by Julius Moravcsik and Philip Temko, pp. 47–78. Totowa, N.J., 1982.
Oates, Whitney J. *Plato's View of Art.* New York, 1972.
Tate, J. "Imitation in Plato's *Republic*." *Classical Quarterly* 22 (1928): 16–23.
Verdenius, W. J. *Mimesis: Plato's Doctrine of Artistic Imitation and Its Meaning for Us.* Leiden, 1949.
Woodruff, Paul. "Aristotle on Mimesis." In *Essays on Aristotle's Poetics,* edited by Amelie Oksenberg Rorty, pp. 73–95. Princeton, N.J., 1992.

PAUL WOODRUFF

Plato's Use of Poetry

Plato condemns or severely restricts the use of poetry in education, yet he uses poetry extensively in his own works, citing verses with approval, imitating poetic style and imagery, or subjecting poems to critical study. In this Plato follows to some extent the custom of his time and place, for poetry loomed large in a culture to which writing itself, to say nothing of composition in prose, was a relative novelty. Still, Plato makes more use of poetry than any other prose writer of his age, and this calls for explanation. Plato is uniquely interested in evaluating and criticizing Greek culture, and this interest partly explains the efforts he makes to come to grips with both rhetoric and poetry. The poets he uses most are the ones who constituted a canon in his time, the ones who had the most secure places in traditional education—Hesiod, Simonides, and Pindar, but most of all Homer. The author of *On the Sublime* classifies Plato among those writers who drew on Homer: "Plato, above all, diverted for himself thousands on thousands of channels from the Homeric river" (Pseudo-Longinus 13.3). Yet, Homer is the poet Plato singles out for the most criticism.

General Criticism. Plato's explicit reasons for keeping poetry out of education are well known, and are based mainly on his view that poetry disarms reason, both in poets and in their audiences.

1. Poetry emphasizes and appeals to the emotions, thus weakening reason (*Republic* 605c–606d).
2. Living poets cannot explain their work, and therefore must write from inspiration rather than from knowledge (*Apology* 22bc; cf. *Ion* 534a and *Laws* 719c).
3. Dead poets cannot discuss their work at all, but serious discussions require interlocutors who can respond to questioning ("I think you and I should . . . set the poets aside and exchange words entirely on our own, testing the truth and ourselves"; *Protagoras* 348a).
4. Poetry is mimetic (*Republic* 597e) or tends to include *mimēsis* (392d–398b).
5. Poets seem often to represent gods and heroes improperly (*Republic* 377d–392c).

This last is the main point at issue in the "ancient quarrel" between philosophy and poetry.

Citations. It is not surprising that speakers in Plato's dialogues who are marked for refutation frequently appeal to the authority of poets in support of their own views. Their use of poetry may be seen as one of the marks against them. But Socrates and the Athenian Stranger cite poetry as well. At *Meno* 81b, Socrates quotes Pindar in support of the immortality of the soul. In the *Laws,* the Athenian cites Theognis (630ac) and Hesiod (690e) in support of his views. Such an appeal is not uncritical, however: in the *Meno* Socrates adds, "see if you think this is true," and in the *Laws* the Athenian says that poets "often enough hit on" the truth (682a). Plato appeals to poets not because they are poets, but because he thinks they tell the truth on some occasions. Truth therefore matters more than accuracy of quotation, and Plato holds it wrong to care who is the author of a line that turns out to be true (*Phaedrus* 275bc). In fact, Plato is not above inventing lines from Homer, or adjusting them to suit his need, as he does at *Phaedrus* 252b.

Still, Plato treats individual poets as hitting the truth more reliably than do the speakers who cite them. Glaucon and Adeimantus in *Republic*, book 2, Callicles in the *Gorgias,* and Agathon in the *Symposium* all appeal to poetry that they have misunderstood, and that would, if carefully interpreted, undermine their positions. Plato means to exclude the uncritical use of poetry by those who do not question the apparent meaning of the verses they cite. The general danger of poetry is due to its power to weaken our ability to examine its subjects in a rational way.

Imitations. Plato frequently takes over the language and imagery of poets for his own purposes. Homer's influence on Plato's writing pervades much of the corpus. We are told that Ammonius (pupil of the second-century Homeric scholar Aristarchus) picked out the many passages in which Plato drew on Homer (Pseudo-Longinus 13.3). In some instances, Plato seems to pay homage to the wisdom of a poet by imitating him; in others the matter is more complex.

The *Republic,* for example, may be seen to offer implicit homage to Aeschylus. Its guiding metaphor, the ship of state, comes from traditional poetry but is especially significant in *Seven against Thebes.* This play supports Plato's main thesis in the *Republic* and provides a poetic backdrop for its entire argument. By contrast, in the *Phaedrus,* Plato's explicit homage to the poets of love (235c) is undermined by later discussion. Still, Socrates' account of how it feels to be in love probably owes much to Sappho's imagery from such poems as the one now designated fragment 31 (251b ff.). Although the Platonic Socrates cites her with approval before launching into his first speech attacking love (235c), he later retracts that speech as a horrible attack on a god (242d). Sappho, he implies, may have been right to treat love as madness, but wrong not to see that madness can be a valuable gift from the gods.

As for Homer, Plato loves him as the best and most poetic of tragedians but makes reluctant war against him over the enormous influence he has in classical Greek culture (*Republic* 606e–607a). The weight of Homer's canonical authority lay heavily on writers of this era. Plato is not the first Greek prose writer to set himself against Homer while imitating him; the historian Thucydides tries to outdo Homer in the magnitude of the events he recounts while developing a narrative style replete with set-piece speeches reminiscent of Homer's. Both Plato and Thucydides are reaching for scraps of Homer's mantle of authority. Such imitation of Homer is homage not to the poet's wisdom but to his power over the minds of Plato's contemporaries (*Republic* 607e). From time to time, Plato allows that even Homer gets something right (389e with *Iliad* 4.412ff.).

Critical Study of Poetry. Although Socrates has said that dead poets cannot be cross-examined (*Protagoras* 347c–348a), Plato does occasionally examine dead poets with what he regards as success; in other passages he examines poets indirectly through refuting their representatives—speakers who quote or recite their work. Platonic examinations of poetry lead to positive interpretation in some cases, and to outright refutation in others.

Interpretation. Plato's method for interpreting poets, similar to the one he uses for oracles, is a type of cross-examination or *elenchus.* His procedure is to test interpretations by attempting to refute them until he finds one that he cannot refute, and thus to reject any interpretation under which the verse is false. The result is similar to an *elenchus* of a person. When you first answer Socrates you think you mean one thing, but if you survive his questioning you will find you believe something quite different and much more Socratic. And in some sense of *believe,* you will admit that you have believed what Socrates says all along—you were at least logically committed in that direction from the start, without knowing it. Thus it is with a gobbet of poetry: on its surface it means one thing; but since that is not true, a wise poet would be led by questioning to agree that he or she had meant something else by it all along.

So, for example, at *Republic* 424c, Socrates quotes Homer (in a version differing slightly from ours): "People like best the song that comes newest from the singer's lips" (*Odyssey* 1.351), and proceeds to rule out any interpretation of this that would recommend the introduction of new types of poetry—a kind of innovation he abhors. Socrates thus treats a poetic text as an oracular utterance that must be rendered true by interpretation (cf. *Apology* 21bc).

Socrates uses a similar procedure at *Protagoras* 342a–347a, where he examines a supposed contradiction in a fragment of Simonides, which is brought up by Protagoras as a subject for an exercise in critical thinking relating to virtue or moral goodness. Socrates rejects Protagoras's claim that the poem contains a contradiction; properly interpreted, he argues, it is consistent. The poem begins thus:

> It is hard to be a truly good man
> foursquare in hands and feet and purpose,
> made without blame.
> [*Here seven lines of the poem have been lost.*]
> And Pittacus' proverb does not ring true to me,
> though it was said by a wise man:
> that it is hard to be noble.

Protagoras and Socrates have taken the poem out of context, since its main subject is the vicissitudes of good and bad fortune, and the sort of goodness it treats along the way is more aristocratic than moral in Socrates' sense. The point is that it is not hard to be noble (i.e., rich and powerful) if you are fortunate; but it is hard to be *secure* in this good fortune (i.e., foursquare), since your luck can change (Gagarin-Woodruff, 1995). But, Socrates' resolution of the conflict is possible and accepted by some scholars (Taylor, 1991). The words translated as "be" in the first and last lines quoted above look different, and, although they are usually treated as aspects of the same verb *to be,* the first can carry the different meaning "becomes"—a distinction Socrates (unlike poets) frequently uses for philosophical purposes. If the word means "becomes" in this case, there is no contradiction, as Socrates points out: it is not hard to be good; the difficulty is to become good (343d).

So far so good, but Socrates interprets a later part of the poem in a way that is impossible:

> But I praise and love all those
> who willingly do
> nothing shameful. Not even gods fight necessity.

Socrates believes that this would be nonsense as stated, since on his view no one willingly does anything shameful—and, moreover, no intelligent person would disagree (345d). Accordingly, he transposes the adverb *willingly* to modify *praise* rather than *do:* "I willingly praise . . ." Although grammatically possible, this makes odd Greek and even odder sense. On this reading, we would need an example of a god yielding to necessity and praising someone unwillingly; but we have many examples in poetry of gods being forced to act shamefully. In any case, hardly anyone does agree with Socrates that no one willingly does wrong.

It is tempting to read this passage as a parody on Socrates' part of bad methods of interpretation practiced by Sophists (Taylor, 1991), but we cannot let Socrates off so easily. He has done this sort of interpretation before and will do it again. He is not discussing the text as such at this point; he is, rather, talking about Simonides, because it is the poet (not the poem) who would be brought by *elenchus* to agree with Socrates. Whatever words Simonides uses, Socrates believes that at root the poet must mean what is true, and charity compels him to find a way to construe the words as carrying that meaning (Brickhouse and Smith, 1994, pp. 82–83).

As a method of interpretation this appears to take texts lightly, but it takes their authors with the utmost seriousness. That is why Socrates steers the conversation away from poetry at just this point: "Usually, when people bring up poets, some of them say the poet has certain things in mind; others disagree; and they are conversing on a matter which they cannot possibly put to the test" (347e). If Socrates meant by this that no one could be certain what was meant by any text, he would be plainly wrong. But that is not what he says; his point, rather, is that we cannot know what poets have in mind unless we are able to lead them—the living, present poets—through the stages of questioning that might reveal—to them as well as to us—what it is they have in mind. This is not a question about what might have crossed their minds when writing the poem (that would merely be a matter of recall); it is, rather, a question of what they believe in the last analysis, in the most timeless sense in which a human being may be said to believe anything.

In the *Republic,* Plato uses a similar treatment of the thesis that it is just to render every man his due, attributed to the same poet, Simonides. Here, as in the case of the oracle in the *Apology,* we have no exact quotation. And as in the *Apology,* Socrates sets out to refute vulnerable readings of the text, on the assumption that Simonides could not have meant anything that could be refuted (335e). Later in the *Republic,* Socrates will give new meaning to "render every man his due," but without mention of Simonides.

In the *Laws,* the Athenian gives us an imaginary cross-examination of Tyrtaeus, the legendary poet who celebrated Spartan heroism. This *elenchus* leads to a better theory than the one Tyrtaeus's verses originally expressed (629a; see

667a and 858e). What Tyrtaeus said was that he would not set any value on a man, no matter how rich he was, unless he always excelled in war. The Athenian then imagines a conversation with Tyrtaeus in which he leads the poet to agree that there are two forms of war, foreign and civil, and that civil war *(stasis)* is the more dangerous of the two. He concludes that a man whose loyalty prevents him from taking part in a civil war is more praiseworthy than one who shows his mettle only in foreign wars, bolstering his point with a quotation from Theognis, and implying that he could coax agreement with this from Tyrtaeus himself—an important result in an argument aimed at impressing a Spartan.

Refutation. In the *Laws,* the Athenian addresses Pindar directly and seems to propose to refute him (at 690b; see 714e). In the *Ion,* Socrates refutes the claim to wisdom of a rhapsode, or professional reciter of Homer; the same argument, used directly against Homer, would show that Homer is not wise but (at most) inspired.

Elsewhere, Plato refutes those who quote poetry without implying an attack on the poets. The speakers in these cases are at fault for not examining the verses they quote. Agathon, for example, uses a Homeric couplet about *atē* (madness) without seeing that it undermines his view of love as a gentle peacemaker (*Symposium* 195de, with Agamemnon's excuse for the action that led to the wrath of Achilles at *Iliad* 19.92ff.).

Callicles quotes or cites a number of poems each of which is, in its larger context, disastrous for his case. He identifies himself, for example, with Zethus in Euripides' *Antiope,* a play that features a debate between the herdsman Zethus and the musician Amphion over the value of Amphion's contemplative life (484e, 485e, 486b). As we know from surviving fragments, Amphion is the winner in this play, but Callicles quotes only out of context from Zethus's attack on Amphion and supposes that he has Euripides' support.

The most famous poem Callicles quotes is the "Custom Is King" fragment of Pindar (*Gorgias* 484b; Pindar Fr. 169, *nomosbasileus*).

> Custom, king of all,
> of mortals and immortals,
> brings on the greatest violence
> with a supreme hand
> and makes it just—or so I learn
> from the deeds of Heracles . . .

No two scholars agree on what Pindar meant, but everyone agrees that Callicles has it wrong, and some hold that Plato had it wrong as well: Pindar is not singing the praises of Heracles for stealing the cattle by stealth and violence. He is impressed by the power of custom to render violence into justice, but if Pindar admires anyone in this story, it is not Heracles, but the brave defender Diomedes. To make matters worse, the poem reverses the point about custom and nature that Callicles wanted to make. He wanted to contrast the natural justice of naked power against the conventional concept of a justice that seeks to curb aggression. But on Pindar's view such a contrast is impossible: it is custom, he says, making no mention of nature, that turns violent crime into justice. Callicles has not examined the poems he cites; if he had, he would see how they provide material for an *elenchus* that would destroy his position.

Glaucon and Adeimantus fall into a similar trap in book 2 of the *Republic.* Glaucon sets up as his ideal the hero who is the opposite of Aeschylus' Amphiaraus, the one good man among the *Seven against Thebes,* of whom it is said that he does not seem, but actually is, just. Glaucon's straw man is the character who wishes "not to seem, but to be unjust" (361b). Here again, the poem refutes the man who cites it: Eteocles, who is, but does not seem to be, unjust—Glaucon's model—is punished; whereas Amphiaraus, who is, but does not seem to be, just, is given the highest of all rewards and becomes a blessing to the people of Thebes.

Adeimantus does no better. He quotes Homer, Hesiod, Pindar, and Archilochus in support of his view that justice is honored only for its consequences; but the poets do not consistently bear him out. Homer and Hesiod are especially damaging to his case. One passage he takes from Homer says that the rewards of the gods are evidence of justice in a ruler (*Odyssey* 19.109 at 363bc—Odysseus in disguise to Penelope, on her good name), while he understands the other to imply that the gods can be bribed to reward the unjust (*Iliad* 9.497 at 364e). The passages are inconsistent: if gods are readily bribed to deliver prosperity to the unjust, then prosperity is not evidence for justice. Worse for Adeimantus, neither passage really supports his position at all, since neither bears on why people should pursue justice.

In two cases, even Socrates seems to have Homer wrong. In the *Hippias Minor* (369e–371d), Socrates argues that Homer makes Achilles a liar, and, in the *Republic* (390e), that he makes Achilles subject to bribes. In both cases, Socrates examines a broad Homeric context to support his unpopular conclusion, but does so without sympathy for the values Homer represents. In the embassy scene of book 9, Achilles does indeed say he will do things that we will not do, but in this he would have seemed more impulsive than devious to a sympathetic reader. In the last book of the *Iliad,* it is Achilles' sense of honor, not greed, that compels him to accept Priam's treasure in return for the body of Hector (*Iliad,* 24.502–594), but such honor is not to be dreamed of in Plato's philosophy. Sensitivity to cultural differences has no place in Plato's interpretations of poetry.

BIBLIOGRAPHY

Works by Plato

Platonis Protagoras. Edited by J. Adam and A. M. Adam. Cambridge, 1893.

Protagoras. Translated and edited by C. C. W. Taylor. Rev. ed. Oxford, 1991.

Phaedrus. Translated and edited by Alexander Nehamas and Paul Woodruff. Indianapolis, 1995.

Other Sources

Annas, Julia. "Plato on the Triviality of Literature." In *Plato on Beauty, Wisdom, and the Arts,* edited by Julius Moravcsik and Philip Temko, pp. 1–28. Totowa, N.J., 1982.

Brickhouse, Thomas C., and Nicholas D. Smith. *Plato's Socrates.* New York and Oxford, 1994.

Gagarin, Michael, and Paul Woodruff. *Early Greek Political Thought from Homer to the Sophists.* Cambridge and New York, 1995.

Gould, Thomas. *The Ancient Quarrel between Poetry and Philosophy.* Princeton, N.J., 1990.

Kennedy, George A., ed. *Cambridge History of Literary Criticism,* vol. 1, *Classical Criticism.* Cambridge and New York, 1989.

Moravcsik, Julius, and Philip Temko, eds. *Plato on Beauty, Wisdom, and the Arts.* Totowa, N.J., 1982.

Nightingale, Andrea Wilson. "Plato's *Gorgias* and Euripides' *Antiope:* A Study in Generic Transformation." *Classical Antiquity* (1992): 121–141.

Nightingale, Andrea Wilson. *Genres in Dialogue: Plato and the Construct of Philosophy.* Cambridge and New York, 1995.

Ostwald, Martin. "Pindar, nomos, and Heracles." *Harvard Studies in Classical Philology* 69 (1965): 109–138.

Page, Denys Lionel, ed. *Poetae melici Graeci.* Oxford, 1962.

Parry, Hugh. "An Interpretation of Simonides 4 (Diehl)." *Transactions of the American Philological Association* 96 (1965): 297–320.

Rosen, Stanley. "The Quarrel between Philosophy and Poetry." In *The Quarrel between Philosophy and Poetry: Studies in Ancient Thought,* pp. 1–26. New York and London, 1988.

Urmson, J. "Plato and the Poets." In *Plato on Beauty, Wisdom, and the Arts,* edited by Julius Moravcsik and Philip Temko, pp. 125–136. Totowa, N.J., 1982.

Woodruff, Paul. "What Could Go Wrong with Inspiration? Why Plato's Poets Fail." In *Plato on Beauty, Wisdom, and the Arts,* edited by Julius Moravcsik and Philip Temko, pp. 137–150. Totowa, N.J., 1982.

PAUL WOODRUFF

Plato on the Effects of Art

Popular conceptions of Plato's attitude concerning art focus on *Republic* 398a1–8, where Plato urges us to honor the poet but send him to another city. Behind this famous quotation, however, lurk a number of complex issues involving the natures of different art forms, their expected effects on audiences, various notions of freedom and responsibility, and conceptions of what constitutes a healthy community.

Plato develops a seminormative concept of *technē* or "rational legitimate discipline" in the *Gorgias.* Two of the necessary conditions for being a *technē* in Plato's sense are dealing with genuine and fundamental elements of reality, and being concerned with the public good. Plato blames the rhetorician for not meeting these conditions. This not only denies rhetoric the status of being a *technē,* but also shows that Plato holds practitioners responsible for meeting or not meeting the conditions in question. A putative practitioner of a discipline chooses whether to practice a genuine or only a sham "art." The implicit notion of responsibility in this context is being concerned with the effects of one's actions on the welfare of others.

One can conclude from this that according to Plato an artist is as responsible for the effects his or her work has on audiences as anyone else is responsible for harming or helping a community through actions that emerge out of choice.

How much freedom to create does this leave the artist? This question can only be answered when we agree on a conception of freedom.

As Plato's famous cave allegory (*Republic,* book 7) shows, his notion of freedom entails the following:

1. attaining self-knowledge (this is partly indirect, not purely introspective or behavior);
2. understanding the fundamental elements of reality, and our relations to these; and
3. being able to form attitudes such as interest, orientation, respect, or cooperation on the basis of having met conditions 1 and 2.

If we attain Plato's freedom, then we also have freedom in a more modern sense; that is, we can choose between alternatives, since being able to form attitudes and act on them on the basis of 1 and 2 entails this capacity. Plato's notion of freedom admits of matters of degrees. To the extent that an agent has this kind of freedom she can participate in a legitimate *technē.* Since music meets the *technē*-warranting conditions, it is not subject to Plato's strictures, but literature and painting are. Their practitioners, according to Plato, typically do not have the right kind of freedom, at least not to a sufficient extent. But they are still responsible for this condition, in our sense of this notion. The artists of these "lower" arts therefore have freedom in a minimal modern sense, but not in the Platonic sense. This would be one of Plato's objections to the artists and their activities.

Let us now look at Plato's specific charges against the "lower" arts. These charges rest on two assumptions:

1. Poetry and painting can be, and typically are, beneficial or harmful to audiences.
2. Literature and painting typically function in communal contexts, and in many such contexts are taken to provide guidance or inspiration for our lives.

The second point should be stressed, even if it seems obvious. The artist's functioning in a community and not in a human vacuum is not always part of modern theories of aesthetics. The artist functions in a community, and his or her effects on the community need to be taken into consideration, like the effects of anyone else. This by itself says nothing about censorship. How a community and the artist involved deal with the relevant responsibilities is a separate question. The claim about possible harm is a psychological one. Products of the art forms under consideration please, and pleasures—as Plato keeps pointing out—may be good or harmful for us.

With this much understood, let us look at Plato's charges. One of these is that the poet has a harmful effect on the audience (378c–d, 386a–b). He can do this by drawing attention away from what is ontologically fundamental, or by causing pleasures that will make us less than ideal agents, and in many other ways. The second charge is that the poet does not fit into the educational framework whose development and maintenance are the primary responsibilities of the state (377a4–b10). One might respond, Why should art be expected to fit into this grand educational scheme? Plato's response would be that the educational scheme *(paideia)* is designed to help the citizens toward self-improvement and freedom—in the Platonic sense—and that every institution has to fit itself somewhere in this scheme. If art does not contribute to what all justified practices contribute, it loses its legitimacy. For of what use can it be? If the answer is that it brings us pleasure, we run up against Plato's attack on hedonism, which says—among other things—that pleasure as such is neither good nor bad. The enjoyments that go with the life of a good person are good, and those that prevent us from approximating that life are bad. The arts in question, when considered on their own merit, are construed by Plato as causing the wrong kinds of pleasure.

Another response to this charge could be that the artist does not determine how the audience will respond to the work of art. The audience is constituted by humans who have choices, and thus they can determine how to respond to different features in a work of art. One would, however, have to admit that only to a certain extent does the audience have control over its response to different kinds of artworks. If art caters to what are for Plato our "lower" desires, this will work to prevent us from applying appropriate criteria in assessing products, and hence in responding to them. (This issue raises the same psychological problems as modern debates about the harm television violence can do to the audience.) There are many issues here that Plato does not take up. To what extent are we aware of how a given artwork affects us? Even if we are in some cases aware of this, to what extent do we have control over the effects?

As a further response to Plato's charges one might say that the artist merely describes human action, emotion, and agency, and does not present normative conceptions of these items. Plato disagrees. He thinks that artists present normative conceptions of human agency, and he scolds some for, as an example, presenting the agent as doing too much crying and lamenting (387b11–c5). The notion that human agency, seen from the first person point of view, is necessarily normative pervades all of Plato's moral psychology (e.g., book 4 of the *Republic*). Herewith the implicit assumptions supporting this stance.

Kinds that we describe partly in terms of their basic potentialities must be given a partly normative characterization. For example, biological kinds are characterized partly in terms of basic potentialities. Spiders weave webs, beavers build dams, and so forth. But these species also have other dispositional characteristics. It is a partly normative assessment to claim that web weaving and dam building are gen-

uine species-defining natural potentialities rather than one among many other dispositional properties that many or most members of these species might have. It is a matter of deciding what is a healthy specimen, a challenge that may be theoretically complex but normally does not cause much headache to physicians or biologists. As Plato stresses throughout the dialogues, health is a partly normative and partly descriptive property.

Further arguments apply more specifically to the conception of human agency from a first person point of view. The basic question of Greek drama is, "Ti dran?" ("what is to be done?") presented from the point of view of a hero or heroine. So the question becomes, "What shall I do?" There are two elements in this question that need to be analyzed from a partly normative standpoint. One is the *what* in the question. This calls for a conception of what is good—derivatively, what will lead to happiness and what will lead to suffering. But from Plato's point of view, there is a less obvious but equally normative component in the characterization of the self, or "I," as an agent. Implicit in a decision will be some conception of how I construe the self. Which elements have priorities over others? One cannot make decisions without some assumptions about priorities. We might assume that reason has priorities over certain emotions, or some kind of reasoning capacity over others, and so on. Furthermore, the way we make a decision (e.g., calmly or overcome by emotion) implicitly presents a partial conception of the self.

These implicit assumptions about agency can be seen clearly both in Greek literature and in Plato's dialogues. In the *Iliad*, Achilles is held up as the main hero, and his key decisions are made in fits of passion, as he is overwhelmed and driven by some powerful force such as wrath. In contrast, in Plato's *Phaedo*, Socrates is portrayed as making key decisions in a calm, reasonable mood, and the source of his way of deciding is presented as his commitment to detached, rational investigation of choices to be made. One could go on, beyond the Platonic text, and show that similar implicit conceptions underlie the portraits of agency in the works of William Shakespeare, Friedrich von Schiller, and others, up to Samuel Beckett's *Endgame*.

If we accept the claim that the representation of an agent's dilemma and her response is always partly normative in literature, be it philosophical or dramatic, then we can hardly deny that such portraits should be subjects of critical evaluation. We engage in such evaluations in other walks of life—for example, when we assess the activities of physicians, judges, politicans, and parents. Why should literature be exempt? The response that nothing really happens, it is all make-believe, hardly meets the point. The portrayal affects other humans for better or worse. Hence, it should be subjected to criticism. To Plato, as to most of us, it would sound strange for someone to say that the play of one's imagination should not be subject to moral criticism.

If it is expressed in a communal setting, and affects the welfare of others, why should it be exempt from the critical reflection that we apply to all other activities with the same effects?

Plato's stance is echoed by recent writers such as Albert Camus (*L'homme révolté*) who maintain that the artist, like anyone else, is responsible for predictable effects on his or her audiences. We can summarize Plato's conclusions about the effect of art and the artist's responsibility in two layers.

1. In a community such as the Athens of Plato's time, the presentation of literature and the plastic arts would have a predictable effect on the audience, even if we ascribe to it free choice concerning alternative modes of reaction. These effects can be harmful or beneficial, and can be judged as such by the community. The artist is responsible for the nature of the products and their normative implications, and thus for the consequences of what happens when these are influencing the values of the community.

As we saw, this conclusion presupposes the communal setting in which art takes place and that a typical artwork of a literary or plastic sort will have normative implications. But it is also crucial to see that the artist should understand the ways in which art can be used. Plato uses aesthetic qualities in his work so as to have the sensual and visual point beyond itself—toward higher layers of reality. The artist is responsible for not availing himself of that mode of presentation, but for appealing instead to the taste of the "lovers of sights and sounds."

We can attempt to abstract from the Athenian setting and Plato's times, and restate Plato's position in its most general terms.

2. In any communal context C, products of poetry, drama, and painting will have certain predictable effects $E' \ldots E_n$ on the audience, taking into account their choices and preferences of interpretation. It is a matter of objective evaluation whether these effects are harmful or beneficial, and the artist is responsible for the nature of his product, and for the consequences of its presentations for whatever audience can be reasonably predicted.

Stating the conclusion about artistic responsibility in this manner shows the obvious legitimacy of some responsibility to be assigned to the artist. At the same time, it shows the difficulty of assessing harm or benefit. For given the longevity of some artworks, it is difficult for the artist to project the nature of future audiences. In order to see the plausibility of Plato's stance, one must keep in mind his rich conception of what is permanent and basic in human nature. For him, audiences do not differ that much. This is probably one of the key points on which Plato and many modern aestheticians disagree. Keeping this in mind, let us restate—speculatively—how Plato's view would be applied to modern industrial societies.

As we saw, his view on the artist's responsibilities depends on certain presuppositions. Many of these are not met by modern societies. First, we do not stress the communal context of art. In fact, there are even aesthetic theories stressing the separateness of what they call the art world. Plato would find such a notion incomprehensible. The communal context for him is the city, the state, and so on—in short, the political unit within which art develops. Second, Plato would insist on the need of at least a partial agreement on communal values and conceptions of how art products and their effects relate to these. Finally, his conception of the main task of a political community as educational, and hence the politician as an educator, is not met by modern societies.

Still, Plato's view that anyone who chooses to create certain items that can harm or benefit people is responsible for the predictable effects of his or her work is relevant even to our world. It should be the key issue underlying discussions of freedom and censorship.

BIBLIOGRAPHY

Collingwood, R. G. "Plato's Philosophy of Art." *Mind* (1952): 154–172.

Lodge, Rupert C. *Plato's Theory of Art.* London, 1953.

Moravcsik, Julius. "On Correcting the Poets." *Oxford Studies in Ancient Philosophy* 4 (1986): 35–47.

Tigerstedt, E. N. *Plato's Idea of Poetical Inspiration.* Commentationes Humanarum Litterarum, no. 44. Helsinki, 1969.

Urmson, J. "Plato and the Poets." In *Plato on Beauty, Wisdom, and the Arts,* edited by Julius Moravcsik and Philip Temko, pp. 125–136. Totowa, N.J., 1982.

JULIUS MORAVCSIK

Plato and Modern Aesthetics

The view that has dominated modern philosophy of art assumes that there is conceptual unity binding together what we call the fine arts, and that the same is true of aesthetic qualities, with beauty assumed as the highest genus, as well as aesthetic appreciation. According to this view the major task of aesthetics is to define art, beauty, and aesthetic appreciation. Defining aesthetic appreciation is assumed to be centered on articulating the concept of taste as a distinct human faculty.

Plato belongs to what one would broadly label the essentialist camp—those who attempt to define art in terms of necessary and jointly sufficient conditions—but he draws the conceptual map in a, to us, unfamiliar way. In particular, he has a lot to say about the arts and about their understanding, without having a general concept corresponding to our notion of fine art, and he does not have a concept corresponding to that of taste. Let us sketch briefly how one can "do" aesthetics without these two pillars of the modern approaches.

In addition to not having a generic notion of the "fine arts," Plato also lacks a generic and autonomous notion of beauty, and he has no autonomous concept of aesthetic taste. To be sure, English translations use "beauty" as an equivalent to the Greek *kalon* in many places, but this is misleading. The Greek word designates a wide genus that applies to much of what we might call "outstanding," such as work in mathematics, geometry, political institutions, or character, in addition to items we would describe as beautiful. Something that is *kalon* is taken to have intrinsic value, but this value need not have either strictly aesthetic or moral connotations. Since it is used in what we might call moral contexts, translators at times render *kalon* as "noble"; but this is just as bad a translation as "beautiful." Plato has no autonomous domains for either the aesthetic or the moral.

"Fine" is probably the best equivalent for *kalon* in modern English. Plato uses it in that sense in *Symposium* 210–212, where he includes the theoretical sciences, political and civic institutions, as well as items with a fine appearance in his list of species of this notion. The examples listed suggest that our "beauty" corresponds in Plato to what he regards as fine in appearance. But this is not a mere genus-species articulation. The "species," if we may call them such, are hierarchically arranged, with what is fine in appearance (only fine in appearance?) at the lowest rank. Thus, items that we would call beautiful occupy the lowest rank of a wider genus that includes items we would typically describe as fine, for example, a fine mathematical proof, fine character, or a fine painting. As a common denominator, Plato singles out the elements of order and harmony, which although they do not yield a definition, do permeate everything that is *kalon;* together they constitute the mark of what it is to be *kalon.*

Before we push on with further elucidation of what is *kalon,* let us consider what can be said about the fine arts in Plato's framework. The Greek *technē* is often translated as "art," but this too is misleading. *Technē,* like *kalon,* is a wide genus that includes just about anything that one would regard as a rational and legitimate discipline, or complex of skills, ranging from the production of artifacts to mathematics and the *technē* of living. In *Gorgias,* Plato exploits the normative implications of this notion and argues that, for example, rhetoric is not a *technē,* and hence it should not have the honorific status that it occupied in Athenian public life. According to Greek mythological tradition, all *technai* are gifts from Prometheus. Plato thinks that mathematics should be included among such gifts but not rhetoric. Do the various art forms qualify as *technai?* As we shall see, some do more so than others. Hence, what is a unified genus in modern aesthetics appears as a scattered collection within the Platonic landscape.

Plato does not define *technē,* nor does he define the various art forms. But we know from the *Republic* 474–475 that he would define such items in terms of the objects with which they deal or produce. Thus, music would be the art that deals with sound and harmony; painting, perceptible objects; and literature, human passion and action. From the Platonic point of view, these items constitute an ontologically heterogeneous list; hence, no strong conceptual unity would be expected. This, in turn, reflects on their respective status as *technai.* The *technē*-making conditions include being concerned with what is ontologically fundamental and with the public good. For Plato, music meets these conditions, but literature does not. Painting and literature deal with "sights and sound," the lovers of which are described in pejorative terms in *Republic* 475; musical harmony deals with the Forms, as we see in *Philebus.*

Plato finds different features uniting different subsets of art forms. In *Republic* 398–399 he points out that music and literature both have some concern with rhythm and sounds, but later at 597e literature is paired with painting because both represent the objects of the senses. These differences reflect differences in terms of what an art form leads us to, and in terms of whether it will have negative effects on us. Music can focus on the appropriate objects and can thus enable us to develop attitudes leading toward harmony within ourselves and in relation to others. But this is not unique to music; mathematics has the same effect. Since keeping our minds on the most fundamental elements of reality is, for Plato, a necessary condition of moral improvement, most of the art forms receive low grades on that score.

Stepping back for a moment from Plato's own ontology and ethics, we should note that the questions of what music is about and what the ontological status of tone and harmony is, as well as how painting and literature represent, are still with us. Plato thinks that similarity plays an important role in representation. Today some philosophers try to characterize representation without ascribing a key role to similarity. This difference is yet to be resolved.

In turning to the characterization of appreciation we should ask whether Plato's questions are the same as those of modern aesthetics, and whether his explanatory notions are the same as ours. We can start addressing these issues by considering whether the alleged aesthetic capacity of taste could be a genuine human capacity in Plato's framework. In the *Republic,* book 5, 474–477, Plato says that cognitive capacities are distinguished by their respective domains of objects and by their characteristic results. This characterization is important also in its omissions. It does not regard behavioral or introspective data as definitive for these individuations. In the text Plato distinguishes on this basis the capacity to have insights and to understand from the capacity to process beliefs and pieces of information. Given the ontological heterogeneity of the arts for Plato, he could not have a concept of taste uniting aesthetic appreciation. His approach involves, rather, various analyses of the appropriate responses to specific art forms. The appreciation of the kind of music he respects—namely, that which is based on harmony—involves the ability to discover and understand harmonious structures and to derive enjoyment from that.

Unfortunately, he does not offer details concerning how one discovers and understands harmony. For him this is a basic capacity, but it is not a purely aesthetic one; he sees it also in mathematical work. He points to being able to think of representations as real, and of being affected by the passions expressed in drama as crucial to the enjoyment of literature and the plastic arts. Again, it was left to his successors to attempt to give more detailed characterizations. In summary, there is no property running through the appreciation of all art forms, and the properties Plato singles out with respect to appreciating specific art forms are for him applicable also to what we would call various nonaesthetic modes of appreciation.

Looking at this brief review of what Plato says about the objects, about "beauty," and about appreciation, we see that a salient feature of Platonic aesthetics is its strong links with both metaphysics and ethics. His ontological conception involves not only priorities in terms of what accounts for what, but also a tie between these priorities and the human task of self-improvement. If one ignores these facts, one ends up with shallow interpretations according to which Plato is just "moralizing" about art or subordinating art to politics. He does not, however, subordinate art to what we today would call politics, but insists on art being analyzed in a communal setting, and thinks of the ideal community as dedicated to helping citizens in their task of self-improvement.

There are two kinds of audiences: the ones that do and the ones that do not understand the ontological status of any given art form. Assigning to literature, for example, the ontological status Plato deems as proper clashes with how most artists view their own work. They think of a poem or painting as having intrinsic value and thus being self-contained. Aesthetic appreciation is meant to be interpreting and enjoying the work of art within its own rights and merits.

Plato can see merit in similes, metaphors, or certain types of graphic illustrations. But this is instrumental merit. We can see this in his own employment of such devices. The Divided Line is a helpful image, the cave allegory an effective literary device. But in all such instances the artistic device is meant to point beyond itself. It functions to direct the mind to elements on higher ontological levels, and by analogy make items on those higher levels more intelligible. A Sophoclean tragedy is meant to be understood and appreciated on its own terms; the literary devices employed by Plato are meant to be merely tools and aids for the imagination in areas of understanding in which the mind has difficulties grasping directly the natures of certain abstract entities and their interrelations. One might think that at least in this role one could locate a distinctive place for artifacts in Plato's scheme. But this is false. Plato assigns the same "pointing to beyond itself" role to diagrams in geometry, as we see in *Meno*.

Why could Plato not see drama as having intrinsic merit? For this to be possible, drama would have to have a vital and unique role in our coming to understand our nature and virtues. Such a role seems plausible when we think of kindness, sympathy—in short, virtues whose application does not depend on some merit possessed by the object. Respect or approval must be earned, but kindness or sympathy need not be. Plato does not have among his virtues, however, the sort that can be directed even at undeserving objects. Hence, the person who should command respect can be described in general terms, indicating something about her that warrants respect. But it might be difficult to teach and articulate the concept of kindness without relying to some extent on individual examples, and this is the place at which drama and poetry can enter as part of the wider educational process.

Underlying Plato's views is a very deep intuition. It shows that some attitudes are rational in the sense that directing these toward certain humans depends on quality; that is, the person who is the object must possess certain good characteristics. But the states of character, feelings, and passions that are in the focus of literature are not of this sort. These (e.g., hatred) can be, and often are, directed toward specific persons, without consideration of their good or bad characteristics. This explains not only Plato's stance but also why we cannot have a drama about wisdom or about respect. Painting and literature have their own domains, even more narrowly describable than what Plato offers.

These remarks should show us why Plato neither has nor needs a concept of taste. That concept is invoked to help explain what underlies the unity of aesthetic appreciation. But Plato has no such unity in his aesthetics. As we saw, different capacities are needed to appreciate different art forms, and singly these capacities are exercised also with respect to the nonaesthetic. He still succeeds in giving interesting characterizations of salient cognitive and affective attributes needed for appreciating this or that art form. Reading Plato and contrasting him with modern aestheticians yields the following contrast. One conception tries to find a common feature in all fine arts, posits a corresponding capacity of aesthetic appreciation, and tries to explain this in terms of a putative faculty of taste. The other approach construes what we call aesthetic appreciation as a series of partly interwoven capacities, each strand of which applies also to some nonaesthetic context. The difference is not a matter of analytic definitions, but rather one of differing general hypotheses about parts of cognitive psychology. For Plato, given the link of this material to metaphysics and ethics in his philosophy, he *must* be right. We can detach the psychology, take it on its own merit, and see it as an interesting and challenging alternative to taste-oriented philosophical explanations of our enjoying different art forms.

[*See also* Beauty, *article on* Classical Concepts; *and* Taste, *article on* Early History.]

BIBLIOGRAPHY

Cross, R. C., and A. D. Woozley. *Plato's Republic: A Philosophical Commentary.* New York, 1964.

Moravcsik, Julius. "Noetic Aspiration and Artistic Inspiration." In *Plato on Beauty, Wisdom, and the Arts,* edited by Julius Moravcsik and Philip Temko, pp. 29–46. Totowa, N.J., 1982.

Moravcsik, Julius. "Why Philosophy of Art in Cross-Cultural Perspectives?" *Journal of Aesthetics and Art Criticism* 51.3 (Summer 1993): 425–435.

Nehamas, Alexander. "Plato on Imitation and Poetry in *Republic* 10." In *Plato on Beauty, Wisdom, and the Arts,* edited by Julius Moravcsik and Philip Temko, pp. 47–78. Totowa, N.J., 1982.

Oates, Whitney J. *Plato's View of Art.* New York, 1972.

Tate, J. "Imitation in Plato's *Republic*." *Classical Quarterly* 22 (1928): 16–23.

Verdenius, Willem Jacob. *Mimesis: Plato's Doctrine of Artistic Imitation, and Its Meaning to Us.* Leiden, 1949.

JULIUS MORAVCSIK

PLAY. From the perspective of many contemporary theorists, especially literary theorists, the concept of play seems to be internally connected to the concept of the artwork. A brief glance at the history of the concept of play reveals that this was not always the case: it was first by means of a detour through the cultural theories of play, above all through those of Johan Huizinga and Roger Caillois, on the one hand, and the sign theories of the structuralists and the deconstructionists, on the other, that the concept moved, if not to the center, then to the most interesting margins of contemporary aesthetic theory. From there it was possible to rediscover the idealist concept of play in the aesthetic theory of Immanuel Kant and Friedrich von Schiller as well as that of the early Romantics critically based on it.

Reference to the renaissance of the aesthetic concept of play in the twentieth century should not, however, be mistaken for the thesis that modern and postmodern works of art exhibit more of a play character than do so-called traditional artworks. The most interesting theories of play concerning the aesthetic strive rather to describe the structure of the artwork itself in terms of play—not to designate specific epochs or genres. This implies that the aesthetic concept of play should be limited neither to so-called nonsense poetry—for example, of the Dadaists or Surrealists—nor to play as the content of artworks or any particular games that are not intrinsic to the structure of the artwork such as anagrams, palindromes, or plays with numbers or names (see Hutchinson, 1983, and its wealth of examples). Games at the level of content take on a totally different status if the artwork itself is understood as a play unity; when this is the case, those games are no longer to be understood as isolated events but rather as a reflection of the structure of the artwork as a whole and, as such, as part of that structure. An extreme example of games as the content of artworks is François Rabelais's *Gargantua* in which 217 names for different games are listed and on which Mikhail Bakhtin remarks:

This famous enumeration had a considerable resonance. Rabelais' first German translator, Fischart, completed the long list with 372 German card games and dance tunes. The English seventeenth-century translator, Thomas Urquhart, also increased the lists of recreations by adding English names. . . . the Dutch version initiated research in the field of children's games, resulting in the greatest work ever undertaken in world folk studies.

(Bakhtin, 1968, p. 125)

This zeal on the part of the translators is no accident. Not a few of those theorists who describe the artwork as play see an advantage to their strategy in the fact that their description of the structure of the artwork already accounts for the activity of the recipient in such a way that reception does not carry a mere secondary or contingent status: if something is a game, it is oriented toward other players for conceptual reasons—that is, in order to be a game at all—and it suggests a configuration that provokes activity on the part of its recipient. Among the most prominent theoreticians to assert this argument, alongside Karl Wilhelm Friedrich Von Schlegel and Novalis, are Hans-Georg Gadamer, Wolfgang Iser, and Jacques Derrida. The latter did not develop his position in correspondence to Stéphane Mallarmé without reason. Mallarmé wrote the celebrated text on a throw of the dice and precedes his *Igitur* with an epigram that can be read as bringing those aestheticians who inscribe the recipient as a constitutive element within the structure of the artwork to their point. It also qualifies Mallarmé as a theoretician of play in his own right. Loosely translated (the English edition did not include the epigram), it says, "This tale is addressed to the intelligence of the reader, which stages the scenes itself."

The explosive power of such curious forms of knowledge as those cited by Bakhtin or in learned collections detailing motifs and themes in the concept of play (see Hutchinson, Bakhtin, and Guinness and Hurley, 1986) depends on whether they can be brought into connection with the structure of the work of art. That is also true, by the way, of the clownish, circuslike, and comical aspects of the artwork that Theodor W. Adorno addressed in *Aesthetic Theory*—an attention that should be reason enough to read these together with a theory of play and not to mistake them as isolated elements. Because it is clear that the concept of play can have a significant role for aesthetics only if it indicates more than just a motif or theme within particular works of art, those aestheticians will be discussed here for whom the structure of the artwork is a game and, in many cases, one that comprehends the recipient as one who plays along.

Despite the fact that the concept of play, as stated before, has at least since Kant always reappeared in a prominent role, systematic consideration of the various levels on which this concept plays a role (operates) in the aesthetic process and as to the status of different types of play was undertaken only at a much later date. In this regard, Huizinga's nondifferentiation of the various types of play was paradoxically influential because of the responses it provoked. His one-dimensional characterization of all kinds of play as agonal actions left in its wake a whole series of interesting classifications. The best-known system of classification, critically but also sympathetically based on Huizinga, is that proposed by Caillois in *Man, Play, and Games* between competitions, games of chance, those of disguise, and imitation and ecstatic games. In Caillois's terminology they are called *agon, alea, mimicry,* and *ilinx.* It is astounding how many aestheticians have taken up these categories originally elaborated for the cultural sciences, even though they are not, at least not immediately, applicable to aesthetics (see Hutchinson, pp. 9ff.). Clearly, the cultural theorists named here furnished the decisive incentive and instigation for bringing the concept of play back into the theoretical discussion of art. This is reflected most strikingly in the nearly canon-establishing special volume in the Yale French Studies series from 1968, *Game, Play, Literature,* in which almost all authors cite Huizinga, Caillois, and the phenomenologist Eugen Fink; but also in Iser's much later work, *The Fictive and the Imaginary,* in which he makes a not very enlightening effort to render Caillois's four categories productive for the analysis of the literary artwork (Iser, 1993, pp. 445ff.). Iser's own four-part division of aesthetic play, which has nothing to do with Caillois's, should be considered as much more important and illuminating: namely, the distinction he makes between games with the referential worlds of a text, plays on the assembled positions within a text, plays on possible worlds, and plays on the reader's expectations. Another system of ordering tailored to aesthetic texts is that offered by Robert Detweiler between play as subject matter or content, play as fiction, and play with the reader. Susan Stewart, on the other hand, elaborates five nonsense games when she separates aesthetically understood nonsense from common sense. Inasmuch as these and comparable systems of differentiation of aesthetic play have shown the good sense to claim neither totality nor exhaustiveness, it is not a matter of the number of differentiations made, but rather of whether they touch on what is decisive in the artwork and thereby facilitate a departure from categories primarily relevant to the social sciences and social philosophy. Before taking up this problem again, it is, in any case, important to mention the play between the semantic and material elements in the artwork that Martin Heidegger places at the center of his consideration of the mode of being *(Seinsweise)* of the artwork when he calls it the "opposition" *(Gegeneinander)* or "striving" of "world and earth" (Heidegger, 1971, p. 49).

For the preceding reasons, the games as content that came back into play with Detweiler's categories will not be discussed here. Also omitted will be the play of fiction, as it has nothing to do with specifically literary plays. Insane fictions and speculations are one possible content for literary texts, but they also exist in the sciences: there one finds fictions concerning the origin of the world and of language,

and speculations on worlds run by computers or on how our lives would look if we were bats. What remains, then, of the previously cited aesthetic plays is that on reference, that between different positions within a text and that with readers, and—if one includes Heidegger here—that between meaning and materials. At first glance, it would seem we are very close to the traditional, frequently proposed binary between play internal to a text and play between the text and something external to it. In this distinction, the play between meaning and materials counts as internal to the text, readers belong to those things external, and the issue of reference remains undecided: according to Iser, for example, artworks can refer to "reference worlds" or to the "real" world beyond the domain of texts, but their reference can just as easily proceed "from the return of other texts" (p. 449). The following discussion of Romantic and idealist theories of play describing the aesthetic as inherently playful in its structure should, however, illustrate that this distinction is unproductive, if not indeed misleading.

In Kant's *Critique of Judgment,* play—the "free . . . play . . . of imagination and understanding" (Kant, 1987, p. 132)—appears, for the most part, to provide the basis of aesthetic pleasure and its peculiar subjective universality: such free play is "the basis of this pleasure in the harmony of the cognitive powers" (ibid.). In other passages, Kant calls it the "harmony between the cognitive powers in a judgment of taste" (p. 133). Apart from the fact that Kant describes the free play as harmony without any statement as to causes—in striking contrast not only to Huizinga, who characterizes all play as agonal, or Heidegger, who immediately speaks of a striving—the remarkable aspect of Kantian play theory is its localization of play in the subject alone. The question as to whether the play structure in the experiencing subject corresponds to something in the object is left problematically open in Kantian aesthetics, as is well known. Kant describes neither the aesthetic object, nor the relation between the work of art and its recipient in terms of play, but only the relation between two faculties within the subject in those terms.

One encounters a similarly subject-centered account of aesthetic play in a popularized variant of Kant's theory, namely, Schiller's letters *On the Aesthetic Education of Man.* In this case, play is described not as a balance achieved between two cognitive faculties, but rather as the harmony between two drives. When Schiller writes that "it (beauty) is the object common to both drives, that is to say, the object of the play-drive" (Schiller, 1967, p. 106), it is clear that the play drive forms not a third drive but rather the correct relation—one could almost say play relation—between the sensuous drive and the formal drive that otherwise tend to exclude one another. Schiller grants the aesthetic object even less attention than does Kant, because for Schiller the prime issue is the idea of a human being who falls victim neither to the senses nor to understanding. This is the human being who only plays with beauty and plays with beauty only. "For, to mince matters no longer, man only plays when he is in the fullest sense of the word a human being, and he is only fully a human being when he plays" (p. 102)

The early Romantics, especially the brothers Friedrich and August Wilhelm von Schlegel and Novalis, react critically to this idealistic—because harmonious and subject centered—concept of play in a twofold fashion. They universalize play by elevating it to the sole mode of relation with the world, with others and with oneself, such that (aesthetic) play is not differentiated from the spheres of nature, cognition, or morality, nor can it reconcile these spheres—the main project of the aesthetics of Kant and Schiller. For the aforementioned early Romantics, "All of the sacred plays of art are only a remote imitation of the infinite play of the universe, the work of art which eternally creates itself anew" (Schlegel, 1968, p. 89). The early Romantics have for so long gone unrecognized in the discussion of play because the word *play* does not appear with the same frequency in their work as it does in that of Schiller and Kant. Further, the play described by Kant and Schiller between a sensuous-imaginative faculty, on the one hand, and a reasoning-classificatory faculty, on the other, has taken on the character of a general definition to such an extent that philosophical aesthetics has for a long time regarded play as a reconciling third between two mediated or, indeed, reconciled faculties. The play of the early Romantics is, in fact, something else. Their play of repetition is diametrically opposed to the play of mediation favored by the idealists.

What the early Romantics thematize as the special case of aesthetic play is precisely not the issue—as in Kant and Schiller—of play between faculties and drives in the subject. They are much more concerned with describing the aesthetic object as an infinite play. Because it assumes derivations, it is characterized—largely in musical (Naumann, 1990), grammatical, and philosophically reflective *(reflexionsphilosophisch)* terms—as an impure repetition or reflection. As Gadamer argues later in conscious reference to Friedrich Schlegel, aesthetic play comprises the to-and-fro of self-representation to the extent that it represents nothing but itself and always refers back to itself (Gadamer, 1986, pp. 111ff.; Adorno also emphatically relates aesthetic play to the concept of repetition when he states, "Forms of play are invariably forms of repetition"; 1997).

The best philosophical and literary texts are represented by the Schlegels and Novalis as having developed from a self-contradicting—or, to express it musically, dissonant—seed out of which an endless series of variations and reflections unfolds (see Naumann, pp. 162ff., and Menninghaus, 1987, especially pp. 132–207). "Every seed is a *dissonance*—an incongruity which should not immediately reconcile itself. This first moment comprehends the changing elements in a relation which cannot remain as it is—as, for instance,

in *Meister*" (Novalis, 1965, p. 581). This play of variation is not to be understood simply as developing or departing from a particular motif or medium—on the contrary, the point of departure is represented as having itself been constituted by variation. It is obvious that in a theoretical framework such as this, play becomes a counterconcept to the representative and mimetic conception of art. In opposition to this representative conception of art, an emphasis is placed on self-referentiality that simultaneously carries reflexive and musicorhythmic implications. It is no accident that reflection, rhyme, sequence, symmetry, dissonance, and grammar become central aesthetic categories and synonyms for *play*. Self-referentiality is not meant here as self-presence or transparence, but rather should be taken in an open structural sense: the individual moments generate one another reciprocally. Further, it is not a case of a closed structure but of the opening or possibility of a play that, like all good games, can be played endlessly even though the playing field and the rules—and one could just as well say the two covers of the book or the framed canvas—function as boundaries. The outstanding example of textual play of this variety was *Wilhelm Meister* for the early Romantics. They read *Wilhelm Meister* not as a bildungsroman but as a novel about the formation *(Bildung)* of a self-composing and self-reflective work out of itself (Novalis, 1983).

In this capricious bildungsroman those categories of play-as-content relevant to aesthetics—and in *Wilhelm Meister* it is always a question of plays (drama) and the world of the theater in relation to the world of economic affairs—are elucidated. When games form a part of a "musical" play of repetition and also reflect this, they become aesthetically relevant. Wilhelm's playacting is simultaneously a part of the whole and a reflection of the whole of the textual weave as play. One could make a similar claim for play with fictions. According to Friedrich Schlegel and Novalis, to the extent that the artwork never simply completes itself as an illustration of familiar "worlds of reference" (Iser), but also essentially refers to itself and to other texts (and always in the mode of a replay/repetition), the question of fiction assumes a role in aesthetic play and can, among other things, be reflected in the form of a fictive world. The theater, as the uncanny site where a real event takes place before the eyes of the audience and simultaneously spins a fiction, stands as the most prominent topos in literature through which to reflect on fictionality. Friedrich Schlegel stressed above all else the *parekbase*, the apparent breaking down of the illusion—for instance, in the form of a direct address to the audience—as the outstanding locus of the thematization of fiction and connected it with irony, a further figure that reflects on the status of the artwork.

The early Romantic theories of play as the play of repetition *(Wiederholungsspiel)* through which the discrete moments of the artwork reciprocally constitute themselves—offered as a countermove to what was established by Kant and Schiller—should, nonetheless, not be taken for theories exclusively concerned with aesthetic objects. The persistently demanded infinity of the Romantic artwork expresses the insight that the work of art can only be theoretically formulated in its essential character—as infinite—through reference to other potential players. As text or painting, every play is limited. Games and subjects playing with them, however, are, in the best cases, limitless. As soon as one interprets the artwork as play it becomes necessary—as was also made clear at the beginning with the epigram from Mallarmé—to think of play in terms of players rather than to separate the two as in the case of the customary differentiation between the aesthetic subject and the aesthetic object. The infinite processual character of aesthetic play that Kant and Schiller bring into play on the side of the subject is installed in advance in the play character of the artwork by Novalis and the Schlegels.

The tradition of repetition play is continued in the twentieth century by Derrida. He shares with the early Romantics not only the concept of an infinitely playable *(spielbaren)* play of repetition that reflects itself as such but also the sense that literary textual play is only one possible expression of a more general play of the (sign)world (see Derrida, 1978). In this move, Derrida accords problematic distinction to the play of art in a manner similar to the way the Romantics mark off Romantic poetry. The early Romantics, who expected a great deal from the advent of universal poetry, assumed that in Romantic poetry the original, foundational play already and most appropriately takes place. One could take a critical stance toward this using Schiller's dictum, "With only beauty shall he play" (Schiller, p. 614). Derrida developed his theory of the aesthetic play of repetition in a discussion of Mallarmé and Philippe Sollers, and set the associative play on words and word fields, the micrological and musical play of syllables, vowels, and consonants as well as the intertextual play of repetition at the center of his theory (Derrida, 1981; on theory and praxis of intertextual plays of repetition, see Genette, 1982).

Retrospectively, the following ought to have become clear. The differentiation between that which is internal to a text and the play between text and recipient should be regarded as obfuscating and ill conceived by aestheticians who ascribe to the concept of play a central role within the field of aesthetics, since they—as no one else—know that play and playing can only be explained through reference to one another. The decisive split between theories that conceive the aesthetic in terms of play is that between plays of repetition, on the one hand, and the free play of two faculties, on the other—the difference between the early Romantic repetition play and idealist mediation play *(Wiederholungsspiel* vs. *Vermittlungsspiel)*. The early Romantics would certainly concur with Kant and Schiller that a conceptual faculty adheres to aesthetic play as much as do the senses of sight, sound, and so on. What remains in question

for them, however, is whether a relation of harmony is thereby necessarily won. They would also agree that one could infinitely pursue this productive exchange between two modes of observation trained on the same object—and to that extent Schiller and Kant are self-consistent when they waste hardly a word on the object, because the main issue remains that a subject brings both faculties into play with one another in response to a thing *(Gegenstand)*. This should not, on the other hand, give the mistaken impression that the early Romantics are interested in this infinite alternation of engagement. In contrast, to the idealists' openness with respect to objects, the early Romantics set apart those play objects that are a provocation and invitation to play because they construct and reflect themselves as play.

One could say the mediative play of the two faculties/ drives outlines a theory of the aesthetic gaze for which an infinite performability *(Inszenierbarkeit,* literally, "stageability") is postulated, at least in the case of Kant and Schiller, but never demonstrated. Beyond the triviality of the fact that one can play through this playful exchange indefinitely, the debate arises as to why it does not become a boring and joyless game over time and, further, why one is playing it at all. The theory of play associated with repetition, on the other hand, is not one of the aesthetic gaze but rather of the artwork that has always already provided for the desired, necessary, and not only possible infinity on conceptual grounds—at least to the extent that those theories refer to play with an object that is in itself an infinite play. Kant's arabesques and shell and wallpaper patterns can be thought of as rather boring because they are purely repetitive precursors to the constantly deferring and transcending structure of repetition envisioned by the early Romantics, provided one regards them retrospectively from the vantage point of the early Romantics.

In many passages of *The Pleasure of the Text,* Roland Barthes brought both kinds of play, that of mediation between two faculties and that of repetition, together exactly where the ruptures—from which in his opinion the pleasures of reading derive—are at the same time ruptures between the repeated elements and ruptures that split meaning and material asunder.

It is clear that artworks understood as play are poor candidates for any gains in terms of experience and cognition. This is most manifest in Gadamer's aesthetics, which claims to be one of repetition play and of world disclosure at the same time. Involuntarily, his aesthetics makes clear that disclosure is only to be gained at the cost of the termination of play. This can naturally be effected at any time in favor of experience and cognition, but one should understand that at that moment one has left the artwork behind and has ceased to play.

[*See also* Fiction; Gadamer; Imagination; Kant; Romanticism; *and* Schiller.]

BIBLIOGRAPHY

Adorno, Theodor W. *Aesthetic Theory*. Edited by Gretel Adorno and Rolf Tiedemann, translated by Robert Hullot-Kentor. Minneapolis, 1997.

Bakhtin, Mikhail M. "The Role of Games in Rabelais." In *Game, Play, Literature*, edited by Jacques Ehrmann, pp. 124–132. Yale French Studies, vol. 41. New Haven, 1968.

Barthes, Roland. *The Pleasure of the Text*. Translated by Richard Miller. New York, 1975.

Caillois, Roger. *Man, Play, and Games*. Translated by Meyer Barash. London, 1962.

Derrida, Jacques. "Structure, Sign, and Play in the Discourse of the Human Sciences." In *Writing and Difference*, translated by Alan Bass, pp. 278–293. Chicago, 1978.

Derrida, Jacques. "The Double Seance." In *Dissemination*, translated by Barbara Johnson, pp. 173–286. Chicago, 1981.

Detweiler, Robert. "Games and Play in Modern American Fiction." *Contemporary Literature* 17.1 (Winter 1976): 44–62.

Ehrmann, Jacques, ed. *Game, Play, Literature*. Yale French Studies, vol. 41. New Haven, 1968.

Fink, Eugen. *Spiel als Weltsymbol*. Stuttgart, 1960.

Gadamer, Hans-Georg. *The Relevance of the Beautiful and Other Essays*. Edited by Robert Bernasconi, translated by Nicholas Walker. Cambridge and New York, 1986.

Gadamer, Hans-Georg. *Truth and Method*. 2d rev. ed. Translation revised by Joel Weinsheimer and Donald G. Marshall. New York, 1989.

Genette, Gérard. *Palimpsestes*. Paris, 1982.

Guinness, Gerald, and Andrew Hurley, eds. *Auctor Ludens: Essays on Play in Literature*. Philadelphia, 1986.

Huizinga, Johan. *Homo Ludens: A Study of the Play-Element in Culture*. Translated by R. F. C. Hull. London, 1949.

Hutchinson, Peter. *Games Authors Play*. London and New York, 1983.

Iser, Wolfgang. *The Fictive and the Imaginary: Charting Literary Anthropology*. Baltimore, 1993.

Kant, Immanuel. *Critique of Judgment*. Translated by Werner S. Pluhar. Indianapolis, 1987.

Kowatzki, Irmgard. *Der Begriff des Spiels als ästhetisches Phänomen: Von Schiller bis Benn*. Bern, 1973.

Novalis. *Schriften*, vol. 2, 2d ed., *Das philosophische Werk I*. Edited by Richard Samuel in collaboration with Hans-Joachim Mähl and Gerhard Schulz. Darmstadt, 1965.

Novalis. *Schriften*, vol. 3, 3d ed., *Das philosophische Werk II*. Edited by Richard Samuel in collaboration with Hans-Joachim Mähl and Gerhard Schulz. Darmstadt, 1983.

Schiller, Friedrich von. *On the Aesthetic Education of Man in a Series of Letters*. Translated by Elizabeth M. Wilkinson and L. A. Willoughby. Oxford, 1967.

Schlegel, Karl Wilhelm Friedrich von. *Dialogue on Poetry and Literary Aphorisms*. Translated by Ernest Behler and Roman Struc. University Park, Pa., 1968.

Stewart, Susan. *Nonsense: Aspects of Intertextuality in Folklore and Literature*. Baltimore, 1979.

RUTH SONDEREGGER